DATE DUE

THE WORD STUDY CONCORDANCE

A modern, improved, and enlarged version of both *The Englishman's Greek Concordance* and *The New Englishman's Greek Concordance*

By
GEORGE V. WIGRAM
and
RALPH D. WINTER

expanded to include key numbering, an Alpha-Numeric Index, a Word Family Index and the cross-reference headings.

William Carey Library
1705 North Sierra Bonita
Pasadena, California, U.S.A. 91104
TEL (213) 798-0819

For many years Samuel Bagster and Sons, Limited, have provided to students and scholars the basic text of this book. This edition differs in the addition of: (1) the numerical apparatus which allows instant consultation by number from either *Strong's Exhaustive Concordance of the Bible* or the totally new companion *Word Study New Testament*; (2) a number for the frequency of each word; (3) the page numbers tying each entry to the place where it is discussed in the following reference tools: *A Concordance to the Greek New Testament* (W. F. Moulton and A. S. Geden, editors), *A Greek-English Lexicon of the New Testament and Other Early Christian Literature* (William F. Arndt and F. Wilbur Gingrich, editors), *A Theological Dictionary of the New Testament* (Gerhard Kittel and Gerhard Friedrich, editors), in this latter case both volume and page being given; (4) the numbers for the roots and components of each word; (5) a special index of word roots, showing all the words derived therefrom, called "A Word Family Index," and (6) the Alpha-Numeric Index.

Published cooperatively by: Tyndale House Publishers, Inc., Wheaton, Illinois; William Carey Library, Pasadena, California.

Library of Congress Catalog Card Number 78-68107 ISBN 0-87808-751-6

CONTENTS

PREFACE

When I first studied Greek, it was taught by an oral method similar to the approach in World War II known as the Army Language Training Program, and it was taught by a former missionary. Acting as college president at Westmont College, Dr. Elbert McCreary did not have time to work out a full-fledged course on an oral basis, but he did share some of the excitement of the Greek New Testament to those fortunate students who were in his classes during that brief period before he retired. Unlike many former seminary students, Dr. McCreary had continued to study the New Testament a verse a day throughout his many years of missionary labors in Ethiopia and had gained an appreciation for Greek as a real *language*, not just as a subject to be studied. Naturally, in Ethopia he had to learn a second and a third language to do his work, and he gradually came to look at the Greek language as simply another tongue, not a special academic study.

Thus, when I later attended seminary, I did so with impossibly high expectations. I felt drawn possibly as a career to further the task Dr. McCreary had attempted. I left seminary to study linguistics with the Wycliffe Bible Translators at Norman, Oklahoma. I was the only one there not intending to become a missionary. Although I had graduated from Cal Tech as an engineer, I eventually got a Ph.D. degree at Cornell University in Structural Linguistics. The teaching of New Testament Greek and language teaching in general was one of my keen interests as a possible area of contribution for my life work. My dissertation was in the area of vocabulary statistics.

Having a Ph.D. in linguistics, I returned to seminary where I was allowed to bypass the usual course work in Hebrew and gained the credit by examination and independent study. My wife had studied Hebrew with me and joined me and one of my seminary professors in the preparation of some lexical aids for the study of Hebrew. In 1956 I authored with that professor a paper which was presented to the Society of Biblical Literature in the area of biblical language teaching.[1].

But the idealistic reflections of students do not always materialize, and adulthood consists quite commonly of the heartless destruction of many earlier hopes and plans. Thus in the inevitable shakedown of priorities, my wife and I felt led, despite our continuing concern in this area, to pursue as a major career a task that put us in touch for over a decade with an indigenous tribal group in the western mountains of Guatemala. There some of the Indian young men helped from time to time to carry forward some of this work. I became involved directly in the development and design of theological education, not only in Guatemala but in other parts of Latin America, for a time as the executive secretary of the Latin American Association of Theological Schools, Northern Region. Then my work (and that of others) in theological education was put into global orbit through what came to be known as the *theological education by extension movement.*

What finally brought some of these things to fruition was the creation of the William Carey Library publishing company. The Library focused on the production of technical books that had to do with the development of all aspects of a worldwide Christian movement. Its specific interest was in those things that would contribute to the biblical studies which inevitably must underlie the growth of a healthy church around the world.

The first thing the William Carey Library published was *The New Englishman's Greek Concordance.* which adapted the Strong set of numbers to the *Englishman's Greek Concordance,* the latter having been virtually unusable for over a hundred years because of the absence of a numerical index. I was much encouraged in this project by Robert Funk, then the executive secretary of the Society of Biblical Literature, a man who continues to be an innovator of much courage in many areas, including the study of Greek.

Now *The Word Study Concordance* and its companion, *The Word Study New Testament,* appear after an additional six years. Many people have aided in the production of these two works. I refer at least to the students at the Bethany Missionary Fellowship in Minneapolis, who worked thousands of hours preparing a file for over 200,000 slips which were necessary for the preparation of the *Word Study New Testament;* to Mrs. Lyle Storey at Melodyland, who compiled the index in *The Word Study New Testament* to the three reference tools; to Wayland Wong, missionary professor extraordinary in Hong Kong, who early and constantly has promoted this project; to my daughters, who spent at least one Easter vacation helping in the transfer of the Strong numbers to the basic text; to various seminarians, friends, and relatives who donated many hours here and there.

I am especially indebted to my wife who has borne the lion's share of the labor from the inception of this task. She supervised and worked not only with our daughters as we were beginning the task, but has checked and rechecked the work of others, singlehandedly composed and pasted up the Alpha-Numeric Index, and edited introductions and explanatory sections. Throughout, she has been the general overseer of the final preparation of these two manuscripts, which without her involvement at every point would certainly not have come into existence.

She joins me in my very earnest desIre that God will make these volumes a great contribution to the effective study of the New Testament, to the end that perhaps even a whole new era is before us in the churches, colleges, and seminaries as we all take the Bible more seriously. Certainly there has been no time in history when such a breakthrough has been more urgent.

RALPH D. WINTER

1. Charles T. Fritsch and Ralph D. Winter, "A New Approach to the Hebrew Lexical Problem," *Doron: Hebraic Studies,* Israel T. Naamani, David Rudavsky and Carl F. Ehle, Jr., eds. (New York: The National Association of Professors of Hebrew in American Institutions of Higher Learning, 1956), pp. 49-61.

Guide to the Numbers in the Headings

The following is a typical vocabulary entry:

```
 A     B    C   D    E           F
 |     |    |   |    |           |
2842  20  439/552 3:789        2844
```

κοινωνία, *koinōnia*.

Acts 2:42. and *fellowship*, and in breaking of bread,
Ro. 15:26. to make a certain *contribution*
1Co. 1: 9. called unto the *fellowship* of his Son
10:16. is it not the *communion* of the blood
— is it not the *communion* of the body
2Co. 6:14. what *communion* hath light
8: 4. and (take upon us) the *fellowship*
9:13. for (your) liberal *distribution*
13:14(13). the *communion* of the Holy Ghost,
Gal. 2: 9. the right hands of *fellowship*;
Eph 3: 9. what (is) the *fellowship* of the mystery,
Phi. 1: 5. For your *fellowship* in the gospel
2: 1. if any *fellowship* of the Spirit,
3:10. and the *fellowship* of his sufferings,
Philem 6. That the *communication* of thy faith
Heb 13:16. and *to communicate* forget not:
1Joh. 1: 3. may have *fellowship* with us: and truly our *fellowship* (is) with
6. If we say that we have *fellowship*
7. we have *fellowship* one with another,

FIGURE A

A. The number 2842 at the extreme left is the key number assigned to *koinonia* by Strong in his *Exhaustive Concordance of the Bible.* These numbers to the left are arranged in sequence except for those assigned to proper names, which are listed sequentially in a separate section (pp. 817-872). In some cases where a number is missing from the section where it would be expected, a footnote on that page indicates where it is to be found. (See for example the footnote on page 582.)

B. The number 20 indicates the frequency (e.g., the number of occurrences) of the Greek word *koinonia* in the New Testament.

C. The number 439 is the *page* on which the word *koinonia* is discussed in Arndt and Gingrich (editors), *A Greek Lexicon of the New Testament and Other Early Christian Literature,* probably the most widely used Greek lexicon.

D. The number 552 is the *page* in *The Concordance to the Greek New Testament* (edited by W.F. Moulton and A.S. Geden) on which the word *koinonia* may be found. (The new edition of this book also carries the same Strong numbering system as this volume.)

E. Number 3:789 gives the volume (3) and page number (789) where *koinonia* is found in Kittel's famous *Theological Dictionary of the New Testament.* The index volume of Kittel (Volume 10) carries an index which employs the same (Strong's) numbering system.

F. The number to the far right (2844) indicates the root or base (or "parent") of the word *koinonia.* The word indicated by this number is that suggested by Strong as the most likely root, but is not always etymologically exact, and will be found in the "Word Family Index" (pp. xix to xxxv) along with all the words related to it. A number preceded by *rt* (*from the root of*) indicates that the entry has the same base as another word. If this number to the far right is preceded by *cf* (*compare with*), it is a synonym or is somehow related to the entry. If preceded by *eq*, the number refers to a word which is *equivalent to* or another form of the entry.

At times the number to the far right is in brackets (for example, see entry #4526). The brackets indicate that the root of this entry is a Hebrew word and may be investigated further by referring to Strong's "Hebrew and Chaldee Dictionary" in the appendix to Strong's *Exhaustive Concordance of the Bible*. It may also be investigated by checking the *New Englishman's Hebrew and Chaldee Concordance.*

The number occurring on the outer margin at the very top of each page, as in a dictionary or encyclopedia, is for quick reference. The left hand page carries the number to the first vocabulary entry on that page, and the right hand page carries the number to the last vocabulary entry on that page.

INTRODUCTION to the Word Study Concordance

The Englishman's Greek Concordance has never been widely known or used at any time since its first appearance in 1840. Only in 1972, when an improved version developed by Dr. Ralph D. Winter was published, did it become feasible for popular use by Sunday School teachers, pastors, scholars, and students. Now *The Word Study Concordance* is a dramatically improved and expanded version of both of the earlier volumes. It not only includes all of the original work but also is published along with a revolutionary companion volume, *The Word Study New Testament,* which reduces by 90 percent the labors connected with the use of even the 1972 version.

AN INVALUABLE TOOL FOR THE LAY PERSON

The Word Study Concordance, as well as its two predecessors, is different from ordinary concordances based on English translations in that it traces not English but *Greek words* and tells—in English—for a given word just how the translators interpreted it in all the passages in which the Greek word appears. This means you can find listed in *The Word Study Concordance* every passage where a given Greek word occurs in the New Testament, regardless of how many different ways it may be translated into English. We will see in a moment how important this is.

You don't have to understand Greek, however, in order to use The Word Study Concordance. This is because every entry in the concordance is numbered. Once you have the right number, you can find what you want in just a matter of seconds. Since we have employed the same key numbers developed originally by James Strong in his well-known reference work, *An Exhaustive Concordance of the Bible,* it is possible for you to find these key numbers if you have a copy of *Strong's Concordance.* But we have made it very much easier for you than that. *The Word Study New Testament,* the companion volume to *The Word Study Concordance,* is a regular King James Version of the New Testament except that, as you see below, it has the key numbers of the Greek words printed right under practically every word—every noun, verb, adjective, and adverb. For example, Acts 2:40-42 looks like this:

390 ACTS 2, 3

40 And with many other words did he
4118-4119 2087 3056 1263
testify and exhort, saying, Save yourselves
1263 3870 4982 4982
from this untoward generation.
575 4646 1074
41 Then they that gladly received his word
588...780 588 3056
were baptized: and the same day there were
907....... 2250 4369...
added unto them about three thousand souls.
...... 5153........ 5590
42 And they continued steadfastly in the
4342..............
apostles' doctrine and fellowship, and in
652 1322 2842
breaking of bread, and in prayers.
2800 740 4335

FIGURE B

Thus, suppose you want to know what is really behind the word *fellowship* in verse 42 above. Can you see the number *2842* under *fellowship*? This is the key number! It refers to the Greek word from which *fellowship* is translated. By using *The Word Study New Testament* you do not need to look up anything in *Strong's Concordance*. You can go directly to entry #2842 in your *Word Study Concordance*.

The Number on the Left

In *The Word Study Concordance* the key numbers appear (as in the illustration below) in numerical order in the far left column of each entry. Number 2842, for example, is on page 427. In a moment we will explain the series of numbers in the heading, but right now note that beneath this line of numbers you find the Greek word *koinonia* printed in both the Greek alphabet and in English letters. Under *koinonia* are references and brief quotations from all twenty passages in the New Testament that use the word *koinonia:*

2842 20 439/552 3:789 2844

κοινωνία, *koinōnia.*

Acts 2:42. and *fellowship*, and in breaking of bread,
Ro. 15:26. to make a certain *contribution*
1Co. 1: 9. called unto the *fellowship* of his Son
10:16. is it not the *communion* of the blood
— is it not the *communion* of the body
2Co. 6:14. what *communion* hath light
8: 4. and (take upon us) the *fellowship*
9:13. for (your) liberal *distribution*
13:14(13). the *communion* of the Holy Ghost,
Gal. 2: 9. the right hands of *fellowship;*
Eph 3: 9. what (is) the *fellowship* of the mystery,
Phi. 1: 5. For your *fellowship* in the gospel
2: 1. if any *fellowship* of the Spirit,
3:10. and the *fellowship* of his sufferings,
Philem 6. That the *communication* of thy faith
Heb 13:16. and *to communicate* forget not:
1Joh. 1: 3. may have *fellowship* with us: and truly our *fellowship* (is) with
6. If we say that we have *fellowship*
7. we have *fellowship* one with another,

FIGURE C

Incidentally, did you know, before you glanced down through this entry, that the Greek word *koinonia,* while translated "fellowship" in Acts 2:42, is translated "contribution" in Romans 15:26?

How many other ways is *koinonia* translated? In each case the italicized words indicate the various English translations of the same Greek word *koinonia: fellowship, contribution, communion, distribution, communication, communicate*—six different words. These references are, therefore, scattered in six different places in *Strong's* or *Young's Concordances* but are all collected together here in *The Word Study Concordance*. This book is basically a concordance of the *Greek* New Testament, not an English translation, and accordingly must group citations under Greek words, not English words. Note that eight out of the twenty times it appears, the word *koinonia* is not translated "fellowship." This is a very important difference because only as you read down the list of passages that use *koinonia* can you get a feel for the way the New Testament uses this word. This way you suddenly find that the New Testament itself is teaching you that the Greek word is not quite the same as our English word *fellowship*!

Now let's look at the series of numbers in the heading of this word *koinonia*.

The Number on the Far Right

At the far right in Figure C you see the number *2844*. This is the key number of the word from which the Greek word *koinonia* is derived— its root word. That entry happens to be found on the same page (427). It turns out to be the key number for the Greek word *koinonos.*

2844 10 440/553 3:789 2839

κοινωνός, ***koinōnos.***

Mat 23:30. we would not have been *partakers*
Lu. 5:10. which were *partners* with Simon.
1Co.10:18. *partakers* of the altar?
20. ye should have *fellowship* with
2Co. 1: 7. as ye are *partakers* of the sufferings,
8:23. (he is) my *partner* and fellowhelper
Philem 17. If thou count me therefore a *partner*,
Heb 10:33. ye became *companions* of them
1Pet.5: 1. and also a *partaker* of the glory
2Pet.1: 4. be *partakers* of the divine nature, having escaped

FIGURE D

The Scripture references under *koinonos* are all different from the ones under *koinonia. Koinonos,* the root word of *koinonia,* is translated "fellowship" only once out of ten times. At this point in our study we begin to see we're bumping into a concept that is significantly more meaningful than mere "fellowship."

But we're not finished with *koinonos* yet. The idea of "partnership" comes in here very strongly—maybe not legal, business-style partnership, but something a good deal more serious, exciting and lasting than mere *fellowship.* If this second word, #2844, is the word from which *koinonia* comes, then it is a root word or a "parent" word. Why don't we see if there are other members in this word family? This is often the most exciting study of all.

The Word Family Index

Number 2844 is also to be found on page xxviii in the "Word Family Index." There you find the following:

```
2844 koinōnos                10
       2841  koinōneo            8
       2842  koinōnia           20
       2843  koinōnikos          1
       4791  sunkoinōnos         4
```

FIGURE E

The number to the right of each word indicates the number of times the word appears in the New Testament. In this example *koinonos* appears ten times. The four derivatives occur eight, twenty, one and four times respectively, a total of forty-three occurrences for the whole family if you add these up. Four of the family members are huddled close together in the body of the concordance—2844, 2841, 2842, and 2843—because they all start with the same letter. The fourth word, #4791, will only take an extra ten seconds to look up. On page 704 you find:

4791 4 782/924 3:789 4862,2844
συγκοινωνός, *sunkoinōnos.*

Ro. 11:17. and *with* them *partakest* of the root
1Co. 9:23. I might be *partaker* thereof *with* (you).
Phi. 1: 7. ye all are *partakers* of my grace.
Rev. 1: 9. and *companion* in tribulation,

FIGURE F

Now, as you read through all the wealth of Bible texts in this word family, again the "partaking" kind of companionship is the feel you get in these additional four passages. In a Bible study group you can ask different ones to look up each of these verses and read the whole verse and even look at the total context. You may not need to. Your *Word Study Concordance* quotes quite a bit of the verse from the Authorized King James Version, and you may in many cases recognize the full intent of the verse.

Is this now the end of the road? Have you received all the insight you can? By no means! Now you can see what someone else has decided who may have looked at many of the same passages you have just now consulted. Who would that person be? That is the job of anyone who has made a dictionary (often called *lexicon*) of the New Testament. Thus, after (not before) you have done your own quick study you can, if you desire, check a Greek lexicon. Note, very carefully, however, that once you have read through these Bible passages yourself, you have acquired something no dictionary can easily give you—you now have a certain instinctive *feel* for the word. You have become conditioned by the actual use of the word (which is the most normal and reliable way to learn any word in any language) not to equate it to some other word. Students often try to short-circuit this process and go directly to a lexicon, but they do not gain as much that way. However, one reason they do not take the time to read the biblical passages is that until now they have not had the great facility for such a quest as you have as the owner of *The Word Study New Testament* and *The Word Study Concordance.*

On the other hand, it is certainly of great value to go on and consult with the writers of reference works. Even that process is greatly speeded up by use of *The Word Study Concordance.* One of the additional reference books to which we will refer will be of use only to students of Greek; but two others which are constantly consulted by advanced students can be used with profit by anyone.

A GOLD MINE FOR THE ADVANCED BIBLE STUDENT AND THE STUDENT OF GREEK

A primary feature of *The Word Study Concordance* is the addition of a series of reference numbers. While the 1972 *New Englishman's Greek Concordance* added the key number and the root word number, this improved and enlarged edition, called now *The Word Study Concordance,* adds a series of numbers that refer to three additional reference works.

key number-[2842 | 20 439/552 3:789 | 2844]-*root word number*

Added in 1978 edition

FIGURE G

The new series of numbers above appears in the heading for the word *koinonia*. The number *20* indicates the frequency or number of occurrences of the Greek word *koinonia* in the New Testament, and there are accordingly twenty citations in this entry. Just to the right of #20 are the numbers *439* followed by a slash, *522,* and 3:789. These numbers are for the benefit of advanced students. Number 439, the first number in this series of three, is the *page* on which the word *koinonia* is discussed in Arndt and Gingrich's *A Greek Lexicon of the New Testament and Other Early Christian Literature,* probably the most widely-used Greek lexicon. You do not need to know Greek once you find the right entry, using the page number.

Number 552 is the *page* in *The Concordance to the Greek New Testament* (edited by W.F. Moulton and A.S. Geden) on which the word *koinonia* may be found. (The 1978 edition of *Moulton and Geden's Concordance* carries the same Strong numbering system as does this volume, so that you can go directly from *The Word Study New Testament* to the word in *Moulton and Geden.* This concordance is useful only to those who read Greek—it is entirely in Greek, but is the only tool *requiring* Greek.

Number 3:789 gives the volume (3) and page number (789) where *koinonia* is found in Kittel's famous *Theological Dictionary of the New Testament.* You do not need to know Greek to profit from this ten-volume commentary on the vocabulary of the Greek New Testament. The tenth volume, the Index volume, carries an index employing the same system of numbers we have used.

The Word Study New Testament has a special "Key Number Index to Standard Reference Works" located in the back. This gives for each key number all the same items as are found in the headings of the entries in this concordance. Thus either *The Word Study New Testament* or *The Word Study Concordance* will help you locate any word quickly in *Arndt and Gingrich, Moulton and Geden* or *Kittel*.

How Does the Word Study Concordance Compare with Ordinary Concordances?

Why is this book uniquely superior to the best concordances of English translations? Both Strong and Young have produced tools which, by a fairly tedious procedure, allow a diligent person to ferret out the same list of occurrences of a given Greek word as we found gathered all together under a single key number. The amazing way in which the present work short-circuits those tedious processes may not be appreciated unless we first discuss briefly the built-in limitations of all concordances which are built from *translations* of the Bible. Strong, Young, and Cruden all base their concordances on the King James Version.

The first great value of concordances of *translations* of the Bible is that they allow you to find where a verse is when all you can remember is the wording or part of the wording. Naturally, however, since people are increasingly using a great variety of modern-speech translations, a problem arises because most of these new versions do not yet have their own concordances. Thus, as time goes on, the finding of verse references by means of any concordance of the King James Version is going to be less and less easy for many people.

By contrast, the present work leans on the King James Version only to identify the references of a given Greek word. This is true because this book is a concordance of the *Greek* New Testament, not of an English translation. The amazing difference is that the lists of references this book gives will be of permanent value all around the world, even for those who speak neither English nor Greek! We hope, for example, that pastors in many other countries will find it a treasure at their elbow. Thus we should not let the fact that the citations are from the King James Version obscure the crucial fact that the *lists of references* are references to *Greek* words in the *Greek* New Testament. The significance of this type of information is not affected by new translations and will never even get out of date.

A second great value of a traditional concordance of an English translation is that it allows a person to follow key words throughout the Bible. At this point, however, a very grave limitation of any *English* concordance appears. What happens is this: as the appearance of a certain English word like *love* is traced through the New Testament, perhaps without knowing it the English reader is switching back and forth between half a dozen different Greek words, all of which are sometimes translated *love*. If each of those Greek words were then followed out through the New Testament, one would find the English translation for them also switching back and forth between the word *love* and various other English words like *desire, will, kiss,* etc. This is not necessarily because the English translation is faulty. It is simply because no English word is the exact equivalent of any Greek word. Linguistic scientists will tell you that no two words between any two languages are likely to be exact equivalents. It would actually be a bizarre translation, not a good one, in which the same English word was given for every appearance in the Greek New Testament of a certain Greek word. The confusion may be seen in the case of the word *love.*

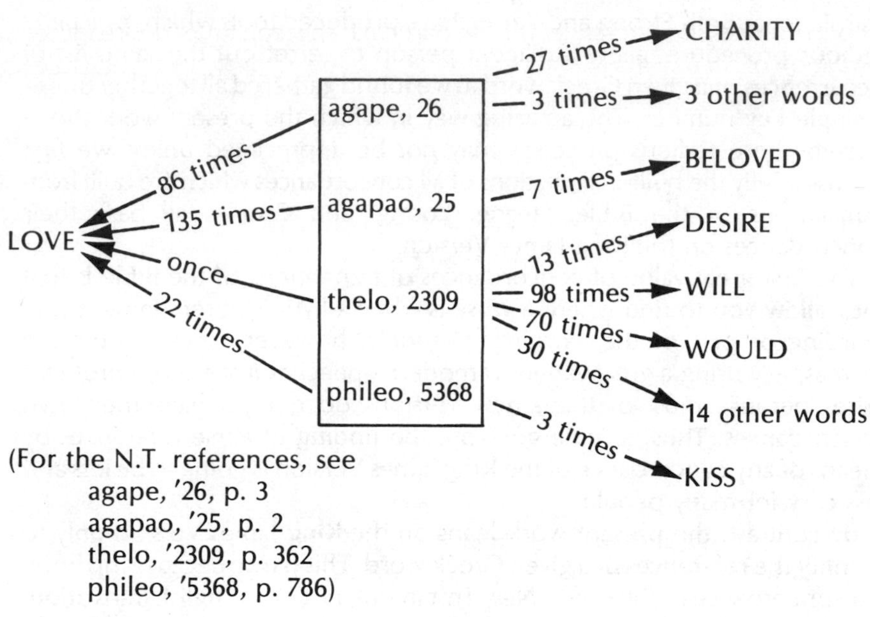

FIGURE H

In the middle of the figure above we have indicated four of the Greek words which are sometimes translated *love.* On the right you see reference to twenty-three English words, which are sometimes employed to translate one or the other of these four Greek words. These words on the right, of course, are used not merely to translate the four Greek words in the center but are employed in translating more than a dozen other Greek words. If these were followed out the picture would become even more complicated.

The concordances of *Strong* and *Young* also refer to the original Greek words. But when you look up *love* in *Strong* and *Young,* you are led eventually to the four Greek words in the middle of the figure above. But these concordances will naturally give you only those Bible references where those four Greek words happen to be translated by the English word *love*. On the other hand, if a person wants to know, for example, all the places where the Greek word *agape* appears, he would find eighty-six of its references under the word *love* and thirty more references under *charitably, charity, feast of charity,* and *dear*. What a treat to find all 116 occurrences of *agape* all in one place in this concordance: See word #26, pp. 3-4.

Or, suppose one desires to find all the places where the Greek word *thelo* occurs. There are eighteen different words: *love, desire, will, would,* and fourteen less frequent words that are used by the King James translators for *thelo*. Furthermore, this task of looking up eighteen words is not easy. But (using *Strong's Concordance*), once he finds one of those words, say *desire*, which occurs 111 times, he would have an additional task finding among the 111 occurrences the references for the particular thirteen times *desire* is the translation of *thelo*. Finally, the person has to cope with the fact that while he can eventually collect a total of 209 references in eighteen groups, he may still have to sift and collate these all together in a single series in biblical order running from Matthew to Revelation in order to get a good grasp the pattern in which the word *thelo* is employed by the biblical writers.

Imagine, *The Word Study Concordance* puts all those 209 references in one place, in order, only ten seconds away from him under the key number 2309, p. 362. Furthermore, this book identifies the passages by English citations, italicizing that particular English word in a given passage which is used to translate the Greek word.

So again, neither *Young* nor *Strong* gives in any one place all the references for any one Greek word. The stubborn fact is simply this: an English concordance quite naturally organizes the Greek words around *English* words and concepts, while the present work gathers English words around *Greek* words and concepts. It is clearly the Greek concordance that will help the Bible student to think the way the Greeks thought—the way the New Testament writers thought. The difference, ultimately, is profound.

How Does The Word Study Concordance
Compare with Greek Lexicons?

In reality, even the best lexicons or dictionaries are basically some scholar's reflections on the data drawn from a concordance. The most famous dictionary of any language is the monumental twelve-volume *Oxford English Dictionary*. It is so thorough and authoritative because it consists primarily of a concordance of citations from important English authors down through history. Similarly, the largest lexicons of the vocabulary of the Greek New Testament must actually cite, at least by reference, every New Testament occurrence of a word (except for highly frequent words). They also cite other illuminating occurrences in the ancient Greek translation of the Old Testament (called the *Septuagint*) and contemporary papyrus manuscripts, etc.

A lexicon, however, is still basically a human scholar's commentary on a concordance. Human commentaries are helpful, even vital, but the concordance is more basic. The concordance in one sense is totally objective—it merely tells the various places where a word occurs and makes a brief quotation including the word. The detailed lexicon goes on to try to classify different modes of meaning, giving references to back up its conclusions. But in most cases the lexicon only gives references, not citations from the Bible. Thus unless you happen to recognize the various passages referred to solely by verse reference, you have to look up all those references to see just what it is upon which the lexicographer is basing his conclusions. But there is a much more profound point here.

It is not that we feel we must always check up on the lexicographer, and that giving just verse references makes that task difficult. It is also as important to assimilate and remember the sense of the words of scripture as it is to verify them. This concordance performs both functions because it cites not only the Biblical references but, in English, the entire phrase in which the word studied occurs.

Thus nothing will give the Bible student a sure *feel* for a word like a concordance. Language teachers know that new words are best learned by seeing how they are used in a number of different situations, and how other members of the same word family are used. When a Greek student memorizes one or two English "equivalents" for each of 100 important New Testament Greek terms, he has in reality less than a translation already gives him. A better method would be to use this concordance to get acquainted with a number of key passages in the New Testament where each of these words occurs and begin to associate with the words those key contexts. You can see how this works in the case of the examples given in the next section.

NOTES ON THE FOUR SMALLER SECTIONS

A. *Proper Names Concordance.* The Proper Names Concordance is part and parcel of the main body of the Concordance. If you are looking up a number which you know refers to a proper name of a person or place, you must go directly to this section.

B. *English-Greek Index*. This index starts out with an English word, perhaps a concept you are especially interested in—e.g., *meek, master, Lord*. It lists all the Greek words which happen to be translated by the English concept you are studying. An ordinary concordance tells you only those reference where this particular English word is found. This index leads you to Greek words and in turn to a number of passages with associated meanings that may not always be translated by that same English word.

C. *Greek-English Index*. This index is in effect a brief summary of the material found in the body of the Concordance.

D. *Comparative Concordance*. If you want to make absolutely sure you are not missing anything, check the number of the word you are studying in this Concordance because it collects together all of the evidence from all of the more recently discovered Greek texts.

Ralph D. Winter
Roberta H. Winter

Word Family Index

As you consult this index, the numbers off to the right of the Greek words indicate in each case the frequency of that word. The numbers to the left are the regular key numbers used for identification and quick reference. The words listed in each group belong to a "word family" according to the relationships suggested originally by Strong in his concordance. Words having only one declension or related form are not included in this list.

The determination of what words should be grouped with which roots has been based entirely on Strong's "Greek Dictionary of the New Testament" appended to his *Exhaustive Concordance of the Bible.* While the latest etymological research may differ in some particulars from Strong's determinations, the grouping here, based on his original suggestions, will be found to be of great practical value, and will be improved as scholarship provides additional insights.

ROOT NO.	DRVT. NO.	TRANSLITERATION	FRQ.
1		alpha	4
	4	abaress	1
	12	abussos	9
	22	agamos	4
	35	agenealogeetos	1
	36	agenees	1
	46	agnaphos	2
	50	agnoeo	22
	56	agnōsia	2
	57	agnōstos	1
	62	agrammatos	1
	69	agrupmeo	4
	77	adapanos	1
	80	adelphos	346
	82	adeelos	1
	86	hadees	11
	87	adiakritos	1
	88	adialiptos	2
	90	adiaphthoria	1
	94	adikos	12
	96	adokimos	8
	97	adolos	1
	102	adunatos	10
	106	azumos	9
	110	athanasia	3
	111	athemitos	2
	112	atheos	1
	113	athesmos	2
	114	atheteo	16
	120	athumeo	1
	121	athōos	2
	127	adiōs	2
	160	aiphnidios	2
	169	akathartos	30
	170	akaireomai	1
	172	akakos	2
	175	akarpos	7
	176	akatagnōstos	1
	177	akatakaluptos	2
	178	akatakritos	2
	179	akatalutos	1
	180	akatapautos	1
	182	akatastatos	1
	183	akatasketos	1
	185	akeraios	3
	186	aklinees	1
	190	akoloutheo	92
	193	akratees	1
	194	akraton	1
	208	akuroō	3
	209	akōlutōs	1
	210	akōn	1
	215	alaleetos	1
	216	alalos	3
	218	alipho	9
	227	aleethees	25
	249	alogos	3
	253	alupoteros	1
	255	alusitelees	1
	261	amathees	1
	263	amarantos	1
	264	hamartano	43
	267	amarturos	1
	269	amakos	2
	271	amethustos	1
	272	ameleo	5
	273	amemptos	5
	275	amerimnos	2
	276	ametathetos	2
	277	ametakineetos	1
	278	ametameleetos	2
	279	ametanoeetos	1
	280	ametros	2
	282	ameetōr	1
	283	amiantos	4
	298	amōmeetos	2
	299	amōmos	7
	335	anaidīa	1
	338	anaitios	2
	358	analos	1
	361	anamarteetos	1
	368	anantirreetos	1
	370	anaxios	1
	379	anapologeetos	2
	382	anarithmeetos	1
	410	anenkleetos	5
	411	anekdieegeetos	11
	412	aneklaleetos	1
	413	aneklīptos	1
	415	anele-eemon	1
	418	anendekton	2
	419	anexerūneetos	1
	421	anexikniastos	2
	422	anepaiskuntos	1
	423	anepileeptos	3
	428	anuthetos	1
	431	anepsios	1
	434	aneemeros	1
	448	anileōs	1
	449	aniptos	3
	453	anoeetos	6
	454	anoia	2
	459	anomos	10
	462	anosios	2
	504	anudros	4
	505	anupokritos	6
	506	anupotaktos	4
	512	anophelees	2
	517	aoratos	5
	521	apaidutos	1
	531	aparabatos	1
	532	aparaskūastos	1
	537	hapas	44
	540	apator	1
	545	apithees	6
	551	apirastos	1
	552	apīros	1
	562	aperantos	1
	563	aperispastōs	1
	564	aperitmeetos	1
	571	apistos	23
	573	haplous	2
	639	aporeomai	4
	676	aprositos	1
	677	aproskopos	3
	678	aprosōpoleeptōs	1
	679	apaistos	1
	692	argos	8
	720	arneomai	31
	729	arraphos	1
	731	arreetos	1
	732	arrostos	5
	761	asalūtos	2
	762	asbestos	4
	765	asebees	9
	766	aselgīa	9
	767	aseemos	1
	772	asthenees	25
	777	asitos	1
	781	asophos	1
	782	aspazomai	60
	784	aspilos	4
	786	aspondos	2
	790	astateo	1
	793	asteeriktos	2
	794	astorgos	2
	795	astokeo	3
	799	Asumkritos	1
	800	asumphōnos	4
	801	asunetos	5
	802	asunthetos	1
	804	asphalees	5
	809	askeemōn	1
	810	asōtia	3
	811	asōtōs	1
	813	ataktos	1
	815	ateknos	3
	816	atenizo	14
	820	atimos	4
	823	atomos	1
	824	atopos	3
	852	aphanees	1
	855	aphantos	1
	857	aphīdia	1
	858	aphelotees	1
	862	aphthartos	7
	865	aphilagathos	1
	866	aphilarguros	1
	870	aphobōs	4
	878	aphrōn	11
	880	aphōnes	4
	884	akaristos	2
	886	akīropoi-eetos	3
	888	akrīos	2
	890	akreetos	1
	893	apsūdees	1
	895	apsukos	1
	1819	exapina	1
17		agathopoyos	1
	15	agathopoyeo	11
	16	agathopoiya	1
18		agathos	102
	14	agathoergeo	1
	17	agathopoyos	1
	19	agathōsunee	4
	5358	philagathos	1
25		agapao	142
	26	agapee	16
	27	agapeetos	62
32		angelos	186
	31	angelia	1
	312	anangello	18
	518	apangello	44
	743	arkangelos	2
	1229	diangello	3
	1804	exangello	1
	1861	epangellomai	15
	2097	ūangelizo,-omai	55
	2098	ūangelion	77
	2465	isangelos	1
	2605	kantangello	17
	3853	parangello	30
40		hagios	229
	37	hagiazo	29
	39	hagion	11
	41	hagiotees	1
	42	hagiosunee	3
	53	hagnos	8
43		ankalai	1
	44	ankistron	1
	45	ankura	4
	318	anankee	18
	1723	enankalizomai	2
	3591	onkos	1
50		agnoeo	22
	51	agnoeema	1
	52	agnoia	4
53		hagnos	8
	47	hagnīa	2
	48	hagnizo	7
	54	hagnotees	1
	55	hagnōs	1
58		agora	11
	59	agorazo	31
	60	agoraios	2
	1215	deemeegoreo	1
	2725	kateegoros	7
	3831	paneeguris	1
	3931	pareegoria	1
	4316	prosagorūomai	1
66		agrios	3
	65	agrielaios	2
	67	Agrippas	12
68		agros	36
	63	agrauleo	1
	66	agrias	3
71		ago	71
	33	age	2
	34	agelee	8
	61	agra	1
	68	agros	36
	72	agōgee	1
	73	agōn	6
	321	anago	24
	514	axios	41
	520	apago	16
	747	arkeegos	4
	1236	diago	2
	1396	doulagōgeo	1
	1521	īsago	10
	1806	exago	13
	2233	heegeomai	28
	2609	katago	10
	3329	metago	2
	3489	nauageo	2
	3807	paidagōgos	3
	3855	parago	10
	4013	periago	6
	4254	proago	18
	4317	prosago	4
	4755	strateegos	10
	4812	sulagōgeo	1
	4863	sunago	62
	5217	hupago	81
	5468	kalinagōgeo	2
	5497	kīragōgos	1
	5524	koreegeo	2
73		agōn	6
	74	agōnia	1
	75	agonizomai	7
75		agōnizomai	7
	464	antagonizomai	1
	1864	epagōnizomai	1
	2596	katagōnizomai	1
	4865	sunagōnizomai	1
80		adelphos	396
	79	adelphee	24
	81	adelphotees	2
	5361	philadelphos	1
	5569	psūdadelphos	2
82		adeelos	1
	83	adeelotees	1
	84	adeelōs	1
94		adikos	12
	91	adikeo	27
	93	adikia	26
	95	adikos	1
104		aī	8
	126	aīdios	2
	165	aiōn	128
109		aeer	7
	105	aetos	4
	417	anemos	31
	833	aulee	12
	836	aulos	1
	839	aurion	15
	840	austeeros	2
	846	autos	5117
	5594	psukomai	1
118		athleo	2
	119	athleesis	1
	4866	sunathleo	2
129		haima	99
	130	haimatekkusia	1
	131	haimorroeo	1
134		aineo	9
	133	ainesis	1
	1867	epaineo	6
	1868	epainos	11
	3867	paraineo	2
136		ainos	2
	134	aineo	9
	135	ainigma	1
138		haireomai	3
	139	hairesis	9
	140	hairetizo	1
	337	anaireo	23
	355	analisko	3
	726	harpazo	13
	851	aphaireo	10
	1244	diaireo	2
	1807	exaireo	8
	2507	kathaireo	9
	4014	periaireo	4
	4255	proaireomai	1
142		airo	102
	522	apairomai	3
	685	ara	1
	686	ara	51
	700	aresko	17
	703	aretee	5
	704	areen	1
	706	arithmos	18
	712	ariston	3
	716	harma	4
	730	arreen	3
	730	arseen	6
	737	arti	36
	740	artos	100
	741	artao	3
	759	arōma	4
	1808	exairo	2
	1869	epairo	19
	3332	metairo	2
	3349	meteōrizomai	1
	4868	sunairo	3
	5229	huperairomai	3
143		aisthanomai	1
	144	aistheesis	1
	145	aistheeteerion	1
150		aiskros	1
	146	aiskrokerdees	3
	148	aiskrologia	1
	149	aiskron	3
	151	aiskrotees	1
153		aiskunomai	5
	150	aiskros	1
	152	aiskunee	6
	422	anepaiskuntos	1
	1870	epaiskunomai	11
	2617	kataiskuno	13
154		aiteo	71
	155	aiteema	3
	156	aitia	20
	159	aitios	1
	523	apaiteo	2
	1809	exaiteomai	1
	1871	epaiteo	1
	3868	paraiteomai	11
	4319	prosaiteo	3
156		aitia	20
	157	aitiama	1

ROOT NO.	DRVT. NO.	TRANSLITERATION	FRQ.
	4256	proaitiaomai	1
159		aitios	1
	158	aition	4
	338	anaitios	2
164		aikmalōtos	1
	161	aikmalosia	3
	162	aikmalōtūo	2
	163	aikmalōtizo	3
	4869	sunaikmalōtos	3
169		akathartos	30
	167	akatharsia	10
	168	akathartees	1
188		akmeen	1
	173	akantha	14
	187	akmazo	1
	206	akron	6
	2391	oxus	8
	5230	huperakmos	1
190		akoloutheo	92
	1811	exakoloutheo	3
	1872	epakoloutheo	4
	2628	katakoloutheo	2
	3877	parakoloutheo	4
	4870	sunakoloutheo	2
191		akouo	437
	189	akoee	24
	202	akroatees	4
	1251	diakou-omai	1
	1522	īsakouo	5
	1873	epakouo	1
	3878	parakouo	2
	4257	proakouo	1
	5219	hupakouo	21
196		akribestatos	1
	195	akribīa	1
	197	akribesteron	4
	198	akriboō	1
	199	akribōs	5
202		akroatees	4
	201	akroateerion	1
	1874	epakroaomai	1
206		akron	6
	196	akribestos	1
	200	akris	4
	203	akrobustia	20
	204	akrogoniaios	2
	205	akrothinion	1
220		alektōr	12
	219	alektorophōnia	1
	223	Alexandros	6
227		aleethees	25
	225	aleethīs	110
	226	aleethūo	2
	228	aleethinos	27
	230	aleethōs	21
236		allatto	6
	465	antallagma	2
	525	apallasso	3
	1259	diallattomai	1
	2644	katallasso	6
	3337	metallatto	2
	3883	parallagee	1
242		hallomai	3
	21	agalliao	11
	1814	exallomai	1
	2177	ephallomai	1
243		allos	160
	235	alla	636
	236	allatto	6
	237	allakothen	1
	238	alleegoreō	1
	240	alleelōn	100
	241	allogenees	1
	245	allotrios	14
	246	allophulos	1
	247	allōs	1
245		allotrios	14
	244	allotrioepiskopos	1
	526	apallotrioō	3
251		hals	1
	123	aigialos	6
	217	halas	8
	231	halius	5
	233	halizo	3
	252	halukos	1
	358	analos	1
	1724	enalios	1
	2281	thalassa	92
	3882	paralios	1
257		halōn	2
	248	aloaō	3
	288	ampelos	8
	3389	meetralōees	2
260		hama	10
	270	amao	1
	285	ammos	5
	2438	himas	4
264		hamartano	43
	265	hamarteema	4
	266	hamartia	174
	268	hamartōlos	47
	361	anamarteetos	1
	4258	proamartano	2
288		ampelos	8
	289	ampelourgos	1
	290	ampelōn	23
297		amphoteros	14
	288	ampelos	8
	295	Amphilpolis	1
302		an	191
	1875	epan	3
	3752	hotan	122
303		ana (adv.)	10
303		ana (prep.)	5
	305	anabaino	81
	306	anaballomai	6
	307	anabibazo	1
	308	anablepo	26
	310	anaboao	3
	312	anangello	18
	313	anagennao	2
	314	anaginōsko	33
	318	anankee	18
	319	anagnōrizomai	1
	321	anago	24
	322	anadiknumi	2
	324	anadekomai	2
	325	anadidōmi	1
	326	anazao	5
	327	anazeeteo	2
	328	anazōnnumi	1
	329	anazōpureo	1
	330	anathallo	1
	333	anatheōreo	2
	337	anaireo	23
	339	anakathizo	2
	340	anakainizo	1
	341	anakainoō	2
	343	anakalupto	2
	344	anakampto	4
	345	anakīmai	14
	346	anakephalaio-omai	2
	347	anaklino	8
	348	anakopto	1
	349	anakrazo	5
	350	anakrino	16
	352	anakupto	4
	353	analambano	13
	355	analisko	3
	356	analogia	1
	360	analuo	2
	362	anameno	1
	363	anamimneesko	6
	365	ananeoō	1
	366	ananeepho	1
	373	anapauo	12
	374	anapītho	1
	375	anapempo	4
	376	anapeeros	2
	377	anapipto	11
	378	anapleeroō	6
	380	anaptusso	1
	381	anapto	3
	383	anasīo	2
	384	anaskūazo	1
	385	anaspao	2
	388	anastauroō	1
	389	anastenazo	1
	390	anastrepho	11
	392	anatassomai	1
	393	anatello	9
	394	anatitheemi	2
	396	anatrepo	2
	397	anatrepho	3
	398	anaphainomai	2
	399	anaphero	10
	400	anaphōneo	1
	401	anakusis	1
	402	anakōreo	14
	404	anapsuko	1
	424	anerkomai	3
	426	anetazo	2
	429	anūrisko	2
	430	anekomai	15
	433	aneeko	3
	447	anieemi	4
	450	anisteemi	112
	455	anoiga	77
	461	anorthoō	3
	4874	sunamignumi	3
305		anabaino	81
	304	anabathmos	2
	4320	prosanabaino	1
	4872	sunanabaino	2
318		anankee	18
	315	anankazo	9
	316	anankaios	8
	1876	epanankes	1
331		anathema	6
	332	anathematizo	4
	2652	katanathema	2
363		anamimneesko	6
	364	anamneesis	4
	1878	epanamimneesko	1
373		anapauo	12
	372	anapausis	5
	1879	epanapauomai	2
	4875	sunanapauomai	1
378		anapleeroō	6
	466	antanapleeroō	1
	4322	prosanapleeroō	2
393		anatello	9
	395	anatolee	10
	1816	exanatello	2
394		anatitheemi	2
	331	anathema	6
	334	anatheema	1
	4323	prosanatitheemi	2
430		anekomai	15
	414	anaktoteros	6
	420	anexikakos	1
	463	anokee	2
435		aneer	215
	223	Alexandros	6
	405	andrapodistees	1
	406	Andreas	13
	407	andrizomai	1
	408	Andronikos	1
	409	androphonos	1
	444	anthrōpos	559
	5362	philandros	1
444		anthrōpos	559
	441	anthrōpareskos	2
	442	anthrōpinos	7
	443	anthrōpoktonos	3
	5364	philanthrōpōs	1
450		anisteemi	112
	386	anastasis	42
	387	anastatoō	3
	1817	exanisteemi	3
	1881	epanistamai	2
459		anomos	10
	458	anomia	15
	460	anomōs	2
467		antapodidōmi	7
	468	antapodoma	2
	469	antapodosis	1
473		anti	22
	368	anantirreetos	1
	436	anthisteemi	14
	437	anthomologeomai	1
	446	anthupatos	4
	464	antagonizomai	1
	465	antallagma	2
	466	antanapleeroō	1
	467	antapodidōmi	7
	470	antapokrinomai	2
	471	antepo	2
	472	antekomai	4
	474	antiballo	1
	475	antidiatithemenos	1
	476	antidikos	5
	477	antithesis	1
	478	antikathisteemi	1
	479	antikaleō	1
	480	antikimai	8
	481	antikru	1
	482	antilambanomai	3
	483	antilego	10
	486	antiloidoreo	1
	487	antilutron	1
	488	antimetreo	2
	489	antimisthia	2
	492	antiparerkomai	2
	493	Antipas	1
	495	antiperan	1
	496	antipipto	1
	497	antistratūomai	1
	498	antitassomai	5
	499	antitupon	2
	500	antikristos	5
	503	antophthalmeo	1
	507	ano	9
	528	apantao	7
	1725	enanti	1
	2658	katantao	14
	4876	sunantao	6
	5220	hupandros	1
	5221	hupantao	5
482		antilambanomai	3
	484	antileepsis	1
	4878	sunantilambanomai	2
507		ano	9
	508	anōgeon	2
	509	anōthen	13
	511	anōteron	2
	1883	epano	20
	5231	huperano	3
514		axios	41
	370	anaxios	1
	515	axioō	7
	516	axiōs	6
538		apatao	4
	539	apatee	7
	1818	exapatao	5
545		apīthees	6
	543	apīthia	7
	544	apītheo	16
546		apīleo	2
	547	apīlee	4
	4324	prosapīleomai	1
568		apeko	11
	566	apekī	1
	567	apekomai	6
571		apistos	23
	569	apisteo	7
	570	apistia	12
573		haplous	2
	572	haplotees	8
	574	haplōs	1
575		apo	656
	518	apangello	44
	519	apankomai	1
	520	apago	16
	522	apairomai	3
	523	apaiteo	2
	524	apalgeo	1
	525	apallasso	3
	526	apallotrioō	3
	528	apantao	7
	533	aparneomai	13
	534	aparti	1
	536	aparkee	8
	541	apaugasma	1
	548	apīmi	7
	549	apimi	1
	550	apīpin	1
	553	apekdekomai	7
	554	apekduomai	2
	556	apelao	1
	557	apelegmos	1
	558	apelutheros	1
	560	apelpizp	1
	561	apenanti	6
	565	aperkomai	120
	568	apeko	11
	576	apobaino	4
	577	apoballo	2
	578	apoblepo	1
	581	apogenomenos	1
	583	apographo	4
	584	apodīknumi	4
	586	apodekatoō	4
	588	apodekomai	6
	590	apodeemos	1
	591	apodidōmi	48
	592	apodiorizo	1
	593	apodokimazo	9
	597	apotheesaurizo	1
	598	apothlibo	1
	599	apothneesko	111
	600	apokathist-ao, -ano,-eemi	8
	601	apokalupto	26
	603	apokaradokia	2
	604	apokatallatto	3
	606	apokīmai	4
	607	apokephalizo	4
	608	apoklīo	1
	609	apokopto	6
	611	apokrinomai	249
	613	apokrupto	6

ROOT NO.	DRVT. NO.	TRANSLITERATION	FRQ.
575		apo (cont.)	
	615	apoktīno	75
	616	apokueo	2
	617	apolulizo	4
	618	apolambano	12
	619	apolausis	2
	620	apolīpo	6
	621	apolīko	1
	622	apollumi	92
	626	apologeomai	10
	628	apolouō	2
	629	apolutrōsis	10
	630	apoluo	69
	631	apomassomai	1
	632	aponemo	1
	633	aponipto	1
	634	apopipto	1
	635	apoplanao	2
	636	apopleo	4
	637	apopluno	1
	638	apopnigo	3
	641	aporripto	1
	642	aporphanizomai	1
	643	aposkūazomai	1
	644	aposkiasma	1
	645	apospao	4
	648	apostegazo	1
	649	apostello	133
	650	apostereo	6
	653	apostomatizo	1
	654	apostrepho	10
	655	apostugeo	1
	656	aposunagōgos	3
	657	apotassomai	6
	658	apoteleo	1
	659	apotitheemi	8
	660	apotinasso	2
	661	apotio	1
	662	apotolmaō	1
	664	apotomōs	2
	665	apotrepomai	1
	667	apophero	5
	668	apophūgo	3
	669	apopthengomai	3
	670	apophortizomai	1
	671	apokreesis	1
	672	apokōreo	3
	673	apokōrizomai	2
	674	apopsuko	1
	683	apōtheomai	6
	683	apōthomai	6
	851	aphaireo	10
	856	aphedrōn	2
	863	aphieemi	146
	864	aphikneomai	1
	868	aphisteemi	15
	871	aphomoi-oō	1
	872	aphoraō	2
	873	aphorizo	10
	874	aphormee	7
	879	aphupnoō	1
577		apoballo	2
	579	apobleetos	1
	580	apobolee	2
588		apodekomai	6
	587	apodektos	2
	594	apodokee	2
591		apodidōmi	48
	467	antapodidōmi	7
	3406	misthapodotees	1
611		apokrinomai	249
	470	antapokrinomai	2
	610	apokrima	1
	612	apokrisis	4
622		apollumi	92
	623	Apolluōn	1
	684	apōlia	20
	4881	sunapollumai	1
626		apologeomai	10
	379	anapologeetos	2
	627	apologia	8
639		aporeomai	4
	640	aporia	1
	1820	exaporeomai	2
649		apostello	133
	651	apostolee	4
	652	apostolos	81
	1821	exapostello	11
	4882	sunapostello	1
659		apotitheemi	8
	595	apothesis	2
	596	apotheekee	7
680		haptomai	36

ROOT NO.	DRVT. NO.	TRANSLITERATION	FRQ.
	860	haphee	2
	2358	thriambuo	2
	2510	kathapto	1
681		hapto	4
	381	anapto	3
	680	haptomai	36
696		arguros	5
	694	argurion	20
	695	argurokopos	1
	5366	philarguros	2
700		aresko	17
	441	anthrōpareskos	2
	699	areskīa	1
	701	arestos	4
705		arithmeo	3
	382	anarithmeetos	1
	2674	katarithmeomai	1
712		ariston	3
	708	Aristarkos	5
	709	aristaō	3
	710	aristeros	3
	711	Aristoboulos	1
714		arkeo	8
	713	arketos	8
	715	arktos	1
	842	autarkees	1
	1884	eparkeo	3
719		harmos	1
	718	harmozo	1
	4883	sunarmologeomai	2
726		harpazo	13
	724	harpagee	3
	725	harpagmos	1
	727	harpax	5
	2590	karpos	66
	2897	kraipalee	1
	4884	sunarpazo	4
737		arti	36
	534	aparti	1
	736	artemōn	1
	738	artigenneetos	1
	739	artios	1
739		artios	1
	1822	exartizo	2
	2675	katartizo	13
746		arkee	58
	744	arkaios	12
	747	arkeegos	4
	748	arkieratikos	1
	749	arkierūs	143
	750	arkipoimeen	1
	751	Arkippos	2
	752	arkisunagōgos	2
	753	arkitektōn	1
	754	arkitelōnees	1
	755	arkitriklinos	3
	775	Asiarkees	1
756		arkomai	184
	536	aparkee	8
	746	arkee	58
	1728	enarkomai	2
	5225	huparko	48
757		arko	2
	708	Aristarkos	5
	743	arkangelos	2
	745	Arkelaos	1
	756	arkomai	84
	758	arkōn	37
	1543	hekatontarkos	16
	1885	eparkia	2
	3966	patriarkees	4
	3980	pītharkeo	4
	4173	politarkees	2
	4759	stratopedarkees	1
	5076	tetrarkees	4
	5506	kiliarkos	22
765		asebees	9
	763	asebīa	6
	764	asebeo	2
772		asthenees	25
	769	asthenīa	24
	770	astheneo	36
773		Asia	19
	774	Asianos	1
	775	Asiarkees	1
792		asteer	24
	797	astrapto	2
	798	astron	4
797		astrapto	2
	796	astrapee	9
	1823	exastrapto	1
	1833	exetazo	3
	4015	periastrapto	2

ROOT NO.	DRVT. NO.	TRANSLITERATION	FRQ.
804		asphalees	5
	803	asphalīa	3
	805	asphalizo	3
	806	asphalōs	3
809		askeemōn	1
	807	askeemoneo	2
	808	askeemosunee	2
813		ataktos	1
	812	atakteo	1
	814	ataktōs	2
820		atimos	4
	818	atimazo	6
	819	atimia	7
	821	atimoō	1
827		augee	1
	826	augazo	1
	5081	teelaugōs	1
832		auleo	3
	63	agrauleo	1
	834	auleetees	2
833		aulee	12
	835	aulizomai	2
	4259	proaulion	1
837		auxano & auxo	22
	838	auxeesis	2
	4885	sunauxanomai	1
	5199	hugiees	14
	5232	huperauxanō	1
846		autos	5117
	829	authadees	2
	830	authairetos	2
	831	authenteo	1
	842	autarkees	1
	843	autokatakritos	1
	844	automatos	2
	845	autoptees	1
	847	autou	4
	849	autokīr	1
	1683	emautou,-to,-ton	37
	1824	exautees	6
	1888	epautophōro	1
	3778	houtoi	80
	3778	houtos	192
	3778	hautee	81
	3778	hautai	3
	3910	parautika	1
	4572	seautou,-to,-ton	40
	5024	tauta	247
	5367	philautos	1
	5615	hōsautōs	17
852		aphanees	1
	853	aphanizo	5
	869	aphno	3
906		ballo	125
	293	amphibleestron	2
	306	anaballomai	6
	474	antiballo	1
	577	apoballo	2
	956	belos	1
	957	beltion	1
	992	bleeteos	2
	1000	bolee	1
	1002	bolis	1
	1225	diaballomai	1
	1544	ekballo	82
	1685	emballo	1
	1911	epiballo	18
	2598	kataballo	3
	3036	lithoboleo	9
	3328	metaballomai	1
	3846	paraballo	2
	4016	periballo	24
	4261	proballo	2
	4657	skubalon	1
	4820	sumballo	6
	5235	huperballo	5
	5260	hupoballo	1
907		baptizo	80
	908	baptisma	22
	909	baptismos	4
	910	baptistees	14
911		bapto	3
	907	baptizo	80
	1686	embapto	3
916		bareo	6
	1912	epibareo	3
	2599	katabareo	1
922		baros	6
	4	abarees	1
	926	barus	6
926		barus	6
	916	bareo	6
	917	bareōs	2

ROOT NO.	DRVT. NO.	TRANSLITERATION	FRQ.
	925	baruno	1
	927	barutīmos	1
928		basanizo	12
	929	basanismos	6
	930	basanistees	1
935		basilūs	118
	932	basilīa	162
	934	basilīos	1
	936	basilūo	22
	937	basilikos	5
936		basilūo	21
	938	basilissa	4
	4821	sumbasilūo	2
939		basis	1
	305	anabaino	81
	307	anabibazo	1
	901	bathus	3
	902	bai-on	1
	922	baros	6
	931	basanos	3
	935	basilūs	118
	941	bastazo	27
	949	bebaios	9
	952	bebeelos	5
	968	beema	12
	1041	bōmos	1
	1224	diabaino	3
	1684	embaino	18
	1687	embatūo	1
	1910	epibaino	6
	1913	epibibazo	3
	2597	katabaino	80
	2601	katabibazomai	2
	3326	meta	473
	3327	metabaino	12
	3845	parabaino	4
	4260	probaino	5
	4819	sumbaino	8
	5233	huperbaino	1
948		bdelussomai	2
	946	bdelugma	6
	947	bdeluktos	1
950		bebaioō	8
	951	bebaiōsis	2
	1226	diabebaio-omai	2
970		bia	4
	971	biazomai	2
	972	biaios	1
971		biazomai	2
	973	biastees	1
	3849	parabiazomai	2
	4264	probibazo	2
977		brōsko	1
	1033	brōma	17
	1035	brōsis	11
	4598	seetobrotos	1
	4662	skoleekobiotos	1
979		bios	11
	980	bioō	1
	3969	Patrobas	1
980		bioō	1
	981	biōsis	1
	982	biōtikos	3
984		blapto	2
	983	blaberos	1
	989	blaspheemos	5
989		blaspheemos	5
	987	blaspheemeo	35
	988	blaspheemia	19
991		blepo	135
	308	anablepo	26
	578	apoblepo	1
	990	blemma	1
	1227	diablepo	2
	1689	emblepo	12
	1914	epiblepo	3
	4017	periblepo	7
	4265	problepo	1
994		boaō	11
	310	anaboao	3
	995	boee	1
	1916	epiboao	1
998		boeethos	1
	996	boeethīa	2
	997	boeetheo	8
1006		bosko	9
	1008	botanee	1
	1016	bous	8
1011		boulūomai	8
	1010	boulūtees	2
	3851	paraboulūomai	1
	4823	sumbaulūo	5

ROOT NO.	DRVT. NO.	TRANSLITERATION	FRQ.
1012		boulee	12
	711	Aristoboulos	1
	1011	boulūomai	8
	4825	sumboulos	1
1014		boulomai	35
	1012	boulee	12
	1013	bouleema	2
	1917	epiboulee	4
	2103	Ūboulos	1
1021		bradus	3
	1019	braduno	2
	1020	braduploeō	1
	1022	bradutees	1
1037		buthos	1
	12	abussos	9
	1036	buthizo	2
1053		Galatia	4
	1052	Galatai	1
	1054	Galatikos	2
1061		gamiskomai	1
	1547	ekgamizo	5
	1548	ekgamiskomai	2
1062		gamos	16
	22	agamos	4
	1060	gameo	29
	1061	gamiskomai	1
	1918	epigambrūo	1
1065		ge	11
	5	īge	5
	3304	menounge	4
1073		gemo	11
	1072	gemizo	9
	1117	gomos	3
1074		genea	42
	1075	genealogeomai	1
	1076	genealogia	2
	1078	genesis	3
	1079	genetee	1
1078		genesis	3
	1077	genesia	2
	3824	palingenesia	2
1080		gennao	97
	313	anagennao	2
	1081	genneema	9
	1083	genneesis	2
	1084	genneetos	2
1085		genos	21
	36	agenees	1
	241	allogenees	1
	1074	genea	42
	2225	zōogoneo	2
	4773	sungenees	12
1092		geōrgos	19
	1090	geōrgeomai	1
	1091	geōrgion	1
1093		gee	252
	508	anōgeon	2
	1069	gīton	4
	1092	geōrgos	19
	1919	epigīos	7
1096		ginomai	677
	581	apogenomenos	1
	1085	genos	21
	1118	gonūs	19
	1135	gunee	221
	1549	ekgona	1
	1920	epiginomai	1
	2061	Hermogenees	1
	2104	ūgenees	3
	3439	monogenees	9
	4266	proginomai	1
	5041	teknogoneo	1
1097		ginōsk-ō & -omai	223
	303	anaginōsko	33
	1106	gnōmee	9
	1107	gnōrizo	24
	1108	gnōsis	29
	1109	gnōstees	1
	1110	gnōstos	15
	1231	diaginōsko	2
	1921	epiginōsko	42
	2589	kardiognōstees	89
	2607	kataginōsko	3
	3563	nous	24
	3686	onoma	230
	4267	proginōsko	5
	4774	sungnōmee	1
1100		glōssa	50
	1101	glōssokomon	2
	2084	heteroglōssos	1
1107		gnōrizo	24
	319	anagnōrizomai	1
	1232	diagnōrizo	1

ROOT NO.	DRVT. NO.	TRANSLITERATION	FRQ.
1111		gonguzo	8
	1112	gongusmos	5
	1113	gongustees	1
1121		gramma	15
	61	agrammatos	1
	1122	grammatūs	67
1125		grapho	194
	583	apographo	4
	1121	gramma	15
	1123	graptos	1
	1124	graphee	51
	1449	engrapho	2
	1924	epigrapho	5
	4270	prographo	5
	5261	hupogrammos	1
	5498	kīrographon	1
1131		gumnos	15
	1128	gumnazo	4
	1130	gumneetūmai	1
	1132	gumnotees	3
1135		gunee	221
	1133	gunaikarion	1
	1134	gunaikīos	1
1137		gōnia	9
	204	akrogōniaios	2
	5068	tetragōnos	1
1142		daimōn	5
	1139	diamonizomai	13
	1140	daimonion	60
	1141	daimoniōdees	1
	1174	dīsidaimonia	1
1159		dapanao	5
	1550	ekdapano	1
	4325	prosdapanao	1
1160		dapanee	1
	77	adapanos	1
	1159	dapanao	5
	1173	dīpnon	16
	1174	dīsidaimonesteros	1
1161		de	398
	1490	ī de meege	14
	3366	meede	57
	3592	hode,heede,tode	12
	3761	oude	137
	5107	toisde	1
1166		dīkno-o & -umi	33
	322	anadīknumi	2
	584	apodīknumi	4
	1164	dīgma	1
	1380	dokeo	63
	1731	endiknumi	11
	1925	epidīknumi	9
	5263	hupodīknumi	6
1169		dīlos	3
	1167	dīlia	1
	1171	dīnos	2
	1174	dīsidaimonia	1
1176		deka	27
	1147	daktulos	8
	1177	dekadao	2
	1178	dekapente	3
	1179	Dekapolis	3
	1180	dekatessares	5
	1182	dekatos	3
	1427	dodeka	72
	1440	hebdomeekonta	5
	1733	hendeka	6
1182		dekatos	3
	1181	dekatee	4
	4003	pentekaidekatos	1
	5065	tessareskaidekatos	2
1189		deomai	22
	1162	de-eesis	19
	4326	prosdeomai	1
1196		desmeo	1
	1195	desmūo	2
	1197	desmee	1
	1230	diaginomai	3
1199		ho desmos & ta desma	20
	1196	desmeo	1
	1198	desmios	16
	1200	desmophulax	3
	1201	desmōteerion	4
	1202	desmotees	2
	4884	sundesmos	4
1208		dūteros	43
	1206	dūteraios	1
	1207	duteroprōtos	1
1209		dekomai	59
	324	anadekomai	2
	588	apodekomai	6
	1184	dektos	5
	1188	dexios	73

ROOT NO.	DRVT. NO.	TRANSLITERATION	FRQ.
	1237	diadekomai	1
	1403	dokee	2
	1523	īsdekomai	1
	1551	ekdekomai	8
	1735	endeketai	1
	1926	epidekomai	2
	3580	xenodokeo	1
	3829	pandokīon	1
	3858	paradekomai	5
	4327	prosdekomai	14
1210		deo	44
	1163	dī	105
	1189	deomai	22
	1199	ho demos & ta desma	20
	1203	despotees	10
	1218	deemos	4
	1238	diadeema	3
	1401	doulos	125
	1729	ende-ees	1
	2611	katadeo	1
	4019	perideomai	1
	5264	hupodekomai	4
1211		dee	6
	1221	deepote	1
	1894	epīdee	11
	2235	eedee	59
1212		deelos	4
	82	adeelos	1
	1213	deeloō	7
	1552	ekdeelos	1
	2612	katadeelos	1
	4271	prodeelos	3
1218		deemos	4
	590	apodeemos	1
	1215	deemeegoreo	1
	1219	deemosios	4
	1553	ekdeemeo	3
	1739	endomeesis	1
	1927	epideemeo	2
	3530	Nikodeemos	5
1223		dia	640
	88	adialiptos	2
	592	apodiorizo	1
	1224	diabaino	3
	1225	diaballomai	1
	1226	diabebaio-omai	2
	1227	diablepo	2
	1229	diangello	3
	1230	diaginomai	3
	1231	diaginōsko	2
	1235	diagreegoreo	1
	1236	diago	2
	1237	diadekomai	1
	1238	diadeema	3
	1239	diadidōmi	5
	1241	diazōnnumi	3
	1244	diaireo	2
	1245	diakatharizo	2
	1246	diakatelenkomai	1
	1251	diakou-omai	1
	1252	diakrino	19
	1254	diakōluo	2
	1255	dialaleo	2
	1256	dialegomai	13
	1257	dialīpo	1
	1259	diallattomai	1
	1260	dialogizomai	16
	1262	dialuomai	1
	1263	diamarturomai	15
	1264	diamakomai	1
	1265	diameno	5
	1266	diamerizo	12
	1555	ekdieegeomai	2
1249		diakonos	30
	1247	diakoneo	37
	1248	diakonia	34
1252		diakrino	19
	87	adiakritos	1
	1253	diakrisis	3
1303		diatithemai	7
	475	antidiatithemenos	1
	1242	diatheekee	33
1320		didaskalos	58
	2085	heterodidaskaleo	2
	2567	kalodidaskalos	1
	3547	nomodidaskalos	3
	5572	psūdodidaskalos	1
1325		didōmi	413
	325	anadidōmi	1
	591	apodidōmi	48
	1156	danīon	1
	1239	diadidōmi	5

ROOT NO.	DRVT. NO.	TRANSLITERATION	FRQ.
	1390	doma	4
	1394	dosis	2
	1395	dotees	1
	1554	ekdidōmi	4
	1560	ekdotos	1
	1929	epididōmi	11
	2624	katakleerodoteo	1
	3330	metadidōmi	5
	3860	paradidōmi	121
	4272	prodidōmi	1
1349		dikee	4
	94	adikos	12
	476	antidikos	5
	1558	ekdikos	2
	1738	endikos	3
	2613	katadikazo	5
	2993	Laodikīa	5
	5267	hupodikos	1
1364		dis	6
	1250	diakosioi	8
	1324	Didumos	3
1377		diōko	44
	1559	ekdioko	2
	2614	katadiōko	1
1380		dokeo	63
	603	apokaradokia	2
	1378	dogma	5
	1391	doxa	168
	2106	ūdokeo	21
	2107	ūdokia	9
1388		dolos	12
	97	adolos	1
	1185	deleazo	3
1391		doxa	168
	1741	endoxos	4
	2755	kenodoxous	1
	3861	paradoxos	1
1401		doulos	125
	1396	doulagōgeo	1
	1398	doulūo	25
	1399	doulee	3
	1400	doulon	2
	1402	douloō	8
	4889	sundoulos	10
1410		dunamai	210
	1411	dunamis	120
	1413	dunastees	3
	1415	dunatos	35
1415		dunatos	35
	102	adunatos	10
	1414	dunateo	1
1416		duno & dumi	2
	931	epiduo	1
	1424	dusmee	5
	1562	ekduo	5
	3601	odunee	2
	3821	parīsduno	1
1417		duo	135
	1177	dekadao	2
	1208	dūteros	43
	1427	dōdeka	72
1418		dus-	
	1419	dusbastaktos	2
	1420	dusenteria	1
	1421	dusermeenūtos	1
	1422	duskolos	1
	1426	duspheemia	1
1427		dōdeka	72
	1428	dōdekato	1
	1429	dōdekaphulon	1
1435		dōron	19
	734	Artemis	1
	1431	dōrea	11
	1433	dōreo	3
	2211	Zeenas	1
	3564	Numphas	1
1437		ean	341
	302	an	191
	2579	kan	13
	3362	ean mee	60
1439		eao	13
	1436	ea	2
	4330	proseao	1
1443		Heber	1
	1444	Hebraikos	1
	1445	Hebraios	4
	1446	Hebraīs	3
1451		engus	30
	1448	engizo	43
	1452	enguteron	1
1453		egīro	141
	1127	greegoreo	23
	1454	egersis	1

ROOT NO.	DRVT. NO.	TRANSLITERATION	FRQ.
1453		egīro (cont.)	
	1825	exegīro	2
	1892	epegīro	2
	4891	sunegīro	1
1458		enkaleo	7
	410	anenkleetos	5
	1462	enkleema	2
1468		enkratees	1
	1466	enkratīa	4
	1467	enkratūomai	2
1473		ego	370
	1699	emos	78
	2248	heemas	178
	2249	heemis	127
	2254	heemin	177
	2257	heemōn	410
	2504	kago,kamoi,kame	72
1476		hedraios	3
	856	aphedrōn	2
	1475	edaphos	1
	1477	hedraiōma	1
	1747	enedra	1
	1749	enedron	1
	2272	heesukios	2
	2515	kathedra	3
	2516	kathezomai	6
	4332	prosedrūo	1
	4892	sunedrion	22
1484		ethnos	164
	1481	ethnarkees	1
	1482	ethnikos	2
1485		ethos	12
	1480	ethizo	1
	2239	eethos	1
1486		īōtha	4
	1484	ethnos	164
	1485	ethos	12
1487		ī, from īmi	310
	1437	ean	341
	1489	īge	5
	1490	i de mee & i de meege	14
	1499	ī kan	22
	1508	ī mee	92
	1512	ī per	6
	1513	ī pōs	4
	1535	īte	65
	1536	ītis	79
	1893	epī	27
	5616	hosī	34
	5619	hōsperī	1
1491		īdos	5
	1126	graōdees	1
	1497	īdōlon	11
	2264	Heerōdees	44
	2306	thīōdees	1
	4075	petrōdees	14
	5472	kalkeedon	1
1492		īdeo, īdo, oida	663
	86	hadees	11
	127	aidōs	2
	1491	īdos	5
	1896	ephorao	2
	2396	ide	27
	2397	idea	1
	2400	idou	213
	2470	isos	8
	2477	historeo	1
	4275	proīdeo	2
	4894	sunīdeo	14
	5237	huperīdo	1
1497		īdōlon	11
	712	katīdōlos	1
	1493	īdōlīon	1
	1494	īdōlothuton	10
	1495	īdōlolatrīa	4
	1496	īdōlolatrees	7
1503		īko	2
	1504	īkōn	23
	1933	epi-īkees	5
1507		hīlisso	1
	257	halōn	2
	1667	helisso	1
	1750	enīleo	1
1510		īmi	141
	548	apīmi	7
	1488	ī	92
	1498	īeen, īees, īee	12
	1511	īnaī	126
	1526	īsi	163
	1751	enīmi	1
	2070	esmen	53
	2071	esomai, etc.	193

ROOT NO.	DRVT. NO.	TRANSLITERATION	FRQ.
	2075	este	92
	2076	esti	906
	2258	een,ees,eestha	454
	2277	eeto	2
	2468	isthi	5
	3603	ho esti	11
	3689	ontōs	10
	3918	parīmi	23
	4041	periousios	1
	4895	sunīmi	3
	5600	ō, ees, ee	166
	5607	ōn, ousa, on	154
1515		īreenee	92
	1514	īreenūo	4
	1516	īreenikos	2
	1517	īreenopoyeō	1
1519		īs	1773
	1521	īsago	10
	1522	īsakouo	5
	1523	īsdekomai	1
	1524	īsīmi	4
	1525	īserkomai	198
	1528	īskaleo	1
	1529	īsodos	5
	1530	īspeedao	1
	1531	īsporūomai	17
	1532	īstreko	1
	1533	īsphero	7
	2072	esoptron	2
	2080	eso	8
	3921	parīsduno	1
	4657	skubalon	1
1520		hīs, hen	271
	1527	hīs kath hīs	2
	1733	hendeka	6
	1775	henotees	2
	3367	meedīs, meedemia, meeden	92
	3391	mia	80
	3762	oudīs	235
1521		īsago	10
	1898	epīsagōgee	1
	3819	parīsago	1
1525		īserkomai	198
	3922	parīserkomai	2
	4897	sunīserkomai	2
1537		ek, ex	921
	421	anexikniastos	2
	1544	ekballo	82
	1545	ekbasis	2
	1547	ekgamizo	5
	1548	ekgamiskomai	2
	1549	ekgona	1
	1550	ekdapano	1
	1551	ekdekomai	8
	1552	ekdeelos	1
	1553	ekdeemeo	3
	1554	ekdidōmi	4
	1555	ekdieegeomai	2
	1558	ekdikos	2
	1559	ekdioko	2
	1560	ekdotos	1
	1562	ekduo	5
	1567	ekzeeteo	7
	1569	ekthambos	1
	1570	ekthetos	1
	1571	ekkathairo	2
	1573	ekkakeo	6
	1574	ekkenteo	2
	1575	ekklazo	3
	1577	ekkleesia	115
	1577	ekklīo	2
	1578	ekklino	3
	1579	ekkolumbao	1
	1580	ekkopto	11
	1582	ekkremamai	1
	1583	eklaleo	1
	1584	eklampo	1
	1585	eklanthanomai	1
	1586	eklegomai	21
	1587	eklīpo	3
	1590	ekluo	6
	1591	ekmasso	5
	1592	ekmukteerizo	2
	1593	eknūo	1
	1594	ekneepho	1
	1597	ekpalai	2
	1598	ekpīrozo	4
	1599	ekpempo	2
	1600	ekpetannumi	1
	1601	ekpipto	13
	1602	ekpleo	3
	1603	ekpleeroō	1

ROOT NO.	DRVT. NO.	TRANSLITERATION	FRQ.
	1605	ekpleesso	13
	1606	ekpneo	3
	1607	ekporūomai	34
	1608	ekpornūo	1
	1609	ekptuo	1
	1610	ekrizoō	4
	1612	ekstrephomai	1
	1613	ektarasso	1
	1614	ektīno	16
	1615	ekteleo	2
	1620	ektitheemi	4
	1621	ektinasso	2
	1622	hekos	9
	1624	ektrepomai	5
	1625	ektrepho	2
	1626	ektrōma	1
	1627	ekphero	7
	1628	ekphūgo	7
	1629	ekphobeo	1
	1630	ekphobos	2
	1631	ekphuo	2
	1632	ekkuno	10
	1632	ekkeo	18
	1633	ekkōreo	1
	1634	ekpsuko	3
	1804	exangello	1
	1805	exagorazo	4
	1806	exago	13
	1807	exaireo	8
	1808	exairo	2
	1809	exaiteoman	1
	1810	exaiphnees	5
	1811	exakoloutheo	3
	1813	exalīpho	5
	1814	exallomai	1
	1816	exanatello	2
	1817	exanisteemi	3
	1818	exapatao	5
	1819	exapina	1
	1820	exaporeomai	2
	1821	exapastello	11
	1822	exartizo	2
	1823	exastrapto	1
	1824	exautees	6
	1825	exegīro	2
	1826	exīmi	4
	1827	exelenko	1
	1828	exelkomai	1
	1829	exorama	1
	1830	exerūnao	1
	1831	exerkomai	222
	1833	exetazo	3
	1834	exeegeomai	6
	1837	exeekeomai	1
	1839	existeemi	17
	1840	exiskuo	1
	1841	exodus	3
	1842	exolothrūomai	1
	1843	exomologeomai	11
	1844	exorkizo	1
	1846	exorutto	2
	1847	exoudenoō	1
	1851	exokee	1
	1853	exupnos	1
	1854	exo	65
	1856	exōtho	2
1540		hekaton	17
	1250	diakosioi	8
	1541	hekatontaetees	1
	1542	hekatontaplasiōn	3
	1543	hekatontarkos	16
	1812	hexakosioi	2
	4001	pentakosioi	2
	5071	tetrakosioi,-sia	4
	5145	triakosioi	2
1551		ekdekomai	8
	553	apekedkomai	7
	1561	ekdokee	1
1553		ekdeemeo	3
	3923	parīsphero	1
	4898	sunekdeemos	2
1563		ekī	98
	1564	ekīthen	27
	1565	ekīnos	251
	1566	ekīse	2
	2546	kakī	11
1565		ekīnos	251
	1900	epekīna	1
	2548	kakīnos	23
	5238	huperekīna	1
1586		eklegomai	21
	1588	eklektos	23
	1589	eklogee	7

ROOT NO.	DRVT. NO.	TRANSLITERATION	FRQ.
	4899	sunekleklōs	1
1614		ektīno	16
	1618	ektenees	2
	1901	epektīnomai	1
	5239	huperktīno	1
1618		ektenees	2
	1616	ektenīa	1
	1617	ektenesteron	1
	1619	ektenōs	1
1632		ekkuno	10
	130	haimatekkusia	1
	5240	huperekkunomai	1
1635		hekōn	2
	210	akōn	1
	1595	hekousios	1
	1596	hekousios	2
1636		elaia	15
	65	agrielaios	2
	1637	elaion	12
	1638	elaiōn	1
	2565	kallielaios	1
1640		elassōn & elattōn	4
	1641	elattoneo	1
	1642	elattoō	3
	1645	elaphros	2
1643		elauno	5
	556	apelao	1
	4900	sunelauno	1
1651		elenko	17
	557	apelgmos	1
	1246	diakatelenkomai	1
	1649	elenxis	1
	1650	elenkos	2
	1827	exelenko	1
1656		eleos	28
	1652	ele-īnos	2
	1653	eleeo	31
	1654	ele-eemosunee	14
1658		elūtheros	23
	558	apelutheros	1
	1657	elūtheria	11
	1659	elūtheroō	7
1670		helkuo	6
	1668	helkos	3
	1828	exelkomai	1
1672		Helleen	27
	1673	Helleenikos	2
	1674	Helleenis	2
	1675	Helleenistees	3
1679		elpizo	31
	560	apelpizo	1
	4276	proelpizo	1
1691		eme	88
	1699	emos	78
	3165	me	301
1698		emoi	95
	1699	emos	78
	3427	moi	241
1700		emou	109
	1683	emautou,-to,-ton	37
	1699	emos	78
	3450	mou	586
1702		empaizo	13
	1701	empaigmos	1
	1703	empaiktai	2
1722		en	2781
	1449	engrapho	2
	1450	enguos	1
	1455	enkathetos	1
	1456	enkainia	1
	1458	enkaleo	7
	1459	enkatalīpo	9
	1460	ankatoikeo	1
	1461	enkentrizo	6
	1463	enkombo-omai	1
	1465	enkopto	5
	1468	enkratees	1
	1469	enkrino	1
	1470	enkrupto	2
	1471	enkuos	1
	1472	enkrio	1
	1677	ellogeo	2
	1684	embaino	18
	1685	emballo	1
	1686	embapto	3
	1687	embatūo	1
	1688	embibazo	1
	1689	emblepo	12
	1690	embrimaomai	5
	1693	emmainomai	1
	1696	emmeno	3
	1702	empaizo	13
	1704	emperipateo	1

ROOT NO.	DRVT. NO.	TRANSLITERATION	FRQ.
1722		en (cont.)	
	1705	empleetho	4
	1705	empiplao	1
	1706	empipto	7
	1707	empleko	2
	1709	empneo	1
	1710	emporūomai	2
	1713	emporos	5
	1714	empreetho	1
	1715	emprosthen	48
	1716	emptuo	6
	1717	emphanees	2
	1719	emphobos	6
	1720	emphusao	1
	1721	emphutos	1
	1723	enankalizomai	2
	1724	enalios	1
	1725	enanti	1
	1728	enarkomai	2
	1729	ende-ees	1
	1731	endiknumi	11
	1735	endeketai	1
	1738	endikos	2
	1739	endomeesis	1
	1741	endoxos	4
	1747	enedra	1
	1747	enedron	1
	1756	energees	3
	1757	enūlogeomai	2
	1758	eneko	3
	1759	enthade	8
	1760	enthumeomai	3
	1764	enisteemi	7
	1765	eniskuo	2
	1770	ennūo	1
	1771	ennoia	2
	1772	ennomos	2
	1774	enoikeo	5
	1776	enkleo	1
	1779	entaphiazo	2
	1781	entellomai	17
	1784	entimos	5
	1786	entopios	1
	1787	entos	2
	1788	entrepo,-omai	9
	1790	entromos	3
	1793	entunkano	5
	1794	entulitto	3
	1795	entupoō	1
	1796	enubrizo	1
	1798	enupnion	1
	1799	enōpian	97
	1801	enōtizomai	1
1725		enanti	1
	561	apenanti	6
	713	katenanti	5
	1727	enantios	8
1727		enantios	8
	1726	enantion	5
	5227	hupenantios	2
1731		endīknumi	11
	1730	endīgma	1
	1732	endīxis	4
1746		enduo	28
	1737	endiduskomai	2
	1902	ependuomai	2
1756		energees	3
	1753	energīa	8
	1754	energeo	21
1767		ennea	1
	1766	ennatos	10
	1768	enneneekontaennea	4
1772		ennomos	2
	1750	enīleo	1
	1751	enīmi	1
1781		entellomai	17
	1778	entalma	3
	1785	entolee	71
1793		entunkano	5
	1783	entūxis	2
	5241	huperentunkano	1
1803		hex	13
	1623	ektos	14
	1812	hexakosioi	2
	1835	hexeekonta	9
1854		exo	65
	1855	exōthen	11
	1857	exōteros	3
1861		epangellomai	15
	1860	epangelia	53
	1863	epago	3
	4279	proepangellomai	1
1893		epī	27

ROOT NO.	DRVT. NO.	TRANSLITERATION	FRQ.
	1894	epīdee	11
	1897	epīper	1
1909		epi	895
	422	anepaiskuntos	1
	1861	epangellomai	15
	1864	epagōnizomai	1
	1867	epaineo	6
	1868	epainos	11
	1869	epairo	19
	1870	epaiskunomai	12
	1871	epaiteo	1
	1872	epakoloutheo	4
	1873	epakouo	1
	1874	epakroaomai	1
	1875	epan	3
	1876	epanankes	1
	1877	epanago	3
	1878	epanamimneesko	1
	1879	epanapauomai	2
	1880	epanerkomai	2
	1881	epanistamai	2
	1882	epanorthōsis	1
	1883	epano	20
	1884	eparkeo	3
	1885	eparkia	2
	1886	epaulis	1
	1887	epaulis	17
	1888	epautophōro	1
	1890	epaphrizo	1
	1891	Epaphroditos	2
	1892	epegīro	2
	1893	epī	27
	1896	ephorao	2
	1898	epīsagōgee	1
	1899	epīta	16
	1900	epekīna	1
	1901	epektīnomai	1
	1902	ependuomai	2
	1904	eperkomai	10
	1905	eperotao	59
	1907	epeko	5
	1908	epeereazo	3
	1910	epibaino	6
	1911	epiballo	18
	1912	epibareo	3
	1913	epibibazo	3
	1914	epiblepo	3
	1916	epiboao	1
	1917	epiboulee	4
	1918	epigambrūo	1
	1919	epigīos	7
	1920	epiginomai	1
	1921	epiginōsko	42
	1924	epigrapho	5
	1925	epidīknumi	9
	1926	epidekomai	2
	1927	epideemeo	2
	1928	epidiatassomai	1
	1929	epididōmi	11
	1931	epiduo	1
	1933	epi-īkees	5
	1934	epīzeeteo	14
	1935	epithanatios	1
	1937	epithumeo	16
	1940	epikathizo	1
	1941	epikaleomai	32
	1943	epikalupto	1
	1944	epikataratos	3
	1945	epikīmai	7
	1947	epikouria	1
	1948	epikrino	1
	1949	epilambanomai	19
	1950	epilanthanomai	8
	1951	epilegomai	2
	1952	epilīpo	1
	1954	epiloipos	1
	1956	epiluo	2
	1957	epimartureo	1
	1959	epimeleomai	3
	1961	epimeno	18
	1962	epinūo	1
	1963	epinoia	1
	1965	epiorkos	1
	1966	epiousa	5
	1967	epiousios	2
	1968	epipipto	13
	1969	epipleetto	1
	1970	epipnigo	1
	1971	epipotheo	9
	1973	epipotheetos	1
	1975	epiporūomai	1
	1976	epirrapto	1
	1977	epirripto	2

ROOT NO.	DRVT. NO.	TRANSLITERATION	FRQ.
	1978	episeemos	2
	1979	episitismos	1
	1980	episkeptomai	11
	1981	episkeenoō	1
	1982	episkiazo	5
	1983	episkopeo	2
	1985	episkopos	5
	1986	epispaomai	1
	1988	epistatees	7
	1989	epistello	3
	1991	episteerizo	4
	1993	epistomizo	1
	1994	epistrepho	39
	1996	episunago	7
	1998	episuntreko	1
	1999	episustasis	2
	2000	episphalees	1
	2001	episkuo	1
	2002	episōrūo	1
	2004	epitasso	10
	2005	epiteleo	11
	2007	epititheemi	42
	2009	epitimia	1
	2010	epitrepo	19
	2012	epitropos	3
	2013	epitunkano	5
	2014	epiphaino	4
	2018	epiphero	5
	2019	epiphōneo	3
	2021	epikireo	3
	2022	epikeo	1
	2023	epikoreegeo	5
	2025	epikrio	2
	2026	epoikodomeo	8
	2027	epokello	1
	2028	eponomazomai	1
	2029	epoptūo	2
	2030	epoptees	1
	2032	epouranios	2
	2177	ephallomai	1
	2178	ephapax	5
	2182	ephūretees	1
	2184	epheemoros	1
	2185	ephikneomai	2
	2186	ephisteemi	21
1937		epithumeo	16
	1938	epithumeetees	1
	1939	epithumia	38
1959		epimeleomai	3
	1958	epimelīa	1
	1960	epimelōs	1
1971		epipotheo	9
	1972	epipotheesis	2
	1973	epipotheetos	1
	1974	epipothia	1
2014		epiphaino	4
	2016	epiphanees	1
	2017	epiphauo	1
2031		epos	1
	2261	eepios	2
	3516	neepios	14
2033		hepta	87
	1442	hebdomos	9
	2034	heptakis	4
2036		epo	976
	471	antepo	2
	550	apīpīn	1
	2031	epos	1
	2046	ereo	71
	4277	proēpo	3
2038		ergazomai	39
	2716	katergazomai	24
	4020	periergazomai	1
	4333	prosergazomai	1
2041		ergon	176
	14	agathoergeo	1
	289	ampelourgos	1
	692	argos	8
	1092	geōrgos	19
	1093	geōrgos	19
	1756	energees	3
	2038	ergazomai	39
	2040	ergatees	16
	2410	hierourgeo	1
	2557	kakourgos	4
	3011	litourgos	5
	3835	panourgos	1
	4021	periergos	2
	4904	sunergos	3
	4943	sunupourgeo	1
2046		ereo	71
	2036	epo	976
	2045	erūnao	6

ROOT NO.	DRVT. NO.	TRANSLITERATION	FRQ.
	2060	Hermees	2
	2065	erōtao	58
	2463	iris	20
	4280	proereo	9
2048		ereemos (subst.)	35
2048		ereemos (adj.)	15
	2047	ereemia	4
	2049	ereemoō	5
	2263	eeremos	1
2054		eris	9
	2042	erethizo	2
	2051	erizo	1
2059		hermeenūo	4
	1421	dusermeenūtos	1
	3177	methermeenūomai	7
2060		Hermees	2
	2057	Hermas	1
	2058	hermeenia	2
	2059	hermeenūo	5
	2061	Hermogenees	1
2064		erkomai	642
	424	anerkomai	3
	565	aperkomai	120
	1525	īserkomai	198
	1831	exerkomai	222
	1904	eperkomai	10
	2718	katerkomai	13
	3928	parerkomai	31
	4022	perierkomai	4
	4281	proerkomai	9
	4334	proserkomai	86
	4905	sunerkomai	32
2068		esthio	65
	2719	katesthio	6
	3523	neestis	2
	3599	odous	12
	4906	sunesthio	5
2087		heteros	99
	2084	heterglōssos	1
	2085	heterodidaskaleo	2
	2086	heterozugeo	1
	2088	heterōs	1
2089		eti	119
	3371	meeketi	21
	3765	ouketi or ouk eti	48
2090		hetoimazo	40
	2091	hetoimasia	1
	2141	ūporeomai	1
	4282	proetoimazo	2
2092		hetoimos	17
	2090	hetoimazo	40
	2093	hetoimōs	3
2094		etos	49
	1541	hekatontaetees	1
	5063	tessarakontaetees	2
	5148	trietia	1
2095		ū	6
	2097	ūangelizo,-omai	55
	2098	ūangelion	77
	2101	ūarestos	3
	2103	Ūboulos	1
	2104	ūgenees	3
	2105	ūdia	1
	2106	ūdokeo	21
	2107	ūdokia	9
	2110	ūergetees	1
	2111	ūthetos	3
	2115	ūthumos	2
	2117	ūthus	8
	2117	ūthus (adv.)	8
	2121	ūkairos	2
	2123	ūkopoteros	7
	2126	ūlabees	3
	2127	ūlogeo	44
	2129	ūlogia	16
	2130	ūmetadotos	1
	2131	Ūnīkee	1
	2132	ūnoeo	1
	2133	ūnoia	2
	2137	ūodoumai	4
	2138	ūpīthees	1
	2139	ūperistatos	1
	2140	ūpoiya	1
	2143	ūprepia	1
	2144	ūprosdektos	5
	2145	ūprosedros	1
	2146	ūprosōpeo	1
	2152	ūsebees	4
	2154	ūseemos	1
	2155	ūsplanknos	2
	2158	ūskeemōn	5
	2159	ūtonos	2
	2160	ūtrapelia	1

ROOT NO.	DRVT. NO.	TRANSLITERATION	FRQ.
2095		ū (cont.)	
	2161	ūtukos	1
	2163	ūpheemos	1
	2164	ūphoreo	1
	2165	ūphraino,-omai	14
	2170	ūkaristos	1
	2173	ūkreestos	3
	2175	ūōdia	3
	2176	ūōnumos	10
	4910	sunūōkeomai	2
2097		ūangelizo,-omai	55
	2099	ūangelistees	3
	4283	proūangelizomai	1
2101		ūarestos	3
	2100	ūaresteo	3
	2102	ūarestōs	1
2110		ūergetees	1
	2108	ūergesia	2
	2109	ūergeteo	1
2117		ūthus	8
	2112	ūtheōs	80
	2113	ūthudromeo	2
	2116	ūthuno	2
	2118	ūthutees	1
2121		ūkairos	2
	2119	ūkaireo	3
	2120	ūkairia	2
	2122	ūkairōs	2
2126		ūlabees	3
	2124	ūlabiā	2
	2125	ūlabeomai	2
2127		ūlogeo	44
	1757	enūlogeomai	2
	2128	ūlogeetos	8
2147		hurisko	178
	429	anūrisko	2
	2182	ephūretees	1
2152		ūsebees	4
	2150	ūsebīa	15
	2151	ūsebeo	2
	2153	ūsebōs	2
2158		uskeemōn	5
	2156	ūskeemonōs	3
	2157	ūskeemosunee	1
2170		ūkaristos	1
	2168	ūkaristeo	39
	2169	ūkaristia	15
2172		ūkomai	7
	2171	ūkee	3
	4336	prosūkomai	87
2181		Ephesos	15
	2179	Ephesinos	1
	2180	Ephesios	5
2186		ephisteemi	21
	1987	epistamai	14
	2721	katephisteemi	1
	4911	sunephisteemi	1
2192		eko	709
	430	anekomai	15
	471	antekomai	4
	568	apeko	11
	809	askeemōn	1
	1758	eneko	3
	1836	hexees	5
	1838	hexis	1
	1851	exokee	1
	1907	epeko	5
	2078	eskatos	58
	2135	ūnoukos	8
	2272	heesukios	2
	2558	kakoukoumenos	2
	2722	kateko	19
	3348	meteko	8
	3562	nounekōs	1
	3793	oklos	175
	3930	pareko	16
	4023	perieko	3
	4123	pleonektees	4
	4283	proëkomai	1
	4337	proseko	24
	4465	rabdoukos	2
	4910	sunūōkeomai	2
	4912	suneko	12
	4975	skedon	3
	4976	skeema	2
	4981	skolee	2
	5242	hupereko	5
	5254	hupeko	1
2198		zaō	142
	326	anazao	5
	2221	zōgreo	2
	2222	zōee	134
	2225	zōogoneo	2
	2226	zōon	23
	2227	zōopoieo	12
	4800	suzao	3
2203		Zūs	2
	1359	Dioskouroi	1
	1361	Diotrephees	1
	2105	ūdia	1
	2211	Zeenas	1
2204		zeo	2
	2200	zestos	4
	2205	zeelos	17
	2219	zumee	13
2206		zeeloō	12
	2207	zeelōtees	5
	3863	parazeeloō	4
2212		zeeteo	119
	327	anazeeteo	2
	1567	ekzeeteo	7
	1934	epizeeteo	14
	2213	zeeteema	5
	2214	zeeteesis	6
	4802	suzeeteo	10
2218		zugos	6
	2086	heterozugeo	1
	2201	zūgos	2
	2202	zūkteeria	1
	5268	hupozugion	2
2219		zumee	13
	106	azumos	9
	2220	zumoō	4
2224		zōnnuo	2
	328	anazōnnumi	1
	1241	diazōnnumi	3
	4024	perizōnnumi	7
	5269	hupozōnnumi	1
2228		ee	357
	2229	ee meen	1
	2235	eedee	59
	2260	eeper	1
	2273	eetoi	1
2232		heegemōn	22
	2230	heegemonūo	2
	2231	heegemonia	1
2233		heegeomai	28
	1555	ekdieegeomai	2
	1834	exeegeomai	6
	2232	heegemōn	22
	2519	katheegeetees	3
	3595	hodeegos	5
	4285	proeegeomai	1
	4755	strateegos	10
2237		heedonee	5
	780	asmenōs	2
	829	authadees	2
	2234	heedeos	4
	2236	heedista	2
	4913	suneedomai	1
	5369	phileedonos	1
2240		heeko	27
	433	aneeko	3
	2520	katheekon	2
2245		heelikos	2
	2244	heelikia	8
	5082	teelikoutos	4
2250		heemera	389
	2184	epheemeros	1
	2522	katheemerinos	1
	3314	meseembria	2
	3574	nuktheemeron	1
	3637	oktaeemeros	1
	4594	seemeron	41
2255		heemisu	5
	2253	heemithanees	1
	2256	heemiōrion	1
2264		Heerōdees	44
	2265	Heerōdianoi	3
	2266	Heerōdias	6
	2267	Heerōdiōn	1
2272		heesukios	2
	2270	heesukazo	5
	2271	heesukia	4
2279		eekos	3
	2278	eekeo	2
	2727	kateeko	8
2285		thambos	3
	1569	ekthambos	1
	2284	thambeomai	4
2288		thanatos	119
	110	athanasia	3
	1935	epithanatios	1
	2286	thanasimos	1
	2287	thanateephoros	1
	2289	thanatoō	11
2290		thapto	11
	4916	sunthaptomai	2
	5027	taphee	1
	5028	taphos	7
2300		theaomai	24
	2295	thaumazo	46
	2302	theatron	3
	2334	theōreo	57
2304		thīos adj.	3
	2303	thīon	7
	2305	thīotees	1
2309		thelo	209
	1479	ethelothreeskīa	1
	2307	theleema	64
	2308	theleeis	1
2316		Theos	1343
	112	atheos	1
	2299	thea	3
	2304	thīos. adj.	3
	2312	theodidaktos	1
	2314	theomakos	1
	2315	theopnūstos	1
	2318	theosebees	1
	2319	theostugees	1
	2320	theotees	1
	2321	Theophilos	2
	5095	Timotheos	24
	5377	philotheos	1
2325		therizo	21
	2326	therismos	13
	2327	theristees	2
2330		theros	3
	2324	therapōn	1
	2325	therizo	21
	2329	thermee	1
2334		theōreo	47
	333	anatheoreo	2
	2335	theōria	1
	3865	paratheōreo	1
2337		theelazo	1
	2338	theelīa	2
	2338	theelu	3
2339		theera	1
	2340	theerūo	1
	2342	theerion	46
2346		thlibo	10
	598	apothlibo	1
	2347	thlipsis	45
	4918	sunthlibo	2
2348		thneesko	13
	599	apothneesko	111
	2253	heemithanees	1
	2288	thanatos	119
	2349	thneetos	6
2360		throeomai	3
	2351	thorubos	7
	2355	threenos	1
	2357	threeskos	1
	2358	thriambuo	2
2370		thumiao	1
	2368	thumiama	6
	2369	thumiateerion	1
2372		thumos	18
	120	athumeo	1
	1760	enthumeomai	3
	1937	epithumeo	16
	2115	ūthumos	2
	2371	thumomakeo	1
	2373	thumo-omai	1
	3661	homothumadon	12
	4289	prothumos	3
2374		thura	39
	2375	thureos	1
	2376	thuris	2
	2377	thurōros	4
2380		thuo	14
	1494	īdōlothuton	10
	2366	thuella	1
	2367	thuinos	1
	2370	thumiao	1
	2372	thumos	18
	2378	thusia	29
2390		iaomai	28
	2386	iama	3
	2392	iasis	3
	2394	Iasōn	5
	2395	iatros	7
2407		hieratūo	1
	2405	hieratīa	2
	2406	hieratūma	2
2409		hierūs	32
	749	arkierūs	143
	2407	hieratūo	1
2411		hieron	71
	2417	hierosulos	1
	2418	hierourgeo	1
2413		hieros	2
	748	arkieratikos	1
	2404	Hïerapolis	1
	2409	hierūs	32
	2411	hieron	71
	2412	hieroprepees	1
	2420	hierōsunee	4
2425		hikanos	975
	864	aphikneomai	1
	1338	diikneomai	1
	2426	hikanotees	1
	2427	hikanoō	2
	2428	hiketeeria	1
2431		hilaros	1
	2432	hilarotees	1
	2434	hilasmos	2
2436		hileōs	2
	448	anileōs	2
	2431	hilaros	1
	2433	hikaskomai	2
2443		hina	665
	2444	hinati, hina ti	6
	3363	hina mee	97
2453		Īoudaios	198
	2450	ioudaizo	1
	2451	Īoudaïkos	1
2462		hippos	16
	67	Agrippas	67
	751	Arkippos	2
	2460	hippūs	2
	2461	hippikon	1
	5376	Philippos	38
2470		isos	8
	2465	isangelos	1
	2472	isotimos	1
	2473	isopsakos	1
	2481	isōs	1
2476		histeemi	155
	14	anthisteemi	14
	450	anisteemi	112
	790	astateo	1
	868	aphisteemi	15
	1764	enisteemi	7
	1839	existeemi	17
	1988	epistatees	7
	2139	ūperistatos	1
	2186	ephisteemi	21
	2525	kathisteemi	1
	3179	methistano, methisteemi	5
	3936	paristano	2
	3936	paristeemi	39
	4026	periisteemi	4
	4291	proïsteemi	8
	4414	protostatees	1
	4712	stadios, stadion	6
	4713	stamnos	1
	4714	stasis	9
	4715	stateer	1
	4716	stauros	28
	4719	stakus	5
	4724	stellomai	2
	4728	stenos	3
	4731	steros	4
	4738	steethos	5
	4739	steeko	8
	4741	steerizo	13
	4745	stoa	4
	4921	sunistao, sunisteemi	13
	4921	sunistano	3
	5287	hupostasis	5
2479		iskus	11
	2478	iskuros	27
	2480	iskuo	29
2480		iskuo	29
	1765	eniskuo	2
	1840	exiskuo	1
	2001	episkuo	1
	2729	katiskuo	2
2491		Īōannees	133
	2489	Īōanna	2
	2490	Īōannas	1
	2494	Īōnan	1
2508		kathairo	2
	169	akathartos	30
	4027	perikatharma	1
2511		katharizo	30
	1245	diakatharizo	2
	2512	katharismos	7

ROOT NO.	DRVT. NO.	TRANSLITERATION	FRQ.
2513		katharos	28
	2508	kathairo	2
	2511	katharizo	30
	2514	katharotees	1
2523		kathizo	48
	339	anakathizo	2
	1940	epikathizo	1
	4776	sunkathizo	2
2525		kathisteemi	22
	182	akatastatos	1
	478	antikathisteemi	1
	600	apokathist-ao, -ano, -eemi	8
	2688	katasteema	1
	2723	kateegoreo	22
2532		kai	766
	1499	i kai	22
	2504	kago,kamoi,kame	72
	2539	kaiper	6
	2543-2544	kaitoi, kai-toige	4
	2546	kakī	11
	2547	kakīthen	9
	2548	kakīnos	23
	2579	kan	13
	4003	pentekaidekatos	1
	5065	tessareskaidekatos	2
2537		kainos	44
	340	anakainizo	1
	341	anakainoō	2
	1456	enkainia	1
	2538	kainotees	2
2540		kairos	86
	170	akaireomai	1
	2121	ukairos	2
	4340	proskairos	4
2545		kaio	12
	1572	ekkaiomai	1
	2575	kaminos	4
	2618	katakaio	12
	2738	kauma	2
	2740	kausis	1
	2743	kauteeriazomai	1
	3646	holokautōma	3
2556		kakos & to kakon	51
	172	akakos	2
	420	anexikakos	1
	1573	ekkakeo	6
	2549	kakia	11
	2550	kakoeethīa	1
	2551	kakologeo	4
	2555	kakopoyos	5
	2557	kakourgos	4
	2558	kakoukoumenos	2
	2559	kakoō	6
	2560	kakōs	16
2564		kaleo	106
	479	antikaleō	1
	1458	enkaleo	7
	1528	īskaleo	1
	1577	ekkleesia	115
	1941	epikaleomai	32
	2811	kleos	1
	2821	kleesis	11
	2823	klibanos	2
	3333	metakaleomai	4
	3870	parakaleo	108
	4292	prokaloomai	1
	4341	proskaleomai	30
	4779	sunkaleo	8
2570		kalos	102
	2565	kallielaios	1
	2566	kalōs	1
	2567	kalodidaskalos	1
	2568	Kaloi Limenes	1
	2569	kalopoiōn	1
	2573	kalōs & kallion	37
2572		kalupto	8
	177	akatakaluptos	2
	343	anakalupto	2
	601	apokalupto	26
	1943	epikalupto	1
	2571	kalumma	4
	2619	katakaluptomai	3
	3871	parakalupto	1
	4028	perikalupto	3
	4780	sunkaluptomai	1
2578		kampto	4
	344	anakampto	4
	345	anakimai	14
	4625	scandalon	15
	4781	sunkampto	1
2588		kardia	160

ROOT NO.	DRVT. NO.	TRANSLITERATION	FRQ.
	2589	kardiognōstees	89
	4641	skleerokardia	3
2590		karpos	66
	175	akarpos	7
	2591	karpos	1
	2593	karpophoros	1
2596		kata prep.	481
	177	akatakaluptos	2
	266	kataklao or kataklazo	2
	712	katīdōlos	1
	1246	diakatelenkomai	1
	1527	hīs kath hīs	3
	2505	katha	1
	2507	kathaireo	9
	2510	kathapto	1
	2515	kathedra	3
	2516	kathezomai	6
	2517	kathexees	5
	2518	kathūdo	22
	2519	katheegeetees	3
	2520	katheekon	2
	2521	katheemai	89
	2522	katheemerinos	1
	2524	kathieemi	4
	2525	kathisteemi	1
	2526	katho	4
	2527	katholou	1
	2528	kathoplizomai	1
	2529	kathorao	1
	2530	kathoti	5
	2531	kathōs	182
	2576	kammuo	2
	2597	katabaino	80
	2598	kataballo	3
	2599	katabareo	1
	2601	katabibazomai	2
	2603	katabrabūo	1
	2605	kantangello	17
	2607	kataginōsko	3
	2608	katagnumi	4
	2609	katago	10
	2610	katagōnizomai	1
	2611	katadeo	1
	2612	katadeelos	1
	2613	katadikazo	5
	2614	katadiōko	1
	2615	katadouloō	2
	2617	kataiskuno	13
	2618	katakaio	12
	2619	katakaluptomai	3
	2620	katakaukaomai	4
	2621	katakīmai	11
	2623	katakliō	2
	2624	katakleerodoteo	1
	2625	kataklino	3
	2626	katakluzomai	2
	2628	katakoloutheo	2
	2629	katakopto	1
	2630	katakreemnizo	1
	2632	katakrino	19
	2634	katakuriūo	4
	2637	katalalos	1
	2638	katalambano	15
	2639	kataleogomai	1
	2641	katalipo	25
	2642	katalithazo	1
	2644	katallasso	6
	2645	kataloipos	1
	2647	kataluo	17
	2648	katamanthano	1
	2649	katamartureo	4
	2650	katameno	1
	2651	katamonas	2
	2652	katanathema	2
	2653	katanathematizo	1
	2654	katanalisko	1
	2656	katanūo	1
	2657	katanoeo	15
	2658	katantao	13
	2660	katdnusso	1
	2661	kataxio-omai	4
	2662	katapateo	5
	2664	katapauo	4
	2665	katapetasma	6
	2666	katapino	7
	2667	katapipto	2
	2668	katapleo	1
	2669	kataponeomai	2
	2670	katapontizomai	2
	2671	katara	6
	2673	katargeo	27
	2674	katarithmeomai	1

ROOT NO.	DRVT. NO.	TRANSLITERATION	FRQ.
	2675	katartizo	13
	2678	katasīo	4
	2679	kataskapto	2
	2680	kataskūazo	11
	2681	kataskeenoō	4
	2683	kataskiazo	1
	2685	kataskopos	1
	2686	katasophizomai	1
	2687	katastello	2
	2690	katastrepho	2
	2691	katastreeniazo	1
	2693	katastrōnnumi	1
	2694	katasuro	1
	2695	katasphatto	1
	2696	katasphragizomai	1
	2698	katatitheemi	3
	2699	katatomee	1
	2700	katatoxūomai	1
	2701	katatreko	1
	2702	kataphero	3
	2703	kataphūgo	2
	2704	kataphthīro	2
	2705	kataphileo	6
	2706	kataphroneo	9
	2708	katakeo	2
	2709	katakthonios	1
	2710	katakraomai	2
	2711	katupsuko	1
	2713	katenanti	5
	2714	katenōpion	5
	2715	katexousiazo	2
	2716	katergazomai	24
	2718	katerkomai	13
	2719	katesthio	6
	2720	katūthuno	3
	2721	katephisteemi	1
	2722	kateko	19
	2725	kateegoros	7
	2726	kateephīa	1
	2727	kateekeo	8
	2728	katio-omai	1
	2729	katiskuo	2
	2730	katoikeo	47
	2734	katoptrizomai	1
	2735	katorthōma	1
	2736	kato, katōtero	11
	4785	sunkataseephizomai	1
2597		katabaino	80
	2600	katabasis	1
	4782	sunkatabaino	1
2605		katangello	17
	2604	katangelūs	1
	4293	prokatangello	4
2632		katakrino	19
	178	akatakritos	2
	843	autokatakritos	1
	2631	katakrima	3
	2633	katakrisis	2
2637		katalalos	1
	2635	katalaleo	5
	2636	katalalia	2
2641		katalīpo	25
	1459	enkalīpo	9
	2640	katalīmma	1
2644		katallasso	6
	604	apokatallatto	3
	2643	katallagee	4
2647		kataluo	17
	179	akatalutos	1
	2646	katuluma	3
2664		katapauo	4
	180	akatapaustos	1
	2663	katapausis	9
2675		katartizo	13
	2676	katartisis	1
	2677	katartismos	1
	4294	prokatarizo	1
2698		katatitheemi	3
	3872	parakatatheekee	2
	4784	sunkatathesis	1
2722		kateko	19
	183	akatasketos	1
	2697	kataskesis	1
2730		katoikeo	47
	1460	enkatoikeo	1
	2731	katoikeesis	1
	2732	katoikeeteerion	2
2736		kato, katōtero	11
	2737	katōteros	1
	5270	hupokato	9
2744		kaukaomai	38
	2620	katakaukaomai	4
	2745	kaukeema	11

ROOT NO.	DRVT. NO.	TRANSLITERATION	FRQ.
	2746	kaukeesis	12
2749		kīmai	26
	480	antikimai	8
	606	apokaīmai	4
	1945	epikīmai	7
	2621	katakīmai	11
	2837	koimaomai	18
	2845	koitee	4
	2968	kōmee	28
	2970	kōmos	3
	3873	parakīmai	2
	4029	perikīmai	5
	4295	prokīmai	5
2756		kenos	18
	2755	kenodoxous	1
	2757	kenophōnia	2
	2758	kenoō	5
	2761	kenōs	1
2759		kentron	5
	1461	enkentrizo	6
	1574	ekkenteo	3
	2971	kōnōps	1
2766		keramos	1
	2763	keramūs	3
	2764	keramikos	1
	2765	keramion	2
2767		kerannumi, kerao	3
	185	akeraios	3
	194	akraton	1
	2766	keramos	1
	4786	sunkerannumi	2
2768		keras	11
	2762	keraia	2
	2769	keration	1
	2898	kranion	4
2776		kephalee	76
	607	apokephalizo	4
	2774	kephalaion	2
	2777	kephalis	1
	4030	perikephalaia	2
	4344	proskephalaion	1
2784		keerusso	61
	2782	keerugma	8
	2783	keerux	3
	4296	prokeerusso	2
2788		kithara	4
	2789	kitharizo	2
	2790	kitharōdos	2
2795		kineo	8
	2796	kineesis	1
	3334	metakineo	1
	4787	sunkineo	1
2806		klazo, klao	15
	1575	ekklazo	3
	2622	kataklao or kataklazo	2
	2798	klados	11
	2800	klasis	2
	2801	klasma	9
	2814	kleema	4
	2819	kleeros	13
2808		klio	16
	608	apoklīo	1
	2623	katakliō	2
	2807	klīs	6
	4788	sunklīo	4
2813		klepto	12
	2809	klemma	1
	2812	kleptees	16
	2829	klopee	2
2818		kleeronomos	15
	2816	kleeronomeo	18
	2817	kleeronomia	14
	4789	sunkleeronomos	4
2819		kleeros	13
	2624	katakleerodoteo	1
	2818	kleeronomos	15
	2820	kleero-omai	1
	3490	naukleeros	1
	3648	holokleeros	2
2827		klino	7
	186	aklinees	1
	347	anaklino	8
	755	arkitriklīnos	3
	1578	ekklino	3
	2625	kataklino	3
	2824	klima	3
	2825	klinee	10
	2828	klisia	1
	4346	prosklisis	1
2830		kludōn	2
	2148	Ūrokludōn	1
	2626	katakluzomai	2

ROOT NO.	DRVT. NO.	TRANSLITERATION	FRQ.
2830		kludōn (cont.)	
	2831	kludōnizomai	1
2839		koinos	12
	2840	koinoō	15
	2844	koinōnos	10
2844		koinōnos	10
	2841	koinōneo	8
	2842	koinōnia	20
	2843	koinōnikos	1
	4791	sunkoinōnos	4
2845		koitee	4
	733	arsenokoitees	2
	2846	koitōn	1
2849		kolazomai	2
	2851	kolasis	2
	2966	kōlon	1
	2967	kōluo	23
2860		kolumbao	1
	1597	ekklino	3
	2861	kolumbeethra	5
2865		komizo	11
	2864	komee	1
	2889	kosmos	187
	4792	sunkomizo	1
2873		kopos	19
	2123	ūkopoteros	7
	2869	kopazo	3
	2872	kopiao	23
2875		kopto	8
	348	anakopto	1
	609	apokopto	6
	695	argurokopos	1
	1465	enkopto	5
	1581	ekkopto	11
	2629	katakopto	1
	2870	kopetos	1
	2871	kopee	1
	2873	kopos	19
	4298	prokopto	6
	4350	proskopto	8
2877		korasion	8
	1359	Dioskouroi	1
	1947	epikouria	1
2889		kosmos	187
	1101	glōssokomon	2
	2885	kosmeo	10
	2886	kosmikos	2
	2887	kosmios	2
	2888	kosmokratōr	1
2896		krazo	59
	349	anakrazo	5
	2906	kraugee	6
	2987	lamprotees	1
2904		kratos	12
	193	akratees	1
	1468	enkratees	1
	2594	kartereo	1
	2900	krataios	1
	2902	krateō	47
	2903	kratistos	4
	2909	krīssōn, krīttōn	19
	3841	pantokrator	10
	4031	perikratees	1
2910		kremamai, kremao	7
	1582	ekkremamai	1
	2911	kreemnos	3
2919		krino	114
	350	anakrino	16
	1252	diakrino	19
	1469	enkrino	1
	1506	īlikrinees	2
	1948	epikrino	1
	2632	katakrino	19
	2917	krima	21
	2923	kritees	17
	4299	prokrima	1
	4793	sunkrino	3
	5271	hupokrinomai	1
2923		kritees	17
	2922	kriteerion	3
	2924	kritikos	1
2928		krupto	16
	613	apokrupto	6
	1470	enkrupto	2
	2926-2927	kruptos	20
	2931	kruphee	1
	4032	perikrupto	1
2932		ktaomai	7
	2933	kteema	4
	2934	kteenos	4
	2935	kteetōr	1
2936		ktizo	14
	2938	ktisma	4
	2939	ktistees	1
2945		kuklo	7
	2943	kuklothen	4
	2944	kukloō	5
2947		kuliomai	1
	617	apokulizo	4
	2946	kulisma	1
	4351	proskulio	2
2949		kuma	4
	616	apokueo	2
	1471	enkrio	1
	2947	kuliomai	1
	2948	kullos	4
	2950	kumbalon	2
	2955	kupto	3
2955		kupto	3
	352	anakupto	4
	3879	parakupto	5
	4794	sunkupto	1
2962		kurios	749
	2959	kuria	2
	2960	kuriakos	2
	2961	kuriūo	7
	2963	kuriotees	4
	2964	kuroō	2
	5181	Turannos	1
2964		kuroō	2
	208	akuroō	3
	4300	prokuroōmai	1
2965		kuōn	5
	2952	kunarion	4
	4352	proskuneo	60
	4657	skubalon	1
2967		kōluo	23
	209	akōlutos	1
	1254	diakōluo	1
2980		laleo	295
	216	alalos	3
	1255	dialaleo	2
	1583	eklaleo	1
	2637	katalalos	2
	2981	lalia	4
	3424	mogilalos	1
	4354	proslaleo	2
	4814	sullaleo	6
2983		lambano	263
	353	analambano	13
	482	antilambanomai	3
	618	apolambano	12
	678	aprosōpoleeptōs	1
	1187	dexiolabos	1
	1949	epilambanomai	19
	2126	ūlabees	3
	2638	katalambano	15
	3028	leepsis	1
	3334	metalambano	6
	3880	paralambano	50
	4301	prolambano	3
	4355	proslambano	14
	4381	prosopoleeptees	1
	4815	sullambano	16
	4843	sumperilambano	1
	5274	hupolambano	4
2989		lampo	7
	1584	eklampo	1
	2985	lampas	9
	4034	perilampo	2
2990		lanthano	6
	227	aleethees	25
	1585	eklanthanomai	1
	1950	epilanthanomai	8
	2977	lathra	4
	3024	leethee	1
2992		laos	143
	2993	Laodikīa	5
	3011	litourgos	5
2994		Laodikus	2
	745	Arkelaos	1
	3532	Nilolaos	1
3000		latrūo	21
	1496	īdōlolatrees	7
	2999	latrīa	5
3004		lego	1343
	483	antilego	10
	1256	dialegomai	13
	1586	ekleogomai	21
	1951	epilegomai	2
	2639	kataleogomai	1
	3056	logos	330
	3151	mataiologos	1
	3473	mōrologia	1
	3881	paralegomai	2
	4302	prolego	3
	4691	spermologos	1
	4758	stratologeo	1
	4816	sullego	8
	4883	sunarmologeomai	2
	5542	kreestologia	1
	5573	psūdologos	1
3007		līpo	6
	88	adialiptos	2
	620	apolīpo	6
	1257	dialīpo	1
	1587	eklīpo	3
	1952	epilīpo	1
	2641	katalīpo	25
	3005	līmma	1
	3042	limos	12
	3062	loipos	41
	4035	perilīpomai	2
	5275	hupolīpomai	1
3008		lītourgeo	3
	3009	lītourgia	6
	3010	lītourgikos	1
3013		lepis	1
	3014	lepra	4
	3016	lepton	3
3017		Lūi	5
	3018	Lūi	1
	3018	Lūis	3
	3019	Lūitees	3
3022		lūkos	25
	3021	lūkaino	2
	3074	lukos	6
	3088	luknos	14
3030		libanos	2
	3031	libanōton	2
	5474	kalkolibanon	2
3037		lithos	60
	3034	lithazo	8
	3035	lithinos	3
	3036	lithoboleo	9
	3038	Lithostrōtos	1
	5555	krusolithos	1
3040		limeen	3
	2568	Kaloi Limenes	1
	3041	limnee	10
3049		logizomai	41
	1260	dialogizomai	16
	3053	logismos	2
	3884	paralogizomai	2
	4817	sullogizomai	1
3056		logos	330
	148	aiskrologia	1
	249	alogos	3
	356	analogia	1
	626	apologeomai	10
	945	battologeo	1
	1075	genealogeomai	1
	1076	genealogia	2
	1677	ellogeo	2
	2127	ūlogeo	44
	2129	ūlogia	16
	2551	kakologeo	4
	3048	logia	2
	3049	logizomai	41
	3050	logikos	2
	3052	logios	1
	3054	logomakeo	1
	3670	homologeo	23
	4086	pithanologia	1
	4180	polulogia	1
3060		loidoros	2
	3058	loidoreo	4
	3059	loidoria	3
3062		loipos	41
	1954	epiloipos	1
	2645	kataloipos	1
	3063	to loipon, ho loipon & loipon	14
	3064	tou loipou	1
3068		louo	6
	628	apolouō	2
	3067	loutron	2
3077		lupee	16
	253	alupoteros	1
	3076	lupeo	26
	4036	perilupos	5
3080		lusis	1
	3078	Lusanias	1
	3081	lusitelī	1
3083		lutron	2
	487	antilutron	1
	629	apolutrōsis	10
	3084	lutroō	3
3084		lutroō	3
	3085	lutrōsis	3
	3086	lutrōtees	1
3089		luo	43
	360	analuo	2
	630	apoluo	69
	1262	dialuomai	1
	1590	ekluo	6
	1956	epiluo	2
	2647	kataluo	17
	3075	lumainomai	1
	3083	lutron	2
	3886	paraluomai	5
3101		matheetees	268
	3100	matheetūo	4
	3102	matheetria	1
3105		mainomai	5
	1693	emmainomai	1
	3130	mania	1
	3132	manna	5
3116		makrothumōs	1
	3114	makrothumeo	10
	3115	makrothumia	14
3117		makros	5
	3112	makran	10
	3113	makrothen	5
	3116	makrothumōs	1
	3118	makrokronios	1
3129		manthano	25
	261	amathees	1
	2596	katamanthano	1
	4827	summatheethees	1
3133		marianomai	1
	263	amarantos	1
	264	hamartano	43
3140		martureo -eomai	79
	1263	diamarturomai	15
	1957	epimartureo	1
	2649	katamartureo	4
	4828	summartureo	4
3144		martur & martus	34
	267	amarturos	1
	3140	martureo -eomai	79
	3141	marturia	37
	3142	marturion	20
	3143	marturomai	3
	5575	psūdomartur	3
3145		massaomai	1
	1591	ekmasso	5
	3148	mastix	6
	3149	mastos	3
	3155	mateen	2
3152		mataios	6
	3151	mataiologos	1
	3153	mataiotees	3
	3154	mataiōmai	1
3161		Mattathias	2
	3156	Matthaios	5
	3158	Matthat	2
	3159	Matthias	2
	3160	Mattatha	1
3163		makee	4
	269	amakos	2
	3162	makaira	29
3164		makomai	4
	1264	diamakomai	1
	2314	themakos	1
	2371	thumomakeo	1
	3054	logomakeo	1
	3163	makee	4
3173		megas	195
	3167	megalīa	2
	3169	megaloprepees	1
	3170	megaluno	8
	3171	megalōs	1
	3172	megalōsunee	3
	3174	megethos	1
	3176	megistos	1
	3187	mīzōn, mīzon	45
3184		methuo	7
	271	amethustos	1
	3182	methuskomai	3
	3183	methusos	2
3187		mīzōn, mīzon	45
	3173	megas	195
	3185	mīzon adv.	1
	3186	mīzoteros	1
3189		melas	3
	3188	melan subs.	3
	3435	moluno	3
3199		melī	10
	272	ameleo	5
	1959	epimeleomai	3
	3191	meletao	3

ROOT NO.	DRVT. NO.	TRANSLITERATION	FRQ.
3199		melī (cont.)	
	3195	mello	110
	3338	metamelomai	6
3201		memphomai	3
	273	amemptos	5
	3202	mempsimoiros	1
	3437	momphee	1
	3470	momos	1
3303		men	195
	3304	menounge	4
	3305	mentio	8
3306		meno	120
	362	anameno	1
	1265	diameno	5
	1696	emmeno	3
	1961	epimeno	18
	2650	katameno	1
	3438	monee	2
	3441	monos	47
	3887	parameno	3
	4037	perimeno	1
	4357	prasmeno	6
	5278	hupomeno	17
3307		merizo	14
	1266	diamerizo	12
	3308	merimna	6
	3311	merismos	2
	3312	meristees	1
	4829	summerizomai	1
3308		merimna	6
	1275	amerimnos	2
	3309	merimnao	19
3313		meros	43
	3307	merizo	14
	3310	meris	10
	3444	morphee	3
	4181	polumerōs	1
3319		mesos	61
	3314	meseembria	2
	3316	mesitees	6
	3317	mesonuktion	4
	3318	Mesopotamia	2
	3320	mesotoikon	1
	3321	mesouraneema	3
	3322	mesoō	1
3326		meta	473
	3177	methermeenūomai	7
	3179	methistano, methisteemi	5
	3180	methodīa	2
	3181	methoria	1
	3319	mesos	61
	3327	metabaino	12
	3328	metaballomai	1
	3329	metago	2
	3330	metadidōmi	5
	3332	metairo	2
	3333	metakaleomai	4
	3334	metakineo	1
	3335	metalambano	6
	3337	metallatto	2
	3338	metamelomai	6
	3339	metamorphŏomai	4
	3340	metanŏeo	34
	3342	metaxu	9
	3343	metapempo	8
	3344	metastrepho	3
	3345	metaskeematizo	5
	3346	metatitheemi	6
	3347	metepīta	1
	3348	meteko	8
	3349	meteōrizomai	1
	3350	metoikesia	4
	3359	metōpon	8
3340		metanŏeo	34
	279	ametanoeetos	1
	3341	metanoya	24
3346		metatitheemi	6
	276	ametathetos	2
	3331	metathesis	3
3348		meteko	8
	3352	metokee	1
	3353	metokos	6
3354		metreo	10
	488	antimetreo	2
	3355	metreetees	1
3358		metron	13
	280	ametros	2
	3354	metreo	10
	3357	metriōs	1
3361		mee	675
	1490	i de mee, i de meege	14
	1508	ī mee	92
	3362	ean mee	60
	3363	hina mee	97
	3364	mee ouk & ou mee	5
	3365	meedamōs	2
	3366	meede	57
	3367	meedīs, meedemia, meeden	92
	3371	meeketi	21
	3378	mee ouk & ou mee	5
	3379	meepotee or mee potee	25
	3380	meepo	2
	3381	meepos or mee pōs	12
	3383	meeti	37
	3385	meeti	16
	3386	meeti	1
	3387	meetis or mee tis	4
3366		meede	57
	3368	meedepote	1
	3369	meedepo	1
3372		meekos	3
	3117	makros	5
	3360	mekri & mekris	17
	3373	meekunomai	1
3376		meen	18
	3561	noumeenia	1
	5072	tetrameenon	1
	5150	trimeenon	1
3384		meeteer	85
	282	ameetōr	1
	3388	meetra	2
	3389	meetralōees	1
3392		miaino	5
	283	amiantos	4
	3393	miasma	1
	3394	miasmos	1
3396		mignumi	4
	3395	migma	1
	4874	sunamignumi	3
3401		mimeomai	4
	3402	mimeetees	7
	4831	summineetes	1
3403		mimneeskomai	2
	363	anamimneesko	6
	3417	mnīa	7
	3420	mneemee	1
	5279	hupomimneesko	7
3408		misthos	29
	489	antimisthia	2
	3407	misthios	2
	3409	mistho-omai	2
3409		mistho-omai	2
	3406	misthapodotees	1
	3410	misthōma	1
3415		mnaomai	21
	3403	mimneeskomai	2
	3417	mnīa	7
	3418	mneema	7
	3423	mneestūomai	3
3420		mneemee	1
	3419	mneemīon	42
	3421	mneemonūo	21
3425		mogis	1
	3424	mogilalos	1
	3433	molis	6
	3449	mokthos	3
3432		moikos	4
	3428	moikalis	7
	3429	moikaomai	6
	3431	moikūo	14
3441		monos	47
	2651	katamonas	2
	3439	monogenees	9
	3440	monon	66
	3442	monophthalomos	2
	3443	monŏomai	1
3444		morphee	3
	3445	morphŏomai	1
	4832	summorphŏomai	2
3445		morphŏomai	1
	3339	metamorphŏomai	4
	3446	morphōsis	2
3453		mueomai	1
	3454	muthos	5
	3504	neophutos	1
3458		mulos	4
	3457	mudikos	1
	3459	mulōn	1
3464		muron	14
	3462	murizo	1
	4666	smurna	2
3466		musteerion	27
	2576	kammuo	2
	3453	mueomai	1
	3467	muōpazo	1
3470		mōmos	1
	299	amōmos	7
	3469	mōmeomai	2
3474		mōros	13
	3471	mōraino	4
	3472	mōria	5
3491		naus	1
	3489	nauageo	2
	3490	naukleeros	1
	3492	nautees	3
	3517	Neerūs	1
3501		neos, neōteros	24
	365	ananeoō	1
	3494	neanias	5
	3496	Neapolis	1
	3502	neossos	1
	3503	neotees	5
	3504	neophutos	1
	3512	neōterikos	1
	3561	noumeenia	1
3502		neossos	1
	3555	nossia	1
	3556	nossion	1
3506		nūo	2
	1593	eknūo	1
	1770	ennūo	1
	1962	epinūo	1
	2656	katanūo	1
	3573	nustazo	2
3525		neepho	6
	366	ananeepho	1
	1594	ekneepho	1
	3524	neephaleos & nephalios	3
3528		nikao	28
	3527	Nikanōr	1
	5245	hupernikao	1
3529		nikee	1
	959	Bernikee	3
	2131	Ūnīkee	1
	2332	Thessabnikee	5
	3528	nikao	28
	3534	nikos	4
3534		nikos	4
	408	Andronikos	1
	3530	Nikodeemos	5
	3532	Nikolaos	1
	3533	Nikopolis	1
3538		nipto	17
	449	aniptos	3
	633	aponipto	1
	3537	nipteer	1
3539		noeo	14
	50	agnoeo	22
	453	anoeetos	6
	1425	dusoneetos	1
	2657	katanoeo	15
	3340	metanŏeo	34
	3540	noeema	6
	4306	pronoeo	3
	5282	huponoeo	3
3550		nomothetees	1
	3548	nomothesia	1
	3549	nomotheteo	2
3551		nomos	197
	459	anomos	10
	632	aponemo	1
	1268	dianemomai	1
	1772	ennomos	2
	2818	kleeronomos	15
	3542	nomee	2
	3543	nomizo	15
	3544	nomikos	9
	3545	nomimōs	2
	3547	nomodidaskalos	3
	3550	nomothetees	1
	3623	oikonomos	10
	3891	paranomeo	1
3563		nous	24
	454	anoia	2
	1771	ennoia	2
	1963	epinoia	1
	2132	ūnoeo	1
	3539	noeo	14
	3559	nouthesia	3
	3562	nounekōs	1
3565		numphee	8
	3564	Numphas	1
	3566	numphios	16
	3567	numphōn	3
3568		nun	139
	3569	ta nun or tanun	520
	3570	nuni	20
	5106	toinun	4
3571		nux	65
	3317	mesonuktion	4
	3574	nuktheemeron	1
3581		xenos	14
	3578	xenia	2
	3580	xenodokeo	1
	5382	philoxenos	3
3582		xestees	2
	3584	xeeros	7
	3586	xulon	19
3584		xeeros	7
	2991	laxūtos	1
	3583	xeeraino	16
3588		ho, hee, to	543
	3569	ta nun or tanun	520
	3592	hode,heede,tode	12
	3739	hos, hee, ho	1393
	3778	houtos	192
	3778	houtoi	80
	3778	hautee	82
	3778	hautai	3
	5024	tauta	247
	5082	teelikoutos	4
	5104	toi	1
	5119	tote	159
	5120	tou	1
	5121	tounantion	3
	5122	tounoma	1
3593		hodūo	1
	3180	methodīa	2
	4922	sunodūo	1
3598		hodos	102
	296	amphodon	1
	1526	īsodos	5
	1841	exodos	3
	2137	ūodoumai	4
	3593	hudūo	1
	3595	hodeegos	5
	3596	hodoiporeo	1
	3938	parodos	1
	4923	sunodia	1
3605		ozo	1
	2175	ūōdia	3
	3744	osmee	6
	3750	osphreesis	1
3611		oikeo	9
	1774	enoikeo	5
	2730	katoikeo	47
	3610	oidetees	4
	3612	oikeema	1
	3613	oikeeteerion	2
	3625	oikoumence	16
	3939	paroikeo	2
	4039	perioikeo	1
	4924	sunoikeo	1
3618		oikodomeo	39
	456	anoikodomeō	2
	2026	epoikodomeo	8
	4925	sunoikodomeomai	1
3623		oikonomos	10
	3621	oikonomeo	1
	3622	oikonomia	7
3624		oikos	114
	3350	metoikesia	4
	3609	oikīos	3
	3611	oikeo	9
	3614	oikia	95
	3617	oikodespotees	12
	3619	oikodomee	18
	3623	oikonomos	10
	3633	oimai	1
	3832	panoiki	1
	3941	paroikos	4
	4040	perioikos	1
3627		oiktīro, oiktīreo	2
	3628	oiktirmos	5
	3629	oiktirmōn	3
3631		oinos	33
	3632	oinophlugia	1
	3943	paroinos	2
3634		hoios	15
	3633	oiomai	2
	4169	poios	34
3638		okto	9
	3590	ogdoos	5
	3637	oktaeemeros	1
3639		olethros	4
	622	apollumi	92
	3645	olothrūo	1

ROOT NO.	DRVT. NO.	TRANSLITERATION	FRQ.
3641		oligos	43
	3640	oligopistos	5
	3642	oligopsukos	1
	3643	oligōreo	1
3645		olothrūo	1
	1842	exolothrūomai	1
	3644	olothrūtees	1
3650		holos	112
	2527	katholou	1
	3646	holokautōma	3
	3648	holokleeros	2
	3651	holotelees	1
	3654	holōs	4
3658		homilos	1
	3656	homileo	4
	3657	homilia	1
3660		omnumi, omnuo	27
	3728	horkōmosia	4
	4945	sunōmosia	1
3664		homoios	47
	3662	homoiazo	1
	3665	homoiotees	2
	3666	homoioō	15
	3668	homoiōs	30
	3946	paromoios	2
3666		homoioō	15
	871	aphomoi-oō	1
	3667	homoiōma	6
	3669	homoiōsis	1
3670		homologeo	23
	437	anthomologeomai	1
	1843	exomologeomai	11
	3671	homologia	6
	3672	homologuomenos	1
3674		homou	3
	3661	homothumadon	12
	3664	homoios	47
	3670	homologeo	23
	3673	homoteknos	1
	3675	homophrōn	1
	3676	homōs	3
	4927	sunomoreo	1
3685		oneemi	1
	3682	Oneesimos	2
	3683	Oneesiphoros	2
3686		onoma	230
	2176	ūōnumos	10
	3687	onomazo	10
	5122	tounoma	1
	5581	psūdōnumos	1
3688		onos	6
	3678	onarion	1
	3684	onikos	2
3691		oxus	8
	3690	oxos	7
	3947	paroxunomai	2
3696		hopla	6
	3695	hoplizomai	1
	3833	panoplia	3
3700		optanomai	1
	845	autoptees	1
	1799	enōpion	97
	2029	epoptūo	2
	2030	epoptees	1
	2072	esoptron	2
	2596	katoptrizomai	1
	3659	omma	1
	3692	opee	2
	3701	optasia	4
	3788	ophthalmos	102
	3789	ophis	14
	3790	ophrus	1
	3799	opsis	3
	4647	skolops	1
	4659	sukthropos	2
	5203	hudropikos	1
	5299	hupōpiazo	2
3708		horao	59
	872	aphoraō	2
	2529	kathorao	1
	3700	optomai	58
	3705	horama	12
	3706	horasis	4
	3707	horatos	1
	4308	proŏrao	2
	5432	phroureo	4
3709		orgee	36
	3710	orgizomai	8
	3711	orgilos	1
3713		oregomai	3
	3709	orgee	36
	3712	orgwya	2
	3715	orexis	1
3717		orthos	2
	461	anorthoō	3
	2735	katorthōma	1
	3716	orthopodeo	1
	3718	orthotomeo	1
	3723	orthōs	4
3722		orthros	3
	3719	orthrizo	1
	3720	orthrinos	1
	3721	orthrios	1
3724		horizo	8
	592	apodiorizo	1
	873	aphorizo	10
	4309	proŏrizo	6
3725		horia	11
	3181	methoria	1
	3724	horizo	9
	3734	horothesia	1
	4927	sunomoreo	1
3727		horkos	10
	1965	epiorkos	1
	3726	horkizo	3
	3728	horkōmosia	4
3730		hormee	2
	3729	hormao	5
	3731	hormeema	1
	4358	prosormizomai	1
3735		oros	65
	3714	orinos	2
	3717	orthos	2
	3722	orthros	3
	3733	ornis	2
	3772	ouranos	284
3739		hos, hee, ho	1393
	2505	katha	1
	2526	katho	4
	2530	kathoti	5
	3603	ho esti	11
	3606	hothen	15
	3697	hopoios	5
	3698	hopote	1
	3699	hopou	82
	3704	hopōs	56
	3740	hosakis	3
	3745	hosos	115
	3748	hostis	153
	3753	hote	105
	3757	hou	27
	4214	posos	27
	5613	hōs	492
3741		hosios	8
	462	anosios	2
	3742	hosiotees	2
	3743	hosiōs	1
3748		hostis	153
	3754	hoti	1293
	3755	hotou	6
3753		hote	105
	3752	hotan	122
	3842	pantote	42
3756		lu, ouk, ouk	1453
	3364	mee ouk & ou mee	5
	3378	mee ouk & ou mee	5
	3761	oude	137
	3765	ouketi or ouk eti	48
	3766	oukoun	1
	3777	oute	94
	3780	ouki	56
3761		oude	137
	3762	oudīs	235
	3763	oudepote	16
	3764	oudepo	5
3762		oudīs	235
	1847	exoudenoō	1
	3760	oudamōs	1
3767		oun	526
	3304	menounge	4
	3766	oukoun	1
	5105	toigaroun	2
3772		ouranos	284
	2032	epouranios	2
	3321	mesouraneema	3
	3770	ouranios	8
	3771	ouranothen	2
3775		ous	37
	1801	enōtizomai	1
	5621	ōtion	5
3778		houtos	192
3778		houtoi	80
3778		hautee	81
3778		hautai	3
	3779	houto, houtōs	213
	5022	tauros	4
	5025	tautais	12
	5025	tautas	9
	5026	tautee	31
	5026	tauteen	57
	5026	tautees	34
	5082	teelikoutos	4
	5118	tosoutos	21
	5124	touto	320
	5125	toutois	19
	5126	touton	64
	5127	toutou	77
	5128	toutous	27
	5129	touto	89
	5130	toutōn	69
3784		ophīlo	136
	3781	ophīletees	7
	3782	ophīlee	2
	3783	ophīleema	2
	3785	ophelon	4
	4359	prosphīlo	1
3786		ophelos	3
	3784	ophīlo	136
	5624	ōphelimos	4
3788		ophthalmos	102
	503	antophthalmeo	1
	3442	monophthalmos	2
	3787	ophthalmodoulīa	2
3793		oklos	175
	3791	okleomai	2
	3792	oklopoyeo	1
3795		opsarion	5
	3800	opsōnion	4
	3953	paropsis	2
3796		opse	3
	3703	opōra	1
	3797	opsimos	1
	3798	opsia	15
3806		pathos	3
	2552	kakopathīa	1
	3356	metriopatheo	1
	3804	patheema	16
3811		paidūo	13
	521	apaidūtos	1
	3809	paidīa	6
	3810	paidūtees	2
3816		pais	24
	3807	paidagōgos	3
	3808	paidarīon	2
	3811	paidūo	13
	3814	paidiskee	13
	3815	paizo	1
3817		paio	5
	3816	pais	24
	3960	patasso	10
	3961	pateo	5
3819		palai	6
	1597	ekpalai	2
	3820	palaios	19
3820		palaios	19
	3821	palaiotees	1
	3822	palaioō	4
3844		para	200
	3845	parabaino	4
	3846	paraballo	2
	3849	parabiazomai	2
	3851	paraboulūomai	1
	3853	parangello	30
	3854	paraginomai	37
	3855	parago	10
	3856	paradīgmatizo	2
	3858	paradekomai	5
	3859	paradiatribee	1
	3860	paradidōmi	121
	3861	paradoxos	1
	3863	parazeeloō	4
	3864	parathalassios	1
	3865	paratheoreo	1
	3867	paraineo	2
	3868	paraiteomai	11
	3869	parakathizo	1
	3870	parakaleo	108
	3871	parakalupto	1
	3872	parakatatheekee	2
	3873	parakīmai	2
	3877	parakoloutheo	4
	3878	parakouo	2
	3879	parakupto	5
	3880	paralambano	50
	3881	paralegomai	2
	3882	paralios	1
	3883	parallagee	1
	3884	paralogizomai	2
	3886	paraluomai	5
	3887	parameno	3
	3891	paranomeo	1
	3893	parapikraino	1
	3895	parapipto	1
	3896	parapleo	1
	3897	parapleesion	1
	3899	paraporūomai	5
	3901	pararrueo	1
	3902	paraseemos	1
	3903	paraskūazo	4
	3906	parateereo	6
	3908	paratitheemi	1
	3909	paratunkano	1
	3910	parautika	1
	3911	paraphero	2
	3912	paraphroneo	1
	3914	parakīmazo	4
	3916	parakreema	19
	3918	parīmi	23
	3919	parīsago	1
	3921	parīsduno	1
	3922	parīserkomai	2
	3923	parīsphero	1
	3925	parembolee	10
	3926	parenokleo	2
	3927	parepideemos	3
	3928	parerkomai	31
	3930	pareko	16
	3931	pareegoria	1
	3935	pariemai	1
	3936	paristeemi	39
	3936	paristano	2
	3938	parodos	1
	3939	paroikeo	2
	3941	paroikos	4
	3942	paroimia	5
	3943	paroinos	2
	3946	paromoios	2
	3947	paroxunomai	2
	3949	parorgizo	2
	3953	paropsis	2
3845		parabaino	4
	531	aparabatos	1
	3847	parabasis	7
	3848	parabatees	5
3860		paradidōmi	121
	3862	paradosis	13
	3970	patroparadotos	1
3870		parakaleo	108
	3874	parakleesis	29
	4837	sumparakaleomai	1
3903		paraskūazo	4
	532	aparaskūastos	1
	3904	paraskūee	6
3918		parīmi	23
	3952	parousia	24
	4840	sumparīmi	1
3956		pas, pasa, pan	1243
	3826	pampleethī	1
	3827	pampolus	1
	3828	Pamphulia	5
	3829	pandokīon	1
	3831	paneeguris	1
	3832	panoiki	1
	3833	panoplia	3
	3835	panourgos	1
	3837	pantakou	7
	3838	panteles	2
	3839	pantee	1
	3840	pantothen	3
	3841	pantokrator	10
	3842	pantote	42
	3843	pantōs	9
	3954	parreesia	51
3958		pasko	42
	3806	pathos	3
	3997	penthos	5
	4310	propasko	1
	4841	sumpasko	2
3961		pateo	5
	2662	katapateo	5
	4043	peripateo	96
3962		pateer	418
	493	Antipas	1
	540	apator	1
	2810	Kleopas	1
	3964	patralōees	1
	3965	patria	3
	3967	patrikos	1
	3968	patris	8
	3969	Patrobas	1
	3970	patroparadotos	1
	3971	patrōos	3

ROOT NO.	DRVT. NO.	TRANSLITERATION	FRQ.
3962		pateer (cont.)	
	4986	Sōpatros	1
3973		pauomai	15
	373	anapauo	12
	2664	katapauo	4
3979		pezee	2
	3978	pezūo	1
	5132	trapeza	15
3982		pītho, pepoitha	55
	374	anapitho	1
	545	apīthees	6
	2138	ūpīthees	1
	3980	pītharkeo	4
	3981	pīthos	1
	3988	pīsmonee	1
	4006	pepoitheeis	6
	4086	pithanologia	1
	4102	pistis	244
	4103	pistos	66
3984		pīra	2
	552	apīros	1
	3985	pīrazo	39
	3987	pīrao	2
	5005	talaipōros	2
3985		pīrazo	39
	1598	ekpīrozo	4
	3986	pīrasmos	21
3992		pempo	81
	375	anapempo	4
	1599	ekpempo	2
	3343	metapempo	8
	4311	propempo	9
	4842	sumpempo	2
3993		penees	1
	3983	pīnao	23
	3998	penikros	1
	4192	ponos	3
4002		pente	38
	1178	dekapente	3
	3991	pemptos	4
	3999	pentakis	1
	4001	pentakosioi	2
	4003	pentekaidekatos	1
	4004	penteekonta	1
4007		per	4
	1512	ī per	6
	1895	epīdeeper	1
	1897	epīper	1
	2260	eeper	1
	2509	kathaper	13
	2539	kaiper	6
	5618	hōsper	42
4008		peran	23
	495	antiperan	1
	562	aperantos	1
	960	Beroya	2
	1276	diaperao	6
	3984	pīra	2
	4007	per	4
	4009	peras	4
	4012	peri	331
	4044	peripiro	1
	5327	pharanx	1
4012		peri	331
	2139	ūperistatos	1
	4013	periago	6
	4014	periaireo	4
	4015	periastrapto	2
	4016	periballo	24
	4017	periblepo	7
	4019	perideomai	1
	4020	periergazomai	1
	4021	periergos	2
	4022	perierkomai	4
	4023	perieko	3
	4024	perizōnnumi	7
	4026	periisteemi	4
	4027	perikatharma	1
	4028	perikalupto	3
	4029	perikīmai	5
	4030	perikephalaia	2
	4031	perikratees	1
	4032	perikrupto	1
	4033	perikukloō	1
	4034	perilampo	2
	4035	perilīpomai	2
	4036	perilupos	5
	4037	perimeno	1
	4038	perix	1
	4039	perioikeo	1
	4040	perioikos	1
	4041	periousios	1
	4043	peripateo	96

ROOT NO.	DRVT. NO.	TRANSLITERATION	FRQ.
	4044	peripīro	1
	4045	peripipto	3
	4046	peripoyeomai	2
	4048	perirreegnumi	1
	4049	perispaomai	1
	4053	perissos, perissoteros	22
	4059	peritemno	18
	4060	perititheemi	8
	4062	peritrepo	1
	4063	peritreko	1
	4064	periphero	5
	4065	periphroneo	1
	4066	perikōros	10
	4067	peripseema	1
	4843	sumperilambano	1
4052		perissūo	39
	4050	perissīa	5
	4051	perissūma	5
	5248	huperperissūo	2
4053		perissos & perissoteros	22
	4044	perissoterōs	13
	4052	perissuo	39
	4056	perissoterōs	13
	4057	perissōs	3
4059		peritemno	18
	564	aperitmeetos	1
	4061	peritomee	36
4072		petomai	1
	1600	ekpetannumi	1
	2596	katapetasma	6
	4071	petīnon	14
	4420	peterux	5
4078		peegnumi	1
	697	Arīos pagos	2
	3803	pagis	5
	3975	pakunomai	2
	4076	peeganon	1
	4077	peegee	12
	4089	pikros	2
	4362	prospeegnumi	1
	4634	skeenopeegia	1
4089		pikros	2
	4087	pikraino	4
	4088	pikria	4
	4090	pikrōs	2
4095		pino, pio, piomai	75
	2666	katapino	7
	4188	poma	2
	4213	posis	3
	4222	potizo	15
	4224	potos	1
	4844	sumpino	1
	5202	hudropoteo	1
4098		pipto, epeson	90
	377	anapipto	11
	496	antipipto	1
	634	apopipto	1
	1601	ekpipto	13
	1706	empipto	7
	1968	epipipto	13
	2667	katapipto	2
	3895	parapipto	1
	4045	peripipto	3
	4312	propetees	2
	4363	prospipto	8
	4430	ptoma	5
	4431	ptosis	2
4102		pistis	244
	3640	oligopistos	5
	4100	pistūo	248
	4101	pistikos	2
4103		pistos	66
	571	apistos	23
	4104	pistoō	1
4108		planos	5
	4106	planee	10
	4107	planeetees	1
4111		plasso	2
	1542	hekatontaplasiōn	3
	4109	plax	3
	4110	plasma	1
	4112	plastos	1
	4116	platus	1
	4141	pleesso	1
4116		platus	1
	4113	platīa	9
	4114	platos	4
	4115	platuno	3
4118		plīstos	3
	1705	empiplao	1
	1705	empleetho	4
	5073	tetraploōs	1

ROOT NO.	DRVT. NO.	TRANSLITERATION	FRQ.
4119		pleiōn, pleion, pleon	56
	4121	pleonazo	9
	4123	pleonektees	4
	4133	pleen	31
4120		pleko	3
	573	haplous	2
	1707	empleko	2
	4117	plegma	1
	4179	pollaplasiōn	1
4123		pleonektees	4
	4122	pleonekteo	5
	4124	pleonexia	10
4126		pleo	5
	636	apopleo	4
	1020	braduploeō	1
	1602	ekpleo	3
	2668	katapleo	1
	3896	parapleo	1
	4130	pleetho	24
	4143	ploion	67
	4144	ploōs	3
	5284	hupopleo	2
4130		pleetho	24
	4128	pleethos	32
	4132	pleemmura	1
	4134	pleerees	17
	4140	pleesmonee	1
	4149	poutos	1
4134		pleerees	17
	4135	pleerophoreo	5
	4137	pleeroō	90
4137		pleeroō	90
	378	anapleerōo	6
	1603	ekpleeroō	1
	4138	pleerōma	17
	4862	sumpleeroō	3
4141		pleesso	1
	1605	ekpleesso	13
	1969	epipleetto	1
	3990	pelekizomai	1
	4127	pleegee	21
	4131	pleektees	2
4149		ploutos	1
	4145	plousios	28
	4148	ploutizo	3
4150		pluno	1
	637	apopluno	1
	4126	pleo	5
4154		pneo	7
	1606	ekpneo	3
	1709	empneo	1
	2315	theopnūstos	1
	4151	pnūma	385
	4155	pnigo	2
	4157	pnoee	2
	5285	hupopneo	1
4155		pnigo	2
	638	apopnigo	3
	1970	epipnigo	1
	4156	pniktos	3
	4856	sumpnigo	5
4160		poyeo	576
	17	agathopoyos	1
	2140	ūpoiya	1
	2227	zōopoieo	12
	2555	kakopoyos	5
	2569	kalopoiōn	1
	3447	moskopoyeo	1
	3792	oklopoyeo	1
	4046	peripoyeomai	2
	4161	poyeema	2
	4162	poyeesis	1
	4163	poyeetees	6
	4364	prospoyeomai	1
	4635	skeenopoyos	1
	5499	kiropoyeetos	6
4166		poimeen	18
	750	arkipoimeen	1
	4165	poimaino	11
4171		polemos	18
	4170	polemeo	7
	4172	polis	164
4172		polis	164
	295	Amphipolis	1
	1179	Dekapolis	3
	2404	Hīerapolis	1
	2969	kōmopolis	1
	3496	Neapolis	1
	3533	Nikopolis	1
	4173	politarkees	2
	4177	politees	3
4177		politees	3
	4174	politīa	2

ROOT NO.	DRVT. NO.	TRANSLITERATION	FRQ.
	4176	politūomai	2
	4847	sumpolitees	1
4183		polus	365
	3827	pampolus	1
	4118	plistos	3
	4119	pleiōn, pleion, pleon	59
	4178	pollakis	18
	4179	pollaplasiōn	1
	4180	polulogia	1
	4181	polumerōs	1
	4182	polupoikilos	1
	4184	polusplanknos	1
	4185	polutelees	3
	4186	polutimos	2
	4187	polutropōs	1
4192		ponos	3
	2669	kataponeomai	2
	4190	poneeros	78
4195		Pontos	2
	2670	katapontizomai	2
	4193	Pontikos	1
4198		porūomai	154
	639	aporeomai	4
	1531	īsporuomai	17
	1607	ekporūomai	34
	1710	emporūomai	3
	1713	emporos	5
	1975	epiporūomai	1
	3596	hodoiporeo	1
	3899	paraporūomai	5
	4197	poria	2
	4313	proporūomai	2
	4365	prosporūomai	1
	4848	sumporūomai	4
4203		pornūo	8
	1608	ekpornūo	1
	4202	pornīa	26
4209		porphura	5
	4210	porphureos, porphurous	3
	4211	porphuropōlis	1
4215		potamos	16
	3318	Mesopotamia	2
	4216	potamophoreetos	1
4218		pote	32
	1221	deepote	1
	3368	meedepote	1
	3379	meepotee or mee potee	25
	3698	hopote	1
	3763	oudepote	16
	4455	popote	6
4225		pou	3
	3699	hopou	82
	4080	peelikos	2
	4218	pote	32
	4458	pōs	16
4226		pou	47
	4169	poios	34
	4217	potapos	7
	4219	pote	19
	4220	poteron	1
	4459	pos	103
4228		pous	93
	405	andrapodistees	1
	3716	orthopodeo	1
	3976	pedee	3
	3977	pedinos	1
	3979	pezee	2
	4158	podeerees	1
	4692	spūdo	6
	5074	tretrapous	3
	5286	hupopodion	9
4238		prasso, pratto	38
	4233	practōr	2
	4234	praxis	6
4239		praūs	3
	4235	praos	1
	4240	praūtees	3
4241		prepī	7
	2143	ūprepīa	1
	3169	megaloprepees	1
4245		presbuteros, -tera	67
	4243	presbūo	2
	4244	presbuterion	3
	4246	presbutees	3
	4850	sumpresbuteros	1
4253		pro	49
	4206	porro	2
	4208	ponōtero	2
	4248	preenees	1
	4250	prin, prinee	14

ROOT NO.	DRVT. NO.	TRANSLITERATION	FRQ.
4253		pro (cont.)	
	4254	proago	18
	4255	proaireomai	1
	4256	proaitiaomai	1
	4257	proakouo	1
	4258	proamartano	2
	4259	proaulion	1
	4260	probaino	5
	4261	proballo	2
	4264	probibazo	2
	4265	problepo	1
	4266	proginomai	1
	4267	proginōsko	5
	4270	prographo	5
	4271	prodeelos	3
	4272	prodidōmi	1
	4274	prodromos	1
	4275	proīdea	2
	4276	proelpizo	1
	4277	proēpo	3
	4278	proenarkomai	2
	4279	proepangellomai	1
	4280	proereo	9
	4281	proerkomai	9
	4282	proetoimazo	2
	4283	proūangelizomai	1
	4284	prôêkomai	1
	4285	proeegeomai	1
	4287	prothesmia	1
	4289	prothumos	3
	4291	proīsteemi	8
	4292	prokaleomai	1
	4293	prokatangello	4
	4294	prokatarizo	1
	4295	prokīmai	5
	4296	prokeerusso	2
	4298	prokopto	6
	4299	prokrima	1
	4300	prokuroômai	1
	4301	prolambano	3
	4302	prolego	3
	4303	promarturomai	1
	4304	promeletao	1
	4305	promerimnao	1
	4306	pronoeo	3
	4308	prôôrao	2
	4309	prôôrizo	6
	4310	propasko	1
	4311	propempo	9
	4312	propetees	2
	4313	proporūomai	2
	4314	pros	711
	4315	prosabbaton	1
	4372	prosphatos	1
	4384	protassomai	1
	4385	protīno	1
	4387	proteros	1
	4388	protitheemi	3
	4389	protrepomai	1
	4390	protreko	2
	4391	prouparko	2
	4392	prophasis	7
	4393	prophero	2
	4396	propheetees	149
	4399	prophthano	1
	4400	prokīrizomai	2
	4401	prokīrotoneomai	1
	4402	Prokoros	1
	4404	prōī	10
	4408	prōra	2
	4413	prōtos	100
	5432	phroureo	4
4289		prothumos	3
	4288	prothumia	5
	4290	prothumōs	1
4314		pros	711
	676	aprositos	1
	1715	emprosthen	48
	2145	ūprosedros	1
	4316	prosagorūomai	1
	4317	prosago	4
	4319	prosaiteo	3
	4320	prosanabaino	1
	4321	prosanalisko	1
	4322	prosanapleeroō	2
	4323	prosanatitheemi	2
	4324	prosapīleomai	1
	4325	prosdapano	1
	4326	prosdeomai	1
	4327	prosdekomai	14
	4328	prosdokao	16
	4330	proseao	1
	4331	prosengizo	1

ROOT NO.	DRVT. NO.	TRANSLITERATION	FRQ.
	4332	prosedrūo	1
	4333	prosergazomai	1
	4334	proserkomai	86
	4336	prosūkomai	87
	4337	prosko	24
	4338	prosseeloō	1
	4340	proskairos	4
	4341	proskalemai	30
	4342	proskartereo	10
	4344	proskephalaion	1
	4345	proskleeroômai	1
	4346	prosklisis	1
	4347	proskollaomai	4
	4350	proskopto	8
	4351	proskulio	2
	4352	proskuneo	60
	4354	proslaleo	2
	4355	proslambano	14
	4357	prosmeno	7
	4358	prosormizomai	1
	4359	prosophīlo	1
	4360	prosokthizo	2
	4361	prospīnos	1
	4362	prospeegnumi	1
	4363	prospipto	8
	4364	prospoyeomai	1
	4365	prosporuomai	1
	4366	prosreegnumi	2
	4367	prostasso	7
	4369	prostitheemi	18
	4370	prostreko	3
	4371	prosphagion	1
	4374	prosphero, proseenenka	48
	4375	prosphilees	1
	4377	prosphoneo	7
	4378	proskusis	1
	4379	prospsauo	1
	4383	prosopon	78
4350		proskopto	8
	677	aproskopos	3
	4348	proskomma	6
	4349	proskopee	1
4381		prosōpoleeptees	1
	4380	prosopoleepteo	1
	4382	prosopoleepsia	4
4383		prosōpon	78
	678	aprosōpoleeptōs	1
	2146	uprosōpeo	1
	4381	prosōpoleeptees	1
4396		propheetees	149
	4394	propheetīa	19
	4395	propheetūo	38
	4397	propheetikos	2
	4398	propheetis	2
	5578	psūdopropheetees	11
4404		prōī	10
	4405	prōīa	4
	4406	prōīmos	10
	4407	prōīnos	1
4413		prōtos	100
	1207	duteroprōtos	1
	4409	prōtūo	1
	4410	prōtoklisia	4
	4412	prōton & to prōton	60
	4414	prōtostatees	1
	4416	prōtotokos	9
	5383	philoprōtūo	1
4429		ptuo	3
	1609	ekptuo	1
	1716	emptuo	6
	4425	ptuon	2
	4426	pturomai	1
	4427	ptusma	1
4442		pur	74
	329	anazopureo	1
	4443	pura	2
	4448	purôômai	6
	4450	purros	2
4443		pura	2
	4445	puresso	2
	4447	purinos	1
4452		pō	
	3369	meedepo	1
	3380	meepo	2
	3764	oudepo	5
	4455	pōpote	6
4458		pōs	16
	1513	ī pōs	4
	3381	meepōs or mee pōs	12
	4452	po	
4464		rabdos	12
	4463	rabdizo	2

ROOT NO.	DRVT. NO.	TRANSLITERATION	FRQ.
	4465	rabdoukos	2
4474		rapizo	2
	4464	rabdos	12
	4475	rapisma	3
	4495	ripto	8
4482		reo	1
	131	haimorroeo	1
	3901	pararrueo	1
	5493	kīmarros	1
4483		reo	26
	368	anantirreetos	1
	720	arneomai	31
	731	arreetos	1
	2036	epo	976
	2046	ereo	71
	3954	parreesia	51
	4487	reema	70
	4489	reetor	1
	4490	reetos	1
4486		reegnumi & reesso	7
	2608	katagnumi	4
	4048	perirreegnumi	1
	4366	prosreegnumi	2
	4470	rakos	2
	4485	reegma	1
	5138	trakus	2
	5327	pharanx	1
4496		ripto	8
	641	aporripto	1
	1977	epirripto	2
	4493	ripee	1
	4494	ripizomai	1
4506		ruomai	18
	4505	rumee	4
	4511	rusis	3
	4512	rutis	1
4509		rupos	1
	4508	ruparos	1
	4510	rupoō	2
4521		sabbaton & sabbata	68
	4315	prosabbaton	1
	4520	sabbatismos	1
4531		salūo	15
	761	asalūtos	2
	4530	Salīm	1
4535		salos	1
	4529	Salamis	1
	4531	saluo	15
	4536	salpinx	11
4556		sardios	1
	4555	sardinos	1
	4557	sardonux	1
4561		sarx	151
	4559	sarkikos	11
	4560	sarkinos	1
4573		sebazomai	1
	4574	sebasma	2
	4575	sebastos	3
4576		sebomai	10
	765	asebees	9
	2152	ūsebees	4
	2318	theosebees	1
	4573	sebazomai	1
	4586	semnos	4
4579		sīo	5
	383	anasīo	2
	2678	katasīo	4
	4578	sīsmos	14
4591		seemaino	6
	767	aseemos	1
	1978	episeemos	2
	2154	ūseemos	1
	3902	paraseemos	1
	4592	seemion	77
	4953	susseemon	1
4599		sthenoō	1
	772	asthenees	25
	4988	Sōsthenees	2
4621		sitos	14
	777	asitos	1
	1979	episitismos	1
	4618	sitūtos	3
	4619	sitistos	1
	4620	sitometrion	1
4628		skelos	3
	4642	skleeros	6
	4646	skolios	4
	4647	skolops	1
4632		skūos	23
	384	anaskūazo	1
	643	aposkūazomai	1
	2680	kataskūazo	11
	3903	paraskūazo	4

ROOT NO.	DRVT. NO.	TRANSLITERATION	FRQ.
	4631	skūee	1
4633		skeenee	20
	4635	skeenopoyos	1
	4636	skeenos	2
4636		skeenos	2
	4634	skeenopeegia	1
	4637	skeenoō	5
4637		skeenoō	5
	1981	episkeenoō	1
	2596	kataskeenoō	4
	4638	skeenōma	3
4639		skia	7
	644	aposkiasma	1
	1982	episkiazo	5
	2683	kataskiazo	1
	4655	skotos	32
4642		skleeros	6
	4641	skleerokardia	3
	4643	skleerotees	1
	4644	skleerotrakeelos	1
	4645	skleeruno	6
4649		skopos	1
	1980	episkeptomai	11
	1985	episkopos	5
	2685	kataskopos	1
	4648	skopeo	6
4655		skotos	32
	4652	skotīnos	4
	4653	skotia	16
	4654	skotizomai	8
	4656	skotôômai	1
4667		Smurna	1
	4668	Smurnaios	1
	4669	smurnizomai	1
4680		sophos	22
	781	asophos	1
	4678	sophis	51
	4679	sophizo	2
	5386	philosophos	1
4682		sparasso	4
	4787	sunkineo	1
	4952	susparasso	1
4685		spaomai	2
	385	anaspao	2
	645	apospao	4
	782	aspazomai	60
	1986	epispaomai	1
	4049	perispaomai	1
	4687	spiro	53
4687		spīro	53
	4690	sperma	44
	4701	spora	1
	4703	sporos	5
	4711	spuris	5
4698		splankna	11
	2155	ūsplankos	2
	4184	polusplanknos	1
	4697	splanknizomai	12
4710		spoudee	12
	4704	spoudazo	11
	4705	spoudaios	3
	4707	spoudaios	3
4717		stauroō	46
	388	anaotauroō	1
	4957	sustauroō	5
4721		stegee	3
	648	apostegazo	1
	4722	stego	4
	5152	tristegon	1
4724		stellomai	2
	649	apostello	133
	1989	epistello	3
	2687	katastello	2
	4749	stolee	9
	4958	sustello	2
	5288	hupostello	4
4727		stenazo	6
	389	anastenazo	1
	4726	stenagmos	2
	4959	sustenazo	1
4728		stenos	3
	4727	stenazo	6
	4730	stenokōria	4
4731		stereos	4
	4723	stīra	4
	4732	stereoō	3
4735		stephanos	8
	4718	stapholee	3
	4725	stemma	1
	4737	stephanoō	3
4741		steerizo	13
	793	asteeriktos	2
	1991	episteerizo	4

ROOT NO.	DRVT. NO.	TRANSLITERATION	FRQ.
4741		steerizo (cont.)	
	4740	steerigmos	1
4748		stoikeo	5
	4747	stoikīon	7
	4960	sustoikeo	1
4750		stoma	78
	653	apostomatizo	1
	1993	epistomizo	1
	4751	stomakos	1
4754		stratūomai	7
	497	antistratūomai	1
	4752	stratīa	2
	4753	stratūma	8
4756		stratia	2
	4754	stratūomai	7
	4755	strateegos	10
	4757	statiōtees	26
	4758	stratologeo	1
	4760	stratopedarkees	1
4762		strepho	18
	390	anastrepho	11
	654	apostrepho	10
	1612	ekstrephomai	1
	1994	epistrepho	39
	2690	katastrepho	2
	3344	metastrepho	3
	4761	strebloō	1
	4962	sustrepho	1
	5290	hupostrepho	35
4766		strōnnumi, strōnnuo	7
	792	asteer	24
	3038	Lithostrōtos	1
	5291	hupostrōnnumi	1
4767		stugeetos	1
	655	apostugeo	1
	2319	theostugees	1
	4768	stugnazo	2
4771		su	178
	4571	se	196
	4671	soi	221
	4674	sos	27
	4675	sou	498
	5210	humīs	243
4802		suzeeteo	10
	4803	suzeeteesis	3
	4804	suzeeteesis	1
4810		sukon	4
	4808	sukee	16
	4811	sukophanteo	2
4813		sulao	1
	2417	hierosulos	1
	4812	sulagōgeo	1
4859		sumphōnos	1
	800	asumphōnos	4
	4856	sumphōneo	6
	4858	sumphōnia	1
4862		sun	125
	2839	koinos	12
	3342	metaxu	9
	4773	sungenees	12
	4774	sungnōmee	1
	4775	sunkatheemai	2
	4776	sunkathizo	2
	4777	sunkakopatheo	1
	4778	sunkakoukeomai	1
	4779	sunkaleo	8
	4780	sunkaluptomai	1
	4781	sunkampto	1
	4782	sunkatabaino	1
	4784	sunkatathesis	1
	4785	sunkataseephizomai	1
	4786	sunkerannumi	2
	4788	sunklīo	4
	4789	sunkleeronomos	4
	4790	sunkoinōneo	3
	4791	sunkoinōnos	4
	4792	sunkomizo	1
	4793	sunkrino	3
	4794	sunkupto	1
	4795	sunkuria	1
	4796	sunkairo	7
	4797	sunkeo	1
	4798	sunkraomai	1
	4800	suzaō	3
	4801	suzūgnuo	2
	4802	suzeeteo	10
	4806	suzōōpoyeo	2
	4814	sullaleo	6
	4815	sullambano	16
	4816	sullego	8
	4817	sullogizomai	1
	4818	sullupeomai	1
	4819	sumbaino	8
	4820	sumballo	6
	4821	sumbasilūo	2
	4822	sumbibazo	6
	4823	sumbaulūo	5
	4825	sumbaulos	1
	4827	summatheethees	1
	4828	summartureo	4
	4829	summerizomai	1
	4830	summetokos	2
	4831	summineetes	1
	4832	summorphoōmai	2
	4836	sumparaginomai	2
	4837	sumparakaleomai	1
	4838	sumparalambano	4
	4839	sumparameno	1
	4840	sumparīmī	1
	4841	sumpasko	2
	4842	sumpempo	2
	4843	sumperilambano	1
	4844	sumpino	2
	4845	sumpleeroō	3
	4846	sumpnigo	5
	4847	sumpolitees	1
	4848	sumporūomai	4
	4850	sumpresbuteros	1
	4851	sumphero	17
	4852	sumpheemi	1
	4853	sumphuletees	1
	4854	sumphutos	1
	4855	sumphuomai	1
	4860	sumpseephizo	1
	4863	sunago	62
	4865	sunagōnizomai	1
	4866	sunathleo	2
	4867	sunathroizo	3
	4868	sunairo	3
	4869	sunaikmalōtos	3
	4870	sunakoloutheo	2
	4871	sunalizomai	1
	4872	sunanabaino	2
	4873	sunanakīmai	9
	4874	sunamignumi	3
	4875	sunanapauomai	1
	4876	sunantao	6
	4878	sunantilambanomai	2
	4879	sunapagomai	3
	4880	sunapothneesko	3
	4881	sunapollumai	1
	4882	sunapostello	1
	4883	sunarmologeomai	2
	4884	sunarpazo	4
	4885	sunauxanomai	1
	4886	sundesmos	4
	4888	sundoxazomai	1
	4889	sundoulos	10
	4891	sunegīro	1
	4892	sunedrion	22
	4894	sunīdeo	14
	4895	sunīmi	2
	4896	sunīmi	1
	4897	sunīserkomai	2
	4898	sunekdeemos	2
	4899	suneklektos	1
	4900	sunelauno	1
	4901	sunepimartureo	1
	4902	sunepomai	1
	4904	sunergos	3
	4905	sunerkomai	32
	4906	sunesthio	5
	4909	sunūdokeo	6
	4910	sunūokeomai	2
	4911	sunephisteemi	1
	4912	suneko	12
	4913	suneedomai	1
	4915	suneelikiōtees	1
	4916	sunthaptomai	2
	4917	sunthlaomai	2
	4918	sunthlibo	2
	4919	sunthrupto	1
	4920	sunieemi	26
	4921	sunistao, sunisteemi	13
	4921	sunistano	3
	4922	sunodūo	1
	4923	sunodia	1
	4924	sunoikeo	1
	4925	sunoikodomeomai	1
	4926	sunomileo	1
	4927	sunomoreo	1
	4929	suntasso	2
	4931	sunteleo	7
	4932	suntemno	2
	4933	sunteereo	4
	4934	suntitheemi	4
	4936	suntreko	3
	4937	suntribo	8
	4939	suntrophos	1
	4940	suntunkano	1
	4942	sunupokrinomai	1
	4943	sunupourgeo	1
	4944	sunōdino	1
	4945	sunōmosia	1
	4952	susparasso	1
	4953	susseemon	1
	4954	sussōma	1
	4955	sustasiastees	1
	4957	sustauroō	5
	4958	sustello	2
	4959	sustenazo	1
	4960	sustoikeo	1
	4961	sustratiōtees	2
	4962	sustrepho	1
	4964	suskeematizomai	2
4863		sunago	62
	1996	episunago	7
	4864	sunagōgee	57
4864		sunagōgee	57
	656	aposunagōgos	3
	752	arkisunagōgos	2
4920		sunieemi	26
	4907	sunesis	7
	4908	sunetos	4
4921		sunistano	3
4921		sunistao,sunisteemi	13
	1999	episustasis	2
	4956	sustatikos	2
4936		suntreko	3
	1998	episuntreko	1
	4890	sundromee	1
4951		suro	5
	2694	katasuro	1
	4577	sira	1
	4950	surtis	1
4969		sphatto	10
	2695	katasphatto	1
	4372	prosphatos	1
	4967	sphagee	3
4976		skeema	2
	2158	uskeemōn	5
	3345	metaskeematizo	5
	4964	suskeematizomai	2
4982		sōzo	111
	810	asotia	3
	811	asotos	1
	4983	sōma	146
	4986	Sōpatros	1
	4988	Sōsthenees	2
	4990	soteer	24
	4998	sōphrōn	4
4983		sōma	146
	4954	sussōma	1
	4984	sōmatikos	2
4991		soteeria	45
	4992	sōteerion	4
	4993	sōteerios	1
4998		sōphrōn	4
	4993	sōphroneo	6
	4994	sōphronizo	1
	4996	sōphronōs	1
	4997	sōphrosunee	3
5005		talaipōros	2
	5003	talaipōreo	1
	5004	talaipōria	2
5007		talanton	15
	5005	talaipōros	2
	5506	talantiaios	1
5011		tapīnos	8
	5012	tapinophrosunee	7
	5013	tapīnoō	14
5015		tarasso	17
	5016	tarakee	2
	5017	tarakos	2
5021		tasso	8
	392	anatossomai	1
	498	antitassomai	5
	657	apostassomai	6
	813	ataktos	1
	2004	epitasso	10
	4367	prostasso	7
	4384	protassomai	1
	4929	suntasso	2
	5001	tagma	1
	5002	taktos	1
	5010	taxis	10
	5293	hupotasso	40
5036		takus	1
	5029	taka	2
	5030	takeōs	10
	5032	takion	5
	5033	takista	1
	5034	takos	7
	5035	taku	13
5037		te	209
	1535	īte	65
	3361	meete	37
	3753	hote	105
	3777	oute	94
	4218	pote	32
	4219	pote	19
	5620	hōste	83
5043		teknon	99
	815	ateknos	3
	5040	teknion	9
	5041	teknogoneo	1
	5044	teknotropheo	1
	5388	philoteknos	1
5046		telīos	19
	5047	telīotees	2
	5048	telīoō	24
	5049	telīōs	1
5055		teleo	26
	658	apoteleo	1
	1615	ekteleo	2
	2005	epiteleo	12
	4931	sunteleo	7
	5053	telūtao	12
5056		telos	42
	393	anatello	9
	1781	entellomai	17
	3081	lusitelī	1
	3651	holotelees	1
	3838	panteles	2
	4185	polutelees	3
	5046	telīos	19
	5052	telesphoreo	1
	5055	teleo	26
	5057	telōnees	22
	5081	teelaugōs	1
5057		telōnees	22
	754	arkitelōnees	1
	5058	telōnion	3
5064		tessares, -ra	42
	1180	dekatessares	5
	5062	tessarakonta	22
	5065	tessareskaidekatos	2
	5066	tetartaios	1
	5067	tetartos	10
	5068	tetragōnos	1
	5070	tetrakiskilioi	5
	5071	tetrakosioi,-sia	4
	5072	tetrameenon	1
	5073	tetraplōōs	1
	5074	tetrapous	3
	5076	tetrarkees	4
	5132	trapeza	15
5078		teknee	3
	3673	homoteknos	1
	5079	teknitees	4
5083		teereo	75
	3906	parateereo	6
	4933	sunteereo	4
	5084	teereesis	3
5087		titheemi, etheeka, ethemeen, tho, &c.	96
	113	athesmos	2
	114	atheteo	16
	121	athōos	2
	394	anatitheemi	2
	477	antithesis	1
	659	apotitheemi	8
	1570	ekthetos	1
	1620	ektitheemi	4
	2111	ūthetos	3
	2117	ūthus	8
	2117	ūthus adv.	8
	2310	themelios	16
	2336	theekee	1
	2344	theesauros	18
	2698	katatitheemi	3
	3346	metatitheemi	6
	3550	nomothetees	1
	3559	nouthesia	3
	3734	horothesia	1
	4060	perititheemi	8
	4287	prothesmia	1
	4369	prostitheemi	18
	4388	protitheemi	3
	4934	suntitheemi	4
	5206	whyothesia	5

ROOT NO.	DRVT. NO.	TRANSLITERATION	FRQ.
5087		titheemi, &c. (cont.)	
	5294	hupotitheemi	2
5088		tikto, etekon	19
	5043	teknon	99
	5045	tektōn	2
	5078	teknee	3
	5110	tokos	2
	5115	toxon	1
5092		timee	43
	820	atimos	4
	927	barutimos	1
	1784	entimos	5
	2009	epitimia	1
	4186	polutimos	2
	5093	timios	14
	5095	Timotheos	24
	5096	Timōn	1
	5389	philotimeomai	3
5093		timios	14
	5091	timao	21
	5094	timiotees	1
5098		timōria	1
	5043	teknon	99
	5045	tektōn	2
5099		tio	1
	661	apotio	1
	5092	timee	43
5100		tis	452
	1509	i mee ti	3
	1536	ītis	79
	2530	kathoti	5
	3385	meeti	15
	3386	meeti	1
	3387	meetis or mee tis	4
	3748	hostis	153
	5101	tis	538
5104		toi	1
	2273	eetoi	1
	2543	kaitoi, kai-toige	4
	2544	kaitoi, kai-toige	4
	3305	mentio	8
	5105	toigaroun	2
	5106	toinun	4
	5107	toisde	1
5111		tolmao	16
	662	apotolmaō	1
	5112	tolmeeroteron	1
	5113	tolmeetees	1
5114		tomōteros	1
	823	atomos	1
	2998	latomeo	2
	3718	orthotomeo	1
	4059	peritemno	18
	4750	stoma	78
	4932	suntemno	2
5117		topos	92
	824	atopos	3
	1786	entopios	1
5137		trakeelos	7
	4644	skleerotrakeelos	1
	5136	trakeelizomai	1
5140		trīs, tria	68
	755	arkitriklinos	3
	5144	triakonta	11
	5145	triakosioi	2
	5146	tribolos	2
	5148	trietia	1
	5150	trimeenon	1
	5151	tris	12
	5152	tristegon	1
	5154	tritos	57
5142		trepho	8
	397	anatrepho	3
	1361	Diotrephees	1
	1625	ektrepho	2
	1790	entromos	3
	2353	thremma	1
	2361	thrombos	1
	5044	teknotropheo	1
	5160	trophee	16
	5162	trophos	1
5143		treko	20
	1532	īstreko	1
	2701	katatreko	1
	4063	peritreko	1
	4370	prostreko	3
	4390	protreko	2
	4936	suntreko	3
	5137	trakeelos	7
	5164	trokos	1
	5295	hupotreko	1
5147		tribos	3
	1304	diatribo	10
2346		thlibo	10
	4937	suntribo	8
	5551	kronotribeo	1
5157		tropee	1
	396	anatrepo	2
	665	apotrepomai	1
	1624	ektrepomai	5
	1788	entrepo, -omai	9
	2010	epitrepo	19
	2160	ūtrapelia	1
	4062	peritrepo	1
	4389	protrepomai	1
	4762	strepho	18
	5142	trepho	8
	5158	tropos	13
5158		tropos	13
	2012	epitropos	3
	4187	polutropōs	1
	5159	tropophoreo	1
5172		truphee	2
	5170	Truphaina	1
	5171	truphao	1
	5173	Truphōsa	2
5177		tunkano	13
	1793	entunkano	5
	1794	entulitto	3
	2013	epitunkano	5
	2161	Ūtokos	1
	3909	paratunkano	1
	4940	suntunkano	1
	5190	Tukikos	5
5179		tupos	16
	499	antitupon	2
	1795	entupoō	1
	5296	hopotupōsis	2
5180		tupto	14
	5178	tumpanizomai	1
	5179	tupos	16
5188		tuphomai	1
	5187	tuphoomai	3
	5189	tuphōnikos	1
5195		hubrizo	5
	1796	enubrizo	1
	5197	hubristees	2
5204		hudōr	79
	504	anudros	4
	5201	hudria	3
	5202	hudropoteo	1
	5203	hudrōpikos	1
5205		huetos	6
	5194	hualos	2
	5200	hugros	1
	5204	hudōr	79
5210		humīs	243
	5209	humas	437
	5212	humeteros	10
	5213	humin	621
	5216	humōn	583
5219		hupakouo	21
	5218	hupakoee	15
	5255	hupeekōos	3
5225		huparko	48
	4391	prouparko	2
	5223	huparxis	2
	5224	huparkonta	14
5228		huper	160
	446	anthupatos	4
	5196	hubris	3
	5229	huperairomai	3
	5230	huperakmos	1
	5231	huperano	3
	5232	huperauxano	1
	5233	huperbaino	1
	5235	huperballo	5
	5237	huperīdo	1
	5238	huperekīna	1
	5239	huperektīno	1
	5240	huperekkunomai	1
	5241	huperentunkano	1
	5242	hupereko	5
	5244	hupereephanos	5
	5245	hupernikao	1
	5246	huperonkos	2
	5248	huperperissūo	2
	5249	huperperissōs	1
	5250	huperpleonazo	1
	5251	huperupsoō	1
	5252	huperphroneo	1
	5253	huperōon	4
	5289	hupostolee	1
	5311	hupsos	6
5235		huperballo	5
	5234	huperballontōs	1
	5234	huperbolee	8
5257		hupeeretees	20
	5221	hupantao	5
	5256	hupeereteo	3
5258		hupnos	6
	69	agrupneo	4
	879	aphupnoō	1
	1798	enupnion	1
	1853	exupnos	1
5259		hupo	230
	278	hupomeno	17
	4943	sunupourgeo	1
	5217	hupago	81
	5219	hupakouo	21
	5225	huparko	48
	5226	hupīko	1
	5227	hupenantios	2
	5254	hupeko	1
	5257	hupeeretees	20
	5260	hupoballo	1
	5261	hupogrammos	1
	5263	hupodiknumi	6
	5265	hupodeomai	3
	5267	hupodikos	1
	5268	hupozugion	2
	5269	hupozōnnumi	1
	5270	hupokato	9
	5271	hupokrinomai	1
	5274	hupolambano	4
	5276	hupoleenion	1
	5279	hupomimneesko	7
	5282	huponoeo	3
	5284	hupopleo	2
	5285	hupopneo	1
	5286	hupopodion	9
	5287	hupostasis	5
	5288	hupostello	4
	5290	hupostrepho	35
	5291	hupostrōnnumi	1
	5293	hupotasso	40
	5294	hupotitheemi	2
	5295	hupotreko	1
	5296	hupotupōsis	2
	5297	hupophero	3
	5298	hupokōreo	2
	5299	hupōpiazo	2
	5306	husteros	1
5271		hupokrinomai	1
	505	anupokritos	6
	4942	sunupokrinomai	1
	5272	hupokrisis	7
	5273	hupokritees	20
5293		hupotasso	40
	506	anupotaktos	4
	5292	hupotagee	4
5302		hustereo	16
	5303	hustereema	9
	5304	hustereesis	2
5306		husteros	1
	5302	hustereo	16
	5305	husteron	12
5311		hupsos	6
	5308	hupseelos	11
	5310	hupsistos	13
	5312	hupsoō	20
5312		hupsoō	20
	5251	huperaupsoō	1
	5313	hupsōma	2
5315		phago	97
	2068	esthio	65
	4371	prosphagion	1
	5314	phagos	2
5316		phaino	31
	160	aiphnidios	2
	398	anaphainomai	2
	852	aphanees	1
	855	aphantos	1
	1717	emphanees	2
	1819	exapina	1
	2014	epiphaino	4
	2726	kateephīa	1
	4392	prophasis	7
	4811	sukophanteo	2
	5244	hupereephanos	5
	5318	phaneros	21
	5322	phanos	1
	5324	phantazomai	1
5318		phaneros	21
	5319	phaneroō	49
	5320	phanerōs	3
5324		phantazomai	1
	5325	phantasia	1
	5326	phantasma	2
5332		pharmakūs	1
	5331	pharmakīa	3
	5333	pharmakos	1
5338		phengos	3
	5348	phthano	7
	5350	phthengomai	3
5339		phīdomai	10
	857	aphīdia	1
	5340	phīdomenōs	2
5342		phero, oiso, eenenka	64
	399	anaphero	10
	667	apophero	5
	959	Bernikee	3
	1533	īsphero	7
	1627	ekphero	7
	2018	epiphero	5
	2287	thanateephoros	1
	2593	karpophoros	1
	2702	kataphero	3
	3911	paraphero	2
	4064	periphero	5
	4374	prosphero, proseenenka	48
	4393	prophero	2
	4851	sumphero	17
	5052	telesphoreo	1
	5297	hupophero	3
	5411	phoros	5
	5414	phortos	1
	5459	phōsphoros	1
	5606	ōmos	3
5343		phūgo	31
	668	apophūgo	3
	1628	ekphūgo	7
	2703	kataphūgo	2
	5436	Phugellos	1
	5437	phugee	2
5345		pheemee	2
	989	blaspheemos	5
	1426	duspheemia	1
	2163	ūpheemos	1
5346		pheemi	58
	2036	epo	976
	4396	propheetees	149
	4852	sumpheemi	1
	5334	phasis	1
	5335	phasko	4
	5345	pheemee	2
	5350	phthengomai	3
5350		phthengomai	3
	669	apopthengomai	3
	5353	phthongos	2
5351		phthīro	8
	862	aphthartos	7
	2704	kataphthīro	2
	5349	phthartos	6
	5355	phthonos	9
	5356	phthora	9
5361		philadelphos	1
	5359	Philadelphia	2
	5360	philadelphia	6
5366		philarguros	2
	866	aphilarguros	2
	5365	philarguria	1
5368		phileo	25
	2705	kataphileo	6
	4375	prosphilees	1
	5370	phileema	7
	5371	Phileemōn	1
	5372	Phileetos	1
5384		philos	29
	2321	Theophilos	2
	5358	philagathos	1
	5361	philadelphos	1
	5362	philandros	1
	5364	philanthrōpōs	1
	5366	philarguros	2
	5367	philautos	1
	5368	phileo	25
	5369	phileedonos	1
	5373	philia	1
	5376	Philippos	38
	5377	philotheos	1
	5382	philoxenos	3
	5383	philoprōtūo	1
	5386	philosophos	1
	5387	philostorgos	1
	5388	philoteknos	1
	5389	philotimeomai	3
	5391	philophrōn	1
5395		phlox	7
	5393	Phlegōn	1
	5394	phlogizo	2

ROOT NO.	DRVT. NO.	TRANSLITERATION	FRQ.
5397		phluaros	1
	3632	oinophlugia	1
	5396	phluareo	1
5399		phobeomai	93
	1629	ekphobeo	1
	5400	phobeetron	1
5401		phobos	47
	870	aphobōs	4
	1630	ekphobus	2
	1719	emphobos	6
	5398	phoberos	3
	5399	phubeomai	93
5404		phoinix	2
	5403	Phoinikee	3
	5405	Phoinix	1
5408		phonos	10
	409	androphonos	1
	5406	phonūs	7
5409		phoreo	6
	2164	ūphoreo	1
	4135	pleerophoreo	5
	4216	potamophoreetos	1
	5159	tropophoreo	1
5411		phoros	5
	3683	Oneesiphoros	2
	5409	phoreo	6
5414		phortos	1
	5412	phortizo	2
	5413	phortion	5
5420		phrasso	2
	4973	sphragis	16
	5418	phragmos	4
5424		phrenes	2
	878	aphrōn	11
	2165	ūphraino, -omai	14
	3675	homophrōn	1
	4998	sōphrōn	4
	5012	tapinophrosunee	7
	5309	hupseelophroneo	2
	5391	philophrōn	1
	5420	phrasso	2
	5423	phrenapatees	1
	5426	phroneo	29
	5429	phronimos	14
	5431	phrontizo	1
5426		phroneo	29
	2706	kataphroneo	9
	3912	paraphroneo	1
	4065	periphroneo	1
	5252	huperphroneo	1
	5427	phroneema	4
	5428	phroneesis	2
5441		phulax	3
	1200	desmophulax	3
	5439	phulakizo	1
5442		phulasso	30
	5438	phulakee	7
	5440	phulakteerion	1
	5441	phulax	3
5443		phulee	31
	246	allophulos	1
	1429	dodekaphulon	1
	3828	Pamphulia	5
	4853	sumphuletees	1
	5442	phulasso	30
	5444	phullon	6
5448		phussioō	7
	5050	telīōsīs	2
	5450	phusiōsis	1
5449		phusis	14
	5446	phusikos	3
	5448	phusioō	7
5453		phuo	3
	1721	emphutos	1
	4855	sumphuomai	1
	5443	phulee	31
	5449	phusis	14
	5452	phutūo	11
5455		phōneo	42
	400	anaphōneo	1
	2019	epiphōneo	3
	4377	prosphōneo	7
5456		phōnee	141
	219	alektorophōnia	1
	880	aphōnos	4
	2757	kenophōnia	2
	5455	phōneo	42
5457		phōs	70
	5316	phaino	31
	5346	pheemi	58
	5458	phōsteer	2
	5459	phōsphoros	1
	5460	phōtīnos	5
	5461	phōtizo	11
5463		kairo	74
	4796	sunkairo	7
	5479	kara	59
	5485	karis	156
5465		kalao	7
	5464	kalaza	4
	5467	kalepos	2
	5469	kalinos	2
	5475	kalkos	5
5475		kalkos	5
	5470	kalkeos	1
	5471	kalkūs	1
	5472	kalkeedon	1
	5473	kalkion	1
	5474	kalkolibanon	2
5482		karax	1
	5480	karagma	9
	5481	karakteer	1
	5489	kartees	11
5483		karizomai	23
	884	Apsinthos	2
	884	akaristos	3
	2170	ūkaristos	1
	5486	karisma	17
5485		karis	156
	5483	karizomai	23
	5484	karin	9
	5487	karitoō	2
5490		kasma	1
	2785	keetos	1
	5465	kalao	7
	5476	kamai	2
	5491	kīlos	7
	5510	kiōn	3
	5561	kōra	27
5494		kīmōn	6
	5492	kīmazomai	1
	5493	kīmarros	1
	5495	kīr	779
	5522	hōōs	2
5495		kīr	779
	849	autokīr	1
	2021	epikīreo	3
	4400	prokīrizomai	2
	5497	kīragōgos	1
	5498	kīrographon	1
	5499	kīropoyeetos	6
	5500	kirotoneo	2
5507		kilioi	11
	2035	heptakiskilioi	1
	4000	pentakiskilioi	6
	5070	tetrakiskilioi	5
	5153	triskilioi	1
	5505	kiliades	23
	5506	kiliarkos	22
5525		koros	1
	4402	Prokoros	1
	5524	koreegeo	2
5530		kraomai	11
	761	apokreesis	1
	2710	katakraomai	2
	4798	sunkraomai	1
	5531	krao	1
	5532	krīa	89
	5534	kree	1
	5540	kreesis	2
	5543	kreestos	7
	5557	krusos	13
	5559	krōs	1
5531		krao	1
	5533	kreōphīletees	2
	5534	kree	1
5536		kreema	7
	3916	parakreema	19
	5537	kreematizo	9
5543		kreestos	7
	890	akreetos	1
	2173	ūkreestos	3
	5541	kreestūomai	1
	5542	kreestologia	1
	5544	kreestotees	10
5547		Kristos	569
	500	antikristos	5
	5546	Kristianos	3
	5580	psūdokristos	2
5548		krio	5
	1472	enkrio	1
	2025	epikrio	2
	5545	krīsma	3
	5547	Kristos	569
5550		kronos	53
	3118	makrokronios	1
	5549	kronizo	5
	5551	kronotribeo	1
5557		krusos	13
	5552	kruseos	18
	5553	krusion	9
	5554	krusodaktulios	1
	5555	krusolithos	1
	5556	krusoprasos	1
	5558	krusoō	2
5561		kōra	27
	2149	urukōros	1
	4066	perikōros	10
	4730	stenokōria	4
	5562	kōreo	10
	5563	kōrizo	13
	5564	kōrion	10
	5565	kōris	39
5562		kōreo	10
	402	anakōreo	14
	672	apokōreo	3
	1633	ekkōreo	1
	5298	hupokōreo	2
5567		psallo	5
	5568	psalmos	7
	5584	pseelaphao	4
	5589	psikion	3
	5597	psōko	1
5571		psūdees	3
	5569	psūdadelphos	2
	5570	psūdapostolos	1
	5572	psūdodidaskalos	1
	5573	psūdologos	1
	5575	psūdomartur	4
	5578	psūdopropheetees	11
	5580	psūdokristos	2
	5581	psūdōnumos	1
5574		psūdomai	12
	5571	psūdees	3
	5579	psūdos	9
	5582	psūsma	1
	5583	psūstees	10
5575		psūdomartur	3
	5576	psūdomartureo	6
	5577	psūdomarturia	2
5585		pseephizo	2
	4785	sunkataseephizomai	1
	4860	sumpseephizo	1
5590		psukee	105
	895	apsukos	1
	2473	isopsukos	1
	3563	nous	24
	3642	oligopsukos	1
	5591	psukikos	6
5594		psukomai	1
	404	anapsuko	1
	674	apopsuko	1
	1634	ekpsuko	3
	2711	katupsuko	1
	5592	psukos	3
5607		ōn, ousa, on	154
	3689	ontōs	10
	3776	ousia	2
5610		hōra	108
	2256	heemiōrion	1
	3703	opōra	1
	5611	hōraios	4
5613		hōs	492
	2531	kathōs	182
	5615	hōsautōs	17
	5616	hosī	34
	5618	hōsper	42
	5620	hōste	83
5624		ōphelimos	4
	512	anōphelees	2
	5622	ōphelīa	2

Main Concordance

1 4 1/46 1:1

A, alpha.

Rev. 1: 8. I am *Alpha* and Omega, the beginning
11. I am *Alpha* and Omega, the first and the
21: 6. I am *Alpha* and Omega, the beginning
22:13. I am *Alpha* and Omega, the beginning

4 1 1/1 1,922

ἀβαρής, abarees.

2Co.11: 9. kept myself *from being burdensome*

5 3 1/1 1:5 [2]

ἀββᾶ, abba.

Mar 14:36. And he said, *Abba*, Father,
Ro. 8:15. whereby we cry, *Abba*, Father.
Gal. 4: 6. into your hearts, crying, *Abba*, Father.

12 9 2/2 1:9 1,1037

ἄβυσσος, abussos.

Lu. 8:31. command them to go out into the *deep*.
Ro. 10: 7. Who shall descend into the *deep*?
Rev. 9: 1. the key of the *bottomless* pit.
2. And he opened the *bottomless* pit;
11. the angel of the *bottomless pit*,
11: 7. that ascendeth out of the *bottomless pit*
17: 8. shall ascend out of the *bottomless pit*,
20: 1. having the key of the *bottomless pit*
3. cast him into the *bottomless pit*,

14 1 2/2 1:10 18,2041

ἀγαθοεργέω, agathoergeo.

1Ti. 6:18. *That* they *do good*, that they be rich in

15 10 /2 1:10 17

ἀγαθοποιέω, agathopoyeo.

Mar. 3: 4. *to do good* on the sabbath days,
Lu. 6: 9. on the sabbath days *to do good*,
33. ye *do good* to them *which do good*
35. and *do good*, and lend,
Acts14:17. in that he *did good*, and gave us
1Pet 2:15. *with well doing* ye may put to silence
20. *when* ye *do well*, and suffer (for it),
3: 6. as long as ye *do well*, and are not afraid
17. ye suffer for *well doing*, than for evil
3Joh. 11. He *that doeth good* is of God:

16 1 2/2 1:10 17

ἀγαθοποιΐα, agathopoiya.

1Pet. 4. 19: their souls (to him) in *well doing*,

17 1 2/2 1:10 18,4160

ἀγαθοποιός, agathopoyos.

1Pet. 2:14. for the praise of them *that do well*.

18 102 2/2 1:10 cf 2570

ἀγαθός, agathos.

Mat. 5:45. to rise on the evil and on the *good*,
7:11. give *good* gifts unto your children,
— which is in heaven give *good things*
17. every *good* tree bringeth forth good fruit;
18. A *good* tree cannot bring forth evil
12:34. ye, being evil, speak *good things*?
35. A *good* man out of the *good* treasure of the heart bringeth forth *good things*:
19:16. *Good* Master, what *good thing* shall I do,
17. Why callest thou me *good*? (there is) none *good*
20:15. Is thine eye evil, because I am *good*?
22:10. many as they found, both bad and *good*:
25:21. Well done, (thou) *good* and faithful
23. Well done, *good* and faithful servant;
Mar 10:17. *Good* Master, what shall I do that I
18. Why callest thou me *good*? (there is) none *good*
Lu. 1:53. hath filled the hungry with *good things*;
6:45. A *good* man out of the *good* treasure of his heart bringeth forth that which is *good*;
8: 8. And other fell on *good* ground,
15. which in an honest and *good* heart,
10:42. Mary hath chosen that *good* part,
11:13. know how to give *good* gifts unto your
12:18. will I bestow all my fruits and my *goods*
19. Soul, thou hast much *goods* laid up
16:25. thy lifetime receivedst thy *good things*,
18:18. *Good* Master, what shall I do to inherit
19. Why callest thou me *good*? none (is) *good*,
19:17. Well, thou *good* servant. because thou
23:50. (he was) a *good* man, and a just:
Joh. 1:46(47). Can there any *good thing* come out
5:29. they that have done *good*, unto the
7:12. some said, He is a *good* man: others
Acts 9:36. this woman was full of *good* works
11:24. For he was a *good* man, and full of the
23: 1. I have lived in all *good* conscience
Ro. 2: 7. by patient continuance in *well* doing
10. peace, to every man that worketh *good*,
3: 8. Let us do evil, that *good* may come?
5: 7. for a *good* man some would even dare
7:12. commandment holy, and just, and *good*.
13. Was then that which is *good* made death
— working death in me by that which is *good*
18. in my flesh, dwelleth no *good thing*:

Ro. 7:19. For the *good* that I would I do not:
8:28. all things work together for *good*
9:11. neither having done any *good* or evil,
10:15. and bring glad tidings of *good things!*
12: 2. ye may prove what (is) that *good*, and
9. cleave to that which is *good*.
21. overcome evil with *good*.
13: 3. rulers are not a terror to *good* works,
— do that which is *good*,
4. the minister of God to thee for *good*.
14:16. Let not then your *good* be evil spoken of:
15: 2. please (his) neighbour for (his) *good* to
16:19. wise unto that which is *good*,
2Co. 5:10. whether (it be) *good* or bad.
9: 8. may abound to every *good* work:
Gal. 6: 6. him that teacheth in all *good things*.
10. let us do *good* unto all (men),
Eph. 2:10. created in Christ Jesus unto *good* works,
4:28. with (his) hands the thing which is *good*,
29. but that which is *good* to the use
6: 8. whatsoever *good* thing any man doeth,
Phi. 1: 6. he which hath begun a *good* work
Col. 1:10. being fruitful in every *good* work,
1Th. 3: 6. ye have *good* remembrance of us
5:15. ever follow that which is *good*,
2Th. 2:16. consolation and *good* hope through grace,
17. stablish you in every *good* word and work.
1Ti. 1: 5. a pure heart, and (of) a *good* conscience.
19. Holding faith, and a *good* conscience;
2:10. professing godliness with *good* works.
5:10. have diligently followed every *good* work.
2 Ti. 2:21. (and) prepared unto every *good* work.
3:17. throughly furnished unto all *good* works.
Tit. 1:16. and unto every *good* work reprobate.
2: 5. keepers at home, *good*, obedient to
10. shewing all *good* fidelity;
3: 1. to be ready to every *good* work,
Philem. 6. the acknowledging of every *good thing*
14. that thy *benefit* should not be as
Heb. 9:11. an high priest of *good things* to come,
10: 1. having a shadow of *good things* to come,
13:21. Make you perfect in every *good* work
Jas. 1:17. Every *good* gift and every perfect gift
3:17. full of mercy and *good* fruits,
1 Pet. 2:18. not only to the *good* and gentle,
3:10. he that will love life, and see *good* days
11. Let him eschew evil, and do *good*;
13. be followers of that which is *good*?
16. Having a *good* conscience; that,
— falsely accuse your *good* conversation
21. the answer of a *good* conscience toward
3 Joh. 11. but that which is *good*.

19 4 3/4 1:10 18

ἀγαθωσύνη, agathōsunee.

Ro. 15:14. ye also are full of *goodness*, filled
Gal. 5:22. longsuffering, gentleness, *goodness*, faith,
Eph. 5: 9. the fruit of the Spirit (is) in all *goodness*
2Th. 1:11. all the good pleasure of (his) *goodness*,

20 5 3/4 1:19 21

ἀγαλλίασις, agalliasis.

Luke 1:14. thou shalt have joy and *gladness*;
44. the babe leaped in my womb for *joy*.
Acts 2:46. with *gladness* and singleness of heart,
Heb. 1: 9. hath anointed thee with the oil of *gladness*
Jude 24. presence of his glory with *exceeding joy*,

21 11 3/4 1:19 242
agan (much)

ἀγαλλιάω, agalliao.

Mat. 5:12. Rejoice, and *be exceeding glad*: for great
Lu. 1:47. my spirit *hath rejoiced* in God my Saviour
10:21. In that hour Jesus *rejoiced* in spirit,
Joh. 5:35. willing for a season *to rejoice* in his light.
8:56. Your father Abraham *rejoiced* to see my
Acts 2:26. heart rejoice, and my tongue *was glad*;
16:34. set meat before them, and *rejoiced*,
1Pet. 1: 6. Wherein ye *greatly rejoice*, though now for a season,
8. ye *rejoice* with joy unspeakable and
4:13. ye may be glad also *with exceeding joy*
Rev.19: 7. *Let* us be glad and *rejoice*, and give

22 4 4/4 1,1062

ἄγαμος, agamos.

1Cor.7: 8. I say therefore to the *unmarried* and
11. if she depart, let her remain *unmarried*,
32. He that is *unmarried* careth for
34. The *unmarried* woman careth for the

23 7 4/4 agan (much), achthos (grief)

ἀγανακτέω, aganakteo.

Mat.20:24. they *were moved with indignation* against
21:15. they *were sore displeased*,
26: 8. they *had indignation*, saying, To what
Mar 10:14. Jesus saw (it), he *was much displeased*,
41. they began *to be much displeased*
14: 4 some *that had indignation* within
Lu. 13:14. answered *with indignation*, because

24 1 4/4 23

ἀγανάκτησις, aganakteesis.

2Cor.7:11. yea, (what) *indignation*, yea, (what) fear

25 142 4/4 1:21 [cf 5689]
cf 5368

ἀγαπάω, agapao.

Mat. 5:43. Thou *shalt love* thy neighbour, and
44. I say unto you, *Love* your enemies,
46. For if ye *love* them *which love* you,
6:24. will hate the one, and *love* the other;
19:19. Thou *shalt love* thy neighbour as thyself.
22:37. Thou *shalt love* the Lord thy God with all thy heart,
39. Thou *shalt love* thy neighbour as
Mar 10:21. Jesus beholding him *loved* him, and
12:30. thou *shalt love* the Lord thy God with
31. Thou *shalt love* thy neighbour as thyself.
33. *to love* him with all the heart, and
— *to love* (his) neighbour as himself, is
Lu. 6:27. you which hear, *Love* your enemies,
32. if ye *love* them *which love* you, what
— sinners also *love* those *that love* them.
35. *love* ye your enemies, and do good,
7: 5. he *loveth* our nation, and he hath
42. which of them *will love* him most?
47. are forgiven; for she *loved* much:
— little is forgiven, (the same) *loveth* little.
10:27. Thou *shalt love* the Lord thy God with
11:43. for ye *love* the uppermost seats in
16:13. will hate the one, and *love* the other,
Joh. 3:16. For God so *loved* the world, that he gave
19. men *loved* darkness rather than light.
35. The Father *loveth* the Son, and hath
8:42. If God were your Father, ye would *love* me:
10:17. Therefore *doth* my Father *love* me,
11: 5. Now Jesus *loved* Martha, and her
12:43. they *loved* the praise of men more
13: 1. *having loved* his own which were in the world, he *loved* them unto the end.
23 one of his disciples, whom Jesus *loved*.

Joh. 13:34. That ye *love* one another; as I *have loved* you, that ye also *love* one another.
14:15. If ye *love* me, keep my commandments.
21. he it is *that loveth* me: and he *that loveth* me *shall be loved* of my Father, and I *will love* him,
23. If a man *love* me, he will keep my words: and my Father *will love* him,
24. He *that loveth* me not keepeth not
28. If ye *loved* me, ye would rejoice,
31. world may know that I *love* the Father;
15: 9. As the Father *hath loved* me, so *have* I *loved* you: continue ye
12. my commandment, That ye *love* one another, as I *have loved* you.
17. I command you, that ye *love* one another.
17:23. *hast loved* them, as thou *hast loved* me.
24. thou *lovedst* me before the foundation
26. the love wherewith thou *hast loved* me
19:26. the disciple standing by, whom he *loved*,
21: 7. that disciple whom Jesus *loved* saith
15. (son) of Jonas, *lovest* thou me more than
16. Simon, (son) of Jonas, *lovest* thou me?
20. the disciple whom Jesus *loved* following;
Ro. 8:28. for good to them *that love* God,
37. than conquerors through him *that loved* us.
9:13. As it is written, Jacob *have* I *loved*,
25. her *beloved*, which was not *beloved*.
13: 8. to *love* one another: for he *that loveth* another
9. Thou *shalt love* thy neighbour as thyself.
1Co. 2: 9. prepared for them *that love* him.
8: 3. if any man *love* God, the same is
2Co. 9: 7. for God *loveth* a cheerful giver.
11:11. Wherefore? because I *love* you not?
12:15. abundantly I *love* you, the less I *be loved*.
Gal. 2:20. the Son of God, who *loved* me, and
5:14. Thou *shalt love* thy neighbour as thyself.
Eph. 1: 6. hath made us accepted in the *beloved*.
2: 4. his great love wherewith he *loved* us,
5: 2. walk in love, as Christ also *hath loved* us,
25. Husbands, *love* your wives, even as Christ also *loved* the church,
28. So ought men *to love* their wives as
— He *that loveth* his wife *loveth* himself.
33. so *love* his wife even as himself;
6:24. with all them *that love* our Lord Jesus
Col. 3:12. the elect of God, holy and *beloved*,
19. Husbands, *love* (your) wives, and
1Th. 1: 4. Knowing, brethren *beloved*, your
4: 9. taught of God *to love* one another.
2Th. 2:13. for you, brethren *beloved* of the Lord,
16. even our Father, which *hath loved* us,
2Ti. 4: 8. unto all them also *that love* his appearing.
10. *having loved* this present world,
Heb. 1: 9. Thou *hast loved* righteousness, and
12: 6. For whom the Lord *loveth* he chasteneth,
Jas. 1:12. hath promised to them *that love* him.
2: 5. hath promised to them *that love* him?
8. Thou *shalt love* thy neighbour as
1Pet. 1: 8. Whom having not seen, ye *love*;
22. (see that ye) *love* one another with a
2:17. *Love* the brotherhood. Fear God.
3:10. For he that will *love* life, and see
2Pet. 2:15. who *loved* the wages of unrighteousness;
1Joh. 2:10. He *that loveth* his brother abideth
15. *Love* not the world, neither the
— If any man *love* the world, the
3:10. neither he *that loveth* not his brother.
11. that we *should love* one another.
14. because we *love* the brethren. He *that loveth* not (his) brother
1Joh. 3:18. little children, *let* us not *love* in word,
23. his Son Jesus Christ, and *love* one another,
4: 7. Beloved, *let* us *love* one another:
— every one *that loveth* is born of God,
8. He *that loveth* not knoweth not God;
10. Herein is love, not that we *loved* God, but that he *loved* us, and sent his Son
11. Beloved, if God so *loved* us, we ought also *to love* one another.
12. If we *love* one another, God dwelleth
19. We *love* him, because he first *loved* us.
20. If a man say, I *love* God, and
— for he *that loveth* not his brother
— how can he *love* God whom he
21. That he *who loveth* God *love* his brother
5: 1. every one *that loveth* him that begat *loveth* him also that is begotten
2. we know that we *love* the children of God, when we *love* God,
2 Joh. 1. her children, whom I *love* in the truth;
5. from the beginning, that we *love* one
3 Joh. 1. wellbeloved Gaius, whom I *love* in the truth.
Rev. 1: 5. Unto him *that loved* us, and
3: 9. to know that I *have loved* thee.
12:11. they *loved* not their lives unto the
20: 9. the saints about, and the *beloved* city:

---

26 116 5/6 1:21 25

ἀγάπη, *agapee*.

Mat. 24:12. the *love* of many shall wax cold.
Lu. 11:42. pass over judgment and the *love* of God:
Joh. 5:42. ye have not the *love* of God in you.
13:35. if ye have *love* one to another.
15: 9. I loved you: continue ye in my *love*.
10. ye shall abide in my *love*;
— commandments, and abide in his *love*.
13. Greater *love* hath no man than this,
17:26. the *love* wherewith thou hast loved
Ro. 5: 5. because the *love* of God is shed
8. God commendeth his *love* toward us,
8:35. separate us from the *love* of Christ?
39. to separate us from the *love* of God,
12: 9. (Let) *love* be without dissimulation.
13:10. *Love* worketh no ill to his neighbour: therefore *love* (is) the fulfilling of the law.
14:15. now walkest thou not *charitably*.
15:30. Christ's sake, and for the *love* of the Spirit,
1Cor. 4:21. with a rod, or in *love*, and (in) the
8: 1. Knowledge puffeth up, but *charity* edifieth.
13: 1. of angels, and have not *charity*, I
2. remove mountains, and have not *charity*,
3. body to be burned, and have not *charity*,
4. *Charity* suffereth long, (and) is kind; *charity* envieth not; *charity* vaunteth not itself, is not
8. *Charity* never faileth: but whether
13. now abideth faith, hope, *charity*,
— the greatest of these (is) *charity*.
14: 1. Follow after *charity*, and desire spiritua.
16:14. Let all your things be done with *charity*.
24. My *love* (be) with you all in Christ Jesus
2Cor. 2: 4. that ye might know the *love* which I
8. confirm (your) *love* toward him.
5:14. For the *love* of Christ constraineth us;
6: 6. by the Holy Ghost, by *love* unfeigned,
8: 7. (in) all diligence, and (in) your *love* to us.
8. to prove the sincerity of your *love*.
24. before the churches, the proof of your *love*
13:11. the God of *love* and peace shall be
14(13). and the *love* of God, and the

Gal. 5: 6. faith which worketh by *love*.
13. but by *love* serve one another.
22. the fruit of the Spirit is *love*, joy, peace,
Eph. 1: 4. without blame before him in *love* :
15. faith in the Lord Jesus, and *love* unto all
2: 4. for his great *love* wherewith he
3:17(18). being rooted and grounded in *love*,
19. to know the *love* of Christ, which
4: 2. forbearing one another in *love* ;
15. speaking the truth in *love*, may
16. the edifying of itself in *love*.
5: 2. walk in *love*, as Christ also hath
6:23. to the brethren, and *love* with faith,
Phil. 1: 9. that your *love* may abound yet
17. the other of *love*, knowing that
2: 1. in Christ, if any comfort of *love*,
2. be likeminded, having the same *love*,
Col. 1: 4. of the *love* (which ye have) to all the
8. Who also declared unto us your *love*
13. kingdom of his *dear* Son: (lit. Son of his *love*)
2: 2. be comforted, being knit together in *love*,
3:14. above all these things (put on) *charity*,
1Th. 1: 3. work of faith, and labour of *love*,
3: 6. good tidings of your faith and *charity*,
12. abound in *love* one toward another,
5: 8. putting on the breastplate of faith and *love* ;
13. highly in *love* for their work's sake.
2Th. 1: 3. the *charity* of every one of you all
2:10. they received not the *love* of the truth,
3. 5. direct your hearts into the *love* of God,
1Ti. 1 : 5. the commandment is *charity* out of a
14. abundant with faith and *love* which
2:15. in faith and *charity* and holiness
4:12. in conversation, in *charity*, in spirit,
6:11. faith, *love*, patience, meekness.
2Ti. 1: 7. of power, and of *love*, and of a sound
13. in faith and *love* which is in Christ
2:22. follow righteousness, faith, *charity*,
3:10. faith, longsuffering, *charity*, patience,
Tit. 2: 2. sound in faith, in *charity*, in patience.
Philem. 5. Hearing of thy *love* and faith,
7. great joy and consolation in thy *love*,
9. for *love's* sake I rather beseech
Heb. 6:10. to forget your work and labour of *love*,
10:24. to provoke unto *love* and to good
1 Pet. 4: 8. have fervent *charity* among yourselves: for *charity* shall cover the multitude
5:14. Greet ye one another with a kiss of *charity*.
2 Pet 1: 7. to brotherly kindness *charity*.
1 Joh 2: 5. verily is the *love* of God perfected :
15. the *love* of the Father is not in him.
3: 1. what manner of *love* the Father hath
16. Hereby perceive we the *love* (of God)
17. how dwelleth the *love* of God in him?
: 7. love one another: for *love* is of God ;
8. knoweth not God ; for God is *love*.
9. manifested the *love* of God toward us,
10. Herein is *love*, not that we loved God,
12. his *love* is perfected in us.
16. *love* that God hath to us. God is *love* ; and he that dwelleth in *love* dwelleth in God,
17. Herein is our *love* made perfect,
18. There is no fear in *love* ; but perfect *love* casteth out fear :
— feareth is not made perfect in *love*.
5: 3. this is the *love* of God, that we
2 Joh. 3. the Son of the Father, in truth and *love*.
6. this is *love*, that we walk after
3 Joh. 6. have borne witness of thy *charity*
Jude 2. Mercy unto you, and peace, and *love*,
12. spots in your *feasts of charity*,
Jude 21. Keep yourselves in the *love* of God,
Rev. 2: 4. thou hast left thy first *love*.
19. I know thy works, and *charity*,

---

27 62 , 6/7, 1:21 25
ἀγαπητός, *agapeetos*.

Mat. 3:17. saying, This is my *beloved* Son,
12:18. whom I have chosen ; my *beloved*,
17: 5. which said, This is my *beloved* Son,
Mar. 1:11. (saying), Thou art my *beloved* Son,
9: 7. saying, This is my *beloved* Son :
12: 6. one son, his *wellbeloved*, he sent
Lu. 3:22. which said, Thou art my *beloved* Son;
9:35. saying, This is my *beloved* Son :
20:13. I will send my *beloved* son :
Acts15:25. chosen men unto you with our *beloved*
Rom. 1: 7. To all that be in Rome, *beloved* of God,
11:28. touching the election, (they are) *beloved*
12:19. *Dearly beloved*, avenge not yourselves,
16: 5. Salute my *wellbeloved* Epenetus,
8. Greet Amplias my *beloved* in the Lord.
9. Salute Urbane,...and Stachys my *beloved*.
12. Salute the *beloved* Persis, which laboured
1Cor 4:14. as my *beloved* sons I warn (you).
17. who is my *beloved* son, and
10:14. Wherefore, my *dearly beloved*, flee from idolatry.
15:58. Therefore, my *beloved* brethren,
2Cor 7: 1. *dearly beloved*, let us cleanse ourselves
12:19. (we do) all things, *dearly beloved*,
Eph. 5: 1. followers of God, as *dear* children ;
6:21. a *beloved* brother and faithful
Phil. 2:12. Wherefore, my *beloved*, as ye have
4: 1. my brethren *dearly beloved* and longed for
— stand fast in the Lord, (my) *dearly beloved*.
Col. 1: 7. our *dear* fellowservant, who is
4: 7. unto you, (who is) a *beloved* brother,
9. a faithful and *beloved* brother,
14. Luke, the *beloved* physician, and Demas,
1Th. 2: 8. because ye were *dear* unto us.
1Ti. 6: 2. because they are faithful and *beloved*,
2Ti. 1: 2. To Timothy, (my) *dearly beloved* son:
Philem. 1. unto Philemon our *dearly beloved*, and
2. to (our) *beloved* Apphia, and Archippus
16. above a servant, a brother *beloved*,
Heb. 6: 9. *beloved*, we are persuaded better things
Jas. 1:16. Do not err, my *beloved* brethren.
19. Wherefore, my *beloved* brethren, let every
2: 5. Hearken, my *beloved* brethren,
1Pet. 2:11. *Dearly beloved*, I beseech (you) as strangers
4:12. *Beloved*, think it not strange
2Pet. 1:17. This is my *beloved* Son, in whom
3: 1. This second epistle, *beloved*, I now write
8. *beloved*, be not ignorant of this
14. Wherefore, *beloved*, seeing that ye look
15. even as our *beloved* brother Paul
17. Ye therefore, *beloved*, seeing ye know
1Joh. 3:2. *Beloved*, now are we the sons of God,
21. *Beloved*, if our heart condemn us not,
4: 1. *Beloved*, believe not every spirit
7. *Beloved*, let us love one another
11. *Beloved*, if God so loved us,
3 Joh. 1. The elder unto the *wellbeloved* Gaius,
2. *Beloved*, I wish above all things
5. *Beloved*, thou doest faithfully
11. *Beloved*, follow not that which is evil,
Jude 3. *Beloved*, when I gave all diligence
17. *beloved*, remember ye the words
20. But ye, *beloved*, building up yourselves

---

29 3 , 6/8,
ἀγγαρεύω, *angaruo*.

Mat 5:41. whosoever *shall compel* thee *to go* a mile.

Mat 27:32. him they *compelled* to bear his cross.
Mar 15:21. they *compel* one Simon a Cyrenian,

---

30 2 6/8 *aggos* (pail)

ἀγγεῖον, *angīon.*

Mat 13:48. gathered the good into *vessels*, but
25: 4. But the wise took oil in their *vessels*

---

31 1 7/8 1:56 32

ἀγγελία, *angelia.*

1Joh. 3:11. For this is the *message* that ye heard

---

32 186 7/8 1:74 *aggellō*

ἄγγελος, *angelos.*

Mat. 1:20. the *angel* of the Lord appeared unto
24. did as the *angel* of the Lord had bidden
2:13. *angel* of the Lord appeareth to Joseph
19. behold, an *angel* of the Lord appeareth
4: 6. He shall give his *angels* charge
11. behold, *angels* came and ministered
11:10. Behold, I send my *messenger*
13:39. and the reapers are the *angels*.
41. The Son of man shall send forth his *angels*,
49. the *angels* shall come forth, and sever
16:27. the glory of his Father with his *angels*;
18:10. That in heaven their *angels* do
22:30. are as the *angels* of God in heaven.
24:31. And he shall send his *angels* with
36. no, not the *angels* of heaven,
25:31. all the holy *angels* with him,
41. prepared for the devil and his *angels*.
26:53. more than twelve legions of *angels*?
28: 2. for the *angel* of the Lord descended
5. the *angel* answered and said
Mar. 1: 2. Behold, I send my *messenger* before
13. and the *angels* ministered unto him.
8:38. of his Father with the holy *angels*.
12:25. are as the *angels* which are in heaven.
13:27. then shall he send his *angels*,
32. not the *angels* which are in heaven,
Lu. 1:11. appeared unto him an *angel* of the
13. the *angel* said unto him, Fear not,
18. Zacharias said unto the *angel*,
19. the *angel* answering said unto him,
26. the sixth month the *angel* Gabriel
28. And the *angel* came in unto her,
30. *angel* said unto her, Fear not, Mary.
34. Then said Mary unto the *angel*,
35. the *angel* answered and said unto her,
38. And the *angel* departed from her.
2: 9. the *angel* of the Lord came upon them,
10. the *angel* said unto them, Fear not:
13. with the *angel* a multitude of
15. as the *angels* were gone away
21. which was so named of the *angel*
4:10. He shall give his *angels* charge over thee,
7:24. when the *messengers* of John were departed,
27. Behold, I send my *messenger* before
9:26. (in his) Father's, and of the holy *angels*.
52. And sent *messengers* before his face:
12: 8. confess before the *angels* of God:
9. denied before the *angels* of God.
15:10. in the presence of the *angels* of God
16:22. carried by the *angels* into Abraham's bosom:
22:43. there appeared an *angel* unto him
24:23. had also seen a vision of *angels*,
Joh. 1:51. (52) the *angels* of God ascending and
5: 4. For an *angel* went down at
12:29. others said, An *angel* spake to him.
20:12. seeth two *angels* in white sitting,

Acts 5:19. the *angel* of the Lord by night
6:15. as it had been the face of an *angel*.
7:30. mount Sina an *angel* of the Lord in
35. by the hand of the *angel* which
38. with the *angel* which spake to him
53. the law by the disposition of *angels*,
8:26. *angel* of the Lord spake unto Philip,
10: 3. an *angel* of God coming in to him,
7. when the *angel* which spake unto Cornelius
22. warned from God by an holy *angel*
11:13. had seen an *angel* in his house,
12: 7. the *angel* of the Lord came upon
8. the *angel* said unto him, Gird thyself,
9. which was done by the *angel*;
10. forthwith the *angel* departed
11. the Lord hath sent his *angel*,
15. said they, It is his *angel*.
23. the *angel* of the Lord smote him,
23: 8. no resurrection, neither *angel*, nor spirit:
9. if a spirit or an *angel* hath spoken
27:23. by me this night the *angel* of God.
Rom 8:38. nor life, nor *angels*, nor principalities,
1Co 4: 9. the world, and to *angels*, and to men.
6: 3. Know ye not that we shall judge *angels*?
11:10. on (her) head because of the *angels*.
13: 1. the tongues of men and of *angels*,
2Co 11:14. transformed into an *angel* of light.
12: 7. in the flesh, the *messenger* of Satan
Gal 1: 8. we, or an *angel* from heaven,
3: 9. (and it was) ordained by *angels* in
4:14. received me as an *angel* of God,
Col. 2:18. humility and worshipping of *angels*,
2Th. 1: 7. from heaven with his mighty *angels*
1Ti. 3:16. in the Spirit, seen of *angels*,
5:21. Jesus Christ, and the elect *angels*,
Heb. 1: 4. made so much better than the *angels*,
5. unto which of the *angels* said he
6(7). let all the *angels* of God worship him.
7. *angels* he saith, Who maketh his *angels*
13. to which of the *angels* said he at
2: 2. if the word spoken by *angels* was stedfast,
5. unto the *angels* hath he not put
7. a little lower than the *angels*;
9. made a little lower than the *angels*
16. not on (him the nature of) *angels*;
12:22. an innumerable company of *angels*,
13: 2. some have entertained *angels* unawares.
Jas. 2:25. she had received the *messengers*,
1Pet. 1:12. which things the *angels* desire to look into
3:22. *angels* and authorities and powers
2Pet. 2: 4. spared not the *angels* that sinned,
11. Whereas *angels*, which are greater
Jude 6. the *angels* which kept not their
Rev. 1: 1. he sent and signified (it) by his *angel*
20. the *angels* of the seven churches:
2: 1. Unto the *angel* of the church of Ephesus
8. unto the *angel* of the church
12. to the *angel* of the church in Pergamos
18. unto the *angel* of the church
3. 1. unto the *angel* of the church
5. my Father, and before his *angels*.
7. to the *angel* of the church in
14. unto the *angel* of the church
5: 2. I saw a strong *angel* proclaiming
11. I heard the voice of many *angels*
7: 1. I saw four *angels* standing
2. I saw another *angel* ascending
— a loud voice to the four *angels*,
11. all the *angels* stood round
8: 2. I saw the seven *angels* which
3. another *angel* came and stood at the altar
4. before God out of the *angel's* hand.

Rev. 8: 5. the *angel* took the censer, and filled
6. seven *angels* which had the seven trumpets
7. The first *angel* sounded, and there followed
8. the second *angel* sounded, and as it were
10. the third *angel* sounded, and there fell
12. the fourth *angel* sounded, and the third part
13. heard an *angel* flying through the midst
— the trumpet of the three *angels*,
9: 1. the fifth *angel* sounded, and I saw
11. (which is) the *angel* of the bottomless pit,
13. And the sixth *angel* sounded,
14. Saying to the sixth *angel* which had the trumpet, Loose the four *angels*
15. And the four *angels* were loosed,
10: 1. And I saw another mighty *angel*
5. the *angel* which I saw stand
7. of the voice of the seventh *angel*,
8. open in the hand of the *angel*
9. I went unto the *angel*, and said
10. the little book out of the *angel's* hand,
11: 1. and the *angel* stood, saying, Rise,
15. And the seventh *angel* sounded;
12: 7. Michael and his *angels* fought against the dragon; and the dragon fought and his *angels*,
9. his *angels* were cast out with him.
14: 6. I saw another *angel* fly in the
8. And there followed another *angel*, saying,
9. the third *angel* followed them,
10. in the presence of the holy *angels*,
15. another *angel* came out of the temple,
17. another *angel* came out of the temple
18. another *angel* came out from the altar,
19. the *angel* thrust in his sickle
15: 1. seven *angels* having the seven last plagues;
6. the seven *angels* came out of
7. gave unto the seven *angels*
8. plagues of the seven *angels* were fulfilled.
16: 1. saying to the seven *angels*,
3. the second *angel* poured out his vial
4. the third *angel* poured out his vial
5. I heard the *angel* of the waters
8. the fourth *angel* poured out his vial
10. the fifth *angel* poured out his vial
12. the sixth *angel* poured out his vial
17. the seventh *angel* poured out his vial
17: 1. one of the seven *angels* which
7. And the *angel* said unto me,
18: 1. I saw another *angel* come down
21. a mighty *angel* took up a stone
19:17. I saw an *angel* standing in the sun;
20: 1. And I saw an *angel* come down
21: 9. one of the seven *angels* which
12. at the gates twelve *angels*,
17. measure of a man, that is, of the *angel*.
22: 6. sent his *angel* to shew unto
8. before the feet of the *angel*
16. have sent mine *angel* to testify

---

33 2 8/10 71

ἄγε, *age*, adv.

Jas. 4:13. *Go to* now, ye that say, To day
5: 1. *Go to* now, (ye) rich men, weep

---

34 8 8/10 71 (cf 32)

ἀγέλη, *agelee*.

Mat. 8:30. an *herd* of many swine feeding.
31. go away into the *herd* of swine.
32. they went into the *herd* of swine: and, behold, the whole *herd* of swine ran
Mar 5:11. a great *herd* of swine feeding.
13. the *herd* ran violently down
Lu. 8:32. an *herd* of many swine feeding
33. the *herd* ran violently down a steep

---

35 1 8/10 1:662 1,1075

ἀγενεαλόγητος, *agenealogeetos*.

Heb 7: 3. father, without mother, *without descent*,

---

36 1 8/10 1,1085

ἀγενής, *agenees*.

1Co. 1:28. *base things* of the world, and things

---

37 29 8/10 1:88 40

ἁγιάζω, *hagiazo*.

Mat. 6: 9. in heaven, *Hallowed be* thy name.
23:17. or the temple *that sanctifieth* the gold?
19. or the altar *that sanctifieth* the gift?
Lu. 11: 2. in heaven, *Hallowed be* thy name.
Joh.10:36. whom the Father *hath sanctified*,
17:17. *Sanctify* them through thy truth:
19. for their sakes I *sanctify* myself, that they also might be *sanctified* through the
Acts20:32. among all them *which are sanctified*.
26:18. among them *which are sanctified*
Ro. 15:16. *being sanctified* by the Holy Ghost.
1Co. 1: 2. *that are sanctified* in Christ Jesus,
6:11. are washed, but ye *are sanctified*,
7:14. husband *is sanctified* by the wife, and the unbelieving wife *is sanctified*
Eph 5:26. That he *might sanctify* and cleanse
1Th. 5:23. God of peace *sanctify* you wholly;
1Ti. 4: 5. it *is sanctified* by the word of God
2Ti. 2:21. unto honour, *sanctified*, and meet
Heb 2:11. *that sanctifieth* and they *who are sanctified*
9:13. unclean, *sanctifieth* to the purifying
10:10. By the which will we are *sanctified*
14. for ever them *that are sanctified*.
29. the covenant, wherewith he *was sanctified*.
13:12. that he *might sanctify* the people
1Pet 3:15. *sanctify* the Lord God in your hearts:
Jude 1. them that are *sanctified* by God
Rev.22:11. that is holy, *let him be holy* still.

---

38 10 9/11 1:88 37

ἁγιασμός, *hagiasmos*.

Ro. 6:19. servants to righteousness unto *holiness*.
22. ye have your fruit unto *holiness*,
1Co. 1:30. and *sanctification*, and redemption:
1Th. 4: 3. will of God, (even) your *sanctification*,
4. his vessel in *sanctification* and honour;
7. unto uncleanness, but unto *holiness*.
2Th. 2:13. through *sanctification* of the Spirit
1Ti. 2:15. charity and *holiness* with sobriety.
Heb 12:14. peace with all (men), and *holiness*,
1Pet. 1: 2. through *sanctification* of the Spirit,

---

39 11 9/ 40

ἅγιον, *hagion*.

Observe. † Holies (pl). § Holy (sing.) of Holies (pl)

Heb 8: 2. A minister of the *sanctuary*,† and
9: 1. divine service, and a worldly *sanctuary*.
2. which is called the *sanctuary*.
3. which is called the *Holiest of all*;§
8. the way into the *holiest of all*† was
12. entered in once into the *holy place*,†
24. into the *holy places*† made with hands
25. into the *holy place*† every year

Heb 10:19. to enter into the *holiest*† by the blood
13:11. brought into the *sanctuary*† by the

40 229 9/11 1:88 [cf 2282]
ἅγιος, *hagios.* *hagos* (awful thing)

Mat 1:18. found with child of the *Holy* Ghost.
20. in her is of the *Holy* Ghost.
3:11. baptize you with the *Holy* Ghost,
4: 5. him up into the *holy* city,
7: 6. Give not that which is *holy* unto
12:32. speaketh against the *Holy* Ghost,
24:15. the prophet, stand in the *holy* place,
25:31. all the *holy* angels with him,
27:52. bodies of the *saints* which slept arose,
53. and went into the *holy* city,
28:19. of the Son, and of the *Holy* Ghost:
Mar. 1: 8. baptize you with the *Holy* Ghost.
24. thou art, the *Holy One* of God.
3:29. blaspheme against the *Holy* Ghost
6:20. was a just man and an *holy*,
8:38. his Father with the *holy* angels.
12:36. himself said by the *Holy* Ghost,
13:11. not ye that speak, but the *Holy* Ghost.
Lu. 1:15. be filled with the *Holy* Ghost,
35. The *Holy* Ghost shall come upon thee,
— also that *holy thing* which shall
41. filled with the *Holy* Ghost:
49. great things; and *holy* (is) his name.
67. was filled with the *Holy* Ghost,
70. the mouth of his *holy* prophets,
72. to remember his *holy* covenant;
2:23. shall be called *holy* to the Lord;
25. and the *Holy* Ghost was upon him.
26. unto him by the *Holy* Ghost,
3:16. baptize you with the *Holy* Ghost
22. the *Holy* Ghost descended in
4: 1. Jesus being full of the *Holy* Ghost
34. thou art; the *Holy One* of God.
9:26. (in his) Father's, and of the *holy* angels.
11:13. Father give the *Holy* Spirit to them
12:10. blasphemeth against the *Holy* Ghost
12. For the *Holy* Ghost shall teach
Joh. 1:33. which baptizeth with the *Holy* Ghost.
7:39. for the *Holy* Ghost was not yet
14:26. the Comforter, (which is) the *Holy* Ghost,
17:11. I come to thee. *Holy* Father, keep
20:22. unto them, Receive ye the *Holy* Ghost:
Acts 1: 2. that he through the *Holy* Ghost
5. be baptized with the *Holy* Ghost
8. that the *Holy* Ghost is come upon
16. which the *Holy* Ghost by the mouth
2: 4. were all filled with the *Holy* Ghost,
33. the promise of the *Holy* Ghost,
38. shall receive the gift of the *Holy* Ghost.
3:14. ye denied the *Holy One* and the Just,
21. the mouth of all his *holy* prophets
4: 8. filled with the *Holy* Ghost,
27. against thy *holy* child Jesus,
30. name of thy *holy* child Jesus.
31. they were all filled with the *Holy* Ghost,
5: 3. heart to lie to the *Holy* Ghost,
32. (so is) also the *Holy* Ghost,
6: 3. full of the *Holy* Ghost and wisdom,
5. of faith and of the *Holy* Ghost,
13. words against this *holy* place,
7:33. where thou standest is *holy* ground.
51. ye do always resist the *Holy* Ghost:
55. being full of the *Holy* Ghost,
8:15. that they might receive the *Holy* Ghost:
17. they received the *Holy* Ghost.
18. the *Holy* Ghost was given,
Acts 8:19. he may receive the *Holy* Ghost.
9:13. he hath done to thy *saints* at
17. be filled with the *Holy* Ghost.
31. in the comfort of the *Holy* Ghost,
32. came down also to the *saints*
41. when he had called the *saints*
10:22. warned from God by an *holy* angel
38. with the *Holy* Ghost and with power:
44. the *Holy* Ghost fell on all them
45. poured out the gift of the *Holy* Ghost
47. have received the *Holy* Ghost as
11:15. the *Holy* Ghost fell on them,
16. be baptized with the *Holy* Ghost.
24. full of the *Holy* Ghost and of faith:
13: 2. the *Holy* Ghost said, Separate me
4. sent forth by the *Holy* Ghost,
9. filled with the *Holy* Ghost, set
52. with joy, and with the *Holy* Ghost.
15: 8. giving them the *Holy* Ghost,
28. seemed good to the *Holy* Ghost,
16: 6. were forbidden of the *Holy* Ghost
19: 2. Have ye received the *Holy* Ghost
— whether there be any *Holy* Ghost.
6. the *Holy* Ghost came on them;
20:23. Save that the *Holy* Ghost witnesseth
28. the *Holy* Ghost hath made you
21:11. Thus saith the *Holy* Ghost,
28. and hath polluted this *holy* place.
26:10. many of the *saints* did I shut up
28:25. Well spake the *Holy* Ghost by Esaias
Ro. 1: 2. his prophets in the *holy* scriptures,
7. beloved of God, called (to be) *saints*:
5: 5. our hearts by the *Holy* Ghost
7:12. the law (is) *holy*, and the commandment *holy*,
8:27. he maketh intercession for the *saints*
9: 1. me witness in the *Holy* Ghost,
11:16. For if the firstfruit (be) *holy*,
— if the root (be) *holy*, so (are)
12: 1. a living sacrifice, *holy*, acceptable
13. to the necessity of *saints*;
14:17. peace, and joy in the *Holy* Ghost.
15:13. through the power of the *Holy* Ghost.
16. sanctified by the *Holy* Ghost.
25. Jerusalem to minister unto the *saints*.
26. for the poor *saints* which are
31. may be accepted of the *saints*;
16: 2. in the Lord, as becometh *saints*
15. all the *saints* which are with them.
16. Salute one another with an *holy* kiss
1Co. 1: 2. called (to be) *saints*, with all
2:13. which the *Holy* Ghost teacheth;
3:17. for the temple of God is *holy*,
6: 1. and not before the *saints*?
2. that the *saints* shall judge the world?
19. is the temple of the *Holy* Ghost
7:14. unclean; but now are they *holy*.
34. may be *holy* both in body and
12: 3. is the Lord, but by the *Holy* Ghost
14:33. in all churches of the *saints*.
16: 1. concerning the collection for the *saints*
15. to the ministry of the *saints*,
20. Greet ye one another with an *holy* kiss.
2Co. 1: 1. with all the *saints* which are
6: 6. by kindness, by the *Holy* Ghost,
8: 4. of the ministering to the *saints*.
9: 1. the ministering to the *saints*,
12. supplieth the want of the *saints*,
13:12. Greet one another with an *holy* kiss.
13(12). All the *saints* salute you.
14(13). communion of the *Holy* Ghost,
Eph. 1: 1. to the *saints* which are at Ephesus,

Eph. 1: 4. we should be *holy* and without
13. with that *holy* Spirit of promise,
15. and love unto all the *saints,*
18. his inheritance in the *saints,*
2:19. fellowcitizens with the *saints,*
21. groweth unto an *holy* temple
3: 5. unto his *holy* apostles and prophets
8. less than the least of all *saints,*
18. to comprehend with all *saints*
4:12. For the perfecting of the *saints,*
30. grieve not the *holy* Spirit
5: 3. among you, as becometh *saints;*
27. be *holy* and without blemish.
6:18. supplication for all *saints;*
Phil. 1: 1. to all the *saints* in Christ Jesus
4:21. Salute every *saint* in Christ Jesus.
22. All the *saints* salute you,
Col. 1: 2. To the *saints* and faithful
4. (which ye have) to all the *saints.*
12. the inheritance of the *saints* in light
22. through death, to present you *holy*
26. made manifest to his *saints:*
3:12. elect of God, *holy* and beloved,
1Th. 1: 5. in power, and in the *Holy* Ghost,
6. with joy of the *Holy* Ghost:
3:13. Jesus Christ with all his *saints.*
4. 8. given unto us his *holy* Spirit.
5:26. Greet all the brethren with an *holy* kiss
27. unto all the *holy* brethren
2Th. 1:10. to be glorified in his *saints,*
1Ti. 5:10. if she have washed the *saints'* feet,
2Ti. 1: 9. called (us) with an *holy* calling,
14. by the *Holy* Ghost which dwelleth
Tit. 3: 5. and renewing of the *Holy* Ghost;
Philem. 5. Lord Jesus, and toward all *saints;*
7. the bowels of the *saints* are
Heb 2: 4. miracles, and gifts of the *Holy* Ghost,
3: 1. Wherefore, *holy* brethren, partakers
7. as the *Holy* Ghost saith, To day
6: 4. made partakers of the *Holy* Ghost,
10. have ministered to the *saints,*
9: 8. The *Holy* Ghost this signifying,
10:15. the *Holy* Ghost also is a witness
13:24. over you, and all the *saints.*
1Pet 1:12. with the *Holy* Ghost sent down
15. called you is *holy,* so be ye *holy*
16. Be ye *holy;* for I am *holy.*
2: 5. spiritual house, an *holy* priesthood,
9. a royal priesthood, an *holy* nation,
3: 5. in the old time the *holy* women
2Pet 1:18. with him in the *holy* mount.
21. *holy* men of God spake (as they were) moved by the *Holy* Ghost.
2:21. from the *holy* commandment delivered
3: 2. spoken before by the *holy* prophets,
11. in (all) *holy* conversation and
1Joh. 2:20. have an unction from the *Holy One,*
5: 7. the Word, and the *Holy* Ghost:
Jude 3. once delivered unto the *saints.*
14. with ten thousands of his *saints,*
20. on your *most holy* faith, praying in the *Holy* Ghost,
Rev. 3: 7. saith he that is *holy,* he that
4: 8. and night, saying, *Holy, holy, holy,*
5: 8. which are the prayers of *saints.*
6:10. How long, O Lord, *holy* and true,
8: 3. with the prayers of all *saints* upon
4. with the prayers of the *saints,*
11: 2. the *holy* city shall they tread under
18. the prophets, and to the *saints,*
13: 7. to make war with the *saints,*
10. patience and the faith of the *saints.*
Rev. 14:10. the presence of the *holy* angels,
12. Here is the patience of the *saints:*
15: 3. (are) thy ways, thou King of *saints.*
16: 6. they have shed the blood of *saints*
17: 6. drunken with the blood of the *saints,*
18:20. (ye) *holy* apostles and prophets;
24. blood of prophets, and of *saints,*
19: 8. fine linen is the righteousness of *saints.*
20: 6. Blessed and *holy* (is) he that
9. compassed the camp of the *saints*
21: 2. And I John saw the *holy* city,
10. great city, the *holy* Jerusalem,
22: 6. God of the *holy* prophets sent his angel
11. that is *holy,* let him be holy still.
19. of life, and out of the *holy* city,

---

41 1 10/14 1:88 40
ἁγιότης, *hagiotees.*

Heb 12:10. might be partakers of his *holiness.*

---

42 3 10/14 1:88 40
ἁγιωσύνη, *hagiōsunee.*

Ro. 1: 4. according to the spirit of *holiness,*
2Co. 7: 1. perfecting *holiness* in the fear of God.
1Th. 3:13. unblameable in *holiness* before

---

43 1 10/14 *agkos* (bend)
ἀγκάλαι, *ankalai.*

Lu. 2:28. took he him up in his *arms,*

---

44 1 10/14 rt 43
ἄγκιστρον, *ankistron.*

Mat. 17:27. go thou to the sea, and cast an *hook,*

---

45 4 10/14 rt 43
ἄγκυρα, *ankura.*

Acts 27:29. they cast four *anchors* out of the stern,
30. would have cast *anchors* out
40. they had taken up the *anchors,*
Heb 6:19. Which (hope) we have as an *anchor*

---

46 2 10/14 1,rt 1102
ἄγναφος, *agnaphos.*

Mat. 9:16. a piece of *new* cloth unto an old garment,
Mar 2:21. a piece of *new* cloth on an old garment:

---

47 2 10/14 1:122 53
ἁγνεία, *hagnīa.*

1Ti. 4:12. in spirit, in faith, in *purity.*
5: 2. the younger as sisters, with all *purity.*

---

48 7 11/14 1:122 53
ἁγνίζω, *hagnizo.*

Joh. 11:55. the passover, to *purify* themselves.
Acts 21:24. Them take, and *purify thyself*
26. next day *purifying himself* with them
24:18. found me *purified* in the temple,
Jas. 4: 8. (ye) sinners; and *purify* (your) hearts,
1Pet. 1:22. Seeing ye have *purified* your souls
1Joh. 3: 3. *purifieth* himself, even as he

---

49 1 11/14 1:122 48
ἁγνισμός, *hagnismos.*

Acts 21:26. of the days of *purification,* until

---

50 22 11/14 1:115 1,3539
ἀγνοέω, *agnoeo.*

Mar 9:32. they *understood not* that saying,

Lu. 9·45. they *understood not* this saying,
Acts13:27. *because* they *knew* him *not*,
17:23. Whom therefore ye *ignorantly* worship,
Ro. 1:13. Now I would not have you *ignorant*,
2: 4. *not knowing* that the goodness
6: 3. *Know* ye *not*, that so many of
7: 1. *Know* ye *not*, brethren, for I speak
10: 3. For they *being ignorant* of God's
11:25. that ye *should be ignorant* of this
1Co.10: 1. not that ye *should be ignorant*,
12: 1. I would not have you *ignorant*.
14:38. *be ignorant, let* him *be ignorant*.
2Co. 1: 8. not, brethren, have you *ignorant* of
2:11. for we *are* not *ignorant* of his devices.
6: 9. As *unknown*, and (yet) well known;
Gal. 1:22. was *unknown* by face unto the
1Th. 4:13. not have you *to be ignorant*,
1Ti. 1:13. I did (it) *ignorantly* in unbelief.
Heb. 5: 2. have compassion on the *ignorant*,
2Pet.2:12. things that they *understand not*;

51 1 11/14 1:115 50

ἀγνόημα, agnoeema.

Heb. 9: 7. himself, and (for) the *errors* of the people:

52 4 11/14 1:115 50

ἄγνοια, agnoia.

Acts 3:17. I wot that through *ignorance* ye did
17:30. the times of this *ignorance* God
Eph 4:18. through the *ignorance* that is in
1Pet.1:14. former lusts in your *ignorance*·

53 8 11/14 1:122 rt 40

ἁγνός, hagnos.

2Co. 7:11. yourselves to be *clear* in this matter.
11: 2. present (you as) a *chaste* virgin
Phil. 4: 8. (are) just, whatsoever things (are) *pure*,
1Ti. 5:22. keep thyself *pure*.
Tit. 2: 5. discreet, *chaste*, keepers at home,
Jas. 3:17. from above is first *pure*,
1Pet.3: 2. behold your *chaste* conversation
1Joh.3: 3. purifieth himself, even as he is *pure*.

54 1 12/14 1:122 53

ἁγνότης, hagnotees.

2Co. 6: 6. By *pureness*, by knowledge, by

55 1 12/14 53

ἁγνῶς, hagnōs.

Phil. 1:16. preach Christ of contention, not *sincerely*.

56 2 12/14 1:115 1,1108

ἀγνωσία, agnōsia.

1Co.15:34. some have *not the knowledge* of God:
1 Pet.2:15. silence the *ignorance* of foolish men:

57 1 12/14 1:115 1,1110

ἄγνωστος, agnōstos.

Acts17:23. To The *Unknown* God.

58 11 12/15 cf 1453
ageirō (to gather)

ἀγορά, agora.

Mat.11:16. children sitting in the *markets*,
20: 3. standing idle in the *marketplace*,
23: 7. greetings in the *markets*, and
Mar. 6:56. they laid the sick in the *streets*,
7: 4. (when they come) from the *market*
Mar.12:38. salutations in the *marketplaces*,
Lu. 7:32. children sitting in the *marketplace*,
11:43. and greetings in the *markets*.
20:46. love greetings in the *markets*,
Acts16:19. drew (them) into the *marketplace*
17:17. in the *market* daily with them

59 31 12/15 1:124 58

ἀγοράζω, agorazo.

Mat.13:44. that he hath, and *buyeth* that field.
46. all that he had, and *bought* it.
14:15. villages, and *buy* themselves victuals.
21:12. sold and *bought* in the temple,
25: 9. that sell, and *buy* for yourselves.
10. while they went *to buy*, the
27: 7. *bought* with them the potter's field,
Mar. 6:36. villages, and *buy* themselves bread:
37. go and *buy* two hundred pennyworth
11:15. sold and *bought* in the temple,
15:46. he *bought* fine linen, and
16: 1. *had bought* sweet spices, that they
Lu. 9:13. we should go and *buy* meat for
14:18. I *have bought* a piece of ground,
19. I *have bought* five yoke of oxen,
17:28(27). did eat, they drank, they *bought*.
19:45. sold therein, and them *that bought*·
22:36. sell his garment, and *buy* one.
Joh. 4: 8. away unto the city to *buy* meat.
6: 5. Whence *shall* we *buy* bread,
13:29. *Buy* (those things) that we have
1Co. 6:20. For ye *are bought* with a price:
7:23. Ye *are bought* with a price;
30. they *that buy*, as though they
2Pet. 2: 1. denying the Lord *that bought* them,
Rev. 3:18. I counsel thee *to buy* of me gold tried
5: 9. *redeemed* us to God by thy blood
13:17. that no man might *buy* or sell,
14: 3. which *were redeemed* from the earth.
4. These *were redeemed* from among men
18:11. for no man *buyeth* their merchandise

60 2 12/15 58

ἀγοραιος, agoraios.

Acts17: 5. certain lewd fellows of the *baser sort*, (lit. *frequenters of the markets*)
19:38. against any man, the *law* is open, (lit. *court days* go on)

61 1 13/15 71

ἄγρα, agra.

Lu. 5: 4. let down your nets for a *draught*.
9. at the *draught* of the fishes which

62 1 13/15 1,1121

ἀγράμματος, agrammatos.

Acts 4:13. they were *unlearned* and ignorant men,

63 1 13/15 68,832

ἀγραυλέω, agrauleo.

Lu. 2: 8. shepherds *abiding in the field*,

64 1 13/15 61

ἀγρεύω, agrūo.

Mar.12:13. *to catch* him in (his) words.

65 2 13/15 66,1636

ἀγριέλαιος, agrielaios.

Ro. 11:17. thou, being a *wild olive tree*,
24. cut out of the *olive tree which is wild*

66 3 13/15 68

αγριος, agrios.

Mat. 3 4. meat was locusts and *wild* honey.
Mar. 1: 6. did eat locusts and *wild* honey;
Jude 13. *Raging* waves of the sea, foaming

68 36 13/15 71

ἀγρός, agros.

Mat. 6:28. Consider the lilies of the *field*, how
30. so clothe the grass of the *field*, which
13:24. which sowed good seed in his *field:*
27. sow good seed in thy *field?*
31. took, and sowed in his *field:*
36. parable of the tares of the *field*.
38. The *field* is the world; the good
44. like unto treasure hid in a *field;*
— he hath, and buyeth that *field*.
19:29. or wife, or children, or *lands*,
22: 5. went their ways, one to his *farm*,
24:18. let him which is in the *field*
40. Then shall two be in the *field;*
27: 7. bought with them the potter's *field*,
8. that *field* was called, The *field*
10. gave them for the potter's *field*,
Mar. 5:14. in the city, and in the *country*.
6:36. go into the *country* round about,
56. into villages, or cities, or *country*,
10:29. or wife, or children, or *lands*, for
30. mothers, and children, and *lands*,
13:16. let him that is in the *field* not
15:21. coming out of the *country*, the father
16:12. walked, and went into the *country*.
Lu. 8:34. in the city and in the *country*.
9:12. into the towns and *country* round
12:28. which is to day in the *field*,
14:18. I have bought a *piece of ground*,
15:15. sent him into his *fields* to feed
25. his elder son was in the *field:*
17: 7. when he is come from the *field*,
31. he that is in the *field*, let
36. Two (men) shall be in the *field;*
23:26. coming out of the *country*,
Acts 4:37. Having *land*, sold (it), and brought

69 4 13/16 2:333 1,5258

αγρυπνέω agrupneo.

Mar. 13:33. Take ye heed, *watch* and pray:
Lu. 21:36. *Watch* ye therefore, and pray always,
Eph. 6:18. and *watching* thereunto with all
Heb. 13:17. for they *watch* for your souls,

70 2 14/16 69

ἀγρυπνία, agrupnia.

2Co. 6: 5. in tumults, in labours, in *watchings*,
11:27. painfulness, in *watchings* often,

71 71 14/16

ἄγω, ago.

Mat. 10:18. ye *shall be brought* before governors
14: 6. when Herod's birthday *was kept*,
21: 2. loose (them), and *bring* (them) unto me.
7. *brought* the ass, and the colt,
26:46. Rise, *let us be going:* behold, he
Mar. 1:38. *Let us go* into the next towns,
11: 2. never man sat; loose him, and *bring* (him).
7. they *brought* the colt to Jesus,
13:11. when they *shall lead* (you),
14:42. Rise up, *let us go;* lo, he that
Lu. 4: 1. *was led* by the Spirit into the
Lu. 4: 9. And he *brought* him to Jerusalem,
29. *led* him unto the brow of the hill
40. diseases *brought* them unto him;
10:34. *brought* him to an inn, and
18:40. commanded him *to be brought* unto him
19:27. reign over them, *bring* hither, and
30. loose him, and *bring* (him hither).
35. And they *brought* him to Jesus:
21:12. *being brought* before kings and rulers
22:54. Then took they him, and *led* (him),
23: 1. of them arose, and *led* him unto Pilate.
32. malefactors, *led* with him to be put
24:21. to day *is* the third day since these
Joh. 1:42(43). he *brought* him to Jesus.
7:45. Why *have* ye not *brought* him?
8: 3. the scribes and Pharisees *brought* unto
9:13. They *brought* to the Pharisees him
10:16. of this fold: them also I must *bring*,
11. 7. *Let* us *go* into Judæa again.
15. nevertheless *let* us *go* unto him.
16. *Let* us also *go*, that we may die
14:31. Arise, *let* us *go* hence.
18:28. Then *led* they Jesus from Caiaphas
19: 4. Behold, I *bring* him forth to you,
13. he *brought* Jesus forth, and sat down
Acts 5:21. to the prison *to have* them *brought*.
26. the officers, and *brought* them without
27. And *when* they *had brought* them,
6:12. caught him, and *brought* (him)
8:32. He *was led* as a sheep to the
9: 2. he *might bring* them bound
21. he *might bring* them bound
27. took him, and *brought* (him) to
11:26(25). had found him, he *brought* him
17: 5. sought *to bring* them out to the
15. conducted Paul *brought* him unto Athens:
19. took him, and *brought* him unto
18:12. against Paul, and *brought* him
19:37. For ye *have brought* hither these men,
38. against any man, the law *is open*,
20:12. they *brought* the young man alive,
21:16. *brought* with them one Mnason
34. commanded him *to be carried*
22: 5. *to bring* them which were there bound
24. commanded him *to be brought*
23:10. *to bring* (him) into the castle.
18. took him, and *brought* (him) to
— *to bring* this young man unto thee,
31. took Paul, and *brought* (him) by night
25: 6. commanded Paul *to be brought*.
17. commanded the man *to be brought forth*.
23. commandment Paul *was brought forth*.
Ro. 2: 4. God *leadeth* thee to repentance?
8:14. many as *are led* by the Spirit of God,
1Co. 12: 2. dumb idols, even as ye *were led*.
Gal. 5:18. if ye *be led* of the Spirit, ye are not
1 Th. 4:14. in Jesus *will* God *bring* with him.
2 Ti. 3: 6. *led away* with divers lusts,
4:11. Take Mark, and *bring* him with thee.
Heb. 2:10. *bringing* many sons unto glory,

72 1 14/17 1:128 71

ἀγωγή, agōgee.

2 Ti. 3:10. my doctrine, *manner of life*, purpose,

73 6 14/17 1:134 71

ἀγών, agōn.

Phil. 1:30. Having the same *conflict* which ye saw
Col. 2: 1. what great *conflict* I have for you,
1Th. 2: 2. gospel of God with much *contention*.
1 Ti. 6:12. Fight the good *fight* of faith.

2 Ti. 4: 7. I have fought a good *fight*, I have
Heb. 12: 1. the *race* that is set before us.

74 1 15/17 1:134 73

ἀγωνία, *agōnia.*

Lu. 22:44. being in an *agony* he prayed

75 7 15/17 1:134 73

ἀγωνίζομαι, *agōnizomai.*

Lu. 13:24. *Strive* to enter in at the strait
Joh. 18:36. then *would* my servants *fight*,
1 Co. 9:25. And every man *that striveth* for
Col. 1:29. *striving* according to his working,
4:12. *labouring fervently* for you in prayers.
1 Ti. 6:12. *Fight* the good fight of faith,
2 Ti. 4: 7. I *have fought* a good fight,

77 1 15/17 1,1160

ἀδάπανος, *adapanos.*

1 Co. 9:18. the gospel of Christ *without charge*,

79 24 15/17 1:144 80

ἀδελφή, *adelphee.*

Mat. 12:50. the same is my brother, and *sister*,
13:56. his *sisters*, are they not all with us?
19:29. forsaken houses, or brethren, or *sisters*
Mar. 3:35. is my brother, and my *sister*,
6: 3. are not his *sisters* here with us?
10:29. house, or brethren, or *sisters*, or father,
30. houses, and brethren, and *sisters*,
Lu. 10:39. she had a *sister* called Mary,
40. not care that my *sister* hath left
14:26. children, and brethren, and *sisters*,
Joh. 11: 1. town of Mary and her *sister* Martha.
3. Therefore his *sisters* sent unto him,
5. loved Martha, and her *sister*,
28. called Mary her *sister* secretly,
39. the *sister* of him that was dead,
19:25. his mother, and his mother's *sister*,
Acts 23:16. when Paul's *sister's* son heard of
Ro. 16: 1. I commend unto you Phebe our *sister*,
15. and Julia, Nereus, and his *sister*,
1 Co. 7:15. A brother or a *sister* is not under
9: 5. to lead about a *sister*, a wife,
1 Ti. 5: 2. as mothers; the younger as *sisters*,
Jas. 2:15. If a brother or *sister* be naked,
2 Joh. 13. The children of thy elect *sister* greet

80 346 15/17 1:144 1 *delphus* (womb)

ἀδελφός, *adelphos.*

Mat. 1: 2. begat Judas and his *brethren*;
11. begat Jechonias and his *brethren*,
4:18. the sea of Galilee, saw two *brethren*, Simon called Peter, and Andrew his *brother*,
21. he saw other two *brethren*, James (the son) of Zebedee, and John his *brother*,
5:22. whosoever is angry with his *brother*
— whosoever shall say to his *brother*,
23. that thy *brother* hath ought against thee;
24. first be reconciled to thy *brother*,
47. if ye salute your *brethren* only,
7: 3. the mote that is in thy *brother's* eye,
4. wilt thou say to thy *brother*,
5. mote out of thy *brother's* eye.
10: 2. called Peter, and Andrew his *brother*;
—(3). (son) of Zebedee, and John his *brother*;
21. And the *brother* shall deliver up the *brother* to

Mat. 12:46. (his) mother and his *brethren*
47. thy mother and thy *brethren*
48. and who are my *brethren*?
49. Behold my mother and my *brethren*!
50. the same is my *brother*, and sister.
13:55. his *brethren*, James, and Joses,
14: 3. Herodias' sake, his *brother* Philip's wife.
17: 1. James, and John his *brother*,
18:15. if thy *brother* shall trespass
— thou hast gained thy *brother*.
21. how oft shall my *brother* sin
35. forgive not every one his *brother* their
19:29. houses, or *brethren*, or sisters,
20:24. indignation against the two *brethren*.
22:24. his *brother* shall marry his wife, and raise up seed unto his *brother*.
25. there were with us seven *brethren*:
— left his wife unto his *brother*:
23: 8. (even) Christ; and all ye are *brethren*.
25:40. the least of these my *brethren*,
28:10. go tell my *brethren* that they go
Mar. 1:16. saw Simon and Andrew his *brother*
19. (son) of Zebedee, and John his *brother*,
3:17. and John the *brother* of James;
31. There came then his *brethren* and
32. thy mother and thy *brethren* without
33. Who is my mother, or my *brethren*?
34. Behold my mother and my *brethren*!
35. will of God, the same is my *brother*,
5:37. and John the *brother* of James.
6: 3. son of Mary, the *brother* of James,
17. Herodias' sake, his *brother* Philip's wife:
18. for thee to have thy *brother's* wife.
10:29. left house, or *brethren*, or sisters,
30. houses, and *brethren*, and sisters,
12:19. If a man's *brother* die, and leave
— that his *brother* should take his wife, and raise up seed unto his *brother*.
20. Now there were seven *brethren*:
13:12. the *brother* shall betray the *brother*
Lu. 3: 1. and his *brother* Philip tetrarch of
19. for Herodias his *brother* Philip's wife,
6:14. named Peter, and Andrew his *brother*,
41. mote that is in thy *brother's* eye,
42. say to thy *brother*, *Brother*, let me
— mote that is in thy *brother's* eye.
8:19. (his) mother and his *brethren*,
20. Thy mother and thy *brethren*
21. My mother and my *brethren* are
12:13. Master, speak to my *brother*, that
14:12. not thy friends, nor thy *brethren*,
26. children, and *brethren*, and sisters,
15:27. said unto him, Thy *brother* is come;
32. for this thy *brother* was dead, and
16:28. For I have five *brethren*; that
17: 3. If thy *brother* trespass against thee,
18:29. house, or parents, or *brethren*, or wife,
20:28. If any man's *brother* die, having
— that his *brother* should take his wife, and raise up seed unto his *brother*.
29. There were therefore seven *brethren*
21:16. by parents, and *brethren*, and kinsfolks,
22:32. art converted, strengthen thy *brethren*.
Joh. 1:40(41). was Andrew, Simon Peter's *brother*.
41(42). findeth his own *brother* Simon,
2:12. his mother, and his *brethren*
6: 8. Andrew, Simon Peter's *brother*, saith
7: 3. His *brethren* therefore said unto him,
5. neither did his *brethren* believe
10. But when his *brethren* were gone up, then
11: 2. whose *brother* Lazarus was sick.
19. to comfort them concerning their *brother*

Joh. 11:21. been here, my *brother* had not died.
23. Thy *brother* shall rise again.
32. been here, my *brother* had not died.
20:17. go to my *brethren*, and say unto them,
21:23. saying abroad among the *brethren*,
Acts 1:14. of Jesus, and with his *brethren*.
16. Men (and) *brethren*, this scripture
2:29. Men (and) *brethren*, let me freely
37. Men (and) *brethren*, what shall we do?
3:17. now, *brethren*, I wot that through
22. unto you of your *brethren*, like
6: 3. Wherefore, *brethren*, look ye out among
7: 2. said, Men, *brethren*, and fathers,
13. was made known to his *brethren*;
23. to visit his *brethren* the children
25. his *brethren* would have understood
26. saying, Sirs, ye are *brethren*;
37. unto you of your *brethren*, like
9:17. said, *Brother* Saul, the Lord, (even)
30. (Which) when the *brethren* knew,
10:23. certain *brethren* from Joppa accompanied
11: 1. the apostles and *brethren* that
12. these six *brethren* accompanied me,
29. to send relief unto the *brethren* which
12: 2. he killed James the *brother* of John
17. unto James, and to the *brethren*.
13:15. saying, (Ye) men (and) *brethren*,
26. Men (and) *brethren*, children of
38. unto you therefore, men (and) *brethren*,
14: 2. minds evil affected against the *brethren*.
15: 1. from Judæa taught the *brethren*,
3. caused great joy unto all the *brethren*.
7. said unto them, Men (and) *brethren*,
13. Men (and) *brethren*, hearken
22. chief men among the *brethren*:
23. and elders and *brethren* (send) greeting unto the *brethren*.
32. exhorted the *brethren* with many words,
33. from the *brethren* unto the apostles.
36. go again and visit our *brethren*
40. being recommended by the *brethren*
16: 2. reported of by the *brethren* that were
40. and when they had seen the *brethren*,
17: 6. they drew Jason and certain *brethren*
10. the *brethren* immediately sent away Paul
14. the *brethren* sent away Paul
18:18. then took his leave of the *brethren*,
27. the *brethren* wrote, exhorting the
20:32. now, *brethren*, I commend you
21: 7. saluted the *brethren*, and abode with them one day.
17. the *brethren* received us gladly.
20. Thou seest, *brother*, how many thousands
22: 1. Men, *brethren*, and fathers, hear ye
5. I received letters unto the *brethren*,
13. *Brother* Saul, receive thy sight.
23: 1. Men (and) *brethren*, I have lived
5. I wist not, *brethren*, that he was
6. Men (and) *brethren*, I am a Pharisee,
28:14. Where we found *brethren*, and were
15. And from thence, when the *brethren*
17. Men (and) *brethren*, though I have
21. any of the *brethren* that came
Ro. 1:13. not have you ignorant, *brethren*,
7: 1. Know ye not, *brethren*, for I speak
4. Wherefore, my *brethren*, ye also are
8:12. Therefore, *brethren*, we are debtors,
29. the firstborn among many *brethren*.
9: 3. accursed from Christ for my *brethren*,
10: 1. *Brethren*, my heart's desire and prayer
11:25. *brethren*, that ye should be ignorant
12: 1. I beseech you therefore, *brethren*,

Ro. 14:10. why dost thou judge thy *brother*? or why dost thou set at nought thy *brother*?
13. to fall in (his) *brother's* way.
15. if thy *brother* be grieved with
21. (any thing) whereby thy *brother* stumbleth
15:14. persuaded of you, my *brethren*,
15. *brethren*, I have written the more
30. Now I beseech you, *brethren*,
16:14. the *brethren* which are with them.
17. I beseech you, *brethren*, mark them
23. saluteth you, and Quartus a *brother*.
1Co. 1: 1. will of God, and Sosthenes (our) *brother*,
10. I beseech you, *brethren*, by the name
11. declared unto me of you, my *brethren*,
26. ye see your calling, *brethren*.
2: 1. I, *brethren*, when I came to you,
3: 1. I, *brethren*, could not speak unto you
4: 6. And these things, *brethren*, I have
5:11. that is called a *brother* be a
6: 5. be able to judge between his *brethren*?
6. *brother* goeth to law with *brother*.
8. defraud, and that (your) *brethren*,
7:12. If any *brother* hath a wife that
15. A *brother* or a sister is not under
24. *Brethren*, let every man, wherein
29. this I say, *brethren*, the time (is)
8:11. shall the weak *brother* perish, for
12. ye sin so against the *brethren*,
13. meat make my *brother* to offend,
— lest I make my *brother* to offend.
9: 5. (as) the *brethren* of the Lord, and
10: 1. *brethren*, I would not that ye should
11: 2. I praise you, *brethren*, that ye
33. Wherefore, my *brethren*, when ye come
12: 1. Now concerning spiritual (gifts), *brethren*,
14: 6. Now, *brethren*, if I come unto you
20. *Brethren*, be not children in underst.:
26. How is it then, *brethren*? when
39. Wherefore, *brethren*, covet to prophesy,
15: 1. Moreover, *brethren*, I declare unto you
6. above five hundred *brethren* at once;
50. this I say, *brethren*, that flesh and
58. Therefore, my beloved *brethren*,
16:11. I look for him with the *brethren*.
12. As touching (our) *brother* Apollos,
— unto you with the *brethren*:
15. I beseech you, *brethren*, ye know
20. All the *brethren* greet you.
2Co. 1: 1. will of God, and Timothy (our) *brother*,
8. not, *brethren*, have you ignorant of
2:13. I found not Titus my *brother*:
8: 1. Moreover, *brethren*, we do you to wit
18. have sent with him the *brother*,
22. have sent with them our *brother*,
23. or our *brethren* (be enquired of),
9: 3. Yet have I sent the *brethren*,
5. necessary to exhort the *brethren*,
11: 9. the *brethren* which came from
12:18. with (him) I sent a *brother*.
13:11. Finally, *brethren*, farewell. Be perfect,
Gal. 1: 2. all the *brethren* which are with me,
11. I certify you, *brethren*, that the gospel
19. save James the Lord's *brother*.
3:15. *Brethren*, I speak after the manner
4:12. *Brethren*, I beseech you, be as I (am)
28. Now we, *brethren*, as Isaac was,
31. So then, *brethren*, we are not children
5:11. And I, *brethren*, if I yet preach
13. For, *brethren*, ye have been called
6: 1. *Brethren*, if a man be overtaken
18. *Brethren*, the grace of our Lord
Eph. 6:10. Finally, my *brethren*, be strong

Eph. 6:21. a beloved *brother* and faithful minister
23. Peace (be) to the *brethren*, and love
Phil. 1:12. ye should understand, *brethren*,
14. many of the *brethren* in the Lord,
2:25. send to you Epaphroditus, my *brother*,
3: 1. Finally, my *brethren*, rejoice in
13. *Brethren*, I count not myself to
17. *Brethren*, be followers together
4: 1. my *brethren* dearly beloved and
8. Finally, *brethren*, whatsoever things
21. The *brethren* which are with me
Col. 1: 1. will of God, and Timotheus (our) *brother*,
2. saints and faithful *brethren*
4: 7. you (who is) a beloved *brother*,
9. a faithful and beloved *brother*,
15. Salute the *brethren* which are
1Th. 1: 4. Knowing, *brethren* beloved, your
2: 1. For yourselves, *brethren*, know
9. ye remember, *brethren*, our
14. For ye, *brethren*, became followers
17. we, *brethren*, being taken from
3: 2. sent Timotheus, our *brother*,
7. Therefore, *brethren*, we were comforted
4: 1. we beseech you, *brethren*, and
6. defraud his *brother* in (any) matter:
10. toward all the *brethren* which
— we beseech you, *brethren*, that
13. not have you to be ignorant, *brethren*,
5: 1. the times and the seasons, *brethren*,
4. ye, *brethren*, are not in darkness,
12. we beseech you, *brethren*, to know
14. we exhort you, *brethren*, warn
25. *Brethren*, pray for us.
26. Greet all the *brethren* with
27. read unto all the holy *brethren*.
2Th. 1: 3. thank God always for you, *brethren*,
2: 1. we beseech you, *brethren*, by
13. for you, *brethren* beloved of the
15. Therefore, *brethren*, stand fast,
3: 1. Finally, *brethren*, pray for us,
6. we command you, *brethren*,
— from every *brother* that walketh
13. ye, *brethren*, be not weary in
15. admonish (him) as a *brother*.
1Ti. 4: 6. put the *brethren* in remembrance
5: 1. the younger men as *brethren*;
6: 2. because they are *brethren*;
2Ti. 4:21. Claudia, and all the *brethren*.
Philem. 1. Timothy (our) *brother*, unto
7. the saints are refreshed by thee, *brother*.
16. above a servant, a *brother* beloved,
20. Yea, *brother*, let me have
Heb. 2:11. not ashamed to call them *brethren*,
12. declare thy name unto my *brethren*,
17. made like unto (his) *brethren*,
3: 1. Wherefore, holy *brethren*,
12. Take heed, *brethren*, lest there
7: 5. that is, of their *brethren*,
8:11. neighbour, and every man his *brother*,
10:19. Having therefore, *brethren*, boldness
13:22. I beseech you, *brethren*, suffer
23. Know ye that (our) *brother*
Jas. 1: 2. My *brethren*, count it all joy
9. Let the *brother* of low degree
16. Do not err, my beloved *brethren*.
19. Wherefore, my beloved *brethren*,
2: 1. My *brethren*, have not the faith
5. Hearken, my beloved *brethren*,
14. What (doth it) profit, my *brethren*,
15. If a *brother* or sister be naked,
3: 1. My *brethren*, be not many masters,
10. My *brethren*, these things ought
Jas. 3:12. Can the figtree, my *brethren*,
4:11. of another, *brethren*. He that speaketh evil of (his) *brother*, and judgeth his *brother*,
5: 7. Be patient therefore, *brethren*,
9. Grudge not one against another, *brethren*,
10. Take, my *brethren*, the prophets,
12. above all things, my *brethren*,
19. *Brethren*, if any of you do err
1Pet. 5:12. a faithful *brother* unto you,
2Pet. 1:10. the rather, *brethren*, give diligence
3:15. as our beloved *brother* Paul also
1Joh. 2: 7. *Brethren*, I write no new commandment
9. in the light, and hateth his *brother*,
10. He that loveth his *brother* abideth
11. he that hateth his *brother*
3:10. that loveth not his *brother*.
12. wicked one, and slew his *brother*.
— works were evil, and his *brother's* righteous.
13. Marvel not, my *brethren*, if
14. because we love the *brethren*. He that loveth not (his) *brother* abideth
15. Whosoever hateth his *brother*
16. (our) lives for the *brethren*.
17. seeth his *brother* have need,
4:20. hateth his *brother*, he is a liar: for he that loveth not his *brother*
21. loveth God love his *brother* also.
5:16. If any man see his *brother* sin
3 Joh. 3. when the *brethren* came and
5. thou doest to the *brethren*, and
10. he himself receive the *brethren*,
Jude 1. of Jesus Christ, and *brother* of James,
Rev. 1: 9. I John, who also am your *brother*,
6:11. fellowservants also and their *brethren*,
12:10. the accuser of our *brethren* is cast
19:10. of thy *brethren* that have the
22: 9. of thy *brethren* the prophets, and

81 2 16/21 1:144 80

ἀδελφότης, *adelphotees.*

1Pet. 2:17. Love the *brotherhood*. Fear God.
5: 9. accomplished in your *brethren*

82 1 16/21 1,1212

ἄδηλος, *adeelos.*

Lu. 11:44. are as graves which *appear not*,
1Co. 14: 8. the trumpet give an *uncertain* sound,

83 1 16/21 82

ἀδηλότης, *adeelotees.*

1Ti. 6:17. nor trust in *uncertain* riches,

84 1 16/21 82

ἀδήλως, *adeelōs.*

1Co. 9:26. so run, not as *uncertainly*,

85 3 16/21 *adeō* (to be sated)

ἀδημονέω, *adeemoneo.*

Mat. 26:37. to be sorrowful and *very heavy*.
Mar 14:33. sore amazed, and *to be very heavy*;
Phil. 2:26. after you all, and was *full of heaviness*,

86 11 16/21 1:146 1,1492

ᾅδης, *hadees.*

Mat. 11:23. shalt be brought down to *hell*:
16:18. the gates of *hell* shall not prevail
Lu. 10:15. shalt be thrust down to *hell*.
16:23. in *hell* he lift up his eyes.

Acts 2:27. wilt not leave my soul in *hell*,
* 31. his soul was not left in *hell*,
1Co.15:55. O *grave*, where (is) thy victory?
Rev. 1:18. have the keys of *hell* and of death.
6: 8. was Death, and *Hell* followed
20:13. death and *hell* delivered up the
14. death and *hell* were cast into

87 1 16/21 3:921 1,1252

ἀδιάκριτος, *adiakritos.*

Jas. 3:17. *without partiality*, and without hypocrisy.

88 2 17/21 1,1223 3007

ἀδιάλειπτος, *adialiptos.*

Ro. 9: 2. great heaviness and *continual* sorrow
2Ti. 1: 3. that *without ceasing* I have

89 4 17/21 88

ἀδιαλείπτως, *adialiptōs.*

Ro. 1: 9. that *without ceasing* I make mention
1Th. 1: 3. Remembering *without ceasing*
2:13. thank we God *without ceasing*,
5:17. Pray *without ceasing*.

90 1 17/ 1,1311

ἀδιαφθορία, *adiaphthoria.*

Tit. 2: 7. in doctrine (shewing) *uncorruptness*,

91 27 17/21 1:149 94

ἀδικέω, *adikeo.*

Mat.20:13. Friend, I *do* thee no *wrong*:
Lu. 10:19. nothing *shall* by any means *hurt* you.
Acts 7:24. seeing one (of them) *suffer wrong*,
26. why *do* ye *wrong* one to another?
27. he *that did* his neighbour *wrong*
25:10. to the Jews *have I done* no *wrong*,
11. For if I *be an offender*, or have
1Co. 6: 7. Why *do* ye not rather *take wrong*?
8. Nay, ye *do wrong*, and defraud,
2Co. 7: 2. we *have wronged* no man,
12. his cause *that had done the wrong*, nor for his cause *that suffered wrong*,
Gal. 4:12. ye *have* not *injured* me at all.
Col. 3:25. he *that doeth wrong* shall receive for the *wrong* which he *hath done*:
Philem 18. If he *hath wronged* thee, or oweth
Rev. 2:11. *shall* not *be hurt* of the second
6: 6. (see) thou *hurt* not the oil and
7: 2. it was given *to hurt* the earth
3. Saying, *Hurt* not the earth, neither
9: 4. *should* not *hurt* the grass of
10. (was) *to hurt* men five months.
19. with them they *do hurt*.
11: 5. if any man will *hurt* them,
— and if any man will *hurt* them,
22:11. He *that is unjust, let* him *be unjust*

92 3 17/22 1:149 91

ἀδίκημα, *adikeema.*

Acts18:14. If it were a *matter of wrong* or
24:20. found any *evil doing* in me,
Rev.18: 5. God hath remembered her *iniquities*.

93 25 17/22 1:149 94

ἀδικία, *adikia.*

Lu. 13:27. from me, all (ye) workers of *iniquity*.
16: 8. commended the *unjust* steward,
Lu. 16: 9. of the mammon of *unrighteousness*;
18: 6. Hear what the *unjust* judge saith.
Joh. 7:18. no *unrighteousness* is in him.
Acts 1:18. with the reward of *iniquity*;
8:23. (in) the bond of *iniquity*.
Ro. 1:18. ungodliness and *unrighteousness* of men, who hold the truth in *unrighteousness*;
29. filled with all *unrighteousness*,
2: 8. the truth, but obey *unrighteousness*,
3: 5. if our *unrighteousness* commend the
6:13. instruments of *unrighteousness* unto
9:14. (Is there) *unrighteousness* with God?
1Co.13: 6. Rejoiceth not in *iniquity*, but
2Co.12:13. forgive me this *wrong*.
2Th. 2:10. deceivableness of *unrighteousness* in
12. had pleasure in *unrighteousness*.
2Ti. 2:19. name of Christ depart from *iniquity*.
Heb. 8:12. merciful to their *unrighteousness*,
Jas. 3: 6. tongue (is) a fire, a world of *iniquity*:
2Pet. 2:13. the reward of *unrighteousness*,
15. loved the wages of *unrighteousness*;
1Joh. 1: 9. cleanse us from all *unrighteousness*.
5:17. All *unrighteousness* is sin:

94 12 17/22 1:149 1,1349

ἄδικος, *adikos.*

Mat. 5:45. rain on the just and on the *unjust*.
Lu. 16:10. he that is *unjust* in the least is *unjust*
11. faithful in the *unrighteous* mammon,
18:11. extortioners, *unjust*, adulterers, or
Acts24:15. both of the just and *unjust*.
Ro. 3: 5. (Is) God *unrighteous* who taketh
1Co. 6: 1. go to law before the *unjust*, and
9. the *unrighteous* shall not inherit the
Heb. 6:10. For God (is) not *unrighteous* to forget
1Pet. 3:18. for sins, the just for the *unjust*,
2Pet. 2: 9. to reserve the *unjust* unto the day

95 1 18/22 94

ἀδίκως, *adikōs.*

1Pet. 2:19. endure grief, suffering *wrongfully*.

96 8 18/22 2:255 1,1384

ἀδόκιμος, *adokimos.*

Ro. 1:28. gave them over to a *reprobate* mind,
1Co. 9:27. I myself should be *a castaway*.
2Co.13: 5. Christ is in you, except ye be *reprobates*?
6. that we are not *reprobates*.
7. though we be as *reprobates*.
2Ti. 3: 8. *reprobate* concerning the faith.
Tit. 1:16. unto every good work *reprobate*.
Heb. 6: 8. beareth thorns and briers (is) *rejected*,

97 1 18/22 1,1388

ἄδολος, *adolos.*

1Pet. 2: 2. desire the *sincere* milk of the word.

100 1 18/22 *hadros* (stout)

ἁδρότης, *hadrotees.*

2Co. 8:20. blame us in this *abundance*

101 2 18/22 2:284 102

ἀδυνατέω, *adunateo.*

Mat.17:20. nothing *shall be impossible* unto
Lu. 1:37. with God nothing *shall be impossible*.

102 10 18/23 2:284 1,1415

ἀδύνατος, adunatos.

Mat.19:26. With men this is *impossible*;
Mar10:27. With men (it is) *impossible*,
Lu. 18:27. things which are *impossible* with
Acts14: 8. man at Lystra, *impotent* in his feet,
Ro. 8: 3. For what the law *could not do*,
15: 1. bear the infirmities of the *weak*,
Heb. 6: 4. For (it is) *impossible* for those
18. in which (it was) *impossible* for
10: 4. (it is) *not possible* that the blood
11: 6. without faith (it is) *impossible* to

103 5 18/23 1:163

ᾄδω, ado.

Eph. 5:19. *singing* and making melody
Col. 3:16. *singing* with grace in your
Rev. 5: 9. they *sung* a new song, saying,
14: 3. they *sung* as it were a new
15: 3. they *sing* the song of Moses

104 8 19/23

ἀεί, aï.

Mar15: 8. as he had *ever* done unto them.
Acts 7:51. ye do *always* resist the Holy Ghost:
2Co. 4:11. we which live are *alway* delivered
6:10. As sorrowful, yet *alway* rejoicing;
Tit. 1:12. The Cretians (are) *alway* liars.
Heb. 3:10. They do *alway* err in (their) heart;
1Pet. 3:15. (be) ready *always* to (give) an
2Pet. 1:12. to put you *always* in remembrance

105 4 19/23 rt 109

ἀετός, aetos.

Mat.24:28. there will the *eagles* be gathered
Lu. 17:37. thither will the *eagles* be gathered
Rev. 4: 7. fourth beast (was) like a flying *eagle*.
12:14. given two wings of a great *eagle*,

106 9 19/23 2:902 1,2219

ἄζυμος, azumos.

Mat.26:17. the (feast of) *unleavened bread*
Mar.14: 1. the passover, and of *unleavened bread*:
12. the first day of *unleavened bread*,
Lu. 22: 1. Now the feast of *unleavened bread*
7. came the day of *unleavened bread*,
Acts12: 3. were the days of *unleavened bread*.
20: 6. after the days of *unleavened bread*,
1Co. 5: 7. a new lump, as ye are *unleavened*.
8. *unleavened* (bread) of sincerity and

109 7 19/23 1:165 cf 5594
aēmi (to breathe)

ἀήρ, aeer.

Acts22:23. (their) clothes, and threw dust into the *air*,
1Co. 9:26. not as one that beateth the *air*:
14: 9. for ye shall speak into the *air*.
Eph. 2: 2. prince of the power of the *air*,
1Th. 4:17. to meet the Lord in the *air*: and
Rev. 9: 2. the sun and the *air* were darkened
16:17. poured out his vial into the *air*.

110 3 20/23 3:7 1,2288

ἀθανασία, athanasia.

1Co.15:53. this mortal (must) put on *immortality*.
54. shall have put on *immortality*,
1Ti. 6:16. Who only hath *immortality*.

111 2 20/23 1:166 1
themis (statute)

ἀθέμιτος, athemitos.

Acts10:28. it is an *unlawful thing* for a
1Pet.4: 3. banquetings, and *abominable* idolatries.

112 1 20/23 3:65 1,2316

ἄθεος, atheos.

Eph. 2:12. no hope, and *without God* in the world:

113 2 20/23 1:167 1,5087

ἄθεσμος, athesmos.

2Pet. 2: 7. filthy conversation of the *wicked*:
3:17. with the error of the *wicked*,

114 16 20/23 8:152 1,5087

ἀθετέω, atheteo.

Mar. 6:26. he would not *reject* her.
7: 9. ye *reject* the commandment of
Lu. 7:30. lawyers *rejected* the counsel of
10:16. he *that despiseth* you *despiseth* me; and he *that despiseth* me *despiseth* him that sent me.
Joh.12:48. He *that rejecteth* me, and receiveth
1Co. 1:19. *will bring to nothing* the understanding
Gal. 2:21. I *do* not *frustrate* the grace of God:
3:15. confirmed, no man *disannulleth*,
1Th. 4: 8. therefore *that despiseth*, *despiseth* not man,
1Ti. 5:12. they *have cast off* their first faith.
Heb10:28. He *that despised* Moses' law
Jude 8. defile the flesh, *despise* dominion,

115 2 20/23 8:152 114

ἀθέτησις, atheteesis.

Heb. 7:18. verily a *disannulling* of the
9:26. to *put away* sin by the sacrifice

118 2 20/24 1:167
athlos (contest)

ἀθλέω, athleo.

2Ti. 2: 5. if a man also *strive* for
— except he *strive* lawfully.

119 1 20/24 1:167 118

ἄθλησις, athleesis.

Heb10:32. endured a great *fight* of afflictions;

120 1 21/24 1,2372

ἀθυμέω, athumeo.

Col. 3:21. (to anger), lest they *be discouraged*.

121 2 21/24 1,5087

ἀθῶος, athōos.

Mat.27: 4. I have betrayed the *innocent* blood.
24. I am *innocent* of the blood of

122 1 21/24 *aix* (goat)

αἴγειος, aigios.

Heb11:37. about in sheepskins and *goat*skins;

123 6 21/24 251
aissō (to rush)

αἰγιαλός, aigialos.

Mat.13: 2. whole multitude stood on the *shore*.
48. was full, they drew to *shore*,
Joh.21: 4. Jesus stood on the *shore*:
Acts21: 5. kneeled down on the *shore*, and prayed.
27:39. discovered a certain creek with a *shore*,
40. to the wind, and made toward *shore*.

126 2 21/24 1:168 104

ἀΐδιος, aidios.

Rom. 1:20. (even) his *eternal* power and
Jude 6. reserved in *everlasting* chains

127 2 21/24 1:169 1,1492

αἰδώς, aidōs.

1Ti. 2: 9. with *shamefacedness* and sobriety;
Heb12:28. acceptably with *reverence* and godly fear:

129 99 22/25 1:172

αἷμα, haima.

Mat.16:17. for flesh and *blood* hath not
23:30. in the *blood* of the prophets.
35. the righteous *blood* shed upon the earth, from the *blood* of righteous Abel
— unto the *blood* of Zacharias son of
26:28. For this is my *blood* of the new
27: 4. I have betrayed the innocent *blood*.
6. because it is the price of *blood*.
8. was called, The field of *blood*,
24. I am innocent of the *blood* of this
25. His *blood* (be) on us, and on our
Mar. 5:25. which had an issue of *blood*
29. the fountain of her *blood* was
14:24. This is my *blood* of the new
Lu. 8:43. having an issue of *blood* twelve
44. her issue of *blood* stanched.
11:50. the *blood* of all the prophets,
51. From the *blood* of Abel unto the *blood* of Zacharias,
13: 1. whose *blood* Pilate had mingled
22:20. new testament in my *blood*,
44. great drops of *blood* falling down
Joh. 1:13. Which were born, not of *blood*, nor
6:53. Son of man, and drink his *blood*,
54. eateth my flesh, and drinketh my *blood*,
55. my *blood* is drink indeed.
56. eateth my flesh, and drinketh my *blood*,
19:34. came thereout *blood* and water.
Acts 1:19. to say, The field of *blood*.
2:19. *blood*, and fire, and vapour of
20. into darkness, and the moon into *blood*.
5:28. bring this man's *blood* upon us.
15:20. things strangled, and (from) *blood*.
29. offered to idols, and from *blood*,
17:26. hath made of one *blood* all nations
18: 6. Your *blood* (be) upon your own
20:26. from the *blood* of all (men).
28. purchased with his own *blood*.
21:25. from *blood*, and from strangled,
22:20. when the *blood* of thy martyr
Ro. 3:15. Their feet (are) swift to shed *blood*:
25. through faith in his *blood*, to
5: 9. being now justified by his *blood*,
1Co.10:16. communion of the *blood* of Christ?
11:25. the new testament in my *blood*:
27. the body and *blood* of the Lord.
15:50. that flesh and *blood* cannot
Gal. 1:16. I conferred not with flesh and *blood*:
Eph. 1: 7. have redemption through his *blood*,
2:13. nigh by the *blood* of Christ.
6:12. wrestle not against flesh and *blood*,
Col. 1:14. redemption through his *blood*,
20. peace through the *blood* of his
Heb 2:14. partakers of flesh and *blood*, he
9: 7. once every year, not without *blood*,
12. Neither by the *blood* of goats and calves, but by his own *blood*
13. For if the *blood* of bulls and of
14. more shall the *blood* of Christ,
Heb. 9:18. (testament) was dedicated without *blood*.
19. he took the *blood* of calves and
20. Saying, This (is) the *blood* of the
21. sprinkled with *blood* both the tabernacle
22. are by the law purged with *blood*
25. every year with *blood* of others;
10: 4. that the *blood* of bulls and of
19. the holiest by the *blood* of Jesus,
29. counted the *blood* of the covenant,
11:28. the passover, and the sprinkling of *blood*,
12: 4. not yet resisted unto *blood*,
24. to the *blood* of sprinkling, that
13:11. those beasts, whose *blood* is
12. sanctify the people with his own *blood*,
20. through the *blood* of the everlasting
1Pet. 1: 2. sprinkling of the *blood* of Jesus Christ·
19. with the precious *blood* of Christ,
1Joh.1: 7. the *blood* of Jesus Christ his Son
5: 6. came by water and *blood*, (even) Jesus Christ: not by water only, but by water and *blood*.
8. the spirit, and the water, and the *blood*:
Rev. 1: 5. from our sins in his own *blood*,
5: 9. redeemed us to God by thy *blood*
6:10. not judge and avenge our *blood*
12. the moon became as *blood*;
7:14. white in the *blood* of the Lamb.
8: 7. hail and fire mingled with *blood*,
8. part of the sea became *blood*;
11: 6. over waters to turn them to *blood*,
12:11. by the *blood* of the Lamb, and
14:20. *blood* came out of the winepress,
16: 3. it became as the *blood* of a dead
4. of waters; and they became *blood*.
6. shed the *blood* of saints and prophets, and thou hast given them *blood* to drink;
17: 6. drunken with the *blood* of the saints, and with the *blood* of the martyrs of Jesus:
18:24. was found the *blood* of prophets,
19: 2. avenged the *blood* of his servants
13. with a vesture dipped in *blood*:

130 1 22/26 1:172 129,1632

αἱματεκχυσία, haimatekhusia.

Heb 9:22. without *shedding of blood* is no

131 1 23/26 129,4482

αἱμοῤῥοέω, haimorroeo.

Mat. 9:20. *diseased with an issue of blood* twelve

133 1 23/26 134

αἴνεσις, ainesis.

Heb13:15. let us offer the sacrifice *of praise* to

134 9 23/26 1:177 136

αἰνέω, aineo.

Lu. 2:13. the heavenly host, *praising* God,
20. glorifying and *praising* God for
19:37. to rejoice and *praise* God with a
24:53. *praising* and blessing God.
Acts 2:47. *Praising* God, and having favour
3: 8. walking, and leaping, and *praising* God.
9. saw him walking and *praising* God:
Ro. 15:11. again, *Praise* the Lord, all ye
Rev.19: 5. saying, *Praise* our God, all ye

135 1 23/26 1:178 136

αἴνιγμα, ainigma.

1Co.13:12. now we see through a glass, *darkly*;

136 2 23/26

αἶνος, ainos.

Mat.21:16. thou hast perfected *praise?*
Lu. 18:43. saw (it), gave *praise* unto God.

138 3 23/26 1:180 cf 142

αἱρέομαι, haireomai.

Phil. 1:22. what I *shall choose* I wot not.
2Th.2:13. *hath* from the beginning *chosen* you
Heb 11:25. *Choosing* rather to suffer

139 9 23/26 1:180 138

αἵρεσις, hairesis.

Acts 5:17. which is the *sect* of the Sadducees
15: 5. certain of the *sect* of the Pharisees
24: 5. of the *sect* of the Nazarenes:
14. the way which they call *heresy*,
26: 5. straitest *sect* of our religion
28:22. for as concerning this *sect*,
1Co.11:19. there must be also *heresies*
Gal. 5:20. strife, seditions, *heresies*,
2Pet.2: 1. shall bring in damnable *heresies*,

140 1 23/26 1:180 138

αἱρετίζω, hairetizo.

Mat.12:18. my servant, whom I *have chosen*;

141 1 23/26 1:180 rt 140

αἱρετικός, hairetikos.

Tit. 3:10. A man that is an *heretick*

142 102 23/ 1:185 [cf 5375]

αἴρω, airo.

Mat. 4: 6. in (their) hands they *shall bear* thee *up*
9: 6. Arise, *take up* thy bed, and go
16. to fill it up *taketh* from the garment,
11:29. *Take* my yoke upon you, and
13:12. from him *shall be taken away*
14:12. came, and *took up* the body,
20. they *took up* of the fragments
15:37. they *took up* of the broken (meat)
16:24. *take up* his cross, and follow me.
17:27. *take up* the fish that first
20:14. *Take* (that) thine (is), and go thy
21:21. *Be* thou *removed*, and be thou cast into
43. of God *shall be taken* from you,
22:13. hand and foot, and *take* him *away*,
24:17. *to take* any thing out of his house:
18. return back *to take* his clothes.
39. came, and *took* them all away;
25:28. *Take* therefore the talent from him,
29. that hath not *shall be taken away*
27:32. they compelled *to bear* his cross.
Mar 2: 3. which was *borne* of four.
9. Arise, and *take up* thy bed,
11. Arise, and *take up* thy bed,
12. he arose, *took up* the bed, and went
21. filled it up *taketh away* from the
4:15. *taketh away* the word that was
25. from him *shall be taken* even
6: 8. they *should take* nothing for
29. they came and *took up* his corpse,
43. they *took up* twelve baskets full
8: 8. they *took up* of the broken (meat)
19. baskets full of fragments *took* ye *up?*
20. baskets full of fragments *took* ye *up?*
34. deny himself, and *take up* his cross,
10:21. come, *take up* the cross, and follow
11:23. *Be* thou *removed*, and be thou cast into
13:15. *to take* anything out of his house:
Mar 13:16. for *to take up* his garment.
15:21. of Alexander and Rufus, to *bear* his
24. what every man *should take*.
16:18. They *shall take up* serpents.
Lu. 4:11. in (their) hands they *shall bear* thee *up*,
5:24. Arise, and *take up* thy couch, and go
25. before them, and *took up* that whereon
6:29. him *that taketh away* thy cloke
30. of him *that taketh away* thy goods
8:12. the devil, and *taketh away* the word out
18. from him *shall be taken* even that
9: 3. *Take* nothing for (your) journey, neither
17. there *was taken up* of fragments
23. deny himself, and *take up* his cross daily,
11:22. he *taketh* from him all his armour
52. ye *have taken away* the key of knowledge
17:13. they *lifted up* (their) voices, and said,
31. let him not come down *to take* it *away*:
19:21. thou *takest up* that thou layedst
22. *taking up* that I laid not down,
24. *Take* from him the pound, and
26. that he hath *shall be taken away*
22:36. that hath a purse, *let* him *take* (it),
23:18. saying, *Away with* this (man),
Joh. 1:29. Lamb of God, which *taketh away*
2:16. *Take* these things hence; make
5: 8. Rise, *take up* thy bed, and walk.
9. was made whole, and *took up* his bed,
10. not lawful for thee *to carry* (thy) bed.
11. said unto me, *Take up* thy bed,
12. said unto thee, *Take up* thy bed, and
8:59. Then *took* they *up* stones to cast
10:18. No man *taketh* it from me, but
24. How long dost thou make us to doubt? (lit. *suspend* our souls)
11:39. Jesus said, *Take* ye *away* the stone.
41. Then they *took away* the stone (from)
— Jesus *lifted up* (his) eyes, and said,
48. Romans shall come and *take away* both
15: 2. beareth not fruit he *taketh away*:
16:22. your joy no man *taketh* from you.
17:15. that thou *shouldest take* them out
19:15. cried out, *Away with* (him), *away with* (him),
31. (that) they *might be taken away*.
38. *might take away* the body of Jesus:
— came therefore, and *took* the body of Jesus.
20. 1. the stone *taken away* from the
2. They *have taken away* the Lord
13. they *have taken away* my Lord,
15. laid him, and I *will take* him *away*.
Acts 4:24. they *lifted up* their voice to
8:33. his judgment *was taken away*.
— his life *is taken* from the earth.
20: 9. the third loft, and *was taken up* dead.
21:11. come unto us, he *took* Paul's girdle
36. followed after, crying, *Away with* him.
22:22. said, *Away with* such a (fellow)
27:13. *loosing* (thence), they sailed close
17. Which when they *had taken up*,
1Co. 6:15. shall I then *take* the members
Eph. 4:31. evil speaking, *be put away* from you,
Col. 2:14. contrary to us, and *took* it out of the way
1Joh.3: 5. was manifested to *take away* our sins:
Rev.10: 5. *lifted* up his hand to heaven,
18:21. a mighty angel *took up* a stone

143 1 26/27 1:187

αἰσθάνομαι, aisthanomai.

Lu. 9:45. hid from them, that they *perceived* it not;

144 1 24/27 1:187 143

αἴσθησις, aistheesis.

Phil. 1: 9. in knowledge and (in) all *judgment;*

145 1 24/27 1:187 143

αἰσθητήριον, aistheeteerium.

Heb. 5:14. have their *senses* exercised to

146 3 24/27 150
kerdos (gain)

αἰσχροκερδής, aiskrokerdees.

1Ti. 3: 3. no striker, not *greedy of filthy lucre;*
8. to much wine, not *greedy of filthy lucre;*
Tit. 1: 7. no striker, not *given to filthy lucre;*

147 1 24/27 146

αἰσχροκερδῶς, aiskrokerdōs.

1Pet. 5: 2. willingly; not *for filthy lucre,*

148 1 24/27 150,3056

αἰσχρολογία, aiskrologia.

Col. 3: 8. *filthy communication* out of your

149 3 24/27 150

αἰσχρόν, aiskron.

1Co. 11: 6. if it be a *shame* for a woman to
14:35. for it is a *shame* for women to
Eph. 5:12. For it is a *shame* even to speak

150 1 24/27 1:189 rt 153

αἰσχρός, aiskros.

Tit. 1:11. ought not, for *filthy* lucre's sake.

151 1 24/28 1:189 150

αἰσχρότης, aiskrotees.

Eph. 5: 4. Neither *filthiness,* nor foolish talking,

152 6 24/28 1:189 153

αἰσχύνη, aiskunee.

Lu. 14: 9. thou begin with *shame* to take
2Co. 4: 2. the hidden things of *dishonesty,*
Phil. 3:19. (whose) glory (is) in their *shame,*
Heb 12: 2. endured the cross, despising the *shame,*
Jude 13. foaming out their own *shame;*
Rev. 3:18. the *shame* of thy nakedness do

153 5 25/28 1:189
aischos (disfigurement)

αἰσχύνομαι, aiskunomai.

Lu. 16: 3. I cannot dig; to beg I *am ashamed.*
2Co. 10: 8. your destruction, I *should* not *be ashamed:*
Phil. 1:20. in nothing I *shall be ashamed,*
1Pet. 4:16. a Christian, *let* him not *be ashamed;*
1Joh. 2:28. not *be ashamed* before him

154 71 25/28 1:191 cf 4441

αἰτέω, aiteo.

Mat. 5:42. Give to him *that asketh* thee, and
6: 8. have need of, before ye *ask* him.
7: 7. *Ask,* and it shall be given you;
8. every one *that asketh* receiveth;
9. if his son *ask* bread, will he
10. Or if he *ask* a fish, will he give
11. good things to them *that ask* him?
14: 7. give her whatsoever she *would ask.*
18:19. any thing that they *shall ask,*
20:20. *desiring* a certain thing of him.
22. said, Ye know not what ye *ask.*
Mat. 21:22. whatsoever ye *shall ask* in prayer
27:20. that they *should ask* Barabbas.
58. to Pilate, and *begged* the body of Jesus.
Mar. 6:22. *Ask* of me whatsoever thou wilt;
23. Whatsoever thou *shalt ask* of me,
24. unto her mother, What *shall* I *ask?*
25. unto the king, and *asked,* saying,
10:35. for us whatsoever we *shall desire.*
38. Ye know not what ye *ask:*
11:24. What things soever ye *desire,* when
15: 6. one prisoner, whomsoever they *desired.*
8. began *to desire* (him to do) as he
43. unto Pilate, and *craved* the body of Jesus.
Lu. 1:63. he *asked* for a writing table, *and* wrote.
6:30. Give to every man *that asketh* of thee;
11. 9. *Ask,* and it shall be given you;
10. every one *that asketh* receiveth;
11. If a son *shall ask* bread of any
12. Or if he *shall ask* an egg, will
13. Holy Spirit to them *that ask* him?
12:48. of him they *will ask* the more.
23:23. *requiring* that he might be
25. into prison, whom they *had desired;*
52. unto Pilate, and *begged* the body of Jesus.
Joh. 4: 9. being a Jew, *askest* drink of me,
10. thou *wouldest have asked* of him,
11:22. whatsoever thou *wilt ask* of God,
14:13. whatsoever ye *shall ask* in my
14. If ye *shall ask* any thing in
15: 7. abide in you, ye *shall ask* what
16. whatsoever ye *shall ask* of the
16:23. Whatsoever ye *shall ask* the Father
24. *have* ye *asked* nothing in my name: *ask,*
26. At that day ye *shall ask* in my
Acts 3: 2. *to ask* alms of them that entered
14. the Just, and *desired* a murderer to
7:46. *desired* to find a tabernacle for
9: 2. *desired* of him letters to Damascus
12:20. their friend, *desired* peace; because
13:21. afterward they *desired* a king:
28. yet *desired* they Pilate that he
16:29. Then he *called for* a light, and sprang
25: 3. *desired* favour against him, that
15. *desiring* (to have) judgment against
1Co. 1:22. For the Jews *require* a sign, and
Eph. 3:13. I *desire* that ye faint not at my
20. above all that we *ask* or think,
Col. 1: 9. to *desire* that ye might be filled
Jas. 1: 5. you lack wisdom, *let* him *ask* of God,
6. But *let* him *ask* in faith, nothing
4: 2. ye have not, because ye *ask* not.
3. Ye *ask,* and receive not, because ye *ask* amiss, that ye may
1Pet. 3:15. every man *that asketh* you a
1Joh. 3:22. whatsoever we *ask,* we receive
5:14. if we *ask* any thing according
15. we *ask,* we know that we have the petitions that we *desired* of him.
16. not unto death, he *shall ask,* and

155 3 25/28 1:191 154

αἴτημα, aiteema.

Lu. 23:24. it should be as they *required.* (lit. their *request*)
Phil. 4: 6. let your *requests* be made known
1Joh. 5:15. we have the *petitions* that we

156 20 25/28 rt 154

αἰτία, aitia.

Mat. 19: 3. to put away his wife for every *cause?*
10. If the *case* of the man be so with

Mat.27:37. over his head his *accusation* written,
Mar 15:26. his *accusation* was written over,
Lu. 8:47. for what *cause* she had touched
Joh. 18:38. I find in him no *fault* (at all).
19: 4. I find no *fault* in him.
6. for I find no *fault* in him.
Acts 10:21. what (is) the *cause* wherefore
13:28. they found no *cause* of death (in)
22:24. he might know *where*fore (lit. for what *cause*) they
23:28. I would have known the *cause*
25:18. they brought none *accusation* of
27. the *crimes* (laid) against him.
28:18. there was no *cause* of death in me.
20. For this *cause* therefore have I
2Ti. 1: 6. *Where*fore (lit. for which *cause*) I put thee in remembrance
12. For the which *cause* I also suffer
Tit. 1:13. witness is true. *Where*fore rebuke
Heb. 2:11. for which *cause* he is not ashamed

157 1 26/28 156

αἰτίαμα, aitiama.

Acts 25: 7. many and grievous *complaints* against

158 4 26/29 159 cf 156

αἴτιον, aition.

Lu. 23: 4. I find no *fault* in this man.
14. have found no *fault* in this man
22. I have found no *cause* of death in
Acts 19:40. there being no *cause* whereby

159 1 26/29 rt 154

αἴτιος, aitios.

Heb. 5: 9. he became the *author* of eternal

160 2 26/29 1,5316

αἰφνίδιος, aiphnidios.

Lu. 21:34. that day come upon you *unawares.*
1Th. 5: 3. then *sudden* destruction cometh

161 3 26/29 1:195 164

αἰχμαλωσία, aikmalōsia.

Eph. 4: 8. he led *captivity* captive, and gave
Rev. 13:10. He that leadeth into *captivity* shall go into *captivity:*

162 2 26/29 1:195 164 cf163

αἰχμαλωτεύω, aikmalōtuo

Eph. 4: 8. up on high, he *led* captivity *captive,*
2Ti. 3: 6. *lead captive* silly women laden

163 3 26/29 1:195 164

αἰχμαλωτίζω, aikmalōtizo.

Lu. 21:24. *shall be led away captive* into
Ro. 7:23. *bringing* me *into captivity* to
2Co. 10: 5. *bringing into captivity* every

164 1 26/29 1:195 rt 259 *aichme* (spear)

αἰχμάλωτος, aikmalōtos.

Lu. 4:18(19). to preach deliverance to the *captives,*

165 128 26/29 1:197 rt 104 cf 5550

αἰών, aiōn.

NOTE.—[1] εις τον α. [2] εις τους α. [3] εις τȣς α. των α.

Mat. 6:13. the power, and the glory, for *ever.*[2]
12:32. forgiven him, neither in this *world,*
13:22. heareth the word; and the care of this *world,*
39. the harvest is the end of the *world*
40. it be in the end of this *world.*
49. So shall it be at the end of the *world:*
21:19. grow on thee henceforward for *ever.*[1]
24: 3. thy coming, and of the end of the *world?*
28:20. (even) unto the end of the *world.*
Mar. 3:29. against the Holy Ghost hath never (lit. not for *ever*)[1]
4:19. the cares of this *world,* and the
10:30. in the *world* to come eternal life.
11:14. No man eat fruit of thee hereafter for *ever*[1]
Lu. 1:33. over the house of Jacob for *ever;*[2] and
55. to Abraham, and to his seed for *ever.*[1]
70. which have been since the *world began* (lit. from *ever*) (απ' αιωνος)
16: 8. the children of this *world* are in
18:30. in the *world* to come life
20:34. The children of this *world* marry,
35. worthy to obtain that *world,* and
Joh. 4:14. shall give him shall never thirst; (lit. not for *ever*)[1]
6:51. of this bread, he shall live for *ever:*[1]
58. eateth of this bread shall live for *ever.*[1]
8:35. abideth not in the house for *ever:*[1] (but) the Son abideth for *ever.*[1]
51. my saying, he shall never see death. (lit. not for *ever*)[1]
52. my saying, he shall never taste of (lit. not for *ever*)[1]
9:32. Since the *world began* was it (εκ τȣ α.)
10:28. they shall never perish, neither (lit. not for *ever*)[1]
11:26. believeth in me shall never die. (lit. not for *ever*)[1]
12:34. that Christ abideth for *ever:*[1]
13: 8. Thou shalt never wash my feet. (lit. not for *ever*)[1]
14:16. he may abide with you for *ever;*[1]
Acts 3:21. holy prophets since the *world began.* (lit. from *ever*) (απ' αιωνος)
15:18. from the *beginning of the world.* (απ' αιωνος)
Ro. 1:25. the Creator, who is blessed for *ever.*[2]
9: 5. is over all, God blessed for *ever.*[2]
11:36. to whom (be) glory for *ever.*[2]
12: 2. be not conformed to this *world:*
16:27. (be) glory through Jesus Christ for *ever*
1Co. 1:20. where (is) the disputer of this *world?*
2: 6. yet not the wisdom of this *world,* nor of the princes of this *world,*
7. God ordained before the *world* (προ των)
8. none of the princes of this *world* knew
3:18. seemeth to be wise in this *world,*
8:13. no flesh *while the world standeth,* (lit. *ever*)[1]
10:11. the ends of the *world* are come. (των α.
2Co. 4: 4. the god of this *world* hath blinded
9: 9. his righteousness remaineth for *ever.*[1]
11:31. Christ, which is blessed for *evermore,*[2]
Gal. 1: 4. deliver us from this present evil *world,*
5. To whom (be) glory for *ever* and *ever.*[3]
Eph. 1:21. named, not only in this *world,*
2: 2. according to the *course* of this world,
7. That in the *ages* to come he might
3: 9. the *beginning of the world* (απο των α.)
11. According to the *eternal* purpose (των α.)
21. throughout all ages, *world* without *end* (τȣ α. των α.)
6:12. of the darkness of this *world.*

Phi. 4:20. our Father (be) glory for *ever* and *ever*.[3]
Col. 1:26. hid from *ages* and from generations, (απο των α.)
1Ti. 1:17. Now unto the King *eternal*, (των α.)
— (be) honour and glory for *ever* and *ever*.[3]
6:17. that are rich in this *world*,
2Ti. 4:10. having loved this present *world*,
18. to whom (be) glory for *ever* and *ever*.[3]
2:12. godly, in this present *world* ;
Heb 1: 2. by whom also he made the *worlds* ;
8. Thy throne, O God, (is) for *ever* and *ever*: (τον α. τȣ α.)
5: 6. Thou (art) a priest for *ever*[1] after
6: 5. the powers of the *world* to come,
20. made an high priest for *ever*[1] after
7:17. Thou (art) a priest for *ever*[1] after
21. Thou (art) a priest for *ever*[1] after
24. this (man), because he continueth *ever*,[1]
28. Son, who is consecrated for *evermore*.[1]
9:26. now once in the end of the *world* (των α.)
11: 3. the *worlds* were framed by the
13: 8. yesterday, and to day, and for *ever*.[2]
21. to whom (be) glory for *ever* and *ever*.[3]
1Pet. 1:23. which liveth and abideth for *ever*.[1]
25. word of the Lord endureth for *ever*.[1]
4:11. praise and dominion for *ever* and *ever*.[3]
5:11. (be) glory and dominion for *ever* and *ever*.[3]
2Pet. 2:17. of darkness is reserved for *ever*. (εις αιωνα)
3:18. (be) glory both now and for *ever*. (εις ημεραν αιωνος)
1Joh. 2:17. the will of God abideth for *ever*.[1]
2Joh. 2. shall be with us for *ever*.[1]
Jude 13. the blackness of darkness for *ever*.[1]
25. both now and *ever*. (εις παντας τȣς α.)
Rev. 1: 6. (be) glory and dominion for *ever* and *ever*.[3]
18. behold, I am alive for *evermore*,[3]
4: 9. who liveth for *ever* and *ever*,[3]
10. worship him that liveth for *ever* and *ever*,[3]
5:13. unto the Lamb for *ever* and *ever*.[3]
14. worshipped him that liveth for *ever* and *ever*.[3]
7:12. might, (be) unto our God for *ever* and *ever*.[3]
10: 6. sware by him that liveth for *ever* and *ever*,[3]
11:15. he shall reign for *ever* and *ever*.[3]
14:11. their torment ascendeth up for *ever* and *ever* : (εις αιωνας αιωνων)
15: 7. God, who liveth for *ever* and *ever*.[3]
19: 3. her smoke rose up for *ever* and *ever*.[3]
20:10. tormented day and night for *ever* and *ever*.[3]
22: 5. they shall reign for *ever* and *ever*.[3]

166 71 27/30 1:197 165

αἰώνιος, aiōnios.

Mat. 18: 8. to be cast into *everlasting* fire.
19:16. that I may have *eternal* life?
29. shall inherit *everlasting* life.
25:41. ye cursed, into *everlasting* fire,
46. go away into *everlasting* punishment: but the righteous into life *eternal*.
Mar. 3:29. in danger of *eternal* damnation:
10:17. that I may inherit *eternal* life?
30. in the world to come *eternal* life.
Lu. 10:25. what shall I do to inherit *eternal* life?
16: 9. receive you into *everlasting* habitations.
18:18. what shall I do to inherit *eternal* life?
30. in the world to come life *everlasting*.
Joh. 3:15. not perish, but have *eternal* life.
16. not perish, but have *everlasting* life.
36. believeth on the Son hath *everlasting* life.
Joh. 4:14. springing up into *everlasting* life.
36. gathereth fruit unto life *eternal* :
5:24. that sent me, hath *everlasting* life,
39. ye think ye have *eternal* life:
6:27. which endureth unto *everlasting* life,
40. on him, may have *everlasting* life:
47. believeth on me hath *everlasting* life.
54. drinketh my blood, hath *eternal* life;
68. thou hast the words of *eternal* life.
10:28. I give unto them *eternal* life ;
12:25. shall keep it unto life *eternal*.
50. his commandment is life *everlasting* :
17: 2. he should give *eternal* life to as
3. this is life *eternal*, that they
Acts 13:46. unworthy of *everlasting* life, lo,
48. as many as were ordained to *eternal* life
Ro. 2: 7. honour and immortality, *eternal* life:
5:21. through righteousness unto *eternal* life
6:22. unto holiness, and the end *everlasting* life
23. the gift of God (is) *eternal* life
16:25. kept secret since the *world* began, (χρονοις αιωνιοις)
26. commandment of the *everlasting* God,
2Co. 4:17. exceeding (and) *eternal* weight of glory;
18. things which are not seen (are) *eternal*.
5: 1. with hands, *eternal* in the heavens.
Gal. 6: 8. shall of the Spirit reap life *everlasting*.
2Th. 1: 9. be punished with *everlasting* destruction
2:16. hath given (us) *everlasting* consolation
1Ti. 1:16. believe on him to life *everlasting*.
6:12. lay hold on *eternal* life, whereunto
16. (be) honour and power *everlasting*.
19. they may lay hold on *eternal* life.
2Ti. 1: 9. in Christ Jesus before the *world* began; (προ χρονων αιωνιων)
2:10. in Christ Jesus with *eternal* glory.
Tit. 1: 2. hope of *eternal* life, which God, that cannot lie, promised before the *world* began ; (προ χρ. αι.)
3: 7. to the hope of *eternal* life.
Philem. 15. thou shouldest receive him *for ever* ;
Heb 5: 9. the author of *eternal* salvation
6: 2. the dead, and of *eternal* judgment.
9:12. having obtained *eternal* redemption
14. who through the *eternal* Spirit offered
15. the promise of *eternal* inheritance.
13:20. blood of the *everlasting* covenant,
1Pet. 5:10. called us unto his *eternal* glory
2Pet. 1:11. into the *everlasting* kingdom of our
1Joh. 1: 2. shew unto you that *eternal* life.
2:25. promised us, (even) *eternal* life.
3:15. no murderer hath *eternal* life
5:11. God hath given to us *eternal* life,
13. know that ye have *eternal* life,
20. the true God, and *eternal* life.
Jude 7. suffering the vengeance of *eternal* fire.
21. Lord Jesus Christ unto *eternal* life.
Rev. 14: 6. having the *everlasting* gospel to

167 10 28/31 3:413 169

ἀκαθαρσία, akatharsia.

Mat. 23:27. dead (men's) bones, and of all *uncleanness*
Ro. 1:24. gave them up to *uncleanness* through
6:19. your members servants to *uncleanness*
2Co. 12:21. have not repented of the *uncleanness*
Gal. 5:19. Adultery, fornication, *uncleanness*,
Eph. 4:19. to work all *uncleanness* with greediness.
5: 3. fornication, and all *uncleanness*, or
Col. 3: 5. upon the earth : fornication, *uncleanness*,
1Th. 2: 3. not of deceit, nor of *uncleanness*, nor
4: 7. God hath not called us unto *uncleanness*.

168 1 28/ 169

ἀκαθάρτης, akathartees.

Rev.17: 4. abominations and *filthiness* of her fornication:

169 30 28/31 3:413 1,2508

ἀκάθαρτος, akathartos.

Mat.10: 1. power (against) *unclean* spirits,
12:43. When the *unclean* spirit is gone
Mar 1:23. a man with an *unclean* spirit;
26. when the *unclean* spirit had torn
27. commandeth he even the *unclean* spirits,
3:11. *unclean* spirits, when they saw
30. said, He hath an *unclean* spirit.
5: 2. a man with an *unclean* spirit,
8. Come out of the man, (thou) *unclean* spirit.
13. the *unclean* spirits went out,
6: 7. gave them power over *unclean* spirits;
7:25. young daughter had an *unclean* spirit,
9:25. he rebuked the *foul* spirit, saying
Lu. 4:33. had a spirit of an *unclean* devil,
36. he commandeth the *unclean* spirits,
6:18. that were vexed with *unclean* spirits:
8:29. had commanded the *unclean* spirit
9:42. Jesus rebuked the *unclean* spirit,
11:24. When the *unclean* spirit is gone
Acts 5:16. which were vexed with *unclean* spirits:
8: 7. For *unclean* spirits, crying with
10:14. any thing that is common or *unclean*.
28. not call any man common or *unclean*.
11: 8. nothing common or *unclean* hath at
1Co. 7:14. else were your children *unclean*;
2Co. 6:17. touch not the *unclean* (thing);
Eph. 5: 5. nor *unclean* person, nor covetous man,
Rev.16:13. I saw three *unclean* spirits like
18: 2. the hold of every *foul* spirit, and a cage of every *unclean* and hateful bird.

170 1 28/32 3:455 1,2540

ἀκαιρέομαι, akaireomai.

Phil. 4:10. careful, but ye *lacked opportunity*.

171 1 28/32 3:455 rt 170

ἀκαίρως, akairōs.

2Ti. 4: 2. be instant in season, *out of season*;

172 2 28/32 3:469 1,2556

ἄκακος, akakos.

Ro. 16:18. deceive the hearts of the *simple*.
Heb 7:26. (who is) holy, *harmless*, undefiled,

173 14 28/32 rt 188

ἄκανθα, akantha.

Mat. 7:16. Do men gather grapes of *thorns*, or figs
13: 7. some fell among *thorns*; and the *thorns*
22. seed among the *thorns* is he that
27:29. had platted a crown of *thorns*,
Mar 4: 7. some fell among *thorns*, and the *thorns*
18. they which are sown among *thorns*;
Lu. 6:44. For of *thorns* men do not gather
8: 7. some fell among *thorns*; and the *thorns* sprang up with it, and
14. that which fell among *thorns* are
Joh.19: 2. the soldiers platted a crown of *thorns*,
Heb 6: 8. that which beareth *thorns* and

174 2 29/32 173

ἀκάνθινος, akanthinos.

Mar 15:17. platted a crown *of thorns*, and put it
Joh.19: 5. wearing the crown *of thorns*, and the

175 7 29/32 3:614 1,2590

ἄκαρπος, akarpos.

Mat.13:22. choke the word, and he becometh *unfruitful*.
Mar 4:19. the word, and it becometh *unfruitful*
1Co.14:14. my understanding is *unfruitful*.
Eph. 5:11. with the *unfruitful* works of
Tit. 3:14. that they be not *unfruitful*.
2Pet. 1: 8. neither (be) barren nor *unfruitful* in
Jude 12. whose fruit withereth, *without fruit*,

176 1 29/32 1:689 1,2607

ἀκατάγνωστος, akatagnōstos.

Tit. 2: 8. Sound speech, that *cannot be condemned*;

177 2 29/32 1,2596,2572

ἀκατακάλυπτος, akatakaluptos.

1Co.11: 5. prophesieth with (her) head *uncovered*
13. that a woman pray unto God *uncovered*?

178 2 29/32 3:921 1,2632

ἀκατάκριτος, akatakritos.

Acts16:37. have beaten us openly *uncondemned*,
22:25. a man that is a Roman, and *uncondemned*?

179 1 29/32 4:328 1,2647

ἀκατάλυτος, akatalutos.

Heb 7:16. after the power of an *endless* life.

180 1 29/32 1,2664

ἀκατάπαυστος, akatapaustos.

2Pet. 2:14. that *cannot cease* from sin; beguiling

181 5 29/32 3:444 182

ἀκαταστασία, akatastasia.

Lu. 21: 9. shall hear of wars and *commotions*,
1Co.14:33. God is not (the author) of *confusion*,
2Co. 6: 5. in imprisonments, in *tumults*, in
12:20. whisperings, swellings, *tumults*:
Jas. 3:16. there (is) *confusion* and every evil work.

182 1 29/32 3:444 1,2525

ἀκατάστατος, akatastatos.

Jas. 1: 8. A double minded man (is) *unstable* in

183 1 29/32 1,2722

ἀκατάσχετος, akatasketos.

Jas. 3: 8. (it is) an *unruly* evil, full of deadly

185 3 29/32 1:209 1,2767

ἀκέραιος, akeraios.

Mat.10:16. wise as serpents, and *harmless* as doves.
Ro. 16:19. is good, and *simple* concerning evil.
Phil. 2:15. ye may be blameless and *harmless*,

186 1 30/32 1,2827

ἀκλινής, aklinees.

Heb 10:23. profession of (our) faith *without wavering*

187 1 30/33 rt 188

ακμάζω, akmazo.

Rev.14:18. for her grapes *are fully ripe.*

188 1 30/33

ἀκμήν, akmeen
akē (point)

Mat.15:16. Are ye also *yet* without understanding?

189 24 30/33 1:216 191

ἀκοή, akoee.

Mat. 4:24. his *fame* went througnout all Syria:
13:14. By *hearing* ye shall hear, and
14: 1. heard of the *fame* of Jesus,
24: 6. hear of wars and *rumours* of wars:
Mar 1:28. immediately his *fame* spread
7:35. straightway his *ears* were opened,
13: 7. hear of wars and *rumours* of wars,
Lu. 7: 1. sayings in the *audience* of the people,
Joh.12:38. who hath believed our *report?*
Acts17:20. certain strange things to our *ears:*
28:26. *Hearing* ye shall hear, and shall not
Ro. 10:16. who hath believed our *report?*
17. faith (cometh) by *hearing*, and *hearing*
1Co.12:17. the *hearing?* If the whole (were) *hearing*, where
Gal. 3: 2. or by the *hearing* of faith?
5. the law, or by the *hearing* of faith?
1Th. 2:13. the word of God *which ye heard* of us, ye
2Ti. 4: 3. to themselves teachers, having itching *ears;*
4. shall turn away (their) *ears* from
Heb 4: 2. the word *preached* did not profit
5:11. seeing ye are dull of *hearing.*
2Pet.2: 8. among them, in seeing and *hearing*,

190 92 30/33 1:210 1
keleuthos (road)

ἀκολουθέω, akoloutheo.

Mat. 4:20. left (their) nets, and *followed* him.
22. left the ship and their father, and *followed* him.
25. there *followed* him great multitudes
8: 1. great multitudes *followed* him.
10. said to them *that followed*, Verily
19. I *will follow* thee whithersoever
22. Jesus said unto him, *Follow* me;
23 into a ship, his disciples *followed* him.
9: 9. *Follow* me. And he arose, and *followed*
19. Jesus arose, and *followed* him,
27. two blind men *followed* him, crying,
10:38. taketh not his cross, and *followeth* after me, is not worthy
12:15. great multitudes *followed* him,
14:13. they *followed* him on foot out of the
16:24. take up his cross, and *follow* me.
19: 2. great multitudes *followed* him;
21. treasure in heaven: and come (and) *follow* me.
27. have forsaken all, and *followed* thee;
28. That ye which *have followed* me,
20:29. a great multitude *followed* him.
34. received sight, and they *followed* him.
21: 9. multitudes that went before, and *that followed*,
26:58. Peter *followed* him afar off unto
27:55. which *followed* Jesus from Galilee,
Mar 1:18. forsook their nets, and *followed* him.
2:14. *Follow* me. And he arose and *followed*
15. there were many, and they *followed* him.
3: 7. a great multitude from Galilee *followed*
Mar 5:24. with him; and much people *followed* him.
6: 1. own country; and his disciples *fo ow* him
8:34. take up his cross, and *follow* me.
9:38. in thy name, and he *followeth* not us. and we forbad him, because he *followeth* not
10:21. take up the cross, and *follow* me.
28. have left all, and *have followed* thee.
32. *as they followed*, they were afraid.
52. received his sight, and *followed* Jesus
11: 9. went before, and they *that followed*,
14:13. bearing a pitcher of water: *follow* him.
51. there *followed* him a certain young
54. Peter *followed* him afar off, even
15:41. he was in Galilee, *followed* him. and
Lu. 5:11. they forsook all, and *followed* him.
27. custom: and he said unto him, *Follow* me.
28. he left all, rose up, and *followed* him.
7: 9. unto the people *that followed* him,
9:11. when they knew (it), *followed* him:
23. take up his cross daily, and *follow* me.
49. because he *followeth* not with us
57. I *will follow* thee whithersoever
59. he said unto another, *Follow* me.
61. also said, Lord, I *will follow* thee;
18:22. treasure in heaven: and come, *follow* me.
28. we have left all, and *followed* thee.
43. received his sight, and *followed* him,
22:10. *follow* him into the house where
39. his disciples also *followed* him.
54. priest's house. And Peter *followed* afar off
23:27. there *followed* him a great company
Joh. 1:37. heard him speak, and they *followed*
38. Jesus turned, and saw them *following*,
40 (41) heard John (speak), and *followed* him
43 (44) findeth Philip, and saith unto him *Follow* me.
6: 2. a great multitude *followed* him,
8:12. he *that followeth* me shall not
10: 4. before them, and the sheep *follow* him:
5. a stranger *will* they not *follow*,
27. I know them, and they *follow* me:
11:31. up hastily and went out, *followed* her,
12:26. If any man serve me, *let* him *follow* me;
13:36. not *follow* me now; but thou *shalt follow*
37. why cannot I *follow* thee now?
18:15. Simon Peter *followed* Jesus, and (so)
20: 6. cometh Simon Peter *following* him,
21:19. he saith unto him, *Follow* me.
20. disciple whom Jesus loved *following;*
22. what (is that) to thee? *follow* thou me.
Acts12: 8. thy garment about thee, and *follow* me.
9. he went out, and *followed* him;
13:43. religious proselytes *followed* Paul and
21:36. the multitude of the people *followed* after,
1Co 10: 4. spiritual Rock *that followed* them:
Rev. 6: 8. was Death, and Hell *followed* with him.
14: 4. are they *which follow* the Lamb
8. there *followed* another angel, saying,
9. the third angel *followed* them,
13. their works *do follow* them.
18: 5. her sins *have reached* unto heaven,
19:14. *followed* him upon white horses,

191 437 31/34 1:216

ἀκούω, akouo.

Mat. 2: 3. *When* Herod the king *had heard* (these things),
9. *When* they *had heard* the king, they
18. In Rama *was* there a voice *heard*,
22. *when* he *heard* that Archelaus did
4:12. *when* Jesus *had heard* that John

Mat. 5:21. Ye *have heard* that it was said
27. Ye *have heard* that it was said
33. Ye *have heard* that it hath been
38 Ye *have heard* that it hath been said
43. Ye *have heard* that it hath been
7:24. whosoever *heareth* these sayings
26. every one *that heareth* these sayings
8:10. *When* Jesus *heard* (it), he marvelled,
9:12. *when* Jesus *heard* (that), he said
10:14. not receive you, nor *hear* your words,
27. what ye *hear* in the ear, (that) preach
11: 2. *when* John *had heard* in the prison
4. things which ye *do hear* and see:
5. lepers are cleansed, and the deaf *hear*, the
15. He that hath ears *to hear, let* him *hear*.
12:19. *shall* any man *hear* his voice in
24. *when* the Pharisees *heard* (it), they
42. *to hear* the wisdom of Solomon; and,
13: 9. Who hath ears *to hear, let* him *hear*.
13. seeing, see not; and *hearing* they *hear* not,
14. By hearing ye *shall hear*, and shall
15. (their) ears are dull of *hearing*, and
— with (their) eyes, and *hear* with (their) ears,
16. they see: and your ears, for they *hear*
17. *to hear* (those things) which ye *hear*, and *have* not *heard* them.
18. *Hear* ye therefore the parable of
19. *When* any one *heareth* the word
20. same is he *that heareth* the word,
22. is he *that heareth* the word; and the
23. good ground is he *that heareth* the
43. Who hath ears *to hear, let* him *hear*.
14: 1. Herod the tetrarch *heard* of the fame
13. *When* Jesus *heard* (of it), he departed
— *when* the people *had heard* (thereof),
15:10. said unto them, *Hear*, and understand·
12. offended, *after they heard* this saying?
17: 5 I am well pleased; *hear* ye him.
6. *when* the disciples *heard* (it), they
18:15. if he *shall hear* thee, thou hast gained
16. if he *will* not *hear* (thee, then) take
19:22. *when* the young man *heard* that
25. *When* his disciples *heard* (it), they
20:24. *when* the ten *heard* (it), they were
30. *when* they *heard* that Jesus passed
21:16. said unto him, *Hearest* thou what
33. *Hear* another parable: There was
45. *when* the chief priests and Pharisees *had heard*
22: 7. *when* the king *heard* (thereof), he
22. *When* they *had heard* (these words),
33. *when* the multitude *heard* (this),
34. *when* the Pharisees *had heard*
24: 6. ye shall *hear* of wars and rumours
26:65. now ye *have heard* his blasphemy
27:13. *Hearest* thou not how many things
47. *when* they *heard* (that), said,
28:14. if this *come to* the governor's *ears*, (lit. *be heard* by)
Mar 2: 1. it *was noised* that he was in
17. *When* Jesus *heard* (it), he saith
3: 8. *when* they *had heard* what great
21. *when* his friends *heard* (of it),
4: 3. *Hearken*; Behold, there went out
9. that hath ears *to hear, let* him *hear*.
12. *hearing* they *may hear*, and not
15. when they *have heard*, Satan
16. who, when they *have heard* the
18. among thorns; such *as hear* the word,
20. such as *hear* the word, and receive

Mar 4:23. have ears *to hear, let* him *hear*.
24. Take heed what ye *hear*; with
— unto you *that hear* shall more
33. as they were able *to hear* (it).
5:27. *When* she *had heard* of Jesus, came
36. As soon as Jesus *heard* the word
6: 2. many *hearing* (him) were astonished,
11. shall not receive you, nor *hear* you,
14. king Herod *heard* (of him); for
16. *when* Herod *heard* (thereof), he said,
20. *when* he *heard* him, he did many things and *heard* him gladly.
29. *when* his disciples *heard* (of it), they
55. were sick, where they *heard* he was.
7:14. *Hearken* unto me every one (of you),
16. If any man have ears *to hear, let* him *hear*,
25. had an unclean spirit, *heard* of him,
37. he maketh both the deaf *to hear*, and
8.18. see ye not? having ears, *hear* ye not?
9: 7. This is my beloved Son: *hear* him.
10:41. *when* the ten *heard* (it), they began
47. *when* he *heard* that it was Jesus
11:14. hereafter for ever. And his disciples *heard* (it).
18. the scribes and chief priests *heard* (it),
12:28. *having heard* them reasoning
29. *Hear*, O Israel; The Lord our God is
37. the common people *heard* him gladly.
13: 7. ye *shall hear* of wars and rumours of wars,
14:11. *when* they *heard* (it), they were glad,
58. We *heard* him say, I will destroy
64. Ye *have heard* the blasphemy:
15:35. *when* they *heard* (it), said, Behold,
16·11. *when* they *had heard* that he was
Lu. 1:41. when Elisabeth *heard* the salutation
58. her cousins *heard* how the Lord
66. all they *that heard* (them) laid
2:18. all they *that heard* (it) wondered
20. things that they *had heard* and seen,
46. both *hearing* them, and asking them
47. all *that heard* him were astonished
4:23. whatsoever we *have heard* done
28. *when* they *heard* these things, were
5: 1. upon him *to hear* the word of God,
15. great multitudes came together *to hear* and to be healed
6:17(18). which came *to hear* him, and to be
27. I say unto you *which hear*, Love your
47. cometh to me, and *heareth* my sayings,
49. he *that heareth*, and doeth not, is like
7: 3. *when* he *heard* of Jesus, he sent
9. *When* Jesus *heard* these things,
22. what things ye have seen and *heard*;
— lepers are cleansed, the deaf *hear*,
29. all the people *that heard* (him),
8: 8. He that hath ears *to hear, let* him *hear*.
10. *hearing* they might not understand.
12. by the way side are they *that hear*;
13. which, when they *hear*, receive the
14. which, *when* they *have heard*, go
15. *having heard* the word, keep (it),
18. Take heed therefore how ye *hear*:
21. are these *which hear* the word of God,
50. *when* Jesus *heard* (it), he answered
9: 7. Herod the tetrarch *heard* of all that
9. who is this, of whom I *hear* such things?
35. This is my beloved Son: *hear* him.
10:16. He *that heareth* you *heareth* me;
24. *to hear* those things which ye *hear*, and *have* not *heard* (them)
39. sat at Jesus feet, and *heard* his word.
11:28. blessed (are) they *that hear* the word

Lu. 11:31. *to hear* the wisdom of Solomon;
12: 3. in darkness *shall be heard* in the
14:15. at meat with him *heard* these things,
35. He that hath ears *to hear*, *let* him *hear*.
15: 1. publicans and sinners for *to hear* him.
25. he *heard* musick and dancing.
16: 2. How is it that I *hear* this of thee?
14. were covetous, *heard* all these things:
29. Moses and the prophets; *let* them *hear* them.
31. If they *hear* not Moses and the prophets,
18: 6. *Hear* what the unjust judge saith.
22. *when* Jesus *heard* these things,
23. *when* he *heard* this, he was very
26. they *that heard* (it) said, Who then
36. *hearing* the multitude pass by,
19:11. *as* they *heard* these things, he added
48. people were very attentive to *hear* him.
20:16. *when* they *heard* (it), they said,
45. *in the audience of* all the people
21: 9. ye *shall hear* of wars and commotions,
38. in the temple, for *to hear* him.
22:71. ourselves *have heard* of his own
23: 6. *When* Pilate *heard* of Galilee, he
8. he had *heard* many things of him;
Joh. 1:37. the two disciples *heard* him speak,
40(41). One of the two *which heard* John
3: 8. thou *hearest* the sound thereof,
29. which standeth and *heareth* him,
32. what he hath seen and *heard*, that
4: 1. the Pharisees *had heard* that Jesus
42. for we *have heard* (him) ourselves,
47. *When* he *heard* that Jesus was
5:24. He *that heareth* my word, and believeth
25. when the dead *shall hear* the voice
— they *that hear* shall live.
28. in the graves *shall hear* his voice,
30. as I *hear*, I judge: and my judgment
37. Ye *have* neither *heard* his voice
6:45. Every man therefore that *hath heard*,
60. *when* they *had heard* (this),
— an hard saying; who can *hear* it?
7:32. The Pharisees *heard* that the people
40. *when* they *heard* this saying,
51. judge (any) man, before it *hear* him,
8: 9. they *which heard* (it), being convicted
26. things which I *have heard* of him.
40. the truth, which I *have heard* of God:
43. because ye cannot *hear* my word.
47. He that is of God *heareth* God's words: ye therefore *hear* (them) not,
9:27. told you already, and ye *did* not *hear*: wherefore would ye *hear* (it) again?
31. we know that God *heareth* not sinners:
— doeth his will, him he *heareth*.
32. *was* it not *heard* that any man
35. Jesus *heard* that they had cast
40. Pharisees which were with him *heard*
10: 3. the sheep *hear* his voice: and he calleth
8. the sheep *did* not *hear* them.
16. they *shall hear* my voice; and there
20. a devil, and is mad; why *hear* ye him?
27. My sheep *hear* my voice, and I know
11: 4. *When* Jesus *heard* (that), he said,
6. When he *had heard* therefore that
20. as soon as she *heard* that Jesus
29. As soon as she *heard* (that), she
41. I thank thee that thou *hast heard* me.
42. I knew that thou *hearest* me always:
12:12. *when* they *heard* that Jesus was
18. for that they *heard* that he had
29. that stood by, and *heard* (it), said

Joh.12:34. We *have heard* out of the law
47. if any man *hear* my words,
14:24. the word which ye *hear* is not
28. Ye *have heard* how I said unto
15:15. things that I *have heard* of my
16:13. whatsoever he *shall hear*, that
18:21. ask them *which heard* me,
37. Every one that is of the truth *heareth*
19: 8. When Pilate therefore *heard* that
13. *When* Pilate therefore *heard* that
21: 7. *when* Simon Peter *heard* that it was
Acts 1: 4. which, (saith he), ye *have heard* of me.
2: 6. every man *heard* them speak in
8. how *hear* we every man in our
11. we *do hear* them speak in our
22. men of Israel, *hear* these words;
33. which ye now see and *hear*.
37. *when* they *heard* (this), they were
3:22. him *shall* ye *hear* in all things
23. which *will* not *hear* that prophet,
4: 4. many of them *which heard* the
19. in the sight of God *to hearken* unto
20. things which we have seen and *heard*.
24. *when* they *heard* that, they lifted
5: 5. Ananias *hearing* these words
— on all them *that heard* these things
11. upon as many *as heard* these things.
21. *when* they *heard* (that), they entered
24. the chief priests *heard* these things,
33. *When* they *heard* (that), they were
6:11. We *have heard* him speak blasphemous
14. For we *have heard* him say, that
7: 2. Men, brethren, and fathers, *hearken*;
12. *when* Jacob *heard* that there was
34. I *have heard* their groaning, and am
37. like unto me; him *shall* ye *hear*.
54. *When* they *heard* these things, they
8: 6. Philip spake, *hearing* and seeing the
14. at Jerusalem *heard* that Samaria
30. *heard* him read the prophet Esaias,
9: 4. fell to the earth, and *heard* a voice saying
7. stood speechless, *hearing* a voice, but
13. I *have heard* by many of this man,
21. all *that heard* (him) were amazed,
38. the disciples had *heard* that Peter
10:22. into his house, and *to hear* words of thee.
33. *to hear* all things that are commanded
44. fell on all them *which heard* the word.
46. For they *heard* them speak with tongues,
11: 1. in Judæa *heard* that the Gentiles
7. I *heard* a voice saying unto me,
18. *When* they *heard* these things, they
22. Then tidings of these things *came* unto
13: 7. desired *to hear* the word of God.
16. ye that fear God, *give audience*.
44. together, *to hear* the word of God.
48. *when* the Gentiles *heard* this, they
14: 9. The same *heard* Paul speak: who
14. Barnabas and Paul, *heard* (of), they rent
15: 7. should *hear* the word of the gospel,
12. *gave audience to* Barnabas and Paul,
13. Men (and) brethren, *hearken* unto me:
24. as we *have heard*, that certain which
16:14. which worshipped God, *heard* (us):
38. *when* they *heard* that they were Romans.
17: 8. *when* they *heard* these things.
21. to tell, or to *hear* some new thing.
32. *when* they *heard* of the resurrection
— We *will hear* thee again of this
18: 8. the Corinthians *hearing* believed,
26. *when* Aquila and Priscilla *had heard*,
19: 2. We *have* not so much as *heard* whether

Acts 19: 5. *When* they *heard* (this), they were
10. in Asia *heard* the word of the Lord
26. ye see and *hear*, that not alone
28. *when* they *heard* (these sayings),
21: 12. when we *heard* these things, both
20. *when* they *heard* (it), they glorified
22. for they *will hear* that thou art
22: 1. brethren, and fathers, *hear* ye my defence
2. *when* they *heard* that he spake
7. *heard* a voice saying unto me,
9. they *heard* not the voice of him
14. shouldest *hear* the voice of his
15. of what thou hast seen and *heard*.
22. they *gave* him *audience* unto
26. *When* the centurion *heard* (that), he went
23: 16. *when* Paul's sister's son *heard* of their lying
24: 4. thou wouldest *hear* us of thy clemency
22. *when* Felix *heard* these things, having
24. sent for Paul, and *heard* him concerning
25: 22. I would also *hear* the man myself. To morrow, said he, thou *shalt hear* him.
26: 3. I beseech thee *to hear* me patiently.
14. I *heard* a voice speaking unto me,
29. also all *that hear* me this day,
28: 15. *when* the brethren *heard* of us,
22. we desire *to hear* of thee what thou
26. Hearing ye *shall hear*, and shall not
27. their ears are dull of *hearing*, and their
— see with (their) eyes, and *hear* with (their) ears,
28. unto the Gentiles, and (that) they *will hear* it.
Ro. 10: 14. of whom they *have* not *heard?* and how *shall* they *hear* without a preacher?
18. I say, *Have* they not *heard?* Yes verily,
11: 8. ears that they should not *hear;* unto
15: 21. they that *have* not *heard* shall
1Co. 2: 9. Eye hath not seen, nor ear *heard*,
5: 1. It *is reported* commonly (that there)
11: 18. I *hear* that there be divisions among
14. 2. for no man *understandeth* (him);
2Co. 12: 4. into paradise, and *heard* unspeakable
6. seeth me (to be), or (that) he *heareth* of me.
Gal. 1: 13. ye *have heard* of my conversation
23. they had *heard* only, That he
4: 21. under the law, *do* ye not *hear* the law?
Eph. 1: 13. *after that* ye *heard* the word of truth,
15. *after* I *heard* of your faith in the Lord
3: 2. If ye *have heard* of the dispensation
4: 21. If so be that ye *have heard* him,
29. may minister grace unto the *hearers*.
Phi. 1: 27. I *may hear* of your affairs, that ye
30. saw in me, (and) now *hear* (to be) in me.
2: 26. because that ye *had heard* that he
4: 9. both learned, and received, and *heard*, and seen
Col. 1: 4. *Since* we *heard* of your faith in
6. since the day ye *heard* (of it), and knew
9. we also, since the day we *heard* (it),
23. the gospel, which ye *have heard*,
2Th. 3: 11. For we *hear* that there are some
1Ti. 4: 16. save thyself, and them *that hear* thee.
2Ti. 1: 13. words, which thou *hast heard* of me,
2: 2. things that thou *hast heard* of me
14. to the subverting of the *hearers*.
4: 17. (that) all the Gentiles *might hear*:
Philem. 5. *Hearing* of thy love and faith, which thou
Heb. 2: 1. to the things *which we have heard*,
3. unto us by them *that heard* (him);
3: 7. To day if ye *will hear* his voice,
15. To day if ye *will hear* his voice,

Heb 3: 16. some, *when* they *had heard*, did
4: 2. with faith in them *that heard* (it).
7. To day if ye *will hear* his voice,
12: 19. which (voice) they *that heard*
Jas. 1: 19. let every man be swift *to hear*,
2: 5. *Hearken*, my beloved brethren, Hath
5: 11. Ye *have heard* of the patience of Job,
2Pet. 1: 18. voice which came from heaven we *heard*
1Joh 1: 1. which we *have heard*, which we
3. That which we have seen and *heard*
5. the message which we *have heard*
2: 7. the word which ye *have heard* from
18. as ye *have heard* that antichrist
24. which ye *have heard* from the beginning. If that which ye *have heard* from
3: 11. the message that ye *heard* from
4: 3. ye *have heard* that it should come;
5. of the world, and the world *heareth* them.
6. he that knoweth God *heareth* us; he that is not of God *heareth* not us.
5: 14. according to his will, he *heareth* us:
15. if we know that he *hear* us,
2Joh. 6. as ye *have heard* from the beginning,
3Joh. 4. I have no greater joy than to *hear*
Rev. 1: 3. they *that hear* the words of this prophecy
10. *heard* behind me a great voice,
2: 7. He that hath an ear, *let* him *hear*
11. He that hath an ear, *let* him *hear*
17. He that hath an ear, *let* him *hear*
29. He that hath an ear, *let* him *hear*
3: 3. how thou hast received and *heard*,
6. He that hath an ear, *let* him *hear*
13. He that hath an ear, *let* him *hear*
20. if any man *hear* my voice, and open
22. He that hath an ear, *let* him *hear*
4: 1. the first voice which I *heard* (was)
5: 11. I *heard* the voice of many angels
13. that are in them, *heard* I saying,
6: 1. I *heard*, as it were the noise of
3. I *heard* the second beast say, Come
5. I *heard* the third beast say, Come and see
6. I *heard* a voice in the midst of
7. I *heard* the voice of the fourth beast
7: 4. I *heard* the number of them which
8: 13. I beheld, and *heard* an angel flying
9: 13. I *heard* a voice from the four horns
16. I *heard* the number of them.
20. neither can see, nor *hear*, nor walk:
10: 4. I *heard* a voice from heaven saying
8. the voice which I *heard* from heaven
11: 12. they *heard* a great voice from heaven
12: 10. I *heard* a loud voice saying in
13: 9. If any man have an ear, *let* him *hear*.
14: 2. I *heard* a voice from heaven, as the
— I *heard* the voice of harpers harping
13. I *heard* a voice from heaven
16: 1. I *heard* a great voice out of the
5. I *heard* the angel of the waters say,
7. I *heard* another out of the altar say,
18: 4. I *heard* another voice from heaven,
22. trumpeters, *shall be heard* no more
— the sound of a millstone *shall be heard* more
23. the bride *shall be heard* no more
19: 1. I *heard* a great voice of much people
6. I *heard* as it were the voice of a
21: 3. I *heard* a great voice out of heaven
22: 8. I John saw these things, and *heard* (them). And when I *had heard* and seen,
17. let him *that heareth* say, Come.
18. every man *that heareth* the words of the prophecy of this book,

192 2 32/38 2:339 193

ακρασία, akrasia.

Mat.23:25. they are full of extortion and *excess*.
1Co. 7: 5. tempt you not for your *incontinency*.

193 1 32/38 2:339 1,2904

ἀκρατής, akratees.

2Ti. 3: 3. false accusers, *incontinent*, fierce,

194 1 32/38 1,2767

ἄκρατον, akraton.

Rev.14:10. which is poured out *without mixture*

195 1 32/38 rt 196

ἀκρίβεια, akribīa.

Acts22: 3. according to the *perfect manner* of the

196 1 32/38 rt 206

ἀκριβέστατος, akribestatos.

Acts26: 5. after the *most straitest* sect of our

197 4 32/38 rt 196

ἀκριβέστερον, akribesteron, adv.

Acts18:26. him the way of God *more perfectly*.
23:15. enquire something *more perfectly*
20. enquire somewhat of him *more perfectly*.
24:22. having *more perfect* knowledge

198 1 32/38 rt 196

ἀκριβόω, akriboō.

Mat. 2. 7. *enquired* of them *diligently* what
16. he *had diligently enquired* of the wise

199 5 32/38 rt 196

ἀκριβῶς, akribōs.

Mat. 2. 8. Go and search *diligently* for the young
Lu. 1: 3. having had *perfect* understanding of all
Acts18:25. he spake and taught *diligently* the things
Eph. 5:15. that ye walk *circumspectly*, not
1Th. 5: 2. yourselves know *perfectly* that the

200 4 32/39 rt 206

ἀκρίς, akris.

Mat. 3: 4. his meat was *locusts* and wild honey.
Mar. 1: 6. he did eat *locusts* and wild honey;
Rev. 9: 3. out of the smoke *locusts* upon the
7. the shapes of the *locusts* (were) like unto

201 1 33/39 202

ἀκροατήριον, akroateerion.

Acts25:23. was entered into the *place of hearing*,

202 4 33/39 191

ἀκροατής, akroatees.

Ro. 2:13. For not the *hearers* of the law (are) just
Jas. 1:22. doers of the word, and not *hearers* only,
23. if any be a *hearer* of the word, and not
25. he being not a forgetful *hearer*, but

203 20 33/39 1:225 206 *posthē*

ἀκροβυστία, akrobustia.

Acts11: 3. Thou wentest in to men uncircumcised, (lit. having *uncircumcision*)

Ro. 2:25. thy circumcision is made *uncircumcision*.
26. if the *uncircumcision* keep the
— shall not his *uncircumcision* be
27. shall not *uncircumcision* which is
3:30. by faith, and *uncircumcision* through
4: 9. or upon the *uncircumcision* also?
10. in circumcision, or in *uncircumcision*? Not in circumcision, but in *uncircumcision*.
11. (he had yet) being uncircumcised: (lit. in *uncircumcision*)
— though they be *not circumcised*; that
12. (he had) being (yet) *uncircumcised*.
1Co. 7:18. Is any called in *uncircumcision*?
19. *uncircumcision* is nothing, but
Gal. 2: 7. gospel of the *uncircumcision* was
5: 6. any thing, nor *uncircumcision*;
6:15. nor *uncircumcision*, but a new creature.
Eph. 2:11. who are called *Uncircumcision* by
Col. 2:13. the *uncircumcision* of your flesh,
3:11. circumcision nor *uncircumcision*,

204 2 33/39 1:791 206,1137

ἀκρογω ōniaios.

Eph. 2:20. Christ himself being the *chief corner* (stone;)
1Pet. 2: 6. I lay in Sion a *chief corner* stone, elect,

205 1 33/39 206 *this* (heap)

ἀκροθίνιον, akrothinion.

Heb. 7. 4. Abraham gave the tenth of the *spoils*.

206 6 33/39 cf rt 188

ἄκρον, akron.

Mat.24.31. from *one end* of heaven to the *other*.
Mar.13:27. from the *uttermost part* of the earth to the *uttermost part* of heaven.
Lu. 16:24. may dip the *tip* of his finger in water,
Heb 11:21. (leaning) upon the *top* of his staff.

208 3 33/39 3:1098 1,2964

ἀκυρόω, akuroō.

Mat.15: 6. Thus *have* ye *made* the commandment of God *of none effect*
Mar. 7:13. *Making* the word of God *of none effect*
Gal. 3:17. years after, cannot *disannul*, that

209 1 33/39 1,2967

ἀκωλύτως, akōlutōs.

Acts28:31. all confidence, *no man forbidding him*.

210 1 33/39 2:469 1,1635

ἄκων, akōn.

1Co. 9:17. if *against my will*, a dispensation

211 4 33/39

ἀλάβαστρον, alabastron.

Mat.26: 7. having an *alabaster box* of very
Mar 14: 3. having an *alabaster box* of ointment
— she brake the *box*, and poured (it) on
Lu. 7:37. brought an *alabaster box* of ointment,

212 2 34/39 1:226 213

ἀλαζονεία, alazonīa.

Jas. 4:16. now ye rejoice in your *boastings*:
1Joh.2:16. lust of the eyes, and the *pride* of life

213 2 34/39 1:226

ἀλαζών, *alazōn.* *alē* (vagrancy)

Ro. 1:30. spiteful, proud, *boasters*, inventors
2Ti. 3: 2. covetous, *boasters*, proud, blasphemers,

214 2 34/39 1:227 *alalē* (shout)

ἀλαλάζω, *alalazo.*

Mar. 5:38. them that wept and *wailed* greatly.
1Co 13: 1. (as) sounding brass, or a *tinkling* cymbal.

215 1 34/39 1,2980

ἀλάλητος, *alaleetos.*

Ro. 8:26. with groanings *which cannot be uttered.*

216 3 34/39 1,2980

ἄλαλος, *alalos.*

Mar. 7:37. the deaf to hear, and the *dumb* to speak.
9:17. my son, which hath a *dumb* spirit;
25. (Thou) *dumb* and deaf spirit, I charge thee,

217 8 34/40 1:228 251

ἅλας, *halas.*

Mat. 5:13. Ye are the *salt* of the earth: but if the *salt* have lost his savour,
Mar. 9:50. *Salt* (is) good: but if the *salt* have
— Have *salt* in yourselves, and have
Lu. 14:34. *Salt* (is) good: but if the *salt* have
Col. 4: 6. grace, seasoned with *salt*, that ye

218 9 34/40 1:229 1,rt 3045

ἀλείφω, *alīpho.*

Mat. 6:17. *anoint* thine head, and wash thy face;
Mar. 6:13. *anointed* with oil many that were
16: 1. they might come and *anoint* him.
Lu. 7:38. *anointed* (them) with the ointment.
46. My head with oil thou *didst* not *anoint:* but this woman *hath anointed* my feet
Joh. 11: 2. Mary *which anointed* the Lord
12: 3. *anointed* the feet of Jesus, and wiped
Jas. 5:14. *anointing* him with oil in the

219 1 34/40 220,5456

ἀλεκτοροφωνία, *alektorophōnia.*

Mar 13:35. at midnight, or at the *cockcrowing,*

220 12 34/40 *alekō* (to ward off)

ἀλέκτωρ, *alektōr.*

Mat. 26:34. this night, before the *cock* crow,
74. I know not the man. And immediately the *cock* crew.
75. Before the *cock* crow, thou shalt deny
Mar 14:30. before the *cock* crow twice, thou
68. into the porch; and the *cock* crew.
72. the second time the *cock* crew.
— Before the *cock* crow twice, thou
Lu. 22:34. the *cock* shall not crow this day,
60. while he yet spake, the *cock* crew.
61. Before the *cock* crow, thou shalt deny
Joh. 13:38. The *cock* shall not crow, till thou
18:27. denied again: and immediately the *cock* crew.

224 2 35/40 *aleō* (to grind)

ἄλευρον, *alūron.*

Mat. 13:33. hid in three measures of *meal*, till
Lu. 13:21. took and hid in three measures of *meal*,

225 110 35/40 1:232 227

ἀλήθεια, *aleethīa.*

Mat. 22:16. teachest the way of God in *truth*,
Mar. 5:33. before him, and told him all the *truth.*
12:14. teachest the way of God in *truth:*
32. Master, thou hast said the *truth:*
Lu. 4:25. I tell you of a *truth*, many widows
20:21. teachest the way of God truly: (lit. in *truth*)
22:59. Of a *truth* this (fellow) also was
Joh. 1:14. of the Father, full of grace and *truth.*
17. grace and *truth* came by Jesus Christ.
3:21. he that doeth *truth* cometh to the
4:23. worship the Father in spirit and in *truth:*
24. worship (him) in spirit and in *truth.*
5:33. he bare witness unto the *truth.*
8:32. ye shall know the *truth*, and the *truth* shall make you free.
40. a man that hath told you the *truth*,
44. abode not in the *truth*, because there is no *truth* in him.
45. because I tell (you) the *truth*, ye
46. if I say the *truth*, why do ye not
14: 6. I am the way, the *truth*, and the life.
17. (Even) the Spirit of *truth;* whom the
15:26. (even) the Spirit of *truth*, which
16: 7. Nevertheless I tell you the *truth;*
13. when he, the Spirit of *truth*, is come, he will guide you into all *truth:*
17:17. Sanctify them through thy *truth:* thy word is *truth.*
19. be sanctified through the *truth.*
18:37. I should bear witness unto the *truth.* Every one that is of the *truth* heareth
38. Pilate saith unto him, What is *truth?*
Acts 4:27. For of a *truth* against thy holy
10:34. said, Of a *truth* I perceive that
26:25. the words of *truth* and soberness.
Ro. 1:18. who hold the *truth* in unrighteousness,
25. Who changed the *truth* of God into
2: 2. judgment of God is according to *truth*
8. contentious, and do not obey the *truth*,
20. knowledge and of the *truth* in the law.
3: 7. For if the *truth* of God hath more
9: 1. I say the *truth* in Christ, I lie not,
15: 8. circumcision for the *truth* of God,
1Co. 5: 8. unleavened (bread) of sincerity and *truth.*
13: 6. in iniquity, but rejoiceth in the *truth;*
2Co. 4: 2. by manifestation of the *truth*
6: 7. By the word of *truth*, by the power
7:14. we spake all things to you in *truth*,
— (I made) before Titus, is found a *truth.*
11:10. As the *truth* of Christ is in me,
12: 6. for I will say the *truth:* but (now)
13: 8. we can do nothing against the *truth*, but for the *truth.*
Gal. 2: 5. that the *truth* of the gospel might
14. according to the *truth* of the gospel,
3: 1. that ye should not obey the *truth*,
5: 7. that ye should not obey the *truth?*
Eph. 1:13. after that ye heard the word of *truth*,
4:21. taught by him, as the *truth* is in Jesus:
24. created in righteousness and *true* holiness.
25. speak every man *truth* with his neighbour:
5: 9. in all goodness and righteousness and *truth;*
6:14. your loins girt about with *truth*,
Phi. 1:18. whether in pretence, or in *truth*,
Col. 1: 5. the word of the *truth* of the gospel;
6. knew the grace of God in *truth:*
2Th. 2:10. received not the love of the *truth*,

2Th. 2:12. damned who believed not the *truth*,
13. of the Spirit and belief of the *truth:*
1Ti. 2: 4. unto the knowledge of the *truth*.
7. I speak the *truth* in Christ, (and) lie not; a teacher of the Gentiles in faith and *verity*.
3:15. the pillar and ground of the *truth*.
4: 3. which believe and know the *truth*.
6: 5. corrupt minds, and destitute of the *truth*,
2Ti. 2:15. rightly dividing the word of *truth*.
18. Who concerning the *truth* have erred,
25. to the acknowledging of the *truth*;
3: 7. come to the knowledge of the *truth*.
8. so do these also resist the *truth:*
4: 4. turn away (their) ears from the *truth*,
Tit. 1: 1. the acknowledging of the *truth* which
14. men, that turn from the *truth*.
Heb 10:26. received the knowledge of the *truth*,
Jas. 1:18. begat he us with the word of *truth*,
3:14. glory not, and lie not against the *truth*.
5:19. if any of you do err from the *truth*,
1Pet. 1:22. purified your souls in obeying the *truth*
2Pet. 1:12. be established in the present *truth*.
2: 2. the way of *truth* shall be evil spoken
1Joh. 1: 6. we lie, and do not the *truth:*
8. ourselves, and the *truth* is not in us.
2: 4. is a liar, and the *truth* is not in him.
21. the *truth*, but because ye know it, and that no lie is of the *truth*.
3:18. neither in tongue; but in deed and in *truth*.
19. we know that we are of the *truth*,
4: 6. Hereby know we the Spirit of *truth*,
5: 6. witness, because the Spirit is *truth*.
2 Joh. 1. her children, whom I love in the *truth*;
— they that have known the *truth*;
2. For the *truth's* sake, which dwelleth
3. Son of the Father, in *truth* and love.
4. of thy children walking in *truth*,
3 Joh. 1. Gaius, whom I love in the *truth*.
3. testified of the *truth* that is in thee, even as thou walkest in the *truth*.
4. that my children walk in *truth*.
8. might be fellowhelpers to the *truth*.
12. report of all (men), and of the *truth* itself:

226 2 36/41 1:232 227

ἀληθεύω, *aleethŭo.*

Gal. 4:16. your enemy, *because* I *tell* you *the truth?*
Eph. 4:15. *speaking the truth* in love, may

227 25 36/41 1:232 1,2990

ἀληθής, *aleethees.*

Mat22:16. Master, we know that thou art *true*,
Mar12:14. Master, we know that thou art *true*,
Joh. 3:33. set to his seal that God is *true*.
4:18. hast is not thy husband: in that saidst thou *truly*.
5:31. of myself, my witness is not *true*.
32. which he witnesseth of me is *true*.
7:18. glory that sent him, the same is *true*,
8:13. of thyself; thy record is not *true*.
14. of myself, (yet) my record is *true:*
16. if I judge, my judgment is *true:*
17. the testimony of two men is *true*.
26. he that sent me is *true;* and I speak
10:41. that John spake of this man were *true*.
19:35. he knoweth that he saith *true*,
21:24. we know that his testimony is *true*.
Acts12: 9. wist not that it was *true* which
Ro. 3: 4. yea, let God be *true*, but every man
2Co. 6: 8. as deceivers, and (yet) *true:*
Phi. 4: 8. brethren, whatsoever things are *true*,
Tit. 1:13. This witness is *true*. Wherefore
1Pet.5:12. this is the *true* grace of God wherein
2Pet.2:22. according to the *true* proverb,
1Joh.2: 8. which thing is *true* in him and in you:
27. of all things, and is *truth*, and is no lie,
3 Joh. 12. ye know that our record is *true*.

228 27 36/42 1:232 227

ἀληθινός, *aleethinos.*

Lu. 16:11. commit to your trust the *true* (riches)?
Joh. 1: 9. (That) was the *true* Light, which lighteth
4:23. when the *true* worshippers shall
37. herein is that saying *true*, One
6:32. my Father giveth you the *true* bread
7:28. he that sent me is *true*, whom
15: 1. I am the *true* vine, and my Father
17: 3. might know thee the only *true* God,
19:35. bare record, and his record is *true:*
1Th. 1: 9. to serve the living and *true* God;
Heb. 8: 2. the sanctuary, and of the *true* tabernacle,
9:24. (which are) the figures of the *true;*
10:22. Let us draw near with a *true* heart
1Joh 2: 8. darkness is past, and the *true* light now
5:20. we may know him that is *true*, and we are in him that is *true*,
— This is the *true* God, and eternal life.
Rev. 3: 7. he that is holy, he that is *true*,
14. the faithful and *true* witness, the
6:10. How long, O Lord, holy and *true*,
15: 3. just and *true* (are) thy ways, thou
16: 7. *true* and righteous (are) thy judgments.
19: 2. *true* and righteous (are) his judgments
9. These are the *true* sayings of God.
11. sat upon him (was) called Faithful and *True*,
21: 5. these words are *true* and faithful.
22: 6. These sayings (are) faithful and *true*

229 2 36/42 224

ἀλήθω, *aleetho.*

Mat.24:41. Two (women shall be) *grinding* at the
Lu. 17:35. Two (women) shall be *grinding* together;

230 21 36/42 227

ἀληθῶς, *aleethōs.*

Mat.14:33. *Of a truth* thou art the Son of God.
26:73. *Surely* thou also art (one) of them;
27:54. *Truly* this was the Son of God.
Mar 14:70. *Surely* thou art (one) of them: for
15:39. *Truly* this man was the Son of God.
Lu. 9:27. I tell you *of a truth*, there be some
12:44. *Of a truth* I say unto you, that he
21: 3. *Of a truth* I say unto you, that this
Joh. 1:47(48). Behold an Israelite *indeed*, in
4:42. this is *indeed* the Christ, the Saviour
6:14. This is *of a truth* that prophet that
55. For my flesh is meat *indeed*, and my blood is drink *indeed*.
7:26. Do the rulers know *indeed* that this is the *very* Christ?
40. *Of a truth* this is the prophet.
8:31. (then) are ye my disciples *indeed;*
17: 8. have known *surely* that I came
Acts12:11. I know *of a surety*, that the Lord
1Th. 2:13. as it is *in truth*, the word of God,
1Joh.2: 5. in him *verily* is the love of God

231 5 37/40 251

ἁλιεύς, haliūs.

Mat. 4:18. a net into the sea: for they were *fishers*.
19. I will make you *fishers* of men.
Mar 1:16. a net into the sea: for they were *fishers*.
17. make you to become *fishers* of men.
Lu. 5: 2. but the *fishermen* were gone out

232 1 37/42 231

ἁλιεύω, haliūo.

Joh. 21: 3. Peter saith unto them, I go *a fishing*.

233 3 37/42 251

ἁλίζω, halizo.

Mat. 5:13. lost his savour, wherewith *shall* it *be salted*?
Mar 9:49. every one *shall be salted* with fire, and every sacrifice *shall be salted* with salt.

234 1 37/42

alisgeo (to soil)

ἀλίσγημα, alisgeema.

Acts 15:20. abstain from *pollutions* of idols, and

235 636 37/42 243

ἀλλά, alla.

Mat. 4: 4. *but* by every word that proceedeth out of
5:15. under a bushel, *but* on a candlestick;
17. not come to destroy, *but* to fulfil.
&c. &c.

Note.—It is always rendered in E. T. "*but*," with the exception of the following passages.:—

Mat. 19:11. *save* (they) to whom it is given.
Mar 9: 8. they saw no man any more, *save* Jesus
14:29. all shall be offended, *yet* (will) not I.
36. cup from me: *nevertheless* not what I will,
Lu. 16:21. moreover (lit. *but* even) the dogs came and licked
17: 8. *And* will not rather say
23:15. *No*, nor yet Herod: for I sent you
24:21. and (αλλα γε) beside all this
22. *Yea*, and certain women also of our
Joh 7:27. *Howbeit* we know this man whence he is:
11:15. *nevertheless* let us go unto him.
16: 2. *yea*, the time cometh, that whosoever
7. *Nevertheless* I tell you the truth;
Acts 7:48. *Howbeit* the most High dwelleth
10:20. Arise *therefore*, and get thee down,
19: 2. We have not so much as heard (αλλ' ουδε)
Ro 3:31. God forbid: *yea*, we establish the law.
5:14. *Nevertheless* death reigned from Adam
6: 5. we shall be also (αλλα και)
7: 7. *Nay*, I had not known sin, but
8:37. *Nay*, in all these things we are more
1Co. 3: 2. neither (αλλ' ουτε) yet now are ye able.
4: 3. *yea*, I judge not mine own self.
4. *yet* am I not hereby justified:
15. instructers in Christ, *yet* (have ye) not
6: 8. *Nay*, ye do wrong, and defraud,
8: 7. *Howbeit* (there is) not in every man
9: 2. unto others, *yet* doubtless I am to you:
12. *Nevertheless* we have not used this power;
12:22. *Nay*, much more those members of
14:19. *Yet* in the church I had rather speak
20. *howbeit* in malice be ye children,
15:46. *Howbeit* that (was) not first which is
2Co. 1:13. unto you, than (αλλ' η) what ye read or
4: 8. troubled on every side, *yet* not distressed;
16. our outward man perish, *yet* the inward
5:16. *yet* now henceforth know we (him) no
2Co. 7: 6. *Nevertheless* God, that comforteth those
11. *yea*, (what) clearing of yourselves, *yea* (what) indignation, *yea*, (what) fear, *yea*, (what) vehement desire, *yea*, (what) zeal, *yea*, (what) revenge!
8: 7. *Therefore*, as ye abound in every (thing),
11: 1. in (my) folly: and *indeed* bear with me.
6. rude in speech, *yet* not in knowledge;
12:16. *nevertheless*, being crafty, I caught you
13: 4. crucified through weakness, *yet* he liveth
Gal. 4: 8. *Howbeit* then, when ye knew not
17. *yea*, they would exclude you, that ye
30. *Nevertheless* what saith the scripture?
Eph. 5:24. *Therefore* as the church is subject unto Christ,
Phi. 1:18. therein do rejoice, *yea*, and will rejoice.
2:17. *Yea*, and if I be offered upon the
3: 8. *Yea* doubtless, and I count all things
Col. 2: 5. absent in the flesh, *yet* am I with you
1Ti. 1:16. *Howbeit* for this cause I obtained mercy,
2Ti. 1:12. *nevertheless* I am not ashamed:
Heb 3:16. *howbeit* not all that came out of Egypt
Jas. 2:18. *Yea*, a man may say, Thou hast faith,
Rev. 2: 4. *Nevertheless* I have (somewhat) against thee,
20. *Notwithstanding* I have a few things

236 6 38/43 1:251 243

ἀλλαττω, allatto.

Acts 6:14. *shall change* the customs which
Ro. 1:23. *changed* the glory of the uncorruptible
1Co. 15:51. all sleep, but we *shall* all *be changed*,
52. incorruptible, and we *shall be changed*.
Gal. 4:20. with you now, and *to change* my voice
Heb 1:12. fold them up, and they *shall be changed*.

237 1 38/43 243

ἀλλαχόθεν, allakothen.

Joh. 10. 1. sheepfold, but climbeth up *some other way*,

238 1 38/43 1:260 243

agoreō

ἀλληγορέω, alleegoreō. (to harangue)

Gal. 4:24. Which things are an allegory (lit. *allegorized*): for these

239 4 38/43 1:264 [1984] [3050]

ἀλληλούια, alleelouya.

Rev. 19: 1. much people in heaven, saying, *Alleluia*;
3. again they said, *Alleluia*. And her
4. on the throne, saying, Amen; *Alleluia*.
6. of mighty thunderings, saying, *Alleluia*.

240 100 38/43 243

ἀλλήλων, alleelōn.

Mat. 24:10. offended, and shall betray *one another*, and shall hate *one another*.
25:32. shall separate them *one* from *another*,
Mar 4:41. feared exceedingly, and said *one* to *another*
8:16. they reasoned among *themselves*, saying,
9:34. they had disputed among *themselves*,
50. have peace *one* with *another*.
15:31. mocking said among *themselves* with
Lu. 2:15. the shepherds said *one* to *another*,
4:36. all amazed, and spake among *themselves*,
6:11. communed *one* with *another* what
7:32. in the marketplace, and calling *one* to *another*,
8:25. wondered, saying *one* to *another*. What

Lu. 22: 1 that they trode *one* upon *another*, he
23:12. Pilate and Herod were made friends *together:*
24:14. they talked *together* of all these things
17. these that ye have *one* to *another*, as
32. they said *one* to *another*, Did not our
Joh. 4:33. said the disciples *one* to *another*,
5:44. which receive honour *one* of *another*,
6:43. Murmur not among *yourselves*.
52. The Jews therefore strove among *themselves*,
11:56. spake among *themselves*, as they
13:14. ought to wash *one another's* feet.
22. the disciples looked *one* on *another*,
34. unto you, That ye love *one another;* as I have loved you, that ye also love *one another*.
35. if ye have love *one* to *another*.
15:12. That ye love *one another*, as I have
17. I command you, that ye love *one another*.
16:17. his disciples among *themselves*, What
19. Do ye enquire among *yourselves* of
19:24. said therefore among *themselves*,
Acts 2: 7. marvelled, saying *one* to *another*,
4:15. they conferred among *themselves*,
7:26. why do ye wrong *one* to *another?*
15:39. departed asunder *one* from *the other:*
19:38. deputies: let them implead *one another*.
21: 6. had taken our leave *one* of *another*,
26:31. they talked between *themselves*,
28: 4. they said among *themselves*, No doubt
25. when they agreed not among *themselves*,
Ro. 1:12. by the *mutual* faith both of you and me.
27. in their lust *one* toward *another;*
2:15. accusing or else excusing *one another;*
12: 5. every one members *one* of *another*.
10. affectioned *one* to *another* with brotherly love; in honour preferring *one another;*
16. (Be) of the same mind *one* toward *another*.
13: 8. to love *one another:* for he that loveth
14:13. not therefore judge *one another* any more:
19. things wherewith *one* may edify *another*.
15: 5. be likeminded *one* toward *another*
7. Wherefore receive ye *one another*, as
14. able also to admonish *one another*.
16:16. Salute *one another* with an holy kiss.
1Co. 7: 5. Defraud ye not *one the other*, except
11:33. together to eat, tarry *one* for *another*.
12:25. have the same care *one* for *another*.
16:20. Greet ye *one another* with an holy kiss.
2Co. 13:12. Greet *one another* with an holy kiss.
Gal. 5:13. by love serve *one another*.
15. if ye bite and devour *one another*, take heed that ye be not consumed *one* of *another*.
17. these are contrary *the one* to *the other:*
26. provoking *one another*, envying *one another*.
6: 2. Bear ye *one another's* burdens, and so
Eph 4: 2. forbearing *one another* in love;
25. for we are members *one* of *another*.
32. ye kind *one* to *another*, tenderhearted,
5:21. Submitting yourselves *one* to *another*
Phi. 2: 3. let *each* esteem *other* better than
Col. 3: 9. Lie not *one* to *another*, seeing that
13. Forbearing *one another*, and forgiving one
1Th. 3:12. abound in love *one* toward *another*,
4: 9. are taught of God to love *one another*.
18. comfort *one another* with these words.
5:11. Wherefore comfort *yourselves together*,
15. both among *yourselves*, and to all (men).
2Th. 1: 3. you all toward *each other* aboundeth;
Tit. 3: 3. envy, hateful, (and) hating *one another*.
Heb 10:24. let us consider *one another* to provoke
Jas. 4:11. Speak not evil *one* of *another*, brethren.
5: 9. Grudge not *one* against *another*, brethren
16. Confess (your) faults *one* to *another*, and pray *one* for *another*, that ye may
1Pet. 1:22. (see that ye) love *one another* with
4: 9. Use hospitality *one* to *another* without
5: 5. all (of you) be subject *one* to *another*.
14. Greet ye *one another* with a kiss of
1Joh. 1: 7. we have fellowship *one* with *another*.
3:11. that we should love *one another*.
23. love *one another*, as he gave us
4: 7. Beloved, let us love *one another:*
11. we ought also to love *one another*.
12. If we love *one another*, God dwelleth
2Joh. 5. the beginning, that we love *one another*.
Rev. 6: 4. that they should kill *one another:*
11:10. shall send gifts *one* to *another;*

---

241 1 39/44 1:264 243,1085

ἀλλογενής, *allogenees*.

Lu. 17:18. to give glory to God, save this *stranger*.

---

242 3 39/44

ἅλλομαι, *hallomai*.

Joh. 4:14. water *springing up* into everlasting life.
Acts 3: 8. into the temple, walking, and *leaping*, and
14:10. on thy feet. And he *leaped* and walked.

---

243 .160 39/44 1:264

ἄλλος, *allos*.

Mat. 2:12. into their own country *another* way.
4:21. he saw *other* two brethren, James
5:39. right cheek, turn to him the *other* also.
8: 9. he goeth; and to *another*, Come, and he cometh;
10:23. persecute you in this city, flee ye into *another:*
12:13. restored whole, like as the *other*.
13: 5. *Some* fell upon stony places, where
7. *some* fell among thorns; and the
8. *other* fell into good ground, and
24. *Another* parable put he forth unto
31. *Another* parable put he forth unto
33. *Another* parable spake he unto them;
16:14. John the Baptist: *some*, Elias; and *others*,
19: 9. fornication, and shall marry *another*,
20: 3. saw *others* standing idle in the
6. found *others* standing idle, and saith
21: 8. *others* cut down branches from the
33. Hear *another* parable: There was a
36. Again, he sent *other* servants more
41. (his) vineyard unto *other* husbandmen,
22: 4. Again, he sent forth *other* servants,
25:16. made (them) *other* five talents.
17. (received) two, he also gained *other* two.
20. brought *other* five talents, saying,
— gained beside them five talents *more*.
22. I have gained two *other* talents
26:71. into the porch, *another* (maid) saw
27:42. He saved *others;* himself he cannot
61. Mary Magdalene, and the *other* Mary,
28: 1. came Mary Magdalene and the *other* Mary
Mar. 3: 5. hand was restored whole as the *other*
4: 5. *some* fell on stony ground, where
7. *some* fell among thorns, and the
8. *other* fell on good ground, and did
36. were also with him *other* little ships.

Mar. 6:15. *Others* said, That it is Elias. And *others* said, That it is a prophet,
7: 4. many *other* things there be, which
8. many *other* such like things ye
8: 28. *some* (say), Elias; and *others*, One of the
10: 11. put away his wife, and marry *another*,
12. her husband, and be married to *another*,
11: 8. *others* cut down branches off the
12: 4. he sent unto them *another* servant;
5. again he sent *another*; and him they killed, and many *others*;
9. will give the vineyard unto *others*.
31. There is none *other* commandment
32. one God; and there is none *other* but he:
14:19. (Is) it I? and *another* (said), (Is) it I?
58. three days I will build *another*
15:31. He saved *others*; himself he cannot
41. many *other* women which came
Lu. 5:29. publicans and of *others* that sat down
6:10. was restored whole as the *other*.
29. on the (one) cheek offer also the *other*;
7: 8. to *another*, Come, and he cometh;
19. that should come? or look we for *another*?
20. that should come? or look we for *another*?
9: 8. that Elias had appeared; and of *others*,
19. *some* (say), Elias; and *others* (say),
20:16. shall give the vineyard to *others*.
22:59. one hour after *another* confidently
23:35. He saved *others*; let him save
Joh. 4:37. true, *One* soweth, and *another* reapeth.
38. *other* men laboured, and ye are
5: 7. *another* steppeth down before me.
32. There is *another* that beareth witness
43. if *another* shall come in his
6:22. there was none *other* boat there,
23. there came *other* boats from
7:12. He is a good man: *others* said,
41. *Others* said, This is the Christ. But *some* said, Shall Christ come
9: 9. *Some* said, This is he: *others* (said),
16. *Others* said, How can a man
10:16. *other* sh[illegible] I have, which are
21. *Others* said, These are not the words
12:29. *others* said, An angel spake to him.
14:16. he shall give you *another* Comforter,
15:24. works which none *other* man did,
18:15. followed Jesus, and (so did) *another* disciple:
16. Then went out that *other* disciple,
34. or did *others* tell it thee of me?
19:18. crucified him, and two *other* with him,
32. the first, and of the *other* which was
20: 2. to the *other* disciple, whom Jesus loved,
3. went forth, and that *other* disciple,
4. the *other* disciple did outrun Peter,
8. Then went in also that *other* disciple,
25. The *other* disciples therefore said
30. many *other* signs truly did Jesus
21: 2. the (sons) of Zebedee, and two *other* of his
8. the *other* disciples came in a little
18. *another* shall gird thee, and carry (thee)
25. there are also many *other* things
Acts 2:12. were in doubt, saying *one* to *another*,
4:12. Neither is there salvation in any *other*:
15: 2. Paul and Barnabas, and certain *other* of them,
19:32. *Some* therefore cried one thing, and some *another*;
21:34. *some* cried one thing, some *another*,
1Co. 1:16. whether I baptized any *other*.
3:10. foundation, and *another* buildeth thereon.
1Co. 3:11. For *other* foundation can no man
9: 2. If I be not a[illegible]postle unto *others*,
12. If *others* be partakers of (this) power
27. when I have preached to *others*,
10:29. my liberty judged of *another* (man's)
12: 8. to *another* the word of knowledge
9. to *another* the gifts of healing by
10. To *another* the working of miracles; to *another* prophecy; to *another* discerning of spirits;
— to *another* the interpretation of tongues:
14:19. (by my voice) I might teach *others*
29. two or three, and let the *other* judge.
30. revealed to *another* that sitteth by,
15:39. *one* (kind of) flesh of men, *another* flesh of beasts, *another* of fishes, (and) *another* of birds.
41. *one* glory of the sun, and *another* glory of the moon, and *another* glory of the stars:
2Co. 1:13. For we write none *other* things
8:13. (I mean) not that *other* men be
11: 4. if he that cometh preacheth *another*
8. I robbed *other* churches, taking
Gal. 1: 7. Which is not *another*; but there
5:10. ye will be none *otherwise* minded:
Phi. 3: 4. If any *other* man thinketh that
1Th. 2: 6. neither of you, nor (yet) of *others*,
Heb. 4: 8. afterward have spoken of *another* day.
11:35. *others* were tortured, not accepting
Jas. 5:12. by the earth, neither by any *other* oath:
Rev. 2:24. I will put upon you none *other* burden.
6: 4. there went out *another* horse
7: 2. I saw *another* angel ascending
8: 3. *another* angel came and stood at
10: 1. I saw *another* mighty angel
12: 3. there appeared *another* wonder in
13:11. I beheld *another* beast coming
14: 6. I saw *another* angel fly in the
8. there followed *another* angel, saying
15. *another* angel came out of the
17. *another* angel came out of the
18. *another* angel came out from
15: 1. I saw *another* sign in heaven,
16: 7. I heard *another* out of the altar
17:10. one is, (and) the *other* is not yet come;
18: 1. I saw *another* angel come down
4. I heard *another* voice from heaven,
20:12. *another* book was opened, which

244 1 39/46 2:599 245,1985

ἀλλοτριοεπίσκοπος, *allotrioepiskopos.*

1Pet. 4:15. or as *a busybody in other men's matters*.

245 14 40/46 1:264 243

ἀλλότριος, *allotrios.*

Mat. 17:25. of their own children, or of *strangers*?
26. Peter saith unto him, Of *strangers*.
Lu. 16:12. faithful in that which is *another man's*,
Joh. 10: 5. *a stranger* will they not follow,
— they know not the voice of *strangers*.
Acts 7: 6. should sojourn in a *strange* land;
Ro. 14: 4. that judgest *another man's* servant?
15:20. build upon *another man's* foundation.
2Co. 10:15. (that is), of *other men's* labours;
16. not to boast in *another man's* line
1Ti. 5:22. neither be partaker of *other men's* sins:
Heb. 9:25. every year with blood *of others*;
11: 9. land of promise, as (in) a *strange* country,
34. to flight the armies of the *aliens*.

246 1 40/46 1:264 243,5443

ἀλλόφυλος, *allophulos.*

Acts10:28. or come unto *one of another nation*.

247 1 40/46 243

ἄλλως, *allōs.*

1Ti. 5:25. they that are *otherwise* cannot be hid.

248 3 40/46 rt 257

ἀλοάω, *aloaō.*

1Co. 9: 9. of the ox that *treadeth out the corn.*
10. that he that *thresheth* in hope should
1Ti. 5:18. the ox that *treadeth out the corn.*

249 3 40/46 4:69 1,3056

ἄλογος, *alogos.*

Acts 25:27. For it seemeth to me *unreasonable* to
2Pet. 2:12. these, as natural *brute* beasts, made
Jude 10. know naturally, as *brute* beasts, in

250 1 40/46 [cf 174]

ἀλόη, *aloee.*

Joh. 19:39. brought a mixture of myrrh and *aloes*,

251 1 40/46

ἅλς, *hals.*

Mar. 9:49. every sacrifice shall be salted with *salt*.

252 1 40/46 251

ἁλυκός, *halukos.*

Jas. 3:12. no fountain both yield *salt* water and fresh.

253 1 40/46 4:313 1,3077

ἀλυπότερος, *alupoter*

Phil. 2: 28. that I may be the *less sorrowful*

254 11 40/46

ἅλυσις, *halusis.*

Mar. 5: 3. could bind him, no, not with *chains:*
4. often bound with fetters and *chains*, and the *chains* had been plucked asunder
Lu. 8:29. he was kept bound with *chains* and
Acts12: 6. bound with two *chains:* and the
7. his *chains* fell off from (his) hands.
21:33. (him) to be bound with two *chains;*
28:20. of Israel I am bound with this *chain.*
Eph. 6:20. For which I am an ambassador in *bonds:*
2Ti. 1:16. was not ashamed of my *chain:*
Rev.20: 1. bottomless pit and a great *chain* in his hand.

255 1 40/46 1,rt 3081

ἀλυσιτελής, *alusitelees.*

Heb 13:17. for that (is) *unprofitable* for you.

257 2 41/47 rt 1507

ἅλων, *halōn.*

Mat. 3:12. he will throughly purge his *floor*, and
Lu. 3:17. he will throughly purge his *floor*

258 3 41/47

ἀλώπηξ, *alōpeex.*

Mat. 8:20. The *foxes* have holes, and the birds of the
Lu. 9:58. Jesus said unto him, *Foxes* have holes,
13:32. Go ye, and tell that *fox*, Behold, I cast

259 1 41/47 eq 138

ἅλωσις, *halōsis.*

2Pet. 2:12. beasts, made to *be taken* and destroyed, (lit. for *capture*)

260 10 41/47

ἅμα, *hama.*

Mat.13:29. ye root up also the wheat *with* them.
20: 1. which went out early (lit. *with* the early dawn) in the morning
Acts24:26. He hoped *also* that money should
27:40. unto the sea, *and* loosed the rudder bands,
Ro. 3:12. they are *together* become unprofitable;
Col. 4: 3. *Withal* praying also for us, that God
1Th. 4:17. shall be caught up *together* with
5:10. we should live *together* with him.
1Ti. 5:13. *withal* they learn (to be) idle,
Philem.22. *withal* prepare me also a lodging:

261 1 41/47 1,3129

ἀμαθής, *amathees.*

2Pet. 3:16. which they that are *unlearned* and

262 1 41/47 263

ἀμαράντινος, *amarantinos.*

1Pet. 5: 4. a crown of glory *that fadeth not away*.

263 1 41/47 1,3133

ἀμάραντος, *amarantos.*

1Pet. 1: 4. undefiled, and *that fadeth not away*,

264 43 41/47 1:267 1,3133

ἁμαρτάνω, *hamartano.*

Mat.18:15. if thy brother *shall trespass* against
21. how oft *shall* my brother *sin* against
27. 4. I *have sinned* in that I have
Lu. 15:18. Father, I *have sinned* against heaven,
21. Father, I *have sinned* against heaven,
17: 3. If thy brother *trespass* against thee,
4. if he *trespass* against thee seven times
Joh. 5:14. thou art made whole: *sin* no more,
8:11. condemn thee: go, and *sin* no more.
9: 2. Master, who *did sin*, this man, or
3. Neither *hath* this man *sinned*, nor
Acts25: 8. *have* I *offended* any thing at all.
Ro. 2:12. as many as *have sinned* without law
— as many as *have sinned* in the law
3:23. For all *have sinned*, and come short
5:12. upon all men, for that all *have sinned:*
14. them *that had* not *sinned* after
16. not as (it was) by one *that sinned*,
6:15. *shall* we *sin*, because we are not
1Co. 6:18. fornication *sinneth* against his own
7:28. if thou marry, thou *hast* not *sinned*; and if a virgin marry, she *hath* not *sinned*.
36. do what he will, he *sinneth* not:
8:12. ye *sin* so against the brethren, and wound their weak conscience, ye *sin* against Christ.

1Co.15:34. Awake to righteousness, and *sin* not;
Eph. 4:26. Be ye angry, and *sin* not: let not
1Ti. 5:20. Them that *sin* rebuke before all,
Tit. 3:11. is subverted, and *sinneth*, being condemned
Heb. 3:17. with them *that had sinned*,
10:26. For if we *sin* wilfully after that
1Pet. 2:20. if, when ye be buffeted *for your faults*, (lit. *having sinned*)
2Pet. 2: 4. spared not the angels *that sinned*,
1Joh. 1:10. If we say that we *have* not *sinned*,
2: 1. that ye *sin* not. And if any man *sin*,
3: 6. Whosoever abideth in him *sinneth* not: whosoever *sinneth* hath not seen him,
8. for the devil *sinneth* from the
9. he cannot *sin*, because he is
5:16. see his brother *sin* a sin (which)
— them *that sin* not unto death.
18. whosoever is born of God *sinneth* not;

265 4 42/47 1:267 264

ἁμάρτημα, hamarteema.

Mar. 3:28. All *sins* shall be forgiven unto
4:12. (their) *sins* should be forgiven them.
Ro. 3:25. for the remission of *sins* that are
1Co. 6:18. Every *sin* that a man doeth is

266 174 42/47 1:267 264

ἁμαρτία, hamartia.

Mat. 1:21. shall save his people from their *sins*.
3: 6. in Jordan, confessing their *sins*.
9: 2. good cheer; thy *sins* be forgiven thee.
5. to say, (Thy) *sins* be forgiven thee;
6. hath power on earth to forgive *sins*,
12:31. All manner of *sin* and blasphemy
26:28. for many for the remission of *sins*.
Mar. 1: 4. repentance for the remission of *sins*.
5. river of Jordan, confessing their *sins*.
2: 5. Son, thy *sins* be forgiven thee.
7. who can forgive *sins* but God
9. (Thy) *sins* be forgiven thee; or to
10. hath power on earth to forgive *sins*,
Lu. 1:77. by the remission of their *sins*,
3: 3. repentance for the remission of *sins*;
5:20. Man, thy *sins* are forgiven thee.
21. Who can forgive *sins*, but God
23. to say, Thy *sins* be forgiven thee;
24. hath power upon earth to forgive *sins*,
7:47. Her *sins*, which are many, are
48. said unto her, Thy *sins* are forgiven.
49. Who is this that forgiveth *sins* also?
11: 4. forgive us our *sins*; for we also
24:47. repentance and remission of *sins*
Joh. 1:29. which taketh away the *sin* of the world.
8:21. seek me, and shall die in your *sins*·
24. that ye shall die in your *sins*:
— I am (he), ye shall die in your *sins*.
34. Whosoever committeth *sin* is the servant of *sin*.
46. Which of you convinceth me of *sin*?
9:34. Thou wast altogether born in *sins*,
41. ye should have no *sin*: but now ye say, We see; therefore your *sin* remaineth.
15:22. unto them, they had not had *sin*: but now they have no cloke for their *sin*.
24. man did, they had not had *sin*:
16: 8. he will reprove the world of *sin*, and
9. Of *sin*, because they believe not
19:11. unto thee hath the greater *sin*.
20:23. Whose soever *sins* ye remit, they

Acts 2:38. for the remission of *sins*, and ye
3:19. that your *sins* may be blotted out,
5:31. repentance to Israel, and forgiveness of *sins*.
7:60. lay not this *sin* to their charge.
10:43. shall receive remission of *sins*.
13:38. unto you the forgiveness of *sins*:
22:16. be baptized, and wash away thy *sins*,
26:18. they may receive forgiveness of *sins*,
Ro. 3: 9. that they are all under *sin*;
20. by the law (is) the knowledge of *sin*.
4: 7. forgiven, and whose *sins* are covered.
8. to whom the Lord will not impute *sin*.
5:12. by one man *sin* entered into the world, and death by *sin*; and so death
13. until the law *sin* was in the world: but *sin* is not imputed when
20. where *sin* abounded, grace did
21. That as *sin* hath reigned
6: 1. Shall we continue in *sin*, that grace
2. shall we, that are dead to *sin*, live
6. the body of *sin* might be destroyed, that henceforth we should not serve *sin*.
7. he that is dead is freed from *sin*.
10. he died unto *sin* once: but in
11. to be dead indeed unto *sin*, but alive
12. Let not *sin* therefore reign in your
13. instruments of unrighteousness unto *sin*.
14. For *sin* shall not have dominion
16. whether of *sin* unto death, or of
17. that ye were the servants of *sin*,
18. Being then made free from *sin*,
20. when ye were the servants of *sin*,
22. now being made free from *sin*,
23. For the wages of *sin* (is) death;
7: 5. the motions of *sins*, which were by
7. we say then? (Is) the law *sin*?
— I had not known *sin*, but by
8. *sin*, taking occasion by the
— For without the law *sin* (was) dead.
9. *sin* revived, and I died.
11. For *sin*, taking occasion by the
13. *sin*, that it might appear *sin*,
— that *sin* by the commandment
14. I am carnal, sold under *sin*.
17. *sin* that dwelleth in me.
20. I that do it, but *sin* that dwelleth
23. to the law of *sin* which is in
25. but with the flesh the law of *sin*.
8: 2. free from the law of *sin* and death.
3. likeness of *sinful* flesh, and for *sin*, condemned *sin* in the flesh:
10. the body (is) dead because of *sin*;
11:27. when I shall take away their *sins*.
14:23. whatsoever (is) not of faith is *sin*.
1Co. 15: 3. that Christ died for our *sins*
17. ye are yet in your *sins*.
56. The sting of death (is) *sin*; and the strength of *sin* (is) the law.
2Co. 5:21. hath made him (to be) *sin* for us, who knew no *sin*;
11: 7. Have I committed an *offence* in
Gal. 1: 4. Who gave himself for our *sins*,
2:17. (is) therefore Christ the minister of *sin*?
3:22. scripture hath concluded all under *sin*,
Eph. 2: 1. were dead in trespasses and *sins*;
Col. 1:14. his blood, (even) the forgiveness of *sins*:
2:11. the body of the *sins* of the flesh by
1Th. 2:16. to fill up their *sins* alway: for
2Th. 2: 3. that man of *sin* be revealed, the
1Ti. 5:22. partaker of other men's *sins*: keep
24. Some men's *sins* are open beforehand,

D

2Ti. 3: 6. captive silly women laden with *sins*,
Heb. 1: 3. had by himself purged our *sins*,
2:17. reconciliation for the *sins* of the
3:13. through the deceitfulness of *sin*.
4:15. like as (we are, yet) without *sin*.
5: 1. both gifts and sacrifices for *sins*.
3. also for himself, to offer for *sins*.
7:27. sacrifice, first for his own *sins*,
8:12. their *sins* and their iniquities will
9:26. to put away *sin* by the sacrifice
28. offered to bear the *sins* of many;
— second time without *sin* unto
10: 2. had no more conscience of *sins*.
3. again (made) of *sins* every year.
4. bulls and of goats should take away *sins*.
6. (sacrifices) for *sin* thou hast
8. (offering) for *sin* thou wouldest not.
11. which can never take away *sins*:
12. had offered one sacrifice for *sins*,
17. their *sins* and iniquities will I
18. (there is) no more offering for *sin*.
26. remaineth no more sacrifice for *sins*
11:25. the pleasures of *sin* for a season;
12: 1. the *sin* which doth so easily beset
4. unto blood, striving against *sin*.
13:11. by the high priest for *sin*, are
Jas. 1:15. it bringeth forth *sin*: and *sin*, when
2: 9. respect to persons, ye commit *sin*,
4:17. doeth (it) not, to him it is *sin*.
5:15. if he have committed *sins*,
20. shall hide a multitude of *sins*.
1Pet. 2:22. Who did no *sin*, neither was
24. Who his own self bare our *sins* in
— that we, being dead to *sins*,
3:18. hath once suffered for *sins*,
4: 1. in the flesh hath ceased from *sin*;
8. shall cover the multitude of *sins*.
2Pet. 1: 9. was purged from his old *sins*.
2:14. that cannot cease from *sin*;
1Joh. 1: 7. his Son cleanseth us from all *sin*.
8. If we say that we have no *sin*,
9. If we confess our *sins*, he is faithful and just to forgive us (our) *sins*,
2: 2. he is the propitiation for our *sins*:
12. because your *sins* are forgiven
3: 4. Whosoever committeth *sin*
— *sin* is the transgression of the law.
5. manifested to take away our *sins*; and in him is no *sin*.
8. He that committeth *sin* is of the
9. born of God doth not commit *sin*;
4:10. the propitiation for our *sins*.
5:16. see his brother sin a *sin* (which)
— There is a *sin* unto death: I do
17. All unrighteousness is *sin*: and there is a *sin* not unto death.
Rev. 1: 5. washed us from our *sins* in his
18: 4. ye be not partakers of her *sins*,
5. For her *sins* have reached unto

267	1	43/49		1,3144

ἀμάρτυρος, *amarturos.*

Acts 14:17. he left not himself *without witness*,

268	47	43/50	1:317	264

ἁμαρτωλός, *hamartōlos.*

Mat. 9:10. many publicans and *sinners* came and
11. your Master with publicans and *sinners*?
13. the righteous, but *sinners* to repentance.
11:19. a friend of publicans and *sinners*.
26:45. is betrayed into the hands of *sinners*.
Mar. 2:15. many publicans and *sinners* sat also
16. eat with publicans and *sinners*, they
— eateth and drinketh with publicans and *sinners*?
17. the righteous, but *sinners* to repentance.
8:38. this adulterous and *sinful* generation;
14:41. is betrayed into the hands of *sinners*.
Lu. 5: 8. for I am a *sinful* man, O Lord.
30. eat and drink with publicans and *sinners*?
32. the righteous, but *sinners* to repentance.
6:32. for *sinners* also love those that
33. for *sinners* also do even the same.
34. for *sinners* also lend to *sinners*,
7:34. a friend of publicans and *sinners*!
37. a woman in the city, which was a *sinner*,
39. toucheth him: for she is a *sinner*.
13: 2. were *sinners* above all the Galilæans,
15: 1. the publicans and *sinners* for to hear
2. This man receiveth *sinners*, and
7. over one *sinner* that repenteth,
10. over one *sinner* that repenteth.
18:13. God be merciful to me a *sinner*.
19: 7. guest with a man that is a *sinner*.
24: 7. into the hands of *sinful* men,
Joh. 9:16. can a man that is a *sinner* do
24. we know that this man is a *sinner*.
25. Whether he be a *sinner* (or no), I
31. that God heareth not *sinners*:
Ro. 3: 7. am I also judged as a *sinner*?
5: 8. that, while we were yet *sinners*,
19. disobedience many were made *sinners*.
7:13. might become exceeding *sinful*.
Gal. 2:15. Jews by nature, and not *sinners* of
17. we ourselves also are found *sinners*,
1Ti. 1: 9. for the ungodly and for *sinners*, for
15. into the world to save *sinners*;
Heb. 7:26. undefiled, separate from *sinners*,
12: 3. such contradiction of *sinners* against
Jas. 4: 8. Cleanse (your) hands, (ye) *sinners*,
5:20. which converteth the *sinner*
1Pet. 4:18. where shall the ungodly and the *sinner* appear?
Jude 15. which ungodly *sinners* have

269	2	44/50	4:527	1,3163

ἄμαχος, *amakos.*

1Ti. 3: 3. patient, *not a brawler*, not covetous;
Tit. 3: 2. evil of no man, to be *no brawlers*, (but)

270	1	44/50		260

ἀμάω, *amao.*

Jas. 5: 4. the labourers *who have reaped down*

271	1	44/50		1,3184

ἀμέθυστος, *amethustos.*

Rev 21:20. a jacinth; the twelfth, *an amethyst*.

272	5	44/50		1,3199

ἀμελέω, *ameleo.*

Mat. 22: 5. they *made light of* (it), and went their
1Ti. 4:14. *Neglect* not the gift that is in thee,
Heb. 2: 3. *if* we *neglect* so great salvation; which
8: 9. I *regarded* them *not*, saith the Lord.
2Pet. 1:12. I *will* not *be negligent* to put you

273	5	44/50	4:571	1,3201

ἄμεμπτος, *amemptos.*

Lu. 1: 6. ordinances of the Lord *blameless*.

Phil. 2:15. That ye may be *blameless* and
3: 6. which is in the law, *blameless.*
1Th. 3:13. stablish your hearts *unblameable* in
Heb. 8: 7. that first (covenant) had been *faultless,*

274 2 44/50 273

ἀμέμπτως, amemptōs.

1Th. 2:10. justly and *unblameably* we behaved
5:23. be preserved *blameless* unto the

275 2 44/50 4:589 1,3308

ἀμέριμνος, amerimnos.

Mat. 28:14. we will persuade him, and secure (lit. make *without care*) you.
1Co. 7:32. I would have you *without carefulness.*

276 2 44/50 1,3346

ἀμετάθετος, ametathetos.

Heb. 6:17. the *immutability* of his counsel,
18. That by two *immutable* things,

277 1 44/50 1,3334

ἀμετακίνητος, ametakineetos.

1Co. 15:58. be ye stedfast, *unmoveable,* always

278 2 44/51 4:626 1,3338

ἀμεταμέλητος, ametameleetos.

Ro. 11:29. gifts and calling of God (are) *without repentance.*
2Co. 7:10. to salvation *not to be repented of:*

279 1 45/51 4:948 1,3340

ἀμετανόητος, ametanoeetos.

Ro. 2: 5. thy hardness and *impenitent* heart

280 2 45/51 4:632 1,3358

ἄμετρος, ametros.

2Co. 10:13. boast of *things without* (our) *measure,*
15. Not boasting of *things without* (our) *measure,*

281 152 45/51 1:335 [543]

ἀμήν, ameen.

Mat. 5:18. For *verily* I say unto you, Till heaven
26. *Verily* I say unto thee, Thou shalt
6: 2. *Verily* I say unto you, They have their reward.
5. *Verily* I say unto you, They have
13. the power, and the glory, for ever *Amen.*
16. *Verily* I say unto you, They have
8:10. *Verily* I say unto you, I have not
10:15. *Verily* I say unto you, It shall be
23. for *verily* I say unto you, Ye shall
42. *verily* I say unto you, he shall in
11:11. *Verily* I say unto you, Among them that
13:17. For *verily* I say unto you, That many
16:28. *Verily* I say unto you, There be some
17:20. for *verily* I say unto you, If ye
18: 3. And said, *Verily* I say unto you,
13. And if so be that he find it, *verily*
18. *Verily* I say unto you, Whatsoever
19:23. *Verily* I say unto you, That a rich man
28. *Verily* I say unto you That ye which
21:21. *Verily* I say unto you, If ye have faith,
31. *Verily* I say unto you, That the publicans
23:36. *Verily* I say unto you, All these things
24: 2. See ye not all these things? *verily* I say
34. *Verily* I say unto you, This generation
47. *Verily* I say unto you, That he
25:12. *Verily* I say unto you, I know you not.
40. King shall answer and say unto them, *Verily*
45. shall he answer them, saying, *Verily*
26:13. *Verily* I say unto you, Wheresoever this gospel
21. *Verily* I say unto you. that one of you
34. *Verily* I say unto thee, That this night,
28:20. (even) unto the end of the world. *Amen.*
Mar 3:28. *Verily* I say unto you, All sins shall
6:11. *Verily* I say unto you, It shall be more
8:12. seek after a sign? *verily* I say unto you,
9: 1. *Verily* I say unto you, That there be some
41. because ye belong to Christ, *verily* I sav unto
10:15. *Verily* I say unto you, Whosoever
29. *Verily* I say unto you, There is no man
11:23. For *verily* I say unto you, That whosoever
12:43. *Verily* I say unto you, That this poor widow
13:30. *Verily* I say unto you, that this generation
14: 9. *Verily* I say unto you, Wheresoever
18. *Verily* I say unto you, One of you which
25. *Verily* I say unto you, I will drink
30. *Verily* I say unto thee, That this day,
16:20. confirming the word with signs following. *Amen.*
Lu. 4:24. *Verily* I say unto you, No prophet is
12:37. shall find watching: *verily* I say unto you,
13:35. left unto you desolate: and *verily* I say
18:17. *Verily* I say unto you, Whosoever
29. *Verily* I say unto you, There is no
21:32. *Verily* I say unto you, This generation
23:43. *Verily* I say unto thee, To day shalt thou
24:53. in the temple, praising and blessing God. *Amen.*
Joh. 1:51(52). *Verily, verily,* I say unto you, Hereafter ye shall
3: 3. *Verily, verily,* I say unto thee, Except a
5. *Verily, verily,* I say unto thee, Except a
11. *Verily, verily,* I say unto thee, We speak
5:19. *Verily, verily,* I say unto you, The Son
24. *Verily, verily,* I say unto you, He that
25. *Verily, verily,* I say unto you, The
6:26. *Verily, verily,* I say unto you, Ye seek
32. *Verily, verily,* I say unto you, Moses gave
47. *Verily, verily,* I say unto you, He
53. *Verily, verily,* I say unto you, Except
8:34. *Verily, verily,* I say unto you, Whosoe[illegible]
51. *Verily, verily,* I say unto you, If a
58. *Verily, verily,* I say unto you, Befor[illegible]
10: 1. *Verily, verily,* I say unto you, He
7. *Verily, verily,* I say unto you,
12:24. *Verily, verily,* I say unto you, Except
13:16. *Verily, verily,* I say unto you, The servan
20. *Verily, verily,* I say unto you, He
21. testified, and said, *Verily, verily,* I say
38. for my sake? *Verily, verily,* I say unto
14:12. *Verily, verily,* I say unto you,
16:20. *Verily, verily,* I say unto you, That
23. ask me nothing. *Verily, verily,* I say unto
21:18. *Verily, verily,* I say unto thee, When
25. contain the books that should be written *Amen.*
Ro. 1:25. the Creator, who is blessed for ever. *Amen.*
9: 5. over all, God blessed for ever. *Amen.*

Ro. 11:36. to whom (be) glory for ever. *Amen.*
15:33. God of peace (be) with you all. *Amen.*
16:20. (be) with you. *Amen.*
24. Jesus Christ (be) with you all. *Amen.*
27. glory through Jesus Christ for ever. *Amen.*
1Co.14:16. unlearned say *Amen* at thy giving of thanks,
16:24. you all in Christ Jesus. *Amen.*
2Co. 1:20. (are) yea, and in him *Amen*, unto the
13:14(13). of the Holy Ghost, (be) with you all. *Amen.*
Gal. 1: 5. (be) glory for ever and ever. *Amen.*
6:18. Christ (be) with your spirit. *Amen.*
Eph. 3:21. throughout all ages, world without end. *Amen.*
6:24. Jesus Christ in sincerity. *Amen.*
Phi. 4:20. (be) glory for ever and ever. *Amen.*
23. (be) with you all. *Amen.*
Col. 4:18. Remember my bonds. Grace (be) with you. *Amen.*
1Th. 5:28. Christ (be) with you. *Amen.*
2Th. 3:18. Christ (be) with you all. *Amen.*
1Ti. 1:17. and glory for ever and ever. *Amen.*
6:16. (be) honour and power everlasting. *Amen.*
21. Grace (be) with thee. *Amen.*
2Ti. 4:18. to whom (be) glory for ever and ever. *Amen.*
22. Grace (be) with you. *Amen.*
Tit. 3:15. Grace (be) with you all. *Amen.*
Philem. 25. Christ (be) with your spirit. *Amen.*
Heb 13:21. to whom (be) glory for ever and ever. *Amen.*
25. Grace (be) with you all. *Amen.*
1Pet. 4:11. be praise and dominion for ever and ever. *Amen.*
5:11. glory and dominion for ever and ever. *Amen.*
14. all that are in Christ Jesus. *Amen.*
2Pet. 3:18. (be) glory both now and for ever. *Amen.*
1Joh. 5:21. Little children, keep yourselves from idols. *Amen.*
2Joh. 13. of thy elect sister greet thee. *Amen.*
Jude 25. dominion and power, both now and ever. *Amen.*
Rev. 1. 6. and dominion for ever and ever. *Amen.*
7. shall wail because of him. Even so, *Amen.*
18. I am alive for evermore, *Amen*;
3:14. These things saith the *Amen*,
5:14. And the four beasts said, *Amen.*
7:12. Saying, *Amen*: Blessing, and glory,
— might, (be) unto our God for ever and ever. *Amen.*
19: 4. sat on the throne, saying, *Amen*; Alleluia.
22:20. *Amen.* Even so, come, Lord Jesus.
21. Jesus Christ (be) with you all. *Amen.*

282 1 45/52 1,3384

ἀμήτωρ, *ameetōr.*

Heb 7: 3. Without father, *without mother*,

283 4 45/52 4:644 1,3392

ἀμίαντος, *amiantos.*

Heb 7:26. (who is) holy, harmless, *undefiled*,
13: 4. honourable in all, and the bed *undefiled*:
Jas. 1:27. Pure religion and *undefiled* before God
1Pet. 1: 4. an inheritance incorruptible, and *undefiled*,

285 5 45/52 260

ἄμμος, *ammos.*

Mat. 7 26. which built his house upon the *sand*:
Ro. 9:27. Israel be as the *sand* of the sea,
Heb 11:12. as the *sand* which is by the sea shore
Rev. 13: 1(12:18). I stood upon the *sand* of the sea,
20: 8. number of whom (is) as the *sand* of the sea,

286 4 45/52 1:338

ἀμνός, *amnos.*

Joh. 1:29. Behold the *Lamb* of God, which
36. he saith, Behold the *Lamb* of God!
Acts 8:32. like a *lamb* dumb before his shearer,
1Pet. 1:19. blood of Christ, as of a *lamb* without

287 1 46/52
ameibo (to exchange)

ἀμοιβή, *amoibee.*

1Ti. 5: 4. piety at home, and to requite (lit. return recompences to) their parents:

288 8 46/52 1:342 rt 297
rt 257

ἄμπελος, *ampelos.*

Mat. 26:29. of this fruit of the *vine*, until that
Mar 14:25. drink no more of the fruit of the *vine*,
Lu. 22:18. I will not drink of the fruit of the *vine*,
Joh. 15: 1. I am the true *vine*, and my Father is
4. except it abide in the *vine*; no more
5. I am the *vine*, ye (are) the branches:
Jas. 3:12. bear olive berries? either a *vine*, figs?
Rev. 14:19. gathered the *vine* of the earth, and cast

289 1 46/52 288,2041

ἀμπελουργός, *ampelourgos.*

Lu. 13: 7. said he unto the *dresser of his vineyard*,

290 23 46/52 288

ἀμπελών, *ampelōn.*

Mat. 20: 1. to hire labourers into his *vineyard.*
2. he sent them into his *vineyard.*
4. Go ye also into the *vineyard*, and
7. Go ye also into the *vineyard*; and
8. the lord of the *vineyard* saith
21:28. work to day in my *vineyard.*
33. housholder, which planted a *vineyard*,
39. cast (him) out of the *vineyard*, and
40. the lord therefore of the *vineyard*
41. will let out (his) *vineyard* unto
Mar 12: 1. A (certain) man planted a *vineyard*,
2. of the fruit of the *vineyard.*
8. cast (him) out of the *vineyard.*
9. therefore the lord of the *vineyard* do?
— will give the *vineyard* unto others.
Lu. 13: 6. had a fig tree planted in his *vineyard*;
20: 9. A certain man planted a *vineyard*,
10. give him of the fruit of the *vineyard*
13. said the lord of the *vineyard*,
15. they cast him out of the *vineyard*,
— shall the lord of the *vineyard* do
16. shall give the *vineyard* to others.
1Co. 9: 7. who planteth a *vineyard*, and eateth

292 1 46/53

ἀμύνομαι, *amunomai.*

Acts 7:24. suffer wrong, he *defended* (him), and

293 2 46/53 906
amphi (round)

ἀμφίβληστρον, *amphibleestron.*

Mat. 4:18. casting a *net* into the sea, for they

Mar 1:16. Andrew his brother casting a *net* into the sea:

294 4 46/53 *amphi* (round) *hennumi* (to invest)

αμφιέννυμι, *amphiennumi.*

Mat. 6:30. if God so *clothe* the grass of the field,
11: 8. A man *clothed* in soft raiment?
Lu. 7:25. A man *clothed* in soft raiment?
12:28. If then God so *clothe* the grass,

296 1 47/53 3598 *amphi* (round)

ἄμφοδον, *amphodon.*

Mar 11: 4. in a place *where two ways met;*

297 14 47/53 *amphi* (around)

ἀμφότερος, *amphoteros.*

Mat. 9:17. into new bottles, and *both* are preserved.
13:30. Let *both* grow together until the
15:14. *both* shall fall into the ditch.
Lu. 1: 6. they were *both* righteous before God,
7. they *both* were (now) well stricken
5: 7. they came, and filled *both* the ships,
38. into new bottles; and *both* are preserved.
6:39. shall they not *both* fall into the
7:42. he frankly forgave them *both.*
Acts 8:38. went down *both* into the water,
23: 8. angel, nor spirit: but the Pharisees confess *both.*
Eph. 2:14. our peace, who hath made *both* one,
16. he might reconcile *both* unto God
18. through him we *both* have access

298 2 47/53 4:829 1,3469

ἀμώμητος, *amōmeetos.*

Phi. 2:15. the sons of God, *without rebuke,*
2Pet. 3:14. in peace, without spot, and *blameless.*

299 7 47/53 4:829 1,3470

ἄμωμος, *amōmos.*

Eph. 1: 4. *without blame* before him in love:
5:27. that it should be holy and *without blemish.*
Col. 1:22. to present you holy and *unblameable*
Heb 9:14. offered himself *without spot* to God,
1Pet. 1 19. as of a lamb *without blemish* and
Jude 24. to present (you) *faultless* before the
Rev.14: 5. for they are *without fault* before the

302 191 47/53 1437

ἄν, *an.*

OBSERVE.—The place where, ἄν stands is marked thus)(

Mat. 2:13. and be thou there until)(I bring thee word:
5:18. Till)(heaven and earth pass, one jot or one tittle shall in no wise pass from the law, till)(all be fulfilled.
19. whosoever)(shall do and teach (them),
21. and whosoever)(shall kill shall be in danger
22. and whosoever)(shall say to his brother, Raca,
— but whosoever)(shall say, Thou fool, shall be
26. come out thence, till)(thou hast paid
31. said, Whosoever)(shall put away his wife,

Mat. 5:32. whosoever)(shall put away his wife, saving
6: 5. the streets, that)(they may be seen
7:12. all things whatsoever)(ye would that men
10:11. whatsoever)(city or town ye shall enter,
— and there abide till)(ye go thence.
23. Israel, till)(the Son of man be come.
33. But whosoever)(shall deny me before men,
11:21. Sidon, they would have repented long ago)(in sackcloth
23. Sodom, it would have remained)(until this day.
12: 7. sacrifice,)(ye would not have condemned
20. not quench, till)(he send forth judgment
32. whosoever)(speaketh a word against the Son
— but whosoever)(speaketh against the Holy Ghost,
50. whosoever)(shall do the will of my
15: 5. Whosoever)(shall say to (his) father
16:25. whosoever)(will save his life shall lose it; and whosoever)(will lose his life
28. death, till)(they see the Son of man
18: 6. But whoso)(shall offend one of these
19. 9. Whosoever)(shall put away his wife,
21:22. all things, whatsoever)(ye shall ask
44. on whomsoever)(it shall fall, it will
22: 9. as many as)(ye shall find, bid to
44. right hand, till)(I make thine enemies
23: 3. All therefore whatsoever)(they bid you observe,
16. Whosoever)(shall swear by the temple, it is nothing; but whosoever)(shall swear by the gold
18. but whosoever)(sweareth by the gift
30. we)(would not have been partakers with them
39. henceforth, till)(ye shall say,
24:22. shortened, there)(should no flesh be saved:
34. shall not pass, till)(all these things
43. he)(would have watched, and)(would not have suffered his house
25:27. coming I)(should have received mine
26:48. Whomsoever I)(shall kiss, that same is he:
Mar 3:28. blasphemies wherewith soever)(they shall blaspheme:
29. But he that)(shall blaspheme against the
35. For whosoever)(shall do the will of God,
4:25. For he that)(hath, to him shall be
6:10. there abide till)(ye depart from that place.
11. And whosoever)(shall not receive you,
56. And whithersoever)(he entered, into villages,
— as many as)(touched him were made whole.
8:35. For whosoever)(will save his life shall lose it; but whosoever)(shall lose his
38. Whosoever therefore)(shall be ashamed of me
9: 1. death, till)(they have seen the kingdom
18. wheresoever)(he taketh him, he teareth him:
41. For whosoever)(shall give you a cup
42. And whosoever)(shall offend one of (these)
10:44. And whosoever of you)(will be the chiefest,
11:23. whosoever)(shall say unto this mountain,
24. What things soever)(ye desire, when ye

Mar 12:36. right hand, till)(I make thine enemies
13:20. those days, no flesh)(should be saved.
14: 9. Wheresoever this gospel)(shall be preached
44. Whomsoever)(I shall kiss, that same is he;
Lu. 1:62. father, how)(he would have him called.
2:35. thoughts of many hearts)(may be revealed.
6:11. communed one with another what)(they might do
7:39. a prophet,)(would have known who
8:18. for whosoever)(hath, to him shall be given; and whosoever)(hath not, from him shall
9: 4. And whatsoever)(house ye enter into,
5. And whosoever)(will not receive you,
24. For whosoever)(will save his life shall lose it: but whosoever)(will lose his life
26. For whosoever)(shall be ashamed of me
27. till)(they see the kingdom of God.
46. which of them)(should be greatest.
57. I will follow thee whithersoever)(thou goest.
10: 5. whatsoever)(house ye enter, first say, Peace
8. And into whatsoever)(city ye enter,
10. But into whatsoever)(city ye enter, and
13. they had)(a great while ago repented, sitting
35. and whatsoever)(thou spendest more, when I
12: 8. Whosoever)(shall confess me before men,
39. thief would come, he)(would have watched, and)(not have suffered his house
13:25. When once the master of the house)(is risen up,
35. not see me, until)((the time) come when
17: 6. faith as a grain of mustard seed,)(ye might say unto
— planted in the sea; and)(it should obey you.
19:23. coming)(I might have required mine own
20:18. on whomsoever)(it shall fall, it will
43. Till)(I make thine enemies thy footstool.
21:32. not pass away, till)(all be fulfilled.
Joh. 1:33. Upon whom)(thou shalt see the Spirit descending,
2: 5. Whatsoever)(he saith unto you, do (it).
4:10. thou)(wouldest have asked of him, and)(he would have given thee living water.
14. But whosoever)(drinketh of the water
5:19. what things soever)(he doeth, these also
46. believed Moses, ye would have believed)(me:
8:19. me,)(ye should have known my Father
39. Abraham's children,)(ye would do the works
42. your Father, ye)(would love me:
9:41. If ye were blind, ye)(should have no sin:
11:21. hadst been here, my brother)(had not died.
22. whatsoever)(thou wilt ask of God, God
32. if thou hadst been here, my brother)(had
13:24. ask who)(it should be of whom
14: 2. if (it were) not (so),)(I would have
7. If ye had known me,)(ye should have known
13. whatsoever)(ye shall ask in my name,
28. If ye loved me,)(ye would rejoice,
15:16. whatsoever)(ye shall ask of the Father
Joh. 15:19. of the world, the world)(would love
16:13. but whatsoever)(he shall hear, (that) shall
23. Whatsoever)(ye shall ask the Father in
18:30. not a malefactor,)(we would not have delivered
36. if my kingdom were of this world, then)(would my servants fight,
20:23. Whose soever sins)(ye remit, they are remitted unto them; (and) whose soever (sins))(ye retain,
Acts 2:12. What)(meaneth this?
21. whosoever)(shall call on the name
35. Until)(I make thy foes thy footstool.
39. as many as)(the Lord our God shall
45. to all (men), as)(every man had ne[illegible]
3:19. blotted out, when)(the times of refreshing shall come
22. in all things whatsoever)(he shall say
23. soul, which)(will not hear that prophet,
4:35. unto every man according as)(he had
5:24. doubted of them whereunto this)(would grow.
7: 3. into the land which)(I shall shew thee.
8:19. power, that on)(whomsoever I lay hands,
31. How)(can I, except some man should guide
10:17. what this vision which he had seen)(should mean,
15:17. That the residue of men)(might seek after
17:18. some said, What)(will this babbler say?
20. know therefore what these things)(mean.
18:14. reason would that)(I should bear with you:
21:33. and demanded who)(he was, and what
26:29. And Paul said, I would)(to God, that not
Ro. 3: 4. That)(thou mightest be justified in thy sayings,
9:15. mercy on whom)(I will have mercy, and I will have compassion on whom)(I will
29. had left us a seed,)(we had been as Sodoma, and)(been made like unto
10:13. For whosoever)(shall call upon the name
16: 2. whatsoever business)(she hath need of you:
1Co. 2: 8. had they known (it), they)(would not have
4: 5. before the time, until)(the Lord come,
7: 5. not one the other, except (it))((be) with consent
11:25. this do ye, as oft as)(ye drink (it), in
26. For as often as)(ye eat this bread, and
— shew the Lord's death till)(he come.
27. Wherefore whosoever)(shall eat this bread,
31. judge ourselves, we)(should not be judged.
34. the rest will I set in order when)(I come.
12: 2. dumb idols, even as)(ye were led.
15:25. For he must reign, till he)(hath put all
16: 2. in store, as (God))(hath prospered him,
2Co. 3:16. when it)(shall turn to the Lord,
10: 9. not seem as if I)(would terrify
11:21. Howbeit whereinsoever any)(is bold,
Gal. 1:10. men, I)(should not be the servant of Christ.
3:21. righteousness)(should have been by the law.
4:15. out your own eyes, and)(have given them

Gal. 5:10. shall bear his judgment, whosoever)(he be.
17. cannot do the things that ye)(would.
Phi. 2:23. so soon as I)(shall see how it will
Col. 3:17. And whatsoever)(ye do in word or deed,
1Th. 2: 7. among you, even as a nurse)(cherisheth
Heb 1:13. right hand, until)(I make thine enemies
4: 8. then)(would he not afterward have spoken
8: 4. on earth, he)(should not be a priest,
7. faultless, then)(should no place have been sought for the second.
10: 2. For then)(would they not have ceased to
11:15. came out, they)(might have had opportunity
Jas. 3: 4. whithersoever)(the governor listeth.
4: 4. whosoever)(therefore will be a friend
5: 7. patience for it, until)(he receive the early
1Joh. 2: 5. But whoso)(keepeth his word, in him
19. of us, they)(would (no doubt) have continued
3:17. whoso)(hath this world's good,
4:15. Whosoever)(shall confess that Jesus is the Son
5:15. whatsoever)(we ask, we know that we
Rev. 2:25. which ye have (already) hold fast till)(I come.
13:15. that as many as)(would not worship
14: 4. the Lamb whithersoever)(he goeth.

303 10 49/55

ἀνά, *ana.* adv.

Mat. 20: 9. they received *every man* a penny.
10. likewise received *every man* a penny.
Mar. 6:40. in ranks, *by* hundreds, and *by* fifties.
Lu. 9: 3. money; neither have two coats *apiece.*
14. sit down *by* fifties in a company.
10: 1. sent them two *and* two before
Joh. 2: 6. containing two or three firkins *apiece.*
Rev. 4: 8. the four beasts had *each* of them
21:21 every *several* gate was of one pearl:

303 5 49/55

ἀνά, *ana.* prep.

Mat. 13:25. sowed tares among (lit. *in* the midst of) the wheat,
Mar. 7:31. *through* the midst of the coasts
1Co. 6: 5. to judge between (lit. *in* the midst of) his brethren?
14:27. most (by) three, and (that) *by* course;
Rev. 7:17. the Lamb which is *in* the midst

304 2 49/56 305(cf 898)

ἀναβαθμός, *anabathmos.*

Acts 21:35. when he came upon the *stairs,* so
40. Paul stood on the *stairs,* and beckoned

305 81 49/56 1:518 303,rt939

ἀναβαίνω, *anabaino.*

Mat. 3:16. *went up* straightway out of the water:
5: 1. he *went up* into a mountain: and
13: 7. the thorns *sprung up,* and choked them:
14:23. he *went up* into a mountain apart
15:29. *went up* into a mountain, and sat
17:27. the fish that first *cometh up*; and
20:17. Jesus *going up* to Jerusalem
18. Behold, we *go up* to Jerusalem;
Mar. 1:10. straightway *coming up* out of the water,
3:13. he *goeth up* into a mountain, and
4: 7. the thorns *grew up,* and choked it,
8. fruit *that sprang up* and increased;
32. when it is sown, it *groweth up,*
6:51. he *went up* unto them into the ship;
10:32. in the way *going up* to Jerusalem;
33. Behold, we *go up* to Jerusalem;
Lu. 2: 4. Joseph also *went up* from Galilee,
42. they *went up* to Jerusalem after
5:19. they *went up*on the housetop, and let
9:28. *went up* into a mountain to pray.
18:10. Two men *went up* into the temple
31. Behold, we *go up* to Jerusalem, and
19: 4. *climbed up* into a sycomore tree
28. he went before, *ascending up* to
24:38. why do thoughts *arise* in your hearts?
Joh. 1:51(52). the angels of God *ascending* and
2:13. was at hand, and Jesus *went up* to Jerusalem,
3:13. no man *hath ascended up* to heaven,
5: 1. of the Jews; and Jesus *went up* to Jerusalem.
6:62. ye shall see the Son of man *ascend up*
7: 8. *Go* ye *up* unto this feast: I *go* not *up* yet unto this feast;
10. when his brethren *were gone up,* then *went* he also *up* unto the feast,
14. Jesus *went up* into the temple,
10: 1. *climbeth up* some other way, the
11:55. *went* out of the country *up* to Jerusalem
12:20. Greeks among them *that came up* to
20:17. for I am not yet *ascended* to my
— I *ascend* unto my Father, and your
21: 3. They went forth, and *entered* into a ship
11. Simon Peter *went up,* and drew the
Acts 1:13. they *went up* into an upper room,
2:34. For David is not *ascended* into the
3: 1. Peter and John *went up* together into
7:23. it *came* into his heart to visit his
8:31. that he would *come up* and sit with him.
39. *were come up* out of the water,
10: 4. thine alms *are come up* for a
9. Peter *went up* upon the housetop
11: 2. when Peter *was come up* to Jerusalem,
15: 2. should *go up* to Jerusalem unto
18:22. landed at Cæsarea, *and gone up,* and saluted
20:11. therefore *was come up* again, and had
21: 4. he should not *go up* to Jerusalem.
12. besought him not *to go up* to Jerusalem.
15. our carriages, and *went up* to Jerusalem.
31. tidings *came* unto the chief captain
24:11. since I *went up* to Jerusalem for
25: 1. he *ascended* from Cæsarea to Jerusalem.
9. said, Wilt thou *go up* to Jerusalem,
Ro. 10: 6. Who shall *ascend* into heaven?
1Co. 2: 9. neither *have entered* into the heart
Gal. 2: 1. I *went up* again to Jerusalem
2. I *went up* by revelation, and
Eph 4: 8. When he *ascended up* on high,
9. Now that he *ascended,* what is
10. the same also *that ascended up*
Rev. 4: 1. which said, *Come up* hither, and I will
7: 2. another angel *ascending* from the
8: 4. *ascended up* before God out of
9: 2. there *arose* a smoke out of the pit,
11: 7. the beast *that ascendeth* out of the
12. saying unto them, *Come up* hither. And they *ascended up* to heaven in a
13: 1. saw a beast *rise up* out of the sea,
11. another beast *coming up* out of
14:11. their torment *ascendeth up* for ever

Rev 17: 8. shall *ascend* out of the bottomless
19: 3. her smoke *rose up* for ever and
20: 9. they *went up* on the breadth of

306 6 50/57 303,906

ἀναβάλλομαι, *anaballomai.*

Acts24:22. of (that) way, he *deferred* them, and

307 1 50/57 303,rt 939

ἀναβιβάζω, *anabibazo.*

Mat.13:48. they *drew* to shore, and sat down,

308 26 50/57 303,991

ἀναβλέπω, *anablepo.*

Mat.11: 5. The blind *receive* their *sight*, and
14:19. *looking up* to heaven, he blessed,
20:34. their eyes *received sight*, and they
Mar. 6:41. he *looked up* to heaven, *and* blessed,
7:34. *looking up* to heaven, he sighed,
8:24. he *looked up, and* said, I see men
25. upon his eyes, and made him *look up:*
10:51. Lord, that I *might receive* my *sight*.
52. immediately he *received* his *sight*,
16: 4. when they *looked*, they saw that
Lu. 7:22. how that the blind *see*, the lame
9:16. *looking up* to heaven, he blessed
18:41. Lord, that I *may receive* my *sight*.
42. said unto him, *Receive* thy *sight:*
43. immediately he *received* his *sight*,
19: 5. came to the place, he *looked up, and*
21: 1. he *looked up, and* saw the rich men
Joh. 9:11. I went and washed, and I *received sight*.
15. how he *had received* his *sight*.
18. had been blind, and *received* his *sight*,
— of him *that had received* his *sight*.
Acts 9:12. that he *might receive* his *sight*.
17. that thou *mightest receive* thy *sight*,
18. he *received sight* forthwith, and arose,
22:13. Brother Saul, *receive* thy *sight*. And the same hour I *looked up* upon him.

309 1 50/57 308

ἀνάβλεψις, *anablepsis.*

Lu. 4:18. *recovering of sight* to the blind,

310 3 50/57 303,994

ἀναβοάω, *anaboao.*

Mat.27:46. Jesus *cried* with a loud voice.
Mar.15: 8. the multitude *crying aloud*
Lu. 9:38. a man of the company *cried out*,

311 1 50/57 306

ἀναβολή, *anabolee.*

Acts25:17. without any *delay* on the morrow

312 18 50/57 1:56 303,rt 32

ἀναγγέλλω, *anangello.*

Mar. 5:14. *told* (it) in the city, and in the country.
19. *tell* them how great things the
Joh. 4:25. he *will tell* us all things.
5:15. *told* the Jews that it was Jesus,
16:13. he *will shew* you things to come.
14. of mine, and *shall shew* (it) unto you.
15. mine, and *shall shew* (it) unto you.
Joh 16:25. I *shall shew* you plainly of the
Acts14:27. they *rehearsed* all that God
15: 4. they *declared* all things that
16:38. the serjeants *told* these words unto
19:18. came, and confessed, and *shewed* their deeds.
20:20. *have shewed* you, and have taught you
27. to *declare* unto you all the counsel
Ro. 15:21. To whom he *was* not *spoken* of, they
2Co. 7: 7. *when* he *told* us your earnest desire,
1Pet. 1:12. things, which *are* now *reported* unto you
1Joh.1: 5. *declare* unto you, that God is light,

313 2 51/57 1:665 303,1080

ἀναγεννάω, *anagennao.*

1Pet. 1: 3. *which*...hath *begotten* us *again* unto a lively
23. *Being born again*, not of corruptible

314 33 51/57 1:343 303,1097

ἀναγινώσκω, *anaginōsko.*

Mat.12: 3. *Have* ye not *read* what David did, when
5. Or *have* ye not *read* in the law, how
19: 4. *Have* ye not *read*, that he which made
21:16. *have* ye never *read*, Out of the mouth of
42. *Did* ye never *read* in the scriptures,
22:31. *have* ye not *read* that which was
24:15. whoso *readeth*, let him understand:
Mar. 2:25. *Have* ye never *read* what David did,
12:10. *have* ye not *read* this scripture; The
26. *have* ye not *read* in the book of Moses,
13:14. let him *that readeth* understand,
Lu. 4:16. sabbath day, and stood up for *to read*.
6: 3. *Have* ye not *read* so much as this,
10:26. What is written in the law? how *readest* thou?
Joh.19:20. This title then *read* many of the Jews:
Acts 8:28. in his chariot *read* Esaias the prophet.
30. heard him *read* the prophet Esaias, and said, Understandest thou what thou *readest?*
32. the scripture which he *read* was this,
13:27. the prophets *which are read* every sabbath
15:21. *being read* in the synagogues every
31. (Which) *when* they *had read*, they rejoiced
23:34. *when* the governor *had read* (the letter),
2Co. 1:13. than what ye *read* or acknowledge;
3: 2. in our hearts, known and *read* of all men:
15. unto this day, when Moses *is read*,
Eph 3: 4. *when* ye *read*, ye may understand
Col. 4:16. when this epistle *is read* among you, cause that it *be read* also in the church
— that ye likewise *read* the (epistle)
1Th. 5:27. that this epistle *be read* unto all
Rev. 1: 3. Blessed (is) he *that readeth*, and they that
5: 4. worthy to open and *to read* the book,

315 9 51/58 1:344 318

ἀναγκάζω, *anankazo.*

Mat.14:22. Jesus *constrained* his disciples to get
Mar. 6:45. he *constrained* his disciples to get
Lu. 14:23. *compel* (them) to come in, that my
Acts26:11. *compelled* (them) to blaspheme;
28:19. I *was constrained* to appeal unto
2Co.12:11. a fool in glorying; ye *have compelled* me
Gal. 2: 3. being a Greek, *was compelled* to be
14. why *compellest* thou the Gentiles
6:12. they *constrain* you to be circumcised;

316 8 51/58 1:344 318

ἀναγκαῖος, anankaios.

Acts10:24. together his kinsmen and *near* friends.
13:46. It was *necessary* that the word of
1Co.12:22. seem to be more feeble, are *necessary:*
2Co. 9: 5. Therefore I thought it *necessary* to exhort
Phi. 1:24. in the flesh (is) *more needful* for you.
2:25. Yet I supposed it *necessary* to send
Tit. 3:14. maintain good works for *necessary* uses,
Heb 8: 3. (it is) *of necessity* that this man have

317 1 52/58 315

ἀναγκαστῶς, anankastōs.

1Pet.5: 2. not *by constraint*, but willingly;

318 18 52/58 1:344 303,rt 43

ἀνάγκη, anankee.

Mat.18: 7. for it *must needs* be that offences
Lu. 14:18. ground, and I *must needs* go and see it:
21:23. there shall be great *distress* in the land,
23:17. For of *necessity* he must release one
Ro. 13: 5. (ye) *must needs* be subject, not
1Co. 7:26. this is good for the present *distress*,
37. in his heart, having no *necessity*,
9:16. for *necessity* is laid upon me; yea,
2Co. 6: 4. much patience, in afflictions, in *necessities*,
9: 7. not grudgingly, or of *necessity:* for
12:10. in reproaches, in *necessities*, in persecutions,
1Th. 3: 7. in all our affliction and *distress* by
Philem.14. not be as it were of *necessity*, but
Heb. 7:12. there is made of *necessity* a change
27. Who *needeth* not daily, as those
9:16. there must also of *necessity* be the
23. therefore *necessary* that the patterns
Jude 3. it was *needful* for me to write unto

319 1 /58 303,1107

ἀναγνωρίζομαι, anagnōrizomai.

Acts 7:13. Joseph *was made known* to his

320 3 52/58 1:343 314

ἀνάγνωσις, anagnōsis.

Acts13:15. after the *reading* of the law and the
2Co. 3:14. in the *reading* of the old testament;
1Ti. 4:13. give attendance *to reading*, to exhortation,

321 24 52/58 303,71

ἀνάγω, anago.

Mat. 4: 1. Then *was* Jesus *led up* of the spirit into
Lu. 2:22. they *brought* him to Jerusalem,
4: 5. the devil, *taking* him *up* into an
8:22. And they *launched forth*.
22:66. *led* him into their council, saying,
Acts 7:41. *offered* sacrifice unto the idol, and
9:39. they *brought* him into the upper
12: 4. after Easter *to bring* him *forth* to the
13:13. *when* Paul and his company *loosed* from Paphos,
16:11. Therefore *loosing* from Troas, we came
34. *when* he *had brought* them into
18:21. if God will. And he *sailed* from Ephesus.
20: 3. he was about *to sail* into Syria, he
13. to ship, and *sailed* unto Assos, there
21: 1. after we were gotten from them and *had launched*,
2. we went aboard, and *set forth*.
27: 2. we *launched*, meaning to sail
4. *when* we *had launched* from
12. part advised *to depart* thence
21. not *have loosed* from Crete, and to have
28:10. *when* we *departed*, they laded
11. we *departed* in a ship of Alexandria,
Ro. 10: 7. *to bring up* Christ *again* from the dead.
Heb 13:20. *that brought again* from the dead

322 2 53/59 2:25 303,1166

ἀναδείκνυμι, anadīknumi.

Lu. 10: 1. the Lord *appointed* other seventy
Acts 1:24. *shew* whether of these two thou

323 1 53/59 2:25 322

ἀνάδειξις, anadīxis.

Lu. 1:80. till the day of his *shewing* unto Israel.

324 2 53/59 303,1209

ἀναδέχομαι, anadekomai.

Acts28: 7. name was Publius; who *received* us, *and*
Heb 11:17. he *that had received* the promises

325 1 53/59 303,1325

ἀναδίδωμι, anadidōmi.

Acts23:33. *when...delivered* the epistle to the governor,

326 5 53/59 2:832 303,2198

ἀναζάω, anazao.

Lu. 15:24. my son was dead, and *is alive again;*
32. thy brother was dead, and *is alive again;*
Ro. 7: 9. the commandment came, sin *revived*,
14: 9. Christ both died, and rose, and *revived*, that
Rev.20: 5. rest of the dead *lived* not *again* until

327 2 53/59 303,2212

ἀναζητέω, anazeeteo.

Lu. 2:44. they *sought* him among (their)
Acts11:25. Barnabas to Tarsus, for *to seek* Saul:

328 1 53/59 303,2224

ἀναζώννυμι, anazōnnumi.

1Pet. 1:13. Wherefore *gird up* the loins of your

329 1 53/59 303,4442
rt2226

ἀναζωπυρέω, anazōpureo.

2Ti. 1: 6. that thou *stir up* the gift of God,

330 1 53/59 303
thallō (to flourish)

ἀναθάλλω, anathallo.

Phi. 4:10. your care of me *hath flourished again;*

331 6 53/59 1:353 394

ἀνάθεμα, anathema.

Acts23:14. We have bound ourselves under a *great* curse, (lit. under a curse *by a curse*)
Ro. 9: 3. that myself were *accursed* from
1Co.12: 3. calleth Jesus *accursed:* and (that) no
16:22. let him be *Anathema* Maran-atha.
Gal. 1: 8. preached unto you, let him be *accursed*.
have received; let him be *accursed*.

332 4 54/59 331

ἀναθεματίζω, anathematizo.

Mar 14:71. he began *to curse* and to swear, (saying),
Acts23:12. *bound* themselves *under a curse*,
14. *bound* ourselves *under a* great *curse*,
21. *have bound* themselves *with an oath*,

333 2 54/59 303,2334

ἀναθεωρέω, anatheōreo.

Acts17:23. *as* I passed by, and *beheld* your devotions,
Heb13: 7. *considering* the end of (their) conversation:

334 1 54/59 1:353 394,cf331

ἀνάθημα, anatheema.

Lu. 21: 5. was adorned with goodly stones and *gifts*,

335 1 54/59 1,127

ἀναίδεια, anaidīa.

Lu. 11: 8. because of his *importunity* he will rise

336 2 54/59 337

ἀναίρεσις, anairesis.

Acts 8: 1. Saul was consenting unto his *death*.
22:20. standing by, and consenting unto his *death*,

337 23 54/59 303,138

ἀναιρέω, anaireo.

Mat. 2:16. sent forth, and *slew* all the children that
Lu. 22: 2. sought how they *might kill* him;
23:32. led with him *to be put to death*.
Acts 2:23. by wicked hands have crucified and *slain*:
5:33. took counsel *to slay* them.
36. who *was slain*; and all, as many as
7:21. Pharaoh's daughter *took* him *up*, and
28. Wilt thou *kill* me, as thou *diddest* (lit. *killedst*) the Egyptian
9:23. the Jews took counsel *to kill* him.
24. watched the gates day and night to *kill* him.
29. they went about *to slay* him.
10:39. whom they *slew* and hanged on a tree:
12: 2. he *killed* James the brother of John
13:28. that he should *be slain*.
16:27. his sword, and would *have killed* himself,
22:20. the raiment of them *that slew* him.
23:15. he come near, are ready *to kill* him.
21. nor drink till they *have killed* him:
27. should have *been killed* of them:
25. 3. laying wait in the way *to kill*
26:10. *when* they *were put to death*, I gave
Heb 10: 9. He *taketh away* the first, that he

338 2 54/59 1,159

ἀναίτιος, anaitios.

Mat.12: 5. profane the sabbath, and are *blameless*?
7. would not have condemned the *guiltless*.

339 2 55/59 303,2523

ἀνακαθίζω, anakathizo.

Lu. 7:15. he that was dead *sat up*, and began
Acts 9:40. when she saw Peter, she *sat up*.

340 1 55/60 3:447 303,2537

ἀνακαινίζω, anakainizo.

Heb. 6: 6. *to renew* them again unto repentance;

341 2 55/60 3:447 303,2537

ἀνακαινόω, anakainoō.

2Co. 4:16. the inward (man) *is renewed* day by day.
Col. 3:10. *which is renewed* in knowledge

342 2 55/60 3:447 341

ἀνακαίνωσις, anakainōsis.

Ro. 12: 2. transformed by the *renewing* of your
Tit. 3: 5. regeneration, and *renewing* of the Holy Ghost;

343 2 55/60 3:556 303,2572

ἀνακαλύπτω, anakalupto.

2Co. 3:14. remaineth the same vail un*taken away*
18. we all, with *open* face beholding as

344 4 55/60 303,2578

ἀνακάμπτω, anakampto.

Mat. 2:12. that they should not *return* to Herod,
Lu. 10: 6. if not, it *shall turn* to you *again*.
Acts18:21. I *will return* again unto you,
Heb11:15. had opportunity *to have returned*.

345 14 55/60 3:654 303,2749

ἀνάκειμαι anakīmai.

Mat. 9:10. *as* Jesus *sat at meat* in the house,
22:10. the wedding was furnished with *guests*.
11. the king came in to see the *guests*,
26: 7. on his head, *as* he *sat* (at meat).
20. he *sat down* with the twelve.
Mar. 5:40. entereth in where the damsel was *lying*.
14:18. *as* they *sat* and did eat, Jesus said,
16:14. the eleven *as* they *sat at meat*,
Lu. 7:37. knew that (Jesus) *sat at meat* in
22:27. (is) greater, he *that sitteth at meat*
— (is) not he *that sitteth at meat*?
Joh. 6:11. disciples to them *that were set down*;
13:23. there was *leaning* on Jesus' bosom
28. no man *at the table* knew for (lit. of those *reclining*)

346 2 55/60 3:673 303,2775

ἀνακεφαλαιόομαι, anakephalaio-omai.

Ro. 13: 9. it *is briefly comprehended* in this saying,
Eph. 1:10. he might *gather together in one* all

347 8 55/60 303,2827

ἀνακλίνω, anaklino.

Mat. 8:11. *shall sit down* with Abraham, and
14:19. commanded the multitude *to sit down*
Mar. 6:39. *to make* all *sit down* by companies
Lu. 2: 7. *laid* him in a manger; because
7:36. Pharisee's house, and *sat down to meat*.
9:15. they did so, and *made* them all *sit down*.
12:37. *make* them *to sit down to meat*, and will
13:29. *shall sit down* in the kingdom of God.

348 1 55/ 303,2875

ἀνακόπτω, anakopto.

Gal. 5: 7. who *did hinder* you that ye should

349 5 55/60 3:898 303,2896

ἀνακράζω, anakrazo.

Mar. 1:23. with an unclean spirit; and he *cried out*,
6:49. it had been a spirit, and *cried out*

Lu. 4:33. unclean devil, and *cried out* with a loud voice,
8:28. When he saw Jesus, he *cried out, and* fell
23:18. they *cried out* all at once, saying,

350 16 56/60 3:921 303,2919

ἀνακρίνω, anakrino.

Lu. 23:14. I, *having examined* (him) before
Acts 4: 9. If we this day *be examined* of the
12:19. him not, he *examined* the keepers, *and*
17:11. *searched* the scriptures daily, whether
24: 8. *by examining* of whom thyself
28:18. Who, *when* they *had examined* me,
1Co. 2:14. because they *are* spiritually *discerned.*
15. he that is spiritual *judgeth* all things, yet he himself *is judged* of no man.
4: 3. that I *should be judged* of you,
— yea, I *judge* not mine own self.
4. he *that judgeth* me is the Lord.
9: 3. to them *that do examine* me is this,
10:25. *asking* no *question* for conscience
27. eat, *asking* no *question* for conscience
14:24. convinced of all, he *is judged* of all·

351 1 56/60 3:921 350

ἀνάκρισις, anakrisis.

Acts25:26. that, after *examination* had, I might

352 4 56/60 303,2955

ἀνακύπτω, anakupto.

Lu. 13:11. could in no wise *lift up* (herself).
21:28. then *look up,* and lift up your heads
Joh. 8: 7. he *lifted up* himself, *and* said unto
10. *When* Jesus *had lifted up* himself, and

353 13 56/60 4:5 303,2983

ἀναλαμβάνω, analambano.

Mar 16:19. he *was received up* into heaven,
Acts 1: 2. the day in which he *was taken up,*
11. Jesus, which *is taken up* from you
22. day that he *was taken up* from us,
7:43. Yea, ye *took up* the tabernacle of
10:16. the vessel *was received up* again
20:13. there intending *to take in* Paul: for
14. we *took* him *in, and* came to Mitylene.
23:31. *took* Paul, *and* brought (him) by night
Eph. 6:13. *take unto* you the whole armour of
16. *taking* the shield of faith, wherewith
1Ti. 3:16. in the world, *received up* into glory.
2Ti. 4:11. *Take* Mark, *and* bring him with thee:

354 1 /61 4:5 353

ἀνάληψις, analeepsis.

Lu. 9:51. *that* he *should be received up,* (lit. of his *taking up*)

355 3 56/61 303,138

ἀναλίσκω, analisko.

Lu. 9:54. come down from heaven, and *consume* them,
Gal. 5:15. that ye *be* not *consumed* one of
2Th. 2: 8. whom the Lord *shall consume* with

356 1 56/61 1:347 303,3056

ἀναλογία, analogia.

Ro. 12: 6. according to the *proportion* of faith;

357 1 56/61 356

ἀναλογίζομαι, analogizomai.

Heb12: 3. For *consider* him that endured

358 1 57/61 1,251

ἄναλος, analos.

Mar. 9:50. if the salt have *lost* his *saltness,*

359 1 57/61 4:328 360

ἀνάλυσις, analusis.

2Ti. 4: 6. the time of my *departure* is at hand.

360 2 57/61 4:328 303,3089

ἀναλύω, analuo.

Lu. 12:36. when he *will return* from the wedding;
Phil. 1:23. having a desire *to depart,* and to be with

361 1 57/61 1:317 1,264

ἀναμάρτητος, anamarteetos.

Joh. 8: 7. He *that is without sin* among you,

362 1 57/61 303,3306

ἀναμένω, anameno.

1Th. 1:10. *to wait for* his Son from heaven,

363 6 57/61 303,3403

ἀναμιμνήσκω, anamimneesko.

Mar11:21. Peter *calling to remembrance* saith
14:72. Peter *called to mind* the word that
1Co. 4:17. *bring* you *into remembrance* of my
2Co. 7:15. he *remembereth* the obedience of
2Ti. 1: 6. I *put* thee *in remembrance* that
Heb10:32. *call to remembrance* the former

364 4 57/61 1:348 363

ἀνάμνησις, anamneesis.

Lu. 22:19. this do in *remembrance* of me.
1Co.11:24. this do in *remembrance* of me.
25. drink (it), in *remembrance* of me.
Heb 10: 3. (there is) a *remembrance again* (made)

365 1 57/61 4:896 303,3501

ἀνανεόω, ananeoō.

Eph. 4:23. *be renewed* in the spirit of your

366 1 57/61 303,3525

ἀνανήφω, ananeepho.

2Ti. 2:26. they *may recover* themselves out of

368 1 58/61 1,473,4483

ἀναντίῤῥητος, anantirreetos.

Acts19:36. these things *cannot be spoken against,*

369 1 58/61 368

ἀναντιρρήτως, anantirreetōs.

Acts10:29. came I (unto you) *without gainsaying*,

370 1 58/61 1,514

ἀνάξιος, anaxios.

1Co. 6 2. are ye *unworthy* to judge the smallest

371 2 58/61 370

ἀναξίως, anaxiōs.

1Co.11:27. cup of the Lord, *unworthily*, shall be
29. he that eateth and drinketh *unworthily*,

372 5 58/61 1:350 373

ἀνάπαυσις, anapausis.

Mat.11:29. ye shall find *rest* unto your souls.
12:43. through dry places, seeking *rest*, and
Lu. 11:24. through dry places, seeking *rest*; and
Rev. 4: 8. they *rest* not day and night, saying,
14:11. they have no *rest* day nor night, who

373 12 58/61 1:350 303,3973

ἀναπαύω, anapauo.

Mat.11:28. are heavy laden, and I *will give* you *rest*.
26:45. Sleep on now, and *take* (your) *rest*: behold,
Mar. 6:31. into a desert place, and *rest* a while:
14:41. Sleep on now, and *take* (your) *rest*: it is
Lu. 12:19. *take* thine *ease*, eat, drink, (and)
1Co.16:18. they *have refreshed* my spirit and your's:
2Co. 7:13. his spirit *was refreshed* by you all.
Philem. 7. bowels of the saints *are refreshed* by thee,
20. *refresh* my bowels in the Lord.
1Pet.4:14. of glory and of God *resteth* upon you:
Rev. 6:11. they *should rest* yet for a little
14:13. that they *may rest* from their labours;

374 1 58/62 303,3982

ἀναπείθω, anapitho.

Acts18:13. This (fellow) *persuadeth* men to worship

375 4 58/62 303,3992

ἀναπέμπω, anapempo.

Lu. 23: 7. he *sent* him to Herod, who himself
11. a gorgeous robe, and *sent* him *again* to Pilate.
15. nor yet Herod: for I *sent* you to him;
Philem 12. Whom I *have sent again*: thou

376 2 59/62 303
peros (maimed)

ἀνάπηρος, anapeeros.

Lu. 14:13. call the poor, the *maimed*, the lame,
21. hither the poor, and the *maimed*, and the

377 11 59/62 303,4098

ἀναπίπτω, anapipto.

Mat.15:35. the multitude *to sit down* on the
Mar. 6:40. they *sat down* in ranks, by hundreds,
8: 6. the people *to sit down* on the ground:
Lu. 11:37. he went in, and *sat down to meat*.
14:10. go and *sit down* in the lowest room;
17: 7. Go and *sit down to meat*?
22:14. he *sat down*, and the twelve apostles
Joh. 6:10. Jesus said, Make the men *sit down*.
Joh. 6:10. So the men *sat down*, in number
13:12. his garments, *and was set down* again.
21:20. which also *leaned* on his breast

378 6 59/62 6:283 303,4137

ἀναπληρόω, anapleeroō.

Mat.13:14. in them *is fulfilled* the prophecy
1Co.14:16. shall he *that occupieth* the room
16:17. lacking on your part they *have supplied*.
Gal. 6: 2. so *fulfil* the law of Christ.
Phi. 2:30. to *supply* your lack of service
1Th. 2:16. *to fill up* their sins alway: for

379 2 59/62 1,626

ἀναπολόγητος, anapologeetos.

Ro. 1:20. so that they are *without excuse*:
2: 1. Therefore thou art *inexcusable*,

380 1 59/62 303,4428

ἀναπτύσσω, anaptusso.

Lu. 4:17. *when* he *had opened* the book,

381 3 59/62 303,681

ἀνάπτω, anapto.

Lu. 12:49. will I, if it *be* already *kindled*?
Acts28: 2. for they *kindled* a fire, *and* received
Jas. 3: 5. how great a matter a little fire *kindleth*!

382 1 59/62 1,705

ἀναρίθμητος, anarithmeetos.

Heb 11:12. sand which is by the sea shore *innumerable*.

383 2 59/62 303,4579

ἀνασείω, anasīo.

Mar 15:11. the chief priests *moved* the people.
Lu. 23: 5. saying, He *stirreth up* the people,

384 1 59/62 303,4632

ἀνασκευάζω, anaskūazo.

Acts15:24. with words, *subverting* your souls,

385 2 59/62 303,4685

ἀνασπάω, anaspao.

Lu. 14: 5. straightway *pull him out* on the sabbath
Acts11:10. all *were drawn up* again into heaven.

386 42 59/62 1:368 450

ἀνάστασις, anastasis.

Mat.22:23. which say that there is no *resurrection*,
28. in the *resurrection* whose wife
30. For in the *resurrection* they neither
31. touching the *resurrection* of the
Mar 12:18. which say there is no *resurrection*;
23. In the *resurrection* therefore,
Lu. 2:34. for the fall and *rising again* of many
14:14. at the *resurrection* of the just.
20:27. deny that there is any *resurrection*;
33. Therefore in the *resurrection* whose
35. that world, and the *resurrection* from
36. being the children of the *resurrection*.
Joh. 5:29. the *resurrection* of life; and they that have done evil, unto the *resurrection*

Joh. 11:24. rise again in the *resurrection* at
25. I am the *resurrection*, and the life:
Acts 1:22. a witness with us of his *resurrection*.
2:31. spake of the *resurrection* of Christ,
4: 2. through Jesus the *resurrection* from
33. the *resurrection* of the Lord Jesus:
17:18. unto them Jesus, and the *resurrection*.
32. heard of the *resurrection* of the dead,
23: 6. of the hope and *resurrection* of the dead
8. say that there is no *resurrection*,
24:15. there shall be a *resurrection* of the
21. Touching the *resurrection* of the dead
26:23. the first *that should rise* (lit. of *the res.*) from the dead,
Ro. 1: 4. by the *resurrection* from the dead:
6: 5. (in the likeness) of (his) *resurrection*:
1Co.15:12. there is no *resurrection* of the dead?
13. if there be no *resurrection* of the
21. also the *resurrection* of the dead.
42. So also (is) the *resurrection* of the dead
Phi. 3:10. the power of his *resurrection*, and
2Ti. 2:18. that the *resurrection* is past already;
Heb. 6: 2. of *resurrection* of the dead, and of
11:35. their dead *raised to life again*: (lit. from *res.*)
— might obtain a better *resurrection*:
1Pet. 1: 3. hope by the *resurrection* of Jesus Christ
3:21. by the *resurrection* of Jesus Christ:
Rev 20: 5. This (is) the first *resurrection*.
6. hath part in the first *resurrection*:

387 3 60/63 450

ἀναστατόω, anastatoō.

Acts17: 6. *that have turned* the world *upside down*
21:38. before these days *madest an uproar*,
Gal. 5:12. were even cut off *which trouble* you.

388 1 60/63 7:572 303,4717

ἀνασταυρόω, anastauroō.

Heb. 6: 6. seeing they *crucify* to themselves the Son of God *afresh*,

389 1 60/63 303,4727

ἀναστενάζω, anastenazo.

Mar. 8:12. he *sighed deeply* in his spirit, *and*

390 11 60/63 7:714 303,4762

ἀναστρέφω, anastrepho.

Mat.17:22. *while* they *abode* in Galilee, Jesus
Joh. 2:15. changers' money, and *overthrew* the tables;
Acts 5:22. not in the prison, they *returned, and*
15:16. After this I *will return*, and will build
2Co. 1:12. *had* our *conversation* in the world,
Eph. 2. 3. we all *had* our *conversation* in
1Ti. 3:15. *to behave* thyself in the house of God,
Heb10:33. whilst ye became companions of them *that were so used*.
13:18. in all things willing *to live* honestly.
1Pet. 1:17. *pass* the time of your sojourning
2Pet. 2:18. from them *who live* in error.

391 13 61/63 7:714 390

ἀναστροφή, anastrophee.

Gal. 1:13. ye have heard of my *conversation* in
Eph. 4:22. concerning the former *conversation*
1Ti 4:12. in word, in *conversation*, in charity,
Heb 13: 7. the end of (their) *conversation*:
Jas. 3:13. shew out of a good *conversation* his
1Pet. 1:15. holy in all manner of *conversation*;
18. from your vain *conversation*
2:12. Having your *conversation* honest
3: 1. won by the *conversation* of the wives;
2. they behold your chaste *conversation*
16. your good *conversation* in Christ.
2Pet. 2: 7. the filthy *conversation* of the wicked:
3:11. in (all) holy *conversation* and godliness,

392 1 61/63 8:27 303,5021

ἀνατάσσομαι, anatassomai.

Lu. 1: 1. *to set forth in order* a declaration of

393 9 61/63 1:351 303 rt 5056

ἀνατέλλω, anatello.

Mat. 4:16. shadow of death light *is sprung up*.
5:45. *maketh* his sun *to rise* on the evil and on
13: 6. *when* the sun *was up*, they were scorched;
Mar. 4: 6. *when* the sun *was up*, it was scorched;
16: 2. unto the sepulchre *at the rising of* the sun.
Lu. 12:54. When ye see a cloud *rise* out of the west,
Heb 7:14. our Lord *sprang* out of Juda; of
Jas. 1:11. For the sun is no sooner *risen* with
2Pet. 1:19. the day star *arise* in your hearts:

394 2 61/63 1:353 303,5087

ἀνατίθημι, anatitheemi.

Acts25:14. Festus *declared* Paul's cause unto
Gal. 2: 2. *communicated* unto them that

395 10 64/64 1:351 393

ἀνατολή, anatolee.

Mat. 2: 1. wise men from the *east* to Jerusalem,
2. we have seen his star in the *east*,
9. the star, which they saw in the *east*,
8:11. shall come from the *east* and west, and
24:27. the lightning cometh out of the *east*,
Lu. 1:78. the *dayspring* from on high hath
13:29. they shall come from the *east*, and
Rev. 7: 2. angel ascending from the east, (lit. from the *rising* of the sun)
16:12. the way of the kings of the east (lit. from the *rising* of the sun) might
21:13. On the *east* three gates; on the north

396 2 62/64 303,rt 5157

ἀνατρέπω, anatrepo.

2Ti. 2:18. *overthrow* the faith of some.
Tit. 1:11. who *subvert* whole houses, teaching

397 3 62/64 303,5142

ἀνατρέφω, anatrepho.

Acts 7.20. *nourished up* in his father's house
21. *nourished* him for her own son.
22: 3. yet *brought up* in this city at the

398 2 62/64 303,5316

ἀναφαίνομαι, anaphainomai.

Lu. 19:11. kingdom of God should immediately *appear*.
Acts21: 3. *when we had discovered* Cyprus.

399 10 62/64 9:56 303,5342

ἀναφέρω, anaphero.

Mat.17: 1. *bringeth* them *up* into an high
Mar. 9: 2. *leadeth* them *up* into an high
Lu. 24:51. from them, and *carried up* into heaven.
Heb. 7:27. those high priests, *to offer up* sacrifice,
— *when* he *offered up* himself.
9:28. once offered *to bear* the sins of many;
13:15. *let* us *offer* the sacrifice of praise
Jas. 2:21. *when* he *had offered* Isaac his son upon
1Pet.2: 5. *to offer up* spiritual sacrifices,
24. his own self *bare* our sins in

400 1 62/64 303,5455

ἀναφωνέω, anaphōneo.

Lu. 1:42. she *spake out* with a loud voice,

401 1 62/64 303 *cheo* (to pour)

ἀνάχυσις, anakusis.

1Pet.4: 4. to the same *excess* of riot, speaking

402 14 62/64 303,5562

ἀναχωρέω, anakōreo.

Mat. 2:12. they *departed* into their own country
13. *when* they *were departed*, behold,
14. by night, and *departed* into Egypt
22. he *turned aside* into the parts
4:12. into prison, he *departed* into Galilee;
9:24. He said unto them, *Give place*:
12:15. he *withdrew* him*self* from thence.
14:13. he *departed* thence by ship into a
15:21. *departed* into the coasts of Tyre and Sidon.
27: 5. in the temple, and *departed*, and went
Mar. 3: 7. Jesus *withdrew* him*self* with his
Joh. 6:15. he *departed* again into a mountain
Acts23:19. *went* (with him) *aside* privately, and
26:31. *when* they *were gone aside*, they

403 1 63/64 9:608 404

ἀνάψυξις, anapsuxis.

Acts 3:19(20). the times of *refreshing* shall

404 1 63/64 9:608 303,5594

ἀναψύχω, anapsuko.

2Ti. 1:16. for he oft *refreshed* me, and was not

405 1 63/64 435,4228

ἀνδραποδιστής, andrapodistees.

1Ti. 1:10. for *menstealers*, for liars, for perjured

407 1 63/64 1:360 435

ἀνδρίζομαι, andrizomai.

1Co.16:13. *quit* you *like men*, be strong.

409 1 63/65 435,5408

ἀνδροφόνος, androphonos.

1Ti. 1: 9. murderers of mothers, for *manslayers*

410 5 63/65 1:356 1,1458

ἀνέγκλητος, anenkleetos.

1Co.1: 8. (that ye may be) *blameless* in the
Col. 1:22. holy and unblameable and *unreprovable*
1Ti. 3:10. office of a deacon, being (found) *blameless*.
Tit. 1: 6. If any be *blameless*, the husband
7. For a bishop must be *blameless*,

411 11 63/65 1,1555

ἀνεκδιήγητος, anekdieegeetos.

2Co. 9:15. Thanks (be) unto God for his *unspeakable* gift.

412 1 63/65 1,1583

ἀνεκλάλητος, aneklaleetos.

1Pet. 1: 8. with joy *unspeakable* and full of glory:

413 1 63/65 1,1587

ἀνέκλειπτος, aneklīptos.

Lu. 12:33. treasure in the heavens *that faileth not*,

414 6 63/65 1:359 430

ἀνεκτότερος, anektoteros.

Mat.10:15. It shall be *more tolerable* for the
11:22. It shall be *more tolerable* for Tyre and
24. it shall be *more tolerable* for the land.
Mar. 6:11. It shall be *more tolerable* for Sodom
Lu. 10:12. it shall be *more tolerable* in that day
14. it shall be *more tolerable* for Tyre and

415 1 63/65 2:477 1,1655

ἀνελεήμων, anele-eemōn.

Ro. 1:31. natural affection, implacable, *unmerciful*:

416 1 64/65 417

ἀνεμίζομαι, anemizomai.

Jas. 1: 6. *driven with the wind* and tossed.

417 31 64/65 rt 109

ἄνεμος, anemos.

Mat. 7:25. floods came, and the *winds* blew,
27. the floods came, and the *winds* blew, and
8:26. rebuked the *winds* and the sea;
27. that even the *winds* and the sea obey him
11. 7. A reed shaken with the *wind*?
14:24. for the *wind* was contrary.
30. when he saw the *wind* boisterous,
32. come into the ship, the *wind* ceased.
24:31. his elect from the four *winds*,
Mar. 4:37. there arose a great storm of *wind*,
39. he arose, and rebuked the *wind*,
— the *wind* ceased, and there was a
41. that even the *wind* and the sea obey
6:48. for the *wind* was contrary unto
51. into the ship; and the *wind* ceased:
13:27. his elect from the four *winds*,
Lu. 7:24. A reed shaken with the *wind*?
8:23. there came down a storm of *wind*
24. he arose, and rebuked the *wind* and the
25. commandeth even the *winds* and water,
Joh. 6:18. by reason of a great *wind* that blew.
Acts27: 4. because the *winds* were contrary.
7. the *wind* not suffering us, we
14. arose against it a tempestuous *wind*,
15. could not bear up into the *wind*,
Eph. 4:14. carried about with every *wind*
Jas. 3: 4. (are) driven of fierce *winds*, yet
Jude 12. without water, carried about of *winds*;

Rev. 6:13. when she is shaken of a mighty *wind*.
7: 1. holding the four *winds* of the earth, that the *wind* should not blow

418 1 64/65 1,rt 1735

ἀνένδεκτον, anendekton.

Lu. 17: 1. It is *impossible* but that offences

419 1 64/65 1:357 1,1830

ἀνεξερεύνητος, anexerūneetos.

Ro. 11:33. how *unsearchable* (are) his judgments,

420 1 64/65 3:469 430,2556

ἀνεξίκακος, anexikakos.

2Ti. 2:24. gentle unto all (men), apt to teach, *patient*,

421 2 64/65 1:358 1,1537 2487

ἀνεξιχνίαστος, anexikniastos.

Ro. 11:33. his ways *past finding out!*
Eph. 3: 8. the *unsearchable* riches of Christ;

422 1 64/65 1,1909,153

ἀνεπαίσχυντος, anepaiskuntos.

2Ti. 2:15. a workman *that needeth not to be ashamed,*

423 3 64/65 4:5 1,1949

ἀνεπίληπτος, anepileeptos.

1Ti. 3: 2. A bishop then must be *blameless*,
5: 7. that they may be *blameless*.
6:14. without spot, *unrebukeable*, until

424 3 64/65 303,2064

ἀνέρχομαι, anerkomai.

Joh. 6: 3. Jesus *went up* into a mountain,
Gal. 1:17. Neither *went* I *up* to Jerusalem to
18. after three years I *went up* to Jerusalem

425 5 64/66 1:367 447

ἄνεσις, anesis.

Acts24:23. to let (him) have *liberty*, and that he
2Co. 2:13. I had no *rest* in my spirit,
7: 5. our flesh had no *rest*, but we were
8:13. (I mean) not that other men be *eased*,
2Th. 1: 7. you who are troubled *rest* with us,

426 2 64/66 303
etazō (to test)

ἀνετάζω, anetazō.

Acts22:24. should *be examined* by scourging,
29. which should *have examined* him:

427 3 64/66 cf 1

ἄνευ, anū.

Mat.10:29. fall on the ground *without* your Father.
1Pet. 3: 1. may *without* the word be won
4: 9. hospitality one to another *without* grudging.

428 1 65/66 1,2111

ἀνεύθετος, anūthetos.

Acts27:12. the haven was *not commodious* to

429 2 65/66 303,2147

ἀνευρίσκω, anūriskō.

Lu. 2:16. with haste, and *found* Mary, and Joseph,
Acts21: 4. *finding* disciples, we tarried there

430 15 65/66 1:359 303,2192

ἀνέχομαι, anekomai.

Mat.17:17. how long *shall* I *suffer* you?
Mar. 9:19. how long *shall* I *suffer* you?
Lu. 9:41. shall I be with you, and *suffer* you?
Acts18:14. would that I *should bear with* you:
1Co. 4:12. being persecuted, we *suffer* it:
2Co.11: 1. could *bear with* me a little in (my) folly: and indeed *bear with* me.
4. ye might well *bear with* (him).
19. For ye *suffer* fools gladly, seeing
20. For ye *suffer*, if a man bring
Eph. 4: 2. *forbearing* one another in love;
Col. 3:13. *Forbearing* one another, and forgiving
2Th. 1: 4. persecutions and tribulations that ye *endure:*
2Ti. 4: 3. when they *will* not *endure* sound
Heb13:22. brethren, *suffer* the word of exhortation:

431 1 65/66 1
nepos (brood)

ἀνεψιός, anepsios.

Col. 4:10. Marcus, *sister's son* to Barnabas,

432 1 65/66

ἄνηθον, aneethon.

Mat.23:23. tithe of mint, and *anise* and cummin,

433 3 65/66 1:360 303,2240

ἀνήκω, aneeko.

Eph. 5: 4. nor jesting, which are not *convenient:*
Col. 3:18. own husbands, as *it is fit* in the Lord.
Philem. 8. injoin thee that *which is convenient*,

434 1 65/66 1
hemeros (lame)

ἀνήμερος, aneemeros.

2Ti. 3: 3. false accusers, incontinent, *fierce*,

435 215 65/66 1:360 cf 444

ἀνήρ, aneer.

Mat. 1:16. begat Joseph the *husband* of Mary,
19. Then Joseph her *husband*, being
7:24. I will liken him unto a wise *man*,
26. be likened unto a foolish *man*,
12:41. The *men* of Nineveh shall rise
14:21. were about five thousand *men*,
35. when the *men* of that place had
15:38. that did eat were four thousand *men*.
Mar. 6:20. that he was a just *man* and an holy,
44. were about five thousand *men*.
10: 2. Is it lawful for a *man* to put
12. a woman shall put away her *husband*,
Lu. 1:27. espoused to a *man* whose name
34. this be, seeing I know not a *man*?
2:36. lived with an *husband* seven
5: 8. for I am a sinful *man*, O Lord.
12. behold a *man* full of leprosy:
18. behold, *men* brought in a bed
7:20. When the *men* were come unto
8:27. a certain *man*, which had devils
38. Now the *man* out of whom the
41. there came a *man* named Jairus,
9:14. were about five thousand *men*.

Lu. 9:30. there talked with him two *men*,
32. the two *men* that stood with him.
33. behold, a *man* of the company
11:31. with the *men* of this generation,
32. The *men* of Nineve shall rise
14:24. none of those *men* which were
16:18. is put away from (her) *husband*
17:12. ten *men* that were lepers, which
19: 2. (there was) a *man* named Zacchæus,
7. guest with a *man* that is a sinner.
22:63. the *men* that held Jesus mocked
23:50. (there was) a *man* named Joseph, (and he was) a good *man*, and a just:
24: 4. two *men* stood by them in
19. which was a prophet mighty in (lit. a *man*, a prophet)
Joh. 1:13. nor of the will of *man*, but of God.
30. After me cometh a *man* which
4:16. Go, call thy *husband*, and come
17. answered and said, I have no *husband*.
— hast well said, I have no *husband*:
18. For thou hast had five *husbands*; and he whom thou now hast is not thy *husband*:
6:10. So the *men* sat down, in number
Acts 1:10. two *men* stood by them in white
11. Ye *men* of Galilee, why stand ye
16. *Men* (and) brethren, this scripture
21. these *men* which have companied
2: 5. Jews, devout *men*, out of every nation
14. Ye *men* of Judæa, and all (ye) that dwell
22. Ye *men* of Israel, hear these words; Jesus of Nazareth, a *man* approved of God
29. *Men* (and) brethren, let me freely
37. *Men* (and) brethren, what shall we do?
3: 2. a certain *man* lame from his
12. Ye *men* of Israel, why marvel
14. desired a murderer (lit. a *man* a murderer) to be granted
4: 4. the number of the *men* was about
5: 1. a certain *man* named Ananias,
9. have buried thy *husband* (are)
10. buried (her) by her *husband*.
14. multitudes both of *men* and women.
25. the *men* whom ye put in prison
35. Ye *men* of Israel, take heed to
36. to whom a number of *men*, about
6: 3. seven *men* of honest report,
5. a *man* full of faith and of the Holy
11. Then they suborned *men*, which
7: 2. *Men*, brethren, and fathers, hearken,
26. saying, *Sirs*, ye are brethren; why
8: 2. devout *men* carried Stephen
3. haling *men* and women committed
9. was a certain *man*, called Simon,
12. were baptized, both *men* and women.
27. behold, a *man* of Ethiopia,
9: 2. whether they were *men* or women,
7. the *men* which journeyed
12. a *man* named Ananias coming
13. heard by many of this *man*,
38. they sent unto him two *men*,
10: 1. There was a certain *man* in
5. now send *men* to Joppa, and call
17. the *men* which were sent from
19. Behold, three *men* seek thee.
21. down to the *men* which were sent
22. the centurion, a just *man*, and one
28. for a *man* that is a Jew to keep
30. behold, a *man* stood before me
11: 3. in to *men* uncircumcised,
11. there were three *men* already come
12. we entered into the *man's* house:
Acts 11:13. said unto him, Send *men* to Joppa,
20. were *men* of Cyprus and Cyrene, which,
24. he was a good *man*, and full of the Holy
13: 7. Sergius Paulus, a prudent *man*; who
15. saying, (Ye) *men* (and) brethren,
16. said, *Men* of Israel, and ye that fear God,
21. a *man* of the tribe of Benjamin,
22. a *man* after mine own heart,
26. *Men* (and) brethren, children of the
38. therefore, *men* (and) brethren, that
14: 8. there sat a certain *man* at Lystra,
15. *Sirs*, why do ye these things?
15: 7. said unto them, *Men* (and) brethren,
13. *Men* (and) brethren, hearken unto
22. to send chosen *men* of their own
— chief *men* among the brethren:
25. to send chosen *men* unto you
16: 9. There stood a *man* of Macedonia,
17: 5. certain lewd *fellows* of the baser
12. were Greeks, and of *men*, not a few.
22. said, (Ye) *men* of Athens, I perceive
31. by (that) *man* whom he hath
34. certain *men* clave unto him, and
18:24. an eloquent *man*, (and) mighty
19: 7. all the *men* were about twelve.
25. *Sirs*, ye know that by this
35. he said, (Ye) *men* of Ephesus,
37. ye have brought hither these *men*,
20:30. of your own selves shall *men* arise,
21:11. bind the *man* that owneth this
23. We have four *men* which have a
26. Then Paul took the *men*, and the
28. Crying out, *Men* of Israel, help:
38. four thousand *men* that were
22: 1. *Men*, brethren, and fathers, hear ye
3. I am verily a *man* (which am) a Jew,
4. into prisons both *men* and women.
12. a devout *man* according to the law,
23: 1. said, *Men* (and) brethren, I have
6. *Men* (and) brethren, I am a Pharisee,
21. of them more than forty *men*,
27. This *man* was taken of the Jews,
30. the Jews laid wait for the *man*,
24: 5. we have found this *man* (a)
25: 5. with (me), and accuse this *man*, if
14. There is a certain *man* left in
17. commanded the *man* to be brought
23. chief captains, and principal *men*
24. all *men* which are here present
27:10. *Sirs*, I perceive that this voyage
21. *Sirs*, ye should have hearkened
25. Wherefore, *sirs*, be of good cheer.
28:17. *Men* (and) brethren, though I have
Ro. 4: 8. Blessed (is) the *man* to whom the
7: 2. by the law to (her) *husband* so long
— if the *husband* be dead, she is loosed from the law of (her) *husband*.
3. if, while (her) *husband* liveth, she be married to another *man*,
— if her *husband* be dead, she is
— she be married to another *man*.
11: 4. to myself seven thousand *men*,
1Co. 7: 2. let every woman have her own *husband*.
3. Let the *husband* render unto the
— also the wife unto the *husband*.
4. of her own body, but the *husband*: and likewise also the *husband* hath not power
10. Let not the wife depart from (her) *husband*:
11. or be reconciled to (her) *husband*: and let not the *husband* put away (his) wife.
13. the woman which hath an *husband*
14. the unbelieving *husband* is

1Co. 7:14. wife is sanctified by the *husband:*
16. whether thou shalt save (thy) *husband?* or how knowest thou, O *man*, whether
34. how she may please (her) *husband.*
39. as long as her *husband* liveth; but if her *husband* be dead,
11: 3. the head of every *man* is Christ; and the head of the woman (is) the *man;*
4. Every *man* praying or prophesying,
7. For a *man* indeed ought not to
— woman is the glory of the *man.*
8. For the *man* is not of the woman; but the woman of the *man.*
9. Neither was the *man* created for the woman; but the woman for the *man.*
11. neither is the *man* without the woman, neither the woman without the *man*,
12. as the woman (is) of the *man*, even so (is) the *man* also by the
14. that, if a *man* have long hair, it
13:11. when I became a *man*, I put away
14:35. let them ask their *husbands* at home:
2Co.11: 2. I have espoused you to one *husband*,
Gal. 4:27. than she which hath an *husband.*
Eph. 4:13. unto a perfect *man*, unto the measure
5:22. yourselves unto your own *husbands*,
23. the *husband* is the head of the wife,
24. (be) to their own *husbands* in every
25. *Husbands*, love your wives, even
28. So ought *men* to love their wives
33. that she reverence (her) *husband.*
Col. 3:18. yourselves unto your own *husbands*,
19. *Husbands*, love (your) wives, and
1Ti. 2: 8. that *men* pray every where, lifting
12. nor to usurp authority over the *man*,
3: 2. the *husband* of one wife, vigilant,
12. be the *husbands* of one wife, ruling
5: 9. having been the wife of one *man*,
Tit. 1: 6. the *husband* of one wife, having
2: 5. good, obedient to their own *husbands*,
Jas. 1: 8. A double minded *man* (is) unstable
12. Blessed (is) the *man* that endureth
20. the wrath of *man* worketh not the
23. he is like unto a *man* beholding
2: 2. assembly a *man* with a gold ring,
3: 2. the same (is) a perfect *man*, (and)
1Pet.3: 1. in subjection to your own *husbands;*
5. subjection unto their own *husbands:*
7. Likewise, ye *husbands*, dwell with
Rev.21: 2. as a bride adorned for her *husband.*

---

436 14 66/69 473,2476

ἀνθίστημι, anthisteemi.

Mat. 5:39. unto you, That ye *resist* not evil:
Lu. 21:15. not be able to gainsay nor *resist.*
Acts 6:10. were not able *to resist* the wisdom
13: 8. *withstood* them, seeking to turn
Ro. 9:19. For who *hath resisted* his will?
13: 2. *resisteth* the ordinance of God: and they *that resist* shall receive
Gal. 2:11. I *withstood* him to the face,
Eph. 6:13. able *to withstand* in the evil day,
2Ti. 3: 8. Jannes and Jambres *withstood* Moses,
— *do* these also *resist* the truth:
4:15. he hath greatly *withstood* our words.
Jas. 4: 7. *Resist* the devil, and he will flee
1Pet.5: 9. Whom *resist* stedfast in the faith,

---

437 1 66/69 5:199 473,3670

ἀνθομολογέομαι, anthomologeomai.

Lu. 2:38. *gave thanks* likewise unto the Lord,

---

438 4 66/69

ἄνθος, anthos

Jas. 1:10. because as the *flower* of the grass
11. the grass, and the *flower* thereof falleth,
1Pet. 1:24. the glory of man as the *flower* of grass.
— the *flower* thereof falleth away:

---

439 2 66/69 440

ἀνθρακία, anthrakia.

Joh. 18:18. who had made a *fire of coals;* for
21: 9. they saw a *fire of coals* there, and fish

---

440 1 66/69

ἄνθραξ, anthrax.

Ro. 12:20. thou shalt heap *coals* of fire on his

---

441 2 67/69 1:455 444,700

ἀνθρωπάρεσκος, anthrōpareskos.

Eph. 6: 6. Not with eyeservice, as *menpleasers;*
Col. 3:22. not with eyeservice, as *menpleasers;*

---

442 7 67/69 1:364 444

ἀνθρώπινος, anthrōpinos.

Ro. 6:19. I speak *after the manner of men*
1Co. 2: 4. with enticing words *of man's* wisdom,
13. not in the words which *man's* wisdom
4: 3. of you, or of *man's* judgment:
10:13. such as is *common to man:*
Jas. 3: 7. hath been tamed of *man*kind: (lit. *human* nature)
1Pet. 2:13. to every ordinance *of man* for the

---

443 3 67/69 444 *kteinō* (to kill) cf 5406

ἀνθρωποκτόνος, anthrōpoktonos.

Joh. 8:44. He was a *murderer* from the beginning,
1Joh. 3:15. hateth his brother is a *murderer:* and ye know that no *murderer* hath eternal life

---

444 559 67/69 1:364 435 _*ops* (countenance)

ἄνθρωπος, anthrōpos.

Mat. 4: 4. *Man* shall not live by bread
19. I will make you fishers of *men.*
5:13. to be trodden under foot of *men.*
16. Let your light so shine before *men*,
19. shall teach *men* so, he shall be
6: 1. do not your alms before *men*,
2. that they may have glory of *men.*
5. that they may be seen of *men.*
14. if ye forgive *men* their trespasses,
15. if ye forgive not *men* their trespasses
16. that they may appear unto *men*
18. That thou appear not unto *men*
7: 9. what *man* is there of you, whom
12. ye would that *men* should do to you,
8: 9. For I am a *man* under authority
20. the Son of *man* hath not where
27. the *men* marvelled, saying,
9: 6. know that the Son of *man* hath
8. had given such power unto *men.*
9. he saw a *man*, named Matthew,
32. brought to him a dumb *man*
10:17. beware of *men:* for they will deliver
23. till the Son of *man* be come.
32. shall confess me before *men*,
33. shall deny me before *men*, him
35. to set a *man* at variance against
36. a *man's* foes (shall be) they of

Mat.11: 8. A *man* clothed in soft raiment?
19. The Son of *man* came eating and drinking,
and they say, Behold a *man* gluttonous,
12: 8. For the Son of *man* is Lord even
10. behold, there was a *man* which
11. What *man* shall there be among
12. then is a *man* better than a sheep?
13. Then saith he to the *man*, Stretch
31. blasphemy shall be forgiven unto *men*:
— shall not be forgiven unto *men*.
32. speaketh a word against the Son of *man*,
35. A good *man* out of the good
— an evil *man* out of the evil
36. idle word that *men* shall speak,
40. so shall the Son of *man* be three
43. unclean spirit is gone out of a *man*,
45. the last (state) of that *man* is
13:24. is likened unto a *man* which
25. while *men* slept, his enemy
28. unto them, An (lit. a *man* an) enemy hath
done this.
31. which a *man* took, and sowed in
37. soweth the good seed is the Son of *man*;
41. The Son of *man* shall send forth
44. which when a *man* hath found,
45. is like unto a merchant *man*,
52. like unto a *man* (that is) an
15: 9. doctrines the commandments of *men*.
11. goeth into the mouth defileth a *man*;
— out of the mouth, this defileth a *man*.
18. the heart; and they defile the *man*.
20. defile a *man*: but to eat with unwashen
hands defileth not a *man*.
16: 13. Whom do *men* say that I the Son of *man* am?
23. of God, but those that be of *men*.
26. For what is a *man* profited, if
— or what shall a *man* give in
27. For the Son of *man* shall come
28. till they see the Son of *man*
17: 9. until the Son of *man* be risen
12. shall also the Son of *man* suffer
14. came to him a (certain) *man*,
22. The Son of *man* shall be betrayed into the
hands of *men*:
18: 7. woe to that *man* by whom the
11. For the Son of *man* is come to
12. if a *man* have an hundred
23. heaven likened unto a *certain* king,
19: 3. Is it lawful for a *man* to put
5. this cause shall a *man* leave
6. together, let not *man* put asunder.
10. If the case of the *man* be so with
12. which were made eunuchs of *men*:
26. With *men* this is impossible;
28. when the Son of *man* shall sit
20: 1. like unto a *man* (that is) an
18. the Son of *man* shall be betrayed
28. Even as the Son of *man* came not
21:25. from heaven, or of *men*? And
26. if we shall say, Of *men*; we fear
28. A (certain) *man* had two sons;
33. There was a certain (lit. a certain *man* a)
housholder,
22: 2. heaven is like unto a *certain* king,
11. saw there a *man* which had not
16. regardest not the person of *men*.
23: 4. lay (them) on *men's* shoulders;
5. they do for to be seen of *men*:
7. to be called of *men*, Rabbi, Rabbi.
13(14). the kingdom of heaven against *men*:
28. appear righteous unto *men*, but
24:27. the coming of the Son of *man* be.
Mat.24:30. sign of the Son of *man* in heaven.
— shall see the Son of *man* coming
37. the coming of the Son of *man* be.
39. the coming of the Son of *man* be.
44. the Son of *man* cometh.
25:13. wherein the Son of *man* cometh.
14. as a *man* travelling into a far
24. that thou art an hard *man*,
31. When the Son of *man* shall come
26: 2. the Son of *man* is betrayed to be
24. Son of *man* goeth as it is written of him:
but woe unto that *man* by whom the Son
of *man* is betrayed! it had been good for
that *man* if he had not
45. the Son of *man* is betrayed into
64. shall ye see the Son of *man* sitting
72. with an oath, I do not know the *man*.
74. (saying), I know not the *man*.
27:32. they found a *man* of Cyrene,
57. there came a rich *man* of
Mar. 1:17. you to become fishers of *men*.
23. a *man* with an unclean spirit;
2:10. that the Son of *man* hath power
27. The sabbath was made for *man*, and not
man for the sabbath:
28. the Son of *man* is Lord also of
3: 1. there was a *man* there which
3. he saith unto the *man* which
5. he saith unto the *man*, Stretch
28. forgiven unto the sons of *men*,
4:26. as if a *man* should cast seed
5: 2. out of the tombs a *man* with an
8. said unto him, Come out of the *man*,
7: 7. doctrines the commandments of *men*.
8. ye hold the tradition of *men*,
11. If a *man* shall say to his father
15. There is nothing from without a *man*,
— are they that defile the *man*.
18. without entereth into the *man*,
20. That which cometh out of the *man*, that
defileth the *man*.
21. out of the heart of *men*, proceed evil
23. from within, and defile the *man*.
8:24. said, I see *men* as trees, walking.
27. Whom do *men* say that I am?
31. that the Son of *man* must suffer
33. the things that be of *men*.
36. For what shall it profit a *man*,
37. what shall a *man* give in exchange
38. of him also shall the Son of *man* be
9: 9. till the Son of *man* were risen from
12. it is written of the Son of *man*, that
31. The Son of *man* is delivered into the hands
of *men*,
10: 7. this cause shall a *man* leave his
9. together, let not *man* put asunder.
27. With *men* (it is) impossible, but not
33. the Son of *man* shall be delivered
45. For even the Son of *man* came
11: 2. a colt tied, whereon never *man* sat;
30. was (it) from heaven, or of *men*?
32. if we shall say, Of *men*; they
12: 1. A (certain) *man* planted a vineyard,
14. regardest not the person of *men*, but
13:26. shall they see the Son of *man* coming
34. (Son of man is) as a *man* taking a far
14:13. there shall meet you a *man* bearing
21. The Son of *man* indeed goeth,
— woe to that *man* by whom the Son of *man* is
betrayed! good were it for that *man* if he
41. the Son of *man* is betrayed into
62. ye shall see the Son of *man* sitting

Mar.14:71. I know not this *man* of whom
15:39. Truly this *man* was the Son of God.
Lu. 1:25. take away my reproach among *men*.
2:14. peace, good will toward *men*.
15. the (lit. the *men* the) shepherds said one to another,
25. there was a *man* in Jerusalem,
— the same *man* (was) just and devout,
52. stature, and in favour with God and *man*.
4: 4. That *man* shall not live by bread
33. there was a *man*, which had a
5:10. henceforth thou shalt catch *men*.
18. brought in a bed a *man* which
20. said unto him, *Man*, thy sins are
24. that the Son of *man* hath power
6: 5. That the Son of *man* is Lord also
6. there was a *man* whose right hand
8. said to the *man* which had the
10. he said unto the *man*, Stretch
22. Blessed are ye, when *men* shall
— as evil, for the Son of *man's* sake.
26. when all *men* shall speak well
31. as ye would that *men* should do
45. A good *man* out of the good treasure
— an evil *man* out of the evil treasure
48. He is like a *man* which built
49. is like a *man* that without a foundation
7: 8. I also am a *man* set under authority,
25. A *man* clothed in soft raiment?
31. shall I liken the *men* of this generation?
34. The Son of *man* is come eating
— Behold a gluttonous *man*, and a
8:29. spirit to come out of the *man*.
33. Then went the devils out of the *man*,
35. came to Jesus, and found the *man*,
9:22. The Son of *man* must suffer
25. For what is a *man* advantaged, if
26. of him shall the Son of *man* be
44. for the Son of *man* shall be delivered into the hands of *men*.
56. For the Son of *man* is not come to destroy *men's* lives,
58. the Son of *man* hath not where
10:30. A certain *man* went down from
11:24. unclean spirit is gone out of a *man*,
26. the last (state) of that *man* is worse
30. so shall also the Son of *man* be to this
44. the *men* that walk over (them) are
46. (ye) lawyers! for ye lade *men* with
12: 8. Whosoever shall confess me before *men*, him shall the Son of *man* also
9. he that denieth me before *men*
10. a word against the Son of *man*,
14. said unto him, *Man*, who made me
16. The ground of a certain rich *man*
36. ye yourselves like unto *men* that
40. for the Son of *man* cometh at
13: 4. they were sinners above all *men*
19. mustard seed, which a *man* took,
14: 2. there was a certain *man* before
16. A certain *man* made a great supper,
30. Saying, This *man* began to build,
15: 4. What *man* of you, having an
11. he said, A certain *man* had two
16: 1. There was a certain rich *man*,
15. which justify yourselves before *men*;
— esteemed among *men* is abomination
19. There was a certain rich *man*,
17:22. one of the days of the Son of *man*,
24. so shall also the Son of *man* be
26. in the days of the Son of *man*.
30. when the Son of *man* is revealed.

Lu. 18: 2. feared not God, neither regarded *man*:
4. I fear not God, nor regard *man*;
8. when the Son of *man* cometh,
10. Two *men* went up into the temple
11. that I am not as other *men* (are),
27. which are impossible with *men* are
31. concerning the Son of *man* shall
19:10. For the Son of *man* is come to seek
12. A certain noble*man* went into
21. because thou art an austere *man*:
22. knewest that I was an austere *man*,
30. whereon yet never *man* sat:
20: 4. was it from heaven, or of *men*?
6. if we say, Of *men*; all the people
9. A certain *man* planted a vineyard,
21:26. *Men's* hearts failing them for fear,
27. see the Son of *man* coming in a cloud
36. to stand before the Son of *man*.
22:10. there shall a *man* meet you, bearing
22. Son of *man* goeth, as it was determined: but woe unto that *man* by whom
48. betrayest thou the Son of *man*
58. Peter said, *Man*, I am not.
60. Peter said, *Man*, I know not what
69. shall the Son of *man* sit on the
23: 4. I find no fault in this *man*.
6. whether the *man* were a Galilæan.
14. Ye have brought this *man* unto me,
— have found no fault in this *man*
47. Certainly this was a righteous *man*.
24: 7. The Son of *man* must be delivered into the hands of sinful *men*,
Joh. 1: 4. the life was the light of *men*.
6. There was a *man* sent from God,
9. which lighteth every *man* that
51(52). descending upon the Son of *man*.
2:10. Every *man* at the beginning doth
25. that any should testify of *man*: for he knew what was in *man*.
3: 1. There was a *man* of the Pharisees,
4. How can a *man* be born when
13. (even) the Son of *man* which is
14. so must the Son of *man* be
19. *men* loved darkness rather than
27. A *man* can receive nothing,
4:28. into the city, and saith to the *men*,
29. Come, see a *man*, which told me
50. the *man* believed the word that
5: 5. a certain *man* was there, which
7. Sir, I have no *man*, when the
9. immediately the *man* was made
12. What *man* is that which said
15. The *man* departed, and told the
27. because he is the Son of *man*.
34. I receive not testimony from *man*:
41. I receive not honour from *men*.
6:10. Said, Make the *men* sit down.
14. Then those *men*, when they had
27. which the Son of *man* shall
53. the flesh of the Son of *man*, and
62. ye shall see the Son of *man* ascend
7:22. ye on the sabbath day circumcise a *man*.
23. If a *man* on the sabbath day receive
— I have made a *man* every whit
46. Never *man* spake like this *man*.
51. Doth our law judge (any) *man*, before
8:17. the testimony of two *men* is true.
28. have lifted up the Son of *man*,
40. a *man* that hath told you the
9: 1. he saw a *man* which was blind
11. A *man* that is called Jesus
16. This *man* is not of God, because

Joh. 9:16. Others said, How can a *man* that
24. again called they the *man*
— we know that this *man* is a
30. The *man* answered and said unto
10:33. thou, being a *man*, makest
11:47. this *man* doeth many miracles.
50. that one *man* should die for
12:23. that the Son of *man* should be
34. The Son of *man* must be lifted up? who is this Son of *man*?
43. loved the praise of *men* more
13:31. Now is the Son of *man* glorified,
16:21. for joy that a *man* is born into
17: 6. manifested thy name unto the *men*
18:14. that one *man* should die for the
17. also (one) of this *man's* disciples?
29. accusation bring ye against this *man*?
19: 5. saith unto them, Behold the *man*!
Acts 4: 9. deed done to the impotent *man*,
12. given among *men*, whereby we
13. were unlearned and ignorant *men*,
14. beholding the *man* which was
16. What shall we do to these *men*?
17. henceforth to no *man* in this
22. the *man* was above forty years
5: 4. thou hast not lied unto *men*, but
28. to bring this *man's* blood upon us.
29. to obey God rather than *men*.
35. to do as touching these *men*.
38. Refrain from these *men*, and let them
— counsel or this work be of *men*,
6:13. This *man* ceaseth not to speak
7:56. the Son of *man* standing on the
9:33. he found a certain *man* named
10:26. Stand up; I myself also am a *man*.
28. should not call any *man* common
12:22. voice of a god, and not of a *man*.
14:11. down to us in the likeness of *men*.
15. We also are *men* of like passions
15:17. the residue of *men* might seek
26. *Men* that have hazarded their
16:17. These *men* are the servants of
20. saying, These *men*, being Jews,
35. saying, Let those *men* go.
37. uncondemned, being Romans, (lit. Roman *men*) and
17:25. Neither is worshipped with *men's* hands,
26. made of one blood all nations of *men*
29. graven by art and *man's* device.
30. commandeth all *men* every where
18:13. This (fellow) persuadeth *men* to
19:16. the *man* in whom the evil spirit
35. what *man* is there that knoweth
21:28. This is the *man*, that teacheth all
39. Paul said, I am a *man* (which am)
22:15. shalt be his witness unto all *men*
25. scourge a *man* that is a Roman,
26. thou doest: for this *man* is a Roman.
23: 9. We find no evil in this *man*:
24:16. offence toward God, and (toward) *men*.
25:16. to deliver any *man* to die, before
22. I would also hear the *man* myself.
26:31. This *man* doeth nothing worthy
32. This *man* might have been set
28: 4. No doubt this *man* is a murderer,
Ro. 1:18. ungodliness and unrighteousness of *men*,
23. image made like to corruptible *man*,
2: 1. inexcusable, O *man*, whosoever
3. thinkest thou this, O *man*, that
9. every soul of *man* that doeth evil,
16. shall judge the secrets of *men*
29 whose praise (is) not of *men*, but of God.
Ro. 3: 4. God be true, but every *man* a liar;
5. taketh vengeance? I speak as a *man*
28. that a *man* is justified by faith
4: 6. the blessedness of the *man*, unto whom
5:12. as by one *man* sin entered into
— so death passed upon all *men*,
15. gift by grace, (which is) by one *man*,
18. (judgment came) upon all *men*
— (the free gift came) upon all *men* unto
19. as by one *man's* disobedience many
6: 6. that our old *man* is crucified
7: 1. dominion over a *man* as long as
22. law of God after the inward *man*:
24. O wretched *man* that I am!
9:20. O *man*, who art thou that repliest
10: 5. the *man* which doeth those things
12:17. honest in the sight of all *men*.
18. live peaceably with all *men*.
14:18. acceptable to God, and approved of *men*.
20. (it is) evil for that *man* who eateth
1Co. 1:25. foolishness of God is wiser than *men*; and the weakness of God is stronger than *men*.
2: 5. not stand in the wisdom of *men*,
9. entered into the heart of *man*, the
11. what *man* knoweth the things of a *man*, save the spirit of *man*
14. the natural *man* receiveth not
3: 3. are ye not carnal, and walk as *men*?
21. Therefore let no man glory in *men*.
4: 1. Let a *man* so account of us, as
9. unto the world, and to angels, and to *men*.
6:18. Every sin that a *man* doeth is
7: 1. (It is) good for a *man* not to touch
7. I would that all *men* were even
23. be not ye the servants of *men*.
26. (it is) good for a *man* so to be.
9: 8. Say I these things as a *man*?
11:28. let a *man* examine himself,
13: 1. with the tongues of *men* and of angels,
14: 2. speaketh not unto *men*, but unto
3. speaketh unto *men* (to) edification,
15:19. we are of all *men* most miserable.
21. since by *man* (came) death, by *man* (came) also the resurrection
32. If after the manner of *men* I have
39. (there is) one (kind of) flesh of *men*,
45. The first *man* Adam was made
47. The first *man* (is) of the earth, earthy: the second *man* (is) the Lord
2Co. 3: 2. known and read of all *men*:
4: 2. to every *man's* conscience in
16. though our outward *man* perish,
5:11. we persuade *men*; but we are
8:21. also in the sight of *men*.
12: 2. I knew a *man* in Christ above
3. I knew such a *man*, whether
4. is not lawful for a *man* to utter.
Gal. 1: 1. Paul, an apostle, not of *men*, neither by *man*,
10. For do I now persuade *men*, or God? or do I seek to please *men*? for if I yet pleased *men*, I
11. preached of me is not after *man*.
12. I neither received it of *man*,
2: 6. God accepteth no *man's* person:
16. a *man* is not justified by the
3:12. The *man* that doeth them shall
15. I speak after the manner of *men*; Though (it be) but a *man's* covenant,
5: 3. I testify again to every *man*
6: 1. if a *man* be overtaken in a
7. for whatsoever a *man* soweth,
Eph. 2:15. himself of twain one new *man*,

Eph. 3: 5. known unto the sons of *men*,
16. by his Spirit in the inner *man*;
4: 8. captivity captive, and gave gifts unto *men*.
14. by the sleight of *men*, (and) cunning
22. the old *man*, which is corrupt
24. that ye put on the new *man*,
5:31. shall a *man* leave his father
6: 7. as to the Lord, and not to *men*:
Phi. 2: 7. was made in the likeness of *men*:
8. being found in fashion as a *man*,
4: 5. moderation be known unto all *men*.
Col. 1:28. Whom we preach, warning every *man*, and teaching every *man* in all wisdom; that we may present every *man*
2: 8. vain deceit, after the tradition of *men*,
22. commandments and doctrines of *men*?
3: 9. ye have put off the old *man* with
23. to the Lord, and not unto *men*;
1Th. 2: 4. not as pleasing *men*, but God,
6. Nor of *men* sought we glory, neither
13. received (it) not (as) the word of *men*,
15. please not God, and are contrary to all *men*:
4: 8. despiseth not *man*, but God,
2Th. 2: 3. that *man* of sin be revealed, the
3: 2. from unreasonable and wicked *men*:
1Ti. 2: 1. of thanks, be made for all *men*;
4. Who will have all *men* to be saved,
5. one mediator between God and *men*, the *man* Christ Jesus;
4:10. who is the saviour of all *men*,
5:24. Some *men's* sins are open beforehand,
6: 5. disputings of *men* of corrupt minds,
9. which drown *men* in destruction
11. But thou, O *man* of God, flee
16. whom no *man* hath seen, nor
2Ti. 2: 2. commit thou to faithful *men*,
3: 2. For *men* shall be lovers of their
8. *men* of corrupt minds, reprobate
13. evil *men* and seducers shall wax
17. That the *man* of God may be
Tit. 1:14. commandments of *men*, that
2:11. salvation hath appeared to all *men*,
3: 2. shewing all meekness unto all *men*.
8. are good and profitable unto *men*.
10. A *man* that is an heretick after
Heb 2: 6. What is *man*, that thou art
— or the son of *man*, that thou
5: 1. priest taken from among *men* is ordained for *men* in things
6:16. For *men* verily swear by the greater:
7: 8. here *men* that die receive tithes;
28. maketh *men* high priests which
8: 2. the Lord pitched, and not *man*.
9:27. as it is appointed unto *men*
13: 6. I will not fear what *man* shall
Jas. 1: 7. let not that *man* think that he
19. let every *man* be swift to hear,
2:20. wilt thou know, O vain *man*,
24. that by works a *man* is justified,
3: 8. the tongue can no *man* tame;
9. therewith curse we *men*, which
5:17. Elias was a *man* subject to like
1Pet. 1:24. all the glory of *man* as the flower
2: 4. disallowed indeed of *men*, but
15. silence the ignorance of foolish *men*
3: 4. the hidden *man* of the heart,
4: 2. in the flesh to the lusts of *men*.
6. according to *men* in the flesh,
2Pet. 1:21. not in old time by the will of *man*: but holy *men* of God spake (as they were)
2:16. dumb ass speaking with *man's* voice
2Pet. 3: 7. judgment and perdition of ungodly
1Joh. 5: 9. If we receive the witness of *men*,
Jude 4. there are certain *men* crept in
Rev. 1:13. (one) like unto the Son of *man*.
4: 7. third beast had a face as a *man*,
8:11. many *men* died of the waters,
9: 4. only those *men* which have not
5. a scorpion, when he striketh a *man*.
6. those days shall *men* seek death.
7. faces (were) as the faces of *men*.
10. their power (was) to hurt *men*
15. to slay the third part of *men*.
18. was the third part of *men* killed,
20. the rest of the *men* which were
11:13. were slain of *men* seven thousand:
13:13. on the earth in the sight of *men*,
18. for it is the number of a *man*,
14: 4. were redeemed from among *men*,
14. sat like unto the Son of *man*,
16: 2. grievous sore upon the *men*
8. unto him to scorch *men* with fire.
9. *men* were scorched with great
18. as was not since *men* were
21. there fell upon *men* a great hail
— and *men* blasphemed God
18:13. chariots, and slaves, and souls of *men*.
21: 3. tabernacle of God (is) with *men*,
17. (according to) the measure of a *man*,

445 1 68/75 446

ἀνθυπατεύω, anthupatūo.

Acts 18:12. *when* Gallio *was the deputy* of

446 4 68/75 473,5228

ἀνθύπατος, anthupatos.

Acts 13: 7. was with the *deputy* of the country,
8. to turn away the *deputy* from the
12. Then the *deputy*, when he saw
19:38. the law is open, and there are *deputies*,

447 4 69/75 1:367 303
hiemi (to send)

ἀνίημι, anieemi.

Acts 16:26. every one's bands *were loosed*.
27:40. *loosed* the rudder bands, and hoised
Eph. 6: 9. unto them, *forbearing* threatening:
Heb 13: 5. he hath said, I *will* never *leave* thee,

448 1 69/65 1,2436

ἀνίλεως, anileōs.

Jas. 2:13. shall have judgment *without mercy*,

449 3 69/75 4:946 1,3538

ἄνιπτος, aniptos.

Mat. 15:20. to eat with *unwashen* hands
Mar 7: 2. to say, with *unwashen*, hands,
5. eat bread with *unwashen* hands?

450 112 69/75 1:368 303,2476

ἀνίστημι, anisteemi.

Mat. 9: 9. Follow me. And he *arose, and* followed him.
12:41. men of Nineveh *shall rise* in
17: 9. the Son of man *be risen again* from
20:19. the third day he *shall rise again*.
22:24. *raise up* seed unto his brother.
26:62. the high priest *arose, and* said
Mar 1:35. *rising up* a great while before

Mar. 2:14. Follow me. And he *arose and* followed
3:26. if Satan *rise up* against himself,
5:42. the damsel *arose*, and walked;
7:24. from thence he *arose, and* went into
8:31. after three days *rise again.*
9: 9. the Son of man *were risen* from the
10. what *the rising* from the dead (lit. *to rise*)
27. lifted him up; and he *arose.*
31. he *shall rise* the third day.
10: 1. he *arose* from thence, *and* cometh
34. the third day he *shall rise again.*
50. *rose, and* came to Jesus.
12:23. therefore, when they *shall rise,*
25. when they *shall rise* from the
14:57. there *arose* certain, *and* bare false
60. priest *stood up* in the midst, *and*
16: 9. *when* (Jesus) *was risen* early
Lu. 1:39. Mary *arose* in those days, *and*
4:16. sabbath day, and *stood up* for to read,
29. *rose up, and* thrust him out of the
38. he *arose* out of the synagogue, *and*
39. she *arose and* ministered unto them.
5:25. immediately he *rose up* before them, *and*
28. he left all, *rose up, and* followed him.
6: 8. he *arose and* stood forth.
8:55. came again, and she *arose* straightway:
9: 8. one of the old prophets *was risen again.*
19. one of the old prophets *is risen again.*
10:25. behold, a certain lawyer *stood up,*
11: 7. I cannot *rise and* give thee.
8. Though he will not *rise and* give him,
32. *shall rise up* in the judgment
15:18. I will *arise and* go to my father,
20. he *arose, and* came to his father.
16:31. though one *rose* from the dead.
17:19. said unto him, *Arise,* go thy way:
18:33. the third day he *shall rise again.*
22:45. *when* he *rose up* from prayer,
46. *rise and* pray, lest ye enter into
23: 1. whole multitude of them *arose, and*
24: 7. the third day *rise again.*
12. Then *arose* Peter, *and* ran unto the
33. they *rose up* the same hour, *and*
46. *to rise* from the dead the third day:
Joh. 6:39. should *raise* it *up again* at the
40. I *will raise* him *up* at the last
44. I *will raise* him *up* at the last day.
54. I *will raise* him *up* at the last day.
11:23. Thy brother *shall rise again.*
24. I know that he *shall rise again*
31. that she *rose up* hastily and went
20: 9. that he must *rise again* from the
Acts 1:15. Peter *stood up* in the midst of...*and*
2:24. Whom God *hath raised up,* having
30. he would *raise up* Christ to sit
32. This Jesus *hath* God *raised up,*
3:22. your God *raise up* unto you of your
26. God, *having raised up* his Son
5: 6. the young men *arose,* wound...*and*
17. Then the high priest *rose up, and*
34. *Then stood* there *up* one in the
36. before these days *rose up* Theudas,
37. After this man *rose up* Judas
6: 9. Then there *arose* certain of the
7:18. Till another king *arose,* which
37. A prophet *shall* the Lord your God *raise up*
8:26. *Arise,* and go toward the south
27. he *arose and* went: and, behold, a
9: 6. *Arise,* and go into the city, and it shall
11. *Arise, and* go into the street which
18. *arose, and* was baptized.
34. *arise,* and make thy bed. And he *arose*

Acts 9:39. *Then* Peter *arose* and went with them
40. the body said, Tabitha, *arise.*
41. her (his) hand, and *lifted* her *up,*
10:13. *Rise,* Peter; kill, and eat.
20. *Arise* therefore, and get thee down,
26. saying, *Stand up;* I myself also
41. after he *rose* from the dead.
11: 7. *Arise,* Peter; slay and eat.
28. there *stood up* one of them...*and*
12: 7. raised him up, saying, *Arise up*
13:16. *Then* Paul *stood up,* and beckoning
33(32). he *hath raised up* Jesus *again;*
34. he *raised* him *up* from the dead,
14:10. *Stand* upright on thy feet.
20. he *rose up, and* came into the city:
15: 7. Peter *rose up, and* said unto them,
17: 3. suffered, and *risen again* from the dead;
31. he *hath raised* him from the dead.
20:30. of your own selves *shall* men *arise,*
22:10. said unto me, *Arise, and* go into
16. *arise, and* be baptized, and wash
23: 9. of the Pharisees' part *arose, and*
26:16. *rise,* and stand upon thy feet:
30. the king *rose up,* and the governor,
Ro. 14: 9. Christ both died, and *rose,* and revived,
15:12. he *that shall rise* to reign over
1Co. 10: 7. eat and drink, and *rose up* to play.
Eph. 5:14. *arise* from the dead, and Christ shall
1Th. 4:14. Jesus died *and rose again,* even so
16. the dead in Christ *shall rise* first:
Heb 7:11. another priest should *rise* after
15. there *ariseth* another priest,

453 6 70/77 4:948 1,3539

ἀνόητος, *anoeetos.*

Lu. 24:25. O *fools,* and slow of heart to believe
Ro. 1:14. both to the wise, and to the *unwise.*
Gal. 3: 1. O *foolish* Galatians, who hath
3. Are ye so *foolish?* having begun
1Ti. 6: 9. (into) many *foolish* and hurtful
Tit. 3: 3. ourselves also were sometimes *foolish,*

454 2 70/77 4:948 1,3563

ἄνοια, *anoia.*

Lu. 6:11. they were filled with *madness;*
2Ti: 3: 9. their *folly* shall be manifest

455 77 70/77 303 *oigō* (to open)

ἀνοίγω, *anoigo.*

Mat. 2:11. *when* they *had opened* their treasures,
3:16. the heavens *were opened* unto him,
5: 2. he *opened* his mouth, *and* taught
7: 7. knock, and it *shall be opened* unto you:
8. that knocketh it *shall be opened.*
9:30. their eyes *were opened;* and Jesus
13:35. I *will open* my mouth in parables;
17:27. *when* thou *hast opened* his mouth,
20:33. Lord, that our eyes *may be opened.*
25:11. saying, Lord, Lord, *open* to us.
27:52. the graves *were opened;* and many
Lu. 1:64. his mouth *was opened* immediately,
3:21. praying, the heaven was *opened,*
11: 9. knock, and it *shall be opened* unto you.
10. that knocketh it *shall be opened.*
12:36. they *may open* unto him immediately
13:25. saying, Lord, Lord, *open* unto us;
Joh. 1:51(52). ye shall see heaven *open,* and
9:10. How *were* thine eyes *opened?*
14. Jesus made the clay, and *opened* his eyes.
17. that he *hath opened* thine eyes?

Joh. 9:21. or who *hath opened* his eyes,
26. how *opened* he thine eyes?
30. (yet) he *hath opened* mine eyes.
32. that any man *opened* the eyes
10: 3. To him the porter *openeth*; and
21. Can a devil *open* the eyes of the
11:37. *which opened* the eyes of the blind,
Acts 5:19. by night *opened* the prison doors,
23. *when* we *had opened*, we found
7:56. Behold, I see the heavens *opened*,
8:32. so *opened* he not his mouth:
35. Then Philip *opened* his mouth, *and*
9: 8. *when* his eyes *were opened*, he
40. she *opened* her eyes: and when
10:11. saw heaven *opened*, and a certain
34. *Then* Peter *opened* (his) mouth, *and*
12:10. which *opened* to them of his
14. she *opened* not the gate for gladness,
16. *when* they *had opened* (the door),
14:27. how he *had opened* the door of
16:26. all the doors *were opened*, and every
27. seeing the prison doors *open*,
18:14. was now about *to open* (his) mouth,
26:18. *To open* their eyes, (and) to turn
Ro. 3:13. Their throat (is) an *open* sepulchre;
1Co.16: 9. a great door and effectual *is opened* unto
2Co. 2:12. *when*...a door *was opened* unto me of the
6:11. our mouth *is open* unto you, our
Col. 4: 3. that God *would open* unto us a door
Rev. 3: 7. he *that openeth*, and no man shutteth; and shutteth, and no man *openeth*;
8. I have set before thee an *open* door,
20. hear my voice, and *open* the door,
4: 1. a door (was) *opened* in heaven:
5: 2. Who is worthy *to open* the book, and
3. was able *to open* the book, neither
4. found worthy *to open* and to read the
5. hath prevailed *to open* the book,
9. *to open* the seals thereof: for thou
6: 1. when the Lamb *opened* one of the
3. when he *had opened* the second
5. when he *had opened* the third
7. when he *had opened* the fourth
9. when he *had opened* the fifth
12. when he *had opened* the sixth
8: 1. when he *had opened* the seventh
9: 2. he *opened* the bottomless pit;
10: 2. in his hand a little book *open*:
8. take the little book which is *open*
11:19. temple of God *was opened* in
12:16. the earth *opened* her mouth, and
13: 6. he *opened* his mouth in blasphemy
15: 5. the testimony in heaven *was opened*:
19:11. I saw heaven *opened*, and behold
20:12. the books *were opened*: and another book was *opened*, which is

456 2 70/78 303,3618

ἀνοικοδομέω, anoikodomeō.

Acts15:16. *will build again* the tabernacle
I *will build again* the ruins thereof,

457 1 71/78 455

ἄνοιξις, anoixis.

Eph. 6:19. that I may open (lit. in the *opening* of) my mouth boldly,

458 15 71/78 4:1022 459

ἀνομία, anomia.

Mat. 7:23. depart from me, ye that work *iniquity*.
13:41. that offend, and them which do *iniquity*;
23:28. are full of hypocrisy and *iniquity*.
24:12. because *iniquity* shall abound,
Ro. 4: 7. they whose *iniquities* are forgiven,
6:19. servants to uncleanness and *to iniquity* unto *iniquity*;
2Co. 6:14. hath righteousness with *unrighteousness*?
2Th. 2: 7. the mystery of *iniquity* doth already
Tit. 2:14. might redeem us from all *iniquity*,
Heb 1: 9. loved righteousness, and hated *iniquity*;
8:12. their *iniquities* will I remember no
10:17. their sins and *iniquities* will I remember
1Joh.3: 4. Whosoever committeth sin transgresseth also (lit. commits *transgression of*) *the law*: for sin is the *transgression of the law*.

459 10 71/78 4:1022 1,3551

ἄνομος, anomos.

Mar 15:28. numbered with the *transgressors*.
Lu. 22:37. reckoned among the *transgressors*:
Acts 2:23. by *wicked* hands have crucified
1Co. 9:21. that are *without law*, as *without law*, being not *without law* to God,
— gain them that are *without law*.
2Th. 2: 8. then shall that *Wicked* be revealed,
1Ti. 1: 9. for the *lawless* and disobedient,
2Pet.2: 8. to day with (their) *unlawful* deeds;

460 2 71/78 459

ἀνόμως, anomōs.

Ro. 2:12. as many as have sinned *without law* shall also perish *without law*:

461 3 71/78 303,rt 3717

ἀνορθόω, anorthoō.

Lu. 13:13. she *was made straight*, and
Acts15:16. the ruins thereof, and I *will set* it *up*:
Heb 12:12. *lift up* the hands which hang

462 2 71/78 5:489 1,3741

ἀνόσιος, anosios.

1Ti. 1: 9. for *unholy* and profane, for
2Ti. 3: 2. disobedient to parents, unthankful, *unholy*,

463 2 72/78 1:359 430

ἀνοχή, anokee.

Ro. 2: 4. riches of his goodness and *forbearance*
3:25(26). through the *forbearance* of God;

464 1 72/78 1:134 473,75

ἀνταγωνίζομαι, antagōnizomai.

Heb 12: 4. unto blood, *striving against* sin.

465 2 72/78 1:251 473,236

ἀντάλλαγμα, antallagma.

Mat.16:26. what shall a man give *in exchange*
Mar. 8:37. shall a man give *in exchange* for

466 1 72/78 6:283 473,378

ἀνταναπληρόω, antanapleeroō.

Col. 1:24. *fill up* that which is behind of the

467 7 72/78 2:166 473,591

ἀνταποδίδωμι, antapodidōmi.

Lu. 14:14. they cannot *recompense* thee: for thou *shalt be recompensed*
Ro. 11:35. it *shall be recompensed* unto him *again*
12:19. I *will repay*, saith the Lord.
1Th. 3: 9. what thanks can we *render* to God *again*
2Th. 1: 6. with God *to recompense* tribulation
Heb 10:30. I *will recompense*, saith the Lord.

---

468 2 72/78 2:166 467

ἀνταπόδομα, antapodoma.

Lu. 14:12. again, and a *recompence* be made thee.
Ro. 11: 9. a stumblingblock, and a *recompence* unto

---

469 1 72/78 2:166 467

ἀνταπόδοσις, antapodosis.

Col. 3:24. ye shall receive the *reward* of the inheritance:

---

470 2 72/79 3:921 473,611

ἀνταποκρίνομαι, antapokrinomai.

Lu. 14: 6. could not *answer* him *again* to
Ro. 9:20. thou *that repliest against* God?

---

471 2 72/79 473,2036

ἀντέπω, antepo.

Lu. 21:15. shall not be able *to gainsay* nor
Acts 4:14. they could *say* nothing *against it.*

---

472 4 72/79 2:816 473,2192

ἀντέχομαι, antekomai.

Mat. 6:24. or else he *will hold to* the one, and
Lu. 16:13. or else he *will hold to* the one, and despise
1Th. 5:14. *support* the weak, be patient
Tit. 1: 9. *Holding fast* the faithful word

---

473 22 72/79 1:372

ἀντί, anti.

Mat. 2:22. *in the room* of his father Herod,
5:38. An eye *for* an eye, and a tooth *for*
17:27. give unto them *for* me and thee.
20:28. give his life a ransom *for* many.
Mar 10:45. to give his life a ransom *for* many.
Lu. 1:20. because (lit. *for* that) thou believest not my words,
11:11. will he *for* a fish give him a
12: 3. Therefore (lit. *for* that) whatsoever ye have spoken
19:44. because (lit. *for* that) thou knewest not the
Joh. 1:16. all we received, and grace *for* grace.
Acts 12:23. because (lit. *for* that) he gave not God the glory:
Ro. 12:17. Recompense to no man evil *for* evil.
1Co 11:15. (her) hair is given her *for* a covering.
Eph. 5:31. *For* this cause shall a man leave
1Th. 5:15. none render evil *for* evil unto any
2Th. 2:10. because (lit. *for* that) they received not the love
Heb 12: 2. who *for* the joy that was set
16. who *for* one morsel of meat sold
Jas. 4:15. *For* that ye (ought) to say, If the
1Pet. 3: 9. Not rendering evil *for* evil, or railing *for* railing:

---

474 1 73/79 473,906

ἀντιβάλλω, antiballo.

Lu. 24:17. (are) these *that* ye *have* one to another,

---

475 1 73/79 473,1303

ἀντιδιατιθέμενος, antidiatithemenos.

2Ti. 2:25. instructing those *that oppose themselves;*

---

476 5 73/79 1:373 473,1349

ἀντίδικος, antidikos.

Mat. 5:25. Agree with thine *adversary* quickly,
— at any time the *adversary* deliver
Lu. 12:58. goest with thine *adversary* to the
18: 3. saying, Avenge me of mine *adversary.*
1Pet. 5: 8. because your *adversary* the devil,

---

477 1 73/79 473,5087

ἀντίθεσις, antithesis.

1Ti. 6:20. *oppositions* of science falsely so called:

---

478 1 73/79 473,2525

ἀντικαθίστημι, antikathisteemi.

Heb 12: 4. Ye *have* not yet *resisted* unto blood,

---

479 1 73/79 3:487 473,2564

ἀντικαλέω, antikaleō.

Lu. 14:12. lest they also *bid* thee *again*, and

---

480 8 73/79 3:654 473,2749

ἀντίκειμαι, antikimai.

Lu. 13:17. all his *adversaries* were ashamed:
21:15. which all your *adversaries* shall
1Co 16: 9. unto me, and (there are) many *adversaries.*
Gal. 5:17. these *are contrary* the one to the other:
Phi. 1:28. nothing terrified by your *adversaries.*
2Th. 2: 4. Who *opposeth* and exalteth himself
1Ti. 1:10. that *is contrary* to sound doctrine;
5:14. give none occasion to the *adversary*

---

481 1 73/79 473

ἀντικρύ, antikru.

Acts 20:15. came the next (day) *over against* Chios;

---

482 3 73/79 1:375 473,2983

ἀντιλαμβάνομαι, antilambanomai.

Lu. 1:54. He *hath holpen* his servant Israel,
Acts 20:35. ye ought *to support* the weak, and
1Ti. 6: 2. beloved, *partakers* of the benefit.

---

483 10 74/79 473,3004

ἀντιλέγω, antilego.

Lu. 2:34. a sign *which shall be spoken against;*
20:27. *which deny* that there is any resurrection;
Joh. 19:12. himself a king *speaketh against* Cæsar.
Acts 13:45. *spake against* those things which were spoken by Paul, *contradicting* and blaspheming.
28:19. *when* the Jews *spake against* (it),
22. every where it *is spoken against.*
Ro. 10:21. a disobedient and *gainsaying* people.
Tit. 1: 9. exhort and to convince the *gainsayers.*
2: 9. well in all (things); not *answering again;*

484 1 74/80 1:375 482

ἀντίληψις, antileepsis.

1Co.12:28. gifts of healings, *helps*, governments,

485 4 74/80 483

ἀντιλογία, antilogia.

Heb. 6:16. (is) to them an end of all *strife*.
7: 7. without all *contradiction* the less is
12: 3. endured such *contradiction* of
Jude 11. perished in the *gainsaying* of Core.

486 1 74/80 4:293 473,3058

ἀντιλοιδορέω, antiloidoreo.

1Pet.2:23. when he was reviled, *reviled* not *again*;

487 1 74/80 4:328 473,3083

ἀντίλυτρον, antilutron.

1Ti. 2: 6. Who gave himself a *ransom* for all,

488 2 74/80 473,3354

ἀντιμετρέω, antimetreo.

Mat. 7: 2. it *shall be measured* to you *again*.
Lu. 6:38. it *shall be measured* to you *again*.

489 2 74/80 4:695 473,3408

ἀντιμισθία, antimisthia.

Ro. 1:27. that *recompence* of their error which
2Co. 6:13. Now for a *recompence* in the same,

492 2 75/80 473,3928

ἀντιπαρέρχομαι, antiparerkomai.

Lu. 10:31. he *passed by on the other side*.
32. looked (on him), and *passed by on the other side*.

495 1 75/80 473,4008

ἀντιπέραν, antiperan.

Lu. 8:26. Gadarenes, which is *over against* Galilee.

496 1 75/80 473,4098

ἀντιπίπτω, antipipto.

Acts 7:51. ye *do* always *resist* the Holy Ghost:

497 1 75/80 473,4754

ἀντιστρατεύομαι, antistratūomai.

Ro. 7:23. *warring against* the law of my mind,

498 5 75/80 473,5021

ἀντιτάσσομαι, antitassomai.

Acts18: 6. *when* they *opposed* them*selves*, and
Ro. 13: 2. Whosoever therefore *resisteth* the power,
Jas. 4: 6. he saith, God *resisteth* the proud, but
5: 6. the just; (and) he *doth* not *resist* you.
1Pet.5: 5. for God *resisteth* the proud, and giveth

499 2 75/80 8:246 473,5179

ἀντίτυπον, antitupon.

Heb. 9:24. (which are) the *figures* of the true;
1Pet.3:21. The *like figure whereunto*, (even) baptism

500 5 75/80 9:493 473,5547

ἀντιχρίστος, antikristos.

1Joh 2:18. have heard that *antichrist* shall come, even now are there many *antichrists*;
22. He is *antichrist*, that denieth the Father
4: 3. this is that (spirit) of *antichrist*, whereof
2Joh. 7. This is a deceiver and an *antichrist*.

501 4 75/80 *antlos* (hold of a ship)

ἀντλέω, antleo.

Joh. 2: 8. saith unto them, *Draw out* now, and bear unto
9. the servants *which drew* the water knew;
4: 7. cometh a woman of Samaria *to draw* water:
15. I thirst not, neither come hither *to draw*.

502 1 75/80 501

ἄντλημα, antleema.

Joh. 4:11. Sir, thou hast no*thing to draw with*,

503 1 75/80 473,3788

ἀντοφθαλμέω, antophthalmeo.

Acts27:15. could not *bear up into* the wind,

504 4 75/80 1,5204

ἄνυδρος, anudros.

Mat.12:43. he walketh through *dry* places, seeking
Lu. 11:24. walketh through *dry* places, seeking rest;
2Pet.2:17. These are wells *without water*, clouas
Jude 12. clouds (they are) *without water*,

505 6 76/81 8:559 1,5271

ἀνυπόκριτος, anupokritos.

Ro. 12: 9. (Let) love be *without dissimulation*.
2Co. 6: 6. by the Holy Ghost, by love *unfeigned*,
1Ti. 1: 5. a good conscience, and (of) faith *unfeigned*:
2Ti. 1: 5. the *unfeigned* faith that is in thee,
1Pet.1:22. unto *unfeigned* love of the brethren,
Jas. 3:17. without partiality, and *without hypocrisy*.

506 4 76/81 8:27 1,5293

ἀνυπότακτος, anupotaktos.

1Ti. 1: 9. for the lawless and *disobedient*, for the
Tit. 1: 6. not accused of riot, or *unruly*.
10. there are many *unruly* and vain
Heb. 2: 8. nothing *that is not put under* him.

507 9 76/81 1:376 473

ἄνω, ano.

Joh. 2: 7. they filled them up to *the brim*.
8:23. Ye are from beneath; I am from *above*:
11:41. Jesus lifted *up* (his) eyes, and said,
Acts 2:19. I will shew wonders in heaven *above*,
Gal. 4:26. Jerusalem which is *above* is free,
Phi. 3:14. prize of the *high* calling of God
Col. 3: 1. seek those things which are *above*,
2. Set your affection on things *above*,
Heb 12:15. of bitterness springing *up* trouble (you),

508 2 76/57 507,1093

ἀνώγεον anōgeon.

Mar 14:15. shew you a large *upper room* furnished
Lu. 22:12. shew you a large *upper room* furnished:

509 13 76/81 1:376 507

ἄνωθεν, anōthen.

Mat.27:51. in twain from *the top* to the bottom;
Mar 15:38. in twain from *the top* to the bottom.
Lu. 1: 3. of all things *from the very first*,
Joh. 3: 3. Except a man be born *again*,
7. Ye must be born *again*.
31. He that cometh *from above* is
19:11. except it were given thee *from above*:
23. woven from the *top* throughout.
Acts26: 5. knew me *from the beginning*,
Gal. 4: 9. ye desire *again* (lit. a second time *again* παλιν ανωθεν) to be in bondage?
Jas. 1:17. every perfect gift is *from above*,
3:15. descendeth not *from above*, but
17. the wisdom that is *from above* is

510 1 76/81 511

ἀνωτερικός, anōterikos.

Acts19: 1. having passed through the *upper* coasts

511 2 76/81 1:376 507

ἀνώτερον, anōteron.

Lu. 14:10. say unto thee, Friend, go up *higher*:
Heb10: 8. *Above* when he said, Sacrifice and

512 2 76/81 1,rt 5624

ἀνωφελής, anōphelees.

Tit. 3: 9. for they are *unprofitable* and vain.
Heb. 7:18. the weakness and *unprofitableness* thereof.

513 2 77/81 *agnumi* (to break)

ἀξίνη, axinee.

Mat. 3:10. now also the *ax* is laid unto the root
Lu. 3: 9. now also the *axe* is laid unto the root

514 41 77/81 1:379 71

ἄξιος, axios.

Mat. 3: 8. therefore fruits *meet* for repentance:
10:10. the workman is *worthy* of his meat.
11. enquire who in it is *worthy*; and there
13. if the house be *worthy*, let your peace
— if it be not *worthy*, let your peace return
37. more than me is not *worthy* of me:
— than me is not *worthy* of me.
38. followeth after me, is not *worthy* of me.
22: 8. they which were bidden were not *worthy*.
Lu. 3: 8. therefore fruits *worthy* of repentance,
7: 4. That he was *worthy* for whom he
10: 7. for the labourer is *worthy* of his hire.
12:48. did commit things *worthy* of stripes,
15:19. am no more *worthy* to be called
21. am no more *worthy* to be called thy
23:15. nothing *worthy* of death is done unto
41. for we receive the *due reward* of our
Joh. 1:27. shoe's latchet I am not *worthy* to unloose.
Acts13:25. of (his) feet I am not *worthy* to loose.
46. judge yourselves un*worthy* of
23:29. laid to his charge *worthy* of death
25:11. committed any thing *worthy* of death,
25. committed nothing *worthy* of death,
26:20. do works *meet* for repentance.
31. doeth nothing *worthy* of death or of
Ro. 1:32. such things are *worthy* of death,
8:18. present time (are) not *worthy* (to be)
1Co16: 4. if it be *meet* that I go also, they shall
2Th. 1: 3. for you, brethren, as it is *meet*, because
1Ti. 1:15. faithful saying, and *worthy* of all acceptation,
4: 9. This (is) a faithful saying and *worthy* of all
5:18. The labourer (is) *worthy* of his reward.
6: 1. their own masters *worthy* of all
Heb 11:38. Of whom the world was not *worthy*:
Rev. 3: 4. in white: for they are *worthy*.
4:11. Thou art *worthy*, O Lord, to receive
5: 2. Who is *worthy* to open the book,
4. no man was found *worthy* to open
9. Thou art *worthy* to take the book,
12. *Worthy* is the Lamb that was slain
16: 6. blood to drink; for they are *worthy*.

515 7 77/82 1:379 514

ἀξιόω, axioō.

Lu. 7: 7. neither *thought* I myself *worthy* to
Acts15:38. Paul *thought* not *good* to take him
28:22. we *desire* to hear of thee what thou
2Th. 1:11. God *would count* you *worthy* of (this)
1Ti. 5:17. *be counted worthy* of double honour,
Heb. 3: 3. *was counted worthy* of more glory
10:29. *shall* he *be thought worthy*, who hath

516 6 78/82 514

ἀξίως, axiōs.

Ro. 16: 2. her in the Lord, *as becometh* saints,
Eph. 4: 1. that ye walk *worthy* of the vocation
Phil. 1:27. be *as* it *becometh* the gospel of Christ:
Col. 1:10. might walk *worthy* of the Lord unto
1Th. 2:12. That ye would walk *worthy* of God,
3 Joh. 6. their journey after a godly sort, (lit. *worthily* of God) thou

517 5 78/82 5:315 1,3707

ἀόρατος, aoratos.

Ro. 1:20. For the *invisible things* of him from
Col. 1:15. Who is the image of the *invisible* God,
16. that are in earth, visible and *invisible*,
1Ti. 1:17. the King eternal, immortal, *invisible*,
Heb11:27. as seeing him who is *invisible*.

518 44 78/82 1:56 575,rt 32

ἀπαγγέλλω, apangello.

Mat. 2: 8. *bring* me *word again*, that I may
8:33. into the city, and *told* every thing,
11: 4. Go and *shew* John *again* those things
12:18. he *shall shew* judgment to the
14:12. buried it, and went and *told* Jesus.
28: 8. did run *to bring* his disciples *word*.
9. And as they went *to tell* his disciples,
10. go *tell* my brethren that they go
11. *shewed* unto the chief priests all
Mar. 6:30. *told* him all things, both what
16:10. she went and *told* them that had
13. they went and *told* (it) unto the residue:
Lu. 7:18. *shewed* him of all these things.
22. Go your way, and *tell* John what things
8:20. it *was told* him (by certain) which
34. went and *told* (it) in the city and in the
36. which saw (it) *told* them by what
47. she *declared* unto him before
9:36. kept (it) close, and *told* no man in those
13: 1. some *that told* him of the Galilæans.
14:21. came, and *shewed* his lord these things.
18:37. they *told* him, that Jesus of
24: 9. *told* all these things unto the

Joh. 4:51. his servants met him, and *told* (him),
20.18. came *and told* the disciples that
Acts 4:23. *reported* all that the chief priests
5:22. not in the prison, they returned, and *told*,
25. Then came one and *told* them, saying,
11:13. he *shewed* us how he had seen
12:14. ran in, and *told* how Peter stood before
17. Go *shew* these things unto James,
15:27. *who shall* also *tell* (you) the same
16:36. keeper of the prison *told* this saying
22:26. he went and *told* the chief captain,
23:16. entered into the castle, and *told* Paul.
17. he hath a certain thing *to tell* him.
19. What is that thou hast *to tell* me?
26:20. *shewed* first unto them of Damascus,
28:21. that came *shewed* or spake any
1 Co.14:25. *and report* that God is in you of a truth.
1Th. 1: 9. themselves *shew* of us what
Heb. 2:12. I *will declare* thy name unto
1Joh.1: 2. bear witness, and *shew* unto you that
3. seen and heard *declare* we unto you,

519 1 78/82 575
agchō (to choke)

ἀπάγχομαι, *apankomai*.

Mat.27: 5. departed, and went and *hanged himself*.

520 16 78/82 575,71

ἀπάγω, *apago*.

Mat. 7:13. the way, *that leadeth* to destruction,
14. narrow (is) the way, *which leadeth* unto
26:57. laid hold on Jesus *led* (him) *away*
27: 2. bound him, they *led* (him) *away*,
31. *led* him *away* to crucify (him).
Mar 14:44. take him, and *lead* (him) *away* safely.
53. they *led* Jesus *away* to the high
15:16. the soldiers *led* him *away* into
Lu. 13:15. from the stall, and *lead* (him) *away* to
23:26. as they *led* him *away*, they laid
Joh. 18:13. *led* him *away* to Annas first;
19:16. they took Jesus, and *led* (him) *away*.
Acts12:19. commanded that (they) should *be put to death*.
23:17. *Bring* this young man unto the
24: 7. *took* (him) *away* out of our hands,
1Co 12: 2. *carried away* unto these dumb idols, even

521 1 79/83 5:596 1,3811

ἀπαίδευτος, *apaidūtos*.

2Ti. 2:23. foolish and *unlearned* questions avoid,

522 3 79/83 575,142

ἀπαίρομαι, *apairomai*.

Mat. 9:15. bridegroom *shall be taken* from them,
Mar. 2:20. bridegroom *shall be taken away* from
Lu. 5:35. bridegroom *shall be taken away* from

523 3 79/83 1:191 575,154

ἀπαιτέω, *apaiteo*.

Lu. 6:30. away thy goods *ask* (them) not *again*.
12:20. thy soul *shall be required* of thee:

524 1 79/83 575
algeō (to smart)

ἀπαλγέω, *apalgeo*.

Eph. 4:19. Who *being past feeling* have given

525 3 79/83 1:251 575,236

ἀπαλλάσσω, *apallasso*.

Lu. 12.58. that thou mayest *be delivered* from him;
Acts19:12. the diseases *departed* from them,
Heb. 2:15. and *deliver* them who through fear of

526 3 79/83 1:264 575,245

ἀπαλλοτριόω, *apallotrioō*.

Eph. 2:12. *being aliens* from the commonwealth
4:18. being *alienated* from the life of
Col. 1:21. that were sometime *alienated*

527 2 79/83

ἁπαλός, *hapalos*.

Mat.24:32. When his branch is yet *tender*,
Mar 13:28. When her branch is yet *tender*,

528 7 79/83 575,473

ἀπαντάω, *apantao*.

Mat.28: 9. behold, Jesus *met* them, saying,
Mar. 5: 2. there *met* him out of the tombs a
14:13. there *shall meet* you a man bearing
Lu. 14:31. *to meet* him that cometh against
17:12. there *met* him ten men that were
Joh. 4:51. his servants *met* him, and told (him),
Acts16:16. with a spirit of divination *met* us,

529 4 79/83 1:38 528

ἀπάντησις, *apanteesis*.

Mat.25: 1. went forth to *meet* (lit. the *meeting* of) the bridegroom.
6. bridegroom cometh; go ye out to *meet* him.
Acts28: 15. they came to *meet* us as far as
1Th. 4:17. to *meet* the Lord in the air: and

530 15 80/83 1:381 537

ἅπαξ, *hapax*.

2Co 11:25. beaten with rods, *once* was I stoned,
Phi. 4:16. ye sent *once* and again unto my
1Th. 2:18. come unto you, even I Paul, *once* and again;
Heb. 6: 4. those who were *once* enlightened,
9: 7. the high priest alone *once* every year,
26. now *once* in the end of the world
27. it is appointed unto men *once* to die,
28. Christ was *once* offered to bear the
10: 2. worshippers *once* purged should
12:26. Yet *once* more I shake not the
27. this (word) Yet *once* more, signifieth
1Pet. 3:18. Christ also hath *once* suffered for sins,
20. when *once* the longsuffering of God
Jude 3. faith which was *once* delivered
5. though ye *once* knew this, how that

531 1 80/83 5:736 1,3845

ἀπαράβατος, *aparabatos*.

Heb. 7.24. hath an *unchangeable* priesthood.

532 1 80/83 1,3903

ἀπαρασκεύαστος, *aparaskūastos*.

2Co. 9: 4. with me, and find you *unprepared*,

533 13 80/83 575,720

ἀπαρνέομαι, *aparneomai*.

Mat.16:24. come after me, *let* him *deny* himself.

Mat.26:34. cock crow, thou *shalt deny* me thrice.
35. yet *will* I not *deny* thee.
75. cock crow, thou *shalt deny* me thrice.
Mar. 8:34. *let* him *deny* himself, and take
14:30. crow twice, thou *shalt deny* me thrice.
31. I *will* not *deny* thee in any wise.
72. twice, thou *shalt deny* me thrice.
Lu. 9:23. come after me, *let* him *deny* himself,
12: 9. *shall be denied* before the angels
22:34. thou *shalt* thrice *deny* that thou
61. cock crow, thou *shalt deny* me thrice.
Joh.13:38. crow, till thou *hast denied* me

534 1 80/83 575,737

ἀπάρτι, aparti.

Rev.14:13. die in the Lord *from henceforth:*

535 1 80/83 534

ἀπαρτισμός, apartismos.

Lu. 14:28. whether he have (sufficient) to finish (it)? (lit. the *finishing*)

536 8 80/83 1:478 575,756

ἀπαρχή, aparkee.

Ro. 8:23. which have the *firstfruits* of the Spirit,
11:16. For if the *firstfruit* (be) holy, the
16: 5. who is the *firstfruits* of Achaia
1Co.15:20. become the *firstfruits* of them that
23. Christ the *firstfruits;* afterward
16:15. that it is the *firstfruits* of Achaia,
Jas. 1:18. a kind of *firstfruits* of his creatures.
Rev.14: 4. (being) the *firstfruits* unto God and

537 44 81/84 5:886 1,3956

ἅπας, hapas.

Mat. 6:32. ye have need of *all* these things.
24:39. the flood came, and took them *all* away;
28:11. unto the chief priests *all* the things that
Mar 5:40. when he had put them *all* out, he
8:25. restored, and saw *every* man clearly.
11:32. for *all* (men) counted John, that he was
16:15. Go ye into *all* the world, and preach
Lu. 2:39. had performed *all things* according
3:16. John answered, saying unto (them) *all*,
21. when *all* the people were baptized,
4: 6. *All* this power will I give thee,
5:11. they forsook *all*, and followed him.
26. they were *all* amazed, and they glorified
28. he left *all*, rose up, and followed him.
7:16. there came a fear on *all:* and they
8:37. Then the *whole* multitude of the
9:15. they did so, and made them *all* sit
15:13. younger son gathered *all* together,
17:27. the flood came, and destroyed them *all*.
29. from heaven, and destroyed (them) *all*.
19: 7. when they saw (it), they *all* murmured,
37. the *whole* multitude of the disciples
48. for *all* the people were very attentive
21: 4. For *all* these have of their abundance
— hath cast in *all* the living that
12. before *all* these, they shall lay
23: 1. the *whole* multitude of them arose,
Acts 2: 1. they were *all* with one accord in
4. they were *all* filled with the Holy
14. *all* (ye) that dwell at Jerusalem,
44. together, and had *all* things common;
4:31. they were *all* filled with the Holy
32. they had *all* things common.
5:12. they were *all* with one accord in
Acts. 5:16. they were healed *every one*.
6:15. *all* that sat in the council, looking
10: 8. he had declared *all* (these) *things*
11:10. *all* were drawn up again into heaven.
13:29. had fulfilled *all* that was written
16: 3. they knew *all* that his father was
28. Do thyself no harm: for we are *all* here.
27:33. Paul besought (them) *all* to take
Eph. 6:13. having done *all*, to stand.
Jas. 3: 2. in many things we offend *all*.

538 4 81/84 1:384

ἀπατάω, apatao.

Eph. 5: 6. *Let* no man *deceive* you with
1Ti. 2:14. Adam *was* not *deceived*, but the woman *being deceived* was in the
Jas. 1:26. his tongue, but *deceiveth* his own

539 7 81/84 1:384 538

ἀπάτη, apatee.

Mat.13:22. the *deceitfulness* of riches, choke
Mar. 4:19. the *deceitfulness* of riches, and the
Eph. 4:22. corrupt according to the *deceitful*
Col. 2: 8. through philosophy and vain *deceit*,
2Th. 2:10. with all *deceivableness* of
Heb 3:13. through the *deceitfulness* of sin.
2Pet. 2:13. with their own *deceivings* while

540 1 81/84 5:590 1,3962

ἀπάτωρ, apatōr.

Heb 7: 3. *Without father*, without mother,

541 1 81/84 1:507 575,826

ἀπαύγασμα, apaugasma.

Heb 1: 3. Who being the *brightness* of (his)

543 7 81/84 6:1 545

ἀπείθεια, apīthīa.

Ro. 11:30. obtained mercy through their *unbelief:*
32. concluded them all in *unbelief*,
Eph. 2: 2. in the children of *disobedience:*
5: 6. upon the children of *disobedience*.
Col. 3: 6. on the children of *disobedience:*
Heb 4: 6. entered not in because of *unbelief:*
11. the same example of *unbelief*.

544 16 82/85 6:1 545

ἀπειθέω, apītheo.

Joh. 3:36. he *that believeth not* the Son shall
Acts14: 2. the *unbelieving* Jews stirred up the
17: 5. the Jews *which believed not*, moved
19: 9. when divers were hardened, and *believed not*,
Ro. 2: 8. *do not obey* the truth, but obey
10:21. unto a *disobedient* and gainsaying people.
11:30. in times past *have not believed* God,
31. have these also now *not believed*,
15:31. from them *that do not believe* in
Heb 3:18. to them *that believed not?*
11:31. not with them *that believed not*,
1Pet. 2: 7. unto them *which be disobedient*, the
8. stumble at the word, *being disobedient:*
3: 1. that, if any *obey not* the word, they
20. Which sometime *were disobedient*,
4:17. them *that obey not* the gospel of God?

542. See 872

545 6 82/85 6:1 1,3982

ἀπειθής, apīthees.

Lu. 1:17. the *disobedient* to the wisdom of the just;
Acts26:19. I was not *disobedient* unto the heavenly
Ro. 1:30. of evil things, *disobedient* to parents,
2Ti. 3: 2. blasphemers, *disobedient* to parents,
Tit. 1:16. being abominable, and *disobedient*, and
3: 3. were sometimes foolish, *disobedient*,

546 2 82/85

ἀπειλέω, apīleo.

Acts 4:17. *let* us straitly *threaten* them, that they
1Pet. 2:23. when he suffered, he *threatened* not;

547 4 82/85 546

ἀπειλή, apīlee.

Acts 4:17. let us *straitly* (lit. with *threatening*) threaten them, that
29. Lord, behold their *threatenings*:
9: 1. breathing out *threatenings* and
Eph. 6: 9. unto them, forbearing *threatening*:

548 7 82/85 575,1510
cf 549

ἄπειμι, apīmi.

1Co. 5: 3. For I verily, as *absent* in body, but
2Co.10: 1. *being absent* am bold toward you:
11. by letters *when* we *are absent*, such
13: 2. *being absent* now I write to them
10. I write these things *being absent*,
Phi. 1:27. I come and see you, or else *be absent*,
Col. 2: 5. though I *be absent* in the flesh,

549 1 82/85 575
eimi (to go)
cf 548

ἀπεῖμι, apīmi.

Acts17:10. *went* into the synagogue of the Jews.

550 1 82/85 575,2036

ἀπειπεῖν, apīpin.

2Co. 4: 2. *have renounced* the hidden things

551 1 82/85 6:23 1,3987

ἀπείραστος, apīrastos.

Jas. 1:13. for God *cannot be tempted* with

552 1 82/85 1,3984

ἄπειρος, apīros.

Heb. 5:13. (is) *unskilful* in the word of

553 7 82/85 2:50 575,1551

ἀπεκδέχομαι, apekdekomai.

Ro. 8:19. *waiteth for* the manifestation of the
23. ourselves, *waiting for* the adoption,
25. (then) do we with patience *wait for* (it).
1Co. 1: 7. *waiting for* the coming of our
Gal. 5: 5. *wait for* the hope of righteousness
Phi. 3:20. whence also we *look for* the Saviour,
Heb 9:28. unto them *that look for* him shall

554 2 82/85 2:318 575,1562

ἀπεκδύομαι, apekduomai.

Col. 2:15. *having spoiled* principalities and
3: 9. that ye *have put off* the old man

555 1 83/85 2:318 554

ἀπέκδυσις, apekdusis.

Col. 2:11. in *putting off* the body of the sins

556 1 83/85 575,1643

ἀπελάω, apelao.

Acts18:16. he *drave* them from the judgment seat.

557 1 83/85 575,1651

ἀπελεγμός, apelegmos.

Acts19:27. our craft is in danger to be set at *nought*;

558 1 83/85 2:487 575,1658

ἀπελεύθερος, apelūtheros.

1Co. 7:22. (being) a servant, is the Lord's *freeman*:

560 1 83/85 2:517 575,1679

ἀπελπίζω, apelpizo.

Lu. 6:35. lend, *hoping for* nothing *again*;

561 6 83/85 575,1725

ἀπέναντι, apenanti.

Mat.21: 2. Go into the village *over against* you,
27:24. washed (his) hands *before* the multitude,
61. sitting *over against* the sepulchre.
Acts 3:16. soundness *in the presence* of you all.
17: 7. these all do *contrary* to the decrees of
Ro. 3:18. no fear of God *before* their eyes.

562 1 83/86 1,4008

ἀπέραντος, aperantos.

1Ti. 1: 4. to fables and *endless* genealogies, which

563 1 83/86 1,4049

περισπάστως, aperispastōs.

1Co. 7:35. upon the Lord *without distraction*.

564 1 83/86 6:72 1,4059

ἀπερίτμητος, aperitmeetos.

Acts 7:51. stiffnecked and *uncircumcised* in heart

565 120 83/86 2:666 575,2064

ἀπέρχομαι, aperkomai.

Mat. 2:22. he was afraid *to go* thither:
4:24. his fame *went* throughout all Syria:
8:18. commandment *to depart* unto the
19. will follow thee whithersoever thou *goest*
21. suffer me first *to go* and bury my father
31. suffer us *to go away* into the herd
32. they *went* into the herd of swine:
33. fled, and *went* their *ways* into the city, *and*
9: 7. he arose, and *departed* to his house.
10: 5. *Go* not into the way of the Gentiles,
13:25. tares among the wheat, and *went* his *way*
28. that we *go and* gather them up?
46. *went and* sold all that he had, and
14:15. that they *may go* into the villages, *and*
16. said unto them, They need not *depart*;
25. Jesus *went* unto them, walking
16: 4. he left them, and *departed*.
21. how that he must *go* unto Jerusalem.
18:30. *went and* cast him into prison, till
19:22. that saying, he *went away* sorrowful.

Mat.20: 4(5). And they *went* their *way*.
21:29. afterward he repented, and *went*.
30. said, I (go), Sir: and *went* not.
22: 5. *went* their *ways*, one to his farm,
22. left him, and *went* their *way*.
25:10. *while* they *went* to buy, the bridegroom
18. *went and* digged in the earth, and hid
25. *went and* hid thy talent in the earth:
46. these *shall go away* into everlasting
26:36. Sit ye here, while I *go and* pray yonder.
42. He *went away* again the second time, *and*
44. he left them, *and went away* again,
27: 5. departed, and *went and* hanged himself.
60. the door of the sepulchre, and *departed*.
28:10. my brethren that they *go* into
Mar 1:20. the hired servants, and *went* after him.
35. he went out, and *departed* into a
42. the leprosy *departed* from him,
3:13. whom he would: and they *came* unto
5:17. to pray him *to depart* out of their
20. he *departed*, and began to publish
24. (Jesus) *went* with him; and much
6:27(28). he *went and* beheaded him in
32. they *departed* into a desert place
36. that they *may go* into the country
37. Shall we *go and* buy two hundred
46. he *departed* into a mountain
7:24. he arose, and *went* into the borders
30. *when* she *was come* to her
8:13. again *departed* to the other side.
9:43. having two hands *to go* into hell,
10:22. sad at that saying, and *went away*
11: 4. they *went* their *way*, and found
12:12. they left him, and *went* their *way*.
14:10. one of the twelve, *went* unto the
12. Where wilt thou *that* we *go and*
39. again he *went away, and* prayed
16:13. they *went and* told (it) unto the
Lu. 1:23. he *departed* to his own house.
38. the angel *departed* from her.
2:15. as the angels *were gone away* from
5:13. the leprosy *departed* from him.
14. *go, and* shew thyself to the priest,
25. *departed* to his own house,
7:24. *when* the messengers of John were *departed*,
8:31. command them *to go out* into
34. *went and* told (it) in the city and in
37. besought him *to depart* from them;
39. he *went* his *way*, and published
9:12. that they may *go* into the towns...*and*
57. I will follow thee whithersoever thou *goest*.
59. suffer me first *to go* and bury my father.
60. *go* thou *and* preach the kingdom of God.
10:30. *departed*, leaving (him) half dead.
17:23. *go* not after (them), nor follow (them).
19:32. that were sent *went* their *way*,
22: 4. he *went* his *way, and* communed
13. they *went, and* found as he had
23:33. when they *were come* to the place,
24:12. clothes laid by themselves, and *departed*,
24. *went* to the sepulchre, and found
Joh. 4: 3. He left Judæa, and *departed* again into
8. For his disciples *were gone away*
28. *went* her *way* into the city, and
43. and *went* into Galilee.
47. he *went* unto him, and besought
5:15. The man *departed*, and told the Jews
6: 1. Jesus *went* over the sea of Galilee,
22. (that) his disciples *were gone away*
66. many of his disciples *went* back,
68. Lord, to whom *shall* we *go?*
9: 7. He *went his way* therefore, and
Joh. 9:11. I *went and* washed, and I received sight.
10:40. *went away* again beyond Jordan
11:28. had so said, she *went* her *way*,
46. some of them *went* their *ways* to the
54. *went* thence unto a country
12:19. behold, the world *is gone* after him.
36. These things spake Jesus, and *departed and*
16: 7. expedient for you that I *go away*: for if I *go not away*,
18: 6. they *went* backward, and fell to
20:10. the disciples *went away* again
Acts 4:15. commanded them *to go aside* out
5:26. Then *went* the captain with
9:17. Ananias *went* his *way*, and entered
10: 7. spake unto Cornelius *was departed*,
28:29. the Jews *departed*, and had great
Ro. 15:28. I *will come* by you into Spain.
Gal. 1:17. I *went* into Arabia, and returned
Jas. 1:24. beholdeth himself, and *goeth* his *way*,
Jude 7. *going* after strange flesh, are
Rev. 9:12. One woe *is past*; (and), behold,
10: 9. I *went* unto the angel, and said unto
11:14. The second woe *is past*; (and), behold.
12:17. *went* to make war with the
16: 2. the first *went*, and poured out his
18:14. lusted after *are departed* from thee,
— goodly *are departed* from thee, and
21: 4. the former things *are passed away*.

566 1 84/87 568

ἀπέχει, apekī.

Mar.14:41. *it is enough*, the hour is come;

567 6 84/87 568

ἀπέχομαι, apekomai.

Acts15:20. that they *abstain* from pollutions
29. That ye *abstain* from meats offered
1Th. 4: 3. that ye should *abstain* from fornication:
5:22. *Abstain* from all appearance of evil.
1Ti. 4: 3. (commanding) *to abstain* from meats,
1Pet. 2:11. *abstain* from fleshly lusts, which

568 11 84/87 2:816 575,2192

ἀπέχω, apeko.

Mat. 6: 2. I say unto you, They *have* their reward.
5. I say unto you, They *have* their reward.
16. I say unto you, They *have* their reward.
15: 8. their heart *is* far from me.
Mar. 7: 6. their heart *is* far from me.
Lu. 6:24. ye *have received* your consolation.
7: 6. *when* he *was* now not far from the house,
15:20. *when* he *was* yet a great way off,
24:13. *which was* from Jerusalem (about)
Phi. 4:18. But I *have* all, and abound:
Philem.15. that thou *shouldest receive* him for

569 7 84/87 6:174 571

ἀπιστέω, apisteo.

Mar.16:11. had been seen of her, *believed not*.
16. he *that believeth not* shall be damned.
Lu. 24:11. as idle tales, and they *believed* them *not*.
41. *while* they yet *believed not* for joy, and
Acts28:24. were spoken, and some *believed not*
Ro. 3: 3. what if some *did not believe?*
2Ti. 2:13. If we *believe not*, (yet) he abideth

570 12 84/87 6:174 571

ἀπιστία, apistia.

Mat. 13:58. works there because of their *unbelief.*
17:20. said unto them, Because of your *unbelief:*
Mar. 6: 6. he marvelled because of their *unbelief.*
9:24. I believe; help thou mine *unbelief.*
16:14. upbraided them with their *unbelief*
Ro. 3: 3. shall their *unbelief* make the
4:20. promise of God through *unbelief;*
11:20. because of *unbelief* they were broken
23. if they abide not in *unbelief,*
1Ti. 1:13. I did (it) ignorantly in *unbelief.*
Heb. 3:12. you an evil heart of *unbelief,*
19. not enter in because of *unbelief.*

571 23 85/88 6:174 1,4103

ἄπιστος, apistos.

Mat. 17:17. O *faithless* and perverse generation,
Mar. 9:19. O *faithless* generation, how long shall
Lu. 9:41. O *faithless* and perverse generation,
12:46. his portion with the *unbelievers.*
Joh. 20:27. be not *faithless,* but believing.
Acts 26: 8. thought a *thing incredible* with you,
1Cor. 6: 6. that before the *unbelievers.*
7:12. hath a wife *that believeth not,*
13. hath an husband *that believeth not,*
14. For the *unbelieving* husband
— the *unbelieving* wife is sanctified
15. if the *unbelieving* depart, let him
10:27. If any of them *that believe not*
14:22. to them *that believe not:* but
— not for them *that believe not,*
23. (that are) unlearned, or *unbelievers,*
24. there come in one *that believeth not,*
2Co. 4: 4. minds of them *which believe not,*
6:14. yoked together with *unbelievers:*
15. hath he that believeth with an *infidel?*
1Ti. 5: 8. is worse than an *infidel.*
Tit. 1:15. defiled and *unbelieving* (is) nothing
Rev. 21: 8. But the fearful, and *unbelieving,*

572 8 85/88 1:386 573

ἁπλότης, haplotees.

Ro. 12: 8. (let him do it) with *simplicity;*
2Co. 1:12. that in *simplicity* and godly sincerity
8: 2. unto the riches of their *liberality.*
9:11. in every thing to all *bountifulness,*
13. for (your) *liberal* distribution unto
11: 3. from the *simplicity* that is in Christ.
Eph. 6: 5. in *singleness* of your heart, as
Col. 3:22. in *singleness* of heart, fearing God:

573 2 85/88 1:386 1,4120

ἁπλοῦς, haplous.

Mat. 6:22. if therefore thine eye be *single,*
Lu. 11:34. therefore when thine eye is *single,*

574 1 85/88 573

ἁπλῶς, haplōs.

Jas. 1: 5. that giveth to all (men) *liberally,*

575 656 85/88

ἀπό, apo.

Note.—Only with a genitive.

Mat. 1:17. the generations *from* Abraham
— *from* David until the carrying
— *from* the carrying away into
1:21. shall save his people *from* their sins.
24. Then Joseph being raised *from* sleep
2: 1. came wise men *from* the east
16. *from* two years old and under, according
3: 4. had his raiment *of* camel's hair,
7. to flee *from* the wrath to come?
13. cometh Jesus *from* Galilee to Jordan
16. went up straightway *out of* the water:
4:17. *From* that time Jesus began to
25. multitudes of people *from* Galilee, and
5:18. shall in no wise pass *from* the law,
29. pluck it out, and cast (it) *from* thee:
30. cut it off, and cast (it) *from* thee: for
42. from him that would borrow *of* thee
6:13. temptation, but deliver us *from* evil:
7: 4. pull out the mote *out of* thine eye;
15. Beware *of* false prophets, which come
16. Ye shall know them *by* their fruits. Do men gather grapes *of* thorns, or figs *of* thistles?
20. Wherefore *by* their fruits ye shall
23. depart *from* me, ye that work iniquity.
8: 1. was come down *from* the mountain,
11. many shall come *from* the east and
30. a good way off *from* them an herd
34. he would depart *out of* their coasts.
9:15. bridegroom shall be taken *from* them,
16. to fill it up taketh *from* the garment,
22. was made whole *from* that hour.
10:17. But beware *of* men: for they will
28. fear not them (lit. *for* them) which kill the body,
11:12. *from* the days of John the Baptist
19. wisdom is justified *of* her children.
25. hast hid these things *from* the wise
29. my yoke upon you, and learn *of* me;
12:38. we would see a sign *from* thee.
43. the unclean spirit is gone *out of* a man,
13: 1. same day went Jesus *out of* the house,
12. *from* him shall be taken away
35. kept secret *from* the foundation of
44. *for* joy thereof goeth and selleth all
14: 2. he is risen *from* the dead; and
13. followed him on foot *out of* the cities.
26. they cried out *for* fear.
29. Peter was come down *out of* the ship,
15: 1. which were *of* Jerusalem, saying,
8. their heart is far *from* me.
22. came *out of* the same coasts, and
27. dogs eat *of* the crumbs which fall *from*
28. made whole *from* that very hour
16: 6. beware *of* the leaven of the Pharisees
11. ye should beware *of* the leaven of
12. bade (them) not beware *of* the leaven of bread, but *of* the doctrine of the Pharisees,
21. *From* that time *forth* began Jesus
— suffer many things *of* the elders
17: 9. as they came down *from* the mountain,
18. the devil; and he departed *out of* him: and the child was cured *from* that very
25. *of* whom do the kings of the earth
— *of* their own children, or *of* strangers?
26. Peter saith unto him, *Of* strangers.
18: 7. Woe unto the world *because of* offences!
8. cut them off, and cast (them) *from* thee:
9. pluck it out, and cast (it) *from* thee:
35. if ye *from* your hearts forgive not
19: 1. he departed *from* Galilee, and came
4. which made (them) *at* the beginning
8. *from* the beginning it was not so.
20: 8. beginning *from* the last unto the
29. as they departed *from* Jericho,

Mat.21: 8. cut down branches *from* the trees,
11. the prophet *of* Nazareth of Galilee.
43. shall be taken *from* you, and given
22:46. durst any (man) *from* that day
23:33. can ye escape (lit. *from*) the damnation of hell?
34. persecute (them) *from* city to city:
35. *from* the blood of righteous Abel unto
39. Shall not see me hence*forth*, till ye
24: 1. went out, and departed *from* the temple:
21. not *since* the beginning of the world
27. lightning cometh *out of* the east,
29. the stars shall fall *from* heaven,
31. *from* one end of heaven to the other
32. Now learn a parable *of* the fig tree;
25:28. Take therefore the talent *from* him,
29. *from* him that hath not shall be taken away (lit. *from* him) even
32. separate them one *from* another, as a shepherd divideth (his) sheep *from* the goats:
34. *from* the foundation of the world:
41. Depart *from* me, ye cursed, into
26:16. *from* that time he sought opportunity
29. I will not drink hence*forth* of this
39. let this cup pass *from* me: nevertheless
42. cup may not pass away *from* me;
47. *from* the chief priests and elders of
58. Peter followed him afar *off* (lit. *from* far)
64. Here*after* shall ye see the Son of man
27: 9. they *of* the children of Israel did
21. Whether *of* the twain will ye that
24. I am innocent *of* the blood of
40. come down *from* the cross.
42. now come down *from* the cross,
45. Now *from* the sixth hour there
51. rent in twain *from* the top to the
55. were there beholding afar *off*, which followed Jesus *from* Galilee,
57. came a rich man *of* Arimathæa,
64. He is risen *from* the dead: so the
28: 2. rolled back the stone *from* the
4. *for* fear of him the keepers did
7. that he is risen *from* the dead;
8. departed quickly *from* the sepulchre
Mar. 1: 9. that Jesus came *from* Nazareth
10. coming up *out of* the water, he saw
42. the leprosy departed *from* him,
2:20. shall be taken away *from* them,
3: 7. a great multitude *from* Galilee followed him, and *from* Judæa,
8. *from* Jerusalem, and *from* Idumæa,
22. scribes which came down *from* Jerusalem
4:25. *from* him shall be taken even that
5: 6. when he saw Jesus afar *off*, he
17. him to depart *out of* their coasts.
29. that she was healed *of* that plague.
34. in peace, and be whole *of* thy plague.
35. there came *from* the ruler of the
6:33. ran afoot thither *out of* all cities, and
43. of the fragments, and *of* the fishes.
7: 1. scribes, which came *from* Jerusalem.
4. (when they come) *from* the market,
6. their heart is far *from* me.
15. but the things which come *out of* him,
17. entered into the house *from* the people,
28. under the table eat *of* the children's
33. he took him aside *from* the multitude,
8:11. seeking of him a sign *from* heaven,
15. beware *of* the leaven of the Pharisees,
31. be rejected *of* the elders, and (of) the chief
9: 9. as they came down *from* the mountain,
10: 6. *from* the beginning of the creation

Mar.10:46. as he went *out of* Jericho with his
11:12. when they were come *from* Bethany,
12: 2. *of* the fruit of the vineyard.
34. not far *from* the kingdom of God.
38. Beware *of* the scribes, which love
13:19. as was not *from* the beginning of
27. *from* the uttermost part of the
28. Now learn a parable *of* the fig tree;
14:35. the hour might pass *from* him.
36. take away this cup *from* me:
52. linen cloth, and fled *from* them naked.
54. Peter followed him afar *off*, even
15:21. who passed by, coming *out of* the country,
30. Save thyself, and come down *from* the cross.
32. descend now *from* the cross, that
38. rent in twain *from* the top to the
40. also women looking on afar *off*:
43. Joseph *of* Arimathæa, an
45. when he knew (it) *of* the centurion,
16: 8. out quickly, and fled *from* the sepulchre;
9. Mary Magdalene, *out of* whom he
Lu. 1: 2. which *from* the beginning were
38. the angel departed *from* her.
48. *from* henceforth all generations shall
52. put down the mighty *from* (their) seats,
70. which have been *since* the world began:
2: 4. Joseph also went up *from* Galilee,
15. were gone away *from* them into
36. seven years *from* her virginity;
37. which departed not *from* the temple,
3: 7. to flee *from* the wrath to come?
4: 1. returned *from* Jordan, and was led
13. he departed *from* him for a season.
35. in the midst, he came *out of* him,
41. devils also came *out of* many,
42. that he should not depart *from* them.
5: 2. the fishermen were gone *out of* them,
3. thrust out a little *from* the land.
8. saying, Depart *from* me; for
10. *from* henceforth thou shalt catch
13. immediately the leprosy departed *from* him.
15. healed by him *of* their infirmities.
35. shall be taken away *from* them,
36. that was (taken) *out of* the new agreeth
6:13. *of* them he chose twelve, whom
17. multitude of people *out of* all Judæa
— to be healed *of* their diseases;
29. and him (lit. *from* him) that taketh away thy cloke
30. *of* him that taketh away thy goods
7: 6. was now not far *from* the house,
21. cured many *of* (their) infirmities and
35. wisdom is justified *of* all her children.
45. this woman, *since* the time I came
8: 2. had been healed *of* evil spirits and
— *out of* whom went seven devils,
3. ministered unto him *of* their substance.
12. the word *out of* their hearts, lest
18. *from* him shall be taken even
29. the unclean spirit to come *out of* the
33. Then went the devils *out of* the man,
35. *out of* whom the devils were
37. besought him to depart *from* them;
38. the man *out of* whom the devils
43. an issue of blood twelve (lit. *from* twelve) years,
46. I perceive that virtue is gone *out of* me.
9: 5 when ye go *out of* that city, shake off the very dust *from* your feet
22. be rejected *of* the elders and chief priests

Lu. 9:33. as they departed *from* him,
37. they were come down *from* the
38. behold, a man *of* the company
39. bruising him hardly departeth *from* him.
45. it was hid *from* them, that they
54. fire to come down *from* heaven,
10:21. hid these things *from* the wise and
30. went down *from* Jerusalem to Jericho,
42. shall not be taken away *from* her.
11: 4. temptation; but deliver us *from* evil.
24. the unclean spirit is gone *out of* a
50. was shed *from* the foundation of the world,
may be required *of* this generation;
51. *From* the blood of Abel unto the
— be required *of* this generation.
12: 1. Beware ye *of* the leaven of the Pharisees,
4. Be not afraid *of* them that kill
15. Take heed, and beware *of* covetousness:
20. thy soul shall be required *of* thee:
52. For *from* henceforth there shall be
54. When ye see a cloud rise *out of* the west,
57. why even *of* yourselves judge ye
58. thou mayest be delivered *from* him;
13:15. loose his ox or (his) ass *from* the stall,
16. be loosed *from* this bond on the
25. When *once* (lit. *from* when) the master of the house
27. depart *from* me, all (ye) workers
29. they shall come *from* the east, and (from) the west, and *from* the north,
14:18. all *with* one (consent) began to make
15:16. filled his belly *with* the husks that
16: 3. taketh away *from* me the stewardship:
16. *since* that time the kingdom of
18. that is put away *from* (her) husband
21. *with* the crumbs which fell *from* the
23. seeth Abraham afar *off*, and
30. went unto them *from* the dead,
17:25. be rejected *of* this generation.
29. day that Lot went *out of* Sodom it rained fire and brimstone *from* heaven,
18: 3. Avenge me *of* mine adversary.
34. this saying was hid *from* them,
19: 3. could not *for* the press, because he
24. Take *from* him the pound, and give
26. *from* him that hath not, even
— shall be taken away *from* him.
39. Pharisees *from* among the multitude
42. now they are hid *from* thine eyes.
20:10. should give him *of* the fruit of the
46. Beware *of* the scribes, which desire
21:11. signs shall there be *from* heaven.
26. Men's hearts failing them *for* fear,
30. know *of* your own selves that summer
22:18. not drink *of* the fruit of the vine,
41. he was withdrawn *from* them about
42. remove this cup *from* me:
43. an angel unto him *from* heaven,
45. when he rose up *from* prayer,
— found them sleeping *for* sorrow,
69. Here*after* shall the Son of man
71. ourselves have heard *of* his own mouth.
23: 5. beginning *from* Galilee to this place.
26. coming *out of* the country, and on him
49. women that followed him *from* Galilee,
51. (he was) *of* Arimathæa, a city of the
24: 2. stone rolled away *from* the sepulchre.
9. returned *from* the sepulchre, and
13. which was *from* Jerusalem
21. third day *since* these things were
27. beginning *at* Moses and (lit. and *at*) all the

Lu. 24:31. he vanished *out of* their sight.
41. they yet believed not *for* joy, and
42. broiled fish, and *of* an honeycomb.
47. all nations, beginning *at* Jerusalem.
51. he was parted *from* them, and carried
Joh. 1:44(45). Philip was *of* Bethsaida, the
45(46). Jesus *of* Nazareth the son of Joseph
51(52). Here*after* ye shall see heaven open,
3: 2. thou art a teacher come *from* God:
5:19. The Son can do nothing *of* himself,
30. I can *of* mine own self do nothing:
7:17. or (whether) I speak *of* myself.
18. He that speaketh *of* himself seeketh
28. I am not come *of* myself, but he
42. *out of* the town of Bethlehem, where
8: 9. beginning *at* the eldest, (even)
28. (that) I do nothing *of* myself, but
42. neither came I *of* myself, but he
44. He was a murderer *from* the beginning,
10: 5. not follow, but will flee *from* him:
18. No man taketh it *from* me, but I lay it down *of* myself. I have
11: 1. (named) Lazarus, *of* Bethany, the
18. unto Jerusalem, about fifteen furlongs *off*:
51. this spake he not *of* himself: but
53. Then *from* that day forth they took
12:21. which (was) *of* Bethsaida of Galilee,
36. departed, and did hide himself *from* them.
13: 3. that he was come *from* God, and
19. Now (lit. *from* now) I tell you before it come,
14: 7. *from* henceforth ye know him,
10. unto you I speak not *of* myself:
15: 4. the branch cannot bear fruit *of* itself,
27. been with me *from* the beginning.
16:13. for he shall not speak *of* himself;
22. your joy no man taketh *from* you.
30. that thou camest forth *from* God.
18:28. led they Jesus *from* Caiaphas unto
34. Sayest thou this thing *of* thyself,
19:27. *from* that hour that disciple took
38. after this Joseph *of* Arimathæa,
21: 2. Nathanael *of* Cana in Galilee, and
6. to draw it *for* the multitude of fishes.
8. they were not far *from* land, but as it were two hundred cubits, (lit. *off*)
10. Bring *of* the fish which ye have now
Acts 1: 4. should not depart *from* Jerusalem,
9. a cloud received him *out of* their sight.
11. is taken up *from* you into heaven,
12. *from* the mount called Olivet,
22. Beginning *from* the baptism of
— that he was taken up *from* us,
2: 5. *out of* every nation under heaven.
17. I will pour out *of* my Spirit upon
18. in those days *of* my Spirit; and
22. a man approved *of* God among
40. yourselves *from* this untoward generation.
3:19. *from* the presence of the Lord;
21. holy prophets *since* the world began,
24. all the prophets *from* Samuel
26. every one of you *from* his iniquities.
5: 2. kept back (part) *of* the price, his
3. to keep back (part) *of* the price of the
38. Refrain *from* these men, and let
41. departed *from* the presence of the
6: 9. Alexandrians, and of them *of* Cilicia
7:45. God drave out *before* the face of
8:10. *from* the least to the greatest,
22. Repent therefore *of* this thy wickedness,
26. that goeth down *from* Jerusalem
33. his life is taken *from* the earth.

Acts 8:35. began *at* the same scripture, and
9: 3. round about him a light *from* heaven:
8. Saul arose *from* the earth; and when
13. I have heard *by* many of this man,
18. there fell *from* his eyes as it had
10:17. men which were sent *from* Cornelius
21. were sent unto him *from* Cornelius;
23. certain brethren *from* Joppa
30. Four days *ago* I was fasting until
37. all Judæa, and began *from* Galilee,
38. God anointed Jesus *of* Nazareth
11:11. I was, sent *from* Cæsarea unto me.
19. Now they which were scattered abroad *upon* the
27. came prophets *from* Jerusalem
12: 1. to vex certain *of* the church.
10. the angel departed *from* him.
14. opened not the gate *for* gladness,
19. he went down *from* Judæa to
20. was nourished *by* the king's
13: 8. turn away the deputy *from* the faith.
13. his company loosed *from* Paphos,
— John departing *from* them
14. when they departed *from* Perga,
23. *Of* this man's seed hath God
29. they took (him) down *from* the tree
31. with him *from* Galilee to
39. *from* which ye could not be
50. expelled them *out of* their coasts.
14:15. should turn *from* these vanities
19. thither (certain) Jews *from* Antioch
15: 1. men which came down *from*
5. certain *of* the sect of the Pharisees
7. how that a good while *ago*
18. *from* the beginning of the world.
19. which *from among* the Gentiles
20. that they abstain *from* pollutions
33. *from* the brethren unto the apostles.
38. departed *from* them *from* Pamphylia,
39. departed asunder one *from* the other:
16:11. Therefore loosing *from* Troas,
18. to come *out of* her. And he
33. of the night, and washed (their) (lit. *from* their) stripes;
17: 2. with them *out of* the scriptures,
13. when the Jews *of* Thessalonica had
27. he be not far *from* every one of us:
18: 2. lately come *from* Italy, with his
5. Timotheus were come *from* Macedonia,
6. *from* henceforth I will go unto
16. drave them *from* the judgment seat.
21. if God will. And he sailed *from* Ephesus.
19: 9. he departed *from* them, and separated
12. So that *from* his body were brought
— the diseases departed *from* them, and the evil spirits went *out of* them.
13. Then certain *of* the vagabond Jews,
20: 6. we sailed away *from* Philippi
9. *with* sleep, and fell down *from* the third loft, and
17. *from* Miletus he sent to Ephesus,
18. know, *from* the first day that (lit. *from* which) I
26. that I (am) pure *from* the blood of
21: 1. after we were gotten *from* them,
7. we had finished (our) course *from* Tyre,
10. there came down *from* Judæa
16. (certain) of the disciples *of* Cæsarea,
21. the Gentiles to forsake Moses, (lit. apostasy *from*)
27. the Jews which were *of* Asia, when
22:11. I could not see *for* the glory of

Acts 22:22. Away with such a (fellow) *from* the earth
29. straightway they departed *from* him
30. he loosed him *from* (his) bands,
23:21. looking for a promise *from* thee.
23. *at* the third hour of the night;
34. he understood that (he was) *of* Cilicia;
24:11. twelve days since (lit. *from* that) I went up to
18. certain Jews *from* Asia found
25: 1. he ascended *from* Cæsarea to
7. Jews which came down *from*
26: 4. from my youth, which was *at* the first
18. to turn (them) *from* darkness to
27:21. not have loosed *from* Crete, and
44. some on (broken pieces) *of* the ship.
28:21. neither received letters *out of* Judæa
23. both *out of* the law of Moses, and
— *from* morning till evening.
Ro. 1: 7. Grace to you and peace *from* God
18. revealed *from* heaven against
20. of him *from* the creation of the world
5: 9. we shall be saved *from* wrath
14. death reigned *from* Adam to Moses,
6: 7. he that is dead is freed *from* sin.
18. Being then made free *from* sin,
22. now being made free *from* sin,
7: 2. she is loosed *from* the law of
3. she is free *from* that law;
6. now we are delivered *from* the law,
8: 2. free *from* the law of sin and death.
21. delivered *from* the bondage of
35. separate us *from* the love of Christ?
39. able to separate us *from* the love of
9: 3. myself were accursed *from* Christ
11:25. blindness *in* part is happened
26. turn away ungodliness *from* Jacob:
13: 1. For there is no power but *of* God:
15:15. more boldly unto you *in* some sort,
19. so that *from* Jerusalem, and round
23. a great desire these (lit. *from*) many years
24. somewhat (lit. *in* part) filled with your (company).
31. be delivered *from* them that do not
16:17. ye have learned; and avoid (lit. bend *from*) them.
1Co 1: 3. Grace (be) unto you, and peace, *from* God
30. who *of* God is made unto us wisdom,
4: 5. shall every man have praise *of* God.
6:19. which ye have *of* God, and ye are
7:10. not the wife depart *from* (her) husband.
27. Art thou loosed *from* a wife? seek
10:14. my dearly beloved, flee *from* idolatry.
11:23. For I have received *of* the Lord that
14:36. came the word of God out *from* you?
2Co. 1: 2. Grace (be) to you and peace *from* God our
14. ye have acknowledged us *in* part,
16. to come again *out of* Macedonia unto
2: 3. sorrow (from them) *of* whom I ought
5. he hath not grieved me, but *in* part:
3: 5. to think any thing as *of* ourselves.
18. into the same image *from* glory to glory (even) as *by* the Spirit of the Lord.
5: 6. we are absent *from* the Lord:
16. Wherefore hence*forth* know we no
7: 1. cleanse ourselves *from* all filthiness
13. his spirit was refreshed *by* you all.
8:10. also to be forward a year *ago*.
9: 2. that Achaia was ready a year *ago*;
10: 7. let him *of* himself think this again,

2Co.11 3. corrupted *from* the simplicity
9. brethren which came *from* Macedonia
12: 8. that it might depart *from* me.
Gal. 1: 1. Paul, an apostle, not *of* men,
3. Grace (be) to you and peace *from* God the
6. so soon removed *from* him that called
2: 6. *of* those who seemed to be somewhat,
12. before that certain came *from* James,
3: 2. This only would I learn *of* you,
4:24. the one *from* the mount Sinai,
5: 4. Christ is become of no effect (lit. ye cease *from* Christ) unto you,
Eph. 1: 2. Grace (be) to you, and peace, *from* God
3: 9. *from* the beginning of the world
4:31. evil speaking, be put away *from* you,
6:23. love with faith, *from* God the Father
Phi. 1: 2. Grace (be) unto you, and peace, *from* God our
5. the gospel *from* the first day, until
28. to you of salvation, and that *of* God.
4:15. when I departed *from* Macedonia,
Col. 1: 2. Grace (be) unto you, and peace, *from* God
6. *since* the day ye heard (of it),
7. As ye also learned *of* Epaphras
9. we also, *since* the day we heard (it),
23. moved away *from* the hope of the
26. been hid *from* ages and *from* generations,
2:20. with Christ *from* the rudiments
3:24. that *of* the Lord ye shall receive
1Th. 1: 1. Grace (be) unto you, and peace, *from* God
8. For *from* you sounded out the word
9. how ye turned to God *from* idols
10. which delivered us *from* the wrath to
2: 6. neither *of* you, nor (yet) *of* others, when
17. being taken *from* you for a short
3: 6. Timotheus came *from* you unto us,
4: 3. ye should abstain *from* fornication:
16. shall descend *from* heaven with a
5:22. Abstain *from* all appearance of evil.
2Th. 1: 2. Grace unto you, and peace, *from* God our
7. shall be revealed *from* heaven with
9. destruction *from* the presence of the Lord, and *from* the glory of his power;
2: 2. That ye be not soon shaken *in* mind,
13. God hath *from* the beginning chosen
3: 2. delivered *from* unreasonable and
3. stablish you, and keep (you) *from* evil.
6. *from* every brother that walketh disorderly,
1Ti. 1: 2. Grace, mercy, (and) peace, *from* God
3: 7. a good report *of* them which are without;
6: 5. *from* such withdraw thyself.
10. they have erred *from* the faith,
2Ti. 1: 2. Grace, mercy, (and) peace, *from* God
3. I serve *from* (my) forefathers with
2:19. name of Christ depart *from* iniquity.
21. If a man therefore purge himself *from* these,
3:15. that *from* a child thou hast known
4: 4. turn away (their) ears *from* the truth,
18. deliver me *from* every evil work,
Tit. 1: 4. Grace, mercy, (and) peace, *from* God the
2:14. might redeem us *from* all iniquity,
Philem. 3. Grace to you, and peace, *from* God our
Heb 3:12. in departing *from* the living God.
4: 3. finished *from* the foundation of
4. the seventh day *from* all his works.
10. hath ceased *from* his own works, as God (did) *from* his.
5: 7. was heard *in* that he feared;
8. *by* the things which he suffered;
6: 1. of repentance *from* dead works,
7. receiveth blessing *from* God:
Heb 7: 1. returning *from* the slaughter
2. Abraham gave a tenth part *of* all;
13. *of* which no man gave attendance at
26. undefiled, separate *from* sinners,
8:11. *from* the least to the greatest.
9:14. purge your conscience *from* dead work
26. *since* the foundation of the world:
10:22. sprinkled *from* an evil conscience,
11:12. Therefore sprang there even *of* one,
15. that (country) *from* whence they came
34. *out of* weakness were made strong,
12:15. lest any man fail *of* the grace of God;
25. away from him that (speaketh) *from* heaven:
13:24. They *of* Italy salute you.
Jas. 1:13. tempted, I am tempted *of* God:
17. cometh down *from* the Father of
27. himself unspotted *from* the world.
4: 7. Resist the devil, and he will flee *from* you.
5: 4. which is *of* you kept back by fraud,
19. any of you do err *from* the truth,
1Pet. 1:12. Holy Ghost sent down *from* heaven;
3:10. let him refrain his tongue *from* evil,
11. Let him eschew (lit. depart *from*) evil, and do good;
4:17. must begin *at* the house of God: and if (it) first (begin) *at* us, what shall
2Pet. 3: 4. for since (lit *from* that) the fathers fell asleep,
— *from* the beginning of the creation.
1Joh. 1: 1. which was *from* the beginning,
5. message which we have heard *of* him,
7. his Son cleanseth us *from* all sin.
9. to cleanse us *from* all unrighteousness.
2: 7. which ye had *from* the beginning.
— ye have heard *from* the beginning.
13. (that is) *from* the beginning.
14. him (that is) *from* the beginning.
20. have an unction *from* the Holy One,
24. heard *from* the beginning. If that which ye have heard *from* the beginning
27. which ye have received *of* him
28. ashamed *before* him at his coming.
3: 8. the devil sinneth *from* the
11. that ye heard *from* the beginning,
17. shutteth up his bowels (of compassion) *from*
4:21. commandment have we *from* him,
5:21. children, keep yourselves *from* idols.
2Joh. 5. which we had *from* the beginning,
6. ye have heard *from* the beginning,
3Joh. 7. taking nothing *of* the Gentiles.
Jude 14. Enoch also, the seventh *from* Adam,
23. the garment spotted *by* the flesh.
Rev. 1: 4. *from* him which is, and which was,
— *from* the seven spirits which
5. *from* Jesus Christ, (who is) the
— washed us *from* our sins in his
2:17. I give to eat *of* the hidden manna,
3:12. down out of heaven *from* my God:
6: 4. to take peace *from* the earth, and
10. avenge our blood *on* them that
16. hide us *from* the face of him
— *from* the wrath of the Lamb;
7: 2. angel ascending *from* the east,
17. wipe away all tears *from* their eyes.
9: 6. death shall flee *from* them.
12: 6. she hath a place prepared *of* God,
14. *from* the face of the serpent.
13: 8. slain *from* the foundation of the
14: 3. which were redeemed *from* the earth.
4. These were redeemed *from* among

Rev.14:20. *by the space of* a thousand (and)
16:12. the way of the kings *of* the east
17. voice *out of* the temple of heaven, *from* the throne,
18. such as was not since (lit. *from* that) men were
17: 8. life *from* the foundation of the world,
18:10. Standing afar *off* for the fear of
14. lusted after are departed *from* thee,
— and goodly are departed *from* thee,
15. *by* her, shall stand afar *off* for the fear
17. as trade by sea, stood afar *off*,
20: 9. fire came down *from* God out of
11. *from* whose face the earth and the
21: 2. coming down *from* God out of
4. wipe away all tears *from* their eyes;
10. descending out of heaven *from* God,
13. *On* the east three gates; *on* the north three gates; *on* the south three gates; and *on* the west three gates.
22:19. shall take away *from* the words
— away his part *out of* the book of

576 4 88/89 575 *bainō* (to walk)

ἀποβαίνω, *apobaino.*

Lu. 5: 2. the fishermen *were gone out* of them, and
21:13. it *shall turn* to you for a testimony.
Joh.21: 9. then as they *were come* to land,
Phi. 1:19. that this *shall turn* to my salvation

577 2 88/89 575,906

ἀποβάλλω, *apoballo.*

Mar 10:50. he, *casting away* his garment,
Heb 10:35. *Cast* not *away* therefore your

578 1 88/89 575,991

ἀποβλέπω, *apoblepo.*

Heb 11:26. for he *had respect* unto the

579 1 88/89 577

ἀπόβλητος, *apobleetos.*

1Ti. 4: 4. nothing *to be refused*, if it be received

580 2 88/89 577

ἀποβολή, *apobolee.*

Acts27:22. there shall be no *loss* of (any man's) life
Ro. 11:15. For if the *casting away* of them (be)

581 1 88/89 575,1096

ἀπογενόμενος, *apogenomenos.*

1Pet.2:24. that we, *being dead* to sins, should

582 2 88/89 583

απογραφή, *apographee.*

Lu. 2: 2. this *taxing* was first made when
Acts 5:37. in the days of the *taxing*, and drew

583 4 89/89 575,1125

ἀπογράφω, *apographo.*

Lu. 2: 1. that all the world should *be taxed.*
3. all went *to be taxed*, every one into
5. *To be taxed* with Mary his espoused
Heb 12:23. firstborn, *which are written* in heaven

584 4 89/89 575,1166

ἀποδείκνυμι, *apodiknumi.*

Acts 2:22. a man *approved* of God among you
25: 7. against Paul, which they could not *prove.*
1Co. 4: 9. that God hath *set forth* us the apostles
2Th. 2: 4. *shewing* himself that he is God.

585 1 89/89 584

ἀπόδειξις, *apodixis.*

1Co. 2: 4. in *demonstration* of the Spirit and of

586 4 89/89 575,1183

ἀποδεκατόω, *apodekatoō.*

Mat.23:23. for ye *pay tithe* of mint and anise
Lu. 11:42. for ye *tithe* mint and rue and all manner
18:12. I *give tithes* of all that I possess.
Heb. 7: 5. *to take tithes* of the people according

587 2 89/89 2:50 588

ἀπόδεκτος, *apodektos.*

1Ti. 2: 3. For this (is) good and *acceptable* in the
5: 4. good and *acceptable* before God.

588 6 89/89 2:50 575,1209

ἀποδέχομαι, *apodekomai.*

Lu. 8:40. the people gladly *received* him:
Acts 2:41. they *that* gladly *received* his word
15: 4. they *were received* of the church,
18:27. exhorting the disciples *to receive* him:
24: 3. We *accept* (it) always, and in all
28:30. *received* all that came in unto

589 6 89/89 590

ἀποδημέω, *apodeemeō.*

Mat.21:33. *went into a far country:*
25:14. a man *travelling into a far country,*
15. ability; and straightway *took* his *journey.*
Mar 12: 1. husbandmen, and *went into a far country.*
Lu. 15:13. *took* his *journey* into a far country,
20: 9. *went into a far country* for a long

590 1 89/89 575,1218

ἀπόδημος, *apodeemos.*

Mar 13:34. as a man *taking a far journey,*

591 48 89/89 2:166 575,1325

ἀποδίδωμι, *apodidōmi.*

Mat. 5:26. till thou *hast paid* the uttermost
33. *shalt perform* unto the Lord
6: 4. himself *shall reward* thee openly.
6. seeth in secret *shall reward* thee openly.
18. in secret, *shall reward* thee openly.
12:36. they *shall give* account thereof
16:27. then he *shall reward* every man
18:25. forasmuch as he had not *to pay*,
— that he had, and *payment to be made.*
26. with me, and I *will pay* thee all.
28. saying, *Pay* me that thou owest.
29. patience with me, and I *will pay* thee all.
30. till he *should pay* the debt.
34. till he *should pay* all that was
20: 8. Call the labourers, and *give* them (their) hire,
21:41. which *shall render* him the
22:21. *Render* therefore unto Cæsar the

Mat.27:58. commanded the body *to be delivered.*
Mar 12:17. *Render* to Cæsar the things that
Lu. 4:20. he *gave* (it) *again* to the minister, *and*
7:42. when they had nothing *to pay,*
9:42. *delivered* him *again* to his father.
10:35. I come again, I *will repay* thee.
12:59. till thou *hast paid* the very
16: 2. *give* an account of thy stewardship;
19: 8. accusation, I *restore* (him) fourfold.
20:25. *Render* therefore unto Cæsar the
Acts 4:33. *gave* the apostles witness of the
5: 8. whether ye *sold* the land for
7: 9. with envy, *sold* Joseph into Egypt:
19:40. we may *give* an account of
Ro 2: 6. Who *will render* to every man
12:17. *Recompense* to no man evil
13: 7. *Render* therefore to all their dues:
1Co. 7: 3. *Let* the husband *render* unto the
1Th. 5:15. See that none *render* evil for evil
1Ti. 5: 4. piety at home, and to requite (lit. *to render* recompence to) their parents:
2Ti. 4: 8. *shall give* me at that day:
14. the Lord *reward* him according
Heb 12:11. afterward it *yieldeth* the peaceable
16. morsel of meat *sold* his birthright.
13:17. as they *that* must *give* account,
1Pet.3: 9. Not *rendering* evil for evil, or
4: 5. Who *shall give* account to him
Rev.18: 6. *Reward* her even as she *rewarded*
22: 2. *yielded* her fruit every month:
12. *to give* every man according

592 1 90/90 5:452 575,1223 3724

ἀποδιορίζω, *apodiorizo.*

Jude 19. These be they *who separate themselves,*

593 9 90/90 2:255 575,1381

ἀποδοκιμάζω, *apodokimazo.*

Mat.21:42. The stone which the builders *rejected,*
Mar. 8:31. *be rejected* of the elders, and (of) the
12:10. The stone which the builders *rejected*
Lu. 9:22. *be rejected* of the elders and chief
17:25. *be rejected* of this generation.
20:17. The stone which the builders *rejected*
Heb 12:17. inherited the blessing, he *was rejected:*
1Pet.2: 4. *disallowed* indeed of men, but
7. the stone which the builders *disallowed,*

594 2 90/90 2:50 588

ἀποδοχή, *apodokee.*

1Ti. 1:15. worthy of all *acceptation,* that
4: 9. saying and worthy of all *acceptation.*

595 2 90/90 659

ἀπόθεσις, *apothesis.*

1Pet.3:21. not the *putting away* of the filth
2Pet.1:14. I must put off (this) my tabernacle, (lit. my *putting off* of)

596 6 90/90 659

ἀποθήκη, *apotheekee.*

Mat. 3:12. gather his wheat into the *garner;*
6:26. do they reap, nor gather into *barns;*
13:30. gather the wheat into my *barn.*
Lu. 3:17. gather the wheat into his *garner;*
12:18. I will pull down my *barns,*
24. which neither have storehouse nor *barn;*

597 1 90/90 575,2343

ἀποθησαυρίζω, *apotheesaurizo.*

1Ti. 6:19. *Laying up in store* for themselves

598 1 90/90 575,2346

ἀποθλίβω, *apothlibo.*

Lu. 8:45. the multitude throng thee and *press* (thee),

599 111 90/90 3:7 575,2348

ἀποθνήσκω, *apotheesko.*

Mat. 8:32. into the sea, and *perished* in the waters.
9:24. for the maid *is* not *dead,* but sleepeth.
22:24. Master, Moses said, If a man *die,*
27. last of all the woman *died* also.
26:35. Though I should *die* with thee, yet
Mar. 5:35. which said, Thy daughter *is dead:*
39. the damsel *is* not *dead,* but sleepeth.
9:26. that many said, He *is dead.*
12:19. If a man's brother *die,* and leave (his)
20. took a wife, and *dying* left no seed.
21. the second took her, and *died,* neither
22. last of all the woman *died* also.
15:44. he asked him whether he *had been* any while *dead.*
Lu. 8:42. twelve years of age, and she *lay a dying.*
52. Weep not; she *is* not *dead,* but sleepeth.
53. knowing that she *was dead.*
16:22. it came to pass, that the beggar *died,*
— the rich man also *died,* and was
20:28. If any man's brother *die,* having a wife
— and he *die* without children, that his
29. took a wife, and *died* without children.
30. her to wife, and he *died* childless.
31. they left no children, and *died.*
32. Last of all the woman *died* also.
36. Neither can they *die* any more:
Joh. 4:47. for he was at the point *of death.*
49. Sir, come down ere my child *die.*
6:49. eat manna in the wilderness, and *are dead.*
50. a man may eat thereof, and not *die.*
58. fathers did eat manna, and *are dead:*
8:21. shall seek me, and *shall die* in your
24. that ye *shall die* in your sins:
— ye *shall die* in your sins:
52. Abraham *is dead,* and the prophets;
53. which *is dead?* and the prophets *are dead:*
11:14. unto them plainly, Lazarus *is dead*
16. that we *may die* with him.
25. though he *were dead,* yet shall
26. believeth in me *shall* never *die.*
32. been here, my brother *had* not *died.*
37. this man should not *have died?*
50. one man *should die* for the people,
51. that Jesus should *die* for that
12:24. of wheat fall into the ground and *die* it abideth alone: but if it *die,* it
33. signifying what death he should *die.*
18:32. what death he should *die.*
19: 7. by our law he ought *to die,*
21:23. that disciple *should* not *die:* yet Jesus said not unto him, He *shall* not *die,*
Acts 7: 4. thence, when his father was *dead,*
9:37. that she was sick, and *died:*
21:13. also *to die* at Jerusalem for the
25:11. worthy of death, I refuse not *to die*
Ro. 5: 6. in due time Christ *died* for the
7. for a righteous man *will* one *die*·

Ro. 5: 7. some would even dare *to die*.
8. yet sinners, Christ *died* for us.
15. the offence of one many *be dead*,
6: 2. How shall we, that *are dead* to sin,
7. For he that *is dead* is freed from
8. Now if we *be dead* with Christ,
9. raised from the dead, *dieth* no more;
10. For in that he *died*, he *died* unto
7: 2. if the husband *be dead*, she is
3. if her husband *be dead*, she is
6. that *being dead* wherein we
9(10). sin revived, and I *died*.
8:13. live after the flesh, ye shall *die:*
34. (It is) Christ *that died*, yea rather,
14: 7. no man *dieth* to himself.
8. whether we *die*, we *die* unto
— live therefore, or *die*, we are the Lord's.
9. to this end Christ both *died*, and rose,
15. thy meat, for whom Christ *died*.
1Co. 8:11. brother perish, for whom Christ *died?*
9:15. better for me *to die*, than that any
15: 3. how that Christ *died* for our sins
22. For as in Adam all *die*, even so
31. Jesus our Lord, I *die* daily.
32. eat and drink; for to morrow we *die*.
36. is not quickened, except it *die:*
2Co. 5:14(15). that if one *died* for all, then were all *dead:* (lit. *died*)
15. (that) he *died* for all, that they
— unto him *which died* for them,
6: 9. as *dying*, and, behold, we live;
Gal. 2:19. I through the law *am dead* to
21. then Christ *is dead* in vain.
Phi. 1:21. to live (is) Christ, and *to die* (is) gain.
Col. 2:20. if ye *be dead* with Christ from
3: 3. For ye *are dead*, and your life is hid
1Th. 4:14. that Jesus *died* and rose again, even
5:10. *Who died* for us, that, whether we
Heb. 7: 8. here men *that die* receive tithes;
9:27. it is appointed unto men once *to die*,
10:28. despised Moses' law *died* without
11: 4. by it he *being dead* yet speaketh.
13. These all *died* in faith, not having
21. Jacob, when he was *a dying*,
37. were slain with (lit. *died by* the death of) the sword:
Jude 12. without fruit, twice *dead*, plucked
Rev. 3: 2. remain, that are ready *to die:*
8: 9. in the sea, and had life, *died;*
11. many men *died* of the waters,
9: 6. not find it; and shall desire *to die*,
14:13. Blessed (are) the dead *which die* in the Lord
16: 3. every living soul *died* in the sea.

600 8 91/91 1:387 575,2525

ἀποκαθιστ-άω, -άνω, -ημι, *apokathist-ao, -ano, -eemi.*

Mat.12:13. it *was restored* whole, like as the other.
17:11. first come, and *restore* all things.
Mar. 3: 5. his hand *was restored* whole as
8:25. he *was restored*, and saw every man
9:12. cometh first, and *restoreth* all things;
Lu. 6:10. his hand *was restored* whole as the
Acts 1: 6. at this time *restore again* the kingdom
Heb 13:19. that I *may be restored* to you the

601 26 91/92 3:556 575,2572

ἀποκαλύπτω, *apokalupto.*

Mat.10:26. that shall not *be revealed;* and
Mat.11:25. *hast revealed* them unto babes.
27. to whomsoever the Son will *reveal* (him).
16:17. flesh and blood *hath* not *revealed* (it) unto
Lu. 2:35. of many hearts *may be revealed*.
10:21. *hast revealed* them unto babes:
22. (he) to whom the Son will *reveal* (him).
12: 2. covered, that *shall* not *be revealed;*
17:30. when the Son of man *is revealed*.
Joh. 12:38. arm of the Lord *been revealed?*
Ro. 1:17. *is* the righteousness of God *revealed* from
18. the wrath of God *is revealed* from
8:18. glory which shall *be revealed* in us.
1Co. 2:10. God *hath revealed* (them) unto us
3:13. because it *shall be revealed* by fire;
14:30. If (any thing) *be revealed* to another
Gal. 1:16. *To reveal* his son in me, that
3:23. which should afterwards *be revealed*.
Eph. 3: 5. as it *is* now *revealed* unto his holy
Phi. 3:15. God *shall reveal* even this unto you.
2Th. 2: 3. that man of sin *be revealed*, the
6. that he *might be revealed* in his
8. then *shall* that Wicked *be revealed*,
1Pet. 1: 5. ready *to be revealed* in the last
12. Unto whom it *was revealed*, that
5: 1. the glory that shall *be revealed:*

602 18 91/92 3:556 601

ἀποκάλυψις, *apokalupsis.*

Lu. 2:32. A light *to lighten* the Gentiles, and
Ro. 2: 5. *revelation* of the righteous judgment
8:19. *manifestation* of the sons of God.
16:25. according to the *revelation* of the mystery,
1Co. 1: 7. waiting for the *coming* of our Lord
14: 6. speak to you either by *revelation*,
26. hath a tongue, hath a *revelation*,
2Co. 12: 1. to visions and *revelations* of the Lord.
7. the abundance of the *revelations*,
Gal. 1:12. by the *revelation* of Jesus Christ.
2: 2. I went up by *revelation*, and
Eph. 1:17. the spirit of wisdom and *revelation*
3: 3. How that by *revelation* he made
2Th. 1: 7. *when* the Lord Jesus *shall be revealed* (lit. in the *revelation* of &c.) from
1Pet. 1: 7. glory at the *appearing* of Jesus
13. at the *revelation* of Jesus Christ;
4:13. *when* his glory *shall be revealed*,
Rev. 1: 1. The *Revelation* of Jesus Christ,

603 2 92/92 1:393 575,1380 *kara* (head)

ἀποκαραδοκία, *apokaradokia.*

Ro. 8:19. the *earnest expectation* of the
Phi. 1:20. According to my *earnest expectation*

604 3 92/92 1:251 575,2644

ἀποκαταλλάττω, *apokatallatto.*

Eph. 2:16. that he *might reconcile* both unto
Col. 1:20. by him *to reconcile* all things unto
21. yet now *hath* he *reconciled*

605 1 92/92 1:387 600

ἀποκατάστασις, *apokatastasis.*

Acts 3:21. the times of *restitution* of all things,

606 4 92/92 3:654 575,2749

ἀπόκειμαι, *apokeimai.*

Lu. 19:20. which I have kept *laid up* in

Col. 1: 5. the hope *which is laid up* for you
2Ti. 4: 8. there *is laid up* for me a crown of
Heb. 9:27. as it *is appointed* unto men

607 4 92/92 575,2776

ἀποκεφαλίζω, apokephalizo.

Mat.14:10. he sent, and *beheaded* John in
Mar. 6:16. It is John, whom I *beheaded:*
27(28). he went and *beheaded* him in the
Lu. 9: 9. Herod said, John *have* I *beheaded:*

608 1 92/92 575,2808

ἀποκλείω, apoklīo.

Lu. 13:25. is risen up, and *hath shut to* the door,

609 6 92/92 3:830 575,2875

ἀποκόπτω, apokopto. cf 2699

Mar. 9:43. if thy hand offend thee, *cut* it *off:*
45. if thy foot offend thee, *cut* it *off:*
Joh.18:10. priest's servant, and *cut off* his right ear.
26. (his) kinsman whose ear Peter *cut off,*
Acts27:32. the soldiers *cut off* the ropes of
Gal. 5:12. I would they were even *cut off*

610 1 92/92 3:921 611

ἀπόκριμα, apokrima.

2Co. 1: 9. we had the *sentence* of death in

611 249 92/93 3:921 575 *krinō*

ἀποκρίνομαι, apokrinomai.

Mat. 3:15. Jesus *answering* said unto him,
4: 4. he *answered and* said, It is written,
8: 8. The centurion *answered and* said,
11. 4. Jesus *answered and* said unto them,
25. At that time Jesus *answered and*
12:38. scribes and of the Pharisees *answered,*
39. he *answered and* said unto them,
48. he *answered and* said unto him
13:11. He *answered and* said unto them,
37. He *answered and* said unto them,
14:28. Peter *answered* him *and* said, Lord,
15: 3. he *answered and* said unto them,
13. he *answered and* said, Every plant,
15. Then *answered* Peter *and* said unto
23. he *answered* her not a word.
24. he *answered and* said, I am not sent
26. he *answered and* said, It is not meet
28. Then Jesus *answered and* said unto her,
16: 2. He *answered and* said unto them,
16. Simon Peter *answered and* said,
17. Jesus *answered and* said unto him,
17: 4. Then *answered* Peter, *and* said unto
11. Jesus *answered and* said unto them,
17. Then Jesus *answered and* said,
19: 4. he *answered and* said unto them,
27. Then *answered* Peter *and* said unto
20:13. he *answered* one of them, *and* said,
22. Jesus *answered and* said, Ye know
21:21. Jesus *answered and* said unto them,
24. Jesus *answered and* said unto them,
27. they *answered* Jesus, *and* said,
29. He *answered and* said, I will not:
30. he *answered and* said, I (go), sir:
22: 1. Jesus *answered and* spake unto
29. Jesus *answered and* said unto them,
46. no man was able *to answer* him
24: 4. Jesus *answered and* said unto them,

Mat.25. 9. the wise *answered,* saying, (Not so);
12. he *answered and* said, Verily I say
26. His lord *answered and* said unto
37. Then *shall* the righteous *answer* him
40. the King shall *answer and* say unto
44. Then *shall* they also *answer* him,
45. Then *shall* he *answer* them,
26:23. he *answered and* said, He that
25. which betrayed him, *answered and* said,
33. Peter *answered and* said unto him,
62. unto him, *Answerest thou* nothing?
63. the high priest *answered and* said
66. They *answered and* said, He is guilty
27:12. priests and elders, he *answered* nothing
14. he *answered* him to never a
21. The governor *answered and* said
25. Then *answered* all the people, *and*
28: 5. the angel *answered and* said
Mar. 3:33. he *answered* them, saying,
5: 9. he *answered,* saying, My name
6:37. He *answered and* said unto them,
7: 6. He *answered and* said unto them,
28. she *answered* and said unto him,
8: 4. his disciples *answered* him,
28. they *answered,* John the Baptist.
29. Peter *answereth and* saith unto him,
9: 5. Peter *answered and* said to Jesus,
12. he *answered and* told them, Elias
17. one of the multitude *answered and*
19. He *answereth* him, *and* saith,
38. John *answered* him, saying,
10: 3. he *answered and* said unto them,
5. Jesus *answered and* said unto
20. he *answered and* said unto him,
24. Jesus *answereth* again, *and* saith
29. Jesus *answered and* said, Verily
51. Jesus *answered and* said unto him,
11:14. Jesus *answered and* said unto it,
22. Jesus *answering* saith unto
29. Jesus *answered and* said unto
— ask of you one question, and *answer* me
30. from heaven, or of men? *answer* me.
33. they *answered and* said unto Jesus,
— Jesus *answering* saith unto
12:17. Jesus *answering* said unto them,
24. Jesus *answering* said unto
28. that he *had answered* them well,
29. Jesus *answered* him, The first
34. saw that he *answered* discreetly,
35. Jesus *answered and* said, while
13: 2. Jesus *answering* said unto him,
5. Jesus *answering* them began
14:20. he *answered and* said unto them,
40. wist they what to *answer* him.
48. Jesus *answered and* said unto
60. saying, *Answerest* thou nothing?
61. held his peace, and *answered* nothing
15: 2. he *answering* said unto him,
4. saying, *Answerest* thou nothing?
5. Jesus yet *answered* nothing;
9. Pilate *answered* them, saying,
12. Pilate *answered and* said again
Lu. 1:19. the angel *answering* said unto
35. the angel *answered and* said unto
60. his mother *answered and* said,
3:11. He *answereth and* saith unto them,
16. John *answered,* saying unto (them)
4: 4. Jesus *answered* him, saying,
8. Jesus *answered and* said unto him,
12. Jesus *answering* said unto him,
5: 5. Simon *answering* said unto him,
22. he *answering* said unto them,

5:31. Jesus *answering* said unto them,
6: 3. Jesus *answering* them said,
7:22. Then Jesus *answering* said unto
40. Jesus *answering* said unto him,
43. Simon *answered and* said, I suppose
8:21. he *answered and* said unto them,
50. he *answered* him, saying, Fear not:
9:19. They *answering* said, John the
20. Peter *answering* said, The Christ
41. Jesus *answering* said, O faithless
49. John *answered and* said, Master,
10:27. he *answering* said, Thou shalt
28. unto him, Thou *hast answered* right:
41. Jesus *answered and* said unto her,
11: 7. from within shall *answer and* say,
45. Then *answered* one of the lawyers, *and*
13: 2. Jesus *answering* said unto them
8. he *answering* said unto him,
14. the ruler of the synagogue *answered...and*
15. The Lord then *answered* him,
25. he shall *answer and* say unto you,
14: 3. Jesus *answering* spake unto the
5. *answered* them, saying, Which
15:29. he *answering* said to (his) father,
17:17. Jesus *answering* said, Were there
20. he *answered* them and said,
37. they *answered and* said unto him,
19:40. he *answered and* said unto them,
20: 3. he *answered and* said unto them,
7. they *answered*, that they could
24. They *answered and* said, Cæsar's.
34. Jesus *answering* said unto them,
39. certain of the scribes *answering*
22:51. Jesus *answered and* said, Suffer
68. ye *will* not *answer* me, nor let
23: 3. he *answered* him *and* said,
9. he *answered* him nothing.
40. the other *answering* rebuked him,
24:18. Cleopas, *answering* said unto him,
Joh. 1:21. Art thou that prophet? And he *answered*, No.
26. John *answered* them, saying,
48(49). Jesus *answered* and said unto him,
49(50). Nathanael *answered* and saith
50(51). Jesus *answered* and said unto
2:18. Then *answered* the Jews and said
19. Jesus *answered* and said unto them,
3: 3. Jesus *answered* and said unto him,
5. Jesus *answered*, Verily, verily,
9. Nicodemus *answered* and said
10. Jesus *answered* and said unto
27. John *answered* and said, A man
4:10. Jesus *answered* and said unto her,
13. Jesus *answered* and said unto her,
17. The woman *answered* and said,
5: 7. The impotent man *answered*
11. He *answered* them, He that
17. Jesus *answered* them, My Father
19. Then *answered* Jesus and said
6: 7. Philip *answered* him, Two
26. Jesus *answered* them and said,
29. Jesus *answered* and said unto them,
43. Jesus therefore *answered* and said
68. Then Simon Peter *answered* him,
70. Jesus *answered* them, Have not
7:16. Jesus *answered* them, and said,
20. The people *answered* and said,
21. Jesus *answered* and said unto them,
46. The officers *answered*, Never man
47. Then *answered* them the Pharisees,
52. They *answered* and said unto him,
8:14. Jesus *answered* and said unto them,
19. Jesus *answered*, Ye neither know

Joh. 8:33. They *answered* him, We be Abraham's
34. Jesus *answered* them, Verily,
39. They *answered* and said unto him,
48. Then *answered* the Jews, and said
49. Jesus *answered*, I have not a devil;
54. Jesus *answered*, If I honour
9: 3. Jesus *answered*, Neither hath this
11. He *answered* and said, A man that
20. His parents *answered* them
25. He *answered* and said, Whether he
27. He *answered* them, I have told
30. The man *answered* and said unto
34. They *answered* and said unto him,
36. He *answered* and said, Who is he,
10:25. Jesus *answered* them, I told you,
32. Jesus *answered* them, Many
33. The Jews *answered* him, saying,
34. Jesus *answered* them, Is it not
11: 9. Jesus *answered*, Are there not
12:23. Jesus *answered* them, saying,
30. Jesus *answered* and said, This voice
34. The people *answered* him,
13: 7. Jesus *answered* and said unto him,
8. Jesus *answered* him, If I wash
26. Jesus *answered*, He it is, to whom
36. Jesus *answered* him, Whither
38. Jesus *answered* him, Wilt thou
14:23. Jesus *answered* and said unto him,
16:31. Jesus *answered* them, Do ye now
18: 5. They *answered* him, Jesus of Nazareth.
8. Jesus *answered*, I have told you
20. Jesus *answered* him, I spake
22. *Answerest* thou the high priest so?
23. Jesus *answered* him, If I have
30. They *answered* and said unto him,
34. Jesus *answered* him, Sayest
35. Pilate *answered*, Am I a Jew?
36. Jesus *answered*, My kingdom
37. Jesus *answered*, Thou sayest
19: 7. The Jews *answered* him, We have
11. Jesus *answered*, Thou couldest
15. The chief priests *answered*, We
22. Pilate *answered*, What I have
20:28. Thomas *answered* and said unto
21: 5. They *answered* him, No.
Acts 3:12. he *answered* unto the people,
4:19. Peter and John *answered and* said unto
5: 8. Peter *answered* unto her, Tell me
29. Peter and the (other) apostles *answered and*
8:24. Then *answered* Simon, *and* said,
34. the eunuch *answered* Philip, *and*
37. he *answered and* said, I believe
9:13. Then Ananias *answered*, Lord,
10:46. magnify God. Then *answered* Peter,
11: 9. the voice *answered* me again
15:13. James *answered*, saying, Men
19:15. the evil spirit *answered and* said,
21:13. Then Paul *answered*, What mean
22: 8. I *answered*, Who art thou, Lord?
28. the chief captain *answered*, With
24:10. *answered*, Forasmuch as I know
25. Felix trembled, and *answered*,
25: 4. Festus *answered*, that Paul
9. *answered* Paul, *and* said, Wilt thou
12. *answered*, Hast thou appealed
16. To whom I *answered*, It is not
Col. 4: 6. how ye ought *to answer* every
Rev. 7:13. one of the elders *answered*, saying

612 4 93/95 3:921 611

ἀπόκρισις, *apokrisis*.

Lu. 2:47. at his understanding and *answers*.
20:26. they marvelled at his *answer*.

Joh. 1:22. that we may give an *answer*
19: 9. Jesus gave him no *answer*.

613 6 93/95 3:957 575,2928

ἀποκρύπτω, *apokrupto*.

Mat. 11:25. because thou *hast hid* these things
25:18. in the earth, and *hid* his lord's money.
Lu. 10:21. that thou *hast hid* these things
1Co. 2: 7. (even) the *hidden* (wisdom), which
Eph. 3: 9. *hath been hid* in God, who
Col. 1:26. which *hath been hid* from ages

614 3 93/95 3:957 613

ἀπόκρυφος, *apokruphos*.

Mar. 4:22. neither was any thing *kept secret*,
Lu. 8:17. neither (any thing) *hid*, that shall
Col. 2: 3. In whom are *hid* all the treasures

615 75 93/95 575
kteinō (to slay)

ἀποκτείνω, *apoktino*.

Mat. 10:28. fear not them *which kill* the body, but are not able *to kill* the soul:
14: 5. he would *have put* him *to death*,
16:21. *be killed*, and be raised again the
17:23. they *shall kill* him, and the third
21:35. beat one, and *killed* another, and stoned
38. come, *let* us *kill* him, and let us
39. out of the vineyard, and *slew* (him).
22: 6. entreated (them) spitefully, and *slew* (them).
23:34. (some) of them ye *shall kill* and crucify;
37. (thou) *that killest* the prophets, and
24: 9. to be afflicted, and *shall kill* you:
26: 4. take Jesus by subtilty, and *kill* (him)
Mar. 3: 4. to save life, or *to kill*? But they
6:19. would *have killed* him; but
8:31. chief priests, and scribes, and *be killed*,
9:31. they *shall kill* him; and *after that* he *is killed*,
10:34. spit upon him, and *shall kill* him:
12: 5. him they *killed*, and many others; beating some, and *killing* some.
7. come, *let* us *kill* him, and
8. they took him, and *killed* (him)
14: 1. by craft, and *put* (him) *to death*.
Lu. 9:22. *be slain*, and be raised the third
11:47. prophets, and your fathers *killed* them.
48. for they indeed *killed* them, and
49. (some) of them they *shall slay* and
12: 4. afraid of them *that kill* the body,
5. after he *hath killed* hath power
13: 4. fell, and *slew* them, think ye that
31. for Herod will *kill* thee.
34. Jerusalem, *which killest* the prophets,
18:33. scourge (him), and *put* him *to death*.
20:14. come, *let* us *kill* him, that the
15. out of the vineyard, and *killed* (him).
Joh. 5:16. persecute Jesus, and sought *to slay* him,
18. sought the more *to kill* him,
7: 1. the Jews sought *to kill* him.
19. Why go ye about *to kill* me?
20. who goeth about *to kill* thee?
25. he, whom they seek *to kill*?
8:22. *Will* he *kill* himself? because
37. ye seek *to kill* me, because
40. now ye seek *to kill* me, a man
11:53. together for to *put* him *to death*.
12:10. *might put* Lazarus also *to death*;
16: 2. that whosoever *killeth* you will
Joh. 18:31. for us *to put* any man *to death*.
Acts 3:15. and *killed* the Prince of life, whom
7:52. they *have slain* them which
21:31. they went about *to kill* him,
23:12. till they *had killed* Paul.
14. nothing until we *have slain* Paul.
27:42. counsel was to *kill* the prisoners,
Ro. 7:11. deceived me, and by it *slew* (me).
11: 3. Lord, they *have killed* thy prophets,
2Co. 3: 6. for the letter *killeth*, but the spirit
Eph. 2:16. *having slain* the enmity thereby:
1Th. 2:15. *Who* both *killed* the Lord Jesus,
Rev. 2:13. who *was slain* among you,
23. I *will kill* her children with
6: 8. *to kill* with sword, and with hunger,
11. that should *be killed* as they
9: 5. that they *should* not *kill* them,
15. for to *slay* the third part of men.
18. *was* the third part of men *killed*,
20. men which *were* not *killed* by these
11: 5. he must in this manner *be killed*.
7. shall overcome them, and *kill* them
13. *were slain* of men seven thousand:
13:10. he that *killeth* with the sword must *be killed* with the sword.
15. image of the beast *should be killed*.
19:21. the remnant *were slain* with

616 2 93/96 575,rt 2949

ἀποκυέω, *apokueo*.

Jas. 1:15. is finished, *bringeth forth* death.
18. Of his own will *begat* he us with

617 4 93/96 575,2947

ἀποκυλίζω, *apokulizo*.

Mat. 28: 2. came and *rolled back* the stone
Mar 16: 3. Who *shall roll* us *away* the stone
4. that the stone *was rolled away*:
Lu. 24: 2. found the stone *rolled away* from

618 12 93/96 575,2983

ἀπολαμβάνω, *apolambano*.

Mar. 7:33. *took* him *aside* from the multitude, *and*
Lu. 6:34. of whom ye hope *to receive*, what
— lend to sinners, *to receive...again*.
15:27. because he *hath received* him
16:25. in thy lifetime *receivedst* thy
18:30. Who *shall* not *receive* manifold
23:41. for we *receive* the due reward
Ro. 1:27. *receiving* in themselves that
Gal. 4: 5. that we *might receive* the
Col. 3:24. ye *shall receive* the reward of the
2Joh. 8. that *we receive* a full reward.
3Joh. 8. We therefore ought *to receive* such,

619 2 94/96 575
lauō (to enjoy)

ἀπόλαυσις, *apolausis*.

1Ti. 6:17. to us richly all things to enjoy; (lit. for *enjoyment*)
Heb 11:25. than *to enjoy* the pleasures of sin

620 6 94/96 575,3007

ἀπολείπω, *apolipo*.

2Ti. 4:13. The cloke that I *left* at Troas with
20. Trophimus *have I left* at Miletum
Heb. 4: 6. Seeing therefore it *remaineth* that
9. There *remaineth* therefore a rest to
10:26. there *remaineth* no more sacrifice
Jude 6. but *left* their own habitation, he hath

621 1 94/369 575, leichō (to lick)

ἀπολείχω, apoliko.

Lu. 16:21. the dogs came and *licked* his sores.

622 92 94/96 1:394 575 rt 3639

ἀπόλλυμι, apollumi.

Mat. 2:13. the young child *to destroy* him.
5:29. one of thy members *should perish*,
30. one of thy members *should perish*,
8:25. Lord, save us: *we perish*.
9:17. wine runneth out, and the bottles *perish*:
10: 6. go rather to the *lost* sheep of the house
28. able *to destroy* both soul and body in hell.
39. that findeth his life *shall lose* it: and he *that loseth* his life for my sake
42. *shall* in no wise *lose* his reward.
12:14. how they *might destroy* him.
15:24. unto the *lost* sheep of the house
16:25. will save his life *shall lose* it: and whosoever *will lose* his life
18:11. come to save that *which was lost*.
14. of these little ones *should perish*.
21:41. *will* miserably *destroy* those wicked
22: 7. *destroyed* those murderers, and
26:52. *shall perish* with the sword.
27:20. ask Barabbas, and *destroy* Jesus.
Mar. 1:24. art thou come *to destroy* us?
2:22. the bottles *will be marred*:
3: 6. how they *might destroy* him.
4:38. carest thou not that we *perish*?
8:35. will save his life *shall lose* it; but whosoever *shall lose* his life
9:22. into the waters, to *destroy* him:
41. he *shall* not *lose* his reward.
11:18. how they *might destroy* him:
12: 9. will come and *destroy* the husbandmen,
Lu. 4:34. art thou come *to destroy* us?
5:37. spilled, and the bottles *shall perish*
6: 9. to save life, or *to destroy* (it)?
8:24. saying, Master, master, we *perish*.
9:24. will save his life *shall lose* it: but whosoever *will lose* his life for my
25. *and lose* himself, or be cast away
56. not come *to destroy* men's lives,
11:51. *which perished* between the altar
13: 3. ye *shall* all likewise *perish*.
5. ye *shall* all likewise *perish*.
33. that a prophet *perish* out of Jerusalem.
15: 4. *if* he *lose* one of them, doth not
— go after that *which is lost*, until
6. found my sheep *which was lost*.
8. if she *lose* one piece, doth not
9. found the piece which I *had lost*.
17. to spare, and I *perish* with hunger!
24. he was *lost*, and is found.
32. and was *lost*, and is found.
17:27. flood came, and *destroyed* them all.
29. from heaven, and *destroyed* (them) all.
33. to save his life *shall lose* it; and whosoever *shall lose* his life
19:10. to save that *which was lost*.
47. people sought *to destroy* him,
20:16. come and *destroy* these husbandmen,
21:18. not an hair of your head *perish*.
Joh. 3:15. believeth in him *should* not *perish*,
16. believeth in him *should* not *perish*,
6:12. that remain, that nothing *be lost*.
27. for the meat *which perisheth*,
39. given me I *should lose* nothing,
10:10. for to steal, and to kill, and to *destroy*:
28. they *shall* never *perish*, neither
Joh. 11:50. that the whole nation *perish* not.
12:25. that loveth his life *shall lose* it;
17:12. I have kept, and none of them *is lost*,
18: 9. thou gavest me *have* I *lost* none.
14. one man should *die* for the people
Acts 5:37. he also *perished*; and all, (even) as
Ro. 2:12. *shall* also *perish* without law:
14:15. *Destroy* not him with thy meat,
1Co. 1:18. to them *that perish* foolishness;
19. I *will destroy* the wisdom of the
8:11. *shall* the weak brother *perish*,
10: 9. tempted, and *were destroyed* of serpents.
10. *were destroyed* of the destroyer.
15:18. fallen asleep in Christ *are perished*.
2Co. 2:15. are saved, and in them *that perish*:
4: 3. it is hid to them *that are lost*:
9. cast down, but not *destroyed*;
2Th. 2:10. unrighteousness in them *that perish*;
Heb. 1:11. They *shall perish*; but thou remainest;
Jas. 1:11. grace of the fashion of it *perisheth*:
4:12. is able to save and *to destroy*:
1Pet. 1: 7. precious than of gold *that perisheth*,
2Pet. 3: 6. being overflowed with water, *perished*:
9. not willing that any should *perish*,
2Joh. 8. that we *lose* not those things
Jude 5. afterward *destroyed* them that
11. *perished* in the gainsaying of Core.

626 10 95/97 575,3056

ἀπολογέομαι, apologeomai.

Lu. 12:11. how or what thing ye *shall answer*,
21:14. meditate before what ye shall *answer*:
Acts 19:33. would *have made* his *defence* unto
24:10. more cheerfully *answer* for myself
25: 8. *While* he *answered for* himself,
26: 1. the hand, and *answered for* himself:
2. I shall *answer for* myself this
24. *as* he thus *spake for* himself,
Ro. 2:15. accusing or else *excusing* one another
2Co. 12:19. that we *excuse* ourselves unto you?

627 8 95/97 626

ἀπολογία, apologia.

Acts 22: 1. hear ye my *defence*, (which I make)
25:16. have licence *to answer for* himself
1Co. 9: 3. Mine *answer* to them that
2Co. 7:11. yea, (what) *clearing of* yourselves,
Phi. 1: 7. in the *defence* and confirmation
17. for the *defence* of the gospel.
2Ti. 4:16. At my first *answer* no man
1Pet. 3:15. to (give) an *answer* to every

628 2 95/97 4:295 575,3068

ἀπολούω, apolouō.

Acts 22:16. be baptized, and *wash away* thy sins,
1Co. 6:11. ye *are washed*, but ye are sanctified,

629 10 95/97 4:328 575,3083

ἀπολύτρωσις, apolutrōsis.

Lu. 21:28. for your *redemption* draweth nigh.
Ro. 3:24. through the *redemption* that is in
8:23. the *redemption* of our body.
1Co. 1:30. sanctification, and *redemption*:
Eph. 1: 7. In whom we have *redemption*
14. until the *redemption* of the
4:30. unto the day of *redemption*.
Col. 1:14. In whom we have *redemption*

Heb. 9:15. for the *redemption* of the transgressions
11:35. tortured, not accepting *deliverance;*

630 69 95/98 575,3089

ἀπολύω, apoluo.

Mat. 1:19. was minded *to put* her *away* privily.
5:31. Whosoever *shall put away* his wife,
32. whosoever *shall put away* his wife,
— shall marry her *that is divorced*
14:15. *send* the multitude *away*, that
22. while he *sent* the multitudes *away*.
23. *when* he *had sent* the multitudes *away*,
15:23. saying, *Send* her *away;* for she
32. I will not *send* them *away* fasting,
39. he *sent away* the multitude, *and*
18:27. *loosed* him, and forgave him the
19: 3. for a man *to put away* his wife
7. divorcement, and *to put* her *away?*
8. you *to put away* your wives:
9. Whosoever *shall put away* his wife,
— marrieth her *which is put away*
27:15. was wont *to release* unto the people
17. Whom will ye that I *release* unto you?
21. will ye that I *release* unto you?
26. Then *released* he Barabbas unto
Mar. 6:36. *Send* them *away*, that they may
45. while he *sent away* the people.
8: 3. if I *send* them *away* fasting
9. he *sent* them *away*.
10: 2. for a man *to put away* (his) wife?
4. divorcement, and *to put* (her) *away*.
11. Whosoever *shall put away* his wife,
12. If a woman *shall put away* her
15: 6. he *released* unto them one prisoner,
9. Will ye that I *release* unto you
11. he *should* rather *release* Barabbas
15. *released* Barabbas unto them,
Lu. 2:29. *lettest* thou thy servant *depart* in
6:37. *forgive*, and ye *shall be forgiven:*
8:38. Jesus *sent* him *away*, saying,
9:12. *Send* the multitude *away*, that
13:12. thou *art loosed* from thine infirmity.
14: 4. healed him, and *let* him *go;*
16:18. Whosoever *putteth away* his wife,
— marrieth her *that is put away* from
22:68. ye will not answer me, nor *let* (me) *go*.
23:16. therefore chastise him, and *release* (him).
17. he must *release* one unto them
18. *release* unto us Barabbas:
20. therefore, willing *to release* Jesus,
22. chastise him, and *let* (him) *go*.
25. he *released* unto them him
Joh. 18:39. that I *should release* unto you
— that I *release* unto you the King
19:10. have power *to release* thee?
12. Pilate sought *to release* him:
— If thou *let* this man *go*, thou art
Acts 3:13. determined *to let* (him) *go*.
4:21. they *let* them *go*, finding nothing
23. *being let go*, they went to their
5:40. the name of Jesus, and *let* them *go*.
13: 3. on them, they *sent* (them) *away*.
15:30. *when* they *were dismissed*, they
33. they *were let go* in peace from
16:35. saying, *Let* those men *go*.
36. have sent to *let* you *go:* now
17: 9. of the other, they *let* them *go*.
19:41. thus spoken, he *dismissed* the assembly.
23:22. *let* the young man *depart*, and
26:32. might *have been set at liberty*,
28:18. would *have let* (me) *go*, because

Acts28:25. among themselves, they *departed*,
Heb 13:23. brother Timothy *is set at liberty;*

631 1 96/98 575 *massō* (to press)

ἀπομάσσομαι, apomassomai.

Lu. 10:11. we *do wipe off* against you:

632 1 96/98 575,rt 3551

ἀπονέμω, aponemo.

1Pet. 3: 7. *giving* honour unto the wife, as

633 1 96/98 575,3538

ἀπονίπτω, aponipto.

Mat.27:24. *washed* (his) hands before the

634 1 96/98 575,4098

ἀποπίπτω, apopipto.

Acts 9:18. there *fell from* his eyes as it had

635 2 96/98 6:228 575,4105

ἀποπλανάω, apoplanao.

Mar 13:22. *to seduce*, if (it were) possible,
1Ti. 6:10. they *have erred* from the faith,

636 4 96/98 575,4126

ἀποπλέω, apopleo.

Acts13: 4. from thence they *sailed* to Cyprus.
14:26. thence *sailed* to Antioch, from
20:15. we *sailed* thence, *and* came the
27: 1. that we should *sail* into Italy,

637 1 96/819 575,4150

ἀποπλύνω, apopluno.

Lu. 5: 2. *were washing* (their) nets.

638 3 96/99 6:455 575,4155

ἀποπνίγω, apopnigo.

Mat.13: 7. the thorns sprung up, and *choked* them:
Lu. 8: 7. sprang up with it, and *choked* it.
33. place into the lake, and *were choked*.

639 4 97/99 1,rt 4198

ἀπορέομαι, aporeomai.

Joh.13:22. another, *doubting* of whom he spake.
Acts25:20. because I *doubted* of such manner
2Co. 4: 8. (we are) *perplexed*, but not in despair;
Gal. 4:20. for I *stand in doubt* of you.

640 1 97/99 rt 639

ἀπορία, aporia.

Lu. 21:25. distress of nations, with *perplexity;*

641 1 97/99 6:991 575,4496

ἀποῤῥίπτω, aporripto.

Acts27:43. should *cast* (themselves) first

642 1 97/99 575,3737

ἀπορφανίζομαι, aporphanizomai.

1Th. 2:17. *being taken* from you for a short

643 1 97/370 575,4632

αποσκευάζομαι, aposkūazomai.

Acts21:15. we *took up our carriages* (lit. *made ourselves ready*), *and* went up

644 1 97/99 7:394 575,4639

ἀποσκίασμα, aposkiasma.

Jas. 1:17. variableness, neither *shadow* of turning.

645 4 97/99 575,4685

ἀποσπάω, apospao.

Mat.26:51. *drew* his sword, and struck a servant
Lu. 22:41. he *was withdrawn* from them
Acts20:30. *to draw away* disciples after them.
21: 1. *after* we *were gotten* from them,

646 2 97/99 1:512 868

ἀποστασία, apostasia.

Acts21:21. among the Gentiles *to forsake* Moses,
2Th. 2: 3. except there come a *falling away* first,

647 3 97/99 868

ἀποστάσιον, apostasion.

Mat. 5:31. give her a *writing of divorcement*:
19: 7. to give a writing of *divorcement*,
Mar10: 4. to write a bill of *divorcement*, and

648 1 97/99 575,4721

ἀποστεγάζω, apostegazo.

Mar 2: 4. they *uncovered* the roof where

649 133 98/99 1:398 575,4724

ἀποστέλλω, apostello.

Mat. 2:16. *sent forth, and* slew all the children
10: 5. These twelve Jesus *sent forth*,
16. I *send* you *forth* as sheep in the
40. receiveth him *that sent* me.
11:10. I *send* my messenger before thy
13:41. The Son of man *shall send forth*
14:35. they *sent out* into all that country
15:24. I *am* not *sent* but unto the
20: 2. he *sent* them into his vineyard.
21: 1. then *sent* Jesus two disciples,
3. straightway he *will send* them.
34. he *sent* his servants to the
36. he *sent* other servants more
37. last of all he *sent* unto them
22: 3. *sent forth* his servants to call
4. Again, he *sent forth* other servants,
16. they *sent out* unto him their
23:34. I *send* unto you prophets, and wise
37. stonest them *which are sent* unto
24:31. he *shall send* his angels with
27:19. his wife *sent* unto him, saying,
Mar 1: 2. I *send* my messenger before thy
3:14. that he *might send* them *forth*
31. standing without, *sent* unto him,
4:29. immediately he *putteth in* the sickle,
5:10. that he *would* not *send* them *away*
6: 7. began *to send* them *forth* by two and two;
17. *had sent forth and* laid hold upon
27. the king *sent* an executioner, *and*
8:26. he *sent* him *away* to his house,
9:37. not me, but him *that sent* me.
11: 1. he *sendeth forth* two of his disciples,
3. straightway he *will send* him
Mar12: 2. he *sent* to the husbandmen a
3. beat him, and *sent* (him) *away* empty.
4. he *sent* unto them another
— *sent* (him) *away* shamefully
5. again he *sent* another; and
6. he *sent* him also last unto them,
13. they *send* unto him certain
13:27. then *shall* he *send* his angels,
14:13. he *sendeth forth* two of his disciples
Lu. 1:19. *am sent* to speak unto thee,
26. the angel Gabriel *was sent* from
4:18. he *hath sent* me to heal the
— *to set* at liberty them that are
43. for therefore *am* I *sent*.
7: 3. he *sent* unto him the elders of
20. John Baptist *hath sent* us unto
27. I *send* my messenger before thy
9: 2. he *sent* them to preach the
48. receiveth him *that sent* me:
52. *sent* messengers before his face:
10: 1. *sent* them two and two before
3. I *send* you *forth* as lambs among
16. despiseth him *that sent* me.
11:49. I *will send* them prophets and
13:34. stonest them *that are sent* unto
14:17. *sent* his servant at supper time
32. he *sendeth* an ambassage, *and*
19:14. *sent* a message after him, saying,
29. he *sent* two of his disciples,
32. they *that were sent* went their
20:10. he *sent* a servant to the husbandmen,
20. *sent forth* spies, which should
22: 8. he *sent* Peter and John, saying, Go
35. When I *sent* you without purse,
24:49 I *send* the promise of my Father
Joh. 1: 6. There was a man *sent* from God,
19. when the Jews *sent* priests and
24. they *which were sent* were of the
3:17. For God *sent* not his Son into the
28. that I am *sent* before him.
34. he whom God *hath sent* speaketh
4:38. I *sent* you to reap that whereon
5:33. Ye *sent* unto John, and he bare witness
36. that the Father *hath sent* me.
38. for whom he *hath sent*, him
6:29. on him whom he *hath sent*.
57. As the living Father *hath sent* me,
7:29. from him, and he *hath sent* me.
32. chief priests *sent* officers to take
8:42. came I of myself, but he *sent* me.
9. 7. which is by interpretation, *Sent*.
10:36. sanctified, and *sent* into the world,
11: 3. Therefore his sisters *sent* unto him,
42. believe that thou *hast sent* me.
17: 3. Jesus Christ, whom thou *hast sent*.
8. that thou *didst send* me.
18. As thou *hast sent* me into the world, even so *have* I also *sent* them into
21. believe that thou *hast sent* me.
23. know that thou *hast sent* me,
25. have known that thou *hast sent* me
18:24. Now Annas *had sent* him bound
20:21. as (my) Father *hath sent* me, even
Acts 3:20. he *shall send* Jesus Christ, which
26. *sent* him to bless you, in turning
5:21. *sent* to the prison to have them
7:14. Then *sent* Joseph, *and* called his
34. I *will send* thee into Egypt.
35. the same *did* God *send* (to be)
8:14. they *sent* unto them Peter and John
9:17. *hath sent* me, that thou mightest
38. they *sent* unto him two men,

Acts10: 8. he *sent* them to Joppa.
17. the men *which were sent* from
20. for I *have sent* them.
21. to the me[illegible]ich *were sent* unto
36. The word which (God) *sent* unto
11:11. *sent* from Cæsarea unto me.
13. *Send* men to Joppa, and call for
30. *and sent* it to the elders by the hands
13:15. rulers of the synagogue *sent* unto
26. the word of this salvation *sent*.
15:27. We *have sent* therefore Judas
16:35. the magistrates *sent* the serjeants,
36. The magistrates *have sent* to let
19:22. *So* he *sent* into Macedonia two
26:17. unto whom now I *send* thee,
28:28. salvation of God *is sent* unto the
Ro. 10:15. preach, except they *be sent?*
1Co. 1:17. For Christ *sent* me not to baptize,
2Co.12:17. of them whom I *sent* unto you?
2Ti. 4:12. Tychicus *have* I *sent* to Ephesus.
Heb 1:14. *sent forth* to minister for them
1Pet. 1:12. Holy Ghost *sent* down from heaven;
1Joh.4: 9. God *sent* his only begotten Son
10. he loved us, and *sent* his Son (to be)
14. that the Father *sent* the Son
Rev. 1: 1. he *sent and* signified (it) by his
5: 6. *sent forth* into all the earth.
22: 6. *sent* his angel to shew unto

650 6 98/101 575
stereō (to deprive)
ἀποστερέω, *apostereo*.

Mar10:19. *Defraud* not, Honour thy father
1Co. 6: 7. rather (suffer yourselves to) *be defrauded?*
8. Nay, ye do wrong, and *defraud*,
7: 5. *Defraud* ye not one the other,
1Ti. 6: 5. corrupt minds, and *destitute* of the truth,
Jas. 5: 4. which *is* of you *kept back by fraud*,

651 4 98/101 1:398 649
ἀποστολή, *apostolee*.

Acts 1:25. of this ministry and *apostleship*,
Ro. 1: 5. received grace and *apostleship*, for
1Co. 9: 2. the seal of mine *apostleship* are
Gal. 2: 8. to the *apostleship* of the circumcision,

652 81 99/101 1:398 649
ἀπόστολος, *apostolos*.

Mat.10: 2. the names of the twelve *apostles*
Mar 6:30. the *apostles* gathered themselves
Lu. 6:13. whom also he named *apostles;*
9:10. the *apostles*, when they were
11:49. send them prophets and *apostles*
17: 5. the *apostles* said unto the Lord,
22:14. the twelve *apostles* with him.
24:10. told these things unto the *apostles*.
Joh. 13:16. neither *he that is sent* greater
Acts 1: 2. commandments unto the *apostles*
26. numbered with the eleven *apostles*.
2:37. Peter, and to the rest of the *apostles*,
42. in the *apostles'* doctrine and fellowship,
43. were done by the *apostles*.
4:33. gave the *apostles* witness of the
35. laid (them) down at the *apostles'* feet:
36. who by the *apostles* was surnamed
37. laid (it) at the *apostles'* feet.
5: 2. laid (it) at the *apostles'* feet.
12. by the hands of the *apostles* were
18. laid their hands on the *apostles*,
29. Peter and the (other) *apostles* answered
Acts 5:34. to put the *apostles* forth a little
40. they had called the *apostles*,
6: 6. Whom they set before the *apostles:*
8: 1. Judæa and Samaria, except the *apostles*.
14. Now when the *apostles* which
18. laying on of the *apostles'* hands
9:27. brought (him) to the *apostles*, and
11: 1. the *apostles* and brethren that were
14: 4. with the Jews, and part with the *apostles*.
14. (Which) when the *apostles*, Barnabas
15: 2. unto the *apostles* and elders about
4. (of) the *apostles* and elders, and they
6. the *apostles* and elders came together
22. Then pleased it the *apostles* and
23. The *apostles* and elders and brethren
33. the brethren unto the *apostles*.
16: 4. were ordained of the *apostles* and
Ro. 1: 1. called (to be) an *apostle*, separated
11:13. as I am the *apostle* of the Gentiles,
16: 7. are of note among the *apostles*,
1Co. 1: 1. called (to be) an *apostle* of Jesus
4: 9. set forth us the *apostles* last,
9: 1. Am I not an *apostle?* am I not
2. If I be not an *apostle* unto others,
5. as well as other *apostles*, and
12:28. first *apostles*, secondarily
29. (Are) all *apostles?* (are) all
15: 7. of James; then of all the *apostles*.
9. I am the least of the *apostles*, that am not meet to be called an *apostle*,
2Co. 1. 1. Paul, an *apostle* of Jesus Christ
8:23. (they are) the *messengers* of the
11: 5. behind the very chiefest *apostles*.
13. themselves into the *apostles* of Christ.
12:11. the very chiefest *apostles*,
12. the signs of an *apostle* were
Gal. 1: 1. Paul, an *apostle*, not of men,
17. to them which were *apostles*
19. others of the *apostles* saw I none,
Eph. 1: 1. Paul, an *apostle* of Jesus Christ
2:20. the foundation of the *apostles* and
3: 5. revealed unto his holy *apostles* and
4:11. he gave some, *apostles;* and some,
Phi. 2:25. your *messenger*, and he that
Col. 1: 1. Paul, an *apostle* of Jesus Christ
1Th. 2: 6. as the *apostles* of Christ.
1Ti. 1: 1. Paul, an *apostle* of Jesus Christ
2: 7. ordained a preacher, and an *apostle*,
2Ti. 1: 1. Paul, an *apostle* of Jesus Christ
11. appointed a preacher, and an *apostle*,
Tit. 1: 1. an *apostle* of Jesus Christ,
Heb 3: 1. consider the *apostle* and high priest
1Pet. 1: 1. Peter, an *apostle* of Jesus Christ, to
2Pet. 1: 1. a servant and an *apostle* of Jesus
3: 2. of us the *apostles* of the Lord and Saviour:
Jude 17. before of the *apostles* of our Lord
Rev. 2: 2. them which say they are *apostles*,
18:20. (ye) holy *apostles* and prophets;
21:14. the names of the twelve *apostles*

653 1 99/102 575,4750
ἀποστοματίζω, *apostomatizo*.

Lu. 11:53. *to provoke* him *to speak* of many things:

654 10 99/102 7:714 575,4762
ἀποστρέφο, *apostrepho*.

Mat. 5:42. borrow of thee *turn* not thou *away*.
26:52. *Put up again* thy sword into his
27: 3. *brought again* the thirty pieces
Lu. 23:14. as one *that perverteth* the people:
Acts 3:26. in *turning away* every one of you

Ro. 11:26. *shall turn away* ungodliness from
2Ti. 1:15. in Asia *be turned away from* me;
4: 4. they *shall turn away* (their) ears
Tit. 1:14. men, *that turn from* the truth.
Heb 12:25. if we *turn away from* him that

655 1 100/102 575,rt 4767

ἀποστυγέω, apostugeo.

Ro. 12: 9. *Abhor* that which is evil; cleave

656 3 100/102 7:798 575,4864

ἀποσυνάγωγος, aposunagōgos.

Joh. 9:22. be *put out of the synagogue.*
12:42. should be *put out of the synagogue:*
16: 2. shall put you *out of the synagogues:*

657 6 100/102 575,5021

ἀποτάσσομαι, apotassomai.

Mar 6:46. *when* he *had sent* them *away*,
Lu. 9:61. let me first go *bid* them *farewell*,
14:33. that *forsaketh* not all that he hath,
Acts18:18. *then took* his *leave* of the brethren,
21. *bade* them *farewell*, saying, I
2Co. 2:13. *taking* my *leave* of them, I went

658 1 100/102 575,5055

ἀποτελέω, apoteleo.

Jas. 1:15. sin, *when* it is *finished*, bringeth

659 8 100/102 575,5087

ἀποτίθημι, apotitheemi.

Acts 7:58. the witnesses *laid down* their clothes
Ro. 13:12. therefore *cast off* the works of darkness,
Eph. 4:22. That ye *put off* concerning the former
25. Wherefore *putting away* lying, speak
Col. 3: 8. now ye also *put off* all these; anger,
Heb 12: 1. let us *lay aside* every weight, and
Jas. 1:21. Wherefore *lay apart* all filthiness
1Pet. 2: 1. Wherefore *laying aside* all malice,

660 2 100/102 575 *tinassō* (to jostle)

ἀποτινάσσω, apotinasso.

Lu. 9: 5. *shake off* the very dust from your
Acts28: 5. he *shook off* the beast into the fire,

661 1 100/102 575,5099

ἀποτίω, apotio.

Philem. 19. with mine own hand, I *will repay* (it):

662 1 100/102 8:181 575,5111

ἀποτολμάω, apotolmaō.

Ro. 10:20. Esaias *is very bold*, and saith,

663 2 101/102 8:106 rt 664

ἀποτομία, apotomia.

Ro. 11:22. therefore the goodness and *severity* of God: on them which fell, *severity*; but

664 2 101/102 8:106 575 *temnō* (to cut)

ἀποτόμως, apotomos.

2Co. 13:10. being present I should use *sharpness*,
Tit. 1:13. Wherefore rebuke them *sharply*.

665 1 101/102 575,rt 5157

ἀποτρέπομαι, apotrepomai.

2Ti. 3: 5. power thereof: from such *turn away*.

666 1 101/102 548

ἀπουσία, apousia.

Phi. 2:12. now much more in my *absence*,

667 5 101/102 575,5342

ἀποφέρω, apophero.

Mar 15: 1. bound Jesus, and *carried* (him) *away*,
Lu. 16:22. was *carried* by the angels into
1Co. 16: 3. them will I send *to bring* your
Rev. 17: 3. So he *carried* me *away* in the spirit
21:10. he *carried* me *away* in the spirit

668 3 101/102 575,5343

ἀποφεύγω, apophūgo.

2Pet. 1: 4. *having escaped* the corruption
2:18. *that were* clean *escaped* from them
20. For if *after* they *have escaped* the

669 3 101/102 1:447 575,5350

ἀποφθέγγομαι, apophthengomai.

Acts 2: 4. as the Spirit gave them *utterance*.
14. lifted up his voice, and *said* unto them,
26:25. *speak forth* the words of truth

670 1 101/103 575,5412

ἀποφορτίζομαι, apophortizomai.

Acts21: 3. the ship was to *unlade* her burden.

671 1 101/103 575,5530

ἀπόχρησις, apokreesis.

Col. 2:22. all are to perish with the *using*,

672 3 101/103 575,5562

ἀποχωρέω, apokōreo.

Mat. 7:23. *depart* from me, ye that work
Lu. 9:39. him hardly *departeth* from him.
Acts13:13. John *departing* from them

673 2 101/103 575,5563

ἀποχωρίζομαι, apokōrizomai.

Acts15:39. they *departed asunder* one from
Rev. 6:14. the heaven *departed* as a scroll

674 1 101/102 575,5594

ἀποψύχω, apopsuko.

Lu. 21:26. Men's *hearts failing* them for fear,

676 1 102/103 1,4314 *eimi* (to "go")

ἀπρόσιτος, aprositos.

1Ti. 6:16. the light *which no man can approach*

677 3 102/103 6:745 1,4350

ἀπρόσκοπος, aproskopos.

Acts24:16. a conscience *void of offence* toward
1Co. 10:32. Give *none offence*, neither to the Jews,
Phi. 1:10. *without offence* till the day of Christ:

678 1 102/103 6:768 1,4383 2983

ἀπροσωπολήπτως, aprosōpoleeptōs.

1Pet. 1:17. who *without respect of persons* judgeth

679 1 102/103 1,4417

ἄπταιστος, aptaistos.

Jude 24. is able to keep you *from falling,*

680 36 102/103 681

ἅπτομαι, haptomai.

Mat. 8: 3. Jesus put forth (his) hand, and *touched* him,
15. he *touched* her hand, and the fever
9:20. *touched* the hem of his garment:
21. If I *may* but *touch* his garment,
29. Then *touched* he their eyes,
14:36. *might* only *touch* the hem of his garment: and as many as *touched* were made
17: 7. Jesus came and *touched* them, and said,
20:34. compassion (on them), and *touched* their eyes:
Mar. 1:41. *touched* him, and saith unto him,
3:10. upon him for to *touch* him,
5:27. behind, and *touched* his garment.
28. If I *may touch* but his clothes,
30. said, Who *touched* my clothes?
31. sayest thou, Who *touched* me?
6:56. that they *might touch* if it were
— as many as *touched* him were
7:33. he spit, and *touched* his tongue;
8:22. besought him to *touch* him.
10:13. that he *should touch* them:
Lu. 5:13. put forth (his) hand, and *touched* him,
6:19. multitude sought *to touch* him:
7:14. he came and *touched* the bier:
39. woman (this is) that *toucheth* him:
8:44. *touched* the border of his garment:
45. Jesus said, Who *touched* me?
— sayest thou, Who *touched* me?
46. Jesus said, Somebody *hath touched* me:
47. what cause she *had touched* him,
18:15. that he *would touch* them:
22:51. he *touched* his ear, and healed him.
Joh. 20:17. *Touch* me not; for I am not
1Co. 7: 1. for a man not *to touch* a woman.
2Co. 6:17. *touch* not the unclean (thing);
Col. 2:21. *Touch* not; taste not; handle not;
1Joh. 5:18. that wicked one *toucheth* him not.

681 4 102/103

ἅπτω, hapto.

Lu. 8:16. No man, *when* he *hath lighted* a
11:33. No man, *when* he *hath lighted* a
15: 8. *doth* not *light* a candle, and sweep
22:55. *when* they *had kindled* a fire in

683 6 102/103 1:448 575 ōtheō (to shove)

ἀπωθέομαι, apōtheomai.

Acts 13:46. seeing ye *put* it *from* you, and judge

683 6 102/103 1:448 575 ōthō (to shove)

ἀπώθομαι, apōthomai.

Acts 7:27. his neighbour wrong *thrust* him *away*
39. not obey, but *thrust* (him) *from* them,
Ro. 11: 1. *Hath* God *cast away* his people?
2. God *hath* not *cast away* his people
1Ti. 1:19. which some *having put away*

684 20 103/103 1:394 622

ἀπώλεια, apōlia.

Mat. 7:13. that leadeth to *destruction*, and
26: 8. To what purpose (is) this *waste*?
Mar. 14: 4. Why was this *waste* of the ointment
Joh. 17:12. the son of *perdition*; that the
Acts 8:20. Thy money perish (lit. be to *destruction*) with thee,
25:16. Romans to deliver any man to *die*,
Ro. 9:22. vessels of wrath fitted to *destruction*:
Phi. 1:28. an evident token of *perdition*, but
3:19. Whose end (is) *destruction*, whose
2Th. 2: 3. be revealed, the son of *perdition*;
1Ti. 6: 9. drown men in destruction and *perdition*.
Heb 10:39. who draw back unto *perdition*; but
2Pet 2: 1. shall bring in *damnable* heresies,
— upon themselves swift *destruction*.
2. shall follow their *pernicious ways*;
3. their *damnation* slumbereth not.
3: 7. judgment and *perdition* of ungodly
16. unto their own *destruction*.
Rev. 17: 8. bottomless pit, and go into *perdition*:
11. is of the seven, and goeth into *perdition*.

685 1 103/104 1:448 142

ἀρά, ara.

Ro. 3:14. Whose mouth (is) full of *cursing* and bitterness:

686 51 103/104 142 cf 687

ἄρα, ara.

ἄραγε[2]. Those passages in which οὖν is combined in translation, are marked [3].

Mat. 7:20. *Wherefore* by their fruits ye shall [2]
12:28. *then* the kingdom of God is come
17:26. unto him, *Then* are the children free.[2]
18: 1. Who (lit. who *then*) is the greatest in the kingdom of
19:25. saying, Who *then* can be saved?
27. what shall we have *therefore*?
24:45. Who *then* is a faithful and wise
Mar. 4:41. What *manner of man* is this,
11:13. if *haply* he might find any thing
Lu. 1:66. What *manner* of child shall this be!
8:25. What *manner of man* is this!
11:20. *no doubt* the kingdom of God is
48. *Truly* ye bear witness that ye
12:42. Who *then* is that faithful and wise
22:23. which (lit. which *then*) of them it was that should
Acts 7: 1. priest, Are these things so? (lit. *indeed* so)
8:22. if *perhaps* the thought of thine
11:18. *Then* hath God also to the Gentiles[2]
12:18. what (lit. what *indeed*) was become of Peter.
17:27. if *haply* they might feel after[2]
21:38. Art not thou (lit. thou *then*) that Egyptian, which
Ro. 5:18. *Therefore* as by the offence of one[3]
7: 3. So *then* if, while (her) husband
21. I find *then* a law, that,
25. So *then* with the mind I myself
8: 1. (There is) *therefore* now no condemnation
12. *Therefore*, brethren, we are[3]
9:16. So *then* (it is) not of him that
18. *Therefore* hath he mercy on whom[3]
10:17. So *then* faith (cometh) by hearing,
14:12. So *then* every one of us shall
19. Let us *therefore* follow after the
1Co. 5:10. for *then* must ye needs go out

1Co. 7:14. else (lit. else *indeed*) were your children unclean;
15:14. *then* (is) our preaching vain, and
15. if *so be* that the dead rise not.
18. *Then* they also which are fallen
2Co. 1:17. thus minded, did I (lit. I *indeed*) use lightness?
5:14(15). died for all, *then* were all dead:
7:12. *Wherefore,* though I wrote unto you,
Gal. 2·21. *then* Christ is dead in vain.
3: 7. Know ye *therefore* that they
29. *then* are ye Abraham's seed,
4:31. So *then,* brethren, we are not
5:11. *then* is the offence of the cross
6:10. As we have *therefore* opportunity,
Eph. 2:19. Now *therefore* ye are no more
1Th. 5: 6. *Therefore* let us not sleep, as[3]
2Th. 2:15. *Therefore,* brethren, stand fast,[3]
Heb 4: 9. There remaineth *therefore* a
12: 8. *then* are ye bastards, and not sons.

687 3 103/104 686

ἆρα, *ara,* adv. whether.

Lu. 18: 8.)(shall he find faith on the earth?
Acts 8:30.)(Understandest thou what thou readest?
Gal. 2:17. (is) *therefore* Christ the minister

691 1 104/104 1:452 692

ἀργέω, *argeo.*

2Pet. 2: 3. of a long time *lingereth* not,

692 8 104/104 1:452 1,2041

ἀργός, *argos.*

Mat.12:36. That every *idle* word that men
20: 3. saw others standing *idle* in the
6. standing *idle,* and saith unto them, Why stand ye here all the day *idle?*
1Ti. 5:13. withal they learn (to be) *idle,*
— not only *idle,* but tattlers also
Tit. 1:12. alway liars, evil beasts, *slow* bellies.
2Pet. 1: 8. neither (be) *barren* nor unfruitful

694 20 104/105 696

ἀργύριον, *argurion.*

Mat.25:18. in the earth, and hid his lord's *money.*
27. therefore to have put my *money*
26:15. for thirty *pieces of silver.*
27. 3. the thirty *pieces of silver* to the
5. he cast down the *pieces of silver* in
6. chief priests took the *silver pieces,*
9. took the thirty *pieces of silver,*
28:12. they gave large *money* unto the
15. So they took the *money,* and did
Mar.14:11. promised to give him *money.*
Lu. 9: 3. neither bread, neither *money;*
19:15. to whom he had given the *money,*
23. gavest not thou my *money* into
22: 5. covenanted to give him *money.*
Acts 3: 6. *Silver* and gold have I none; but
7:16. Abraham bought for a sum of *money*
8:20. Thy *money* perish with thee,
19:19. fifty thousand (*pieces*) *of silver.*
20:33. I have coveted no man's *silver,*
1Pet. 1:18. corruptible things, (as) *silver* and gold,

695 1 104/105 696,2875

ἀργυροκόπος, *argurokopos.*

Acts19·24. Demetrius, a *silversmith,* which

696 5 104/105

ἄργυρος, *arguros.* *argos* (shining)

Mat.10: 9. Provide neither gold, nor *silver.*
Acts17:29. like unto gold, or *silver,* or stone,
1Co. 3:12. this foundation gold, *silver,*
Jas. 5: 3. Your gold and *silver* is cankered:
Rev.18:12. merchandise of gold, and *silver,*

693 3 104/105

ἀργυροῦς, *argurous.* *argos* (shining)

Acts19:24. which made *silver* shrines for
2 Ti. 2:20. not only vessels of gold and *of silver,*
Rev. 9:20. idols of gold, and *silver,* and brass, and stone,

699 1 105/105 1:455 700

ἀρέσκεια, *areskīa.*

Col. 1:10. worthy of the Lord unto all *pleasing,*

700 17 105/105 1:455 142

ἀρέσκω, *aresko.*

Mat.14: 6. danced before them, and *pleased* Herod.
Mar. 6:22. danced, *and pleased* Herod and them that
Acts 6: 5. the saying *pleased* the whole multitude:
Ro. 8: 8. they that are in the flesh cannot *please* God.
15: 1. the weak, and not *to please* ourselves.
2. *Let* every one of us *please* (his) neighbour
3. even Christ *pleased* not himself;
1Co. 7:32. how he *may please* the Lord:
33. how he *may please* (his) wife.
34. how she *may please* (her) husband.
10:33. as I *please* all (men) in all (things),
Gal. 1:10. do I seek *to please* men? for if I yet *pleased* men, I should
1Th. 2: 4. not as *pleasing* men, but God,
15. have persecuted us; *and* they *please* not God,
4: 1. how ye ought to walk and *to please* God,
2Ti. 2: 4. that he *may please* him who hath

701 4 105/105 1:455 700

ἀρεστός, *arestos.*

Joh. 8:29. I do always those *things that please* him.
Acts 6: 2. It is not *reason* that we should
12: 3. because he saw it *pleased* the Jews,
1Joh 3:22. *things that are pleasing* in his sight.

703 5 105/105 1:457 142

ἀρετή, *aretee.*

Phi. 4: 8. if (there be) any *virtue,* and if (there be) any praise,
1Pet. 2: 9. shew forth the *praises* of him who
2Pet. 1: 3. hath called us to glory and *virtue:*
5. add to your faith *virtue;* and to *virtue* knowledge;

704 1 105/105 1:338 142

ἀρήν, *areen.*

Lu. 10: 3. I send you forth as *lambs* among wolves.

705 3 105/105 1:461 706

ἀριθμεω, *arithmeo.*

Mat 10:30. hairs of your head are all *numbered.*
Lu. 12: 7. hairs of your head *are* all *numbered.*
Rev. 7: 9. multitude, which no man could *number,*

706 18 105/106 1:461 142
ἀριθμός, arithmos.

Lu. 22: 3. being of the *number* of the twelve.
Joh. 6:10. in *number* about five thousand.
Acts 4: 4. the *number* of the men was about
5:36. a *number* of men, about four hundred,
6: 7. the *number* of the disciples multiplied
11:21. a great *number* believed, and turned
16: 5. in the faith, and increased in *number* daily.
Ro. 9:27. Though the *number* of the children
Rev. 5:11 & 7:4. the *number* of them
9:16. the *number* of the army of the
— I heard the *number* of them.
13:17. name of the beast, or the *number* of his name.
18. count the *number* of the beast: for it is the *number* of a man; and his *number* is (χξϛ')
15: 2. over the *number* of his name,
20: 8. the *number* of whom (is) as the sand

709 3 106/106 712
ἀριστάω, aristaō.

Lu. 11:37. besought him to *dine* with him:
Joh.21:12. Jesus saith unto them, Come (and) *dine*.
15. So when they *had dined*, Jesus

710 3 106/106 rt 712
ἀριστερός, aristeros

Mat. 6: 3. let not thy *left hand* know what
Lu. 23:33. one on the right hand, and the other on the *left*.
2Co. 6: 7. on the right hand and on the *left*,

712 3 106/106 142
ἄριστον, ariston.

Mat.22: 4. Behold, I have prepared my *dinner*:
Lu. 11:38. had not first washed before *dinner*.
14:12. When thou makest a *dinner* or a supper,

713 3 106/106 714
ἀρκετός, arketos.

Mat. 6:34. *Sufficient* unto the day (is) the evil thereof.
10:25. It is *enough* for the disciple that he
1Pet. 4: 3. the time past of (our) life may *suffice* us

714 8 106/106 1:464 cf 142
ἀρκέω, arkeo.

Mat.25: 9. lest there *be* not *enough* for us and you.
Lu. 3:14. *be content* with your wages.
Joh. 6: 7. of bread *is* not *sufficient* for them,
14: 8. shew us the Father, and it *sufficeth* us.
2Co 12: 9. My grace *is sufficient* for thee:
1 Ti. 6: 8. food and raiment *let us be* therewith *content*.
Heb 13: 5. (be) *content* with such things as ye have:
3Joh. 10. malicious words: and not *content* therewith,

715 1 107/106 1:464 714
ἄρκτος, arktos.

Rev. 13: 2. his feet were as (the feet) of a *bear*,

716 4 102/106 142
ἅρμα, harma.

Acts 8:28. returning, and sitting in his *chariot*
29. Go near, and join thyself to this *chariot*.
38. he commanded the *chariot* to stand
Rev. 9: 9. as the sound of *chariots* of many

719 1 107/106 rt 716
ἁρμός, harmos.

Heb. 4:12. of the *joints* and marrow, and (is)

718 1 107/106 719
ἁρμόζω, harmozo.

2Co.11: 2. for I *have espoused* you to one husband,

720 31 107/107 1:469 1,4483
ἀρνέομαι, arneomai.

Mat 10:33. whosoever *shall deny* me before men, him *will* I also *deny* before my Father
26:70. he *denied* before (them) all,
72. again he *denied* with an oath,
Mar 14:68. he *denied*, saying, I know not,
70. he *denied* it again. And a little
Lu. 8:45. *When* all *denied*, Peter and they
12: 9. he *that denieth* me before men
22:57. he *denied* him, saying, Woman,
Joh. 1:20. he confessed, and *denied* not; but
18:25. He *denied* (it), and said, I am not.
27. Peter then *denied* again:
Acts 3:13. *denied* him in the presence of Pilate,
14. ye *denied* the Holy One and the Just,
4:16. in Jerusalem; and we cannot *deny* (it).
7:35. Moses whom they *refused*, saying,
1 Ti. 5: 8. he *hath denied* the faith, and is
2 Ti. 2:12. if we *deny* (him), he also *will deny* us:
13. he cannot *deny* himself.
3: 5. form of godliness, but *denying* the power
Tit. 1:16. in works they *deny* (him),
2:12. *denying* ungodliness and worldly lusts,
Heb 11:24. *refused* to be called the son of
2Pet. 2: 1. even *denying* the Lord that bought
1Joh 2:22. he *that denieth* that Jesus is the Christ?
— *that denieth* the Father and the Son.
23. Whosoever *denieth* the Son, the
Jude 4. *denying* the only Lord God, and our
Rev. 2:13. *hast* not *denied* my faith,
3: 8. *hast* not *denied* my name.

721 30 107/107 1:338 704
ἀρνίον, arnion.

Joh.21:15. He saith unto him, Feed my *lambs*.
Rev. 5: 6. in the midst of the elders, stood a *Lamb*
8. elders fell down before the *Lamb*,
12. Worthy is the *Lamb* that was slain
13. upon the throne, and unto the *Lamb* for ever
6: 1. when the *Lamb* opened one of the seals,
16. from the wrath of the *Lamb*:
7: 9. before the *Lamb*, clothed with white
10. upon the throne, and unto the *Lamb*.
14. white in the blood of the *Lamb*.
17. For the *Lamb* which is in the
12:11. by the blood of the *Lamb*, and by the
13: 8. book of life of the *Lamb* slain
11. he had two horns like a *lamb*,
14: 1. lo, a *Lamb* stood on the mount
4. they which follow the *Lamb*
— the firstfruits unto God and to the *Lamb*.
10. in the presence of the *Lamb*:
15: 3. of God, and the song of the *Lamb*, saying.
17:14. These shall make war with the *Lamb*, and the *Lamb* shall overcome them:
19: 7. the marriage of the *Lamb* is come.
9. unto the marriage supper of the *Lamb*.
21: 9. shew thee the bride, the *Lamb's* wife.
14. the twelve apostles of the *Lamb*.
22. Lord God Almighty, and the *Lamb*

Rev 21:23. the *Lamb* (is) the light thereof.
27. written in the *Lamb's* book of life.
22: 1. the throne of God and of the *Lamb*.
3. the throne of God and of the *Lamb*

756 See also p. 85 /113

ἀρξάμενος, arxamenos.

Lu. 24:47. among all nations, *beginning* at Jerusalem.
Acts10:37. *and began* from Galilee, after the

722 3 108/107 723

ἀροτριάω, arotriao.

Lu. 17: 7. which of you, having a servant *plowing*
1Co. 9:10. he *that ploweth* should *plow* in hope;

723 1 108/107

ἄροτρον, arotron.

Lu. 9:62. having put his hand to the *plough*,

724 3 108/107 726

ἁρπαγή, harpagee.

Mat.23:25. are full of *extortion* and excess.
Lu. 11:39. inward part is full of *ravening* and
Heb 10:34. took joyfully the *spoiling* of your goods,

725 1 108/107 726

ἁρπαγμός, harpagmos.

Phil. 2: 6. thought it not *robbery* to be equal with God:

726 13 108/107 1:472 138

ἁρπάζω, harpazo.

Mat 11:12. the violent *take* it *by force*.
13:19. cometh the wicked (one), and *catcheth away*
Joh. 6:15. would come and *take* him *by force*,
10:12. the wolf *catcheth* them, and scattereth
28. any (man) *pluck* them out of my hand.
29. *to pluck* (them) out of my Father's hand.
Acts 8:39. Spirit of the Lord *caught away* Philip,
23:10. *to take* him *by force* from among
2Co 12: 2. such an one *caught up* to the third heaven.
4. that he *was caught up* into paradise,
1Th. 4:17. *shall be caught up* together with
Jude 23. with fear, *pulling* (them) out of the fire;
Rev 12: 5. her child *was caught up* unto God,

727 5 108/108 726

ἅρπαξ, harpax.

Mat. 7:15. inwardly they are *ravening* wolves.
Lu. 18:11. as other men (are), *extortioners*, unjust,
1Co. 5:10. with the covetous, or *extortioners*, or
11. a railer, or a drunkard, or an *extortioner*;
6:10. revilers, nor *extortioners*, shall inherit

728 3 109/108 1:475 [6162]

ἀῤῥαβών, arrabōn.

2Co. 1:22. given the *earnest* of the Spirit in
5: 5. hath given unto us the *earnest* of the Spirit.
Eph. 1:14. Which is the *earnest* of our inheritance

729 1 109/104

ἄῤῥαφος, arraphos.

Joh 19:23. now the coat was *without seam*,

730 3 109/108 142

ἄῤῥην, arreen.

Ro. 1:27. likewise also the *men*, leaving

Rev 12: 5. she brought forth a *man* child,
13. woman which brought forth the *man* (child).

731 1 109/108 1,4483

ἄῤῥητος, arreetos.

2Co 12: 4. into paradise, and heard *unspeakable* words,

732 5 109/108 1,4517

ἄῤῥωστος, arrōstos.

Mat 14:14. toward them, and he healed their *sick*.
Mar. 6: 5. laid his hands upon a few *sick folk*,
13. anointed with oil many *that were sick*,
16:18. they shall lay hands on the *sick*, and
1Co 11:30. many (are) weak and *sickly* among you,

733 2 109/108 730,2845

ἀρσενοκοίτης, arsenokoitees.

1Co 6: 9. effeminate, nor *abusers of themselves with mankind*,
1Ti. 1:10. *that defile themselves with mankind*,

730 6 109/108 142
See above

ἄρσην, arseen.

Mat 19: 4. made them *male* and female,
Mar 10: 6. God made them *male* and female.
Lu. 2:23. Every *male* that openeth the womb
Ro. 1:27. *men* with *men* working that
Gal. 3:28. there is neither *male* nor female:

736 1 109/108 737

ἀρτέμων, artemōn.

Acts27:40. hoised up the *mainsail* to the wind,

737 36 109/108 142(cf 740)

ἄρτι, arti.

Mat. 3:15. Suffer (it to be so) *now*: for thus it
9:18. My daughter is *even now* dead:
11:12. until *now* the kingdom of heaven
23:39. Ye shall not see me *hence*forth, till
26:29. I will not drink *hence*forth of this fruit
53. that I cannot *now* pray to my Father,
64. *Here*after shall ye see the Son of man
Joh. 1:51(52). *Here*after ye shall see heaven open,
2:10. hast kept the good wine until *now*.
5:17. My Father worketh *hitherto*, and I work.
9:19. how then doth he *now* see?
25. whereas I was blind, *now* I see.
13: 7. What I do thou knowest not *now*;
19. *Now* (lit. *hence*forth) I tell you before it come,
33. cannot come; so *now* I say to you.
37. why cannot I follow thee *now*?
14: 7. from *hence*forth ye know him,
16:12. ye cannot bear them *now*.
24. *Hitherto* have ye asked nothing
31. Jesus answered them, Do ye *now* believe
1Co. 4:11. Even unto this *present* hour we both
13. the offscouring of all things unto *this day*.
8: 7. conscience of the idol unto *this hour*
13:12. For *now* we see through a glass,
— *now* I know in part; but then
15: 6. greater part remain unto *this present*,
16: 7. I will not see you *now* by the way.
Gal. 1: 9. we said before, so say I *now* again,

Gal 1:10. For do I *now* persuade men, or God?
4:20. I desire to be present with you *now*,
1Th. 3: 6. *now* when Timotheus came
2Th. 2: 7. only he who *now* letteth, (will let),
1Pet. 1: 6. though *now* for a season, if need be,
8. whom, though *now* ye see (him) not,
1Joh. 2: 9. is in darkness even until *now*.
Rev. 12:10. *Now* is come salvation, and strength,

738 1 110/109 1:665 737,1084

ἀρτιγέννητος, *artigenneetos*.

1Pet. 2: 2. As *newborn* babes, desire the

739 1 110/109 1:475 737

ἄρτιος, *artios*.

2Ti. 3:17. That the man of God may be *perfect*,

740 100 110/109 1:477 142

ἄρτος, *artos*.

Mat. 4: 3. command that these stones be made *bread*.
4. Man shall not live by *bread* alone,
6:11. Give us this day our daily *bread*.
7: 9. whom if his son ask *bread*, will
12: 4. did eat the shew*bread*, which
14:17. We have here but five *loaves*,
19. took the five *loaves*, and the two fishes,
— gave the *loaves* to (his) disciples,
15: 2. their hands, when they eat *bread*.
26. not meet to take the children's *bread*,
33. should we have so much *bread*
34. How many *loaves* have ye?
36. he took the seven *loaves* and the fishes,
16: 5. they had forgotten to take *bread*.
7. because we have taken no *bread*.
8. because ye have brought no *bread*?
9. neither remember the five *loaves*
10. Neither the seven *loaves* of the
11. not to you concerning *bread*,
12. not beware of the leaven of *bread*,
26:26. Jesus took *bread*, and blessed (it),
Mar. 2:26. did eat the shew*bread*, which
3:20. could not so much as eat *bread*.
6: 8. no scrip, no *bread*, no money
36. into the villages, and buy themselves *bread*:
37. two hundred pennyworth of *bread*,
38. How many *loaves* have ye?
41. when he had taken the five *loaves*
— blessed, and brake the *loaves*,
44. they that did eat of the *loaves*
52. not (the miracle) of the *loaves*:
7: 2. saw some of his disciples eat *bread*
5. eat *bread* with unwashen hands?
27. not meet to take the children's *bread*,
8: 4. satisfy these (men) with *bread*
5. How many *loaves* have ye?
6. he took the seven *loaves*, and
14. (disciples) had forgotten to take *bread*,
— with them more than one *loaf*.
16. because we have no *bread*.
17. because ye have no *bread*?
19. When I brake the five *loaves*
14:22. Jesus took *bread*, and blessed,
Lu. 4: 3. this stone that it be made *bread*.
4. man shall not live by *bread* alone.
6: 4. did take and eat the shew*bread*,
7:33. neither eating *bread* nor drinking
Lu. 9: 3. nor scrip, neither *bread*, neither
13. We have no more but five *loaves*
16. Then he took the five *loaves* and
11: 3. Give us day by day our daily *bread*.
5. Friend, lend me three *loaves*;
11. If a son shall ask *bread* of any
14: 1. to eat *bread* on the sabbath day,
15. he that shall eat *bread* in the
15:17. servants of my father's have *bread*,
22:19. he took *bread*, and gave thanks,
24:30. he took *bread*, and blessed (it),
35. known of them in breaking of *bread*.
Joh. 6: 5. Whence shall we buy *bread*,
7. Two hundred pennyworth of *bread*
9. which hath five barley *loaves*,
11. Jesus took the *loaves*; and when
13. fragments of the five barley *loaves*,
23. place where they did eat *bread*,
26. because ye did eat of the *loaves*,
31. He gave them *bread* from heaven
32. Moses gave you not that *bread*
— my Father giveth you the true *bread*,
33. For the *bread* of God is he which
34. Lord, evermore give us this *bread*.
35. I am the *bread* of life: he that
41. I am the *bread* which came down
48. I am that *bread* of life.
50. This is the *bread* which cometh
51. I am the living *bread* which
— if any man eat of this *bread*,
— the *bread* that I will give
58. This is that *bread* which came
— he that eateth of this *bread* shall
13:18. He that eateth *bread* with me
21: 9. fish laid thereon, and *bread*.
13. Jesus then cometh, and taketh *bread*,
Acts 2:42. in breaking of *bread*, and in prayers.
46. breaking *bread* from house to house,
20: 7. came together to break *bread*,
11. had broken *bread*, and eaten,
27:35. he took *bread*, and gave thanks
1Co. 10:16. The *bread* which we break, is it
17. we (being) many are one *bread*, (and)
— all partakers of that one *bread*.
11:23. in which he was betrayed took *bread*:
26. as often as ye eat this *bread*,
27. whosoever shall eat this *bread*,
28. so let him eat of (that) *bread*,
2Co. 9:10. minister *bread* for (your) food,
2Th. 3: 8. Neither did we eat any man's *bread*
12. they work, and eat their own *bread*.
Heb. 9: 2. the table, and the shew*bread*;

741 3 110/110 142

ἀρτύω, *artuo*.

Mar. 9:50. wherewith *will* ye *season* it?
Lu. 14:34. wherewith *shall* it *be seasoned*?
Col. 4: 6. alway with grace, *seasoned* with salt,

743 2 110/110 1:74 757,32

ἀρχάγγελος, *arkangelos*.

1Th. 4:16. with the voice of the *archangel*,
Jude 9. Yet Michael the *archangel*,

744 12 110/110 1:478 746

ἀρχαῖος, *arkaios*.

Mat. 5:21. was said by *them of old time*,
27. was said by *them of old time*,
33. been said by *them of old time*.

G 2

Lu. 9: 8. one of the *old* prophets was risen
19. one of the *old* prophets is risen
Acts15: 7. how that a good while ago (lit. from days *of old*)
21. For Moses of *old* time hath in
21:16. one Mnason of Cyprus, an *old* disciple
2Co. 5:17. *old* things are passed away;
2Pet.2: 5. spared not the *old* world, but
Rev.12: 9. that *old* serpent, called the Devil,
20: 2. that *old* serpent, which is the devil,

746 58 111/110 1:478 756

ἀρχή, arkee.

Mat.19: 4. which made (them) at the *beginning*
8. from the *beginning* it was not so.
24: 8. these (are) the *beginning* of sorrows.
21. since the *beginning* of the world
Mar. 1: 1. The *beginning* of the gospel of
10: 6. from the *beginning* of the creation
13: 8(9). these (are) the *beginnings* of sorrows.
19. as was not from the *beginning*
Lu. 1: 2. from the *beginning* were eyewitnesses,
12:11. unto the synagogues, and (unto) *magistrates*,
20:20. might deliver him unto the *power* and authority of the governor.
Joh. 1: 1. In the *beginning* was the Word,
2. The same was in the *beginning*
2:11. This *beginning* of miracles did
6:64. Jesus knew from the *beginning* who
8:25. I said unto you from the *beginning*.
44. was a murderer from the *beginning*,
15:27. with me from the *beginning*.
16: 4. not unto you at the *beginning*,
Acts10:11. knit at the four *corners*, and let
11: 5. down from heaven by four *corners*;
15. as on us at the *beginning*.
26: 4. which was at *the first* among
Ro. 8:38. nor *principalities*, nor powers, nor
1Co.15:24. have put down all *rule* and all
Eph. 1:21. above all *principality*, and power,
3:10. now unto the *principalities* and
6:12. against *principalities*, against powers,
Phil. 4:15. that in the *beginning* of the gospel,
Col. 1:16. dominions, or *principalities*, or
18. who is the *beginning*, the
2:10. the head of all *principality* and
15. having spoiled *principalities* and
2Th. 2:13. God hath from the *beginning* chosen
Tit. 3: 1. subject to *principalities* and powers,
Heb. 1:10. Thou, Lord, in the *beginning*
2: 3. which *at the first* began to
3:14. if we hold the *beginning* of
5:12. the *first* principles of the oracles
6: 1. leaving the *principles* of the doctrine
7: 3. having neither *beginning* of days,
2Pet.3: 4. from the *beginning* of the creation.
1Joh.1: 1. which was from the *beginning*,
2: 7. which ye had from the *beginning*.
— ye have heard from the *beginning*.
13. him (that is) from the *beginning*.
14. known him (that is) from the *beginning*.
24. have heard from the *beginning*.
— ye have heard from the *beginning*
3: 8. the devil sinneth from the *beginning*.
11. that ye heard from the *beginning*,
2Joh. 5. which we had from the *beginning*,
6. as ye have heard from the *beginning*,
Jude 6. angels which kept not their *first estate*,
Rev. 1: 8. the *beginning* and the ending,
3:14. the *beginning* of the creation of God;
Rev.21: 6. the *beginning* and the end. I will
22:13. Alpha and Omega, the *beginning* and the end,

747 4 112/111 1:478 746,71

ἀρχηγός, arkeegos.

Acts 3:15. killed the *Prince* of life, whom
5:31. (to be) a *Prince* and a Saviour, for to
Heb. 2:10. to make the *captain* of their salvation
12: 2. Jesus the *author* and finisher of (our) faith;

748 1 112/111 746,2413

ἀρχιερατικός, arkieratikos.

Acts 4: 6. of the kindred *of the high priest*,

749 143 112/111 3:221 746,2409

ἀρχιερεύς, arkierūs.

Mat. 2: 4. gathered all the *chief priests* and
16:21. the elders and *chief priests* and scribes,
20:18. betrayed unto the *chief priests*
21:15. when the *chief priests* and scribes
23. the *chief priests* and the elders of the
45. the *chief priests* and Pharisees had
26: 3. assembled together the *chief priests*,
— unto the palace of the *high priest*,
14. Iscariot, went unto the *chief priests*,
47. from the *chief priests* and elders of
51. struck a servant of the *high priest's*,
57. away to Caiaphas the *high priest*,
58. unto the *high priest's* palace, and
59. Now the *chief priests*, and elders, and all
62. the *high priest* arose, and said
63. the *high priest* answered and said
65. the *high priest* rent his clothes,
27: 1. all the *chief priests* and elders of
3. silver to the *chief priests* and elders,
6. the *chief priests* took the silver
12. he was accused of the *chief priests*
20. the *chief priests* and elders persuaded
41. also the *chief priests* mocking (him),
62. the *chief priests* and Pharisees came
28:11. shewed unto the *chief priests* all
Mar. 2:26. days of Abiathar the *high priest*,
8:31. (of) the *chief priests*, and scribes,
10:33. be delivered unto the *chief priests*,
11:18. the scribes and *chief priests* heard
27. there come to him the *chief priests*,
14: 1. the *chief priests* and the scribes sought
10. went unto the *chief priests*, to
43. from the *chief priests* and the scribes
47. smote a servant of the *high priest*,
53. led Jesus away to the *high priest*:
— assembled all the *chief priests* and the
54. into the palace of the *high priest*:
55. the *chief priests* and all the council
60. the *high priest* stood up in the
61. Again the *high priest* asked him,
63. the *high priest* rent his clothes,
66. one of the maids of the *high priest*:
15: 1. the *chief priests* held a consultation
3. the *chief priests* accused him
10. the *chief priests* had delivered him
11. the *chief priests* moved the people,
31. also the *chief priests* mocking
Lu. 3: 2. Annas and Caiaphas being the *high priests*
9:22. *chief priests* and scribes, and be slain,
19:47. the *chief priests* and the scribes
20: 1. the *chief priests* and the scribes

Lu. 20:19. the *chief priests* and the scribes the
22: 2. the *chief priests* and scribes sought
4. communed with the *chief priests*
50. smote the servant of the *high priest*,
52. Jesus said unto the *chief priests*,
54. into the *high priest's* house.
66. the *chief priests* and the scribes
23: 4. said Pilate to the *chief priests*
10. the *chief priests* and scribes stood
13. together the *chief priests* and the rulers
23. of them and of the *chief priests*
24:20. how the *chief priests* and our rulers
Joh. 7:32. the Pharisees and the *chief priests*
45. came the officers to the *chief priests*
11:47. gathered the *chief priests* and the
49. being the *high priest* that same
51. being *high priest* that year,
57. both the *chief priests* and the Pharisees
12:10. the *chief priests* consulted that
18: 3. from the *chief priests* and Pharisees,
10. smote the *high priest's* servant,
13. was the *high priest* that same year.
15. known unto the *high priest*, and
— into the palace of the *high priest*.
16. known unto the *high priest*,
19. The *high priest* then asked Jesus
22. Answerest thou the *high priest* so?
24. bound unto Caiaphas the *high priest*.
26. the servants of the *high priest*,
35. Thine own nation and the *chief priests*
19: 6. the *chief priests* therefore and officers
15. The *chief priests* answered,
21. Then said the *chief priests* of the
Acts 4: 6. Annas the *high priest*, and Caiaphas,
23. the *chief priests* and elders had said
5:17. the *high priest* rose up, and all they
21. the *high priest* came, and they that
24. the *chief priests* heard these things,
27. the *high priest* asked them,
7: 1. Then said the *high priest*, Are
9: 1. went unto the *high priest*,
14. authority from the *chief priests*
21. bound unto the *chief priests*?
19:14. a Jew, (and) *chief of the priests*,
22: 5. also the *high priest* doth bear
30. commanded the *chief priests* and
23: 2. the *high priest* Ananias commanded
4. Revilest thou God's *high priest*?
5. that he was the *high priest*:
14. they came to the *chief priests*
24: 1. Ananias the *high priest* descended
25: 2. the *high priest* and the chief of the
15. the *chief priests* and the elders of
26:10. authority from the *chief priests*;
12. commission from the *chief priests*,
Heb 2:17. merciful and faithful *high priest*
3: 1. apostle and *high priest* of our
4:14. we have a great *high priest*, that
15. we have not an *high priest* which
5: 1. every *high priest* taken from
5. to be made an *high priest*;
10. Called of God an *high priest*
6:20. made an *high priest* for ever
7:26. For such an *high priest* became
27. not daily, as those *high priests*,
28. maketh men *high priests* which
8: 1. We have such an *high priest*,
3. For every *high priest* is ordained
9: 7. (went) the *high priest* alone once
11. Christ being come an *high priest*
25. as the *high priest* entereth into
13:11. by the *high priest* for sin, are

750 1 112/112 746,4166

ἀρχιποίμην, arkipoimeen.

1Pet. 5: 4. when the *chief Shepherd* shall

752 2 112/112 6:485 746,4864

ἀρχισυνάγωγος, arkisunagōgos. 7:798

Mar. 5:22. one of the *rulers of the synagogue*,
35. from the *ruler of the synagogue's* (house)
36. unto the *ruler of the synagogue*,
38. house of the *ruler of the synagogue*,
Lu. 8:49. from the *ruler of the synagogue's* (house)
13:14. the *ruler of the synagogue* answered
Acts13:15. the *rulers of the synagogue* sent
18: 8. the *chief ruler of the synagogue*,
17. the *chief ruler of the synagogue*,

753 1 112/112 746,5045

ἀρχιτέκτων, arkitektōn.

1Co. 3:10. as a wise *masterbuilder*, I have

754 1 112/113 746,5057

ἀρχιτελώνης, arkitelōnees.

Lu. 19: 2. was the *chief among the publicans*,

755 3 112/113 746,5140

ἀρχιτρίκλινος, arkitriklinos. 2827

Joh. 2: 8. bear unto the *governor of the feast*.
9. When the *ruler of the feast* had
— the *governor of the feast* called the

756 84 113/113 757, See also p. 82

ἄρχομαι, arkomai.

Mat. 4:17. Jesus *began* to preach, and to say,
11: 7. Jesus *began* to say unto the
20. Then *began* he to upbraid the
12: 1. *began* to pluck the ears of corn,
14:30. *beginning* to sink, he cried,
16:21. *began* Jesus to shew unto his
22. *began* to rebuke him, saying,
18:24. *when* he *had begun* to reckon.
20: 8. *beginning* from the last unto
24:49. *shall begin* to smite (his)
26:22. *began* every one of them to say
37. *began* to be sorrowful and very heavy.
74. Then *began* he to curse and to swear,
Mar. 1:45. *began* to publish (it) much,
2:23. his disciples *began*, as they went,
4: 1. he *began* again to teach by the
5:17. they *began* to pray him to depart
20. *began* to publish in Decapolis
6: 2. he *began* to teach in the synagogue.
7. *began* to send them forth by two
34. *began* to teach them many things.
55. *began* to carry about in beds
8:11. *began* to question with him,
31. he *began* to teach them, that
32. Peter took him, and *began* to rebuke
10.28. Then Peter *began* to say unto him,
32. *began* to tell them what things
41. they *began* to be much displeased
47. he *began* to cry out, and say, Jesus,
11:15. *began* to cast out them that sold
12: 1. he *began* to speak unto them
13: 5. Jesus answering them *began* to say,
14:19. they *began* to be sorrowful, and to
33. *began* to be sore amazed, and to be
65 some *began* to spit on him,

Mar.14:69. *began* to say to them that stood by,
71. he *began* to curse and to swear, (saying),
15: 8. crying aloud, *began* to desire (him)
18. *began* to salute him, Hail,
Lu. 3: 8. *begin* not to say within yourselves,
23. Jesus himself began (lit. was *beginning*) to be about
4:21. he *began* to say unto them, This
5:21. scribes and the Pharisees *began* to reason,
7:15. he that was dead sat up, and *began* to
24. he *began* to speak unto the people
38. *began* to wash his feet with tears,
49. *began* to say within themselves,
9:12. when the day *began* to wear away,
11:29. gathered thick together, he *began* to say,
53. scribes and the Pharisees *began* to
12: 1. he *began* to say unto his disciples
45. *shall begin* to beat the menservants
13:25. ye *begin* to stand without, and to knock
26. Then *shall* ye *begin* to say, We
14: 9. thou *begin* with shame to take
18. with one (consent) *began* to make excuse.
29. behold (it) *begin* to mock him,
30. Saying, This man *began* to build,
15:14. he *began* to be in want.
24. they *began* to be merry.
19:37. multitude of the disciples *began* to
45. *began* to cast out them that sold
20: 9. Then *began* he to speak to the people
21:28. *when* these things *begin* to come
22:23. they *began* to enquire among
23: 2. they *began* to accuse him, saying,
5. *beginning* from Galilee to this
30. Then *shall* they *begin* to say to
24:27 47. *beginning* at
Joh. 8: 9. *beginning* at the eldest, (even)
13: 5. *began* to wash the disciples' feet,
Acts 1: 1. all that Jesus *began* both to do and teach,
22. *Beginning* from the baptism of
2: 4. *began* to speak with other tongues,
8:35. *began* at the same scripture, *and*
10:37. and *began* from Galilee
11: 4. *rehearsed* (the matter) *from the beginning,*
15. as I *began* to speak, the Holy
18:26. he *began* to speak boldly in the
24: 2. Tertullus *began* to accuse (him),
27:35. had broken (it), he *began* to eat.
2Co. 3: 1. *Do* we *begin* again to commend
1Pet. 4:17. judgment must *begin* at the house

757 2 113/113 1:478

ἄρχω, *arko.*

Mar.10:42. accounted *to rule over* the Gentiles
Ro. 15:12. he that shall rise *to reign over* the

758 37 113/113 1:478 757

ἄρχων, *arkōn.*

Mat. 9:18. there came a certain *ruler*,
23. Jesus came into the *ruler's* house,
34. through the *prince* of the devils.
12:24. by Beelzebub the *prince* of the devils.
20:25. the *princes* of the Gentiles exercise
Mar. 3:22. by the *prince* of the devils casteth
Lu. 8:41. he was a *ruler* of the synagogue:
11:15. through Beelzebub the *chief* of the devils.
12:58. with thine adversary to the *magistrate*,
14: 1. house of one of the *chief* Pharisees
18:18. a certain *ruler* asked him,
23:13. chief priests and the *rulers* and the people,
35. the *rulers* also with them derided (him).
Lu. 24:20. the chief priests and our *rulers* delivered
Joh. 3: 1. Nicodemus, a *ruler* of the Jews:
7:26. Do the *rulers* know indeed that
48. Have any of the *rulers* or of the
12:31. now shall the *prince* of this world
42. among the *chief rulers* also
14:30. the *prince* of this world cometh,
16:11. the *prince* of this world is judged.
Acts 3:17. ye did (it) as (did) also your *rulers*.
4: 5. that their *rulers*, and elders, and scribes,
8. Ye *rulers* of the people, and elders
26. the *rulers* were gathered together
7:27. Who made thee a *ruler* and a judge
35. Who made thee a *ruler* and a judge?
— God send (to be) a *ruler* and a
13:27. dwell at Jerusalem, and their *rulers*,
14: 5. also of the Jews with their *rulers*,
16:19. into the marketplace unto the *rulers*
23: 5. not speak evil of the *ruler* of thy
Ro. 13: 3. For *rulers* are not a terror to good
1Co. 2: 6. nor of the *princes* of this world,
8. none of the *princes* of this world
Eph. 2: 2. the *prince* of the power of the air,
Rev. 1: 5. the *prince* of the kings of the earth.

759 4 113/114 142

ἄρωμα, *arōma.*

Mar.16: 1. bought *sweet spices*, that they
Lu. 23:56. prepared *spices* and ointments;
24: 1. bringing the *spices* which they
Joh. 19:40. in linen clothes with the *spices*,

761 2 113/114 1,4531

ἀσάλευτος, *asalūtos.*

Acts27:41. stuck fast, and remained *unmoveable*,
Heb 12:28. a kingdom *which cannot be moved*,

762 4 114/114 1,4570

ἄσβεστος, *asbestos.*

Mat. 3:12. the chaff with *unquenchable* fire.
Mar. 9:43. fire that *never shall be quenched:*
45. fire that *never shall be quenched:*
Lu. 3:17. will burn with fire *unquenchable*.

763 6 114/114 7:168 765

ἀσέβεια, *asebīa.*

Ro. 1:18. against all *ungodliness* and
11:26. shall turn away *ungodliness*
2Ti. 2:16. will increase unto more *ungodliness*.
Tit. 2:12. denying *ungodliness* and worldly
Jude 15. their *ungodly* deeds which they have
18. after their own *ungodly* lusts.

764 2 114/114 7:168 765

ἀσεβέω, *asebeo.*

2Pet. 2: 6. that after should *live ungodly*;
Jude 15. deeds which they *have ungodly committed*.

765 9 114/114 7:168 1,4576

ἀσεβής, *asebees.*

Ro. 4: 5. him that justifieth the *ungodly*,
5: 6. Christ died for the *ungodly*.
1Ti. 1: 9. for the *ungodly* and for sinners, for
1Pet. 4:18. where shall the *ungodly* and the
2Pet. 2: 5. upon the world of the *ungodly*;

2Pet. 3: 7. judgment and perdition of *ungodly* men.
Jude 4. *ungodly men*, turning the grace
15. convince all *that are ungodly*
— which *ungodly* sinners have

766 9 114/114 1:490 1 selges

ἀσέλγεια, aselgia. (self-restraint)

Mar. 7:22. deceit, *lasciviousness*, an evil eye,
Ro. 13:13. not in chambering and *wantonness*,
2Co.12:21. *lasciviousness* which they have
Gal. 5:19. fornication, uncleanness, *lasciviousness*.
Eph. 4:19. themselves over unto *lasciviousness*,
1Pet 4: 3. we walked in *lasciviousness*,
2Pet. 2: 7. vexed with the *filthy* conversation of
18. (through much) *wantonness*, those
Jude 4. grace of our God into *lasciviousness*,

767 1 114/115 5:200 1,rt 4591

ἄσημος, aseemos.

Acts21:39. in Cilicia, a citizen of no *mean* city:

769 24 114/115 1:490 772

ἀσθένεια, asthenia.

Mat. 8:17. Himself took our *infirmities*, and
Lu. 5:15. healed by him of their *infirmities*.
8: 2. healed of evil spirits and *infirmities*,
13:11. which had a spirit of *infirmity*
12. thou art loosed from thine *infirmity*.
Joh. 5: 5. had an *infirmity* thirty and eight years.
11: 4. This *sickness* is not unto death,
Acts28: 9. which had *diseases* in the island,
Ro. 6:19. because of the *infirmity* of your flesh:
8:26. the Spirit also helpeth our *infirmities*:
1Co. 2: 3. I was with you in *weakness*, and in
15:43. it is sown in *weakness*; it is raised
2Co.11:30. things which concern mine *infirmities*.
12: 5. not glory, but in mine *infirmities*.
9. is made perfect in *weakness*.
— I rather glory in my *infirmities*,
10. I take pleasure in *infirmities*,
13: 4. he was crucified through *weakness*,
Gal. 4:13. through *infirmity* of the flesh
1Ti. 5:23. stomach's sake and thine often *infirmities*.
Heb. 4:15. with the feeling of our *infirmities*;
5: 2. also is compassed with *infirmity*.
7:28. high priests which have *infirmity*;
11:34. out of *weakness* were made strong,

770 36 115/115 1:490 772

ἀσθενέω, astheneo.

Mat.10: 8. Heal the *sick*, cleanse the lepers,
25:36. I *was sick*, and ye visited me:
Mar. 6:56. they laid the *sick* in the streets,
Lu. 4:40. all they that had any *sick* with
7:10. servant whole *that had been sick*.
9: 2. kingdom of God, and to heal the *sick*.
Joh. 4:46. whose son *was sick* at Capernaum.
5: 3. a great multitude of *impotent folk*,
7. The *impotent man* answered him,
6: 2. did on them *that were diseased*.
11: 1. Now a certain (man) was *sick*,
2. whose brother Lazarus *was sick*.
3. he whom thou lovest *is sick*.
6. heard therefore that he *was sick*,
Acts 9:37. that she *was sick, and* died:
19:12. were brought unto the *sick*
20:35. ye ought to support the *weak*,
Ro. 4:19. *being* not *weak* in faith, he
8: 3. that it *was weak* through the flesh
14: 1. Him *that is weak* in the faith
2. another, *who is weak*, eateth herbs.
21. is offended, or *is made weak*.
1Co. 8: 9. stumblingblock to them *that are weak*.
11. shall the *weak* brother perish,
12. wound their *weak* conscience
2Co.11:21. as though we *had been weak*.
29. Who *is weak*, and I *am* not *weak*?
12:10. for when I *am weak*, then am
13: 3. to you-ward *is* not *weak*, but
4. For we also *are weak* in him,
9. we are glad, when we *are weak*,
Phil. 2:26. heard that he *had been sick*.
27. he *was sick* nigh unto death:
2Ti. 4:20. Trophimus have I left at Miletum *sick*.
Jas. 5:14. *Is* any *sick* among you? let

771 1 115/115 1:490 770

ἀσθένημα, astheneema.

Ro. 15: 1. to bear the *infirmities* of the weak,

772 25 115/115 1:490 1,rt 4599

ἀσθενής, asthenees.

Mat.25:39. Or when saw we thee *sick*, or in
43. *sick*, and in prison, and ye visited
44. naked, or *sick*, or in prison, and
26:41. willing, but the flesh (is) *weak*.
Mar14:38. ready, but the flesh (is) *weak*.
Lu. 10: 9. heal the *sick* that are therein,
Acts 4: 9. done to the *impotent* man,
5:15. brought forth the *sick* into the
16. bringing *sick* folks, and them
Ro. 5: 6. we were yet *without strength*,
1Co. 1:25. the *weakness* of God is stronger
27. the *weak things* of the world
4:10. we (are) *weak*, but ye (are) strong;
8: 7. their conscience being *weak*
10. conscience of him which is *weak*
9:22. To the *weak* became I as *weak*, that I might gain the *weak*
11:30. many (are) *weak* and sickly among
12:22. which seem to be *more feeble*,
2Co.10:10. (his) bodily presence (is) *weak*,
Gal. 4: 9. to the *weak* and beggarly elements,
1Th. 5:14. support the *weak*, be patient
Heb. 7:18. for the *weakness* and unprofitableness
1Pet.3: 7. as unto the *weaker* vessel, and

776 1 115/116 777

ἀσιτία, asitia.

Acts27:21. after long *abstinence* Paul stood

777 1 115/116 1,4621

ἄσιτος, asitos.

Acts27:33. ye have tarried and continued *fasting*,

778 1 115/116 1:494 cf 4632

ἀσκέω, askeo.

Acts24:16. herein *do* I *exercise* myself, to

779 12 116/116 cf 4632

ἀσκός, askos.

Mat. 9:17. put new wine into old *bottles*;
— else the *bottles* break, and the wine

Mat. 9:17. wine runneth out, and the *bottles* perish:
— put new wine into new *bottles*,
Mar. 2:22. putteth new wine into old *bottles:*
— new wine doth burst the *bottles*,
— the *bottles* will be marred:
— wine must be put into new *bottles*.
Lu. 5:37. putteth new wine into old *bottles*;
— new wine will burst the *bottles*,
— spilled, and the *bottles* shall perish.
38. new wine must be put into new *bottles*;

780 2 116/116 rt 2237

ἀσμένως, *asmenōs*.

Acts 2:41. they that *gladly* received his word
21:17. the brethren received us *gladly*.

781 1 116/116 1,4680

ἄσοφος, *asophos*.

Eph. 5:15. circumspectly, not as *fools*, but as wise,

782 60 116/116 1:496 1,4685

ἀσπάζομαι, *aspazomai*.

Mat. 5:47. if ye *salute* your brethren
10:12. when ye come into an house, *salute* it.
Mar. 9:15. running to (him) *saluted* him.
15:18. began *to salute* him, Hail,
Lu. 1:40. house of Zacharias, and *saluted* Elisabeth.
10: 4. *salute* no man by the way.
Acts18:22. *when*...gone up, and *saluted* the church,
20: 1. the disciples, and *embraced* (them),
21: 6. *when* we *had taken* our *leave* one of another,
7. *saluted* the brethren, *and* abode
19. *when* he *had saluted* them,
25:13. came unto Cæsarea, to *salute* Festus.
Ro. 16: 3. *Greet* Priscilla and Aquila my
5. *Salute* my wellbeloved Epenetus,
6. *Greet* Mary; who bestowed much
7. *Salute* Andronicus and Junia,
8. *Greet* Amplias my beloved
9. *Salute* Urbane, our helper
10. *Salute* Apelles, approved in Christ. *Salute* them which are of
11. *Salute* Herodion my kinsman. *Greet* them that be of the (houshold)
12. *Salute* Tryphena and Tryphosa,
— *Salute* the beloved Persis, which
13. *Salute* Rufus chosen in the
14. *Salute* Asyncritus, Phlegon,
15. *Salute* Philologus, and Julia,
16. *Salute* one another with an holy kiss. The churches of Christ *salute* you.
21. Jason, and Sosipater, my kinsmen, *salute* you.
22. I, Tertius, who wrote (this) epistle, *salute* you
23. the whole church, *saluteth* you.
— chamberlain of the city *saluteth* you,
1Co.16:19(18). The churches of Asia *salute* you.
— Aquila and Priscilla *salute* you
20. All the brethren *greet* you. *Greet* ye one another with an
2Co.13:12. *Greet* one another with an holy kiss.
13(12). All the saints *salute* you.
Phi. 4:21. *Salute* every saint in Christ Jesus. The brethren which are with me *greet* you.
22. All the saints *salute* you,
Col. 4:10. my fellowprisoner *saluteth* you,
12. a servant of Christ, *saluteth* you,
14. beloved physician, and Demas, *greet* you.
Col. 4:15. *Salute* the brethren which are
1Th. 5:26. *Greet* all the brethren with an
2Ti. 4:19. *Salute* Prisca and Aquila, and the
21. Eubulus *greeteth* thee, and Pudens,
Tit. 3:15(14). All that are with me *salute* thee. *Greet* them that love us in the
Philem 23. There *salute* thee Epaphras, my
Heb 11:13. *embraced* (them), and confessed that
13:24. *Salute* all them that have
— They of Italy *salute* you.
1Pet. 5:13. elected together with (you), *saluteth* you
14. *Greet* ye one another with a
2Joh. 13. children of thy elect sister *greet* thee.
3Joh 14(15). (Our) friends *salute* thee.
—(—) *Greet* the friends by name.

783 10 116/117 1:496 782

ἀσπασμός, *aspasmos*.

Mat.23: 7. *greetings* in the markets, and to be
Mar 12:38. *salutations* in the marketplaces,
Lu. 1:29. what manner of *salutation* this
41. when Elisabeth heard the *salutation* of
44. the voice of thy *salutation* sounded
11:43. *greetings* in the markets.
20:46. love *greetings* in the markets,
1Co.16:21. The *salutation* of (me) Paul with
Col. 4:18. The *salutation* by the hand of
2Th. 3:17. The *salutation* of Paul with mine

784 4 116/117 1:502 1,4695

ἄσπιλος, *aspilos*.

1Ti. 6:14. (this) commandment *without spot*,
Jas. 1:27. to keep himself *unspotted* from
1Pet.1:19. a lamb without blemish and *without spot:*
2Pet.3:14. in peace, *without spot*, and blameless.

785 1 116/117

ἀσπίς, *aspis*.

Ro. 3:13. the poison of *asps* (is) under their lips:

786 2 116/117 1,4689

ἄσπονδος, *aspondos*.

Ro. 1:31. without natural affection, *implacable*,
2Ti. 3: 3. Without natural affection, *trucebreakers*,

787 2 117/117

ἀσσάριον, *assarion*.

Mat.10:29. two sparrows sold for a *farthing*?
Lu. 12: 6. five sparrows sold for two *farthings*,

788 1 117/117 *agchō* (to squeeze)

ἆσσον, *asson*.

NOTE.—Considered by Stephens as a proper name.

Acts27:13. they sailed *close* by Crete.

790 1 117/117 1:503 1,2476

ἀστατέω, *astateo*.

1Co. 4:11. *have no certain dwellingplace*;

791 2 117/117 *astu* (city)

ἀστεῖος, *astīos*.

Acts 7:20. Moses was born, and was exceeding *fair*,
Heb 11:23. they saw (he was) a *proper* child;

792 24 117/117 1:503 rt 4766

ἀστήρ, asteer.

Mat. 2: 2. we have seen his *star* in the east,
7. what time the *star* appeared.
9. lo, the *star*, which they saw in the east,
10. When they saw the *star*, they
24:29. the *stars* shall fall from heaven,
Mar 13:25. the *stars* of heaven shall fall,
1Co.15:41. another glory of the *stars:* for (one) *star* differeth from (another) *star* in glory.
Jude 13. wandering *stars*, to whom is
Rev. 1:16. had in his right hand seven *stars:*
20. The mystery of the seven *stars*
— The seven *stars* are the angels
2: 1. that holdeth the seven *stars* in
28. I will give him the morning *star*.
3: 1. Spirits of God, and the seven *stars;*
6:13. the *stars* of heaven fell unto
8:10. there fell a great *star* from heaven,
11. the name of the *star* is called
12. the third part of the *stars;* so as
9: 1. I saw a *star* fall from heaven
12: 1. upon her head a crown of twelve *stars:*
4. the third part of the *stars* of heaven,
22:16. the bright and morning *star*.

793 2 117/118 7:653 1,4741

ἀστήρικτος, asteeriktos.

2Pet. 2:14. beguiling *unstable* souls: an
3:16. they that are unlearned and *unstable*

794 2 117/118 1 stergō (to cherish)

ἄστοργος, astorgos.

Ro. 1:31. *without natural affection*, implacable,
2Ti. 3: 3. *Without natural affection*, truce-breakers,

795 3 117/118 1 stoichos (aim)

ἀστοχέω, astokeo.

1Ti. 1: 6. From which some *having swerved*
6:21. *have erred* concerning the faith.
2Ti. 2:18. Who concerning the truth *have erred*,

796 9 117/118 1:505 797

ἀστραπή, astrapee.

Mat.24:27. For as the *lightning* cometh
28: 3. His countenance was like *lightning*,
Lu. 10:18. I beheld Satan as *lightning* fall
11:36. as when the *bright shining* of a
17:24. For as the *lightning*, that lighteneth
Rev. 4: 5. proceeded *lightnings* and thunderings
8: 5. thunderings, and *lightnings*, and an
11:19. there were *lightnings*, and voices,
16:18. voices, and thunders, and *lightnings*

797 2 117/118 792

ἀστράπτω, astrapto.

Lu. 17:24. the lightning, *that lighteneth* out
24: 4. stood by them in *shining* garments:

798 4 117/118 1:503 792

ἄστρον, astron.

Lu. 21:25. in the moon, and in the *stars;* and upon
Acts 7:43. the *star* of your god Remphan,
27:20. when neither sun nor *stars* in
Heb 11:12. as the *stars* of the sky in multitude,

800 4 118/118 1,4859

ἀσύμφωνος, asumphōnos.

Acts28:25. when they *agreed not* among themselves,

801 5 118/118 7:888 1,4908

ἀσύνετος, asunetos.

Mat.15:16. Are ye also yet *without understanding?*
Mar. 7:18. Are ye so *without understanding*
Ro. 1:21. their *foolish* heart was darkened.
31. *Without understanding*, covenantbreakers,
10:19. by a *foolish* nation I will anger you.

802 1 118/118 1,4934

ἀσύνθετος, asunthetos.

Ro. 1:31. *covenantbreakers*, without natural affection,

803 3 118/118 1:506 804

ἀσφάλεια, asphalīa.

Lu. 1: 4. know the *certainty* of those things,
Acts 5:23. found we shut with all *safety*,
1Th. 5: 3. when they shall say, Peace and *safety;*

804 5 118/118 1:506 1 sphallō (to fail)

ἀσφαλής, asphalees.

Acts21:34. could not know the *certainty* for
22:30. he would have known the *certainty*
25:26. Of whom I have no *certain* thing
Phi. 3: 1. not grievous, but for you (it is) *safe*,
Heb. 6:19. the soul, both *sure* and stedfast,

805 3 118/118 1:506 804

ἀσφαλίζω, asphalizo.

Mat.27:64. the sepulchre *be made sure*
65. *make* (it) as *sure* as ye can.
66. they went, and *made* the sepulchre *sure*,
Acts16:24. *made* their feet *fast* in the stocks.

806 3 118/118 1:506 804

ἀσφαλῶς, asphalōs.

Mar 14:44. take him, and lead (him) away *safely*.
Acts 2:36. house of Israel know *assuredly*,
16:23. the jailor to keep them *safely:*

807 2 118/118 809

ἀσχημονέω, askeemoneo.

1Co. 7:36. he *behaveth* himself *uncomely*
13: 5. *Doth* not *behave* itself *unseemly*,

808 2 118/118 809

ἀσχημοσύνη, askeemosunee.

Ro. 1:27. men working *that which is unseemly*,
Rev.16:15. walk naked, and they see his *shame*.

809 1 119/118 1,2192

ἀσχήμων, askeemōn.

1Co.12:23. our *uncomely* (parts) have more

810 3 119/118 1:506 1,4982

ἀσωτία, asōtia.

Eph. 5:18. drunk with wine, wherein is *excess;*
Tit. 1: 6. not accused of *riot*, or unruly.
1Pet.4: 4. to the same excess of *riot*, speaking

811 1 119/119 1:506 1,4982

ἀσώτως, asōtos.

Lu. 15:13. wasted his substance with *riotous* living.

812 1 119/119 8:27 813

ἀτακτέω, atakteo.

2 Th. 3: 7. *behaved* not ourselves *disorderly*

813 1 119/119 8:27 1,5021

ἄτακτος, ataktos.

1 Th. 5:14. warn them that are *unruly,*

814 2 119/119 8:27 813

ἀτάκτως, ataktōs.

2Th. 3: 6. every brother that walketh *disorderly,*
11. which walk among you *disorderly,*

815 3 119/119 1,5043

ἄτεκνος, ateknos.

Lu. 20:28. he die *without children,* that
29. took a wife, and died *without children.*
30. to wife, and he died *childless.*

816 14 119/119 1 *teinō* (to stretch)

ἀτενίζω, atenizo.

Lu. 4:20. eyes of all them that...were *fastened* on him.
22:56. *earnestly looked* upon him, *and* said,
Acts 1:10. they *looked stedfastly* toward
3: 4. Peter, *fastening* his *eyes* upon him
12. why *look* ye so *earnestly* on us,
6:15. *looking stedfastly* on him, saw
7:55. *looked up stedfastly* into heaven, and
10: 4. *when* he *looked* on him, he was
11: 6. *when* I *had fastened* mine *eyes,*
13: 9. *Then...set* his *eyes* on him,
14: 9. who *stedfastly beholding* him,
23: 1. Paul, *earnestly beholding* the council,
2Co. 3: 7. could not *stedfastly behold* the
13. could not *stedfastly look* to the

817 2 119/119 cf 427

ἄτερ, ater.

Lu. 22: 6. *in the absence* of the multitude.
35. When I sent you *without* purse,

818 6 119/119 820

ἀτιμάζω, atimazo.

Lu. 20:11. *entreated* (him) *shamefully, and* sent
Joh. 8:49. I honour my Father, and ye *do dishonour* me.
Acts 5:41. worthy *to suffer shame* for his name.
Ro. 1:24. *to dishonour* their own bodies
2:23. the law *dishonourest* thou God?
Jas. 2: 6. ye *have despised* the poor. Do not

819 7 119/119 820

ἀτιμία, atimia.

Ro. 1:26. God gave them up unto *vile* affections:
9:21. honour, and another unto *dishonour?*
1Co.11:14. long hair, it is a *shame* unto him?
15:43. It is sown in *dishonour;* it is
2Co. 6: 8. By honour and *dishonour,* by evil
11:21. I speak as concerning *reproach,*
2Ti. 2:20. some to honour, and some to *dishonour.*

820 4 119/119 1,5092

ἄτιμος, atimos.

Mat.13:57. A prophet is not *without honour,*
Mar 6: 4. A prophet is not *without honour,*
1Co. 4:10. honourable, but we (are) *despised.*
12:23. we think to be *less honourable,*

821 1 119/119 820

ἀτιμόω, atimoō.

Mar12: 4. sent (him) away *shamefully handled.*

822 2 120/119

ἀτμίς, atmis.

Acts 2:19. blood, and fire, and *vapour* of smoke.
Jas. 4:14. It is even a *vapour,* that appeareth

823 1 120/119 1,rt 5114

ἄτομος, atomos.

1Co.15:52. In a *moment,* in the twinkling

824 3 120/119 1,5117

ἄτοπος, atopos.

Lu. 23:41. this man hath done nothing *amiss.*
Acts28: 6. saw no *harm* come to him, they
2Th. 3: 2. from *unreasonable* and wicked men:

826 1 120/119 1:507 827

αὐγάζω, augazo.

2Co. 4: 4. should *shine* unto them.

827 1 120/119

αὐγή, augee.

Acts20:11. a long while, even till *break of day,*

829 2 120/119 1:508 rt 2237 846

αὐθάδης, authadees.

Tit. 1: 7. not *selfwilled,* not soon angry,
2Pet. 2:10. Presumptuous (are they), *selfwilled,*

830 2 120/119 846 *handanō* (to please)

αὐθαίρετος, authairetos.

2Co. 8: 3. (they were) *willing of* them*selves;*
17. *of* his *own accord,* he went unto you.

831 1 120/119 846 *hentes* (worker)

αὐθεντέω, authenteo.

1Ti. 2:12. nor *to usurp authority over* the man,

832 3 120/119 836

αὐλέω, auleo.

Mat.11:17. We *have piped* unto you, and ye have
Lu. 7:32. We *have piped* unto you, and ye
1Co.14: 7. known *what is piped* or harped?

833 12 120/120 rt 109

αὐλή, aulee.

Mat.26: 3. unto the *palace* of the high priest,
58. unto the high priest's *palace,*
69. Peter sat without in the *palace*
Mar14:54. into the *palace* of the high priest.

Mar 14:66. Peter was beneath in the *palace*,
15:16. into the *hall*, called Prætorium;
Lu. 11:21. man armed keepeth his *palace*,
22:55. a fire in the midst of the *hall*,
Joh.10: 1. the door into the sheep*fold*,
16. which are not of this *fold*.
18:15. into the *palace* of the high priest.
Rev 11: 2. the *court* which is without the

834 2 121/120 832

αὐλητής, auleetees.

Mat. 9:23. saw the *minstrels* and the people
Rev 18:22. harpers, and musicians, and of *pipers*,

835 2 121/120 833

αὐλίζομαι, aulizomai.

Mat 21:17. into Bethany; and he *lodged* there.
Lu. 21:37. he went out, and *abode* in the mount

836 1 121/120 rt109

αὐλός, aulos.

1Co 14: 7. whether *pipe* or harp, except they

837 22 121/120 8:517

ξάνω & αὔξω, auxano & auxo.

Mat. 6:28 of the field, how they *grow*;
13:32. when it *is grown*, it is the greatest
Mar 4: 8. fruit that sprang up and *increased*,
Lu. 1:80. the child *g w*, and waxed strong
2:40. the child *grew*, and waxed strong
12:27. Consider the lili how they *grow*
13:19. it *grew*, and waxed a great tree:
Joh. 3:30. He must *increase*, but I (must)
Acts 6: 7. the word of God *increased*;
7:17. the people *grew* and multiplied
12:24. the word of God *grew* and multi
19:20. So mightily *grew* the word of God
1Co. 3: 6. God *gave the increase*.
7. God *that giveth the increase*.
2Co. 9:10. *increase* the fruits of your
10:15. *when* your faith *is increased*,
Eph. 2:21. *groweth* unto an holy temple
4:15. *may grow up* into him in all
Col. 1:10. *increasing* in the knowledge of God;
2:19. *increaseth* with the increase of God.
1Pet. 2: 2. the word, that ye *may grow* thereby:
2Pet. 3:18. *grow* in grace, and (in) the knowledge

838 2 121/120 837

αὔξησις, auxeesis.

Eph. 4:16. maketh *increase* of the body
Col. 2:19. increaseth with the *increase* of God.

839 15 121/120 rt 109

αὔριον, aurion.

Mat. 6:30. *to morrow* is cast into the oven,
34. no thought for the *morrow*: for the *morrow* shall take thought
Lu. 10:35. on the *morrow* when he departed,
12:28. *to morrow* is cast into the oven;
13:32. I do cures to day and *to morrow*, and
33. I must walk to day, and *to morrow*,
Acts 4: 3. in hold unto the *next day*:
5. it came to pass on the *morrow*,
23:15. him down unto you *to morrow*.
20. bring down Paul *to morrow*
Acts25:22. *To morrow*, said he, thou shalt
1Co 15:32. eat and drink; for *to morrow* we die.
Jas. 4:13. To day or *to morrow* we will go
14. what (shall be) on the *morrow*.

840 2 121/120 rt 109

αὐστηρός, austeeros.

Lu. 19:21. because thou art an *austere* man:
22. that I was an *austere* man,

αὗται & αὕτη see οὗτος. 3778

841 2 121/120 1:464 842

αὐτάρκεια, autarkīa.

2Co. 9: 8. having all *sufficiency* in all
1Ti. 6: 6. godliness with *contentment* is

842 1 122/120 1:464 846,714

αὐτάρκης, autarkees.

Phi. 4:11. state I am, (therewith) to be *content*.

843 1 122/120 3:921 846,2632

αὐτοκατάκριτος, autokatakritos.

Tit. 3:11. sinneth, being *condemned of* him*self*.

844 2 122/120 846,3154

αὐτόματος, automatos.

Mar 4:28. earth bringeth forth fruit of her*self*;
Acts12:10. opened to them *of* his *own accord*:

845 1 122/120 5:315 846,3700

αὐτόπτης, autoptees.

Lu. 1: 2. beginning were *eyewitnesses*,

846 5117 122/120-130 rt 109

αὐτός, autos. cf 848

[2] marks those combined with the definite article.

Mat. 1:20. that which is conceived in *her* is
2:16. and in all the coasts *there*of,
3: 5. Then went out to *him*
7. He said unto *them*,
5: 3. for *their's* is the kingdom
4. for *they* shall be comforted.
10. for *their's* is the kingdom
7:13. many there be that go in *there*at:
10:11. enquire who in *it* is worthy;
13: 2. so that *he* went into a ship,
4. And when *he* sowed,
16:21. how that *he* must go unto Jerusalem,
17:18. Jesus rebuked the devil (lit. *him*); and he (lit. the devil) departed
21:19. and found nothing *there*on, but leaves
41. destroy *those* wicked men,
24:32. fig tree; When *his* branch is
25:16. went and traded with *the same*,
Mar 1:19. who (lit. and *they*) also were in the ship
2:15. that, as Jesus (lit. *he*) sat at meat in *his*
6:22. daughter of the *said* Herodias[2]
31. Come ye your*selves* apart
7:25. whose young (lit. of whom *her*) daughter
12:37. David therefore him*self* calleth *him* Lord;
44. of *their* abundance;
13:28. fig tree: When *her* branch is yet
16:14. as *they* sat at meat,
Lu. 1:57. time came that *she* should be delivered;
2:22. the days of her (lit. *their*) purification

Lu. 2:35. through thy *own* soul also,
38. she coming in *that* instant gave thanks[2]
6:42. when thou thy*self* beholdest not
7:12. mother, and *she* was a widow:
21. And in *that same* hour he cured[2]
10: 9. heal the sick that are *there*in,
10. into the streets of *the same*,
11: 4. for we (lit. we our*selves*) also forgive
14:32. while *the other* is yet a great way
19:23. have required *mine own* (lit. *it*) with
21:21. countries enter *there*into.
24:18. which are come to pass there (lit. in *it*)
39. that it is I my*self*:
Joh. 11: 4. might be glorified *there*by.
12: 7. burying hath she kept *this*.
14:17. because it seeth *him* not,
15: 2. he taketh (lit. taketh *it*) away:
17:11. *those* whom thou hast given me,
18:28. and they them*selves* went not into
Acts 3:12. had made *this man* to walk?
9:37. whom (lit. and *her*) when they had washed,
11:22. Then tidings of *these things*
Ro. 8:16. The Spirit *itself* beareth[2]
9:17. for this *same* purpose
13: 6. upon this *very* thing.
2Co. 2: 3. I wrote this *same* unto you,
5: 5. for the self*same* thing (is) God,
13:11. be of one mind, (lit. think the *same* thing[2])
1Th. 5:23. And the *very* God of peace[2]
Heb 3: 3. who hath builded the house (lit. *it*) hath more honour than the house.
9:19. both the book, (lit. both the book *itself*[2])
10: 1. not the *very* image of the things,[2]
Jas. 3: 9. *There*with bless we God, even the Father;
1Pet. 1:12. unto us they did minister the *things*,
2:24. Who his own *self* bare our sins
4:14. on *their* part he is evil spoken of,
2Pet. 1: 5. And beside this, (Gr. Even this *very* thing)
3Joh. 12. and of the truth *itself*:[2]
Rev. 17: 9. on *which* the woman sitteth.
&c. &c.

OBSERVE the meaning of ἐπι & κατα...το αὐτο.

Mat. 22:34. were gathered *together*.
Lu. 17:35. Two (women) shall be grinding *together*;
Acts 14: 1. they went both *together*
&c. &c.

847 4 123/130 846

αὐτοῦ, *autou*, adv.

Mat. 26:36. Sit ye *here*, while I go and pray
Acts 15:34. it pleased Silas to abide *there* still.
18:19. to Ephesus, and left them *there*:
21: 4. we tarried *there* seven days:

848 659 122/122 1438

αὑτοῦ, *hautou*.

Mat. 1:21. he shall save *his* people from
24. took unto him *his* wife:
25. brought forth *her* firstborn son:
2:11. they had opened *their* treasures,
12. departed into *their own* country
18. Rachel weeping (for) *her* children,
3: 4. had *his* raiment of camel's hair, and a leathern girdle about *his* loins;
6. in Jordan, confessing *their* sins.
7. Sadducees come to *his* baptism,
12. he will throughly purge *his* floor, and gather *his* wheat into the garner;
4: 6. He shall give *his* angels charge
21. in a ship with Zebedee *their* father,
Mat. 4:22. left the ship and *their* father, and
5: 2. he opened *his* mouth, and taught
22. is angry with *his* brother without
— whosoever shall say to *his* brother,
28. adultery with her already in *his* heart.
31. Whosoever shall put away *his* wife,
32. whosoever shall put away *his* wife,
45. he maketh *his* sun to rise on
6: 2. They have *their* reward.
5. I say unto you, They have *their* reward.
16. for they disfigure *their* faces,
— I say unto you, They have *their* reward.
27. add one cubit unto *his* stature?
29. Solomon in all *his* glory was
7: 6. trample them under *their* feet,
24. which built *his* house upon a rock:
26. which built *his* house upon the sand:
8:18. Jesus saw great multitudes about *him*,
9: 7. he arose, and departed to *his* house.
37. Then saith he unto *his* disciples,
38. send forth labourers into *his* harvest.
10:10. workman is worthy of *his* meat.
17. scourge you in *their* synagogues;
24. nor the servant above *his* lord.
38. he that taketh not *his* cross, and
39. He that findeth *his* life shall
— he that loseth *his* life for my
42. shall in no wise lose *his* reward.
11: 1. of commanding *his* twelve disciples,
2. he sent two of *his* disciples,
16. calling unto *their* fellows,
19. wisdom is justified of *her* children.
12:49. forth *his* hand toward *his* disciples,
13:15. *their* eyes they have closed; lest
24. which sowed good seed in *his* field:
31. a man took, and sowed in *his* field:
41. shall send forth *his* angels, and
43. in the kingdom of *their* Father.
52. bringeth forth out of *his* treasure
54. he was come into *his* own country,
57. save in *his* own country, and in *his* own house.
14: 2. said unto *his* servants, This is
3. Herodias' sake, *his* brother Philip's wife.
8. before instructed of *her* mother,
11. she brought (it) to *her* mother.
22. Jesus constrained *his* disciples
15: 2. they wash not *their* hands
6(5). and honour not *his* father or *his* mother
8. nigh unto me with *their* mouth,
27. fall from *their* master's table.
32. Then Jesus called *his* disciples
36. brake (them), and gave to *his* disciples,
16:13. he asked *his* disciples, saying,
20. Then charged he *his* disciples
21. to shew unto *his* disciples, how that
24. Then said Jesus unto *his* disciples,
— take up *his* cross, and follow me.
25. whosoever will save *his* life shall
— whosoever will lose *his* life for my
26. whole world, and lose *his own* soul?
— give in exchange for *his* soul?
27. come in the glory of *his* Father
28. Son of man coming in *his* kingdom
17: 6. they fell on *their* face, and were
8. they had lifted up *their* eyes,
25. of *their own* children, or of strangers?
18:23. would take account of *his* servants.
28. found one of *his* fellowservants,
31. came and told unto *their* lord all
35. every one *his* brother their trespasses.
19: 3. a man to put away *his* wife for

Mat.19: 5. shall cleave to *his* wife: and they
9. Whosoever shall put away *his* wife,
23. Then said Jesus unto *his* disciples,
28. shall sit in the throne of *his* glory,
20: 1. to hire labourers into *his* vineyard.
2. he sent them into *his* vineyard.
8. saith unto *his* steward, Call the
20. of Zebedee's children with *her* sons,
28. to give *his* life a ransom for many.
21: 7. put on them *their* clothes, and
34. he sent *his* servants to the
37. he sent unto them *his* son, saying,
22: 2. which made a marriage for *his* son,
3. sent forth *his* servants to call
5. his farm, another to *his* merchandise:
7. he sent forth *his* armies, and destroyed
8. Then saith he to *his* servants, The
16. sent out unto him *their* disciples
24. raise up seed unto *his* brother.
25. left *his* wife unto *his* brother:
23: 1. the multitude, and to *his* disciples,
4. move them with one of *their* fingers.
5. all *their* works they do for to
— they make broad *their* phylacteries,
— the borders of *their* garments,
37. them which are sent unto *thee*,
24:17. take any thing out of *his* house:
18. return back to take *his* clothes.
29. the moon shall not give *her* light,
31. he shall send *his* angels with
43. have suffered *his* house to be
45. made ruler over *his* houshold,
47. ruler over all *his* goods.
48. evil servant shall say in *his* heart,
25: 1. ten virgins, which took *their* lamps,
4. the wise took oil in *their* vessels with *their* lamps.
7. virgins arose, and trimmed *their* lamps.
14. delivered unto them *his* goods.
18. in the earth, and hid *his* lord's money.
31. Son of man shall come in *his* glory,
— sit upon the throne of *his* glory:
33. set the sheep on *his* right hand,
34. say unto them on *his* right hand,
26: 1. he said unto *his* disciples,
39. a little farther, and fell on *his* face,
45. Then cometh he to *his* disciples,
51. drew *his* sword, and struck a
65. the high priest rent *his* clothes,
27:39. reviled him, wagging *their* heads,
60. laid it in *his own* new tomb,
Mar. 1: 5. of Jordan, confessing *their* sins.
6. a girdle of a skin about *his* loins;
18. straightway they forsook *their* nets,
20. they left *their* father Zebedee
27. they questioned among *themselves*,
2: 6. reasoning in *their* hearts,
8. Jesus perceived in *his* spirit that
3: 7. himself with *his* disciples to the sea:
9. he spake to *his* disciples, that a
34. on them which sat about *him*,
4: 2. said unto them in *his* doctrine,
34. expounded all things to *his* disciples.
5:30. that virtue had gone out of *him*,
6: 1. came into *his* own country; and his
4. without honour, but in *his* own country,
— own kin, and in *his own* house.
17. Herodias' sake, *his* brother Philip's wife:
21. that Herod on *his* birth day made a supper to *his* lords, high captains,
24. went forth, and said unto *her* mother,
28. the damsel gave it to *her* mother.

Mar. 6:41. gave (them) to *his* disciples to set
45. he constrained *his* disciples to get
7:12. to do ought for *his* father or *his*
26. the devil out of *her* daughter.
30. when she was come to *her* house,
33. put *his* fingers into his ears, and he
8: 1. Jesus called *his* disciples (unto him),
3. fasting to *their* own houses
6. gave to *his* disciples to set before
10. entered into a ship with *his* disciples.
12. sighed deeply in *his* spirit, and saith,
27. by the way he asked *his* disciples,
33. turned about, and looked on *his* disciples
34. with *his* disciples also, he said
— take up *his* cross, and follow me.
35. whosoever will save *his* life shall
— whosoever shall lose *his* life for
36. whole world, and lose *his own* soul?
37. a man give in exchange for *his* soul?
38. cometh in the glory of *his* Father
9:16. What question ye with *them*?
18. he foameth, and gnasheth with *his* teeth,
31. For he taught *his* disciples, and said
41. He shall not lose *his* reward.
10: 7. shall a man leave *his* father and mother, and cleave to *his* wife;
11. Whosoever shall put away *his* wife,
12. a woman shall put away *her* husband,
23. saith unto *his* disciples, How
45. to give *his* life a ransom for many.
50. he, casting away *his* garment,
11: 1. he sendeth forth two of *his* disciples,
7. cast *their* garments on him;
8. many spread *their* garments in
23. shall not doubt in *his* heart, but
12: 6. one son, *his* wellbeloved, he sent
19. raise up seed unto *his* brother.
38. said unto them in *his* doctrine,
43. he called (unto him) *his* disciples,
44. she of *her* want did cast in all that she had, (even) all *her* living.
13:15. to take any thing out of *his* house:
16. for to take up *his* garment.
24. the moon shall not give *her* light,
27. then shall he send *his* angels, and shall gather together *his* elect from
34. taking a far journey, who left *his* house, and gave authority to *his* servants, and to every man *his* work, and commanded
14:13. sendeth forth two of *his* disciples,
32. he saith to *his* disciples, Sit ye here,
46. they laid *their* hands on him,
63. the high priest rent *his* clothes,
15:29. railed on him, wagging *their* heads,
Lu. 1: 7. were (now) well stricken in years. (lit. in *their* days)
15. even from *his* mother's womb.
18. wife well stricken in years. (lit. in *her* days)
23. he departed to *his own* house.
36. conceived a son in *her* old age.
48. the low estate of *his* handmaiden:
51. hath shewed strength with *his* arm,
54. He hath holpen *his* servant Israel,
56. returned to *her own* house.
58. had shewed great (lit. *his own*) mercy upon her;
66. laid (them) up in *their* hearts,
68. hath visited and redeemed *his* people,
69. in the house of *his* servant David;
70. by the mouth of *his* holy prophets.
72. to remember *his* holy covenant;
2: 7. brought forth *her* firstborn son,

Lu. 2: 8. keeping watch over *their* flock
19. pondered (them) in *her* heart.
28. took he him up in *his* arms,
36. seven years from *her* virginity;
39. to *their own* city Nazareth.
51. all these sayings in *her* heart.
3:15. all men mused in *their* hearts
17. and he will throughly purge *his* floor, and will gather the wheat into *his* garner;
4:10. He shall give *his* angels charge
24. is accepted in *his* own country.
5:15. healed by him of *their* infirmities.
25. departed to *his own* house,
29. a great feast in *his own* house:
6:13. he called (unto him) *his* disciples:
17. and to be healed of *their* diseases;
20. he lifted up *his* eyes on *his* disciples,
40. The disciple is not above *his* master:
45. the good treasure of *his* heart
— out of the evil treasure of *his* heart
7: 1. he had ended all *his* sayings in
3. would come and heal *his* servant.
12. the only son of *his* mother, and she
16. God hath visited *his* people.
19. calling (unto him) two of *his* disciples
35. wisdom is justified of all *her* children.
38. wipe (them) with the hairs of *her* head,
44. wiped (them) with the hairs of *her* head.
8: 5. A sower went out to sow *his* seed:
41. that he would come into *his* house:
9: 1. Then he called *his* twelve disciples
14. he said to *his* disciples, Make
23. take up *his* cross daily, and follow me.
24. whosoever will save *his* life
— whosoever will lose *his* life
26. he shall come in *his own* glory,
43. he said unto *his* disciples,
51. set *his* face to go to Jerusalem,
52. sent messengers before *his* face:
62. having put *his* hand to the plough,
10: 1. two and two before *his* face into
2. send forth labourers into *his* harvest.
7. the labourer is worthy of *his* hire.
38. Martha received him into *her* house.
11: 1. as John also taught *his* disciples.
12: 1. began to say unto *his* disciples
22. he said unto *his* disciples,
25. can add to *his* stature one cubit?
27. Solomon in all *his* glory was
39. not have suffered *his* house
42. make ruler over *his* houshold,
44. ruler over all that he hath. (lit. is *his*)
45. that servant say in *his* heart,
53. against *her* daughter in law,
— against *her* mother in law.
13. 6. a fig tree planted in *his* vineyard;
15. on the sabbath loose *his* ox or
34. stonest them that are sent unto *thee*;
14:17. sent *his* servant at supper
21. shewed *his* lord these things.
— being angry, said to *his* servant,
27. whosoever doth not bear *his* cross,
15:13. there wasted *his* substance with
15. he sent him into *his* fields to
16. have filled *his* belly with the husks
22. the father said to *his* servants,
16: 1. he said also unto *his* disciples,
18. Whosoever putteth away *his* wife,
23. in hell he lift up *his* eyes, being
24. may dip the tip of *his* finger in
17:24. the Son of man be in *his* day.
33. shall seek to save *his* life shall

Lu. 18: 7. shall not God avenge *his own* elect,
13. smote upon *his* breast, saying,
14. This man went down to *his* house
40. him to be brought unto *him*.
19:15. servants to be called unto *him*,
29. he sent two of *his* disciples,
36. spread *their* clothes in the way.
20:28. raise up seed unto *his* brother.
45. he said unto *his* disciples,
21: 1. casting *their* gifts into the treasury.
4. she of *her* penury hath cast
12. shall lay *their* hands on you,
22:36. let him sell *his* garment, and buy
23:11. Herod with *his* men of war set
24:26. to enter into *his* glory?
50. he lifted up *his* hands, and blessed
Joh. 1:47(48). Jesus saw Nathanael coming to *him*.
2:11. manifested forth *his* glory; and
21. he spake of the temple of *his* body.
3: 4. second time into *his* mother's womb,
16. gave *his* only begotten Son, that
17. God sent not *his* Son into the
4: 5. Jacob gave to *his* son Joseph.
28. The woman then left *her* waterpot,
5: 9. took up *his* bed, and walked:
6: 3. there he sat with *his* disciples.
5. a great company come unto *him*,
12. he said unto *his* disciples,
22. Jesus went not with *his* disciples
7:53. every man went unto *his own* house.
9:21. he shall speak for *himself*.
10:11. the good shepherd giveth *his* life
11: 2. wiped his feet with *her* hair,
28. called Mary *her* sister secretly,
54. there continued with *his* disciples.
12: 3. wiped his feet with *her* hair:
25. He that loveth *his* life shall lose it; and he that hateth *his* life in this
13:12. had taken *his* garments, and was
16. servant is not greater than *his* Lord;
18. lifted up *his* heel against me.
15:13. a man lay down *his* life for *his* friends
20. servant is not greater than *his* lord.
22. have no cloke for *their* sin.
17: 1. lifted up *his* eyes to heaven,
13. my joy fulfilled in *themselves*.
18: 1. he went forth with *his* disciples
2. resorted thither with *his* disciples.
19:12. whosoever maketh *himself* a king
17. he bearing *his* cross went forth
26. he saith unto *his* mother, Woman,
20:20. shewed unto them (his) hands and *his* side
30. in the presence of *his* disciples,
21:14. Jesus shewed himself to *his* disciples,
Acts 2:14. lifted up *his* voice, and said unto them,
3: 2. lame from *his* mother's womb
13. hath glorified *his* Son Jesus;
18. by the mouth of all *his* prophets,
21. by the mouth of all *his* holy prophets
26. God, having raised up *his* Son Jesus,
5: 1. Ananias, with Sapphira *his* wife,
18. laid *their* hands on the apostles,
31. God exalted with *his* right hand
37. drew away much people after *him*:
7:10. over Egypt and all *his* house.
13. was made known to *his* brethren;
14. sent Joseph, and called *his* father Jacob
— all *his* kindred, threescore and fifteen
19. cast out *their* young children,
20. nourished up in *his* father's house
23. to visit *his* brethren the children
25. he supposed *his* brethren would

Acts 7:39. in *their* hearts turned back again
41. in the works of *their own* hands.
54. they were cut to the (lit. *their*) heart, and
57. stopped *their* ears, and ran upon
58. witnesses laid down *their* clothes
8:28. returning, and sitting in *his* chariot
32. so opened he not *his* mouth:
35. Then Philip opened *his* mouth,
39. he went on *his* way rejoicing.
9: 4. heard a voice saying unto *him*,
8. when *his* eyes were opened, he
40. she opened *her* eyes: and when
10: 2. feared God with all *his* house,
7. called two of *his* houshold servants,
22. to send for thee into *his* house, and
24. had called together *his* kinsmen
12:11. the Lord hath sent *his* angel,
13:36. was laid unto *his* fathers,
42. might be preached to *them* the next sabbath.
50. expelled them out of *their* coasts.
51. shook off the dust of *their* feet
14: 3. unto the word of *his* grace,
8. a cripple from *his* mother's womb,
11. they lifted up *their* voices, saying
14. they rent *their* clothes, and ran in
16. to walk in *their own* ways.
15:14. out of them a people for *his* name.
18. Known unto God are all *his* works
26. hazarded *their* lives for the name of
16: 3. Paul have to go forth with *him*;
16. brought *her* masters much gain
19. the hope of *their* gains was gone,
34. he had brought them into *his* house,
18: 8. on the Lord with all *his* house;
19:18. confessed, and shewed *their* deeds.
20:30. to draw away disciples after *them*.
36. he kneeled (lit. bending *his* knees) down,
21:11. bound *his own* hands and feet,
22:14. that thou shouldest know *his* will,
22. (then) lifted up *their* voices, and said,
23: 2. them that stood by *him* to
24:24. Felix came with *his* wife
25:21. I commanded *him* to be kept till
27:27. *they* drew near to some country;
28:27. *their* eyes have they closed; lest
Ro. 1: 2. promised afore by *his* prophets
3. Concerning *his* Son Jesus Christ
21. became vain in *their* imaginations,
27. burned in *their* lust one toward
— recompence of *their* error which
2:15. the law written in *their* hearts,
3:13. with *their* tongues they have
25. to declare *his* righteousness for
8:29. conformed to the image of *his* Son,
9:22. to make *his* power known,
23. the riches of *his* glory on the
11: 1. Hath God cast away *his* people?
2. God hath not cast away *his* people
1Co. 2:10. revealed (them) unto us by *his* Spirit:
6: 5. to judge between *his* brethren?
14. also raise up us by *his own* power.
7:36. himself uncomely toward *his* virgin,
37. hath so decreed in *his* heart
9:10. should be partaker of *his* hope.
11: 4. covered, dishonoureth *his* head.
15:25. all enemies under *his* feet.
2Co. 2:14. the savour of *his* knowledge
11: 3. beguiled Eve through *his* subtilty,
Gal. 1:15. called (me) by *his* grace,
16. To reveal *his* Son in me, that
4: 4. God sent forth *his* Son, made
6. sent forth the Spirit of *his* Son
25. is in bondage with *her* children.

Eph. 1: 5. by Jesus Christ to *himself*, acco good pleasure of *his* will,
6. the praise of the glory of *his* grace,
9. unto us the mystery of *his* will, according to *his* good pleasure which he hath purposed in *himself*
11. after the counsel of *his own* will:
17. revelation in the knowledge *of him*.
20. set (him) at *his own* right hand
2: 4. for *his* great love wherewith he
7. the exceeding riches of *his* grace
15. Having abolished in *his* flesh the
3:16. according to the riches of *his* glory,
— by *his* Spirit in the inner man;
4:17. in the vanity of *their* mind,
25. speak every man truth with *his* neighbour:
5:31. shall a man leave *his* father and mother, and shall be joined unto *his* wife,
Phi. 4:19. according to *his* riches in glory
Col. 1:13. into the kingdom of *his* dear Son:
20. to reconcile all things unto *himself*;
22. In the body of *his* flesh through
— unreprovable in *his* sight:
2:18. puffed up by *his* fleshly mind,
1Th. 2:16. to fill up *their* sins alway:
4: 6. defraud *his* brother in (any) matter:
8. given unto us *his* holy Spirit.
2Th. 1: 7. from heaven with *his* mighty angels
10. to be glorified in *his* saints,
2: 8. consume with the spirit of *his* mouth,
— with the brightness of *his* coming:
1Ti. 5:18. The labourer (is)worthy of *his* reward
2Ti. 2:19. The Lord knoweth them that are *his*.
4: 1. at *his* appearing and *his* kingdom;
18. preserve (me) unto *his* heavenly kingdom:
Tit. 1: 3. manifested *his* word through preaching,
3: 5. according to *his* mercy he saved us,
Heb. 1: 3. all things by the word of *his* power,
7. Who maketh *his* angels spirits, and *his* ministers a flame of fire.
2: 4. according to *his* own will?
3: 6. Christ as a son over *his own* house;
18. should not enter into *his* rest,
4: 4. seventh day from all *his* works.
10. hath ceased from *his own* works,
5: 7. Who in the days of *his* flesh, when
6:17. the immutability of *his* counsel,
7: 5. to the law, that is, of *their* brethren,
8:11. not teach every man *his* neighbour, and every man *his* brother, saying,
9:26. by the sacrifice *of himself*.
10:20. the veil, that is to say, *his* flesh;
30. The Lord shall judge *his* people.
11: 7. an ark to the saving of *his* house;
22. commandment concerning *his* bones.
23. was hid three months of *his* parents.
35. Women received *their* dead raised
12: 2. the joy that was set before *him*
3. contradiction of sinners against *himself*,
10. chastened (us) after *their own* pleasure;
16. morsel of meat sold *his* birthright.
13:21. which is wellpleasing in *his* sight,
Jas. 1: 8. A double minded man (is) unstable in all *his* ways.
9. rejoice in that he is exalted: (lit in *his* exaltation)
10. the rich, in that he is made low: (lit. in *his*, &c.)
11. rich man fade away in *his* ways.
18. a kind of firstfruits of *his* creatures.
23. a man beholding *his* natural face
25. shall be blessed in *his* deed

Jas. 1:26. bridleth not *his* tongue, but deceiveth *his* *own* heart, this
2:21. he had offered Isaac *his* son upon
3:13. *his* works with meekness of wisdom.
4:11. judgeth *his* brother, speaketh evil
5:18. the earth brought forth *her* fruit.
1Pet. 1: 3. according to *his* abundant mercy
2: 9. into *his* marvellous light:
24. bare our sins in *his own* body
3:10. let him refrain *his* tongue from evil, and *his* lips that they speak no guile:
5:10. called us unto *his* eternal glory
2Pet. 1: 9. was purged from *his* old sins.
2:12. perish in *their* own corruption;
13. with *their* own deceivings while
3: 3. walking after *their* own lusts,
16. unto *their* own destruction.
1Joh. 2: 9. hateth *his* brother, is in darkness
10. He that loveth *his* brother abideth
11. he that hateth *his* brother is in
3:10. he that loveth not *his* brother.
12. that wicked one, and slew *his* brother.
15. Whosoever hateth *his* brother is
16. he laid down *his* life for us.
17. seeth *his* brother have need, and shutteth up *his* bowels (of compassion)
4: 9. God sent *his* only begotten Son
10. sent *his* Son (to be) the propitiation
13. he hath given us of *his* Spirit.
20. I love God, and hateth *his* brother,
— he that loveth not *his* brother
21. who loveth God love *his* brother also.
5: 9. he hath testified of *his* Son.
10. record that God gave of *his* Son.
16. If any man see *his* brother sin
Jude 14. with ten thousands of *his* saints,
16. walking after *their own* lusts;
24. before the presence of *his* glory
Rev. 1: 1. to shew unto *his* servants things
— sent and signified (it) by *his* angel unto *his* servant John:
5. from our sins in *his own* blood,
6. priests unto God and *his* Father;
16. he had in *his* right hand seven
— as the sun shineth in *his* strength.
17. he laid *his* right hand upon me,
2: 1. seven stars in *his* right hand,
18. who hath *his* eyes like unto a flame
21. to repent of *her* fornication;
22. except they repent of *their* deeds.
3: 4. have not defiled *their* garments;
4: 4. had on *their* heads crowns of gold.
10. cast *their* crowns before the throne,
6: 5. a pair of balances in *his* hand.
13. a fig tree casteth *her* untimely figs,
14. were moved out of *their* places.
7:11. before the throne on *their* faces,
14. have washed *their* robes, and made them (lit. *their* robes) white in the blood
8:12. shone not for a third part *of it*,
9: 4. seal of God in *their* foreheads.
11. they had a king over *them*,
20. not of the works of *their* hands,
21. Neither repented they of *their* murders, nor of *their* sorceries, nor of *their* fornication, nor of *their* thefts.
10: 2. he had in *his* hand a little book open: and he set *his* right foot upon the sea,
5. lifted up *his* hand to heaven,
11: 7. shall have finished *their* testimony,
11. they stood upon *their* feet; and
16. sat before God on *their* seats, fell upon *their* faces, and worshipped
Rev 12: 3. seven crowns upon *his* heads.
11. by the word of *their* testimony; and they loved not *their* lives unto
14. into *her* place, where she is
15. the serpent cast out of *his* mouth
16. the earth opened *her* mouth,
— the dragon cast out of *his* mouth.
13: 2. the dragon gave him *his* power, and *his* seat,
6. he opened *his* mouth in blasphemy
14: 1. name written in *their* foreheads.
2. harpers harping with *their* harps:
8. the wrath of *her* fornication.
9. mark in *his* forehead, or in *his* hand,
13. they may rest from *their* labours;
14. having on *his* head a golden crown, and in *his* hand a sharp sickle.
16. thrust in *his* sickle on the earth;
19. the angel thrust in *his* sickle
16: 2. poured out *his* vial upon the earth;
3. poured out *his* vial upon the sea;
4. poured out *his* vial upon the rivers
8. poured out *his* vial upon the sun;
10. poured out *his* vial upon the seat
— they gnawed *their* tongues for pain,
11. because of *their* pains and *their* sores, and repented not of *their* deeds.
12. poured out *his* vial upon the great river
15. watcheth, and keepeth *his* garments,
17. poured out *his* vial into the air;
19. wine of the fierceness of *his* wrath.
17: 4. a golden cup in *her* hand full
— filthiness of *her* fornication:
5. upon *her* forehead (was) a name
17. in their hearts to fulfil *his* will,
— give *their* kingdom unto the beast,
18: 7. for she saith in *her* heart,
19. they cast dust on *their* heads,
19: 2. the earth with *her* fornication,
— avenged the blood of *his* servants
16. on *his* thigh a name written,
20: 1. a great chain in *his* hand.
4. mark upon *their* foreheads, or in *their* hands;
7. Satan shall be loosed out of *his* prison,
21: 2. a bride adorned for *her* husband.
24. bring *their* glory and honour into it.
22: 2. yielded *her* fruit every month:
6. sent *his* angel to shew unto *his* servants

---

849 1 123/131 846,5495

αὐτόχειρ, autokīr.

Acts27:19. we cast out *with* our *own hands*

---

850 1 123/131 *auchmos* (dust)

αὐχμηρός, aukmeeros.

2Pet. 1:19. light that shineth in a *dark* place,

---

851 10 123/131 575,138

ἀφαιρέω, aphaireo.

Mat 26:51. high priest's, and *smote off* his ear.
Mar 14:47. high priest, and *cut off* his ear.
Lu. 1:25. *to take away* my reproach among men.
10:42. *shall* not *be taken away* from her.
16: 3. my lord *taketh away* from me
22:50. high priest, and *cut off* his right ear.
Ro. 11:27. when I *shall take away* their sins.
Heb 10: 4. should *take away* sins.
Rev 22:19. if any man *shall take away*
— God *shall take away* his part

852 1 124/131 1,5316

ἀφανής, aphanees.

Heb. 4:13. *that is not manifest* in his sight:

853 5 124/131 852

ἀφανίζω, aphanizo.

Mat. 6:16. for they *disfigure* their faces,
19. where moth and rust *doth corrupt,*
20. neither moth nor rust *doth corrupt,*
Acts13:41. Behold, ye despisers, and wonder, and *perish:*
Jas. 4:14. a little time, and then *vanisheth away.*

854 1 124/131 853

ἀφανισμός, aphanismos.

Heb. 8:13. waxeth old (is) ready *to vanish away.*

855 1 124/131 1,5316

ἄφαντος, aphantos.

Lu. 24:31. he (lit. he was) *vanished out of* their *sight.*

856 2 124/131 575,rt 1476

ἀφεδρών, aphedrōn.

Mat.15:17. is cast out into the *draught?*
Mar. 7:19. goeth out into the *draught,* purging

857 1 124/131 1,5339

ἀφειδία, aphīdia.

Col. 2:23. humility, and *neglecting* of the body;

858 1 124/131 1 phellos (stone)

ἀφελότης, aphelotees.

Acts 2:46. with gladness and *singleness* of heart,

859 17 124/131 1:509 863

ἄφεσις, aphesis.

Mat 26:28. for many for the *remission* of sins.
Mar. 1: 4. repentance for the *remission* of sins.
3:29. hath never *forgiveness,* but is in
Lu. 1:77. by the *remission* of their sins,
3: 3. repentance for the *remission* of sins;
4:18(19). to preach *deliverance* to the captives,
—(—). to set at *liberty* them that are bruised,
24:47. repentance and *remission* of sins
Acts 2:38. for the *remission* of sins, and ye
5:31. repentance to Israel, and *forgiveness* of sins.
10:43. shall receive *remission* of sins.
13:38. unto you the *forgiveness* of sins:
26:18. may receive *forgiveness* of sins,
Eph. 1: 7. the *forgiveness* of sins, according
Col. 1:14. (even) the *forgiveness* of sins:
Heb. 9:22. without shedding of blood is no *remission.*
10:18. Now where *remission* of these (is),

860 2 124/132 680

ἁφή, haphee.

Eph. 4:16. that which every *joint* supplieth,
Col. 2:19. all the body by *joints* and bands

861 8 124/132 9:93 862

ἀφθαρσία, aphtharsia.

Ro. 2: 7. glory and honour and *immortality,*
1 Co. 15:42. it is raised in *incorruption:*
50. doth corruption inherit *incorruption.*
1Co 15:53. must put on *incorruption,* and
54. shall have put on *incorruption,*
Eph. 6:24. love our Lord Jesus Christ in *sincerity.*
2Ti. 1:10. brought life and *immortality* to
Tit. 2: 7. uncorruptness, gravity, *sincerity,*

862 7 125/131 9:93 1,5351

ἄφθαρτος, aphthartos.

Ro. 1:23. the glory of the *uncorruptible* God
1Co. 9:25. crown; but we an *incorruptible.*
15:52. dead shall be raised *incorruptible,*
1Ti. 1:17. unto the King eternal, *immortal,*
1 Pet 1: 4. To an inheritance *incorruptible,*
23. *incorruptible,* by the word of God,
3: 4. that which is *not corruptible,*

863 146 125/131 1:509 575 hiemi (to send)

ἀφίημι, aphieemi.

Mat. 3:15. *Suffer* (it to be so) now: for thus it
— Then he *suffered* him.
4:11. Then the devil *leaveth* him,
20. they straightway *left* (their) nets, *and*
22. they immediately *left* the ship *and*
5:24. *Leave* there thy gift before the
40. *let* him *have* (thy) cloke also.
6:12. *forgive* us our debts, as we *forgive* our debtors.
14. For if ye *forgive* men their trespasses. your heavenly Father *will* also *forgive* you:
15. if ye *forgive* not men their
— *will* your Father *forgive* your trespasses.
7: 4. *Let* me pull out the mote out of
8:15. the fever *left* her: and she arose,
22. *let* the dead bury their dead.
9: 2. of good cheer; thy sins *be forgiven* thee.
5. to say (Thy) sins *be forgiven* thee;
6. power on earth *to forgive* sins,
12:31. blasphemy *shall be forgiven*
— *shall* not *be forgiven* unto men
32. it *shall be forgiven* him:
— it *shall* not *be forgiven* him,
13:30. *Let* both grow together until the
36. Jesus *sent* the multitude *away, and*
15:14. *Let* them *alone:* they be blind
18:12. *doth* he not *leave* the ninety and
21. sin against me, and I *forgive* him?
27. loosed him, and *forgave* him the
32. I *forgave* thee all that debt,
35. *forgive* not every one his brother
19:14. *Suffer* little children, and forbid them not,
27. Behold, we *have forsaken* all,
29. every one that *hath forsaken* houses,
22:22. *left* him, *and* went their way.
25. *left* his wife unto his brother:
23:13(14). neither *suffer* ye them that
23. *have omitted* the weightier
— not *to leave* the other undone.
38. your house *is left* unto you desolate.
24: 2. There *shall* not *be left* here one
40. one shall be taken, and the other *left.*
41. one shall be taken, and the other *left.*
26:44. he *left* them, *and* went away
56. the disciples *forsook* him, *and* fled.
27:49. The rest said, *Let be,* let us see
50. a loud voice, *yielded up* the ghost.
Mar. 1:18. straightway they *forsook* their nets, *and*
20. they *left* their father Zebedee...*and*
31. immediately the fever *left* her,
34. *suffered* not the devils to speak,
2: 5. Son, thy sins *be forgiven* thee.

Mar. 2: 7. who can *forgive* sins but God
9. (Thy) sins *be forgiven* thee; or to say,
10. power on earth *to forgive* sins,
3:28. All sins *shall be forgiven* unto
4:12. (their) sins *should be forgiven* them.
36. *when* they *had sent away* the multitude,
5:19. Howbeit Jesus *suffered* him not,
37. he *suffered* no man to follow
7: 8. *laying aside* the commandment
12. ye *suffer* him no more to do
27. *Let* the children first be filled:
8:13. he *left* them, *and* entering into
10:14. *Suffer* the little children to come
28. Lo, we *have left* all, and have followed
29. no man that *hath left* house, or
11: 6. commanded: and they *let* them *go*.
16. *would* not *suffer* that any man
25. *forgive*, if ye have ought against
— *may forgive* you your trespasses.
26. if ye *do* not *forgive*, neither
— in heaven *forgive* your trespasses.
12:12. they *left* him, *and* went their way.
19. wife (behind him), and *leave* no children,
20. dying *left* no seed.
21. neither *left* he any seed. and
22. the seven had her, and *left* no seed:
13: 2. there *shall* not *be left* one stone
34. who *left* his house, *and* gave
14: 6. Jesus said, *Let* her *alone;*
50. they all *forsook* him, *and* fled.
15:36. saying, *Let alone;* let us see
37. Jesus *cried* with a loud voice, *and* gave up the ghost.
Lu. 4:39. rebuked the fever; and it *left* her:
5:11. they *forsook* all, *and* followed him.
20. Man, thy sins *are forgiven* thee.
21. Who can *forgive* sins, but God
23. Thy sins *be forgiven* thee; or
24. power upon earth *to forgive* sins,
6:42. Brother, *let* me pull out the mote
7:47. Her sins, which are many, *are forgiven*
— to whom little *is forgiven*,
48. said unto her, Thy sins *are forgiven*.
49. Who is this that *forgiveth* sins also?
8:51. he *suffered* no man to go in,
9:60. *Let* the dead bury their dead:
10:30. departed, *leaving* (him) half dead.
11:4. *forgive* us our sins; for we also *forgive* every one
42. not *to leave* the other undone.
12:10. it *shall be forgiven* him: but
— it *shall* not *be forgiven*.
39. not *have suffered* his house to be
13: 8. Lord, *let* it *alone* this year also,
35. your house *is left* unto you desolate:
17: 3. if he repent, *forgive* him.
4. saying, I repent; thou *shalt forgive* him.
34. taken, the other *shall be left*.
35. one shall be taken, and the other *left*.
36. one shall be taken, and the other *left*.
18:16. *Suffer* little children to come unto me,
28. Peter said, Lo, we *have left* all,
29. no man that *hath left* house,
19:44. they *shall* not *leave* in thee one stone
21: 6. there *shall* not *be left* one stone
23:34. said Jesus, Father, *forgive* them;
Joh. 4: 3. He *left* Judæa, and departed again
28. The woman then *left* her waterpot,
52. the seventh hour the fever *left* him.
8:29. the Father *hath* not *left* me alone;
10:12. *leaveth* the sheep, and fleeth:
11:44. Loose him, and *let* him go.
11:48. If we *let* him thus *alone*, all (men)
12: 7. Then said Jesus, *Let* her *alone:*
14:18. I *will* not *leave* you comfortless:
27. Peace I *leave* with you, my peace
16:28. again, I *leave* the world, and go to
32. *shall leave* me alone: and yet I
18: 8. *let* these go their way:
20:23. sins ye *remit*, they *are remitted*
Acts 8:22. of thine heart *may be forgiven* thee.
14:17. he *left* not himself without witness,
Ro. 1:27. *leaving* the natural use of the woman,
4: 7. they whose iniquities *are forgiven*,
1Co. 7:11. let not the husband *put away* (his) wife.
12. *let* him not *put* her *away*.
13. dwell with her, *let* her not *leave* him.
Heb. 2: 8. he *left* nothing (that is) not put
6: 1. *leaving* the principles of the doctrine
Jas. 5:15. they *shall be forgiven* him.
1 Joh 1: 9. faithful and just to *forgive* us (our) sins,
2:12. because your sins *are forgiven*
Rev. 2: 4. thou *hast left* thy first love.
11: 9. *shall* not *suffer* their dead

---

864 1 126/133 575,rt 2425

ἀφικνέομαι, *aphikneomai*.

Ro. 16:19. your obedience *is come abroad*

---

865 1 126/133 1:10 1,5358

ἀφιλάγαθος, *aphilagathos*.

2Ti. 3: 3. *despisers of those that are good*,

---

866 2 126/134 1,5366

ἀφιλάργυρος, *aphilarguros*.

1Ti. 3: 3. not a brawler, *not covetous;*
Heb 13: 5. conversation (be) *without covetousness;*

---

867 1 126/134 864

ἄφιξις, *aphixis*.

Acts 20:29. I know this, that after my *departing*

---

868 15 126/134 1:512 575,2476

ἀφίστημι, *aphisteemi*.

Lu. 2:37. which *departed* not from the temple,
4:13. he *departed* from him for a season.
8:13. in time of temptation *fall away*.
13:27. *depart* from me, all (ye) workers of iniquity.
Acts 5:37. *drew away* much people after him:
38. *Refrain* from these men, and let them
12:10. the angel *departed* from him.
15:38. *who departed* from them from
19: 9. he *departed* from them, *and* separated
22:29. straightway they *departed* from him
2Co 12: 8. that it *might depart* from me.
1Ti. 4: 1. some *shall depart* from the faith,
6: 5. from such *withdraw thyself*.
2Ti. 2:19. name of Christ *depart* from iniquity.
Heb. 3:12. in *departing* from the living God.

---

869 3 126/134 852

ἄφνω, *aphno*.

Acts 2: 2. *suddenly* there came a sound
16:26. *suddenly* there was a great earthquake,
28: 6 swollen, or fallen down dead *suddenly;*

870 4 126/134 1,5401

ἀφόϐως, aphobōs.

Lu. 1:74. might serve him *without fear,*
1Co 16:10. he may be with you *without fear:*
Phi. 1:14. bold to speak the word *without fear.*
Jude 12. feeding themselves *without fear:*

871 1 126/134 5:186 575,3666

ἀφομοιόω, aphomoi-oō.

Heb. 7: 3. *made like* unto the Son of God;

872 2 126/134 575,3708

ἀφοράω, aphoraō.

Phi. 2:23. so soon as *I shall see*
Heb12: 2. *Looking* unto Jesus the author and

873 10 126/134 5:452 575,3724

ἀφορίζω, aphorizo.

Mat 13:49. *sever* the wicked from among the just,
25:32. he *shall separate* them one from another,
as a shepherd *divideth* (his) sheep
Lu. 6:22. when they *shall separate* you (from)
Acts13: 2. *Separate* me Barnabas and Saul for
19: 9. from them, and *separated* the disciples,
Ro. 1: 1. *separated* unto the gospel of God,
2Co. 6:17. *be* ye *separate,* saith the Lord,
Gal. 1:15. *who separated* me from my mother's
2:12. he withdrew and *separated* himself,

874 7 127/134 5:467 575,3729

ἀφορμή, aphormee.

Ro. 7: 8. taking *occasion* by the commandment,
11. taking *occasion* by the commandment,
2Co. 5:12. give you *occasion* to glory on our behalf,
11:12. that I may cut off *occasion* from them
which desire *occasion;*
Gal. 5:13. (use) not liberty for an *occasion* to
1Ti. 5:14. give none *occasion* to the adversary

875 2 127/134 876

ἀφρίζω, aphrizo.

Mar. 9:18. he *foameth,* and gnasheth with his teeth,
20. fell on the ground, and wallowed *foaming.*

876 1 127/134

ἀφρός, aphros.

Lu. 9:39. teareth him that he foameth again, (lit. with *foaming*)

877 4 127/134 9:220 878

ἀφροσύνη, aphrosunee.

Mar. 7:22. blasphemy, pride, *foolishness:*
2Co.11: 1. bear with me a little in (my) *folly:*
17. as it were foolishly (lit. in *folly*), in this
confidence
21. I speak *foolishly,* I am bold also.

878 11 127/134 9:220 1,5424

ἄφρων, aphrōn.

Lu. 11:40. (Ye) *fools,* did not he that made
12:20. (Thou) *fool,* this night thy soul
Ro. 2:20. An instructor of the *foolish,* a
1Co.15:36. (Thou) *fool,* that which thou sowest
2Co.11:16 Let no man think me a *fool;*
16. yet as a *fool* receive me.
19. For ye suffer *fools* gladly, seeing
12: 6. I shall not be a *fool;* for I
11. I am become a *fool* in glorying;
Eph. 5:17. Wherefore be ye not *unwise,*
1Pet.2:15. silence the ignorance of *foolish* men

879 1 127/134 8:545 575,5258

ἀφυπνόω, aphupnoō.

Lu. 8:23. as they sailed he *fell asleep:*

880 4 127/134 1,5456

ἄφωνος, aphōnos.

Acts 8:32. like a lamb *dumb* before his shearer,
1Co.12: 2. carried away unto these *dumb* idols,
14:10. none of them (is) *without signification.*
2Pet.2:16. the *dumb* ass speaking with man's voice

884 2 127/135 9:359 1,5483

ἀχάριστος, akaristos.

Lu. 6:35. he is kind unto the *unthankful* and (to)
2Ti. 3: 2. disobedient to parents, *unthankful,*

886 3 127/135 9:424 1,5499

ἀχειροποίητος, akīropoi-eetos.

Mar 14:58. will build another *made without hands*
2Co. 5: 1. an house *not made with hands,*
Col. 2:11. the circumcision *made without hands,*

887 1 127/135

ἀχλύς, aklus.

Acts13:11. there fell on him a *mist* and

889 1 128/135 888

ἀχρειόομαι, akrīo-omai.

Ro. 3:12. they *are together become unprofitable;*

888 2 128/135 1,5534

ἀχρεῖος, akrīos.

Mat.25:30. cast ye the *unprofitable* servant
Lu. 17:10. say, We are *unprofitable* servants:

890 1 128/135 1,5543

ἄχρηστος, akreestos.

Philem 11. in time past was to thee *unprofitable,*

891 49 128/135 cf 206 cf 3360

ἄχρι & ἄχρις, akri & akris.

Observe.—Those marked [2] are ἀχρις.

Mat.24:38. *until* the day that Noe entered
Lu. 1:20. *until* the day that these things
4:13. departed from him *for* a season.
17:27. *until* the day that Noe entered
21:24. *until* the times of the Gentiles
Acts 1: 2. *Until* the day in which he was
2:29. his sepulchre is with us *unto* this day.
3:21. *until* the times of restitution of
7:18. *Till* another king arose, which knew[2]
11: 5. four corners; and it came *even to* me:[2]
13: 6. through the isle *unto* Paphos,
11. not seeing the sun *for* a season.

Acts20: 4. there accompanied him *into* Asia
6. unto them to Troas *in* five days ;[2]
11. even *till* break of day, so he departed.[2]
22: 4. I persecuted this way *unto* the death,
22. gave him audience *unto* this word,
23: 1. conscience before God *until* this day.
26:22. I continue *unto* this day, witnessing
27:33. *while* the day was coming on,
28:15. to meet us *as far as* Appii forum,[2]
Ro. 1:13. come unto you, but was let hither*to*,
5:13. For *until* the law sin was in
8:22. travaileth in pain together *until* now.
11:25. *until* the fulness of the Gentiles be[2]
1 Co. 4:11. Even *unto* this present hour we
11:26. shew the Lord's death *till* he come.[2]
15:25. *till* he hath put all enemies under[2]
2Co. 3:14. for *until* this day remaineth the
10:13. a measure to reach even *unto* you.
14. we are come *as far as to* you also in
Gal. 3:19. *till* the seed should come to whom[2]
4 : 2. *until* the time appointed of the father.
19. *until* Christ be formed in you,[2]
Phi. 1: 5. from the first day *until* now ;
6. *until* the day of Jesus Christ:[2]
Heb. 3:13. *while* it is called To day ;[2]
4:12. *even to* the dividing asunder of soul
6:11. full assurance of hope *unto* the end:
Rev. 2:10. be thou faithful *unto* death,
25. have (already) hold fast *till* I come:[2]
26. keepeth my works *unto* the end,
7: 3. *till* we have sealed the servants[2]
12:11. loved not their lives *unto* the death.
14:20. even *unto* the horse bridles,
15: 8. *till* the seven plagues of the seven
17:17. *until* the words of God shall
18: 5. her sins have reached *unto* heaven,
20: 3. *till* the thousand years should

---

892 2 128/136

cheō (to shed)

ἄχυρον, akuron.

Mat. 3:12. he will burn up the *chaff* with
Lu. 3:17. the *chaff* he will burn with fire

---

893 1 128/136 9:594 1,5579

ἀψευδής, apsūdees.

Tit. 1: 2. which God, *that cannot lie*,

---

894 2 129/136

ἄψινθος, apsinthos.

Rev. 8:11. third part of the waters became *wormwood*;

---

895 1 129/136 1,5590

ἄψυχος, apsukos.

1Co.14: 7. things *without life* giving sound,

---

898 1 129/136 rt 899

βαθμός, bathmos.

1Ti. 3:13. purchase to themselves a good *degree*,

---

899 9 129/136 1:517 cf 939

βάθος, bathos.

Mat.13: 5. they had no *deepness* of earth:
Mar. 4: 5. because it had no *depth* of earth:
Lu. 5: 4. Launch out into the *deep*, and let
Ro. 8:39. Nor height, nor *depth*, nor any other
11:33. O the *depth* of the riches both of
1Co. 2:10. yea, the *deep things* of God.
2Co. 8: 2. their *deep* poverty abounded
Eph. 3:18. the breadth, and length, and *depth*, and
Rev. 2:24. have not known the *depths* of Satan,

---

900 1 130/136 901

βαθύνω, bathuno.

Lu. 6:48. which built an house, and digged deep (lit. and *deepened*)

---

901 3 130/136 rt 939

βαθύς, bathus.

Lu. 24: 1. *very early* in the morning, they came
Joh. 4:11. to draw with, and the well is *deep*:
Acts20: 9. being fallen into a *deep* sleep:

---

902 1 130/136 rt 939

βαΐον, bai-on.

Joh.12:13. Took *branches* of palm-trees, and went

---

905 4 130/137 1:525 cf 906

βαλάντιον, balantion.

Lu. 10: 4. Carry neither *purse*, nor scrip,
12:33. provide yourselves *bags* which wax no old,
22:35. I sent you without *purse*, and scrip,
36. he that hath a *purse*, let him take (it),

---

906 125 130/137 1:526 cf 4496

βάλλω, ballo.

Mat. 3:10. hewn down, and *cast* into the fire.
4: 6. the Son of God, *cast* thyself down:
18. *casting* a net into the sea: for
5:13. good for nothing, but *to be cast* out,
25. to the officer, and thou *be cast* into prison
29. pluck it out, and *cast* (it) from thee:
— whole body *should be cast* into hell.
30. cut it off, and *cast* it from thee:
— whole body *should be cast* into hell.
6:30. to morrow is *cast* into the oven,
7: 6. neither *cast* ye your pearls before swine,
19. hewn down, and *cast* into the fire.
8: 6. my servant *lieth* at home sick
14. he saw his wife's mother *laid*, and sick
9: 2. sick of the palsy, *lying* on a bed:
17. Neither *do* men *put* new wine into
— they *put* new wine into new bottles,
10:34. that I am come *to send* peace on earth
I come not *to send* peace,
13:42. *shall cast* them into a furnace
47. a net, that was *cast* into the sea,
48. good into vessels, but *cast* the bad away.
50. *shall cast* them into the furnace
15:26. children's bread, and *to cast* (it) to dogs.
17:27. go thou to the sea, and *cast* an hook,
18: 8. cut them off, and *cast* (them) from thee
— *to be cast* into everlasting fire.
9. pluck it out, and *cast* (it) from thee:
— two eyes *to be cast* into hell fire.
30. went and *cast* him into prison,
21:21. *be* thou *cast* into the sea ;
25:27. therefore *to have put* my money
26:12. *in that* she *hath poured* this

Mat.27: 6. for *to put* them into the treasury,
35. parted his garments, *casting* lots:
— upon my vesture *did* they *cast* lots.
Mar. 1:16. *casting* a net into the sea:
2:22. no man *putteth* new wine into
4:26. a man *should cast* seed into the ground;
7:27. children's bread, and *to cast* (it) unto the dogs.
30. her daughter *laid* upon the bed.
33. *put* his fingers into his ears, and
9:22. it *hath cast* him into the fire,
42. his neck, and he *were cast* into the sea.
45. two feet *to be cast* into hell,
47. two eyes *to be cast* into hell fire:
11:23. removed, and *be* thou *cast* into the sea;
12:41. people *cast* money into the treasury: and many that were rich *cast* in much.
42. she *threw* in two mites, which make
43. this poor widow hath *cast* more in, than all they which *have cast* into
44. (they) *did cast* in of their abundance; but she of her want *did cast* in all
14:65. the servants *did strike* him
15:24. parted his garments, *casting* lots
Lu. 3: 9. is hewn down, and *cast* into the fire.
4: 9. *cast* thyself down from hence·
5:37. no man *putteth* new wine into
12:28. to morrow is *cast* into the oven;
49. I am come *to send* fire on the earth;
58. the officer *cast* thee into prison.
13: 8. till I shall dig about it, and dung (it): (lit. *cast in* dung)
19. a man took, and *cast* into his garden;
14:35. for the dunghill; (but) men *cast* it *out*.
16:20. Lazarus, which *was laid* at his gate,
21: 1. the rich men *casting* their gifts
2. a certain poor widow *casting* in
3. this poor widow *hath cast* in more
4. of their abundance *cast* in unto
— she of her penury *hath cast* in
23:19. for murder, was *cast* into prison.
25. for sedition and murder was *cast* into prison,
34. parted his raiment, and *cast* lots.
Joh. 3:24. John was not yet *cast* into prison.
5: 7. to *put* me into the pool: but while
8: 7. *let* him first *cast* a stone at her.
59. took they up stones to *cast* at him:
12: 6. the bag, and bare *what was put* therein.
13: 2. devil *having* now *put* into the heart
5. he *poureth* water into a bason,
15: 6. he *is cast* forth as a branch, and is
— *cast* (them) into the fire, and they are
18:11. *Put up* thy sword into the sheath:
19:24. and for my vesture they *did cast* lots.
20:25. *put* my finger into the print of the nails, and *thrust* my hand into his side,
27. *thrust* (it) into my side: and be
21: 6. *Cast* the net on the right side of
— They *cast* therefore, and now they
7. *did cast* himself into the sea.
Acts16:23. they *cast* (them) into prison,
24. *thrust* them into the inner prison,
37. *have cast* (us) into prison; and now
22:23. *as* they...cast (off) their clothes, and *threw* dust into the air,
27:14. there *arose* against it a tempestuous wind,
Jas. 3: 3. *we put* bits in the horses' mouths,
1 Joh.4:18. perfect love *casteth* out fear:
Rev. 2:10. the devil shall *cast* (some) of you
14. Balac *to cast* a stumblingblock
22. Behold, I *will cast* her into a bed,
Rev. 2:24. I *will put* upon you none other
4:10. *cast* their crowns before the throne,
6:13. as a fig tree *casteth* her untimely figs.
8: 5. *cast* (it) into the earth: and there were
7. they *were cast* upon the earth:
8. with fire *was cast* into the sea:
12: 4. stars of heaven, and *did cast* them to the earth
9. the great dragon *was cast out*,
— he *was cast out* into the earth, and his angels *were cast out* with him.
13. dragon saw that he *was cast* unto
15. the serpent *cast* out of his mouth
16. the dragon *cast* out of his mouth.
14:16. *thrust* in his sickle on the earth;
19. the angel *thrust* in his sickle
— *cast* (it) into the great winepress
18:19. they *cast* dust on their heads,
21. millstone, and *cast* (it) into the sea,
— great city Babylon *be thrown down*,
19:20. These both *were cast* alive into
20: 3. *cast* him into the bottomless pit,
10. *was cast* into the lake of fire and
14. death and hell *were cast* into the lake
15. *was cast* into the lake of fire.

907 80 131/138 1:529 911

βαπτίζω, baptizo.

Mat. 3: 6. *were baptized* of him in Jordan,
11. I indeed *baptize* you with water
— he *shall baptize* you with the
13. unto John, *to be baptized* of him.
14. I have need *to be baptized* of thee,
16. Jesus, *when* he *was baptized*,
20:22. *to be baptized*, with the baptism that I *am baptized* with?
23. and *be baptized* with the baptism that I *am baptized* with:
28:19. *baptizing* them in the name
Mar. 1: 4. John did *baptize* in the wilderness,
5. *were* all *baptized* of him in the
8. I indeed *have baptized* you with water: but he *shall baptize* you with the
9. *was baptized* of John in Jordan.
6:14. That John the *Baptist* was risen
7: 4. except they *wash*, they eat not.
10:38. and *be baptized* with the baptism that I *am baptized* with?
39. and with the baptism that I *am baptized* withal *shall* ye *be baptized:*
16:16. He that believeth and is *baptized* shall
Lu. 3: 7. came forth *to be baptized* of him,
12. came also publicans *to be baptized*,
16. I indeed *baptize* you with water;
— he *shall baptize* you with the
21. when all the people were *baptized*, it came to pass, that Jesus also *being baptized*,
7:29. *being baptized* with the baptism
30. themselves, *being* not *baptized* of him.
11:38. *had* not first *washed* before dinner.
12:50. I have a baptism *to be baptized* with;
Joh. 1:25. said unto him, Why *baptizest* thou then,
26. saying, I *baptize* with water:
28. Jordan, where John was *baptizing*.
31. therefore am I come *baptizing* with
33. sent me *to baptize* with water,
— *which baptizeth* with the Holy Ghost.
3:22. there he tarried with them, and *baptized*
23. John also was *baptizing* in Ænon
— they came, and *were baptized*.
26. behold, the same *baptizeth*, and all

Joh. 4: 1. that Jesus made and *baptized* more disciples
2. Though Jesus himself *baptized* not,
10:40. place where John at first *baptized;*
Acts 1: 5. John truly *baptized* with water;
— ye *shall be baptized* with the Holy Ghost
2:38. Repent, and *be baptized* every one of you
41. received his word *were baptized:*
8:12. *were baptized,* both men and women.
13. *when* he *was baptized,* he continued
16. only they were *baptized* in the name
36. what doth hinder me *to be baptized?*
38. Philip and the eunuch; and he *baptized* him.
9:18. forthwith, and arose, and *was baptized.*
10:47. that these should not *be baptized,*
48. commanded them *to be baptized*
11:16. John indeed *baptized* with water;
— ye *shall be baptized* with the Holy Ghost.
16:15. when she *was baptized,* and her
33. *was baptized,* he and all his,
18: 8. hearing believed, and *were baptized.*
19: 3. Unto what then *were* ye *baptized?*
4. John verily *baptized* with the
5. they *were baptized* in the name
22:16. arise, and *be baptized,* and wash away
Ro. 6: 3. so many of us as *were baptized* into Jesus Christ *were baptized* into his death?
1Co. 1:13. *were* ye *baptized* in the name
14. that I *baptized* none of you,
15. that I *had baptized* in mine own name.
16. I *baptized* also the houshold of Stephanas: besides, I know not whether I *baptized* any other.
17. Christ sent me not *to baptize,*
10: 2. were all *baptized* unto Moses
12:13. by one Spirit *are* we all *baptized*
15:29. which are *baptized* for the dead,
— why *are* they then *baptized* for
Gal. 3:27. *have been baptized* into Christ

908 22 132/139 1:529 907

βάπτισμα, baptisma.

Mat. 3: 7. Pharisees and Sadducees come to his *baptism,*
20:22. the *baptism* that I am baptized with?
23. with the *baptism* that I am
21:25. The *baptism* of John, whence was it?
Mar. 1: 4. preach the *baptism* of repentance
10:38. the *baptism* that I am baptized with?
39. with the *baptism* that I am
11:30. The *baptism* of John, was (it) from
Lu. 3: 3. preaching the *baptism* of repentance
7:29. baptized with the *baptism* of John.
12:50. I have a *baptism* to be baptized
20: 4. The *baptism* of John, was it from
Acts 1:22. Beginning from the *baptism* of John,
10:37. the *baptism* which John preached;
13:24. the *baptism* of repentance to all
18:25. knowing only the *baptism* of John.
19: 3. they said, Unto John's *baptism.*
4. with the *baptism* of repentance,
Ro. 6: 4. with him by *baptism* into death:
Eph. 4: 5. One Lord, one faith, one *baptism,*
Col. 2:12. Buried with him in *baptism,*
1Pet.3:21. (even) *baptism,* doth also now save us

909 4 132/139 1:529 907

βαπτισμός, baptismos.

Mar. 7: 4. (as) the *washing* of cups, and pots,
Mar. 7: 8. (as) the *washing* of pots and cups:
Heb. 6: 2. Of the doctrine of *baptisms,* and of
9:10. meats and drinks, and divers *washings,*

910 14 132/139 1:529 907

βαπτιστής, baptistees.

Mat. 3: 1. In those days came John the *Baptist,*
11:11. a greater than John the *Baptist:*
12. from the days of John the *Baptist*
14: 2. This is John the *Baptist;*
8. Give me here John *Baptist's* head
16:14. (that thou art) John the *Baptist:*
17:13. spake unto them of John the *Baptist.*
Mar. 6:24. The head of John the *Baptist.*
25. the head of John the *Baptist.*
8:28. they answered, John the *Baptist:*
Lu. 7:20. John *Baptist* hath sent us
28. a greater prophet than John the *Baptist:*
33. John the *Baptist* came neither
9:19. answering said, John the *Baptist;*

911 3 132/139 1:529

βάπτω, bapto.

Lu. 16:24. that he *may dip* the tip of his finger
Joh.13:26. shall give a sop *when I have dipped* (it).
Rev.19:13. clothed with a vesture *dipped* in blood:

915 6 132/140 1:546

βάρβαρος, barbaros.

Acts28: 2. the *barbarous* people shewed us
4. when the *barbarians* saw the (venomous)
Ro. 1:14. to the Greeks, and to the *Barbarians;*
1Co.14:11. unto him that speaketh a *barbarian,*
— (shall be) a *barbarian* unto me.
Col. 3:11. *Barbarian,* Scythian, bond (nor) free:

916 6 133/140 1:553 926

βαρέω, bareo.

Mat.26:43. asleep again: for their eyes were *heavy.*
Mar.14:40. asleep again: for their eyes were *heavy,*
Lu. 9:32. were with him were *heavy* with sleep:
2Co. 1: 8. we *were pressed* out of measure,
5: 4. do groan, *being burdened:* not
1Ti. 5:16. let not the church *be charged;*

917 2 133/140 926

βαρέως, bareōs.

Mat.13:15. (their) ears are *dull* of hearing,
Acts28:27. their ears are *dull* of hearing, and their

922 6 133/140 1:553 rt 939

βάρος, baros.

Mat.20:12. have borne the *burden* and heat of the day.
Acts15:28. upon you no greater *burden* than
2Co. 4:17. exceeding (and) eternal *weight* of glory;
Gal. 6: 2. Bear ye one another's *burdens,*
1Th. 2: 6. we might have been *burdensome,* as
Rev. 2:24. put upon you none other *burden.*

925 1 133/140 926

βαρύνω, baruno.

Lu. 21:34. your hearts *be overcharged* with

926 6 133/140 1:553 rt 922

βαρύς, barus.

Mat.23: 4. For they bind *heavy* burdens and

Mat.23:23. omitted the *weightier* (matters) of the law,
Acts20:29. shall *grievous* wolves enter in among
25. 7. laid many and *grievous* complaints
2Co.10:10. letters, say they, (are) *weighty* and powerful,
1Joh.5. 3. his commandments are not *grievous*.

927 1 134/141 926,5092

βαρύτιμος, barutimos.

Mat.26: 7. box of *very precious* ointment, and

928 12 134/141 1:561 931

βασανίζω, basanizo.

Mat. 8: 6. sick of the palsy, grievously *tormented*.
29. art thou come hither *to torment* us
14:24. midst of the sea, *tossed* with waves
Mar. 5: 7. that thou *torment* me not.
6:48. he saw them *toiling* in rowing,
Lu. 8:28. I beseech thee, *torment* me not.
2Pet. 2: 8. *vexed* (his) righteous soul from
Rev. 9: 5. *should be tormented* five months:
11:10. these two prophets *tormented* them
12: 2. in birth, *and pained* to be delivered.
14:10. he *shall be tormented* with fire
20:10. *shall be tormented* day and night

929 6 134/141 1:561 928

βασανισμός, basanismos.

Rev. 9: 5. their *torment* (was) as the *torment* of
14:11. the smoke of their *torment* ascendeth
18: 7. so much *torment* and sorrow give her:
10. afar off for the fear of her *torment*,
15. for the fear of her *torment*, weeping

930 1 134/141 1:561 928

βασανιστής, basanistees.

Mat.18:34. delivered him to the *tormentors*,

931 3 134/141 1:561 cf rt 939

βάσανος, basanos.

Mat. 4:24. taken with divers diseases and *torments*,
Lu. 16:23. he lift up his eyes, being in *torments*,
28. also come into this place of *torment*.

932 162 134/141 1:564 935

βασιλεία, basilīa.

Mat. 3: 2. for the *kingdom* of heaven is at hand.
4: 8. all the *kingdoms* of the world,
17. for the *kingdom* of heaven is at hand.
23. preaching the gospel of the *kingdom*,
5: 3. their's is the *kingdom* of heaven.
10. for their's is the *kingdom* of heaven.
19. least in the *kingdom* of heaven:
— called great in the *kingdom* of heaven.
20. enter into the *kingdom* of heaven.
6:10. Thy *kingdom* come. Thy will be
13. For thine is the *kingdom*, and the
33. seek ye first the *kingdom* of God,
7:21. shall enter into the *kingdom* of heaven;
8:11. Isaac, and Jacob, in the *kingdom* of heaven.
12. the children of the *kingdom* shall
9:35. preaching the gospel of the *kingdom*,
10: 7. The *kingdom* of heaven is at hand.
11:11. least in the *kingdom* of heaven
12. until now the *kingdom* of heaven
Mat.12:25. Every *kingdom* divided against
26. how shall then his *kingdom* stand?
28. then the *kingdom* of God is come
13:11. mysteries of the *kingdom* of heaven
19. any one heareth the word of the *kingdom*
24. The *kingdom* of heaven is likened
31. The *kingdom* of heaven is like
33. The *kingdom* of heaven is like
38. are the children of the *kingdom*;
41. shall gather out of his *kingdom*
43. in the *kingdom* of their Father.
44. the *kingdom* of heaven is like
45. Again, the *kingdom* of heaven is
47. the *kingdom* of heaven is like
52. instructed unto the *kingdom* of heaven
16:19. the keys of the *kingdom* of heaven:
28. Son of man coming in his *kingdom*.
18: 1. greatest in the *kingdom* of heaven?
3. shall not enter into the *kingdom* of heaven
4. greatest in the *kingdom* of heaven.
23. Therefore is the *kingdom* of heaven
19:12. for the *kingdom* of heaven's sake.
14. for of such is the *kingdom* of heaven.
23. hardly enter into the *kingdom* of heaven.
24. a rich man to enter into the *kingdom* of God.
20: 1. For the *kingdom* of heaven is
21. the other on the left, in thy *kingdom*.
21:31. go into the *kingdom* of God before you.
43. The *kingdom* of God shall be taken
22: 2. The *kingdom* of heaven is like
23:13(14). ye shut up the *kingdom* of heaven
24: 7. nation, and *kingdom* against *kingdom*:
14. this gospel of the *kingdom* shall
25: 1. Then shall the *kingdom* of heaven
34. inherit the *kingdom* prepared for
26:29. with you in my Father's *kingdom*.
Mar 1:14. the gospel of the *kingdom* of God,
15. the *kingdom* of God is at hand:
3:24. if a *kingdom* be divided against itself, that *kingdom* cannot stand.
4:11. the mystery of the *kingdom* of God:
26. So is the *kingdom* of God, as if a
30. shall we liken the *kingdom* of God?
6:23. unto the half of my *kingdom*.
9: 1. have seen the *kingdom* of God
47. to enter into the *kingdom* of God
10:14. for of such is the *kingdom* of God.
15. shall not receive the *kingdom* of God
23. enter into the *kingdom* of God!
24. to enter into the *kingdom* of God!
25. to enter into the *kingdom* of God.
11:10. Blessed (be) the *kingdom* of our father
12:34. not far from the *kingdom* of God.
13: 8. *kingdom* against *kingdom*: and
14:25. I drink it new in the *kingdom* of God.
15:43. also waited for the *kingdom* of God,
Lu 1:33. of his *kingdom* there shall be no end.
4: 5. all the *kingdoms* of the world
43. I must preach the *kingdom* of God
6:20. for your's is the *kingdom* of God.
7:28. he that is least in the *kingdom* of God
8: 1. glad tidings of the *kingdom* of God:
10. the mysteries of the *kingdom* of God:
9: 2. to preach the *kingdom* of God,
11. spake unto them of the *kingdom* of God
27. till they see the *kingdom* of God.
60. preach the *kingdom* of God.
62. is fit for the *kingdom* of God.
10: 9. The *kingdom* of God is come nigh
11. the *kingdom* of God is come nigh unto you.

11: 2. Thy *kingdom* come. Thy will
17. Every *kingdom* divided against
18. how shall his *kingdom* stand?
20. the *kingdom* of God is come upon you.
12:31. seek ye the *kingdom* of God;
32. pleasure to give you the *kingdom*.
13:18. what is the *kingdom* of God like?
20. shall I liken the *kingdom* of God?
28. the prophets, in the *kingdom* of God,
29. shall sit down in the *kingdom* of God.
14:15. eat bread in the *kingdom* of God.
16:16. the *kingdom* of God is preached.
17:20. when the *kingdom* of God should come,
— The *kingdom* of God cometh not
21. the *kingdom* of God is within you.
18:16. of such is the *kingdom* of God.
17. shall not receive the *kingdom* of God
24. enter into the *kingdom* of God!
25. enter into the *kingdom* of God.
29. for the *kingdom* of God's sake,
19:11. thought that the *kingdom* of God
12. to receive for himself a *kingdom*,
15. returned, having received the *kingdom*,
21:10. nation, and *kingdom* against *kingdom*:
31. the *kingdom* of God is nigh at hand.
22:16. fulfilled in the *kingdom* of God.
18. until the *kingdom* of God shall come.
29. I appoint unto you a *kingdom*, as
30. drink at my table in my *kingdom*,
23:42. when thou comest into thy *kingdom*.
51. waited for the *kingdom* of God.
Joh. 3: 3. cannot see the *kingdom* of God.
5. enter into the *kingdom* of God.
18:36. My *kingdom* is not of this world: if my *kingdom* were of this world,
— now is my *kingdom* not from hence.
Acts 1: 3. pertaining to the *kingdom* of God:
6. restore again the *kingdom* to Israel?
8:12. concerning the *kingdom* of God,
14:22. enter into the *kingdom* of God.
19: 8. concerning the *kingdom* of God.
20:25. gone preaching the *kingdom* of God.
28:23. testified the *kingdom* of God,
31. Preaching the *kingdom* of God,
Ro. 14:17. For the *kingdom* of God is not
1Co. 4:20. the *kingdom* of God (is) not in word,
6: 9. shall not inherit the *kingdom* of God?
10. shall inherit the *kingdom* of God
15:24. delivered up the *kingdom* to God,
50. cannot inherit the *kingdom* of God;
Gal. 5:21. shall not inherit the *kingdom* of God
Eph. 5: 5. inheritance in the *kingdom* of Christ
Col. 1:13. into the *kingdom* of his dear Son:
4:11. into the *kingdom* of God, which
1Th. 2:12. called you unto his *kingdom* and glory.
2Th. 1: 5. worthy of the *kingdom* of God,
2Ti. 4: 1. at his appearing and his *kingdom*;
18. unto his heavenly *kingdom*:
Heb 1: 8. righteousness (is) the sceptre of thy *kingdom*.
11:33. through faith subdued *kingdoms*,
12:28. receiving a *kingdom* which cannot
Jas. 2: 5. heirs of the *kingdom* which he
2Pet. 1:11. the everlasting *kingdom* of our Lord
Rev. 1: 9. in the *kingdom* and patience of
11:15. The *kingdoms* of this world are
12:10. strength, and the *kingdom* of our God,
16:10. his *kingdom* was full of darkness;
17:12. have received no *kingdom* as yet;
17. give their *kingdom* unto the beast,
18. which reigneth (lit. having *dominion*) over the kings of the earth.

933 1 135/143 934

βασίλειον, *basilīon*.

Lu. 7:25. live delicately, are in *kings' courts*.

934 1 135/143 1:564 935

βασίλειος, *basilīos*.

1Pet. 2: 9. a *royal* priesthood, an holy nation.

935 118 135/143 1:564 939

βασιλεύς, *basilūs*.

Mat. 1: 6. Jesse begat David the *king*; and David the *king* begat Solomon of her
2: 1. in the days of Herod the *king*.
2. he that is born *King* of the Jews?
3. When Herod the *king* had heard
9. When they had heard the *king*,
5:35. for it is the city of the great *King*.
10:18. before governors and *kings* for my sake,
11: 8. soft (clothing) are in *kings'* houses.
14: 9. the *king* was sorry: nevertheless
17:25. the *kings* of the earth take custom
18:23. likened unto a certain *king*, which
21: 5. Behold, thy *King* cometh unto thee,
22: 2. like unto a certain *king*, which
7. when the *king* heard (thereof), he
11. when the *king* came in to see
13. Then said the *king* to the servants,
25:34. Then shall the *King* say unto them
40. the *King* shall answer and say
27:11. Art thou the *king* of the Jews?
29. saying, Hail, *king* of the Jews!
37. THIS IS JESUS THE *KING* OF THE JEWS.
42. If he be the *King* of Israel,
Mar 6:14. *king* Herod heard (of him); for
22. the *king* said unto the damsel,
25. with haste unto the *king*, and asked
26. the *king* was exceeding sorry;
27. immediately the *king* sent an
13: 9. before rulers and *kings* for my sake,
15: 2. Art thou the *King* of the Jews?
9. I release unto you the *King* of the Jews?
12. whom ye call the *King* of the Jews?
18. salute him, Hail, *King* of the Jews!
26. written over, THE *KING* OF THE JEWS.
32. Let Christ the *King* of Israel
Lu. 1: 5. days of Herod, the *king* of Judæa,
10:24. many prophets and *kings* have
14:31. Or what *king*, going to make war against another *king*,
19:38. Blessed (be) the *King* that cometh
21:12. before *kings* and rulers for my name's sake.
22:25. The *kings* of the Gentiles exercise
23: 2. that he himself is Christ a *King*.
3. Art thou the *King* of the Jews?
37. If thou be the *King* of the Jews,
38. THIS IS THE *KING* OF THE JEWS.
Joh. 1:49(50). thou art the *King* of Israel.
6:15. by force, to make him a *king*,
12:13. Blessed (is) the *King* of Israel
15. thy *King* cometh, sitting on an ass's colt.
18:33. Art thou the *King* of the Jews?
37. said unto him, Art thou a *king* then? Jesus answered, Thou sayest that I am a *king*.
39. release unto you the *King* of the Jews?
19: 3. said, Hail, *King* of the Jews!
12. whosoever maketh himself a *king*

Joh. 19:14. saith unto the Jews, Behold your *King!*
15. Shall I crucify your *King?*
— We have no *king* but Cæsar.
19. JESUS OF NAZARETH THE *KING* OF THE JEWS.
21. Write not, The *King* of the Jews; but that he said, I am *King* of the Jews.
Acts 4:26. The *kings* of the earth stood up,
7:10. sight of Pharaoh *king* of Egypt;
18. Till another *king* arose, which
9:15. my name before the Gentiles, and *kings*,
12: 1. Herod the *king* stretched forth
20. Blastus the *king's* chamberlain
13:21. afterward they desired a *king*:
22. unto them David to be their *king*;
17: 7. saying that there is another *king*,
25:13. *king* Agrippa and Bernice came
14. declared Paul's cause unto the *king*,
24. Festus said, *King* Agrippa, and all
26. before thee, O *king* Agrippa,
26: 2. I think myself happy, *king* Agrippa,
7. For which hope's sake, *king* Agrippa,
13. At midday, O *king*, I saw in
19. Whereupon, O *king* Agrippa,
26. the *king* knoweth of these things,
27. *King* Agrippa, believest thou
30. the *king* rose up, and the governor,
2Co. 11:32. the governor under Aretas the *king*
1Ti. 1:17. Now unto the *King* eternal,
2: 2. For *kings*, and (for) all that are in
6:15. the *King* of kings, and Lord of lords;
Heb 7: 1. Melchisedec, *king* of Salem,
— from the slaughter of the *kings*,
2. interpretation *King* of righteousness, and after that also *King* of Salem, which is, *King* of peace;
11:23. afraid of the *king's* commandment.
27. fearing the wrath of the *king*: for
1Pet. 2:13. whether it be to the *king*, as supreme;
17. Fear God. Honour the *king*.
Rev 1: 5. the prince of the *kings* of the earth.
6. hath made us *kings* and priests unto
5:10. made us unto our God *kings* and priests:
6:15. the *kings* of the earth, and the great
9:11. they had a *king* over them, (which is)
10:11. peoples, and nations, and tongues, and *kings*.
15: 3. true (are) thy ways, thou *King* of saints.
16:12. the way of the *kings* of the east might
14. go forth unto the *kings* of the earth
17: 2. With whom the *kings* of the earth
10. there are seven *kings*: five are fallen,
12. horns which thou sawest are ten *kings*,
— receive power as *kings* one hour
14. Lord of lords, and *King* of *kings*:
18. reigneth over the *kings* of the earth.
18: 3. the *kings* of the earth have committed
9. the *kings* of the earth, who have
19:16. written, *KING* OF *KINGS*, AND LORD OF LORDS.
18. That ye may eat the flesh of *kings*,
19. I saw the beast, and the *kings* of the earth,
21:24. the *kings* of the earth do bring their

936 21 136/144 1:564 935

βασιλεύω, basilūo.

Mat. 2:22. that Archelaus *did reign* in Judæa
Lu. 1:33. he *shall reign* over the house of Jacob
19:14. We will not have this (man) *to reign* over us.
27. not that I should *reign* over them,
Ro. 5:14. death *reigned* from Adam to Moses,
17. by one man's offence death *reigned*
— *shall reign* in life by one, Jesus Christ.
21. as sin *hath reigned* unto death, even so *might* grace *reign* through
6:12. *Let* not sin therefore *reign* in
1Co. 4: 8. ye *have reigned* as kings without us: and I would to God ye *did reign*,
15:25. For he must *reign*, till he hath put
1Ti. 6:15. the King of *kings* (lit. of *them that reign*), and Lord of lords;
Rev. 5:10. we *shall reign* on the earth.
11:15. his Christ; and he *shall reign* for ever and ever.
17. to thee thy great power, and *hast reigned*.
19: 6. the Lord God omnipotent *reigneth*.
20: 4. they lived and *reigned* with Christ
6. *shall reign* with him a thousand years.
22: 5. they *shall reign* for ever and ever.

937 5 136/144 1:564 935

βασιλικός, basilikos.

Joh. 4:46. there was a certain *nobleman*, whose
49. The *nobleman* saith unto him,
Acts 12:20. was nourished by the *king's* (country).
21. Herod, arrayed in *royal* apparel, sat
Jas. 2: 8. If ye fulfil the *royal* law according

938 4 136/144 1:564 936

βασίλισσα, basilissa.

Mat 12 42. The *queen* of the south shall rise
Lu. 11:31. The *queen* of the south shall rise up
Acts 8:27. under Candace *queen* of the Ethiopians,
Rev 18: 7. she saith in her heart, I sit a *queen*,

939 1 136/144 *bainō* (to walk)

βάσις, basis.

Acts 3: 7. his *feet* and ancle bones received strength

940 1 136/145 1:594 cf 5335

βασκαίνω, baskaino.

Gal. 3: 1. O foolish Galatians, who *hath bewitched* you,

941 27 136/145 1:596 cf rt 939

βαστάζω, bastazo.

Mat. 3:11. whose shoes I am not worthy *to bear*
8:17. our infirmities, and *bare* (our) sicknesses.
20:12. *which have borne* the burden and heat
Mar 14:13. a man *bearing* a pitcher of water:
Lu. 7:14. they *that bare* (him) stood still.
10: 4. *Carry* neither purse, nor scrip, nor shoes.
11:27. Blessed (is) the womb *that bare* thee,
14:27. whosoever *doth not bear* his cross,
22:10. a man meet you, *bearing* a pitcher
Joh. 10:31. the Jews *took up* stones again to stone him
12: 6. had the bag, and *bare* what was put
16:12. ye cannot *bear* them now.
19:17. he *bearing* his cross went forth
20:15. Sir, if thou *have borne* him (hence),
Acts 3: 2. from his mother's womb *was carried*,
9:15. *to bear* my name before the Gentiles,
15:10. our fathers nor we were able *to bear*
21:35. that he was *borne* of the soldiers
Ro. 11:18. thou *bearest* not the root, but the
15: 1. ought *to bear* the infirmities of the
Gal. 5:10. *shall bear* his judgment, whosoever
6: 2. *Bear* ye one another's burdens,
5. every man *shall bear* his own burden

Gal. 6:17. for I *bear* in my body the marks
Rev. 2: 2. how thou canst not *bear* them
3. *hast borne*, and hast patience, and for
17: 7. the woman, and of the beast *that carrieth* her,

943 5 137/145 [1324]

ὁ βάτος, batos, m.

Lu. 16: 6. he said, An hundred *measures* of oil.

942 1 137/145

ἡ βάτος, batos, f.

Mar 12:26. how in the *bush* God spake unto him,
Lu. 6:44. nor of a *bramble bush* gather they grapes.
20:37. even Moses shewed at the *bush*,
Acts 7:30. in a flame of fire in a *bush*.
35. which appeared to him in the *bush*.

944 1 137/145

βάτραχος, batrakos.

Rev 16:13. I saw three unclean spirits like *frogs*

945 1 137/145 1:597 3056 *Battos*

βαττολογέω, battologeo.

Mat. 6: 7. when ye pray, *use not vain repetitions*,

946 6 137/145 1:598 948

βδέλυγμα, bdelugma.

Mat 24:15. see the *abomination* of desolation,
Mar 13:14. shall see the *abomination* of desolation,
Lu. 16:15. is *abomination* in the sight of God.
Rev 17: 4. full of *abominations* and filthiness of
5. MOTHER OF HARLOTS AND *ABOMINATIONS* OF THE EARTH.
21:27. (whatsoever) worketh *abomination*,

947 1 137/145 1:598 948

βδελυκτός, bdeluktos.

Tit. 1:16. being *abominable*, and disobedient,

948 2 137/145 1:598 *bdeō* (to stink)

βδελύσσομαι, bdelussomai.

Ro. 2:22. thou that *abhorrest* idols, dost thou
Rev 21: 8. unbelieving, and the *abominable*, and

949 9 137/145 1:600 rt 939

βέβαιος, bebaios.

Ro. 4:16. the promise might be *sure* to all
2Co. 1: 7(6). our hope of you (is) *stedfast*, knowing,
Heb. 2: 2. word spoken by angels was *stedfast*,
3: 6. rejoicing of the hope *firm* unto the end.
14. our confidence *stedfast* unto the end;
6:19. anchor of the soul, both sure and *stedfast*,
9:17. a testament (is) *of force* after men
2Pet. 1:10. make your calling and election *sure*:
19. also a *more sure* word of prophecy;

950 8 138/145 1:600 949

βεβαιόω, bebaioō.

Mar 16:20. *confirming* the word with signs
Ro. 15: 8. to *confirm* the promises (made)
1Co. 1: 6. testimony of Christ *was confirmed*
8. Who *shall* also *confirm* you unto
2Co. 1:21. he *which stablisheth* us with you
Col. 2: 7. *stablished* in the faith, as ye
Heb. 2: 3. *was confirmed* unto us by them
13: 9. the heart *be established* with grace

951 2 138/145 1:600 950

βεβαίωσις, bebaiōsis.

Phi. 1: 7. defence and *confirmation* of the gospel,
Heb. 6:16. an oath for *confirmation* (is) to them

952 5 138/145 1:604 rt 939 *belos* (threshold)

βέβηλος, bebeelos.

1Ti. 1: 9. sinners, for unholy and *profane*,
4: 7. refuse *profane* and old wives' fables,
6:20. avoiding *profane* (and) vain babblings,
2Ti. 2:16. shun *profane* (and) vain babblings:
Heb 12:16. any fornicator, or *profane person*,

953 2 138/145 1:604 952

βεβηλόω, bebeeloō.

Mat 12: 5. priests in the temple *profane* the sabbath,
Acts 24: 6. hath gone about *to profane* the temple:

956 1 138/145 1:608 906

βέλος, belos.

Eph. 6:16. to quench all the fiery *darts* of the wicked

957 1 138/146 906

βέλτιον, beltion.

2Ti. 1:18. at Ephesus, thou knowest *very well*.

968 12 139/147 rt 939

βῆμα, beema.

Mat 27:19. was set down on the *judgment seat*,
Joh. 19:13. sat down in the *judgment seat*
Acts 7: 5. no, not (so much as) *to set* his foot *on* (lit. foot-*room*)
12:21. sat upon his *throne*, and made an
18:12. brought him to the *judgment seat*.
16. drave them from the *judgment seat*.
17. beat (him) before the *judgment seat*.
25: 6. next day sitting on the *judgment seat*
10. I stand at Cæsar's *judgment seat*,
17. I sat on the *judgment seat*, and
Ro. 14:10. before the *judgment seat* of Christ.
2Co. 5:10. before the *judgment seat* of Christ;

969 1 139/147

βήρυλλος, beerullos.

Rev 21:20. seventh, chrysolite; the eighth, *beryl*;

970 4 140/147 cf 979

βία, bia.

Acts 5:26. brought them without *violence*:
21:35. for the *violence* of the people.
24: 7. with great *violence* took (him)
27:41. with the *violence* of the waves.

971 2 140/147 1:609 970

βιάζομαι, biazomai.

Mat 11:12. kingdom of heaven *suffereth violence*,
Lu. 16:16. preached, and every man *presseth* into it.

972 1 140/147 970

βίαιος, biaios.

Acts 2: 2. as of a rushing *mighty* wind,

973 1 140/147 1:609 971

βιαστής, biastees.

Mat 11:12. the *violent* take it by force.

974 4 140/147 975

βιβλαρίδιον, biblaridion.

Rev 10: 2. had in his hand a *little book* open:
8. Go (and) take the *little book* which is open
9. said unto him, Give me the *little book*.
10. I took the *little book* out of the angel's hand,

975 32 140/147 1:615 976

βιβλίον, biblion.

Mat 19: 7. to give a *writing* of divorcement,
Mar 10: 4. to write a *bill* of divorcement, and to
Lu. 4:17. delivered unto him the *book* of the prophet Esaias. And when he had opened the *book*, he
20. he closed the *book*, and he gave (it) again
Joh. 20:30. which are not written in this *book*:
21:25. could not contain the *books* that
Gal. 3:10. all things which are written in the *book*
2Ti. 4:13. bring (with thee), and the *books*, (but)
Heb. 9:19. sprinkled both the *book*, and all the people,
10: 7. in the volume of the *book* it is written
Rev. 1:11. What thou seest, write in a *book*,
5: 1. on the throne a *book* written within
2. Who is worthy to open the *book*, and
3. was able to open the *book*, neither
4. worthy to open and to read the *book*,
5. hath prevailed to open the *book*,
7. he came and took the *book* out of the
8. when he had taken the *book*, the
9. Thou art worthy to take the *book*,
6:14. the heaven departed as a *scroll* when
17: 8. whose names were not written in the *book*
20:12. the *books* were opened: and another *book* was opened, which
— which were written in the *books*,
21:27. written in the Lamb's *book* of life.
22: 7. sayings of the prophecy of this *book*.
9. which keep the sayings of this *book*:
10. sayings of the prophecy of this *book*:
18. words of the prophecy of this *book*,
— plagues that are written in this *book*:
19. things which are written in this *book*.

976 13 140/147 1:615

βίβλος, biblos.

Mat. 1: 1. The *book* of the generation of Jesus Christ,
Mar 12:26. have ye not read in the *book* of Moses,
Lu. 3: 4. As it is written in the *book* of the words
20:42. David himself saith in the *book* of Psalms,
Acts 1:20. it is written in the *book* of Psalms,
7:42. written in the *book* of the prophets,
19:19. brought their *books* together, and burned
Phi. 4: 3. whose names (are) in the *book* of life.
Rev. 3: 5. blot out his name out of the *book* of life.
13: 8. not written in the *book* of life of
20:15. found written in the *book* of life
22:19. take away from the words of the *book*
— take away his part out of the *book* of life,

979 11 141/148

βίος, bios.

Mar 12:44. all that she had, (even) all her *living*.
Lu. 8:14. riches and pleasures of (this) *life*,
43. spent all her *living* upon physicians
Lu. 15:12. he divided unto them (his) *living*.
30. hath devoured thy *living* with harlots,
21: 4. cast in all the *living* that she had.
1Ti. 2: 2. a quiet and peaceable *life* in all
2Ti. 2: 4. himself with the affairs of (this) *life*;
1Pet. 4: 3. the time past of (our) *life* may
1Joh. 2:16. the pride of *life*, is not of the Father,
3:17. whoso hath this world's *good*,

980 1 140/148 979

βιόω, bioō.

1Pet. 4: 2. should *live* the rest of (his) time in

981 1 141/148 980

βίωσις, biōsis.

Acts 26: 4. My *manner of life* from my youth,

982 3 141/148 980

βιωτικός, biōtikos.

Lu. 21:34. drunkenness, and cares *of this life*,
1Co. 6: 3. *things that pertain to this life*?
4. *things pertaining to this life*,

983 1 141/148 984

βλαβερός, blaberos.

1Ti. 6: 9. (into) many foolish and *hurtful* lusts,

984 2 141/148

βλάπτω, blapto.

Mar 16:18. deadly thing, it *shall* not *hurt* them;
Lu. 4:35. he came out of him, and *hurt* him not.

985 4 141/148

blastos (sprout)

βλαστάνω, blastano.

Mat 13:26. when the blade *was sprung up*,
Mar 4:27. the seed *should spring* and grow up,
Heb. 9: 4. Aaron's rod *that budded*, and the tables
Jas. 5:18. the earth *brought forth* her fruit.

987 35 142/148 1:621 989

βλασφημέω, blaspheemeo.

Mat. 9: 3. within themselves, This (man) *blasphemeth*
26:65. saying, He *hath spoken blasphemy*;
27:39. they that passed by *reviled* him,
Mar. 3:28. wherewith soever they *shall blaspheme*
29. he that *shall blaspheme* against
15:29. they that passed by *railed on* him,
Lu. 12:10. unto him that *blasphemeth* against
22:65. *blasphemously* spake they against him.
23:39. which were hanged *railed on* him,
Joh. 10:36. Thou *blasphemest*; because I said,
Acts 13:45. contradicting and *blaspheming*.
18: 6 when they opposed themselves, and *blasphemed*,
19:37. nor yet *blasphemers* of your goddess.
26:11. compelled (them) *to blaspheme*;
Ro. 2:24. the name of God *is blasphemed*
3: 8. as we *be slanderously reported*,
14:16. *Let* not then your good *be evil spoken of*
1Co. 4:13. *Being defamed*, we intreat: we
10:30. why *am I evil spoken of* for that
1Ti. 1:20. that they may learn not *to blaspheme*
6: 1. (his) doctrine *be not blasphemed*.
Tit. 2: 5. the word of God *be not blasphemed*.
3: 2. *To speak evil of* no man, to be no

977. See p. 111

Jas. 2: 7. *Do* not they *blaspheme* that worthy
1Pet.4: 4. excess of riot, *speaking evil* of (you):
14. on their part he *is evil spoken of,*
2Pet.2: 2. the way of truth *shall be evil spoken of.*
10. are not afraid *to speak evil of* dignities.
12. *speak evil of* the things that they
Jude 8. despise dominion, and *speak evil of*
10. these *speak evil of* those things
Rev 13: 6. *to blaspheme* his name, and his
16: 9. *blasphemed* the name of God,
11. *blasphemed* the God of heaven
21. men *blasphemed* God because

988 19 142/148 1:621 989

βλασφημία, *blaspheemia.*

Mat. 12:31. All manner of sin and *blasphemy*
— the *blasphemy* (*against*) the (Holy)
15:19. thefts, false witness, *blasphemies;*
26:65. now ye have heard his *blasphemy.*
Mar. 2: 7. doth this (man) thus speak *blasphemies?*
3:28. *blasphemies* wherewith soever
7:22. an evil eye, *blasphemy,* pride,
14:64. Ye have heard the *blasphemy:*
Lu. 5:21. Who is this which speaketh *blasphemies?*
Joh. 10:33. for *blasphemy;* and because that
Eph. 4:31. clamour, and *evil speaking,* be put away
Col. 3: 8. anger, wrath, malice, *blasphemy,*
1Ti. 6: 4. whereof cometh envy, strife, *railings,*
Jude 9. against him a *railing* accusation,
Rev. 2: 9. (I know) the *blasphemy* of them
13: 1. upon his heads the name of *blasphemy.*
5. speaking great things and *blasphemies;*
6. opened his mouth in *blasphemy*
17: 3. full of names of *blasphemy,*

989 5 142/149 1:621 984,5345

βλάσφημος, *blaspheemos.*

Acts 6:11. heard him speak *blasphemous* words
13. to speak *blasphemous* words
1Ti. 1:13. Who was before a *blasphemer,*
2Ti. 3: 2. covetous, boasters, proud, *blasphemers,*
2Pet. 2:11. bring not *railing* accusation

990 1 142/149 991

βλέμμα, *blemma.*

2Pet. 2: 8. among them, in *seeing* and hearing,

991 135 142/149 5:315 cf 3700

βλέπω, *blepo.*

Mat. 5:28. whosoever *looketh on* a woman to lust
6: 4. thy Father *which seeth* in secret
6. thy Father *which seeth* in secret
18. thy Father, *which seeth* in secret,
7: 3. why *beholdest* thou the mote that
11: 4. things which ye do hear and *see:*
12:22. blind and dumb both spake and *saw.*
13:13. because they *seeing see* not;
14. *seeing* ye *shall see,* and shall not
16. blessed (are) your eyes, for they *see.*
17. desired to see (those things) which ye *see,*
14:30. *when* he *saw* the wind boisterous,
15:31. *when* they *saw* the dumb to speak,
— lame to walk, and the blind to *see*·
18:10. do always *behold* the face of my Father
22:16. for thou *regardest* not the person
24: 2. *See* ye not all these things?
4. *Take heed* that no man deceive
Mar. 4:12. That *seeing* they *may see,* and not
24. *Take heed* what ye hear: with what
5:31. Thou *seest* the multitude thronging
Mar. 8:15. Take heed, *beware* of the leaven of
18. Having eyes, *see* ye not? and having
23. he asked him if he *saw* ought.
24. said, I *see* men as trees, walking.
12:14. for thou *regardest* not the person
38. *Beware* of the scribes, which love
13: 2. *Seest* thou these great buildings?
5. *Take heed* lest any (man) deceive
9. *take heed* to yourselves: for they
23. *take* ye *heed:* behold, I have
33. *Take* ye *heed,* watch and pray:
Lu. 6:41. why *beholdest* thou the mote
42. *when* thou thyself *beholdest* not the beam
7:21. many (that were) blind he gave *sight.*
44. said unto Simon, *Seest* thou this woman?
8:10. that *seeing* they *might* not *see,*
16. which enter in *may see* the light.
18. *Take heed* therefore how ye hear:
9:62. hand to the plough, and *looking* back,
10:23. Blessed (are) the eyes *which see* the things that ye *see:*
24. to see those things which ye *see,*
11:33. which come in *may see* the light.
21: 8. *Take heed* that ye be not deceived:
30. ye *see and* know of your own selves
24:12. he *beheld* the linen clothes
Joh. 1:29. John *seeth* Jesus coming unto
5:19. what he *seeth* the Father do:
9: 7. therefore, and washed, and came *seeing.*
15. clay upon mine eyes, and I washed, and *do see.*
19. how then *doth* he now *see?*
21. by what means he now *seeth,* we
25. whereas I was blind, now I *see.*
39. that they *which see* not *might see;* and that they *which see* might be made blind.
41. now ye say, We *see;* therefore
11: 9. because he *seeth* the light of this
13:22. the disciples *looked* one on another,
20: 1. *seeth* the stone taken away from
5. *saw* the linen clothes lying;
21: 9. they *saw* a fire of coals there,
20. *seeth* the disciple whom Jesus loved
Acts 1: 9. *while* they *beheld,* he was taken up;
2:33. which ye now *see* and hear.
3: 4. upon him with John, said, *Look* on us.
4:14. *beholding* the man which was
8: 6. *seeing* the miracles which he did.
9: 8. eyes were opened, he *saw* no man:
9. days without sight, (lit. not *seeing*)
12: 9. the angel; but thought he *saw* a vision.
13:11. blind, not *seeing* the sun for a season.
40. *Beware* therefore, lest that come
27:12. *lieth* toward the south west and
28:26. *seeing* ye *shall see,* and not perceive:
Ro. 7:23. I *see* another law in my members,
8:24. hope *that is seen* is not hope: for what a man *seeth,* why doth
25. if we hope for that we *see* not, (then)
11: 8. eyes that they should not see, (lit. *of* not *seeing*)
10. darkened, that they may not *see,*
1Co. 1:26. For ye *see* your calling, brethren,
3:10. *let* every man *take heed* how he
8: 9. *take heed* lest by any means this
10:12. *let*...standeth *take heed* lest he fall.
18. *Behold* Israel after the flesh:
13:12. For now we *see* through a glass,
16:10. *see* that he may be with you
2Co. 4:18. *which are seen,* but at the things *which are* not *seen:* for the things *which are seen* (are) temporal; but the things *which are* not *seen* are eternal.

2Co. 7: 8. for I *perceive* that the same epistle
10: 7. *Do* ye *look on* things after the outward
12. 6. that which he *seeth* me (to be), or
Gal. 5:15. *take heed* that ye be not consumed
Eph. 5:15. *See* then that ye walk circumspectly,
Phi. 3: 2. *Beware* of dogs, *beware* of evil workers, *beware* of the concision.
Col. 2: 5. joying and *beholding* your order,
8. *Beware* lest any man spoil you
4:17. *Take heed* to the ministry which
Heb. 2: 9. we *see* Jesus, who was made a
3:12. *Take heed*, brethren, lest there be
19. So we *see* that they could not enter
10:25. more, as ye *see* the day approaching
11: 1. the evidence of things not *seen*.
3. things *which are seen* were not
7. of things not *seen* as yet, moved
12:25. *See* that ye refuse not him that
Jas. 2:22. *Seest* thou how faith wrought
2Joh. 8. *Look to* yourselves, that we lose
Rev. 1:11. What thou *seest*, write in a book,
12. I turned *to see* the voice that
3:18. with eyesalve, that thou *mayest see*.
5: 3. open the book, neither *to look* thereon.
4. the book, neither *to look* thereon.
6: 1. four beasts saying, Come and *see*.
3. second beast say, Come and *see*.
5. the third beast say, Come and *see*.
7. the fourth beast say, Come and *see*.
9:20. which neither can *see*, nor hear,
11: 9. nations *shall see* their dead bodies
16:15. lest he walk naked, and they *see*
17: 8. *when* they *behold* the beast that was,
18: 9. when they *shall see* the smoke of her
22: 8. I John *saw* these things, *and* heard (them). And when I had heard and *seen*, I fell

---

992 2 143/150 906

βλητέος, bleeteos.

Mar. 2:22. new wine *must be put* into new bottles.
Lu. 5:38. new wine *must be put* into new

---

994 11 143/150 1:625

βοάω, boaō.

Mat. 3: 3. The voice of one *crying* in the wilderness,
Mar. 1: 3. The voice of one *crying* in the wilderness,
15:34. ninth hour Jesus *cried* with a loud voice,
Lu. 3: 4. The voice of one *crying* in the wilderness,
18: 7. his own elect, *which cry* day and night
38. he *cried*, saying, Jesus, (thou) son of David,
Joh. 1:23. the voice of one *crying* in the wilderness,
Acts 8: 7. unclean spirits, *crying* with loud voice,
17: 6. unto the rulers of the city, *crying*,
21:34. some *cried* one thing, some another,
Gal. 4:27. break forth and *cry* thou that travailest

---

995 1 144/150 994

βοή, boee.

Jas. 5: 4. the *cries* of them which have reaped

---

996 2 144/150 1:628 998

βοήθεια, boeethia.

Acts27:17. had taken up, they used *helps*,
Heb. 4:16. find grace *to help* in time of need. (lit. for seasonable *help*)

---

997 8 144/150 1:628 998

βοηθέω, boeetheo.

Mat.15:25. worshipped him, saying, Lord, *help* me.
Mar. 9:22. have compassion on us, and *help* us.
24. I believe; *help* thou mine unbelief.
Acts16: 9. Come over into Macedonia, and *help* us.
21:28. Crying out, Men of Israel, *help*:
2Co. 6: 2. in the day of salvation *have* I *succoured* thee:
Heb. 2:18. he is able *to succour* them that are
Rev.12:16. the earth *helped* the woman, and the

---

998 1 144/150 1:628 995 *theō* (to run)

βοηθός, boeethos.

Heb13: 6. The Lord (is) my *helper*, and I will

---

999 3 144/150 cf 900

βόθυνος, bothunos.

Mat.12:11. if it fall into a *pit* on the sabbath day,
15:14. the blind, both shall fall into the *ditch*.
Lu. 6:39. shall they not both fall into the *ditch*?

1000 1 144/151 906

βολή, bolee.

Lu. 22:41. withdrawn from them about a stone's *cast*,

1001 2 144/151 1002

βολίζω, bolizo.

Acts27:28. *sounded, and* found (it) twenty fathoms:
— gone a little further, they *sounded* again, *and*

1002 1 144/ 906

βολίς, bolis.

Heb 12:20. stoned, or thrust through with a *dart*:

1004 1 144/151

βόρβορος, borboros.

2Pet. 2:22. to her wallowing in the *mire*.

1005 2 144/151

βοῤῥᾶς, borras.

Lu. 13:29. from the *north*, and (from) the south,
Rev.21:13. on the *north* three gates; on the south

1006 9 144/151 cf977 cf1016

βόσκω, bosko.

Mat. 8:30. an herd of many swine *feeding*.
33. they *that kept* them fled, *and* went
Mar. 5:11. a great herd of swine *feeding*.
14. they *that fed* the swine fled, and told
Lu. 8:32 an herd of many swine *feeding* on
34. they *that fed* (them) saw what was done,
15:15. he sent him into his fields *to feed* swine.
Joh.21:15. He saith unto him, *Feed* my lambs.
17. Jesus saith unto him, *Feed* my sheep.

1008 1 144/151 1006

βοτάνη, botanee.

Heb. 6: 7. bringeth forth *herbs* meet for them

1009 1 145/151

βότρυς, botrus.

Rev.14:18. gather the *clusters of the vine* of the earth;

1011 8 145/151 1012

βουλεύομαι, boulūomai.

Lu. 14:31. *consulteth* whether he be able with
Joh. 12:10. the chief priests *consulted* that
Acts 5:33. *took counsel* to slay them.
15:37. Barnabas *determined* to take
27:39. a shore, into the which they *were minded*,
2Co. 1:17. *When* I therefore was thus *minded*,
— that I *purpose*, *do* I *purpose* according

1010 2 145/151 1011

βουλεύτης, boulūtees.

Mar 15:43. Joseph of Arimathæa, an honourable *counsellor*,
Lu. 23:50. (there was) a man named Joseph, a *counsellor*;

1012 12 145/151 1:629 1014

βουλή, boulee.

Lu. 7:30. lawyers rejected the *counsel* of God
23:51. consented to the *counsel* and deed of them;
Acts 2:23. by the determinate *counsel* and
4:28. to do whatsoever thy hand and thy *counsel*
5:38. for if this *counsel* or this work be
13:36. by the *will* of God, fell on sleep,
20:27. unto you all the *counsel* of God.
27:12. the more part advised (lit. gave *counsel*) to depart
42. the soldiers' *counsel* was to kill
1Co. 4: 5. manifest the *counsels* of the hearts:
Eph. 1:11. after the *counsel* of his own will:
Heb 6:17. the immutability of his *counsel*,

1013 2 145/151 1:629 1014

βούλημα, bouleema.

Acts 27:43. kept them from (their) *purpose*;
Ro. 9:19. For who hath resisted his *will*?

1014 35 145/151 1:629 cf 2309

βούλομαι, boulomai.

Mat. 1:19. *was minded* to put her away privily.
11:27. to whomsoever the Son *will* reveal (him).
Mar 15:15. Pilate, *willing* to content the people,
Lu. 10:22. (he) to whom the Son *will* reveal (him).
22:42. Father, if thou *be willing*, remove
Joh. 18:39. *will* ye therefore that I release
Acts 5:28. *intend* to bring this man's blood upon us.
12: 4. *intending* after Easter to bring
17:20. we *would* know therefore what
18:15. for I *will* be no judge of such
27. *when* he *was disposed* to pass
19:30. *when* Paul *would* have entered
22:30. *because* he *would* have known the
23:28. *when* I *would* have known the cause
25:20. I asked (him) whether he *would* go to
22. I *would* also hear the man myself.
27:43. the centurion, *willing* to save Paul,
28:18. *would* have let (me) go, because
1Co. 12:11. to every man severally as he *will*.
2Co. 1:15. I *was minded* to come unto you
Phi. 1:12. I *would* ye should understand,
1Ti. 2: 8. I *will* therefore that men pray
5:14. I *will* therefore that the younger
6: 9. they *that will* be rich fall into temptation
Tit. 3: 8. these things I *will* that thou affirm
Philem 13. Whom I *would* have retained with me,
Heb. 6:17. God, *willing* more abundantly to shew
Jas. 1:18. *Of* his *own will* begat he us with the
3: 4. whithersoever the governor *listeth*.
4: 4. whosoever therefore *will* be a friend of
2Pet. 3: 9. not *willing* that any should perish,
2Joh. 12. I *would* not (write) with paper and ink
3Joh. 10. forbiddeth them *that would*, and casteth
Jude 5. I *will* therefore put you in remembrance,

1015 2 146/152

βουνός, bounos.

Lu. 3: 5. every mountain and *hill* shall be brought
23:30. Fall on us; and to the *hills*, Cover us.

1016 8 146/152 rt 1006

βοῦς, bous.

Lu. 13:15. loose his *ox* or (his) ass from the stall,
14: 5. have an ass or an *ox* fallen into a pit,
19. I have bought five yoke of *oxen*,
Joh. 2:14. those that sold *oxen* and sheep and doves,
15. out of the temple, and the sheep, and the *oxen*;
1Co. 9: 9. not muzzle the mouth of the *ox* that
— Doth God take care for *oxen*?
1Ti. 5:18. Thou shalt not muzzle the *ox* that

1017 2 146/152 1:637

βραβεῖον, brabīon. *brabeus* (umpire)

1Co. 9:24. run all, but one receiveth the *prize*?
Phi. 3:14. I press toward the mark for the *prize*

1018 1 146/152 1:637

βραβεύω, brabūo. *brabeus* (umpire)

Col. 3:15. the peace of God *rule* in your hearts,

1019 2 146/152 1021

βραδύνω, braduno.

1Ti. 3:15. if I *tarry* long, that thou mayest
2Pet. 3: 9. The Lord *is* not *slack* concerning

1020 1 146/152 1021,4126

βραδυπλοέω, braduploeō.

Acts 27: 7. *when* we *had sailed slowly* many days,

1021 3 146/152

βραδύς, bradus.

Lu. 24:25. O fools, and *slow* of heart to believe all
Jas. 1:19. swift to hear, *slow* to speak, *slow* to wrath:

1022 1 146/152 1021

βραδυτής, bradutees.

2Pet. 3: 9. as some men count *slackness*;

1023 3 146/152 1:639 1024

βραχιων, brakiōn.

Lu. 1:51. He hath shewed strength with his *arm*;
Joh. 12:38. to whom hath the *arm* of the Lord been
Acts 13:17. with an high *arm* brought he

1024 7 146/152

βραχύς, brakus.

Lu. 22:58. after a *little while* another saw him,
Joh. 6: 7. every one of them may take a *little*.
Acts 5:34. to put the apostles forth a *little space*,
27:28. when they had gone a *little* further.

Heb. 2: 7. madest him a *little* lower than the angels;
9. made a *little* lower than the angels
13:22. written a letter unto you in *few words.*

1025 8 146/152 5:636

βρέφος, brephos.

Lu. 1:41. the *babe* leaped in her womb;
44. the *babe* leaped in my womb
2:12. the *babe* wrapped in swaddling clothes,
16. Mary, and Joseph, and the *babe* lying in a
18:15. they brought unto him also *infants,*
Acts 7:19. they cast out their *young children,*
2Ti. 3:15. from a *child* thou hast known
1Pet. 2: 2. As newborn *babes,* desire the sincere

1026 7 147/152

βρέχω, breko.

Mat. 5:45. *sendeth rain* on the just and on the
Lu. 7:38. began *to wash* his feet with tears,
44. she *hath washed* my feet with tears,
17:29. *it rained* fire and brimstone from
Jas. 5:17. that it might not *rain:* and it *rained* not
Rev 11: 6. that it *rain* not in the days of

1027 12 147/152 1:640

βροντή, brontee.

Mar. 3:17. which is, The sons of *thunder:*
Joh. 12:29. heard (it), said that it thundered: (lit. that there was *thunder*)
Rev. 4: 5. lightnings and *thunderings* and voices:
6: 1. as it were the noise of *thunder,*
8: 5. voices, and *thunderings,* and lightnings,
10: 3. seven *thunders* uttered their voices.
4. when the seven *thunders* had uttered
— things which the seven *thunders* uttered,
11:19. lightnings, and voices, and *thunderings,*
14: 2. as the voice of a great *thunder:*
16:18. were voices, and *thunders,* and lightnings;
19: 6. as the voice of mighty *thunderings,*

1028 2 147/153 1026

βροχή, brokee.

Mat. 7:25. the *rain* descended, and the floods came,
27. the *rain* descended, and the floods came,

1029 1 147/153

βρόχος, brokos.

1Co. 7:35. not that I may cast a *snare* upon you.

1030 7 147/153 1:641 1031

βρυγμός, brugmos.

Mat. 8:12. shall be weeping and *gnashing* of teeth.
13:42. shall be wailing and *gnashing* of teeth.
50. shall be wailing and *gnashing* of teeth.
22:13. shall be weeping and *gnashing* of teeth.
24:51. shall be weeping and *gnashing* of teeth.
25:30. shall be weeping and *gnashing* of teeth.
Lu. 13:28. shall be weeping and *gnashing* of teeth,

1031 1 147/153 1:641

βρύχω, bruko.

Acts 7:54. they *gnashed* on him with (their) teeth.

1032 1 147/153

βρύω, bruo.

Jas. 3:11. Doth a fountain *send forth* at the

1033 17 147/153 1:642 rt 977

βρῶμα, brōma.

Mat. 14:15. the villages, and buy themselves *victuals.*
Mar. 7:19. into the draught, purging all *meats?*
Lu. 3:11. he that hath *meat,* let him do likewise.
9:13. except we should go and buy *meat* for
Joh. 4:34. My *meat* is to do the will of him
Ro. 14:15. brother be grieved with (thy) *meat,*
— Destroy not him with thy *meat,*
20. For *meat* destroy not the work of God.
1Co. 3: 2. fed you with milk, and not with *meat:*
6:13. *Meats* for the belly, and the belly for *meats:*
8: 8. *meat* commendeth us not to God:
13. if *meat* make my brother to offend,
10: 3. did all eat the same spiritual *meat;*
1Ti. 4: 3. (commanding) to abstain from *meats,*
Heb. 9:10. (Which stood) only in *meats* and drinks,
13: 9. not with *meats,* which have not

1034 1 147/153 1035

βρώσιμος, brōsimos.

Lu. 24:41. said unto them, Have ye here any *meat?* (lit. *thing eatable*)

1035 11 147/153 1:642 rt 977

βρῶσις, brōsis.

Mat. 6:19. where moth and *rust* doth corrupt,
20. where neither moth nor *rust* doth corrupt,
Joh. 4:32. I have *meat* to eat that ye know
6:27. Labour not for the *meat* which perisheth, but for that *meat* which endureth
55. For my flesh is *meat* indeed,
Ro. 14:17. the kingdom of God is not *meat* and
1Co. 8: 4. the *eating* of those things that are
2Co. 9:10. both minister bread for (your) *food,*
Col. 2:16. no man therefore judge you in *meat,*
Heb 12:16. for one *morsel of meat* sold his birthright.

977 1 141/148

βρώσκω, brōsko.

Joh. 6:13. over and above unto them *that had eaten.*

1036 2 147/153 1037

βυθίζω, buthizo.

Lu. 5: 7. the ships, so that they *began to sink.*
1Ti. 6: 9. which *drown* men in destruction

1037 1 148/153 eq 899

βυθός, buthos.

2Co. 11:25. night and a day I have been in the *deep;*

1038 3 148/153 *bursa* (hide)

βυρσεύς, bursūs.

Acts 9:43. days in Joppa with one Simon a *tanner.*
10: 6. He lodgeth with one Simon a *tanner,*
32. in the house of (one) Simon a *tanner*

1039 4 148/153 1040

βύσσινος, bussinos.

Rev. 18:16. city, that was clothed in *fine linen,*
19: 8. she should be arrayed in *fine linen,* clean and white: for the *fine linen* is the
14. clothed in *fine linen,* white and clean.

1040 2 148/153 [948]

βύσσος, bussos.

Lu. 16:19. was clothed in purple and *fine linen,*
Rev. 18:12. pearls, and *fine linen,* and purple and

1041 1 148/153 rt 939

βωμός, bōmos.

Acts17:23. I found an *altar* with this inscription.

1044 1 148/153 *grainō* (to gnaw)

γάγγραινα, gangraina.

2Ti. 2:17. their word will eat as doth a *canker*:

1047 1 148/154

γάζα, gaza.

Acts 8:27. had the charge of all her *treasure*,

1049 5 148/154 1047,5438

γαζοφυλάκιον, gazophulakion.

Mar 12:41. Jesus sat over against the *treasury*,
— people cast money into the *treasury*:
43. which have cast into the *treasury*:
Lu. 21: 1. casting their gifts into the *treasury*.
Joh. 8:20. These words spake Jesus in the *treasury*,

1051 5 149/154 1:645

γάλα, gala.

1Co. 3: 2. I have fed you with *milk*, and not with
9: 7. eateth not of the *milk* of the flock?
Heb. 5:12. become such as have need of *milk*,
13. For every one that useth *milk* (is)
1Pet.2: 2. desire the sincere *milk* of the word,

1055 3 149/154

γαλήνη, galeenee.

Mat. 8.26. the sea; and there was a great *calm*.
Mar. 4:39. wind ceased, and there was a great *calm*.
Lu. 8:24. they ceased, and there was a *calm*.

1060 29 150/155 1:648 1062

γαμέω, gameo.

Mat. 5:32. whosoever *shall marry* her that
19: 9. *shall marry* another, committeth adul-
— tery: and *whoso marrieth* her which
10. with (his) wife, it is not good *to marry*.
22:25. the first, *when* he *had married a wife*,
30. in the resurrection they neither *marry*,
24.38. *marrying* and giving in marriage,
Mar. 6:17. Philip's wife: for he *had married* her.
10:11. whosoever shall put away his wife, and *marry*
12. her husband, and *be married* to another,
12:25. they neither *marry*, nor are given in
Lu. 14:20. another said, I *have married* a wife,
16:18. putteth away his wife, and *marrieth*
— whosoever *marrieth* her that is put away
17:27. they drank, they *married wives*, they
20:34. The children of this world *marry*,
35. neither *marry*, nor are given in
1Co. 7: 9. if they cannot contain, *let* them *marry*:
— for it is better *to marry* than to burn.
10. unto the *married* I command,
28. if thou *marry*, thou hast not sinned; and if a virgin *marry*, she hath not sinned.
33. he *that is married* careth for the
34. she *that is married* careth for the
36. he sinneth not: *let* them *marry*.
39. she is at liberty *to be married* to whom
1Ti. 4: 3. Forbidding *to marry*, (and commanding)
5:11. wanton against Christ, they will *marry*;
14. therefore that the younger women *marry*,

1061 1 150/155 1062

γαμίσκομαι, gamiskomai.

Mar.12:25. neither marry, nor *are given in marriage*;

1062 16 150/155 1:648

γάμος, gamos.

Mat.22: 2. a certain king, which made a *marriage*
3. them that were bidden to the *wedding*:
4. (are) ready: come unto the *marriage*.
8. The *wedding* is ready, but they which
9. shall find, bid to the *marriage*.
10. the *wedding* was furnished with guests.
11. which had not on a *wedding* garment:
12. in hither not having a *wedding* garment
25:10. went in with him to the *marriage*:
Lu. 12:36. when he will return from the *wedding*
14: 8. bidden of any (man) to a *wedding*,
Joh. 2: 1. the third day there was a *marriage*
2. called, and his disciples, to the *marriage*.
Heb 13: 4. *Marriage* (is) honourable in all, and the
Rev.19: 7. for the *marriage* of the Lamb is come,
9. unto the *marriage* supper of the Lamb.

1063 1069 151/156

γάρ, gar.

Mat. 1:20. *for* that which is conceived in her
&c. &c.

Note.—Always rendered "*for*," except in,

Mat. 1:18. When *as* his mother Mary was
15:27. Truth, Lord: yet (και γαρ) the dogs
27:23. *Why*, what evil hath he done?
Mar 7:28. yet (και γαρ) the dogs under
8:38. Whosoever *therefore* shall be ashamed
15:14. *Why*, what evil
Lu. 12:58. When)(thou goest with thine adversary
20:36. Neither)(can they die any more:
23:22. *Why*, what evil hath he done?
Joh. 3:19. *because* their deeds were evil.
4:37. *And* herein is that saying true,
7:41. Shall)(Christ come
8:42. neither)(came I of myself,
9:30. *Why* herein is a marvellous thing,
10:26. *because* ye are not of my sheep, as
Acts 2:15. *seeing* it is (but) the third hour
4:34. Neither)(was there any among them
8:31. said, How)(can I,
39. *and* he went on his way rejoicing.
16:37. nay *verily*; but let them come
19:35. what)(man is there that knoweth not
28:20. *because that* for the hope of Israel
Ro. 3: 2. chiefly,)(because that unto them were
4:15. *Because* the law worketh wrath:
5: 7. *yet* peradventure for a good man some
8: 7. law of God, neither *indeed* can be.
15: 2. Let)(every one of us please (his)
27. It hath pleased them *verily*; and their
1Co. 9:10. For our sakes, *no doubt*, (this) is written
11: 9. Neither)(was the man created for the
22. *What?* have ye not houses to eat
2Co.12: 1. I)(will come to visions and revelations
Phi. 1:18. What *then?* notwithstanding, every
2: 5. Let)(this mind be in you, which was
1Th. 4:10. And *indeed* ye do it toward all the
2Ti. 2: 7. *and* the Lord give thee understanding
Jas. 4:14. It is *even* a vapour, that appeareth for
1Pet.4:15. *But* let none of you suffer as a
2Pet.1: 9. *But* he that lacketh these things
3Joh 7. *Because that* for his name's sake they

1064 9 151/157

γαστήρ, gasteer.

Mat. 1:18. she was found with child (lit. **having in** the *womb*)
23. Behold, a virgin shall be with **child, (lit.** having &c.)
24:19. woe unto them that are with **child, (lit.** having &c.)
Mar 13:17. woe to them that are with child, (lit. ...)
Lu. 1:31. thou shalt conceive in thy *womb,*
21:23. woe unto them that are with child, (lit. having &c.)
1Th. 5: 3. as travail upon a woman with child; (lit. having &c.)
Tit. 1:12. alway liars, evil beasts, slow *bellies.*
Rev.12: 2. she being with child (lit. ...) cried, travailing

1065 11 152/157

γέ, ge.

See also ἄραγε, εἴγε, εἰ δὲ μήγε, καίτοιγε, μενοῦνγε.

Lu. 11: 8. *yet* because of his importunity he
18: 5. *Yet* because this widow troubleth
19:42. even thou, *at least* in this thy day,
24:21. *and beside* (ἀλλα γε) all this, to day **is the** third
Acts 2:18. and)(on my servants and on my
8:30.)(Understandest thou what thou
11:18. Then hath)(God also to the Gentiles
Ro. 8:32. He that)(spared not his own Son,
1Co. 4: 8. I would)(to God ye did reign,
6: 3. how much more)(things that **pertain**
9: 2. apostle unto others, yet *doubtless* **I am to** you.

1067 12 152/157 1:657 [1516] [2011]

γέεννα, ge-enna.

Mat. 5:22. shall be in danger of *hell* **fire.**
29. whole body should be cast into *hell.*
30. whole body should be cast into *hell.*
10:28. to destroy both soul and body in *hell.*
18: 9. two eyes to be cast into *hell* fire.
23:15. more the child of *hell* than yourselves.
33. can ye escape the damnation of *hell?*
Mar 9:43. having two hands to go into *hell,*
45. having two feet to be cast into *hell,*
47. having two eyes to be cast into *hell* **fire:**
Lu. 12: 5. hath power to cast into *hell;*
Jas. 3: 6. of nature; and it is set on fire of *hell.*

1069 4 152/157 1093

γείτων, giton.

Lu. 14:12. thy kinsmen, nor (thy) rich *neighbours;*
15: 6. calleth together (his) friends and *neighbours,*
9. calleth (her) friends and (her) *neighbours*
Joh. 9: 8. The *neighbours* therefore, and they which

1070 2 152/157 1:658

γελάω, gelao.

Lu. 6:21. (ye) that weep now: for ye *shall laugh.*
25. Woe unto you *that laugh* now!

1071 1 152/157 1:658 1070

γέλως, gelos.

Jas. 4: 9. let your *laughter* be turned to

1072 9 152/158 1073

γεμίζω, gemizo.

Mar 4:37. into the ship, so that it *was* now *full.*
15:36. one ran and *filled* a spunge *full* of
Lu. 14:23. that my house *may be filled.*
15:16. he would fain *have filled* his belly
Joh. 2: 7. *Fill* the waterpots with water. And they *filled* them up to the brim.
6:13. *filled* twelve baskets with the
Rev. 8: 5. *filled* it with fire of the altar, and cast (it)
15: 8. the temple *was filled* with smoke

1073 11 153/158

γέμω, gemo.

Mat.23:25. within they *are full* of extortion
27. *are* within *full* of dead (men's) bones,
Lu. 11:39. your inward part *is full* of ravening
Ro. 3:14. Whose mouth (*is*) *full* of cursing
Rev. 4: 6. *full* of eyes before and behind.
8. (they were) *full* of eyes within: and they
5: 8. harps, and golden vials *full* of odours,
15: 7. *full* of the wrath of God, who liveth
17: 3. *full* of names of blasphemy,
4. cup in her hand *full* of abominations
21: 9. seven vials *full* of the seven last plagues,

1074 42 153/158 1:662 1085

γενεά, genea.

Mat. 1:17. all the *generations* from Abraham to David (are) fourteen *generations;*
— into Babylon (are) fourteen *generations*
— unto Christ (are) fourteen *generations.*
11:16. whereunto shall I liken this *generation?*
12:39. An evil and adulterous *generation*
41. in judgment with this *generation,*
42. in the judgment with this *generation,*
45. also unto this wicked *generation.*
16: 4. A wicked and adulterous *generation*
17:17. O faithless and perverse *generation,*
23:36. shall come upon this *generation.*
24:34. This *generation* shall not pass,
Mar 8:12. Why doth this *generation* seek
— no sign be given unto this *generation.*
38. this adulterous and sinful *generation;*
9:19. O faithless *generation,* how long
13:30. that this *generation* shall not pass,
Lu. 1:48. all *generations* shall call me blessed.
50. from *generation* to *generation.*
7:31. liken the men of this *generation?*
9:41. O faithless and perverse *generation,*
11:29. to say, This is an evil *generation:*
30. Son of man be to this *generation.*
31. with the men of this *generation,*
32. in the judgment with this *generation,*
50. may be required of this *generation;*
51. It shall be required of this *generation.*
16: 8. are in their *generation* wiser than
17:25. be rejected of this *generation.*
21:32. This *generation* shall not pass
Acts 2:40. yourselves from this untoward *generation.*
8:33. who shall declare his *generation?*
13:36. he had served his own *generation*
14:16. Who in *times* past suffered all
15:21. For Moses of old *time* hath in
Eph. 3: 5. Which in other *ages* was not made known
21. throughout all *ages,* world without end.
Phi. 2:15. in the midst of a crooked and perverse *nation,*

Col. 1:26. hid from ages and from *generations*,
Heb 3:10. I was grieved with that *generation*,

1075 1 153/158 1:662 1074,3056

γενεαλογέομαι, *genealogeomai.*

Heb. 7: 6. whose *descent is* not *counted* from them

1076 2 153/158 1:662 1074,3056

γενεαλογία, *genealogia.*

1Ti. 1: 4. heed to fables and endless *genealogies*,
Tit. 3: 9. avoid foolish questions, and *genealogies*,

1077 2 153/158 1078

γενέσια, *genesia.*

Mat.14: 6. when Herod's *birthday* was kept,
Mar 6:21. Herod on his *birthday* made a supper

1078 3 154/158 1:681 rt 1074

γένεσις, *genesis.*

Mat. 1: 1. The book of the *generation* of Jesus Christ,
Jas. 1:23. a man beholding his *natural* face in a glass:
3: 6. setteth on fire the course of *nature*;

1079 1 154/158 rt 1074

γενετή, *genetee.*

Joh. 9: 1. a man which was blind from (his) *birth*.

1080 97 154/159 1:665 eq 1085

γεννάω, *gennao.*

Mat. 1: 2. Abraham *begat* Isaac; and Isaac *begat* Jacob; and Jacob *begat* Judas
3. Judas *begat* Phares...and Phares *begat* Esrom; and Esrom *begat* Aram;
4. Aram *begat* Aminadab; and Aminadab *begat* Naasson; and Naasson *begat* Salmon;
5. Salmon *begat* Booz...Booz *begat* Obed of Ruth; and Obed *begat* Jesse;
6. Jesse *begat* David
— David the king *begat* Solomon
7. Solomon *begat* Roboam; and Roboam *begat* Abia; and Abia *begat* Asa;
8. Asa *begat* Josaphat; and Josaphat *begat* Joram; and Joram *begat* Ozias;
9. Ozias *begat* Joatham; and Joatham *begat* Achaz; and Achaz *begat* Ezekias;
10. Ezekias *begat* Manasses; and Manasses *begat* Amon; and Amon *begat* Josias;
11. Josias *begat* Jechonias
12. Jechonias *begat* Salathiel; and Salathiel *begat* Zorobabel;
13. Zorobabel *begat* Abiud; and Abiud *begat* Eliakim; and Eliakim *begat* Azor;
14. Azor *begat* Sadoc; and Sadoc *begat* Achim; and Achim *begat* Eliud;
15. Eliud *begat* Eleazar; and Eleazar *begat* Matthan; and Matthan *begat* Jacob;
16. Jacob *begat* Joseph the husband of Mary, of whom *was born* Jesus, who is
20. that which is *conceived* in her is
: 1. *when* Jesus *was born* in Bethlehem
4. where Christ *should be born*.
Mat.19:12. which *were* so *born* from (their) mother's womb:
26:24. that man if he *had* not *been born*.
Mar 14:21. that man if he *had* never *been born*.
Lu. 1:13. thy wife Elisabeth *shall bear* thee a son,
35. that holy thing which *shall be born*
57. delivered; and she *brought forth* a son.
23:29. barren, and the wombs that never *bare*,
Joh. 1:13. Which *were born*, not of blood, nor of
3: 3. Except a man *be born* again, he
4. How can a man be *born* when he is old?
— into his mother's womb, and be *born*?
5. Except a man *be born* of water
6. That *which is born* of the flesh is flesh; and that *which is born* of the Spirit is spirit.
7. Ye must *be born* again.
8. every one *that is born* of the Spirit.
8:41. We *be* not *born* of fornication; we
9: 2. or his parents, that he *was born* blind?
19. your son, who ye say *was born* blind?
20. our son, and that he *was born* blind:
32. the eyes of one *that was born* blind.
34. Thou *wast* altogether *born* in sins,
16:21. as soon as she *is delivered of* the child,
— that a man *is born* into the world.
18:37. To this end *was* I *born*, and for this cause
Acts 2: 8. our own tongue, wherein we *were born*?
7: 8. so (Abraham) *begat* Isaac, and circumcised
20. In which time Moses *was born*,
29. Madian, where he *begat* two sons.
13:33. my Son, this day *have* I *begotten* thee.
22: 3. a man (which am) a Jew, *born* in Tarsus,
28. Paul said, But I *was* (free) *born*.
Ro. 9:11. For (the children) *being* not yet *born*,
1Co. 4:15. I *have begotten* you through the gospel.
Gal. 4:23. bondwoman *was born* after the flesh;
24. *which gendereth* to bondage, which
29. he *that was born* after the flesh
2Ti. 2:23. knowing that they *do gender* strifes.
Philem.10. whom I *have begotten* in my bonds:
Heb 1: 5. my Son, this day *have* I *begotten* thee?
5: 5. my Son, to day *have* I *begotten* thee.
11:12. Therefore *sprang* there even of one, and him
23. By faith Moses, *when* he *was born*,
2Pet. 2:12. beasts, *made* to be taken and destroyed,
1Joh. 2:29. doeth righteousness *is born* of him.
3: 9. Whosoever is *born* of God doth not
— because he *is born* of God.
4: 7. every one that loveth *is born* of God,
5: 1. Jesus is the Christ *is born* of God: and every one that loveth him *that begat* loveth him also *that is begotten* of him.
4. For whatsoever is *born* of God
18. whosoever is *born* of God sinneth not; but he that is *begotten* of God keepeth

1081 9 155/159,160 1:665 1080

γέννημα, *genneema.*

Mat. 3: 7. O *generation* of vipers, who hath
12:34. O *generation* of vipers, how can ye,
23:33. (Ye) serpents, (ye) *generation* of vipers,
26:29. henceforth of this *fruit* of the vine,
Mar 14:25. drink no more of the *fruit* of the vine,
Lu. 3: 7. O *generation* of vipers, who hath
12:18. there will I bestow all my *fruits* and
22:18. I will not drink of the *fruit* of the vine,
2Co. 9:10. increase the *fruits* of your righteousness,

1083 2 155/158 1080

γέννησις, genneesis.

Mat. 1:18. Now the *birth* of Jesus Christ was on
Lu. 1:14. gladness; and many shall rejoice at his *birth*.

1084 2 155/160 1:665 1080

γεννητός, genneetos.

Mat.11:11. Among *them that are born* of women
Lu. 7:28. Among *those that are born* of women

1085 21 155/160 1:681 1096

γένος, genos.

Mat.13:47. into the sea, and gathered of every *kind:*
17:21. Howbeit this *kind* goeth not out
Mar. 7:26. a Greek, a Syrophenician by *nation;*
9:29. This *kind* can come forth by nothing,
Acts 4: 6. of the *kindred* of the high priest,
36. a Levite, (and) of the *country* of Cyprus,
7:13. Joseph's *kindred* was made known
19. same dealt subtilly with our *kindred,*
13:26. children of the *stock* of Abraham,
17:28. For we are also his *offspring.*
29. then as we are the *offspring* of God,
18: 2. Aquila, *born* in (lit. by *birth* of) Pontus,
24. Jew named Apollos, *born* at Alexandria,
1Co.12:10. to another (divers) *kinds* of tongues;
28. governments, *diversities* of tongues.
14:10. many *kinds* of voices in the world,
2Co.11:26. (in) perils by (mine own) *countrymen,*
Gal. 1:14. many my equals in mine own *nation,*
Phi. 3: 5. of the *stock* of Israel, (of) the tribe of
1Pet.2: 9. ye (are) a chosen *generation,* a royal
Rev.22:16. I am the root and the *offspring* of David,

1087 1 155/160 1088

γερουσία, gerousia.

Acts 5:21. all the *senate* of the children of Israel,

1088 1 156/160 cf 1094

γέρων, gerōn.

Joh. 3: 4. can a man be born when he is *old?*

1089 15 156/160 1:675

γεύομαι, gūomai.

Mat.16:28. which *shall* not *taste* of death, till
27:34. *when* he *had tasted* (thereof), he would
Mar. 9: 1. here, which *shall* not *taste* of death,
Lu. 9:27. *shall* not *taste* of death, till they see
14:24. were bidden *shall taste* of my supper.
Joh. 2: 9. ruler of the feast *had tasted* the water
8:52. saying, he *shall* never *taste* of death.
Acts10:10. very hungry, and would *have eaten:*
20:11. had broken bread, and *eaten,* and talked
23:14. that we will *eat* nothing until we
Col. 2:21. Touch not; *taste* not; handle not;
Heb. 2: 9. *should taste* death for every man.
6: 4. *have tasted* of the heavenly gift, and were
5. *have tasted* the good word of God,
1Pet.2: 3. If so be ye *have tasted* that the Lord

1090 1 156/160 1092

γεωργέομαι, geōrgeomai.

Heb. 6: 7. for them by whom it *is dressed,* receiveth

1091 1 156/160 1092

γεώργιον, geōrgion.

1Co. 3: 9. with God: ye are God's *husbandry,*

1092 19 156/161 rt 2041,1093

γεωργός, geōrgos.

Mat.21:33. let it out to *husbandmen,* and went
34. sent his servants to the *husbandmen,*
35. the *husbandmen* took his servants,
38. when the *husbandmen* saw the son,
40. will he do unto those *husbandmen?*
41. (his) vineyard unto other *husbandmen,*
Mar.12: 1. let it out to *husbandmen,* and went
2. he sent to the *husbandmen*
— might receive from the *husbandmen*
7. those *husbandmen* said among
9. will come and destroy the *husbandmen,*
Lu. 20: 9. a vineyard, and let it forth to *husbandmen,*
10. sent a servant to the *husbandmen,*
— the *husbandmen* beat him,
14. when the *husbandmen* saw him,
16. shall come and destroy these *husbandmen,*
Joh.15: 1. my Father is the *husbandman.*
2Ti. 2: 6. The *husbandman* that laboureth
Jas. 5: 7. the *husbandman* waiteth for the

1093 252 156/161 1:677

γῆ, gee.

Mat. 2: 6. thou Bethlehem, (in) the *land* of Juda,
20. go into the *land* of Israel: for they
21. came into the *land* of Israel.
4:15. The *land* of Zabulon, and the *land* of N.
5: 5. the meek: for they shall inherit the *earth.*
13. Ye are the salt of the *earth:* but if
18. Till heaven and *earth* pass, one jot or
35. Nor by the *earth;* for it is his footstool:
6:10. Thy will be done in *earth,* as (it is)
19. for yourselves treasures upon *earth,*
9: 6. man hath power on *earth* to forgive
26. fame hereof went abroad into all that *land.*
31. abroad his fame in all that *country.*
10:15. for the *land* of Sodom and Gomorrha in
29. shall not fall on the *ground* without
34. I am come to send peace on *earth:*
11:24. more tolerable for the *land* of Sodom
25. O Father, Lord of heaven and *earth,*
12:40. three nights in the heart of the *earth.*
42. from the uttermost parts of the *earth* to
13: 5. where they had not much *earth:*
— they had no deepness of *earth:*
8. other fell into good *ground,*
23. received seed into the good *ground*
14:34. came into the *land* of Gennesaret.
15:35. multitude to sit down on the *ground.*
16:19. whatsoever thou shalt bind on *earth*
— whatsoever thou shalt loose on *earth*
17:25. of whom do the kings of the *earth* take
18:18. Whatsoever ye shall bind on *earth*
— whatsoever ye shall loose on *earth*
19. if two of you shall agree on *earth* as
23: 9. call no (man) your father upon the *earth:*
35. righteous blood shed upon the *earth,*
24:30. then shall all the tribes of the *earth*
35. Heaven and *earth* shall pass away,
25:18. received one went and digged in the *earth,*
25. went and hid thy talent in the *earth:*
27:45. there was darkness over all the *land*
51. the *earth* did quake, and the rocks rent:
28:18. given unto me in heaven and in *earth.*
Mar. 2:10. Son of man hath power on *earth* to

Mar. 4: 1. multitude was by the sea on the *land*.
5. where it had not much *earth;*
— because it had no depth of *earth:*
8. other fell on good *ground*, and did
20. which are sown on good *ground;*
26. should cast seed into the *ground;*
28. the *earth* bringeth forth fruit of herself;
31. when it is sown in the *earth*, is less than all the seeds that be in the *earth:*
6:47. the sea, and he alone on the *land*.
53. came into the *land* of Gennesaret,
8: 6. people to sit down on the *ground.*
9: 3. as no fuller on *earth* can white them.
20. he fell on the *ground*, and wallowed
13:27. from the uttermost part of the *earth*
31. Heaven and *earth* shall pass away:
14:35. fell on the *ground*, and prayed that,
15:33. there was darkness over the whole *land*
Lu. 2:14. on *earth* peace, good will toward men.
4:25. famine was throughout all the *land;*
5: 3. thrust out a little from the *land*.
11. had brought their ships to *land*,
24. Son of man hath power upon *earth*
6:49. built an house upon the *earth;*
8: 8. other fell on good *ground*, and sprang
15. that on the good *ground* are they,
27. when he went forth to *land*, there met
10:21. O Father, Lord of heaven and *earth*, that
11: 2. be done, as in heaven, so in *earth*.
31. from the utmost parts of the *earth*
12:49. I am come to send fire on the *earth;*
51. come to give peace on *earth?* I tell
56. ye can discern the face of the sky and of the *earth;* but how
13: 7. why cumbereth it the *ground?*
14:35. It is neither fit for the *land*, nor
16:17. easier for heaven and *earth* to pass,
18: 8. shall he find faith on the *earth?*
21:23. shall be great distress in the *land*,
25. upon the *earth* distress of nations,
33. Heaven and *earth* shall pass away:
35. dwell on the face of the whole *earth*.
22:44. of blood falling down to the *ground*.
23:44. there was a darkness over all the *earth*
24: 5. bowed down (their) faces to the *earth*,
Joh. 3:22. his disciples into the *land* of Judæa;
31. he that is of the *earth* is *earthly*, and speaketh of the *earth:*
6:21. the ship was at the *land* whither
8: 6. with (his) finger wrote on the *ground*,
8. he stooped down, and wrote on the *ground*.
12:24. a corn of wheat fall into the *ground* and die,
32. if I be lifted up from the *earth*,
17: 4. I have glorified thee on the *earth:*
21: 8. they were not far from *land*, but
9. then as they were come to *land*,
11. drew the net to *land* full of great
Acts 1: 8. unto the uttermost part of the *earth*.
2:19. signs in the *earth* beneath;
3:25. the kindreds of the *earth* be blessed.
4:24. which hast made heaven, and *earth*,
26. The kings of the *earth* stood up,
7: 3. Get thee out of thy *country*,
— come into the *land* which I shall
4. Then came he out of the *land*
— he removed him into this *land*,
6. seed should sojourn in a strange *land;*
11. a dearth over all the *land* of Egypt
29. was a stranger in the *land* of Madian,
33. where thou standest is holy *ground*.
36. signs in the *land* of Egypt, and in

Acts 7:40. brought us out of the *land* of Egypt,
49. my throne, and *earth* (is) my footstool:
8:33. his life is taken from the *earth*.
9: 4. he fell to the *earth*, and heard a voice
8. Saul arose from the *earth;* and when
10:11. four corners, and let down to the *earth:*
12. fourfooted beasts of the *earth*.
11: 6. saw fourfooted beasts of the *earth*,
13:17. as strangers in the *land* of Egypt,
19. seven nations in the *land* of Chanaan, he divided their *land* to them by lot.
47. salvation unto the ends of the *earth*.
14:15. God, which made heaven, and *earth*,
17:24. he is Lord of heaven and *earth*, dwelleth
26. to dwell on all the face of the *earth*,
22:22. Away with such a (fellow) from the *earth*.
26:14. when we were all fallen to the *earth*,
27:39. was day, they knew not the *land:*
43. first (into the sea), and get to *land:*
44. that they escaped all safe to *land*.
Ro. 9:17. be declared throughout all the *earth*.
28. will the Lord make upon the *earth*.
10:18. their sound went into all the *earth*,
1Co. 8: 5. whether in heaven or in *earth*,
10:26. For the *earth* (is) the Lord's, and the fulness
28. for the *earth* (is) the Lord's, and the fulness
15:47. The first man (is) of the *earth*, earthy:
Eph. 1:10. are in heaven, and which are on *earth;*
3:15. the whole family in heaven and *earth* is named,
4: 9. into the lower parts of the *earth?*
6: 3. thou mayest live long on the *earth*.
Col. 1:16. are in heaven, and that are in *earth*,
20. whether (they be) things in *earth*, or
3: 2. things above, not on things on the *earth*.
5. your members which are upon the *earth;*
Heb 1:10. hast laid the foundation of the *earth;*
6: 7. For the *earth* which drinketh in
8: 4. For if he were on *earth*, he should
9. to lead them out of the *land* of Egypt;
11: 9. he sojourned in the *land* of promise,
13. were strangers and pilgrims on the *earth*.
38. (in) dens and caves of the *earth*.
12:25. refused him that spake on *earth*,
26. Whose voice then shook the *earth:*
— once more I shake not the *earth* only,
Jas. 5: 5. Ye have lived in pleasure on the *earth*,
7. the precious fruit of the *earth*,
12. neither by heaven, neither by the *earth*,
17. it rained not on the *earth* by the
18. the *earth* brought forth her fruit.
2Pet. 3: 5. the *earth* standing out of the water
7. the heavens and the *earth*, which are
10. the *earth* also and the works that
13. for new heavens and a new *earth*,
1Joh. 5: 8. there are three that bear witness in *earth*,
Jude 5. the people out of the *land* of Egypt,
Rev. 1: 5. prince of the kings of the *earth*.
7. all kindreds of the *earth* shall
3:10. them that dwell upon the *earth*.
5: 3. nor in *earth*, neither under the *earth*,
6. of God sent forth into all the *earth*.
10. we shall reign on the *earth*.
13. on the *earth*, and under the *earth*,
6: 4. to take peace from the *earth*, and that
8. over the fourth part of the *earth*,
— death, and with the beasts of the *earth*.
10. on them that dwell on the *earth?*
13. the stars of heaven fell unto the *earth*,
15. the kings of the *earth*, and the great men,

7: 1. standing on the four corners of the *earth*,
holding the four winds of the *earth*, that
the wind should not blow on the *earth*,
2. it was given to hurt the *earth*
3. Saying, Hurt not the *earth*, neither
8: 5. cast (it) into the *earth:* and there were
7. blood, and they were cast upon the *earth:*
13. woe, to the inhabiters of the *earth* by
9: 1. a star fall from heaven unto the *earth:*
3. of the smoke locusts upon the *earth:*
— as the scorpions of the *earth* have power.
4. should not hurt the grass of the *earth*,
10: 2. (his) left (foot) on the *earth*,
5. stand upon the sea and upon the *earth*
6. the *earth*, and the things that therein are,
8. standeth upon the sea and upon the *earth*.
11: 4. standing before the God of the *earth*.
6. to smite the *earth* with all plagues,
10. they that dwell upon the *earth* shall
— tormented them that dwelt on the *earth*.
18. destroy them which destroy the *earth*.
12: 4. did cast them to the *earth:*
9. he was cast out into the *earth*,
12. Woe to the inhabiters of the *earth*
13. saw that he was cast unto the *earth*,
16. the *earth* helped the woman, and the *earth*
opened her mouth,
13: 3. all the *world* wondered after
8. all that dwell upon the *earth*
11. beast coming up out of the *earth;*
12. causeth the *earth* and them which
13. from heaven on the *earth* in the
14. deceiveth them that dwell on the *earth*
14: 3. which were redeemed from the *earth*.
6. unto them that dwell on the *earth*,
7. him, that made heaven, and *earth*,
15. for the harvest of the *earth* is ripe.
16. thrust in his sickle on the *earth;* and the
earth was reaped.
18. the clusters of the vine of the *earth;*
19. angel thrust in his sickle into the *earth*,
and gathered the vine of the *earth*,
16: 1. the wrath of God upon the *earth*.
2. poured out his vial upon the *earth;*
14. unto the kings of the *earth* and of
18. not since men were upon the *earth*,
17: 2. With whom the kings of the *earth*
— the inhabitants of the *earth* have
5. OF HARLOTS AND ABOMINATIONS
OF THE *EARTH*
8. they that dwell on the *earth* shall
18. reigneth over the kings of the *earth*.
18: 1. the *earth* was lightened with his glory.
3. the kings of the *earth* have committed
— the merchants of the *earth* are waxed
9. the kings of the *earth*, who have
11. the merchants of the *earth* shall weep
23. were the great men of the *earth;* for
24. all that were slain upon the *earth*.
19: 2. which did corrupt the *earth* with
19. the beast, and the kings of the *earth*,
20: 8. in the four quarters of the *earth*,
9. up on the breadth of the *earth*,
11. the *earth* and the heaven fled away;
21: 1. I saw a new heaven and a new *earth:* for
the first heaven and the first *earth* were
24. the kings of the *earth* do bring their

1094 1 156/163 cf 1088

γῆρας, *geeras.*

Lu. 1:36. also conceived a son in her *old age*.

1095 /163 1094

γηράσκω, *geerasko.*

Joh. 21:18. when thou *shalt be old*, thou shalt
Heb. 8:13. that which decayeth and *waxeth old*

1096 677 157/164 1:681

γίνομαι, *ginomai.*

Mat. 1:22. Now all this *was done*, that it
4: 3. command that these stones *be made* bread.
5:18. from the law, till all *be fulfilled*.
45. ye *may be* the children of your Father
6:10. Thy will *be done* in earth, as (it is)
16. when ye fast, *be* not, as the hypocrites,
7:28. it *came to pass*, when Jesus had
8:13. thou hast believed, (so) *be* it *done* unto
thee.
16. *When* the even *was come*, they brought
24. *there arose* a great tempest in the sea,
26. the sea; and there *was* a great calm.
9:10. it *came to pass*, as Jesus sat at
16. the garment, and the rent *is made* worse.
29. According to your faith *be* it unto you.
10:16. *be* ye therefore wise as serpents,
25. the disciple that he *be* as his master,
11: 1. it *came to pass*, when Jesus had made
20. most of his mighty works *were done*,
21. the mighty works, *which were done* in you,
had been done in Tyre
23. mighty works, *which have been done* in thee,
had been done in Sodom,
26. for so it *seemeth* good in thy sight.
12:45. the last (state) of that man *is* worse
13:21. *when* tribulation or persecution *ariseth*
22. choke the word, and he *becometh* unfruitful
32. greatest among herbs, and *becometh* a tree
53. it *came to pass*, (that) when Jesus
14:15. *when* it *was* evening, his disciples
23. *when* the evening *was come*, he was
15:28. *be* it unto thee even as thou wilt.
16: 2. said unto them, *When* it *is* evening,
17: 2. his raiment *was* white as the light.
18: 3. converted, and *become* as little children,
12. if a man *have* an hundred sheep,
13. if so *be* that he find it, verily I say
19. it *shall be done* for them of my Father
31. his fellowservants saw *what was done*,
— unto their lord all *that was done*.
19: 1. it *came to pass*, (that) when Jesus
8. from the beginning it *was* not so.
20: 8. So *when* even *was come* the lord of
26. whosoever will *be* great among you,
21: 4. All this *was done*, that it might
19. *Let* no fruit *grow* on thee henceforward
21. thou cast into the sea; it *shall be done*.
42. the same *is become* the head of the corner:
this *is* the Lord's *doing*, and it is marvellous
23:15. when he *is made*, ye make him
26. the outside of them *may be* clean also
24: 6. (these things) must *come to pass*,
20. that your flight *be* not in the winter,
21. such as *was* not since the beginning
— to this time, no, nor ever *shall be*.
32. When his branch *is* yet tender,
34. till all these things *be fulfilled*.
44. Therefore *be* ye also ready: for in
25: 6. at midnight there *was* a cry *made*,
26: 1. it *came to pass*, when Jesus had
2. after two days *is* (the feast of) the
5. lest there *be* an uproar among the people.
6. *when* Jesus *was* in Bethany, in the
20. Now *when* the even *was come*,

Mat.26:42. except I drink it, thy will *be done.*
54. scriptures be fulfilled, that thus it must *be?*
56. all this *was done,* that the scriptures
27: 1. *When* the morning *was come,*
24. (that) rather a tumult *was made,*
45. there *was* darkness over all the land
54. those things *that were done,* they
57. *When* the even *was come,* there
28: 2. behold, there *was* a great earthquake:
4. keepers did shake, and *became* as dead (men).
11. all the things *that were done.*
Mar.1. 4. John *did* baptize in the wilderness
9. it *came to pass* in those days,
11. there *came* a voice from heaven,
17. I will make you *to become* fishers of men.
32. at (lit. *when* it *was*) even, when the sun
2:15. it *came to pass,* that, as Jesus sat
21. the rent *is made* worse.
23. it *came to pass,* that he went
27. The sabbath *was made* for man,
4: 4. it *came to pass,* as he sowed, some
10. when he *was* alone, they that were
11. all (these) things *are done* in parables:
17. *when* affliction or persecution *ariseth* for
19. choke the word, and it *becometh* unfruitful.
22. neither *was* any thing *kept* secret,
32. *becometh* greater than all herbs,
35. same day, *when* the even *was come,*
37. there *arose* a great storm of wind,
39. wind ceased, and there *was* a great calm.
5:14. to see what it was *that was done.*
16. *befell* to him that was possessed with the
33. knowing what *was done* in her,
6: 2. *when* the sabbath day *was come,*
— mighty works *are wrought* by his hands?
14. for his name *was* spread abroad:
21. *when* a convenient day *was come,*
26. the king *was* exceeding sorry; (yet)
35. *when* the day *was* now far spent,
47. *when* even *was come,* the ship
9: 3. his raiment *became* shining,
7. there *was* a cloud that overshadowed
21. since this *came* unto him? And he said,
26. out of him: and he *was* as one dead;
33. *being* in the house he asked them,
50. if the salt have lost his saltness, (lit. *be* saltless)
10:43. whosoever will *be* great among you,
44. whosoever of you will *be* the chiefest,
11:19. when even *was come,* he went out
23. things which he saith *shall come to pass;*
12:10. *is become* the head of the corner:
11. This *was* the Lord's *doing,* and it is
13: 7. for (such things) must needs *be;*
18. that your flight *be* not in the winter.
19. such as *was* not from the beginning
— unto this time, neither *shall be.*
28. When her branch *is* yet tender,
29. shall see these things *come to pass,*
30. till all these things *be done.*
14: 4. Why *was* this waste of the ointment *made?*
17. in the evening (lit. *when* it *was*) he cometh with
15:33. *when* the sixth hour *was come,* there *was*
42. now *when* the even *was come,*
16:10. them that *had been* with him, as
Lu. 1: 2. *which* from the beginning *were*
5. There *was* in the days of Herod, the
8. it *came to pass,* that while he
20. these things *shall be performed,*
23. it *came to pass,* that, as soon as the

Lu. 1:38. *be* it unto me according to thy word.
41. it *came to pass,* that, when Elisabeth
44. as soon as the voice...sounded (lit. *was*) in mine ears,
59. it *came to pass,* that on the eighth
65. fear *came* on all that dwelt round
2: 1. it *came to pass* in those days, that
2. this taxing *was* first *made*
6. so it *was,* that, while they were there,
13. suddenly there *was* with the angel
15. it *came to pass,* as the angels were
— this thing *which is come to pass,*
42. when he *was* twelve years old, they
46. it *came to pass,* that after three days
3: 2. the word of God *came* unto John the
21. it *came to pass,* that Jesus also being
22. a voice *came* from heaven, which said,
4: 3. this stone that it *be made* bread.
23. we have heard *done* in Capernaum,
25. great famine *was* throughout all the land;
36. they *were* all amazed, and spake among
42. *when* it *was* day, he departed and went
5: 1. it *came to pass,* that, as the people pressed
12. it *came to pass,* when he was in a
17. it *came to pass* on a certain day, as he was
6: 1. it *came to pass* on the second sabbath
6. it *came to pass* also on another sabbath,
12. it *came to pass* in those days, that he
13. when it *was* day, he called (unto him)
16. Judas Iscariot, which also *was* the traitor.
36. *Be* ye therefore merciful, as your Father
48. *when* the flood *arose,* the stream beat
49. the ruin of that house *was* great.
7:11. it *came to pass* the day after, that
8: 1. it *came to pass* afterward, that he
17. that *shall* not *be made* manifest;
22. Now it *came to pass* on a certain day,
24. they ceased, and there *was* a calm.
34. that fed (them) saw *what was done,*
35. they went out to see *what was done;*
40. it *came to pass,* that, when Jesus
56. should tell no man *what was done.*
9: 7. heard of all *that was done* by him:
18. it *came to pass,* as he was alone
28. it *came to pass* about an eight days
29. as he prayed, the fashion of his countenance *was*
33. it *came to pass,* as they departed from him,
34. there *came* a cloud, and overshadowed them:
35. there *came* a voice out of the cloud,
36. when the voice *was past,* Jesus
37. it *came to pass,* that on the next day,
51. it *came to pass,* when the time was come
57. it *came to pass,* that, as they went
10:13. the mighty works *had been done* in Tyre and Sidon, *which have been done* in you,
21. for so it seemed (lit. *was*) good in thy
32. a Levite, *when* he *was* at the place,
36. *was* neighbour unto him that fell
38. it *came to pass,* as they went, that
11: 1. it *came to pass,* that, as he was
2. Thy will *be done,* as in heaven, so in earth.
14. it *came to pass,* when the devil was
26. last (state) of that man *is* worse than the first.
27. it *came to pass,* as he spake these
30. as Jonas *was* a sign unto the Ninevites,
12:40. *Be* ye therefore ready also: for the Son of
54. ye say, There cometh a shower; and so it *is.*

Lu. 12:55. There will be heat; and it *cometh to pass.*
13: 2. *were* sinners above all the Galilæans,
4. think ye that they *were* sinners above
17. glorious things *that were done* by him.
19. it grew, and *waxed* a great tree; and the
14: 1. it *came to pass,* as he went into the
12. bid thee again, and a recompence *be made* thee.
22. Lord, it *is done* as thou hast commanded,
15:10. there *is* joy in the presence of the angels
14. there *arose* a mighty famine in that
16:11. If therefore ye *have* not *been* faithful in
12. if ye *have* not *been* faithful in that
22. it *came to pass,* that the beggar died.
17:11. it *came to pass,* as he went to
14. it *came to pass,* that, as they went,
26. as it *was* in the days of Noe, so shall
28. also as it *was* in the days of Lot;
18:23. heard this, he *was* very sorrowful:
24. Jesus saw *that* he *was* very sorrowful,
35. it *came to pass,* that as he was come
19: 9. This day *is* salvation *come* to this house,
15. it *came to pass,* that when he was
17. because thou *hast been* faithful
19. *Be* thou also over five cities.
29. it *came to pass,* when he was come
20: 1. it *came to pass,* (that) on one of those
14. that the inheritance *may be* our's.
16. they heard (it), they said, God forbid. (lit. *be it* not)
17. the same *is become* the head of the
33. whose wife of them *is* she? for
21: 7. when these things shall *come to pass?*
9. these things must first *come to pass;*
28. these things begin to *come to pass,*
31. see these things *come to pass,* know
32. not pass away, till all *be fulfilled.*
36. these things that shall *come to pass,*
22:14. when the hour *was come,* he sat down,
24. there *was* also a strife among them,
26. *let* him *be* as the younger; and he
40. *when* he *was* at the place, he said
42. not my will, but thine, *be done.*
44. *being* in an agony he prayed more earnestly: and his sweat *was* as it were great drops
66. as soon as it *was* day, the elders
23. 8. have seen some miracle *done* by him.
12. Pilate and Herod *were made* friends together:
19. a certain sedition *made* in the city,
24. that it should *be* as they required.
31. what *shall be done* in the dry?
44. there *was* a darkness over all the earth
47. the centurion saw *what was done,*
48. beholding the things *which were done,*
24: 4. it *came to pass,* as they were much
5. *as* they *were* afraid, and bowed down
12. at that *which was come to pass.*
15. it *came to pass,* that, while they communed
18. things *which are come to pass* there
19. which *was* a prophet mighty in deed
21. third day since these things *were done.*
22. *which were* early at the sepulchre;
30. it *came to pass,* as he sat at meat
31. he vanished out of their sight. (lit. he *was* vanished)
37. they *were* terrified and affrighted, *and*
51. it *came to pass,* while he blessed
Joh. 1: 3. All things *were made* by him; .... *was* not any thing *made* that *was made.*
Joh. 1: 6. There *was* a man sent from God,
10. the world *was made* by him, and the
12. power *to become* the sons of God,
14. the Word *was made* flesh, and dwelt
15. after me *is preferred* before me:
17. grace and truth *came* by Jesus Christ.
27. coming after me *is preferred* before me,
28. These things *were done* in Bethabara
30. a man which *is preferred* before me,
2: 1. the third day there *was a* marriage
9. tasted the water *that was made* wine,
3: 9. unto him, How can these things *be?*
25. there *arose* a question between (some)
4:14. *shall be* in him a well of water
5: 4. *was made* whole of whatsoever disease
6. unto him, Wilt thou *be made* whole?
9. immediately the man *was made* whole,
14. Behold, thou *art made* whole: sin no more, lest a worse thing *come* unto thee.
6:16. when even *was* (now) *come,* his
17. it *was* now dark, and Jesus was not
19. on the sea, and *drawing* nigh unto the ship:
21. immediately the ship *was* at the land
25. Rabbi, when *camest* thou hither?
7:43. there *was* a division among the people
8:33. sayest thou, Ye *shall be made* free?
58. Before Abraham *was,* I am.
9:22. he *should be* put out of the synagogue.
27. will ye also *be* his disciples?
39. they which see *might be made* blind.
10:16. there *shall be* one fold, (and) one shepherd.
19. There *was* a division therefore again
22. it *was* at Jerusalem the feast of
35. unto whom the word of God *came,*
12:29. heard (it), said that it thundered: (lit. that there *was* thunder)
30. This voice *came* not because of me,
36. that ye *may be* the children of light.
42. lest they *should be* put out of the
13: 2. supper *being ended,* the devil having
19. Now I tell you before it *come,* that, when it *is come to pass,* ye may
14:22. Lord, how *is* it that thou wilt manifest
29. I have told you before it *come to pass,* that, when it *is come to pass,* ye might
15: 7. it *shall be done* unto you.
8. so *shall* ye *be* my disciples.
16:20. your sorrow *shall be turned* into joy.
19:36. these things *were done,* that the
20:27. *be* not faithless, but believing.
21: 4. *when* the morning *was* now *come,*
Acts 1:16. Judas, *which was* guide to them
18. *falling* headlong, he burst asunder
19. it *was* known unto all the dwellers
20. *Let* his habitation *be* desolate, and let
22. must one *be ordained to be* a witness
2: 2. suddenly there *came* a sound from
6. *when* this *was* noised abroad, the
43. fear *came* upon every soul: and many wonders and signs *were done* by the apostles.
4: 4. the number of the men *was* about
5. it *came to pass* on the morrow,
11. *which is become* the head of the corner.
16. miracle *hath been done* by them
21. glorified God for that *which was done.*
22. this miracle of healing *was shewed.*
28. counsel determined before *to be done.*
30. signs and wonders may *be done* by the

Acts 5: 5. great fear *came* on all them
7. it *was* about the space of three hours
— not knowing *what was done*,
11. great fear *came* upon all the church,
12. *were* many signs and wonders *wrought*
24. of them whereunto this *would grow*.
36. were scattered, *and brought* to nought.
6: 1. there *arose* a murmuring of the
7: 13. Joseph's kindred *was made* known
29. *was* a stranger in the land of Madian,
31. voice of the Lord *came* unto him,
32. Then Moses trembled (lit. *was* trembling), *and* durst not behold.
38. This is he, *that was* in the church
39. To whom our fathers would not obey, (lit. *be* obedient)
40. we wot not what *is become* of him.
52. of whom ye *have been* now the betrayers
8: 1. at that time there *was* a great
8. there *was* great joy in that city.
13. the miracles and signs *which were done*.
9: 3. as he journeyed,)(he came near
19. Then *was* Saul certain days with
32. it *came to pass*, as Peter passed
37. it *came to pass* in those days,
42. it *was* known throughout all Joppa;
43. it *came to pass*, that he tarried many
10: 4. when he looked on him, he *was* afraid, *and*
10. he *became* very hungry, and would
13. there *came* a voice to him, Rise,
16. This *was done* thrice: and the vessel
25. as Peter *was* coming in, Cornelius
37. *which was published* throughout
40. third day, and shewed him openly; (lit. made him *to be* manifest)
11: 10. this *was done* three times: and all
19. scattered abroad upon the persecution *that arose* about Stephen
26. it *came to pass*, that a whole year
28. which *came to pass* in the days of
12: 5. prayer was *made* without ceasing
9. *which was done* by the angel;
11. *when* Peter *was come* to himself,
18. *as soon as* it *was* day, there was
— the soldiers, what *was become* of Peter.
23. he *was* eaten of worms, *and* gave up the ghost.
13: 5. *when* they *were* at Salamis, they
12. when he saw *what was done*, believed,
32. the promise *which was made*
14: 1. it *came to pass* in Iconium, that
3. signs and wonders *to be done* by their hands.
5. there *was* an assault *made* both of the
15: 2. *When* therefore Paul and Barnabas *had* no small
7. *when* there *had been* much disputing,
25. *being assembled* with one accord,
39. the contention *was* so sharp between
16: 16. it *came to pass*, as we went to prayer,
26. suddenly there *was* a great earthquake,
27. keeper of the prison awaking (lit. *being* awaked) out of his sleep,
29. sprang in, and *came* trembling, *and*
35. *when* it *was* day, the magistrates
19: 1. it *came to pass*, that, while Apollos
10. this *continued* by the space of two years,
17. this *was* known to all the Jews
21. After I *have been* there, I must
23. same time there *arose* no small
26. no gods, *which are made* with hands:
28. they *were* full of wrath, and cried out,

Acts 19: 34. was a Jew, all with one voice ..cried o (lit. there *was* from all &c.)
20: 3. when the Jews laid wait for him, (lit. *when* there *was* a laying in wait)
— he purposed (lit. there *was* the purpose) to return through
16. he *would* not spend the time in
— *to be* at Jerusalem the day of
18. I *have been* with you at all seasons,
37. they all wept (lit. there *was* a weeping) sore,
21: 1. it *came to pass*, that after we were
5. when we (lit. it *was* that we) had accomplished those
14. The will of the Lord *be done*.
17. *when* we *were come* to Jerusalem,
30. city was moved, and the people ran (lit. there *was* a concourse) together:
35. when he *came* upon the stairs,
40. *when* there *was made* a great silence,
22: 6. it *came to pass*, that, as I made my
9. saw indeed the light, and *were* afraid;
17. it *came to pass*, that, when I was
— in the temple, I *was* in a trance;
23: 7. there *arose* a dissension between the
9. there *arose* a great cry: and the scribes
10. *when* there *arose* a great dissension,
12. *when* it *was* day, certain of the Jews
24: 2. very worthy deeds are *done* unto this
25. Felix trembled (lit. *having become* alarmed), and answered, Go thy way
25: 15. About whom, *when* I *was* at Jerusalem,
26. *after* examination *had*, I might
26: 4. *which was* at the first among mine
6. hope of the promise *made* of God
19. I *was* not disobedient unto the
22. prophets and Moses did say should *come*.
28. thou persuadest me *to be* a Christian.
29. *were* both almost, and altogether such as I am,
27: 7. scarce *were come* over against Cnidus,
16. much work *to come* by the boat:
27. when the fourteenth night *was come*,
29. of the stern, and wished for (lit. it *to be*) the day.
33. while the day was coming on, (lit. about *to be*)
36. *Then were* they all of good cheer,
39. when it *was* day, they knew not
42. the soldiers' counsel *was* to kill
44. so it *came to pass*, that they
28: 6. saw no harm *come* to him,
8. it *came to pass*, that the father
9. So *when* this *was done*, others also,
17. it *came to pass*, that after three

Ro. 1: 3. *which was made* of the seed of David
2: 25. thy circumcision *is made* uncircumcision.
3: 4. God forbid (lit. *let* it not *be*): *let* God *be* true, but every man a liar;
6. God forbid (lit. *let &c.*): for then how
19. all the world *may become* guilty
31. God forbid (lit. *let &c.*): yea, we establish
4: 18. that he might *become* the father
6: 2. God forbid (lit. *let &c*). How shall we, that
5. if we *have been* planted together
15. but under grace? God forbid. (lit. *let &c.*)
7: 3. she *be married* to another man,
— *though* she *be married* to another
4. that ye should *be married* to another,
7. (Is) the law sin? God forbid. (lit. *let &c.*)
13. *made* death unto me? God forbid. (lit. *let &c.*)

Ro. 7:13. *might become* exceeding sinful.
9:14. unrighteousness with God? God forbid. (lit. *may* it not *be*)
29. we *had been* as Sodoma,
10:20. I *was made* manifest unto them
11: 1. God cast away his people? God forbid. (lit. *may, &c.*)
5. there *is* a remnant according
6. otherwise grace *is* no more grace.
9. *Let* their table *be made* a snare, and a
11. stumbled that they should fall? God forbid: (lit. *may, &c.*)
17. and with them partakest (lit. *be* partaker) of the root
25. blindness in part *is happened* to Israel,
34. or who *hath been* his counsellor?
12:16. *Be* not wise in your own conceits.
15: 8. Jesus Christ *was* a minister of the
16. offering up of the Gentiles *might be*
31. *may be* accepted of the saints;
16: 2. she *hath been* a succourer of many,
7. who also *were* in Christ before me.
1Co. 1:30. who of God *is made* unto us wisdom,
2: 3. I *was* with you in weakness, and in
3:13. Every man's work *shall be made*
18. *let* him *become* a fool, that he *may be* wise.
4: 5. then *shall* every man *have* praise
9. we *are made* a spectacle unto the
13. we *are made* as the filth of the world,
16. I beseech you, *be* ye followers of me.
6:15. the members of an harlot? God forbid. (lit. *may, &c.*)
7:21. if thou mayest *be made* free,
23. *be* not ye the servants of men.
36. need so require, (lit. it so *to be*) let him do what
8: 9. *become* a stumblingblock to them
9:15. that it *should be* so *done* unto me:
20. unto the Jews I *became* as a Jew,
22. To the weak *became* I as weak,
— I *am made* all things to all
23. that I *might be* partaker thereof
27. I myself *should be* a castaway.
10: 6. these things *were* our examples,
7. Neither *be* ye idolaters, as (were)
20. ye should have fellowship (lit. *be* partakers)
32. Give none offence (lit. *be* without offence), neither to the Jews,
11. 1. *Be* ye followers of me, even as
19. *may be made* manifest among you.
13: 1. I *am become* (as) sounding brass,
11. when I *became* a man, I put
14:20. *be* not children in understanding:
— in understanding *be* men.
25. *are* the secrets of his heart *made* manifest;
26. *Let* all things *be done* unto edifying.
40. *Let* all things *be done* decently
15:10. (bestowed) upon me *was* not in vain;
20. (and) *become* the firstfruits of them
37. thou sowest not that body *that shall be*,
45. Adam *was made* a living soul;
54. then *shall be brought to pass* the
58. my beloved brethren, *be* ye stedfast,
16: 2. that there *be* no gatherings when
10. that he *may be* with you without
14 *Let* all your things *be done* with charity.
2Co. 1: 8. trouble *which came* to us in Asia,
18. our word toward you *was* not yea and nay.
19. *was* not yea and nay, but in him *was* yea.
3: 7. written (and) engraven in stones *was* glorious,
5:17. behold, all things *are become* new
2Co. 5:21. we *might be made* the righteousness
6:14. *Be* ye not unequally yoked together
7:14. which (I made) before Titus, *is found* a truth.
8:14. that their abundance also *may be*
— that there *may be* equality:
12:11. I *am become* a fool in glorying;
Gal. 2:17. minister of sin? God forbid. (lit. *may, &c.*)
3:13. *being made* a curse for us: for it is
14. blessing of Abraham *might come* on the
17. the law, *which was* four hundred
21. against the promises of God? God forbid (lit. *may, &c.*)
24. the law *was* our schoolmaster
4: 4. his Son, *made* of a woman, *made* under
12. Brethren, I beseech you, *be* as I (am);
16. *Am* I therefore *become* your enemy,
5. 26. *Let* us not *be* desirous of vain glory,
6:14. God forbid (lit. *may* it not *be*) that I should glory,
Eph. 2:13. *are made* nigh by the blood of Christ.
3: 7. Whereof I *was made* a minister,
4:32. *be* ye kind one to another, tenderhearted,
5: 1. *Be* ye therefore followers of God, as
7. *Be* not ye therefore partakers with
12. those things *which are done* of them
17. Wherefore *be* ye not unwise but
6: 3. That it *may be* well with thee,
Phi. 1:13. my bonds in Christ *are* manifest
2: 7. *and was made* in the likeness of men:
8. *and became* obedient unto death,
15. That ye *may be* blameless and harmless,
3: 6. which is in the law,)(blameless.
17. Brethren, *be* followers together of me,
21. that it may *be* fashioned like unto
Col. 1:18. he *might have* the preeminence.
23. whereof I Paul *am made* a minister;
25. Whereof I *am made* a minister,
3:15. called in one body; and *be* ye thankful.
4:11. which *have been* a comfort unto me.
1Th. 1: 5. our gospel *came* not unto you
— what manner of men we *were*
6. ye *became* followers of us, and of the
7. So that ye *were* ensamples to all
2: 1. unto you, that it *was* not in vain:
5. at any time used we (lit. *were* we in) flattering words,
7. we *were* gentle among you,
8. because ye *were* dear unto us.
10. unblameably we *behaved ourselves*
14. ye, brethren, *became* followers of the
3: 4. even as it *came to pass*, and ye know.
5. tempted you, and our labour *be* in vain.
2Th. 2: 7. until he *be taken* out of the way.
1Ti. 2:14. deceived *was* in the transgression.
4:12. *be* thou an example of the believers,
5: 9. *having been* the wife of one man,
6: 4. strifes of words, whereof *cometh* envy, strife,
2Ti. 1:17. *when* he was in Rome, he sought me
2:18. that the resurrection is *past* already;
3: 9. manifest unto all (men), as their's also *was*.
11. afflictions, which *came* unto me at Antioch,
Tit. 3: 7. we *should be made* heirs according
Philem. 6. thy faith *may become* effectual by
Heb 1: 4. *Being made* so much better than
2: 2. word spoken by angels *was* stedfast.
17. that he *might be* a merciful and faithful
3:14. we *are made* partakers of Christ,
4: 3. although the works *were finished* from
5: 5. himself *to be made* an high priest:

Heb. 5: 9. he *became* the author of eternal
11. seeing ye *are* dull of hearing.
12. *are become* such as have need of milk,
6: 4. *were made* partakers of the Holy Ghost,
12. That ye *be* not slothful, but followers
20. Jesus, *made* an high priest for ever
7:12. there *is made* of necessity a change
16. Who *is made* not after the law of a
18. For there *is* verily a disannulling of
21(20). those priests *were made* without an oath;
22. By so much *was* Jesus *made* a surety
23. they truly were (lit. are *made*) many priests,
26. *made* higher than the heavens;
9:15. that by means of death (lit. death *having taken place*), for the
22. without shedding of blood *is* no remission.
10:33. *whilst* ye *became* companions of
11: 3. *were* not *made* of things which do appear.
6. he *is* a rewarder of them that
7. *became* heir of the righteousness
24. Moses, *when* he *was come* to years,
34. made strong, *waxed* valiant in fight,
12: 8. whereof all *are* partakers, then
Jas. 1:12. for *when* he *is* tried, he shall receive
22. *be* ye doers of the word, and not hearers
25. he *being* not a forgetful hearer,
2: 4. *are become* judges of evil thoughts?
10. in one (point), he *is* guilty of all.
11. thou *art become* a transgressor of the law.
3: 1. My brethren, *be* not many masters,
9. *which are made* after the similitude
10. these things ought not so *to be*.
5: 2. your garments *are* motheaten.
1Pet. 1:15. so *be* ye holy in all manner of
16. Because it is written, *Be* ye holy;
2: 7. the same *is made* the head of the
3: 6. whose daughters ye *are*, as long
13. if ye *be* followers of that which is good?
4:12. the fiery trial *which is* to try you,
5: 3. *being* ensamples to the flock.
2Pet. 1: 4. by these ye *might be* partakers of the
16. *were* eyewitnesses of his majesty.
20. no prophecy of the scripture *is* of any private
2: 1. there *were* false prophets also among
20. the latter end *is* worse with them
1Joh. 2:18. even now *are* there many antichrists;
3Joh. 8. that we *might be* fellowhelpers
Rev. 1: 1. things which must shortly *come to pass*;
9. *was* in the isle that is called Patmos,
10. I *was* in the Spirit on the Lord's day,
18. (I am) he that liveth, and *was* dead;
19. the things which shall *be* hereafter;
2: 8. which *was* dead, and is alive;
10. *be* thou faithful unto death, and I will
3: 2. *Be* watchful, and strengthen the things
4: 1. things which must *be* hereafter.
2. immediately I *was* in the spirit:
6:12. *there was* a great earthquake; and the sun *became* black as sackcloth of hair, and the moon *became* as blood;
8: 1. there *was* silence in heaven about
5. there *were* voices, and thunderings,
7. there *followed* hail and fire mingled
8. third part of the sea *became* blood;
11. part of the waters *became* wormwood;
11:13. same hour *was* there a great earthquake,
— the remnant *were* affrighted,
15. there *were* great voices in heaven, saying, The kingdoms of this world *are become*
Rev. 11:19. there *were* lightnings, and voices,
12: 7. there *was* war in heaven:
10. Now *is come* salvation, and strength,
16: 2. there *fell* a noisome and grievous
3. it *became* as the blood of a dead (man).
4. fountains of waters; and they *became* blood.
10. his kingdom *was* full of darkness;
17. from the throne, saying, It *is done*.
18. there *were* voices, and thunders,
— there *was* a great earthquake, such as *was* not since men *were* upon the earth,
19. the great city *was divided* into
18: 2. *is become* the habitation of devils,
21: 6. he said unto me, It *is done*.
22: 6. things which must shortly *be done*.

1097 223 159/170 1:689

γινώσκ-ω & -ομαι, *ginōsk-ō* & *-omai*.

Mat. 1:25. *knew* her not till she had brought
6: 3. *let* not thy left hand *know* what
7:23. profess unto them, I never *knew* you.
9:30. saying, See (that) no man *know* (it).
10:26. hid, that *shall* not *be known*.
12: 7. if ye *had known* what (this) meaneth,
15. *when* Jesus *knew* (it), he withdrew
33. the tree *is known* by (his) fruit.
13:11. given unto you *to know* the mysteries
16: 3. ye can (lit. *know* how to) discern the face of the sky;
8. (Which) *when* Jesus *perceived*, he said
21:45. they *perceived* that he spake of them.
22:18. Jesus *perceived* their wickedness, *and*
24:32. ye *know* that summer (is) nigh:
33. these things, *know* that it is near,
39. *knew* not until the flood came,
43. *know* this, that if the goodman
50. in an hour that he *is* not *aware of*,
25:24. Lord, I *knew* thee that thou art an
26:10. *When* Jesus *understood* (it), he said
Mar 4:11. *to know* the mystery of the kingdom
13. how then *will* ye *know* all parables?
5:29. she *felt* in (her) body that she was
43. that no man *should know* it;
6:38. And *when* they *knew*, they say, Five,
7:24. would have no man *know* (it):
8:17. *when* Jesus *knew* (it), he saith unto
9:30. that any man *should know* (it).
12:12. they *knew* that he had spoken the
13:28. ye *know* that summer is near:
29. come to pass, *know* that it is nigh,
15:10. he *knew* that the chief priests
45. *when* he *knew* (it) of the centurion,
Lu. 1:18. Whereby *shall* I *know* this?
34. this be, seeing I *know* not a man?
2:43. Joseph and his mother *knew* not (of it).
6:44. every tree *is known* by his own
7:39. would *have known* who and what
8:10. Unto you it is given *to know*
17. that *shall* not *be known* and come
46. for I *perceive* that virtue is gone
9:11. the people, *when* they *knew* (it),
10:11. *be* ye *sure* of this, that the kingdom
22. no man *knoweth* who the Son is,
12: 2. neither hid, that *shall* not *be known*.
39. this *know*, that if the goodman
46. at an hour when he *is* not *aware*,
47. servant, *which knew* his lord's will,
48. he *that knew* not, and did commit
16: 4. I *am resolved* what to do,
15. God *knoweth* your hearts: for

Lu. 18:34. neither *knew* they the things which
19:15. that he *might know* how much
42. Saying, If thou *hadst known*,
44. thou *knewest* not the time of thy
20:19. they *perceived* that he had spoken
21:20. then *know* that the desolation
30. ye see and *know* of your own selves
31. *know* ye that the kingdom of God
24:18. *hast* not *known* the things
35. how he *was known* of them in
Joh 1:10. the world *knew* him not.
48(49). unto him, Whence *knowest* thou me?
2:24. unto them, because he *knew* all
25. for he *knew* what was in man.
3:10. a master of Israel, and *knowest* not these things?
4: 1. When therefore the Lord *knew* how
53. So the father *knew* that (it was)
5: 6. and *knew* that he had been now a
42. I *know* you, that ye have not
6:15. *When* Jesus therefore *perceived* that
69. we believe and *are sure* that thou
7:17. he *shall know* of the doctrine,
26. Do the rulers *know* indeed that
27. no man *knoweth* whence he is.
49. this people *who knoweth* not the law
51. before it hear him, and *know*
8:27. They *understood* not that he
28. then *shall* ye *know* that I am
32. ye *shall know* the truth, and the truth
43. Why do ye not *understand* my speech?
52. Now we *know* that thou hast a devil.
55. Yet ye *have* not *known* him;
10: 6. they *understood* not what things
14. *know* my (sheep), and *am known* of mine.
15. As the Father *knoweth* me, even so *know* I the Father:
27. I *know* them, and they follow me:
38. believe the works: that ye *may know*,
11:57. if any man *knew* where he were,
12: 9. of the Jews therefore *knew* that he
16. These things *understood* not his disciples
13: 7. thou *shalt know* hereafter.
12. *Know* ye what I have done
28. no man at the table *knew*
35. this *shall* all (men) *know* that
14: 7. If ye *had known* me, ye should *have known* my Father also: and from henceforth ye *know* him,
9. *hast* thou not *known* me,
17. neither *knoweth* him: but ye *know*
20. At that day ye *shall know* that
31. that the world *may know* that
15:18. ye *know* that it hated me
16: 3. they *have* not *known* the Father,
19. Jesus *knew* that they were desirous
17: 3. that they *might know* thee the only true
7. they *have known* that all things
8. and *have known* surely that I
23. that the world *may know* that
25. the world *hath* not *known* thee: but I *have known* thee, and these *have known* that
19: 4. that ye *may know* that I find no fault
21:17. thou *knowest* that I love thee.
Acts 1: 7. not for you *to know* the times
2:36. *let* all the house of Israel *know* assuredly,
8:30. *Understandest* thou what thou
9:24. their laying await *was known*
17:13. Jews of Thessalonica *had knowledge*
19. May we *know* what this new
20. we would *know* therefore what these
19:15. evil spirit answered and said. Jesus I *know*.

Acts 19:35. that *knoweth* not how that the city
20:34. ye yourselves *know*, that these hands
21:24. all *may know* that those things,
34. when he could not *know* the certainty
37. Who said, *Canst* thou *speak* Greek?
22:14. that thou shouldest *know* his will,
30. would *have known* the certainty
23: 6. *when* Paul *perceived* that the one
28. when I would *have known* the cause
24:11. Because that thou mayest *understand*,
Ro. 1:21. *when* they *knew* God, they glorified
2:18. *knowest* (his) will, and approvest the
3:17. way of peace *have* they not *known*:
6: 6. *Knowing* this, that our old man
7: 1. I speak to them *that know* the law,
7. I *had* not *known* sin, but by the
15. that which I do I *allow* not: for what
10:19. I say, *Did* not Israel *know*?
11:34. who *hath known* the mind of the Lord?
1Co. 1:21. the world by wisdom *knew* not God,
2: 8. none of the princes of this world *knew*: for *had* they *known* (it) they would not
14. neither can he *know* (them), because
16. who *hath known* the mind of the Lord,
3:20. The Lord *knoweth* the thoughts of
4:19. *will know*, not the speech of them
8: 2. he *knoweth* nothing yet as he ought *to know*.
3. the same *is known* of him.
13: 9. For we *know* in part, and we prophesy
12. now I *know* in part; but then
14: 7. how *shall* it *be known* what
9. how *shall* it *be known* what is
2Co. 2: 4. that ye *might know* the love
9. that I *might know* the proof of
3: 2. *known* and read of all men:
5:16. though we *have known* Christ after the flesh, yet now henceforth *know* we (him) no more.
21. *who knew* no sin; that we
8: 9. ye *know* the grace of our Lord
13: 6. I trust that ye *shall know* that
Gal. 2: 9. *when...perceived* the grace that was
3: 7. *Know* ye therefore that they which
4: 9. *after* that ye *have known* God, or rather *are known* of God,
Eph. 3:19. *to know* the love of Christ, which
5: 5. this ye *know*, that no whoremonger,
6:22. that ye *might know* our affairs,
Phi. 1:12. I would ye should *understand*,
2:19. good comfort, *when* I *know* your state.
22. ye *know* the proof of him, that,
3:10. That I may *know* him, and the
4: 5. *Let* your moderation *be known*
Col. 4: 8. that he *might know* your estate,
1Th. 3: 5. I sent *to know* your faith, lest by
2Ti. 1:18. at Ephesus, thou *knowest* very well.
2:19. The Lord *knoweth* them that are his.
3: 1. This *know* also, that in the last
Heb. 3:10. they *have* not *known* my ways.
8:11. his brother, saying, *Know* the Lord:
10:34. *knowing* in yourselves that ye have
13:23. *Know* ye that (our) brother Timothy
Jas. 1: 3. *Knowing* (this), that the trying of
2:20. wilt thou *know*, O vain man,
5:20. *Let* him *know*, that he which
2Pet. 1:20. *Knowing* this first, that no prophecy
3: 3. *Knowing* this first, that there shall
1Joh. 2: 3. we *do know* that we *know* (lit. *have kn.*) him,
4. He that saith, I *know* (lit. *have kn.*) him,
5. hereby *know* we that we are in him.
13. because ye *have known* him

1Joh.2: 13. because ye *have known* the Father.
14. because ye *have known* him (that is)
18. we *know* that it is the last time.
29. ye *know* that every one that doeth
3: 1. the world *knoweth* us not, because it *knew* him not.
6. not seen him, neither *known* him.
16. Hereby *perceive* (lit. *have perceived*) we the love (of God),
19. hereby we *know* that we are of
20. than our heart, and *knoweth* all things.
24. hereby we *know* that he abideth
4: 2. Hereby *know* ye the Spirit of God:
6. he *that knoweth* God heareth us;
— Hereby *know* we the spirit of truth,
7. is born of God, and *knoweth* God.
8. He that loveth not *knoweth* (lit. *hath known*) not God;
13. Hereby *know* we that we dwell
16. we *have known* and believed the
5: 2. By this we *know* that we love
20. that we *may know* him that is true,
2Joh. 1. they *that have known* the truth;
Rev. 2:17. which no man *knoweth* saving
23. all the churches *shall know*
24. which *have* not *known* the depths
3: 3. thou shalt not *know* what hour
9. and to *know* that I have loved thee.

1098 1 161/172 cf 1099

γλεῦκος, glūkos.

Acts 2:13. These men are full of *new wine*.

1099 4 161/172

γλυκύς, glukus.

Jas. 3:11. the same place *sweet* (water) and bitter?
12. fountain both yield salt water and *fresh*.
Rev.10: 9. be in thy mouth *sweet* as honey.
10. it was in my mouth *sweet* as honey:

1100 50 161/172 1:719

γλῶσσα, glōssa.

Mar. 7:33. he spit, and touched his *tongue*;
35. the string of his *tongue* was loosed,
16:17. they shall speak with new *tongues*;
Lu. 1:64. his *tongue* (loosed), and he spake, and
16:24. his finger in water, and cool my *tongue*;
Acts 2: 3. there appeared unto them cloven *tongues*
4. began to speak with other *tongues*,
11. hear them speak in our *tongues* the
26. heart rejoice, and my *tongue* was glad;
10:46. they heard them speak with *tongues*
19: 6. they spake with *tongues*, and prophesied.
Ro. 3:13. with their *tongues* they have used deceit;
14:11. every *tongue* shall confess to God.
1Co.12:10. to another (divers) kinds of *tongues*; to another the interpretation of *tongues*:
28. governments, diversities of *tongues*:
30. do all speak with *tongues*? do all
13: 1. I speak with the *tongues* of men and of
8. whether (there be) *tongues*, they shall
14: 2. he that speaketh in an (unknown) *tongue*
4. He that speaketh in an (unknown) *tongue*
5. that ye all spake with *tongues*,
— than he that speaketh with *tongues*,
6. if I come unto you speaking with *tongues*,
9. except ye utter by the *tongue* words
13. that speaketh in an (unknown) *tongue*
1Co.14: 14. if I pray in an (unknown) *tongue*,
18. I speak with *tongues* more than
19. thousand words in an (unknown) *tongue*
22. Wherefore *tongues* are for a sign,
23. all speak with *tongues*, and there
26. hath a doctrine, hath a *tongue*,
27. any man speak in an (unknown) *tongue*,
39. forbid not to speak with *tongues*.
Phi. 2:11. (that) every *tongue* should confess
Jas. 1:26. bridleth not his *tongue*, but
3: 5. so the *tongue* is a little member,
6. the *tongue* (is) a fire, a world of iniquity: so is the *tongue* among our members,
8. the *tongue* can no man tame;
1Pet.3:10. let him refrain his *tongue* from evil,
1Joh.3:18. not love in word, neither in *tongue*;
Rev. 5: 9. out of every kindred, and *tongue*, and
7: 9. kindreds, and people, and *tongues*, stood
10:11. many peoples, and nations, and *tongues*,
11: 9. kindreds and *tongues* and nations shall
13: 7. over all kindreds, and *tongues*, and nations.
14: 6. to every nation, and kindred, and *tongue*,
16:10. they gnawed their *tongues* for pain,
17:15. multitudes, and nations, and *tongues*.

1101 2 161/173 1100,rt2889

γλωσσόκομον, glōssokomon.

Joh.12: 6. he was a thief, and had the *bag*,
13:29. thought, because Judas had the *bag*,

1102 1 162/173 *knaptō* (to tease)

γναφεύς, gnaphūs.

Mar. 9: 3. so as no *fuller* on earth can white them.

1103 4 162/173 1:727 rt 1077

γνήσιος, gneesios.

2Co. 8: 8. to prove the *sincerity* of your love.
Phi. 4: 3. I intreat thee also, *true* yokefellow,
1Ti. 1: 2. Unto Timothy, (my) *own* son in the faith:
Tit. 1: 4. Titus, (mine) *own* son after the common

1104 1 162/173 1103

γνησίως, gneesiōs.

Phi. 2:20. who will *naturally* care for your state. (lit. *sincerely* or *truly*)

1105 1 162/173 cf 3509

γνόφος, gnophos.

Heb 12:18. nor unto *blackness*, and darkness, and

1106 9 162/173 1:689 1097

γνώμη, gnōmee.

Acts20: 3. he purposed (lit. it was his *purpose*) to return
1Co 1:10. same mind and in the same *judgment*.
7:25. yet I give my *judgment*, as one
40. if she so abide, after my *judgment*:
2Co. 8:10. herein I give (my) *advice*: for
Philem 14. without thy *mind* would I do
Rev.17:13. These have one *mind*, and shall
17. in their hearts to fulfil his *will*, and to agree (lit. to form one *judgment*)

1107 24 162/173 1:689 1097

γνωρίζω, *gnōrizo.*

Lu. 2:15. which the Lord *hath made known* unto us.
Joh 15:15. I *have made known* unto you.
17:26. I *have declared* unto them thy name, and *will declare* (it):
Acts 2:28. Thou *hast made known* to me the
Ro. 9:22. *to make* his power *known*, endured
23. that he *might make known* the riches
16:26. *made known* to all nations for
1Co 12: 3. Wherefore I *give you to understand*,
15: 1. brethren, I *declare* unto you the gospel
2Co. 8: 1. we *do* you *to wit* of the grace of God
Gal. 1:11. I *certify* you, brethren, that the
Eph. 1: 9. *Having made known* unto us
3: 3. he *made known* unto me the mystery;
5. *was* not *made known* unto the sons
10. *might be known* by the church
6:19. *to make known* the mystery of
21. *shall make known* to you all things:
Phi. 1:22. what I shall choose I *wot* not.
4: 6. *let* your requests *be made known* unto God.
Col. 1:27. To whom God would *make known*
4: 7. *shall* Tychicus *declare* unto you,
9. They *shall make known* unto you
2Pet. 1:16. when we *made known* unto you

1108 29 162/173 1:689 1097

γνῶσις, *gnōsis.*

Lu. 1:77. To give *knowledge* of salvation
11:52. have taken away the key of *knowledge:*
Ro. 2:20. which hast the form of *knowledge*
11:33. of the wisdom and *knowledge* of God!
15:14. filled with all *knowledge*, able
1Co. 1: 5. all utterance, and (in) all *knowledge;*
8: 1. we know that we all have *knowledge. Knowledge* puffeth up, but charity edifieth.
7. not in every man that *knowledge:*
10. see thee which hast *knowledge* sit
11. through thy *knowledge* shall the
12: 8. to another the word of *knowledge*
13: 2. all mysteries, and all *knowledge;*
8. whether (there be) *knowledge*, it
14: 6. either by revelation, or by *knowledge*,
2Co. 2:14. manifest the savour of his *knowledge*
4: 6. the light of the *knowledge* of the glory
6: 6. by *knowledge*, by longsuffering, by kindness,
8: 7. (in) faith, and utterance, and *knowledge*,
10: 5. against the *knowledge* of God,
11: 6. rude in speech, yet not in *knowledge;*
Eph. 3:19. love of Christ, which passeth *knowledge*,
Phi. 3: 8. excellency of the *knowledge* of Christ
Col. 2: 3. treasures of wisdom and *knowledge*.
1Ti. 6:20. oppositions of *science* falsely so called:
1Pet. 3: 7. dwell with (them) according to *knowledge*,
2Pet. 1: 5. your faith, virtue; and to virtue *knowledge;*
6. to *knowledge* temperance; and to
3:18. (in) the *knowledge* of our Lord and Saviour

1109 1 163/174 1097

γνώστης, *gnōstees.*

Acts 26: 3. to be *expert* in all customs and questions

1110 15 163/174 1097

γνωστός, *gnōstos.*

Lu. 2:44. among (their) kinsfolk and *acquaintance*
23:49. all his *acquaintance*, and the women
Joh. 18:15. that disciple was *known* unto the
16. which was *known* unto the high priest,
Acts 1:19. it was *known* unto all the dwellers
2:14. be this *known* unto you, and hearken
4:10. Be it *known* unto you all, and to all
16. a *notable* miracle hath been done
9:42. it was *known* throughout all Joppa;
13:38. Be it *known* unto you therefore, men
15:18. *Known* unto God are all his works
19.17. this was *known* to all the Jews
28:22. we *know* that every where it is spoken
28. Be it *known* therefore unto you,
Ro. 1:19. that *which may be known* of God

1111 8 163/174 1:728

γογγύζω, *gonguzo.*

Mat. 20:11. they *murmured* against the goodman
Lu. 5:30. their scribes and Pharisees *murmured*
Joh. 6:41. The Jews then *murmured* at him,
43. *Murmur* not among yourselves.
61. that his disciples *murmured* at it,
7:32. Pharisees heard that the people *murmured*
1Co. 10:10. Neither *murmur* ye, as some of them also *murmured*, and were destroyed of

1112 4 163/174 1:728 1111

γογγυσμός, *gongusmos.*

Joh. 7:12. there was much *murmuring* among
Acts 6: 1. there arose a *murmuring* of the Grecians
Phi. 2:14. Do all things without *murmurings*
1Pet. 4: 9. hospitality one to another without *grudging*.

1113 1 163/174 1:728 1111

γογγυστής, *gongustees.*

Jude. 16. These are *murmurers*, complainers,

1114 1 163/174 1:737

goaō (to wail)

γόης, *goees.*

2Ti. 3:13. evil men and *seducers* shall wax worse

1117 3 164/174 1073

γόμος, *gomos.*

Acts 21: 3. the ship was to unlade her *burden*.
Rev. 18:11. no man buyeth their *merchandise*
12. The *merchandise* of gold, and silver,

1118 19 164/174 rt 1096

γονεύς, *gonūs.*

Mat. 10:21. children shall rise up against (their) *parents*,
Mar 13:12. children shall rise up against (their) *parents*,
Lu. 2:27. when the *parents* brought in the
41. his *parents* went to Jerusalem every
8:56. her *parents* were astonished: but he
18:29. hath left house, or *parents*, or brethren,
21:16. shall be betrayed both by *parents*, and
Joh. 9: 2. who did sin, this man, or his *parents*,
3. this man sinned, nor his *parents:*
18. they called the *parents* of him that

Joh. 9:20. His *parents* answered them and said,
22. These (words) spake his *parents*,
23. Therefore said his *parents*, He is of age;
Ro. 1:30. evil things, disobedient to *parents*,
2Co.12:14. ought not to lay up for the *parents*, but the *parents* for the children.
Eph. 6: 1. obey your *parents* in the Lord:
Col. 3:20. obey (your) *parents* in all things:
2Ti. 3: 2. blasphemers, disobedient to *parents*,

1119 12 164/175 1:738

γόνυ, gonu.

Mar 15:19. bowing (their) *knees* worshipped him.
Lu. 5: 8. he fell down at Jesus' *knees*, saying,
22:41. stone's cast, and *kneeled* (lit. placing the *knees*) down,
Acts 7:60. he *kneeled* down, and cried with a
9:40. put them all forth, and *kneeled* down,
20:36. he *kneeled* down, and prayed with
21: 5. we *kneeled* down on the shore,
Ro. 11: 4. who have not bowed the *knee* to
14:11. every *knee* shall bow to me,
Eph. 3:14. I bow my *knees* unto the Father
Phi. 2:10. name of Jesus every *knee* should bow,
Heb 12:12. hands which hang down, and the feeble *knees*;

1120 4 164/175 1:738 1119 petō

γονυπετέω, gonupeteo.

Mat.17:14. a (certain) man, *kneeling down*
27:29. they *bowed the knee* before him, *and*
Mar. 1:40. beseeching him, and *kneeling down*
10:17. running, and *kneeled* to him, *and* asked

1121 15 164/175 1:742 1125

γράμμα, gramma.

Lu. 16: 6. he said unto him, Take thy *bill*,
7. he said unto him, Take thy *bill*,
23:38. written over him in *letters* of Greek,
Joh. 5:47. if ye believe not his *writings*,
7:15. How knoweth this man *letters*,
Acts26:24. much *learning* doth make thee mad.
28:21. We neither received *letters* out of Judæa
Ro. 2:27. who by the *letter* and circumcision
29. in the spirit, (and) not in the *letter*;
7: 6. not (in) the oldness of the *letter*.
2Co. 3: 6. not of the *letter*, but of the spirit: for the *letter* killeth, but the spirit
7. written (lit. in *letters*,) (and) engraven in stones,
Gal. 6:11. Ye see how large a *letter* I have
2Ti. 3:15. thou hast known the holy *scriptures*,

1122 67 164/175 1:740 1121

γραμματεύς, grammatūs.

Mat. 2: 4. chief priests and *scribes* of the people
5:20. (righteousness) of the *scribes* and Pharisees,
7:29. having authority, and not as the *scribes*.
8:19. a certain *scribe* came, and said unto
9: 3. behold, certain of the *scribes* said
12:38. certain of the *scribes* and of the Pharisees
13:52. every *scribe* (which is) instructed
15: 1. came to Jesus *scribes* and Pharisees,
16:21. the elders and chief priests and *scribes*,
17:10. Why then say the *scribes* that
20:18. the chief priests and unto the *scribes*,
Mat.21:15. when the chief priests and *scribes* saw
23: 2. The *scribes* and the Pharisees sit in
13. woe unto you, *scribes* and Pharisees,
14. Woe unto you, *scribes* and Pharisees,
15. Woe unto you, *scribes* and Pharisees,
23. Woe unto you, *scribes* and Pharisees,
25. Woe unto you, *scribes* and Pharisees,
27. Woe unto you, *scribes* and Pharisees,
29. Woe unto you, *scribes* and Pharisees,
34. unto you prophets, and wise men, and *scribes*:
26: 3. the chief priests, and the *scribes*, and the
57. where the *scribes* and the elders were
27:41. with the *scribes* and elders, said,
Mar. 1:22. had authority, and not as the *scribes*.
2: 6. certain of the *scribes* sitting there,
16. when the *scribes* and Pharisees saw
3:22. the *scribes* which came down
7: 1. certain of the *scribes*, which came
5. the Pharisees and *scribes* asked him,
8:31. (of) the chief priests, and *scribes*, and be
9:11. Why say the *scribes* that Elias
14. the *scribes* questioning with them.
16. he asked the *scribes*, What question
10:33. the chief priests, and unto the *scribes*;
11:18. the *scribes* and chief priests heard (it),
27. the chief priests, and the *scribes*, and the
12:28. one of the *scribes* came, and having
32. the *scribe* said unto him, Well,
35. How say the *scribes* that Christ
38. Beware of the *scribes*, which love
14: 1. the chief priests and the *scribes* sought
43. from the chief priests and the *scribes*
53. chief priests and the elders and the *scribes*.
15: 1. the elders and *scribes*, and the whole council,
31. said among themselves with the *scribes*,
Lu. 5:21. the *scribes* and the Pharisees began to reason,
30. their *scribes* and Pharisees murmured
6: 7. the *scribes* and Pharisees watched him,
9:22. the elders and chief priests and *scribes*,
11:44. Woe unto you, *scribes* and Pharisees,
53. the *scribes* and the Pharisees began
15: 2. the Pharisees and *scribes* murmured,
19:47. the chief priests and the *scribes* and the
20: 1. the chief priests and the *scribes* came
19. the chief priests and the *scribes* the same
39. certain of the *scribes* answering said,
46. Beware of the *scribes*, which desire to
22: 2. the chief priests and *scribes* sought
66. the chief priests and the *scribes* came together,
23:10. the chief priests and *scribes* stood
Joh. 8: 3. the *scribes* and Pharisees brought unto
Acts 4: 5. that their rulers, and elders, and *scribes*,
6:12. the elders, and the *scribes*, and came upon (him),
19:35. when the *townclerk* had appeased the
23: 9. the *scribes* (that were) of the Pharisees,
1Co. 1:20. Where (is) the wise? where (is) the *scribe*?

1123 1 165/176 1125

γραπτός, graptos.

Ro. 2:15. the work of the law *written* in their

1124 51 165/176 1:742 1125

γραφή, graphee.

Mat.21:42. Did ye never read in the *scriptures*.

Mat.22:29. Ye do err, not knowing the *scriptures*,
26:54. shall the *scriptures* be fulfilled,
56. that the *scriptures* of the prophets
Mar 12:10. have ye not read this *scripture*;
24. because ye know not the *scriptures*,
14:49. the *scriptures* must be fulfilled.
15:28. the *scripture* was fulfilled, which saith,
Lu. 4:21. This day is this *scripture* fulfilled
24:27. in all the *scriptures* the things
32. he opened to us the *scriptures*?
45. they might understand the *scriptures*,
Joh. 2:22. they believed the *scripture*, and the
5:39. Search the *scriptures*; for in them
7:38. as the *scripture* hath said, out of
42. Hath not the *scripture* said,
10:35. the *scripture* cannot be broken;
13:18. that the *scripture* may be fulfilled,
17:12. that the *scripture* might be fulfilled.
19:24. that the *scripture* might be fulfilled,
28. that the *scripture* might be fulfilled,
36. that the *scripture* should be fulfilled,
37. again another *scripture* saith,
20: 9. as yet they knew not the *scripture*,
Acts 1:16. this *scripture* must needs have
8:32. The place of the *scripture* which
35. began at the same *scripture*,
17: 2. reasoned with them out of the *scriptures*,
11. searched the *scriptures* daily,
18:24. eloquent man, (and) mighty in the *scriptures*,
28. shewing by the *scriptures* that
Ro. 1: 2. by his prophets in the holy *scriptures*,
4: 3. For what saith the *scripture*?
9:17. For the *scripture* saith unto Pharaoh,
10:11. For the *scripture* saith, Whosoever
11: 2. Wot ye not what the *scripture* saith
15: 4. through patience and comfort of the *scriptures*
16:26. by the *scriptures* of the prophets,
1Co.15: 3. for our sins according to the *scriptures*;
4. the third day according to the *scriptures*:
Gal. 3: 8. the *scripture*, foreseeing that God
22. the *scripture* hath concluded all
4:30. Nevertheless what saith the *scripture*?
1Ti. 5:18. For the *scripture* saith, Thou shalt
2Ti. 3:16. All *scripture* (is) given by inspiration
Jas. 2: 8. according to the *scripture*, Thou shalt love
23. the *scripture* was fulfilled which
4: 5. Do ye think that the *scripture* saith in
1Pet.2: 6. also it is contained in the *scripture*,
2Pet.1:20. that no prophecy of the *scripture* is of
3:16. as (they do) also the other *scriptures*,

1125 194 165/176 1:742

γράφω, *grapho*.

Mat. 2: 5. for thus it *is written* by the prophet,
4: 4. he answered and said, It *is written*,
6. cast thyself down: for it *is written*,
7. Jesus said unto him, It *is written* again,
10. Get thee hence, Satan: for it *is written*,
11:10. this is (he), of whom it *is written*,
21:13. It *is written*, My house shall be called
26:24. as it *is written* of him: but woe
31. for it *is written*, I will smite the
27:37. over his head his accusation *written*,
Mar 1: 2. As it *is written* in the prophets,
7: 6. of you hypocrites, as it *is written*,
9:12. how it *is written* of the Son of man,
13. whatsoever they listed, as it *is written*
10: 4. *to write* a bill of divorcement,
5. he *wrote* you this precept.
Mar 11:17. saying unto them, *Is* it not *written*
12:19. Master, Moses *wrote* unto us,
14:21. indeed goeth, as it *is written* of him:
27. it *is written*, I will smite the shepherd,
Lu. 1: 3. from the very first, *to write* unto thee
63. *wrote*, saying, His name is John.
2:23. it *is written* in the law of the Lord,
3: 4. it *is written* in the book of the words
4: 4. It *is written*, That man shall not live
8. it *is written*, Thou shalt worship the Lord
10. it *is written*, He shall give his angels
17. the place where it was *written*,
7:27. This is (he), of whom it *is written*,
10:20. your names *are written* in heaven.
26. What *is written* in the law? how readest thou?
16: 6. sit down quickly, and *write* fifty.
7. Take thy bill, and *write* fourscore.
18:31. all things *that are written* by the
19:46. Saying unto them, It *is written*,
20:17. What is this then *that is written*,
28. Saying, Master, Moses *wrote* unto us,
21:22. all things *which are written*
22:37. this *that is written* must yet be
23:38. a superscription also was *written*
24:44. must be fulfilled, *which were written*
46. said unto them, Thus it *is written*,
Joh. 1:45(46). in the law, and the prophets, *did write*,
2:17. remembered that it was *written*,
5:46. have believed me: for he *wrote* of me.
6:31. as it is *written*, He gave them bread
45. It is *written* in the prophets, And
8: 6. with (his) finger *wrote* on the ground,
8. stooped down, and *wrote* on the ground.
17. It *is* also *written* in your law,
10:34. Is it not *written* in your law,
12:14. sat thereon; as it is *written*,
16. these things were *written* of him,
15:25. fulfilled *that is written* in their law,
19:19. Pilate *wrote* a title, and put (it) on the cross. And the *writing* was, JESUS OF NAZARETH
20. it was *written* in Hebrew, (and) Greek,
21. *Write* not, The King of the Jews;
22. What I *have written* I *have written*.
20:30. which are not *written* in this book:
31. these *are written*, that ye might
21:24. and *wrote* these things: and we know
25. if they *should be written* every one,
— the books *that should be written*.
Acts 1:20. it *is written* in the book of Psalms,
7:42. it *is written* in the book of the prophets,
13:29. all *that was written* of him,
33. it *is* also *written* in the second
15:15. words of the prophets; as it *is written*,
23. *And* they *wrote* (letters) by them after
18:27. the brethren *wrote*, exhorting the
23: 5. for it *is written*, Thou shalt not
25. *And* he *wrote* a letter after this manner:
24:14. all things *which are written* in
25:26. I have no certain thing *to write*
— I might have somewhat *to write*.
Ro. 1:17. as it *is written*, The just shall live
2:24. through you, as it *is written*.
3: 4. every man a liar; as it *is written*,
10. as it *is written*, There is none righteous
4:17. as it *is written*, I have made thee
23. it *was* not *written* for his sake
8:36. as it *is written*, For thy sake we are
9:13. as it *is written*, Jacob have I loved,
33. as it *is written*, Behold, I lay in Sion

Ro. 10:5. Moses *describeth* the righteousness
15. as it *is written*, How beautiful are
11: 8. According as it *is written*, God hath
26. as it *is written*, There shall come
12:19. it *is written*, Vengeance (is) mine;
14:11. For it *is written*, (As) I live, saith
15: 3. as it *is written*, The reproaches of
9. as it *is written*, For this cause I will
15. I *have written* the more boldly
21. as it *is written*, To whom he was
16:22. I Tertius, *who wrote* (this) epistle,
1Co. 1:19. For it *is written*, I will destroy the
31. according as it *is written*, He that
2: 9. as it *is written*, Eye hath not seen,
3:19. For it *is written*, He taketh the wise
4: 6. above that which *is written*, that no
14. I *write* not these things to shame you,
5: 9. I *wrote* unto you in an epistle
11. now I *have written* unto you
7: 1. things whereof ye *wrote* unto me:
9: 9. it *is written* in the law of Moses,
10. For our sakes, no doubt, (this) *is written*:
15. neither *have* I *written* these things,
10: 7. as it *is written*, The people sat
11. they *are written* for our admonition,
14:21. In the law it *is written*, With (men)
37. the things that I *write* unto you
15:45. so it *is written*, The first man
54. to pass the saying *that is written*,
2Co. 1:13. we *write* none other things unto you,
2: 3. I *wrote* this same unto you, lest,
4. I *wrote* unto you with many tears;
9. to this end also *did* I *write*, that
4:13. according *as* it *is written*, I believed,
7:12. Wherefore, though I *wrote* unto you,
8:15. As it *is written*, He that (had gathered)
9: 1. superfluous for me *to write* to you:
9. As it *is written*, He hath dispersed
13: 2. being absent now I *write* to them
10. I *write* these things being absent,
Gal. 1:20. the things which I *write* unto you,
3:10. for it *is written*, Cursed (is) every
— things *which are written* in the book
13. for it *is written*, Cursed (is) every one
4:22. For it *is written*, that Abraham had
27. For it *is written*, Rejoice, (thou) barren
6:11. I *have written* unto you with
Phi. 3: 1. *To write* the same things to you,
1Th. 4: 9. need not that I *write* unto you:
5: 1. have no need that I *write* unto you.
2Th. 3:17. token in every epistle: so I *write*.
1Ti. 3:14. These things *write* I unto thee,
Philem.19. I Paul *have written* (it) with
21. I *wrote* unto thee, knowing that
Heb 10: 7. in the volume of the book it *is written*
1Pet. 1:16. Because it *is written*, Be ye holy;
5:12. I *have written* briefly, exhorting,
2Pet.3: 1. beloved, I now *write* unto you;
15. given unto him *hath written* unto you;
1Joh.1: 4. these things *write* we unto you,
2: 1. these things *write* I unto you,
7. I *write* no new commandment
8. a new commandment I *write* unto you,
12. I *write* unto you, little children,
13. I *write* unto you, fathers, because ye
— I *write* unto you, young men, because
— I *write* unto you, little children,
14. I *have written* unto you, fathers,
— I *have written* unto you, young men,
21. I *have* not *written* unto you because
26. These (things) *have* I *written* unto you
5:13. These things *have* I *written* unto you
2Joh. 5. as *though* I *wrote* a new commandment
12. Having many things *to write* unto you,
3Joh. 9. I *wrote* unto the church: but Diotrephes
13. I had many things *to write*, but I will not with ink and pen *write* unto thee:
Jude 3. *to write* unto you of the common
— needful for me *to write* unto you,
Rev. 1: 3. those things *which are written* therein:
11. What thou seest, *write* in a book,
19. *Write* the things which thou hast
2: 1. angel of the church of Ephesus *write*;
8. angel of the church in Smyrna *write*;
12. angel of the church in Pergamos *write*;
17. in the stone a new name *written*,
18. angel of the church in Thyatira *write*;
3: 1. angel of the church in Sardis *write*;
7. angel of the church in Philadelphia *write*;
12. I *will write* upon him the name
14. angel of the church of the Laodiceans *write*;
5: 1. a book *written* within and on the backside,
10: 4. their voices, I was about *to write*:
— thunders uttered, and *write* them not.
13: 8. names *are* not *written* in the book
14: 1. his Father's name *written* in their foreheads.
13. *Write*, Blessed (are) the dead which
17: 5. upon her forehead (was) a name *written*,
8. whose names *were* not *written*
19: 9. he saith unto me, *Write*, Blessed (are)
12. he had a name *written*, that no
16. on his thigh a name *written*,
20:12. out of those things *which were written*
15. not found *written* in the book of life
21: 5. he said unto me, *Write*: for these
27. they *which are written* in the Lamb's
22:18. plagues *that are written* in this book:
19. things *which are written* in this

1126 1 166/179 1491
graus (old woman)

γραώδης, *graōdees.*

1Ti. 4: 7. refuse profane and *old wives'* fables,

1127 23 166/179 2:333 1453

γρηγορέω, *greegoreo.*

Mat.24:42. *Watch* therefore: for ye know not what
43. he would *have watched*, and would not have
25:13. *Watch* therefore, for ye know neither the
26:38. tarry ye here, and *watch* with me.
40. could ye not *watch* with me one hour?
41. *Watch* and pray, that ye enter not into
Mar 13:34. commanded the porter to *watch*.
35. *Watch* ye therefore: for ye know not
37. unto you I say unto all, *Watch*.
14:34. tarry ye here, and *watch*.
37. couldest not thou *watch* one hour?
38. *Watch* ye and pray, lest ye enter into
Lu. 12:37. when he cometh shall find *watching*:
39. would come, he would *have watched*,
Acts20:31. Therefore *watch*, and remember, that
1Co.16:13. *Watch* ye, stand fast in the faith,
Col. 4: 2. *and watch* in the same with thanksgiving;
1Th. 5: 6. *let* us *watch* and be sober.
10. whether we *wake* or sleep, we should
1Pet.5: 8. Be sober, *be vigilant*; because your
Rev. 3: 2. Be *watchful*, and strengthen the things
3. If therefore thou *shalt* not *watch*,
16:15. Blessed (is) he *that watcheth*, and keepeth

1128 4 166/179 1:773 1131

γυμνάζω, gumnazo.

1Ti. 4: 7. *exercise* thyself (rather) unto godliness.
Heb 5:14. have their senses *exercised* to discern
12:11. unto them *which are exercised* thereby.
2Pet.2:14. an heart they have *exercised* with

1129 1 166/179 1:773 1128

γυμνασία, gumnasia.

1Ti. 4: 8. For bodily *exercise* profiteth little:

1130 1 166/179 1131

γυμνητεύομαι, gumneetuomai.

1Co. 4:11. we both hunger, and thirst, and *are naked*,

1131 15 166/179 1:773

γυμνός, gumnos.

Mat.25:36. *Naked*, and ye clothed me: I was sick,
38. took (thee) in? or *naked*, and clothed (thee)?
43. *naked*, and ye clothed me not: sick,
44. a stranger, or *naked*, or sick, or in prison,
Mar14:51. a linen cloth cast about (his) *naked* (body);
52. linen cloth, and fled from them *naked*.
Joh.21: 7. for he was *naked*, and did cast himself
Acts19:16. out of that house *naked* and wounded.
1Co.15:37. body that shall be, but *bare* grain,
2Co. 5: 3. we shall not be found *naked*
Heb 4:13. all things (are) *naked* and opened unto
Jas. 2:15. If a brother or sister be *naked*, and
Rev. 3:17. miserable, and poor, and blind, and *naked*:
16:15. lest he walk *naked*, and they see his shame.
17:16. shall make her desolate and *naked*,

1132 3 167/179 1:773 1131

γυμνότης, gumnotees.

Ro. 8:35. famine, or *nakedness*, or peril, or sword?
2Co.11:27. fastings often, in cold and *nakedness*.
Rev. 3:18. the shame of thy *nakedness* do not appear;

1133 1 167/179 1135

γυναικάριον, gunaikarion.

2Ti. 3: 6. lead captive *silly women* laden with

1134 1 167/179 1135

γυναικεῖος, gunaikios.

1Pet.3: 7. giving honour unto the *wife*, as unto the

1135 221 167/179 1:776 rt 1096

γυνή, gunee.

Mat. 1:20. to take unto thee Mary thy *wife*:
24. bidden him, and took unto him his *wife*:
5:28. whosoever looketh on a *woman* to lust
31. Whosoever shall put away his *wife*, let
32. That whosoever shall put away his *wife*,
9:20. behold, a *woman*, which was diseased
22. the *woman* was made whole from
11:11. them that are born of *women* there
13:33. leaven, which a *woman* took, and hid
14: 3. Herodias' sake, his brother Philip's *wife*.
21. five thousand men, beside *women*
15:22. behold, a *woman* of Canaan came
28. O *woman*, great (is) thy faith:
Mat.15:38. four thousand men, beside *women*
18:25. to be sold, and his *wife*, and children,
19: 3. lawful for a man to put away his *wife*
5. shall cleave to his *wife*: and they
8. suffered you to put away your *wives*:
9. Whosoever shall put away his *wife*,
10. case of the man be so with (his) *wife*,
29. father, or mother, or *wife*, or children
22:24. his brother shall marry his *wife*
25. left his *wife* unto his brother:
27. last of all the *woman* died also.
28. whose *wife* shall she be of the seven?
26: 7. There came unto him a *woman*
10. Why trouble ye the *woman*? for she
27:19. his *wife* sent unto him, saying,
55. many *women* were there beholding
28: 5. angel answered and said unto the *women*
Mar. 5:25. a certain *woman*, which had an
33. the *woman* fearing and trembling,
6:17. Herodias' sake, his brother Philip's *wife*:
18. for thee to have thy brother's *wife*.
7:25. For a (certain) *woman*, whose young
26. The *woman* was a Greek, a Syrophenician
10: 2. for a man to put away (his) *wife*?
7. father and mother, and cleave to his *wife*
11. Whosoever shall put away his *wife*,
12. if a *woman* shall put away her husband,
29. or father, or mother, or *wife*, or children,
12:19. die, and leave (his) *wife* (behind him),
— his brother should take his *wife*,
20. the first took a *wife*, and dying left no seed.
22. last of all the *woman* died also.
23. whose *wife* shall she be of them? for the seven had her to *wife*.
14: 3. there came a *woman* having an
15:40. There were also *women* looking on
Lu. 1: 5. his *wife* (was) of the daughters of Aaron,
13. thy *wife* Elisabeth shall bear
18. man, and my *wife* well stricken in years
24. those days his *wife* Elisabeth conceived
28. blessed (art) thou among *women*.
42. said, Blessed (art) thou among *women*.
2: 5. taxed with Mary his espoused *wife*,
3:19. Herodias his brother Philip's *wife*,
4:26. unto a *woman* (that was) a widow.
7:28. Among those that are born of *women*
37. behold, a *woman* in the city,
39. who and what manner of *woman*
44. he turned to the *woman*, and said unto Simon, Seest thou this *woman*?
50. he said to the *woman*, Thy faith
8: 2. certain *women*, which had been
3. Joanna the *wife* of Chuza
43. a *woman* having an issue of blood
47. when the *woman* saw that she
10:38. a certain *woman* named Martha
11:27. a certain *woman* of the company
13:11. there was a *woman* which had a
12. *Woman*, thou art loosed from thine
21. like leaven, which a *woman* took
14:20. another said, I have married a *wife*,
26. his father, and mother, and *wife*, children,
15: 8. what *woman* having ten pieces
16:18. Whosoever putteth away his *wife*,
17:32. Remember Lot's *wife*.
18:29. left house, or parents, or brethren, *wife*,
20:28. If any man's brother die, having a *wife*,
— his brother should take his *wife*,
29. seven brethren, and the first took a *wife*,

Lu. 20:30. the second took her to *wife*,
32. Last of all the *woman* died also.
33. whose *wife* of them is she? for seven had her to *wife*.
22 57. saying, *Woman*, I know him not.
23:27. a great company of people, and of *women*,
49. the *women* that followed him
55. the *women* also, which came with him
24:22. certain *women* also of our company
24. even so as the *women* had said:
Joh. 2: 4. *Woman*, what have I to do with thee?
4: 7. There cometh a *woman* of Samaria
9. Then saith the *woman* of Samaria
— which am a *woman* of Samaria?
11. The *woman* saith unto him, Sir,
15. The *woman* saith unto him, Sir,
17. The *woman* answered and said, I have
19. The *woman* saith unto him, Sir,
21. Jesus saith unto her, *Woman*, believe me,
25. The *woman* saith unto him, I know
27. that he talked with the *woman*:
28. The *woman* then left her waterpot,
39. the saying of the *woman*, which testified,
42. said unto the *woman*, Now we believe,
8: 3. brought unto him a *woman* taken
4. this *woman* was taken in adultery,
9. the *woman* standing in the midst.
10. and saw none but the *woman*, he said
— *Woman*, where are those thine accusers?
16:21. A *woman* when she is in travail hath
19:26. his mother, *Woman*, behold thy son!
20:13. they say unto her, *Woman*, why weepest thou?
15. *Woman*, why weepest thou? whom
Acts 1:14. prayer and supplication, with the *women*,
5: 1. Ananias, with Sapphira his *wife*,
2. his *wife* also being privy (to it),
7. his *wife*, not knowing what was
14. multitudes both of men and *women*.
8: 3. haling men and *women* committed
12. were baptized, both men and *women*.
9: 2. whether they were men or *women*,
13:50. the devout and honourable *women*,
16: 1. the son of a certain *woman*,
13. spake unto the *women* which
14. a certain *woman* named Lydia,
17: 4. of the chief *women* not a few.
12. also of honourable *women* which were
34. a *woman* named Damaris, and others
18: 2. from Italy, with his *wife* Priscilla;
21: 5. on our way, with *wives* and children,
22: 4. into prisons both men and *women*.
24:24. Felix came with his *wife* Drusilla,
Ro. 7. 2. the *woman* which hath an husband
1Co. 5: 1. that one should have his father's *wife*.
7: 1. good for a man not to touch a *woman*.
2. let every man have his own *wife*,
3. Let the husband render unto the *wife*
— also the *wife* unto the husband.
4. The *wife* hath not power of her own body,
— power of his own body, but the *wife*.
10. Let not the *wife* depart from (her) husband:
11. let not the husband put away (his) *wife*.
12. If any brother hath a *wife* that believeth not,
13. the *woman* which hath an husband
14. husband is sanctified by the *wife*, and the unbelieving *wife* is sanctified by
16. For what knowest thou, O *wife*,
— whether thou shalt save (thy) *wife*?
27. Art thou bound unto a *wife*?

1Co. 7:27. Art thou loosed from a *wife*? seek not a *wife*.
29. they that have *wives* be as though
33. how he may please (his) *wife*.
34. difference (also) between a *wife* and a virgin.
39. The *wife* is bound by the law
9: 5. to lead about a sister, a *wife*, as
11: 3. the head of the *woman* (is) the man;
5. every *woman* that prayeth or
6. if the *woman* be not covered,
— a shame for a *woman* to be shorn
7. the *woman* is the glory of the man.
8. the man is not of the *woman*, but the *woman* of the man.
9. created for the *woman*, but the *woman* for
10. For this cause ought the *woman*
11. neither is the man without the *woman*, neither the *woman* without the man,
12. as the *woman* (is) of the man, even so (is) the man also by the *woman*;
13. that a *woman* pray unto God uncovered?
15. if a *woman* have long hair, it is
14:34. Let your *women* keep silence in
35. a shame for *women* to speak in the church
Gal. 4: 4. sent forth his Son, made of a *woman*,
Eph 5:22. *Wives*, submit yourselves unto
23. the husband is the head of the *wife*,
24. so (let) the *wives* (be) to their own
25. Husbands, love your *wives*, even
28. So ought men to love their *wives*
— He that loveth his *wife* loveth himself.
31. shall be joined unto his *wife*,
33. so love his *wife* even as himself; and the *wife* (see) that she reverence
Col. 3:18. *Wives*, submit yourselves unto
19. Husbands, love (your) *wives*, and be not
1Ti. 2: 9. that *women* adorn themselves in
10. which becometh *women* professing
11. Let the *woman* learn in silence
12. I suffer not a *woman* to teach,
14. the *woman* being deceived was
3: 2. the husband of one *wife*, vigilant,
11. Even so (must their) *wives* (be) grave,
12. deacons be the husbands of one *wife*,
5: 9. having been the *wife* of one man,
Tit. 1: 6. be blameless, the husband of one *wife*,
Heb 11:35. *Women* received their dead raised to
1Pet. 3: 1. ye *wives*, (be) in subjection to your own
— won by the conversation of the *wives*;
5. the holy *women* also, who trusted in God,
Rev. 2:20. thou sufferest that *woman* Jezebel,
9: 8. they had hair as the hair of *women*,
12: 1. a *woman* clothed with the sun,
4. the dragon stood before the *woman*
6. the *woman* fled into the wilderness,
13. he persecuted the *woman* which brought
14. to the *woman* were given two wings
15. water as a flood after the *woman*.
16. the earth helped the *woman*, and the
17. the dragon was wroth with the *woman*;
14: 4. they which were not defiled with *women*.
17: 3. I saw a *woman* sit upon a scarlet coloured beast,
4. the *woman* was arrayed in purple
6. I saw the *woman* drunken with the
7. tell thee the mystery of the *woman*,
9. seven mountains, on which the *woman* sitteth.
18. the *woman* which thou sawest
19: 7. his *wife* hath made herself ready.
21: 9. I will shew thee the bride, the Lamb's *wife*.

1137 9 167/182 1:791 cf 1119

γωνία, gōnia.

Mat. 6: 5. in the *corners* of the streets, that they
21:42. is become the head of the *corner*.
Mar.12:10. is become the head of the *corner*:
Lu. 20:17. same is become the head of the *corner*?
Acts 4:11. which is become the head of the *corner*.
26:26. for this thing was not done in a *corner*.
1Pet.2: 7. same is made the head of the *corner*,
Rev. 7: 1. standing on the four *corners* of the earth,
20: 8. which are in the four *quarters* of the earth,

1139 13 168/182 2:1 1142

δαιμονίζομαι, daimonizomai.

Mat. 4:24. those which were *possessed with devils*,
8:16. many that were *possessed with devils*:
28. there met him two *possessed with devils*,
33. befallen to the *possessed of the devils*.
9:32. a dumb man *possessed with a devil*.
12:22. one *possessed with a devil*, blind, and dumb:
15:22. my daughter *is* grievously *vexed with a devil*.
Mar. 1:32. them *that were possessed with devils*.
5:15. him *that was possessed with the devil*,
16. to him *that was possessed with the devil*,
18. he *that had been possessed with the devil*
Lu. 8:36. he *that was possessed of the devils*
Joh.10:21. not the words of him *that hath a devil*.

1140 60 168/182 2:1 1142

δαιμόνιον, daimonion.

Mat. 7:22. in thy name have cast out *devils*?
9:33. when the *devil* was cast out, the
34. Pharisees said, He casteth out *devils* through the prince of the *devils*.
10: 8. raise the dead, cast out *devils*:
11:18. nor drinking, and they say, He hath a *devil*.
12:24. This (fellow) doth not cast out *devils*, but by Beelzebub the prince of the *devils*.
27. if I by Beelzebub cast out *devils*,
28. if I cast out *devils* by the Spirit
17:18. Jesus rebuked the *devil*; and he departed
Mar. 1:34. divers diseases, and cast out many *devils*; and suffered not the *devils* to speak,
39. throughout all Galilee, and cast out *devils*.
3:15. to heal sicknesses, and to cast out *devils*:
22. by the prince of the *devils* casteth he out *devils*.
6:13. they cast out many *devils*, and anointed
7:26. that he would cast forth the *devil*
29. the *devil* is gone out of thy daughter.
30. she found the *devil* gone out,
9:38. we saw one casting out *devils*
16: 9. out of whom he had cast seven *devils*.
17. In my name shall they cast out *devils*;
Lu. 4:33. which had a spirit of an unclean *devil*,
35. when the *devil* had thrown him
41. *devils* also came out of many,
7:33. ye say, He hath a *devil*.
8: 2. out of whom went seven *devils*,
27. a certain man, which had *devils*
30. because many *devils* were entered
33. Then went the *devils* out of the man,
35. out of whom the *devils* were departed,
38. the man out of whom the *devils* were
Lu. 9: 1. power and authority over all *devils*,
42. the *devil* threw him down, and tare (him).
49. Master, we saw one casting out *devils*
10:17. Lord, even the *devils* are subject unto us
11:14. he was casting out a *devil*, and it was
— when the *devil* was gone out,
15. He casteth out *devils* through Beelzebub the chief of the *devils*.
18. that I cast out *devils* through Beelzebub.
19. if I by Beelzebub cast out *devils*,
20. with the finger of God cast out *devils*,
13:32. Behold, I cast out *devils*, and I do cures
Joh. 7:20. people answered and said, Thou hast a *devil*:
8:48. thou art a Samaritan, and hast a *devil*?
49. Jesus answered, I have not a *devil*;
52. Now we know that thou hast a *devil*.
10:20. many of them said, He hath a *devil*,
21. Can a *devil* open the eyes of the blind?
Acts17:18. to be a setter forth of strange *gods*:
1Co.10:20. they sacrifice to *devils*, and not to God:
— that ye should have fellowship with *devils*
21. cup of the Lord, and the cup of *devils*:
— the Lord's table, and of the table of *devils*.
1Ti. 4: 1. heed to seducing spirits, and doctrines of *devils*;
Jas. 2:19. the *devils* also believe, and tremble.
Rev. 9:20. that they should not worship *devils*,

1141 1 168/183 2:1 1140,1142

δαιμονιώδης, daimoniōdees.

Jas. 3:15. not from above, but (is) earthly, sensual *devilish*.

1142 5 168/183 2:1

daiō (to distribute)

δαίμων, daimōn.

Mat. 8:31. So the *devils* besought him, saying,
Mar. 5:12. all the *devils* besought him, saying,
Lu. 8:29. was driven of the *devil* into the wilderness
Rev.16:14. For they are the spirits of *devils*,
18: 2. is become the habitation of *devils*,

1143 1 168/183

δάκνω, dakno.

Gal. 5:15. if ye *bite* and devour one another,

1144 11 168/183

δάκρυ & δάκρυον, dakru & dakruon.

NOTE.—[2]marks those which are obviously from δακρυον.

Mar. 9:24. said with *tears*, Lord, I believe;
Lu. 7:38. began to wash his feet with *tears*,
44. she hath washed my feet with *tears*,
Acts20:19. humility of mind, and with many *tears*.
31. warn every one night and day with *tears*.
2Co. 2: 4. I wrote unto you with many *tears*;
2Ti. 1: 4. being mindful of thy *tears*, that
Heb. 5: 7. supplications with strong crying and *tears*
12:17. though he sought it carefully with *tears*.
Rev. 7:17. God shall wipe away all *tears*[2]
21: 4. God shall wipe away all *tears* from[2]

1145 1 169/183 1144 cf 2799

δακρύω, dakruo.

Joh.11:35. Jesus *wept*.

1146 1 169/183 1147

δακτύλιος, daktulios.

Lu. 15:22. put a *ring* on his hand, and shoes on

1147 8 169/183 2:20 1176

δάκτυλος, daktulos.

Mat.23: 4. move them with one of their *fingers*.
Mar. 7:33. put his *fingers* into his ears, and he spit,
Lu. 11:20. if I with the *finger* of God cast out
46. the burdens with one of your *fingers*.
16:24. may dip the tip of his *finger* in water,
Joh. 8: 6. with (his) *finger* wrote on the ground,
20:25. put my *finger* into the print of the nails,
27. Reach hither thy *finger*, and behold

1150 4 169/183

δαμάζω, damazo.

Mar. 5: 4. neither could any (man) *tame* him.
Jas. 3. 7. things in the sea, *is tamed*, and *hath been tamed* of mankind:
8. the tongue can no man *tame*; (it is)

1151 1 169/183 cf 1150

δάμαλις, damalis.

Heb. 9:13. the ashes of an *heifer* sprinkling

1155 4 169/184 1156

δανείζω, danīzo.

Mat. 5:42. from him that would *borrow* of thee
Lu. 6:34. if ye *lend* (to them) of whom ye hope
— for sinners also *lend* to sinners,
35. do good, and *lend*, hoping for nothing

1156 1 169/184 cf rt 1325 *danos* (gift)

δάνειον, danīon.

Mat.18:27. loosed him, and forgave him the *debt*.

1157 1 169/184 1155

δανειστής, danīstees.

Lu. 7:41. There was a certain *creditor* which

1159 5 169/184 1160

δαπανάω, dapanao.

Mar. 5:26. *had spent* all that she had, and was
Lu. 15:14. *when* he *had spent* all, there arose
Acts21:24. *be at charges* with them, that they
2Co.12:15. I *will* very gladly *spend* and be spent
Jas. 4: 3. that ye *may consume* (it) upon your lusts.

1160 1 170/184

daptō (to devour)

δαπάνη, dapanee.

Lu. 14:28. sitteth not down first, and counteth the *cost*,

1161 398 170/

δέ

1162 19 170/185 2:40 1189

δέησις, de-eesis.

Lu. 1:13. Zacharias: for thy *prayer* is heard;
2:37. served (God) with fastings and *prayers* night and day.
5:33. disciples of John fast often, and make *prayers*,
Acts 1:14. with one accord in prayer and *supplication*,
Ro. 10: 1. my heart's desire and *prayer* to God for
2Co. 1:11. helping together by *prayer* for us,
9:14. by their *prayer* for you, which long
Eph. 6:18. Praying always with all prayer and *supplication*
— perseverance and *supplication* for all saints;
Phil. 1: 4. Always in every *prayer* of mine for you all making *request* with joy,
19. to my salvation through your *prayer*,
4: 6. every thing by prayer and *supplication*
1Ti. 2: 1. that, first of all, *supplications*,
5: 5. continueth in *supplications* and prayers
2Ti. 1: 3. of thee in my *prayers* night and day;
Heb. 5: 7. when he had offered up *prayers* and
Jas. 5:16. fervent *prayer* of a righteous man
1Pet.3:12. his ears (are open) unto their *prayers*:

1163 105 171/185 2:21 1210

δεῖ, dī, an impersonal verb.

Mat.16:21. how that he *must* go unto Jerusalem,
17:10. that Elias *must* first come?
18:33. *Should*est not thou also have had
23:23. these *ought* ye to have done, and not
24: 6. all (these things) *must* come to pass,
25:27. Thou *ought*est therefore to have put
26:35. Though I *should* die with thee,
54. scriptures be fulfilled, that thus it *must* be?
Mar. 8:31. the Son of man *must* suffer many
9:11. the scribes that Elias *must* first come?
13: 7. for (such things) *must needs* be;
10. the gospel *must* first be published
14. standing where it *ought* not,
14:31. If I *should* die with thee, I will not
Lu. 2:49. I *must* be about my Father's business?
4:43. I *must* preach the kingdom of God
9:22. The Son of man *must* suffer many things
11:42. these *ought* ye to have done, and not to
12:12. in the same hour what ye *ought* to say.
13:14. six days in which men *ought* to work.
16. *ought* not this woman, being a
33. Nevertheless I *must* walk to day,
15:32. It *was meet* that we should make merry
17:25. first *must* he suffer many things,
18: 1. that men *ought* always (to) pray,
19: 5. to day I *must* abide at thy house.
21: 9. these things *must* first come to pass;
22: 7. when the passover *must* be killed.
37. that is written *must* yet be accomplished
24: 7. The Son of man *must* be delivered into
26. *Ought* not Christ to have suffered these
44. that all things *must* be fulfilled,
46. thus it *behoved* Christ to suffer,
Joh. 3: 7. Ye *must* be born again.
14. so *must* the Son of man be lifted up:
30. He *must* increase, but I (must) decrease.
4: 4. he *must needs* go through Samaria.
20. place where men *ought* to worship.
24. *must* worship (him) in spirit and in truth.
9: 4. I *must* work the works of him that
10:16. them also I *must* bring, and they
12:34. The Son of man *must* be lifted up?
20: 9. that he *must* rise again from the dead.
Acts 1:16. scripture *must needs* have been fulfilled
22(21). *must* one be ordained
3:21. Whom the heaven *must* receive until
4:12. among men, whereby we *must* be saved.
5:29. We *ought* to obey God rather than men.
9: 6. shall be told thee what thou *must* do.
16. he *must* suffer for my name's sake

Acts10: 6. tell thee what thou *ought*est to do.
14:22. we *must* through much tribulation
15: 5. That it was *needful* to circumcise
16:30. Sirs, what *must* I do to be saved?
17: 3. that Christ *must needs* have suffered,
18:21. I *must* by all means keep this feast
19:21. been there, I *must* also see Rome.
36. ye *ought* to be quiet, and to do nothing rashly.
20:35. labouring ye *ought* to support the weak,
21:22. multitude *must* needs come together:
23:11. so *must* thou bear witness also at Rome.
24:19. Who *ought* to have been here before
25:10. where I *ought* to be judged:
24. crying that he *ought* not to live
26: 9. that I *ought* to do many things
27:21. Sirs, ye *should* have hearkened unto me,
24. thou *must* be brought before Cæsar:
26. we *must* be cast upon a certain island.
Ro. 1:27. recompence of their error which *was meet.*
8:26. what we should pray for as we *ought:*
12: 3. more highly than he *ought* to think;
1Co. 8: 2. nothing yet as he *ought* to know.
11:19. For there *must* be also heresies among
15:25. For he *must* reign, till he hath put all
53. this corruptible *must* put on incorruption,
2Co. 2: 3. from them of whom I *ought* to rejoice;
5:10. we *must* all appear before the judgment seat
11:30. If I *must needs* glory, I will glory of the
Eph.6:20. may speak boldly, as I *ought* to speak.
Col. 4: 4. manifest, as I *ought* to speak.
6. how ye *ought* to answer every man.
1Th. 4: 1. how ye *ought* to walk and to please
2Th 3: 7. know how ye *ought* to follow us:
1Ti. 3: 2. A bishop then *must* be blameless,
7. Moreover he *must* have a good report
15. how thou *ought*est to behave thyself
5:13. speaking things which they *ought* not.
2Ti. 2: 6. that laboureth *must* be first partaker
24. the servant of the Lord *must* not strive;
Tit. 1: 7. For a bishop *must* be blameless,
11. Whose mouths *must* be stopped,
— teaching things which they *ought* not,
Heb. 2: 1. we *ought* to give the more earnest heed
9:26. then *must* he often have suffered
11: 6. he that cometh to God *must* believe
1Pet.1: 6. though now for a season, if *need* be,
2Pet.3:11. what manner (of persons) *ought* ye to be
Rev. 1: 1. things which *must* shortly come to pass;
4: 1. things which *must* be hereafter.
10:11. said unto me, Thou *must* prophesy
11: 5. he *must* in this manner be killed.
13:10. *must* be killed with the sword.
17:10. he *must* continue a short space.
20: 3. after that he *must* be loosed a little
22: 6. the things which *must* shortly be done.

1164 1 171/186 rt 1166

δεῖγμα, dīgma.

Jude 7. are set forth for an *example,* suffering

1165 1 171/186 2:25 1164

δειγματίζω, dīgmatizo.

Col. 2:15. he *made a shew* of them openly.

1166 33 171/186 2:25

δεικνύ-ω & -υμι dīknu-o & -umi.

Mat. 4: 8. *sheweth* him all the kingdoms of the

Mat. 8: 4. go thy way, *shew* thyself to the priest,
16:21. began Jesus *to shew* unto his disciples,
Mar. 1:44. go thy way, *shew* thyself to the priest,
14:15. he *will shew* you a large upper room
Lu. 4: 5. *shewed* unto him all the kingdoms
5:14. go, and *shew* thyself to the priest, and offer
22:12. he *shall shew* you a large upper room
Joh. 2:18. What sign *shewest* thou unto us,
5:20. *sheweth* him all things that himself doeth. and he *will shew* him greater works than
10:32. Many good works *have* I *shewed* you
14: 8. Lord, *shew* us the Father, and it sufficeth
9. sayest thou (then), *Shew* us the Father?
20:20. he *shewed* unto them (his) hands
Acts 7: 3. into the land which I *shall shew* thee.
10:28. God *hath shewed* me that I should
1Co.12:31. *shew* I unto you a more excellent way
1Ti. 6:15. Which in his times he *shall shew,*
Heb. 8: 5. the pattern *shewed* to thee in the mount.
Jas. 2:18. *shew* me thy faith without thy works and I *will shew* thee my faith by my
3:13. *let* him *shew* out of a good conversation
Rev. 1: 1. *to shew* unto his servants things
4: 1. I *will shew* thee things which must
17: 1. I *will shew* unto thee the judgment
21: 9. I *will shew* thee the bride, the Lamb's
10. *shewed* me that great city, the holy
22: 1. he *shewed* me a pure river of water
6. *to shew* unto his servants the things
8. the angel *which shewed* me these things.

1167 1 172/186 1169

δειλία, dīlia.

2Ti. 1: 7. God hath not given us the spirit of *fear;*

1168 1 172/186 1167

δειλιάω, dīliao.

Joh.14:27. heart be troubled, neither *let* it *be afraid.*

1169 3 172/186 deos (dread)

δειλός, dīlos.

Mat. 8:26. Why are ye *fearful,* O ye of little faith?
Mar. 4:40. said unto them, Why are ye so *fearful?*
Rev.21: 8. the *fearful,* and unbelieving, and the abominable,

1170 1 172/187 rt 1171

δεῖνα, dīna.

Mat.26:18. Go into the city to *such a man.*

1171 2 172/187 rt 1169

δεινῶς, dīnōs.

Mat. 8: 6. of the palsy, *grievously* tormented,
Lu. 11:53. Pharisees began to urge (him) *vehemently*

1172 4 172/187 2:34 1173

δειπνέω, dīpneo.

Lu. 17: 8. Make ready wherewith I *may sup,*
22:20. Likewise also the cup after *supper,* (lit. the *supping*)
1Co.11:25. (took) the cup, when he *had supped,*
Rev. 3:20. *will sup* with him, and he with me.

1173 16 172/187 2:34 rt 1160

δεῖπνον, dīpnon.

Mat.23: 6. love the uppermost rooms at *feasts*,
Mar. 6:21. made a *supper* to his lords, high captains,
12:39. the uppermost rooms at *feasts:*
Lu. 14:12. When thou makest a dinner or a *supper*,
16. A certain man made a great *supper*,
17. sent his servant at *supper* time
24. were bidden shall taste of my *supper*.
20:46. the chief rooms at *feasts;*
Joh. 12: 2. There they made him a *supper;*
13: 2. *supper* being ended, the devil having
4. He riseth from *supper*, and laid aside his
21:20. also leaned on his breast at *supper*,
1Co.11:20. (this) is not to eat the Lord's *supper*.
21. one taketh before (other) his own *supper:*
Rev.19: 9. unto the marriage *supper* of the Lamb.
17. unto the *supper* of the great God;

1174 1 172/187 rt 1169,1142

δεισιδαιμονέστερος, dīsidaimonesteros.

Acts17:22. in all things ye are *too superstitious*.

1175 1 172/187 2:1 rt 1174

δεισιδαιμονία, dīsidaimonia.

Acts25:19. questions against him of their own *superstition*,

---

1176 27 172/187 2:36

δέκα, deka.

Mat.20:24. when the *ten* heard (it), they were
25: 1. heaven be likened unto *ten* virgins,
28. and give (it) unto him which hath *ten* talents.
Mar 10:41. when the *ten* heard (it), they began
Lu. 13: 4. Or those eighteen (lit. eight and *ten*), upon whom the
11. a spirit of infirmity eighteen (lit. eight &c.) years,
16. whom Satan hath bound, lo, these eighteen (lit. eight &c.) years,
14:31. be able with *ten* thousand to meet him
15: 8. what woman having *ten* pieces of silver,
17:12. there met him *ten* men that were lepers,
17. said, Were there not *ten* cleansed?
19:13. he called his *ten* servants, and delivered them *ten* pounds, and said unto them,
16. Lord, thy pound hath gained *ten* pounds.
17. have thou authority over *ten* cities.
24. give (it) to him that hath *ten* pounds.
25. said unto him, Lord, he hath *ten* pounds.
Acts25: 6. tarried among them more than *ten* days,
Rev. 2:10. ye shall have tribulation *ten* days:
12: 3. red dragon, having seven heads and *ten*
13: 1. out of the sea, having seven heads and *ten* horns, and upon his horns *ten* crowns, and upon
17: 3. blasphemy, having seven heads and *ten* horns
7. which hath the seven heads and *ten* horns.
12. the *ten* horns which thou sawest are *ten* kings, which have received
16. the *ten* horns which thou sawest

1177 2 173/ 1176,1417

δεκαδύο, dekaduo.

Acts19: 7. all the men were about *twelve*. (lit. *ten* (&) *two*)
24:11. *twelve* days since I went up to (lit. *ten* &c.)

1178 3 173/187 1176,4002

δεκαπέντε, dekapente.

Joh. 11:18. nigh unto Jerusalem, about *fifteen* furlongs
Acts27:28. sounded again, and found (it) *fifteen* fathoms.
Gal. 1:18. to see Peter, and abode with him *fifteen* days.

1180 5 173/187 1176,5064

δεκατέσσαρες, dekatessares.

Mat. 1:17. Abraham to David (are) *fourteen* (lit. *four* (&) *ten*) generations;
— Babylon (are) *fourteen* generations;
— unto Christ (are) *fourteen* generations.
2Co.12: 2. a man in Christ about *fourteen* years ago,
Gal. 2: 1. *fourteen* years after I went up again

1181 4 173/187 1182

δεκάτη, dekatee, subst.

Heb. 7: 2. Abraham gave a *tenth part* of all;
4. Abraham gave the *tenth* of the spoils.
8. here men that die receive *tithes;*
9. Levi also, who receiveth *tithes*,

1182 3 173/188 1176

δέκατος, dekatos.

Joh. 1:39(40). for it was about the *tenth* hour.
Rev 11:13. the *tenth* part of the city fell,
21:20. ninth, a topaz; the *tenth*, a chrysoprasus;

1183 2 173/188 1181

δεκατόω, dekatoō.

Heb. 7: 6. *received tithes* of Abraham, and blessed
9. Levi also, who receiveth tithes, *payed tithes*

1184 5 173/188 2:50 1209

δεκτός, dektos.

Lu. 4:19. To preach the *acceptable* year of the Lord.
24. No prophet is *accepted* in his own country
Acts10:35. worketh righteousness, is *accepted*
2Co. 6: 2. I have heard thee in a time *accepted*,
Phi. 4:18. a sweet smell, a sacrifice *acceptable*,

1185 3 173/188 rt 1388

δελεάζω, deleazo.

Jas. 1:14. drawn away of his own lust, and *enticed*.
2Pet.2:14. *beguiling* unstable souls: an heart
18. they *allure* through the lusts of the flesh,

1186 26 173/188

drus (oak)

δένδρον, dendron.

Mat. 3:10. the ax is laid unto the root of the *trees:* therefore every *tree* which bringeth not
7:17. every good *tree* bringeth forth good fruit; but a corrupt *tree* bringeth forth evil
18. A good *tree* cannot bring forth evil fruit, neither (can) a corrupt *tree* bring forth
19. Every *tree* that bringeth not forth
12:33. Either make the *tree* good, and his fruit good; or else make the *tree* corrupt, and
— for the *tree* is known by (his) fruit.
13:32. greatest among herbs, and becometh a *tree*

Mat.21: 8. others cut down branches from the *trees*,
Mar. 8:24. said, I see men as *trees*, walking.
11: 8. others cut down branches off the *trees*,
Lu. 3: 9. the axe is laid unto the root of the *trees*: every *tree* therefore which bringeth not
6:43. a good *tree* bringeth not forth corrupt fruit; neither doth a corrupt *tree* bring forth
44. every *tree* is known by his own fruit.
13:19. it grew, and waxed a great *tree*;
21:29. Behold the fig tree, and all the *trees*;
Jude 12. *trees* whose fruit withereth, without
Rev. 7: 1. nor on the sea, nor on any *tree*.
3. the earth, neither the sea, nor the *trees*,
8: 7. the third part of *trees* was burnt
9: 4. neither any green thing, neither any *tree*;

1187 1 173/188 1188,2983

δεξιολάβος, dexiolabos.

Acts23:23. *spearmen* two hundred, at the third

1188 53 173/188 2:37 1209

δεξιός, dexios.

[2] marks those which have χεῖρ understood and [3] those which have μέρη understood.

Mat. 5:29. if thy *right* eye offend thee, pluck
30. if thy *right* hand offend thee,
39. shall smite thee on thy *right* cheek,
6: 3. know what thy *right hand* doeth:[2]
20:21. may sit, the one on thy *right hand*,[3]
23. to sit on my *right hand*, and on my left,[3]
22:44. Sit thou on my *right hand*, till I make[3]
25:33. set the sheep on his *right hand*,[3]
34. say unto them on his *right hand*,[3]
26:64. sitting on the *right hand* of power,[3]
27:29. a reed in his *right hand*: and they[2]
38. one on the *right hand*, and another on[3]
Mar 10:37. we may sit, one on thy *right hand*,[3]
40. to sit on my *right hand* and on my left[3]
12:36. Sit thou on my *right hand*, till I make[3]
14:62. sitting on the *right hand* of power,[3]
15:27. the one on his *right hand*, and the other[3]
16: 5. a young man sitting on the *right side*,[3]
19. sat on the *right hand* of God.[3]
Lu. 1:11. standing on the *right side* of the altar[3]
6: 6. a man whose *right* hand was withered.
20:42. Sit thou on my *right hand*,[3]
22:50. cut off his *right* ear.
69. sit on the *right hand* of the power of God.[3]
23:33. one on the *right hand*, and the other on[3]
Joh. 18:10. priest's servant, and cut off his *right* ear.
21: 6. Cast the net on the *right* side of the ship,
Acts 2:25. for he is on my *right hand*, that[3]
33. being by the *right hand* of God[2]
34. Sit thou on my *right hand*,[3]
3: 7. he took him by the *right* hand,
5:31. Him hath God exalted with his *right hand*[2]
7:55. Jesus standing on the *right hand* of God,[3]
56. standing on the *right hand* of God.[3]
Ro. 8:34. even at the *right hand* of God,[2]
2Co. 6: 7. on the *right hand* and on the left,[3]
Gal. 2: 9. the *right hands* of fellowship; that[2]
Eph. 1:20. set (him) at his own *right hand*[2]
Col. 3: 1. Christ sitteth on the *right hand* of God.[2]
Heb. 1: 3. the *right hand* of the Majesty on high;[2]
13. Sit on my *right hand*, until I make[3]
8: 1. set on the *right hand* of the throne[2]
10:12. sat down on the *right hand* of God;[2]
12: 2. is set down at the *right hand* of the[2]
1Pet. 3:22. is on the *right hand* of God;[2]
Rev. 1:16. he had in his *right* hand seven stars:
17. he laid his *right* hand upon me,
20. which thou sawest in my *right hand*,[2]
2: 1. the seven stars in his *right hand*,[2]
5: 1. I saw in the *right hand* of him[2]
7. took the book out of the *right hand*[2]
10: 2. he set his *right* foot upon the sea,
13:16. to receive a mark in their *right* hand.

1189 22 174/189 2:40 1210cf4441

δέομαι, deomai.

Mat. 9:38. *Pray* ye therefore the Lord of the harvest,
Lu. 5:12. seeing Jesus fell on (his) face, and *besought* him, saying,
8:28. I *beseech* thee, torment me not.
38. *besought* him that he might be
9:38. I *beseech* thee, look upon my son:
40. I *besought* thy disciples to cast him out;
10: 2. *pray* ye therefore the Lord of the harvest.
21:36. Watch ye therefore, and *pray* always,
22:32. I *have prayed* for thee, that thy faith
Acts 4:31. *when* they *had prayed*, the place
8:22. *pray* God, if perhaps the thought
24. *Pray* ye to the Lord for me, that none
34. I *pray* thee, of whom speaketh the
10: 2. alms to the people, and *prayed to* God alway.
21:39. I *beseech* thee, suffer me to speak
26: 3. I *beseech* thee to hear me patiently
Ro. 1:10. *Making request*, if by any means
2Co. 5:20. we *pray* (you) in Christ's stead,
8: 4. *Praying* us with much intreaty
10: 2. I *beseech* (you), that I may not
Gal. 4:12. Brethren, I *beseech* you, be as I (am)
1Th. 3:10. Night and day *praying* exceedingly

1192 1 174/189 1194

δέρμα, derma.

Heb 11:37. wandered about in sheepskins and goat-*skins*;

1193 2 174/189 1192

δερμάτινος, dermatinos.

Mat. 3: 4. a *leathern* girdle about his loins;
Mar. 1: 6. with a girdle *of a skin* about his loins;

1194 15 174/189

δέρω, dero.

Mat.21:35. husbandmen took his servants, and *beat* one,
Mar 12: 3. they caught (him), and *beat* him,
5. many others; *beating* some, and killing some.
13: 9. in the synagogues ye *shall be beaten*:
Lu. 12:47. *shall be beaten* with many (stripes).
48. *shall be beaten* with few (stripes).
20:10. the husbandmen *beat* him, *and*
11. another servant: *and* they *beat* him also.
22:63. that held Jesus mocked him, *and smote* (him).
Joh. 18:23. if well, why *smitest* thou me?
Acts 5:40. called the apostles, *and beaten* (them),
16:37. They *have beaten* us openly uncondemned, ...*and*
22:19. imprisoned *and beat* in every synagogue
1Co. 9:26. not as *one that beateth* the air:
2Co. 11:20. if a man *smite* you on the face.

1195 2 174/189 1196

δεσμεύω, desmūo.

Mat.23: 4. For they *bind* heavy burdens
Acts22: 4. *binding* and delivering into prisons

1196 1 174/189 1199

δεσμέω, desmeo.

Lu. 8:29. he *was* kept *bound* with chains

1197 1 174/189 1196

δέσμη, desmee.

Mat.13:30. bind them in *bundles* to burn

1198 16 175/189 2:43 1199

δέσμιος, desmios.

Mat.27:15. to release unto the people a *prisoner*,
16. they had then a notable *prisoner*,
Mar.15: 6. he released unto them one *prisoner*,
Acts16:25. praises unto God: and the *prisoners* heard them.
27. supposing that the *prisoners* had been fled.
23:18. Paul the *prisoner* called me unto (him),
25:14. a certain man left *in bonds* by Felix:
27. unreasonable to send a *prisoner*,
28:16. the centurion delivered the *prisoners*
17. yet was I delivered *prisoner* from
Eph. 3: 1. I Paul, the *prisoner* of Jesus Christ
4: 1. I therefore, the *prisoner* of the Lord,
2Ti. 1: 8. of our Lord, nor of me his *prisoner:*
Philem. 1. Paul, a *prisoner* of Jesus Christ,
9. now also a *prisoner* of Jesus Christ.
Heb 13: 3. Remember them *that are in bonds*,

1199 20 175/190 2:43 1210

ὁ δεσμὸς & τὰ δεσμά,
ho desmos & ta desma.

Always masculine in the singular. In the plural, the masculine and neuter forms are found: Those obviously neuter are thus marked [3].

Mar. 7:35. the *string* of his tongue was loosed,
Lu. 8:29. he brake the *bands*, and was driven[3]
13:16. be loosed from this *bond* on the
Acts16:26. every one's *bands* were loosed.[3]
20:23. saying that *bonds* and afflictions abide me.[3]
22:30. he loosed him from (his) *bands*,
23:29. worthy of death or of *bonds*.
26:29. such as I am, except these *bonds*.
31. nothing worthy of death or of *bonds*.
Phi. 1: 7. inasmuch as both in my *bonds*,
13. So that my *bonds* in Christ are
14. waxing confident by my *bonds*,
16. to add affliction to my *bonds:*
Col. 4:18. Remember my *bonds*. Grace (be) with you.
2Ti. 2: 9. as an evil doer, (even) unto *bonds;*
Philem.10. whom I have begotten in my *bonds:*
13. have ministered unto me in the *bonds*
Heb 10:34. had compassion of me in my *bonds*,
11:36. moreover of *bonds* and imprisonment.
Jude 6. hath reserved in everlasting *chains*

1200 3 175/190 1199,5441

δεσμοφύλαξ, desmophulax.

Acts16:23. charging the *jailor* to keep them safely:
27. the *keeper of the prison* awaking out
36. the *keeper of the prison* told this saying

1201 4 175/190 1199

δεσμωτήριον, desmōteerion.

Mat.11: 2. when John had heard in the *prison*
Acts 5:21. sent to the *prison* to have them brought
23. The *prison* truly found we shut
16:26. foundations of the *prison* were shaken:

1202 2 175/190 1199

δεσμώτης, desmotees.

Acts27: 1. delivered Paul and certain other *prisoner*
42. soldiers' counsel was to kill the *prisoners*,

1203 10 175/190 2:44 1210
posis (husband)

δεσπότης, despotees.

Lu. 2:29. *Lord*, now lettest thou thy servant
Acts 4:24. *Lord*, thou (art) God, which hast made
1Ti. 6: 1. their own *masters* worthy of all honour,
2. they that have believing *masters*,
2Ti. 2:21. sanctified, and meet for the *master*'s use,
Tit. 2: 9. to be obedient unto their own *masters*,
1Pet.2:18. (be) subject to (your) *masters* with all fear;
2Pet.2: 1. denying the *Lord* that bought them,
Jude 4. denying the only *Lord* God, and our
Rev. 6:10. How long, O *Lord*, holy and true, dost

1204 1 175/190

δεῦρο, dūro.

Mat.19:21. treasure in heaven: and *come* (and) follow me.
Mar.10:21. *come*, take up the cross, and follow me.
Lu. 18:22. treasure in heaven: and *come*, follow me.
Joh.11:43. with a loud voice, Lazarus, *come* forth.
Acts 7: 3. *come* into the land which I shall
34. now *come*, I will send thee into Egypt.
Ro. 1:13. come unto you, but was let *hitherto*,
Rev.17: 1. *Come hither;* I will shew unto
21: 9. *Come hither*, I will shew thee the bride,

1205 13 175/190 1204
eimi (to go)

δεῦτε, dūte.

Mat. 4:19. he saith unto them, Follow (lit. *come* after) me
11:28. *Come* unto me, all (ye) that labour
21:38. *come*, let us kill him, and let us
22: 4. things (are) ready: *come* unto the marriage.
25:34. *Come*, ye blessed of my Father, inherit
28: 6. *Come*, see the place where the Lord l[illegible]
Mar. 1:17. *Come* ye after me, and I will make
6:31. *Come* ye yourselves apart into a
12: 7. the heir; *come*, let us kill him,
Lu. 20:14. the heir: *come*, let us kill him,
Joh. 4:29. *Come*, see a man, which told me
21:12. Jesus saith unto them, *Come* (and) dine.
Rev.19:17. *Come* and gather yourselves together

1206 1 175/190 1208

δευτεραῖος, dūteraios

Acts28:13. we came the *next day* to Puteoli:

1207 1 176/191 1208,4413

δευτερόπρωτος, duteroprōtos.

Lu. 6: 1. it came to pass on the *second* sabbath *after the first*,

1208 43 176/191 1417

δεύτερος, dūteros.

Mat.21:30. he came to the *second*, and said
22:26. Likewise the *second* also, and the third,
39. the *second* (is) like unto it, Thou
26:42. He went away again the *second time*,
Mar 12:21. the *second* took her, and died,
31. the *second* (is) like, (namely) this,
14:72. the *second time* the cock crew.
Lu. 12:38. he shall come in the *second* watch,
19:18. the *second* came, saying, Lord,
20:30. the *second* took her to wife, and he died
Joh. 3: 4. can he enter the *second time* into his
4:54. This (is) again the *second* miracle
9:24. Then *again* called they the man
21:16. He saith to him again the *second time*,
Acts 7:13. at the *second* (time) Joseph was
10:15. (spake) unto him again the *second time*,
11: 9. voice answered me *again* from heaven,
12:10. past the first and the *second* ward,
13:33. also written in the *second* psalm,
1Co.12:28. first apostles, *secondarily* prophets,
15:47. the *second* man (is) the Lord
2Co. 1:15. that ye might have a *second* benefit;
13: 2. as if I were present, the *second time*;
Tit. 3:10. after the first and *second* admonition
Heb 8: 7. have been sought for the *second*.
9: 3. after the *second* veil, the tabernacle
7. into the *second* (went) the high priest
28. shall he appear the *second time*
10: 9. that he may establish the *second*.
2Pet.3: 1. This *second* epistle, beloved, I now
Jude 5. *afterward* destroyed them that
Rev. 2:11. shall not be hurt of the *second* death.
4: 7. the *second* beast like a calf,
6: 3. when he had opened the *second* seal, I heard the *second* beast say, Come and see.
8: 8. the *second* angel sounded, and as it
11:14. The *second* woe is past; (and), behold,
16: 3. the *second* angel poured out his vial
19: 3. *again* they said, Alleluia.
20: 6. the *second* death hath no power,
14. This is the *second* death.
21: 8. fire and brimstone: which is the *second* death.
19. foundation (was) jasper; the *second*,

1209 59 176/191 2:50 cf 2983

δέχομαι, dekomai.

Mat.10:14. whosoever shall not *receive* you,
40. He *that receiveth* you *receiveth* me, and he *that receiveth* me *receiveth* him that sent me.
41. He *that receiveth* a prophet in the
— he *that receiveth* a righteous man
11:14. if ye will *receive* (it), this is Elias,
18: 5. whoso shall *receive* one such little child in my name *receiveth* me.
Mar. 6:11. whosoever shall not *receive* you,
9:37. Whosoever shall *receive* one of such children in my name, *receiveth* me: and whosoever shall *receive* me, *receiveth*
10:15. Whosoever shall not *receive* the kingdom
Lu. 2:28. Then *took* he him up in his arms,
8:13. when they hear, *receive* the word with joy;
9: 5. whosoever will not *receive* you,
11. he *received* them, *and* spake unto them
48. Whosoever shall *receive* this child in my name *receiveth* me: and whosoever shall *receive* me *receiveth* him that sent me:
Lu. 9:53. they *did* not *receive* him, because
10: 8. whatsoever city ye enter, and they *receive* you,
10. city ye enter, and they *receive* you not,
16: 4. they *may receive* me into their houses.
6. he said unto him, *Take* thy bill,
7. *Take* thy bill, and write fourscore.
9. they *may receive* you into everlasting
18:17. Whosoever shall not *receive* the
22:17. he *took* the cup, *and* gave thanks,
Joh. 4:45. the Galilæans *received* him, having
Acts 3:21. Whom the heaven must *receive*
7:38. who *received* the lively oracles
59. saying, Lord Jesus, *receive* my spirit.
8:14. that Samaria *had received* the word
11: 1. Gentiles *had* also *received* the word
17:11. in that they *received* the word
21:17. the brethren *received* us gladly.
22: 5. from whom also I *received* letters...*and*
28:21. We neither *received* letters out of
1Co. 2:14. the natural man *receiveth* not
2Co. 6: 1. *receive* not the grace of God in vain.
7:15. with fear and trembling ye *received* him.
8: 4. that we would *receive* the gift,
17. For indeed he *accepted* the exhortation;
11: 4. gospel, which ye *have* not *accepted*,
16. yet as a fool *receive* me, that I
Gal. 4:14. *received* me as an angel of God,
Eph. 6:17. *take* the helmet of salvation, and the
Phi. 4:18. *having received* of Epaphroditus
Col. 4:10. if he come unto you, *receive* him;
1Th. 1: 6. *having received* the word in much
2:13. ye *received* (it) not (as) the word of men,
2Th. 2:10. they *received* not the love of the truth,
Heb 11:31. *when* she *had received* the spies with peace,
Jas. 1:21. *receive* with meekness the engrafted word

1210 44 176/192 2:60 cf 1163
cf 1189

δέω, deo.

Mat.12:29. except he first *bind* the strong man
13:30. *bind* them in bundles to burn
14: 3. laid hold on John, and *bound* him,
16:19. whatsoever thou shalt *bind* on earth shall be *bound* in heaven:
18:18. Whatsoever ye shall *bind* on earth shall be *bound* in heaven:
21: 2. straightway ye shall find an ass *tied*,
22:13. *Bind* him hand and foot, *and* take
27: 2. *when* they *had bound* him,
Mar. 3:27. except he will first *bind* the strong
5: 3. no man could *bind* him, no,
4. had been often *bound* with fetters
6:17. laid hold upon John, and *bound* him
11: 2. ye shall find a colt *tied*, whereon
4. found the colt *tied* by the door
15: 1. *bound* Jesus, *and* carried (him) away,
7. Barabbas, (which lay) *bound* with
Lu. 13:16. whom Satan *hath bound*, lo, these
19:30. ye shall find a colt *tied*, whereon
Joh.11:44. *bound* hand and foot with graveclothes
18:12. the Jews took Jesus, and *bound* him
24. Now Annas had sent him *bound*
19:40. *wound* it in linen clothes
Acts 9: 2. bring them *bound* unto Jerusalem
14. *to bind* all that call on thy name.
21. he might bring them *bound*
10:11. a great sheet *knit* at the four corners,
12: 6. *bound* with two chains: and the
20:22. I go *bound* in the spirit unto
21:11. *bound* his own hands and feet, *and*

Act 21:11. Jews at Jerusalem *bind* the man
13. I am ready not *to be bound* only,
33. commanded (him) *to be bound* with
22: 5. *bound* unto Jerusalem, for to be punished.
29. because he had *bound* him.
24:27. the Jews a pleasure, left Paul *bound*.
Rom. 7: 2. which hath an husband *is bound* by
1Co 7:27. *Art* thou *bound* unto a wife?
39. The wife *is bound* by the law as
Col. 4: 3. for which I *am* also *in bonds:*
2Ti. 2: 9. the word of God *is* not *bound*.
Rev. 9:14. Loose the four angels *which are bound*
20: 2. Satan, and *bound* him a thousand years,

1211 6 177/192 cf 1161

δή, dee.

Mat.13:23. which *also* beareth fruit, and bringeth
Lu. 2:15. Let us *now* go even unto Bethlehem,
Acts13: 2. Separate)(me Barnabas and Saul
15:36. Let us go again *and* visit our brethren
1Co. 6:20. *therefore* glorify God in your body,
2Co.12: 1. not expedient for me *doubtless* to glory.

1212 4 177/192

δῆλος, deelos.

Mat.26:73. thy speech bewrayeth thee. (lit. maketh thee *manifest*)
1Co.15:27. (it is) *manifest* that he is excepted,
Gal. 3:11. (it is) *evident:* for, The just shall live
1Ti. 6: 7. (it is) *certain* we can carry nothing out.

1213 7 177/192 2:61 1212

δηλόω, deeloō.

1Co. 1:11. it *hath been declared* unto me
3:13. for the day *shall declare* it, because
Col. 1: 8. *Who* also *declared* unto us your love
Heb 9: 8. The Holy Ghost this *signifying*,
12:27. *signifieth* the removing of those
1Pet.1:11. which was in them *did signify*,
2Pet.1:14. our Lord Jesus Christ *hath shewed* me.

1215 1 177/192 1218,58

δημηγορέω, deemeegoreo.

Acts12:21. sat upon his throne, and *made an oration*

1217 1 177/192 2:62 1218,2041

δημιουργός, deemiourgos.

Heb11:10. hath foundations, whose builder and *maker* (is) God.

1218 4 178/193 2:63 1210

δῆμος, deemos.

Acts12:22. the *people* gave a shout, (saying),
17: 5. to bring them out to the *people*.
19:30. have entered in unto the *people*,
33. have made his defence unto the *people*.

1219 4 178/193 1218

δημόσιος, deemosios.

In the passages marked [2] δημοσιᾳ (χωρᾳ *in a place*, being understood) is used as an adverb.

Acts 5:18. put them in the *common* prison.
Acts16:37. They have beaten us *openly* [2]
18:28. convinced the Jews, (and that) *publickly*,[2]
20:20. have taught you *publickly*, and from [2]

1220 16 178/193

δηνάριον, deenarion.

Mat.18:28. which owed him an hundred *pence:*
20: 2. agreed with the labourers for a *penny* a day,
9. they received every man a *penny*.
10. likewise received every man a *penny*.
13. didst not thou agree with me for a *penny*?
22:19. they brought unto him a *penny*.
Mar. 6:37. buy two hundred *penny*worth of bread,
12:15. bring me a *penny*, that I may see (it).
14: 5. sold for more than three hundred *pence*,
Lu. 7:41. the one owed five hundred *pence*,
10:35. he took out two *pence*, and gave (them) to the
20:24. Shew me a *penny*. Whose image
Joh. 6: 7. Two hundred *penny*worth of bread
12: 5. ointment sold for three hundred *pence*,
Rev. 6: 6. A measure of wheat for a *penny*, and three measures of barley for a *penny*;

1221 1 178/193 1211,4218

δήποτε, deepote.

Joh. 5: 4. made whole of what*soever* disease

1222 1 178/193 1211,4225

δήπου, deepou.

Heb. 2:16. For *verily* he took not on (him)

1223 640 178/193 2:65

διά, dia.

Followed by an accusative and a genitive;—the cases in which it is followed by a genitive are marked with a *g*.

Mat. 1:22. spoken of the Lord *by* the prophet, saying,*g*
2: 5. for thus it is written *by* the prophet,*g*
12. into their own country another (lit. *by* another) way.*g*
15. spoken of the Lord *by* the prophet, saying,*g*
23. which was spoken *by* the prophets,*g*
4: 4. proceedeth out *of* the mouth of God.*g*
14. which was spoken *by* Esaias the prophet,*g*
6:25. There*fore* I say unto you, Take no
7:13. Enter ye in *at* the strait gate:*g*
— many there be which go in there*at*:*g*
8:17. which was spoken *by* Esaias the prophet,*g*
28. no man might pass *by* that way.*g*
10:22. hated of all (men) *for* my name's *sake:*
12: 1. on the sabbath day *through* the corn;*g*
17. which was spoken *by* Esaias the prophet,*g*
27. there*fore* they shall be your judges.
31. Where*fore* I say unto you, All manner
43. he walketh *through* dry places, seeking rest,*g*
13: 5. *because* they had no deepness of earth:
6. *because* they had no root, they withered
13. There*fore* speak I to them in parables:
21. persecution ariseth *because of* the word,
35. which was spoken *by* the prophet,*g*
52. There*fore* every scribe (which is) instructed
58. works there, *because of* their unbelief.

Mat.14: 2. there*fore* mighty works do shew forth
3. put (him) in prison *for* Herodias' *sake*,
9. nevertheless *for* the oath's *sake*,
15: 3. of God *by* your tradition?
6. of none effect *by* your tradition.
17:20. said unto them, *Because of* your unbelief:
18: 7. that man *by* whom the offence cometh! g
10. their angels do always (lit. *through* all
(time)) behold the face g
23. There*fore* is the kingdom of heaven
19:12. *for* the kingdom of heaven's *sake*.
24. a camel to go *through* the eye of a needle, g
21: 4. which was spoken *by* the prophet, g
43. There*fore* say I unto you, The kingdom
23:14(13). there*fore* ye shall receive the greater
34. Where*fore*, behold, I send unto you
24: 9. hated of all nations *for* my name's *sake*.
12. *because* iniquity shall abound,
15. spoken of *by* Daniel the prophet, stand g
22. *for* the elect's *sake* those days shall
44. There*fore* be ye also ready: for in such
26:24. *by* whom the Son of man is betrayed! g
61. to build it *in* three days. g
27: 9. that which was spoken *by* Jeremy the
prophet, g
18. he knew that *for* envy they had delivered
19. this day in a dream *because of* him.
Mar. 2: 1. into Capernaum *after* (some) days; g
4. come nigh unto him *for* the press,
23. that he went *through* the corn fields g
27. The sabbath was made *for* man, and not
man *for* the sabbath:
3: 9. wait on him *because of* the multitude,
4: 5. *because* it had no depth of earth:
6. *because* it had no root, it withered
17. persecution ariseth *for* the word's *sake*,
5: 4. *Because* that he had been often bound
6: 2. mighty works are wrought *by* his hands? g
6. he marvelled *because of* their unbelief.
14. there*fore* mighty works do shew forth
17. in prison *for* Herodias' *sake*,
26. (yet) *for* his oath's *sake*, and for their
7:29. *For* this saying go thy way; the
9:30. departed thence, and passed *through* Galilee; g
10: 1. Judæa *by* the farther side of Jordan: g
25. a camel to go *through* the eye of a needle, g
11:16. should carry (any) vessel *through* the
temple. g
24. There*fore* I say unto you, What
12:24. Do ye not there*fore* err, because ye
13:13. hated of all (men) *for* my name's *sake*:
20. *for* the elect's *sake*, whom he hath
14:21. *by* whom the Son of man is betrayed! g
58. *within* three days I will build another g
15:10. chief priests had delivered him *for* envy
16:20. confirming the word *with* signs following g
Lu. 1:70. spake *by* the mouth of his holy prophets, g
78. *Through* the tender mercy of our God;
2: 4. *because* he was of the house and lineage
4:30. he passing *through* the midst of them g
5: 5. Master, we have toiled all (lit. *through* all)
the night, g
19. could not find *by* g what (way) they might
bring him in *because of* the multitude,
— let him down *through* the tiling g
6: 1. that he went *through* the corn fields; g
8: 4. of every city, he spake *by* a parable: g
6. withered away, *because* it lacked moisture.
19. could not come at him *for* the press.
47. *for* what cause she had touched him,
9: 7. *because* that it was said of some, that

Lu. 11: 8. give him, *because* he is his friend, yet
because of his importunity he
19. there*fore* shall they be your judges.
24. he walketh *through* dry places, seeking g
49. There*fore* also said the wisdom of God,
12:22. There*fore* I say unto you, Take no thought
13:24. Strive to enter in *at* the strait gate: g
14:20. a wife, and there*fore* I cannot come.
17: 1. woe (unto him), *through* whom they
come! g
11. passed *through* the midst of Samaria g
18: 5. Yet *because* this widow troubleth me,
25. a camel to go *through* a needle's eye, g
31. things that are written *by* the prophets g
19: 4. for he was to pass (that (way). g
11. *because* he was nigh to Jerusalem,
21:17. hated of all (men) *for* my name's *sake*.
22:22. that man *by* whom he is betrayed! g
23: 8. *because* he had heard many things
19. Who *for* a certain sedition made in
25. him that *for* sedition and murder was
Joh 1: 3. All things were made *by* him; g
7. all (men) *through* him might believe g
10. the world was made *by* him, and the g
17. For the law was given *by* g Moses, (but)
grace and truth came *by* g Jesus Christ.
31. there*fore* am I come baptizing with
2:24. unto them, *because* he knew all (men),
3:17. the world *through* him might be saved.
29. *because of* the bridegroom's voice:
4: 4. he must needs go *through* Samaria. g
39. *for* the saying of the woman, which
41. more believed *because of* his own word;
42. we believe, not *because of* thy saying:
5:16. there*fore* did the Jews persecute Jesus,
18. There*fore* the Jews sought the more
6:57. sent me, and I live *by* the Father:
— eateth me, even he shall live *by* me.
65. There*fore* said I unto you, that no
7:13. openly of him *for* fear of the Jews.
22. Moses there*fore* gave unto you circumcision;
43. a division among the people *because of*
8:47. ye there*fore* hear (them) not, because ye
59. going *through* the midst of them, g
9:23. There*fore* said his parents, He is of age:
10: 1. He that entereth not *by* the door into the g
2. he that entereth in *by* the door is the g
9. *by* me if any man enter in, he shall g
17. There*fore* doth my Father love me,
19. among the Jews *for* these sayings.
32. *for* which of those works do ye stone me?
11: 4. Son of God might be glorified there*by*. g
15. I am glad *for* your *sakes* that I was
42. *because of* the people which stand by
12: 9. they came not *for* Jesus' *sake* only,
11. Because that *by reason of* him many
18. *For* this *cause* the people also met him,
27. *for* this *cause* came I unto this hour.
30. This voice came not *because of* me, but *for*
your *sakes*.
39. There*fore* they could not believe.
42. *because of* the Pharisees they did not
13:11. there*fore* said he, Ye are not all clean.
14: 6. no man cometh unto the Father, but
by me. g
11. believe me *for* the very works' *sake*.
15: 3. Now ye are clean *through* the word
19. there*fore* the world hateth you.
21. do unto you *for* my name's *sake*,
16:15. there*fore* said I, that he shall take
21. *for* joy that a man is born into

Joh. 17:20. believe on me *through* their word ;g
19:11. there*fore* he that delivered me unto
23. woven from the top *through*out.g
38. secretly *for* fear of the Jews, besought
42. *because of* the Jews' preparation (day);
20:19. were assembled *for* fear of the Jews,
Act. 1: 2. he *through* the Holy Ghost had giveng
3. being seen of them (lit. *through*) forty days,g
16. *by* the mouth of David spake beforeg
2:16. which was spoken *by* the prophet Joel ;g
22. which God did *by* him in theg
23. *by* wicked hands have crucifiedg
25. the Lord always (lit. *through* all (time)) before my face,g
26. There*fore* did my heart rejoice,
43. wonders and signs were done *by* the apostles.g
3:16. the faith which is *by* him hath giveng
18. *by* the mouth of all his prophets,g
21. *by* the mouth of all his holy prophetsg
4: 2. grieved *that* (lit. *because that*) they taught the people,
16. miracle hath been done *by* themg
21. punish them, *because of* the people:
25. *by* the mouth of thy servant Davidg
30. *by* the name of thy holy child Jesus.g
5:12. *by* the hands of the apostles were manyg
19. Lord *by* night opened the prison doors,g
7:25. God *by* his hand would deliver them:g
8:11. *because that* of long time he had
18. *through* laying on of the apostles' handsg
20. may be purchased *with* money.g
9:25. let (him) down *by* the wall, in a basket.g
32. Peter passed *throughout* all (quarters),g
10:21. what (is) the cause where*fore* ye are come?
36. preaching peace *by* Jesus Christ:g
43 *through* his name whosoever believethg
11:28. signified *by* the spirit that thereg
30. *by* the hands of Barnabas and Saul.g
12: 9. which was done *by* the angel ;g
20. *because* their country was nourished
13:38. *through* this man is preached untog
49. published *throughout* all the region.g
14: 3. wonders to be done *by* their hands.g
22. we must *through* much tribulationg
15: 7. the Gentiles *by* my mouth shouldg
11. *through* the grace of the Lord Jesusg
12. wrought among the Gentiles *by* them.g
23. they wrote (letters) *by* them after thisg
27. tell (you) the same things *by* mouth.g
32. exhorted the brethren *with* many words,g
16: 3. circumcised him *because of* the Jews
9. a vision appeared to Paul *in* the night ;g
17:10. Paul and Silas *by* night unto Berea:g
18: 2. *because that* Claudius had commanded
3. *because* he was of the same craft,
9. to Paul in the night *by* a vision,g
27. which had believed *through* grace:g
28. shewing *by* the scriptures thatg
19:11. miracles *by* the hands of Paul:g
26. no gods, which are made *with* hands:g
20: 3. purposed to return *through* Macedonia.g
28. hath purchased *with* his own blood.g
21: 4. who said to Paul *through* the Spirit,g
19. among the Gentiles *by* his ministry.g
34. not know the certainty *for* the tumult,
35. *for* the violence of the people.
22:24. might know where*fore* they cried so
23:28. the cause where*fore* they accused him,
31. brought (him) *by* night to Antipatris.g
Acts24: 2. Seeing that *by* thee we enjoy greatg
— unto this nation *by* thy providence,g
17. Now *after* many years I cameg
27: 4. *because* the winds were contrary.
9. *because* the fast was now already
28: 2. *because of* the present rain, and *because* of the cold.
18. *because* there was no cause of death
20. *For* this cause therefore have I called
25. Well spake the Holy Ghost *by* Esaias prophet g
Ro. 1: 2. had promised afore *by* his prophetsg
5. *By* whom we have received graceg
8. I thank my God *through* Jesus Christ g
12. *by* the mutual faith both of you and me.g
26. *For* this cause God gave them up
2:12. shall be judged *by* the law;g
16. judge the secrets of men *by* Jesus Christg
23. *through* breaking the law dishonourestg
24. blasphemed among the Gentiles *through*
27. who *by* the letter and circumcision dostg
3:20. for *by* the law (is) the knowledge of sin.g
22. (which is) *by* faith of Jesus Christg
24. *through* the redemption that is ing
25. *through* faith in his blood,g
— *for* the remission of sins.
27. It is excluded. *By* what law?g
— *by* the law of faith.g
30. uncircumcision *through* faith.g
31. make void the law *through* faith?g
4:11. *though*g they be not circumcised; (lit. *through*g uncircumcision)
13. or to his seed, *through*g the law, but *through*g the righteousness of faith.
16. There*fore* (it is) of faith, that (it might be)
23. not written *for* his *sake* alone,
24. *for* us also, to whom it shall be
25. Who was delivered *for* our offences, and was raised again *for* our justification.
5: 1. *through* our Lord Jesus Christ:g
2. *By* whom also we have accessg
5. in our hearts *by* the Holy Ghostg
9. shall be saved from wrath *through* him.g
10. reconciled to God *by* the death of his Son,g
11. *through*g our Lord Jesus Christ, *by*g whom we have now received
12. Where*fore*, as *by*g one man sin entered into the world, and death *by*g sin;
16. not as (it was) *by* one that sinned,g
17. one man's offence death reigned *by* one ;g
— shall reign in life *by* one, Jesus Christ.g
18. as *by* the offence of one (judgment)g
— even so *by* the righteousness of oneg
19. as *by* one man's disobedienceg
— so *by* the obedience of one shall g
21. *through*g righteousness unto eternal life *by*g Jesus Christ our Lord.
6: 4. buried with him *by* baptism intog
— from the dead *by* the glory of the Father,g
19. *because of* the infirmity of your flesh:
7: 4. dead to the law *by* the body of Christ;g
5. which were *by* the law,g
7. had not known sin, but *by* the law:g
8. taking occasion *by* the commandment,g
11. taking occasion *by*g the commandment, deceived me, and *by*g it slew (me).
13. death in me *by*g that which is good; that sin *by*g the commandment might
25. *through* Jesus Christ our Lord.g
8: 3. that it was weak *through* the flesh,g
10. the body (is) dead *because of* sin; but the Spirit (is) life *because of* righteousness

Ro. 8:11. *by* his Spirit that dwelleth in you.
20. *by reason of* him who hath subjected
25. do we *with* patience wait for (it).g
37. conquerors *through* him that loved us.g
10:17. hearing *by* the word of God.g
11:8. (they are) enemies *for* your *sakes:*
— (they are) beloved *for* the fathers' *sakes.*
36. For of him, and *through* him, and to him,g
12: 1. brethren, *by* the mercies of God, thatg
3. *through* the grace given unto me,g
13: 5. be subject, not only *for* wrath, but also *for* conscience *sake.*
6. For *for* this *cause* pay ye tribute
14:14. (there is) nothing unclean *of* itself:g
15. thy brother be grieved *with* (thy) meat,
20. that man who eateth *with* offence.g
15: 4. that we *through* patience and comfortg
9. *For* this *cause* I will confess to thee
15. *because of* the grace that is given
18. which Christ hath not wrought *by* me,g
28. I will come *by* you into Spain.g
30. *for*g the Lord Jesus Christ's sake, and *for*g the love of the Spirit, that ye
32. with joy *by* the will of God,g
16:18. *by* good words and fair speeches deceiveg
26. *by* the scriptures of the prophets,g
27. (be) glory *through* Jesus Christ for ever.g
1Co. 1: 1. *through* the will of God,g
9. *by* whom ye were called untog
10. *by* the name of our Lord Jesus Christ,g
21. the world *by*g wisdom knew not God, it pleased God *by*g the foolishness of
2:10. revealed (them) unto us *by* his Spirit:g
3: 5. ministers *by* whom ye believed,g
15. shall be saved; yet so as *by* fire.g
4: 6. to myself and (to) Apollos *for* your *sakes;*
10. We (are) fools *for* Christ's *sake,*
15. I have begotten you *through* the gospel.g
17. *For* this *cause* have I sent unto you
6:14. raise up us *by* his own power.g
7: 2. Nevertheless, (to avoid) (lit. *on account of*) fornication,
5. Satan tempt you not *for* your incontinency.
26. this is good *for* the present distress,
8: 6. Jesus Christ, *by*g whom (are) all things, and we *by*g him.
11. brother perish, *for* whom Christ died?
9:10. saith he (it) altogether *for* our *sakes? For* our *sakes*, no doubt,
23. this I do *for* the gospel's *sake,*
10: 1. all passed *through* the sea;g
25. asking no question *for* conscience *sake:*
27. asking no question *for* conscience *sake.*
28. eat not *for* his *sake* that shewed it,
11: 9. Neither was the man created *for* the woman; but the woman *for* the man.
10. *For* this *cause* ought the woman to have power on (her) head *because of* the angels.
12. so (is) the man also *by* the woman;g
30. *For* this *cause* many (are) weak
12: 8. *by* the Spirit the word of wisdom;g
13:12. For now we see *through* a glass, darkly;g
14: 9. except ye utter *by* the tongue wordsg
19. rather speak five words *with* myg
15: 2. *By* which also ye are saved, if yeg
21. For since *by*g man (came) death, *by*g man (came) also the resurrection
57. victory *through* our Lord Jesus Christ.g
16: 3. whomsoever ye shall approve *by* (your)g
2Co. 1: 1. of Jesus Christ *by* the will of God,g
4. *by* the comfort, wherewith we ourselvesg

2Co. 1: 5. consolation also aboundeth *by* Christ.g
11. thanks may be given *by* many ong
16. to pass *by* you into Macedonia, and tog
19. who was preached among you *by*g us, (even) *by*g me and Silvanus and
20. unto the glory of God *by* us.g
2: 4. I wrote unto you *with* many tears;g
10. *for* your *sakes* (forgave I it) in the
14. his knowledge *by* us in every place.g
3: 4. such trust have we *through* Christg
7. *for* the glory of his countenance;
11. that which is done away (was) gloriousg (lit. *through* glory)
4: 1. There*fore* seeing we have this ministry,
5. your servants *for* Jesus' *sake.*
11. delivered unto death *for* Jesus' *sake,*
14. shall raise up us also *by* Jesus,g
15. all things (are) *for* your *sakes,*
— *through* the thanksgiving of manyg
5: 7. For we walk *by*g faith, not *by*g sightg
10. receive the things (done) *in* (his) body,g
18. reconciled us to himself *by* Jesus Christ,g
20. as though God did beseech (you) *by* us:g
6: 7. *by* the armour of righteousnessg
8. *By*g honour and dishonour, *by*g evil
7:13. There*fore* we were comforted in your
8: 5. unto us *by* the will of God.g
8. *by occasion of* the forwardness of others,g
9. yet *for* your *sakes* he became poor,
18. the gospel *throughout* all the churches;g
9:11. causeth *through* us thanksgivingg
12. *by* many thanksgivings unto God;g
13. Whiles *by* the experiment of thisg
14. *for* the exceeding grace of God
10: 1. *by* the meekness and gentleness of Christ.g
9. as if I would terrify you *by* letters.g
11. *by* letters when we are absent,g
11:33. *through*g a window in a basket was I let down *by*g the wall, and escaped
12:17. *by* any of them whom I sent unto you?g
13:10. There*fore* I write these things being
Gal. 1: 1. not of men, neither *by*g man, but *by*g Jesus Christ, and God the Father,
12. *by* the revelation of Jesus Christ.g
15. mother's womb, and called (me) *by* his grace,g
2: 1. Then fourteen years *after* I went upg
4. that *because of* false brethren unawares
16. *by* the faith of Jesus Christ, even weg
19. For I *through* the law am dead to the law,g
21. for if righteousness (come) *by* the law,g
3:14. the promise of the Spirit *through* faith.g
18. God gave (it) to Abraham *by* promise.g
19. ordained *by* angels in the hand ofg
26. children of God *by* faith in Christ Jesus.g
4: 7. then an heir of God *through* Christ.g
13. Ye know how *through* infirmity of
23. he of the freewoman (was) *by* promise.g
5: 6. faith which worketh *by* love.g
13. *by* love serve one another.g
6:14. Jesus Christ, *by* whom the world is crucifiedg
Eph. 1: 1. apostle of Jesus Christ *by* the will of God,g
5. adoption of children *by* Jesus Christg
7. we have redemption *through* his blood,g
15. Where*fore* I also, after I heard of
2: 4. *for* his great love wherewith he loved us,
8. by grace are ye saved *through* faith;g
16. unto God in one body *by* the cross,g
18. For *through* him we both haveg
3: 6. of his promise in Christ *by* the gospel:g
9. who created all things *by* Jesus Christ:g
10. might be known *by* the churchg

3:12. with confidence *by* the faith of him.g
16. be strengthened with might *by* his Spiritg
17. Christ may dwell in your hearts *by* faith;g
4: 6. who (is) above all, and *through* all,g
16. *by* that which every joint supplieth,g
18. *through* the ignorance that is in them, *because of* the blindness of their heart:
5: 6. for *because of* these things cometh
17. Where*fore* be ye not unwise,
6:13. Where*fore* take unto you the whole
18. Praying always *with* all prayer g
Phil. 1: 7. *because* I have you in my heart;
11. which are *by* Jesus Christ, unto theg
15. preach Christ even *of* envy and strife; and some also *of* good will:
19. to my salvation *through* your prayer,g
20. whether (it be) *by*g life, or *by*g death.
24. in the flesh (is) more needful *for* you.
26. *by* my coming to you again.g
2:30. Because *for* the work of Christ
3: 7. those I counted loss *for* Christ.
8. *for* the excellency of the knowledge
— *for* whom I have suffered the loss
9. which is *through* the faith of Christ,g
Col. 1: 1. of Jesus Christ *by* the will of God,g
5. *For* the hope which is laid up for
9. *For* this *cause* we also, since the
14. we have redemption *through* his blood,g
16. all things were created *by* him, and for him:g
20. peace *through*g the blood of his cross, *by*g him to reconcile all things unto himself; *by*g him, (I say), whether (they be)
22. In the body of his flesh *through* death,g
2: 8. lest any man spoil you *through* philosophyg
12. *through* the faith of the operation ofg
19. from which all the body *by* jointsg
3: 6. *For* which things' *sake* the wrath of
17. thanks to God and the Father *by* him.g
4: 3. *for* which I am also in bonds:
1Th. 1: 5. we were among you *for* your *sake*.
2:13. *For* this *cause* also thank we God
3: 5. *For* this *cause*, when I could no longer
7. There*fore*, brethren, we were comforted
— affliction and distress *by* your faith:g
9. we joy *for* your *sakes* before our God;
4: 2. we gave you *by* the Lord Jesus.g
14. them also which sleep *in* Jesusg
5: 9. obtain salvation *by* our Lord Jesus Christ,g
13. highly in love *for* their work's *sake*.
2Th. 2: 2. be troubled, neither *by*g spirit, nor *by*g word, nor *by*g letter as *from*g us, as that the day of
11. *for* this *cause* God shall send them
14. Whereunto he called you *by* our gospel,g
15. whether *by*g word, or (lit. or *by*g) our epistle.
3:12. exhort *by* our Lord Jesus Christ,g
14. obey not our word *by* this epistle,g
16. you peace always (lit. *through*g all time) by all means.
1Ti. 1:16. *for* this *cause* I obtained mercy,
2:10. professing godliness *with* good works.g
15. she shall be saved *in* childbearing,g
4: 5. sanctified *by* the word of Godg
14. which was given thee *by* prophecy,g
5:23. a little wine *for* thy stomach's *sake*
2Ti. 1: 1. *by* the will of God, according tog
6. Where*fore* I put thee in remembrance
— *by* the putting on of my hands.g
10. *by* the appearing of our Saviourg
— immortality to light *through* the gospel:g
2Ti. 1:12. *For* the which cause I also suffer
14. keep *by* the Holy Ghost whichg
2: 2. heard of me *among* many witnesses,g
10. There*fore* I endure all things *for* the elect's *sakes*.
3:15. *through* faith which is in Christ Jesus.g
4:17. that *by* me the preaching mightg
Tit. 1:13. Where*fore* rebuke them sharply,
3: 5. *by* the washing of regeneration,g
6. *through* Jesus Christ our Saviour;g
Philem. 7. saints are refreshed *by* thee, brother.g
9. Yet *for* love's *sake* I rather beseech (thee),
15. For perhaps he there*fore* departed for
22. I trust that *through* your prayersg
Heb. 1: 2. *by* whom also he made the worlds;g
3. when he had *by* himself purged our sins,g
9. there*fore* God, (even) thy God, hath
14. sent forth to minister *for* them
2: 1. There*fore* we ought to give the more
2. For if the word spoken *by* angelsg
3. began to be spoken *by* the Lord,g
9. *for* the suffering of death, crowned
10. *for* whom (are) all things, and *by*g whom
— their salvation perfect *through* sufferingsg
11. *for* which cause he is not ashamed to
14. that *through* death he might destroyg
15. through fear of death were all (lit. *through*g all) their lifetime
3:16. all that came out of Egypt *by* Moses.g
19. could not enter in *because of* unbelief.
4: 6. entered not in *because of* unbelief:
5: 3. *by reason* here*of* he ought, as for the
12. *for* the time ye ought to be teachers,
14. those who *by reason of* use have
6: 7. meet for them *by* whom it is dressed,
12. them who *through* faith and patience g
18. That *by* two immutable things,g
7: 9. receiveth tithes, payed tithes *in* Abraham.g
11. perfection were *by* the Leviticalg
18. *for* the weakness and unprofitableness
19. *by* the which we draw nigh unto God.g
21. *by* him that said unto him,g
23. *because* they were not suffered
24. this (man), *because* he continueth
25. that come unto God *by* him,g
9:11. *by* a greater and more perfect tabernacle,g
12. Neither *by*g the blood of goats and calves, but *by*g his own blood he entered in
14. who *through* the eternal Spirit g
15. *for* this *cause* he is the mediator
26. *by* the sacrifice of himself.g
10: 2. *because* that the worshippers
10. *through* the offering of the body ofg
20. consecrated for us, *through* the veil,g
11: 4. *by* which he obtained witness g
— *by* it he being dead yet speaketh.g
7. *by* the which he condemned the world,g
29. through the Red sea as *by* dry (land):g
33. Who *through* faith subdued kingdoms,g
39. obtained a good report *through* faith,g
12: 1. let us run *with* patience the race g
11. them which are exercised there*by*.g
15. there*by* many be defiled;g
28. let us have grace, where*by* we may serve g
13: 2. for there*by* some have entertainedg
11. into the sanctuary *by* the high priestg
12. sanctify the people *with* his own blood,g
15. *By* him therefore let us offer g
21. in his sight, *through* Jesus Christ;g
22. written a letter unto you *in* few words.g
Jas. 2:12. be judged *by* the law of liberty.g
4: 2. ye have not, *because* ye ask not.

1Pet. 1: 3. *by* the resurrection of Jesus Christ[g]
5. *through* faith unto salvation[g]
7. though it be tried *with* fire, might[g]
12. *by* them that have preached the gospel[g]
20. manifest in these last times *for* you,
21. Who *by* him do believe in God, that[g]
22. obeying the truth *through* the Spirit[g]
23. *by* the word of God, which liveth[g]
2: 5. acceptable to God *by* Jesus Christ.[g]
13. ordinance of man *for* the Lord's *sake*.
14. unto them that are sent *by* him[g]
19. a man *for* conscience toward God
3: 1. won *by* the conversation of the wives;[g]
14. if ye suffer *for* righteousness' *sake*,
20. eight souls were saved *by* water.[g]
21. *by* the resurrection of Jesus Christ:[g]
4:11. may be glorified *through* Jesus Christ,[g]
5:12. *By* Silvanus, a faithful brother[g]
— I have written briefly (lit. *with*[g] a few words), exhorting,

2Pet. 1: 3. *through*[g] the knowledge of him that hath called us *to*[g] glory and virtue:
4. Where*by* are given unto us exceeding[g]
— that *by* these ye might be[g]
2: 2. *by reason of* whom the way of truth
3: 5. out of the water and *in* the water:[g]
6. Where*by* the world that then[g]
12. where*in* the heavens being on fire

1Joh. 2:12. forgiven you *for* his name's *sake*.
3: 1. there*fore* the world knoweth us
4: 5. there*fore* speak they of the world,
9. that we might live *through* him.[g]
5: 6. is he that came *by* water and blood.[g]

2Joh. 2. *For* the truth's *sake*, which dwelleth
12. I would not (write) *with* paper and ink:[g]

3Joh. 10. Where*fore*, if I come, I will remember
13. I will not *with* ink and pen write[g]

Rev. 1: 1. sent and signified (it) *by* his angel[g]
9. called Patmos, *for* the word of God, and *for* the testimony
2: 3. hast patience, and *for* my name's *sake*
4:11. *for* thy pleasure they are and were
6: 9. were slain *for* the word of God, and *for* the testimony which they held:
7:15. There*fore* are they before the throne
12:11. overcame him *by* the blood of the Lamb, and *by* the word of their testimony;
12. There*fore* rejoice, (ye) heavens, and ye
13:14. *by* (the means of) those miracles
18: 8. There*fore* shall her plagues come
10. afar off *for* the fear of her torment,
15. afar off *for* the fear of her torment,
20: 4. were beheaded *for* the witness of Jesus, and *for* the word of God, and which had

1224 3 180/200 1223,rt 939

διαβαίνω, *diabaino.*

Lu. 16:26. they which would *pass* from hence
Acts16: 9. saying, *Come over* into Macedonia, *and*
Heb11:29. By faith they *passed through* the Red sea

1225 1 180/200 2:71 1223,906

διαβάλλομαι, *diaballomai.*

Lu. 16: 1. the same *was accused* unto him

1226 2 180/200 1223,950

διαβεβαιόομαι, *diabebaio-omai.*

1Ti. 1: 7. what they say, nor whereof they *affirm*.
Tit. 3: 8. things I will that thou *affirm constantly*,

1227 2 180/200 1223,991

διαβλέπω, *diablepo.*

Mat. 7: 5. then *shalt* thou *see clearly* to cast
Lu. 6:42. then *shalt* thou *see clearly* to pull

1228 38 181/200 2:71 [cf 7854] 1225

διάβολος, *diabolos.*

Mat. 4: 1. to be tempted of the *devil*.
5. Then the *devil* taketh him up into
8. Again the *devil* taketh him up
11. Then the *devil* leaveth him,
13:39. The enemy that sowed them is the *devil*
25:41. prepared for the *devil* and his angels:

Lu. 4: 2. Being forty days tempted of the *devil*.
3. the *devil* said unto him, If thou
5. the *devil*, taking him up into
6. the *devil* said unto him, All this
13. when the *devil* had ended all
8:12. then cometh the *devil* and taketh

Joh. 6:70. you twelve, and one of you is a *devil*?
8:44. Ye are of (your) father the *devil*,
13: 2. the *devil* having now put into

Acts10:38. all that were oppressed of the *devil*;
13:10. (thou) child of the *devil*, (thou) enemy

Eph. 4:27. Neither give place to the *devil*.
6:11. to stand against the wiles of the *devil*.

1Ti. 3: 6. the condemnation of the *devil*.
7. reproach and the snare of the *devil*.
11. wives (be) grave, not *slanderers*, sober,

2Ti. 2:26. out of the snare of the *devil*, who
3: 3. trucebreakers, *false accusers*, incontinent,

Tit. 2: 3. not *false accusers*, not given to much wine

Heb 2:14. power of death, that is, the *devil*;

Jas. 4: 7. Resist the *devil*, and he will flee

1Pet. 5: 8. because your adversary the *devil*,

1Joh. 3: 8. He that committeth sin is of the *devil*; for the *devil* sinneth from the beginning.
— might destroy the works of the *devil*.
10. manifest, and the children of the *devil*:

Jude 9. when contending with the *devil*

Rev. 2:10. the *devil* shall cast (some) of you
12: 9. that old serpent, called the *Devil*,
12. the *devil* is come down unto you,
20: 2. that old serpent, which is the *devil*,
10. the *devil* that deceived them was

1229 3 181/201 1:56 1223,rt 32

διαγγέλλω, *diangello.*

Lu. 9:60. go thou and *preach* the kingdom of God.
Acts21:26. to *signify* the accomplishment of the
Ro. 9:17. that my name *might be declared*

1230 3 181/201 1223,1096

διαγίνομαι, *diaginomai.*

Mar.16: 1. *when* the sabbath *was past*,
Acts25:13. *after* (lit. *when were past*) certain days king Agrippa
27: 9. Now *when* much time *was spent*,

1231 2 181/201 1223,1097

διαγινώσκω, *diaginōsko.*

Acts23:15. ye would *enquire* something more perfectly
24:22. I *will know the uttermost* of your matter.

1232 1 181/173 1123,1107

διαγνωρίζω, diagnōrizo.

Lu. 2:17. they *made known abroad* the

1233 /201 1231

διάγνωσις, diagnōsis.

Acts25:21. reserved unto the *hearing* of Augustus,

1234 /201 1:728 1223,1111

διαγογγύζω, diagonguzo.

Lu. 15: 2. the Pharisees and scribes *murmured,*
19: 7. when they saw (it), they all *murmured,*

1235 1 181/201 1223,1127

διαγρηγορέω, diagreegoreo.

Lu. 9:32. *when* they *were awake,* they saw

1236 2 181/201 1223,71

διάγω, diago.

1 Ti. 2: 2. that we *may lead* a quiet and peaceable life
Tit. 3: 3. *living* in malice and envy, hateful,

1237 1 181/201 1223,1209

διαδέχομαι, diadekomai.

Acts 7:45. also our fathers *that came after*

1238 3 181/201 1223,1210

διάδημα, diadeema.

Rev.12: 3. seven *crowns* upon his heads.
13: 1. upon his horns ten *crowns,* and upon
19:12. on his head (were) many *crowns;*

1239 5 181/201 1223,1325

διαδίδωμι, diadidōmi.

Lu. 11:22. wherein he trusted, and *divideth* his spoils.
18:22. *distribute* unto the poor, *and* thou shalt
Joh. 6:11. he *distributed* to the disciples, and the
Acts 4:35. *distribution was made* unto every
Rev.17:13. *shall give* their power and strength

1240 1 181/201 1237

διάδοχος, diadokos.

Acts24:27. Porcius Festus came into Felix' *room:* (lit. Felix received a *successor* Porcius Festus)

1241 3 182/201 5:292 1223,2224

διαζώννυμι, diazōnnumi.

Joh.13: 4. took a towel, and *girded* himself.
5. the towel wherewith he was *girded.*
21: 7. he *girt* (his) fisher's coat (unto him),

1242 33 182/201 2:104 1303

διαθήκη, diatheekee.

Mat.26:28. my blood of the new *testament,*
Mar.14:24. my blood of the new *testament,*
Lu. 1:72. to remember his holy *covenant;*
22:20. This cup (is) the new *testament* in
Acts 3:25. of the *covenant* which God made
7: 8. he gave him the *covenant* of
Ro. 9: 4. the glory, and the *covenants,* and the giving
Ro. 11:27. this (is) my *covenant* unto them,
1Co.11:25. This cup is the new *testament* in
2Co. 3: 6. able ministers of the new *testament;*
14. in the reading of the old *testament;*
Gal. 3:15. Though (it be) but a man's *covenant,*
17. the *covenant,* that was confirmed
4:24. for these are the two *covenants;*
Eph. 2:12. strangers from the *covenants* of
Heb 7:22. made a surety of a better *testament.*
8: 6. the mediator of a better *covenant,*
8. when I will make a new *covenant*
9. Not according to the *covenant* that
— they continued not in my *covenant,*
10. this (is) the *covenant* that I will make
9: 4. the ark of the *covenant* overlaid
— the tables of the *covenant;*
15. the mediator of the new *testament,*
— (that were) under the first *testament,*
16. For where a *testament* (is), there must
17. For a *testament* (is) of force after
20. This (is) the blood of the *testament*
10:16. This (is) the *covenant* that I will make
29. counted the blood of the *covenant,*
12:24. the mediator of the new *covenant,*
13:20. the blood of the everlasting *covenant,*
Rev.11:19. his temple the ark of his *testament:*

1243 3 182/202 1:180 1244

διαίρεσις, diairesis.

1Co.12: 4. Now there are *diversities* of gifts,
5. there are *differences* of administrations,
6. there are *diversities* of operations,

1244 2 182/202 1:180 1223,138

διαιρέω, diaireo.

Lu. 15:12. he *divided* unto them (his) living.
1Co.12:11. *dividing* to every man severally as

1245 2 183/202 1223,2511

διακαθαρίζω, diakatharizo.

Mat. 3:12. he *will throughly purge* his floor,
Lu. 3:17. he *will throughly purge* his floor,

1246 1 183/202 1223,2596,1651

διακατελέγχομαι, diakatelenkomai.

Acts18:28. For he mightily *convinced* the Jews,

1247 37 183/202 2:81 1249

διακονέω, diakoneo.

Mat. 4:11. angels came and *ministered unto* him.
8:15. she arose, and *ministered unto* them.
20:28. came not *to be ministered unto,* but *to minister,* and to give his life a
25:44. in prison, and *did* not *minister unto* thee?
27:55. from Galilee, *ministering unto* him:
Mar. 1:13. the angels *ministered unto* him.
31. left her, and she *ministered unto* them.
10:45. not *to be ministered unto,* but *to minister,*
15:41. followed him, and *ministered unto* him;
Lu. 4:39. she arose and *ministered unto* them.
8: 3. others, which *ministered unto* him
10:40. my sister hath left me *to serve* alone?
12:37. will come forth and *serve* them.
17: 8. I may sup, and gird thyself, and *serve* me,
22:26. he that is chief, as he *that doth serve.*
27. that sitteth at meat, or he *that serveth?*

Lu. 22:27. I am among you as he *that serveth.*
Joh. 12: 2. made him a supper; and Martha *served:*
26. If any man *serve* me, let him follow me;
— if any man *serve* me, him will (my)
Acts 6: 2. leave the word of God, and *serve* tables.
19:22. two of them *that ministered unto* him,
Ro. 15:25. unto Jerusalem to *minister unto* the saints.
2Co. 3: 3. the epistle of Christ *ministered* by us.
8:19. *which is administered* by us to the
20. *which is administered* by us:
1Ti. 3:10. *let* them *use the office of a deacon,*
13. For they *that have used the office of a deacon* well
2Ti. 1:18. how many things he *ministered unto*
Philem. 13. he *might have ministered unto* me
Heb. 6:10. *in that* ye *have ministered to* the saints, and do *minister.*
1Pet. 1:12. unto us they *did minister* the things,
4:10. (even so) *minister* the same one to another,
11. if any man *minister,* (let him do it)

1248 34 183/202 2:81 1249

διακονία, diakonia.

Lu. 10:40. Martha was cumbered about much *serving,*
Acts 1:17. had obtained part of this *ministry.*
25. he may take part of this *ministry*
6: 1. neglected in the daily *ministration.*
4. to prayer, and to the *ministry* of the word.
11:29. determined to send *relief* unto the
12:25. they had fulfilled (their) *ministry,*
20:24. the *ministry,* which I have received
21:19. among the Gentiles by his *ministry.*
Ro. 11:13. I magnify mine *office:*
12: 7. Or *ministry,* (let us wait) on (our) *ministering:*
15:31. that my *service* which (I have)
1Co. 12: 5. are differences of *administrations,*
16:15. themselves to the *ministry* of the saints,
2Co 3: 7. if the *ministration* of death, written
8. shall not the *ministration* of the spirit
9. if the *ministration* of condemnation
— doth the *ministration* of righteousness
4: 1. seeing we have this *ministry,*
5:18. to us the *ministry* of reconciliation;
6: 3. that the *ministry* be not blamed:
8: 4. the fellowship of the *ministering* to
9: 1. touching the *ministering* to the saints,
12. For the *administration* of this service
13. by the experiment of this *ministration*
11: 8. wages (of them), to *do* you *service.* (lit. for *ministering* to you)
Eph. 4:12. for the work of the *ministry,*
Col. 4:17. Take heed to the *ministry* which
1Ti. 1:12. putting me into the *ministry;*
2Ti. 4: 5. make full proof of thy *ministry.*
11. profitable to me for the *ministry.*
Heb. 1:14. spirits, sent forth to *minister* for them
Rev. 2:19. I know thy works, and charity, and *service,*

1249 30 183/203 2:81 diakō (to run errands)

διάκονος, diakonos.

Mat. 20:26. let him be your *minister;*
22:13. Then said the king to the *servants,*
23:11. greatest among you shall be your *servant.*
Mar. 9:35. be last of all, and *servant* of all.
10:43. among you, shall be your *minister:*
Joh. 2: 5. His mother saith unto the *servants,*
9. the *servants* which drew the water
Joh. 12:26. there shall also my *servant* be:
Ro. 13: 4. For he is the *minister* of God to thee
— he is the *minister* of God, a revenger
15: 8. a *minister* of the circumcision for
16: 1. Phebe our sister, which is a *servant*
1Co. 3: 5. *ministers* by whom ye believed,
2Co. 3: 6. also hath made us able *ministers*
6: 4. ourselves as the *ministers* of God,
11:15. if his *ministers* also be transformed as the *ministers* of righteousness;
23. Are they *ministers* of Christ?
Gal. 2:17. (is) therefore Christ the *minister* of sin?
Eph 3: 7. Whereof I was made a *minister,*
6:21. beloved brother and faithful *minister*
Phi. 1: 1. with the bishops and *deacons:*
Col. 1: 7. for you a faithful *minister* of Christ;
23. I Paul am made a *minister;*
25. Whereof I am made a *minister,*
4: 7. a faithful *minister* and fellowservant
1Th. 3: 2. Timotheus, our brother, and *minister* of God,
1Ti. 3: 8. Likewise (must) the *deacons* (be) grave,
12. *deacons* be the husbands of one wife,
4: 6. thou shalt be a good *minister* of

1250 8 184/203 1364,1540

διακόσιοι, diakosioi.

Mar. 6:37. *two hundred* pennyworth of bread,
Joh. 6: 7. *Two hundred* pennyworth of bread
21: 8. as it were *two hundred* cubits,
Acts 23:23. Make ready *two hundred* soldiers
— spearmen *two hundred,* at the third
27:37. *two hundred* threescore and sixteen
Rev 11: 3. a thousand *two hundred* (and) threescore
12: 6. a thousand *two hundred* (and) threescore days.

1251 1 184/203 1223,191

διακούομαι, diakou-omai.

Acts 23:35. I *will hear* thee, said he, when

1252 19 184/203 3:921 1223,2919

διακρίνω, diakrino.

Mat. 16: 3. ye can *discern* the face of the sky;
21:21. If ye have faith, and *doubt* not, ye
Mar. 11:23. shall not *doubt* in his heart,
Acts 10:20. go with them, *doubting* nothing:
11: 2. of the circumcision *contended* with him,
12. bade me go with them, nothing *doubting.*
15: 9. *put* no *difference* between us and them,
Ro. 4:20. He *staggered* not at the promise of God
14:23. he *that doubteth* is damned if he eat,
1Co. 4: 7. For who *maketh* thee *to differ*
6: 5. able *to judge* between his brethren?
11:29. not *discerning* the Lord's body.
31. For if we would *judge* ourselves,
14:29. speak two or three, and *let* the other *judge*
Jas. 1: 6. nothing *wavering.* For he that *wavereth*
2: 4. *Are* ye not then *partial* in yourselves
Jude 9. when *contending* with the devil
22. of some have compassion, *making a difference:*

1253 3 184/203 3:921 1252

διάκρισις, diakrisis.

Ro. 14: 1. not to doubtful *disputations*
1Co. 12:10. to another *discerning* of spirits; to
Heb 5:14. exercised to *discern* both good and evil.

1254 1 184/203 1223,2967

διακωλύω, diakōluō.

Mat. 3:14. John *forbad* him, saying, I have

1255 2 184/203 1223,2980

διαλαλέω, dialaleo.

Lu. 1:65. these sayings *were noised abroad*
6:11. *communed* one with another what

1256 13 184/203 2:93 1223,3004

διαλέγομαι, dialegomai.

Mar 9:34. they *had disputed* among themselves,
Acts 17: 2. *reasoned with* them out of the scriptures,
17. Therefore *disputed* he in the synagogue
18: 4. he *reasoned* in the synagogue every
19. the synagogue, and *reasoned with* the Jews.
19: 8. three months, *disputing* and persuading
9. *disputing* daily in the school
20: 7. Paul *preached unto* them, ready
9. *as* Paul *was* long *preaching*, he sunk
24:12. in the temple *disputing* with any man,
25. *as* he *reasoned* of righteousness,
Heb 12: 5. which *speaketh* unto you as unto
Jude 9. he *disputed* about the body of Moses,

1257 1 184/204 4:194 1223,3007

διαλείπω, dialīpo.

Lu. 7:45. *hath* not *ceased* to kiss my feet.

1258 6 184/204 1256

διάλεκτος, dialektos.

Acts 1:19. field is called in their proper *tongue*,
2: 6. heard them speak in his own *language*.
8. hear we every man in our own *tongue*,
21:40. spake unto (them) in the Hebrew *tongue*,
22: 2. he spake in the Hebrew *tongue* to them,
26:14. saying in the Hebrew *tongue*, Saul,

1259 1 185/204 1:251 1223,236

διαλλάττομαι, diallattomai.

Mat. 5:24. first *be reconciled* to thy brother,

1260 16 185/204 2:93 1223,3049

διαλογίζομαι, dialogizomai.

Mat. 16: 7. they *reasoned* among themselves,
8. why *reason* ye among yourselves,
21:25. they *reasoned* with themselves, saying,
Mar 2: 6. sitting there, and *reasoning* in their hearts,
8. that they so *reasoned* within themselves,
— Why *reason* ye these things in your
8:16. they *reasoned* among themselves,
17. Why *reason* ye, because ye have no bread?
9:33. that ye *disputed* among yourselves
Lu. 1:29. *cast in* her *mind* what manner
3:15. And *as*...all men *mused* in their hearts
5:21. scribes and the Pharisees began *to reason*,
22. What *reason* ye in your hearts?
12:17. he *thought* within himself, saying,
20:14. they *reasoned* among themselves,
Joh. 11:50. Nor *consider* that it is expedient

1261 14 185/204 2:93 1260

διαλογισμός, dialogismos.

Mat 15:19. out of the heart proceed evil *thoughts*,
Mar 7:21. heart of men, proceed evil *thoughts*,
Lu. 2:35. that the *thoughts* of many hearts
5:22. when Jesus perceived their *thoughts*,
6: 8. he knew their *thoughts*, and said to
9:46. there arose a *reasoning* among them,
47. perceiving the *thought* of their heart,
24:38. why do *thoughts* arise in your hearts?
Ro. 1:21. became vain in their *imaginations*,
14: 1. not to *doubtful* disputations.
1Co. 3:20. The Lord knoweth the *thoughts* of
Phi. 2:14. Do all things without murmurings and *disputings*:
1Ti. 2: 8. holy hands, without wrath and *doubting*
Jas. 2: 4. become judges of evil *thoughts*?

1262 1 185/204 1223,3089

διαλύομαι, dialuomai.

Acts 5:36. *were scattered*, and brought to nought.

1263 15 185/204 4:474 1223,3140

διαμαρτύρομαι, diamarturomai.

Lu. 16:28. that he *may testify unto* them,
Acts 2:40. many other words *did* he *testify* and exhort,
8:25. *when* they *had testified* and preached
10:42. *to testify* that it is he which was
18: 5. *and testified* to the Jews (that) Jesus (was) Christ.
20:21. *Testifying* both to the Jews, and also to
23. Holy Ghost *witnesseth* in every city,
24. *to testify* the gospel of the grace of God.
23:11. for as thou *hast testified* of me in
28:23. expounded *and testified* the kingdom of God,
1Th. 4: 6. have forewarned you and *testified*.
1Ti. 5:21. I *charge* (thee) before God, and the Lord
2Ti. 2:14. *charging* (them) before the Lord that
4: 1. I *charge* (thee) therefore before God,
Heb 2: 6. one in a certain place *testified*, saying,

1264 1 185/204 1223,3164

διαμάχομαι, diamakomai.

Acts 23: 9. the Pharisees' part arose, and *strove*, saying,

1265 5 185/205 1223,3306

διαμένω, diameno.

Lu. 1:22. beckoned unto them, and *remained* speechless.
22:28. they *which have continued* with me
Gal. 2: 5. the truth of the gospel *might continue*
Heb 1:11. They shall perish; but thou *remainest*;
2Pet. 3: 4. all things *continue* as (they were)

1266 12 185/205 1223,3307

διαμερίζω, diamerizo.

Mat. 27:35. *parted* his garments, casting lots:
— They *parted* my garments among
Mar 15:24. they *parted* his garments, casting lots
Lu. 11:17. Every kingdom *divided* against itself
18. If Satan also *be divided* against himself,
12:52. shall be five in one house *divided*,
53. The father *shall be divided* against
22:17. Take this, and *divide* (it) among yourselves:
23:34. they *parted* his raiment, *and* cast lots.
Joh. 19:24. They *parted* my raiment among them,

Acts 2: 3. appeared unto them *cloven* tongues
45. *parted* them to all (men), as every

1267 1 186/205 1266

διαμερισμός, *diamerismos.*

Lu. 12:51. I tell you, Nay; but rather *division*.

1268 1 186/205 1223,rt 3551

διανέμομαι, *dianemomai.*

Acts 4:17. that it *spread* no further among the people,

1269 1 186/205 1223,3506

διανεύω, *dianūo.*

Lu. 1:22. for he beckoned (lit. was *beckoning*) unto them, and remained

1270 1 186/205 4:948 1223,3539

διανόημα, *dianoeema.*

Lu. 11:17. he, knowing their *thoughts*, said

1271 13 186/205 4:948 1223,3563

διάνοια, *dianoya.*

Mat.22:37. with all thy soul, and with all thy *mind*.
Mar 12:30. all thy soul, and with all thy *mind*,
Lu. 1:51. in the *imagination* of their hearts.
10:27. all thy strength, and with all thy *mind*;
Eph. 1:18. The eyes of your *understanding* being
2: 3. desires of the flesh and of the *mind*;
4:18. Having the *understanding* darkened,
Col. 1:21. enemies in (your) *mind* by wicked
Heb 8:10. I will put my laws into their *mind*,
10:16. in their *minds* will I write them;
1Pet. 1:13. gird up the loins of your *mind*,
2Pet. 3: 1. I stir up your pure *minds* by way
1Joh. 5:20. hath given us an *understanding*,

1272 8 186/205 1223,455

διανοίγω, *dianoigo.*

Mar 7:34. saith unto him, Ephphatha, that is, *Be opened*.
35. straightway his ears *were opened*,
Lu. 2:23. Every male *that openeth* the womb
24:31. their eyes *were opened*, and they knew him;
32. while he *opened* to us the scriptures?
45. Then *opened* he their understanding,
Acts16:14. whose heart the Lord *opened*, that
17: 3. *Opening* and alleging, that Christ

1273 1 186/205 1223,3571

διανυκτερεύω, *dianukterūo.*

Lu. 6:12. *continued all night* in prayer to God.

1274 1 186/205 1223 anuō(to effect)

διανύω, *dianuo.*

Acts21: 7. *when* we *had finished* (our) course

1275 7 186/193 1223,3956

διαπαντός, *diapantos.*

Mar 5: 5. *always*, night and day, he was in
Lu. 24:53. were *continually* in the temple,
Acts10. 2. alms to the people, and prayed to God *alway*.
24:16. to have *always* a conscience void of
Ro. 11:10. bow down their back *alway*.
Heb 9: 6. the priests went *always* into the first tabernacle,
13:15. sacrifice of praise to God *continually*,

1276 6 186/205 1223,rt 4008

διαπεράω, *diaperao.*

Mat. 9: 1. he entered into a ship, and *passed over*,
14:34. *when* they *were gone over*, they
Mar 5:21. *when* Jesus *was passed over* again
6:53. *when* they *had passed over*, they came
Lu. 16:26. neither *can* they *pass* to us, that (would come)
Acts21: 2. finding a ship *sailing over* unto

1277 1 186/205 1223,4126

διαπλέω, *diapleo.*

Acts27: 5. *when* we *had sailed over* the sea of

1278 2 186/205 1223,4192

διαπονέομαι, *diaponeomai.*

Acts 4: 2. *Being grieved* that they taught the people,
16:18. Paul, *being grieved*, turned and said

1279 5 186/205 1223,4198

διαπορεύομαι, *diaporūomai.*

Lu. 6: 1. that he *went through* the corn fields;
13:22. he *went through* the cities and villages.
18:36. hearing the multitude *pass by*,
Acts16: 4. as they *went through* the cities,
Ro. 15:24. for I trust to see you *in my journey*.

1280 5 186/206 1223,639

διαπορέω, *diaporeo.*

Lu. 9: 7. he *was perplexed*, because that it was
24: 4. as they were *much perplexed* thereabout,
Acts 2:12. they were all amazed, and *were in doubt*,
5:24. they *doubted* of them whereunto
10:17. while Peter *doubted* in himself what

1281 1 186/206 6:632 1223,4231

διαπραγματεύομαι, *diapragmatūomai.*

Lu. 19:15. how much every man *had gained by trading*.

1282 2 187/206 1223,rt 4249

διαπρίομαι, *diapriomai.*

Acts 5:33. heard (that), they *were cut* (to the heart)
7:54. they *were cut* to the heart, and they

1283 4 187/206 1223,726

διαρπάζω, *diarpazo.*

Mat.12:29. into a strong man's house, and *spoil* his goods,
— then he *will spoil* his house.
Mar 3:27. a strong man's house, and *spoil* his goods,
— then he *will spoil* his house.

1284 5 187/206 1223,4486

διαῤῥήσσω & διαῤῥήγνυμι,
diarreesso & diarreegnumi.

Mat.26:65. Then the high priest *rent* his clothes,
Mar 14:63. Then the high priest *rent* his clothes, *and*
Lu. 5: 6. multitude of fishes: and their net *brake.*
8:29. he *brake* the bands, *and* was driven
Acts14:14. they *rent* their clothes, *and* ran in

1285 1 187/206 1223 saphes (clear)

διασαφέω, diasapheo.

Mat.18:31. came and *told unto* their lord all that

1286 1 187/206 1223,4579

διασείω, diasīo.

Lu. 3:14. *Do violence to* no man, neither accuse

1287 9 187/206 7:418 1223,4650

διασκορπίζω, diaskorpizo.

Mat 25:24. gathering where thou *hast* not *strawed:*
26. gather where I *have* not *strawed:*
26:31. the flock *shall be scattered abroad.*
Mar 14:27. the shepherd, and the sheep *shall be scattered.*
Lu. 1:51. he *hath scattered* the proud in the
15:13. there *wasted* his substance with
16: 1. that he had *wasted* his goods.
Joh. 11:52. children of God *that were scattered abroad.*
Acts 5:37. as many as obeyed him, *were dispersed.*

1288 2 187/206 1223,4685

διασπάω, diaspao.

Mar 5: 4. the chains had been *plucked asunder*
Acts23:10. lest Paul *should have been pulled in pieces*

1289 3 187/206 1223,4687

διασπείρω, diaspīro.

Acts 8: 1. they *were* all *scattered abroad* throughout
4. they *that were scattered abroad* went
11:19. they *which were scattered abroad* upon

1290 3 187/206 2:98 1289

διασπορά, diaspora.

Joh. 7:35. unto the *dispersed* (lit. the *dispersion*) among the Gentiles,
Jas. 1: 1. twelve tribes *which are scattered abroad,*
1Pet.1: 1. strangers *scattered* throughout Pontus,

1291 8 187/206 7:588 1223,4724

διαστέλλομαι, diastellomai.

Mat 16:20. Then *charged* he his disciples
Mar 5:43. he *charged* them straitly that no
7:36. he *charged* them that they should
— the more he *charged* them, so much
8:15. he *charged* them, saying, Take heed,
9: 9. he *charged* them that they should
Acts15:24. we *gave* no (such) *commandment:*
Heb 12:20. not endure *that which was commanded,*

1292 1 187/206 1339

διάστημα, diasteema.

Acts 5: 7. it was about the *space* of three hours

1293 3 188/206 7:588 1291

διαστολή, diastolee.

Ro. 3:22. for there is no *difference:*
10:12. no *difference* between the Jew and the
1Co.14: 7. except they give a *distinction* in the sounds,

1294 7 188/206 7:714 1223,4762

διαστρέφω, diastrepho.

Mat.17:17. O faithless and *perverse* generation, how
Lu. 9:41. O faithless and *perverse* generation, how
23: 2. We found this (fellow) *perverting* the nation,
Acts13: 8. seeking *to turn away* the deputy from
10. cease to *pervert* the right ways of the Lord?
20:30. men arise, speaking *perverse* things,
Phi. 2:15. midst of a crooked and *perverse* nation,

1295 8 188/207 1223,4982

διασώζω, diasōzo.

Mat.14:36. many as touched *were made perfectly whole.*
Lu. 7: 3. that he would come and *heal* his servant.
Acts23:24. *bring* (him) *safe* unto Felix the governor
27:43. the centurion, willing *to save* Paul,
44. that they *escaped* all *safe* to land.
28: 1. *when* they *were escaped,* then they
4. *though* he *hath escaped* the sea, yet
1Pet.3:20. eight souls *were saved* by water.

1296 2 188/207 8:27 1299

διαταγή, diatagee.

Acts 7:53. the law by the *disposition* of angels,
Ro. 13: 2. resisteth the *ordinance* of God: and they

1297 1 188/207 1299

διάταγμα, diatagma.

Heb 11:23. not afraid of the king's *commandment.*

1298 1 188/207 1223,5015

διαταράττω, diataratto.

Lu. 1:29. she *was troubled* at his saying, and cast

1299 16 188/207 8:27 1223,5021

διατάσσω, diatasso.

Mat.11: 1. of *commanding* his twelve disciples,
Lu. 3:13. than that *which is appointed* you.
8:55. he *commanded* to give her meat.
17: 9. things *that were commanded* him?
10. those things *which are commanded* you,
Acts 7:44. as he *had appointed,* speaking
18: 2. Claudius *had commanded* all
20:13. for so had he *appointed,* minding
23:31. the soldiers, as it *was commanded*
24:23. he *commanded* a centurion to keep
1Co. 7:17. so *ordain* I in all churches.
9:14. Even so hath the Lord *ordained*
11:34. the rest *will* I *set in order* when
16: 1. as I *have given order* to the churches
Gal. 3:19. (it was) *ordained* by angels in
Tit. 1: 5. as I *had appointed* thee·

1300 1 188/207 1223,5055

διατελέω, diateleo.

Acts27:33. *continued* fasting, having taken nothing.

1301 2 188/207 8:140 1223,5083

διατηρέω, diateereo.

Lu. 2:51. his mother *kept* all these sayings in
Acts15:29. from which *if* ye *keep* yourselves, ye

1302 27 188/197 1223,5101

διατί, diati.

Mat. 9:11 *Why* eateth your Master with publicans
14. *Why* do we and the Pharisees fast oft,
13:10. *Why* speakest thou unto them in parables?
15: 2. *Why* do thy disciples transgress
3. *Why* do ye also transgress the
17:19. *Why* could not we cast him out?
21:25. *Why* did ye not then believe him?
Mar. 2:18. *Why* do the disciples of John and of the
7: 5. *Why* walk not thy disciples according
11:31. *Why* then did ye not believe him?
Lu. 5:30. *Why* do ye eat and drink with publicans
33. *Why* do the disciples of John fast often,
19:23. *Wherefore* then gavest not thou my
31. ask you, *Why* do ye loose (him)?
20: 5. *Why* then believed ye him not?
24:38. *why* do thoughts arise in your hearts?
Joh. 7:45. *Why* have ye not brought him?
8:43. *Why* do ye not understand my speech?
46. *why* do ye not believe me?
12: 5. *Why* was not this ointment sold
13:37. Lord, *why* cannot I follow thee now?
Acts 5: 3. *why* hath Satan filled thine heart
Ro. 9:32. *Wherefore?* Because (they sought it)
1Co. 6: 7. *Why* do ye not rather take wrong? *why* do ye not rather (suffer yourselves)
2Co.11:11. *Wherefore?* because I love you not?
Rev.17: 7. *Wherefore* didst thou marvel?

1303 7 188/207 2:104 1223,5087

διατιθεμαι, diatithemai.

Lu. 22:29. I *appoint* unto you a kingdom, as my Father *hath appointed* unto me;
Acts 3:25. the covenant which God *made*
Heb. 8:10. the covenant that I *will make* with
9:16. be the death of the *testator*.
17. strength at all while the *testator* liveth.
10:16. the covenant that I *will make* with

1304 10 189/207 1223,rt 5147

διατρίβω, diatribo.

Joh. 3:22. there he *tarried* with them, and baptized.
11:54. there *continued* with his disciples.
Acts12:19. from Judæa to Cæsarea, and (there) *abode*.
14: 3. Long time therefore *abode* they speaking
28. there they *abode* long time with
15:35. Paul also and Barnabas *continued* in Antioch,
16:12. we were in that city *abiding* certain days.
20: 6. where we *abode* seven days.
25: 6. And *when* he *had tarried* among them
14. when they *had been* there many days,

1305 1 189/207 1223,5142

διατροφή, diatrophee.

Ti. 6: 8. having *food* and raiment let us be

1306 1 189/207 1223,826

διαυγάζω, diaugazo.

2Pet. 1:19. until the day *dawn*, and the day star

1307 1 189/207 1223,5316

διαφανής, diaphanees.

Rev.21:21. as it were *transparent* glass.

1308 13 189/207 9:56 1223,5342

διαφέρω, diaphero.

Mat. 6:26. *Are* ye not much *better* than they?
10:31. ye *are of more value* than many sparrows.
12:12. How much then *is* a man *better* than a sheep?
Mar11:16. that any man *should carry* (any) vessel
Lu. 12: 7. ye *are of more value* than many sparrows.
24. more *are* ye *better* than the fowls?
Acts13:49. word of the Lord *was published* throughout
27:27. *as* we *were driven up and down* in
Ro. 2:18. the things *that are more excellent*,
1Co.15:41. for (one) star *differeth from* (another)
Gal. 2: 6. it *maketh* no *matter* to me:
4: 1. *differeth* nothing *from* a servant,
Phi. 1:10. ye may approve things *that are excellent*;

1309 1 189/208 1223,5343

διαφεύγω, diaphūgo.

Acts27:42. any of them should swim out, and *escape*

1310 3 189/208 1223,5345

διαφημίζω, diapheemizo.

Mat. 9:31. *spread abroad* his *fame* in all that country.
28:15. this saying *is commonly reported* among
Mar. 1:45. *to blaze abroad* the matter, insomuch

1311 6 189/208 9:93 1225,5351

διαφθείρω, diapthīro.

Lu. 12:33. no thief approacheth, neither moth *corrupteth*.
2Co. 4:16. though our outward man *perish*,
1Ti. 6: 5. disputings of men of *corrupt* minds,
Rev. 8: 9. third part of the ships *were destroyed*.
11:18. shouldest *destroy* them *which destroy* the earth.

1312 6 189/208 9:93 1311

διαφθορά, diaphthora.

Acts 2:27. suffer thine Holy One to see *corruption*.
31. neither his flesh did see *corruption*.
13:34. no more to return to *corruption*,
35. suffer thine Holy One to see *corruption*.
36. laid unto his fathers, and saw *corruption*:
37. God raised again, saw no *corruption*.

1313 4 190/208 9:56 1308

διάφορος, diaphoros.

Ro. 12: 6. gifts *differing* according to the grace
Heb. 1: 4. obtained a *more excellent* name
8: 6. obtained a *more excellent* ministry,
9:10. in meats and drinks, and *divers* washings,

1314 1 190/208 1223,5442

διαφυλάττω, diaphulatto.

Lu. 4:10. his angels charge over thee, *to keep* thee.

1315 2 190/208 1223,5495

διαχειρίζομαι, diakirizomai.

Acts 5:30. Jesus, whom ye *slew* and hanged on a tree.
26:21. the temple, and went about *to kill* (me).

1316 1 190/208 1223,5563

διαχωρίζομαι, diakōrizomai.

Lu. 9:33. as they *departed* from him, Peter said

1317 2 190/208 2:135 1318

διδακτικός, didaktikos.

1Ti. 3: 2. given to hospitality, *apt to teach;*
2Ti. 2:24. gentle unto all (men), *apt to teach,*

1318 3 190/208 2:135 1321

διδακτός, didaktos.

Joh. 6:45. they shall be all *taught* of God.
1Co. 2:13. words *which* man's wisdom *teacheth*, but *which* the Holy Ghost *teacheth;*

1319 21 190/208 2:135 1320

διδασκαλία, didaskalia.

Mat.15: 9. teaching (for) *doctrines* the commandments
Mar. 7: 7. teaching (for) *doctrines* the commandments of men.
Ro. 12: 7. or he that teacheth, on *teaching;*
15: 4. aforetime were written for our *learning,*
Eph. 4:14. about with every wind of *doctrine,*
Col. 2:22. the commandments and *doctrines* of men?
1Ti. 1:10. that is contrary to sound *doctrine;*
4: 1. to seducing spirits, and *doctrines* of devils;
6. words of faith and of good *doctrine,*
13. to reading, to exhortation, to *doctrine.*
16. Take heed unto thyself, and unto the *doctrine;*
5:17. who labour in the word and *doctrine.*
6: 1. the name of God and (his) *doctrine* be
3. to the *doctrine* which is according
2Ti. 3:10. thou hast fully known my *doctrine,*
16. profitable for *doctrine*, for reproof,
4: 3. will not endure sound *doctrine;*
Tit. 1: 9. may be able by sound *doctrine*
2: 1. things which become sound *doctrine:*
7. in *doctrine* (shewing) uncorruptness,
10. may adorn the *doctrine* of God

1320 58 190/208 2:135 1321

διδάσκαλος, didaskalos.

Mat. 8:19. said unto him, *Master*, I will
9:11. Why eateth your *Master* with publicans
10:24. The disciple is not above (his) *master,*
25. the disciple that he be as his *master,*
12:38. *Master*, we would see a sign from thee.
17:24. Doth not your *master* pay tribute?
19:16. Good *Master*, what good thing
22:16. *Master*, we know that thou art true,
24. Saying, *Master*, Moses said, If a
36. *Master*, which (is) the great commandment
26:18. say unto him, The *Master* saith,
Mar. 4:38. *Master*, carest thou not that we perish?
5:35. why troublest thou the *Master*
9:17. said, *Master*, I have brought
38. *Master*, we saw one casting out
10:17. Good *Master*, what shall I do
20. *Master*, all these have I observed
Mar.10:35. saying, *Master*, we would that
12:14. they say unto him, *Master*, we know
19. *Master*, Moses wrote unto us,
32. Well, *master*, thou hast said the
13: 1. *Master*, see what manner of stones
14:14. The *master* saith, Where is the
Lu. 2:46. sitting in the midst of the *doctors,*
3:12. *Master*, what shall we do?
6:40. The disciple is not above his *master:*
— perfect shall be as his *master.*
7:40. he saith, *Master*, say on.
8:49. is dead; trouble not the *Master.*
9:38. saying, *Master*, I beseech thee,
10:25. *Master*, what shall I do to inherit
11:45. said unto him, *Master*, thus saying
12:13. said unto him, *Master*, speak
18:18. saying, Good *Master*, what shall
19:39. said unto him, *Master*, rebuke thy disciples.
20:21. *Master*, we know that thou sayest
28. Saying, *Master*, Moses wrote unto us,
39. said, *Master*, thou hast well said.
21: 7. saying, *Master*, but when shall
22:11. The *Master* saith unto thee, Where
Joh. 1:38(39). to say, being interpreted, *Master,*
3: 2. we know that thou art a *teacher*
10. Art thou a *master* of Israel,
8: 4. They say unto him, *Master*, this
11:28. saying, The *Master* is come,
13:13. Ye call me *Master* and Lord: and ye
14. If I then, (your) Lord and *Master,*
20:16. Rabboni; which is to say, *Master.*
Acts13: 1. at Antioch certain prophets and *teachers;*
Ro. 2:20. a *teacher* of babes, which hast the
1Co.12:28. secondarily prophets, thirdly *teachers,*
29. (are) all prophets? (are) all *teachers?*
Eph. 4:11. evangelists; and some, pastors and *teachers;*
1Ti. 2: 7. a *teacher* of the Gentiles in faith
2Ti. 1:11. an apostle, and a *teacher* of the Gentiles.
4: 3. they heap to themselves *teachers,*
Heb. 5:12. for the time ye ought to be *teachers,*
Jas. 3: 1. My brethren, be not many *masters,*

1321 97 191/209 2:135 *daō* (to learn)

διδάσκω, didasko.

Mat. 4:23. *teaching* in their synagogues, and preaching
5: 2. he opened his mouth, and *taught* them,
19. *shall teach* men so, he shall be
— whosoever shall do and *teach* (them),
7:29. he taught (lit. was *teaching*) them as (one) having authority,
9:35. *teaching* in their synagogues,
11: 1. *to teach* and to preach in their cities.
13:54. he *taught* them in their synagogue,
15: 9. *teaching* (for) doctrines the commandments
21:23. came unto him *as* he *was teaching,*
22:16. and *teachest* the way of God in truth,
26:55. with you *teaching* in the temple,
28:15. did as they *were taught:* and this
20. *Teaching* them to observe all things
Mar. 1:21. entered into the synagogue, and *taught.*
22. for he taught (lit. was *teaching*) them as one that had
2:13. resorted unto him, and he *taught* them.
4: 1. he began again *to teach* by the
2. he *taught* them many things
6: 2. began *to teach* in the synagogue:
6. round about the villages, *teaching.*

Mar. 6:30. had done, and what they *had taught*.
34. he began *to teach* them many things.
7: 7. *teaching* (for) doctrines the commandments
8:31. he began *to teach* them, that the
9:31. For he *taught* his disciples, and said
10: 1. as he was wont, he *taught* them
11:17. he *taught*, saying unto them,
12:14. but *teachest* the way of God in truth:
35. *while* he *taught* in the temple,
14:49. daily with you in the temple *teaching*,
Lu. 4:15. he *taught* in their synagogues,
31. taught (lit. was *teaching*) them on the sabbath days.
5: 3. *taught* the people out of the ship.
17. on a certain day, as he was *teaching*,
6: 6. entered into the synagogue and *taught*:
11: 1. said unto him, Lord, *teach* us to pray, as John also *taught* his disciples.
12:12. the Holy Ghost *shall teach* you in the
13:10. he was *teaching* in one of the synagogues
22. went through the cities and villages, *teaching*,
26. thou *hast taught* in our streets.
19:47. he taught (lit. was *teaching*) daily in the temple.
20: 1. *as* he *taught* the people in the temple,
21. we know that thou sayest and *teachest* rightly,
— *teachest* the way of God truly:
21:37. in the day time he was *teaching* in the
23: 5. *teaching* throughout all Jewry,
Joh. 6:59. *as* he *taught* in Capernaum.
7:14. Jesus went up into the temple, and *taught*.
28. cried Jesus in the temple *as* he *taught*,
35. among the Gentiles, and *teach* the Gentiles?
8: 2. he sat down, and *taught* them.
20. *as* he *taught* in the temple: and no
28. as my Father *hath taught* me, I
9:34. born in sins, and dost thou *teach* us?
14:26. he *shall teach* you all things,
18:20. I ever *taught* in the synagogue,
Acts 1: 1. Jesus began both to do and *teach*,
4: 2. grieved that they *taught* the people,
18. not to speak at all nor *teach* in
5:21. early in the morning, and *taught*.
25. in the temple, and *teaching* the people.
28. ye should not *teach* in this name?
42. they ceased not to *teach* and preach
11:26. with the church, and *taught* much people.
15: 1. down from Judæa *taught* the brethren,
35. *teaching* and preaching the word
18:11. *teaching* the word of God among them.
25. he spake and *taught* diligently the
20:20. have shewed you, and *have taught* you
21:21. that thou *teachest* all the Jews
28. This is the man, *that teacheth* all
28:31. *teaching* those things which
Ro. 2:21. Thou therefore *which teachest* another, *teachest* thou not thyself?
12: 7. or he *that teacheth*, on teaching;
1Co. 4:17. as I *teach* every where in every church.
11:14. Doth not even nature itself *teach* you,
Gal. 1:12. neither *was* I *taught* (it), but by
Eph. 4:21. heard him, and *have been taught* by him,
Col. 1:28. *teaching* every man in all wisdom;
2: 7. as ye *have been taught*, abounding
3:16. *teaching* and admonishing one another
2Th. 2:15. traditions which ye *have been taught*,
1Ti. 2:12. I suffer not a woman *to teach*,
4:11. These things command and *teach*.
6: 2. These things *teach* and exhort.
2Ti. 2: 2. who shall be able *to teach* others also.
Tit. 1:11. *teaching* things which they ought not,
Heb. 5:12. ye have need that one *teach* you
8:11. they shall not *teach* every man
1Joh. 2:27. ye need not that any man *teach* you:
— the same anointing *teacheth* you
— even as it *hath taught* you, ye
Rev. 2:14. who *taught* Balac to cast a stumblingblock
20. *to teach* and to seduce my servants

1322 /210 2:135 1321

διδαχή, *didakee.*

Mat. 7:28. were astonished at his *doctrine*:
16:12. of the *doctrine* of the Pharisees and of
22:33. they were astonished at his *doctrine*.
Mar. 1:22. they were astonished at his *doctrine*:
27. what new *doctrine* (is) this? for
4: 2. said unto them in his *doctrine*,
11:18. the people was astonished at his *doctrine*.
12:38. he said unto them in his *doctrine*,
Lu. 4:32. they were astonished at his *doctrine*.
Joh. 7:16. My *doctrine* is not mine, but his
17. he shall know of the *doctrine*,
18:19. of his disciples, and of his *doctrine*.
Acts 2:42. in the apostles' *doctrine* and fellowship,
5:28. filled Jerusalem with your *doctrine*,
13:12. astonished at the *doctrine* of the Lord.
17:19. what this new *doctrine*, whereof
Ro. 6:17. form of *doctrine* which was delivered
16:17. offences contrary to the *doctrine*
1Co. 14: 6. or by prophesying, or by *doctrine*?
26. hath a psalm, hath a *doctrine*,
2Ti. 4: 2. with all longsuffering and *doctrine*.
Tit. 1: 9. Holding fast the faithful word as he *hath been taught*,
Heb. 6: 2. Of the *doctrine* of baptisms, and of
13: 9. about with divers and strange *doctrines*.
2Joh. 9. abideth not in the *doctrine* of Christ,
— He that abideth in the *doctrine* of Christ,
10. bring not this *doctrine*, receive him
Rev. 2:14. that hold the *doctrine* of Balaam,
15. that hold the *doctrine* of the Nicolaitanes
24. as many as have not this *doctrine*,

1323 2 191/211 1364,1406

δίδραχμον, *didrakmon.*

Mat. 17:24. they that received *tribute* (money)
— Doth not your master pay *tribute*?

1325 413 191/211 2:166

δίδωμι, *didōmi.*

Mat. 4: 9. All these things *will* I *give* thee,
5:31. *let* him *give* her a writing of divorcement.
42. *Give* to him that asketh thee,
6:11. *Give* us this day our daily bread.
7: 6. *Give* not that which is holy unto
7. Ask, and it *shall be given* you;
11. know how to *give* good gifts unto
— *shall* your Father which is in heaven *give*
9: 8. which *had given* such power unto men.
10: 1. he *gave* them power (against) unclean
8. freely ye have received, freely *give*.
19. it *shall be given* you in that same
12:39. there *shall* no sign *be given* to it,
13: 8. into good ground, and *brought forth* fruit,
11. Because it *is given* unto you to know
— to them it *is not given*.
12. whosoever hath, to him *shall be given*.

Mat.14: 7. *to give* her whatsoever she would ask.
8. *Give* me here John Baptist's head
9. he commanded (it) *to be given* (her).
11. in a charger, and *given* to the damsel:
16. need not depart; *give* ye them to eat.
19. *gave* the loaves to (his) disciples,
15:36. brake (them), and *gave* to his disciples,
16: 4. there *shall* no sign *be given* unto it,
19. I *will give* unto thee the keys of the
26. what *shall* a man *give* in exchange
17:27. that take, and *give* unto them for me and thee.
19: 7. command *to give* a writing of divorcement,
11. save (they) to whom it *is given.*
21. *give* to the poor, and thou shalt have
20: 4. whatsoever is right I *will give* you.
14. I will *give* unto this last, even
23. on my left, is not mine *to give,*
28. *to give* his life a ransom for many.
21:23. who *gave* thee this authority?
43. shall be taken from you, and *given* to
22:17. Is it lawful *to give* tribute unto
24:24. *shall shew* great signs and wonders;
29. the moon *shall* not *give* her light,
45. *to give* them meat in due season?
25: 8. *Give* us of your oil; for our lamps
15. unto one he *gave* five talents,
28. *give* (it) unto him which hath ten
29. every one that hath *shall be given,*
35. an hungred, and ye *gave* me meat:
42. an hungred, and ye *gave* me no meat:
26: 9. sold for much, and *given* to the poor.
15. said (unto them), What will ye *give* me,
26. brake (it), and *gave* (it) to the disciples,
27. gave thanks, and *gave* (it) to them, saying,
48. he that betrayed him *gave* them
27:10. *gave* them for the potter's field,
34. They *gave* him vinegar to drink
28:12. they *gave* large money unto
18. All power *is given* unto me in heaven
Mar. 2:26. *gave* also to them which were with him?
4: 7. choked it, and it *yielded* no fruit.
8. *did yield* fruit that sprang up
11. Unto you it *is given* to know the
25. he that hath, to him *shall be given:*
5:43. something should *be given* her to eat.
6: 2. this *which is given* unto him,
7. *gave* them power over unclean spirits;
22. whatsoever thou wilt, and I *will give* (it)
23. I *will give* (it) thee, unto the half
25. I will that thou *give* me by and by
28. in a charger, and *gave* it to the damsel: and the damsel *gave* it to her mother.
37. *Give* ye them to eat. And they
— of bread, and *give* them to eat?
41. *gave* (them) to his disciples to set
8: 6. brake, and *gave* to his disciples to set
12. There *shall* no sign *be given* unto
37. what *shall* a man *give* in exchange
10:21. *give* to the poor, and thou shalt have
37. *Grant* unto us that we may sit,
40. is not mine *to give;* but (it shall be)
45. *to give* his life a ransom for many.
11:28. who *gave* thee this authority to do
12: 9. *will give* the vineyard unto others.
14. Is it lawful *to give* tribute to Cæsar,
15(14). Shall we *give*, or shall we not *give?*
13:11. shall *be given* you in that hour,
22. *shall shew* signs and wonders, to
24. the moon *shall* not *give* her light,
34. *gave* authority to his servants.

Mar 14: 5. and *have been given* to the poor.
11. promised *to give* him money.
22. brake (it), and *gave* to them, and said,
23. had given thanks, he *gave* (it) to them,
44. betrayed him *had given* them a
15:23. they *gave* him to drink wine
Lu. 1:32. the Lord God *shall give* unto him the
74(73). That he would *grant* unto us,
77. *To give* knowledge of salvation
2:24. *to offer* a sacrifice according to that
4: 6. All this power *will I give* thee,
— to whomsoever I will I *give* it.
6: 4. *gave* also to them that were with him;
30. *Give* to every man that asketh of thee;
38. *Give*, and it *shall be given* unto you;
— *shall* men *give* into your bosom.
7:15. he *delivered* him to his mother.
44. thou *gavest* me no water for my feet:
45. Thou *gavest* me no kiss: but this
8:10. Unto you it *is given* to know the
18. whosoever hath, to him *shall be given*,
55. he commanded *to give* her meat.
9: 1. *gave* them power and authority over all
13. said unto them, *Give* ye them to eat.
16. *gave* to the disciples to set before
10:19. I *give* unto you power to tread on
35. two pence, and *gave* (them) to the host,
11: 3. *Give* us day by day our daily bread.
7. I cannot rise and *give* thee.
8. Though he will not rise and *give* him,
— he will rise and *give* him as many
9. Ask, and it *shall be given* you; seek,
13. *to give* good gifts unto your children:
— *shall* (your) heavenly Father *give* the
29. there *shall* no sign *be given* it, but
41. rather *give* alms of such things
12:32. your Father's good pleasure *to give* you
33. Sell that ye have, and *give* alms;
42. *to give* (them their) portion of meat
48. unto whomsoever much *is given,* of
51. that I am come *to give* peace on earth?
58. *give* diligence that thou mayest be
14: 9. say to thee, *Give* this man place;
15:12. Father, *give* me the portion of goods
16. no man *gave* unto him.
22. *put* a ring on his hand, and shoes on
29. yet thou never *gavest* me a kid,
16:12. who *shall give* you that which is
17:18. that returned *to give* glory to God,
18:43. when they saw(it), *gave* praise unto God.
19: 8. my goods I *give* to the poor;
13. *delivered* them ten pounds, and said
15. to whom he *had given* the money,
23. Wherefore then *gavest* not thou my
24. *give* (it) to him that hath ten pounds.
26. unto every one which hath *shall be given*
20: 2. who is he *that gave* thee this authority?
10. they *should give* him of the fruit
16. *shall give* the vineyard to others.
22. Is it lawful for us *to give* tribute
21:15. For I *will give* you a mouth
22: 5. covenanted *to give* him money.
19. brake (it), and *gave* unto them, saying This is my body *which is given* for you.
23: 2. forbidding *to give* tribute to Cæsar,
Joh. 1:12. to them *gave* he power to become
17. the law *was given* by Moses,
22. that we *may give* an answer to
3:16. that he *gave* his only begotten Son,
27. except it be *given* him from heaven.
34. God *giveth* not the Spirit by measure
35. *hath given* all things into his hand

Joh. 4: 5. that Jacob *gave* to his son Joseph.
7. Jesus saith unto her, *Give* me to drink.
10. saith to thee, *Give* me to drink;
— he would *have given* thee living water.
12. Jacob, which *gave* us the well,
14. the water that I *shall give* him
— the water that I *shall give* him shall
15. Sir, *give* me this water, that I thirst not,
5:22. *hath committed* all judgment unto
26. so *hath* he *given* to the Son to have
27. *hath given* him authority to execute
36. which the Father *hath given* me
6:27. the Son of man *shall give* unto you:
31. He *gave* them bread from heaven
32. Moses *gave* you not that bread
— my Father *giveth* you the true
33. *giveth* life unto the world.
34. Lord, evermore *give* us this bread.
37. All that the Father *giveth* me
39. of all which he *hath given* me
51. bread that I *will give* is my flesh, which I *will give* for the life of the world.
52. How can this man *give* us (his) flesh
65. were *given* unto him of my Father.
7:19. *Did* not Moses *give* you the law,
22. Moses therefore *gave* unto you circumcision;
9:24. said unto him, *Give* God the praise:
10:28. I *give* unto them eternal life;
29. My Father, which *gave* (them) me,
11:22. God *will give* (it) thee.
57. the Pharisees *had given* a commandment,
12: 5. three hundred pence, and *given* to the poor?
49. he *gave* me a commandment,
13: 3. the Father *had given* all things into
15. For I *have given* you an example,
26. the sop, he *gave* (it) to Judas Iscariot,
29. that he *should give* something to
34. A new commandment I *give* unto you,
14:16. he *shall give* you another Comforter,
27. my peace I *give* unto you: not as the world *giveth, give* I unto you.
15:16. in my name, he *may give* it you.
16:23. in my name, he *will give* (it) you.
17: 2. As thou *hast given* him power
— that he *should give* eternal life to as many as thou *hast given* him.
4. work which thou *gavest* me to do.
6. which thou *gavest* me out of the world: thine they were, and thou *gavest* them me;
7. whatsoever thou *hast given* me
8. I *have given* unto them the words which thou *gavest* me;
9. for them which thou *hast given* me;
11. those whom thou *hast given* me,
12. those that thou *gavest* me I have kept,
14. I *have given* them thy word; and the
22. the glory which thou *gavest* me I *have given* them;
24. they also, whom thou *hast given* me,
— my glory, which thou *hast given* me:
18: 9. Of them which thou *gavest* me have I
11. cup which my Father *hath given* me,
22. struck Jesus (lit. *gave* a blow to) with the palm of his hand,
19: 3. they *smote* him with their hands.
9. Jesus *gave* him no answer.
11. except it were *given* thee from above:
21:13. taketh bread, and *giveth* them, and fish
Acts 1:26. they *gave* forth their lots; and the lot
2: 4. as the Spirit *gave* them utterance.

Acts 2:19. I *will shew* wonders in heaven above,
27. neither *wilt* thou *suffer* thine Holy
3: 6. such as I have *give* I thee: In the
16. *hath given* him this perfect soundness
4:12. name under heaven *given* among men,
29. *grant* unto thy servants, that with
5:31. for *to give* repentance to Israel,
32. whom God *hath given* to them that
7: 5. he *gave* him none inheritance in it,
— promised that he would *give* it to him
8. he *gave* him the covenant of circumcision:
10. *gave* him favour and wisdom in the sight
25. God by his hand would deliver (lit. *give* salvation to) them:
38. the lively oracles *to give* unto us:
8:18. the Holy Ghost *was given*, he offered
19. Saying, *Give* me also this power, that
9:41. he *gave* her (his) hand, *and* lifted her
10:40. the third day, and shewed him openly; (lit. *gave* him to be manifested)
11:17. as God *gave* them the like gift as
18. to the Gentiles *granted* repentance
12:23. because he *gave* not God the glory:
13:20. after that he *gave* (unto them) judges
21. God *gave* unto them Saul the son of Cis,
34. I *will give* you the sure mercies of David.
35. *shalt* not *suffer* thine Holy One to see
14: 3. and *granted* signs and wonders to be done
17. *and gave* us rain from heaven, and fruitful
15: 8. *giving* them the Holy Ghost, even
17:25. *seeing* he *giveth* to all life, and breath,
19:31. not *adventure* himself into the theatre.
20:32. *to give* you an inheritance among
35. It is more blessed *to give* than to receive.
24:26. money should *have been given* him
Ro 4:20. strong in faith, *giving* glory to God;
5: 5. Holy Ghost *which is given* unto us.
11: 8. God *hath given* them the spirit of
12: 3. through the grace *given* unto me,
6. the grace *that is given* to us, whether
19. *give* place unto wrath: for it is written,
14:12. *shall give* account of himself to God.
15: 5. *grant* you to be likeminded one
15. the grace *that is given* to me of God,
1Co. 1: 4. the grace of God *which is given*
3: 5. even as the Lord *gave* to every man?
10. grace of God *which is given* unto me,
7:25. yet I *give* my judgment, as one
9:12. lest we should hinder (lit. *give* any hindrance to) the gospel
11:15. hair *is given* her for a covering.
12: 7. manifestation of the Spirit *is given* to every
8. to one *is given* by the Spirit the word
24. *having given* more abundant honour
14: 7. things without life *giving* sound,
— except they *give* a distinction in the
8. if the trumpet *give* an uncertain sound,
9. except ye *utter* by the tongue words easy
15:38. God *giveth* it a body as it hath pleased
57. God, *which giveth* us the victory through
2Co. 1:22. and *given* the earnest of the Spirit
5: 5. *who* also *hath given* unto us the earnest
12. *give* you occasion to glory on our behalf,
18. and *hath given* to us the ministry of
6: 3. *Giving* no offence in any thing,
8: 1. grace of God *bestowed* on the churches
5. first *gave* their own selves to the Lord,
10. herein I *give* (my) advice: for this
16. God, *which put* the same earnest care
9: 9. he *hath given* to the poor: his
10: 8. the Lord *hath given* us for edification,

2Co 12: 7. there *was given* to me a thorn in
13:10. power which the Lord *hath given* me
Gal. 1: 4. *Who gave* himself for our sins,
2: 9. the grace *that was given* unto me, they *gave* to me and Barnabas the
3:21. if there *had been* a law *given* which
22. *might be given* to them that believe.
4:15. your own eyes, and *have given* them to me.
Eph. 1:17. *may give* unto you the spirit of
22. *gave* him (to be) the head over all
3: 2. *which is given* me to you-ward:
7. the grace of God *given* unto me by
8. *is* this grace *given*, that I should
16. That he *would grant* you, according
4: 7. unto every one of us *is given* grace
8. captivity captive, and *gave* gifts unto men.
11. he *gave* some, apostles; and some,
27. Neither *give* place to the devil.
29. that it *may minister* grace unto
6:19. that utterance *may be given* unto me,
Col. 1:25. *which is given* to me for you,
1Th. 4: 2. we *gave* you by the Lord Jesus.
8. *who hath* also *given* unto us his holy Spirit.
2Th. 1: 8. *taking* vengeance on them that
2:16. and *hath given* (us) everlasting consolation
3: 9. to *make* ourselves an ensample
16. *give* you peace always by all means.
1Ti. 2: 6. *Who gave* himself a ransom for
4:14. which *was given* thee by prophecy,
5:14. *give* none occasion to the adversary
2Ti. 1: 7. God *hath* not *given* us the spirit of fear;
9. grace, *which was given* us in Christ
16. The Lord *give* mercy unto the house
18. The Lord *grant* unto him that he
2: 7. the Lord *give* thee understanding
25. if God peradventure will *give* them
Tit. 2:14. Who *gave* himself for us, that he
Heb 2:13. the children which God *hath given* me.
7: 4. Abraham *gave* the tenth of the spoils.
8:10. I will *put* my laws into their mind,
10:16. I will *put* my laws into their hearts,
Jas. 1: 5. ask of God, *that giveth* to all (men)
— upbraideth not; and it *shall be given* him.
2:16. notwithstanding ye *give* them not
4: 6. he *giveth* more grace. Wherefore
— *giveth* grace unto the humble.
5:18. the heaven *gave* rain, and the earth
1Pet. 1:21. from the dead, and *gave* him glory,
5: 5. *giveth* grace to the humble.
2Pet. 3:15. according to the wisdom *given* unto him
1Joh. 3: 1. of love the Father *hath bestowed* upon us,
23. as he *gave* us commandment.
24. by the Spirit which he *hath given* us.
4:13. because he *hath given* us of his Spirit.
5:11. God *hath given* to us eternal life,
16. he *shall give* him life for them
20. *hath given* us an understanding,
Rev. 1: 1. which God *gave* unto him, to shew
2: 7. *will* I *give* to eat of the tree of life,
10. I *will give* thee a crown of life.
17. To him that overcometh *will* I *give* to eat
— and *will give* him a white stone,
21. I *gave* her space to repent of her
23. I *will give* unto every one of you
26. to him *will* I *give* power over
28. I *will give* him the morning star.
3: 8. I *have set* before thee an open door,
9. Behold, I will *make* them of the
21. that overcometh *will* I *grant* to sit
4: 9. when those beasts *give* glory
6: 2. a crown *was given* unto him:
Rev. 6: 4. (power) *was given* to him that sat
— there *was given* unto him a great sword.
8. power *was given* unto them over
11. white robes *were given* unto every
7: 2. to whom it *was given* to hurt
8: 2. to them *were given* seven trumpets.
3. there *was given* unto him much incense, that he *should offer* (it) with the prayers
9: 1. to him *was given* the key of the
3. unto them *was given* power, as the
5. to them it *was given* that they
10: 9. said unto him, *Give* me the little book.
11: 1. there *was given* me a reed like
2. for it *is given* unto the Gentiles:
3. I *will give* (power) unto my two
13. *gave* glory to the God of heaven.
18. that thou shouldest *give* reward
12:14. to the woman *were given* two wings
13: 2. the dragon *gave* him his power,
4. which *gave* power unto the beast:
5. there *was given* unto him a mouth
— power *was given* unto him to continue
7. it *was given* unto him to make war
— power *was given* him over all
14. miracles which he *had power* to do
15. he had power (lit. it *was given* him) *to give* life unto the image of
16. to receive (lit. that he *should give* them) a mark in their right hand,
14: 7. Fear God, and *give* glory to him;
15: 7. *gave* unto the seven angels seven
16: 6. thou *hast given* them blood to drink;
8. power *was given* unto him to scorch
9. they repented not *to give* him glory.
19. *to give* unto her the cup of the wine
17:17. For God *hath put* in their hearts to
— and *give* their kingdom unto the beast,
18: 7. so much torment and sorrow *give* her:
19: 7. be glad and rejoice, and *give* honour to him:
8. to her *was granted* that she should
20: 4. judgment *was given* unto them:
13. the sea *gave up* the dead which
— death and hell *delivered up* the dead which
21: 6. I *will give* unto him that is athirst

1326 7 193/215 1223,1453

διεγείρω, *diëgiro.*

Mat. 1:24. Then Joseph *being raised* from sleep
Mar 4:38. they *awake* him, and say unto him,
39. he *arose, and* rebuked the wind,
Lu. 8:24. they came to him, and *awoke* him,
Joh. 6:18. the sea *arose* by reason of a great
2Pet. 1:13. in this tabernacle, *to stir* you *up*
3: 1. I *stir up* your pure minds by

1327 1 193/216 5:42 1223,1841

διέξοδος, *diexodos.*

Mat.22: 9. Go ye therefore into the *high*ways,

1328 1 193/216 2:661 1329

διερμηνευτής, *diermeenütees.*

1Co.14:28. if there be no *interpreter*, let him

1329 6 193/216 2:661 1223,2059

διερμηνεύω, *diermeenüo.*

Lu. 24:27. he *expounded* unto them in all

Acts 9:36. which *by interpretation* is called
1Co.12:30. do all speak with tongues? *do* all *interpret?*
14: 5. except he *interpret*, that the church
13. pray that he *may interpret*.
27. (that) by course; and *let* one *interpret*.

1330 42 193/216 2:666 1223,2064

διέρχομαι, dierkomai.

Mat.12:43. he *walketh through* dry places, seeking
19:24. easier for a camel *to go through* the eye
Mar 4:35. *Let* us *pass over* unto the other side.
10:25. *to go through* the eye [some copies read εἰσελθεῖν]
Lu. 2:15. *Let* us now *go* even unto Bethlehem,
35. a sword *shall pierce through* thy
4:30. he *passing through* the midst of them
5:15. the more *went* there a fame *abroad*
8:22. *Let* us *go over* unto the other side
9: 6. they departed, and *went through* the towns,
11:24. he *walketh through* dry places, seeking
17:11. he *passed through* the midst of Samaria
19: 1. (Jesus) entered and *passed through* Jericho.
4. for he was *to pass* that (way).
Joh. 4: 4. he must needs *go through* Samaria.
8:59. *going through* the midst of them,
Acts 8: 4. *went every where* preaching the word.
40. *passing through* he preached in all
9:32. *as* Peter *passed through*out all (quarters),
38. would not delay *to come* to them.
10:38. who *went about* doing good, and healing
11:19. *travelled* as far as Phenice, and Cyprus,
22. that he should *go* as far as Antioch.
12:10. *When* they *were past* the first and the
13: 6. *when* they *had gone through* the isle
14. *when* they *departed* from Perga,
14:24. *after* they *had passed throughout* Pisidia,
15: 3. they *passed through* Phenice
41. he *went through* Syria and Cilicia,
16: 6. *when* they *had gone throughout* Phrygia
17:23. For *as* I *passed by*, and beheld your
18:23. *and went over* (all) the country of Galatia
27. when he was disposed *to pass* into Achaia,
19: 1. Paul *having passed through* the
21. *when* he *had passed through* Macedonia
20: 2. *when* he *had gone over* those parts,
25. among whom I *have gone* preaching
Ro. 5:12. so death *passed* upon all men,
1Co.10: 1. all *passed through* the sea;
16: 5. when I shall *pass through* Macedonia: for I *do pass through* Macedonia.
2Co. 1:16. *to pass* by you into Macedonia,
Heb 4:14. high priest, *that is passed* into the heavens,

1331 1 193/216 1223,2065

διερωτάω, dierōtao.

Acts10:17. *had made enquiry for* Simon's house, *and*

1332 1 193/216 1364,2094

διετής, dietees.

Mat. 2:16. from *two years old* and under, according

1333 2 194/216 1332

διετία, dietia.

Acts24:27. after *two years* Porcius Festus came
28:30. Paul dwelt *two* whole *years* in his own

1334 8 194/216 1223,2233

διηγέομαι, dieegeomai.

Mar 5:16. they that saw (it) *told* them how it
9: 9. that they *should tell* no man what
Lu. 8:39. *shew* how great things God hath done
9:10. *told* him all that they had done.
Acts 8:33. who *shall declare* his generation?
9:27. *declared* unto them how he had seen
12:17. *declared* unto them how the Lord
Heb 11:32. the time would fail me to *tell* of

1335 1 194/216 2:907 1334

διήγησις, dieegeesis.

Lu. 1: 1. to set forth in order a *declaration*

1336 4 194/216 1223,5342

(εἰς τὸ) διηνεκές, dieenekes.

Heb 7: 3. of God; abideth a priest *continually*.
10: 1. offered year by year *continually* make
12. *for ever* sat down on the right hand
14. he hath perfected *for ever* them that

1337 1 194/216 1364,2281

διθάλασσος, dithalassos.

Acts27:41. falling into a place *where two seas met*,

1338 3 194/216 1223,rt 2425

διϊκνέομαι, diikneomai.

Heb 4:12. *piercing* even to the dividing asunder

1339 3 194/217 1223,2476

διΐστημι, diisteemi.

Lu. 22:59. about the space of one hour after (lit. about one hour *having intervened*)
24:51. he *was parted* from them, and carried
Acts27:28. *when* they *had gone* a little *further*,

1340 2 194/217 1223,2478

διϊσχυρίζομαι, diiskurizomai.

Lu. 22:59. another *confidently affirmed*, saying,
Acts12:15. she *constantly affirmed* that it was

1341 1 194/217 2:174 1342,2920

δικαιοκρισία, dikaiokrisia.

Ro. 2: 5. revelation of the *righteous judgment* of God;

1342 81 194/217 2:174 1349

δίκαιος, dikaios.

Mat. 1:19. Joseph her husband, being a *just* (man),
5:45. sendeth rain on the *just* and on the unjust.
9:13. not come to call the *righteous*, but sinners
10:41. he that receiveth a *righteous* man in the name of a *righteous* man shall receive a *righteous* man's reward
13:17. many prophets and *righteous* (men) have
43. Then shall the *righteous* shine forth
49. sever the wicked from among the *just*,
20: 4. whatsoever is *right* I will give you.
7. whatsoever is *right*, (that) shall ye receive.
23:28. outwardly appear *righteous* unto men,
29. garnish the sepulchres of the *righteous*,
35. the *righteous* blood shed upon the earth, from the blood of *righteous* Abel unto
25:37. Then shall the *righteous* answer him,

Mat.25:46. the *righteous* into life eternal.
27:19. nothing to do with that *just* man:
24. innocent of the blood of this *just* person:
Mar. 2:17. I came not to call the *righteous*, but
6:20. knowing that he was a *just* man
Lu. 1: 6. they were both *righteous* before God,
17. disobedient to the wisdom of the *just;*
2:25. the same man (was) *just* and devout,
5:32. I came not to call the *righteous*, but
12:57. yourselves judge ye not what is *right?*
14:14. at the resurrection of the *just*.
15: 7. more than over ninety and nine *just* persons,
18: 9. in themselves that they were *righteous*,
20:20. which should feign themselves *just* men,
23:47. Certainly this was a *righteous* man.
50. (he was) a good man, and a *just:*
Joh. 5:30. my judgment is *just;* because I
7:24. appearance, but judge *righteous* judgment
17:25. O *righteous* Father, the world hath
Acts 3:14. ye denied the Holy One and the *Just*,
4:19. Whether it be *right* in the sight
7:52. of the coming of the *Just* One;
10:22. Cornelius the centurion, a *just* man,
22:14. know his will, and see that *Just* One,
24:15. of the dead, both of the *just* and unjust.
Ro. 1:17. written, The *just* shall live by faith.
2:13. hearers of the law (are) *just* before God,
3:10. There is none *righteous*, no, not one:
26. might be *just*, and the justifier
5: 7. scarcely for a *righteous* man will one die:
19. shall many be made *righteous*.
7:12. the commandment holy, and *just*, and good.
Gal. 3:11. The *just* shall live by faith.
Eph. 6: 1. in the Lord: for this is *right*.
Phi. 1: 7. Even as it is *meet* for me to think
4: 8. whatsoever things (are) *just*, whatsoever
Col. 4: 1. that which is *just* and equal;
2Th. 1: 5. of the *righteous* judgment of God,
6. Seeing (it is) a *righteous* thing
1Ti. 1: 9. law is not made for a *righteous* man,
2Ti. 4: 8. which the Lord, the *righteous* judge,
Tit. 1: 8. a lover of good men, sober, *just*, holy,
Heb 10:38. Now the *just* shall live by faith:
11: 4. obtained witness that he was *righteous*,
12:23. to the spirits of *just* men made perfect,
Jas. 5: 6. have condemned (and) killed the *just;*
16. prayer of a *righteous* man availeth much.
1Pet. 3:12. eyes of the Lord (are) over the *righteous*,
18. suffered for sins, the *just* for the unjust,
4:18. if the *righteous* scarcely be saved,
2Pet. 1:13. Yea, I think it *meet*, as long as I am
2: 7. delivered *just* Lot, vexed with the filthy
8. For that *righteous* man dwelling
— vexed (his) *righteous* soul from day
1Joh. 1: 9. he is faithful and *just* to forgive us
2: 1. with the Father, Jesus Christ the *righteous:*
29. If ye know that he is *righteous*,
3: 7. is *righteous*, even as he is *righteous*.
12. works were evil, and his brother's *righteous*.
Rev.15: 3. *just* and true (are) thy ways, thou King
16: 5. Thou art *righteous*, O Lord, which art,
7. true and *righteous* (are) thy judgments.
19: 2. true and *righteous* (are) his judgments:
22:11. he that is *righteous*, let him be righteous

1343 92 195/218 2:174 1342

δικαιοσύνη, *dikaiosunee.*

Mat. 3:15. becometh us to fulfil all *righteousness*.
Mat. 5: 6. do hunger and thirst after *righteousness:*
10. persecuted for *righteousness'* sake:
20. except your *righteousness* shall exceed
6:33. kingdom of God, and his *righteousness;*
21:32. in the way of *righteousness*,
Lu. 1:75. In holiness and *righteousness* before him,
Joh.16: 8. of *righteousness*, and of judgment:
10. Of *righteousness*, because I go to
Acts10:35. feareth him, and worketh *righteousness*,
13:10. (thou) enemy of all *righteousness*,
17:31. will judge the world in *righteousness*
24:25. as he reasoned of *righteousness*,
Ro. 1:17. therein is the *righteousness* of God
3. 5. commend the *righteousness* of God,
21. now the *righteousness* of God
22. Even the *righteousness* of God (which)
25. to declare his *righteousness* for
26. at this time his *righteousness:*
4: 3. counted unto him for *righteousness*.
5. his faith is counted for *righteousness*.
6. God imputeth *righteousness* without works,
9. reckoned to Abraham for *righteousness*.
11. a seal of the *righteousness* of the
— that *righteousness* might be imputed
13. through the *righteousness* of faith.
22. was imputed to him for *righteousness*.
5:17. of the gift of *righteousness*
21. might grace reign through *righteousness*
6:13. instruments of *righteousness* unto God.
16. or of obedience unto *righteousness?*
18. became the servants of *righteousness*.
19. your members servants to *righteousness*
20. ye were free from *righteousness*.
8:10. Spirit (is) life because of *righteousness*.
9:28. cut (it) short in *righteousness:*
30. which followed not after *righteousness*, have attained to *righteousness*, even the *righteousness* which is of faith.
31. followed after the law of *righteousness*, hath not attained to the law of *righteousness*.
10: 3. being ignorant of God's *righteousness*, and going about to establish their own *righteousness*, have not submitted themselves unto the *righteousness* of God.
4. of the law for *righteousness* to
5. Moses describeth the *righteousness*
6. the *righteousness* which is of faith
10. man believeth unto *righteousness;*
14:17. but *righteousness*, and peace, and joy in
1Co. 1:30. made unto us wisdom, and *righteousness*,
2Co. 3: 9. the ministration of *righteousness*
5:21. be made the *righteousness* of God in him.
6: 7. by the armour of *righteousness* on
14. what fellowship hath *righteousness* with
9: 9. his *righteousness* remaineth for ever.
10. increase the fruits of your *righteousness;*
11:15. as the ministers of *righteousness;*
Gal. 2:21. for if *righteousness* (come) by the law,
3: 6. was accounted to him for *righteousness*.
21. verily *righteousness* should have been
5: 5. the hope of *righteousness* by faith.
Eph. 4:24. created in *righteousness* and true holiness.
5: 9. in all goodness and *righteousness*
6:14. the breastplate of *righteousness;*
Phi. 1:11. filled with the fruits of *righteousness*,
3: 6. touching the *righteousness* which
9. not having mine own *righteousness*,
— *righteousness* which is of God by faith:
1Ti. 6:11. follow after *righteousness*, godliness,
2Ti. 2:22. follow *righteousness*, faith, charity
3:16. for instruction in *righteousness*:

2Ti. 4: 8. for me a crown of *righteousness*,
Tit. 3: 5. Not by works of *righteousness* which
Heb 1: 9. Thou hast loved *righteousness*,
5:13. unskilful in the word of *righteousness:*
7: 2. King of *righteousness*, and after that
11: 7. the *righteousness* which is by faith.
33. wrought *righteousness*, obtained
12:11. the peaceable fruit of *righteousness*
Jas. 1:20. worketh not the *righteousness* of God.
2:23. imputed unto him for *righteousness:*
3:18. the fruit of *righteousness* is sown
1Pet. 2:24. should live unto *righteousness:*
3:14. if ye suffer for *righteousness'* sake,
2Pet. 1: 1. through the *righteousness* of God
2: 5. a preacher of *righteousness*, bringing
21. known the way of *righteousness*,
3:13. wherein dwelleth *righteousness*.
1Joh. 2:29. every one that doeth *righteousness*
3: 7. he that doeth *righteousness* is
10. whosoever doeth not *righteousness*
Rev. 19:11. in *righteousness* he doth judge and make war.

1344 60 196/219 2:174 1342

δικαιόω, *dikaioō*.

Mat. 11:19. wisdom *is justified* of her children.
12:37. by thy words thou *shalt be justified*,
Lu. 7:29. the publicans, *justified* God, being
35. wisdom *is justified* of all her children.
10:29. he, willing *to justify* himself, said
16:15. Ye are they *which justify* yourselves
18:14. went down to his house *justified*
Acts 13:39. by him all that believe *are justified*
— ye could not *be justified* by the
Ro. 2:13. the doers of the law *shall be justified*.
3: 4. That thou *mightest be justified* in
20. there *shall* no flesh *be justified* in his
24. *Being justified* freely by his grace
26. the *justifier* of him which believeth
28. that a man is *justified* by faith
30. one God, which *shall justify* the
4: 2. if Abraham *were justified* by works,
5. believeth on him that *justifieth* the
5: 1. Therefore *being* (lit. *having been*) *justified* by faith,
9. *being* now *justified* (lit. *having been j.*) by his blood,
6: 7. he that is dead *is freed* (lit. *is justified*), from sin.
8:30. whom he called, them he also *justified:* and whom he *justified*, them he also glorified.
33. of God's elect? (It is) God *that justifieth*.
1Co. 4: 4. yet *am* I not hereby *justified:*
6:11. ye *are* (lit. *have been*) *justified* in the name of
Gal. 2:16. a man *is* not *justified* by the works
— that we *might be justified* by the
— *shall* no flesh *be justified*.
17. while we seek *to be justified* by Christ,
3: 8. that God *would justify* the heathen
11. no man *is justified* by the law
24. that we *might be justified* by faith.
5: 4. whosoever of you *are justified* by
1Ti. 3:16. was manifest in the flesh, *justified* in the Spirit,
Tit. 3: 7. That *being justified* (lit. *having been j.*) by his grace,
Jas. 2:21. *Was* not Abraham our father *justified* by works,
24. that by works a man *is justified*,
25. *was* not Rahab the harlot *justified* by works,
Rev. 22:11. righteous, *let* him *be righteous* still:

1345 10 197/219 2:174 1344

δικαίωμα, *dikaiōma*.

Lu. 1: 6. commandments and *ordinances* of the Lord
Ro. 1:32. Who knowing the *judgment* of God,
2:26. keep the *righteousness* of the law,
5:16. of many offences unto *justification*.
18. by the *righteousness* of one
8: 4. That the *righteousness* of the law
Heb. 9: 1. had also *ordinances* of divine service,
10. divers washings, and carnal *ordinances*,
Rev. 15: 4. thy *judgments* are made manifest.
19: 8. fine linen is the *righteousness* of saints.

1346 5 197/219 1342

δικαίως, *dikaiōs*.

Lu. 23:41. we indeed *justly;* for we receive
1Co. 15:34. Awake *to righteousness*, and sin not;
1Th. 2:10. how holily and *justly* and unblameably we
Tit. 2:12. we should live soberly, *righteously*, and
1Pet. 2:23. to him that judgeth *righteously:*

1347 2 197/219 2:174 1344

δικαίωσις, *dikaiōsis*.

Ro. 4:25. was raised again for our *justification*.
5:18. upon all men unto *justification* of life.

1348 3 197/219 1349

δικαστής, *dikastees*.

Lu. 12:14. who made me a *judge* or a divider
Acts 7:27. Who made thee a ruler and a *judge* over us?
35. Who made thee a ruler and a *judge*?

1349 4 197/219 2:174 1166

δίκη, *dikee*.

Acts 25:15. (to have) *judgment* against him.
28: 4. yet *vengeance* suffereth not to live.
2Th. 1: 9. Who shall be punished (lit. suffer *vengeance*) with
Jude 7. suffering the *vengeance* of eternal fire.

1350 12 197/220 *dikō* (to cast a net)

δίκτυον, *diktuon*.

Mat. 4:20. they straightway left (their) *nets*,
21. mending their *nets;* and he called them
Mar. 1:18. straightway they forsook their *nets*,
19. in the ship mending their *nets*.
Lu. 5: 2. were washing (their) *nets*.
4. let down your *nets* for a draught.
5. at thy word I will let down the *net*.
6. of fishes: and their *net* brake.
Joh. 21: 6. Cast the *net* on the right side
8. dragging the *net* with fishes.
11. drew the *net* to land full of
— yet was not the *net* broken.

1351 1 197/220 1364, 3056

δίλογος, *dilogos*.

1 Ti. 3: 8. not *doubletongued*, not given to

1352 53 197/220 · 1223,3739

δıό, dio.

Mat.27: 8. *Wherefore* that field was called,
Lu. 1:35. *therefore* also that holy thing which
7: 7. *Wherefore* neither thought I myself
Acts10:29. *Therefore* came I (unto you) without
13:35. *Wherefore* he saith also in another
15:19. *Wherefore* my sentence is, that we
20:26. *Wherefore* I take you to record this
31. *Therefore* watch, and remember, that
24:26. *wherefore* he sent for him the oftener,
25:26. *Wherefore* I have brought him
26: 3. *wherefore* I beseech thee to hear me
27:25. *Wherefore*, sirs, be of good cheer.
34. *Wherefore* I pray you to take (some)
Ro. 1:24. *Wherefore* God also gave them up to
2: 1. *Therefore* thou art inexcusable, O man,
4:22. *therefore* it was imputed to him
13: 5. *Wherefore* (ye) must needs be subject,
15: 7. *Wherefore* receive ye one another,
22. *For which cause* also I have been
1Co.12: 3. *Wherefore* I give you to understand,
2Co. 2: 8. *Wherefore* I beseech you that ye
4:13. I believed, *and therefore* have I spoken;
— we also believe, and *therefore* speak;
16. *For which cause* we faint not;
5: 9. *Wherefore* we labour, that, whether
6:17. *Wherefore* come out from among them,
12:10. *Therefore* I take pleasure in infirmities,
Eph. 2:11. *Wherefore* remember, that ye (being)
3:13. *Wherefore* I desire that ye faint not
4: 8. *Wherefore* he saith, When he
25. *Wherefore* putting away lying,
5:14. *Wherefore* he saith, Awake thou that
Phi. 2: 9. *Wherefore* God also hath highly
1Th. 2:18. *Wherefore* we would have come unto
3: 1. *Wherefore* when we could no longer
5:11. *Wherefore* comfort yourselves
Philem. 8. *Wherefore*, though I might be much
Heb. 3: 7. *Wherefore* as the Holy Ghost saith,
10. *Wherefore* I was grieved with that
6: 1. *Therefore* leaving the principles
10: 5. *Wherefore* when he cometh into
11:12. *Therefore* sprang there even of one,
16. *wherefore* God is not ashamed to
12:12. *Wherefore* lift up the hands which
28. *Wherefore* we receiving a kingdom
13:12. *Wherefore* Jesus also, that he might
Jas. 1:21. *Wherefore* lay apart all filthiness
4: 6. *Wherefore* he saith, God resisteth
1Pet.1:13. *Wherefore* gird up the loins of your
2: 6. *Wherefore* also it is contained in
2Pet.1:10. *Wherefore* the rather, brethren,
12. *Wherefore* I will not be negligent
3:14. *Wherefore*, beloved, seeing that ye

1353 2 197/220 1223,3593

δıοδεύω, diodūo.

Lu. 8: 1. he *went throughout* every city and village,
Acts17: 1. *when* they *had passed through* Amphipolis

1355 3 198/220 1352,4007

δıόπερ, dioper.

1Co. 8:13. *Wherefore*, if meat make my
10:14. *Wherefore*, my dearly beloved, flee
14:13. *Wherefore* let him that speaketh

1356 1 198/220 cf 2203 *petō* (to fall)

δıοπετής, diopetees.

Acts19:35. the (image) which *fell down from Jupiter?*

1357 1 198/220 5:449 1223,3717

δıόρθωσıς, diorthōsis.

Heb. 9:10. until the time of *reformation*.

1358 4 198/220 1223,3736

δıορύσσω, diorusso.

Mat. 6:19. where thieves *break through* and steal:
20. where thieves *do* not *break through* nor steal:
24:43. suffered his house *to be broken up*.
Lu. 12:39. suffered his house *to be broken through*.

1360 22 198/221 1223,3754

δıότı, dioti.

Lu. 1:13. *for* thy prayer is heard; and thy wife
2: 7. *because* there was no room for them
21:28. *for* your redemption draweth nigh.
Acts10:20. doubting nothing: *for* I have sent them.
17:31. *Because* he hath appointed a day,
18:10. *For* I am with thee, and no man
— *for* I have much people in this city.
22:18. *for* they will not receive thy testimony
Ro. 1:19. *Because* that which may be known
21. *Because that*, when they knew God,
3:20. *Therefore* (lit. *because*) by the deeds of the law there
8: 7. *Because* the carnal mind (is) enmity
1Co.15: 9. *because* I persecuted the church of God.
Gal. 2:16. *for* by the works of the law shall no
Phi. 2:26. *because that* ye had heard that he
1Th. 2: 8. *because* ye were dear unto us.
4: 6. *because that* the Lord (is) the avenger
Heb11: 5. *because* God had translated him:
23. *because* they saw (he was) a proper
Jas. 4: 3. receive not, *because* ye ask amiss,
1Pet.1:16. *Because* it is written, Be ye holy;
24. *For* all flesh (is) as grass, and all

1362 4 198/221 1364,rt 4119

δıπλοῦς, diplous.

Mat.23:15. *twofold more* the child of hell than
1Ti. 5:17. be counted worthy of *double* honour,
Rev.18: 6. double unto her *double* according to
— which she hath filled fill to her *double*.

1363 1 198/221 1362

δıπλόω, diploō.

Rev.18: 6. *double* unto her double according to

1364 6 198/221 1417

δίς, dis.

Mar.14:30. this night, before the cock crow *twice*,
72. Before the cock crow *twice*, thou shalt
Lu. 18:12. I fast *twice* in the week, I give
Phi. 4:16. sent once and *again* unto my necessity.
1Th. 2:18. even I Paul, once and *again*;
Jude 12. without fruit, *twice* dead, plucked up

1365 2 199/221 1364

δıστάζω, distazo.

Mat.14:31. wherefore *didst* thou *doubt*?
28:17. they worshipped him: but some *doubted*.

1366 3 199/221 1364,4750

δίστομος, distomos.

Heb. 4:12. sharper than any *twoedged* sword,

Rev. 1:16. went a sharp *twoedged* sword:
2:12. hath the sharp sword *with two edges*;

1367 1 199/221 1364,5507

διςχίλιοι, diskilioi.

Mar. 5:13. they were about *two thousand*;

1368 1 199/221 1223 *hulizō* (to filter)

διϋλίζω, diulizo.

Mat.23:24. (Ye) blind guides, which *strain at* a gnat, (lit. *strain out*)

1369 1 199/221 1364

διχάζω, dikazo.

Mat.10:35. *to set* a man *at variance* against

1370 3 199/221 1:512 1364,4714

διχοστασία, dikostasia.

Ro. 16:17. mark them which cause *divisions*
1Co. 3: 3. among you envying, and strife, and *divisions*,
Gal. 5:20. emulations, wrath, strife, *seditions*,

1371 2 199/221 2:225 1364 *temnō* (to cut)

διχοτομέω, dikotomeo.

Mat.24:51. *shall cut* him *asunder*, and appoint
Lu. 12:46. *will cut* him *in sunder*, and will appoint

1372 16 199/221 2:226 eq 1373

διψάω, dipsao.

Mat. 5: 6. which do hunger and *thirst* after righteousness:
25:35. I *was thirsty*, and ye gave me drink:
37. fed (thee)? or *thirsty*, and gave (thee) drink?
42. I *was thirsty*, and ye gave me no drink:
44. Lord, when saw we thee an hungred, or *athirst*,
Joh. 4:13. drinketh of this water *shall thirst* again:
14. water that I shall give him *shall* never *thirst*;
15. give me this water, that I *thirst* not,
6:35. believeth on me shall never *thirst*.
7:37. If any man *thirst*, let him come unto me,
19:28. scripture might be fulfilled, saith, I *thirst*.
Ro. 12:20. feed him; if he *thirst*, give him drink:
1Co. 4:11. both hunger, and *thirst*, and are naked,
Rev. 7:16. hunger no more, neither *thirst* any more;
21: 6. I will give unto him *that is athirst*
22:17. let him *that is athirst* come.

1373 1 199/221 2:226

δίψος, dipsos.

2Co.11:27. in watchings often, in hunger and *thirst*,

1374 2 200/222 9:608 1364,5590

δίψυχος, dipsukos.

1: 8. A *double minded* man (is) unstable
4: 8. purify (your) hearts, (ye) *double minded*.

1375 10 200/222 1377

διωγμός, diogmos.

Mat. 13:21. or *persecution* ariseth because of the word,
Mar.4:17. or *persecution* ariseth for the word's sake.
Mar 10:30. children, and lands, with *persecutions*;
Acts 8: 1. a great *persecution* against the church
13:50. raised *persecution* against Paul and
Ro. 8:35. distress, or *persecution*, or famine,
2Co.12:10. in necessities, in *persecutions*, in distresses
2Th. 1: 4. faith in all your *persecutions* and tribulations
2Ti. 3:11. *Persecutions*, afflictions, which came — at Lystra; what *persecutions* I endured.

1376 1 200/222 2:229 1377

διώκτης, diōktees.

1Ti. 1:13. a blasphemer, and a *persecutor*, and injurious:

1377 44 200/222 *diō* (to flee)

διώκω, diōko.

Mat. 5:10. *which are persecuted* for righteousness' sake:
11. when (men) shall revile you, and *persecute* (you),
12. for so *persecuted* they the prophets
44. despitefully use you, and *persecute* you;
10:23. when they *persecute* you in this city,
23:34. and *persecute* (them) from city to city:
Lu. 17:23. go not after (them), nor *follow* (them).
21:12. lay their hands on you, and *persecute* (you),
Joh. 5:16. therefore did the Jews *persecute* Jesus,
15:20. If they *have persecuted* me, they *will* also *persecute* you;
Acts 7:52. *have* not your fathers *persecuted*?
9: 4. Saul, Saul, why *persecutest* thou me?
5. I am Jesus whom thou *persecutest*:
22: 4. I *persecuted* this way unto the death,
7. Saul, Saul, why *persecutest* thou me?
8. Jesus of Nazareth, whom thou *persecutest*.
26:11. I *persecuted* (them) even unto strange cities.
14. Saul, Saul, why *persecutest* thou me?
15. I am Jesus whom thou *persecutest*.
Ro. 9:30. *which followed* not *after* righteousness,
31. Israel, *which followed after* the law
12:13. necessity of saints; *given to* hospitality.
14. Bless them *which persecute* you:
14:19. therefore *follow after* the things which
1Co. 4:12. *being persecuted*, we suffer it:
14: 1. *Follow after* charity, and desire spiritual
15: 9. because I *persecuted* the church of God
2Co. 4: 9. *Persecuted*, but not forsaken; cast
Gal. 1:13. beyond measure I *persecuted* the church
23. he *which persecuted* us in times past
4:29. *persecuted* him (that was born) after
5:11. why do I yet *suffer persecution*?
6:12. *should suffer persecution* for the cross
Phi. 3: 6. Concerning zeal, *persecuting* the church
12. I *follow after*, if that I may
14. I *press* toward the mark for the
1Th. 5:15. ever *follow* that which is good,
1Ti. 6:11. *follow after* righteousness, godliness,
2Ti. 2:22. *follow* righteousness, faith, charity,
3:12. in Christ Jesus *shall suffer persecution*.
Heb 12:14. *Follow* peace with all (men), and holiness,
1Pet.3:11. let him seek peace, and *ensue* it.
Rev.12:13. he *persecuted* the woman which

1378 5 200/222 2:230 rt 1380

δογμα, dogma.

Lu. 2: 1. there went out a *decree* from Cæsar

Acts.16: 4. they delivered them the *decrees* for
17: 7. all do contrary to the *decrees* of Cæsar,
Eph. 2:15. commandments(contained)in *ordinances;*
Col. 2:14. the handwriting of *ordinances* that

1379 1 200/222 2:230 1378

δογματίζομαι, *dogmatizomai.*

Col. 2:20. in the world, *are ye subject to ordinances,*

1380 63 200/222 2:232 cf rt1166

δοκέω, *dokeo.*

NOTE.—In many of the passages the form is that of the impersonal verb.

Mat. 3: 9. *think* not to say within yourselves,
6: 7. for they *think* that they shall be heard
17:25. saying, What *thinkest* thou, Simon?
18:12. How *think* ye? if a man have
21:28. what *think* ye? A (certain) man had
22:17. Tell us therefore, What *thinkest* thou?
42. Saying, What *think* ye of Christ?
24:44. in such an hour as ye *think* not
26:53. *Thinkest* thou that I cannot now
66. What *think* ye? They answered and said,
Mar. 6:49. they *supposed* it had been a spirit,
10:42. they *which are accounted* to rule over
Lu. 1: 3. It *seemed good* to me also, having
8:18. even that which he *seemeth* to have.
10:36. Which now of these three, *thinkest* thou,
12:40. at an hour when ye *think* not.
51. *Suppose* ye that I am come to give
13: 2. *Suppose* ye that these Galilæans were
4. *think* ye that they were sinners
17: 9. were commanded him? I *trow* not.
19:11. they *thought* that the kingdom of God
22:24. of them *should be accounted* the greatest.
24:37. *supposed* that they had seen a spirit.
Joh. 5:39. in them ye *think* ye have eternal life:
45. Do not *think* that I will accuse
11:13. they *thought* that he had spoken
56. What *think* ye, that he will not come
13:29. For some (of them) *thought*, because
16: 2. *will think* that he doeth God service.
20:15. She, *supposing* him to be the gardener,
Acts 12: 9. by the angel; but *thought* he saw a vision.
15:22. Then *pleased* it the apostles
25. It *seemed good* unto us, being
28. For it *seemed good* to the Holy Ghost,
34. it *pleased* Silas to abide there still.
17:18. He *seemeth* to be a setter forth of
25:27. For it *seemeth* to me unreasonable
26: 9. I verily *thought* with myself,
27:13. *supposing* that they had obtained
1 Co. 3:18. *seemeth* to be wise in this world,
4: 9. For I *think* that God hath set
7:40. I *think* also that I have the Spirit
8: 2. if any man *think* that he knoweth
10:12. let him *that thinketh* he standeth
11:16. if any man *seem* to be contentious,
12:22. members of the body, *which seem* to be
23. which we *think* to be less honourable,
14:37. If any man *think* himself to be
2Co.10: 9. That I *may* not *seem* as if I would
11:16. *Let* no man *think* me a fool;
12:19. *think* ye that we excuse ourselves
Gal. 2: 2. to them *which were of reputation*,
6. of those *who seemed* to be somewhat,
— for they *who seemed* (to be somewhat)
9. *who seemed* to be pillars, perceived
6: 3. if a man *think* himself to be something,
Phi. 3: 4. If any other man *thinketh* that he
Heb. 4: 1. any of you *should seem* to come
10:29. how much sorer punishment, *suppose* ye,
12:10. chastened (us) after their *own pleasure*
11. the present *seemeth* to be joyous,
Jas. 1:26. If any man among you *seem* to be
4: 5. *Do* ye *think* that the scripture saith

1381 23 201/223 2:255 1384

δοκιμάζω, *dokimazo.*

Lu. 12:56. ye can *discern* the face of the sky and
— that ye *do* not *discern* this time?
14:19. five yoke of oxen, and I go *to prove* them:
Ro. 1:28. they *did* not *like* to retain God in (their)
2:18. *approvest* the things that are more
12: 2. that ye may *prove* what (is) that good,
14:22. in that thing which he *alloweth*.
1Co. 3:13. the fire *shall try* every man's work
11:28. *let* a man *examine* himself,
16: 3. whomsoever ye shall *approve* by
2Co. 8: 8. to *prove* the sincerity of your love.
22. whom we *have* oftentimes *proved*
13: 5. in the faith; *prove* your own selves.
Gal. 6: 4. *let* every man *prove* his own work,
Eph. 5:10. *Proving* what is acceptable unto the Lord
Phi. 1:10. That ye may *approve* things that
1Th. 2: 4. as we *were allowed* of God to be
— God, *which trieth* our hearts.
5:21. *Prove* all things; hold fast that
1Ti. 3:10. *let* these also first *be proved;*
Heb. 3: 9. your fathers tempted me *proved* me,
1Pet. 1: 7. *though* it *be tried* with fire,
1Joh. 4: 1. *try* the spirits whether they are

1382 7 201/223 2:255 1380

δοκιμή, *dokimee.*

Ro. 5: 4. *experience;* and *experience*, hope
2Co. 2: 9. I might know the *proof* of you,
8: 2. that in a great *trial* of affliction
9:13. by the *experiment* of this ministration
13: 3. Since ye seek a *proof* of Christ
Phi. 2:22. ye know the *proof* of him,

1383 2 202/223 2:255 1382

δοκίμιον, *dokimion.*

Jas. 1: 3. the *trying* of your faith worketh
1Pet. 1: 7. That the *trial* of your faith, being

1384 7 202/224 2:255 1380

δόκιμος, *dokimos.*

Ro. 14:18. acceptable to God, and *approved* of men.
16:10. Salute Appelles *approved* in Christ.
1Co.11:19. they *which are approved* may be
2Co.10:18. he that commendeth himself is *approved*,
13: 7. not that we should appear *approved*,
2Ti. 2:15. Study to shew thyself *approved* unto God,
Jas. 1:12. for when he is *tried*, he shall receive

1385 6 202/224 1209

δοκός, *dokos.*

Mat. 7: 3. considerest not the *beam* that is in
4. behold, a *beam* (is) in thine own eye?
5. first cast out the *beam* out of thine
Lu. 6:41. perceivest not the *beam* that is in
42. beholdest not the *beam* that is in
— cast out first the *beam* out of thine

1386 1 202/224 1388

δόλιος, *dolios.*

2Co.11: 3. false apostles, *deceitful* workers.

1387 1 202/224 1386

δολιόω, *dolioō.*

Ro. 3:13. with their tongues they *have used deceit;*

1388 12 202/224 *dellō* (to decoy) cf 1185

δόλος, *dolos.*

Mat.26: 4. they might take Jesus by *subtilty,*
Mar. 7:22. wickedness, *deceit,* lasciviousness,
14: 1. they might take him by *craft,*
Joh. 1:47(48) Israelite indeed, in whom is no *guile!*
Acts13:10. O full of all *subtilty* and all mischief,
Ro. 1:29. full of envy, murder, debate, *deceit,*
2Co.12:16. being crafty, I caught you with *guile.*
1Th. 2: 3. nor of uncleanness, nor in *guile:*
1Pet.2: 1. laying aside all malice, and all *guile,*
22. neither was *guile* found in his mouth:
3:10. his lips that they speak no *guile:*
Rev.14: 5. in their mouth was found no *guile*

1389 1 202/224 1388

δολόω, *doloō.*

2Co. 4: 2. nor *handling* the word of God *deceitfully,*

1390 4 202/224 rt 1325

δόμα, *doma.*

Mat. 7:11. know how to give good *gifts* unto
Lu. 11:13. to give good *gifts* unto your children:
Eph. 4: 8. captivity captive, and gave *gifts* unto men.
Phil. 4:17. Not because I desire a *gift:*

1391 168 202/224 2:232 rt 1380

δόξα, *doxa.*

Mat. 4: 8. of the world, and the *glory* of them;
6:13. the power, and the *glory,* for ever.
29. even Solomon in all his *glory* was
16:27. in the *glory* of his Father with
19:28. shall sit in the throne of his *glory,*
24:30. with power and great *glory.*
25:31. Son of man shall come in his *glory,*
— sit upon the throne of his *glory:*
Mar. 8:38. cometh in the *glory* of his Father
10:37. on thy left hand, in thy *glory.*
13:26. in the clouds with great power and *glory.*
Lu. 2: 9. the *glory* of the Lord shone round
14. *Glory* to God in the highest, and on
32. the *glory* of thy people Israel.
4: 6. will I give thee, and the *glory* of them:
9:26. when he shall come in his own *glory,*
31. Who appeared in *glory,* and spake of his
32. they saw his *glory,* and the two men
12:27. Solomon in all his *glory* was not
14:10. then shalt thou have *worship* in the
17:18. returned to give *glory* to God, save
19:38. peace in heaven, and *glory* in the highest.
21:27. in a cloud with power and great *glory.*
24:26. to enter into his *glory?*
Joh. 1:14. we beheld his *glory,* the *glory* as of the
2:11. Galilee, and manifested forth his *glory;*
5:41. I receive not *honour* from men.
44. which receive *honour* one of another,
— the *honour* that (cometh) from God only?
7:18. himself seeketh his own *glory:* but he that seeketh his *glory* that sent him.
Joh. 8:50. I seek not mine own *glory.*
54. If I honour myself, my *honour* is nothing
9:24. said unto him, Give God the *praise:*
11: 4. for the *glory* of God, that the Son
40. thou shouldest see the *glory* of God?
12:41. said Esaias, when he saw his *glory,*
43. they loved the *praise* of men more than the *praise* of God.
17: 5. with the *glory* which I had
22. the *glory* which thou gavest me
24. that they may behold my *glory,*
Acts 7 2. The God of *glory* appeared unto
55. saw the *glory* of God, and Jesus
12:23. because he gave not God the *glory:*
22:11. for the *glory* of that light, being
Ro. 1:23. the *glory* of the uncorruptible God
2: 7. in well doing seek for *glory* and honour
10. *glory,* honour, and peace, to every man
3: 7. through my lie unto his *glory;*
23. come short of the *glory* of God;
4:20. was strong in faith, giving *glory* to God
5: 2. rejoice in hope of the *glory* of God.
6: 4. by the *glory* of the Father,
8:18. the *glory* which shall be revealed
21. into the *glorious* liberty (lit. liberty of the *glory*) of the children of God.
9: 4. the adoption, and the *glory,* and the covenants,
23. make known the riches of his *glory* on
— had afore prepared unto *glory,*
11:36. to whom (be) *glory* for ever.
15: 7. received us to the *glory* of God.
16:27. To God only wise, (be) *glory* through
1Co. 2: 7. before the world unto our *glory:*
8. not have crucified the Lord of *glory.*
10:31. do all to the *glory* of God.
11: 7. as he is the image and *glory* of God: but the woman is the *glory* of the man.
15. have long hair, it is a *glory* to her:
15:40. the *glory* of the celestial (is) one, and the
41. one *glory* of the sun, and another *glory* of
— another *glory* of the stars: for (one) star differeth from (another) star in *glory.*
43. sown in dishonour; it is raised in *glory:*
2Co. 1:20. unto the *glory* of God by us.
3: 7. engraven in stones, was *glorious,* (lit. in *glory*)
— for the *glory* of his countenance;
8. ministration of the spirit be rather *glorious?* (lit. in *glory*)
9. ministration of condemnation (be) *glory*
— of righteousness exceed in *glory.*
10. by reason of the *glory* that excelleth.
11. which is done away (was) *glorious* (lit. through *glory*), much more that which remaineth (is) *glorious.* (lit. in *glory*)
18. as in a glass the *glory* of the Lord,
— the same image from *glory* to *glory,*
4: 4. the light of the *glorious* gospel of Christ. (lit. gospel of the *glory*)
6. the knowledge of the *glory* of God
15. redound to the *glory* of God.
17. exceeding (and) eternal weight of *glory;*
6: 8. By *honour* and dishonour, by evil
8:19. to the *glory* of the same Lord,
23. messengers of the churches, (and) the *glory* of Christ.
Gal. 1: 5. To whom (be) *glory* for ever and ever.
Eph. 1: 6. To the praise of the *glory* of his grace,
12. should be to the praise of his *glory.*
14. unto the praise of his *glory.*
17. the Father of *glory,* may give unto

Eph 1:18. the riches of the *glory* of his inheritance
3:13. tribulations for you, which is your *glory.*
16. according to the riches of his *glory,*
21. Unto him (be) *glory* in the church
Phi. 1:11. unto the *glory* and praise of God.
2:11. to the *glory* of God the Father.
3:19. (whose) *glory* (is) in their shame,
21. fashioned like unto his *glorious* body, (lit. the body of his *glory*)
4:19. his riches in *glory* by Christ Jesus.
20. our Father (be) *glory* for ever and ever.
Col. 1:11. according to his *glorious* power, (lit. power of his *glory*)
27. the riches of the *glory* of this mystery
— Christ in you, the hope of *glory:*
3: 4. shall ye also appear with him in *glory.*
1Th. 2: 6. Nor of men sought we *glory,*
12. called you unto his kingdom and *glory.*
20. For ye are our *glory* and joy.
2Th. 1: 9. from the *glory* of his power;
2:14. the *glory* of our Lord Jesus Christ.
1Ti. 1:11. According to the *glorious* gospel (lit. gospel of the *glory*) of
17. (be) honour and *glory* for ever and ever.
3:16. in the world, received up into *glory.*
2Ti. 2:10. in Christ Jesus with eternal *glory.*
4:18. to whom (be) *glory* for ever and ever.
Tit. 2:13. the *glorious* appearing (lit. appearing of the *glory*) of the great God
Heb. 1: 3. Who being the brightness of (his) *glory,*
2: 7. thou crownedst him with *glory*
9. the suffering of death, crowned with *glory,*
10. in bringing many sons unto *glory,*
3: 3. counted worthy of more *glory* than Moses,
9: 5. over it the cherubims of *glory*
13:21. to whom (be) *glory* for ever and ever.
Jas. 2: 1. our Lord Jesus Christ, (the Lord) of *glory,*
1Pet. 1: 7. praise and honour and *glory* at the appearing
11. the *glory* (lit. *glories*) that should follow
21. up from the dead, and gave him *glory;*
24. the *glory* of man as the flower of grass.
4:11. to whom be *praise* and dominion for ever
13. when his *glory* shall be revealed,
14. for the spirit of *glory* and of God resteth
5: 1. a partaker of the *glory* that shall be
4. ye shall receive a crown of *glory*
10. hath called us unto his eternal *glory*
11. To him (be) *glory* and dominion for ever
2Pet. 1: 3. hath called us to *glory* and virtue:
17. from God the Father honour and *glory,*
— a voice to him from the excellent *glory,*
2:10. not afraid to speak evil of *dignities.*
3:18. To him (be) *glory* both now and for ever.
Jude 8. speak evil of *dignities.*
24. faultless before the presence of his *glory*
25. God our Saviour, (be) *glory* and majesty,
Rev. 1: 6. to him (be) *glory* and dominion for ever
4: 9. when those beasts give *glory* and honour
11. to receive *glory* and honour and power:
5:12. strength, and honour, and *glory*, and blessing.
13. Blessing, and honour, and *glory*, and power,
7:12. Saying, Amen: Blessing, and *glory,*
11:13. gave *glory* to the God of heaven.
14: 7. Fear God, and give *glory* to him;
15: 8. with smoke from the *glory* of God,
16: 9. they repented not to give him *glory.*
18: 1. the earth was lightened with his *glory.*
19: 1. Salvation, and *glory* and honour, and power,
7. be glad and rejoice, and give *honour* to
Rev.21:11. Having the *glory* of God: and her
23. the *glory* of God did lighten it,
24. do bring their *glory* and honour into it
26. they shall bring the *glory* and honour

1392 62 203/226 2:232 1391

δοξάζω, *doxazo.*

Mat. 5:16. may see your good works, and *glorify*
6: 2. that they *may have glory* of men.
9: 8. they marvelled, and *glorified* God,
15:31. they *glorified* the God of Israel.
Mar. 2:12. were all amazed, and *glorified* God,
Lu. 2:20. *glorifying* and praising God for all
4:15. *being glorified* of all.
5:25. to his own house, *glorifying* God.
26. were all amazed, and they *glorified* God,
7:16. they *glorified* God, saying,
13:13. she was made straight, and *glorified* God.
17:15. *and* with a loud voice *glorified* God,
18:43. followed him, *glorifying* God:
23:47. saw what was done, he *glorified* God,
Joh. 7:39. because that Jesus *was* not yet *glorified.*
8:54. If I *honour* myself, my honour is nothing it is my Father *that honoureth* me:
11: 4. the Son of God *might be glorified*
12:16. when Jesus *was glorified,* then
23. the Son of man *should be glorified.*
28. Father, *glorify* thy name.
— I *have* both *glorified* (it), and *will glorify* (it)
13:31. Now *is* the Son of man *glorified*, and God *is glorified* in him.
32. If God *be glorified* in him, God *shall* also *glorify* him in himself, and *shall* straightway *glorify* him.
14:13. the Father *may be glorified* in the Son.
15: 8. Herein *is* my Father *glorified,*
16:14. He *shall glorify* me: for he
17: 1. *glorify* thy Son, that thy Son also *may glorify* thee:
4. I *have glorified* thee on the earth:
5. O Father, *glorify* thou me with
10. I *am glorified* in them.
21:19. by what death he should *glorify* God.
Acts 3:13. *hath glorified* his Son Jesus;
4:21. for all (men) *glorified* God for that
11:18. held their peace, and *glorified* God,
13:48. *glorified* the word of the Lord:
21:20. they *glorified* the Lord, and said
Ro. 1:21. they *glorified* (him) not as God,
8:30. justified, them he also *glorified.*
11:13. I *magnify* mine office:
15: 6. with one mind (and) one mouth *glorify* God,
9. the Gentiles might *glorify* God
1Co. 6:20. therefore *glorify* God in your body.
12:26. or one member *be honoured,* all
2Co. 3:10. that *which was made glorious had* no *glory* in this respect,
9:13. *Whiles...*they *glorify* God for your professed
Gal. 1:24. they *glorified* God in me.
2Th. 3: 1. *be glorified,* even as (it is) with you:
Heb 5: 5. Christ *glorified* not himself
1Pet. 1: 8. joy unspeakable and *full of glory:*
2:12. they *may...glorify* God in the day of visitation.
4:11. *may be glorified* through Jesus Christ,
14. on your part he *is glorified.*
16. *let* him *glorify* God on this behalf.
Rev. 15: 4. Who shall not fear thee, O Lord, and *glorify* thy name?

Rev.18. 7. How much she *hath glorified* herself,

1394 2 204/227 rt 1325

δόσις, *dosis.*

Phi. 4:15. concerning *giving* and receiving, but
Jas. 1:17. Every good *gift* (lit. *giving*) and every perfect gift is

1395 1 204/227 rt 1325

δότης, *dotees.*

2Co. 9: 7. for God loveth a cheerful *giver.*

1396 1 204/227 2:261 1401,71

δουλαγωγέω, *doulagōgeo.*

1Co. 9:27. under my body, and *bring* (it) *into subjection:*

1397 5 204/227 2:261 1398

δουλεία, *doulīa.*

Ro. 8:15. received the spirit of *bondage* again
21. shall be delivered from the *bondage* of
Gal. 4:24. which gendereth to *bondage,*
5: 1. again with the yoke of *bondage.*
Heb 2:15. all their lifetime subject to *bondage.*

1398 25 204/227 2:261 1401

δουλεύω, *doulūo.*

Mat. 6:24. No man can *serve* two masters:
— Ye cannot *serve* God and mammon.
Lu. 15:29. these many years *do I serve* thee,
16:13. No servant can *serve* two masters:
— Ye cannot *serve* God and mammon.
Joh. 8:33. *were* never *in bondage* to any
Acts 7: 7. to whom they *shall be in bondage*
20:19. *Serving* the Lord with all humility
Ro. 6: 6. henceforth we should not *serve* sin.
7: 6. we should *serve* in newness of spirit,
25. I myself *serve* the law of God;
9:12. The elder *shall serve* the younger.
12:11. fervent in spirit; *serving* the Lord;
14:18. *that* in these things *serveth* Christ
16:18. such *serve* not our Lord Jesus Christ,
Gal. 4: 8. ye *did service* unto them which
9. ye desire again *to be in bondage?*
25. *is in bondage* with her children.
5:13. by love *serve* one another.
Eph. 6: 7. With good will *doing service,* as to
Phi. 2:22. he *hath served* with me in the gospel.
Col. 3:24. for ye *serve* the Lord Christ.
1Th. 1: 9. *to serve* the living and true God;
1Ti. 6: 2. *let* them not...but rather *do* (them) *service,*
Tit. 3: 3. *serving* divers lusts and pleasures, living

1399 3 204/227 2:261 1401

δούλη, *doulee.*

Lu. 1:38. Behold the *handmaid* of the Lord;
48. regarded the low estate of his *handmaiden:*
Acts 2:18. on my servants and on my *handmaidens*

1400 2 204/227 1401

δοῦλον, *doulon.*

Ro. 6:19. yielded your members *servants* to
— your members *servants* to righteousness

1401 125 204/227 2:261 1210

δοῦλος, *doulos.*

Mat. 8: 9. to my *servant,* Do this, and he doeth (it)
10:24. nor the *servant* above his lord.
25. as his master, and the *servant* as his lord.
13:27. the *servants* of the housholder came
28. The *servants* said unto him, Wilt thou
18:23. which would take account of his *servants*
26. The *servant* therefore fell down,
27. the lord of that *servant* was moved
28. the same *servant* went out, and found
32. O thou wicked *servant,* I forgave thee
20:27. chief among you, let him be your *servant:*
21:34. sent his *servants* to the husbandmen,
35. the husbandmen took his *servants,*
36. Again, he sent other *servants* more
22: 3. sent forth his *servants* to call
4. Again, he sent forth other *servants,*
6. the remnant took his *servants,*
8. Then saith he to his *servants,*
10. those *servants* went out into the
24:45. Who then is a faithful and wise *servant,*
46. Blessed (is) that *servant,* whom his lord
48. if that evil *servant* shall say
50. The lord of that *servant* shall come
25:14. called his own *servants,* and delivered
19. the lord of those *servants* cometh,
21. Well done, (thou) good and faithful *servant:*
23. Well done, good and faithful *servant;*
26. (Thou) wicked and slothful *servant,*
30. cast ye the unprofitable *servant* into
26:51. drew his sword, and struck a *servant*
Mar 10:44. the chiefest, shall be *servant* of all.
12: 2. sent to the husbandmen a *servant,*
4. he sent unto them another *servant;*
13:34. gave authority to his *servants,*
14:47. smote a *servant* of the high priest,
Lu. 2:29. now lettest thou thy *servant* depart in peace,
7: 2. a certain centurion's *servant,* who was
3. that he would come and heal his *servant.*
8. to my *servant,* Do this, and he doeth (it).
10. found the *servant* whole that had
12:37. Blessed (are) those *servants,* whom
38. find (them) so, blessed are those *servants.*
43. Blessed (is) that *servant,* whom his
45. if that *servant* say in his heart,
46. The lord of that *servant* will come
47. that *servant,* which knew his lord's will,
14:17. sent his *servant* at supper time
21. So that *servant* came, and shewed his lord
— said to his *servant,* Go out quickly into
22. the *servant* said, Lord, it is done
23. the lord said unto the *servant,*
15:22. the father said to his *servants,*
17: 7. which of you, having a *servant* plowing
9. Doth he thank that *servant* because
10. say, We are unprofitable *servants:*
19:13. he called his ten *servants,* and delivered
15. commanded these *servants* to be called
17. said unto him, Well, thou good *servant:*
22. will I judge thee, (thou) wicked *servant*
20:10. sent a *servant* to the husbandmen,
11. again he sent another *servant:*
22:50. smote the *servant* of the high priest.
Joh. 4:51. going down, his *servants* met him
8:34. Whosoever committeth sin is the *servant*
35. the *servant* abideth not in the house
13:16. The *servant* is not greater than his lord
15:15. I call you not *servants;* for the *servant*

Joh.15:20. The *servant* is not greater than his lord.
18:10. drew it, and smote the high priest's *servant*,
— The *servant's* name was Malchus.
18. the *servants* and officers stood there,
26. One of the *servants* of the high priest,
Acts 2:18. on my *servants* and on my handmaidens.
4:29. grant unto thy *servants*, that with
16:17. the *servants* of the most high God,
Ro. 1: 1. Paul, a *servant* of Jesus Christ, called
6:16. yield yourselves *servants* to obey, his *servants* ye are to whom ye obey;
17. that ye were the *servants* of sin,
20. when ye were the *servants* of sin,
1Co. 7:21. Art thou called (being) a *servant?*
22. (being) a *servant*, is the Lord's freeman:
— (being) free, is Christ's *servant*.
23. be not ye the *servants* of men.
12:13. whether (we be) *bond* or free; and have
2Co. 4: 5. ourselves your *servants* for Jesus' sake.
Gal. 1:10. I should not be the *servant* of Christ.
3:28. there is neither *bond* nor free, there
4: 1. a child, differeth nothing from a *servant*,
7. Wherefore thou art no more a *servant*,
Eph. 6: 5. *Servants*, be obedient to them that
6. as the *servants* of Christ, doing the
8. whether (he be) *bond* or free.
Phi. 1: 1. the *servants* of Jesus Christ, to all
2: 7. took upon him the form of a *servant*,
Col. 3:11. Barbarian, Scythian, *bond* (nor) free:
22. *Servants*, obey in all things (your)
4: 1. give unto (your) *servants* that which
12. a *servant* of Christ, saluteth you,
1Ti. 6: 1. many *servants* as are under the yoke
2Ti. 2:24. the *servant* of the Lord must not strive;
Tit. 1: 1. Paul, a *servant* of God, and an apostle
2: 9. (Exhort) *servants* to be obedient
Philem.16. Not now as a *servant*, but above a *servant*,
Jas. 1: 1. a *servant* of God and of the Lord Jesus Christ,
1Pet.2:16. but as the *servants* of God.
2Pet.1: 1. a *servant* and an apostle of Jesus Christ,
2:19. themselves are the *servants* of corruption:
Jude 1. Jude, the *servant* of Jesus Christ,
Rev. 1: 1. to shew unto his *servants* things
— by his angel unto his *servant* John:
2:20. to teach and to seduce my *servants*
6:15. the mighty men, and every *bondman*,
7: 3. have sealed the *servants* of our God
10: 7. declared to his *servants* the prophets.
11:18. shouldest give reward unto thy *servants*
13:16. rich and poor, free and *bond*, to receive
15: 3. the song of Moses the *servant* of God,
19: 2. avenged the blood of his *servants* at
5. Praise our God, all ye his *servants*,
18. flesh of all (men, both) free and *bond*,
22: 3. his *servants* shall serve him:
6. to shew unto his *servants* the things

1402 8 205/229 2:261 [1401]

δουλόω, douloō.

Acts 7: 6. they should *bring* them *into bondage*,
Ro. 6:18. ye *became* the *servants* of righteousness.
22. and *become servants* to God, ye have
1Co. 7:15. *is* not *under bondage* in such (cases):
9:19. have I *made* myself *servant* unto all,
Gal. 4: 3. were *in bondage* under the elements
Tit. 2: 3. not *given* to much wine, teachers
2Pet. 2:19. of the same *is* he *brought in bondage*.

1403 2 205/229 2:50 1209

δοχή, dokee.

Lu. 5:29. Levi made him a great *feast* in his
14:13. when thou makest a *feast*, call the poor,

1404 13 205/229 2:281 *derkomai* (to look)

δράκων, drakōn.

Rev.12: 3. behold a great red *dragon*, having
4. the *dragon* stood before the woman
7. his angels fought against the *dragon*; and the *dragon* fought and his angels,
9. the great *dragon* was cast out, that
13. when the *dragon* saw that he was
16. the flood which the *dragon* cast out
17. the *dragon* was wroth with the woman,
13: 2. the *dragon* gave him his power,
4. they worshipped the *dragon* which
11. like a lamb, and he spake as a *dragon*.
16:13. out of the mouth of the *dragon*,
20: 2. he laid hold on the *dragon*, that old

1405 1 205/229 cf rt 1404

δράσσομαι, drassomai.

1Co. 3:19. He *taketh* the wise in their own craftiness.

1406 3 205/229 1405

δραχμή, drakmee.

Lu. 15: 8. what woman having ten *pieces of silver*, if she lose one *piece*, (lit. *drachma*)
9. I have found the *piece* which I had lost.

δρέμω see τρέχω. 5143

1407 8 205/229 *drepō* (to pluck)

δρέπανον, drepanon.

Mar 4:29. immediately he putteth in the *sickle*,
Rev.14:14. in his hand a sharp *sickle*.
15. Thrust in thy *sickle*, and reap:
16. thrust in his *sickle* on the earth;
17. he also having a sharp *sickle*.
18. to him that had the sharp *sickle*, saying, Thrust in thy sharp *sickle*,
19. the angel thrust in his *sickle*

1408 3 205/229 8:226 eq 5143

δρόμος, dromos.

Acts13:25. as John fulfilled his *course*, he said,
20:24. that I might finish my *course* with joy,
2Ti. 4: 7. I have finished (my) *course*, I have

δῦμι see δύνω. 1416

1410 210 206/229 2:284

δύναμαι, dunamai.

Mat. 3: 9. God *is able* of these stones to raise up
5:14. A city that is set on an hill *can*not be hid.
36. thou *canst* not make one hair white
6:24. No man *can* serve two masters:
– Ye *can*not serve God and mammon.
27. by taking thought *can* add one cubit
7:18. A good tree *can*not bring forth evil
8: 2. if thou wilt, thou *canst* make me clean,

Mat. 9:15. *Can* the children of the bridechamber
28. Believe ye that I *am able* to do this?
10:28. but *are* not *able* to kill the soul:
— fear him *which is able* to destroy both
12:29. how *can* one enter into a strong man's
34. how *can* ye, being evil, speak good things?
16: 3. *can* ye not (discern) the signs of the times?
17:16. thy disciples, and they *could* not cure him.
19. Why *could* not we cast him out?
19:12. He *that is able* to receive (it), let him
25. saying, Who then *can* be saved?
20:22. *Are* ye *able* to drink of the cup that
— They say unto him, We *are able*.
22:46. no man *was able* to answer him
26: 9. this ointment *might* have been sold
42. if this cup *may* not pass away from me,
53. that I *can*not now pray to my Father,
61. said, I *am able* to destroy the temple
27:42. He saved others; himself he *can*not save.
Mar 1:40. If thou wilt, thou *canst* make me clean.
45. that Jesus *could* no more openly enter
2: 4. *when* they *could* not come nigh unto
7. who *can* forgive sins but God only?
19. *Can* the children of the bridechamber
— bridegroom with them, they *can*not fast.
3:20. they *could* not so much as eat bread.
23. How *can* Satan cast out Satan?
24. that kingdom *can*not stand.
25. against itself, that house *can*not stand.
26. he *can*not stand, but hath an end.
27. No man *can* enter into a strong
4:32. the fowls of the air *may* lodge under
33. as they *were able* to hear (it).
5: 3. no man *could* bind him, no,
6: 5. he *could* there do no mighty work,
19. would have killed him; but she *could* not:
7:15. that entering into him *can* defile him:
18. into the man, (it) *can*not defile him;
24. know (it): but he *could* not be hid.
8: 4. whence *can* a man satisfy these
9: 3. as no fuller on earth *can* white them.
22. if thou *canst do* any thing, have
23. If thou *canst* believe, all things
28. Why *could* not we cast him out?
29. This kind *can* come forth by nothing,
39. that *can* lightly speak evil of me.
10:26. Who then *can* be saved?
38. *can* ye drink of the cup that I
39. they said unto him, We *can*.
14: 5. it *might* have been sold for
7. whensoever ye will ye *may* do them good.
15:31. He saved others; himself he *can*not save.
Lu. 1:20. thou shalt be dumb, and not *able* to speak,
22. he *could* not speak unto them:
3: 8. God *is able* of these stones to raise up
5:12. if thou wilt, thou *canst* make me clean.
21. Who *can* forgive sins, but God alone?
34. *Can* ye make the children of the
6:39. *Can* the blind lead the blind?
42. how *canst* thou say to thy brother,
8:19. *could* not come at him for the press.
9:40. to cast him out; and they *could* not.
11: 7. I *can*not rise and give thee.
12:25. taking thought *can* add to his stature
26. If ye then *be* not *able* to do that
13:11. and *could* in no wise lift up (herself).
14:20. married a wife, and therefore I *can*not come.
26. own life also, he *can*not be my disciple.
27. come after me, *can*not be my disciple.
33. he hath, he *can*not be my disciple.
Lu. 16: 2. for thou *mayest* be no longer steward.
13. No servant *can* serve two masters.
— Ye *can*not serve God and mammon.
26. so that they which would pass...*can*not;
18:26. Who then *can* be saved?
19: 3. *could* not for the press, because he
20:36. Neither *can* they die any more
21:15. *shall* not *be able* to gainsay nor resist.
Joh. 1:46(47). *Can* there any good thing come
3: 2. for no man *can* do these miracles
3. he *can*not see the kingdom of God.
4. How *can* a man be born when he is old? *can* he enter the second time into
5. he *can*not enter into the kingdom of God.
9. How *can* these things be?
27. A man *can* receive nothing, except it be
5:19. The Son *can* do nothing of himself,
30. I *can* of mine own self do nothing:
44. How *can* ye believe, which receive
6:44. No man *can* come to me, except
52. How *can* this man give us (his) flesh
60. an hard saying; who *can* hear it?
65. that no man *can* come unto me,
7: 7. The world *can*not hate you; but me
34. where I am, (thither) ye *can*not come.
36. where I am, (thither) ye *can*not come?
8:21. whither I go, ye *can*not come.
22. saith, Whither I go, ye *can*not come.
43. because ye *can*not hear my word.
9: 4. night cometh, when no man *can* work.
16. How *can* a man that is a sinner do
33. were not of God, he *could* do nothing.
10:21. *Can* a devil open the eyes of the blind?
29. no (man) *is able* to pluck (them) out of
35. the scripture *can*not be broken;
11:37. *Could* not this man, which opened
12:39. Therefore they *could* not believe,
13:33. Whither I go, ye *can*not come;
36. Whither I go, thou *canst* not follow me
37. Lord, why *can*not I follow thee now?
14: 5. how *can* we know the way?
17. whom the world *can*not receive,
15: 4. the branch *can*not bear fruit of itself,
5. without me ye *can* do nothing.
16:12. ye *can*not bear them now.
Acts 4:16. in Jerusalem; and we *can*not deny (it)
20. For we *can*not but speak the things
5:39. be of God, ye *can*not overthrow it; lest
8:31. How *can* I, except some man should
10:47. *Can* any man forbid water, that
13:39. from which ye *could* not be justified by
15: 1. the manner of Moses, ye *can*not be saved.
17:19. *May* we know what this new
19:40. we *may* give an account of this concourse.
20:32. to the word of his grace, *which is able* to
21:34. *when* he *could* not know the certainty
24: 8. thyself *mayest* take knowledge of all
11. *Because that* thou *mayest* understand,
13. Neither *can* they prove the things
25:11. no man *may* deliver me unto them.
26:32. This man *might* have been set at liberty,
27:12. if by any means they *might* attain
15. *And when* the ship...*could* not bear up
31. abide in the ship, ye *can*not be saved.
39. if it *were possible*, to thrust in the ship.
43. they *which could* swim should
Ro. 8: 7. law of God, neither indeed *can* be.
8. they that are in the flesh *can*not please
39. creature, *shall be able* to separate
15:14. *able* also to admonish one another.
16:25. to him *that is of power* to stablish you

1Co. 2:14. neither *can* he know (them), because
3: 1. I, brethren, *could* not speak unto you
2. hitherto ye *were* not *able* (to bear it), neither yet now *are* ye *able*.
11. other foundation *can* no man lay
6: 5. not one that *shall be able* to judge
7:21. if thou *mayest* be made free,
10:13. tempted above that ye *are able*;
— that ye may *be able* to bear (it).
21. Ye *can*not drink the cup of the Lord,
— ye *can*not be partakers of the Lord's table,
12: 3. (that) no man *can* say that Jesus
21. the eye *can*not say unto the hand,
14:31. ye *may* all prophesy one by one,
15:50. flesh and blood *can*not inherit the
2Co. 1: 4. we may *be able* to comfort them
3: 7. *could* not stedfastly behold the face
13: 8. we *can do* nothing against the truth
Gal. 3:21. a law given *which could* have given
Eph. 3: 4. when ye read, ye *may* understand
20. Now unto him *that is able* to do
6:11. that ye may *be able* to stand against
13. that ye *may be able* to withstand in
16. wherewith ye *shall be able* to quench
Phi. 3:21. whereby he *is able* even to subdue all
1Th. 2: 6. *when* we *might* have been burdensome,
3: 9. what thanks *can* we render to God
1Ti. 5:25. they that are otherwise *can*not be hid.
6: 7. certain we *can* carry nothing out.
16. whom no man hath seen, nor *can* see:
2Ti. 2:13. faithful: he *can*not deny himself.
3: 7. and never *able* to come to the knowledge
15. scriptures, *which are able* to make thee wise
Heb. 2:18. he *is able* to succour them that are
3:19. we see that they *could* not enter in
4:15. an high priest *which can*not be touched
5: 2. *Who can* have compassion on the
7. unto him *that was able* to save him
7:25. Wherefore he *is able* also to save them to
9: 9. sacrifices, *that could* not make him that
10: 1. *can* never with those sacrifices
11. which *can* never take away sins:
Jas. 1:21. word, *which is able* to save your souls.
2:14. have not works? *can* faith save him?
3: 8. the tongue *can* no man tame;
12. *Can* the fig tree, my brethren,
4: 2. desire to have, and *can*not obtain:
12. lawgiver, *who is able* to save and to
1Joh. 3: 9. he *can*not sin, because he is born of God.
4:20. how *can* he love God whom he
Jude 24. Now unto him *that is able* to keep
Rev. 2: 2. how thou *canst* not bear them
3: 8. an open door, and no man *can* shut it:
5: 3. *was able* to open the book, neither
6:17. who *shall be able* to stand?
7: 9. multitude, which no man *could* number,
9:20. which neither *can* see, nor hear,
13: 4. who *is able* to make war with him?
17. that no man *might* buy or sell,
14: 3. no man *could* learn that song
15: 8. no man *was able* to enter into

1411 120 206/231 2:284 1410

δύναμις, dunamis.

Mat. 6:13. thine is the kingdom, and the *power*,
7:22. in thy name done many *wonderful works*?
11:20. most of his *mighty works* were done,
21. for if the *mighty works*, which were
23. if the *mighty works*, which have been
13:54. this wisdom, and (these) *mighty works*?
58. he did not many *mighty works* there because of their unbelief.
14: 2. therefore *mighty works* do shew forth
22:29. the scriptures, nor the *power* of God.
24:29. the *powers* of the heavens shall be shaken:
30. with *power* and great glory.
25:15. according to his several *ability*;
26:64. sitting on the right hand of *power*,
Mar. 5:30. that *virtue* had gone out of him,
6: 2. even such *mighty works* are wrought
5. could there do no *mighty work*,
14. therefore *mighty works* do shew forth
9: 1. kingdom of God come with *power*.
39. no man which shall do a *miracle*
12:24. the scriptures, neither the *power* of God?
13:25. the *powers* that are in heaven shall
26. in the clouds with great *power* and glory.
14:62. sitting on the right hand of *power*,
Lu. 1:17. in the spirit and *power* of Elias, to
35. the *power* of the Highest shall overshadow thee:
4:14. Jesus returned in the *power* of the Spirit
36. with authority and *power* he commandeth
5:17. the *power* of the Lord was (present) to heal
6:19. for there went *virtue* out of him,
8:46. I perceive that *virtue* is gone out of me.
9: 1. gave them *power* and authority over all
10:13. if the *mighty works* had been done
19. over all the *power* of the enemy:
19:37. the *mighty works* that they had seen;
21:26. the *powers* of heaven shall be shaken.
27. in a cloud with *power* and great glory.
22:69. the right hand of the *power* of God.
24:49. until ye be endued with *power*
Acts 1: 8. ye shall receive *power*, after that
2:22. by *miracles* and wonders and signs,
3:12. as though by our own *power* or
4: 7. By what *power*, or by what name,
33. with great *power* gave the apostles
6: 8. Stephen, full of faith and *power*,
8:10. This man is the great *power* of God.
13. the *miracles* and signs which were done.
10:38. with the Holy Ghost and with *power*:
19:11. God wrought special *miracles*
Ro. 1: 4. (to be) the Son of God with *power*,
16. for it is the *power* of God unto
20. (even) his eternal *power* and Godhead,
8:38. nor principalities, nor *powers*,
9:17. that I might shew my *power*
15:13. through the *power* of the Holy Ghost.
19. through mighty (lit. by the *power* of) signs and wonders, by the *power* of
1Co. 1:18. saved it is the *power* of God.
24. Christ the *power* of God, and the wisdom
2: 4. demonstration of the Spirit and of *power*
5. in the *power* of God.
4:19. which are puffed up, but the *power*.
20. not in word, but in *power*.
5: 4. with the *power* of our Lord Jesus Christ,
6:14. raise up us by his own *power*.
12:10. To another the working of *miracles*;
28. thirdly teachers, after that *miracles*,
29. (are) all *workers of miracles*?
14:11. know not the *meaning* of the voice,
15:24. all rule and all authority and *power*.
43. in weakness; it is raised in *power*:
56. the *strength* of sin (is) the law.
2Co. 1: 8. pressed out of measure, above *strength*,
4: 7. excellency of the *power* may be of God,
6: 7. word of truth, by the *power* of God.

2Co. 8: 3. For to (their) *power*, I bear record, yea, and beyond (their) *power* (they were) willing of themselves,
12: 9. for my *strength* is made perfect
— the *power* of Christ may rest upon me.
12. signs, and wonders, and *mighty deeds*.
13: 4. he liveth by the *power* of God.
— by the *power* of God toward you.
Gal. 3: 5. worketh *miracles* among you,
Eph. 1:19. the exceeding greatness of his *power*
21. all principality, and power, and *might*,
3: 7. the effectual working of his *power*.
16. be strengthened with *might* by
20. according to the *power* that worketh
Phi. 3:10. the *power* of his resurrection, and the
Col. 1:11. Strengthened with all *might*,
29. which worketh in me *mightily*.
1Th. 1: 5. in word only, but also in *power*,
2Th. 1: 7. from heaven with his *mighty* angels, (lit. angels of *power* of him)
11. the work of faith with *power*:
2: 9. with all *power* and signs and lying
2Ti. 1: 7. of *power*, and of love, and of a sound mind.
8. according to the *power* of God;
3: 5. godliness, but denying the *power*
Heb. 1: 3. all things by the word of his *power*,
2: 4. signs and wonders, and with divers *miracles*,
6: 5. the *powers* of the world to come,
7:16. after the *power* of an endless life.
11:11. received *strength* to conceive seed,
34. Quenched the *violence* of fire,
1Pet. 1: 5. Who are kept by the *power* of God
3:22. authorities and *powers* being made
2Pet. 1: 3. According as his divine *power*
16. the *power* and coming of our Lord
2:11. which are greater in power and *might*,
Rev. 1:16. as the sun shineth in his *strength*.
3: 8. for thou hast a little *strength*,
4:11. to receive glory and honour and *power*:
5:12. to receive *power*, and riches, and wisdom,
7:12. honour, and *power*, and might, (be) unto
11:17. hast taken to thee thy great *power*,
12:10. Now is come salvation, and *strength*,
13: 2. the dragon gave him his *power*,
15: 8. the glory of God, and from his *power*;
17:13. shall give their *power* and strength unto
18: 3. the *abundance* of her delicacies.
19: 1. honour, and *power*, unto the Lord our God:

1412 1 207/233 2:284 1411

δυναμόω, dunamoō.

Col. 1:11. *Strengthened* with all might,

1413 3 207/233 2:284 1410

δυνάστης, dunastees.

Lu. 1:52. hath put down the *mighty* from (their) seats,
Acts 8:27. an eunuch *of great authority* under Candace
1Ti. 6:15. (who is) the blessed and only *Potentate*,

1414 1 207/233 2:284 1415

δυνατέω, dunateo.

2Co.13: 3. is not weak, but is *mighty* in you.

1415 35 207/233 2:284 1410

δυνατός, dunatos.

Mat.19:26. with God all things are *possible*.
24:24. insomuch that, if (it were) *possible*,
26:39. O my Father, if it be *possible*, let this
Mar. 9:23. all things (are) *possible* to him that believeth.
10:27. with God all things are *possible*.
13:22. if (it were) *possible*, even the elect.
14:35. if it were *possible*, the hour might pass
36. Father, all things (are) *possible* unto thee.
Lu. 1:49. he *that is mighty* hath done to me
14:31. whether he be *able* with ten thousand
18:27. impossible with men are *possible* with God.
24:19. a prophet *mighty* in deed and word
Acts 2:24. it was not *possible* that he should
7:22. was *mighty* in words and in deeds.
11:17. that I *could* (lit. should be *able*) withstand God?
18:24. an eloquent man, (and) *mighty* in the scriptures,
20:16. he hasted, if it were *possible* for him,
25: 5. said he, which among you are *able*,
Ro. 4:21. promised, he was *able* also to perform.
9:22. (his) wrath, and to make his *power* known,
11:23. for God is *able* to graff them in again.
12:18. If it be *possible*, as much as lieth in you,
14: 4. for God is *able* to make him stand.
15: 1. We then that are *strong* ought to
1Co. 1:26. not many *mighty*, not many noble,
2Co. 9: 8. God (is) *able* to make all grace abound
10: 4. *mighty* through God to the pulling down
12:10. for when I am weak, then am I *strong*.
13: 9. when we are weak, and ye are *strong*:
Gal. 4:15. that, if (it had been) *possible*, ye would
2Ti. 1:12. persuaded that he is *able* to keep
Tit. 1: 9. he may be *able* by sound doctrine
Heb 11:19. that God (was) *able* to raise (him) up,
Jas. 3: 2. *able* also to bridle the whole body.
Rev. 6:15. the chief captains, and the *mighty men*,

1416 /233

δύνω & δῦμι, duno & dumi.

Mar. 1:32. at even, when the sun *did set*,
Lu. 4:40. Now *when* the sun *was setting*, all they

1417 135 208/233 2:318

δύο, duo.

Mat. 4:18. saw *two* brethren, Simon called Peter,
21. from thence, he saw other *two* brethren,
5:41. compel thee to go a mile, go with him *twain*.
6:24. No man can serve *two* masters:
8:28. there met him *two* possessed with devils,
9:27. *two* blind men followed him, crying,
10:10. neither *two* coats, neither shoes,
29. Are not *two* sparrows sold for a farthing?
11: 2. he sent *two* of his disciples,
14:17. We have here but five loaves, and *two* fishes.
19. took the five loaves, and the *two* fishes,
18: 8. having *two* hands or *two* feet to be
9. having *two* eyes to be cast into hell fire.
16. (then) take with thee one or *two* more, that in the mouth of *two* or three witnesses
19. if *two* of you shall agree on earth as
20. where *two* or three are gathered
19: 5. they *twain* shall be one flesh?
6. Wherefore they are no more *twain*,

Mat.20:21. Grant that these my *two* sons may
24. with indignation against the *two* brethren.
30. *two* blind men sitting by the way side,
21: 1. then sent Jesus *two* disciples,
28. A (certain) man had *two* sons;
31. Whether of them *twain* did the
22:40. On these *two* commandments
24:40. Then shall *two* be in the field;
41. *Two* (women shall be) grinding at
25:15. to another *two*, and to another one;
17. (had received) *two*, he also gained other *two*.
22. He also that had received *two* talents
— thou deliveredst unto me *two* talents: behold, I have gained *two* other talents beside them.
26: 2. Ye know that after *two* days is
37. with him Peter and the *two* sons of Zebedee,
60. At the last came *two* false witnesses,
27:21. Whether of the *twain* will ye that I
38. *two* thieves crucified with him,
51. the temple was rent in *twain*
Mar. 6: 7. to send them forth by *two* and *two*;
9. shod with sandals; and not put on *two* coats.
38. they say, Five, and *two* fishes.
41. taken the five loaves and the *two* fishes,
— the *two* fishes divided he among them all.
9:43. having *two* hands to go into hell,
45. having *two* feet to be cast into hell,
47. having *two* eyes to be cast into hell fire:
10: 8. they *twain* shall be one flesh: so then they are no more *twain*,
11: 1. he sendeth forth *two* of his disciples,
12:42. poor widow, and she threw in *two* mites,
14: 1. After *two* days was (the feast of) the
13. he sendeth forth *two* of his disciples,
15:27. with him they crucify *two* thieves;
38. the veil of the temple was rent in *twain*
16:12. in another form unto *two* of them,
Lu. 2:24. pair of turtledoves, or *two* young pigeons.
3:11. He that hath *two* coats, let him impart
5: 2. saw *two* ships standing by the lake:
7:19. John calling (unto him) *two* of his disciples
41. a certain creditor which had *two* debtors:
9: 3. neither have *two* coats apiece.
13. no more but five loaves and *two* fishes;
16. took the five loaves and the *two* fishes,
30. behold, there talked with him *two* men,
32. the *two* men that stood with him.
10: 1. sent them *two* and two (lit. by *twos*) before his face
35. when he departed, he took out *two* pence,
12: 6. five sparrows sold for *two* farthings,
52. three against *two*, and *two* against three.
15:11. he said, A certain man had *two* sons:
16:13. No servant can serve *two* masters:
17:34. there shall be *two* (men) in one bed;
35. *Two* (women) shall be grinding together;
36. *Two* (men) shall be in the field;
18:10. *Two* men went up into the temple
19:29. he sent *two* of his disciples,
21: 2. poor widow casting in thither *two* mites.
22:38. Lord, behold, here (are) *two* swords.
23:32. there were also *two* other, malefactors,
24: 4. *two* men stood by them in shining garments:
13. *two* of them went that same day
Joh 1:35. John stood, and *two* of his disciples;
37 the *two* disciples heard him speak,
Joh. 1:40(41). One of the *two* which heard John
2: 6. containing *two* or three firkins
4:40. with them: and he abode there *two* days.
43. after *two* days he departed thence,
6: 9. five barley loaves, and *two* small fishes:
8:17. that the testimony of *two* men is true.
11: 6. he abode *two* days still in the same
19:18. crucified him, and *two* other with him,
20: 4. So they ran *both* together: and the
12. seeth *two* angels in white sitting,
21 2. the (sons) of Zebedee, and *two* other of his disciples.
Acts 1:10. *two* men stood by them in white apparel,
23. they appointed *two*, Joseph called
24. whether of these *two* thou hast chosen,
7:29. land of Madian, where he begat *two* sons.
9:38. they sent unto him *two* men,
10: 7. called *two* of his houshold servants,
12: 6. Peter was sleeping between *two* soldiers, bound with *two* chains: and the keepers
19:10. continued by the space of *two* years;
22. he sent into Macedonia *two* of them that
34. about the space of *two* hours cried out,
21:33. to be bound with *two* chains;
23:23. he called unto (him) *two* centurions,
1Co. 6:16. for *two*, saith he, shall be one flesh.
14:27. (let it be) by *two*, or at the most (by) three,
29. Let the prophets speak *two* or three, and let
2Co.13: 1. In the mouth of *two* or three witnesses
Gal. 4:22. that Abraham had *two* sons,
24. for these are the *two* covenants; the
Eph. 2:15. to make in himself of *twain* one new man,
5:31. they *two* shall be one flesh
Phi. 1:23. For I am in a strait betwixt *two*,
1Ti. 5:19. before *two* or three witnesses.
Heb 6:18. That by *two* immutable things,
10:28. without mercy under *two* or three witnesses:
Rev. 9:12. there come *two* woes more hereafter.
16. *two* hundred thousand thousand:
11: 2. tread under foot forty (and) *two* months.
3. (power) unto my *two* witnesses,
4. the *two* olive trees, and the *two* candlesticks
10. these *two* prophets tormented them
12:14. to the woman were given *two* wings of a great eagle,
13: 5. to continue forty (and) *two* months.
11. he had *two* horns like a lamb,
19:20. These *both* were cast alive into a lake

1419 2 208/235 1418,941

δυσβάστακτος, *dusbastaktos*.

Mat.23: 4. heavy burdens and *grievous to be borne*,
Lu. 11:46. with burdens *grievous to be borne*,

1420 1 208/235 1418,1787

δυσεντερία, *dusenteria*.

Acts28: 8. sick of a fever and of a *bloody flux*: (lit. a *dysentery*)

1421 1 208/235 1418,2059

δυσερμήνευτος, *dusermeenūtos*.

Heb 5:11 things to say, and *hard to be uttered*, seeing

1422 1 208/235 1418

δύσκολος, duskolos. kolon (food)

Mar.10:24. how *hard* is it for them that trust

1423 3 208/235 1422

δυσκόλως, duskolōs.

Mat.19:23. a rich man shall *hardly* enter into
Mar.10:23. How *hardly* shall they that have riches
Lu. 18:24. How *hardly* shall they that have riches

1424 5 209/235 1416

δυσμή, dusmee.

Mat. 8:11. many shall come from the east and *west*, (lit. *setting*)
24:27. shineth even unto the *west;* so
Lu. 12:54. When ye see a cloud rise out of the *west*,
13:29. come from the east, and (from) the *west*,
Rev.21:13. on the *west* three gates.

1425 1 209/235 4:948 1418,3539

δυσνόητος, dusnoeetos.

2Pet.3:16. are some things *hard to be understood*,

1426 1 209/235 1418/5345

δυσφημία, duspheemia.

2Co. 6: 8. by *evil report* and good report: as

1427 72 209/235 2:321 1417,1176

δώδεκα, dōdeka.

Mat. 9:20. with an issue of blood *twelve* years,
10: 1. called unto (him) his *twelve* disciples,
2. the names of the *twelve* apostles are
5. These *twelve* Jesus sent forth,
11: 1. of commanding his *twelve* disciples,
14:20. fragments that remained *twelve* baskets full.
19:28. ye also shall sit upon *twelve* thrones, judging the *twelve* tribes of Israel.
20:17. took the *twelve* disciples apart
26:14. Then one of the *twelve*, called
20. he sat down with the *twelve*.
47. lo, Judas, one of the *twelve*, came,
53. more than *twelve* legions of angels?
Mar. 3:14. he ordained *twelve*, that they
4:10. were about him with the *twelve*
5:25. had an issue of blood *twelve* years,
42. she was (of the age) of *twelve* years.
6: 7. he called (unto him) the *twelve*,
43. they took up *twelve* baskets full
8:19. They say unto him, *Twelve*.
9:35. he sat down, and called the *twelve*,
10:32. he took again the *twelve*, and began
11:11. went out unto Bethany with the *twelve*.
14:10. Judas Iscariot, one of the *twelve*,
17. in the evening he cometh with the *twelve*.
20. (It is) one of the *twelve*, that dippeth
43. cometh Judas, one of the *twelve*,
Lu. 2:42. when he was *twelve* years old,
6:13. of them he chose *twelve*, whom
8: 1. the *twelve* (were) with him,
42. one only daughter, about *twelve* years
43. having an issue of blood *twelve* years,
9: 1. he called his *twelve* disciples together,
12. then came the *twelve*, and said unto him,
17. that remained to them *twelve* baskets.
18:31. Then he took (unto him) the *twelve*,
22: 3. being of the number of the *twelve*.
Lu. 22:14. sat down, and the *twelve* apostles with him.
30. judging the *twelve* tribes of Israel
47. called Judas, one of the *twelve*, went
Joh. 6:13. filled *twelve* baskets with the fragments
67. Then said Jesus unto the *twelve*,
70. Have not I chosen you *twelve*,
71. betray him, being one of the *twelve*.
11: 9. Are there not *twelve* hours in the day?
20:24. Thomas, one of the *twelve*, called
Acts 6: 2. Then the *twelve* called the multitude
7: 8. Jacob (begat) the *twelve* patriarchs.
1Co.15: 5. seen of Cephas, then of the *twelve:*
Jas. 1: 1. to the *twelve* tribes which are
Rev. 7: 5. of Juda (were) sealed *twelve* thousand.
— of Reuben (were) sealed *twelve* thousand.
— of Gad (were) sealed *twelve* thousand.
6. of Aser (were) sealed *twelve* thousand.
— of Nepthalim (were) sealed *twelve* thousand. Of the tribe of Manasses (were) sealed *twelve* thousand.
7. of Simeon (were) sealed *twelve* thousand.
— of Levi (were) sealed *twelve* thousand.
— of Issachar (were) sealed *twelve* thousand.
8. of Zabulon (were) sealed *twelve* thousand.
— of Joseph (were) sealed *twelve* thousand.
— of Benjamin (were) sealed *twelve* thousand.
12: 1. upon her head a crown of *twelve* stars:
21:12. high, (and) had *twelve* gates, and at the gates *twelve* angels, and names
— the *twelve* tribes of the children of Israel:
14. wall of the city had *twelve* foundations,
— the names of the *twelve* apostles
16. with the reed, *twelve* thousand furlongs.
21. the *twelve* gates (were) *twelve* pearls;
22: 2. which bare *twelve* (manner of) fruits,

1428 1 209/236 2:321 1427

δωδέκατος, dōdekatos.

Rev.21:20. the *twelfth*, an amethyst.

1429 1 209/236 2:321 1427,5443

δωδεκάφυλον, dōdekaphulon.

Acts26: 7. Unto which (promise) our *twelve tribes*,

1430 7 209/236

δῶμα, dōma. demō (to build)

Mat.10:27. (that) preach ye upon the *housetops*.
24:17. him which is on the *housetop* not
Mar.13:15. let him that is on the *housetop* not
Lu. 5:19. they went upon the *housetop*,
12: 3. shall be proclaimed upon the *housetops*.
17:31. he which shall be upon the *housetop*,
Acts10: 9. Peter went up upon the *housetop*

1431 11 209/236 2:166 1435

δωρεά, dōrea.

Joh. 4:10. If thou knewest the *gift* of God,
Acts 2:38. ye shall receive the *gift* of the Holy Ghost.
8:20. hast thought that the *gift* of God may
10:45. poured out the *gift* of the Holy Ghost.
11:17. as God gave them the like *gift* as
Ro. 5:15. the grace of God, and the *gift* by grace,
17. of the *gift* of righteousness shall

2Co. 9:15. Thanks (be) unto God for his unspeakable *gift*.
Eph. 3: 7. according to the *gift* of the grace of
4: 7. the measure of the *gift* of Christ.
Heb. 6: 4. have tasted of the heavenly *gift*,

1432 9 209/236 2:166 1431

δωρεάν, dōrean.

Mat.10: 8. *freely* ye have received, *freely* give
Joh.15:25. They hated me *without a cause*.
Ro. 3:24. Being justified *freely* by his grace
2Co.11: 7. to you the gospel of God *freely*?
Gal. 2:21. the law, then Christ is dead *in vain*.
2Th. 3: 8. did we eat any man's bread *for nought*;
Rev.21: 6. fountain of the water of life *freely*.
22:17. let him take the water of life *freely*.

1433 3 209/236 1435

δωρέω, dōreo.

Mar.15:45. he *gave* the body to Joseph.
2Pet. 1: 3. his divine power hath *given* unto us
4. Whereby *are given* unto us exceeding

1434 2 209/236 2:166 1433

δώρημα, dōreema.

Ro. 5:16. by one that sinned, (so is) the *gift*:
Jas. 1:17. Every good gift and every perfect *gift*

1435 19 210/237 2:166

δῶρον, dōron.

Mat. 2:11. They presented unto him *gifts*;
5:23. if thou bring thy *gift* to the altar,
24. Leave there thy *gift* before the altar,
— then come and offer thy *gift*.
8: 4. offer the *gift* that Moses commanded,
15: 5. (It is) a *gift*, by whatsoever thou
23:18. whosoever sweareth by the *gift* that
19. whether (is) greater, the *gift*, or the altar that sanctifieth the *gift*?
Mar. 7:11. Corban, that is to say, a *gift*, by whatsoever
Lu. 21: 1. casting their *gifts* into the treasury.
4. cast in unto the *offerings* of God:
Eph. 2: 8. not of yourselves: (it is) the *gift* of God:
Heb. 5: 1. may offer both *gifts* and sacrifices for
8: 3. to offer *gifts* and sacrifices: wherefore
4. there are priests that offer *gifts*
9: 9. were offered both *gifts* and sacrifices,
11: 4. God testifying of his *gifts*: and by it
Rev.11:10. shall send *gifts* one to another;

1436 2 210/237 1439

ἔα, ea.

Mar. 1:24. Saying, *Let* (us) *alone*; what have we
Lu. 4:34. Saying, *Let* (us) *alone*; what have we

1437 341 210/237,240 1487,302

ἐάν, ean.

NOTE.—Those in which it is combined with *μή*, & is mostly rendered *except*, or lit. *if...not*, are marked thus ².

Mat. 4: 9. *if* thou wilt fall down and worship me.
5:13. but *if* the salt have lost his savour,
19. Who*soever* therefore shall break one
20. *except*² your righteousness shall exceed
23. *if* thou bring thy gift to the altar,
32. who*soever* shall marry her that is
46. For *if* ye love them which love you,
47. *if* ye salute your brethren only,
6:14. For *if* ye forgive men their trespasses,
15. *if*² ye forgive not men their trespasses.
22. *if* therefore thine eye be single, thy
23. But *if* thine eye be evil, thy whole
7: 9. whom *if* his son ask bread, will he
10. Or *if* he ask a fish, will he give him
8: 2. Lord, *if* thou wilt, thou canst make me clean.
19. follow thee whither*soever* thou goest.
9:21. *If* I may but touch his garment,
10:13. *if* the house be worthy, let your
— but *if*² it be not worthy, let your peace
14. who*soever*² shall not receive you,
42. who*soever* shall give to drink unto one
11: 6. who*soever*² shall not be offended in me.
27. to whom*soever* the Son will reveal (him)
12:11. *if* it fall into a pit on the sabbath day,
29. *except*² he first bind the strong man?
36. every idle word that)(men shall speak,
14: 7. to give her what*soever* she would ask.
15: 5. by what*soever* thou mightest be profited
14. *if* the blind lead the blind, both
16:19. what*soever* thou shalt bind on earth
— what*soever* thou shalt loose on earth
26. *if* he shall gain the whole world,
17:20. *If* ye have faith as a grain of mustard
18: 3. *Except*² ye be converted, and become as
5. who*so* shall receive one such little child
12. *if* a man have an hundred sheep,
13. *if so* be that he find it, verily I say
15. *if* thy brother shall trespass against thee,
— *if* he shall hear thee, thou hast gained
16. But *if*² he will not hear (thee, then) take
17. And *if* he shall neglect to hear them,
— but *if* he neglect to hear the church,
18. What*soever* ye shall bind on earth
— what*soever* ye shall loose on earth
19. That *if* two of you shall agree on earth as touching any thing that)(they shall ask,
35. *if*² ye from your hearts forgive not
20: 4. what*soever* is right I will give you.
7. what*soever* is right, (that) shall ye receive
26. who*soever* will be great among you,
27. who*soever* will be chief among you,
21: 3. *if* any (man) say ought unto you,
21. *If* ye have faith, and doubt not, ye
24. one thing, which *if* ye tell me, I in
25. *If* we shall say, From heaven; he
26. But *if* we shall say, Of men; we fear
22:24. *If* a man die, having no children,
23:18. Who*soever* shall swear by the altar,
24:23. *if* any man shall say unto you,
26. Wherefore *if* they shall say unto you,
28. For where*soever* the carcase is, there
48. But and *if* that evil servant shall say in
26:13. Where*soever* this gospel shall be preached
42. *except*² I drink it, thy will be done.
28:14. *if* this come to the governor's ears,
Mar. 1:40. *If* thou wilt, thou canst make me clean.
3:24. *if* a kingdom be divided against itself,
25. *if* a house be divided against itself,
27. *except*² he will first bind the strong
4:22. which)(²shall not be manifested;
26. as *if* a man should cast seed into
6:10. In what place *soever* ye enter into

Mar 6:22. Ask of me what*soever* thou wilt,
23. What*soever* thou shalt ask of me,
7: 3. *except*[2] they wash (their) hands oft,
4. *except*[2] they wash, they eat not.
11. *If* a man shall say to his father or
— by what*soever* thou mightest be profited
8: 3. *if* I send them away fasting to their
36. *if* he shall gain the whole world,
9:37. Who*soever* shall receive one of such
— who*soever* shall receive me, receiveth
43. *if* thy hand offend thee, cut it off:
45. *if* thy foot offend thee,
47. *if* thine eye offend thee, pluck it out:
50. but *if* the salt have lost his saltness,
10:11. Who*soever* shall put away his wife,
12. *if* a woman shall put away her husband,
15. Who*soever*[2] shall not receive the kingdom
30. *But*[2] he shall receive an hundredfold
35. do for us what*soever* we shall desire.
43. who*soever* will be great among you,
11: 3. *if* any man say unto you,
23. he shall have what*soever* he saith.
31. saying, *If* we shall say, From heaven;
32. But *if* we shall say, Of men; they
12:19. *If* a man's brother die, and leave
13:11. what*soever* shall be given you in
21. And then *if* any man shall say to you,
14:14. where*soever* he shall go in, say ye
31. *If* I should die with thee, I will not deny
Lu. 4: 6. to whom*soever* I will I give it.
7. *If* thou therefore wilt worship me,
5:12. *if* thou wilt, thou canst make me clean.
6:33. *if* ye do good to them which do good
34. *if* ye lend (to them) of whom ye hope
7:23. who*soever*[2] shall not be offended in me.
9:48. Who*soever* shall receive this child
— who*soever* shall receive me receiveth
10: 6. *if* the son of peace be there, your peace
22. to whom)(the Son will reveal (him).
11:12. Or *if* he shall ask an egg, will he
12:38. *if* he shall come in the second watch,
45. But *and if* that servant say in his heart,
13: 3. *except*[2] ye repent, ye shall all likewise perish.
5. but, *except*[2] ye repent, ye shall all
14:34. but *if* the salt have lost his savour,
15: 8. *if* she lose one piece, doth not
16:30. *if* one went unto them from the dead,
31. *though* (lit. *if*) one rose from the dead.
17: 3. *If* thy brother trespass against thee,
— *if* he repent, forgive him.
4. *if* he trespass against thee seven times
33. Who*soever* shall seek to save his life
— who*soever* shall lose his life shall
18:17. Who*soever*[2] shall not receive the
19:31. *if* any man ask you, Why do ye
40. *if* these should hold their peace,
20: 5. *If* we shall say, From heaven;
6. But *and if* we say, Of men; all the people
28. *If* any man's brother die, having
22:67. *If* I tell you, ye will not believe:
68. *if* I also ask (you), ye will not
Joh. 3: 2. *except*[2] God be with him.
3. *Except*[2] a man be born again,
5. *Except*[2] a man be born of water
12. *if* I tell you (of) heavenly things?
27. *except*[2] it be given him from heaven.
4:48. *Except*[2] ye see signs and wonders, ye
5:19. *but*[2] what he seeth the Father do:
31. *If* I bear witness of myself, my
43. *if* another shall come in his own
6:44. can come to me, *except*[2] the Father

Joh. 6:51. *if* any man eat of this bread,
53. *Except*[2] ye eat the flesh of the Son of man,
62. (What) *and if* ye shall see the Son of man
65. *except*[2] it were given unto him
7:17. *If* any man will do his will,
37. *If* any man thirst, let him come
51. judge (any) man, before it (lit. *unless*[2] it previously) hear him,
8:16. yet *if* I judge, my judgment is
24. *if*[2] ye believe not that I am (he).
31. *If* ye continue in my word,
36. *If* the Son therefore shall make
51. *If* a man keep my saying, he shall
52. thou sayest, *If* a man keep my saying,
54. *If* I honour myself, my honour is nothing.
55. *if* I should say, I know him not,
9:22. that *if* any man did confess that
31. but *if* any man be a worshipper of God,
10: 9. by me *if* any man enter in, he
11: 9. *If* any man walk in the day, he
10. But *if* a man walk in the night, he
40. *if* thou wouldest believe, thou shouldest
48. *If* we let him thus alone, all (men)
57. that, *if* any man knew where he were,
12:24. *Except*[2] a corn of wheat fall into the
— *if* it die, it bringeth forth much fruit.
26. *If* any man serve me, let him follow
— *if* any man serve me, him will
32. *if* I be lifted up from the earth, will
47. *if* any man hear my words, and believe
13: 8. *If*[2] I wash thee not, thou hast no
17. happy are ye *if* ye do them.
20. He that receiveth whom*soever* I send
35. *if* ye have love one to another.
14: 3. *if* I go and prepare a place for you, I will
14. *If* ye shall ask any thing in my name,
15. *If* ye love me, keep my commandments.
23. *If* a man love me, he will keep my words:
15: 4. *except*[2] it abide in the vine; no more can ye, *except*[2] ye abide in me.
6. *If*[2] a man abide not in me, he is
7. *If* ye abide in me, and my words abide in you, ye shall ask what)(ye will, and it shall
10. *If* ye keep my commandments,
14. *if* ye do whatsoever I command you.
16: 7. for *if*[2] I go not away, the Comforter
— but *if* I depart, I will send him unto you
19:12. saying, *If* thou let this man go,
20:25. *Except*[2] I shall see in his hands the
21:22. *If* I will that he tarry till I come,
23. *If* I will that he tarry till I come,
25. which, *if* they should be written
Acts 5:38. for *if* this counsel or this work be
7: 7. the nation to whom)(they shall be
8:31. *except*[2] some man should guide me?
9: 2. that *if* he found any of this way,
13:41. *though* a man declare it unto you.
15: 1. *Except*[2] ye be circumcised after the
26: 5. *if* they would testify, that after the
27:31. *Except*[2] these abide in the ship,
Ro. 2:25. profiteth, *if* thou keep the law: but *if* thou be a breaker of the law,
26. Therefore *if* the uncircumcision keep
7: 2. but *if* the husband be dead, she is
3. *if*, while (her) husband liveth, she be
— but *if* her husband be dead, she is free
9:27. *Though* the number of the children
10: 9. *if* thou shalt confess with thy mouth
15. shall they preach, *except*[2] they be sent
11:22. *if* thou continue in (his) goodness:
23. *if*[2] they abide not in unbelief, shall

1437

Ro. 12:20. if thine enemy hunger, feed him; *if* he thirst, give him drink:
13: 4. But *if* thou do that which is evil, be afraid;
14: 8. For *whether* we live, we live unto the Lord; and *whether* we die, we die unto the Lord: *whether* we live therefore, *or* die, we are the Lord's.
23. he that doubteth is damned *if* he eat,
15:24. When*soever* I take my journey into
— *if* first I be somewhat filled with
1Co. 4:15. *though* ye have ten thousand instructers
19. come to you shortly, *if* the Lord will,
5:11. *if* any man that is called a brother
6: 4. *If* then ye have judgments of things
18. Every sin that)(a man doeth is without
7: 8. for them *if* they abide even as I.
11. But and *if* she depart, let her remain
28. But and *if* thou marry, thou hast not sinned; and *if* a virgin marry, she hath not sinned.
36. *if* she pass the flower of (her) age,
39. but *if* her husband be dead, she is at
40. she is happier *if* she so abide,
8: 8. neither, *if* we eat, are we the better; neither, *if*[2] we eat not, are we the worse.
10. For *if* any man see thee which
9:16. *though* I preach the gospel, I have
— woe is unto me, *if*[2] I preach not the gospel!
10:28. *if* any man say unto you, This
11:14. that, *if* a man have long hair, it is
15. But *if* a woman have long hair, it is
12:15. *If* the foot shall say, Because I am
16. *if* the ear shall say, Because I am
13: 1. *Though* I speak with the tongues
2. *though* I have (the gift of) prophecy,
— *though* I have all faith, so that I
3. *though* I bestow all my goods
— *though* I give my body to be burned,
14: 6. *if* I come unto you speaking
— *except*[2] I shall speak to you either
7. *except*[2] they give a distinction in
8. *if* the trumpet give an uncertain
9. *except*[2] ye utter by the tongue words
11. Therefore *if*[2] I know not the meaning
14. For *if* I pray in an (unknown) tongue,
16. *when* thou shalt bless with the spirit,
23. *If* therefore the whole church be come
24. But *if* all prophesy, and there come in one
28. But *if*[2] there be no interpreter, let him
30. *If* (any thing) be revealed to another
15:36. is not quickened, *except*[2] it die:
16: 3. whom*soever* ye shall approve by
4. *if* it be meet that I go also, they shall
6. on my journey whither*soever* I go.
7. a while with you, *if* the Lord permit.
10. *if* Timotheus come, see that he may
2Co. 5: 1. we know that *if* our earthly house •
8:12. accepted according to that)(a man hath,
9: 4. *if* they of Macedonia come with me,
10: 8. For *though* I should boast somewhat
12: 6. For *though* I would desire to glory,
13: 2. that, *if* I come again, I will not spare:
Gal. 1: 8. though (lit. even *if*) we, or an angel from heaven,
2:16. but (lit. *if*[2] not) by the faith of Jesus Christ,
5: 2. that *if* ye be circumcised, Christ
6: 1. *if* a man be overtaken in a fault,
7. what*soever* a man soweth, that shall
Eph. 6: 8. what*soever* good thing any man doeth,
Col. 3:13. *if* any man have a quarrel against
23. what*soever* ye do, do (it) heartily,
4:10. *if* he come unto you, receive him,
1Th. 3: 8. we live, *if* ye stand fast in the Lord.
2Th. 2: 3. *except*[2] there come a falling away first,
1Ti. 1: 8. law (is) good, *if* a man use it lawfully;
2:15. *if* they continue in faith and charity
3:15. But *if* I tarry long, that thou mayest
2Ti. 2: 5. *if* a man also strive for masteries,
— *except*[2] he strive lawfully.
21. *If* a man therefore purge himself
Heb. 3: 6. *if* we hold fast the confidence and the
7. To day *if* ye will hear his voice,
14. *if* we hold the beginning of our
15. To day *if* ye will hear his voice,
4: 7. To day *if* ye will hear his voice,
6: 3. this will we do, *if* God permit.
10:38. *if* (any man) draw back, my
13:23. *if* he come shortly, I will see
Jas. 2: 2. For *if* there come unto your
14. *though* a man say he hath faith,
15. *If* a brother or sister be naked,
17. faith, *if*[2] it hath not works, is dead,
4:15. *If* the Lord will, we shall live,
5:19. *if* any of you do err from the truth,
1Pet.3:13. *if* ye be followers of that which is good?
1Joh.1: 6. *If* we say that we have fellowship
7. But *if* we walk in the light, as he is
8. *If* we say that we have no sin,
9. *If* we confess our sins, he is faithful
10. *If* we say that we have not sinned,
2: 1. *if* any man sin, we have an advocate
3. *if* we keep his commandments.
15. *If* any man love the world, the
24. *If* that which ye have heard from
29. *If* ye know that he is righteous,
3: 2. we know that, *when* he shall appear,
20. For *if* our heart condemn us,
21. *if*[2] our heart condemn us not,
22. what*soever* we ask, we receive of him,
4:12. *If* we love one another, God dwelleth in us,
20. *If* a man say, I love God, and hateth
5:14. *if* we ask any thing according to his
15. *if* we know that he hear us,
16. *If* any man see his brother sin
3Joh. 5. what*soever* thou doest to the brethren,
10. Wherefore, *if* I come, I will remember
Rev. 2: 5. out of his place, *except*[2] thou repent.
22. *except*[2] they repent of their deeds.
3: 3. *If*[2] therefore thou shalt not watch,
19. As many as)(I love, I rebuke
20. *if* any man hear my voice, and open
11: 6. all plagues, as often as)(they will.
22:18. *If* any man shall add unto these
19. And *if* any man shall take away

1438 339 211/240

ἑαυτ-οῦ, -ῷ, -ὸν, &c, *heaut-ou, -o, -on,* &c.

NOTE.—See also the contracted form of this word under αὐτοῦ.

Mat. 3: 9. think not to say within *yourselves,*
6:34. take thought for the things of *itself.*
8:22. let the dead bury *their* dead.
9: 3. the scribes said within *themselves,*
21. For she said within *herself,* If I may
12:25. Every kingdom divided against *itself*
— or house divided against *itself*
26. he is divided against *himself;*
45. taketh with *himself* seven other spirits more wicked than *himself,*

Mat.13:21. Yet hath he not root in *himself*,
14:15. villages, and buy *themselves* victuals.
15:30. having with *them* (those that were) lame,
16: 7. they reasoned among *themselves*,
8. why reason ye among *yourselves*,
24. let him deny *himself*, and take up
18: 4. Whosoever therefore shall humble *himself*
19:12. have made *themselves* eunuchs for
21: 8. spread *their* garments in the way;
25. they reasoned with *themselves*, saying,
38. they said among *themselves*,
23:12. whosoever shall exalt *himself* shall
— he that shall humble *himself* shall
31. ye be witnesses unto *yourselves*, that
37. as a hen gathereth *her* chickens under
25: 3. They that (were) foolish took *their* lamps, and took no oil with *them*:
9. them that sell, and buy for *yourselves*.
26:11. ye have the poor always with *you*;
27:35. parted my garments among *them*,
42. He saved others; *himself* he cannot save.
Mar. 2: 8. they so reasoned within *themselves*,
19. they have the bridegroom with *them*,
3:24. if a kingdom be divided against *itself*,
25. if a house be divided against *itself*,
26. if Satan rise up against *himself*,
4:17. have no root in *themselves*, and so
5: 5. crying, and cutting *himself* with stones.
26. had spent all that she had (lit. all things from *herself*), and was nothing
30. Jesus, immediately knowing in *himself*
6:36. villages, and buy *themselves* bread: for
51. they were sore amazed in *themselves*
8:14. with *them* more than one loaf.
34. let him deny *himself*, and take up
9: 8. save Jesus only with *themselves*.
10. they kept that saying with *themselves*,
33. that ye disputed among *yourselves*
50. Have salt in *yourselves*, and have peace
10:26. saying among *themselves*, Who then
11:31. they reasoned with *themselves*, saying
12: 7. husbandmen said among *themselves*,
33. to love (his) neighbour as *himself*,
13: 9. take heed to *yourselves*: for they shall
14: 4. that had indignation within *themselves*,
7. ye have the poor with *you* always,
33. he taketh with *him* Peter and James
15:31. He saved others; *himself* he cannot save.
16: 3. they said among *themselves*, Who shall
Lu. 1:24. hid *herself* five months, saying,
3: 8. begin not to say within *yourselves*,
7:30. the counsel of God against *themselves*,
39. he spake within *himself*, saying,
49. began to say within *themselves*,
9:23. let him deny *himself*, and take up
25. gain the whole world, and lose *himself*,
47. took a child, and set him by *him*,
60. Let the dead bury *their* dead:
10:29. he, willing to justify *himself*,
11:17. Every kingdom divided against *itself*
18. If Satan also be divided against *himself*,
21. man armed keepeth *his* palace,
26. other spirits more wicked than *himself*;
12: 1. Beware ye)(of the leaven of the Pharisees,
17. he thought within *himself*, saying,
21. that layeth up treasure for *himself*,
33. provide *yourselves* bags which
36. like unto men that wait for *their* lord,
47. servant, which knew *his* lord's will,
57. why even of *yourselves* judge ye
13:19. a man took, and cast into *his* garden;

Lu. 13:34. as a hen (doth gather) *her* brood
14:11. whosoever exalteth *himself* shall
— he that humbleth *himself* shall
26. come to me, and hate not *his* father,
— yea, and *his own* life also, he cannot
33. forsaketh not all that he hath (lit. all the things of *himself*), he
15: 5. he layeth (it) on *his* shoulders, rejoicing.
17. when he came to *himself*, he said,
20. he arose, and came to *his* father. But when
16: 3. Then the steward said within *himself*,
5. called every one of *his* lord's debtors
8. are in *their* generation wiser than the children
9. Make to *yourselves* friends of the mammon
15. Ye are they which justify *yourselves*
17: 3. Take heed to *yourselves*: If thy brother
14. Go shew *yourselves* unto the priests.
18: 4. afterward he said within *himself*,
9. certain which trusted in *themselves*
11. stood and prayed thus with *himself*,
14. every one that exalteth *himself* shall be
— he that humbleth *himself* shall be
19:12. to receive for *himself* a kingdom,
13. he called *his* ten servants, and delivered
35. they cast *their* garments upon the colt,
20: 5. they reasoned with *themselves*, saying,
14. they reasoned among *themselves*,
20. which should feign *themselves* just
21:30. ye see and know of *your own selves* that
34. take heed to *yourselves*, lest at any
22:17. divide (it) among *yourselves*:
23. began to enquire among *themselves*,
66. led him into *their* council, saying,
23: 2. saying that *he himself* is Christ
12. at enmity between *themselves*.
28. weep for *yourselves*, and for your children.
35. He saved others; let him save *himself*,
48. smote *their* breasts, and returned.
24:12. departed, wondering in *himself* at
27. the scriptures the things concerning *himself*.
Joh. 2:24. Jesus did not commit *himself* unto
5:18. making *himself* equal with God.
19. Son can do nothing of *himself*,
26. as the Father hath life in *himself*;
— the Son to have life in *himself*;
42. ye have not the love of God in *you*.
6:53. his blood, ye have no life in *you*.
61. When Jesus knew in *himself* that
7:18. He that speaketh of *himself* seeketh
35. said the Jews among *themselves*,
8:22. said the Jews, Will he kill *himself*?
11:33. groaned in the spirit, and was troubled, (lit. disturbed *himself*)
38. therefore again groaning in *himself*
51. this spake he not of *himself*: but
55. before the passover, to purify *themselves*.
12: 8. the poor always ye have with *you*;
19. Pharisees therefore said among *themselves*
13: 4. took a towel, and girded *himself*.
32. God shall also glorify him in *himself*,
15: 4. the branch cannot bear fruit of *itself*,
16:13. for he shall not speak of *himself*;
18:34. Sayest thou this thing of *thyself*,
19: 7. he made *himself* the Son of God.
24. They parted my raiment among *them*,
20:10. went away again unto their own home. (lit. to *themselves*)
21: 1. Jesus shewed *himself* again to the

Joh.21: 7. did cast *himself* into the sea.
Acts 1: 3. To whom also he shewed *himself* alive
5:35. take heed to *yourselves* what ye intend
36. Theudas, boasting *himself* to be somebody;
7:21. nourished him for *her own* son.
8: 9. that *himself* was some great one:
34. of *himself*, or of some other man?
10:17. while Peter doubted in *himself*
12:11. when Peter was come to *himself*,
13:46. judge *yourselves* unworthy of everlasting life,
14:17. he left not *himself* without witness,
15:29. from which if ye keep *yourselves*,
16:27. would have killed *himself*,
19:31. not adventure *himself* into the theatre.
20:28. Take heed therefore unto *yourselves*,
21:23. men which have a vow on *them*;
23:12. bound *themselves* under a curse,
14. We have bound *ourselves* under a
21. which have bound *themselves* with
25: 4. that *he himself* would depart shortly
28:16. Paul was suffered to dwell by *himself*
29. had great reasoning among *themselves*.
Ro. 1:24. their own bodies between *themselves*:
27. receiving in *themselves* that recompence
2:14. are a law unto *themselves*:
4:19. considered not *his own* body now dead,
5: 8. God commendeth *his* love toward us,
6:11. reckon ye also *yourselves* to be dead
13. yield *yourselves* unto God, as
16. to whom ye yield *yourselves* servants
8: 3. God sending *his own* Son in the
23. we ourselves groan within *ourselves*,
11:25. should be wise in your own conceits; (lit. in or by *yourselves*)
12:16. Be not wise in your own conceits. (lit. in or by *yourselves*)
19. Dearly beloved, avenge not *yourselves*,
13: 2. shall receive to *themselves* damnation.
9. Thou shalt love thy neighbour as *thyself*.
14: 7. none of us liveth to *himself*, and no man dieth to *himself*.
12. shall give account of *himself* to God.
14. (there is) nothing unclean of *itself*:
22. he that condemneth not *himself*
15: 1. and not to please *ourselves*.
3. For even Christ pleased not *himself*;
16: 4. laid down *their own* necks:
18. *their own* belly; and by good words
1Co. 3:18. Let no man deceive *himself*.
6: 7. ye go to law *one* with *another*.
19. have of God, and ye are not *your own*?
7: 2. let every man have *his own* wife,
37. in his heart that he will keep *his* virgin,
10:24. Let no man seek *his own*, but
29. Conscience, I say, not *thine own*, but
11: 5. head uncovered dishonoureth *her* head:
28. let a man examine *himself*, and so
29. eateth and drinketh damnation to *himself*,
31. if we would judge *ourselves*, we
13: 5. seeketh not *her own*, is not easily
14: 4. in an (unknown) tongue edifieth *himself*;
28. Let him speak to *himself*, and to God.
16: 2. every one of you lay by *him* in store,
15. they have addicted *themselves* to the
2Co. 1: 9. the sentence of death in *ourselves*, that we should not trust in *ourselves*,
3: 1. Do we begin again to commend *ourselves*?
5. Not that we are sufficient of *ourselves* to think any thing as of *ourselves*;
13. (which) put a vail over *his* face,
4: 2. commending *ourselves* to every man's
2Co. 4: 5. For we preach not *ourselves*, but Christ
— *ourselves* your servants for Jesus' sake.
5:12. For we commend not *ourselves* again
15. not henceforth live unto *themselves*,
18. reconciled us to *himself* by Jesus
19. reconciling the world unto *himself*,
6: 4. approving *ourselves* as the ministers
7: 1. let us cleanse *ourselves* from all
11. ye have approved *yourselves* to be
8: 5. first gave *their own selves* to the Lord,
10: 7. If any man trust to *himself* that
— let him of *himself* think this again,
12. or compare *ourselves* with some that commend *themselves*: but they measuring *themselves* by *themselves*, and comparing *themselves* among *themselves*,
14. we stretch not *ourselves* beyond
18. not he that commendeth *himself*
13: 5. Examine *yourselves*, whether ye be in the faith; prove *your own selves*. Know ye not *your own selves*,
Gal. 1: 4. Who gave *himself* for our sins,
2:12. he withdrew and separated *himself*,
20. loved me, and gave *himself* for me.
5:14. Thou shalt love thy neighbour as *thyself*.
6: 3. he is nothing, he deceiveth *himself*.
4. let every man prove *his own* work,
— have rejoicing in *himself* alone,
8. he that soweth to *his* flesh shall
Eph. 2:15. for to make in *himself* of twain
4:16. unto the edifying of *itself* in love.
19. have given *themselves* over unto
32. tenderhearted, forgiving *one another*,
5: 2. hath given *himself* for us an offering
19. Speaking to *yourselves* in psalms
25. Husbands, love *your* wives, even
— loved the church, and gave *himself* for it;
27. present it to *himself* a glorious church,
28. So ought men to love *their* wives as *their own* bodies. He that loveth *his* wife loveth *himself*.
29. no man ever yet hated *his own* flesh;
33. in particular so love *his* wife even as *himself*; and the wife
Phi. 2: 3. esteem other better than *themselves*.
4. Look not every man on *his own* things,
7. made *himself* of no reputation,
8. he humbled *himself*, and became obedient
12. work out *your own* salvation with fear
21. For all seek *their own*, not the things
3:21. to subdue all things unto *himself*.
Col. 3:13. forgiving *one another*, if any man
16. teaching and admonishing *one another* in
1Th. 2: 7. as a nurse cherisheth *her* children:
8. also *our own* souls, because ye were
11. as a father (doth) *his* children,
12. hath called you unto *his* kingdom
4: 4. know how to possess *his* vessel in
5:13. be at peace among *yourselves*.
2Th. 2: 4. shewing *himself* that he is God.
6. might be revealed in *his* time.
3: 9. to make *ourselves* an ensample
12. they work, and eat *their own* bread.
1Ti. 2: 6. Who gave *himself* a ransom for all,
9. women adorn *themselves* in modest
3:13. purchase to *themselves* a good degree,
6:10. pierced *themselves* through with
19. Laying up in store for *themselves*
2Ti 2:13. faithful: he cannot deny *himself*.
21. If a man therefore purge *himself*
4: 3. they heap to *themselves* teachers,
Tit 2:14. Who gave *himself* for us, that he

Tit. 2:14. purity unto *himself* a peculiar people,
Heb 1: 3. had by *himself* purged our sins,
3:13. exhort *one another* daily, while
5: 3. so also for *himself*, to offer for sins.
4. no man taketh this honour unto *himself*,
5. Christ glorified not *himself*
6: 6. crucify to *themselves* the Son of God
13. by no greater, he sware by *himself*,
7:27. when he offered up *himself*.
9: 7. which he offered for *himself*,
14. offered *himself* without spot
25. that he should offer *himself* often,
10:25. the assembling of *ourselves* together,
34. knowing in *yourselves* that ye
Jas. 1:22. hearers only, deceiving *your own selves*.
24. For he beholdeth *himself*, and goeth
27. to keep *himself* unspotted from the world.
2: 4. Are ye not then partial in *yourselves*,
17. Even so faith, if it hath not works, is dead, being alone. (lit. by *itself*)
1 Pet. 1:12. that not unto *themselves*, but unto
3: 5. adorned *themselves*, being in
4: 8. have fervent charity among *yourselves*:
10. minister the same *one* to *another*,
19. commit the keeping of *their* souls
2Pet. 2: 1. bring upon *themselves* swift destruction.
1Joh. 1: 8. have no sin, we deceive *ourselves*,
3: 3. purifieth *himself*, even as he is pure.
5:10. hath the witness in *himself*:
18. begotten of God keepeth *himself*,
21. Little children, keep *yourselves* from idols.
2Joh. 8. Look to *yourselves*, that we lose not
Jude 6. angels which kept not *their* first estate,
12. feeding *themselves* without fear:
13. foaming out *their own* shame;
18. walk after *their own* ungodly lusts.
19. they who separate *themselves*,
20. building up *yourselves* on your
21. Keep *yourselves* in the love of God,
Rev. 2: 9. of them which say *they* are Jews,
20. which calleth *herself* a prophetess,
3: 9. which say *they* are Jews, and are not,
4: 8. beasts had each of them (lit. each by *itself*) six wings
6:15. hid *themselves* in the dens
8: 6. prepared *themselves* to sound.
10: 3. seven thunders uttered *their* voices.
4. seven thunders had uttered *their* voices.
7. declared to *his* servants the prophets.
17:13. shall give *their* power and strength
18: 7. How much she hath glorified *herself*,
19: 7. his wife hath made *herself* ready.

1439 13 211/244 cf 1436

ἐάω, eao.

Mat.24:43. would not *have suffered* his
Lu. 4:41. *suffered* them not to speak:
22:51. *Suffer* ye thus far. And he touched
Acts 5:38. Refrain from these men, and *let* them *alone*:
14:16. *suffered* all nations to walk in
16: 7. the Spirit *suffered* them not.
19:30. the disciples *suffered* him not.
23:32. they *left* the horsemen to go with him, *and*
27:32. ropes of the boat, and *let* her fall off.
40. they *committed* (themselves) unto the sea,
28: 4. yet vengeance *suffereth* not to live.
1Co.10:13. who *will* not *suffer* you to be tempted
Rev. 2:20. because thou *sufferest* that woman Jezebel, which calleth

---

1440 5 212/244 2:627 1442,1176

ἑβδομήκοντα, hebdomeekonta.

Lu. 10: 1. the Lord appointed other *seventy*
17. the *seventy* returned again with joy, saying, Lord, even the devils
Acts 7:14. kindred, threescore and fifteen (lit. *seventy* five) souls.
23:23. horsemen *threescore and ten*, and spearmen
27:37. threescore and sixteen (lit. *seventy* six) souls.

1441 1 212/244 2:627 1440

ἑβδομηκοντάκις, hebdomeekontakis.

Mat.18:22. Until seven times: but, Until *seventy times* seven.

1442 9 212/244 2:627 2033

ἕβδομος, hebdomos.

Joh. 4:52. Yesterday at the *seventh* hour the fever left him.
Heb 4: 4. of the *seventh* (day) on this wise, and God did rest the *seventh* day from all his works.
Jude 14. Enoch also, the *seventh* from Adam
Rev. 8: 1. when he had opened the *seventh* seal,
10: 7. the days of the voice of the *seventh* angel, when he shall begin to sound,
11:15. the *seventh* angel sounded; and there
16:17. the *seventh* angel poured out his vial
21:20. the *seventh*, chrysolite; the eighth, beryl, the ninth, a topaz;

ἑβραϊκός, hebraïkos.

See among Proper Names.

ἑβραΐς, hebraïs.

See among Proper Names.

ἑβραϊστί, hebraïsti.

See among Proper Names.

1448 43 212/245 2:330 1451

ἐγγίζω, engizo.

Mat. 3: 2. for the kingdom of heaven *is at hand*.
4:17. for the kingdom of heaven *is at hand*.
10: 7. The kingdom of heaven *is at hand*.
15: 8. *draweth nigh* unto me with their mouth,
21: 1. when they *drew nigh* unto Jerusalem,
34. when the time of the fruit *drew near*,
26:45. behold, the hour *is at hand*, and the
46. he *is at hand* that doth betray me.
Mar. 1:15. the kingdom of God *is at hand*:
11: 1. when they *came nigh* to Jerusalem,
14:42. lo, he that betrayeth me *is at hand*.
Lu. 7:12. when he *came nigh* to the gate of the city,
10: 9. The kingdom of God *is come nigh* unto you.
11. the kingdom of God *is come nigh* unto
12:33. where no thief *approacheth*, neither
15: 1. Then *drew near* unto him all the
25. as he came and *drew nigh* to the house,
18:35. as he was *come nigh* unto Jericho,

Lu. 18:40. *when* he *was come near*, he asked him,
19 29. when he *was come nigh* to Bethphage
37. *when* he *was come nigh*, even now
41. when he *was come near*, he beheld
21: 8. the time *draweth near:* go ye not
20. that the desolation thereof *is nigh*.
28. for your redemption *draweth nigh*.
22: 1. the feast of unleavened bread *drew nigh*,
47. *drew near* unto Jesus to kiss him.
24:15. Jesus himself *drew near, and* went with them.
28. they *drew nigh* unto the village,
Acts 7:17. the time of the promise *drew nigh*,
9: 3. as he journeyed, he *came near* Damascus:
10: 9. *as* they went...and *drew nigh* unto the city,
21:33. chief captain *came near, and* took him,
22: 6. *as* I made my journey, and *was come nigh*
23:15. we, or ever he *come near*, are ready
Ro. 13:12. night is far spent, the day *is at hand:*
Phi. 2:30. work of Christ he *was nigh* unto death,
Heb. 7:19. by the which we *draw nigh* unto God.
10:25. the more, as ye see the day *approaching*.
Jas. 4: 8. *Draw nigh* to God, and he will *draw nigh*
5: 8. the coming of the Lord *draweth nigh*.
1Pet. 4: 7. the end of all things *is at hand:*

1449 2 213/333 1722,1125

ἐγγράφω, *engrapho*.

2Co. 3: 2. Ye are our epistle *written in* our hearts,
3. ministered by us, *written* not with ink,

1450 1 213/245 2:329 1722 *guion* (limb)

ἔγγυος, *enguos*.

Heb. 7:22. Jesus made a *surety* of a better testament.

1451 30 213/245 2:330 *agchō* (to squeeze)

ἐγγύς, *engus*.

Mat. 24:32. ye know that summer (is) *nigh:*
33. know that it is *near*, (even) at the doors.
26:18. The Master saith, My time is *at hand*,
Mar. 13:28. ye know that summer is *near:*
29. know that it is *nigh*, (even) at the doors.
Lu. 19:11. because he was *nigh* to Jerusalem,
21:30. that summer is now *nigh at hand*.
31. kingdom of God is *nigh at hand*.
Joh. 2:13. the Jews' passover was *at hand*,
3:23. was baptizing in Ænon *near* to Salim,
6: 4. the passover, a feast of the Jews, was *nigh*.
19. on the sea, and drawing *nigh* unto the ship:
23. *nigh* unto the place where they
7: 2. Jews' feast of tabernacles was *at hand*.
11:18. Bethany was *nigh* unto Jerusalem,
54. unto a country *near* to the wilderness,
55. the Jews' passover was *nigh at hand:*
19:20. was crucified was *nigh* to the city:
42. the sepulchre was *nigh at hand*.
Acts 1:12. *from* Jerusalem a sabbath day's journey.
9:38. as Lydda was *nigh* to Joppa,
27: 8. *nigh* whereunto was the city (of) Lasea.
Ro. 10: 8. The word is *nigh* thee, (even) in thy
Eph. 2:13. are made *nigh* by the blood of Christ.
17. were afar off, and to them that were *nigh*.
Phi. 4: 5. unto all men. The Lord (is) *at hand*.
Heb. 6: 8. rejected, and (is) *nigh unto* cursing;
8:13. waxeth old (is) *ready* to vanish away.
Rev. 1: 3. for the time (is) *at hand*.
22:10. for the time is *at hand*.

1452 1 213/245 1451

ἐγγύτερον, *enguteron*.

Ro. 13:11. now (is) our salvation *nearer*

1453 141 213/245 2:333 cf rt 58

ἐγείρω, *egīro*.

Mat. 2:13. *Arise, and* take the young child
14. *When* he *arose*, he took the young
20. *Arise, and* take the young child
21. he *arose, and* took the young child
3: 9. *to raise up* children unto Abraham.
8:15. she *arose*, and ministered unto them.
25. *awoke* him, saying, Lord, save us:
26. Then he *arose, and* rebuked the winds
9: 5. or to say, *Arise*, and walk?
6. *Arise*, take up thy bed, and go unto
7. he *arose, and* departed to his house.
19. Jesus *arose, and* followed him,
25. took her by the hand, and the maid *arose*.
10: 8. *raise* the dead, cast out devils:
11: 5. the dead *are raised up*, and the poor
11. there *hath* not *risen* a greater than John
12:11. will he not lay hold on it, and *lift* (it) *out?*
42. The queen of the south *shall rise up* in
14: 2. John the Baptist; he *is risen* from the dead;
16:21. and *be raised again* the third day.
17: 7. said, *Arise*, and be not afraid.
23. the third day he *shall be raised again*.
24: 7. nation *shall rise* against nation,
11. many false prophets *shall rise*,
24. For there *shall arise* false Christs,
25: 7. Then all those virgins *arose*, and trimmed
26:32. after I *am risen again*, I will go
46. *Rise*, let us be going: behold, he is
27:52. bodies of the saints which slept *arose*,
63. After three days I will *rise again*.
64. He *is risen* from the dead: so the
28: 6. He is not here: for he *is risen*, as he said.
7. tell his disciples that he *is risen* from
Mar. 1:31. by the hand, and *lifted* her *up*
2: 9. or to say, *Arise*, and take up thy bed,
11. I say unto thee, *Arise*, and take up thy bed,
12. immediately he *arose*, took up the bed,
3: 3. had the withered hand, *Stand* forth.
4:27. should sleep, and *rise* night and day,
5:41. Damsel, I say unto thee, *arise*.
6:14. That John the Baptist *was risen*
16. he *is risen* from the dead.
9:27. *lifted* him *up;* and he arose.
10:49. Be of good comfort, *rise;* he calleth thee.
12:26. as touching the dead, that they *rise:*
13: 8. nation *shall rise* against nation,
22. false Christs and false prophets *shall rise*,
14:28. after that I *am risen*, I will go
42. *Rise up*, let us go; lo, he that
16: 6. he *is risen;* he is not here:
14. had seen him *after* he *was risen*.
Lu. 1:69. *hath raised up* an horn of salvation
3: 8. *to raise up* children unto Abraham.
5:23. or to say, *Rise up* and walk?
24. I say unto thee, *Arise*, and take up
6: 8. *Rise up*, and stand forth in the midst.
7:14. Young man, I say unto thee, *Arise*.
16. a great prophet *is risen up* among us
22. the deaf hear, the dead *are raised*,
8:24. Then *he arose, and* rebuked the wind
54. called, saying, Maid, *arise*.
9: 7. that John *was risen* from the dead

Lu. 9:22. and *be raised* the third day.
11: 8. he will not *rise and* give him as many
31. The queen of the south *shall rise up*
13:25. the master of the house *is risen up*,
20:37. Now that the dead *are raised*,
21:10. Nation *shall rise* against nation,
24: 6. He is not here, but *is risen:*
34. Saying, The Lord *is risen* indeed.
Joh. 2:19. in three days I *will raise* it *up*.
20. *wilt* thou *rear* it *up* in three days?
22. When therefore he *was risen* from the dead,
5: 8. Jesus saith unto him, *Rise*, take up
21. as the Father *raiseth up* the dead,
7:52. for out of Galilee *ariseth* no prophet.
11:29. she *arose* quickly, and came unto him.
12: 1. whom he *raised* from the dead.
9. whom he *had raised* from the dead.
17. *raised* him from the dead, bare record.
13: 4. He *riseth* from supper, and laid aside his
14:31. even so I do. *Arise*, let us go hence.
21:14. *after that* he *was risen* from the dead.
Acts 3: 6. name of Jesus Christ of Nazareth *rise up* and walk.
7. by the right hand, and *lifted* (him) *up:*
15. whom God *hath raised* from the dead;
4:10. whom God *raised* from the dead,
5:30. The God of our fathers *raised up* Jesus,
9: 8. Saul *arose* from the earth; and when
10:26. Peter *took* him *up*, saying, Stand up;
40. Him God *raised up* the third day,
12: 7. *raised* him *up*, saying, Arise up
13:22. he *raised up* unto them David
23. *raised* unto Israel a Saviour, Jesus:
30. God *raised* him from the dead:
37. he, whom God *raised again*, saw no
26: 8. that God should *raise* the dead?
Ro. 4:24. we believe on him *that raised up* Jesus
25. and *was raised again* for our justification.
6: 4. as Christ *was raised up* from the dead
9. Christ *being raised* from the dead
7: 4. to him *who is raised* from the dead,
8:11. Spirit of him *that raised up* Jesus
— he *that raised up* Christ from the dead
34. yea rather, *that is risen again*,
10: 9. God *hath raised* him from the dead,
13:11. high time *to awake* out of sleep:
1Co. 6:14. God *hath* both *raised up* the Lord,
15: 4. that he *rose again* the third day
12. preached that he *rose* from the dead,
13. then *is* Christ not *risen:*
14. if Christ *be* not *risen*, then
15. of God that he *raised up* Christ: whom he *raised* not *up*, if so be that the dead *rise* not.
16. For if the dead *rise* not, then *is* not Christ *raised:*
17. if Christ *be* not *raised*, your faith
20. now *is* Christ *risen* from the dead,
29. for the dead, if the dead *rise* not at all?
32. advantageth it me, if the dead *rise* not?
35. How *are* the dead *raised up?*
42. it *is raised* in incorruption:
43. sown in dishonour; it *is raised* in glory: it is sown in weakness; it *is raised* in power:
44. it *is raised* a spiritual body.
52. the dead *shall be raised* incorruptible,
2Co. 1: 9. in God *which raiseth* the dead:
4:14. he *which raised up* the Lord Jesus *shall raise up* us also by Jesus,
nto him *which* died for them, and *rose again*.

Gal. 1: 1. the Father, *who raised* him from the dead
Eph. 1:20. *when* he *raised* him from the dead.
5:14. he saith, *Awake* thou that sleepest,
Col. 2:12. of God, *who hath raised* him from the dead
1Th. 1:10. whom he *raised* from the dead,
2Ti. 2: 8. was *raised* from the dead according to
Heb 11:19. that God (was) able *to raise* (him) *up*,
Jas. 5:15. the Lord *shall raise* him *up;*
1Pet. 1:21. God, *that raised* him *up* from the dead,
Rev. 11: 1. *Rise*, and measure the temple of God,

1454 1 214/247 2:333 1453

ἔγερσις, *egersis.*

Mat. 27:53. came out of the graves after his *resurrection*,

1455 1 214/337 1722,2524

ἐγκάθετος, *enkathetos.*

Lu. 20:20. they watched (him), and sent forth *spies*,

1456 1 214/337 1722,2537

ἐγκαίνια, *enkainia.*

Joh. 10:22. at Jerusalem the *feast of the dedication*,

1457 2 214/337 3:447 1456

ἐγκαινίζω, *enkainizo.*

Heb. 9:18. (testament) *was dedicated* without blood.
10:20. way, which he *hath consecrated* for us,

1458 7 214/247 3:487 1722,2564

ἐγκαλέω, *enkaleo.*

Acts 19:38. *let* them *implead* one another.
40. we are in danger *to be called in question*
23:28. the cause wherefore they *accused* him,
29. to be *accused* of questions of their law,
26: 2. the things whereof I *am accused* of the Jews:
7. king Agrippa, I *am accused* of the Jews.
Ro. 8:33. Who *shall lay* any thing *to the charge* of God's elect?

1459 9 214/247 1722,2641

ἐγκαταλείπω, *enkatalīpo.*

Mat. 27:46. my God, why *hast* thou *forsaken* me?
Mar 15:34. my God, why *hast* thou *forsaken* me?
Acts 2:27. thou *wilt* not *leave* my soul in hell,
Ro. 9:29. the Lord of Sabaoth *had left* us a seed,
2Co. 4: 9. Persecuted, but not *forsaken;* cast
2Ti. 4:10. For Demas *hath forsaken* me,
16. with me, but all (men) *forsook* me:
Heb 10:25. Not *forsaking* the assembling of ourselves together,
13: 5. I will never leave thee, nor *forsake* thee.

1460 1 215/337 1722,2730

ἐγκατοικέω, *enkatoikeo.*

2Pet. 2: 8. that righteous man *dwelling among* them,

1461 6 215/337 1722,2759

ἐγκεντρίζω, *enkentrizo.*

Ro. 11:17. *wert graffed in* among them,
19. broken off, that I *might be graffed in.*
23. abide not in unbelief, *shall be graffed in* for God is able *to graff* them in again.

11:24. and *wert graffed* contrary to nature into a
— *shall* these...*be graffed into* their own olive tree?

1462 2 215/247 3:487 1458

ἔγκλημα, *enkleema.*

Acts23:29. to have nothing *laid to* his *charge* worthy
25:16. concerning the *crime laid against* him.

1463 1 215/247 2:339 1722 *komboō* (to gird)

ἐγκομβόομαι, *enkombo-omai.*

1Pet.5: 5. *be clothed with* humility: for God

1464 1 215/337 3:830 1465

ἐνκοπή, *enkopee.*

1Co. 9:12. lest we should hinder (lit. give any *hindrance*) the gospel of Christ.

1465 5 215/337 3:830 1722,2875

ἐγκόπτω, *enkopto.*

Acts24: 4. that I *be* not further *tedious unto* thee,
Ro. 15:22. I *have been* much *hindered* from coming
Gal. 5: 7. Ye did run well; who *did hinder* (lit. *hath hindered*) you
1Th. 2:18. once and again; but Satan *hindered* us.
1Pet.3: 7. that your prayers *be* not *hindered*.

1466 4 215/247 2:339 1468

ἐγκράτεια, *enkratīa.*

Acts24:25. reasoned of righteousness, *temperance*,
Gal. 5:23. Meekness, *temperance:* against such
2Pet. 1: 6. to knowledge *temperance;* and to *temperance*

1467 2 215/247 2:339 1468

ἐγκρατεύομαι, *enkratūomai.*

1Co. 7: 9. if they *cannot contain*, let them marry:
9:25. striveth for the mastery *is temperate* in

1468 1 215/247 2:339 1722,2904

ἐγκρατής, *enkratees.*

Tit. 1: 8. sober, just, holy, *temperate;*

1469 1 215/337 3:921 1722,2919

ἐγκρίνω, *enkrino.*

2Co.10:12. we dare not *make* ourselves *of the number*,

1470 2 216/247 1722,2928

ἐγκρύπτω, *enkrupto.*

Mat.13:33. took, and *hid in* three measures of meal,
Lu. 13:21. took and *hid in* three measures of meal,

1471 1 216/337 1722,rt 2949

ἔγκυος, *enkuos.*

Lu. 2: 5. his espoused wife, being *great with child.*

1472 1 216/247 1722,5548

ἐγχρίω, *enkrio.*

Rev. 3 18. *anoint* thine eyes with eyesalve, that

1473 370 216/247 2:343 cf **1691, 1698, 1700, 2248, 2249, 2254, 2257,** etc.

ἐγώ, *ego*

Mat. 3:11. *I* indeed baptize you with water
14. *I* have need to be baptized of thee,
5:22. *I* say unto you, That whosoever
28. *I* say unto you, That whosoever
32. *I* say unto you, That whosoever
34. *I* say unto you, Swear not at all,
39. *I* say unto you, That ye resist not evil:
44. *I* say unto you, Love your enemies,
8: 7. unto him, *I* will come and heal him.
9. For *I* am a man under authority,
10:16. Behold, *I* send you forth as sheep in
11:10. Behold, *I* send my messenger before
12:27. if *I* by Beelzebub cast out devils,
28. if *I* cast out devils by the Spirit of God,
14:27. Be of good cheer; it is *I;* be not afraid.
18:33. even as *I* had pity on thee?
20:15. Is thine eye evil, because *I* am good?
22. the cup that *I* shall drink of,
— the baptism that *I* am baptized with?
23. the baptism that *I* am baptized with:
21:27. Neither tell *I* you by what authority
30. he answered and said, *I* (go), sir:
22:32. *I* am the God of Abraham,
23:34. behold, *I* send unto you prophets,
24: 5. in my name, saying, *I* am Christ;
25:27. *I* should have received mine own
26:22. to say unto him, Lord, is it *I?*
25. answered and said, Master, is it *I?*
33. (yet) will *I* never be offended.
39. not as *I* will, but as thou (wilt).
28:20. lo, *I* am with you alway,
Mar 1: 2. Behold, *I* send my messenger
8. *I* indeed have baptized you with water:
6:16. It is John, whom *I* beheaded:
50. Be of good cheer: it is *I;* be not afraid.
9:25. *I* charge thee, come out of him,
10:38. drink of the cup that *I* drink of?
— the baptism that *I* am baptized with?
39. drink of the cup that *I* drink of; and with the baptism that *I* am baptized withal
11:33. Neither do *I* tell you by what
12:26. saying, *I* (am) the God of Abraham,
13: 6. in my name, saying, *I* am (Christ);
14:19. (Is) it *I?* and another (said), (Is) it *I?*
29. be offended, yet (will) not *I.*
36. not what *I* will, but what thou wilt.
58. *I* will destroy this temple that is
62. Jesus said, *I* am: and ye shall see
Lu. 1:18. for *I* am an old man, and my wife
19. said unto him, *I* am Gabriel,
3:16. *I* indeed baptize you with water;
7: 8. For *I* also am a man set under
27. Behold, *I* send my messenger before
8:46. for *I* perceive that virtue is gone out of me.
9: 9. Herod said, John have *I* beheaded:
— of whom *I* hear such things?
10: 3. behold, *I* send you forth as lambs
35. when I come again, *I* will repay thee.
11:19. if *I* by Beelzebub cast out devils,
15:17. to spare, and *I* perish with hunger!
19:22. Thou knewest that *I* was an austere man,
23. *I* might have required mine own
20: 8. Neither tell *I* you by what authority
21: 8. in my name, saying, *I* am (Christ);
15. For *I* will give you a mouth and wisdom,
22:27. *I* am among you as he that serveth.
32. *I* have prayed for thee, that thy
70. said unto them Ye say that *I* am.

Lu. 23:14. *I*, having examined (him) before you,
24:39. that it is *I* myself: handle me,
49. *I* send the promise of my Father
Joh. 1:20. confessed, *I* am not the Christ.
23. *I* (am) the voice of one crying in the
26. saying, *I* baptize with water:
27. *I* am not worthy to unloose.
30. This is he of whom *I* said, After
31. am *I* come baptizing with water.
3:28. said, *I* am not the Christ, but that
4:14. of the water that *I* shall give him
26. *I* that speak unto thee am (he).
32. *I* have meat to eat that ye
38. *I* sent you to reap that whereon ye
5: 7. while *I* am coming, another steppeth
30. *I* can of mine own self do nothing:
31. If *I* bear witness of myself, my
34. *I* receive not testimony from man:
36. *I* have greater witness than (that)
— the same works that *I* do, bear
43. *I* am come in my Father's name,
45. Do not think that *I* will accuse you
6:20. he saith unto them, It is *I*; be not
35. *I* am the bread of life: he that
40. *I* will raise him up at the last day.
41. *I* am the bread which came down
44. *I* will raise him up at the last day.
48. *I* am that bread of life.
51. *I* am the living bread which
— bread that *I* will give is my flesh, which *I* will give for the life of
54. *I* will raise him up at the last day.
63. the words that *I* speak unto you,
70. Have not *I* chosen you twelve,
7. 7. me it hateth, because *I* testify of it,
8. *I* go not up yet unto this feast;
17. or (whether) *I* speak of myself.
29. *I* know him: for I am from him,
34. where *I* am, (thither) ye cannot come.
36. where *I* am, (thither) ye cannot come?
8:11. Neither do *I* condemn thee:
12. *I* am the light of the world: he
14. Though *I* bear record of myself,
15. after the flesh; *I* judge no man.
16. yet if *I* judge, my judgment
— *I* and the Father that sent me
18. *I* am one that bear witness
21. *I* go my way, and ye shall seek me,
— whither *I* go, ye cannot come.
22. Whither *I* go, ye cannot come.
23. Ye are from beneath; *I* am from above:
— *I* am not of this world.
24. if ye believe not that *I* am (he),
28. then shall ye know that *I* am (he),
29. for *I* do always those things that
38. *I* speak that which I have seen with
42. for *I* proceeded forth and came from God;
45. because *I* tell (you) the truth, ye
49. Jesus answered, *I* have not a devil;
50. *I* seek not mine own glory:
54. If *I* honour myself, my honour
55. *I* know him: and if I should say,
58. Before Abraham was, *I* am.
9: 9. like him: (but) he said, *I* am (he).
39. *I* am come into this world,
10: 7. *I* am the door of the sheep.
9. *I* am the door: by me if any
10. *I* am come that they might
11. *I* am the good shepherd: the
14. *I* am the good shepherd, and know
17. because *I* lay down my life,

Joh. 10:18. *I* lay it down of myself. I have
25. works that *I* do in my Father's name,
30. *I* and (my) Father are one.
34. in your law, *I* said, Ye are gods?
11:25. *I* am the resurrection, and the life:
27. *I* believe that thou art the Christ,
42. *I* knew that thou hearest me
12:26. where *I* am, there shall also
46. *I* am come a light into the world,
47. believe not, *I* judge him not:
49. *I* have not spoken of myself;
50. whatsoever *I* speak therefore, even
13: 7. What *I* do thou knowest not now;
14. If *I* then (your) Lord and Master,
15. that ye should do as *I* have done to you.
18. *I* know whom I have chosen:
19. ye may believe that *I* am (he).
26. *I* shall give a sop, when I have dipped (it).
33. Whither *I* go, ye cannot come;
14: 3. that where *I* am, (there) ye may
4. whither *I* go ye know, and the way
6. *I* am the way, the truth, and the life:
10. Believest thou not that *I* am in the Father
— the words that *I* speak unto you
11. Believe me that *I* (am) in the Father,
12. works that *I* do shall he do also;
— because *I* go unto my Father.
14. any thing in my name, *I* will do (it).
16. *I* will pray the Father, and he shall
19. because *I* live, ye shall live also.
20. know that *I* (am) in my Father,
21. *I* will love him, and will manifest
27. not as the world giveth, give *I* unto you
28. Ye have heard how *I* said unto you,
15: 1. *I* am the true vine, and my Father
5. *I* am the vine, ye (are) the branches:
10. even as *I* have kept my Father's
14. if ye do whatsoever *I* command you.
16. *I* have chosen you, and ordained you,
19. *I* have chosen you out of the world,
20. Remember the word that *I* said
26. whom *I* will send unto you
16: 4. remember that *I* told you of them.
7. Nevertheless *I* tell you the truth; It is expedient for you that *I* go away:
16. because *I* go to the Father.
17. Because *I* go to the Father?
26. not unto you, that *I* will pray
27. believed that *I* came out from God.
33. *I* have overcome the world.
17: 4. *I* have glorified thee on the earth:
9. *I* pray for them: I pray not for
11. in the world, and *I* come to thee.
12. *I* kept them in thy name:
14. *I* have given them thy word;
— even as *I* am not of the world.
16. even as *I* am not of the world.
19. for their sakes *I* sanctify myself,
22. thou gavest me *I* have given them;
23. *I* in them, and thou in me,
24. be with me where *I* am;
25. *I* have known thee, and these have
18: 5. Jesus saith unto them, *I* am (he).
6. as he had said unto them, *I* am (he),
8. I have told you that *I* am (he):
20. *I* spake openly to the world; *I* ever taught in the synagogue,
21. behold, they know what *I* said.
26. Did not *I* see thee in the garden
35. Pilate answered, Am *I* a Jew?
37. Thou sayest that *I* am a king. To this end was *I* born, and for this

Joh.18:38. I find in him no fault (at all).
19: 6. for I find no fault in him.
Acts 7: 7. shall be in bondage will I judge,
32. (Saying), I (am) the God of thy fathers,
9: 5. I am Jesus whom thou persecutest:
10. he said, Behold, I (am here), Lord.
16. I will shew him how great things
10:20. for I have sent them.
21. I am he whom ye seek:
11: 5. I was in the city of Joppa praying:
17. what was I that I could withstand God?
13:25. I am not (he). But, behold, there
33. my Son, this day have I begotten thee
41. I work a work in your days,
15:19. Wherefore my sentence is (lit. I judge), that we
17: 3. Jesus, whom I preach unto you,
23. him declare I unto you.
18: 6. I (am) clean: from henceforth I will go
10. For I am with thee, and no man shall
15. for I will be no judge of such (matters).
20:22. I go bound in the spirit unto Jerusalem,
25. now, behold, I know that ye all,
26. that I (am) pure from the blood
29. For I know this, that after my departing
21:13. for I am ready not to be bound only,
39. I am a man (which am) a Jew
22. . I am verily a man (which am) a Jew,
8. I answered, Who art thou, Lord? and he said unto me, I am Jesus of Nazareth,
19. they know that I imprisoned and beat
21. for I will send thee far hence
28. With a great sum obtained I this freedom.
And Paul said, But I was (free) born.
23. 1. I have lived in all good conscience
6. Men (and) brethren, I am a Pharisee,
— of the dead I am called in question.
24:21. I am called in question by you this day.
25:18. of such things as I supposed:
20. because I doubted of such manner
25. when I found that he had committed
26: 9. I verily thought with myself, that
10. the saints did I shut up in prison,
15. I said, Who art thou, Lord? And he said, I am Jesus whom thou persecutest.
28:17. nothing...yet was I delivered prisoner
Ro. 7: 9. I was alive without the law once:
— but...sin revived, and I died.
14. I am carnal, sold under sin.
17. then it is no more I that do it,
20. if I do that I would not, it is no more I that do it, but sin
24. O wretched man that I am!
25. I myself serve the law of God;
9: 3. For I could wish that)(myself
10:19. I will provoke you to jealousy by
11: 1. For I also am an Israelite,
13. as I am the apostle of the Gentiles,
19. that I might be graffed in.
12:19. I will repay, saith the Lord.
14:11. (As) I live, saith the Lord, every
15:14. I myself also am persuaded of you,
16: 4. unto whom not only I give thanks,
22. I Tertius, who wrote (this) epistle,
1Co. 1:12. I am of Paul; and I of Apollos; and I of Cephas; and I of Christ.
2: 3. I was with you in weakness,
3: 1. I, brethren, could not speak unto you
4. while one saith, I am of Paul; and another, I (am) of Apollos;
6. I have planted, Apollos watered;
4:15. I have begotten you through the gospel.
1Co. 5: 3. For I verily, as absent in body,
6:12. I will not be brought under the power
7:10. I command, (yet) not I, but the Lord,
12. to the rest speak I, not the Lord:
28. in the flesh: but I spare you.
9: 6. Or I only and Barnabas, have not we
15. I have used none of these things:
26. I therefore so run, not as uncertainly;
10:30. For if I by grace be a partaker,
— that for which I give thanks?
11:23. I have received of the Lord
15: 9. For I am the least of the apostles,
10. yet not I, but the grace of God
11. Therefore whether (it were) I or they,
16:10. the work of the Lord, as I also (do).
2Co. 1:23. Moreover I call God for a record
2: 2. For if I make you sorry, who
10. I (forgive) also: for if I forgave any
10: 1. Now I Paul myself beseech you
11:23. I speak as a fool I (am) more;
29. who is offended, and I burn not?
12:11. I ought to have been commended
13. that I myself was not burdensome
15. I will very gladly spend and be
16. be it so, I did not burden you:
Gal. 1:12. For I neither received it of man,
2:19. For I through the law am dead
20. nevertheless I live; yet not I,
4:12. Brethren, I beseech you, be as I (am);
5: 2. Behold, I Paul say unto you.
10. I have confidence in you
11. I, brethren, if I yet preach
6:17. I bear in my body the marks
Eph. 3: 1. For this cause I Paul, the prisoner
4: 1. I therefore, the prisoner of the Lord,
5:32. I speak concerning Christ and the church.
Phi. 3: 4. Though I might also have
— might trust in the flesh, I more:
13. I count not myself to have apprehended.
4:11. for I have learned, in whatsoever
Col. 1:23. whereof I Paul am made a minister;
25. Whereof I am made a minister,
1Th. 2:18. even I Paul, once and again;
1Ti. 1:11. which was committed to *my* trust.
15. to save sinners; of whom I am chief.
2: 7. Whereunto I am ordained a preacher,
2Ti. 1:11. Whereunto I am appointed a preacher,
4: 1. I charge (thee) therefore before God,
6. I am now ready to be offered,
Tit. 1: 3. preaching, which is committed unto *me*
5. in every city, as I had appointed thee:
Philem 13. Whom I would have retained with me,
19. I Paul have written (it) with mine
— I will repay (it): albeit I do not
20. let *me* have joy of thee in the Lord:
Heb. 1: 5. this day have I begotten thee? And again I will be to him a Father,
2:13. again, I will put my trust in him.
— Behold I and the children which God
5: 5. my Son, to day have I begotten thee.
10:30. I will recompense, saith the Lord.
12:26. I shake not the earth only,
1Pet. 1:16. Be ye holy; for I am holy.
2Pet. 1:17. in whom I am well pleased.
2Joh. 1. whom I love in the truth; and not I only but also all they
3Joh. 1. Gaius, whom I love in the truth.
Rev. 1: 8. I am Alpha and Omega, the
9. I John, who also am your brother,
11. Saying, I am Alpha and Omega,
17. Fear not; I am the first and the last:
2:22. Behold, I will cast her into a bed,

Rev. 2:23. that *I* am he which searcheth the
3: 9. to know that *I* have loved thee.
19. As many as I love, *I* rebuke and chasten:
5: 4. *I* wept much, because no man
17: 7. *I* will tell thee the mystery of the
21: 2. *I* John saw the holy city, new Jerusalem,
6. *I* am Alpha and Omega, the beginning
— *I* will give unto him that is athirst
22: 8. *I* John saw these things, and heard
13. *I* am Alpha and Omega, the beginning and the end,
16. *I* Jesus have sent mine angel
— *I* am the root and the offspring of David,

See also in κἀγώ.

1474 1 216/255 1475

ἐδαφίζω, *edaphizo.*

Lu. 19:44. *shall lay* thee *even with the ground,*

1475 1 216/255 rt 1476

ἔδαφος, *edaphos.*

Acts 22: 7. I fell unto the *ground,* and heard

1476 3 217/255 2:362 *hezomai*

ἑδραῖος, *hedraios.* (to sit)

1Co. 7:37. he that standeth *stedfast* in his heart,
15:58. my beloved brethren, be ye *stedfast,*
Col. 1:23. continue in the faith grounded and *settled,*

1477 1 217/255 2:362 1476

ἑδραίωμα, *hedraiōma.*

1Ti. 3:15. the pillar and *ground* of the truth.

1479 1 217/255 3:155 2309,2356

ἐθελοθρησκεία, *ethelothreeskīa.*

Col. 2:23. a shew of wisdom in *will worship,*

ἐθέλω see θέλω. 2309

1480 1 217/256 1485

ἐθίζω, *ethizo.*

2:27. to do for him after the *custom* of the law, (lit. *that which was wont to be done*)

1481 1 217/256 1484,746

ἐθνάρχης, *ethnarkees.*

2Co. 11:32. the *governor* under Aretas the king

1482 2 217/256 2:364 1484

ἐθνικός, *ethnikos.*

Mat. 6: 7. use not vain repetitions, as the *heathen*
18:17. let him be unto thee as an *heathen man*

1483 1 217/256 1482

ἐθνικῶς, *ethnikōs.*

Gal. 2:14. livest *after the manner of Gentiles,*

1484 164 217/256 2:364 1486

ἔθνος, *ethnos.*

Mat. 4:15. beyond Jordan, Galilee of the *Gentiles*
Mat. 6:32. after all these things do the *Gentiles* seek:
10: 5. Go not into the way of the *Gentiles,*
18. a testimony against them and the *Gentiles.*
12:18. shall shew judgment to the *Gentiles.*
21. in his name shall the *Gentiles* trust
20:19. shall deliver him to the *Gentiles*
25. the princes of the *Gentiles* exercise dominion
21:43. given to a *nation* bringing forth the
24: 7. For *nation* shall rise against *nation,*
9. ye shall be hated of all *nations* for
14. for a witness unto all *nations;*
25:32. before him shall be gathered all *nations:*
28:19. Go ye therefore, and teach all *nations,*
Mar 10:33. shall deliver him to the *Gentiles:*
42. accounted to rule over the *Gentiles*
11:17. called of all *nations* the house of prayer?
13: 8. For *nation* shall rise against *nation,*
10. first be published among all *nations*
Lu 2:32. A light to lighten the *Gentiles,*
7: 5. For he loveth our *nation,* and he hath
12:30. do the *nations* of the world seek after:
18:32. he shall be delivered unto the *Gentiles,*
21:10. *Nation* shall rise against *nation,*
24. led away captive into all *nations:*
— shall be trodden down of the *Gentiles,* until
— the times of the *Gentiles* be fulfilled.
25. upon the earth distress of *nations,*
22:25. The kings of the *Gentiles* exercise lordship
23: 2. We found this (fellow) perverting the *nation,*
24:47. preached in his name among all *nations,*
Joh. 11:48. take away both our place and *nation.*
50. that the whole *nation* perish not.
51. that Jesus should die for that *nation;*
52. not for that *nation* only, but that
18:35. Thine own *nation* and the chief priests
Acts 2: 5. out of every *nation* under heaven.
4:25. Why did the *heathen* rage, and the people
27. with the *Gentiles,* and the people of Israel,
7: 7. the *nation* to whom they shall be
45. into the possession of the *Gentiles,*
8: 9. bewitched the *people* of Samaria,
9:15. to bear my name before the *Gentiles,*
10:22. among all the *nation* of the Jews,
35. in every *nation* he that feareth him,
45. on the *Gentiles* also was poured out
11: 1. the *Gentiles* had also received the word
18. hath God also to the *Gentiles* granted
13:19. when he had destroyed seven *nations*
42. the *Gentiles* besought that these words
46. lo, we turn to the *Gentiles.*
47. thee to be a light of the *Gentiles,*
48. when the *Gentiles* heard this, they
14: 2. the unbelieving Jews stirred up the *Gentiles,*
5. of the *Gentiles,* and also of the Jews
16. all *nations* to walk in their own ways.
27. the door of faith unto the *Gentiles.*
15: 3. declaring the conversion of the *Gentiles:*
7. that the *Gentiles* by my mouth should hear
12. wrought among the *Gentiles* by them.
14. did visit the *Gentiles,* to take out of
17. all the *Gentiles,* upon whom my name
19. which from among the *Gentiles* are
23. the brethren which are of the *Gentiles*
17:26. made of one blood all *nations* of men
18: 6. I will go unto the *Gentiles.*
21:11. into the hands of the *Gentiles.*
19. God had wrought among the *Gentiles*
21. the Jews which are among the *Gentiles*
25. As touching the *Gentiles* which believe,

Acts22:21. send thee far hence unto the *Gentiles*.
24: 2. worthy deeds are done unto this *nation*
10. many years a judge unto this *nation*,
17. I came to bring alms to my *nation*,
26: 4. among mine own *nation* at Jerusalem,
17. from the people, and (from) the *Gentiles*,
20. (then) to the *Gentiles*, that they should repent
23. light unto the people, and to the *Gentiles*.
28:19. had ought to accuse my *nation* of.
28. salvation of God is sent unto the *Gentiles*,
Ro. 1: 5. to the faith among all *nations*,
13. even as among other *Gentiles*.
2:14. the *Gentiles*, which have not the law,
24. God is blasphemed among the *Gentiles*
3:29. also of the *Gentiles*? Yes, of the *Gentiles* also:
4:17. made thee a father of many *nations*,
18. become the father of many *nations*,
9:24. Jews only, but also of the *Gentiles*?
30. That the *Gentiles*, which followed not
10:19. no *people*, (and) by a foolish *nation* I wil
11:11. salvation (is come) unto the *Gentiles*,
12. diminishing of them the riches of the *Gentiles*;
13. For I speak to you *Gentiles*, inasmuch as I am the apostle of the *Gentiles*,
25. until the fulness of the *Gentiles* be
15: 9. that the *Gentiles* might glorify God
— I will confess to thee among the *Gentiles*,
10. he saith, Rejoice, ye *Gentiles*,
11. Praise the Lord, all ye *Gentiles*;
12. shall rise to reign over the *Gentiles*; in him shall the *Gentiles* trust.
16. minister of Jesus Christ to the *Gentiles*,
— the offering up of the *Gentiles* might
18. to make the *Gentiles* obedient,
27. if the *Gentiles* have been made partakers
16: 4. all the churches of the *Gentiles*.
26. made known to all *nations* for
1Co. 5: 1. not so much as named among the *Gentiles*,
10.20. the things which the *Gentiles* sacrifice,
12: 2. Ye know that ye were *Gentiles*,
2Co.11:26. (in) perils by the *heathen*, (in) perils
Gal. 1:16. I might preach him among the *heathen*;
2: 2. gospel which I preach among the *Gentiles*,
8. mighty in me toward the *Gentiles*:
9. we (should go) unto the *heathen*,
12. he did eat with the *Gentiles*
14. the *Gentiles* to live as do the Jews?
15. not sinners of the *Gentiles*,
3: 8. that God would justify the *heathen*
— In thee shall all *nations* be blessed.
14. might come on the *Gentiles* through
Eph. 2:11. ye (being) in time past *Gentiles* in
3: 1. prisoner of Jesus Christ for you *Gentiles*,
6. That the *Gentiles* should be fellowheirs,
8. I should preach among the *Gentiles*
4:17. walk not as other *Gentiles* walk,
Col. 1:27. this mystery among the *Gentiles*;
1Th. 2:16. Forbidding us to speak to the *Gentiles*
4: 5. as the *Gentiles* which know not God:
1Ti. 2: 7. a teacher of the *Gentiles* in faith
3:16. preached unto the *Gentiles*, believed
2Ti. 1:11. an apostle, and a teacher of the *Gentiles*.
4:17. (that) all the *Gentiles* might hear:
1Pet.2: 9. a royal priesthood, an holy *nation*,
12. conversation honest among the *Gentiles*:
4: 3. wrought the will of the *Gentiles*,
3Joh. 7. taking nothing of the *Gentiles*.
Rev. 2:26. to him will I give power over the *nations*
Rev 5: 9. every kindred, and tongue, and people and *nation*;
7: 9. no man could number, of all *nations*,
10:11. before many peoples, and *nations*, and tongues,
11: 2. for it is given unto the *Gentiles*:
9. people and kindreds and tongues and *nations*
18. the *nations* were angry, and thy wrath
12: 5. was to rule all *nations* with a rod of iron:
13: 7. over all kindreds, and tongues, and *nations*.
14: 6. to every *nation*, and kindred, and tongue,
8. she made all *nations* drink of the wine
15: 4. all *nations* shall come and worship
16:19. the cities of the *nations* fell:
17:15. peoples, and multitudes, and *nations*,
18: 3. For all *nations* have drunk of the wine
23. by thy sorceries were all *nations* deceived.
19:15. with it he should smite the *nations*:
20: 3. should deceive the *nations* no more,
8. shall go out to deceive the *nations*
21:24. the *nations* of them which are saved
26. glory and honour of the *nations* into it.
22: 2. (were) for the healing of the *nations*.

1485 12 217/258 2:372 1486

ἔθος, *ethos*.

Lu. 1: 9. According to the *custom* of the priest's office,
2:42. after the *custom* of the feast.
22:39. came out, and went, as he *was wont*,
Joh.19:40. as the *manner* of the Jews is to bury.
Acts 6:14. change the *customs* which Moses delivered us.
15: 1. circumcised after the *manner* of Moses,
16:21. teach *customs*, which are not lawful for us
21:21. neither to walk after the *customs*.
25:16. It is not the *manner* of the Romans
26: 3. to be expert in all *customs* and questions
28:17. against the people, or *customs* of our fathers,
Heb 10:25. as the *manner* of some (is);

1486 4 217/307

ἔθω, εἴωθα, *etho, ĕōtha*.

Mat 27:15. the governor *was wont* to release unto
Mar 10: 1. as he *was wont*, he taught them again.
Lu. 4:16. as his *custom was*, he went into the
Acts17: 2. Paul, as his *manner was*, went in

1487 310 217/272 cf 1437

εἶ, from εἰμί, ī, from ĭmi.

Mat. 2: 6. *art* not the least among the princes
4: 3. If thou *be* the Son of God, command
6. If thou *be* the Son of God, cast thyself down:
5:25. whiles thou *art* in the way with him;
11: 3. *Art* thou he that should come, or do
14:28. Lord, if it *be* thou, bid me come
33. Of a truth thou *art* the Son of God.
16:16. Thou *art* the Christ, the Son of the living God.
17. Blessed *art* thou, Simon Bar-jona:
18. I say also unto thee, That thou *art* Peter
23. thou *art* an offence unto me: for thou
22:16. Master, we know that thou *art* true,
25:24. I knew thee that thou *art* an hard man,

Mat.26:63. whether thou *be* the Christ, the Son of God.
73. Surely thou also *art* (one) of them;
27:11. saying, *Art* thou the King of the Jews?
40. If thou *be* the Son of God, come down
Mar. 1:11. Thou *art* my beloved Son, in whom
24. I know thee who thou *art*, the Holy One of God
3:11. saying, Thou *art* the Son of God.
8:29. saith unto him, Thou *art* the Christ.
12:14. Master, we know that thou *art* true,
34. Thou *art* not far from the kingdom of God.
14:61. *Art* thou the Christ, the Son of the Blessed?
70. to Peter, Surely thou *art* (one) of them: for thou *art* a Galilæan, and thy speech
15: 2. *Art* thou the King of the Jews?
Lu. 3:22. which said, Thou *art* my beloved Son;
4: 3. If thou *be* the Son of God, command this
9. If thou *be* the Son of God, cast thyself down
34. who thou *art*; the Holy One of God.
41. Thou *art* Christ the Son of God.
7:19. saying, *Art* thou he that should come?
20. saying, *Art* thou he that should come?
15:31. unto him, Son, thou *art* ever with me,
19:21. because thou *art* an austere man:
22:58. saw him, and said, Thou *art* also of them.
67(66). *Art* thou the Christ? tell us.
70. *Art* thou then the Son of God?
23: 3. *Art* thou the King of the Jews?
37. If thou *be* the king of the Jews, save thyself.
39. If thou *be* Christ, save thyself and us.
40. seeing thou *art* in the same condemnation?
Joh. 1:19. from Jerusalem to ask him, Who *art* thou?
21. What then? *Art* thou Elias?
— *Art* thou that prophet? And he answered, No.
22. said they unto him, Who *art* thou?
25. if thou *be* not that Christ, nor Elias,
42(43). Thou *art* Simon the son of Jona:
49(50). Rabbi, thou *art* the Son of God; thou *art* the King of Israel.
3:10. *Art* thou a master of Israel,
4:12. *Art* thou greater than our father Jacob,
19. I perceive that thou *art* a prophet.
6:69. are sure that thou *art* that Christ,
7:52. said unto him, *Art* thou also of Galilee?
8:25. said they unto him, Who *art* thou?
48. that thou *art* a Samaritan and hast a devil?
53. *Art* thou greater than our father Abraham,
9:28. reviled him, and said, Thou *art* his disciple;
10:24. If thou *be* the Christ, tell us plainly.
11:27. I believe that thou *art* the Christ,
18:17. *Art* not thou also (one) of this man's
25. *Art* not thou also (one) of his disciples?
33. *Art* thou the King of the Jews?
37. said unto him, *Art* thou a king then?
19: 9. saith unto Jesus, Whence *art* thou?
12. thou *art* not Cæsar's friend:
21:12. durst ask him, Who *art* thou?
Acts 9: 5. he said, Who *art* thou, Lord?
13:33. in the second psalm, Thou *art* my Son,
21:38. *Art* not thou that Egyptian,
22: 8. I answered, Who *art* thou, Lord?
27. Tell me, *art* thou a Roman?
26:15. I said, Who *art* thou, Lord?
Ro. 2: 1. Therefore thou *art* inexcusable, O man,
9:20. who *art* thou that repliest against God?
14: 4. Who *art* thou that judgest another
Gal. 4: 7. Wherefore thou *art* no more a servant,
Heb 1: 5. Thou *art* my Son, this day have I
12. thou *art* the same, and thy years
5: 5. said unto him, Thou *art* my Son,
Jas. 4:11. thou *art* not a doer of the law,
12. who *art* thou that judgest another?
Rev. 2: 9. tribulation, and poverty, but thou *art* rich
3: 1. hast a name that thou livest, and *art* dead.
15. that thou *art* neither cold nor hot:
16. So then because thou *art* lukewarm,
17. knowest not that thou *art* wretched,
4:11. Thou *art* worthy, O Lord, to receive glory
5: 9. Thou *art* worthy to take the book,
16: 5. Thou *art* righteous, O Lord, which art,

1488 92 217/258 1510

εἰ, ī, conj.

Mat. 4: 3. *If* thou be the Son of God, command
6. *If* thou be the Son of God, cast thyself down.
5:29. And *if* thy right eye offend thee, pluck
30. *if* thy right hand offend thee,
6:23. *If* therefore the light that is in thee
30. Wherefore, *if* God so clothe the grass
7:11. *If* ye then, being evil, know how
8:31. *If* thou cast us out, suffer us to go
10:25. *If* they have called the master of
11:14. And *if* ye will receive (it), this is Elias,
21. for *if* the mighty works, which were
23. for *if* the mighty works, which have
12: 7. But *if* ye had known what (this) meaneth,
10.)(Is it lawful to heal on the sabbath
26. *if* Satan cast out Satan, he is divided
27. *if* I by Beelzebub cast out devils,
28. But *if* I cast out devils by the Spirit of God,
14:28. Lord, *if* it be thou, bid me come
17: 4. *if* thou wilt, let us make here three
18: 8. Wherefore *if* thy hand or thy foot offend thee,
9. *if* thine eye offend thee, pluck it out,
19: 3.)(Is it lawful for a man to put away
10. *If* the case of the man be so with (his) wife,
17. *if* thou wilt enter into life, keep the
21. *If* thou wilt be perfect, go (and) sell that
22:45. *If* David then call him Lord,
23:30. *If* we had been in the days of our fathers,
24:24. *if* (it were) possible, they shall deceive
43. *if* the goodman of the house had known
26:24. *if* he had not been born.
39. O my Father, *if* it be possible, let
42. *if* this cup may not pass away
63. tell us *whether* thou be the Christ,
27:40. save thyself. *If* thou be the Son of God,
42. *If* he be the King of Israel, let
43. deliver him now, *if* he will have him:
49. let us see *whether* Elias will come
Mar. 3: 2. *whether* he would heal him on the sabbath day;
26. *if* Satan rise up against himself,
8:12. There shall no sign be given (lit *if* a sign shall be given)
9:23. *If* thou canst believe, all things (are).
42. that (lit. *if*) a millstone were hanged
10: 2.)(Is it lawful for a man to put away
11:13. *if* haply he might find any thing
25. forgive, *if* ye have ought against any:
26. But *if* ye do not forgive, neither will
13:22. to seduce, *if* (it were) possible, even the elect.
14:21. that man *if* he had never been born.
29. Al*though* all shall be offended,

Mar 14:35. prayed that, *if* it were possible,
15:36. let us see *whether* Elias will come
44. marvelled *if* he were already dead:
Lu. 4: 3. *If* thou be the Son of God, command
9. *If* thou be the Son of God, cast
6: 7. *whether* he would heal on the sabbath day;
32. For *if* ye love them which love you,
7:39. This man, *if* he were a prophet,
9:23. *If* any (man) will come after me,
10:13. *if* the mighty works had been done
11:13. *If* ye then, being evil, know how to give good gifts
19. *if* I by Beelzebub cast out devils,
20. But *if* I with the finger of God
36. *If* thy whole body therefore (be) full
12:26. *If* ye then be not able to do that
28. *If* then God so clothe the grass,
39. that *if* the goodman of the house
49. what will I, *if* it be already kindled?
13:23. Lord,)(are there few that be saved?
14: 3.)(Is it lawful to heal on the sabbath day?
28. *whether* he have (sufficient) to finish (it)?
31. *whether* he be able with ten thousand
16:11. *If* therefore ye have not been faithful
12. *if* ye have not been faithful in that
31. *If* they hear not Moses and the prophets,
17: 2. that (lit. *if*) a millstone were hanged
6. *If* ye had faith as a grain of mustard seed,
19:42. *If* thou hadst known, even thou,
22:42. *if* thou be willing, remove this cup
49. Lord,)(shall we smite with the sword?
67.)(Art thou the Christ? tell us.
23: 6. *whether* the man were a Galilæan.
31. *if* they do these things in a green tree,
35. *if* he be Christ, the chosen of God.
37. *If* thou be the king of the Jews,
39. *If* thou be Christ, save thyself and us.
Joh 1:25. Why baptizest thou then, *if* thou be not
3:12. *If* I have told you earthly things,
4:10. *If* thou knewest the gift of God,
5:46. For)(had ye believed Moses, ye
47. *if* ye believe not his writings, how
7: 4. *If* thou do these things, shew thyself
23. *If* a man on the sabbath day
8:19. *if* ye had known me, ye should
39. *If* ye were Abraham's children,
42. *If* God were your Father,
46. *if* I say the truth, why do ye not believe
9:25. *Whether* he be a sinner (or no),
41. *If* ye were blind, ye should have no sin:
10:24. *If* thou be the Christ, tell us plainly.
35. *If* he called them gods, unto whom
37. *If* I do not the works of my Father,
38. But *if* I do, though ye believe not me,
11:12. Lord, *if* he sleep, he shall do well.
21. Lord, *if* thou hadst been here,
32. Lord, *if* thou hadst been here,
13:14. *If* I then, (your) Lord and Master,
17. *If* ye know these things, happy
32. *If* God be glorified in him,
14: 7. *If* ye had known me, ye should
28. *If* ye loved me, ye would rejoice,
15:18. *If* the world hate you, ye know that
19. *If* ye were of the world, the world
20. *If* they have persecuted me, they
— *if* they have kept my saying, they will
18: 8. *if* therefore ye seek me, let these go
23. Jesus answered him, *If* I have spoken evil,
— but *if* well, why smitest thou me?
36. *if* my kingdom were of this world,
20:15. Sir, *if* thou have borne him hence,
Acts 1: 6.)(wilt thou at this time restore again
Acts 4: 9. *If* we this day be examined of the
19. *Whether* it be right in the sight of God
5: 8. *whether* ye sold the land for so much?
39. But *if* it be of God, ye cannot overthrow
7: 1. said the high priest,)(Are these things
8:22. *if* perhaps the thought of thine heart
37. *If* thou believest with all thine heart,
10:18. *whether* Simon, which was surnamed
11:17. *Forasmuch* then *as* God gave them
13:15. *if* ye have any word of exhortation
16:15. *If* ye have judged me to be faithful
17:11. *whether* those things were so.
27. *if* haply they might feel after him,
18:14. *If* it were a matter of wrong or
15. But *if* it be a question of words
19: 2.)(Have ye received the Holy Ghost
— *whether* there be any Holy Ghost.
38. Wherefore *if* Demetrius, and the craftsmen
39. But *if* ye enquire any thing concerning
20:16. he hasted, *if* it were possible for him,
21:37.)(May I speak unto thee?
22:25.)(Is it lawful for you to scourge a man
27. Tell me,)(art thou a Roman?
23: 9. *if* a spirit or an angel hath spoken
25:11. For *if* I be an offender, or have committed
— but *if* there be none of these things
20. *whether* he would go to Jerusalem,
26: 8. incredible with you, *that* God should raise the dead?
23. *That* Christ should suffer, (and) *that* he should be the first that should rise
27:39. *if* it were possible, to thrust in the ship.
Ro. 3. 3. For what *if* some did not believe?
5. But *if* our unrighteousness commend
7. *if* the truth of God hath more abounded
4: 2. For *if* Abraham were justified by works,
14. *if* they which are of the law (be) heirs,
5:10. For *if*, when we were enemies,
15. For *if* through the offence of one many
17. For *if* by one man's offence death
6: 5. For *if* we have been planted together
8. Now *if* we be dead with Christ,
7:16. *If* then I do that which I would not,
20. Now *if* I do that I would not,
8: 9. *if* any man have not the Spirit of Christ,
10. *if* Christ (be) in you, the body (is)
11. *if* the Spirit of him that raised up
13. For *if* ye live after the flesh, ye shall die: but *if* ye through the Spirit do mortify
17. *if* children, then heirs; heirs of God,
25. *if* we hope for that we see not,
31. *If* God (be) for us, who (can be) against us?
9:22. *if* God, willing to shew (his) wrath,
11: 6. *if* by grace, then (is it) no more of works.
— But *if* (it be) of works, then is it no more grace:
12. Now *if* the fall of them (be) the riches
15. For *if* the casting away of them
16. For *if* the firstfruit (be) holy, the
— *if* the root (be) holy, so (are) the branches.
17. *if* some of the branches be broken off,
18. *if* thou boast, thou bearest not the root,
21. *if* God spared not the natural branches,
24. For *if* thou wert cut out of the olive tree,
12:18. *If* it be possible, as much as lieth in you,
14:15. *if* thy brother be grieved with (thy) meat,
15:27. For *if* the Gentiles have been made
1Co. 2: 8. for)(had they known (it), they would not
3:12. *if* any man build upon this foundation

1Co. 6: 2. *if* the world shall be judged by you, are ye unworthy to judge
7: 9. *if* they cannot contain, let them
15. *if* the unbelieving depart, let him depart.
16. *whether* thou shalt save (thy) husband?
— how knowest thou, O man, *whether* thou shalt save (thy) wife?
36. *if* any man think that he
8: 2. *if* any man think that he knoweth
3. *if* any man love God, the same
13. *if* meat make my brother to offend,
9: 2. *If* I be not an apostle unto others,
11. *If* we have sown unto you spiritual
— *if* we shall reap your carnal things?
12. *If* others be partakers of (this) power
17. For *if* I do this thing willingly,
— *if* against my will, a dispensation
10:27. *If* any of them that believe not
30. For *if* I by grace be a partaker,
11: 6. For *if* the woman be not covered,
— *if* it be a shame for a woman to
16. *if* any man seem to be contentious,
31. For *if* we would judge ourselves,
34. *if* any man hunger, let him eat at home;
12:17. *If* the whole body (were) an eye,
— *If* the whole (were) hearing, where
19. *if* they were all one member,
14:10. There are,)(it may be, so many kinds
35. *if* they will learn any thing,
38. *if* any man be ignorant, let him
15: 2. *if* ye keep in memory what I preached
12. Now *if* Christ be preached that he rose
13. But *if* there be no resurrection of the dead,
14. *if* Christ be not risen, then (is) our
16. *if* the dead rise not, then is not Christ raised:
17. *if* Christ be not raised, your faith (is) vain;
19. *If* in this life only we have hope in Christ,
29. *if* the dead rise not at all? why are
32. *If* after the manner of men I have
— what advantageth it me, *if* the dead rise not?
37.)(it may chance of wheat, or of some
2Co. 2: 2. For *if* I make you sorry, who is he
5. *if* any have caused grief, he hath
9. *whether* ye be obedient in all things.
3: 7. *if* the ministration of death,
9. *if* the ministration of condemnation
11. For *if* that which is done away
5:14(15). that *if* one died for all,
8:12. For *if* there be first a willing mind,
11: 4. For *if* he that cometh preacheth another Jesus, whom we have not
30. *If* I must needs glory, I will glory
13: 4. For *though* he was crucified through weakness,
5. Examine yourselves, *whether* ye be in
Gal. 1:10. for *if* I yet pleased men, I should not
2:14. *If* thou, being a Jew, livest after
17. *if*, while we seek to be justified
18. For *if* I build again the things
21. for *if* righteousness (come) by the law
3:18. For *if* the inheritance (be) of the law,
21. for *if* there had been a law given
29. *if* ye (be) Christ's, then are ye
4: 7. *if* a son, then an heir of God
15. *if* (it had been) possible, ye would
5:11. brethren, *if* I yet preach circumcision,
15. But *if* ye bite and devour one another,
18. But *if* ye be led of the Spirit, ye are not
25. *If* we live in the Spirit, let us also
6: 3. *if* a man think himself to be something,
Phi. 1:22. *if* I live in the flesh, this (is) the fruit of my labour:
Col. 2:20. Wherefore *if* ye be dead with Christ
3: 1. *If* ye then be risen with Christ,
1Th. 4:14. For *if* we believe that Jesus died
2Th. 3:14. *if* any man obey not our word
1Ti. 3: 5. For *if* a man know not how to
5: 4. *if* any widow have children or
8. *if* any provide not for his own,
10. *if* she have brought up children, *if* she have lodged strangers, *if* she have washed the saints' feet, *if* she have relieved the afflicted, *if* she have diligently followed
2Ti. 2:11. For *if* we be dead with (him), we
12. *If* we suffer, we shall also reign with (him): *if* we deny (him), he also will deny us:
13. *If* we believe not, (yet) he abideth faithful:
Philem 17. *If* thou count me therefore a partner
18. *If* he hath wronged thee,
Heb. 2: 2. For *if* the word spoken by angels
3:11. They shall not (lit. *if* they shall) enter into my rest.
4: 3. *if* they shall enter into my rest:
5. *If* they shall enter into my rest.
8. For *if* Jesus had given them rest,
7:11. *If* therefore perfection were by the
15. for that (lit. *if*) after the similitude of
8: 4. For *if* he were on earth, he should not
7. For *if* that first (covenant) had been
9:13. For *if* the blood of bulls and of goats,
11:15. truly, *if* they had been mindful
12: 7. *If* ye endure chastening, God dealeth
8. But *if* ye be without chastisement,
25. For *if* they escaped not who refused
Jas. 1: 5. *If* any of you lack wisdom, let him ask of God,
26. *If* any man among you seem to
2: 8. *If* ye fulfil the royal law according
9. *if* ye have respect to persons, ye commit
11. Now *if* thou commit no adultery, yet
3:14. But *if* ye have bitter envying
4:11. *if* thou judge the law, thou art not
1Pet. 1: 6. though now for a season, *if* need be,
17. *if* ye call on the Father, who without
2:19. *if* a man for conscience toward
20. *if*, when ye be buffeted for your faults, ye shall take it patiently? but *if*, when ye do well, and suffer (for it),
3:17. *if* the will of God be so, that ye
4:14. *If* ye be reproached for the name
16. Yet *if* (any man suffer) as a Christian.
17. *if* (it) first (begin) at us, what shall
18. *if* the righteous scarcely be saved,
2Pet. 2: 4. For *if* God spared not the angels
20. For *if* after they have escaped the
1Joh. 2:19. for *if* they had been of us, they would
3:13. my brethren, *if* the world hate you.
4: 1. the spirits *whether* they are of God:
11. *if* God so loved us, we ought also
5: 9. *If* we receive the witness of men,

1489 5 152/258 1487,1065

εἴγε, *ige.*

2Co. 5: 3. *If so be that* being clothed we
Gal. 3: 4. many things in vain? *if* (it be) *yet* in vain.
Eph. 3: 2. *If* ye have heard of the dispensation
4:21. *If so be that* ye have heard him,
Col. 1:23. *If* ye continue in the faith

1490 14 217/261 1487,1161,3361

εἰ δὲ μή,[2] & εἰ δὲ μήγε,

ī de mee, & *ī de meege.*

Mat. 6: 1. *otherwise* ye have no reward of your
9:17. *else* the bottles break, and the wine
Mar. 2:21. *else* the new piece that filled it up[2]
22. *else* the new wine doth burst the bottles,[2]
Lu. 5:36. *if otherwise,* then both the new maketh
37. *else* the new wine will burst the
10: 6. *if not,* it shall turn to you again.
13: 9. if it bear fruit, (well): *and if not,* (then)
14:32. *Or else,* while the other is yet a great
Joh.14: 2. *if* (it were) *not* (so), I would have told[2]
11. *or else* believe me for the very works' sake.[2]
2Co.11:16. *if otherwise,* yet as a fool receive me,
Rev. 2: 5. *or else* I will come unto thee quickly,[2]
16. Repent; *or else* I will come unto thee[2]

1499 22 217/258 1487,2532

εἰ καὶ, *ī kai.*

Mat.26:33. *Though* all (men) shall be offended
Lu. 11: 8. *Though* he will not rise and give him,
18. *If* Satan also be divided
18: 4. *Though* I fear not God, nor regard man;
1Co. 4: 7. now *if* thou didst receive (it), why dost
7:21. *if* thou mayest be made free,
2Co. 4: 3. But *if* our gospel be hid, it is hid to them
16. *though* our outward man perish,
5:16. yea, *though* we have known Christ after
7: 8. For *though* I made you sorry with a letter, I do not repent, *though* I did repent:
— *though* (it were) but for a season.
12. Wherefore, *though* I wrote unto you,
11: 6. *though* (I be) rude in speech, yet
15. *if* his ministers *also* be transformed
12:11. chiefest apostles, *though* I be nothing.
15. *though* the more abundantly I love you,
Phi. 2:17. Yea, *and if* I be offered upon the sacrifice
3:12. *if that* I may apprehend that
Col. 2: 5. For *though* I be absent in the flesh,
Heb. 6: 9. accompany salvation, *though* we thus
1Pet.3:14. But *and if* ye suffer for righteousness'

1508 92 /261 1487,3361

εἰ μή, *ī mee.*

Mat. 5:13. good for nothing, *but* to be cast out
11:27. knoweth the Son, *but* the Father; neither knoweth any man the Father, *save* the
12: 4. with him, *but* only for the priests?
24. *but* by Beelzebub the prince of the devils.
39. *but* the sign of the prophet Jonas:
13:57. without honour, *save* in his own country,
14:17. We have here *but* five loaves,
15:24. I am not sent *but* unto the lost sheep
16: 4. *but* the sign of the prophet Jonas.
17: 8. they saw no man, *save* Jesus only.
21. goeth not out *but* by prayer and fasting.
19: 9. *except* (it be) for fornication,
17. (there is) none good *but* one, (that is),
21:19. found nothing thereon, *but* leaves only,
24:22. *except* those days should be shortened,
36. of heaven, *but* my Father only.
Mar 2: 7. who can forgive sins *but* God only?
26. not lawful to eat *but* for the priests,
5:37. suffered no man to follow him, *save* Peter,
6: 4. without honour, *but* in his own country,
5. *save that* he laid his hands upon a
8. nothing for (their) journey, *save* a staff
8.14. with them *more than* one loaf.
9: 9. till (lit. *except* when) the Son of man
Mar 9:29. by nothing, *but* by prayer and fasting.
10:18. (there is) none good *but* one, (that is), God.
11:13. he found nothing *but* leaves;
13:20. *except that* the Lord had shortened
32. neither the Son, *but* the Father.
Lu. 4:26. was Elias sent, *save* unto Sarepta,
27. was cleansed, *saving* Naaman the Syrian.
5:21. Who can forgive sins, *but* God alone?
6: 4. not lawful to eat *but* for the priests alone?
8:51. no man to go in, *save* Peter, and James, and John,
10:22. knoweth who the Son is, *but* the Father; and who the Father is, *but* the Son,
11:29. *but* the sign of Jonas the prophet.
17:18. to give glory to God, *save* this stranger.
18:19. none (is) good, *save* one, (that is), God.
Joh. 3:13. *but* he that came down from heaven,
6:22. *save* that one whereinto his disciples
46. *save* he which is of God, he hath
9:33. *If* this man were *not* of God, he
10:10. The thief cometh not, *but* for to steal,
14: 6. no man cometh unto the Father, *but* by me.
15:22. *If* I had *not* come and spoken unto them,
24. *If* I had *not* done among them the
17:12. is lost, *but* the son of perdition;
18:30. *If* he were *not* a malefactor, we
19:11. *except* it were given thee from above:
15. We have no king *but* Cæsar.
Acts11:19. to none *but* unto the Jews only.
21:25. *save only that* they keep themselves
26:32. *if* he had *not* appealed unto Cæsar.
Ro. 7: 7. I had not known sin, *but* by the law:
— *except* the law had said, Thou
9:29. *Except* the Lord of Sabaoth had
11:15. (of them be), *but* life from the dead?
13: 1. For there is no power *but* of God:
8. any thing, *but* to love one another.
14:14. *but* to him that esteemeth any
1Co. 1:14. none of you, *but* Crispus and Gaius;
2: 2. *save* Jesus Christ, and him crucified.
11. *save* the spirit of man which is
— knoweth no man, *but* the Spirit of God.
7:17. *But* as God hath distributed to every man,
8: 4. (there is) none other God *but* one.
10:13. *but* such as is common to man:
12: 3. *but* by the Holy Ghost.
14: 5. except)(he interpret, that the church
15: 2. unless)(ye have believed in vain.
2Co. 2: 2. *but* the same which is made sorry
3: 1. or need we (lit. *if* we need *not*), as some (others), epistles
12: 5. I will not glory, *but* in mine infirmities.
13. *except* (it be) that I myself was not
Gal 1: 7. *but* there be some that trouble you,
19. saw I none, *save* James the Lord's brother.
6:14. that I should glory, *save* in the cross of
Eph. 4: 9. what is it *but* that he also descended
Phi. 4:15. concerning giving and receiving, *but* ye only.
1Ti. 5:19. but (lit. unless *with this exception*) before two or three witnesses.
Heb. 3:18. *but* to them that believed not?
1Joh.2:22. Who is a liar *but* he that denieth
5: 5. *but* he that believeth that Jesus is
Rev. 2:17. no man knoweth *saving* he that
9: 4. *but* only those men which have not
13:17. buy or sell, *save* he that had the mark,
14: 3. *but* the hundred (and) forty (and) four thousand,
19:12. that no man knew, *but* he himself.

1491–1507 pp. 192–193

Rev.21:27. *but* they which are written in the Lamb's book

1509 3 217/261 1508,5100

εἰ μή τι, ī mee ti.

Lu. 9:13. *except* we should go and buy meat
1Co. 7: 5. *except* (it be) with consent for a time,
2Co.13: 5. Christ is in you, *except* ye be reprobates?

1512 6 225/262 1487,4007

εἴ περ, ī per.

Ro. 8: 9. *if so be that* the Spirit of God dwell in you.
17. *if so be that* we suffer with (him),
1Co. 8: 5. For *though* there be that are called gods,
15:15. *if* so be *that* the dead rise not.
2Th. 1: 6. *Seeing* (it is) a righteous thing with God
1Pet.2: 3. *If so be* ye have tasted that the Lord

1513 4 226/258 1487,4458

εἴ πως, ī pōs.

Acts27:12. *if by any means* they might attain
Ro. 1:10. *if by any means* now at length
11:14. *If by any means* I may provoke to
Phi. 3:11. *If by any means* I might attain unto

1535 65 233/306 1487,5037

εἴτε, īte.

Ro. 12: 6. *whether* prophecy, (let us prophesy) according
7. *Or* ministry, (let us wait) on (our) ministering: *or* he that teacheth, on teaching;
8. *Or* he that exhorteth, on exhortation:
1Co. 3:22. *Whether* Paul, *or* Apollos, *or* Cephas, *or* the world, *or* life, *or* death, *or* things present, *or* things to come;
8: 5. *whether* in heaven *or* in earth,
10:31. *Whether* therefore ye eat, *or* drink, *or* whatsoever
12:13. *whether* (we be) Jews *or* Gentiles, *whether* (we be) bond *or* free;
26. *whether* one member suffer, all the members suffer with it; *or* one member be honoured,
13: 8. *whether* (there be) prophecies, they shall fail; *whether* (there be) tongues, they shall cease; *whether* (there be) knowledge, it shall
14: 7. *whether* pipe *or* harp, except they give
27. *If* any man speak in an (unknown) tongue,
15:11. Therefore *whether* (it were) I *or* they, so
2Co. 1: 6. And *whether* we be afflicted, (it is) for your
— *or whether* we be comforted, (it is) for your
5: 9. *whether* present *or* absent, we may be
10. hath done, *whether* (it be) good *or* bad.
13. *whether* we be beside ourselves, (it is) to God, *or whether* we be sober,
8:23. *Whether* (any do enquire) of Titus,
— *or* our brethren (be enquired of),
12: 2. *whether* in the body, I cannot tell; *or whether*
3. *whether* in the body, *or* out of the body,
Eph. 6: 8. of the Lord, *whether* (he be) bond *or* free.
Phi. 1:18. *whether* in pretence, *or* in truth,
20. *whether* (it be) by life, *or* by death.
27. *whether* I come and see you, *or* else be absent,
Col. 1:16. *whether* (they be) thrones, *or* dominions, *or* principalities, *or* powers:
20. *whether* (they be) things in earth, *or* things
1Th. 5:10. *whether* we wake *or* sleep, we should
2Th. 2:15. taught, *whether* by word, *or* our epistle.
1Pet. 2:13. *whether* it be to the king, as supreme;
14. *Or* unto governors, as unto them that

1536 79 /262 1487,5100

εἴ τις, ī tis.

Mat.16:24. *If any* (man) will come after me,
Mar. 4:23. *If any* man have ears to hear,
7:16. *If any* man have ears to hear,
8:23. he asked him *if* he saw *ought*.
9:22. *if* thou canst do *any thing*, have compassion
35. *If any* man desire to be first,
Lu. 14:26. *If any* (man) come to me, and hate not
19: 8. *if* I have taken any thing *from any* man
Acts24:19. *if* they had *ought* against me.
20. *if* they have found *any* evil doing in me,
25: 5. *if* there be *any* wickedness in him.
Ro. 13: 9. *if* (there be) *any* other commandment,
1Co. 1:16. I know not *whether* I baptized *any* other.
3:14. *If any man's* work abide which
15. *If any man's* work shall be burned,
17. *If any* man defile the temple of God,
18. *If any* man among you seemeth to be
7:12. *If any* brother hath a wife that believeth not,
14:37. *If any* man think himself to be a prophet,
16:22. *If any* man love not the Lord Jesus Christ,
2Co. 2:10. for *if* I forgave *any thing*, to whom
5:17. Therefore *if any* man (be) in Christ,
7:14. *if* I have boasted *any thing* to him
10: 7. *If any* man trust to himself
11:20. *if a man* bring you into bondage, *if a man* devour (you), *if a man* take (of you), *if a man* exalt himself, *if a man* smite
Gal. 1: 9. *If any* (man) preach any other gospel
Eph. 4:29. but that which (lit. *if any*) is good to the use of
Phi. 2: 1. *If* (there be) therefore *any* consolation in Christ, *if any* comfort of love, *if any* fellowship of the Spirit, *if any* bowels and mercies,
3: 4. *If any* other man thinketh that
15. *if* in *any thing* ye be otherwise
4: 8. *if* (there be) *any* virtue, and *if* (there be) *any* praise,
2Th. 3:10. that *if any* would not work,
1Ti. 1:10. *if* there be *any* other thing that
3: 1. *If a man* desire the office of a bishop,
5:16. *If any* man or woman that
6: 3. *If any* man teach otherwise,
Tit. 1: 6. *If any* be blameless, the husband
Jas. 1:23. For *if any* be a hearer of the word,
3: 2. *If any* man offend not in word,
1Pet.3: 1. that, *if any* obey not the word, they
4:11. *If any* man speak, (let him speak)
— *if any* man minister, (let him do it)
2Joh. 10. *If* there come *any* unto you, and bring
Rev.11: 5. *if any* man will hurt them, fire
— *if any* man will hurt them, he must
13: 9. *If any* man have an ear, let him hear.
10. He that (lit. *if any*) leadeth into captivity shall go into captivity: he that (lit. *if any*) killeth with the sword
14. 9. *If any* man worship the beast
11. *whosoever* receiveth the mark of his name.
20.15. *whosoever* was not found written

1510, p. 194 1511, p. 195 1514-1534, pp. 196-214

1492 663 219/263,267 5:315

εἰδέω, εἴδω, οἶδα, *ideo, ido, oida.* eq 3700, eq 3708, cf 3700

Mat. 2: 2. for we *have seen* his star in the east,
9. the star, which they *saw* in the east,
10. *When* they *saw* the star, they rejoiced
16. Herod, *when* he *saw* that he was
3: 7. *when* he *saw* many of the Pharisees
16. he *saw* the spirit of God descending
4: 16. which sat in darkness *saw* great light;
18. by the sea of Galilee, *saw* two brethren,
21. from thence, he *saw* other two brethren,
5: 1. *seeing* the multitudes, he went up
16. that they *may see* your good works,
6: 8. your Father *knoweth* what things
32. your heavenly Father *knoweth* that ye
7: 11. If ye then,...*know how* to give good
8: 14. he *saw* his wife's mother laid, and sick
18. Now *when* Jesus *saw* great multitudes
34. *when* they *saw* him, they besought
9: 2. Jesus *seeing* their faith said unto
4. Jesus *knowing* their thoughts said,
6. that ye *may know* that the Son of man
8. But *when* the multitudes *saw* (it), they
9. he *saw* a man, named Matthew,
11. And *when* the Pharisees *saw* (it), they
22. and *when* he *saw* her, he said, Daughter,
23. and *saw* the minstrels and the people
36. But *when* he *saw* the multitudes, he was
11: 8. what went ye out *for to see?* A man
9. what went ye out *for to see?* A prophet?
12: 2. But *when* the Pharisees *saw* (it), they said
25. Jesus *knew* their thoughts, *and* said
38. Master, we would *see* a sign from thee.
13: 14. ye shall see, and shall not *perceive:*
15. lest at any time they *should see* with
17. righteous (men) have desired *to see* (those things) which ye see, and *have* not *seen* (them);
14: 14. Jesus went forth, and *saw* a great
26. And *when* the disciples *saw* him walking
15: 12. *Knowest* thou that the Pharisees were
16: 28. till they *see* the Son of man coming
17: 8. they *saw* no man, save Jesus only.
18: 31. So *when* his fellowservants *saw* what
20: 3. and *saw* others standing idle in the
22. said, Ye *know* not what ye ask.
25. Ye *know* that the princes of the Gentiles
21: 15. And *when* the chief priests and scribes *saw*
19. And *when* he *saw* a fig tree in the way,
20. And *when* the disciples *saw* (it) they marvelled,
27. they answered Jesus, and said, We *cannot tell.*
32. ye, *when* ye *had seen* (it), repented not
38. But *when* the husbandmen *saw* the son,
22: 11. he *saw* there a man which had not
16. Master, we *know* that thou art true,
29. Ye do err, not *knowing* the scriptures,
23: 39. Ye shall not *see* me henceforth, till
24: 15. shall *see* the abomination of desolation,
33. when ye shall *see* all these things,
36. of that day and hour *knoweth* no (man),
42. ye *know* not what hour your Lord
43. man of the house *had known* in what
25: 12. Verily I say unto you, I *know* you not.
13. ye *know* neither the day nor the hour
26. thou *knewest* that I reap where
37. Lord, when *saw* we thee an hungred,
38. When *saw* we thee a stranger,
39. Or when *saw* we thee sick, or in prison,

Mat. 25: 44. Lord, when *saw* we thee an hungred,
26: 2. Ye *know* that after two days is (the feast)
8. But *when* his disciples *saw* (it), they had
58. sat with the servants, *to see* the end.
70. I *know* not what thou sayest.
71. another (maid) *saw* him, and said
72. I *do* not *know* the man.
74. to swear, (saying), I *know* not the man.
27: 3. *when* he *saw* that he was condemned,
18. For he *knew* that for envy they had
24. *When* Pilate *saw* that he could prevail
49. *let* us *see* whether Elias will come
54. *saw* the earthquake, and those things
65. make (it) as sure as ye *can.* (lit. *know*)
28: 5. for I *know* that ye seek Jesus,
6. Come, *see* the place where the Lord lay.
17. And *when* they *saw* him, they worshipped
Mar. 1: 10. he *saw* the heavens opened, and the
16. he *saw* Simon and Andrew his brother
19. he *saw* James the (son) of Zebedee,
24. I *know* thee who thou art, the
34. devils to speak, because they *knew* him.
2: 5. *When* Jesus *saw* their faith, he said
10. that ye *may know* that the Son of man
12. saying, We never *saw* it on this fashion.
14. he *saw* Levi the (son) of Alphæus
16. And *when* the scribes and Pharisees *saw*
4: 12. they may see, and not *perceive;*
13. *Know* ye not this parable? and how
27. grow up, he *knoweth* not how.
5: 6. But *when* he *saw* Jesus afar off, he ran
14. they went out *to see* what it was
16. they *that saw* (it) told them how it
22. and *when* he *saw* him, he fell at his feet,
32. he looked round about *to see* her that
33. *knowing* what was done in her,
6: 20. *knowing* that he was a just man
33. the people *saw* them departing,
34. And Jesus, when he came out, *saw*
38. How many loaves have ye? go and *see.*
48. he *saw* them toiling in rowing;
49. But *when* they *saw* him walking upon
50. For they all *saw* him, and were troubled.
7: 2. And *when* they *saw* some of his disciples
8: 33. when he had turned about and *looked on*
9: 1. till they *have seen* the kingdom of God
6. For he *wist* not what to say; for they
8. they *saw* no man any more, save Jesus
9. tell no man what things they *had seen,*
14. he *saw* a great multitude about them,
15. the people, *when* they *beheld* him,
20. and *when* he *saw* him, straightway the
25. *When* Jesus *saw* that the people came
38. we *saw* one casting out devils in thy name,
10: 14. But *when* Jesus *saw* (it), he was much
19. Thou *knowest* the commandments,
38. Ye *know* not what ye ask:
42. Ye *know* that they which are accounted
11: 13. *seeing* a fig tree afar off having leaves,
20. they *saw* the fig tree dried up
33. answered and said unto Jesus, We *canno tell.*
12: 14. Master, we *know* that thou art true,
15. he, *knowing* their hypocrisy,
— bring me a penny, that I *may see* (it).
24. *because* ye *know* not the scriptures,
28. *perceiving* that he had answered
34. *when* Jesus *saw* that he answered discreetly,
13: 14. when ye shall *see* the abomination of
29. when ye shall *see* these things come to pass,
32. But of that day and (that) hour *knoweth* no
33. for ye *know* not when the time is.

Mar 13:35. ye *know* not when the master of the house
14:40. neither *wist* they what to answer him.
67. *when* she *saw* Peter warming himself,
68. he denied, saying, I *know* not, neither
69. a maid *saw* him again, *and* began
71. I *know* not this man of whom ye speak.
15:32. that we *may see* and believe.
36. *let* us *see* whether Elias will come
39. *when* the centurion...*saw* that he so cried out,
16: 5. they *saw* a young man sitting on the
Lu. 1:12. *when* Zacharias *saw* (him), he was
29. *when* she *saw* (him), she was troubled
2:15. Let us now go...and *see* this thing which is come to pass,
17. *when* they *had seen* (it), they made
20. things that they had heard and *seen*,
26. that he should not *see* death, before he *had seen* the Lord's Christ.
30. For mine eyes *have seen* thy salvation,
48. *when* they *saw* him, they were amazed:
49. *wist* ye not that I must be about
4:34. I *know* thee who thou art; the Holy
41. for they *knew* that he was Christ.
5: 2. *saw* two ships standing by the lake:
8. *When* Simon Peter *saw* (it), he fell down
12. who *seeing* Jesus fell on (his) face,
20. *when* he *saw* their faith, he said
24. that ye *may know* that the Son of man
26. We *have seen* strange things to day.
6: 8. he *knew* their thoughts, and said to the man
7:13. *when* the Lord *saw* her, he had compassion
22. tell John what things ye *have seen*
25. what went ye out *for to see?*
26. what went ye out *for to see?* A prophet?
39. Now *when* the Pharisee...*saw* (it),
8:20. stand without, desiring *to see* thee.
28. *When* he *saw* Jesus, he cried out,
34. *When* they that fed (them) *saw* what
35. they went out *to see* what was done;
36. They also *which saw* (it) told them
47. *when* the woman *saw* that she was not hid,
53. *knowing* that she was dead.
9: 9. he desired *to see* him.
27. till they *see* the kingdom of God.
32. they *saw* his glory, and the two men
33. one for Elias: not *knowing* what he said.
47. Jesus, *perceiving* the thought of their heart,
49. we *saw* one casting out devils in thy name;
54. *when* his disciples James and John *saw*
55. Ye *know* not what manner of spirit
10:24. kings have desired *to see* those things which ye see, and *have* not *seen* (them);
31. *when* he *saw* him, he passed by on the
32. came and *looked* (*on* him), *and* passed by
33. *when* he *saw* him, he had compassion (on him),
11:13. *know* to give good gifts unto
17. he, *knowing* their thoughts, said
38. And *when* the Pharisee *saw* (it), he
44. that walk over (them) *are* not *aware* (of them).
12:30. and your Father *knoweth* that ye have need
39. goodman of the house *had known* what
54. When ye *see* a cloud rise out of the west,
56. ye *can* discern the face of the sky and of the earth;
13:12. *when* Jesus *saw* her, he called (her to him),
25. I *know* you not whence ye are:
27. I *know* you not whence ye are; depart
35. say unto you, Ye shall not *see* me, until
14:18. I must needs go and *see* it: I pray thee

Lu. 15:20. his father *saw* him, and had compassion,
17:14. *when* he *saw* (them), he said unto them
15. *when* he *saw* that he was healed,
22. ye shall desire *to see* one of the days of
18:15. *when* (his) disciples *saw* (it), they rebuked
20. Thou *knowest* the commandments
24. *when* Jesus *saw* that he was very
43. all the people, *when* they *saw* (it),
19: 3. he sought *to see* Jesus who he was;
4. up into a sycomore tree to *see* him:
5. he looked up, and *saw* him, and said
7. *when* they *saw* (it), they all murmured,
22. Thou *knewest* that I was an austere man
37. the mighty works that they *had seen;*
41. he *beheld* the city, *and* wept over it,
20: 7. that they could not *tell* whence (it was).
13. reverence (him) *when* they *see* him.
14. *when* the husbandmen *saw* him,
21. we *know* that thou sayest and teachest
21: 1. And he looked up, and *saw* the rich
2. he *saw* also a certain poor widow
20. when ye shall *see* Jerusalem compassed
29. *Behold* the fig tree, and all the trees;
31. when ye *see* these things come to pass,
22:34. shalt thrice deny that thou *knowest* me.
49. *When* they which were about him *saw*
56. a certain maid *beheld* him...*and* said,
57. saying, Woman, I *know* him not.
58. another *saw* him, *and* said,
60. Man, I *know* not what thou sayest.
23: 8. And *when* Herod *saw* Jesus, he
— was desirous *to see* him of a long (season),
— he hoped *to have seen* some miracle
34. for they *know* not what they do.
47. *when* the centurion *saw* what was done,
24:24. had said: but him they *saw* not.
39. *Behold* my hands and my feet, that it is I myself: handle me, and *see;*
Joh. 1:26. one among you, whom ye *know* not;
31. I *knew* him not: but that he should
33. I *knew* him not: but he that sent
— Upon whom thou shalt *see* the Spirit
39(40). He saith unto them, Come and *see*. They came and *saw* where he dwelt,
46(47). Philip saith unto him, Come and *see*.
47(48). Jesus *saw* Nathanael coming to him,
48(49). thou wast under the fig tree, I *saw* thee.
50(51). I *saw* thee under the fig tree,
2: 9. *knew* not whence it was: but the servants which drew the water *knew;*
3: 2. we *know* that thou art a teacher
3. he cannot *see* the kingdom of God.
8. *canst* not *tell* whence it cometh,
11. We speak that we *do know*, and testify
4:10. If thou *knewest* the gift of God, and who
22. Ye worship ye *know* not what: we *know* what we worship:
25. I *know* that Messias cometh, which is
29. Come, *see* a man, which told me
32. meat to eat that ye *know* not *of*.
42. we have heard (him) ourselves, and *know*
48. Except ye *see* signs and wonders, ye will
5: 6. *When* Jesus *saw* him lie, and knew that
13. he that was healed *wist* not who it was:
32. I *know* that the witness which he
6: 6. he himself *knew* what he would do.
14. *when* they *had seen* the miracle
22. *when* the people...*saw* that there was
24. the people therefore *saw* that Jesus was
26. not because ye *saw* the miracles,
30. that we *may see*, and believe thee?

Joh. 6:42. whose father and mother we *know*?
61. *When* Jesus *knew* in himself that
64. For Jesus *knew* from the beginning
7:15. saying, How *knoweth* this man letters,
27. we *know* this man whence he is.
28. Ye both *know* me, and ye *know* whence I am:
— sent me is true, whom ye *know* not.
29. I *know* him: for I am from him,
52. Search, and *look:* for out of Galilee ariseth no prophet.
8:14. I *know* whence I came, and whither I go; but ye *cannot tell* whence
19. Ye neither *know* me, nor my Father:
— if ye *had known* me, ye should *have known* my Father also.
37. I *know* that ye are Abraham's seed;
55. I *know* him: and if I should say, I *know* him not,
— I *know* him, and keep his saying.
56. Abraham rejoiced to *see* my day: and he *saw* (it), and was glad.
9: 1. he *saw* a man which was blind from
12. Where is he? He said, I *know* not.
20. We *know* that this is our son,
21. what means he now seeth, we *know* not; or who hath opened his eyes, we *know* not:
24. we *know* that this man is a sinner.
25. I *know* not: one thing I *know*, that,
29. We *know* that God spake unto Moses:
— we *know* not from whence he is.
30. that ye *know* not from whence he is,
31. we *know* that God heareth not sinners:
10: 4. sheep follow him: for they *know* his voice.
5. they *know* not the voice of strangers.
11:22. I *know*, that even now, whatsoever
24. I *know* that he shall rise again
31. *when* they *saw* Mary, that she rose
32. was come where Jesus was, *and saw* him,
33. When Jesus therefore *saw* her weeping,
34. said unto him, Lord, come and *see*.
42. I *knew* that thou hearest me always:
49. Ye *know* nothing at all,
12: 9. that they *might see* Lazarus also,
21. saying, Sir, we would *see* Jesus.
35. in darkness *knoweth* not whither he
40. that they *should* not *see* with
41. when he *saw* his glory, and spake of him.
50. I *know* that his commandment
13: 1. *when* Jesus *knew* that his hour
3. Jesus *knowing* that the Father had
7. What I do thou *knowest* not now;
11. For he *knew* who should betray him;
17. If ye *know* these things, happy are ye if
18. I *know* whom I have chosen:
14: 4. whither I go ye *know*, and the way ye *know*.
5. Lord, we *know* not whither thou goest; and how can we *know* the way?
15:15. the servant *knoweth* not what his lord doeth:
21. they *know* not him that sent me.
16:18. we *cannot tell* what he saith.
30. Now *are* we *sure* that thou *knowest* all
18: 2. Judas also, which betrayed him, *knew*
4. *knowing* all things that should come
21. behold, they *know* what I said.
26. Did not I *see* thee in the garden
19: 6. priests therefore and officers *saw* him,
10. *knowest* thou not that I have power
26. *When* Jesus therefore *saw* his mother,
28. Jesus *knowing* that all things were
33. *saw* that he was dead already,
35. he *knoweth* that he saith true,

Joh. 20: 2. we *know* not where they have laid him.
8. to the sepulchre, and he *saw*, and believed.
9. as yet they *knew* not the scripture,
13. I *know* not where they have laid him.
14. *knew* not that it was Jesus.
20. disciples glad, *when* they *saw* the Lord.
25. Except I shall *see* in his hands the
27. Reach hither thy finger, and *behold* my hands;
29. they *that have* not *seen*, and (yet)
21: 4. disciples *knew* not that it was Jesus.
12. *knowing* that it was the Lord.
15. Lord; thou *knowest* that I love thee
16. Yea, Lord; thou *knowest* that I love thee.
17. Lord, thou *knowest* all things;
21. Peter *seeing* him saith to Jesus,
24. we *know* that his testimony is true.
Acts 2:22. as ye yourselves also *know:*
27. thine Holy One *to see* corruption.
30. *knowing* that God had sworn with
31. neither his flesh *did see* corruption.
3: 3. Who *seeing* Peter and John about to go
9. all the people *saw* him walking
12. *when* Peter *saw* (it), he answered
16. this man strong, whom ye see and *know*.
17. I *wot* that through ignorance ye did (it),
4:20. things which we *have seen* and heard.
5: 7. his wife, not *knowing* what was done,
6:15. *saw* his face as it had been the face
7:18. another king arose, which *knew* not Joseph.
24. *seeing* one (of them) suffer wrong,
31. *When* Moses *saw* (it), he wondered
34. I have seen, I *have seen* (lit. *seeing* I *have seen*) the affliction of my people
40. we *wot* not what is become of him.
55. *saw* the glory of God, and Jesus standing
8:39. that the eunuch *saw* him no more:
9:12. *hath seen* in a vision a man
27. how he *had seen* the Lord in the way,
35. all that dwelt at Lydda and Saron *saw*
40. *when* she *saw* Peter, she sat up.
10: 3. He *saw* in a vision evidently
17. what this vision which he *had seen*
37. That word, (I say), ye *know*,
11: 5. in a trance I *saw* a vision,
6. I considered, and *saw* fourfooted
13. he *had seen* an angel in his house,
23. *when* he came, and *had seen* the grace
12: 3. *because* he *saw* it pleased the Jews,
9. *wist* not that it was true which
11. Now I *know* of a surety, that the Lord
16. had opened (the door), and *saw* him,
13:12. the deputy, *when* he *saw* what was done,
35. thine Holy One *to see* corruption.
36. laid unto his fathers, and *saw* corruption:
37. God raised again, *saw* no corruption.
41. *Behold*, ye despisers, and wonder, and perish:
45. *when* the Jews *saw* the multitudes,
14: 9. *perceiving* that he had faith to be healed,
11. *when* the people *saw* what Paul had done,
15: 6. came together for *to consider* of this matter.
16: 3. they *knew* all that his father was a Greek.
10. after he *had seen* the vision, immediately
19. And *when* her masters *saw* that the hope
27. *seeing* the prison doors open, he drew
40. *when* they *had seen* the brethren,
19:21. I have been there, I must also *see* Rome.
32. the more part *knew* not wherefore
20:22. not *knowing* the things that shall
25. now, behold, I *know* that ye all,
29. I *know* this, that after my departing

Acts21:32. *when* they *saw* the chief captain
22:14. know his will, and *see* that Just One,
18. And *saw* him saying unto me, Make
23: 5. Then said Paul, I *wist* not, brethren,
24:22. *having* more perfect *knowledge* of (that) way,
26:13. I *saw* in the way a light from heaven,
16. these things which thou *hast seen*,
27. I *know* that thou believest.
28: 4. when the barbarians *saw* the
15. whom *when* Paul *saw*, he thanked God,
20. *to see* (you), and to speak with (you):
26. seeing ye shall see, and not *perceive:*
27. lest they *should see* with (their) eyes,
Ro. 1:11. For I long *to see* you, that I may
2: 2. we *are sure* that the judgment
3:19. Now we *know* that what things
5: 3. *knowing* that tribulation worketh patience;
6: 9. *Knowing* that Christ being raised
16. *Know* ye not, that to whom ye yield
7: 7. for I *had* not *known* lust, except
14. we *know* that the law is spiritual:
18. For I *know* that in me that is,
8:22. we *know* that the whole creation
26. we *know* not what we should pray
27. *knoweth* what (is) the mind of the Spirit,
28. we *know* that all things work together
11: 2. *Wot* ye not what the scripture saith
22. *Behold* therefore the goodness and severity
13:11. *knowing* the time, that now (it is)
14:14. I *know*, and am persuaded by the Lord Jesus,
15:29. I *am sure* that, when I come
1Co. 1:16. I *know* not whether I baptized any other.
2: 2. not *to know* any thing among you,
9. Eye *hath* not *seen*, nor ear heard,
11. what man *knoweth* the things of
— the things of God *knoweth* no man,
12. that we *might know* the things
3:16. *Know* ye not that ye are the temple
5: 6. *Know* ye not that a little leaven
6: 2. *Do* ye not *know* that the saints shall
3. *Know* ye not that we shall judge angels?
9. *Know* ye not that the unrighteous
15. *Know* ye not that your bodies are
16. *know* ye not that he which is joined
19. *know* ye not that your body is the temple
7:16. For what *knowest* thou, O wife,
— or how *knowest* thou, O man, whether
8: 1. we *know* that we all have knowledge.
2. if any man think that he *know*eth any
4. we *know* that an idol (is) nothing
10. if any man *see* thee which hast knowledge
9:13. *Do* ye not *know* that they which
24. *Know* ye not that they which run
11: 3. I would have you *know*, that the
12: 2. Ye *know* that ye were Gentiles,
13: 2. though I have...prophecy, and *understand*
14:11. if I *know* not the meaning of the voice,
16. he *understandeth* not what thou sayest?
15:58. *forasmuch as* ye *know* that your labour
16: 7. I will not *see* you now by the way;
15. ye *know* the house of Stephanas,
2Co. 1: 7. *knowing*, that as ye are partakers
4:14. *Knowing* that he which raised up
5: 1. we *know* that if our earthly house
6. *knowing* that, whilst we are at home
11. *Knowing* therefore the terror of the Lord,
16. henceforth *know* we no man after the flesh:
9: 2. I *know* the forwardness of your mind,
11:11. because I love you not? God *knoweth*.
2Co.11:31. *knoweth* that I lie not.
12: 2. I *knew* a man in Christ above
— in the body, I *cannot tell;* or whether out of the body, I *cannot tell:* God *knoweth;*
3. I *knew* such a man, whether in
— I *cannot tell:* God *knoweth;*
Gal. 1:19. other of the apostles *saw* I none,
2: 7. *when* they *saw* that the gospel of
14. when I *saw* that they walked not uprightly
16. *Knowing* that a man is not justified
4: 8. then, *when* ye *knew* not God,
13. Ye *know* how through infirmity
6:11. Ye *see* how large a letter I have written
Eph. 1:18. that ye may *know* what is the hope
6: 8. *Knowing* that whatsoever good thing
9. *knowing* that your Master also is
21. that ye also *may know* my affairs,
Phi. 1:17. *knowing* that I am set for the defence
19. For I *know* that this shall turn
25. I *know* that I shall abide and continue
27. that whether I come and *see* you, or
30. the same conflict which ye *saw* in me,
2:28. *when* ye *see* him again, ye may rejoice,
4: 9. received, and heard, and *seen* in me, do:
12. I *know* both how to be abased, and I *know*
15. Now ye Philippians *know* also,
Col. 2: 1. I would that ye *knew* what great
3:24. *Knowing* that of the Lord ye shall
4: 1. *knowing* that ye also have a Master
6. that ye may *know* how ye ought
1Th. 1: 4. *Knowing*, brethren beloved, your
5. ye *know* what manner of men we were
2: 1. yourselves, brethren, *know* our entrance
2. were shamefully entreated, as ye *know*,
5. used we flattering words, as ye *know*,
11. As ye *know* how we exhorted
17. *to see* your face with great desire.
3: 3. yourselves *know* that we are appointed
4. even as it came to pass, and ye *know*.
6. desiring greatly *to see* us, as we also
10. that we might *see* your face, and might
4: 2. ye *know* what commandments we gave
4. That every one of you should *know* how
5. the Gentiles *which know* not God:
5: 2. yourselves *know* perfectly that the day of the Lord
12. *to know* them which labour among you,
2Th. 1: 8. vengeance on them *that know* not God,
2: 6. now ye *know* what withholdeth
3: 7. yourselves *know* how ye ought to follow us:
1Ti. 1: 8. we *know* that the law (is) good, if a
9. *Knowing* this, that the law is not made for
3: 5. if a man *know* not how to rule his
15. that thou *mayest know* how thou oughtest
6:16. whom no man *hath seen*, nor can *see:*
2Ti. 1: 4. Greatly desiring *to see* thee, being
12. for I *know* whom I have believed,
15. This thou *knowest*, that all they
2:23. *knowing* that they do gender strifes.
3:14. *knowing* of whom thou hast learned
15. thou *hast known* the holy scriptures,
Tit. 1:16. They profess that they *know* God;
3:11. *Knowing* that he that is such
Philem.21. *knowing* that thou wilt also do
Heb 3: 9. proved me, and *saw* my works forty years.
8:11. for all *shall know* me, from the least
10:30. For we *know* him that hath said,
11: 5. translated that he should not *see* death;
13. *having seen* them afar off, and were
23. because they *saw* (he was) a proper child;
Jas. 3: 1. *knowing* that we shall receive the

Jas. 4 4. *know* ye not that the friendship of
17. to him *that knoweth* to do good,
5:11. *have seen* the end of the Lord; that
1Pet. 1: 8. Whom *having* not *seen*, ye love:
18. *Forasmuch as* ye *know* that ye were not
3: 9. *knowing* that ye are thereunto called,
10. he that will love life, and *see* good days,
5: 9. *knowing* that the same afflictions
2Pet. 1:12. these things, though ye *know* (them),
14. *Knowing* that shortly I must put
2: 9. The Lord *knoweth how* to deliver the
1Joh. 2:11. *knoweth* not whither he goeth, because
20. from the Holy One, and ye *know* all things.
21. ye *know* not the truth, but because ye *know*
29. If ye *know* that he is righteous,
3: 1. *Behold*, what manner of love the
2. we *know* that, when he shall appear,
5. ye *know* that he was manifested to
14. We *know* that we have passed from
15. ye *know* that no murderer hath eternal life
5:13. that ye *may know* that ye have eternal life,
15. if we *know* that he hear us,
— we *know* that we have the petitions
16. If any man *see* his brother sin a sin
18. We *know* that whosoever is born of God
19. we *know* that we are of God, and the whole
20. we *know* that the Son of God is come,
3Joh. 12. ye *know* that our record is true.
14. I trust I shall shortly *see* thee,
Jude 5. *though* ye once *knew* this, how that
10. those things which they *know* not:
Rev. 1: 2. of all things that he *saw*.
12. being turned, I *saw* seven golden candlesticks;
17. when I *saw* him, I fell at his feet
19. Write the things which thou *hast seen*,
20. the seven stars which thou *sawest* in my
— the seven candlesticks which thou *sawest*
2: 2. I *know* thy works, and thy labour,
9. I *know* thy works, and tribulation,
13. I *know* thy works, and where thou dwellest,
19. I *know* thy works, and charity, and service,
3: 1. I *know* thy works, that thou hast a
8. I *know* thy works: behold, I have
15. I *know* thy works, that thou art
17. *knowest* not that thou art wretched,
4: 1. After this I *looked*, and, behold, a
4. I *saw* four and twenty elders sitting,
5: 1. I *saw* in the right hand of him
2. I *saw* a strong angel proclaiming
6. I *beheld*, and, lo, in the midst of
11. I *beheld*, and I heard the voice of
6: 1. I *saw* when the Lamb opened one
2. I *saw*, and behold a white horse:
5. I *beheld*, and lo a black horse;
8. I *looked*, and behold a pale horse:
9. I *saw* under the altar the souls
12. I *beheld* when he had opened the sixth
7: 1. after these things I *saw* four angels
2. I *saw* another angel ascending from
9. After this I *beheld*, and, lo, a great
14. I said unto him, Sir, thou *knowest*.
8: 2. I *saw* the seven angels which stood
13. I *beheld*, and heard an angel flying
9: 1. I *saw* a star fall from heaven
17. thus I *saw* the horses in the vision,
10: 1. I *saw* another mighty angel come down
5. the angel which I *saw* stand upon the sea
12:12. *because* he *knoweth* that he hath but
13. when the dragon *saw* that he was cast
13: 1. *saw* a beast rise up out of the sea,
2. the beast which I *saw* was like unto

Rev. 13: 3. I *saw* one of his heads as it were wounded
11. I *beheld* another beast coming
14: 1. I *looked*, and, lo, a Lamb stood on
6. I *saw* another angel fly in the midst
14. I *looked*, and behold a white cloud,
15: 1. I *saw* another sign in heaven,
2. I *saw* as it were a sea of glass
5 after that I *looked*, and, behold, the temple
16:13. I *saw* three unclean spirits like frogs
17: 3. I *saw* a woman sit upon a scarlet coloured beast,
6. I *saw* the woman drunken with
— *when* I *saw* her, I wondered with
8. The beast that thou *sawest* was, and is
12. the ten horns which thou *sawest* are
15. The waters which thou *sawest*,
16. the ten horns which thou *sawest* upon
18. the woman which thou *sawest* is
18: 1. after these things I *saw* another angel
7. am no widow, and shall *see* no sorrow.
19:11. I *saw* heaven opened, and behold
12. that no man *knew*, but he himself.
17. I *saw* an angel standing in the sun;
19. I *saw* the beast, and the kings of the earth,
20: 1. I *saw* an angel come down from heaven,
4. I *saw* thrones, and they sat upon them,
11. I *saw* a great white throne, and him
12. I *saw* the dead, small and great,
21: 1. I *saw* a new heaven and a new earth
2. I John *saw* the holy city, new Jerusalem,
22. I *saw* no temple therein: for the

See also ἴδε and ἰδού for passages where used adverbially.

1491 5 220/270 2:373 1492

εἶδος, *īdos.*

Lu. 3:22. in a bodily *shape* like a dove
9:29. the *fashion* of his countenance was
Joh. 5:37. at any time, nor seen his *shape*.
2Co. 5: 7. For we walk by faith, not by *sight*:
1Th. 5:22. Abstain from all *appearance* of evil

εἴδω see εἰδέω. p. 188

1493 1 220/270 2:375 1497

εἰδωλεῖον, *īdōlīon.*

1Co. 8:10. sit at meat in the *idol's temple*, shall

1494 10 221/270 2:375 1497,2380

εἰδωλόθυτον, *īdōlothuton.*

Acts 15:29. abstain from *meats offered to idols*,
21:25. from (things) *offered to idols*, and from blood,
1Co. 8: 1. as touching *things offered unto idols*,
4. eating of those *things that are offered in sacrifice unto idols*,
7. eat (it) as a *thing offered unto an idol*;
10. to eat those *things which are offered to idols*
10:19. or that *which is offered in sacrifice to idols* is any thing?
28. This is *offered in sacrifice unto idols*,
Rev. 2:14. to eat *things sacrificed unto idols*,
20. to eat *things sacrificed unto idols*.

1495 4 220/270 2:375 1497,2999

εἰδωλολατρεία, *īdōlolatrīa.*

1Co. 10:14. my dearly beloved, flee from *idolatry*.

Gal. 3:20. *Idolatry* witchcraft, hatred, variance,
Col. 3. 5. and covetousness, which is *idolatry:*
1Pet. 4. 3. banquetings, and abominable *idolatries:*

1496 7 220/270 2:375 rt 3000

εἰδωλολάτρης, *īdōlolatrees.* 1497

1Co. 5 10. or extortioners, or with *idolaters ;*
11. a fornicator, or covetous, or an *idolater,*
6: 9. neither fornicators, nor *idolaters,* nor adulterers,
10: 7. Neither be ye *idolaters,* as (were) some
Eph. 5: 5. nor covetous man, who is an *idolater,*
Rev. 21: 8. *idolaters,* and all liars, shall have their part
22: 15. and murderers, and *idolaters,*

1497 11 220/270 2:375 1491

εἴδωλον, *īdōlon.*

Acts 7:41. offered sacrifice unto the *idol,*
15:20. that they abstain from pollutions of *idols,*
Ro. 2:22. thou that abhorrest *idols,* dost thou
1Co. 8: 4. we know that an *idol* (is) nothing
7. with conscience of the *idol* unto this hour
10:19. that the *idol* is any thing,
12: 2. carried away unto these dumb *idols,*
2Co. 6:16. hath the temple of God with *idols?*
1Th. 1: 9. how ye turned to God from *idols*
1Joh. 5:21. Little children, keep yourselves from *idols.*
Rev. 9:20. *idols* of gold, and silver, and brass,

1498 12 221/278 1510

εἴην, εἴης, εἴη, &c. *īeen, īees, īee.* optat. from εἰμί.

Lu. 1:29. what manner of salutation this *should be.*
3:15. whether he *were* the Christ, or not;
8: 9. saying, What *might* this parable *be?*
9:46. which of them *should be* greatest.
15:26. asked what these things *meant.*
18:36. pass by, he asked what it *meant.*
22:23. which of them it *was* that should do
Joh. 13:24. who it *should be* of whom he spake.
Acts 8:20. Thy money perish (lit. *be* to destruction) with thee, because
10:17. this vision which he had seen *should mean,*
21:33. demanded who he *was,* and what he
Rev. 3:15. I would thou *wert* cold or hot.

εἰ καί. p. 186

See after εἰ.

1500 7 221/270 2:380 1502

εἰκῆ, *īkee.*

Mat. 5:22. angry with his brother *without a cause*
Ro. 13: 4. he beareth not the sword *in vain:*
1Co. 15: 2. unless ye have believed *in vain.*
Gal. 3: 4. so many things *in vain?* if (it be) yet *in vain.*
4:11. bestowed upon you labour *in vain.*
Col. 2:18. *vainly* puffed up by his fleshly mind,

1501 12 221/270

εἴκοσι, *īkosi.*

Lu. 14:31. cometh against him with *twenty* thousand:
Joh. 6:19. about five and *twenty* or thirty furlongs,
Acts 1:15. were about an hundred and *twenty,*
27:28. sounded, and found (it) *twenty* fathoms:
1Co. 10: 8. fell in one day three and *twenty* thousand.
Rev. 4: 4. the throne (were) four and *twenty* seats:
— I saw four and *twenty* elders sitting,
10. The four and *twenty* elders fall down
5: 8. four (and) *twenty* elders fell down before
14. the four (and) *twenty* elders fell down
11:16. the four and *twenty* elders, which sat
19: 4. four and *twenty* elders and the four beasts

1502 1 221/270

εἴκω, *īko.*

Gal. 2: 5. To whom we *gave place* by subjection,

1503 2 221/349

εἴκω, *īko.*

Jas. 1: 6. he that wavereth, *is like* a wave of the sea
23. he *is like* unto a man beholding his

1504 23 221/270 2:381 1503

εἰκών, *īkōn.*

Mat. 22:20. Whose (is) this *image* and superscription?
Mar. 12:16. Whose (is) this *image* and superscription?
Lu. 20:24. Whose *image* and superscription hath it?
Ro. 1:23. into an *image* made like to corruptible man,
8:29. conformed to the *image* of his Son,
1Co. 11: 7. as he is the *image* and glory of God:
15:49. have borne the *image* of the earthy, we shall also bear the *image* of the heavenly.
2Co. 3:18. into the same *image* from glory to glory,
4: 4. of Christ, who is the *image* of God,
Col. 1:15. Who is the *image* of the invisible God,
3:10. the *image* of him that created him:
Heb 10: 1. not the very *image* of the things,
Rev. 13:14. should make an *image* to the beast,
15. to give life unto the *image* of the beast, that the *image* of the beast
— as would not worship the *image*
14: 9. worship the beast and his *image,*
11. who worship the beast and his *image,*
15: 2. victory over the beast, and over his *image*
16: 2. them which worshipped his *image.*
19:20. them that worshipped his *image.*
20: 4. not worshipped the beast, neither his *image,*

1505 3 221/271 2:397 1506

εἰλικρίνεια, *īlikrinīa.*

1Co. 5: 8. with the unleavened (bread) of *sincerity*
2Co. 1:12. that in simplicity and godly *sincerity,*
2:17. as of *sincerity,* but as of God, in the

1506 2 221/271 2:397 2919

εἰλικρινής, *īlikrinees.* *heilē* (ray)

Phi. 1:10. that ye may be *sincere* and without offence
2Pet. 3: 1. in (both) which I stir up your *pure* minds

1507 1 221/325 cf 1667

εἱλίσσω, *hīlisso.* *heilō* (to coil)

Rev. 6:14. as a scroll *when* it is *rolled together;*

εἰ μή. p. 186

See after εἰ.

1510 141 221/271 2:398

εἰμί, imi.

Mat. 3:11. whose shoes I *am* not worthy to bear:
8: 8. Lord, I *am* not worthy that thou
9. For I *am* a man under authority,
11:29. for I *am* meek and lowly in heart:
14:27. Be of good cheer; it is I (lit. I *am*); be not afraid.
18:20. there *am* I in the midst of them.
20:15. Is thine eye evil, because I *am* good?
22:32. I *am* the God of Abraham, and the God
24: 5. in my name, saying, I *am* Christ;
26:22. to say unto him, Lord. is it I? (lit. *am* I)
25. answered and said, Master, is it I? (lit. *am* I)
27:24. I *am* innocent of the blood of this just person:
43. for he said, I *am* the Son of God.
28:20. I *am* with you alway, (even) unto the end
Mar. 1: 7. I *am* not worthy to stoop down and unloose.
6:50. Be of good cheer: it is I (lit. I *am*); be not afraid.
13: 6. in my name, saying, I *am* (Christ);
14:62. Jesus said, I *am*: and ye shall see
Lu. 1:18. for I *am* an old man, and my wife
19. answering said unto him, I *am* Gabriel,
3:16. whose shoes I *am* not worthy to unloose:
5: 8. for I *am* a sinful man, O Lord.
7: 6. I *am* not worthy that thou shouldest
8. For I also *am* a man set under authority,
15:19. *am* no more worthy to be called thy son:
21. *am* no more worthy to be called thy son.
18:11. that I *am* not as other men (are),
19:22. Thou knewest that I *was* an austere man,
21: 8. in my name, saying, I *am* (Christ);
22:27. I *am* among you as he that serveth.
33. Lord, I *am* ready to go with thee,
58. Peter said, Man, I *am* not.
70. he said unto them, Ye say that I *am*.
24:39. that it is I myself (lit. I *am* myself): handle me,
Joh. 1:20. confessed, I *am* not the Christ.
21. Art thou Elias? And he saith, I *am* not.
27. whose shoe's latchet I *am* not worthy to unloose.
3:28. that I said, I *am* not the Christ, but that I *am* sent before him.
4:26. I that speak unto thee *am* (he).
6:20. saith unto them, It is I; (lit. I *am*)
35. said unto them, I *am* the bread of life:
41. I *am* the bread which came down
48. I *am* that bread of life.
51. I *am* the living bread which came
7:28. know me, and ye know whence I *am*:
29. I know him: for I *am* from him,
33. Yet a little while *am* I with you,
34. where I *am*, (thither) ye cannot come.
36. where I *am*, (thither) ye cannot come?
8:12. saying, I *am* the light of the world:
16. for I *am* not alone, but I and the Father
18. I *am* one that bear witness of myself,
23. Ye are from beneath; I *am* from above: — I *am* not of this world.
24. If ye believe not that I *am* (he),
28. then shall ye know that I *am* (he),
58. Before Abraham was, I *am*.
9: 5. I *am* the light of the world.
9. He is like him: (but) he said, I *am* (he).
10: 7. I say unto you, I *am* the door of the sheep.
9. I *am* the door: by me if any man
11. I *am* the good shepherd: the good

Joh. 10:14. I *am* the good shepherd, and know
36. because I said, I *am* the Son of God?
11:25. I *am* the resurrection, and the life:
12:26. where I *am*, there shall also my servant
13:13. ye say well; for (so) I *am*.
19. ye may believe that I *am* (he).
33. yet a little while I *am* with you.
14: 3. that where I *am*, (there) ye may be also.
6. I *am* the way, the truth, and the life:
9. *Have* I *been* so long time with you,
15: 1. I *am* the true vine, and my Father
5. I *am* the vine, ye (are) the branches:
16:32. yet I *am* not alone, because the Father
17:11. now I *am* no more in the world,
14. even as I *am* not of the world.
16. even as I *am* not of the world.
24. be with me where I *am*; that they
18: 5. Jesus saith unto them, I *am* (he).
6. as he had said unto them, I *am* (he),
8. I have told you that I *am* (he):
17. this man's disciples? He saith, I *am* not.
25. He denied (it), and said, I *am* not.
35. Pilate answered, *Am* I a Jew?
37. Thou sayest that I *am* a king.
19:21. that he said, I *am* King of the Jews.
Acts 9: 5. I *am* Jesus whom thou persecutest:
10:21. Behold, I *am* he whom ye seek:
26. Stand up; I myself also *am* a man.
13:25. I *am* not (he). But, behold, there cometh — shoes of (his) feet I *am* not worthy to loose.
18:10. For I *am* with thee, and no man shall
21:39. I *am* a man (which am) a Jew of
22: 3. I *am* verily a man (which am) a Jew,
8. I *am* Jesus of Nazareth, whom thou
23: 6. Men (and) brethren, I *am* a Pharisee,
25:10. I stand (lit. *am* standing) at Cæsar's judgment seat,
26:15. I *am* Jesus whom thou persecutest.
29. almost, and altogether such as I *am*,
27:23. of God, whose I *am*, and whom I serve,
Ro. 1:14. I *am* debtor both to the Greeks,
7:14. I *am* carnal, sold under sin.
11: 1. For I also *am* an Israelite,
13. as I *am* the apostle of the Gentiles,
1Co. 1:12. every one of you saith, I *am* of Paul;
3: 4. while one saith, I *am* of Paul;
9: 1. *Am* I not an apostle? *am* I not free?
2. If I *be* not an apostle unto others, yet doubtless I *am* to you:
12:15. Because I *am* not the hand, I *am* not of
16. Because I *am* not the eye, I *am* not of
13: 2. have not charity, I *am* nothing.
15: 9. For I *am* the least of the apostles, that *am* not meet to be called an apostle,
10. by the grace of God I *am* what I *am*:
2Co.12:10. when I am weak, then *am* I strong.
11. chiefest apostles, though I *be* nothing.
Phi. 4:11. in whatsoever state I *am*,
Col. 2: 5. yet *am* I with you in the spirit,
1Ti. 1:15. to save sinners; of whom I *am* chief.
Heb 12:21. Moses said, I exceedingly fear (lit. I *am* exceedingly afraid) and quake:
1Pet.1:16. Be ye holy; for I *am* holy.
2Pet.1:13. as long as I *am* in this tabernacle,
Rev. 1: 8. I *am* Alpha and Omega, the
11. Saying, I *am* Alpha and Omega,
17. Fear not; I *am* the first and the last.
18. behold, I *am* alive for evermore.
2:23. I *am* he which searcheth the reins
3:17. Because thou sayest, I *am* rich,
18: 7. *am* no widow and shall see no sorrow.

Rev.19:10. I *am* thy fellowservant, and of thy brethren
21: 6. It is done. I *am* Alpha and Omega,
22: 9. for I *am* thy fellowservant, and of
13. I *am* Alpha and Omega, the beginning
16. I *am* the root and the offspring of David,

See persons and tenses from this verb severally arranged under—

Εἶ, ἐστί, ἐσμέν, ἐστέ, εἰσί.

Ἦν, ἦς, ἦσθα, ἦν, &c. *Imp.*

Ἤμην, ἦσο, ἦτο, &c. *Plup.*

Ἔσομαι, ἔσῃ, ἔσται, &c. *Fut.*

Ἔστω, ἔστε, ἔστωσαν, ἴσθι, ἤτω.

Εἴην, εἴης, εἴη.

Ὦ, ᾖς, ᾖ, ὦμεν, ἦτε, ὦσι.

Εἶναι, ἔσεσθαι, ἐσόμενος.

1511 126 221/278 1510

εἶναι, *inai*, from εἰμί.

Mat.16:13. Whom do men say that I the Son of man *am?*
15. whom say ye that I *am?*
17: 4. Lord, it is good for us *to be* here:
19:21. If thou wilt *be* perfect, go (and) sell
20:27. whosoever will *be* chief among you,
22:23. which say that there *is* no resurrection,
Mar. 6:49. they supposed it *had been* a spirit,
8:27. Whom do men say that I *am?*
29. whom say ye that I *am?*
9: 5. Master, it is good for us *to be* here:
35. If any man desire *to be* first,
12:18. which say there *is* no resurrection;
14:64. condemned him *to be* guilty of death.
Lu. 2: 4. because he *was* of the house and lineage
6. so it was, that, while they *were* there,
44. supposing him *to have been* in the company,
49. that I must *be* about my Father's business?
4:41. for they knew that he *was* Christ.
5:12. when he *was* in a certain city,
8:38. besought him that he might *be* with him:
9:18. came to pass, as he *was* alone praying,
— Whom say the people that I *am?*
20. whom say ye that I *am?*
33. it is good for us *to be* here:
11. 1. as he *was* praying in a certain place,
8. give him, because he *is* his friend,
14:26. own life also, he cannot *be* my disciple.
27. come after me, cannot *be* my disciple.
33. that he hath, he cannot *be* my disciple.
19:11. because he *was* nigh to Jerusalem,
20: 6. they be persuaded that John *was* a prophet.
20. should feign themselves)(just men,
27. which deny that there *is* any resurrection;
41. How say they that Christ *is* David's son?
22:24. should be accounted)(the greatest.
23: 2. that he himself *is* Christ a King.
Joh. 1:46(47). Can there any good thing *come* out
7: 4. himself seeketh *to be* known openly.
17: 5. I had with thee before the world *was*.
Acts 2:12. saying one to another, What meaneth this? (lit. might this *be*)
4:32. which he possessed *was* his own;
5:36. Theudas, boasting himself *to be* somebody;
8: 9. that himself *was* some great one:
37. I believe that Jesus Christ *is* the Son of God.

Acts13:25. he said, Whom think ye that I *am?*
47. that thou *shouldest be* for salvation
16:13. where prayer was wont *to be made;*
15. judged me *to be* faithful to the Lord,
17: 7. saying that *there is* another king,
18. He seemeth *to be* a setter forth of strange
20. therefore what these things mean. (lit. would *be*)
29. that the Godhead *is* like unto gold,
18: 3. because he *was* of the same craft,
15. for I will *be* no judge of such (matters).
28. by the scriptures that Jesus *was* Christ.
19: 1. that, while Apollos *was* at Corinth,
23: 8. say that there *is* no resurrection,
27: 4. because the winds *were* contrary.
28: 6. said that he *was* a god.
Ro. 1:20. so that they *are* without excuse:
22. Professing themselves *to be* wise,
2:19. thou thyself *art* a guide of the blind,
3: 9. that they *are* all under sin;
26. that he might *be* just, and the justifier
4:11. that he might *be* the father of all
13. that he should *be* the heir of the world,
16. the promise might *be* sure to all the seed;
6:11. yourselves *to be* dead indeed unto sin,
7: 3. so that she *is* no adulteress, though
8:29. that he might *be* the firstborn among
9: 3. I could wish that myself *were* accursed from
14:14. esteemeth any thing *to be* unclean,
15:16. That I should *be* the minister of Jesus
16:19. yet I would have you)(wise unto that
1Co. 3:18. seemeth *to be* wise in this world,
7: 7. I would that all men *were* even as I myself.
25. obtained mercy of the Lord *to be* faithful.
26. that (it is) good for a man so *to be*.
32. I would have you)(without carefulness.
10: 6. we should not lust after (lit. *be* desirers)
11:16. if any man seem *to be* contentious,
19. there must *be* also heresies among you,
12:23. which we think *to be* less honourable,
14:37. If any man think himself *to be* a prophet,
2Co. 5: 9. or absent, we may *be* accepted of him.
7:11. have approved yourselves *to be* clear
9: 5. that the same might *be* ready, as
10: 7. trust to himself that he *is* Christ's,
11:16. Let no man think me)(a fool;
Gal. 2: 6. of those who seemed *to be* somewhat,
9. Cephas, and John, who seemed *to be* pillars,
4:21. ye that desire *to be* under the law,
6: 3. if a man think himself *to be* something,
Eph. 1: 4. that we should *be* holy and without blame
12. we should *be* to the praise of his glory,
3: 6. That the Gentiles should *be* fellowheirs,
Phi. 1:23. a desire to depart, and *to be* with Christ;
2: 6. not robbery *to be* equal with God:
3: 8. I count all things)((but) loss for the
— do count them)((but) dung, that I
4:11. whatsoever state I am, (therewith) *to be* content.
1Th. 2: 6. when we might *have been* burdensome,
1Ti. 1: 7. Desiring *to be* teachers of the law;
2:12. over the man, but *to be* in silence.
3: 2. A bishop then must *be* blameless,
6: 5. supposing that gain *is* godliness:
18. ready to distribute, (lit. *to be* distributors)
2Ti. 2:24. not strive; but *be* gentle unto all (men),
Tit. 1: 7. For a bishop must *be* blameless,
2: 2. That the aged men *be* sober, grave,
4. to love their husbands, (lit. *to be* loving their husbands)
9. to please (them) well (lit. *to be* well pleasing) in all (things);

o 2

Tit. 3: 1. *to be* ready to every good work,
2. *to be* no brawlers, (but) gentle,
Heb 5:12. when for the time ye ought *to be* teachers,
11: 4. obtained witness that he *was* righteous,
12:11. for the present seemeth *to be* joyous,
Jas. 1:18. we should *be* a kind of firstfruits
26. man among you seem *to be* religious,
4: 4. will *be* a friend of the world
1Pet. 1:21. your faith and hope might *be* in God.
5:12. that this *is* the true grace of God
1Joh. 2: 9. He that saith he *is* in the light,
Rev. 2: 2. them which say they *are* apostles,
9. of them which say they *are* Jews,
3: 9. which say they *are* Jews, and are not,

εἵνεκεν see ἕνεκα. 1752

εἶπα, εἶπον, see ἔπω. 2036

1512 6 225/262

εἴπερ. p. 187

See after εἰ.

1513 4 226/258

εἴπως. p. 187

See after εἰ.

1514 4 226/297 2:400 1515

εἰρηνεύω, īreenūo.

Mar. 9:50. *have peace* one with another.
Ro. 12:18. *live peaceably* with all men.
2Co. 13:11. be of one mind, *live in peace*;
1Th. 5:13. *be at peace* among yourselves.

1515 92 226/297 2:400 eirō (to join)

εἰρήνη, īreenee.

Mat. 10:13. let your *peace* come upon it: but if it be not worthy, let your *peace* return to you.
34. *peace* on earth: I came not to send *peace*,
Mar. 5:34. go in *peace*, and be whole of thy plague.
Lu. 1:79. to guide our feet into the way of *peace*.
2:14. on earth *peace*, good will toward men.
29. lettest thou thy servant depart in *peace*,
7:50. Thy faith hath saved thee; go in *peace*.
8:48. thy faith hath made thee whole; go in *peace*.
10: 5. first say, *Peace* (be) to this house.
6. And if the son of *peace* be there, your *peace* shall rest upon it:
11:21. his goods are in *peace*:
12:51. I am come to give *peace* on earth?
14:32. an ambassage, and desireth conditions of *peace*.
19:38. *peace* in heaven, and glory in the highest.
42. things (which belong) unto thy *peace*!
24:36. saith unto them, *Peace* (be) unto you.
Joh. 14:27. *Peace* I leave with you, my *peace* I give
16:33. that in me ye might have *peace*.
20:19. saith unto them, *Peace* (be) unto you.
21. to them again, *Peace* (be) unto you:
26. said, *Peace* (be) unto you.
Acts 7:26. would have set them *at one* again.
Acts 9:31. Then had the churches *rest*
10:36. preaching *peace* by Jesus Christ:
12:20. their friend, desired *peace*;
15:33. they were let go in *peace* from the
16:36. now therefore depart, and go in *peace*.
24: 2. by thee we enjoy great *quietness*,
Ro. 1: 7. Grace to you and *peace* from God
2:10. glory, honour, and *peace*, to every man
3:17. the way of *peace* have they not known:
5: 1. by faith, we have *peace* with God
8: 6. spiritually minded (is) life and *peace*.
10:15. them that preach the gospel of *peace*,
14:17. righteousness, and *peace*, and joy in the
19. the things which make for *peace*,
15:13. with all joy and *peace* in believing,
33. the God of *peace* (be) with you all.
16:20. the God of *peace* shall bruise Satan
1Co. 1: 3. Grace (be) unto you, and *peace*,
7:15. God hath called us to *peace*.
14:33. not (the author) of confusion, but of *peace*,
16:11. conduct him forth in *peace*, that
2Co. 1: 2. Grace (be) to you and *peace* from God
13:11. the God of love and *peace* shall be with you.
Gal. 1: 3. Grace (be) to you and *peace* from God the
5:22. love, joy, *peace*, longsuffering, gentleness,
6:16. *peace* (be) on them, and mercy, and upon
Eph. 1: 2. Grace (be) to you, and *peace*, from God
2:14. For he is our *peace*, who hath made
15. one new man, (so) making *peace*;
17. came and preached *peace* to you
4: 3. unity of the Spirit in the bond of *peace*.
6:15. the preparation of the gospel of *peace*;
23. *Peace* (be) to the brethren, and love with faith,
Phi. 1: 2. Grace (be) unto you, and *peace*, from God
4: 7. the *peace* of God, which passeth all
9. the God of *peace* shall be with you.
Col. 1: 2. Grace (be) unto you, and *peace*, from God
3:15. let the *peace* of God rule in your hearts,
1Th. 1: 1. Grace (be) unto you, and *peace*, from God
5: 3. when they shall say, *Peace* and safety;
23. the very God of *peace* sanctify you
2Th. 1. 2. Grace unto you, and *peace*, from God
3:16. the Lord of *peace* himself give you *peace*
1Ti. 1: 2. Grace, mercy, (and) *peace*, from God
2Ti. 1: 2. Grace, mercy, (and) *peace*, from God
2:22. follow righteousness, faith, charity, *peace*,
Tit. 1: 4. Grace, mercy, (and) *peace*, from God
Philem. 3. Grace to you, and *peace*, from God
Heb 7: 2. King of Salem, which is, King of *peace*;
11:31. she had received the spies with *peace*.
12:14. Follow *peace* with all (men), and holiness,
13:20. the God of *peace*, that brought again
Jas. 2:16. say unto them, Depart in *peace*,
3:18. fruit of righteousness is sown in *peace* of them that make *peace*.
1Pet. 1: 2. Grace unto you, and *peace*, be multiplied.
3:11. let him seek *peace*, and ensue it.
5:14. *Peace* (be) with you all that are in Christ Jesus.
2Pet. 1: 2. Grace and *peace* be multiplied unto you
3:14. ye may be found of him in *peace*,
2Joh. 3. Grace be with you, mercy, (and) *peace*
3Joh. 14(15). *Peace* (be) to thee. (Our) friends, salute thee.
Jude 2. Mercy unto you, and *peace*, and love,
Rev. 1: 4. Grace (be) unto you, and *peace*, from him
6: 4. to take *peace* from the earth.

1516 2 227/298 2:400 1515

εἰρηνικός, īreenikos.

Heb 12:11. the *peaceable* fruit of righteousness unto
Jas. 3:17. first pure, then *peaceable*, gentle,

1517 1 227/298 2:400 1515,4160

εἰρηνοποιέω, īreenopoyeō.

Col. 1:20. *having made peace* through the blood

1518 1 227/298 2:400

εἰρηνοποιός, īreenopoyos.

Mat. 5: 9. Blessed (are) the *peacemakers* : for they

εἴρω, see ἐρέω. 2046

1519 1773 227/298 2:420,434

εἰς, īs.

Mat. 2: 1. came wise men from the east *to* Jerusalem,
8. he sent them *to* Bethlehem, and said,
11. when they were come *into* the house,
12. they departed *into* their own country
13. flee *into* Egypt, and be thou there until
14. by night, and departed *into* Egypt:
20. go *into* the land of Israel:
21. came *into* the land of Israel.
22. he turned aside *into* the parts of Galilee:
23. came and dwelt *in* a city called Nazareth
3:10. hewn down, and cast *into* the fire.
11. baptize you with water *unto* repentance:
12. gather his wheat *into* the garner;
4: 1. led up of the spirit *into* the wilderness
5. devil taketh him up *into* the holy city,
8. up *into* an exceeding high mountain,
12. he departed *into* Galilee;
13. he came and dwelt *in* Capernaum,
18. casting a net *into* the sea: for they
24. his fame went *throughout* (lit. *into*) all Syria:
5: 1. he went up *into* a mountain:
13. it is thenceforth good *for* nothing,
20. enter *into* the kingdom of heaven.
22. shall be in danger *of* (lit. *unto*) hell fire.
25. the officer, and thou be cast *into* prison.
29. thy whole body should be cast *into* hell.
30. thy whole body should be cast *into* hell.
35. neither *by* Jerusalem; for it is
6: 6. when thou prayest, enter *into* thy closet,
13. lead us not *into* temptation,
— the power, and the glory, *for* ever.
26. Behold)(the fowls of the air:
— reap, nor gather *into* barns;
30. to morrow is cast *into* the oven,
34. therefore no thought *for* the morrow:
7:13. the way, that leadeth *to* destruction,
14. the way, which leadeth *unto* life,
19. is hewn down, and cast *into* the fire.
21. shall enter *into* the kingdom of heaven,
8: 4. *for* a testimony unto them.
5. when Jesus was entered *into* Capernaum,
12. shall be cast out *into* outer darkness:
14. when Jesus was come *into* Peter's house,
18. to depart *unto* the other side.
23. when he was entered *into* a ship,
28. *to* the other side *into* the country of the
31. to go away *into* the herd of swine.
32. they went *into* the herd of swine:

Mat. 8:32. ran violently down a steep place *into* the sea,
33. went their ways *into* the city, and told
34. the whole city came out *to* meet Jesus:
9: 1. he entered *into* a ship, and passed over, and came *into* his own city.
6. take up thy bed, and go *unto* thine house.
7. he arose, and departed *to* his house.
13. the righteous, but sinners *to* repentance.
17. do men put new wine *into* old bottles:
— they put new wine *into* new bottles,
23. when Jesus came *into* the ruler's house,
26. fame hereof went abroad *into* all that land.
28. when he was come *into* the house,
38. send forth labourers *into* his harvest.
10: 5. Go not *into* the way of the Gentiles, and *into* (any) city of the Samaritans
9. nor silver, nor brass *in* your purses,
10. Nor scrip *for* (your) journey, neither
11. *into* whatsoever city or town ye shall enter,
12. when ye come *into* an house, salute it.
17. will deliver you up *to* the councils,
18. *for* a testimony against them
21. shall deliver up the brother *to* death,
22. he that endureth *to* the end shall
23. this city, flee ye *into* another:
27. what ye hear *in* the ear, (that)
41. receiveth a prophet *in* the name of a prophet
— *in* the name of a righteous man
42. (water) only *in* the name of a disciple,
11: 7. What went ye out *into* the wilderness to see?
12: 4. he entered *into* the house of God,
9. he went *into* their synagogue:
11. if it fall *into* a pit on the sabbath day,
18. *in* whom my soul is well pleased:
20. till he send forth judgment *unto* victory.
29. can one enter *into* a strong man's house,
41. they repented *at* the preaching of Jonas;
44. I will return *into* my house
13: 2. so that he went *into* a ship, and sat;
22. He also that received seed *among* the thorns
30. bind them *in* bundles to burn them: but gather the wheat *into* my barn.
33. hid *in* three measures of meal,
36. multitude away, and went *into* the house.
42. shall cast them *into* a furnace of fire:
47. a net, that was cast *into* the sea,
48. gathered the good *into* vessels,
50. shall cast them *into* the furnace of fire:
52. instructed *unto* the kingdom of heaven
54. he was come *into* his own country,
14:13. by ship *into* a desert place apart:
15. that they may go *into* the villages,
19. looking up *to* heaven, he blessed,
22. his disciples to get *into* a ship, and to go before him *unto* the other side,
23. he went up *into* a mountain apart
31. where*fore* didst thou doubt?
32. when they were come *into* the ship,
34. they came *into* the land of Gennesaret.
35. they sent out *into* all that country
15:11. Not that which goeth *into* the mouth
14. both shall fall *into* the ditch.
17. entereth *in at* the mouth goeth *into* the belly, and is cast out *into* the draught?
21. departed *into* the coasts of Tyre and Sidon.
24. I am not sent but *unto* the lost sheep
29. went up *into* a mountain

Mat.15:39. took ship (lit. entered *into* a ship), and came *into* the coasts
16: 5. his disciples were come *to* the other side,
13. Jesus came *into* the coasts of Cæsarea
21. that he must go *unto* Jerusalem,
17: 1. up *into* an high mountain apart,
15. falleth *into* the fire, and oft *into* the water.
22. shall be betrayed *into* the hands of men:
24. when they were come *to* Capernaum,
25. when he was come *into* the house,
27. go thou *to* the sea, and cast an hook,
18: 3. ye shall not enter *into* the kingdom of heaven.
6. of these little ones which believe *in* me,
8. better for thee to enter *into* life halt
— to be cast *into* everlasting fire.
9. thee to enter *into* life with one eye,
— having two eyes to be cast *into* hell fire.
15. thy brother shall trespass *against* thee,
20. are gathered together *in* my name,
21. how oft shall my brother sin *against* me,
29. his fellowservant fell down *at* his feet,
30. went and cast him *into* prison,
19: 1. came *into* the coasts of Judæa
5. they twain shall be)(one flesh?
17. if thou wilt enter *into* life,
23. hardly enter *into* the kingdom of heaven.
24. to enter *into* the kingdom of God.
20: 1. to hire labourers *into* his vineyard.
2. he sent them *into* his vineyard.
4. Go ye also *into* the vineyard,
7. Go ye also *into* the vineyard;
17. Jesus going up *to* Jerusalem
18. Behold, we go up *to* Jerusalem;
19. to the Gentiles)(to mock, and to scourge,
21: 1. when they drew nigh *unto* Jerusalem, and were come *to* Bethphage,
2. Go *into* the village over against you,
10. when he was come *into* Jerusalem,
12. Jesus went *into* the temple of God,
17. went out of the city *into* Bethany;
18. as he returned *into* the city,
19. no fruit grow on thee henceforward *for* ever.
21. be thou cast *into* the sea; it shall be done.
23. when he was come *into* the temple,
31. go *into* the kingdom of God before you.
42. same is become)(the head of the corner:
22: 3. that were bidden *to* the wedding:
4. all things (are) ready: come *unto* the marriage.
5. one *to* his farm, another *to* his merchandise:
9. as ye shall find, bid *to* the marriage.
10. servants went out *into* the highways,
13. cast (him) *into* outer darkness;
16. thou regardest not)(the person of men.
23:34. persecute (them) from city *to* city:
24: 9. deliver you up to be afflicted, (lit. *unto* affliction)
13. he that shall endure *unto* the end,
14. *for* a witness unto all nations;
38. the day that Noe entered *into* the ark,
25: 1. went forth to meet (lit. *unto* the meeting) the bridegroom.
6. go ye out to meet him. (lit. *unto* &c.)
10. went in with him *to* the marriage:
21. enter thou *into* the joy of thy lord.
23. enter thou *into* the joy of thy lord.
30. unprofitable servant *into* outer darkness.
41. ye cursed, *into* everlasting fire,
46. go away *into* everlasting punishment: but the righteous *into* life eternal.

Mat.26: 2. Son of man is betrayed *to* be crucified.
3. *unto* the palace of the high priest,
8. *To* what purpose (is) this waste?
10. she hath wrought a good work *upon* me.
13. be told *for* a memorial of her.
18. Go *into* the city to such a man,
28. shed for many *for* the remission of sins
30. they went out *into* the mount of Olives.
32. I will go before you *into* Galilee.
36. *unto* a place called Gethsemane,
41. that ye enter not *into* temptation:
45. betrayed *into* the hands of sinners.
52. Put up again thy sword *into* his place:
67. Then did they spit *in* his face,
71. when he was gone out *into* the porch,
27: 6. to put them *into* the treasury,
7. the potter's field, to bury strangers in. (lit. *for* the burial of strangers)
10. gave them *for* the potter's field,
27. took Jesus *into* the common hall,
30. they spit *upon* him, and took the reed, and smote him *on* the head.
31. led him away)(to crucify (him).
33. were come *unto* a place called Golgotha,
51. the veil of the temple was rent *in* twain
53. went *into* the holy city, and appeared
28: 1. as it began to dawn *toward* the first
7. he goeth before you *into* Galilee;
10. tell my brethren that they go *into* Galilee,
11. some of the watch came *into* the city,
16. went away *into* Galilee, *into* a mountain
19. baptizing them *in* the name of the Father,
Mar. 1: 4. repentance *for* the remission of sins.
9. was baptized of John *in* Jordan.
12. the spirit driveth him *into* the wilderness.
14. Jesus came *into* Galilee, preaching
21. they went *into* Capernaum;
— he entered *into* the synagogue, and taught.
28. *throughout* all the region round about
29. they entered *into* the house of Simon
35. departed *into* a solitary place,
38. Let us go *into* the next towns,
— for there*fore* came I forth.
39. *throughout* all Galilee, and cast out devils.
44. *for* a testimony unto them.
45. no more openly enter *into* the city,
2: 1. again he entered *into* Capernaum
— it was noised that he was *in* the house.
11. go thy way *into* thine house.
17. the righteous, but sinners *to* repentance.
22. no man putteth new wine *into* old bottles.
— new wine must be put *into* new bottles.
26. How he went *into* the house of God
3: 1. he entered again *into* the synagogue;
3. withered hand, Stand forth. (lit. *into* the midst)
13. he goeth up *into* a mountain,
19(20). they went *into* an house.
27. No man can enter *into* a strong
29. shall blaspheme *against* the Holy Ghost
— hath never (εις τον αιωνα) forgiveness, but is in danger of eternal damnation:
4: 1. so that he entered *into* a ship,
7. some fell *among* thorns.
8. other fell *on* good ground, and did
18. they which are sown *among* thorns;
22. that it should come abroad. (lit. *unto* manifestation)
35. Let us pass over *unto* the other side.
37. the waves beat *into* the ship,
5: 1. *unto* the other side of the sea, *into* the

Mar. 5:12. *into* the swine, that we may enter *into* them.
13. went out, and entered *into* the swine:
— down a steep place *into* the sea,
14. told (it) *in* the city, and *in* the country.
18. when he was come *into* the ship,
19. Go home *to* thy friends, and tell them
21. over again by ship *unto* the other side,
26. nothing bettered, but rather grew)(worse,
34. go *in* peace, and be whole of thy plague.
38. he cometh *to* the house of the ruler
6: 1. came *into* his own country;
8. should take nothing *for* (their) journey,
— no bread, no money *in* (their) purse:
10. what place soever ye enter *into* an house,
11. *for* a testimony against them.
31. ye yourselves apart *into* a desert place,
32. they departed *into* a desert place
36. that they may go *into* the country
41. he looked up *to* heaven, and blessed,
45. to get *into* the ship, and to go *to* the other side
46. he departed *into* a mountain to pray.
51. he went up unto them *into* the ship;
56. whithersoever he entered, *into* villages,
7:15. that entering *into* him can defile him:
17. when he was entered *into* the house
18. entereth *into* the man, (it) cannot defile him;
19. it entereth not *into* his heart, but *into* the belly, and goeth out *into* the draught,
24. went *into* the borders of Tyre
— entered *into* an house, and would have
30. when she was come *to* her house,
33. put his fingers *into* his ears,
34. looking up *to* heaven, he sighed,
8: 3. away fasting *to* their own houses,
10. straightway he entered *into* a ship
— came *into* the parts of Dalmanutha.
13. entering *into* the ship again departed *to* the
19. I brake the five loaves *among* five thousand.
20. when the seven *among* four thousand,
22. he cometh *to* Bethsaida; and they
23. when he had spit *on* his eyes, and put
26. *to* his house, saying, Neither go *into* the town,
27. *into* the towns of Cæsarea Philippi:
9: 2. leadeth them up *into* an high mountain
22. cast him *into* the fire, and *into* the waters,
25. enter no more *into* him.
28. when he was come *into* the house,
31. delivered *into* the hands of men,
33. he came *to* Capernaum:
42. (these) little ones that believe *in* me,
— he were cast *into* the sea.
43. for thee to enter *into* life maimed,
— to go *into* hell, *into* the fire that
45. better for thee to enter halt *into* life,
— to be cast *into* hell, *into* the fire that
47. to enter *into* the kingdom of God
— having two eyes to be cast *into* hell fire:
10: 1. cometh *into* the coasts of Judæa
8. they twain shall be)(one flesh:
15. he shall not enter there*in*.
17. when he was gone forth *into* the way,
23. enter *into* the kingdom of God!
24. in riches to enter *into* the kingdom of God!
25. a rich man to enter *into* the kingdom of God.
32. in the way going up *to* Jerusalem;
33. Behold, we go up *to* Jerusalem;
46. they came *to* Jericho: and as he went
11: 1. they came nigh *to* Jerusalem, *unto*
Mar. 11: 2. Go your way *into* the village
— as soon as ye be entered *into* it,
8. many spread their garments *in* the way:
— branches off the trees, and strawed (them) *in* the way.
11. Jesus entered *into* Jerusalem, and *into* the temple:
— he went out *unto* Bethany with
14. No man eat fruit of thee hereafter *for* ever.
15. they come *to* Jerusalem: and Jesus went *into* the
23. removed, and be thou cast *into* the sea;
27. they come again *to* Jerusalem:
12:10. is become)(the head of the corner:
14. thou regardest not)(the person of men,
41. people cast money *into* the treasury:
43. which have cast *into* the treasury:
13: 3. as he sat *upon* the mount of Olives
9. deliver you up *to* councils; and *in* the synagogues (lit. *unto* the synagogues)
— *for* a testimony against them.
10. first be published *among* all nations.
12. brother shall betray the brother *to* death,
13. he that shall endure *unto* the end,
14. in Judæa flee *to* the mountains:
15. not go down *into* the house,
16. him that is *in* the field not turn)(back
14: 4. Why (lit. *for* what) was this waste of the
6. she hath wrought a good work *on* me.
8. to anoint my body *to* the burying.
9. preached *throughout* the whole world,
— spoken of *for* a memorial of her.
13. saith unto them, Go ye *into* the city,
16. disciples went forth, and came *into* the city,
20. that dippeth with me *in* the dish.
26. they went out *into* the mount of Olives.
28. I will go before you *into* Galilee.
32. they came *to* a place which was
38. lest ye enter *into* temptation.
41. is betrayed *into* the hands of sinners.
54. even *into* the palace of the high priest:
55.)(to put him to death; and found none.
60. the high priest stood up *in* the midst,
68. he went out *into* the porch;
15:34. why (lit. *for* what) hast thou forsaken me?
38. the veil of the temple was rent *in* twain
41. came up with him *unto* Jerusalem.
16: 5. entering *into* the sepulchre,
7. that he goeth before you *into* Galilee:
12. as they walked, and went *into* the country
15. Go ye *into* all the world,
19. he was received up *into* heaven,
Lu. 1: 9. he went *into* the temple of the Lord.
20. which shall be fulfilled *in* their season.
23. he departed *to* his own house.
26. sent from God *unto* a city of Galilee,
33. reign over the house of Jacob *for* ever;
39. went *into* the hill country with haste, *into* a city of Juda;
40. entered *into* the house of Zacharias,
44. thy salutation sounded *in* mine ears,
50. from generation to generation. (lit. *unto* generations of g.)
55. to Abraham, and to his seed *for* ever.
56. three months, and returned *to* her own house.
79. to guide our feet *into* the way of peace.
2: 3. every one *into* his own city.
4. *into* Judæa, *unto* the city of David,
15. gone away from them *into* heaven,
22. they brought him *to* Jerusalem.

Lu. 2:27. he came by the Spirit *into* the temple:
28. took he him up *in* his arms,
32. A light to lighten (lit. *toward* the enlightening) the Gentiles,
34. *for* the fall and rising again of many
— *for* a sign which shall be spoken against;
39. returned *into* Galilee, *to* their own city
41. his parents went *to* Jerusalem
42. they went up *to* Jerusalem
45. they turned back again *to* Jerusalem,
51. with them, and came *to* Nazareth,
3: 3. came *into* all the country about Jordan,
— repentance *for* the remission of sins;
5. crooked shall be made straight, (lit. *into*) and the rough ways (shall be) made smooth; (lit. *into* smooth ways)
9. hewn down, and cast *into* the fire.
17. gather the wheat *into* his garner;
4: 1. led by the Spirit *into* the wilderness,
5. taking him up *into* an high mountain,
9. he brought him *to* Jerusalem,
14. in the power of the Spirit *into* Galilee:
16. he came *to* Nazareth, where he
— he went *into* the synagogue
26. save *unto* Sarepta, (a city) of Sidon,
29. that they might cast him down headlong. (lit. *for* to cast &c.)
31. came down *to* Capernaum,
35. had thrown him *in* the midst,
37. *into* every place of the country
38. entered *into* Simon's house.
42. went *into* a desert place:
43. for there*fore* am I sent.
5: 3. he entered *into* one of the ships.
4. Launch out *into* the deep, and let down your nets *for* a draught.
14. *for* a testimony unto them.
17. was (present) to heal them. (lit. *for* their being healed)
19. *into* the midst before Jesus.
24. go *unto* thine house.
25. departed *to* his own house,
32. righteous, but sinners *to* repentance.
37. new wine *into* old bottles;
38. new wine must be put *into* new bottles,
6: 4. he went *into* the house of God,
6. he entered *into* the synagogue
8. stand forth *in* the midst.
12. he went out *into* a mountain
20. he lifted up his eyes *on* his disciples,
38. shall men give *into* your bosom.
39. both fall *into* the ditch?
7: 1. *in* the audience of the people, he entered *into* Capernaum.
10. returning *to* the house, found
11. he went *into* a city called Nain;
24. What went ye out *into* the wilderness
30. counsel of God *against* themselves, (lit. *towards* themselves.)
36. he went *into* the Pharisee's house,
44. I entered *into* thine house, thou
50. faith hath saved thee; go *in* peace.
8:14. that which fell *among* thorns
17. be known and come abroad. (lit. *unto* manifestation)
22. he went *into* a ship with his disciples.
— Let us go over *unto* the other side
23. a storm of wind *on* the lake;
26. *at* the country of the Gadarenes,
29. driven of the devil *into* the wilderness.
30. many devils were entered *into* him.
31. to go out *into* the deep.

Lu. 8:32. suffer them to enter *into* them.
33. entered *into* the swine:
— down a steep place *into* the lake,
34. told (it) *in* the city and *in* the country.
37. he went up *into* the ship.
39. Return *to* thine own house,
41. that he would come *into* his house:
43. spent all her living *upon* physicians
48. made thee whole; go *in* peace.
51. when he came *into* the house,
9: 3. Take nothing *for* (your) journey,
4.)(whatsoever house ye enter into,
5. *for* a testimony against them.
10. aside privately *into* a desert place
12. that they may go *into* the towns
13. buy meat *for* all this people.
16. looking up *to* heaven, he
28. went up *into* a mountain to pray.
34. as they entered *into* the cloud.
44. these sayings sink down *into* your ears.
— delivered *into* the hands of men.
51. set his face to go *to* Jerusalem,
52. *into* a village of the Samaritans,
53. though he would go *to* Jerusalem.
56. they went *to* another village.
61. which are at home *at* my house.
62. hand to the plough, and looking)(back is fit *for* the kingdom of God.
10: 1. *into* every city and place, whither
2. send forth labourers *into* his harvest.
5. *into* whatsoever house ye enter,
7. Go not from house *to* house.
8. *into* whatsoever city ye enter,
10. *into* whatsoever city ye enter,
— go your ways out *into* the streets
30. down from Jerusalem *to* Jericho,
34. brought him *to* an inn,
36. him that fell *among* the thieves?
38. he entered *into* a certain village:
— Martha received him *into* her house.
11: 4. lead us not *into* temptation;
7. my children are with me *in* bed;
24. I will return *unto* my house whence
32. they repented *at* the preaching of
33. putteth (it) *in* a secret place,
49. I will send)(them prophets and apostles,
12: 5. hath power to cast *into* hell;
10. speak a word *against* the Son of man,
— blasphemeth *against* the Holy Ghost
19. goods laid up *for* many years;
21. is not rich *toward* God.
28. to morrow is cast *into* the oven;
49. come to send fire *on* the earth;
58. the officer cast thee *into* prison.
13: 9. if not, (then) after that (lit. *for* afterwards) thou shalt cut it down.
11. bowed together, and could *in* no wise lift up (herself).
19. took, and cast *into* his garden; and it grew, and waxed)(a great tree;
21. hid *in* three measures of meal,
22. teaching, and journeying *toward* Jerusalem.
14: 1. as he went *into* the house of one
5. an ass or an ox fallen *into* a pit,
8. bidden of any (man) *to* a wedding, sit not down *in* the highest
10. sit down *in* the lowest room;
21. Go out quickly *into* the streets
23. Go out *into* the highways and hedges,
31. to make war (lit. to enter *upon* war) against another king,
35: fit *for* the land, nor yet *for* the dunghill;

Lu. 15: 6. when he cometh)(home, he calleth
13. took his journey *into* a far country,
15. he sent him *into* his fields to feed swine.
17. when he came *to* himself,
18. I have sinned *against* heaven,
21. I have sinned *against* heaven,
22. put a ring *on* his hand, and shoes *on* (his) feet:
16: 4. may receive me *into* their houses.
8. are *in* (lit. *towards*) their generation wiser
9. receive you *into* everlasting habitations.
16. every man presseth *into* it.
22. by the angels *into* Abraham's bosom:
27. send him *to* my father's house:
28. come *into* this place of torment.
17: 2. about his neck, and he cast *into* the sea,
3. If thy brother trespass *against* thee,
4. if he trespass *against* thee seven
11. as he went *to* Jerusalem, that
12. he entered *into* a certain village,
24. shineth *unto* the other (part) under
27. that Noe entered *into* the ark,
31. let him likewise not return)(back.
18: 5. by her continual coming (lit. coming *for* ever) she weary me.
10. Two men went up *into* the temple to pray;
13. so much as (his) eyes *unto* heaven, but smote *upon* his breast, saying,
14. this man went down *to* his house
17. shall in no wise enter there*in*.
24. enter *into* the kingdom of God!
25. a rich man to enter *into* the kingdom
31. Behold, we go up *to* Jerusalem,
35. he was come nigh *unto* Jericho,
19: 12. nobleman went *into* a far country
28. ascending up *to* Jerusalem.
29. he was come nigh *to* Bethphage
30. Go ye *into* the village over against
45. he went *into* the temple, and began
20: 17. the same is become)(the head of the
20. that so they might deliver (lit. *for* to deliver) him unto the
21: 1. casting their gifts *into* the treasury.
4. cast *in unto* the offerings of God·
12. *to* the synayogues, and into prisons,
13. it shall turn to you *for* a testimony.
14. Settle (it) therefore *in* your hearts,
21. in Judæa flee *to* the mountains;
— are in the countries enter there*into*.
24. led away captive *into* all nations:
37. went out, and abode *in* the mount
22: 3. Then entered Satan *into* Judas
10. when ye are entered *into* the city,
— follow him *into* the house
19. this do *in* (lit. *unto*) remembrance of me.
33. both *into* prison, and *to* death.
39. *to* the mount of Olives;
40. that ye enter not *into* temptation.
46. lest ye enter *into* temptation.
54. him *into* the high priest's house.
65. blasphemously spake they *against* him.
66. led him *into* their council,
23: 19. for murder, was cast *into* prison.
25. for sedition and murder was cast *into* prison,
46. *into* thy hands I commend my
24: 5. down (their) faces *to* the earth,
7. delivered *into* the hands of sinful men,
13. went that same day *to* a village
20. delivered him *to* be condemned to death,
26. and to enter *into* his glory?

Lu. 24: 28. they drew nigh *unto* the village,
33. returned *to* Jerusalem, and found
47. in his name *among* all nations,
50. led them out as far as *to* Bethany,
51. from them, and carried up *into* heaven.
52. returned *to* Jerusalem with great joy:
Joh. 1: 7. The same came *for* a witness,
9. that cometh *into* the world.
11. He came *unto* his own,
12. them that believe *on* his name.
18. which is *in* the bosom of the Father,
43(44). Jesus would go forth *into* Galilee,
2: 2. called, and his disciples, *to* the marriage
11. his disciples believed *on* him.
12. he went down *to* Capernaum,
13. Jesus went up *to* Jerusalem,
23. many believed *in* his name,
3: 4. second time *into* his mother's womb,
5. enter *into* the kingdom of God.
13. no man hath ascended up *to* heaven,
15. That whosoever believeth *in* him
16. that whosoever believeth *in* him
17. sent not his Son *into* the world to
18. He that believeth *on* him is not
— hath not believed *in* the name of
19. that light is come *into* the world,
22. his disciples *into* the land of Judæa;
24. John was not yet cast *into* prison
36. He that believeth *on* the Son hath
4: 3. departed again *into* Galilee.
5. Then cometh he *to* a city of Samaria,
8. gone away *unto* the city to buy
14. I shall give him shall never (lit. not *for* ever) thirst;
— springing up *into* everlasting life.
28. went her way *into* the city,
36. gathereth fruit *unto* life eternal:
38. ye are entered *into* their labours.
39. believed *on* him for the saying
43. went *into* Galilee.
45. when he was come *into* Galilee,
— they also went *unto* the feast.
46. So Jesus came again *into* Cana
47. was come out of Judæa *into* Galilee,
54. was come out of Judæa *into* Galilee.
5: 1. Jesus went up *to* Jerusalem.
7. to put me *into* the pool:
24. shall not come *into* condemnation; but is passed from death *unto* life.
29. *unto* the resurrection of life;
— *unto* the resurrection of damnation.
45. (even) Moses, *in* whom ye trust.
6: 3. Jesus went up *into* a mountain,
9. what are they *among* so many?
14. that should come *into* the world.
15. he departed again *into* a mountain
17. entered *into* a ship, and went over the sea *toward* Capernaum.
21. received him *into* the ship:
— at the land whither (lit. *unto* which) they went.
22. where*into* his disciples were entered.
— with his disciples *into* the boat,
24. took shipping (lit. entered *into* ships), and came *to* Capernaum,
27. endureth *unto* everlasting life,
29. believe *on* him whom he hath sent.
35. he that believeth *on* me shall never thirst
40. seeth the Son, and believeth *on* him
47. He that believeth *on* me hath
51. he shall live *for* ever: and the bread
58. eateth of this bread shall live *for* ever.

Joh. 6:66. many of his disciples went)(back.
7: 3. Depart hence, and go *into* Judæa,
5. neither did his brethren believe *in* him.
8. Go ye up *unto* this feast: I go not up yet *unto* this feast:
10. went he also up *unto* the feast,
14. Jesus went up *into* the temple,
31. many of the people believed *on* him,
35. will he go *unto* the dispersed among
38. He that believeth *on* me, as the
39. they that believe *on* him should
48. the Pharisees believed *on* him?
53. every man went *unto* his own house.
8 1. Jesus went *unto* the mount of Olives.
2. he came again *into* the temple,
6. with (his) finger wrote *on* the ground,
8. stooped down, and wrote *on* the ground.
26. I speak *to* (lit. *into*) the world those things
30. many believed *on* him.
35. abideth not in the house *for* ever: (but) the Son abideth)(ever.
51. he shall never see death. (εις τον αιωνα)
52. he shall never taste of death. (εις &c.)
9: 7. Go, wash *in* the pool of Siloam,
11. Go *to* the pool of Siloam, and wash:
35. Dost thou believe *on* the Son of God?
36. that I might believe *on* him?
39. *For* judgment I am come *into* this
10: 1. by the door *into* the sheepfold,
28. shall never perish, (εις τον αιωνα)
36. sanctified, and sent *into* the world,
40. *into* the place where John at first
42. many believed *on* him there.
11: 7. Let us go *into* Judæa again.
25. he that believeth *in* me,
26. whosoever liveth and believeth *in* me shall never die. (εις τον αιωνα)
27. which should come *into* the world.
30. Jesus was not yet come *into* the town,
31. She goeth *unto* the grave to weep
32. she fell down *at* his feet, saying
38. himself cometh *to* the grave.
45. which Jesus did, believed *on* him.
48. all (men) will believe *on* him:
52. he should gather together *in* one
54. went thence *unto* a country near
— *into* a city called Ephraim,
55. up *to* Jerusalem before the passover,
56. that he will not come *to* the feast?
12: 1. before the passover came *to* Bethany,
7. *against* the day of my burying
11. went away, and believed *on* Jesus.
12. people that were come *to* the feast,
— that Jesus was coming *to* Jerusalem,
13. went forth to meet (lit. *to* the meeting) him, and cried,
24. a corn of wheat fall *into* the ground
25. shall keep it *unto* life eternal.
27. for this cause came I *unto* this hour.
34. that Christ abideth *for* ever:
36. believe *in* the light, that ye may
37. yet they believed not *on* him:
42. rulers also many believed *on* him;
44. believeth *on* me, believeth not *on* me, but *on* him that sent me.
46. I am come a light *into* the world, that whosoever believeth *on* me
13: 1. he loved them *unto* the end.
2. put *into* the heart of Judas Iscariot,
3. had given all things *into* his hands,
5. he poureth water *into* a bason,
8. Thou shalt never (lit. not *for* ever) wash

Joh. 13:22. disciples looked one *on* another,
27. after the sop Satan entered *into* him.
29. we have need of *against* the feast;
14: 1. believe *in* God, believe also *in* me.
12. He that believeth *on* me, the works
16. he may abide with you *for* ever;
15: 6. cast (them) *into* the fire, and they
16: 9. because they believe not *on* me;
13. he will guide you *into* all truth:
20. your sorrow shall be turned *into* joy.
21. that a man is born *into* the world.
28. am come *into* the world:
32. scattered, every man *to* his own,
17: 1. lifted up his eyes *to* heaven,
18. thou hast sent me *into* the world,
— I also sent them *into* the world.
20. which shall believe *on* me through
23. they may be made perfect *in* one;
18: 1. a garden, *into* the which he entered,
6. they went back*ward*, and fell to the
11. Put up thy sword *into* the sheath:
15. *into* the palace of the high priest.
28. *unto* the hall of judgment:
— went not *into* the judgment hall,
33. Pilate entered *into* the judgment hall
37. *To* this end was I born, and *for* this cause came I *into* the world,
19: 9. went again *into* the judgment hall,
13. *in* a place that is called the Pavement,
17. went forth *into* a place called
27. took her *unto* his own (home).
37. They shall look *on* him whom
20: 1. *unto* the sepulchre, and seeth the
3. that other disciple, and came *to* the
4. came first *to* the sepulchre.
6. went *into* the sepulchre,
7. wrapped together *in* a place by itself.
8. came first *to* the sepulchre,
11. (looked) *into* the sepulchre,
14. she turned herself)(back, and saw
19. came Jesus and stood *in* the midst,
25. my finger *into* the print of the nails, and thrust my hand *into* his side,
26. stood *in* the midst, and said,
27. thrust (it) *into* my side: and be
21: 3. entered *into* a ship immediately;
4. Jesus stood *on* the shore:
6. Cast the net *on* the right side of the
7. did cast himself *into* the sea.
9. then as they were come *to* land,
23. this saying abroad *among* the brethren,
Acts 1:10. looked stedfastly *toward* heaven
11. why stand ye gazing up *into* heaven?
— is taken up from you *into* heaven,
— have seen him go *into* heaven.
12. returned they *unto* Jerusalem
13. they went up *into* an upper room,
25. he might go *to* his own place.
2:20. The sun shall be turned *into* darkness, and the moon *into* blood,
22. a man approved of God *among* you by miracles
25. David speaketh *concerning* him,
27. thou wilt not leave my soul *in* hell.
31. his soul was not left *in* hell,
34. not ascended *into* the heavens:
38. *for* the remission of sins,
39. to all that are afar off, (lit. *at* a distance)
3: 1. up together *into* the temple
2. them that entered *into* the temple;
3. Peter and John about to go *into* the temple
4. fastening his eyes *upon* him with John

Acts 3: 8. entered with them *into* the temple,
19. that your sins may be blotted out, (lit. *unto* your sins being blotted out)
4: 3. put (them) *in* hold *unto* the next day:
6. gathered together *at* Jerusalem.
11. is become)(the head of the corner.
17. spread no further *among* the people,
30. stretching forth thine hand to heal; (lit. *to* the healing)
5:16. round about *unto* Jerusalem,
21. they entered *into* the temple
— sent *to* the prison to have them
36. were scattered, and brought *to* nought.
6:11. blasphemous words *against* Moses,
12. brought (him) *to* the council.
15. looking stedfastly *on* him,
7: 3. come *into* the land which I
4. he removed him *into* this land, wherein ye now dwell
5. give it to him *for* a possession,
9. with envy, sold Joseph *into* Egypt:
15. Jacob went down *into* Egypt,
16. were carried over *into* Sychem,
19. *to the end* they might not live.
21. nourished him *for* her own son.
26. have set them *at* one again,
34. I will send thee *into* Egypt.
39. hearts turned back again *into* Egypt,
53. *by* the disposition of angels,
55. looked up stedfastly *into* heaven,
8: 3. committed (them) *to* prison.
5. Philip went down *to* the city of Samaria,
16. *in* the name of the Lord Jesus.
20. Thy money perish (lit. be *unto* destruction) with thee,
23. thou art *in* the gall of bitterness,
25. the Lord, returned *to* Jerusalem,
26. down from Jerusalem *unto* Gaza,
27. had come *to* Jerusalem for to
38. went down both *into* the water,
40. Philip was found *at* Azotus:
— till he came *to* Cæsarea.
9: 1. *against* the disciples of the Lord,
2. desired of him letters *to* Damascus
— bring them bound *unto* Jerusalem.
6. Arise, and go *into* the city, and it
8. brought (him) *into* Damascus.
17. went his way, and entered *into* the house;
21. came hither *for* that *intent*, that he
26. when Saul was come *to* Jerusalem,
30. *to* Cæsarea, and sent him forth *to* Tarsus.
39. brought him *into* the upper chamber:
10: 4. are come up *for* a memorial
5. now send men *to* Joppa,
8. unto them, he sent them *to* Joppa.
16. was received up again *into* heaven.
22. to send for thee *into* his house,
24. after they entered *into* Cæsarea.
32. Send therefore *to* Joppa, and call
43. whosoever believeth *in* him
11: 2. when Peter was come up *to* Jerusalem,
6. *Upon* the which when I had fastened
8. at any time entered *into* my mouth.
10. all were drawn up again *into* heaven.
12. we entered *into* the man's house:
13. Send men *to* Joppa, and call
18. granted repentance *unto* life.
20. when they were come *to* Antioch,
22. came *unto* the ears of the church
25. Then departed Barnabas *to* Tarsus,
26(25). he brought him *unto* Antioch.
27. prophets from Jerusalem *unto* Antioch.

Acts11:29. to send)(relief unto the brethren
12: 4. put (him) *in* prison, and delivered
10. gate that leadeth *unto* the city;
17. departed, and went *into* another place.
19. went down from Judæa *to* Cæsarea,
13: 2. *for* the work whereunto I have
4. departed *unto* Seleucia; and from thence they sailed *to* Cyprus.
9. Holy Ghost, set his eyes *on* him,
13. they came *to* Perga in Pamphylia
— from them returned *to* Jerusalem.
14. they came *to* Antioch in Pisidia, and went *into* the synagogue on the
22. raised up unto them David to be their king; (lit. *for* a king)
29. laid (him) *in* a sepulchre.
31. with him from Galilee *to* Jerusalem,
34. no more to return *to* corruption,
42. preached to them)(the next sabbath.
46. lo, we turn *to* the Gentiles.
47. I have set thee to be a light (lit. *for* a light)
— that thou shouldest be *for* salvation unto
48. as were ordained *to* eternal life
51. against them, and came *unto* Iconium.
14: 1. *into* the synagogue of the Jews,
6. fled *unto* Lystra and Derbe, cities of
14. ran *in among* the people, crying
20. rose up, and came *into* the city:
— he departed with Barnabas *to* Derbe.
21. they returned again *to* Lystra,
22. enter *into* the kingdom of God.
23. the Lord, *on* whom they believed.
24. they came *to* Pamphylia.
25. they went down *into* Attalia:
26. thence sailed *to* Antioch,
— *for* the work which they fulfilled.
15: 2. should go up *to* Jerusalem
4. when they were come *to* Jerusalem
22. of their own company *to* Antioch
30. were dismissed, they came *to* Antioch:
38. went not with them *to* the work.
39. took Mark, and sailed *unto* Cyprus;
16: 1. Then came he *to* Derbe and Lystra:
8. by Mysia came down *to* Troas.
9. saying, Come over *into* Macedonia,
10. to go *into* Macedonia,
11. with a straight course *to* Samothracia, and the next (day) *to* Neapolis;
12. from thence *to* Philippi,
15. come *into* my house, and abide
16. came to pass, as we went *to* prayer,
19. drew (them) *into* the marketplace
23. they cast (them) *into* prison,
24. thrust them *into* the inner prison, and made their feet fast *in* the stocks.
34. had brought them *into* his house,
37. have cast (us) *into* prison;
40. entered *into* (the house of) Lydia:
17: 1. they came *to* Thessalonica,
5. to bring them out *to* the people.
10. Paul and Silas by night *unto* Berea:
— *into* the synagogue of the Jews.
20. certain strange things *to* our ears:
21. spent their time *in* nothing else,
18: 1. departed from Athens, and came *to* Corinth;
6. I will go *unto* the Gentiles.
7. entered *into* a certain (man's) house,
18. sailed thence *into* Syria,
19. he came *to* Ephesus, and left them
— himself entered *into* the synagogue,
21. this feast that cometh *in* Jerusalem:

Acts18:22. when he had landed *at* Cæsarea,
— he went down *to* Antioch.
24. mighty in the scriptures, came *to* Ephesus.
27. was disposed to pass *into* Achaia,
1. through the upper coasts came *to* Ephesus:
3. *Unto* what then were ye baptized? and they said, *Unto* John's baptism.
4. believe *on* him which should come after him, that is, *on* Christ Jesus.
5. *in* the name of the Lord Jesus.
8. he went *into* the synagogue,
21. to go *to* Jerusalem, saying,
22. So he sent *into* Macedonia two
— he himself stayed *in* Asia
27. in danger to be set at nought; (lit. should come *into* reprobation)
— goddess Diana should be despised, (lit. be reckoned *for* nothing)
29. rushed with one accord *into* the theatre.
30. entered *in unto* the people,
31. not adventure himself *into* the theatre.
20: 1. for to go *into* Macedonia.
2. he came *into* Greece,
3. was about to sail *into* Syria,
6. came unto them *to* Troas
13. before to ship, and sailed *unto* Assos,
14. when he met with us *at* Assos, we took him in, and came *to* Mitylene.
15. next (day) we arrived *at* Samos,
— next (day) we came *to* Miletus.
16. for him, to be *at* Jerusalem
17. from Miletus he sent *to* Ephesus,
18. the first day that I came *into* Asia,
21. repentance *toward* God, and faith
22. bound in the spirit *unto* Jerusalem,
29. grievous wolves enter *in among* you,
38. they accompanied him *unto* the ship.
21: 1. course *unto* Coos, and the (day) following *unto* Rhodes, and from thence *unto* Patara:
2. a ship sailing over *unto* Phenicia,
3. sailed *into* Syria, and landed *at* Tyre.
4. should not go up *to* Jerusalem.
6. leave one of another, we took (lit. embarked *into*) ship; and they returned)(home again.
7. from Tyre, we came *to* Ptolemais,
8. *unto* Cæsarea. and we entered *into* the house
11. *into* the hands of the Gentiles.
12. not to go up *to* Jerusalem.
13. also to die *at* Jerusalem for the
15. went up *to* Jerusalem.
17. when we were come *to* Jerusalem,
26. with them entered *into* the temple,
28. brought Greeks also *into* the temple,
29. Paul had brought *into* the temple.
34. to be carried *into* the castle.
37. Paul was to be led *into* the castle,
38. leddest out *into* the wilderness
22: 4. delivering *into* prisons both men
5. unto the brethren, and went *to* Damascus,
— were there bound *unto* Jerusalem,
7. I fell *unto* the ground, and heard
10. Arise, and go *into* Damascus;
11. with me, I came *into* Damascus.
13. same hour I looked up *upon* him.
17. when I was come again *to* Jerusalem,
21. send thee far hence *unto* the Gentiles.
23. threw dust *into* the air,
24. to be brought *into* the castle,
30. set him *before* them.

Acts23:10. to bring (him) *into* the castle.
11. hast testified of me *in* Jerusalem,
— must thou bear witness also *at* Rome.
16. went and entered *into* the castle,
20. to morrow *into* the council,
28. I brought him forth *into* their council:
30. the Jews laid wait *for* the man,
31. by night *to* Antipatris.
32. with him, and returned *to* the castle:
33. when they came *to* Cæsarea,
24:15. have hope *toward* God, which
17. to bring alms *to* my nation,
24. concerning the faith *in* Christ
25: 1. ascended from Cæsarea *to* Jerusalem.
3. send for him *to* Jerusalem,
6. he went down *unto* Cæsarea;
8. *against* the law of the Jews, neither *against* the temple, nor yet *against* Cæsar,
9. Wilt thou go up *to* Jerusalem,
13. Agrippa and Bernice came *unto* Cæsarea
15. when I was *at* Jerusalem,
16. to deliver any man to die, (lit. *unto* death)
20. I doubted of such manner *of* questions, (lit. *as to* the investigation about this)
— whether he would go *to* Jerusalem,
21. *unto* the hearing of Augustus,
23. entered *into* the place of hearing,
26: 7. *Unto* which (promise) our twelve
11. even *unto* strange cities.
12. as I went *to* Damascus with
14. we were all fallen *to* the earth,
16. appeared unto thee *for* this *purpose*,
17. *unto* whom now I send thee,
18. turn (them) from darkness *to* light,
— sanctified by faith that is *in* me.
20. *throughout* all the coasts of Judæa,
24. much learning doth make thee mad. (lit. perverts thee *to* madness)
27: 1. that we should sail *into* Italy,
3. next (day) we touched *at* Sidon.
5. we came *to* Myra, (a city) of Lycia.
6. ship of Alexandria sailing *into* Italy; and he put us there*in*.
8. came *unto* a place which is called
12. they might attain *to* Phenice,
17. should fall *into* the quicksands,
26. must be cast *upon* a certain island.
29. should have fallen *upon* rocks,
30. let down the boat *into* the sea,
38. cast out the wheat *into* the sea.
39. *into* the which they were minded,
40. committed (themselves) *unto* the sea,
— to the wind, and made *toward* shore.
41. *into* a place where two seas met,
28: 5. shook off the beast *into* the fire,
6. saw no harm come *to* him,
12. landing *at* Syracuse, we
13. fetched a compass, and came *to* Rhegium.
— we came the next day *to* Puteoli:
14. so we went *toward* Rome.
15. they came to meet (lit. *unto* the meeting) us as far
16. when we came *to* Rome,
17. *into* the hands of the Romans.
23. came many to him *into* (his) lodging;
Ro 1: 1. separated *unto* the gospel of God,
5. *for* obedience to the faith
11. *to the end* ye may be established;
16. *unto* salvation to every one
17. revealed from faith *to* faith:
20. *so that* they are without excuse
24. gave them up *to* uncleanness

Ro. 1:25. who is blessed *for* ever.
26. them up *unto* vile affections:
— *into* that which is against nature:
27. lust one *toward* another;
28. over *to* a reprobate mind,
2: 4. God leadeth thee *to* repentance?
26. be counted *for* circumcision?
3: 7. through my lie *unto* his glory,
22. *unto* all and upon all them
25. to declare (lit. *unto* the demonstration of) his righteousness
26. that he might be (lit. *unto* his being) just,
4: 3. counted unto him *for* righteousness.
5. faith is counted *for* righteousness.
9. reckoned to Abraham *for* righteousness.
11. that he might be the father (lit. *unto* his being the father)
— that righteousness might be imputed (lit. *unto* righteousness being imputed)
16. *to the end* the promise might be
18. that he might become the father (lit. *unto* his becoming)
20. staggered not *at* the promise of God
22. imputed to him *for* righteousness.
5: 2. access by faith *into* this grace
8. commendeth his love *toward* us,
12. sin entered *into* the world,
— so death passed *upon* (lit. *towards*) all men,
15. hath abounded *unto* many.
16. (was) by one *to* condemnation,
— of many offences *unto* justification.
18. *upon* all men *to* condemnation;
— *upon* all men *unto* justification
21. through righteousness *unto* eternal life
6: 3. baptized *into* Jesus Christ were baptized *into* his death?
4. with him by baptism *into* death:
12. that ye should obey it (lit. *unto* obeying it)
16. servants to obey, (lit. *unto* obedience)
— whether of sin *unto* death, or of obedience *unto* righteousness?
17. that form of doctrine which was delivered you. (lit. *unto* which you were delivered)
19. uncleanness and to iniquity *unto* iniquity;
— servants to righteousness *unto* holiness.
22. have your fruit *unto* holiness,
7: 4. that ye should be married to another, (lit. *unto* your becoming another's)
5. to bring (lit. *unto* bringing) forth fruit unto death.
10. which (was ordained) to life (lit. *unto* life), I found (to be) *unto* death.
8: 7. carnal mind (is) enmity *against* God:
15. spirit of bondage again *to* (lit. *unto*) fear;
18. which shall be revealed *in* us.
21. *into* the glorious liberty of the
28. all things work together *for* good
29. that he might be (lit. *unto* his being) the firstborn
9. 5. over all, God blessed *for* ever.
8. the children of the promise are counted *for* the seed.
17. Even *for* this same *purpose* have I raised
21. *unto* honour, and another *unto* dishonour?
22. of wrath fitted *to* (lit. *unto*) destruction:
23. had afore prepared *unto* glory,
31. *to* the law of righteousness.
10: 1. that they might be saved. (lit. is *unto* their salvation)
4. the law *for* righteousness to every
6. Who shall ascend *into* heaven?
7. Who shall descend *into* the deep?

Ro. 10:10. man believeth *unto* righteousness,
— confession is made *unto* salvation.
12. rich *unto* all that call upon him.
14. *in* whom they have not believed?
18. their sound went *into* all the earth,
— words *unto* the ends of the world.
11: 9. their table be made)(a snare, and)(a trap, and)(a stumblingblock, and)(a recompence
11. *for* to provoke them to jealousy.
24. *into* a good olive tree:
32. hath concluded them all *in* unbelief,
36. through him, and *to* (lit. *for* or *unto*) him, (are) all things: to whom (be) glory *for* ever.
12: 2. that ye may prove (lit. *unto* your proving)
3. to think soberly, (lit. *unto* being soberminded)
10. kindly affectioned one *to* another
16. the same mind one *toward* another.
13: 4. minister of God to thee *for* good.
— a revenger *to* (execute) wrath upon him
6. attending continually *upon* this
14. for the flesh, to (fulfil) the lusts (lit. *unto* lusts)
14: 1. not *to* doubtful disputations.
9. For *to* this *end* Christ both died,
19. wherewith one may edify another. (lit. of edification *towards* each other)
15: 2. *for* (his) good to edification.
4. were written *for* our learning,
7. received us *to* the glory of God.
8. to confirm (lit. *unto* confirming) the promises (made)
13. that ye may abound (lit. *unto* your abounding) in hope,
16. That I should be (lit. *unto* my being) the minister of Jesus Christ *to* the Gentiles,
18. to make the Gentiles obedient, (lit. *unto* the obedience of the Gentiles)
24. I take my journey *into* Spain,
25. now I go *unto* Jerusalem
26. contribution *for* the poor saints
28. I will come by you *into* Spain.
31. my service which (I have) *for* Jerusalem
16: 5. the firstfruits of Achaia *unto* Christ.
6. bestowed much labour *on* us.
19. obedience is come abroad *unto* all
— wise *unto* that which is good, and simple concerning evil. (lit. *unto* that which is evil)
26. known *to* all nations *for* the obedience of faith:
27. glory through Jesus Christ *for* ever.
1Co. 1: 9. *unto* the fellowship of his Son
13. baptized *in* the name of Paul?
15. baptized *in* mine own name.
2: 7. before the world *unto* our glory:
4: 3. with me it is)(a very small thing
6. transferred *to* myself and (to) Apollos
5: 5. *for* the destruction of the flesh,
6:16. for two, saith he, shall be)(one flesh.
18. sinneth *against* his own body.
8: 6. (are) all things, and we *in* him;
10. to eat (lit. *unto* eating) those things which are offered to idols;
12. ye sin so *against* the brethren,
— ye sin *against* Christ.
13. no flesh while the world standeth, (*εις τον αιωνα*)
9:18. *that* I abuse not my power
10: 2. were all baptized *unto* Moses

1Co.10: 6. *to the intent* we should not lust
11. *upon* whom the ends of the world
31. do all *to* the glory of God.
11:17. not *for* the better, but *for* the worse.
22. houses to eat and to drink in? (lit. *for* eating and drinking)
24. this do *in* (lit. *unto*) remembrance of me.
25. drink (it), *in* (lit. *unto*) remembrance of me.
33. when ye come together *to* eat,
34. not together *unto* condemnation.
12:13. all baptized *into* one body,
— made to drink *into* one Spirit.
14: 8. prepare himself *to* the battle?
9. for ye shall speak *into* the air.
22. Wherefore tongues are *for* a sign,
36. or came it *unto* you only?
15:10. his grace which was (bestowed) *upon* me
45. Adam was made)(a living soul;
— (was made))(a quickening spirit.
54. Death is swallowed up *in* victory.
16: 1. the collection *for* the saints,
3. bring your liberality *unto* Jerusalem.
15. *to* the ministry of the saints,
2Co. 1: 4. that we may be able (lit. *unto* our being able) to comfort
5. as the sufferings of Christ abound *in* us,
10. *in* whom we trust that he will
11. *upon* us by the means of many
16. to pass by you *into* Macedonia,
— brought on my way *toward* Judæa.
21. stablisheth us with you *in* Christ,
23. I came not as yet *unto* Corinth.
2: 4. have more abundantly *unto* you.
8. confirm (your) love *toward* him.
9. *to this end* also did I write,
— ye be obedient *in* all things.
12. when I came *to* Troas to (preach) Christ's gospel, (lit. *for* the gospel of)
13. I went from thence *into* Macedonia.
16. the savour of death *unto* death;
— the savour of life *unto* life.
3: 7. stedfastly behold)(the face of Moses
13. *to* the end of that which is abolished:
18. same image from glory *to* glory,
4: 4. lest the light...should shine unto them. (lit. *unto* the light...not shining unto them)
11. delivered *unto* death for Jesus' sake,
15. redound *to* the glory of God.
17. worketh for us a far more exceeding (lit. according to excess *unto* excess)
5: 5. *for* the selfsame thing (is) God,
6: 1. receive not the grace of God *in* vain.
18. will be)(a Father unto you, and ye shall be my sons (lit. to me *for* sons)
7: 3. to die and live with (you). (lit. *unto* dying together and living with you)
5. when we were come *into* Macedonia,
9. that ye sorrowed *to* repentance:
10. worketh repentance *to* salvation
15. affection is more abundant *toward* you,
8: 2. poverty abounded *unto* the riches
4. the ministering *to* the saints.
6. *Insomuch that* we desired Titus,
— finish *in* you the same grace also.
14(13). (may be a supply) *for* their want,
— may be (a supply) *for* your want:
22. confidence which (I have) *in* you.
23. partner and fellowhelper *concerning* you:
24. *to* them, and *before* (lit. *unto* the face of) the churches,
9: 1. the ministering *to* the saints,

2Co. 9: 5. they would go before *unto* you,
8. all grace abound *toward* you;
— may abound *to* every good work
9. his righteousness remaineth *for* ever.
10. both minister bread *for* (your) food,
11. every thing *to* all bountifulness.
13. subjection *unto* the gospel of Christ,
— distribution *unto* them, and *unto* all
10: 1. being absent am bold *toward* you:
5. *to* the obedience of Christ;
8. *for* edification, and not *for* your destruction,
13. not boast *of* things without (our) measure,
14. though we reached not *unto* you:
15. boasting *of* things without (our) measure,
— according to our rule abundant*ly*,
16. the gospel *in* the (regions) beyond you,
— *of* things made ready to our hand.
11: 3. the simplicity that is *in* Christ.
6. manifest *among* you in all things.
10. no man shall stop me of this boasting (lit. this boasting shall not be stopped *unto* me)
13. themselves *into* the apostles of Christ.
14. transformed *into* an angel of light.
20. if a man smite you *on* the face.
31. Christ, which is blessed *for* evermore,
12: 1. I will come *to* visions and revelations
4. he was caught up *into* paradise,
6. should think *of* me above that
13: 2. that, if I come again, (lit. *to* a return)
3. which *to* you-*ward* is not weak,
4. by the power of God *toward* you.
10. *to* edification, and not *to* destruction.
Gal. 1: 5. To whom (be) glory *for* ever and ever.
6. grace of Christ *unto* another gospel:
17. Neither went I up *to* Jerusalem
— I went *into* Arabia, and returned again *unto* Damascus.
18. I went up *to* Jerusalem to see
21. I came *into* the regions of Syria
2: 1. I went up again *to* Jerusalem
2. I should run, or had run, *in* vain.
8. in Peter *to* the apostleship
— mighty in me *toward* the Gentiles:
9. (should go) *unto* the heathen, and they *unto* the circumcision
11. when Peter was come *to* Antioch,
16. we have believed *in* Jesus Christ,
3: 6. accounted to him *for* righteousness.
14. might come *on* the Gentiles
17. confirmed before of God *in* Christ,
— that it should make (lit. *unto* making) the promise of none effect.
23. shut up *unto* the faith which
24. schoolmaster (to bring us) *unto* Christ,
27. have been baptized *into* Christ
4: 6. Spirit of his Son *into* your hearts,
11. bestowed *upon* you labour in vain.
24. which gendereth *to* bondage,
5:10. I have confidence *in* you through
13. liberty *for* an occasion to the flesh,
6: 4. have rejoicing *in* himself alone, and not *in* another.
8. he that soweth *to* his flesh
— he that soweth *to* the Spirit
Eph. 1: 5. *unto* the adoption of children...*to* himself,
6. *To* the praise of the glory of his
8. hath abounded *toward* us
10. That *in* the dispensation of the
12. That we should be (lit. *unto* our being) *to* the praise of his glory,
14. *until* the redemption of the purchased

Eph. 1:14. *unto* the praise of his glory.
15. love *unto* all the saints,
18. *that* ye may know what is the
19. greatness of his power *to* us-*ward*
2:15. of twain)(one new man, (so)
21. *unto* an holy temple in the Lord:
22. *for* an habitation of God
3: 2. which is given me *to* you-*ward:*
16. his Spirit *in* the inner man;
19. *with* (lit. *into*) all the fulness of God.
21. *throughout* all ages, world without end.
4: 8. When he ascended up *on* high,
9. descended first *into* the lower
12. *for* the work of the ministry, *for* the edifying
13. all come *in* the unity of the faith,
— *unto* a perfect man, *unto* the measure
15. may grow up *into* him in all
16. *unto* the edifying of itself in love.
19. *to* work (lit. *unto* working) all uncleanness
30. sealed *unto* the day of redemption.
32. be ye kind one *to* another,
5: 2. *for* a sweetsmelling savour.
31. they two shall be)(one flesh.
32. I speak *concerning* Christ and)(the church.
6:18. watching there*unto* with all
22. I have sent unto you *for* the same
Phi. 1: 5. For your fellowship *in* the gospel
10. *That* ye may approve things
— *till* the day of Christ;
11. *unto* the glory and praise of God.
12. *unto* the furtherance of the gospel;
17. *for* the defence of the gospel.
19. this shall turn *to* my salvation
23. having a desire to depart, (lit. *for* departing)
25. *for* your furtherance and joy of faith;
29. not only to believe *on* him,
2:11. *to* the glory of God the Father.
16. that I may rejoice (lit. *for* a rejoicing to me) *in* the day of Christ, that I have not run *in* vain, neither laboured *in* vain.
22. hath served with me *in* the gospel.
3:11. *unto* the resurrection of the dead.
16. Nevertheless, where*to* we have already
21. that it may be (lit. *unto* being) fashioned like unto his glorious body,
4:15. *as* concerning (lit. *to* account of) giving and receiving,
16. once and again *unto* my necessity.
17. that may abound *to* your account.
20. (be) glory *for* ever and ever.
Col. 1: 4. love (which ye have) *to* all the saints,
6. Which is come *unto* you, as (it is) in
10. worthy of the Lord *unto* all pleasing,
— increasing *in* the knowledge of God;
11. *unto* all patience and longsuffering
12. to be partakers of (lit. *unto* the sharing) the inheritance
13. *into* the kingdom of his dear Son:
16. were created by him, and *for* him.
20. to reconcile all things *unto* himself;
25. which is given to me *for* you,
29. Where*unto* I also labour, striving
2: 2. *unto* all riches of the full assurance
— *to* the acknowledgement of the
5. stedfastness of your faith *in* Christ.
22. Which all are to perish (lit. *unto* perishing) with the using;
3: 9. Lie not one *to* another, seeing

Col. 3:10. renewed *in* knowledge after
15. *to* the which also ye are called
4: 8. *for* the same *purpose*, that he
11. fellowworkers *unto* the kingdom of God
1Th. 1: 5. came not *unto* you in word only,
2: 9. we preached *unto* you the gospel
12. That ye would walk (lit. *unto* your walking) worthy of God, who hath called you *unto* his kingdom
16. to fill up (lit. *unto* filling up) their sins
— come upon them *to* the uttermost.
3: 2. *to* establish you, and to comfort you
3. that we are appointed there*unto*.
5. I sent *to* know your faith,
— our labour be *in* vain.
10. *that* we might see your face,
12. in love one *toward* another, and *toward* all (men), even as we (do) *toward* you:
13. *To the end* he may stablish
4: 8. also given *unto* us his holy Spirit.
9. taught of God *to* love one another.
10. do it *toward* all the brethren
15. remain *unto* the coming of the Lord
17. to meet (lit. *unto* meeting) the Lord *in* the air:
5: 9. appointed us *to* wrath, but to obtain salvation (lit. *unto* acquisition of salvation)
15. both *among* yourselves, and *to* all
18. in Christ Jesus *concerning* you.
2Th. 1: 3. of you all *toward* each other aboundeth;
5. *that* ye may be counted worthy
11. Where*fore* also we pray always
2: 2. *That* ye be not soon shaken in
4. sitteth *in* the temple of God,
6. *that* he might be revealed in his time.
10. that they might be (lit. *unto* their being) saved.
11. *that* they should believe a lie:
13. chosen you *to* salvation through
14. Where*unto* he called you by our gospel *to* the obtaining of the glory of our
3. 5. *into* the love of God, and *into* the patient
9. an ensample unto you *to* follow us.
1Ti. 1: 3. when I went *into* Macedonia,
6. turned aside *unto* vain jangling;
12. putting me *into* the ministry;
15. came *into* the world to save sinners;
16. believe on him *to* life everlasting.
17. (be) honour and glory *for* ever and ever.
2: 4. to come *unto* the knowledge of the
7. Where*unto* I am ordained a preacher,
3: 6. *into* the condemnation of the devil.
7. lest he fall *into* reproach and the
4: 3. created to be (lit. *unto* being) received with thanksgiving
10. For there*fore* we both labour and suffer
5:24. going before *to* judgment;
6: 7. we brought nothing *into* (this) world,
9. fall *into* temptation and a snare,
— which drown men *in* destruction
12. where*unto* thou art also called,
17. giveth us richly all things *to* enjoy:
19. *against* the time to come,
2Ti. 1:11. Where*unto* I am appointed a
12. committed unto him *against* that day.
2:14. strive not about words *to* no profit,
20. some *to* honour, and some *to* dishonour.
21. he shall be a vessel *unto* honour
— prepared *unto* every good work.
25. *to* the acknowledging of the truth;
26. taken captive by him *at* his will.
3: 6. they which creep *into* houses,

2Ti. 3: 7. never able to come *to* the knowledge
15. to make thee wise *unto* salvation
4: 10. is departed *unto* Thessalonica; Crescens *to* Galatia, Titus *unto* Dalmatia.
11. profitable to me *for* the ministry.
12. Tychicus have I sent *to* Ephesus.
18. *unto* his heavenly kingdom: to whom (be) glory *for* ever and ever.
Tit. 3:12. to come unto me *to* Nicopolis:
14. maintain good works *for* necessary uses,
Philem 5. the Lord Jesus, and *toward* all saints;
6. which is in you *in* Christ Jesus.
Heb. 1: 5. to him)(a Father, and he shall be to me)(a Son?
6. the firstbegotten *into* the world,
8. Thy throne, O God, (is) *for* ever and ever:
14. sent forth *to* minister (lit. *unto* ministering)
2: 3. was confirmed *unto* us by them
10. bringing many sons *unto* glory,
17. to make (lit. *unto* making) reconciliation
3: 5. *for* a testimony of those things
11. They shall not enter *into* my rest.
18. they should not enter *into* his rest,
4: 1. of entering *into* his rest, any of
3. have believed do enter *into* rest,
— if they shall enter *into* my rest:
5. If they shall enter *into* my rest.
6. that some must enter there*in*,
10. he that is entered *into* his rest,
11. labour therefore to enter *into* that rest,
16. grace to (lit. *unto*) help in time of need.
5: 6. Thou (art) a priest *for* ever after
6: 6. renew them again *unto* repentance;
8. end (is) to be burned: (lit. *unto* burning)
10. ye have shewed *toward* his name,
16. an oath *for* confirmation (is) to them
19. entereth *into* that within the veil;
20. made an high priest *for* ever
7: 3. abideth a priest continually. (lit. *for* a continuance)
14. *of* which tribe Moses spake nothing
17. Thou (art) a priest *for* ever after the
21. Thou (art) a priest *for* ever after
24. because he continueth)(ever,
25. to save them *to* the uttermost
— *to* make intercession for them.
28. who is consecrated *for* evermore.
8: 3. high priest is ordained *to* offer gifts
10. will put my laws *into* their mind,
— I will be to them)(a God, and they shall be to me)(a people:
9: 6. went always *into* the first tabernacle,
7. *into* the second (went) the high priest
9. a figure *for* the time then present,
12. entered in once *into* the holy place,
14. *to* serve the living God?
15. *for* the redemption of the transgressions
24. not entered *into* the holy places made
— *into* heaven itself, now to appear
25. entereth *into* the holy place every
26. *to* put away (lit. *unto* the putting away) sin
28. offered *to* bear the sins of many;
— without sin *unto* salvation.
10: 1. offered year by year continually
5. when he cometh *into* the world,
12. *for* ever sat down on the right
14. perfected *for* ever them that
19. boldness *to* enter into the holiest
24. *to* provoke unto love and to good works:
31. to fall *into* the hands of the living God.
39. who draw back *unto* perdition,
Heb 10:39. believe *to* the saving of the soul.
11: 3. *so that* things which are seen
7. an ark *to* the saving of his house,
8. called to go out *into* a place which
— after receive *for* an inheritance.
9. sojourned *in* the land of promise.
11. received strength *to* conceive seed,
26. had respect *unto* the recompence
12: 2. Looking *unto* Jesus the author and
3. contradiction of sinners *against* himself,
10. *that* (we) might be partakers of
13: 8. same yesterday, and to day, and *for* ever
11. blood is brought *into* the sanctuary
21. every good work *to* do his will,
— to whom (be) glory *for* ever and ever.
Jas. 1:18. *that* we should be a kind of
19. swift *to* hear, slow *to* speak, slow *to* wrath.
25. whoso looketh *into* the perfect law
2: 2. if there come *unto* your assembly
6. draw you *before* the judgment seats?
23. imputed unto him *for* righteousness.
3: 3. we put bits *in* the horses' mouths,
4: 9. your laughter be turned *to* mourning, and (your) joy *to* heaviness.
13. we will go *into* such a city,
5: 3. shall be)(a witness against you,
4. entered *into* the ears of the Lord
12. lest ye fall *into* condemnation.
1Pet. 1: 2. *unto* obedience and sprinkling
3. again *unto* a lively hope by the
4. *To* an inheritance incorruptible,
— reserved in heaven *for* you,
5. through faith *unto* salvation
7. be found *unto* praise and honour
8. *in* whom, though now ye see (him) not,
10. grace (that should come) *unto* you:
11. Searching)(what, or what manner of time
— testified beforehand the sufferings *of* Christ,
12. which things the angels desire to look *into*.
21. Who by him do believe *in* God,
— your faith and hope might be *in* God.
22. *unto* unfeigned love of the brethren,
23. which liveth and abideth *for* ever.
25. word of the Lord endureth *for* ever
— the gospel is preached *unto* you.
2: 7. the same is made)(the head of the
8. where*unto* also they were appointed.
9. a peculiar people; (lit. a people *unto* acquisition)
— of darkness *into* his marvellous light:
14. *for* the punishment of evildoers,
21. For even here*unto* were ye called.
3: 7. *that* your prayers be not hindered.
9. that ye are there*unto* called,
12. his ears (are open) *unto* their prayers:
20. where*in* few, that is, eight souls
21. of a good conscience *toward* God,
22. Who is gone *into* heaven, and is on
4: 2. *That* he no longer should live
4. run not with (them) *to* the same excess
6. For *for* this *cause* was the gospel
7. therefore sober, and watch *unto* prayer.
8. fervent charity *among* yourselves.
9. Use hospitality one *to* another
10. minister the same one *to* another,
11. praise and dominion *for* ever and ever
5: 10. called us *unto* his eternal glory
11. glory and dominion *for* ever and ever
12. grace of God where*in* ye stand.
2Pet. 1. 8. *in* the knowledge of our Lord Jesus

2Pet.1:11. *in* the everlasting kingdom of
17. *in* whom I am well pleased.
4. to be reserved *unto* judgment;
9. *unto* the day of judgment to
12. made *to* be taken and destroyed,
17. darkness is reserved *for* ever.
22. *to* her wallowing in the mire.
3: 7. *against* the day of judgment
9. is longsuffering *to* us-*ward*,
— that all should come *to* repentance.
18. To him (be) glory both now and *for* ever.
1Joh.2:17. the will of God abideth *for* ever.
3: 8. *For* this *purpose* the Son of God was
14. have passed from death *unto* life,
4: 1. are gone out *into* the world.
9. only begotten Son *into* the world,
5: 8. these three agree *in* one.
10. He that believeth *on* the Son
— believeth not)(the record that God
13. believe *on* the name of the Son
— believe *on* the name of the Son of God.
2Joh. 2. shall be with us *for* ever.
7. deceivers are entered *into* the world,
10. receive him not *into* (your) house,
3Joh. 5. doest *to* the brethren, and *to* strangers,
Jude 4. ordained *to* this condemnation,
— grace of our God *into* lasciviousness,
6. *unto* the judgment of the great day.
13. the blackness of darkness *for* ever.
21. *unto* eternal life.
25. and power, both now and)(ever.
Rev. 1: 6. glory and dominion *for* ever and ever.
11. What thou seest, write *in* a book,
— *unto* Ephesus, and *unto* Smyrna, and *unto* Pergamos, and *unto* Thyatira, and *unto* Sardis, and *unto* Philadelphia, and *unto* Laodicea.
18. behold, I am alive *for* evermore,
2:10. shall cast (some) of you *into* prison,
22. Behold, I will cast her *into* a bed,
— with her *into* great tribulation,
4: 9. who liveth *for* ever and ever,
10. worship him that liveth *for* ever
5: 6. sent forth *into* all the earth.
13. unto the Lamb *for* ever and ever.
14. him that liveth *for* ever and ever.
6:13. stars of heaven fell *unto* the earth,
15. *in* the dens and *in* the rocks of the
7:12. unto our God *for* ever and ever.
8: 5. of the altar, and cast (it) *into* the earth:
7. they were cast *upon* the earth:
8. with fire was cast *into* the sea:
11. part of the waters became)(wormwood;
9: 1. a star fall from heaven *unto* the earth:
3. of the smoke locusts *upon* the earth:
7. like unto horses prepared *unto* battle;
9. of many horses running *to* battle.
15. were prepared *for* an hour, and a day,
10: 5. lifted up his hand *to* heaven,
6. by him that liveth *for* ever and ever,
11: 6. over waters to turn them *to* blood,
9. suffer their dead bodies to be put *in* graves.
12. they ascended up *to* heaven in
15. he shall reign *for* ever and ever.
12: 4. did cast them *to* the earth:
6. the woman fled *into* the wilderness,
9. he was cast out *into* the earth,
13. that he was cast *unto* the earth.
14. fly *into* the wilderness, *into* her place,
13: 3. as it were wounded *to* death;
6. *in* blasphemy against God,
10. shall go *into* captivity:
Rev.13:13. down from heaven *on* the earth
14:11. ascendeth up *for* ever and ever:
19. thrust in his sickle *into* the earth.
— and cast (it) *into* the great wine press
15: 7. God, who liveth *for* ever and ever.
8. was able to enter *into* the temple,
16: 1. the wrath of God *upon* the earth
2. grievous sore *upon* the men
3. poured out his vial *upon* the sea;
4. poured out his vial *upon* the rivers and)(fountains of waters;
14. *to* the battle of that great day
16. together *into* a place called in
17. poured out his vial *into* the air;
19. city was divided *into* three parts,
17: 3. in the spirit *into* the wilderness:
8. go *into* perdition: and they that
11. of the seven, and goeth *into* perdition.
17. God hath put *in* their hearts
18:21. a great millstone, and cast (it) *into* the sea,
19: 3. her smoke rose up *for* ever and ever.
9. called *unto* the marriage supper
17. *unto* the supper of the great God;
20. both were cast alive *into* a lake
20: 3. cast him *into* the bottomless pit,
8. to gather them together *to* battle:
10. was cast *into* the lake of fire
— day and night *for* ever and ever.
14. death and hell were cast *into* the lake
15. was cast *into* the lake of fire.
21:24. bring their glory and honour *into* it.
26. glory and honour of the nations *into* it.
27. shall in no wise enter *into* it
22: 2. *for* the healing of the nations.
5. they shall reign *for* ever and ever.
14. in through the gates *into* the city.

1520 271 229/299 3391,3762
cf 1527,3367

εἷς, ἕν, *heis, hen.*

(μία, see in its place.)

Mat. 5:18. *one* jot or one tittle shall in no wise
29. that *one* of thy members should perish,
30. that *one* of thy members should
41. shall compel thee to go *a* mile
6:24. for either he will hate the *one*,
— or else he will hold to the *one*,
27. can add *one* cubit unto his stature?
29. was not arrayed like *one* of these.
8:19. *a certain* scribe came, and said
10:29. *one* of them shall not fall on the
42. unto *one* of these little ones a cup
12:11. that shall have *one* sheep, and if it
13:46. when he had found *one* pearl
16:14. Jeremias, or *one* of the prophets.
18: 5. shall receive *one* such little child
6. shall offend *one* of these little ones
10. despise not *one* of these little ones;
12. *one* of them be gone astray,
14. that *one* of these little ones should
16. take with thee *one* or two more.
24. *one* was brought unto him,
28. found *one* of his fellowservants,
19:16. behold, *one* came and said unto him,
17. none good but *one*, (that is), God:
20:13. he answered *one* of them, and said,
21. the *one* on thy right hand, and the *other*
21:24. I also will ask you *one* thing,
22:35. Then *one* of them, (which was) a lawyer
23: 8. for *one* is your Master, (even) Christ;

Mat.23: 9. for *one* is your Father, which is
10. for *one* is your Master, (even) Christ.
15. sea and land to make *one* proselyte,
24:40. the *one* shall be taken, and the *other* left.
25:15. to another two, and to another *one;*
18. he that had received *one* went
24. he which had received the *one*
40. unto *one* of the least of these
45. to *one* of the least of these, ye did
26:14. Then *one* of the twelve, called
21. that *one* of you shall betray me.
47. lo, Judas, *one* of the twelve, came,
51. *one* of them which were with Jesus
27:14. answered him to never *a* word;
15. release unto the people *a* prisoner,
38. *one* on the right hand, and *another*
48. straightway *one* of them ran,
Mar. 2: 7. who can forgive sins but God *only?*
4: 8. *some* (lit. *one*) thirty, and *some* sixty, and *some* an
20. *some* thirtyfold, *some* sixty, and *some*
5:22. there cometh *one* of the rulers of
6:15. a prophet, or as *one* of the prophets.
8:14. with them more than *one* loaf.
28. others, *One* of the prophets.
9:17. *one* of the multitude answered
37. shall receive *one* of such children
42. whosoever shall offend *one* of (these)
10:17. there came *one* running, and kneeled
18. none good but *one*, (that is), God.
21. said unto him, *One* thing thou lackest:
37. *one* on thy right hand, and the *other*
11:29. I will also ask of you *one* question,
12: 6. Having yet therefore *one* son,
28. *one* of the scribes came, and having heard
29. The Lord our God is *one* Lord:
32. for there is *one* God; and there is none other but he:
13: 1. *one* of his disciples saith unto him,
14:10. Judas Iscariot, *one* of the twelve,
18. *One* of you which eateth with me
20. (It is) *one* of the twelve, that dippeth
43. cometh Judas, *one* of the twelve,
47. *one* of them that stood by drew
51. followed him *a* certain young man,
15: 6. he released unto them *one* prisoner,
27. *one* on his right hand, and the *other*
36. *one* ran and filled a spunge full
Lu. 4:40. laid his hands on every *one* of them,
5: 3. he entered into *one* of the ships,
7:41. the *one* owed five hundred pence,
9: 8. that *one* of the old prophets was
10:42. *one* thing is needful: and Mary
11:46. with *one* of your fingers.
12: 6. not *one* of them is forgotten before God?
25. can add to his stature *one* cubit?
27. was not arrayed like *one* of these.
52. there shall be five in *one* house
15: 4. if he lose *one* of them, doth not
7. over *one* sinner that repenteth,
10. over *one* sinner that repenteth.
15. joined himself to *a* citizen (lit. *one* of the citizens)
19. as *one* of thy hired servants.
26. he called *one* of the servants,
16: 5. every *one* of his lord's debtors
13. for either he will hate the *one*,
— or else he will hold to the *one*,
17: 2. should offend *one* of these little ones.
15. *one* of them, when he saw
34. the *one* shall be taken, and the other
18:10. the *one* a Pharisee, and the other a

Lu. 18:19. none (is) good, save *one*, (that is), God.
22. Yet lackest thou *one* thing.
20: 3. I will also ask you *one* thing;
22:47. Judas, *one* of the twelve, went
50. *one* of them smote the servant
23:17. he must release *one* unto them
39. *one* of the malefactors which were
24:18. the *one* of them, whose name was
Joh. 1: 3. was not *any* thing made that was
40(41). *One* of the two which heard John
6: 8. *One* of his disciples, Andrew,
9. There is *a* lad here, which hath
22. save that *one* whereinto his disciples
70. *one* of you is a devil?
71. betray him, being *one* of the twelve.
7:21. I have done *one* work, and ye all
50. to Jesus by night, being *one* of them,
8:41. we have *one* Father, (even) God.
9:25. *one* thing I know, that, whereas
10:16. shall be one fold, (and) *one* shepherd.
30. I and (my) Father are *one*.
11:49. *one* of them, (named) Caiaphas,
50. that *one* man should die for the
52. together in *one* the children of God
12: 2. Lazarus was *one* of them that sat
4. Then saith *one* of his disciples,
13:21. that *one* of you shall betray me.
23. on Jesus' bosom *one* of his disciples,
17:11. that they may be *one*, as we (are).
21. That they all may be *one;*
— that they also may be *one* in us:
22. they may be *one*, even as we are *one:*
23. may be made perfect in *one;*
18:14. *one* man should die for the people.
22. *one* of the officers which stood by
26. *One* of the servants of the high priest,
39. release unto you *one* at the passover:
19:34. *one* of the soldiers with a spear
20: 7. together in a place by itself. (lit. *one* place)
12. the *one* at the head, and the *other* at the feet,
24. Thomas, *one* of the twelve,
21:25. if they should be written every *one*,
Acts 1:22. must *one* be ordained to be
24. shew whether of these two (lit. out of these two *one* which) thou
2: 3. it sat upon each)(of them.
6. because that every *man* (lit. *one*) heard
4:32. neither said *any* (of them) that
11:28. there stood up *one* of them
17:26. hath made of *one* blood all
27. not far from every *one* of us:
20:31. to warn every *one* night and day
21:19. he declared particularly (lit. by each *one*) what things
26. offered for every *one* of them.
23: 6. that the *one* part were Sadducees,
17. Paul called *one* of the centurions
28:25. after that Paul had spoken *one* word,
Ro. 3:10. There is none righteous, no, not *one:*
12. none that doeth good, no, not *one*.
30. Seeing (it is) *one* God, which shall
5:12. as by *one* man sin entered into
15. if through the offence of *one* many
— (which is) by *one* man, Jesus Christ,
16. not as (it was) by *one* that sinned,
— the judgment (was) by *one* to
17. For if by *one* man's offence death reigned by *one;*
— shall reign in life by *one*, Jesus Christ.
18. as by the offence of *one* (or, by *one* offence)

Ro. 5:18. by the righteousness of *one* (or, by *one* righteousness)
19. as by *one* man's disobedience
— so by the obedience of *one* shall
9:10. Rebecca also had conceived by *one*,
12: 4. have many members in *one* body,
5. (being) many, are *one* body in Christ,
15: 6. may with one mind (and) *one* mouth
1Co. 3: 8. planteth and he that watereth are *one*:
4: 6. no *one* of you be puffed up for *one*
6: 5. not *one* that shall be able
16. joined to an harlot is *one* body?
17. joined unto the Lord is *one* spirit.
8: 4. (there is) none other God but *one*.
6. to us (there is but) *one* God,
— *one* Lord Jesus Christ, by whom
9:24. run all, but *one* receiveth the prize?
10:17. (being) many are *one* bread, (and) *one* body: for we are all partakers of that *one* bread.
11: 5. for that is even all *one* as if
12:11. that *one* and the selfsame Spirit,
12. For as the body is *one*,
— the members of that *one* body, being many, are *one* body:
13. For by *one* Spirit are we all baptized into *one* body, whether
— all made to drink into *one* Spirit.
14. the body is not *one* member,
18. every *one* of them in the body,
19. if they were all *one* member,
20. many members, yet but *one* body.
26. whether *one* member suffer,
— or *one* member be honoured,
14:27. by course; and let *one* interpret.
31. ye may all prophesy one by *one*,
2Co. 5:14(15). that if *one* died for all, then
11: 2. have espoused you to *one* husband,
Gal. 3:16. as of many; but as of *one*,
20. not (a mediator) of *one*, but God is *one*.
28. ye are all *one* in Christ Jesus.
4:22. the *one* by a bondmaid, the *other* by
5:14. the law is fulfilled in *one* word,
Eph. 2:14. who hath made both *one*, and hath
15. in himself of twain *one* new man,
16. both unto God in *one* body by
18. by *one* Spirit unto the Father.
4: 4. (There is) *one* body, and *one* Spirit,
5. *One* Lord, one faith, *one* baptism,
6. *One* God and Father of all, who
7. unto every *one* of us is given grace
16. working in the measure of every)(part,
5:33. every one of you in particular (lit. you one by *one*)
Phi. 1:27. that ye stand fast in *one* spirit,
2: 2. (being) of one accord, of *one* mind.
3:13(14). (this) *one* thing (I do), forgetting
Col. 3:15. also ye are called in *one* body;
4: 6. to answer every *man*. (lit. *one*)
1Th. 2:11. comforted and charged every *one* of you,
5:11. edify *one another*, even as also ye do.
2Th. 1: 3. the charity of every *one* of you
1Ti. 2: 5. (there is) *one* God, and *one* mediator
5: 9. having been the wife of *one* man,
Heb. 2:11. who are sanctified (are) all of *one*:
11:12. Therefore sprang there even of *one*,
Jas. 2:10. yet offend in *one* (point), he is
19. Thou believest that there is *one* God;
4:12. There is *one* lawgiver, who is
13. continue there *a* year, and buy and sell,
2Pet. 3: 8. be not ignorant of this *one* thing,
1Joh. 5: 7. these three are *one*.
1Joh. 5: 8. these three agree in *one*.
Rev. 4: 8. the four beasts had each of them (lit. *one* by itself)
5: 5. *one* of the elders saith unto me,
6: 1. *one* of the four beasts saying,
7:13. *one* of the elders answered, saying
8:13. heard *an* angel flying through
15: 7. *one* of the four beasts gave unto
17: 1. there came *one* of the seven angels
10. five are fallen, and *one* is,
18:21. *a* mighty angel took up a stone
19:17. I saw *an* angel standing in
21: 9. came unto me *one* of the seven
21. every)(several gate was of *one* pearl:
22: 2. yielded her fruit every)(month:

1527 2 /299 1520,2596

εἷς καθ' εἷς, *hīs kath hīs*.

Mar 14:19. to say unto him *one by one*,
Joh. 8: 9. went out *one by one*, beginning

1521 10 231/303 1519,71

εἰσάγω, *īsago*.

Lu. 2:27. when the parents *brought in* the
14:21. *bring in* hither the poor, and the
22:54. *brought* him *into* the high priest's
Joh. 18:16. the door, and *brought in* Peter.
Acts 7:45. Which also our fathers...*brought in* with Jesus
9: 8. *brought* (him) *into* Damascus.
21:28. *brought* Greeks also *into* the temple,
29. Paul had *brought into* the temple.
37. as Paul was *to be led into* the castle,
Heb. 1: 6. when he *bringeth in* the firstbegotten

1522 5 231/303 1:216 1519,191

εἰσακούω, *īsakouo*.

Mat. 6: 7. they think that they *shall be heard*
Lu. 1:13. for thy prayer *is heard*; and thy
Acts 10:31. said, Cornelius, thy prayer *is heard*,
1Co. 14:21. for all that *will* they not *hear* me,
Heb. 5: 7. *was heard* in that he feared;

1523 1 231/303 2:50 1519,1209

εἰσδέχομαι, *īsdekomai*.

2Co. 6:17. unclean (thing); and I *will receive*

1524 4 231/303 1519 *eimi* (to go)

εἴσειμι, *īsīmi*.

Acts 3: 3. Peter and John about *to go into* the
21:18. Paul *went in* with us unto James;
26. with them *entered into* the temple,
Heb. 9: 6. the priests *went* always *into* the first

1525 198 231/303 2:666 1519,2064

εἰσέρχομαι, *īserkomai*.

Mat. 5:20. ye shall in no case *enter into*
6: 6. when thou prayest, *enter into* thy
7:13. *Enter* ye *in* at the strait gate:
— many there be *which go in* thereat:
21. *shall enter into* the kingdom of heaven;
8: 5. *when* Jesus *was entered into* Capernaum,
8. thou *shouldest come* under my roof:
9:25. put forth, he *went in*, *and* took her
10: 5. city of the Samaritans *enter* ye not:
11. whatsoever city or town ye shall *enter*

Mat. 10:12. *when* ye *come into* an house,
12: 4. How he *entered into* the house of God,
29. how can one *enter into* a strong
45. *they enter in and* dwell there:
15:11. Not that *which goeth into* the mouth
17:25. when he *was come into* the house,
18: 3. ye shall not *enter into* the kingdom
8. *to enter into* life halt or maimed,
9. *to enter into* life with one eye,
19:17. if thou wilt *enter into* life,
23. *shall* hardly *enter into* the kingdom
24. *to enter into* the kingdom of God.
21:10. *when* he *was come into* Jerusalem,
12. Jesus *went into* the temple of God,
22:11. *when* the king *came in* to see the
12. Friend, how *camest* thou *in* hither
23:13. ye neither *go in* (yourselves), neither suffer ye them *that are entering to go in.*
24:38. day that Noe *entered into* the ark,
25:10. *went in* with him to the marriage:
21. *enter* thou into the joy of thy lord.
23. *enter* thou into the joy of thy lord.
26:41. that ye *enter* not into temptation:
58. high priest's palace, and *went* in, *and*
27:53. *went into* the holy city, and appeared
Mar. 1:21. he *entered into* the synagogue, *and*
45. no more openly *enter into* the city,
2: 1. again he *entered into* Capernaum
26. How he *went into* the house of God
3: 1. he *entered* again *into* the synagogue;
27. can *enter into* a strong man's house, *and*
5:12. that we *may enter into* them.
13. went out, and *entered into* the swine:
39. *when* he *was come in*, he saith
6:10. place soever ye *enter into* an house,
22. *when* the daughter of the said H...*came in,*
25. *came in* straightway with haste...*and*
7:17. when he *was entered into* the house
24. *entered into* an house, *and* would
8:26. Neither *go into* the town, nor tell (it)
9:25. *enter* no more *into* him.
28. *when* he *was come into* the house,
43. *to enter into* life maimed,
45. for thee *to enter* halt *into* life,
47. *to enter into* the kingdom of God
10:15. he shall not *enter* therein.
23. *shall...enter into* the kingdom of God
24. *to enter into* the kingdom of God!
25. a camel *to go through* the eye of a needle,
— *to enter into* the kingdom of God.
11:11. Jesus *entered into* Jerusalem,
15. Jesus *went into* the temple, *and*
13:15. neither *enter* (therein), to take any
14:14. wheresoever he shall *go in*, say
38. lest ye *enter into* temptation.
15:43. came, and *went in* boldly unto Pilate,
16: 5. *entering into* the sepulchre,
Lu. 1: 9. *when* he *went into* the temple of the Lord.
28. the angel *came in* unto her, *and*
40. *entered into* the house of Zacharias,
4:16. he *went into* the synagogue
38. *entered into* Simon's house.
6: 4. How he *went into* the house of God,
6. that he *entered into* the synagogue
7: 1. he *entered into* Capernaum.
6. thou *shouldest enter* under my roof:
36. *went into* the Pharisee's house, *and*
44. I *entered into* thine house,
45. since the time I *came in*
8:30. many devils *were entered into* him.
32. suffer them *to enter into* them.
33. *entered into* the swine: and the herd

Lu. 8:41. that he would *come into* his house·
51. *when* he *came into* the house, he suffered no man *to go in*,
9: 4. whatsoever house ye *enter into*,
34. feared as they *entered into* the cloud.
46. there *arose* a reasoning among them,
52. they went, and *entered into* a village
10: 5. into whatsoever house ye *enter*,
8. into whatsoever city ye *enter*,
10. into whatsoever city ye *enter*,
38. he *entered into* a certain village:
11:26. they *enter in, and* dwell there:
37. he *went in, and* sat down to meat.
52. ye *entered* not *in* yourselves, and then *that were entering* in ye hindered.
13:24. Strive *to enter in* at the strait gate:
— will seek *to enter in*, and shall not
14:23. compel (them) *to come in*, that my
15:28. was angry, and would not *go in:*
17: 7. *when* he *is come* from the field,
12. *as* he *entered into* a certain village,
27. that Noe *entered into* the ark,
18:17. shall in no wise *enter* therein.
24. *shall* they that have riches *enter into* the
25. a camel *to go* through a needle's eye,
— *to enter into* the kingdom of God.
19: 1. (Jesus) *entered and* passed through
7. he *was gone* to be guest with a
45. he *went into* the temple, *and* began
21:21. *let* not them that are in the countries *enter* thereinto.
22: 3. Then *entered* Satan into Judas
10. *when* ye *are entered* into the city,
40. that ye *enter* not into temptation.
46. lest ye *enter* into temptation.
24: 3. they *entered in, and* found not the
26. *to enter into* his glory?
29. he *went in* to tarry with them.
Joh. 3: 4. can he *enter* the second time into
5. he cannot *enter into* the kingdom
4:38. ye *are* (lit. *have*) *entered into* their labours.
10: 1. He *that entereth* not by the door
2. he *that entereth in* by the door
9. by me if any man *enter in*,
— *shall go in* and out, and find pasture.
13:27. Satan *entered into* him.
18: 1. a garden, into the which he *entered*,
28. *went* not *into* the judgment hall,
33. Pilate *entered into* the judgment hall
19: 9. *went* again *into* the judgment hall,
20: 5. clothes lying; yet *went* he not *in.*
6. *went into* the sepulchre,
8. *went in* also that other disciple,
Acts 1:13. when they *were come in*, they went
21. the Lord Jesus *went in* and out among us
3: 8. *entered* with them *into* the temple,
5: 7. not knowing what was done, *came in.*
10. the young men *came in, and* found
21. they *entered into* the temple early
9: 6. Arise, and *go into* the city, and it shall
12. a man named Ananias *coming in*,
17. went his way, and *entered into* the house
10: 3. an angel of God *coming in* to him,
24. after they *entered into* Cæsarea.
25. as Peter was *coming in*,
27. talked with him, he *went in*,
11: 3. Thou *wentest in* to men uncircumcised,
8. at any time *entered into* my mouth.
12. we *entered into* the man's house:
20. *when* they *were come* to Antioch,
13:14. *went into* the synagogue...*and* sat
14: 1. that they *went* both together *into* the

Acts14:20. he rose up, and *came into* the city:
22. *enter into* the kingdom of God.
16:15. *come into* my house, *and* abide (there).
40. *entered into* (the house of) Lydia:
17: 2. as his manner was, *went in* unto them,
18:19. *entered into* the synagogue, *and*
19: 8. he *went into* the synagogue, *and* spake
30. have *entered in* unto the people,
20:29. *shall* grievous wolves *enter in*
21: 8. we *entered into* the house...*and*
23:16. *entered into* the castle, *and*
33. Who, *when* they *came* to Cæsarea,
25:23. *when...was entered into* the place of hearing,
28: 8. to whom Paul *entered in,...and* healed him.
Ro. 5:12. sin *entered into* the world,
11:25. fulness of the Gentiles *be come in.*
1Co.14:23. there *come in* (those that are) unlearned,
24. there *come in* one that believeth not,
Heb. 3:11. They *shall* not *enter into* my rest.
18. should not *enter into* his rest,
19. that they could not *enter in*
4: 1. left (us) of *entering into* his rest,
3. have believed *do enter into* rest,
— if they *shall enter into* my rest:
5. If they *shall enter into* my rest.
6. that some must *enter* therein,
— *entered* not *in* because of unbelief
10. he *that is entered into* his rest,
11. therefore *to enter into* that rest,
6:19. and *which entereth into* that within
20. the forerunner *is* for us *entered,*
9:12. *entered in* once into the holy place,
24. For Christ *is* not *entered into* the holy
25. as the high priest *entereth into* the
10: 5. *when* he *cometh into* the world,
Jas. 2: 2. if there *come* unto your assembly
— there *come in* also a poor man
5: 4. *are entered into* the ears of the Lord
2Joh. 7. deceivers *are entered into* the world,
Rev. 3:20. open the door, I *will come in* to him,
11:11. life from God *entered* into them,
15: 8. was able *to enter into* the temple,
21:27. shall in no wise *enter into* it
22:14. *may enter in* through the gates into

1526 163 221/275

εἰσί, isi, from εἰμί.

Mat. 2:18. comforted, because they *are* not.
7:13. many there *be* which go in thereat:
14. few there *be* that find it.
15. inwardly they *are* ravening wolves.
10:30. hairs of your head *are* all numbered.
11: 8. wear soft (clothing) *are* in kings' houses.
12: 5. profane the sabbath, and *are* blameless?
48. who *are* my brethren?
13:38. the good seed *are* the children of the
— the tares *are* the children of the
39. the reapers *are* the angels.
56. *are* they not all with us?
15:14. they *be* blind leaders of the blind.
16:28. There *be* some standing here, which
17:26. Then *are* the children free.
18:20. two or three *are* gathered together
19: 6. Wherefore they *are* no more twain,
12. For there *are* some eunuchs,
— and there *are* some eunuchs, which
— and there *be* eunuchs, which have
20:16. for many *be* called, but few chosen.
22:14. many *are* called, but few (are) chosen.
Mat.22:30. *are* as the angels of God in heaven.
Mar. 4:15. these *are* they by the way side,
16. these *are* they likewise which
17. endure but for a time: (lit. *are* temporary)
18. these *are* they which are sown among thorns;)(such as hear the word,
20. these *are* they which are sown on good
6: 3. *are* not his sisters here with us?
9: 1. there *be* some of them that stand
10: 8. then they *are* no more twain,
12:25. *are* as the angels which are in
Lu. 7:25. live delicately, *are* in kings' courts.
31. to what *are* they like?
32 They *are* like unto children
8:12. by the way side *are* they that hear;
14. which fell among thorns *are* they, which,
15. that on the good ground *are* they,
21. *are* these which hear the word
9:13. We have no (lit. There *are* not to us) more
27. there *be* some standing here,
11: 7. my children *are* with me in bed;
12:38. so, blessed *are* those servants.
13:14. There *are* six days in which men
30. there *are* last which shall be first, and
— there *are* first which shall be last.
16: 8. *are* in their generation wiser than
18: 9. that they *were* righteous, and despised
20:36. they *are* equal unto the angels; and *are*
— the children of God, being
21:22. these *be* the days of vengeance,
Joh. 4:35. for they *are* white already to harvest.
5:39. they *are* they which testify of me.
6:64. there *are* some of you that believe not.
— who they *were* that believed not,
7:49. who knoweth not the law *are* cursed.
8:10. where *are* those thine accusers?
10: 8. came before me *are* thieves and robbers:
12. whose own the sheep *are* not,
11: 9. *Are* there not twelve hours in the day?
14: 2. In my Father's house *are* many mansions.
17: 9. given me; for they *are* thine.
11. these *are* in the world, and I come
14. they *are* not of the world,
16. They *are* not of the world, even as
Acts 2: 7. *are* not all these which speak
13. These men *are* full of new wine.
4:13. that they *were* unlearned and ignorant
5:25. *are* standing in the temple,
13:31. who *are* his witnesses unto the people.
16:17. *are* the servants of the most high God,
38. they heard that they *were* Romans.
19:26. that they *be* no gods, which
38. law is open, and there *are* deputies:
21:20. thousands of Jews there *are* which
23. We have (lit. There *are* to us) four men
23:21. now *are* they ready, looking for
24:11. there *are* yet but twelve days
Ro. 1:32. such things *are* worthy of death,
2:14. *are* a law unto themselves:
8:14. they *are* the sons of God.
9: 4. Who *are* Israelites; to whom
7. they *are* the seed of Abraham,
13: 1. powers that be *are* ordained of God.
3. rulers *are* not a terror to good works,
6. for they *are* God's ministers,
15:27. their debtors they *are.*
16: 7. who *are* of note among the apostles,
1Co. 1:11. there *are* contentions among you.
3: 8. planteth and he that watereth *are*
20. thoughts of the wise, that they *ar*
8: 5. there *be* that are called gods,
— as there *be* gods many, and lords

1Co.10:18. *are* not they which eat of the sacrifices partakers of the altar?
12: 4. there *are* diversities of gifts,
5. there *are* differences of administrations,
6. there *are* diversities of operations,
14:22. Wherefore tongues *are* for a sign,
37. *are* the commandments of the Lord.
2Co.11:22. *Are* they Hebrews? so (am) I. *Are* they Israelites? so (am) I. *Are* they the seed of Abraham?
23. *Are* they ministers of Christ?
Gal. 1: 7. there *be* some that trouble you,
3: 7. same *are* the children of Abraham.
10. as many as *are* of the works of the law *are* under the curse: for it is
4:24. for these *are* the two covenants;
Eph. 5:16. because the days *are* evil.
Col. 2: 3. In whom *are* hid all the treasures
1Ti. 5:24. Some men's sins *are* open beforehand,
6: 1. as many servants as *are* under
2. because they *are* brethren; but rather do (them) service, because they *are* faithful
2Ti. 3: 6. For of this sort *are* they which
Tit. 1:10. there *are* many unruly and vain
3: 9. for they *are* unprofitable and vain.
Heb 1:10. the heavens *are* the works of thine
14. *Are* they not all ministering
7:21. priests *were* made without an oath;
23. they truly *were* many priests,
11:13. they *were* strangers and pilgrims on the
2Pet.2:17. These *are* wells without water,
3: 7. by the same word *are* kept in store,
1Joh.2:19. that they *were* not all of us.
4: 5. They *are* of the world: therefore speak they of the world,
5: 3. his commandments *are* not grievous.
7. there *are* three that bear record
— these three *are* one.
8. there *are* three that bear witness
— and these three *agree* in one.
Jude 12. These *are* spots in your feasts
16. These *are* murmurers,
19. These *be* they who separate
Rev. 1:19. the things which *are*, and the
20. The seven stars *are* the angels
— *are* the seven churches.
2: 2. say they are apostles, and *are* not,
9. which say they are Jews, and *are* not,
3: 4. in white: for they *are* worthy.
9. which say they are Jews, and *are* not,
4: 5. which *are* the seven Spirits of God.
11. and for thy pleasure they *are*
5: 6. which *are* the seven Spirits of God
8. which *are* the prayers of saints.
7:13. What *are* these which are arrayed
14. These *are* they which came
15. Therefore *are* they before the throne of God,
9:19. their power *is* in their mouth,
11: 4. These *are* the two olive trees,
14: 4. These *are* they which were not defiled with women; for they *are* virgins. These *are* they which follow the Lamb
5. for they *are* without fault before
16: 6. blood to drink; for they *are* worthy.
14. they *are* the spirits of devils,
17: 9. The seven heads *are* seven mountains,
10. there *are* seven kings: five
12. which thou sawest *are* ten kings,
15. *are* peoples, and multitudes, and nations,
19: 9. These *are* the true sayings of God.
21: 5. these words *are* true and faithful.

1527, p. 211

1528 1 231/306 3:487 1519,2564

εἰσκαλέω, *īskaleo.*

Acts10:23. Then *called* he them *in, and* lodged

1529 5 232/306 5:42 1519,3598

εἴσοδος, *īsodos.*

Acts13:24. had first preached before his *coming*
1Th. 1: 9. what manner of *entering in* we
2: 1. know our *entrance in* unto you,
Heb 10:19. boldness to *enter into* (lit. for *entrance into*) the holiest
2Pet. 1:11. an *entrance* shall be ministered

1530 1 232/306 1519 *pedaō* (to leap)

εἰσπηδάω, *īspeedao.*

Acts14:14. *ran in* among the people, crying
16:29. called for a light, and *sprang in,*

1531 17 232/306 6:566 1519,4198

εἰσπορεύομαι, *īsporūomai.*

Mat.15:17. *whatsoever entereth in* at the mouth
Mar. 1:21. they *went into* Capernaum;
4:19. the lusts of other things *entering in,*
5:40. *entereth in* where the damsel
6:56. whithersoever he *entered,*
7:15. *that entering into* him can defile
18. *whatsoever* thing from without *entereth into*
19. it *entereth* not *into* his heart,
11: 2. as soon *as* ye *be entered into* it,
Lu. 8:16. they *which enter in* may see
11:33. they *which come in* may see
19:30. in the which *at* your *entering*
22:10. the house where he *entereth in.*
Acts 3: 2. of them *that entered into* the temple;
8: 3. As for Saul,...*entering into* every house,
9:28. he was with them *coming in*
28:30. received all *that came in* unto him,

1532 1 232/306 1519,5143

εἰστρέχω, *īstreko.*

Acts12:14. she opened not...but *ran in, and* told

1533 7 233/306 9:56 1519,5342

εἰσφέρω, *īsphero.*

Mat. 6:13. *lead* us not *into* temptation,
Lu. 5:18. sought (means) *to bring* him *in,*
19. they *might bring* him *in* because
11: 4. *lead* us not *into* temptation;
Acts17:20. *bringest* certain strange things to
1Ti. 6: 7. we *brought* nothing *into* (this)
Heb 13:11. whose blood *is brought into* the

1534 16 233/306 cf 1899

εἶτα, *īta.*

Mar. 4:17. *afterward,* when affliction or persecution
28. *then* the ear, *after that* the full
8:25. *After that* he put (his) hands again
Lu. 8:12. *then* cometh the devil, and taketh
Joh.13: 5. *After that* he poureth water into
19:27. *Then* saith he to the disciple,
20:27. *Then* saith he to Thomas, Reach
1Co.12:28. *then* gifts of healings, helps,
15: 5. seen of Cephas, *then* of the twelve:
7. *then* of all the apostles.
24. *Then* (cometh) the end, when he

1Ti. 2:13. Adam was first formed, *then* Eve.
3:10. *then* let them use the office of a
Heb 12: 9. *Furthermore* we have had fathers
Jas. 1:15. *Then* when lust hath conceived,

1535 65 233/306

εἴτε, ite. p. 187
See after εἰ.

1536 79 - /262

εἴ τις. p. 187
See after εἰ.

1486 4 217/307

εἴωθα see ἔθω. p. 188

1537 921 233/307

ἐκ, ἐξ, ek, ex.

Mat. 1: 3. Judas begat Phares and Zara *of* Thamar;
5. Salmon begat Booz *of* Rachab; and Booz begat Obed *of* Ruth;
6. the king begat Solomon *of* her
16. *of* whom was born Jesus,
18. with child *of* the Holy Ghost.
20. in her is *of* the Holy Ghost.
2: 6. for *out of* thee shall come a
15. *Out of* Egypt have I called my son.
3: 9. God is able *of* these stones to
17. lo a voice *from* heaven, saying,
5:37. more than these cometh *of* evil.
6:27. Which *of* you by taking thought
7: 5. the beam *out of* thine own eye;
— the mote *out of* thy brother's eye.
9. Or what man is there *of* you,
8:28. devils, coming *out of* the tombs,
10:29. one *of* them shall not fall on the
12:11. What man shall there be *among*
33. the tree is known *by* (his) fruit.
34. *out of* the abundance of the heart
35. *out of* the good treasure of the heart
— evil man *out of* the evil treasure
37. *by* thy words thou shalt be justified, and *by* thy words thou shalt be condemned.
42. *from* the uttermost parts of the earth
13:41. *out of* his kingdom all things
47. gathered *of* every kind:
49. the wicked *from* among the just,
52. *out of* his treasure (things) new
15: 5. thou mightest be profited *by* me;
11. that which cometh *out of* the mouth,
18. which proceed *out of* the mouth come forth *from* the heart;
19. *out of* the heart proceed evil thoughts,
16: 1. shew them a sign *from* heaven.
17: 5. behold a voice *out of* the cloud,
9. be risen again *from* the dead.
18:12. one *of* them be gone astray, doth
19:12. so born *from* (their) mother's womb
20. have I kept *from* my youth *up*:
20: 2. with the labourers *for* a penny a day,
21. the one *on* thy right...the other *on* the left,
23. to sit *on* my right hand, and *on* my
21:16. *Out of* the mouth of babes and
19. *on* thee henceforward for ever.
25. *from* heaven, or *of* men?
— If we shall say, *From* heaven;
26. if we shall say, *Of* men;
31. Whether *of* them twain did

Mat.22:35. Then one *of* them, (which was)
44. Sit thou *on* my right hand,
23:25. are full *of* extortion and excess.
34. (some) *of* them ye shall kill
— (Some) *of* them shall ye scourge
24:17. take any thing *out of* his house:
31. his elect *from* the four winds,
25: 2. five *of* them were wise, and five
8. Give us *of* your oil; for our
33. sheep *on* his right hand, but the goats *on* the left.
34. unto them *on* his right hand,
41. unto them *on* the left hand,
26:21. that one *of* you shall betray me.
27. Saying, Drink ye all *of* it;
29. henceforth *of* this fruit of the vine,
42. went away again)(the second time,
44. prayed)(the third time, saying
64. sitting *on* the right hand of power,
73. Surely thou also art (one) *of* them;
27: 7. bought *with* them the potter's field,
29. they had platted a crown *of* thorns,
38. one *on* the right hand, and another *on* the left.
48. straightway one *of* them ran,
53. came *out of* the graves after his
28: 2. descended *from* heaven, and came
Mar. 1:11. there came a voice *from* heaven,
25. Hold thy peace, and come *out of* him.
26. he came *out of* him.
29. were come *out of* the synagogue,
5: 2. when he was come *out of* the ship, immediately there met him *out of* the tombs
8. Come *out of* the man,
30. that virtue had gone *out of* him,
6:14. the Baptist was risen *from* the dead,
16. he is risen *from* the dead.
51. amazed in themselves *beyond* (lit. *out of*) measure,
54. they were come *out of* the ship,
7:11. mightest be profited *by* me;
20. That which cometh *out of* the man,
21. *out of* the heart of men, proceed
26. the devil *out of* her daughter.
29. devil is gone *out of* thy daughter
31. departing *from* the coasts of Tyre
9: 7. a voice came *out of* the cloud,
9. were risen *from* the dead.
10. rising *from* the dead should mean.
17. one *of* the multitude answered
25. I charge thee, come *out of* him,
10:20. these have I observed *from* my youth.
37. one *on* thy right hand, and the other *on* thy left
40. to sit *on* my right hand and *on* my left
11: 8. cut down branches *off* the trees,
14. No man eat fruit *of* thee hereafter
20. fig tree dried up *from* the roots.
30. *from* heaven, or *of* men?
31. If we shall say, *From* heaven;
32. if we shall say, *Of* men;
12:25. when they shall rise *from* the dead,
30. thou shalt love the Lord thy God *with* all thy heart, and *with* all thy soul, and *with* all thy mind, and *with* all thy strength:
33. And to love him *with* all the heart, and *with* all the understanding, and *with* a the soul, and *with* all the strength,
36. Sit thou *on* my right hand,
44. did cast in *of* their abundance; but she o her want did cast in
13: 1. as he went *out of* the temple,
15. take any thing *out of* his house.

Mar 13:27. his elect *from* the four winds,
14:18. One *of* you which eateth with
20. one *of* the twelve, that dippeth
23. they all drank *of* it.
25. I will drink no more *of* the fruit
31. he spake the more vehemently, (lit. *of* excess)
62. sitting *on* the right hand of power,
69. that stood by, This is (one) *of* them.
70. Surely thou art (one) *of* them:
72.)(the second time the cock crew.
15:27. one *on* his right hand, and the other *on*
39. which stood over against (lit. *on* the opposite) him,
46. hewn *out of* a rock,
16: 3. roll us away the stone *from* the door
12. in another form unto two *of* them,
19. sat *on* the right hand of God.
Lu. 1: 5. Zacharias, *of* the course of Abia: and his wife (was) *of* the daughters of Aaron,
11. *on* the right side of the altar
15. even *from* his mother's womb.
27. was Joseph, *of* the house of David;
35. which shall be born *of* thee
71. saved *from* our enemies, and *from* the hand
74. *out of* the hand of our enemies
78. the dayspring *from* on high
2: 4. *out of* the city of Nazareth,
— *of* the house and lineage of David:
35. that the thoughts *of* many hearts
36. of Phanuel, *of* the tribe of Aser:
3: 8. God is able *of* these stones to raise
22. a voice came *from* heaven,
4:22. proceeded *out of* his mouth.
35. Hold thy peace, and come *out of* him.
38. he arose *out of* the synagogue,
5: 3. taught the people *out of* the ship.
17. *out of* every town of Galilee,
6:42. the beam *out of* thine own eye,
44. tree is known *by* his own fruit. For *of* thorns men do not gather figs, nor *of* a bramble bush gather
45. *out of* the good treasure of his
— evil man *out of* the evil treasure
— for *of* the abundance of the heart
8:27. there met him *out of* the city
— which had devils)(long time,
9: 7. that John was risen *from* the dead;
35. there came a voice *out of* the cloud,
10: 7. Go not *from* house to house.
11. the very dust *of* your city,
18. Satan as lightning fall *from* heaven.
27. *with* all thy heart, and *with* all thy soul, and *with* all thy strength, and *with* all
11: 5. Which *of* you shall have a friend,
6. a friend of mine *in* his journey
13. (your) heavenly Father (lit. your Father *from* heaven)
15. some *of* them said, He casteth
16. sought of him a sign *from* heaven.
27. a certain woman *of* the company
31. *from* the utmost parts of the earth
49. (some) *of* them they shall slay
54. something *out of* his mouth,
12: 6. not one *of* them is forgotten
13. one *of* the company said unto
15. in the abundance *of* the things which he possesseth.
25. which *of* you with taking thought
36. he will return *from* the wedding;
14:28. which *of* you, intending to build
33. whosoever he be *of* you that forsaketh

Lu. 15: 4. What man *of* you, having an hundred sheep, if he lose one *of* them.
16: 9. *of* the mammon of unrighteousness;
31. though one rose *from* the dead.
17: 7. which *of* you, having a servant
— when he is come *from* the field,
15. one *of* them, when he saw
24. *out of* the one (part) under heaven.
18:21. these have I kept *from* my youth *up*.
19:22. *Out of* thine own mouth will I
20: 4. was it *from* heaven, or *of* men?
5. If we shall say, *From* heaven;
6. if we say, *Of* men;
35. the resurrection *from* the dead,
42. Sit thou *on* my right hand,
21: 4. these have *of* their abundance
— she *of* her penury hath cast in
16. (some) *of* you shall they cause to be
18. not an hair *of* your head perish.
22: 3. being *of* the number of the twelve.
16. I will not any more eat there*of*
23. which *of* them it was that should
50. one *of* them smote the servant
58. Thou art also *of* them.
69. the Son of man sit *on* the right hand
23: 7. he belonged *unto* Herod's jurisdiction,
8. desirous to see him *of* a long (season),
33. one *on* the right hand, and the other *on* the
55. which came with him *from* Galilee,
24:13. two *of* them went that same day
22. certain women also *of* our company
46. to rise *from* the dead the third day:
49. endued with power *from* on high.
Joh. 1:13. Which were born, not *of* blood, nor *of* the will of the flesh, nor *of* the will of man, but *of* God.
16. *of* his fulness have all we
19. sent priests and Levites *from* Jerusalem
24. sent were *of* the Pharisees.
32. descending *from* heaven like
35. John stood, and two *of* his disciples;
40(41). One *of* the two which heard
44(45). the city (lit. *of* the city) of Andrew
46(47). thing come *out of* Nazareth?
2:15. made a scourge *of* small cords, he drove them all *out of* the temple,
22. he was risen *from* the dead,
3: 1. There was a man *of* the Pharisees,
5. Except a man be born *of* water
6. That which is born *of* the flesh
— that which is born *of* the Spirit
8. every one that is born *of* the Spirit.
13. he that came down *from* heaven,
25. question between (some) *of* John's disciples and (lit. *of* John's disciples with)
27. it be given him *from* heaven.
31. he that is *of* the earth is *earthly*, (lit. *of* the earth) and speaketh *of* the earth: he that cometh *from* heaven
34. giveth not the Spirit *by* measure
4: 6. being wearied *with* (his) journey,
7. There cometh a woman *of* Samaria
12. the well, and drank there*of* himself,
13. Whosoever drinketh *of* this water
14. whosoever drinketh *of* the water
22. for salvation is *of* the Jews.
30. Then they went *out of* the city,
39. the Samaritans *of* that city believed
47. come *out of* Judæa into Galilee,
54. when he was come *out of* Judæa
5:24. is passed *from* death unto life.
6: 8. One *of* his disciples, Andrew

Joh. 6:11. likewise *of* the fishes as much
13. fragments *of* the five barley loaves,
23. came other boats *from* Tiberias
26. because ye did eat *of* the loaves,
31. gave them bread *from* heaven to eat.
32. that bread *from* heaven; but my Father giveth you the true bread *from* heaven.
33. he which cometh down *from* heaven,
38. For I came down *from* heaven,
39. given me I should lose nothing, (lit. not lose *of* it)
41. which came down *from* heaven.
42. saith, I came down *from* heaven?
50. bread which cometh down *from* heaven, that a man may eat there*of*
51. came down *from* heaven: if any man eat *of* this
58. bread which came down *from* heaven:
60. Many therefore *of* his disciples,
64. some *of* you that believe not. For Jesus knew *from* the beginning
65. given unto him *of* my Father.
66. *From* that (time) many of his
70. one *of* you is a devil?
71. being one *of* the twelve.
7:17. whether it be *of* God, or
19. none *of* you keepeth the law?
22. not because it is *of* Moses, but *of* the fathers;
25. some *of* them of Jerusalem,
31. many *of* the people believed
38. *out of* his belly shall flow rivers
40. Many *of* the people therefore,
41. Shall Christ come *out of* Galilee?
42. cometh *of* the seed of David,
44. some *of* them would have taken
48. Have any *of* the rulers or *of* the Pharisees believed on him?
50. to Jesus by night, being one *of* them,
52. Art thou also *of* Galilee?
— *out of* Galilee ariseth no prophet.
8:23. Ye are *from* beneath; I am *from* above: ye are *of* this world; I am not *of* this world.
41. We be not born *of* fornication;
42. proceeded forth and came *from* God;
44. Ye are *of* (your) father the devil,
— he speaketh *of* his own:
46. Which *of* you convinceth me of sin?
47. He that is *of* God heareth God's words:
— because ye are not *of* God.
59. went *out of* the temple, going
9: 1. which was blind *from* (his) birth.
6. made clay *of* the spittle, and he
16. said some *of* the Pharisees,
24. Then again (lit. *of* a second time) called
32. *Since* the world began (εκ του αιωνος) was it not heard that
40. (some) *of* the Pharisees which were
10:16. which are not *of* this fold:
20. many *of* them said, He hath
26. because ye are not *of* my sheep,
28. pluck them *out of* my hand.
29. *out of* my Father's hand.
32. I shewed you *from* my Father,
39. he escaped *out of* their hand,
11: 1. of Bethany,)(the town of Mary
19. many *of* the Jews came to
37. some *of* them said, Could not
45. many *of* the Jews which came
46. some *of* them went their ways
49. one *of* them, (named) Caiaphas,

Joh. 11:55. many went *out of* the country
12: 1. whom he raised *from* the dead.
3. *with* the odour of the ointment.
4. Then saith one *of* his disciples,
9. Much people *of* the Jews
— he had raised *from* the dead.
17. called Lazarus *out of* his grave, and raised him *from* the dead,
20. Greeks *among* them that came up to
27. Father, save me *from* this hour:
28. came there a voice *from* heaven,
32. if I be lifted up *from* the earth,
34. We have heard *out of* the law
42. *among* the chief rulers also many
49. I have not spoken *of* myself;
13: 1. should depart *out of* this world
4. He riseth *from* supper, and laid
21. that one *of* you shall betray me.
15:19. If ye were *of* the world, the
— because ye are not *of* the world, but I have chosen you *out of* the world,
16: 4. I said not unto you *at* the beginning,
5. none *of* you asketh me,
14. for he shall receive *of* mine,
15. that he shall take *of* mine,
17. Then said (some) *of* his disciples
17: 6. gavest me *out of* the world:
12. none *of* them is lost, but the
14. they are not *of* the world, even as I am not *of* the world.
15. take them *out of* the world,
— shouldest keep them *from* the evil.
16. They are not *of* the world, even as I am not *of* the world.
18: 3. *from* the chief priests and Pharisees,
9. *Of* them which thou gavest me
17. also (one) *of* this man's disciples?
25. Art not thou also (one) *of* his disciples?
26. One *of* the servants of the high priest,
36. My kingdom is not *of* this world: if my kingdom were *of* this world,
37. Every one that is *of* the truth
19: 2. soldiers platted a crown *of* thorns,
12. *from* thence*forth* Pilate sought
23. woven *from* the top throughout.
20: 1. stone taken away *from* the sepulchre.
2. the Lord *out of* the sepulchre,
9. he must rise again *from* the dead.
24. Thomas, one *of* the twelve,
21: 2. two other *of* his disciples.
14. that he was risen *from* the dead.
Acts 1:18. *with* the reward of iniquity;
24. shew whether *of* these two thou
25. *from* which Judas by transgression
2: 2. there came a sound *from* heaven
25. for he is *on* my right hand,
30. that *of* the fruit of his loins,
34. Sit thou *on* my right hand,
3: 2. lame *from* his mother's womb
15. God hath raised *from* the dead;
22. raise up unto you *of* your brethren,
23. destroyed *from among* the people.
4: 2. the resurrection *from* the dead.
6. *of* the kindred of the high priest,
10. whom God raised *from* the dead,
5:38. counsel or this work be *of* men,
39. if it be *of* God, ye cannot
6: 3. look ye *out among* you seven men
9. arose certain *of* the synagogue, which
7: 3. Get thee *out of* thy country, and *from* thy kindred,
4. *out of* the land of the Chaldæans.

Acts 7:10. *out of* all his afflictions,
37. unto you *of* your brethren,
40. *out of* the land of Egypt,
55. standing *on* the right hand of God,
56. standing *on* the right hand of God.
8:37. believest *with* all thine heart,
39. were come up *out of* the water,
9:33. had kept his bed)(eight years,
10: 1. a centurion *of* the band called
15. unto him again)(the second time,
41. after he rose *from* the dead.
45. they *of* the circumcision which
11: 2. they that were *of* the circumcision
5. a great sheet, let down *from* heaven
9. answered me again (lit. *of* a second time) *from* heaven,
20. some *of* them were men of Cyprus
28. there stood up one *of* them named
12: 7. his chains fell *off from* (his) hands.
11. *out of* the hand of Herod, and (from)
17. had brought him *out of* the prison.
25. Barnabas and Saul returned *from* Jerusalem,
13:17. brought he them *out of* it.
21. a man *of* the tribe of Benjamin,
30. God raised him *from* the dead:
34. he raised him up *from* the dead,
42. were gone *out of* the synagogue,
14: 8. a cripple *from* his mother's womb,
15: 2. certain other *of* them, should go up
14. take *out of* them (lit. *out of* the nations)
21. Moses *of* old time hath in every
22. to send chosen men *of* their own
23. which are *of* the Gentiles in Antioch
24. certain which went *out from* us
29. *from* which if ye keep yourselves,
16:40. they went *out of* the prison,
17: 3. suffered, and risen again *from* the dead;
4. some *of* them believed, and consorted
12. Therefore many *of* them believed;
26. hath made *of* one blood all nations
31. he hath raised him *from* the dead.
33. Paul departed *from* among them.
18: 1. Paul departed *from* Athens, and came
2. all Jews to depart *from* Rome:
19:16. fled *out of* that house
25. ye know that *by* this craft
33. drew Alexander *out of* the multitude,
34. all with one voice (lit. one voice *from* all)
20:30. Also *of* your own selves shall
21: 8. which was (one) *of* the seven;
22: 6. there shone *from* heaven a great
14. hear the voice *of* (lit. *from*) his mouth
18. get thee quickly *out of* Jerusalem:
23:10. by force *from* among them,
21. *of* them more than forty men,
34. asked *of* what province he was.
24: 7. took (him) away *out of* our hands,
10. thou hast been *of* many years
26: 4. My manner of life *from* my youth,
17. Delivering thee *from* the people,
23. first that should rise from the dead, (lit. first *from* the resurrection of the dead)
27:22. no loss of (any man's) life *among* you,
29. four anchors *out of* the stern,
30. about to flee *out of* the ship,
— cast anchors *out of* the foreship,
34. not an hair fall *from* the head
28: 3. came a viper *out of* the heat,
4. beast hang *on* his hand,
— though he hath escaped)(the sea,
17. was I delivered prisoner *from* Jerusalem

Ro. 1: 3. made *of* the seed of David
4. *by* the resurrection from the dead:
17. revealed *from* faith to faith:
— The just shall live *by* faith.
2: 8. unto them that *are* contentious, (lit. *of* contention)
18. being instructed *out of* the law;
27. uncircumcision which is *by* nature,
29. whose praise (is) not *of* men, but *of* God
3:20. *by* the deeds of the law there shall
26. justifier of him which believeth (lit. him *of* faith)
30. justify the circumcision *by* faith,
4: 2. if Abraham were justified *by* works,
12. not *of* the circumcision only,
14. they which are *of* the law
16. Therefore (it is) *of* faith, that
— not to that only which is *of* the law, but to that also which is *of* the faith of A.;
24. raised up Jesus our Lord *from* the dead;
5: 1. Therefore being justified *by* faith,
16. the judgment (was) *by* one to
— the free gift (is) *of* many offences
6: 4. Christ was raised up *from* the dead
9. Christ being raised *from* the dead
13. those that are alive *from* the dead,
17. ye have obeyed *from* the heart
7: 4. him who is raised *from* the dead,
24. deliver me *from* the body of this death?
8:11. raised up Jesus *from* the dead
— that raised up Christ *from* the dead
9: 5. Whose (are) the fathers, and *of* whom
6. not all Israel, which are *of* Israel:
10. Rebecca also had conceived *by* one,
11. not *of* works, but *of* him that calleth;
21. *of* the same lump to make
24. not *of* the Jews only, but also *of* the Gentiles?
30. righteousness which is *of* faith.
32. not *by* faith, but as it were *by* the
10: 5. righteousness which is *of* the law,
6. righteousness which is *of* faith
7. bring up Christ again *from* the dead.
9. hath raised him *from* the dead,
17. So then faith (cometh) *by* hearing,
11: 1. *of* the seed of Abraham,
6. then (is it) no more *of* works:
— if (it be) *of* works, then is it
14. might save some *of* them.
15. but life *from* the dead?
24. *out of* the olive tree which is wild
26. There shall come *out of* Sion the
36. For *of* him, and through him,
12:18. as much as lieth in you, (lit. as is *of* you)
13: 3. thou shalt have praise *of* the same
11. time to awake *out of* sleep.
14:23. because (he eateth) not *of* faith. for whatsoever (is) not *of* faith is sin.
16:10. which are *of* Aristobulus' (houshold).
11. be *of* the (houshold) of Narcissus,

1Co. 1:30. *of* him are ye in Christ Jesus,
2:12. the spirit which is *of* God;
5: 2. be taken away *from* among you.
10. needs go *out of* the world.
13. put away *from among* yourselves
7: 5. except (it be) *with* consent for a time,
7. hath his proper gift *of* God,
8: 6. the Father, *of* whom (are) all things,
9: 7. eateth not *of* the fruit thereof?
— eateth not *of* the milk of the flock?
13. live (of the things) *of* the temple?
14. should live *of* the gospel.

1Co. 9:19. though I be free *from* all (men),
10: 4. they drank *of* that spiritual Rock
17. all partakers *of* that one bread.
11: 8. man is not *of* the woman; but the woman *of* the man.
12. as the woman (is) *of* the man,
— by the woman; but all things *of* God.
28. eat *of* (that) bread, and drink *of* (that) cup.
12:15. I am not *of* the body; is it therefore not *of* the body?
16. not the eye, I am not *of* the body; is it therefore not *of* the body?
27. body of Christ, and members *in* particular.
13: 9. we know *in* part, and we prophesy *in* part.
10. then that which is *in* part
12. now I know *in* part;
15: 6. *of* whom the greater part remain
12. that he rose *from* the dead,
20. now is Christ risen *from* the dead,
47. The first man (is) *of* the earth, earthy: the second man (is) the Lord *from* heaven.
2Co. 1:10. delivered us *from* so great a death,
11. *by the means of* many persons
2: 2. same which is made sorry *by* me?
4. For *out of* much affliction and
17. as *of* sincerity, but as *of* God,
3: 1. (letters) of commendation *from* you?
5. think any thing as *of* ourselves; but our sufficiency (is) *of* God;
4: 6. the light to shine *out of* darkness,
7. may be of God, and not *of* us.
5: 1. we have a building *of* God,
2. our house which is *from* heaven:
8. rather to be absent *from* the body,
18. all things (are) *of* God, who hath
6:17. come out *from* among them,
7: 9. receive damage *by* us in nothing.
8: 7. and (in) your love (lit. love *from* you) to us,
11. a performance also *out of* that
14(13). *by* an equality, (that) now
9: 2. your zeal (lit. the zeal *of* you) hath provoked
7. not grudgingly (lit. *of* grief), or *of* necessity:
11:26. (in) perils *by* (mine own) countrymen, (in) perils *by* the heathen,
12: 6. or (that) he heareth *of* me.
13: 4. he was crucified *through* weakness, yet he liveth *by* the power of God.
— live with him *by* the power of God
Gal. 1: 1. who raised him *from* the dead;
4. *from* this present evil world,
8. though we, or an angel *from* heaven,
15. separated me *from* my mother's womb,
2:12. which were *of* the circumcision.
15. not sinners *of* the Gentiles,
16. not justified *by* the works of the law, but by the faith of Jesus Christ,
— that we might be justified *by* the faith of Christ, and not *by* the works of the law: for *by* the works of the law shall no
3: 2. the Spirit *by* the works of the law, or *by* the hearing of faith?
5. *by* the works of the law, or *by* the
7. that they which are *of* faith,
8. justify the heathen *through* faith,
9. then they which be *of* faith
10. as are *of* the works of the law
11. The just shall live *by* faith.
12. the law is not *of* faith·

Gal. 3:13. hath redeemed us *from* the curse
18. if the inheritance (be) *of* the law, (it is) no more *of* promise:
21. should have been *by* the law.
22. the promise *by* faith of Jesus Christ
24. we might be justified *by* faith.
4: 4. his Son, made *of* a woman,
22. one *by* a bondmaid, the other *by* a freewoman.
23. he (who was) *of* the bondwoman
— he *of* the freewoman (was) by
5: 5. hope of righteousness *by* faith.
8. (cometh) not *of* him that calleth you.
6: 8. shall *of* the flesh reap corruption;
— shall *of* the Spirit reap life
Eph. 1:20. he raised him *from* the dead,
2: 8. that not *of* yourselves:
9. Not *of* works, lest any man should
3:15. *Of* whom the whole family
20. exceeding abundantly (lit. *of* abundance) above all that
4:16. *From* whom the whole body
29. proceed *out of* your mouth,
5:14. that sleepest, and arise *from* the dead,
30. For we are members of his body, *of* his flesh, and *of* his bones.
6: 6. the will of God *from* the heart;
Phil. 1:16. one preach Christ *of* contention,
17. the other *of* love, knowing that
23. I am in a strait *betwixt* two, (lit. am held in a strait *by* the two)
3: 5. *of* the stock of Israel,
— an Hebrew *of* the Hebrews;
9. righteousness, which is *of* the law
— righteousness which is *of* God
20. *from* whence also we look for
4:22. they that are *of* Cæsar's houshold.
Col. 1:13. delivered us *from* the power of
18. the firstborn *from* the dead;
2:12. hath raised him *from* the dead.
14. took it *out of* the way, nailing it
19. *from* which all the body by
3: 8. filthy communication *out of* your mouth.
23. ye do, do (it) heartily, (lit. *from* the heart)
4: 9. beloved brother, who is (one) *of* you.
11. who are *of* the circumcision.
12. who is (one) *of* you, a servant of Christ,
16. read the (epistle) *from* Laodicea.
1Th. 1:10. to wait for his Son *from* heaven, whom he raised *from* the dead,
2: 3. (was) not *of* deceit, nor *of* uncleanness,
6. Nor *of* men sought we glory,
3:10. praying exceedingly (lit. above *of* excess)
5:13. esteem them very highly (lit. above *of* excess) in love
2Th. 2: 7. until he be taken *out of* the way.
1Ti. 1: 5. charity *out of* a pure heart,
6: 4. of words, where*of* cometh envy,
2Ti. 2: 8. Jesus Christ *of* the seed of David was raised *from* the dead according
22. on the Lord *out of* a pure heart.
26. *out of* the snare of the devil,
3: 6. For *of* this sort are they which
11. *out of* (them) all the Lord delivered me.
4:17. delivered *out of* the mouth of the lion.
Tit. 1:10. specially they *of* the circumcision:
12. One *of* themselves, (even) a prophet
2: 8. he that is *of* the contrary part
3: 5. Not *by* works of righteousness
Heb. 1:13. Sit *on* my right hand, until
2:11. sanctified (are) all *of* one:
3:13. lest any *of* you be hardened

Heb 3:16. not all that came *out of* Egypt
4: 1. any *of* you should seem to come
5: 1. high priest taken *from among* men
7. able to save him *from* death,
7: 4. Abraham gave)(the tenth of the spoils.
5. they that are *of* the sons of Levi.
— come *out of* the loins of Abraham:
6. descent is not counted *from* them
12. there is made *of* necessity a change
14. our Lord sprang *out of* Juda;
8: 9. to lead them *out of* the land of Egypt;
9:28. shall he appear)(the second time
10:38. the just shall live *by* faith:
11: 3. not made *of* things which do appear.
19. to raise (him) up, even *from* the dead;
35. received their dead raised to life again: (lit. their dead *of* or by resurrection)
13:10. where*of* they have no right to eat
20. *from* the dead our Lord Jesus,
Jas. 2:16. one *of* you say unto them,
18. shew me thy faith *without* thy works, and I will shew thee my faith *by* my works.
21. Abraham our father justified *by* works,
22. *by* works was faith made perfect?
24. see then how that *by* works a man is justified, and not *by* faith only.
25. Rahab the harlot justified *by* works,
3:10. *Out of* the same mouth proceedeth
11. send *forth at* the same place
13. shew *out of* a good conversation
4: 1. *of* your lusts that war in your
5:20. the sinner *from* the error of his way shall save a soul *from* death,
1Pet. 1: 3. of Jesus Christ *from* the dead,
18. *from* your vain conversation
21. that raised him up *from* the dead,
22. love one another *with* a pure heart
23. not *of* corruptible seed, but of
2: 9. hath called you *out of* darkness
12. they may *by* (your) good works,
4:11. as *of* the ability which God giveth:
2Pet. 1:18. this voice which came *from* heaven
2: 8. soul from day to day (lit. day *after* day)
9. deliver the godly *out of* temptations,
21. turn *from* the holy commandment
3: 5. earth standing *out of* the water
1Joh. 2:16. is not *of* the Father, but is *of* the world.
19. They went out *from* us, but they were not *of* us; for if they had been *of* us,
— that they were not all *of* us.
21. that no lie is *of* the truth.
29. doeth righteousness is born *of* him.
3: 8. that committeth sin is *of* the devil;
9. Whosoever is born *of* God doth
— because he is born *of* God.
10. doeth not righteousness is not *of* God,
12. Cain, (who) was *of* that wicked one,
14. passed *from* death unto life,
19. we know that we are *of* the truth,
24. *by* the Spirit which he hath given us
4: 1. whether they are *of* God:
2. come in the flesh is *of* God:
3. in the flesh is not *of* God:
4. Ye are *of* God, little children,
5. They are *of* the world: therefore speak they *of* the world,
6. We are *of* God: he that knoweth
— he that is not *of* God heareth not us. Hereby know we the spirit of
7. love one another: for love is *of* God; and every one that loveth is born *of* God,
13. he hath given us *of* his Spirit.
1Joh. 5: 1. Jesus is the Christ is born *of* God:
— also that is begotten *of* him.
4. whatsoever is born *of* God
18. whosoever is born *of* God sinneth not, but he that is begotten *of* God keepeth
19. we know that we are *of* God,
2Joh. 4. that I found *of* thy children
3Joh. 10. casteth (them) *out of* the church.
11. He that doeth good is *of* God:
Jude 5. people *out of* the land of Egypt,
23. pulling (them) *out of* the fire;
Rev. 1: 5. the first begotten *of* the dead,
16. *out of* his mouth went a sharp
2: 5. thy candlestick *out of* his place,
7. to eat *of* the tree of life, which is
10. the devil shall cast (some) *of* you
11. shall not be hurt *of* the second death.
17. I give to eat *of* the hidden manna,
21. to repent *of* her fornication;
22. except they repent *of* their deeds.
3: 5. his name *out of* the book of life,
9. them *of* the synagogue of Satan,
10. thee *from* the hour of temptation,
12. which cometh down *out of* heaven
16. I will spue thee *out of* my mouth.
18. buy of me gold tried *in* the fire,
4: 5. *out of* the throne proceeded lightnings
5: 5. one *of* the elders saith unto me,
— the Lion *of* the tribe of Juda,
7. *out of* the right hand of him
9. *out of* every kindred, and tongue,
6: 1. the Lamb opened one *of* the seals,
— one *of* the four beasts saying,
14. were moved *out of* their places
7: 4. *of* all the tribes of the children
5. *Of* the tribe of Juda (were) sealed
— *Of* the tribe of Reuben... *Of* the tribe of Gad
6. *Of* the tribe of Aser... *Of* the tribe of Nepthalim... *Of* the tribe of Manasses
7. *Of* the tribe of Simeon... *Of* the tribe of Levi... *Of* the tribe of Issachar
8. *Of* the tribe of Zabulon... *Of* the tribe of Joseph... *Of* the tribe of Benjamin
9. *of* all nations, and kindreds, and people,
13. one *of* the elders answered,
14. came *out of* great tribulation,
8: 4. *out of* the angel's hand.
5. filled it *with* fire of the altar,
10. fell a great star *from* heaven,
11. many men died *of* the waters,
13. *by reason of* the other voices
9: 1. I saw a star fall *from* heaven
2. there arose a smoke *out of* the pit,
— *by reason of* the smoke of the pit.
3. there came *out of* the smoke
13. I heard a voice *from* the four horns
17. *out of* their mouths issued fire
18. *by* the fire, and *by* the smoke, and *by* the brimstone, which issued *out of* their mouths.
20. repented not *of* the works of their
21. repented they *of* their murders, nor *of* their sorceries, nor *of* their fornication, nor *of* their thefts.
10: 1. angel come down *from* heaven,
4. I heard a voice *from* heaven
8. the voice which I heard *from* heaven
10. little book *out of* the angel's hand,
11: 5. fire proceedeth *out of* their mouth
7. *out of* the bottomless pit
9. they *of* the people and kindreds

Rev.11:11. the Spirit of life *from* God
12. they heard a great voice *from* heaven
12:15. the serpent cast *out of* his mouth
16. the dragon cast *out of* his mouth.
13: 1. a beast rise up *out of* the sea,
11. coming up *out of* the earth;
13. maketh fire come down *from* heaven
14: 2. I heard a voice *from* heaven,
8. made all nations drink *of* the wine
10. same shall drink *of* the wine of
13. I heard a voice *from* heaven
— they may rest *from* their labours;
15. angel came *out of* the temple,
17. another angel came *out of* the temple
18. angel came out *from* the altar,
20. blood came *out of* the winepress,
15: 2. *over* the beast, and *over* his image, and *over* his mark, (and) *over* the number of
6. seven angels came *out of* the temple,
7. one *of* the four beasts gave unto
8. *from* the glory of God, and *from* his power;
16: 1. a great voice *out of* the temple
7. I heard another *out of* the altar
10. they gnawed their tongues *for* pain,
11. *because of* their pains and)(their sores, and repented not *of* their deeds.
13. *out of* the mouth of the dragon, and *out of* the mouth of the beast, and *out of* the mouth of the false prophet.
21. a great hail *out of* heaven,
— *because of* the plague of the hail;
17: 1. came one *of* the seven angels
2. *with* the wine of her fornication.
6. *with* the blood of the saints, and *with* the blood of the martyrs of Jesus:
8. ascend *out of* the bottomless pit,
11. is *of* the seven, and goeth into
18: 1. another angel come down *from* heaven,
— was lightened *with* his glory.
3. have drunk *of* the wine of the
— *through* the abundance of her
4. I heard another voice *from* heaven, saying, Come *out of* her, my people,
— receive not *of* her plagues.
12. vessels *of* most precious wood,
19. *by reason of* her costliness!
20. God hath avenged you *on* (lit. *of*) her.
19: 2. blood of his servants *at* her hand.
5. a voice came *out of* the throne,
15. *out of* his mouth goeth a sharp
21. (sword) proceeded *out of* his mouth: and all the fowls were filled *with* their flesh.
20: 1. an angel come down *from* heaven,
7. shall be loosed *out of* his prison,
9. down from God *out of* heaven,
12. judged *out of* those things which were
21: 2. down from God *out of* heaven,
3. I heard a great voice *out of* heaven
6. *of* the fountain of the water of life
10. descending *out of* heaven from God,
21. every several gate was *of* one pearl:
22: 1. proceeding *out of* the throne
19. *out of* the holy city, and (from) the

1538 83 236/308

ἕκαστος, *hekastos.*

Mat.16:27. shall reward *every man* according
18:35. forgive not *every one* his brother
25:15. to *every man* according to his
26:22 began *every one* of them to say
Mar 13:34. to *every* man his work,
Lu. 2: 3. *every one* into his own city.
4:40. his hands on *every* one of them,
6:44. For *every* tree is known by
13:15. doth not *each one* of you on the
16: 5. called *every* one of his lord's debtors
Joh. 6: 7. that *every one* of them may take
7:53. *every man* went unto his own house.
16:32. scattered, *every man* to his own,
19:23. four parts, to *every* soldier a part;
Acts 2: 3. it sat upon *each* of them.
6. *every* man heard them speak
8. how hear we *every man* in our
38. be baptized *every one* of you
3:26. turning away *every one* of you
4:35. made unto *every man* according
11:29. *every man* according to his ability,
17:27. not far from *every* one of us:
20:31. to warn *every* one night and day
21:19. he declared *particularly* (lit. by *each* one)
26. offered for *every* one of them.
Ro. 2: 6. render to *every man* according
12: 3. as God hath dealt to *every* man
14: 5. Let *every man* be fully persuaded
12. So then *every one* of us shall
15: 2. Let *every one* of us please
1Co. 1:12. that *every one* of you saith,
3: 5. as the Lord gave to *every man?*
8. *every man* shall receive his own
10. let *every man* take heed how
13. *Every man's* work shall be
— fire shall try *every man's* work
4: 5. *every man* have praise of God.
7: 2. let *every man* have his own wife, and let *every woman* have her own husband.
7. *every* man hath his proper gift
17. hath distributed to *every man*, as the Lord hath called *every one*,
20. Let *every man* abide in the same
24. let *every man*, wherein he is called,
10:24. *every man* another's (wealth).
11:21. in eating *every one* taketh before
12: 7. given to *every man* to profit
11. dividing to *every man* severally
18. *every* one of them in the body,
14:26. *every one* of you hath a psalm,
15:23. *every man* in his own order·
38. to *every* seed his own body.
16: 2. let *every one* of you lay by him
2Co. 5:10. that *every one* may receive the
9: 7. *Every man* according as he purposeth
Gal. 6: 4. let *every man* prove his own work,
5. *every man* shall bear his own burden.
Eph. 4: 7. unto *every* one of us is given grace
16. in the measure of *every* part,
25. speak *every man* truth with
5:33. let *every one* of you in particular
6: 8. good thing *any man* doeth,
Phi. 2: 4. Look not *every man* on his own things, but *every man* also on the things
Col. 4: 6. ought to answer *every* man.
1Th. 2:11. charged *every* one of you,
4: 4. That *every one* of you should
2Th. 1: 3. the charity of *every* one of you
Heb. 3:13. exhort one another daily, (lit. on *every* day)
6:11. we desire that *every one* of you
8:11. teach *every man* his neighbour, and *every man* his brother,
11:21. blessed *both* (lit. *each* of) the sons of Joseph;
Jas. 1:14. *every man* is tempted, when

1Pet. 1:17. according to *every man's* work,
4:10. As *every man* hath received the
Rev. 2:23. I will give unto *every one* of you
5: 8. having *every one* of them harps,
6:11. given unto *every one* of them;
20:13. they were judged *every man*
21:21. *every* several gate was of one
22: 2. yielded her fruit *every* month:
12. to give *every man* according

1539 1 236/309 1538,5119

ἑκάστοτε, hekastote.

2Pet. 1:15. able...to have these things *always* in remembrance.

1540 17 236/309

ἑκατόν, hekaton.

Mat. 13: 8. some an *hundredfold*, some
23. bringeth forth, some an *hundredfold*,
18:12. if a man have an *hundred* sheep,
28. owed him an *hundred* pence:
Mar. 4: 8. some sixty, and some an *hundred*.
20. some sixty, and some an *hundred*.
6:40. by *hundreds*, and by fifties.
Lu. 15: 4. having an *hundred* sheep,
16: 6. An *hundred* measures of oil.
7. An *hundred* measures of wheat.
Joh. 19:39. about an *hundred* pound (weight).
21:11. fishes, an *hundred* and fifty and three:
Acts 1:15. about an *hundred* and twenty,
Rev. 7: 4. sealed an *hundred* (and) forty (and) four
14: 1. an *hundred* forty (and) four thousand,
3. the *hundred* (and) forty (and) four thousand,
21:17. an *hundred* (and) forty (and) four cubits,

1541 1 236/309 1540,2094

ἑκατονταέτης, hekatontaetees.

Ro. 4:19. was about an *hundred years old*,

1542 3 236/309 1540,4111

ἑκατονταπλασίων, hekatontaplasiōn.

Mat. 19:29. shall receive an *hundredfold*,
Mar 10:30. he shall receive an *hundredfold*
Lu. 8: 8. bare fruit an *hundredfold*.

1543 5 236/309 1540,757

ἑκατοντάρχης, hekatontarkees.

Acts 10: 1. a *centurion* of the band called
22. they said, Cornelius the *centurion*,
24:23. commanded a *centurion* to
27: 1. a *centurion* of Augustus' band.
31. Paul said to the *centurion*

1543 16 236/309 1540,757

ἑκατόνταρχος, hekatontarkos.

Mat. 8: 5. there came unto him a *centurion*,
8. The *centurion* answered and said,
13. Jesus said unto the *centurion*,
27:54. when the *centurion*, and they that
Lu. 7: 2. a certain *centurion's* servant,
6. the *centurion* sent friends to him,
23:47. when the *centurion* saw what
Acts 21:32. immediately took soldiers and *centurions*,
22:25. Paul said unto the *centurion*
Acts 22:26. When the *centurion* heard (that),
23:17. Paul called one of the *centurions*
23. he called unto (him) two *centurions*.
27: 6. there the *centurion* found a ship
11. the *centurion* believed the master
43. the *centurion*, willing to save Paul,
28:16. the *centurion* delivered the prisoners

1544 82 236/309 1:526 1537,906

ἐκβάλλω, ekballo.

Mat. 7: 4. Let me *pull out* the mote out of
5. first *cast out* the beam out of
— see clearly *to cast out* the mote out of
22. in thy name *have cast out* devils?
8:12. *shall be cast out* into outer darkness:
16. he *cast out* the spirits with (his) word,
31. saying, If thou *cast* us *out*,
9:25. when the people *were put forth*,
33. *when* the devil *was cast out*,
34. He *casteth out* devils through
38. that he will *send forth* labourers
10: 1. unclean spirits, *to cast* them *out*,
8. raise the dead, *cast out* devils:
12:20. till he *send forth* judgment unto
24. *doth* not *cast out* devils,
26. if Satan *cast out* Satan, he is
27. if I by Beelzebub *cast out* devils,
— *do* your children *cast* (them) *out?*
28. if I *cast out* devils by the Spirit
35. *bringeth forth* good things:
— *bringeth forth* evil things.
13:52. *bringeth forth* out of his treasure
15:17. *is cast out* into the draught?
17:19. Why could not we *cast* him *out?*
21:12. *cast out* all them that sold
39. they caught him, and *cast* (him) out
22:13. *cast* (him) into outer darkness;
25:30. *cast* ye the unprofitable servant into outer
Mar. 1:12. *driveth* him into the wilderness.
34. and *cast out* many devils;
39. throughout all Galilee, and *cast out* devils.
43. forthwith *sent* him *away;*
3:15. *to cast out* devils:
22. of the devils *casteth* he *out* devils.
23. How can Satan *cast out* Satan?
5:40. *when* he *had put* them all *out*,
6:13. they *cast out* many devils,
7:26. he *would cast forth* the devil
9:18. that they *should cast* him *out;*
28. Why could not we *cast* him *out?*
38. we saw one *casting out* devils
47. thine eye offend thee, *pluck* it *out*.
11:15. began *to cast out* them that
12: 8. *cast* (him) out of the vineyard.
16: 9. out of whom he *had cast* seven devils.
17. *shall* they *cast out* devils;
Lu. 4:29. *thrust* him out of the city,
6:22. shall reproach (you), and *cast out* your name
42. let me *pull out* the mote
— *cast out* first the beam out of
— see clearly *to pull out* the mote
8:54. *put* them all out, and took her by the hand and
9:40. thy disciples to *cast* him *out;*
49. we saw one *casting out* devils
10: 2. that he *would send forth* labourers into his harvest.
35. he *took out* two pence, *and* gave
11:14. he was *casting out* a devil,
15. He *casteth out* devils through

Lu. 11:18. I *cast out* devils through Beelzebub.
19. if I by Beelzebub *cast out* devils, by whom *do* your sons *cast* (them) *out?*
20. But if I with the finger of God *cast out*
13:28. you (yourselves) *thrust* out.
32. Behold, I *cast out* devils,
19:45. *to cast out* them that sold therein,
20:12. wounded him also, and *cast* (him) *out.*
15. *cast* him out of the vineyard, *and*
Joh. 2:15. he *drove* them all *out* of the temple,
6:37. I *will* in no wise *cast* out.
9:34. thou teach us? And they *cast* him out.
35. that they *had cast* him out;
10: 4. he *putteth forth* his own sheep,
12:31. *shall* the prince of this world *be cast* out.
Acts 7:58. *cast* (him) out of the city, *and*
9:40. *put* them all forth, and kneeled down, *and*
13:50. *expelled* them out of their coasts.
16:37. now do they *thrust* us *out* privily?
27:38. *and cast out* the wheat into the sea.
Gal. 4:30. *Cast out* the bondwoman
Jas. 2:25. and *had sent* (them) *out* another way?
3Joh. 10. *casteth* (them) *out* of the church.
Rev. 11: 2. without the temple *leave* out,

1545 2 237/310 1537 *bainō* (to walk)

ἔκβασις, *ekbasis.*

1Co. 10:13. also make a *way to escape*,
Heb 13: 7. considering the *end* of (their) conversation:

1546 1 237/310 1544

ἐκβολή, *ekbolee.*

Acts 27:18. next (day) they lightened the ship; (lit. they made a *casting out*)

1547 5 237/155 1537,1061

ἐκγαμίζω, *ekgamizo.*

Mat. 22:30. neither marry, nor *are given in marriage*,
24:38. marrying and *giving in marriage*,
Lu. 17:27. they *were given in marriage*,
1Co. 7:38. he *that giveth* (her) *in marriage* doeth well; but he *that giveth* (her) not *in marriage*

1548 2 237/155 1537,1061

ἐκγαμίσκομαι, *ekgamiskomai.*

Lu. 20:34. marry, and *are given in marriage:*
35. neither marry, nor *are given in marriage:*

1549 1 237/310 1537,1096

ἔκγονα, *ekgona.*

1Ti. 5: 4. have children or *nephews*, (lit. *descendants*)

1550 1 237/310 1537,1159

ἐκδαπανάω, *ekdapanao.*

2Co. 12:15. I will very gladly spend and *be spent*

1551 8 237/311 1537,1209

ἐκδέχομαι, *ekdekomai.*

Joh. 5: 3. withered, *waiting for* the moving
Acts 17:16. *while* Paul *waited for* them at Athens,
1Co. 11:33. to eat, *tarry* one *for* another.
1Co. 16:11. I *look for* him with the brethren.
Heb 10:13. *expecting* till his enemies be
11:10. he *looked for* a city which hath
Jas. 5: 7. the husbandman *waiteth for* the
1Pet. 3:20. *waited* in the days of Noah,

1552 1 237/311 1537,1212

ἔκδηλος, *ekdeelos.*

2Ti. 3: 9. folly shall be *manifest* unto all

1553 3 237/311 2:63 1537,1218

ἐκδημέω, *ekdeemeo.*

2Co. 5: 6. we *are absent* from the Lord:
8. rather *to be absent* from the body,
9. that, whether present or *absent*,

1554 4 237/311 1537,1325

ἐκδίδωμι, *ekdidōmi.*

Mat. 21:33. built a tower, and *let* it *out* to
41. *will let out* (his) vineyard unto
Mar 12: 1. *let* it *out* to husbandmen,
Lu. 20: 9. *let* it *forth* to husbandmen,

1555 2 238/311 1537,1223,2233

ἐκδιηγέομαι, *ekdieegeomai.*

Acts 13:41. though a man *declare* it unto you.
15: 3. *declaring* the conversion of the

1556 6 238/311 2:442 1558

ἐκδικέω, *ekdikeo.*

Lu. 18: 3. saying, *Avenge* me of mine adversary.
5. I *will avenge* her, lest by her
Ro. 12:19. Dearly beloved, *avenge* not yourselves,
2Co. 10: 6. *to revenge* all disobedience,
Rev. 6:10. dost thou not judge and *avenge* our blood
19: 2. *hath avenged* the blood of his

1557 9 238/311 2:442 1556

ἐκδίκησις, *ekdikeesis.*

Lu. 18: 7. shall not God *avenge* (lit. make *vengeance for*) his own
8. that he will *avenge* (lit. make, &c.) them speedily.
21:22. these be the days of *vengeance*,
Acts 7:24. *avenged* (lit. made *v.* &c.) him that was oppressed,
Ro. 12:19. it is written, *Vengeance* (is) mine;
2Co. 7:11. (what) zeal, yea, (what) *revenge!*
2Th. 1: 8. taking *vengeance* on them that
Heb 10:30. said, *Vengeance* (belongeth) unto me,
1Pet. 2:14. for the *punishment* of evildoers,

1558 2 238/311 2:442 1537,1349

ἔκδικος, *ekdikos.*

Ro. 13: 4. a *revenger* to (execute) wrath upon
1Th. 4: 6. the Lord (is) the *avenger* of all such,

1559 2 238/311 1537,1377

ἐκδιώκω, *ekdioko.*

Lu. 11:49. them they shall slay and *persecute:*
1Th. 2:15. own prophets, and *have persecuted* us;

1560 1 238/311 1537,1325

ἔκδοτος, ekdotos.

Acts 2:23. being *delivered* by the determinate

1561 1 238/311 2:50 1551

ἐκδοχή, ekdokee.

Heb 10:27. a certain fearful *looking for* of judgment

1562 5 238/311 2:318 rt 1416 1537

ἐκδύω, ekduo.

Mat.27:28. they *stripped* him, *and* put on him
31. they *took* the robe *off from* him,
Mar 15:20. they *took off* the purple *from* him,
Lu. 10:30. which *stripped* him... *of his raiment and*
2Co. 5: 4. that we would *be unclothed*,

1563 98 238/311

ἐκεῖ, ekī.

Mat. 2:13. be thou *there* until I bring thee word:
15. was *there* until the death of Herod:
22. he was afraid to go *thither:*
5:24. Leave *there* thy gift before the
6:21. *there* will your heart be also.
8:12. *there* shall be weeping and gnashing
12:45. they enter in and dwell *there:*
13:42. *there* shall be wailing and gnashing
50. *there* shall be wailing and gnashing
58. did not many mighty works *there*
14:23. evening was come, he was *there* alone.
15:29. into a mountain, and sat down *there*.
17:20. Remove hence *to yonder place;*
18:20. *there* am I in the midst of them.
19: 2. he healed them *there*.
21:17. into Bethany; and he lodged *there*.
22:11. he saw *there* a man which had
13. *there* shall be weeping and gnashing
24:28. *there* will the eagles be gathered
51. *there* shall be weeping and gnashing
25:30. *there* shall be weeping and gnashing
26:36. while I go and pray *yonder*.
71. said unto them that were *there*,
27:36. they watched him *there;*
47. Some of them that stood *there*,
55. many women were *there*
61. *there* was Mary Magdalene,
28: 7. *there* shall ye see him:
Mar 1:13. he was *there* in the wilderness
2: 6. certain of the scribes sitting *there*,
3: 1. there was a man *there* which
5:11. Now there was *there* nigh unto
6: 5. could *there* do no mighty work,
10. *there* abide till ye depart from
33. ran afoot *thither* out of all cities,
55. where they heard he was)(.
11: 5. them that stood *there* said
13:21. Lo, here (is) Christ; or, lo, (he is) *there*,
14:15. *there* make ready for us.
16: 7. *there* shall ye see him, as he said
Lu. 2: 6. that, while they were *there*,
6: 6. *there* was a man whose right
8:32. there was *there* an herd of many
9: 4. *there* abide, and thence depart.
10: 6. if the son of peace be *there*,
11:26. they enter in, and dwell *there:*
12:18. *there* will I bestow all my
34. *there* will your heart be also.
13:28. *There* shall be weeping and gnashing
15:13. *there* wasted his substance
17:21. Lo here! or, lo *there!*
Lu. 17:23. See here; or, see *there*
37. *thither* will the eagles be gathered
21: 2. casting in *thither* two mites.
22:12. room furnished: *there* make ready
23:33. *there* they crucified him,
Joh. 2: 1. the mother of Jesus was *there:*
6. were set *there* six waterpots
12. they continued *there* not many
3:22. *there* he tarried with them,
23. there was much water *there:*
4: 6. Now Jacob's well was *there*.
40. he abode *there* two days.
5: 5. a certain man was *there*,
6: 3. *there* he sat with his disciples.
22. was none other boat *there*,
24. saw that Jesus was not *there*,
10:40. first baptized; and *there* he abode.
42. many believed on him *there*.
11: 8. goest thou *thither* again?
15. that I was not *there*, to the
31. unto the grave to weep *there*.
12: 2. *There* they made him a supper;
9. knew that he was *there*.
26. *there* shall also my servant be.
18: 2. Jesus ofttimes resorted *thither*
3. cometh *thither* with lanterns
19:42. *There* laid they Jesus therefore
Acts 9:33. *there* he found a certain man
14:28. *there* they abode long time with
16: 1. a certain disciple was *there*,
17:14. Timotheus abode *there* still.
19:21. After I have been *there*,
25: 9. *there* be judged of these things
14. they had been *there* many days,
Ro 9:26. *there* shall they be called the
15:24. brought on my way *thitherward*
2Co 3:17. Spirit of the Lord (is), *there* (is) liberty.
Tit. 3:12. I have determined *there* to winter.
Heb. 7: 8. *there* he (receiveth them), of whom
Jas. 2: 3. to the poor, Stand thou *there*,
3:16. *there* (is) confusion and every evil work.
4:13. continue *there* a year, and buy and sell
Rev. 2:14. thou hast *there* them that hold
12: 6. they should feed her *there*
14. where she is nourished)(for
21:25. there shall be no night *there*.
22: 5. there shall be no night *there;*

See also κἀκεῖ.

1564 27 238/312 1563

ἐκεῖθεν, ekīthen.

Mat. 4:21. going on *from thence*, he saw
5:26. by no means come out *thence*,
9: 9. as Jesus passed forth *from thence*,
27. when Jesus departed *thence*,
11: 1. he departed *thence* to teach
12: 9. when he was departed *thence*,
15. he withdrew himself *from thence:*
13:53. finished these parables, he departed *thence*
14:13. he departed *thence* by ship
5:21. went *thence*, and departed into
29. Jesus departed *from thence*,
19:15. hands on them, and departed *thence*,
Mar. 1:19. had gone a little farther *thence*,
6: 1. he went out *from thence*,
10. till ye depart *from that place*.
11. when ye depart *thence*, shake
7:24. *from thence* he arose, and went
9:30. they departed *thence*, and passed
Lu. 9: 4. there abide, and thence depart.

Lu. 12:59. thou shalt not depart *thence*,
16:26. that (would come) *from thence*.
Joh. 4:43 after two days he departed *thence*,
11:54. went *thence* unto a country near
Acts13: 4. *from thence* they sailed to Cyprus.
16:12. *from thence* to Philippi, which
18: 7. he departed *thence*, and entered
20:13. *there* (lit. *thence*) intending to take in Paul:

See also κἀκεῖθεν.

1565 251 238/313 1563 cf 3778

ἐκεῖνος, *ekinos*.

Mat. 3: 1. In *those* days came John the Baptist,
7:22. Many will say to me in *that* day,
25. winds blew, and beat upon *that* house;
27. winds blew, and beat upon *that* house;
8:13. healed in the *selfsame* hour.
28. no man might pass by *that* way.
9:22. was made whole from *that* hour.
26. went abroad into all *that* land.
31. abroad his fame in all *that* country.
10:14. depart out of *that* house or city,
15. than for *that* city.
19. be given you in *that same* hour
11:25. At *that* time Jesus answered
12: 1. At *that* time Jesus went on the
45. the last (state) of *that* man
13: 1. *The same* day went Jesus out
11. to *them* it is not given.
44. that he hath, and buyeth *that* field.
14: 1. At *that* time Herod the tetrarch
35. when the men of *that* place
— sent out into all *that* country
15:22. came out of *the same* coasts,
28. made whole from *that very* hour.
17:18. child was cured from *that very* hour.
27. *that* take, and give unto them
18: 1. At *the same* time came the
7. woe to *that* man by whom
27. Then the lord of *that* servant
28. *the same* servant went out,
32. I forgave thee all *that* debt,
21:40. do unto *those* husbandmen?
22: 7. destroyed *those* murderers,
10. So *those* servants went out
23. *The same* day came to him
46. from *that* day forth ask him
24:19. them that give suck in *those* days!
22. except *those* days should be shortened,
— elect's sake *those* days shall be shortened.
29. the tribulation of *those* days
36. of *that* day and hour knoweth
43. know *this*, that if the goodman
46. Blessed (is) *that* servant, whom
48. if *that* evil servant shall say
50. The lord of *that* servant shall
25: 7. Then all *those* virgins arose,
19. the lord of *those* servants cometh,
26:24. woe unto *that* man by whom
— it had been good for *that* man
29. until *that* day when I drink it
55. In *that same* hour said Jesus
27: 8. Wherefore *that* field was called,
19. nothing to do with *that* just man:
63. we remember that *that* deceiver said,
Mar. 1: 9. it came to pass in *those* days,
2:20. shall they fast in *those* days.
3:24. *that* kingdom cannot stand.
25. *that* house cannot stand.
4:11. unto *them* that are without,
35. *the same* day, when the even
Mar. 6:11. judgment, than for *that* city.
55. ran through *that* whole region
7:15. *those* are they that defile the man.
20. *that* defileth the man.
8: 1. In *those* days the multitude being
12: 7. *those* husbandmen said among
13:11. shall be given you in *that* hour,
17. that give suck in *those* days!
19. (in) *those* days shall be affliction,
24. in *those* days, after *that* tribulation, the
32. of *that* day and (that) hour knoweth
14:21. woe to *that* man by whom
— good were it for *that* man
25. until *that* day that I drink it
16:10. *she* went and told them that had
13. neither believed they *them*.
20. *they* went forth, and preached
Lu. 2: 1. it came to pass in *those* days,
4: 2. in *those* days he did eat nothing:
5:35. shall they fast in *those* days.
6:23. Rejoice ye in *that* day, and leap
48. beat vehemently upon *that* house,
49. the ruin of *that* house was great.
8:32. suffer them to enter into *them*.
9: 5. when ye go out of *that* city,
34. as *they* entered into the cloud.
36. told no man in *those* days
10:12. more tolerable in *that* day for Sodom than for *that* city.
31. came down a certain priest *that* way:
11:26. the last (state) of *that* man
12:37. Blessed (are) *those* servants, whom
38. blessed are *those* servants.
43. Blessed (is) *that* servant, whom
45. if *that* servant say in his heart, My lord delayeth his coming;
46. The lord of *that* servant will
47. *that* servant, which knew his
13: 4. Or *those* eighteen, upon whom
14:21. So *that* servant came, and shewed
24. none of *those* men which were
15:14. a mighty famine in *that* land;
15. to a citizen of *that* country;
17: 9. Doth he thank *that* servant
31. In *that* day, he which shall be
18: 3. there was a widow in *that* city;
14. justified (rather) than *the other*:
19: 4. for he was to pass *that* (way).
27. *those* mine enemies, which
20: 1. on one of *those* days, as he taught
18. Whosoever shall fall upon *that* stone
35. worthy to obtain *that* world,
21:23. that give suck, in *those* days!
34. (so) *that* day come upon you unawares.
22:22. woe unto *that* man by whom
Joh. 1: 8. *He* was not that Light, but (was)
18. of the Father, *he* hath declared (him).
33. *the same* said unto me,
39(40). abode with him *that* day:
2:21. *he* spake of the temple of his body
3:28. that I am sent before *him*.
30. *He* must increase, but I (must)
4:25. when *he* is come, he will tell
39. the Samaritans of *that* city
53. at *the same* hour, in the which
5: 9. on *the same* day was the sabbath.
11. *the same* said unto me,
19. for what things soever *he* doeth,
35. *He* was a burning and a shining light:
38. for whom *he* hath sent,
39. *they* are they which testify of me.
43. his own name, *him* ye will receive.

Joh. 5:46. for *he* wrote of me.
47. if ye believe not *his* writings,
6:22. save *that* one whereinto his
29. believe on him whom *he* hath sent.
7:11. said, Where is *he?*
45. *they* said unto them,
8:10. where are *those* thine accusers?
42. neither came I of myself, but *he* sent me.
44. *He* was a murderer from the
9: 9. *he* said, I am (he).
11. *He* answered and said, A man
12. said they unto him, Where is *he?*
25. *He* answered and said, Whether
28. said, Thou art *his* disciple;
36. *He* answered and said, Who is he,
37. it is *he* that talketh with thee.
10: 1. *the same* is a thief and a robber.
6. *they* understood not what
35. If he called *them* gods, unto
11:13. *they* thought that he had spoken
29. As soon as *she* heard (that),
49. the high priest *that same* year,
51. being high priest *that* year,
53. Then from *that* day forth they
12:48. *the same* shall judge him in
13: 6. Peter (lit. *he*) saith unto him, Lord,
25. *He* then lying on Jesus' breast
26. *He* it is, to whom I shall give
27. Satan entered into *him*.
30. *He* then having received the sop
14:20. At *that* day ye shall know
21. *he* it is that loveth me:
26. *he* shall teach you all things,
15:26. *he* shall testify of me:
16: 8. when he is come, *he* will reprove
13. Howbeit when *he*, the Spirit of truth,
14. *He* shall glorify me: for he shall
23. in *that* day ye shall ask me
26. At *that* day ye shall ask in my
18:13. the high priest *that same* year.
15. *that* disciple was known unto
17. *He* saith, I am not.
25. *He* denied (it), and said, I am not.
19:21. that *he* said, I am King of the Jews.
27. from *that* hour that disciple took
31. for *that* sabbath day was an high day,
20:13. *they* say unto her, Woman,
15. *She*, supposing him to be the
16. *She* turned herself, and saith unto
19. *the same* day at evening,
21: 3. *that* night they caught nothing.
7. *that* disciple whom Jesus loved
23. that *that* disciple should not die:
Acts 1:19. *that* field is called in their
2:18. I will pour out in *those* days
41. *the same* day there were added
3:13. *he* was determined to let (him) go.
23. which will not hear *that* prophet,
7:41. they made a calf in *those* days,
8: 1. at *that* time there was a great
8. there was great joy in *that* city.
9:37. it came to pass in *those* days,
10: 9. as *they* went on their journey,
10. while *they* made ready, he
12: 1. Now about *that* time Herod
6. *the same* night Peter was sleeping
14:21. preached the gospel to *that* city,
16: 3. which were in *those* quarters:
33. *the same* hour of the night,
35. saying, Let *those* men go.
19:16. they fled out of *that* house
23. *the same* time there arose no

Acts20: 2. he had gone over *those* parts,
21: 6. *they* returned home again.
22:11. for the glory of *that* light, being
28: 7. In *the same* quarters were
Ro. 6:21. the end of *those* things (is) death.
11:23. *they* also, if they abide not in
14:14. to *him* (it is) unclean.
15. Destroy not *him* with thy meat,
1Co. 9:25. *they* (do it) to obtain a corruptible
10:11. these things happened unto *them*
28. for *his* sake that shewed it,
15:11. whether (it were) I or *they*, so we
2Co. 7: 8. I perceive that *the same* epistle
8: 9. that ye through *his* poverty might
14(13). (be a supply) for *their* want,
— *their* abundance also may be
10:18. not *he* that commendeth himself is
Eph. 2:12. That at *that* time ye were
2Th. 1:10. was believed in *that* day.
2Ti. 1:12. unto him against *that* day.
18. mercy of the Lord in *that* day:
2:13. believe not, (yet) *he* abideth faithful:
26. taken captive by him at *his* will.
3: 9. unto all (men), as *their's* also was.
4: 8. shall give me at *that* day:
Tit. 3: 7. being justified by *his* grace,
Heb. 3:10. I was grieved with *that* generation,
4: 2. but the word preached did not profit *them*,
11. to enter into *that* rest, lest
6: 7. herbs meet for *them* by whom
8: 7. if *that* first (covenant) had been
10. after *those* days, saith the Lord;
10:16. after *those* days, saith the Lord,
11:15. if they had been mindful of *that* (country)
12:25. For if *they* escaped not who
Jas. 1: 7. let not *that* man think
4:15. we shall live, and do this, or *that*
2Pet. 1:16. were eyewitnesses of *his* majesty.
1Joh. 2: 6. even as *he* walked.
3: 3. himself, even as *he* is pure.
5. ye know that *he* was manifested
7. righteous, even as *he* is righteous.
16. *he* laid down his life for us:
4:17. because as *he* is, so are we in
5:16. I do not say that he shall pray for *it*.
Rev. 9: 6. in *those* days shall men seek
11:13. *the same* hour was there a
16:14. to the battle of *that* great day

See also κἀκεῖνος.

1566 2 239/315 1563

εκεῖσε, ekīse.

Acts21: 3. for *there* the ship was to unlade
22: 5. to bring them which were *there*

1567 7 239/315 2:892 1537,2212

ἐκζητέω, ekzeeteo.

Lu. 11:50. *may be required* of this generation;
51. It *shall be required* of this generation.
Acts15:17. men *might seek after* the Lord,
Ro. 3:11. none *that seeketh after* God.
Heb11: 6. them *that diligently seek* him.
12:17. though he *sought* it *carefully*
1Pet. 1:10. *have enquired* and searched diligently

1568 4 239/316 3:4 1569

ἐκθαμβέω, ekthambeo.

Mar. 9:15. when they beheld him, *were greatly amazed*,
14:33. began *to be sore amazed*,

ar 16: 5. they *were affrighted.*
6. he saith unto them, *Be* not *affrighted:*

1569 1 239/316 3:4 1537,2285

ἔκθαμβος, ekthambos.

Acts 3:11. is called Solomon's, *greatly wondering.*

1570 1 239/316 1537,5087

ἔκθετος, ekthetos.

Acts 7:19. cast out their young children, (lit. in making their young children *exposed*)

1571 2 239/316 3:413 1537,2508

ἐκκαθαίρω, ekkathairo.

1Co. 5: 7. *Purge out* therefore the old leaven,
2Ti. 2:21. If a man therefore *purge* himself

1572 1 240/316 1537,2545

ἐκκαίομαι, ekkaiomai.

Ro. 1:27. *burned* in their lust one toward another;

1573 6 240/337 1537,2556

ἐκκακέω, ekkakeo.

Lu. 18: 1. ought always (to) pray, and not *to faint;*
2Co. 4: 1. received mercy, we *faint* not;
16. For which cause we *faint* not;
Gal. 6: 9. *let* us not *be weary* in well doing:
Eph. 3:13. I desire that ye *faint* not
2Th. 3:13. *be* not *weary* in well doing.

1574 2 240/316 2:446 rt2759 1537

ἐκκεντέω, ekkenteo.

Joh. 19:37. look on him whom they *pierced.*
Rev. 1: 7. they (also) which *pierced* him:

1575 3 240/316 1537,2806

ἐκκλάζω, ekklazo.

Ro. 11:17. if some of the branches *be broken off,*
19. The branches *were broken off,*
20. of unbelief they *were broken off,*

1576 2 240/316 1537,2808

ἐκκλείω, ekklīo.

Ro. 3:27. Where (is) boasting then? It *is excluded.*
Gal. 4:17. yea, they would *exclude* you,

1577 115 240/316 3:487 1537,2564

ἐκκλησία, ekkleesia.

Mat. 16:18. I will build my *church;*
18:17. tell (it) unto the *church:* but if he neglect to hear the *church,*
Acts 2:47. the Lord added to the *church* daily
5:11. fear came upon all the *church,*
7:38. he, that was in the *church*
8: 1. the *church* which was at Jerusalem;
3. he made havock of the *church,*
9:31. Then had the *churches* rest
11:22. the *church* which was in Jerusalem:
26. assembled themselves with the *church,*
12: 1. to vex certain of the *church.*
5. without ceasing of the *church* unto God
13: 1. Now there were in the *church*
14:23. elders in every *church,* and had
27. had gathered the *church* together,
Acts 15: 3. on their way by the *church,*
4. they were received of the *church,*
22. elders, with the whole *church,*
41. confirming the *churches.*
16: 5. so were the *churches* established
18:22. gone up, and saluted the *church,*
19:32. for the *assembly* was confused;
39. determined in a lawful *assembly.*
41. thus spoken, he dismissed the *assembly.*
20:17. called the elders of the *church.*
28. to feed the *church* of God,
Ro. 16: 1. is a servant of the *church*
4. all the *churches* of the Gentiles.
5. the *church* that is in their house.
16. The *churches* of Christ salute you.
23. mine host, and of the whole *church,*
1Co. 1: 2. Unto the *church* of God which
4:17. I teach every where in every *church.*
6: 4. least esteemed in the *church.*
7:17. so ordain I in all *churches.*
10:32. nor to the *church* of God.
11:16. neither the *churches* of God.
18. come together in the *church,*
22. or despise ye the *church* of God,
12:28. God hath set some in the *church,*
14: 4. that prophesieth edifieth the *church.*
5. the *church* may receive edifying.
12. to the edifying of the *church.*
19. in the *church* I had rather speak
23. the whole *church* be come together
28. keep silence in the *church;*
33. as in all *churches* of the saints.
34. keep silence in the *churches:*
35. for women to speak in the *church.*
15: 9. I persecuted the *church* of God.
16: 1. to the *churches* of Galatia,
19. The *churches* of Asia salute you.
— with the *church* that is in their house.
2Co. 1: 1. unto the *church* of God which
8: 1. on the *churches* of Macedonia;
18. gospel throughout all the *churches*
19. was also chosen of the *churches*
23. the messengers of the *churches,*
24. to them, and before the *churches,*
11: 8. I robbed other *churches,* taking
28. the care of all the *churches.*
12:13. were inferior to other *churches,*
Gal. 1: 2. unto the *churches* of Galatia:
13. I persecuted the *church* of God
22. unto the *churches* of Judæa
Eph. 1:22. gave him (to be) the head over all (things) to the *church,*
3:10. might be known by the *church*
21. glory in the *church* by Christ Jesus
5:23. Christ is the head of the *church:*
24. the *church* is subject unto Christ,
25. as Christ also loved the *church,*
27. to himself a glorious *church,*
29. even as the Lord the *church:*
32. concerning Christ and the *church.*
Phi. 3: 6. Concerning zeal, persecuting the *church*
4:15. no *church* communicated with me
Col. 1:18. the head of the body, the *church:*
24. body's sake, which is the *church:*
4:15. the *church* which is in his house.
16. in the *church* of the Laodiceans;
1Th. 1: 1. unto the *church* of the Thessalonians
2:14. followers of the *churches* of God
2Th. 1: 1. unto the *church* of the Thessalonians
4. in you in the *churches* of God
1Ti. 3: 5. take care of the *church* of God?
15. the *church* of the living God,

1Ti. 5:16. let not the *church* be charged;
Philem 2. to the *church* in thy house:
Heb. 2:12. in the midst of the *church*
12:23. assembly and *church* of the firstborn,
Jas. 5:14. call for the elders of the *church*;
3Joh. 6. thy charity before the *church*:
9. I wrote unto the *church*:
10. casteth (them) out of the *church*.
Rev. 1: 4. John to the seven *churches*
11. unto the seven *churches* which
20. the angels of the seven *churches*:
— are the seven *churches*.
2: 1. the angel of the *church* of Ephesus
7. the Spirit saith unto the *churches*;
8. the angel of the *church* in Smyrna
11. the Spirit saith unto the *churches*;
12. to the angel of the *church* in Pergamos
17. the Spirit saith unto the *churches*;
18. the angel of the *church* in Thyatira
23. all the *churches* shall know
29. the Spirit saith unto the *churches*.
3: 1. angel of the *church* in Sardis
6. the Spirit saith unto the *churches*.
7. to the angel of the *church* in
13. the Spirit saith unto the *churches*.
14. unto the angel of the *church* of
22. the Spirit saith unto the *churches*.
22:16. these things in the *churches*.

1578 3 241/317 1537,2827

ἐκκλίνω, ekklino.

Ro. 3:12. They *are* all *gone out of the way*,
16:17. which ye have learned; and *avoid* them.
1Pet. 3:11. Let him *eschew* evil, and do good;

1579 1 241/317 1537,2860

ἐκκολυμβάω, ekkolumbao.

Acts27:42. lest any of them should *swim out*, and

1580 1 241/317 1537,2865

ἐκκομίζομαι, ekkomizomai.

Lu. 7:12. there *was* a dead man *carried out*,

1581 11 241/318 3:830 1537,2875

ἐκκόπτω, ekkopto.

Mat. 3:10. *is hewn down*, and cast into the fire.
5:30. *cut* it *off*, and cast (it) from thee:
7:19. *is hewn down*, and cast into the fire.
18: 8. *cut* them *off*, and cast (them) from thee:
Lu. 3: 9. *is hewn down*, and cast into the fire.
13: 7. find none: *cut* it *down*;
9. after that thou *shalt cut* it *down*.
Ro. 11:22. thou also *shalt be cut off*.
24. *wert cut out* of the olive tree
2Co. 11:12. that I *may cut off* occasion
1Pet. 3: 7. your prayers *be* not *hindered*.
Some read here εγκοπτ.

1582 1 241/318 3:915 1537,2910

ἐκκρέμαμαι, ekkremamai.

Lu. 19:48. were very attentive to hear (lit. *hung* on him hearing) him.

1583 1 241/318 1537,2980

ἐκλαλέω, eklaleo.

Acts23:22. *tell* no man that thou hast

1584 1 241/318 4:16 1537,2989

ἐκλάμπω, eklampo.

Mat. 13:43. Then *shall* the righteous *shine forth* as the

1585 1 241/318 1537,2990

ἐκλανθάνομαι, eklanthanomai.

Heb. 12: 5. ye *have forgotten* the exhortation

1586 21 241/318 4:69 1537,3004

ἐκλέγομαι, eklegomai.

Mar. 13:20. elect's sake, whom he *hath chosen*,
Lu. 6:13. of them he *chose* twelve, whom
10:42. Mary *hath chosen* that good part,
14: 7. they *chose out* the chief rooms;
Joh. 6:70. *Have* not I *chosen* you twelve,
13:18. I know whom I *have chosen*:
15:16. Ye *have* not *chosen* me, but I *have chosen* you, and
19. I *have chosen* you out of the world,
Acts 1: 2. the apostles whom he *had chosen*:
24. of these two thou *hast chosen*,
6: 5. they *chose* Stephen, a man full
13:17. *chose* our fathers, and exalted the
15: 7. God *made choice* among us,
22. to send *chosen* men of their own
25. to send *chosen* men unto you
1Co. 1:27. God *hath chosen* the foolish things of
— and God *hath chosen* the weak
28. which are despised, *hath* God *chosen*,
Eph. 1: 4. as he *hath chosen* us in him
Jas. 2: 5. *Hath* not God *chosen* the poor of

1587 3 242/318 1537,3007

ἐκλείπω, eklīpo.

Lu. 16: 9. that, when ye *fail*, they may
22:32. for thee, that thy faith *fail* not:
Heb. 1:12. thy years *shall* not *fail*.

1588 23 243/318 4:69 1586

ἐκλεκτός, eklektos.

Mat. 20:16. many be called, but few *chosen*.
22:14. many are called, but few (are) *chosen*.
24:22. for the *elect's* sake those days
24. shall deceive the very *elect*.
31. shall gather together his *elect*
Mar. 13:20. for the *elect's* sake, whom he hath
22. if (it were) possible, even the *elect*.
27. shall gather together his *elect*
Lu. 18: 7. shall not God avenge his own *elect*,
23:35. if he be Christ, the *chosen* of God.
Ro. 8:33. to the charge of God's *elect*?
16:13. Salute Rufus *chosen* in the Lord,
Col. 3:12. therefore, as the *elect* of God,
1Ti. 5:21. Jesus Christ, and the *elect* angels,
2Ti. 2:10. all things for the *elect's* sakes,
Tit. 1: 1. to the faith of God's *elect*,
1Pet. 1: 2(1). *Elect* according to the foreknowledge
2: 4. *chosen* of God, (and) precious,
6. a chief corner stone, *elect*, precious:
9. ye (are) a *chosen* generation,
2Joh. 1. The elder unto the *elect* lady
13. The children of thy *elect* sister
Rev. 17:14. (are) called, and *chosen*, and faithful.

1589 7 242/314 4:69 1586

ἐκλογή, eklogee.

Acts 9:15. he is a chosen vessel (lit. a vessel of *election*) unto me,

Ro. 9:11. purpose of God according to *election*
11: 5. according to the *election* of grace.
7. the *election* hath obtained it,
28. as touching the *election*,
1Th. 1: 4. beloved, your *election* of God.
2Pet. 1:10. your calling and *election* sure:

1590 6 242/319 1537,3089

ἐκλύω, ekluo.

Mat. 9:36. because they fainted (lit. were *faint*), and
15:32. lest they *faint* in the way.
Mar. 8: 3. they *will faint* by the way;
Gal. 6: 9. we shall reap, *if* we *faint* not.
Heb 12: 3. wearied *and faint* in your minds.
5. nor *faint* when thou art rebuked

1591 5 242/319 1537,rt 3145

ἐκμάσσω, ekmasso.

Lu. 7:38. *did wipe* (them) with the hairs of
44. *wiped* (them) with the hairs of her head.
Joh. 11: 2. and *wiped* his feet with her hair,
12: 3. *wiped* his feet with her hair:
13: 5. *to wipe* (them) with the towel

1592 2 242/319 4:796 1537,3456

ἐκμυκτηρίζω, ekmukteerizo.

Lu. 16:14. all these things: and they *derided* him.
23:35. rulers also with them *derided* (him),

1593 1 242/319 1537,3506

ἐκνεύω, eknūo.

Joh. 5:13. Jesus *had conveyed himself away*,

1594 1 242/319 4:936 1537,3525

ἐκνήφω, ekneepho.

1Co.15:34. *Awake* to righteousness, and sin not;

1595 1 242/319 2:469 1635

ἑκούσιος, hekousios.

Philem.14. it were of necessity, but willingly. (lit. according to *willing*)

1596 2 242/319 1635

ἑκουσίως, hekousiōs.

Heb 10:26. For if we sin *wilfully* after
1Pet.5: 2. not by constraint, but *willingly*,

1597 2 242/319 1537,3819

ἔκπαλαι, ekpalai.

2Pet.2: 3. whose judgment now *of a long time*
3: 5. the heavens were *of old*. and the

1598 4 243/319 6:1 1537,3985

ἐκπειράζω, ekpīrazo.

Mat. 4: 7. Thou *shalt* not *tempt* the Lord
Lu. 4:12. Thou *shalt* not *tempt* the Lord
10:25. stood up, *and tempted* him, saying,
1Co.10: 9. Neither *let* us *tempt* Christ,

1599 2 243/319 1537,3992

ἐκπέμπω, ekpempo.

Acts13: 4. So they, *being sent forth* by the Holy Ghost,
17:10. *sent away* Paul and Silas by night

1600 1 242/319 1537,4072

ἐκπετάννυμι, ekpetannumi.

Ro. 10:21. I *have stretched forth* my hands

1601 13 243/319 6:161 1537,4098

ἐκπίπτω, ekpipto.

Mar.13:25. the stars of heaven shall *fall*,
Acts12: 7. his chains *fell off* from (his) hands.
27:17. lest they *should fall* into the
26. we must *be cast* upon a certain island.
29. lest we *should have fallen* upon rocks,
32. of the boat, and let her *fall off*.
Ro. 9: 6. word of God *hath taken none effect*.
1Co.13: 8. Charity never *faileth*: but whether
Gal. 5: 4. ye *are fallen* from grace.
Jas. 1:11. the flower thereof *falleth*,
1Pet. 1:24. the flower thereof *falleth away*:
2Pet.3:17. lest ye also,...*fall* from your
Rev. 2: 5. from whence thou *art fallen*,

1602 3 243/319 1537,4126

ἐκπλέω, ekpleo.

Acts15:39. took Mark, and *sailed* unto Cyprus;
18:18. *sailed thence* into Syria,
20: 6. we *sailed away* from Philippi

1603 1 243/319 6:283 1537,4137

ἐκπληρόω, ekpleeroō.

Acts13:33(32). God *hath fulfilled* the same

1604 1 243/319 6:283 1603

ἐκπλήρωσις, ekpleerōsis.

Acts21:26. the *accomplishment* of the days

1605 13 243/320 1537,4141

ἐκπλήσσω, ekpleesso.

Mat. 7:28. the people *were astonished* at
13:54. insomuch that they were astonished, (lit. so as for them *to be astonished*)
19:25. they *were* exceedingly *amazed*,
22:33. they *were astonished* at his doctrine.
Mar. 1:22. they *were astonished* at his doctrine:
6: 2. many hearing (him) *were astonished*,
7:37. *were* beyond measure *astonished*,
10:26. they *were astonished* out of measure,
11:18. the people *was astonished* at his
Lu. 2:48. saw him, they *were amazed*:
4:32. they *were astonished* at his doctrine:
9:43. they *were* all *amazed* at the
Acts13:12. *being astonished* at the doctrine

1606 3 243/320 6:332 1537,4154

ἐκπνέω, ekpneo.

Mar.15:37. with a loud voice, and *gave up the ghost*.
39. so cried out, and *gave up the ghost*,
Lu. 23:46. said thus, he *gave up the ghost*.

1607 34 243/320 6:566 1537,4198

ἐκπορεύομαι, ekporūomai.

Mat. 3: 5. Then *went out* to him Jerusalem,
4: 4. every word *that proceedeth out of* the
15:11. that *which cometh* out of the mouth
18. *which proceed out* of the mouth
17:21. this kind *goeth* not *out* but by
20:29. *as* they *departed* from Jericho,

Mar. 1: 5. there *went out* unto him all the
6:11. *when* ye *depart* thence, shake off
7:15. the things *which come* out of him,
19. *goeth out* into the draught,
20. That *which cometh* out of the man,
21. of men, *proceed* evil thoughts,
23. these evil things *come* from within,
10:17. *when* he *was gone forth* into
46. *as* he *went* out of Jericho with
11:19. he *went* out of the city.
13: 1. *as* he *went* out of the temple,
Lu. 3: 7. to the multitude *that came forth*
4:22. *which proceeded* out of his mouth.
37. the fame of him *went out* into every place of the country
Joh. 5:29. *shall come forth*; they that have
15:26. which *proceedeth* from the Father,
Acts 9:28. he was with them coming in and *going out* at Jerusalem.
25: 4. he himself would *depart* shortly
Eph. 4:29. *Let* no corrupt communication *proceed* out of your mouth,
Rev 1:16. out of his mouth went (lit. *coming forth*) a sharp twoedged sword:
4: 5. out of the throne *proceeded* lightnings
9:17. out of their mouths *issued* fire
18. *which issued* out of their mouths.
11: 5. fire *proceedeth* out of their mouth,
16:14. (which) *go forth* unto the kings
19:15. out of his mouth *goeth* a sharp
21. *which* (sword) *proceeded* out of his mouth:
22: 1. clear as crystal, *proceeding* out of the throne of God

1608 1 244/320 6:579 1537,4203

ἐκπορνεύω, ekpornūo.

Jude 7. in like manner, *giving themselves over to fornication,*

1609 1 244/320 2:448 1537,4429

ἐκπτύω, ekptuo.

Gal. 4:14. ye despised not, nor *rejected*;

1610 4 244/320 1537,4492

ἐκριζόω, ekrizoō.

Mat.13:29. lest...ye *root up* also the wheat
15:13. hath not planted, *shall be rooted up.*
Lu. 17: 6. *Be* thou *plucked up by the root,*
Jude 12. twice dead, *plucked up by the roots;*

1611 7 244/320 2:449 1839

ἔκστασις, ekstasis.

Mar. 5:42. astonished with a great *astonishment.*
16: 8. and were amazed: (lit. *astonishment* took them)
Lu. 5:26. were all amazed, (lit. *amazement* took them)
Acts 3:10. filled with wonder and *amazement*
10:10. made ready, he fell into a *trance*, (lit. a *trance* fell upon him)
11: 5. in a *trance* I saw a vision,
22:17. in the temple, I was in a *trance*;

1612 1 244/320 1537,4762

ἐκστρέφομαι, ekstrephomai.

Tit. 3:11. he that is such *is subverted,*

1613 1 244/320 1537,5015

ἐκταράσσω, ektarasso.

Acts16:20. *do exceedingly trouble* our city,

1614 16 244/320 2:460 1537 + teinō (to stretch)

ἐκτείνω, ektīno.

Mat. 8: 3. Jesus *put forth* (his) hand, *and*
12:13. *Stretch forth* thine hand. And he *stretched* (it) *forth*;
49. he *stretched forth* his hand toward his disciples, *and*
14:31. Jesus *stretched forth* (his) hand, *and*
26:51. *stretched out* (his) hand, *and* drew
Mar. 1:41. *put forth* (his) hand, *and* touched
3: 5. *Stretch forth* thine hand. And he *stretched* (it) *out*:
Lu. 5:13. he *put forth* (his) hand, *and* touched
6:10. *Stretch forth* thy hand.
22:53. ye *stretched forth* no hands against
Joh.21:18. thou *shalt stretch forth* thy hands,
Acts 4:30. By *stretching forth* thine hand
26: 1. Then Paul *stretched forth* the hand, *and*
27:30. as though they would have cast anchors out (lit. were about *to cast* out a.)

1615 2 244/321 1537,5055

ἐκτελέω, ekteleo.

Lu. 14:29. is not able *to finish* (it),
30. was not able *to finish.*

1616 1 245/321 2:460 1618

ἐκτένεια, ektenīa.

Acts26: 7. *instantly* (lit. in *intensity*) serving, (God) day and night,

1617 1 245/321 1618

ἐκτενέστερον, ektenesteron.

Lu. 22:44. he prayed *more earnestly:*

1618 2 245/321 1614

ἐκτενής, ektenees.

Acts12: 5. prayer was made *without ceasing* (lit. *intense*)
1Pet.4: 8. *fervent* charity among yourselves:

1619 1 245/321 1618

ἐκτενῶς, ektenōs.

1Pet.1:22. with a pure heart *fervently:*

1620 4 245/321 1537,5087

ἐκτίθημι, ektitheemi.

Acts 7:21. *when* he *was cast out*, Pharaoh's daughter
11: 4. and *expounded* (it) by order unto them,
18:26. and *expounded* unto him the way of God
28:23. to whom he *expounded* and testified

1621 2 245/321 1537 + tinassō (to swing)

ἐκτινάσσω, ektinasso.

Mat.10:14. *shake off* the dust of your feet.
Mar. 6:11. *shake off* the dust under your feet
Acts13:51. they *shook off* the dust of their feet against them, *and*
18: 6. he *shook* (his) raiment, *and* said

1622 9 245/321 1537

ἕκτος hektos.

Mat.20: 5. about the *sixth* and ninth hour,
27:45. from the *sixth* hour there was
Mar.15:33. when the *sixth* hour was come,
Lu. 1:26. in the *sixth* month the angel
36. this is the *sixth* month with her,
23:44. it was about the *sixth* hour,
Joh. 4: 6. it was about the *sixth* hour.
19:14. about the *sixth* hour: and he saith
Acts10: 9. to pray about the *sixth* hour:
Rev. 6:12. he had opened the *sixth* seal,
9:13. the *sixth* angel sounded,
14. Saying to the *sixth* angel which
16:12. the *sixth* angel poured out his vial
21:20. fifth, sardonyx; the *sixth*, sardius;

1623 14 245/321 1803

ἐκτός, ektos.

Mat.23:26. that the *outside* of them may be
Acts26:22. none *other* things *than* those which the prophets and Moses
1Co. 6:18. that a man doeth is *without* the body;
14: 5. with tongues, except (lit. *unless* with the exception that) he interpret,
15: 2. *unless* ye have believed in vain.
27. that he is excepted (lit. that this is *with the exception* of him), which did put
2Co.12: 2. or whether *out of* the body, I cannot tell:
3. in the body, or *out of* the body,
1Ti. 5:19. *but* (lit. *unless* with the exception) before two or three witnesses.

1624 5 245/321 1537,rt 5157

ἐκτρέπομαι, ektrepomai.

1Ti. 1: 6. *have turned aside* unto vain
5:15. some *are* already *turned aside*
6:20. *avoiding* profane (and) vain babblings,
2Ti. 4: 4. and *shall be turned* unto fables.
Heb 12:13. lest that which is lame *be turned out of the way;*

1625 2 245/321 1537,5142

ἐκτρέφω, ektrepho.

Eph. 5:29. *nourisheth* and cherisheth it, even as the
6: 4. *bring them up* in the nurture and

1626 1 246/321 2:465 1537 titroskō (to wound)

ἔκτρωμα, ektrōma.

1Co.15: 8. seen of me also, as of one *born out of due time.*

1627 7 246/321 1537,5342

ἐκφέρω, ekphero.

Lu. 15:22. *Bring forth* the best robe,
Acts 5: 6. *carried* (him) *out, and* buried (him).
9. at the door, and *shall carry* thee *out.*
10. *carrying* (her) *forth*, buried (her)
15. they *brought forth* the sick into
1Ti. 6: 7. certain we can *carry* nothing *out.*
Heb. 6: 8. that *which beareth* thorns

1628 7 246/322 1537,5343

ἐκφεύγω, ekphūgo.

Lu. 21:36. worthy *to escape* all these things
Acts16:27. that the prisoners had been fled. (lit. *to have escaped*)
Acts19:16. they *fled* out of that house naked
Ro. 2: 3. that thou *shalt escape* the judgment of God?
2Co.11:33. was I let down by the wall, and *escaped* his hands.
1Th. 5: 3. with child; and they shall not *escape.*
Heb. 2: 3. How *shall* we *escape*, if we neglect

1629 1 246/322 1537,5399

ἐκφοβέω, ekphobeo.

2Co.10: 9. as if I would *terrify* you by letters.

1630 2 246/322 1537,5401

ἔκφοβος, ekphobos.

Mar. 9: 6. for they were *sore afraid.*
Heb.12:21. said, I exceedingly fear (lit. am *exceedingly fearful*) and quake:

1631 2 246/322 1537,5453

ἐκφύω, ekphuo.

Mat.24:32. When his branch is yet tender, and *putteth forth* leaves,
Mar.13:28. yet tender, and *putteth forth* leaves,

1632 18 246/322 2:467 1537 cheō (to pour)

ἐκχέω, ekheo.

Mat. 9:17. bottles break, and the wine *runneth out,*
Mar. 2:22. the wine *is spilled,*
Joh. 2:15. *poured out* the changers' money,
Acts 2:17. I *will pour out* of my Spirit
18. I *will pour out* in those days
33. he *hath shed forth* this, which
22:20. blood of thy martyr Stephen *was shed,*
Ro. 3:15. Their feet (are) swift *to shed* blood:
Tit. 3: 6. Which he *shed* on us abundantly
Rev.16: 1. *pour out* the vials of the wrath
2. *poured out* his vial upon the earth;
3. second angel *poured out* his vial
4. third angel *poured out* his vial
6. they *have shed* the blood of saints
8. fourth angel *poured out* his vial
10. fifth angel *poured out* his vial
12. sixth angel *poured out* his vial
17. seventh angel *poured out* his vial

1632 10 247/322 2:467 1537 cheō (to pour)

ἐκχύνω, ekkuno.

Mat.23:35. righteous blood *shed* upon the earth,
26:28. *which is shed* for many for
Mar.14:24. blood of the new testament, *which is shed* for many
Lu. 5:37. will burst the bottles, and *be spilled*
11:50. prophets, *which was shed* from the foundation
22:20. my blood, *which is shed* for you.
Acts 1:18. all his bowels *gushed out.*
10:45. on the Gentiles also *was poured out* the gift of the Holy Ghost.
Ro. 5: 5. the love of God *is shed abroad*
Jude 11. and *ran greedily* after the error of

1633 1 247/322 1537,5562

ἐκχωρέω, ekkōreo.

Lu. 21:21. *let* them which are in the midst of it depart out;

1634 3 247/322 1537,5594

ἐκψύχω, *ekpsuko.*

Acts 5: 5. fell down, and *gave up the ghost:*
10. at his feet, and *yielded up the ghost:*
12:23. eaten of worms, and *gave up the ghost.*

1635 2 247/322 2:469

ἑκών, **hekōn.**

Ro. 8:20. subject to vanity, not willingly, (lit. not *willing*)
1Co. 9:17. if I do this thing *willingly*,

1636 15 247/322

ἐλαία, *elaia.*

Mat.21: 1. unto the mount of *Olives*,
24: 3. he sat upon the mount of *Olives*,
26:30. went out into the mount of *Olives*.
Mar.11: 1. at the mount of *Olives*, he sendeth
13: 3. as he sat upon the mount of *Olives*
14:26. went out into the mount of *Olives*.
Lu. 19:29. called (the mount) of *Olives*,
37. the descent of the mount of *Olives*,
21:37. that is called (the mount) of *Olives*.
22:39. to the mount of *Olives*;
Joh. 8: 1. Jesus went unto the mount of *Olives*.
Ro. 11:17. root and fatness of the *olive tree*;
24. graffed into their own *olive tree*?
Jas. 3:12. fig tree, my brethren, bear *olive berries*?
Rev.11: 4. These are the two *olive trees*,

1637 11 247/322 2:470 1636

ελαιον, *elaion.*

Mat.25: 3. took no *oil* with them:
4. the wise took *oil* in their vessels
8. Give us of your *oil*; for our lamps
Mar. 6:13. anointed with *oil* many that
Lu. 7:46. My head with *oil* thou didst
10:34. pouring in *oil* and wine,
16: 6. An hundred measures of *oil*.
Heb. 1: 9. with the *oil* of gladness above
Jas. 5:14. anointing him with *oil* in the name
Rev. 6: 6. hurt not the *oil* and the wine.
18:13. wine, and *oil*, and fine flour,

1638 1 247/323 1636

ἐλαιών, *elaiōn.*

Acts 1:12. from the mount called *Olivet*,

1640 4 247/323 4:648 *elachus* (short)

ἐλάσσων, & ἐλάττων, *elassōn*, & *elattōn.*

Joh. 2:10. then that which is *worse*.
Ro. 9:12. The elder shall serve the *younger*.
1Ti. 5: 9. into the number *under* threescore years
Heb. 7: 7. the *less* is blessed of the better.

1641 1 247/323 1640

ἐλαττονέω, *elattoneo.*

2Co. 8:15. he that (had gathered) little *had* no *lack*.

1642 3 247/323 1640

ἐλαττόω, *elattoō.*

Joh. 3:30. He must increase, but I (must) *decrease*.
Heb. 2: 7. Thou *madest* him a little *lower*
9. Jesus, *who was made* a little *lower*

1643 5 248/323

ἐλαύνω, *elauno.*

Mar 6:48. he saw them toiling in *rowing*;
Lu. 8:29. *was driven* of the devil into the
Joh. 6:19. *when* they *had rowed* about five
Jas. 3: 4. (are) *driven* of fierce winds, yet
2Pet. 2:17. clouds *that are carried* with a tempest;

1644 1 248/323 1645

ἐλαφρία, *elaphria.*

2Co. 1:17. thus minded, did I use *lightness*?

1645 2 248/323 cf 1643,rt 1640

ἐλαφρός, *elaphros.*

Mat.11:30. easy, and my burden is *light*.
2Co. 4:17. For our *light* affliction, which is but for a moment,

---

1646 13 248/323 4:648 *elachus* (short)

ἐλάχιστος, *elakistos.*

Mat. 2: 6. art not the *least* among the
5:19. one of these *least* commandments,
— he shall be called the *least* in the
25:40. the *least* of these my brethren,
45. to one of the *least* of these,
Lu. 12:26. to do that thing which is *least*,
16:10. faithful in that which is *least*
— he that is unjust in the *least*
19:17. thou hast been faithful in a *very little*,
1Co. 4: 3. with me it is a *very small* thing
6: 2. to judge the *smallest* matters?
15: 9. I am the *least* of the apostles,
Jas. 3: 4. turned about with a *very small* helm,

1647 1 248/323 1646

ἐλαχιστότερος, *elakistoteros.*

Eph. 3: 8. who am *less than the least* of all saints.

ἐλάω, see ἐλαύνω. 1643

1649 1 248/323 2:473 1651

ἔλεγξις, *elenxis.*

2Pet.2:16. But was rebuked (lit. had *rebuke*) for his

1650 2 248/323 2:473 1651

ἔλεγχος, *elenkos.*

2Ti. 3:16. for doctrine, for *reproof*, for
Heb11: 1. the *evidence* of things not seen.

1651 17 248/323 2:473

ἐλέγχω, *elenko.*

Mat.18:15. go and *tell* him his *fault* between
Lu. 3:19. *being reproved* by him for Herodias
Joh. 3:20. lest his deeds *should be reproved*.
8: 9. *being convicted* by (their own)
46. Which of you *convinceth* me of sin?
16: 8. he *will reprove* the world of sin,
1Co.14.24. unlearned, he *is convinced* of all,
Eph. 5:11. of darkness, but rather *reprove* (them).

Eph. 5:13. all things *that are reproved* are
1Ti. 5:20. Them that sin *rebuke* before all,
2Ti. 4: 2. *reprove*, rebuke, exhort with all
Tit. 1: 9. to exhort and *to convince* the gainsayers.
13. Wherefore *rebuke* them sharply,
2:15. *rebuke* with all authority.
Heb 12: 5. *when* thou *art rebuked* of him:
Jas. 2: 9. *and are convinced* (lit. *being convicted*) of the law as transgressors.
Rev. 3:19. As many as I love, I *rebuke*

1652 2 249/324 1656

ἐλεεινός, ele-īnos.

Co.15:19. we are of all men most miserable. (lit. *more miserable* than all)
Rev. 3:17. thou art wretched, and *miserable*.

1653 31 249/324 2:477 1656

ἐλεέω, eleëo.

Mat. 5: 7. for they *shall obtain mercy*.
9:27. son of David, *have mercy on* us.
15:22. *Have mercy on* me, O Lord,
17:15. Lord, *have mercy on* my son:
18:33. Shouldest not thou also *have had compassion on* thy fellowservant, even as I *had pity on* thee?
20:30. *Have mercy on* us, O Lord,
31. saying, *Have mercy on* us, O Lord,
Mar 5:19. and *hath had* compassion *on* thee.
10:47. son of David, *have mercy on* me.
48. son of David, *have mercy on* me.
Lu. 16:24. Father Abraham, *have mercy on* me,
17:13. Master, *have mercy on* us.
18:38. son of David, *have mercy on* me.
39. son of David, *have mercy on* me.
Ro. 9:15. I will *have mercy on* whom I *will have mercy*,
16. of God *that sheweth mercy*.
18. Therefore *hath* he *mercy on* whom he will (have mercy)
11:30. yet *have* now *obtained mercy*
31. they also *may obtain mercy*.
32. that he *might have mercy upon* all.
12: 8. he *that sheweth mercy*, with
1Co. 7:25. as one *that hath obtained mercy*
2Co. 4: 1. as we *have received mercy*,
Phi. 2:27. God *had mercy on* him;
1Ti. 1:13. I *obtained mercy*, because I did
16. for this cause I *obtained mercy*,
1Pet.2:10. *which had* not *obtained mercy*, but now *have obtained mercy*.
Jude 22. *of* some *have compassion*,

1654 14 249/324 2:477 1656

ἐλεημοσύνη, ele-eemosunee.

Mat. 6: 1. do not your *alms* before men,
2. Therefore when thou doest (thine) *alms*,
3. when thou doest *alms*, let not
4. That thine *alms* may be in secret:
Lu. 11:41. rather give *alms* of such things
12:33. Sell that ye have, and give *alms*;
Acts 3: 2. to ask *alms* of them that entered
3. into the temple asked an *alms*.
10. it was he which sat for *alms*
9:36. full of good works and *almsdeeds*
10: 2. gave much *alms* to the people,
4. Thy prayers and thine *alms* are come
Acts10:31. thine *alms* are had in remembrance
24:17. I came to bring *alms* to my nation,

1655 2 249/324 2:477 1653

ἐλεήμων, ele-eemōn.

Mat. 5: 7. Blessed (are) the *merciful*: for they
Heb. 2:17. a *merciful* and faithful high priest

1656 28 249/324 2:477

ἔλεος, eleos.

Generally neuter, but those marked [2] are masculine.

Mat. 9:13. I will have *mercy*,[2] and not sacrifice:
12: 7. I will have *mercy*,[2] and not sacrifice,
23:23. judgment, *mercy*,[2] and faith:
Lu. 1:50. his *mercy* (is) on them that fear him
54. in remembrance of (his) *mercy*;
58. shewed great *mercy* upon her;
72. To perform the *mercy* (promised)
78. the tender *mercy* of our God;
10:37. He that shewed *mercy* on him.
Ro. 9:23. glory on the vessels of *mercy*,
11:31. that through your *mercy* they
15: 9. might glorify God for (his) *mercy*;
Gal. 6:16. peace (be) on them, and *mercy*,
Eph. 2: 4. God, who is rich in *mercy*,
1Ti. 1: 2. Grace, *mercy*, (and) peace, from
2Ti. 1: 2. Grace, *mercy*, (and) peace, from God
16. The Lord give *mercy* unto the
18. may find *mercy* of the Lord
Tit. 1: 4. Grace, *mercy*, (and) peace, from God
3: 5. according to his *mercy*[2] he saved
Heb. 4:16. that we may obtain *mercy*,[2]
Jas. 2:13. that hath shewed no *mercy*; and *mercy* rejoiceth against judgment.
3:17. full of *mercy* and good fruits,
1Pet. 1: 3. according to his abundant *mercy*
2Joh. 3. Grace be with you, *mercy*, (and) peace,
Jude 2. *Mercy* unto you, and peace, and love,
21. the *mercy* of our Lord Jesus Christ

1657 11 259/324 2:487 1658

ἐλευθερία, elūtheria.

Ro. 8:21. glorious *liberty* of the children of God.
1Co.10:29. why is my *liberty* judged of
2Co. 3:17. the Lord (is), there (is) *liberty*.
Gal. 2: 4. to spy out our *liberty* which we
5: 1. in the *liberty* wherewith Christ
13. ye have been called unto *liberty*; only (use) not *liberty* for an occasion
Jas. 1:25. the perfect law of *liberty*,
2:12. judged by the law of *liberty*.
1Pet.2:16. free, and not using (your) *liberty*
2Pet.2:19. While they promise them *liberty*,

1658 23 250/325 2:487 *eleuthomai* (to come, go)

ἐλεύθερος, elūtheros.

Mat.17:26. Then are the children *free*.
Joh. 8:33. sayest thou, Ye shall be made *free*?
36. ye shall be *free* indeed.
Ro. 6:20. ye were *free* from righteousness.
7: 3. she is *free* from that law;
1Co. 7:21. if thou mayest be made *free*,
22. he that is called, (being) *free*,
39. she is *at liberty* to be married
9: 1. an apostle? am I not *free*?
19. though I be *free* from all (men),
12:13. whether (we be) bond or *free*;

Gal. 3:28. there is neither bond nor *free*,
4:22. the other by a *freewoman*.
23. he of the *freewoman* (was) by
26. Jerusalem which is above is *free*,
30. with the son of the *freewoman*.
31. bondwoman, but of the *free*.
Eph. 6: 8. whether (he be) bond or *free*.
Col. 3:11. Barbarian, Scythian, bond (nor) *free*:
1Pet. 2:16. As *free*, and not using (your) liberty
Rev. 6:15. every bondman, and every *free man*,
13:16. rich and poor, *free* and bond, to receive
19:18. all (men, both) *free* and bond,

1659 7 250/325 2:487 1658

ἐλευθερόω, elūtheroō.

Joh. 8:32. the truth *shall make* you *free*.
36. the Son therefore *shall make* you *free*,
Ro. 6:18. *Being* then *made free* from sin,
22. now *being made free* from sin,
8: 2. *hath made* me *free* from the law
21. *shall be delivered* from the bondage
Gal. 5: 1. wherewith Christ *hath made* us *free*,

1660 1 250/325 2:666 eleuthomai (to come, go)

ἔλευσις, elūsis.

Acts 7:52. of the *coming* of the Just One;

1661 1 250/325

ἐλεφάντινος, elephantinos.

Rev. 18:12. all manner vessels *of ivory*,

1667 1 250/325 1507

ἑλίσσω, helisso.

Heb. 1:12. as a vesture *shalt* thou *fold them up*,

1669 1 251/325 1668

ἑλκόομαι, helko-omai.

Lu. 16:20. laid at his gate, *full of sores*,

1668 3 251/325 1670

ἕλκος, helkos.

Lu. 16:21. the dogs came and licked his *sores*.
Rev. 16: 2. fell a noisome and grievous *sore*
11. because of their pains and their *sores*,

1670 6 251/325 cf 138,cf 1667

ἑλκύω, helkuo.

Joh. 6:44. which hath sent me *draw* him:
12:32. *will draw* all (men) unto me.
18:10. Peter having a sword *drew* it,
21: 6. they were not able *to draw* it
11. Peter went up, and *drew* the net to land
Acts 16:19. they caught...and *drew* (them) into

1670 2 251/325 2:503 cf 1667 cf 138

ἕλκω, helko.

Acts 21:30. they took Paul, and *drew* him out of the
Jas. 2: 6. Do not rich men...and *draw* you before

1677 2 251/326 2:516 1722,3056

ἐλλογέω, ellogeo.

Ro. 5:13. sin is not *imputed* when there
Philem 18. *put that on* mine *account*;

1679 31 251/326 2:517 1680

ἐλπίζω, elpizo.

Mat. 12:21. in his name *shall* the Gentiles *trust*.
Lu. 6:34. of whom ye *hope* to receive,
23: 8. he *hoped* to have seen some miracle
24:21. we *trusted* that it had been
Joh. 5:45. (even) Moses, in whom ye *trust*.
Acts 24:26. He *hoped* also that money should
26: 7. serving (God) day and night, *hope* to come.
Ro. 8:24. why doth he yet *hope for*?
25. if we *hope for* that we see not,
15:12. in him *shall* the Gentiles *trust*.
24. for I *trust* to see you in my
1Co. 13: 7. believeth all things, *hopeth* all things,
15:19. only we have hope (lit. are *hoping*) in Christ,
16: 7. I *trust* to tarry a while with you,
2Co. 1:10. in whom we *trust* that he will
13. I *trust* ye shall acknowledge
5:11. I *trust* also are made manifest
8: 5. not as we *hoped*, but first gave their own selves to the Lord,
13: 6. I *trust* that ye shall know
Phi. 2:19. I *trust* in the Lord Jesus
23. Him therefore I *hope* to send
1Ti. 3:14. *hoping* to come unto thee shortly:
4:10. because we *trust* in the living God,
5: 5. *trusteth* in God, and continueth
6:17. nor *trust* in uncertain riches,
Philem 22. for I *trust* that through your
Heb 11: 1. substance of *things hoped for*,
1Pet. 1:13. *hope* to the end for the grace
3: 5. women also, *who trusted* in God,
2Joh. 12. I *trust* to come unto you,
3Joh. 14. I *trust* I shall shortly see thee,

1680 54 252/327 2:517 elpō (to anticipate)

ἐλπίς, elpis.

Acts 2:26. also my flesh shall rest in *hope*:
16:19. the *hope* of their gains was gone,
23: 6. of the *hope* and resurrection of the
24:15. have *hope* toward God, which
26: 6. for the *hope* of the promise made
7. For which *hope's* sake, king
27:20. all *hope* that we should be
28:20. that for the *hope* of Israel
Ro. 4:18. Who against *hope* believed in *hope*,
5: 2. rejoice in *hope* of the glory of God.
4. experience; and experience, *hope*.
5. *hope* maketh not ashamed;
8:20. subjected (the same) in *hope*,
24. we are saved by *hope*: but *hope* that is seen is not *hope*:
12:12. Rejoicing in *hope*; patient in
15: 4. of the scriptures might have *hope*.
13. Now the God of *hope* fill you with
— that ye may abound in *hope*, through the power of the Holy Ghost.
1Co. 9:10. should plow in *hope*; and that he that thresheth in *hope* should be partaker of his *hope*.
13:13. now abideth faith, *hope*, charity,
2Co. 1: 7(6). our *hope* of you (is) stedfast,
3:12. Seeing then that we have such *hope*,
10:15. having *hope*, when your faith is
Gal. 5: 5. through the Spirit wait for the *hope* of righteousness by faith.
Eph. 1:18. what is the *hope* of his calling,
2:12. having no *hope*, and without God
4: 4. called in one *hope* of your calling;

Phi. 1:20. earnest expectation and (my) *hope*
Col. 1: 5. the *hope* which is laid up for you
23. from the *hope* of the gospel,
27. Christ in you, the *hope* of glory.
Th. 1: 3. and patience of *hope* in our Lord Jesus Christ,
2:19. For what (is) our *hope*, or joy,
4:13. even as others which have no *hope*.
5: 8. an helmet, the *hope* of salvation.
2Th. 2:16. consolation and good *hope* through grace,
1Ti. 1: 1. Jesus Christ, (which is) our *hope*;
Tit. 1: 2. In *hope* of eternal life, which
2:13. Looking for that blessed *hope*, and the glorious appearing
3: 7. to the *hope* of eternal life.
Heb. 3: 6. the confidence and the rejoicing of the *hope* firm unto
6:11. full assurance of *hope* unto the end:
18. upon the *hope* set before us:
7:19. bringing in of a better *hope*
10:23. the profession of (our) *faith*
1Pet. 1: 3. a lively *hope* by the resurrection
21. your faith and *hope* might be in God.
3:15. a reason of the *hope* that is in you
1Joh. 3: 3. every man that hath this *hope* in him purifieth himself,

---

ἕλω, ἕλομαι, *helo, helomai*. 138

See in **αἱρέομαι**.

1682 2 253/327 [426]

Ἐλωΐ, *Elōi*.

Mar15:34. *Eloi, Eloi*, lama sabachthani?

1683 37 253/327 1700,846

ἐμαυτοῦ, -τῷ, -τὸν, *emautou, -to, -ton*.

Mat. 8: 9. having soldiers under *me*: (lit. *myself*)
Lu. 7: 7. neither thought I *myself* worthy
8. having under *me* soldiers,
Joh. 5:30. I can of *mine own self* do nothing:
31. If I bear witness of *myself*,
7:17. or (whether) I speak of *myself*.
28. I am not come of *myself*, but he
8:14. Though I bear record of *myself*,
18. I am one that bear witness of *myself*,
28. (that) I do nothing of *myself*;
42. neither came I of *myself*,
54. answered, If I honour *myself*,
10:18. I lay it down of *myself*.
12:32. will draw all (men) unto *me*.
49. I have not spoken of *myself*;
14: 3. again, and receive you unto *myself*;
10. I speak not of *myself*: but the
21. will manifest *myself* to him.
17:19. for their sakes I sanctify *myself*,
Acts20:24. count I my life dear unto *myself*,
24:10. more cheerfully answer for *myself*:
26: 2. I think *myself* happy, king
9. I verily thought with *myself*,
Ro. 11: 4. I have reserved to *myself* seven
1Co. 4: 3. yea, I judge not *mine own self*.
4. For I know nothing by *myself*;
6. in a figure transferred to *myself*
7: 7. all men were even as *I myself*.
9:19. have I made *myself* servant
10:33. not seeking *mine own* profit,
2Co. 2: 1. I determined this with *myself*,
11: 7. in abasing *myself* that ye
2Co.11: 9. I have kept *myself* from being
12: 5. yet of *myself* I will not glory,
Gal. 2:18. I make *myself* a transgressor.
Phi. 3:13. I count not *myself* to have
Philem 13. Whom I would have retained with *me*,

1684 18 253/328 1722,rt 939

ἐμβαίνω, *embaino*.

Mat. 8:23. *when* he *was entered* into a ship,
9: 1. he *entered into* a ship, *and* passed
13: 2. so that he *went into* a ship, *and* sat;
14:22. his disciples *to get into* a ship,
32. *when* they *were come into* the ship,
15:39. took ship, (lit. *entered* into a ship)
Mar. 4: 1. so that he *entered* into a ship, *and* sat
5:18. *when* he *was come into* the ship,
6:45. his disciples *to get into* the ship,
8:10. he *entered* into a ship with his...*and*
13. *entering* into the ship again
Lu. 5: 3. he *entered* into one of the ships, which was Simon's, *and*
8:22. that he *went into* a ship with
37. he *went up into* the ship, *and*
Joh. 5: 4. *whosoever* then first after...*stepped in*
6:17. *entered* into a ship, *and* went over
22. whereinto his disciples *were entered*,
24. took shipping, (lit. *entered* into ships)

1685 1 253/328 1722,906

ἐμβάλλω, *emballo*.

Lu. 12: 5. hath power *to cast into* hell;

1686 3 253/328 1722,911

ἐμβάπτω, *embapto*.

Mat.26:23. He *that dippeth* (his) hand with
Mar.14:20. *that dippeth* with me in the dish.
Joh.13:26. *when* he *had dipped* the sop,

1687 1 253/328 2:535 1722
rt 939 eq 1684

ἐμβατεύω, *embatuo*.

Col. 2:18. *intruding into* those things which he hath not seen,

---

1688 1 253/328 1722
bibazō (to mount)

ἐμβιβάζω, *embibazo*.

Acts27: 6. sailing into Italy; and he put us therein. (lit. *caused* us *to enter* into it)

1689 12 253/328 1722,991

ἐμβλέπω, *emblepo*.

Mat. 6:26. *Behold* the fowls of the air: for they
19:26. Jesus *beheld* (them), *and* said unto
Mar. 8:25. *saw* every man clearly.
10:21. Jesus *beholding* him loved him, and said
27. Jesus *looking upon* them
14:67. she *looked upon* him, *and* said,
Lu. 20:17. *he beheld* them, *and* said,
22:61. the Lord turned, and *looked upon* Peter.
Joh. 1:36. *looking upon* Jesus as he walked,
42(43). *when* Jesus *beheld* him,
Acts 1:11. why stand ye *gazing up* into heaven?
22:11. when I *could* not *see* for the glory

1690 5 254/328 1722
brimaomai (to snort)

ἐμβριμάομαι, *embrimaomai*.

Mat. 9:30. Jesus *straitly charged* them,

Mar. 1:43. he *straitly charged* him, *and* forthwith
14: 5. they *murmured against* her.
Joh. 11:33. *he groaned* in the spirit, and was troubled,
38. therefore again *groaning* in himself

1691 88 216/252 3165

ἐμέ, *eme*, from ἐγώ.

Mat. 10:37. loveth father or mother more than *me*
— loveth son or daughter more than *me*
40. He that receiveth you receiveth *me*, and he that receiveth *me*
18: 5. in my name receiveth *me*.
6. little ones which believe in *me*,
21. shall my brother sin against *me*,
26:10. hath wrought a good work upon *me*.
11. *me* ye have not always.
Mar. 9:37. in my name, receiveth *me*: and whosoever shall receive *me*, receiveth not *me*, but him that sent me.
42. little ones that believe in *me*,
14: 6. hath wrought a good work on *me*.
7. *me* ye have not always.
Lu. 4:18. The Spirit of the Lord (is) upon *me*,
9:48. in my name receiveth *me*: and whosoever shall receive *me*
10:16. despiseth you despiseth *me*; and he that despiseth *me* despiseth
22:53. stretched forth no hands against *me*:
23:28. weep not for *me*, but weep for
24:39. as ye see *me* have.
Joh. 3:30. He must increase, but *I* (must) decrease.
6:35. he that believeth on *me* shall
37. giveth me shall come to *me*;
47. He that believeth on *me* hath
57. even he shall live by *me*.
7: 7. *me* it hateth, because I testify of it,
38. He that believeth on *me*, as the
8:19. Ye neither know *me*, nor my Father: if ye had known *me*, ye should
42. ye would love *me*:
9: 4. *I* must work the works of him
11:25. he that believeth in *me*, though
26. whosoever liveth and believeth in *me*
12: 8. *me* ye have not always.
30. This voice came not because of *me*,
44. He that believeth on *me*, believeth not on *me*, but on
45. he that seeth *me* seeth him that
46. that whosoever believeth on *me*
48. He that rejecteth *me*, and receiveth not
13:18. lifted up his heel against *me*.
20. whomsoever I send receiveth *me*; and he that receiveth *me* receiveth
14: 1. believe also in *me*.
9. he that hath seen *me* hath
12. He that believeth on *me*,
15:18. ye know that it hated *me*
20. If they have persecuted *me*,
23. He that hateth *me* hateth
24. hated both *me* and my Father.
16: 3. not known the Father, nor *me*.
9. because they believe not on *me*,
14. He shall glorify *me*: for he
23. in that day ye shall ask *me* nothing,
27. because ye have loved *me*
32. shall leave *me* alone:
17:18. As thou hast sent *me* into
20. them also which shall believe on *me* through their word;
23. loved them, as thou hast loved *me*.
8: 8. if therefore ye seek *me*, let

Acts 3:22. of your brethren, like unto *me*;
7:37. of your brethren, like unto *me*;
8:24. ye have spoken come upon *me*.
13:25. there cometh one after *me*,
22: 6. a great light round about *me*.
26:18. inheritance among them which are sanctified by faith that is in *me*.
Ro. 1:15. So, as much as in *me* is,
10:20. of them that sought *me* not;
— them that asked not after *me*.
15: 3. that reproached thee fell on *me*
1Co. 9: 3. to them that do examine *me*
15:10. grace which (was bestowed) upon *me*
2Co. 2: 5. he hath not grieved *me*,
11:10. no man shall stop *me* of this
12: 6. lest any man should think of *me*
9. power of Christ may rest upon *me*.
Eph. 6:21. ye also may know my affairs, (lit. the things as to *me*)
Phi. 1:12. things (which happened) unto *me* (lit. the &c.)
2:23. see how it will go with *me*.
27. not on him only, but on *me* also,
Col. 4: 7. All *my* state (lit. the &c.) shall Tychicus
2Ti. 1: 8. nor of *me* his prisoner:
Philem 17. If thou count *me* therefore a partner, receive him as *myself*.
Rev. 1:17. laid his right hand upon *me*,

1692 1 254/328

ἐμέω, *emeo*.

Rev. 3:16. I will *spue* thee out of my mouth.

1693 1 254/328 1722,3105

ἐμμαίνομαι, *emmainomai*.

Acts 26:11. *being* exceedingly *mad against* them,

1696 3 254/328 4:574 1722,3306

ἐμμένω, *emmeno*.

Acts 14:22. *to continue* in the faith,
Gal. 3:10. every one that *continueth* not in
Heb. 8: 9. they *continued* not in my covenant,

1698 95 216/252 3427

ἐμοί, *emoi*, from ἐγώ.

Mat. 10:32. Whosoever therefore shall confess *me*
11: 6. shall not be offended in *me*.
18:26. Lord, have patience with *me*,
29. saying, Have patience with *me*,
25:40. ye have done (it) unto *me*.
45. ye did (it) not to *me*.
26:31. shall be offended because of *me*
Mar. 5: 7. What have *I* to do with thee,
14:27. shall be offended because of *me*
Lu. 4: 6. for that is delivered unto *me*;
7:23. shall not be offended in *me*.
8:28. What have *I* to do with thee, Jesus
12: 8. Whosoever shall confess *me* before
15:29. yet thou never gavest *me* a kid,
22:37. must yet be accomplished in *me*,
Joh. 2: 4. what have *I* to do with thee?
5:46. ye would have believed *me*:
6:56. dwelleth in *me*, and I in him.
7:23. are ye angry at *me*, because
8:12. he that followeth *me* shall not
10:38. though ye believe not *me*,
— believe, that the Father (is) in *me*,
12:26. If any man serve *me*, let him follow *me*
— if any man serve *me*, him

Joh.14 10. and the Father in *me?* the words
— the Father that dwelleth in *me*,
11. the Father in *me:* or else
20. in my Father, and ye in *me*,
30. cometh, and hath nothing in *me*.
15: 2. Every branch in *me* that beareth not
4. Abide in *me*, and I in you.
— except ye abide in *me*.
5. He that abideth in *me*, and I in him,
6. If a man abide not in *me*,
7. If ye abide in *me*, and my words
16:33. that in *me* ye might have peace.
17: 6. thou gavest them *me;*
21. as thou, Father, (art) in *me*,
23. I in them, and thou in *me*,
18:35. have delivered thee unto *me:*
19:10. Speakest thou not unto *me?*
Acts10:28. God hath shewed *me* that I
11:12. these six brethren accompanied *me*,
22: 9. they that were with *me* saw
24:20. found any evil doing in *me*,
26:13. them which journeyed with *me*.
28:18. there was no cause of death in *me*.
Ro. 7: 8. wrought in *me* all manner of
13. made death unto *me?*
17. sin that dwelleth in *me*.
18. For I know that in *me* that
20. sin that dwelleth in *me*.
21. when *I* would do good, evil is present with *me*.
12:19. Vengeance (is) *mine;* (lit. to *me*)
14:11. every knee shall bow to *me*,
1Co. 4: 3. with *me* it is a very small thing
9:15. should be so done unto *me:*
14:11. (shall be) a barbarian unto *me*.
15:10. grace of God which was with *me*.
16: 4. they shall go with *me*.
2Co. 1:17. that with *me* there should be
9: 4. they of Macedonia come with *me*,
11:10. the truth of Christ is in *me*,
13: 3. a proof of Christ speaking in *me*,
Gal. 1: 2. the brethren which are with *me*,
16. To reveal his Son in *me*,
24. they glorified God in *me*.
2: 3. neither Titus, who was with *me*,
6. in conference added nothing to *me:*
8. mighty in *me* toward the Gentiles:
9. they gave to *me* and Barnabas
20. not I, but Christ liveth in *me:*
6:14. God forbid that *I* should glory, (lit. be it not to *me* to glory)
— the world is crucified unto *me*,
Eph. 3: 8. Unto *me*, who am less than the least
Phi. 1: 7. as it is meet for *me* to think this
21. For to *me* to live (is) Christ,
26. abundant in Jesus Christ for *me*
30. same conflict which ye saw in *me*, (and) now hear (to be) in *me*.
2:16. *I* may rejoice in the day of Christ,
22. served with *me* in the gospel.
3: 1. to *me* indeed (is) not grievous,
4: 9. heard, and seen in *me*, do:
21. The brethren which are with *me*
Col. 1:29. which worketh in *me* mightily
1Ti. 1:16. that in *me* first Jesus Christ
2Ti. 4: 8. not to *me* only, but unto all them
Philem 11. profitable to thee and to *me:*
16. a brother beloved, specially to *me*,
18. put that on mine account; (lit. on account to *me*)
Heb 10:30. Vengeance (belongeth) unto *me*,
13: 6. The Lord (is) *my* helper, and I will

1699 78 254/329 1473 (1698, 1700, 1691)
ἐμός, *emos.*

Mat.18:20. gathered together in *my* name,
20:15. do what I will with *mine own?*
23. is not *mine* to give, but (it)
25:27. received *mine own* with usury.
Mar. 8:38. ashamed of me and of *my* words
10:40. is not *mine* to give;
Lu. 9:26. ashamed of me and of *my* words,
15:31. all that I have (lit. *mine*) is thine.
22:19. this do in remembrance *of me*.
Joh. 3:29. this *my* joy therefore is fulfilled.
4:34. *My* meat is to do the will of him
5:30. I judge: and *my* judgment is just; because I seek not *mine own* will,
47. how shall ye believe *my* words?
6:38. not to do *mine own* will,
7: 6. *My* time is not yet come:
8. for *my* time is not yet full come.
16. *My* doctrine is not *mine*,
8:16. I judge, *my* judgment is true:
31. If ye continue in *my* word,
37. *my* word hath no place in you.
43. do ye not understand *my* speech? (even) because ye cannot hear *my* word.
51. If a man keep *my* saying,
56. Abraham rejoiced to see *my* day:
10:14. know *my* (sheep), and am known of *mine*.
26. ye are not of *my* sheep,
27. *My* sheep hear my voice, and I know
12:26. there shall also *my* servant be:
13:35. that ye are *my* disciples,
14:15. keep *my* commandments.
24. word which ye hear is not *mine*,
27. *my* peace I give unto you:
15: 8. so shall ye be *my* disciples.
9. continue ye in *my* love.
11. that *my* joy might remain in you, (lit. that *my* joy in you might remain)
12. This is *my* commandment,
16:14. for he shall receive of *mine*,
15. that the Father hath are *mine*.
— that he shall take of *mine*,
17:10. all *mine* are thine, and thine are *mine;*
13. *my* joy fulfilled in themselves.
24. they may behold *my* glory,
18:36. *My* kingdom is not of this world: if *my* kingdom were of this world, then would *my* servants fight,
— but now is *my* kingdom not from hence.
Ro. 3: 7. through *my* lie unto his glory;
10: 1. *my* heart's desire and prayer to God
1Co. 1:15. had baptized in *mine own* name.
5: 4. gathered together, and *my* spirit,
7:40. so abide, after *my* judgment:
9: 2. the seal of *mine* apostleship are
3. *Mine* answer...that do examine me
11:24. this do in remembrance *of me*.
25. new testament in *my* blood:
— in remembrance *of me*.
16:18. have refreshed *my* spirit and your's.
21. Paul with *mine own* hand.
2Co. 1:23. for a record upon *my* soul,
2: 3. that *my* joy is (the joy) of you all.
8:23. *my* partner and fellowhelper
Gal. 1:13. have heard of *my* conversation
6:11. unto you with *mine own* hand.
Phi. 1:26. by *my* coming to you again.
3: 9. not having *mine own* righteousness.
Col. 4:18. by the hand *of me* Paul.
2Th. 3:17. of Paul with *mine own* hand,
2Ti. 4: 6. the time of *my* departure is

Philem.10. I beseech thee for *my* son
12. that is, *mine own* bowels:
19. written (it) with *mine own* hand,
2Pet.1:15. may be able after *my* decease
3Joh. 4. that *my* children walk in truth.
Rev. 2:20. to teach and to seduce *my* servants

1700 109 216/251 3449

ἐμοῦ, *emou*, from ἐγώ.

Mat. 5:11. against you falsely, for *my* sake. (lit. on account of *me*)
7:23. depart from *me*, ye that work
0:18. kings for *my* sake, (lit. on account of *me*)
39. loseth his life for *my* sake shall
1:29. my yoke upon you, and learn of *me*;
2:30. He that is not with *me* is against *me*; and he that gathereth not with *me*
5: 5. mightest be profited by *me*;
8. their heart is far from *me*.
6:25. will lose his life for *my* sake
17:27. give unto them for *me* and thee.
25:41. Depart from *me*, ye cursed, into
26:23. dippeth (his) hand with *me* in the
38. tarry ye here, and watch with *me*.
39. let this cup pass from *me*
40. could ye not watch with *me* one hour?
42. may not pass away from *me*,
Mar. 7: 6. their heart is far from *me*.
11. thou mightest be profited by *me*;
8:35. shall lose his life for *my* sake and the gospel's, (lit. on account of *me* and)
10:29. for *my* sake, and the gospel's,
:3: 9. before rulers and kings for *my* sake,
4:18. One of you which eateth with *me*
20. that dippeth with *me* in the dish.
36. take away this cup from *me*:
Lu. 5: 8. saying, Depart from *me*;
8.46. that virtue is gone out of *me*.
9:24. will lose his life for *my* sake,
10:16. He that heareth you heareth *me*;
11: 7. my children are with *me* in bed;
23. He that is not with *me* is against *me*: and he that gathereth not with *me* scattereth.
12:13. divide the inheritance with *me*.
13:27. depart from *me*, all (ye) workers
15:31. Son, thou art ever with *me*,
16: 3. my lord taketh away from *me*
22:21. with *me* on the table.
28. which have continued with *me*
37. for the things concerning *me*
42. remove this cup from *me*:
23:43. shalt thou be with *me* in paradise.
24:44. (in) the psalms, concerning *me*.
oh. 4: 9. askest drink of *me*, which am
5: 7. another steppeth down before *me*.
32. another that beareth witness of *me*;
— which he witnesseth of *me*
36. that I do, bear witness of *me*,
37. hath borne witness of *me*.
39. they are they which testify of *me*.
46. for he wrote of *me*.
8:18. that sent me beareth witness of *me*.
29. he that sent me is with *me*:
10: 8. All that ever came before *me*
9. by *me* if any man enter in,
18. No man taketh it from *me*,
25. they bear witness of *me*.
13. 8. thou hast no part with *me*.
18. He that eateth bread with *me* hath
38. down thy life for *my* sake? (lit. for *me*)
14: 6. cometh unto the Father, but by *me*.
Joh.15: 5. without *me* ye can do nothing.
26. he shall testify of *me*:
27. ye have been with *me* from the beginning.
16:32. because the Father is with *me*.
17:24. be with *me* where I am;
18:34. did others tell it thee of *me*?
19:11. no power (at all) against *me*,
Acts 8:24. Pray ye to the Lord for *me*,
11: 5. it came even to *me*:
20:34. to them that were with *me*.
22:18. receive thy testimony concerning *me*.
23:11. hast testified of *me* in Jerusalem,
25: 9. judged of these things before *me*?
Ro. 1:12. mutual faith both of you and *me*.
11:27. this (is) *my* covenant unto them,
15:18. Christ hath not wrought by *me*,
30. in (your) prayers to God for *me*;
16: 2. of many, and of *my*self also.
7. also were in Christ before *me*.
13. his mother and *mine*.
2Co. 1:19. by *me* and Silvanus and Timotheus,
2: 2. which is made sorry by *me*?
7: 7. your fervent mind toward *me*;
12: 6. or (that) he heareth of *me*.
8. that it might depart from *me*.
Gal. 1:11. which was preached of *me*
17. which were apostles before *me*;
2:20. loved me, and gave himself for *me*.
Eph. 6:19. for *me*, that utterance may
Phil. 4:10. at the last your care of *me*
2Ti. 1:13. which thou hast heard of *me*,
2: 2. that thou hast heard of *me*
4:11. Only Luke is with *me*.
17. that by *me* the preaching might
Tit. 3:15. All that are with *me* salute thee.
Heb 10: 7. the book it is written of *me*,
Rev. 1:12. the voice that spake with *me*.
3: 4. shall walk with *me* in white:
18. I counsel thee to buy of *me* gold
20. will sup with him, and he with *me*.
21. to sit with *me* in my throne,
4: 1. of a trumpet talking with *me*;
10: 8. spake unto *me* again, and said,
17: 1. talked with *me*, saying unto me,
21: 9. talked with *me*, saying, Come
15. he that talked with *me* had
22:12. my reward (is) with *me*, to give

1701 1 255/329 5:625 1702

ἐμπαιγμός, *empaigmos*.

Heb 11:36. trial of (cruel) *mockings* and scourgings,

1702 13 255/329 5:625 1722,3815

ἐμπαίζω, *empaizo*.

Mat. 2:16. he *was mocked* of the wise men,
20:19. deliver him to the Gentiles *to mock*,
27:29. before him, and *mocked* him, saying,
31. after that they *had mocked* him,
41. the chief priests *mocking* (him),
Mar 10:34. they *shall mock* him, and shall
15:20. when they *had mocked* him,
31. also the chief priests *mocking*
Lu. 14:29. that behold (it) begin *to mock* him.
18:32. *shall be mocked*, and spitefully
22:63. men that held Jesus *mocked* him,
23:11. set him at nought, and *mocked* (him),
36. the soldiers also *mocked* him.

1703 2 255/329 5:625 1702
ἐμπαῖκται, *empaiktai.*

2Pet.3: 3. shall come in the last day *scoffers,*
Jude 18. should be *mockers* in the last time,

1704 1 255/338 5:940 1722,4043
ἐμπεριπατέω, *emperipateo.*

2Co. 6:16. I will dwell in them, and *walk in* (them);

1705 1 255/330 1722,rt 4118
ἐμπιπλάω, *empiplao.*

Acts14:17. *filling* our hearts with food and

1706 7 255/330 1722,4098
ἐμπίπτω, *empipto.*

Mat.12:11. if it *fall into* a pit on the sabbath day,
Lu. 10:36. unto him *that fell among* the thieves?
14: 5. an ass or an ox fallen into (lit. *shall fall into*) a pit,
Ti. 3: 6. he *fall into* the condemnation
7. lest he *fall into* reproach
6: 9. *fall into* temptation and a snare,
Heb 10:31. *to fall into* the hands of the

1707 2 256/330 1722,4120
ἐμπλέκω, *empleko.*

Ti. 2: 4. *entangleth himself with* the
2Pet.2:20. they are again *entangled* therein, *and*

1705 4 255/330 1722,rt 4118
ἐμπλήθω, *empleetho.*

Lu. 1:53. He *hath filled* the hungry with
6:25. Woe unto you *that are full!*
Joh. 6:12. When they *were filled,* he said
Ro. 15:24. somewhat *filled* with your (company).

1708 1 256/330 1707
ἐμπλοκή, *emplokee.*

1Pet.3: 3. (adorning) of *plaiting* the hair,

1709 1 256/338 1722,4154
ἐμπνέω, *empneo.*

Acts 9: 1. Saul, yet *breathing* out threatenings

1710 2 256/330 1722,4198
ἐμπορεύομαι, *emporuomai.*

Jas. 4:13. and *buy and sell,* and get gain:
2Pet. 2: 3. *shall* they...*make merchandise of* you:

1711 1 256/330 1713
ἐμπορία, *emporia.*

Mat.22: 5. another to his *merchandise:*

1712 1 256/330 1713
ἐμπόριον, *emporion.*

Joh. 2:16. Father's house an house of *merchandise.*

1713 5 256/330 1722,rt 4198
ἔμπορος, *emporos.*

Mat.13:45. like unto a *merchant* man,
Rev.18: 3. the *merchants* of the earth are
11. the *merchants* of the earth shall
15. The *merchants* of these things,
23. thy *merchants* were the great men

1714 1 255/330 1722 pretho (to blow)
ἐμπρήθω, *empreetho.*

Mat.22: 7. those murderers, and *burned up* their city.

1715 48 256/330 1722,4314
ἔμπροσθεν, *emprosthen.*

Mat. 5:16. Let your light so shine *before* men,
24. Leave there thy gift *before* the altar.
6: 1. do not your alms *before* men,
2. do not sound a trumpet *before* thee,
7: 6. cast ye your pearls *before* swine,
10:32. shall confess me *before* men, him will I confess also *before* my Father
33. shall deny me *before* men, him will I also deny *before* my
11:10. shall prepare thy way *before* thee.
26. it seemeth good *in* thy *sight.*
17: 2. was transfigured *before* them:
18:14. it is not the will *of* (lit. *before*) your Father
23:13(14). the kingdom of heaven *against* (lit. *before*) men:
25:32. *before* him shall be gathered all
26:70. he denied *before* (them) all,
27:11. Jesus stood *before* the governor:
29. they bowed the knee *before* him,
Mar. 1: 2. shall prepare thy way *before* thee.
9: 2. he was transfigured *before* them.
Lu. 5:19. into the midst *before* Jesus.
7:27. shall prepare thy way *before* thee.
10:21. so it seemed good *in* thy *sight.*
12: 8. shall confess me *before* men, him shall the Son of man also confess *before* the angels of God:
14: 2. there was a certain man *before* him
19: 4. he ran *before,* and climbed up
27. bring hither, and slay (them) *before* me.
28. had thus spoken, he went *before,*
21:36. to stand *before* the Son of man.
Joh. 1:15. after me is preferred *before* me:
27. coming after me is preferred *before* me,
30. a man which is preferred *before* me:
3:28. that I am sent *before* him.
10: 4. he goeth *before* them, and the sheep
12:37. done so many miracles *before* them,
Acts18:17. beat (him) *before* the judgment seat.
2Co. 5:10. all appear *before* the judgment seat
Gal. 2:14. I said unto Peter *before* (them) all,
Phi. 3:13(14). unto those things which are *before,*
1Th. 1: 3. *in the sight of* God and our Father;
2:19. *in the presence of* our Lord Jesus
3: 9. for your sakes *before* our God;
13. unblameable in holiness *before* God,
1Joh.3:19. shall assure our hearts *before* him.
Rev. 4: 6. full of eyes *before* and behind.
19:10. I fell *at* his feet to worship
22: 8. *before* the feet of the angel

1716 6 256/331 1722,4429
ἐμπτύω, *emptuo.*

Mat.26:67. Then *did* they *spit* in his face,
27:30. they *spit upon* him, *and* took

Mar 10:34. scourge him, and *shall spit upon* him,
14:65. some began *to spit on* him,
15:19. *did spit upon* him, and bowing
Lu. 18:32. shall be mocked, and spitefully entreated, and *spitted on:*

1717 2 257/331 1722,5316

ἐμφανής, emphanees.

Acts10. 40. shewed him *openly;* (lit. gave him to be *manifest*)
Ro. 10:20. I was made *manifest* unto them

1718 10 257/331 9:1 1717

ἐμφανίζω, emphanizo.

Mat.27:53. into the holy city, and *appeared* unto
Joh.14:21. *will manifest* myself to him.
22. that thou wilt *manifest* thyself
Acts23:15. *signify* to the chief captain
22. thou *hast shewed* these things to me.
24: 1. who *informed* the governor against Paul.
25: 2. the Jews *informed* him against Paul,
15. elders of the Jews *informed* (me),
Heb 9:24. now *to appear* in the presence of
11:14. *declare plainly* that they seek a country.

1719 6 257/331 1722,5401

ἔμφοβος, emphobos.

Lu. 24: 5. as they were *afraid,* and bowed down
37. they were terrified and *affrighted,*
Acts10: 4. looked on him, he was *afraid,*
22: 9. saw indeed the light, and were *afraid;*
24:25. Felix trembled, and (lit. becoming *afraid*) answered,
Rev.11:13. the remnant were *affrighted,*

1720 1 257/331 2:536 1722 *phusaō* (to puff)

ἐμφυσάω, emphusao.

Joh. 20:22. said this, he *breathed on* (them),

1721 1 252/331 1722,5453

ἔμφυτος, emphutos.

Jas. 1:21. with meekness the *engrafted* word,

1722 2781 257/331 2:537

ἐν, en.

Mat. 1:18. she was found with child (lit. having *in* the womb) of the
20. that which is conceived *in* her is
23. a virgin shall be with child, (lit. shall have *in* the womb)
2: 1. born *in* Bethlehem of Judæa *in* the days of Herod
2. have seen his star *in* the east,
5. *In* Bethlehem of Judæa:
6. not the least *among* the princes
9. which they saw *in* the east,
16. children that were *in* Bethlehem, and *in* all the coasts thereof,
18. *In* Rama was there a voice
19. in a dream to Joseph *in* Egypt,
3: 1. *In* those days came John the Baptist, preaching *in* the wilderness of
3. of one crying *in* the wilderness, Prepare
6. baptized of him *in* Jordan,
9. think not to say *within* yourselves,
11. I indeed baptize you *with* water

Mat. 3:11. baptize you *with* the Holy Ghost
12. Whose fan (is) *in* his hand,
17. *in* whom I am well pleased.
4:13. *in* the borders of Zabulon
16. people which sat *in* darkness
— *in* the region and shadow of death,
21. *in* a ship with Zebedee their
23. teaching *in* their synagogues,
— all manner of disease *among* the people.
5:12. for great (is) your reward *in* heaven:
13. where*with* shall it be salted?
15. unto all that are *in* the house.
16. your Father which is *in* heaven.
19. least *in* the kingdom of heaven.
— great *in* the kingdom of heaven.
25. whiles thou art *in* the way with
28. with her already *in* his heart.
34. Swear not at all; neither *by* heaven;
35. Nor *by* the earth; for it is his
36. Neither shalt thou swear *by* thy head,
45. your Father which is *in* heaven:
48. Be ye therefore perfect, even as your Father which is *in* heaven
6: 1. your Father which is *in* heaven.
2. *in* the synagogues and *in* the streets,
4. alms may be *in* secret: and thy Father which seeth *in* secret himself shall reward thee open*ly*. (lit. *in* open way)
5. *in* the synagogues and *in* the corners of
6. thy Father which is *in* secret; and thy Father which seeth *in* secret shall reward thee open*ly*.
7. be heard *for* their much speaking.
9. Our Father which art *in* heaven,
10. in earth as (it is) *in* heaven.
18. thy Father which is *in* secret: and thy Father, which seeth *in* secret, shall reward thee open*ly*.
20. for yourselves treasures *in* heaven,
23. the light that is *in* thee be
29. even Solomon *in* all his glory
7: 2. *with* what judgment ye judge,
— *with* what measure ye mete,
3. mote that is *in* thy brother's eye,
— beam that is *in* thine own eye?
4. a beam (is) *in* thine own eye?
6. they trample them *under* their feet,
11. your Father which is *in* heaven
15. come to you *in* sheep's clothing,
21. my Father which is *in* heaven.
22. Many will say to me *in* that day,
8: 6. my servant lieth *at* home sick
10. so great faith, no, not *in* Israel
11. *in* the kingdom of heaven.
13. was healed *in* the selfsame hour.
24. there arose a great tempest *in* the sea,
32. into the sea, and perished *in* the waters.
9: 3. the scribes said *within* themselves,
4. think ye evil *in* your hearts?
10. Jesus sat at meat *in* the house,
21. For she said *within* herself,
31. his fame *in* all that country.
33. It was never so seen *in* Israel.
34. *through* the prince of the devils.
35. teaching *in* their synagogues,
— every disease *among* the people.
10:11. enquire who *in* it is worthy;
15. *in* the day of judgment,
16. as sheep *in* the midst of wolves:
17. will scourge you *in* their synagogues,
19. be given you *in* that same hour
20. your Father which speaketh *in* you.

Mat.10 23. when they persecute you *in* this city,
27. What I tell you *in* darkness, (that) speak ye *in* light:
28. destroy both soul and body *in* hell.
32. shall confess)(me before men,)(him will I confess also before my Father which is *in* heaven.
33. my Father which is *in* heaven.
11: 1. to preach *in* their cities.
2. John had heard *in* the prison
6. shall not be offended *in* me.
8. A man clothed *in* soft raiment?
— soft (clothing) are *in* kings' houses.
11. *Among* them that are born of women
— he that is least *in* the kingdom
16. children sitting *in* the markets,
20. where*in* most of his mighty works
21. works, which were done *in* you, had been done *in* Tyre and Sidon, they would have repented long ago *in* sackcloth
22. *at* the day of judgment,
23. works, which have been done *in* thee, had been done *in* Sodom, it would
24. *in* the day of judgment, than for thee.
25. *At* that time Jesus answered and said,
12: 1. *At* that time Jesus went on the
2. to do *upon* the sabbath day.
5. have ye not read *in* the law,
— the priests *in* the temple profane
19. hear his voice *in* the streets.
21. *in* his name shall the Gentiles trust.
24. *by* Beelzebub the prince of the devils.
27. if I *by* Beelzebub cast out devils, *by* whom do your children cast
28. cast out devils *by* the Spirit of God,
32. neither *in* this world, neither *in* the (world) to come.
36. *in* the day of judgment.
40. three nights *in* the whale's belly;
— three nights *in* the heart of the earth.
41. shall rise *in* judgment with
42. shall rise up *in* the judgment
50. my Father which is *in* heaven,
13: 1.)(The same day went Jesus out
3. many things unto them *in* parables,
4. when he sowed, (lit. *in* his sowing)
10. speakest thou unto them *in* parables?
13. speak I to them *in* parables:
19. which was sown *in* [illegible] heart.
21. Yet hath he not root *in* [illegible]self,
24. sowed good seed *in* his field:
25. while men slept (lit. *in* men's sleeping), his enemy
27. sow good seed *in* thy field?
30. *in* the time of harvest I will say to the
31. a man took, and sowed *in* his field:
32. lodge *in* the branches thereof.
34. unto the multitude *in* parables;
35. I will open my mouth *in* parables;
40. shall it be *in* the end of this world.
43. *in* the kingdom of their Father.
44. like unto treasure hid *in* a field;
49. *at* the end of the world:
54. taught them *in* their synagogue,
57. they were offended *in* him.
— without honour, save *in* his own country, and *in* his own house.
14: 1. *At* that time Herod the tetrarch
2. do shew forth themselves *in* him.
3. put (him) *in* prison for Herodias' sake,
6. danced before them (lit. *in* the midst), and pleased Herod.

Mat.14: 10. beheaded John *in* the prison.
13. he departed thence *by* ship into
33. they that were *in* the ship came
15: 32. lest they faint *in* the way.
33. so much bread *in* the wilderness,
16: 7. they reasoned *among* themselves,
8. why reason ye *among* yourselves,
17. but my Father which is *in* heaven.
19. shall be bound *in* heaven:
— shall be loosed *in* heaven.
27. For the Son of man shall come *in* the glory of his Father with
28. Son of man coming *in* his kingdom.
17: 5. This is my beloved Son, *in* whom I am well pleased;
12. have done *unto* him whatsoever
21. goeth not out but *by* prayer
22. while they abode *in* Galilee,
18: 1. *At* the same time came the
— greatest *in* the kingdom of heaven?
2. set him *in* the midst of them,
4. greatest *in* the kingdom of heaven.
6. drowned *in* the depth of the sea.
10. *in* heaven their angels do always
— my Father which is *in* heaven.
14. your Father which is *in* heaven,
18. Whatsoever ye shall bind on earth shall be bound *in* heaven:
— shall be loosed *in* heaven.
19. my Father which is *in* heaven.
20. am I *in* the midst of them.
19: 21. and thou shalt have treasure *in* heaven.
28. *in* the regeneration when the Son of man shall sit in the throne
20: 3. standing idle *in* the marketplace,
15. what I will *with* mine own?
17. twelve disciples apart *in* the way
21. on the left, *in* thy kingdom.
26. it shall not be so *among* you: but whosoever will be great *among* you,
27. whosoever will be chief *among* you,
21: 8. spread their garments *in* the way;
— strawed (them) *in* the way.
9. Blessed (is) he that cometh *in* the name of the Lord; Hosanna *in* the highest.
12. that sold and bought *in* the temple,
14. blind and the lame came to him *in* the temple;
15. children crying *in* the temple,
19. came to it, and found nothing there*on*,
22. whatsoever ye shall ask *in* prayer
23. *By* what authority doest thou these
24. will tell you *by* what authority
27. Neither tell I you *by* what authority
28. work to day *in* my vineyard.
32. *in* the way of righteousness,
33. digged a winepress *in* it, and built
38. they said *among* themselves,
41. render him the fruits *in* their seasons.
42. Did ye never read *in* the scriptures,
— it is marvellous *in* our eyes?
22: 1. spake unto them again *by* parables,
15. might entangle him *in* (his) talk
16. teachest the way of God *in* truth
23.)(The same day came to him the
28. Therefore *in* the resurrection
30. For *in* the resurrection they neither
— as the angels of God *in* heaven.
36. the great commandment *in* the law?
37. *with* all thy heart, and *with* all thy soul, and *with* all thy mind.
40. *On* these two commandments

Mat. 22:43. How then doth David *in* spirit call
23: 6. the uppermost rooms *at* feasts, and the chief seats *in* the synagogues,
7. greetings *in* the markets, and to be
9. your Father, which is *in* heaven.
16. Whosoever shall swear *by* the temple,
— whosoever shall swear *by* the gold
18. Whosoever shall swear *by* the altar,
— whosoever sweareth *by* the gift
20. shall swear *by* the altar, sweareth *by* it, and *by* all
21. whoso shall swear *by* the temple, sweareth *by* it, and *by* him
22. he that shall swear *by* heaven, sweareth *by* the throne of God, and *by* him
30. If we had been *in* the days
— *in* the blood of the prophets.
34. scourge *in* your synagogues,
39. shall say, Blessed (is) he that cometh *in* the name of the Lord.
24:14. be preached *in* all the world
15. stand *in* the holy place,
16. let them which be *in* Judæa
18. let him which is *in* the field
19. woe unto them that are with child (lit. have *in* the womb), and to them that give suck *in* those days!
20. neither *on* the sabbath day:
26. Behold, he is *in* the desert;
— (he is) *in* the secret chambers;
30. And then shall appear the sign of the Son of man *in* heaven:
38. For as *in* the days that were before the flood they
40. Then shall two be *in* the field;
41. (shall be) grinding *at* the mill;
45. to give them meat *in* due season?
48. evil servant shall say *in* his heart,
50. The lord of that servant shall come *in* a day when he looketh not for (him), and *in* an hour
25: 4. the wise took oil *in* their vessels
13. where*in* the Son of man cometh.
16. went and traded *with* the same,
18. went and digged *in* the earth,
25. went and hid thy talent *in* the earth:
31. When the Son of man shall come *in* his glory, and all the
36. I was *in* prison, and ye came unto me.
39. when saw we thee sick, or *in* prison,
43. sick, and *in* prison, and ye visited me not.
44. or naked, or sick, or *in* prison,
26: 5. they said, Not *on* the feast (day), lest there be an uproar *among* the people.
6. when Jesus was *in* Bethany, *in* the house of Simon
13. be preached *in* the whole world,
23. (his) hand with me *in* the dish,
29. with you *in* my Father's kingdom.
31. All ye shall be offended *because of* me)(this night:
33. shall be offended *because of* thee, (lit. *in* thee)
34. That)(this night, before the cock crow,
52. shall perish *with* the sword.
55. *In* that same hour said Jesus
— with you teaching *in* the temple,
69. Peter sat without *in* the palace:
27: 5. the pieces of silver *in* the temple,
12. when he was accused (lit. *in* his being acc.) of the chief priests
40. buildest (it) *in* three days,

Mat. 27:56. *Among* which was Mary Magdalene,
60. laid it *in* his own new tomb, which he had hewn out *in* the rock:
28:18. power is given unto me *in* heaven and in
Mar. 1: 2. As it is written *in* the prophets,
3. voice of one crying *in* the wilderness,
4. John did baptize *in* the wilderness,
5. *in* the river of Jordan,
8. have baptized you *with* water.
— baptize you *with* the Holy Ghost.
9. it came to pass *in* those days,
11. *in* whom I am well pleased.
13. he was there *in* the wilderness
15. repent ye, and believe)(the gospel.
16. casting a net *into* the sea:
19. *in* the ship mending their nets.
20. *in* the ship with the hired
23. there was *in* their synagogue a man *with* an unclean spirit;
39. he preached *in* their synagogues
45. was without *in* desert places:
2: 6. reasoning *in* their hearts,
8. they so reasoned *within* themselves,
— reason ye these things *in* your hearts?
15. it came to pass, that, as Jesus sat (lit. *in* his sitting) at meat *in* his house,
19. while (lit. *in* which time) the bridegroom is with
20. then shall they fast *in* those days.
23. through the corn fields *on* the sabbath day;
24. why do they *on* the sabbath day
3:22. *by* the prince of the devils casteth
23. said unto them *in* parables,
4: 1. entered into a ship, and sat *in* the sea;
2. taught them many things *by* parables, and said unto them *in* his doctrine,
4. it came to pass, as he sowed, (lit. *in* sowing)
11. things are done *in* parables:
15. that was sown *in* their hearts.
17. have no root *in* themselves,
24. *with* what measure ye mete,
28. after that the full corn *in* the ear.
30. or *with* what comparison shall
35. And)(the same day, when
36. even as he was *in* the ship.
5: 2. a man *with* an unclean spirit,
3. had (his) dwelling *among* the tombs;
5. he was *in* the mountains, and *in*
13. were choked *in* the sea.
20. began to publish *in* Decapolis
21. was passed over again *by* ship
25. which had (lit. being *in*) an issue of blood
27. came *in* the press behind,
30. immediately knowing *in* himself
— turned him about *in* the press,
6: 2. to teach *in* the synagogue:
3. they were offended *at* him.
4. *in* his own country, and *among* his own kin, and *in* his own house.
11. *in* the day of judgment,
14. do shew forth themselves *in* him.
17. upon John, and bound him *in* prison
27(28). beheaded him *in* the prison,
29. his corpse, and laid it *in* a tomb.
47. ship was *in* the midst of the sea,
48. he saw them toiling *in* rowing;
51. were sore amazed *in* themselves
56. they laid the sick *in* the streets,
8: 1. *In* those days the multitude
3. they will faint *by* the way:
14. neither had they *in* the ship

Mar. 8:26. nor tell (it) to any *in* the town.
27. *by* the way he asked his disciples,
38. *in* this adulterous and sinful generation;
— cometh *in* the glory of his Father
9: 1. kingdom of God come *with* power.
29. come forth *by* nothing, but *by* prayer
33. being *in* the house he asked them,
— disputed among yourselves *by* the way?
34. *by* the way they had disputed
36. set him *in* the midst of them:
41. water to drink *in* my name,
50. where*with* will ye season it? Have salt *in* yourselves, and have peace one with another. (lit. *in* one another)
10:10. *in* the house his disciples asked
21. thou shalt have treasure *in* heaven:
30. hundredfold now *in* this time,
— *in* the world to come eternal life.
32. they were *in* the way going up
37. on thy left hand, *in* thy glory.
43. so shall it not be *among* you: but whosoever will be great *among* you,
52. followed Jesus *in* the way.
11: 9. cometh *in* the name of the Lord.
10. cometh *in* the name of the Lord: Hosanna *in* the highest.
13. he might find any thing there*on*:
15. that sold and bought *in* the temple,
23. shall not doubt *in* his heart,
25. your Father also which is *in* heaven
26. your Father which is *in* heaven
27. as he was walking *in* the temple,
28. *By* what authority doest thou
29. I will tell you *by* what authority
33. *by* what authority I do these things.
12: 1. to speak unto them *by* parables.
11. it is marvellous *in* our eyes?
23. *In* the resurrection therefore,
25. as the angels which are *in* heaven.
26. not read *in* the book of Moses,
35. while he taught *in* the temple,
36. himself said *by* the Holy Ghost,
38. said unto them *in* his doctrine,
— which love to go *in* long clothing, and (love) salutations *in* the marketplaces,
39. chief seats *in* the synagogues, and the uppermost rooms *at* feasts:
13:11. shall be given you *in* that hour,
14. let them that be *in* Judæa flee
17. woe to them that are with child (lit. have *in* the womb), and to them that give suck *in* those days!
24. *in* those days, after that tribulation,
25. the powers that are *in* heaven
26. Son of man coming *in* the clouds
32. not the angels which are *in* heaven,
14: 1. might take him *by* craft,
2. they said, Not *on* the feast (day)
3. being *in* Bethany *in* the house
25. new *in* the kingdom of God.
27. offended *because of* (lit. *in*) me)(this night:
30. this day, (even) *in* this night,
49. I was daily with you *in* the temple
66. Peter was beneath *in* the palace,
15: 7. committed murder *in* the insurrection.
29. buildest (it) *in* three days,
40. *among* whom was Mary
41. Who also, when he was *in* Galilee,
46. laid him *in* a sepulchre
16: 5. a young man sitting *on* the right side.
12. he appeared *in* another form

Mar. 16:17. *In* my name shall they cast
Lu. 1: 1. are most surely believed *among us*,
5. *in* the days of Herod, the king
6. walking *in* all the commandments
7. were (now) well stricken *in* years
8. that while he executed the priest's office (lit. *in* his executing, &c.) before God *in* the order of his course,
17. *in* the spirit and power of Elias,
— disobedient *to* the wisdom of the just;
18. my wife well stricken *in* years.
21. that he tarried (lit. *at* his tarrying) so long *in* the temple.
22. had seen a vision *in* the temple:
25. *in* the days wherein he looked on (me), to
— take away my reproach *among* men.
26. *in* the sixth month the angel
28. blessed (art) thou *among* women.
31. thou shalt conceive *in* thy womb,
36. conceived a son *in* her old age:
39. Mary arose *in* those days,
41. the babe leaped *in* her womb;
42. Blessed (art) thou *among* women,
44. the babe leaped *in* my womb *for* joy.
51. hath shewed strength *with* his arm;
59. that *on* the eighth day they came
61. There is none *of* thy kindred that
65. *throughout* all the hill country
66. laid (them) up *in* their hearts,
69. *in* the house of his servant David;
75. *In* holiness and righteousness before
77. *by* the remission of their sins,
78. where*by* the dayspring from on
79. to them that sit *in* darkness
80. was *in* the deserts till the day
2: 1. it came to pass *in* those days,
6. while they were (lit. *in* their being) there,
7. laid him *in* a manger; because there was no room for them *in* the inn.
8. there were *in* the same country
11. this day *in* the city of David a Saviour,
12. lying *in* a manger.
14. Glory to God *in* the highest,
— peace, good will *toward* men.
16. the babe lying *in* a manger.
19. pondered (them) *in* her heart.
21. he was conceived *in* the womb.
23. written *in* the law of the Lord,
24. is said *in* the law of the Lord,
25. there was a man *in* Jerusalem,
27. he came *by* the Spirit into
— when the parents brought in (lit. *on* the parents bringing in) the child Jesus,
29. thy servant depart *in* peace,
34. rising again of many *in* Israel;
36. she was of a great (lit. advanced *in*) age,
38. looked for redemption *in* Jerusalem.
43. as they returned (lit. *in* their ret.), the child Jesus tarried behind *in* Jerusalem;
44. to have been *in* the company,
— *among* (their) kinsfolk and)(acquaintance.
46. *in* the temple, sitting *in* the midst
49. I must be *about* my Father's business?
51. kept all these sayings *in* her heart.
3: 1. Now *in* the fifteenth year of the
2. of Zacharias *in* the wilderness.
4. As it is written *in* the book of the
— one crying *in* the wilderness.
8. begin not to say *within* yourselves,
15. all men mused *in* their hearts
16. *with* the Holy Ghost and with fire:

Lu. 3:17. Whose fan (is) *in* his hand,
20. that he shut up John *in* prison.
21. when all the people were baptized, (lit. *in all*, &c. being baptized)
22. *in* thee I am well pleased.
4: 1. was led *by* the Spirit into the
2. *in* those days he did eat nothing:
5. the world *in* a moment of time.
14. Jesus returned *in* the power of the
15. he taught *in* their synagogues,
16. *on* the sabbath day, and stood
18(19). to set *at* liberty them that are
20. that were *in* the synagogue
21. this scripture fulfilled *in* your ears.
23. have heard done *in* Capernaum, do also here *in* thy country.
24. accepted *in* his own country.
25. many widows were *in* Israel *in* the days of Elias,
27. many lepers were *in* Israel
28. all they *in* the synagogue,
31. taught them *on* the sabbath days.
32. for his word was *with* power.
33. *in* the synagogue there was a man,
36. for *with* authority and power
44. he preached *in* the synagogues
5: 1. it came to pass, that, as the people pressed (lit. *in* the p. pressing)
7. which were *in* the other ship,
12. came to pass, when he was (lit. *in* his being) *in* a certain city,
16. withdrew himself *into* the wilderness,
17. came to pass *on* a certain day,
22. What reason ye *in* your hearts?
29. a great feast *in* his own house:
34. while (lit. *in* which time) the bridegroom is with them?
35. shall they fast *in* those days.
6: 1. came to pass *on* the second sabbath
2. to do *on* the sabbath days?
6. came to pass also *on* another
7. would heal *on* the sabbath day,
12. came to pass *in* those days,
— continued all night *in* prayer
23. Rejoice ye *in* that day, and leap
— your reward (is) great *in* heaven.
41. mote that is *in* thy brother's eye,
— beam that is *in* thine own eye?
42. the mote that is *in* thine eye,
— beam that is *in* thine own eye?
— mote that is *in* thy brother's eye.
7: 9. so great faith, no, not *in* Israel.
11. it came to pass)(the day after,
16. prophet is risen up *among* us;
17. went forth *throughout* all Judæa, and *throughout* all the region round
21. *in* the same hour he cured many
23. shall not be offended *in* me.
25. A man clothed *in* soft raiment?
— which are gorgeously apparelled (lit. *in* gorgeous apparel), and live delicately, are *in* kings' courts.
28. *Among* those that are born of women
— least *in* the kingdom of God
32. sitting *in* the marketplace,
37. behold, a woman *in* the city,
— sat at meat *in* the Pharisee's house,
39. he spake *within* himself, saying,
49. began to say *within* themselves,
8: 1. it came to pass afterward, (lit. *in* after time)
5. as he sowed (lit. *in* his sowing), some fell

Lu. 8: 7. some fell *among* thorns; and the
10. to others *in* parables; that seeing
13. *in* time of temptation fall away.
15. that *on* the good ground are they, which *in* an honest and good heart, having
— bring forth fruit *with* patience.
22. came to pass *on* a certain day,
27. neither abode *in* (any) house, but *in* the tombs.
32. swine feeding *on* the mountain:
40. came to pass, that, when Jesus was returned, (lit. *on* Jesus's having returned)
42. as he went (lit. *in* his going) the people thronged
43. having (lit. being *in*))(an issue of blood
9: 12. we are here *in* a desert place.
18. as he was alone (lit. *in* his being alone)
26. he shall come *in* his own glory,
29. as he prayed, (lit. *in* his praying)
31. Who appeared *in* glory, and spake
— should accomplish *at* Jerusalem.
33. came to pass, as they departed (lit. *in* their departure)
34. they feared as they entered (lit. *in* their entering)
36. when the voice was past, (lit. *in* the &c.)
— told no man *in* those days
37. came to pass, that *on* the next
46. arose a reasoning *among* them,
48. that is least *among* you all,
51. came to pass, when the time was come (lit. *in* the, &c.)
57. as they went *in* the way,
10: 3. forth as lambs *among* wolves.
7. *in* the same house remain,
9. heal the sick that are there*in*,
12. more tolerable *in* that day for
13. had been done *in* Tyre and Sidon, which have been done *in* you, they had...repented, sitting *in* sackcloth and
14. Tyre and Sidon *at* the judgment,
17. subject unto us *through* thy name.
20. *in* this rejoice not, that the spirits
— your names are written *in* heaven.
21. *In* that hour Jesus rejoiced in spirit,
26. What is written *in* the law?
31. came down a certain priest)(that way:
35. when I come again (lit. *in* my coming again), I will repay thee.
38. it came to pass, as they went, (lit. *in* their going)
11: 1. that, as he was praying (lit. *in* his being praying) *in* a certain place,
2. Our Father which art *in* heaven,
— Thy will be done, as *in* heaven,
15. *through* Beelzebub the chief of the
18. I cast out devils *through* Beelzebub.
19. if I *by* Beelzebub cast out devils, *by* whom do your sons cast (them)
20. if I *with* the finger of God cast
21. his goods are *in* peace:
27. it came to pass, as he spake (lit. *in* his, &c.)
31. shall rise up *in* the judgment
32. shall rise up *in* the judgment
35. the light which is *in* thee be not
37. as he spake (lit. *in* his, &c.), a certain
43. uppermost seats *in* the synagogues, and greetings *in* the markets.
12: 1. *In* the mean time, when there
3. ye have spoken *in* darkness shall be heard *in* the light;
— have spoken in the ear *in* closets

Lu. 12: 8. Whosoever shall confess)(me before men,)(him shall the Son of man
12. shall teach you *in* the same hour
15. not *in* the abundance of the
17. he thought *within* himself,
27. Solomon *in* all his glory was
28. which is to day *in* the field,
33. a treasure *in* the heavens
38. shall come *in* the second watch, or come *in* the third
42. portion of meat *in* due season?
45. if that servant say *in* his heart,
46. will come *in* a day when...and *at* an hour
51. come to give peace *on* earth?
52. there shall be five *in* one house
58. (as thou art) *in* the way, give
13: 1. There were present *at* that season
4. the tower *in* Siloam fell,
— men that dwelt *in* Jerusalem?
6. a fig tree planted *in* his vineyard; and he came and sought fruit there*on*,
7. seeking fruit *on* this fig tree,
10. teaching *in* one of the synagogues *on* the sabbath.
14. six days *in* which men ought to work: *in* them therefore come
19. lodged *in* the branches of it.
26. thou hast taught *in* our streets.
28. prophets, *in* the kingdom of God,
29. sit down *in* the kingdom of God.
31.)(The same day there came certain
35. cometh *in* the name of the Lord.
14: 1. it came to pass, as he went (lit. *in* his going) into
5. pull him out *on* the sabbath day?
14. *at* the resurrection of the just.
15. *in* the kingdom of God.
31. be able *with* ten thousand
34. where*with* shall it be seasoned?
15: 4. the ninety and nine *in* the wilderness,
7. likewise joy shall be *in* heaven
25. his elder son was *in* the field:
16: 3. the steward said *within* himself,
10. faithful *in* that which is least is faithful also *in* much: and he that is unjust *in* the least is unjust also *in* much.
11. *in* the unrighteous mammon,
12. have not been faithful *in* that which is
15. highly esteemed *among* men
23. *in* hell he lift up his eyes, being *in* torments, and seeth Abraham afar off, and Lazarus *in* his bosom.
24. I am tormented *in* this flame.
25. remember that thou *in* thy lifetime
17: 6. be thou planted *in* the sea;
11. came to pass, as he went (lit. *in* his &c.)
14. pass, that, as they went, (lit. *in* their &c.)
24. the Son of man be *in* his day.
26. as it was *in* the days of Noe,
— *in* the days of the Son of man.
28. as it was *in* the days of Lot;
31. *In* that day, he which shall
— his stuff *in* the house,
— he that is *in* the field, let him
36. Two (men) shall be *in* the field,
18: 2. There was *in* a city a judge,
3. there was a widow *in* that city;
4. afterward he said *within* himself,
8. he will avenge them speedi*ly*.
22. thou shalt have treasure *in* heaven:
30. more *in* this present time, and *in* the world to come

Lu. 18:35. it came to pass, that as he was come nigh (lit. *in* his coming nigh)
19: 5. I must abide *at* thy house
15. it came to pass, that when he was returned, (lit. *on* his returning)
17. hast been faithful *in* a very little,
20. have kept laid up *in* a napkin:
30. *in* the which at your entering
36. spread their clothes *in* the way.
38. cometh *in* the name of the Lord: peace *in* heaven, and glory *in* the highest.
42. at least *in* this thy day,
44. thy children *within* thee; and they shall not leave *in* thee
45. cast out them that sold there*in*,
47. he taught daily *in* the temple.
20: 1. (that) *on* one of those days, as he taught the people *in* the temple,
2. *by* what authority doest thou
8. *by* what authority I do these
10. *at* the season he sent a servant
19. and the scribes)(the same hour sought
33. Therefore *in* the resurrection whose
42. saith *in* the book of Psalms,
46. desire to walk *in* long robes, and love greetings *in* the markets, and the highest seats *in* the synagogues, and the chief rooms *at* feasts;
21: 6. *in* the which there shall not be
19. *In* your patience possess ye your
21. them which are *in* Judæa flee
— them which are *in* the midst of it
— them that are *in* the countries
23. unto them that are with child (lit. have *in* the womb), and to them that give suck, *in* those days!
— wrath *upon* this people.
25. shall be signs *in* the sun, and
— distress of nations, *with* perplexity;
27. coming *in* a cloud with power
34. be overcharged *with* surfeiting,
36. Watch ye therefore, and pray always, (lit. *at* all times)
37. he was teaching *in* the temple;
38. to him *in* the temple, for to hear
22: 7. when (lit. *in* which) the passover must be killed.
16. fulfilled *in* the kingdom of God.
20. new testament *in* my blood,
24. was also a strife *among* them,
26. he that is greatest *among* you,
27. I am *among* (lit. *in* the midst of) you as he that serveth.
28. with me *in* my temptations.
30. at my table *in* my kingdom,
37. must yet be accomplished *in* me,
44. being *in* an agony he prayed
49. shall we smite *with* the sword?
53. daily with you *in* the temple,
55. a fire *in* the midst of the hall,
— Peter sat down *among* (lit. *in* the midst of) them.
23: 4. I find no fault *in* this man.
7. was *at* Jerusalem *at* that time.
9. questioned with him *in* many words;
12. And)(the same day Pilate and Herod were made friends together: for before they were *at* enmity
14. found no fault *in* this man
19. sedition made *in* the city,
22. found no cause of death *in* him
29. *in* the which they shall say,

Lu. 23 31. do these things *in* a green tree, what shall be done *in* the dry?
40. art *in* the same condemnation?
42. thou comest into (lit. *in*) thy kingdom.
43. shalt thou be with me *in* paradise.
53. laid it *in* a sepulchre that was hewn
24: 4. it came to pass, as they were much perplexed (lit. *in* their being per.)
— stood by them *in* shining garments:
6. when he was yet *in* Galilee,
13. went)(that same day to a village
15. it came to pass, that, while they communed (lit. *in* their c.)
18. thou only a stranger *in* Jerusalem,
— come to pass there (lit. *in* it) *in* these days?
19. a prophet mighty *in* deed and word
27. unto them *in* all the scriptures
30. it came to pass, as he sat (lit. *in* his sitting) at meat
32. our heart burn *within* us, while he talked with us *by* the way,
35. things (were done) *in* the way,
— of them *in* breaking of bread.
36. stood *in* the midst of them,
38. do thoughts arise *in* your hearts?
44. written *in* the law of Moses,
49. tarry ye *in* the city of Jerusalem,
51. came to pass, while he blessed (lit. *in* his blessing) them,
53. were continually *in* the temple,
Joh. 1: 1. *In* the beginning was the Word,
2. The same was *in* the beginning
4. *In* him was life; and the life
5. the light shineth *in* darkness;
10. He was *in* the world, and the
14. was made flesh, and dwelt *among* us,
23. of one crying *in* the wilderness,
26. saying, I baptize *with* water:
28. These things were done *in* Bethabara
31. I come baptizing *with* water.
33. sent me to baptize *with* water,
— baptizeth *with* the Holy Ghost.
45(46). of whom Moses *in* the law,
47(48). *in* whom is no guile!
2: 1. a marriage *in* Cana of Galilee;
11. did Jesus *in* Cana of Galilee,
14. found *in* the temple those
19. *in* three days I will raise it up.
20. thou rear it up *in* three days?
23. when he was *in* Jerusalem *at* the passover, *in* the feast
25. for he knew what was *in* man.
3: 13. Son of man which is *in* heaven.
14. the serpent *in* the wilderness,
21. that they are wrought *in* God.
23. also was baptizing *in* Ænon
35. given all things *into* his hand.
4: 14. shall be *in* him a well of water
20. Our fathers worshipped *in* this
— that *in* Jerusalem is the place
21. neither *in* this mountain, nor yet *at* Jerusalem,
23. worship the Father *in* spirit and
24. worship (him) *in* spirit and in truth.
31. *In* the mean while his disciples
37. here*in* is that saying true,
44. no honour *in* his own country.
45. he did *at* Jerusalem *at* the feast:
46. whose son was sick *at* Capernaum.
52. the hour when (lit. *in* which) he began to amend.

Joh. 4: 53. *at* the same hour, *in* the which
5: 2. Now there is *at* Jerusalem
3. *In* these lay a great multitude
4. at a certain season *into* the pool,
5. had an infirmity (lit. having *in* infirmity) thirty and eight years.
7. while (lit. *in* which time) I am coming,
9. and *on* the same day was the sabbath.
13. a multitude being *in* (that) place.
14. Jesus findeth him *in* the temple.
16. had done these things *on* the sabbath day.
26. the Father hath life *in* himself;
— the Son to have life *in* himself;
28. *in* the which all that are *in* the
35. a season to rejoice *in* his light.
38. his word abiding *in* you:
39. *in* them ye think ye have eternal
42. have not the love of God *in* you.
43. I am come *in* my Father's name,
— shall come *in* his own name,
6: 10. there was much grass *in* the place.
31. did eat manna *in* the desert;
39. raise it up again *at* the last day.
45. It is written *in* the prophets,
49. did eat manna *in* the wilderness,
53. ye have no life *in* you.
56. dwelleth *in* me, and I *in* him.
59. *in* the synagogue, as he taught *in*
61. When Jesus knew *in* himself
7: 1. Jesus walked *in* Galilee: for he would not walk *in* Jewry,
4. doeth any thing *in* secret,
— seeketh to be known open*ly*.
9. he abode (still) *in* Galilee.
10. as it were *in* secret.
11. Jews sought him *at* the feast,
12. murmuring *among* the people
18. no unrighteousness is *in* him.
22. ye *on* the sabbath day circumcise
23. If a man *on* the sabbath day
— whole *on* the sabbath day?
28. Then cried Jesus *in* the temple
37. *In* the last day, that great (day)
43. was a division *among* the people
8: 3. a woman taken *in* adultery; and when they had set her *in* the midst,
5. Moses *in* the law commanded
9. the woman standing *in* the midst.
12. shall not walk *in* darkness,
17. It is also written *in* your law,
20. spake Jesus *in* the treasury, as he taught *in* the temple:
21. shall die *in* your sins:
24. die *in* your sins: for if ye believe not that I am (he), ye shall die *in* your sins.
31. If ye continue *in* my word,
35. servant abideth not *in* the house
37. my word hath no place *in* you.
44. abode not *in* the truth, because there is no truth *in* him.
9: 3. be made manifest *in* him.
5. As long as I am *in* the world,
16. there was a division *among* them.
30. Why here*in* is a marvellous thing,
34. wast altogether born *in* sins,
10: 19. again *among* the Jews for these
22. it was *at* Jerusalem the feast
23. *in* the temple *in* Solomon's porch.
25. that I do *in* my Father's name,
34. Is it not written *in* your law,
38. that the Father (is) *in* me, and I *in* him.
11: 6. two days still *in* the same place

Joh.11: 9. If any man walk *in* the day,
10. if a man walk *in* the night,
— because there is no light *in* him.
17. *in* the grave four days already.
20. Mary sat (still) *in* the house.
24. *in* the resurrection *at* the last day.
30. was *in* that place where
31. were with her *in* the house.
38. again groaning *in* himself
54. no more openly *among* the Jews;
56. as they stood *in* the temple,
12:13. cometh *in* the name of the Lord.
20. came up to worship *at* the feast:
25. hateth his life *in* this world
35. he that walketh *in* darkness
46. should not abide *in* darkness.
48. shall judge him *in* the last day.
13: 1. his own which were *in* the world,
23. there was leaning *on* Jesus' bosom
31. God is glorified *in* him.
32. If God be glorified *in* him, God shall also glorify him *in* himself,
35. *By* this shall all (men) know
— if ye have love one *to* another.
14: 2. *In* my Father's house are
10. that I am *in* the Father, and the Father *in* me?
— the Father that dwelleth *in* me,
11. I (am) *in* the Father, and the Father *in* me:
13. ye shall ask *in* my name,
— Father may be glorified *in* the Son.
14. ask any thing *in* my name,
17. dwelleth with you, and shall be *in* you.
20. *At* that day ye shall know that I (am) *in* my Father, and ye *in* me, and I *in* you.
26. Father will send *in* my name,
30. cometh, and hath nothing *in* me.
15: 2. Every branch *in* me that
4. Abide *in* me, and I *in* you.
— except it abide *in* the vine;
— except ye abide *in* me.
5. He that abideth *in* me, and I *in* him,
6. If a man abide not *in* me,
7. If ye abide *in* me, and my words abide *in* you, ye
8. Here*in* is my Father glorified,
9. continue ye *in* my love.
10. ye shall abide *in* my love,
— abide *in* his love
11. my joy might remain *in* you,
16. ask of the Father *in* my name,
24. If I had not done *among* them
25. that is written *in* their law,
16:23. *in* that day ye shall ask me
— ask the Father *in* my name,
24. ye asked nothing *in* my name:
25. have I spoken unto you *in* proverbs:
— no more speak unto you *in* proverbs,
26. *At* that day ye shall ask *in* my
30. *by* this we believe that thou
33. *in* me ye might have peace. *In* the world ye shall have tribulation:
17:10. I am glorified *in* them.
11. I am no more *in* the world, but these are *in* the world,
— keep *through* thine own name
12. I was with them *in* the world, I kept them *in* thy name:
13. these things I speak *in* the world,
— my joy fulfilled *in* themselves.
17. Sanctify them *through* thy truth.

Joh.17:19. be sanctified *through* the truth.
21. thou, Father, (art) *in* me, and I *in* thee, that they also may be one *in* us.
23. I *in* them, and thou *in* me,
26. may be *in* them, and I *in* them.
18:20. *in* the synagogue, and *in* the temple.
— *in* secret have I said nothing.
26. thee *in* the garden with him.
38. I find *in* him no fault (at all).
39. release unto you one *at* the passover:
19: 4. that I find no fault *in* him.
6. for I find no fault *in* him.
31. upon the cross *on* the sabbath day,
41. Now *in* the place where he was
— *in* the garden a new sepulchre, where*in* was never man yet laid.
20:12. seeth two angels *in* white sitting,
25. Except I shall see *in* his hands
30. are not written *in* this book:
31. have life *through* his name.
21: 3. and)(that night they caught nothing.
20. leaned on his breast *at* supper,
Acts 1: 3. *by* many infallible proofs,
5. baptized *with* the Holy Ghost
6. wilt thou *at* this time restore
7. hath put *in* his own power.
8. *in* Jerusalem, and *in* all Judæa,
10. stood by them *in* white apparel;
15. *in* those days Peter stood up *in* the midst of the disciples,
20. written *in* the book of Psalms,
— let no man dwell there*in*:
21. all the time that (lit. *in* all the time *in* which) the Lord Jesus
2: 1. when the day of Pentecost was fully come (lit. *in* the day of P. being fully come)
5. were dwelling *at* Jerusalem
8. where*in* we were born?
17. come to pass *in* the last days,
18. I will pour out *in* those days
19. shew wonders *in* heaven above,
22. by him *in* the midst of you,
29. his sepulchre is *with* us unto
46. with one accord *in* the temple,
— did eat their meat *with* gladness
3: 6. *In* the name of Jesus Christ
26. *in* turning away every one of you
4: 2. *through* Jesus the resurrection
7. had set them *in* the midst, they asked, *By* what power, or *by* what name,
9. *by* what *means* he is made whole;
10. *by* the name of Jesus Christ of
— *by* him doth this man stand
12. is there salvation *in* any other:
— given *among* men, where*by* we
24. the sea, and all that *in* them is:
30. *By* stretching forth thine hand
31. where (lit. *in* which) they were assembled together;
34. any *among* them that lacked:
5: 4. was it not *in* thine own power?
— this thing *in* thine heart?
12. wrought *among* the people;
— one accord *in* Solomon's porch.
18. put them *in* the common prison.
20. stand and speak *in* the temple
22. found them not *in* the prison,
23. shut *with* all safety,
25. whom ye put *in* prison are standing *in* the temple,
27. set (them) *before* the council:
34. stood there up one *in* the council.

Acts 5:37. *in* the days of the taxing,
42. daily *in* the temple,
6: 1. *in* those days, when the number
— neglected *in* the daily ministration.
7. multiplied *in* Jerusalem
8. wonders and miracles *among* the people.
15. all that sat *in* the council,
7: 2. when he was *in* Mesopotamia, before he dwelt *in* Charran,
4. dwelt *in* Charran: and from
5. none inheritance *in* it,
6. should sojourn *in* a strange land;
7. serve me *in* this place.
12. that there was corn *in* Egypt,
13. *at* the second (time) Joseph was
14.)(threescore and fifteen souls.
16. laid *in* the sepulchre that Abraham
17. grew and multiplied *in* Egypt,
20. *In* which time Moses was born,
— nourished up *in* his father's house
22. mighty *in* words and *in* deeds.
29. fled Moses *at* this saying, and was a stranger *in* the land of Madian,
30. *in* the wilderness of mount Sina
— *in* a flame of fire in a bush.
33. place where (lit. *in* which) thou standest
34. my people which is *in* Egypt,
35. *by* the hand of the angel which appeared to him *in* the bush.
36. *in* the land of Egypt, and *in* the Red sea, and *in* the wilderness
38. *in* the church *in* the wilderness
— spake to him *in* the mount Sina,
41. made a calf *in* those days,
— rejoiced *in* the works of their own
42. written *in* the book of the prophets,
— forty years *in* the wilderness?
44. Our fathers had the tabernacle of witness (lit. the tab. &c. was *among* our fathers)
— *in* the wilderness,
45. *into* the possession of the Gentiles,
48. not *in* temples made with hands;
8: 1. *at* that time there was a great
— church which was *at* Jerusalem;
6.)(hearing and seeing the miracles
8. there was great joy *in* that city.
9. beforetime *in* the same city
14. apostles which were *at* Jerusalem
21. part nor lot *in* this matter:
33. *In* his humiliation his judgment
9: 3. as he journeyed, (lit. *in* his journeying)
10. a certain disciple *at* Damascus,
— said the Lord *in* a vision,
11. enquire *in* the house of Judas
12. hath seen *in* a vision a man
13. to thy saints *at* Jerusalem:
17. *in* the way as thou camest,
19. disciples which were *at* Damascus.
20. preached Christ *in* the synagogues,
21. called on this name *in* Jerusalem,
22. Jews which dwelt *at* Damascus,
25. down by the wall *in* a basket.
27. had seen the Lord *in* the way,
— preached boldly *at* Damascus *in* the name of Jesus.
28. coming in and going out *at* Jerusalem.
29(28). And he spake boldly *in* the name of the Lord Jesus,
36. there was *at* Joppa a certain
37. it came to pass *in* those days,
— laid (her) *in* an upper chamber.
38. heard that Peter was there, (lit. *in* it)

Acts 9:43. he tarried many days *in* Joppa
10: 1. a certain man *in* Cæsarea
3. He saw *in* a vision evidently
12. Where*in* were all manner of
17. while Peter doubted *in* himself
30. I prayed *in* my house,
— before me *in* bright clothing,
32. he is lodged *in* the house of (one)
35. *in* every nation he that feareth
39. *in* the land of the Jews, and *in* Jerusalem,
48. *in* the name of the Lord.
11: 5. I was *in* the city of Joppa praying: and *in* a trance I saw a vision,
11. unto the house where (lit. *in* which) I
13. seen an angel *in* his house,
14. where*by* thou and all thy house
15. as I began (lit. *on* my beginning) to speak, the Holy Ghost fell on them, as on us *at* the beginning.
16. baptized *with* the Holy Ghost.
22. church which was *in* Jerusalem:
26. assembled themselves *with* the church,
— called Christians first *in* Antioch.
27. *in* these days came prophets
29. brethren which dwelt *in* Judæa:
12: 5. Peter therefore was kept *in* prison:
7. a light shined *in* the prison:
— saying, Arise up quick*ly*.
11. when Peter was come *to* himself,
18. no small stir *among* the soldiers,
13: 1. church that was *at* Antioch
5. when they were *at* Salamis,
— *in* the synagogues of the Jews:
15. if ye have (lit. if there is *in* you) any
17. when they dwelt as strangers (lit. *in* the sojourning) *in* the land of Egypt,
18. their manners *in* the wilderness.
19. *in* the land of Chanaan,
26. whosoever *among* you feareth
27. they that dwell *at* Jerusalem,
33. written *in* the second psalm,
35. he saith also *in* another (psalm),
39. *by* him all that believe are
— justified *by* the law of Moses.
40. spoken of *in* the prophets;
41. I work a work *in* your days,
14: 1. it came to pass *in* Iconium,
8. sat a certain man *at* Lystra,
15. all things that are there*in*.
16. Who *in* times past suffered
25. preached the word *in* Perga,
15: 7. God made choice *among* us,
12. had wrought *among* the Gentiles
21. being read *in* the synagogues
22. chief men *among* the brethren:
35. Barnabas continued *in* Antioch,
36. every city where (lit. *in* which) we have
16: 2. brethren that were *at* Lystra
3. which were *in* those quarters:
4. elders which were *at* Jerusalem.
6. to preach the word *in* Asia,
12. we were *in* that city abiding
18. *in* the name of Jesus Christ
32. all that were *in* his house.
33.)(the same hour of the night,
36. therefore depart, and go *in* peace.
17: 11. than those *in* Thessalonica,
13. was preached of Paul *at* Berea,
16. Paul waited for them *at* Athens, his spirit was stirred *in* him,
17. *in* the synagogue with the Jews,
— *in* the market daily with them

Acts17:22. Paul stood *in* the midst of
23. an altar with this inscription, (lit. *on* which was inscribed)
24. the world and all things there*in*,
— not *in* temples made with hands;
28. For *in* him we live, and move,
31. a day, *in* the which he will judge the world *in* righteousness *by* (that) man
34. *among* the which (was) Dionysius
18: 4. he reasoned *in* the synagogue
9. *in* the night by a vision,
10. I have much people *in* this city.
11. the word of God *among* them.
18. having shorn (his) head *in* Cenchrea:
24. mighty *in* the scriptures,
26. to speak boldly *in* the synagogue:
19: 1. that, while Apollos was (lit. *in* Apollos's being) *at* Corinth,
9. disputing daily *in* the school
16. the man *in* whom the evil
21. Paul purposed *in* the spirit,
39. determined *in* a lawful assembly.
20: 5. tarried for us *at* Troas.
7. *upon* the first (day) of the week,
8. many lights *in* the upper chamber,
10. for his life is *in* him.
15. tarried *at* Trogyllium; and the
16. not spend the time *in* Asia:
19. *by* the lying in wait of the Jews:
22. that shall befall me there: (lit. *in* it)
25. *among* whom I have gone
26. I take you to record)(this day,
28. *over* the which the Holy Ghost
32. an inheritance *among* all them
21:11. So shall the Jews *at* Jerusalem
19. had wrought *among* the Gentiles
27. they saw him *in* the temple,
29. before with him *in* the city
34. some another, *among* the multitude,
22: 3. a Jew, born *in* Tarsus,
— yet brought up *in* this city
17. *in* the temple, I was *in* a trance;
18. quick*ly* out of Jerusalem:
23: 6. he cried out *in* the council,
9. We find no evil *in* this man:
35. kept *in* Herod's judgment hall.
24:11. since I went up *to* Jerusalem for to worship. (lit. I went up to worship *in* Jerusalem)
12. neither found me *in* the temple
— neither *in* the synagogues,
14. in the law and *in* the prophets:
16. here*in* do I exercise myself,
18. Where*upon* certain Jews from Asia found me purified *in* the temple,
20. found any evil doing *in* me,
21. I cried standing *among* them,
25: 4. Paul should be kept *at* Cæsarea, and that he himself would depart short*ly*
5. which *among* you are able, go
— if there be any wickedness *in* him.
6. he had tarried *among* them
24. both *at* Jerusalem, and (also) here,
26: 4. *among* mine own nation *at* Jerusalem,
7. instant*ly* (lit. *in* intensity) serving (God) day and night,
10. I also did *in* Jerusalem:
12. Where*upon* as I went to Damascus
18. inheritance *among* them which
20. first unto them *of* Damascus,
21. the Jews caught me *in* the temple,
26. was not done *in* a corner.

Acts26:28. Almost (lit. *in* part) thou persuadest me to be a Christian.
29. were both almost, and altogether such (lit. both *in* part, and *in* whole)
27: 7. when we had sailed slowly)(many days,
21. Paul stood forth *in* the midst
27. driven up and down *in* Adria,
31. Except these abide *in* the ship,
37. we were in all *in* the ship
28: 7. *In* the same quarters were
9. which had diseases *in* the island,
11. we departed *in* a ship of Alexandria, which had wintered *in* the isle,
18. was no cause of death *in* me.
29. great reasoning *among* themselves.
30. *in* his own hired house,
Ro. 1: 2. prophets *in* the holy scriptures,
4. the Son of God *with* power,
5. to the faith *among* all nations,
6. *Among* whom are ye also the
7. To all that be *in* Rome,
8. *throughout* the whole world.
9. *with* my spirit *in* the gospel
10. *by* the will of God to come
12. together *with* you by the mutual faith (lit. by the faith *in* the one and the other)
13. *among* you also, even as *among* other
15. to you that are *at* Rome also.
17. For there*in* is the righteousness
18. hold the truth *in* unrighteousness;
19. of God is manifest *in* them;
21. became vain *in* their imaginations,
23. *into* an image made like to
24. *through* the lusts of their own
— their own bodies *between* themselves:
25. the truth of God *into* a lie,
27. burned *in* their lust one toward another; men *with* men working that
— receiving *in* themselves that
28. to retain God *in* (their) knowledge,
2: 1. for where*in* thou judgest another,
5. wrath *against* the day of wrath
12. as have sinned *in* the law
15. the law written *in* their hearts.
16. *In* the day when God shall judge
17. makest thy boast *of* God,
19. of them which are *in* darkness,
20. of the truth *in* the law.
23. makest thy boast *of* the law,
24. blasphemed *among* the Gentiles
28. which is one outward*ly*;
— which is outward (lit. *in* outward manifestation) *in* the flesh:
29. a Jew, which is one inward*ly*;
— of the heart, *in* the spirit, (and) not
3: 4. justified *in* thy sayings, and mightest overcome when thou art judged. (lit. *in* being judged)
7. *through* my lie unto his glory;
16. misery (are) *in* their ways:
19. them who are *under* the law.
24. redemption that is *in* Christ Jesus:
25. through faith *in* his blood,
—(26). *through* the forbearance of God;
26. *at* this time his righteousness:
4:10. *in* circumcision, or *in* uncircumcision? Not *in* circumcision, but *in* uncircumcision
11. (yet) being uncircumcised: (lit. *in* unc.)
12. which (he had) being (yet) uncircumcised. (lit. *in* uncircumcision)

Ro. 5: 2. this grace wherein we stand,
3. we glory *in* tribulations also:
5. shed abroad *in* our hearts
9. now justified *by* his blood,
10. we shall be saved *by* his life.
11. we also joy *in* God through
13. sin was *in* the world:
15. the gift *by* grace, (which is)
17. shall reign *in* life by one,
21. as sin hath reigned *unto* (lit. *in*) death,
6: 2. live any longer there*in*?
4. should walk *in* newness of life.
11. *through* Jesus Christ our Lord.
12. reign *in* your mortal body, that ye should obey it *in* the lusts thereof.
23. the gift of God (is) eternal life *through* Jesus Christ our Lord.
7: 5. when we were *in* the flesh,
— did work *in* our members
6. dead where*in* we were held;
— serve *in* newness of spirit,
8. wrought *in* me all manner
17. sin that dwelleth *in* me.
18. *in* me that is, *in* my flesh,
20. sin that dwelleth *in* me.
23. another law *in* my members,
— of sin which is *in* my members.
8: 1. them which are *in* Christ Jesus,
2. Spirit of life *in* Christ Jesus
3. *in* that it was weak through
— *in* the likeness of sinful flesh, and for sin, condemned sin *in* the flesh:
4. law might be fulfilled *in* us,
8. they that are *in* the flesh cannot
9. ye are not *in* the flesh, but *in* the Spirit,
— the Spirit of God dwell *in* you.
10. if Christ (be) *in* you, the body
11. dwell *in* you, he that raised
— his Spirit that dwelleth *in* you.
15. where*by* we cry, Abba, Father.
23. ourselves groan *within* ourselves,
29. firstborn *among* many brethren.
34. *at* the right hand of God,
37. *in* all these things we are more
39. which is *in* Christ Jesus our Lord.
9: 1. I say the truth *in* Christ,
— me witness *in* the Holy Ghost,
7. *In* Isaac shall thy seed be called.
17. I might shew my power *in* thee,
— declared *throughout* all the earth.
22. endured *with* much longsuffering
25. As he saith also *in* Osee,
26. *in* the place where it was said
28. cut (it) short *in* righteousness:
33. I lay *in* Sion a stumblingstone
10: 5. those things shall live *by* them.
6. Say not *in* thine heart,
8. *in* thy mouth, and *in* thy heart:
9. shalt confess *with* thy mouth the Lord Jesus, and shalt believe *in* thine heart
11: 2. the scripture saith *of* Elias?
5. so then *at* this present time
17. wert graffed in *among* them,
12: 3. to every man that is *among* you,
4. have many members *in* one body,
5. are one body *in* Christ,
7. (let us wait) *on* (our) ministering: or he that teacheth, *on* teaching;
8. that exhorteth, *on* exhortation: he that giveth, (let him do it) *with* simplicity; he that ruleth, *with* diligence; he that sheweth mercy *with* cheerfulness.

Ro. 12:21. overcome evil *with* good.
13: 9. comprehended *in* this saying, namely (lit. *in* this), Thou shalt love thy
13. Let us walk honestly, as *in* the day;
14: 5. fully persuaded *in* his own mind.
14. persuaded *by* the Lord Jesus,
17. peace, and joy *in* the Holy Ghost.
18. *in* these things serveth Christ
21. where*by* thy brother stumbleth,
22. *in* that thing which he alloweth.
15: 5. likeminded one toward another (lit. *toward* one another)
6. with one mind (and))(one mouth
9. to thee *among* the Gentiles,
13. all joy and peace *in* believing,
— abound *in* hope, *through* the power
16. sanctified *by* the Holy Ghost.
17. I may glory *through* Jesus Christ
19. *Through* mighty signs and wonders, *by* the power of the Spirit of God;
23. no more place *in* these parts,
26. saints which are *at* Jerusalem.
27. minister unto them *in* carnal things.
29. *in* the fulness of the blessing
30. together with me *in* (your) prayers
31. that do not believe *in* Judæa;
32. *with* joy by the will of God,
16: 1. church which is *at* Cenchrea:
2. That ye receive her *in* the Lord,
— *in* whatsoever business she hath
3. my helpers *in* Christ Jesus:
7. are of note *among* the apostles, who also were *in* Christ before me.
8. my beloved *in* the Lord.
9. Urbane, our helper *in* Christ,
10. Salute Apelles approved *in* Christ.
11. which are *in* the Lord.
12. who labour *in* the Lord.
— laboured much *in* the Lord.
13. Rufus chosen *in* the Lord,
16. Salute one another *with* an holy kiss.
20. under your feet short*ly*.
22. salute you *in* the Lord.
1Co. 1: 2. church of God which is *at* Corinth,
— sanctified *in* Christ Jesus,
— that *in* every place call upon
4. is given you *by* Jesus Christ;
5. *in* every thing ye are enriched *by* him *in* all utterance,
6. was confirmed *in* you:
7. ye come behind *in* no gift;
8. *in* the day of our Lord Jesus
10. no divisions *among* you;
— *in* the same mind and *in* the same judgment.
11. there are contentions *among* you.
17. not *with* wisdom of words,
21. *in* the wisdom of God
30. of him are ye *in* Christ Jesus,
31. let him glory *in* the Lord.
2: 2. to know any thing *among* you,
3. with you *in* weakness, and *in* fear, and *in* much trembling.
4. *with* enticing words of man's wisdom, but *in* demonstration of the Spirit
5. not stand *in* the wisdom of men, but *in* the power of God.
6. wisdom *among* them that are perfect:
7. wisdom of God *in* a mystery,
11. spirit of man which is *in* him?
13. not *in* the words which man's
— but which (lit. *in* the which) the Holy Ghost teacheth;

1 Co. 3: 1. as unto babes *in* Christ.
3. *among* you envying, and strife,
13. it shall be revealed *by* fire;
16. Spirit of God dwelleth *in* you?
18. If any man *among* you seemeth to be wise *in* this world,
19. the wise *in* their own craftiness.
21. let no man glory *in* men.
4: 2. it is required *in* stewards,
4. yet am I not here*by* justified:
6. that ye might learn *in* us
10. ye (are) wise *in* Christ;
15. ten thousand instructers *in* Christ,
— for *in* Christ Jesus I have begotten
17. faithful *in* the Lord, who shall
— my ways which be *in* Christ, as I teach every where *in* every church.
20. not *in* word, but *in* power.
21. unto you *with* a rod, or *in* love, and
5: 1. (there is) fornication *among* you,
— as named *among* the Gentiles,
4. *In* the name of our Lord Jesus
5. saved *in* the day of the Lord Jesus.
8. not *with* old leaven, neither *with* the leaven of malice and wickedness; but *with* the unleavened (bread) of
9. I wrote unto you *in* an epistle
6: 2. shall be judged *by* you,
4. least esteemed *in* the church.
5. is not a wise man *among* you?
7. utterly a fault *among* you,
11. *in* the name of the Lord Jesus, and *by* the Spirit
19. the Holy Ghost (which is) *in* you,
20. glorify God *in* your body, and *in* your spirit, which are God's.
7: 14. is sanctified *by* the wife,
— wife is sanctified *by* the husband:
15. under bondage *in* such (cases): but God hath called us *to* peace.
17. so ordain I *in* all churches.
18. Is any called *in* uncircumcision?
20. Let every man abide *in* the same calling where*in* he was called. (lit. Let every man *in* the calling wherein he was called remain *in* the same)
22. he that is called *in* the Lord,
24. every man, where*in* he is called, there*in* abide
37. standeth stedfast *in* his heart,
— hath so decreed *in* his heart
39. whom she will; only *in* the Lord.
8: 4. an idol (is) nothing *in* the world,
5. whether *in* heaven or in earth,
7. not *in* every man that knowledge:
10. at meat *in* the idol's temple,
9: 1. are not ye my work *in* the Lord?
2. are ye *in* the Lord.
9. written *in* the law of Moses,
15. that it should be so done *unto* me:
18. not my power *in* the gospel.
24. they which run *in* a race run
10: 2. *in* the cloud and *in* the sea;
5. *with* many of them God was not
— overthrown *in* the wilderness.
8. fell *in* one day three and twenty thousand.
25. is sold *in* the shambles,
11: 11. without the man, *in* the Lord.
13. Judge *in* yourselves: is it comely
18. come together *in* the church,
— there be divisions *among* you;
19. be also heresies *among* you,

1Co. 11: 19. be made manifest *among* you.
21. For *in* eating every one taketh before
22. shall I praise you *in* this?
23.)(the (same) night in which he was betrayed
25. new testament *in* my blood.
30. many (are) weak and sickly *among* you.
34. let him eat *at* home;
12: 3. speaking *by* the Spirit of God
— but *by* the Holy Ghost.
6. God which worketh all *in* all.
9. faith *by* the same Spirit; to another the gifts of healing *by* the same Spirit;
13. For *by* one Spirit are we all
18. every one of them *in* the body,
25. be no schism *in* the body;
28. God hath set some *in* the church,
13: 12. we see through a glass, dark*ly*;
14: 6. either *by* revelation, or *by* knowledge, or *by* prophesying, or *by* doctrine?
10. many kinds of voices *in* the world,
11. (shall be) a barbarian *unto* me.
19. Yet *in* the church I had rather
— words *in* an (unknown) tongue.
21. *In* the law it is written, *With* (men of) other tongues and)(other lips will I
25. that God is *in* you of a truth.
28. keep silence *in* the church;
33. as *in* all churches of the saints.
34. women keep silence *in* the churches.
35. ask their husbands *at* home.
— women to speak *in* the church.
15: 1. have received, and where*in* ye stand;
3. I delivered unto you first of all (lit. *in* the first)
12. how say some *among* you
17. ye are yet *in* your sins.
18. which are fallen asleep *in* Christ
19. If *in* this life only we have hope *in* Christ, we are of all men most miserable.
22. For as *in* Adam all die, even so *in* Christ shall all be made alive.
23. every man *in* his own order:
— that are Christ's *at* his coming.
28. that God may be all *in* all.
31. which I have *in* Christ Jesus
32. I have fought with beasts *at* Ephesus,
41. for (one) star differeth from (another) star *in* glory.
42. sown *in* corruption; it is raised *in* incorruption:
43. sown *in* dishonour; it is raised *in* glory: it is sown *in* weakness; it is raised *in* power:
52. *In* a moment, *in* the twinkling of an eye, *at* the last trump:
58. *in* the work of the Lord,
— labour is not in vain *in* the Lord.
16: 7. will not see you now *by* the way;
8. I will tarry *at* Ephesus until
11. but conduct him forth *in* peace,
13. stand fast *in* the faith,
14. your things be done *with* charity.
19. salute you much *in* the Lord,
20. one another *with* an holy kiss.
24. with you all *in* Christ Jesus.
2Co. 1: 1. church of God which is *at* Corinth, with all the saints which are *in* all Achaia:
4. them which are *in* any trouble
6. *in* the enduring of the same
8. which came to us *in* Asia,
9. sentence of death *in* ourselves

2Co. 1:12. *in* simplicity and godly sincerity, not *with* fleshly wisdom, but *by* the grace of God, we have had our conversation *in* the world,
14. *in* the day of the Lord Jesus.
19. who was preached *among* you
— not yea and nay, but *in* him was yea.
20. *in* him (are) yea, and *in* him Amen,
22. of the Spirit *in* our hearts.
2: 1. come again to you *in* heaviness.
10. *in* the person of Christ;
12. opened unto me *of* the Lord,
14. causeth us to triumph *in* Christ,
— by us *in* every place.
15. *in* them that are saved, and *in* them
17. speak we *in* Christ.
3: 2. epistle written *in* our hearts,
3. not *in* tables of stone, but *in*
7. ministration of death, written (and) engraven *in* stones, was glorious, (lit. *in* letters, engraven *in* stones, was *in* glory)
8. the spirit be rather)(glorious? (lit. *in* g.)
9. righteousness exceed *in* glory.
10. had no glory *in* this respect,
11. that which remaineth (is) glorious. (lit. that which remaineth *in* glory)
14. is done away *in* Christ.
4: 2. not walking *in* craftiness,
3. it is hid *to* them that are lost:
4. *In* whom the god of this world
6. hath shined *in* our hearts,
— *in* the face of Jesus Christ.
7. this treasure *in* earthen vessels,
8. (We are) troubled *on* every side,
10. bearing about *in* the body
— be made manifest *in* our body.
11. manifest *in* our mortal flesh.
12. death worketh *in* us, but life *in* you.
5: 1. eternal *in* the heavens.
2. For *in* this we groan, earnestly
4. we that are *in* (this) tabernacle
6. we are at home *in* the body,
11. made manifest *in* your consciences.
12. which glory *in* appearance,
17. if any man (be) *in* Christ,
19. that God was *in* Christ, reconciling
— hath committed *unto* us the word
21. righteousness of God *in* him.
6: 2. *in* the day of salvation have I
3. Giving no offence *in* any thing,
4. *in* all (things) approving ourselves
— *in* much patience, *in* afflictions, *in* necessities, *in* distresses,
5. *In* stripes, *in* imprisonments, *in* tumults, *in* labours, *in* watchings, *in* fastings;
6. *By* pureness, *by* knowledge, *by* long-suffering, *by* kindness, *by* the Holy Ghost, *by* love unfeigned,
7. *By* the word of truth, *by* the power of
12. not straitened *in* us, but ye are straitened *in* your own bowels.
16. God hath said, I will dwell *in* them,
7: 1. holiness *in* the fear of God.
3. that ye are *in* our hearts to die
5. we were troubled *on* every side;
6. *by* the coming of Titus;
7. not *by* his coming only, but *by* the consolation wherewith
8. I made you sorry *with* a letter,
9. receive damage by us *in* nothing.
11. *In* all (things) ye have approved yourselves to be clear *in* this matter.

2Co. 7:14. spake all things to you *in* truth,
16. confidence *in* you *in* all (things)
8: 1. bestowed *on* the churches of
2. *in* a great trial of affliction
7. as ye abound *in* every (thing),
— diligence, and (in) your love *to* us, (see) that ye abound *in* this grace also.
10. here*in* I give (my) advice:
14(13). *at* this time your abundance
16. *into* the heart of Titus for you.
18. whose praise (is) *in* the gospel
20. blame us *in* this abundance
22. proved diligent *in* many things,
9: 3. be in vain *in* this behalf;
4. should be ashamed *in* this
8. always having all sufficiency *in* all (things),
11. Being enriched *in* every thing
10: 1. in presence (am) base *among* you,
3. though we walk *in* the flesh,
6. having *in* a readiness to revenge
12. measuring themselves *by* themselves,
14. *in* (preaching) the gospel of Christ:
15. Not boasting...*of* other men's labours;
— we shall be enlarged *by* you
16. not to boast *in* another man's
17. let him glory *in* the Lord.
11: 3. beguiled Eve *through* his subtilty,
6. we have been through*ly* made manifest among you *in* all things.
9. *in* all (things) I have kept myself from
10. the truth of Christ is *in* me,
— boasting *in* the regions of Achaia.
12. that where*in* they glory,
17. as it were foolish*ly*, *in* this confidence
21. where*in*soever any is bold, I speak foolish*ly*, I am bold also.
23. *in* labours more abundant, *in* stripes above measure, *in* prisons more frequent, *in* deaths oft.
25. I have been *in* the deep;
26. perils *in* the city, (in) perils *in* the wilderness, (in) perils *in* the sea, (in) perils *among* false brethren;
27. *In* weariness and painfulness, *in* watchings often, *in* hunger and thirst, *in* fastings often, *in* cold and nakedness.
32. *In* Damascus the governor under
33. through a window *in* a basket
12: 2. I knew a man *in* Christ about
— whether *in* the body, I cannot tell;
3. whether *in* the body, or out of the
5. not glory, but *in* mine infirmities.
9. is made perfect *in* weakness.
— I rather glory *in* my infirmities,
10. I take pleasure *in* infirmities, *in* reproaches, *in* necessities, *in* persecutions, *in* distresses for Christ's sake:
12. *among* you *in* all patience, *in* signs, and wonders, and mighty deeds.
19. we speak before God *in* Christ:
13: 3. of Christ speaking *in* me,
— not weak, but is mighty *in* you.
4. we also are weak *in* him,
5. whether ye be *in* the faith;
— that Jesus Christ is *in* you,
12. Greet one another *with* an holy kiss.
Gal. 1: 6. *into* the grace of Christ unto
13. in time past *in* the Jews' religion,
14. profited *in* the Jews' religion above many my equals *in* mine own nation,
16. To reveal his Son *in* me, that I might preach him *among* the

Gal. 1:22. churches of Judæa which were *in* Christ:
24. they glorified God *in* me.
2: 2. which I preach *among* the Gentiles,
4. which we have *in* Christ Jesus,
17. seek to be justified *by* Christ,
20. not I, but Christ liveth *in* me: and the life which I now live *in* the flesh I live *by* the faith of the Son of God,
3: 1. set forth, crucified *among* you?
5. worketh miracles *among* you,
8. *In* thee shall all nations be blessed.
10. *in* all things which are written *in* the book
11. no man is justified *by* the law
12. doeth them shall live *in* them.
14. on the Gentiles *through* Jesus Christ;
19. *in* the hand of a mediator.
26. by faith *in* Christ Jesus.
28. ye are all one *in* Christ Jesus.
4:14. which was *in* my flesh
18. affected always *in* (a) good (thing), and not only when I am present with you. (lit. *in* my being present with you)
19. until Christ be formed *in* you,
20. for I stand in doubt *of* you.
25. Agar is mount Sinai *in* Arabia,
5: 4. are justified *by* the law;
6. For *in* Jesus Christ neither
10. confidence in you *through* the Lord,
14. law is fulfilled *in* one word, (even) *in* this;
6: 1. a man be overtaken *in* a fault,
— *in* the spirit of meekness;
6. teacheth *in* all good things.
12. to make a fair shew *in* the flesh,
13. that they may glory *in* your flesh.
14. save *in* the cross of our Lord
15. For *in* Christ Jesus neither
17. I bear *in* my body the marks

Eph. 1: 1. which are *at* Ephesus, and to the faithful *in* Christ Jesus:
3. *with* all spiritual blessings *in* heavenly (places) *in* Christ:
4. he hath chosen us *in* him
— without blame before him *in* love:
6. where*in* he hath made us accepted *in* the beloved.
7. *In* whom we have redemption
8. *in* all wisdom and prudence;
9. he hath purposed *in* himself:
10. all things *in* Christ, both which are *in* heaven, and which are on earth; (even) *in* him:
11. *In* whom also we have obtained
12. who first trusted *in* Christ.
13. *In* whom ye also (trusted),
— *in* whom also after that ye
15. your faith *in* the Lord Jesus,
17. *in* the knowledge of him:
18. his inheritance *in* the saints,
20. Which he wrought *in* Christ,
— *at* his own right hand *in* the heavenly
21. not only *in* this world, but also *in*
23. of him that filleth all *in* all.
2: 2. Where*in* in time past ye walked
— *in* the children of disobedience:
3. *Among* whom also we all had
— *in* the lusts of our flesh,
4. God, who is rich *in* mercy,
6. *in* heavenly (places) *in* Christ Jesus:
7. That *in* the ages to come he
— *in* (his) kindness toward us *through* Christ Jesus.
10. created *in* Christ Jesus unto

Eph. 2:10. that we should walk *in* them.
11. in time past Gentiles *in* the flesh,
— Circumcision *in* the flesh made
12. That *at* that time ye were
— without God *in* the world:
13. now *in* Christ Jesus ye who
— nigh *by* the blood of Christ.
15. Having abolished *in* his flesh the enmity, (even) the law of commandments (contained) *in* ordinances; for to make *in* himself of twain one new man,
16. both unto God *in* one body
— having slain the enmity there*by*:
18. have access *by* one Spirit unto
21. *In* whom all the building
— unto an holy temple *in* the Lord:
22. *In* whom ye also are builded
— habitation of God *through* the Spirit.
3: 3. as I wrote afore *in* few words,
4. *in* the mystery of Christ
5. Which *in* other ages was not
— apostles and prophets *by* the Spirit
6. his promise *in* Christ by the gospel:
8. I should preach *among* the Gentiles
9. hath been hid *in* God, who
10. powers *in* heavenly (places) might
11. which he purposed *in* Christ Jesus
12. *In* whom we have boldness and access *with* confidence by the
13. faint not *at* my tribulations for you,
15. the whole family *in* heaven
17. Christ may dwell *in* your hearts by faith,
—(18). that ye, being rooted and grounded *in* love,
20. the power that worketh *in* us,
21. glory *in* the church *by* Christ Jesus
4: 1. the prisoner *of* the Lord,
2. forbearing one another *in* love;
3. Spirit *in* the bond of peace.
4. as ye are called *in* one hope
6. through all, and *in* you all.
14. *by* the sleight of men, (and) cunning craftiness, (lit. *in* cunning craftiness)
15. speaking the truth *in* love,
16. *in* the measure of every part,
— the edifying of itself *in* love.
17. testify *in* the Lord, that ye
— *in* the vanity of their mind,
18. the ignorance that is *in* them,
19. all uncleanness *with* greediness.
21. have been taught *by* him, as the truth is *in* Jesus:
24. which after God is created *in* righteousness and
30. where*by* ye are sealed unto
32. as God *for* Christ's *sake* hath
5: 2. walk *in* love, as Christ also
3. not be once named *among* you,
5. inheritance *in* the kingdom of
8. now (are ye) light *in* the Lord:
9. *in* all goodness and righteousness
18. drunk with wine, where*in* is excess; but be filled *with* the Spirit;
19. melody *in* your heart to the Lord;
20. *in* the name of our Lord Jesus
21. one to another *in* the fear of God.
24. own husbands *in* every thing.
26. washing of water *by* the word,
6: 1. obey your parents *in* the Lord:
2. first commandment *with* promise;
4. *in* the nurture and admonition
5. *in* singleness of your heart,

Eph. 6: 9. your Master also is *in* heaven
10. be strong *in* the Lord, and *in* the power of
12. spiritual wickedness *in* high (places).
13. to withstand *in* the evil day,
14. your loins girt about *with* truth,
15. shod *with* the preparation of the
16. where*with* ye shall be able to
18. Praying always (lit. *in* all times) with all prayer and supplication *in* the Spirit,
— *with* all perseverance and supplication
19. that I may open (lit. *in* the opening of) my mouth bold*ly*,
20. an ambassador *in* bonds: that there*in* I may speak boldly,
21. faithful minister *in* the Lord,
24. love our Lord Jesus Christ *in* sincerity.

Phi. 1: 1. to all the saints *in* Christ Jesus which are *at* Philippi,
4. Always *in* every prayer of mine
6. begun a good work *in* you
7. I have you *in* my heart; inasmuch as both *in* my bonds,
8. *in* the bowels of Jesus Christ.
9. yet more and more *in* knowledge
13. my bonds *in* Christ are manifest *in* all the palace,
14. many of the brethren *in* the Lord,
18. I there*in* do rejoice, yea, and will
20. *in* nothing I shall be ashamed, but (that) *with* all boldness,
— be magnified *in* my body,
22. if I live *in* the flesh, this
24. to abide *in* the flesh (is) more
26. abundant *in* Jesus Christ *for* me
27. that ye stand fast *in* one spirit,
28. *in* nothing terrified by your
30. ye saw *in* me, (and) now hear (to be) *in* me.

2: 1. any consolation *in* Christ,
5. this mind be *in* you, which was also *in*
6. being *in* the form of God,
7. was made *in* the likeness of men:
10. *at* the name of Jesus every
12. not as *in* my presence only, but now much more *in* my absence,
13. God which worketh *in* you
15. *in* the midst of a crooked
— *among* whom ye shine as lights *in* the world;
19. I trust *in* the Lord Jesus to send
24. I trust *in* the Lord that I
29. *in* the Lord with all gladness;

3: 1. rejoice *in* the Lord.
3. rejoice *in* Christ Jesus, and have no confidence *in* the flesh.
4. have confidence *in* the flesh.
— he might trust *in* the flesh,
6. righteousness which is *in* the law,
9. be found *in* him, not having
14. calling of God *in* Christ Jesus.
19. (whose) glory (is) *in* their shame,
20. our conversation is *in* heaven;

4: 1. so stand fast *in* the Lord,
2. of the same mind *in* the Lord.
3. laboured with me *in* the gospel,
— names (are) *in* the book of life.
4. Rejoice *in* the Lord alway:
6. *in* every thing by prayer and
7. hearts and minds *through* Christ Jesus.
9. heard, and seen *in* me, do:
10. I rejoiced *in* the Lord greatly,
11. *in* whatsoever state I am,

Phi. 4:12 every where (lit. *in* all) and *in* all things
13. Christ which strengtheneth (lit. *in* Christ strengthening) me.
15. that *in* the beginning of the gospel,
16. For even *in* Thessalonica ye
19. riches *in* glory *by* Christ Jesus.
21. Salute every saint *in* Christ Jesus.

Col. 1: 2. brethren *in* Christ which are *at* Colosse:
4. your faith *in* Christ Jesus,
5. laid up for you *in* heaven,
— before *in* the word of the truth
6. as (it is) *in* all the world;
— as (it doth) also *in* you, since the
— the grace of God *in* truth:
8. your love *in* the Spirit.
9. *in* all wisdom and spiritual understanding;
10. fruitful *in* every good work,
11. Strengthened *with* all might,
12. inheritance of the saints *in* light:
14. *In* whom we have redemption
16. *by* him were all things created, that are *in* heaven,
17. *by* him all things consist.
18. that *in* all (things) he might have
19. *in* him should all fulness dwell;
20. in earth, or things *in* heaven.
21. in (your) mind *by* wicked works,
22. *In* the body of his flesh through
23. was preached *to* every creature
24. now rejoice *in* my sufferings
— *in* my flesh for his body's sake, which is the church:
27. mystery *among* the Gentiles; which is Christ *in* you,
28. teaching every man *in* all wisdom;
— every man perfect *in* Christ Jesus:
29. which worketh *in* me mighti*ly*.

2: 1. (for) them *at* Laodicea,
— not seen my face *in* the flesh;
2. being knit together *in* love,
3. *In* whom are hid all the
4. beguile you *with* enticing words.
6. the Lord, (so) walk ye *in* him:
7. Rooted and built up *in* him, and stablished *in* the faith,
— abounding there*in with* thanksgiving.
9. For *in* him dwelleth all
10. ye are complete *in* him,
11. *In* whom also ye are circumcised
— *in* putting off the body of the
— *by* the circumcision of Christ:
12. Buried with him *in* baptism, where*in*
13. you, being dead *in* your sins
15. made a shew of them open*ly*, triumphing over them *in* it.
16. *in* meat, or *in* drink, or *in* respect
18. *in* a voluntary humility and
20. as though living *in* the world,
23. shew of wisdom *in* will worship,
— not *in* any honour to the satisfying

3: 1. sitteth *on* the right hand of God.
3. life is hid with Christ *in* God.
4. ye also appear with him *in* glory.
7. *In* the which ye also walked some time, when ye lived *in* them.
11. Christ (is) all, and *in* all.
15. peace of God rule *in* your hearts,
— ye are called *in* one body;
16. dwell *in* you richly *in* all wisdom;
— *with* grace *in* your hearts to the Lord.
17. *in* word or)(deed, (do) all *in* the name
18. as it is fit *in* the Lord.

Col. 3:22. not *with* eyeservice, as
— *in* singleness of heart, fearing God:
4: 1. ye also have a Master *in* heaven.
2. watch *in* the same *with* thanksgiving;
5. Walk *in* wisdom toward them
6. your speech (be) alway *with* grace,
7. fellowservant *in* the Lord:
12. labouring fervently for you *in* prayers,
— complete *in* all the will of God.
13. *in* Laodicea, and them *in* Hierapolis.
15. the brethren which are *in* Laodicea,
16. *in* the church of the Laodiceans;
17. thou hast received *in* the Lord,
1Th. 1: 1. *in* God the Father and (in) the Lord
5. not unto you *in* word only, but also *in* power, and *in* the Holy Ghost, and *in* much assurance;
— we were *among* you for your sake.
6. the word *in* much affliction,
7. to all that believe *in* Macedonia
8. not only *in* Macedonia and Achaia, but also *in* every place your faith
2: 2. as ye know, *at* Philippi, we were bold *in* our God to speak unto you the gospel of God *with* much contention.
3. nor of uncleanness, nor *in* guile:
5. at any time used we flattering words (lit. were we *in* fl. w.), as ye know, nor a cloke (lit. *in* a cloke) of covetousness;
6(7). we might have been burdensome, (lit. *in* or *for* a burden)
7. we were gentle *among* you,
13. worketh also *in* you that believe.
14. which *in* Judæa are *in* Christ Jesus:
17. to see your face *with* great desire.
19. Lord Jesus Christ *at* his coming?
3: 1. to be left *at* Athens alone;
2. labourer *in* the gospel of Christ,
3. moved *by* these afflictions:
8. if ye stand fast *in* the Lord.
13. unblameable *in* holiness before
— *at* the coming of our Lord Jesus
4: 1. exhort (you) *by* the Lord Jesus,
4. *in* sanctification and honour;
5. Not *in* the lust of concupiscence,
6. defraud his brother *in* (any) matter;
7. unto uncleanness, but *unto* holiness.
10. which are *in* all Macedonia:
15. unto you *by* the word of the Lord,
16. *with* a shout, *with* the voice of the archangel, and *with* the trump of God: and the dead *in* Christ shall rise first:
17. together with them *in* the clouds,
18. comfort one another *with* these words.
5: 2. cometh as a thief *in* the night.
3. as travail upon a woman with child; (lit. having *in* the womb)
4. But ye, brethren, are not *in* darkness,
12. *among* you, and are over you *in* the Lord,
13. *in* love for their work's sake. (And) be at peace *among* yourselves.
18. *In* every thing give thanks: for this is the will of God *in* Christ Jesus
23. *unto* the coming of our Lord Jesus
26. all the brethren *with* an holy kiss.
2Th. 1: 1. *in* God our Father and the Lord
4. glory *in* you *in* the churches
faith *in* all your persecutions
7. when the Lord Jesus shall be revealed (lit. *in* the revelation of the Lord Jesus)
8. *In* flaming fire taking vengeance

2Th. 1:10. to be glorified *in* his saints, and to be admired *in* all them that believe
— was believed *in* that day.
11. the work of faith *with* power:
12. glorified *in* you, and ye *in* him,
2: 6. might be revealed *in* his time.
9. *with* all power and signs
10. *with* all deceivableness of unrighteousness *in* them that perish;
12. had pleasure *in* unrighteousness.
13. *through* sanctification of the
16. consolation and good hope *through* grace,
17. stablish you *in* every good word
3: 4. we have confidence *in* the Lord
6. *in* the name of our Lord Jesus
7. not ourselves disorderly *among* you;
8. wrought *with* labour and travail
11. which walk *among* you disorderly,
16. peace always *by* all means.
17. is the token *in* every epistle:
1Ti. 1: 2. (my) own son *in* the faith:
3. thee to abide still *at* Ephesus.
4. godly edifying which is *in* faith.
13. I did (it) ignorantly *in* unbelief.
14. love which is *in* Christ Jesus.
16. that *in* me first Jesus Christ
18. that thou *by* them mightest
2: 2. (for) all that are *in* authority;
— *in* all godliness and honesty.
7. I speak the truth *in* Christ,
— a teacher of the Gentiles *in* faith
8. that men pray every where, (lit. *in* every place)
9. adorn themselves *in* modest apparel,
— not *with* broidered hair, or gold,
11. learn *in* silence *with* all subjection.
12. over the man, but to be *in* silence.
14. was *in* the transgression.
15. if they continue *in* faith and charity
3: 4. having his children *in* subjection
9. the faith *in* a pure conscience.
11. sober, faithful *in* all things.
13. *in* the faith which is *in* Christ Jesus.
15. behave thyself *in* the house of God,
16. God was manifest *in* the flesh, justified *in* the Spirit,
— preached *unto* the Gentiles, believed on *in* the world, received up *into* glory.
4: 1. that *in* the latter times some shall
2. Speaking lies *in* hypocrisy;
12. *in* word, *in* conversation, *in* charity, *in* spirit, *in* faith, *in* purity.
14. the gift that is *in* thee, which
15. give thyself wholly *to* them (lit. be *in* them); that thy profiting may appear *to* all.
5: 2. younger as sisters, *with* all purity.
10. Well reported of *for* good works;
17. they who labour *in* the word
6:17. that are rich *in* this world,
— *in* the living God, who giveth
18. that they be rich *in* good works,
2Ti. 1: 1. life which is *in* Christ Jesus,
3. *with* pure conscience, that
— *in* my prayers night and day;
5. unfeigned faith that is *in* thee, which dwelt first *in* thy grandmother
— I am persuaded that *in* thee also.
6. the gift of God, which is *in* thee
9. was given us *in* Christ Jesus
13. *in* faith and love which is *in* Christ
14. Holy Ghost which dwelleth *in* us

2Ti. 1:15. all they which are *in* Asia
17. when he was *in* Rome,
18. mercy of the Lord *in* that day:
— ministered unto me *at* Ephesus,
2: 1. *in* the grace that is *in* Christ Jesus.
7. understanding *in* all things.
9. Where*in* I suffer trouble,
10. salvation which is *in* Christ Jesus
20. *in* a great house there are not
25. *In* meekness instructing those
3: 1. that *in* the last days perilous
11. unto me *at* Antioch, *at* Iconium, *at* Lystra;
12. will live godly *in* Christ Jesus
14. *in* the things which thou hast
15. faith which is *in* Christ Jesus.
16. for instruction *in* righteousness:
4: 2. *with* all longsuffering and doctrine.
5. watch thou *in* all things,
8. shall give me *at* that day:
13. The cloke that I left *at* Troas
16. *At* my first answer no man
20. Erastus abode *at* Corinth: but Trophimus have I left *at* Miletum
Tit. 1: 3. manifested his word *through* preaching,
5. this cause left I thee *in* Crete,
6. not accused (lit. not *in* accusation) of riot, or unruly.
9. may be able *by* sound doctrine
13. they may be sound *in* the faith;
2: 3. *in* behaviour as becometh holiness,
7. *in* doctrine (shewing) uncorruptness,
9. to please (them) well *in* all (things);
10. God our Saviour *in* all things.
12. righteously, and godly, *in* this present world;
3: 3. living *in* malice and envy, hateful,
5. Not by works *of* righteousness which
15. them that love us *in* the faith.
Philem. 6. *by* the acknowledging of every good thing which is *in* you
8. might be much bold *in* Christ
10. whom I have begotten *in* my bonds:
13. *in* the bonds of the gospel:
16. both *in* the flesh, and *in* the Lord?
20. have joy of thee *in* the Lord: refresh my bowels *in* the Lord.
23. my fellowprisoner *in* Christ Jesus;
Heb. 1: 1. unto the fathers *by* the prophets,
2(1). spoken unto us *by* (his) Son,
3. *on* the right hand of the Majesty *on* high;
2: 8. For *in* that he put all
12. *in* the midst of the church
18. For *in* that he himself hath
3: 2. Moses (was faithful) *in* all his house.
5. faithful *in* all his house,
8. as *in* the provocation, in the day of temptation *in* the wilderness;
11. So I sware *in* my wrath,
12. lest there be *in* any of you
– *in* departing from the living God.
15. While it is said (lit. *in* its being said), To day if ye
— as *in* the provocation.
17. carcases fell *in* the wilderness?
4: 3. As I have sworn *in* my wrath,
4. God did rest)(the seventh day
5. *in* this (place) again, If they
7. a certain day, saying *in* David,
11. *after* the same example of unbelief.
5: 6. he saith also *in* another (place),
7. Who *in* the days of his flesh,
6:17. Where*in* God, willing more

Heb 6:18. *in* which (it was) impossible
7:10. yet *in* the loins of his father,
8: 1. who is set *on* the right hand
— of the Majesty *in* the heavens;
5. shewed to thee *in* the mount.
9. *in* the day when I took them
— they continued not *in* my covenant,
13. *In* that he saith, A new (covenant),
9: 2. where*in* (was) the candlestick,
4. where*in* (was) the golden pot that
22. by the law purged *with* blood;
23. patterns of things *in* the heavens
25. every year *with* blood of others;
10: 3. *in* those (sacrifices there is) a remembrance
7. *in* the volume of the book it is
10. *By* the which will we are sanctified
12. *on* the right hand of God;
19. the holiest *by* the blood of Jesus,
22. *in* full assurance of faith,
29. where*with* he was sanctified,
32. the former days, *in* which, after
34. knowing *in* yourselves that ye have *in* heaven a better and an
38. shall have no pleasure *in* him.
11: 2. For *by* it the elders obtained
9. dwelling *in* tabernacles
18. *in* Isaac shall thy seed be called:
19. he received him *in* a figure.
26. than the treasures *in* Egypt:
34. made strong, waxed valiant *in* fight,
37. were slain *with* the sword: (lit. died *in* the slaughter of the sword)
— *in* sheepskins (and))(goatskins;
38. they wandered *in* deserts,
12: 2. set down *at* the right hand
23. which are written *in* heaven,
13: 3. being yourselves also *in* the body.
4. Marriage (is) honourable *in* all,
9. that have been occupied there*in*.
18. *in* all things willing to live
20. *through* the blood of the everlasting
21. perfect *in* every good work to do his will, working *in* you that which
Jas. 1: 1. tribes which are scattered abroad, (lit. *in* the dispersion)
4. perfect and entire, wanting)(nothing.
6. let him ask *in* faith, nothing wavering:
8. unstable *in* all his ways.
9. rejoice in that he is exalted: (lit. *in* his exaltation)
10. in that he is made low: (lit. *in* his humiliation)
11. the rich man fade away *in* his ways.
21. receive *with* meekness the
23. beholding his natural face *in* a glass:
25. shall be blessed *in* his deed.
26. If any man *among* you seem
27. fatherless and widows *in* their affliction,
2: 1. *with* respect of persons.
2. with a gold ring, *in* goodly apparel,
— also a poor man *in* vile raiment;
4. not then partial *in* yourselves.
5. poor of this world rich *in* faith,
10. yet offend *in* one (point),
16. say unto them, Depart *in* peace,
3: 2. If any man offend not *in* word,
6. so is the tongue *among* our members,
9. There*with* bless we God, even the Father; and there*with* curse we men.
13. endued with knowledge *among* you?
— *with* meekness of wisdom.
14. envying and strife *in* your hearts,

Jas. 3:18. righteousness is sown *in* peace
4: 1. wars and fightings *among* you?
— lusts that war *in* your members?
3. may consume (it) *upon* your lusts.
5. The spirit that dwelleth *in* us
16. ye rejoice *in* your boastings:
5: 3. treasure together *for* the last days.
5. as *in* a day of slaughter.
13. Is any *among* you afflicted?
14. Is any sick *among* you?
— *in* the name of the Lord:
19. if any *of* you do err from the truth,
1Pet. 1: 2. *through* sanctification of the Spirit,
4. reserved *in* heaven for you,
5. kept *by* the power of God
— to be revealed *in* the last time.
6. Where*in* ye greatly rejoice, though
— in heaviness *through* manifold temptations:
7. *at* the appearing of Jesus Christ:
11. which was *in* them did signify,
12. unto you *with* the Holy Ghost
13. *at* the revelation of Jesus Christ;
14. former lusts *in* your ignorance:
15. holy *in* all manner of conversation;
17. of your sojourning (here) *in* fear:
22. purified your souls *in* obeying the
2: 2. that ye may grow there*by*:
6. it is contained *in* the scripture, Behold, I lay *in* Sion a chief
12. honest *among* the Gentiles: that, whereas (lit. *in* that which) they speak against
— glorify God *in* the day of visitation.
18. subject to (your) masters *with* all fear;
22. was guile found *in* his mouth:
24. bare our sins *in* his own body
3: 2. conversation (coupled) *with* fear.
4. *in* that which is not corruptible,
15. sanctify the Lord God *in* your
— of the hope that is *in* you
16. whereas (lit. *in* that which) they speak evil of you,
— your good conversation *in* Christ.
19. *By* which also he went and preached unto the spirits *in* prison;
20. waited *in* the days of Noah,
22. is *on* the right hand of God
4: 1. hath suffered *in* the flesh
2. rest of (his) time *in* the flesh
3. we walked *in* lasciviousness,
4. Where*in* they think it strange
11. that God *in* all things may be
12. strange concerning the fiery trial which is to try you, (lit. the fiery trial *in* you which is to try you)
13. when his glory shall be revealed, (lit. *in* the revelation of his glory)
14. reproached *for* the name of Christ,
16. glorify God *on* this behalf.
19. (to him) *in* well doing,
5: 1. The elders which are *among* you
2. flock of God which is *among* you,
6. he may exalt you *in* due time:
9. your brethren that are *in* the world.
10. his eternal glory *by* Christ Jesus,
13. The (church that is) *at* Babylon,
14. one another *with* a kiss of charity.
— all that are *in* Christ Jesus.
2Pet. 1: 1. *through* the righteousness of God
2. *through* the knowledge of God,
4. that is *in* the world *through* lust.
5. add *to* your faith virtue; and *to* virtue
2Pet. 1: 6. *to* knowledge temperance; and *to* temperance patience; and *to* patience
7. *to* godliness brotherly kindness; and *to* brotherly kindness charity.
12. established *in* the present truth.
13. as long as I am *in* this tabernacle,
— *by* putting (you) in remembrance;
18. with him *in* the holy mount.
19. a light that shineth *in* a dark place,
— the day star arise *in* your hearts:
2: 1. there were false prophets also *among* the people, even as there shall be false teachers *among* you,
3. *through* covetousness shall they
7. vexed *with* the filthy conversation
8. righteous man dwelling *among* them,
10. *in* the lust of uncleanness,
12. speak evil *of* the things that they understand not; and shall utterly perish *in* their own corruption;
13. to riot *in* the day time.
— *with* their own deceivings
16. speaking *with* man's voice
18. they allure *through* the lusts of the
— from them who live *in* error.
20. *through* the knowledge of the Lord
3: 1. *in* (both) which I stir up your pure minds *by way of* remembrance;
10. as a thief *in* the night; *in* the which the heavens
— the works that are there*in*
11. *in* (all) holy conversation
13. where*in* dwelleth righteousness.
14. ye may be found of him *in* peace,
16. *in* all (his) epistles, speaking *in* them of these things; *in* which are some things hard
18. grow *in* grace, and (in) the knowledge
1Joh. 1: 5. *in* him is no darkness
6. with him, and walk *in* darkness,
7. walk *in* the light, as he is *in*
8. the truth is not *in* us.
10. his word is not *in* us.
2: 3. here*by* we do know that we
4. the truth is not *in* him.
5. *in* him verily is the love of God perfected: here*by* know we that we are *in* him.
6. that saith he abideth *in* him
8. is true *in* him and *in* you:
9. that saith he is *in* the light,
— is *in* darkness even until now.
10. abideth *in* the light, and there is none occasion of stumbling *in* him.
11. is *in* darkness, and walketh *in* darkness,
14. word of God abideth *in* you,
15. things (that are) *in* the world.
— the Father is not *in* him.
16. For all that (is) *in* the world,
24. Let that therefore abide *in* you,
— shall remain *in* you, ye also shall continue *in* the Son, and *in* the Father.
27. received of him abideth *in* you,
— ye shall abide *in* him.
28. little children, abide *in* him;
— ashamed before him *at* his coming
3: 5. and *in* him is no sin.
6. Whosoever abideth *in* him sinneth not;
9. his seed remaineth *in* him:
10. *In* this the children of God are manifest.
14. not (his) brother abideth *in* death.
15. hath eternal life abiding *in* him.
16. Here*by* perceive we the love

1Joh. 3:17. the love of God *in* him?
19. here*by* we know that we are
24. dwelleth *in* him, and he *in* him. And here*by* we know that he abideth *in* us,
4: 2. Here*by* know ye the Spirit
— come *in* the flesh is of God:
3. come *in* the flesh is not of God:
— now already is it *in* the world.
4. greater is he that is *in* you, than he that is *in* the world.
9. *In* this was manifested the love of God *toward* us,
10. Here*in* is love, not that we
12. God dwelleth *in* us, and his love is perfected *in* us.
13. Here*by* know we that we dwell *in* him, and he *in* us,
15. God dwelleth *in* him, and he *in* God.
16. the love that God hath *to* us.
— he that dwelleth *in* love dwelleth *in* God, and God *in* him.
17. Here*in* is our love made perfect,
— boldness *in* the day of judgment:
— so are we *in* this world.
18. There is no fear *in* love;
— is not made perfect *in* love.
5: 2. *By* this we know that we
6. not *by* water only, but *by* water and blood.
7. three that bear record *in* heaven,
8. three that bear witness *in* earth,
10. hath the witness *in* himself:
11. this life is *in* his Son.
19. whole world lieth *in* wickedness.
20. we are *in* him that is true, (even) *in* his Son Jesus Christ

2Joh. 1. whom I love *in* the truth;
2. truth's sake, which dwelleth *in* us,
3. the Father, *in* truth and love.
4. thy children walking *in* truth,
6. ye should walk *in* it.
7. Jesus Christ is come *in* the flesh.
9. abideth not *in* the doctrine of
— He that abideth *in* the doctrine

3Joh. 1. whom I love *in* the truth.
3. as thou walkest *in* the truth.
4. that my children walk *in* truth.

Jude 1. sanctified *by* God the Father,
10. as brute beasts, *in* those things they corrupt themselves.
12. These are spots *in* your feasts of
14. the Lord cometh *with* ten thousands
18. be mockers *in* the last time,
20. praying *in* the Holy Ghost,
21. Keep yourselves *in* the love of God,
23. And others save *with* fear,
24. before the presence of his glory *with* exceeding joy,

Rev. 1: 1. must short*ly* come to pass;
3. things which are written there*in*:
4. churches which are *in* Asia:
5. from our sins *in* his own blood,
9. companion *in* tribulation, and *in* the
— was *in* the isle that is called
10. I was *in* the Spirit *on* the Lord's day,
11. seven churches which are *in* Asia;
13. *in* the midst of the seven
15. as if they burned *in* a furnace;
16. he had *in* his right hand
— as the sun shineth *in* his strength.
2: 1. seven stars *in* his right hand, who walketh *in* the midst of
7. *in* the midst of the paradise
12. the church *in* Pergamos write;
13. even *in* those days where*in*
14. who taught)(Balac to cast a stumblingblock
16. *with* the sword of my mouth.
18. of the church *in* Thyatira write;
23. I will kill her children *with* death;
24. unto the rest *in* Thyatira,
27. rule them *with* a rod of iron;
3: 1. of the church *in* Sardis write;
4. hast a few names even *in* Sardis
— shall walk with me *in* white:
5. shall be clothed *in* white raiment;
7. of the church *in* Philadelphia
12. a pillar *in* the temple of my God,
21. to sit with me *in* my throne, with my Father *in* his throne.
4: 1. a door (was) opened *in* heaven:
2. immediately I was *in* the spirit: and, behold, a throne was set *in* heaven,
4. sitting, clothed *in* white raiment;
6. *in* the midst of the throne,
5: 3. no man *in* heaven, nor
6. *in* the midst of the throne
— *in* the midst of the elders,
9. redeemed us to God *by* thy blood
13. which is *in* heaven, and *on* the earth,
— the sea, and all that are *in* them,
6: 5. a pair of balances *in* his hand.
6. *in* the midst of the four beasts
8. *with* sword, and *with* hunger, and *with* death,
7: 9. palms *in* their hands;
14. white *in* the blood of the Lamb.
15. day and night *in* his temple:
8: 1. there was silence *in* heaven
9. creatures which were *in* the sea,
13. *through* the midst of heaven,
9: 6. *in* those days shall men seek
10. there were stings *in* their tails:
11. *in* the Greek tongue hath (his)
17. thus I saw the horses *in* the vision,
19. power is *in* their mouth, and *in* their
— *with* them they do hurt.
20. were not killed *by* these plagues
10: 2. he had *in* his hand a little book
6. sware *by* him that liveth for ever and ever who created heaven, and the things that there*in* are, and the earth, and the things that there*in* are, and the sea, and the things which are there*in*,
7. *in* the days of the voice
8. open *in* the hand of the angel
9. it shall be *in* thy mouth sweet
10. it was *in* my mouth sweet
11: 1. them that worship there*in*.
6. *in* the days of their prophecy:
12. ascended up to heaven *in* a cloud;
13.)(the same hour was there a great earthquake,
— *in* the earthquake were slain
15. there were great voices *in* heaven,
19. temple of God was opened *in* heaven, and there was seen *in* his temple
12: 1. appeared a great wonder *in* heaven;
2. she being with child (lit. having *in* the womb) cried, travailing
3. another wonder *in* heaven;
5. all nations *with* a rod of iron:
7. there was war *in* heaven:
8. found any more *in* heaven.

Rev.12:10. a loud voice saying *in* heaven,
12. ye that dwell *in* them.
13: 3. all the world wondered after (lit. *in* all the world it was wondered)
6. them that dwell *in* heaven.
8. written *in* the book of life
10. he that killeth *with* the sword must be killed *with* the sword.
12. them which dwell there*in*
14: 2. harpers harping *with* their harps:
5. *in* their mouth was found no
6. fly *in* the midst of heaven,
7. Saying *with* a loud voice,
9. saying *with* a loud voice,
10. *into* the cup of his indignation;
— tormented *with* fire and brimstone
13. the dead which die *in* the Lord
14. *in* his hand a sharp sickle.
15. crying *with* a loud voice to him
17. the temple which is *in* heaven,
15: 1. I saw another sign *in* heaven,
— *in* them is filled up the wrath
5. the testimony *in* heaven was
16: 3. every living soul died *in* the sea.
8. to scorch men *with* fire.
17: 3. carried me away *in* the spirit
4. having a golden cup *in* her hand
16. eat her flesh, and burn her *with* fire.
18: 2. cried might*ily* with a strong voice,
6. *in* the cup which she hath filled
7. for she saith *in* her heart,
8. her plagues come *in* one day,
— shall be utterly burned *with* fire
10. *in* one hour is thy judgment come
16. purple, and scarlet, and decked *with* gold,
19. where*in* were made rich all that had ships *in* the sea by
22. heard no more at all *in* thee;
— shall be found any more *in* thee;
— shall be heard no more at all *in* thee;
23. shine no more at all *in* thee;
— heard no more at all *in* thee:
— for *by* thy sorceries were all
24. *in* her was found the blood
19: 1. voice of much people *in* heaven,
2. corrupt the earth *with* her fornication,
11. *in* righteousness he doth judge
14. the armies (which were) *in* heaven
15. *with* it he should smite the nations: and he shall rule them *with* a rod of iron:
17. an angel standing *in* the sun;
— fowls that fly *in* the midst of heaven,
20. *with* which he deceived them
— lake of fire burning *with* brimstone.
21. remnant were slain *with* the sword
20: 6. hath part *in* the first resurrection:
8. which are *in* the four quarters
12. which were written *in* the books,
13. the dead which were *in* it;
— the dead which were *in* them:
15. found written *in* the book of life
21: 8. shall have their part *in* the lake
10. he carried me away *in* the spirit
14. *in* them the names of the twelve
22. I saw no temple there*in*:
23. the moon, to shine *in* it:
24. shall walk *in* the light of it:
27. are written *in* the Lamb's book
22: 2. *In* the midst of the street of it,
3. the Lamb shall be *in* it;
6. things which must short*ly* be done.
18. that are written *in* this book:
Rev.22:19. which are written *in* this book.

1723 2 261/333 1722,43

ἐναγκαλίζομαι, enankalizomai.

Mar. 9:36. *when* he had *taken* him *in* his *arms*
10:16. he *took* them *up in* his *arms*, put (his) hands upon them, *and* blessed them.

1724 1 261/333 1722,251

ἐνάλιος, enalios.

Jas. 3: 7. and of *things in the sea*, is tamed,

1725 1 261/333 1722,473

ἔναντι, enanti.

Lu. 1: 8. *before* God in the order of his course,

1726 5 261/333 1727

ἐναντίον, enantion.

Mar. 2:12. went forth *before* them all;
Lu. 20:26. his words *before* the people:
24:19. *before* God and all the people
Acts 7:10. wisdom *in the sight of* Pharaoh
8:32. like a lamb dumb *before* his shearer,

1727 8 261/333 1725

ἐναντίος, enantios.

Mat.14:24. for the wind was *contrary*.
Mar. 6:48. for the wind was *contrary* unto
15:39. which stood *over against* him, (lit. from or on the *opposite* side)
Acts26: 9. many things *contrary* to the name of Jesus
27: 4. because the winds were *contrary*.
28:17. committed nothing *against* the people,
1Th. 2:15. are *contrary* to all men:
Tit. 2: 8. he that is of the *contrary* part

1728 2 261/333 1722,756

ἐνάρχομαι, enarkomai.

Gal. 3: 3. *having begun* in the Spirit,
Phi. 1: 6. that he *which hath begun* a good work in you

1729 1 261/334 1722,1210

ἐνδεής, ende-ees.

Acts 4:34. any among them that lacked: (lit. *needy*)

1730 1 261/334 1731

ἔνδειγμα, endīgma.

2Th. 1: 5. a *manifest token* of the righteous

1731 11 262/334 1722,1166

ἐνδείκνυμι, endīknumi.

Ro. 2:15. Which *shew* the work of the law
9:17. that I *might shew* my power
22. willing *to shew* (his) wrath,
2Co. 8:24. Wherefore *shew* ye to them,
Eph. 2: 7. he *might shew* the exceeding riches
1Ti. 1:16. Jesus Christ *might shew forth*
2Ti. 4:14. the coppersmith *did* me much evil
Tit. 2:10. *shewing* all good fidelity:
3: 2. *shewing* all meekness unto all men.
Heb. 6:10. ye *have shewed* toward his name,
11. desire that every one of you *do* same diligence

1732 4 262/334 1731

ἔνδειξις, endixis.

Ro. 3:25. to declare (lit. for *declaration* of) his righteousness
26. To declare (lit. for *declaration* &c.), (I say), at this time
2Co. 8:24. the *proof* of your love, and of our
Phi. 1:28. to them an *evident token* of perdition,

1733 6 262/334 1520,1176

ἕνδεκα, hendeka.

Mat.28:16. Then the *eleven* disciples went away
Mar 16:14. he appeared unto the *eleven*
Lu. 24: 9. told all these things unto the *eleven*,
33. found the *eleven* gathered together,
Acts 1:26. numbered with the *eleven* apostles.
2:14. Peter, standing up with the *eleven*,

1734 3 262/334 1733

ἑνδέκατος, hendekatos.

Mat.20: 6. about the *eleventh* hour he
9. (were hired) about the *eleventh* hour,
Rev.21:20. the *eleventh*, a jacinth;

1735 1 262/334 1722,1209

ἐνδέχεται, endeketai.

Lu. 13:33. for it *cannot be* that a prophet

1736 3 262/334 1722,1218

ἐνδημέω, endeemeo.

2Co. 5: 6. *whilst* we *are at home* in the
8. *to be present* with the Lord.
9. that, whether *present* or absent, we may

1737 2 262/334 1746

ἐνδιδύσκομαι, endiduskomai.

Lu. 8:27. long time, and *ware* no clothes,
16:19. which *was clothed in* purple

1738 2 262/334 1722,1349

ἔνδικος, endikos.

Ro. 3: 8. whose damnation is *just*.
Heb. 2: 2. received a *just* recompence

1739 1 262/335 1722,rt 1218

ἐνδόμησις, endomeesis.

Rev.21:18. the *building* of the wall of it

1740 2 262/334 2:232 1741

ἐνδοξάζομαι, endoxazomai.

2Th. 1:10. he shall come *to be glorified* in
12. That the name of our Lord Jesus Christ *may be glorified*

1741 4 262/334 2:232 1722,1391

ἔνδοξος, endoxos.

Lu. 7:25. they which are *gorgeous*ly apparelled,
13:17. for all the *glorious* things that were done by him.
1Co. 4:10. ye (are) strong; ye (are) *honourable*,
Eph. 5:27. That he might present it to himself a *glorious* church,

1742 8 263/334 1746

ἔνδυμα, enduma.

Mat. 3: 4. John had his *raiment* of camel's hair,
6:25. than meat, and the body than *raiment*?
28. why take ye thought for *raiment*?
7:15. come to you in sheep's *clothing*,
22:11. had not on a wedding *garment*:
12. not having a wedding *garment*?
28: 3. his *raiment* white as snow:
Lu. 12:23. the body (is more) than *raiment*.

1743 8 263/334 2:284 1722,1412

ἐνδυναμόω, endunamoō.

Acts 9:22. Saul *increased* the more *in strength*,
Ro. 4:20. *was strong* in faith, giving glory
Eph. 6:10. brethren, *be strong* in the Lord,
Phi. 4:13. Christ *which strengtheneth* me.
1Ti. 1:12. Jesus our Lord, *who hath enabled* me,
2Ti. 2: 1. my son, *be strong* in the grace that
4:17. with me, and *strengthened* me;
Heb 11:34. out of weakness *were made strong*,

1744 1 263/334 1772,1416

ἐνδύνω, enduno.

2Ti. 3: 6. they *which creep* into houses,

1745 1 263/334 1746

ἔνδυσις, endusis.

1Pet. 3: 3. or of *putting on* of apparel;

1746 28 263/334 2:318 1722,1416

ἐνδύω, enduo.

Mat. 6:25. your body, what ye *shall put on*.
22:11. a man *which had* not *on* a wedding garment:
27:31. and *put* his own raiment *on* him,
Mar. 1: 6. John was *clothed with* camel's hair,
6: 9. not *put on* two coats.
15:17. they *clothed* him with purple,
20. *put* his own clothes *on* him,
Lu. 12:22. the body, what ye *shall put on*.
15:22. the best robe, and *put* (it) *on* him;
24:49. until ye *be endued* with power
Acts12:21. Herod, *arrayed* in royal apparel,
Ro. 13:12. *let us put on* the armour of light.
14. *put* ye *on* the Lord Jesus Christ,
1Co.15:53. For this corruptible must *put on* incorruption,
— (must) *put on* immortality.
54. *shall have put on* incorruption,
— *shall have put on* immortality,
2Co. 5: 3. If so be that *being clothed*
Gal. 3:27. into Christ *have put on* Christ.
Eph. 4:24. that ye *put on* (lit. *have put on*) the new man,
6:11. *Put on* the whole armour of God,
14. *having on* the breastplate of
Col. 3:10. *have put on* the new (man),
12. *Put on* therefore, as the elect of God,
1Th. 5: 8. *putting on* the breastplate of faith
Rev. 1:13. *clothed with* a garment down to the foot,
15: 6. *clothed in* pure and white linen,
19:14. *clothed in* fine linen, white and clean.

ἐνέγκω see φέρω. 5342

1747 1 263
1749 1 264/335 1722,rt 1476

ἐνέδρα & -δρον, *enedra & -dron.*

Acts23:16. heard of their *lying in wait,*
25: 3. laying wait (lit. making a *lying in wait*) in the way to kill him.

1748 2 264/335 1747

ἐνεδρεύω, *enedrūo.*

Lu. 11:54. *Laying wait for* him, and seeking
Acts23:21. for there *lie in wait for* him

1750 1 264/335 1772,rt 1507

ἐνειλέω, *enīleo.*

Mar 15:46. and *wrapped* him *in* the linen,

1751 1 264/335 1772,1510

ἔνειμι, *enīmi.*

Lu. 11:41. But rather give alms of *such things as* ye *have;* (lit. but as to *things that are in*)

1752 25 264/335

ἕνεκα, ἕνεκεν, εἵνεκεν,
heneka, heneken, hīneken.

Mat. 5:10. persecuted *for* righteousness' *sake.*
11. against you falsely, *for* my *sake.*
10:18. *for* my *sake,* for a testimony against
39. loseth his life *for* my *sake* shall
16:25. will lose his life *for* my *sake*
19: 5. *For* this *cause* shall a man
29. *for* my name's *sake,* shall receive
Mar. 8:35. shall lose his life *for* my *sake*
10: 7. *For* this *cause* shall a man leave
29. *for* my *sake,* and the gospel's,
13: 9. before rulers and kings *for* my *sake,*
Lu. 4:18. *because* (or lit. *in* that) he hath anointed
6:22. *for* the Son of man's *sake.*
9:24. will lose his life *for* my *sake,*
18:29. *for* the kingdom of God's *sake,*
21:12. *for* my name's *sake.*
Acts19:32. knew not where*fore* they were come
26:21. *For* these *causes* the Jews caught me
28:20. because that *for* the hope of Israel
Ro. 8:36. *For* thy *sake* we are killed all the day
14:20. *For* meat destroy not the work of God.
2Co. 3:10. *by reason of* the glory that excelleth.
7:12. not *for* his *cause* that had done the wrong, nor *for* his *cause* that suffered wrong, but *that* (lit. *for that*) our care

1753 8 264/335 2:635 1756

ἐνέργεια, *energīa.*

Eph. 1:19. the *working* of his mighty power,
3: 7. by the *effectual working* of his power
4:16. the *effectual working* in the
Phi. 3:21. according to the *working* whereby
Col. 1:29. striving according to his *working,*
2:12. through the faith of the *operation* of
2Th. 2: 9. is after the *working* of Satan
11. shall send them strong delusion, (lit. *working* of error)

1754 21 264/336 2:635 1756

ἐνεργέω, *energeo.*

Mat.14. 2. works *do shew forth* them*selves* in him.
Mar 6:14. mighty works *do shew forth* them*selves*
Ro 7 5. *did work* in our members
1Co.12: 6. God *which worketh* all in all.
1Co.12:11. all these *worketh* that one and the selfsame Spirit,
2Co. 1: 6. *which is effectual* (lit. *that worketh*) in the enduring
4:12. So then death *worketh* in us,
Gal. 2: 8. For he *that wrought effectually in* Peter — the same *was mighty in* me
3: 5. and *worketh* miracles among you,
5: 6. faith *which worketh* by love.
Eph. 1:11. of him *who worketh* all things
20. Which he *wrought* in Christ,
2: 2. the spirit *that* now *worketh in*
3:20. the power *that worketh in us,*
Phi. 2:13. God *which worketh in* you both to will and *to do* of (his) good
Col. 1:29. *which worketh in* me mightily.
1Th. 2:13. which *effectually worketh* also *in* you
2Th. 2: 7. mystery of iniquity *doth* already *work:*
Jas. 5:16. The *effectual fervent* prayer of a righteous man availeth much.

1755 2 265/336 2:635 1754

ἐνέργημα, *energeema.*

1Co.12: 6. there are diversities of *operations,*
10. To another the *working* of miracles;

1756 3 265/336 2:635 1722,2041

ἐνεργής, *energees.*

1Co.16: 9. a great door and *effectual* is opened
Philem 6. become *effectual* by the acknowledging
Heb. 4:12. word of God (is) quick, and *powerful.*

ἐνεστῶτα see ἐνίστημι. 1764

1757 2 265/336 1722,2127

ἐνευλογέομαι, *enūlogeomai.*

Acts 3:25. in thy seed *shall* all the kindreds of the earth *be blessed.*
Gal. 3: 8. In thee *shall* all nations *be blessed.*

1758 3 265/336 1722,2192

ἐνέχω, *eneko.*

Mar. 6:19. Herodias *had a quarrel against* him,
Lu. 11:53. began *to urge* (him) vehemently,
Gal. 5: 1. *be* not *entangled* again *with* the

1759 8 265/336 1722

ἐνθάδε, *enthade.*

Lu. 24:41. Have ye *here* any meat?
Joh. 4:15. neither come *hither* to draw.
16. call thy husband, and come *hither.*
Acts10:18. Peter, were lodged *there.*
16:28. for we are all *here.*
17: 6. are come *hither* also;
25:17. when they were come *hither,*
24. both at Jerusalem, and (also) *here,*

1760 3 265/336 3:167 1722,2372

ἐνθυμέομαι, *enthumeomai.*

Mat. 1:20. *while* he *thought* on these things,
9: 4. Wherefore *think* ye evil in your
Acts10:19. *While* Peter *thought* on the vision,

1761 4 265/336 3:167 1760

ἐνθύμησις, enthumeesis.

Mat. 9: 4. Jesus knowing their *thoughts*
12:25. Jesus knew their *thoughts*.
Acts17:29. graven by art and man's *device*.
Heb. 4:12. a discerner of the *thoughts* and intents

1762 5 265/336 1751

ἔνι for ἔνεστι.

Gal. 3:28. *There is* neither Jew nor Greek, *there is* neither bond nor free, *there is* neither male nor female:
Col. 3:11. Where *there is* neither Greek nor Jew,
Jas. 1:17. with whom *is* no variableness,

1763 14 265/336 enos (year)

ἐνιαυτός, eniautos.

Lu. 4:19. the acceptable *year* of the Lord.
Joh. 11:49. the high priest that same *year*,
51. being high priest that *year*,
18·13. the high priest that same *year*.
Acts11:26. a whole *year* they assembled
18:11. continued (there) a *year* and six months,
Gal. 4:10. days, and months, and times, and *years*.
Heb. 9: 7. high priest alone once every *year*,
25. into the holy place every *year*
10: 1. they offered year by *year*
3. again (made) of sins every *year*.
Jas. 4:13. continue there a *year*, and buy
5:17. by the space of three *years*
Rev. 9:15. an hour, and a day, and a month, and a *year*,

1764 7 266/337 2:543 1722,2476

ἐνίστημι, enisteemi.

Ro. 8:38. nor powers, nor things *present*,
1Co. 3:22. things *present*, or things to come;
7:26. good for the *present* distress,
Gal. 1: 4. from this *present* evil world,
2Th. 2: 2. the day of Christ *is at hand*.
2Ti. 3: 1. perilous times *shall come*.
Heb. 9: 9. for the time then *present*,

1765 2 266/337 1722,2480

ἐνισχύω, eniskuo.

Lu. 22:43. from heaven, *strengthening* him.
Acts 9:19. received meat, he *was strengthened*.

1766 10 261/333 1767

ἔνvατος, ennatos.

Mat.20: 5. about the sixth and *ninth* hour,
27:45. all the land unto the *ninth* hour.
46. about the *ninth* hour Jesus cried
Mar.15:33. whole land until the *ninth* hour.
34. at the *ninth* hour Jesus cried
Lu. 23:44. all the earth until the *ninth* hour.
Acts 3: 1. (being) the *ninth* (hour).
10: 3. about the *ninth* hour of the day
30. at the *ninth* hour I prayed
Rev.21:20. the *ninth*, a topaz; the tenth, a

1767 1 266/337

ἐννέα, ennea.

Lu. 17:17. where (are) the *nine?*

1768 4 264/335,337 1767

ἐννενηκονταεννέα, enneneekontaennea.

Mat.18:12. doth he not leave the *ninety* and *nine*.
Mat.18:13. the *ninety* and *nine* which went not
Lu. 15: 4. doth not leave the *ninety* and *nine*.
7. than over *ninety* and *nine* just persons,

1769 1 266/335 1770

ἐννεός, enneos.

Acts 9: 7. stood *speechless*, hearing a voice,

1770 1 266/337 1722,3506

ἐννεύω, ennüo.

Lu. 1:62. they *made signs* to his father.

1771 2 266/337 4:948 1722,3563

ἔννοια, ennoia.

Heb. 4:12. thoughts and *intents* of the heart.
1Pet.4: 1. arm yourselves likewise with the same *mind*;

1772 2 266/337 4:1022 1722 3551

ἔννομος, ennomos.

Acts19:39. determined in a *lawful* assembly.
1Co. 9:21. but *under* the *law* to Christ,

1773 1 266/337 1722,3571

ἔννυχον, ennukon.

Mar. 1:35. in the morning, rising up a great while before day, (lit. while yet much *in the night*)

1774 5 266/338 1722,3611

ἐνοικέω, enoikeo.

Ro. 8:11. his Spirit *that dwelleth in* you.
2Co. 6:16. God hath said, I *will dwell in* them,
Col. 3:16. *Let* the word of Christ *dwell in* you
2Ti. 1: 5. which *dwelt* first *in* thy grandmother
14. Holy Ghost *which dwelleth in* us.

ἐνόντα see **ἔνειμι**. 1751

1775 2 267/338 1520

ἑνότης, henotees.

Eph. 4: 3. to keep the *unity* of the Spirit
13. come in the *unity* of the faith,

1776 1 267/338 1722,3791

ἐνοχλέω, enokleo.

Heb12:15. lest any root of bitterness springing up *trouble*

1777 10 267/338 2:816 1758

ἔνοχος, enokos.

Mat. 5:21. shall be *in danger of* the judgment:
22. shall be *in danger of* the judgment:
— shall be *in danger of* the council:
— shall be *in danger of* hell fire.
26:66. said, He is *guilty of* death.
Mar. 3:29. is *in danger of* eternal damnation:
14:64. condemned him to be *guilty of* death.
1Co.11:27. shall be *guilty of* the body and blood
Heb. 2:15. their lifetime *subject to* bondage.
Jas. 2:10. offend in one (point), he is *guilty of* all.

1778 3 267/338 1781

ἔνταλμα, entalma.

Mat.15: 9. the *commandments* of men.
Mar. 7: 7. the *commandments* of men.
Col. 2:22. the *commandments* and doctrines of men?

1779 2 267/338 1722,5028

ἐνταφιάζω, entaphiazo.

Mat.26:12. she did (it) for my burial. (lit. unto *burying* me)
Joh.19:40. manner of the Jews is *to bury*.

1780 2 267/338 1779

ἐνταφιασμός, entaphiasmos.

Mar 14: 8. to anoint my body to the *burying*.
Joh.12: 7. against the day of my *burying*

1781 17 267/338 2:544 1722

ἐντέλλομαι, entellomai. rt 5056

Mat. 4: 6. He *shall give* his angels *charge* concerning thee:
15: 4. For God *commanded*, saying,
17: 9. Jesus *charged* them, saying,
19: 7. Why *did* Moses then *command* to
28:20. whatsoever I *have commanded* you:
Mar 10: 3. What did Moses *command* you?
11: 6. even as Jesus *had commanded*:
13:34. *commanded* the porter to watch.
Lu. 4:10. He *shall give* his angels *charge* over thee,
Joh. 8: 5. Moses in the law *commanded* us,
14:31. the Father *gave* me *commandment*,
15:14. do whatsoever I *command* you.
17. These things I *command* you,
Acts 1: 2. *after that* he...*had given commandments* unto the apostles
13:47. the Lord *commanded* us,
Heb. 9:20. which God *hath injoined* unto you.
11:22. *gave commandment* concerning his bones.

1782 13 268/338 rt 1759

ἐντεῦθεν, entūthen.

Mat.17:20. Remove *hence* to yonder place;
Lu. 4: 9. cast thyself down *from hence*:
13:31. Get thee out, and depart *hence*.
16:26. would pass *from hence* to you
Joh. 2:16. Take these things *hence*;
7: 3. Depart *hence*, and go into Judæa,
14:31. Arise, let us go *hence*.
18:36. my kingdom not *from hence*.
19:18. two other with him, on either side (lit. *hence* and *hence*)
Jas. 4: 1. (come they) not *hence*, (even) of
Rev.22: 2. *on* either side (lit. *hence* &c.) of the river, (was there)

1783 2 268/338 8:238 1793

ἔντευξις, entuxis.

1Ti. 2: 1. *intercessions*, (and) giving of thanks,
4: 5. sanctified by the word of God and *prayer*.

1784 5 268/338 1722,5092

ἔντιμος, entimos.

Lu. 7: 2. who was *dear* unto him,
14: 8. lest a *more honourable* man
Phi. 2:29. hold such *in reputation*:
1Pet.2: 4. chosen of God, (and) *precious*,
6. a chief corner stone, elect, *precious*:

1785 71 268/339 2:544 1781

ἐντολή, entolee.

Mat. 5:19. one of these least *commandments*,
15: 3. transgress the *commandment*
6. made the *commandment* of God
19:17. keep the *commandments*.
22:36. which (is) the great *commandment*
38. first and great *commandment*.
40. On these two *commandments*
Mar. 7: 8. laying aside the *commandment*
9. ye reject the *commandment*
10: 5. he wrote you this *precept*.
19. Thou knowest the *commandments*,
12:28. the first *commandment* of all?
29. first of all the *commandments*
30. this (is) the first *commandment*.
31. none other *commandment* greater
Lu. 1: 6. in all the *commandments*
15:29. at any time thy *commandment*:
18:20. Thou knowest the *commandments*,
23:56. according to the *commandment*.
Joh.10:18. This *commandment* have I
11:57. had given a *commandment*,
12:49. he gave me a *commandment*,
50. his *commandment* is life
13:34. A new *commandment* I give
14:15. keep my *commandments*.
21. that hath my *commandments*,
15:10. If ye keep my *commandments*,
— my Father's *commandments*,
12. This is my *commandment*,
Acts17:15. receiving a *commandment*
Ro. 7: 8. occasion by the *commandment*,
9. when the *commandment* came,
10. the *commandment*, which
11. occasion by the *commandment*,
12. the *commandment* holy, and just,
13. sin by the *commandment* might
13: 9. any other *commandment*, it
1Co. 7:19. keeping of the *commandments*
14:37. the *commandments* of the Lord.
Eph. 2:15. the law of *commandments*
6: 2. which is the first *commandment*
Col. 4:10. ye received *commandments*.
1Ti. 6:14. keep (this) *commandment* without
Tit. 1:14. *commandments* of men, that
Heb 7: 5. have a *commandment* to take
16. law of a carnal *commandment*,
18. of the *commandment* going before
9:19. Moses had spoken every *precept*
2Pet.2:21. to turn from the holy *commandment*
3: 2. the *commandment* of us the
1Joh.2: 3. if we keep his *commandments*.
4. keepeth not his *commandments*,
7. I write no new *commandment* but an old *commandment*
— The old *commandment* is the
8. a new *commandment* I write
3:22. we keep his *commandments*,
23. this is his *commandment*,
— as he gave us *commandment*
24. keepeth his *commandments*
4:21. this *commandment* have we
5: 2. keep his *commandments*.
3. that we keep his *commandments*. and his *commandments* are not grievous
2Joh. 4. have received a *commandment*
5. not as though I wrote a new *commandment*
6. walk after his *commandments*. This is the *commandment*, That,
Rev.12:17. keep the *commandments* of God

Rev.14:12. keep the *commandments* of God,
22:14. that do his *commandments*,

1786 1 268/339 1722,5117

ἐντόπιος, entopios.

Acts21:12. both we, and they *of that place*,

1787 2 268/339 1722

ἐντός, entos.

Mat.23:26. that (which is) *within* the cup
Lu. 17:21. kingdom of God is *within* you.

1788 9 269/339 1722,rt 5157

ἐντρέπω, -ομαι, entrepo, -omai.

Mat.21:37. saying, They *will reverence* my son.
Mar.12: 6. saying, They *will reverence* my son.
Lu. 18: 2. which feared not God, neither *regarded* man:
4. I fear not God, nor *regard* man;
20:13. may be they *will reverence* (him)
1Co. 4:14. I write not these things to *shame* you,
2Th. 3:14. that he *may be ashamed*.
Tit. 2: 8. of the contrary part *may be ashamed*,
Heb12: 9. we *gave* (them) *reverence*:

1789 1 269/339 1722,5142

ἐντρέφομαι, entrephomai.

1Ti. 4: 6. *nourished up in* the words of faith

1790 3 269/340 1722,5156

ἔντρομος, entromos.

Acts 7:32. Then Moses *trembled* (lit. being *trembling*), and durst not
16:29. sprang in, and came *trembling*,
Heb12:21. I exceedingly fear and *quake*: (lit. am fearful and *quaking*)

1791 2 269/340 1788

ἐντροπή, entropee.

1Co. 6: 5. I speak to your *shame*. Is it so,
15:34. I speak (this) to your *shame*.

1792 1 269/340 1722,5171

ἐντρυφάω, entruphao.

2Pet.2:13. *sporting themselves* with their own

1793 5 269/340 8:238 1722,5177

ἐντυγχάνω, entunkano.

Acts25:24. the Jews *have dealt* with me,
Ro. 8:27. *maketh intercession* for the saints
34. also *maketh intercession* for us.
11: 2. he *maketh intercession* to God
Heb 7:25. *to make intercession* for them.

1794 3 269/340 1722,5177

ἐντυλίττω, entulitto.

Mat.27:59. he *wrapped* it *in* a clean linen cloth,
Lu. 23:53. *wrapped* it *in* linen, and laid it in
Joh.20: 7. *wrapped together* in a place by itself.

1795 1 269/340 1722,5179

ἐντυπόω, entupoō.

2Co. 3: 7. written (and) *engraven* in stones,

1796 1 269/340 8:295 1722,5195

ἐνυβρίζω, enubrizo.

Heb 10:29. and *hath done despite unto* the Spirit

1797 2 270/340 8:545 1798

ἐνυπνιάζομαι, enupniazomai.

Acts 2:17. your old men *shall dream* dreams:
Jude 8. Likewise also these (filthy) *dreamers* defile the flesh,

1798 1 270/340 8:545 1722,5258

ἐνύπνιον, enupnion.

Acts 2:17. your old men shall dream *dreams*:

1799 97 270/340 1722,3700

ἐνώπιον, enōpion.

Lu. 1: 6. were both righteous *before* God,
15. great *in the sight of* the Lord,
17. shall go *before* him in the spirit
19. that stand *in the presence of* God;
75. In holiness and righteousness *before* him,
4: 7. If thou therefore wilt worship)(me,
5:18. to lay (him) *before* him.
25. he rose up *before* them, and took
8:47. unto him *before* all the people
12: 6. of them is forgotten *before* God?
9. he that denieth me *before* men shall be denied *before* the angels of God.
13:26. have eaten and drunk *in* thy *presence*,
14:10. *in the presence of* them that sit
15:10. joy *in the presence of* the angels
18. sinned against heaven, and *before* thee,
21. against heaven, and *in* thy *sight*,
16:15. which justify yourselves *before* men;
— abomination *in the sight of* God.
23:14. having examined (him) *before* you
24:11. their words seemed *to* them
43. did eat *before* them.
Joh.20:30. *in the presence of* his disciples,
Acts 2:25. the Lord always *before* my face,
4:10. stand here *before* you whole.
19. be right *in the sight of* God
6: 5. saying pleased)(the whole multitude:
6. Whom they set *before* the apostles:
7:46. Who found favour *before* God,
8:21. not right *in the sight of* God.
9:15. my name *before* the Gentiles,
10: 4. up for a memorial *before* God.
30. a man stood *before* me in bright clothing,
31. remembrance *in the sight of* God.
33. we all here present *before* God,
19: 9. that way *before* the multitude,
19. burned them *before* all (men):
27:35. to God *in presence of* them all:
Ro. 3:20. no flesh be justified *in* his *sight*:
12:17. honest *in the sight of* all men.
14:22. have (it) to thyself *before* God.
1Co. 1:29. no flesh should glory *in* his *presence*.
2Co. 4: 2. conscience *in the sight of* God
7:12. for you *in the sight of* God
8:21. only *in the sight of* the Lord, but also *in the sight of* men.
Gal. 1:20. behold, *before* God, I lie not.
1Ti. 2: 3. *in the sight of* God our Saviour;
5: 4. good and acceptable *before* God,
20. Them that sin rebuke *before* all,
21. I charge (thee) *before* God, and the
6:12. profession *before* many witnesses.

1Ti. 5:13. charge *in the sight of* God,
2Ti 2:14. charging (them) *before* the Lord
4: 1. therefore *before* God, and the Lord Jesus
Heb. 4:13. is not manifest *in* his *sight:*
13:21. is wellpleasing *in* his *sight,*
Jas. 4:10. *in the sight of* the Lord,
1Pet. 3: 4. which is *in the sight of* God
1Joh. 3:22. that are pleasing *in* his *sight.*
3Joh. 6. of thy charity *before* the church:
Rev. 1: 4. which are *before* his throne;
2:14. *before* the children of Israel,
3: 2. thy works perfect *before* God.
5. *before* my Father, and *before* his angels.
8. set *before* thee an open door,
9. come and worship *before* thy feet,
4: 5. burning *before* the throne,
6. *before* the throne (there was) a sea
10. elders fall down *before* him
— their crowns *before* the throne,
5: 8. fell down *before* the Lamb,
7: 9. *before* the throne, and *before* the Lamb,
11. fell *before* the throne on their faces,
15. they *before* the throne of God,
8: 2. angels which stood *before* God;
3. which was *before* the throne.
4. ascended up *before* God out of
9:13. golden altar which is *before* God,
11: 4. *before* the God of the earth.
16. sat *before* God on their seats,
12: 4. the dragon stood *before* the woman
10. accused them *before* our God
13:12. the first beast *before* him,
13. on the earth *in the sight of* men,
14. to do *in the sight of* the beast;
14: 3. *before* the throne, and *before* the four
5. without fault *before* the throne of God.
10. *in the presence of* the holy angels, and *in the presence of* the Lamb:
15: 4. shall come and worship *before* thee;
16:19. came in remembrance *before* God,
19:20. that wrought miracles *before* him,
20:12. small and great, stand *before* God;

1801 1 270/341 5:543 1722,3775

ἐνωτίζομαι, *enōtizomai.*

Acts 2:14. unto you, and *hearken to* my words:

ἐξ see above ἐκ. 1537

1803 13 270/341

ἕξ, *hex.*

Mat. 17: 1. after *six* days Jesus taketh Peter,
Mar 9: 2. after *six* days Jesus taketh
Lu. 4:25. shut up three years and *six* months,
13:14. There are *six* days in which men
Joh. 2: 6. were set there *six* waterpots
20. Forty and *six* years was this temple
12: 1. *six* days before the passover
Acts 11:12. these *six* brethren accompanied
18:11. continued (there) a year and *six* months,
27:37. two hundred threescore and *six*teen (lit. seventy *six*)
Jas. 5:17. space of three years and *six* months,
Rev. 4: 8. each of them *six* wings about
13:18. Six hundred threescore (and) *six*.

1804 1 270/341 1:56 1537,rt 32

ἐξαγγέλλω, *exangello.*

1Pet. 2: 9. ye *should shew forth* the praises

1805 4 271/341 1:124 1537,39

ἐξαγοράζω, *exagorazo.*

Gal. 3:13. Christ *hath redeemed* us from the
4: 5. To *redeem* them that were under the law,
Eph 5:16. *Redeeming* the time, because
Col. 4: 5. *redeeming* the time.

1806 13 271/341 1537,71

ἐξάγω, *exago.*

Mar 8:23. and *led* him *out* of the town;
15:20. *led* him *out* to crucify him.
Lu. 24:50. he *led* them *out* as far as to Bethany,
Joh. 10: 3. by name, and *leadeth* them *out.*
Acts 5:19. *brought* them *forth, and* said,
7:36. He *brought* them *out,* after that
40. Moses, which *brought* us *out* of the
12:17. the Lord *had brought* him *out* of the prison.
13:17. *brought* he them *out* of it.
16:37. let them come themselves and *fetch* us *out.*
39. *brought* (them) *out, and* desired
21:38. *which* before...*leddest out* into the wilderness
Heb 8: 9. *to lead* them *out* of the land of Egypt;

1807 8 271/342 1537,138

ἐξαιρέω, *exaireo.*

Mat. 5:29. *pluck* it *out,* and cast (it) from thee:
18: 9. *pluck* it *out,* and cast (it) from thee:
Acts 7:10. And *delivered* him out of all his afflictions,
34. am come down *to deliver* them.
12:11. *hath delivered* me out of the hand
23:27. came I with an army and *rescued* him,
26:17. *Delivering* thee from the people,
Gal. 1: 4. that he *might deliver* us from

1808 2 271/342 1537,142

ἐξαίρω, *exairo.*

1Co. 5: 2. *might be taken away* from among you.
13. *put away* from among yourselves

1809 1 271/342 1:191 1537,154

ἐξαιτέομαι, *exaiteomai.*

Lu. 22:31. Satan *hath desired* (to have) you,

1810 5 271/342 rt160 cf1819 1537

ἐξαίφνης, *exaiphnees.*

Mar. 13:36. Lest coming *suddenly* he find
Lu. 2:13. *suddenly* there was with the angel
9:39. he *suddenly* crieth out;
Acts 9: 3. *suddenly* there shined round about
22: 6. *suddenly* there shone from heaven

1811 3 271/342 1:210 1537,190

ἐξακολουθέω, *exakoloutheo.*

2Pet. 1:16. For we *have* not *followed* cunningly devised fables, *when*
2: 2. many *shall follow* their pernicious
15. *following* the way of Balaam

1812 2 271/342 1803,1540
ἑξακόσιοι, hexakosioi.

Rev.13:18. *Six hundred* threescore (and) six.
14:20. a thousand (and) *six hundred* furlongs.

1813 5 272/342 1537,218
ἐξαλείφω, exalīpho.

Acts 3:19. your sins may *be blotted out,*
Col. 2:14. *Blotting out* the handwriting of
Rev. 3: 5. I *will* not *blot out* his name
7:17. God *shall wipe away* all tears
21: 4. God *shall wipe away* all tears

1814 1 272/342 1537,242
ἐξάλλομαι, exallomai.

Acts 3: 8. he *leaping up* stood, and walked,

1815 1 272/342 1:368 1817
ἐξανάστασις, exanastasis.

Phi. 3:11. unto the *resurrection* of the dead.

1816 2 272/342 1537,393
ἐξανατέλλω, exanatello.

Mat.13: 5. forthwith they *sprung up,*
Mar. 4: 5. immediately it *sprang up,*

1817 3 272/342 1:368 1537,450
ἐξανίστημι, exanisteemi.

Mar 12:19. should take his wife, and *raise up* seed
Lu. 20:28. and *raise up* seed unto his brother.
Acts15: 5. there *rose up* certain of the sect

1818 5 272/342 1:384 1537,538
ἐξαπατάω, exapatao.

Ro. 7:11. *deceived* me, and by it slew (me).
16:18. *deceive* the hearts of the simple.
1Co. 3:18. *Let* no man *deceive* himself.
2Co.11: 3. as the serpent *beguiled* Eve
2Th. 2: 3. Let no man *deceive* you by any

1819 1 272/342 1 1537,5316 1,cf 1810
ἐξάπινα, exapina.

Mar. 9: 8. *suddenly*, when they had looked

1820 2 272/342 1537,639
ἐξαπορέομαι, exaporeomai.

2Co. 1: 8. that we *despaired* even of life:
4: 8. perplexed, but not *in despair;*

1821 11 272/342 1:398 1537,649
ἐξαποστέλλω, exapostello.

Lu. 1:53. the rich he *hath sent* empty *away.*
20:10. beat him, and *sent* (him) *away* empty.
11. shamefully, and *sent* (him) *away* empty.
Acts 7:12. he *sent out* our fathers first.
9:30. *sent* him *forth* to Tarsus.
11:22. they *sent forth* Barnabas, that
12:11. the Lord *hath sent* his angel,
17:14. the brethren *sent away* Paul
22:21. for I *will send* thee far hence
Gal. 4: 4. God *sent forth* his Son,
6. God *hath sent forth* the Spirit of

1822 2 273/343 1:475 1537,739
ἐξαρτίζω, exartizo.

Acts21: 5. when we *had accomplished* those days,
2Ti. 3:17. *throughly furnished* unto all good

1823 1 273/343 1537,797
ἐξαστράπτω, exastrapto

Lu. 9:29. his raiment (was) white (and) *glistering*

1824 6 273/343 1537,846
ἐξαυτῆς, exautees.

Mar. 6:25. that thou give me *by and by* in a
Acts10:33. *Immediately* therefore I sent to thee;
11:11. *immediately* there were three men
21:32. Who *immediately* took soldiers
23:30. I sent *straightway* to thee, and gave
Phi. 2:23. therefore I hope to send *presently*

1825 2 273/343 2:333 1537,1453
ἐξεγείρω, exegīro.

Ro. 9:17. same purpose *have I raised* thee *up,*
1Co. 6:14. *will* also *raise up* us by his own power.

1826 4 273/343
ἔξειμι, exīmi.

Acts13:42. *when* the Jews *were gone out* of the
17:15. with all speed, they *departed.*
20: 7. ready *to depart* on the morrow;
27:43. first (into the sea), and *get* to land:

1827 1 273/323 1537,1651
ἐξελέγχω, exelenko.

Jude 15. *to convince* all that are ungodly

1828 1 273/343 1537,1670
ἐξέλκομαι, exelkomai.

Jas. 1:14. *when* he *is drawn away* of his own

ἐξέλω see ἐξαιρέω. 1807

1829 1 273/343
ἐξέραμα, exerama.

2Pet.2:22. turned to his own *vomit* again;

1830 1 273/343 2:655 1537,2045
ἐξερευνάω, exerūnao.

1Pet.1:10. have enquired and *searched diligently,*

1831 222 273/343 2:666 1537,2064
ἐξέρχομαι, exerkomai.

Mat. 2: 6. out of thee *shall come* a Governor,
5:26. shalt by no means *come out*
8:28. *coming out* of the tombs,
32. *when* they *were come out,* they went
34. city *came out* to meet Jesus:
9:26. fame hereof *went abroad* into
31. *when* they *were departed,*
32. *As* they *went out,* behold, they
10:11. there abide till ye *go thence.*
14. *when* ye *depart out of* that house
11: 7. What *went* ye *out* into the wilderness

Mat.11: 8. what *went* ye *out* for to see ?
9. what *went* ye *out* for to see ?
12:14. Then the Pharisees *went out, and*
43. unclean spirit *is gone out* of a man,
44. from whence I *came out*;
13: 1. same day *went* Jesus *out* of the house. *and*
3. a sower *went forth* to sow ;
49. the angels *shall come forth,*
14:14. Jesus *went forth, and* saw a great
15:18. *come forth* from the heart ;
19. For out of the heart *proceed* evil
21 Then Jesus *went* thence, *and*
22. a woman of Canaan *came out of* the same coasts, *and* cried
17:18. he *departed out of* him:
18:28. the same servant *went out, and* found
20: 1. which *went out* early in the morning
3. he *went out* about the third hour, *and*
5. Again he *went out*...*and* did
6. the eleventh hour he *went out, and* found
21:17. *went out of* the city into Bethany ;
22:10. those servants *went out*...*and* gathered
24: 1. Jesus *went out, and* departed from
26. he is in the desert; *go* not *forth*:
27. lightning *cometh out of* the east,
25: 1. *went forth* to meet the bridegroom.
6. *go* ye *out* to meet him.
26:30. they *went out* into the mount
55. *Are* ye *come out* as against a thief
71. *when* he *was gone out* into the
75. he *went out, and* wept bitterly.
27:32. *as* they *came out,* they found
53. *came out* of the graves...*and* went
28: 8. they *departed*...*and* did run
Mar. 1:25. Hold thy peace, and *come out of* him.
26. he *came out of* him.
28. his fame *spread abroad* throughout
29. *when* they *were come out* of the synagogue,
35. before day, he *went out,*
38. for therefore *came* I *forth.*
45. he *went out, and* began to publish
2:12. *went forth* before them all ;
13. he *went forth* again by the sea side ;
3: 6. the Pharisees *went forth, and* straightway
21. they *went out* to lay hold on him:
4: 3. there *went out* a sower to sow:
5: 2. *when* he *was come out* of the ship,
8. *Come out* of the man, (thou) unclean
13. the unclean spirits *went out, and*
14. they *went out* to see what it was
30. *that* virtue *had gone out* of him,
6: 1. he *went out* from thence,
10. till ye *depart* from that place.
12. they *went out, and* preached that
24. she *went forth, and* said unto her
34. Jesus, *when* he *came out,* saw
54. *when* they *were come out* of the
7:29. the devil *is gone out* of thy daughter.
30. she found the devil *gone out,*
31. again, *departing* from the coasts
8:11. the Pharisees *came forth,*
27. Jesus *went out,* and his disciples.
9:25. I charge thee, *come out* of him,
26. rent him sore, and *came out* of him:
29. This kind can *come forth* by nothing,
30. they *departed* thence, *and* passed
11.11. he *went out* unto Bethany with
12. *when* they *were come* from Bethany,
14:16. his disciples *went forth,* and came
26. sung an hymn, they *went out* into
48. *Are* ye *come out,* as against
68. he *went out* into the porch ;

Mar 16: 8. they *went out* quickly, *and* fled
20. they *went forth, and* preached every where,
Lu. 1:22. *when* he *came out,* he could
2: 1. that there *went out* a decree
4:14. there *went out* a fame of him
35. Hold thy peace, and *come out* of him.
— he *came out* of him, and hurt him not.
36. unclean spirits, and they *come out.*
41. devils also *came out* of many,
42. was day, he *departed and* went into
5: 8. saying, *Depart* from me ;
27. after these things he *went forth,*
6:12. he *went out* into a mountain
19. there *went* virtue *out* of him,
7:17. this rumour of him *went forth*
24. What *went* ye *out* into the
25. what *went* ye *out* for to see ?
26. what *went* ye *out* for to see ?
8: 2. *out* of whom *went* seven devils,
5. A sower *went out* to sow his seed:
27. *when* he *went forth* to land,
29. *to come out* of the man.
33. *went* the devils *out* of the man, *and*
35. they *went out* to see what was
— out of whom the devils *were departed,*
38. out of whom the devils *were departed*
46. *that* virtue *is gone out* of me.
9: 4. there abide, and thence *depart.*
5. *when* ye *go out* of that city,
6. they *departed, and* went through
10:10. *go* your ways *out* into the streets of the same, *and*
35. on the morrow *when* he *departed,*
11:14. *when* the devil *was gone out,*
24. unclean spirit *is gone out* of a man,
— unto my house whence I *came out.*
12:59. thou *shalt* not *depart* thence,
13:31. *Get* thee *out,* and depart hence:
14:18. I must needs *go* and see it:
21. *Go out* quickly into the streets
23. *Go out* into the highways and hedges,
15:28. therefore *came* his father *out, and* intreated him.
17:29. same day that Lot *went out* of Sodom
21:37. at night he *went out, and* abode
22:39. he *came out, and* went, as he was wont,
52. *Be* ye *come out,* as against a thief,
62. Peter *went out, and* wept bitterly.
Joh. 1:43(44). Jesus would *go forth* into Galilee,
4:30. Then they *went out* of the city,
43. after two days he *departed* thence,
8: 9. *went out* one by one,
42. I *proceeded forth* and came from God ;
59. and *went out* of the temple,
10: 9. *shall go* in and *out,* and find pasture.
39. he *escaped* out of their hand,
11:31. she rose up hastily and *went out,*
44. he that was dead *came forth,*
12:13. and *went forth* to meet him,
13: 3. that he *was come* from God,
30. the sop *went* immediately *out*:
31(30). Therefore, when he *was gone out,*
16:27. that I *came out* from God.
28. I *came forth* from the Father,
30. that thou *camest forth* from God.
17: 8. that I *came out* from thee,
18: 1. he *went forth* with his disciples
4. *went forth, and* said unto them,
16. Then *went out* that other disciple,
29. Pilate then *went out* unto them,
38. he *went out* again unto the Jews,
19: 4. Pilate therefore *went forth* again.

Joh. 19: 5. Then *came* Jesus forth, wearing
17. *went forth* into a place called
34. forthwith *came* there*out* blood and water.
20: 3. Peter therefore *went forth*,
21: 3. They *went forth*, and entered into
23. Then *went* this saying *abroad*
Acts 1: 21. *went* in and *out* among us,
7: 3. *Get* thee *out* of thy country,
4. Then *came* he *out* of the land...*and*
7. after that *shall* they *come forth*,
8: 7. *came out* of many that were
10: 23. Peter *went away* with them,
11: 25. Then *departed* Barnabas to Tarsus,
12: 9. he *went out, and* followed him;
10. they *went out, and* passed on through
17. he *departed, and* went into another
14: 20. he *departed* with Barnabas to Derbe.
15: 24. certain *which went out* from us have
40. Paul chose Silas, and *departed*,
16: 3. Paul have *to go forth* with him;
10. *to go* into Macedonia,
13. on the sabbath we *went out* of the city
18. in the name of Jesus Christ *to come out* of her. And he *came out*
19. hope of their gains *was gone*.
36. therefore *depart, and* go in peace.
39. *to depart out* of the city.
40. they *went out* of the prison, *and* entered
— they comforted them, and *departed*.
17: 33. Paul *departed* from among them.
18: 23. he *departed*, and went over (all)
19: 12. the evil spirits *went out* of them.
20: 1. *departed* for to go into Macedonia.
11. break of day, so he *departed*.
21: 5. we *departed and* went our way;
8. were of Paul's company *departed, and* came unto
22: 18. *get* thee quickly *out* of Jerusalem:
28: 3. *came* a viper *out* of the heat, *and*
15. they *came* to meet us as far
Ro. 10: 18. their sound *went* into all the
1Co. 5: 10. needs *go out* of the world.
14: 36. *came* the word of God *out* from
2Co. 2: 13. I *went from thence* into Macedonia.
6: 17. *come out* from among them,
8: 17. his own accord he *went* unto you.
Phi. 4: 15. when I *departed* from Macedonia,
1Th. 1: 8. faith to God-ward *is spread abroad*;
Heb. 3: 16. howbeit not all *that came out* of Egypt by Moses.
7: 5. though they *come out* of the loins of
11: 8. he was called *to go out* into a
— he *went out*, not knowing whither
15. from whence they *came out*,
13: 13. *Let* us *go forth* therefore unto
Jas. 3: 10. *proceedeth* blessing and cursing.
1Joh. 2: 19. They *went out* from us,
4: 1. false prophets *are gone out* into
3Joh. 7. for his name's sake they *went forth*,
Rev. 3: 12. he *shall go* no more *out*:
6: 2. he *went forth* conquering, and to conquer.
4. there *went out* another horse
9: 3. there *came out* of the smoke locusts
14: 15. another angel *came out* of the temple,
17. And another angel *came out* of the
18. another angel *came out* from the
20. blood *came out* of the winepress,
15: 6. seven angels *came out* of the temple,
16: 17. *came* a great voice *out* of the temple
18: 4. saying, *Come out* of her,
19: 5. a voice *came out* of the throne,
20: 8. *shall go out* to deceive the nations

1832 32 274/345 2:560 1537,1510

ἔξεστι, exesti.

Mat. 12: 2. that which *is* not *lawful* to do
4. was not *lawful* for him to eat,
10. *Is* it *lawful* to heal on the sabbath
12. Wherefore it *is lawful* to do well
14: 4. It *is* not *lawful* for thee to have her.
19: 3. *Is* it *lawful* for a man to put
20: 15. *Is* it not *lawful* for me to do
22: 17. *Is* it *lawful* to give tribute
27: 6. It *is* not *lawful* for to put them
Mar. 2: 24. that which *is* not *lawful*?
26. which *is* not *lawful* to eat
3: 4. *Is* it *lawful* to do good on the
6: 18. It *is* not *lawful* for thee to have
10: 2. *Is* it *lawful* for a man to put
12: 14. *Is* it *lawful* to give tribute
Lu. 6: 2. that which *is* not *lawful* to do
4. which it *is* not *lawful* to eat
9. *Is* it *lawful* on the sabbath days
14: 3. *Is* it *lawful* to heal on the
20: 22. *Is* it *lawful* for us to give tribute
Joh. 5: 10. it *is* not *lawful* for thee to carry
18: 31. It *is* not *lawful* for us to put
Acts 2: 29. let me freely speak unto you (lit. it *being permitted* me to freely speak)
8: 37. all thine heart, thou mayest. (lit. it *is permitted*)
16: 21. which *are* not *lawful* for us to receive,
21: 37. May I speak (lit. *Is* it *permitted* me to speak) unto thee?
22: 25. *Is* it *lawful* for you to scourge
1Co. 6: 12. All things *are lawful* unto me, but all
— all things *are lawful* for me, but I
10: 23. All things *are lawful* for me,
— all things *are lawful* for me, but all
2Co. 12: 4. which it *is* not *lawful* for a man

1833 3 275/346 1537,797

ἐξετάζω, exetazo.

Mat. 2: 8. *search* diligently for the young child;
10: 11. *enquire* who in it is worthy;
Joh. 21: 12. none of the disciples durst *ask* him,

1834 6 275/346 2:907 1537,2233

ἐξηγέομαι, exeegeomai.

Lu. 24: 35. they *told* what things (were done)
Joh. 1: 18. of the Father, he *hath declared* (him).
Acts 10: 8. *when* he *had declared* all
15: 12. *declaring* what miracles and wonders
14. Simeon *hath declared* how
21: 19. he *declared* particularly what

1835 9 275/346 1803

ἑξήκοντα, hexeekonta.

Mat. 13: 8. some *sixtyfold*, some thirtyfold.
23. some an hundredfold, some *sixty*,
Mar. 4: 8. some thirty, and some *sixty*,
20. some thirtyfold, some *sixty*,
Lu. 24: 13. from Jerusalem (about) *threescore* furlongs.
1Ti. 5: 9. number under *threescore* years old,
Rev. 11: 3. a thousand two hundred (and) *threescore*
12: 6. a thousand two hundred (and) *threescore*
13: 18. Six hundred *threescore* (and) six.

1836 5 275/346 2192

ἑξῆς, hexees.

Lu. 7: 11. it came to pass *the* day *after*,
9: 37. it came to pass, that on *the next* day,

Acts21: 1. the (day) *following* unto Rhodes,
25:17. *on the morrow* I sat on the
27:18. *the next* (day) they lightened the

1837 1 275/346 1537,2278

ἐξηχέομαι, exeekeomai.

1Th. 1: 8. from you *sounded out* the word

1838 1 275/346 2192

ἕξις, hexis.

Heb. 5:14. those who by reason of *use*

1839 17 275/346 2:449 1537,2476

ἐξίστημι, existeemi.

Mat.12:23. all the people *were amazed,*
Mar. 2:12. that they *were* all *amazed,*
3:21. they said, He *is beside himself.*
5:42. they *were astonished* with a great astonishment.
6:51. they *were* sore *amazed*
Lu. 2:47. *were astonished* at his understanding
8:56. her parents *were astonished:*
24:22. *made* us *astonished,* which were early
Acts 2: 7. they *were* all *amazed*
12. they *were* all *amazed,*
8: 9. *bewitched* the people of Samaria,
11. he *had bewitched* them with
13. *wondered,* beholding the miracles
9:21. all that heard (him) *were amazed,*
10:45. *were astonished,* as many as
12:16. saw him, they *were astonished.*
2Co. 5:13. whether we *be beside ourselves,*

1840 1 276/346 1537,2480

ἐξισχύω, exiskuo.

Eph. 3:18. *May be able* to comprehend

1841 3 276/346 5:42 1537,3598

ἔξοδος, exodos.

Lu. 9:31. spake of his *decease* which he
Heb11:22. the *departing* of the children of Israel;
2Pet.1:15. may be able after my *decease*

1842 1 276/346 5:167 1537,3645

ἐξολοθρεύομαι, exolothrūomai.

Acts 3:23. *shall be destroyed* from among

1843 11 276/346 5:199 1537,3670

ἐξομολογέομαι, exomologeomai.

Mat. 3: 6. in Jordan, *confessing* their sins.
11:25. said, I *thank* thee, O Father,
Mar. 1: 5. of Jordan, *confessing* their sins.
Lu. 10:21. said, I *thank* thee, O Father,
22: 6. he *promised,* and sought opportunity
Acts19:18. came, *and confessed,* and shewed
Ro. 14:11. every tongue *shall confess* to God.
15: 9. I *will confess* to thee among the Gentiles,
Phi. 2:11. every tongue *should confess* that
Jas. 5:16. *Confess* (your) faults one to another,
Rev. 3: 5. I *will confess* his name before

ἐξόν see in ἔξεστι 1832

1844 1 277/346 5:457 1537,3726

ἐξορκίζω, exorkizo.

Mat.26:63. I *adjure* thee by the living God,

1845 1 277/347 5:457 1844

ἐξορκιστής, exorkistees.

Acts19:13. of the vagabond Jews, *exorcists,*

1846 2 277/347 1537,3736

ἐξορύττω, exorutto.

Mar. 2: 4. *when* they *had broken* (it) *up,*
Gal. 4:15. ye *would have plucked out* your own eyes, *and*

1847 1 277/347 1537,3762

ἐξουδενόω, exoudenoō. cf 1848

Mar. 9:12. that he must suffer many things, and *be set at nought.*

1848 11 277/347 eq 1847

ἐξουθενέω, exoutheneo.

Lu. 18: 9. were righteous, and *despised* others:
23:11. *set* him *at nought,* and mocked
Acts 4:11. the stone *which was set at nought* of you builders,
Ro. 14: 3. *Let* not him that eateth *despise*
10. why dost thou *set at nought* thy brother?
1Co. 1:28. things *which are despised,* hath God chosen,
6: 4. set them to judge *who are least esteemed* in the church.
16:11. Let no man therefore *despise* him:
2Co.10:10. (his) speech *contemptible.*
Gal. 4:14. in my flesh ye *despised* not, nor
1Th. 5:20. *Despise* not prophesyings.

1849 103 277/347 2:560 1832

ἐξουσία, exousia.

Mat. 7:29. as (one) having *authority,*
8: 9. For I am a man under *authority,*
9: 6. Son of man hath *power* on earth
8. had given such *power* unto men.
10: 1. he gave them *power* (against)
21:23. By what *authority* dost thou these things? and who gave thee this *authority?*
24. by what *authority* I do these things.
27. by what *authority* I do these things.
28:18. All *power* is given unto me
Mar. 1:22. as one that had *authority,*
27. for with *authority* commandeth
2:10. Son of man hath *power* on earth
3:15. to have *power* to heal sicknesses,
6: 7. gave them *power* over unclean spirits;
11:28. By what *authority* dost thou these things? and who gave thee this *authority*
29. by what *authority* I do these things.
33. by what *authority* I do these things.
13:34. gave *authority* to his servants,
Lu. 4: 6. All this *power* will I give thee,
32. for his word was with *power.*
36. for with *authority* and power
5:24. the Son of man hath *power*
7: 8. am a man set under *authority,*
9: 1. gave them power and *authority*
10:19. I give unto you *power* to tread
12: 5. hath *power* to cast into hell;
11 (unto) magistrates, and *powers,*

Lu. 19:17. have thou *authority* over ten cities.
20: 2. by what *authority* doest thou these things? or who is he that gave thee this *authority?*
8. by what *authority* I do these things.
20. power and *authority* of the governor.
22:53. your hour, and the *power* of darkness.
23: 7. belonged unto Herod's *jurisdiction*,
Joh. 1:12. to them gave he *power* to become
5:27. hath given him *authority* to
10:18. I have *power* to lay it down, and I have *power* to take it again.
17: 2. hast given him *power* over all flesh.
19:10. I have *power* to crucify thee, and have *power* to release thee?
11. Thou couldest have no *power*
Acts 1: 7. Father hath put in his own *power*.
5: 4. was it not in thine own *power?*
8:19. Give me also this *power*,
9:14. here he hath *authority* from
26:10. having received *authority* from
12. with *authority* and commission from
18. (from) the *power* of Satan unto God,
Ro 9:21. Hath not the potter *power* over
13: 1. be subject unto the higher *powers*. For there is no *power* but of God: the *powers* that be are ordained
2. Whosoever therefore resisteth the *power*,
3. not be afraid of the *power?*
1Co. 7:37. hath *power* over his own will,
8: 9. lest by any means this *liberty*
9: 4. Have we not *power* to eat and to drink?
5. Have we not *power* to lead about
6. have not we *power* to forbear
12. partakers of (this) *power* over you,
— we have not used this *power*;
18. that I abuse not my *power*
11:10. the woman to have *power*
15:24. all rule and all *authority* and power.
2Co.10: 8. somewhat more of our *authority*,
13:10. according to the *power* which
Eph. 1:21. all principality, and *power*, and might,
2: 2. prince of the *power* of the air,
3:10. principalities and *powers* in heavenly
6:12. against principalities, against *powers*,
Col. 1:13. from the *power* of darkness,
16. dominions, or principalities, or *powers*:
2:10. head of all principality and *power*:
15. spoiled principalities and *powers*,
2Th. 3: 9. Not because we have not *power*,
Tit. 3: 1. subject to principalities and *powers*,
Heb 13:10. whereof they have no *right* to eat
1Pet.3:22. *authorities* and powers being made
Jude 25. majesty, dominion and *power*,
Rev. 2:26. will I give *power* over the nations:
6: 8. *power* was given unto them
9: 3. unto them was given *power*, as the scorpions of the earth have *power*.
10. their *power* (was) to hurt men
19. their *power* is in their mouth,
11: 6. These have *power* to shut heaven,
— have *power* over waters to turn
12:10. the *power* of his Christ: for the
13: 2. his seat, and great *authority*.
4. which gave *power* unto the beast:
5. *power* was given unto him
7. *power* was given him over all
12. he exerciseth all the *power* of
14:18. which had *power* over fire;
16: 9. hath *power* over these plagues
17:12. receive *power* as kings one hour
13. shall give their power and *strength*

Rev.18: 1. from heaven, having great *power*;
20: 6. second death hath no *power*,
22:14. that they may have *right* to the tree of life

1850 4 278/348 2:560 1849

ἐξουσιάζω, *exousiazo*.

Lu. 22:25. they *that exercise authority upon* them
1Co. 6:12. I *will* not *be brought under the power* of
7: 4. *hath* not *power of* her own body, the husband *hath* not *power of* his own body,

---

1851 1 278/348 1537,2192

ἐξοχή, *exokee*.

Acts25:23. and principal men (lit. the men which were of *eminence*) of the city,

---

1852 1 278/348 8:545 1853

ἐξυπνίζω, *exupnizo*.

Joh. 11:11. that I *may awake* him *out of sleep*.

1853 1 278/348 8:545 1537,5258

ἔξυπνος, *exupnos*.

Acts16:27. awaking (lit. being *awakened*) *out of* his *sleep*, and seeing

---

1854 65 278/348 2:575 1537

ἔξω, *exo*.

Mat. 5:13. for nothing, but to be cast *out*,
12:46. his brethren stood *without*,
47. thy brethren stand *without*,
13:48. but cast the bad *away*
21:17. went *out of* the city into Bethany;
39. cast (him) *out of* the vineyard,
26:69. Peter sat *without* in the palace:
75. he went *out*, and wept bitterly.
Mar. 1:45. was *without* in desert places:
3:31. standing *without*, sent unto him,
32. thy brethren *without* seek for thee
4:11. unto them that are *without*,
5:10. send them away *out of* the country.
8:23. led him *out of* the town;
11: 4. tied by the door *without*
19. he went *out of* the city.
12: 8. cast (him) *out of* the vineyard.
14:68. he went *out* into the porch.
Lu. 1:10. the people were praying *without*
4:29. thrust him *out of* the city,
8:20. thy brethren stand *without*,
54. he put them all *out*, and took
13:25. ye begin to stand *without*,
28. you (yourselves) thrust *out*.
33. a prophet perish *out of* Jerusalem.
14:35. men cast it *out*.
20:15. they cast him *out of* the vineyard,
22:62. Peter went *out*, and wept bitterly.
24:50. he led them *out* as far as
Joh. 6:37. I will in no wise cast *out*.
9:34. And they cast him *out*.
35. that they had cast him *out*;
11:43. loud voice, Lazarus, come *forth*.
12:31. prince of this world be cast *out*.
15: 6. he is cast *forth* as a branch,
18:16. Peter stood at the door *without*.
19: 4. Pilate therefore went *forth* again,
— I bring him *forth* to you,
5. Then came Jesus *forth*,
13. he brought Jesus *forth*,

Joh.20:11. Mary stood *without* at the sepulchre
Acts 4:15. aside *out of* the council,
5:23. the keepers standing *without*
34. to put the apostles *forth* a little
7:58. cast (him) *out of* the city,
9:40. Peter put them all *forth*,
14:19. drew (him) *out of* the city,
16:13. we went *out of* the city
30. brought them *out*, and said,
21: 5. till (we were) *out of* the city:
30. drew him *out of* the temple:
26:11. even unto strange cities. (lit. cities *without*)
1Co. 5:12. judge them also that are *without*?
13. them that are *without* God judgeth
2Co. 4:16. though our *outward* man perish,
Col. 4: 5. toward them that are *without*,
1Th. 4:12. toward them that are *without*,
Heb 13:11. are burned *without* the camp.
12. suffered *without* the gate.
13. unto him *without* the camp,
1Joh. 4:18. perfect love casteth *out* fear:
Rev. 3:12. he shall go no more *out*:
11: 2. which is without the temple leave *out*,
14:20. was trodden *without* the city,
22:15. For *without* (are) dogs

1855 11 279/349 1854

ἔξωθεν, exōthen.

NOTE.—In Rev. xi. 2, ἔσωθεν is the reading of some copies.

Mat 23:25. ye make clean the *outside* of the
27. which indeed appear beautiful *outward*,
28. Even so ye also *outwardly* appear
Mar. 7:15. nothing *from without* a man,
18. whatsoever being *from without*
Lu. 11:39. the *outside* of the cup and the platter;
40. made that which is *without*
2Co. 7: 5. *without* (were) fightings, within
1Ti. 3: 7. of them which are *without*;
1Pet. 3: 3. adorning let it not be that *outward*
Rev. 11: 2. the court which is *without* the

1856 2 279/349 1537
otheō (to push)

ἐξωθώ, exōtho.

Acts 7:45. whom God *drave out* before
27:39. were possible, *to thrust in* the ship,

1857 3 279/349 1854

ἐξώτερος, exōteros.

Mat. 8:12. be cast out into *outer* darkness:
22:13. cast (him) into *outer* darkness;
25:30. unprofitable servant into *outer* darkness:

1858 1 279/349 1859

ἑορτάζω, heortazo.

1Co. 5: 8. Therefore *let us keep the feast*,

1859 27 279/349

ἑορτή, heortee.

Mat 26: 5. they said, Not on the *feast* (day),
27:15. at (that) *feast* the governor was
Mar 14: 2. they said, Not on the *feast* (day),
15. 6 Now at (that) *feast* he released unto
Lu. 2:41. at the *feast* of the passover.
42. after the custom of the *feast*.
22: 1. the *feast* of unleavened bread
23:17. release one unto them at the *feast*.
Joh. 2:23. at the passover, in the *feast* (day
4:45. at Jerusalem at the *feast*: for they also went unto the *feast*.
5: 1. there was a *feast* of the Jews;
6: 4. a *feast* of the Jews, was nigh.
7: 2. the Jews' *feast* of tabernacles was
8. Go ye up unto this *feast*: I go not up yet unto this *feast*;
10. went he also up unto the *feast*,
11. Jews sought him at the *feast*,
14. about the midst of the *feast*
37. that great (day) of the *feast*,
11:56. he will not come to the *feast*?
12:12. were come to the *feast*,
20. to worship at the *feast*:
13: 1. before the *feast* of the passover,
29. need of against the *feast*;
Acts18:21. by all means keep this *feast*
Col. 2:16. or in respect of an *holyday*,

1860 53 280/350 2:576 1861

ἐπαγγελία, epangelia.

Lu. 24:49. I send the *promise* of my Father
Acts 1: 4. for the *promise* of the Father,
2:33. the *promise* of the Holy Ghost,
39. the *promise* is unto you,
7:17. the time of the *promise* drew nigh,
13:23. according to (his) *promise*
32. the *promise* which was made
23:21. looking for a *promise* from thee.
26: 6. for the hope of the *promise* made
Ro. 4:13. For the *promise*, that he should
14. the *promise* made of none effect:
16. the *promise* might be sure to
20. not at the *promise* of God
9: 4. service (of God), and the *promises*;
8. the children of the *promise*
9. this (is) the word of *promise*,
15: 8. to confirm the *promises* (made)
2Co. 1:20. For all the *promises* of God
7: 1. Having therefore these *promises*,
Gal. 3:14. the *promise* of the Spirit through
16. were the *promises* made.
17. make the *promise* of none effect.
18. (it is) no more of *promise*: but God gave (it) to Abraham by *promise*.
21. against the *promises* of God?
22. that the *promise* by faith of Jesus
29. heirs according to the *promise*.
4:23. the freewoman (was) by *promise*.
28. are the children of *promise*.
Eph. 1:13. that holy Spirit of *promise*,
2:12. from the covenants of *promise*,
3: 6. partakers of his *promise* in Christ
6: 2. first commandment with *promise*;
1Ti. 4: 8. having *promise* of the life
2Ti. 1: 1. according to the *promise* of life
Heb. 4: 1. lest, a *promise* being left
6:12. faith and patience inherit the *promises*
15. he obtained the *promise*.
17. unto the heirs of *promise*
7: 6. blessed him that had the *promises*.
8: 6. established upon better *promises*.
9:15. might receive the *promise*
10:36. ye might receive the *promise*.
11: 9. sojourned in the land of *promise*.

Heb 11: 9. of the same *promise*:
13. not having received the *promises*,
17. that had received the *promises*
33. obtained *promises*, stopped the
39. received not the *promise*:
2Pet. 3: 4. Where is the *promise* of his coming?
9. not slack concerning his *promise*.
1Joh. 1: 5. This then is the *message* which
2:25. this is the *promise* that he

1861 15 280/350 2:576 1909,rt32

ἐπαγγέλλομαι, *epangellomai*.

Mar 14:11. they were glad, and *promised* to give
Acts 7: 5. he *promised* that he would give
Ro. 4:21. that, what he *had promised*,
Gal. 3:19. to whom the *promise was made*;
1Ti. 2:10. women *professing* godliness
6:21. Which some *professing* have
Tit. 1: 2. which God, that cannot lie, *promised*
Heb. 6:13. *when* God *made promise* to Abraham,
10:23. he (is) faithful *that promised*;
11:11. him faithful *who had promised*.
12:26. now he *hath promised*, saying,
Jas. 1:12. which the Lord *hath promised*
2: 5. which he *hath promised* to them
2Pet. 2:19. *While* they *promise* them liberty,
1Joh. 2:25. that he *hath promised* us,

1862 2 280/350 2:576 1861

ἐπάγγελμα, *epangelma*.

2Pet. 1: 4. exceeding great and precious *promises*:
3:13. according to his *promise*,

1863 3 280/350 1909,71

ἐπάγω, *epago*.

Acts 5:28. *to bring* this man's blood *upon* us.
2Pet. 2: 1. *and bring upon* themselves swift
5. *bringing in* the flood *upon* the

1864 1 281/350 1:134 1909,75

ἐπαγωνίζομαι, *epagōnizomai*.

Jude 3. should *earnestly contend for* the faith

1865 1 281/351 1909 athroizō (to assemble)

ἐπαθροίζομαι, *epathro-izomai*.

Lu. 11 29. *when* the people *were gathered thick together*,

1867 6 281/351 1909,134

ἐπαινέω, *epaineo*.

Lu. 16: 8. the lord *commended* the unjust
Ro. 15:11. *laud* him, all ye people.
1Co. 11: 2. Now I *praise* you, brethren,
17. I *praise* (you) not, that ye come together
22. *shall* I *praise* you in this? I *praise* (you) not.

1868 11 281/351 2:586 1909rt134

ἔπαινος, *epainos*.

Ro. 2:29. whose *praise* (is) not of men,
13: 3 thou shalt have *praise* of the same:
1Co. 4: 5 every man have *praise* of God.
2Co. 8:18. whose *praise* (is) in the gospel
Eph. 1: 6. To the *praise* of the glory of his
12. to the *praise* of his glory,
14. unto the *praise* of his glory.
Phi. 1:11. the glory and *praise* of God.
4: 8. if (there be) any *praise*,
1Pet. 1: 7. be found unto *praise* and honour
2:14. the *praise* of them that do well.

1869 19 281/351 1:185 1909,142

ἐπαίρω, *epairo*.

Mat. 17: 8. *when* they *had lifted up* their eyes,
Lu. 6:20. he *lifted up* his eyes on his disciples, *and*
11:27. *lifted up* her voice, *and* said
16:23. *lift up* his eyes, being in torments, *and*
18:13. would not *lift up* so much as
21:28. *lift up* your heads; for your redemption
24:50. *lifted up* his hands, *and* blessed them.
Joh. 4:35. *Lift up* your eyes, and look on the
6: 5. *When* Jesus then *lifted up* (his) eyes,
13:18. *hath lifted up* his hee against me.
17: 1. *lifted up* his eyes to heaven,
Acts 1: 9. he *was taken up*; and a cloud
2:14. *lifted up* his voice, and said
14:11. they *lifted up* their voices,
22:22. and (then) *lifted up* their voices,
27:40. *hoised up* the mainsail to the wind, *and*
2Co. 10: 5. every high thing *that exalteth itself*
11:20. if a man *exalt himself*,
1Ti. 2: 8. *lifting up* holy hands,

1870 11 281/351 1909,153

ἐπαισχύνομαι, *epaiskunomai*.

Mar. 8:38. therefore *shall be ashamed* of me
— *shall* the Son of man *be ashamed*,
Lu. 9:26. whosoever *shall be ashamed* of me
— of him *shall* the Son of man *be ashamed*,
Ro. 1:16. For I *am* not *ashamed* of the
6:21. whereof ye *are* now *ashamed*?
2Ti. 1: 8. *Be* not thou therefore *ashamed*
12. nevertheless I *am* not *ashamed*:
16. and *was* not *ashamed* of my chain:
Heb. 2:11. *is* not *ashamed* to call them brethren,
11:16. God *is* not *ashamed* to be called

1871 1 282/351 1909,154

ἐπαιτέω, *epaiteo*.

Lu. 16: 3. *to beg* I am ashamed.

1872 4 282/351 1:210 1909,190

ἐπακολουθέω, *epakoloutheo*.

Mar. 16:20. the word with signs *following*.
1Ti. 5:10. if she *have* diligently *followed* every
24. some (men) they *follow after*.
1Pet. 2:21. that ye *should follow* his steps:

1873 1 282/351 1:216 1909,191

ἐπακούω, *epakouo*.

2Co. 6: 2. I *have heard* thee in a time

1874 1 282/351 1909,rt 202

ἐπακροάομαι, *epakroaomai*.

Acts 16:25. the prisoners *heard* them

1875 3 282/351 1909,302

ἐπάν, epan.

Mat. 2: 8. *when* ye have found (him),
Lu. 11:22. *when* a stronger than he shall
34. *when* (thine eye) is evil, thy

1876 1 282/351 1909,318

ἐπάναγκες, epananches.

Acts15:28. than these *necessary* things;

1877 3 282/351 1909,321

ἐπανάγω, epanago.

Mat.21:18. *as* he *returned* into the city,
Lu. 5: 3. that he would *thrust out* a little
4. *Launch out* into the deep,

1878 1 282/351 1909,363

ἐπαναμιμνήσκω, epanamimneesko.

Ro. 15:15. as *putting* you *in mind*, because

1879 2 282/351 1:350 1909,373

ἐπαναπαύομαι, epanapauomai.

Lu. 10: 6. your peace *shall rest upon* it:
Ro. 2:17. a Jew, and *restest in* the law,

1880 2 282/352 1909,424

ἐπανέρχομαι, epanerkomai.

Lu. 10:35. when I *come again*, I will repay thee.
19:15. that when he was *returned*,

1881 2 282/352 1909,450

ἐπανίσταμαι, epanistamai.

Mat.10:21. the children *shall rise up against*
Mar.13:12. children *shall rise up against* (their) parents,

1882 1 282/352 5:449 1909,461

ἐπανόρθωσις, epanorthōsis.

2Ti. 3:16. for reproof, for *correction*,

1883 20 283/352 1909,507

ἐπάνω, epano.

Mat. 2: 9. stood *over* where the young
5:14. A city that is set *on* an hill
21: 7. put *on* them their clothes, and they set (him) there*on*.
23:18. by the gift that is *upon* it
20. by all things there*on*.
22. by him that sitteth there*on*.
27:37. set up *over* his head his
28: 2. from the door, and sat *upon* it.
Mar.14: 5. *more than* three hundred pence,
Lu. 4:39. he stood *over* her, and rebuked
10:19. to tread *on* serpents and scorpions,
11:44. the men that walk *over* (them)
19:17. have thou authority *over* ten cities.
19. Be thou also *over* five cities.
Joh. 3:31. cometh from above is *above* all:
— cometh from heaven is *above* all.
1Co.15: 6. seen of *above* five hundred brethren
Rev. 6: 8. his name that sat *on* him,
20: 3. set a seal *upon* him,

1884 3 283/352 1909,714

ἐπαρκέω, eparkeo.

1Ti. 5:10. if she *have relieved* the afflicted,
1Ti. 5:16. *let* them *relieve* them,
— that it *may relieve* them that are widows indeed.

1885 2 283/352 1909,757

ἐπαρχία, eparkia.

Acts23:34. he asked of what *province* he was.
25: 1. Festus was come into the *province*,

1886 1 283/352 1909,cf 833

ἔπαυλις, epaulis.

Acts 1:20. Let his *habitation* be desolate,

1887 17 283/352 1909,839

ἐπαύριον, epaurion.

Mat.27:62. Now the *next day*, that followed
Mar 11:12. on the *morrow*, when they were
Joh. 1:29. The *next day* John seeth Jesus
35. the *next day after* John stood,
43(44). The *day following* Jesus would
6:22. The *day following*, when the people
12:12. On the *next day* much people that
Acts10: 9. On the *morrow*, as they went
23. on the *morrow* Peter went away
24. the *morrow* after they entered
14:20. the *next day* he departed with
20: 7. ready to depart on the *morrow*;
21: 8. the *next* (*day*) we that were
22:30. On the *morrow*, because he
23:32. On the *morrow* they left the
25: 6. the *next day* sitting on the
23. on the *morrow*, when Agrippa

1888 1 123/131 1909, 846
phŏr (thief)

ἐπαυτοφώρῳ, epautophōro.

Joh. 8: 4. taken in adultery, *in the very act*.

1890 1 283/352 1909,875

ἐπαφρίζω, epaphrizo.

Jude 13. *foaming out* their own shame.

1892 2 283/352 1909,1453

ἐπεγείρω, epegīro.

Acts13:50. and *raised* persecution against Paul
14: 2. Jews *stirred up* the Gentiles.

1893 27 283/352 1909,1487

ἐπεί, epī.

Mat.18:32. *because* thou desiredst me:
27: 6. *because* it is the price of blood.
Mar 15:42. *because* it was the preparation,
Lu. 1:34. *seeing* I know not a man?
7: 1. *when* he had ended all his
Joh.13:29. *because* Judas had the bag,
19:31. *because* it was the preparation,
Ro. 3: 6. *for then* how shall God judge
11: 6. *otherwise* grace is no more grace.
— *otherwise* work is no more work.
22. *otherwise* thou also shalt be cut off.
1Co. 5:10. *for* then must ye needs go out of
7:14. *else* were your children unclean;
14:12. *forasmuch as* ye are zealous of
16. *Else* when thou shalt bless
15:29. *Else* what shall they do which

*Co.11:18. *Seeing that* many glory after the
13: 3. *Since* ye seek a proof of Christ
Heb 2:14. *Forasmuch* then *as* the children
4: 6. *Seeing* therefore it remaineth that some
5: 2. *for that* he himself also is compassed
11. *seeing* ye are dull of hearing.
6:13. *because* he could swear by no
9:17. *otherwise* it is of no strength
26. *For then* must he often have
10: 2. *For then* would they not have
11:11. *because* she judged him faithful

1897 1 284/ 1893,4007

ἐπείπερ, *epīper.*

Ro. 3:30. *Seeing* (it is) one God, which

1894 11 284/353 1893,1211

ἐπειδή, *epīdee.*

Mat.21:46. *because* they took him for a
Lu. 11: 6. *For* a friend of mine in his
Acts13:46. *seeing* ye put it from you,
14:12. *because* he was the chief speaker.
15:24. *Forasmuch as* we have heard,
1Co. 1:21. For *after that* in the wisdom
22. *For* the Jews require a sign,
14:16. *seeing* he understandeth not what
15:21. For *since* by man (came) death,
2Co. 5: 4. not *for that* we would be unclothed,
Phi. 2:26. *For* he longed after you all,

1895 1 284/353 1894,4007

ἐπειδήπερ, *epīdeeper.*

Lu. 1: 1. *Forasmuch as* many have

1896 2 284/

ἐπείδω see ἐφοράω.

1898 1 284/353 1909,1521

ἐπεισαγωγή, *epīsagōgee.*

Heb 7:19. the *bringing in* of a better hope

1899 16 284/353 1909,1534

ἔπειτα, *epīta.*

Mar 7: 5. *Then* the Pharisees and scribes asked
Lu. 16: 7. *Then* said he to another,
Joh.11: 7. *Then* after that saith he to (his)
1Co.12:28. *after that* miracles, then gifts
15: 6. *After that*, he was seen of above five hundred
7. *After that*, he was seen of James;
23. *afterward* they that are Christ's
46. *afterward* that which is spiritual.
Gal. 1:18. *Then* after three years I went up
21. *Afterwards* I came into the regions
2: 1. *Then* fourteen years after I went
1Th. 4:17. *Then* we which are alive (and) remain
Heb 7: 2. *after that* also King of Salem,
27. for his own sins, and *then* for the people's:
Jas. 3:17. is first pure, *then* peaceable,
4:14. a little time, and *then* vanisheth away.

1900 1 284/353 1909,1565

ἐπέκεινα, *epekīna.*

Acts 7:43. carry you away *beyond* Babylon.

1901 1 284/353 1909,1614

ἐπεκτείνομαι, *epektīnomai.*

Phi. 3:13(14). *reaching forth unto* those things

1902 2 284/353 2:318 1909,1746

ἐπενδύομαι, *ependuomai.*

2Co. 5: 2. earnestly desiring *to be clothed upon*
4. would be unclothed, but *clothed upon*.

1903 1 284/353 1902

ἐπενδύτης, *ependutees.*

Joh.21: 7. he girt (his) *fisher's coat* (unto him)

1904 10 284/353 2:666 1909,2064

ἐπέρχομαι, *eperkomai.*

Lu 1:35. The Holy Ghost *shall come upon* thee,
11:22. he shall *come upon* him *and* overcome
21:26. looking after those things *which are coming on* the earth:
35. as a snare *shall* it *come on* all
Acts 1: 8. *after that* the Holy Ghost *is come upon* you
8:24. which ye have spoken *come upon* me.
13:40. lest that *come upon* you, which
14:19. there *came thither* (certain) Jews
Eph. 2: 7. in the ages *to come* he might
Jas. 5: 1. miseries *that shall come upon* (you).

1905 59 284/354 2:685 1909,2065

ἐπερωτάω, *eperōtao.*

Mat.12:10. they *asked* him, saying,
16: 1. *desired* him that he would
17:10. his disciples *asked* him, saying,
22:23. is no resurrection, and *asked* him,
35. a lawyer, *asked* (him a question),
41. gathered together, Jesus *asked* them,
46. durst any (man) from that day forth *ask*
27:11. the governor *asked* him, saying,
Mar 5: 9. he *asked* him, What (is) thy name?
7: 5. Pharisees and scribes *asked* him,
17. his disciples *asked* him
8: 5. he *asked* them, How many loaves
23. he *asked* him if he saw ought.
27. by the way he *asked* his disciples,
9:11. they *asked* him, saying, Why say the scribes
16. he *asked* the scribes, What question ye
21. he *asked* his father, How long is it ago
28. his disciples *asked* him privately,
32. were afraid *to ask* him.
33. in the house he *asked* them,
10: 2. came to him, and *asked* him,
10. his disciples *asked* him again
17. kneeled to him, and *asked* him,
11:29. I *will* also *ask* of you one question.
12:18. they *asked* him, saying,
28. *asked* him, Which is the first
34. no man after that durst *ask* him
13: 3. John and Andrew *asked* him
14:60. in the midst, and *asked* Jesus,
61. Again the high priest *asked* him,
15: 2. Pilate *asked* him, Art thou
4. Pilate *asked* him again,
44. he *asked* him whether he had been
Lu. 2:46. hearing them, and *asking* them *questions*.
3:10. the people *asked* him, saying,
14. soldiers likewise *demanded* of him,
6: 9. I *will ask* you one thing;
8: 9. his disciples *asked* him,
30. Jesus *asked* him, saying,

Lu. 9:18. he *asked* them, saying,
17:20. *when* he *was demanded* of
18:18. a certain ruler *asked* him,
40. was come near, he *asked* him.
20:21. they *asked* him, saying, Master.
27. and they *asked* him.
40. they durst not *ask* him
21: 7. they *asked* him, saying,
22:64. struck him on the face, and *asked* him.
23: 3. Pilate *asked* him, saying,
6. he *asked* whether the man
9. he *questioned* with him in many words;
Joh. 18: 7. Then *asked* he them again,
21. Why *askest* thou me? *ask* them which heard
Acts 1: 6. they *asked* of him, saying, Lord,
5:27. the high priest *asked* them.
23:34. he *asked* of what province he was.
Ro. 10:20. unto them *that asked* not *after* me.
1Co.14:35. *let* them *ask* their husbands at home:

1906 1 285/354 2:685 1905

ἐπερώτημα, *eperōteema.*

1Pet.3:21. the *answer* of a good conscience

1907 5 285/354 1909,2192

ἐπέχω, *epeko.*

Lu. 14: 7. *when* he *marked* how they chose
Acts 3: 5. he *gave heed unto* them,
19:22. he himself *stayed* in Asia
Phi. 2:16. *Holding forth* the word of life:
1Ti. 4:16. *Take heed unto* thyself, and unto

1908 3 285/354 1909 areia (threats)

ἐπηρεάζω, *epeereazo.*

Mat. 5:44. pray for them *which despitefully use* you,
Lu. 6:28. for them *which despitefully use* you.
1Pet.3:16. ashamed *that falsely accuse* your good

1909 895 285/354

ἐπί, *epi.*

Followed by a genitive, a dative, or an accusative; which are severally distinguished by [g], [d], [a]

Mat. 1:11. *about the time*[g] they were carried away to Babylon:
2:22. Archelaus did reign *in*[g] Judæa
3: 7. Sadducees come *to*[a] his baptism,
13. cometh Jesus from Galilee *to*[a] Jordan
16. like a dove, and lighting *upon*[a] him:
4: 4. Man shall not live *by*[d] bread alone, but *by*[d] every word that proceedeth
5. *on*[a] a pinnacle of the temple.
6. *in*[g] (their) hands they shall bear
5:15. under a bushel, but *on*[a] a candlestick
23. bring thy gift *to*[a] the altar,
39. smite thee *on*[a] thy right cheek,
45. his sun to rise *on*[a] the evil and on the good, and sendeth rain *on*[a] the just and on the unjust.
6:10. Thy will be done *in*[g] earth, as
19. for yourselves treasures *upon*[g] earth,
27. add one cubit *unto*[a] his stature?
7:24. built his house *upon*[a] a rock:
25. for it was founded *upon*[a] a rock.
26. built his house *upon*[a] the sand:
28. astonished *at*[d] his doctrine:
9: 2. sick of the palsy, lying *on*[g] a bed:

Mat. 9: 6. hath power *on*[g] earth to forgive
9. sitting *at*[a] the receipt of custom.
15. as long as (lit. *for*[a] as long as) the bridegroom is
16. new cloth *unto*[d] an old garment,
18. lay thy hand *upon*[a] her, and she
10:13. let your peace come *upon*[a] it:
18. brought *before*[a] governors and kings
21. children shall rise up *against*[a] (their
27. preach ye *upon*[g] the housetops.
29. shall not fall *on*[a] the ground
34. come to send peace *on*[a] earth:
11:29. Take my yoke *upon*[a] you, and learn
12:18. I will put my spirit *upon*[a] him,
26. he is divided *against*[a] himself;
28. kingdom of God is come *unto*[a] you.
49. forth his hand *toward*[a] his disciples,
13: 2. whole multitude stood *on*[a] the shore.
5. Some fell *upon*[a] stony places,
7. some fell *among*[a] thorns;
8. other fell *into*[a] good ground,
14. *in*[d] them is fulfilled the prophecy
20. received the seed *into*[a] stony places,
23. received seed *into*[a] the good ground
48. they drew *to*[a] shore, and sat down,
14: 8. John Baptist's head *in*[d] a charger.
11. head was brought *in*[d] a charger,
14. with compassion *toward*[a] them,
19. to sit down *on*[a] the grass,
25. went unto them, walking *on*[g] the sea.
26. saw him walking *on*[a] the sea,
28. come unto thee *on*[a] the water.
29. he walked *on*[a] the water,
15:32. I have compassion *on*[a] the multitude,
35. to sit down *on*[a] the ground.
16:18. *upon*[d] this rock I will build
19. thou shalt bind *on*[g] earth
— thou shalt loose *on*[g] earth
17: 6. they fell *on*[a] their face,
18: 5. such little child *in*[d] my name
6. were hanged *about*[a] his neck,
12. goeth *into*[a] the mountains,
13. he rejoiceth more *of*[d] that (sheep), than *of*[d] the ninety and nine
16. that *in*[g] the mouth of two or three
18. Whatsoever ye shall bind *on*[g] earth
— whatsoever ye shall loose *on*[g] earth
19. two of you shall agree *on*[g] earth
26. Lord, have patience *with*[d] me,
29. saying, Have patience *with*[d] me,
19: 9. except (it be) *for*[d] fornication,
28. shall sit *in*[g] the throne of his glory, ye also shall sit *upon*[a] twelve thrones,
21: 5. meek, and sitting *upon*[a] an ass,
19. a fig tree *in*[g] the way, he came *to*[a] it,
44. whosoever shall fall *on*[a] this stone
— *on*[a] whomsoever it shall fall,
22: 9. therefore *into*[a] the highways
33. were astonished *at*[d] his doctrine.
34. were gathered *together*.[a]
23: 2. the Pharisees sit *in*[g] Moses' seat:
4. lay (them) *on*[a] men's shoulders;
9. call no (man) your father *upon*[g] the earth:
35. That *upon*[a] you may come all the righteous blood shed *upon*[g] the earth,
36. shall come *upon*[a] this generation
24: 2. one stone *upon*[a] another,
3. sat *upon*[g] the mount of Olives,
5. many shall come *in*[d] my name,
7. nation shall rise *against*[a] nation, and kingdom *against*[a] kingdom:
16. flee *into*[a] the mountains:

1909

Mat.24:17. him which is *on*[g] the housetop
30. coming *in*[g] the clouds of heaven
33. it is near, (even) *at*[d] the doors.
45. hath made ruler *over*[g] his houshold,
47. make him ruler *over*[d] all his goods.
25:20. I have gained *beside*[d] them five
21. faithful *over*[a] a few things, I will make thee ruler *over*[g] many things:
22. two other talents *beside*[d] them.
23. faithful *over*[a] a few things, I will make thee ruler *over*[g] many things:
31. sit *upon*[g] the throne of his glory:
40. *In*asmuch[a] as ye have done (it)
45. *In*asmuch[a] as ye did (it) not
26: 7. poured it *on*[a] his head, as he sat
12. poured this ointment *on*[g] my body,
39. fell *on*[a] his face, and prayed,
50. where*fore*[d] art thou come?
— laid hands *on*[a] Jesus, and took him.
55. come out as *against*[a] a thief
64. coming *in*[g] the clouds of heaven.
27:19. set down *on*[g] the judgment seat,
25. and said, His blood (be) *on*[a] us, and *on*[a] our children.
27. gathered *unto*[a] him the whole
29. they put (it) *upon*[a] his head, and a reed *in*[a] his right hand:
35. *upon*[a] my vesture did they cast
43. He trusted *in*[a] God; let him
45. darkness *over*[a] all the land
28:14. if this come *to*[g] the governor's ears,
18. unto me in heaven and *in*[g] earth.
Mar. 1:10. like a dove descending *upon*[a] him:
22. were astonished *at*[d] his doctrine:
2: 4. the bed where*in*[d] the sick of the palsy
10. power *on*[g] earth to forgive sins,
14. sitting *at*[a] the receipt of custom,
21. new cloth *on*[d] an old garment:
26. *in the days of*[g] Abiathar
3: 5. grieved *for*[d] the hardness of their hearts,
24. kingdom be divided *against*[a] itself,
25. a house be divided *against*[a] itself,
26. if Satan rise up *against*[a] himself,
4: 1. was by the sea *on*[g] the land.
5. some fell *on*[a] stony ground,
16. which are sown *on*[a] stony ground;
20. are sown *on*[a] good ground;
21. not to be set *on*[a] a candlestick?
26. should cast seed *into*[g] the ground;
31. when it is sown *in*[g] the earth,
— the seeds that be *in*[g] the earth:
38. was *in*[d] the hinder part of the ship, asleep *on*[a] a pillow:
5:21. much people gathered *unto*[a] him:
33. knowing what was done *in*[d] her,
6:25. give me by and by *in*[d] a charger
28. And brought his head *in*[d] a charger,
34. moved with compassion *toward*[d] them,
39. by companies *upon*[d] the green grass.
47. he alone *on*[g] the land.
48. walking *upon*[g] the sea,
49. saw him walking *upon*[g] the sea,
52. not (the miracle) of (lit. *upon*[d]) the
53. they came *into*[a] the land of Gennesaret,
55. began to carry about *in*[d] beds
7:30. her daughter laid *upon*[g] the bed.
8: 2. I have compassion *on*[a] the multitude,
4. with bread here *in*[g] the wilderness?
6. to sit down *on*[g] the ground:
25. put (his) hands again *upon*[a] his eyes,
9: 3. so as no fuller *on*[g] earth can
12. how it is written *of*[a] the Son of man,
Mar. 9:13. as it is written *of*[a] him.
20. he fell *on*[g] the ground, and wallowed
22. have compassion *on*[a] us, and help us.
37. one of such children *in*[d] my name
39. shall do a miracle *in*[d] my name,
10:11. committeth adultery *against*[a] her
16. put (his) hands *upon*[a] them,
22. he was sad *at*[d] that saying,
24. were astonished *at*[d] his words.
— for them that trust *in*[d] riches
11: 2. where*on*[a] never man sat;
4. in a place (lit. *at*[g]) where two ways met;
7. he sat *upon*[d] him.
13. when he came *to*[a] it,
18. was astonished *at*[d] his doctrine.
12:14. teachest the way of God *in*[g] truth:
17. they marvelled *at*[d] him.
26. how *in*[g] the bush God spake
32. Master, thou hast said)([g] the truth:
13: 2. left one stone *upon*[d] another,
6. many shall come *in*[d] my name,
8. nation shall rise *against*[a] nation, and kingdom *against*[a] kingdom:
9. brought *before*[g] rulers and kings
12. shall rise up *against*[a] (their) parents,
15. him that is *on*[g] the housetop
29. it is nigh, (even) *at*[d] the doors.
14:35. fell *on*[g] the ground, and prayed
46. they laid their hands *on*[a] him,
48. Are ye come out, as *against*[a] a thief,
51. a linen cloth cast *about*[g] (his) naked
15: 1. straightway *in*[a] the morning
22. *unto*[a] the place Golgotha,
24. casting lots *upon*[a] them,
33. darkness *over*[a] the whole land
46. *unto*[a] the door of the sepulchre.
16: 2. they came *unto*[a] the sepulchre
18. they shall lay hands *on*[a] the sick.
Lu. 1:12. troubled, and fear fell *upon*[a] him.
14. many shall rejoice *at*[d] his birth.
16. shall he turn *to*[a] the Lord their God.
17. hearts of the fathers *to*[a] the children,
29. was troubled *at*[d] his saying,
33. reign *over*[a] the house of Jacob
35. Holy Ghost shall come *upon*[a] thee,
47. hath rejoiced *in*[d] God my Saviour.
48. hath regarded)([a] the low estate of
59. *after*[d] the name of his father.
65. fear came *on*[a] all that dwelt
2: 8. keeping watch *over*[a] their flock
14. *on*[g] earth peace, good will toward
20. *for*[d] all the things that they had
25. the Holy Ghost was *upon*[a] him.
33. marvelled *at*[d] those things which
40. the grace of God was *upon*[a] him.
47. astonished *at*[d] his understanding
3: 2. Annas and Caiaphas being the high priests, (lit. *in the time of*[g] the high priests A. and C.) the word of God came *unto*[a] John
20. Added yet this *above*[d] all,
22. like a dove *upon*[a] him,
4: 4. shall not live *by*[d] bread alone, but *by*[d] every word of God.
9. set him *on*[a] a pinnacle of the
11. *in*[g] (their) hands they shall bear
18. Spirit of the Lord (is) *upon*[a] me,
22. wondered *at*[d] the gracious words
25. I tell you *of*[g] a truth,
— was shut up)([a] three years and six
— famine was *throughout*[a] all the land;
27. *in the time of*[g] Eliseus the

Lu. 4:29. where*on*[g] their city was built,
32. were astonished *at*[d] his doctrine:
36. they were all amazed, (lit. amazement was *upon*[a] all)
5: 5. nevertheless *at*[d] thy word I will
9. *at*[d] the draught of the fishes
11. had brought their ships *to*[a] land,
12. seeing Jesus fell *on*[a] (his) face,
18. men brought *in*[g] a bed a man
19. they went *upon*[a] the housetop
24. hath power *upon*[g] earth to
25. took up that where*on*[d] he lay,
27. sitting *at*[a] the receipt of custom:
36. a new garment *upon*[a] an old;
6:17. with them, and stood *in*[g] the plain,
29. smiteth thee *on*[a] the (one) cheek
35. he is kind *unto*[a] the unthankful
48. laid the foundation *on*[a] a rock:
— it was founded *upon*[a] a rock.
49. built an house *upon*[a] the earth;
7:13. he had compassion *on*[d] her,
44. gavest me no water *for*[a] my feet:
8: 6. some fell *upon*[a] a rock;
8. other fell *on*[a] good ground,
13. They *on*[g] the rock (are they), which,
16. setteth (it) *on*[g] a candlestick,
27. when he went forth *to*[a] land,
9: 1. power and authority *over*[a] all devils,
5. for a testimony *against*[a] them.
38. I beseech thee, look *upon*[a] my son:
43. *at*[d] the mighty power of God.
— *at*[d] all things which Jesus did,
48. receive this child *in*[d] my name
49. casting out devils *in*[d] thy name;
62. put his hand *to*[a] the plough,
10: 6. your peace shall rest *upon*[a] it: if not, it shall turn *to*[a] you again.
9. is come nigh *unto*[a] you.
11. is come nigh *unto*[a] you.
19. *over*[a] all the power of the enemy:
34. set him *on*[a] his own beast,
35. *on*[a] the morrow when he departed,
11: 2. be done, as in heaven, so *in*[g] earth.
17. Every kingdom divided *against*[a] itself
— a house (divided) *against*[a] a house
18. Satan also be divided *against*[a] himself,
20. kingdom of God is come *upon*[a] you.
22. his armour where*in*[d] he trusted,
33. under a bushel, but *on*[a] a candlestick,
12: 3. proclaimed *upon*[g] the housetops.
11. bring you *unto*[a] the synagogues,
14. a judge or a divider *over*[a] you?
25. can add *to*[a] his stature one
42. make ruler *over*[g] his houshold,
44. ruler *over*[d] all that he hath.
52. divided, three *against*[d] two, and two *against*[d] three.
53. *against*[d] the son, and the son *against*[d] the father; the mother *against*[d] the daughter, and the daughter *against*[d] the mother; the mother in law *against*[a] her daughter in law, and the daughter in law *against*[a]
58. thine adversary *to*[a] the magistrate,
13: 4. *upon*[a] whom the tower in Siloam fell,
17. *for*[d] all the glorious things that
14:31. him that cometh *against*[a] him
15: 4. go *after*[a] that which is lost,
5. he layeth (it) *on*[a] his shoulders,
7. *over*[d] one sinner that repenteth, more than *over*[d] ninety and nine
10. *over*[d] one sinner that repenteth.

Lu. 15:20. fell *on*[a] his neck, and kissed him.
16:26. *beside*[d] all this, between us and you
17: 4. turn again *to*[a] thee, saying,
16. fell down *on*[a] (his) face at his feet,
31. shall be *upon*[g] the housetop,
34. shall be two (men) *in*[g] one bed;
35. shall be grinding together; (lit. *at*[a] the same)
18: 4. he would not *for*[a] a while:
7. though he bear long *with*[d] them?
8. shall he find faith *on*[g] the earth?
9. which trusted *in*[d] themselves
19: 4. climbed up *into*[a] a sycomore tree
5. when Jesus came *to*[a] the place,
14. this (man) to reign *over*[a] us.
23. my money *into*[a] the bank,
27. that I should reign *over*[a] them,
30. where*on*[a] yet never man sat:
35. cast their garments *upon*[a] the colt,
41. beheld the city, and wept *over*[d] it,
43. the days shall come *upon*[a] thee,
44. in thee one stone *upon*[d] another;
20:18. Whosoever shall fall *upon*[a] that stone
— *on*[a] whomsoever it shall fall,
19. sought to lay hands *on*[a] him;
21. teachest the way of God truly: (lit. *in*[g] truth)
26. they marvelled *at*[d] his answer,
37. even Moses shewed *at*[g] the bush,
21. 6. be left one stone *upon*[d] another,
8. many shall come *in*[d] my name,
10. Nation shall rise *against*[a] nation, and kingdom *against*[a] kingdom:
12. they shall lay their hands *on*[a] you,
— brought *before*[a] kings and rulers
23. great distress *in*[g] the land,
25. *upon*[g] the earth distress of nations,
34. that day come *upon*[a] you unawares.
35. shall it come *on*[a] all them that dwell *on*[a] the face of the whole earth.
22:21. with me *on*[g] the table.
30. may eat and drink *at*[g] my table in my kingdom, and sit *on*[g] thrones judging the
40. when he was *at*[g] the place,
44. falling down *to*[a] the ground.
52. which were come *to*[a] him, Be ye come out, as *against*[a] a thief,
53. no hands *against*[a] me:
59. *Of*[g] a truth this (fellow) also
23: 1. led him *unto*[a] Pilate.
28. weep not *for*[a] me, but weep *for*[a] yourselves, and *for*[a] your children.
30. to the mountains, Fall *on*[a] us;
33. when they were come *to*[a] the place,
38. also was written *over*[d] him
44. darkness *over*[a] all the earth
48. came together *to*[a] that sight,
24: 1. they came *unto*[a] the sepulchre,
12. Peter, and ran *unto*[a] the sepulchre;
22. were early *at*[a] the sepulchre;
24. with us went *to*[a] the sepulchre,
25. to believe)([d] all that the prophets
47. should be preached *in*[d] his name
49. promise of my Father *upon*[a] you:
Joh. 1:32. it abode *upon*[a] him.
33. *Upon*[a] whom thou shalt see the Spirit descending, and remaining *on*[a] him,
51(52). descending *upon*[a] the Son of man.
3:36. but the wrath of God abideth *on*[a] him.
4: 6. sat thus *on*[d] the well:
27. *upon*[d] this came his disciples,
5: 2. *by*[d] the sheep (market) a pool.

Joh. 6: 2. which he did *on*[g] them that were
16. went down *unto*[a] the sea,
19. they see Jesus walking *on*[g] the sea.
21. the ship was *at*[g] the land
7:30. no man laid hands *on*[a] him,
44. no man laid hands *on*[a] him.
8: 7. let him first cast a stone *at*[d] her.
59. took they up stones to cast *at*[a] him:
9: 6. he anointed)([a] the eyes of the blind
15. He put clay *upon*[a] mine eyes,
11:38. a stone lay *upon*[d] it.
12:14. found a young ass, sat there*on*;[a]
15. sitting *on*[a] an ass's colt.
16. these things were written *of*[d] him,
13:18. lifted up his heel *against*[a] me.
25. lying *on*[a] Jesus' breast
17: 4. I have glorified thee *on*[g] the earth:
18: 4. that should come *upon*[a] him,
19:13. sat down *in*[g] the judgment seat
19. put (it) *on*[g] the cross.
24. *for*[a] my vesture they did cast lots.
31. not remain *upon*[g] the cross
33. when they came *to*[a] Jesus,
20: 7. napkin, that was *about*[g] his head,
21: 1. *at*[g] the sea of Tiberias;
11. drew the net *to*[g] land full
20. leaned *on*[a] his breast at supper,
Acts 1: 8. Holy Ghost is come *upon*[a] you:
15. the number of the names together (lit. *at*[a] one)
21. went in and out *among*[a] us,
26. the lot fell *upon*[a] Matthias;
2: 1. with one accord *in*[a] one place.
3. it sat *upon*[a] each of them.
17. my Spirit *upon*[a] all flesh:
18. And *on*[a] my servants and *on*[a] my handmaidens I will pour
19. signs *in*[g] the earth beneath;
26. my flesh shall rest *in*[d] hope:
30. Christ to sit *on*[g] his throne;
38. *in*[d] the name of Jesus Christ
44. all that believed were together, (lit. *at*[a] one place)
3: 1. Now Peter and John went up together (lit. *at*[a] the same)
10. *at*[d] the Beautiful gate of the
— *at*[d] that which had happened
11. *in*[d] the porch that is called
12. why marvel ye *at*[d] this?
16. *through*[d] faith in his name
4: 5. it came to pass *on*[a] the morrow,
9. examined *of*[d] the good deed done
17. that it spread no further (lit. spread not *unto*[a] more)
— to no man *in*[d] this name.
18. teach *in*[d] the name of Jesus.
21. glorified God *for*[d] that which was done.
22. *on*[a] whom this miracle of
26. gathered together (lit. *at*[a] one) against
27. For *of*[g] a truth *against*[a] thy holy child Jesus, whom
29. Lord, behold)([a] their threatenings:
33. great grace was *upon*[a] them all.
5: 5. great fear came *on*[a] all them
9. (are) *at*[d] the door, and shall carry
11. great fear came *upon*[a] all the church, and *upon*[a] as many as heard these
15. laid (them) *on*[g] beds and couches,
18. laid their hands *on*[a] the apostles.
28. should not teach *in*[d] this name?
— this man's blood *upon*[a] us.
30. ye slew and hanged *on*[g] a tree

Acts 5:35. to do *as touching*[d] these men.
40. not speak *in*[d] the name of Jesus,
6: 3. may appoint *over*[g] this business.
7:10. made him governor *over*[a] Egypt
11. a dearth *over*[a] all the land
23. it came *into*[a] his heart
27. a ruler and a judge *over*[a] us?
54. gnashed *on*[a] him with (their) teeth.
57. ran *upon*[a] him with one accord,
8: 1. persecution *against*[a] the church
2. made great lamentation *over*[d] him.
16. was fallen *upon*[d] none of them:
17. laid they (their) hands *on*[a] them,
24. have spoken come *upon*[a] me.
26. *unto*[a] the way that goeth down
27. who had the charge of all her treasure (lit. who was *over*[g] all her)
28. sitting *in*[g] his chariot
32. as a sheep *to*[a] the slaughter;
36. they came *unto*[a] a certain water
9: 4. he fell *to*[a] the earth,
11. go *into*[a] the street which is
17. putting his hands *on*[a] him
21. bound *unto*[a] the chief priests?
33. had kept his bed (lit. lain *on*[d] his bed) eight years,
35. turned *to*[a] the Lord.
42. many believed *in*[a] the Lord.
10: 9. Peter went up *upon*[a] the housetop
10. he fell into a trance, (lit. a trance fell *upon*[a] him)
11. vessel descending *unto*[a] him,
— let down *to*[g] the earth:
16. This was done)([a] thrice:
17. stood *before*[a] the gate,
25. fell down *at*[a] his feet,
34. *Of*[g] a truth I perceive that
39. slew and hanged *on*[g] a tree:
44. Holy Ghost fell *on*[a] all them
45. that *on*[a] the Gentiles also was
11:10. this was done)([a] three times:
11. already come *unto*[a] the house
15. the Holy Ghost fell *on*[a] them, as *on*[a] us at the beginning.
17. who believed *on*[a] the Lord Jesus
19. persecution that arose *about*[d] Stephen
21. turned *unto*[a] the Lord.
28. dearth *throughout*[a] all the world.
— *in the days of*[g] Claudius Cæsar
12:10. they came *unto*[a] the iron gate
12. he came *to*[a] the house of Mary
20. Blastus the king's chamberlain (lit. that was *over*[g] the king's bedchamber)
21. sat *upon*[g] his throne,
13:11. hand of the Lord (is) *upon*[a] thee.
— there fell *on*[a] him a mist
12. *at*[d] the doctrine of the Lord.
31. he was seen)([a] many days of them
40. lest that come *upon*[d] you,
50. raised persecution *against*[a] Paul
51. dust of their feet *against*[a] them.
14: 3. speaking boldly *in*[d] the Lord,
10. Stand upright *on*[a] thy feet.
13. oxen and garlands *unto*[a] the gates,
15. *unto*[a] the living God,
15:10. to put a yoke *upon*[a] the neck
14. a people *for*[d] his name.
17. *upon*[a] whom my name is called, (lit *upon*[a] whom my name is called *upon*[a] them)
19. are turned *to*[a] God:
31. they rejoiced *for*[d] the consolation.

Acts16:18 this did she)([a] many days.
19. marketplace *unto*[a] the rulers,
31. Believe *on*[a] the Lord Jesus Christ,
17: 2.)([a] three sabbath days reasoned
6. *unto*[a] the rulers of the city,
14. to go as it were *to*[a] the sea:
19. brought him *unto*[a] Areopagus,
26. to dwell *on*[a] all the face of the
18: 6. *upon*[a] your own heads;
12. brought him *to*[a] the judgment seat,
20. desired (him) to tarry)([a] longer time
19: 6. Holy Ghost came *on*[a] them;
8. *for the space of*[a] three months,
10. *by the space of*[a] two years,
12. were brought *unto*[a] the sick
13. to call *over*[a] them which had
16. leaped *on*[a] them, and overcame
17. fear fell *on*[a] them all,
34. about *the space of*[a] two hours
20: 9. there sat *in*[g] a window
— as Paul was)([a] long preaching,
11. talked)([a] a long while, even till
13. we went before *to*[a] ship,
37. fell *on*[a] Paul's neck, and kissed him,
38. *for*[d] the words which he spake
21: 5. kneeled down *on*[a] the shore,
23. which have a vow *on*[g] them;
24. be at charges *with*[d] them,
27. laid hands *on*[a] him,
32. ran down *unto*[a] them:
35. when he came *upon*[a] the stairs,
40. Paul stood *on*[g] the stairs,
22:19. them that believed *on*[a] thee:
23:30. also to say *before*[g] thee what
24: 4. not)([a] further tedious unto thee,
8. his accusers to come *unto*[a] thee:
19. to have been here *before*[g] thee,
20. while I stood *before*[g] the council,
25: 6. sitting *on*[g] the judgment seat
9. judged of these things *before*[g] me?
10. I stand *at*[g] Cæsar's judgment seat,
12. *unto*[a] Cæsar shalt thou go.
17. I sat *on*[g] the judgment seat,
26. brought him forth *before*[g] you, and specially *before*[g] thee, O king Agrippa,
26: 2. for myself this day *before*[g] thee
6. *for*[d] the hope of the promise
16. stand *upon*[a] thy feet:
18. (from) the power of Satan *unto*[a] God,
20. should repent and turn *to*[a] God,
27:20. nor stars *in*[a] many days appeared,
43. (into the sea), and get *to*[a] land:
44. the rest, some *on*[d] boards, and some *on*[g] (broken pieces) of the ship.
— they escaped all safe *to*[a] land.
28: 3. laid (them) *on*[a] the fire,
6. after they had looked)([a] a great while,
14. were desired to tarry *with*[d] them
Ro. 1: 9(10). of you always *in*[g] my prayers;
18. *against*[a] all ungodliness
2: 2. *against*[a] them which commit
9. *upon*[a] every soul of man that
3:22. *upon*[a] all them that believe:
4: 5. believeth *on*[a] him that justifieth
9. *upon*[a] the circumcision (only), or *upon*[a] the uncircumcision also?
18. against hope believed *in*[d] hope,
24. we believe *on*[a] him that raised
5: 2. rejoice *in*[d] hope of the glory
12. *for*[d] that all have sinned:
14. even *over*[a] them that had not sinned *after*[d] the similitude of Adam's
Ro. 6:21. where*of*[d] ye are now ashamed?
7: 1.)([a] as long as he liveth?
8:20. subjected (the same) *in*[d] hope,
9: 5. who is *over*[g] all, God blessed
23. his glory *on*[a] the vessels of mercy,
28. the Lord make *upon*[g] the earth.
33. whosoever believeth *on*[d] him
10:11. Whosoever believeth *on*[d] him
19. to jealousy *by*[d] (them that are) no people, (and) *by*[d] a foolish nation
11:13. *in*asmuch[a] as I am the apostle
22. *on*[a] them which fell, severity; but *toward*[a] thee, goodness,
12:20. heap coals of fire *on*[a] his head.
15: 3. that reproached thee fell *on*[a] me.
12. *in*[d] him shall the Gentiles trust.
20. build *upon*[a] another man's foundation:
16:19. therefore *on* your *behalf*[d]:
1Co. 1: 4. *for*[d] the grace of God which is
2: 9. *into*[a] the heart of man,
3:12. build *upon*[a] this foundation
6: 1. against another, go to law *before*[g] the unjust, and not *before*[g] the saints?
6. that *before*[g] the unbelievers.
7: 5. come together again (lit. *to*[a] one), that Satan
36. uncomely *toward*[a] his virgin,
39.)([a] as long as her husband liveth;
8: 5. whether in heaven or *in*[g] earth,
11. *through*[d] thy knowledge shall
9:10. should plow *in*[d] hope; and that he that thresheth *in*[d] hope
11:10. to have power *on*[g] (her) head
20. together therefore *into*[a] one place,
13: 6. Rejoiceth not *in*[d] iniquity,
14:16. *at*[d] thy giving of thanks,
23. be come together *into*[a] one place,
25. falling down *on*[a] (his) face
16:17. I am glad *of*[d] the coming of Stephanas
2Co. 1: 4. *in*[d] all our tribulation,
9. that we should not trust *in*[d] ourselves, but *in*[d] God which raiseth the dead:
23. for a record *upon*[a] my soul,
2: 3. having confidence *in*[a] you all,
3:13. put a vail *over*[a] his face,
14. *in*[d] the reading of the old testament;
15. the vail is *upon*[a] their heart.
7: 4. joyful *in*[d] all our tribulation.
7. he was comforted *in*[d] you,
13. were comforted *in*[d] your comfort;
— *for*[d] the joy of Titus, because
14. which (I made) *before*[g] Titus,
9: 6. he which soweth bountifully shall reap also bountifully. (lit. he which soweth *of*[d] blessings, or in bounties, shall reap *of*[d] blessings, or bounties)
13. *for*[d] your professed subjection
14. exceeding grace of God *in*[d] you.
15. *for*[d] his unspeakable gift.
10: 2. to be bold *against*[a] some,
12: 9. power of Christ may rest *upon*[a] me.
21. not repented *of*[d] the uncleanness
13: 1. *In*[g] the mouth of two or three
Gal. 3:13. every one that hangeth *on*[g] a tree:
16. saith not, And to seeds, as *of*[g] many; but as *of*[g] one,
4: 1.)([a] as long as he is a child,
9. turn ye again *to*[a] the weak
5:13. ye have been called *unto*[d] liberty;
6:16. peace (be) *on*[a] them, and mercy, and *upon*[a] the Israel of God.
Eph. 1:10. which are *on*[g] earth; (even) in him:

Eph. 1:16 mention of you *in*[g] my prayers;
2: 7. in (his) kindness *toward*[a] us
10. in Christ Jesus *unto*[d] good works,
20. built *upon*[d] the foundation of
3:15. in heaven and)([g] earth is named,
4: 6. who (is) *above*[g] all, and through all,
26. down *upon*[d] your wrath:
5: 6. wrath of God *upon*[a] the children of
6: 3. live long *on*[g] the earth.
16. *Above*[d] all, taking the shield of
Phi. 1: 3. *upon*[d] every remembrance of you,
5. *For*[d] your fellowship in the gospel
2:17. offered *upon*[d] the sacrifice
27. should have sorrow *upon*[d] sorrow.
3: 9. which is of God *by*[d] faith:
12. that *for*[d] which also I am apprehended
14. *for*[a] the prize of the high calling
4:10. where*in*[d] ye were also careful.
Col. 1:16. in heaven, and that are *in*[g] earth,
20. whether (they be) things *in*[g] earth,
3: 2. not on things *on*[g] the earth.
5. which are *upon*[g] the earth;
6. cometh *on*[a] the children of
14. *above*[d] all these things
1Th. 1: 2. mention of you *in*[g] our prayers;
2:16. wrath is come *upon*[a] them
3: 7. brethren, we were comforted *over*[d] you *in*[d] all our affliction
9. *for*[d] all the joy wherewith we
4: 7. not called us *unto*[d] uncleanness,
2Th. 1:10. our testimony *among*[a] you
2: 1. gathering together *unto*[a] him,
4. *above*[a] all that is called God,
3: 4. confidence in the Lord *touching*[a] you,
1Ti. 1:16. should hereafter believe *on*[d] him
18. which went before *on*[a] thee,
4:10. we trust *in*[d] the living God,
5: 5. trusteth *in*[a] God, and continueth
19. *before*[g] two or three witnesses.
6:13. who *before*[g] Pontius Pilate
17. nor trust *in*[g] uncertain riches,
2Ti. 2:14. *to*[d] the subverting of the hearers.
16. will increase *unto*[a] more ungodliness.
3: 9. they shall proceed no)([a] further:
13. shall wax)([a] worse and worse,
4: 4. shall be turned *unto*[a] fables.
Tit. 1: 2. *In*[d] hope of eternal life,
3: 6. he shed *on*[a] us abundantly
Philem. 4. of thee always *in*[g] my prayers,
7. consolation *in*[d] thy love,
Heb 1: 2(1). Hath *in*[g] these last days spoken
2: 7. *over*[a] the works of thy hands:
13. I will put my trust *in*[d] him.
3: 6. as a son *over*[a] his own house;
6: 1. let us go on *unto*[a] perfection;
— of faith *toward*[a] God,
7. rain that cometh oft *upon*[g] it,
7:11. for *under*[d] it the people received
13. For he *of*[a] whom these things
8: 1. Now *of*[d] the things which we have spoken
4. For if he were *on*[g] earth,
6. established *upon*[d] better promises.
8. a new covenant *with*[a] the house of Israel and *with*[a] the house of Judah:
10. write them *in*[g] their hearts:
9:10. (Which stood) only *in*[d] meats and drinks,
15. *under*[d] the first testament,
17. of force after men are dead· (lit. *upon the basis of*[d] dead ones)
26. *in*[d] the end of the world
10:16. I will put my laws *into*[g] their hearts, and *in*[g] their minds will I write them:

Heb 10:21. priest *over*[a] the house of God,
28. *under*[d] two or three witnesses:
11: 4. God testifying *of*[d] his gifts:
13. strangers and pilgrims *on*[g] the earth.
21. *upon*[a] the top of his staff.
30. were compassed about)([a] seven days.
12:10. he *for*[a] (our) profit, that (we)
25. refused him that spake *on*[g] earth.
Jas. 2: 3. ye have respect *to*[a] him that weareth
7. by the which ye are called? (lit. which is called *upon*[a] you)
21. offered Isaac his son *upon*[a] the altar?
5: 1. *for*[d] your miseries that shall come upon (you).
5. lived in pleasure *on*[g] the earth,
7. hath long patience *for*[d] it,
14. let them pray *over*[a] him,
17. it rained not *on*[g] the earth
1Pet. 1:13. hope to the end *for*[a] the grace that
20. *in*[g] these last times for you,
2: 6. he that believeth *on*[d] him shall
24. in his own body *on*[a] the tree,
25. now returned *unto*[a] the Shepherd
3: 5. women also, who trusted *in*[a] God,
12. eyes of the Lord (are) *over*[a] the righteous,
— *against*[a] them that do evil.
4:14. of God resteth *upon*[a] you:
5: 7. Casting all your care *upon*[a] him;
2Pet. 1:13.)([a] as long as I am in this tabernacle,
2:22. turned *to*[a] his own vomit again;
3: 3. shall come *in*[g] the last days
1Joh. 3: 3. that hath this hope *in*[d] him
3Joh. 10. and not content there*with*,[d] neither doth
Rev. 1: 7. shall wail *because of*[a] him.
17. laid his right hand *upon*[a] me,
20. sawest *in*[g] my right hand,
2:17. *in*[a] the stone a new name written,
24. I will put *upon*[a] you none
26. will I give power *over*[g] the nations:
3: 3. I will come *on*[a] thee as a thief,
— what hour I will come *upon*[a] thee.
10. come *upon*[g] all the world, to try them that dwell *upon*[g] the earth.
12. I will write *upon*[a] him the name
20. Behold, I stand *at*[a] the door,
4: 2. (one) sat *on*[g] the throne.
4. *upon*[a] the seats I saw four
— *on*[a] their heads crowns of gold.
9. to him that sat *on*[g] the throne,
10. him that sat *on*[g] the throne,
5: 1. And I saw *in*[a] the right hand of him that sat *on*[g] the throne
3. no man in heaven, nor *in*[g] earth
7. him that sat *upon*[g] the throne.
10. we shall reign *on*[g] the earth.
13. such as are *in*[g] the sea,
— him that sitteth *upon*[g] the throne,
6: 2. he that sat *on*[d] him had a bow;
4. to him that sat there*on*[d] to
5. he that sat *on*[d] him had a pair
8. *over*[a] the fourth part of the earth,
10. them that dwell *on*[g] the earth?
16. mountains and rocks, Fall *on*[a] us,
— of him that sitteth *on*[g] the throne.
7: 1. standing *on*[a] the four corners of
— wind should not blow *on*[g] the earth, nor *on*[g] the sea, nor *on*[a] any tree.
3. servants of our God *in*[g] their foreheads
10. which sitteth *upon*[g] the throne.
11. before the throne *on*[a] their faces,
15 and he that sitteth *on*[g] the throne shall dwell *among*[a] them.

Rev 7:16. shall the sun light *on*[a] them,
17. *unto*[a] living fountains of waters:
8: 3. came and stood *at*[a] the altar,
— of all saints *upon*[a] the golden altar
10. fell *upon*[a] the third part of the rivers, and *upon*[a] the fountains of waters;
13. to the inhabiters *of*[g] the earth
9: 4. seal of God *in*[g] their foreheads.
7. *on*[a] their heads (were) as it were
11. they had a king *over*[g] them,
14. are bound *in*[d] the great river
17. them that sat *on*[g] them, having
10: 1. a rainbow (was) *upon*[g] his head,
2. he set his right foot *upon*[a] the sea, and (his) left (foot) *on*[a] the earth,
5. the angel which I saw stand *upon*[g] the sea and *upon*[g] the earth
8. of the angel which standeth *upon*[g] the sea and *upon*[g] the earth.
11. prophesy again *before*[d] many peoples,
11: 6. have power *over*[g] waters to turn
8. *in*[g] the street of the great city,
10. they that dwell *upon*[g] the earth shall rejoice *over*[d] them,
— them that dwelt *on*[g] the earth.
11. of life from God entered *into*[a] them, and they stood *upon*[a] their feet; and great fear fell *upon*[a] them which saw them.
16. which sat before God *on*[a] their seats, fell *upon*[a] their faces,
12: 1. *upon*[g] her head a crown
3. seven crowns *upon*[a] his heads.
17. dragon was wroth *with*[d] the woman,
13: 1(12:18). I stood *upon*[a] the sand of the sea,
— *upon*[g] his horns ten crowns, and *upon*[a] his heads the name
7. given him *over*[a] all kindreds,
8. all that dwell *upon*[g] the earth
14. them that dwell *on*[g] the earth
— to them that dwell *on*[g] the earth,
16. to receive a mark *in*[g] their right hand, or *in*[g] their foreheads:
14: 1. stood *on*[a] the mount Sion,
— name written *in*[g] their foreheads.
6. them that dwell *on*[g] the earth,
9. and receive (his) mark *in*[g] his forehead, or *in*[a] his hand,
14. *upon*[a] the cloud (one) sat like
— having *on*[g] his head a golden
15. to him that sat *on*[g] the cloud,
16. he that sat *on*[a] the cloud thrust in his sickle *on*[a] the earth;
18. which had power *over*[g] fire;
15: 2. stand *on*[a] the sea of glass,
16: 2. poured out his vial *upon*[a] the earth;
8. his vial *upon*[a] the sun;
9. hath power *over*[a] these plagues:
10. *upon*[a] the seat of the beast;
12. *upon*[a] the great river Euphrates;
14. *unto*[a] the kings of the earth
18. since men were *upon*[g] the earth,
21. there fell *upon*[a] men a great hail
17: 1. whore that sitteth *upon*[g] many waters:
3. sit *upon*[a] a scarlet coloured beast,
5. *upon*[a] her forehead (was) a name
8. they that dwell *on*[g] the earth
— not written *in*[a] the book of life
9. *on* which (lit. where *on*[g] them) the woman sitteth.
16. which thou sawest *upon*[a] the beast,
18. *over*[g] the kings of the earth.
18: 9. bewail her, and lament *for*[d] her,
Rev.18:11. shall weep and mourn *over*[d] her;
17. all the company *in*[g] ships,
19. they cast dust *on*[a] their heads,
20. Rejoice *over*[a] her, (thou) heaven,
24. that were slain *upon*[g] the earth.
19: 4. God that sat *on*[g] the throne,
11. he that sat *upon*[a] him
12. *on*[a] his head (were) many crowns;
14. followed him *upon*[d] white horses,
16. And he hath *on*[a] (his) vesture and *on*[a] his thigh a name written,
18. of them that sit *on*[g] them,
19. him that sat *on*[g] the horse,
21. of him that sat *upon*[g] the horse,
20: 1. a great chain *in*[a] his hand.
4. thrones, and they sat *upon*[a] them,
— received (his) mark *upon*[a] their foreheads or *in*[a] their hands;
6. *on*[g] such the second death
9. up *on*[a] the breadth of the earth,
11. throne, and him that sat *on*[g] it,
21: 5. he that sat *upon*[g] the throne
10. *to*[a] a great and high mountain,
12. *at*[d] the gates twelve angels,
16. the reed,)([g] twelve thousand furlongs.
22: 4. name (shall be) *in*[g] their foreheads.
14. may have right *to*[a] the tree of life,
16. these things *in*[d] the churches.
18. God shall add *unto*[a] him

1910 6 289/364 1909, rt 939

ἐπιβαίνω, *epibaino.*

Mat.21: 5. meek, and *sitting upon* an ass,
Acts20:18. first day that I *came* into Asia,
21: 2. we *went aboard, and* set forth.
6. we *took* ship; and they returned
25: 1. *when* Festus *was come into* the province,
27: 2. And *entering into* a ship

1911 18 289/364 1:526 1909,906

ἐπιβάλλω, *epiballo.*

Mat. 9:16. No man *putteth* a piece of new cloth *unto*
26:50. Then came they, and *laid* hands
Mar 4:37. and the waves *beat into* the ship,
11: 7. and *cast* their garments *on* him;
14:46. they *laid* their hands *on* him,
72. *when* he *thought thereon*, he wept.
Lu. 5:36. No man *putteth* a piece of a new garment
9:62. *having put* his hand to the plough,
15:12. the portion of goods *that falleth* (to me).
20:19. *to lay* hands *on* him;
21:12. they *shall lay* their hands *on* you,
Joh. 7:30. no man *laid* hands *on* him,
44. no man *laid* hands *on* him.
Acts 4: 3. they *laid* hands *on* them,
5:18. And *laid* their hands *on* the apostles,
12: 1. Herod the king *stretched forth* (his) hands to vex
21:27. and *laid* hands *on* him,
1Co. 7:35. not that I *may cast* a snare *upon* you,

1912 3 290/364 1909,916

ἐπιβαρέω, *epibareo.*

2Co. 2: 5. that I *may* not *overcharge* you all
1Th. 2: 9. would not *be chargeable unto* any
2Th. 3: 8. might not *be chargeable to* any

1913 3 290/365 1909,rt 939

ἐπιβιβάζω, epibibazo

Lu. 10:34. and *set* him *on* his own beast, *and*
19:35. and they *set* Jesus thereon.
Acts23:24. that they may *set* Paul *on, and*

1914 3 290/365 1909,991

ἐπιβλέπω, epiblepo.

Lu. 1:48. he *hath regarded* the low estate
9:38. *look upon* my son:
Jas. 2: 3. And ye *have respect to* him that weareth

1915 4 290/365 1911

ἐπίβλημα, epibleema.

Mat. 9:16. putteth a *piece* of new cloth
Mar. 2:21. seweth a *piece* of new cloth
Lu. 5:36. No man putteth a *piece* of a new garment
— and the *piece* that was (taken) out of the

1916 1 290/150 1909,994

ἐπιβοάω, epiboao.

Acts25:24. *crying* that he ought not to live

1917 4 290/365 1909,1014

ἐπιβουλή, epiboulee.

Acts 9:24. their *laying await* was known of Saul.
20: 3. when the Jews *laid wait* (lit. when there was a *lying in wait* of the Jews)
19. befell me by the *lying in wait* of the Jews:
23:30. told me how that the Jews *laid wait* (lit. when the *lying in wait* of the Jews, was told me)

1918 1 290/365 1909,1062

ἐπιγαμβρεύω, epigambrŭo.

Mat.22:24. his brother *shall marry* his wife,

1919 7 290/365 1:677 1909,1093

ἐπίγειος, epigīos.

Joh 3:12. If I have told you *earthly* things,
1Co.15:40. and bodies *terrestrial:* but the
— the (glory) of the *terrestrial* (is) another.
2Co. 5: 1. if our *earthly* house of (this)
Phi. 2:10. (things) *in earth*, and (things) under the earth;
3:19. who mind *earthly* things.
Jas. 3:15. but (is) *earthly*, sensual, devilish.

1920 1 290/365 1909,1096

ἐπιγίνομαι, epiginomai.

Acts28:13. and after one day the south wind *blew, and*

1921 42 290/365 1:689 1909,1097

ἐπιγινώσκω, epiginōsko.

Mat. 7:16. Ye *shall know* them by their fruits.
20. by their fruits ye *shall know* them.
11:27. no man *knoweth* the Son, but the Father; neither *knoweth* any man the Father,
14:35. *when* the men of that place *had knowledge of* him,
17:12. and they *knew* him not, but have
Mar. 2: 8. And immediately *when* Jesus *perceived*
5:30. Jesus, immediately *knowing* in himself
6:33. and many *knew* him, and ran afoot
54. the ship, straightway they *knew* him,
Lu. 1: 4. That thou *mightest know* the certainty
22. they *perceived* that he had seen a vision
5:22. *when* Jesus *perceived* their thoughts,
7:37. *when* she *knew* that (Jesus) sat at meat
23: 7. And *as soon as* he *knew* that he belonged
24:16. holden that they should not *know* him.
31. opened, and they *knew* him;
Acts 3:10. And they *knew* that it was he which sat for
4:13. and they *took knowledge of* them, that they
9:30. (Which) *when* the brethren *knew*, they brought
12:14. And *when* she *knew* Peter's voice, she
19:34. *when* they *knew* that he was a Jew,
22:24. that he *might know* wherefore they cried
29. *after* he *knew* that he was a Roman,
24: 8. thyself mayest *take knowledge of* all
25:10. as thou very well *knowest.*
27:39. they *knew* not the land: but they
28: 1. then they *knew* that the island
Ro. 1:32. Who *knowing* the judgment of God,
1Co.13:12. but then *shall* I *know* even as also I *am known.*
14:37. *let* him *acknowledge* that the things
16:18. therefore *acknowledge* ye them that
2Co. 1:13. than what ye read or *acknowledge;*
— ye *shall acknowledge* even to the end;
14. ye *have acknowledged* us in part,
6: 9. unknown, and (yet) *well known,*
13: 5. *Know* ye not your own selves, how
Col. 1: 6. and *knew* the grace of God in truth:
1Ti. 4: 3. which believe and *know* the truth.
2Pet.2.21. for them not *to have known* the way
— than, *after* they *have known* (it), to turn

1922 20 291/366 1:689 1921

ἐπίγνωσις, epignōsis.

Ro. 1:28. to retain God in (their) *knowledge*,
3:20. by the law (is) the *knowledge* of sin.
10: 2. zeal of God, but not according to *knowledge.*
Eph. 1:17. in the *knowledge* of him:
4:13. and of the *knowledge* of the Son of God,
Phi. 1: 9. in *knowledge* and (in) all judgment;
Col. 1: 9. with the *knowledge* of his will in all
10. increasing in the *knowledge* of God;
2: 2. to the *acknowledgement* of the mystery
3:10. renewed in *knowledge* after the image
1Ti. 2: 4. to come unto the *knowledge* of the truth.
2Ti. 2:25. repentance to the *acknowledging* of the truth,
3: 7. never able to come to the *knowledge* of the truth.
Tit. 1: 1. the *acknowledging* of the truth
Philem. 6. by the *acknowledging* of every
Heb 10:26. received the *knowledge* of the truth,
2Pet.1: 2. through the *knowledge* of God,
3. through the *knowledge* of him that hath
8. in the *knowledge* of our Lord
2:20. the *knowledge* of the Lord and Saviour

1923 5 291/366 1:742 1924

ἐπιγραφή, epigraphee.

Mat.22:20. Whose (is) this image and *superscription?*
Mar 12:16. this image and *superscription?*
15:26. the *superscription* of his accusation
Lu. 20:24. Whose image and *superscription*
23:38. a *superscription* also was written

1924 5 291/366 1:742 1909,1125
ἐπιγράφω, epigrapho.

Mar 15:26. of his accusation was *written over*,
Acts17:23. an altar with this inscription, (lit. on which *had been inscribed*)
Heb. 8:10. and *write* them *in* their hearts:
10:16. and *in* their minds *will* I *write* them;
Rev.21:12. and names *written thereon*,

1925 9 291/366 1909,1166
ἐπιδείκνυμι, epidīknumi.

Mat.16: 1. that he would *shew* them a sign
22:19. *Shew* me the tribute money.
24: 1. *to shew* him the buildings
Lu. 17:14. *shew* yourselves unto the priests.
20:24. *Shew* me a penny.
24:40. he *shewed* them (his) hands and (his) feet.
Acts 9:39. *shewing* the coats and garments
18:28. *shewing* by the scriptures that Jesus
Heb. 6:17. *to shew* unto the heirs of promise

1926 2 292/366 1909,1209
ἐπιδέχομαι, epidekomai.

3Joh. 9. but Diotrephes,...*receiveth* us not.
10. neither *doth* he himself *receive* the brethren,

1927 2 292/366 1909,1218
ἐπιδημέω, epideemeo.

Acts 2:10. and strangers of Rome, (lit. Romans *there dwelling*)
17:21. and strangers *which were there*

1928 1 292/366 1909,1299
ἐπιδιατάσσομαι, epidiatassomai.

Gal. 3:15. disannulleth, or *addeth thereto*.

1929 11 292/366 1909,1325
ἐπιδίδωμι, epididōmi.

Mat. 7: 9. *will* he *give* him a stone?
10. *will* he *give* him a serpent?
Lu. 4:17. *was delivered unto* him the book
11:11. *will* he *give* him a stone?
— *will* he for a fish *give* him
12. *will* he *offer* him a scorpion?
24:30. blessed (it), and brake, and *gave* to them.
42. they *gave* him a piece of
Joh. 13:26. to whom I *shall give* a sop,
Acts15:30. they *delivered* the epistle:
27:15. we let (her) drive. (lit. *giving* her up we were borne)

1930 1 292/366 1909,3717
ἐπιδιορθόω, epidiorthoō.

Tit. 1: 5. that thou *shouldest set in order*

1931 1 292/366 1909,1416
ἐπιδύω, epiduo.

Eph. 4:26. *let* not the sun *go down* upon your wrath:

1932 2 292/366 2:588 1933
ἐπιείκεια, epi-īkīa.

Acts24: 4. wouldest hear us of thy *clemency*
2Co.10: 1. and *gentleness* of Christ,

1933 5 292/366 2:588 1909,1503
ἐπιεικής, epi-īkees.

Phi. 4: 5. Let your *moderation* be known
1Ti. 3: 3. but *patient*, not a brawler,
Tit. 3: 2. to be no brawlers, (but) *gentle*,
Jas. 3:17. *gentle*, (and) easy to be intreated,
1Pet.2:18. not only to the good and *gentle*,

ἐπίειμι see **ἐπιοῦσα**. 1966

1934 14 292/367 2:892 1909,2212
ἐπιζητέω, epizeeteo.

Mat. 6:32. *after* all these things *do* the Gentiles *seek*:
12:39. generation *seeketh after* a sign,
16: 4. adulterous generation *seeketh after*
Mar. 8:12 Why *doth* this generation *seek after*
Lu. 11:29. they *seek* a sign; and there shall no
12:30. *do* the nations of the world *seek after*:
Acts12:19. *when* Herod *had sought for* him,
13: 7. and *desired* to hear the word of God.
19:39. if ye *enquire* any thing concerning
Ro. 11: 7. not obtained that which he *seeketh for*,
Phi. 4:17. Not because I *desire* a gift: but I *desire* fruit that may abound
Heb 11:14. plainly that they *seek* a country
13:14. city, but we *seek* one to come.

1935 1 292/367 1909,2288
ἐπιθανάτιος, epithanatios.

1Co. 4. 9. as it were *appointed to death*:

1936 4 292/367 8:152 2007
ἐπίθεσις, epithesis.

Acts 8:18. through *laying on* of the apostles' hands
1Ti. 4:14. with the *laying on* of the hands
2Ti. 1: 6. by the *putting on* of my hands.
Heb. 6: 2. and of *laying on* of hands, and of

1937 16 293/367 3:167 1909,2372
ἐπιθυμέω, epithumeo.

Mat. 5:28. looketh on a woman *to lust after* her
13:17. righteous (men) *have desired* to see
Lu. 15:16. he *would fain* have filled his belly
16:21. *desiring* to be fed with the crumbs
17:22. ye *shall desire* to see one of the days
22:15. desire I *have desired* to eat this passover
Acts20:33. I *have coveted* no man's silver,
Ro. 7: 7. Thou *shalt* not *covet*.
13: 9. Thou *shalt* not *covet*; and if
1Co.10: 6. after evil things, as they also *lusted*.
Gal. 5:17. For the flesh *lusteth* against the Spirit,
1Ti. 3: 1. he *desireth* a good work.
Heb. 6:11. And we *desire* that every one of you
Jas. 4: 2. Ye *lust*, and have not: ye kill,
1Pet. 1:12. which things the angels *desire* to look
Rev. 9: 6. and *shall desire* to die, and death

1938 1 293/367 3:167 1937
ἐπιθυμητής, epithumeetees.

1Co.10: 6. intent we should not lust after evil things, (lit. be *desirers* of evil things)

1939 38 293/367 3:167 1937
ἐπιθυμία, epithumia.

Mar. 4:19. the *lusts* of other things

Lu. 22:15. With *desire* I have desired
Joh. 8:44. the *lusts* of your father ye will do.
Ro. 1:24. through the *lusts* of their own hearts,
6:12. should obey it in the *lusts* thereof.
7: 7. for I had not known *lust*,
8. in me all manner of *concupiscence*.
13:14. to (fulfil) the *lusts* (thereof).
Gal. 5:16. shall not fulfil the *lust* of the flesh.
24. with the affections and *lusts*.
Eph. 2: 3. in the *lusts* of our flesh,
4:22. according to the deceitful *lusts*;
Phi. 1:23. having a *desire* to depart,
Col. 3: 5. evil *concupiscence*, and covetousness,
1Th. 2:17. endeavoured...with great *desire*.
4: 5. Not in the lust of *concupiscence*,
1Ti. 6: 9. (into) many foolish and hurtful *lusts*,
2Ti. 2:22. Flee also youthful *lusts*:
3: 6. led away with divers *lusts*,
4: 3. after their own *lusts* shall they heap
Tit. 2:12. denying ungodliness and worldly *lusts*,
3: 3. serving divers *lusts* and pleasures,
Jas. 1:14. when he is drawn away of his own *lust*,
15. Then when *lust* hath conceived,
1Pet. 1:14. according to the former *lusts*.
2:11. abstain from fleshly *lusts*, which war
4: 2. should live...to the *lusts* of men,
3. *lusts*, excess of wine, revellings,
2Pet. 1: 4. that is in the world through *lust*.
2:10. in the *lust* of uncleanness,
18. allure through the *lusts* of the flesh,
3: 3. walking after their own *lusts*,
1Joh. 2:16. *lust* of the flesh, and the *lust* of the eyes,
17. world passeth away, and the *lust* thereof:
Jude 16. walking after their own *lusts*;
18. after their own ungodly *lusts*.
Rev. 18:14. the fruits that thy soul lusted after (lit. of thy soul's *desire*)

1940 1 293/367 1909,2523

ἐπικαθίζω, *epikathizo*.

Mat. 21: 7. and they *set* (him) there*on*.

1941 32 293/367 3:487 1909,2564

ἐπικαλέομαι, *epikaleomai*.

Mat. 10: 3. whose surname was Thaddæus; (lit. *surnamed* T.)
Lu. 22: 3. into Judas *surnamed* Iscariot,
Acts 1:23. who *was surnamed* Justus,
2:21. whosoever *shall call on* the name
4:36. *who* by the apostles *was surnamed* Barnabas,
7:59. stoned Stephen, *calling upon* (God),
9:14. all *that call on* thy name.
21. them *which called on* this name
10: 5. Simon, whose surname is (lit. who *is surnamed*) Peter:
18. Simon, *which was surnamed* Peter,
32. whose surname is (lit. who *is surnamed*) Peter;
11:13. Simon, whose surname is (lit. *who is surnamed*) Peter;
12:12. of John, whose surname was (lit. *who was surnamed*) Mark;
25. John, whose surname was (lit. *who was surnamed*) Mark.
15:17. upon whom my name *is called*,
22. Judas *surnamed* Barsabas,
22:16. *calling on* the name of the Lord.
25:11. I *appeal unto* Cæsar.
12. *Hast* thou *appealed unto* Cæsar?
Acts 25:21. But *when* Paul *had appealed*
25. himself *hath appealed to* Augustus,
26:32. if he *had* not *appealed unto*
28:19. constrained *to appeal unto* Cæsar;
Ro. 10:12. unto all *that call upon* him.
13. whosoever *shall call upon* the name
14. How then *shall* they *call on* him
1Co. 1: 2. with all *that* in every place *call upon* the name
2Co. 1:23. I *call* God for a record upon my soul,
2 Ti. 2:22. with them *that call on* the Lord
Heb. 11:16. *to be called* their God:
Jas. 2: 7. name by the which ye are called? (lit. *called upon* you)
1 Pet. 1:17. And if ye *call on* the Father,

1942 1 294/368 1943

ἐπικάλυμμα, *epikalumma*.

1Pet. 2:16. not using (your) liberty for a *cloke* of

1943 1 294/368 1909,2572

ἐπικαλύπτω, *epikalupto*.

Ro. 4: 7. and whose sins *are covered*.

1944 3 294/368 1:448 1909,2672

ἐπικατάρατος, *epikataratos*.

Joh. 7:49. people who knoweth not the law are *cursed*.
Gal. 3:10. *Cursed* (is) every one that continueth not
13. *Cursed* (is) every one that hangeth on

1945 7 294/368 3:654 1909,2749

ἐπίκειμαι, *epikīmai*.

Lu. 5: 1. as the people *pressed upon* him
23:23. And they *were instant* with loud voices,
Joh. 11:38. and a stone *lay* upon it.
21: 9. and fish *laid thereon*, and bread.
Acts 27:20. *when*...no small tempest *lay on* (us),
1Co. 9:16. for necessity *is laid upon* me;
Heb. 9:10. *imposed* (*on* them) until the time

1947 1 294/368 1909,rt 2877

ἐπικουρία, *epikouria*.

Acts 26:22. Having therefore obtained *help* of God,

1948 1 294/368 1909,2919

ἐπικρίνω, *epikrino*.

Lu. 23:24. Pilate *gave sentence* that it should be

1949 19 295/368 4:5 1909,2983

ἐπιλαμβάνομαι, *epilambanomai*.

Mat. 14:31. *caught* him, and said unto him,
Mar. 8:23. he *took* the blind man *by* the hand, *and*
Lu. 9:47. *took* a child, *and* set him by him,
14: 4. he *took* (him), *and* healed him,
20:20. that they *might take hold of* his words,
26. they could not *take hold of* his words
23:26. they *laid hold upon* one Simon,
Acts 9:27. But Barnabas *took* him, *and* brought
16:19. they *caught* Paul and Silas, *and* drew
17:19. And they *took* him, *and* brought him
18:17. Then all the Greeks *took* Sosthenes,
21:30. and they *took* Paul, *and* drew him
33. and *took* him, and commanded

Acts23:19. the chief captain *took* him *by* the hand,
1Ti. 6:12. *lay hold on* eternal life,
19. that they *may lay hold on* eternal life.
Heb. 2:16. he *took* not *on* (him the nature of) angels; but he *took on* (him) the seed of Abraham.
8: 9. *when* I *took* them *by* the hand

1950 8 295/368 1909,2990

ἐπιλανθάνομαι, epilanthanomai.

Mat.16: 5. they *had forgotten* to take bread.
Mar. 8:14. *had forgotten* to take bread,
Lu. 12: 6. not one of them is *forgotten*
Phi. 3:13(14). *forgetting* those things which are
Heb. 6:10. *to forget* your work and labour
13: 2. *Be* not *forgetful* to entertain
16. and to communicate *forget* not:
Jas. 1:24. *forgetteth* what manner of man

1951 2 295/369 1909,3004

ἐπιλέγομαι, epilegomai.

Joh. 5: 2. *which is called* in the Hebrew tongue
Acts15:40. And Paul *chose* Silas, *and*

1952 1 295/369 1909,3007

ἐπιλείπω, epilīpo.

Heb 11:32. the time *would fail* me to tell

1953 1 295/369 1950

ἐπιλησμονή, epileesmonee.

Jas. 1:25. he being not a forgetful hearer, (lit. a hearer of *forgetfulness*)

1954 1 295/369 1909,3062

ἐπίλοιπος, epiloipos.

1Pet.4: 2. should live the rest of (his) time in the flesh (lit. the *remaining* time, &c.)

1955 1 295/369 4:328 1956

ἐπίλυσις, epilusis.

2Pet.1:20. is of any private *interpretation*.

1956 2 295/369 4:328 1909,3089

ἐπιλύω, epiluo.

Mar. 4:34. he *expounded* all things to his disciples.
Acts19:39. it *shall be determined* in a

1957 1 295/369 4:474 1909,3140

ἐπιμαρτυρέω, epimartureo.

1Pet.5:12. exhorting, and *testifying*

1958 1 295/369 1959

ἐπιμέλεια, epimelīa.

Acts27: 3. go unto his friends to refresh himself. (lit. to have their *care*)

1959 3 296/369 1909,3199

ἐπιμελέομαι, epimeleomai.

Lu. 10:34. to an inn, and *took care of* him.
35. *Take care of* him; and whatsoever
1Ti. 3: 5. how *shall* he *take care of* the church

1960 1 296/369 1959

ἐπιμελῶς, epimelōs.

Lu. 15: 8. seek *diligently* till she find (it)?

1961 18 296/369 1909,3306

ἐπιμένω, epimeno.

Joh. 8: 7. So when they *continued* asking
Acts10:48. prayed they him to *tarry* certain days.
12:16. But Peter *continued* knocking:
13:43. *to continue in* the grace of God.
15:34. it pleased Silas *to abide* there still.
21: 4. we *tarried* there seven days:
10. And *as* we *tarried* (there) many days,
28:12. we *tarried* (there) three days.
14. *to tarry* with them seven days:
Ro. 6: 1. *Shall* we *continue in* sin, that grace
11:22. if thou *continue in* (his) goodness:
23. if they *abide* not *in* unbelief,
1Co.16: 7. I trust *to tarry* a while with you,
8. But I *will tarry* at Ephesus
Gal. 1:18. and *abode* with him fifteen days.
Phil. 1:24. *to abide in* the flesh (is) more needful
Col. 1:23. If ye *continue in* the faith
1Ti. 4:16. *continue in* them: for in doing this

1962 1 296/369 1909,3506

ἐπινεύω, epinūo.

Acts18:20. time with them, he *consented* not;

1963 1 296/369 1909,3563

ἐπίνοια, epinoia.

Acts 8:22. the *thought* of thine heart may

1964 1 296/369 5:457 1965

ἐπιορκέω, epiorkeo.

Mat. 5:33. Thou *shalt* not *forswear thyself*,

1965 1 296/369 5:457 1909,3727

ἐπίορκος, epiorkos.

1Ti. 1:10. for liars, for *perjured persons*,

1966 5 296/353 1909 *heimi* (to go)

ἐπιοῦσα, epiousa.

Acts 7:26. And the *next* day he shewed himself
16:11. and the *next* (day) to Neapolis;
20:15. came the *next* (day) over against Chios;
21:18. And the (day) *following* Paul went in
23:11. And the night *following* the Lord

1967 2 296/369 2:590 1909 *heimi* (to go)

ἐπιούσιος, epiousios.

Mat. 6:11. Give us this day our *daily* bread
Lu. 11: 3. day by day our *daily* bread.

1968 13 297/369 1909,4098

ἐπιπίπτω, epipipto.

Mar. 3:10. insomuch that they *pressed upon* him
Lu. 1:12. and fear *fell upon* him.
15:20. and ran, and *fell on* his neck,
Joh.13:25. He then *lying on* Jesus' breast
Acts 8:16. he was *fallen upon* none of them:
10:10. made ready, he fell into a trance, (lit. a trance *fell upon* him)

Acts10:44. the Holy Ghost *fell on* all
11:15. the Holy Ghost *fell on* them,
13:11. there *fell on* him a mist
19:17. and fear *fell on* them all,
20:10. Paul went down, and *fell on* him,
37. and *fell on* Paul's neck, *and*
Ro. 15: 3. them that reproached thee *fell on* me.

1969 1 297/370 1909,4141

ἐπιπλήττω, epipleetto.

1Ti. 5: 1. *Rebuke* not an elder, but intreat

1970 1 /99 1909,4155

ἐπιπνίγω, epipnigo.

(Most copies have ἀπέπνιξαν.)

Lu. 8: 7. thorns sprang up with it, and *choked* it.

1971 9 297/370 1909 *potheō* (to yearn)

ἐπιποθέω, epipotheo.

Ro. 1:11. For I *long* to see you, that
2Co. 5: 2. *earnestly desiring* to be clothed upon
9:14. *which long after* you for the
Phi. 1: 8. how *greatly* I *long after* you all
2:26. For he *longed after* you all,
1Th. 3: 6. *desiring greatly* to see us,
2Ti. 1: 4. *Greatly desiring* to see thee,
Jas. 4: 5. spirit that dwelleth in us *lusteth* to envy?
1Pet. 2: 2. *desire* the sincere milk of the word,

1972 2 297/370 1971

ἐπιπόθησις, epipotheesis.

2Co. 7: 7. he told us your *earnest desire*,
11. yea, (what) *vehement desire*,

1973 1 298/370 1909,1971

ἐπιπόθητος, epipotheetos.

Phi. 4: 1. dearly beloved and *longed for*,

1974 1 298/370 1971

ἐπιποθία, epipothia.

Ro. 15:23. having a *great desire* these many years

1975 1 298/370 1909,4198

ἐπιπορεύομαι, epiporūomai.

Lu. 8: 4. and *were come* to him out of

1976 1 298/370 1909,rt 4476

ἐπιῤῥάπτω, epirrapto.

Mar. 2:21. *seweth* a piece of new cloth *on*

1977 2 298/370 6:991 1909,4496

ἐπιῤῥίπτω, epirripto.

Lu. 19:35. they *cast* their garments *upon* the colt, *and*
1Pet. 5: 7. *Casting* all your care *upon* him;

1978 2 298/370 7:200 1909 rt 4591

ἐπίσημος, episeemos.

Mat. 27:16. a *notable* prisoner, called Barabbas.
Ro. 16: 7. who are *of note* among the apostles,

1979 1 298/370 1909,4621

ἐπισιτισμός, episitismos.

Lu. 9:12. and lodge, and get *victuals*:

1980 11 298/370 2:599 1909 rt 4649

ἐπισκέπτομαι, episkeptomai.

Mat. 25:36. sick, and ye *visited* me:
43. and ye *visited* me not.
Lu. 1:68. for he *hath visited* and redeemed
78. dayspring from on high *hath visited* us,
7:16. That God *hath visited* his people.
Acts 6: 3. *look* ye *out* among you seven men
7:23. *to visit* his brethren the children
15:14. how God at the first *did visit*
36. Let us go again and *visit* our brethren
Heb. 2: 6. that thou *visitest* him?
Jas. 1:27. *To visit* the fatherless and widows

1981 1 298/370 7:368 1909,4637

ἐπισκηνόω, episkeenoō.

2Co. 12: 9. that the power of Christ *may rest upon* me.

1982 5 298/370 7:394 1909,4639

ἐπισκιάζω, episkiazo.

Mat. 17: 5. a bright cloud *overshadowed* them:
Mar. 9: 7. there was a cloud *that overshadowed* them:
Lu. 1:35. the power of the Highest *shall overshadow* thee:
9:34. came a cloud, and *overshadowed* them:
Acts 5:15. *might overshadow* some of them.

1983 2 298/370 2:599 1909,4648

ἐπισκοπέω, episkopeo.

Heb 12:15. *Looking diligently* lest any man
1Pet. 5: 2. *taking the oversight* (thereof), not by constraint,

1984 4 299/370 2:599 1980

ἐπισκοπή, episkopee.

Lu. 19:44. knewest not the time of thy *visitation*.
Acts 1:20. his *bishoprick* let another take.
1Ti. 3: 1. If a man desire *the office of a bishop*,
1Pet. 2:12. glorify God in the day of *visitation*.

1985 5 299/370 2:599 1909,4649

ἐπίσκοπος, episkopos.

Acts 20:28. the Holy Ghost hath made you *overseers*,
Phi. 1: 1. with the *bishops* and deacons:
1Ti. 3: 2. A *bishop* then must be blameless,
Tit. 1: 7. For a *bishop* must be blameless,
1Pet. 2:25. Shepherd and *Bishop* of your souls.

1986 1 299/371 1909,4685

ἐπισπάομαι, epispaomai.

1Co. 7:18. *let* him not *become uncircumcised*.

1987 14 300/371 2186

ἐπίσταμαι, epistamai.

Mar 14:68. neither *understand* I what thou sayest.
Acts 10:28. Ye *know* how that it is an unlawful thing
15: 7. Men (and) brethren, ye *know*
18:25. *knowing* only the baptism of John.
19:15. Paul I *know*, but who are ye?

Acts19:25. ye *know* that by this craft
20:18. Ye *know*, from the first day
22:19. they *know* that I imprisoned
24:10. *as* I *know* that thou hast been
26:26. For the king *knoweth* of these things,
1Ti. 6: 4. He is proud, *knowing* nothing,
Heb 11: 8. not *knowing* whither he went.
Jas. 4:14. Whereas ye *know* not what (shall be)
Jude 10. but what they *know* naturally,

1988 7 300/371 2:622 1909,2476

ἐπιστάτης, epistatees.

Lu. 5: 5. *Master*, we have toiled all the night,
8:24. *Master, master*, we perish.
45. *Master*, the multitude throng thee
9:33. *Master*, it is good for us to be here:
49. *Master*, we saw one casting out devils
17:13. Jesus, *Master*, have mercy on us.

1989 3 300/371 7:588 1909,4724

ἐπιστέλλω, epistello.

Acts15:20. But that we *write unto* them,
21:25. we *have written* (and) concluded
Heb 13:22. I *have written a letter unto* you in few words.

1990 1 300/371 1987

ἐπιστήμων, episteemōn.

Jas. 3:13. and *endued with knowledge* among you?

1991 4 300/371 7:653 1909,4741

ἐπιστηρίζω, episteerizo.

Acts14:22. *Confirming* the souls of the disciples,
15:32. with many words, and *confirmed* (them).
41. *confirming* the churches.
18:23. *strengthening* all the disciples.

1992 24 300/371 7:588 1989

ἐπιστολή, epistolee.

Acts 9: 2. *letters* to Damascus to the synagogues,
15:30. they delivered the *epistle*:
22: 5. I received *letters* unto the brethren,
23:25. he wrote a *letter* after this manner:
33. and delivered the *epistle* to the
Ro. 16:22. I Tertius, who wrote (this) *epistle*,
1Co. 5. 9. I wrote unto you in an *epistle*
16: 3. ye shall approve by (your) *letters*,
2Co. 3: 1. *epistles* of commendation to you,
2. Ye are our *epistle* written
3. to be the *epistle* of Christ
7: 8. I made you sorry with a *letter*
— I perceive that the same *epistle*
10: 9. as if I would terrify you by *letters*.
10. For (his) *letters*, say they, (are) weighty
11. by *letters* when we are absent,
Col. 4:16. when this *epistle* is read among you,
1Th. 5:27. that this *epistle* be read unto all
2Th. 2: 2. nor by *letter* as from us,
15. whether by word, or our *epistle*.
3:14. our word by this *epistle*, note that man,
17. the token in every *epistle*:
2Pet.3: 1. This second *epistle*, beloved, I now write
16. As also in all (his) *epistles*,

1993 1 301/371 1909,4750

ἐπιστομίζω, epistomizo.

Tit. 1: 11. Whose *mouths* must *be stopped*,

1994 39 301/371 7:714 1909,4762

ἐπιστρέφω, epistrepho.

Mat. 9:22. But Jesus *turned* him *about*,
10:13. *let* your peace *return* to you.
12:44. I *will return* into my house
13:15. and *should be converted*,
24:18. Neither *let* him...*return* back
Mar 4:12. lest...they *should be converted*,
5:30. *turned* him *about* in the press, and
8:33. But *when* he *had turned about*
13:16 *let* him...not *turn* back *again*
Lu. 1:16. of the children of Israel *shall* he *turn*
17. *to turn* the hearts of the fathers
2:20. the shepherds *returned*, glorifying
8:55. And her spirit *came again*,
17: 4. *turn again* to thee, saying,
31. *let* him likewise not *return*
22:32. and when thou *art converted*, strengthen
Joh. 12:40. and *be converted*, and I should heal
21:20. Then Peter, *turning about*,
Acts 3:19. Repent ye therefore, and *be converted*
9:35. and *turned* to the Lord.
40. *turning* (him) to the body said,
11:21. believed, and *turned* unto the Lord.
14:15. that ye should *turn* from these vanities
15:19. which from among the Gentiles *are turned* to God:
36. Let us *go again and* visit
16:18. Paul, being grieved, *turned and* said
26:18. *to turn* (them) from darkness
20. should repent and *turn* to God,
28:27. *should be converted*, and I should heal them.
2Co. 3:16. Nevertheless when it *shall turn* to the Lord,
Gal. 4: 9. how *turn* ye again to the weak
1Th. 1: 9. how ye *turned* to God from idols
Jas. 5:19. from the truth, and one *convert* him;
20. he *which converteth* the sinner
1Pet. 2:25. *are* now *returned* unto the Shepherd
2Pet. 2:21. after they have known (it), *to turn*
22. The dog (is) *turned* to his own vomit *again*;
Rev. 1:12. I *turned* to see the voice that spake with me. And *being turned*, I saw seven

1995 1 301/372 7:714 1994

ἐπιστροφή, epistrophee.

Acts15: 3. declaring the *conversion* of the Gentiles

1996 7 301/372 1909,4863

ἐπισυνάγω, episunago.

Mat.23:37. would I *have gathered* thy children together, even as a hen *gathereth*
24:31. they *shall gather together* his elect
Mar. 1:33. was *gathered together* at the door.
13:27. *shall gather together* his elect
Lu. 12: 1. *when* there *were gathered together* an innumerable multitude
13:34. would I *have gathered* thy children *together*.

1997 2 301/372 7:798 1996

ἐπισυναγωγή, episunagōgee.

2Th. 2: 1. (by) our *gathering together* unto him,
Heb 10:25. the *assembling* of ourselves *together*,

1998 1 301/372 1909,4936

ἐπισυντρέχω, episuntreko.

Mar. 9:25. that the people *came running together*

1999 2 301/371 1909,4921

ἐπισύστασις, *episustasis.*

Acts24:12. neither raising up the people, (lit. making a *tumultuous assembly*)
2Co.11:28. *that which cometh upon* me daily,

2000 1 301/372 1909 *sphallō* (to trip)

ἐπισφαλής, *episphalees.*

Acts27: 9. when sailing was now *dangerous*,

2001 1 302/372 1909,2480

ἐπισχύω, *episkuo*

Lu. 23: 5. And they *were the more fierce*, saying,

2002 1 302/372 7:1094 1909 4987

ἐπισωρεύω, *episōrūo.*

2Ti. 4: 3. *shall* they *heap* to themselves

2003 7 302/372 8:27 2004

ἐπιταγή, *epitagee.*

Ro. 16:26. the *commandment* of the everlasting God,
1Co. 7: 6. (and) not of *commandment*.
25. I have no *commandment* of the Lord:
2Co. 8: 8. I speak not by *commandment*,
1Ti. 1: 1. by the *commandment* of God our Saviour,
Tit. 1: 3. according to the *commandment* of God our Saviour;
2:15. exhort, and rebuke with all *authority*.

2004 10 302/372 1909,5021

ἐπιτάσσω, *epitasso.*

Mar. 1:27. *commandeth* he even the unclean spirits,
6:27. *commanded* his head to be brought:
39. he *commanded* them to make all sit down
9:25. I *charge* thee, come out of him,
Lu. 4:36. he *commandeth* the unclean spirits,
8:25. he *commandeth* even the winds
31. that he *would* not *command* them
14:22. it is done as thou *hast commanded*,
Acts23: 2. Ananias *commanded* them that stood by
Philem. 8. *to injoin* thee that which is convenient,

2005 11 302/372 8:49 1909,5055

ἐπιτελέω, *epiteleo.*

Lu. 13:32. I *do* cures to day and to morrow,
Ro. 15:28. *When* therefore I *have performed* this, and
2Co. 7: 1. *perfecting* holiness in the fear of God.
8: 6. so he *would* also *finish* in you the same
11. *perform* the doing (of it);
— so (there may be) a performance also (lit. *to perform*)
Gal. 3: 3. *are* ye now *made perfect* by the flesh?
Phi. 1: 6. *will perform* (it) until the day
Heb. 8: 5. when he was about *to make* the tabernacle:
9: 6. *accomplishing* the service (of God).
1Pet. 5: 9. *are accomplished* in your brethren

2006 1 302/372 *epitēdes* (enough)

ἐπιτήδειος, *epiteedīos.*

Jas. 2:16. *things which are needful to* the body;

2007 42 302/372 8:152 1909,5087

ἐπιτίθημι, *epititheemi.*

Mat. 9.18. *lay* thy hand *upon* her,
Mat.19:13. that he *should put* (his) hands on them,
15. he *laid* (his) hands *on* them, *and*
21: 7. and *put on* them their clothes,
23: 4. and *lay* (them) *on* men's shoulders;
27:29. they *put* (it) *upon* his head,
37. And *set up* over his head his accusation
Mar. 3:16. Simon he surnamed (lit. he *added* the name of) Peter;
17. he surnamed (lit. he, &c.) them Boanerges
4:21. and not to *be set on* a candlestick?
5:23. come and *lay* thy hands *on* her,
6: 5. he *laid* his hands *upon* a few sick folk, *and*
7:32. beseech him to *put* his hand *upon* him
8:23. *and put* his hands *upon* him,
25. he *put* (his) hands again *upon* his eyes,
16:18. they *shall lay* hands *on* the sick,
Lu. 4:40. he *laid* his hands *on* every one of them, *and*
8:16. but *setteth* (it) *on* a candlestick,
10:30. and wounded (him), (lit. *having inflicted* wounds)
13:13. he *laid* (his) hands *on* her:
15: 5. he *layeth* (it) *on* his shoulders,
23:26. *on* him they *laid* the cross,
Joh. 9:15. He *put* clay *upon* mine eyes,
19: 2. and *put* (it) *on* his head,
Acts 6: 6. they *laid* (their) hands *on* them.
8:17. *laid* they (their) hands *on* them,
19. *on* whomsoever I *lay* hands,
9:12. *putting* (his) hand *on* him,
17. *putting* his hands *on* him
13: 3. and *laid* (their) hands *on* them,
15:10. *to put* a yoke *upon* the neck
28. *to lay upon* you no greater burden
16:23. *when* they *had laid* many stripes *upon* them,
18:10. no man *shall set on* thee
19: 6. *when* Paul *had laid* (his) hands *upon* them,
28: 3. and *laid* (them) *on* the fire, there came
8. and *laid* his hands *on* him, *and*
10. they *laded* (us) with such things as
1Ti. 5:22. *Lay* hands suddenly *on* no man,
Rev. 1:17. he *laid* his right hand *upon* me,
22:18. If any man shall *add unto* these things, God *shall add unto* him the plagues

2008 29 303/373 2:623 2909,5091

ἐπιτιμάω, *epitimao.*

Mat. 8:26. he arose, and *rebuked* the winds
12:16. And *charged* them that they should not.
16:22. and began *to rebuke* him,
17:18. And Jesus *rebuked* the devil;
19:13. the disciples *rebuked* them.
20:31. the multitude *rebuked* them,
Mar. 1:25. Jesus *rebuked* him, saying, Hold
3:12. And he straitly *charged* them
4:39. he arose, and *rebuked* the wind,
8:30. And he *charged* them that they should tell
32. and began *to rebuke* him.
33. he *rebuked* Peter, saying, Get thee
9:25. he *rebuked* the foul spirit,
10:13. (his) disciples *rebuked* those that brought (them).
48. many *charged* him that he should hold
Lu. 4:35. Jesus *rebuked* him, saying, Hold
39. and *rebuked* the fever; and it left her:
41. he *rebuking* (them) suffered them not.
8:24. he arose, and *rebuked* the wind
9:21. And he *straitly charged* them, *and*
42. Jesus *rebuked* the unclean spirit,
55. he turned, and *rebuked* them,
17: 3. trespass against thee, *rebuke* him;
18:15. disciples saw (it), they *rebuked* them.

Lu. 18:39. they which went before *rebuked* him,
19.39. Master, *rebuke* thy disciples.
23:40 answering *rebuked* him, saying,
2Ti. 4: 2. reprove, *rebuke*, exhort with all
Jude 9. but said, The Lord *rebuke* thee.

2009 1 303/373 2:623 1909,5092

ἐπιτιμία, epitimia.

2Co. 2: 6. Sufficient to such a man (is) this *punishment*,

2010 19 303/373 1909,rt 5157

ἐπιτρέπω, epitrepo.

Mat. 8:21. *suffer* me first to go and bury
31. *suffer* us to go away into the
19: 8. *suffered* you to put away your wives:
Mar. 5:13. forthwith Jesus *gave* them *leave*.
10: 4. Moses *suffered* to write a bill
Lu. 8:32. that he *would suffer* them to enter into them. And he *suffered* them.
9:59. *suffer* me first to go and bury
61 but *let* me first go bid them
Joh. 19:38. and Pilate *gave* (him) *leave*.
Acts21:39. *suffer* me to speak unto the people.
40. And *when* he *had given* him *licence*,
26: 1. Thou art permitted (lit. it *is permitted* thee) to speak for thyself.
27: 3. and *gave* (him) *liberty* to go unto his friends
28:16. but Paul was suffered (lit. it *was permitted* Paul) to dwell
1Co.14:34. for it *is* not *permitted* unto them
16: 7. a while with you, if the Lord *permit*.
1Ti. 2:12. I *suffer* not a woman to teach,
Heb. 6: 3. this will we do, if God *permit*.

2011 1 303/373 2010

ἐπιτροπή, epitropee.

Acts26:12. with authority and *commission*

2012 3 303/374 1909,5158

ἐπίτροπος, epitropos.

Mat.20: 8. saith unto his *steward*,
Lu. 8: 3. wife of Chuza Herod's *steward*,
Gal. 4: 2. is under *tutors* and governors

2013 5 303/374 1909,5177

ἐπιτυγχάνω, epitunkano.

Ro. 11: 7. Israel *hath* not *obtained*
— but the election *hath obtained* it,
Heb. 6:15. he *obtained* the promise.
11:33. *obtained* promises, stopped the mouths
Jas. 4: 2. desire to have, and cannot *obtain*:

2014 4 304/374 9:1 1909,5316

ἐπιφαίνω, epiphaino.

Lu. 1:79. *To give light* to them that sit in
Acts27:20. nor stars in many days *appeared*,
Tit. 2:11. bringeth salvation *hath appeared*
3: 4. love of God our Saviour toward man *appeared*,

2015 6 304/374 9:1 2016

ἐπιφανεια, epiphania.

2Th. 2: 8. with the *brightness* of his coming.
1Ti. 6:14. until the *appearing* of our Lord Jesus Christ:
2Ti. 1:10. by the *appearing* of our Saviour Jesus Christ,
4: 1. at his *appearing* and his kingdom;
8. them also that love his *appearing*.
Tit. 2:13. the glorious *appearing* of the great God and our Saviour Jesus Christ;

2016 1 304/374 9:1 2014

ἐπιφανής, epiphanees.

Acts 2:20. that great and *notable* day of

2017 1 2017/374 9:310 2014

ἐπιφαύω, epiphauo.

Eph. 5:14. Christ *shall give* thee *light*.

2018 5 304/374 1909,5342

ἐπιφέρω, epiphero.

Acts19:12. So that from his body *were brought*
25:18. they *brought* none accusation
Ro. 3: 5. unrighteous *who taketh* vengeance?
Phi. 1:16. *to add* affliction to my bonds:
Jude 9. durst not *bring against* him

2019 3 304/374 1909,5455

ἐπιφωνέω, epiphōneo.

Lu. 23:21. But they *cried*, saying, Crucify
Acts12:22. the people *gave a shout*,
22:24. wherefore they *cried* so *against* him.

2020 2 304/374 9:310 2017

ἐπιφώσκω, epiphosko.

Mat.28: 1. *as* it *began to dawn* toward the first (day)
Lu. 23:54. and the sabbath *drew on*.

2021 3 304/374 1909,5495

ἐπιχειρέω, epikīreo.

Lu. 1: 1. many *have taken in hand*
Acts 9:29. they *went about* to slay him.
19:13. *took upon* them to call over them

2022 1 304/374 1909 *cheō* (to pour)

ἐπιχέω, epikeo.

Lu. 10:34. *pouring in* oil and wine,

2023 5 305/374 1909,5524

ἐπιχορηγέω, epikoreegeo.

2Co. 9.10. he *that ministereth* seed to the sower
Gal. 3: 5. He therefore *that ministereth* to you
Col. 2:19. *having nourishment ministered*, and
2Pet. 1: 5. *add* to your faith virtue;
11. *shall be ministered unto* you

2024 2 305/374 2023

ἐπιχορηγία, epikoreegia.

Eph. 4:16. by that which every joint supplieth, (lit. by the *supply* of every joint)
Phi. 1:19. the *supply* of the Spirit of Jesus Christ,

2025 2 305/374 1909,5548

ἐπιχρίω, epikrio.

Joh. 9: 6. he *anointed* the eyes of the blind man with the clay,
11. and *anointed* mine eyes, and said

2026 8 305/374 5:119 1909,3618

ἐποικοδομέω, epoikodomeo.

Acts20:32. *to build* you *up*, and to give you
1Co. 3:10. and another *buildeth thereon*.
— take heed how he *buildeth thereupon*.
12. Now if any man *build upon* this
14. abide which he *hath built thereupon*,
Eph. 2:20. *And are built upon* the foundation
Col. 2: 7. Rooted and *built up* in him,
Jude 20. *building up* yourselves *on* your

2027 1 305/368 1909 okello (to urge)

ἐποκέλλω, epokello.

Acts27:41. they *ran* the ship *aground*;

2028 1 305/374 5:242 1909,3687

ἐπονομάζομαι, eponomazomai.

Ro. 2:17. Behold, thou *art called* a Jew.

2030 1 305/374 5:315 1909,3700

ἐπόπτης, epoptees.

2Pet. 1:16. but were *eyewitnesses*

2029 2 305/374 5:315 1909,3700

ἐποπτεύω, epoptūo.

1Pet.2:12. by (your) good works, which they shall behold, (lit. *beholding*)
3: 2. *While* they *behold* your chaste

2031 1 305/374 2036

ἔπος, epos.

Heb. 7: 9. And as I may so say, (lit. to say the *word*)

2032 20 305/375 5:497 1909,3772

ἐπουράνιος, epouranios.

Mat.18:35. shall my *heavenly* Father do
Joh. 3:12. if I tell you (of) *heavenly* things?
1Co.15:40. (There are) also *celestial* bodies,
— but the glory of the *celestial* (is) one,
48. as (is) the *heavenly*, such (are) they also that are *heavenly*.
49. the image of the *heavenly*.
Eph. 1: 3. in *heavenly* (places) in Christ:
20. at his own right hand in the *heavenly* (places),
2: 6. in *heavenly* (places) in Christ Jesus:
3:10. powers in *heavenly* (places)
6:12. wickedness in *high* (places).
Phi. 2:10. of (things) *in heaven*, and (things) in earth,
2Ti. 4:18. unto his *heavenly* kingdom:
Heb. 3: 1. partakers of the *heavenly* calling,
6: 4. tasted of the *heavenly* gift,
8: 5. serve unto the example and shadow of *heavenly* things,
Heb 9:23. but the *heavenly* things themselves
11:16. a better (country), that is, an *heavenly*.
12:22. the *heavenly* Jerusalem.

2033 87 306/375 2:627

ἑπτά, hepta.

Mat.12:45. *seven* other spirits more wicked
15:34. *Seven*, and a few little fishes.
36. And he took the *seven* loaves
37. that was left *seven* baskets full.
16:10. Neither the *seven* loaves of
18:22. but, Until seventy times *seven*.
22:25. there were with us *seven* brethren:
26. unto the *seventh*.
28. whose wife shall she be of the *seven*?
Mar. 8: 5. loaves have ye? And they said, *Seven*.
6. and he took the *seven* loaves,
8. that was left *seven* baskets.
20. And when the *seven* among four
— And they said, *Seven*.
12:20. there were *seven* brethren:
22. And the *seven* had her, and left
23. for the *seven* had her to wife.
16: 9. out of whom he had cast *seven* devils.
Lu. 2:36. lived with an husband *seven* years
8: 2. out of whom went *seven* devils,
11:26. *seven* other spirits more wicked
20:29. There were therefore *seven* brethren:
31. in like manner the *seven* also:
33. for *seven* had her to wife.
Acts 6: 3. *seven* men of honest report,
13:19. destroyed *seven* nations in the land
19:14. there were *seven* sons of (one) Sceva,
20: 6. where we abode *seven* days.
21: 4. we tarried there *seven* days:
8. which was (one) of the *seven*;
27. And when the *seven* days were
28:14. to tarry with them *seven* days:
Heb 11:30. compassed about *seven* days.
Rev. 1: 4. John to the *seven* churches which
— and from the *seven* spirits
12. I saw *seven* golden candlesticks;
13. in the midst of the *seven* candlesticks
16. in his right hand *seven* stars:
20. The mystery of the *seven* stars
— *seven* golden candlesticks. The *seven* stars are the angels of the *seven* churches: and the *seven* candlesticks which thou sawest are the *seven* churches.
2: 1. he that holdeth the *seven* stars
— in the midst of the *seven* golden
3: 1. that hath the *seven* Spirits of God, and the *seven* stars;
4: 5. (there were) *seven* lamps of fire
— which are the *seven* Spirits
5: 1. sealed with *seven* seals.
5. to loose the *seven* seals thereof.
6. having *seven* horns and *seven* eyes, which are the *seven* Spirits
8: 2. I saw the *seven* angels
— to them were given *seven* trumpets.
6. the *seven* angels which had the *seven* trumpets
10: 3. *seven* thunders uttered their voices.
4. when the *seven* thunders had uttered
— which the *seven* thunders uttered,
11:13. were slain of men *seven* thousand:
12: 3. having *seven* heads and ten horns, and *seven* crowns

Rev.13: 1. having *seven* heads and ten horns,
15: 1. *seven* angels having the *seven* last plagues;
6. the *seven* angels came out of the temple, having the *seven* plagues,
7. gave unto the *seven* angels *seven* golden vials.
8. till the *seven* plagues of the *seven* angels were fulfilled.
16: 1. saying to the *seven* angels,
17: 1. one of the *seven* angels which had the *seven* vials,
3. having *seven* heads and ten horns.
7. which hath the *seven* heads
9. The *seven* heads are *seven* mountains, on which
10. there are *seven* kings: five are fallen,
11. and is of the *seven*, and goeth
21: 9. came unto me one of the *seven* angels which had the *seven* vials full of the *seven* last plagues,

---

2034 4 306/376 2:627 2033

ἑπτάκις, *heptakis.*

Mat.18:21. I forgive him? till *seven times?*
22. unto thee, Until *seven times:*
Lu. 17: 4. trespass against thee *seven times* in a day, and *seven times* in a day turn

---

2035 1 305/376 2:627 2034,5507

ἑπτακισχίλιοι, *heptakiskilioi.*

Ro. 11: 4. reserved to myself *seven thousand* men,

2036 976 225/288(2046,4483,5346) cf 3004

ἔπω, *epo.*

Mat. 2: 5. they *said* unto him, In Bethlehem
8. he sent them to Bethlehem, and *said,*
13. until I *bring* thee *word:*
3: 7. he *said* unto them, O generation of
15. *said* unto him, Suffer (it to be)
4: 3. when the tempter came to him, he *said,* If
— *command* that these stones be made
4. *said,* It is written, Man
5. 11. and shall *say* all manner of evil
22. whosoever shall *say* to his brother,
— but whosoever shall *say,* Thou fool,
8: 4. See thou *tell* no man;
8. but *speak* the word only,
10. and *said* to them that followed,
13. Jesus *said* unto the centurion,
19. and *said* unto him, Master,
21. another of his disciples *said*
22. Jesus *said* unto him, Follow me;
32. he *said* unto them, Go.
9: 2. *said* unto the sick of the palsy;
3. *said* within themselves,
4. *said,* Wherefore think ye evil
5. whether is easier, *to say,* (Thy) sins
— or *to say,* Arise, and walk?
11. they *said* unto his disciples,
12. heard (that), he *said* unto them,
15. Jesus *said* unto them,
22. and when he saw her, he *said,*
10:27. (that) *speak* ye in light:
11: 3. And *said* unto him, Art thou he
4. answered and *said* unto them, Go
25. and *said,* I thank thee, O Father,
12: 2. Pharisees saw (it), they *said* unto him,

Mat.12: 3. he *said* unto them, Have ye not read
11. And he *said* unto them, What man
24. when the Pharisees heard (it), they *said,*
25. and *said* unto them, Every kingdom
32. And whosoever *speaketh* a word
— but whosoever *speaketh* against the Holy Ghost,
39. But he answered and *said* unto them,
47. Then one *said* unto him, Behold, thy mother
48. But he answered and *said* unto him that *told* him,
49. and *said,* Behold my mother
13:10. and *said* unto him, Why speakest thou
11. He answered and *said* unto them,
27. and *said* unto him, Sir, didst not thou sow
28. The servants *said* unto him,
37. He answered and *said* unto them,
52. Then *said* he unto them, Therefore
57. *said* unto them, A prophet
14: 2. And *said* unto his servants,
16. *said* unto them, They need not
18. He *said,* Bring them hither to me.
28. And Peter answered him and *said,*
29. And he *said,* Come.
15: 3. he answered and *said* unto them,
5. Whosoever shall *say* to (his) father or (his) mother,
10. and *said* unto them, Hear,
12. and *said* unto him, Knowest thou that
13. But he answered and *said,*
15. answered Peter and *said* unto him,
16. Jesus *said,* Are ye also yet
24. and *said,* I am not sent
26. and *said,* It is not meet
27. And she *said,* Truth, Lord:
28. Jesus answered and *said* unto her,
32. and *said,* I have compassion
34. And they *said,* Seven,
16: 2. He answered and *said* unto them,
6. Then Jesus *said* unto them,
8. Jesus perceived, he *said* unto them,
11. that I *spake* (it) not to you concerning bread,
12. understood they how that he *bade* (them) not
14. they *said,* Some (say that thou art) John
16. And Simon Peter answered and *said,*
17. And Jesus answered and *said* unto him,
20. that they *should tell* no man
23. he turned, and *said* unto Peter,
24. Then *said* Jesus unto his disciples,
17: 4. and *said* unto Jesus, Lord
7. and *said,* Arise, and be not afraid.
9. *Tell* the vision to no man,
11. Jesus answered and *said* unto them,
13. he *spake* unto them of John
17. Then Jesus answered and *said,*
19. and *said,* Why could not we cast
20. And Jesus *said* unto them,
22. Jesus *said* unto them,
24. and *said,* Doth not your master
18: 3. And *said,* Verily I say unto you,
17. *tell* (it) unto the church:
21. and *said,* Lord, how oft
19: 4. he answered and *said* unto them,
5. And *said,* For this cause
11. But he *said* unto them,
14. But Jesus *said,* Suffer
16. one came and *said* unto him,
17. And he *said* unto him, Why
18. Jesus *said,* Thou shalt do no murder,

Mat.19:23. Then *said* Jesus unto his disciples,
26. But Jesus beheld (them), and *said* unto them,
27. answered Peter and *said* unto him,
28. And Jesus *said* unto them,
20: 4. And *said* unto them; Go
13. one of them, and *said*, Friend,
17. and *said* unto them,
21. he *said* unto her, What wilt thou?
— *Grant* that these my two sons may sit,
22. But Jesus answered and *said*,
25. and *said*, Ye know that the princes
32. and *said*, What will ye that
21: 3. if any (man) *say* ought unto you,
5. *Tell* ye the daughter of Sion,
16. And *said* unto him, Hearest thou
21. Jesus answered and *said* unto them,
— if ye shall *say* unto this mountain,
24. And Jesus answered and *said* unto them,
— which if ye *tell* me,
25. If we shall *say*, From heaven;
26. But if we shall *say*, Of men;
27. and *said*, We cannot tell.
28. he came to the first, and *said*, Son,
29. He answered and *said*, I will not:
30. to the second, and *said* likewise. And he answered and *said*,
38. they *said* among themselves,
22: 1. and *spake* unto them again by parables,
4. *Tell* them which are bidden,
13. Then *said* the king to the servants,
17. *Tell* us therefore, What thinkest thou?
18. and *said*, Why tempt ye me,
24. Moses *said*, If a man die,
29. Jesus answered and *said* unto them,
37. Jesus *said* unto him,
44. The Lord *said* unto my Lord,
23: 3. whatsoever they *bid* you observe,
39. till ye shall *say*, Blessed
24: 2. And Jesus *said* unto them,
3. *Tell* us, when shall these things be?
4. Jesus answered and *said* unto them,
23. if any man shall *say* unto you,
26. Wherefore if they shall *say* unto you,
48. But and if that evil servant shall *say*
25: 8. the foolish *said* unto the wise,
12. But he answered and *said*,
22. and *said*, Lord, thou deliveredst
24. and *said*, Lord, I knew thee
26. His lord answered and *said* unto him,
26: 1. he *said* unto his disciples,
10. understood (it), he *said* unto them,
15. *said* (unto them), What will ye give me,
18. And he *said*, Go into the city to such a man, and *say* unto him,
21. as they did eat, he *said*,
23. And he answered and *said*,
25. and *said*, Master, is it I? He said unto him, Thou *hast said*.
26. and *said*, Take, eat;
33. Peter answered and *said* unto him,
35. Likewise also *said* all the disciples.
44. *saying* the same words.
49. and *said*, Hail, master;
50. And Jesus *said* unto him,
55. *said* Jesus to the multitudes,
61. And *said*, This (fellow) said,
62. priest arose, and *said* unto him,
63. priest answered and *said* unto him,
— that thou *tell* us whether thou be
64. Thou *hast said*: nevertheless
66. They answered and *said*,

Mat.26:73. and *said* to Peter, Surely
27: 4. And they *said*, What (is that) to us?
6. took the silver pieces, and *said*,
17. Pilate *said* unto them, Whom will ye
21. The governor answered and *said* unto them,
— They *said*, Barabbas.
25. all the people, and *said*, His blood
43. for he *said*, I am the Son of God.
63. remember that that deceiver *said*,
64. him away, and *say* unto the people,
28: 5. and *said* unto the women,
6. for he is risen, as he *said*.
7. *tell* his disciples that he is risen
— lo, I *have told* you.
13. *Say* ye, His disciples came by night,
Mar 1:17. Jesus *said* unto them,
42. And *as soon as* he *had spoken*,
44. See thou *say* nothing to any
2: 8. he *said* unto them, Why reason ye
9. *to say* to the sick of the palsy,
— or *to say*, Arise, and take up
19. Jesus *said* unto them,
3: 9. And he *spake* to his disciples,
32. and they *said* unto him, Behold, thy mother
4:39. and *said* unto the sea, Peace,
40. *said* unto them, Why are ye so fearful?
5: 7. cried with a loud voice, and *said*,
33. and *told* him all the truth.
34. And he *said* unto her, Daughter,
43. *commanded* that something should be
6:16. Herod...*said*, It is John, whom
22. the king *said* unto the damsel,
24. and *said* unto her mother,
— And she *said*, The head of John
31. And he *said* unto them, Come
37. He answered and *said* unto them,
7: 6. He answered and *said* unto them,
10. For Moses *said*, Honour
11. If a man shall *say* to his father
27. But Jesus *said* unto her,
29. And he *said* unto her, For this saying
36. that they *should tell* no man:
8: 5. And they *said*, Seven.
7. *commanded* to set them also before (them)
20. And they *said*, Seven.
26. nor *tell* (it) to any in the town.
34. he *said* unto them, Whosoever will
9:12. he answered and *told* them,
17. and *said*, Master, I have brought
18. and I *spake* to thy disciples
21. And he *said*, Of a child.
23. Jesus *said* unto him,
29. And he *said* unto them, This
36. in his arms, he *said* unto them,
39. But Jesus *said*, Forbid him not:
10: 3. he answered and *said* unto them,
4. And they *said*, Moses
5. Jesus answered and *said* unto them,
14. and *said* unto them, Suffer
18. And Jesus *said* unto him,
20. he answered and *said* unto him,
21. *said* unto him, One thing thou lackest:
29. And Jesus answered and *said*,
36. And he *said* unto them, What would ye
37. They *said* unto him, Grant
38. But Jesus *said* unto them,
39. they *said* unto him, We can. And Jesus *said* unto them,
49. *commanded* him to be called
51. The blind man *said* unto him,
52. And Jesus *said* unto him,

Mar 11: 3. if any man *say* unto you, Why do ye this?
say ye that the Lord
6. And they *said* unto them
14. Jesus answered and *said* unto it,
23. whosoever shall *say* unto this mountain,
— he shall have whatsoever he *saith.*
29. Jesus answered and *said* unto them,
31. If we shall *say*, From heaven;
32. But if we shall *say*, Of men;
12: 7. *said* among themselves,
12. that he *had spoken* the parable
15. *said* unto them, Why tempt ye me?
16. And they *said* unto him, Cæsar's.
17. Jesus answering *said* unto them,
24. Jesus answering *said* unto them,
26. how in the bush God *spake* unto him,
32. the scribe *said* unto him, Well, Master,
thou *hast said* the truth:
34. discreetly, he *said* unto him,
36. For David himself *said*
— The Lord *said* to my Lord,
13: 2. Jesus answering *said* unto him,
4. *Tell* us, when shall these things be?
21. if any man shall *say* to you,
14: 6. And Jesus *said*, Let her alone;
14. *say* ye to the goodman of the house,
16. and found as he *had said* unto them:
18. Jesus *said*, Verily I say
20. he answered and *said* unto them,
22. gave to them, and *said*,
24. And he *said* unto them,
39. prayed, *and spake* the same words.
48. Jesus answered and *said* unto them,
62. And Jesus *said*, I am:
72. that Jesus *said* unto him,
15: 2. he answering *said* unto him,
12. *said* again unto them,
39. he *said*, Truly this man
16: 7. go your way, *tell* his disciples
— as he *said* unto you.
8. neither *said* they any thing to any
15. he *said* unto them, Go ye
Lu. 1: 13. But the angel *said* unto him,
18. Zacharias *said* unto the angel,
19. the angel answering *said* unto him,
28. the angel came in unto her, and *said*,
30. And the angel *said* unto her,
34. Then *said* Mary unto the angel,
35. the angel answered and *said* unto her
38. And Mary *said*, Behold
42. and *said*, Blessed (art) thou
46. And Mary *said*, My soul
60. his mother answered and *said*,
61. And they *said* unto her,
2: 10. And the angel *said* unto them,
15. the shepherds *said* one to another,
28. and blessed God, and *said*,
34. and *said* unto Mary
48. and his mother *said* unto him,
49. he *said* unto them, How is
3: 12. and *said* unto him,
13. And he *said* unto them,
14. And he *said* unto them,
4: 3. the devil *said* unto him,
— *command* this stone that it
6. the devil *said* unto him,
8. Jesus answered and *said* unto him,
9. and *said* unto him, If thou
12. Jesus answering *said* unto him,
23. And he *said* unto them,
24. And he *said*, Verily I say
43. And he *said* unto them,

Lu. 5: 4. he *said* unto Simon, Launch
5. Simon answering *said* unto him.
10. Jesus *said* unto Simon,
13. *saying*, I will: be thou clean.
14. charged him *to tell* no man:
20. their faith, he *said* unto him,
22. he answering *said* unto them,
23. Whether is easier, *to say*,
— or *to say*, Rise up
24. he *said* unto the sick of the palsy,
27. and he *said* unto him,
31. Jesus answering *said* unto them,
33. And they *said* unto him,
34. And he *said* unto them,
6: 2. of the Pharisees *said* unto them,
3. Jesus answering them *said*,
8. and *said* to the man
9. Then *said* Jesus unto them,
10. he *said* unto the man,
26. when all men shall *speak*
39. And he *spake* a parable unto them,
7: 7. but *say* in a word, and
9. and *said* unto the people that followed
13. and *said* unto her, Weep not.
14. And he *said*, Young man,
20. they *said*, John Baptist
22. Jesus answering *said* unto them,
31. And the Lord *said*,
39. he *spake* within himself, saying,
40. Jesus answering *said* unto him, Simon, I
have somewhat *to say* unto thee. And
he saith, Master, *say on.*
42. *Tell* me therefore, which of them
43. Simon answered and *said*,
— And he *said* unto him,
48. *said* unto her, Thy sins are forgiven.
50. And he *said* to the woman,
8: 4. he *spake* by a parable:
10. And he *said*, Unto you it is given
21. answered and *said* unto them,
22. and he *said* unto them,
25. And he *said* unto them, Where is your
faith?
28. with a loud voice *said*,
30. And he *said*, Legion:
45. And Jesus *said*, Who touched me?
— Peter and they that were with him *said*,
46. And Jesus *said*, Somebody hath
48. And he *said* unto her, Daughter,
52. but he *said*, Weep not;
56 that they should *tell* no man what was
done.
9: 3. And he *said* unto them,
9. And Herod *said*, John have I
12. the twelve, and *said* unto him,
13. But he *said* unto them,
— And they *said*, We have no more
14. And he *said* to his disciples,
19. They answering *said*,
20. He *said* unto them, But whom say ye that
I am? Peter answering *said*,
21. *to tell* no man that thing;
22. *Saying*, The Son of man must suffer
33. Peter *said* unto Jesus,
41. And Jesus answering *said*,
43. he *said* unto his disciples,
48. And *said* unto them, Whosoever
49. John answered and *said*,
50. And Jesus *said* unto him,
54. James and John saw (this), they *said*,
— Lord, wilt thou that we *command*
55. and *said*, Ye know not what

Lu. 9:57. a certain (man) *said* unto him,
58. And Jesus *said* unto him,
59. And he *said* unto another, Follow me. But he *said*, Lord,
60. Jesus *said* unto him,
61. And another also *said*,
62. And Jesus *said* unto him,
10:10. into the streets of the same, and *say*,
18. And he *said* unto them, I beheld
21. and *said*, I thank thee,
23. and *said* privately, Blessed
26. He *said* unto him,
27. And he answering *said*,
28. And he *said* unto him, Thou hast answered
29. willing to justify himself, *said*
30. Jesus answering *said*, A certain
35. and *said* unto him, Take care of him;
37. And he *said*, He that shewed mercy on him. Then *said* Jesus unto him,
40. and came to him, and *said*,
— *bid* her therefore that she help me.
41. And Jesus answered and *said* unto her,
11: 1. one of his disciples *said*
2. he *said* unto them, When ye pray,
5. And he *said* unto them,
— at midnight, and *say* unto him,
7. shall answer and *say*,
15. But some of them *said*,
17. *said* unto them, Every kingdom
27. and *said* unto him, Blessed
28. But he *said*, Yea rather, blessed
39. And the Lord *said* unto him,
46. And he *said*, Woe unto you also,
49. *said* the wisdom of God,
12: 3. whatsoever ye *have spoken* in darkness
11. or what ye shall *say*:
12. what ye ought *to say*.
13. And one of the company *said* unto him, Master, *speak* to my brother,
14. And he *said* unto him,
15. And he *said* unto them,
16. And he *spake* a parable
18. And he *said*, This will I do:
20. But God *said* unto him,
22. And he *said* unto his disciples,
41. Then Peter *said* unto him,
42. And the Lord *said*,
45. But and if that servant *say*
13: 2. Jesus answering *said* unto them,
7. Then *said* he unto the dresser of his vineyard,
12. and *said* unto her, Woman,
15. and *said*, (Thou) hypocrite,
20. And again he *said*, Whereunto
23. Then *said* one unto him, Lord,
— And he *said* unto them,
32. And he *said* unto them, Go ye, and *tell* that fox, Behold, I cast out
35. until (the time) come when ye shall *say*,
14: 3. *spake* unto the lawyers
5. answered them, saying, (lit. 'answering them *said*)
10. he *may say* unto thee, Friend,
15. he *said* unto him, Blessed
16. Then *said* he unto him,
17. *to say* to them that were bidden,
18. The first *said* unto him,
19. And another *said*, I have
20. another *said*, I have married a wife,
21. *said* to his servant,
22. And the servant *said*, Lord.

Lu. 14:23. the lord *said* unto the servant,
25. he turned, and *said* unto them,
15: 3. And he *spake* this parable
11. And he *said*, A certain man
12. And the younger of them *said* to (his) father,
17. he came to himself, he *said*,
21. And the son *said* unto him,
22. But the father *said* to his servants,
27. And he *said* unto him, Thy brother
29. *said* to (his) father, Lo,
31. And he *said* unto him, Son,
16: 2. he called him, and *said* unto him,
3. the steward *said* within himself,
6. And he *said*, An hundred measures of oil. And he *said* unto him, Take
7. Then *said* he to another,
— And he *said*, An hundred
15. And he *said* unto them, Ye
24. he cried and *said*, Father
25. But Abraham *said*, Son,
27. Then he *said*, I pray thee therefore,
30. And he *said*, Nay, father
31. And he *said* unto him, If they hear not Moses
17: 1. Then *said* he unto the disciples,
5. the apostles *said* unto the Lord,
6. And the Lord *said*, If ye had faith
14. when he saw (them), he *said* unto them,
17. And Jesus answering *said*,
19. he *said* unto him, Arise,
20. he answered them and *said*,
22. And he *said* unto the disciples,
37. he *said* unto them, Wheresoever
18: 4. he *said* within himself,
6. And the Lord *said*, Hear
9. And he *spake* this parable
16. and *said*, Suffer little children
19. And Jesus *said* unto him,
21. he *said*, All these have I kept
22. heard these things, he *said* unto him,
24. he *said*, How hardly
26. And they that heard (it) *said*,
27. he *said*, The things which are impossible
28. Then Peter *said*, Lo,
29. And he *said* unto them, Verily
31. and *said* unto them, Behold,
41. And he *said*, Lord, that I may receive
42. And Jesus *said* unto him,
19: 5. and *said* unto him,
8. and *said* unto the Lord;
9. and Jesus *said* unto him,
11. he added and *spake* a parable,
12. He *said* therefore, A certain
13. and *said* unto them,
15. he *commanded* these servants to be
17. And he *said* unto him, Well,
19. And he *said* likewise to him,
24. he *said* unto them that stood by,
25. And they *said* unto him, Lord,
28. And *when* he *had* thus *spoken*,
30. *Saying*, Go ye into the village
32. even as he *had said* unto them.
33. the owners thereof *said*
34. And they *said*, The Lord
39. *said* unto him, Master,
40. he answered and *said* unto them,
20: 2. *spake* unto him, saying, *Tell* us, by what authority
3. and *said* unto them,
— and *answer* me:
5. If we shall *say*, From heaven,

Lu. 20: 6. But and if we *say*, Of men;
8. And Jesus *said* unto them,
13. Then *said* the lord of the vineyard,
16. when they heard (it), they *said*,
17. he beheld them, and *said*,
19. that he *had spoken* this parable
23. and *said* unto them,
24. They answered and *said*, Cæsar's.
25. And he *said* unto them,
34. Jesus answering *said* unto them,
39. certain of the scribes answering *said*, Master, thou *hast* well *said*.
41. And he *said* unto them,
42. The Lord *said* unto my Lord,
45. he *said* unto his disciples,
21: 3. And he *said*, Of a truth
5. goodly stones and gifts, he *said*,
8. And he *said*, Take heed
29. And he *spake* to them a parable;
22: 8. *saying*. Go and prepare
9. And they *said* unto him,
10. And he *said* unto them,
15. And he *said* unto them,
17. gave thanks, and *said*,
25. And he *said* unto them,
31. And the Lord *said*, Simon,
33. And he *said* unto him,
34. And he *said*, I tell thee,
35. And he *said* unto them,
— And they *said*, Nothing.
36. Then *said* he unto them
38. And they *said*, Lord,
— And he *said* unto them,
40. he *said* unto them, Pray
46. And *said* unto them, Why sleep ye?
48. But Jesus *said* unto him,
49. they *said* unto him, Lord,
51. And Jesus answered and *said*,
52. Then Jesus *said* unto
56. looked upon him, and *said*,
58. And Peter *said*, Man, I am not.
60. And Peter *said*, Man, I know not
61. how he *had said* unto him, Before
67(66 & 67). *tell* us. And he *said* unto them, If I *tell* you,
70. Then *said* they all,
71. And they *said*, What need we
23: 4. *said* Pilate to the chief priests
14. *Said* unto them, Ye have
22. he *said* unto them the third time,
28. *said*, Daughters of Jerusalem,
43. And Jesus *said* unto him,
46. had cried with a loud voice, he *said*,
— *having said* thus, he gave up the ghost.
24: 5. they *said* unto them,
17. And he *said* unto them,
18. Cleopas, answering *said* unto him,
19. And he *said* unto them, What things? And they *said* unto him,
24. even so as the women *had said*.
25. Then he *said* unto them,
32. they *said* one to another,
38. And he *said* unto them, Why
40. *when* he *had* thus *spoken*, he shewed
41. and wondered, he *said* unto them,
44. he *said* unto them, These (are) the words
46. And *said* unto them,

Joh. 1: 15. This was he *of* whom I *spake*,
22. Then *said* they unto him, Who art thou?
23. as *said* the prophet Esaias.
25. and *said* unto him, Why baptizest
30. he of whom I *said*,
33. the same *said* unto me,
38(39). They *said* unto him, Rabbi,
42(43). And when Jesus beheld him, he *said*,
46(47). And Nathanael *said* unto him,
48(49). Jesus answered and *said* unto him,
50(51). Jesus answered and *said* unto him, Because I *said* unto thee, I saw thee
2: 16. *said* unto them that sold doves,
18. Then answered the Jews and *said* unto
19. Jesus answered and *said* unto them,
20. Then *said* the Jews,
22. the word which Jesus *had said*,
3: 2. and *said* unto him, Rabbi,
3. Jesus answered and *said* unto him,
7. that I *said* unto thee, Ye must
9. Nicodemus answered and *said* unto him,
10. Jesus answered and *said* unto him,
12. If I *have told* you earthly things,
— if I *tell* you (of) heavenly things?
26. and *said* unto him, Rabbi,
27. John answered and *said*,
28. bear me witness, that I *said*,
4: 10. Jesus answered and *said* unto her,
13. Jesus answered and *said* unto her,
17. The woman answered and *said*,
— Thou *hast* well *said* I have no
27. yet no man *said*, What seekest thou?
29. a man, which *told* me all things
32. But he *said* unto them, I
39. He *told* me all that ever I did.
48. Then *said* Jesus unto him,
50. the word that Jesus *had spoken* unto him,
52. And they *said* unto him, Yesterday
53. in the which Jesus *said* unto him,
5: 11. the same *said* unto me,
12. What man is that *which said* unto thee,
14. and *said* unto him, Behold,
19. and *said* unto them, Verily, verily,
6: 10. And Jesus *said*, Make the men
25. they *said* unto him, Rabbi,
26. and *said*, Verily, verily,
28. Then *said* they unto him,
29. and *said* unto them, This is
30. They *said* therefore unto him, What
32. Then Jesus *said* unto them,
34. Then *said* they unto him,
35. And Jesus *said* unto them,
36. But I *said* unto you, That
41. because he *said*, I am
43. *said* unto them, Murmur not
53. Then Jesus *said* unto them,
59. These things *said* he in the synagogue,
60. disciples, when they had heard (this), *said*,
61. he *said* unto them, Doth this offend
67. Then *said* Jesus unto the twelve,
7: 3. His brethren therefore *said* unto him,
9. *When* he *had said* these words unto them,
16. Jesus answered them, and *said*, My
20. and *said*, Thou hast a devil:
21. and *said* unto them, I have done
33. Then *said* Jesus unto them,
35. Then *said* the Jews among themselves,
36. What (manner of) saying is this that he *said*,
38. as the scripture *hath said*,
39. But this *spake* he of the Spirit,
42. Hath not the scripture *said*,
45. and they *said* unto them,
52. and *said* unto him, Art thou also
8: 7. he lifted up himself, and *said*
10. he *said* unto her, Woman,
11. She *said*, No man, Lord. And Jesus *said* unto her,
13. The Pharisees therefore *said* unto him,

Joh. 8:14. and *said* unto them, Though I bear
21. Then *said* Jesus again unto them,
23. And he *said* unto them, Ye
24. I *said* therefore unto you, that
25. And Jesus *saith* unto them,
28. Then *said* Jesus unto them,
39. They answered and *said* unto him,
41. Then *said* they to him, We
42. Jesus *said* unto them,
48. *said* unto him, Say we not well
52. Then *said* the Jews unto him,
55. and if I *should say*, I know him not,
57. Then *said* the Jews unto him,
58. Jesus *said* unto them,
9: 6. *When* he *had* thus *spoken*, he spat
7. And *said* unto him, Go,
11. He answered and *said*,
— and *said* unto me, Go
12. Then *said* they unto him, Where is he?
15. He *said* unto them, He put clay
17. He *said*, He is a prophet.
20. His parents answered them and *said*,
22. These (words) *spake* his parents,
23. Therefore *said* his parents,
24. blind, and *said* unto him,
25. and *said*, Whether he be a sinner
26. Then *said* they to him again,
27. I *have told* you already,
28. Then they reviled him, and *said*,
30. The man answered and *said* unto
34. They answered and *said* unto him,
35. found him, he *said* unto him,
36. He answered and *said*,
37. And Jesus *said* unto him,
39. And Jesus *said*, For judgment
40. heard these words, and *said* unto him,
41. Jesus *said* unto them,
10: 6. *spake* Jesus unto them:
7. Then *said* Jesus unto them again,
24. be the Christ, *tell* us plainly.
25. I *told* you, and ye believed not:
26. as I *said* unto you.
34. I *said*, Ye are gods?
35. If he *called* them gods,
36. because I *said*, I am the Son of God?
41. all things that John *spake*
11: 4. When Jesus heard (that), he *said*,
11. These things *said* he: and after
12. Then *said* his disciples,
14. *said* Jesus unto them plainly,
16. Then *said* Thomas, which is called
21. Then *said* Martha unto Jesus,
25. Jesus *said* unto her,
28. And *when* she *had* so *said*,
— *saying*, The Master is come,
34. And *said*, Where have ye laid him?
37. And some of them *said*,
40. *Said* I not unto thee, that, if
41. and *said*, Father, I thank thee
42. because of the people...I *said*
43. And *when* he thus *had spoken*,
46. and *told* them what things Jesus
49. *said* unto them, Ye know nothing
51. this *spake* he not of himself:
12: 6. This he *said*, not that he cared
7. Then *said* Jesus, Let her alone:
19. therefore *said* among themselves,
27. and what shall I *say*? Father,
30. and *said*, This voice came not because of
35. Then Jesus *said* unto them,
38. which he *spake*, Lord, who hath
39. because that Esaias *said* again,

Joh. 12:41. These things *said* Esaias,
44. Jesus cried and *said*,
49. what I *should say*, and what I should
13: 7. Jesus answered and *said* unto him,
11. therefore *said* he,
12. again, he *said* unto them,
21. *When* Jesus *had* thus *said*,
— and testified, and *said*,
28. for what intent he *spake* this
33. as I *said* unto the Jews,
14: 2. I would *have told* you.
23. Jesus answered and *said* unto him,
26. whatsoever I *have said*
28. how I *said* unto you,
— ye would rejoice, because I *said*,
15:20. the word that I *said* unto you,
16: 4. that I *told* you of them.
— I *said* not unto you at the beginning,
15. therefore *said* I, that he shall
17. Then *said* (some) of his disciples
19. and *said* unto them,
— of that I *said*, A little while,
17: 1. to heaven, and *said*,
18: 1. *When* Jesus *had spoken* these words,
4. went forth, and *said* unto them,
6. As soon then as he *had said*
7. they *said*, Jesus of Nazareth.
8. I *have told* you that I am (he):
9. saying might be fulfilled, which he *spake*
11. Then *said* Jesus unto Peter,
16. and *spake* unto her that kept the door,
21. they know what I *said*.
22. And *when* he *had* thus *spoken*,
— with the palm of his hand, *saying*,
25. They *said* therefore unto him, Art not
— He denied (it), and *said*,
29. and *said*, What accusation
30. They answered and *said* unto him,
31. Then *said* Pilate unto them,
— The Jews therefore *said* unto him,
32. which he *spake*, signifying
33. called Jesus, and *said* unto him,
34. or did others *tell* it thee of me?
37. Pilate therefore *said* unto him,
38. And *when* he *had said* this, he went
19:21. but that he *said*,
24. They *said* therefore among themselves,
30. he *said*, It is finished:
20:14. And *when* she *had* thus *said*,
15. *tell* me where thou hast laid him,
17. and *say* unto them,
18. and (that) he *had spoken* these
20. And *when* he *had* so *said*, he shewed
21. Then *said* Jesus to them
22. *when* he *had said* this, he breathed
25. But he *said* unto them,
26. and *said*, Peace (be) unto you.
28. and *said* unto him, My Lord
21: 6. And he *said* unto them, Cast
17. because he *said* unto him the third time,
— And he *said* unto him, Lord,
19. This *spake* he, signifying
— And *when* he *had spoken* this, he saith
20. and *said*, Lord, which is he
23. yet Jesus *said* not unto him,
Acts 1: 7. And he *said* unto them,
9. And *when* he *had spoken* these things,
11. Which also *said*, Ye men of Galilee,
15. midst of the disciples, and *said*,
24. they prayed, and *said*,
2:29. let me freely *speak* unto you
34. The Lord *said* unto my Lord,

Acts 2:37. and *said* unto Peter
3: 4. *said*, Look on us.
6. Then Peter *said*, Silver and gold
22. *said* unto the fathers,
4: 8. filled with the Holy Ghost, *said* unto
19. and *said* unto them,
23. and elders *had said* unto them.
24. and *said*, Lord, thou (art) God,
25. *Who* by the mouth of thy servant David *hast said*,
5: 3. But Peter *said*, Ananias,
8. *Tell* me whether ye sold the land for so much? And she *said*, Yea, for so much.
9. Peter *said* unto her,
19. and brought them forth, and *said*,
29. apostles answered and *said*,
35. And *said* unto them,
6: 2. and *said*, It is not reason
7: 1. Then *said* the high priest,
3. And *said* unto him,
7. will I judge, *said* God:
26. *saying*, Sirs, ye are brethren;
27. thrust him away, *saying*,
33. Then *said* the Lord to him,
35. whom they refused, *saying*,
37. *which said* unto the children of Israel,
40. *Saying* unto Aaron,
56. And *said*, Behold, I see
60. *when* he *had said* this, he fell asleep.
8:20. But Peter *said* unto him,
24. Then answered Simon, and *said*,
29. Then the Spirit *said* unto Philip,
30. and *said*, Understandest thou
31. And he *said*, How can I,
34. and *said*, I pray thee,
37. And Philip *said*, If thou
— And he answered and *said*,
9: 5. And he *said*, Who art thou, Lord? the Lord *said*,
6. and astonished *said*,
10. and to him *said* the Lord
— he *said*, Behold, I (am here), Lord.
15. But the Lord *said* unto him,
17. *said*, Brother Saul, the Lord,
34. And Peter *said* unto him,
40. to the body *said*, Tabitha, arise.
10: 3. and *saying* unto him, Cornelius.
4. he was afraid, and *said*,
— And he *said* unto him, Thy prayers
14. But Peter *said*, Not so,
19. the Spirit *said* unto him,
21. and *said*, Behold, I am he whom
22. And they *said*, Cornelius
34. and *said*, Of a truth I perceive
11: 8. But I *said*, Not so, Lord:
12. And the spirit *bade* me go
13. which stood and *said* unto him,
12: 8. And the angel *said* unto him,
11. was come to himself, he *said*,
15. they *said* unto her, Thou art mad.
17. And he *said*, Go shew
13: 2. the Holy Ghost *said*,
10. And *said*, O full of all subtilty
16. beckoning with (his) hand *said*, Men
22. he gave testimony, and *said*,
46. and *said*, It was necessary
14:10. *Said* with a loud voice,
15: 7. Peter rose up, and *said* unto them,
36. Paul *said* unto Barnabas,
16:18. and *said* to the spirit,
20. brought them to the magistrates, saying, (lit. having brought them...*said*)

Acts16:31. And they *said*, Believe
17:32. some mocked: and others *said*,
18: 6. and *said* unto them, Your blood
9. Then *spake* the Lord to Paul
14. Gallio *said* unto the Jews,
21. bade them farewell, *saying*,
19: 2. He *said* unto them, Have ye received
— And they *said* unto him,
3. And he *said* unto them
— And they *said*, Unto John's baptism.
4. Then *said* Paul, John verily
15. the evil spirit answered and *said*,
21. *saying*, After I have been there,
25. and *said*, Sirs, ye know
41. *when* he *had* thus *spoken*, he dismissed
20:10. *said*, Trouble not yourselves;
18. he *said* unto them, Ye know,
35. he *said*, It is more blessed to give
36. *when* he *had* thus *spoken*, he kneeled
21:11. and *said*, Thus saith the Holy Ghost,
14. *saying*, The will of the Lord
20. and *said* unto him, Thou seest,
37. May I *speak* unto thee?
39. But Paul *said*, I am a man
22: 8. And he *said* unto me, I am Jesus
10. And I *said*, What shall I do, Lord? And the Lord *said* unto me,
13. and stood, and *said* unto me,
14. he *said*, The God of our fathers
19. And I *said*, Lord,
21. And he *said* unto me,
24. *and bade* that he should be examined
25. Paul *said* unto the centurion
27. captain came, and *said* unto him,
23: 1. beholding the council, *said*,
3. Then *said* Paul unto him,
4. they that stood by *said*,
11. and *said*, Be of good cheer, Paul:
14. and *said*, We have bound ourselves
20. And he *said*, The Jews
23. called unto (him) two centurions, saying, (lit. he having called...*said*)
24:20. *let* these same (here) *say*, if they have found any
22. *and said*, When Lysias
25: 9. answered Paul, and *said*,
10. Then *said* Paul, I stand
26:15. And I *said*, Who art thou, Lord? And he *said*,
29. And Paul *said*, I would to God,
30. And *when* he *had* thus *spoken*,
27:21. in the midst of them, and *said*,
31. Paul *said* to the centurion
35. And *when* he *had* thus *spoken*,
28:21. And they *said* unto him,
25. *after that* Paul *had spoken* one word,
26. and *say*, Hearing ye shall hear,
29. And *when* he *had said* these words,
Ro. 10: 6. *Say* not in thine heart,
1 Co. 1:15. Lest any *should say* that
10:28. But if any man *say* unto you,
11:22. What shall I *say* to you?
24. he brake (it), and *said*,
12: 3. no man can *say* that Jesus is the Lord,
15. If the foot shall *say*,
16. And if the ear shall *say*,
21. the eye cannot *say* unto the hand,
15:27. But when he *saith*, All things
2Co. 4: 6. For God, *who commanded* the light to shine
6:16. as God *hath said*, I will dwell in them,
Gal. 2:14. I *said* unto Peter before (them) all,

Col 4:17. And *say* to Archippus, Take heed to
Tit. 1:12. a prophet of their own, *said*,
Heb. 1: 5. For unto which of the angels *said* he
3:10. that generation, and *said*, They do alway
7: 9. And as I may so *say*,
10: 7. Then *said* I, Lo, I come
30. For we know him *that hath said*,
12:21. Moses *said*, I exceedingly fear
Jas. 2: 3. and *say* unto him, Sit thou here
— and *say* to the poor,
11. For he *that said*, Do not commit adultery, *said* also, Do not kill.
16. And one of you *say* unto them,
1Joh. 1: 6. If we *say* that we have fellowship
8 If we *say* that we have no sin,
10. If we *say* that we have not sinned,
4:20. If a man *say*, I love God,
Jude 9. but *said*, The Lord rebuke thee.
Rev. 7:14. And he *said* to me, These are they
17: 7. And the angel *said* unto me,
21: 5. he that sat upon the throne *said*,
6. And he *said* unto me, It is done.
22: 6. And he *said* unto me, These sayings
17. And *let* him that heareth *say*,

2038 39 306/376 2:635 2041

ἐργάζομαι, *ergazomai.*

Mat. 7:23. ye *that work* iniquity.
21:28. go *work* to day in my vineyard.
25:16. went and *traded* (lit. *worked for himself gain*) with the same,
26:10. for she *hath wrought* a good work
Mar 14: 6. she *hath wrought* a good work on me.
Lu. 13:14. in which men ought *to work:*
Joh. 3:21. that they are *wrought* in God.
5:17. answered them, My Father *worketh* hitherto, and I *work*.
6:27. *Labour* not *for* the meat
28. that we *might work* the works
30. what *dost* thou *work?*
9: 4. I must *work* the works
— when no man can *work*.
Acts 10:35. and *worketh* righteousness,
13:41. I *work* a work in your days,
18: 3. he abode with them, and *wrought:*
Ro. 2:10. to every man *that worketh* good,
4: 4. Now to him *that worketh* is the reward
5. But to him *that worketh* not,
13:10. Love *worketh* no ill to his neighbour:
1Cor. 4:12. *working* with our own hands:
9: 6. power to forbear working? (lit. not *to work*)
13. they *which minister about* holy things
16:10. he *worketh* the work of the Lord,
Gal. 6:10. *let* us *do* good unto all
Eph. 4:28. *working* with (his) hands the thing which
Col. 3:23. *do* (it) heartily,
1Th. 2: 9. *labouring* night and day, because we would not be chargeable
4:11. and *to work* with your own hands,
2Th. 3: 8. but *wrought* (lit. *working*) with labour
10. if any would not *work*,
11. *working* not at all,
12. that with quietness they *work*, *and* eat their
Heb 11:33. *wrought* righteousness, obtained promises,
Jas. 2: 9. ye *commit* sin, and are convinced
2Joh. 8. those things which we *have wrought*, (lit. *have gained*)
3Joh. 5. whatsoever thou *doest* to the brethren,
Rev. 18:17. as many as *trade by* (lit. *work for themselves gain by*) sea,

2039 6 307/376 2:635 2040

ἐργασία, *ergasia.*

Lu. 12:58. in the way, give *diligence*
Acts 16:16. brought her masters much *gain*
19. the hope of their *gains*
19:24. brought no small *gain*
25. by this *craft* we have our wealth.
Eph. 4:19. to work (lit. to the *working* of) all uncleanness

2040 16 307/377 2:635 2041

ἐργάτης, *ergatees.*

Mat. 9:37. but the *labourers* (are) few;
38. that he will send forth *labourers*
10:10. for the *workman* is worthy
20: 1. to hire *labourers* into his vineyard.
2. agreed with the *labourers* for a penny
8. Call the *labourers*, and give them
Lu. 10: 2. but the *labourers* (are) few:
— that he would send forth *labourers*
7. for the *labourer* is worthy of
13:27. (ye) *workers* of iniquity.
Acts 19:25. the *workmen* of like occupation,
2Co. 11:13. false apostles, deceitful *workers*,
Phi. 3: 2. beware of evil *workers*,
1Ti. 5:18. The *labourer* (is) worthy of his reward
2Ti. 2:15. a *workman* that needeth not to be
Jas. 5: 4. the hire of the *labourers*

2041 176 307/377 2:635 *ergo* (to work)

ἔργον, *ergon.*

Mat. 5:16. they may see your good *works*,
11: 2. heard in the prison the *works* of Christ,
23: 3. but do not ye after their *works:*
5. But all their *works* they do
26:10. for she hath wrought a good *work*
Mar 13:34. to every man his *work*,
14: 6. she hath wrought a good *work* on me.
Lu. 11:48. the *deeds* of your fathers:
24:19. mighty in *deed* and word
Joh. 3:19. their *deeds* were evil.
20. lest his *deeds* should be reproved.
21. his *deeds* may be made manifest,
4:34. and to finish his *work*.
5:20. shew him greater *works* than these,
36. for the *works* which the Father
— the same *works* that I do,
6:28. that we might work the *works* of God?
29. This is the *work* of God,
7: 3. the *works* that thou doest.
7. the *works* thereof are evil.
21. I have done one *work*,
8:39. the *works* of Abraham.
41. the *deeds* of your father.
9: 3. the *works* of God should be made manifest in him.
4. work the *works* of him that
10:25. the *works* that I do
32. Many good *works* have I shewed you from my Father; for which of those *works*
33. For a good *work* we stone thee not;
37. If I do not the *works* of my Father,
38. believe not me, believe the *works:*
14:10. dwelleth in me, he doeth the *works*.
11. believe me for the very *works'* sake.
12. the *works* that I do
15:24. If I had not done among them the *works*
17: 4. I have finished the *work*
Acts 5:38. this *work* be of men, it will come to nought:
7:22. mighty in words and in *deeds*.

Acts 7:41. in the *works* of their own hands.
9:36. this woman was full of good *works*
13: 2. for the *work* whereunto I have called
41. I work a *work* in your days, a *work* which ye shall in no wise believe,
14:26. for the *work* which they fulfilled.
15:18. Known unto God are all his *works*
38. and went not with them to the *work*.
26:20. *works* meet for repentance.
Ro 2: 6. to every man according to his *deeds*:
7. patient continuance in well *doing*
15. shew the *work* of the law
3:20. by the *deeds* of the law there shall no flesh be justified
27. By what law? of *works*?
28. without the *deeds* of the law.
4: 2. were justified by *works*,
6. righteousness without *works*,
9:11. not of *works*, but of him that calleth;
32. but as it were by the *works* of the law.
11: 6. then (is it) no more of *works*:
— But if (it be) of *works*, then is it no more grace: otherwise *work* is no more *work*.
13: 3. a terror to good *works*,
12. the *works* of darkness,
14:20. destroy not the *work* of God.
15:18. by word and *deed*,
1Co. 3:13. Every man's *work* shall be made manifest:
— every man's *work* of what sort it is.
14. If any man's *work* abide
15. If any man's *work* shall be burned,
5: 2. he that hath done this *deed*
9: 1. are not ye my *work*
15:58. abounding in the *work* of the Lord,
16:10. for he worketh the *work* of the Lord,
2Co. 9: 8. to every good *work*:
10:11. in *deed* when we are present.
11:15. according to their *works*.
Gal. 2:16. by the *works* of the law, but
— not by the *works* of the law: for by the *works* of the law shall no flesh
3: 2. the Spirit by the *works* of the law,
5. by the *works* of the law, or by the hearing
10. For as many as are of the *works* of the law
5:19. the *works* of the flesh
6: 4. But let every man prove his own *work*,
Eph. 2: 9. Not of *works*, lest any man should boast.
10. created in Christ Jesus unto good *works*,
4:12. for the *work* of the ministry,
5:11. with the unfruitful *works*
Phi. 1: 6. he which hath begun a good *work* in you
22. the fruit of my *labour*:
2:30. for the *work* of Christ
Col. 1:10. in every good *work*,
21. enemies in (your) mind by wicked *works*,
3:17. do in word or *deed*,
1Th. 1: 3. your *work* of faith,
5:13. for their *work's* sake.
2Th. 1:11. the *work* of faith with power:
2:17. good word and *work*.
1Ti. 2:10. with good *works*.
3: 1. he desireth a good *work*.
5:10. Well reported of for good *works*;
— diligently followed every good *work*.
25. also the good *works* (of some) are manifest beforehand;
6:18. that they be rich in good *works*,
2Ti. 1: 9. not according to our *works*,
2:21. prepared unto every good *work*
3:17. throughly furnished unto all good *works*.
2Ti. 4: 5. do the *work* of an evangelist,
14. according to his *works*:
18. from every evil *work*,
Tit. 1:16. but in *works* they deny (him),
— unto every good *work* reprobate.
2: 7. a pattern of good *works*:
14. zealous of good *works*.
3: 1. to be ready to every good *work*,
5. Not by *works* of righteousness
8. to maintain good *works*.
14. to maintain good *works*
Heb. 1:10. the *works* of thine hands:
2: 7. over the *works* of thy hands:
3: 9. and saw my *works* forty years.
4: 3. although the *works* were finished from the foundation of the world.
4. rest the seventh day from all his *works*.
10. hath ceased from his own *works*,
6: 1. of repentance from dead *works*,
10. your *work* and labour of love,
9:14. purge your conscience from dead *works*
10:24. to provoke unto love and to good *works*:
13:21. Make you perfect in every good *work*
Jas. 1: 4. let patience have (her) perfect *work*,
25. but a doer of the *work*,
2:14. say he hath faith, and have not *works*?
17. faith, if it hath not *works*, is dead,
18. and I have *works*: shew me thy faith without thy *works*, and I will shew thee my faith by my *works*.
20. faith without *works* is dead?
21. Was not Abraham our father justified by *works*,
22. faith wrought with his *works*, and by *works* was faith made perfect?
24. that by *works* a man is justified, and not by faith only.
25. was not Rahab the harlot justified by *works*,
26. so faith without *works* is dead also.
3:13. his *works* with meekness of wisdom.
1Pet. 1:17. according to every man's *work*,
2:12. by (your) good *works*, which they shall behold,
2Pet. 2: 8. with (their) unlawful *deeds*;
3:10. and the *works* that are therein
1Joh. 3: 8. might destroy the *works* of the devil.
12. his own *works* were evil,
18. but in *deed* and in truth.
2Joh. 11. is partaker of his evil *deeds*.
3Joh. 10. his *deeds* which he doeth,
Jude 15. of all their ungodly *deeds*
Rev. 2: 2. I know thy *works*, and thy labour,
5. repent, and do the first *works*;
6. the *deeds* of the Nicolaitanes,
9. I know thy *works*, and tribulation,
13. I know thy *works*, and where
19. I know thy *works*, and charity,
— thy patience, and thy *works*;
22. they repent of their *deeds*.
23. unto every one of you according to your *works*.
26. keepeth my *works* unto the end,
3: 1. I know thy *works*, that thou hast
2. for I have not found thy *works*
8. I know thy *works*: behold, I
15. I know thy *works*, that thou art
9:20. repented not of the *works* of their hands.
14:13. and their *works* do follow them.
15: 3. and marvellous (are) thy *works*,
16:11. repented not of their *deeds*.
18: 6. double according to her *works*.

Rev 20:12. according to their *works*.
13. according to their *works*.
22:12. according as his *work* shall be.

2042 2 308/379 2054

ἐρεθίζω, *erethizo.*

2Co. 9: 2. zeal *hath provoked* very many.
Col. 3:21. *provoke* not your children (*to anger*),

2043 1 308/379

ἐρείδω, *erīdo.*

Acts27:41. the forepart *stuck fast, and* remained

2044 1 308/379

ἐρεύγομαι, *erūgomai.*

Mat.13:35. I *will utter* things which have been kept secret

2045 6 308/376 2:655 2046

ἐρευνάω, *erūnao.*

Joh. 5:39. *Search* the scriptures; for in them
7:52. *Search*, and look: for out of Galilee
Ro. 8:27. And he *that searcheth* the hearts
1Co. 2:10. the Spirit *searcheth* all things,
1Pet. 1:11. *Searching* what, or what manner
Rev. 2:23. I am he *which searcheth* the reins

2046 71 /387 4483 (2036)

ἐρέω, *ereo.*

Mat. 7: 4. Or how *wilt* thou *say* to thy brother,
22. Many *will say* to me
13:30. I *will say* to the reapers,
17:20. ye *shall say* unto this mountain,
21: 3. ye *shall say*, The Lord hath need of them;
24. I in like wise *will tell* you by what
25. he *will say* unto us, Why
25:34. Then *shall* the King *say* unto them
40. the King shall answer and *say* unto them,
41. Then *shall* he *say* also unto them on the
26:75. of Jesus, *which said* unto him,
Mar 11:29. and I *will tell* you by what authority
31. he *will say*, Why then did ye not
Lu. 2:24. according to that *which is said* in the
4:12. It *is said*, Thou shalt not tempt
23. Ye *will* surely *say* unto me this proverb,
12:10. whosoever *shall speak* a word
19. And I *will say* to my soul,
13:25. he shall answer and *say* unto you,
27. he *shall say*, I tell you, I know you not.
14: 9. come and *say* to thee, Give this man place;
15:18. and *will say* unto him, Father,
17: 7. *will say* unto him by and by, when he is
8. And *will* not rather *say* unto him,
21. Neither *shall* they *say*, Lo here!
23. And they *shall say* to you, See
19:31. thus *shall* ye *say* unto him,
20: 5. he *will say*, Why then believed ye him not?
22:11. And ye *shall say* unto the goodman of
13. and found as he *had said* unto them:
23:29. in the which they *shall say*, Blessed
Joh. 4:18. in that *saidst* thou truly.
6:65. Therefore *said* I unto you,
11:13. Howbeit Jesus *spake* of his death:
12:50. even as the Father *said* unto me,
14:29. I *have told* you before it come to pass,
15:15. but I *have called* you friends;
Acts 2:16. this is that *which was spoken*
8:24. of these things which ye *have spoken*
13:34. he *said* on this wise, I will give
40. *which is spoken of* in the prophets.
17:28. certain also of your own poets *have said*,
20:38. for the words which he *spake*,
23: 5. Thou *shalt* not *speak* evil *of* the ruler
Ro. 3: 5. righteousness of God, what *shall* we *say*?
4: 1. What *shall* we then *say* that Abraham,
18. according to that *which was spoken*,
6: 1. What *shall* we *say* then? Shall we continue
7: 7. What *shall* we *say* then? (Is) the law sin?
8:31. What *shall* we then *say* to these things?
9:14. What *shall* we *say* then? (Is there)
19. Thou *wilt say* then unto me, Why doth he
20. *Shall* the thing formed *say* to him that
30. What *shall* we *say* then? That the Gentiles,
11:19. Thou *wilt say* then, The branches were
1Co.14:16. how *shall* he that occupieth the room of the unlearned *say* Amen
23. *will* they not *say* that ye are mad?
15:35. But some (man) *will say*, How
2Co.12: 6. for I *will say* the truth:
9. And he *said* unto me, My grace is
Phi. 4: 4. again I *say*, Rejoice.
Heb 1:13. *said* he at any time, Sit on my right hand,
4: 3. as he *said*, As I have sworn
4. For he *spake* in a certain place of the
7. as it *is said*, To day if ye will hear his
10: 9. Then *said* he, Lo, I come
13: 5. for he *hath said*, I will never leave thee, nor forsake thee.
Jas. 2:18. Yea, a man may *say*, Thou hast faith,
Rev. 7:14. And I *said* unto him, Sir,
17: 7. I *will tell* thee the mystery
19: 3. And again they *said*, Alleluia.

2047 4 308/379 2:657 2048

ἐρημία, *ereemia.*

Mat.15:33. so much bread in the *wilderness*, as to
Mar 8: 4. with bread here in the *wilderness*?
2Co.11:26. (in) perils in the *wilderness*,
Heb 11:38. they wandered in *deserts*,

2048 35 308/379 2:657

ἔρημος, ἡ, *ereemos.* subst.

Mat. 3: 1. in the *wilderness* of Judæa,
3. crying in the *wilderness*, Prepare ye
4: 1. led up of the spirit into the *wilderness*
11: 7. What went ye out into the *wilderness* to
24:26. Behold, he is in the *desert*;
Mar 1: 3. voice of one crying in the *wilderness*,
4. John did baptize in the *wilderness*,
12. driveth him into the *wilderness*.
13. he was there in the *wilderness*
Lu. 1:80. and was in the *deserts* till the day of
3: 2. the son of Zacharias in the *wilderness*.
4. of one crying in the *wilderness*,
4: 1. by the Spirit into the *wilderness*,
5:16. withdrew himself into the *wilderness*,
7:24. ye out into the *wilderness* for to see?
8:29. driven of the devil into the *wilderness*.
15: 4. the ninety and nine in the *wilderness*,
Joh. 1:23. of one crying in the *wilderness*,
3:14. lifted up the serpent in the *wilderness*,
6:31. fathers did eat manna in the *desert*;
49. did eat manna in the *wilderness*,
11:54. unto a country near to the *wilderness*,
Acts 7:30. in the *wilderness* of mount Sina
36. in the *wilderness* forty years.
38. in the church in the *wilderness*
42. forty years in the *wilderness*?
44. of witness in the *wilderness*,
13:18. their manners in the *wilderness*.

Acts21:38. leddest out into the *wilderness*
1Co.10: 5. were overthrown in the *wilderness*.
Heb 3: 8. day of temptation in the *wilderness*:
17. carcases fell in the *wilderness*?
Rev.12: 6. fled into the *wilderness*,
14. that she might fly into the *wilderness*,
17: 3. away in the spirit into the *wilderness*:

2048 15 308/379

ἔρημος, *ereemos*. adj.

Mat.14:13. into a *desert* place apart:
15. This is a *desert* place,
23:38. your house is left unto you *desolate*.
Mar 1:35. departed into a *solitary* place,
45. was without in *desert* places:
6:31. apart into a *desert* place,
32. they departed into a *desert* place
35. This is a *desert* place,
Lu. 4:42. and went into a *desert* place:
9:10. into a *desert* place belonging to the city
12. here in a *desert* place.
13:35. your house is left unto you *desolate*:
Acts 1:20. Let his habitation be *desolate*,
8:26. Jerusalem unto Gaza, which is *desert*.
Gal. 4:27. the desolate hath many more children (lit. many the children of the *desolate* rather)

2049 5 309/380 2:657 2048

ἐρημόω, *ereemoō*.

Mat.12:25. kingdom...*is brought to desolation*;
Lu. 11:17. divided against itself *is brought to desolation*;
Rev.17:16. shall make her *desolate*
18:17(16). For in one hour so great riches *is come to nought*.
19. in one hour *is she made desolate*.

2050 5 309/380 2:657 2049

ἐρήμωσις, *ereemōsis*.

Mat.24:15. the abomination of *desolation*,
Mar 13:14. the abomination of *desolation*,
Lu. 21:20. the *desolation* thereof is nigh.

2051 1 309/380 2054

ἐρίζω, *erizo*.

Mat.12:19. He *shall* not *strive*, nor cry;

2052 7 309/380 2:660 rt 2042

ἐριθεία, *erithīa*.

Ro. 2: 8. But unto them that are contentious, (lit. of *contention*)
2Co.12:20. envyings, wraths, *strifes*,
Gal. 5:20. emulations, wrath, *strife*,
Phi. 1:16. The one preach Christ of *contention*,
2: 3. (Let) nothing (be done) through *strife*
Jas. 3:14. envying and *strife* in your hearts,
16. For where envying and *strife*

2053 2 309/380

ἔριον, *erion*.

Heb 9:19. scarlet *wool*, and hyssop,
Rev. 1:14. and (his) hairs (were) white like *wool*,

2054 9 309/380

ἔρις, *eris*.

Ro. 1:29. of envy, murder, *debate*,
13:13. not in *strife* and envying.
1Co. 1:11. there are *contentions* among you.
3: 3. *strife*, and divisions, are ye not carnal,
2Co.12:20. lest (there be) *debates*, envyings,
Gal. 5:20. *variance*, emulations, wrath,
Phi. 1:15. preach Christ even of envy and *strife*;
1Ti. 6: 4. cometh envy, *strife*, railings,
Tit. 3: 9. genealogies, and *contentions*, and strivings about the law;

2055 1 309/380 2056

ἐρίφιον, *eriphion*.

Mat.25:33. but the *goats* on the left.

2056 2 309/380 cf 2053

ἔριφος, *eriphos*.

Mat.25:32. divideth (his) sheep from the *goats*
Lu. 15:29. thou never gavest me a *kid*,

2058 2 309/380 2:661 2060

ἑρμηνεία, *hermeenīa*.

1Co.12:10. the *interpretation* of tongues:
14:26. a revelation, hath an *interpretation*

2059 4 3059/380 2:661 2060

ἑρμηνεύω, *hermeenūo*.

Joh. 1:38(39). which is to say, *being interpreted*,
42(43). which *is by interpretation*, A stone.
9: 7. which *is by interpretation*, Sent.
Heb 7: 2. *being by interpretation* King of righteousness,

2062 4 310/380 *herpō* (to creep)

ἑρπετόν, *herpeton*.

Acts10:12. wild beasts, and *creeping things*,
11: 6. wild beasts, and *creeping things*,
Ro. 1:23. fourfooted beasts, and *creeping things*.
Jas. 3: 7. and of *serpents*, and of things in the sea.

2064 642 310/381 2:666

ἔρχομαι, *erkomai*.

Mat. 2: 2. and *are come* to worship him.
8. I *may come and* worship him also.
9. till it *came and* stood over where
11. *when* they *were come* into the house,
21. and *came* into the land of Israel.
23. he *came and* dwelt in a city called
3: 7. saw many of the Pharisees and Sadducees *come* to his baptism,
11. but he *that cometh* after me is mightier
14. and *comest* thou to me?
16. like a dove, and *lighting* upon him:
4:13. he *came and* dwelt in Capernaum,
5:17. that I *am come* to destroy
— I *am* not *come* to destroy,
24. and then *come and* offer thy gift.
6:10. Thy kingdom *come*. Thy will be done
7:15. which *come* to you in sheep's clothing,
25. and the floods *came*,
27. and the floods *came*,
8: 2. there *came* a leper *and* worshipped
7. I will *come and* heal him
9. and to another, *Come*, and he *cometh*; and to my
14. And *when* Jesus *was come*
28. *when* he *was come* to the other side
29. *art* thou *come* hither to torment us before
9: 1. and *came* into his own city.
10. sinners *came and* sat down with him
13. for I *am* not *come* to call
15. but the days *will come*,
18. there *came* a certain ruler, *and* worshipped
— *come and* lay thy hand upon her,
23. And *when* Jesus *came* into the

2063. See p. 829

Mat. 9:28. And *when* he *was come* into the house,
10:13. *let* your peace *come* upon it:
23. till the Son of man *be come*.
34. that I *am come* to send peace on earth: I *came* not to send peace,
35. For I *am come* to set a man at variance
11: 3. Art thou he *that should come*,
14. which was for *to come*.
18. For John *came* neither eating
19. The Son of man *came* eating
12: 9. he *went* into their synagogue:
42. for she *came* from the uttermost parts
44. and *when* he *is come*, he findeth (it) empty,
13: 4. and the fowls *came* and devoured
19. then *cometh* the wicked (one), and
25. his enemy *came* and sowed tares
32. so that the birds of the air *come*
36. and *went* into the house:
54. *when* he *was come* into his own country,
14:12. and *went and* told Jesus.
28. bid me *come* unto thee on the water.
29. And he said, *Come*.
— walked on the water, *to go* to Jesus.
33. *came and* worshipped him,
34. when they were gone over, they *came* into
15:25. Then *came* she *and* worshipped
29. *came* nigh unto the sea
39. and *came* into the coasts of Magdala.
16: 5. *when* his disciples *were come*
13. *When* Jesus *came* into the coasts
24. If any (man) will *come* after me,
27. Son of man shall *come* in the glory
28. see the Son of man *coming* in his kingdom.
17:10. Elias must first *come?*
11. Elias truly shall first *come*,
12. That Elias *is come* already,
14. *when* they *were come* to the multitude,
24. And *when* they *were come* to Capernaum,
18: 7. that offences *come;* but woe to that man by whom the offence *cometh!*
11. For the Son of man *is come*
31. and *came and* told unto their lord
19: 1. *came* into the coasts of Judæa
14. forbid them not, *to come* unto me:
20: 9. *when* they *came* that (were hired) about the eleventh hour,
10. But *when* the first *came*, they supposed
28. *came* not to be ministered unto,
21: 1. and *were come* to Bethphage,
5. *cometh* unto thee, meek,
9. Blessed (is) he *that cometh* in the name of the Lord;
19. he *came* to it, and found nothing thereon,
23. *when* he *was come* into the temple,
32. For John *came* unto you
40. When the lord therefore of the vineyard *cometh*,
22: 3 they would not *come*.
23:35. That upon you *may come*
39. Blessed (is) he *that cometh* in the name of the Lord.
24: 5. For many *shall come* in my name,
30. and they shall see the Son of man *coming* in the clouds of heaven
39. until the flood *came*.
42. your Lord *doth come*.
43. the thief would *come*,
44. the Son of man *cometh*.
46. whom his lord *when* he *cometh*
48. My lord delayeth his coming; (lit. *to come*)
25: 6. Behold, the bridegroom *cometh;*

Mat.25:10. went to buy, the bridegroom *came;*
11. Afterward *came* also the other
13. the Son of man *cometh*.
19. the lord of those servants *cometh*,
27. at my *coming* I should have received
31. When the Son of man *shall come*
36. and ye *came* unto me.
39. in prison, and *came* unto thee?
26:36. Then *cometh* Jesus with them
40. And he *cometh* unto the disciples,
43. he *came and* found them
45. Then *cometh* he to his disciples,
47. one of the twelve, *came*,
64. and *coming* in the clouds of heaven.
27:33. *when* they *were come* unto a place called
49. whether Elias *will come* to save him.
57. there *came* a rich man
64. lest his disciples *come* by night, and
28: 1. *came* Mary Magdalene
11. *came* into the city, *and* shewed
13. *came* by night, *and* stole him (away)
Mar 1: 7. There *cometh* one mightier than I
9. Jesus *came* from Nazareth
14. Jesus *came* into Galilee,
24. *art* thou *come* to destroy us?
29. they *entered* into the house of Simon
40. there *came* a leper to him,
45. they *came* to him from every quarter.
2: 3. And they *come* unto him,
13. the multitude *resorted* unto him,
17. I *came* not to call the righteous,
18. they *come* and say
20. But the days *will come*,
3: 8. what great things he did, *came* unto him
19. and they *went* into an house.
31. There *came* then his brethren
4: 4. and the fowls of the air *came*
15. Satan *cometh* immediately,
21. *Is* a candle *brought* to be put
22. that it *should come* abroad.
5: 1. they *came* over unto the other side
15. they *come* to Jesus,
22. there *cometh* one of the rulers of the
23. (I pray thee), *come and* lay thy hands on her,
26. nothing bettered, but rather *grew* worse,
27. *came* in the press behind, *and* touched
33. *came* and fell down before him,
35. there *came* from the ruler of the
38. he *cometh* to the house of the ruler
6: 1. and *came* into his own country;
29. when his disciples heard (of it), they *came*
31. for there were many *coming*
48. he *cometh* unto them,
53. when they had passed over, they *came*
7: 1. certain of the scribes, *which came*
25. *came and* fell at his feet:
31. he *came* unto the sea
8:10. *came* into the parts of Dalmanutha.
22. he *cometh* to Bethsaida;
34. Whosoever will *come* after me,
38. when he *cometh* in the glory
9: 1. have seen the kingdom of God *come* with power.
7. a voice *came* out of the cloud,
11. Elias must first *come?*
12. Elias verily *cometh* first, *and*
13. That Elias *is* indeed *come*,
14. *when* he *came* to (his) disciples,
33. And he *came* to Capernaum:
10: 1. and *cometh* into the coasts
14. Suffer the little children *to come* unto me,

Mar 10:30. in the world *to come*
45. *came* not to be ministered unto,
46. they *came* to Jericho:
50. rose, and *came* to Jesus.
11: 9. he *that cometh* in the name of the Lord:
10. the kingdom of our father David, *that cometh*
13. he *came*, if haply he might find any thing thereon: and *when* he *came* to it,
15. And they *come* to Jerusalem:
27. they *come* again to Jerusalem:
— there *come* to him the chief priests,
12: 9. he *will come* and destroy
14. And *when* they *were come*, they say
18. Then *come* unto him the Sadducees,
42. there *came* a certain poor widow, *and*
13: 6. For many *shall come* in my name,
26. see the Son of man *coming* in the clouds
35. the master of the house *cometh*,
36. Lest *coming* suddenly he find
14: 3. there *came* a woman having an alabaster box
16. and *came* into the city,
17. he *cometh* with the twelve.
32. And they *came* to a place
37. he *cometh*, and findeth them
41. And he *cometh* the third time,
— it is enough, the hour *is come;*
45. And *as soon as* he *was come*, he goeth straightway
62. *coming* in the clouds of heaven.
66. there *cometh* one of the maids
15:21. *coming* out of the country,
36. whether Elias *will come*
43. also waited for the kingdom of God, *came*,
16: 1. that they might *come and* anoint him.
2. they *came* unto the sepulchre
Lu. 1:43. that the mother of my Lord *should come*
59. they *came* to circumcise the child;
2:16. And they *came* with haste,
27. he *came* by the Spirit into
44. in the company, *went* a day's journey;
51. and *came* to Nazareth,
3: 3. he *came* into all the country
12. Then *came* also publicans to be baptized,
16. but one mightier than I *cometh*,
4:16. he *came* to Nazareth,
34. *art* thou *come* to destroy us?
42. and *came* unto him,
5: 7. that they should *come and* help them. And they *came*, and filled
17. which were *come* out of every town
32. I *came* not to call the righteous,
35. But the days *will come*,
6:17. which *came* to hear him,
47. *Whosoever cometh* to me,
7: 3. that he would *come and* heal his servant.
7. thought I myself worthy *to come* unto thee:
8. and to another, *Come*, and he *cometh*; and to my
19. Art thou he *that should come?*
20. Art thou he *that should come?*
33. For John the Baptist *came* neither
34. The Son of man *is come* eating and
8:12. then *cometh* the devil,
17. not be known and *come* abroad.
35. and *came* to Jesus,
41. behold, there *came* a man
47. that she was not hid, she *came* trembling,
49. there *cometh* one from the ruler
9:23. If any (man) will *come* after me,
26. when he shall *come* in his own glory,

Lu. 9:56. is not *come* to destroy men's lives,
10: 1. he himself would *come*.
32. *came* and looked (on him), *and* passed by
33. as he journeyed, *came* where he was:
11: 2. Thy kingdom *come*. Thy will be done
25. And *when* he *cometh*, he findeth (it) swept
31. she *came* from the utmost parts
12:36. *when* he *cometh* and knocketh,
37. whom the lord *when* he *cometh* shall find
38. And if he shall *come* in the second watch or *come* in the third watch,
39. the thief would *come*,
40. the Son of man *cometh*
43. whom his lord *when* he *cometh*
45. My lord delayeth his coming; (lit. *to come*)
49. I *am come* to send fire on the earth;
54. There *cometh* a shower;
13: 6. he *came* and sought fruit
7. I *come* seeking fruit
14. in them therefore *come and* be healed,
35. Blessed (is) he *that cometh* in the name of the Lord.
14: 1. as he *went* into the house
9. he that bade thee and him *come and* say
10. when he that bade thee *cometh*,
17. *Come;* for all things are now ready.
20. and therefore I cannot *come*.
26. If any (man) *come* to me,
27. doth not bear his cross, and *come* after me.
31. meet him *that cometh* against him
15: 6. And *when* he *cometh* home, he calleth
17. And *when* he *came* to himself,
20. and *came* to his father.
25. as he *came and* drew nigh
30. But as soon as this thy son *was come*,
16:21. the dogs *came and* licked his sores.
28. lest they also *come* into this place of torment.
17: 1. but that offences will *come*: but woe (unto him), through whom they *come!*
20. when the kingdom of God should *come*,
— The kingdom of God *cometh* not with observation:
22. The days *will come*, when ye shall desire
27. the flood *came*, and destroyed them all.
18: 3. she *came* unto him, saying, Avenge
5. by her continual *coming* she weary me.
8. *when* the Son of man *cometh*, shall he
16. little children *to come* unto me,
30. in the world *to come* life everlasting.
19: 5. when Jesus *came* to the place,
10. For the Son of man *is come*
13. Occupy till I *come*.
18. And the second *came*,
20. And another *came*, saying,
23. at my *coming* I might have required mine
38. Blessed (be) the King *that cometh* in the name of the Lord:
20:16. He *shall come* and destroy
21: 6. the days *will come*, in the which
8. for many *shall come* in my name,
27. then shall they see the Son of man *coming* in a cloud with power
22: 7. Then *came* the day of unleavened bread,
18. until the kingdom of God shall *come*.
45. *and was come* to his disciples,
23:26. laid hold upon one Simon, a Cyrenian, *coming* out of the country,
29. behold, the days *are coming*.
42. when thou *comest* into thy kingdom.
24: 1. very early in the morning, they *came*

Lu. 24:23. found not his body, they *came*, saying,
Joh. 1: 7. The same *came* for a witness,
9. *that cometh* into the world.
11. He *came* unto his own,
15. He *that cometh* after me
27. who *coming* after me
29. John seeth Jesus *coming* unto him,
30. After me *cometh* a man
31. *am* I *come* baptizing with water.
39(40). He saith unto them, *Come* and see. They *came* and saw
46(47). Philip saith unto him, *Come* and see.
47(48). Jesus saw Nathanael *coming* to him,
3: 2. The same *came* to Jesus by night,
— thou art a teacher *come* from God: (lit. that thou *art come* a teacher from God)
8. canst not tell whence it *cometh*,
19. light *is come* into the world,
20. neither *cometh* to the light,
21. he that doeth truth *cometh* to the light,
22. After these things *came* Jesus
26. they *came* unto John,
— all (men) *come* to him.
31. He *that cometh* from above is above all:
— he *that cometh* from heaven
4: 5. Then *cometh* he to a city of Samaria,
7. There *cometh* a woman of Samaria
15. that I thirst not, neither *come* hither to draw.
16. call thy husband, and *come* hither.
21. the hour *cometh*, when
23. But the hour *cometh*, and now is,
25. I know that Messias *cometh*, which is called Christ: when he *is come*,
27. upon this *came* his disciples,
30. and *came* unto him.
35. and (then) *cometh* harvest?
40. So when the Samaritans *were come* unto him,
45. Then when he *was come* into Galilee,
— for they also *went* unto the feast.
46. So Jesus *came* again
54. *when* he *was come* out of Judæa
5: 7. but while I *am coming*,
24. and shall not *come* into condemnation;
25. The hour *is coming*, and now is,
28. for the hour *is coming*,
40. ye will not *come* to me,
43. I *am come* in my Father's name,
— if another shall *come* in his own name,
6: 5. a great company *come* unto him,
14. of a truth that prophet *that should come* into the world.
15. they would *come* and take him
17. and *went* over the sea
— Jesus *was* not *come* to them.
23. Howbeit there *came* other boats
24. and *came* to Capernaum,
35. he *that cometh* to me shall never hunger;
37. him *that cometh* to me I will in no wise cast out.
44. No man can *come* to me, except
45. learned of the Father, *cometh* unto me.
65. no man can *come* unto me, except
7:27. when Christ *cometh*, no man
28. I *am* not *come* of myself,
30. his hour *was* not yet *come*.
31. When Christ *cometh*, will he do
34. where I am, (thither) ye cannot *come*.
36. ye cannot *come*?
37 *let* him *come* unto me, and
41. Shall Christ *come* out of Galilee?

Joh. 7:42. Christ *cometh* of the seed of David.
45. Then *came* the officers
50. he *that came* to Jesus by night,
8: 2. the people *came* unto him;
14. for I know whence I *came*,
— ye cannot tell whence I *come*,
20. his hour was not yet *come*.
21. whither I go, ye cannot *come*.
22. Whither I go, ye cannot *come*.
42. *came* I of myself, but he sent me.
9: 4. the night *cometh*, when no man
7. washed, and *came* seeing.
39. I *am come* into this world,
10: 8. All that ever *came* before me
10. The thief *cometh* not, but for
— I *am come* that they might have life,
12. seeth the wolf *coming*,
41. many *resorted* unto him,
11:17. Then *when* Jesus *came*, he found
19. And many of the Jews *came*
20. as soon as she heard that Jesus was coming, (lit. *cometh*)
27. *which should come* into the world.
29. she arose quickly, and *came* unto him.
30. Now Jesus *was* not yet *come*
32. when Mary *was come* where Jesus was,
34. Lord, *come* and see.
38. groaning in himself *cometh* to the grave.
45. many of the Jews *which came* to Mary,
48. the Romans *shall come*
56. that he will not *come* to the feast?
12: 1. before the passover *came* to Bethany,
9. and they *came* not for Jesus' sake
12. much people *that were come* to the feast,
— that Jesus *was coming* (lit. *cometh*)
13. *that cometh* in the name of the Lord.
15. behold, thy King *cometh*, sitting on
22. Philip *cometh* and telleth Andrew:
23. The hour *is come*, that the Son of man
27. *came* I unto this hour.
28. Then *came* there a voice from heaven,
46. I *am come* a light into the world,
47. for I *came* not to judge
13: 1. when Jesus knew that his hour *was come*
6. Then *cometh* he to Simon Peter:
33. Whither I go, ye cannot *come*;
14: 3. I will *come* again, and receive you
6. no man *cometh* unto the Father,
18. I will *come* to you.
23. we *will come* unto him, and make our abode
28. and *come* (again) unto you.
30. for the prince of this world *cometh*,
15:22. If I *had* not *come* and spoken
26. But when the Comforter *is come*,
16: 2. the time *cometh*, that whosoever killeth
4. when the time shall *come*,
7. the Comforter *will* not *come*
8. And *when* he *is come*, he will reprove
13. Howbeit when he, the Spirit of truth, *is come*,
— he will shew you things *to come*.
21. because her hour *is come*:
25. but the time *cometh*, when I shall no more
28. and *am come* into the world:
32. Behold, the hour *cometh*, yea, *is* now *come*, that ye shall
17: 1. Father, the hour *is come*; glorify
11. these are in the world, and I *come* to thee.
13. And now *come* I to thee;
18: 3. *cometh* thither with lanterns
4. all things *that should come* upon him,
37. for this cause *came* I into the world,

Joh.19:32. Then *came* the soldiers,
33. But when they *came* to Jesus,
38. He *came* therefore, and took the body
39. And there *came* also Nicodemus, *which* at the first *came* to Jesus by night,
20: 1. *cometh* Mary Magdalene early,
2. she runneth, and *cometh* to Simon Peter,
3. and *came* to the sepulchre.
4. and *came* first to the sepulchre.
6. Then *cometh* Simon Peter
8. that other disciple, *which came* first to the
18. Mary Magdalene *came*
19. *came* Jesus and stood
24. Didymus, was not with them when Jesus *came*.
26. *came* Jesus, the doors being shut,
21: 3. We also *go* with thee.
8. the other disciples *came* in a little ship;
13. Jesus then *cometh*, and taketh bread,
22. that he tarry till I *come*,
23. he tarry till I *come*, what (is that) to thee?
Acts 1:11. *shall* so *come* in like manner as
2:20. before that great and notable day of the Lord *come*:
3:19. the times of refreshing shall *come*
4:23. they *went* to their own company,
5:15. the shadow of Peter *passing by*
7:11. Now there *came* a dearth over
8:27. and *had come* to Jerusalem for to worship,
36. they *came* unto a certain water:
40. till he *came* to Cæsarea.
9:17. in the way as thou *camest*,
21. and *came* hither for that intent, that he
10:29. Therefore *came* I (unto you) without gainsaying,
11: 5. by four corners; and it *came* even to me:
12. Moreover these six brethren accompanied (lit. *went* with) me,
12:10. they *came* unto the iron gate
12. he *came* to the house of Mary the mother
13:13. they *came* to Perga in Pamphylia:
25. there *cometh* one after me,
44. the *next* (lit. *following*) sabbath day
51. and *came* unto Iconium.
14:24. they *came* to Pamphylia.
15:30. they *came* to Antioch:
16: 7. *After* they *were come* to Mysia,
37. but let them *come* themselves *and* fetch us
39. they *came and* besought them,
17: 1. they *came* to Thessalonica,
13. they *came* thither also, and stirred up
15. for to *come* to him with all speed,
18: 1. from Athens, and *came* to Corinth;
2. lately *come* from Italy, with his wife
7. and *entered* into a certain (man's) house,
21. keep this feast that *cometh*
19: 1. having passed through the upper coasts *came* to Ephesus:
4. on him *which should come* after him,
6. the Holy Ghost *came* on them;
18. And many that believed *came*,
27. our craft is in danger to be set at nought; (lit. *to come* into censure)
20: 2. he *came* into Greece,
6. and *came* unto them to Troas
14. we took him in, and *came* to Mitylene.
15. we *came* to Miletus.
21: 1. we *came* with a straight course unto Coos,
8. departed, and *came* unto Cæsarea:
11. And *when* he *was come* unto us, he took
2 they will hear that thou *art come*.
22:11. I *came* into Damascus.

Acts22:13. *Came* unto me, and stood, *and*
30. commanded the chief priests and all their council *to appear*,
24: 8. Commanding his accusers *to come* unto
25:23. *when* Agrippa *was come*,
27: 8. And, hardly passing it, *came* unto a place
28:13. we *came* the next day to Puteoli:
14. we *went* toward Rome.
16. we *came* to Rome,
Ro. 1:10. by the will of God *to come* unto you.
13. oftentimes I purposed *to come* unto you,
3: 8. evil, that good *may come?*
7: 9. but *when* the commandment *came*,
9: 9. At this time *will* I *come*,
15:22. much hindered from *coming* to you.
23. desire these many years *to come* unto you;
24. my journey into Spain, I *will come* to
29. *when* I *come* unto you, I *shall come* in the fulness of the blessing of the gospel
32. That I *may come* unto you with joy
1Co. 2: 1. And I, brethren, *when* I *came* to you, *came* not with excellency of speech
4: 5. until the Lord *come*, who both will bring
18. as though I would not *come*
19. But I *will come* to you shortly,
21. shall I *come* unto you with a rod,
11:26. shew the Lord's death till he *come*.
34. the rest will I set in order when I *come*.
13:10. But when that which is perfect *is come*,
14: 6. if I *come* unto you speaking with tongues,
15:35. and with what body *do* they *come?*
16: 2. that there be no gatherings when I *come*.
5. Now I *will come* unto you, when I
10. Now if Timotheus *come*, see that
11. conduct him forth in peace, that he *may come* unto me:
12. I greatly desired him *to come* unto you
— but his will was not at all *to come* at this time; but he *will come* when he
2Co. 1:15. I was minded *to come* unto you before,
16. *to come* again out of Macedonia
23. I *came* not as yet unto Corinth.
2: 1. that I would not *come* again to you in
3. lest, *when* I *came*, I should have sorrow
12. Furthermore, *when* I *came* to Troas
7: 5. *when* we *were come* into Macedonia,
9: 4. Lest haply if they of Macedonia *come*
11: 4. For if he *that cometh* preacheth
9. the brethren *which came* from Macedonia
12: 1. I *will come* to visions
14. I am ready *to come* to you;
20. lest, *when* I *come*, I shall not find you such
21. lest, *when* I *come* again, my God will
13: 1. This (is) the third (time) I *am coming* to
2. if I *come* again, I will not spare:
Gal. 1:21. Afterwards I *came* into the regions
2:11. But when Peter *was come*
12. For before that certain *came*
— but when they *were come*,
3:19. till the seed *should come*
23. But before faith *came*,
25. But *after that* faith *is come*,
4: 4. But when the fulness of the time *was come*,
Eph. 2:17. And *came and* preached peace
5: 6. for because of these things *cometh* the
Phi. 1:12. *have fallen out* rather unto the furtherance of the gospel;
27. that whether I *come* (lit. *coming*)
2:24. that I also myself *shall come* shortly.
Col. 3: 6. the wrath of God *cometh* on the
4:10. if he *come* unto you, receive

1Th. 1:10. delivered us from the wrath *to come.*
2:18. we would *have come* unto you,
3: 6. But now *when* Timotheus *came*
5: 2. the day of the Lord so *cometh* as a thief
2Th. 1:10. When he shall *come* to be glorified
2: 3. except there *come* a falling away
1Ti. 1:15. Christ Jesus *came* into the world
2: 4. *to come* unto the knowledge of the truth.
3:14. hoping *to come* unto thee shortly:
4:13. Till I *come*, give attendance to reading,
2Ti. 3: 7. never able *to come* to the knowledge of
4: 9. Do thy diligence *to come* shortly unto me:
13. *when* thou *comest*, bring (with thee),
21. thy diligence *to come* before winter.
Tit. 3:12. be diligent *to come* unto me
Heb. 6: 7. drinketh in the rain *that cometh* oft
8: 8. Behold, the days *come*,
10:37. and he *that* shall *come* will come,
11: 8. not knowing whither he *went.*
13:23. with whom, if he *come* shortly,
2Pet. 3: 3. there *shall come* in the last days
1Joh. 2:18. have heard that antichrist shall *come*,
4: 2. *that* Jesus Christ *is come* in the flesh
3. *that...is come* in the flesh
— ye have heard that it should *come;* (lit. *cometh*)
5: 6. This is he that *came* by water and blood,
2Joh. 7. *that* Jesus Christ *is come* in the flesh.
10. If there *come* any unto you,
12. I trust *to come* unto you,
3Joh. 3. *when* the brethren *came*
10. Wherefore, if I *come*, I will remember
Jude 14. the Lord *cometh* with ten thousands of his
Rev. 1: 4. which is, and which was, and *which is to come;*
7. he *cometh* with clouds;
8. which is, and which was, and *which is to come,*
2: 5. or else I will *come* unto thee
16. I will *come* unto thee quickly,
3:10. hour of temptation, which shall *come*
11. Behold, I *come* quickly:
4: 8. which was, and is, and *is to come.*
5: 7. And he *came* and took
6: 1. one of the four beasts saying, *Come* and
3. I heard the second beast say, *Come* and
5. the third beast say, *Come* and see.
7. the fourth beast say, *Come* and see.
17. For the great day of his wrath *is come;*
7:13. in white robes? and whence *came* they?
14. These are they *which came* out of great
8: 3. another angel *came* and stood
9:12. there *come* two woes more
11:14. the third woe *cometh*
17. which art, and wast, and *art to come;*
18. thy wrath *is come,*
14: 7. the hour of his judgment *is come:*
15. the time *is come* for thee to reap;
16:15. I *come* as a thief.
17: 1. And there *came* one of the seven
10. the other *is* not yet *come;* and when he *cometh*, he must continue a short space.
18:10. for in one hour *is* thy judgment *come.*
19: 7. the marriage of the Lamb *is come,*
21: 9. And there *came* unto me one of the seven
22: 7. Behold, I *come* quickly:
12. behold, I *come* quickly;
17. the Spirit and the bride say, *Come.* And let him that heareth say, *Come.* And *let* him that is athirst *come.*
20. Surely I *come* quickly; Amen. Even so *come*, Lord Jesus.

2065 58 311/388 2:685 2046

ἐρωτάω, *erōtao.*

Mat. 15:23. his disciples came and *besought* him,
16:13. he *asked* his disciples, saying, Whom do
21:24. I also *will ask* you one thing,
Mar. 4:10. they that were about him with the twelve *asked of* him
7:26. and she *besought* him that he would cast
Lu. 4:38. they *besought* him for her.
5: 3. *prayed* him that he would thrust
7: 3. *beseeching* him that he would come
36. And one of the Pharisees *desired* him
8:37. *besought* him to depart from them;
9:45. they feared *to ask* him of that saying.
11:37. a certain Pharisee *besought* him
14:18. I *pray* thee have me excused.
19. I *pray* thee have me excused.
32. and *desireth* conditions of peace.
16:27. I *pray* thee therefore, father,
19:31. if any man *ask* you,
20: 3. I *will* also *ask* you
22:68. And if I also *ask* (you),
Joh. 1:19. from Jerusalem to *ask* him, Who art thou
21. And they *asked* him, What then?
25. they *asked* him, and said
4:31. his disciples *prayed* him,
40. they *besought* him that he would tarry
47. *besought* him that he would come down,
5:12. Then *asked* they him, What man is that
8: 7. So when they continued *asking* him, he
9: 2. his disciples *asked* him,
15. the Pharisees also *asked* him
19. they *asked* them, saying, Is this your son,
21. he is of age; *ask* him: he shall speak
23. said his parents, He is of age; *ask* him.
12:21. *desired* him, saying, Sir, we would see
14:16. I *will pray* the Father,
16: 5. none of you *asketh* me,
19. they were desirous *to ask* him,
23. ye *shall ask* me nothing.
26. that I *will pray* the Father for you:
30. that any man *should ask* thee:
17: 9. I *pray* for them: I *pray* not for the world,
15. I *pray* not that thou shouldest take
20. Neither *pray* I for these alone,
18:19. The high priest then *asked* Jesus of his
19:31. *besought* Pilate that their legs
38. *besought* Pilate that he might take
Acts 3: 3. about to go into the temple *asked* an alms.
10:48. *prayed* they him to tarry
16:39. brought (them) out, and *desired* (them)
18:20. *When* they *desired* (him) to tarry
23:18. called me unto (him), and *prayed* me
20. The Jews have agreed *to desire* thee
Phi. 4: 3. I *intreat* thee also, true yokefellow,
1Th. 4: 1. we *beseech* you, brethren, and exhort
5:12. And we *beseech* you, brethren, to know
2Th. 2: 1. Now we *beseech* you, brethren, by the coming of our Lord
1Joh. 5:16. I do not say that he *shall pray* for it.
2Joh. 5. now I *beseech* thee, lady,

ἔσεσθαι, *esesthai.*

From εἰμί. 1510

Acts 11:28. that there should *be* great dearth throughout all
23:30. that the Jews laid wait (lit. that there was about *to be* a lying in wait of the Jews)
24:15. that there shall *be* a resurrection

Acts24:25. and judgment to come, (lit. about *to be*)
27:10. I perceive that this voyage will *be*

2066 7 312/389 *hennumi* (to clothe)

ἐσθής, esthees.

Lu. 23:11. and arrayed him in a gorgeous *robe*,
Acts 1:10. two men stood by them in white *apparel*,
10:30. stood before me in bright *clothing*,
12:21. Herod, arrayed in royal *apparel*,
Jas. 2: 2. gold ring, in goodly *apparel*, and there come in also a poor man in vile *raiment*;
3. to him that weareth the gay *clothing*,

2067 1 312/389 2066

ἔσθησις, estheesis.

Lu. 24: 4. stood by them in shining *garments*:

2068 65 312/389 2:689 (5315) *edō* (to eat)

ἐσθίω, esthio.

Mat. 9:11. Why *eateth* your Master with publicans
11:18. John came neither *eating* nor drinking,
19. The Son of man came *eating* and drinking,
12: 1. began to pluck the ears of corn, and *to eat*.
14:21. And they *that had eaten* were about
15: 2. wash not their hands when they *eat* bread.
27. the dogs *eat* of the crumbs
38. And they *that did eat* were four
24:49. and *to eat* and drink with the drunken;
26:21. *as* they *did eat*, he said, Verily
26. And *as* they *were eating*, Jesus took
Mar. 1: 6. he did eat (lit. *eating*) locusts and
2:16. saw him *eat* with publicans and
— How is it that he *eateth* and drinketh
7: 2. saw some of his disciples *eat* bread
3. *eat* not, holding the tradition
4. except they wash, they *eat* not.
5. but *eat* bread with unwashen hands?
28. yet the dogs under the table *eat* of the
14:18. as they sat and *did eat*, Jesus said, Verily I say unto you, One of you *which eateth*
22. *as* they *did eat*, Jesus took
Lu. 5:30. Why *do* ye *eat* and drink with
33. but thine *eat* and drink?
6: 1. and *did eat*, rubbing (them) in
7:33. the Baptist came neither *eating* bread
34. The Son of man is come *eating* and
10: 7. remain, *eating* and drinking such
8. *eat* such things as are set before you:
12:45. and *to eat* and drink, and to be
15:16. that the swine *did eat*:
17:27. They *did eat*, they drank, they married
28. they *did eat*, they drank, they bought,
22:30. That ye *may eat* and drink at my table
Acts27:35. when he had broken (it), he began *to eat*.
Ro. 14: 2. another, who is weak, *eateth* herbs.
3. Let not him *that eateth* despise him *that eateth* not; and let not him *which eateth* not judge him *that eateth*:
6. He *that eateth*, *eateth* to the Lord, for he giveth God thanks; and he *that eateth* not, to the Lord he *eateth* not,
20. (it is) evil for that man *who eateth* with offence.
1Co. 8: 7. *eat* (it) as a thing offered unto an idol;
10. *to eat* those things which are offered to
9: 7. and *eateth* not of the fruit thereof?
— and *eateth* not of the milk of the flock?
1Co. 9:13. *live* (of the things) of the temple?
10:18. they *which eat* of the sacrifices
25. Whatsoever is sold in the shambles, (that *eat*,
27. whatsoever is set before you, *eat*,
28. *eat* not for his sake that shewed
31. Whether therefore ye *eat*, or drink,
11:22. have ye not houses *to eat* and to drink in?
26. as often as ye *eat* this bread,
27. whosoever shall *eat* this bread,
28. *let* him *eat* of (that) bread,
29. For he *that eateth* and drinketh unworthily, *eateth* and drinketh
34. *let* him *eat* at home;
2Th. 3:10. neither should he *eat*.
12. that with quietness they work, and *eat* their own bread.
Heb 10:27. which shall *devour* the adversaries.

2070 53 221/274 1510

ἐσμέν, esmen.

From εἰμί.

Mar. 5: 9. Legion: for we *are* many.
Lu. 9:12. we *are* here in a desert place.
17:10. We *are* unprofitable servants:
Joh. 8:33. We *be* Abraham's seed,
9:28. we *are* Moses' disciples.
40. *Are* we blind also?
10:30. I and (my) Father *are* one.
17:22. even as we *are* one:
Acts 2:32. whereof we all *are* witnesses.
3:15. whereof we *are* witnesses.
5:32. we *are* his witnesses
10:39. And we *are* witnesses of all things
14:15. We also *are* men of like passions with you,
16:28. for we *are* all here.
17:28. live, and move, and *have our being*;
— For we *are* also his offspring.
23:15. *are* ready to kill him.
Ro. 6:15. we *are* not under the law,
8:12. brethren, we *are* debtors,
16. that we *are* the children of God:
12: 5. *are* one body in Christ,
14: 8. we *are* the Lord's,
1Co. 3: 9. For we *are* labourers together with God:
10:17. we (being) many *are* one bread, (and) one body:
22. *are* we stronger than he?
15:19. we have hope (lit. we *are* hoping) in Christ, we *are* of all men most
2Co. 1:14. we *are* your rejoicing,
24. but *are* helpers of your joy:
2:15. we *are* unto God a sweet savour of Christ
17. For we *are* not as many,
3: 5. Not that we *are* sufficient
10:11. that, such as we *are* in word
13: 6. we *are* not reprobates.
Gal. 3:25. we *are* no longer under a schoolmaster.
4:28. we, brethren, as Isaac was, *are* the children of promise.
31. we *are* not children of the bondwoman
Eph. 2:10. For we *are* his workmanship,
4:25. we *are* members one of another.
5:30. For we *are* members of his body,
Phi. 3: 3. For we *are* the circumcision,
1Th. 5: 5. we *are* not of the night, nor
Heb. 3: 6. whose house *are* we,
4: 2. For unto us was the gospel preached, (lit we *are* evangelized)
10:10. we *are* sanctified through

Heb 10:39. we *are* not of them who draw back unto
1Joh.2: 5. that we *are* in him.
3: 2. now *are* we the sons of God,
19. that we *are* of the truth,
4: 6. We *are* of God: he that knoweth
17. as he is, so *are* we in this world.
5:19. we know that we *are* of God,
20. and we *are* in him that is true,

2071 193 221/285 1510

See also p. 309

ἔσομαι, ἔσῃ, ἔσται, ἐσόμεθα, ἔσεσθε, ἔσονται, esomai, &c.

From εἰμί.

Mat. 5:21. *shall be* in danger of the judgment:
22. *shall be* in danger of the judgment:
— *shall be* in danger of the council:
— *shall be* in danger of hell fire.
48. *Be* ye therefore perfect,
6: 5. thou *shalt* not *be* as the hypocrites (are):
21. there *will* your heart *be* also.
22. thy whole body *shall be* full of light.
23. thy whole body *shall be* full of darkness.
8:12. there *shall be* weeping
10:15. It *shall be* more tolerable for the land of Sodom
22. ye *shall be* hated of all
11:22. It *shall be* more tolerable for Tyre and
24. it *shall be* more tolerable for the land of
12:11. What man *shall* there *be* among you,
27. they *shall be* your judges.
40. so *shall* the Son of man *be* three days
45. so *shall* it *be* also unto this wicked
13:40. so *shall* it *be* in the end
42. there *shall be* wailing
49. So *shall* it *be* at the end
50. there *shall be* wailing
16:19. *shall be* bound in heaven:
— *shall be* loosed in heaven.
22. this *shall* not *be* unto thee.
17:17. how long *shall* I *be* with you?
18:18. *shall be* bound in heaven:
— *shall be* loosed in heaven.
19: 5. they twain *shall be* one flesh?
27. what shall we have therefore? (lit. what *shall be* to us therefore)
30. But many (that are) first *shall be* last;
20:16. So the last *shall be* first,
26. But it *shall* not *be* so among you:
22:13. there *shall be* weeping
28. whose wife *shall* she *be* of the seven?
23:11. among you *shall be* your servant.
24: 3. when *shall* these things *be?*
7. there *shall be* famines, and pestilences,
9. ye *shall be* hated of all nations for
21. For then *shall be* great tribulation,
27. so *shall* also the coming of the Son of man *be.*
37. *shall* also the coming of the Son of man *be.*
39. so *shall* also the coming of the Son of man *be.*
40. Then *shall* two *be* in the field;
51. there *shall be* weeping
25:30. there *shall be* weeping
27:64. so the last error *shall be* worse
Mar. 6:11. It *shall be* more tolerable for Sodom
9:19. *shall* I *be* with you?
35. (the same) *shall be* last of all,
10: 8. they twain *shall be* one flesh:
Mar.10:31. But many (that are) first *shall be* last:
43. But so *shall* it not *be* among you:
— *shall be* your minister:
44. *shall be* servant of all.
11:23. he shall have (lit. it *shall be* to him) whatsoever he saith.
24. that ye receive (them), and ye shall have (them). (lit. they *shall be* to you)
12: 7. the inheritance *shall be* our's.
23. whose wife *shall* she *be* of them?
13: 4. when *shall* these things *be?*
8. there *shall be* earthquakes in divers places, and there *shall be* famines and troubles:
13. ye *shall be* hated of all
19. For (in) those days *shall be* affliction,
25. the stars of heaven shall fall, (lit. *shall be* falling)
14: 2. lest there *be* an uproar
Lu. 1:14. And thou shalt have joy (lit. joy *shall be* to thee)
15. For he *shall be* great in the sight
20. And, behold, thou *shalt be* dumb,
32. He *shall be* great, and shall
33. of his kingdom there *shall be* no end.
34. How *shall* this *be*, seeing I know not
45. there *shall be* a performance
66. What manner of child *shall* this *be!*
2:10. which *shall be* to all people.
3: 5. the crooked *shall be* made straight,
4: 7. wilt worship me, all *shall be* thine.
5:10. thou shalt catch men. (lit. thou *shalt be* catching men)
6:35. your reward *shall be* great, and ye *shall be* the children of the Highest:
40. every one that is perfect *shall be* as
9:41. how long *shall* I *be* with you,
48. the same *shall be* great.
10:12. it *shall be* more tolerable in that day
14. it *shall be* more tolerable for Tyre
11:19. *shall* they *be* your judges.
30. so *shall* also the Son of man *be* to this
36. the whole *shall be* full of light,
12:20. then whose *shall* those things *be*,
34. there *will* your heart *be* also.
52. For from henceforth there *shall be*
55. There *will be* heat; and
13:28. There *shall be* weeping
30. there are last which *shall be* first, and there are first which *shall be* last.
14:10. then shalt thou have (lit. *shall be* to thee)
14. And thou *shalt be* blessed;
15: 7. likewise joy *shall be* in heaven
17:24. so *shall* also the Son of man *be* in his
26. so *shall* it *be* also in the days of the Son
30. Even thus *shall* it *be* in the day
31. he which *shall be* upon the housetop,
34. there *shall be* two (men) in one bed;
35. Two (women) *shall be* grinding
36. Two (men) *shall be* in the field;
21: 7. but when *shall* these things *be?*
11. And great earthquakes *shall be* in divers
— great signs *shall* there *be* from heaven.
17. ye *shall be* hated of all
23. for there *shall be* great distress
24. Jerusalem *shall be* trodden down of
25. there *shall be* signs in the sun,
22:69. Hereafter shall the Son of man sit (lit. *shall be* sitting)
23:43. *shalt* thou *be* with me in paradise.
Joh. 6:45. they *shall be* all taught of God.
8:36. ye *shall be* free indeed.
55. I *shall be* a liar like unto you:

Joh. 12:26. *shall* also my servant *be:*
14:17. and *shall be* in you.
19:24. but cast lots for it, whose it *shall be:*
Acts 1: 8. ye *shall be* witnesses unto me
2:17. it *shall come to pass* in the last days,
21. it *shall come to pass,* (that) whosoever
3:23. And it *shall come to pass,* (that) every
7: 6. That his seed should sojourn (lit. *shall be* sojourning)
13:11. and thou *shalt be* blind,
22:15. thou *shalt be* his witness
27:22. there *shall be* no loss of (any man's) life
25. that it *shall be* even as it was told me.
Ro. 4:18. So *shall* thy seed *be.*
6: 5. likeness of his death, we *shall be* also
9: 9. Sarah *shall have* a son.
26. it *shall come to pass,* (that) in the place
15:12. There *shall be* a root of Jesse,
1Co. 6:16. for two, saith he, *shall be* one flesh.
11:27. *shall be* guilty of the body
14: 9. for ye shall speak (lit. *shall be* speaking)
11. I *shall be* unto him that speaketh
2Co. 3: 8. How *shall* not the ministration of the spirit *be* rather glorious?
6:16. I *will be* their God, and they *shall be* my
18. And *will be* a Father unto you, and ye *shall be* my sons and daughters,
11:15. whose end *shall be* according to their
12: 6. I *shall* not *be* a fool;
13:11. God of love and peace *shall be* with you.
Eph. 5:31. and they two *shall be* one flesh.
6: 3. and thou mayest live long (lit. thou *shalt be* long lived)
Phi. 4: 9. the God of peace *shall be* with you.
Col. 2: 8. lest any man spoil you (lit. *shall be* making spoil of you)
1Th. 4:17. *shall* we ever *be* with the Lord.
1Ti. 4: 6. thou *shalt be* a good minister
2Ti. 2: 2. who *shall be* able to teach others also.
21. he *shall be* a vessel unto honour,
3: 2. For men *shall be* lovers of their own
9. their folly *shall be* manifest unto all
4: 3. For the time *will come* when
Heb. 1: 5. I *will be* to him a Father, and he *shall be*
2:13. I will put my trust (lit. I *will be* trusting)
3:12. lest there *be* in any of you
8:10. I *will be* to them a God, and they *shall be* to me a people:
12. I *will be* merciful to their unrighteousness,
Jas. 1:25. *shall be* blessed in his deed.
5: 3. *shall be* a witness against you,
2Pet. 2: 1. there *shall be* false teachers
1Joh. 3: 2. it doth not yet appear what we *shall be.*
— we *shall be* like him;
2Joh. 2. and *shall be* with us for ever.
3. Grace *be* with you,
Jude 18. they told you there should *be* mockers
Rev. 10: 6. there should *be* time no longer:
9. it *shall be* in thy mouth sweet as honey.
20: 6. they *shall be* priests of God and of Christ,
21: 3. they *shall be* his people, and God himself *shall be* with them, (and be) their God.
4. there *shall be* no more death,
— neither *shall* there *be* any more pain:
7. and I *will be* his God, and he *shall be* my
25. for there *shall be* no night there.
22: 3. *shall be* no more curse: but the throne of God and of the Lamb *shall be* in it;
5. And there *shall be* no night there;
12. according as his work *shall be.*
14. that they *may have* right to the tree (lit. that right to the t. of l. *shall be* theirs)

2071 /288 See also p. 308

ἐσόμενος, *esomenos.*

Lu. 22:49. When they which were about him saw *what would follow,*

2072 2 313/391 2:696 1519,3700 cf 2734

ἔσοπτρον, *esoptron.*

1Co. 13:12. now we see through a *glass,* darkly;
Jas. 1:23. beholding his natural face in a *glass:*

2073 3 313/391 *hesperos* (evening)

ἑσπέρα, *hespera.*

Lu. 24:29. it is toward *evening,*
Acts 4: 3. for it was now *eventide.*
28:23. from morning till *evening.*

2075 92 221/274 1510

ἐστέ, *este.*

From εἰμί.

Mat. 5:11. Blessed *are* ye, when (men) shall revile
13. Ye *are* the salt of the earth: but if
14. Ye *are* the light of the world.
8:26. Why *are* ye fearful, O ye of little faith?
10:20. For it is not ye (lit. ye *are* not) that speak,
15:16. *Are* ye also yet without understanding?
23: 8. and all ye *are* brethren.
28. but within ye *are* full of hypocrisy
31. ye *are* the children of them which killed
Mar. 4:40. Why *are* ye so fearful?
7:18. *Are* ye so without understanding also?
9:41. because ye *belong* to Christ,
13:11. for it is not ye (lit. ye *are* not) that speak,
Lu. 6:22. Blessed *are* ye, when men shall hate you,
9:55. what manner of spirit ye *are* of.
11:44. for ye *are* as graves
13:25. I know you not whence ye *are:*
27. I know you not whence ye *are;*
16:15. Ye *are* they which justify yourselves
22:28. Ye *are* they which have continued
24:17. as ye walk, and *are* sad?
38. Why *are* ye troubled?
48. And ye *are* witnesses of these things.
Joh. 8:23. Ye *are* from beneath; I am from above: ye *are* of this world;
31. (then) *are* ye my disciples indeed;
37. ye *are* Abraham's seed;
44. Ye *are* of (your) father the devil,
47. ye *are* not of God.
10:26. because ye *are* not of my sheep,
34. I said, Ye *are* gods?
13:10. ye *are* clean, but not all.
11. Ye *are* not all clean.
17. happy *are* ye if ye do them.
35. that ye *are* my disciples,
15: 3. Now ye *are* clean
14. Ye *are* my friends,
19. ye *are* not of the world,
27. ye *have been* with me from the beginning.
Acts 3:25. Ye *are* the children of the prophets,
7:26. Sirs, ye *are* brethren; why do ye wrong
19:15. Paul I know; but who *are* ye?
22: 3. zealous toward God, as ye all *are* this day.
Ro. 1: 6. Among whom *are* ye also
6:14. for ye *are* not under the law,
16. his servants ye *are* to whom ye obey;
8: 9. But ye *are* not in the flesh,
15:14. ye also *are* full of goodness,
1Co. 1:30. But of him *are* ye in Christ Jesus.
3: 3. For ye *are* yet carnal:

1Co. 3: 3. *are* ye not carnal,
4. *are* ye not carnal?
9. (ye *are*) God's building.
16. that ye *are* the temple of God,
17. which (temple) ye *are*.
4: 8. Now ye *are* full, now ye
5: 2. ye *are* puffed up, and have not
7. as ye *are* unleavened.
6: 2. *are* ye unworthy to judge the smallest
19. and ye *are* not your own?
9: 1. *are* not ye my work in the Lord?
2. of mine apostleship *are* ye in the Lord.
12:27. Now ye *are* the body of Christ,
14:12. ye *are* zealous of spiritual (gifts),
15:17. ye *are* yet in your sins.
2Co. 1: 7. as ye *are* partakers of the sufferings,
2: 9. whether ye *be* obedient in all things.
3: 2. Ye *are* our epistle written in
3. declared *to be* the epistle of Christ ·
6:16. ye *are* the temple of the living God;
7: 3. ye *are* in our hearts
13: 5. whether ye *be* in the faith;
— except ye *be* reprobates?
Gal. 3: 3. *Are* ye so foolish?
26. ye *are* all the children of God by faith
28. for ye *are* all one
29. *are* ye Abraham's seed,
4: 6. And because ye *are* sons,
5:18. ye *are* not under the law.
Eph. 2: 5. by grace ye *are* saved;
8. For by grace *are* ye saved
19. Now therefore ye *are* no more strangers
5: 5. For this ye know, (lit. ye *are* aware of)
Col. 2:10. And ye *are* complete in him,
1Th. 2:20. For ye *are* our glory
4: 9. ye yourselves *are* taught of God
5: 4. ye, brethren, *are* not in darkness,
5. Ye *are* all the children of light,
Heb 12: 8. But if ye *be* without chastisement,
— *are* ye bastards, and not sons.
1Joh 2:14. because ye *are* strong,
4: 4. Ye *are* of God, little children,

2076 906 221/273 2:21 1510

ἐστί, esti.

From εἰμί.

Mat. 1:20. conceived in her *is* of the Holy Ghost.
23. which being interpreted *is*,
2: 2. Saying, Where *is* he
3: 3. For this *is* he that was spoken of
11. cometh after me *is* mightier than I,
15. for thus it becometh us (lit. *is* becoming for us) to fulfil
17. This *is* my beloved Son,
5: 3. for their's *is* the kingdom of heaven.
10. for their's *is* the kingdom of heaven.
34. by heaven; for it *is* God's throne:
35. earth; for it *is* his footstool: neither by Jerusalem; for it *is* the city of
37. whatsoever is more than these *cometh* of
48. Father which is in heaven *is* perfect.
6:13. For thine *is* the kingdom,
21. For where your treasure *is*,
22. The light of the body *is* the eye:
23. the light that is in thee *be* darkness,
25. *Is* not the life more than meat,
7: 9. Or what man *is* there of you,
12. for this *is* the law and the prophets.
8:27. What manner of man *is* this,
9: 5. For whether *is* easier

Mat. 9:13. learn what (that) *meaneth*, I will have
15. the bridegroom *is* with them?
10: 2. names of the twelve apostles *are* these;
10. the workman *is* worthy of his meat.
11. who in it *is* worthy;
24. The disciple *is* not above (his) master,
26. for there *is* nothing covered,
37. more than me *is* not worthy of me:
— *is* not worthy of me.
38. followeth after me, *is* not worthy of me.
11: 6. And blessed *is* (he), whosoever shall
10. For this *is* (he), of whom it is
11. he that is least in the kingdom of heaven *is*
14. receive (it), this *is* Elias,
16. It *is* like unto children sitting in
30. and my burden *is* light.
12: 6. in this place *is* (one) greater
7. But if ye had known what (this) *meaneth*,
8. For the Son of man *is* Lord even of the sabbath day.
23. *Is* not this the son of David?
30. He that is not with me *is* against me;
48. Who *is* my mother?
50. the same *is* my brother, and sister, and mother.
13:19. This *is* he which received seed by
20. the same *is* he that heareth the word,
21. but dureth for a while: (lit. *is* temporary)
22. *is* he that heareth the word; and the care
23. *is* he that heareth the word, and
31. The kingdom of heaven *is* like to a grain
32. Which indeed *is* the least of all seeds: but when it is grown, it *is*
33. The kingdom of heaven *is* like unto
37. that soweth the good seed *is* the Son of
38. The field *is* the world;
39. The enemy that sowed them *is* the devil; the harvest *is* the end of the world;
44. Again, the kingdom of heaven *is* like unto treasure
45. of heaven *is* like unto a merchant man,
47. kingdom of heaven *is* like unto a net,
52. *is* like unto a man (that is) an
55. *Is* not this the carpenter's son?
57. A prophet *is* not without honour,
14: 2. This *is* John the Baptist;
15. This *is* a desert place,
26. were troubled, saying, It *is* a spirit;
15:20. These *are* (the things) which defile
26. It *is* not meet to take the children's
16:20. that he *was* Jesus the Christ.
17: 4. Lord, it *is* good for us to be here:
5. This *is* my beloved Son, in whom I
18: 1. Who *is* the greatest in the kingdom
4. as this little child, the same *is* greatest
7. for it must needs be (lit. it *is* a necessity that offences come;
8. it *is* better for thee to enter into
9. it *is* better for thee to enter into life with
14. Even so it *is* not the will
19:10. If the case of the man *be* so
14. of such *is* the kingdom
24. It *is* easier for a camel to go through
26. this *is* impossible; but with God all things *are* possible.
20: 1. kingdom of heaven *is* like unto a man
15. *Is* thine eye evil,
23. *is* not mine to give,
21:10. was moved, saying, Who *is* this?
11. This *is* Jesus the prophet of Nazareth
38. This *is* the heir;
42. and it *is* marvellous in our eyes?

Mat. 22: 8. The wedding *is* ready,
32. God *is* not the God of the dead,
38. This *is* the first and great commandment.
42. whose son *is* he?
45. how *is* he his son?
23: 8. for one *is* your Master, (even) Christ; and all ye are brethren.
9. for one *is* your Father,
10. for one *is* your Master, (even) Christ.
16. swear by the temple, it *is* nothing;
17. for whether *is* greater,
18. swear by the altar, it *is* nothing;
24: 6. but the end *is* not yet.
26. he *is* in the desert;
33. it *is* near, (even) at the doors.
45. Who then *is* a faithful and wise servant,
26: 18. My time *is* at hand;
26. Take, eat; this *is* my body.
28. For this *is* my blood of the new
38. My soul *is* exceeding sorrowful,
39. if it *be* possible, let this cup
48. I shall kiss, that same *is* he:
66. He *is* guilty of death.
68. Who *is* he that smote thee?
27: 6. it *is* the price of blood.
33. that *is* to say, a place of a skull,
37. THIS *IS* JESUS THE KING OF THE JEWS.
42. If he *be* the King of Israel,
62. Now the next day, that followed (lit. which *is* after) the day of the
28: 6. He *is* not here: for he is risen,
Mar. 1: 27. saying, What thing *is* this?
2: 1. that he *was* in the house.
9. Whether *is* it easier to say
19. while the bridegroom *is* with them?
28. Therefore the Son of man *is* Lord
3: 17. Boanerges, which *is*, The sons of thunder:
29. but *is* in danger of eternal damnation:
33. Who *is* my mother, or my brethren?
35. *is* my brother, and my sister, and mother.
4: 22. For there *is* nothing hid,
26. So *is* the kingdom of God, as if a man
31. *is* less than all the seeds
41. What manner of man *is* this,
5: 14. to see what it *was* that was done.
41. which *is*, being interpreted, Damsel, I
6: 3. *Is* not this the carpenter,
4. A prophet *is* not without honour,
15. Others said, That it *is* Elias. And others said, That it *is* a prophet, or
16. he said, It *is* John, whom I beheaded:
35. This *is* a desert place,
55. where they heard he *was*.
7: 4. And many other things there *be*,
11. Corban, that *is to say*, a gift,
15. There *is* nothing from without a man,
— those *are* they that defile
27. for it *is* not meet to take the children's
34. that *is*, Be opened.
9: 5. it *is* good for us to be here:
7. This *is* my beloved Son:
10. what the rising from the dead should *mean*.
21. How long *is* it ago since this
39. for there *is* no man which shall do
40. For he that *is* not against us *is* on our
42. it *is* better for him that a millstone
43. it *is* better for thee to enter into
45. it *is* better for thee to enter
47. it *is* better for thee to enter
10: 14. of such *is* the kingdom of God.

Mar. 10: 24. how hard *is* it for them that
25. It *is* easier for a camel
27. with God all things *are* possible.
29. There *is* no man that hath left
40. *is* not mine to give;
47. it *was* Jesus of Nazareth,
12: 7. This *is* the heir;
11. and it *is* marvellous in our eyes?
27. He *is* not the God of the dead,
28. Which *is* the first commandment of all?
29. The Lord our God *is* one Lord:
31. There *is* none other commandment
32. for there *is* one God; and there *is* none other but he:
33. *is* more than all whole burnt offerings
35. that Christ *is* the son of David?
37. whence *is* he (then) his son?
42. two mites, which *make* a farthing.
13: 28. ye know that summer *is* near:
29. it *is* nigh, (even) at the doors.
33. for ye know not when the time *is*.
14: 14. Where *is* the guestchamber,
22. Take, eat: this *is* my body.
24. This *is* my blood of the new
34. My soul *is* exceeding sorrowful
35. that, if it *were* possible, the hour might
44. Whomsoever I shall kiss, that same *is* he;
69. This *is* (one) of them.
15: 16. into the hall, *called* Prætorium;
22. which *is*, being interpreted, The place
34. which *is*, being interpreted, My God,
42. that *is*, the day before the sabbath,
16: 6. he is risen; he *is* not here:
Lu. 1: 36. this *is* the sixth month with her,
61. There *is* none of thy kindred
63. His name *is* John.
2: 11. which *is* Christ the Lord.
4: 22. *Is* not this Joseph's son?
24. No prophet *is* accepted
5: 21. Who *is* this which speaketh blasphemies?
23. Whether *is* easier, to say,
34. while the bridegroom *is* with them?
39. The old *is* better.
6: 5. the Son of man *is* Lord also
20. your's *is* the kingdom of God.
32. what thank *have* ye? (lit. *is* to you)
33. what thank *have* ye? (lit. *is* to you)
34. what thank *have* ye? (lit. *is* to you)
35. he *is* kind unto the unthankful and
36. as your Father also *is* merciful.
40. The disciple *is* not above his master:
43. For a good tree bringeth not forth (lit. *is* not bringing forth) corrupt fruit;
47. I will shew you to whom he *is* like:
48. He *is* like a man which built an house,
49. *is* like a man that without a foundation
7: 4. he *was* worthy for whom he should do
23. blessed *is* (he), whosoever shall not be
27. This *is* (he), of whom it is written,
28. there *is* not a greater prophet than John
— *is* greater than he.
39. for she *is* a sinner.
49. Who *is* this that forgiveth sins also?
8: 11. Now the parable *is* this: The seed *is* the
17. For nothing *is* secret,
25. Where *is* your faith?
— What manner of man *is* this!
26. which *is* over against Galilee.
30. What *is* thy name?
9: 9. but who *is* this, of whom I hear such
33. it *is* good for us to be here:
35. This *is* my beloved Son:

Lu. 9:38. for he *is* mine only child.
50. Forbid (him) not: for he that *is* not against us *is* for us.
62. *is* fit for the kingdom of God.
10: 7. for the labourer *is* worthy of his hire.
22. knoweth who the Son *is*, but the Father; and who the Father *is*, but the Son, and (he) to
29. And who *is* my neighbour?
42. But one thing *is* needful:
11:21. his goods *are* in peace:
23. not with me *is* against me:
29. This *is* an evil generation:
34. The light of the body *is* the eye:
— thy whole body also *is* full of light;
35. light which is in thee *be* not darkness.
41. all things *are* clean unto you.
12: 1. which *is* hypocrisy.
2. there *is* nothing covered,
6. not one of them *is* forgotten
15. a man's life *consisteth* not
23. The life *is* more than meat,
24. which neither *have* storehouse
34. For where your treasure *is*,
42. Who then *is* that faithful and wise
13:18. Unto what *is* the kingdom of God like?
19. It *is* like a grain of mustard seed,
21. It *is* like leaven,
14:17. all things *are* now ready.
22. and yet there *is* room.
31. whether he *be* able with ten thousand
35. It *is* neither fit for the land, nor yet for the dunghill;
15:31. all that I have *is* thine.
16:10. *is* faithful also in much:
— *is* unjust also in much.
15. *is* abomination in the sight of God.
17. And it *is* easier for heaven and
17: 1. It *is* impossible but that offences
21. the kingdom of God *is* within you.
18:16. of such *is* the kingdom of God.
25. For it *is* easier for a camel
27. *are* possible with God.
29. There *is* no man that hath left
19: 3. to see Jesus who he *was*;
9. *is* a son of Abraham.
46. *is* the house of prayer:
20: 2. who *is* he that gave thee
6. for they *be* persuaded
14. This *is* the heir:
17. What *is* this then that is written,
38. he *is* not a God of the dead, but
44. how *is* he then his son?
21:30. summer *is* now nigh at hand.
31. the kingdom of God *is* nigh at hand.
22:11. Where *is* the guestchamber,
19. This *is* my body which is given
38. he said unto them, It *is* enough.
53. but this *is* your hour, and the power
59. for he *is* a Galilæan.
64. who *is* it that smote thee?
23: 6. whether the man *were* a Galilæan.
7. he *belonged* unto Herod's jurisdiction,
15. nothing worthy of death *is* done unto
35. let him save himself, if he *be* Christ,
38. THIS *IS* THE KING OF THE JEWS.
24: 6. He *is* not here, but is risen:
21. that it *had been* he which should have
29. it *is* toward evening,
Joh. 1:19. this *is* the record of John,
27. He it *is*, who coming after
30. This *is* he of whom I said,

Joh. 1:33. the same *is* he which baptizeth
34. this *is* the Son of God.
42. which *is* by interpretation,
47(48). in whom *is* no guile!
2: 9. and knew not whence it *was*:
17. remembered that it *was* written,
3: 6. born of the flesh *is* flesh; and that which is born of the Spirit *is* spirit.
8. so *is* every one that is born of the Spirit.
19. And this *is* the condemnation,
21. they *are* wrought in God.
29. that hath the bride *is* the bridegroom:
31. that cometh from above *is* above all: he that is of the earth *is* earthly,
— that cometh from heaven *is* above all.
33. hath set to his seal that God *is* true.
4:10. who it *is* that saith to thee,
11. the well *is* deep:
18. *is* not thy husband:
20. in Jerusalem *is* the place
22. salvation *is* of the Jews.
23. the hour cometh, and now *is*,
29. *is* not this the Christ?
34. My meat *is* to do the will of him that
35. There *are* yet four months,
37. herein *is* that saying true, One soweth, and another reapeth. (lit. one *is* the sower, and another the reaper)
42. this *is* indeed the Christ, the Saviour of the world.
5: 2. Now there *is* at Jerusalem
10. It *is* the sabbath day: it is not lawful
12. What man *is* that which said
13. wist not who it *was*:
15. that it *was* Jesus, which had made
25. The hour is coming, and now *is*,
27 because he *is* the Son of man.
30. my judgment *is* just;
31 of myself, my witness *is* not true.
32. There *is* another that beareth witness
— that the witness which he witnesseth of me *is* true.
45. there *is* (one) that accuseth you,
6: 9. There *is* a lad here,
— what *are* they among so many?
14. This *is* of a truth that prophet
24. that Jesus *was* not there,
29. This *is* the work of God,
31. as it *is* written, He gave them bread from
33. the bread of God *is* he which cometh
39. And this *is* the Father's will
40. And this *is* the will
42. *Is* not this Jesus, the son
45. It *is* written in the prophets,
50. This *is* the bread which
51. the bread that I will give *is* my flesh,
55. For my flesh *is* meat indeed, and my blood *is* drink indeed.
58. This *is* that bread which came down
60. This *is* an hard saying;
63. It *is* the spirit that quickeneth;
— words that I speak unto you, (they) *are* spirit, and (they) *are* life.
64. and who should betray (lit. who it *was* that should betray) him.
70. one of you *is* a devil?
7: 6. but your time *is* alway ready.
7. the works thereof *are* evil.
11. and said, Where *is* he?
12. some said, He *is* a good man:
16. My doctrine *is* not mine,
17. whether it *be* of God,

Joh. 7: 18. the same *is* true, and no unrighteousness *is* in him.
22. not because it *is* of Moses,
25. *Is* not this he, whom they seek
26. that this *is* the very Christ?
27. we know this man whence he *is*:
— no man knoweth whence he *is*.
28. but he that sent me *is* true,
36. What (manner of) saying *is* this
40. Of a truth this *is* the prophet.
41. This *is* the Christ.
8: 13. thy record *is* not true.
14. (yet) my record *is* true:
16. my judgment *is* true:
17. the testimony of two men *is* true.
19. Where *is* thy Father?
26. he that sent me *is* true;
29. And he that sent me *is* with me:
34. *is* the servant of sin.
39. Abraham *is* our father.
44. there *is* no truth in him.
— for he *is* a liar,
50. there *is* one that seeketh and judgeth.
54. If I honour myself, my honour *is* nothing: it *is* my Father that honoureth me; of whom ye say, that he *is* your God:
9: 4. the works of him that sent me, while it *is*
8. *Is* not this he that sat
9. Some said, This *is* he: others (said), He *is* like him:
12. Where *is* he? He said,
16. This man *is* not of God, because he
17. He *is* a prophet.
19. *Is* this your son,
20. this *is* our son,
24. this man *is* a sinner.
25. Whether he *be* a sinner (or no),
29. we know not from whence he *is*.
30. herein *is* a marvellous thing, that ye know not from whence he *is*,
36. Who *is* he, Lord, that I might believe
37. it *is* he that talketh with thee.
10: 1. *is* a thief and a robber.
2. *is* the shepherd of the sheep.
13. because he *is* an hireling,
16. which *are* not of this fold:
21. *are* not the words of him that hath a devil.
29. My Father, which gave (them) me, *is* greater than all;
34. *Is* it not written in your law,
11: 4. This sickness *is* not unto death,
10. there *is* no light in him.
39. for he hath been (dead) four days. (lit. *is* of the fourth day)
57. if any man knew where he *were*,
12: 9. of the Jews therefore knew that he *was*
14. sat thereon; as it *is* written,
31. Now *is* the judgment of this world:
34. who *is* this Son of man?
35. Yet a little while *is* the light with you.
50. that his commandment *is* life everlasting:
13: 10. but *is* clean every whit:
16. The servant *is* not greater
25. saith unto him, Lord, who *is* it?
26. He it *is*, to whom I shall give a sop,
14: 10. and the Father in me? (lit. *is* in me)
21. he it *is* that loveth me:
24. the word which ye hear *is* not mine, but
28. *is* greater than I.
15: 1. my Father *is* the husbandman.
12. This *is* my commandment,
20. The servant *is* not greater

Joh. 16: 15. All things that the Father hath *are* mine:
17. What *is* this that he saith unto us,
18. What *is* this that he saith, A little while?
32. the Father *is* with me.
17: 3. And this *is* life eternal,
7. whatsoever thou hast given me *are* of
10. all mine *are* thine,
17. thy word *is* truth.
18: 36. My kingdom *is* not of this world:
— but now *is* my kingdom not from hence.
38. Pilate saith unto him, What *is* truth?
39. But ye *have* a custom,
19: 35. his record *is* true:
40. as the manner of the Jews *is*
20: 14. knew not that it *was* Jesus.
15. She, supposing him to *be* the gardener,
30. which *are* not written in this book:
31. might believe that Jesus *is* the Christ,
21: 4. knew not that it *was* Jesus.
7. It *is* the Lord. Now when Simon Peter heard that it *was* the Lord,
12. knowing that it *was* the Lord.
20. said, Lord, which *is* he that betrayeth
24. This *is* the disciple which testifieth
— know that his testimony *is* true.
25. And there *are* also many other things
Acts 1: 7. It *is* not for you to know
12. which *is* from Jerusalem a sabbath day's
2: 15. seeing it *is* (but) the third hour
16. this *is* that which was spoken
25. he *is* on my right hand,
29. his sepulchre *is* with us
39. For the promise *is* unto you,
4: 11. This *is* the stone which was set at nought
12. Neither *is* there salvation in any other: for there *is* none other name
19. Whether it *be* right in the sight
36. which *is*, being interpreted, The son of
5: 39. But if it *be* of God,
6: 2. It *is* not reason that we
7: 33. the place where thou standest *is* holy
37. This *is* that Moses, which said
38. This *is* he, that was in the church in
8: 10. This man *is* the great power of God.
21. Thou *hast* neither part nor lot in this matter: for thy heart *is* not right in the sight of God.
26. Jerusalem unto Gaza, which *is* desert.
9: 15. he *is* a chosen vessel unto me,
20. that he *is* the Son of God.
21. *Is* not this he that destroyed
22. that this *is* very Christ.
26. that he *was* a disciple.
38. that Peter *was* there,
10: 4. What *is* it, Lord?
6. whose house *is* by the sea side:
28. it *is* an unlawful thing for a man that is a
34. that God *is* no respecter of persons:
35. *is* accepted with him.
36. he *is* Lord of all:
42. it *is* he which was ordained
12: 3. it pleased (lit. *was* pleasing to) the Jews,
9. that it *was* true which was done
15. It *is* his angel.
13: 15. if ye *have* any word of exhortation for the people, say on.
15: 18. Known unto God *are* all his works from the beginning of the world.
16: 12. which *is* the chief city of that part
17: 3. Jesus, whom I preach unto you, *is* Christ.
18: 10. I *have* much people
15. But if it *be* a question

Acts19: 2. whether there *be* any Holy Ghost.
25. we *have* our wealth.
34. that he *was* a Jew,
35. what man *is* there that knoweth not
36. ye ought (lit. it *is* fit for you) to be quiet,
20:10. his life *is* in him.
35. It *is* more blessed to give
21:11. that owneth this girdle, (lit. whose this girdle *is*)
22. What *is* it therefore? the multitude
24. informed concerning thee, *are* nothing;
28. This *is* the man, that teacheth all
33. and what he had done. (lit. he *were* the doer of)
22:26. thou doest: for this man *is* a Roman.
29. after he knew that he *was* a Roman,
23: 5. that he *was* the high priest:
6. that the one part *were* Sadducees,
19. What *is* that thou hast to tell
27. having understood that he *was* a Roman.
34. of what province he *was*.
25: 5. if there *be* any wickedness in him.
11. but if there *be* none of these things
14. There *is* a certain man left
16. It *is* not the manner of the Romans
26:26. for this thing *was* not done in a corner.
28: 4. No doubt this man *is* a murderer,
22. we know that (lit. it *is* known to us)
Ro. 1: 9. For God *is* my witness,
12. That *is*, that I may be comforted
16. for it *is* the power of God
19. that which may be known of God *is* manifest in them;
25. who *is* blessed for ever.
2: 2. the judgment of God *is* according to
11. For there *is* no respect of persons
28. he *is* not a Jew, which is one outwardly;
3: 8. whose damnation *is* just.
10. There *is* none righteous, no, not one:
11. There *is* none that understandeth, there *is* none that seeketh after God.
12. there *is* none that doeth good, no, not one. (lit. there *is* not even one)
18. There *is* no fear of God
22. for there *is* no difference:
4:15. for where no law *is*,
16. who *is* the father of us all,
21. he *was* able also to perform.
5:14. who *is* the figure of him that was to come.
7: 3. she *is* free from that law;
14. the law *is* spiritual:
8: 9. he *is* none of his.
24. but hope that is seen *is* not hope:
34. who *is* even at the right hand
9: 2. I *have* great heaviness
10: 1. prayer to God for Israel *is*, that they
8. The word *is* nigh thee,
12. For there *is* no difference
11: 6. then *is* it no more grace: otherwise work *is* no more work.
23. for God *is* able to graff them in again.
13: 1. For there *is* no power but of God:
4. For he *is* the minister of God to thee
— for he *is* the minister of God, a revenger
14: 4. for God *is* able to make him stand.
17. For the kingdom of God *is* not
23. whatsoever (is) not of faith *is* sin.
16: 5. who *is* the firstfruits of Achaia
1Co 1:18. *is* to them that perish foolishness;
— it *is* the power of God.
25. the foolishness of God *is* wiser than men; and the weakness of God *is* stronger

1 Co. 2:14. for they *are* foolishness unto him:
3: 5. Who then *is* Paul,
7. neither *is* he that planteth any thing,
11. than that is laid, which *is* Jesus Christ.
13. every man's work of what sort it *is*.
17. the temple of God *is* holy,
19. wisdom of this world *is* foolishness
21. For all things *are* your's;
22. present, or things to come; all *are* your's;
4: 3. But with me it *is* a very small thing
4. he that judgeth me *is* the Lord.
17. who *is* my beloved son,
6: 5. that there *is* not a wise man among you?
7. there *is* utterly a fault among you,
15. *are* the members of Christ?
16. joined to an harlot *is* one body?
17. joined unto the Lord *is* one spirit.
18. a man doeth *is* without the body;
19. your body *is* the temple of the Holy Ghost
20. in your body, and in your spirit, which *are* God's.
7: 8. *is* good for them if they abide even as I.
9. for it *is* better to marry
14. else *were* your children unclean; but now *are* they holy.
19. Circumcision *is* nothing, and uncircumcision *is* nothing,
22. *is* the Lord's freeman:
— *is* Christ's servant.
29. it remaineth (lit. what remains *is*), that both they that have wives
39. she *is* at liberty to be married to whom
40. But she *is* happier if she so abide, after my judgment:
9: 3. Mine answer to them that do examine me *is* this,
16. I *have* nothing to glory of:
— yea, woe *is* unto me,
18. What *is* my reward then?
10:16. *is* it not the communion of the blood of Christ?
— *is* it not the communion of the body of Christ?
19. that the idol *is* any thing, or that which is offered in sacrifice to idols *is* any thing?
28. This *is* offered in sacrifice unto idols,
11: 3. the head of every man *is* Christ;
5. for that *is* even all one as if she were
7. but the woman *is* the glory of the man.
8. For the man *is* not of the woman;
13. *is* it comely that a woman
14. it *is* a shame unto him?
15. it *is* a glory to her:
20. (this) *is* not to eat the Lord's supper.
24. Take, eat: this *is* my body,
25. This cup *is* the new testament in my
12: 6. but it *is* the same God which worketh
12. For as the body *is* one, and hath
— being many, *are* one body:
14. *is* not one member, but
15. *is* it therefore not of the body?
16. *is* it therefore not of the body?
22. seem to be more feeble, *are* necessary:
14:10. There *are*, it may be, so many kinds of
14. my understanding *is* unfruitful.
15. What *is* it then? I will pray
25. God *is* in you of a truth.
26. How *is* it then, brethren?
33. For God *is* not (the author) of confusion,
35. for it *is* a shame for women to speak in the church.

1Co.15:12. that there *is* no resurrection of
13. there *be* no resurrection of the dead,
44. There *is* a natural body, and there *is* a spiritual body.
58. *is* not in vain in the Lord.
16:15. that it *is* the firstfruits of Achaia,
2Co. 1:12. our rejoicing *is* this,
2: 2. who *is* he then that maketh me glad,
3. my joy *is* (the joy) of you all.
3:17. Now the Lord *is* that Spirit:
4: 3. But if our gospel *be* hid, it *is* hid to them that are lost:
4. who *is* the image of God,
7:15. *is* more abundant toward you,
9: 1. it *is* superfluous for me to write
12. not only supplieth (lit. *is* supplying)
10:18. For not he that commendeth himself *is* approved,
11:10. As the truth of Christ *is* in me,
12:13. For what *is* it wherein you were
13: 5. how that Jesus Christ *is* in you, except
Gal. 1: 7. Which *is* not another; but
11. preached of me *is* not after man.
3:12. And the law *is* not of faith:
16. And to thy seed, which *is* Christ.
20. a mediator *is* not (a mediator) of one, but God *is* one.
4: 1. the heir, as long as he *is* a child,
2. But *is* under tutors and
24. Which things *are* an allegory:
— which *is* Agar.
25. *is* mount Sinai in Arabia,
26. But Jerusalem which is above *is* free, which *is* the mother of us all.
5: 3. he *is* a debtor to do the whole
19. Now the works of the flesh *are* manifest, which *are* (these);
22. the fruit of the Spirit *is* love, joy,
23. against such there *is* no law.
Eph. 1:14. Which *is* the earnest of our inheritance
18. that ye may know what *is* the hope
23. Which *is* his body,
2:14. For he *is* our peace,
3:13. for you, which *is* your glory.
4: 9. Now that he ascended, what *is* it but
10. *is* the same also that ascended up
15. which *is* the head, (even) Christ:
21. as the truth *is* in Jesus:
5: 5. who *is* an idolater, hath any
10. what *is* acceptable unto the Lord.
12. For it *is* a shame even to speak of
13. whatsoever doth make manifest *is* light.
18. wherein *is* excess;
23. the husband *is* the head of the wife,
— he *is* the saviour of the body.
32. This *is* a great mystery:
6: 1. in the Lord: for this *is* right.
2. which *is* the first commandment
9. your Master also *is* in heaven; neither *is* there respect of persons with him.
12. we wrestle not against (lit. The wrestling *is* not to us against)
17. which *is* the word of God:
Phi. 1: 7. Even as it *is* meet for me to
8. For God *is* my record,
28. which *is* to them an evident token
2:13. For it *is* God which worketh in you both
4: 8. whatsoever things *are* true, whatsoever
Col. 1: 6. and bringeth forth fruit, (lit. *is* fruit-bearing)
7. who *is* for you a faithful minister
15. Who *is* the image of the invisible God,
Col. 1: 17. he *is* before all things,
18. he *is* the head of the body, the church: who *is* the beginning, the firstborn
24. for his body's sake, which *is* the church.
27. which *is* Christ in you,
2:10. which *is* the head of all
17. Which *are* a shadow of things to come;
22. Which all *are* to perish
23. Which things have indeed a shew (lit. which *are* holding some account of wisdom)
3: 1. where Christ sitteth (lit. *is* sitting) on the right hand of God.
5. and covetousness, which *is* idolatry:
14. which *is* the bond of perfectness.
20. for this *is* well pleasing
25. there *is* no respect of persons.
4: 9. who *is* (one) of you.
1Th. 2:13. as it *is* in truth,
4: 3. For this *is* the will of God,
2Th. 1: 3. as it *is* meet, because that
2: 4. himself that he *is* God.
9. whose coming *is* after the working of Satan
3: 3. But the Lord *is* faithful,
17. which *is* the token in every epistle:
1Ti. 1: 5. the end of the commandment *is* charity
20. Of whom *is* Hymenæus
3:15. in the house of God, which *is* the church
16. great *is* the mystery of godliness:
4: 8. profiteth (lit. *is* pr. for) little: but godliness *is* profitable unto all things,
10. who *is* the saviour of all men,
5: 4. parents: for that *is* good and
8. and *is* worse than an infidel.
25. the good works (of some) *are* manifest beforehand;
6: 6. with contentment *is* great gain.
10. the love of money *is* the root of all evil:
2Ti. 1: 6. which *is* in thee by the putting on
12. he *is* able to keep that which I
15. of whom *are* Phygellus
2:17. of whom *is* Hymenæus and Philetus;
20. there *are* not only vessels
4:11. Only Luke *is* with me.
— for he *is* profitable to me
Tit. 1: 6. If any *be* blameless, the husband of one
13. This witness *is* true. Wherefore
3: 8. These things *are* good and profitable
Heb. 2: 6. What *is* man, that thou art mindful
4:13. Neither *is* there any creature that
5:13. for he *is* a babe.
14. But strong meat *belongeth to* them that
7: 2. which *is*, King of peace;
15. it *is* yet far more evident: for that
8: 6. he *is* the mediator of a better covenant,
9: 5. of which we cannot now speak (lit. it *is* not now to speak)
15. he *is* the mediator of the new testament,
11: 1. Now faith *is* the substance of things hoped for,
6. cometh to God must believe that he *is*,
12: 7. for what son *is* he whom the father
Jas. 1:13. cannot be tempted (lit. *is* not to be tempted) with evil,
17. perfect gift *is* from above, and
23. if any *be* a hearer of the word, and not
27. before God and the Father *is* this,
2:17. hath not works, *is* dead, being alone.
19. Thou believest that there *is* one God;
20. faith without works *is* dead?
26. the body without the spirit *is* dead, so faith without works *is* dead also.

Jas. 3: 5. the tongue *is* a little member,
15. This wisdom descendeth not (lit. this *is* not the wisdom that descendeth)
17. wisdom that is from above *is* first pure,
4: 4. the friendship of the world *is* enmity with God?
12. There *is* one lawgiver, who is able
14. It *is* even a vapour, that
16. all such rejoicing *is* evil.
17. to him it *is* sin.
5: 11. the Lord *is* very pitiful, and of tender mercy.
1Pet. 1: 6. if need *be*, ye are in heaviness
25. And this *is* the word which
2: 15. so *is* the will of God,
3: 4. which *is* in the sight of God
22. *is* on the right hand of God;
4: 11. to whom *be* praise and dominion
2Pet. 1: 9. *is* blind, and cannot see afar off,
14. shortly I must put off (this) my tabernacle, (lit. the putting off my tabernacle *is* at hand)
17. This *is* my beloved Son,
3: 4. Where *is* the promise of his coming?
16. in which *are* some things hard to be understood,
1Joh. 1: 5. This then *is* the message
— God *is* light, and in him *is* no darkness at all.
7. as he *is* in the light,
8. and the truth *is* not in us.
9. he *is* faithful and just
10. his word *is* not in us.
2: 2. And he *is* the propitiation for our sins:
4. and keepeth not his commandments, *is* a liar, and the truth *is* not in him.
7. The old commandment *is* the word
8. which thing *is* true in him and in you:
9. hateth his brother, *is* in darkness
10. there *is* none occasion of stumbling in
11. he that hateth his brother *is* in darkness,
15. the love of the Father *is* not in him.
16. and the pride of life, *is* not of the Father, but *is* of the world.
18. children, it *is* the last time:
— whereby we know that it *is* the last time.
21. and that no lie *is* of the truth.
22. Who *is* a liar but he that denieth that Jesus *is* the Christ? He *is* antichrist, that denieth
25. And this *is* the promise that he
27. teacheth you of all things, and *is* truth, and *is* no lie,
29. If ye know that he *is* righteous,
3: 2. we shall see him as he *is*.
3. purifieth himself, even as he *is* pure.
4. sin *is* the transgression of
5. in him *is* no sin.
7. he that doeth righteousness *is* righteous, even as he *is* righteous.
8. He that committeth sin *is* of the devil:
10. the children of God *are* manifest,
— doeth not righteousness *is* not of God,
11. For this *is* the message that ye heard
15. hateth his brother *is* a murderer:
20. God *is* greater than our heart,
23. this *is* his commandment,
4: 1. whether they *are* of God:
2. come in the flesh *is* of God:
3. *is* not of God: and this *is* that (spirit) of antichrist,
— even now already *is* it in the world.
4. greater is he that *is* in you,
1Joh. 4: 6. he that *is* not of God
7. let us love one another: for love *is* of God;
8. for God *is* love.
10. Herein *is* love, not that we loved God,
12. and his love *is* perfected in us.
15. confess that Jesus *is* the Son of God,
16. God *is* love; and he that dwelleth in
17. because as he *is*, so are we in this world.
18. There *is* no fear in love;
20. and hateth his brother, he *is* a liar: for
5: 1. that Jesus *is* the Christ is born
3. For this *is* the love of God, that we
4. this *is* the victory that overcometh
5. Who *is* he that overcometh the world, but he that believeth that Jesus *is* the Son of God?
6. This *is* he that came by water and
— it *is* the Spirit that beareth witness, because the Spirit *is* truth.
9. the witness of God *is* greater: for this *is* the witness of God
11. *is* the record, that God hath given to us eternal life, and this life *is* in his Son.
14. this *is* the confidence that we have
16. There *is* a sin unto death:
17. All unrighteousness *is* sin: and there *is* a sin not unto death.
20. This *is* the true God, and eternal life.
2Joh. 6. this *is* love, that we walk after his commandments. This *is* the commandment,
7. This *is* a deceiver and
3Joh. 11. He that doeth good *is* of God:
12. ye know that our record *is* true.
Rev. 1: 4. which *are* before his throne;
2: 7. which *is* in the midst of the paradise
5: 2. Who *is* worthy to open the book, and
12. Worthy *is* the Lamb that was slain to
13. every creature which *is* in heaven,
— such as *are* in the sea, and all
13: 10. Here *is* the patience and the faith of the
18. Here *is* wisdom. Let him that
— for it *is* the number of a man;
14: 12. Here *is* the patience of the saints:
16: 21. plague thereof *was* exceeding great.
17: 8. beast that thou sawest was, and *is* not;
— behold the beast that was, and *is* not, and yet *is*.
10. one *is*, (and) the other is not yet come;
11. the beast that was, and *is* not, even he *is* the eighth, and *is* of the seven,
14. he *is* Lord of lords, and King of kings:
18. thou sawest *is* that great city, which
19: 8. *is* the righteousness of saints.
10. the testimony of Jesus *is* the spirit of
20: 2. serpent, which *is* the devil, and Satan,
12. which *is* (the book) of life:
14. This *is* the second death.
21: 1. there *was* no more sea.
8. which *is* the second death.
12. which *are* (the names) of the twelve tribes
16. the length *is* as large as the breadth:
— and the height of it *are* equal.
17. measure of a man, that *is*, of the angel.
22. the Lord God Almighty and the Lamb *are* the temple of it.
22: 10. for the time *is* at hand.

See also *τουτέστι*.

2077 16 221/278 1510

ἔστω, ἔστωσαν, esto, estōsan.

Mat. 5: 37. But *let* your communication *be*, Yea, yea;

Mat. 18:17. *let* him *be* unto thee as an heathen man
20:26. *let* him *be* your minister;
27. chief among you, *let* him *be* your servant:
Lu. 12:35. *Let* your loins *be* girded about, and
Acts 1:20. let no man dwell therein: (lit. *let* there not *be* one dwelling in it)
2:14. *be* this known unto you, and hearken
4:10. *Be* it known unto you all,
13:38. *Be* it known unto you therefore,
28:28. *Be* it known therefore unto you,
2Co.12:16. But *be* it so, I did not burden
Gal. 1: 8. *let* him *be* accursed.
9. than that ye have received, *let* him *be* accursed.
1Ti. 3:12. *Let* the deacons *be* the husbands of one
Jas. 1:19. *let* every man *be* swift to hear, slow
1Pet.3: 3. *let* it not *be* that outward (adorning)

2078 58 313/391 2:697 2192

ἔσχατος, eskatos.

Mat. 5:26. till thou hast paid the *uttermost* farthing.
12:45. the *last* (state) of that man is worse than
19:30. many (that are) first shall be *last;* and the *last* (shall be) first.
20: 8. beginning from the *last* unto the first.
12. These *last* have wrought (but) one hour,
14. I will give unto this *last*, even as
16. So the *last* shall be first, and the first *last:* for many be
27:64. the *last* error shall be worse than
Mar. 9:35. (the same) shall be *last* of all,
10:31. But many (that are) first shall be *last;* and the *last* first.
12: 6. he sent him also *last* unto them,
22. *last* of all the woman died
Lu. 11:26. the *last* (state) of that man is worse
12:59. till thou hast paid the very *last* mite.
13:30. there are *last* which shall be first, and there are first which shall be *last.*
14: 9. with shame to take the *lowest* room.
10. go and sit down in the *lowest* room;
Joh. 6:39. raise it up again at the *last* day.
40. I will raise him up at the *last* day.
44. I will raise him up at the *last* day.
54. and I will raise him up at the *last* day.
7:37. In the *last* day, that great (day)
8: 9. at the eldest, (even) unto the *last:*
11:24. in the resurrection at the *last* day.
12:48. the same shall judge him in the *last* day.
Acts 1: 8. unto the *uttermost* (part) of the earth.
2:17. shall come to pass in the *last* days,
13:47. unto the ends of the earth. (lit. unto the *uttermost part* of the earth)
1Co. 4: 9. hath set forth us the apostles *last*, as it were appointed to death:
15: 8. And *last* of all he was seen of me
26. The *last* enemy (that) shall be destroyed
45. the *last* Adam (was made) a quickening
52. at the *last* trump:
2Ti. 3: 1. in the *last* days perilous times
Heb 1: 2(1). Hath in these *last* days spoken
Jas. 5: 3. treasure together for the *last* days.
1Pet. 1: 5. ready to be revealed in the *last* time.
20. was manifest in these *last* times
2Pet. 2:20. the *latter end* is worse with them than
3: 3. shall come in the *last* days scoffers,
1Joh. 2:18. children, it is the *last* time:
— whereby we know that it is the *last* time.
Jude 18. should be mockers in the *last* time,
Rev. 1:11. I am Alpha and Omega, the first and the *last*
17. Fear not; I am the first and the *last:*
2: 8. saith the first and the *last*,
19. the *last* (to be) more than the first.
15: 1. having the seven *last* plagues;
21: 9. vials full of the seven *last* plagues,
22:13. the first and the *last*.

2079 1 314/392 2078

ἐσχάτως, eskatōs.

Mar. 5:23. lieth at the point of death: (lit. is *in the last* state)

2080 8 314/392 2:698 1519

ἔσω, eso.

Mat.26:58. went *in*, and sat with the servants,
Mar.14:54. even into (lit. even *within* into) the palace
15:16. led him away *into* the hall,
Joh.20:26. his disciples were *within*, and Thomas
Acts 5:23. opened, we found no man *within*.
Ro. 7:22. I delight in the law of God after the *inward* man:
1Co. 5:12. do not ye judge them that are *within?*
Eph. 3:16. to be strengthened with might by his Spirit in the *inner* man;

2081 14 314/392 2080

ἔσωθεν, esōthen.

Mat. 7:15. but *inwardly* they are ravening wolves.
23:25. but *within* they are full of extortion
27. but are *within* full of dead
28. but *within* ye are full of hypocrisy
Mar. 7:21. For *from within*, out of the heart
23. come *from within*, and defile the man.
Lu. 11: 7. And he *from within* shall answer
39. your *inward* part is full of ravening
40. make that which is *within* also?
2Co. 4:16. yet the *inward* (man) is renewed
7: 5. without (were) fightings, *within* (were)
Rev. 4: 8. (they were) full of eyes *within:*
5: 1. a book written *within* and on the
11: 2. But the court which is *without* the temple (in some copies ἔξωθεν)

2082 2 314/392 2080

ἐσώτερος, esōteros.

Acts16:24. thrust them into the *inner* prison,
Heb. 6:19. into that *within* the veil;

2083 4 314/392 2:699 etes (clansman)

ἑταῖρος, hetairos.

Mat.11:16. and calling unto their *fellows*,
20:13. *Friend*, I do thee no wrong:
22:12. *Friend*, how camest thou in
26:50. *Friend*, wherefore art thou come?

2084 1 314/392 1:719 2087,1100

ἑτερόγλωσσος, heteroglōssos.

1Co.14:21. With (*men of*) *other tongues*

2085 2 314/392 2:135 2087,1320

ἑτεροδιδασκαλέω, heterodidaskaleo.

1Ti. 1: 3. that they *teach* no *other doctrine*,
6: 3. If any man *teach otherwise*,

2086 1 315/392 2:896 2087,2218

ἑτεροζυγέω, heterozugeo.

2Co. 6:14. *unequally yoked together with* unbelievers:

2087 99 315/392 2:702

ἕτερος, heteros.

Mat. 6:24. for either he will hate the one, and love the *other*; or else he will hold to the one, and despise the *other*.
8:21. And *another* of his disciples said
11: 3. or do we look for *another*?
12:45. taketh with himself seven *other* spirits more wicked
15:30. dumb, maimed, and many *others*,
16:14. and *others*, Jeremias,
Mar 16:12. he appeared in *another* form
Lu. 3:18. And many *other* things in his exhortation preached he
4:43. to *other* cities also:
5: 7. which were in the *other* ship,
6: 6. also on *another* sabbath,
7:41. and the *other* fifty.
8: 3. and many *others*, which ministered
6. And *some* fell upon a rock;
7. And *some* fell among thorns;
8. And *other* fell on good ground,
9:29. the fashion of his countenance was *altered*, (lit. became *other*)
56. And they went to *another* village.
59. And he said unto *another*,
61. And *another* also said,
10: 1. appointed *other* seventy also,
11:16. And *others*, tempting (him),
26. seven *other* spirits
14:19. *another* said, I have bought
20. And *another* said,
31. to make war against *another* king,
16: 7. said he to *another*, And how much
13. and love the *other*; or else he will hold to the one, and despise the *other*.
18. and marrieth *another*,
17:34. and the *other* shall be left.
35. be taken, and the *other* left.
18:10. and the *other* a publican.
19:20. And *another* came, saying,
20:11. he sent *another* servant:
22:58. *another* saw him, and said,
65. many *other* things blasphemously
23:32. there were also two *other*, malefactors, led with him
40. But the *other* answering
Joh. 19:37. again *another* scripture saith,
Acts 1:20. let *another* take.
2: 4. to speak with *other* tongues,
13. *Others* mocking said, These men
40. And with many *other* words
4:12. there is none *other* name under
7:18. *another* king arose, which
8:34. or of some *other* man?
12:17. and went into *another* place.
13:35. Wherefore he saith also in *another* (psalm),
15:35. with many *others* also.
17: 7. that there is *another* king, (one) Jesus.
21. spent their time in nothing *else*, but
34. and *others* with them.
19:39. But if ye enquire any thing concerning *other* matters,
20:15. and the *next* (day) we arrived
23: 6. the one part were Sadducees, and the *other* Pharisees,
27: 1. and certain *other* prisoners
3. And the *next* (day) we touched
Ro. 2: 1. thou judgest *another*,
21. Thou therefore which teachest *another*,
7: 3. she be married to *another* man,
— though she be married to *another* man.
4. that ye should be married to *another*,
23. *another* law in my members,
8:39. nor any *other* creature,
13: 8. he that loveth *another* hath fulfilled
9. if (there be) any *other* commandment,
1Co. 3: 4. and *another*, I (am) of Apollos;
4: 6. be puffed up for one against *another*.
6: 1. having a matter against *another*,
8: 4. (there is) none *other* God
10:24. but every man *another's* (wealth).
29. not thine own, but of the *other*:
12: 9. To *another* faith by the same Spirit;
10. to *another* (divers) kinds of tongues;
14:17. but the *other* is not edified.
21. and *other* lips will I speak unto this
15:40. the glory of the celestial (is) *one*, and the (glory) of the terrestrial (is) *another*.
2Co. 8: 8. by occasion of the forwardness of *others*,
11: 4. or (if) ye receive *another* spirit,
— or *another* gospel, which ye have not
Gal. 1: 6. unto *another* gospel:
19. But *other* of the apostles
6: 4. in himself alone, and not in *another*.
Eph. 3: 5. Which in *other* ages was not made known
Phi. 2: 4. every man also on the things of *others*.
1Ti. 1:10. and if there be any *other* thing
2Ti. 2: 2. who shall be able to teach *others* also.
Heb. 5: 6. As he saith also in *another* (place),
7:11. that *another* priest should rise
13. pertaineth to *another* tribe,
15. there ariseth *another* priest,
11:36. And *others* had trial of (cruel) mockings
Jas. 2:25. and had sent (them) out *another* way?
4:12. who art thou that judgest *another*?
Jude 7. and going after *strange* flesh,

2088 1 315/393 2087

ἑτέρως, heterōs.

Phi. 3:15. if in any thing ye be *otherwise* minded,

2089 119 315/393 cf 2094

ἔτι, eti.

Mat. 5:13. it is *thenceforth* good for nothing,
12:46. While he *yet* talked to the people,
17: 5. While he *yet* spake, behold, a bright
18:16. (then) take with thee one or two *more*,
19:20. what lack I *yet*?
26:47. And while he *yet* spake,
65. what *further* need have we
27:63. said, while he was *yet* alive,
Mar. 5:35. While he *yet* spake, there came from
— troublest thou the Master any *further*?
8:17. have ye your heart *yet* hardened?
12 6. Having *yet* therefore one son,
14:43. immediately, while he *yet* spake,
63. What need we *any further* witnesses?
Lu. 1:15. *even* from his mother's womb.
8:49. While he *yet* spake, there cometh
9:42. And as he was *yet* a coming,
14:22. and *yet* there is room.
26. yea, and his own life *also*,
32. while the other is *yet* a great way off,
15:20. But when he was *yet* a great way off,
16: 2. for thou mayest be no *longer* steward.
18:22. *Yet* lackest thou one thing:

Lu. 20:36. can they die *any more:*
40. And *after that* they durst not ask
22:37. that this that is written must *yet* be accomplished in me,
47. And while he *yet* spake,
60. while he *yet* spake, the cock crew.
71. What need we *any further* witness?
24: 6. when he was *yet* in Galilee,
41. And while they *yet* believed not
44. while I was *yet* with you,
Joh. 4:35. There are *yet* four months,
7:33. *Yet* a little while am I with you,
11:54. no *more* openly among the Jews;
12:35. *Yet* a little while is the light
13:33. *yet* a little while I am with you.
14:19. *Yet* a little while, and the world seeth me no *more;*
30. *Hereafter* I will not talk much
16:10. ye see me no *more;*
12. I have *yet* many things to say
21. she remembereth no *more* the anguish,
25. no *more* speak unto you in proverbs,
17:11. I am no *more* in the world,
20: 1. when it was *yet* dark,
21: 6. *now* they were not able to draw it
Acts 2:26. *moreover* also my flesh shall rest in hope:
9: 1. *yet* breathing out threatenings
10:44. While Peter *yet* spake
18:18. Paul (after this) tarried (there) *yet* a good while,
21:28. and *further* brought Greeks also
Ro. 3: 7. why *yet* am I also judged as a sinner?
5: 6. For when we were *yet* without strength,
8. while we were *yet* sinners,
6: 2. dead to sin, live *any longer* therein?
9. raised from the dead dieth no *more;* death hath no *more* dominion over him.
7:17. then it is no *more* I that do it, but sin
20. I would not, it is no *more* I that do it,
9:19. Why doth he *yet* find fault?
11: 6. then (is it) no *more* of works: otherwise grace is no *more* grace. But if (it be) of works, then is it no *more* grace: otherwise work is no *more* work.
14:15. *now* walkest thou not charitably.
1Co. 3: 2. neither *yet* now are ye able.
3. For ye are *yet* carnal:
12:31. and *yet* shew I unto you a more excellent
15:17. ye are *yet* in your sins.
2Co. 1:10. that he will *yet* deliver (us);
5:16. yet now *henceforth* know we (him) no *more.* (lit. we know him no *more henceforth*)
Gal. 1:10. for if I *yet* pleased men,
2:20. nevertheless I live; *yet* not I, (lit. live no *more* I,) but Christ liveth in me:
3:18. (it is) no *more* of promise:
25. we are no *longer* under a schoolmaster.
4: 7. thou art no *more* a servant,
5:11. if I *yet* preach circumcision, why do I *yet* suffer persecution?
Phi. 1: 9. your love may abound *yet* more and more
2Th. 2: 5. when I was *yet* with you,
Heb 7:10. he was *yet* in the loins of his father,
11. what *further* need (was there)
15. it is *yet* far more evident:
8:12. will I remember no *more.*
9: 8. the first tabernacle was *yet* standing
10: 2. should have had no *more* conscience
17. will I remember no *more.*
18. (there is) no *more* offering for sin.
26. remaineth no *more* sacrifice for sins,
Heb 10:37. For *yet* a little while, and he that
11: 4. he being dead *yet* speaketh.
32. And what shall I *more* say?
36. yea, *moreover* of bonds and
12:26. saying, *Yet* once *more* I shake
27. And this (word), *Yet* once *more,*
Rev. 3:12. he shall go no *more* out:
6:11. they should rest *yet* for a little
7:16. They shall hunger no *more,* neither thirst *any more;*
9:12. there come two woes *more*
10: 6. there should be time no *longer:*
12: 8. their place found *any more* in heaven.
18:21. shall be found no *more* at all.
22. shall be heard no *more* at all in thee;
— shall be found *any more* in thee;
— shall be heard no *more* at all in thee;
23. shall shine no *more* at all in thee;
— shall be heard no *more* at all
20: 3. should deceive the nations no *more,*
21: 1. there was no *more* sea.
4. there shall be no *more* death,
— shall there be *any more* pain:
22: 3. there shall be no *more* curse:
11. him be unjust *still:* and he which is filthy, let him be filthy *still:* and he that is righteous, let him be righteous *still:* and he that is holy, let him be holy *still.*

See also οὐκέτι.

2090 40 316/394 2:704 cf 2680
ἑτοιμάζω, hetoimazo. 2092

Mat. 3: 3. *Prepare* ye the way of the Lord.
20:23. for whom it *is prepared* of my Father.
22: 4. I *have prepared* my dinner:
25:34. inherit the kingdom *prepared* for you
41. *prepared* for the devil
26:17. that we *prepare* for thee to eat
19. they *made ready* the passover.
Mar. 1: 3. *Prepare* ye the way of the Lord.
10:40. for whom it *is prepared.*
14:12. Where wilt thou that we go and *prepare*
15. there *make ready* for us.
16. and they *made ready* the passover.
Lu. 1:17. *to make ready* a people prepared for the Lord.
76. face of the Lord *to prepare* his ways;
2:31. Which thou *hast prepared* before the face of all people;
3: 4. *Prepare* ye the way of the Lord,
9:52. to *make ready* for him.
12:20. which thou *hast provided?*
47. which knew his lord's will, and *prepared* not (himself),
17: 8. *Make ready* wherewith I may sup,
22: 8. Go and *prepare* us the passover,
9. Where wilt thou that we *prepare?*
12. there *make ready.*
13. they *made ready* the passover.
23:56. *prepared* spices and ointments;
24: 1. the spices which they *had prepared,*
Joh. 14: 2. I go *to prepare* a place for you.
3. if I go and *prepare* a place for you,
Acts 23:23. *Make ready* two hundred soldiers
1Co. 2: 9. the things which God *hath prepared* for them that love him.
2Ti. 2:21. *prepared* unto every good work.
Philem 22. *prepare* me also a lodging:
Heb 11:16. for he *hath prepared* for them a city
Rev. 8: 6. *prepared* themselves to sound

Rev. 9: 7. like unto horses *prepared* unto battle;
15. *which were prepared* for an hour,
12: 6. a place *prepared* of God,
16: 12. that the way of the kings of the east *might be prepared.*
19: 7. and his wife *hath made* herself *ready.*
21: 2. out of heaven, *prepared* as a bride adorned for her husband.

2091 1 316/395 2:704 2090

ἑτοιμασία, *hetoimasia.*

Eph. 6:15. with the *preparation* of the gospel

2092 17 316/395 2:704 *heteos* (fitness)

ἕτοιμος, *hetoimos.*

Mat.22: 4. and all things (are) *ready:*
8. The wedding is *ready*, but they
24:44. be ye also *ready:* for in such an hour as
25:10. they that were *ready* went in with him
Mar.14:15. upper room furnished (and) *prepared:*
Lu. 12:40. Be ye therefore *ready* also: for the Son
14:17. all things are now *ready.*
22:33. Lord, I am *ready* to go with thee,
Joh. 7: 6. but your time is alway *ready.*
Acts23:15. ever he come near, are *ready* to kill him.
21. and now are they *ready*, looking for
2Co. 9: 5. that the same might be *ready*,
10: 6. And having in a *readiness* to revenge
16. of things *made ready to our hand.*
Tit. 3: 1. to be *ready* to every good work,
1Pet. 1: 5. unto salvation *ready* to be revealed
3:15. and (be) *ready* always to (give) an answer ...with meekness and fear:

2093 3 316/395 2092

ἑτοίμως, *hetoimōs.*

Acts21:13. I am *ready* (lit. hold myself *preparedly*)
2Co.12:14. the third time I am *ready* (lit. hold, &c.)
1Pet.4: 5. to him that is *ready* (lit. hold, &c.)

2094 49 317/395

ἔτος, *etos.*

Mat. 9:20. which was diseased with an issue of blood twelve *years*,
Mar 5:25. an issue of blood twelve *years*,
42. for she was (of the age) of twelve *years.*
Lu. 2:36. had lived with an husband seven *years*
37. of about fourscore and four *years*,
41. parents went to Jerusalem every *year*
42. when he was twelve *years* old,
3: 1. Now in the fifteenth *year* of the reign
23. began to be about thirty *years* of age,
4:25. three *years* and six months,
8:42. about twelve *years* of age,
43. having an issue of blood twelve *years*,
12:19. laid up for many *years;*
13: 7. these three *years* I come
8. Lord, let it alone this *year* also,
11. a spirit of infirmity eighteen *years*,
16. Satan hath bound, lo, these eighteen *years*,
15:29. these many *years* do I serve thee,
Joh. 2:20. Forty and six *years* was this temple in
5: 5. an infirmity thirty and eight *years.*
8:57. Thou art not yet fifty *years* old,
Acts 4:22. the man was above forty *years* old,
7: 6. entreat (them) evil four hundred *years*,
30. when forty *years* were expired,
Acts 7:36. and in the wilderness forty *years.*
42. forty *years* in the wilderness?
9:33. had kept his bed eight *years*,
13:20. four hundred and fifty *years*,
21. by the space of forty *years.*
19:10. continued by the space of two *years;*
24:10. thou hast been of many *years*
17. Now after many *years* I came
Ro. 15:23. a great desire these many *years* to
2Co.12: 2. about fourteen *years* ago,
Gal. 1:18. Then after three *years* I went up
2: 1. Then fourteen *years* after I went
3:17. four hundred and thirty *years* after,
1Ti. 5: 9. into the number under threescore *years* old,
Heb 1:12. thy *years* shall not fail.
3: 9. my works forty *years.*
17. was he grieved forty *years?*
2Pet. 3: 8. one day (is) with the Lord as a thousand *years*, and a thousand *years* as one day.
Rev.20: 2. bound him a thousand *years*,
3. the thousand *years* should be fulfilled:
4. lived and reigned with Christ a thousand *years.*
5. until the thousand *years* were finished.
6. shall reign with him a thousand *years.*
7. when the thousand *years* are expired,

2095 6 317/396 *eus* (good)

εὖ, *ū.*

Mat.25:21. *Well done*, (thou) good and faithful servant:
23. *Well done*, good and faithful servant;
Mar 14: 7. whensoever ye will ye may do them *good:*
Lu. 19:17. *Well*, thou good servant:
Acts15:29. ye shall do *well.* Fare ye well.
Eph 6: 3. That it may be *well* with thee,

2097 55 317/396 2:707 2095,32

εὐαγγελίζω, -ομαι, *ūangelizo, -omai.*

Mat.11: 5. the poor *have the gospel preached* to them.
Lu. 1:19. to *shew* thee these *glad tidings.*
2:10. I *bring* you *good tidings* of great joy,
3:18. *preached* he unto the people.
4:18. *to preach the gospel* to the poor;
43. I must *preach* the kingdom of God to
7:22. to the poor *the gospel is preached.*
8: 1. preaching and *shewing the glad tidings*
9: 6. *preaching the gospel*, and healing
16:16. the kingdom of God *is preached*,
20: 1. in the temple, and *preached the gospel*,
Acts 5:42. to teach and *preach* Jesus Christ.
8: 4. went every where *preaching* the word.
12. *preaching* the things concerning
25. *preached the gospel* in many villages
35. and *preached* unto him Jesus.
40. he *preached* in all the cities,
10:36. *preaching* peace by Jesus Christ:
11:20. *preaching* the Lord Jesus.
13:32. we *declare* unto you *glad tidings*,
14: 7. And there they preached the gospel. (lit. were *preaching the gospel*)
15. *and preach* unto you that ye should turn
21. And *when* they *had preached the gospel*
15:35. and *preaching* the word of the Lord,
16:10. *to preach the gospel* unto them.
17:18. he *preached* unto them
Ro. 1:15. *to preach the gospel* to you that are at Rome
10:15. of them *that preach the gospel* of peace, and *bring glad tidings* of good things!

Ro. 15:20. have I strived *to preach the gospel,*
1Co. 1:17. but *to preach the gospel:*
9:16. For though I *preach the gospel,*
— if I *preach* not *the gospel!*
18. *when* I *preach the gospel,* I may make the
15: 1. which I *preached* unto you,
2. in memory what I *preached* unto you,
2Co.10:16. *To preach the gospel* in the (regions) beyond you,
11 7. I *have preached* to you the gospel
Gal. 1: 8. *preach* any other *gospel* unto you than that which we *have preached* unto you,
9. if any (man) *preach* any other *gospel*
11. the gospel *which was preached* of me
16. that I *might preach* him
23. now *preacheth* the faith
4:13. I *preached the gospel* unto you
Eph. 2:17. And came and *preached*
3: 8. that I should *preach* among the Gentiles
1Th. 3: 6. and *brought* us *good tidings* of your
Heb. 4: 2. unto us *was the gospel preached,* (lit. we are *addressed with the gospel*)
6. they to whom it was first preached (lit. those first *addressed with the gospel*) entered not
1Pet. 1:12. by them *that have preached the gospel*
25. the word *which by the gospel is preached* unto you.
4: 6. *was the gospel preached* also to them that are dead,
Rev.10: 7. as he *hath declared* to his servants the prophets.
14: 6. *to preach* unto them that dwell on the earth, and to every nation, and

2098 77 318/397 2:707 2095,32

εὐαγγέλιον, *ūangelion.*

Mat. 4:23. preaching the *gospel* of the kingdom,
9:35. and preaching the *gospel*
24:14. this *gospel* of the kingdom
26:13. Wheresoever this *gospel* shall be preached
Mar. 1: 1. The beginning of the *gospel* of Jesus Christ,
14. the *gospel* of the kingdom of God,
15. repent ye, and believe the *gospel.*
8:35. for my sake and the *gospel's,*
10:29. for my sake, and the *gospel's,*
13:10. the *gospel* must first be published
14: 9. this *gospel* shall be preached
16:15. preach the *gospel* to every creature.
Acts15: 7. should hear the word of the *gospel,*
20:24. to testify the *gospel* of the grace of God.
Ro. 1: 1. separated unto the *gospel*
9. in the *gospel* of his Son,
16. For I am not ashamed of the *gospel*
2:16. according to my *gospel.*
10:16. they have not all obeyed the *gospel.*
11:28. As concerning the *gospel,*
15:16. ministering the *gospel* of God, that
19. I have fully preached the *gospel*
29. of the blessing of the *gospel*
16:25. according to my *gospel,*
1Co. 4:15. I have begotten you through the *gospel.*
9:12. lest we should hinder the *gospel* of Christ.
14. that they which preach the *gospel* should live of the *gospel.*
18. I may make the *gospel* of Christ without charge, that I abuse not my power in the *gospel.*
23. I do for the *gospel's* sake,
15: 1. the *gospel* which I preached
2Co. 2:12. to (preach) Christ's *gospel,*
4: 3. if our *gospel* be hid, it is hid to
4. the light of the glorious *gospel*
8:18. whose praise (is) in the *gospel*
9:13. unto the *gospel* of Christ,
10:14. in (preaching) the *gospel* of Christ:
11: 4. or another *gospel,* which ye have not accepted,
7. I have preached to yon the *gospel* of God freely?
Gal. 1: 6. unto another *gospel:*
7. would pervert the *gospel* of Christ.
11. that the *gospel* which was preached
2: 2. communicated unto them that *gospel*
5. that the truth of the *gospel* might
7. the *gospel* of the uncircumcision
14. according to the truth of the *gospel,*
Eph. 1:13. the *gospel* of your salvation:
3: 6. in Christ by the *gospel:*
6:15. with the preparation of the *gospel*
19. the mystery of the *gospel,*
Phi. 1: 5. For your fellowship in the *gospel*
7. and confirmation of the *gospel,* ye all
12. unto the furtherance of the *gospel;*
17. for the defence of the *gospel.*
27. your conversation be as it becometh the *gospel* of Christ:
— striving together for the faith of the *gospel;*
2:22. he hath served with me in the *gospel.*
4: 3. laboured with me in the *gospel,*
15. in the beginning of the *gospel,*
Col. 1: 5. in the word of the truth of the *gospel;*
23. from the hope of the *gospel,*
1Th. 1: 5. For our *gospel* came not unto you
2: 2. to speak unto you the *gospel* of God
4. to be put in trust with the *gospel,*
8. not the *gospel* of God only,
9. we preached unto you the *gospel* of God.
3: 2. fellowlabourer in the *gospel* of Christ,
2Th. 1: 8. and that obey not the *gospel* of our
2:14. he called you by our *gospel,* to the
1Ti. 1:11. According to the glorious *gospel*
2Ti. 1: 8. be thou partaker of the afflictions of the *gospel*
10. immortality to light through the *gospel:*
2: 8. according to my *gospel:*
Philem 13. in the bonds of the *gospel:*
1Pet. 4:17. of them that obey not the *gospel* of God?
Rev.14: 6. having the everlasting *gospel*

2099 3 318/398 2:707 2097

εὐαγγελιστής, *ūangelistees.*

Acts21: 8. the house of Philip the *evangelist,*
Eph. 4:11. and some, *evangelists;* and some,
2Ti. 4: 5. do the work of an *evangelist,*

2100 3 318/398 1:455 2101

εὐαρεστέω, *ūaresteo.*

Heb11: 5. had this testimony, that he *pleased* God.
6. (it is) impossible *to please* (him):
13:16. for with such sacrifices God *is well pleased.*

2101 3 319/398 1:455 2095,701

εὐάρεστος, *ūarestos.*

Ro. 12: 1. a living sacrifice, holy, *acceptable* (lit. *well-pleasing*) unto God,
2. that good, and *acceptable,* and
14:18. *acceptable* to God, and approved of men.
2Co. 5: 9. we may be accepted of him. (lit. to be *well pleasing* unto him)
Eph. 5:10. what is *acceptable* unto the Lord

Phi. 4:18. *wellpleasing* to God.
Col. 3:20. for this is *wellpleasing* unto the Lord.
Tit. 2: 9. (and) to please (them) well (lit. to be *well-pleasing*) in all (things);
Heb 13:21. working in you that which is *wellpleasing* in his sight, through Jesus Christ;

2102 1 319/398 2101
εὐαρέστως, ūarestōs.

Heb 12:28. we may serve God *acceptably*

2104 3 319/398 2095,1096
εὐγενὴς, ūgenees.

Lu. 19:12. A certain *noble*man went into a far
Acts17:11. These were *more noble* than
1Cor. 1:26. not many *noble*, (are called):

2105 1 319/398 2095,2203
εὐδία, ūdia.

Mat.16: 2. ye say, (It will be) *fair weather:*

2106 21 319/398 2:738 2095,1380
εὐδοκέω, ūdokeo.

Mat. 3:17. in whom I *am well pleased.*
12:18. in whom my soul *is well pleased:*
17: 5. in whom I *am well pleased;*
Mar. 1:11. in whom I *am well pleased.*
Lu. 3:22. in thee I *am well pleased.*
12:32. it is your Father's good pleasure (lit. your Father *is well pleased*) to give
Ro. 15:26. it *hath pleased* them of Macedonia and Achaia (lit. Macedonia and Achaia *have been pleased*)
27. It *hath pleased* them verily; and
1Co. 1:21. it *pleased* God (lit. God *has been pleased*) by the foolishness of preaching
10: 5. with many of them God *was* not *well pleased:*
2Co. 5: 8. We are confident, (I say), and *willing*
12:10. Therefore I *take pleasure* in infirmities,
Gal. 1:15. But when it *pleased* God,
Col. 1:19. it *pleased* (the Father) that in him should all fulness dwell;
1Th. 2: 8. we *were willing* to have imparted
3: 1. we *thought* it *good* to be left
2Th. 2:12. but *had pleasure* in unrighteousness.
Heb 10: 6. thou *hast had* no *pleasure.*
8. neither *hadst pleasure* (therein);
38. my soul shall *have* no *pleasure* in him.
2Pet. 1:17. in whom I *am well pleased.*

2107 9 319/399 2:738 rt 1380 2095
εὐδοκία, ūdokia.

Mat.11:26. for so it seemed good (lit. it was *well-seeming*) in thy sight.
Lu. 2:14. *good will* toward men.
10:21. for so it seemed *good* (lit. was, &c.) in thy sight.
Ro. 10: 1. Brethren, my heart's *desire*
Eph. 1: 5. according to the *good pleasure* of his will,
9. according to his *good pleasure*
Phi. 1:15. and some also of *good will:*
2:13. to will and to do of (his) *good pleasure.*
2Th. 1:11. all the *good pleasure* of (his) goodness,

2108 2 320/399 2:635 2110
εὐεργεσία, ūergesia.

Acts 4: 9. of the *good deed done* to the impotent man,
1Ti 6: 2. are faithful and beloved, partakers of the *benefit*

2109 1 320/399 2:635 2110
εὐεργετέω, ūergeteo.

Acts10:38. who went about *doing good,*

2110 1 320/399 2:635 2095 *ergō* (to work)
εὐεργέτης, ūergetees.

Lu. 22:25. they that exercise authority upon them are called *benefactors.*

2111 3 320/399 2095,5087
εὔθετος, ūthetos.

Lu. 9:62. looking back, is *fit* for the kingdom of God.
14:35. It is neither *fit* for the land, nor yet for the dunghill;
Heb. 6: 7. bringeth forth herbs *meet* for them by whom it is dressed,

2112 80 320/399 2117
εὐθέως, ūtheōs.

Mat. 4:20. *straightway* left (their) nets,
22. *immediately* left the ship
8: 3. *immediately* his leprosy was cleansed.
13: 5. *forthwith* they sprung up,
14:22. *straightway* Jesus constrained
27. But *straightway* Jesus spake
31. And *immediately* Jesus stretched forth
20:34. *immediately* their eyes received sight,
21: 2. *straightway* ye shall find an ass
3. and *straightway* he will send them.
24:29. *Immediately* after the tribulation
25:15. and *straightway* took his journey.
26:49. And *forthwith* he came to Jesus,
74. *immediately* the cock crew.
27:48. *straightway* one of them ran,
Mar. 1:10. *straightway* coming up out of the water,
18. *straightway* they forsook their nets,
20. And *straightway* he called them:
21. and *straightway* on the sabbath day
29. *forthwith*, when they were come out of the synagogue,
30. *anon* they tell him of her.
31. *immediately* the fever left her,
42. *immediately* the leprosy departed from him,
43. *forthwith* sent him away;
2: 2. *straightway* many were gathered
8. *immediately* when Jesus perceived
12. And *immediately* he arose,
3: 6. *straightway* took counsel with the Herodians
4: 5. and *immediately* it sprang up,
15. Satan cometh *immediately,*
16. *immediately* receive it with gladness;
17. *immediately* they are offended.
29. *immediately* he putteth in the sickle,
5: 2. *immediately* there met him
13. *forthwith* Jesus gave them leave.
29. *straightway* the fountain of her blood
30. Jesus, *immediately* knowing in himself
36. *As soon as* Jesus heard the word
42. *straightway* the damsel arose,
6:25. she came in *straightway* with haste
27. *immediately* the king sent
45. *straightway* he constrained his
50. *immediately* he talked with them,
54. *straightway* they knew him,
7:35. *straightway* his ears were opened,
8:10. *straightway* he entered into a ship
9:15. *straightway* all the people, when they beheld

Mar 9:20. *straightway* the spirit tare
24. *straightway* the father of the child
10:52. And *immediately* he received his sight,
11: 2. *as soon as* ye be entered into it,
3. *straightway* he will send him
14:43. *immediately*, while he yet spake,
45. he goeth *straightway* to him, and saith,
15: 1. *straightway* in the morning
Lu. 5:13. *immediately* the leprosy departed
39. *straightway* desireth new:
6:49. and *immediately* it fell;
12:36. they may open unto him *immediately*.
54. *straightway* ye say, There cometh a shower;
14: 5. will not *straightway* pull him out
17. 7. will say unto him *by and by*,
21. 9. but the end (is) not *by and by*.
Joh. 5: 9. *immediately* the man was made whole,
6:21. *immediately* the ship was at the
13:30. received the sop went *immediately* out:
18:27. *immediately* the cock crew.
Acts 9:18. *immediately* there fell from his eyes
20. And *straightway* he preached Christ
34. And he arose *immediately*.
12:10. *forthwith* the angel departed
16:10. *immediately* we endeavoured to go
17:10. the brethren *immediately* sent away
14. And then *immediately* the brethren
21:30. *forthwith* the doors were shut.
22:29. Then *straightway* they departed
Gal. 1:16. *immediately* I conferred not
Jas. 1:24. *straightway* forgetteth what manner
3Joh. 14. But I trust I shall *shortly* see thee,
Rev. 4: 2. *immediately* I was in the spirit:

2113 2 321/399 2117,1408

εὐθυδρομέω, ūthudromeo.

Acts16:11. we *came with a straight course* to Samothracia
21: 1. we came *with a straight course* (lit. *having run with &c.* we came)

2114 3 321/399 2115

εὐθυμέω, ūthumeo.

Acts27:22. I exhort you *to be of good cheer*:
25. Wherefore, sirs, *be of good cheer*
Jas. 5:13. *Is* any *merry?* let him sing psalms.

2115 2 321/399 2095,2372

εὔθυμος, ūthumos.

Acts27:36. Then were they all *of good cheer*,

2115 /399

εὐθυμότερον, ūthumoteron.

Acts24:10. the *more cheerfully* answer for myself:

2116 2 321/399 2117

εὐθύνω, ūthuno.

Joh. 1:23. *Make straight* the way of the Lord,
Jas. 3: 4. whithersoever the governor listeth: (lit. wh. the purpose of the *helmsman* willeth)

2117 8 321/399 2095,5087

εὐθύς, ūthus.

Mat. 3: 3. make his paths *straight*.
Mar 1: 3. make his paths *straight*.
Lu. 3: 4. make his paths *straight*.
5. the crooked shall be made *straight*,

Acts 8:21. thy heart is not *right* in the sight of God.
9:11. into the street which is called *Straight*.
13:10. cease to pervert the *right* ways of the Lord?
2Pet.2:15. which have forsaken the *right* way,

2117 8 321/400 2095,5087

εὐθυς, ūthus. adv.

Mat. 3:16. went up *straightway* out of the water:
13:20. and *anon* with joy receiveth it;
21. *by and by* he is offended.
Mar 1:12. *immediately* the spirit driveth him
28. *immediately* his fame spread abroad
Joh.13:32. shall *straightway* glorify him.
19:34. *forthwith* came thereout blood
21: 3. entered into a ship *immediately*,

2118 1 321/400 2117

εὐθύτης, ūthutees.

Heb 1: 8. a sceptre of *righteousness* (is) the sceptre

2119 3 321/400 3:455 2121

εὐκαιρέω, ūkaireo.

Mar 6:31. they *had* no *leisure* so much as to eat.
Acts17:21. *spent* their *time* in nothing else,
1Co.16:12. when he *shall have convenient time*.

2120 2 321/400 3:455 2121

εὐκαιρία, ūkairia.

Mat.26:16. he sought *opportunity* to betray
Lu. 22: 6. sought *opportunity* to betray him

2121 2 321/400 3:455 2095,2540

εὔκαιρος, ūkairos.

Mar 6:21. when a *convenient* day was come,
Heb 4:16. find grace to help in time of need. (lit. for *seasonable* assistance)

2122 2 321/400 2121

εὐκαίρως, ūkairōs.

Mar 14:11. how he might *conveniently* betray him.
2Ti. 4: 2. be instant *in season*, out of season;

2123 7 322/400 2095,2873

εὐκοπώτερος, ūkopōteros.

Mat. 9: 5. For whether is *easier*, to say,
19:24. It is *easier* for a camel
Mar 2: 9. Whether is it *easier*
10:25. It is *easier* for a camel
Lu. 5:23. Whether is *easier*, to say, Thy sins
16:17. And it is *easier* for heaven and earth
18:25. For it is *easier* for a camel to go

2124 2 322/400 2126

εὐλάβεια, ūlabia.

Heb 5: 7. was heard in that he feared; (lit. for his *fearing*)
12:28. with reverence and *godly fear*:

2125 2 322/401 2:751 2126

εὐλαβέομαι, ūlabeomai.

Acts23:10. the chief captain, *fearing* lest Paul
Heb 11: 7. *moved with fear*, prepared an ark

2126 3 322/401 2:751 2095,2983

εὐλαβής, ūlabees.

Lu. 2:25. the same man (was) just and *devout*,
Acts 2: 5. Jews, *devout* men, out of every nation
8: 2. And *devout* men carried Stephen

2127 44 322/401 2:754 2095,3056

εὐλογέω, ūlogeo.

Mat. 5:44. *bless* them that curse you,
14:19. to heaven, he *blessed*, and brake,
21: 9. *Blessed* (is) he that cometh in the name
23:39. *Blessed* (is) he that cometh
25:34. ye *blessed* of my Father,
26:26. *blessed* (it), *and* brake (it),
Mar 6:41. to heaven, and *blessed*,
8: 7. and he *blessed*, *and* commanded
10:16. hands upon them and *blessed* them
11: 9. *Blessed* (is) he that cometh
10. *Blessed* (be) the kingdom of our father
14:22. and *blessed*, *and* brake (it),
Lu. 1:28. *blessed* (art) thou among women.
42. *Blessed* (art) thou among women, and *blessed* (is) the fruit of thy womb.
64. and he spake, *and praised* God.
2:28. him up in his arms, and *blessed* God,
34. And Simeon *blessed* them, and said
6:28. *Bless* them that curse you,
9:16. he *blessed* them, and brake, and gave
13:35. *Blessed* (is) he that cometh
19:38. *Blessed* (be) the King that cometh
24:30. he took bread, and *blessed* (it),
50. he lifted up his hands, and *blessed* them.
51. while he blessed (lit. in his *blessing*) them,
53. praising and *blessing* God.
Joh. 12:13. *Blessed* (is) the King of Israel that
Acts 3:26. sent him to *bless* you, in turning
Ro. 12:14. *Bless* them which persecute you: *bless*, and curse not.
1Co. 4:12. being reviled, we *bless*;
10:16. The cup of blessing which we *bless*,
14:16. Else when thou *shalt bless* with the spirit,
Gal. 3: 9. *are blessed* with faithful Abraham.
Eph. 1: 3. Father of our Lord Jesus Christ, *who hath blessed* us with all
Heb 6:14. Saying, Surely *blessing* I *will bless* thee, and multiplying
7: 1. and *blessed* him;
6. *blessed* him that had the promises.
7. the less *is blessed* of the better.
11:20. Isaac *blessed* Jacob and Esau
21. *blessed* both the sons of Joseph;
Jas. 3: 9. Therewith *bless* we God, even the
1Pet.3: 9. but contrariwise *blessing*;

2128 8 323/401 2127

εὐλογητός, ūlogeetos.

Mar 14:61. the Son of the *Blessed*?
Lu. 1:68. *Blessed* (be) the Lord God
Ro. 1:25. the Creator, who is *blessed* for ever.
9: 5. Christ (came), who is over all, God *blessed* for ever.
2Co. 1: 3. *Blessed* (be) God, even the Father of
11:31. which is *blessed* for evermore,
Eph. 1: 3. *Blessed* (be) the God and Father of
1Pet. 1: 3. *Blessed* (be) the God and Father of our Lord Jesus Christ,

2129 16 323/401 2:754 2095,3056

εὐλογία, ūlogia.

Ro. 15:29. in the fulness of the *blessing*
16:18. by good words and *fair speeches* deceive
1Co.10:16. The cup of *blessing* which we
2Co. 9: 5. your *bounty*, whereof ye had notice before,
— as (*a matter of*) *bounty*,
6. he which soweth *bountifully* shall reap also *bountifully*.
Gal. 3:14. That the *blessing* of Abraham might come on the Gentiles through Jesus
Eph. 1: 3. with all spiritual *blessings*
Heb 6: 7. receiveth *blessing* from God:
12:17. would have inherited the *blessing*,
Jas. 3:10. proceedeth *blessing* and cursing.
1Pet. 3: 9. that ye should inherit a *blessing*.
Rev. 5:12. and glory, and *blessing*.
13. *Blessing*, and honour, and glory,
7:12. *Blessing*, and glory, and wisdom,

2130 1 323/401 2095,3330

εὐμετάδοτος, ūmetadotos.

1Ti. 6:18. *ready to distribute*, willing to communicate;

2132 1 323/401 4:948 2095,3563

εὐνόεω, ūnoeo.

Mat. 5:25. Agree (lit. be thou *agreeing*) with thine adversary quickly,

2133 2 323/401 4:948 2095,3563

εὔνοια, ūnoia.

1Co. 7: 3. unto the wife due *benevolence*:
Eph. 6: 7. With *good will* doing service,

2134 2 323/402 2135

εὐνουχίζω, ūnoukizo.

Mat.19:12. *were made eunuchs* of men:
— *have made* themselves *eunuchs* for the kingdom of heaven's sake.

2135 8 323/402 2:765 2192

εὐνοῦχος, ūnoukos. eune (bed)

Mat.19:12. For there are some *eunuchs*, which
— and there are some *eunuchs*, which were
— and there be *eunuchs*, which have
Acts 8:27. an *eunuch* of great authority under Candace
34. And the *eunuch* answered Philip,
36. the *eunuch* said, See, (here is) water;
38. into the water, both Philip and the *eunuch*;
39. the *eunuch* saw him no more:

2137 4 324/402 2095,3598

εὐοδοῦμαι, ūodoumai.

Ro. 1:10. now at length I might *have a prosperous journey*
1Co.16: 2. lay by him in store, as (God) hath prospered him, (lit. whatever he *be prospered* in)
3Joh. 2. that thou mayest *prosper* and be in health, even as thy soul *prospereth*.

2138 1 324/402 2095,3982

εὐπειθής, ūpitheeS.

Jas. 3:17. *easy to be intreated*, full of mercy

2139 1 324/402 2095,4012,2476

εὐπερίστατος, ūperistatos.

Heb 12: 1. the sin *which doth so easily beset* (us),

2140 1 324/402 2095,4160

εὐποιΐα, ūpoiya.

Heb 13:16. But *to do good* and to communicate forget not: (lit. forget not the *doing-good*, &c.)

2141 1 324/402 2090,rt 4197

εὐπορέομαι, ūporeomai.

Acts11:29. every man according to his ability, (lit. as he *abounded*)

2142 1 324/402 rt 2141

εὐπορία, ūporia.

Acts19:25. by this craft we have our *wealth*.

2143 1 324/402 2095,4241

εὐπρέπεια, ūprepīa.

Jas. 1:11. the *grace* of the fashion of it perisheth:

2144 5 324/402 2:50 2095,4327

εὐπρόσδεκτος, ūprosdektos.

Ro. 15:16. the offering up of the Gentiles might be *acceptable*,
31. may be *accepted* of the saints;
2Co. 6: 2. behold, now (is) the *accepted* time;
8:12. (it is) *accepted* according to that a man
1Pet. 2: 5. *acceptable* to God by Jesus Christ.

2145 1 324/402 2095, 4314
dokeuō (to watch)

εὐπρόσεδρος, ūprosedros.

1Co. 7:35. that ye may attend upon the Lord (lit. with a view to *assiduous*ness unto the Lord)

2146 1 324/402 6:768 2095,4383

εὐπροσωπέω, uprosōpeo.

Gal. 6:12. *to make a fair shew* in the flesh,

2147 178 325/402 2:769

εὑρίσκω, hurisko.

Mat. 1:18. she *was found* with child of the Holy Ghost.
2: 8. and when ye *have found* (him),
11. they *saw* the young child
7: 7. seek, and ye *shall find*;
8. he that seeketh *findeth*.
14. and few there be *that find* it.
8:10. I *have* not *found* so great faith,
10:39. He *that findeth* his life shall
— loseth his life for my sake *shall find* it.
11:29. ye *shall find* rest unto your souls.
12:43. seeking rest, and *findeth* none.
44. he *findeth* (it) empty,
13:44. the which *when* a man *hath found*,
46. Who, *when* he *had found* one pearl of great price,
16:25. lose his life for my sake *shall find* it.
17:27. thou *shalt find* a piece of money:
18:13. if so be that he *find* it,
28. *found* one of his fellowservants,
20: 6. and *found* others standing
21: 2. ye *shall find* an ass tied,
19. *found* nothing thereon,
22: 9. as many as ye shall *find*,
10. all as many as they *found*,
Mat.24:46. when he cometh *shall find* so doing.
26:40. *findeth* them asleep,
43. and *found* them asleep again:
60. But *found* none: yea, though many false witnesses came, (yet) *found* they none.
27:32. they *found* a man of Cyrene,
Mar. 1:37. And *when* they *had found* him,
7:30. she *found* the devil gone out,
11: 2. ye shall *find* a colt tied,
4. and *found* the colt tied
13. if haply he might *find* any thing thereon.
— he *found* nothing but leaves;
13:36. he *find* you sleeping.
14:16. *found* as he had said unto them:
37. and *findeth* them sleeping,
40. he *found* them asleep again,
55. to put him to death; and *found* none.
Lu. 1:30. for thou *hast found* favour with God.
2:12. Ye *shall find* the babe wrapped in swaddling clothes,
45. And *when* they *found* him not,
46. they *found* him in the temple,
4:17. he *found* the place where it was written,
5:19. *when* they could not *find* by what (way)
6: 7. that they *might find* an accusation against him.
7: 9. I *have* not *found* so great faith,
10. *found* the servant whole that had been
8:35. and *found* the man, out of whom
9:12. and lodge, and *get* victuals:
36. Jesus *was found* alone.
11: 9. seek, and ye *shall find*;
10. and he that seeketh *findeth*;
24. and *finding* none, he saith, I will
25. he *findeth* (it) swept
12:37. when he cometh *shall find* watching:
38. and *find* (them) so, blessed are those
43. *shall find* so doing.
13: 6. sought fruit thereon, and *found* none.
7. on this fig tree, and *find* none:
15: 4. until he *find* it?
5. *when* he *hath found* (it), he layeth (it)
6. I *have found* my sheep
8. till she *find* (it)?
9. *when* she *hath found* (it), she calleth
— for I *have found* the piece
24. he was lost, and *is found*.
32. was lost, and *is found*.
17:18. There *are* not *found* that returned
18: 8. *shall* he *find* faith on the earth?
19:30 ye *shall find* a colt tied,
32. and *found* even as he had said
48. *could* not *find* what they might do:
22:13. and *found* as he had said
45. he *found* them sleeping
23: 2. We *found* this (fellow) perverting
4. I *find* no fault in this man.
14. *have found* no fault in this man
22. I *have found* no cause of death in him
24: 2. And they *found* the stone rolled away
3. and *found* not the body of the Lord
23. And *when* they *found* not his body, they came,
24. and *found* (it) even so as the women
33. *found* the eleven gathered together,
Joh. 1:41(42). He first *findeth* his own brother Simon, and saith unto him, We *have found*
43(44). and *findeth* Philip, and saith unto him,
45(46). Philip *findeth* Nathanael, and saith unto him, We *have found*

Joh. 2:14. And *found* in the temple those
5:14. Afterward Jesus *findeth* him in the temple,
6:25. *when* they *had found* him on the other side
7:34. and *shall* not *find* (me):
35. we *shall* not *find* him?
36. and *shall* not *find* (me):
9:35. and *when* he *had found* him, he said
10: 9. shall go in and out, and *find* pasture.
11:17. he *found* that he had (lain) in the grave four days already.
12:14. And Jesus, *when* he *had found* a young ass,
18:38. I *find* in him no fault (at all).
19: 4. may know that I *find* no fault in him.
6. I *find* no fault in him.
21: 6. right side of the ship, and ye *shall find*.
Acts 4:21. *finding* nothing how they might punish
5:10. came in, and *found* her dead,
22. *found* them not in the prison,
23. The prison truly *found* we shut
— we *found* no man within.
39. ye *be found* even to fight against God.
7:11. and our fathers *found* no sustenance.
46. Who *found* favour before God, and desired *to find* a tabernacle for the God
8:40. But Philip *was found* at Azotus:
9: 2 if he *found* any of this way,
33. And there he *found* a certain man
10:27. *found* many that were come together.
11:26(25). *when* he *had found* him, he brought
12:19. and *found* him not, he examined
13: 6. they *found* a certain sorcerer, a false prophet,
22. I *have found* David the (son) of Jesse,
28. And *though* they *found* no cause of death
17: 6. And *when* they *found* them not,
23. I *found* an altar with this inscription,
27. they might feel after him, and *find* him,
18: 2. And *found* a certain Jew named
19: 1. and *finding* certain disciples,
19. and *found* (it) fifty thousand (pieces) of silver.
21: 2. And *finding* a ship sailing over
23: 9. We *find* no evil in this man:
29. Whom I *perceived* to be accused
24: 5. For we *have found* this man
12 they neither *found* me in the temple
18. Jews from Asia *found* me purified
20. if they *have found* any evil doing in me,
27: 6. And there the centurion *found* a ship
28. and *found* (it) twenty fathoms:
— and *found* (it) fifteen fathoms.
28:14. Where we *found* brethren, *and* were
Ro. 4: 1. as pertaining to the flesh, *hath found*?
7:10. the commandment,...I found (lit. *was found* to me)
18. but (how) to perform that which is good I *find* not.
21. I *find* then a law, that, when I
10:20. I *was found* of them that sought me not;
1Co. 4: 2. that a man *be found* faithful.
15:15. Yea, and we *are found* false witnesses
2Co. 2:13(12). because I *found* not Titus
5: 3. we *shall* not *be found* naked.
9: 4. come with me, and *find* you unprepared,
11:12. they *may be found* even as we.
12:20. lest,...I shall not *find* you such as I would, and (that) I shall *be found* unto you such
Gal. 2:17. we ourselves also *are found*
Phi. 2: 8. *being found* in fashion as
3: 9. And *be found* in him, not having mine
2Ti. 1:17. very diligently, and *found* (me).
18. that he may *find* mercy of the Lord in
Heb 4 16. that we may obtain mercy, and *find* grace
9:12. *having obtained* eternal redemption (for us).
11: 5. and *was* not *found*, because God
12:17. for he *found* no place of repentance,
1Pet.1: 7. *might be found* unto praise
2:22. neither *was* guile *found*
2Pet.3:14. that ye may *be found* of him in peace,
2Joh. 4. I *found* of thy children walking in truth,
Rev. 2: 2. and *hast found* them liars.
3: 2. for I *have* not *found* thy works perfect
5: 4. no man *was found* worthy to open
9. 6. seek death, and *shall* not *find* it;
12: 8. neither *was* their place *found*
14: 5. in their mouth *was found* no guile
16:20. the mountains *were* not *found*.
18:14. thou *shalt find* them no more at all.
21. and *shall be found* no more at all.
22. *shall be found* any more in thee;
24. *was found* the blood of prophets, and of saints,
20:11. there *was found* no place for them
15. And whosoever *was* not *found*

2149 1 326/404 5561 *eurus* (wide)

εὐρύχωρος, *urukōros*

Mat. 7:13. *broad* (is) the way,

2150 15 326/404 7:168 2152

εὐσέβεια, *ūsebīa.*

Acts 3:12. as though by our own power or *holiness*
1Ti. 2: 2. in all *godliness* and honesty.
3:16. the mystery of *godliness*:
4: 7. and exercise thyself (rather) unto *godliness*.
8. but *godliness* is profitable unto all things,
6: 3. to the doctrine which is according to *godliness*;
5. that gain is *godliness*:
6. *godliness* with contentment
11. *godliness*, faith, love, patience,
2Ti. 3: 5. Having a form of *godliness*,
Tit. 1: 1. of the truth which is after *godliness*;
2Pet.1: 3. unto life and *godliness*,
6. and to patience *godliness*;
7. And to *godliness* brotherly kindness;
3:11. in (all) holy conversation and *godliness*,

2151 2 326/404 7:168 2152

εὐσεβέω, *ūsebeo.*

Acts17:23. Whom therefore ye ignorantly *worship*,
1Ti. 5: 4. let them learn first *to shew piety* at home, (lit. to *care piously for* their own house)

2152 4 326/404 7:168 2095,4576

εὐσεβής, *ūsebees.*

Acts10: 2. (A) *devout* (man), and one that feared God
7. and a *devout* soldier of them that waited on him
22:12. a *devout* man according to the law.
2Pet.2: 9. The Lord knoweth how to deliver the *godly*

2153 2 326/404 2152
εὐσεβῶς, ūsebōs.

2Ti. 3:12. all that will live *godly* in Christ
Tit. 2:12. we should live soberly, righteously, and *godly*,

2154 1 326/404 2:770 2095
7:200 rt 4591
εὔσημος, ūseemos.

1Co.14: 9. except ye utter...words *easy to be understood,* (lit. *well-significant*)

2155 2 326/404 7:548 2095,4698
εὔσπλαγχνος, ūsplanknos.

Eph. 4:32. *tenderhearted,* forgiving one another,
1Pet.3: 8. love as brethren, (be) *pitiful,*

2156 3 327/404 2158
εὐσχημόνως, ūskeemonōs.

Ro. 13:13. Let us walk *honestly,*
1Co.14:40. be done *decently* and in order.
1Th. 4:12. That ye may walk *honestly* toward them that are without,

2157 1 327/404 2158
εὐσχημοσύνη, ūskeemosunee.

1Co.12.23. have more abundant *comeliness.*

2158 5 327/405 2:770 2095,4976
εὐσχήμων, uskeemōn.

Mar 15:43. of Arimathæa, an *honourable* counsellor,
Acts13:50. the devout and *honourable* women,
17:12. also of *honourable* women which
1Co. 7:35. but for that which is *comely,*
12:24. For our *comely* (parts) have no need:

2159 2 327/405 2095
teinō (to stretch)
εὐτόνως, ūtonōs.

Lu. 23:10. and *vehemently* accused him.
Acts18:28. For he *mightily* convinced the Jews,

2160 1 327/405 2095,rt 5157
εὐτραπελία, ūtrapelia.

Eph. 5: 4. foolish talking, nor *jesting,*

2162 1 327/405 2163
εὐφημία, ūpheemia.

2Co. 6: 8. by evil report and *good report:*

2163 1 327/405 2095,5345
εὔφημος, ūpheemos.

Phi. 4: 8. whatsoever things (are) *of good report;*

2164 1 327/405 2095,5409
εὐφορέω, ūphoreo.

Lu. 12:16. The ground of a certain rich man *brought forth plentifully:*

2165 14 327/405 2:772 2095,5424
εὐφραίνω -ομαι, ūphraino -omai.

Lu. 12:19. eat, drink, (and) *be merry.*
15:23. let us eat, and *be merry:*
24. they began *to be merry.*
Lu. 15:29. I *might make merry* with my friends:
32. that we should *make merry,* and be glad:
16:19. *and fared* sumptuously every day:
Acts 2:26. Therefore *did* my heart *rejoice,*
7:41. unto the idol, and *rejoiced* in the works of their own hands.
Ro. 15:10. *Rejoice,* ye Gentiles, with his people.
2Co. 2: 2. who is he then *that maketh* me *glad,*
Gal. 4:27. *Rejoice,* (thou) barren that bearest not;
Rev.11:10. shall rejoice over them, and *make merry,*
12:12. Therefore *rejoice,* (ye) heavens, and ye
18:20. *Rejoice* over her, (thou) heaven, and (ye) holy apostles and

2167 2 328/405 2:772 rt 2165
εὐφροσύνη, ūphrosunee.

Acts 2:28. thou shalt make me full of *joy*
14:17. with food and *gladness.*

2168 39 328/405 9:359 2170
εὐχαριστέω, ūkaristeo.

Mat.15:36. and *gave thanks, and* brake (them),
26:27. the cup, and *gave thanks, and* gave
Mar. 8: 6. and *gave thanks, and* brake,
14:23. and *when he had given thanks,* he gave
Lu. 17:16. *giving* him *thanks:*
18:11. God, I *thank* thee, that I am not as
22:17. and *gave thanks, and* said,
19. and *gave thanks, and* brake (it),
Joh. 6:11. *when he had given thanks,* he distributed to the disciples,
23. did eat bread, *after that* the Lord *had given thanks:*
11:41. Father, I *thank* thee that thou hast heard me.
Acts27:35. *gave thanks* to God in presence of them all:
28:15. he *thanked* God, *and* took courage.
Ro. 1: 8. I *thank* my God through Jesus Christ
21. they glorified (him) not as God, neither *were thankful;*
7:25. I *thank* God through Jesus Christ
14: 6. for he *giveth* God *thanks;*
— eateth not, and *giveth* God *thanks.*
16: 4. not only I *give thanks,* but also all
1Co. 1: 4. I *thank* my God always on your behalf,
14. I *thank* God that I baptized none
10:30. for that for which I *give thanks?*
11:24. *when* he *had given thanks,* he brake (it)
14:17. thou verily *givest thanks* well,
18. I *thank* my God, I speak with tongues
2Co. 1:11. *thanks may be given* by many on our behalf.
Eph. 1:16. Cease not to *give thanks* for you,
5.20. *Giving thanks* always for all things
Phi. 1: 3. I *thank* my God upon every remembrance
Col. 1: 3. We *give thanks* to God and the
12. *Giving thanks* unto the Father,
3:17. *giving thanks* to God and the Father
1Th. 1: 2. We *give thanks* to God always for you
2:13. For this cause also *thank* we God
5:18. In every thing *give thanks:*
2Th. 1: 3. We are bound *to thank* God always
2:13. are bound *to give thanks* alway
Philem. 4. I *thank* my God, making mention
Rev 11:17. We *give* thee *thanks,* O Lord God Almighty

2169 15 328/406 9:359 2170
εὐχαριστία, ūkaristia.

Acts24: 3. most noble Felix, with all *thankfulness.*
1Co.14:16. say Amen at thy *giving of thanks.*

2Co. 4:15. might through the *thanksgiving* of many redound
9:11. causeth through us *thanksgiving* to
12. by many *thanksgivings* unto God;
Eph. 5: 4. but rather *giving of thanks.*
Phi. 4: 6. prayer and supplication with *thanksgiving*
Col. 2: 7. abounding therein with *thanksgiving.*
4: 2. watch in the same with *thanksgiving;*
1Th. 3: 9. For what *thanks* can we render to God again for you,
1Ti. 2: 1. intercessions, (and) *giving of thanks,* be made for all men;
4: 3. to be received with *thanksgiving*
4. if it be received with *thanksgiving:*
Rev. 4: 9. and *thanks* to him that sat on the throne,
7:12. and *thanksgiving,* and honour,

2170 1 329/406 9:359 2095,5483

εὐχάριστος, ūkaristos.

Col. 3:15. and be ye *thankful.*

2171 3 329/406 2:775 2172

εὐχή, ūkee.

Acts18:18. head in Cenchrea: for he had a *vow.*
21:23. which have a *vow* on them;
Jas. 5:15. And the *prayer* of faith shall save

2172 7 329/406 2:775

εὔχομαι, ūkomai.

Acts26:29. I *would* to God, that not only thou,
27:29. and *wished* for the day.
Ro. 9: 3. For I could wish (lit *used to wish*) that myself
2Co.13: 7. Now I *pray* to God that
9. this also we *wish,* (even) your perfection.
Jas. 5:16. *pray* one for another, that ye may be healed.
3Joh. 2. I *wish* above all things that thou mayest prosper

2173 3 329/406 2095,5543

εὔχρηστος, ūkreestos.

2Ti. 2:21. *meet for* the master's *use,*
4:11. *profitable* to me for the ministry.
Philem 11. *profitable* to thee and to me:

2174 1 330/406 2095,5590

εὐψυχέω, ūpsukeo.

Phi. 2:19. that I also *may be of good comfort,*

2175 3 330/406 2:808 2095,3605

εὐωδία, ūodia.

2Co. 2:15. we are...a *sweet savour* of Christ,
Eph. 5: 2. for a *sweetsmelling* savour.
Phi. 4:18. odour of a *sweet smell,* a sacrifice

2176 10 330/406 2095,3686

εὐώνυμος, ūonumos.

Mat.20:21. and the other on the *left,*
23. to sit on my right hand, and on my *left,*
25:33. but the goats on the *left.*
41. say also unto them on the *left* hand,
27:38. and another on the *left.*
Mar.10:37. and the other on thy *left* hand,
40. and on my *left* hand is not mine
Mar 15:27. and the other on his *left.*
Acts21: 3. we left it *on the left* hand,
Rev.10: 2. and (his) *left* (foot) on the earth,

2177 1 330/406 1909,242

ἐφάλλομαι, ephallomai.

Acts19:16. *leaped on* them,...*and* prevailed against

2178 5 330/406 1:381 1909,530

ἐφάπαξ, ephapax.

Ro. 6:10. he died unto sin *once:*
1Co.15: 6. five hundred brethren *at once;*
Heb 7:27. for this he did *once,* when he offered up himself.
9:12. he entered in *once* into the holy place,
10:10. through the offering of the body of Jesus Christ *once (for all).*

2182 1 330/407 1909,2147

ἐφευρετής, ephūretees.

Ro. 1:30. *inventors* of evil things,

2183 2 330/407 2184

ἐφημερία, epheemeria.

Lu. 1: 5. Zacharias, of the *course* of Abia:
8. before God in the order of his *course,*

2184 1 330/407 1909,2250

ἐφήμερος, epheemeros.

Jas. 2:15. be naked, and destitute of *daily* food,

2185 2 330/407 1909,cf 2240

ἐφικνέομαι, ephikneomai.

2Co.10:13. *to reach* even unto you.
14. as *though* we *reached* not unto you:

2186 21 330/407 1909,2476

ἐφίστημι, ephisteemi.

Lu. 2: 9. the angel of the Lord *came upon* them,
38. And she *coming in* that instant
4:39. he *stood* over her, and rebuked
10:40. and *came to* him, *and* said, Lord,
20: 1. the chief priests and the scribes *came upon* (him)
21:34. that day *come upon* you unawares.
24: 4. two men *stood by* them in shining garments:
Acts 4: 1. and the Sadducees, *came upon* them,
6:12. *came upon* (him), *and* caught him,
10:17. and *stood before* the gate,
11:11. there *were* three men already *come unto* the house
12: 7. the angel of the Lord *came upon* (him),
17: 5. *assaulted* the house of Jason, *and* sought
22:13. Came unto me, and *stood, and* said
20. I also was *standing by,* and consenting
23:11. the Lord *stood by* him, *and* said, Be of good
27. then *came* I with an army, *and* rescued
28: 2. because of the *present* rain,
1Th. 5: 3. destruction *cometh upon* them.
2Ti 4: 2. *be instant* in season out of season;
6. the time of my departure *is at hand*

1896 2 284/353 1909,1492

ἐφοράω, *ephorao.*

Lu. 1:25. wherein he *looked on* (me),
Acts 4:29. Lord, *behold* their threatenings:

2188 1 331/407 [6606]

ἐφφαθά, *ephphatha.*

Mar. 7:34. *Ephphatha,* that is, Be opened.

2189 6 331/407 2:811 2190

ἔχθρα, *ekthra.*

Lu. 23:12. they were at *enmity* between themselves.
Ro. 8: 7. the carnal mind (is) *enmity* against God:
Gal. 5:20. witchcraft, *hatred,* variance,
Eph. 2:15. abolished in his flesh the *enmity,*
16. having slain the *enmity* thereby:
Jas. 4: 4. the friendship of the world is *enmity* with

2190 32 331/407 2:811 *echthō* (to hate)

ἐχθρός, *ekthros.*

Mat. 5:43. and hate thine *enemy.*
44. Love your *enemies,* bless
10:36. And a man's *foes* (shall be) they of his
13:25. his *enemy* came and sowed tares
28. An *enemy* hath done this.
39. The *enemy* that sowed them is the devil;
22:44. till I make thine *enemies* thy
Mar 12:36. thine *enemies* thy footstool.
Lu. 1:71. That we should be saved from our *enemies,*
74. out of the hand of our *enemies*
6:27. Love your *enemies,* do good to
35. love ye your *enemies,*
10:19. and over all the power of the *enemy:*
19:27. But those mine *enemies,* which
43. that thine *enemies* shall cast a trench about
20:43. Till I make thine *enemies* thy footstool.
Acts 2:35. thy *foes* thy footstool.
13:10. (thou) *enemy* of all righteousness,
Ro. 5:10. For if, when we were *enemies,*
11:28. (they are) *enemies* for your sakes·
12:20. if thine *enemy* hunger, feed him;
1Co.15:25. till he hath put all *enemies*
26. The last *enemy* (that) shall be destroyed
Gal. 4:16. Am I therefore become your *enemy,*
Phi. 3:18. (that they are) the *enemies* of the cross
Col. 1:21. and *enemies* in (your) mind
2Th. 3:15. count (him) not as an *enemy,*
Heb 1:13. I make thine *enemies* thy footstool?
10:13. till his *enemies* be made
Jas. 4: 4. will be a friend of the world is the *enemy* of God.
Rev.11: 5. and devoureth their *enemies:*
12. and their *enemies* beheld them.

2191 5 332/408 2:815

ἔχιδνα, *ekidna.*

Mat. 3: 7. O generation of *vipers,* who hath
12:34. O generation of *vipers,* how can ye,
23:33. (ye) generation of *vipers,* how
Lu. 3: 7. O generation of *vipers,*
Acts28: 3. a *viper* out of the heat,

2192 709 332/408 2:816,6:1091

ἔχω, *eko.*

Mat. 1:18. she was found with child (lit. *having* in the womb)
23. a virgin shall be with child, (lit. *shall have,* &c.)
Mat. 3: 4. *had* his raiment of camel's hair,
9. We *have* Abraham to (our) father:
14. I *have* need to be baptized of thee,
4:24. sick people (lit. *that had* themselves sickly)
5:23. *hath* ought against thee;
46. what reward *have* ye?
6: 1. otherwise ye *have* no reward
8. what things ye *have* need of,
7:29. as (one) *having* authority,
8: 9. *having* soldiers under me:
16. all that were sick: (lit. *that had* themselves sickly)
20. The foxes *have* holes, and the birds of the air (have) nests; but the Son of man *hath* not where to lay (his) head.
9: 6. the Son of man *hath* power
12. They that be whole need not (lit. *have* not need of) a physician, but they *that are* sick.
36. as sheep *having* no shepherd.
11:15. He *that hath* ears to hear, let him hear
18. and they say, He *hath* a devil.
12:10. *which had* (his) hand withered.
11. that *shall have* one sheep,
13: 5. they *had* not much earth:
— because they *had* no deepness
6. because they *had* no root,
9. *Who hath* ears to hear, let
12. For whosoever *hath,* to him shall
— but whosoever *hath* not, from him shall be taken away even that he *hath.*
21. Yet *hath* he not root in himself,
27. from whence then *hath* it tares?
43. *Who hath* ears to hear, let him hear.
44. selleth all that he *hath,* and
46. sold all that he *had,* and bought it.
14: 4. It is not lawful for thee *to have* her.
5. they *counted* him as a prophet.
16. They need not depart; (lit. *have* not need to depart)
17. We *have* here but five loaves, and
35. all that were diseased; (lit. *that had* themselves sickly)
15:30. came unto him, *having* with them
32. three days, and *have* nothing to eat:
34. How many loaves *have* ye?
17:20. If ye *have* faith as a grain of
18: 8. rather than *having* two hands or two feet
9. rather than *having* two eyes to be cast
25. But *forasmuch as* he *had* not
— and all that he *had,* and payment.
19:16. that I *may have* eternal life?
21. thou *shalt have* treasure in heaven:
22. for he had great possessions. (lit. was *having*)
21: 3. The Lord *hath* need of them;
21. If ye *have* faith, and doubt not,
26. for all *hold* John as a prophet.
28. A (certain) man *had* two sons;
46. they *took* him *for* a prophet.
22:12. not *having* a wedding garment?
24. If a man die, *having* no children,
25. *having* no issue, left his wife unto
28. for they all *had* her.
24:19. unto them that are with child, (lit. *that have* in the womb)
25:25. lo, (there) thou *hast* (that is) thine.
28. unto him *which hath* ten talents.
29. For unto every one *that hath* shall
— but from him *that hath* not shall be taken away even that which he *hath.*

Mat.26: 7. *having* an alabaster box of very
11. ye *have* the poor always with you; but me ye *have* not always.
65. what further need *have* we of
27:16. And they *had* then a notable prisoner,
65. Pilate said unto them, Ye *have* a watch:
Mar 1:22. as one *that had* authority,
32. that were diseased, (lit. *that had* themselves sickly)
34. many that were sick (lit. *that had*, &c.)
38. into the next towns, (lit. towns *holding nigh*)
2:10. the Son of man *hath* power
17. They that are whole *have* no need
— but they *that are* sick:
19. as long as they *have* the bridegroom
25. what David did, when he *had* need,
3: 1. a man there *which had* a withered hand.
3. unto the man *which had* the
10. as many as *had* plagues.
15. And *to have* power to heal
22. He *hath* Beelzebub, and by
26. he cannot stand, but *hath* an end.
29. *hath* never forgiveness,
30. He *hath* an unclean spirit.
4: 5. it *had* not much earth;
— because it *had* no depth
6. because it *had* no root,
9. He *that hath* ears to hear,
17. *have* no root in themselves,
23. If any man *have* ears to hear,
25. For he that *hath*, to him shall be given: and he that *hath* not, from him shall be taken even that which he *hath*.
40. how is it that ye *have* no faith?
5: 3. Who *had* (his) dwelling among
15. *and had* the legion,
23. lieth (lit. *hath* herself) at the point of
6:18. *to have* thy brother's wife.
34. were as sheep not *having* a shepherd:
36. for they *have* nothing to eat.
38. How many loaves *have* ye?
55. to carry about...those *that were* sick,
7:16. If any man *have* ears to hear,
25. daughter *had* an unclean spirit,
8: 1. and *having* nothing to eat,
2. *have* nothing to eat:
5. How many loaves *have* ye?
7. they *had* a few small fishes:
14. neither *had* they in the ship with them
16. (It is) because we *have* no bread.
17. because ye *have* no bread?
— *have* ye your heart yet hardened?
18. *Having* eyes, see ye not? and *having* ears,
9:17. my son, *which hath* a dumb spirit;
43. than *having* two hands to go
45. than *having* two feet to be cast
47. with one eye, than *having* two eyes
50. *Have* salt in yourselves,
10:21. sell whatsoever thou *hast*, and give to the poor, and thou *shalt have* treasure in
22. for he *had* great possessions.
23. shall they *that have* riches enter
11: 3. that the Lord *hath* need of him;
13. seeing a fig tree afar off *having* leaves,
22. *Have* faith in God.
25. if ye *have* ought against any:
32. *counted* John, that he was a prophet
12: 6. *Having* yet therefore one son, his
23. for the seven *had* her to wife.
44. did cast in all that she *had*,
13:17. them that are with child, (lit. *that have*, &c.)

Mar 14: 3. *having* an alabaster box of ointment.
7. ye *have* the poor with you always,
— but me ye *have* not always.
8. She hath done what she could: (lit. what she *had* in her power, &c.)
63. What need we any further witnesses? (lit. What further *have* we need of witnesses?)
16: 8. for they trembled (lit. trembling *took* them)
18. and they shall recover. (lit. *shall have* themselves well)
Lu. 3: 8. We *have* Abraham to (our) father:
11. He *that hath* two coats, let him impart to him *that hath* none; and he *that hath*
4:33. a man, *which had* a spirit of an unclean
40. all they that *had* any sick
5:24. the Son of man *hath* power
31. They that are whole need not (lit. *have* not need of) a physician; but they *that are* sick.
6: 8. to the man *which had* the withered
7: 2. centurion's servant,...*was* sick, *and*
8. *having* under me soldiers,
33. and ye say, He *hath* a devil.
40. I *have* somewhat to say unto thee.
42. And *when* they *had* nothing
8: 6. because it lacked (lit. *had* not) moisture.
8. He *that hath* ears to hear,
13. and these *have* no root, which for a
18. *hath*, to him shall be given; and whosoever *hath* not, from him shall be taken even that which he seemeth *to have*.
27. man, which *had* devils long time,
9: 3. neither *have* two coats apiece.
11. healed them *that had* need of healing.
58. Foxes *have* holes, and birds of the air (have) nests; but the Son of man *hath* not where to lay (his) head.
11: 5. Which of you *shall have* a friend,
6. I *have* nothing to set before him?
36. full of light, *having* no part dark,
12: 4. and after that *have* no more that they
5. Fear him, *which* after he hath killed *hath* power to cast into hell;
17. I *have* no room where to bestow
19. Soul, thou *hast* much goods
50. But I *have* a baptism to be baptized with;
13: 6. A certain (man) *had* a fig tree
11. a woman *which had* a spirit of infirmity
33. to morrow, and the (day) *following*:
14:14. they cannot recompense thee: (lit. they *have* not to recompense thee)
18. I must needs go (lit. I *have* need to go) and see it: I pray thee *have* me excused.
19. I go to prove them: I pray thee *have* me
28. whether he *have* (sufficient) to finish (it)?
35. He *that hath* ears to hear,
15: 4. *having* an hundred sheep,
7. need no repentance. (lit. *have* no need of)
8. *having* ten pieces of silver,
11. A certain man *had* two sons:
16: 1. rich man, which *had* a steward;
28. For I *have* five brethren;
29. They *have* Moses and the prophets;
17: 6. If ye *had* faith as a grain
7. which of you, *having* a servant plowing
9. Doth he thank that servant (lit. *hath* he favour, or thanks, to)
18:22. sell all that thou *hast*, and distribute unto the poor, and thou *shalt have* treasure in heaven:
24. How hardly shall they *that have* riches

Lu. 19:17. have thou (lit. be thou *having*) authority over
20. thy pound, which I *have kept* laid up
24. give (it) to him *that hath* ten pounds.
25. Lord, he *hath* ten pounds.
26. unto every one *which hath* shall be given; and from him *that hath* not, even that he *hath* shall be taken
31. the Lord *hath* need of him.
34. The Lord *hath* need of him.
20:24. Whose image and superscription *hath* it?
28. any man's brother die, *having* a wife,
33. for seven *had* her to wife.
21: 4. hath cast in all the living that she *had*.
23. unto them that are with child, (lit. *that have* in the womb)
22:36. he *that hath* a purse,
— he *that hath* no sword, let him sell
37. the things concerning me *have* an end.
71. What need we any further witness? (lit. what further *have* we need of witnessing)
23:17. For of necessity he must release (lit. he *had* necessity to release)
24:39. for a spirit *hath* not flesh and bones, as ye see me *have*.
41. *Have* ye here any meat?
Joh. 2: 3. They *have* no wine.
25. needed not (lit. *had* not need) that any should testify of man:
3:15. should not perish, but *have* eternal
16. should not perish, but *have* everlasting life.
29. He *that hath* the bride is the
36. on the Son *hath* everlasting life:
4:11. thou *hast* nothing to draw with, and the well is deep: from whence then *hast* thou
17. and said, I *have* no husband.
— Thou hast well said, I *have* no husband:
18. For thou *hast had* five husbands; and he whom thou now *hast* is not
32. I *have* meat to eat that ye know not of.
44. *hath* no honour in his own country.
52. when he began to amend. (lit. he *had* himself better)
5: 2. Bethesda, *having* five porches.
5. *which had* an infirmity thirty and
6. he *had been* now a long time
7. I *have* no man, when the water is troubled,
24. *hath* everlasting life, and shall
26. Father *hath* life in himself; so hath he given to the Son *to have* life in himself;
36. I *have* greater witness
38. ye *have* not his word
39. ye *have* eternal life:
40. that ye *might have* life.
42. ye *have* not the love of God
6: 9. which *hath* five barley loaves,
40. *may have* everlasting life:
47. on me *hath* everlasting life.
53. ye *have* no life in you.
54. my blood, *hath* eternal life;
68. thou *hast* the words of eternal life,
7:20. Thou *hast* a devil:
8: 6. that they *might have* to accuse him.
12. but *shall have* the light of life.
26. I *have* many things to say and to judge of you:
41. we *have* one Father, (even) God.
48. and *hast* a devil?
49. I *have* not a devil;

Joh. 8:52. that thou *hast* a devil.
57. Thou art not yet fifty years old, (lit. *hast* not yet fifty years)
9:21. he is of age; (lit. he *hath* due age)
23. He is of age; (lit: *hath* &c.)
41. ye should *have* no sin:
10:10. that they *might have* life, and that they *might have* (it) more abundantly.
16. And other sheep I *have*,
18. I *have* power to lay it down, and I *have* power to take it again.
20. He *hath* a devil, and is mad;
11:17. he found that he *had* (lain) in the grave four days
12: 6. *had* the bag, and bare what was put
8. ye *have* with you; but me ye *have* not always.
35. while ye *have* the light,
36. While ye *have* light,
48. *hath* one that judgeth him:
13: 8. thou *hast* no part with me.
10. needeth not (lit. *hath* not need) save to wash (his) feet,
29. because Judas *had* the bag, that Jesus
— that we *have* need of against the feast;
35. if ye *have* love one to another.
14:21. He *that hath* my commandments,
30. cometh, and *hath* nothing in me.
15:13. Greater love *hath* no man than this,
22. they *had* not *had* sin: but now they *have* no
24. they *had* not *had* sin:
16:12. I *have* yet many things to say unto you.
15. All things that the Father *hath* are mine:
21. *hath* sorrow, because her hour is come:
22. ye now therefore *have* sorrow:
30. and needest not (lit. *hast* not need)
33. ye *might have* peace. In the world ye *shall have* tribulation:
17: 5. which I *had* with thee before the world
13. that they *might have* my joy
18:10. Simon Peter *having* a sword
19: 7. We *have* a law, and by our law
10. knowest thou not that I *have* power to crucify thee, and *have* power to
11. Thou couldest have (lit. *hadst*) no power
— *hath* the greater sin.
15. We *have* no king but Cæsar.
20:31. believing ye *might have* life
21: 5. Children, *have* ye any meat?
Acts 1:12. which is from Jerusalem a sabbath day's journey. (lit. which is near Jerusalem, *having* a sabbath day's journey)
2:44. were together, and *had* all things common;
45. as every man *had* need.
47. *having* favour with all the people.
3: 6. but such as I *have* give I thee:
4:14. they could say nothing (lit. *had* nothing to say) against it.
35. according as he *had* need.
7: 1. *Are* these things so?
8: 7. came out of many that were possessed (with them): (lit. *that had* them)
9:14. he *hath* authority from the chief priests
31. Then *had* the churches rest
11: 3. to men uncircumcised, (lit. men *having* uncircumcision)
12:15. constantly affirmed that it *was* even so.
13: 5. and they *had* also John
14: 9. that he *had* faith to be healed,
15:21. *hath* in every city them that preach him,
36. where we have preached the word of the Lord, (and see) how they *do*.

Acts16. 16 *possessed with* a spirit of divination
17:11. whether those things *were* so.
18: 18 for he *had* a vow.
19: 13. over them *which had* evil spirits
38. *have* a matter against any man,
20: 15. and the *next* (day) we came
24. neither *count* I my life dear
21: 13. I *am* ready not to be bound only,
23. men *which have* a vow on them;
26. and the *next* day purifying himself
23: 17. for he *hath* a certain thing to tell
18. *who hath* something to say unto thee.
19. that thou *hast* to tell me?
29. to *have* nothing laid to his charge worthy
24: 9. that these things *were* so.
15. And *have* hope toward God,
16. *to have* always a conscience void of offence
19. if they *had* ought against me.
23. and to let (him) *have* liberty,
25. Go thy way for this time; (lit. for the time *that* now *is*)
25: 16. *have* the accusers face to face,
19. But *had* certain questions against him
26. I *have* no certain thing to write unto my
— I *might have* somewhat to write.
27: 39. a certain creek with a shore, (lit. *having* a shore)
28: 9. others also, *which had* diseases.
19. not that I *had* ought to accuse
29. *and had* great reasoning among themselves.
Ro. 1: 13. that I *might have* some fruit
28. *to retain* God in (their) knowledge,
2: 14. the Gentiles, *which have* not the law,
— these, *having* not the law, are a law
20. *which hast* the form of knowledge
4: 2. he *hath* (whereof) to glory; but not before
5: 1. we *have* peace with God through
2. By whom also we *have* access by faith
6: 21. What fruit *had* ye then in those things
22. ye *have* your fruit unto holiness,
8: 9. if any man *have* not the Spirit of Christ,
23. ourselves also, *which have* the firstfruits of the Spirit,
9: 10. Rebecca also had conceived by one, (lit. *having* conception)
21. *Hath* not the potter power over the clay,
10: 2. they *have* a zeal of God,
12: 4. we *have* many members in one body, and all members *have* not the same office:
6. *Having* then gifts differing
13: 3. thou *shalt have* praise of the same:
14: 22. *Hast* thou faith? *have* (it) to thyself before God.
15: 4. that we...*might have* hope.
17. I *have* therefore whereof I may glory
23. *having* no more place in these parts, and *having* a great desire
1Co. 2: 16. we *have* the mind of Christ.
4: 7. and what *hast* thou that thou didst not
15. For though ye *have* ten thousand instructers in Christ,
5: 1. that one should *have* his father's wife.
6: 1. *having* a matter against another,
4. If then ye *have* judgments of things
7. ye go to law (lit. ye *have* law suits) one with another.
19. Holy Ghost (which is) in you, which ye *have* of God,
7: 2. *let* every man *have* his own wife, and *let* every woman *have* her own husband.
7. every man *hath* his proper gift
12. If any brother *hath* a wife
1Co. 7: 13. which *hath* an husband that believeth not,
25. I *have* no commandment of the Lord:
28. Nevertheless such *shall have* trouble in the
29. that both they *that have* wives be as though they *had* none;
37. *having* no necessity, but *hath* power over his own will,
40. that I *have* the Spirit of God.
8: 1. we all *have* knowledge.
10. any man see thee *which hast* knowledge
9: 4. *Have* we not power to eat and
5. *Have* we not power to lead
6. *have* not we power to forbear
17. willingly, I *have* a reward:
11: 4. *having* (his) head covered,
10. *to have* power on (her) head
16. we *have* no such custom,
22. *have* ye not houses
— and shame them *that have* not?
12: 12. is one, and *hath* many members,
21. I *have* no need of thee:
— I *have* no need of you.
23. *have* more abundant comeliness.
24. our comely (parts) *have* no need:
30. *Have* all the gifts of healing?
13: 1. and *have* not charity, I am become
2. though I *have* (the gift of) prophecy,
— though I *have* all faith,
— and *have* not charity,
3. to be burned, and *have* not charity,
14: 26. every one of you *hath* a psalm, *hath* a doctrine, *hath* a tongue, *hath* a revelation, *hath* an interpretation.
15: 31. which I *have* in Christ Jesus
34. for some *have* not the knowledge of God:
2Co. 1: 9. we *had* the sentence of death
15. that ye *might have* a second benefit;
2: 3. lest, when I came, I should *have* sorrow
4. which I *have* more abundantly unto you.
13. I *had* no rest in my spirit,
3: 4. And such trust *have* we
12. *Seeing* then *that* we *have* such hope,
4: 1. *seeing* we *have* this ministry,
7. But we *have* this treasure in
13. We *having* the same spirit
5: 1. we *have* a building of God,
12. that ye *may have* somewhat to (answer) them which
6: 10. as *having* nothing, and (yet)
7: 1. *Having* therefore these promises,
5. our flesh *had* no rest, but we were
8: 11. out of that which ye *have*.
12. according to that a man *hath*, (and) not according to that he *hath* not.
9: 8. that ye, always *having* all sufficiency
10: 6. And *having* in a readiness
15. but *having* hope, when your faith
12: 14. I *am* ready to come to you;
Gal. 2: 4. which we *have* in Christ Jesus,
4: 22. that Abraham *had* two sons,
27. than she *which hath* an husband.
6: 4. *shall* he *have* rejoicing
10. As we *have* therefore opportunity,
Eph. 1: 7. In whom we *have* redemption
2: 12. *having* no hope, and without God
18. we both *have* access by one Spirit unto the Father.
3: 12. In whom we *have* boldness
4: 28. that he *may have* to give to him *that* needeth. (lit. *that hath* need)
5: 5. *hath* any inheritance in the
27. a glorious church, not *having* spot,

Phi. 1: 7. because I *have* you in my heart;
23. *having* a desire to depart,
30. *Having* the same conflict
2: 2. *having* the same love.
20. For I *have* no man likeminded,
27. lest I *should have* sorrow upon sorrow.
29. *hold* such in reputation:
3: 4. I might also *have* confidence
9. not *having* mine own righteousness,
17. as ye *have* us for an ensample.
Col. 1:14. In whom we *have* redemption
2: 1. what great conflict I *have* for you,
23. Which things *have* indeed a shew of wisdom
3:13. if any man *have* a quarrel against any
4: 1. ye also *have* a Master in heaven.
13. he *hath* a great zeal for you,
1Th. 1: 8. that we need not (lit. *have* not need)
9. of entering in we *had* unto you,
3: 6. that ye *have* good remembrance of us
4: 9. ye need not (lit. *have* not need) that I write
12. ye *may have* lack of nothing.
13. as others *which have* no hope.
5: 1. ye *have* no need that I write unto you.
3. upon a woman with child; (lit. *having* in the womb)
2Th. 3: 9. Not because we *have* not power,
1Ti. 1:12. And I thank (lit. *have* thanks to) Christ
19. *Holding* faith, and a good conscience;
3: 4. *having* his children in subjection
7. he must *have* a good report
9. *Holding* the mystery of the faith
4: 8. *having* promise of the life
5: 4. But if any widow *have* children or
12. *Having* damnation, because they
16. If any man or woman that believeth *have* widows,
20. that others also may fear. (lit. *may have* fear)
25. and they *that are* otherwise
6: 2. they *that have* believing masters,
8. And *having* food and raiment let us
16. *Who* only *hath* immortality,
2Ti. 1: 3. I thank God, (lit. I *have* thanks to)
— without ceasing I *have* remembrance of
13. *Hold fast* the form of sound words,
2:17. will eat (lit. *will have* corrosion) as doth a canker:
19. standeth sure, *having* this seal,
3: 5. *Having* a form of godliness,
Tit. 1: 6. *having* faithful children,
2: 8. *having* no evil thing to say of you.
Philem. 5. faith, which thou *hast* toward the Lord
7. For we *have* great joy and
8. though I might be much bold (lit. *having* much boldness) in Christ
17. If thou *count* me therefore a partner,
Heb. 2:14. might destroy him *that had* the power of death, that is, the devil;
3: 3. *hath* more honour than
4:14. *Seeing* then *that* we *have* a great high priest,
15. we *have* not an high priest which
5:12. ye *have* need that one teach you again
— are become *such as have* need of milk,
14. those *who* by reason of use *have* their senses exercised
6: 9. things *that accompany* salvation,
13. he could swear by no greater, (lit. he *had* by no greater to swear)
18. we *might have* a strong consolation,
19. we *have* as an anchor of the soul,
7: 3. *having* neither beginning of days,
5. *have* a commandment to take tithes

Heb. 7: 6. blessed him *that had* the promises.
24. *hath* an unchangeable priesthood.
27. Who needeth not daily, (lit. *hath* not need, &c.)
28. high priests *which have* infirmity;
8: 1. We *have* such an high priest,
3. that this man *have* somewhat also
9: 1. Then verily the first (covenant) *had* also
4. *Which had* the golden censer,
— the golden pot *that had* manna,
8. was yet standing: (lit. yet *had* standing)
10: 1. For the law *having* a shadow
2. because that the worshippers...should have had (lit. through the worshippers... *having*) no more conscience
19. *Having* therefore, brethren, boldness
34. knowing in yourselves that ye *have*
35. which *hath* great recompence of reward.
36. For ye *have* need of patience,
11:10. a city *which hath* foundations,
15. they might have *had* opportunity to have returned.
25. than to enjoy the pleasures of sin for a season; (lit. *to have* temporary enjoyment of sin)
12: 1. seeing we also are compassed about with so great a cloud (lit. *having* so great a cloud of w. encompassing us)
9. we *have had* fathers of our flesh
28. *let* us *have* grace, whereby we may
13:10. We *have* an altar, whereof they *have* no right to eat
14. For here *have* we no continuing city,
18. we *have* a good conscience,
Jas. 1: 4. *let* patience *have* (her) perfect work,
2: 1. *have* not the faith of our Lord
14. though a man say he *hath* faith, and *have* not works?
17. faith, if it *hath* not works, is dead,
18. a man may say, Thou *hast* faith, and I *have* works:
3:14. if ye *have* bitter envying and strife
4: 2. Ye lust, and *have* not:
— yet ye *have* not, because ye ask not.
1Pet. 2:12. *Having* your conversation honest
16. *using* (your) liberty for a cloke
3:16. *Having* a good conscience;
4: 5. give account to him *that is* ready
8. *And* above all things *have* fervent
2Pet. 1:15. that ye may *be able* after my decease
19. We *have* also a more sure word
2:14. *Having* eyes full of adultery,
— an heart they *have* exercised with
16. But was rebuked (lit. *had* rebuke) for his iniquity:
1Joh. 1: 3. that ye also *may have* fellowship
6. we *have* fellowship with him,
7. we *have* fellowship one with another,
8. If we say that we *have* no sin,
2: 1. we *have* an advocate with
7. which ye *had* from the beginning.
20. ye *have* an unction from
23. the same *hath* not the Father:
27. and ye need not (lit. *have* not need)
28. we *may have* confidence,
3: 3. And every man *that hath* this hope
15. murderer *hath* eternal life abiding
17. But whoso *hath* this world's good, and seeth his brother *have* need,
21. (then) *have* we confidence toward God.
4:16. the love that God *hath* to us.
17. perfect, that we *may have* boldness

1Joh. 4:18. because fear *hath* torment.
21. this commandment *have* we from him,
5:10. *hath* the witness in himself:
12. He *that hath* the Son *hath* life; (and) he *that hath* not the Son of God *hath* not life.
13. may know that ye *have* eternal life,
14. the confidence that we *have* in him,
15. we know that we *have* the petitions
2 Joh. 5. that which we *had* from the beginning,
9. *hath* not God. He that abideth in the doctrine of Christ, he *hath* both
12. *Having* many things to write unto you,
3Joh. 4. I *have* no greater joy than to hear
13. I *had* many things to write,
Jude 3. it was needful for me to write (lit. I *had* need)
19. sensual, *having* not the Spirit.
Rev. 1:16. he *had* in his right hand
18. and *have* the keys of hell and
2: 3. And hast borne, and *hast* patience,
4. Nevertheless I *have* (somewhat) against
6. But this thou *hast*, that thou
7. He *that hath* an ear, let him hear
10. and ye *shall have* tribulation ten days.
11. He *that hath* an ear, let him hear
12. he *which hath* the sharp sword
14. I *have* a few things against thee, because thou *hast* there them that hold
15. So *hast* thou also them that
17. He *that hath* an ear, let him hear
18. the Son of God, *who hath* his eyes like
20. I *have* a few things against thee,
24. as many as *have* not this doctrine,
25. that which ye *have* (already) hold fast
29. He *that hath* an ear, let him hear
3: 1. he *that hath* the seven Spirits
— thou *hast* a name that thou livest,
4. Thou *hast* a few names even
6. He *that hath* an ear, let him hear
7. he *that hath* the key of David,
8. thou *hast* a little strength,
11. hold that fast which thou *hast*,
13. He *that hath* an ear, let him hear
17. and *have* need of nothing;
22. He *that hath* an ear, let him hear
4: 4. they *had* on their heads crowns
7. the third beast *had* a face
8. beasts *had* each of them six wings
— and they rest not (lit. *have* not rest)
5: 6. *having* seven horns and seven eyes,
8. *having* every one of them harps,
6: 2. he that sat on him *had* a bow;
5. *had* a pair of balances in his hand.
9. the testimony which they *held:*
7: 2. *having* the seal of the living God:
8: 3. *having* a golden censer;
6. angels *which had* the seven trumpets
9. which were in the sea, *and had* life,
9: 3. as the scorpions of the earth *have* power.
4. which *have* not the seal of God
8. they *had* hair as the hair of women,
9. And they *had* breastplates,
10. they *had* tails like unto
11. they *had* a king over them,
-- *hath* (his) name Apollyon.
14. which *had* the trumpet,
17. *having* breastplates of fire,
19. and *had* heads, and with them
10: 2. he *had* in his hand a little book
11: 6. These *have* power to shut heaven,
— and *have* power over waters to turn

Rev.12 2. And she being with child (lit. *having* in the womb)
3. red dragon, *having* seven heads
6. where she *hath* a place prepared
12. *having* great wrath, because he knoweth that he *hath* but a short time.
17. and *have* the testimony of Jesus Christ.
13: 1. *having* seven heads and ten horns,
9. If any man *have* an ear, let him hear.
11. he *had* two horns like a lamb,
14. which *had* the wound by a sword;
17. no man might buy or sell, save he *that had* the mark,
18. Let him *that hath* understanding count
14: 1. thousand, *having* his Father's name
6. *having* the everlasting gospel
11. they *have* no rest
14. *having* on his head a golden crown,
17. he also *having* a sharp sickle.
18. *which had* power over fire;
-- to him *that had* the sharp sickle,
15: 1. angels *having* the seven last plagues;
2. *having* the harps of God.
6. *having* the seven plagues,
16: 2. upon the men *which had* the mark of
9. of God, *which hath* power over
17: 1. one of the seven angels *which had* the
3. *having* seven heads and ten horns.
4. *having* a golden cup in her hand
7. *which hath* the seven heads
9. the mind *which hath* wisdom.
13. These *have* one mind, and shall give
18. which reigneth over (lit. *which hath* reign over)
18: 1. from heaven, *having* great power;
19. all *that had* ships in the sea
19:10. brethren *that have* the testimony of Jesus
12. *and* he *had* a name written,
16. he *hath* on (his) vesture
20: 1. *having* the key of the bottomless
6. Blessed and holy (is) he *that hath* part in the first resurrection: on such the second death *hath* no power,
21: 9. of the seven angels *which had* the
11. *Having* the glory of God:
12. And *had* a wall great and high, (and) *had*
14. wall of the city *had* twelve foundations,
15. *had* a golden reed to measure
23. the city *had* no need of the sun,
22: 5. they need no candle, (lit. they *have* not need)

2193 148 334/415

ἕως, *heōs*.

Mat. 1:17. from Abraham *to* David (are) fourteen generations; and from David *until* the
— *unto* Christ (are) fourteen generations.
25. *till* she had brought forth her firstborn
2: 9. *till* it came and stood
13. *until* I bring thee word:
15. *until* the death of Herod:
5:18. *Till* heaven and earth pass,
— *till* all be fulfilled.
25. *whiles* thou art in the way
26. *till* thou hast paid the uttermost
10:11. and there abide *till* ye go thence,
23. *till* the Son of man be come.
11:12. And from the days of John the Baptist *until* now
13. and the law prophesied *until* John

Mat.11:23. art exalted *unto* heaven, shalt be brought down *to* hell.
12:20. *till* he send forth judgment unto victory.
13:33. *till* the whole was leavened.
14:22. *while* he sent the multitudes away.
16:28. *till* they see the Son of man
17: 9. *until* the Son of man be risen again
17. how long (lit. *until* when) shall I be with you? *how long* shall I suffer you?
18:21. *till* seven times?
22. I say not unto thee, *Until* seven times: but, *Until* seventy times seven.
30. *till* he should pay the debt.
34. *till* he should pay all that was due
20: 8. beginning from the last *unto* the first.
22:26. also, and the third, *unto* the seventh.
44. *till* I make thine enemies
23:35. *unto* the blood of Zacharias
39. henceforth, *till* ye shall say,
24:21. beginning of the world *to* this time,
27. shineth even *unto* the west;
31. one end of heaven *to* the other.
34. *till* all these things be fulfilled.
39. *until* the flood came,
26:29. of this fruit of the vine, *until* that day
36. *while* I go and pray yonder.
38. My soul is exceeding sorrowful, *even unto* death:
58. *unto* the high priest's palace,
27: 8. field of blood, *unto* this day.
45. over all the land *unto* the ninth hour.
51. from the top *to* the bottom;
64. be made sure *until* the third day,
28:20. (even) *unto* the end of the world.
Mar. 6:10. there abide *till* ye depart from that place.
23. *unto* the half of my kingdom,
45. *while* he sent away the people.
9: 1. *till* they have seen the kingdom
19. *how long* (lit. *until* when) shall I be with you? *how long* shall I suffer you?
12:36. *till* I make thine enemies
13:19. which God created *unto* this time,
27. *to* the uttermost part of heaven.
14:25. *until* that day that I drink it
32. here, *while* I shall pray.
34. My soul is exceeding sorrowful *unto* death.
54. *even* into the palace of the
15:33. the whole land *until* the ninth hour.
38. from the top *to* the bottom.
Lu. 1:80. *till* the day of his shewing
2:15. Let us now go even *unto* Bethlehem,
4:29. and led him *unto* the brow of the hill
42. sought him, and came *unto* him,
9:27. *till* they see the kingdom
41. *how long* (lit. *until* when) shall I be with
10:15. art exalted *to* heaven, shalt be thrust down *to* hell.
11:51. *unto* the blood of Zacharias,
12:50. *till* it be accomplished!
59. *till* thou hast paid the very last
13: 8. *till* I shall dig about it,
21. *till* the whole was leavened.
35. *until* (the time) come when ye shall say,
15: 4. *until* he find it?
8. and seek diligently *till* she find (it)?
16:16. prophets (were) *until* John:
17: 8. *till* I have eaten and drunken;
19:13. Occupy *till* I come.
20:43. *Till* I make thine enemies
21:32. *till* all be fulfilled.
22:16. *until* it be fulfilled in the kingdom
18. *until* the kingdom of God

Lu. 22:51. Suffer ye thus *far*.
23: 5. beginning from Galilee *to* this place
44. *until* the ninth hour.
24:49. *until* ye be endued with power
50. *as far as* to Bethany,
Joh. 2: 7. they filled them *up to* the brim.
10. hast kept the good wine *until* now.
5:17. My Father worketh hitherto, (lit. *until* now)
8: 9. (even) *unto* the last:
9: 4. *while* it is day:
18. *until* they called the parents
10:24. How long (lit. *till* when) dost thou make
12:35. *while* ye have the light,
36. *While* ye have light, believe
13:38. *till* thou hast denied me thrice.
16:24. Hither*to* have ye asked nothing
21:22. If I will that he tarry *till* I come.
23. tarry *till* I come, what (is that) to thee?
Acts 1: 8. *unto* the uttermost part of the earth.
22. *unto* that same day that
2:35. *Until* I make thy foes
7:45. *unto* the days of David;
8:10. from the least *to* the greatest,
40. *till* he came to Cæsarea.
9:38. he would not delay to come *to* them
11:19. travelled *as far as* Phenice,
22. that he should go *as far as* Antioch.
13:20. *until* Samuel the prophet.
47. *unto* the ends of the earth.
17:15. brought him *unto* Athens:
21: 5. *till* (we were) out of the city:
26. *until* that an offering should be offered
23:12. *till* they had killed Paul.
14. eat nothing *until* we have slain Paul.
21. *till* they have killed him:
23. soldiers to go *to* Cæsarea,
25:21. *till* I might send him
26:11. even *unto* strange cities.
28:23. from morning *till* evening.
Ro. 3:12. no, not one. (lit. there is not *even* one)
11: 8. should not hear; *unto* this day.
1Co. 1: 8. shall also confirm you *unto* the end,
4: 5. *until* the Lord come,
13. the offscouring of all things *unto* this day.
8: 7. *unto* this hour eat (it) as a thing offered unto an idol;
15: 6. the greater part remain *unto* this present,
16: 8. will tarry at Ephesus *until* Pentecost.
2Co. 1:13. ye shall acknowledge even *to* the end;
3:15. But *even unto* this day,
12: 2. caught up *to* the third heaven.
2Th. 2: 7. *until* he be taken out of the way.
1Ti. 4:13. *Till* I come, give attendance
Heb. 1:13. *until* I make thine enemies
8:11. know me, from the least *to* the greatest.
10:13. *till* his enemies be made
Jas. 5: 7. *unto* the coming of the Lord.
— *until* he receive the early and latter rain.
2Pet. 1:19. *until* the day dawn,
1Joh. 2: 9. is in darkness *even until* now.
Rev. 6:10. How long (lit. *till* when) O Lord, holy
11. *until* their fellowservants also and
20: 5. *until* the thousand years were finished.

2198 142 336/417 2:832

ζάω, zao.

Mat. 4: 4. Man *shall* not *live* by bread alone,
9:18. upon her, and she *shall live.*

Mat. 16:16. the Son of the *living* God.
22:32. of the dead, but of the *living*.
26:63. I adjure thee by the *living* God,
27:63. said, *while* he *was* yet *alive*,
Mar. 5:23. that she may be healed; and she *shall live*.
12:27. but the God of the *living*:
16:11. when they had heard that he *was alive*,
Lu. 2:36. *and had lived* with an husband seven years
4: 4. man *shall* not *live* by bread alone,
10:28. this do, and thou *shalt live*.
15:13. with riotous *living*. (lit *living* riotously)
20:38. of the dead, but of the *living*: for all *live* unto him.
24: 5. the *living* among the dead?
23. which said that he *was alive*.
Joh. 4:10. he would have given thee *living* water.
11. hast thou that *living* water?
50. Go thy way; thy son *liveth*.
51. and told (him), saying, Thy son *liveth*.
53. said unto him, Thy son *liveth*:
5:25. they that hear *shall live*.
6:51. I am the *living* bread which came down
— he *shall live* for ever:
57. As the *living* Father hath sent me, and I *live* by the Father:
— even he *shall live* by me.
58. eateth of this bread *shall live* for ever.
69. the Son of the *living* God.
7:38. shall flow rivers of *living* water.
11:25. though he were dead, yet *shall* he *live*:
26. *whosoever liveth* and believeth
14:19. I *live*, ye *shall live* also.
Acts 1: 3. he shewed himself *alive*
7:38. the *lively* oracles to give unto us:
9:41. saints and widows, presented her *alive*.
10:42. (to be) the Judge of *quick* and dead.
14:15. unto the *living* God,
17:28. For in him we *live*,
20:12. they brought the young man *alive*,
22:22. for it is not fit that he should *live*.
25:19. whom Paul affirmed *to be alive*.
24. that he ought not *to live* any longer.
26: 5. I *lived* a Pharisee.
28: 4. yet vengeance suffereth not *to live*.
Ro. 1:17. *shall live* by faith.
6: 2. How *shall* we,...*live* any longer therein?
10. once: but in that he *liveth*, he *liveth* unto God.
11. dead indeed unto sin, but *alive* unto God
13. as *those that are alive* from the dead,
7: 1. as long as he *liveth*?
2. is bound by the law to (her) husband *so long as* he *liveth*;
3. So then if, *while* (her) husband *liveth*,
9. I *was alive* without the law once:
8:12. *to live* after the flesh.
13. For if ye *live* after the flesh,
— deeds of the body, ye *shall live*.
9:26. the children of the *living* God.
10: 5. which doeth those things *shall live* by
12: 1. present your bodies a *living* sacrifice,
14: 7. For none of us *liveth* to himself,
8. For whether we *live*, we *live* unto the
— whether we *live* therefore, or die,
9. he might be Lord both of the dead and *living*.
11. (As) I *live*, saith the Lord,
1Co. 7:39. as long as her husband *liveth*;
9:14. should *live* of the gospel.
15:45. The first man Adam was made a *living*
2Co. 1: 8. we despaired even of *life*: (lit. *to live*)
2Co. 3: 3. with the Spirit of the *living* God;
4:11. For we *which live* are alway delivered
5:15. that they *which live should* not henceforth *live* unto themselves,
6: 9. as dying, and, behold, we *live*;
16. ye are the temple of the *living* God;
13: 4. yet he *liveth* by the power of God.
— we *shall live* with him by the power of
Gal. 2:14. *livest* after the manner of Gentiles,
19. that I *might live* unto God.
20. nevertheless I live; yet not I (lit. and *live* no more I), but Christ *liveth* in me: and the life which I now *live* in the flesh I *live* by the faith of the Son of God,
3:11. The just *shall live* by faith.
12. man that doeth them *shall live* in them.
5:25. If we *live* in the Spirit,
Phi. 1:21. For to me *to live* (is) Christ,
22. But if I *live* in the flesh,
Col. 2:20. why, as though *living* in the world,
3: 7. also walked some time, when ye *lived* in them.
1Th 1: 9. to serve the *living* and true God;
3: 8. For now we *live*, if ye stand fast
4:15. we *which are alive* (and) remain
17. we *which are alive* (and) remain
5:10. we *should live* together with him.
1Ti. 3:15. the church of the *living* God,
4:10. we trust in the *living* God,
5: 6. is dead *while* she *liveth*.
6:17. but in the *living* God,
2Ti. 3:12. and all that will *live* godly in Christ
4: 1. who shall judge the *quick* and the dead
Tit. 2:12. we *should live* soberly, righteously,
Heb 2:15. were all their *life*time subject to bondage
3:12. in departing from the *living* God.
4:12. the word of God (is) *quick*, and powerful,
7: 8. of whom it is witnessed that he *liveth*.
25. *seeing* he ever *liveth* to make intercession
9:14. to serve the *living* God?
17. while the testator *liveth*.
10:20. By a new and *living* way,
31. into the hands of the *living* God.
38. Now the just *shall live* by faith:
12: 9. unto the Father of spirits, and *live*?
22. unto the city of the *living* God,
Jas. 4:15. If the Lord will, we *shall live*, and do this, or that.
1Pet. 1: 3. begotten us again unto a *lively* hope
23. by the word of God, *which liveth* and
2: 4. To whom coming, (as unto) a *living*
5. as *lively* stones, are built up
24. *should live* unto righteousness:
4: 5. to judge the *quick* and the dead.
6. but *live* according to God in the spirit.
1Joh. 4: 9. that we *might live* through him.
Rev. 1:18. (I am) he *that liveth*, and was dead; and, behold, I am *alive*
2: 8. which was dead, and *is alive*;
3: 1. that thou *livest*, and art dead.
4: 9. *who liveth* for ever and ever,
10. worship him *that liveth* for ever and
5:14. worshipped him *that liveth* for ever
7: 2. the seal of the *living* God:
17. unto *living* fountains of waters:
10: 6. sware by him *that liveth* for ever
13:14. had the wound by a sword, and *did live*.
15: 7. of the wrath of God, *who liveth* for ever
16: 3. every *living* soul died in the sea.
19:20. both were cast *alive* into a lake of fire
20: 4. they *lived* and reigned with Christ a

2200 3 337/419 2:875 2204

Ζεστός, zestos.

Rev. 3:15. thou art neither cold nor *hot*: I would thou wert cold or *hot*.
16. lukewarm, and neither cold nor *hot*,

2201 2 337/419 rt 2218

ζεῦγος, zūgos.

Lu. 2:24. A *pair* of turtledoves,
14:19. I have bought five *yoke* of oxen,

2202 1 337/419 rt 2218

ζευκτηρία, zūkteeria.

Acts27:40. and loosed the rudder *bands*,

2204 2 338/419 2:875

ζέω, zeo.

Acts18:25. *being fervent* in the spirit,
Ro. 12:11. *fervent* in spirit; serving the Lord;

2205 17 338/419 2:877 2204

ζῆλος, zeelos.

Joh. 2:17. The *zeal* of thine house hath eaten me up.
Acts 5:17. were filled with *indignation*,
13:45. they were filled with *envy*,
Ro. 10: 2. they have a *zeal* of God,
13:13. not in strife and *envying*.
1Co. 3: 3. *envying*, and strife, and divisions,
2Co. 7: 7. your *fervent mind* toward me;
11. yea, (what) *zeal*, yea, (what) revenge!
9: 2. your *zeal* hath provoked very many.
11: 2. For I am jealous over you with godly *jealousy*:
12:20. *envyings*, wraths, strifes,
Gal. 5.20. variance, *emulations*, wrath, strife,
Phi. 3: 6. Concerning *zeal*, persecuting the
Col. 4:13. he hath a great *zeal* for you,
Heb 10:27. fiery *indignation*, which shall devour
Jas. 3:14. But if ye have bitter *envying*
16. For where *envying* and strife (is),

2206 12 338/419 2:877 2205

ζηλόω, zeeloō.

Acts 7: 9. the patriarchs, *moved with envy*,
17: 5. But the Jews which believed not, *moved with envy*, took
1Co.12:31. But *covet earnestly* the best gifts
13: 4. charity *envieth* not;
14: 1. and *desire* spiritual (gifts),
39. *covet* to prophesy, and forbid not
2Co.11: 2. For I *am jealous over* you with godly
Gal. 4:17. They *zealously affect* you, (but) not well;
— that ye *might affect* them.
18. good *to be zealously affected* always in (a) good (thing),
Jas. 4: 2. ye kill, and *desire to have*,
Rev. 3:19. *be zealous* therefore, and repent.

2207 5 338/419 2:877 2206

ζηλωτής, zeelōtees.

Acts21:20. and they are all *zealous* of the law:
22: 3. and was *zealous* toward God,
1Co.14:12. as ye are *zealous* of spiritual (gifts),
Gal. 1:14. *zealous* of the traditions of my fathers.
Tit. 2:14. a peculiar people, *zealous* of good works.

2209 4 338/419 2:888 cf rt1150

ζημία, zeemia.

Acts27:10. will be with hurt and much *damage*,
21. to have gained this harm and *loss*.
Phi. 3: 7. I counted *loss* for Christ.
8. I count all things (but) *loss*

2210 6 339/419 2:888 2209

ζημιόω, zeemioō.

Mat.16:26. if he shall gain the whole world, and *lose* his own soul?
Mar. 8:36. and *lose* his own soul?
Lu. 9:25. and lose himself, or *be cast away*?
1Co. 3:15. he *shall suffer loss*: but he himself
2Co. 7: 9. ye *might receive damage* by us in nothing.
Phi. 3: 8. I *have suffered the loss* of all things,

2212 119 339/419 2:892 cf 4441

ζητέω, zeeteo.

Mat. 2:13. for Herod will *seek* the young child
20. they are dead *which sought* the young child's life.
6:33. But *seek* ye first the kingdom
7: 7. *seek*, and ye shall find;
8. he *that seeketh* findeth;
12:43. *seeking* rest, and findeth none.
46. *desiring* to speak with him.
47. *desiring* to speak with thee.
13:45. unto a merchant man, *seeking* goodly
18:12. and *seeketh* that which is gone astray?
21:46. *when* they *sought* to lay hands on him,
26:16. he *sought* opportunity to betray him.
59. and all the council, *sought* false witness
28: 5. ye *seek* Jesus, which was crucified.
Mar. 1:37. All (men) *seek for* thee.
3:32. without *seek for* thee.
8:11. *seeking* of him a sign from heaven,
11:18. *sought* how they might destroy him:
12:12 they *sought* to lay hold on him,
14: 1. the chief priests and the scribes *sought*
11. he *sought* how he might conveniently
55. *sought for* witness against Jesus
16: 6. Ye *seek* Jesus of Nazareth,
Lu. 2:45. back again to Jerusalem, *seeking* him.
48. *have sought* thee sorrowing.
49. How is it that ye *sought* me?
4:42. and the people *sought* him,
5:18. they *sought* (*means*) to bring him in,
6:19. multitude *sought* to touch him: for
9: 9. he *desired* to see him.
11: 9. *seek*, and ye shall find;
10. he *that seeketh* findeth;
16. *sought* of him a sign from heaven.
24. through dry places, *seeking* rest;
54. *seeking* to catch something
12:29. *seek* not ye what ye shall eat, or
31. *seek* ye the kingdom of God;
48. of him *shall be* much *required*:
13: 6. *and sought* fruit thereon,
7. these three years I come *seeking* fruit
24. many, I say unto you, *will seek* to enter
15: 8. and *seek* diligently till she find
17:33. Whosoever *shall seek* to save his life
19: 3. he *sought* to see Jesus
10. is come *to seek* and to save that which was
47. *sought* to destroy him,
20:19. scribes the same hour *sought* to lay
22: 2. the chief priests and scribes *sought*
6. he promised, and *sought* opportunity
24: 5. Why *seek* ye the living among

Joh. 1:38(39). and saith unto them, What *seek* ye?
4:23. the Father *seeketh* such to worship
27. said, What *seekest* thou?
5:16. and *sought* to slay him,
18. the Jews *sought* the more to kill him,
30. I *seek* not mine own will,
44. and *seek* not the honour that
6:24. came to Capernaum, *seeking for* Jesus.
26. Ye *seek* me, not because ye saw
7: 1. because the Jews *sought* to kill him.
4. he himself *seeketh* to be known openly.
11. *sought* him at the feast,
18. *seeketh* his own glory: but he *that seeketh* his glory that sent him,
19. Why *go* ye *about* to kill me?
20. who *goeth about* to kill thee?
25. whom they *seek* to kill?
30. Then they *sought* to take him:
34. Ye *shall seek* me, and shall not find
36. Ye *shall seek* me, and shall not find (me)
8:21. ye *shall seek* me, and shall die in your
37. but ye *seek* to kill me,
40. But now ye *seek* to kill me,
50. I *seek* not mine own glory: there is one *that seeketh* and judgeth.
10:39. Therefore they *sought* again to take him:
11: 8. the Jews of late *sought* to stone thee;
56. Then *sought* they for Jesus,
13:33. Ye *shall seek* me: and as
16:19. *Do* ye *enquire* among yourselves
18: 4. said unto them, Whom *seek* ye?
7. asked he them again, Whom *seek* ye?
8. if therefore ye *seek* me,
19:12. thenceforth Pilate *sought* to release
20:15. why weepest thou? whom *seekest* thou?
Acts 9:11. *enquire* in the house of Judas *for* (one) called Saul,
10:19. Behold, three men *seek* thee.
21. I am he whom ye *seek*:
13: 8. *seeking* to turn away the deputy
11. *seeking* some to lead him by the hand.
16:10. we *endeavoured* to go into Macedonia,
17: 5. and *sought* to bring them out
27. That they should *seek* the Lord,
21:31. And *as* they *went about* to kill him,
27:30. And *as* the shipmen *were about* to flee
Ro. 2: 7. To them *who* by patient continuance in well doing *seek for* glory and
10: 3. and *going about* to establish their own righteousness,
20. I was found of them *that sought* me not;
11: 3. am left alone, and they *seek* my life.
1Co. 1:22. and the Greeks *seek after* wisdom:
4: 2 it *is required* in stewards,
7:27. *seek* not to be loosed. Art thou loosed from a wife? *seek* not a wife.
10:24. *Let* no man *seek* his own,
33. not *seeking* mine own profit, but
13: 5. *seeketh* not her own, is not easily
14:12. *seek* that ye may excel
2Co.12:14. for I *seek* not your's, but you:
13: 3. ye *seek* a proof of Christ speaking in me,
Gal. 1:10. or *do* I *seek* to please men?
2:17. But if, *while* we *seek* to be justified
Phi. 2:21. all *seek* their own, not the things
Col. 3: 1. *seek* those things which are above,
1Th. 2: 6. Nor of men *sought* we glory,
2Ti. 1:17. he *sought* me out very diligently,
Heb 8: 7. then should no place *have been sought* for
1Pet. 3:11. *let* him *seek* peace, and ensue it.
5: 8. *seeking* whom he may devour:
Rev. 9: 6. in those days *shall* men *seek* death.

2213 5 339/421 2212

ζήτημα, zeeteema.

Acts15: 2. apostles and elders about this *question.*
18:15. But if it be a *question* of words and
23:29. accused of *questions* of their law,
25:19. But had certain *questions* against him
26: 3. expert in all customs and *questions*

2214 6 339/421 2:892 2212

ζήτησις, zeeteesis.

Joh. 3:25. Then there arose a *question* between
Acts25:20. I doubted of such manner of questions, (lit. I was at a loss about *inquiry* into this)
1Ti. 1: 4. genealogies, which minister *questions*,
6: 4. about *questions* and strifes of words,
2Ti. 2:23. foolish and unlearned *questions* avoid,
Tit. 3: 9. But avoid foolish *questions*, and

2215 8 340/421

ζιζάνια, zizania.

Mat.13:25. his enemy came and sowed *tares*
26. then appeared the *tares* also.
27. from whence then hath it *tares*?
29. while ye gather up the *tares*,
30. Gather ye together first the *tares*,
36. the parable of the *tares* of the field.
38. but the *tares* are the children of the wicked
40. As therefore the *tares* are gathered and

2217 4 340/421 cf rt3509

ζόφος, zophos.

2Pet. 2: 4. delivered (them) into chains of *darkness*,
17 to whom the *mist* of darkness is reserved
Jude 6. he hath reserved in everlasting chains under *darkness*
13. to whom is reserved the *blackness* of darkness for ever.

2218 6 340/421 2:896 rt *zeugnumi* (to join)

ζυγός, zugos.

Mat.11:29. Take my *yoke* upon you, and
30. For my *yoke* (is) easy,
Acts15:10. to put a *yoke* upon the neck of the
Gal. 5: 1. entangled again with the *yoke* of bondage.
1Ti. 6: 1. servants as are under the *yoke*
Rev. 6: 5. had a *pair of balances* in his hand.

2219 13 340/421 2:902 2204

ζύμη, zumee.

Mat.13:33. unto *leaven*, which a woman took,
16: 6. beware of the *leaven* of the Pharisees
11. beware of the *leaven* of the Pharisees
12. not beware of the *leaven* of bread,
Mar. 8:15. of the *leaven* of the Pharisees, and (of) the *leaven* of Herod.
Lu. 12: 1. of the *leaven* of the Pharisees,
13:21. It is like *leaven*,
1Co. 5: 6. a little *leaven* leaveneth the whole lump?
7. Purge out therefore the old *leaven*,
8. let us keep the feast, not with old *leaven*, neither with the *leaven* of malice
Gal. 5: 9. A little *leaven* leaveneth the whole lump.

2220 4 340/421 2:902 2219

ζυμόω, zumoo.

Mat.13:33. till the whole *was leavened*.

Lu. 13:21. till the whole *was leavened*.
1Co. 5: 6. a little leaven *leaveneth* the whole lump?
Gal. 5: 9. *leaveneth* the whole lump.

2221 2 340/421 2198,64

ζωγρέω, zōgreo.

Lu. 5:10. henceforth thou shalt *catch* men.
2Ti. 2:26. *who are taken captive* by him at his will.

2222 134 340/422 2:832 2198 cf 5590

ζωή, zōee.

Mat. 7:14. the way, which leadeth unto *life*,
18: 8. is better for thee to enter into *life*
9. to enter into *life* with one eye,
19:16. that I may have eternal *life*?
17. but if thou wilt enter into *life*,
29. shall inherit everlasting *life*.
25:46. the righteous into *life* eternal.
Mar. 9:43. for thee to enter into *life* maimed,
45. to enter halt into *life*,
10:17. that I may inherit eternal *life*?
30. and in the world to come eternal *life*.
Lu. 1:75. before him, all the days of our *life*
10:25. to inherit eternal *life*?
12:15. a man's *life* consisteth not in
16:25. thou in thy *lifetime* receivedst
18:18. to inherit eternal *life*?
30. in the world to come *life* everlasting.
Joh. 1: 4. In him was *life*; and the *life* was the light of men.
3:15. but have eternal *life*.
16. but have everlasting *life*.
36. He that believeth on the Son hath everlasting *life*:
— shall not see *life*;
4:14. into everlasting *life*.
36. fruit unto *life* eternal:
5:24. hath everlasting *life*,
— is passed from death unto *life*.
26. Father hath *life* in himself; so hath he given to the Son to have *life* in himself;
29. unto the resurrection of *life*;
39. in them ye think ye have eternal *life*:
40. that ye might have *life*.
6:27. endureth unto everlasting *life*,
33. giveth *life* unto the world.
35. I am the bread of *life*:
40. may have everlasting *life*:
47. He that believeth on me hath everlasting *life*.
48. I am that bread of *life*.
51. for the *life* of the world.
53. ye have no *life* in you.
54. hath eternal *life*;
63. (they) are spirit, and (they) are *life*.
68. thou hast the words of eternal *life*.
8:12. shall have the light of *life*.
10:10. am come that they might have *life*,
28. give unto them eternal *life*;
11:25. the resurrection, and the *life*:
12:25. shall keep it unto *life* eternal.
50. his commandment is *life* everlasting:
14: 6. am the way, the truth, and the *life*:
17: 2. he should give eternal *life* to
3. And this is *life* eternal,
20:31. believing ye might have *life*
Acts 2:28. made known to me the ways of *life*;
3:15. And killed the Prince of *life*,
5:20. all the words of this *life*.
8:33. his *life* is taken from the earth.
Acts11:18. granted repentance unto *life*,
13:46. unworthy of everlasting *life*,
48. ordained to eternal *life*
17:25. he giveth to all *life*,
Ro. 2: 7. To them who by patient...eternal *life*:
5:10. we shall be saved by his *life*.
17. shall reign in *life* by one,
18. unto justification of *life*.
21. through righteousness unto eternal *life*
6: 4. we also should walk in newness of *life*.
22. and the end everlasting *life*.
23. (is) eternal *life* through Jesus Christ
7:10. the commandment, which (was ordained to *life*,
8: 2. the law of the Spirit of *life*
6. to be spiritually minded (is) *life* and
10. (is) *life* because of righteousness.
38. that neither death, nor *life*,
11:15. but *life* from the dead?
1Co. 3:22. or *life*, or death, or things present,
15:19. If in this *life* only we have hope in Christ,
2Co. 2:16. and to the other the savour of *life* unto *life*.
4:10. that the *life* also of Jesus might be
11. the *life* also of Jesus might be made manifest in our mortal flesh.
12. death worketh in us, but *life* in you.
5: 4. mortality might be swallowed up of *life*.
Gal. 6: 8. shall of the Spirit reap *life* everlasting.
Eph. 4:18. alienated from the *life* of God
Phi. 1:20. whether (it be) by *life*, or by death.
2:16. Holding forth the word of *life*;
4: 3. names (are) in the book of *life*.
Col. 3: 3. and your *life* is hid with Christ in God.
4. When Christ, (who is) our *life*,
1Ti. 1:16. believe on him to *life* everlasting.
4: 8. having promise of the *life* that now is,
6:12. lay hold on eternal *life*,
19. may lay hold on eternal *life*.
2Ti. 1: 1. of *life* which is in Christ Jesus,
10. brought *life* and immortality to light
Tit. 1: 2. In hope of eternal *life*,
3: 7. according to the hope of eternal *life*.
Heb. 7: 3. having neither beginning of days, nor end of *life*;
16. after the power of an endless *life*.
Jas. 1:12. he shall receive the crown of *life*,
4:14. For what (is) your *life*?
1Pet.3: 7. heirs together of the grace of *life*;
10. For he that will love *life*,
2Pet.1: 3. that (pertain) unto *life* and godliness,
1Joh.1: 1. of the Word of *life*;
2. the *life* was manifested,
— and shew unto you that eternal *life*,
2:25. hath promised us, (even) eternal *life*.
3:14. we have passed from death unto *life*,
15. hath eternal *life* abiding in him.
5:11. that God hath given to us eternal *life*, and this *life* is in his Son.
12. He that hath the Son hath *life*; (and) he that hath not the Son of God hath not *life*.
13. that ye have eternal *life*,
16. and he shall give him *life*
20. This is the true God, and eternal *life*.
Jude 21. of our Lord Jesus Christ unto eternal *life*.
Rev. 2: 7. will I give to eat of the tree of *life*,
10. I will give thee a crown of *life*.
3: 5. out of the book of *life*,
11:11. the Spirit of *life* from God
13: 8. in the book of *life* of the Lamb
17: 8. in the book of *life*

Rev.20: 12. which is (the book) of *life*
15. written in the book of *life*
21: 6. of the water of *life* freely.
27. the Lamb's book of *life*.
22: 1. river of water of *life*,
2. (was there) the tree of *life*,
14. they may have right to the tree of *life*,
17. whosoever will, let him take the water of *life* freely.
19. his part out of the book of *life*,

2223 8 341/423 5:292 cf *zeugnumi* (to join)

ζώνη, *zōnee.*

Mat. 3: 4. a leathern *girdle* about his loins;
10: 9. silver, nor brass in your *purses*,
Mar. 1: 6. a *girdle* of a skin about his loins;
6: 8. no money in (their) *purse:*
Acts21: 11. he took Paul's *girdle*,
— bind the man that owneth this *girdle*,
Rev. 1: 13. about the paps with a golden *girdle*.
15: 6. girded with golden *girdles*.

2224 2 342/423 5:292 2223

ζωννύω, *zōnnuo.*

Joh.21: 18. When thou wast young, thou *girdedst*
— and another *shall gird* thee,

2225 2 342/423 2:832 2198,1085

ζωογονέω, *zōogoneo.*

Lu. 17: 33. lose his life *shall preserve* it.
Acts 7: 19. to the end they might not *live*.

2226 23 342/423 2:832 2198

ζῶον, *zōon.*

Heb 13: 11. of those *beasts*, whose blood is brought
2Pet. 2: 12. as natural brute *beasts*,
Jude 10. know naturally, as brute *beasts*,
Rev. 4: 6. (were) four *beasts* full
7. the first *beast* (was) like a lion, and the second *beast* like a calf, and the third *beast* had a face as a man, and the fourth *beast*
8. And the four *beasts* had each of them
9. when those *beasts* give glory
5: 6. and of the four *beasts*,
8. the four *beasts* and
11. round about the throne and the *beasts*
14. And the four *beasts* said, Amen.
6: 1. I heard,...one of the four *beasts* saying,
3. I heard the second *beast* say,
5. I heard the third *beast* say,
6. in the midst of the four *beasts*
7. the voice of the fourth *beast*
7: 11. (about) the elders and the four *beasts*,
14: 3. before the four *beasts*,
15: 7. one of the four *beasts* gave
19: 4. elders and the four *beasts* fell down

2227 12 342/424 2:832 2198,4160

ζωοποιέω, *zōopoieo.*

Joh. 5: 21. raiseth up the dead, and *quickeneth* (them); even so the Son *quickeneth* whom he
6: 63. It is the spirit *that quickeneth*;
Ro. 4: 17. God, *who quickeneth* the dead,
8: 11. *shall* also *quicken* your mortal bodies
1Co.15: 22. *shall* all *be made alive*.
1Co.15: 36. that which thou sowest *is* not *quickened*,
45. (was made) a *quickening* spirit.
2Co. 3: 6. but the spirit *giveth life*.
Gal. 3: 21. which could *have given life*,
1Ti. 6: 13. of God, *who quickeneth* all things,
1Pet. 3: 18. but *quickened* by the Spirit:

2228 357 342/424 cf2235,cf 2260, cf 2273

ἤ, *ee.*

Mat. 1: 18. before)(they came together,
5: 17. to destroy the law, *or* the prophets:
18. one jot *or* one tittle shall in no wise
36. not make one hair white *or* black.
6: 24. for *either* he will hate the one,...*or else* he will hold to the one,
31. *or*, What shall we drink? *or*, Wherewithal shall we be clothed?
7: 4. *Or* how wilt thou say to thy brother,
9. *Or* what man is there of you,
16. grapes of thorns, *or* figs of thistles?
9: 5. *or* to say, Arise, and walk?
10: 11. And into whatsoever city *or* town
14. depart out of that house *or* city,
15. *than* for that city.
19. how *or* what ye shall speak:
37. He that loveth father *or* mother
— he that loveth son *or* daughter
11: 3. *or* do we look for another?
22. at the day of judgment, *than* for you.
24. in the day of judgment, *than* for thee.
12: 5. *Or* have ye not read in the law,
25. and every city *or* house divided
29. *Or else* how can one enter into
33. *Either* make the tree good,
— *or else* make the tree corrupt,
13: 21. *or* persecution ariseth because of the
15: 4. He that curseth father *or* mother,
5. say to (his) father *or* (his) mother,
6(5). honour not his father *or* his mother.
16: 14. *or* one of the prophets.
26. *or* what shall a man give
17: 25. custom *or* tribute? of their own children, *or* of strangers?
18: 8. if thy hand *or* thy foot
— halt *or* maimed, *rather than* having two hands *or* two feet
9. *rather than* having two eyes
13. *than* of the ninety and nine
16. take with thee one *or* two more, that in the mouth of two *or* three witnesses
20. For where two *or* three are gathered
19: 24. *than* for a rich man to enter into the
29. that hath forsaken houses, *or* brethren, *or* sisters, *or* father, *or* mother, *or* wife, *or* children, *or* lands, for my name's sake,
20: 15.)(Is it not lawful for me
—)(Is thine eye evil,
21: 25. from heaven, *or* of men?
22: 17. tribute unto Cæsar, *or* not?
23: 17. whether is greater, the gold, *or* the temple
19. greater, the gift, *or* the altar
24: 23. here (is) Christ, *or* there;
25: 37. *or* thirsty, and gave (thee) drink?
38. *or* naked, and clothed (thee)?
39. sick, *or* in prison,
44. when saw we thee an hungred, *or* athirst, *or* a stranger, *or* naked, *or* sick, *or* in

Mat.26:53.)(Thinkest thou that I cannot
— more *than* twelve legions of angels?
27:17. Barabbas, *or* Jesus which is called
Mar. 2: 9. (Thy) sins be forgiven thee; *or* to say,
3: 4. to do good on the sabbath days, *or* to do evil? to save life, *or* to kill?
33. my mother, *or* my brethren?
4:21. under a bushel, *or* under a bed?
30. *or* with what comparison
6:11. for Sodom *and* Gomorrha in the day of judgment, *than* for that city.
15. it is a prophet, *or* as one of the prophets.
56. *or* cities, *or* country,
7:10. Whoso curseth father *or* mother,
11. say to his father *or* mother,
12. for his father *or* his mother;
8:37. *Or* what shall a man give
9:43. *than* having two hands
45. *than* having two feet
47. *than* having two eyes
10:25. *than* for a rich man to enter into the
29. hath left house, *or* brethren, *or* sisters, *or* father, *or* mother, *or* wife, *or* children, *or* lands,
11:30. was (it) from heaven, *or* of men?
12:14. to give tribute to Cæsar, *or* not?
15(14). Shall we give, *or* shall we not give?
13:21. here (is) Christ; *or*, lo, (he is) there;
35. at even, *or* at midnight, *or* at the cock-crowing, *or* in the morning:
14:30. before)(the cock crow twice,
Lu. 2:24. *or* two young pigeons.
26. before)(he had seen the Lord's Christ.
5:23. *or* to say, Rise up
6: 9. to do good, *or* to do evil? to save life, *or* to destroy (it)?
42. *Either* how canst thou say
7:19. *or* look we for another?
20. *or* look we for another?
8:16. *or* putteth (it) under a bed;
9:13. We have no more *but* five loaves
25. lose himself, *or* be cast away?
10:12. more tolerable in that day for Sodom, *than* for that city.
14. at the judgment, *than* for you.
11:12. *Or* if he shall ask an egg,
12:11. how *or* what thing ye shall answer, *or* what ye shall say:
14. who made me a judge *or* a divider
29. what ye shall eat, *or* what ye shall drink,
41. unto us, *or* even to all?
51. I tell you, Nay; but *rather* division:
13: 4. *Or* those eighteen, upon whom
15. loose his ox *or* (his) ass from the stall,
14: 5. an ass *or* an ox fallen into a pit,
12. thou makest a dinner *or* a supper,
31. *Or* what king, going to make war
15: 7. more *than* over ninety and nine
8. *Either* what woman having ten pieces of
16:13. for *either* he will hate the one,
— *or else* he will hold to the one,
17. *than* one tittle of the law
17: 2. *than* that he should offend
7. a servant plowing *or* feeding cattle,
21. Lo here! *or*, lo there!
23. See here; *or*, see there:
18:11. *or* even as this publican.
14. to his house justified (rather) *than* the
25. *than* for a rich man to enter into the
29. *or* parents, *or* brethren, *or* wife, *or*
20: 2. *or* who is he that gave thee this
4. was it from heaven, *or* of men?

Lu. 20:22. to give tribute unto Cæsar, *or* no?
22:27. he that sitteth at meat, *or* he that serveth?
34. before *that* thou shalt thrice deny
68. ye will not answer me, *nor* let (me) go.
Joh. 2: 6. two *or* three firkins
3:19. loved darkness rather *than* light,
4: 1. baptized more disciples *than* John,
27. What seekest thou? *or*, Why talkest thou
6:19. five and twenty *or* thirty furlongs,
7:17. be of God, *or* (whether) I speak of
48. any of the rulers *or* of the Pharisees
9: 2. this man, *or* his parents,
21. *or* who hath opened his eyes,
13:10. needeth not *save* to wash (his) feet,
29. *or*, that he should give something to the
18:34. *or* did others tell it thee of me?
Acts 1: 7. the times *or* the seasons, which
2:20. before)(that great and notable day of the Lord come:
3:12. *or* why look ye so earnestly on us, as though by our own power *or* holiness
4: 7. *or* by what name, have ye done this?
19. hearken unto you more *than* unto God,
34. possessors of lands *or* houses
5:29. We ought to obey God rather *than* men.
38. if this counsel *or* this work be of men,
7: 2. before)(he dwelt in Charran,
49. *or* what (is) the place of my rest?
8:34. of himself, *or* of some other
10:14. any thing that is common *or* unclean,
28. *or* come unto one of another nation;
— not call any man common *or* unclean,
11: 8. nothing common *or* unclean
17:21. *but either* to tell, or to hear some new
29. unto gold, *or* silver, *or* stone,
18:14. a matter of wrong *or* wicked lewdness,
19:12. unto the sick handkerchiefs *or* aprons,
20:33. no man's silver, *or* gold, *or* apparel.
35. more blessed to give *than* to receive.
23: 9. if a spirit *or* an angel hath spoken to him,
29. worthy of death *or* of bonds.
24:11. there are yet but (lit. not more *than*) twelve days
12. *neither* raising up the people,
20. *Or else* let these same (here) say
21. *Except it be* for this one voice,
23. to minister *or* come unto him.
25: 6. among them more *than* ten days,
16. before *that* he which is accused
26:31. nothing worthy of death *or* of bonds.
27:11. more *than* those things which
28: 6. *or* fallen down dead suddenly:
17. *or* customs of our fathers,
21. *or* spake any harm of thee.
Ro. 1:21. they glorified (him) not as God, *neither* were thankful;
2: 4. *Or* despisest thou the riches of his
15. accusing *or* else excusing one another
3: 1. *or* what profit (is there)
29.)((Is he) the God of the Jews only?
4: 9. *or* upon the uncircumcision also?
10. *or* in uncircumcision?
13. to Abraham, *or* to his seed,
6: 3.)(Know ye not, that so many
16. *or* of obedience unto righteousness?
7: 1.)(Know ye not, brethren,
8:35. *or* distress, *or* persecution, *or* famine, *or* nakedness, *or* peril, *or* sword?
9:11. having done any good *or* evil,
21.)(Hath not the potter power
10: 7. *Or*, Who shall descend
11: 2.)(Wot ye not what the scripture saith of

Ro. 11:34. *or* who hath been his counsellor:
35. *Or* who hath first given to him,
13:11. *than* when we believed.
14: 4. to his own master he standeth *or* falleth.
10. *or* why dost thou set at nought
13. *or* an occasion to fall
21. *or* is offended, *or* is made weak.
1Co. 1:13. *or* were ye baptized in the name of Paul?
2: 1. excellency of speech *or* of wisdom,
3: 5. but ministers by whom (lit. but *rather*, &c.)
4: 3. *or* of man's judgment:
21. *or* in love, and (in) the spirit
5:10. *or* with the covetous, *or* extortioners, *or*
11.)(a fornicator, *or* covetous, *or* an idolater, *or* a railer, *or* a drunkard, *or* an
6: 9.)(Know ye not that the unrighteous
16. *What?* know ye not that he which is
19. *What?* know ye not that your body
7: 9. it is better to marry *than* to burn.
11. *or* be reconciled to (her) husband.
15. A brother *or* a sister is not under
16. *or* how knowest thou, O man, whether
9: 6. *Or* I only and Barnabas.
7. *or* who feedeth a flock,
8. *or* saith not the law the same also?
10. *Or* saith he (it) altogether for our sakes?
15. *than* that any man should make my
10:19. *or* that which is offered in sacrifice to idols is any thing?
22.)(Do we provoke the Lord to jealousy?
11: 4. Every man praying *or* prophesying,
5. that prayeth *or* prophesieth
6. for a woman to be shorn *or* shaven,
14.)(Doth not even nature itself
22. *or* despise ye the church of God,
27. *and* drink (this) cup of the Lord,
12:21. *nor* again the head to the feet,
13: 1. *or* a tinkling cymbal.
14: 5. *than* he that speaketh with tongues,
6. *either* by revelation, *or* by knowledge, *or* by prophesying, *or* by doctrine?
7. be known what is piped *or* harped?
19. *than* ten thousand words in an (unknown)
23. unlearned, *or* unbelievers,
24. that believeth not, *or* (one) unlearned.
27. (let it be) by two, *or* at the most
29. the prophets speak two *or* three,
36. *What?* came the word of God out from you? *or* came it unto you only?
37. to be a prophet, *or* spiritual,
15:37. *or* of some other (grain):
16: 6. *yea*, and winter with you,
2Co. 1:13. *than* what ye read *or* acknowledge;
17. *or* the things that I purpose,
3: 1. to you, *or* (letters) of commendation from
6:15. *or* what part hath he that believeth with
9: 7. not grudgingly, *or* of necessity:
10:12. *or* compare ourselves with some
11: 4. *or* (if) ye receive another spirit,
— *or* another gospel, which ye have not
7.)(Have I committed an offence
12: 6. *or* (that) he heareth of me.
13: 5.)(Know ye not your own selves,
Gal. 1: 8. *or* an angel from heaven,
10. do I now persuade men, *or* God? *or* do I seek to please men?
2: 2. I should run, *or* had run, in vain.
3: 2. *or* by the hearing of faith?
5. *or* by the hearing of faith?
15. disannulleth, *or* addeth thereto.
4:27. more children *than* she which hath
Eph. 3:20. above all that we ask *or* think,
Eph. 5: 3. *or* covetousness, let it not be once named
4. foolish talking, *nor* jesting.
5. *nor* unclean person, *nor* covetous man,
27. *or* wrinkle, *or* any such thing;
Phi. 2: 3. through strife *or* vainglory;
3:12. *either* were already perfect:
Col. 2:16. *or* in drink, *or* in respect of an holyday, *or* of the new moon, *or* of the sabbath (days):
3:17. And whatsoever ye do in word *or* deed,
1Th. 2:19. our hope, *or* joy, *or* crown of rejoicing?)((Are) not even ye
2Th. 2: 4. is called God, *or* that is worshipped;
1Ti. 1: 4. rather *than* godly edifying
2: 9. *or* gold, *or* pearls, *or* costly array;
5: 4. have children *or* nephews,
16. any man *or* woman that believeth have
19. before two *or* three witnesses.
2Ti. 3: 4. lovers of pleasures more *than* lovers of
Tit. 1: 6. not accused of riot, *or* unruly.
3:12. unto thee, *or* Tychicus,
Philem. 18. he hath wronged thee, *or* oweth
Heb. 2: 6. *or* the son of man, that
10:28. under two *or* three witnesses:
11:25. *than* to enjoy the pleasures of sin for a
12:16. *or* profane person, as Esau,
20. *or* thrust through with a dart:
Jas. 1:17. *neither* shadow of turning.
2: 3. *or* sit here under my footstool:
15. a brother *or* sister be naked,
3:12. *either* a vine, figs?
4: 5.)(Do ye think that the scripture saith in
15. we shall live, and do this, *or* that.
1Pet. 1:11. *or* what manner of time the Spirit of Christ which was in them did signify,
18. (as) silver *and* gold, from your vain
3: 3. *or* of putting on of apparel;
9. *or* railing for railing:
17. *than* for evil doing.
4:15. *or* (as) a thief, *or* (as) an evildoer, *or* as a busybody in other men's matters.
2Pet. 2:21. *than*, after they have known (it), to turn
1Joh. 4: 4. *than* he that is in the world.
Rev. 3:15. thou wert cold *or* hot.
13:16. *or* in their foreheads:
17. buy *or* sell, save he that had the mark, *or* the name of the beast, *or* the number of his name.
14: 9. in his forehead, *or* in his hand,

2229 1 334/ 2228

ἦ μήν, ee meen.

Heb. 6:14. *Surely* blessing I will bless

2260 1 149/432 2228,4007

ἤπερ, eeper.

Joh. 12:43. more *than* the praise of God.

2273 1 350/424,434 2228,5104

ἤτοι, eetoi.

Ro. 6:16. *whether* of sin unto death, or

2231 1 343/425 2232

ἡγεμονία, heegemonia.

Lu. 3: 1. of the *reign* of Tiberius Cæsar.

2230 2 343/424 2232

ἡγεμονεύω, heegemonūo.

Lu. 2: 2. *when* Cyrenius *was governor* of Syria.
3: 1. Pontius Pilate *being governor* of Judæa,

2232 22 344/425 2233
ἡγεμών, heegemōn.

Mat. 2: 6. art not the least among the *princes* of
10:18. ye shall be brought before *governors*
27: 2. him to Pontius Pilate the *governor*.
11. Jesus stood before the *governor:* and the *governor* asked him,
14. the *governor* marvelled greatly.
15. the *governor* was wont to release
21. The *governor* answered and said unto
23. And the *governor* said, Why, what evil
27. Then the soldiers of the *governor*
28:14. if this come to the *governor's* ears,
Mar13: 9. ye shall be brought before *rulers*
Lu. 20:20. the power and authority of the *governor*.
21:12. before kings and *rulers*
Acts23:24. unto Felix the *governor*.
26. unto the most excellent *governor* Felix (sendeth) greeting.
33. delivered the epistle to the *governor*,
34. And when the *governor* had read
24: 1. who informed the *governor* against Paul.
10. after that the *governor* had beckoned unto
26:30. the king rose up, and the *governor*,
1Pet.2:14. Or unto *governors*, as unto them that are sent by him

2233 28 344/425 2:907 71
ἡγέομαι, heegeomai.

Mat. 2: 6. shall come a *Governor*,
Lu. 22:26. he *that is chief*, as he that doth serve.
Acts 7:10. he made him *governor* over Egypt
14:12. the *chief* speaker. (lit. *leading* in speech)
15:22. *chief* men among the brethren:
26: 2. I *think* myself happy, king Agrippa,
2Co. 9: 5. Therefore I *thought* it necessary
Phi. 2: 3 *let* each *esteem* other better than themselves.
6. *thought* it not robbery to be equal
25. Yet I *supposed* it necessary
3: 7. those I *counted* loss
8. I *count* all things (but) loss
— *do count* them (but) dung,
1Th. 5:13. And *to esteem* them very highly in love
2Th. 3:15. *count* (him) not as an enemy,
1Ti. 1:12. for that he *counted* me faithful,
6: 1. *Let* as many servants...*count* their own masters worthy
Heb 10:29. and *hath counted* the blood of the covenant,
11:11. she *judged* him faithful who had promised.
26. *Esteeming* the reproach of Christ greater
13: 7. Remember them *which have the rule over*
17. Obey them *that have the rule over* you,
24. Salute all them *that have the rule over* you,
Jas. 1: 2. *count* it all joy when ye fall into
2Pet.1:13. Yea, I *think* it meet, as long as
2:13. (as) they *that count* it pleasure to riot
3: 9. as some men *count* slackness;
15. And *account* (that) the longsuffering of our Lord (is) salvation;

2234,2236 4,2 344/425 rt 2237
ἡδέως, ἥδιστα, heedeōs, heedista.

Mar. 6:20. and heard him *gladly*.
12:37. the common people heard him *gladly*
2Co.11:19. For ye suffer fools *gladly*,
12: 9. *Most gladly* therefore will I rather
15. I will *very gladly* spend and be spent for

2235 59 344/425 2228,1211
ἤδη, eedee.

Mat. 3:10. And *now* also the ax is laid
5:28. hath committed adultery with her *already*
14:15. the time is *now* past;
24. was *now* in the midst of the sea,
15:32. they continue with me *now* three days,
17:12. Elias is come *already*,
24:32. When his branch is *yet* tender,
Mar. 4:37. into the ship, so that it was *now* full.
6:35. when the day was *now* far spent,
— and *now* the time (is) far passed:
8: 2. they have *now* been with me three days,
11:11. and *now* the eventide was come,
13:28. When her branch is *yet* tender,
15:42. And *now* when the even was come,
44. if he were *already* dead:
Lu. 3: 9. And *now* also the axe
7: 6. And when he was *now* not far
11: 7. the door is *now* shut,
12:49. if it be *already* kindled?
14:17. for all things are *now* ready.
19:37. when he was come nigh, *even now* at the
21:30. When they *now* shoot forth,
— that summer is *now* nigh at hand.
Joh. 3:18. believeth not is condemned *already*,
4:35. they are white *already* to harvest.
51. And as he was *now* going down,
5: 6. that he had been *now* a long time
6:17. it was *now* dark,
7:14. *Now* about the midst of the feast
9:22. for the Jews had agreed *already*,
27. I have told you *already*,
11:17. that he had (lain) in the grave four days *already*.
39. Lord, *by this time* he stinketh·
13: 2. the devil having *now* put
15: 3. *Now* ye are clean through the word
19:28. all things were *now* accomplished,
33. that he was dead *already*.
21: 4. But when the morning was *now* come,
14. This is *now* the third time
Acts 4: 3. for it was *now* eventide.
27: 9. when sailing was *now* dangerous, because the fast was *now already* past,
Ro. 1:10. if by any means *now* at length I might have a prosperous journey
4:19. considered not his own body *now* dead,
13:11. *now* (it is) high time to awake out of
1Co. 4: 8. *Now* ye are full, *now* ye are rich,
5: 3. have judged *already*, as though I were
6: 7. *Now* therefore there is utterly
Phi. 3:12. Not as though I had *already* attained, either were *already* perfect:
4:10. that *now* at the last your care of me hath flourished again;
2Th. 2: 7. the mystery of iniquity doth *already* work:
1Ti. 5:15. For some are *already* turned aside
2Ti. 2:18. that the resurrection is past *already*;
4: 6. For I am *now* ready to be offered,
2Pet.3: 1. This second epistle, beloved, I *now*
1Joh.2: 8. the true light *now* shineth.
4: 3. *already* is it in the world.

ἥδιστα see ἡδέως. 2234

2237 5 344/426 2:909 handanō (to please)
ἡδονή, heedonee.

Lu. 8:14. and riches and *pleasures* of (this) life,
Tit. 3: 3. serving divers lusts and *pleasures*,
Jas. 4: 1. (come they) not hence, (even) of your *lusts*

Jas. 4 3. ye may consume (it) upon your *lusts*.
2Pet.2:13. (as) they that count it *pleasure* to riot

2238 2 345/426 3744
hēdomai (to delight)
ἡδύοσμον, *heeduosmon.*

Mat.23:23. ye pay tithe of *mint*
Lu. 11:42. tithe *mint* and rue and all manner

2239 1 345/426 1485
ἦθος, *eethos.*

1Co.15:33. communications corrupt good *manners.*

2240 27 335/426 2:926
ἥκω, *heeko.*

Mat. 8:11. *shall come* from the east and west,
23:36. All these things *shall come* upon
24:14. then *shall* the end *come*.
50. The lord of that servant *shall come*
Mar 8: 3. for divers of them *came* from far.
Lu. 12:46. The lord of that servant *will come*
13:29. they *shall come* from the east,
35. until (the time) *come* when ye shall say,
15:27. Thy brother *is come*;
19:43. the days *shall come* upon thee,
Joh. 2: 4. mine hour *is* not yet *come*.
4:47. When he heard that Jesus *was come*
6:37. *shall come* to me;
8:42. I proceeded forth and *came* from God;
Acts28:23. there *came* many to him
Ro. 11:26. There *shall come* out of Sion the Deliverer,
Heb10: 7. Then said I, Lo, I *come*
9. Lo, I *come* to do thy will, O God.
37. and he that shall come *will come*,
2Pet.3:10. But the day of the Lord *will come* as a
1Joh.5:20. that the Son of God *is come*,
Rev. 2:25. hold fast till I *come*.
3: 3. I *will come* on thee as a thief, and thou shalt not know what hour I *will come* upon thee.
9. I will make them to *come* and worship
15: 4. all nations *shall come* and worship before
18: 8. *shall* her plagues *come* in one day,

2241 2 345/426 [410]
Ἠλί, *Eli.*

Mat.27:46. *Eli, Eli*, lama sabachthani? that is to say, My God, My God, why hast thou forsaken me?

2244 8 345/427 2:941 rt 2245
ἡλικία, *heelikia.*

Mat. 6:27. can add one cubit unto his *stature*?
Lu. 2:52. in wisdom and *stature*,
12:25. to his *stature* one cubit?
19: 3. he was little of *stature*.
Joh. 9:21. we know not: he is of *age*; ask him:
23. said his parents, He is of *age*; ask him.
Eph. 4:13. unto the measure of the *stature* of the fulness of Christ:
Heb11:11. when she was past *age*,

2245 2 346/427
hēlix (comrade)
ἡλίκος, *heelikos.*

Col. 2: 1. that ye knew *what great* conflict I have
Jas. 3: 5. *how great* a matter a little fire kindleth!

2246 32 346/427
helē (ray)
ἥλιος, *heelios.*

Mat. 5:45. he maketh his *sun* to rise
13: 6. And when the *sun* was up,
43. Then shall the righteous shine forth as the *sun*
17: 2. his face did shine as the *sun*,
24:29. shall the *sun* be darkened,
Mar 1:32. when the *sun* did set,
4: 6. But when the *sun* was up,
13:24. the *sun* shall be darkened,
16: 2. at the rising of the *sun*.
Lu. 4:40. Now when the *sun* was setting,
21:25. there shall be signs in the *sun*,
23:45. the *sun* was darkened,
Acts 2:20. The *sun* shall be turned into darkness,
13:11. thou shalt be blind, not seeing the *sun*
26:13. the brightness of the *sun*,
27:20. And when neither *sun* nor stars
1Co.15:41. (There is) one glory of the *sun*,
Eph. 4:26. let not the *sun* go down upon your wrath:
Jas. 1:11. For the *sun* is no sooner risen
Rev. 1:16. as the *sun* shineth in his strength.
6:12. the *sun* became black as sackcloth of
7: 2. from the east, (lit. from the rising of the *sun*)
16. shall the *sun* light on them,
8:12. the third part of the *sun* was smitten,
9: 2. the *sun* and the air were darkened
10: 1. his face (was) as it were the *sun*,
12: 1. clothed with the *sun*,
16: 8. poured out his vial upon the *sun*.
12. kings of the east (lit. kings from the rising of the *sun*)
19:17. an angel standing in the *sun*;
21:23. had no need of the *sun*,
22: 5. neither light of the *sun*; for the Lord God giveth them light:

2247 2 346/427
ἧλος, *heelos.*

Joh.20:25. the print of the *nails*, and put my finger into the print of the *nails*,

2248 178 216/255 1473
ἡμᾶς, *heemas*, from ἐγώ.

Mat. 6:13. lead *us* not into temptation, but deliver *us* from
8:25. Lord, save *us*: we perish.
29. to torment *us* before the time?
31. If thou cast *us* out, suffer
9:27. (Thou) son of David, have mercy on *us*.
13:56. are they not all with *us*?
17: 4. it is good for *us* to be here.
20: 7. no man hath hired *us*.
30. Have mercy on *us*, O Lord,
31. Have mercy on *us*, O Lord,
27: 4. What (is that) to *us*?
25. His blood (be) on *us*,
Mar. 1:24. art thou come to destroy *us*?
5:12. Send *us* into the swine,
6: 3. are not his sisters here with *us*?
9: 5. it is good for *us* to be here:
22. have compassion on *us*,
Lu. 1:71. from the hand of all that hate *us*,
78. from on high hath visited *us*,
4:34. art thou come to destroy *us*?
7:20. hath sent *us* unto thee,
9:33. for *us* to be here:
11: 1. Lord, teach *us* to pray, as John also

Lu. 11: 4. lead *us* not into temptation; but deliver *us* from evil.
45. thou reproachest *us* also.
12:41. this parable unto *us*,
16:26. can they pass to *us*,
17:13. have mercy on *us*.
19:14. will not have this (man) to reign over *us*.
20: 6. all the people will stone *us*:
23:30. say to the mountains, Fall on *us*; and to the hills, Cover *us*.
39. save thyself and *us*.
24:22. of our company made *us* astonished,
Joh. 1:22. to them that sent *us*.
9:34. and dost thou teach *us*?
Acts 1:21. went in and out among *us*,
3: 4. said, Look on *us*.
4:12. whereby *we* must be saved.
5:28. to bring this man's blood upon *us*.
6: 2. It is not reason that *we* should leave
7:27. a ruler and a judge over *us*?
40. which brought *us* out of the land of
11:15. fell on them, as on *us* at the beginning.
14:11. are come down to *us*
22. *we* must through much tribulation enter
16:10. the Lord had called *us*
15. And she constrained *us*.
37. They have beaten *us* openly
— do they thrust *us* out privily?
— come themselves and fetch *us* out.
20: 5. tarried for *us* at Troas.
21: 1. after *we* were gotten from them, and had launched,
5. when *we* had accomplished those days,
— and they all brought *us* on our way,
11. when he was come unto *us*,
17. the brethren received *us*
27: 1. that *we* should sail into Italy,
6. and he put *us* therein.
7. the wind not suffering *us*,
20. that *we* should be saved
26. *we* must be cast upon a certain island.
28: 2. and received *us* every one,
7. who received us, and lodged *us*
10. Who also honoured *us*
Ro. 3: 8. as some affirm that *we* say,
4:24. But for *us* also, to whom it shall be
5: 8. commendeth his love toward *us*,
6: 6. henceforth *we* should not serve
7: 6. *we* should serve in newness
8:18. the glory which shall be revealed in *us*.
35. Who shall separate *us* from
37. through him that loved *us*.
39. shall be able to separate *us*
9:24. Even *us*, whom he hath called,
13:11. now (it is) high time)(to awake out of
15: 7. as Christ also received *us*
16: 6. bestowed much labour on *us*.
1Co. 4: 1. Let a man so account of *us*,
9. that God hath set forth *us* the apostles
6:14. and will also raise up *us*
7:15. God hath called *us*
8: 8. But meat commendeth *us* not
9:10. Or saith he (it) altogether for *our* sakes? For *our* sakes, no doubt, (this) is
10: 6. to the intent *we* should not lust after
2Co. 1: 4. Who comforteth *us* in all our tribulation, that *we* may be able to
5. the sufferings of Christ abound in *us*,
8. that *we* despaired even of life:
10. Who delivered *us* from so great a death,
11. the gift (bestowed) upon *us*
14. ye have acknowledged *us* in part,
2Co. 1:21. Now he which stablisheth *us* with you in Christ, and hath anointed *us*, (is) God;
22. Who hath also sealed *us*,
2:14. which always causeth *us* to triumph in
3: 6. hath made *us* able ministers
4:14. shall raise up *us* also by Jesus,
5: 5. Now he that hath wrought *us*
10. For *we* must all appear before
14. the love of Christ constraineth *us*;
18. hath reconciled *us* to himself
7: 2. Receive *us*; we have wronged no man,
6. comforted *us* by the coming of Titus;
8: 4. that *we* would receive the gift,
6. Insomuch that *we* desired
20. that no man should blame *us*
10: 2. which think of *us* as if we walked
Gal. 1: 4. that he might deliver *us*
23. he which persecuted *us* in times past
2: 4. that they might bring *us* into bondage:
3:13. Christ hath redeemed *us*
5: 1. wherewith Christ hath made *us* free,
Eph. 1: 3. who hath blessed *us* with all
4. According as he hath chosen *us*
— that *we* should be holy and
5. Having predestinated *us* unto the adoption
6. wherein he hath made *us* accepted
8. Wherein he hath abounded toward *us*
12. That *we* should be to the praise
19. to *us*-ward who believe,
2: 4. wherewith he loved *us*,
5. when *we* were dead in sins,
7. in (his) kindness toward *us*
5: 2. Christ also hath loved *us*,
Phi. 3:17. as ye have *us* for an ensample.
Col. 1:12. which hath made *us* meet
13. Who hath delivered *us*
1Th. 1: 8. so that *we* need not
10. Jesus, which delivered *us* from the wrath to come.
2:15. and have persecuted *us*;
16. Forbidding *us* to speak to the Gentiles
18. Satan hindered *us*.
3: 6. when Timotheus came from you unto *us*,
— desiring greatly to see *us*,
4: 7. For God hath not called *us*
8. given unto *us* his holy Spirit.
5: 9. God hath not appointed *us* to
2Th. 1: 4. So that *we* ourselves glory in you
2:16. which hath loved *us*,
3: 7. how ye ought to follow *us*:
9. an ensample unto you to follow *us*.
2Ti. 1: 9. Who hath saved *us*, and called
2:12. if we deny (him), he also will deny *us*:
Tit. 2:12. Teaching *us* that, denying ungodliness
14. that he might redeem *us*
3: 5. he saved *us*, by the washing
6. Which he shed on *us* abundantly
15. that love *us* in the faith.
Heb. 2: 1. *we* ought to give the more earnest heed
3. unto *us* by them that heard (him);
13: 6. So that *we* may boldly say,
Jas. 1:18. Of his own will begat he *us* with the word of truth, that *we* should be
1Pet. 1: 3. hath begotten *us* again unto
3:18. that he might bring *us*
21. The like figure whereunto (even) baptism doth also now save *us*
5:10. who hath called *us*
2Pet. 1: 3. of him that hath called *us*
3: 9. is longsuffering to *us*-ward,
1Joh. 1: 7. cleanseth *us* from all sin.
9. and to cleanse *us* from all

1Joh.3: 1. the world knoweth *us* not,
4:10. but that he loved *us*,
11. if God so loved *us*, we ought also
19. because he first loved *us*.
3Joh. 9. among them, receiveth *us* not.
10. prating against *us* with malicious
Rev. 1: 5. Unto him that loved *us*, and washed *us* from our sins in his own blood,
6. And hath made *us* kings and priests
5: 9. hast redeemed *us* to God
10. And hast made *us* unto our God kings and priests:
6:16. Fall on *us*, and hide *us* from the face of him that sitteth on the throne,

2249 127 346/253 1473

ἡμεῖς, heemīs.

From ἐγώ.

Mat. 6:12. as *we* forgive our debtors.
9:14. Why do *we* and the Pharisees fast oft,
17:19. Why could not *we* cast him out?
19:27. Behold, *we* have forsaken all,
28:14. *we* will persuade him,
Mar. 9:28. Why could not *we* cast him out?
10:28. Lo, *we* have left all, and have
14:58. *We* heard him say, I will destroy
Lu. 3:14. And what shall *we* do?
9:13. except *we* should go and buy meat
18:28. *we* have left all,
23:41. And *we* indeed justly;
24:21. But *we* trusted that it had been he which
Joh. 1:16. of his fulness have all *we* received,
4:22. we know what *we* worship:
6:42. whose father and mother *we* know?
69. And *we* believe and are sure that thou art that Christ,
7:35. that *we* shall not find him?
8:41. *We* be not born of fornication;
48. Say *we* not well that thou art
9:21. who hath opened his eyes, *we* know not:
24. *we* know that this man
28. but *we* are Moses' disciples.
29. *We* know that God spake unto Moses:
40. Are *we* blind also?
11:16. Let *us* also go, that we may die
12:34. *We* have heard out of the law
17:11. that they may be one, as *we* (are).
22. even as *we* are one:
19: 7. *We* have a law,
21: 3. *We* also go with thee.
Acts 2: 8. how hear *we* every man
32. whereof *we* all are witnesses.
3:15. whereof *we* are witnesses.
4: 9. If *we* this day be examined
20. For *we* cannot but speak the things
5:32. And *we* are his witnesses
6: 4. But *we* will give ourselves continually to
10:33. *we* all here present before God,
39. And *we* are witnesses of all things
47. received the Holy Ghost as well as *we*?
13:32. And *we* declare unto you glad tidings,
14:15. *We* also are men of like passions.
15:10. nor *we* were able to bear?
20: 6. And *we* sailed away
13. And *we* went before
21: 7. And when *we* had finished (our) course
12. both *we*, and they of that place,
25. *we* have written (and) concluded
23:15. and *we*, or ever he come near,
24: 8. whereof *we* accuse him.
Acts28:21. *We* neither received letters
Ro. 6: 4. even so *we* also should walk in newness of life.
8:23. even *we* ourselves groan within ourselves,
15: 1. *We* then that are strong ought
1Co. 1:23. But *we* preach Christ crucified,
2:12. Now *we* have received, not the spirit of the world, but
16. But *we* have the mind of Christ.
4: 8. that *we* also might reign with you.
10. *We* (are) fools for Christ's sake,
— *we* (are) weak, but ye
— but *we* (are) despised.
8: 6. of whom (are) all things, and *we* in him;
— by whom (are) all things, and *we* by him.
9:11. If *we* have sown unto you spiritual things, (is it) a great thing if *we* shall reap your carnal
12. (are) not *we* rather?
25. but *we* an incorruptible.
11:16. *we* have no such custom,
12:13. are *we* all baptized into one body,
15:30. And why stand *we* in jeopardy
52. and *we* shall be changed.
2Co. 1: 6. which *we* also suffer:
3:18. But *we* all, with open face
4:11. For *we* which live are alway
13. *we* also believe, and therefore speak;
5:16. henceforth know *we* no man
21. that *we* might be made the righteousness
9: 4. *we* that we say not, ye should be
10: 7. even so (are) *we* Christ's.
13. But *we* will not boast of things
11:12. they may be found even as *we*.
21. as though *we* had been weak.
13: 4. For *we* also are weak in
6. that *we* are not reprobates.
7. not that *we* should appear approved,
— though *we* be as reprobates.
9. when *we* are weak,
Gal. 1: 8. But though *we*, or an angel
2: 9. that *we* (should go) unto the heathen,
15. *We* (who are) Jews by nature,
16. even *we* have believed in Jesus Christ,
4: 3. Even so *we*, when we were
28. Now *we*, brethren, as Isaac
5: 5. For *we* through the Spirit
Eph. 2: 3(2). Among whom also *we* all
Phi. 3: 3. For *we* are the circumcision,
Col. 1: 9. For this cause *we* also, since
28. Whom *we* preach, warning every man,
1Th. 2:13. For this cause also thank *we* God
17. But *we*, brethren, being taken from you
3: 6. as *we* also (to see) you:
12. even as *we* (do) toward you:
4:15. that *we* which are alive (and) remain
17. Then *we* which are alive
5: 8. But let *us*, who are of the day,
2Th. 2:13. But *we* are bound to give thanks
Tit. 3: 3. For *we ourselves* also were sometimes
5. Not by works of righteousness which *we* have done,
Heb. 2: 3. How shall *we* escape,
3: 6. whose house are *we*,
10:39. But *we* are not of them who draw back
12: 1. Wherefore seeing we also are compassed about...let *us*
25. much more (shall not) *we* (escape),
2Pet. 1:18. this voice which came from heaven *we* heard, when
1Joh. 3:14. We know that *we* have passed
16. and *we* ought to lay down (our) lives

1Joh.4 6. *We* are of God:
10. not that *we* loved God, but that he
11. *we* ought also to love one another.
14. And *we* have seen and do testify
16. And *we* have known and believed
17. so are *we* in this world.
19. *We* love him, because he first loved us.
3Joh. 8. *We* therefore ought to receive such,
12. yea, and *we* (also) bear record;

2250 389 346/427 2:943
ἡμέρα, heemera. *hēmai* (to sit)

Mat. 2: 1. in the *days* of Herod the king,
3: 1. In those *days* came John
4: 2. when he had fasted forty *days*
6:34. Sufficient unto the *day* (is) the evil
7:22. Many will say to me in that *day*,
9:15. but the *days* will come,
10:15. in the *day* of judgment,
11:12. And from the *days* of John
22. at the *day* of judgment,
24. in the *day* of judgment,
12:36. account thereof in the *day* of judgment.
40. Jonas was three *days* and three nights
— three *days* and three nights in the heart of the earth.
13: 1. The same *day* went Jesus out
15:32. they continue with me now three *days*,
16:21. be raised again the third *day*.
17: 1. And after six *days* Jesus taketh
23. the third *day* he shall be raised again.
20: 2. for a penny a *day*,
6. all the *day* idle?
12. borne the burden and heat of the *day*.
19. the third *day* he shall rise again.
22:23. The same *day* came to him
46. from that *day* forth
23:30. If we had been in the *days* of our fathers,
24:19. to them that give suck in those *days*!
22. except those *days* should be shortened,
— those *days* shall be shortened.
29. after the tribulation of those *days*
36. But of that *day* and hour
37. But as the *days* of Noe (were),
38. For as in the *days* that were before the
— until the *day* that Noe entered
50. in a *day* when he looketh not for (him),
25:13. ye know neither the *day* nor
26: 2. after two *days* is (the feast of) the passover,
29. until that *day* when I drink it new with you
55. *daily* with you teaching
61. to build it in three *days*.
27:40. and buildest (it) in three *days*,
63. After three *days* I will rise again.
64. until the third *day*,
28:20. I am with you alway, (lit. all the *days*)
Mar. 1: 9. in those *days*, that Jesus came
13. there in the wilderness forty *days*,
2: 1. into Capernaum after (some) *days*;
20. But the *days* will come, when
— then shall they fast in those *days*.
4:27. sleep, and rise night and *day*,
35. the same *day*, when the even
5: 5. And always, night and *day*, he was
6:11. in the *day* of judgment,
21. when a convenient *day* was come,
8: 1. In those *days* the multitude being
2. they have now been with me three *days*,
31. after three *days* rise again.
9: 2. after six *days* Jesus taketh
31. he shall rise the third *day*.

Mar 10:34. the third *day* he shall rise again.
13:17. to them that give suck in those *days*!
19. For (in) those *days* shall be
20. had shortened those *days*,
— he hath shortened the *days*.
24. But in those *days*, after that tribulation,
32. But of that *day* and (that) hour
14: 1. After two *days* was (the feast of)
12. the first *day* of unleavened bread,
25. until that *day* that I drink it new
49. I was *daily* with you in the temple
58. within three *days* I will build another made without hands.
15:29. and buildest (it) in three *days*,
Lu. 1: 5. There was in the *days* of Herod,
7. were (now) well stricken in *years*.
18. my wife well stricken in *years*.
20. not able to speak, until the *day* that
23. that, as soon as the *days* of his ministration were accomplished,
24. And after those *days* his wife
25. in the *days* wherein he looked on (me),
39. Mary arose in those *days*, and went
59. that on the eighth *day*
75. all the *days* of our life.
80. was in the deserts till the *day* of his
2: 1. in those *days*, that there went out a decree
6. the *days* were accomplished that she
21. eight *days* were accomplished
22. when the *days* of her purification
36. she was of a great *age*,
37. with fastings and prayers night and *day*.
43. when they had fulfilled the *days*,
44. went a *day's* journey;
46. that after three *days* they found
4: 2. forty *days* tempted of the devil. And in those *days* he did eat nothing:
16. into the synagogue on the sabbath *day*,
25. were in Israel in the *days* of Elias,
42. And when it was *day*,
5:17. on a certain *day*, as he was teaching,
35. But the *days* will come, when
— then shall they fast in those *days*.
6:12. it came to pass in those *days*,
13. when it was *day*,
23. Rejoice ye in that *day*,
8:22. it came to pass on a certain *day*,
9:12. And when the *day* began to wear away,
22. be raised the third *day*.
23. and take up his cross *daily*,
28. about an eight *days*
36. told no man in those *days*
37. that on the next *day*,
51. when the *time* was come that he should be received up,
10:12. shall be more tolerable in that *day*
11: 3. Give us day by *day* (καθ' ἡμέραν)
12:46. in a *day* when he looketh not for (him),
13:14. There are six *days* in which
— and not on the sabbath *day*.
16. on the sabbath *day*?
31. The same *day* there came
14: 5. on the sabbath *day*?
15:13. not many *days* after
16:19. fared sumptuously every *day*:
17: 4. seven times in a *day*, and seven times in a *day* turn again to thee,
22. The *days* will come, when ye shall desire to see one of the *days*
24. so shall also the Son of man be in his *day*.
26. as it was in the *days* of Noe, so shall it be also in the *days* of the Son of man.

Lu. 17:27. until the *day* that Noe entered
28. in the *days* of Lot;
29. But the same *day* that Lot went out
30. in the *day* when the Son of man
31. In that *day*, he which shall be upon
18: 7 which cry *day* and night unto him,
33. the third *day* he shall rise again.
19:42. at least in this thy *day*,
43. For the *days* shall come upon thee,
47. he taught *daily* in the temple.
20: 1. (that) on one of those *days*,
21: 6. the *days* will come, in the which
22. For these be the *days* of vengeance,
23. that give suck, in those *days*!
34. and (so) that *day* come upon you
37. And in the *day time* he was teaching in the temple;
22: 7. the *day* of unleavened bread,
53. When I was *daily* with you in the temple,
66. as soon as it was *day*,
23: 7. was at Jerusalem at that *time*.
12. the same *day* Pilate and Herod
29. behold, the *days* are coming,
54. that *day* was the preparation,
24: 7. the third *day* rise again.
13. went that same *day* to a village
18. come to pass there in these *days*?
21. to day is the third *day*
29. the *day* is far spent.
46. from the dead the third *day*:
Joh. 1:39(40). abode with him that *day*:
2: 1. And the third *day* there was a marriage
12. they continued there not many *days*.
19. in three *days* I will raise it up.
20. wilt thou rear it up in three *days*
4:40. and he abode there two *days*.
43. Now after two *days*
5: 9. on the same *day*
6:39. raise it up again at the last *day*.
40. I will raise him up at the last *day*.
44. him up at the last *day*.
54. him up at the last *day*.
7:37. In the last *day*, that great
8:56. Abraham rejoiced to see my *day*:
9: 4. while it is *day*:
11: 6. two *days* still in the same place where he
9. Are there not twelve hours in the *day*? If any man walk in the *day*,
17. he had (lain) in the grave four *days*
24. in the resurrection at the last *day*.
53. Then from that *day* forth
12: 1. six *days* before the passover
7. against the *day* of my burying
48. the same shall judge him in the last *day*.
14:20. At that *day* ye shall know that I
16:23. in that *day* ye shall ask me nothing.
26. At that *day* ye shall ask in my name:
19:31. for that sabbath day was an high *day*,
20:19. the same *day* at evening,
26. And after eight *days* again his
Acts 1: 2. Until the *day* in which he was taken up,
3. being seen of them forty *days*,
5. not many *days* hence.
15. And in those *days* Peter stood up
22. unto that same *day* that he was
2: 1. the *day* of Pentecost
15. the third hour of the *day*.
17. it shall come to pass in the last *days*,
18. I will pour out in those *days* of my Spirit;
20. before that great and notable *day* of the Lord come:
29. his sepulchre is with us unto this *day*.

Acts 2:41. the same *day* there were added
46. And they, continuing *daily*
47. the Lord added to the church *daily*
3: 2. whom they laid *daily* at the gate
24. have likewise foretold of these *days*.
5:36. For before these *days* rose up Theudas,
37. in the *days* of the taxing,
42. And *daily* in the temple,
6: 1. And in those *days*,
7: 8. circumcised him the eighth *day*;
26. And the next *day* he shewed himself
41. they made a calf in those *days*,
45. unto the *days* of David;
8: 1. at that *time* there was a great persecution
9: 9. three *days* without sight,
19. Then was Saul certain *days* with
23. many *days* were fulfilled,
24. watched the gates *day* and night
37. to pass in those *days*, that she
43. he tarried many *days* in Joppa
10: 3. the ninth hour of the *day*
30. Four *days* ago I was fasting
40. raised up the third *day*,
48. to tarry certain *days*.
11:27. And in these *days* came prophets
12: 3. Then were the *days* of unleavened bread.
18. Now as soon as it was *day*,
21. And upon a set *day* Herod,
13:14. on the sabbath *day*,
31. he was seen many *days* of them
41. I work a work in your *days*,
15: 7. a good *while* ago God made choice
36. And some *days* after
16: 5. increased in number *daily*.
12. abiding certain *days*.
13. And on the sabbath)(we went
18. did she many *days*.
35. And when it was *day*,
17:11. and searched the scriptures *daily*,
17. and in the market *daily* with them that met with him.
31. Because he hath appointed a *day*,
18:18. tarried (there) yet a good *while*,
19: 9. disputing *daily* in the school of
20: 6. from Philippi after the *days* of unleavened bread, and came unto them to Troas in five *days*; where we abode seven *days*.
16. the *day* of Pentecost.
18. from the first *day*
26. I take you to record this *day*,
31. I ceased not to warn every one night and *day* with tears.
21: 4. we tarried there seven *days*:
5. we had accomplished those *days*,
7. with them one *day*.
10. And as we tarried (there) many *days*,
15. And after those *days*
26. and the next *day* purifying
— the accomplishment of the *days* of
27. the seven *days* were almost ended,
38. that Egyptian, which before these *days*
23: 1. before God until this *day*.
12. And when it was *day*,
24: 1. And after five *days*
11. there are yet but twelve *days*
24. And after certain *days*,
25: 1. after three *days* he ascended
6. more than ten *days*,
13. And after certain *days*
14. they had been there many *days*,
26: 7. serving (God) *day* and night,
13. At mid*day*, O king, I saw

Acts26:22. I continue unto this *day*,
27: 7. And when we had sailed slowly many *days*, and scarce were come
20. neither sun nor stars in many *days*
29. and wished for the *day*.
33. while the *day* was coming on,
— the fourteenth *day* that ye have tarried
39. And when it was *day*,
28: 7. lodged us three *days* courteously.
12. we tarried (there) three *days*.
13. after one *day* the south wind blew,
14. to tarry with them seven *days*:
17. that after three *days*
23. And when they had appointed him a *day*,
Ro. 2: 5. wrath against the *day* of wrath
16. In the *day* when God shall judge
8:36. we are killed all the *day* long;
10:21. All *day* long I have stretched forth
11: 8. unto this *day*.
13:12. the *day* is at hand:
13. honestly, as in the *day*;
14: 5. esteemeth one *day* above another)(: another esteemeth every *day* (alike).
6. He that regardeth the *day*,
— and he that regardeth not the *day*,
1Co. 1: 8. in the *day* of our Lord
3:13. for the *day* shall declare it,
4: 3. that I should be judged of you, or of man's *judgment*: (lit. man's *day*)
5: 5. in the *day* of the Lord Jesus.
10: 8. and fell in one *day*
15: 4. he rose again the third *day*
31. Jesus our Lord, I die *daily*.
2Co. 1:14. in the *day* of the Lord Jesus.
4:16. the inward (man) is renewed *day* by *day*.
6: 2. in the *day* of salvation have I succoured
— behold, now (is) the *day* of salvation.
11:28. that which cometh upon me *daily*,
Gal. 1:18. abode with him fifteen *days*.
4:10. Ye observe *days*,
Eph. 4:30. unto the *day* of redemption.
5:16. the *days* are evil.
6:13. to withstand in the evil *day*,
Phi. 1: 5. from the first *day* until now;
6. until the *day* of Jesus Christ:
10. without offence till the *day* of Christ;
2:16. in the *day* of Christ,
Col. 1: 6. since the *day* ye heard (of it),
9. since the *day* we heard (it),
1Th. 2: 9. for labouring night and *day*,
3:10. Night and *day* praying exceedingly
5: 2. the *day* of the Lord so cometh as a thief
4. that that *day* should overtake you as a
5. and the children of the *day*:
8. But let us, who are of the *day*,
2Th. 1:10. among you was believed in that *day*.
2: 2. the *day* of Christ is at hand.
3: 8. wrought with labour and travail night and *day*,
1Ti. 5: 5. continueth in supplications and prayers night and *day*
2Ti. 1: 3. in my prayers night and *day*;
12. committed unto him against that *day*.
18. may find mercy of the Lord in that *day*:
3: 1. that in the last *days*
4: 8. shall give me at that *day*.
Heb. 1: 2(1). Hath in these last *days* spoken
3: 8. in the *day* of temptation
13. But exhort one another *daily*,
4: 4. And God did rest the seventh *day*
7. Again, he limiteth a certain *day*,
8. have spoken of another *day*.

Heb. 5: 7. in the *days* of his flesh,
7: 3. neither beginning of *days*,
27. needeth not *daily*, as those
8: 8. Behold, the *days* come, saith the Lord,
9. in the *day* when I took them
10. that I will make with the house of Israel after those *days*,
10:11. And every priest standeth *daily*
16. that I will make with them after those *days*,
25. as ye see the *day* approaching.
32. call to remembrance the former *days*,
11:30. were compassed about seven *days*.
12:10. For they verily for a few *days*
Jas. 5: 3. Ye have heaped treasure together for the last *days*.
5. as in a *day* of slaughter.
1Pet. 2:12. in the *day* of visitation.
3:10. he that will love life, and see good *days*,
20. in the *days* of Noah,
2Pet. 1:19. in a dark place, until the *day* dawn,
2: 8. (his) righteous soul from *day* to *day*
9. unto the *day* of judgment
13. to riot in the *day* time.
3: 3. that there shall come in the last *days*
7. against the *day* of judgment
8. one *day* (is) with the Lord as a thousand years, and a thousand years as one *day*.
10. But the *day* of the Lord will come
12. unto the coming of the *day* of God,
18. To him (be) glory both now and for ever. (εἰς ἡμέραν αἰῶνος)
1Joh. 4:17. in the *day* of judgment:
Jude 6. unto the judgment of the great *day*.
Rev. 1:10. I was in the Spirit on the Lord's *day*,
2:10. ye shall have tribulation ten *days*:
13. in those *days* wherein Antipas
4: 8. and they rest not *day* and night,
6:17. the great *day* of his wrath is come;
7:15. and serve him *day* and night
8:12. the *day* shone not for a third part
9: 6. And in those *days* shall men seek
15. a *day*, and a month, and
10: 7. But in the *days* of the voice
11: 3. a thousand two hundred (and) threescore *days*.
6. in the *days* of their prophecy:
9. three *days* and an half,
11. after three *days* and an half
12: 6. a thousand two hundred (and) threescore *days*.
10. before our God *day* and night.
14:11. and they have no rest *day* nor night,
16:14. of that great *day* of God Almighty.
18: 8. shall her plagues come in one *day*,
20:10. *day* and night for ever and ever.
21:25. shall not be shut at all by *day*.

2251 9 348/432 2349

ἡμέτερος, *heemeteros*.

Acts 2:11. we do hear them speak in *our* tongues
24: 6. according to *our* law.
26: 5. sect of *our* religion
Ro. 15: 4. were written for *our* learning.
1Co.15:31. I protest by your rejoicing (some read, *our* rejoicing)
2Ti. 4:15. he hath greatly withstood *our* words.
Tit. 3:14. And let *our's* also learn

1Joh. 1: 3. and truly *our* fellowship (is) with the Father, and with his Son Jesus Christ.
2: 2. and not for *our's* only, but also

ἡ μήν see after ἤ. 2229

2252 16 348/281 2358

ἤμην, *eemeen.*

From εἰμί.

Mat.25:35. I *was* a stranger, and ye took me in:
36. I *was* in prison, and ye came unto me.
43. I *was* a stranger, and ye took me not in:
Mar 14:49. I *was* daily with you in the temple
Joh.11:15. that I *was* not there,
16: 4. because I *was* with you.
17.12. While I *was* with them
Acts10:30. I *was* fasting until this hour;
11: 5. I *was* in the city of Joppa praying:
11. the house where I *was*,
17. what *was* I, that I could withstand God?
22:19. that I imprisoned (lit. *was* imprisoning)
20. I also *was* standing by,
1Co.13:11. When I *was* a child,
Gal. 1:10. I should not *be* the servant of Christ.
22. And *was* unknown by face

2253 1 348/432 rt 2255,2348

ἡμιθανής, *heemithanees.*

Lu. 10:30. leaving (him) *half dead*

2254 177 216/255 1473

ἡμῖν, *heemin.*

From ἐγώ.

Mat. 3:15. it becometh *us* to fulfil
6:11. Give *us* this day
12. forgive *us* our debts,
8:29. What have *we* to do with thee, Jesus,
31. suffer *us* to go away
13:36. Declare unto *us* the parable
15:15. Declare unto *us* this parable.
33. Whence should *we* have so much
19:27. what shall *we* have therefore?
20:12. thou hast made them equal unto *us*,
21:25. he will say unto *us*, Why
22:17. Tell *us* therefore, What thinkest thou?
25. Now there were with *us* seven
24: 3. Tell *us*, when shall these things
25: 8. Give *us* of your oil;
9. there be not enough for *us* and you:
11. Lord, Lord, open to *us*.
26:63. that thou tell *us* whether thou be
68. Prophesy unto *us*, thou Christ,
Mar. 1:24. what have *we* to do with thee, thou Jesus
9:22. compassion on us, and help *us*.
38. and he followeth not *us*: and we forbad him, because he followeth not *us*.
10:35. thou shouldest do for *us*
37. Grant unto *us* that we may sit, one on
12:19. Moses wrote unto *us*,
13: 4. Tell *us*, when shall these things
14:15. there make ready for *us*.
16: 3. Who shall roll *us* away the stone
Lu. 1: 1. are most surely believed among *us*,
2 Even as they delivered them unto *us*,
69. an horn of salvation *for us*
74(73). That he would grant unto *us*,
2:15. which the Lord hath made known unto *us*.
Lu. 2:48. why hast thou thus dealt with *us*?
4:34. what have *we* to do with thee, (thou) Jesus
7: 5. he hath built *us* a synagogue.
16. is risen up among *us*;
9:13. *We* have no more but five loaves
10:11. dust of your city, which cleaveth on *us*,
17. even the devils are subject unto *us*
11: 3. Give *us* day by day
4. forgive *us* our sins; for we also forgive every one that is indebted to *us*.
13:25. Lord, Lord, open unto *us*;
17: 5. Increase our (lit. to *us*) faith.
20: 2. Tell *us*, by what authority
22. Is it lawful for *us* to give tribute unto Cæsar,
28. Moses wrote unto *us*,
22: 8. and prepare *us* the passover,
67(66). Art thou the Christ? tell *us*.
23:18. and release unto *us* Barabbas:
24:24. certain of them which were with *us*
32. Did not our heart burn within *us*, while he talked with *us* by the way, and while he opened to *us* the scriptures?
Joh. 1:14. and dwelt among *us*,
2:18. What sign shewest thou unto *us*
4:12. which gave *us* the well,
25. he will tell *us* all things.
6:34. evermore give *us* this bread.
52. give *us* (his) flesh to eat?
8: 5. Moses in the law commanded *us*,
10:24. be the Christ, tell *us* plainly.
11:50. that it is expedient for *us*, that
14: 8. shew *us* the Father, and it sufficeth *us*.
9. Shew *us* the Father?
22. that thou wilt manifest thyself unto *us*,
16:17. What is this that he saith unto *us*,
17:21. they also may be one in *us*:
18:31. It is not lawful for *us* to put any man to
Acts 1:17. he was numbered with *us*,
21. which have companied with *us*.
22. be ordained to be a witness with *us*
2:29. is with *us* unto this day.
3:12. or why look ye so earnestly on *us*,
6:14. which Moses delivered *us*.
7:38. the lively oracles to give unto *us*:
40. Make *us* gods to go before us:
10:41. (even) to *us*, who did eat and drink
42. And he commanded *us*
11:13. And he shewed *us*
17. as (he did) unto *us*, who believed
13:33(32). unto *us* their children,
47. hath the Lord commanded *us*,
14:17. gave *us* rain from heaven,
15: 7. God made choice among *us*,
8. even as (he did) unto *us*;
25. It seemed good unto *us*, being
28. to the Holy Ghost, and to *us*,
16: 9. Come over into Macedonia, and help *us*.
16. possessed with a spirit of divination met *us*,
17. The same followed Paul and *us*,
— shew unto *us* the way
21. which are not lawful for *us* to receive,
19:27. this *our* craft is in danger
20:14. And when he met with *us*
21:16. with *us* also (certain)
18. with *us* unto James;
23. *We* have four men which have a vow
25:24. men which are here present with *us*,
27: 2. (one) Aristarchus...being with *us*.
28: 2. shewed *us* no little kindness:
15. they came to meet *us*.
22. for as concerning this sect, *we* know

Ro. 5: 5. which is given unto *us*.
8: 4. might be fulfilled in *us*,
32. freely give *us* all things?
9:29. had left *us* a seed,
12: 6. the grace that is given to *us*,
1 Co. 1:18. unto *us* which are saved it is the power
30. who of God is made unto *us* wisdom,
2:10. But God hath revealed (them) unto *us*
12. that are freely given to *us*
4: 6. that ye might learn in *us*
8: 6. But to *us* (there is but) one God, the
15:57. which giveth *us* the victory
2Co. 1: 8. which came to *us* in Asia,
4:12. So then death worketh in *us*,
17. worketh for *us* a far more exceeding
5: 5. hath given unto *us* the earnest
18. hath given to *us* the ministry
19. hath committed unto *us*
6:12. Ye are not straitened in *us*,
7: 7. when he told *us* your earnest desire,
8: 5. and unto *us* by the will of God.
7. (in) your love to *us*,
10: 8. hath given *us* for edification,
13. which God hath distributed to *us*,
Eph. 1: 9. Having made known unto *us* the mystery
3:20. that worketh in *us*,
6:12. *we* wrestle not against flesh
Col. 1: 8. Who also declared unto *us*
2:14. which was contrary to *us*,
4: 3. would open unto *us* a door of utterance,
1 Th. 2: 8. ye were dear unto *us*.
3: 6. brought *us* good tidings of
1 Ti. 6:17. giveth *us* richly all things to enjoy;
2Ti. 1: 7. For God hath not given *us*
9. which was given *us* in
14. which dwelleth in *us*.
Heb. 1: 2(1). spoken unto *us* by (his) Son,
4:13. with whom *we* have to do.
5:11. Of whom *we* have many things to say
7:26. For such an high priest became *us*,
10:15. also is a witness to *us*:
20. way, which he hath consecrated for *us*,
12: 1. *we* also are compassed about with
— the race that is set before *us*,
Jas. 3: 3. that they may obey *us*;
4: 5. that dwelleth in *us*
5:17. subject to like passions as *we* are,
1 Pet. 1:12. but unto *us* they did minister the things,
2:21. leaving *us* an example,
4: 3. time past of (our) life may suffice *us*
2 Pet. 1: 1. that have obtained like precious faith with *us*
3. given unto *us* all things
4. Whereby are given unto *us* exceeding
1 Joh. 1: 2. and was manifested unto *us*;
8. the truth is not in *us*.
9. to forgive *us* (our) sins,
10. his word is not in *us*.
2:25. he hath promised *us*,
3: 1. the Father hath bestowed upon *us*,
23. as he gave *us* commandment.
24. that he abideth in *us*, by the Spirit which he hath given *us*.
4: 9. the love of God toward *us*,
12. God dwelleth in *us*, and his love is perfected in *us*.
13. that we dwell in him, and he in *us*, because he hath given *us* of his Spirit.
16. that God hath to *us*.
5:11. God hath given to *us*
20. hath given *us* an understanding,
2 Joh. 2 the truth's sake, which dwelleth in *us*,

2255 5 348/ cf 260

ἥμισυ, heemisu.

Mar. 6:23. unto the *half* of my kingdom.
Lu. 19: 8. the *half* of my goods I give to the poor;
Rev. 11: 9. three days and an *half*,
11. three days and an *half*
12:14. for a time, and times, and *half* a time,

2256 1 348/432 rt 2255,5610

ἡμιώριον, heemiōrion.

Rev. 8: 1. about the space of *half an hour*.

2257 410 216/254 1473

ἡμῶν, heemōn.

From ἐγώ.

Mat. 1:23. being interpreted is, God with *us*.
6: 9. *Our* Father which art in heaven,
11. Give us this day *our* daily bread.
12. forgive us *our* debts, as we forgive *our* debtors.
8:17. Himself took *our* infirmities,
15:23. she crieth after *us*.
20:33. *our* eyes may be opened.
21:42. marvellous in *our* eyes?
23:30. the days of *our* fathers,
25: 8. *our* lamps are gone out.
27:25. and on *our* children.
28:13. and stole him (away) while *we* slept.
Mar. 9:40. For he that is not against *us* is on *our*
11:10. of *our* father David,
12: 7. and the inheritance shall be *our's*.
11. marvellous in *our* eyes?
29. The Lord *our* God is one Lord:
Lu. 1:55. As he spake to *our* fathers,
71. That we should be saved from *our*
72. (promised) to *our* fathers,
73. to *our* father Abraham,
74. out of the hand of *our* enemies
75. the days of *our* life.
78. Through the tender mercy of *our* God;
79. to guide *our* feet into the way
7: 5. For he loveth *our* nation,
9:49. he followeth not with *us*.
50. Forbid (him) not: for he that is not against *us* is for *us*.
11: 2. *Our* Father which art in heaven,
3. Give us day by day *our* daily bread
4. And forgive us *our* sins;
13:26. thou hast taught in *our* streets.
16:26. between *us* and you there is
20:14. that the inheritance may be *our's*.
24:20. and *our* rulers delivered him
22. certain women also of *our company* (lit. of *us*)
29. saying, Abide with *us*:
32. Did not *our* heart burn
Joh. 3:11. ye receive not *our* witness.
4:12. than *our* father Jacob,
20. *Our* fathers worshipped in this
6:31. *Our* fathers did eat manna
7:51. Doth *our* law judge
8:39. Abraham is *our* father.
53. than *our* father Abraham,
9:20. We know that this is *our* son.
10:24. dost thou make us (lit. *our* soul) to
11:11. *Our* friend Lazarus sleepeth;
48. take away both *our* place
12:38. hath believed *our* report?
19: 7. by *our* law he ought
Acts 1:22. that he was taken up from *us*,

Acts 2:8. in *our* own tongue,
39. the Lord *our* God
3:13 the God of *our* fathers,
25. which God made with *our* fathers,
5:30. The God of *our* fathers
7: 2. unto *our* father Abraham,
11. *our* fathers found no sustenance.
12. he sent out *our* fathers first.
15. he, and *our* fathers,
19. dealt subtilly with *our* kindred, and evil entreated *our* fathers,
38. and (with) *our* fathers:
39. *our* fathers would not obey,
40. Make us gods to go before *us:*
44. *Our* fathers had the tabernacle
45. *our* fathers that came after
— before the face of *our* fathers,
13:17. chose *our* fathers, and exalted
14:17. *our* hearts with food and gladness.
15: 9. between *us* and them,
10. neither *our* fathers nor we
24. which went out from *us*
25. with *our* beloved Barnabas and Paul,
26. of *our* Lord Jesus Christ.
36. and visit *our* brethren
16:16. as *we* went to prayer,
20. do exceedingly trouble *our* city,
17:20. strange things to *our* ears:
27. from every one of *us:*
19:25. we have *our* wealth.
20:21. toward *our* Lord Jesus Christ.
21:10. And as *we* tarried (there)
17. And when *we* were come
22:14. The God of *our* fathers
24: 4. that thou wouldest hear *us*
7. took (him) away out of *our* hands,
26: 7. *our* twelve tribes,
14. when *we* were all fallen to the earth,
27:10. but also of *our* lives.
18. *we* being exceedingly tossed
27. as *we* were driven up and down in
28:15. when the brethren heard of *us*,
25. Esaias the prophet unto *our* fathers,
Ro. 1: 3(4). Jesus Christ *our* Lord,
7. from God *our* Father,
3: 5. But if *our* unrighteousness
4: 1. that Abraham, *our* father
12. of *our* father Abraham,
16. who is the father of *us* all,
24. Jesus *our* Lord from the dead;
25. for *our* offences, and was raised again for *our* justification.
5: 1. through *our* Lord Jesus Christ:
5. is shed abroad in *our* hearts
6. when *we* were yet without strength,
8. in that, while *we* were yet sinners, Christ died for *us*.
11. through *our* Lord Jesus
21. by Jesus Christ *our* Lord.
6: 6. that *our* old man is crucified with
11. through Jesus Christ *our* Lord.
23. through Jesus Christ *our* Lord.
7: 5. did work in *our* members
25. through Jesus Christ *our* Lord.
8:16. beareth witness with *our* spirit,
23. the redemption of *our* body.
26. helpeth *our* infirmities:
— maketh intercession for *us*
31. If God (be) for *us*, who (can be) against *us?*
32. but delivered him up for *us* all.
34. maketh intercession for *us*

Ro. 8:39. in Christ Jesus *our* Lord.
9:10. (even) by *our* father Isaac;
10:16. who hath believed *our* report?
13:11. (is) *our* salvation nearer
14: 7. For none of *us* liveth to himself,
12. So then every one of *us*
15: 2. Let every one of *us* please
6. the Father of *our* Lord Jesus
30. for the (lit. *our*) Lord Jesus Christ's sake,
16: 1. I commend unto you Phebe *our* sister,
9. *our* helper in Christ,
18. *our* Lord Jesus Christ,
20. The grace of *our* Lord Jesus
24. The grace of *our* Lord Jesus
1Co. 1: 2. the name of Jesus Christ *our* Lord, both theirs and *our's:*
3. from God *our* Father,
7. the coming of *our* Lord
8. the day of *our* Lord Jesus Christ.
9. Jesus Christ *our* Lord.
10. the name of *our* Lord
2: 7. before the world unto *our* glory:
4: 8. ye have reigned as kings without *us:*
5: 4. name of *our* Lord Jesus
— the power of *our* Lord Jesus Christ,
7. Christ *our* passover is sacrificed for *us:*
6:11. by the Spirit of *our* God.
9: 1. have I not seen Jesus Christ *our* Lord?
10: 1. all *our* fathers were under the cloud,
6. were *our* examples, to the intent
11. they are written for *our* admonition,
12:23. and *our* uncomely (parts)
24. For *our* comely (parts)
15: 3. that Christ died for *our* sins
14. then (is) *our* preaching vain,
31. in Christ Jesus *our* Lord,
57. through *our* Lord Jesus Christ.
2Co. 1: 2. from God *our* Father,
3. of *our* Lord Jesus Christ,
4. in all *our* tribulation,
5. *our* consolation also aboundeth
7(6). And *our* hope of you
8. have you ignorant of *our* trouble
11. helping together by prayer for *us*,
— thanks may be given by many on *our* behalf.
12. *our* rejoicing is this, the testimony of *our* conscience,
14. even as ye also (are) *our's*
18. *our* word toward you was not
19. who was preached among you by *us*,
20. unto the glory of God by *us*.
22. given the earnest of the Spirit in *our* hearts.
2:14. the savour of his knowledge by *us*
3: 2. Ye are *our* epistle written in *our* hearts,
3. the epistle of Christ ministered by *us*,
5. *our* sufficiency (is) of God;
4: 3. But if *our* gospel be hid,
6. hath shined in *our* hearts,
7. may be of God, and not of *us*.
10. might be made manifest in *our* body.
11. be made manifest in *our* mortal flesh.
16. though *our* outward man perish,
17. *our* light affliction, which is but
18. While *we* look not at the things
5: 1. we know that if *our* earthly house
2. with *our* house which is from heaven:
12. to glory on *our* behalf,
20. did beseech (you) by *us:*
21. he hath made him (to be) sin for *us*,
6:11. *our* mouth is open unto you, *our* heart enlarged.
7: 3. that ye are in *our* hearts

2Co. 7: 4. in all *our* tribulation.
5. For, when *we* were come into Macedonia, *our* flesh had no rest,
9. ye might receive damage by *us*
12. that *our* care for you (many copies read "your care for *us*")
14. *our* boasting, which (I made) before
8: 4. Praying *us* with much intreaty
9. the grace of *our* Lord Jesus Christ,
19. to travel with *us* with this grace, which is administered by *us*
20. which is administered by *us*:
22. with them *our* brother,
23. or *our* brethren (be enquired of),
24. and of *our* boasting
9: 3. *our* boasting of you
11. causeth through *us* thanksgiving
10: 4. the weapons of *our* warfare
8. boast somewhat more of *our* authority,
15. according to *our* rule
11:31. Father of *our* Lord Jesus
Gal. 1: 3. the Father, and (from) *our* Lord Jesus
4. Who gave himself for *our* sins,
— the will of God and *our* Father:
2: 4. to spy out *our* liberty
3:13. being made a curse for *us*:
24. the law was *our* schoolmaster
4:26. the mother of *us* all.
6:14. the cross of *our* Lord Jesus
18. the grace of *our* Lord Jesus Christ
Eph. 1: 2. from God *our* Father,
3. Father of *our* Lord Jesus Christ,
14. the earnest of *our* inheritance
17. the God of *our* Lord Jesus Christ,
2: 3. the lusts of *our* flesh,
14. For he is *our* peace,
3:11. in Christ Jesus *our* Lord:
14. the Father of *our* Lord Jesus Christ,
4: 7. But unto every one of *us*
5: 2. hath given himself for *us* an offering
20. in the name of *our* Lord Jesus
6:22. that ye might know *our* affairs,
24. *our* Lord Jesus Christ
Phi. 1: 2. from God *our* Father,
3:20. For *our* conversation is in heaven;
21. Who shall change *our* vile body,
4:20. unto God and *our* Father (be) glory
23. The grace of *our* Lord Jesus Christ
Col. 1: 2. from God *our* Father
3. the Father of *our* Lord Jesus
7. *our* dear fellowservant,
2:14. that was against *us*,
3: 4. Christ, (who is) *our* life, shall appear,
4: 3. Withal praying also for *us*,
1Th. 1: 1. from God *our* Father,
2. making mention of you in *our* prayers;
3. of hope in *our* Lord Jesus Christ, in the sight of God and *our* Father;
5. *our* gospel came not unto you in word
6. And ye became followers of *us*,
9. themselves shew of *us* what manner
2: 1. *our* entrance in unto you,
2. we were bold in *our* God to speak unto you
3. For *our* exhortation (was) not of
4. but God, which trieth *our* hearts.
9. ye remember, brethren, *our* labour and
13. the word of God which ye heard of *us*,
19. For what (is) *our* hope,
— in the presence of *our* Lord Jesus Christ
20. For ye are *our* glory and joy.
3: 2. *our* brother, and minister of God, and *our* fellowlabourer in
1Th. 3: 5. *our* labour be in vain.
6. that ye have good remembrance of *us*
7. *our* affliction and distress
9. we joy for your sakes before *our* God,
11. God himself and *our* Father, and *our* Lord Jesus Christ, direct *our* way unto you.
13. even *our* Father, at the coming of *our*
4: 1. ye have received of *us*
5: 9. by *our* Lord Jesus
10. Who died for *us*,
23. of *our* Lord Jesus Christ.
25. Brethren, pray for *us*.
28. The grace of *our* Lord Jesus Christ
2Th. 1: 1. in God *our* Father
2. from God *our* Father
7. to you who are troubled rest with *us*,
8. of *our* Lord Jesus Christ:
10. *our* testimony among you
11. *our* God would count you worthy of (this) calling,
12. the name of *our* Lord Jesus Christ
— according to the grace of *our* God
2: 1. by the coming of *our* Lord Jesus Christ, and (by) *our* gathering together unto
2. by letter as from *us*,
14. by *our* gospel, to the obtaining of the glory of *our* Lord Jesus Christ.
15. whether by word, or *our* epistle.
16. *our* Lord Jesus Christ himself, and God, even *our* Father,
3: 1. pray for *us*, that the word
6. in the name of *our* Lord Jesus
— the tradition which he received of *us*.
12. by *our* Lord Jesus Christ,
14. And if any man obey not *our* word
18. The grace of *our* Lord Jesus
1Ti. 1: 1. of God *our* Saviour, and Lord Jesus Christ, (which is) *our* hope;
2. from God *our* Father and Jesus Christ *our*
12. And I thank Christ Jesus *our* Lord,
14. the grace of *our* Lord was exceeding
2: 3. in the sight of God *our* Saviour;
6: 3. the words of *our* Lord Jesus Christ,
14. the appearing of *our* Lord Jesus Christ:
2Ti. 1: 2. Christ Jesus *our* Lord.
8. the testimony of *our* Lord,
9. not according to *our* works,
10. of *our* Saviour Jesus Christ,
Tit. 1: 3. the commandment of God *our* Saviour;
4. Jesus Christ *our* Saviour.
2:10. the doctrine of God *our* Saviour
13. and *our* Saviour Jesus Christ;
14. Who gave himself for *us*,
3: 4. love of God *our* Saviour
6. through Jesus Christ *our* Saviour;
Philem. 1. *our* dearly beloved, and fellowlabourer,
2. and Archippus *our* fellowsoldier,
3. from God *our* Father
25. The grace of *our* Lord Jesus
Heb 1: 3. when he had by himself purged *our* sins,
3: 1. and high priest of *our* profession,
4:15. with the feeling of *our* infirmities;
6:20. the forerunner is for *us* entered,
7:14. *our* Lord sprang out of Juda;
9:24. in the presence of God for *us*.
10:26. if *we* sin wilfully after that we have
11:40. some better thing for *us*, that they without *us* should not
12: 9. we have had fathers of *our* flesh
29. *our* God (is) a consuming fire.
13:18. Pray for *us*: for we trust
20. again from the dead *our* Lord Jesus,

Jas. 2: 1. the faith of *our* Lord Jesus Christ,
21. Was not Abraham *our* father justified
3: 6. so is the tongue among *our* members.
1Pet. 1: 3. Father of *our* Lord Jesus
2:21. because Christ also suffered for *us*.
24. Who his own self bare *our* sins
4: 1. hath suffered for *us*
17. and if (it) first (begin) at *us*,
2Pet. 1: 1. of God and *our* Saviour
2. and of Jesus *our* Lord,
8. the knowledge of *our* Lord Jesus Christ.
11. of *our* Lord and Saviour Jesus
14. *our* Lord Jesus Christ hath shewed
16. the power and coming of *our* Lord
3: 2. of the commandment of *us* the apostles
15. the longsuffering of *our* Lord (is) salvation: even as *our* beloved brother Paul
18. of *our* Lord and Saviour Jesus
1Joh. 1: 1. with *our* eyes, which we have looked upon, and *our* hands have handled,
3. may have fellowship with *us*:
9. If we confess *our* sins, he is faithful
2: 2. he is the propitiation for *our* sins:
19. They went out from *us*, but they were not of *us*; for if they had been of *us*, they would (no doubt) have continued with *us*:
— they were not all of *us*.
3: 5. to take away *our* sins;
16. because he laid down his life for *us*
19. and shall assure *our* hearts
20. if our heart condemn *us*, God is greater than *our* heart, and
21. Beloved, if *our* heart condemn *us* not,
4: 6. heareth *us*; he that is not of God heareth not *us*.
10. (to be) the propitiation for *our* sins.
17. Herein is *our* love (lit. love with *us*) made perfect,
5: 4. (even) *our* faith.
14. according to his will, he heareth *us*:
15. And if we know that he hear *us*,
2Joh. 2. and shall be with *us* for ever.
12. that *our* joy may be full.
3Joh. 12. ye know that *our* record is true.
Jude 4. turning the grace of *our* God into
— and *our* Lord Jesus Christ.
17. the apostles of *our* Lord Jesus Christ;
21. the mercy of *our* Lord Jesus Christ
25. To the only wise God *our* Saviour, (be)
Rev. 1: 5. washed us from *our* sins in his own blood,
5:10. And hast made us unto *our* God kings and
6:10. avenge *our* blood on them that dwell
7: 3. the servants of *our* God
10. Salvation to *our* God (τῷ θεῷ ἡμῶν most copies omit this) which sitteth upon the throne, (some copies read, to him which sitteth upon the throne of *our* God)
12. power, and might, (be) unto *our* God
11: 8. where also *our* Lord was crucified.
15. (the kingdoms) of *our* Lord, and of
12:10. and the kingdom of *our* God,
— the accuser of *our* brethren is cast down, which accused them before *our* God
19: 1. and power, unto the Lord *our* God:
5. Praise *our* God, all ye his servants,
22:21. The grace of *our* Lord Jesus Christ

2258 454 221/281 1510

ἦν, ἦς, ἦσθα, &c., *een, ees, eestha*, &c.

From εἰμί.

Mat. 1:18. the birth of Jesus Christ *was* on this wise:
2: 9. where the young child *was*.
15. And *was* there until
3: 4. and his meat *was* locusts and
4:18. for they *were* fishers.
7:27. great *was* the fall of it.
29. For he taught (lit. *was* teaching) them
8:30. there *was* a good way off from them an
9:36. because they fainted, (lit. *were* fainting)
12: 4. which *was* not lawful for him to eat,
10. there *was* a man which had (his) hand
40. For as Jonas *was* three days
14:21. *were* about five thousand men,
23. he *was* there alone.
24. *was* now in the midst of the sea, tossed with waves: for the wind *was* contrary.
15:38. *were* four thousand men,
19:22. for he had (lit. *was* having) great
21:25. The baptism of John, whence *was* it?
33. There *was* a certain housholder,
22: 8. they which were bidden *were* not worthy.
25. Now there *were* with us
23:30. If we *had been* in the days of our fathers, we would not *have been* partakers
24:38. before the flood they *were* eating and
25: 2. And five of them *were* wise,
21. thou *hast been* faithful over a few things,
23. thou *hast been* faithful over a few things,
26:24. it *had been* good for that man if
43. for their eyes *were* heavy.
69. Thou also *wast* with Jesus
71. This (fellow) *was* also with Jesus
27:54. this *was* the Son of God.
55. And many women *were* there,
56. Among which *was* Mary Magdalene,
61. And there *was* Mary Magdalene,
28: 3. His countenance *was* like lightning,
Mar. 1: 6. And John *was* clothed with camel's hair,
13. And he *was* there in the wilderness
— and *was* with the wild beasts;
16. for they *were* fishers.
22. for he taught (lit. *was* teaching) them
23. And there *was* in their synagogue
33. all the city *was* gathered together
39. And he preached (lit. *was* preaching) in
45. *was* without in desert places:
2: 4. the roof where he *was*:
6. But there *were* certain of the scribes
15. for there *were* many,
18. the disciples of John and of the Pharisees *used* to fast: (lit. *were* fasting)
3: 1. and there *was* a man there
4: 1. multitude *was* by the sea on the land.
36. even as he *was* in the ship. And there *were* also with him other little ships.
38. And he *was* in the hinder part of the
5: 5. he *was* in the mountains, and in the tombs
11. Now there *was* there nigh unto the
13. they *were* about two thousand;
21. and he *was* nigh unto the sea.
40. where the damsel *was* lying.
42. for she *was* (of the age) of twelve years.
6:31. for there *were* many coming
34. they *were* as sheep not
44. that did eat of the loaves *were* about
47. the ship *was* in the midst of the sea,
48. for the wind *was* contrary
52. for their heart *was* hardened.
7:26. The woman *was* a Greek,
8: 9. And they that had eaten *were* about
9: 4. and they *were* talking with
6. for they *were* sore afraid.
10:22. for he had (lit. *was* having) great

Mar.10:32. they *were* in the way going up to Jerusalem; and Jesus went before them: (lit. *was* going before)
11:13. for the time of figs *was* not (yet).
30. *was* (it) from heaven, or of men?
32. that he *was* a prophet indeed.
12:20. Now there *were* seven brethren:
14: 1. *was* (the feast of) the passover,
4. And there *were* some that had indignation
21. good *were* it for that man if he had
40. for their eyes *were* heavy,
54. and he sat (lit. *was* sitting) with the servants,
56. their witness agreed not together. (lit. *were* not commensurate)
59. neither so did their witness agree together. (lit. *was* not commensurate)
67. And thou also *wast* with
15: 7. And there *was* (one) named Barabbas,
25. And it *was* the third hour,
26. the superscription of his accusation *was*
39. *was* the Son of God.
40. There *were* also women looking on afar off: among whom *was* Mary
41. when he *was* in Galilee,
42. because it *was* the preparation,
43. which also waited for (lit. who also himself *was* waiting for) the kingdom of God,
46. which *was* hewn out of a rock,
16: 4. for it *was* very great.
Lu. 1: 6. And they *were* both righteous
7. And they had no child (lit. there *was* not a child to them), because that Elisabeth *was* barren, and they both *were*
10. *were* praying without
21. And the people waited for (lit. *was* waiting for)
22. he beckoned (lit. *was* beckoning) unto them,
66. the hand of the Lord *was* with him.
80. and *was* in the deserts
2: 7. because there *was* no room for them
8. there *were* in the same country shepherds
25. there *was* a man in Jerusalem,
— the Holy Ghost *was* upon him.
26. it *was* revealed unto him
33. And Joseph and his mother marvelled (lit. *were* marvelling)
36. And there *was* one Anna, a prophetess,
40. the grace of God *was* upon him.
51. *was* subject unto them:
3:23. Jesus himself began to be (lit. *was*) about
4:16. where he *had been* brought up:
17. where it *was* written,
20. *were* fastened on him.
25. many widows *were* in Israel in the
27. And many lepers *were* in Israel
31. and taught them (lit. *was* teaching)
32. his word *was* with power.
33. in the synagogue there *was* a man,
38. *was* taken with a great fever;
44. And he preached (lit. *was* preaching) in the synagogues
5: 1. he stood (lit. *was* standing) by the lake of Gennesaret,
3. of the ships, which *was* Simon's,
10. which *were* partners with Simon.
16. And he withdrew (lit. *was* withdrawing) himself
17. as he *was* teaching, that there *were* Pharisees and doctors of the law sitting by, which *were* come out of

Lu. 5:17. the power of the Lord *was* (present) to heal them.
18. which *was* taken with a palsy:
29. and there *was* a great company of publicans and of others that sat down (lit. *were* sitting down) with them.
6: 6. and there *was* a man whose right hand *was* withered.
12. and continued all night (lit *was* cont.)
7: 2. who *was* dear unto him,
12. a widow: and much people of the city *was* with her.
37. which *was* a sinner,
39. This man, if he *were* a prophet,
41. There was a certain creditor which *had* two
8: 2. which *had been* healed
32. And there *was* there an herd of many
40. for they *were* all waiting
42. he *had* one only daughter
9:14. For they *were* about five thousand men.
30. which *were* Moses and Elias:
32. *were* heavy with sleep:
45. and it *was* hid from them,
53. his face *was* as though he would go to
10:39. And she *had* a sister
11:14. And he *was* casting out a devil, and it *was* dumb.
13:10. And he *was* teaching in one.
11. *was* a woman which had a spirit of infirmity eighteen years, and *was* bowed
14: 1. they watched him. (lit. *were* watching)
2. there *was* a certain man before him which had the dropsy.
15: 1. Then drew near (lit. *were* &c.) unto him
24. this my son *was* dead, and is alive again he *was* lost, and is found.
25. Now his elder son *was* in the field:
32. this thy brother *was* dead, and is alive again; and *was* lost, and is found.
16: 1. There *was* a certain rich man,
19. There *was* a certain rich man,
20. there *was* a certain beggar named Lazarus
17:16. and he *was* a Samaritan.
18: 2. There *was* in a city a judge,
3. And there *was* a widow in that city;
23. for he *was* very rich.
34. and this saying *was* hid
19: 2. which *was* the chief among the publicans, and he *was* rich.
3. he *was* little of stature.
47. And he taught (lit. *was* teaching) daily
20: 4. *was* it from heaven, or of men?
29. There *were* therefore seven brethren:
21:37. And in the day time he *was* teaching in the temple;
22:56. This man *was* also with him.
59. this (fellow) also *was* with him:
23: 8. for he *was* desirous to see him of a long (season),
19. and for murder, *was* cast into prison.
38. And a superscription also *was* written
44. And it *was* about the sixth hour,
47. Certainly this *was* a righteous man.
51. The same had not consented (lit. *was* not consenting)
53. wherein never man before *was* laid.
54. And that day *was* the preparation,
55. the women also, which came (lit. *were* come) with him
24:10. It *was* Mary Magdalene, and Joanna,
13. behold, two of them went (lit. *were* going) that same day

Lu. 24:32. Did not our heart burn within us, (lit. *was* not...burning)
53. And *were* continually in the temple,
Joh. 1: 1. In the beginning *was* the Word, and the Word *was* with God, and the Word *was*
2. The same *was* in the beginning with
4. In him *was* life; and the life *was* the light
8. He *was* not that Light,
9. (That) *was* the true Light,
10. He *was* in the world,
15. This *was* he of whom I spake,
— he *was* before me.
24. *were* of the Pharisees.
28. where John *was* baptizing.
30. for he *was* before me.
39(40). for it *was* about the tenth hour.
40(41). *was* Andrew, Simon Peter's brother.
44(45). Now Philip *was* of Bethsaida,
2: 1. and the mother of Jesus *was*
6. And there *were* set there six waterpots
13. And the Jews' passover *was* at hand,
23. Now when he *was* in Jerusalem
25. for he knew what *was* in man.
3: 1. There *was* a man of the Pharisees,
19. because their deeds *were* evil.
23. John also *was* baptizing in Ænon near to Salim, because there *was* much water
24. For John *was* not yet cast
26. he that *was* with thee beyond
4: 6. Now Jacob's well *was* there.
— (and) it *was* about the sixth hour.
46. And there *was* a certain nobleman,
5: 1. After this there *was* a feast
5. And a certain man *was* there,
9. and on the same day *was* the sabbath.
35. He *was* a burning and a shining light:
6: 4. And the passover, a feast of the Jews, *was*
10. Now there *was* much grass
22. there *was* none other boat there,
62. where he *was* before?
7: 2. Now the Jews' feast of tabernacles *was* at
12. there *was* much murmuring
39. for the Holy Ghost *was* not yet (given);
42. town of Bethlehem, where David *was*?
8:39. If ye *were* Abraham's children,
42. If God *were* your Father,
44. He *was* a murderer from
9: 8. before had seen him that he *was* blind,
14. And it *was* the sabbath day when
16. And there *was* a division among them.
18. that he *had been* blind,
24. the man that *was* blind,
33. If this man *were* not of God,
41. If ye *were* blind, ye should
10: 6. what things they *were* which he spake unto them.
22. and it *was* winter.
40. where John at first baptized; (lit. *was* baptizing)
41. that John spake of this man *were* true.
11: 1. a certain (man) *was* sick, (named) Lazarus,
2. It *was* (that) Mary which anointed
6. he abode two days still in the same place where he *was*.
15. that I *was* not there,
18. Now Bethany *was* nigh
21. if thou *hadst been* here, my brother
30. but *was* in that place where
32. when Mary was come where Jesus *was*,
— if thou *hadst been* here,
38. It *was* a cave, and a stone lay upon it.
41. where the dead *was* laid.

Joh. 11:55. And the Jews' passover *was* nigh at hand:
12: 1. where Lazarus *was* which had been dead.
2. *was* one of them that sat at the table with.
6. but because he *was* a thief,
16. that these things *were* written of him,
20. And there *were* certain Greeks
13: 5. wherewith he *was* girded.
23. Now there *was* leaning
30. and it *was* night.
15:19. If ye *were* of the world,
17: 6. thine they *were*, and thou gavest them me;
18: 1. the brook Cedron, where *was* a garden,
10. The servant's name *was* Malchus.
13. for he *was* father in law to Caiaphas, which *was* the high priest
14. Now Caiaphas *was* he, which gave counsel
15. *was* known unto the high priest,
16. which *was* known unto the high priest,
18. for it *was* cold:
— and Peter stood (lit. *was* standing) with
25. And Simon Peter stood (lit. *was* &c.)
28. and it *was* early;
30. If he *were* not a malefactor,
36. if my kingdom *were* of this world,
40. Now Barabbas *was* a robber.
19:11. except it *were* given thee from above:
14. And it *was* the preparation of the passover,
19. And the writing *was*,
20. *was* nigh to the city: and it *was* written in Hebrew,
23. now the coat *was* without seam,
31. because it *was* the preparation,
— for that sabbath day *was* an high day,
41. Now in the place where he was crucified there *was* a garden;
42. the sepulchre *was* nigh at hand.
20: 7. the napkin, that *was* about his head,
19. where the disciples *were* assembled
24. *was* not with them
26. again his disciples *were* within,
21: 2. There *were* together Simon Peter, and
7. for he *was* naked,
8. for they *were* not far from land,
18. When thou *wast* young, thou girdedst
Acts 1:10. while they looked stedfastly (lit. *were* looking st.)
13. where abode (lit. *were* abiding) both Peter and James, and
14. These all continued (lit. *were* continuing) with one accord in prayer and
15. the number of the names together *were* about an hundred and twenty,
17. For he *was* numbered with us,
2: 1. they *were* all with one accord in one
2. where they *were* sitting.
5. And there *were* dwelling at Jerusalem
24. because it *was* not possible that he
42. And they continued (lit. *were* c.) stedfastly in
44. all that believed *were* together,
3:10. that it *was* he which sat for alms
4: 3. for it *was* now eventide.
6. as many as *were* of the kindred of the high priest,
13. that they *had been* with Jesus.
22. For the man *was* above forty years old,
31. where they *were* assembled together;
32. *were* of one heart and of one soul:
— they had (lit. to them *were*) all things common.
33. and great grace *was* upon them all.
5:12. and they *were* all with one accord

Acts 7: 9. but God *was* with him,
20. and *was* exceeding fair,
22. and *was* mighty in words and in deeds.
44. Our fathers *had* the tabernacle
8: 1. *was* consenting unto his death.
13. he continued (lit. *was* c.) with Philip,
16. For as yet he *was* fallen upon none
27. who had the charge of (lit. who *was* over) all her treasure,
28. *Was* returning, and sitting in his
32. the scripture which he read *was* this,
9: 9. And he *was* three days
10. And there *was* a certain disciple
28. he *was* with them coming in
33. and *was* sick of the palsy.
36. there *was* at Joppa a certain disciple
— this woman *was* full of good works
10: 1. There *was* a certain man in Cæsarea
24. Cornelius waited for them, (lit. *was* w.)
38. God *was* with him.
11:20. And some of them *were* men of
21. And the hand of the Lord *was* with them:
24. For he *was* a good man,
12: 3. Then *were* the days of unleavened bread.
5. but prayer *was* made without ceasing
6. Peter *was* sleeping
12. where many *were* gathered together
18. there *was* no small stir
20. And Herod *was* highly displeased
13: 1. Now there *were* in the church that was at Antioch certain
7. Which *was* with the deputy of the country,
46. It *was* necessary that the word of God
48. as many as *were* ordained
14: 4. part *held* with the Jews,
7. And there they preached (lit. *were* preaching) the gospel.
12. he *was* the chief speaker.
26. from whence they *had been* recommended
16: 1. a certain disciple *was* there,
9. There stood (lit. *was* standing) a man of Macedonia,
12. and we *were* in that city
17: 1. where *was* a synagogue
11. These *were* more noble
18: 3. they *were* tentmakers.
7. joined hard (lit. *was* adjacent) to the synagogue.
14. If it *were* a matter of wrong
25. This man *was* instructed
19: 7. And all the men *were* about twelve.
14. And there *were* seven sons
16. in whom the evil spirit *was*
32. for the assembly *was* confused;
20: 8. there *were* many lights in the upper chamber, where they *were* gathered
13. for so had (lit. *was*) he appointed,
16. if it *were* possible for him,
21: 3. for there the ship *was* to unlade.
9. And the same man *had* four daughters,
29. For they had seen before (lit. *were* having seen before)
22:29. because he had bound him. (lit. *was* having bound)
23:13. And they *were* more than forty
27: 8. nigh whereunto *was* the city (of) Lasea.
37. And we *were* in all in the ship
Ro. 5:13. sin *was* in the world:
6:17. that ye *were* the servants
20. For when ye *were* the servants of sin, ye *were* free from
7: 5. For when we *were* in the flesh,

1Co. 6:11. And such *were* some of you.
10: 1. *were* under the cloud,
4. and that Rock *was* Christ.
12: 2. Ye know that ye *were* Gentiles,
19. And if they *were* all one member,
16:12. but his will *was* not at all
2Co. 5:19. that God *was* in Christ,
Gal. 1:23. But they had heard (lit. *were* hearing)
2: 6. whatsoever they *were*,
11. because he *was* to be blamed.
3:21. righteousness should *have been* by the law.
4: 3. Even so we, when we *were* children, *were* in bondage
15. Where *is* then the blessedness
Eph. 2: 3. and *were* by nature the children of wrath,
12. That at that time ye *were*
5: 8. For ye *were* sometimes darkness,
Phi. 2:26. he longed after (lit. *was* longing after) you all,
3: 7. what things *were* gain to me,
Col. 2:14. that *was* against us,
1Th. 3: 4. when we *were* with you,
2Th. 3:10. when we *were* with you,
Tit. 3: 3. For we ourselves also *were* sometimes
Heb 2:15. *were* all their lifetime subject to bondage.
7:10. he *was* yet in the loins of his father,
11. If therefore perfection *were* by the
8: 4. For if he *were* on earth, he should not *be* a priest,
7. if that first (covenant) *had been* faultless,
11:38. Of whom the world *was* not worthy:
12:21. And so terrible *was* the sight,
Jas. 1:24. forgetteth what manner of man he *was*.
5:17. *was* a man subject to like passions as we
1Pet. 2:25. For ye *were* as sheep going astray;
2Pet. 2:21. For it *had been* better for them
3: 5. the heavens *were* of old,
1Joh. 1: 1. That which *was* from the beginning,
2. which *was* with the Father,
2:19. but they *were* not of us; for if they *had been* of us,
3:12. (who) *was* of that wicked one,
— Because his own works *were* evil,
Rev. 1: 4. which is, and which *was*, and which is to
8. the Lord, which is, and which *was*, and
4: 3. *was* to look upon like a
8. which *was*, and is, and is to come.
9: 8. *were* as (the teeth) of lions.
10. there *were* stings in their tails:
10:10. and it *was* in my mouth
11:17. which art, and *wast*, and art to come;
13: 2. *was* like unto a leopard,
16: 5. O Lord, which art, and *wast*, and shalt be,
17: 8. The beast that thou sawest *was*, and is
— the beast that *was*, and is not, and yet is.
11. the beast that *was*, and is not,
18:23. *were* the great men of the earth;
21:18. And the building of the wall of it *was* (of)
21. every several gate *was* of one pearl:

2259 2 348/432

ἡνίκα, *heenika.*

2Co. 3:15. *when* Moses is read,
16. Nevertheless *when* it shall turn to the

2260 1 349/

ἤπερ see after ἤ. p. 342

2261 2 349/432 2031

ἤπιος, *eepios.*

1Th. 2: 7. But we were *gentle* among you,
2Ti. 2:24. must not strive; but be *gentle* unto all

2263 1 349/432 2048

ἤρεμος, *eeremos.*

1 Ti. 2: 2. that we may lead a *quiet* and peaceable

2270 5 349/434 rt 2272

ἡσυχάζω, *heesukazo.*

Lu. 14: 4(3). And they *held* their *peace.*
23:56. and *rested* the sabbath day according
Acts11:18. they *held* their *peace,* and glorified God,
21:14. not be persuaded, we *ceased,* saying,
1Th. 4:11. that ye study *to be quiet,*

2271 4 350/434 2272

ἡσυχία, *heesukia.*

Acts22: 2. they kept the more *silence:*
2Th. 3:12. that with *quietness* they work,
1Ti. 2:11. Let the woman learn in *silence*
12. but to be in *silence.*

2272 2 350/434 rt 1476,2192

ἡσύχιος, *heesukios.*

1Ti. 2: 2. we may lead a quiet and *peaceable* life
1Pet.3: 4. of a meek and *quiet* spirit,

2273 1 350/

ἤτοι see after ἤ. p. 342

2274 3 350/434 rt 2276

ἡττάομαι, *heetaomai.*

2Co.12:13. For what is it wherein you *were inferior*
2Pet.2:19. for of whom a man *is overcome,*
20. they are again entangled therein, and *overcome.*

2275 2 350/434 2274

ἥττημα, *heeteema.*

Ro. 11:12. and the *diminishing* of them
1Co. 6. 7. there is utterly a *fault* among you,

2276 2 350/433 hēka (slightly) cf 2556

ἧττον, *heeton.*

1Co.11·17. ye come together not for the better, but for the *worse.*
2Co.12:15. the *less* I be loved.

2277 2 221/278 1510

ἤτω, *eeto.*

From εἰμί.

1Co.16:22. *let* him *be* Anathema Maran-atha.
Jas. 5:12. but *let* your yea *be* yea;

2278 2 350/434 2:954 2279

ἠχέω, *eekeo.*

Lu. 21:25. the sea and the waves *roaring;*
1Co.13: 1. I am become (as) *sounding* brass,

2279 3 350/434

ἦχος, *eekos.*

Lu. 4:37. the *fame* of him went out
Acts 2: 2. a *sound* from heaven
Heb12:19. And the *sound* of a trumpet,

2281 92 350/434 251

θάλασσα, *thalassa.*

Mat. 4:15. (by) the way of the *sea,* beyond
18. by the *sea* of Galilee,
— a net into the *sea:*
8:24. there arose a great tempest in the *sea.*
26. rebuked the winds and the *sea.*
27. the winds and the *sea* obey him!
32. down a steep place into the *sea,*
13: 1. and sat by the *sea* side.
47. that was cast into the *sea,*
14:24. was now in the midst of the *sea,*
25, 26. walking on the sea.
15:29. nigh unto the *sea* of Galilee;
17:27. go thou to the *sea,*
18: 6. in the depth of the *sea.*
21:21. be thou cast into the *sea;*
23:15. for ye compass *sea* and land
Mar 1:16. by the *sea* of Galilee,
— a net into the *sea:*
2:13. he went forth again by the *sea* side;
3: 7. with his disciples to the *sea:*
4: 1. to teach by the *sea* side:
— sat in the *sea;* and the whole multitude was by the *sea*
39. and said unto the *sea,*
41 the wind and the *sea* obey
5: 1. over unto the other side of the *sea,*
13. down a steep place into the *sea,*
— were choked in the *sea.*
21. and he was nigh unto the *sea.*
6:47. in the midst of the *sea,*
48. walking upon the *sea.*
49. walking upon the *sea,*
7:31 unto the *sea* of Galilee,
9:42. he were cast into the *sea.*
11:23. be thou cast into the *sea,*
Lu. 17: 2. about his neck, and he cast into the *sea,*
6. be thou planted in the *sea;*
21:25. the *sea* and the waves roaring;
Joh. 6: 1. Jesus went over the *sea* of Galilee,
16. his disciples went down unto the *sea,*
17 and went over the *sea*
18. And the *sea* arose by reason of a great wind
19. walking on the *sea,*
22. which stood on the other side of the *sea*
25. found him on the other side of the *sea,*
21: 1. at the *sea* of Tiberias;
7. did cast himself into the *sea.*
Acts 4:24. hast made heaven, and earth, and the *sea*
7:36. in the Red *sea,* and in the wilderness
10: 6. house is by the *sea* side:
32. a tanner by the *sea* side:
14:15. made heaven, and earth, and the *sea,*
17:14. as it were to the *sea:*
27:30. the boat into the *sea,*
38. the wheat into the *sea.*
40. they committed (themselves) unto the *sea,*
28: 4. though he hath escaped the *sea,*
Ro. 9:27. as the sand of the *sea,*
1Co.10: 1. passed through the *sea;*
2. in the cloud and in the *sea;*
2Co.11:26. (in) perils in the *sea,*
Heb 11:12. by the *sea* shore innumerable.
29. they passed through the Red *sea*
Jas. 1: 6. that wavereth is like a wave of the *sea*
Jude 13. Raging waves of the *sea,*
Rev. 4: 6. a *sea* of glass like unto crystal:
5:13. and such as are in the *sea,*
7: 1. not blow on the earth, nor on the *sea,*
2. the earth and the *sea,*
3. neither the *sea,* nor the trees,
8: 8. was cast into the *sea:* and the third part of the *sea* became blood;
9. which were in the *sea,*
10: 2. right foot upon the *sea,*

Rev 10: 5. upon the *sea* and
6. and the *sea*, and the things which are
8. standeth upon the *sea*
12:12. the earth and of the *sea!*
13: 1. (12:18). upon the sand of the *sea*, and saw a beast rise up out of the *sea*,
14: 7. and earth, and the *sea*,
15: 2. as it were a *sea* of glass
— stand on the *sea* of glass,
16: 3. his vial upon the *sea;*
— every living soul died in the *sea*.
18:17. as many as trade by *sea*,
19. that had ships in the *sea*
21. and cast (it) into the *sea*,
20: 8. as the sand of the *sea*.
13. And the *sea* gave up
21: 1. and there was no more *sea*.

2282 2 351/435 cf *thallō* (to warm)

θάλπω, thalpo.

Eph. 5:29. but nourisheth and *cherisheth* it,
1 Th. 2: 7. even as a nurse *cherisheth* her children:

2284 4 351/435 3:4 2285

θαμβέομαι, thambeomai.

Mar 1:27. And they *were* all *amazed*,
10:24. *were astonished* at his words.
32. and they *were amazed;*
Acts 9: 6. And he trembling and *astonished*

2285 3 351/435 3:4 (to dumbfound)

θάμβος, thambos. cf *taphō*

Lu. 4:36. And they were all amazed, (lit. *amazement* was upon all)
5: 9. For he was astonished, (lit. *astonishment* came upon him)
Acts 3:10. they were filled with *wonder* and

2286 1 351/435 2288

θανάσιμος, thanasimos.

Mar 16:18. and if they drink any *deadly* thing,

2287 1 351/435 2288,5342

θανατηφόρος, thanateephoros.

Jas. 3: 8. full of *deadly* poison.

2288 119 351/435 3:7 2348

θάνατος, thanatos.

Mat. 4:16. in the region and shadow of *death*
10:21. brother shall deliver up the brother to *death*,
15: 4. let him die the *death*.
16:28. shall not taste of *death*,
20:18. they shall condemn him to *death*,
26:38. exceeding sorrowful, even unto *death:*
66. He is guilty of *death*.
Mar 7:10. let him die the *death:*
9: 1. shall not taste of *death*,
10:33. shall condemn him to *death*,
13:12. brother shall betray the brother to *death*,
14:34. soul is exceeding sorrowful unto *death:*
64. condemned him to be guilty of *death*.
Lu. 1:79. and (in) the shadow of *death*,
2:26. that he should not see *death*, before
9:27. which shall not taste of *death*,
22:33. with thee, both into prison, and to *death*
23:15. nothing worthy of *death*
22. no cause of *death* in him:
24:20. to be condemned to *death*,
Joh. 5:24. from *death* unto life.
8:51. he shall never see *death*.
52. he shall never taste of *death*.
11: 4. This sickness is not unto *death*,
13. Jesus spake of his *death:*
12:33. what *death* he should die.
18:32. what *death* he should die.
21:19. by what *death* he should glorify God.
Acts 2:24. having loosed the pains of *death:*
13:28. though they found no cause of *death* (in him),
22: 4. I persecuted this way unto the *death*,
23:29. worthy of *death* or of bonds.
25:11. have committed any thing worthy of *death*,
25. nothing worthy of *death*,
26:31. worthy of *death* or of bonds.
28:18. no cause of *death* in me.
Ro. 1:32. commit such things are worthy of *death*,
5:10. by the *death* of his Son,
12. and *death* by sin; and so *death* passed
14. *death* reigned from Adam
17. *death* reigned by one;
21. sin hath reigned unto *death*,
6: 3. were baptized into his *death?*
4. by baptism into *death:*
5. in the likeness of his *death*,
9. *death* hath no more dominion over him.
16. whether of sin unto *death*,
21. the end of those things (is) *death*.
23. the wages of sin (is) *death;*
7: 5. to bring forth fruit unto *death*.
10. I found (to be) unto *death*.
13. which is good made *death* unto me?
— sin, working *death* in me
24. from the body of this *death?*
8: 2. the law of sin and *death*.
6. to be carnally minded (is) *death;*
38. neither *death*, nor life,
1Co. 3:22. or life, or *death*,
11:26. ye do shew the Lord's *death*
15:21. by man (came) *death*,
26. (that) shall be destroyed (is) *death*.
54. *Death* is swallowed up in victory.
55. O *death*, where (is) thy sting?
56. The sting of *death* (is) sin;
2Co. 1: 9. we had the sentence of *death* in ourselves,
10. Who delivered us from so great a *death*,
2:16. To the one (we are) the savour of *death* unto *death;*
3: 7. the ministration of *death*,
4:11. are alway delivered unto *death*
12. then *death* worketh in us,
7:10. the sorrow of the world worketh *death*.
11:23. in prisons more frequent, in *deaths* oft.
Phi. 1:20. whether (it be) by life, or by *death*.
2: 8. and became obedient unto *death*, even the *death* of the cross.
27. he was sick nigh unto *death:*
30. he was nigh unto *death*,
3:10. being made conformable unto his *death;*
Col. 1:22. In the body of his flesh through *death*,
2Ti. 1:10. who hath abolished *death*,
Heb. 2: 9. for the suffering of *death*,
— should taste *death* for every man.
14. through *death* he might destroy him that had the power of *death*.

Heb. 2:15. through fear of *death*
5: 7. to save him from *death*,
7:23. they were not suffered to continue by reason of *death*:
9:15. by means of *death*, for the redemption
16. there must also of necessity be the *death*
11: 5. that he should not see *death*;
Jas 1:15. sin, when it is finished, bringeth forth *death*.
5:20. shall save a soul from *death*,
1Joh. 3:14. we have passed from *death* unto life,
— brother abideth in *death*.
5:16. a sin (which is) not unto *death*,
— that sin not unto *death*. There is a sin unto *death*:
17. there is a sin not unto *death*.
Rev. 1:18. the keys of hell and of *death*.
2:10. be thou faithful unto *death*,
11. shall not be hurt of the second *death*
23. I will kill her children with *death*;
6: 8. his name that sat on him was *Death*,
— with hunger, and with *death*,
9: 6. men seek *death*, and shall not
— *death* shall flee from them.
12:11. their lives unto the *death*.
13: 3. as it were wounded to *death*; and his deadly wound (lit. w. of *death*) was healed:
12. whose deadly wound (lit. w. of *death*) was healed.
18: 8. *death*, and mourning, and famine;
20: 6. the second *death* hath no power,
13. *death* and hell delivered up the dead
14. *death* and hell were cast into the lake of fire. This is the second *death*.
21: 4. there shall be no more *death*,
8. which is the second *death*.

2289 11 352/437 3:7 2288

ϑανατόω, thanatoō.

Mat. 10:21. and *cause* them *to be put to death*.
26:59. against Jesus, to *put* him *to death*;
27: 1. against Jesus *to put* him *to death*:
Mar 13:12. and *shall cause* them *to be put to death*.
14:55. against Jesus *to put* him *to death*;
Lu. 21:16. (some) of you *shall* they *cause to be put to death*.
Ro. 7: 4. ye also *are become dead* to the law
8:13. if ye through the Spirit *do mortify* the deeds of the body,
36. For thy sake we *are killed*
2Co. 6: 9. as chastened, and not *killed*;
1Pet. 3:18. *being put to death* in the flesh,

2290 11 352/437

ϑάπτω, thapto.

Mat. 8:21. first to go and *bury* my father.
22. let the dead *bury* their dead.
14:12. and *buried* it, and went and told Jesus.
Lu. 9:59. and *bury* my father.
60. Let the dead *bury* their dead:
16:22. rich man also died, and *was buried*;
Acts 2:29. he is both dead and *buried*,
5: 6. carried (him) out, and *buried* (him).
9. the feet of them *which have buried* thy husband
10. *buried* (her) by her husband.
1Co. 15: 4. And that he *was buried*,

2292 6 352/437 3:25 eq 2293

ϑαῤῥέω, tharreo.

2Co. 5: 6. Therefore (we are) always *confident*,
8. We *are confident*, (I say), and willing
7:16. I *have confidence* in you in all (things).
10: 1. but being absent *am bold* toward you:
2. that I may not *be bold* when I
Heb 13: 6. So that we may *boldly* (lit. *being confident*) say,

2293 8 352/437 3:25 2294cf2292

ϑαρσέω, tharseo.

Mat. 9: 2. Son, *be of good cheer*;
22. Daughter, *be of good comfort*; thy faith
14:27. *Be of good cheer*; it is I;
Mar. 6:50. *Be of good cheer*: it is I;
10:49. *Be of good comfort*, rise; he calleth thee.
Lu. 8:48. Daughter, *be of good comfort*:
Joh. 16:33. but *be of good cheer*; I have overcome the
Acts 23:11. *Be of good cheer*, Paul: for as

2294 1 352/437 *thrasos* (daring)

ϑάρσος, tharsos.

Acts 28:15. he thanked God, and took *courage*.

2295 1 352/437 3:27 2300

ϑαῦμα, thauma.

Rev. 17: 6. and when I saw her, I wondered with great *admiration*.

2296 46 352/437 3:27 2295

ϑαυμάζω, thaumazo.

Mat. 8:10. Jesus heard (it), he *marvelled*, and said
27. the men *marvelled*, saying,
9: 8. the multitudes saw (it), they *marvelled*.
33. the multitudes *marvelled*, saying,
15:31. that the multitude *wondered*,
21:20. they *marvelled*, saying, How soon
22:22. When they had heard (these words), they *marvelled*,
27:14. insomuch that the governor *marvelled*
Mar 5:20. and all (men) *did marvel*.
6: 6. he *marvelled* because of their unbelief.
51. amazed in themselves beyond measure, and *wondered*.
12:17. they *marvelled* at him.
15: 5. so that Pilate *marvelled*.
44. Pilate *marvelled* if he were already dead:
Lu. 1:21. and *marvelled* that he tarried
63. And they *marvelled* all.
2:18. they that heard (it) *wondered*
33. Joseph and his mother marvelled (lit. were *marvelling*)
4:22. and *wondered* at the gracious words
7: 9. he *marvelled* at him, and turned him about,
8:25. And they being afraid *wondered*,
9:43. But while they *wondered* every one
11:14. and the people *wondered*.
38. when the Pharisee saw (it), he *marvelled*
20:26. they *marvelled* at his answer, *and* held
24:12. *wondering* in himself at that
41. believed not for joy, and *wondered*,
Joh. 3: 7. *Marvel* not that I said unto thee,
4:27. *marvelled* that he talked with the woman:
5:20. greater works than these, that ye may *marvel*.
28. *Marvel* not at this:
7:15. And the Jews *marvelled*,
21. and ye all *marvel*.

Acts 2: 7. and *marvelled*, saying one to another,
3:12. why *marvel* ye at this?
4:13. they *marvelled*; and they took knowledge
7:31. he *wondered* at the sight.
13:41. ye despisers, and *wonder*, and perish.
Gal. 1: 6. I *marvel* that ye are so soon
2Th 1:10. and *to be admired* in all them that
1 Joh.3:13. *Marvel* not, my brethren,
Jude 16. *having* men's persons *in admiration*
Rev 13: 3. the world wondered (lit. it *was wondered* in all the world) after the beast.
17: 6. when I saw her, I *wondered*
7. Wherefore *didst* thou *marvel?*
8. they that dwell on the earth *shall wonder*,

2297 1 353/438 3:27 2295

ϑαυμάσιος, *thaumasios*.

Mat 21:15. the *wonderful* things that he did,

2298 7 357/438 3:27 2296

ϑαυμαστός, *thaumastos*.

Mat 21:42. it is *marvellous* in our eyes?
Mar 12:11. it is *marvellous* in our eyes?
Joh. 9:30. Why herein is a *marvellous* thing,
2Co.11:14. And no *marvel*; for Satan himself
1Pet. 2: 9. out of darkness into his *marvellous* light:
Rev 15: 1. sign in heaven, great and *marvellous*,
3. and *marvellous* (are) thy works,

2299 3 353/438 2316

Θεά, *thea*.

Acts19:27. of the great *goddess* Diana
35. of the great *goddess* Diana,
37. nor yet blasphemers of your *goddess*.

2300 24 353/438 5:315 cf 3700

ϑεάομαι, *theaomai*.

Mat 6: 1. *to be seen* of them:
11: 7. *to see?* A reed shaken with the wind?
22:11. the king came in *to see* the guests,
23: 5. for *to be seen* of men:
Mar 16:11. and *had been seen* of her,
14. they believed not them *which had seen* him
Lu. 5:27. and *saw* a publican, named Levi,
7:24. into the wilderness for *to see?*
23:55. and *beheld* the sepulchre, and how his
Joh. 1:14. we *beheld* his glory, the glory
32. I *saw* the Spirit descending
38. *saw* them following, *and* saith
4:35. and *look* on the fields;
6: 5. *saw* a great company come unto him,
8:10. and *saw* none but the woman,
11:45. and *had seen* the things which Jesus did,
Acts 1:11. in like manner as ye *have seen* him
8:18. And *when* Simon *saw* that
21:27. *when* they *saw* him in the temple,
22: 9. that were with me *saw* indeed the light,
Ro. 15:24. *to see* you in my journey,
1Joh.1: 1. which we *have looked upon*, and our hands
4:12(11). No man *hath seen* God at any time.
14. And we *have seen* and do testify

2301 1 354/438 3:42 2302

ϑεατρίζομαι, *theatrizomai*.

Heb 10:33. *whilst* ye *were made a gazingstock* both by reproaches and afflictions;

2302 3 354/438 3:42 2300

ϑέατρον, *theatron*.

Acts19:29. with one accord into the *theatre*.
31. that he would not adventure himself into the *theatre*.
1Co. 4: 9. for we are made a *spectacle*

2303 7 354/438 2304

ϑεῖον, *thīon*.

Lu. 17:29. fire and *brimstone* from heaven,
Rev 9:17. issued fire and smoke and *brimstone*.
18. the smoke, and by the *brimstone*,
14:10. with fire and *brimstone*
19:20. lake of fire burning with *brimstone*.
20:10. the lake of fire and *brimstone*,
21: 8. burneth with fire and *brimstone*:

2304 3 354/439 3:65 2316

ϑεῖος, *thīos*. adj.

Acts17:29. that the Godhead (lit. the *Divine*) is like
2Pet 1: 3. According as his *divine* power
4. might be partakers of the *divine* nature,

2305 1 354/439 3:65 2304

ϑειότης, *thīotees*.

Ro. 1:20. his eternal power and *Godhead*;

2306 1 354/439 2303,1491

ϑειώδης, *thīodees*.

Rev 9:17. of fire, and of jacinth, and *brimstone*:

2307 64 354/439 3:44 2309

ϑέλημα, *theleema*.

Mat. 6:10. Thy *will* be done in earth,
7:21. but he that doeth the *will*
12:50. For whosoever shall do the *will*
18:14. it is not the *will* of your Father
21:31. of them twain did the *will* of (his) father?
26:42. except I drink it, thy *will* be done.
Mar. 3:35. shall do the *will* of God,
Lu. 11: 2. Thy *will* be done, as in heaven,
12:47. which knew his lord's *will*,
— did according to his *will*,
22:42. nevertheless not my *will*,
23:25. he delivered Jesus to their *will*.
Joh. 1:13. nor of the *will* of the flesh, nor of the *will* of man,
4:34. the *will* of him that sent me,
5:30. I seek not mine own *will*, but the *will* of the Father which hath sent me.
6:38. not to do mine own *will*, but the *will* of him that sent me.
39. the Father's *will* which hath sent me,
40. the *will* of him that sent me,
7:17. do his *will*, he shall know of the doctrine,
9:31. doeth his *will*, him he heareth.
Acts13:22. shall fulfil all my *will*. (lit. *desires*)
21:14. The *will* of the Lord be done.
22:14. that thou shouldest know his *will*,
Ro. 1:10. by the *will* of God
2:18. knowest (his) *will*, and approvest
12: 2. that good, and acceptable, and perfect, *will* of God,
15:32. by the *will* of God,
1Co. 1: 1. through the *will* of God,
7:37. over his own *will*,
16:12. his *will* was not at all to come at this time

2Co. 1: 1. an apostle of Jesus Christ by the *will* of
8: 5. by the *will* of God.
Gal. 1: 4. according to the *will* of God
Eph. 1: 1. by the *will* of God,
5. the good pleasure of his *will*,
9. the mystery of his *will*,
11. the counsel of his own *will*:
2: 3. fulfilling the *desires* of the flesh
5:17. what the *will* of the Lord (is).
6: 6. doing the *will* of God
Col. 1: 1. by the *will* of God,
9. the knowledge of his *will*
4:12. in all the *will* of God.
1Th. 4: 3. this is the *will* of God, (even) your sanctification,
5:18. for this is the *will* of God in Christ
2Ti. 1: 1. by the *will* of God,
2:26. taken captive by him at his *will*.
Heb 10: 7. to do thy *will*, O God.
9. I come to do thy *will*, O God.
10. By the which *will* we are sanctified
36. after ye have done the *will* of God,
13:21. every good work to do his *will*,
1Pet.2:15. so is the *will* of God, that with well doing
3:17. if the *will* of God be so,
4: 2. but to the *will* of God.
3. the *will* of the Gentiles,
19. according to the *will* of God
2Pet.1:21. prophecy came not in old time by the *will* of man:
1Joh.2:17. that doeth the *will* of God
5:14. according to his *will*,
Rev. 4:11. for thy *pleasure* they are

2308 1 355/439 3:44 2309

θέλησις, *theleesis.*

Heb. 2: 4. gifts of the Holy Ghost, according to his own *will*?

2309 209 355/439 3:44 cf rt138

θέλω, *thelo.* cf 1014

Mat. 1:19. not *willing* to make her a publick example,
2:18. and *would* not be comforted, because
5:40. *if* any man *will* sue thee at the law,
42. him *that would* borrow of thee
7:12. whatsoever ye *would* that men should do
8: 2. if thou *wilt*, thou canst
3. I *will*; be thou clean.
9:13. I *will have* mercy, and not sacrifice:
11:14. if ye *will* receive (it),
12: 7. I *will have* mercy, and not sacrifice,
38. we *would* see a sign from thee.
13:28. *Wilt* thou then that we go
14: 5. *when* he *would* have put him to death,
15:28. be it unto thee even as thou *wilt*.
32. I *will* not send them away fasting,
16:24. If any (man) *will* come after me,
25. For whosoever *will* save his life
17: 4. if thou *wilt*, let us make
12. unto him whatsoever they *listed*.
18:23. which *would* take account
30. And he *would* not: but went and cast him
19:17. but if thou *wilt* enter
21. If thou *wilt* be perfect,
20:14. I *will* give unto this last,
15. to do what I *will* with mine own?
21. said unto her, What *wilt* thou?
26. whosoever *will* be great among you,
27. whosoever *will* be chief among you,
32. What *will* ye that I shall do unto you?
Mat.21:29. and said, I *will* not:
22: 3. and they *would* not come.
23: 4. *will* not move them with one of their
37. how often *would* I have gathered
— and ye *would* not!
26:15. What *will* ye give me,
17. Where *wilt* thou that we prepare
39. nevertheless not as I *will*,
27:15. a prisoner, whom they *would*.
17. Whom *will* ye that I release
21. Whether of the twain *will* ye that I release
34. tasted (thereof), he *would* not drink.
43. deliver him now, if he *will have* him:
Mar. 1:40. If thou *wilt*, thou canst
41. I *will*; be thou clean.
3:13. calleth (unto him) whom he *would*.
6:19. *would* have killed him;
22. Ask of me whatsoever thou *wilt*,
25. I *will* that thou give me
26. he *would* not reject her.
48. *would* have passed by them.
7:24. and *would* have no man know (it):
8:34. Whosoever *will* come after me,
35. For whosoever *will* save his life
9:13. unto him whatsoever they *listed*,
30. he *would* not that any man should know (it).
35. If any man *desire* to be first,
10:35. we *would* that thou shouldest do for us whatsoever we shall desire.
36. What *would* ye that I should do for you?
43. whosoever *will* be great among you,
44. whosoever of you *will* be the chiefest,
51. What *wilt* thou that I should do unto thee?
12:38. which *love* to go in long clothing,
14: 7. and whensoever ye *will* ye may
12. Where *wilt* thou that we go
36. not what I *will*, but what thou
15: 9. *Will* ye that I release unto you
12. What *will* ye then that I shall do (unto him) whom
Lu. 1:62. how he *would* have him called.
4: 6. to whomsoever I *will* I give it.
5:12. if thou *wilt*, thou canst make me clean.
13. I *will*: be thou clean.
39. straightway *desireth* new:
6:31. And as ye *would* that men
8:20. *desiring* to see thee.
9:23. if any (man) *will* come after me,
24. For whosoever *will* save his life
54. Lord, *wilt* thou that we command
10:24. prophets and kings *have desired* to see those things which ye see,
29. *willing* to justify himself,
12:49. what *will* I, if it be already kindled.
13:31. for Herod *will* kill thee.
34. how often *would* I have gathered
— and ye *would* not!
14:28. *intending* to build a tower,
15:28. he was angry, and *would* not go in:
16:26. they *which would* pass from hence
18: 4. And he *would* not for a while:
13. *would* not lift up so much as (his) eyes
41. What *wilt* thou that I shall do unto thee?
19:14. We *will* not have this (man) to reign over
27. mine enemies, *which would* not that I
20:46. the scribes, *which desire* to walk in long
22: 9. Where *wilt* thou that we prepare?
23: 8. for he was *desirous* to see him of a long
20. *willing* to release Jesus,
Joh. 1:43(44). Jesus *would* go forth
3: 8. bloweth where it *listeth*.

Joh 5: 6. *Wilt* thou be made whole?
21. quickeneth whom he *will*.
35. ye *were willing* for a season to rejoice
40. ye *will* not come to me,
6:11. of the fishes as much as they *would*.
21. Then they willingly received (lit. they *willed* to receive) him into the ship:
67. *Will* ye also go away?
7: 1. for he *would* not walk in Jewry,
17. If any man *will* do his will,
44. And some of them *would* have taken him;
8:44. the lusts of your father ye *will* do.
9:27. wherefore *would* ye hear (it) again? *will* ye also be his disciples?
12:21. we *would* see Jesus.
15: 7. ye shall ask what ye *will*,
16:19. they *were desirous* to ask him,
17:24. I *will* that they also, whom thou hast given me, be with me where I am;
21:18. walkedst whither thou *wouldest*:
— carry (thee) whither thou *wouldest* not.
22. If I *will* that he tarry till I come,
23. If I *will* that he tarry
Acts 2:12. one to another, What *meaneth* this?
7:28. *Wilt* thou kill me,
39. To whom our fathers *would* not obey,
9: 6. what *wilt* thou *have* me to do?
10:10. and *would* have eaten:
14:13. and *would* have done sacrifice
16: 3. Him *would* Paul *have* to go
17:18. What *will* this babbler say?
20. what these things *mean*.
18:21. return again unto you, *if* God *will*.
19:33. and *would* have made his defence
24: 6. and *would* have judged according to our
27. *willing* to shew the Jews a pleasure,
25: 9. *willing* to do the Jews a pleasure,
— *Wilt* thou go up to Jerusalem,
26: 5. if they *would* testify,
Ro. 1:13. Now I *would* not *have* you ignorant,
7:15. for what I *would*, that do I not;
16. If then I do that which I *would* not,
18. for *to will* is present with me;
19. For the good that I *would* I do not: but the evil which I *would* not,
20. I do that I *would* not,
21. *when* I *would* do good, evil is
9:16. So then (it is) not of him *that willeth*,
18. hath he mercy on whom he *will* (have mercy), and whom he *will* he hardeneth.
22. (What) if God, *willing* to shew
11:25. For I *would* not, brethren, that ye should be ignorant of
13: 3. *Wilt* thou then not be afraid
16:19. but yet I *would* have you wise
1Co. 4:19. come to you shortly, if the Lord *will*,
21. What *will* ye?...with a rod,
7: 7. For I *would* that all men
32. But I *would* have you without carefulness.
36. let him do what he *will*,
39. to be married to whom she *will*;
10: 1. Moreover, brethren, I *would* not that ye should be ignorant,
20. and I *would* not that ye should have
27. and ye *be disposed* to go;
11: 3. But I *would have* you know,
12: 1. I *would* not *have* you ignorant.
18. as it *hath pleased* him. (lit. he *hath willed*)
14: 5. I *would* that ye all spake with tongues,
19. I *had rather* speak five words
35. And if they *will* learn any thing,
15:38. as it *hath pleased* him, (lit. he *hath*, &c.)
1Co.16: 7. For I *will* not see you now
2Co. 1: 8. For we *would* not, brethren, have you
5: 4. not for that we *would* be unclothed,
8:10. have begun before,...*to be forward* a year
11. a readiness *to will*,
11:12. from them *which desire* occasion;
32. *desirous* to apprehend me:
12: 6. For though I *would desire* to glory,
20. I shall not find you such as I *would*,
— such as ye *would* not:
Gal. 1: 7. that trouble you, and *would* pervert the gospel of Christ.
3: 2. This only *would* I learn of you,
4: 9. ye *desire* again to be in bondage?
17. they *would* exclude you,
20. I *desire* to be present with you
21. Tell me, ye that *desire* to be under the law,
5:17. ye cannot do the things that ye *would*.
6:12. As many as *desire* to make a fair shew
13. *desire* to have you circumcised,
Phi. 2:13. worketh in you both *to will* and to do of (his) good pleasure.
Col. 1:27. To whom God *would* make known
2: 1. For I *would* that ye knew
18. Let no man beguile you of your reward in a voluntary humility (lit. beguile you *willing*, or at his will)
1Th. 2:18. we *would* have come unto you,
4:13. But I *would* not *have* you to be ignorant,
2Th 3:10. if any *would* not work,
1Ti. 1: 7. *Desiring* to be teachers of the law;
2: 4. Who *will have* all men to be saved,
5:11. wanton against Christ, they *will* marry;
2Ti. 3:12. all *that will* live godly in Christ
Philem. 14. *would* I do nothing;
Heb 10: 5. offering thou *wouldest* not,
8. thou *wouldest* not, neither hadst pleasure
12:17. *when* he *would* have inherited
13:18. in all things *willing* to live honestly.
Jas. 2:20. But *wilt* thou know,
4:15. If the Lord *will*, we shall live,
1Pet. 3:10. For he *that will* love life,
3:17. if the will of God *be so*,
2Pet. 3: 5. For this they *willingly* are ignorant of,
3Joh. 13. but I *will* not with ink
Rev. 11: 5. (*bis*) if any man *will* hurt them,
6. as often as they *will*.
22:17. And whosoever *will*, let him take the

2310 16 356/442 3:63 5087

θεμέλιος, themelios.

Acts 16:26. it is θεμέλια, i. e. neut. pl.

Lu. 6:48. laid the *foundation* on a rock:
49. without a *foundation* built
14:29. after he hath laid the *foundation*,
Acts 16:26. the *foundations* of the prison were shaken:
Ro. 15:20. upon another man's *foundation*:
1Co. 3:10. I have laid the *foundation*,
11. For other *foundation* can no man
12. upon this *foundation* gold,
Eph 2:20. upon the *foundation* of the apostles
1Ti. 6:19. for themselves a good *foundation* against
2Ti. 2:19. the *foundation* of God standeth sure,
Heb 6: 1. laying again the *foundation*
11:10. a city which hath *foundations*,
Rev 21:14. wall of the city had twelve *foundations*,
19. the *foundations* of the wall of the city
— The first *foundation* (was) jasper;

2311 6 356/442 3:63 2310

θεμελιόω, themelioō.

Mat 7:25. for it *was founded* upon a rock.

Lu. 6:48. for it *was founded* upon a rock.
Eph 3:17(18). being rooted and *grounded* in love,
Col. 1:23. continue in the faith *grounded* and
Heb 1:10. *hast laid the foundation of* the earth;
1Pet 5:10. stablish, strengthen, *settle* (you).

2312 1 356/442 3:65 2316,1321

ϑεοδίδακτος, *theodidaktos.*

Th 4: 9. ye yourselves are *taught of God* to love one another.

2313 1 357/ 4:527 2314

ϑεομαχέω, *theomakeo.*

Acts23: 9. *let* us not *fight against God.*

2314 1 357/442 4:527 2316,3164

ϑεομάχος, *theomakos*, adj.

Acts 5:39. ye be found even *to fight against God.*

2315 1 357/442 6:332 2316,4154

ϑεόπνευστος, *theopnūstos.*

2Ti. 3:16. scripture (is) *given by inspiration of God,*

2316 1343 357/442 3:65

Θεός, *Theos.*

Mat. 1:23. being interpreted is, *God* with us.
3: 9. *God* is able of these stones
16. he saw the Spirit of *God*
4: 3. If thou be the Son of *God,*
4. out of the mouth of *God.*
6. If thou be the Son of *God,* cast
7. shalt not tempt the Lord thy *God.*
10. Thou shalt worship the Lord thy *God,*
5: 8. for they shall see *God.*
9. they shall be called the children of *God.*
34. for it is *God's* throne:
6:24. serve *God* and mammon.
30. *God* so clothe the grass of the field,
33. first the kingdom of *God,*
8:29. Jesus, thou Son of *God?*
9: 8. and glorified *God,* which had
12: 4. into the house of *God,*
28. cast out devils by the Spirit of *God,* then the kingdom of *God*
14:33. Of a truth thou art the Son of *God.*
15: 3. the commandment of *God*
4. For *God* commanded, saying,
6. the commandment of *God*
31. they glorified the *God* of Israel.
16:16. the Son of the living *God.*
23. savourest not the things that be of *God,*
19: 6. What therefore *God* hath joined together,
17. but one, (that is), *God:*
24. into the kingdom of *God.*
26. but with *God* all things
21:12. into the temple of *God,*
31. into the kingdom of *God*
43. The kingdom of *God* shall be taken
22:16. and teachest the way of *God*
21. and unto *God* the things that are *God's.*
29. nor the power of *God.*
30. but are as the angels of *God*
31. which was spoken unto you by *God,*
32. the *God* of Abraham, and the *God* of Isaac, and the *God* of Jacob? *God* is not the *God* of the dead,
37. Thou shalt love the Lord thy *God*

Mat23:22. sweareth by the throne of *God,*
26:61. to destroy the temple of *God,*
63. I adjure thee by the living *God,*
— the Christ, the Son of *God.*
27:40. If thou be the Son of *God,* come down
43. He trusted in *God;*
— I am the Son of *God.*
46. My *God,* my *God,* why hast thou forsaken
54. Truly this was the Son of *God.*
Mar 1: 1. of Jesus Christ, the Son of *God;*
14. the gospel of the kingdom of *God,*
15. the kingdom of *God* is at hand:
24. who thou art, the Holy One of *God.*
2: 7. can forgive sins but *God* only?
12. and glorified *God* saying,
26. into the house of *God*
3:11. Thou art the Son of *God.*
35. shall do the will of *God,*
4:11. the mystery of the kingdom of *God:*
26. So is the kingdom of *God,*
30. shall we liken the kingdom of *God?*
5: 7. (thou) Son of the most high *God?* I adjure thee by *God,*
7: 8. laying aside the commandment of *God,*
9. ye reject the commandment of *God,*
13. Making the word of *God* of none effect
8:33. thou savourest not the things that be of *God,* but
9: 1. they have seen the kingdom of *God*
47. to enter into the kingdom of *God*
10: 6. *God* made them male
9. What therefore *God* hath joined together,
14. of such is the kingdom of *God.*
15. Whosoever shall not receive the kingdom of *God*
18. none good but one, (that is), *God.*
23. enter into the kingdom of *God!*
24. to enter into the kingdom of *God!*
25. to enter into the kingdom of *God.*
27. but not with *God:* for with *God* all things
11:22. Have faith in *God.*
12:14. teachest the way of *God*
17. and to *God* the things that are *God's.*
24. neither the power of *God?*
26. *God* spake unto him, saying, I (am) the *God* of Abraham, and the *God* of Isaac, and the *God* of Jacob?
27. He is not the *God* of the dead, but the *God* of the living:
29. The Lord our *God* is one Lord:
30. thou shalt love the Lord thy *God*
32. for there is one *God;* and
34. from the kingdom of *God.*
13:19. which *God* created unto this time,
14:25. new in the kingdom of *God.*
15:34. My *God,* my *God,* why hast
39. this man was the Son of *God.*
43. waited for the kingdom of *God,*
16:19. on the right hand of *God.*
Lu. 1: 6. they were both righteous before *God,*
8. before *God* in the order of his course,
16. to the Lord their *God.*
19. that stand in the presence of *God;*
26. Gabriel was sent from *God*
30. hast found favour with *God.*
32. the Lord *God* shall give unto him
35. shall be called the Son of *God.*
37. with *God* nothing shall be impossible.
47. in *God* my Saviour.
64. he spake, and praised *God.*
68. Blessed (be) the Lord *God* of Israel;
78. the tender mercy of our *God;*

Lu. 2:13. praising *God*, and saying,
14. Glory to *God* in the highest,
20. and praising *God*
28. and blessed *God*, and said,
40. the grace of *God* was upon him.
52. with *God* and man.
3: 2. the word of *God* came unto John
6. the salvation of *God*.
8. *God* is able of these stones
38. of Adam, which was (the son) of *God*.
4: 3. If thou be the Son of *God*, command
4. by every word of *God*.
8. Thou shalt worship the Lord thy *God*,
9. If thou be the Son of *God*, cast
12. Thou shalt not tempt the Lord thy *God*.
34. the Holy One of *God*.
41. Thou art Christ the Son of *God*.
43. the kingdom of *God* to other cities also:
5: 1. to hear the word of *God*,
21. Who can forgive sins, but *God* alone?
25. to his own house, glorifying *God*.
26. and they glorified *God*,
6: 4. into the house of *God*,
12. in prayer to *God*.
20. your's is the kingdom of *God*.
7:16. and they glorified *God*,
— *God* hath visited his people.
28. in the kingdom of *God*
29. justified *God*, being baptized
30. the counsel of *God* against
8: 1. shewing the glad tidings of the kingdom of *God*:
10. the mysteries of the kingdom of *God*:
11. The seed is the word of *God*.
21. which hear the word of *God*,
28. (thou) Son of *God* most high?
39. how great things *God* hath done unto
9: 2. to preach the kingdom of *God*,
11. of the kingdom of *God*,
20. The Christ of *God*.
27. see the kingdom of *God*.
43. at the mighty power of *God*.
60. preach the kingdom of *God*.
62. is fit for the kingdom of *God*.
10: 9. The kingdom of *God* is come nigh unto
11. the kingdom of *God* is come nigh unto
27. Thou shalt love the Lord thy *God*
11:20. But if I with the finger of *God* cast out devils, no doubt the kingdom of *God* is
28. they that hear the word of *God*,
42. and the love of *God*:
49. said the wisdom of *God*,
12: 6. not one of them is forgotten before *God*?
8. before the angels of *God*:
9. before the angels of *God*.
20. But *God* said unto him,
21. and is not rich toward *God*.
24. *God* feedeth them: how much more
28. *God* so clothe the grass,
31. But rather seek ye the kingdom of *God*;
13: 13. she was made straight, and glorified *God*.
18. is the kingdom of *God* like?
20. shall I liken the kingdom of *God*?
28. the prophets, in the kingdom of *God*,
29. shall sit down in the kingdom of *God*.
14:15. bread in the kingdom of *God*.
15: 10. in the presence of the angels of *God*
16:13. serve *God* and mammon.
15. but *God* knoweth your hearts:
— abomination in the sight of *God*.
16. the kingdom of *God* is preached,
17:15. with a loud voice glorified *God*.

Lu. 17:18. to give glory to *God*,
20. when the kingdom of *God* should come,
— The kingdom of *God* cometh not
21. the kingdom of *God* is within you.
18: 2. which feared not *God*,
4. Though I fear not *God*,
7. And shall not *God* avenge
11. *God*, I thank thee, that I am not
13. *God* be merciful to me a sinner.
16. for of such is the kingdom of *God*.
17. shall not receive the kingdom of *God*
19. save one, (that is), *God*.
24. enter into the kingdom of *God*!
25. to enter into the kingdom of *God*.
27. are possible with *God*.
29. for the kingdom of *God's* sake,
43. followed him, glorifying *God*:
— gave praise unto *God*.
19:11. the kingdom of *God* should immediately
37. and praise *God* with a loud voice
20:21. teachest the way of *God* truly:
25. and unto *God* the things which be *God's*.
36. and are the children of *God*,
37. he calleth the Lord the *God* of Abraham, and the *God* of Isaac, and the *God* of Jacob.
38. For he is not a *God* of the dead,
21: 4. unto the offerings of *God*:
31. the kingdom of *God* is nigh at hand.
22:16. in the kingdom of *God*.
18. the kingdom of *God* shall come.
69. of the power of *God*.
70. Art thou then the Son of *God*?
23:35. if he be Christ, the chosen of *God*.
40. Dost not thou fear *God*,
47. he glorified *God*, saying,
51. also himself waited for the kingdom of *God*.
24:19. before *God* and all the people:
53. praising and blessing *God*.
Joh. 1: 1. the Word was with *God*, and the Word was *God*.
2. was in the beginning with *God*.
6. sent from *God*, whose name (was) John.
12. to become the sons of *God*,
13. Which were born, not...but of *God*.
18. No man hath seen *God*
29. Behold the Lamb of *God*,
34. this is the Son of *God*.
36. Behold the Lamb of *God*!
49(50). thou art the Son of *God*;
51(52). the angels of *God* ascending
3: 2. thou art a teacher come from *God*:
— except *God* be *with* him.
3. see the kingdom of *God*.
5. into the kingdom of *God*.
16. *God* so loved the world,
17. For *God* sent not
18. of the only begotten Son of *God*.
21. that they are wrought in *God*.
33. that *God* is true.
34. For he whom *God* hath sent speaketh the words of *God*: for *God* giveth not the
36. the wrath of *God* abideth on him.
4:10. If thou knewest the gift of *God*,
24. *God* (is) a Spirit: and they that
5:18. said also that *God* was his Father, making himself equal with *God*.
25. the voice of the Son of *God*:
42. ye have not the love of *God*
44. the honour that (cometh) from *God* only?
6:27. hath *God* the Father sealed.

Joh. 6:28. we might work the works of *God?*
29. This is the work of *God,*
33. For the bread of *God* is he which
45. they shall be all taught of *God.*
46. save he which is of *God,*
69. the Son of the living *God.*
7:17. whether it be of *God,*
8:40. which I have heard of *God:*
41. we have one Father, (even) *God.*
42. If *God* were your Father,
— proceeded forth and came from *God;*
47. He that is of *God* heareth *God's* words:
— because ye are not of *God.*
54. that he is your *God:*
9: 3. the works of *God*...in him.
16. This man is not of *God,*
24. Give *God* the praise:
29. *God* spake unto Moses:
31. *God* heareth not sinners:
33. If this man were not of *God,*
35. on the Son of *God?*
10:33. being a man, makest thyself *God.*
34. I said, Ye are *gods?*
35. he called them *gods,* unto whom the word of *God* came,
36. I am the Son of *God?*
11: 4. for the glory of *God,* that the Son of *God* might be glorified
22. whatsoever thou wilt ask of *God, God* will give (it) thee.
27. the Christ, the Son of *God,*
40. thou shouldest see the glory of *God?*
52. the children of *God* that were scattered abroad.
12:43. more than the praise of *God.*
13: 3. he was come from *God,* and went to *God;*
31. and *God* is glorified in him.
32. *God* be glorified in him, *God* shall also glorify him
14: 1. ye believe in *God,*
16: 2. that he doeth *God* service.
27. came out from *God.*
30. that thou camest forth from *God.*
17: 3. the only true *God,*
19: 7. he made himself the Son of *God.*
20:17. (to) my *God,* and your *God.*
28. My Lord and my *God.*
31. the Christ, the Son of *God;*
21:19. death he should glorify *God.*
Acts 1: 3. the things pertaining to the kingdom of *God:*
2:11. the wonderful works of *God.*
17. saith *God,* I will pour out
22. approved of *God* among you
— *God* did by him in the midst
23. delivered by...and foreknowledge of *God,*
24. Whom *God* hath raised up,
30. *God* had sworn with an oath to him,
32. Jesus hath *God* raised up,
33. Therefore being by the right hand of *God*
36. *God* hath made that same...both Lord and Christ.
39. the Lord our *God* shall call.
47. Praising *God,* and having favour
3: 8. leaping, and praising *God.*
9. walking and praising *God:*
13. The *God* of Abraham, and of Isaac, and of Jacob, the *God* of our fathers,
15. whom *God* hath raised from the dead;
18. But those things, which *God* before had
21. which *God* hath spoken
22. the Lord your *God*

Acts 3:25. covenant which *God* made
26. *God,* having raised up his Son
4:10. whom *God* raised from the dead,
19. right in the sight of *God* to hearken unto you more than unto *God,*
21. all (men) glorified *God*
24. they lifted up their voice to *God*
— *God,* which hast made heaven,
31. they spake the word of *God*
5: 4. not lied unto men, but unto *God.*
29. We ought to obey *God* rather than men.
30. The *God* of our fathers
31. Him hath *God* exalted...a Prince and a Saviour,
32. whom *God* hath given to them that obey
39. But if it be of *God,*
6: 2. should leave the word of *God,*
7. the word of *God* increased;
11. against Moses, and (against) *God.*
7: 2. The *God* of glory appeared
6. And *God* spake on this wise,
7. will I judge, said *God:*
9. but *God* was with him,
17. which *God* had sworn to Abraham,
20. and was exceeding (lit. to *God*) fair,
25. how that *God* by his hand
32. (Saying), I (am) the *God* of thy fathers, the *God* of Abraham, and the *God* of Isaac, and the *God* of Jacob.
35. the same did *God* send (to be) a ruler and
37. the Lord your *God* raise
40. Make us *gods* to go before us:
42. Then *God* turned, and gave
43. the star of your *god* Remphan,
45. whom *God* drave out
46. favour before *God,* and desired to find a tabernacle for the *God* of Jacob.
55. saw the glory of *God,* and Jesus standing on the right hand of *God,*
56. standing on the right hand of *God.*
8:10. the great power of *God.*
12. things concerning the kingdom of *God,*
14. Samaria had received the word of *God,*
20. thou hast thought that the gift of *God*
21. right in the sight of *God.*
22. and pray *God,* if perhaps
37. that Jesus Christ is the Son of *God,*
9:20. he is the Son of *God.*
10: 2. one that feared *God*
— prayed to *God* alway.
3. an angel of *God* coming in
4. for a memorial before *God.*
15. What *God* hath cleansed,
22. and one that feareth *God,*
28. but *God* hath shewed me
31. had in remembrance in the sight of *God.*
33. are we all here present before *God,*
— that are commanded thee of *God.*
34. *God* is no respecter of persons:
38. How *God* anointed Jesus
— *God* was with him.
40. Him *God* raised up
41. chosen before of *God,*
42. was ordained of *God*
46. speak with tongues, and magnify *God.*
11: 1. received the word of *God.*
9. What *God* hath cleansed,
17. *God* gave them the like gift
— that I could withstand *God?*
18. glorified *God,* saying, Then hath *God* also to the Gentiles granted repentance
23. had seen the grace of *God,*

Acts12: 5. church unto *God* for him.
22. (It is) the voice of a *god*, and not of a
23. he gave not *God* the glory:
24. the word of *God* grew
13: 5. they preached the word of *God*
7. to hear the word of *God*.
16. ye that fear *God*,
17. The *God* of this people
21. *God* gave unto them Saul
23. Of this man's seed hath *God*
26. whosoever among you feareth *God*,
30. But *God* raised him
33(32). *God* hath fulfilled the same
36. by the will of *God*, fell on sleep,
37. But he, whom *God* raised again,
43. to continue in the grace of *God*.
44. to hear the word of *God*.
46. the word of *God* should first have been
14:11. The *gods* are come down to us in the
15. unto the living *God*,
22. into the kingdom of *God*.
26. to the grace of *God*
27. all that *God* had done with
15: 4. all things that *God* had done with them.
7. *God* made choice among us,
8. And *God*, which knoweth the hearts,
10. why tempt ye *God*,
12. miracles and wonders *God* had wrought among the Gentiles by them.
14. how *God* at the first did visit
18. Known unto *God* are all his works from the beginning of the world.
19. Gentiles are turned to *God*:
40. by the brethren unto the grace of *God*.
16:14. which worshipped *God*, heard (us):
17. the servants of the most high *God*,
25. and sang praises unto *God*:
34. believing in *God* with all his house.
17:13. the word of *God* was preached of Paul
23. TO THE UNKNOWN *GOD*.
24. *God* that made the world
29. Forasmuch then as we are the offspring of *God*,
30. *God* winked at; but now
18: 7. (one) that worshipped *God*,
11. the word of *God* among them.
13. to worship *God* contrary to the law.
21. return again unto you, if *God* will.
26. the way of *God* more perfectly.
19: 8. things concerning the kingdom of *God*.
11. *God* wrought special miracles by the hands of Paul:
26. they be no *gods*, which are made with
20:21. repentance toward *God*, and faith toward
24. the gospel of the grace of *God*.
25. preaching the kingdom of *God*,
27. all the counsel of *God*.
28. to feed the church of *God*,
32. to *God*, and to the word of his grace,
21:19. what things *God* had wrought among
22: 3. and was zealous toward *God*,
14. The *God* of our fathers hath chosen
23: 1. have lived in all good conscience before *God*
3. *God* shall smite thee,
4. Revilest thou *God's* high priest?
24:14. worship I the *God* of my fathers,
15. And have hope toward *God*,
16. to have always a conscience void of offence toward *God*,
26: 6. the promise made of *God*
8. that *God* should raise the dead?

Acts26:18. of Satan unto *God*,
20. repent and turn to *God*,
22. Having therefore obtained help of *God*
29. I would to *God*, that not only
27:23. the angel of *God*, whose I am.
24. *God* hath given thee all them
25. for I believe *God*,
35. and gave thanks to *God*
28: 6. and said that he was a *god*.
15. he thanked *God*, and took courage.
23. and testified the kingdom of *God*,
28. the salvation of *God*
31. Preaching the kingdom of *God*,
Ro. 1: 1. unto the gospel of *God*,
4. And declared (to be) the Son of *God*
7. be in Rome, beloved of *God*,
— from *God* our Father,
8. I thank my *God* through Jesus
9. For *God* is my witness,
10. by the will of *God* to come
16. for it is the power of *God*
17. For therein is the righteousness of *God*
18. the wrath of *God*...from heaven
19. that which may be known of *God*
— *God* hath shewed (it) unto them.
21. when they knew *God*, they glorified (him) not as *God*,
23. the glory of the uncorruptible *God*
24. *God* also gave them up
25. the truth of *God*
26. *God* gave them up
28. to retain *God* in (their) knowledge, *God* gave them over to
32. Who knowing the judgment of *God*,
2: 2. that the judgment of *God* is
3. thou shalt escape the judgment of *God*?
4. the goodness of *God*
5. of the righteous judgment of *God*;
11. respect of persons with *God*.
13. (are) just before *God*,
16. when *God* shall judge the secrets
17. and makest thy boast of *God*,
23. breaking the law dishonourest thou *God*
24. For the name of *God*
29. not of men, but of *God*.
3: 2. the oracles of *God*.
3. make the faith of *God* without effect?
4. yea, let *God* be true,
5. commend the righteousness of *God*,
— (Is) *God* unrighteous who taketh vengeance?
6. how shall *God* judge the world?
7. the truth of *God* hath more
11. that seeketh after *God*.
18. There is no fear of *God*
19. may become guilty before *God*.
21. the righteousness of *God*...is manifested,
22. Even the righteousness of *God* (which is) by faith
23. come short of the glory of *God*;
25. Whom *God* hath set forth (to be) a
—(26). through the forbearance of *God*;
29. (Is he) the *God* of the Jews only?
30. Seeing (it is) one *God*,
4: 2. but not before *God*.
3. Abraham believed *God*,
6. unto whom *God* imputeth righteousness
17. (even) *God*, who quickeneth
20. the promise of *God*
— giving glory to *God*;
5: 1. we have peace with *God*
2. in hope of the glory of *God*

Ro. 5: 5. the love of *God* is shed abroad
8. *God* commendeth his love toward us,
10. we were reconciled to *God*
11. we also joy in *God*
15. the grace of *God*, and the gift
6: 10. but in that he liveth, he liveth unto *God*.
11. but alive unto *God* through Jesus
13. yield yourselves unto *God*,
— instruments of righteousness unto *God*.
17. But *God* be thanked,
22. and become servants to *God*,
23. but the gift of *God*
7: 4. we should bring forth fruit unto *God*.
22. For I delight in the law of *God*
25. I thank *God* through Jesus Christ
— serve the law of *God*;
8: 3. *God* sending his own Son
7. (is) enmity against *God*: for it is not subject to the law of *God*,
8. in the flesh cannot please *God*.
9. if so be that the Spirit of *God* dwell
14. are led by the Spirit of *God*, they are the sons of *God*.
16. that we are the children of *God*:
17. heirs of *God*, and joint-heirs
19. the manifestation of the sons of *God*.
21. of the children of *God*.
27. he maketh intercession...according to (the will of) *God*.
28. to them that love *God*,
31. If *God* (be) for us,
33. of *God's* elect? (It is) *God* that justifieth.
34. at the right hand of *God*,
39. from the love of *God*,
9: 5. who is over all, *God*
6. the word of *God* hath taken
8. these (are) not the children of *God*:
11. the purpose of *God* according to election
14. (Is there) unrighteousness with *God*?
16. but of *God* that sheweth mercy.
20. that repliest against *God*?
22. (What) if *God*, willing to shew
26. shall they be called the children of the living *God*.
10: 1. and prayer to *God*
2. they have a zeal of *God*,
3. being ignorant of *God's* righteousness,
— unto the righteousness of *God*.
9. that *God* hath raised him
17. hearing by the word of *God*.
11: 1. Hath *God* cast away his people?
2. *God* hath not cast away his people
— how he maketh intercession to *God*
8. *God* hath given them the spirit
21. For if *God* spared not the natural
22. and severity of *God*:
23. for *God* is able
29. and calling of *God*
30. have not believed *God*,
32. For *God* hath concluded them
33. and knowledge of *God*!
12: 1. by the mercies of *God*,
— acceptable unto *God*,
2. what (is) that...will of *God*.
3. according as *God* hath dealt
13: 1. power but of *God*: the powers that be are ordained of *God*.
2. resisteth the ordinance of *God*:
4. For he is the minister of *God*
— for he is the minister of *God*,
6. for they are *God's* ministers,
14: 3. for *God* hath received him.

Ro. 14: 4. *God* is able to make him stand.
6. for he giveth *God* thanks;
— and giveth *God* thanks.
11. shall confess to *God*.
12. shall give account of himself to *God*.
17. For the kingdom of *God* is not
18. (is) acceptable to *God*,
20. destroy not the work of *God*.
22. have (it) to thyself before *God*.
15: 5. Now the *God* of patience
6. *God*, even the Father of our Lord
7. us to the glory of *God*.
8. for the truth of *God*,
9. the Gentiles might glorify *God* for
13. Now the *God* of hope
15. that is given to me of *God*,
16. the gospel of *God*,
17. through Jesus Christ in those things which pertain to *God*.
19. by the power of the Spirit of *God*;
30. prayers to *God* for me;
32. by the will of *God*,
33. Now the *God* of peace
16: 20. And the *God* of peace
26. the commandment of the everlasting *God*.
27. To *God* only wise,

1Co. 1: 1. through the will of *God*,
2. Unto the church of *God*
3. peace, from *God* our Father,
4. I thank my *God* always on your behalf, for the grace of *God*
9. *God* (is) faithful, by whom ye were
14. I thank *God* that I baptized
18. it is the power of *God*.
20. hath not *God* made foolish the wisdom
21. the wisdom of *God* the world by wisdom knew not *God*, it pleased *God* by the foolishness
24. power of *God*, and the wisdom of *God*.
25. the foolishness of *God* is wiser than men; and the weakness of *God*
27. *God* hath chosen the foolish
— *God* hath chosen the weak
28. which are despised, hath *God* chosen,
30. of *God* is made unto us wisdom,
1. the testimony of *God*.
5. but in the power of *God*.
7. the wisdom of *God* in a mystery,
— which *God* ordained before
9. which *God* hath prepared for them
10. But *God* hath revealed (them)
— yea, the deep things of *God*.
11. the things of *God* knoweth no man, but the Spirit of *God*.
12. the spirit which is of *God*;
— the things that are freely given to us of *God*.
14. the things of the Spirit of *God*
3: 6. but *God* gave the increase.
7. but *God* that giveth the increase.
9. For we are labourers together with *God*. ye are *God's* husbandry, (ye are) *God's* building.
10. According to the grace of *God*
16. that ye are the temple of *God*, and (that) the Spirit of *God* dwelleth
17. If any man defile the temple of *God*, him shall *God* destroy; for the temple of *God* is holy,
19. is foolishness with *God*.
23. and Christ (is) *God's*.
4: 1. stewards of the mysteries of *God*

1 Cor. 4: 5. shall every man have praise of *God*.
9. *God* hath set forth us the apostles
20. For the kingdom of *God* (is) not in word,
5: 13. But them that are without *God* judgeth.
6: 9. shall not inherit the kingdom of *God*?
10. nor extortioners, shall inherit the kingdom of *God*.
11. by the Spirit of our *God*.
13. but *God* shall destroy both it
14. And *God* hath both raised up the Lord,
19. which ye have of *God*,
20. therefore glorify *God* in your body, and in your spirit, which are *God's*
7: 7. hath his proper gift of *God*,
15. *God* hath called us to peace.
17. as *God* hath distributed
19. keeping of the commandments of *God*.
24. therein abide with *God*.
40. that I have the Spirit of *God*.
8: 3. But if any man love *God*,
4. (there is) none other *God*
5. that are called *gods*,
— as there be *gods* many,
6. (there is but) one *God*, the Father,
8. commendeth us not to *God*:
9: 9. Doth *God* take care for oxen?
21. being not without law to *God*,
10: 5. *God* was not well pleased:
13. but *God* (is) faithful, who will not suffer
20. they sacrifice to devils, and not to *God*:
31. do all to the glory of *God*.
32. nor to the church of *God*:
11: 3. and the head of Christ (is) *God*.
7. forasmuch as he is the image and glory of *God*:
12. but all things of *God*.
13. pray unto *God* uncovered?
16. neither the churches of *God*.
22. or despise ye the church of *God*,
12: 3. speaking by the Spirit of *God*
6. but it is the same *God* which worketh
18. But now hath *God* set the members
24. but *God* hath tempered the body together,
28. *God* hath set some in the church,
14: 2. speaketh not unto men, but unto *God*:
18. I thank my *God*,
25. he will worship *God*, and report that *God* is in you of a truth.
28. let him speak to himself, and to *God*.
33. *God* is not (the author) of confusion, but
36. came the word of *God* out from you?
15: 9. because I persecuted the church of *God*.
10. But by the grace of *God* I am what I am:
— but the grace of *God*
15. false witnesses of *God*; because we have testified of *God* that he raised up
24. the kingdom to *God*, even the Father;
28. that *God* may be all
34. for some have not the knowledge of *God*:
38. But *God* giveth it a body
50. inherit the kingdom of *God*;
57. But thanks (be) to *God*, which giveth
2Co. 1: 1. by the will of *God*,
— unto the church of *God*
2. from *God* our Father,
3. Blessed (be) *God*, even the Father
— and the *God* of all comfort;
4. we ourselves are comforted of *God*.
9. in *God* which raiseth the dead:
12. simplicity and *god*ly sincerity,
— but by the grace of *God*,
18. But (as) *God* (is) true, our word

2Co. 1: 19. For the Son of *God*, Jesus Christ,
20. For all the promises of *God*
— unto the glory of *God*
21. and hath anointed us, (is) *God*;
23. I call *God* for a record
2: 14. Now thanks (be) unto *God*,
15. we are unto *God* a sweet savour
17. the word of *God*:
— but as of *God*, in the sight of *God*
3: 3. with the Spirit of the living *God*;
4. through Christ to *God*-ward:
5. our sufficiency (is) of *God*;
4: 2. handling the word of *God* deceitfully;
— in the sight of *God*.
4. the *god* of this world
— who is the image of *God*,
6. For *God*, who commanded
— of the knowledge of the glory of *God*
7. of the power may be of *God*,
15. to the glory of *God*.
5: 1. we have a building of *God*,
5. for the selfsame thing (is) *God*,
11. but we are made manifest unto *God*;
13. For whether we be beside ourselves, (it is) to *God*:
18. And all things (are) of *God*,
19. To wit, that *God* was in Christ,
20. as though *God* did beseech (you)
— be ye reconciled to *God*.
21. the righteousness of *God* in him.
6: 1. that ye receive not the grace of *God*
4. as the ministers of *God*,
7. by the power of *God*,
16. the temple of *God* with idols? for ye are the temple of the living *God*; as *God* hath said,
— I will be their *God*,
7: 1. in the fear of *God*.
6. *God*,...comforted us
9. for ye were made sorry after a *god*ly manner,
10. For *god*ly sorrow worketh
11. that ye sorrowed after a *god*ly sort,
12. for you in the sight of *God*
8: 1. the grace of *God* bestowed
5. by the will of *God*.
16. But thanks (be) to *God*,
9: 7. *God* loveth a cheerful giver.
8. And *God* (is) able to make
11. through us thanksgiving to *God*.
12. many thanksgivings unto *God*;
13. they glorify *God* for your
14. grace of *God* in you.
15. Thanks (be) unto *God* for
10: 4. but mighty through *God*
5. against the knowledge of *God*,
13. *God* hath distributed to us,
11: 2. For I am jealous over you with *god*ly jealousy;
7. the gospel of *God*
11. love you not? *God* knoweth.
31. The *God* and Father of our Lord
12: 2. I cannot tell: *God* knoweth;
3. I cannot tell: *God* knoweth;
19. before *God* in Christ:
21. my *God* will humble me
13: 4. he liveth by the power of *God*.
— by the power of *God* toward you.
7. Now I pray to *God*
11. and the *God* of love
14(13). and the love of *God*,
Gal. 1: 1. and *God* the Father,

Gal. 1: 3. from *God* the Father,
4. according to the will of *God*
10. do I now persuade men, or *God*?
13. persecuted the church of *God*,
15. But when it pleased *God*,
20. behold, before *God*, I lie not.
24. they glorified *God* in me.
2: 6. *God* accepteth no man's person:
19. that I might live unto *God*.
20. of the Son of *God*,
21. I do not frustrate the grace of *God*.
3: 6. Even as Abraham believed *God*,
8. *God* would justify the heathen
11. is justified...in the sight of *God*,
17. that was confirmed before of *God*
18. *God* gave (it) to Abraham
20. but *God* is one.
21. against the promises of *God*?
26. For ye are all the children of *God*
4: 4. *God* sent forth his Son,
6. *God* hath sent forth the Spirit
7. then an heir of *God*
8. when ye knew not *God*,
— by nature are no *gods*.
9. But now, after that ye have known *God*, or rather are known of *God*,
14. but received me as an angel of *God*,
5: 21. shall not inherit the kingdom of *God*.
6: 7. *God* is not mocked:
16. upon the Israel of *God*.
Eph. 1: 1. by the will of *God*,
2. from *God* our Father,
3. Blessed be the *God* and Father
17. the *God* of our Lord
2: 4. But *God*, who is rich in
8. (it is) the gift of *God*:
10. which *God* hath before ordained
16. unto *God* in one body by the cross,
19. and of the houshold of *God*;
22. for an habitation of *God*
3: 2. of the grace of *God* which
7. the gift of the grace of *God*
9. the beginning of the world...in *God*,
10. the manifold wisdom of *God*,
19. with all the fulness of *God*.
4: 6. One *God* and Father of all,
13. of the knowledge of the Son of *God*,
18. the life of *God* through the ignorance
24. which after *God* is created
30. the holy Spirit of *God*,
32. even as *God* for Christ's sake
5: 1. followers of *God*, as dear children;
2. and a sacrifice to *God*
5. in the kingdom of Christ and of *God*.
6. cometh the wrath of *God*
20. unto *God* and the Father
21. in the fear of *God*.
6: 6. the will of *God*
11. the whole armour of *God*,
13. the whole armour of *God*,
17. which is the word of *God*:
23. from *God* the Father
Phi. 1: 2. from *God* our Father,
3. I thank my *God* upon every
8. For *God* is my record,
11. unto the glory and praise of *God*.
28. and that of *God*.
2: 6. being in the form of *God*,
— to be equal with *God*:
9. *God* also hath highly exalted him,
11. to the glory of *God* the Father.
13. For it is *God* which worketh
Phi. 2: 15. the sons of *God*, without rebuke,
27. but *God* had mercy on him;
3: 3. which worship *God* in the spirit,
9. the righteousness which is of *God*
14. of the high calling of *God*
15. *God* shall reveal even this unto you.
19. whose *God* (is their) belly,
4: 6. let your requests be made known unto *God*.
7. And the peace of *God*,
9. and the *God* of peace
18. acceptable, wellpleasing to *God*.
19. But my *God* shall supply
20. Now unto *God* and our Father (be) glory
Col. 1: 1. by the will of *God*,
2. from *God* our Father
3. We give thanks to *God*
6. the grace of *God* in truth:
10. in the knowledge of *God*;
15. Who is the image of the invisible *God*,
25. the dispensation of *God*
— to fulfil the word of *God*;
27. *God* would make known
2: 2. of the mystery of *God*,
12. of *God*, who hath raised him
19. the increase of *God*.
3: 1. on the right hand of *God*.
3. your life is hid with Christ in *God*.
6. the wrath of *God* cometh
12. as the elect of *God*,
15. And let the peace of *God*
17. giving thanks to *God*
22. in singleness of heart, fearing *God*:
4: 3. that *God* would open unto us
11. unto the kingdom of *God*,
12. in all the will of *God*.
1 Th. 1: 1. (which is) in *God* the Father and (in) the Lord
— from *God* our Father,
2. We give thanks to *God*
3. in the sight of *God*
4. your election of *God*.
8. to *God*-ward is spread abroad;
9. ye turned to *God* from idols to serve the living and true *God*;
2: 2. in our *God* to speak unto you the gospel of *God*
4. we were allowed of *God*
— not as pleasing men, but *God*, which trieth our hearts.
5. *God* (is) witness:
8. the gospel of *God*
9. the gospel of *God*.
10. Ye (are) witnesses, and *God* (also),
12. ye would walk worthy of *God*,
13. thank we *God* without ceasing,
— of *God* which ye heard of us,
— as it is in truth, the word of *God*, which
14. of the churches of *God*
15. they please not *God*,
3: 2. and minister of *God*,
9. render to *God* again for you,
— for your sakes before our *God*;
11. Now *God* himself and our Father,
13. before *God*, even our Father,
4: 1. and to please *God*,
3. For this is the will of *God*.
5. which know not *God*:
7. For *God* hath not called us
8. *God*, who hath also given
14. even so them also which sleep...will *God*
16. and with the trump of *God*:

1Th. 5: 9. *God* hath not appointed us to wrath,
18. for this is the will of *God*
23. And the very *God* of peace
2Th. 1: 1. in *God* our Father
2. from *God* our Father
3. We are bound to thank *God* always
4. in the churches of *God*
5. of the righteous judgment of *God*,
of the kingdom of *God*,
6. Seeing (it is) a righteous thing with *God*
8. on them that know not *God*,
11. our *God* would count you worthy of (this)
12. according to the grace of our *God*
2: 4. that is called *God*, or that is worshipped; so that he as *God* sitteth in the temple of *God*, shewing himself that he is *God*.
11. *God* shall send them
13. to give thanks alway to *God*
— *God* hath from the beginning chosen you
16. *God*, even our Father,
3: 5. into the love of *God*,
1Ti. 1: 1. by the commandment of *God* our Saviour,
2. from *God* our Father
4. *god*ly edifying which is in faith:
11. of the blessed *God*,
17. the only wise *God*,
2: 3. in the sight of *God* our Saviour;
5. For (there is) one *God*, and one mediator between *God* and men,
3: 5. shall he take care of the church of *God*?
15. in the house of *God*, which is the church of the living *God*,
16. *God* was manifest in the flesh,
4: 3. which *God* hath created
4. every creature of *God* (is) good,
5. by the word of *God* and prayer.
10. we trust in the living *God*,
5: 4. good and acceptable before *God*.
5. trusteth in *God*, and continueth
21. I charge (thee) before *God*,
6: 1. that the name of *God*
11. But thou, O man of *God*,
13. thee charge in the sight of *God*,
17. but in the living *God*,
2Ti 1: 1. by the will of *God*,
2. from *God* the Father
3. I thank *God*, whom I serve
6. the gift of *God*,
7. For *God* hath not given us
8. according to the power of *God*;
2: 9. the word of *God* is not bound.
15. to shew thyself approved unto *God*,
19. the foundation of *God* standeth
25. *God* peradventure will give them
3: 17. That the man of *God* may be perfect,
4: 1. before *God*, and the Lord
Tit. 1: 1. Paul, a servant of *God*,
— according to the faith of *God's* elect,
2. *God*, that cannot lie,
3. of *God* our Saviour;
4. from *God* the Father
7. as the steward of *God*;
16. They profess that they know *God*;
2: 5. the word of *God* be not blasphemed.
10. of *God* our Saviour
11. the grace of *God* that bringeth salvation
13. glorious appearing of the great *God* and our Saviour Jesus Christ;
3: 4. of *God* our Saviour
8. they which have believed in *God*
Philem. 3. from *God* our Father
4. I thank my *God*,

Heb. 1: 1. *God*, who...spake in time past unto the fathers by the prophets,
6(7). all the angels of *God*
8. Thy throne, O *God*,
9. *God*, (even) thy *God*, hath anointed thee
2: 4. *God* also bearing (them) witness, both with signs
9. that he by the grace of *God*
13. which *God* hath given me.
17. in things (pertaining) to *God*,
3: 4. that built all things (is) *God*.
12. departing from the living *God*.
4: 4. *God* did rest the seventh day
9. a rest to the people of *God*.
10. *God* (did) from his.
12. For the word of *God* (is) quick,
14. Jesus the Son of *God*,
5: 1. in things (pertaining) to *God*,
4. is called of *God*,
10. of *God* an high priest
12. of the oracles of *God*;
6: 1. and of faith toward *God*,
3. will we do, if *God* permit.
5. have tasted the good word of *God*,
6. to themselves the Son of *God*
7. receiveth blessing from *God*:
10. For *God* (is) not unrighteous
13. when *God* made promise
17. *God*, willing more abundantly
18. (it was) impossible for *God* to lie,
7: 1. priest of the most high *God*,
3. unto the Son of *God*;
19. by the which we draw nigh unto *God*.
25. unto *God* by him,
8: 10. I will be to them a *God*,
9: 14. without spot to *God*,
— to serve the living *God*?
20. *God* hath injoined unto you.
24. in the presence of *God*
10: 7. to do thy will, O *God*.
9. to do thy will, O *God*.
12. on the right hand of *God*;
21. over the house of *God*;
29. hath trodden under foot the Son of *God*,
31. into the hands of the living *God*.
36. after ye have done the will of *God*,
11: 3. worlds were framed by the word of *God*,
4. Abel offered unto *God*
— *God* testifying of his gifts:
5. *God* had translated him:
— that he pleased *God*.
6. he that cometh to *God*
10. and maker (is) *God*.
16. *God* is not ashamed to be called their *God*:
19. *God* (was) able to raise (him) up,
25. the people of *God*,
40. *God* having provided some better thing for
12: 2. of the throne of *God*.
7. *God* dealeth with you
15. of the grace of *God*;
22. and unto the city of the living *God*,
23. to *God* the Judge of all,
28. *God* acceptably with reverence
29. For our *God* (is) a consuming fire.
13: 4. and adulterers *God* will judge.
7. unto you the word of *God*:
15. sacrifice of praise to *God* continually,
16. *God* is well pleased.
20. Now the *God* of peace,
Jas. 1: 1. a servant of *God* and of the Lord Jesus Christ,
of *God*, that giveth

2 R 2

Jas. 1:13. I am tempted of *God*: for *God* cannot be tempted with evil,
20. worketh not the righteousness of *God*.
27. before *God* and the Father
2: 5. Hath not *God* chosen
19. Thou believest that there is one *God*;
23. Abraham believed *God*,
— he was called the Friend of *God*.
3: 9. bless we *God*, even
— after the similitude of *God*.
4: 4. is enmity with *God*?
— is the enemy of *God*.
6. *God* resisteth the proud,
7. Submit yourselves therefore to *God*.
8. Draw nigh to *God*,
1Pet 1: 2. according to the foreknowledge of *God*
3. Blessed (be) the *God* and Father
5. Who are kept by the power of *God*
21. do believe in *God*,
— hope might be in *God*.
23. by the word of *God*, which liveth
2: 4. but chosen of *God*,
5. acceptable to *God* by Jesus
10. but (are) now the people of *God*:
12. they may...glorify *God* in the day
15. the will of *God*,
16. but as the servants of *God*.
17. Fear *God*. Honour the king.
19. if a man for conscience toward *God*
20. this (is) acceptable with *God*.
3: 4. in the sight of *God* of great price.
5. trusted in *God*, adorned themselves,
15. But sanctify the Lord *God*
17. if the will of *God* be so,
18. might bring us to *God*,
20. the longsuffering of *God*
21. the answer...toward *God*,
22. on the right hand of *God*;
4: 2. but to the will of *God*.
6. but live according to *God* in the spirit.
10. of the manifold grace of *God*.
11. as the oracles of *God*;
— the ability which *God* giveth: that *God* in all things may be glorified
14. the spirit of glory and of *God*
16. but let him glorify *God*
17. at the house of *God*:
— the gospel of *God*?
19. according to the will of *God*
5: 2. the flock of *God*
5. *God* resisteth the proud,
6. the mighty hand of *God*,
10. But the *God* of all grace,
12. the true grace of *God*
1Pet i: 1. through the righteousness of *God*
2. through the knowledge of *God*,
7. from *God* the Father
21. holy men of *God*
2: 4. For if *God* spared not the angels that
3: 5. that by the word of *God*
12. the coming of the day of *God*,
.Joh. 1: 5. that *God* is light,
2: 5. is the love of *God* perfected:
14. the word of *God* abideth in you,
17. doeth the will of *God*
3: 1. we should be called the sons of *God*:
2. now are we the sons of *God*,
8. the Son of *God* was manifested,
9. is born of *God*
— he is born of *God*.
10. the children of *God* are manifest,
— is not of *God*,.

1Joh. 3:17. how dwelleth the love of *God*
20. *God* is greater than our heart,
21. (then) have we confidence toward *God*.
4: 1. whether they are of *God*:
2. know ye the Spirit of *God*:
— in the flesh is of *God*:
3. is not of *God*:
4. Ye are of *God*, little children,
6. We are of *God*: he that knoweth *God* heareth us; he that is not of *God*
7. love is of *God*;
— is born of *God*, and knoweth *God*.
8. knoweth not *God*; for *God* is love.
9. the love of *God* toward us,
— *God* sent his only begotten Son into
10. not that we loved *God*,
11. if *God* so loved us,
12. No man hath seen *God* at any time.
— *God* dwelleth in us,
15. the Son of *God*, *God* dwelleth in him, and he in *God*.
16. that *God* hath to us. *God* is love;
— dwelleth in *God*, and *God* in him.
20. I love *God*, and hateth his brother,
— *God* whom he hath not seen?
21. That he who loveth *God*
5: 1. is born of *God*:
2. we love the children of *God*, when we love *God*,
3. the love of *God*,
4. is born of *God*
5. Jesus is the Son of *God*?
9. the witness of *God* is greater: for this is the witness of *God*
10. that believeth on the Son of *God*
— he that believeth not *God*
— that *God* gave of his Son.
11. *God* hath given to us eternal life,
12. hath not the Son of *God*
13. on the name of the Son of *God*;
— on the name of the Son of *God*.
18. is born of *God* sinneth not; but he that is begotten of *God*
19. that we are of *God*,
20. that the Son of *God* is come,
— This is the true *God*,
2Joh. 3. (and) peace, from *God* the Father,
9. of Christ, hath not *God*.
3Joh. 6. if thou bring forward on their journey after a *god*ly sort,
11. He that doeth good is of *God*:
— hath not seen *God*.
Jude 1. are sanctified by *God* the Father,
4. the grace of our *God*
— the only Lord *God*,
21. Keep yourselves in the love of *God*,
25. To the only wise *God* our Saviour,
Rev. 1: 1. which *God* gave unto him,
2. the word of *God*, and
6. priests unto *God* and his Father;
9. for the word of *God*,
2: 7. of the paradise of *God*.
18. These things saith the Son of *God*,
3: 1. that hath the seven Spirits of *God*,
2. found thy works perfect before *God*.
12. in the temple of my *God*,
— the name of my *God*, and the name of the city of my *God*,
— out of heaven from my *God*:
14. the beginning of the creation of *God*;
4: 5. the seven Spirits of *God*.
8. Lord *God* Almighty, which was.

Rev. 5: 6. the seven Spirits of *God*
9. hast redeemed us to *God*
10. unto our *God* kings
6: 9. were slain for the word of *God*,
7: 2. the seal of the living *God*:
3. the servants of our *God*
10. Salvation to our *God* which
11. on their faces, and worshipped *God*,
12. and might, (be) unto our *God*
15. before the throne of *God*,
17. *God* shall wipe away all tears
8: 2. which stood before *God*;
4. before *God* out of the angel's hand.
9: 4. have not the seal of *God*
13. which is before *God*,
10: 7. the mystery of *God* should be finished,
11: 1. measure the temple of *God*,
4. before the *God* of the earth.
11. the Spirit of life from *God*
13. glory to the *God* of heaven.
16. which sat before *God*
— upon their faces, and worshipped *God*,
17. O Lord *God* Almighty,
19. the temple of *God* was opened
12: 5. unto *God*, and (to) his throne.
6. she hath a place prepared of *God*,
10. the kingdom of our *God*,
— before our *God* day and night.
17. keep the commandments of *God*,
13: 6. in blasphemy against *God*,
14: 4. unto *God* and to the Lamb.
5. before the throne of *God*.
7. Fear *God*, and give glory to him;
10. the wine of the wrath of *God*,
12. the commandments of *God*,
19. winepress of the wrath of *God*.
15: 1. is filled up the wrath of *God*.
2. the harps of *God*.
3. the song of Moses the servant of *God*,
— thy works, Lord *God* Almighty;
7. full of the wrath of *God*,
8. from the glory of *God*,
16: 1. the vials of the wrath of *God*
7. Even so, Lord *God* Almighty,
9. blasphemed the name of *God*,
11. blasphemed the *God* of heaven
14. great day of *God* Almighty.
19. came in remembrance before *God*,
21. men blasphemed *God* because of the
17:17. For *God* hath put in their hearts
— the words of *God* shall be fulfilled.
18: 5. *God* hath remembered her iniquities.
8. *God* who judgeth her.
20. for *God* hath avenged you
19: 1. unto the Lord our *God*:
4. worshipped *God* that sat on the throne,
5. Praise our *God*, all ye his servants,
6. the Lord *God* omnipotent
9. are the true sayings of *God*.
10. worship *God*: for the testimony
13. The Word of *God*.
15. and wrath of Almighty *God*.
17. the supper of the great *God*;
20: 4. and for the word of *God*,
6. they shall be priests of *God*
9. fire came down from *God* out
12. small and great, stand before *God*;
21: 2. coming down from *God*
3. Behold, the tabernacle of *God*
— and *God* himself shall be with them, (and be) their *God*.
4. *God* shall wipe away all tears

Rev.21: 7. I will be his *God*,
10. out of heaven from *God*,
11. Having the glory of *God*:
22. for the Lord *God* Almighty
23. for the glory of *God* did lighten
22: 1. the throne of *God* and of the Lamb.
3. the throne of *God* and of the Lamb
5. for the Lord *God* giveth them light:
6. and the Lord *God* of the holy prophets
9. sayings of this book: worship *God*.
18. *God* shall add unto him
19. *God* shall take away his part

2317 1 358/457 3:123 2318

θεοσέβεια, *theosebīa*.

1Ti. 2:10. which becometh women professing *godliness*

2318 1 357/457 3:123 2316,4576

θεοσεβής, *theosebees*.

Joh. 9:31. if any man be *a worshipper of God*,

2319 1 359/457 2136,rt 4767

θεοστυγής, *theostugees*.

Ro. 1:30. *haters of God*, despiteful, proud,

2320 1 359/457 3:65 2316

θεότης, *theotees*.

Col. 2: 9. in him dwelleth all the fulness of the *Godhead* bodily.

2322 4 359/457 3:128 2323

θεραπεία, *therapīa*.

Mat.24:45. hath made ruler over his *houshold*,
Lu. 9:11. them that had need of *healing*.
12:42. shall make ruler over his *houshold*,
Rev.22: 2. (were) for the *healing* of the nations.

2323 44 359/457 3:128 rt 2324

θεραπεύω, *therapūo*.

Mat. 4:23. *healing* all manner of sickness
24. and he *healed* them.
8: 7. I *will* come and *heal* him.
16. and *healed* all that were sick:
9:35. *healing* every sickness and every
10: 1. and *to heal* all manner of sickness
8. *Heal* the sick, cleanse the lepers,
12:10. Is it lawful *to heal* on the sabbath days?
15. he *healed* them all;
22. and he *healed* him,
14:14. he *healed* their sick.
15:30. and he *healed* them:
17:16. and they could not *cure* him.
18. the child *was cured*
19: 2. he *healed* them there.
21:14. and he *healed* them.
Mar 1:34. he *healed* many that were sick
3: 2. whether he would *heal* him on the sabbath day;
10. For he *had healed* many;
15. *to heal* sicknesses, and to cast
6: 5. his hands upon a few sick folk, and *healed*
13. that were sick, and *healed* (them).

Lu. 4:23. this proverb, Physician, *heal* thyself :
40. every one of them, and *healed* them.
5:15. to hear, and *to be healed* by him
6: 7. whether he would *heal* on the sabbath day,
18. and they *were healed.*
7:21. he *cured* many of (their) infirmities
8: 2. women, which had been *healed* of evil
43. neither could *be healed* of any,
9: 1. and *to cure* diseases.
6. and *healing* every where.
10: 9. *heal* the sick that are therein,
13: 14. because that Jesus *had healed* on the sabbath day,
— in them therefore come and *be healed,*
14: 3. Is it lawful *to heal* on the sabbath day?
Joh. 5:10. therefore said unto him *that was cured,*
Acts 4:14. beholding the man *which was healed*
5:16. and they *were healed* every one.
8: 7. and that were lame, *were healed.*
17:25. Neither *is worshipped* with men's hands,
28: 9. came, and *were healed:*
Rev.13: 3. his deadly wound *was healed:*
12. whose deadly wound *was healed.*

2324 1 359/457 3:128 rt 2330

θεράπων, *therapōn.*

Heb 3: 5. faithful in all his house, as a *servant,* for a testimony of those things which

---

2325 21 359/457 3:132 2330

θερίζω, *therizo*

Mat. 6:26. neither do they *reap,*
25:24. *reaping* where thou hast not sown,
26. I *reap* where I sowed not,
Lu. 12:24. for they neither sow nor *reap,*
19:21. *reapest* that thou didst not sow.
22. *reaping* that I did not sow:
Joh. 4:36. he *that reapeth* receiveth wages,
— and he *that reapeth* may rejoice
37. One soweth, and another *reapeth*
38. I sent you *to reap*
1Co. 9:11. if we *shall reap* your carnal things?
2Co. 9: 6. *shall reap* also sparingly;
— *shall reap* also bountifully.
Gal. 6: 7. that *shall* he also *reap.*
8. *shall* of the flesh *reap* corruption;
— *shall* of the Spirit *reap* life everlasting.
9. for in due season we *shall reap,*
Jas. 5: 4. the cries of them *which have reaped*
Rev.14:15. *reap:* for the time is come for thee *to reap;*
16. and the earth *was reaped.*

2326 13 360/458 3:132 2325

θερισμός, *therismos.*

Mat. 9:37. The *harvest* truly (is) plenteous,
38. the Lord of the *harvest,*
— labourers into his *harvest.*
13:30. the *harvest:* and in the time of *harvest*
39. the *harvest* is the end of the world;
Mar 4:29. the *harvest* is come.
Lu. 10: 2. The *harvest* truly (is) great,
— pray ye therefore the Lord of the *harvest,*
— labourers into his *harvest.*
Joh. 4:35. and (then) cometh *harvest?*
— they are white already to *harvest.*
Rev.14:15. the *harvest* of the earth is ripe.

2327 2 360/458 2325

θεριστής, *theristees.*

Mat.13:30. I will say to the *reapers,*
39. and the *reapers* are the angels.

2328 6 360/458 2329

θερμαίνομαι, *thermainomai.*

Mar 14:54. *warmed* him*self* at the fire.
67. saw Peter *warming* him*self,*
Joh. 18:18. it was cold: and they *warmed* them*selves*: and Peter stood with them, and *warmed* him*self.*
25. Simon Peter stood and *warmed* him*self.*
Jas. 2:16. *be* (ye) *warmed* and filled;

2329 1 360/458 rt 2330

θέρμη, *thermee.*

Acts28: 3. there came a viper out of the *heat,*

2330 3 360/458 *therō* (to heat)

θέρος, *theros.*

Mat.24:32. ye know that *summer* (is) nigh:
Mar 13:28. that *summer* is near:
Lu. 21:30. that *summer* is now nigh at hand.

2334 57 360/458 5:315 2300

θεωρέω, *theōreo.* cf 3700

Mat 27:55. women were there *beholding* afar off,
28: 1. *to see* the sepulchre.
Mar 3:11. unclean spirits, when they *saw* him,
5:15. and *see* him that was possessed with the devil,
38. and *seeth* the tumult,
12:41. and *beheld* how the people
15:40. women *looking on* afar off:
47. *beheld* where he was laid.
16: 4. when they looked, they *saw*
Lu. 10:18. I *beheld* Satan as lightning
14:29. all *that behold* (it) begin to mock him,
21: 6. (As for) these things which ye *behold,*
23:35. the people stood *beholding.*
48. *beholding* the things which were done,
24:37. and supposed that they had *seen* a spirit.
39. as ye *see* me have.
Joh. 2:23. *when* they *saw* the miracles
4:19. I *perceive* that thou art a prophet.
6:19. they *see* Jesus walking on the sea,
40. every one *which seeth* the Son,
62. (What) and if ye shall *see* the Son
7: 3. that thy disciples also *may see* the works
8:51. he *shall* never *see* death.
9: 8. they *which* before *had seen* him that he was blind,
10:12. *seeth* the wolf coming,
12:19. *Perceive* ye how ye prevail nothing?
45. And he *that seeth* me *seeth* him that sent
14:17. because it *seeth* him not,
19. a little while, and the world *seeth* me no more; but ye *see* me:
16:10. and ye *see* me no more;
16. A little while, and ye shall not *see* me:
17. A little while, and ye shall not *see* me:
19. A little while, and ye shall not *see* me:
17:24. that they *may behold* my glory,
20: 6. *seeth* the linen clothes lie,
12. *seeth* two angels in white
14. *saw* Jesus standing, and
Acts 3:16. this man strong, whom ye *see* and know:
4:13. Now *when* they *saw* the boldness of Peter

Acts 7:56. I *see* the heavens opened,
8:13. *beholding* the miracles and signs
9: 7. hearing a voice, but *seeing* no man.
10:11. And *saw* heaven opened, and a certain
17:16. *when* he *saw* the city wholly given to
22. I *perceive*...ye are too superstitious.
19:26. ye *see* and hear,
20:38. that they should *see* his face no more.
21:20. Thou *seest*, brother, how many
25:24. ye *see* this man, about whom
27:10. I *perceive* that this voyage will be with
28: 6. and *saw* no harm come to him,
Heb 7: 4. Now *consider* how great this
1Joh 3:17. whoso hath this world's good, and *seeth* his brother have need,
Rev 11:11. fear fell upon them *which saw* them.
12. their enemies *beheld* them.

2335 1 360/459 rt 2334

θεωρία, theōria.

Lu. 23:48. came together to that *sight*, beholding the

2336 1 361/459 5087

θήκη, theekee.

Joh 18:11. Put up thy sword into the *sheath*.

2337 1 361/459 *thelē* (nipple)

θηλάζω, theelazo.

Mat 21:16. Out of the mouth of babes and *sucklings*
24:19. woe...and to them *that give suck* in those days
Mar 13:17. and to them *that give suck*
Lu. 11:27. the paps which thou *hast sucked*
21:23. and to them *that give suck*,
23:29. the paps which never *gave suck*

2338 2 361/459 rt 2337

θήλεια, theelīa.

Ro. 1:26. for even their *women*
27. leaving the natural use of the *woman*,

2338 3 361/459 2337

θῆλυ, theelu.

Mat 19: 4. made them male and *female*.
Mar 10: 6. God made them male and *female*.
Gal. 3:28. there is neither male nor *female*.

2339 1 361/459 *ther* (wild animal)

θήρα, theera.

Ro. 11 9. Let their table be made a snare, and a *trap*, and a stumblingblock,

2340 1 361/459 2339

θηρεύω, theerūo.

Lu. 11:54. seeking *to catch* something out of his

2341 1 361/459 2342,3164

θηριομαχέω, theeriomakeo.

1Co.15:32. I *have fought with beasts* at Ephesus,

2342 46 361/459 3:133 rt 2339

θηρίον, theerion.

Mar. 1:13. was with the *wild beasts*.
Acts 10:12. *wild beasts*, and creeping things,
11: 6. *wild beasts*, and creeping things,
28: 4. *the (venomous) beast* hang
5. shook off the *beast*
Tit. 1:12. evil *beasts*, slow bellies.
Heb 12:20. And if so much as a *beast* touch the
Jas. 3: 7. of *beasts*, and of birds,
Rev. 6: 8. with the *beasts* of the earth.
11: 7. the *beast* that ascendeth
13: 1. a *beast* rise up out of the sea,
2. the *beast* which I saw
3. the world wondered after the *beast*.
4. power unto the *beast*: and they worshipped the *beast*, saying, Who (is) like unto the *beast*?
11. I beheld another *beast*
12. all the power of the first *beast*
— to worship the first *beast*,
14. to do in the sight of the *beast*;
— that they should make an image to the *beast*,
15. unto the image of the *beast*, that the image of the *beast* should both speak,
— worship the image of the *beast*
17. or the name of the *beast*,
18. count the number of the *beast*.
14: 9. If any man worship the *beast*
11. who worship the *beast*
15: 2. over the *beast*, and over
16: 2. the mark of the *beast*,
10. upon the seat of the *beast*;
13. out of the mouth of the *beast*,
17: 3. upon a scarlet coloured *beast*,
7. of the *beast* that carrieth her,
8. The *beast* that thou sawest
— the *beast* that was, and is not,
11. And the *beast* that was,
12. received power as kings one hour with the *beast*.
13. shall give their power and strength unto the *beast*.
16. which thou sawest upon the *beast*,
17. their kingdom unto the *beast*.
19:19. And I saw the *beast*,
20. the *beast* was taken,
— the mark of the *beast*,
20: 4. had not worshipped the *beast*,
10. where the *beast* and the false prophet (are),

2343 8 362/460 3:136 2344

θησαυρίζω, theesaurizo.

Mat. 6:19. *Lay* not *up* for yourselves treasures upon earth,
20. But *lay up* for yourselves treasures in heaven,
Lu. 12:21. he *that layeth up treasure* for himself,
Ro 2: 5. *treasurest up* unto thyself wrath
1Co.16: 2. let every one...lay by him in store, as (God) hath prospered him, (lit. lay by him *treasuring* what he be prospered in)
2Co.12.14. ought not *to lay up* for the parents,
Jas. 5: 3. Ye *have heaped treasure together* for the last days.
2Pet.3: 7. are *kept in store*, reserved unto fire

2344 18 362/460 3:136 5087

θησαυρός, theesauros.

Mat. 2:11. when they had opened their *treasures*,
6:19. yourselves *treasures* upon earth,
20. *treasures* in heaven, where

Mat. 6:21. For where your *treasure* is,
12:35. out of the good *treasure* of the heart
— out of the evil *treasure* bringeth forth
13:44. is like unto *treasure* hid in a field;
52. out of his *treasure* (things) new and
19:21. thou shalt have *treasure* in heaven:
Ma 10:21. thou shalt have *treasure* in heaven:
Lu. 6:45. out of the good *treasure* of his heart
— out of the evil *treasure* of his heart
12:33. a *treasure* in the heavens that faileth not,
34. For where your *treasure* is,
18:22. thou shalt have *treasure* in heaven:
2Co. 4: 7. But we have this *treasure*
Col. 2: 3. all the *treasures* of wisdom and knowledge.
Heb 11:26. than the *treasures* in Egypt:

2345 3 362/460 thigō (to touch)

θίγω, thigo.

Col. 2:21. taste not; *handle* not;
Heb 11:28. lest he that destroyed the firstborn *should touch* them.
12:20. And if so much as a beast *touch* the

2346 10 362/460 3:139 cf rt5147

θλίβω, thlibo

Mat. 7:14. and *narrow* (is) the way,
Mar. 3: 9. lest they *should throng* him.
2Co. 1: 6. And whether we *be afflicted*,
4: 8. (We are) *troubled* on every side,
7: 5. but we were *troubled* on every side;
1Th. 3: 4. that we should *suffer tribulation;*
2Th. 1: 6. tribulation to them *that trouble* you;
7. And to you *who are troubled* rest
1Ti. 5:10. if she have relieved the *afflicted*,
Heb 11:37. being destitute, *afflicted*, tormented;

2347 45 362/460 3:139 2346

θλίψις, thlipsis.

Mat.13:21. for when *tribulation* or persecution ariseth
24: 9. shall they deliver you up to *be afflicted*,
21. For then shall be great *tribulation*,
29. after the *tribulation* of those days
Mar 4:17. afterward, when *affliction* or persecution ariseth
13:19. (in) those days shall be *affliction*,
24. after that *tribulation*, the sun
Joh.16:21. she remembereth no more the *anguish*,
33. In the world ye shall have *tribulation:*
Acts 7:10. out of all his *afflictions*,
11. and Chanaan, and great *affliction:*
11:19. upon the *persecution* that arose
14:22. we must through much *tribulation*
20:23. and *afflictions* abide me.
Ro. 2: 9. *Tribulation* and anguish, upon every
5: 3. we glory in *tribulations* also: knowing that *tribulation*
8:35. (shall) *tribulation*, or distress, or
12:12. patient in *tribulation;* continuing
1Co. 7:28. shall have *trouble* in the flesh:
2Co. 1: 4. in all our *tribulation*,
— them which are in any *trouble*
8. of our *trouble* which came
2: 4. For out of much *affliction*
4:17. our light *affliction*, which is
6: 4. in *afflictions*, in necessities,
7: 4. in all our *tribulation*.
8: 2. in a great trial of *affliction*
13. and ye burdened: (lit. *burden* to you)
Eph. 3:13. at my *tribulations* for you,
Phil. 1:16. to add *affliction* to my bonds:
4:14. that ye did communicate with my *affliction*
Col. 1:24. that which is behind of the *afflictions* of Christ
1Th. 1: 6. the word in much *affliction*,
3: 3. should be moved by these *afflictions:*
7. in all our *affliction*
2Th. 1: 4. *tribulations* that ye endure:
6. *tribulation* to them that trouble you,
Heb 10:33. whilst ye were made a gazingstock both by reproaches and *afflictions;*
Jas. 1:27. and widows in their *affliction*,
Rev. 1: 9. brother, and companion in *tribulation*,
2: 9. and *tribulation*, and poverty,
10. ye shall have *tribulation* ten days:
22. with her into great *tribulation*,
7:14. out of great *tribulation*,

2348 13 363/461 3:7 thanō (to die)

θνήσκω, thneesko.

Mat. 2:20. for they *are dead* which sought
Mar 15:44. if he *were* already *dead:*
Lu. 7:12. there was a *dead* man carried out,
8:49. Thy daughter *is dead;*
Joh.11:21. my brother *had* not *died*.
39. the sister of him *that was dead*,
41. where the *dead* was laid.
44. And he *that was dead* came forth,
12: 1. Lazarus was *which had been dead*,
19:33. that he was *dead* already,
Acts14:19. supposing he had *been dead*.
25:19. of one Jesus, *which was dead*, whom Paul affirmed to be alive.
1Ti. 5: 6. *is dead* while she liveth.

2349 6 363/461 3:7 2348

θνητός, thneetos.

Ro. 6:12. in your *mortal* body,
8:11. also quicken your *mortal* bodies
1Co.15:53. and this *mortal* (must) put on
54. this *mortal* shall have put on
2Co. 4:11. in our *mortal* flesh.
5: 4. mortality (lit. the *mortal*) might be swallowed up of life.

2350 4 363/461 2351

θορυβέομαι, thorubeomai.

Mat. 9:23. the people *making a noise*,
Mar 5:39. Why *make* ye this *ado*, and weep?
Acts17: 5. and *set* all the city *on an uproar*,
20:10. *Trouble* not *yourselves;* for his life

2351 7 363/461 rt 2360

θόρυβος, thorubos.

Mat.26: 5. lest there be an *uproar*
27:24. (that) rather a *tumult* was made
Mar 5:38. and seeth the *tumult*,
14: 2. lest there be an *uproar*
Acts20: 1. And after the *uproar* was ceased,
21:34. the certainty for the *tumult*,
24:18. multitude, nor with *tumult*.

2352 4 363/461 cf 4486

θραύω, thrauo.

Lu. 4:18. to set at liberty them *that are bruised*,

2353 1 363/461 5142

θρέμμα, thremma.

Joh. 4:12. his children, and his *cattle?*

2354 4 363/461 3:148 2355

θρηνέω, threeneo.

Mat. 11:17. we *have mourned* unto you, and
Lu. 7:32. we *have mourned* to you, and
23:27. bewailed and *lamented* him.
Joh. 16:20. ye shall weep and *lament,*

2355 1 363/685 3:148 rt 2360

θρῆνος, threenos.

Mat. 2:18. In Rama was there a voice heard, *lamentation,* and weeping,

2356 4 364/461 3:155 2357

θρησκεία, threeskīa.

Acts26: 5. straitest sect of our *religion*
Col. 2:18. and *worshipping* of angels,
Jas. 1:26. this man's *religion* (is) vain.
27. Pure *religion* and undefiled

2357 1 364/461 3:155 rt 2360

θρῆσκος, threeskos.

Jas. 1:26. any man among you seem to be *religious,*

2358 2 364/462 3:159 rt 2360

θριαμβεύω, thriambuo. rt 680

2Co. 2:14. *which...causeth* us *to triumph* in Christ,
Col. 2:15. *triumphing over* them in it.

2359 15 364/462 cf 2864

θρίξ, τριχὸς, thrix, trikos.

Mat. 3: 4. had his raiment of camel's *hair,*
5:36. one *hair* white or black.
10:30. the very *hairs* of your head
Mar 1: 6. John was clothed with camel's *hair,*
Lu. 7:38. with the *hairs* of her head,
44. and wiped (them) with the *hairs* of her
12: 7. the very *hairs* of your head
21:18. But there shall not an *hair* of your head
Joh. 11: 2. and wiped his feet with her *hair,*
12: 3. wiped his feet with her *hair.*
Acts27:34. an *hair* fall from the head
1Pet 3: 3. of plaiting the *hair,*
Rev 1:14. and (his) *hairs* (were) white
9: 8. And they had *hair* as the *hair* of women,

2360 3 364/462 *threomai* (to wail)

θροέομαι, throeomai.

Mat 24: 6. see that ye *be* not *troubled:*
Mar 13: 7. rumours of wars, *be* ye not *troubled:* for
2Th. 2: 2. or *be troubled,* neither by spirit,

2361 1 364/462 5142

θρόμβος, thrombos.

Lu. 22:44. as it were *great drops* of blood

2362 61 364/462 3:160 *thraō* (to sit)

θρόνος, thronos.

Mat 5:34. for it is God's *throne:*
19:28. in the *throne* of his glory, ye also shall sit upon twelve *thrones.*
Mat 23:22. sweareth by the *throne* of God,
25:31. upon the *throne* of his glory:
Lu. 1:32. the *throne* of his father David:
52. the mighty from (their) *seats,*
22:30. sit on *thrones* judging the twelve
Acts 2:30. to sit on his *throne;*
7:49. Heaven (is) my *throne,*
Col. 1:16. whether (they be) *thrones,* or dominions,
Heb 1: 8. Thy *throne,* O God,
4:16. unto the *throne* of grace,
8: 1. on the right hand of the *throne* of the Majesty
12: 2. at the right hand of the *throne* of God.
Rev 1: 4. seven spirits which are before his *throne;*
2:13. (even) where Satan's *seat* (is):
3:21. with me in my *throne,*
— with my Father in his *throne.*
4: 2. a *throne* was set in heaven, and (one) sat on the *throne.*
3. (there was) a rainbow round about the *throne,*
4. round about the *throne* (were) four and twenty *seats:* and upon the *seats* I saw
5. out of the *throne* proceeded
— burning before the *throne,*
6. before the *throne* (there was) a sea
— and in the midst of the *throne,* and round about the *throne,*
9. that sat on the *throne,*
10. that sat on the *throne,*
— cast their crowns before the *throne,*
5: 1. that sat on the *throne*
6. lo, in the midst of the *throne*
7. that sat upon the *throne.*
11. round about the *throne* and
13. unto him that sitteth upon the *throne,*
6:16. of him that sitteth on the *throne,*
7: 9. stood before the *throne,*
10. our God which sitteth upon the *throne,*
11. round about the *throne,*
— fell before the *throne*
15. before the *throne* of God,
— he that sitteth on the *throne*
17. which is in the midst of the *throne*
8: 3. which was before the *throne.*
11:16. sat before God on their *seats,*
12: 5. God, and (to) his *throne.*
13: 2. and his *seat,* and great authority.
14: 3. a new song before the *throne,*
5. before the *throne* of God.
16:10. upon the *seat* of the beast;
17. from the *throne,* saying, It is done.
19: 4. sat on the *throne,*
5. a voice came out of the *throne,*
20: 4. And I saw *thrones,*
11. a great white *throne,*
21: 5. he that sat upon the *throne*
22: 1. out of the *throne* of God and
3. the *throne* of God and of the Lamb shall be in it;

2364 29 365/463

θυγάτηρ, thugateer.

Mat. 9:18. My *daughter* is even now dead:
22. *Daughter,* be of good comfort; thy faith
10:35. and the *daughter* against her mother,
37. loveth son or *daughter* more than me
14: 6. the *daughter* of Herodias danced
15:22. my *daughter* is grievously vexed with a devil.
28. And her *daughter* was made whole from

Mat.21: 5. Tell ye the *daughter* of Sion,
Mar 5:34. *Daughter*, thy faith hath made
35. Thy *daughter* is dead:
6:22. when the *daughter* of the said
7:26. the devil out of her *daughter*.
29. out of thy *daughter*.
30. and her *daughter* laid upon the bed.
Lu. 1: 5. of the *daughters* of Aaron,
2:36. the *daughter* of Phanuel, of
8:42. he had one only *daughter*,
48. *Daughter*, be of good comfort: thy faith
49. Thy *daughter* is dead;
12:53. against the *daughter*, and the *daughter* against the mother;
13:16. being a *daughter* of Abraham,
23:28. *Daughters* of Jerusalem, weep not
Joh. 12:15. Fear not, *daughter* of Sion:
Acts 2:17. and your *daughters* shall prophesy,
7:21. Pharaoh's *daughter* took him up,
21: 9. four *daughters*, virgins, which
2Co. 6:18. ye shall be my sons and *daughters*, saith the Lord Almighty.
Heb 11:24. the son of Pharaoh's *daughter*,

2365 2 365/463 2364

θυγάτριον, thugatrion.

Mar 5:23. My *little daughter* lieth at the point of
7:25. whose *young daughter* had an unclean

2366 1 365/463 2380

θύελλα, thuella.

Heb 12:18. and darkness, and *tempest*,

2367 1 365/463 2380

θύϊνος, thuinos.

Rev. 18:12. *thyine* wood, and all manner vessels

2368 6 365/463 2370

θυμίαμα, thumiama.

Lu. 1:10. at the time of *incense*.
11. of the altar of *incense*.
Rev. 5: 8. full of *odours*, which are the prayers
8: 3. there was given unto him much *incense*,
4. the smoke of the *incense*,...ascended up
18:13. cinnamon, and *odours*, and ointments,

2369 1 365/463 2370

θυμιατήριον, thumiateerion.

Heb 9: 4. Which had the golden *censer*,

2370 1 365/463 2380

θυμιάω, thumiao.

Lu. 1: 9. his lot was *to burn incense*

2371 1 365/463 2372,3164

θυμομαχέω, thumomakeo.

Acts12:20. Herod was *highly displeased* with them of Tyre and

---

2373 1 366/463 2372

θυμόομαι, thumo-omai.

Mat. 2:16. *was* exceeding *wroth*, and sent forth,

2372 18 365/463 3:167 cf 5590

θυμός, thumòs. 2380

Lu. 4:28. were filled with *wrath*,
Acts19:28. they were full of *wrath*,
Ro. 2: 8. but obey unrighteousness, *indignation* and
2Co. 12:20. debates, envyings, *wraths*, strifes,
Gal. 5:20. hatred, variance, emulations, *wrath*,
Eph. 4:31. Let all bitterness, and *wrath*, and anger,
Col. 3: 8. anger, *wrath*, malice, blasphemy,
Heb 11:27. the *wrath* of the king:
Rev. 12:12. having great *wrath*, because
14: 8. drink of the wine of the *wrath* of her
10. of the wine of the *wrath* of God,
19. winepress of the *wrath* of God.
15: 1. is filled up the *wrath* of God.
7. full of the *wrath* of God,
16: 1. the vials of the *wrath* of God
19. of the wine of the *fierceness* of his wrath.
18: 3. of the wine of the *wrath* of her fornication,
19:15. of the *fierceness* and wrath of Almighty God.

2374 39 366/464 3:173

θύρα, thurá.

Mat. 6: 6. when thou hast shut thy *door*,
24:33. it is near, (even) at the *doors*.
25:10. the *door* was shut.
27:60. to the *door* of the sepulchre,
28: 2. the stone from the *door*,
Mar 1:33. was gathered together at the *door*.
2: 2. no, not so much as about the *door*:
11: 4. by the *door* without in
13:29. it is nigh, (even) at the *doors*.
15:46. unto the *door* of the sepulchre.
16: 3. from the *door* of the sepulchre?
Lu. 11: 7. the *door* is now shut,
13:25. hath shut to the *door*,
— to knock at the *door*,
Joh. 10: 1. by the *door* into the sheepfold,
2. by the *door* is the shepherd
7. the *door* of the sheep.
9. I am the *door*:
18:16. at the *door* without.
20:19. when the *doors* were shut
26. the *doors* being shut,
Acts 3: 2. at the *gate* of the temple
5: 9. (are) at the *door*, and shall carry
19. opened the prison *doors*,
23. standing without before the *doors*:
12: 6. before the *door* kept the prison.
13. the *door* of the gate,
14:27. the *door* of faith unto the Gentiles.
16:26. immediately all the *doors*
27. seeing the prison *doors* open,
21:30. the *doors* were shut.
1Co. 16: 9. For a great *door* and effectual is opened
2Co. 2:12. and a *door* was opened unto me
Col. 4: 3. would open unto us a *door* of utterance,
Jas. 5: 9. standeth before the *door*.
Rev. 3: 8. set before thee an open *door*,
20. I stand at the *door*, and knock: if any man hear my voice, and open the *door*,
4: 1. a *door* (was) opened in heaven:

2375 1 366/464 5:292 2374

θυρεός, thureos.

Eph. 6:16. taking the *shield* of faith, wherewith ye shall be able

---

2376 2 366/464 2374

θυρίς, thuris.

Acts20: 9. there sat in a *window* a certain young man
2Co. 11:33. And through a *window* in a basket

2377 4 366/464 2374 ouros (watcher)

θυρωρός, thurōros.

Mar 13:34. and commanded the *porter* to watch.
Joh. 10: 3. To him the *porter* openeth;
18:16. and spake unto her *that kept the door*,
17. the damsel *that kept the door*

2378 29 366/464 3:180 2380

θυσία, thusia.

Mat. 9:13. I will have mercy, and not *sacrifice*:
12: 7. I will have mercy, and not *sacrifice*,
Mar. 9:49. and every *sacrifice* shall be
12:33. whole burnt offerings and *sacrifices*.
Lu. 2:24. And to offer a *sacrifice*
13: 1. mingled with their *sacrifices*.
Acts 7:41. offered *sacrifice* unto the idol,
42. have ye offered to me slain beasts and *sacrifices*
Ro. 12: 1. a living *sacrifice*, holy,
1Co.10:18. they which eat of the *sacrifices*
Eph. 5: 2. an offering and a *sacrifice* to God
Phi. 2:17. upon the *sacrifice* and service of your faith,
4:18. a *sacrifice* acceptable, wellpleasing
Heb. 5: 1. gifts and *sacrifices* for sins:
7:27. to offer up *sacrifice*, first for
8: 3. to offer gifts and *sacrifices*:
9: 9. were offered both gifts and *sacrifices*,
23. with better *sacrifices* than these.
26. by the *sacrifice* of himself.
10: 1. with those *sacrifices* which
5. *Sacrifice* and offering thou
8. *Sacrifice* and offering and
11. offering oftentimes the same *sacrifices*,
12. after he had offered one *sacrifice*
26. there remaineth no more *sacrifice*
11: 4. By faith...a more excellent *sacrifice* than Cain,
13:15. let us offer the *sacrifice* of praise
16. for with such *sacrifices*
1Pet. 2: 5. to offer up spiritual *sacrifices*,

2379 23 367/465 3:180 2378

θυσιαστήριον, thusiasteerion.

Mat. 5:23. bring thy gift to the *altar*,
24. thy gift before the *altar*,
23:18. shall swear by the *altar*.
19. the gift, or the *altar*
20. shall swear by the *altar*,
35. the temple and the *altar*.
Lu. 1:11. of the *altar* of incense.
11:51. between the *altar* and the temple:
Ro 11: 3. and digged down thine *altars*;
1Co. 9:13. and they which wait at the *altar* are partakers with the *altar*?
10:18. partakers of the *altar*?
Heb. 7:13. no man gave attendance at the *altar*
13:10. We have an *altar*, whereof
Jas. 2:21. offered Isaac his son upon the *altar*?
Rev. 6: 9. under the *altar* the souls
8: 3. stood at the *altar*,
— upon the golden *altar*
5. with fire of the *altar*,
9:13. horns of the golden *altar*
11: 1. the temple of God, and the *altar*,
14:18. came out from the *altar*,
16: 7. I heard another out of the *altar* say,

2380 14 367/465 3:180

θύω, thuo.

Mat.22: 4. and (my) fatlings (are) *killed*,
Mar 14:12. when they *killed* the passover,
Lu. 15:23. the fatted calf, and *kill* (it);
27. thy father *hath killed* the fatted calf,
30. thou *hast killed* for him the fatted calf.
22: 7. when the passover must *be killed*.
Joh. 10:10. but for to steal, and to *kill*,
Acts 10:13. Rise, Peter; *kill*, and eat.
11: 7. Arise, Peter; *slay* and eat.
14:13. would *have done sacrifice*
18. the people, that they *had* not *done sacrifice*
1Co. 5: 7. Christ our passover *is sacrificed* for us:
10:20. the things which the Gentiles *sacrifice*, they *sacrifice* to devils,

2382 5 368/465 5:292

θώραξ, thorax.

Eph. 6:14. having on the *breastplate* of righteousness;
1Th. 5: 8. putting on the *breastplate* of faith
Rev. 9: 9. *breastplates*, as it were *breastplates* of iron;
17. *breastplates* of fire, and of jacinth, and brimstone:

2386 3 368/466 3:194 2390

ἴαμα, iama.

1Co.12: 9. to another the gifts of *healing*
28. miracles, then gifts of *healings*,
30. Have all the gifts of *healing*?

2390 28 368/466 3:194

ἰάομαι, iaomai.

Mat. 8: 8. and my servant *shall be healed*.
13. And his servant *was healed*
13:15. and I *should heal* them.
15:28. And her daughter *was made whole*
Mar 5:29. that she was *healed* of that plague.
Lu. 4:18. he hath sent me *to heal* the brokenhearted,
5:17. the Lord was (present) *to heal* them.
6:17. *to be healed* of their diseases;
19. and *healed* (them) all.
7: 7. and my servant *shall be healed*.
8:47. and how she *was healed* immediately.
9: 2. and *to heal* the sick.
11. and *healed* them that had need of healing.
42. and *healed* the child,
14: 4. and *healed* him, and let him go;
17:15. when he saw that he *was healed*,
22:51. touched his ear, and *healed* him.
Joh. 4:47. that he would come down, and *heal* his son:
5:13. And he *that was healed* wist not who it
12:40. and I *should heal* them.
Acts 3:11. the lame man *which was healed*
9:34. Jesus Christ *maketh* thee *whole*:
10:38. and *healing* all that were oppressed
28: 8. and *healed* him.
27. and I *should heal* them.
Heb 12:13. but let it rather *be healed*.
Jas. 5:16. that ye *may be healed*.
1Pet. 2:24. by whose stripes ye *were healed*.

2392 3 369/467 3:194 2390

ἴασις, iasis.

Lu. 13:32. and I do *cures* to day and to morrow,
Acts 4:22. on whom this miracle of *healing* was
30. By stretching forth thine hand *to heal*;

2393 4 369/467 [3471]

ἴασπις, iaspis.

Rev. 4: 3. a *jasper* and a sardine stone:
21: 11. even like a *jasper* stone,
18. of the wall of it was (of) *jasper;*
19. The first foundation (was) *jasper;*

2395 7 369/467 3:194 2390

ἰατρός, iatros.

Mat. 9: 12. They that be whole need not a *physician,*
Mar 2: 17. They that are whole have no need of the *physician,*
5:26. of many *physicians,*
Lu. 4: 23. *Physician,* heal thyself:
5:31. They that are whole need not a *physician;*
8:43. had spent all her living upon *physicians,*
Col. 4: 14. Luke, the beloved *physician,*

2396 27 369/467 1492

ἴδε, ide.

Mat. 25: 20. *behold,* I have gained beside them five
22. *behold,* I have gained two other talents
25. *lo,* (there) thou hast (that is) thine.
26:65. *behold,* now ye have heard
Mar 2: 24. *Behold,* why do they on the sabbath day
3:34. *Behold* my mother and
11:21. *behold,* the fig tree which thou cursedst
13: 1. *see* what manner of stones
15: 4. *behold* how many things they witness against thee.
16: 6. *behold* the place where they laid him.
Joh. 1: 29. *Behold* the Lamb of God,
36. *Behold* the Lamb of God!
47(48). *Behold* an Israelite indeed,
3:26. *behold,* the same baptizeth,
5:14. *Behold,* thou art made whole:
7:26. But, *lo,* he speaketh boldly,
11: 3. *behold,* he whom thou lovest is sick.
36. *Behold* how he loved him!
12:19. *behold,* the world is gone after him.
16:29. *Lo,* now speakest thou plainly,
18:21. *behold,* they know what I said.
19: 4. *Behold,* I bring him forth to you,
5. (Pilate) saith unto them, *Behold* the man!
14. unto the Jews, *Behold* your King!
Ro. 2: 17. *Behold,* thou art called a Jew,
Gal. 5: 2. *Behold,* I Paul say

2397 1 370/263 1492

ἰδέα, idea.

Mat. 28: 3. His *countenance* was like lightning,

2398 113 370/467 2:373

ἴδιος, idios.

Those marked [1] are κατ' ἰδίαν ; [2] the neuter plural.

Mat. 9: 1. and came into *his own* city.
14:13. into a desert place *apart:*[1]
23. into a mountain *apart*[1]
17: 1. into an high mountain *apart,*[1]
19. the disciples to Jesus *apart,*
20:17. took the twelve disciples *apart*[1] in the way,
22: 5. one to *his* farm, another to
24: 3. the disciples came unto him *privately,*[1]
25:14. (who) called *his own* servants,
15. according to *his several* ability;
Mar 4: 34. and *when they were alone,*[1] he expounded all things to his disciples.
6:31. *apart*[1] into a desert place,
32. desert place by ship *privately.*[1]
7:33. *aside*[1] from the multitude,
9: 2. high mountain *apart*[1] by themselves:
28. asked him *privately,*[1] Why could
13: 3. Andrew asked him *privately,*[1]
15:20. and put *his own* clothes on him,
Lu. 2: 3. into *his own* city.
6:41. that is in *thine own* eye?
44. is known by *his own* fruit.
9:10. and went aside *privately*[1]
10:23. and said *privately,*[1] Blessed
34. and set him on *his own* beast,
Joh. 1: 11. He came unto *his own,*[2] and *his own* (masc. plur.) received him not.
41(42). findeth *his own* brother Simon,
4:44. honour in *his own* country.
5:18. said also that God was *his* Father.
43. in *his own* name,
7:18. seeketh *his own* glory:
8:44. he speaketh of *his own.*
10: 3. he calleth *his own* sheep
4. when he putteth forth *his own* sheep,
12. whose *own* the sheep are not,
13: 1. having loved *his own*
15:19. the world would love *his own:*
16:32. shall be scattered, every man to *his own,*[2]
19:27. that disciple took her unto *his own* (home)[2]
Acts 1: 7. the Father hath put in *his own* power.
19. in their *proper* tongue,
25. that he might go to *his own* place.
2: 6. speak in *his own* language.
8. in our *own* tongue,
3:12. as though by *our own* power or
4:23. they went to *their own* (company),
32. said...ought of the things which he possessed was *his own;*
13:36. after he had served *his own* generation
20:28. which he hath purchased with *his own*
21: 6. and they returned *home*[2] again.
23:19. went (with him) aside *privately,*[1]
24:23. he should forbid none of *his acquaintance*
25:19. of *their own* superstition,
28:30. in *his own* hired house,
Ro. 8: 32. spared not *his own* Son,
10: 3. going about to establish *their own*
11:24. be graffed into *their own* olive tree?
14: 4. to *his own* master he standeth or falleth.
5. be fully persuaded in *his own* mind.
1Co. 3: 8. every man shall receive *his own* reward according to *his own* labour.
4:12. working with *our own* hands:
6:18. sinneth against *his own* body.
7: 2. have *her own* husband.
4. hath not power of *her own* body,
— hath not power of *his own* body,
7. every man hath *his proper* gift
37. over *his own* will,
9: 7. Who goeth a warfare any time at *his own* charges?
11:21. every one taketh before (other) *his own* supper:
12:11. dividing to every man *severally* (lit. in *his own* way, or, *his own*)
14:35. let them ask *their* husbands
15:23. in *his own* order:
38. to every seed *his own* body.
Gal. 2: 2. but *privately*[1] to them which were of
6: 5. shall bear *his own* burden.
9. for in *due* season we shall reap,

Eph 5:22. yourselves unto *your own* husbands,
24. to *their own* husbands in every thing.
Col. 3:18. submit yourselves unto *your own*
1Th 2:14. have suffered like things of *your own* countrymen,
15. and *their own* prophets,
4:11. to do *your own business*,[2] and to work with *your own* hands,
1Ti. 2: 6. to be testified in *due* time.
3: 4. One that ruleth well *his own* house,
5. man know not how to rule *his own* house,
12. and *their own* houses well.
4: 2. having *their* conscience seared with
5: 4. shew piety at home, (lit. at *his own* home)
8. But if any provide not for *his own*,
6: 1. count *their own* masters worthy
15. Which in *his* times he shall shew, (who is) the blessed
2Ti. 1: 9. according to *his own* purpose
4: 3. after *their own* lusts
Tit. 1: 3. But hath in *due* times manifested
12. (even) a prophet of their *own*,
2: 5. obedient to *their own* husbands,
9. to be obedient unto *their own* masters,
Heb 4:10. his own works, as God (did) from *his*.
7:27. first for *his own* sins, and then for the
9:12. but by *his own* blood
13:12. that he might sanctify the people with *his own* blood,
Jas. 1:14. drawn away of *his own* lust, and enticed.
1Pet. 3: 1. (be) in subjection to *your own* husbands;
5. in subjection unto *their own* husbands:
2Pet. 1:20. is of any *private* interpretation.
2:16. But was rebuked for *his* iniquity:
22. turned to *his own* vomit again;
3: 3. walking after their *own* lusts,
16. unto their *own* destruction.
17. fall from *your own* stedfastness.
Jude 6. but left *their own* habitation,

2399 5 371/469 3:215 2398

ἰδιώτης, *idiōtees*.

Acts 4:13. and perceived that they were unlearned and *ignorant* men,
1Co. 14:16. occupieth the room of the *unlearned*
23. (those that are) *unlearned*, or
24. there come in one that believeth not, or (one) *unlearned*,
2Co. 11: 6. though (I be) *rude* in speech, yet not in

2400 213 371/469 1492

ἰδού, *idou*.

Mat 1:20. *behold*, the angel of the Lord
23. *Behold*, a virgin shall be with child,
2: 1. *behold*, there came wise men from the east
9. and, *lo*, the star, which they saw
13. *behold*, the angel of the Lord
19. *behold*, an angel of the Lord
3:16. *lo*, the heavens were opened unto him,
17. And *lo* a voice from heaven,
4:11. and, *behold*, angels came
7: 4. and, *behold*, a beam (is) in
8: 2. And, *behold*, there came a leper
24. And, *behold*, there arose a great tempest
29. And, *behold*, they cried out,
32. *behold*, the whole herd of swine ran
34. And, *behold*, the whole city
9: 2. And, *behold*, they brought to him
3. And, *behold*, certain of the scribes
Mat 9:10. *behold*, many publicans and sinners
18. *behold*, there came a certain ruler,
20. And, *behold*, a woman, which was diseased with an issue of blood
32. *behold*, they brought to him
10:16. *Behold*, I send you forth
11: 8. *behold*, they that wear soft (clothing)
10. *Behold*, I send my messenger
19. *Behold* a man gluttonous,
12: 2. *Behold*, thy disciples do
10. And, *behold*, there was a man
18. *Behold* my servant, whom I have chosen,
41. and, *behold*, a greater than Jonas
42. and, *behold*, a greater than Solomon
46. *behold*, (his) mother and his brethren
47. *Behold*, thy mother and thy brethren
49. *Behold* my mother and my brethren!
13: 3. *Behold*, a sower went forth
15:22. *behold*, a woman of Canaan
17: 3. And, *behold*, there appeared unto them
5. *behold*, a bright cloud overshadowed them, and *behold* a voice out of the cloud,
19:16. And, *behold*, one came
27. *Behold*, we have forsaken all,
20:18. *Behold*, we go up to Jerusalem;
30. And, *behold*, two blind men
21: 5. *Behold*, thy King cometh
22: 4. *Behold*, I have prepared my dinner:
23:34. Wherefore, *behold*, I send
38. *Behold*, your house is left unto you
24:23. *Lo*, here (is) Christ,
25. *Behold*, I have told you before.
26. *Behold*, he is in the desert;
— *behold*, (he is) in the secret chambers,
25: 6. *Behold*, the bridegroom cometh;
26:45. *behold*, the hour is at hand,
46. *behold*, he is at hand that doth betray me.
47. *lo*, Judas, one of the twelve,
51. And, *behold*, one of them which were
27:51. And, *behold*, the veil of the temple
28: 2. And, *behold*, there was a great
7. and, *behold*, he goeth before you
— *lo*, I have told you.
9. *behold*, Jesus met them,
11. *behold*, some of the watch
20. and, *lo*, I am with you
Mar. 1: 2. *Behold*, I send my messenger
3:32. *Behold*, thy mother and thy brethren
4: 3. *Behold*, there went out a sower
5:22. And, *behold*, there cometh one of
10:28. *Lo*, we have left all,
33. *Behold*, we go up to Jerusalem;
13:21. *Lo*, here (is) Christ; or, *lo*, (he is) there
23. *behold*, I have foretold you all things.
14:41. *behold*, the Son of man is betrayed
42. *lo*, he that betrayeth me
15:35. *Behold*, he calleth Elias.
Lu. 1:20. And, *behold*, thou shalt be dumb,
31. And, *behold*, thou shalt conceive in thy
36. And, *behold*, thy cousin Elisabeth,
38. *Behold* the handmaid of the Lord;
44. For, *lo*, as soon as the voice of thy salutation sounded
48. for, *behold*, from henceforth
2: 9. And, *lo*, the angel of the Lord
10. for, *behold*, I bring you good tidings
25. And, *behold*, there was a man
34. *Behold*, this (child) is set for the fall
48. *behold*, thy father and I
5:12. *behold* a man full of leprosy:
18. And, *behold*, men brought
6:23. for, *behold*, your reward

Lu. 7:12. *behold*, there was a dead man carried out,
25. *Behold*, they which are gorgeously
27. *Behold*, I send my messenger
34. *Behold* a gluttonous man,
37. And, *behold*, a woman in the city,
8:41. And, *behold*, there came a man
9:30. And, *behold*, there talked with him two
38. And, *behold*, a man of the company
39. And, *lo*, a spirit taketh him,
10: 3. *behold*, I send you forth
19. *Behold*, I give unto you power
25. And, *behold*, a certain lawyer
11:31. and, *behold*, a greater than Solomon
32. and, *behold*, a greater than Jonas
41. and, *behold*, all things are clean
13: 7. *Behold*, these three years I come
11. And, *behold*, there was a woman
16. *lo*, these eighteen years,
30. And, *behold*, there are last
32. *Behold*, I cast out devils,
35. *Behold*, your house is left unto you
14: 2. And, *behold*, there was a certain man
15:29. *Lo*, these many years do I serve thee,
17:21. *Lo* here! or, *lo* there! for, *behold*, the kingdom of God
23. *See* here; or, *see* there.
18:28. *Lo*, we have left all,
31. *Behold*, we go up to
19: 2. And, *behold*, (there was) a man named
8. *Behold*, Lord, the half of my goods
20. *behold*, (here is) thy pound, which I have
22:10. *Behold*, when ye are entered
21. *behold*, the hand of him that betrayeth
31. *behold*, Satan hath desired (to have)
38. *behold*, here (are) two swords.
47. *behold* a multitude, and he that was called
23:14. and, *behold*, I, having examined (him) before you,
15. and, *lo*, nothing worthy of death
29. For, *behold*, the days are coming,
50. And, *behold*, (there was) a man named
24: 4. *behold*, two men stood by them
13. And, *behold*, two of them
49. And, *behold*, I send
Joh. 4:35. *behold*, I say unto you,
12:15. *behold*, thy King cometh,
16:32. *Behold*, the hour cometh,
19:26. Woman, *behold* thy son!
27. *Behold* thy mother! And from
Acts 1:10. *behold*, two men stood by them
2: 7. *Behold*, are not all these
5: 9. *behold*, the feet of them which have buried
25. *Behold*, the men whom
28. and, *behold*, ye have filled
7:56. *Behold*, I see the heavens opened
8:27. and, *behold*, a man of Ethiopia,
36. *See*, (here is) water; what doth hinder
9:10. *Behold*, I (am here), Lord.
11. for, *behold*, he prayeth,
10:17. *behold*, the men which
19. *Behold*, three men seek
21. *Behold*, I am he whom ye seek:
30. and, *behold*, a man stood before
11:11. And, *behold*, immediately there were three
12: 7. And, *behold*, the angel of the Lord
13:11. And now, *behold*, the hand of the Lord
25. But, *behold*, there cometh one after me,
46. *lo*, we turn to the Gentiles.
16: 1. and, *behold*, a certain disciple
20:22. And now, *behold*, I go bound
25. *behold*, I know that
27:24. and, *lo*, God hath given thee

Ro. 9:33. *Behold*, I lay in Sion
1Co.15:51. *Behold*, I shew you a mystery;
2Co. 5:17. *behold*, all things are become new.
6: 2. *behold*, now (is) the accepted time; *behold* now (is) the day of salvation.
9. and, *behold*, we live;
7:11. For *behold* this selfsame thing,
12:14. *Behold*, the third time I am ready
Gal. 1:20. *behold*, before God, I lie not.
Heb. 2:13. *Behold* I and the children
8: 8. *Behold*, the days come,
10: 7. *Lo*, I come, in the volume
9. *Lo*, I come to do thy will,
Jas. 3: 3. *Behold*, we put bits in the horses' mouths,
4. *Behold* also the ships,
5. *Behold*, how great a matter a little fire
5: 4. *Behold*, the hire of the labourers
7. *Behold*, the husbandman waiteth
9. *behold*, the judge standeth before the door.
11. *Behold*, we count them
1Pet. 2: 6. *Behold*, I lay in Sion
Jude 14. *Behold*, the Lord cometh with
Rev. 1: 7. *Behold*, he cometh with clouds;
18. and, *behold*, I am alive
2:10. *behold*, the devil shall cast (some) of you
22. *Behold*, I will cast her
3: 8. *behold*, I have set before thee
9. *Behold*, I will make them of the synagogue
— *behold*, I will make them
11. *Behold*, I come quickly:
20. *Behold*, I stand at the door,
4: 1. and, *behold*, a door (was) opened
2. and, *behold*, a throne was set
5: 5. *behold*, the Lion of the tribe of Juda, hath prevailed
6. and, *lo*, in the midst of the throne
6: 2. and *behold* a white horse:
5. and *lo* a black horse;
8. and *behold* a pale horse:
12. and, *lo*, there was a great earthquake;
7: 9. and, *lo*, a great multitude,
9:12. (and), *behold*, there come two woes more
11:14. (and), *behold*, the third woe
12: 3. and *behold* a great red dragon,
14: 1. And I looked, and, *lo*, a Lamb
14. and *behold* a white cloud,
15: 5. and, *behold*, the temple of the
16:15. *Behold*, I come as a thief.
19:11. and *behold* a white horse;
21: 3. *Behold*, the tabernacle of God
5. *Behold*, I make all things new.
22: 7. *Behold*, I come quickly:
12. And, *behold*, I come quickly;

2402 1 372/471 *idos* (sweat)

ἱδρώς, hidrōs.

Lu. 22:44. and his *sweat* was as it were great drops of blood

---

2405 2 372/471 3:221 2407

ἱερατεία, hieratīa.

Lu. 1: 9. According to the custom of the *priest's office*,
Heb. 7: 5. receive the *office of the priesthood*,

2406 2 372/471 3:221 2407

ἱεράτευμα, hieratūma.

1Pet. 2: 5. an holy *priesthood*, to offer
9. a royal *priesthood*, an holy nation,

2407 1 372/471 3:221 2409
ἱερατεύω, hieratĕuo.

Lu. 1: 8. that while he *executed the priest's office*

2409 32 372/471 3:221 2413
ἱερεύς, hierūs.

Mat. 8: 4. shew thyself to the *priest*,
12: 4. but only for the *priests?*
5. on the sabbath days the *priests*
Mar 1: 44. shew thyself to the *priest*,
2: 26. but for the *priests*,
Lu. 1: 5. a certain *priest* named Zacharias,
5: 14. and shew thyself to the *priest*,
6: 4. but for the *priests* alone?
10: 31. there came down a certain *priest* that way:
17: 14. yourselves unto the *priests*.
Joh. 1: 19. *priests* and Levites from Jerusalem
Acts 4: 1. *priests*, and the captain of the temple
5: 24. the *high priest* and the captain
6: 7. a great company of the *priests* were obedient to the faith.
14: 13. Then the *priest* of Jupiter,
Heb. 5: 6. Thou (art) a *priest* for ever
7: 1. *priest* of the most high God,
3. abideth a *priest* continually.
11. another *priest* should rise after the order of Melchisedec,
15. after the similitude of Melchisedec there ariseth another *priest*,
17. Thou (art) a *priest* for ever
21(20). those *priests* were made without an oath;
— Thou (art) a *priest* for ever
23. they truly were many *priests*,
8: 4. he should not be a *priest*, seeing that there are *priests*
9: 6. the *priests* went always
10: 11. And every *priest* standeth daily ministering
21. And (having) an high *priest* over the house of God;
Rev. 1: 6. kings and *priests* unto God
5: 10. made us unto our God kings and *priests*:
20: 6. they shall be *priests* of God and of Christ,

2411 71 373/472 3:221 cf 3485 2413
ἱερόν, hieron.

Mat. 4: 5. on a pinnacle of the *temple*,
12: 5. in the *temple* profane the sabbath,
6. in this place is (one) greater than the *temple*.
21: 12. into the *temple* of God,
— bought in the *temple*,
14. and the lame came to him in the *temple*;
15. crying in the *temple*,
23. when he was come into the *temple*,
24: 1. and departed from the *temple*:
— the buildings of the *temple*.
26: 55. teaching in the *temple*,
Mar 11: 11. and into the *temple*:
15. Jesus went into the *temple*,
— and bought in the *temple*,
16. (any) vessel through the *temple*.
27. as he was walking in the *temple*,
12: 35. while he taught in the *temple*,
13: 1. as he went out of the *temple*,
3. over against the *temple*,
14: 49. in the *temple* teaching,
Lu. 2: 27. by the Spirit into the *temple*:
37. departed not from the *temple*,
46. they found him in the *temple*,
4: 9. on a pinnacle of the *temple*,
18: 10. went up into the *temple*
19: 45. he went into the *temple*,
47. daily in the *temple*.
20: 1. the people in the *temple*,
21: 5. spake of the *temple*,
37. teaching in the *temple*,
38. in the *temple*, for to hear him.
22: 52. and captains of the *temple*,
53. with you in the *temple*,
24: 53. were continually in the *temple*,
Joh. 2: 14. found in the *temple* those that sold
15. he drove them all out of the *temple*,
5: 14. Jesus findeth him in the *temple*,
7: 14. Jesus went up into the *temple*,
28. Jesus in the *temple* as he taught,
8: 2. he came again into the *temple*,
20. as he taught in the *temple*:
59. went out of the *temple*,
10: 23. Jesus walked in the *temple*
11: 56. as they stood in the *temple*,
18: 20. and in the *temple*, whither
Acts 2: 46. with one accord in the *temple*,
3: 1. went up together into the *temple*
2. at the gate of the *temple*
— that entered into the *temple*;
3. to go into the *temple*
8. with them into the *temple*,
10. the Beautiful gate of the *temple*:
4: 1. the captain of the *temple*, and
5: 20. and speak in the *temple* to the people
21. into the *temple* early in the morning.
24. and the captain of the *temple*
25. are standing in the *temple*,
42. And daily in the *temple*,
19: 27. the *temple* of the great goddess Diana
21: 26. entered into the *temple*, to signify
27. when they saw him in the *temple*,
28. brought Greeks also into the *temple*,
29. had brought into the *temple*.
30. him out of the *temple*:
22: 17. while I prayed in the *temple*,
24: 6. hath gone about to profane the *temple*.
12. they neither found me in the *temple*
18. purified in the *temple*,
25: 8. neither against the *temple*, nor
26: 21. caught me in the *temple*,
1Co. 9: 13. live (of the things) of the *temple*?

2412 1 373/472 3:221 rt 4241 2413
ἱεροπρεπής, hieroprepees.

Tit. 2: 3. that (they be) in behaviour *as becometh holiness*,

2413 2 373/473 3:221
ἱερός, hieros.

1Co. 9: 13. they which minister about *holy* things
2Ti. 3: 15. thou hast known the *holy* scriptures,

2416 1 374/473 3:221 2417
ἱεροσυλέω, hierosuleo.

Ro. 2: 22. thou that abhorrest idols, dost thou *commit sacrilege*?

2417 1 374/473 3:221 2411,4813
ἱερόσυλος, hierosulos.

Acts 19: 37. which are neither *robbers of churches*, nor

2418 1 374/474 3:221 rt 2041 2411
ἱερουργέω, hierourgeo.

Ro. 15: 16. *ministering* the gospel of God,

2420 4 374/475 3:221 2413

ἱερωσύνη, hierōsunee.

Heb 7:11. perfection were by the Levitical *priesthood*,
12. For the *priesthood* being changed, there is
14. of which tribe Moses spake nothing concerning *priesthood*.
24. hath an unchangeable *priesthood*.

2425 975 374/485 3:293 *hikō* (to arrive)

ἱκανός, hikanos.

Mat. 3:11. whose shoes I am not *worthy* to bear:
8: 8. I am not *worthy* that thou shouldest
28:12. gave *large* money unto the soldiers,
Mar 1: 7. shoes I am not *worthy* to stoop down
10:46. his disciples and a *great* number of people,
15:15. Pilate, willing to content (lit. to do what was *enough for*) the people,
Lu. 3:16. shoes I am not *worthy* to unloose:
7: 6. I am not *worthy* that thou shouldest
11. *many* of his disciples went with him,
12. a widow: and *much* people of the city
8:27. a certain man, which had devils *long* time,
32. an herd of *many* swine feeding
20: 9. into a far country for a *long* time.
22:38. he said unto them, It is *enough*.
23: 8. desirous to see him of a *long* (season),
9. he questioned with him in *many* words;
Acts 5:37. drew away *much* people after him:
8:11. of *long* time he had bewitched them
9:23. after that *many* days were fulfilled,
43. he tarried *many* days in Joppa
11:24. *much* people was added unto the Lord.
26. and taught *much* people.
12:12. *many* were gathered together praying.
14: 3. *Long* time therefore abode they
21. and had taught *many*, they returned
17: 9. when they had taken *security* of Jason,
18:18. tarried (there) yet a *good* while,
19:19. *Many* of them also which used curious
26. persuaded and turned away *much* people,
20: 8. *many* lights in the upper chamber,
11. talked a *long while*, even till break
37. they all wept *sore*, and fell on Paul's
22: 6. from heaven a *great* light round about
27: 7. we had sailed slowly *many* days,
9. when *much* time was spent,
1Co.11:30. sickly among you, and *many* sleep.
15: 9. not *meet* to be called an apostle,
2Co. 2: 6. *Sufficient* to such a man (is) this
16. who (is) *sufficient* for these things?
3: 5. Not that we are *sufficient* of ourselves
2Ti. 2: 2. shall be *able* to teach others also.

2426 1 375/486 3:293 2425

ἱκανότης, hikanotees.

2Co. 3: 5. but our *sufficiency* (is) of God;

2427 2 375/486 3:293 2425

ἱκανόω, hikanoō.

2Co. 3: 6. Who also *hath made* us *able* ministers
Col. 1:12. unto the Father, *which hath made* us *meet* to be partakers of

2428 1 375/486 3:296 rt 2425

ἱκετηρία, hiketeeria.

Heb 5: 7. offered up prayers and *supplications*

2429 1 375/486

ἰκμάς, ikmas.

Lu. 8: 6. because it lacked *moisture*.

2431 1 375/486 3:297 rt 2436

ἱλαρός, hilaros.

2Co. 9: 7. God loveth a *cheerful* giver.

2432 1 376/486 3:297 2431

ἱλαρότης, hilarotees.

Ro. 12: 8. he that sheweth mercy, with *cheerfulness*.

2433 2 376/486 3:300 2436

ἱλάσκομαι, hilaskomai.

Lu. 18:13. God *be merciful* to me a sinner.
Heb 2:17. to *make reconciliation for* the sins

2434 2 376/486 3:300 2431

ἱλασμός, hilasmos.

1Joh. 2: 2. he is the *propitiation* for our sins:
4:10. sent his Son (to be) the *propitiation* for our sins.

2435 2 376/486 3:300 2433

ἱλαστήριον, hilasteerion.

Ro. 3:25. a *propitiation* through faith in his blood,
Heb 9: 5. shadowing the *mercyseat*; of which

2436 2 376/486 3:300 *hellomai* (to take)

ἵλεως, hileōs.

Mat.16:22. saying, *Be it far* from thee, Lord:
Heb 8:12. For I will be *merciful* to their

2438 4 376/486 rt 260

ἱμάς, himas.

Mar 1: 7. the *latchet* of whose shoes I am not
Lu. 3:16. the *latchet* of whose shoes I am not
Joh. 1:27. whose shoe's *latchet* I am not worthy
Acts22:25. as they bound him with *thongs*,

2439 2 376/486 2440

ἱματίζομαι, himatizomai.

Mar 5:15. sitting, and *clothed*, and in his right mind:
Lu. 8:35. at the feet of Jesus, *clothed*,

2440 61 376/486 *ennumi* (to put on)

ἱμάτιον, himation.

Mat 5:40. let him have (thy) *cloke* also.
9:16. new cloth unto an old *garment*,
— to fill it up taketh from the *garment*.
20. touched the hem of his *garment*.
21. If I may but touch his *garment*.
11: 8. A man clothed in soft *raiment*?
14:36. only touch the hem of his *garment*.
17: 2. his *raiment* was white as the light.
21: 7. put on them their *clothes*, and they set
8. spread their *garments* in the way;
23: 5. enlarge the borders of their *garments*,
24:18. return back to take his *clothes*.
26:65. Then the high priest rent his *clothes*,
27:31. and put his own *raiment* on him.
35. and parted his *garments*, casting lots:
— They parted my *garments* among them,

ar piece of new cloth on an old *garment:*
. press behind, and touched his *garment.*
28. If I may touch but his *clothes,*
30. and said, Who touched my *clothes?*
6:56. it were but the border of his *garment:*
9: 3. And his *raiment* became shining,
10:50. And he, casting away his *garment,*
11: 7. and cast their *garments* on him;
8. And many spread their *garments*
13:16. not turn back again for to take up his *garment.*
15:20. and put his own *clothes* on him,
24. they parted his *garments,* casting lots
Lu. 5:36. a piece of a new *garment* upon an old)(;
6:29. him that taketh away thy *cloke*
7:25. A man clothed in soft *raiment?*
8:27. and ware no *clothes,* neither abode
44. touched the border of his *garment:*
19:35. they cast their *garments* upon the colt,
36. they spread their *clothes* in the way.
22:36. let him sell his *garment,* and buy one.
23:34. And they parted his *raiment,* and cast lots.
Joh. 13: 4. and laid aside his *garments;*
12. and had taken his *garments,*
19: 2. they put on him a purple *robe,*
5. wearing the crown of thorns, and the purple *robe.*
23. took his *garments,* and made four parts,
24. They parted my *raiment* among them,
Acts 7:58. the witnesses laid down their *clothes*
9:39. shewing the coats and *garments* which
12: 8. Cast thy *garment* about thee,
14:14. they rent their *clothes,* and ran in
16:22. the magistrates rent off their *clothes*
18: 6. he shook (his) *raiment,* and said
22:20. and kept the *raiment* of them that
23. and cast off (their) *clothes,* and threw dust
Heb 1:11. all shall wax old as doth a *garment;*
Jas. 5: 2. your *garments* are motheaten.
1Pet. 3: 3. or of putting on of *apparel;*
Rev 3: 4. which have not defiled their *garments;*
5. shall be clothed in white *raiment;*
18. white *raiment,* that thou mayest be
4: 4. sitting, clothed in white *raiment;*
16:15. that watcheth, and keepeth his *garments,*
19:13. clothed with a *vesture* dipped in blood:
16. And he hath on (his) *vesture* and on his

2441 6 377/487 2439

ἱματισμός, himatismos.

Mat 27:35. upon my *vesture* did they cast lots.
Lu. 7:25. they which are gorgeously *apparel*led,
9:29. his *raiment* (was) white (and) glistering.
Joh 19:24. for my *vesture* they did cast lots.
Acts 20:33. no man's silver, or gold, or *apparel.*
1Ti. 2: 9. or gold, or pearls, or costly *array;*

2442 1 377/693 *himeros* (yearning)

ἱμείρομαι, himīromai.

1Th. 2: 8. So *being affectionately desirous* of you, we were willing to

---

2443 665 377/487 3:323 cf 1438

ἵνα, hina. cf 3363

The mark ² shews that '*lest*' is put for ἱνα μη; ³ shews that '*to*', or '*for to*', is put for '*that*' with a subjunctive.

Mat. 1:22. this was done, *that* it might be fulfilled
2:15. *that* it might be fulfilled which was
4: 3. command *that* these stones be made
14. *That* it might be fulfilled which
5:29. *that* one of thy members should perish,
30. *that* one of thy members should perish,
7: 1. Judge not, *that* ye be not judged.
12. ye would *that* men should do to you,
8: 8. *that* thou shouldest come under my roof
9: 6. But *that* ye may know that the Son
10:25. the disciple *that* he be as his master,
12:10. *that* they might accuse him.
16. *that* they should not make him known:
14:15. *that* they may go into the villages,
36. besought him *that* they might only touch
16:20. *that* they should tell no man that he
17:27. *lest*² we should offend them,
18: 6. better for him *that* a millstone
14. *that* one of these little ones should perish.
16. *that* in the mouth of two or three
19:13. *that* he should put (his) hands on them
16. *that* I may have eternal life?
20:21. Grant *that* these my two sons may sit,
31. *because* they should hold their peace.
33. Lord, *that* our eyes may be opened.
21: 4. *that* it might be fulfilled which was
23:26. *that* the outside of them may be clean
24:20. pray ye *that* your flight be not in
26: 4. consulted *that* they might take Jesus
5. *lest*² there be an uproar
16. opportunity *to*³ betray him.
41. *that* ye enter not into temptation:
56. *that* the scriptures of the prophets might
63. *that* thou tell us whether thou be
27:20. *that* they should ask Barabbas,
26. delivered (him) *to*³ be crucified.
32. compelled *to*³ bear his cross.
35. *that* it might be fulfilled
28:10. *that* they go into Galilee,
Mar 1:38. *that* I may preach there also:
2:10. But *that* ye may know that the Son
3: 2. *that* they might accuse him.
9. *that* a small ship should wait on him
— *lest*² they should throng him.
10. pressed upon him *for*³ *to* touch him,
12. *that* they should not make him known.
14. ordained twelve, *that* they should be with him, and *that* he might send them
4:12. *That* seeing they may see,
21. *to*³ be put under a
— *to*³ be set on a candlestick?
22. but *that* it should come abroad.
5:10. *that* he would not send them away
12. the swine, *that* we may enter into them.
18. prayed him *that* he might be with him.
23. (I pray thee),)(come and lay thy hands on her,
43. *that* no man should know it;
6: 8. *that* they should take nothing
12. preached *that* men should repent.
25. I will *that* thou give me by and by
36. *that* they may go into the country
41. to his disciples *to*³ set before them;
56. *that* they might touch if it were
7: 9. *that* ye may keep your own tradition.
26. *that* he would cast forth the devil
32. beseech him *to*³ put his hand upon him.
36. *that* they should tell no man:
8: 6. gave to his disciples *to*³ set before
22. and besought him *to*³ touch him.
30. *that* they should tell no man
9: 9. *that* they should tell no man
12. *that* he must suffer many things

Mar 9:18. *that* they should cast him out;
22. and into the waters, *to*[3] destroy him:
30. *that* any man should know (it).
10:13. *that* he should touch them:
17. *that* I may inherit eternal life?
35. we would *that* thou shouldest do for us
37. Grant unto us *that* we may sit,
48. *that* he should hold his peace:
51. *that* I might receive my sight.
11:16. not suffer *that* any man should carry
25. *that* your Father also which is in heaven
28. gave thee this authority *to*[3] do these things?
12: 2. *that* he might receive from the
13. *to*[3] catch him in (his) words.
15. a penny, *that* I may see (it).
19. *that* his brother should take his wife,
13:18. *that* your flight be not in the winter.
34. and commanded the porter *to*[3] watch.
14:10. went unto the chief priests, *to*[3] betray
12. *that* thou mayest eat the passover?
35. prayed *that*, if it were possible, the hour might pass from him.
38. Watch ye and pray, *lest*[2] ye enter into
49. but the scriptures must be fulfilled. (lit. but *that* the scriptures be fulfilled)
15:11. *that* he should rather release Barabbas
15. *to*[3] be crucified.
20. led him out *to*[3] crucify him.
21. *to*[3] bear his cross.
32. *that* we may see and believe.
16: 1. *that* they might come and anoint him.
Lu 1: 4. *That* thou mightest know the certainty
43. *that* the mother of my Lord should
4: 3. this stone *that* it be made bread.
5:24. But *that* ye may know that the Son
6: 7. *that* they might find an accusation
31. as ye would *that* men should do
34. lend to sinners, *to*[3] receive as much again.
7: 6. not worthy *that* thou shouldest enter
36. *that* he would eat with him.
8:10. *that* seeing they might not see,
12. *lest*[2] they should believe and be saved.
16. *that* they which enter in may see
31. *that* he would not command them
32. *that* he would suffer them to enter
9:12. *that* they may go into the towns
40. I besought thy disciples *to*[3] cast him out;
45. *that* they perceived it not:
10:40. bid her therefore *that* she help me.
11:33. *that* they which come in may see
50. *That* the blood of all the prophets,
54. *that* they might accuse him.
12:36. *that* when he cometh and knocketh,
14:10. *that* when he that bade thee cometh,
23. *that* my house may be filled.
29. *Lest*[2] haply,...all that behold (it) begin to mock him,
15:29. *that* I might make merry with
16: 4. *that*, when I am put out of the
9. *that*, when ye fail, they may receive
24. *that* he may dip the tip of his finger
27. *that* thou wouldest send him to my
28. *lest*[2] they also come into this place of torment.
17: 2. *that* he should offend one of these
18: 5. *lest*[2] by her continual coming she weary
15. infants, *that* he would touch them:
39. *that* he should hold his peace:
41. *that* I may receive my sight.
19 4. into a sycomore tree *to*[3] see him:
15. *that* he might know how much every
20:10. *that* they should give him of the fruit

Lu. 20:14. *that* the inheritance may be our's.
20. *that* they might take hold of his words,
28. *that* his brother should take his wife.
21:36. *that* ye may be accounted worthy
22: 8. *that* we may eat.
30. *That* ye may eat and drink at my table
32. *that* thy faith fail not:
46. *lest*[2] ye enter into temptation.
Joh. 1: 7. *to*[3] bear witness of the Light, *that* all (men) through him might believe.
8. *to*[3] bear witness of that Light.
19. from Jerusalem *to*[3] ask him,
22. *that* we may give an answer to them
27. I am not worthy *to*[3] unloose.
31. but *that* he should be made manifest
2:25. needed not *that* any should testify
3:15. *That* whosoever believeth in him
16. *that* whosoever believeth in him
17. into the world *to*[3] condemn the world; but *that* the world through him might be
20. *lest*[2] his deeds should be reproved.
21. *that* his deeds may be made manifest,
4: 8. unto the city *to*[3] buy meat.
15. *that* I thirst not, neither come hither
34. My meat is *to*[3] do the will of him that sent me,
36. *that* both he that soweth and he that reapeth may rejoice together.
47. *that* he would come down, and heal
5: 7. *to*[3] put me into the pool:
14. *lest*[2] a worse thing come unto thee.
20. *that* ye may marvel.
23. *That* all (men) should honour the Son,
34. I say, *that* ye might be saved.
36. given me *to*[3] finish,
40. *that* ye might have life.
6: 5. buy bread, *that* these may eat?
7. *that* every one of them may take a little.
12. that remain, *that* nothing be lost.
15. *to*[3] make him a king,
28. *that* we might work the works of God?
29. *that* ye believe on him whom he
30. *that* we may see, and believe thee?
38. not *to*[3] do mine own will, but the will of him that sent me.
39. *that* of all which he hath given me
40. *that* every one which seeth the Son,
50. *that* a man may eat thereof,
7: 3. *that* thy disciples also may see the works
23. *that* the law of Moses should not be
32. priests sent officers *to*[3] take him.
8: 6. *that* they might have to accuse him.
56. rejoiced *to*[3] see my day:
59. took they up stones *to*[3] cast at him:
9: 2. *that* he was born blind?
3. *that* the works of God should be made
22. *that* if any man did confess that he was Christ,
36. *that* I might believe on him?
39. *that* they which see not might see;
10:10. but *for to*[3] steal,
— I am come *that* they might have life,
17. *that* I might take it again.
31. again *to*[3] stone him.
38. *that* ye may know, and believe,
11: 4. *that* the Son of God might be glorified
11. *that* I may awake him out of sleep.
15. *to the intent* ye may believe;
16. Let us also go, *that* we may die
19. *to*[3] comfort them concerning their brother.
31. unto the grave *to*[3] weep
37. *that* even this man should not have died?

Joh. 11:42. I said (it), *that* they may believe
50. *that* one man should die for
52. *that* also he should gather together
53. for *to*[3] put him to death.
55. *to*[3] purify themselves.
57. *that*, if any man knew where he were,
12: 9. *that* they might see Lazarus also,
10. *that* they might put Lazarus also to death;
20. among them that came up *to*[3] worship at the feast:
23. *that* the Son of man should be glorified.
35. *lest*[2] darkness come upon you:
36. *that* ye may be the children of light.
38. *That* the saying of Esaias the prophet
40. *that* they should not see with (their) eyes,
42. *lest*[2] they should be put out of the
46. *that* whosoever believeth on me
47. for I came not *to*[3] judge the world, but *to*[3] save the world.
13: 1. *that* he should depart out of this world
2. *to*[3] betray him;
15. *that* ye should do as I have done
18. *that* the scripture may be fulfilled,
19. *that*, when it is come to pass,
29. *that* he should give something to
34. *That* ye love one another;
— *that* ye also love one another.
14: 3. *that* where I am, (there) ye may be
13. *that* the Father may be glorified
16. *that* he may abide with you for ever;
29. *that*, when it is come to pass,
31. *that* the world may know that I
15: 2. *that* it may bring forth more fruit.
8. *that* ye bear much fruit;
11. *that* my joy might remain in you,
12. *That* ye love one another,
13. *that* a man lay down his life
16. *that* ye should go and bring forth fruit,
— *that* whatsoever ye shall ask
17. *that* ye love one another.
25. *that* the word might be fulfilled
16: 1. *that* ye should not be offended.
2. *that* whosoever killeth you
4. *that* when the time shall come,
7. expedient for you *that* I go away:
24. *that* your joy may be full.
30. *that* any man should ask thee:
32. *that* ye shall be scattered,
33. *that* in me ye might have peace.
17: 1. *that* thy Son also may glorify thee:
2. *that* he should give eternal life
3. *that* they might know thee the only
4. thou gavest me *to*[3] do.
11. *that* they may be one, as we (are).
12. *that* the scripture might be fulfilled.
13. *that* they might have my joy fulfilled
15. *that* thou shouldest take them out
— *that* thou shouldest keep them
19. *that* they also might be sanctified
21. *That* they all may be one;
— *that* they also may be one in us: *that* the world may believe
22. *that* they may be one, even as we
23. *that* they may be made perfect
— *that* the world may know that thou
24. *that* they also, whom thou hast given
— *that* they may behold my glory,
26. *that* the love wherewith thou hast
18: 9. *That* the saying might be fulfilled,
28. *lest*[2] they should be defiled; but *that* they might eat the passover.
32. *That* the saying of Jesus might

Joh. 18:36. *that* I should not be delivered
37. *that* I should bear witness unto
39. *that* I should release unto you one
19: 4. *that* ye may know that I find
16. unto them *to*[3] be crucified.
24. *that* the scripture might be fulfilled,
28. *that* the scripture might be fulfilled,
31. *that* the bodies should not remain
— *that* their legs might be broken,
35. *that* ye might believe.
36. *that* the scripture should be fulfilled,
38. *that* he might take away the body
20:31. *that* ye might believe that Jesus
— *that* believing ye might have life
Acts 2:25. *that* I should not be moved:
4:17. *that* it spread no further
5:15. *that* at the least the shadow of Peter
26. *lest*[2] they should have been stoned.
8:19. *that* on whomsoever I lay hands,
9:21. *that* he might bring them bound
16:30. Sirs, what must I do *to*[3] be saved?
36. magistrates have sent *to*[3] let you go:
17:15. *for to*[3] come to him with all speed,
19: 4. *that* they should believe on him
21:24. *that* they may shave (their) heads:
22: 5. unto Jerusalem, *for to*[3] be punished.
24. *that* he might know wherefore
23:24. *that* they may set Paul on,
24: 4. *that* I be not further tedious
27:42. counsel was *to*[3] kill the prisoners,
Ro. 1:11. *that* I may impart unto you some
13. *that* I might have some fruit
3: 8. do evil, *that* good may come?
19. *that* every mouth may be stopped,
4:16. *that* (it might be) by grace;
5:20. *that* the offence might abound.
21. *That* as sin hath reigned unto death,
6: 1. continue in sin, *that* grace may abound?
4. *that* like as Christ was raised up
6. *that* the body of sin might be destroyed,
7: 4. *that* we should bring forth fruit unto God.
13. But sin, *that* it might appear sin,
— *that* sin by the commandment might
8: 4. *That* the righteousness of the law
17. *that* we may be also glorified
9:11. *that* the purpose of God according to
23. *that* he might make known
11:11. stumbled *that* they should fall?
19. *that* I might be graffed in.
25. *lest*[2] ye should be wise in your own
31. *that* through your mercy they also
32. *that* he might have mercy upon all.
14: 9. *that* he might be Lord both of the dead
15: 4. *that* we through patience and comfort
6. *That* ye may with one mind
16. *that* the offering up of the Gentiles
20. *lest*[2] I should build
31. *That* I may be delivered from them
— *that* my service which
32. *That* I may come unto you with joy
16: 2. *That* ye receive her in the Lord,
1Co. 1:10. *that* ye all speak the same thing,
15. *Lest*[2] any should say that I had baptized in mine own name.
17. *lest*[2] the cross of Christ should be made
27. *to*[3] confound the wise;
— *to*[3] confound the things which are
28. *to*[3] bring to nought things that are:
31. *That*, according as it is written, He that glorieth, let him
2: 5. *That* your faith should not stand

1Co. 2:12. *that* we might know the things
3:18. become a fool, *that* he may be wise.
4: 2. *that* a man be found faithful.
3. *that* I should be judged of you.
6. *that* ye might learn in us
— *that* no one of you be puffed up
8. *that* we also might reign with you.
5: 2. *that* he that hath done this deed might be taken away
5. *that* the spirit may be saved
7. *that* ye may be a new lump,
7: 5. *that* ye may give yourselves to fasting
— *that* Satan tempt you not for your
29. *that* both they that have wives be
34. *that* she may be holy both in body
35. not *that* I may cast a snare upon you,
8:13. *lest*[2] I make my brother to offend.
9:12. *lest*[2] we should hinder the gospel of Christ.
15. *that* it should be so done unto me:
— *that* any man should make my glorying
18. *that*, when I preach the gospel,
19. *that* I might gain the more.
20. *that* I might gain the Jews;
— *that* I might gain them that are
21. *that* I might gain them that are
22. *that* I might gain the weak:
— *that* I might by all means save some.
23. *that* I might be partaker thereof
24. So run, *that* ye may obtain.
25. they (do it) *to*[3] obtain a corruptible crown;
10:33. *that* they may be saved.
11:19. *that* they which are approved may be made manifest
32. *that* we should not be condemned
34. *that* ye come not together unto
12:25. *That* there should be no schism
13: 3. though I give my body *to*[3] be burned,
14: 1. rather *that* ye may prophesy.
5. but rather *that* ye prophesied:
— *that* the church may receive edifying
12. *that* ye may excel to the edifying
13. pray *that* he may interpret.
19. *that* (by my voice) I might teach
31. *that* all may learn, and all
15:28. *that* God may be all in all.
16: 2. *that* there be no gatherings when I come.
6. *that* ye may bring me on
10. see *that* he may be with you
11. *that* he may come unto me:
12. I greatly desired him *to*[3] come unto you
— his will was not at all *to*[3] come at this
16. *That* ye submit yourselves unto such,
2Co. 1: 9. *that* we should not trust in ourselves,
11. *that* for the gift (bestowed) upon us
15. *that* ye might have a second benefit;
17. *that* with me there should be yea
2: 3. *lest*,[2] when I came, I should have sorrow
4. not *that* ye should be grieved, but *that* ye might know the love
5. *that* I may not overcharge you all.
9. *that* I might know the proof of you,
11. *Lest*[2] Satan should get an advantage of us:
4: 7. *that* the excellency of the power
10. *that* the life also of Jesus might be
11. *that* the life also of Jesus might be
15. *that* the abundant grace might
5: 4. *that* mortality might be swallowed
10. *that* every one may receive the things
12. *that* ye may have somewhat to (answer)
15. *that* they which live should not
21. *that* we might be made
6: 3. *that* the ministry be not blamed:
2Co. 7: 9. *that* ye might receive damage by us
8: 6. *that* as he had begun, so he would
7. *that* ye abound in this grace also.
9. *that* ye through his poverty might
13. not *that* other men be eased,
14. *that* their abundance also may be
9: 3. *lest*[2] our boasting of you should be in vain
— *that*, as I said, ye may be ready:
4. we *that* we say not, ye
5. *that* they would go before unto you,
8. *that* ye, always having all sufficiency
10: 9. *That* I may not seem as if I would
11: 7. *that* ye might be exalted,
12. *that* I may cut off occasion
— *that* wherein they glory, they may
16. *that* I may boast myself a little.
12: 7. *lest*[2] I should be exalted
— the messenger of Satan *to*[3] buffet me, *lest*[2] I should be exalted above measure.
8. *that* it might depart from me.
9. *that* the power of Christ may rest
13: 7. not *that* we should appear approved, but *that* ye should do that which is
10. *lest*[2] being present I should use sharpness,
Gal. 1:16. *that* I might preach him among
2: 4. *that* they might bring us into bondage:
5. *that* the truth of the gospel might
9. *that* we (should go) unto the heathen,
10. *that* we should remember the poor;
16. *that* we might be justified by
19. *that* I might live unto God.
3:14. *That* the blessing of Abraham
— *that* we might receive the promise
22. *that* the promise by faith of Jesus
24. *that* we might be justified by faith.
4: 5. *To*[3] redeem them that were under the law, *that* we might receive the adoption of sons.
17. *that* ye might affect them.
5:17. *so that* ye cannot do the things
6:12. *lest*[2] they should suffer persecution
13. *that* they may glory in your flesh.
Eph. 1:17. *That* the God of our Lord Jesus Christ,
2: 7. *That* in the ages to come he might
9. *lest*[2] any man should boast.
10. *that* we should walk in them.
15. *for to*[3] make in himself of twain one new man,
3:10. *To the intent that* now unto the
16. *That* he would grant you, according
17(18). *that* ye, being rooted and grounded in love,
19. *that* ye might be filled with all
4:10. *that* he might fill all things.
14. *That* we (henceforth) be no more children,
28. *that* he may have to give to him
29. *that* it may minister grace
5:26. *That* he might sanctify and cleanse it
27. *That* he might present it to himself
— *that* it should be holy and without blemish.
33. *that* she reverence (her) husband.
6: 3. *That* it may be well with thee,
13. *that* ye may be able to withstand
19. *that* utterance may be given unto me,
20. *that* therein I may speak boldly,
21. *that* ye also may know my affairs,
22. *that* ye might know our affairs,
Phi. 1: 9. *that* your love may abound yet more
10. *that* ye may be sincere and without offence
26. *That* your rejoicing may be more
27. *that* whether I come and see you,
2: 2. *that* ye be likeminded,

Phi. 2:10. *That* at the name of Jesus every knee
15. *That* ye may be blameless and harmless,
19. *that* I also may be of good comfort,
27. *lest*[2] I should have sorrow upon sorrow.
28. *that*, when ye see him again,
30. *to*[3] supply your lack of service
3: 8. *that* I may win Christ,
Col. 1: 9. *that* ye might be filled with
18. *that* in all (things) he might have
28. *that* we may present every man
2: 2. *That* their hearts might be comforted,
4. *lest*[2] any man should beguile you
3:21. *lest*[2] they be discouraged.
4: 3. *that* God would open unto us a door
4. *That* I may make it manifest,
8. *that* he might know your estate,
12. *that* ye may stand perfect and complete
16. cause *that* it be read also in the church
— *that* ye likewise read the (epistle)
17. Take heed to the ministry... *that* thou fulfil it.
1Th. 2:16. the Gentiles *that* they might be saved,
4: 1. *that*...(so) ye would abound more and
12. *That* ye may walk honestly toward
13. *that* ye sorrow not, even as others
5: 4. *that* that day should overtake you
10. *that*, whether we wake or sleep, we should live together with him.
2Th. 1:11. *that* our God would count you worthy
2:12. *That* they all might be damned
3: 1. *that* the word of the Lord may have
2. *that* we may be delivered from
9. but *to*[3] make ourselves an ensample
12. *that* with quietness they work,
14. *that* he may be ashamed.
1Ti. 1: 3. *that* thou mightest charge some that they teach no other doctrine,
16. *that* in me first Jesus Christ might
18. *that* thou by them mightest war a good
20. *that* they may learn not to blaspheme.
2: 2. *that* we may lead a quiet and peaceable
3: 6. *lest*[2] being lifted up with pride he fall
7. *lest*[2] he fall into reproach
15. *that* thou mayest know how
4:15. *that* thy profiting may appear
5: 7. *that* they may be blameless.
16. *that* it may relieve them that are
20. *that* others also may fear.
21. *that* thou observe these things
6: 1. *that* the name of God and (his) doctrine be not blasphemed.
19. *that* they may lay hold on eternal life.
2Ti. 1: 4. *that* I may be filled with joy;
2: 4. *that* he may please him who hath
10. *that* they may also obtain the salvation
3:17. *That* the man of God may be perfect,
4:17. *that* by me the preaching might be fully
Tit. 1: 5. *that* thou shouldest set in order
9. *that* he may be able by sound doctrine
13. *that* they may be sound in the faith;
2: 4. *That* they may teach the young women
5. *that* the word of God be not blasphemed.
8. *that* he that is of the contrary part may be ashamed,
10. *that* they may adorn the doctrine
12. *that*, denying ungodliness and worldly lusts, we should live
14. *that* he might redeem us from all
3: 7. *That* being justified by his grace, we should be made heirs
8. *that* they which have believed in God
13. *that* nothing be wanting unto them.
Tit. 3:14. *that* they be not unfruitful.
Philem. 13. *that* in thy stead he might
14. *that* thy benefit should not be
15. *that* thou shouldest receive him
19. *albeit* I do not say to thee
Heb 2:14. *that* through death he might destroy
17. *that* he might be a merciful
3:13. *lest*[2] any of you be hardened
4:11. *lest*[2] any man fall after
16. *that* we may obtain mercy
5: 1. *that* he may offer both gifts
6:12. *That* ye be not slothful,
18. *That* by two immutable things,
9:25. *that* he should offer himself often,
10: 9. *that* he may establish the second.
36. *that*, after ye have done the will of God, ye might receive the promise.
11:28. *lest*[2] he that destroyed the firstborn should touch them.
35. *that* they might obtain a better
40. *that* they without us should not be made
12: 3. *lest*[2] ye be wearied
13. *lest*[2] that which is lame be turned out of
27. *that* those things which cannot be shaken
13:12. *that* he might sanctify the people
17. *that* they may do it with joy,
19. *that* I may be restored to you
Jas. 1: 4. *that* ye may be perfect and entire,
4: 3. *that* ye may consume (it) upon your
5: 9. *lest*[2] ye be condemned:
12. *lest*[2] ye fall into condemnation.
1Pet. 1: 7. *That* the trial of your faith,
2: 2. *that* ye may grow thereby:
12. *that*, whereas they speak against you
21. *that* ye should follow his steps:
24. *that* we, being dead to sins,
3: 1. *that*, if any obey not the word,
9. *that* ye should inherit a blessing.
16. *that*, whereas they speak evil of you,
18. *that* he might bring us to God,
4: 6. *that* they might be judged according
11. *that* God in all things may be glorified
13. *that*, when his glory shall be revealed,
5: 6. *that* he may exalt you in due time:
2Pet. 1: 4. *that* by these ye might be partakers
3:17. *lest*[2] ye also, being led away
1Joh. 1: 3. *that* ye also may have fellowship
4. *that* your joy may be full.
9. faithful and just *to*[3] forgive us (our) sins,
2: 1. *that* ye sin not.
19. *that* they might be made manifest
27. *that* any man teach you:
28. *that*, when he shall appear,
3: 1. *that* we should be called
5. was manifested *to*[3] take away our sins;
8. *that* he might destroy the works
11. *that* we should love one another.
23. *That* we should believe on the name
4: 9. *that* we might live through him.
17. *that* we may have boldness
21. *That* he who loveth God loveth his
5: 3. *that* we keep his commandments:
13. *that* ye may know that ye have
— *that* ye may believe on the name
16. I do not say *that* he shall pray for it.
20. *that* we may know him that is true,
2Joh. 5. *that* we love one another.
6. *that* we walk after his commandments.
— *That*,...ye should walk in it.
8. *that* we lose not those things
12. *that* our joy may be full.
3Joh. 4. than *to*[3] hear that my children walk

3Joh. 8. *that* we might be fellowhelpers
Rev 2:10. *that* ye may be tried;
21. space *to*[3] repent
3: 9. I will make them *to*[3] come and worship
11. *that* no man take thy crown.
18. *that* thou mayest be rich;
— *that* thou mayest be clothed,
— *that* thou mayest see.
6: 2. conquering, and *to*[3] conquer.
4. *that* they should kill one another:
11. *that* they should rest yet for a little
7: 1. *that* the wind should not blow
8: 3. *that* he should offer (it) with the prayers
6. prepared themselves *to*[3] sound.
12. *so as* the third part of them was
9: 4. *that* they should not hurt the grass
5. *that* they should not kill them, but *that* they should be tormented
15. *for to*[3] slay the third part of men.
20. *that* they should not worship devils,
11: 6. *that* it rain not in the days of
12: 4. *for to*[3] devour her child as soon
6. *that* they should feed her there
14. *that* she might fly into the wilderness,
15. *that* he might cause her to be carried
13:12. *to*[3] worship the first beast,
13. *so that* he maketh fire come down
15. *that* the image of the beast should
— *that* as many as would not worship
16. *to*[3] receive (lit. *that* he should give them) a mark
17. *that* no man might buy or sell,
14:13. *that* they may rest from their labours;
16:12. *that* the way of the kings of the east
15. *lest*[2] he walk naked,
18: 4. *that* ye be not partakers of her sins, and *that* ye receive not of her plagues.
19: 8. *that* she should be arrayed
15. *that* with it he should smite
18. *That* ye may eat the flesh of kings,
20: 3. *that* he should deceive the nations
21:15. *to*[3] measure the city,
23. no need of the sun, neither of the moon, *to*[3] shine in it:
22:14. *that* they may have right to the tree of

2444 6 379/495 2443,5101

ἱνατί or ἵνα τί, hinati, hina ti.

Mat. 9: 4. *Wherefore* think ye evil in your hearts?
27:46. *why* hast thou forsaken me?
Lu. 13: 7. *why* cumbereth it the ground?
Acts 4:25. *Why* did the heathen rage,
7:26. *why* do ye wrong one to another?
1Co.10:29. *why* is my liberty judged of another (man's) conscience?

2447 3 379/496 3:334

hiēmi (to send)

ἰός, ios.

Ro. 3:13. the *poison* of asps (is) under their lips:
Jas. 3: 8. an unruly evil, full of deadly *poison*.
5: 3. the *rust* of them shall be a witness against

2450 1 380/496 3:357 2453

ἰουδαΐζω, ioudaizo.

Gal. 2:14. why compellest thou the Gentiles *to live as do the Jews?*

2454 2 380/498 3:357 2450

ἰουδαϊσμός, ioudaismos.

Gal. 1:13. my conversation in time past in the *Jews religion*,
14. And profited in the *Jews' religion*

2460 2 381/499 2462

ἱππεύς, hippūs.

Acts23:23. and *horsemen* threescore and ten,
32. left the *horsemen* to go with him,

2461 1 381/499 2462

ἱππικόν, hippikon.

Rev. 9:16. number of the army of the *horse*men

2462 16 381/499 3:336

ἵππος, hippos.

Jas. 3: 3. we put bits in the *horses'* mouths,
Rev. 6: 2. I saw, and behold a white *horse*:
4. there went out another *horse*
5. I beheld, and lo a black *horse*;
8. I looked, and behold a pale *horse*:
9: 7. the locusts (were) like unto *horses*
9. chariots of many *horses* running
17. thus I saw the *horses* in the vision,
— and the heads of the *horses* (were)
14:20. even unto the *horse* bridles,
18:13. and *horses*, and chariots, and slaves,
19:11. heaven opened, and behold a white *horse*
14. followed him upon white *horses*,
18. and the flesh of *horses*,
19. against him that sat on the *horse*,
21. him that sat upon the *horse*,

2463 20 381/500 3:339 2046

ἶρις, iris.

Rev. 4: 3. a *rainbow* round about the throne,
10: 1. and a *rainbow* (was) upon his head,

2465 1 381/500 1:74 2470,32

ἰσάγγελος, isangelos.

Lu. 20:36. for they are *equal unto the angels*;

2467 2 /267 cf 1942

ἴσημι, iseemi.

Acts26: 4. My manner of life...*know* all the Jews;
Heb12:17. For ye *know* how that afterward, when he would have

---

2468 5 381/278 1510

ἴσθι, isthi.

From εἰμί.

Mat. 2:13. *be* thou there until I bring thee word:
5:25. Agree (lit. *be* agreeing) with thine
Mar. 5:34. go in peace, and *be* whole of thy plague.
Lu. 19:17. have thou (lit. *be* thou having) authority
1Ti. 4:15. give thyself wholly to (lit. *be* thou in) them;

2470 8 381/500 3:343 1492

ἴσος or ἶσος, isos.

Mat.20:12. thou hast made them *equal* unto us,
Mar14:56. their witness agreed not (lit. was not *competent*)

Mar 14:59. neither so did their witness agree (lit. was not *equal* or *competent*)
Lu. 6:34. to receive *as much* again.
Joh. 5:18. making himself *equal* with God.
Acts11:17. God gave them the *like* gift as (he did) unto us,
Phil. 2: 6. not robbery to be *equal* with God:
Rev.21:16. length and the breadth and the height of it are *equal*.

2471 3 382/500 3:343

ἰσότης, isotees.

2Co. 8:14(13). But by an *equality*, (that) now
14. that there may be *equality*:
Col. 4: 1. give unto (your) servants that which is just and *equal*; (lit. *equity*)

2472 1 382/500 3:343 2470,1592

ἰσότιμος, isotimos.

2Pet. 1: 1. have obtained *like precious* faith with us

2473 1 382/500 2470,5590

ἰσόψυχος, isopsukos.

Phil. 2:20. For I have no man *likeminded*, who will

2476 155 382/501 7:636 *staō* (to stand)

ἵστημι, histeemi.

Mat. 2: 9. came and *stood* over where the young child
4: 5. and *setteth* him on a pinnacle of the temple,
6: 5. they love to pray *standing* in the
12:25. house divided against itself *shall* not *stand*:
26. how *shall* then his kingdom *stand*?
46. (his) mother and his brethren *stood*
47. thy mother and thy brethren *stand* without,
13: 2. multitude *stood* on the shore.
16:28. There be some *standing* here, which shall not taste
18: 2. Jesus called a little child unto him, and *set* him in the midst
16. three witnesses every word *may be established*.
20: 3. and saw others *standing* idle in the
6. and found others *standing* idle,
— Why *stand* ye here all the day idle?
32. And Jesus *stood still, and* called them,
24:15. the abomination of desolation, spoken of by Daniel the prophet, *stand* in the holy place,
25:33. he *shall set* the sheep on his right hand,
26:15. they *covenanted* with him for thirty pieces
73. came unto (him) they *that stood by*,
27:11. Jesus *stood* before the governor:
47. Some of them *that stood* there, when they heard (that),
Mar. 3:24. that kingdom cannot *stand*.
25. that house cannot *stand*.
26. and be divided, he cannot *stand*,
31. and, *standing* without, sent unto him,
9: 1. there be some of them *that stand* here,
36. he took a child, and *set* him in the midst
10:49. Jesus *stood still*, and commanded him
11: 5. certain of them *that stood* there said
13: 9. ye *shall be brought* before rulers and
14. *standing* where it ought not,
Lu. 1:11. an angel of the Lord *standing* on the right
4: 9. and *set* him on a pinnacle of the temple,
5: 1. he stood (lit. was *standing*) by the lake of Gennesaret,
Lu. 5: 2. saw two ships *standing* by the lake:
6: 8. Rise up, and *stand forth* in the midst
— And he arose and *stood forth*.
17. and *stood* in the plain,
7:14. they that bare (him) *stood still*.
38. *stood* at his feet behind (him) weeping, *and* began to wash
8:20. Thy mother and thy brethren *stand* without,
44. immediately her issue of blood *stanched*.
9:27. there be some *standing* here,
47. took a child, and *set* him by him,
11:18. how *shall* his kingdom *stand*?
13:25. ye begin *to stand* without, and to knock
17:12. lepers, which *stood* afar off:
18:11. The Pharisee *stood and* prayed thus
13. the publican, *standing* afar off,
40. Jesus *stood, and* commanded him
19: 8. Zacchæus *stood, and* said unto the Lord
21:36. *to stand* before the Son of man.
23:10. priests and scribes *stood* and
35. the people *stood* beholding.
49. *stood* afar off, beholding these things.
24:36. Jesus himself *stood* in the midst
Joh. 1:26. but there *standeth* one among you,
35. the next day after John *stood*, and two
3:29. *which standeth* and heareth him, rejoiceth
6:22. the people *which stood* on the other side
7:37. Jesus *stood* and cried, saying,
8: 3. *when* they *had set* her in the midst,
9. the woman *standing* in the midst.
44. and *abode* not in the truth,
11:56. spake among themselves, *as* they *stood* in the temple,
12:29. The people therefore, *that stood by*,
18: 5. which betrayed him, *stood* with them.
16. Peter *stood* at the door without.
18. the servants and officers *stood* there,
— and Peter *stood* with them,
25. Simon Peter *stood* and warmed himself.
19:25. Now there *stood* by the cross of Jesus
20:11. Mary *stood* without at the sepulchre
14. saw Jesus *standing*, and knew not
19. came Jesus and *stood* in the midst,
26. and *stood* in the midst, and said,
21: 4. Jesus *stood* on the shore:
Acts 1:11. why *stand* ye gazing up into heaven?
23. they *appointed* two, Joseph called Barsabas,
2:14. Peter, *standing up* with the eleven,
3: 8. he leaping up *stood*, and walked,
4: 7. *when* they *had set* them in the midst,
14. beholding the man which was healed *standing* with them,
5:20. Go, *stand and* speak in the temple
23. and the keepers *standing* without before
25. the men whom ye put in prison are *standing* in the temple,
27. they *set* (them) before the council:
6: 6. Whom they *set* before the apostles:
13. And *set up* false witnesses, which said,
7:33. the place where thou *standest* is holy
55. and Jesus *standing* on the right hand
56. the Son of man *standing* on the right
60. *lay* not this sin to their charge.
8:38. commanded the chariot to *stand still*:
9: 7. journeyed with him *stood* speechless,
10:30. a man *stood* before me in bright clothing,
11:13. *which stood* and said unto him, Send men to Joppa,
12:14. told how Peter *stood* before the gate.
16: 9. There *stood* a man of Macedonia,
17:22. Paul *stood* in the midst of Mars' hill, and
31. Because he *hath appointed* a day,

Acts21·40. Paul *stood* on the stairs, *and* beckoned
22:25. Paul said unto the centurion *that stood by*,
30. brought Paul down, and *set* him before
24:20. *while* I *stood* before the council,
21. that I cried *standing* among them,
25:10. I *stand* at Cæsar's judgment seat,
18. *when* the accusers *stood up*,
26: 6. now I *stand* and am judged for the hope
16. rise, and *stand* upon thy feet:
22. I *continue* unto this day, witnessing
27:21. Paul *stood forth* in the midst of them, and
Ro. 3:31. yea, we *establish* the law.
5: 2. into this grace wherein we *stand*,
10: 3. *to establish* their own righteousness,
11:20. and thou *standest* by faith.
14: 4. Yea, he *shall be holden up*: for God is able to *make* him *stand*.
1Co. 7:37. he that *standeth* stedfast in his heart,
10:12. let him that thinketh he *standeth*
15: 1. and wherein ye *stand*;
2Co. 1:24. for by faith ye *stand*.
13: 1. *shall* every word *be established*.
Eph. 6:11. that ye may be able *to stand* against
13. and having done all, *to stand*.
14. *Stand* therefore, having your loins girt
Col. 4:12. that ye *may stand* perfect and complete
2Ti. 2:19. the foundation of God *standeth* sure,
Heb 10: 9. that he *may establish* the second.
11. And every priest *standeth* daily
Jas. 2: 3. say to the poor, *Stand* thou there,
5: 9. the judge *standeth* before the door.
1Pet. 5:12. grace of God wherein ye *stand*.
Jude 24. *to present* (you) faultless before the
Rev. 3:20. Behold, I *stand* at the door,
5: 6. stood a Lamb (lit. a Lamb *standing*) as it had been slain,
6:17. and who shall be able *to stand*?
7: 1. I saw four angels *standing* on the four
9. a great multitude,...*stood* (lit. *standing*) before the throne,
11. the angels *stood* round about the throne,
8: 2. seven angels which *stood* before God;
3. another angel came and *stood* at the altar,
10: 5. angel which I saw *stand* upon the sea
8. the angel *which standeth* upon the sea
11: 4. two candlesticks *standing* before the God
11. and they *stood* upon their feet;
12: 4. the dragon *stood* before the woman
13: 1(12:18). I *stood* upon the sand of the sea,
14: 1. lo, a Lamb *stood* on the mount Sion,
15: 2. *stand* on the sea of glass,
18:10. *Standing* afar off for the fear of her
15. *shall stand* afar off for the fear
17. as trade by sea, *stood* afar off,
19:17. I saw an angel *standing* in the sun;
20:12. I saw the dead, small and great, *stand* before God;

See also *στήκω*.

2477 1 383/503 3:391 1492

ἱστορέω, *historeo.*

Gal. 1:18. I went up to Jerusalem *to see* Peter, (lit. *to hold inquiry of* Peter)

2478 27 383/503 3:397 2479

ἰσχυρός, *iskuros.*

Mat. 3:11. he that cometh after me is *mightier*
12:29. enter into a *strong man's* house,
— except he first bind the *strong man*?
14:30. when he saw the wind *boisterous*,
Mar. 1: 7. There cometh one *mightier* than I
3:27. can enter into a *strong man's* house,
— he will first bind the *strong man*;
Lu. 3:16. but one *mightier* than I cometh,
11:21. a *strong man* armed keepeth his palace,
22. when a *stronger* than he shall come
15:14. there arose a *mighty* famine
1Co. 1:25. the weakness of God is *stronger* than men
27. to confound the things which are *mighty*;
4:10. we (are) weak, but ye (are) *strong*;
10:22. are we *stronger* than he?
2Co.10:10. (his) letters,...(are) weighty and *powerful*,
Heb 5: 7. with *strong* crying and tears
6:18. we might have a *strong* consolation,
11:34. waxed *valiant* in fight,
1Joh.2:14. young men, because ye are *strong*,
Rev. 5: 2. I saw a *strong* angel proclaiming
10: 1. I saw another *mighty* angel
18: 8. *strong* (is) the Lord God who judgeth her.
10. Babylon, that *mighty* city!
21. a *mighty* angel took up a stone
19: 6. as the voice of *mighty* thunderings,
18. and the flesh of *mighty* men,

2479 11 384/503 3:397 *is* (force)

ἰσχύς, *iskus.*

Mar 12:30. and with all thy *strength*.
33. and with all the *strength*,
Lu. 10:27. and with all thy *strength*,
Eph. 1:19. according to the working of his *mighty* power,
6:10. and in the power of his *might*.
2Th. 1: 9. and from the glory of his *power*;
1Pet. 4:11. as of the *ability* which God giveth:
2Pet. 2:11. which are greater in *power* and might,
Rev. 5:12. to receive power, and riches, and wisdom, and *strength*,
7:12. power, and *might*, (be) unto our God
18: 2. And he cried *might*ily with a strong voice,

2480 29 384/504 3:397 2479

ἰσχύω, *iskuo.*

Mat. 5:13. it *is* thenceforth *good* for nothing,
8:28. no man *might* pass by that way.
9:12. They *that be whole* need not a physician,
26:40. *could* ye not watch with me one hour?
Mar. 2:17. They *that are whole* have no need
5: 4. neither *could* any (man) tame him.
9:18. cast him out; and they *could* not.
14:37. *couldest* not thou watch one hour?
Lu. 6:48. upon that house, and *could* not shake it:
8:43. neither *could* be healed of any,
13:24. will seek to enter in, and *shall* not *be able*.
14: 6. they *could* not answer him again
29. and *is* not *able* to finish (it),
30. and *was* not *able* to finish.
16: 3. I *can*not dig; to beg I am ashamed.
20:26. they *could* not take hold of his words
Joh.21: 6. and now they *were* not *able* to draw it
Acts 6:10. they *were* not *able* to resist the wisdom
15:10. neither our fathers nor we *were able* to bear?
19:16. *prevailed* against them, so that they fled
20. mightily grew the word of God and *prevailed*.
25: 7. which they *could* not prove.
27:16. we had much work to come by (lit. *were able* with difficulty, to become masters of) the boat:
Gal. 5: 6. neither circumcision *availeth* any thing,
6:15. neither circumcision *availeth* any thing,

Phi. 4:13. I *can do* all things through Christ
Heb 9:17. otherwise it *is of* no *strength* at all while
Jas. 5:16. prayer of a righteous man *availeth* much.
Rev. 12: 8. And *prevailed* not; neither was their place

2481 1 384/504 2470

ἴσως, isōs. adv.

Lu. 20:13. *it may be* they will reverence (him)

2485 2 385/504 2486

ἰχθύδιον, ikthudion.

Mat. 15:34. Seven, and a few *little fishes.*
Mar. 8: 7. And they had a few *small fishes:*

2486 20 385/504

ἰχθύς, ikthus.

Mat. 7:10. Or if he ask a *fish,* will he give him
14:17. but five loaves, and two *fishes.*
19. took the five loaves, and the two *fishes,*
15:36. took the seven loaves and the *fishes,*
17:27. take up the *fish* that first cometh up;
Mar. 6:38. they say, Five, and two *fishes.*
41. taken the five loaves and the two *fishes,*
— the two *fishes* divided he among them
43. full of the fragments, and of the *fishes.*
Lu. 5: 6. inclosed a great multitude of *fishes:*
9. at the draught of the *fishes* which
9:13. but five loaves and two *fishes;*
16. took the five loaves and the two *fishes,*
11:11. or if (he ask) a *fish,* will he for a *fish* give him a serpent?
24:42. gave him a piece of a broiled *fish,*
Joh. 21: 6. to draw it for the multitude of *fishes.*
8. dragging the net with *fishes.*
11. drew the net to land full of great *fishes,*
1Co. 15:39. another of *fishes,* (and) another of birds.

2487 3 385/504 3:402 ikneomai (to arrive) (cf 2240)

ἴχνος, iknōs.

Ro. 4:12. but who also walk in the *steps* of that faith
2Co. 12:18. (walked we) not in the same *steps?*
1Pet. 2:21. leaving us an example, that ye should follow his *steps:*

2503 1 386/507

ἰῶτα, iōta.

Mat. 5:18. one *jot* or one tittle shall in no wise pass from the law, till all be fulfilled.

2504 72 386/507 2532,1473

κἀγώ, κἀμοί, κἀμέ, kago, kamoi, kame.

Mat. 2: 8. that *I* may come and worship him *also.*
10:32. him will *I* confess *also* before my Father
33. him will *I also* deny before my Father
11:28. *and I* will give you rest.
16:18. And *I* say *also* unto thee,
21:24. *I also* will ask you one thing
— *I in like wise* will tell you
26:15. *and I* will deliver him unto you.
Mar 11:29. *I* will *also* ask of you one question
Lu. 1: 3. It seemed good to *me also,*
2:48. thy father *and I* have sought thee
Lu. 11: 9. *And I* say unto you, Ask,
16: 9. *And I* say unto you, Make to yourselves friends
20: 3. *I* will *also* ask you one thing;
22:29. *And I* appoint unto you a kingdom,
Joh. 1:31. *And I* knew him not:
33. *And I* knew him not: but he that
34. *And I* saw, and bare record
5:17. My Father worketh hitherto, *and I* work.
6:56. dwelleth in me, *and I* in him.
57. *and I* live by the Father:
7:28. Ye *both* know *me,* and ye know whence I am:
8:26. *and I* speak to the world those things
10:15. *even so* know *I* the Father:
27. *and I* know them, and they follow me:
28. *And I* give unto them eternal life;
38. the Father (is) in me, *and I* in him.
12:32. *And I,* if I be lifted up from the earth,
14:20. and ye in me, *and I* in you.
15: 4. Abide in me, *and I* in you.
5. He that abideth in me, *and I* in him,
9. *so* have *I* loved you:
17:18. *even so* have *I also* sent them
21. as thou, Father, (art) in me, *and I* in
26. *and I* in them.
20:15. *and I* will take him away.
21. *even so* send *I* you.
Acts 8:19. Give *me also* this power,
10:26. *I* myself *also* am a man.
22:13. *And* the same hour *I* looked up upon him.
19. *And I* said, Lord, they know that I
26:29. and altogether such as)(*I* am,
Ro. 3: 7. why yet am *I also* judged as a sinner?
11: 3. *and I* am left alone,
1Co. 2: 1. *And I,* brethren, when I came to you,
7: 8. It is good for them if they abide *even* as *I.*
40. and I think *also* that *I* have the Spirit
10:33. *Even* as *I* please all (men) in all (things),
11: 1. *even* as *I also* (am) of Christ.
15: 8. he was seen of *me also,*
16: 4. And if it be meet that *I* go *also,*
2Co. 6:17. *and I* will receive you,
11:16. that)(*I* may boast myself a little.
18. *I* will glory *also.*
21. *I* am bold *also.*
22. Are they Hebrews? *so* (am) *I.* Are they Israelites? *so* (am) *I.* Are they the seed of Abraham? *so* (am) *I.*
12:20. *and* (that) *I* shall be found unto you
Gal. 4:12. be as I (am); for)(*I* (am) as ye (are):
6:14. *and I* unto the world.
Eph. 1:15. Wherefore *I also,* after I heard of your faith
Phi. 2:19. that *I also* may be of good comfort,
28. *and* that *I* may be the less sorrowful.
1Th. 3: 5. For this cause, when)(*I* could no longer forbear,
Heb 8: 9. *and I* regarded them not, saith the Lord.
Jas. 2:18. *and I* have works:
— *and I* will shew thee my faith by my
Rev. 2: 6. which *I also* hate.
27. *even* as *I* received
3:10. *I also* will keep thee
21. *even* as *I also* overcame, and am set down

2505 1 387/508 2596,3739

καθά, katha.

Mat. 27:10. for the potter's field, *as* the Lord appointed me.

2506 3 387/508 3:411 2507

καθαίρεσις, kathairesis.

2Co.10: 4. to the *pulling down* of strong holds;
8. and not for your *destruction*,
13:10. to edification, and not to *destruction*.

2507 9 387/508 3:411 2596,138

καθαιρέω, kathaireo.

Mar 15:36. whether Elias will come *to take* him *down*.
46. and *took* him *down*, *and* wrapped
Lu. 1:52. He *hath put down* the mighty
12:18. I *will pull down* my barns,
23:53. And he *took* it *down*, *and* wrapped it
Acts13:19. And *when* he *had destroyed* seven nations
29. they *took* (him) *down* from the tree, *and* laid
19:27. and her magnificence should *be destroyed*,
2Co.10: 5. *Casting down* imaginations, and

2508 2 387/508 3:413 2513

καθαίρω, kathairo.

Joh.15: 2. he *purgeth* it, that it may bring
Heb 10: 2. because that the worshippers once *purged*

2509 13 387/508 2505,4007

καθάπερ, kathaper.

Ro. 4: 6. *Even as* David also describeth
12: 4. For *as* we have many members
1Co.12:12. For *as* the body is one,
2Co. 1:14. *even as* ye also (are) our's in the day of
3:13. And not *as* Moses, (which) put a vail
18. (*even*) *as* by the Spirit of the Lord.
8:11. that *as* (there was) a readiness
1Th. 2:11. *As* ye know how we exhorted
3: 6. *as* we also (to see) you:
12. *even as* we (do) toward you:
4: 5. *even as* the Gentiles which know not
Heb 4: 2. *as well as* unto them:
5: 4. called of God, *as* (was) Aaron.

2510 1 387/509 2596,680

καθάπτω, kathapto.

Acts28: 3. and *fastened on* his hand.

2511 30 388/509 3:413 2513

καθαρίζω, katharizo.

Mat. 8: 2. if thou wilt, thou canst *make* me *clean*.
3. I will; *be* thou *clean*. And immediately his leprosy *was cleansed*.
10: 8. *cleanse* the lepers, raise the dead,
11: 5. the lepers *are cleansed*,
23:25. for ye *make clean* the outside of the cup
26. *cleanse* first that (which is) within
Mar 1:40. If thou wilt, thou canst *make* me *clean*.
41. I will; *be* thou *clean*.
42. and he *was cleansed*.
7:19. into the draught, *purging* all meats?
Lu. 4:27. and none of them *was cleansed*, saving
5:12. if thou wilt, thou canst *make* me *clean*.
13. I will: *be* thou *clean*.
7:22. the lepers *are cleansed*,
11:39. ye Pharisees *make clean* the outside
17:14. as they went, they *were cleansed*.
17. *Were* there not ten *cleansed*?
Acts10:15. What God *hath cleansed*, (that) call not thou common.
11: 9. What God *hath cleansed*, (that) call not
15: 9. *purifying* their hearts by faith.
2Co. 7: 1. *let* us *cleanse* ourselves from all
Eph. 5:26. That he might sanctify *and cleanse* it
Tit. 2:14. and *purify* unto himself a peculiar
Heb 9:14. *shall* the blood of Christ,...*purge* your conscience from dead works to serve
22. almost all things *are* by the law *purged* with blood;
23. should *be purified* with these; but
Jas. 4: 8. *Cleanse* (your) hands, (ye) sinners;
1Joh. 1: 7. the blood of Jesus Christ his Son *cleanseth* us from all sin.
9. and to *cleanse* us from all unrighteousness.

2512 7 388/509 3:413 2511

καθαρισμός, katharismos.

Mar 1:44. and offer for thy *cleansing* those things
Lu. 2:22. when the days of her *purification*
5:14. and offer for thy *cleansing*,
Joh. 2: 6. after the manner of the *purifying*
3:25. and the Jews about *purifying*.
Heb 1: 3. when he had by himself purged our sins (lit. having made through himself a *cleansing* of)
2Pet.1: 9. hath forgotten that he was purged from (lit. the *cleansing* of) his old sins.

κάθαρμα, katharma. 4027

1Co. 4:13. we are made as the *filth* of the world,
See also περικάθαρμα, which most copies read.

2513 28 388/509 3:413

καθαρός, katharos.

Mat 5: 8. Blessed (are) the *pure* in heart:
23:26. the outside of them may be *clean* also
27:59. he wrapped it in a *clean* linen cloth,
Lu. 11:41. all things are *clean* unto you.
Joh.13:10. but is *clean* every whit: and ye are *clean*, but not all.
11. Ye are not all *clean*.
15: 3. Now ye are *clean* through the word
Acts18: 6. upon your own heads; I (am) *clean*:
20:26. I (am) *pure* from the blood of all (men).
Ro. 14:20. All things indeed (are) *pure*; but
1Ti. 1: 5. is charity out of a *pure* heart,
3: 9. of the faith in a *pure* conscience.
2Ti. 1: 3. with *pure* conscience,
2:22. out of a *pure* heart.
Tit. 1:15. Unto the *pure* all things (are) *pure*: but unto them that are defiled and unbelieving (is) nothing *pure*;
Heb 10:22(23). washed with *pure* water.
Jas. 1:27. *Pure* religion and undefiled
1Pet. 1:22. with a *pure* heart fervently:
Rev 15: 6. clothed in *pure* and white linen,
19: 8. fine linen, *clean* and white:
14. clothed in fine linen, white and *clean*.
21:18. and the city (was) *pure* gold, like unto *clear* glass.
21. the street of the city (was) *pure* gold,
22: 1. And he shewed me a *pure* river

2514 1 389/509 3:413 2513

καθαρότης, katharotees.

Heb 9:13. to the *purifying* of the flesh:

2515 3 389/509 2596,rt 1476

καθέδρα, kathedra.

Mat21:12. and the *seats* of them that sold doves,

Mat 23: 2. sit in Moses' *seat:*
Mar 11:15. the *seats* of them that sold doves;

2516 6 389/509 3:440 rt 1476

καθέζομαι, *kathezomai.* 2596

Mat 26:55. I *sat* daily with you teaching in the
Lu. 2:46. *sitting* in the midst of the doctors,
Joh. 4: 6. *sat* thus on the well:
11:20. but Mary *sat* (still) in the house.
20:12. And seeth two angels in white *sitting*.
Acts 6:15. And all *that sat* in the council,

2596, 1520

καθεῖς or καθ' εἷς, *kathīs* or *kath' hīs.*

Ro. 12: 5. and *every one* members one of another.

2517 5 389/510 2596,1836

καθεξῆς, *kathexees.*

Lu. 1: 3. to write unto thee *in order*,
8: 1. And it came to pass *afterward*,
Acts 3:24. and those that follow *after*,
11: 4. and expounded (it) *by order* unto them,
18:23. country of Galatia and Phrygia *in order*,

2518 22 389/510 3:431 2596

καθεύδω, *kathūdo.* heudō (to sleep)

Mat 8:24. but he *was asleep*.
9:24. the maid is not dead, but *sleepeth*.
13:25. But while men *slept*,
25: 5. they all slumbered and *slept*.
26:40. and findeth them *asleep*,
43. came and found them *asleep* again;
45. *Sleep* on now, and take (your) rest:
Mar 4:27. And *should sleep*, and rise night
38. *asleep* on a pillow:
5:39. the damsel is not dead, but *sleepeth*.
13:36. he find you *sleeping*.
14:37. and findeth them *sleeping*, and saith unto Peter, Simon, *sleepest* thou?
40. he found them *asleep* again,
41. *Sleep* on now, and take (your) rest:
Lu. 8:52. she is not dead, but *sleepeth*.
22:46. Why *sleep* ye? rise and pray,
Eph 5:14. Awake thou *that sleepest*,
1 Th. 5: 6. let us not *sleep*,
7. For they *that sleep sleep* in the night;
10. whether we wake or *sleep*,

2519 3 389/510 2596,2233

καθηγητής, *katheegeetees.*

Mat 23: 8. for one is your *Master*,
10. Neither be ye called *masters:* for one is your *Master*,

2520 2 389/510 3:437 2596,2240

καθῆκον, *katheekon.*

Acts 22:22. it is not *fit* that he should live.
Ro. 1:28. those things which are not *convenient*;

2521 89 390/410 3:440 2596 hēmai (to sit)

κάθημαι, *katheemai.*

Mat 4:16. The people *which sat* in darkness
— to them *which sat* in the region and
9: 9. he saw a man, named Matthew, *sitting* at the receipt of
11:16. like unto children *sitting* in
13: 1. and *sat* by the sea side.
2. so that he went into a ship, and *sat*;
15:29. a mountain, and *sat down* there.
20:30. *sitting* by the way side,
22:44. *Sit* thou on my right hand,
23:22. and by him *that sitteth* thereon.
24: 3. *as* he *sat* upon the mount of Olives,
26:58. and *sat* with the servants,
64. see the Son of man *sitting* on the right
69. Peter *sat* without in the palace:
27:19. *When* he *was set down* on the judgment seat,
36. And *sitting down* they watched him
61. *sitting* over against the sepulchre.
28: 2. and *sat* upon it.
Mar 2: 6. certain of the scribes *sitting* there,
14. *sitting* at the receipt of custom,
3:32. the multitude *sat* about him,
34. on them *which sat* about him,
4: 1. into a ship, and *sat* in the sea;
5:15. had the legion, *sitting*, and clothed.
10:46. *sat* by the highway side begging.
12:36. *Sit* thou on my right hand,
13: 3. And *as* he *sat* upon the mount of Olives
14:62. ye shall see the Son of man *sitting*
16: 5. they saw a young man *sitting*
Lu. 1:79. to them *that sit* in darkness
5:17. doctors of the law *sitting by*,
27. *sitting* at the receipt of custom:
7:32. like unto children *sitting* in the
8:35. *sitting* at the feet of Jesus,
10:13. repented, *sitting* in sackcloth and
18:35. blind man *sat* by the way side
20:42. *Sit* thou on my right hand,
21:35. on all them *that dwell* on the face of
22:55. Peter *sat down* among them.
56. maid beheld him *as* he *sat*
69. shall the Son of man *sit* on the right
Joh. 2:14. the changers of money *sitting*:
6: 3. and there he *sat* with his disciples.
9: 8. Is not this he *that sat* and begged?
12:15. *sitting* on an ass's colt.
Acts 2: 2. where they were *sitting*.
34. *Sit* thou on my right hand,
3:10. he *which sat* for alms
8:28. and *sitting* in his chariot read
14: 8. there *sat* a certain man at Lystra,
20: 9. And there *sat* in a window
23: 3. for *sittest* thou to judge me
1 Co. 14:30. to another *that sitteth by*,
Col. 3: 1. where Christ *sitteth* on the right
Heb 1:13. *Sit* on my right hand,
Jas. 2: 3. *Sit* thou here in a good place;
— *sit* here under my footstool:
Rev. 4: 2. and (one) *sat* on the throne.
3. And he *that sat* was to look upon
4. four and twenty elders *sitting*,
9. and thanks to him *that sat* on
10. fall down before him *that sat*
5: 1. in the right hand of him *that sat*
7. out of the right hand of him *that sat*
13. unto him *that sitteth* upon the throne,
6: 2. he *that sat* on him had a bow;
4. to him *that sat* thereon
5. he *that sat* on him had
8. his name *that sat* on him was Death,
16. of him *that sitteth* on the throne,
7:10. *which sitteth* upon the throne,
15. he *that sitteth* on the throne
9:17. and them *that sat* on them,
11:16. elders, *which sat* before God

Rev.14:14. (one) *sat* like unto the Son
15. to him *that sat* on the cloud,
16. he *that sat* on the cloud
17: 1. *that sitteth* upon many waters:
3. a woman *sit* upon a scarlet
9. on which the woman *sitteth.*
15. where the whore *sitteth,*
18: 7. I *sit* a queen, and am no widow,
19: 4. worshipped God *that sat* on the
11. he *that sat* upon him (was) called
18. and of them *that sit* on them,
19. against him *that sat* on the horse,
21. with the sword of him *that sat*
20:11. white throne, and him *that sat* on it,
21: 5. *that sat* upon the throne

/427 2296,2250

καθ' ἡμέραν, *kath' heemeran.*

Mat.26:55. I sat *daily* with you teaching
Mar 14:49. I was *daily* with you in the temple
Lu. 11: 3. *day by day* our daily bread.
16:19. fared sumptuously *every day:*
19:47. he taught *daily* in the temple.
22:53. I was *daily* with you in the temple,
Acts 2:46. continuing *daily* with one accord
47. the Lord added to the church *daily*
3: 2. whom they laid *daily* at the gate
16: 5. increased in number *daily.*
17:11. searched the scriptures *daily,*
17. in the market *daily* with them that
19: 9. disputing *daily* in the school
1Co.15:31. I die *daily.*
2Co.11:28. that which cometh upon me *daily,*
Heb 3:13. exhort one another *daily,*
7:27. Who needeth not *daily,*
10:11. every priest standeth *daily* ministering

2522 1 390/511 2596,2250

καθημερινός, *katheemerinos.*

Acts 6: 1. in the *daily* ministration.

2523 48 390/511 3:440 2516

καθίζω, *kathizo.*

Mat. 5: 1. and *when* he *was set,* his disciples
13:48. they drew to shore, and *sat down, and*
19:28. when the Son of man *shall sit* in the throne of his glory, ye also *shall sit*
20:21. my two sons *may sit,* the one on
23. but *to sit* on my right hand, and on
23: 2. the Pharisees *sit* in Moses' seat:
25:31. then *shall* he *sit* upon the throne
26:36. *Sit* ye here, while I go and pray
Mar. 9:35. And he *sat down, and* called the twelve,
10:37. Grant unto us that we *may sit,*
40. But *to sit* on my right hand and on
11: 2. whereon never man *sat;*
7. and he *sat* upon him.
12:41. Jesus *sat* over against the treasury, *and*
14:32. *Sit* ye here, while I shall pray.
16:19. and *sat* on the right hand of God.
Lu. 4:20. to the minister, and *sat down.*
5: 3. And he *sat down, and* taught
14:28. *sitteth* not *down* first, *and* counteth
31. *sitteth* not *down* first, *and* consulteth
16: 6. *sit down* quickly, *and* write
19:30. whereon yet never man *sat:*
22:30. and *sit* on thrones judging
24:49. but *tarry* ye in the city of Jerusalem,
Joh. 8: 2. and he *sat down, and* taught them.
Joh.12:14. found a young ass, *sat* thereon;
19:13. and *sat down* in the judgment
Acts 2: 3. and it *sat* upon each of them.
30. Christ *to sit* on his throne;
8:31. he would come up and *sit* with him.
12:21. *sat* upon his throne, *and* made
13:14. the sabbath day, and *sat down.*
16:13. we *sat down, and* spake unto
18:11. And he *continued* (there) a year
25: 6. *sitting* on the judgment seat
17. I *sat* on the judgment seat, *and*
1Co. 6: 4. *set* them to judge who are least
10: 7. The people *sat down* to eat and drink,
Eph. 1:20. and *set* (him) at his own right hand
2Th. 2: 4. *sitteth* in the temple of God,
Heb 1: 3. *sat down* on the right hand
8: 1. who *is set* on the right hand
10:12. *sat down* on the right hand
12: 2. *is set down* at the right hand
Rev. 3:21. will I grant *to sit* with me
— and *am set down* with my Father
20: 4. and they *sat* upon them,

2524 4 391/512 2596

καθίημι, *kathieemi.*

Lu. 5:19. and *let* him *down* through the tiling
Acts 9:25. and *let* (him) *down* by the wall
10:11. and *let down* to the earth:
11: 5. a great sheet, *let down* from heaven

2525 22 391/512 3:444 2596,2476

καθίστημι, *kathisteemi.*

Mat.24:45. whom his lord *hath made ruler*
47. he *shall make* him *ruler* over all his
25:21. I *will make* thee *ruler* over many things:
23. I *will make* thee *ruler* over many things:
Lu. 12:14. who *made* me a judge or a divider
42. whom (his) lord *shall make ruler* over
44. that he *will make* him *ruler* over
Acts 6: 3. whom we may *appoint* over this
7:10. he *made* him governor over Egypt
27. Who *made* thee a ruler and a judge over us?
35. Who *made* thee a ruler and a judge?
17:15. And they *that conducted* Paul
Ro. 5:19. many *were made* sinners,
— *shall* many *be made* righteous.
Tit. 1: 5. and *ordain* elders in every city,
Heb 2: 7. *didst set* him over the works of
5: 1. high priest...*is ordained* for men in things
7:28. the law *maketh* men high priests
8: 3. every high priest *is ordained* to offer
Jas. 3: 6. so *is* the tongue among our members,
4: 4. *is* the enemy of God.
2Pet.1: 8. they *make* (you that ye shall) neither (be) barren

2526 4 391/512 2596,3739

καθό, *katho.*

Ro. 8:26. not what we should pray for *as* we ought:
2Co. 8:12. *according to that* a man hath, (and) not *according to that* he hath not.
1Pet.4:13. But rejoice, *inasmuch as* ye are partakers

2527 1 391/512 2596,3650

καθόλου, *katholou.*

Acts 4:18. not to speak *at all* nor teach in the name of Jesus.

2528 1 391/512 2596,3695

καθοπλίζομαι, kathoplizomai.

Lu. 11:21. When a strong man *armed* keepeth

2529 1 391/512 5:315 2596,3708

καθοράω, kathorao.

Ro. 1:20. *are clearly seen*, being understood by

2530 5 392/512 2596,3739,5100

καθότι, kathoti.

Lu. 1: 7. *because that* Elisabeth was barren,
19: 9. *forsomuch as* he also is a son
Acts 2:24. *because* it was not possible
45. *as* every man had need.
4:35. unto every man *according as* he had need.

2531 182 392/512 2596,5613

καθώς, kathōs.

Mat.21: 6. and did *as* Jesus commanded
26:24. *as* it is written of him:
28: 6. he is risen, *as* he said.
Mar. 4:33. *as* they were able to hear
9:13. *as* it is written of him.
11: 6. *even as* Jesus had commanded:
14:16. found *as* he had said
21. *as* it is written of him:
15: 8. *as* he had even done unto them.
16: 7. *as* he said unto you.
Lu. 1: 2. *Even as* they delivered them
55. *As* he spake to our fathers,
70. *As* he spake by the mouth of
2:20. *as* it was told unto them.
23. *As* it is written in the law
5:14. *as* Moses commanded,
6:31. *as* ye would that men should
36. *as* your Father also is merciful.
11: 1. *as* John also taught his disciples.
30. For *as* Jonas was a sign
17:26. And *as* it was in the days of Noe,
19:32. *even as* he had said unto them.
22:13. found *as* he had said unto them:
29. *as* my Father hath appointed unto me;
24:24. *even* so *as* the women had said:
39. *as* ye see me have.
Joh. 1:23. *as* said the prophet Esaias.
3:14. And *as* Moses lifted up the serpent
5:23. *even as* they honour the Father.
30. *as* I hear, I judge:
6:31. *as* it is written,
57. *As* the living Father hath sent me,
58. not *as* your fathers did eat manna,
7:38. *as* the scripture hath said,
8:28. but *as* my Father hath taught me,
10:15. *As* the Father knoweth me,
26. not of my sheep, *as* I said unto you.
12:14. *as* it is written,
50. *even as* the Father said unto me,
13:15. do *as* I have done to you.
33. and *as* I said unto the Jews,
34. *as* I have loved you,
14:27. not *as* the world giveth,
31. *as* the Father gave me commandment,
15: 4. *As* the branch cannot bear fruit
9. *As* the Father hath loved me,
10. *even as* I have kept my Father's
12. *as* I have loved you.
17: 2. *As* thou hast given him power over
11. that they may be one, *as* we (are).
14. *even as* I am not of the world.
Joh. 17: 16. *even as* I am not of the world.
18. *As* thou hast sent me into the world,
21. *as* thou, Father, (art) in me,
22. *even as* we are one:
23. *as* thou hast loved me.
19:40. *as* the manner of the Jews is to bury.
20:21. *as* (my) Father hath sent me,
Acts 2: 4. *as* the Spirit gave them utterance.
22. *as* ye yourselves also know:
7:17. But *when* the time of the promise
42. *as* it is written
44. *as* he had appointed,
48. *as* saith the prophet,
10:47. received the Holy Ghost *as* well as we?
11:29. every man *according to* his ability,
15: 8. even *as* (he did) unto us;
14. *how* God at the first did visit
15. *as* it is written,
22: 3. *as* ye all are this day.
Ro. 1:13. even *as* among other Gentiles.
17. *as* it is written,
28. And *even as* they did not like
2:24. *as* it is written.
3: 4. *as* it is written,
8. *as* we be slanderously reported, and *as* some affirm that we say,
10. *As* it is written,
4:17. *As* it is written,
8:36. *As* it is written, For thy sake
9:13. *As* it is written, Jacob
29. And *as* Esaias said before,
33. *As* it is written,
10:15. *as* it is written, How
11: 8. *According as* it is written,
26. *as* it is written,
15: 3. *as* it is written, The reproaches
7. *as* Christ also received us
9. *as* it is written, For this cause
21. *as* it is written, To whom
1Co. 1: 6. *Even as* the testimony of Christ
31. *according as* it is written,
2: 9. *as* it is written, Eye hath
4:17. *as* I teach every where in every
5: 7. *as* ye are unleavened.
8: 2. nothing yet *as* he ought to know.
10: 6. *as* they also lusted.
7. *as* (were) some of them;
8. *as* some of them committed,
9. *as* some of them also tempted,
10. *as* some of them also murmured,
33. *Even as* I please all (men)
11: 1. *even as* I also (am) of Christ.
2. *as* I delivered (them) to you.
12:11. to every man severally *as* he will.
18. *as* it hath pleased him.
13:12. *even as* also I am known.
14:34. *as* also saith the law.
15:38. a body *as* it hath pleased him,
49. And *as* we have borne the image
2Co. 1: 5. For *as* the sufferings of Christ
14. *As* also ye have acknowledged us
4: 1. *as* we have received mercy,
6:16. *as* God hath said,
8: 5. And (this they did), not *as* we hoped,
6. that *as* he had begun,
15. *As* it is written, He that
9: 3. that, *as* I said, ye may be ready:
7. *according as* he purposeth
9. *As* it is written, He hath dispersed
10: 7. *as* he (is) Christ's, even so (are) we
11:12. they may be found even *as* we.
Gal. 2: 7. *as* (the gospel) of the circumcision

Gal. 3: 6. *Even as* Abraham believed God
5:21. *as* I have also told (you)
Eph. 1: 4. *According as* he hath chosen us
3: 3. *as* I wrote afore in few words,
4: 4. even *as* ye are called in one hope
17. walk not *as* other Gentiles
21. *as* the truth is in Jesus:
32. even *as* God for Christ's sake hath
5: 2. *as* Christ also hath loved us,
3. *as* becometh saints;
25. even *as* Christ also loved the church,
29. even *as* the Lord the church:
Phil. 1: 7. *Even as* it is meet for me
2:12. *as* ye have always obeyed,
3:17. *as* ye have us for an ensample.
Col. 1. 6. *as* (it is) in all the world;
— *as* (it doth) also in you,
7. *As* ye also learned of Epaphras
2: 7. *as* ye have been taught,
3:13. even *as* Christ forgave you,
1Th. 1: 5. *as* ye know what manner of men
2: 2. *as* ye know, at Philippi,
4. But *as* we were allowed of God
5. *as* ye know, nor a cloke of covetousness;
13. *as* it is in truth, the word of God,
14. even *as* they (have) of the Jews:
3: 4. even *as* it came to pass, and ye
4: 1. that *as* ye have received of us
6. *as* we also have forewarned
11. *as* we commanded you;
13. even *as* others which have no hope.
5:11. *even as* also ye do.
2Th. 1: 3. *as* it is meet,
3: 1. even *as* (it is) with you:
1Ti. 1: 3. *As* I besought thee to abide
Heb 3: 7. *as* the Holy Ghost saith,
4: 3. *as* he said, As I have sworn
7. *as* it is said, To day
5: 3. *as* for the people, so also
6. *As* he saith also in another
8: 5. *as* Moses was admonished
10:25. *as* the manner of some (is);
11:12. *as* the stars of the sky in multitude,
1Pet.4:10. *As* every man hath received
2Pet.1:14. even *as* our Lord Jesus Christ
3:15. even *as* our beloved brother Paul
1Joh.2: 6. *even as* he walked.
18. *as* ye have heard that antichrist
27. *even as* it hath taught you,
3: 2. for we shall see him *as* he is.
3. *even as* he is pure.
7. *even as* he is righteous.
12. Not *as* Cain, (who) was of that
23. *as* he gave us commandment.
4:17. because *as* he is, so are we
2Joh. 4. *as* we have received a commandment
6. *as* ye have heard from the
3Joh. 2. *even as* thy soul prospereth.
3. *even as* thou walkest in the truth.

2532 766 392/

καί.

2537 44 394/514 3:447 cf 3501

καινός, *kainos*.

Mat. 9:17. they put new wine into *new* bottles,
13:52. treasure (things) *new* and old.
26:28. my blood of the *new* testament,
29. until that day when I drink it *new*
Mat.27:60. in his own *new* tomb.
Mar 1:27. what *new* doctrine (is) this?
2:21. else the *new* piece that filled it
22. must be put into *new* bottles.
14:24. This is my blood of the *new* testament,
25. until that day that I drink it *new*
16:17. speak with *new* tongues;
Lu. 5:36. No man putteth a piece of a *new* garment
— both the *new* maketh a rent,
— out of the *new* agreeth not with
38. must be put into *new* bottles;
22:20. the *new* testament in my blood,
Joh.13:34. A *new* commandment I give
19:41. in the garden a *new* sepulchre,
Acts17:19. what this *new* doctrine,
21. or to hear some *new* (lit. *newer*) thing.
1Co.11:25. This cup is the *new* testament
2Co. 3: 6. able ministers of the *new* testament;
5:17. (he is) a *new* creature:
— all things are become *new*.
Gal. 6:15. but a *new* creature.
Eph. 2:15. of twain one *new* man,
4:24. put on the *new* man,
Heb. 8: 8. I will make a *new* covenant
13. In that he saith, A *new*
9:15. the mediator of the *new* testament,
2Pet.3:13. look for *new* heavens and a *new* earth,
1Joh.2: 7. I write no *new* commandment
8. Again, a *new* commandment
2Joh. 5. as though I wrote a *new* commandment
Rev. 2:17. and in the stone a *new* name
3:12. *new* Jerusalem, which cometh
— my *new* name.
5: 9. And they sung a *new* song,
14: 3. they sung as it were a *new* song
21: 1. And I saw a *new* heaven and a *new* earth:
2. I John saw the holy city, *new* Jerusalem,
5. I make all things *new*.

2538 2 395/515 3:447 2537

καινότης, *kainotees*.

Ro. 6: 4. should walk in *newness* of life.
7: 6. we should serve in *newness* of spirit,

2539 6 395/515 2532,4007

καίπερ, *kaiper*.

Phi. 3: 4. *Though* I might also have confidence
Heb. 5: 8. *Though* he were a Son, yet
7: 5. *though* they come out of the loins of
12:17. *though* he sought it carefully
2Pet.1:12. *though* ye know (them),
Rev.17: 8. that was, and is not, *and yet* is.

2540 86 395/515 3:455 cf 5550

καιρός, *kairos*.

Mat. 8:29. to torment us before the *time*?
11:25. At that *time* Jesus answered
12: 1. At that *time* Jesus went on the
13:30. and in the *time* of harvest
14: 1. At that *time* Herod the tetrarch
16: 3. the signs of the *times*?
21:34. when the *time* of the fruit
41. the fruits in their *seasons*.
24:45. meat in due *season*?
26:18. My *time* is at hand;
Mar 1:15. The *time* is fulfilled,
10:30. now in this *time*, houses,
11:13. for the *time* of figs was not

2534 *kaige*. From 2532 and 1065

Mar 12: 2. And at the *season* he sent
13:33. ye know not when the *time* is.
Lu. 1:20. shall be fulfilled in their *season*.
4:13. he departed from him for a *season*.
8:13. which for a *while* believe, and in *time* of temptation fall away.
12:42. portion of meat in *due season*?
56. that ye do not discern this *time*?
13: 1. were present at that *season*
18:30. manifold more in this present *time*,
19:44. the *time* of thy visitation.
20:10. And at the *season* he sent
21: 8. and the *time* draweth near:
24. until the *times* of the Gentiles be
36. and pray always, (lit. in every *time*)
Joh. 5: 4. at a certain *season* into the pool,
7: 6. My *time* is not yet come: but your *time* is alway ready.
8. my *time* is not yet full come.
Acts 1: 7. to know the times or the *seasons*,
3:19. when the *times* of refreshing
7:20. In which *time* Moses was born,
12: 1. about that *time* Herod
13:11. not seeing the sun for a *season*.
14:17. and fruitful *seasons*,
17:26. hath determined the *times*
19:23. And the same *time* there arose
24:25. when I have a *convenient season*,
Ro. 3:26. To declare, (I say), at this *time*
5: 6. in *due time* Christ died for
8:18. that the sufferings of this present *time*
9: 9. At this *time* will I come,
11: 5. at this present *time* also
12:11. serving the Lord; (some copies read observant of the *time*)
13:11. And that, knowing the *time*,
1Co. 4: 5. judge nothing before the *time*,
7: 5. with consent for a *time*,
29. the *time* (is) short:
2Co. 6: 2. heard thee in a *time* accepted,
— now (is) the accepted *time*;
8:14(13). now at this *time* your
Gal. 4:10. and *times*, and years.
6: 9. for in due *season* we shall reap,
10. have therefore *opportunity*,
Eph 1:10. the dispensation of the fulness of *times*
2:12. at that *time* ye were without Christ,
5:16. Redeeming the *time*, because the
6:18. Praying always (lit. in all *time*) with all prayer
Col. 4: 5. that are without, redeeming the *time*.
1Th. 2:17. from you for a short *time*
5: 1. But of the times and the *seasons*,
2Th. 2: 6. be revealed in his *time*.
1Ti. 2: 6. to be testified in due *time*.
4: 1. that in the latter *times* some shall
6:15. Which in his *times* he shall
2Ti. 3: 1. perilous *times* shall come.
4: 3. For the *time* will come when
6. the *time* of my departure is at hand.
Tit. 1: 3. But hath in due *times* manifested
Heb 9: 9. a figure for the *time* then present,
10. until the *time* of reformation.
11:11. when she was past age, (lit. the *time* of age)
15. have had *opportunity* to have returned.
1Pet.1: 5. to be revealed in the last *time*.
11. or what manner of *time* the Spirit
4:17. For the *time* (is come) that judgment
5: 6. he may exalt you in *due time*:
Rev 1: 3. for the *time* (is) at hand.
11:18. is come, and the *time* of the dead,
12:12. that he hath but a short *time*.
14. nourished for a *time*, and *times*, and half *time*,
22:10. for the *time* is at hand.

2543-2544 4 396/516 2532,5104,1065

καίτοι, καί-τοιγε, *kaitoi, kai-toige*.

Joh. 4: 2. *Though* Jesus himself baptized not,
Acts14:17. *Nevertheless* he left not himself
17:27. *though* he be not far from every one
Heb 4: 3. *although* the works were finished

2545 12 397/516 3:464

καίω, *kaio*.

Mat 5:15. Neither do men *light* a candle,
Lu. 12:35. and (your) lights *burning*;
24:32. Did not our heart *burn*
Joh. 5:35. He was a *burning* and a shining
15: 6. and they are *burned*.
1Co.13: 3. I give my body to *be burned*,
Heb 12:18. and *that burned* with fire,
Rev 4: 5. seven lamps of fire *burning*
8: 8. a great mountain *burning* with fire
10. *burning* as it were a lamp,
19:20. lake of fire *burning* with brimstone.
21: 8. in the lake *which burneth* with fire and

2546 11 397/516 2532,1563

κἀκεῖ, *kakī*.

Mat 5:23. *and there* rememberest that thy brother
10:11. *and there* abide till ye go
28:10. *and there* shall they see me.
Mar 1:35. a solitary place, *and there* prayed.
38. that I may preach *there also*:
Joh. 11:54. *and there* continued with his
Acts14: 7. *And there* they preached
17:13. they came *thither also*,
22:10. *and there* it shall be told thee
25:20. *and there* be judged of these
27: 6. *And there* the centurion found

2547 9 397/516 2532,1564

κἀκεῖθεν, *kakīthen*.

Mar 10: 1. *And* he arose *from thence*,
Acts 7: 4. *and from thence*, when his father was
13:21. *And afterward* they desired a king:
14:26. *And thence* sailed to Antioch,
20:15. *And* we sailed *thence*,
21: 1. *and from thence* unto Patara:
27: 4. *And* when we had launched *from thence*,
12. advised to depart *thence also*,
28:15. *And from thence*, when the brethren

2548 23 397/517 2532,1565

κἀκεῖνος, *kakīnos*.

Mat.15:18. *and they* defile the man.
20: 4. *And* said unto *them*;
23:23. *and* not to leave *the other* undone.
Mar 12: 4. *and at him* they cast stones,
5. *and him* they killed,
16:11. *And they*, when they had heard
13. *And they* went and told (it)
Lu. 11: 7. *And he* from within shall answer
42. *and* not to leave *the other* undone.
20:11. and they beat *him also*,
22:12. *And he* shall shew you a large
Joh. 6:57. *even he* shall live by me.

Joh. 7:29. *and he* hath sent me.
10:16. *them also* I must bring,
14:12. the works that I do shall *he* do *also;*
17:24. I will that *they also,*
19:35. *and he* knoweth that he saith true,
Acts 5:37. *he also* perished; and all,
15:11. we shall be saved, even as)(*they.*
18:19. *and* left *them* there:
1Co.10: 6. as *they also* lusted.
2Ti. 2:12. *he also* will deny us:
Heb. 4: 2. as well as unto)(*them:*

2549 11 397/517 3:469 2556
κακία, *kakia.*

Mat. 6:34. Sufficient unto the day(is) the *evil* thereof.
Acts 8:22. of this thy *wickedness,*
Ro. 1:29. *maliciousness;* full of envy,
1Co. 5: 8. leaven of *malice* and wickedness;
14:20. howbeit in *malice* be ye children,
Eph. 4:31. away from you, with all *malice:*
Col. 3: 8. anger, wrath, *malice,* blasphemy,
Tit. 3: 3. living in *malice* and envy,
Jas. 1:21. and superfluity of *naughtiness,*
1Pet. 2: 1. laying aside all *malice,*
16. for a cloke of *maliciousness,*

2550 1 398/517 3:469 2556,2239
κακοήθεια, *kakoeethīa.*

Ro. 1:29. debate, deceit, *malignity;* (lit. *depravity*)

2551 4 398/517 3:468 2556,3056
κακολογέω, *kakologeo.*

Mat.15: 4. He *that curseth* father or mother,
Mar. 7:10. *Whoso curseth* father or mother,
9:39. that can lightly *speak evil* of me.
Acts19: 9. but *spake evil* of that way

2552 1 398/517 5:904 2256,3806
κακοπάθεια, *kakopathīa.*

Jas. 5:10. an example of *suffering affliction,*

2553 4 398/517 5:904 rt 2552
κακοπαθέω, *kakopatheo.*

2Ti. 2: 3. therefore *endure hardness,*
9. Wherein I *suffer trouble,* as an
4: 5. *endure afflictions,* do the work of
Jas. 5:13. *Is* any among you *afflicted?*

2554 4 398/517 3:469 2555
κακοποιέω, *kakopoyeo.*

Mar. 3: 4. or *to do evil?*
Lu. 6: 9. to do good, or *to do evil?*
1Pet. 3:17. for well doing, than for *evil doing.*
3Joh. 11. he *that doeth evil* hath not seen God.

2555 5 398/517 3:469 2556,4160
κακοποιός, *kakopoyos.*

Joh. 18:30. If he were not a *malefactor,*
1Pet. 2:12. speak against you as *evildoers,*
14. for the punishment of *evildoers,*
3:16. speak evil of you, as of *evildoers,*
:15. or (as) an *evildoer,*

2556 51 398/517 3:469 cf 4190
κακὸς, & τὸ κακὸν, *kakos,* & *to kakon.*

Mat.21:41. miserably destroy those *wicked* men,
Mat 24:48. if that *evil* servant shall say
27:23. Why, what *evil* hath he done?
Mar 7:21. *evil* thoughts, adulteries,
15:14. Why, what *evil* hath he done?
Lu. 16:25. likewise Lazarus *evil* things:
23:22. Why, what *evil* hath he done?
Joh. 18:23. bear witness of the *evil:*
Acts 9:13. of this man, how much *evil* he
16:28. Do thyself no *harm:*
23: 9. We find no *evil* in this man:
28: 5. and felt no *harm.*
Ro. 1:30. inventors of *evil* things,
2: 9. upon every soul of man that doeth *evil*
3: 8. that we say, Let us do *evil,*
7:19. but the *evil* which I would not,
21. *evil* is present with me.
9:11. done any good or *evil,*
12:17. Recompense to no man *evil* for *evil.*
21. Be not overcome of *evil,* but overcome *evil* with good.
13: 3. not a terror to good works, but to the *evil.*
4. But if thou do that which is *evil,*
— wrath upon him that doeth *evil.*
10. Love worketh no *ill*
14:20. but (it is) *evil* for that man
16:19. and simple concerning *evil.*
1Co.10: 6. should not lust after *evil* things,
13: 5. is not easily provoked, thinketh no *evil;*
15:33. *evil* communications corrupt
2Co. 5:10. whether (it be) good or *bad.*
13: 7. that ye do no *evil;*
Phi. 3: 2. beware of *evil* workers,
Col. 3: 5. *evil* concupiscence, and covetousness,
1Th 5:15. See that none render *evil* for *evil*
1Ti. 6:10. love of money is the root of all *evil:*
2Ti. 4:14. did me much *evil:*
Tit. 1:12. *evil* beasts, slow bellies.
Heb 5:14. to discern both good and *evil.*
Jas. 1:13. God cannot be tempted with *evil.*
3: 8. an unruly *evil,* full of deadly poison.
1Pet.3: 9. Not rendering *evil* for *evil,*
10. refrain his tongue from *evil,*
11. Let him eschew *evil,*
12. (is) against them that do *evil.*
3Joh. 11. follow not that which is *evil,*
Rev 2: 2. not bear them which are *evil:*
16: 2. there fell a *noisome* and grievous sore

2557 4 399/518 3:469 rt 2041
κακοῦργος, *kakourgos.*

Lu. 23:32. two other, *malefactors,* led with him
33. crucified him, and the *malefactors,*
39. one of the *malefactors*
2Ti. 2: 9. as an *evil doer,* (even) unto bonds;

2558 2 399/518 2556,2192
κακουχούμενος, *kakoukoumenos.*

Heb 11:37. destitute, afflicted, *tormented;*
13: 3. (and) them *which suffer adversity,*

2559 6 399/518 3:469 2556
κακόω, *kakoō.*

Acts 7: 6. and *entreat* (them) *evil* four hundred years.
19. and *evil entreated* our fathers,
12: 1. *to vex* certain of the church.
14: 2. and *made* their minds *evil affected*
18:10. no man shall set on thee *to hurt* thee:
1Pet. 3:13. who (is) he *that will harm* you.

2560 16 399/518 4:1091 2556

κακῶς, kakōs. adv.

Mat. 4:24. unto him all *sick* people (lit. those having themselves *sickly*)
8:16. and healed all that were *sick:* (lit. those, &c.)
9:12. but they that are *sick.* (lit. those, &c.)
14:35. all that were *diseased;* (lit. those, &c.)
15:22. is *grievously* vexed with a devil.
17:15. and *sore* vexed: for ofttimes
21:41. *miserably* destroy those wicked
Mar 1:32. all that were *diseased,* (lit. those, &c.)
34. he healed many that were *sick*
2:17. but they that are *sick:*
6:55. in beds those that were *sick,*
Lu. 5:31. but they that are *sick.*
7: 2. was *sick,* and ready to die.
Joh. 18:23. If I have spoken *evil,*
Acts 23: 5. Thou shalt not speak *evil* of the
Jas. 4: 3. receive not, because ye ask *amiss,*

2561 1 399/518 2559

κάκωσις, kakōsis.

Acts 7:34. I have seen the *affliction* of my people

2562 1 399/518 2563

καλάμη, kalamee.

1 Co. 3:12. gold, silver, precious stones, wood, hay, *stubble;*

2563 12 399/518

κάλαμος, kalamos.

Mat. 11: 7. A *reed* shaken with the wind?
12:20. A bruised *reed* shall he not break,
27:29. and a *reed* in his right hand:
30. and took the *reed,* and smote him
48. and put (it) on a *reed,*
Mar 15:19. smote him on the head with a *reed,*
36. and put (it) on a *reed,*
Lu. 7:24. A *reed* shaken with the wind?
3Joh. 13. not with ink and *pen* write unto thee:
Rev. 11: 1. given me a *reed* like unto a rod:
21:15. had a golden *reed* to measure
16. he measured the city with the *reed,*

2564 106 399/518 3:487 cf rt2753

καλέω, kaleo.

Mat. 1:21. and thou *shalt call* his name JESUS:
23. they *shall call* his name Emmanuel,
25. and he *called* his name JESUS.
2: 7. privily *called* the wise men,
15. Out of Egypt *have I called* my son.
23. He *shall be called* a Nazarene.
4:21. and he *called* them.
5: 9. they *shall be called* the children of God.
19. he *shall be called* the least in the kingdom
— the same *shall be called* great in
9:13. I am not come *to call* the righteous,
10:25. If they *have called* the master
20: 8. *Call* the labourers, and give them
21:13. My house *shall be called*
22: 3. sent forth his servants *to call* them *that were bidden*
4. Tell them *which are bidden,*
8. they *which were bidden* were not worthy.
9. *bid* to the marriage.
43. *doth* David in spirit *call* him Lord,
45. If David then *call* him Lord,
23: 7. and *to be called* of men, Rabbi,
8. *be* not ye *called* Rabbi:
9. And *call* no (man) your father
Mat. 23:10. Neither *be ye called* masters:
25:14. *called* his own servants,
27: 8. that field *was called,*
Mar 1:20. straightway he *called* them:
2:17. came not *to call* the righteous,
11:17. My house *shall be called* of all
Lu. 1:13. thou *shalt call* his name John.
31. and *shalt call* his name JESUS.
32. and *shall be called* the Son of the
35. *shall be called* the Son of God.
36. with her, *who was called* barren.
59. and they *called* him Zacharias,
60. but he *shall be called* John.
61. kindred that *is called* by this
62. how he would have him *called.*
76. *shalt be called* the prophet
2: 4. which *is called* Bethlehem;
21. his name *was called* JESUS, *which was so named* of the angel
23. *shall be called* holy to the Lord;
5:32. I came not *to call* the righteous,
6:15. and Simon *called* Zelotes,
46. And why *call* ye me, Lord, Lord,
7:11. he went into a city *called* Nain;
39. the Pharisee *which had bidden* him
8: 2. Mary *called* Magdalene, out of
9:10. belonging to the city *called* Bethsaida.
10:39. she had a sister *called* Mary,
14: 7. a parable to those *which were bidden,*
8. When thou *art bidden* of any (man)
— than thou be *bidden* of him;
9. And he *that bade* thee and him come
10. when thou *art bidden,* go and sit
— when he *that bade* thee cometh,
12. Then said he also to him *that bade* him,
13. when thou makest a feast, *call* the poor
16. a great supper, and *bade* many:
17. to say to them *that were bidden,*
24. none of those men *which were bidden*
15:19. no more worthy *to be called* thy son:
21. no more worthy *to be called* thy son.
19: 2. a man *named* (lit. *called*).
13. And he *called* his ten servants, *and*
29. at the mount *called* (the mount) of Olives
20:44. David therefore *calleth* him Lord,
21:37. *that is called* (the mount) of Olives.
22:25. upon them *are called* benefactors.
23:33. *which is called* Calvary,
Joh. 1:42(43). thou *shalt be called* Cephas,
2: 2. Jesus *was called,* and his disciples,
10: 3. and he *calleth* his own sheep by
Acts 1:12. from the mount *called* Olivet,
19. insomuch as that field *is called*
23. Joseph *called* Barsabas, who
3:11. the porch *that is called* Solomon's,
4:18. And they *called* them, and commanded
7:58. at a young man's feet, *whose name was* (lit. *called*) Saul.
9:11. the street *which is called* Straight,
10: 1. *called* the Italian (band),
13: 1. and Simeon *that was called* Niger,
14:12. they *called* Barnabas, Jupiter;
15:37. John, *whose surname was* (lit. *who was called*) Mark.
24: 2. And *when* he *was called forth,*
27: 8. a place *which is called* The fair havens·
14. wind, *called* Euroclydon.
16. island *which is called* Clauda,
28: 1. the island *was called* Melita.
Ro. 4:17. and *calleth* those things which be not
8:30. them he also *called:* and whom he *called,* them he also justified:

D D

Ro. 9: 7. In Isaac *shall* thy seed *be called.*
11. but of him *that calleth ;*
24. Even us, whom he *hath called,*
25. I *will call* them my people,
26. there *shall* they *be called* the
1Co. 1: 9. by whom ye *were called* unto
7:15. but God *hath called* us to peace.
17. as the Lord *hath called* every
18. *Is* any man *called* being circumcised?
— *Is* any *called* in uncircumcision?
20. Let every man abide in the same calling wherein he *was called.*
21. *Art* thou *called* (being) a servant?
22. For he *that is called* in the Lord, (being) a servant,
— he *that is called* (being) free,
24. wherein he *is called,*
10:27. If any of them that believe not *bid* you
15: 9. am not meet *to be called* an apostle,
Gal. 1: 6. from him *that called* you into
15. and *called* (me) by his grace,
5: 8. not of him *that calleth* you.
13. ye *have been called* unto liberty;
Eph. 4: 1. wherewith ye *are called,*
4. even as ye *are called* in one hope of your
Col. 3:15. to the which also ye *are called*
1Th. 2:12. worthy of God, *who hath called* you
4: 7. God *hath* not *called* us unto uncleanness,
5:24. Faithful (is) he *that calleth* you,
2Th. 2:14. he *called* you by our gospel,
1Ti. 6:12. whereunto thou *art* also *called,*
2Ti. 1: 9. and *called* (us) with an holy calling,
Heb 2:11. not ashamed *to call* them brethren,
3:13. while it *is called* To day;
5: 4. but he *that is called* of God,
9:15. they *which are called* might receive
11: 8. Abraham, *when* he *was called*
18. in Isaac *shall* thy seed *be called:*
Jas. 2:23. he *was called* the Friend of God.
1Pet. 1:15. as he *which hath called* you is holy,
2: 9. of him *who hath called* you out of
21: hereunto *were* ye *called:*
3: 6. Sara obeyed Abraham, *calling* him lord:
9. that ye *are* thereunto *called,*
5:10. the God of all grace, *who hath called* us
2Pet. 1: 3. of him *that hath called* us to glory
1Joh. 3: 1. that we *should be called* the sons of God:
Rev. 1: 9. the isle *that is called* Patmos,
11: 8. which spiritually *is called* Sodom
12. 9. that old serpent, *called* the Devil,
16:16. *called* in the Hebrew tongue Armageddon.
19: 9. (are) they *which are called* unto
11. (was) *called* Faithful and True,
13. his name *is called* The Word of God.

2565 1 400/520 2570,1636

καλλιέλαιος, *kallielaios.*

Ro. 11:24. into a *good olive tree:*

2566 1 401/ 2570

κάλλιον see καλῶς.

2567 1 401/520 2:135 2570,1320

καλοδιδάσκαλος, *kalodidaskalos.*

Tit. 2: 3. not given to much wine, *teachers of good things;*

2569 1 401/520 2570,4160

καλοποιῶν, *kalopoiōn.*

2Th. 3:13. be not weary in *well doing.*

2570 102 401/520 3:536 cf 18

καλός, *kalos.*

Mat. 3:10. bringeth not forth *good* fruit
5:16. that they may see your *good* works,
7:17. bringeth forth *good* fruit;
18. a corrupt tree bring forth *good* fruit.
19. that bringeth not forth *good* fruit
12:33. Either make the tree *good,* and his fruit *good;*
13: 8. other fell into *good* ground,
23. seed into the *good* ground
24. a man which sowed *good* seed
27. Sir, didst not thou sow *good* seed
37. He that soweth the *good* seed
38. the *good* seed are the children
45. merchant man, seeking *goodly* pearls:
48. gathered the *good* into vessels,
15:26. It is not *meet* to take the children's
17: 4. Lord, it is *good* for us to be here:
18: 8. it is *better* for thee to enter into
9. it is *better* for thee to enter into life
26:10. she hath wrought a *good* work upon
24. it had been *good* for that man
Mar. 4: 8. And other fell on *good* ground,
20. which are sown on *good* ground;
7:27. it is not *meet* to take the children's
9: 5. it is *good* for us to be here:
42. it is *better* for him that a
43. it is *better* for thee to enter into
45. it is *better* for thee to enter halt
47. it is *better* for thee to enter into
50. Salt (is) *good:* but if the salt
14: 6. she hath wrought a *good* work
21. *good* were it for that man
Lu. 3: 9. not forth *good* fruit is hewn
6:38. *good* measure, pressed down,
43. For a *good* tree bringeth not forth
— bring forth *good* fruit.
8:15. But that on the *good* ground are they, which in an *honest* and good heart,
9:33. it is *good* for us to be here:
14:34. Salt (is) *good:* but if the salt
21: 5. adorned with *goodly* stones
Joh. 2:10. doth set forth *good* wine;
— thou hast kept the *good* wine
10:11. I am the *good* shepherd: the *good* shepherd giveth his life
14. I am the *good* shepherd,
32. Many *good* works have I shewed
33. For a *good* work we stone thee not;
Acts27: 8. which is called The *fair* havens;
Ro. 7:16. I consent unto the law that (it is) *good.*
18. to perform that which is *good*
21. when I would do *good,*
12:17. Provide things *honest* in the
14:21. (It is) *good* neither to eat
1Co. 5: 6. Your glorying (is) not *good.*
7: 1. (It is) *good* for a man not to
8. It is *good* for them if they
26. that this is *good* for the present
— (it is) *good* for a man so to be.
9:15. (it were) better for me to die (lit. *good* for me rather to die), than
2Co. 8:21. Providing for *honest* things,
13: 7. ye should do that which is *honest,*
Gal. 4:18. But (it is) *good* to be zealously affected always in (a) *good* (thing),
6: 9. let us not be weary in *well* doing:
1Th. 5:21. hold fast that which is *good.*
1Ti. 1: 8. we know that the law (is) *good,*
18. mightest war a *good* warfare;
2: 3. For this (is) *good* and acceptable

1Ti. 3: 1. he desireth a *good* work.
7. must have a *good* report of them
13. to themselves a *good* degree,
4: 4. For every creature of God (is) *good*,
6. thou shalt be a *good* minister
— of faith and of *good* doctrine,
5: 4. for that is *good* and acceptable
10. Well reported of for *good* works;
25. also the *good* works (of some)
6:12. Fight the *good* fight of faith,
— professed a *good* profession
13. witnessed a *good* confession;
18. that they be rich in *good* works,
19. a *good* foundation against the time
2Ti. 1:14. That *good* thing which was committed
2: 3. as a *good* soldier of Jesus Christ.
4: 7. I have fought a *good* fight,
Tit. 2: 7. a pattern of *good* works:
14. zealous of *good* works.
3: 8. to maintain *good* works. These things are *good* and profitable
14. to maintain *good* works
Heb 5:14. to discern both *good* and evil
6: 5. have tasted the *good* word
10:24. provoke unto love and to *good* works:
13: 9. a *good* thing that the heart be
18. we trust we have a *good* conscience,
Jas. 2: 7. that *worthy* name by the which
3:13. out of a *good* conversation
4:17. to him that knoweth to do *good*,
1Pet. 2:12. conversation *honest* among the
— they may by (your) *good* works,
4:10. as *good* stewards of the manifold grace of

2571 4 401/521 3:556 2572

κάλυμμα, *kalumma.*

2Co. 3:13. (which) put a *vail* over his face,
14. the same *vail* untaken away
15. the *vail* is upon their heart.
16. the *vail* shall be taken away.

2572 8 401/521 3:556 cf 2813

καλύπτω, *kalupto.* cf 2928

Mat. 8:24. the ship was *covered* with the waves:
10:26. there is nothing *covered*, that shall
Lu. 8:16. *covereth* it with a vessel,
23:30. and to the hills, *Cover* us.
2Co. 4: 3. But if our gospel be *hid*, it is *hid* to them that are lost:
Jas. 5:20. and *shall hide* a multitude of
1Pet. 4: 8. *shall cover* the multitude of sins.

2573 37 402/521 2570

καλῶς & κάλλιον, *kalōs & kallion.*

Mat. 5:44. do *good* to them that hate you,
12:12. it is lawful to do *well* on the
15: 7. *well* did Esaias prophesy of
Mar 7: 6. *Well* hath Esaias prophesied of
9. *Full well* ye reject the commandment
37. He hath done all things *well*:
12:28. that he had answered them *well*,
32. *Well*, Master, thou hast said
16:18. and they shall recover. (lit. shall be *well*)
Lu. 6:26. when all men shall speak *well*
27. do *good* to them which hate you,
20:39. Master, thou hast *well* said.
Joh. 4:17. Thou hast *well* said,
8:48. Say we not *well* that thou art
13:13. ye say *well*; for (so) I am.
18:23. but if *well*, why smitest thou
Acts10:33. thou hast *well* done that thou
Acts25:10. as thou *very well* knowest.
28:25. *Well* spake the Holy Ghost
Ro. 11:20. *Well*; because of unbelief
1Co. 7:37. will keep his virgin, doeth *well*.
38. in marriage doeth *well*;
14:17. thou verily givest thanks *well*,
2Co. 11: 4. ye might *well* bear with (him).
Gal. 4:17. affect you, (but) not *well*;
5: 7. Ye did run *well*;
Phi. 4:14. ye have *well* done,
1Ti. 3: 4. One that ruleth *well* his own
12. and their own houses *well*.
13. used the office of a deacon *well*
5:17. Let the elders that rule *well*
Heb 13:18. willing to live *honestly*.
Jas. 2: 3. Sit thou here *in a good place*;
8. love thy neighbour as thyself, ye do *well*:
19. one God; thou doest *well*:
2Pet. 1:19. ye do *well* that ye take heed,
3Joh. 6. thou shalt do *well*:

κἀμέ see in κἀγώ. 2504

2574 6 402/522 3:592 [1518]

κάμηλος, *kameelos.*

Mat. 3: 4. his raiment of *camel's* hair,
19:24. easier for a *camel* to go through
23:24. and swallow a *camel*.
Mar. 1: 6. clothed with *camel's* hair,
10:25. easier for a *camel* to go through
Lu. 18:25. easier for a *camel* to go through

2575 4 402/522 2545

κάμινος, *kaminos.*

Mat.13:42. into a *furnace* of fire:
50. into the *furnace* of fire:
Rev. 1:15. as if they burned in a *furnace*;
9: 2. as the smoke of a great *furnace*;

2576 2 407/522 2596,rt 3466

καμμύω, *kammuo.*

Mat.13:15. their eyes they *have closed*;
Acts28:27. their eyes *have* they *closed*;

2577 3 403/522

κάμνω, *kamno.*

Heb 12: 3. lest ye *be wearied* and faint
Jas. 5:15. shall save the *sick*,
Rev. 2: 3. hast laboured, and *hast* not *fainted*.

κἀμοί see in κἀγώ. 2504

2578 4 403/522 3:594

κάμπτω, *kampto.*

Ro. 11: 4. who *have* not *bowed* the knee to
14:11. every knee *shall bow* to me,
Eph. 3:14. For this cause I *bow* my knees
Phi. 2:10. of Jesus every knee *should bow*,

2579 13 403/522 2532,1437

κἄν, *kan.*

Mat.21:21. but *also if* ye shall say unto
26:35. *Though* I should die with thee

D D 2

Mar 5:28. *If* I may touch *but* his clothes,
6:56. *if* it were *but* the border of
16:18. *and if* they drink any deadly
Lu. 13: 9. *And if* it bear fruit, (well):
Joh. 8:14. *Though* I bear record of myself,
10:38. *though* ye believe not me,
11:25. *though* he were dead,
Acts 5:15. that *at the least* the shadow
2Co.11:16. if otherwise, *yet* as a fool
Heb 12:20. *And if so much as* a beast touch
Jas. 5:15. *and if* he have committed sins,

2583 5 403/522 3:596 *kanē* (reed)

κανών, kanōn.

2Co.10.13. but according to the measure of the *rule* which God
15. according to our *rule* abundantly,
16. in another man's *line* of things
Gal. 6:16. as walk according to this *rule*,
Phi. 3:16. let us walk by the same *rule*,

2585 1 404/523 3:603 *kapēlos* (huckster)

καπηλεύω, kapeelūo.

2Co. 2:17. not as many, *which corrupt* the word of

2586 13 404/523

καπνός, kapnos.

Acts 2:19. blood, and fire, and vapour of *smoke:*
Rev 8: 4. And the *smoke* of the incense,
9: 2. there arose a *smoke* out of the pit, as the *smoke* of a great furnace;
— by reason of the *smoke* of the pit.
3. there came out of the *smoke* locusts
17. issued fire and *smoke* and brimstone.
18. men killed, by the fire, and by the *smoke*,
14:11. And the *smoke* of their torment
15: 8. was filled with *smoke*
18: 9. shall see the *smoke* of her burning,
18. when they saw the *smoke* of her
19: 3. And her *smoke* rose up for ever and ever.

2588 160 404/523 3:605 *kar* (heart)

καρδία, kardia.

Mat. 5: 8. Blessed (are) the pure in *heart:*
28. adultery with her already in his *heart*.
6:21. there will your *heart* be also.
9: 4. Wherefore think ye evil in your *hearts?*
11:29. I am meek and lowly in *heart*
12:34. of the *heart* the mouth speaketh.
35. out of the good treasure of the *heart*
40. in the *heart* of the earth.
13:15. this people's *heart* is waxed gross,
— understand with (their) *heart*,
19. away that which was sown in his *heart*.
15: 8. but their *heart* is far from me.
18. come forth from the *heart;*
19. out of the *heart* proceed evil
18:35. if ye from your *hearts* forgive not
22:37. the Lord thy God with all thy *heart*,
24:48. if that evil servant shall say in his *heart*,
Mar. 2: 6. and reasoning in their *hearts*,
8. Why reason ye these things in your *hearts?*
3: 5. grieved for the hardness of their *hearts*,
4:15. that was sown in their *hearts*.
6:52. for their *heart* was hardened.
7: 6. but their *heart* is far from me.
19. it entereth not into his *heart*,
21. out of the *heart* of men,
8:17. have ye your *heart* yet hardened?

Mar 11:23. and shall not doubt in his *heart*,
12:30. love the Lord thy God with all thy *heart*,
33. And to love him with all the *heart*.
Lu. 1:17. to turn the *hearts* of the fathers
51. the imagination of their *hearts*.
66. laid (them) up in their *hearts*,
2:19. and pondered (them) in her *heart*.
35. the thoughts of many *hearts* may be
51. kept all these sayings in her *heart*.
3:15. all men mused in their *hearts*
4:18. to heal the broken*hearted*,
5:22. What reason ye in your *hearts?*
6:45. out of the good treasure of his *heart*
— out of the evil treasure of his *heart*
— of the *heart* his mouth speaketh.
8:12. away the word out of their *hearts*,
15. in an honest and good *heart*,
9:47. perceiving the thought of their *heart*,
10:27. love the Lord thy God with all thy *heart*
12:34. there will your *heart* be also.
45. if that servant say in his *heart*,
16:15. God knoweth your *hearts:*
21:14. Settle (it) therefore in your *hearts*,
34. lest at any time your *hearts* be
24:25. slow of *heart* to believe all
32. Did not our *heart* burn
38. why do thoughts arise in your *hearts?*
Joh. 12:40. and hardened their *heart;*
— nor understand with (their) *heart*,
13: 2. now put into the *heart* of Judas
14: 1. Let not your *heart* be troubled:
27. Let not your *heart* be troubled,
16: 6. sorrow hath filled your *heart*.
22. and your *heart* shall rejoice,
Acts 2:26. Therefore did my *heart* rejoice,
37. they were pricked in their *heart*,
46. and singleness of *heart*,
4:32. were of one *heart* and of one soul:
5: 3. why hath Satan filled thine *heart* to lie
4. conceived this thing in thine *heart?*
7:23. it came into his *heart* to visit
39. in their *hearts* turned back
51. and uncircumcised in *heart*
54. they were cut to the *heart*,
8:21. thy *heart* is not right in the
22. the thought of thine *heart* may
37. If thou believest with all thine *heart*,
11:23. that with purpose of *heart*
13:22. a man after mine own *heart*,
14:17. filling our *hearts* with food and
15: 9. purifying their *hearts* by faith.
16:14. whose *heart* the Lord opened,
21:13. to weep and to break mine *heart?*
28:27 For the *heart* of this people
— and understand with (their) *heart*,
Ro. 1:21. and their foolish *heart* was darkened.
24. through the lusts of their own *hearts*,
2: 5. thy hardness and impenitent *heart*
15. the law written in their *hearts*,
29. circumcision (is that) of the *heart*,
5: 5. shed abroad in our *hearts* by
6:17. have obeyed from the *heart*
8:27. he that searcheth the *hearts*
9: 2. and continual sorrow in my *heart*.
10: 1. my *heart's* desire and prayer
6. Say not in thine *heart*,
8. in thy mouth, and in thy *heart:*
9. and shalt believe in thine *heart*
10. For with the *heart* man believeth
16:18. deceive the *hearts* of the simple.
1Co. 2: 9. neither have entered into the *heart* of
4: 5. the counsels of the *hearts:*

1Co. 7:37. he that standeth stedfast in his *heart*,
— and hath so decreed in his *heart*
14:25. are the secrets of his *heart*
2Co. 1:22. the earnest of the Spirit in our *hearts*.
2: 4. and anguish of *heart* I wrote
3: 2. written in our *hearts*,
3. but in fleshy tables of the *heart*.
15. the vail is upon their *heart*.
4: 6. hath shined in our *hearts*,
5:12. in appearance, and not in *heart*.
6:11. our *heart* is enlarged.
7: 3. ye are in our *hearts* to die and
8:16. care into the *heart* of Titus for you.
9: 7. as he purposeth in his *heart*,
Gal. 4: 6. the Spirit of his Son into your *hearts*,
Eph. 3:17. That Christ may dwell in your *hearts*
4:18. of the blindness of their *heart*:
5:19. making melody in your *heart*
6: 5. in singleness of your *heart*,
22. he might comfort your *hearts*.
Phi. 1: 7. I have you in my *heart*;
4: 7. shall keep your *hearts* and minds
Col. 2: 2. That their *hearts* might be comforted,
3:15. let the peace of God rule in your *hearts*,
16. singing with grace in your *hearts*
22. but in singleness of *heart*,
4: 8. and comfort your *hearts*;
1Th. 2: 4. but God, which trieth our *hearts*.
17. in presence, not in *heart*,
3:13. he may stablish your *hearts*
2Th. 2:17. Comfort your *hearts*, and stablish
3: 5. the Lord direct your *hearts*
1Ti. 1: 5. is charity out of a pure *heart*,
2Ti. 2:22. on the Lord out of a pure *heart*.
Heb. 3: 8. Harden not your *hearts*,
10. They do alway err in (their) *heart*;
12. an evil *heart* of unbelief,
15. harden not your *hearts*,
4: 7. harden not your *hearts*.
12. thoughts and intents of the *heart*.
8:10. and write them in their *hearts*:
10:16. I will put my laws into their *hearts*,
22. Let us draw near with a true *heart*
— having our *hearts* sprinkled
13: 9. a good thing that the *heart* be
Jas. 1:26. but deceiveth his own *heart*,
3:14. and strife in your *hearts*,
4: 8. and purify (your) *hearts*,
5: 5. ye have nourished your *hearts*,
8. stablish your *hearts*: for
1Pet. 1:22. love one another with a pure *heart*
3: 4. the hidden man of the *heart*,
15. sanctify the Lord God in your *hearts*:
2Pet. 1:19. the day star arise in your *hearts*:
2:14. an *heart* they have exercised with covetous
1Joh. 3:19. shall assure our *hearts* before him.
20. For if our *heart* condemn us, God is greater than our *heart*,
21. if our *heart* condemn us not,
Rev. 2:23. he which searcheth the reins and *hearts*:
17:17. For God hath put in their *hearts*
18: 7. saith in her *heart*, I sit a queen, and am no widow,

2589 89 405/525 3:605 2588,1097

καρδιογνώστης, *kardiognōstees*.

Acts 1:24. Thou, Lord, *which knowest the hearts*
15: 8. And God, *which knoweth the hearts*,

2590 66 405/525 3:614 rt 726

καρπός, *karpos*.

Mat. 3: 8. Bring forth therefore *fruits* meet
3:10. which bringeth not forth good *fruit*
7:16. Ye shall know them by their *fruits*.
17. good tree bringeth forth good *fruit*; but a corrupt tree bringeth forth evil *fruit*.
18. bring forth evil *fruit*,
— bring forth good *fruit*.
19. that bringeth not forth good *fruit*
20. by their *fruits* ye shall know them.
12:33. tree good, and his *fruit* good;
— tree corrupt, and his *fruit* corrupt: for the tree is known by (his) *fruit*.
13: 8. and brought forth *fruit*,
26. blade was sprung up, and brought forth *fruit*,
21:19. Let no *fruit* grow on thee
34. when the time of the *fruit* drew near,
— might receive the *fruits* of it.
41. render him the *fruits* in their seasons.
43. bringing forth the *fruits* thereof.
Mar 4: 7. and it yielded no *fruit*.
8. and did yield *fruit*
29. when the *fruit* is brought forth,
11:14. No man eat *fruit* of thee hereafter
12: 2. from the husbandmen of the *fruit* of
Lu. 1:42. blessed (is) the *fruit* of thy womb.
3: 8. Bring forth therefore *fruits* worthy
9. bringeth not forth good *fruit* is hewn
6:43. bringeth not forth corrupt *fruit*; neither doth a corrupt tree...good *fruit*.
44. every tree is known by his own *fruit*.
8: 8. sprang up, and bare *fruit* an hundredfold,
12:17. no room where to bestow my *fruits*;
13: 6. he came and sought *fruit* thereon,
7. these three years I come seeking *fruit*
9. And if it bear *fruit*, (well):
20:10. that they should give him of the *fruit*
Joh. 4:36. and gathereth *fruit* unto life eternal:
12:24. if it die, it bringeth forth much *fruit*.
15: 2. that beareth not *fruit* he taketh away:
— that beareth *fruit*, he purgeth it, that it may bring forth more *fruit*.
4. As the branch cannot bear *fruit* of itself,
5. the same bringeth forth much *fruit*:
8. my Father glorified, that ye bear much *fruit*;
16. that ye should go and bring forth *fruit*, and (that) your *fruit* should remain:
Acts 2:30. that of the *fruit* of his loins,
Ro. 1:13. that I might have some *fruit* among you
6:21. What *fruit* had ye then in those things
22. ye have your *fruit* unto holiness,
15:28. and have sealed to them this *fruit*,
1Co. 9: 7. and eateth not of the *fruit* thereof?
Gal. 5:22. But the *fruit* of the Spirit is love,
Eph. 5: 9. For the *fruit* of the Spirit (is) in all
Phi. 1:11. Being filled with the *fruits* of
22. this (is) the *fruit* of my labour:
4:17. but I desire *fruit* that may abound
2Ti. 2: 6. must be first partaker of the *fruits*.
Heb 12:11. it yieldeth the peaceable *fruit* of
13:15. the *fruit* of (our) lips giving thanks
Jas. 3:17. full of mercy and good *fruits*,
18. And the *fruit* of righteousness is sown in
5: 7. waiteth for the precious *fruit* of the earth,
18. the earth brought forth her *fruit*.
Rev. 22: 2. which bare twelve (manner of) *fruits*, (and) yielded her *fruit* every month:

2592 8 406/525 3:614 2593

καρποφορέω, *karpophoreo*.

Mat. 13:23. which also *beareth fruit*,

Mar. 4:20. and *bring forth fruit*, some thirtyfold,
28. the earth *bringeth forth fruit* of herself;
Lu. 8:15. keep (it), and *bring forth fruit* with
Ro. 7: 4. that we *should bring forth fruit* unto God.
5. *to bring forth fruit* unto death,
Col. 1: 6. and *bringeth forth fruit*, as (it doth)
10. *being fruitful* in every good work,

2593 1 406/526 2590,5342

καρποφόρος, *karpophoros.*

Acts14:17. and *fruitful* seasons, filling

2594 1 406/526 3:617 2904

καρτερέω, *kartereo.*

Heb 11:27. he *endured*, as seeing him who is invisible.

2595 6 406/526 *karpho* (to wither)

κάρφος, *karphos.*

Mat. 7: 3. the *mote* that is in thy brother's eye,
4. Let me pull out the *mote*
5. to cast out the *mote* out of
Lu. 6:41. the *mote* that is in thy brother's eye,
42. let me pull out the *mote*
— to pull out the *mote* that is in

2596 481 406/526

κατά, *kata.* prep.

Mat. 1:20. appeared unto him *in*ᵃ a dream,
2:12. warned of God *in*ᵃ a dream
13. appeareth to Joseph *in*ᵃ a dream,
16. *according to*ᵃ the time which
19. appeareth *in*ᵃ a dream to Joseph
22. being warned of God *in*ᵃ a dream,
5:11. say all manner of evil *against*ᵍ you
23. that thy brother hath ought *against*ᵍ thee;
8:32. ran violently *down*ᵍ a steep place
9:29. *According to*ᵃ your faith be it unto you.
10:35. to set a man at variance *against*ᵍ his father,
and the daughter *against*ᵍ her mother,
— *against*ᵍ her mother in law.
12:14. held a council *against*ᵍ him,
25. kingdom divided *against*ᵍ itself
— city or house divided *against*ᵍ itself
30. He that is not with me is *against*ᵍ me;
32. speaketh a word *against*ᵍ the Son of man,
— but whosoever speaketh *against*ᵍ the Holy Ghost,
14:13. into a desert place *apart*:ᵃ (κατ' ἰδιαν)
23. a mountain *apart*ᵃ to pray: (κατ' ἰδιαν)
16:27. reward every man *according to*ᵃ his works.
17: 1. bringeth them up into an high mountain *apart*,ᵃ
19. came the disciples to Jesus *apart*,ᵃ
19: 3. to put away his wife *for*ᵃ every cause?
20:11. murmured *against*ᵍ the goodman of
17. took the twelve disciples *apart*ᵃ
23: 3. but do not ye *after*ᵃ their works:
24: 3. disciples came unto him privat*ely*,ᵃ
7. earthquakes, *in divers* (lit. *throughout*ᵃ) places.
25:15. to every man *according to*ᵃ his several
26:55. I sat dai*ly*ᵃ with you
59. false witness *against*ᵍ Jesus,
63. I adjure thee *by*ᵍ the living God,
27: 1. took counsel *against*ᵍ Jesus
15. Now *at*ᵃ (that) feast the governor
19. I have suffered many things this day *in*ᵃ a dream because of him.

Mar. 1:27. for *with*ᵃ authority commandeth he
3: 6. counsel with the Herodians *against*ᵍ him,
4:34. when they were *alone*,ᵃ (κατ' ἰδιαν) he
5:13. ran violently *down*ᵍ a steep place
6:31. Come ye yourselves *apart*ᵃ
32. into a desert place by ship privat*ely*.ᵃ
7: 5. Why walk not thy disciples *according to*ᵃ the tradition
33. he took him *aside*ᵃ from the
9: 2. mountain *apart*ᵃ by themselves:
28. disciples asked him privat*ely*,ᵃ
40. he that is not *against*ᵍ us is on
11:25. if ye have ought *against*ᵍ any:
13: 3. Andrew asked him privat*ely*,ᵃ
8. be earthquakes *in divers*ᵃ places,
14: 3. and poured (it) *on*ᵍ his head.
49. I was dai*ly*ᵃ with you in the
55. for witness *against*ᵍ Jesus
56. bare false witness *against*ᵍ him,
57. and bare false witness *against*ᵍ him,
15: 6 Now *at*ᵃ (that) feast he released
Lu. 1: 9. *According to*ᵃ the custom of the priest' office,
18. Where*by*ᵃ shall I know this?
38. be it unto me *according to*ᵃ thy word.
2:22. *according to*ᵃ the law of Moses
24. *according to*ᵃ that which is said
27. *after*ᵃ the custom of the law,
29. *according to*ᵃ thy word:
31. *before*ᵃ the face of all people;
39. *according to*ᵃ the law of the Lord,
41. every year (lit. *by*ᵃ year) at the feast
42. *after*ᵃ the custom of the feast.
4:14. *through*ᵍ all the region
16. *as* his custom was, (lit. *according to*ᵃ his custom)
6:23. *in*ᵃ the like manner did their
26. so (lit. *according to*ᵃ these things) did their fathers to the false
8: 1. that he went throughout *every*ᵃ city
4. were come to him out of every city, (lit. *throughout*ᵃ the cities)
33. the herd ran violently *down*ᵍ a steep place
39. published *throughout*ᵃ the whole city
9: 6. and went *through*ᵃ the towns,
10. and went aside privat*ely*ᵃ
23. and take up his cross dai*ly*,ᵃ
50. he that is not *against*ᵍ us·
10: 4. and salute no man *by*ᵃ the way.
23. and said privat*ely*,ᵃ Blessed
31. And *by*ᵃ chance there came down a
32. when he was *at*ᵃ the place,
33. came where he was: (lit. *at*ᵃ it or *by*ᵃ him)
11: 3. Give us day *by*ᵃ day our daily bread.
23. is not with me is *against*ᵍ me:
13:22. And he went *through*ᵃ the cities
15:14. a mighty famine *in*ᵃ that land;
16:19. and fared sumptuously *every*ᵃ day:
17:30. Even thus (lit. *according to*ᵃ these things) shall it be in the day
19:47. And he taught dai*ly*ᵃ in the
21:11. earthquakes shall be *in divers*ᵍ places,
22:22. *as* it was determined: (lit. *according to*ᵃ that which was determined)
39. *as*ᵃ he was wont, to the mount
53. When I was dai*ly*ᵃ with you in
23: 5. teaching *throughout*ᵍ all Jewry
14. whereof ye accuse him: (lit. *against*ᵍ him)
17. release one unto them *at*ᵃ the feast.
56. *according to*ᵃ the commandment.
Joh. 2: 6. *after*ᵃ *the manner of* the purifying

Joh. 5: 4. For an angel went down *at*[a] a certain
7:24. Judge not *according to*[a] the appearance,
8:15. Ye judge *after*[a] the flesh;
10: 3. he calleth his own sheep *by*[a] name,
18:29. bring ye *against*[g] this man?
31. judge him *according to*[a] your law.
19: 7. and *by*[a] our law he ought to die,
11. no power (at all) *against*[g] me,
21:25. if they should be written *every* one, (lit. *by*[a] one)
Acts 2:10. of Lybia *about*[a] Cyrene,
30. *according to*[a] the flesh, he would raise
46. continuing dai*ly*[a] with one accord
— breaking bread from house to house, (lit. *by*[a] house)
47. the Lord added to the church dai*ly*[a]
3: 2. whom they laid dai*ly*[a] at the gate
13. and denied him *in*[a] the presence of Pilate,
17. I wot that *through*[a] ignorance
22. in all things whatsoever (lit. *according to*[a] all things whatsoever) he shall say unto
4:26. gathered together *against*[g] the Lord, and *against*[g] his Christ.
5:15. the sick into the streets, (lit. *along*[a] the streets)
42. and *in every* house, (lit. *by*[a] house)
6:13. *against*[g] this holy place,
7:44. should make it *according to*[a] the fashion that he had seen.
8: 1. *throughout*[a] the regions of Judæa
3. entering into *every*[a] house,
26. Arise, and go *toward*[a] the south
36. as they went *on*[a] (their) way,
9:31. rest *throughout*[g] all Judæa,
42. it was known *throughout*[g] all Joppa;
10:37. was published *throughout*[g] all Judæa,
11: 1. and brethren that were *in*[a] Judæa
12: 1. Now *about*[a] that time Herod
13: 1. Now there were *in*[a] the church that
22. a man *after*[a] mine own heart,
23. *according to*[a] (his) promise
27. which are read)([a] every sabbath
14: 1. that they went both *together* (lit. *at*[a] the same) into
2. evil affected *against*[g] the brethren.
23. had ordained them elders *in every*[a] church,
15:11. we shall be saved, *even as* they, (lit. *by*[a] the same way)
21. *in every*[a] city them that
— in the synagogues every)([a] sabbath
23. *in*[a] Antioch and Syria and Cilicia:
36. *in* every)([a] city where we have
16: 5. and increased in number dai*ly*.[a]
7. After they were come *to*[a] Mysia, they assayed to go *into*[a] Bithynia:
22. rose up together *against*[g] them:
25. And *at*[a] midnight Paul
17: 2. And Paul, *as* his manner was, (lit. *according to*[a] his manner)
11. searched the scriptures dai*ly*,[a]
17. in the market dai*ly*[a] with them
22. I perceive that *in*[a] all things
25. and breath, *and*[a] all things; (some copies read, *according to*[a] all things)
28. as certain also of your own poets (lit. of the poets *among*[a] you) have said,
18: 4. in the synagogue)([a] every sabbath,
14. reason would (lit. *according to*[a] reason) that I should bear
15. (*of*) your law, (lit. of the law *among*[a] you)
19: 9. disputing dai*ly*[a] in the school
16. and prevailed *against*[g] them,
Acts19:20. So mightily (lit. *with*[a] might) grew the word of God
23. And)([a] the same time there arose
20:20. and *from* house *to* house, (lit. *by*[a] houses)
23. the Holy Ghost witnesseth *in every*[a] city,
21:19. he declared particularly (lit. *according to*[a] each one)
21. all the Jews which are *among*[a] the Gentiles
28. every where *against*[g] the people,
22: 3. taught *according to*[a] the perfect
12. a devout man *according to*[a] the law,
19. beat *in every*[a] synagogue
23: 3. to judge me *after*[a] the law,
19. and went (with him) aside private*ly*,[a]
31. as it was commanded them, (lit. *according to*[a] the command)
24: 1. who informed the governor *against*[g] Paul.
5. among all the Jews *throughout*[a] the world,
6. would have judged *according to*[a] our law.
12. nor *in*[a] the city:
14. that *after*[a] the way which they call
— which are written *in*[a] the law
22. the uttermost of your matter. (lit. the things *among*[a] you)
25: 2. informed him *against*[g] Paul,
3. desired favour *against*[g] him,
— laying wait *in*[a] the way to kill him.
7. grievous complaints *against*[g] Paul,
14. Paul's cause unto the king, (lit. the things *about*[a] Paul)
15. (to have) judgment *against*[g] him.
16. face *to*[a] face, and have licence
23. with the chief captains, and principal men of the city, (lit. those *of*[a] eminence)
27. the crimes (laid) *against*[g] him.
26: 3. which are *among*[a] the Jews:
5. that *after*[a] the most straitest
11. oft *in*[a] every synagogue,
13. I saw *in*[a] the way
27: 2. meaning to sail *by* (lit. *along*[a]) the coasts of Asia;
5. sailed over the sea *of* (lit. *near*[a]) Cilicia
7. come *over against*[a] Cnidus,
— Crete, *over against*[a] Salmone;
12. *toward*[a] the south west and)([a] north west.
14. there arose *against*[g] it a tempestuous
25. that it shall be *even as*[a] it was told me.
27. *about*[a] midnight the shipmen
28:16. to dwell *by*[a] himself
Ro. 1: 3. *according to*[a] the flesh;
4. *according to*[a] the spirit
15. as much as *in*[a] me is,
2: 2. the judgment of God is *according to*[a] truth
5. But *after*[a] thy hardness and impenitent
6. *according to*[a] his deeds:
7. *by*[a] patient continuance
16. *according to*[a] my gospel.
3: 2. Much every way: (lit. *by*[a] every way)
5. I speak *as*[a] a man
4: 1. *as pertaining to*[a] the flesh,
4. is the reward not reckoned *of*[a] grace, but *of*[a] debt.
16. that (it might be) *by*[a] grace;
18. *according to*[a] that which was
5: 6. yet without strength, *in*[a] due time
7:13. might become exceeding sinful. (lit. *according to*[a] excess)
22. *after*[a] the inward man:
8: 1. who walk not *after*[a] the flesh, but *after*[a]
4. who walk not *after*[a] the flesh, but *after*[a]
5. that are *after*[a] the flesh
— they that are *after*[a] the Spirit

Ro. 8:12. to live *after*[a] the flesh.
13. if ye live *after*[a] the flesh,
27. *according to*[a] (the will of) God.
28. *according to*[a] (his) purpose.
31. who (can be) *against*[g] us?
33. Who shall lay any thing to the charge *of*[g] God's elect?
9: 3. *according to*[a] the flesh:
5. *as concerning*[a] the flesh
9. *At*[a] this time will I come,
11. *according to*[a] election might
10: 2. but not *according to*[a] knowledge.
11: 2. to God *against*[g] Israel, saying,
5. *according to*[a] the election of
21. spared not the natur*al* branches, (lit. branches *according to*[a] nature)
24. which is wild *by*[a] nature,
— which be the natur*al*[a] (branches),
28. *As concerning*[a] the gospel,
— but *as touching*[a] the election,
12: 6. differing *according to*[a] the grace
— *according to*[a] the proportion of
14:15. now walkest thou not charitab*ly*[a].
22. have (it) *to*[a] thyself before God.
15: 5. *according to*[a] Christ Jesus:
16: 5. that is *in*[a] their house.
25. *according to*[a] my gospel,
— *according to*[a] the revelation
26. *according to*[a] the commandment
1Co. 1:26. wise men *after*[a] the flesh,
2: 1. came not *with*[a] excellency of
3: 3. and walk *as*[a] men?
8. *according to*[a] his own labour.
10. *According to*[a] the grace of God
4: 6. for one *against*[g] another.
7: 6. I speak this *by*[a] permission, (and) not *of*[a] commandment.
40. so abide, *after*[a] my judgment:
9: 8. Say I these things *as*[a] a man?
10:18. Behold Israel *after*[a] the flesh:
11: 4. having (his) head covered, (lit. *over*[g] his head)
12: 8. *by*[a] the same Spirit;
31. shew I unto you a more excellent way. (lit. *according to*[a] excellence)
14:27. (let it be) *by*[a] two,
31. may all prophesy one *by*[a] one,
40. be done decently and *in*[a] order.
15: 3. died for our sins *according to*[a] the scriptures;
4. *according to*[a] the scriptures:
15. we have testified *of*[g] God
31. I die dai*ly*[a].
32. If *after the manner of*[a] men
16: 2. *Upon*[a] the first (day) of the
19. the church that is *in*[a] their house.
2Co. 1: 8. we were pressed)([a] out of measure,
17. do I purpose *according to*[a] the flesh,
4:13. *according as*[a] it is written,
17. a far more exceeding (and) (lit. *as to*[a] excess unto excess)
5:16. know we no man *after*[a] the flesh: yea, though we have known Christ *after*[a] the flesh,
7: 9. were made sorry *after*[a] a godly manner,
10. For god*ly*[a] sorrow worketh
11. ye sorrowed *after*[a] a godly sort,
8: 2. their deep poverty (lit. *according to*[a] depth) abounded
3. For *to*[a] (their) power,
8. I speak not *by*[a] commandment,
10: 1. who *in*[a] presence (am) base
2. as if we walked *according to*[a] the flesh.
2Co.10: 3. we do not war *after*[a] the flesh:
5. exalteth itself *against*[g] the knowledge
7. *after*[a] the outward appearance?
13. but *according to*[a] the measure
15. *according to*[a] our rule
11:15. *according to*[a] their works.
17. I speak (it) not *after*[a] the Lord.
18. that many glory *after*[a] the flesh,
21. speak *as concerning*[a] reproach,
28. that which cometh upon me dai*ly*[a],
13: 8. we can do nothing *against*[g] the truth,
10. *according to*[a] the power which
Gal. 1: 4. *according to*[a] the will of God
11. preached of me is not *after*[a] man.
13. how that beyond measure I (lit. *according to*[a] excess)
2: 2. I went up *by*[a] revelation,
— but private*ly*[a] to them which
11. I withstood him *to*[a] the face,
3: 1. *before*[a] whose eyes Jesus Christ
15. I speak *after the manner of*[a] men;
21. (Is) the law then *against*[g] the promises
29. heirs *according to*[a] the promise.
4:23. was born *after*[a] the flesh;
28. Now we, brethren, *as*[a] Isaac was,
29. he that was born *after*[a] the flesh persecuted him (that was born) *after*[a]
5:17. the flesh lusteth *against*[g] the Spirit, and the Spirit *against*[g] the flesh:
23. *against*[g] such there is no law.
Eph. 1: 5. *according to*[a] the good pleasure
7. *according to*[a] the riches of his grace;
9. *according to*[a] his good pleasure
11. *according to*[a] the purpose of him who worketh all things *after*[a] the
15. after I heard of your faith (lit. *among*[a] you)
19. *according to*[a] the working of his
2: 2. *according to*[a] the course of this world, *according to*[a] the prince of the power
3: 3. How that *by*[a] revelation he
7. *according to*[a] the gift of the grace of God given unto me *by*[a] the effectual
11. *According to*[a] the eternal purpose
16. *according to*[a] the riches of his glory,
20. *according to*[a] the power that
4: 7. grace *according to*[a] the measure
16. *according to*[a] the effectual
22. *concerning*[a] the former conversation
— *according to*[a] the deceitful lusts;
24. which *after*[a] God is created
5:33. let every one of you in (lit. *by*[a] one)
6: 5. *according to*[a] the flesh,
6. Not *with*[a] eyeservice, as menpleasers;
21. that ye also may know my affairs, (lit. the things *with*[a] me)
Phi. 1:12. the things (which happened) *unto*[a] me
20. *According to*[a] my earnest expectation
2: 3. (Let) nothing (be done) *through*[a] strife
3: 5. *as touching*[a] the law, a Pharisee;
6. *Concerning*[a] zeal, persecuting the church; *touching*[a] the righteousness which
14. I press *toward*[a] the mark
21. *according to*[a] the working whereby
4:11. Not that I speak *in respect of*[a] want:
19. *according to*[a] his riches in glory
Col. 1:11. *according to*[a] his glorious power,
25. *according to*[a] the dispensation
29. striving *according to*[a] his working.
2: 8. *after*[a] the tradition of men, *after*[a] the rudiments of the world, and not *after*[a] Christ.

Col. 2:14. of ordinances that was *against*g us,
22. *after*a the commandments and
3:10. *after*a the image of him that
20. obey (your) parents *in*a all things:
22. Servants, obey *in*a all things (your) masters *according to*a the flesh;
4: 7. All my state shall Tychicus (lit. all the things *concerning*a me)
15. the church which is *in*a his house.
2Th. 1:12. *according to*a the grace of our God
2: 3. Let no man deceive you *by*a any means:
9. is *after*a the working of Satan
3: 6. and not *after*a the tradition
1Ti. 1: 1. *by*a the commandment of God
11. *According to*a the glorious gospel
18. *according to*a the prophecies
5:19. *Against*g an elder receive not
21. doing nothing *by*a partiality.
6: 3. which is *according to*a godliness;
2Ti. 1: 1. *according to*a the promise of
8. *according to*a the power of God;
9. not *according to*a our works, but *according to*a his own purpose
2: 8. *according to*a my gospel:
4: 1. and the dead *at*a his appearing and
3. but *after*a their own lusts
14. *according to*a his works:
Tit. 1: 1. *according to*a the faith of God's
— the truth which is *after*a godliness;
3. *according to*a the commandment
4. own son *after*a the common faith:
5. ordain elders *in every*a city,
9. *as*a he hath been taught,
3: 5. but *according to*a his mercy
7. *according to*a the hope of
Philem. 2. and to the church *in*a thy house:
14. be as it were *of*a necessity, but willing*ly*.a
Heb 1:10. And, Thou, Lord, *in*a the beginning
2: 4. *according to*a his own will?
17. Wherefore *in*a all things it
3: 3. a*inasmuch* as he who hath
8. *in*a the day of temptation in
13. exhort one another dai*ly*,a
4:15. but was *in*a all points tempted *like as*a
5: 6. *after*a the order of Melchisedec.
10. an high priest *after*a the order of
6:13. because he could swear *by*g no greater, he sware *by*g himself,
16. men verily swear *by*g the greater:
20. *after*a the order of Melchisedec.
7: 5. *according to*a the law,
11. rise *after*a the order of Melchisedec, and not be called *after*a the order of Aaron?
15. *after*a the similitude of Melchisedec
16. not *after*a the law of a carnal commandment, but *after*a the power of an
17. *after*a the order of Melchisedec.
20. And *in*asmucha as not without
21. *after*a the order of Melchisedec:
22. *By*a so much was Jesus made
27. Who needeth not dai*ly*,a
8: 4. gifts *according to*a the law:
5. *according to*a the pattern
9. Not *according to*a the covenant
9: 5. cannot now speak particular*ly*.a
9. *in*a which were offered
— *as pertaining to*a the conscience;
19. *according to*a the law,
22. almost all things are *by*a the law
25. *as* the high priest entereth...*every* year (lit. *by*a year)
27. And as (lit. And *inasmuch*a as) it is
Heb 10: 1. offered year *by*a year
3. (made) of sins *every*a year.
8. offered *by*a the law;
11. every priest standeth dai*ly*a
11: 7. which is *by*a faith.
13. These all died *in*a faith,
12:10. chastened (us) *after*a their own
Jas. 2: 8. *according to*a the scripture,
17. is dead, being alone. (lit. *by*a itself)
3: 9. *after*a the similitude of God.
14. and lie not *against*g the truth.
5: 9. Grudge not one *against*g another,
1Pet. 1: 2. Elect *according to*a the foreknowledge
3. *according to*a his abundant mercy
15. But *as*a he which hath called
17. judgeth *according to*a every man's
2:11. which war *against*g the soul;
3: 7. *according to*a knowledge, giving
4: 6. judged *according to*a men in the flesh, but live *according to*a God
14. *on* their *part*a he is evil spoken of, but *on* your *part*a he is glorified.
19. that suffer *according to*a the will
2Pet. 2:11. accusation *against*g them
3: 3. walking *after*a their own lusts,
13. we, *according to*a his promise,
15. *according to*a the wisdom
1Joh. 5:14. any thing *according to*a his will,
2Joh. 6. we walk *after*a his commandments.
3Joh. 14. Greet the friends *by*a name.
Jude 15. To execute judgment *upon*g all,
— ungodly sinners have spoken *against*
16. walking *after*a their own lusts;
18. who should walk *after*a their own
Rev. 2: 4. I have (somewhat) *against*g thee,
14. I have a few things *against*g thee,
20. I have a few things *against*g thee,
23. *according to*a your works.
4: 8. the four beasts had each of them (lit. each *by*a itself)
12: 7. fought *against*g the dragon;
18: 6. *according to*a her works:
20:12. *according to*a their works.
13. *according to*a their works.
22: 2. yielded her fruit *every*a month:
See also καθ' εἷς and καθ' ἡμέραν.

2597 80 409/531 1:518 2596rt939

καταβαίνω, *katabaino.*

Mat. 3:16. *descending* like a dove,
7:25. And the rain *descended*,
27. the rain *descended*, and the floods
8: 1. *When* he *was come down* from the
14:29. And *when* Peter *was come down* out
17: 9. *as* they *came down* from the mountain,
24:17. *Let* him which is on the housetop not *come down* to
27:40. *come down* from the cross.
42. *let* him now *come down* from the
28: 2. for the angel of the Lord *descended*
Mar 1:10. the Spirit like a dove *descending*
3:22. the scribes *which came down* from
9: 9. *as* they *came down* from the
13:15. *let* him that is on the housetop not *go down* into the house,
15:30. *come down* from the cross.
32. Let Christ the King of Israel *descend* now
Lu. 2:51. And he *went down* with them,
3:22. the Holy Ghost *descended* in a
6:17. And he *came down* with them, *and*
8:23. and there *came down* a storm

Lu. 9:54. wilt thou that we command fire *to come down*
10:30. (man) *went down* from Jerusalem
31. by chance there *came down* a
17:31. *let* him not *come down* to take it
18:14 this man *went down* to his house
19: 5. make haste, and *come down*; for to day
6. he made haste, and *came down*,
22:44. great drops of blood *falling down*
Joh. 1:32 I saw the Spirit *descending*
33. thou shalt see the Spirit *descending*,
51(52). ascending and *descending* upon thee
2:12. he *went down* to Capernaum,
3:13. but he *that came down* from
4:47. that he *would come down*,
49. *come down* ere my child die.
51. And *as* he was now *going down*,
5: 4. an angel *went down* at a
7. another *steppeth down* before me.
6:16. his disciples *went down* unto
33. is he *which cometh down* from
38. For I *came down* from heaven,
41. the bread *which came down* from heaven.
42. I *came down* from heaven?
50. the bread *which cometh down* from
51. the living bread *which came down* from
58. This is that bread *which came down*
Acts 7:15. So Jacob *went down* into Egypt,
34. and *am come down* to deliver
8:15. *when* they *were come down*,
26. unto the way *that goeth down* from
38. they *went down* both into the
10:11. a certain vessel *descending*
20 *get* thee *down*, and go with them,
21. Then Peter *went down*......*and* said
11: 5. A certain vessel *descend*,
14:11. The gods *are come down*
25. they *went down* into Attalia:
16: 8. *came down* to Troas.
18:22 he *went down* to Antioch.
20:10. And Paul *went down*, and fell on him,
23:10. commanded the soldiers to *go down, and*
24: 1. Ananias the high priest *descended*
22. the chief captain shall *come down*,
25: 6. he *went down* unto Cæsarea;
7. the Jews *which came down*
Ro. 10: 7. Or, who *shall descend* into
Eph. 4: 9. but that he also *descended* first
10. He *that descended* is the same
1Th. 4:16. For the Lord himself *shall descend*
Jas. 1:17. *and cometh down* from the Father
Rev. 3:12. new Jerusalem, which *cometh down* out of heaven
10: 1. I saw another mighty angel *come down*
12:12. the devil *is come down* unto you,
13:13. he maketh fire *come down*
16:21. there *fell* upon men a great hail
18: 1. I saw another angel *come down*
20: 1. I saw an angel *come down*
9. and fire *came down* from God
21: 2. the holy city, new Jerusalem, *coming down*
10. the holy Jerusalem, *descending* out of heaven from God,

2598 3 409/532 2596,906

καταβάλλω, kataballo.

2Co. 4: 9. *cast down*, but not destroyed;
Heb. 6: 1. not *laying* again the foundation
Rev.12:10. the accuser of our brethren *is cast down*,

2599 1 409/532 2596,916

καταβαρέω, katabareo.

2Co.12:16. I *did* not *burden* you;

2600 1 410/532 2597

κατάβασις, katabasis.

Lu. 19:37. at the *descent* of the mount of Olives,

2601 2 410/532 2596,rt 939

καταβιβάζομαι, katabibazomai.

Mat.11:23. *shall be brought down* to hell:
Lu. 10:15. *shalt be thrust down* to hell.

2602 11 410/532 3:620 2598

καταβολή, katabolee.

Mat.13:35. secret from the *foundation* of the
25:34. from the *foundation* of the world:
Lu. 11:50. which was shed from the *foundation*
Joh 17:24. thou lovedst me before the *foundation*
Eph. 1: 4. chosen us in him before the *foundation*
Heb. 4: 3. works were finished from the *foundation*
9:26. often have suffered since the *foundation*
11:11. received strength to *conceive* seed,
1Pet. 1:20. foreordained before the *foundation*
Rev.13: 8. the Lamb slain from the *foundation*
17: 8. book of life from the *foundation* of the

2603 1 410/532 2596,1018

καταβραβεύω, katabrabūo.

Col. 2:18. *Let* no man *beguile* you *of* your *reward*

2604 1 410/532 1:56 2605

καταγγελεύς, katangelūs

Acts17:18. He seemeth to be a *setter forth* of strange gods:

2605 17 410/532 1:56 2596,rt 32

καταγγέλλω, katangello.

Acts 4: 2. *preached* through Jesus the resurrection
13: 5. they *preached* the word of God
38. through this man *is preached* unto you the forgiveness of sins:
15:36. where we *have preached* the word
16:17. which *shew* unto us the way of
21. And *teach* customs, which are
17: 3. Jesus, whom I *preach* unto you, is
13. the word of God *was preached* of Paul
23. him *declare* I unto you.
26:23. and should *shew* light unto
Ro. 1: 8. your faith *is spoken of* throughout
1 Co. 2: 1. *declaring* unto you the testimony
9:14. they which *preach* the gospel
11:26. ye do *shew* the Lord's death
Phi. 1:16. The one *preach* Christ of contention,
18. or in truth, Christ *is preached*;
Col. 1:28. Whom we *preach*, warning

2606 3 410/532 1:658

καταγελάω, katagelao.

Mat. 9:24. they *laughed* him *to scorn*.
Mar. 5:40. they *laughed* him *to scorn*.
Lu. 8:53. they *laughed* him *to scorn*,

2607 3 410/532 1:689 2596,1097
καταγινώσκω, *kataginōsko.*

Gal. 2:11. because he was *to be blamed.*
1Joh.3:20. For if our heart *condemn* us,
21. if our heart *condemn* us not,

2608 4 410/533 2596,rt 4486
κατάγνυμι, *katagnumi.*

Mat.12:20. A bruised reed *shall* he not *break,*
Joh.19:31. that their legs *might be broken,*
32. and *brake* the legs of the first,
33. they *brake* not his legs:

2609 10 411/533 2596,71
κατάγω, *katago.*

Lu. 5:11. *when* they *had brought* their ships to land,
Acts 9:30. they *brought* him *down* to Cæsarea,
21: 3. into Syria, and *landed* at Tyre:
22:30. *brought* Paul *down, and* set
23:15. that he *bring* him *down* unto you
20. that thou *wouldest bring down* Paul
28. I *brought* him *forth* into their
27: 3. the next (day) we *touched* at Sidon.
28:12. And *landing* at Syracuse, we
Ro. 10: 6. that is, *to bring* Christ *down*

2610 1 411/533 1:134 2596,75
καταγωνίζομαι, *katagōnizomai.*

Heb 11:33. Who through faith *subdued* kingdoms,

2611 1 411/533 2596,1210
καταδέω, *katadeo.*

Lu. 10:34. and *bound up* his wounds,

2612 1 411/533 2596,1212
κατάδηλος, *katadeelos.*

Heb. 7:15. it is yet far more *evident:*

2613 5 411/533 3:621 2596,1349
καταδικάζω, *katadikazo.*

Mat.12: 7. ye would not *have condemned* the guiltless.
37. by thy words thou *shalt be condemned.*
Lu. 6:37. *condemn* not, and ye *shall* not *be condemned:*
Jas. 5: 6. Ye *have condemned* (and) killed the just;

2614 1 411/533 2596,1377
καταδιώκω, *katadiōko.*

Mar. 1:36. Simon and they that were with him *followed after* him.

2615 2 411/533 2:261 2596,1402
καταδουλόω, *katadouloō.*

2Co.11:20. if a man *bring* you *into bondage,*
Gal. 2: 4. that they *might bring* us *into bondage;*

καταδρέμω see κατατρέχω. 2701

2616 2 411/533 2596,1413
καταδυναστεύω, *katadunastūo.*

Acts10:38. healing all *that were oppressed* of the devil;
Jas. 2: 6. *Do* not rich men *oppress* you,

2617 13 411/533 1:189 2596,153
καταισχύνω, *kataiskuno.*

Lu. 13:17. all his adversaries *were ashamed*
Ro. 5: 5. hope *maketh* not *ashamed,*
9:33. believeth on him *shall* not *be ashamed.*
10:11. on him *shall* not *be ashamed.*
1Co. 1:27. to *confound* the wise;
— to *confound* the things which
11: 4. head covered, *dishonoureth* his head.
5. uncovered *dishonoureth* her head:
22. and *shame* them that have not?
2Co. 7:14. I *am* not *ashamed;*
9: 4. we...*should be ashamed* in this
1Pet. 2: 6. *shall* not *be confounded.*
3:16. they *may be ashamed* that

2618 12 411/533 2596,2545
κατακαίω, *katakaio.*

Mat 3:12. but he *will burn up* the chaff
13:30. bind them in bundles *to burn*
40. the tares are gathered and *burned*
Lu. 3:17. but the chaff he *will burn* with
Acts19:19. and *burned* them before all
1Co. 3:15. If any man's work *shall be burned,*
Heb 13:11. *are burned* without the camp.
2Pet. 3:10. and the works that are therein *shall be burned up.*
Rev. 8: 7. the third part of trees *was burnt up,* and all green grass *was burnt up.*
17:16. and *burn* her with fire.
18: 8. she *shall be utterly burned* with fire:

2619 3 412/533 3:556 2596,2572
κατακαλύπτομαι, *katakaluptomai.*

1Co.11: 6. For if the woman *be* not *covered,*
— *let* her *be covered.*
7. ought not *to cover* (his) head,

2620 4 412/533 3:645 2596,2744
κατακαυχάομαι, *katakaukaomai.*

Ro. 11:18. *Boast* not *against* the branches. But if thou *boast,* thou bearest not
Jas. 2:13. and mercy *rejoiceth against*
3:14. *glory* not, and lie not against the truth.

2621 11 412/534 3:654 2596,2749
κατάκειμαι, *katakīmai.*

Mar 1:30. Simon's wife's mother *lay* sick
2: 4. wherein the sick of the palsy *lay.*
15. as Jesus *sat at meat* in his
14: 3. *as* he *sat at meat,* there came a woman
Lu. 5:25. took up that whereon he *lay,*
29. and of others *that sat down* with them.
Joh. 5: 3. In these *lay* a great multitude
6. When Jesus saw him *lie,*
Acts 9:33. Æneas, *which had kept* his bed eight
28: 8. that the father of Publius *lay* sick
1Co. 8:10. *sit at meat* in the idol's temple,

2622 2 412/534 2596,2806
κατακλάω or κατακλάζω, *kataklao* or *kataklazo.*

Mar 6:41. and *brake* the loaves,
Lu. 9:16. he blessed them, and *brake*

2623 2 412/534 2596,2808

κατακλείω, kataklīo.

Lu. 3:20. that he *shut up* John in prison.
Acts26:10. saints *did* I *shut up* in prison,

2624 1 412/534 2596,2819,1325

κατακληροδοτέω, katakleerodoteo.

Acts13:19. he *divided* their land to them *by lot*.

2625 3 412/534 2596,2827

κατακλίνω, kataklino.

Lu. 9:14. *Make* them *sit down* by fifties
14: 8. *sit* not *down* in the highest
24:30. as he *sat at meat* with them,

2626 2 412/534 2596,rt 2830

κατακλύζομαι, katakluzomai.

2Pet.3: 6. *being overflowed* with water,

2627 4 412/534 2626

κατακλυσμός, kataklusmos.

Mat 24:38. before the *flood* they were eating
39. until the *flood* came,
Lu. 17:27. and the *flood* came, and destroyed
2Pet.2: 5. bringing in the *flood* upon the world

2628 2 412/534 2596,190

κατακολουθέω, katakoloutheo.

Lu. 23:55. the women also, which...*followed after*, and beheld the sepulchre,
Acts16:17. The same *followed* Paul and us, *and* cried,

2629 1 412/534 2596,2875

κατακόπτω, katakopto.

Mar 5: 5. *cutting* himself with stones.

2630 1 413/534 2596,2911

κατακρημνίζω, katakreemnizo.

Lu. 4:29. that they might *cast* him *down headlong*.

2631 3 413/534 3:921 2632

κατάκριμα, katakrima.

Ro. 5:16. judgment (was) by one to *condemnation*,
18. upon all men to *condemnation*;
8: 1. now no *condemnation* to them which are in Christ Jesus,

2632 19 413/534 3:921 2596,2919

κατακρίνω, katakrino.

Mat 12:41. and *shall condemn* it:
42. and *shall condemn* it:
20:18. they *shall condemn* him to death,
27: 3. when he saw that he *was condemned*,
Mar 10:33. they *shall condemn* him to death,
14:64. they all *condemned* him to be
16:16. believeth not *shall be damned*.
Lu. 11:31. this generation, and *condemn* them:
32. and *shall condemn* it:
Joh. 8:10. *hath* no man *condemned* thee?
11. Neither *do* I *condemn* thee:
Ro. 2: 1. another, thou *condemnest* thyself;
8: 3. *condemned* sin in the flesh:
34. Who (is) he *that condemneth*?
Ro. 14:23. he that doubteth *is damned* it
1Co.11:32. that we *should* not *be condemned* with the
Heb 11: 7. by the which he *condemned* the world,
Jas. 5: 9. lest ye *be condemned*:
2Pet.2: 6. *condemned* (them) with an overthrow,

2633 2 413/534 3:921 2632

κατάκρισις, katakrisis.

2Co. 3: 9. ministration of *condemnation* (be) glory,
7: 3. I speak not (this) to *condemn* (you):

2634 4 413/534 3:1039 2596 2961

κατακυριεύω, katakuriūo.

Mat 20:25. princes of the Gentiles *exercise dominion over* them,
Mar 10:42. *exercise lordship over* them;
Acts19:16. *overcame* them, *and* prevailed against
1Pet.5: 3. Neither as *being lords over* (God's)

2635 5 413/534 4:3 2637

καταλαλέω, katalaleo.

Jas. 4:11. *Speak* not *evil* one *of* another, brethren
He that *speaketh evil of* (his)
— *speaketh evil of* the law,
1Pet.2:12. they *speak against* you as evildoers,
3:16. whereas they *speak evil of* you,

2636 2 413/534 4:3 2637

καταλαλία, katalalia.

2Co.12:20. strifes, *backbitings*, whisperings,
1Pet.2: 1. envies, and all *evil speakings*,

2637 1 413/535 4:3 2596,rt2980

κατάλαλος, katalalos.

Ro. 1:30. *Backbiters*, haters of God,

2638 15 413/535 4:5 2596,2983

καταλαμβάνω, katalambano.

Mar 9:18. wheresoever he *taketh* him,
Joh. 1: 5. the darkness *comprehended* it not.
8: 3. a woman *taken* in adultery;
4. this woman *was taken* in adultery,
12:35. lest darkness *come upon* you:
Acts 4:13. and *perceived* that they were unlearned
10:34. I *perceive* that God is no respecter
25:25. But *when* I *found* that he had
Ro. 9:30. *have attained* to righteousness,
1Co. 9:24. So run, that ye *may obtain*.
Eph. 3:18. able *to comprehend* with all saints
Phi. 3:12. if that I *may apprehend* that for which also I *am apprehended*
13. I count not myself *to have apprehended*:
1Th. 5: 4. *should overtake* you as a thief.

2639 1 414/535 2596,3004

καταλέγομαι, katalegomai.

1Ti. 5: 9. *Let* not a widow *be taken into the number*

2640 1 414/979 4:194 2641

κατάλειμμα, katalimma.

Ro. 9:27. a *remnant* shall be saved.

2641 25 414/535 4:194 2596,3007

καταλείπω, katalīpo.

Mat. 4:13. And *leaving* Nazareth, he came
16: 4. And he *left* them, *and* departed.
19: 5. For this cause *shall* a man *leave*
21:17. he *left* them, *and* went out of the city
Mar 10: 7. For this cause *shall* a man *leave*
12:19. If a man's brother die, and *leave* (his)
14:52. And he *left* the linen cloth, *and* fled
Lu. 5:28. And he *left* all, rose up, *and*
10:40. that my sister *hath left* me to serve
15: 4. *doth* not *leave* the ninety and nine
20:31. and they *left* no children,
Joh. 8: 9. and Jesus *was left* alone,
Acts 2:31. that his soul *was* not *left* in hell,
6: 2. that we should *leave* the word of God, *and* serve tables.
18:19. and *left* them there:
21: 3. we *left* it on the left hand, *and*
24:27. Jews a pleasure, *left* Paul bound.
25:14. a certain man *left* in bonds
Ro. 11: 4. I *have reserved* to myself
Eph. 5:31. *shall* a man *leave* his father
1Th. 3: 1. we thought it good *to be left* at Athens
Tit. 1: 5. For this cause *left* I thee in
Heb 4: 1. lest, a promise *being left* (us)
11:27. By faith he *forsook* Egypt,
2Pet. 2:15. *Which have forsaken* the right way, *and* are gone astray,

2642 1 415/535 4:267 2596,3034

καταλιθάζω, katalithazo.

Lu. 20: 6. all the people *will stone* us:

2643 4 415/535 1:251 2644

καταλλαγή, katallagee.

Ro. 5:11. by whom we have now received the *atonement.* (lit. *reconciliation*)
11:15. the *reconciling* of the world,
2Co. 5:18. the ministry of *reconciliation;*
19. the word of *reconciliation.*

2644 6 415/535 1:251 2596,236

καταλλάσσω, katallasso.

Ro. 5:10. we *were reconciled* to God
— *being reconciled,* we shall
1Co. 7:11. let her remain unmarried, or *be reconciled* to (her) husband:
2Co. 5:18. of God, *who hath reconciled* us to himself by Jesus Christ,
19. *reconciling* the world unto himself,
20. *be* ye *reconciled* to God.

2645 1 415/535 2596,3062

κατάλοιπος, kataloipos.

Acts 15:17. That the *residue* of men might seek after

2646 3 415/535 4:328 2647

κατάλυμα, katuluma.

Mar 14:14. Where is the *guestchamber,*
Lu. 2: 7. no room for them in the *inn.*
22:11. Where is the *guestchamber,*

2647 17 415/535 4:328 2596,3089

καταλύω, kataluo.

Mat. 5:17. Think not that I am come *to destroy* the
Mat. 5:17. I am not come *to destroy,* but to fulfil.
24: 2. that *shall* not *be thrown down.*
26:61. I am able *to destroy* the temple
27:40. Thou *that destroyest* the temple,
Mar 13: 2. that *shall* not *be thrown down.*
14:58. I *will destroy* this temple
15:29. Ah, thou *that destroyest* the temple,
Lu. 9:12. and *lodge,* and get victuals:
19: 7. gone *to be guest* with a man that is a
21: 6. that *shall* not *be thrown down.*
Acts 5:38. be of men, it *will come to nought:*
39. if it be of God, ye cannot *overthrow* it;
6:14. Jesus of Nazareth *shall destroy* this
Ro. 14:20. For meat *destroy* not the work
2Co. 5: 1. of (this) tabernacle *were dissolved,*
Gal. 2:18. the things which I *destroyed,*

2648 1 415/536 4:390 2596,3129

καταμανθάνω, katamanthano.

Mat. 6:28. *Consider* the lilies of the field,

2649 4 415/536 4:474 2596,3140

καταμαρτυρέω, katamartureo.

Mat. 26:62. what (is it which) these *witness against* thee?
27:13. how many things they *witness against*
Mar 14:60. (which) these *witness against* thee?
15: 4. they *witness against* thee.

2650 1 415/536 2596,3306

καταμένω, katameno.

Acts 1:13. where abode both Peter, and James, (lit. were *abiding*)

2651 2 415/526 2596,3441

καταμόνας, katamonas.

Mar 4:10. And when he was *alone,*
Lu. 9:18. as he was *alone* praying,

2652 2 415/533 2596,331

κατανάθεμα, katanathema.

Rev. 22: 3. there shall be no more *curse:*

2653 1 415/533 2596,332

καταναθεματίζω, katanathematizo.

Mat. 26:74. Then began he *to curse* and to swear,

2654 1 415/536 2596,335

καταναλίσκο, katanalisko.

Heb 12:29. For our God (is) a *consuming* fire.

2655 3 415/536 2596 *narkaō* (to be numb)

καταναρκάω, katanarkao.

2Co. 11: 9(8). I *was chargeable* to no man:
12:13. that I myself *was* not *burdensome* to you?
14. I *will* not *be burdensome* to you:

2656 1 416/536 2596,3506

κατανεύω, katanūo.

Lu. 5: 7. they *beckoned* unto (their) partners,

2657 15 416/536 4:948 2596,3539

κατανοέω, katanoeo.

Mat. 7: 3. but *considerest* not the beam
Lu. 6:41. but *perceivest* not the beam
12:24. *Consider* the ravens: for they
27. *Consider* the lilies how they grow:
20:23. he *perceived* their craftiness, and said
Acts 7:31. and as he drew near *to behold* (it),
32. and durst not *behold*.
11: 6. I *considered*, and saw fourfooted
27:39. they *discovered* a certain creek
Ro. 4:19. he *considered* not his own body
Heb 3: 1. *consider* the apostle and high priest
10:24. *let* us *consider* one another
Jas. 1:23. like unto a man *beholding* his natural face
24. For he *beholdeth* himself, and goeth

2658 13 416/536 3:623 2596,473

καταντάω, katantao.

Acts 16: 1. Then *came* he to Derbe and Lystra:
18:19. And he *came* to Ephesus,
24. mighty in the scriptures, *came* to Ephesus.
20:15. *came* the next (day) over against Chios;
21: 7. we *came* to Ptolemais,
25:13. Agrippa and Bernice *came* unto Cæsarea
26: 7. serving (God) day and night, hope *to come*.
27:12. by any means they might *attain* to Phenice, (*and*)
28:13. and *came* to Rhegium:
1Co.10:11. upon whom the ends of the world *are come*.
14:36. *came* it unto you only?
Eph. 4:13. Till we all *come* in the unity
Phi. 3:11. If by any means I *might attain* unto

2659 1 416/536 3:626 2660

κατάνυξις, katanuxis.

Ro. 11:8. God hath given them the spirit of *slumber*,

2660 1 416/536 3:626 2596,3572

κατανύσσω, katanusso.

Acts 2:37. they *were pricked* in their heart,

2661 4 416/536 1:379 2596,515

καταξιόομαι, kataxio-omai.

Lu. 20:35. which shall be *accounted worthy* to obtain
21:36. that ye *may be accounted worthy* to escape
Acts 5:41. that they *were counted worthy* to suffer
2Th. 1: 5. that ye may *be counted worthy* of

2662 5 416/536 5:940 2596,3961

καταπατέω, katapateo.

Mat. 5:13. and *to be trodden under foot* of men.
7: 6. lest they *trample* them under their feet,
Lu. 8: 5. and it *was trodden down*,
12: 1. that they *trode* one upon another,
Heb 10:29. *who hath trodden under foot* the Son of God,

2663 9 416/536 3:627 2664

κατάπαυσις, katapausis.

Acts 7:49. what (is) the place of my *rest?*
Heb. 3:11. They shall not enter into my *rest*.
18. they should not enter into his *rest*,
4: 1. of entering into his *rest*,
3. do enter into *rest*
— if they shall enter into my *rest:*
4:5. If they shall enter into my *rest*.
10. he that is entered into his *rest*,
11. to enter into that *rest*,

2664 4 416/536 3:627 2596,3973

καταπαύω, katapauo.

Acts14:18. scarce *restrained* they the people,
Heb. 4: 4. And God *did rest* the seventh day
8. if Jesus *had given* them *rest*,
10. he also *hath ceased* from his own works,

2665 6 417/537 3:628 2596,4072

καταπέτασμα, katapetasma.

Mat.27:51. behold, the *veil* of the temple was rent
Mar 15:38. And the *veil* of the temple was rent
Lu. 23:45. and the *veil* of the temple was rent
Heb. 6:19. into that within the *veil*;
9: 3. And after the second *veil*,
10:20. through the *veil*, that is to say, his flesh;

2666 7 417/537 6:135 2596,4095

καταπίνω, katapino.

Mat.23:24. and *swallow* a camel.
1Co.15:54. Death *is swallowed up* in victory.
2Co. 2: 7. *should be swallowed up* with overmuch
5: 4. *might be swallowed up* of life.
Heb 11:29. assaying to do *were drowned*.
1Pet. 5: 8. seeking whom he *may devour:*
Rev.12:16. and *swallowed up* the flood which

2667 2 417/537 6:161 2596,4098

καταπίπτω, katapipto.

Acts26:14. *when* we *were* all *fallen* to the earth,
28: 6. or *fallen down* dead suddenly:

2668 1 417/537 2596,4126

καταπλέω, katapleo.

Lu. 8:26. And they *arrived* at the country

2669 2 417/537 2596,4192

καταπονέομαι, kataponeomai.

Acts 7:24. avenged him *that was oppressed*,
2Pet.2: 7. *vexed* with the filthy conversation

2670 2 417/537 2596,rt 4195

καταποντίζομαι, katapontizomai.

Mat.14:30. and beginning *to sink*,
18: 6. and (that) he *were drowned* in the

2671 6 418/537 1:448 2596,685

κατάρα, katara.

Gal. 3:10. are under the *curse:*
13. hath redeemed us from the *curse* of the law, being made a *curse* for us:
Heb. 6: 8. nigh unto *cursing;* whose end
Jas. 3:10. proceedeth blessing and *cursing*.
2Pet.2:14. *cursed* children: (lit. children of *curse*)

2672 6 418/537 1:448 2671

καταράομαι, kataraomai.

Mat. 5:44. bless them *that curse* you.
25:41. Depart from me, ye *cursed*.

Mar 11:21. the fig tree which thou *cursedst*
Lu. 6:28. Bless them *that curse* you,
Ro. 12:14. bless, and *curse* not.
Jas. 3: 9. and therewith *curse* we men,

2673 27 418/537 1:452 2596,691

καταργέω, katargeo.

Lu. 13: 7. why *cumbereth* it the ground?
Ro. 3: 3. *shall* their unbelief *make* the faith of God *without effect?*
31. *Do* we then *make void* the law
4:14. and the promise *made of none effect:*
6: 6. the body of sin *might be destroyed,*
7: 2. she *is loosed* from the law of
6. now we *are delivered* from the law,
1Co. 1:28. to *bring to nought* things that are:
2: 6. of the princes of this world, *that come to nought:*
6:13. God *shall destroy* both it and them.
13: 8. prophecies, they *shall fail;*
— knowledge, it *shall vanish away.*
10. is in part *shall be done away.*
11. I *put away* childish things.
15:24. when he *shall have put down*
26. The last enemy (that) *shall be destroyed*
2Co. 3: 7. *which* (glory) *was to be done away:*
11. if that *which is done away*
13. to the end of that *which is abolished:*
14. which (vail) *is done away* in Christ.
Gal. 3:17. that it should *make* the promise *of none effect.*
5: 4. Christ is *become of no effect* unto you, (lit. ye *are ceased* from Christ)
11. then *is* the offence of the cross *ceased.*
Eph. 2:15. *Having abolished* in his flesh
2Th. 2: 8. and *shall destroy* with the brightness of his coming:
2Ti. 1:10. Christ, *who hath abolished* death,
Heb. 2:14. that through death he *might destroy* him

2674 1 418/537 2596,705

καταριθμέομαι, katarithmeomai.

Acts 1:17. he was *numbered with* us

2675 13 418/537 1:475 2596,739

καταρτίζω, katartizo.

Mat. 4:21. *mending* their nets;
21:16. thou *hast perfected* praise?
Mar 1:19. in the ship *mending* their nets.
Lu. 6:40. every one *that is perfect* shall be
Ro. 9:22. vessels of wrath *fitted* to destruction:
1Co. 1:10. but (that) ye be *perfectly joined together*
2Co.13:11. *Be perfect*, be of good comfort,
Gal. 6: 1. *restore* such an one in the spirit of
1Th. 3:10. and might *perfect* that which is
Heb 10: 5. a body *hast* thou *prepared* me:
11: 3. the worlds *were framed* by the word
13:21. *Make* you *perfect* in every good work
1Pet.5:10. *make* you *perfect*, stablish,

2676 1 419/538 1:475 2675

κατάρτισις, katartisis.

2Co.13: 9. we wish, (even) your *perfection.*

2677 1 419/538 1:475 2675

καταρτισμός, katartismos.

Eph. 4:12. For the *perfecting* of the saints,

2678 4 419/538 2596,4579

κατασείω, katasio.

Acts12:17. *beckoning* unto them with the hand
13:16. and *beckoning* with (his) hand
19:33. Alexander *beckoned* with the hand, *and*
21:40. and *beckoned* with the hand

2679 2 419/538 2596,4626

κατασκάπτω, kataskapto.

Acts15:16. I will build again the *ruins* thereof,
Ro. 11: 3. they have...and *digged down* thine altars;

2680 11 419/538 2596,4632

κατασκευάζω, kataskuazo.

Mat 11:10. which *shall prepare* thy way
Mar 1: 2. which *shall prepare* thy way
Lu. 1:17. a people *prepared* for the Lord.
7:27. which *shall prepare* thy way
Heb 3: 3. as he *who hath builded* the house
4. every house *is builded* by some (man) but he *that built* all things (is) God.
9: 2. there was a tabernacle *made;*
6. *when* these things *were* thus *ordained,*
11: 7. *prepared* an ark to the saving
1Pet.3:20. *while* the ark *was a preparing,*

2681 4 419/538 7:368 2596,4637

κατασκηνόω, kataskeenoo.

Mat 13:32. come and *lodge* in the branches
Mar 4:32. so that the fowls of the air may *lodge*
Lu. 13:19. the fowls of the air *lodged* in the
Acts 2:26. my flesh *shall rest* in hope:

2682 2 419/538 2681

κατασκήνωσις, kataskeenosis.

Mat. 8:20. the birds of the air (have) *nests;*
Lu. 9:58. and birds of the air (have) *nests;*

2683 1 419/538 2596,4639

κατασκιάζω, kataskiazo.

Heb 9: 5. glory *shadowing* the mercyseat;

2684 1 419/538 7:413 2685

κατασκοπέω, kataskopeo.

Gal. 2: 4. privily *to spy out* our liberty

2685 1 419/538 7:413 2596,4649

κατάσκοπος, kataskopos.

Heb 11:31. when she had received the *spies*

2686 1 419/538 2596,4679

κατασοφίζομαι, katasophizomai.

Acts 7:19. The same *dealt subtilly with* our

2687 2 420/538 7:588 2596,4724

καταστέλλω, katastello.

Acts19:35. *when* the townclerk *had appeased*
36. ye ought to be *quiet,*

2688 1 420/538 2525

κατάστημα, katasteema.

Tit. 2: 3. that (they be) in *behaviour* as becometh

2689 1 420/538 7:588 2687
καταστολή, katastolee.

1Ti. 2: 9. adorn themselves in modest *apparel,*

2690 2 420/538 7:714 2596,4762
καταστρέφω, katastrepho.

Mat 21:12. and *overthrew* the tables
Mar 11:15. and *overthrew* the tables

2691 1 420/538 3:631 2596,4763
καταστρηνιάζω, katastreeniazo.

1Ti. 5:11. *have begun to wax wanton against* Christ,

2692 2 420/538 7:714 2690
καταστροφή, katastrophee.

2Ti. 2:14. to the *subverting* of the hearers.
2Pet. 2: 6. condemned (them) with an *overthrow,*

2693 1 420/538 2596,4766
καταστρώννυμι, katastrōnnumi.

1Co. 10: 5. they *were overthrown* in the wilderness.

2694 1 420/538 2596,4951
κατασύρω, katasuro.

Lu. 12:58. lest he *hale* thee to the judge,

2695 1 420/538 2596,4969
κατασφάττω, katasphatto.

Lu. 19:27. and *slay* (them) before me.

2696 1 420/538 7:939 2596,4972
κατασφραγίζομαι, katasphragizomai.

Rev 5: 1. *sealed* with seven seals.

2697 1 420/538 2722
κατάσχεσις, kataskesis.

Acts 7: 5. give it to him for a *possession,*
45. into the *possession* of the Gentiles,

2698 3 420/538 2596,5087
κατατίθημι, katatitheemi.

Mar 15:46. and *laid* him in a sepulchre
Acts 24:27. willing *to shew* the Jews a pleasure,
25: 9. willing *to do* the Jews a pleasure,

2699 1 420/538 8:106 2596 *temno* (to cut) cf 609
κατατομή, katatomee.

Phi. 3: 2. beware of the *concision.*

2700 1 420/ 2596,5115
κατατοξεύομαι, katatoxūomai.

Heb 12:20. it shall be stoned, or *thrust through* with a dart:

2701 1 420/538 2596,5143
κατατρέχω, katatreko.

Acts 21:32. and *ran down* unto them:

2701.5 9 /540 see2719
καταφάγω, kataphago.

Mat. 13: 4. the fowls came and *devoured* them *up:*
Mar 4: 4. came and *devoured* it *up.*
Lu. 8: 5. the fowls of the air *devoured* it.
15:30. which *hath devoured* thy living
Joh. 2:17. The zeal of thine house *hath eaten* me *up.*
Rev 10: 9. Take (it), and *eat* it *up;*
10. I took the little book...and *ate* it *up;*
12: 4. for to *devour* her child as soon
20: 9. out of heaven, and *devoured* them.

2702 3 420/539 2596,5342
καταφέρω, kataphero.

Acts 20: 9. *being fallen* into a deep sleep:
— he *sunk down* with sleep, *and*
26:10. I *gave* my voice against (them).

2703 2 421/539 2596,5343
καταφεύγω, kataphūgo.

Acts 14: 6. and *fled* unto Lystra and Derbe,
Heb 6:18. *who have fled* for refuge to lay hold

2704 2 421/539 9:93 2596,5351
καταφθείρω, kataphthīro.

2Ti. 3: 8. men of *corrupt* minds, (lit. *corrupt* (as to) mind)
2Pet. 2:12. and *shall utterly perish* in their own

2705 6 421/539 9:113 2596,5368
καταφιλέω, kataphileo.

Mat 26:49. Hail, master; and *kissed* him.
Mar 14:45. Master, master; and *kissed* him.
Lu. 7:38. and *kissed* his feet,
45. hath not ceased to *kiss* my feet.
15:20. fell on his neck, and *kissed* him.
Acts 20:37. fell on Paul's neck, and *kissed* him,

2706 9 421/539 3:631 2596,5426
καταφρονέω, kataphroneo.

Mat. 6:24. will hold to the one, and *despise* the other.
18:10. that ye *despise* not one of these
Lu. 16:13. and *despise* the other.
Ro. 2: 4. Or *despisest* thou the riches of
1Co. 11:22. or *despise* ye the church of
1Ti. 4:12. *Let* no man *despise* thy youth;
6: 2. *let* them not *despise* (them),
Heb 12: 2 *despising* the shame, and is
2Pet. 2:10. and *despise* government.

2707 1 421/539 3:631 2706
καταφρονητής, kataphroneetees.

Acts 13:41. Behold, ye *despisers,* and wonder,

2708 2 421/539 2596 *cheō* (to pour)
καταχέω, katakeo.

Mat. 26: 7. and *poured* it on his head,
Mar 14: 3. and *poured* (it) on his head.

2709 1 421/539 3:633 2596 *chthōn* (ground)
καταχθόνιος, katakthonios.

Phi. 2:10. and (things) *under the earth;*

2710 2 421/539 2596,5530
καταχράομαι, katakraomai.

1Co. 7:31. that use this world, as not *abusing* (it):
9:18. that I *abuse* not my power in

2711 1 422/539 2596,5594

καταψύχω, katapsuko.

Lu. 16:24. in water, and *cool* my tongue;

2712 1 422/539 2:375 2596,1497

κατείδωλος, katīdōlos.

Acts17:16. the city *wholly given to idolatry.*

2713 5 422/539 2596,1725

κατέναντι, katenanti.

Mar 11: 2. into the village *over against* you:
12:41. Jesus sat *over against* the treasury,
13: 3. *over against* the temple,
Lu. 19:30. Go ye into the village *over against*
Ro. 4:17. *before* him whom he believed,

2714 5 422/539 2596,1799

κατενώπιον, katenōpion.

2Co. 2:17. *in the sight* of God speak we
12:19. we speak *before* God in Christ:
Eph. 1: 4. and without blame *before* him
Col. 1:22. unreprovable *in his sight:*
Jude 24. faultless *before the presence* of his glory

2715 2 422/539 2:560 2596,1850

κατεξουσιάζω, katexousiazo.

Mat.20:25. *exercise authority* upon them.
Mar 10:42. *exercise authority* upon them.

2716 24 422/539 3:634 2596,2038

κατεργάζομαι, katergazomai.

Ro. 1:27. *working* that which is unseemly,
2: 9. upon every soul of man *that doeth* evil,
4:15. the law *worketh* wrath:
5: 3. tribulation *worketh* patience;
7: 8. *wrought* in me all manner of
13. *working* death in me by that
15. For that which I *do* I allow not:
17. it is no more I that *do* it,
18. but (how) to *perform* that which is good
20. it is no more I that *do* it,
15:18. which Christ *hath* not *wrought* by me,
1Co. 5: 3. him *that hath* so *done this deed,*
2Co. 4:17. *worketh* for us a far more
5: 5. he *that hath wrought* us for
7:10. godly sorrow *worketh* repentance
— sorrow of the world *worketh* death.
11. what carefulness it *wrought* in you,
9:11. which *causeth* through us thanksgiving
12:12. the signs of an apostle *were wrought*
Eph. 6:13. and *having done* all, to stand.
Phi. 2:12. *work out* your own salvation
Jas. 1: 3. trying of your faith *worketh* patience.
20. the wrath of man *worketh* not the righteousness of God.
1Pet.4: 3. suffice us *to have wrought* the

2718 13 423/540 2596,2064

κατέρχομαι, katerkomai.

Lu. 4:31. And *came down* to Capernaum,
9:37. *when* they *were come down* from
Acts 8: 5. Philip *went down* to the city of
9:32. he *came down* also to the saints
11:27. *came* prophets from Jerusalem
12:19. he *went down* from Judæa
Acts13: 4. *departed* unto Seleucia;
15: 1. certain men *which came down* from
18: 5. and Timotheus *were come* from
22. And *when* he *had landed* at
21:10. there *came down* from Judæa
27: 5. we *came* to Myra,
Jas. 3:15. This wisdom *descendeth* not from above.

2719 6 423/540 2596,2068

κατεσθίω, katesthio.

Mat.23:14(13). ye *devour* widows' houses,
Mar 12:40. *Which devour* widows' houses,
Lu. 20:47. Which *devour* widows' houses,
2Co.11:20. if a man *devour* (you),
Gal. 5:15. if ye bite and *devour* one another,
Rev.11: 5. and *devoureth* their enemies:

2720 3 423/540 2596,2116

κατευθύνω, katūthuno.

Lu. 1:79. *to guide* our feet into the way
1Th. 3:11. *direct* our way unto you.
2Th. 3: 5. the Lord *direct* your hearts into the love of God,

2721 1 423/540 2596,2186

κατεφίστημι, katephisteemi.

Acts18:12. the Jews *made insurrection* with one accord *against* Paul,

2722 19 423/540 2:816 2596,2192

κατέχω, kateko.

Mat.21:38. *let* us *seize on* his inheritance.
Lu. 4:42. and *stayed* him, that he should not
8:15. having heard the word, *keep* (it),
14: 9. with shame *to take* the lowest
Joh. 5: 4. of whatsoever disease he had. (lit. he *was held*)
Acts27:40. and *made toward* shore.
Ro. 1:18. *who hold* the truth in unrighteousness,
7: 6. being dead wherein we *were held;*
1Co. 7:30. as though they *possessed* not;
11: 2. and *keep* the ordinances, as I
15: 2. if ye *keep in memory* what I preached
2Co. 6:10. and (yet) *possessing* all things
1Th. 5:21. *hold fast* that which is good.
2Th. 2: 6. ye know *what withholdeth*
7. only he *who* now *letteth* (will let),
Philem13. I would have *retained* with me,
Heb 3: 6. if we *hold fast* the confidence
14. if we *hold* the beginning of
10:23. *Let* us *hold fast* the profession

2723 22 424/540 3:636 2525

κατηγορέω, kateegoreo.

Mat.12:10. that they *might accuse* him.
27:12. when he *was accused* of the
Mar 3: 2. that they *might accuse* him.
15: 3. the chief priests *accused* him of
Lu. 11:54. that they *might accuse* him.
23: 2. they began *to accuse* him,
10. *and* vehemently *accused* him.
14. whereof ye *accuse* him.
Joh. 5:45. Do not think that I *will accuse*
— there is (one) *that accuseth* you.
8: 6. that they might have *to accuse* him.
Acts22:30. wherefore he *was accused* of the Jews.

Acts24: 2. Tertullus began *to accuse* (him),
8 whereof we *accuse* him.
13. whereof they now *accuse* me.
19. and *object*, if they had ought
25: 5. and *accuse* this man,
11. whereof these *accuse* me,
16. before that he *which is accused*
28: 19. *to accuse* my nation of.
Ro. 2: 15. (their) thoughts the mean while *accusing*
Rev 12: 10. *which accused* them before our God

2724 4 424/541 3:636 2725

κατηγορία, kateegoria.

Lu. 6: 7. an *accusation* against him.
Joh. 18:29. What *accusation* bring ye against
1Ti. 5:19. receive not an *accusation*,
Tit. 1: 6. not accused (lit. not under *accusation*) of riot,

2725 7 424/541 3:636 2596,58

κατήγορος, kateegoros.

Joh. 8:10. where are those thine *accusers?*
Acts23:30. gave commandment to his *accusers*
35. when thine *accusers* are also come.
24: 8. Commanding his *accusers* to come
25:16. have the *accusers* face to face,
18. when the *accusers* stood up,
Rev 12:10. for the *accuser* of our brethren is cast

2726 1 424/541 2596,rt 5316

κατήφεια, kateephīa.

Jas. 4: 9. and (your) joy to *heaviness*.

2727 8 424/541 3:638 2596,2279

κατηχέω, kateekeo.

Lu. 1: 4. wherein thou *hast been instructed*.
Acts18:25. This man was *instructed* in the way of
21:21. they *are informed* of thee,
24. they *were informed* concerning thee,
Ro. 2:18. *being instructed* out of the law;
1Co.14:19. I *might teach* others also,
Gal. 6: 6. Let him *that is taught* in the word communicate unto him *that teacheth*

2596, 2398

κατ' 'δίαν see in κατά & ἴδιος.

2728 1 425/541 3:334 2596,2447

κατιόομαι, katio-omai.

Jas. 5: 3. Your gold and silver *is cankered*,

2729 2 425/541 3:397 2596,2480

κατισχύω, katiskuo.

Mat 16:18. of hell *shall* not *prevail against*
Lu. 23:23. and of the chief priests *prevailed*.

2730 47 425/541 5:199 2596,3611

κατοικέω, katoikeo.

Mat. 2:23. and *dwelt* in a city called Nazareth:
4:13. he came and *dwelt* in Capernaum,
12:45. they enter in and *dwell* there:
23:21. and by him *that dwelleth* therein.
Lu. 11:26. they enter in, and *dwell* there:
13: 4. above all men *that dwelt* in Jerusalem?
Acts 1:19. was known unto all the *dwellers* at
20. and let no man *dwell* therein:
2: 5. there were *dwelling* at Jerusalem
9. and the *dwellers* in Mesopotamia.
14. and all (ye) *that dwell* at Jerusalem,
4:16. to all them *that dwell* in Jerusalem;
7: 2. before he *dwelt* in Charran,
4. and *dwelt* in Charran:
— wherein ye now *dwell*.
48. the most High *dwelleth* not in temples
9:22. the Jews *which dwelt* at Damascus,
32. to the saints *which dwelt* at Lydda.
35. all *that dwelt* at Lydda and Saron
11:29. unto the brethren *which dwelt* in Judæa:
13:27. For they *that dwell* at Jerusalem,
17:24. *dwelleth* not in temples made
26. for *to dwell* on all the face of
19:10. all they *which dwelt* in Asia heard
17. Greeks also *dwelling* at Ephesus;
22:12. of all the Jews *which dwelt* (there),
Eph 3:17. That Christ may *dwell* in your hearts
Col. 1:19. that in him should all fulness *dwell*;
2: 9. in him *dwelleth* all the fulness
Heb 11: 9. *dwelling* in tabernacles with Isaac
Jas. 4: 5. The spirit that *dwelleth* in us
2Pet.3:13. wherein *dwelleth* righteousness.
Rev 2:13. and where thou *dwellest*,
— slain among you, where Satan *dwelleth*
3:10. to try them *that dwell* upon the
6:10. on them *that dwell* on the earth?
8:13. Woe, woe, woe, to the *inhabiters* of
11:10. they *that dwell* upon the earth
— them *that dwelt* on the earth.
12:12. Woe to the *inhabiters* of the earth
13: 8. all *that dwell* upon the earth
12. and them *which dwell* therein
14. deceiveth them *that dwell* on
— saying to them *that dwell* on the
14: 6. to preach unto them *that dwell* on
17: 2. and the *inhabitants* of the earth
8. and they *that dwell* on the earth

2731 1 425/541 2730

κατοίκησις, katoikeesis.

Mar 5: 3. Who had (his) *dwelling* among the tombs:

2732 2 425/541 5:119 2730

κατοικητήριον, katoikeeteerion.

Eph 2:22. for an *habitation* of God through the
Rev 18: 2. is become the *habitation* of devils,

2733 1 425/542

κατοικία, katoikia.

Acts17:26. the bounds of their *habitation*;

2734 1 425/542 2:696 2596,3700

κατοπτρίζομαι, katoptrizomai.

2Co. 3:18. *beholding as in a glass* the glory of the Lord,

2735 1 426/220 2596,3717

κατόρθωμα, katorthōma.

Acts24: 2. and that *very worthy deeds* are done unto

2736 11 426/542 3:640 (cf 2737) 2596

κάτω, κατωτέρω, kato, katōtoro.

Mat. 2:16 from two years old and *under*,

Mat. 4: 6. cast thyself *down:* for it is
27:51. from the top to the *bottom;*
Mar 14:66. as Peter was *beneath* in the palace,
15:38. from the top to the *bottom.*
Lu. 4: 9. cast thyself *down* from hence:
Joh. 8: 6. But Jesus stooped *down,*
8. again he stooped *down,* and wrote
23. Ye are from *beneath;* I am from
Acts 2:19. and signs in the earth *beneath;*
20: 9. and fell *down* from the third

2737 1 426/542 3:640 2736

κατώτερος, *katōteros.*

Eph 4: 9. but that he also descended first into the *lower* parts

2738 2 426/542 3:642 2545

καῦμα, *kauma.*

Rev. 7:16. light on them, nor any *heat.*
16: 9. were scorched with great *heat,*

2739 4 426/542 3:642 2738

καυματίζω, *kaumatizo.*

Mat.13: 6. sun was up, they *were scorched;*
Mar 4: 6. it *was scorched;* and because it had
Rev.16: 8. *to scorch* men with fire.
9. And men *were scorched* with great

2740 1 426/542 3:643 2545

καῦσις, *kausis.*

Heb. 6: 8. whose end (is) to *be burned.* (lit: unto *burning*)

2741 2 426/542 2740

καυσόω, *kausoō.*

2Pet. 3:10. shall melt *with fervent heat,* (lit. *being set on fire*)
12. shall melt *with fervent heat?* (lit. *being,* &c.)

2742 3 426/542 3:643 2741

καύσων, *kausōn.*

Mat.20:12. borne the burden and *heat* of the day.
Lu. 12:55. ye say, There will be *heat;*
Jas. 1:11. is no sooner risen with a *burning heat,*

2743 1 426/542 3:643 2545

καυτηριάζομαι, *kauteeriazomai.*

1Ti. 4: 2. conscience *seared with a hot iron;*

2744 38 426/542 3:645 2172 cf *aucheo* (to boast)

καυχάομαι, *kaukaomai.*

Ro. 2:17. and *makest* thy *boast* of God,
23. Thou that *makest* thy *boast* of the
5: 2. *rejoice* in hope of the glory of God.
3. but we *glory* in tribulations
11. we also *joy* in God through our Lord
1Co. 1:29. That no flesh *should glory*
31. He *that glorieth, let* him *glory* in the Lord.
3:21. *let* no man *glory* in men.
4: 7 why do*st* thou *glory,*
2Co. 5:12. them *which glory* in appearance,
7:14. if I *have boasted* any thing
9: 2. for which I *boast* of you
10: 8. though I *should boast* somewhat
13. we *will* not *boast* of things
15. Not *boasting* of things without
16. not *to boast* in another man's line
17. But he *that glorieth, let* him *glory* in the
11:12. that wherein they *glory,*
16. that I *may boast* myself a little.
18. Seeing that many *glory* after the flesh, I *will glory* also.
30. If I must needs *glory,* I *will glory* of the things which concern
12: 1. not expedient for me doubtless *to glory.*
5. Of such an one *will* I *glory:* yet of myself I *will* not *glory,*
6. though I would desire to *glory,*
9. *will* I rather *glory* in my infirmities,
11. I am become a fool in *glorying;*
Gal. 6:13. that they *may glory* in your flesh.
14. God forbid that I should *glory,*
Eph. 2: 9. lest any man *should boast.*
Phi. 3: 3. and *rejoice* in Christ Jesus,
2Th. 1: 4. So that we ourselves *glory* in you
Jas. 1: 9. *Let* the brother of low degree *rejoice* in that he is exalted:
4:16. now ye *rejoice* in your boastings:

2745 11 427/542 3:645 2744

καύχημα, *kaukeema.*

Ro. 4: 2. he hath (*whereof*) *to glory;* but not
1Co. 5: 6. Your *glorying* (is) not good.
9:15. man should make my *glorying* void,
16. I have nothing *to glory of:*
2Co. 1:14. that we are your *rejoicing,*
5:12. give you occasion *to glory* on our
9: 3. lest our *boasting* of you should be in
Gal. 6: 4. shall he have *rejoicing* in himself
Phi. 1:26. That your *rejoicing* may be more
2:16. that I may *rejoice* in the day of
Heb. 3: 6. the *rejoicing* of the hope firm

2746 12 427/543 3:645 2744

καύχησις, *kaukeesis.*

Ro. 3:27. Where (is) *boasting* then?
15:17. I have therefore *whereof I may glory*
1Co.15:31. I protest by your *rejoicing*
2Co. 1:12. For our *rejoicing* is this,
7: 4. great (is) my *glorying* of you:
14. even so our *boasting,* which (I made)
8:24. and of our *boasting* on your behalf.
9: 4. in this same confident *boasting.*
11:10. no man shall stop me of this *boasting*
17. in this confidence of *boasting.*
1Th. 2:19. or crown of *rejoicing?* (Are) not even ye
Jas. 4:16. all such *rejoicing* is evil.

2749 26 427/543 3:654 cf 5087

κεῖμαι, *kīmai.*

Mat. 3:10. the ax *is laid* unto the root
5:14. A city *that is set* on an hill
28: 6. Come, see the place where the Lord *lay.*
Lu. 2:12. *lying* in a manger.
16. and the babe *lying* in a manger.
34. Behold, this (child) *is set* for the
3: 9. the axe *is laid* unto the root
12:19. thou hast much goods *laid up*
23:53. never man before was *laid.*
24:12. the linen clothes *laid* by themselves.
Joh. 2: 6. And there were *set* there six waterpots
11:41. where the dead was *laid.*

Joh. 19:29. Now there *was set* a vessel full of vinegar:
20: 5. saw the linen clothes *lying*;
6. and seeth the linen clothes *lie*,
7. not *lying* with the linen clothes,
12. where the body of Jesus *had lain*.
21: 9. a fire of coals)(there,
1Co. 3:11. other foundation can no man lay than *that is laid*,
2Co. 3:15. the vail *is* upon their heart.
Phi. 1:17. I *am set* for the defence of the
1Th. 3: 3. we *are appointed* thereunto.
1Ti. 1: 9. the law *is* not *made* for a righteous
1Joh. 5:19. the whole world *lieth* in wickedness.
Rev. 4: 2. a throne *was set* in heaven,
21:16. the city *lieth* foursquare,

2750 1 428/543

κειρίαι, kīriai.

Joh. 11:44. bound hand and foot with *graveclothes*:

2751 4 428/543

κείρω, kīro.

Acts 8:32. a lamb dumb before his *shearer*,
18:18. *having shorn* (his) head
1Co. 11: 6. *let* her also *be shorn*: but if it be a shame for a woman *to be shorn*

2752 1 428/543 3:656 2753

κέλευσμα, kelūsma.

1Th. 4:16. shall descend from heaven with a *shout*,

2753 27 428/543 *kellō* (to urge on)

κελεύω, kelūo.

Mat. 8:18. he *gave commandment* to depart
14: 9. he *commanded* (it) to be given (her).
19. he *commanded* the multitude to sit
28. *bid* me come unto thee on the
15:35. he *commanded* the multitude to
18:25. his lord *commanded* him to be sold,
27:58. Pilate *commanded* the body to be
64. *Command* therefore that the
Lu. 18:40. and *commanded* him to be brought
Acts 4:15. *when* they *had commanded* them
5:34. *commanded* to put the apostles forth
8:38. he *commanded* the chariot to stand
12:19. *commanded* that (they) should be
16:22. and *commanded* to beat (them).
21:33. and *commanded* (him) to be bound
34. he *commanded* him to be carried into
22:24. The chief captain *commanded* him
30. *commanded* the chief priests and all
23: 3. and *commandest* me to be smitten
10. *commanded* the soldiers to go down,
35. he *commanded* him to be kept in Herod's
24: 8. *Commanding* his accusers to come
25: 6. *commanded* Paul to be brought.
17. *commanded* the man to be brought
21. I *commanded* him to be kept till
23. *at* Festus' *commandment* Paul was
27:43. *commanded* that they which could swim

2754 1 428/544 3:659 2755

κενοδοξία, kenodoxia.

Phi. 2: 3. through strife or *vainglory*;

2755 1 428/544 3:659 2756,1391

κενόδοξος, kenodoxos.

Gal. 5:26. Let us not be *desirous of vain glory*,

2756 18 428/544 3:659

κενός, kenos.

Mar 12: 3. and sent (him) away *empty*.
Lu. 1:53. the rich he hath sent *empty* away.
20:10. and sent (him) away *empty*.
11. and sent (him) away *empty*.
Acts 4:25. and the people imagine *vain* things?
1Co. 15:10. upon me was not *in vain*;
14. then (is) our preaching *vain*, and your faith (is) also *vain*.
58. your labour is not *in vain* in the
2Co. 6: 1. receive not the grace of God in *vain*.
Gal. 2: 2. or had run, in *vain*.
Eph. 5: 6. Let no man deceive you with *vain* words:
Phi. 2:16. I have not run in *vain*, neither laboured in *vain*.
Col. 2: 8. through philosophy and *vain* deceit,
1Th. 2: 1. that it was not *in vain*:
3: 5. and our labour be in *vain*.
Jas. 2:20. O *vain* man, that faith without

2757 2 429/544 2756,5456

κενοφωνία, kenophōnia.

1Ti. 6:20. avoiding profane (and) *vain babblings*,
2Ti. 2:16. shun profane (and) *vain babblings*:

2758 5 429/544 3:659 2756

κενόω, kenoō.

Ro. 4:14. of the law (be) heirs, faith *is made void*,
1Co. 1:17. lest the cross of Christ *should be made of none effect*.
9:15. *should make* my glorying *void*.
2Co. 9: 3. lest our boasting of you *should be in vain*
Phi. 2: 7. But *made* himself *of no reputation*,

2759 5 429/544 3:663 *kentō* (to prick)

κέντρον, kentron.

Acts 9: 5. hard for thee to kick against the *pricks*.
26:14. hard for thee to kick against the *pricks*.
1Co. 15:55. O death, where (is) thy *sting*?
56. The *sting* of death (is) sin;
Rev. 9:10. there were *stings* in their tails

2760 3 429/544

κεντυρίων, kenturiōn.

Mar 15:39. when the *centurion*, which stood
44. and calling (unto him) the *centurion*,
45. when he knew (it) of the *centurion*,

2761 1 429/544 2756

κενῶς, kenōs.

Jas. 4: 5. Do ye think that the scripture saith *in vain*.

2762 2 429/544 rt 2768

κεραία, keraia.

Mat. 5:18. one jot or one *tittle* shall in no wise
Lu. 16:17. than one *tittle* of the law to fail.

2763 3 430/544 2766

κεραμεύς, keramūs.

Mat. 27: 7. bought with them the *potter's* field,

Mat.27:10. gave them for the *potter's* field,
Ro. 9:21. Hath not the *potter* power over the clay,

2764 1 430/544 2766

κεραμικός, keramikos.

Rev. 2:27. as the vessels *of a potter* shall

2765 2 430/544 2766

κεράμιον, keramion.

Mar 14:13. bearing a *pitcher* of water:
Lu. 22:10. bearing a *pitcher* of water;

2766 1 430/544 rt 2767

κέραμος, keramos.

Lu. 5:19. let him down through the *tiling*

2767 3 430/544 *keraō* cf 3396

κεράννυμι, κεράω, kerannumi, kerao.

Rev.14:10. of the wine of the wrath of God, *which is poured out* without mixture
18: 6. the cup which she hath *filled fill* to her double.

2768 11 430/544 3:669 *kar* (hair)

κέρας, keras.

Lu. 1:69. hath raised up an *horn* of salvation
Rev. 5: 6. having seven *horns* and seven eyes,
9:13. a voice from the four *horns* of the golden
12: 3. having seven heads and ten *horns*,
13: 1. having seven heads and ten *horns*, and upon his *horns* ten crowns,
11. he had two *horns* like a lamb,
17: 3. having seven heads and ten *horns*.
7. which hath the seven heads and ten *horns*.
12. the ten *horns* which thou sawest
16. the ten *horns* which thou sawest

2769 1 430/545 2768

κεράτιον, keration.

Lu. 15:16. have filled his belly with the *husks*

2770 16 430/545 3:672 2771

κερδαίνω, kerdaino.

Mat.16:26. if he *shall gain* the whole world,
18:15. thou *hast gained* thy brother.
25:17. he also *gained* other two.
20. I *have gained* beside them five
22. I *have gained* two other talents
Mar 8:36. if he *shall gain* the whole world,
Lu. 9:25. *if* he *gain* the whole world,
Acts27:21. and *to have gained* this harm and loss.
1Co. 9:19. that I *might gain* the more.
20. that I *might gain* the Jews;
— that I *might gain* them that are under
21. *might gain* them that are without law.
22. that I *might gain* the weak:
Phi. 3: 8. that I *may win* Christ,
Jas. 4:13. and buy and sell, and *get gain*:
1Pet. 3: 1. they also *may...be won* by the conversation of the wives;

2771 3 430/545 3:672

κέρδος, kerdos.

Phi. 1:21. and to die (is) *gain*.
Phi. 3: 7. But what things were *gain* to me,
Tit. 1:11. for filthy *lucre's* sake.

2772 1 430/545 2751

κέρμα, kerma.

Joh. 2:15. and poured out the changers' *money*

2773 1 430/545 2772

κερματιστής, kermatistees.

Joh. 2:14. and the *changers of money* sitting

2774 2 431/545 2776

κεφάλαιον, kephalaion.

Acts22:28. With a great *sum* obtained I
Heb 8: 1. which we have spoken (this is) the *sum*:

2775 1 431/546 rt 2774

κεφαλαιόω, kephalaioō.

Mar 12: 4. and *wounded* (him) *in the head*,

2776 76 431/545 3:673,1:791 *kaptō* (to seize)

κεφαλή, kephalee.

Mat. 5:36. Neither shalt thou swear by thy *head*,
6:17. when thou fastest anoint thine *head*,
8:20. hath not where to lay (his) *head*.
10:30. hairs of your *head* are all numbered.
14: 8. Give me here John Baptist's *head*
11. And his *head* was brought
21:42. the same is become the *head* of the corner)
26: 7. and poured it on his *head*,
27:29. they put (it) upon his *head*,
30. and smote him on the *head*.
37. And set up over his *head*
39. reviled him, wagging their *heads*,
Mar. 6:24. The *head* of John the Baptist.
25. in a charger the *head* of John
27. commanded his *head* to be brought:
28. brought his *head* in a charger,
12:10. is become the *head* of the corner:
14: 3. and poured (it) on his *head*.
15:19. they smote him on the *head*
29. wagging their *heads*, and saying,
Lu. 7:38. did wipe (them) with the hairs of her *head*,
44. wiped (them) with the hairs of her *head*.
46. My *head* with oil thou didst not
9:58. hath not where to lay (his) *head*.
12: 7. hairs of your *head* are all numbered.
20:17. is become the *head* of the corner?
21:18. there shall not an hair of your *head* perish.
28. lift up your *heads*; for
Joh.13: 9. but also (my) hands and (my) *head*.
19: 2. and put (it) on his *head*,
30. and he bowed his *head*, and gave up
20: 7. the napkin, that was about his *head*,
12. the one at the *head*, and the other
Acts 4:11. is become the *head* of the corner.
18: 6. Your blood (be) upon your own *heads*,
18. having shorn (his) *head*
21:24. that they may shave (their) *heads*·
27:34. shall not an hair fall from the *head* of
Ro. 12:20. shalt heap coals of fire on his *head*.
1Co.11: 3. the *head* of every man is Christ; and the *head* of the woman (is) the man; and the *head* of Christ (is) God.
4. or prophesying, having (his) *head* covered, dishonoureth his *head*.

1Co.11: 5. or prophesieth with (her) *head* uncovered dishonoureth her *head:*
7. a man indeed ought not to cover (his) *head,*
10. ought the woman to have power on (her) *head*
12:21. nor again the *head* to the feet, I have no
Eph. 1:22. gave him (to be) *head* over all (things)
4:15. which is the *head,* (even) Christ:
5:23. the husband is the *head* of the wife, even as Christ is the *head* of the church:
Col. 1:18. he is the *head* of the body, the church:
2:10. the *head* of all principality and power:
19. And not holding the *Head,*
1Pet. 2: 7. is made the *head* of the corner,
Rev. 1:14. His *head* and (his) hairs (were) white
4: 4. they had on their *heads* crowns of gold.
9: 7. on their *heads* (were) as it were crowns
17. the *heads* of the horses (were) as the *heads* of lions;
19. and had *heads,* and with them they do hurt.
10: 1. a rainbow (was) upon his *head,*
12: 1. and upon her *head* a crown of
3. having seven *heads* and ten horns, and seven crowns upon his *heads.*
13: 1. having seven *heads* and ten horns,
— upon his *heads* the name of blasphemy.
3. And I saw one of his *heads* as it were
14:14. having on his *head* a golden crown,
17: 3. having seven *heads* and ten horns.
7. which hath the seven *heads* and ten horns.
9. The seven *heads* are seven mountains,
18:19. they cast dust on their *heads,*
19:12. on his *head* (were) many crowns;

2777 1 431/546 2776

κεφαλίς, kephalis.

Heb10: 7. in the *volume* of the book it is

2778 4 431/546

κῆνσος, keensos.

Mat.17:25. take custom or *tribute?*
22:17. Is it lawful to give *tribute* unto
19. Shew me the *tribute* money.
Mar 12:14. Is it lawful to give *tribute* to

2779 5 431/546

κῆπος, keepos.

Lu. 13:19. and cast into his *garden;*
Joh.18: 1. where was a *garden,*
26. Did not I see thee in the *garden*
19:41. there was a *garden;* and in the *garden* a new sepulchre,

2780 1 431/546 2779 *ouros* (warden)

κηπουρός, keepouros.

Joh.20:15. supposing him to be the *gardener,*

2781 1 431/546 *keos* (wax)

κηρίον, keerion.

Lu. 24:42. and of an honey*comb.*

2782 8 432/546 3:683 2784

κήρυγμα, keerugma.

Mat.12:41. at the *preaching* of Jonas,
Lu. 11:32. at the *preaching* of Jonas;
Ro. 16:25. and the *preaching* of Jesus Christ,
1Co. 1:21. by the foolishness of *preaching* to save
2: 4. my *preaching* (was) not with enticing
15:14. then (is) our *preaching* vain,
2Ti. 4:17. by me the *preaching* might be fully known,
Tit. 1: 3. manifested his word through *preaching,*

2783 3 432/546 3:683 2784

κήρυξ, keerux.

1Ti. 2: 7. I am ordained a *preacher,*
2Ti. 1:11. I am appointed a *preacher,*
2Pet.2: 5. a *preacher* of righteousness,

2784 61 432/546 3:683

κηρύσσω, keerusso.

Mat. 3: 1. *preaching* in the wilderness
4:17. Jesus began *to preach,*
23. *preaching* the gospel of the kingdom,
9:35. *preaching* the gospel of the kingdom,
10: 7. as ye go, *preach,*
27. (that) *preach* ye upon the housetops.
11: 1. and *to preach* in their cities.
24:14. *shall be preached* in all the world
26:13. Wheresoever this gospel *shall be preached*
Mar. 1: 4. and *preach* the baptism of repentance
7. And *preached,* saying, There cometh
14. *preaching* the gospel of the
38. that I *may preach* there also:
39. he preached (lit. was *preaching*) in their synagogues
45. began *to publish* (it) much,
3:14. might send them forth *to preach,*
5:20. and began *to publish* in Decapolis
6:12. and *preached* that men should repent.
7:36. the more a great deal they *published* (it);
13:10. must first *be published* among
14: 9. Wheresoever this gospel *shall be preached*
16:15. *preach* the gospel to every
20. and *preached* every where,
Lu. 3: 3. *preaching* the baptism of repentance
4:18(19). *to preach* deliverance to the captives.
19. *To preach* the acceptable year
44. And he preached (lit. was *preaching*) in the synagogues
8: 1. *preaching* and shewing the glad
39. *and published* throughout the whole
9: 2. he sent them *to preach*
12: 3. *shall be proclaimed* upon the housetops.
24:47. should *be preached* in his
Acts 8: 5. and *preached* Christ unto them.
9:20. he *preached* Christ in the
10:37. the baptism which John *preached;*
42. he commanded us *to preach* unto the
15:21. hath in every city them *that preach* him.
19:13. by Jesus whom Paul *preacheth.*
20:25. among whom I have gone *preaching*
28:31. *Preaching* the kingdom of God,
Ro. 2:21. thou *that preachest* a man
10: 8. the word of faith, which we *preach;*
14. how shall they hear without a *preacher?*
15. how *shall* they *preach,* except they be
1Co. 1:23. But we *preach* Christ crucified,
9:27. *when* I have *preached* to others,
15:11. so we *preach,* and so ye believed.
12. if Christ *be preached* that he
2Co. 1:19. Jesus Christ, *who was preached* among you by us,
4: 5. we *preach* not ourselves.

2Co.11: 4. if he that cometh *preacheth* another Jesus, whom we *have* not *preached*,
Gal. 2: 2. that gospel which I *preach*
5:11. if I yet *preach* circumcision,
Phi. 1:15. Some indeed *preach* Christ even of envy
Col. 1:23. *which was preached* to every creature
1Th 2: 9. we *preached* unto you the gospel
1Ti. 3:16. *preached* unto the Gentiles,
2Ti. 4: 2. *Preach* the word; be instant
1Pet.3:19. and *preached* unto the spirits
Rev. 5: 2. I saw a strong angel *proclaiming*

2785 1 432/547 rt 5490

κῆτος, keetos.

Mat.12:40. and three nights in the *whale's* belly;

2787 6 433/547

κιβωτός, kibōtos.

Mat 24:38. the day that Noe entered into the *ark*,
Lu. 17:27. Noe entered into the *ark*, and the
Heb 9: 4. the *ark* of the covenant
11: 7. prepared an *ark* to the saving
1Pet.3:20. while the *ark* was a preparing,
Rev 11:19. there was seen in his temple the *ark* of

2788 4 433/547

κιθάρα, kithara.

1Co.14: 7. giving sound, whether pipe or *harp*,
Rev. 5: 8. having every one of them *harps*,
14: 2. harping with their *harps*:
15: 2. having the *harps* of God.

2789 2 433/547 2788

κιθαρίζω, kitharizo.

1Co.14: 7. be known what is piped or *harped*?
Rev.14: 2. of harpers *harping* with their harps:

2790 2 433/547 2788,5603

κιθαρῳδός, kitharōdos.

Rev.14: 2. I heard the voice of *harpers*
18:22. And the voice of *harpers*,

2792 1 433/548 [cf 7076]

κινάμωμον, kinamōmon.

Rev.18:13. And *cinnamon*, and odours,

2793 4 433/548 2794

κινδυνεύω, kindunūo.

Lu. 8:23. were filled (with water), and *were in jeopardy*.
Acts19:27. not only this our craft *is in danger*
40. we *are in danger* to be called in question
1Co.15:30. why *stand* we *in jeopardy* every hour?

2794 9 433/548

κίνδυνος, kindunos.

Ro. 8:35. or nakedness, or *peril*, or sword?
2Co 11:26. (in) *perils* of waters, (in) *perils* of robbers, (in) *perils* by (mine own) countrymen, (in) *perils* by the heathen, (in) *perils* in the city, (in) *perils* in the wilderness, (in) *perils* in the sea, (in) *perils* among false brethren;

2795 8 433/548 3:718

κινέω, kineo. kiō (to go)

Mat 23: 4. will not *move* them with one of
27:39. reviled him, *wagging* their heads,
Mar 15:29. railed on him, *wagging* their heads,
Acts17:28. in him we live, and *move*,
21:30. all the city *was moved*,
24: 5. a mover of (lit. *moving*) sedition
Rev. 2: 5. and *will remove* thy candlestick
6:14. every mountain and island *were moved* out of their places.

2796 1 433/548 2795

κίνησις, kineesis.

Joh. 5: 3. waiting for the *moving* of the water.

2798 11 434/548 3:720 2806

κλάδος, klados.

Mat.13:32. lodge in the *branches* thereof.
21: 8. others cut down *branches* from the
24:32. When his *branch* is yet tender,
Mar 4:32. shooteth out great *branches*;
13:28. When her *branch* is yet tender,
Lu. 13:19. lodged in the *branches* of it.
Ro. 11:16. the root (be) holy, so (are) the *branches*.
17. if some of the *branches* be broken off,
18. Boast not against the *branches*.
19. The *branches* were broken off, that
21. if God spared not the natural *branches*,

2806 15 434/549

κλάζω, κλάω, klazo, klao.

Mat 14:19. he blessed, and *brake, and* gave
15:36. and gave thanks, and *brake* (them),
26:26. Jesus took bread, and blessed (it), and *brake*
Mar 8: 6. and gave thanks, and *brake*,
19. When I *brake* the five loaves
14:22. Jesus took bread, and blessed, and *brake*
Lu. 22:19. and gave thanks, and *brake* (it),
24:30. took bread, and blessed (it), and *brake*, and
Acts 2:46. and *breaking* bread from house
20: 7. came together *to break* bread,
11. and *had broken* bread, and eaten,
27:35. *when* he *had broken* (it), he began to eat.
1Co.10:16. The bread which we *break*,
11:24. he *brake* (it), and said, Take, eat: this is my body, *which is broken* for you:

2799 40 434/548 3:722 cf 1145

κλαίω, klaio.

Mat. 2:18. Rachel *weeping* (for) her children,
26:75. he went out, and *wept* bitterly.
Mar 5:38. and them *that wept* and wailed
39. Why make ye this ado, and *weep*?
14:72. And when he thought thereon, he *wept*.
16:10. as they mourned and *wept*.
Lu. 6:21. Blessed (are ye) *that weep* now:
25. for ye shall mourn and *weep*.
7:13. and said unto her, *Weep* not.
32. and ye *have* not *wept*.
38. at his feet behind (him) *weeping*,
8:52. And all *wept*, and bewailed her: but he said, *Weep* not;
19:41. he beheld the city, and *wept* over it,
22:62. Peter went out, and *wept* bitterly.
23:28. *weep* not for me, but *weep* for yourselves,

Joh.11:31. She goeth unto the grave to *weep*
33. When Jesus therefore saw her *weeping*, and the Jews also *weeping*
16:20. ye *shall weep* and lament,
20:11. Mary stood without at the sepulchre *weeping*: and as she *wept*,
13. Woman, why *weepest* thou? She
15. Woman, why *weepest* thou? whom
Acts 9:39. all the widows stood by him *weeping*,
21:13. What mean ye to *weep* and to break
Ro. 12:15. and *weep* with them *that weep*.
1Co. 7:30. And they *that weep*, as though they *wept* not;
Phi. 3:18. and now tell you even *weeping*,
Jas. 4: 9. Be afflicted, and mourn, and *weep*:
5: 1. (ye) rich men, *weep* and howl for your
Rev. 5: 4. And I *wept* much, because no
5. *Weep* not: behold, the Lion of the
18: 9. *shall bewail* her, and lament
11. shall *weep* and mourn over her;
15. of her torment, *weeping* and wailing,
19. cried, *weeping* and wailing, saying,

2800 2 434/548 3:726 2806

κλάσις, klasis.

Lu. 24:35. was known of them in *breaking* of bread.
Acts 2:42. and in *breaking* of bread, and in prayers.

2801 9 434/548 3:726 2806

κλάσμα, klasma.

Mat.14:20. they took up of the *fragments*
15:37. they took up of the *broken* (meat)
Mar 6:43. twelve baskets full of the *fragments*,
8: 8. they took up of the *broken* (meat)
19. how many baskets full of *fragments*
20. how many baskets full of *fragments*
Lu. 9:17. there was taken up of *fragments*
Joh. 6:12. Gather up the *fragments* that remain,
13. filled twelve baskets with the *fragments*

2805 9 434/548 3:722 2799

κλαυθμός, klauthmos.

Mat. 2:18. lamentation, and *weeping*, and great
8:12. there shall be *weeping* and gnashing
13:42. there shall be *wailing* and gnashing
50. there shall be *wailing* and gnashing
22:13. there shall be *weeping* and gnashing
24:51. there shall be *weeping* and gnashing
25:30. there shall be *weeping* and gnashing
Lu. 13:28. There shall be *weeping* and gnashing
Acts20:37. And they all wept sore, (lit. there was great *weeping* of all)

2806 15 434/ 3:726

κλάω see κλάζω. p. 423

2807 6 434/549 3:744 2808

κλείς, klis.

Mat.16:19. I will give unto thee the *keys* of the
Lu. 11:52. ye have taken away the *key* of knowledge:
Rev. 1:18. and have the *keys* of hell and of
3: 7. he that hath the *key* of David,
9: 1. to him was given the *key* of the
20: 1. having the *key* of the bottomless

2808 16 435/549

κλείω, klio.

Mat. 6: 6. *when* thou *hast shut* hy door,
23:13(14). ye *shut up* the kingdom of heaven
25:10. and the door *was shut*.
Lu. 4:25. when the heaven *was shut up*
11: 7. the door *is* now *shut*,
Joh.20:19. *when* the doors *were shut*
26. the doors *being shut*,
Acts 5:23. The prison truly found we *shut*
21:30. forthwith the doors *were shut*.
1Joh.3:17. and *shutteth up* his bowels
Rev. 3: 7. he that openeth, and no man *shutteth*; and *shutteth*, and no man openeth;
8. and no man can *shut* it:
11: 6. These have power *to shut* heaven,
20: 3. into the bottomless pit, and *shut* him *up*,
21:25. the gates of it *shall* not *be shut*

2809 1 435/549 2813

κλέμμα, klemma.

Rev. 9:21. Neither repented they of...nor of their *thefts*.

2811 1 435/549 2564

κλέος, kleos.

1Pet.2:20. For what *glory* (is it), if, when

2812 16 435/549 3:754 2813

κλέπτης, kleptees. cf 3027

Mat. 6:19. where *thieves* break through and steal:
20. where *thieves* do not break through
24:43. in what watch the *thief* would come,
Lu. 12:33. where no *thief* approacheth,
39. what hour the *thief* would come,
Joh.10: 1. the same is a *thief* and a robber.
8. All that ever came before me are *thieves* and robbers:
10. The *thief* cometh not, but for
12: 6. but because he was a *thief*,
1Co. 6:10. Nor *thieves*, nor covetous,
1Th. 5: 2. Lord so cometh as a *thief* in the
4. that day should overtake you as a *thief*.
1Pet.4:15. or (as) a *thief*, or (as) an evildoer,
2Pet.3:10. the Lord will come as a *thief*
Rev. 3: 3. I will come on thee as a *thief*,
16:15. Behold, I come as a *thief*.

2813 12 435/549 3:754

κλέπτω, klepto.

Mat. 6:19. where thieves break through and *steal*:
20. do not break through nor *steal*:
19:18. Thou *shalt* not *steal*,
27:64. lest his disciples...and *steal* him away,
28:13. and *stole* him (away) while we slept.
Mar 10:19. *Do* not *steal*, Do not bear false
Lu. 18:20. *Do* not *steal*, Do not bear false
Joh.10:10. but for to *steal*, and to kill,
Ro. 2:21. that preachest a man should not *steal*, *dost* thou *steal*?
13: 9. Thou *shalt* not *steal*,
Eph. 4:28. *Let* him *that stole steal* no more:

2814 4 435/550 3:757 2806

κλῆμα, kleema.

Joh.15: 2. Every *branch* in me that beareth not
4. As the *branch* cannot bear fruit of
5. I am the vine, ye (are) the *branches*:
6. he is cast forth as a *branch*,

2816 18 435/550 3:758 2818

κληρονομέω, kleeronomeo.

Mat. 5: 5 for they *shall inherit* the earth.
19:29. and *shall inherit* everlasting life.
25:34. *inherit* the kingdom prepared
Mar 10:17. that I *may inherit* eternal life?
Lu. 10:25. what shall I do to *inherit* eternal
18:18. what shall I do to *inherit* eternal
1Co. 6. 9. the unrighteous *shall* not *inherit*
10. *shall inherit* the kingdom
15:50. flesh and blood cannot *inherit* the kingdom of God; neither *doth* corruption *inherit*
Gal. 4:30. *shall* not *be heir* with the son
5:21. *shall* not *inherit* the kingdom
Heb 1: 4. he *hath by inheritance obtained*
14. who shall *be heirs of* salvation?
6:12. of them *who* through faith and patience *inherit* the promises.
12:17. when he would have *inherited*
1Pet. 3: 9. that ye *should inherit* a blessing.
Rev. 21: 7. He that overcometh *shall inherit* all

2817 14 436/550 3:758 2818

κληρονομία, kleeronomia.

Mat. 21:38. let us seize on his *inheritance*.
Mar 12: 7. and the *inheritance* shall be our's.
Lu. 12:13. that he divide the *inheritance*
20:14. that the *inheritance* may be our's.
Acts 7: 5. gave him none *inheritance* in
20:32. and to give you an *inheritance*
Gal. 3:18. if the *inheritance* (be) of the law,
Eph. 1:14. the earnest of our *inheritance*
18. the riches of the glory of his *inheritance* in the saints,
5: 5. hath any *inheritance* in the
Col. 3:24. the reward of the *inheritance*:
Heb 9:15. the promise of eternal *inheritance*.
11: 8. after receive for an *inheritance*,
1Pet. 1: 4. To an *inheritance* incorruptible,

2818 15 436/550 3:758 2819

κληρονόμος, kleeronomos. rt 3551

Mat. 21:38. This is the *heir*; come, let us kill him,
Mar 12: 7. This is the *heir*; come, let us
Lu. 20:14. This is the *heir*: come, let us
Ro. 4:13. that he should be the *heir* of the world,
14. if they which are of the law (be) *heirs*,
8:17. And if children, then *heirs*; *heirs* of God, and joint-heirs with Christ;
Gal. 3:29. and *heirs* according to the promise.
4: 1. Now I say, (That) the *heir*, as long
7. then an *heir* of God through Christ.
Tit. 3: 7. we should be made *heirs* according
Heb 1: 2. appointed *heir* of all things,
6:17. to shew unto the *heirs* of promise
11: 7. and became *heir* of the righteousness
Jas. 2: 5. rich in faith, and *heirs* of the kingdom

2820 1 436/550 3:758 2819

κληρόομαι, kleero-omai.

Eph. 1:11. In whom also we *have obtained an inheritance*, (lit. *have been taken as an inheritance*)

2819 13 436/550 3:758 2806

κλῆρος, kleeros.

Mat. 27:35. and parted his garments, casting *lots*: — upon my vesture did they cast *lots*.
Mar 15:24. casting *lots* upon them,
Lu. 23:34. they parted his raiment, and cast *lots*.
Joh. 19:24. for my vesture they did cast *lots*.
Acts 1:17. had obtained *part* of this ministry.
25. That he may take *part* of this ministry and apostleship,
26. And they gave forth their *lots*. and the *lot* fell upon Matthias;
8:21. Thou hast neither part nor *lot*
26:18. and *inheritance* among them which are
Col. 1:12. to be partakers of the *inheritance* of the saints in light:
1Pet. 5: 3. as being lords over (God's) *heritage*,

2821 11 436/550 3:487 2564

κλῆσις, kleesis.

Ro. 11:29. the gifts and *calling* of God (are)
1Co. 1:26. For ye see your *calling*, brethren,
7:20. abide in the same *calling* wherein
Eph. 1:18. what is the hope of his *calling*,
4: 1. walk worthy of the *vocation*
4. in one hope of your *calling*;
Phi. 3:14. for the prize of the high *calling*
2Th. 1:11. count you worthy of (this) *calling*,
2Ti. 1: 9. called (us) with an holy *calling*,
Heb 3: 1. partakers of the heavenly *calling*,
2Pet. 1:10. give diligence to make your *calling*

2822 11 437/551 3:487 2821

κλητός, kleetos.

Mat. 20:16. many be *called*, but few chosen.
22:14. many are *called*, but few (are) chosen.
Ro. 1: 1. *called* (to be) an apostle,
6. are ye also the *called* of Jesus
7. *called* (to be) saints:
8:28. to them who are the *called*
1Co. 1: 1. Paul, *called* (to be) an apostle
2. sanctified in Christ Jesus, *called* (to be) saints,
24. But unto them which are *called*,
Jude 1. preserved in Jesus Christ, (and) *called*:
Rev. 17:14. they that are with him (are) *called*, and chosen, and faithful.

2823 2 437/551 2564 cf 2821

κλίβανος, klibanos.

Mat. 6:30. and to morrow is cast into the *oven*,
Lu. 12:28. and to morrow is cast into the *oven*;

2824 3 437/551 2827

κλῖμα, klima.

Ro. 15:23. having no more place in these *parts*,
2Co. 11:10. in the *regions* of Achaia.
Gal. 1:21. I came into the *regions* of Syria

2825 10 437/551 2827

κλίνη, klinee.

Mat. 9: 2. sick of the palsy, lying on a *bed*:
6. take up thy *bed*, and go unto thine house.
Mar 4:21. or under a *bed*?
7: 4. brasen vessels, and of *tables*.
30. and her daughter laid upon the *bed*.
Lu. 5:18. men brought in a *bed* a man
8:16. or putteth (it) under a *bed*; but
17:34. there shall be two (men) in one *bed*;
Acts 5:15. and laid (them) on *beds* and couches,
Rev. 2:22. I will cast her into a *bed*,

2826 2 437/551 2825

κλινίδιον, klinidion.

Lu. 5:19. through the tiling with (his) *couch*
24. take up thy *couch*, and go unto thine

2827 7 437/551

κλίνω, klino.

Mat. 8:20. not where to *lay* (his) head.
Lu. 9:12. when the day began *to wear away*,
58. hath not where to *lay* (his) head.
24: 5. as they were afraid, and *bowed down* (their) faces
29. and the day *is far spent*.
Joh. 19:30. and he *bowed* his head, *and* gave up
Heb 11:34. *turned to flight* the armies of the aliens.

2828 1 437/551 2827

κλισία, klisia.

Lu. 9:14. them sit down by fifties in a *company*.

2829 2 437/551 2813

κλοπή, klopee.

Mat. 15:19. fornications, *thefts*, false witness,
Mar 7:22. *Thefts*, covetousness, wickedness,

2830 2 437/551 *kluzō* (to dash over)

κλύδων, kludōn.

Lu. 8:24. rebuked the wind and the *raging* of the water:
Jas. 1: 6. is like a *wave* of the sea

2831 1 437/551 2830

κλυδωνίζομαι, kludōnizomai.

Eph 4:14. *tossed to and fro*, and carried about

2833 1 438/551 *knaō* (to scrape)

κνήθω, kneetho.

2Ti. 4: 3. *having itching* ears; (lit. *itching* as to hearing)

2835 2 438/551

κοδράντης, kodrantees.

Mat. 5:26. till thou hast paid the uttermost *farthing*.
Mar 12:42. two mites, which make a *farthing*.

2836 23 438/551 3:786

κοιλία, koilia. *koilos* (hollow)

Mat 12:40. and three nights in the whale's *belly*;
15:17. in at the mouth goeth into the *belly*,
19:12. so born from (their) mother's *womb*:
Mar 7:19. but into the *belly*,
Lu. 1:15. even from his mother's *womb*.
41. the babe leaped in her *womb*;
42. blessed (is) the fruit of thy *womb*.
44. the babe leaped in my *womb* for joy.
2:21. before he was conceived in the *womb*.
11:27. Blessed (is) the *womb* that bare thee,
15:16. he would fain have filled his *belly*
23:29. and the *wombs* that never bare,
Joh. 3: 4. second time into his mother's *womb*,
7:38. out of his *belly* shall flow rivers
Acts 3: 2. lame from his mother's *womb*
14: 8. a cripple from his mother's *womb*,
Ro. 16:18. serve not our Lord Jesus Christ, but their own *belly*;
1Co. 6:13. Meats for the *belly*, and the *belly* for
Gal. 1:15. separated me from my mother's *womb*,
Phi. 3:19. whose God (is their) *belly*,
Rev 10: 9. it shall make thy *belly* bitter,
10. my *belly* was bitter.

2837 18 438/552 2749

κοιμάομαι, koimaomai.

Mat 27:52. many bodies of the saints *which slept*
28:13. and stole him (away) *while* we *slept*.
Lu. 22:45. he found them *sleeping* for sorrow,
Joh. 11:11. Our friend Lazarus *sleepeth*;
12. Lord, if he *sleep*, he shall do well.
Acts 7:60. when he had said this, he *fell asleep*.
12: 6. Peter was *sleeping* between two
13:36. *fell on sleep*, and was laid unto his
1Co. 7:39. but if her husband *be dead*,
11:30. sickly among you, and many *sleep*.
15: 6. but some *are fallen asleep*.
18. Then they also *which are fallen asleep*
20. the firstfruits of them *that slept*.
51. We *shall* not all *sleep*,
1Th. 4:13. concerning them *which are asleep*,
14. them also *which sleep* in Jesus
15. shall not prevent them *which are asleep*.
2Pet. 3: 4. since the fathers *fell asleep*,

2838 1 438/552 2837

κοίμησις, koimeesis.

Joh. 11:13. had spoken of *taking of rest* in sleep.

2839 12 438/552 3:789 4862

κοινός, koinos.

Mar 7: 2. eat bread with *defiled*, that is to say, with unwashen, hands,
Acts 2:44. and had all things *common*;
4:32. but they had all things *common*.
10:14. eaten any thing that is *common* or
28. should not call any man *common* or
11: 8. for nothing *common* or unclean
Ro. 14:14. that (there is) nothing *unclean* of itself;
— esteemeth any thing to be *unclean*, to him (it is) *unclean*.
Tit. 1: 4. (mine) own son after the *common* faith:
Heb 10:29. an *unholy* thing, and hath done despite
Jude 3. to write unto you of the *common* salvation,

2840 15 439/552 3:789 2839

κοινόω, koinoō.

Mat 15:11. into the mouth *defileth* a man;
— this *defileth* a man.
18. and they *defile* the man.
20. These are (the things) *which defile* a man.
— unwashen hands *defileth* not a man.
Mar 7:15. entering into him can *defile* him:
— those are they *that defile* the man.
18. (it) cannot *defile* him;
20. that *defileth* the man.
23. come from within, and *defile* the man.
Acts 10:15. (that) *call* not thou *common*.
11: 9. (that) *call* not thou *common*.
21:28. and *hath polluted* this holy place.
Heb 9:13. ashes of an heifer sprinkling the *unclean*,
Rev 21:27. enter into it any thing *that defileth*,

2841 8 439/552 3:789 2844

κοινωνέω, koinōneo.

Ro. 12:13. *Distributing* to the necessity of saints;

Ro. 15:27. Gentiles *have been partakers* of their
Gal. 6: 6. *Let* him that is taught...*communicate* unto him that teacheth
Phi. 4:15. no church *communicated* with me
1 Ti. 5:22. neither *be partaker* of other men's sins:
Heb 2:14. as the children *are partakers* of
1Pet 4:13. as ye *are partakers* of Christ's
2Joh. 11. *is partaker* of his evil deeds.

2842 20 439/552 3:789 2844

κοινωνία, koinōnia.

Acts 2:42. and *fellowship*, and in breaking of bread,
Ro. 15:26. to make a certain *contribution*
1Co. 1: 9. called unto the *fellowship* of his Son
10:16. is it not the *communion* of the blood
— is it not the *communion* of the body
2Co. 6:14. what *communion* hath light
8: 4. and (take upon us) the *fellowship*
9:13. for (your) liberal *distribution*
13:14(13). the *communion* of the Holy Ghost,
Gal. 2: 9. the right hands of *fellowship*;
Eph 3: 9. what (is) the *fellowship* of the mystery,
Phi. 1: 5. For your *fellowship* in the gospel
2: 1. if any *fellowship* of the Spirit,
3:10. and the *fellowship* of his sufferings,
Philem 6. That the *communication* of thy faith
Heb 13:16. and *to communicate* forget not:
1Joh. 1: 3. may have *fellowship* with us: and truly our *fellowship* (is) with
6. If we say that we have *fellowship*
7. we have *fellowship* one with another,

2843 1 440/553 3:789 2844

κοινωνικός, koinōnikos.

1Ti. 6:18. ready to distribute, *willing to communicate*;

2844 10 440/553 3:789 2839

κοινωνός, koinōnos.

Mat 23:30. we would not have been *partakers*
Lu. 5:10. which were *partners* with Simon.
1Co.10:18. *partakers* of the altar?
20. ye should have *fellowship* with
2Co. 1: 7. as ye are *partakers* of the sufferings,
8:23. (he is) my *partner* and fellowhelper
Philem 17. If thou count me therefore a *partner*,
Heb 10:33. ye became *companions* of them
1Pet. 5: 1. and also a *partaker* of the glory
2Pet. 1: 4. be *partakers* of the divine nature, having escaped

2845 4 440/553 2749

κοίτη, koitee.

Lu. 11: 7. my children are with me in *bed*;
Ro. 9:10. when Rebecca also had *conceived* (κοιτην ἐχουσα)
13:13. not in *chambering* and wantonness,
Heb 13: 4. and the *bed* undefiled:

2846 1 441/553 2845

κοιτών, koitōn.

Acts12:20. Blastus the king's chamberlain (lit. that was over the king's *bedchamber*)

2847 6 441/553 3:810 2848

κόκκινος & τὸ κόκκινον,
kokkinos & to kokkinon.

Mat.27:28. and put on him a *scarlet* robe.
Heb. 9:19. with water, and *scarlet* wool,
Rev.17: 3. upon a *scarlet coloured* beast,
4. in purple and *scarlet colour*,
18:12. purple, and silk, and *scarlet*
16. and purple, and *scarlet*,

2848 2 441/553 3:810

κόκκος, kokkos.

Mat.13:31. like to a *grain* of mustard seed,
17:20. faith as a *grain* of mustard seed,
Mar. 4:31. (It is) like a *grain* of mustard seed,
Lu. 13:19. a *grain* of mustard seed,
17: 6. faith as a *grain* of mustard seed,
Joh. 12:24. Except a *corn* of wheat fall
1Co.15:37. bare *grain*, it may chance of wheat,

2849 2 441/553 3:814 *kolos* (dwarf)

κολάζομαι, kolazomai.

Acts 4:21. nothing how they *might punish* them,
2Pet. 2: 9. unto the day of judgment *to be punished*:

2850 1 441/553 3:817 *kolax* (fawner)

κολακεία, kolakīa.

1Th. 2: 5. used we *flattering* words, (lit. of *flattery*)

2851 2 441/553 3:814 2849

κόλασις, kolasis.

Mat.25:46. into everlasting *punishment*:
1Joh. 4:18. because fear hath *torment*.

2852 5 441/553 3:818 2849

κολαφίζω, kolaphizo.

Mat.26:67. spit in his face, and *buffeted* him;
Mar 14:65. to cover his face, and *to buffet* him,
1Co. 4:11. and *are buffeted*, and have no certain
2Co.12: 7. the messenger of Satan to *buffet* me,
1Pet. 2:20. *when* ye *be buffeted* for your faults,

2853 10 442/553 3:822 *kolla* (glue)

κολλάω, kollao.

Lu. 10:11. dust of your city, *which cleaveth* on us,
15:15. and *joined* him*self* to a citizen
Acts 5:13. durst no man *join* him*self*
8:29. Go near, and *join* thy*self* to this chariot.
9:26. he assayed to *join* him*self* to the
10:28. that is a Jew to *keep company*,
17:34. certain men *clave* unto him, *and* believed
Ro. 12: 9. *cleave* to that which is good.
1Co. 6:16. he *which is joined* to an harlot
17. But he *that is joined* unto the Lord

2854 1 442/553 *kollura* (cake)

κολλούριον, kollourion.

Rev. 3:18. anoint thine eyes with *eyesalve*,

2855 3 442/553 *kollubos* (a small coin)

κολλυβιστής, kollubistees.

Mat.21:12. tables of the *moneychangers*,
Mar 11:15. tables of the *moneychangers*,
Joh. 2:15. poured out the *changers'* money

2856 4 442/553 3:823 *kolos* (dwarf)

κολοβόω, koloboō.

Mat.24:22. those days *should be shortened*,

Mat.24:22. those days *shall be shortened,*
Mar 13:20. except that the Lord *had shortened* those
— he *hath shortened* the days.

2859 6 443/553 3:824

κόλπος, kolpos.

Lu. 6:38. shall men give into your *bosom.*
16:22. by the angels into Abraham's *bosom:*
23. and Lazarus in his *bosom.*
Joh. 1:18. which is in the *bosom* of the Father,
13:23. leaning on Jesus' *bosom*
Acts27:39. a certain *creek* with a shore;

2860 1 443/554 *kolumbos* (diver)

κολυμβάω, kolumbao.

Acts27:43. that they which could *swim*

2861 5 443/554 2860

κολυμβήθρα, kolumbeethra.

Joh. 5: 2. by the sheep (market) a *pool,*
4. at a certain season into the *pool,*
7. to put me into the *pool:*
9: 7. wash in the *pool* of Siloam,
11. Go to the *pool* of Siloam,

2862 1 443/554

κολώνια, kolōnia.

Acts16:12. that part of Macedonia, (and) a *colony:*

2863 2 443/554 2864

κομάω, komao.

1Co.11:14. if a man *have long hair,*
15. But if a woman *have long hair,*

2864 1 443/554 rt 2865

κόμη, komee.

1Co 11.15. for (her) *hair* is given her for a covering.

2865 11 443/554 *komeō* (to take care of)

κομίζω, komizo.

Mat.25:27 I should *have received* mine own
Lu. 7:37. *brought* an alabaster box
2Co. 5:10. every one *may receive* the things
Eph. 6: 8. the same *shall* he *receive* of the
Col. 3:25. *shall receive* for the wrong
Heb 10:36. ye *might receive* the promise.
11:19. from whence also he *received* him in a
39. *received* not the promise:
1Pet. 1: 9. *Receiving* the end of your faith,
5: 4. ye *shall receive* a crown of glory
2Pet. 2: 13. *And shall receive* the reward of

2866 1 443/554 *kompsos*

κομψότερον, kompsoteron.

Joh. 4:52. when he began to amend. (lit. had himself *better*)

2867 2 444/554 3:827 *konia* (dust)

κονιάω, koniao.

Mat.23:27. like unto *whited* sepulchres,
Acts23: 3. smite thee, (thou) *whited* wall:

2868 5 444/554 *konia* (dust), *ornumi* (to "rouse")

κονιορτός, koniortos.

Mat.10:14. shake off the *dust* of your feet.
Lu. 9: 5. shake off the very *dust* from
10:11. the very *dust* of your city, which
Acts13:51. But they shook off the *dust*
22:23. and threw *dust* into the air,

2869 3 444/554 2873

κοπάζω, kopazo.

Mat.14:32. were come into the ship, the wind *ceased.*
Mar. 4:39. the wind *ceased,* and there was a
6:51. the wind *ceased:* and they were sore amazed

2870 1 444/554 3:830 2875

κοπετός, kopetos.

Acts 8: 2. and made great *lamentation*

2871 1 444/554 2875

κοπή, kopee.

Heb 7: 1. from the *slaughter* of the kings,

2872 23 444/554 3:827 2873

κοπιάω, kopiao.

Mat. 6:28. they *toil* not, neither do they spin:
11:28. Come unto me, all (ye) *that labour*
Lu. 5: 5. we *have toiled* all the night, *and* have
12:27. they *toil* not, they spin not;
Joh. 4: 6. Jesus therefore, *being wearied* with (his) journey,
38. whereon ye *bestowed* no *labour:* other men *laboured,* and ye are
Acts20:35. that so *labouring* ye ought to
Ro. 16: 6. who *bestowed* much *labour* on us.
12. and Tryphosa, *who labour* in the Lord.
— which *laboured* much in the Lord.
1Co. 4:12. And *labour,* working with our
15:10. I *laboured* more abundantly
16:16. that helpeth with (us), and *laboureth.*
Gal. 4:11. lest I *have bestowed* upon you *labour* in vain.
Eph. 4:28. but rather *let him labour,*
Phi. 2:16. neither *laboured* in vain.
Col. 1:29. Whereunto I also *labour,*
1Th. 5:12. to know them *which labour* among you,
1Ti. 4:10. we both *labour* and suffer reproach,
5:17. they *who labour* in the word
2Ti. 2: 6. husbandman *that laboureth* must
Rev. 2: 3. for my name's sake *hast laboured,*

2873 19 444/554 3:827 2875

κόπος, kopos.

Mat.26:10. Why trouble ye (lit. give ye *trouble* to) the woman?
Mar.14: 6. why trouble ye her? (lit. give *trouble* to)
Lu. 11: 7. Trouble me not: (lit. give, &c.)
18: 5. this widow troubleth me, (lit. giveth, &c.)
Joh. 4:38. and ye are entered into their *labours.*
1Co. 3: 8. according to his own *labour.*
15:58. that your *labour* is not in vain
2Co. 6: 5. in *labours,* in watchings,
10:15. of other men's *labours:*
11:23. in *labours* more abundant.
27. In *weariness* and painfulness,
Gal. 6:17. let no man trouble me: (lit. give, &c.)

1Th. 1: 3. your work of faith, and *labour* of love,
2: 9. our *labour* and travail:
3: 5. and our *labour* be in vain.
2Th. 3: 8. but wrought with *labour* and travail
Heb 6:10. your work and *labour* of love,
Rev. 2: 2. I know thy works, and thy *labour*,
14:13. they may rest from their *labours*;

2874 2 444/555 *kopros* (ordure)

κοπρία, *kopria.*

Lu. 13: 8. till I shall dig about it, and dung (it): (lit. throw *dung*)
14:35. nor yet for the *dunghill*;

2875 8 444/555 3:830 cf rt5114

κόπτω, *kopto.*

Mat. 11:17. and ye *have* not *lamented*.
21: 8. others *cut down* branches
24:30. *shall* all the tribes of the earth *mourn*,
Mar 11: 8. others *cut down* branches
Lu. 8:52. And all wept, and *bewailed* her:
23:27. which also *bewailed* and lamented
Rev. 1: 7. *shall wail* because of him.
18: 9. shall bewail her, and *lament* for her,

2876 1 445/555 2880

κόραξ, *korax.*

Lu. 12:24. Consider the *ravens*. for they

2877 8 445/555 *korē* (maiden)

κοράσιον, *korasion.*

Mat. 9:24. the *maid* is not dead,
25. and the *maid* arose.
14:11. in a charger, and given to the *damsel*:
Mar. 5:41. *Damsel*, I say unto thee,
42. the *damsel* arose, and walked;
6:22. the king said unto the *damsel*,
28. and gave it to the *damsel*: and the *damsel* gave it to her mother.

2878 2 445/555 3:860 [7133]

κορβᾶν, κορβανᾶν, *korban, korbanan.*

Mat. 27: 6. to put them into the *treasury*,
Mar. 7:11. (It is) *Corban*, that is to say, a gift,

2880 2 445/555

κορέννυμι, *korennumi.*

Acts 27:38. *when* they *had eaten enough*, they lightened the ship,
1Co. 4: 8. Now ye are *full*, now ye are rich,

2884 1 445/555 [3734]

κόρος, *koros.*

Lu. 16: 7. An hundred *measures* of wheat.

2885 10 445/555 3:867 2889

κοσμέω, *kosmeo.*

Mat. 12:44. findeth (it) empty, swept, and *garnished*.
23:29. and *garnish* the sepulchres of the
25: 7. arose, and *trimmed* their lamps.
Lu. 11:25. he findeth (it) swept and *garnished*.
21: 5. how it *was adorned* with goodly stones
1Ti. 2: 9. that women *adorn* themselves in
Tit. 2:10. that they *may adorn* the doctrine
1Pet. 3: 5. *adorned* themselves, being in subjection
Rev. 21: 2. as a bride *adorned* for her
19. of the wall of the city (were) *garnished*

2886 2 446/555 3:867 2889

κοσμικός, *kosmikos.*

Tit. 2:12. denying ungodliness and *worldly* lusts,
Heb 9: 1. and a *worldly* sanctuary.

2887 2 446/555 3:867 2889

κόσμιος, *kosmios.*

1Ti. 2: 9. adorn themselves in *modest* apparel,
3: 2. vigilant, sober, *of good behaviour*,

2888 1 446/555 3:905 2889,2902

κοσμοκράτωρ, *kosmokratōr.*

Eph. 6:12. against the *rulers* of the darkness of this world, (lit. the *world-rulers* of the darkness of this age)

2889 187 446/556 3:867 rt 2865

κόσμος, *kosmos.*

Mat. 4: 8. him all the kingdoms of the *world*,
5:14. Ye are the light of the *world*.
13:35. from the foundation of the *world*.
38. The field is the *world*;
16:26. if he shall gain the whole *world*,
18: 7. Woe unto the *world* because of
24:21. not since the beginning of the *world*
25:34. from the foundation of the *world*:
26:13. preached in the whole *world*,
Mar. 8:36. shall gain the whole *world*,
14: 9. throughout the whole *world*,
16:15. Go ye into all the *world*,
Lu. 9:25. if he gain the whole *world*,
11:50. from the foundation of the *world*,
12:30. do the nations of the *world* seek
Joh. 1: 9. every man that cometh into the *world*.
10. He was in the *world*, and the *world* was made by him, and the *world* knew him not.
29. taketh away the sin of the *world*.
3:16. For God so loved the *world*,
17. God sent not his Son into the *world* to condemn the *world*; but that the *world* through him might
19. light is come into the *world*,
4:42. the Saviour of the *world*.
6:14. that should come into the *world*.
33. and giveth life unto the *world*.
51. give for the life of the *world*.
7: 4. shew thyself to the *world*.
7. The *world* cannot hate you;
8:12. I am the light of the *world*:
23. ye are of this *world*; I am not of this *world*.
26. I speak to the *world* those things
9: 5. As long as I am in the *world*, I am the light of the *world*.
39. I am come into this *world*, that
10:36. sanctified, and sent into the *world*,
11: 9. he seeth the light of this *world*.
27. which should come into the *world*.
12:19. behold, the *world* is gone after him.
25. that hateth his life in this *world*.
31. Now is the judgment of this *world*: now shall the prince of this *world* be cast out

Joh. 12:46. I am come a light into the *world*,
47. I came not to judge the *world*, but to save the *world*.
13: 1. he should depart out of this *world*
— his own which were in the *world*,
14:17. whom the *world* cannot receive,
19. and the *world* seeth me no more;
22. and not unto the *world*?
27. not as the *world* giveth,
30. the prince of this *world* cometh,
31. But that the *world* may know
15:18. If the *world* hate you,
19. If ye were of the *world*, the *world* would love his own: but because ye are not of the *world*, but I have chosen you out of the *world*, therefore the *world* hateth you.
16: 8. he will reprove the *world* of sin,
11. the prince of this *world* is judged.
20. but the *world* shall rejoice:
21. that a man is born into the *world*.
28. and am come into the *world*: again, I leave the *world*, and go
33. In the *world* ye shall have
— I have overcome the *world*.
17: 5. which I had with thee before the *world*
6. which thou gavest me out of the *world*:
9. I pray not for the *world*,
11. I am no more in the *world*, but these are in the *world*,
12. I was with them in the *world*,
13. and these things I speak in the *world*,
14. and the *world* hath hated them, because they are not of the *world*, even as I am not of the *world*.
15. I pray not...take them out of the *world*,
16. They are not of the *world*, even as I am not of the *world*.
18. As thou hast sent me into the *world*, even so have I also sent them into the *world*.
21. that the *world* may believe that thou
23. that the *world* may know that thou
24. before the foundation of the *world*.
25. the *world* hath not known thee:
18:20. I spake openly to the *world*;
36. My kingdom is not of this *world*: if my kingdom were of this *world*,
37. for this cause came I into the *world*,
21:25. I suppose that even the *world* itself
Acts 17:24. God that made the *world* and all things
Ro. 1: 8. spoken of throughout the whole *world*.
20. from the creation of the *world*
3: 6. how shall God judge the *world*?
19. all the *world* may become guilty
4:13. that he should be the heir of the *world*,
5:12. sin entered into the *world*,
13. until the law sin was in the *world*:
11:12. (be) the riches of the *world*,
15. (be) the reconciling of the *world*,
1Co. 1:20. made foolish the wisdom of this *world*?
21. the *world* by wisdom knew not God,
27. the foolish things of the *world*
— the weak things of the *world*
28. And base things of the *world*,
2:12. not the spirit of the *world*,
3:19. For the wisdom of this *world*
22. or the *world*, or life, or death,
4: 9. a spectacle unto the *world*,
13. as the filth of the *world*,
5:10. with the fornicators of this *world*,
— must ye needs go out of the *world*.
6: 2. the saints shall judge the *world*? and if the *world* shall be judged by you,

1Co. 7:31. And they that use this *world*,
— for the fashion of this *world* passeth
33. careth for the things that are of the *world*, how he may please (his) wife.
34. careth for the things of the *world*, how she may please (her) husband.
8: 4. that an idol (is) nothing in the *world*,
11:32. not be condemned with the *world*.
14:10. many kinds of voices in the *world*,
2Co. 1:12. our conversation in the *world*,
5:19. reconciling the *world* unto himself,
7:10. but the sorrow of the *world* worketh death.
Gal. 4: 3. under the elements of the *world*:
6:14. by whom the *world* is crucified unto me, and I unto the *world*.
Eph. 1: 4. before the foundation of the *world*,
2: 2. according to the course of this *world*,
12. without God in the *world*:
Phi. 2:15. ye shine as lights in the *world*;
Col. 1: 6. as (it is) in all the *world*;
2: 8. after the rudiments of the *world*,
20. from the rudiments of the *world*, why, as though living in the *world*,
1Ti. 1:15. came into the *world* to save sinners;
3:16. believed on in the *world*,
6: 7. brought nothing into (this) *world*,
Heb. 4: 3. from the foundation of the *world*.
9:26. since the foundation of the *world*:
10: 5. when he cometh into the *world*,
11: 7. by the which he condemned the *world*,
38. Of whom the *world* was not worthy:
Jas. 1:27. to keep himself unspotted from the *world*.
2: 5. the poor of this *world* rich in faith, and heirs of
3: 6. a fire, a *world* of iniquity:
4: 4. the friendship of the *world* is enmity
— will be a friend of the *world* is the enemy of God.
1Pet. 1:20. before the foundation of the *world*,
3: 3. Whose *adorning* let it not be
5: 9. your brethren that are in the *world*.
2Pet. 1: 4. the corruption that is in the *world*
2: 5. And spared not the old *world*,
— flood upon the *world* of the ungodly;
20. escaped the pollutions of the *world*
3: 6. Whereby the *world* that then was,
1Joh. 2: 2. for (the sins of) the whole *world*.
15. Love not the *world*, neither the things (that are) in the *world*. If any man love the *world*, the love
16. For all that (is) in the *world*, the lust
— is not of the Father, but is of the *world*.
17. And the *world* passeth away,
3: 1. therefore the *world* knoweth
13. if the *world* hate you.
17. whoso hath this *world's* good
4: 1. are gone out into the *world*.
3. now already is it in the *world*.
4. than he that is in the *world*.
5. They are of the *world*: therefore speak they of the *world*, and the *world* heareth
9. only begotten Son into the *world*,
14. the Saviour of the *world*.
17. so are we in this *world*.
5: 4. overcometh the *world* and this is the victory that overcometh the *world*,
5. that overcometh the *world*.
19. and the whole *world* lieth
2Joh. 7. are entered into the *world*,
Rev. 11:15. The kingdoms of this *world*
13: 8. from the foundation of the *world*.
17: 8. from the foundation of the *world*,

2891 1 448/557 [6966]

κουμι, koumi.

Mar. 5:41. said unto her, Talitha *cumi;* which is,... Damsel, I say unto thee, arise.

2892 3 448/557

κουστωδία, koustōdia.

Mat.27:65. Ye have a *watch:* go your way,
66. sealing the stone, and setting a *watch.*
28:11. some of the *watch* came into the city,

2893 1 448/557 *kouphos* (light)

κουφίζω, kouphizo.

Acts27:38. they *lightened* the ship,

2894 6 448/557

κόφινος, kophinos.

Mat.14:20. that remained twelve *baskets* full.
16: 9. and how many *baskets* ye took up?
Mar 6:43. twelve *baskets* full of the fragments,
8:19. how many *baskets* full
Lu. 9:17. remained to them twelve *baskets.*
Joh. 6:13. and filled twelve *baskets*

2895 12 448/558

κράββατος, krabbatos.

Mar 2: 4. they let down the *bed* wherein
9. Arise, and take up thy *bed,* and walk?
11. Arise, and take up thy *bed,* and go
12. he arose, took up the *bed,*
6:55. and began to carry about in *beds*
Joh. 5: 8. Rise, take up thy *bed,*
9 and took up his *bed,*
10. for thee to carry (thy) *bed.*
11. Take up thy *bed,* and walk.
12. Take up thy *bed,* and walk?
Acts 5:15. and laid (them) on beds and *couches.*
9:33. Æneas, which had kept his *bed*

2896 59 448/558 3:898

κράζω, krazo.

Mat. 8:29. behold, they *cried out,* saying,
9:27. *crying,* and saying, (Thou) son of David,
14:26. they *cried out* for fear.
30. he *cried,* saying, Lord, save me.
15:23. for she *crieth* after us.
20:30. *cried out,* saying, Have mercy
31. but they *cried* the more,
21: 9. *cried,* saying, Hosanna
15. and the children *crying* in the temple,
27:23. But they *cried out* the more,
50. *when* he *had cried* again with a loud
Mar 1:26. and *cried* with a loud voice,
3:11. *cried,* saying, Thou art the Son of God.
5: 5. and in the tombs, *crying,* and
7. And *cried* with a loud voice,
9:24. *cried out, and* said with tears,
26. And (the spirit) *cried,* and rent him
10:47. he began *to cry out,* and say, Jesus,
48. but he *cried* the more
11: 9. that followed, *cried,* saying,
15:13. And they *cried out* again,
14. And they *cried out* the more
39. saw that he so *cried out, and* gave up
Lu. 4:41. came out of many, *crying out,* and saying,
9:39. and he suddenly *crieth out;*
18:39. but he *cried* so much the more,
Lu. 19:40. stones would immediately *cry out.*
Joh. 1:15. and *cried,* saying, This was he
7:28. Then *cried* Jesus in the temple as he
37. Jesus stood and *cried,* saying, If any
12:13. to meet him, and *cried,* Hosanna:
44. Jesus *cried* and said, He that
19:12. the Jews *cried out,* saying, If thou let
Acts 7:57. they *cried out* with a loud voice, *and*
60. and *cried* with a loud voice,
14:14. ran in among the people, *crying out*
16:17. and *cried,* saying, These men
19:28. and *cried out,* saying, Great (is)
32. Some therefore *cried* one thing, and
34. *cried out,* Great (is) Diana
21:28. *Crying out,* Men of Israel, help:
36. *crying,* Away with him.
23: 6. he *cried out* in the council,
24:21. I *cried* standing among them,
Ro. 8:15. whereby we *cry,* Abba, Father.
9:27. Esaias also *crieth* concerning
Gal. 4: 6. into your hearts, *crying,* Abba, Father.
Jas. 5: 4. of you kept back by fraud, *crieth:*
Rev. 6:10. they *cried* with a loud voice,
7: 2. and he *cried* with a loud voice
10. And *cried* with a loud voice,
10: 3. And *cried* with a loud voice,
— when he *had cried,* seven thunders
12: 2. And she being with child *cried,*
14:15. *crying* with a loud voice to him
18: 2. And he *cried* mightily with a
18. And *cried* when they saw the smoke
19. and *cried,* weeping and wailing,
19:17. and he *cried* with a loud voice,

2897 1 449/558 rt726

κραιπάλη, kraipalee.

Lu. 21:34. lest at any time your hearts be overcharged with *surfeiting,*

2898 4 449/558 2768

κρανίον, kranion.

Mat.27:33. a place of a *skull,*
Mar 15:22. The place of a *skull.*
Lu. 23:33. which is called *Calvary,* (lit. *skull*)
Joh.19:17. into a place called (the place) of a *skull.*

2899 5 449/559 3:904 *kara* (head)

κράσπεδον, kraspedon.

Mat. 9:20. and touched the *hem* of his garment:
14:36. might only touch the *hem* of his
23: 5. enlarge the *borders* of their garments,
Mar 6:56. if it were but the *border* of his
Lu. 8:44. and touched the *border* of his

2900 1 449/559 3:905 2904

κραταιός, krataios.

1Pet.5: 6. under the *mighty* hand of God,

2901 4 449/558 3:905 2900

κραταιόω, krataioō.

Lu. 1:80. and *waxed strong* in spirit, and was
2:40. *waxed strong* in spirit, filled with
1Co.16:13. quit you like men, *be strong.*
Eph. 3:16. *to be strengthened* with might

2902 47 449/559 3:905 2904

κρατέω, krateō.

Mat. 9:25. and *took* her *by* the hand.

Mat.12:11. *will* he not *lay hold on* it,
14: 3. For Herod *had laid hold on* John, *and*
18:28. and he *laid hands on* him, *and*
21:46. when they sought *to lay hands on* him,
22: 6. the remnant *took* his servants, *and*
26: 4. consulted that they *might take* Jesus
48. that same is he: *hold* him *fast*.
50. laid hands on Jesus, and *took* him.
55. and ye *laid* no *hold on* me.
57. they *that had laid hold on* Jesus
28: 9. and *held* him *by* the feet, and
Mar 1:31. and *took* her *by* the hand,
3:21. they went out *to lay hold on* him:
5:41. he *took* the damsel *by* the hand,
6:17. and *laid hold upon* John,
7: 3. *holding* the tradition of the elders.
4. which they have received *to hold*,
8. ye *hold* the tradition of men,
9:10. they *kept* that saying with themselves,
27. Jesus *took* him by the hand, *and*
12:12. they sought *to lay hold on* him,
14: 1. sought how they might *take* him by craft, *and*
44. *take* him, and lead (him) away
46. their hands on him, and *took* him.
49. and ye *took* me not:
51. the young men *laid hold on* him:
Lu. 8:54. and *took* her *by* the hand, *and*
24:16. But their eyes *were holden*
Joh.20:23. whose soever (sins) ye *retain*, they *are retained*.
Acts 2:24. that he should *be holden* of it.
3:11. *as* the lame man which was healed *held*
24: 6. whom we *took*, and would have judged
27:13. supposing that they *had obtained*
Col. 2:19. And not *holding* the Head,
2Th. 2:15. stand fast, and *hold* the traditions
Heb 4:14. *let* us *hold fast* (our) profession.
6:18. *to lay hold upon* the hope
Rev. 2: 1. saith he *that holdeth* the
13. and thou *holdest fast* my name,
14. them *that hold* the doctrine of Balaam,
15. them *that hold* the doctrine of the
25. that which ye have (already) *hold fast* till I come.
3:11. *hold* that *fast* which thou hast,
7: 1. *holding* the four winds of the earth,
20: 2. And he *laid hold on* the dragon,

2903 4 450/559 2904

κράτιστος, kratistos.

Lu. 1: 3. *most excellent* Theophilus,
Acts23:26. unto the *most excellent* governor
24: 3. *most noble* Felix, with all thankfulness.
26:25. I am not mad, *most noble* Festus;

2904 12 450/559 3:905

κράτος, kratos.

Lu. 1:51. He hath shewed *strength* with
Acts19:20. So *might*ily grew the word of God
Eph 1:19. the working of his mighty *power*,
6:10. and in the *power* of his might.
Col. 1:11. according to his glorious *power*,
1Ti. 6:16. to whom (be) honour and *power*
Heb 2:14. that had the *power* of death,
1Pet. 4:11. and *dominion* for ever and ever.
5:11. To him (be) glory and *dominion*
Jude 25. *dominion* and power, both now
Rev. 1: 6. to him (be) glory and *dominion* for
5:13. and glory, and *power*, (be) unto

2905 7 450/559 3:898 2906

κραυγάζω, kraugazo

Mat.12:19. He shall not strive, nor *cry*:
15:22. and *cried* unto him, saying,
Joh.11:43. he *cried* with a loud voice,
18:40. Then *cried* they all again,
19: 6. they *cried out*, saying, Crucify
15. they *cried out*, Away with (him),
Acts22:23. And *as* they *cried out*, and cast off

2906 6 450/559 3:898 2896

κραυγή, kraugee.

Mat.25: 6. at midnight there was a *cry* made,
Acts23: 9. And there arose a great *cry*:
Eph 4:31. and anger, and *clamour*,
Heb 5: 7. with strong *crying* and tears
Rev.14:18. and cried with a loud *cry*
21: 4. neither sorrow, nor *crying*, neither shall there be any more pain:

2907 2 450/559

κρέας, kreas.

Ro. 14:21. (It is) good neither to eat *flesh*,
1Co. 8:13. I will eat no *flesh* while

2908 1 450/560 2909

κρεῖσσον, krisson. adv.

1Co. 7:38. he that giveth (her) not in marriage doeth *better*.

2909 19 450/560 2904

κρείσσων, κρείττων, krīssōn, krīttōn.

1Co. 7: 9. it is *better* to marry than to burn.
11:17. not for the *better*, but for the
12:31. covet earnestly the *best* gifts:
Phi. 1:23. with Christ; which is far *better*:
Heb 1: 4. Being made so much *better* than
6: 9. we are persuaded *better* things of you,
7: 7. the less is blessed of the *better*.
19. the bringing in of a *better* hope
22. a surety of a *better* testament.
8: 6. the mediator of a *better* covenant, which was established upon *better* promises.
9:23. with *better* sacrifices than these.
10:34. ye have in heaven a *better* and an
11:16. But now they desire a *better* (country),
35. might obtain a *better* resurrection:
40. some *better* thing for us,
12:24. *better* things than (that of) Abel.
1Pet.3:17. For (it is) *better*, if the will of God be so,
2Pet.2:21. For it had been *better* for them

2910 7 451/560 3:915

κρέμαμαι, κρεμάω, kremamai, kremao.

Mat 18: 6. that a millstone *were hanged* about his
22:40. *hang* all the law and the prophets.
Lu. 23:39. one of the malefactors *which were hanged* railed on him,
Acts 5:30. whom ye slew *and hanged* on a tree.
10:39. whom they slew *and hanged* on a tree:
28: 4. (venomous) beast *hang* on his hand,
Gal. 3:13. Cursed (is) every one *that hangeth* on a

2911 3 451/560 2910

κρημνός, kreemnos.

Mat 8:32. ran violently down a *steep place*
Mar 5:13. down a *steep place* into the sea,
Lu. 8:33. herd ran violently down a *steep place*

2915 2 451/560

κριθή, *krithee.*

Rev 6: 6. three measures of *barley* for a penny;

2916 2 451/560 2915

κρίθινος, *krithinos.*

Joh. 6: 9. which hath five *barley* loaves,
13. fragments of the five *barley* loaves,

2917 28 451/560 3:921 2919

κρίμα, *krima.*

Mat. 7: 2. For with what *judgment* ye judge,
23:14(13). ye shall receive the greater *damnation.*
Mar 12:40. these shall receive greater *damnation.*
Lu. 20:47. shall receive greater *damnation.*
23:40. thou art in the same *condemnation?*
24:20. delivered him to be *condemned* to death,
Joh. 9:39. For *judgment* I am come into
Acts24:25. and *judgment* to come, Felix
Ro. 2: 2. we are sure that the *judgment* of God
3. thou shalt escape the *judgment* of God?
3: 8. whose *damnation* is just.
5:16. for the *judgment* (was) by one
11:33. unsearchable (are) his *judgments,*
13: 2. shall receive to themselves *damnation.*
1Co. 6: 7. because ye go to law (lit. ye have *judgments*) one with another.
11:29. eateth and drinketh *damnation* to himself,
34. come not together unto *condemnation.*
Gal. 5:10. shall bear his *judgment,*
1Ti. 3: 6. he fall into the *condemnation*
5:12. Having *damnation,* because they
Heb 6: 2. and of eternal *judgment.*
Jas. 3: 1. the greater *condemnation.*
1Pet.4:17. For the time (is come) that *judgment*
2Pet.2: 3. whose *judgment* now of a long time
Jude 4. ordained to this *condemnation,*
Rev.17: 1. I will shew unto thee the *judgment* of
18:20. for God hath avenged you (lit. avenged your *judgment*) on her.
20: 4. and *judgment* was given unto them:

2918 2 452/560

κρίνον, *krinon.*

Mat. 6:28. Consider the *lilies* of the field,
Lu. 12:27. Consider the *lilies* how they grow:

2919 114 452/560 3:921

κρίνω, *krino.*

Mat. 5:40. if any man will *sue* thee *at the law,*
7: 1. *Judge* not, that ye *be* not *judged.*
2. For with what judgment ye *judge,* ye *shall be judged:*
19:28. *judging* the twelve tribes of Israel.
Lu. 6:37. *Judge* not, and ye *shall* not *be judged:*
7:43. Thou *hast* rightly *judged.*
12:57. *judge* ye not what is right?
19:22. Out of thine own mouth *will I judge* thee,
:30. *judging* the twelve tribes of Israel.
Joh. 3:17. into the world to *condemn* the world;
18. believeth on him *is* not *condemned:* but he that believeth not *is condemned* already,
5:22. the Father *judgeth* no man,
30. as I hear, I *judge:*
7:24. *Judge* not according to the appearance, but *judge* righteous judgment.
51. *Doth* our law *judge* (any) man,

Joh. 8:15. Ye *judge* after the flesh; I *judge* no man
16. And yet if I *judge,* my judgment is true:
26. things to say and to *judge* of you:
50. there is one that seeketh and *judgeth.*
12:47. I *judge* him not: for I came not to *judge* the world,
48. hath one *that judgeth* him:
— the same *shall judge* him in the last day.
16:11. the prince of this world *is judged.*
18:31. Take ye him, and *judge* him
Acts 3:13. *when* he *was determined* to let (him) go.
4:19. more than unto God, *judge* ye.
7: 7. *will* I *judge,* said God:
13:27. fulfilled (them) in *condemning* (him).
46. and *judge* yourselves unworthy
15:19. Wherefore my *sentence is,* that we
16: 4. decrees for to keep, *that were ordained* of the apostles and elders
15. If ye *have judged* me to be faithful
17:31. will *judge* the world in righteousness
20:16. Paul *had determined* to sail
21:25. we have written (*and*) *concluded* that
23: 3. for sittest thou to *judge* me after the
6. of the hope and resurrection of the dead I *am called in question.*
24: 6. and would have *judged* according
21. I *am called in question* by you this day.
25: 9. and there *be judged* of these things
10. where I ought *to be judged:*
20. and there *be judged* of these
25. I *have determined* to send him.
26: 6. And now I stand *and am judged*
8. Why should it *be thought* a thing
27: 1. when it *was determined* that we
Ro. 2: 1. whosoever thou art *that judgest:* for wherein thou *judgest* another, thou condemnest thyself; for thou that *judgest* doest the same
3. O man, *that judgest* them which do
12. *shall be judged* by the law;
16. when God *shall judge* the secrets
27. *shall* not uncircumcision...*judge* thee,
3: 4. overcome when thou art *judged.*
6. how *shall* God *judge* the world?
7. why yet *am* I also *judged* as a sinner?
14: 3. *let* not him which eateth not *judge* him
4. Who art thou *that judgest* another man's
5. One man *esteemeth* one day above another: another *esteemeth* every day (alike).
10. why *dost* thou *judge* thy brother?
13. *Let* us not therefore *judge* one another any more: but *judge* this
22. Happy (is) he *that condemneth* not himself
1Co. 2: 2. For I *determined* not to know any thing
4: 5. *judge* nothing before the time,
5: 3 *have judged* already, as though I
12. what have I to do *to judge* them also that are without? *do* not ye *judge* them that
13. them that are without God *judgeth.*
6: 1. Dare any...*go to law* before the unjust,
2. the saints *shall judge* the world? and if the world *shall be judged* by you,
3. that we *shall judge* angels?
6. But brother *goeth to law* with brother,
7:37. *hath* so *decreed* in his heart
10:15. *judge* ye what I say.
29. why *is* my liberty *judged* of another
11:13. *Judge* in yourselves: is it comely
31. we should not *be judged.*
32. But *when* we are *judged,* we are
2Co. 2: 1. But I *determined* this with myself,
5:14. *because* we thus *judge,* that if one died for

Col. 2:16. *Let* no man therefore *judge* you in meat,
2Th. 2:12. That they all *might be damned*
2Ti. 4: 1. who shall *judge* the quick and
Tit. 3:12. I *have determined* there to
Heb 10:30. The Lord *shall judge* his people.
13: 4. and adulterers God *will judge*.
Jas. 2:12. as they that shall *be judged*
4:11. and *judgeth* his brother, speaketh evil of the law, and *judgeth* the law: but if thou *judge* the law,
12. who art thou that *judgest*
1Pet. 1:17. *who* without respect of persons *judgeth* according to every
2:23. to him *that judgeth* righteously:
4: 5. that is ready *to judge* the quick and
6. that they *might be judged* according to
Rev. 6:10. *dost* thou not *judge* and avenge
11:18. of the dead, that they should *be judged*,
16: 5. because thou *hast judged* thus.
18: 8. (is) the Lord God *who judgeth* her
20. for God *hath avenged* you on her.
19: 2. for he *hath judged* the great whore,
11. in righteousness he *doth judge* and
20:12. the dead *were judged* out of
13. and they *were judged* every man according to their works.

2920 48 453/562 3:921

κρίσις, *krisis.*

Mat. 5:21. kill shall be in danger of the *judgment*:
22. without a cause shall be in danger of the *judgment*:
10:15. in the day of *judgment*, than for that city.
11:22. at the day of *judgment*, than for you.
24. in the day of *judgment*, than for thee.
12:18. he shall shew *judgment* to the Gentiles.
20. till he send forth *judgment* unto victory.
36. account thereof in the day of *judgment*.
41. Nineveh shall rise in *judgment*
42. of the south shall rise up in the *judgment*
23:23. *judgment*, mercy, and faith:
33. how can ye escape the *damnation* of hell?
Mar 3:29. but is in danger of eternal *damnation*:
6:11. in the day of *judgment*, than
Lu. 10:14. at the *judgment*, than for you.
11:31. shall rise up in the *judgment*
32. Nineve shall rise up in the *judgment*
42. pass over *judgment* and the love of God:
Joh. 3:19. And this is the *condemnation*,
5:22. hath committed all *judgment* unto the
24. shall not come into *condemnation*;
27. to execute *judgment* also,
29. the resurrection of *damnation*.
30. and my *judgment* is just;
7:24. but judge righteous *judgment*.
8:16. my *judgment* is true:
12:31. Now is the *judgment* of this world:
16: 8. of righteousness, and of *judgment*:
11. Of *judgment*, because the prince of this
Acts 8:33. his *judgment* was taken away:
2Th. 1: 5. token of the righteous *judgment* of God,
1Ti. 5:24. going before to *judgment*;
Heb 9:27. but after this the *judgment*:
10:27. fearful looking for of *judgment*
Jas. 2:13. he shall have *judgment* without mercy,
— and mercy rejoiceth against *judgment*.
2Pet. 2: 4. to be reserved unto *judgment*;
9. unto the day of *judgment*
11. bring not railing *accusation*
3: 7. against the day of *judgment*
1Joh. 4:17. boldness in the day of *judgment*:
Jude 6. unto the *judgment* of the great day.
9. a railing *accusation*, but said,
15. To execute *judgment* upon all,
Rev. 14: 7. the hour of his *judgment* is come:
16: 7. and righteous (are) thy *judgments*.
18:10. in one hour is thy *judgment* come.
19: 2. true and righteous (are) his *judgments*:

2922 3 454/562 3:921 2923

κριτήριον, *kriteerion.*

1Co. 6. 2. are ye unworthy *to judge* the smallest
4. If then ye have *judgments* of things pertaining to this life,
Jas. 2: 6. before the *judgment seats*?

2923 17 454/562 3:921 2919

κριτής, *kritees.*

Mat. 5:25. deliver thee to the *judge*, and the *judge* deliver thee to the
12:27. they shall be your *judges*.
Lu. 11:19. therefore shall they be your *judges*.
12:58. lest he hale thee to the *judge*, and the *judge* deliver thee to the
18: 2. There was in a city a *judge*,
6. Hear what the unjust *judge* saith.
Acts 10:42. the *Judge* of quick and dead.
13:20. And after that he gave (unto them) *judges*
18:15. I will be no *judge* of such (matters).
24:10. thou hast been of many years a *judge*
2Ti. 4: 8. the Lord, the righteous *judge*,
Heb 12:23. to God the *Judge* of all,
Jas. 2: 4. are become *judges* of evil thoughts?
4:11. not a doer of the law, but a *judge*.
5: 9. the *judge* standeth before the door.

2924 1 454/563 3:921 2923

κριτικός, *kritikos*, adj.

Heb 4:12. and (is) *a discerner* of the thoughts

2925 9 454/563 3:954

κρούω, *krouo.*

Mat. 7: 7. *knock*, and it shall be opened unto you
8. to him *that knocketh* it shall be opened.
Lu. 11: 9. *knock*, and it shall be opened unto you.
10. to him *that knocketh* it shall be opened.
12:36. that when he cometh and *knocketh*,
13:25. and to *knock* at the door, saying,
Acts 12:13. And *as* Peter *knocked* at the door
16. But Peter continued *knocking*:
Rev. 3:20. I stand at the door, and *knock*:

2926-7 20 455/563 3:957 2928

κρυπτός, *kruptos.*

Mat. 6: 4. That thine alms may be in *secret*: and thy Father which seeth in *secret*
6. to thy Father which is in *secret*; and thy Father which seeth in *secret*
18. but unto thy Father which is in *secret*: and thy Father, which seeth in *secret*,
10:26. and *hid*, that shall not be known.
Mar 4:22. For there is nothing *hid*, which shall
Lu. 8:17. For nothing is *secret*, that shall not
11:33. putteth (it) in a *secret* place,
12: 2. neither *hid*, that shall not be known.
Joh. 7: 4. (that) doeth any thing in *secret*,
10. but as it were in *secret*.
18:20. and in *secret* have I said nothing,

Ro. 2:16. when God shall judge the *secrets* of men
29. he (is) a Jew, which is one *inwardly*;
1Co. 4: 5. bring to light the *hidden* things of
14:25. the *secrets* of his heart made manifest;
2Co. 4: 2. renounced the *hidden* things
1Pet.3: 4. the *hidden* man of the heart,

2928 16 455/563 3:957

κρύπτω, krupto.

Mat. 5:14. on an hill cannot *be hid.*
13:35. I will utter things *which have been kept secret*
44. unto treasure *hid* in a field; the which when a man hath found, he *hideth*,
25:25. and *hid* thy talent in the earth:
Lu. 18:34. this saying was *hid* from them,
19:42. now they *are hid* from thine eyes.
Joh. 8:59. but Jesus *hid* him*self*,
12:36. and *did hide* him*self* from them.
19:38. but *secret*ly for fear of the Jews,
Col. 3: 3. your life *is hid* with Christ in God.
1Ti. 5:25. they that are otherwise cannot *be hid.*
Heb 11:23. *was hid* three months of his parents,
Rev. 2:17. give to eat of the *hidden* manna,
6:15. *hid* themselves in the dens
16. *hide* us from the face of him

2931 1 455/563 3:957 2928

κρυφῆ, kruphee.

Eph. 5:12. which are done of them *in secret.*

2929 1 455/563 2930

κρυσταλλίζω, krustallizo.

Rev.21:11. a jasper stone, *clear as crystal;*

2930 2 455/563 *kruos* (frost)

κρύσταλλος, krustallos.

Rev. 4: 6. a sea of glass like unto *crystal:*
22: 1. river of water of life, clear as *crystal,*

2932 7 456/563

κτάομαι, ktaomai.

Mat.10: 9. *Provide* neither gold, nor silver,
Lu. 18:12. of all that I *possess.*
21:19. In your patience *possess* ye your souls.
Acts 1:18. *purchased* a field with the reward of
8:20. that the gift of God may be *purchased*
22:28. With a great sum *obtained* I
1Th. 4: 4. how *to possess* his vessel in sanctification

2933 4 456/563 2932

κτῆμα, kteema.

Mat.19:22. for he had great *possessions.*
Mar 10:22. for he had great *possessions.*
Acts 2:45. And sold their *possessions* and goods,
5: 1. with Sapphira his wife, sold a *possession,*

2934 4 456/563 2932

κτῆνος, kteenos.

Lu. 10:34. and set him on his own *beast,*
Acts23:24. And provide (them) *beasts*, that they
1Co.15:39. another flesh of *beasts,*
Rev.18:13. and *beasts*, and sheep, and horses.

2935 1 456/563 2932

κτήτωρ, kteetōr.

Acts 4:34. as many as were *possessors* of lands or houses sold them,

2936 14 456/564 3:1000 2927

κτίζω, ktizo.

Mar 13:19. which God *created* unto this time,
Ro. 1:25. more than the *Creator*, who is
1Co.11: 9. Neither *was* the man *created* for the
Eph. 2:10. *created* in Christ Jesus unto good works,
15. for to *make* in himself of twain one new man,
3: 9. hid in God, *who created* all things by Jesus
4:24. the new man, *which* after God *is created* in righteousness
Col. 1:16. by him *were* all things *created,*
— all things *were created* by him, and for
3:10. after the image of him *that created* him:
1Ti. 4: 3. which God *hath created* to be received
Rev. 4:11. for thou *hast created* all things, and for thy pleasure they are and *were created.*
10: 6. who *created* heaven, and the things

2937 19 456/564 3:1000 2936

κτίσις, ktisis.

Mar 10: 6. But from the beginning of the *creation* God made them
13:19. from the beginning of the *creation* which God created
16:15. and preach the gospel to every *creature.*
Ro. 1:20. from the *creation* of the world are clearly
25. and served the *creature* more than the
8:19. expectation of the *creature* waiteth
20. For the *creature* was made subject
21. the *creature* itself also shall be
22. the whole *creation* groaneth and
39. nor any other *creature*, shall be able
2Co. 5:17. (be) in Christ, (he is) a new *creature*
Gal. 6:15. but a new *creature.*
Col. 1:15. the firstborn of every *creature:*
23. was preached to every *creature*
Heb 4:13. Neither is there any *creature* that is
9:11. tabernacle, not made with hands, that is to say, not of this *building;*
1Pet.2:13. to every *ordinance* of man for the Lord's
2Pet.3: 4. continue as (they were) from the beginning of the *creation.*
Rev. 3:14. the beginning of the *creation* of God;

2938 4 457/564 3:1000 2936

κτίσμα, ktisma.

1Ti. 4: 4. For every *creature* of God (is) good,
Jas. 1:18. a kind of firstfruits of his *creatures.*
Rev. 5:13. And every *creature* which is in heaven,
8: 9. third part of the *creatures* which were in the sea,

2939 1 457/564 3:1000 2936

κτίστης, ktistees.

1Pet.4:19. as unto a faithful *Creator.*

2940 1 457/564 *kubos* (cube)

κυβεία, kubīa.

Eph. 4:14. by the *sleight* of men (and) cunning craftiness,

2941 1 457/564 3:1035
κυβέρνησις, kuberneesis.
kubernaō (to steer)

1Co.12:28. helps, *governments*, diversities of tongues.

2942 2 457/564 rt 2941
κυβερνήτης, kuberneetees.

Acts27:11. believed the *master* and the owner of the
Rev.18:17. And every *shipmaster*, and all the company in ships,

2943 4 457/564 rt 2945
κυκλόθεν, kuklothen.

Rev. 4: 3. a rainbow *round about* the throne,
4. And *round about* the throne
8. six wings *about* (him);
5:11. angels *round about* the throne

2944 5 457/564 2945
κυκλόω, kukloō.

Lu. 21:20. see Jerusalem *compassed* with armies,
Joh. 10:24. Then *came* the Jews *round about* him,
Acts14:20. *as* the disciples *stood round about* him,
Heb 11:30. *after* they *were compassed about* seven
Rev.20: 9. and *compassed* the camp of the saints *about*,

2945 7 458/564 *kuklos* (ring)
κύκλῳ, kuklo.
Dat. used for adv.

Mar 3:34. he looked *round about* (lit. in a *circle*) on them which sat about him,
6: 6. he went *round* about the villages,
36. into the country *round about*,
Lu. 9:12. and country *round about*, and lodge,
Ro. 15:19. from Jerusalem, and *round about* unto
Rev. 4: 6. and *round about* the throne,
7:11. all the angels stood *round about* the

2947 1 458/564 rt 2949
κυλίομαι, kuliomai.

Mar 9:20. and *wallowed* foaming.

2946 1 458/564 2947
κύλισμα, kulisma.

2Pet.2:22. to her *wallowing* in the mire.

2948 4 458/564 rt 2949
κυλλός, kullos.

Mat.15:30. dumb, *maimed*, and many others,
31. the *maimed* to be whole,
18: 8. to enter into life halt or *maimed*, rather
Mar 9:43. cut it off: it is better for thee to enter into life *maimed*,

2949 5 458/564 *kuō* (to swell, curve)
κῦμα, kuma.

Mat. 8:24. the ship was covered with the *waves*:
14:24. tossed with *waves*: for the wind
Mar 4:37. the *waves* beat into the ship,
Acts27:41. broken with the violence of the *waves*.
Jude 13. Raging *waves* of the sea, foaming out

2950 1 458/565 3:1037 rt 2949
κύμβαλον, kumbalon.

1Co.13: 1. sounding brass, or a tinkling *cymbal*.

2951 1 458/565 cf [3646]
κύμινον, kuminon.

Mat 23:23. tithe of mint and anise and *cummin*,

2952 4 458/565 3:1101 2965
κυνάριον, kunarion.

Mat.15:26. children's bread, and to cast (it) to *dogs*.
27. yet the *dogs* eat of the crumbs
Mar 7:27. and to cast (it) unto the *dogs*.
28. yet the *dogs* under the table eat of the

2955 3 458/565 rt 2949
κύπτω, kupto.

Mar 1: 7. I am not worthy to *stoop down and*
Joh. 8: 6. But Jesus *stooped* down, *and* with
8. And again he *stooped* down, *and* wrote on

2959 2 459/565 3:1039 2962
κυρία, kuria.

2Joh. 1. The elder unto the elect *lady* and her
5. I beseech thee, *lady*, not as though I

2960 2 459/565 3:1039 2962
κυριακός, kuriakos.

1Co.11:20. (this) is not to eat the *Lord's* supper.
Rev. 1:10. in the Spirit on the *Lord's* day,

2961 7 459/565 3:1039 2962
κυριεύω, kuriuo.

Lu. 22:25. The kings of the Gentiles *exercise lordship over* them;
Ro. 6: 9. *hath* no more *dominion over* him.
14. sin *shall* not *have dominion over* you:
7: 1. the law *hath dominion over* a man
14: 9. that he *might be Lord* both *of* the dead
2Co. 1:24. that we *have dominion over* your faith,
1Ti. 6:15. King of kings, and Lord of *lords*;

2962 749 459/565 3:1039
kuros (supremacy)
κύριος, kurios.

Mat. 1:20. behold, the angel of the *Lord* appeared
22. spoken of the *Lord* by the prophet,
24. did as the angel of the *Lord* had bidden
2:13. the angel of the *Lord* appeareth
15. was spoken of the *Lord* by the prophet,
19. an angel of the *Lord* appeareth in a
3: 3. Prepare ye the way of the *Lord*,
4: 7. shalt not tempt the *Lord* thy God.
10. shalt worship the *Lord* thy God,
5:33. shalt perform unto the *Lord*
6:24. No man can serve two *masters*:
7:21. that saith unto me, *Lord, Lord*,
22. *Lord, Lord*, have we not prophesied
8: 2. saying, *Lord*, if thou wilt, thou canst
6. *Lord*, my servant lieth at home
8. *Lord*, I am not worthy that thou
21. *Lord*, suffer me first to go
25. *Lord*, save us: we perish.
9:28. said unto him, Yea, *Lord*.
38. Pray ye therefore the *Lord* of the harvest,
10:24. nor the servant above his *lord*.
25. and the servant as his *lord*.
11:25. O Father, *Lord* of heaven and earth,
12: 8. is *Lord* even of the sabbath day.
13:27. *Sir*, didst not thou sow good seed in
51. They say unto him, Yea, *Lord*.

Mat 14:28. *Lord*, if it be thou, bid me
30. saying, *Lord*, save me.
15:22. O *Lord*, (thou) son of David;
25. saying, *Lord*, help me.
27. Truth, *Lord:* yet the dogs
— from their *masters'* table.
16:22. Be it far from thee, *Lord*.
17: 4. *Lord*, it is good for us to be here:
15. *Lord*, have mercy on my son:
18:21. *Lord*, how oft shall my brother
25. his *lord* commanded him to be sold,
26. saying, *Lord*, have patience with me,
27. Then the *lord* of that servant
31. told unto their *lord* all that was done.
32. Then his *lord*, after that he
34. And his *lord* was wroth,
20: 8. the *lord* of the vineyard saith
30. O *Lord*, (thou) son of David.
31. O *Lord*, (thou) son of David.
33. *Lord*, that our eyes may be opened.
21: 3. The *Lord* hath need of them;
9. that cometh in the name of the *Lord;*
30. I (go), *sir:* and went not.
40. When the *lord* therefore of the vineyard
42. this is the *Lord's* doing, and it is
22:37. Thou shalt love the *Lord* thy God
43. doth David in spirit call him *Lord*,
44. The *Lord* said unto my *Lord*,
45. If David then call him *Lord*,
23:39. (is) he that cometh in the name of the *Lord*.
24:42. what hour your *Lord* doth come.
45. whom his *lord* hath made ruler
46. whom his *lord* when he cometh
48. My *lord* delayeth his coming;
50. The *lord* of that servant shall come
25:11. *Lord, Lord*, open to us.
18. and hid his *lord's* money.
19. After a long time the *lord* of those
20. *Lord*, thou deliveredst unto me
21. His *lord* said unto him,
— enter thou into the joy of thy *lord*.
22. *Lord*, thou deliveredst unto me
23. His *lord* said unto him,
— into the joy of thy *lord*.
24. *Lord*, I knew thee that thou art
26. His *lord* answered and said
37. *Lord*, when saw we thee
44. *Lord*, when saw we thee
26:22. *Lord*, is it I?
27:10. as the *Lord* appointed me.
63. *Sir*, we remember that
28: 2. the angel of the *Lord*
6. the place where the *Lord* lay.
Mar 1: 3. Prepare ye the way of the *Lord*,
2:28. is *Lord* also of the sabbath.
5:19. how great things the *Lord* hath done
7:28. Yes, *Lord:* yet the dogs
9:24. *Lord*, I believe; help thou
11: 3. that the *Lord* hath need of him;
9. cometh in the name of the *Lord:*
10. in the name of the *Lord:*
12: 9. the *lord* of the vineyard do?
11. This was the *Lord's* doing,
29. The *Lord* our God is one *Lord:*
30. thou shalt love the *Lord* thy God
36. The *Lord* said to my *Lord*,
37. David therefore himself calleth him *Lord;*
13:20. except that the *Lord* had shortened
35. when the *master* of the house
16:19. So then after the *Lord* had spoken
20. the *Lord* working with (them),

Lu. 1: 6. ordinances of the *Lord* blameless.
9. into the temple of the *Lord*.
11. an angel of the *Lord* standing on the
15. great in the sight of the *Lord*,
16. shall he turn to the *Lord* their God.
17. a people prepared for the *Lord*.
25. Thus hath the *Lord* dealt with me
28. the *Lord* (is) with thee: blessed
32. and the *Lord* God shall give
38. Behold the handmaid of the *Lord;*
43. the mother of my *Lord* should come
45. which were told her from the *Lord*.
46. My soul doth magnify the *Lord*,
58. how the *Lord* had shewed great
66. the hand of the *Lord* was with him.
68. Blessed (be) the *Lord* God of Israel;
76. go before the face of the *Lord*
2: 9. the angel of the *Lord* came upon them, and the glory of the *Lord* shone
11. which is Christ the *Lord*.
15. which the *Lord* hath made known
22. to present (him) to the *Lord;*
23. in the law of the *Lord*,
— shall be called holy to the *Lord;*
24. in the law of the *Lord*,
26. before he had seen the *Lord's* Christ.
38. gave thanks likewise unto the *Lord*,
39. to the law of the *Lord*,
3: 4. Prepare ye the way of the *Lord*,
4: 8. Thou shalt worship the *Lord* thy God,
12. Thou shalt not tempt the *Lord*
18. The Spirit of the *Lord* (is) upon me,
19. the acceptable year of the *Lord*.
5: 8. I am a sinful man, O *Lord*.
12. *Lord*, if thou wilt, thou canst
17. the power of the *Lord* was (present)
6: 5. the Son of man is *Lord* also of the
46. why call ye me, *Lord, Lord*,
7: 6. *Lord*, trouble not thyself:
13. when the *Lord* saw her, he had
31. And the *Lord* said, Whereunto then
9:54. *Lord*, wilt thou that we command
57. *Lord*, I will follow thee
59. *Lord*, suffer me first to go and
61. *Lord*, I will follow thee;
10: 1. the *Lord* appointed other seventy
2. pray ye therefore the *Lord* of the
17. *Lord*, even the devils are subject
21. O Father, *Lord* of heaven and earth,
27. Thou shalt love the *Lord* thy God
40. *Lord*, dost thou not care that my sister
11: 1. *Lord*, teach us to pray,
39. the *Lord* said unto him, Now do ye
12:36. that wait for their *lord*,
37. whom the *lord* when he cometh shall find
41. *Lord*, speakest thou this parable unto us,
42. the *Lord* said, Who then is that faithful and wise steward, whom (his) *lord*
43. whom his *lord* when he cometh
45. My *lord* delayeth his coming,
46. The *lord* of that servant will
47. which knew his *lord's* will,
13: 8. *Lord*, let it alone this year also,
15. The *Lord* then answered him, and
23. *Lord*, are there few that be saved?
25. *Lord, Lord*, open unto us;
35. cometh in the name of the *Lord*.
14:21. and shewed his *lord* these things.
22. *Lord*, it is done as thou hast
23. the *lord* said unto the servant,
16: 3. my *lord* taketh away from me the
5. called every one of his *lord's* debtors

Lu. 16: 5. How much owest thou unto my *lord?*
8. the *lord* commended the unjust
13. No servant can serve two *masters:*
17: 5. said unto the *Lord*, Increase our faith.
6. And the *Lord* said, If ye had faith as
37. Where, *Lord?* And he said unto them, Wheresoever
18: 6. And tl e *Lord* said, Hear what
41. *Lord*, that I may receive my sight.
19: 8. and said unto the *Lord;* Behold, *Lord*, the half of my goods I give
16. *Lord*, thy pound hath gained ten pounds.
18. *Lord*, thy pound hath gained five pounds.
20. *Lord*, behold, (here is) thy pound,
25. *Lord*, he hath ten pounds.
31. the *Lord* hath need of him.
33. the *owners* thereof said unto them,
34. The *Lord* hath need of him.
38. cometh in the name of the *Lord:*
20: 13. Then said the *lord* of the vineyard,
15. shall the *lord* of the vineyard do
37. when he calleth the *Lord* the God
42. The *Lord* said unto my *Lord*,
44. David therefore calleth him *Lord*,
22: 31. And the *Lord* said, Simon, Simon,
33. *Lord*, I am ready to go with thee,
38. *Lord*, behold, here (are) two swords.
49. *Lord*, shall we smite with the
61. the *Lord* turned, and looked upon
— Peter remembered the word of the *Lord*,
23: 42. *Lord*, remember me when thou comest
24: 3. found not the body of the *Lord* Jesus.
34. The *Lord* is risen indeed,
Joh. 1: 23. Make straight the way of the *Lord*,
4: 1. When therefore the *Lord* knew
11. *Sir*, thou hast nothing to draw with,
15. *Sir*, give me this water,
19. *Sir*, I perceive that thou art a
49. *Sir*, come down ere my child die.
5: 7. *Sir*, I have no man, when
6: 23. after that the *Lord* had given thanks:
34. *Lord*, evermore give us this bread.
68. *Lord*, to whom shall we go?
8: 11. She said, No man, *Lord*.
9: 36. Who is he, *Lord*, that I might
38. *Lord*, I believe. And he worshipped him.
11: 2. which anointed the *Lord*
3. *Lord*, behold, he whom thou lovest
12. *Lord*, if he sleep, he shall do well.
21. *Lord*, if thou hadst been here,
27. Yea, *Lord:* I believe that thou
32. *Lord*, if thou hadst been here,
34(35). *Lord*, come and see.
39. *Lord*, by this time he stinketh:
12: 13. cometh in the name of the *Lord*.
21. *Sir*, we would see Jesus.
38. *Lord*, who hath believed our report? and to whom hath the arm of the *Lord* been
13: 6. *Lord*, dost thou wash my feet?
9. *Lord*, not my feet only,
13. Ye call me Master and *Lord:*
14. If I then, (your) *Lord* and Master,
16. is not greater than his *lord;*
25. *Lord*, who is it?
36. *Lord*, whither goest thou?
37. *Lord*, why cannot I follow thee
14: 5. *Lord*, we know not whither thou
8. *Lord*, shew us the Father, and
22. *Lord*, how is it that thou wilt
15: 15. knoweth not what his *lord*
20. not greater than his *lord*.

Joh. 20: 2. They have taken away the *Lord*
13. Because they have taken away my *Lord*,
15. *Sir*, if thou have borne him hence,
18. that she had seen the *Lord*,
20. glad, when they saw the *Lord*.
25. We have seen the *Lord*.
28. My *Lord* and my God.
21: 7. It is the *Lord*. Now when Simon Peter heard that it was the *Lord*,
12. knowing that it was the *Lord*.
15. Yea, *Lord;* thou knowest that I
16. Yea, *Lord;* thou knowest that I love
17. *Lord*, thou knowest all things;
20. and said, *Lord*, which is he that
21. *Lord*, and what (shall) this man (do)?
Acts 1: 6. *Lord*, wilt thou at this time restore
21. all the time that the *Lord* Jesus
24. Thou, *Lord*, which knowest the
2: 20. notable day of the *Lord* come:
21. on the name of the *Lord* shall be
25. I foresaw the *Lord* always
34. The *Lord* said unto my *Lord*,
36. hath made that same Jesus,...both *Lord*
— and Christ.
39. as many as the *Lord* our God
47. And the *Lord* added to the church
3: 19. from the presence of the *Lord;*
22. A prophet shall the *Lord* your God
4: 26. against the *Lord*, and against his Christ.
29. *Lord*, behold their threatenings:
33. of the resurrection of the *Lord*
5: 9. to tempt the Spirit of the *Lord?*
14. believers were the more added to the *Lord*,
19. the angel of the *Lord* by night
7: 30. an angel of the *Lord* in a flame
31. the voice of the *Lord* came unto him,
33. Then said the *Lord* to him,
37. A prophet shall the *Lord* your God
49. will ye build me? saith the *Lord:*
59. *Lord* Jesus, receive my spirit.
60. *Lord*, lay not this sin to their
8: 16. in the name of the *Lord* Jesus.
24. Pray ye to the *Lord* for me,
25. preached the word of the *Lord*,
26. the angel of the *Lord* spake unto
39. the Spirit of the *Lord* caught away
9: 1. against the disciples of the *Lord*,
5. Who art thou, *Lord?* And the *Lord* said, I am Jesus
6. *Lord*, what wilt thou have me to do? And the *Lord* (said) unto him,
10. said the *Lord* in a vision, Ananias. And
— he said, Behold, I (am here), *Lord*.
11. And the *Lord* (said) unto him, Arise,
13. *Lord*, I have heard by many
15. But the *Lord* said unto him,
17. the *Lord*, (even) Jesus, that appeared
27. how he had seen the *Lord* in the way,
29(28). in the name of the *Lord* Jesus,
31. and walking in the fear of the *Lord*,
35. and turned to the *Lord*.
42. and many believed in the *Lord*.
10: 4. What is it, *Lord?*
14. Not so, *Lord;* for I have never
36. by Jesus Christ: he is *Lord* of all:
48. baptized in the name of the *Lord*.
11: 8. Not so, *Lord;* for nothing
16. the word of the *Lord*, how that he said,
17. who believed on the *Lord* Jesus
20. preaching the *Lord* Jesus.
21. the hand of the *Lord* was with them:

Acts 11:21. and turned unto the *Lord*.
23. they would cleave unto the *Lord*.
24. people was added unto the *Lord*.
12: 7. the angel of the *Lord* came upon (him),
11. I know of a surety, that the *Lord* hath sent his angel,
17. how the *Lord* had brought him out of the
23. the angel of the *Lord* smote him,
13: 2. As they ministered to the *Lord*, and
10. to pervert the right ways of the *Lord*?
11. the hand of the *Lord* (is) upon thee,
12. astonished at the doctrine of the *Lord*.
47. so hath the *Lord* commanded us,
48. glorified the word of the *Lord*:
49. the word of the *Lord* was published
14: 3. speaking boldly in the *Lord*,
23. commended them to the *Lord*,
15:11. through the grace of the *Lord* Jesus
17. might seek after the *Lord*,
— saith the *Lord*, who doeth all these
26. lives for the name of our *Lord* Jesus
35. preaching the word of the *Lord*,
36. preached the word of the *Lord*,
16:10. gathering that the *Lord* had called us
14. whose heart the *Lord* opened,
15. me to be faithful to the *Lord*,
16. brought her *masters* much gain
19. when her *masters* saw that
30. *Sirs*, what must I do to be saved?
31. Believe on the *Lord* Jesus Christ,
32. unto him the word of the *Lord*,
17:24. seeing that he is *Lord* of heaven and earth,
27. That they should seek the *Lord*,
18: 8. believed on the *Lord* with all
9. Then spake the *Lord* to Paul
25. was instructed in the way of the *Lord*;
— taught diligently the things of the *Lord*,
19: 5. baptized in the name of the *Lord*
10. heard the word of the *Lord*
13. the name of the *Lord* Jesus,
17. the name of the *Lord* Jesus was
20. mightily grew the word of *God* and
20:19. Serving the *Lord* with all
21. faith toward our *Lord* Jesus
24. which I have received of the *Lord*
35. remember the words of the *Lord* Jesus,
21:13. for the name of the *Lord* Jesus.
14. The will of the *Lord* be done.
20. they glorified the *Lord*,
22: 8. Who art thou, *Lord*?
10. What shall I do, *Lord*? And the *Lord* said unto me, Arise,
16. calling on the name of the *Lord*.
19. *Lord*, they know that I imprisoned
23:11. the *Lord* stood by him,
25:26. to write unto my *lord*.
26:15. Who art thou, *Lord*?
28:31. which concern the *Lord* Jesus
Ro. 1: 3(4). his Son Jesus Christ our *Lord*,
7. and the *Lord* Jesus Christ.
4: 8. to whom the *Lord* will not impute sin.
24. raised up Jesus our *Lord* from
5: 1. peace with God through our *Lord* Jesus
11. joy in God through our *Lord* Jesus
21. eternal life by Jesus Christ our *Lord*.
6:11. alive unto God through Jesus Christ our *Lord*.
23. eternal life through Jesus Christ our *Lord*.
7:25. I thank God through Jesus Christ our *Lord*.
8:39. which is in Christ Jesus our *Lord*.
9:28. a short work will the *Lord*
29. Except the *Lord* of Sabaoth

Ro. 10: 9. with thy mouth the *Lord* Jesus
12. the same *Lord* over all is rich
13. call upon the name of the *Lord*
16. *Lord*, who hath believed our
11: 3. *Lord*, they have killed thy
34. known the mind of the *Lord*?
12:11. fervent in spirit; serving the *Lord*;
19. I will repay, saith the *Lord*.
13:14. put ye on the *Lord* Jesus Christ,
14: 4. to his own *master* he standeth
6. regardeth (it) unto the *Lord*;
— to the *Lord* he doth not regard (it).
— eateth to the *Lord*, for he giveth
— to the *Lord* he eateth not,
8. we live unto the *Lord*;...we die unto the *Lord*:...we are the *Lord's*.
11. (As) I live, saith the *Lord*,
14. persuaded by the *Lord* Jesus,
15: 6. Father of our *Lord* Jesus Christ.
11. Praise the *Lord*, all ye Gentiles;
30. for the *Lord* Jesus Christ's sake,
16: 2. That ye receive her in the *Lord*,
8. Amplias my beloved in the *Lord*.
11. of Narcissus, which are in the *Lord*.
12. and Tryphosa, who labour in the *Lord*.
— Persis, which laboured much in the *Lord*
13. Rufus chosen in the *Lord*,
18. such serve not our *Lord* Jesus
20. The grace of our *Lord* Jesus Christ
22. salute you in the *Lord*.
24. The grace of our *Lord* Jesus Christ
1Co. 1: 2. the name of Jesus Christ our *Lord*,
3. and (from) the *Lord* Jesus Christ.
7. waiting for the coming of our *Lord*
8. in the day of our *Lord* Jesus Christ.
9. his Son Jesus Christ our *Lord*.
10. by the name of our *Lord* Jesus
31. let him glory in the *Lord*.
2: 8. crucified the *Lord* of glory.
16. who hath known the mind of the *Lord*,
3: 5. even as the *Lord* gave to every
20. The *Lord* knoweth the thoughts
4: 4. he that judgeth me is the *Lord*.
5. until the *Lord* come,
17. and faithful in the *Lord*,
19. if the *Lord* will,
5: 4. In the name of our *Lord* Jesus
— with the power of our *Lord* Jesus Christ,
5. saved in the day of the *Lord*
6:11. in the name of the *Lord* Jesus,
13. but for the *Lord*; and the *Lord* for the body.
14. God hath both raised up the *Lord*,
17. he that is joined unto the *Lord*
7:10. (yet) not I, but the *Lord*,
12. speak I, not the *Lord*:
17. as the *Lord* hath called every one,
22. that is called in the *Lord*, (being) a servant, is the *Lord's* freeman:
25. no commandment of the *Lord*:
— obtained mercy of the *Lord* to
32. that belong to the *Lord*, how he may please the *Lord*:
34. careth for the things of the *Lord*, that
35. that ye may attend upon the *Lord*
39. to whom she will; only in the *Lord*.
8: 5. as there be gods many, and *lords* many,
6. and one *Lord* Jesus Christ,
9: 1. have I not seen Jesus Christ our *Lord*? are not ye my work in the *Lord*?
2. the seal of mine apostleship are ye in the *Lord*.

1Co. 9: 5. and (as) the brethren of the *Lord*, and
14. Even so hath the *Lord* ordained
10:21. cannot drink the cup of the *Lord*, and the
— of the *Lord's* table, and of the table
22. Do we provoke the *Lord* to jealousy?
26. the earth (is) the *Lord's*, and the
28. the *Lord's*, and the fulness thereof:
11:11. without the man, in the *Lord*.
23. I have received of the *Lord*
— That the *Lord* Jesus the (same)
26. ye do shew the *Lord's* death till
27. drink (this) cup of the *Lord*, unworthily,
— guilty of the body and blood of the *Lord*.
29. not discerning the *Lord's* body.
32. we are chastened of the *Lord*,
12: 3. can say that Jesus is the *Lord*, but
5. of administrations, but the same *Lord*.
14:21. will they not hear me, saith the *Lord*.
37. are the commandments of the *Lord*.
15:31. I have in Christ Jesus our *Lord*,
47. the second man (is) the *Lord* from heaven.
57. the victory through our *Lord* Jesus
58. abounding in the work of the *Lord*,
— labour is not in vain in the *Lord*.
16: 7. if the *Lord* permit.
10. he worketh the work of the *Lord*,
19. salute you much in the *Lord*,
22. If any man love not the *Lord*
23. The grace of our *Lord* Jesus
2Co. 1: 2. and (from) the *Lord* Jesus Christ.
3. Father of our *Lord* Jesus Christ,
14. in the day of the *Lord* Jesus.
2:12. was opened unto me of the *Lord*,
3:16. when it shall turn to the *Lord*,
17. Now the *Lord* is that Spirit: and where the Spirit of the *Lord* (is),
18. beholding as in a glass the glory of the *Lord*,
— (even) as by the Spirit of the *Lord*.
4: 5. but Christ Jesus the *Lord*;
10. the dying of the *Lord* Jesus,
14. he which raised up the *Lord*
5: 6. we are absent from the *Lord*:
8. to be present with the *Lord*.
11. Knowing therefore the terror of the *Lord*,
6:17. be ye separate, saith the *Lord*,
18. ye shall be my sons and daughters, saith the *Lord* Almighty.
8: 5. gave their own selves to the *Lord*,
9. ye know the grace of our *Lord* Jesus
19. to the glory of the same *Lord*,
21. not only in the sight of the *Lord*,
10: 8. which the *Lord* hath given us
17. let him glory in the *Lord*.
18. but whom the *Lord* commendeth.
11:17. I speak (it) not after the *Lord*,
31. Father of our *Lord* Jesus Christ,
12: 1. and revelations of the *Lord*.
8. I besought the *Lord* thrice,
13:10. power which the *Lord* hath given me
14(13). The grace of the *Lord* Jesus
Gal. 1: 3. and (from) our *Lord* Jesus
19. save James the *Lord's* brother.
4: 1. though he be *lord* of all;
5:10. confidence in you through the *Lord*,
6:14. save in the cross of our *Lord*
17. the marks of the *Lord* Jesus.
18. the grace of our *Lord* Jesus
Eph. 1: 2. and (from) the *Lord* Jesus
3. Father of our *Lord* Jesus
15. heard of your faith in the *Lord* Jesus,
17. the God of our *Lord* Jesus

Eph. 2:21. an holy temple in the *Lord*:
3:11. in Christ Jesus our *Lord*:
14. Father of our *Lord* Jesus
4: 1. the prisoner of the *Lord*,
5. One *Lord*, one faith,
17. and testify in the *Lord*,
5: 8. now (are ye) light in the *Lord*:
10. Proving what is acceptable unto the *Lord*
17. what the will of the *Lord* (is).
19. melody in your heart to the *Lord*;
20. in the name of our *Lord* Jesus
22. own husbands, as unto the *Lord*.
29. even as the *Lord* the church:
6: 1. obey your parents in the *Lord*:
4. the nurture and admonition of the *Lord*.
5. to them that are (your) *masters*
7. doing service, as to the *Lord*,
8. shall he receive of the *Lord*,
9. And, ye *masters*, do the same things
— your *Master* also is in heaven;
10. be strong in the *Lord*,
21. and faithful minister in the *Lord*,
23. and the *Lord* Jesus Christ.
24. that love our *Lord* Jesus
Phi. 1: 2. and (from) the *Lord* Jesus
14. brethren in the *Lord*, waxing confident
2:11. confess that Jesus Christ (is) *Lord*,
19. I trust in the *Lord* Jesus to
24. I trust in the *Lord* that I
29. Receive him therefore in the *Lord*
3: 1. rejoice in the *Lord*.
8. of Christ Jesus my *Lord*:
20. the Saviour, the *Lord* Jesus Christ:
4: 1. so stand fast in the *Lord*,
2. be of the same mind in the *Lord*.
4. Rejoice in the *Lord* alway:
5. The *Lord* (is) at hand.
10. I rejoiced in the *Lord* greatly,
23(24). The grace of our *Lord* Jesus
Col. 1: 2. and the *Lord* Jesus Christ.
3. Father of our *Lord* Jesus
10. walk worthy of the *Lord* unto
2: 6. received Christ Jesus the *Lord*, (so)
3:16. grace in your hearts to the *Lord*.
17. (do) all in the name of the *Lord* Jesus,
18. as it is fit in the *Lord*.
20. this is well pleasing unto the *Lord*.
22. obey in all things (your) *masters*
23. as to the *Lord*, and not unto men;
24. Knowing that of the *Lord* ye shall
— for ye serve the *Lord* Christ.
4: 1. *Masters*, give unto (your) servants
— ye also have a *Master* in heaven.
7. fellowservant in the *Lord*:
17. which thou hast received in the *Lord*,
1Th. 1: 1. and (in) the *Lord* Jesus Christ:
— from God our Father, and the *Lord* Jesus
3. patience of hope in our *Lord* Jesus Christ,
6. followers of us, and of the *Lord*,
8. sounded out the word of the *Lord*
2:15. Who both killed the *Lord* Jesus,
19. in the presence of our *Lord* Jesus
3: 8. if ye stand fast in the *Lord*.
11. and our *Lord* Jesus Christ,
12. the *Lord* make you to increase
13. at the coming of our *Lord* Jesus
4: 1. exhort (you) by the *Lord* Jesus,
2. we gave you by the *Lord* Jesus.
6. because that the *Lord* (is) the avenger
15. unto you by the word of the *Lord*,
— remain unto the coming of the *Lord*
16. the *Lord* himself shall descend

1Th. 4:17. to meet the *Lord* in the air: and so shall we ever be with the *Lord*.
5: 2. the day of the *Lord* so cometh
9. salvation by our *Lord* Jesus
12. and are over you in the *Lord*,
23. unto the coming of our *Lord*
27. I charge you by the *Lord* that this
28. The grace of our *Lord* Jesus
2Th. 1: 1. in God our Father and the *Lord* Jesus
2. Father and the *Lord* Jesus Christ.
7. when the *Lord* Jesus shall be revealed
8. obey not the gospel of our *Lord* Jesus
9. from the presence of the *Lord*,
12. That the name of our *Lord* Jesus Christ
— to the grace of our God and the *Lord*
2: 1. by the coming of our *Lord* Jesus
8. whom the *Lord* shall consume
13. brethren beloved of the *Lord*,
14. of the glory of our *Lord* Jesus
16. Now our *Lord* Jesus Christ himself,
3: 1. that the word of the *Lord* may have
3. the *Lord* is faithful, who
4. confidence in the *Lord* touching you,
5. the *Lord* direct your hearts
6. in the name of our *Lord* Jesus
12. exhort by our *Lord* Jesus
16. Now the *Lord* of peace himself
— The *Lord* (be) with you all.
18. The grace of our *Lord* Jesus
1Ti. 1: 1. and *Lord* Jesus Christ,
2. and Jesus Christ our *Lord*.
12. I thank Christ Jesus our *Lord*,
14. the grace of our *Lord* was exceeding
5:21. I charge (thee) before God, and the *Lord* Jesus Christ,
6: 3. the words of our *Lord* Jesus
14. until the appearing of our *Lord*
15. the King of kings, and *Lord* of lords;
2Ti. 1: 2. and Christ Jesus our *Lord*.
8. ashamed of the testimony of our *Lord*,
16. The *Lord* give mercy unto the house
18. The *Lord* grant unto him that he may find mercy of the *Lord* in that day:
2: 7. the *Lord* give thee understanding
14. charging (them) before the *Lord*
19. The *Lord* knoweth them that are his,
22. with them that call on the *Lord*
24. the servant of the *Lord* must not strive;
3:11. out of (them) all the *Lord* delivered me.
4: 1. before God, and the *Lord* Jesus
8. which the *Lord*, the righteous judge,
14. the *Lord* reward him according
17. the *Lord* stood with me,
18. the *Lord* shall deliver me
22. The *Lord* Jesus Christ (be) with
Tit. 1: 4. and the *Lord* Jesus Christ our Saviour.
Philem 3. and the *Lord* Jesus Christ.
5. which thou hast toward the *Lord* Jesus,
16. both in the flesh, and in the *Lord*?
20. me have joy of thee in the *Lord*: refresh my bowels in the *Lord*.
25. The grace of our *Lord* Jesus Christ
Heb 1:10. And, Thou, *Lord*, in the beginning
2: 3. began to be spoken by the *Lord*,
7:14. that our *Lord* sprang out of
21. The *Lord* sware and will not
8: 2. tabernacle, which the *Lord* pitched,
8. the days come, saith the *Lord*,
9. I regarded them not, saith the *Lord*.
10. after those days, saith the *Lord*;
11. saying, Know the *Lord*:
10:16. after those days, saith the *Lord*,
Heb 10:30. I will recompense, saith the *Lord*. And again, The *Lord* shall judge his people.
12: 5. despise not thou the chastening of the *Lord*,
6. whom the *Lord* loveth he chasteneth,
14. without which no man shall see the *Lord*.
13: 6. The *Lord* (is) my helper,
20. from the dead our *Lord* Jesus,
Jas. 1: 1. and of the *Lord* Jesus Christ,
7. receive any thing of the *Lord*.
12. which the *Lord* hath promised
2: 1. the faith of our *Lord* Jesus
4:10. in the sight of the *Lord*, and he
15. (ought) to say, If the *Lord* will, we
5: 4. into the ears of the *Lord* of sabaoth.
7. unto the coming of the *Lord*.
8. the coming of the *Lord* draweth nigh.
10. have spoken in the name of the *Lord*,
11. have seen the end of the *Lord*; that the *Lord* is very pitiful,
14. with oil in the name of the *Lord*:
15. the *Lord* shall raise him up;
1Pet. 1: 3. Father of our *Lord* Jesus
25. the word of the *Lord* endureth
2: 3. that the *Lord* (is) gracious.
13. to every ordinance of man for the *Lord's* sake:
3: 6. obeyed Abraham, calling him *lord*:
12. the eyes of the *Lord* (are) over
— the face of the *Lord* is against
15. sanctify the *Lord* God in
2Pet. 1: 2. and of Jesus our *Lord*,
8. knowledge of our *Lord* Jesus
11. into the everlasting kingdom of our *Lord* and Saviour
14. as our *Lord* Jesus Christ hath shewed me.
16. and coming of our *Lord*
2: 9. The *Lord* knoweth how to deliver
11. against them before the *Lord*.
20. through the knowledge of the *Lord* and
3: 2. the apostles of the *Lord* and Saviour:
8. one day (is) with the *Lord* as
9. The *Lord* is not slack concerning
10. the day of the *Lord* will come
15. the longsuffering of our *Lord* (is)
18. and (in) the knowledge of our *Lord* and
2Joh. 3. and from the *Lord* Jesus
Jude 4. God, and our *Lord* Jesus Christ.
5. how that the *Lord*, having saved the
9. The *Lord* rebuke thee.
14. the *Lord* cometh with ten thousands of his
17. of the apostles of our *Lord* Jesus
21. looking for the mercy of our *Lord* Jesus
Rev. 1: 8. and the ending, saith the *Lord*,
4: 8. Holy, holy, holy, *Lord* God Almighty,
11. Thou art worthy, O *Lord*, to receive
7:14. *Sir*, thou knowest.
11: 8. where also our *Lord* was crucified.
15. are become (the kingdoms) of our *Lord*, and of his Christ;
17. give thee thanks, O *Lord* God Almighty,
14:13. the dead which die in the *Lord* from
15: 3. thy works, *Lord* God Almighty;
4. Who shall not fear thee, O *Lord*,
16: 5. Thou art righteous, O *Lord*,
7. Even so, *Lord* God Almighty,
17:14. for he is *Lord* of *lords*,
18: 8. for strong (is) the *Lord* God
19: 1. unto the *Lord* our God:
6. for the *Lord* God omnipotent
16. KING OF KINGS, AND *LORD* OF *LORDS*.

Rev.21 22. for the *Lord* God Almighty and the Lamb
22: 5. for the *Lord* God giveth them light:
6. the *Lord* God of the holy prophets
20. Even so, come, *Lord* Jesus.
21. The grace of our *Lord* Jesus Christ (be) with you all. Amen.

2963 4 461/574 3:1039 2962

κυριότης, kuriotees.

Eph 1:21. and *dominion*, and every name
Col. 1:16. or *dominions*, or principalities, or
2Pet. 2:10. and despise *government*.
Jude 8. despise *dominion*, and speak evil of

2964 2 461/574 3:1098 rt 2962

κυρόω, kuroō.

2Co. 2: 8. that ye would *confirm* (your) love toward
Gal. 3:15. a man's covenant, yet (if it be) *confirmed*, no man disannulleth,

2965 5 462/574 3:1101

κύων, kuōn.

Mat. 7: 6. Give not that which is holy unto the *dogs*,
Lu. 16:21. the *dogs* came and licked his sores.
Phi. 3: 2. Beware of *dogs*, beware of evil workers,
2Pet. 2:22. The *dog* (is) turned to his own vomit
Rev.22:15. For without (are) *dogs*, and sorcerers,

2966 1 462/574 rt 2849

κῶλον, kōlon.

Heb 3:17. that had sinned, whose *carcases* fell in the wilderness?

2967 23 462/574 rt 2849

κωλύω, kōluo.

Mat.19:14. and *forbid* them not,
Mar 9:38. and we *forbad* him,
39. But Jesus said, *Forbid* him not:
10:14. Suffer the little children to come unto me, and *forbid* them not:
Lu 6:29. *forbid* not (to take thy) coat also.
9:49. and we *forbad* him,
50. *Forbid* (him) not:
11:52. that were entering in ye *hindered*.
18:16. and *forbid* them not:
23: 2. *forbidding* to give tribute to Cæsar,
Acts 8:36. what *doth hinder* me to be baptized?
10:47. Can any man *forbid* water,
11:17. that I could *withstand* God?
16: 6. *and were forbidden* of the Holy Ghost to
24:23. and that he should *forbid* none of his
27:43. *kept* them from (their) purpose;
Ro. 1:13. but *was let* hitherto,
1Co.14:39. and *forbid* not to speak with tongues.
1Th. 2:16. *Forbidding* us to speak to the Gentiles
1Ti. 4: 3. *Forbidding* to marry,
Heb 7:23. because they *were not suffered* to
2Pet. 2:16. *forbad* the madness of the prophet.
3Joh. 10. and *forbiddeth* them that would,

2968 28 462/574 2749

κώμη, kōmee.

Mat. 9:35. about all the cities and *villages*,
10:11. city or *town* ye shall enter,
14:15. that they may go into the *villages*,
21: 2. Go into the *village* over against
Mar 6: 6. he went round about the *villages*,
36. and into the *villages*,
56. into *villages*, or cities, or
8:23. and led him out of the *town*;
26. Neither go into the *town*, nor tell (it) to any in the *town*.
27. into the *towns* of Cæsarea Philippi:
11: 2. Go your way into the *village*
Lu. 5:17. were come out of every *town* of
8: 1. every city and *village*,
9: 6. went through the *towns*,
12. that they may go into the *towns* and
52. and entered into a *village* of the
56. they went to another *village*.
10:38. he entered into a certain *village*:
13:22. the cities and *villages*, teaching,
17:12. into a certain *village*,
19:30. Go ye into the *village* over
24:13. that same day to a *village* called Emmaus,
28. they drew nigh unto the *village*,
Joh. 7:42. out of the *town* of Bethlehem,
11: 1. Bethany, the *town* of Mary and her sister
30. Jesus was not yet come into the *town*,
Acts 8:25. the gospel in many *villages* of the

2969 1 462/575 2968,4172

κωμόπολις, kōmopolis.

Mar. 1:38. Let us go into the next *towns*,

2970 3 462/575 2749

κῶμος, kōmos.

Ro. 13:13. not in *rioting* and drunkenness,
Gal. 5:21. *revellings*, and such like:
1Pet. 4: 3. *revellings*, banquetings, and abominable

2971 1 463/575 rt 2759,3700

κώνωψ, kōnōps.

Mat.23:24. which strain at a *gnat*,

2974 14 463/575 2875

κωφός, kōphos.

Mat. 9:32. brought to him a *dumb* man possessed
33. when the devil was cast out, the *dumb*
11: 5. and the *deaf* hear,
12:22. with a devil, blind, and *dumb*:
— that the blind and *dumb* both spake and
15:30. blind, *dumb*, maimed, and many others,
31. when they saw the *dumb* to speak,
Mar. 7:32. one that was *deaf*, and had an impediment in his speech;
37. he maketh both the *deaf* to hear, and
9:25. (Thou) dumb and *deaf* spirit, I charge
Lu. 1:22. and remained *speechless*.
7:22. the *deaf* hear, the dead are raised,
11:14. was casting out a devil, and it was *dumb*
— when the devil was gone out, the *dumb*

2975 4 463/575 4:1

λαγχάνω, lankano.

Lu. 1: 9. *his lot was* to burn incense
Joh. 19:24. Let us not rend it, but *cast lots* for it
Acts 1:17. had *obtained* part of this ministry
2Pet. 1: 1. to them *that have obtained* like precious

2977 4 463/575 2990

λάθρα, *lathra.*

Mat. 1:19. was minded to put her away *privily.*
2: 7. when he had *privily* called the wise men,
Joh. 11:28. called Mary her sister *secretly,*
Acts 16:37. now do they thrust us out *privily?*

2978 3 463/575

λαῖλαψ, *lailaps.*

Mar 4:37. there arose a great *storm* of wind,
Lu. 8:23. there came down a *storm* of wind
2Pet. 2:17. that are carried with a *tempest;*

2997 1 468/584 *laschō*

λακέω, *lakeo.*

Acts 1:18. he *burst asunder* in the midst,

2979 2 462/575 4:3 *lax* (heelwise)

λακτίζω, *laktizo.*

Acts 9: 5. (it is) hard for thee *to kick* against
26:14. for thee *to kick* against the pricks.

2980 295 464/575 4:3,4:69 cf3004

λαλέω, *laleo.*

Mat. 9:18. *While* he *spake* these things
33. the devil was cast out, the dumb *spake*
10:19. or what ye *shall speak:*
— in that same hour what ye *shall speak.*
20. it is not ye *that speak*, but the Spirit of your Father *which speaketh* in
12:22. that the blind and dumb both *spake* and
34. how can ye, being evil, *speak* good
— of the heart the mouth *speaketh.*
36. every idle word that men *shall speak,*
46. *While* he yet *talked* to the people,
— desiring *to speak* with him,
47. desiring *to speak* with thee.
13: 3. And he *spake* many things unto them in parables,
10. Why *speakest* thou unto them in
13. Therefore *speak* I to them
33. Another parable *spake* he
34. All these things *spake* Jesus
— without a parable *spake* he not
14:27. Jesus *spake* unto them,
15:31. when they saw the dumb to *speak,*
17: 5. *While* he yet *spake*, behold,
23: 1. Then *spake* Jesus to the multitude,
26:13. *shall* also this,...*be told* for a memorial of
47. *while* he yet *spake*, lo, Judas,
28:18. Jesus came and *spake* unto them,
Mar. 1:34. suffered not the devils *to speak,*
2: 2. and he *preached* the word
7. Why *doth* this (man) thus *speak* blasphemies?
4:33. many such parables *spake* he the word
34. without a parable *spake* he not
5:35. *While* he yet *spake*, there came
36. heard the word *that was spoken,*
6:50. immediately he *talked* with them,
7:35. and he *spake* plain.
37. and the dumb *to speak.*
8:32. he *spake* that saying openly.
9: 6. For he wist not what to *say;*
13:11. beforehand what ye *shall speak,*
— that *speak* ye: for it is not ye *that speak,*
14: 9. *shall be spoken of* for a memorial
43. *while* he yet *spake*, cometh Judas,

Mar 16:17. they *shall speak* with new tongues;
19. after the Lord *had spoken*
Lu. 1:19. and am sent *to speak* unto thee,
20. and not able *to speak,*
22. he could not *speak*
45. *which were told* her from the Lord.
55. As he *spake* to our fathers,
64. and he *spake*, and praised God.
70. As he *spake* by the mouth of
2:17. the saying *which was told* them concerning
18. at those things *which were told* them by
20. as it *was told* unto them.
33. *which were spoken* of him.
38. and *spake* of him to all them
50. which he *spake* unto them.
4:41. suffered them not *to speak:*
5: 4. when he had left *speaking,*
21. Who is this which *speaketh* blasphemies?
6:45. of the heart his mouth *speaketh.*
7:15. and began *to speak.*
8:49. *While* he yet *spake*, there cometh one
9:11. *spake* unto them of the kingdom of God,
11:14. devil was gone out, the dumb *spake;*
37. as he *spake*, a certain Pharisee
12: 3. ye *have spoken* in the ear in
22:47. *while* he yet *spake*, behold a multitude,
60. *while* he yet *spake*, the cock crew.
24: 6. remember how he *spake* unto you
25. all that the prophets *have spoken:*
32. while he *talked* with us by the way,
36. And *as* they thus *spake*, Jesus
44. These (are) the words which I *spake*
Joh. 1:37. the two disciples heard him *speak,*
3:11. We *speak* that we do know,
31. and *speaketh* of the earth:
34. *speaketh* the words of God:
4:26. I *that speak* unto thee am (he).
27. marvelled that he *talked* with
— Why *talkest* thou with her?
6:63. the words that I *speak* unto you,
7:13. no man *spake* openly of him
17. or (whether) I *speak* of myself.
18. He *that speaketh* of himself
26. lo, he *speaketh* boldly,
46. Never man *spake* like this man.
8:12. Then *spake* Jesus again unto
20. These words *spake* Jesus in the
25. Even (the same) that I *said* unto you
26. I have many things *to say* and
28. hath taught me, I *speak* these things.
30. *As* he *spake* these words, many believed
38. I *speak* that which I have seen
40. a man that *hath told* you the truth,
44. When he *speaketh* a lie, he *speaketh* of his
9:21. he *shall speak* for himself.
29. We know that God *spake* unto Moses:
37. it is he *that talketh* with thee.
10: 6. which he *spake* unto them.
12:29. An angel *spake* to him.
36. These things *spake* Jesus
41. he saw his glory, and *spake* of him.
48. the word that I *have spoken,*
49. I *have* not *spoken* of myself;
— and what I *should speak*
50. whatsoever I *speak* therefore, even as the Father said unto me, so I *speak.*
14:10. the words that I *speak* unto you I *speak* not of myself:
25. These things *have* I *spoken*
30. I *will* not *talk* much with you:
15: 3. which I *have spoken* unto you.
11. These things *have* I *spoken* unto you.

Joh. 15:22. If I had not come and *spoken* unto them,
16: 1. These things *have* I *spoken*
4. these things *have* I *told* you,
6. because I *have said* these things
13. he *shall* not *speak* of himself; but whatsoever he shall hear, (that) *shall* he *speak:*
18. we cannot tell what he *saith.*
25. *have* I *spoken* unto you in proverbs:
— when I *shall* no more *speak* unto you in
29. now *speakest* thou plainly,
33. These things I *have spoken* unto you,
17: 1. These words *spake* Jesus,
13. these things I *speak* in the world,
18:20. I *spake* openly to the world;
— in secret *have* I *said* nothing.
21. what I *have said* unto them:
23. If I *have spoken* evil,
19:10. *Speakest* thou not unto me?
Acts 2: 4. began *to speak* with other
6. heard them *speak* in his own language.
7. are not all these *which speak*
11. we do hear them *speak* in our
31. *spake* of the resurrection of
3:21. God *hath spoken* by the mouth
22. whatsoever he *shall say* unto
24. as many as *have spoken*, have likewise
4: 1. And *as* they *spake* unto the people,
17. that they *speak* henceforth
20. For we cannot but *speak*
29. all boldness they may *speak*
31. they *spake* the word of God
5:20. Go, stand and *speak* in the temple
40. that they should not *speak* in the name
6:10. and the spirit by which he *spake.*
11. We have heard him *speak* blasphemous
13. This man ceaseth not to *speak*
7: 6. God *spake* on this wise,
38. with the angel *which spake* to him
44. *speaking* unto Moses,
8:25. and *preached* the word of the Lord,
26. the angel of the Lord *spake* unto Philip,
9: 6. it *shall be told* thee what thou
27. and that he *had spoken* to him,
29. he *spake* boldly in the name
10: 6. he *shall tell* thee what thou
7. the angel *which spake* unto Cornelius
32. *shall speak* unto thee.
44. *While* Peter yet *spake* these words, the Holy Ghost fell on all
46. For they heard them *speak* with
11:14. Who *shall tell* thee words,
15. as I began *to speak*, the Holy Ghost
19. *preaching* the word to none but
20. *spake* unto the Grecians, preaching
13:42. might *be preached* to them
46. should first *have been spoken*
14: 1. and so *spake*, that a great
9. The same heard Paul *speak:*
25. *when* they *had preached* the word in
16: 6. *to preach* the word in Asia,
13. and *spake* unto the women
14. the things *which were spoken* of Paul.
32. they *spake* unto him the word
17:19. doctrine, whereof thou speakest, (lit. *spoken* by thee)
18: 9. but *speak*, and hold not thy peace:
25. he *spake* and taught diligently
19: 6. they *spake* with tongues, and
20:30. *speaking* perverse things,
21:39. suffer me *to speak* unto the people.
22: 9. the voice of him *that spake* to me.
Acts 22:10. there it *shall be told* thee of
23: 7. And *when* he *had* so *said*, there arose
9. or an angel *hath spoken* to
18. hath something *to say* unto thee.
26:14. I heard a voice *speaking* unto me,
22. and Moses *did say* should come:
26. before whom also I *speak* freely:
31. they *talked* between themselves,
27:25. it shall be even as it *was told* me.
28:21. or *spake* any harm of thee.
25. Well *spake* the Holy Ghost by
Ro. 3:19. it *saith* to them who are under
7: 1. I *speak* to them that know the law,
15:18. I will not dare *to speak* of any
1Co. 2: 6. we *speak* wisdom among them
7. we *speak* the wisdom of God in
13. Which things also we *speak*,
3: 1. I, brethren, could not *speak* unto you as
9: 8. *Say* I these things as a man?
12: 3. no man *speaking* by the Spirit
30. *do* all *speak* with tongues?
13: 1. Though I *speak* with the tongues
11. When I was a child, I *spake* as
14: 2. he *that speaketh* in an (unknown) tongue *speaketh* not unto men,
— in the spirit he *speaketh* mysteries.
3. prophesieth *speaketh* unto men
4. He *that speaketh* in an (unknown)
5. I would that ye all *spake* with
— than he *that speaketh* with tongues,
6. if I come unto you *speaking* with tongues, what shall I profit you, except I *shall speak*
9. how shall it be known *what is spoken?* for ye shall *speak* into the air.
11. I shall be unto him *that speaketh* a barbarian, and he *that speaketh*
13. let him *that speaketh* in an
18. I *speak* with tongues more
19. I had rather *speak* five words
21. *will* I *speak* unto this people;
23. and all *speak* with tongues,
27. If any man *speak* in an
28. *let* him *speak* to himself,
29. *Let* the prophets *speak* two or
34. not permitted unto them *to speak;*
35. a shame for women *to speak* in the
39. and forbid not *to speak* with
2Co. 2:17. *speak* we in Christ.
4:13. and therefore *have* I *spoken;*
— and therefore *speak;*
7:14. as we *spake* all things to you in
11:17. That which I *speak*, I *speak* (it)
23. I *speak* as a fool I (am) more;
12: 4. not lawful for a man *to utter.*
19. we *speak* before God in Christ:
13: 3. a proof of Christ *speaking* in me,
Eph. 4:25. *speak* every man truth
5:19. *Speaking* to yourselves in psalms
6:20. as I ought *to speak.*
Phi. 1:14. more bold *to speak* the word
Col. 4: 3. *to speak* the mystery of Christ,
4. make it manifest, as I ought *to speak.*
1Th. 1: 8. we need not *to speak* any thing.
2: 2. bold in our God *to speak* unto you
4. even so we *speak;*
16. Forbidding us *to speak* to the
1Ti. 5:13. *speaking* things which they ought not.
Tit. 2: 1. But *speak* thou the things
15. These things *speak*, and exhort,
Heb 1: 1. God, *who*...*spake* in time past unto the
2(1). *Hath* in these last days *spoken* unto us

Heb 2: 2. if the word *spoken* by angels
3. began *to be spoken* by the Lord,
5. the world to come, whereof we *speak.*
3: 5. for a testimony of those things *which were to be spoken after ;*
4: 8. would he not afterward *have spoken* of
5: 5. but he *that said* unto him,
6: 9. though we thus *speak.*
7:14. of which tribe Moses *spake* nothing
9:19. when Moses had spoken every precept (lit. every pr. *having been spoken*)
11: 4. being dead yet *speaketh.*
18. Of whom it *was said,* That in Isaac
12:24. *that speaketh* better things than
25. refuse not him *that speaketh.*
13: 7. who *have spoken* unto you
Jas. 1:19. slow *to speak,* slow to wrath:
2:12. So *speak* ye, and so do,
5:10. who *have spoken* in the name
1Pet. 3:10. that they *speak* no guile:
4:11. If any man *speak,* (let him speak) as
2Pet. 1:21. *spake* (as they were) moved
3:16. *speaking* in them of these things;
1Joh. 4: 5. therefore *speak* they of the world,
2Joh. 12. and *speak* face to face,
3Joh. 14. and we *shall speak* face to
Jude 15. which ungodly sinners *have spoken* against
16. mouth *speaketh* great swelling (words),
Rev. 1:12. to see the voice that *spake*
4: 1. of a trumpet *talking* with me;
10: 3. seven thunders *uttered* their voices.
4. thunders *had uttered* their voices,
— which the seven thunders *uttered,*
8. *spake* unto me again,
13: 5. a mouth *speaking* great things
11. he *spake* as a dragon.
15. the image of the beast *should* both *speak,*
17: 1. and *talked* with me,
21: 9. and *talked* with me, saying, Come
15. And he *that talked* with me had

2981 4 465/578 2980

λαλιά, *lalia.*

Mat. 26:73. thy *speech* bewrayeth thee.
Mar 14:70. thy *speech* agreeth (thereto).
Joh. 4:42. not because of thy *saying:*
8:43. Why do ye not understand my *speech?*

2982 2 465/578 [4100]

λαμά or λαμμᾶ, *lama or lamma.*

Mat. 27:46. Eli, Eli, *lama* sabachthani?
Mar 15:34. Eloi, Eloi, *lama* sabachthani?

2983 263 465/578 4:5 cf1209cf138

λαμβάνω, *lambano.*

Mat. 5:40. and *take away* thy coat,
7: 8. every one that asketh *receiveth;*
8:17. Himself *took* our infirmities,
10: 8. freely ye *have received,*
38. And he that *taketh* not his cross,
41. *shall receive* a prophet's reward;
— *shall receive* a righteous man's reward.
12:14. and *held* a council against him,
13:20. anon with joy *receiveth* it;
31. which a man *took, and* sowed
33. which a woman *took, and* hid
14:19. and *took* the five loaves,
15:26. It is not meet *to take* the children's bread,
36. And he *took* the seven loaves
Mat. 16: 5. had forgotten *to take* bread.
7. because we *have taken* no bread.
8. ye *have brought* no bread?
9. how many baskets ye *took up?*
10. and how many baskets ye *took up?*
17:24. they *that received* tribute (money) came
25. of whom *do* the kings of the earth *take* custom or tribute?
27. that *take, and* give unto them
19:29. *shall receive* an hundredfold,
20: 7. whatsoever is right, (that) *shall* ye *receive.*
9. they *received* every man a penny.
10. they should have *received* more; and they likewise *received*
11. *when* they *had received* (it), they murmured
21:22. whatsoever ye shall ask in prayer believing, ye *shall receive.*
34. that they might *receive* the fruits
35. husbandmen *took* his servants, *and*
39. And they *caught* him, *and* cast
22:15. and *took* counsel how they
23:14(13). ye *shall receive* the greater damnation.
25: 1. which *took* their lamps, *and* went forth
3. foolish *took* their lamps, *and took* no oil
4. But the wise *took* oil
16. Then he *that had received* the five
18. But he *that had received* one
20. so he *that had received* five
22. He also *that had received* two
24. Then he *which had received* the one
26:26. Jesus *took* bread, and blessed (it), *and*
— *Take,* eat; this is my body.
27. And he *took* the cup, and
52. all they *that take* the sword shall
27: 1. elders of the people *took* counsel
6. chief priests *took* the silver pieces, *and*
7. And they *took* counsel, *and* bought
9. And they *took* the thirty pieces
24. he *took* water, *and* washed (his) hands
30. and *took* the reed, and smote
48. and *took* a spunge, *and*
59. *when* Joseph *had taken* the body,
28:12. and had *taken* counsel, they gave
15. So they *took* the money, *and* did as
Mar 4:16. immediately *receive* it with gladness;
6:41. And *when* he *had taken* the five loaves
7:27. not meet *to take* the children's bread,
8: 6. and he *took* the seven loaves, *and*
14. had forgotten *to take* bread,
9:36. And he *took* a child, *and* set him in
10:30. But he shall *receive* an hundredfold
11:24. believe that ye *receive* (them),
12: 2. that he *might receive* from the husbandmen
3. And they *caught* (him), *and* beat
8. And they *took* him, *and* killed
19. his brother *should take* his wife,
20. the first *took* a wife,
21. And the second *took* her,
22. And the seven *had* her, and left no seed:
40. these *shall receive* greater damnation.
14:22. Jesus *took* bread, *and* blessed,
— *Take,* eat: this is my body.
23. And he *took* the cup, *and* when
15:23. but he *received* (it) not.
Lu. 5: 5. and *have taken* nothing:
26. And they were all amazed, (lit. amazement *took* all)
6: 4. *did take* and eat the shewbread,
7:16. And there *came* a fear *on* all:
9:16. Then he *took* the five loaves
39. And, lo, a spirit *taketh* him,
11:10. every one that asketh *receiveth*

u. 13:19. which a man *took, and* cast into his garden;
21. which a woman *took and* hid
19:12. *to receive* for himself a kingdom,
15. was returned, *having received* the kingdom,
20:21. neither *acceptest* thou the person (of any),
28. that his brother *should take* his wife,
29. the first *took* a wife, *and* died without children.
30. And the second *took* her to wife,
31. And the third *took* her;
47. the same *shall receive* greater damnation.
22:17. and said, *Take* this,
19. And he *took* bread, *and* gave thanks,
24:30. he *took* bread, *and* blessed (it),
43. And he *took* (it), *and* did eat before them.
Joh 1:12. as many as *received* him,
16. have all we *received*,
3:11. and ye *receive* not our witness.
27. A man can *receive* nothing,
32. no man *receiveth* his testimony.
33. He *that hath received* his testimony
4:36. that reapeth *receiveth* wages,
5:34. I *receive* not testimony from man:
41. I *receive* not honour from men.
43. and ye *receive* me not:
— him ye *will receive*.
44. *which receive* honour one of another,
6: 7. that every one of them *may take*
11. And Jesus *took* the loaves;
21. Then they willingly *received* him
7:23. If a man on the sabbath day *receive* circumcision,
39. they that believe on him should *receive*:
10:17. that I *might take* it again.
18. I have power *to take* it again. This commandment *have* I *received*
12: 3. Then *took* Mary a pound of ointment
13. *Took* branches of palm trees,
48. and *receiveth* not my words,
13: 4. and *took* a towel, *and* girded himself.
12. and *had taken* his garments,
20. He *that receiveth* whomsoever I send *receiveth* me; and he *that receiveth* me *receiveth* him that sent me.
30. He then *having received* the sop
14:17. whom the world cannot *receive*,
16:14. for he *shall receive* of mine,
15. he *shall take* of mine,
24. ask, and ye *shall receive*,
17: 8. and they *have received* (them),
18: 3. Judas then, *having received* a band
31. *Take* ye him, and judge him
19: 1. Pilate therefore *took* Jesus, and scourged
6. *Take* ye him, and crucify
23. *took* his garments, and made
27. that disciple *took* her unto
30. When Jesus therefore *had received*
40. Then *took* they the body of Jesus.
20:22. *Receive* ye the Holy Ghost:
21:13. and *taketh* bread, and giveth
Acts 1: 8. But ye *shall receive* power,
20. bishoprick let another *take*.
25. That he may *take* part
2:23. ye have *taken, and* by wicked hands
33. and *having received* of the Father
38. ye *shall receive* the gift
3: 3. asked)(an alms.
5. expecting *to receive* something
7:53. Who *have received* the law
8:15. that they *might receive* the Holy Ghost:
17. and they *received* the Holy Ghost.
19. he *may receive* the Holy Ghost.

Acts 9:19. And *when* he *had received* meat,
25. the disciples *took* him by night, *and*
10:43. shall *receive* remission of sins.
47. which *have received* the Holy Ghost
15:14. *to take* out of them a people
16: 3. and *took and* circumcised
24. Who, *having received* such a charge.
17: 9. And *when* they *had taken* security
15. and *receiving* a commandment
19: 2. *Have* ye *received* the Holy Ghost
20:24. which I *have received* of the Lord Jesus,
35. more blessed to give than *to receive*.
24:27. Porcius Festus came into Felix' room (lit. Felix *received* Porcius Festus as his successor)
25:16. and *have* licence to answer
26:10. *having received* authority
18. that they may *receive* forgiveness of sins,
27:35. he *took* bread, *and* gave thanks to God
28:15. thanked God, and *took* courage.
Ro. 1: 5. By whom we *have received* grace and
4:11. And he *received* the sign
5:11. by whom we *have* now *received*
17. much more they *which receive* abundance
7: 8. sin, *taking* occasion by the commandment,
11. For sin, *taking* occasion by
8:15. For ye *have* not *received* the spirit of
— but ye *have received* the Spirit of adoption,
13: 2. *shall receive* to themselves
1Co. 2:12. Now we *have received*, not the spirit of the
3: 8. *shall receive* his own reward
14. he *shall receive* a reward.
4: 7. that thou *didst* not *receive*? now if thou *didst receive* (it), why dost thou glory, as *if* thou *hadst* not *received* (it)?
9:24. but one *receiveth* the prize?
25. to *obtain* a corruptible crown;
10:13. There *hath* no temptation *taken* you
11:23. in which he was betrayed *took* bread:
24. *Take*, eat: this is my body,
14: 5. that the church *may receive* edifying.
2Co.11: 4. (if) ye *receive* another spirit, which ye *have* not *received*,
8. *taking* wages (of them),
20. if a man *take* (of you),
24. five times *received* I forty
12:16. I *caught* you with guile.
Gal. 2: 6. God *accepteth* no man's person:
3: 2. *Received* ye the Spirit by the works
14. that we *might receive* the promise of the
Phi. 2: 7. *and took* (upon him) the form of a servant,
3:12. Not as though I *had* already *attained*,
Col. 4:10. whom ye *received* commandments:
1Ti. 4: 4. *if* it *be received* with thanksgiving:
2Ti. 1: 5. When I call to remembrance the (lit. *taking* remembrance)
Heb 2: 2. *received* a just recompence
3. which at the first began to be spoken (lit. *taking* commencement to be spoken) by the Lord,
4:16. that we *may obtain* mercy,
5: 1. every high priest *taken* from among men
4. no man *taketh* this honour
7: 5. *who receive* the office of the priesthood,
8. men that die *receive* tithes;
9. Levi also, *who receiveth* tithes,
9:15. *might receive* the promise
19. he *took* the blood of calves
10:26. after that we *have received*
11: 8. which he should after *receive* for
11. Sara herself *received* strength
13. not *having received* the promises,

Heb 11:29. which the Egyptians assaying to do (lit. *taking* attempt)
35. Women *received* their dead
36. And others *had* trial of (cruel) mockings
Jas. 1: 7. that he *shall receive* any thing
12. he *shall receive* the crown of
3: 1. we *shall receive* the greater condemnation.
4: 3. Ye ask, and *receive* not,
5: 7. until he *receive* the early and latter rain.
10. *Take*, my brethren, the prophets,
1Pet. 4:10. As every man *hath received* the gift,
2Pet. 1: 9. hath forgotten (lit. *having taken* forgetfulness) that he was purged
17. For he *received* from God the Father
1Joh. 2:27. the anointing which ye *have received* of
3:22. whatsoever we ask, we *receive* of him,
5: 9. If we *receive* the witness of men,
2Joh. 4. as we *have received* a commandment
10. *receive* him not into (your) house,
3Joh. 7. *taking* nothing of the Gentiles.
Rev. 2:17. saving he *that receiveth* (it).
27. even as I *received* of my Father.
3: 3. how thou *hast received* and heard,
11. that no man *take* thy crown.
4:11. *to receive* glory and honour and
5: 7. he came and *took* the book
8. when he *had taken* the book,
9. Thou art worthy *to take* the
12. *to receive* power, and riches, and
6: 4. *to take* peace from the earth,
8: 5. the angel *took* the censer,
10: 8. Go (and) *take* the little book
9. *Take* (it), and eat it up;
10. I *took* the little book
11:17. because thou *hast taken to* thee
14: 9. and *receive* (his) mark in
11. *receiveth* the mark of his name.
17:12. which *have received* no kingdom as yet; but *receive* power as kings one hour
18: 4. that ye *receive* not of her plagues.
19:20. them *that had received* the mark
20: 4. neither *had received* (his) mark
22:17. And whosoever will, *let* him *take* the water of life freely.

2982

λαμμᾶ see λαμὰ. p. 445

2985 9 466/581 4:16 2989

λαμπάς, *lampas.*

Mat. 25: 1. which took their *lamps*,
3. that (were) foolish took their *lamps*,
4. the wise took oil in their vessels with their *lamps*.
7. and trimmed their *lamps*.
8. for our *lamps* are gone out.
Joh. 18: 3. with lanterns and *torches* and
Acts 20: 8. And there were many *lights*
Rev. 4: 5. and (there were) seven *lamps* of fire
8:10. star from heaven, burning as it were a *lamp*,

2986 9 467/581 4:16 2985

λαμπρός, *lampros.*

Lu. 23:11. arrayed him in a *gorgeous* robe,
Acts 10:30. stood before me in *bright* clothing,
Jas. 2: 2. if there come...in *goodly* apparel,
3. that weareth the *gay* clothing.
Rev. 15: 6. clothed in pure and *white* linen,
18:14. all things which were dainty and *goodly* are departed
19: 8. in fine linen, clean and *white*:
22: 1. river of water of life, *clear* as crystal,
16. the *bright* and morning star.

2987 1 467/581 2896

λαμπρότης, *lamprotees.*

Acts 26:13. light from heaven, above the *brightness* of the sun,

2988 1 467/581 2986

λαμπρῶς, *lamprōs.*

Lu. 16:19. and fared *sumptuously* every day:

2989 7 467/581 4:16

λάμπω, *lampo.*

Mat. 5:15. and it *giveth light* unto all that are
16. *Let* your light so *shine* before men,
17: 2. and his face *did shine* as the sun,
Lu. 17:24. *shineth* unto the other (part)
Acts 12: 7. a light *shined* in the prison:
2Co. 4: 6. God, who commanded the light *to shine* out of darkness, *hath shined* in our

2990 6 467/582

λανθάνω, *lanthano.*

Mar 7:24. but he could not *be hid.*
Lu. 8:47. saw that she *was* not *hid*,
Acts 26:26. that none of these things *are hidden*
Heb 13: 2. some *have* entertained angels *unawares*.
2Pet. 3: 5. this they willingly are ignorant of, (lit. this *escapes* them willing)
8. be not ignorant of this one thing, (lit. let not this one thing *escape* you)

2991 1 467/582 *las* (stone), rt 3584

λαξευτός, *laxūtos.*

Lu. 23:53. in a sepulchre that was *hewn in stone*,

2992 143 467/582 4:29 cf 1218

λαός, *laos.*

[a] Denotes where the word is used in the plural: *peoples.*

Mat. 1:21. shall save his *people* from their sins.
2: 4. and scribes of the *people* together,
6. shall rule my *people* Israel.
4:16. The *people* which sat in darkness
23. of disease among the *people*.
9:35. every disease among the *people*.
13:15. For this *people's* heart is waxed
15: 8. This *people* draweth nigh unto me
21:23. and the elders of the *people* came
26: 3. and the elders of the *people*,
5. be an uproar among the *people*.
47. the chief priests and elders of the *people*.
27: 1. and elders of the *people* took counsel
25. Then answered all the *people*,
64. steal him away, and say unto the *people*,
Mar 7: 6. This *people* honoureth me with (their)
11:32. they feared the *people*:
14: 2. be an uproar of the *people*.
Lu. 1:10. And the whole multitude of the *people*
17. to make ready a *people* prepared
21. And the *people* waited for Zacharias.

Lu. 1:68. visited and redeemed his *people*,
77. of salvation unto his *people*
2:10. which shall be to all *people*.
31. before the face of all *people*;[2]
32. the glory of thy *people* Israel.
3:15. And as the *people* were in expectation,
18. preached he unto the *people*.
21. when all the *people* were baptized,
6:17. a great multitude of *people*
7: 1. in the audience of the *people*,
16. God hath visited his *people*.
29. And all the *people* that heard
8:47. before all the *people*
9:13. and buy meat for all this *people*.
18:43. and all the *people*, when they saw
19:47. the chief of the *people* sought to
48. all the *people* were very attentive
20: 1. as he taught the *people* in the
6. all the *people* will stone us:
9. speak to the *people* this
19. they feared the *people*:
26. of his words before the *people*:
45. in the audience of all the *people*
21:23. and wrath upon this *people*.
38. all the *people* came early
22: 2. for they feared the *people*.
66. the elders of the *people* and
23: 5. He stirreth up the *people*,
13. and the rulers and the *people*,
14. as one that perverteth the *people*:
27. a great company of *people*,
35. And the *people* stood beholding.
24:19. before God and all the *people*:
Joh. 8: 2. and all the *people* came unto him;
11:50. that one man should die for the *people*,
18:14. that one man should die for the *people*.
Acts 2:47. favour with all the *people*.
3: 9. all the *people* saw him walking
11. all the *people* ran together
12. he answered unto the *people*,
23. destroyed from among the *people*.
4: 1. as they spake unto the *people*,
2. grieved that they taught the *people*,
8. Ye rulers of the *people*,
10. and to all the *people* of Israel,
17. spread no further among the *people*,
21. because of the *people*:
25. and the *people*[2] imagine vain
27. and the *people*[2] of Israel,
5:12. wonders wrought among the *people*;
13. but the *people* magnified them.
20. speak in the temple to the *people*
25. and teaching the *people*.
26. for they feared the *people*,
34. in reputation among all the *people*,
37. and drew away much *people*
6: 8. and miracles among the *people*.
12. And they stirred up the *people*,
7:17. the *people* grew and multiplied
34. the affliction of my *people*
10: 2. gave much alms to the *people*,
41. Not to all the *people*, but
42. to preach unto the *people*,
12: 4. to bring him forth to the *people*.
11. the expectation of the *people* of
13:15. exhortation for the *people*,
17. The God of this *people* of Israel
— and exalted the *people*
24. repentance to all the *people* of
31. his witnesses unto the *people*.
15:14. out of them a *people* for his
18:10. I have much *people* in this city.

Acts19: 4. saying unto the *people*,
21:28. against the *people*, and the law,
30. the *people* ran together:
36. the multitude of the *people*
39. suffer me to speak unto the *people*.
40. with the hand unto the *people*.
23: 5. evil of the ruler of thy *people*.
26:17. Delivering thee from the *people*,
23. should shew light unto the *people*,
28:17. nothing against the *people*,
26. Go unto this *people*, and say,
27. For the heart of this *people*
Ro. 9:25. I will call them my *people*, which were not my *people*;
26. Ye (are) not my *people*; there shall they be called the children of
10:21. and gainsaying *people*.
11: 1. Hath God cast away his *people*?
2. God hath not cast away his *people*
15:10. Rejoice, ye Gentiles, with his *people*
11. and laud him, all ye *people*[2].
1Co.10: 7. The *people* sat down to eat and
14:21. will I speak unto this *people*;
2Co. 6:16. and they shall be my *people*.
Tit. 2:14. a peculiar *people*, zealous
Heb. 2:17. for the sins of the *people*.
4: 9. a rest to the *people* of God.
5: 3. as for the *people*, so also
7: 5. to take tithes of the *people*
11. under it the *people* received
27. and then for the *people's*:
8:10. and they shall be to me a *people*
9: 7. and (for) the errors of the *people*:
19. every precept to all the *people*
— the book, and all the *people*,
10:30. The Lord shall judge his *people*.
11:25. affliction with the *people* of God,
13:12. might sanctify the *people*
1Pet.2: 9. an holy nation, a peculiar *people*;
10. (were) not a *people*, but (are) now the *people* of God:
2Pet.2: 1. false prophets also among the *people*,
Jude 5. having saved the *people*
Rev. 5: 9. and *people*, and nation;
7: 9. and *people*[2], and tongues,
10:11. prophesy again before many *peoples*
11: 9. And they of the *people*[2] and kindreds
14: 6. and tongue, and *people*,
17:15. the whore sitteth, are *peoples*[2],
18: 4. Come out of her, my *people*,
21: 3. they shall be his *people*[2], and God himself shall be with them,

2995 1 468/584 4:57

λάρυγξ, *larunx.*

Ro. 3:13. Their *throat* (is) an open sepulchre;

2998 2 468/584 2991,rt 5114

λατομέω, *latomeo.*

Mat.27:60. in his own new tomb, which he *had hewn* out in the rock:
Mar 15:46. sepulchre *which was hewn* out of a rock,

2999 5 468/584 4:58 3000

λατρεία, *latrīa.*

Joh.16: 2. will think that he doeth God *service*.
Ro. 9: 4. and the *service* (of God), and the promises;
12: 1. (which is) your reasonable *service*.

2997. p. 443

Heb. 9: 1: ordinances of *divine service*,
6. accomplishing the *service* (of God).

3000 21 468/584 4:58 *latris* (menial servant)

λατρεύω, *latrūo.*

Mat. 4:10. and him only *shalt* thou *serve*.
Lu. 1:74. might *serve* him without fear,
2:37. *but served* (God) with fastings
4: 8. and him only *shalt* thou *serve*.
Acts 7: 7. shall they come forth, and *serve* me in this
42. gave them up *to worship* the host of heaven;
24:14. so *worship* I the God of my fathers,
26: 7. instantly *serving* (God) day and night,
27:23. and whom I *serve*,
Ro. 1. 9. whom I *serve* with my spirit
25. and *served* the creature more
Phi. 3: 3. *which worship* God in the spirit,
2Ti. 1: 3. I thank God, whom I *serve* from
Heb. 8: 5. Who *serve* unto the example
9: 9. not make him *that did the service* perfect,
14. *to serve* the living God?
10: 2. the *worshippers* once purged
12:28. we *may serve* God acceptably
13:10. *which serve* the tabernacle.
Rev. 7:15. and *serve* him day and night
22: 3. and his servants *shall serve* him:

3001 4 468/584 4:65 *lachainō* (to dig)

λάχανον, *lakanon.*

Mat.13:32. the greatest among *herbs*,
Mar. 4:32. greater than all *herbs*,
Lu. 11:42. mint and rue and all manner of *herbs*,
Ro. 14: 2. another, who is weak, eateth *herbs*.

3003 4 469/584 4:68

λεγεών, *legeōn.*

Mat.26:53. give me more than twelve *legions* of
Mar 5: 9. My name (is) *Legion*: for we are many.
15. and had the *legion*, sitting,
Lu. 8:30. And he said, *Legion*: because many

3004 1343 469/584 4:69 cf 2036 cf5346, cf2980, cf4483

λέγω, *lego.*

Mat. 1:16. Jesus, *who is called* Christ.
20. in a dream, *saying*, Joseph,
22. by the prophet, *saying*,
2: 2. *Saying*, Where is he that is born
13. in a dream, *saying*, Arise, and
15. *saying*, Out of Egypt have I
17. by Jeremy the prophet, *saying*,
20. *Saying*, Arise, and take the young
23. dwelt in a city *called* Nazareth:
3: 2. And *saying*, Repent ye:
3. *saying*, The voice of one crying
9. think not *to say* within yourselves,
— for I *say* unto you, that God is able
14. John forbad him, *saying*,
17. a voice from heaven, *saying*,
4: 6. And *saith* unto him, If thou be
9. *saith* unto him, All these things will I
10. Then *saith* Jesus unto him
14. by Esaias the prophet, *saying*,
17. and *to say*, Repent: for the
18. Simon *called* Peter, and Andrew
19. And he *saith* unto them,
5:2. and taught them, *saying*
18. verily I *say* unto you,

Mat. 5:20. For I *say* unto you,
22. But I *say* unto you,
26. Verily I *say* unto thee,
28. But I *say* unto you, That whosoever
32. But I *say* unto you, That whosoever shall
34. But I *say* unto you, Swear not at all;
39. But I *say* unto you, That ye resist no
44. But I *say* unto you, Love your enemies.
6: 2. Verily I *say* unto you, They have
5. Verily I *say* unto you, They have their
16. I *say* unto you, They have their reward
25. Therefore I *say* unto you,
29. And yet I *say* unto you,
31. take no thought, *saying*,
7:21. Not every one *that saith* unto me,
8: 2. and worshipped him, *saying*,
3. and touched him, *saying*, I will;
4. And Jesus *saith* unto him,
6. And *saying*, Lord, my servant
7. Jesus *saith* unto him,
9. I *say* to this (man), Go, and he goeth;
10. Verily I *say* unto you,
11. And I *say* unto you,
17. *saying*, Himself took our
20. Jesus *saith* unto him,
25. *saying*, Lord, save us:
26. And he *saith* unto them,
27. *saying*, What manner of man is this,
29. they cried out, *saying*,
31. devils besought him, *saying*,
9: 6. then *saith* he to the sick of
9. a man, *named* Matthew, sitting at the receipt of custom: and he *saith* unto
14. the disciples of John, *saying*,
18. and worshipped him, *saying*,
21. For she *said* within herself,
24(23). He *said* unto them,
27. and *saying*, (Thou) son of David,
28. and Jesus *saith* unto them,
— They *said* unto him, Yea, Lord.
29. Then touched he their eyes, *saying*,
30. *saying*, See (that) no man know (it)
33. multitudes marvelled, *saying*,
34. But the Pharisees *said*,
37. Then *saith* he unto his disciples,
10: 2. Simon, *who is called* Peter,
5. and commanded them, *saying*,
7. And as ye go, preach, *saying*,
15. Verily I *say* unto you,
23. for verily I *say* unto you,
27. What I *tell* you in darkness.
42. verily I *say* unto you,
11: 7. Jesus began *to say*
9. yea, I *say* unto you,
11. Verily I *say* unto you,
17. And *saying*, We have piped
18. and they *say*, He hath a devil.
19. and they *say*, Behold a man
22. But I *say* unto you, It shall be more tole rable for Tyre
24. But I *say* unto you, That it shall be
12: 6. But I *say* unto you, That in this place is
10. And they asked him, *saying*,
13. Then *saith* he to the man,
17. by Esaias the prophet, *saying*,
23. and *said*, Is not this the son
31. Wherefore I *say* unto you,
36. But I *say* unto you,
38. *saying*, Master, we would see
44. Then he *saith*, I will return
13: 3. *saying*, Behold, a sower
14. the prophecy of Esaias, *which saith*,

Mat.13: 17. For verily I *say* unto you,
24. *saying*, The kingdom of heaven
31. put he forth unto them, *saying*, The
35. by the prophet, *saying*,
36. came unto him, *saying*,
51. Jesus *saith* unto them,
— They *say* unto him, Yea,
54. that they were astonished, and *said*,
55. *is* not his mother *called* Mary?
14: 4. For John *said* unto him.
15. came to him, *saying*,
17. And they *say* unto him,
26. *saying*, It is a spirit;
27. *saying*, Be of good cheer;
30. *saying*, Lord, save me.
31. and *said* unto him,
33. worshipped him, *saying*,
15: 1. which were of Jerusalem, *saying*,
4. God commanded, *saying*,
5. But ye *say*, Whosoever shall
7. well did Esaias prophesy of you, *saying*,
22. *saying*, Have mercy on me,
23. *saying*, Send her away;
25. *saying*, Lord, help me.
33. And his disciples *say* unto him,
34. And Jesus *saith* unto them,
16: 2. When it is evening, ye *say*,
7. *saying*, (It is) because we have
13. asked his disciples, *saying*,
— Whom do men *say* that I
15. He *saith* unto them, But whom *say* ye that I am?
18. And I *say* also unto thee,
22. began to rebuke him, *saying*,
28. Verily I *say* unto you,
17: 5. a voice out of the cloud, *which said*, This is my beloved
9. Jesus charged them, *saying*,
10. his disciples asked him, *saying*, Why then *say* the scribes
12. But I *say* unto you,
14. kneeling down to him, and *saying*,
20. verily I *say* unto you,
25. He *saith*, Yes.
— Jesus prevented him, *saying*,
26. Peter *saith* unto him, Of strangers.
18. 1. *saying*, Who is the greatest
3. Verily I *say* unto you,
10. for I *say* unto you,
13. verily I *say* unto you, he rejoiceth more
18. Verily I *say* unto you, Whatsoever ye
19. Again I *say* unto you, That if two
22. Jesus *saith* unto him, I *say* not unto thee,
26. *saying*, Lord, have patience
28. *saying*, Pay me that thou owest.
29. *saying*, Have patience with
32. *said* unto him, O thou wicked servant,
19: 3. and *saying* unto him,
7. They *say* unto him,
8. He *saith* unto them,
9. And I *say* unto you,
10. His disciples *say* unto him,
17. Why *callest* thou me good?
18. He *saith* unto him,
20. The young man *saith* unto him,
23. Verily I *say* unto you,
24. And again I *say* unto you,
25. *saying*, Who then can be saved?
28. Verily I *say* unto you,
20: 6. and *saith* unto them,
7. They *say* unto him, Because no man hath hired us. He *saith* unto them,
Mat.20: 8. *saith* unto his steward,
12. *Saying*, These last have wrought
21. She *saith* unto him,
22. They *say* unto him, We are able.
23. And he *saith* unto them,
30. *saying*, Have mercy on us,
31. but they cried the more, *saying*, Have mercy on us,
33. They *say* unto him, Lord,
21: 2. *Saying* unto them, Go into
4. by the prophet, *saying*,
9. *saying*, Hosanna to the son
10. the city was moved, *saying*, Who is this?
11. the multitude *said*, This is Jesus
13. And *said* unto them, It is written,
15. and *saying*, Hosanna to the son
16. Hearest thou what these *say*? And Jesus *saith* unto them, Yea;
19. and *said* unto it, Let no fruit
20. they marvelled, *saying*, How soon
21. Verily I *say* unto you,
23. *and said*, By what authority
25. *saying*, If we shall say,
27. Neither *tell* I you by what
31. They *say* unto him, The first. Jesus *saith* unto them, Verily I *say* unto you, That the publicans
37. *saying*, They will reverence my son.
41. They *say* unto him,
42. Jesus *saith* unto them,
43. Therefore *say* I unto you,
45. that he *spake* of them.
22: 1. again by parables, *and said*,
4. *saying*, Tell them which are
8. Then *saith* he to his servants,
12. And he *saith* unto him,
16. *saying*, Master, we know that
20. And he *saith* unto them,
21. They *say* unto him, Cæsar's. Then *saith* he unto them,
23. which *say* that there is no resurrection,
24. *Saying*, Master, Moses said,
31. spoken unto you by God, *saying*,
35. tempting him, and *saying*,
42(41). *Saying*, What think ye of Christ? whose son is he? They *say* unto him, (The son) of David.
43. He *saith* unto them, How then doth David in spirit call him Lord, *saying*,
23: 2. *Saying*, The scribes and the Pharisees sit
3. for they *say*, and do not.
16. (ye) blind guides, which *say*,
30. And *say*, If we had been
36. Verily I *say* unto you, All these
39. For I *say* unto you, Ye shall not see me
24: 2. verily I *say* unto you, There shall not
3. *saying*, Tell us, when shall
5. *saying*, I am Christ;
34. Verily I *say* unto you, This generation
47. Verily I *say* unto you, That he shall make
25: 9. the wise answered, *saying*,
11. *saying*, Lord, Lord, open to us.
12. Verily I *say* unto you,
20. *saying*, Lord, thou deliveredst
37. answer him, *saying*, Lord,
40. Verily I *say* unto you,
44. *saying*, Lord, when saw we
45. *saying*, Verily I *say* unto you, Inasmuch
26: 3. high priest, *who was called* Caiaphas,
5. But they *said*, Not on the
8. *saying*, To what purpose (is)
13. Verily I *say* unto you,

Mat.26:14. Then one of the twelve, *called* Judas
17. *saying* unto him, Where wilt
18. The Master *saith*, My time is
21. Verily I *say* unto you,
22. every one of them *to say* unto him,
25. He *said* unto him, Thou hast said.
27. *saying*, Drink ye all of it;
29. But I *say* unto you,
31. Then *saith* Jesus unto them,
34. Verily I *say* unto thee,
35. Peter *said* unto him,
36. unto a place *called* Gethsemane, and *saith* unto the disciples,
38. Then *saith* he unto them,
39. and prayed, *saying*, O my Father,
40. and *saith* unto Peter, What,
42. and prayed, *saying*, O my Father,
45. and *saith* unto them, Sleep on now,
48. *saying*, Whomsoever I shall kiss,
52. Then *said* Jesus unto him,
64. Jesus *saith* unto him, Thou hast said: nevertheless I *say* unto you,
65. *saying*, He hath spoken blasphemy;
68. *Saying*, Prophesy unto us,
69. *saying*, Thou also wast with Jesus
70. *saying*, I know not what thou *sayest*.
71. another (maid) saw him, and *said*
27: 4. *Saying*, I have sinned
9. Jeremy the prophet, *saying*,
11. *saying*, Art thou the King of the Jews? And Jesus said unto him, Thou *sayest*.
13. Then *said* Pilate unto him,
16. prisoner, *called* Barabbas.
17. or Jesus *which is called* Christ?
19. his wife sent unto him, *saying*,
22. Pilate *saith* unto them, What shall I do then with Jesus *which is called* Christ? (They) all *say* unto him, Let
23. *saying*, Let him be crucified.
24. *saying*, I am innocent of the blood
29. *saying*, Hail, king of the Jews!
33. unto a place *called* Golgotha, that is to *say*, a place of a skull,
40. And *saying*, Thou that destroyest
41. with the scribes and elders, *said*,
46. *saying*, Eli, Eli, lama sabachthani?
47. when they heard (that), *said*,
49. The rest *said*, Let be,
54. *saying*, Truly this was the Son of God.
63. *Saying*, Sir, we remember that
28: 9. behold, Jesus met them, *saying*,
10. Then *said* Jesus unto them,
13. *saying*, Say ye, His disciples
18. *saying*, All power is given unto me
Mar 1: 7. And preached, *saying*, There cometh
15. And *saying*, The time is fulfilled,
24. *Saying*, Let (us) alone;
25. Jesus rebuked him, *saying*,
27. *saying*, What thing is this?
30. and anon they *tell* him of her.
37. they *said* unto him,
38. And he *said* unto them,
40. and *saying* unto him, If thou wilt,
41. and *saith* unto him, I will;
44. And *saith* unto him,
2: 5. he *said* unto the sick of the
10. he *saith* to the sick
11. I *say* unto thee, Arise,
12. *saying*, We never saw it on this
14. and *said* unto him, Follow me.
16. they *said* unto his disciples,
17. he *saith* unto them,

Mar 2:18. they come and *say* unto him,
24. the Pharisees *said* unto him,
25. And he *said* unto them,
27. And he *said* unto them,
3: 3. he *saith* unto the man which
4. And he *saith* unto them,
5. he *saith* unto the man,
11. *saying*, Thou art the Son of God.
21. they *said*, He is beside himself.
22. *said*, He hath Beelzebub,
23. and *said* unto them in parables,
28. Verily I *say* unto you,
30. Because they *said*, He hath an
33. he answered them, *saying*, Who is my
34. and *said*, Behold my mother and
4: 2. and *said* unto them in his doctrine,
9. And he *said* unto them, He that
11. he *said* unto them, Unto you it is given
13. he *said* unto them, Know ye not this
21. he *said* unto them, Is a candle
24. And he *said* unto them,
26. And he *said*, So is the kingdom
30. And he *said*, Whereunto shall
35. he *saith* unto them, Let us pass over
38. and *say* unto him, Master,
41. and *said* one to another,
5: 8. For he *said* unto him, Come out
9. *saying*, My name (is) Legion:
12. *saying*, Send us into the swine,
19. but *saith* unto him, Go home
23. *saying*, My little daughter
28. For she *said*, If I may touch
30. and *said*, Who touched my
31. disciples *said* unto him,
— and *sayest* thou, Who touched me?
35. *which said*, Thy daughter is dead:
36. he *saith* unto the ruler
39. he *saith* unto them,
41. and *said* unto her,
— Damsel, I *say* unto thee, arise.
6: 2. *saying*, From whence hath this (man)
4. But Jesus *said* unto them,
10. And he *said* unto them,
11. Verily I *say* unto you,
14. and he *said*, That John the Baptist
15. Others *said*, That it is Elias. And others *said*, That it is a prophet, or
18. For John *had said* unto Herod,
25. *saying*, I will that thou give me
35. and *said*, This is a desert place,
37. And they *say* unto him,
38. He *saith* unto them, How many
— they *say*, Five, and two fishes.
50. and *saith* unto them,
7: 9. he *said* unto them, Full well ye reject
11. But ye *say*, If a man shall say
14. he *said* unto them, Hearken
18. And he *saith* unto them,
20. And he *said*, That which cometh out of the man,
28. she answered and *said* unto him
34. and *saith* unto him, Ephphatha,
37. *saying*, He hath done all things well;
8: 1. and *saith* unto them,
12. and *saith*, Why doth this generation seek after a sign? verily I *say*
15. he charged them, *saying*,
16. *saying*, (It is) because we have no
17. he *saith* unto them,
19. They *say* unto him, Twelve.
21. And he *said* unto them,
24. and *said*, I see men as trees,

G G 2

Mar 8:26. *saying*, Neither go into the town,
27. *saying* unto them, Whom do men *say* that I am?
29. And he *saith* unto them, But whom *say* ye that I am? And Peter answereth and *saith* unto him,
30. that they *should tell* no man
33. he rebuked Peter, *saying*,
9: 1. And he *said* unto them, Verily I *say* unto you, That there be some
5. and *said* to Jesus, Master, it is good
7. *saying*, This is my beloved Son:
11. *saying*, Why *say* the scribes that Elias must first come?
13. But I *say* unto you, That Elias is
19. and *saith*, O faithless generation,
24. and *said* with tears, Lord, I believe; help thou mine unbelief.
25. *saying* unto him, (Thou) dumb and
26. that many *said*, He is dead.
31. and *said* unto them,
35. and *saith* unto them,
38. John answered him, *saying*,
41. verily I *say* unto you,
10:11. And he *saith* unto them,
15. Verily I *say* unto you,
18. Why *callest* thou me good?
23. and *saith* unto his disciples,
24. and *saith* unto them,
26. *saying* among themselves,
27. Jesus looking upon them *saith*,
28. Peter began *to say* unto him,
29. Verily I *say* unto you,
32. and began *to tell* them
35. *saying*, Master, we would
42. and *saith* unto them,
47. and *say*, Jesus, (thou) son of David,
49. *saying* unto him, Be of good comfort, rise; he calleth thee.
51. Jesus answered and *said* unto him,
11: 2. And *saith* unto them, Go your way
5. of them that stood there *said*
9. that followed, cried, *saying*, Hosanna;
17. he taught, *saying* unto them,
21. *saith* unto him; Master,
22. *saith* unto them, Have faith
23. verily I *say* unto you,
— those things which he *saith* shall come
24. Therefore I *say* unto you,
28. And *say* unto him, By what
31. *saying*, If we shall say,
33. and *said* unto Jesus,
— *saith* unto them, Neither do I *tell* you by what authority I
12: 1. And he began *to speak* unto them
6. *saying*, They will reverence my son.
14. they *say* unto him, Master,
16. And he *saith* unto them,
18. which *say* there is no resurrection; and they asked him, *saying*,
26. *saying*, I (am) the God of Abraham,
35. Jesus answered and *said*,
— How *say* the scribes that
37. David therefore himself *calleth* him Lord;
38. And he *said* unto them
43. and *saith* unto them, Verily I *say* unto you, That this poor widow
13: 1. one of his disciples *saith* unto him,
5. began *to say*, Take heed lest
6. *saying*, I am (Christ);
30. Verily I *say* unto you,
37. what I *say* unto you I *say* unto all,

Mar 14: 2. But they *said*, Not on the feast (day),
4. and *said*, Why was this waste
9. Verily I *say* unto you,
12. his disciples *said* unto him,
13. and *saith* unto them,
14. The master *saith*, Where is the
18. Verily I *say* unto you,
19. and *to say* unto him one by one,
25. Verily I *say* unto you,
27. And Jesus *saith* unto them,
30. And Jesus *saith* unto him, Verily I *say* unto thee, That this day,
31. But he *spake* the more
— Likewise also *said* they all.
32. and he *saith* to his disciples,
34. And *saith* unto them, My soul
36. And he *said*, Abba, Father,
37. and *saith* unto Peter,
41. and *saith* unto them,
44. *saying*, Whomsoever I shall kiss,
45. and *saith*, Master, master;
57. false witness against him, *saying*,
58. We heard him *say*,
60. *saying*, Answerest thou nothing?
61. and *said* unto him,
63. and *saith*, What need we
65. and *to say* unto him,
67. she looked upon him, and *said*,
68. But he denied, *saying*, I know not, neither understand I what thou *sayest*.
69. and began *to say* to them
70. they that stood by *said* again
71. I know not this man of whom ye *speak*.
15. 2. said unto him, Thou *sayest* (it).
4. *saying*, Answerest thou nothing?
7. there was (one) *named* Barabbas,
9. Pilate answered them, *saying*,
12. whom ye *call* the King of the Jews?
14. Pilate *said* unto them,
28. scripture was fulfilled, which *saith*,
29. and *saying*, Ah, thou that
31. *said* among themselves with the scribes,
34. *saying*, Eloi, Eloi, lama sabachthani?
35. *said*, Behold, he calleth Elias.
36. *saying*, Let alone; let us see
16: 3. And they *said* among themselves,
6. And he *saith* unto them,
Lu 1:24. and hid herself five months, *saying*,
63. *saying*, His name is John.
66. *saying*, What manner of child
67. and prophesied, *saying*,
2:13. praising God, and *saying*,
3: 4. *saying*, The voice of one crying
7. Then *said* he to the multitude
8. begin not *to say* within yourselves.
— for I *say* unto you,
10. *saying*, What shall we do then?
11. and *saith* unto them,
14. *saying*, And what shall we do?
16. *saying* unto (them) all,
22. a voice came from heaven, *which said*,
4: 4. Jesus answered him, *saying*,
21. he began *to say* unto them,
22. And they *said*, Is not this
24. Verily I *say* unto you,
25. But I *tell* you of a truth,
34. *Saying*, Let (us) alone;
35. rebuked him, *saying*,
36. *saying*, What a word (is) this!
41. crying out, and *saying*,
5: 8. *saying*, Depart from me;
12. besought him, *saying*, Lord,

Lu. 5:21. *saying*, Who is this which
24. I *say* unto thee, Arise,
26. *saying*, We have seen strange
30. *saying*, Why do ye eat and drink
36. And he *spake* also a parable
39. for he *saith*, The old is better.
6: 5. And he *said* unto them,
20. and *said*, Blessed (be ye) poor:
27. But I *say* unto you which hear,
42. how canst thou *say* to thy
46. and do not the things which I *say*?
7: 4. *saying*, That he was worthy
6. *saying* unto him, Lord,
8. and I *say* unto one, Go, and he goeth;
9. I *say* unto you, I have not found
14. I *say* unto thee, Arise.
16. *saying*, That a great prophet
19. *saying*, Art thou he that should
20. hath sent us unto thee, *saying*, Art thou
24. he began *to speak* unto the people
26. Yea, I *say* unto you,
28. For I *say* unto you,
32. *saying*, We have piped unto you,
33. and ye *say*, He hath a devil.
34. and ye *say*, Behold a gluttonous
39. *saying*, This man, if he were
47. Wherefore I *say* unto thee,
49. began *to say* within themselves,
8. 8. *when* he *had said* these things,
9. *saying*, What might this parable be?
20. And it was told him (by certain) *which* *said*,
24. *saying*, Master, master, we perish.
25. *saying* one to another,
30. Jesus asked him, *saying*,
38. but Jesus sent him away, *saying*,
45. and *sayest* thou, Who touched me?
49. *saying* to him, Thy daughter is dead;
50. *saying*, Fear not: believe only,
54. and called, *saying*, Maid, arise.
9: 7. because that it *was said* of some,
18. *saying*, Whom *say* the people
20. But whom *say* ye that I am?
23. And he *said* to (them) all,
27. But I *tell* you of a truth,
31. and *spake* of his decease
33. not knowing what he *said*.
34. *While* he thus *spake*,
35. *saying*, This is my beloved Son:
38. *saying*, Master, I beseech thee,
10: 2. Therefore *said* he unto them,
5. first *say*, Peace (be) to this house.
9. and *say* unto them,
12. But I *say* unto you,
17. *saying*, Lord, even the devils
24. For I *tell* you, that many prophets
25. *saying*, Master, what shall I do
11: 2. When ye pray, *say*, Our Father
8. I *say* unto you, Though he will not
9. I *say* unto you, Ask, and it
18. because ye *say* that I cast out
24. he *saith*, I will return
27. as he *spake* these things,
29. he began *to say*, This is an evil
45. and *said* unto him, Master, thus *saying* thou reproachest us also.
51. verily I *say* unto you,
53. And *as* he *said* these things
12: 1. he began *to say* unto his
4. I *say* unto you my friends,
5. yea, I *say* unto you, Fear him.
8. Also I *say* unto you, Whosoever shall

Lu. 12:16. *saying*, The ground of a certain
17. *saying*, What shall I do,
22. Therefore I *say* unto you,
27. yet I *say* unto you, that Solomon
37. verily I *say* unto you, that he shall gird himself, and
41. *speakest* thou this parable
44. Of a truth I *say* unto you.
51. I *tell* you, Nay; but rather division:
54. And he *said* also to the people,
— straightway ye *say*, There cometh
55. ye *say*, There will be heat;
59. I *tell* thee, thou shalt not depart thence,
13: 3. I *tell* you, Nay: but, except ye repent,
5. I *tell* you, Nay: but, except ye
6. He *spake* also this parable;
8. answering *said* unto him,
14. and *said* unto the people,
17. *when* he *had said* these things,
18. Then *said* he, Unto what is the
24. for many, I *say* unto you,
25. *saying*, Lord, Lord, open unto us;
26. Then shall ye begin *to say*,
27. But he shall say, I *tell* you,
31. *saying* unto him, Get thee out,
35. verily I *say* unto you,
14: 3. *saying*, Is it lawful to heal
7. And he *put forth* a parable
— chief rooms; *saying* unto them,
12. Then *said* he also to him
24. For I *say* unto you, That none of those men which were
30. *Saying*, This man began to
15: 2. *saying*, This man receiveth
3. this parable unto them, *saying*,
6. *saying* unto them, Rejoice with me;
7. I *say* unto you, that likewise joy shall be in heaven over
9. *saying*, Rejoice with me;
10. Likewise, I *say* unto you, there is joy
16: 1. And he *said* also unto his disciples,
5. and *said* unto the first,
7. And he *said* unto him,
9. And I *say* unto you, Make to yourselves
29. Abraham *saith* unto him, They have
17: 4. turn again to thee, *saying*, I repent;
6. ye might *say* unto this sycamine
10. *say*, We are unprofitable
13. *and said*, Jesus, Master,
34. I *tell* you, in that night
37. they answered and *said* unto him,
18: 1. he *spake* a parable
2. *Saying*, There was in a city
3. *saying*, Avenge me of mine adversary.
6. the unjust judge *saith*.
8. I *tell* you that he will avenge
13. *saying*, God be merciful to me
14. I *tell* you, this man went down
17. Verily I *say* unto you,
18. *saying*, Good Master, what shall I do
19. Why *callest* thou me good?
29. Verily I *say* unto you,
34. knew they the things *which were spoken*.
38. And he cried, *saying*, Jesus,
41. *Saying*, What wilt thou
19: 7. they all murmured, *saying*,
14. *saying*, We will not have this (man)
16. *saying*, Lord, thy pound hath
18. the second came, *saying*, Lord, thy pound
20. *saying*, Lord, behold, (here is) thy
22. And he *saith* unto him,
26. For I *say* unto you, That unto every

Lu. 19:38. *Saying*, Blessed (be) the King
40. and said unto them, I *tell* you
42. *Saying*, If thou hadst known,
46. *Saying* unto them, It is written,
20: 2. *saying*, Tell us, by what authority
5. *saying*, If we shall say,
8. Neither *tell* I you by what
9. Then began he *to speak* to the
14. *saying*, This is the heir:
21. *saying*, Master, we know that thou *sayest* and teachest rightly,
28. *Saying*, Master, Moses wrote
37. when he *calleth* the Lord the God of
41. How *say* they that Christ is
42. David himself *saith* in the
21: 3. Of a truth I *say* unto you,
5. *as* some *spake* of the temple,
7. they asked him, *saying*,
8. *saying*, I am (Christ);
10. Then *said* he unto them,
32. Verily I *say* unto you,
22: 1. *which is called* the passover.
11. The Master *saith* unto thee,
16. For I *say* unto you, I will not any more eat thereof,
18. For I *say* unto you, I will not drink
19. *saying*, This is my body
20. *saying*, This cup (is) the new
34. And he said, I *tell* thee, Peter,
37. For I *say* unto you, that this that is
42. *Saying*, Father, if thou be willing,
47. he *that was called* Judas, one of the
57. *saying*, Woman, I know him not
59. *saying*, Of a truth this (fellow)
60. I know not what thou *sayest*.
64. *saying*, Prophesy, who is it that
65. blasphemously *spake* they against
66. led him into their council, *saying*,
70. Ye *say* that I am.
23: 2. began to accuse him, *saying*,
— *saying* that he himself is Christ
3. *saying*, Art thou the King of the
— and said Thou *sayest* (it).
5 *saying*, He stirreth up the people,
18. *saying*, Away with this (man),
21 *saying*, Crucify (him), crucify him.
30 Then shall they begin *to say* to
34. Then *said* Jesus, Father, forgive them;
35. *saying*, He saved others;
37. *saying*, If thou be the king
39. *saying*, If thou be Christ,
40. *saying*, Dost not thou fear God,
42. And he *said* unto Jesus, Lord,
43. Verily I *say* unto thee, To day
47. *saying*, Certainly this was a righteous
24: 7. *Saying*, The Son of man must be
10. which *told* these things unto
23. *saying*, that they had also seen a vision of angels, which *said*
29. *saying*, Abide with us:
34. *Saying*, The Lord is risen indeed,
36. and *saith* unto them,
Joh 1:15. *saying*, This was he of whom I spake,
21. And he *saith*, I am not.
22. What *sayest* thou of thyself?
26. *saying*, I baptize with water:
29. and *saith*, Behold the Lamb of God,
32. And John bare record, *saying*,
36. he *saith*, Behold the Lamb of God!
38. and *saith* unto them,
—(39). Rabbi, which *is to say*,
39(40). He *saith* unto them, Come and see.

Joh. 1:41(42). and *saith* unto him, We have found
43(44). and *saith* unto him, Follow me.
45(46). and *saith* unto him, We have found
46(47). Philip *saith* unto him, Come and see
47(48). and *saith* of him, Behold an Israelite
48(49). Nathanael *saith* unto him,
49(50). Nathanael answered and *saith*
51(52). And he *saith* unto him, Verily, verily, I *say* unto you, Hereafter
2: 3. the mother of Jesus *saith* unto him,
4. Jesus *saith* unto her, Woman,
5. His mother *saith* unto the servants, Whatsoever he *saith* unto
7. Jesus *saith* unto them, Fill
8. And he *saith* unto them,
10. And *saith* unto him,
21. But he *spake* of the temple of
22. that he *had said* this unto them;
3: 3. Verily, verily, I *say* unto thee,
4. Nicodemus *saith* unto him,
5. Verily, verily, I *say* unto thee,
11. I *say* unto thee, We speak that we do
4: 5. to a city of Samaria, *which is called* Sychar
7. Jesus *saith* unto her, Give me
9. Then *saith* the woman
10. and who it is *that saith* to thee,
11. The woman *saith* unto him, Sir,
15. woman *saith* unto him, Sir, give me
16. Jesus *saith* unto her, Go, call
17. Jesus *said* unto her, Thou hast
19. The woman *saith* unto him,
20. and ye *say*, that in Jerusalem
21. Jesus *saith* unto her, Woman,
25. The woman *saith* unto him,
— Messias cometh, *which is called* Christ:
26. Jesus *saith* unto her, I that speak unto thee am (he).
28. and *saith* to the men,
31. *saying*, Master, eat.
33. Therefore *said* the disciples
34. Jesus *saith* unto them,
35. *Say* not ye, There are yet four months,
— behold, I *say* unto you,
42. And *said* unto the woman,
49. The nobleman *saith* unto him,
50. Jesus *saith* unto him,
51. *saying*, Thy son liveth.
5: 6. he *saith* unto him, Wilt thou be
8. Jesus *saith* unto him, Rise,
10. The Jews therefore *said* unto him
18. but *said* also that God was his
19. Verily, verily, I *say* unto you,
24. verily, I *say* unto you, He that heareth
25. verily, I *say* unto you, The hour is
34. but these things I *say*, that
6: 5. he *saith* unto Philip,
6. this he *said* to prove him:
8. Simon Peter's brother, *saith* unto him,
12. he *said* unto his disciples,
14. *said*, This is of a truth that
20. But he *saith* unto them, It is I;
26. Verily, verily, I *say* unto you,
32. verily, I *say* unto you, Moses gave you
42. And they *said*, Is not this Jesus,
— how is it then that he *saith*,
47. Verily, verily, I *say* unto you,
52. *saying*, How can this man give
53. Verily, verily, I *say* unto you,
65. And he *said*, Therefore said I
71. He *spake of* Judas Iscariot
7: 6. Then Jesus *said* unto them,
11. and *said*, Where is he?

Joh. 7:12. some *said*, He is a good man: others *said*, Nay:
15. *saying*, How knoweth this man
25. Then *said* some of them
26. and they *say* nothing unto him.
28. *saying*, Ye both know me, and
31. and *said*, When Christ cometh,
37. *saying*, If any man thirst,
40. *said*, Of a truth this is the prophet.
41. Others *said*, This is the Christ. But some *said*, Shall Christ
50. Nicodemus *saith* unto them,
8: 4. They *say* unto him, Master,
5. but what *sayest* thou?
6. This they *said*, tempting him,
12. *saying*, I am the light of the world:
19. Then *said* they unto him,
22. *said* the Jews, Will he kill himself? because he *saith*,
25. Then *said* they unto him,
26. I *speak* to the world those things which
27. that he *spake* to them of the Father.
31. Then *said* Jesus to those Jews
33. how *sayest* thou, Ye shall be made free?
34. Verily, verily, I *say* unto you,
39. Jesus *saith* unto them,
45. because I *tell* (you) the truth,
46. And if I *say* the truth,
48. *Say* we not well that thou art
51. Verily, verily, I *say* unto you,
52. and thou *sayest*, If a man keep
54. of whom ye *say*, that he is your God:
58. Verily, verily, I *say* unto you,
9: 2. *saying*, Master, who did sin,
8. *said*, Is not this he that sat
9. Some *said*, This is he:
— he *said*, I am (he).
10. Therefore *said* they unto him,
11. A man *that is called* Jesus
12. He *said*, I know not.
16. Therefore *said* some of the Pharisees,
— Others *said*, How can a man
17. They *say* unto the blind man again, What *sayest* thou of him,
19. *saying*, Is this your son, who ye *say* was
41. but now ye *say*, We see;
10: 1. Verily, verily, I *say* unto you,
7. verily, I *say* unto you, I am the door
20. And many of them *said*, He hath
21. Others *said*, These are not the words
24. and *said* unto him, How long dost thou
33. Jews answered him, *saying*,
36. *Say* ye of him, whom the Father
41. and *said*, John did no miracle:
11: 3. *saying*, Lord, behold, he whom
7. Then after that *saith* he to
8. (His) disciples *say* unto him,
11. after that he *saith* unto them,
13. they thought that he had *spoken*
16. Thomas, *which is called* Didymus,
23. Jesus *saith* unto her,
24. Martha *saith* unto him,
27. She *saith* unto him, Yea, Lord.
31. *saying*, She goeth unto the grave
32. *saying* unto him, Lord, if thou
34(35). They *said* unto him, Lord, come and
36. Then *said* the Jews, Behold how he loved
39. Jesus *said*, Take ye away the stone.
— *saith* unto him, Lord, by this time
40. Jesus *saith* unto her, Said I not
44. Jesus *saith* unto them, Loose
47. and *said*, What do we?

Joh. 11:54. into a city *called* Ephraim,
56. and *spake* among themselves,
12: 4. Then *saith* one of his disciples,
21. *saying*, Sir, we would see Jesus.
22. Philip cometh and *telleth* Andrew: and again Andrew and Philip *tell* Jesus.
23. *saying*, The hour is come,
24. Verily, verily, I *say* unto you,
29. *said* that it thundered: others *said*, An angel spake
33. This he *said*, signifying
34. and how *sayest* thou,
13: 6. and Peter *saith* unto him,
8. Peter *saith* unto him,
9. Simon Peter *saith* unto him,
10. Jesus *saith* to him,
13. and ye *say* well; for (so) I am.
16. Verily, verily, I *say* unto you,
18. I *speak* not of you all:
19. Now I *tell* you before it come,
20. Verily, verily, I *say* unto you, He that
21. verily, I *say* unto you, that one of you
22. doubting of whom he *spake*.
24. ask who it should be of whom he *spake*.
25. *saith* unto him, Lord, who is it?
27. Then *said* Jesus unto him,
29. that Jesus had *said* unto him,
31. Jesus *said*, Now is the Son of man
33. so now I *say* to you.
36. Simon Peter *said* unto him,
37. Peter *said* unto him,
38. Verily, verily, I *say* unto thee,
14: 5. Thomas *saith* unto him, Lord,
6. Jesus *saith* unto him, I am the way,
8. Philip *saith* unto him, Lord, shew
9. Jesus *saith* unto him, Have I been
— how *sayest* thou (then), Shew us
12. Verily, verily, I *say* unto you,
22. Judas *saith* unto him,
15: 15. Henceforth I *call* you not servants;
16: 7. Nevertheless I *tell* you the truth;
12. many things *to say* unto you,
17. What is this that he *saith*
18. They *said* therefore, What is this that he *saith*,
20. Verily, verily, I *say* unto you, That ye
23. Verily, verily, I *say* unto you, Whatsoever
26. and I *say* not unto you, that I
29. His disciples *said* unto him, Lo, now speakest thou plainly, and *speakest* no
18: 5. Jesus *saith* unto them, I am (he).
17. Then *saith* the damsel
— He *saith*, I am not.
26. *saith*, Did not I see thee in the
34. *Sayest* thou this thing of thyself,
37. Thou *sayest* that I am a king.
38. Pilate *saith* unto him, What is truth?
— and *saith* unto them, I find in him no fault
40. *saying*, Not this man, but
19: 3. And *said*, Hail, King of the Jews!
4. and *saith* unto them,
5. *saith* unto them, Behold the man!
6. *saying*, Crucify (him), crucify (him). Pilate *saith* unto them,
9. and *saith* unto Jesus, Whence art thou?
10. Then *saith* Pilate unto him,
12. *saying*, If thou let this man go,
13. in a place *that is called* the Pavement,
14. he *saith* unto the Jews, Behold
15. Pilate *saith* unto them, Shall I
17. a place *called* (the place) of a skull, which *is called* in the Hebrew Golgotha:

Joh. 19:21. Then *said* the chief priests
24. which *saith*, They parted my
26. he *saith* unto his mother,
27. Then *saith* he to the disciple, Behold thy
28. scripture might be fulfilled, *saith*, I thirst.
35. he knoweth that he *saith* true,
37. *saith*, They shall look on him
20: 2. and *saith* unto them,
13. they *say* unto her, Woman, why weepest thou? She *saith* unto them,
15. Jesus *saith* unto her, Woman,
— *saith* unto him, Sir, if thou
16. Jesus *saith* unto her, Mary. She turned herself, and *saith* unto him, Rabboni; which *is to say*, Master.
17. Jesus *saith* unto her, Touch me not;
19. and *saith* unto them, Peace
22. and *saith* unto them, Receive ye
24. *called* Didymus, was not with them
25. disciples therefore *said* unto him,
27. Then *saith* he to Thomas,
29. Jesus *saith* unto him,
21: 2. and Thomas *called* Didymus,
3. Simon Peter *saith* unto them, I go a fishing. They *say* unto him, We also
5. Then Jesus *saith* unto them,
7. *saith* unto Peter, It is the Lord.
10. Jesus *saith* unto them, Bring of the fish
12. Jesus *saith* unto them, Come (and) dine.
15. Jesus *saith* to Simon Peter,
— He *saith* unto him, Yea, Lord;
— He *saith* unto him, Feed my lambs.
16. He *saith* to him again the second time,
— He *saith* unto him, Yea, Lord;
— He *saith* unto him, Feed my sheep.
17. He *saith* unto him the third time,
— Jesus *saith* unto him, Feed
18. Verily, verily, I *say* unto thee,
19. he *saith* unto him, Follow me.
21. *saith* to Jesus, Lord, and what
22. Jesus *saith* unto him, If
Acts 1: 3. *speaking* of the things pertaining to
6. *saying*, Lord, wilt thou at this time
2: 7. marvelled, *saying* one to another,
12. were in doubt, *saying* one to another,
13. Others mocking *said*, These men
17. in the last days, *saith* God,
25. For David *speaketh* concerning
34. but he *saith* himself, The Lord said
40. *saying*, Save yourselves from
3: 2. the gate of the temple *which is called* Beautiful,
25. *saying* unto Abraham, And in thy seed
4:16. *Saying*, What shall we do to
32. neither *said* any (of them)
5:23. *Saying*, The prison truly found
25. *saying*, Behold, the men whom
28. *Saying*, Did not we straitly
36. *boasting* himself to be somebody:
38. And now I *say* unto you, Refrain
6: 9. certain of the synagogue, *which is called*
11. they suborned men, *which said*,
13. set up false witnesses, *which said*,
14. For we have heard him *say*,
7:48. as *saith* the prophet,
49. will ye build me? *saith* the Lord:
59. and *saying*, Lord Jesus, receive
8: 6. those things which Philip spake, (lit. *the things spoken* by)
9. *giving out* that himself was some great one.
10. *saying*, This man is the great power of God.
19. *Saying*, Give me also this power,

Acts 8:26. *saying*, Arise, and go toward
34. of whom *speaketh* the prophet
9: 4. a voice *saying* unto him,
21. were amazed, and *said*;
36. by interpretation *is called* Dorcas.
10:26. Peter took him up, *saying*,
28. that I should not *call* any man
11: 3. *Saying*, Thou wentest in to men
4. expounded (it) by order unto them, *saying*,
7. I heard a voice *saying* unto me,
16. how that he *said*, John indeed
18. and glorified God, *saying*,
12: 7. and raised him up, *saying*,
8. And he *saith* unto him, Cast thy
15. Then *said* they, It is his angel.
13:15. *saying*, (Ye) men (and) brethren, if ye have any word of exhortation for the people, *say on*.
25. he *said*, Whom think ye that I am?
35. he *saith* also in another (psalm),
45. against those things *which were spoken* by Paul,
14:11. *saying* in the speech of Lycaonia,
15. And *saying*, Sirs, why do ye
18. And with these sayings (lit. *saying* these things)
15: 5. *saying*, That it was needful
13. James answered, *saying*,
17. *saith* the Lord, who doeth all these
24. *saying*, (Ye must) be circumcised,
16: 9. *saying*, Come over into Macedonia,
15. she besought (us), *saying*,
17. *saying*, These men are the servants
28. *saying*, Do thyself no harm:
35. *saying*, Let those men go.
17: 7. *saying* that there is another king,
18. And some *said*, What will this babbler *say*?
19. *saying*, May we know what this new
21. either *to tell*, or to hear some
18:13. *Saying*, This (fellow) persuadeth
19: 4. *saying* unto the people,
13. *saying*, We adjure you by Jesus
26. *saying* that they be no gods, which are made with hands:
28. *saying*, Great (is) Diana
20:23. *saying* that bonds and afflictions
21: 4. who *said* to Paul through the
11. Thus *saith* the Holy Ghost,
21. *saying* that they ought not to
23. this that we *say* to thee:
37. he *said* unto the chief captain,
40. in the Hebrew tongue, *saying*,
22: 7. and heard a voice *saying*
18. And saw him *saying* unto me,
22. *and said*, Away with such a
26. *saying*, Take heed what thou doest.
27. *Tell* me, art thou a Roman?
23: 8. the Sadducees *say* that there is
9. *saying*, We find no evil in this
12. *saying* that they would neither
30. *to say* before thee what (they had)
24: 2. began to accuse (him), *saying*,
10. beckoned unto him *to speak*,
14. which they *call* heresy,
25:14. Paul's cause unto the king, *saying*,
20. I *asked* (him) whether he would
26: 1. Thou art permitted *to speak*
14. and *saying* in the Hebrew tongue,
22. *saying* none other things than
31. *saying*, This man doeth nothing
27:10. *And said* unto them, Sirs, I perceive
11. than those things *which were spoken* by Paul.

Acts27:24. *Saying*, Fear not, Paul;
33. *saying*, This day is the fourteenth
28: 4. they *said* among themselves,
6. and *said* that he was a god.
17. he *said* unto them, Men (and)
24. believed the things *which were spoken*,
26. *Saying*, Go unto this people,
Ro. 2:22. Thou *that sayest* a man should not
3: 5. I *speak* as a man
8. as some affirm that we *say*,
19. what things soever the law *saith*, it saith
4: 3. For what *saith* the scripture?
6. as David also *describeth*
9. for we *say* that faith
6:19. I *speak* after the manner of men
7: 7. except the law *had said*,
9: 1. I *say* the truth in Christ,
15. For he *saith* to Moses, I will have
17. the scripture *saith* unto Pharaoh,
25. As he *saith* also in Osee, I will
10: 6. of faith *speaketh* on this wise,
8. But what *saith* it? The word is nigh
11. For the scripture *saith*, Whosoever
16. For Esaias *saith*, Lord, who hath
18. But I *say*, Have they not heard?
19. But I *say*, Did not Israel know? First Moses *saith*,
20. But Esaias is very bold, and *saith*,
21. But to Israel he *saith*, All day long
11: 1. I *say* then, Hath God cast away
2. what the scripture *saith* of Elias?
— to God against Israel, *saying*,
4. what *saith* the answer of God
9. And David *saith*, Let their table
11. I *say* then, Have they stumbled that
13. For I *speak* to you Gentiles,
12: 3. For I *say*, through the grace
19. I will repay, *saith* the Lord.
14:11. (As) I live, *saith* the Lord,
15: 8. Now I *say* that Jesus Christ
10. And again he *saith*, Rejoice, ye
12. And again, Esaias *saith*, There shall be
1Co. 1:10. that ye all *speak* the same
12. Now this I *say*, that every one of you *saith*, I am of Paul;
3: 4. For while one *saith*, I am of Paul;
6: 5. I *speak* to your shame.
7: 6. But I *speak* this by permission,
8. I *say* therefore to the unmarried
12. But to the rest *speak* I,
35. And this I *speak* for your
8: 5. there be *that are called* gods,
9: 8. or *saith* not the law the same
10. Or *saith* he (it) altogether for
10:15. I *speak* as to wise men;
29. Conscience, I *say*, not thine own,
11:25. *saying*, This cup is the new testament
12: 3. *calleth* Jesus accursed:
14:16. not what thou *sayest*?
21. will they not hear me, *saith* the Lord.
34. to be under obedience, as also *saith* the
15:12. how *say* some among you
34. I *speak* (this) to your shame.
51. I *shew* you a mystery;
2Co. 6: 2. For he *saith*, I have heard thee
13. I *speak* as unto (my) children,
17. be ye separate, *saith* the Lord,
18. *saith* the Lord Almighty.
7: 3. I *speak* not (this) to condemn
8: 8. I *speak* not by commandment,
9: 3. that, as I *said*, ye may be ready:
4. that we *say* not, ye
2Co.11:16. I *say* again, Let no man think me
21. I *speak* as concerning reproach,
— I *speak* foolishly, I am bold
Gal. 1: 9. so *say* I now again,
3:15. I *speak* after the manner of men;
16. He *saith* not, And to seeds,
17. And this I *say*, (that) the covenant,
4: 1. Now I *say*, (That) the heir,
21. *Tell* me, ye that desire
30. what *saith* the scripture?
5: 2. I Paul *say* unto you,
16. I *say* then, Walk in the Spirit,
Eph 2:11. *who are called* Uncircumcision by that *which is called* the Circumcision
4: 8. Wherefore he *saith*, When he ascended
17. This I *say* therefore, and testify
5:12. even *to speak* of those things
14. Wherefore he *saith*, Awake thou
32. but I *speak* concerning Christ
Phi. 3:18. of whom I *have told* you often, and now *tell* you even weeping,
4:11. Not that I *speak* in respect of
Col. 2: 4. And this I *say*, lest any man should
4:11. Jesus, *which is called* Justus,
1Th. 4:15. For this we *say* unto you by
5: 3. For when they shall *say*, Peace
2Th. 2: 4. above all *that is called* God,
5. I *told* you these things?
1Ti. 1: 7. neither what they *say*, nor
2: 7. I *speak* the truth in Christ,
4: 1. the Spirit *speaketh* expressly,
5:18. For the scripture *saith*, Thou shalt not
2Ti. 2: 7. Consider what I *say*; and the Lord
18. *saying* that the resurrection
Tit. 2: 8. having no evil thing *to say* of you.
Philem.19. albeit I *do* not *say* to thee
21. thou wilt also do more than I *say*.
Heb 1: 6. firstbegotten into the world, he *saith*,
7. of the angels he *saith*,
2: 6. *saying*, What is man,
12. *Saying*, I will declare thy name
3: 7. as the Holy Ghost *saith*,
15. While it *is said*, To day
4: 7. *saying* in David, To day,
5: 6. As he *saith* also in another (place),
11. many things *to say*,
6:14. *Saying*, Surely blessing I will bless
7:11. and not *be called* after the order
13. of whom these things *are spoken*
21. by him *that said* unto him,
8: 1. Now of the *things* which we have *spoken*
8. finding fault with them, he *saith*, Behold, the days come, *saith* the Lord,
9. I regarded them not, *saith* the Lord.
10. of Israel after those days, *saith* the Lord;
11. *saying*, Know the Lord:
13. In that he *saith*, A new (covenant),
9: 2. which *is called* the sanctuary.
3. the tabernacle which *is called* the Holiest
5. we cannot now *speak* particularly.
20. *Saying*, This (is) the blood of
10: 5. he *saith*, Sacrifice and offering
8. Above *when* he *said*, Sacrifice and
16. *saith* the Lord, I will put my laws
30. I will recompense, *saith* the Lord.
11:14. For they *that say* such things
24. refused *to be called* the son
32. what shall I more *say*?
12:26. *saying*, Yet once more
13: 6. So that we may boldly *say*,
Jas. 1:13. *Let* no man *say* when he is
2:14. though a man *say* he hath faith,

Jas. 2:23. was fulfilled *which saith,*
4: 5. that the scripture *saith* in vain,
6. Wherefore he *saith,* God resisteth the
13. Go to now, ye *that say,*
15. For that ye (ought) *to say,*
2Pet.3: 4. And *saying,* Where is the promise
1Joh.2: 4. He *that saith,* I know him,
6. He *that saith* he abideth in him
9. He *that saith* he is in the light,
5:16. I *do* not *say* that he shall pray for it.
2Joh. 10. neither *bid* him God speed:
11. For he *that biddeth* him God
Jude 14. *saying,* Behold, the Lord cometh
18. How that they *told* you
Rev. 1: 8. *saith* the Lord, which is, and which was,
11. *Saying,* I am Alpha and Omega,
17. *saying* unto me, Fear not;
2: 1. These things *saith* he that holdeth
7. let him hear what the Spirit *saith*
8. These things *saith* the first and the last,
9. *which say* they are Jews,
11. let him hear what the Spirit *saith*
12. These things *saith* he which
17. let him hear what the Spirit *saith*
18. These things *saith* the Son of God,
20. *which calleth* herself a prophetess,
24. But unto you I *say,* and unto the
— depths of Satan, as they *speak;*
29. let him hear what the Spirit *saith*
3: 1. These things *saith* he that
6. let him hear what the Spirit *saith*
7. These things *saith* he that is holy,
9. *which say* they are Jews,
13. let him hear what the Spirit *saith*
14. These things *saith* the Amen,
17. Because thou *sayest,* I am rich,
22. let him hear what the Spirit *saith*
4: 1. *which said,* Come up hither,
8. *saying,* Holy, holy, holy,
10. before the throne, *saying,*
5: 5. one of the elders *saith* unto me,
9. they sung a new song, *saying,*
12. *Saying* with a loud voice,
13. heard I *saying,* Blessing, and
14. And the four beasts *said,* Amen.
6: 1. *saying,* Come and see.
3. the second beast *say,* Come and see.
5. the third beast *say,* Come and see.
6. in the midst of the four beasts *say,*
7. the fourth beast *say,* Come and see.
10. *saying,* How long, O Lord, holy and
16. And *said* to the mountains and
7: 3. *Saying,* Hurt not the earth,
10. *saying,* Salvation to our God
12. *Saying,* Amen: Blessing, and
13. one of the elders answered, *saying*
8:11. the star *is called* Wormwood:
13. *saying* with a loud voice,
9:14. *Saying* to the sixth angel
10: 4. I heard a voice from heaven *saying*
8. and *said,* Go (and) take the
9. *and said* unto him, Give me the little book. And he *said* unto me, Take
11. And he *said* unto me, Thou must
11: 1. *saying,* Rise, and measure the
12. *saying* unto them, Come up hither.
15. *saying,* The kingdoms of this
17. *Saying,* We give thee thanks,
12:10. I heard a loud voice *saying* in
13: 4. *saying,* Who (is) like unto the beast?
14. *saying* to them that dwell on
14: 7. *Saying* with a loud voice,
Rev.14: 8. *saying,* Babylon is fallen,
9. *saying* with a loud voice,
13. *saying* unto me, Write,
— Yea, *saith* the Spirit,
18. *saying,* Thrust in thy sharp
15: 3. the song of the Lamb, *saying,*
16: 1. *saying* to the seven angels,
5. I heard the angel of the waters *say,*
7. I heard another out of the altar *say,*
17. *saying,* It is done.
17: 1. *saying* unto me, Come hither;
15. And he *saith* unto me,
18: 2. *saying,* Babylon the great is
4. *saying,* Come out of her, my
7. for she *saith* in her heart,
10. *saying,* Alas, alas that great city
16. *saying,* Alas, alas that great city,
18. *saying,* What (city is) like
19. *saying,* Alas, alas that great city,
21. and cast (it) into the sea, *saying,*
19: 1. *saying,* Alleluia; Salvation,
4. *saying,* Amen; Alleluia.
5. *saying,* Praise our God,
6. *saying,* Alleluia: for the Lord
9. And he *saith* unto me, Write, Blessed
— And he *saith* unto me, These are the
10. And he *said* unto me, See
17. with a loud voice, *saying* to all the fowls
21: 3. *saying,* Behold, the tabernacle of God
5. And he *said* unto me, Write:
9. *saying,* Come hither, I will shew
22: 9. Then *saith* he unto me, See
10. And he *saith* unto me, Seal not
17. the Spirit and the bride *say,* Come
20. *saith,* Surely I come quickly;

3005 1 471/597 4:194 3007

λεῖμμα, *līmma.*

Ro. 11: 5. there is a *remnant* according to the

3006 1 471/597 4:193

λεῖος, *līos.*

Lu. 3: 5. the rough ways (shall be) made *smooth;*

3007 6 471/597

λείπω, *līpo.*

Lu. 18:22. Yet lackest thou one thing: (lit. one thing *is lacking* to thee)
Tit. 1: 5. the things *that are wanting,*
3:13. that nothing *be wanting* unto them.
Jas. 1: 4. that ye may be perfect and entire, *wanting* nothing.
5. If any of you *lack* wisdom,
2:15. and *destitute* of daily food,

3008 3 471/597 4:215 3011

λειτουργέω, *lītourgeo.*

Acts13. 2. *As* they *ministered* to the Lord,
Ro. 15:27. their duty is also *to minister* unto them in carnal things.
Heb 10:11. every priest standeth daily *ministering*

3009 6 472/597 4:215 3008

λειτουργία, *lītourgia.*

Lu. 1:23. as the days of his *ministration* were
2Co. 9:12. For the administration of this *service*
Phi. 2:17. upon the sacrifice and *service* of your

Phi. 2:30. to supply your lack of *service* toward me.
Heb 8: 6. he obtained a more excellent *ministry*,
9:21. sprinkled with blood...and all the vessels of the *ministry*.

3010 1 472/597 4:215 rt 3008
λειτουργικός, lītourgikos.

Heb 1:14. Are they not all *ministering* spirits,

3011 5 472/597 4:215 2992,2041
λειτουργός, lītourgos.

Ro. 13: 6. they are God's *ministers*, attending
15:16. That I should be the *minister* of
Phi. 2:25. and *he that ministered* to my wants.
Heb 1: 7. and his *ministers* a flame of fire.
8: 2. A *minister* of the sanctuary, and of the true tabernacle,

3012 2 472/597
λέντιον, lention.

Joh. 13: 4. and took a *towel*, and girded himself.
5. to wipe (them) with the *towel* wherewith he was girded.

3013 1 472/597 4:232 *lepō* (to peel)
λεπίς, lepis.

Acts 9:18. fell from his eyes as it had been *scales:*

3014 4 473/597 4:233 rt 3013
λέπρα, lepra.

Mat. 8: 3. his *leprosy* was cleansed.
Mar 1:42. immediately the *leprosy* departed
Lu. 5:12. a man full of *leprosy:*
13. immediately the *leprosy* departed

3015 9 473/598 4:233 rt 3014
λεπρός, lepros.

Mat. 8: 2. And, behold, there came a *leper*
10: 8. cleanse the *lepers*, raise the dead,
11: 5. the *lepers* are cleansed,
26: 6. in the house of Simon the *leper*,
Mar 1:40. there came a *leper* to him,
14: 3. in the house of Simon the *leper*,
Lu. 4:27. many *lepers* were in Israel
7:22. the *lepers* are cleansed,
17:12. ten men that were *lepers*,

3016 3 473/598 rt 3013
λεπτόν, lepton.

Mar 12:42. she threw in two *mites*,
Lu. 12:59. till thou hast paid the very last *mite*.
21: 2. casting in thither two *mites*.

3021 2 473/598 4:241 3022
λευκαίνω, lūkaino.

Mar 9: 3. as no fuller on earth can *white* them.
Rev. 7:14. have washed their robes, and *made* them *white* in the blood of the Lamb.

3022 25 473/598 4:241 *lukē* (light)
λευκός, lūkos.

Mat. 5:36. canst not make one hair *white* or black.
17: 2. his raiment was *white* as the light.
28: 3. and his raiment *white* as snow:
Mar 9: 3. exceeding *white* as snow;
Mar 16: 5. clothed in a long *white* garment;
Lu. 9:29. his raiment (was) *white* (and) glistering.
Joh. 4:35. they are *white* already to harvest.
20:12. And seeth two angels in *white*
Acts 1:10. two men stood by them in *white* apparel;
Rev. 1:14. His head and (his) hairs (were) *white* like wool, as *white* as snow;
2:17. will give him a *white* stone,
3: 4. they shall walk with me in *white*.
5. shall be clothed in *white* raiment;
18. and *white* raiment, that thou mayest be
4: 4. elders sitting, clothed in *white* raiment;
6: 2. behold a *white* horse:
11. And *white* robes were given
7: 9. clothed with *white* robes,
13. which are arrayed in *white* robes?
14:14. and behold a *white* cloud
19:11. and behold a *white* horse;
14. followed him upon *white* horses, clothed in fine linen, *white* and clean.
20:11. I saw a great *white* throne,

3023 9 473/598 4:251
λέων, leōn.

2Ti. 4:17. out of the mouth of the *lion*.
Heb 11:33. stopped the mouths of *lions*,
1Pet. 5: 8. as a roaring *lion*, walketh
Rev. 4: 7. the first beast (was) like a *lion*,
5: 5. the *Lion* of the tribe of Juda,
9: 8. were as (the teeth) of *lions*.
17. as the heads of *lions*;
10: 3. as (when) a *lion* roareth:
13: 2. and his mouth as the mouth of a *lion*:

3024 1 474/598 2990
λήθη, leethee.

2Pet. 1: 9. and hath forgotten (lit. having taken *forgetfulness*) that he was purged from

ληκέω see Λακέω 2977, p. 443

3025 5 474/598 4:254
ληνός, leenos.

Mat. 21:33. and digged a *winepress* in it,
Rev. 14:19. cast (it) into the great *winepress*
20. And the *winepress* was trodden without the city, and blood came out of the *winepress*,
19:15. he treadeth the *winepress* of the fierceness

3026 1 474/598
λῆρος, leeros.

Lu. 24:11. seemed to them as *idle tales*,

3027 15 474/599 4:257 *leizomai* (to plunder)
λῃστής, leestees.

Mat. 21:13. ye have made it a den of *thieves*.
26:55. Are ye come out as against a *thief*
27:38. two *thieves* crucified with him,
44. The *thieves* also, which were crucified
Mar 11:17. ye have made it a den of *thieves*.
14:48. Are ye come out, as against a *thief*,
15:27. with him they crucify two *thieves*;
Lu. 10:30. and fell among *thieves*,
36. that fell among the *thieves*?
19:46. ye have made it a den of *thieves*.
22:52. Be ye come out, as against a *thief*,

Jon.10: 1. the same is a thief and a *robber*.
8. before me are thieves and *robbers:*
18:40. Now Barabbas was a *robber*.
2Co.11:26. (in) perils of *robbers*, (in) perils by

3028 1 474/598 2983

λῆψις, leepsis.

Phi. 4:15. communicated with me as concerning giving and *receiving*,

3029 14 474/599

λίαν, lian.

Mat. 2:16. mocked of the wise men, was *exceeding*
4: 8. an *exceeding* high mountain,
8:28. out of the tombs, *exceeding* fierce,
27:14. the governor marvelled *greatly*.
Mar. 1:35. rising up a *great* while before day,
6:51. they were *sore* amazed
9: 3. *exceeding* white as snow;
16: 2. And *very* early in the morning
Lu. 23: 8. he was *exceeding* glad:
2Co.11: 5. the *very* chiefest apostles.
12:11. behind the *very* chiefest apostles,
2Ti. 4:15. he hath *greatly* withstood our words.
2Joh. 4. I rejoiced *greatly* that I found
3Joh. 3. I rejoiced *greatly*, when the brethren

3030 2 474/599 4:263 [3828]

λίβανος, libanos.

Mat. 2:11. gold, and *frankincense*, and myrrh.
Rev.18:13. *frankincense*, and wine, and oil,

3031 2 474/599 4:263 3030

λιβανωτόν, libanōton.

Rev. 8: 3. at the altar, having a golden *censer*;
5. the angel took the *censer*, and filled it

3034 8 475/599 4:267 3037

λιθάζω, lithazo.

Joh.10:31. Jews took up stones again to *stone* him.
32. of those works *do* ye *stone* me?
33. For a good work we *stone* thee not;
11: 8. of late sought *to stone* thee;
Acts 5:26. lest they *should have been stoned*.
14:19. *having stoned* Paul, drew (him) out
2Co.11:25. once *was* I *stoned*,
Heb 11:37. They *were stoned*, they were sawn asunder,

3035 3 475/599 4:268 3037

λίθινος, lithinos.

Joh. 2: 6. six waterpots *of stone*,
2Co. 3: 3. not in tables *of stone*, but in fleshy
Rev. 9:20. *of* gold, and silver, and brass, and *stone*,

3036 9 475/599 4:267 3037,906

λιθοβολέω, lithoboleo.

Mat.21:35. killed another, and *stoned* another.
23:37. and *stonest* them which are sent
Mar 12: 4. *at* him they *cast stones, and*
Lu. 13:34. and *stonest* them that are
Joh. 8: 5. that such should *be stoned:*
Acts 7:58. cast (him) out of the city, and *stoned* (him):
59. And they *stoned* Stephen.

Acts14: 5. to use (them) despitefully, and *to stone*
Heb 12:20. touch the mountain, it *shall be stoned*,

3037 60 475/599 4:268

λίθος, lithos.

Mat. 3: 9. God is able of these *stones* to
4: 3. command that these *stones* be
6. thou dash thy foot against a *stone*.
7: 9. will he give him a *stone?*
21:42. The *stone* which the builders
44. fall on this *stone* shall be
24: 2. not be left here one *stone* upon another, (lit. *stone* upon *stone*)
27:60. rolled a great *stone* to the
66. sealing the *stone*, and setting a watch.
28: 2. and rolled back the *stone*
Mar. 5: 5. cutting himself with *stones*.
9:42. that a mill*stone* were hanged
12:10. The *stone* which the builders
13: 1. what manner of *stones*
2. shall not be left one *stone* upon another, (lit. *stone* upon *stone*)
15:46. and rolled a *stone*
16: 3. Who shall roll us away the *stone*
4. they saw that the *stone* was
Lu. 3: 8. God is able of these *stones*
4: 3. command this *stone* that it
11. thou dash thy foot against a *stone*.
11:11. will he give him a *stone?*
19:40. the *stones* would immediately cry out.
44. one *stone* upon another; (lit. *stone* upon *stone*)
20:17. The *stone* which the builders
18. shall fall upon that *stone*
21: 5. adorned with goodly *stones*
6. not be left one *stone* upon another, (lit. *stone* upon *stone*)
22:41. about a *stone's* cast,
24: 2. they found the *stone* rolled away
Joh. 8: 7. let him first cast a *stone*
59. Then took they up *stones*
10:31. Jews took up *stones* again
11:38. and a *stone* lay upon it.
39. Take ye away the *stone*.
41. they took away the *stone*
20: 1. and seeth the *stone* taken
Acts 4:11. This is the *stone* which was
17:29. unto gold, or silver, or *stone*,
Ro. 9:32. at that stumbling*stone;*
33. in Sion a stumbling*stone*
1Co. 3:12. gold, silver, precious *stones*,
2Co. 3: 7. engraven in *stones*, was glorious,
1Pet.2: 4. (as unto) a living *stone*,
5. Ye also, as lively *stones*,
6. I lay in Sion a chief corner *stone*,
7. the *stone* which the builders disallowed,
8(7). And a *stone* of stumbling,
Rev. 4: 3. like a jasper and a sardine *stone:*
17: 4. decked with gold and precious *stones*
18:12. and silver, and precious *stones*,
16. gold, and precious *stones*,
21. angel took up a *stone* like
21:11. like unto a *stone* most precious, even like a jasper *stone*, clear as crystal;
19. with all manner of precious *stones*.

3039 2 475/600 4:280 *likmos, liknon* (winnowing fan)

λικμάω, likmao.

Mat.21:44. it *will grind* him *to powder*.
Lu 20:18. it *will grind* him *to powder*.

3040 3 476/600 cf 2568

λιμήν, *limeen.*

Acts27: 8. a place which is called The fair *havens;*
12. because the *haven* was not commodious
— (which is) an *haven* of Crete, and lieth

3041 10 476/600 3040

λίμνη, *limnee.*

Lu. 5: 1. he stood by the *lake* of Gennesaret,
2. two ships standing by the *lake:*
8:22. the other side of the *lake.*
23. a storm of wind on the *lake;*
33. steep place into the *lake,*
Rev.19:20. cast alive into a *lake* of fire
20:10. was cast into the *lake* of fire
14. were cast into the *lake* of fire.
15. was cast into the *lake* of fire.
21: 8. their part in the *lake* which burneth

3042 12 476/600 3007

λιμός, *limos.*

Mat.24: 7. there shall be *famines,* and
Mar 13: 8. and there shall be *famines* and troubles:
Lu. 4:25. when great *famine* was
15:14. arose a mighty *famine*
17. I perish with *hunger!*
21:11. and *famines,* and pestilences;
Acts 7:11. there came a *dearth* over all the land
11:28. there should be great *dearth*
Ro. 8:35. or *famine,* or nakedness,
2Co.11:27. in *hunger* and thirst,
Rev. 6: 8. to kill with sword, and with *hunger,*
18: 8. death, and mourning, and *famine;*

3043 2 476/600

λίνον, *linon.*

Mat.12:20. and smoking *flax* shall he not quench,
Rev.15: 6. clothed in pure and white *linen,*

3045 1 478/601 *lipos* (grease)

λιπαρός, *liparos.*

Rev.18:14. all things which were *dainty* and goodly
are departed from thee,

3046 2 476/601 [libra]

λίτρα, *litra.*

Joh.12: 3. Then took Mary a *pound* of ointment of
19:39. about an hundred *pound* (weight).

3047 1 476/601 *leibō* (to pour)

λίψ, *lips.*

Acts27:12. toward the *south west*

3048 2 476/601 4:282 3056

λογία, *logia.*

1Co.16: 1. Now concerning the *collection* for the
2. that there be no *gatherings* when I come.

3049 41 476/601 4:284 3056

λογίζομαι, *logizomai.*

Mar 11:31. they *reasoned* with themselves,
15:28. he *was numbered* with the
Lu. 22:37. he *was reckoned* among the
Acts19:27. Diana should be despised, (lit. should *be counted* for nothing)
Ro. 2: 3. And *thinkest* thou this, O man,
26. *shall* not his uncircumcision *be counted for* circumcision?
3:28. Therefore we *conclude* that
4: 3. it *was counted* unto him for righteousness.
4. *is* the reward not *reckoned* of grace, but
5. his faith *is counted* for righteousness.
6. unto whom God *imputeth*
8. the Lord *will* not *impute*
9. faith *was reckoned* to Abraham
10. How *was* it then *reckoned?*
11. that righteousness might *be imputed* unto
22. it *was imputed* to him for
23. that it *was imputed* to him;
24. to whom it shall *be imputed,*
6:11. *reckon* ye also yourselves to be dead
8:18. For I *reckon* that the sufferings
36. we *are accounted* as sheep for
9: 8. *are counted* for the seed.
14:14. but to him *that esteemeth* any thing
1Co. 4: 1. *Let* a man so *account of* us,
13: 5. not easily provoked, *thinketh* no evil;
11. I *thought* as a child:
2Co. 3: 5. *to think* any thing as of ourselves;
5:19. not *imputing* their trespasses unto them;
10: 2. I *think* to be bold against some, *which think of* us as if we walked
7. *let* him of himself *think* this again,
11. *Let* such an one *think* this, that, such
11: 5. For I *suppose* I was not a whit
12: 6. lest any man *should think of* me above
Gal. 3: 6. it *was accounted* to him for
Phi. 3:13. I *count* not myself to have
4: 8. *think on* these things.
2Ti. 4:16. it *may* not *be laid to* their *charge.*
Heb 11:19. *Accounting* that God (was) able to raise
Jas. 2:23. it *was imputed* unto him for
1Pet.5:12. faithful brother unto you, as I *suppose,*

3050 2 477/601 4:69 3056

λογικός, *logikos.*

Ro. 12: 1. your *reasonable* service.
1Pet. 2: 2. the sincere milk *of the word,*

3051 4 477/601 4:69 3052

λόγιον, *logion,*

Acts 7:38. who received the lively *oracles* to give
Ro. 3: 2. were committed the *oracles* of God.
Heb 5:12. first principles of the *oracles* of God;
1Pet.4:11. (let him speak) as the *oracles* of God;

3052 1 477/601 4:69 3056

λόγιος, *logios.*

Acts18:24. an *eloquent* man, (and) mighty in the

3053 2 477/601 4:284 3049

λογισμός, *logismos.*

Ro. 2:15. also bearing witness, and (their) *thoughts*
2Co.10: 5(4). Casting down *imaginations,*

3054 1 478/601 4:69 3056,3164

λογομαχέω, *logomakeo.*

2Ti. 2:14. that they *strive* not *about words*

3055 1 478/601 4:69 rt 3054

λογομαχία, *logomakia.*

1Ti. 6: 4. about questions and *strifes of words,*

3056 330 478/601 4:69 3004

λόγος, logos.

Mat. 5:32. saving for the *cause* of fornication,
37. let your *communication* be, Yea, yea;
7:24. heareth these *sayings* of mine, and doeth
26. that heareth these *sayings* of mine, and
28. Jesus had ended these *sayings*,
8: 8. but speak the *word* only,
16. cast out the spirits with (his) *word*,
10:14. nor hear your *words*,
12:32. speaketh a *word* against the Son of man,
36. they shall give *account* thereof
37. For by thy *words* thou shalt be justified, and by thy *words*
13:19. heareth the *word* of the kingdom,
20. is he that heareth the *word*,
21. ariseth because of the *word*,
22. he that heareth the *word*; and the care
— riches, choke the *word*,
23. heareth the *word*, and understandeth
15:12. after they heard this *saying*?
23. answered her not a *word*.
18:23. take *account* of his servants.
19: 1. Jesus had finished these *sayings*,
11. All (men) cannot receive this *saying*,
22. the young man heard that *saying*,
21:24. I also will ask you one *thing*,
22:15. might entangle him in (his) *talk*.
46. to answer him a *word*,
24:35. my *words* shall not pass away.
25:19. and reckoneth (lit. taketh *account*) with them.
26: 1. finished all these *sayings*,
44. saying the same *words*.
28:15. this *saying* is commonly reported
Mar 1:45. and to blaze abroad the *matter*,
2: 2. preached the *word* unto them.
4:14. The sower soweth the *word*.
15. where the *word* is sown;
— taketh away the *word*
16. have heard the *word*,
17. for the *word's* sake,
18. such as hear the *word*,
19. entering in, choke the *word*,
20. such as hear the *word*,
33. spake he the *word* unto them,
5:36. As soon as Jesus heard the *word*
7:13. Making the *word* of God of none effect
29. For this *saying* go thy way;
8:32. And he spake that *saying*
38. and of my *words*
9:10. they kept that *saying*
10:22. he was sad at that *saying*,
24. astonished at his *words*.
11:29. ask of you one *question*,
12:13. to catch him in (his) *words*.
13:31. but my *words* shall not pass
14:39. and spake the same *words*.
16:20. confirming the *word* with
Lu. 1: 2. and ministers of the *word*;
4. the certainty of those *things*,
20. thou believest not my *words*,
29. she was troubled at his *saying*,
3: 4. the book of the *words* of Esaias
4:22. wondered at the gracious *words*
32. for his *word* was with power.
36. What a *word* (is) this!
5: 1. to hear the *word* of God,
15. went there a *fame* abroad
6:47. and heareth my *sayings*,
7: 7. but say in a *word*,
17. this *rumour* of him went forth

Lu. 8:11. The seed is the *word* of God.
12. taketh away the *word* out of
13. receive the *word* with joy;
15. having heard the *word*,
21. are these which hear the *word* of God and do it.
9:26. of me and of my *words*,
28. eight days after these *sayings*,
44. Let these *sayings* sink down
10:39. sat at Jesus' feet, and heard his *word*.
11:28. that hear the *word* of God, and keep it.
12:10. shall speak a *word* against the Son
16: 2. give an *account* of thy stewardship;
20: 3. I will also ask you one *thing*;
20. might take hold of his *words*,
21:33. but my *words* shall not pass
22:61. Peter remembered the *word*
23: 9. questioned with him in many *words*;
24:17. What manner of *communications* (are)
19. mighty in deed and *word*
44. These (are) the *words* which I
Joh. 1: 1. In the beginning was the *Word*, and the *Word* was with God, and the *Word* was God.
14. And the *Word* was made flesh.
2:22. and the *word* which Jesus
4:37. herein is that *saying* true,
39. for the *saying* of the woman,
41. because of his own *word*;
50. the man believed the *word*
5:24. He that heareth my *word*,
38. ye have not his *word*
6:60. This is an hard *saying*;
7:36. What (manner of) *saying* is
40. when they heard this *saying*,
8:31. If ye continue in my *word*,
37. my *word* hath no place in you.
43. ye cannot hear my *word*.
51. If a man keep my *saying*,
52. thou sayest, If a man keep my *saying*,
55. and keep his *saying*.
10:19. among the Jews for these *sayings*.
35. unto whom the *word* of God came,
12:38. That the *saying* of Esaias the prophet
48. the *word* that I have spoken,
14:23. he will keep my *words*:
24. keepeth not my *sayings*: and the *word* which ye hear
15: 3. are clean through the *word*
20. Remember the *word* that I said
— if they have kept my *saying*,
25. that the *word* might be fulfilled
17: 6. and they have kept thy *word*.
14. I have given them thy *word*;
17. thy *word* is truth.
20. shall believe on me through their *word*;
18: 9. That the *saying* might be fulfilled,
32. That the *saying* of Jesus might
19: 8. When Pilate therefore heard that *saying*,
13. heard that *saying*, he brought Jesus forth,
21:23. Then went this *saying* abroad
Acts 1: 1. The former *treatise* have I made,
2:22. men of Israel, hear these *words*;
40. And with many other *words*
41. they that gladly received his *word*
4: 4. which heard the *word* believed;
29. they may speak thy *word*,
31. and they spake the *word* of God
5: 5. Ananias hearing these *words*
24. priests heard these *things*,
6: 2. should leave the *word* of God,
4. the ministry of the *word*.

Acts 6: 5. the *saying* pleased the whole
7. the *word* of God increased;.
7:22. mighty in *words* and in deeds.
29. Then fled Moses at this *saying*,
8: 4. preaching the *word*.
14. had received the *word* of God,
21. neither part nor lot in this *matter:*
25. and preached the *word* of the Lord,
10:29. for what *intent* ye have sent for me?
36. The *word* which (God) sent
44. which heard the *word*.
11: 1. had also received the *word* of God.
19. preaching the *word* to none but
22. Then *tidings* of these things
12:24. But the *word* of God grew
13: 5. they preached the *word* of God
7. desired to hear the *word* of God.
15. if ye have any *word* of exhortation
26. to you is the *word* of this salvation sent.
44. to hear the *word* of God.
46. It was necessary that the *word*
48. glorified the *word* of the Lord:
49. the *word* of the Lord was published
14: 3. gave testimony unto the *word* of his grace,
12. he was the chief speaker. (lit. of *speech*)
25. had preached the *word*
15: 6. to consider of this *matter*.
7. should hear the *word* of the gospel,
15. to this agree the *words* of the prophets;
24. troubled you with *words*,
27. the same things by *mouth*.
32. exhorted the brethren with many *words*,
35. preaching the *word* of the Lord,
36. preached the *word* of the Lord,
16: 6. to preach the *word* in Asia,
32. spake unto him the *word* of the Lord,
36. told this *saying* to Paul,
17:11. received the *word* with all readiness
13. had knowledge that the *word* of God
18:11. teaching the *word* of God
14. reason would that (lit. with *reason*) I should bear with you:
15. if it be a question of *words*
19:10. heard the *word* of the Lord
20. So mightily grew the *word* of God
38. have a *matter* against any
40. may give an *account* of this concourse.
20: 2. had given them much exhortation, (lit. had exhorted them in many *words*)
7. continued his *speech* until midnight.
24. none of these *things* move me,
32. and to the *word* of his grace,
35. and to remember the *words*
38. for the *words* which he spake,
22:22. audience unto this *word*,
Ro. 3: 4. justified in thy *sayings*,
9: 6. Not as though the *word* of God
9. For this (is) the *word* of promise,
28. For he will finish the *work*, (lit. *reckoning*)
— a short *work* will the Lord make
13: 9. comprehended in this *saying*, namely,
14:12. every one of us shall give *account*
15:18. by *word* and deed,
1Co. 1: 5. enriched by him, in all *utterance*, and (in)
17. not with wisdom of *words*,
18. For the *preaching* of the cross
2: 1. not with excellency of *speech*
4. And my *speech* and my preaching (was) not with enticing *words*
13. not in the *words* which man's wisdom
4:19. not the *speech* of them which are
20. not in *word*, but in power.

1Co.12: 8. the *word* of wisdom; to another the *word* of knowledge
14: 9. *words* easy to be understood,
19. I had rather speak five *words*
— than ten thousand *words* in an
36. came the *word* of God out from you?
15: 2. keep in memory what)(I preached
54. to pass the *saying* that is written,
2Co. 1:18. our *word* toward you was not
2:17. which corrupt the *word* of God:
4: 2. nor handling the *word* of God
5:19. the *word* of reconciliation.
6: 7. By the *word* of truth,
8: 7. (in) faith, and *utterance*, and knowledge,
10:10. and (his) *speech* contemptible.
11. such as we are in *word* by letters
11: 6. But though (I be) rude in *speech*,
Gal. 5:14. the law is fulfilled in one *word*,
6: 6. Let him that is taught in the *word*
Eph. 1:13. after that ye heard the *word* of truth,
4:29. Let no corrupt *communication*
5: 6. deceive you with vain *words:*
6:19. that *utterance* may be given unto me,
Phi. 1:14. to speak the *word* without fear.
2:16. Holding forth the *word* of life:
4:15. as concerning giving and receiving, (lit as to the *matter* of g. and r.)
17. may abound to your *account*.
Col. 1: 5. in the *word* of the truth
25. to fulfil the *word* of God;
2:23. have indeed a *shew* of wisdom
3:16. Let the *word* of Christ dwell
17. whatsoever ye do in *word* or deed,
4: 3. unto us a door of *utterance*,
6. Let your *speech* (be) alway
1Th. 1: 5. came not unto you in *word* only,
6. having received the *word* in much
8. sounded out the *word* of the Lord
2: 5. used we flattering *words*,
13. the *word* of God which ye heard of us, ye received (it) not (as) the *word* of men, but as it is in truth, the *word* of God,
4:15. unto you by the *word* of the Lord,
18. comfort one another with these *words*.
2Th. 2: 2. neither by spirit, nor by *word*,
15. whether by *word*, or our epistle.
17. in every good *word* and work.
3: 1. the *word* of the Lord may have (free)
14. if any man obey not our *word*
1Ti. 1:15. This (is) a faithful *saying*, and worthy
3: 1. This (is) a true *saying*,
4: 5. sanctified by the *word* of God and prayer.
6. nourished up in the *words* of faith
9. This (is) a faithful *saying*
12. in *word*, in conversation, in charity,
5:17. they who labour in the *word*
6: 3. to wholesome *words*, (even) the words of our Lord
2Ti. 1:13. Hold fast the form of sound *words*,
2: 9. the *word* of God is not bound.
11. (It is) a faithful *saying:*
15. rightly dividing the *word* of truth
17. And their *word* will eat as doth
4: 2. Preach the *word*; be instant
15. greatly withstood our *words*.
Tit. 1: 3. manifested his *word* through preaching,
9. Holding fast the faithful *word*
2: 5. that the *word* of God be not blasphemed.
8. Sound *speech*, that cannot be condemned;
3: 8. (This is) a faithful *saying*,
Heb. 2: 2. For if the *word* spoken by angels
4: 2. but the *word* preached did not profit

Heb. 4:12. For the *word* of God (is) quick, and
13: with whom we have to do. (lit. *account*)
5:11. Of whom we have many *things* to say,
13. unskilful in the *word* of righteousness:
6: 1. leaving the principles of the doctrine (lit. leaving the *word* of the beginning)
7:28. but the *word* of the oath,
12:19. the *word* should not be spoken to them
13: 7. have spoken unto you the *word* of God:
17. as they that must give *account*,
22. suffer the *word* of exhortation:
Jas. 1:18. begat he us with the *word* of truth,
21. with meekness the engrafted *word*,
22. be ye doers of the *word*,
23. if any be a hearer of the *word*,
3: 2. If any man offend not in *word*,
1Pet. 1:23. of incorruptible, by the *word* of God,
2: 8. which stumble at the *word*,
3: 1. if any obey not the *word*, they also may without the *word* be won by
15. a *reason* of the hope that is in you
4: 5. Who shall give *account* to him
Pet. 1:19. We have also a more sure *word*
2: 3. with feigned *words* make merchandise
3: 5. by the *word* of God the heavens
7. by the same *word* are kept in store,
1Joh. 1: 1. have handled, of the *Word* of life;
10. and his *word* is not in us.
2: 5. But whoso keepeth his *word*,
7. The old commandment is the *word*
14. the *word* of God abideth in you,
3:18. let us not love in *word*,
5: 7. the Father, the *Word*, and the HolyGhost:
3Joh. 10. against us with malicious *words*:
Rev. 1: 2. bare record of the *word* of God,
3. that hear the *words* of this prophecy,
9. for the *word* of God, and for the
3: 8. and hast kept my *word*,
10. hast kept the *word* of my patience,
6: 9. were slain for the *word* of God,
12:11. and by the *word* of their testimony;
19: 9. These are the true *sayings* of God.
13. is called The *Word* of God.
20: 4. and for the *word* of God,
21: 5. for these *words* are true and faithful.
22: 6. These *sayings* (are) faithful and true:
7. blessed (is) he that keepeth the *sayings*.
9. of them which keep the *sayings*
10. Seal not the *sayings* of the prophecy
18. the *words* of the prophecy of this book,
19. take away from the *words* of the book of this prophecy, God

---

3057 1 480/605

λόγχη, lonkee.

Joh. 19:34. with a *spear* pierced his side,

3058 4 480/605 4:293 3060

λοιδορέω, loidoreo.

Joh. 9:28. Then they *reviled* him, and said,
Acts23: 4. *Revilest* thou God's high priest?
1Co. 4:12. *being reviled*, we bless;
1Pet. 2:23. Who, *when* he *was reviled*, reviled not

3059 3 480/605 4:293 3060

λοιδορία, loidoria.

1Ti. 5:14. to the adversary to speak *reproachfully*.
1Pet. 3: 9. or *railing* for *railing*:

3060 2 480/605 4:293 loidos (mischief)

λοίδορος, loidoros.

1Co. 5:11. or a *railer*, or a drunkard.
6:10. nor *revilers*, nor extortioners,

3061 3 480/605

λοιμός, loimos.

Mat.24: 7. famines, and *pestilences*,
Lu. 21:11. and famines, and *pestilences*;
Acts24: 5. found this man (a) *pestilent* (*fellow*),

3063 14 481/605 3062

τὸ λοιπόν, ὅ λοιπόν, & λοιπόν, to loipon, ho loipon, & loipon.

(The neut. of the adj. used as an adv.)

Mat.26:45. Sleep on *now*, and take (your) rest:
Mar14:41. Sleep on *now*, and take (your) rest:
Acts27:20. all hope that we should be saved was *then* taken away.
1Co. 1:16. *besides*, I know not whether I baptized any other.
4: 2. *Moreover* it is required in stewards,
7:29. it remaineth, (lit. as *for the rest* it is) that both they that
2Co.13:11. *Finally*, brethren, farewell.
Eph. 6:10. *Finally*, my brethren, be strong
Phi. 3: 1. *Finally*, my brethren, rejoice in the Lord.
4: 8. *Finally*, brethren, whatsoever things
1Th. 4: 1. *Furthermore* then we beseech you,
2Th. 3: 1. *Finally*, brethren, pray for us,
2Ti. 4: 8. *Henceforth* there is laid up for me
Heb10:13. *From henceforth* expecting till his enemies be made his footstool.

3062 41 481/605 3007

λοιπός, loipos.

Mat.22: 6. And the *remnant* took his servants,
25:11. Afterward came also the *other* virgins.
27:49. The *rest* said, Let be,
Mar 4:19. and the lusts of *other* things
16:13. and told (it) unto the *residue*:
Lu. 8:10. but to *others* in parables; that seeing
12:26. why take ye thought for the *rest*?
18. 9. and despised *others*:
11. that I am not as *other* men
24: 9. unto the eleven, and to all the *rest*.
10. and *other* (women that were) with them,
Acts 2:37. unto Peter and to the *rest* of the apostles,
5:13. And of the *rest* durst no man join
17: 9. security of Jason, and of the *other*,
27:44. And the *rest*, some on boards,
28: 9. *others* also, which had diseases
Ro. 1:13. even as among *other* Gentiles.
11: 7. and the *rest* were blinded
1Co. 7:12. But to the *rest* speak I,
9: 5. as well as *other* apostles,
11:34. And the *rest* will I set in order
15:37. of wheat, or of some *other* (grain):
2Co.12:13. were inferior to *other* churches,
13: 2. I write to them which heretofore have sinned, and to all *other*, that,
Gal. 2:13. And the *other* Jews dissembled
Eph 2: 3. children of wrath, even as *others*
4:17. walk not as *other* Gentiles
Phi. 1:13. and in all *other* (places);
4: 3. and (with) *other* my fellowlabourers,
1Th. 4:13. even as *others* which have no hope.
5: 6. let us not sleep, as (do) *others*;
1Ti. 5:20. that *others* also may fear.

2Pet. 3:16. as (they do) also the *other* scriptures,
Rev. 2 24. and unto the *rest* in Thyatira,
3: 2. and strengthen the things *which remain,*
8:13. by reason of the *other* voices
9:20. the *rest* of the men which were not
11:13. and the *remnant* were affrighted,
12:17. to make war with the *remnant* of her
19:21. And the *remnant* were slain
20: 5. But the *rest* of the dead lived not again until

3064 1 481/605 3062

τοῦ λοιποῦ, *tou loipou.*

Gen. of the adj.

Gal. 6:17. *From henceforth* let no man

3067 2 481/606 4:295 3068

λουτρόν, *loutron.*

Eph 5:26. and cleanse it with the *washing* of water
Tit. 3: 5. by the *washing* of regeneration,

3068 6 481/606 4:295 cf 3538 cf 4150

λούω, *louo.*

Joh.13:10. He *that is washed* needeth not
Acts 9:37. whom *when* they *had washed,* they laid
16:33. and *washed* (their) stripes;
Heb.10:22(23). and our bodies *washed* (lit. *washed* as to the body) with pure water.
2Pet. 2:22. the sow *that was washed* to her
Rev. 1: 5. Unto him that loved us, and *washed* us from our sins in his own blood,

---

3074 6 482/606 4:308 cf rt3022

λύκος, *lukos.*

Mat. 7:15. inwardly they are ravening *wolves.*
10:16. as sheep in the midst of *wolves:*
Lu. 10: 3. as lambs among *wolves.*
Joh.10:12. seeth the *wolf* coming, and leaveth
— and the *wolf* catcheth them,
Acts20:29. shall grievous *wolves* enter in among you,

3075 1 482/606 4:312 3089

λυμαίνομαι, *lumainomai.*

Acts 8: 3. As for Saul, he *made havock* of the church,

3076 26 482/606 4:313 3077

λυπέω, *lupeo.*

Mat.14: 9. the king *was sorry:* nevertheless
17:23. And they *were* exceeding *sorry.*
18:31. what was done, they *were* very *sorry,*
19:22. he went away *sorrowful:*
26:22. they *were* exceeding *sorrowful, and*
37. began *to be sorrowful* and very heavy.
Mar10:22. and went away *grieved:*
14:19. they began *to be sorrowful,*
Joh.16:20. and ye *shall be sorrowful,*
21:17. Peter *was grieved* because he said
Ro. 14:15. if thy brother *be grieved* with (thy) meat,
2Co. 2: 2. For if I *make* you *sorry,*
— *which is made sorry* by me?
4. not that ye *should be grieved,*
5. if any *have caused grief,* he *hath* not *grieved* me, but in part:
6:10. As *sorrowful,* yet alway rejoicing;
2Co. 7: 8. though I *made* you *sorry* with a letter,
— epistle *hath made* you *sorry,*
9. not that ye *were made sorry,* but that ye *sorrowed* to repentance: for ye *were made sorry*
11. that ye *sorrowed* after a godly
Eph 4:30. And *grieve* not the holy Spirit
1Th. 4:13. that ye *sorrow* not, even as
1Pet. 1: 6. *though* now...ye *are in heaviness* through

3077 16 483/606 4:313

λύπη, *lupee.*

Lu. 22:45. he found them sleeping for *sorrow,*
Joh.16: 6. *sorrow* hath filled your heart.
20. but your *sorrow* shall be turned into joy.
21. in travail hath *sorrow,*
22. ye now therefore have *sorrow:*
Ro. 9: 2. I have great *heaviness* and
2Co. 2: 1. not come again to you in *heaviness.*
3. I should have *sorrow* from
7. swallowed up with overmuch *sorrow.*
7:10. For godly *sorrow* worketh repentance
— the *sorrow* of the world worketh death.
9: 7. not grudgingly (lit. of *sorrow*), or of
Phi. 2:27. lest I should have *sorrow* upon *sorrow.*
Heb12:11. but grievous: (lit. of *grief*)
1Pet. 2:19. a man for conscience toward God endure *grief,*

3080 1 483/607 3089

λύσις, *lusis.*

1Co. 7:27. seek not *to be loosed.*

3081 1 483/607 3080,5056

λυσιτελεῖ, *lusiteli.*

Lu. 17: 2. It *were better* for him that a millstone

3083 2 483/607 4:328 3089

λύτρον, *lutron.*

Mat.20:28. to give his life a *ransom* for many.
Mar 10:45. to give his life a *ransom* for many.

3084 3 484/607 4:328 3083

λυτρόω, *lutroō.*

Lu. 24:21. which should have *redeemed* Israel:
Tit. 2:14. that he *might redeem* us from
1Pet. 1:18. ye *were* not *redeemed* with corruptible

3085 3 484/607 4:328 3084

λύτρωσις, *lutrōsis.*

Lu. 1:68. and redeemed (lit. wrought *redemption* for) his people,
2:38. that looked for *redemption*
Heb 9:12. having obtained eternal *redemption* (for us).

3086 1 484/607 4:328 3084

λυτρωτής, *lutrōtees.*

Acts 7:35. God send (to be) a ruler and a *deliverer* by the hand of the angel

---

3087 12 484/607 4:324 3088

λυχνία, *luknia.*

Mat. 5:15. but on a *candlestick,* and it giveth

Mar 4:21. to be set on a *candlestick?*
Lu. 8:16. but setteth (it) on a *candlestick,*
11:33. but on a *candlestick,* that they
Heb 9: 2. wherein (was) the *candlestick,* and the
Rev. 1:12. I saw seven golden *candlesticks;*
13. in the midst of the seven *candlesticks*
20. the seven golden *candlesticks.*
— and the seven *candlesticks* which
2: 1. of the seven golden *candlesticks;*
5. remove thy *candlestick* out of his place,
11: 4. and the two *candlesticks* standing before the God of the earth.

3088 14 484/607 4:324 rt 3022

λύχνος, lŭknŏs.

Mat. 5:15. Neither do men light a *candle,*
6:22. The *light* of the body is the eye:
Mar 4:21. Is a *candle* brought to be put
Lu. 8:16. when he hath lighted a *candle,* covereth
11:33. when he hath lighted a *candle,* putteth
34. The *light* of the body is the eye:
36. the bright shining of a *candle*
12:35. and (your) *lights* burning;
15: 8. doth not light a *candle,*
Joh. 5:35. He was a burning and a shining *light:*
2Pet. 1:19. as unto a *light* that shineth
Rev. 18:23. And the light of a *candle* shall shine no
21:23. and the Lamb (is) the *light* thereof.
22: 5. they need no *candle,* neither light of the sun;

3089 43 484/607 4:328 cf 4486

λύω, luo.

Mat. 5:19. *shall break* one of these least
16:19. whatsoever thou *shalt loose* on earth shall be *loosed* in heaven.
18:18. whatsoever ye *shall loose* on earth shall be *loosed* in heaven.
21: 2. *loose* (them), *and* bring (them) unto me.
Mar 1: 7. not worthy to stoop down and *unloose.*
7:35. the string of his tongue *was loosed,*
11: 2. *loose* him, *and* bring (him).
4. and they *loose* him.
5. What do ye, *loosing* the colt?
Lu. 3:16. I am not worthy *to unloose:*
13:15. *doth* not each one of you on the sabbath *loose* his ox
16. *be loosed* from this bond
19:30. *loose* him, *and* bring (him hither).
31. Why *do* ye *loose* (him)?
33. *as* they *were loosing* the
— Why *loose* ye the colt?
Joh. 1:27. I am not worthy to *unloose.*
2:19. *Destroy* this temple, and in three days I will raise it up.
5:18. he not only *had broken* the sabbath,
7:23. that the law of Moses *should* not *be broken;*
10:35. the scripture cannot *be broken;*
11:44. *Loose* him, and let him go.
Acts 2:24. *having loosed* the pains of death:
7:33. *Put off* thy shoes from thy feet:
13:25. I am not worthy *to loose.*
43. Now *when* the congregation *was broken up,*
22:30. he *loosed* him from (his) bands,
24:26. that he *might loose* him:
27:41. the hinder part *was broken*
1Co. 7:27. *Art* thou *loosed* from a wife?
Eph. 2:14. and *hath broken down* the middle wall
2Pet. 3:10. *shall melt* with fervent heat,
2Pet. 3:11. (Seeing) then (that) all these things shall be *dissolved,*
12. heavens being on fire *shall be dissolved,*
1Joh. 3: 8. that he *might destroy* the works of the
Rev. 5: 2. and *to loose* the seals thereof?
5. and *to loose* the seven seals
9:14. *Loose* the four angels which
15. the four angels *were loosed,*
20: 3. he must *be loosed* a little season,
7. Satan *shall be loosed* out of his prison,

3095 1 485/608 4:356 3096

μαγεία, magia.

Acts 8:11. bewitched them with *sorceries*

3096 1 485/608 4:356 3097

μαγεύω, magūo.

Acts 8: 9. *used sorcery,* and bewitched the people of Samaria,

3097 6 486/608 4:356 [7248]

μάγος, magos.

Mat. 2: 1. there came *wise men* from the east
7. had privily called the *wise men,*
16. that he was mocked of the *wise men,*
— enquired of the *wise men.*
Acts 13: 6. they found a certain *sorcerer,* a false
8. But Elymas the *sorcerer*

3100 4 486/608 3101

μαθητεύω, matheetūo.

Mat. 13:52. every scribe (which is) *instructed*
27:57. who also himself *was* Jesus' *disciple:*
28:19. and *teach* (lit. *disciple*) all nations,
Acts 14:21. and *had taught* many, they returned

3101 268 486/608 4:390 3129

μαθητής, matheetees.

Mat. 5: 1. his *disciples* came unto him:
8:21. another of his *disciples* said
23. his *disciples* followed him.
25. his *disciples* came to (him),
9:10. with him and his *disciples.*
11. they said unto his *disciples,*
14. came to him the *disciples* of John, saying,
— but thy *disciples* fast not?
19. and (so did) his *disciples.*
37. saith he unto his *disciples,*
10: 1. had called unto (him) his twelve *disciples*
24. The *disciple* is not above
25. It is enough for the *disciple*
42. only in the name of a *disciple,*
11: 1. of commanding his twelve *disciples,*
2. he sent two of his *disciples,*
12: 1. *disciples* were an hungred,
2. Behold, thy *disciples* do that
49. forth his hand toward his *disciples,*
13:10. And the *disciples* came, and said
36. into the house: and his *disciples* came
14:12. his *disciples* came, and took up the body,
15. his *disciples* came to him,
19. loaves to (his) *disciples,* and the *disciples* to the multitude.

Mat.14:22. constrained his *disciples* to get
26. when the *disciples* saw him
15: 2. Why do thy *disciples* transgress the tradition of the elders?
12. Then came his *disciples*,
23. And his *disciples* came and besought
32. Jesus called his *disciples*
33. his *disciples* say unto him,
36. and gave to his *disciples*, and the *disciples* to the multitude.
16: 5. when his *disciples* were come
13. he asked his *disciples*, saying, Whom do
20. Then charged he his *disciples*
21. to shew unto his *disciples*,
24. Then said Jesus unto his *disciples*,
17: 6. when the *disciples* heard (it),
10. his *disciples* asked him, saying, Why then
13. Then the *disciples* understood
16. I brought him to thy *disciples*,
19. Then came the *disciples*
18: 1. came the *disciples* unto Jesus,
19:10. His *disciples* say unto him,
13. and the *disciples* rebuked them.
23. Then said Jesus unto his *disciples*,
25. When his *disciples* heard (it),
20:17. took the twelve *disciples*
21: 1. then sent Jesus two *disciples*,
6. And the *disciples* went, and did as
20. when the *disciples* saw (it),
22:16. sent out unto him their *disciples*
23: 1. to the multitude, and to his *disciples*,
24: 1. and his *disciples* came to (him) for to shew him
3. the *disciples* came unto him
26: 1. he said unto his *disciples*,
8. But when his *disciples* saw (it),
17. the *disciples* came to Jesus,
18. at thy house with my *disciples*.
19. And the *disciples* did as Jesus
26. and gave (it) to the *disciples*,
35. Likewise also said all the *disciples*.
36. and saith unto the *disciples*,
40. he cometh unto the *disciples*,
45. cometh he to his *disciples*,
56. Then all the *disciples* forsook him,
27:64. lest his *disciples* come by night,
28: 7. and tell his *disciples* that he is risen from the dead;
8. did run to bring his *disciples* word.
9. as they went to tell his *disciples*,
13. Say ye, His *disciples* came
16. Then the eleven *disciples* went
Mar. 2:15. with Jesus and his *disciples*:
16. they said unto his *disciples*,
18. the *disciples* of John and of the
— Why do the *disciples* of John...fast, but thy *disciples* fast not?
23. his *disciples* began, as they went, to pluck
3: 7. with his *disciples* to the sea:
9. And he spake to his *disciples*,
4:34. expounded all things to his *disciples*.
5:31. his *disciples* said unto him,
6: 1. his *disciples* follow him.
29. when his *disciples* heard
35. his *disciples* came unto him,
41. and gave (them) to his *disciples*
45. he constrained his *disciples* to
7: 2. when they saw some of his *disciples*
5. Why walk not thy *disciples*
17. his *disciples* asked him
8: 1. Jesus called his *disciples*
4. his *disciples* answered him,

Mar. 8: 6. gave to his *disciples* to set
10. entered into a ship with his *disciples*,
27. and his *disciples*, into the towns
— he asked his *disciples*,
33. and looked on his *disciples*,
34. with his *disciples* also,
9:14. when he came to (his) *disciples*,
18. I spake to thy *disciples*
28. his *disciples* asked him
31. For he taught his *disciples*,
10:10. in the house his *disciples*
13. and (his) *disciples* rebuked
23. and saith unto his *disciples*,
24. And the *disciples* were astonished
46. went out of Jericho with his *disciples*
11: 1. sendeth forth two of his *disciples*,
14. And his *disciples* heard (it).
12:43. he called (unto him) his *disciples*,
13: 1. one of his *disciples* saith unto him,
14:12. his *disciples* said unto him,
13. two of his *disciples*,
14. eat the passover with my *disciples*?
16. And his *disciples* went forth,
32. and he saith to his *disciples*,
16: 7. tell his *disciples* and Peter
Lu. 5:30. murmured against his *disciples*,
33. Why do the *disciples* of John
6: 1. his *disciples* plucked the ears
13. he called (unto him) his *disciples*:
17. company of his *disciples*,
20. lifted up his eyes on his *disciples*,
40. The *disciple* is not above his
7:11. many of his *disciples* went with him,
18. the *disciples* of John shewed
19(18). two of his *disciples*
8: 9. his *disciples* asked him,
22. into a ship with his *disciples*:
9: 1. he called his twelve *disciples*
14. And he said to his *disciples*,
16. and gave to the *disciples* to
18. his *disciples* were with him:
40. thy *disciples* to cast him out;
43. he said unto his *disciples*,
54. And when his *disciples* James and John
10:23. he turned him unto (his) *disciples*,
11: 1. one of his *disciples* said unto him,
— as John also taught his *disciples*.
12: 1. he began to say unto his *disciples*
22. he said unto his *disciples*,
14:26. he cannot be my *disciple*.
27. cannot be my *disciple*.
33. he cannot be my *disciple*.
16: 1. he said also unto his *disciples*,
17: 1. Then said he unto the *disciples*,
22. he said unto the *disciples*,
18:15. when (his) *disciples* saw (it),
19:29. he sent two of his *disciples*,
37. the *disciples* began to rejoice
39. Master, rebuke thy *disciples*.
20:45. he said unto his *disciples*,
22:11. eat the passover with my *disciples*
39. his *disciples* also followed him.
45. and was come to his *disciples*,
Joh. 1:35. and two of his *disciples*;
37. the two *disciples* heard him
2: 2. and his *disciples*, to the marriage.
11. his *disciples* believed on him.
12. his brethren, and his *disciples*:
17. his *disciples* remembered that it was
22. his *disciples* remembered that he had
3:22. came Jesus and his *disciples*
25. between (some) of John's *disciples*

H H 2

Joh. 4: 1. more *disciples* than John,
2. baptized not, but his *disciples*,
8. For his *disciples* were gone
27. upon this came his *disciples*,
31. his *disciples* prayed him,
33. Therefore said the *disciples*
6: 3. there he sat with his *disciples*.
8. One of his *disciples*, Andrew,
11. distributed to the *disciples*, and the *disciples* to them
12. he said unto his *disciples*,
16. his *disciples* went down
22. his *disciples* were entered, and that Jesus went not with his *disciples*
— his *disciples* were gone away
24. neither his *disciples*, they also
60. Many therefore of his *disciples*,
61. that his *disciples* murmured
66. many of his *disciples* went back,
7: 3. that thy *disciples* also may see
8:31. (then) are ye my *disciples* indeed;
9: 2. his *disciples* asked him,
27. will ye also be his *disciples*?
28. Thou art his *disciple*; but we are Moses' *disciples*.
11: 7. saith he to (his) *disciples*,
8. (His) *disciples* say unto him,
12. Then said his *disciples*,
54. there continued with his *disciples*.
12: 4. Then saith one of his *disciples*,
16. understood not his *disciples*
13: 5. to wash the *disciples*' feet,
22. Then the *disciples* looked
23. one of his *disciples*, whom Jesus loved.
35. know that ye are my *disciples*,
15: 8. so shall ye be my *disciples*.
16:17. Then said (some) of his *disciples*
29. His *disciples* said unto him,
18: 1. went forth with his *disciples*
— into the which he entered, and his *disciples*.
2. resorted thither with his *disciples*.
15. another *disciple*: that *disciple* was known
16. Then went out that other *disciple*.
17. (one) of his *disciples*?
19. asked Jesus of his *disciples*,
25. (one) of his *disciples*?
19:26. and the *disciple* standing by,
27. Then saith he to the *disciple*,
— from that hour that *disciple*
38. being a *disciple* of Jesus,
20: 2. to the other *disciple*, whom Jesus loved,
3. went forth, and that other *disciple*,
4. and the other *disciple*
8. Then went in also that other *disciple*,
10. Then the *disciples* went away
18. Mary Magdalene came and told the *disciples*
19. where the *disciples* were assembled
20. Then were the *disciples* glad,
25. The other *disciples* therefore
26. his *disciples* were within,
30. in the presence of his *disciples*,
21: 1. again to the *disciples*
2. and two other of his *disciples*
4. but the *disciples* knew not
7. Therefore that *disciple* whom Jesus
8. And the other *disciples* came in a
12. none of the *disciples* durst ask him,
14. shewed himself to his *disciples*,
20. seeth the *disciple* whom Jesus loved
23. that that *disciple* should not
24. This is the *disciple* which testifieth of these

Acts 1:15. in the midst of the *disciples*,
6: 1. when the number of the *disciples*
2. multitude of the *disciples*
7. the number of the *disciples*
9: 1. against the *disciples* of the Lord,
10. a certain *disciple* at Damascus,
19. certain days with the *disciples*
25. Then the *disciples* took him
26. to join himself to the *disciples*:
— believed not that he was a *disciple*.
38. and the *disciples* had heard
11:26. And the *disciples* were called
29. Then the *disciples*, every man
13:52. And the *disciples* were filled
14:20. Howbeit, as the *disciples*
22. Confirming the souls of the *disciples*,
28. abode long time with the *disciples*.
15:10. upon the neck of the *disciples*,
16: 1. a certain *disciple* was there,
18:23. strengthening all the *disciples*.
27. exhorting the *disciples* to
19: 1. and finding certain *disciples*,
9. and separated the *disciples*,
30. the *disciples* suffered him not.
20: 1. Paul called unto (him) the *disciples*,
7. when the *disciples* came together
30. to draw away *disciples* after them.
21: 4. And finding *disciples*, we tarried
16. of the *disciples* of Cæsarea,
— an old *disciple*, with whom we should

3102 1 487/611 4:390 3101

μαθήτρια, matheetria.

Acts 9:36. a certain *disciple* named Tabitha,

3105 5 487/611 4:360 *maō* (to crave for)

μαίνομαι, mainomai.

Joh. 10:20. He hath a devil, and *is mad*;
Acts 12:15. they said unto her, Thou *art mad*.
26:24. Paul, thou *art beside thyself*;
25. I *am* not *mad*, most noble Festus;
1Co. 14:23. will they not say that ye *are mad*?

3106 2 487/611 4:362 3107

μακαρίζω, makarizo.

Lu. 1:48. all generations *shall call* me *blessed*.
Jas. 5:11. we *count* them *happy* which endure.

3107 58 487/612 4:362 *makar* (blest)

μακάριος, makarios.

Mat. 5: 3. *Blessed* (are) the poor in spirit:
4. *Blessed* (are) they that mourn:
5. *Blessed* (are) the meek:
6. *Blessed* (are) they which do hunger
7. *Blessed* (are) the merciful:
8. *Blessed* (are) the pure in heart:
9. *Blessed* (are) the peacemakers:
10. *Blessed* (are) they which are persecuted
11. *Blessed* are ye, when (men)
11: 6. And *blessed* is (he), whosoever
13:16. But *blessed* (are) your eyes,
16:17. *Blessed* art thou, Simon
24:46. *Blessed* (is) that servant,
Lu. 1:45. *blessed* (is) she that believed:
6:20. *Blessed* (be ye) poor:
21. *Blessed* (are ye) that hunger now:
— *Blessed* (are ye) that weep now:

Lu. 6:22. *Blessed* are ye, when men shall hate you, and when they
7:23. And *blessed* is (he), whosoever shall not
10:23. *Blessed* (are) the eyes which see
11:27. *Blessed* (is) the womb that
28. Yea rather, *blessed* (are) they
12:37. *Blessed* (are) those servants,
38. *blessed* are those servants.
43. *Blessed* (is) that servant, whom his lord
14:14. And thou shalt be *blessed;*
15. *Blessed* (is) he that shall eat
23:29. they shall say, *Blessed* (are) the barren,
Joh. 13:17. *happy* are ye if ye do them.
20:29. *blessed* (are) they that have not seen,
Acts 20:35. It is more *blessed* to give
26: 2. I think myself *happy,*
Ro. 4: 7. *Blessed* (are) they whose iniquities are
8. *Blessed* (is) the man to whom
14:22. *Happy* (is) he that condemneth not
1Co. 7:40. But she is *happier* if she
1Ti. 1:11. the glorious gospel of the *blessed* God
6:15. the *blessed* and only Potentate,
Tit. 2:13. Looking for that *blessed* hope,
Jas. 1:12. *Blessed* (is) the man that endureth
25. this man shall be *blessed*
1Pet. 3:14. for righteousness' sake, *happy* (are ye):
4:14. for the name of Christ, *happy* (are ye);
Rev. 1: 3. *Blessed* (is) he that readeth,
14:13. Write, *Blessed* (are) the dead
16:15. *Blessed* (is) he that watcheth,
19: 9. Write, *Blessed* (are) they which
20: 6. *Blessed* and holy (is) he that hath
22: 7. *blessed* (is) he that keepeth the sayings
14. *Blessed* (are) they that do his

3108 3 488/612 4:362 3106

μακαρισμός, makarismos.

Ro. 4: 6. describeth the *blessedness* of the man,
9. (Cometh) this *blessedness* then upon
Gal. 4:15. Where is then the *blessedness*

3111 1 488/612 4:370

μάκελλον, makellon.

1Co. 10:25. Whatsoever is sold in the *shambles,*

3112 10 488/612 4:372 3117

μακράν, makran.

(Acc. of the adj.—ὁδὸν being understood.)

Mat. 8:30. there was a *good way off* from them
Mar 12:34. Thou art not *far* from the kingdom of
Lu. 7: 6. when he was now not *far* from the
15:20. when he was yet a *great way off,*
Joh. 21: 8. they were not *far* from land,
Acts 2:39. and to all that are *afar off,*
17:27. though he be not *far* from every one
22:21. I will send thee *far* hence
Eph 2:13. ye who sometimes were *far off*
17. to you which were *afar off,*

3113 14 489/613 4:372 3117

μακρόθεν, makrothen.

Mat. 26:58. Peter followed him *afar off*
27:55. women were there beholding *afar off,*
Mar 5: 6. when he saw Jesus *afar off,*
8: 3. divers of them came *from far.*
11:13. seeing a fig tree *afar off*
14:54. Peter followed him *afar off,*
15:40. women looking on *afar off:*
Lu. 16:23. and seeth Abraham *afar off,*
18:13. the publican, standing *afar off,*
22:54. Peter followed *afar off.*
23:49. stood *afar off,* beholding these things.
Rev. 18:10. Standing *afar off* for the fear
15. shall stand *afar off* for the fear of
17. and as many as trade by sea, stood *afar off,*

3114 10 489/613 4:374 rt 3116

μακροθυμέω, makrothumeo.

Mat. 18:26. Lord, *have patience* with me,
29. *Have patience* with me, and I will
Lu. 18: 7. though he *bear long* with them?
1Co. 13: 4. Charity *suffereth long,* (and) is kind;
1Th. 5:14. *be patient* toward all (men).
Heb 6:15. *after* he *had patiently endured,* he
Jas. 5: 7. *Be patient* therefore,
— and *hath long patience* for it,
8. *Be* ye also *patient;*
2Pet. 3: 9. but *is longsuffering* to us-ward,

3115 14 489/613 4:374 rt 3116

μακροθυμία, makrothumia.

Ro. 2: 4. and forbearance and *longsuffering;*
9:22. endured with much *longsuffering*
2Co. 6: 6. by *longsuffering,* by kindness,
Gal. 5:22. is love, joy, peace, *longsuffering,*
Eph 4: 2. with *longsuffering,* forbearing
Col. 1:11. and *longsuffering* with joyfulness;
3:12. humbleness of mind, meekness, *long-suffering;*
1Ti. 1:16. might shew forth all *longsuffering,*
2Ti. 3:10. faith, *longsuffering,* charity,
4: 2. with all *longsuffering* and doctrine.
Heb 6:12. through faith and *patience* inherit
Jas. 5:10. of suffering affliction, and of *patience.*
1Pet. 3:20. when once the *longsuffering* of God
2Pet. 3:15. account (that) the *longsuffering* of our

3116 1 489/613 4:374 3117,2372

μακροθύμως, makrothumōs.

Acts 26: 3. I beseech thee to hear me *patiently.*

3117 5 489/613 3372

μακρός, makros.

Mat. 23:14(13). for a pretence make *long* prayer:
Mar 12:40. for a pretence make *long* prayers:
Lu. 15:13. his journey into a *far* country,
19:12. went into a *far* country to receive
20:47. for a shew make *long* prayers:

3118 1 489/613 3117,5550

μακροχρόνιος, makrokronios.

Eph 6: 3. mayest *live long* on the earth.

3119 3 489/613 4:1091 3120

μαλακία, malakia.

Mat. 4:23. all manner of *disease* among the people.
9:35. every sickness and every *disease*
10: 1. of sickness and all manner of *disease.*

3120 4 489/613

μαλακός, malakos.

Mat. 11 8. A man clothed in *soft* raiment?

Mat.11: 8. they that wear *soft* (clothing)
Lu. 7:25. A man clothed in *soft* raiment?
1Co. 6: 9. nor adulterers, nor *effeminate*,

3122 12 490/613 *mala* (very)

μάλιστα, *malista.*

Acts20:38. Sorrowing *most of all* for the words
25:26. and *specially* before thee, O king
26: 3. *Especially* (because I know) thee to be
Gal. 6:10. *especially* unto them who are
Phi. 4:22. *chiefly* they that are of Cæsar's
1Ti. 4:10. *specially* of those that believe.
5: 8. and *specially* for those of his own house,
17. *especially* they who labour in
2Ti. 4:13. (but) *especially* the parchments.
Tit. 1:10. *specially* they of the circumcision:
Philem.16. a brother beloved, *specially* to me,
2Pet.2:10. But *chiefly* them that walk after the flesh

3123 85 490/614 *mala* (very)

μᾶλλον, *mallon.*

Mat. 6:26. Are ye not *much* better than they?
30. (shall he) not much *more* (clothe) you,
7:11. how much *more* shall your Father
10: 6. But go *rather* to the lost sheep of
25. how much *more* (shall they call)
28. but *rather* fear him which is able
18:13. he rejoiceth *more* of that (sheep),
25: 9. but go ye *rather* to them that sell,
27:24. but (that) *rather* a tumult was made,
Mar 5:26. nothing bettered, but *rather* grew worse,
7:36. so much *the more* a great deal
9:42. it is better for him (lit. it is good for him *rather*)
10:48. but he cried *the more* a great deal,
14:31. But he spake *the more* vehemently,
15:11. that he should *rather* release Barabbas
Lu. 5:15. But *so much the more* went there
10:20. but *rather* rejoice, because your
11:13. how much *more* shall (your) heavenly
12:24. how much *more* are ye better
28. how much *more* (will he clothe) you,
18:39. but he cried so much *the more*,
Joh. 3:19. men loved darkness *rather* than light,
5:18. Therefore the Jews sought *the more*
12:43. the praise of men *more* than the praise
19: 8. he was *the more* afraid;
Acts 4:19. to hearken unto you *more* than unto God,
5:14. believers were *the more* added to the Lord,
29. to obey God *rather* than men.
9:22. Saul increased *the more* in strength,
20:35. *more* blessed to give than to receive.
22: 2. they kept *the more* silence:
27:11. *more* than those things which were spoken
Ro. 5: 9. Much *more* then, being now justified
10. much *more*, being reconciled,
15. much *more* the grace of God, and the gift
17. much *more* they which receive
8:34. yea *rather*, that is risen again,
11:12. how much *more* their fulness?
24. how much *more* shall these,
14:13. but judge this *rather*, that no man
1Co. 5: 2. and have not *rather* mourned,
6: 7. Why do ye not *rather* take wrong? why do ye not *rather* (suffer yourselves)
7:21. thou mayest be made free, use (it) *rather*.
9:12. of (this) power over you, (are) not we *rather*?
15 better for me to die, than that (lit. it were good for me to die, *rather* than)
1Co.12:22. Nay, much *more* those members
14: 1. but *rather* that ye may prophesy.
5. but *rather* that ye prophesied:
18. with tongues *more* than ye all:
2Co. 2: 7. ye (ought) *rather* to forgive (him),
3: 8. of the spirit be *rather* glorious?
9. much *more* doth the ministration
11. much *more* that which remaineth
5: 8. willing *rather* to be absent from the body,
7: 7. so that I rejoiced *the more*.
13. and exceedingly *the more* joyed we
12: 9. gladly therefore will I *rather* glory
Gal. 4: 9. have known God, or *rather* are known of
27. hath many more children than she (lit. many are the children of the desolate *rather* than of her)
Eph. 4:28. but *rather* let him labour,
5: 4. but *rather* giving of thanks.
11. of darkness, but *rather* reprove (them).
Phi. 1: 9. your love may abound yet *more* and *more*
12. fallen out *rather* unto the furtherance
23. and to be with Christ; which is far better: (lit. which is much *rather* better)
2:12. but now much *more* in my absence,
3: 4. he might trust in the flesh, I *more*:
1Th. 4: 1. (so) ye would abound *more and more*.
10. that ye increase *more and more*;
1Ti. 1: 4. *rather* than godly edifying
6: 2. but *rather* do (them) service,
2Ti. 3: 4. of pleasures *more* than lovers of God;
Philem. 9. for love's sake I *rather* beseech
16. but how much *more* unto thee,
Heb. 9:14. How much *more* shall the blood of Christ,
10:25. and so much *the more*, as ye see
11:25. Choosing *rather* to suffer affliction
12: 9. shall we not much *rather* be in
13. but let it *rather* be healed.
25. much *more* (shall not) we (escape), if
2Pet.1:10. Wherefore *the rather*, brethren, give

3125 1 491/614

μάμμη, *mammee.*

2Ti. 1: 5. dwelt first in thy *grandmother* Lois,

3126 4 491/614 4:388

μαμμωνᾶς & μαμωνᾶς, *mammōnas & mamōnas.*

Mat. 6:24. Ye cannot serve God and *mammon*.
Lu. 16: 9. friends of the *mammon* of unrighteousness;
11. faithful in the unrighteous *mammon*,
13. Ye cannot serve God and *mammon*.

3129 25 491/615 4:390

μανθάνω, *manthano.*

Mat. 9:13. But go ye and *learn* what (that) meaneth,
11:29. Take my yoke upon you, and *learn* of me;
24:32. Now *learn* a parable of the fig tree;
Mar 13:28. Now *learn* a parable of the fig tree;
Joh. 6:45. that hath heard, and *hath learned* of the
7:15. this man letters, *having* never *learned*?
Acts23:27. *having understood* that he was a Roman.
Ro. 16:17. to the doctrine which ye *have learned*;
1Co. 4: 6. that ye *might learn* in us not to think
14:31. that all *may learn*, and all may be
35. And if they will *learn* any thing,
Gal. 3: 2. This only would I *learn* of you,
Eph 4:20. But ye *have* not so *learned* Christ:
Phi. 4: 9. which ye *have* both *learned*,
11. for I *have learned*, in whatsoever

Col. 1: 7. As ye also *learned* of Epaphras
1Ti. 2:11. *Let* the woman *learn* in silence
5: 4. *let* them *learn* first to shew piety
13. withal they *learn* (to be) idle,
2Ti. 3: 7. Ever *learning*, and never able to come
14. in the things which thou *hast learned*
— knowing of whom thou *hast learned*
Tit. 3:14. And *let* our's also *learn* to
Heb 5: 8. yet *learned* he obedience by
Rev.14: 3. no man could *learn* that song but

3130 1 491/615 3105

μανία, mania.

Acts26:24. much learning doth make thee mad. (lit. turn thee unto *madness*)

3131 5 491/615 4:462 [4478]

μάννα, manna.

Joh. 6:31. Our fathers did eat *manna*
49. Your fathers did eat *manna*
58. not as your fathers did eat *manna*,
Heb 9: 4. the golden pot that had *manna*,
Rev. 2:17. to eat of the hidden *manna*,

3132 1 492/615 3105

μαντεύομαι, mantūomai.

Acts16:16. much gain *by soothsaying*

3133 1 492/615

μαραίνομαι, marainomai.

Jas. 1:11. so also *shall* the rich man *fade away*

3134 1 492/615 4:466

μαρὰν ἀθά, maran atha.

Co.16:22. let him be Anathema *Maran-atha*.

3135 9 492/615 4:472 margaros (oyster)

μαργαρίτης, margaritees.

Mat. 7: 6. neither cast ye your *pearls* before
13:45. a merchant man, seeking goodly *pearls*:
46. found one *pearl* of great price,
1Ti. 2: 9. or *pearls*, or costly array;
Rev.17: 4. and precious stones and *pearls*,
18:12. and precious stones, and of *pearls*,
16. and precious stones, and *pearls*!
21:21. the twelve gates (were) twelve *pearls*; every several gate was of one *pearl*:

3139 1 493/616 marmairo (to glisten)

μάρμαρον, marmaron.

Rev.18:12. of brass, and iron, and *marble*,

3144 34 495/618 4:474

μάρτυρ & μάρτυς, martur & martus.

Mat 18:16. in the mouth of two or three *witnesses*
26:65. what further need have we of *witnesses*?
Mar 14:63. What need we any further *witnesses*?
Lu. 24:48. And ye are *witnesses* of these things.
Acts 1: 8. and ye shall be *witnesses* unto me
22. to be a *witness* with us of his resurrection.
2:32. whereof we all are *witnesses*.
3:15. whereof we are *witnesses*.
5:32. we are his *witnesses* of these things;
Acts 6:13. And set up false *witnesses*,
7:58. the *witnesses* laid down their clothes
10:39. we are *witnesses* of all things
41. unto *witnesses* chosen before of God,
13:31. who are his *witnesses* unto the people.
22:15. thou shalt be his *witness*
20. when the blood of thy *martyr*
26:16. and a *witness* both of these things
Ro. 1: 9. For God is my *witness*,
2Co. 1:23. call God for a *record*
13: 1. In the mouth of two or three *witnesses*
Phi. 1: 8. For God is my *record*, how greatly
1Th. 2: 5. God (is) *witness*:
10. Ye (are) *witnesses*, and God (also),
1Ti. 5:19. but before two or three *witnesses*.
6:12. profession before many *witnesses*.
2Ti. 2: 2. of me among many *witnesses*,
Heb 10:28. under two or three *witnesses*:
12: 1. so great a cloud of *witnesses*,
1Pet. 5: 1. a *witness* of the sufferings of Christ,
Rev. 1: 5. Christ, (who is) the faithful *witness*,
2:13. Antipas (was) my faithful *martyr*,
3:14. the faithful and true *witness*,
11: 3. give (power) unto my two *witnesses*,
17: 6. with the blood of the *martyrs*

3140 79 493/616 4:474 3144

μαρτυρέω -έομαι, martureo -eomai.

Mat 23:31. ye *be witnesses* unto yourselves,
Lu. 4:22. all *bare* him *witness*, and wondered
11:48. Truly ye *bear witness* that ye allow
Joh. 1: 7. to *bear witness* of the Light,
8. to *bear witness* of that Light.
15. John *bare witness* of him,
32. And John *bare record*,
34. I saw, and *bare record*
2:25. that any *should testify* of man:
3:11. and *testify* that we have seen;
26. to whom thou *barest witness*,
28. yourselves *bear* me *witness*,
32. seen and heard, that he *testifieth*;
4:39. of the woman, *which testified*, He
44. For Jesus himself *testified*,
5:31. If I *bear witness* of myself,
32. another *that beareth witness* of me;
— which he *witnesseth* of me
33. and he *bare witness* unto the truth.
36. works that I do, *bear witness* of me,
37. *hath borne witness* of me.
39. are they *which testify* of me.
7: 7. because I *testify* of it,
8:13. Thou *bearest record* of thyself;
14. Though I *bear record* of myself,
18. I am one *that bear witness*
— *beareth witness* of me.
10:25. they *bear witness* of me.
12:17. from the dead, *bare record*.
13:21. and *testified*, and said,
15:26. he *shall testify* of me:
27. ye also shall *bear witness*,
18:23. *bear witness* of the evil:
37. I *should bear witness* unto the truth.
19:35. he that saw (it) *bare record*,
21:24. *which testifieth* of these things,
Acts 6: 3. seven men *of honest report*,
10:22. and *of good report* among
43. *give* all the prophets *witness*,
13:22. to whom also he *gave testimony*, *and* said,
14: 3. in the Lord, *which gave testimony* unto
15: 8. *bare* them *witness*, giving them the Holy Ghost,

Acts16: 2. Which *was well reported of*
22: 5. *doth bear* me *witness*, and all
12. *having* a *good report* of all
23:11. so must thou *bear witness* also
26: 5. if they would *testify*, that after
22. *witnessing* both to small and
Ro. 3:21. *being witnessed* by the law and
10: 2. For I *bear* them *record* that they
1Co.15:15. we *have testified* of God
2Co. 8: 3. I *bear record*, yea, and beyond
Gal. 4:15. for I *bear* you *record*, that, if
Col. 4:13. For I *bear* him *record*, that he
1Th. 2:11. and *charged* every one of you,
1Ti. 5:10. *Well reported of* for good works;
6:13. *who* before Pontius Pilate *witnessed* a good confession;
Heb 7: 8. whom it is *witnessed* (lit. *being witnessed*) that
17. For he *testifieth*, Thou (art) a priest
10:15. the Holy Ghost also *is a witness*
11: 2. elders *obtained a good report.*
4. he *obtained witness* that he was righteous, God *testifying* of his gifts:
5. he *had* this *testimony*, that he
39. *having obtained a good report* through
1Joh.1: 2. and *bear witness*, and shew unto
4:14. and *do testify* that the Father
5: 6. it is the Spirit *that beareth witness*,
7. three *that bear record* in heaven,
8. three *that bear witness* in earth,
9. he *hath testified* of his Son.
10. the record that God *gave* (lit. *testified*) of his Son.
3Joh. 3. and *testified* of the truth that
6. Which *have borne witness* of thy
12. *hath good report* of all (men),
— yea, and we (also) *bear record*;
Rev. 1: 2. Who *bare record* of the word
22:16. sent mine angel *to testify* unto you
20. He *which testifieth* these things saith, Surely I come quickly;

3141 37 494/617 4:474 3144

μαρτυρία, marturia.

Mar 14:55. sought for *witness* against Jesus
56. but their *witness* agreed not
59. neither so did their *witness* agree
Lu. 22:71. What need we any further *witness?*
Joh. 1: 7. The same came for a *witness*,
19. this is the *record* of John,
3:11. and ye receive not our *witness*.
32. and no man receiveth his *testimony*.
33. that hath received his *testimony*
5:31. my *witness* is not true.
32. and I know that the *witness*
34. I receive not *testimony* from man:
36. I have greater *witness* than
8:13. thy *record* is not true.
14. my *record* is true:
17. that the *testimony* of two men is true.
19:35. and his *record* is true:
21:24. we know that his *testimony* is true.
Acts22:18. they will not receive thy *testimony*
1Ti. 3: 7. have a good *report* of them which
Tit. 1:13. This *witness* is true. Wherefore
1Joh.5: 9. If we receive the *witness* of men, the *witness* of God is greater: for this is the *witness* of God
10. hath the *witness* in himself:
— believeth not the *record* that God
11. And this is the *record*,
3Joh. 12. ye know that our *record* is true.
Rev. 1: 2. and of the *testimony* of Jesus Christ,
9. for the *testimony* of Jesus Christ.
6: 9. and for the *testimony* which they held:
11: 7. they shall have finished their *testimony*,
12:11. and by the word of their *testimony*;
17. and have the *testimony* of Jesus Christ.
19:10. and of thy brethren that have the *testimony* of Jesus:
— for the *testimony* of Jesus is
20: 4. beheaded for the *witness* of Jesus, and

3142 20 494/617 4:474 3144

μαρτύριον, marturion.

Mat. 8: 4. for a *testimony* unto them.
10:18. for a *testimony* against them
24:14. for a *witness* unto all nations;
Mar 1:44. for a *testimony* unto them.
6:11. for a *testimony* against them.
13: 9. for a *testimony* against them.
Lu. 5:14. for a *testimony* unto them.
9: 5. for a *testimony* against them.
21:13. shall turn to you for a *testimony*.
Acts 4:33. gave the apostles *witness* of the
7:44. had the tabernacle of *witness* in
1Co. 1: 6. Even as the *testimony* of Christ was
2: 1. unto you the *testimony* of God.
2Co. 1:12. the *testimony* of our conscience,
2Th. 1:10. because our *testimony* among you
1Ti. 2: 6. *to be testified* in due time.
2Ti. 1: 8. ashamed of the *testimony* of our Lord,
Heb 3: 5. for a *testimony* of those things
Jas. 5: 3. the rust of them shall be a *witness* against you,
Rev.15: 5. the temple of the tabernacle of the *testimony* in heaven

3143 3 495/618 3144

μαρτύρομαι, marturomai.

Acts20:26. I *take* you *to record* this day,
Gal. 5: 3. For I *testify* again to every man
Eph 4:17. and *testify* in the Lord,

3144 34 495/

μάρτυς see **μάρτυρ.** p. 471

3145 1 496/618 4:514 *massō* (to squeeze)

μασσάομαι, massaomai.

Rev.16:10. they *gnawed* their tongues for pain,

3146 7 496/618 4:515 3148

μαστιγόω, mastigoō.

Mat 10:17. and they *will scourge* you
20:19. to mock, and *to scourge*,
23:34. and (some) of them *shall* ye *scourge*
Mar 10:34. and *shall scourge* him,
Lu. 18:33. And they *shall scourge* (him), *and*
Joh.19: 1. took Jesus, and *scourged* (him).
Heb 12: 6. and *scourgeth* every son whom

3147 1 496/618 4:515 3149

μαστίζω, mastizo.

Acts22:25. Is it lawful for you *to scourge*

3148 6 496/618 4:515 rt 3145

μάστιξ, mastix.

Mar 3:10. as many as had *plagues*.

Mar. 5:29. that she was healed of that *plague*.
34. and be whole of thy *plague*.
Lu. 7:21. of (their) infirmities and *plagues*,
Acts22.24. be examined by *scourging*;
Heb 11:36. of (cruel) mockings and *scourgings*,

3149 3 496/618 rt 3145

μαστός, *mastos.*

Lu. 11:27. and the *paps* which thou hast sucked.
23:29. the *paps* which never gave suck.
Rev. 1:13. girt about the *paps* with a golden girdle.

3150 1 496/619 4:519 3151

ματαιολογία, *mataiologia.*

1Ti. 1: 6. turned aside unto *vain jangling*;

3151 1 496/619 4:519 3152,3004

ματαιολόγος, *mataiologos.*

Tit. 1:10. unruly and *vain talkers*

3154 1 496/619 4:519 3152

ματαιόομαι, *mataiöomai.*

Ro. 1:21. but *became vain* in their imaginations,

3152 6 496/619 4:519 rt 3156

μάταιος, *mataios.*

Acts14:15. turn from these *vanities* unto
1Co. 3:20. thoughts of the wise, that they are *vain*.
15:17. your faith (is) *vain*;
Tit. 3: 9. for they are unprofitable and *vain*.
Jas. 1:26. this man's religion (is) *vain*.
1Pet. 1:18. from your *vain* conversation

3153 3 496/619 4:519 3152

ματαιότης, *mataiotees.*

Ro. 8:20. was made subject to *vanity*,
Eph 4:17. in the *vanity* of their mind,
2Pet. 2:18. swelling (words) of *vanity*,

3155 2 497/619 4:519 rt 3145

μάτην, *mateen.*

Mat.15: 9. But *in vain* they do worship me,
Mar. 7: 7. Howbeit *in vain* do they

3162 29 497/619 4:524 3163

μάχαιρα, *makaira.*

Mat.10:34. not to send peace, but a *sword*.
26:47. with *swords* and staves,
51. and drew his *sword*, and struck
52. Put up again thy *sword* into his place: for all they that take the *sword* shall perish with the *sword*.
55. with *swords* and staves for to take me?
Mar14:43. with *swords* and staves,
47. drew a *sword*, and smote
48. with *swords* and (with) staves
Lu. 21:24. shall fall by the edge of the *sword*,
22:36. he that hath no *sword*,
38. behold, here (are) two *swords*.
49. shall we smite with the *sword*?
52. with *swords* and staves?
Joh. 18:10. Peter having a *sword* drew it,
11. Put up thy *sword* into the sheath:
Acts12: 2. the brother of John with the *sword*.
16:27. he drew out his *sword*,
Ro. 8:35. or peril, or *sword*?
13: 4. beareth not the *sword* in vain:
Eph. 6:17. *sword* of the Spirit, which is the word
Heb 4:12. sharper than any twoedged *sword*,
11:34. escaped the edge of the *sword*,
37. were slain with the *sword*:
Rev. 6: 4. given unto him a great *sword*.
13:10. he that killeth with the *sword* must be killed with the *sword*.
14. which had the wound by a *sword*,

3163 4 497/619 4:527 3164

μάχη, *makee.*

2Co. 7: 5. without (were) *fightings*,
2Ti. 2:23. they do gender *strifes*.
Tit. 3: 9. and *strivings* about the law;
Jas. 4: 1. and *fightings* among you?

3164 4 497/619 4:527

μάχομαι, *makomai.*

Joh. 6:52. The Jews therefore *strove* among themselves,
Acts 7:26. himself unto them *as* they *strove*,
2Ti. 2:24. servant of the Lord must not *strive*;
Jas. 4: 2. ye *fight* and war, yet ye have not,

3165 301 216/252 1691

μέ, *me.*

From ἐγώ.

Mat. 3:14. and comest thou to *me*?
8: 2. thou canst make *me* clean
10:33. whosoever shall deny *me* before men,
40. receiveth him that sent *me*.
11:28. Come unto *me*, all (ye) that labour
14:28. bid *me* come unto thee on the
30. he cried, saying, Lord, save *me*.
15: 8. and honoureth *me* with (their) lips;
9. in vain they do worship *me*,
22. Have mercy on *me*, O Lord,
16:13. Whom do men say that *I*
15. But whom say ye that *I* am?
18:32. because thou desiredst *me*:
19:14. forbid them not, to come unto *me*
17. Why callest thou *me* good?
22:18. Why tempt ye *me*, (ye) hypocrites
23:39. Ye shall not see *me* henceforth,
25:35. and ye gave *me* drink: I was a stranger, and ye took *me* in:
36. Naked, and ye clothed *me*: I was sick, and ye visited *me*: I was in prison, and ye came unto *me*.
42. and ye gave *me* no drink:
43. a stranger, and ye took *me* not in: naked, and ye clothed *me* not: sick, and in prison, and ye visited *me* not.
26:12. she did (it) for my burial. (lit. for the burying *me*)
21. one of you shall betray *me*.
23. the same shall betray *me*.
32. But after *I* am risen again,
34. thou shalt deny *me* thrice.
35. Though *I* should die with thee,
46. he is at hand that doth betray *me*.
55. and staves for to take *me*?
— and ye laid no hold on *me*.
75. thou shalt deny *me* thrice.
27:46. why hast thou forsaken *me*?

Mat.28.10. there shall they see *me*.
Mar. 1:40. thou canst make *me* clean.
5: 7. that thou torment *me* not.
6:22. Ask of *me* whatsoever thou wilt,
23. Whatsoever thou shalt ask of *me*,
7: 6. This people honoureth *me* with
7. in vain do they worship *me*,
8:27. Whom do men say that *I* am?
29. But whom say ye that *I* am?
38. shall be ashamed of *me*
9:19. bring him unto *me*.
37. but him that sent *me*.
39. lightly speak evil of *me*.
10:14. Suffer the little children to come unto *me*,
18. Why callest thou *me* good?
36. that *I* should do for you?
47. have mercy on *me*.
48. son of David, have mercy on *me*.
12:15. Why tempt ye *me*?
14:18. which eateth with me shall betray *me*.
28. But after that *I* am risen,
30. thou shalt deny *me* thrice.
31. If *I* should die with thee,
42. lo, he that betrayeth *me* is at hand.
48. and (with) staves to take *me*?
49. and ye took *me* not:
72. thou shalt deny *me* thrice.
15:34. why hast thou forsaken *me*?
Lu. 1:43. mother of my Lord should come to *me*?
48. shall call *me* blessed.
2:49. How is it that ye sought *me*? wist ye not that *I* must be about my
4:18. anointed *me* to preach the gospel to the poor; he hath sent *me* to heal
43. *I* must preach the kingdom
5:12. thou canst make *me* clean.
6:46. And why call ye *me*, Lord, Lord,
47. Whosoever cometh to *me*,
8:28. I beseech thee, torment *me* not.
9:18. Whom say the people that *I* am?
20. But whom say ye that *I* am?
26. whosoever shall be ashamed of *me*
48. receiveth him that sent *me*:
10:16. despiseth him that sent *me*.
35. when *I* come again, I will repay
40. that my sister hath left *me* to serve
11: 6. in his journey is come to *me*,
18. because ye say that *I* cast out
12: 9. he that denieth *me* before men
14. Man, who made *me* a judge or
13:33. *I* must walk to day,
35. Ye shall not see *me*, until
14:18. I pray thee have *me* excused.
19. I pray thee have *me* excused.
26. If any (man) come to *me*,
15:19. make *me* as one of thy hired
16: 4. they may receive *me* into their
24. Father Abraham, have mercy on *me*,
18: 3. Avenge *me* of mine adversary.
5. by her continual coming she weary *me*.
16. little children to come unto *me*,
19. Why callest thou *me* good?
38. son of David, have mercy on *me*.
39. son of David, have mercy on *me*.
19: 5. for to day *I* must abide at thy house.
27. which would not that *I* should reign
20:23. Why tempt ye *me*?
22:15. with you before *I* suffer:
21. the hand of him that betrayeth *me*
34. thrice deny that thou knowest *me*.
61. thou shalt deny *me* thrice.
24:39. handle *me*, and see;

Joh. 1:33. but he that sent *me* to baptize
48(49). Whence knowest thou *me*?
2:17. hath eaten *me* up.
4:34. is to do the will of him that sent *me*,
5: 7. to put *me* into the pool:
11. He that made *me* whole,
24. and believeth on him that sent *me*,
30. the Father which hath sent *me*.
36. that the Father hath sent *me*.
37. which hath sent *me*,
40. ye will not come to *me*,
43. and ye receive *me* not:
6:26. Ye seek *me*, not because ye
35. he that cometh to *me*
36. ye also have seen *me*, and
37. and him that cometh to *me*
38. but the will of him that sent *me*.
39. Father's will which hath sent *me*,
40. the will of him that sent *me*,
44. No man can come to *me*, except the Father which hath sent *me*
45. of the Father, cometh unto *me*.
57. As the living Father hath sent *me*,
— so he that eateth *me*, even he
65. no man can come unto *me*, except
7:16. but his that sent *me*.
19. Why go ye about to kill *me*?
28. he that sent *me* is true,
29. and he hath sent *me*.
33. (then) I go unto him that sent *me*.
34. Ye shall seek *me*, and shall not find
36. this that he said, Ye shall seek *me*,
37. let him come unto *me*, and drink.
8:16. but I and the Father that sent *me*.
18. the Father that sent *me*
21. and ye shall seek *me*,
26. but he that sent *me* is true;
28. but as my Father hath taught *me*,
29. And he that sent *me* is with me: the Father hath not left *me* alone;
37. but ye seek to kill *me*,
40. But now ye seek to kill *me*,
42. but he sent *me*
46. Which of you convinceth *me* of sin?
49. and ye do dishonour *me*.
54. it is my Father that honoureth *me*;
9: 4. the works of him that sent *me*,
10:15. As the Father knoweth *me*,
16. them also *I* must bring,
17. Therefore doth my Father love *me*,
32. of those works do ye stone *me*?
11:42. that thou hast sent *me*.
12:27. shall I say? Father, save *me* from this hour:
44. but on him that sent *me*.
45. he that seeth me seeth him that sent *me*.
49. but the Father which sent *me*,
13:13. Ye call *me* Master and Lord:
20. receiveth him that sent *me*.
21. one of you shall betray *me*.
33. Ye shall seek *me*:
38. till thou hast denied *me* thrice.
14: 7. If ye had known *me*,
9. yet hast thou not known *me*,
15. If ye love *me*, keep my
19. and the world seeth *me* no more; but ye see *me*:
21. he it is that loveth *me*: and he that loveth *me*
23. If a man love *me*,
24. He that loveth *me* not
— but the Father's which sent *me*.

Joh.14:28. If ye loved *me*, ye would rejoice,
15: 9. As the Father hath loved *me*,
16. Ye have not chosen *me*,
21. they know not him that sent *me*.
25. They hated *me* without a cause.
16: 5. to him that sent *me*; and none of you asketh *me*,
10. and ye see *me* no more;
16. and ye shall not see *me*: and again, a little while, and ye shall see *me*,
17. not see *me*: and again, a little while, and ye shall see *me*:
19. not see *me*: and again, a little while, and ye shall see *me*?
17: 5. O Father, glorify thou *me*
8. believed that thou didst send *me*.
21. may believe that thou hast sent *me*.
23. may know that thou hast sent *me*,
24. for thou lovedst *me* before the
25. have known that thou hast sent *me*.
26. wherewith thou hast loved *me*
18:21. Why askest thou *me*?
23. why smitest thou *me*?
19:11. he that delivered *me* unto thee
20:21. as (my) Father hath sent *me*,
29. Thomas, because thou hast seen *me*,
21:15. lovest thou *me* more than these?
16. (son) of Jonas, lovest thou *me*?
17. (son) of Jonas, lovest thou *me*?
— the third time, Lovest thou *me*?
Acts 2:28. thou shalt make *me* full of joy
7:28. Wilt thou kill *me*,
8:31. except some man should guide *me*?
36. what doth hinder *me* to be
9: 4. why persecutest thou *me*?
6. what wilt thou have *me* to do?
17. hath sent *me*, that thou mightest
10:29. for what intent ye have sent for *me*?
11:11. sent from Cæsarea unto *me*.
15. And as *I* began to speak,
12:11. and hath delivered *me*
13:25. Whom think ye that *I* am?
16:15. If ye have judged *me* to be
30. what must *I* do to be saved?
18:21. *I* must by all means keep
19:21. After *I* have been there, *I* must also see Rome.
20:23. that bonds and afflictions abide *me*.
22: 7. Saul, Saul, why persecutest thou *me*?
8. And he said unto *me*, I am Jesus
10. And the Lord said unto *me*,
13. Came unto *me*, and stood, and said
17. *I* was in a trance;
21. And he said unto *me*, Depart:
23: 3. sittest thou to judge *me* after the law, and commandest *me* to be
18. Paul the prisoner called *me*
22. hast shewed these things to *me*.
24:12. they neither found *me* in the
13. Neither can they prove (lit. establish against *me*)
18. found *me* purified in the
19. if they had ought against *me*.
25:10. where *I* ought to be judged:
11. no man may deliver *me* unto them.
26: 5. Which knew *me* from the beginning,
13. shining round about *me* and them
14. I heard a voice speaking unto *me*,
— why persecutest thou *me*?
21. the Jews caught *me* in the temple,
28. Almost thou persuadest *me* to be
28:18. when they had examined *me*.

Ro. 7:11. by the commandment, deceived *me*,
23. and bringing *me* into captivity
24. who shall deliver *me*
8: 2. hath made *me* free from
9:20. Why hast thou made *me* thus?
15:16. That *I* should be the minister of
19. *I* have fully preached the gospel
1Co. 1:17. Christ sent *me* not to baptize,
4: 4. but he that judgeth *me* is the Lord.
16: 6. ye may bring *me* on my journey
11. that he may come unto *me*:
2Co. 2: 2. who is he then that maketh *me* glad,
3. of whom *I* ought to rejoice;
13. because *I* found not Titus
7: 7. so that *I* rejoiced the more.
11:16. Let no man think *me* a fool;
— yet as a fool receive *me*,
32. desirous to apprehend *me*:
12: 6. above that which he seeth *me* (to be),
7. of Satan to buffet *me*,
11. ye have compelled *me*:
21. lest, when I come again, my God will humble *me*
Gal. 1:15. who separated *me* from my
2:20. the Son of God, who loved *me*,
4:12. ye have not injured *me* at all.
14. but received *me* as an angel of God,
18. not only when *I* am present
Eph. 6:20. as *I* ought to speak.
Phi. 1: 7. because *I* have you in my heart;
2:30. your lack of service toward *me*.
4:13. Christ which strengtheneth *me*.
Col. 4: 4. as *I* ought to speak.
1Ti. 1:12. Jesus our Lord, who hath enabled *me*, for that he counted *me* faithful,
2Ti. 1:15. in Asia be turned away from *me*;
16. for he oft refreshed *me*,
17. he sought *me* out very diligently,
3:11. out of (them) all the Lord delivered *me*
4: 9. to come shortly unto *me*:
16. but all (men) forsook *me*:
17. stood with me, and strengthened *me*,
18. the Lord shall deliver *me*
Tit. 3:12. be diligent to come unto *me* to
Heb. 3: 9. When your fathers tempted *me*; proved *me*,
8:11. for all shall know *me*,
11:32. the time would fail *me* to tell
Rev.17: 3. So he carried *me* away in the
21: 9. And there came unto *me* one of
10. he carried *me* away in the spirit

3166 1 497/131 3173
aucheō (to boast)

μεγαλαυχέω, *megalaukeo.*

Jas. 3: 5. and *boasteth great things*.

3167 2 497/619 4:529 3173

μεγαλεῖα, *megalīa.*

Lu. 1:49. hath done to me *great things*;
Acts 2:11. the *wonderful works* of God.

3168 3 498/619 4:529 3167

μεγαλειότης, *megalīotees*

Lu. 9:43. amazed at the *mighty power* of God.
Acts19:27. her *magnificence* should be destroyed,
2Pet. 1:16. were eyewitnesses of his *majesty*.

3169 1 498/619 4:529 3173,4241

μεγαλοπρεπής, *megaloprepees.*

2Pet. 1:17. a voice to him from the *excellent* glory,

3170 8 498/619 4:529 3173

μεγαλύνω, *megaluno.*

Mat.23: 5. and *enlarge* the borders of their
Lu. 1:46. My soul *doth magnify* the Lord,
58. *had shewed great* mercy upon her;
Acts 5:13. but the people *magnified* them.
10:46. speak with tongues, and *magnify* God.
19:17. name of the Lord Jesus *was magnified.*
2Co.10:15. that we shall *be enlarged* by you
Phi. 1:20. now also Christ *shall be magnified* in my

3171 1 498/620 3173

μεγάλως, *megalōs.*

Phi. 4:10. I rejoiced in the Lord *greatly,*

3172 3 498/620 4:529 3173

μεγαλωσύνη, *megalōsunee.*

Heb. 1: 3. on the right hand of the *Majesty* on high;
8: 1. throne of the *Majesty* in the heavens;
Jude 25. (be) glory and *majesty,* dominion

3173 195 498/620 4:529 3187, cf 3176

μέγας, *megas.*

Mat. 2:10. with exceeding *great* joy.
4:16. which sat in darkness saw *great* light;
5:19. shall be called *great* in the kingdom
35. it is the city of the *great* King.
7:27. and *great* was the fall of it.
8:24. there arose a *great* tempest
26. and there was a *great* calm.
15:28. O woman, *great* (is) thy faith:
20:25. and they that are *great* exercise
26. whosoever will be *great* among you,
22:36. which (is) the *great* commandment
38. the first and *great* commandment.
24:21. then shall be *great* tribulation,
24. and shall shew *great* signs
31. with a *great* sound of a trumpet,
27:46. Jesus cried with a *loud* voice,
50. had cried again with a *loud* voice,
60. he rolled a *great* stone to the door
28: 2. there was a *great* earthquake:
8. with fear and *great* joy;
Mar. 1:26. and cried with a *loud* voice,
4:32. and shooteth out *great* branches;
37. there arose a *great* storm
39. and there was a *great* calm.
41. And they feared exceedingly, (lit. a *great* fear)
5: 7. And cried with a *loud* voice,
11. a *great* herd of swine feeding.
42. with a *great* astonishment.
10:42. and their *great* ones exercise
43. whosoever will be *great* among
13: 2. Seest thou these *great* buildings?
14:15. a *large* upper room furnished
15:34. Jesus cried with a *loud* voice, saying,
37. cried with a *loud* voice, and gave up
16: 4. for it was very *great.*
Lu. 1:15. For he shall be *great* in the
32. He shall be *great,* and shall be
42. she spake out with a *loud* voice,
2: 9. and they were sore afraid. (lit. feared a *great* fear)
Lu. 2:10. I bring you good tidings of *great* joy.
4:25. when *great* famine was
33. and cried out with a *loud* voice,
38. was taken with a *great* fever;
5:29. Levi made him a *great* feast
6:49. the ruin of that house was *great.*
7:16. That a *great* prophet is risen up
8:28. and with a *loud* voice said,
37. they were taken with *great* fear:
9:48. the same shall be *great.*
13:19. and waxed a *great* tree;
14:16. A certain man made a *great* supper,
16:26. there is a *great* gulf fixed:
17:15. and with a *loud* voice glorified God,
19:37. and praise God with a *loud* voice
21:11. And *great* earthquakes shall be
— and *great* signs shall there be
23. there shall be *great* distress
22:12. he shall shew you a *large* upper room
23:23. were instant with *loud* voices,
46. Jesus had cried with a *loud* voice,
24:52. to Jerusalem with *great* joy:
Joh. 6:18. by reason of a *great* wind
7:37. that *great* (day) of the feast,
11:43. he cried with a *loud* voice,
19:31. for that sabbath day was an *high* day,
21:11. the net to land full of *great* fishes,
Acts 2:20. before that *great* and notable day
4:33. And with *great* power gave the
— and *great* grace was upon them
5: 5. and *great* fear came on all
11. And *great* fear came upon all
6: 8. did *great* wonders and miracles
7:11. and Chanaan, and *great* affliction:
57. they cried out with a *loud* voice,
60. and cried with a *loud* voice,
8: 1. there was a *great* persecution
2. and made *great* lamentation
7. crying with *loud* voice,
8. there was *great* joy in that city.
9. that himself was some *great* one:
10. from the least to the *greatest,* saying, This man is the *great* power of God.
13. beholding the miracles and signs (lit. signs and *great* miracles)
10:11. as it had been a *great* sheet
11: 5. as it had been a *great* sheet,
28. that there should be *great* dearth
14:10. Said with a *loud* voice,
15: 3. they caused *great* joy unto all the
16:26. there was a *great* earthquake,
28. Paul cried with a *loud* voice,
19:27. of the *great* goddess Diana
28. *Great* (is) Diana of the Ephesians.
34. *Great* (is) Diana of the Ephesians.
35. of the *great* goddess Diana,
23: 9. And there arose a *great* cry:
26:22. witnessing both to small and *great,*
24. Festus said with a *loud* voice,
Ro 9: 2. That I have *great* heaviness
1Co. 9:11. (is it) a *great* thing if we
16: 9. For a *great* door and effectual
2Co.11:15. (it is) no *great* thing if his ministers
Eph. 5:32. This is a *great* mystery:
1Ti. 3:16. *great* is the mystery of
6: 6. with contentment is *great* gain.
2Ti. 2:20. But in a *great* house there are
Tit. 2:13. glorious appearing of the *great* God
Heb. 4:14. that we have a *great* high priest,
8:11. from the least to the *greatest.*
10:21. And (having) an *high* priest over
35. which hath *great* recompence

Heb11:24. Moses, when he was come *to years*,
13:20. that *great* Shepherd of the sheep,
Jude 6. unto the judgment of the *great* day.
Rev. 1:10. and heard behind me a *great* voice,
2:22. into *great* tribulation,
5: 2. proclaiming with a *loud* voice,
12. Saying with a *loud* voice,
6: 4. there was given unto him a *great* sword.
10. with a *loud* voice, saying,
12. there was a *great* earthquake;
13. is shaken of a *mighty* wind.
17. the *great* day of his wrath is come;
7: 2. he cried with a *loud* voice to
10. And cried with a *loud* voice,
14. which came out of *great* tribulation,
8: 8. as it were a *great* mountain
10. there fell a *great* star from
13. saying with a *loud* voice,
9: 2. as the smoke of a *great* furnace;
14. bound in the *great* river Euphrates.
10: 3. cried with a *loud* voice,
11: 8. in the street of the *great* city,
11. and *great* fear fell upon them
12. they heard a *great* voice
13. there a *great* earthquake,
15. there were *great* voices in heaven,
17. hast taken to thee thy *great* power,
18. that fear thy name, small and *great*,
19. an earthquake, and *great* hail.
12: 1. a *great* wonder in heaven;
3. a *great* red dragon,
9. the *great* dragon was cast out,
10. I heard a *loud* voice
12. having *great* wrath, because he knoweth
14. two wings of a *great* eagle,
13: 2. and his seat, and *great* authority.
5. a mouth speaking *great* things
13. he doeth *great* wonders,
16. he caused all, both small and *great*,
14: 2. as the voice of a *great* thunder:
7. Saying with a *loud* voice,
8. that *great* city, because the
9. saying with a *loud* voice,
15. crying with a *loud* voice to
18. cried with a *loud* cry to
19. into the *great* winepress of the
15: 1. *great* and marvellous, seven angels
3. *Great* and marvellous (are) thy works,
16: 1. I heard a *great* voice out of
9. scorched with *great* heat,
12. his vial upon the *great* river
14. of that *great* day of God Almighty.
17. a *great* voice out of the temple
18. there was a *great* earthquake,
— so mighty an earthquake, (and) so *great*.
19. the *great* city was divided
— *great* Babylon came in remembrance
21. upon men a *great* hail out of
— plague thereof was exceeding *great*.
17: 1. judgment of the *great* whore
5. MYSTERY, BABYLON THE *GREAT*,
6. I wondered with *great* admiration.
18. is that *great* city,
18: 1. having *great* power;
2. cried mightily with a *strong* voice, saying, Babylon the *great* is fallen,
10. Alas, alas that *great* city Babylon,
16. Alas, alas that *great* city,
18. What (city is) like unto this *great*
19. Alas, alas that *great* city,
21. a stone like a *great* millstone,
— shall that *great* city Babylon
Rev.19: 1. I heard a *great* voice of much
2. hath judged the *great* whore,
5. that fear him, both small and *great*.
17. he cried with a *loud* voice,
— unto the supper of the *great* God;
18. both small and *great*.
20: 1. and a *great* chain in his hand.
11. I saw a *great* white throne,
12. I saw the dead, small and *great*,
21: 3. I heard a *great* voice out of
10. to a *great* and high mountain, and shewed me that *great* city,
12. had a wall *great* and high,

See also μείζων and μέγιστος.

3174 1 499/622 4:529 3173

μέγεθος, *megethos*.

Eph. 1:19. And what (is) the exceeding *greatness* of his power to us-ward

---

3175 3 499/622 3176

μεγιστανες, *megistanes*.

Mar 6:21. made a supper to his *lords*,
Rev. 6:15. and the *great men*, and the rich
18:23. thy merchants were the *great men* of the earth;

3176 1 499/622 3173

μέγιστος, *megistos*.

2Pet.1: 4. *exceeding great* and precious promises:

3177 7 499/622 3326,2059

μεθερμηνεύομαι, *mothermeenūomai*.

Mat. 1:23. *being interpreted* is, God with us.
Mar 5:41. which is, *being interpreted*, Damsel,
15:22. *being interpreted*, The place of a skull.
34. which is, *being interpreted*, My God,
Joh. 1:41(42). *being interpreted* the Christ.
Acts 4:36. which is, *being interpreted*, The son of
13: 8. for so *is* his name *by interpretation*

3178 3 500/622 4:545

μέθη, *methee*.

Lu. 21:34. and *drunkenness*, and cares of this life,
Ro. 13:13. not in rioting and *drunkenness*,
Gal. 5:21. murders, *drunkenness*, revellings,

3179 5 500/622 3326,2476

μεθιστάνω, μεθίστημι, *methistano*, *methisteemi*.

Lu. 16: 4. when I *am put out of* the stewardship,
Acts13:22. *when* he *had removed* him,
19:26. and *turned away* much people,
1Co.13: 2. so that I could *remove* mountains,
Col. 1:13. and *hath translated* (us) into

3180 2 500/622 5:42 3326,3593

μεθοδεία, *methodia*.

Eph. 4:14. whereby they lie in wait to deceive; (lit. unto *circumvention* of deceit)
6:11. to stand against the *wiles* of the devil.

3181 1 500/704 3326,3725

μεθόρια, methoria.

Mar. 7:24. went into the *borders* of Tyre and

3182 3 500/622 4:545 3184

μεθύσκομαι, methuskomai.

Lu. 12:45. eat and drink, and *to be drunken;*
Eph. 5:18. And *be* not *drunk* with wine,
1Th. 5: 7. they *that be drunken* are drunken in

3183 2 500/622 4:545 3184

μέθυσος, methusos.

1Co. 5:11. or a *drunkard,* or an extortioner;
6:10. nor *drunkards,* nor revilers, nor

3184 7 500/622 4:545 3178

μεθύω, methuo.

Mat.24:49. and drink with the *drunken;*
Joh. 2:10. when men *have well drunk,*
Acts 2:15. these *are* not *drunken,* as
1Co.11:21. and another *is drunken.*
1Th. 5: 7. *are drunken* in the night.
Rev.17: 2. *have been made drunk* with the wine
6. *drunken* with the blood of the saints,

3185 1 500/622 3187

μεῖζον, mizon. adv.

Mat.20:31. but they cried *the more,*

3186 1 500/622 3187

μειζότερος, mizoteros.

3Joh. 4. I have no *greater* joy than to hear

3187 45 500/622 3173

μείζων, μεῖζον, mizōn, mizon.

Mat.11:11. hath not risen a *greater* than John
— is *greater* than he.
12: 6. is (one) *greater* than the temple.
13:32. is the *greatest* among herbs, (lit. *greater* than herbs)
18: 1. Who is the *greatest* (lit. *greater*) in the kingdom
4. the same is *greatest* in the kingdom
23:11, But he that is *greatest* among you
17. for whether is *greater,* the gold,
19. whether (is) *greater,* the gift, or the
Mar. 4:32. becometh *greater* than all herbs,
9:34. who (should be) the *greatest.*
12:31. commandment *greater* than these.
Lu. 7:28. there is not a *greater* prophet than
— is *greater* than he.
9:46. which of them should be *greatest.*
12:18. pull down my barns, and build *greater;*
22:24. should be accounted the *greatest.*
26. but he that is *greatest* among you,
27. For whether (is) *greater,* he that sitteth
Joh. 1:50(51). thou shalt see *greater* things than
4:12. Art thou *greater* than
5:20. *greater* works than these,
36. But I have *greater* witness
8:53. Art thou *greater* than our father
10:29. is *greater* than all;
13:16. The servant is not *greater* than his lord; neither he that is sent *greater*
14:12. and *greater* (works) than these
28. for my Father is *greater* than I.
Joh.15:13. *Greater* love hath no man than this,
20. The servant is not *greater* than
19:11. hath the *greater* sin.
Ro. 9:12. The *elder* shall serve the younger.
1Co.13:13. but the *greatest* of these (is) charity.
14: 5. for *greater* (is) he that prophesieth
Heb 6:13. could swear by no *greater,*
16. men verily swear by the *greater:*
9:11. by a *greater* and more perfect
11:26. the reproach of Christ *greater* riches
Jas. 3: 1. receive the *greater* condemnation.
4: 6. But he giveth *more* grace.
2Pet.2:11. which are *greater* in power and might,
1Joh.3:20. God is *greater* than our heart,
4: 4. *greater* is he that is in you,
5: 9. the witness of God is *greater:*

3188 3 500/623 3189

μέλαν, melan. subs.

2Co. 3: 3. written not with *ink,*
2Joh. 12. I would not (write) with paper and *ink:*
3Joh. 13. I will not with *ink* and pen write

3189 3 501/623 4:549

μέλας, melas.

Mat. 5:36. one hair white or *black.*
Rev. 6: 5. and lo a *black* horse;
12. sun became *black* as sackcloth of hair,

3199 10 501/623

μέλει, meli. impers. verb.

Mat.22:16. neither *carest* thou for any
Mar. 4:38. Master, *carest* thou not that we
12:14. and *carest* for no man:
Lu. 10:40. Lord, *dost* thou not *care* that
Joh.10:13. and *careth* not for the sheep.
12: 6. not that he *cared* for the poor;
Acts18:17. And Gallio *cared* for none of
1Co. 7:21. *care* not for it:
9: 9. *Doth* God *take care* for oxen?
1Pet.5: 7. for he *careth* for you.

3191 3 501/623 3199

μελετάω, meletao.

Mar 13:11. neither *do* ye *premeditate:*
Acts 4:25. Why did the heathen rage, and the people *imagine* vain things?
1Ti. 4:15. *Meditate* upon these things;

3192 4 501/623 4:552

μέλι, meli.

Mat. 3: 4. his meat was locusts and wild *honey.*
Mar 1: 6. and he did eat locusts and wild *honey;*
Rev.10: 9. in thy mouth sweet as *honey.*
10. in my mouth sweet as *honey:*

3193 1 501/623 3192

μελίσσιος, melissios.

Lu. 24:42. and of an *honeycomb.*

3195 110 501/623 3199

μέλλω, mello.

Mat. 2:13. Herod *will* seek the young child
3: 7. to flee from the wrath *to come?*

Mat.11:14. *which was for* to come.
12:32. neither in the (world) *to come.*
16:27. the Son of man *shall* come in
17:12. Likewise *shall* also the Son of
22. The Son of man *shall* be betrayed
20:22. that I *shall* drink of,
24: 6. And ye *shall* hear of wars
Mar 10:32. *what* things *should* happen unto him,
13: 4. when all these things *shall* be fulfilled?
Lu. 3: 7. from the wrath *to come?*
7: 2. was sick, and *ready* to die.
9:31. which he *should* accomplish
44. the Son of man *shall* be delivered
10: 1. whither he himself *would* come.
13: 9. *after that* thou shalt cut it down.
19: 4. he *was* to pass that (way).
11. of God *should* immediately appear.
21: 7. when these things *shall* come to pass?
36. *that shall* come to pass,
22:23. *that should* do this thing.
24:21. he *which should* have redeemed
Joh. 4:47. for he *was at the point* of death.
6: 6. he himself knew what he *would* do.
15. that they *would* come and take him
71. he it was that *should* betray him,
7:35. Whither *will* he go, that we shall not find him? *will* he go unto
39. that believe on him *should* receive:
11:51. that Jesus *should* die for
12: 4. *which should* betray him,
33. what death he *should* die.
14:22. that thou *wilt* manifest thyself
18:32. what death he *should* die.
Acts 3: 3. seeing Peter and John *about* to go
5:35. what ye *intend* to do as touching
11:28. that there *should* be great dearth
12: 6. when Herod *would* have brought
13:34. no more to return (lit. *being* no more *about* to return) to corruption,
16:27. and *would* have killed himself,
17:31. in the which he *will* judge the world
18:14. *when* Paul *was* now *about to* open
19:27. magnificence *should* be destroyed,
20: 3. for him, *as* he *was about* to sail into
7. *ready* to depart on the morrow;
13. there *intending* to take in Paul:
— *minding* himself to go afoot.
38. that they *should* see his face no more.
21:27. the seven days *were almost* ended,
37. *as* Paul *was* to be led into the
22:16. And now why *tarriest* thou?
26. Take heed what thou doest: (lit. *art about* to do)
29. *which should have* examined him:
23: 3. God *shall* smite thee,
15. as *though* ye *would* enquire something
20. as *though* they *would* enquire somewhat
27. and *should have* been killed
30. told me how that the Jews laid wait (lit. the lying wait being told me as *about* to be)
24:15. that there *shall* be a resurrection
25. and judgment *to come,*
25: 4. he himself *would* depart shortly
26: 2. *because* I *shall* answer for myself
22. did say *should* come:
23. and *should* shew light unto the
27: 2. *meaning* to sail by the coasts of Asia;
10. *will* be with hurt and much damage,
30. as *though* they *would have* cast
33. while the day *was coming* on,
28: 6. they looked when he *should have* swollen,

Ro. 4:24. to whom it *shall* be imputed,
5:14. figure of him *that was to come.*
8:13. after the flesh, ye *shall* die:
18. glory *which shall* be revealed in us.
38. nor *things to come,*
1Co. 3:22. or *things to come;* all are your's;
Gal. 3:23. *which should afterwards* be revealed.
Eph. 1:21. but also in *that which is to come:*
Col. 2:17. a shadow of *things to come;*
1Th. 3: 4. that we *should* suffer tribulation,
1Ti. 1:16. *which should hereafter* believe
4: 8. and of *that which is to come.*
6:19. against the *time to come,*
2Ti. 4: 1. *who shall* judge the quick and
Heb. 1:14. *who shall* be heirs of salvation?
2: 5. put in subjection the world *to come,*
6: 5. the powers of the world *to come,*
8: 5. *when* he *was about* to make the
9:11. an high priest of good things *to come,*
10: 1. a shadow of good things *to come,*
27. which *shall* devour the adversaries.
11: 8. which he *should after* receive
20. concerning *things to come.*
13:14. but we seek one *to come.*
Jas. 2:12. as they *that shall* be judged
1Pet. 5: 1. glory *that shall* be revealed:
2Pet. 2: 6. *that after should* live ungodly;
Rev. 1:19. the things which *shall* be hereafter;
2:10. which thou *shalt* suffer: behold, the devil *shall* cast (some) of you
3: 2. that *are ready* to die:
10. *which shall* come upon all the
16. I *will* spue thee out of my mouth.
6:11. *that should* be killed as they (were),
8:13. angels, *which are yet* to sound!
10: 4. I *was about* to write:
7. when he *shall begin* to sound,
12: 4. *which was ready* to be delivered,
5. who was (lit. *is about*) to rule all nations
17: 8. and *shall* ascend out of the

3196 34 502/625 4:555

μέλος, *melos.*

Mat. 5:29. that one of thy *members* should
30. that one of thy *members* should perish,
Ro. 6:13. Neither yield ye your *members*
— and your *members* (as) instruments
19. for as ye have yielded your *members*
— now yield your *members* servants
7: 5. did work in our *members*
23. another law in my *members,*
— law of sin which is in my *members.*
12: 4. as we have many *members* in one body, and all *members* have not
5. every one *members* one of another.
1Co. 6:15. your bodies are the *members* of Christ: shall I then take the *members* of Christ, and make (them) the *members* of
12:12. and hath many *members,* and all the *members* of that
14. the body is not one *member,*
18. now hath God set the *members*
19. if they were all one *member,*
20. now (are they) many *members,* yet
22. those *members* of the body, which
25. but (that) the *members* should have
26. And whether one *member* suffer, all the *members* suffer with it; or one *member* be honoured, all the *members* rejoice
27. and *members* in particular.
Eph. 4:25. we are *members* one of another

Eph.5:30. we are *members* of his body,
Col. 3: 5. Mortify therefore your *members*
Jas. 3: 5. the tongue is a little *member*,
6. so is the tongue among our *members*,
4: 1. lusts that war in your *members*?

3200 1 503/625

μεμβράνα, *membrana.*

2Ti. 4:13. and the books, (but) especially the *parchments.*

3201 3 503/625 4:571

μέμφομαι, *memphomai.*

Mar. 7: 2. with unwashen, hands, they *found fault.*
Ro. 9:19. Why *doth* he yet *find fault?*
Heb. 8: 8. For *finding fault* with them,

3202 1 503/625 4:571 3201 *moira* (fate)

μεμψίμοιρος, *mempsimoiros.*

Jude 16. These are murmurers, *complainers*,

3303 195 503/625

μέν, *men.*

Found mostly with the first of two words or clauses that are in contrast, the second having δε; but sometimes combined with οὐν, which is denoted by [2].

Mat. 3:11. I *indeed* baptize you with water
9:37. The harvest *truly* (is) plenteous,
10:13. And if)(the house be worthy,
13: 4. some (seeds))(fell by the way side,
8. some)(an hundredfold, some
23. some)(an hundredfold, some sixty,
32. Which *indeed* is the least of all seeds:
16: 3. ye can discern the face)(of the sky;
14. Some)((say that thou art) John the
17:11. Elias *truly* shall first come,
20:23. Ye shall drink *indeed* of my cup,
21:35. and beat one)(, and killed another
22: 5. one)(to his farm, another to his
8. The wedding)(is ready,
23:27. which *indeed* appear beautiful
28. Even so ye also outwardly)(appear
25:15. And unto one)(he gave five talents,
33. And he shall set the sheep)(on his
26:24. The Son of man)(goeth as it is written
41. the spirit *indeed* (is) willing,
Mar 1: 8. I *indeed* have baptized you with
4: 4. some)(fell by the way side,
9:12. Elias *verily* cometh first, and restoreth
10:39. Ye shall *indeed* drink of the cup
12: 5. beating some)(, and killing some.
14:21. The Son of man *indeed* goeth,
38. The spirit *truly* (is) ready, but the flesh
16:19. *So*[2] then after the Lord had spoken
Lu. 3:16. I *indeed* baptize you with
18. And many other things)([2] in his
8: 5. some)(fell by the way side;
10: 2. The harvest *truly* (is) great,
6. And if)(the son of peace be there,
11:48. for they *indeed* killed them, and ye
13: 9. And if)(it bear fruit, (well):
22:22. And *truly* the Son of man goeth, as
23:33. one)(on the right hand, and the other
41. And we *indeed* justly; for we receive
56. and rested)(the sabbath day
Joh. 7:12. for some)(said, He is a good man: others
10:41. and said, John)(did no miracle:
Joh.11: 6. he abode)(two days still in the same
16: 9. Of sin)(, because they believe not
22. And ye)([2] now therefore have sorrow.
19:24. These things)([2] therefore the soldiers did.
32. and brake the legs of the first)(,
20:30. many other signs *truly*[2] did Jesus
Acts 1: 1. The former treatise)(have I made,
5. For John *truly* baptized with
6. When they)([2] therefore were come
18. Now)([2] this man purchased a field
2:41. Then)([2] they that gladly received his
3:21. Whom the heaven)(must receive until
22. For Moses *truly* said unto the fathers,
4:16. for that *indeed* a notable miracle
5:23. The prison *truly* found we shut
41. And they)([2] departed from the presence
8: 4. Therefore)([2] they that were scattered
25. And)([2] they, when they had testified
9: 7. hearing)(a voice, but seeing no man.
31. Then)([2] had the churches rest
11:16. John *indeed* baptized with water;
19. Now)([2] they which were scattered abroad
12: 5. Peter)([2] therefore was kept in prison:
13: 4. So)([2] they, being sent forth by
36. For David)(, after he had served
14: 3. Long time therefore)([2] abode they
4. and part)(held with the Jews,
12. And they called Barnabas)(, Jupiter;
15: 3. And)([2] being brought on their way by
30. So)([2] when they were dismissed,
16: 5. And)([2] so were the churches established
17:12. Therefore)([2] many of them believed;
17. Therefore)([2] disputed he in the
30. And)([2] the times of this ignorance
32. of the dead, some)(mocked: and others
18:14. If)([2] it were a matter of wrong
19: 4. John *verily* baptized with the
32. Some therefore)([2] cried one thing,
38. Wherefore)([2] if Demetrius, and the
21:39. I am)(a man (which am) a Jew of
22: 3. I am *verily* a man (which am) a Jew,
9. they that were with me saw *indeed*
23: 8. For the Sadducees)(say that there is no
18. So)([2] he took him, and brought
22. So)([2] the chief captain (then) let the
31. Then)([2] the soldiers, as it was
25: 4. But)([2] Festus answered, that Paul
11. For if)(I be an offender, or have
26: 4. My manner of life)([2] from my youth,
9. I *verily*[2] thought with myself,
27:21. Sirs, ye should)(have hearkened unto
41. and the forepart)(stuck fast,
44. and some)(on (broken pieces) of the
28: 5. And)([2] he shook off the beast into
22. for as concerning)(this sect,
24. And some)(believed the things
Ro. 1: 8. First,)(I thank my God through Jesus
2: 7. To them)(who by patient continuance
8. and do not obey)(the truth,
25. circumcision *verily* profiteth, if
3: 2. chiefly)(, because that unto them were
5:16. for the judgment)((was) by one
6:11. to be dead *indeed* unto sin,
7:12. Wherefore the law)((is) holy,
25. So then with the mind)(I myself
8:10. the body)((is) dead because of sin;
17. heirs)(of God, and joint-heirs with
9:21. to make one vessel)(unto honour,
10: 1. my heart's desire)(and prayer to God
11:13. inasmuch as)(I am the apostle of the
22. on them which fell)(, severity;
28. As concerning)(the gospel, (they are)

Ro. 14: 2. For one)(believeth that he may eat
5. One man)(esteemeth one day
20. All things *indeed* (are) pure; but
16:19. wise)(unto that which is good, and
1Co. 1:12. every one of you saith, I)(am of Paul;
18. is to them)(that perish foolishness;
23. unto the Jews)(a stumblingblock,
2:15. he that is spiritual judgeth)(all things,
3: 4. For while one saith, I)(am of Paul;
5: 3. For I *verily*, as absent in body,
6: 4. If)([2] then ye have judgments of things
7. Now)([2] therefore there is utterly a fault
7: 7. one)(after this manner, and another
9:24. they which run in a race run all)(,
25.)([2] Now they (do it) to obtain
11: 7. For a man *indeed* ought not to
14. that, if a man)(have long hair,
18. For first)(of all, when ye come
21. and one)(is hungry, and another is
12: 8. For to one)(is given by the Spirit
20. many)(members, yet but one body.
28. And God hath set some)(in the church,
14:17. For thou *verily* givest thanks well,
15:39. but (there is) one)((kind of) flesh of
40. the glory of the celestial (is) one)(,
51. We shall not all)(sleep,
2Co. 2:16. To the one)((we are) the savour of
4:12. So then death)(worketh in us,
8:17. For *indeed* he accepted the exhortation;
9: 1. For as touching)(the ministering
10: 1. who in presence)((am) base among you,
10. For (his) letters)(, say they, (are)
11: 4. For if)(he that cometh preacheth
12 12. *Truly* the signs of an apostle
Gal. 4: 8. Howbeit then)(, when ye knew not God,
23. But he)((who was) of the bondwoman
24. the one)(from the mount Sinai,
Eph. 4:11. he gave *some*)(, apostles; and some,
Phi. 1:15. Some *indeed* preach Christ even of
16. The one)(preach Christ of contention,
28. which is to them)(an evident token
2:23. Him)([2] therefore I hope to send
3: 1. to me *indeed* (is) not grievous,
13(14). forgetting those things)(which are
Col. 2:23. Which things have *indeed* a shew
1Th. 2:18. *even* I Paul, once and again;
2Ti. 1:10. who hath abolished)(death,
2:19. Nevertheless (lit. but *indeed*) the foundation of God
20. and some)(to honour, and some to
4: 4. shall turn away (their) ears from the truth)(,
Tit. 1:15. Unto the pure all things)((are) pure:
Heb. 1: 7. And of the angels)(he saith,
3: 5. And Moses *verily* (was) faithful
6:16. For men *verily* swear by the
7: 2. first)(being by interpretation
5. And *verily* they that are of the sons
8. And here)(men that die receive tithes;
11. If)([2] therefore perfection were by the
18. For there is *verily* a disannulling
21(20). For those priests)(were made without an oath;
23. And they *truly* were many priests,
8: 4. For if)(he were on earth,
9: 1. Then *verily*[2] the first (covenant)
6. the priests went always into the first)(tabernacle,
23. necessary that the patterns)(of things
10:11. And every priest)(standeth daily
33. Partly)(, whilst ye were made a
11:15. And *truly*, if they had been mindful
Heb12: 9. Furthermore we have had fathers)(of our
10. For they *verily* for a few days
11. Now no chastening for the present)(
Jas. 3:17. wisdom that is from above is first)(pure
1Pet. 1:20. Who *verily* was foreordained
2: 4. disallowed *indeed* of men,
14. for the punishment)(of evildoers,
3:18. being put to death)(in the flesh,
4: 6. might be judged)(according to men in the flesh,
14. on their part)(he is evil spoken of,
Jude 8. defile the flesh)(, despise dominion,
10. speak evil of those things)(which they know not:
22. And of some)(have compassion,

See also μενοῦν γε and μέντοι.

3304 4 504/628 3303,3767,1065

μενοῦνγε, *menounge.*

Lu. 11:28. *Yea rather*, blessed (are) they that,
Ro. 9:20. *Nay but*, O man, who art thou that
10:18. *Yes verily*, their sound went into all
Phi. 3: 8. *Yea doubtless*, and I count all things

3305 8 504/628 3303,5104

μέντοι, *mentoi.*

Joh. 4:27. *yet* no man said, What seekest thou?
7:13. *Howbeit* no man spake openly
12:42. *Nevertheless* (ομως μ.) among the chief
20: 5. *yet* went he not in.
21: 4. *but* the disciples knew not that it
2Ti. 2:19. *nevertheless* the foundation of God
Jas. 2:8. If)(ye fulfil the royal law
Jude 8. *Likewise* (ομοιως μ.) also these (filthy)

3306 120 504/628 4:589

μένω, *meno.*

Mat. 10:11. and there *abide* till ye go thence.
11:23. it would *have remained* until this
26:38. *tarry* ye here, and watch with me.
Mar. 6:10. there *abide* till ye depart from
14:34. *tarry* ye here, and watch.
Lu. 1:56. Mary *abode* with her about three
8:27. neither *abode* in (any) house,
9: 4. there *abide*, and thence depart.
10: 7. And in the same house *remain*,
19: 5. for to day I must *abide* at thy house.
24:29. constrained him, saying, *Abide* with us:
— And he went in *to tarry* with them.
Joh. 1:32. and it *abode* upon him.
33. and *remaining* on him,
38(39). Master, where *dwellest* thou?
39(40). They came and saw where he *dwelt*, and *abode* with him that day:
2:12. they *continued* there not many days.
3:36. the wrath of God *abideth* on him.
4:40. that he would *tarry* with them: and he *abode* there two days.
5:38. ye have not his word *abiding* in you:
6:27. for that meat *which endureth* unto
56. *dwelleth* in me, and I in him.
7: 9. he *abode* (still) in Galilee.
8:31. If ye *continue* in my word,
35. the servant *abideth* not in the house for ever: (but) the Son *abideth* ever.
9:41. therefore your sin *remaineth*.
10:40. and there he *abode*.
11: 6. he *abode* two days still in the
12:24. ground and die, it *abideth* alone:
34. that Christ *abideth* for ever.

Joh.12:46. *should* not *abide* in darkness.
14:10 the Father *that dwelleth* in me,
16. that he *may abide* with you for ever;
17. for he *dwelleth* with you,
25. *being* (yet) *present* with you.
15: 4. *Abide* in me, and I in you.
— except it *abide* in the vine; no more can ye, except ye *abide* in me.
5. He *that abideth* in me,
6. If a man *abide* not in me,
7. If ye *abide* in me, and my words *abide* in
9. *continue* ye in my love.
10. ye *shall abide* in my love;
— and *abide* in his love.
11. that my joy *might remain*
16. (that) your fruit *should remain:*
19:31. that the bodies *should* not *remain* upon
21:22. If I will that he *tarry* till I come,
23. If I will that he *tarry* till I come,
Acts 5: 4. *Whiles* it *remained*, was it not thine own? (lit. *did* it not *remain* to thee)
9:43. that he *tarried* many days in Joppa
16:15. come into my house, and *abide*
18: 3. he *abode* with them, and wrought:
20. When they desired (him) *to tarry*
20: 5. These going before *tarried for* us at
15. and *tarried* at Trogyllium; *and*
23. and afflictions *abide* me.
21: 7. *abode* with them one day.
8. and *abode* with him.
27:31. Except these *abide* in the ship,
41. stuck fast, and *remained* unmoveable,
28:16. Paul was suffered *to dwell* by himself
30. Paul *dwelt* two whole years in
Ro. 9:11. the purpose of God according to election *might stand*,
1Co. 3:14. If any man's work *abide*
7: 8. if they *abide* even as I.
11. *let* her *remain* unmarried,
20. *Let* every man *abide* in the same
24. *let* every man,...therein *abide* with God.
40. she is happier if she so *abide*,
13:13. now *abideth* faith, hope, charity,
15: 6. the greater part *remain* unto this
2Co. 3:11. much more that *which remaineth*
14. *remaineth* the same vail
9: 9. his righteousness *remaineth* for ever.
Phi. 1:25. I know that I *shall abide* and
1Ti. 2:15. if they *continue* in faith and
2Ti. 2:13. he *abideth* faithful: he cannot deny
3:14. *continue* thou in the things
4:20. Erastus *abode* at Corinth:
Heb 7: 3. *abideth* a priest continually.
24. because he *continueth* ever,
10:34. and an *enduring* substance.
12:27. cannot be shaken *may remain*.
13: 1. *Let* brotherly love *continue*.
14. here have we no *continuing* city,
1Pet.1:23. which liveth and *abideth* for ever.
25. the word of the Lord *endureth* for ever.
1Joh.2: 6. He that saith he *abideth* in him
10. *abideth* in the light,
14. the word of God *abideth* in you,
17. doeth the will of God *abideth* for ever.
19. they would (no doubt) *have continued* with us:
24. *Let* that therefore *abide* in you,
— shall *remain* in you, ye also *shall continue*
27. received of him *abideth* in you,
— ye *shall abide* in him.
28. little children, *abide* in him;
3: 6. *Whosoever abideth* in him
1Joh.3: 9. his seed *remaineth* in him:
14. He that loveth not (his) brother *abideth* in death.
15. no murderer hath eternal life *abiding* in
17. how *dwelleth* the love of God in him?
24. *dwelleth* in him, and he in him. And hereby we know that he *abideth* in us,
4:12. God *dwelleth* in us,
13. that we *dwell* in him,
15. God *dwelleth* in him,
16. he *that dwelleth* in love *dwelleth* in God, and God in him.
2Joh. 2. For the truth's sake, *which dwelleth* in us,
9. and *abideth* not in the doctrine
— He *that abideth* in the doctrine
Rev.17:10. he must *continue* a short space.

3308 6 506/629 4:589 3307

μέριμνα, *merimna.*

Mat.13:22. the *care* of this world,
Mar. 4:19. the *cares* of this world,
Lu. 8:14. are choked with *cares* and riches
21:34. and *cares* of this life,
2Co.11:28. the *care* of all the churches.
1Pet.5: 7. Casting all your *care* upon him;

3309 19 506/629 4:589 3308

μεριμνάω, *merimnao.*

Mat. 6:25. *Take* no *thought* for your life,
27. Which of you *by taking thought* can
28. why *take* ye *thought* for raiment?
31. Therefore *take* no *thought*,
34. *Take* therefore no *thought* for the morrow: for the morrow *shall take thought*
10:19. *take* no *thought* how or what ye shall
Lu. 10:41. thou *art careful* and troubled
12:11. *take* ye no *thought* how or what thing
22. *Take* no *thought* for your life,
25. which of you *with taking thought*
26. why *take* ye *thought* for the rest?
1Co. 7:32. He that is unmarried *careth* for
33. he that is married *careth* for the
34. *careth* for the things of the Lord,
— *careth* for the things of the world,
12:25. *should have* the same *care* one for
Phi. 2:20. who *will* naturally *care* for your state.
4: 6. *Be careful* for nothing;

3307 14 505/629 3313

μερίζω, *merizo.*

Mat.12:25. Every kingdom *divided* against itself
— city or house *divided* against itself
26. he *is divided* against himself;
Mar. 3:24. if a kingdom *be divided* against
25. if a house *be divided* against itself,
26. and *be divided*, he cannot stand,
6:41. the two fishes *divided* he among them all
Lu. 12:13. that he *divide* the inheritance with me.
Ro. 12: 3. as God *hath dealt* to every man
1Co. 1:13. *Is* Christ *divided?*
7:17. as God *hath distributed* to every man,
34. There *is difference* (also) *between*
2Co.10:13. which God *hath distributed* to us,
Heb 7: 2. Abraham *gave* a tenth *part* of all;

3310 10 506/629 3313

μερίς, *meris.*

Lu. 10:42. Mary hath chosen that good *part*,
Acts 8:21. Thou hast neither *part* nor lot

Acts16:12. the chief city of that *part* of Macedonia,
2Co. 6:15. what *part* hath he that believeth
Col. 1:12. us meet to be partakers of the inheritance (lit. unto the *share* of the inheritance)

3311 2 506/629 3307

μερισμός, *merismos.*

Heb 2: 4. and *gifts* of the Holy Ghost,
4:12. even to the *dividing asunder* of soul and spirit,

3312 1 506/630 3307

μεριστής, *meristees.*

Lu. 12:14. made me a judge or a *divider* over you?

3313 43 506/630 4:594 *meiromai* (to get an allotment)

μέρος, *meros.*

Mat. 2:22. into the *parts* of Galilee:
15:21. departed into the *coasts* of Tyre and
16:13. Jesus came into the *coasts* of Cæsarea
24:51. and appoint (him) his *portion* with
Mar. 8:10. came into the *parts* of Dalmanutha.
Lu. 11:36. full of light, having no *part* dark,
12:46. will appoint him his *portion* with
15:12. give me the *portion* of goods that
24:42. they gave him a *piece* of a broiled fish,
Joh. 13: 8. If I wash thee not, thou hast no *part* with
19:23. and made four *parts*, to every soldier a *part*;
21: 6. Cast the net on the right *side*
Acts 2:10. and in the *parts* of Libya
5: 2. brought a certain *part*, and laid
19: 1. passed through the upper *coasts*
27. not only this our *craft* is in danger
20: 2. when he had gone over those *parts*,
23: 6. one *part* were Sadducees, and
9. of the Pharisees' *part* arose, and
Ro. 11:25. blindness in *part* is happened to Israel,
15:15. boldly unto you in *some sort*,
24. be *somewhat* filled with your
1Co. 11:18. and I partly believe it. (lit. I believe some *part*)
12:27. and members in *particular*.
13: 9. For we know in *part*, and we prophesy in *part*.
10. then that which is in *part* shall
12. now I know in *part*;
14:27. and (that) by *course*, and let one
2Co. 1:14. acknowledged us in *part*,
2: 5. he hath not grieved me, but in *part*:
3:10. had no glory in this *respect*,
9: 3. should be in vain in this *behalf*;
Eph. 4: 9. into the lower *parts* of the earth?
16. in the measure of every *part*,
Col. 2:16. or in *respect* of an holyday,
Heb. 9: 5. we cannot now speak particularly. (lit. according to *part*)
1Pet. 4:16. let him glorify God on this *behalf*.
Rev. 16:19. was divided into three *parts*,
20: 6. hath *part* in the first resurrection:
21: 8. shall have their *part* in the lake
22:19. God shall take away his *part* out of the book of life,

3314 2 507/630 3319,2250

μεσημβρία, *meseembria.*

Acts 8:26. Arise, and go toward the *south*
22: 6. nigh unto Damascus about *noon*,

3315 1 507/630 4:598 3316

μεσιτεύω, *mesituo.*

Heb. 6:17. *confirmed* (it) by an oath:

3316 6 507/630 4:598 3319

μεσίτης, *mesitees.*

Gal. 3:19. in the hand of a *mediator*.
20. Now a *mediator* is not (a mediator) of one
1Ti. 2: 5. one *mediator* between God and men,
Heb. 8: 6. is the *mediator* of a better covenant,
9:15. he is the *mediator* of the new testament,
12:24. And to Jesus the *mediator* of the new

3317 4 508/630 3319,3571

μεσονύκτιον, *mesonuktion.*

Mar 13:35. or at *midnight*, or at the
Lu. 11: 5. and shall go unto him at *midnight*,
Acts16:25. at *midnight* Paul and Silas prayed,
20: 7. continued his speech until *midnight*.

3319 61 508/630 3326

μέσος, *mesos.*

Mat. 10:16. as sheep in the *midst* of wolves:
13:25. sowed tares *among* the wheat,
49. sever the wicked from *among* the just,
14: 6. Herodias danced before them, (lit. in the *midst*)
24. ship was now in the *midst* of the sea,
18: 2. and set him in the *midst* of them,
20. there am I in the *midst* of them.
25: 6. And at *mid*night there was a cry
Mar. 3: 3. had the withered hand, Stand forth. (lit. into the *midst*)
6:47. the ship was in the *midst* of the sea,
7:31. through the *midst* of the coasts of
9:36. and set him in the *midst* of them:
14:60. high priest stood up in the *midst*,
Lu. 2:46. sitting in the *midst* of the doctors,
4:30. passing through the *midst* of them
35. the devil had thrown him in the *midst*,
5:19. into the *midst* before Jesus.
6: 8. and stand forth in the *midst*.
8: 7. And some fell *among* thorns;
10: 3. as lambs *among* wolves.
17:11. he passed through the *midst* of Samaria
21:21. in the *midst* of it depart out;
22:27. I am *among* you as he that serveth.
55. a fire in the *midst* of the hall,
— Peter sat down *among* them.
23:45. was rent in the *midst*.
24:36. Jesus himself stood in the *midst*
Joh. 1:26. there standeth one *among* you,
8: 3. when they had set her in the *midst*,
9. and the woman standing in the *midst*
59. through the *midst* of them,
19:18. and Jesus in the *midst*.
20:19. and stood in the *midst*, and saith
26. stood in the *midst*, and said, Peace
Acts 1:15. Peter stood up in the *midst*
18. he burst asunder in the *midst*,
2:22. God did by him in the *midst* of you,
4: 7. had set them in the *midst*,
17:22. Paul stood in the *midst* of Mars' hill,
33. Paul departed from *among* them.
23:10. by force from *among* them,
26:13. At *mid*day, O king, I saw
27:21. Paul stood forth in the *midst* of them,
27. about *mid*night the shipmen
1Co. 5: 2. be taken away from *among* you

1Co. 6: 5. able to judge *between* his brethren?
2Co. 6:17. come out from *among* them,
Phi. 2:15. in the *midst* of a crooked and
Col. 2:14. and took it out of the *way*,
1Th. 2: 7. But we were gentle *among* you,
2Th. 2: 7. until he be taken out of the *way*.
Heb. 2:12. in the *midst* of the church will I
Rev. 1:13. in the *midst* of the seven candlesticks
2: 1. walketh in the *midst* of the seven
7. which is in the *midst* of the paradise
4: 6. in the *midst* of the throne, and round
5: 6. in the *midst* of the throne and of the four beasts, and in the *midst* of the elders,
6: 6. in the *midst* of the four beasts
7:17. in the *midst* of the throne
22: 2. In the *midst* of the street of it,

3320 1 509/631 4:625 3319,5109

μεσότοιχον, *mesotoikon*.

Eph. 2:14. hath broken down the *middle wall* of

3321 3 509/631 3319,3772

μεσουράνημα, *mesouraneema*.

Rev. 8:13. flying through the *midst of heaven*,
14: 6. angel fly in the *midst of heaven*,
19:17. that fly in the *midst of heaven*,

3322 1 509/631 3319

μεσόω, *mesoō*.

Joh. 7:14. *about* the *midst* of the feast

3324 8 509/631

μεστός, *mestos*.

Mat.23:28. within ye are *full* of hypocrisy
Joh.19:29. was set a vessel *full* of vinegar:
21:11. *full* of great fishes,
Ro. 1:29. *full* of envy, murder, debate,
15:14. that ye also are *full* of goodness,
Jas. 3: 8. unruly evil, *full* of deadly poison.
17. *full* of mercy and good fruits,
2Pet. 2:14. Having eyes *full* of adultery,

3325 1 509/631 3324

μεστόω, *mestoō*.

Acts 2:13. These men are *full* of new wine.

3326 473 509/631 7:766

μετά, *meta*.

[a] marks where it is followed by an accusative, and not a genitive case.

Mat. 1:12. *after*[a] they were brought to Babylon,
23. being interpreted is, God *with* us.
2: 3. and all Jerusalem *with* him.
11. the young child *with* Mary his mother,
4:21. in a ship *with* Zebedee their
5:25. thou art in the way *with* him;
41. go *with* him twain.
8:11. and shall sit down *with* Abraham,
9:11. Why eateth your Master *with* publicans
15. as the bridegroom is *with* them?
12: 3. and they that were *with* him;
4. neither for them which were *with* him,
30. He that is not *with* me is against me; and he that gathereth not *with* me
41. in judgment *with* this generation,
42. in the judgment *with* this generation,
Mat.12:45. and taketh *with* himself seven
13:20. *with* joy receiveth it;
14: 7. promised *with* an oath to give
15:30. having *with* them (those that were)
16:27. in the glory of his Father *with* his angels;
17: 1. And *after*[a] six days Jesus taketh
3. Moses and Elias talking *with* him.
17 how long shall I be *with* you?
18:16. take *with* thee one or two more,
23. which would take account *of* his servants.
19:10. If the case of the man be so *with* (his)
20: 2. when he had agreed *with* the labourers
20. *with* her sons, worshipping
21: 2. and a colt *with* her:
22:16. their disciples *with* the Herodians,
24:29. Immediately *after*[a] the tribulation
30. *with* power and great glory.
31. shall send his angels *with* a great sound
49. to eat and drink *with* the drunken;
51. his portion *with* the hypocrites:
25: 3. and took no oil *with* them:
4. oil in their vessels *with* their lamps.
10. they that were ready went in *with* him
19. *After*[a] a long time the lord of those servants cometh, and reckoneth *with* them.
31. all the holy angels *with* him,
26: 2. Ye know that *after*[a] two days is
11. the poor always *with* you;
18. at thy house *with* my disciples.
20. he sat down *with* the twelve.
23. dippeth (his) hand *with* me in the
29. when I drink it new *with* you in
32. But *after*[a] I am risen again,
36. Then cometh Jesus *with* them unto
38. and watch *with* me.
40. could ye not watch *with* me one
47. and *with* him a great multitude *with* swords and staves,
51. one of them which were *with* Jesus
55. *with* swords and staves for to
58. and sat *with* the servants,
69. Thou also wast *with* Jesus
71. This (fellow) was also *with* Jesus
72. again he denied *with* an oath,
73. And *after*[a] a while came unto (him)
27:34. vinegar to drink mingled *with* gall;
41. *with* the scribes and elders, said,
53. out of the graves *after*[a] his resurrection,
54. and they that were *with* him,
62. that followed (lit. is *after*[a]) the day of the
63. *After*[a] three days I will rise again.
66. and setting a watch. (lit. *with* the watch)
28: 8. *with* fear and great joy;
12. were assembled *with* the elders.
20. I am *with* you alway,
Mar 1:13. and was *with* the wild beasts;
14. Now *after*[a] that John was put in prison,
20. in the ship *with* the hired servants,
29. *with* James and John
36. Simon and they that were *with* him
2:16. saw him eat *with* publicans and
— and drinketh *with* publicans and
19. while the bridegroom is *with* them? as long as they have the bridegroom *with* them,
25. and they that were *with* him?
3: 5. round about on them *with* anger,
6. took counsel *with* the Herodians
7. *with* his disciples to the sea:
14. that they should be *with* him,
4:16. receive it *with* gladness;
36. were also *with* him other little ships.

Mar 5:18. prayed him that he might be *with* him.
24. And (Jesus) went *with* him;
40. and them that were *with* him,
6:25. *with* haste unto the king,
50. he talked *with* them,
8:10. into a ship *with* his disciples,
14. in the ship *with* them more than
31. and *after*[a] three days rise again.
38. *with* the holy angels.
9: 2. And *after*[a] six days Jesus taketh
8. save Jesus only *with* themselves.
24. and said *with* tears,
10:30. *with* persecutions; and in the
11:11. unto Bethany *with* the twelve.
13:24. *after*[a] that tribulation, the sun shall be
26. *with* great power and glory.
14: 1. *After*[a] two days was (the feast of)
7. the poor *with* you always,
14. passover *with* my disciples?
17. he cometh *with* the twelve.
18. which eateth *with* me shall betray me.
20. that dippeth *with* me in the dish.
28. But *after*[a] that I am risen,
33. And he taketh *with* him Peter and
43. *with* him a great multitude *with* swords and staves,
48. *with* swords and (with) staves to take
54. and he sat *with* the servants,
62. and coming *in* the clouds of heaven.
67. thou also wast *with* Jesus of Nazareth.
70. And a little *after*,[a] they that stood by
15: 1. *with* the elders and scribes
7. bound *with* them that had made
28. he was numbered *with* the transgressors.
31. among themselves *with* the scribes,
16:10. told them that had been *with* him,
12. *After*[a] that he appeared in another form
19. *after*[a] the Lord had spoken unto
Lu. 1:24. And *after*[a] those days his wife
28. the Lord (is) *with* thee:
39. into the hill country *with* haste,
58. had shewed great mercy *upon* her;
66. the hand of the Lord was *with* him.
72. To perform the mercy (promised) *to* our fathers,
2:36. had lived *with* an husband seven years
46. *after*[a] three days they found him
51. And he went down *with* them,
5:27. *after*[a] these things he went forth,
29. that sat down *with* them.
30. Why do ye eat and drink *with* publicans
34. while the bridegroom is *with* them?
6: 3. and they which were *with* him;
4. to them that were *with* him;
17. And he came down *with* them,
7:36. that he would eat *with* him.
8:13. receive the word *with* joy;
45. Peter and they that were *with* him said,
9:28. an eight days *after*[a] these sayings,
39. and it teareth him that he foameth again, (lit. *with* foam)
49. because he followeth not *with* us.
10: 1. *After*[a] these things the Lord appointed
17. *with* joy, saying, Lord, even the devils
37. He that shewed mercy *on* him.
11: 7. my children are *with* me in bed;
23. He that is not *with* me is against me: and he that gathereth not *with* me
31. judgment *with* the men of this
32. *with* this generation, and shall condemn
12: 4. and *after*[a] that have no more that they
5. which *after*[a] he hath killed

Lu. 12:13. he divide the inheritance *with* me.
46. his portion *with* the unbelievers.
58. When thou goest *with* thine adversary
13: 1. had mingled *with* their sacrifices.
14: 9. thou begin *with* shame to take
31. against him *with* twenty thousand?
15:13. And not many days *after*[a]
29. might make merry *with* my friends:
30. devoured thy living *with* harlots,
31. Son, thou art ever *with* me,
17: 8. and *after*ward[a] thou shalt eat and
15. and *with* a loud voice glorified God,
20. cometh not *with* observation:
18: 4. but *after*ward[a] he said within himself,
21:27. *with* power and great glory.
22:11. passover *with* my disciples?
15. passover *with* you before I suffer:
20. also the cup *after*[a] supper,
21. (is) *with* me on the table.
28. continued *with* me in my temptations.
33. Lord, I am ready to go *with* thee,
37. reckoned *among* the transgressors:
52. *with* swords and staves?
53. I was daily *with* you in the
58. And *after*[a] a little while another
59. this (fellow) also was *with* him:
23:12. were made friends together: (lit. *with* one another)
43. be *with* me in paradise.
24: 5. the living *among* the dead?
29. Abide *with* us: for it is toward
30. as he sat at meat *with* them,
52. to Jerusalem *with* great joy:
Joh. 2:12. *After*[a] this he went down to Capernaum,
3: 2. except God be *with* him.
22. *After*[a] these things came Jesus
— there he tarried *with* them,
25. *and* (lit. *with*) the Jews about purifying.
26. he that was *with* thee beyond
4:27. talked *with* the woman:
— Why talkest thou *with* her?
43. Now *after*[a] two days he departed
5: 1. *After*[a] this there was a feast of the Jews;
4. first *after*[a] the troubling of the water
14. *After*ward[a] Jesus findeth him
6: 1. *After*[a] these things Jesus went
3. and there he sat *with* his disciples.
43. Murmur not *among* yourselves.
66. walked no more *with* him.
7: 1. *After*[a] these things Jesus walked
33. a little while am I *with* you,
8:29. he that sent me is *with* me:
9:37. it is he that talketh *with* thee.
40. which were *with* him heard
11: 7. Then *after*[a] that saith he
11. and *after*[a] that he saith unto them,
16. that we may die *with* him.
31. which were *with* her in the house,
54. continued *with* his disciples.
56. and spake *among* themselves,
12: 8. the poor always ye have *with* you,
17. that was *with* him when he
35. a little while is the light *with* you.
13: 7. but thou shalt know here*after*.[a]
8. thou hast no part *with* me.
18. He that eateth bread *with* me
27. *after*[a] the sop Satan entered into him.
33. yet a little while I am *with* you.
14: 9. Have I been so long time *with* you,
16. that he may abide *with* you for ever;
30. Hereafter I will not talk much *with* you:
15:27. ye have been *with* me from the

Joh.16: 4. because I was *with* you.
19. Do ye enquire *among* yourselves
32. because the Father is *with* me.
17:12. While I was *with* them in the world,
24. be *with* me where I am;
18: 2. resorted thither *with* his disciples.
3. cometh thither *with* lanterns and
5. which betrayed him, stood *with* them.
18. and Peter stood *with* them,
26. in the garden *with* him?
19:18. and two other *with* him,
28. *After*[a] this, Jesus knowing that
38. *after*[a] this Joseph of Arimathæa,
40. in linen clothes *with* the spices,
20: 7. not lying *with* the linen clothes,
24. was not *with* them when Jesus came.
26. *after*[a] eight days again his disciples were within, and Thomas *with* them:
21: 1. *After*[a] these things Jesus shewed himself
Acts 1: 3. *after*[a] his passion by many infallible
5. not many days *hence.*[a]
26. numbered *with* the eleven
2:28. full of joy *with* thy countenance.
29. let me freely (lit. *with* boldness) speak
4:29. that *with* all boldness they may speak
31. spake the word of God *with* boldness.
5:26. brought them *with*out violence:
37. *After*[a] this man rose up Judas
7: 4. *when*[a] his father was dead,
5. and to his seed *after*[a] him,
7. and *after*[a] that shall they come forth,
9. but God was *with* him,
38. *with* the angel which spake to him
45. brought in *with* Jesus into the
9:19. *with* the disciples which were
28. And he was *with* them coming in
39. Dorcas made, while she was *with* them.
10:37. *after*[a] the baptism which John
38. for God was *with* him.
41. *after*[a] he rose from the dead.
11:21. the hand of the Lord was *with* them:
12: 4. intending *after*[a] Easter to bring him
13:15. And *after*[a] the reading of the law
17. and *with* an high arm brought he
20. And *after*[a] that he gave (unto them)
25. there cometh one *after*[a] me,
14:23. had prayed *with* fasting,
27. all that God had done *with* them,
15: 4. that God had done *with* them.
13. And *after*[a] they had held their peace,
16. *After*[a] this I will return,
33. they were let go *in* peace from
35. *with* many others also.
36. And some days *after*[a] Paul said
17:11. *with* all readiness of mind,
18: 1. *After*[a] these things Paul departed
10. For I am *with* thee,
19: 4. which should come *after*[a] him,
21. *After*[a] I have been there,
20: 1. And *after*[a] the uproar was ceased,
6. *after*[a] the days of unleavened bread,
18. I have been *with* you
19. *with* all humility of mind,
24. I might finish my course *with* joy,
29. that *after*[a] my departing shall
31. night and day *with* tears.
34. and to them that were *with* me.
21:15. And *after*[a] those days we took up
24: 1. And *after*[a] five days Ananias the high priest descended *with* the elders,
3. *with* all thankfulness.
7. and *with* great violence took
Acts24:18. neither *with* multitude, nor *with* tumult.
24. And *after*[a] certain days,
25: 1. *after*[a] three days he ascended from
12. conferred *with* the council,
23. *with* great pomp, and was entered
26:12. *with* authority and commission
27:10. this voyage will be *with* hurt
14. not long *after*[a] there arose
24. all them that sail *with* thee.
28:11. And *after*[a] three months
13. and *after*[a] one day the south wind blew,
17. that *after*[a] three days Paul called
31. *with* all confidence, no man forbidding
Ro. 12:15. Rejoice *with* them that do rejoice, and weep *with* them that weep.
18. live peaceably *with* all men.
15:10. Rejoice, ye Gentiles, *with* his people.
33. God of peace (be) *with* you all.
16:20. of our Lord Jesus Christ (be) *with* you.
24. (be) *with* you all.
1Co. 6: 6. brother goeth to law *with* brother,
7. ye go to law one *with* another.
7:12. and she be pleased to dwell *with* him,
13. if he be pleased to dwell *with* her,
11:25. (he took) the cup, when he had supped, (lit. *after*[a] supping)
16:11. look for him *with* the brethren.
12. unto you *with* the brethren:
23. of our Lord Jesus Christ (be) *with* you
24. My love (be) *with* you all in Christ
2Co. 6:15. hath he that believeth *with* an infidel?
16. the temple of God *with* idols?
7:15. *with* fear and trembling ye received
8: 4. Praying us *with* much intreaty
18. we have sent *with* him the brother,
13:11. and peace shall be *with* you.
14(13). of the Holy Ghost, (be) *with* you
Gal. 1:18. Then *after*[a] three years I went up
2: 1. to Jerusalem *with* Barnabas,
12. he did eat *with* the Gentiles:
3:17. and thirty years *after*,[a] cannot disannul,
4:25. is in bondage *with* her children.
30. *with* the son of the freewoman.
6:18. Jesus Christ (be) *with* your spirit.
Eph. 4: 2. *With* all lowliness and meekness, *with* longsuffering,
25. every man truth *with* his neighbour:
6: 5. *with* fear and trembling,
7. *With* good will doing service,
23. and love *with* faith,
24. Grace (be) *with* all them that love
Phi. 1: 4. making request *with* joy,
2:12. *with* fear and trembling.
29. in the Lord *with* all gladness;
4: 3. *with* Clement also,
6. and supplication *with* thanksgiving
9. the God of peace shall be *with* you.
23. Jesus Christ (be) *with* you all.
Col. 1:11. longsuffering *with* joyfulness;
4:18. Grace (be) *with* you.
1Th. 1: 6. *with* joy of the Holy Ghost:
3:13. Jesus Christ *with* all his saints.
5:28. our Lord Jesus Christ (be) *with* you.
2Th. 1: 7. rest *with* us, when the Lord Jesus shall be revealed from heaven *with* his
3:12. that *with* quietness they work,
16. The Lord (be) *with* you all.
18. our Lord Jesus Christ (be) *with* you all.
1Ti. 1:14. abundant *with* faith and love
2: 9. *with* shamefacedness and sobriety,
15. and holiness *with* sobriety.
3: 4. in subjection *with* all gravity;

1Ti. 4: 3. to be received *with* thanksgiving
4. if it be received *with* thanksgiving:
14. *with* the laying on of the hands
6: 6. godliness *with* contentment is
21. Grace (be) *with* thee.
2Ti. 2:10. in Christ Jesus *with* eternal glory.
22. *with* them that call on the Lord
4:11. Only Luke is *with* me. Take Mark, and bring him *with* thee:
22. The Lord Jesus Christ (be) *with* thy spirit. Grace (be) *with* you.
Tit. 2:15. and rebuke *with* all authority.
3:10. *after*[a] the first and second admonition
15. All that are *with* me salute thee.
— Grace (be) *with* you all.
Philem.25(24) our Lord Jesus Christ (be) *with* your
Heb. 4: 7. *after*[a] so long a time;
8. then would he not *after*ward[a] have
16. Let us therefore come boldly (lit. *with* boldness)
5: 7. *with* strong crying and tears
7:21. but this *with* an oath
28. which was *since*[a] the law,
8:10. *after*[a] those days, saith the Lord;
9: 3. And *after*[a] the second veil,
19. *with* water, and scarlet wool,
27. but *after*[a] this the judgment:
10:15. for *after*[a] that he had said before,
16. *after*[a] those days, saith the Lord,
22. Let us draw near *with* a true heart
26. *after*[a] that we have received the
34. took joyfully (lit. *with* joy) the spoiling
11: 9. *with* Isaac and Jacob,
31. when she had received the spies *with*
12:14. Follow peace *with* all (men),
17. he sought it carefully *with* tears.
28. *with* reverence and godly fear:
13:17. that they may do it *with* joy,
23. *with* whom, if he come shortly,
25. Grace (be) *with* you all.
1Pet. 1:11. glory that should follow. (lit. *after*[a] these)
3:15. *with* meekness and fear:
2Pet. 1:15. that ye may be able *after*[a] my decease
1Joh. 1: 3. may have fellowship *with* us: and truly our fellowship (is) *with* the Father, and *with* his Son
6. that we have fellowship *with* him,
7. we have fellowship one *with* another,
2:19. have continued *with* us:
4:17. Herein is our love (lit. love *with* us) made perfect,
2Joh. 2. and shall be *with* us for ever.
3. Grace be *with* you,
Rev. 1: 7. Behold, he cometh *with* clouds;
12. to see the voice that spake *with* me.
19. the things which shall be here*after*;[a]
2:16. will fight *against* them with the sword of
22. that commit adultery *with* her
3: 4. they shall walk *with* me in white:
20. and will sup *with* him, and he *with* me.
21. to sit *with* me in my throne,
— and am set down *with* my Father
4: 1. *After*[a] this I looked, and, behold,
— of a trumpet talking *with* me;
— things which must be here*after*.[a]
6: 8. and Hell followed *with* him.
7: 1. And *after*[a] these things I saw
9. *After*[a] this I beheld, and, lo,
9:12. two woes more here*after*.[a]
10: 8. spake *unto* me again,
11: 7. shall make war *against* them,
11. And *after*[a] three days and an half
Rev.12: 9. his angels were cast out *with* him.
17. to make war *with* the remnant
13: 4. who is able to make war *with* him?
7. to make war *with* the saints.
14: 1. and *with* him an hundred forty
4. not defiled *with* women;
13. their works do follow)(them.
15: 5. And *after*[a] that I looked
17: 1. and talked *with* me,
2. *With* whom the kings of the earth
12. one hour *with* the beast.
14. shall make war *with* the Lamb,
— they that are *with* him (are) called
18: 1. *after*[a] these things I saw
3. fornication *with* her,
9. lived deliciously *with* her,
19: 1. *after*[a] these things I heard a great
19. war *against* him that sat on the horse and *against* his army.
20. and *with* him the false prophet
20: 3. *after*[a] that he must be loosed
4. they lived and reigned *with* Christ
6. shall reign *with* him a thousand years.
21: 3. the tabernacle of God (is) *with* men, and he will dwell *with* them,
— God himself shall be *with* them,
9. and talked *with* me,
15. he that talked *with* me had
22:12. my reward (is) *with* me,
21. our Lord Jesus Christ (be) *with* you all

3327 12 511/636 1:518 3326

μεταβαίνω, metabaino. rt 939

Mat. 8:34. that he *would depart* out of their
11: 1. he *departed* thence to teach and
12: 9. *when* he *was departed* thence,
15:29. Jesus *departed* from thence, *and*
17:20. *Remove* hence to yonder place; and it *shall remove*;
Lu. 10: 7. *Go* not from house to house.
Joh. 5:24. *is passed* from death unto life.
7: 3. *Depart* hence, and go into Judæa,
13: 1. that he *should depart* out of this
Acts18: 7. he *departed* thence, *and* entered
1Joh.3:14. we *have passed* from death unto life,

3328 1 512/636 3326,906

μεταβάλλομαι, metaballomai.

Acts28: 6. they *changed their minds, and* said

3329 2 512/636 3326,71

μετάγω, metago.

Jas. 3: 3. and we *turn about* their whole body.
4. yet *are* they *turned about* with a very small

3330 5 512/636 3326,1325

μεταδίδωμι, metadidōmi.

Lu. 3:11. *let* him *impart* to him that hath none;
Ro. 1:11. that I *may impart* unto you some
12: 8. he *that giveth*, (let him do it) with
Eph. 4:28. that he may have *to give* to him that
1Th. 2: 8. willing *to have imparted* unto you,

3331 3 512/636 8:152 3346

μετάθεσις, metathesis.

Heb. 7:12. of necessity a *change* also of the law.
11: 5. for before his *translation*
12:27. the *removing* of those things that are

3332 2 512/636 3326,142

μεταίρω, metairo.

Mat.13:53. finished these parables, he *departed* thence.
19: 1. he *departed* from Galilee,

3333 4 512/636 3:487 3326,2564

μετακαλέομαι, metakaleomai.

Acts 7:14. and *called* his father Jacob *to* (him),
10:32. and *call hither* Simon,
20:17. and *called* the elders of the church.
24:25. I *will call for* thee.

3334 1 512/636 3:718 3326,2795

μετακινέω, metakineo.

Col. 1:23. and (be) not *moved away* from the hope of the gospel,

3335 6 512/636 4:5 3326,2983

μεταλαμβάνω, metalambano.

Acts 2:46. *did eat* their meat with gladness
24:25. *when* I *have* a convenient season,
27:33. Paul besought (them) all *to take* meat,
2Ti. 2: 6. must *be* first *partaker* of the fruits.
Heb 6: 7. *receiveth* blessing from God:
12:10. that (we) might *be partakers* of his

3336 1 512/637 4:5 3335

μετάληψις, metaleepsis.

1Ti. 4: 3. which God hath created to be received (lit. for *reception*)

3337 2 512/637 1:251 3326,236

μεταλλάττω, metallatto.

Ro. 1:25. Who *changed* the truth of God
26. even their women *did change* the

3338 6 512/637 4:626 3326,3199

μεταμέλομαι, metamelomai.

Mat.21:29. afterward he *repented, and* went.
32. *repented* not afterward, that ye
27: 3. *repented himself*, and brought
2Co. 7: 8. I *do* not *repent*, though I *did repent*:
Heb 7:21. The Lord sware and *will* not *repent*,

3339 4 513/637 4:742 3326,3445

μεταμορφόομαι, metamorphöomai.

Mat.17: 2. And *was transfigured* before them:
Mar 9: 2. he *was transfigured* before them.
Ro. 12: 2. *be* ye *transformed* by the renewing
2Co. 3:18. we all,...*are changed* into the same image

3340 34 513/637 4:948 3326,3539

μετανοέω, metanöeo.

Mat. 3: 2. And saying, *Repent* ye: for the kingdom
4:17. and to say, *Repent*: for the kingdom
11:20. because they *repented* not:
21. they would *have repented* long ago
12:41. because they *repented* at the preaching
Mar 1:15. *repent* ye, and believe the gospel.
6:12. and preached that men *should repent*.
Lu. 10:13. they *had* a great while ago *repented*,
11:32. for they *repented* at the preaching
13: 3. but, except ye *repent*, ye shall all
5. except ye *repent*, ye shall all
Lu. 15: 7. over one sinner *that repenteth*,
10. over one sinner *that repenteth*.
16:30. from the dead, they *will repent*,
17: 3. and if he *repent*, forgive him.
4. saying, I *repent*; thou shalt forgive
Acts 2:38. *Repent*, and be baptized every one
3:19. *Repent* ye therefore, and be converted.
8:22. *Repent* therefore of this thy
17:30. all men every where *to repent*:
26:20. that they should *repent* and turn to God,
2Co.12:21. and *have* not *repented*
Rev. 2: 5. *repent*, and do the first works;
— except thou *repent*.
16. *Repent*; or else I will come
21. I gave her space to *repent* of her fornication; and she *repented* not.
22. except they *repent* of their deeds.
3: 3. and hold fast, and *repent*.
19. be zealous therefore, and *repent*.
9:20. *repented* not of the works
21. Neither *repented* they of their
16: 9. they *repented* not to give him glory.
11. and *repented* not of their deeds.

3341 24 513/637 4:948 3340

μετάνοια, metanoya.

Mat. 3: 8. fruits meet for *repentance*:
11. baptize you with water unto *repentance*:
9:13. but sinners to *repentance*.
Mar. 1: 4. and preach the baptism of *repentance*
2:17. but sinners to *repentance*.
Lu. 3: 3. preaching the baptism of *repentance*
8. fruits worthy of *repentance*,
5:32. but sinners to *repentance*.
15: 7. which need no *repentance*.
24:47. And that *repentance* and remission
Acts 5:31. for to give *repentance* to Israel,
11:18. granted *repentance* unto life.
13:24. the baptism of *repentance* to all the people of Israel.
19: 4. baptized with the baptism of *repentance*,
20:21. *repentance* toward God, and faith
26:20. do works meet for *repentance*.
Ro. 2: 4. of God leadeth thee to *repentance*?
2Co. 7: 9. ye sorrowed to *repentance*:
10. worketh *repentance* to salvation
2Ti. 2:25. will give them *repentance*
Heb. 6: 1. of *repentance* from dead works,
6. to renew them again unto *repentance*,
12:17. found no place of *repentance*,
2Pet.3: 9. all should come to *repentance*.

3342 9 514/637 3326,4862

μεταξύ, metaxu.

Mat.18:15. tell him his fault *between* thee and him alone:
23:35. *between* the temple and the altar.
Lu. 11:51. *between* the altar and the temple:
16:26. *between* us and you there is a great gulf
Joh. 4:31. In the *mean while* his disciples
Acts12: 6. sleeping *between* two soldiers,
13:42. be preached to them the *next* sabbath.
15: 9. no difference *between* us and them,
Ro. 2:15. (their) thoughts the *mean while* accusing

3343 8 514/638 3326,3992

μεταπέμπω, metapempo.

Acts10: 5. and *call for* (one) Simon,

Acts10:22. *to send for* thee into his house,
29. *as soon as* I *was sent for* : I ask therefore for what intent ye *have sent for* me?
11:13. and *call for* Simon,
24:24. he *sent for* Paul, and heard him
26. he *sent for* him the oftener, *and*
25: 3. that he *would send for* him to Jerusalem,

3344 3 514/638 7:714 3326,4762

μεταστρέφω, *metastrepho.*

Acts 2:20. The sun *shall be turned* into darkness,
Gal. 1: 7. and would *pervert* the gospel of Christ.
Jas. 4: 9. *let* your laughter *be turned* to mourning,

3345 5 514/638 7:954 3326,4976

μετασχηματίζω, *metaskeematizo.*

1Co. 4: 6. I *have in a figure transferred* to myself
2Co.11:13. *transforming themselves* into the apostles
14. for Satan himself *is transformed* into an angel of light.
15. if his ministers also *be transformed* as the ministers of righteousness;
Phi. 3:21. Who *shall change* our vile body,

3346 6 515/638 8:152 3326,5087

μετατίθημι, *metatitheemi.*

Acts 7:16. And *were carried over* into Sychem,
Gal. 1: 6. that ye *are* so soon *removed* from him
Heb 7:12. the priesthood *being changed*,
11: 5. By faith Enoch *was translated*
— because God *had translated* him:
Jude 4. *turning* the grace of our God into

3347 1 515/638 3326,1899

μετέπειτα, *metepīta.*

Heb12:17. For ye know how that *afterward*, when he

3348 8 515/638 2:816 3326,2192

μετέχω, *meteko.*

1Co. 9:10. should *be partaker* of his hope.
12. If others *be partakers* of (this) power
10:17. we *are* all *partakers* of that one bread.
21. ye cannot *be partakers* of the Lord's
30. if I by grace *be a partaker*,
Heb. 2:14. likewise *took part* of the same;
5:13. For every one *that useth* milk
7:13. *pertaineth* to another tribe, of which

3349 1 515/638 4:630 3326,142

μετεωρίζομαι, *meteōrizomai.*

Lu. 12:29. neither *be* ye *of doubtful mind.*

3350 4 515/638 3326,3624

μετοικεσία, *metoikesia.*

Mat. 1:11. about the time they were carried away to (lit. of the *carrying away to*) Babylon:
12. after they were brought (lit. the *bringing*) to Babylon,
17. from David until the *carrying away into*
— and from the *carrying away into* Babylon

3351 2 515/638 rt 3350

μετοικίζω, *metoikizo.*

Acts 7: 4. he *removed* him *into* this land,
43. I *will carry* you *away* beyond Babylon.

3352 1 516/638 3348

μετοχή, *metokee.*

2Co. 6:14. what *fellowship* hath righteousness with unrighteousness?

3353 6 516/638 2:816 3348

μέτοχος, *metokos.*

Lu. 5: 7. they beckoned unto (their) *partners*,
Heb 1: 9. oil of gladness above thy *fellows*.
3: 1. *partakers* of the heavenly calling,
14. we are made *partakers* of Christ,
6: 4. were made *partakers* of the Holy Ghost,
12: 8. whereof all are *partakers*,

3354 10 516/638 4:632 3358

μετρέω, *metreo.*

Mat. 7: 2. with what measure ye *mete*, it shall
Mar. 4:24. with what measure ye *mete*, it *shall be measured* to you:
Lu. 6:38. with the same measure that ye *mete*
2Co.10:12. they *measuring* themselves by themselves,
Rev.11: 1. Rise, and *measure* the temple of God,
2. leave out, and *measure* it not;
21:15. a golden reed to *measure* the city,
16. he *measured* the city with the reed,
17. he *measured* the wall thereof,

3355 1 516/638 3354

μετρητής, *metreetees.*

Joh. 2: 6. two or three *firkins* apiece.

3356 1 516/639 5:904 rt 3357

μετριοπαθέω, *metriopatheo.* rt 3806

Heb. 5: 2. Who can *have compassion on* the ignorant,

3357 1 516/639 3358

μετρίως, *metriōs.*

Acts20:12. were not *a little* comforted.

3358 13 516/639 4:632

μέτρον, *metron.*

Mat. 7: 2. and with what *measure* ye mete,
23:32. Fill ye up then the *measure* of your
Mar. 4:24. with what *measure* ye mete,
Lu. 6:38. good *measure*, pressed down,
— with the same *measure* that ye mete
Joh. 3:34. God giveth not the Spirit by *measure*
Ro. 12: 3. to every man the *measure* of faith.
2Co.10:13. according to the *measure* of the rule
— a *measure* to reach even unto you.
Eph. 4: 7. according to the *measure* of the gift of
13. unto the *measure* of the stature
16. in the *measure* of every part,
Rev.21:17. the *measure* of a man, that is, of the angel

3359 8 516/639 4:635 3326 *ops* (face)

μέτωπον, *metōpon.*

Rev. 7: 3. servants of our God in their *foreheads*.
9: 4. have not the seal of God in their *foreheads*
13:16. or in their *foreheads*:
14: 1. Father's name written in their *foreheads*.
9. and receive (his) mark in his *forehead*,
17: 5. And upon her *forehead* (was) a name
20: 4. (his) mark upon their *foreheads*,
22: 4. his name (shall be) in their *foreheads*.

3360 17 517/639 3372 cf 891

μέχρι & μέχρις, mekri & mekris.

Mat.11:23. would have remained *until* this day.
13:30. grow together *until* the harvest:
28:15. reported among the Jews *until* this day.
Mar 13:30. *till* all these things be done.
Acts10:30. I was fasting *until* this hour;
20: 7. continued his speech *until* midnight.
Ro. 5:14. death reigned from Adam *to* Moses,
15:19. and round about *unto* Illyricum,
Eph. 4:13. *Till* we all come in the unity of
Phi. 2: 8. became obedient *unto* death,
30. he was nigh *unto* death,
1Ti. 6:14. *until* the appearing of our Lord
2Ti. 2: 9. I suffer trouble, as an evil doer, (even) *unto* bonds;
Heb. 3: 6. rejoicing of the hope firm *unto* the end.
14. stedfast *unto* the end;
9:10. *until* the time of reformation.
12: 4. Ye have not yet resisted *unto* blood,

3361 675 517/639 cf 3756

μή, mee.

? shews where it is used interrogatively; || denotes where the double negative of the Greek is omitted; [2] marks passages where it is connected, though not closely, with ἵνα.

Mat. 1:19. *not* willing to make her a publick
20. fear *not* to take unto thee Mary
2:12. that they should *not* return to Herod
3: 9. And think *not* to say within
10. which bringeth *not* forth good fruit
5:17. Think *not* that I am come to destroy
29. and *not*[2] (that) thy whole body should be
30. and *not* (that) thy whole body should be
34. Swear *not* at all;
39. That ye resist *not* evil:
42. turn *not* thou away.
6: 1. Take heed that ye do *not* your alms before
2. do *not* sound a trumpet before thee,
3. let *not* thy left hand know what
7. use *not* vain repetitions,
8. Be *not* ye therefore like unto them:
13. lead us *not* into temptation,
16. be *not*, as the hypocrites, of a sad
18. That thou appear *not* unto men to fast,
19. Lay *not* up for yourselves
25. Take *no* thought for your life,
31. take *no* thought, saying, What shall
34. Take therefore *no* thought for
7: 1. Judge *not*, that ye be not judged.
6. Give *not* that which is holy unto
9. ? will he give him a stone?
10. ? will he give him a serpent?
19. Every tree that bringeth *not* forth
26. and doeth them *not*,
8:28. so that *no* man might pass by
9:15. ? Can the children of the bridechamber
36. as sheep having *no* shepherd.
10: 5. Go *not* into the way of the Gentiles,
— city of the Samaritans enter ye *not*:
9. Provide *neither* gold, nor silver,
10. *Nor* scrip for (your) journey,
19. take *no* thought how or what ye
26. Fear them *not* therefore:
28. And fear *not* them which kill the body, but are *not* able to kill
31. Fear ye *not* therefore,
34. Think *not* that I am come to
12:30. He that is *not* with me is against me; and he that gathereth *not* with me

Mat.13: 5. they had *no* deepness of earth
6. because they had *no* root.
19. and understandeth (it) *not*,
14:27. it is I; be *not* afraid.
17: 7. Arise, and be *not* afraid.
18:10. Take heed that ye despise *not* one of
13. which went *not* astray.
25. forasmuch as he had *not* to pay
19: 6. let *not* man put asunder.
14. and forbid them *not*,
21:21. If ye have faith, and doubt *not*,
22:12. *not* having a wedding garment?
23. that there is *no* resurrection,
24. If a man die, having *no* children,
25. and, having *no* issue,
29. Ye do err, *not* knowing the scriptures
23: 3. but do *not* ye after their works:
8. be *not* ye called Rabbi:
9. call *no* (man) your father
23. and *not* to leave the other undone.
24: 4. Take heed that *no* man deceive you.
6. see that ye be *not* troubled:
17. *not* come down to take any
18. *Neither* let him which is in the field
23. or there; believe (it) *not*.
26. go *not* forth: behold, (he is) in the secret chambers; believe (it) *not*.
25:29. but from him that hath *not*
26: 5. *Not* on the feast (day),
28: 5. said unto the women, Fear *not* ye:
10. Be *not* afraid: go tell my brethren
Mar 2: 4. they could *not* come nigh unto him
19. ? Can the children of the bridechamber
3:20. they could *not* so much as eat bread.
4: 5. because it had *no* depth of earth:
6. because it had *no* root,
12. may see, and *not* perceive; and hearing they may hear, and *not* understand;
5: 7. that thou torment me *not*.
36. Be *not* afraid, only believe.
6: 8. *no* scrip, *no* bread, *no* money in (their)
9. and *not* put on two coats.
11. whosoever shall *not* receive you,
34. as sheep *not* having a shepherd:
50. it is I; be *not* afraid.
8: 1. and having *nothing* to eat,
9:39. But Jesus said, Forbid him *not*:
10: 9. let *not* man put asunder.
14. and forbid them *not*:
19. Do *not* commit adultery, Do *not* kill, Do *not* steal, Do *not* bear false witness, Defraud *not*,
11:23. and shall *not* doubt in his heart,
12:15(14). or shall we *not* give?
18. which say there is *no* resurrection;
19. and leave *no* children,
24. ye know *not* the scriptures,
13: 5. Take heed *lest* any (man) deceive you:
7. be ye *not* troubled:
11. take *no* thought beforehand
15. let him that is on the housetop *not* go down into the house,
16. let him...*not* turn back again
21. (he is) there; believe (him) *not*:
36. *Lest* coming suddenly he find you
14: 2. *Not* on the feast (day),
16: 6. Be *not* affrighted: Ye seek Jesus
Lu. 1:13. Fear *not*, Zacharias:
20. and *not* able to speak,
30. Fear *not*, Mary: for thou hast found
2:10. Fear *not*: for, behold, I bring you
26. that he should *not* see death,

Lu. 2:45. when they found him *not*,
3: 8. and begin *not* to say
9. which bringeth *not* forth good fruit
11. impart to him that hath *none;*
4:42. that he should *not* depart from them.
5:10. Fear *not;* from henceforth thou
19. when they could *not* find by what
34. ? Can ye make the children of the
6:29. forbid *not* (to take thy) coat also.
30. ask (them) *not* again.
37. Judge *not*, and ye shall not be judged: condemn *not*, and ye
49. he that heareth, and doeth *not*,
7: 6. Lord, trouble *not* thyself:
13. and said unto her, Weep *not*.
30. being *not* baptized of him.
42. when they had *nothing* to pay,
8: 6. because it lacked (lit. had *not*) moisture.
10. seeing they might *not*[2] see, and hearing they might *not* understand.
18. and whosoever hath *not*,
28. I beseech thee, torment me *not*.
49. trouble *not* the Master.
50. Fear *not:* believe only,
52. Weep *not;* she is not dead,
9: 5. whosoever will *not* receive you,
33. *not* knowing what he said.
50. Forbid (him) *not:*
10: 4. Carry *neither* purse, *nor* scrip,
7. Go *not* from house to house,
10. and they receive you *not*,
20. in this rejoice *not*,
11: 4. And lead us *not* into temptation;
7. Trouble me *not:* the door is now shut,
11. ? will he give him a stone?
— ? will he for a fish give him a serpent?
12. ? will he offer him a scorpion?
23. He that is *not* with me is against me: and he that gathereth *not* with me
24. and finding *none*, he saith,
35. which is in thee be *not* darkness.
36. having *no* part dark,
42. and *not* to leave the other undone.
12: 4. Be *not* afraid of them that kill
— have *no* more that they can do.
7. Fear *not* therefore:
11. take ye *no* thought how or what thing
21. and is *not* rich toward God.
22. Take *no* thought for your life,
29. And seek *not* ye what ye shall eat,
— *neither* be ye of doubtful mind.
32. Fear *not*, little flock;
33. bags which wax *not* old,
47. knew his lord's will, and prepared *not*
48. But he that knew *not*, and
13:11. could in *no* wise lift up (herself).
14. and *not* on the sabbath day.
14: 8. sit *not* down in the highest room;
12. call *not* thy friends,
29. and is *not* able to finish (it),
16:26. from hence to you can*not;*
17: 1. It is impossible but that offences will come: (lit. for offences *not* to come)
9. ? Doth he thank that servant
23. go *not* after (them),
31. let him *not* come down
— let him likewise *not* return back.
18: 1. and *not* to faint;
2. a judge, which feared *not* God, *neither*
16. and forbid them *not:*
20. Do *not* commit adultery, Do *not* kill, Do *not* steal, Do *not* bear false witness,

Lu. 19:26. from him that hath *not*,
27. which would *not* that I should reign
20: 7. that they could *not* tell
16. said, God forbid. (lit. may it *not* be)
27. deny that there is *any* || resurrection;
21: 8. Take heed *that* ye be *not* deceived:
— go ye *not* therefore after them.
9. and commotions, be *not* terrified:
14. *not* to meditate before
21. and let *not* them that are in the
22:34. deny that thou)(|| knowest me.
35. ? lacked ye any thing?
36. and he that hath *no* sword,
40. Pray that ye enter *not* into
42. *not* my will, but thine, be done.
23:28. weep *not* for me, but weep for yourselves,
24:16. that they should *not* know him.
23. And when they found *not* his body,
Joh. 2:16. make *not* my Father's house
3: 4. ? can he enter the second time into
7. Marvel *not* that I said unto thee,
16. should *not*[2] perish, but have everlasting
18. he that believeth *not* is condemned already, because he hath *not* believed
4:12. ? Art thou greater than our father Jacob,
5:23. He that honoureth *not* the Son
28. Marvel *not* at this:
45. Do *not* think that I will accuse you
6:20. It is I; be *not* afraid.
27. Labour *not* for the meat which
39. I should lose *nothing*,[2]
43. Murmur *not* among yourselves.
64. who they were that believed *not*,
67. ? Will ye also go away?
7:15. this man letters, having *never* learned?
24. Judge *not* according to the
35. ? will he go unto the dispersed
41. ? Shall Christ come out of Galilee?
47. ? Are ye also deceived?
49. who knoweth *not* the law
51. ? Doth our law judge (any) man,
52. ? Art thou also of Galilee?
8:53. ? Art thou greater than our father
9:27. ? will ye also be his disciples?
39. that they which see *not* might see,
40. ? Are we blind also?
10: 1. He that entereth *not* by the door
21. ? Can a devil open the eyes
37. of my Father, believe me *not*.
38. though ye believe *not* me,
11:37. this man should *not*[2] have died?
50. that the whole nation perish *not*.[2]
12:15. Fear *not*, daughter of Sion:
47. hear my words, and believe *not*,
48. and receiveth *not* my words,
13: 9. Lord, *not* my feet only,
14: 1. Let *not* your heart be troubled:
24. He that loveth me *not* keepeth not
27. Let *not* your heart be troubled,
15: 2. that beareth *not* fruit
18:17. Art *not* thou also (one) of this
25. Art *not* thou also (one) of his
40. *Not* this man, but Barabbas.
19:21. Write *not*, The King of the Jews,
24. Let us *not* rend it,
20:17. Touch me *not;* for I am not
27. and be *not* faithless,
29. blessed (are) they that have *not* seen,
Acts 1: 4. that they should *not* depart
20. and let *no* man dwell therein:
3:23. which will *not* hear that prophet,
4:18. commanded them *not* to speak at all

Acts 4:20. For we cannot *but* speak
5: 7. *not* knowing what was done,
28. that ye should *not* teach in this name?
40. that they should *not* speak in the name
7:19. to the end they might *not* live.
28. ? Wilt thou kill me, as thou diddest
42. ? O ye house of Israel, have ye offered
60. Lord, lay *not* this sin to their
9: 9. he was three days *without* sight,
26. believed *not* that he was a disciple.
38. that he would *not* delay to come
10:15. (that) call *not* thou common.
47. that these should *not* be baptized,
11: 9. (that) call *not* thou common.
12:19. and found him *not*,
13:11. *not* seeing the sun for a season.
40. *lest* that come upon you,
14:18. that they had *not* done sacrifice
15:19. that we trouble *not* them,
38. Paul thought *not* good to take him
— and went *not* with them to the work.
17: 6. And when they found them *not*,
18: 9. Be *not* afraid, but speak, and hold *not* thy
19:31. that he would *not* adventure himself
20:10. Trouble *not* yourselves; for his life
16. he would *not* spend the time in Asia:
20. I kept back nothing...but have shewed you, (lit. from *not* shewing to you)
22. *not* knowing the things that shall
27. For I have not shunned to declare (lit. as *not* to declare)
29. *not* sparing the flock.
21: 4. that he should *not* go up to Jerusalem.
12. besought him *not* to go up to Jerusalem.
14. when he would *not* be persuaded,
21. that they ought *not* to circumcise
34. when he could *not* know the certainty
23: 8. say that there is *no* resurrection,
9. let us *not* fight against God.
10. fearing *lest* Paul should have been
21. But do *not* thou yield unto them:
25:24. that he ought *not* to live any longer.
27. and *not* withal to signify the crimes
27: 7. the wind *not* suffering us,
15. and could *not* bear up into the wind,
17. and, fearing *lest* they should fall into
21. and *not* have loosed from Crete,
24. Fear *not*, Paul; thou must be brought
42. *lest* any of them should swim out,
Ro. 1:28. those things which are *not* convenient;
2:14. which have *not* the law,
— these, having *not* the law,
21. preachest a man should *not* steal,
22. a man should *not* commit adultery
3: 3. ? shall their unbelief make the
4. God forbid: (lit. may it *not* be)
5. ? (Is) God unrighteous who taketh
6. God forbid: (lit. may it *not* be)
8. And *not* (rather), as we be slanderously
31. God forbid: (lit. may it *not* be)
4: 5. But to him that worketh *not*,
17. things which be *not* as though they were.
19. And being *not* weak in faith,
5:13. sin is not imputed when there is *no* law.
14. even over them that had *not* sinned
6: 2. God forbid. (lit. may it *not* be)
12. Let *not* sin therefore reign in your
15. God forbid. (lit. may it *not* be)
7: 3. so that she is *no* adulteress,
7. God forbid. (lit. may it *not* be)
13. God forbid. (lit. may it *not* be)
8: 1. who walk *not* after the flesh,

Ro. 8: 4. who walk *not* after the flesh,
9:14. ? (Is there) unrighteousness with God? God forbid. (lit. may it *not* be)
20. ? Shall the thing formed say to him
30. which followed *not* after righteousness,
10: 6. Say *not* in thine heart, Who shall
20. I was found of them that sought me *not*;
— unto them that asked *not* after me.
11: 1. ? Hath God cast away his people? God forbid. (lit. may it *not* be)
8. eyes that they should *not* see, and ears that they should *not* hear;
10. that they may *not* see,
11. ? Have they stumbled that they should fall? God forbid: (lit. may it *not* be)
18. Boast *not* against the branches.
20. Be *not* highminded, but fear:
12: 2. And be *not* conformed to this world:
3. *not* to think (of himself) more highly
11. *Not* slothful in business;
14. bless, and curse *not*.
16. Mind *not* high things,
— Be *not* wise in your own conceits.
19. avenge *not* yourselves,
21. Be *not* overcome of evil,
13: 3. Wilt thou then *not* be afraid of the power?
13. *not* in rioting and drunkenness, *not* in chambering and wantonness, *not* in strife
14. make *not* provision for the flesh,
14: 1. *not* to doubtful disputations.
3. Let *not* him that eateth despise him that eateth *not*; and let *not* him which eateth *not* judge him that eateth:
6. he that regardeth *not* the day,
— and he that eateth *not*, to the Lord
13. that *no* man put a stumblingblock
15. Destroy *not* him with thy meat,
16. Let *not* then your good be evil spoken of:
20. For meat destroy *not* the work of God.
21. (It is) good *neither* to eat flesh,
22. Happy (is) he that condemneth *not* himself
15: 1. and *not* to please ourselves.
1Co. 1: 7. ye come)(|| behind in no gift;
10. (that) there be *no* divisions among you;
13. ? was Paul crucified for you?
28. and things which are *not*,
29. That *no* flesh should glory
2: 5. That your faith should *not*[2] stand in
4: 5. judge *nothing* before the time,
6. that *no* one of you be puffed up
7. as if thou hadst *not* received (it)?
18. as though I would *not* come to you.
5: 8. *not* with old leaven,
9. *not* to company with fornicators:
11. *not* to keep company, if any man that is
6: 9. Be *not* deceived: neither fornicators,
15. God forbid. (lit. may it *not* be)
7: 1. good for a man *not* to touch a woman.
5. Defraud ye *not* one the other,
10. Let *not* the wife depart from (her)
11. and let *not* the husband put away (his)
12. let him *not* put her away.
13. let her *not* leave him.
18. let him *not* become uncircumcised.
— let him *not* be circumcised.
21. (being) a servant? care *not* for it:
23. be *not* ye the servants of men.
27. bound unto a wife? seek *not* to be loosed.
— loosed from a wife? seek *not* a wife.
29. have wives be as though they had *none*;
30. as though they wept *not*;
— as though they rejoiced *not*;

1Co. 7:30. as though they possessed *not;*
31. as *not* abusing (it):
37. stedfast in his heart, having *no* necessity,
38. but he that giveth (her) *not* in marriage
9: 6. power to forbear working? (lit. *not* to work)
8. ? Say I these things as a man?
9. ? Doth God take care for oxen?
18. that I abuse *not* my power in the gospel.
21. being *not* without law to God,
10: 6. to the intent we should *not* lust after evil
12. take heed *lest* he fall.
22. ? are we stronger than he?
28. eat *not* for his sake that shewed it,
33. *not* seeking mine own profit,
11:22. and shame them that have *not?*
29. *not* discerning the Lord's body.
12:29. ? (Are) all apostles? ? (are) all prophets? ? (are) all teachers? ? (are) all workers of miracles?
30. ? Have all the gifts of healing? ? do all speak with tongues? ? do all interpret?
13: 1. and have *not* charity, I am become
2. and have *not* charity, I am nothing.
3. have *not* charity, it profiteth me nothing.
14:20. be *not* children in understanding:
39. and forbid *not* to speak with tongues.
15:33. Be *not* deceived: evil
34. Awake to righteousness, and sin *not;*
16:11. Let *no* man therefore despise him:
2Co. 2: 1. that I would *not* come again to you
13. because I found *not* Titus my brother:
3: 7. could *not* stedfastly behold the face of
13. could *not* stedfastly look to the end
14. the same vail *un*taken away
4: 2. *not* walking in craftiness,
4. *lest* the light of the glorious gospel
7. and *not* of us.
18. we look *not* at the things which are seen, but at the things which are *not* seen:
— things which are *not* seen (are) eternal.
5:19. *not* imputing their trespasses
21. who knew *no* sin;
6: 1. that ye receive *not* the grace of God in
9. as chastened, and *not* killed;
14. Be ye *not* unequally yoked together
17. touch *not* the unclean (thing);
8:20. that *no* man should blame us
9: 5. and *not* as (of) covetousness.
7. *not* grudgingly, or of necessity:
10: 2. that I may *not* be bold when I am
14. as though we reached *not* unto you:
11:16. Let *no* man think me a fool;
12: 6. *lest* any man should think of me above
17. ? Did I make a gain of you by any of them
21. *lest*, when I come again, my God
— and have *not* repented
13: 7. pray to God)(that ye do no evil;
10. *lest*[2] being present I should use
Gal. 2:17. God forbid. (lit. may it *not* be)
3: 1. that ye should *not* obey the truth,
21. God forbid: (lit. may it *not* be)
4: 8. which by nature are *no* gods.
18. and *not* only when I am present
5: 1. and be *not* entangled again
7. that ye should *not* obey the truth?
13. only (use) *not* liberty for an occasion
15. take heed *that* ye be *not* consumed
26. Let us *not* be desirous of vain glory,
6: 1. *lest* thou also be tempted.
7. Be *not* deceived; God is not mocked:
9. let us *not* be weary in well doing: we shall reap, if we faint *not.*

Gal. 6:14. God forbid that I should glory, (lit. be it *not* to me to glory)
Eph. 2:12. having *no* hope, and without God
3:13. I desire that ye faint *not* at my
4:26. Be ye angry, and sin *not:* let *not* the sun go down upon your wrath:
29. Let *no* corrupt communication proceed
30. And grieve *not* the holy Spirit
5: 7. Be *not* ye therefore partakers with them.
11. And have *no* fellowship with the
15. *not* as fools, but as wise,
17. Wherefore be ye *not* unwise,
18. And be *not* drunk with wine,
27. *not* having spot, or wrinkle,
6: 4. provoke *not* your children to wrath:
6. *Not* with eyeservice, as menpleasers;
Phi. 1:28. And in nothing)(‖ terrified by your
2: 4. Look *not* every man on his own things,
12. *not* as in my presence only,
3: 9. *not* having mine own righteousness,
Col. 1:23. and (be) *not* moved away from the hope
2: 8. Beware *lest* any man spoil you
16. Let *no* man therefore judge you
18. into those things which he hath *not* seen.
21. Touch *not;* taste not;
3: 2. *not* on things on the earth.
9. Lie *not* one to another,
19. and be *not* bitter against them.
21. provoke *not* your children (to anger),
22. *not* with eyeservice, as menpleasers;
1Th. 1: 8. so that we need *not* to speak
2: 9. because we would *not* be chargeable
15. and they please *not* God,
4: 5. *Not* in the lust of concupiscence, even as the Gentiles which know *not* God:
6. That *no* (man) go beyond and defraud
13. even as others which have *no* hope.
5. 6. let us *not* sleep, as (do) others;
15. See that *none* render evil for
19. Quench *not* the Spirit.
20. Despise *not* prophesyings.
2Th. 1: 8. vengeance on them that know *not* God, and that obey *not* the gospel of
2: 2. That ye be *not* soon shaken
3. Let *no* man deceive you
12. be damned who believed *not* the truth,
3: 6. and *not* after the tradition which he
8. that we might *not* be chargeable
13. be *not* weary in well doing:
14. and have *no* company with him,
15. Yet count (him) *not* as an enemy,
1Ti. 1: 3. that they teach *no* other doctrine,
7.)(understanding neither what they say,
20. that they may learn *not* to blaspheme.
2: 9. *not* with broidered hair,
3: 3. *Not* given to wine, *no* striker, *not* greedy of filthy lucre;
6. *Not* a novice, lest being lifted up
8. *not* doubletongued, *not* given to much wine, *not* greedy of filthy lucre;
11. wives (be) grave, *not* slanderers,
4:14. Neglect *not* the gift that is in thee,
5: 1. Rebuke *not* an elder,
9. Let *not* a widow be taken into the number
13. speaking things which they ought *not.*
16. and let *not* the church be charged;
19. Against an elder receive *not* an accusation, but before
6: 2. let them *not* despise (them),
3. and consent *not* to wholesome words,
17. that they be *not* highminded,
2Ti. 1: 8. Be *not* thou therefore ashamed of

2Ti. 2:14. that they strive *not* about words
4:16. *that* it may *not* be laid to their charge.
Tit. 1: 6. *not* accused of riot, or unruly.
7. *not* selfwilled, *not* soon angry, *not* given to wine, *no* striker, *not* given to filthy
11. teaching things which they ought *not*,
14. *Not* giving heed to Jewish fables,
2: 3. *not* false accusers, *not* given to much
9. *not* answering again;
10. *Not* purloining, but shewing all good
Heb 3: 8. Harden *not* your hearts, as in
15. harden *not* your hearts, as in
18. that they should *not* enter
4: 2. *not* being mixed with faith in them
7. harden *not* your hearts.
15. an high priest which can*not* be touched
6: 1. *not* laying again the foundation
7: 6. whose descent is *not* counted
9: 9. that could *not* make him that did
10:25. *Not* forsaking the assembling of
35. Cast *not* away therefore your
11: 3. were *not* made of things which do
5. that he should *not* see death;
8. *not* knowing whither he went.
13. *not* having received the promises,
27. *not* fearing the wrath of the king:
12: 5. despise *not* thou the chastening
15. *lest* any man fail of the grace of God; *lest* any root of bitterness
16. *Lest* there (be) any fornicator,
19. should *not* be spoken to them
25. See that ye refuse *not* him that
27. that those things which can*not* be
13: 2. Be *not* forgetful to entertain strangers:
9. Be *not* carried about with divers
16. and to communicate forget *not:*
17. and *not* with grief:
Jas. 1: 5. liberally, and upbraideth *not;*
7. For let *not* that man think that he
16. Do *not* err, my beloved brethren.
22. and *not* hearers only,
26. and bridleth *not* his tongue,
2: 1. have *not* the faith...with respect of persons.
11. Do *not* commit adultery, said also, Do *not*
13. that hath shewed *no* mercy;
14. and have *not* works? ? can faith save him?
16. ye give them *not* those things which
3: 1. be *not* many masters,
12. ? Can the fig tree, my brethren,
14. glory *not*, and lie not against the truth.
4: 2. because ye ask *not*.
11. Speak *not* evil one of another,
17. and doeth (it) *not*, to him it is sin.
5: 9. Grudge *not* one against another,
12. above all things, my brethren, swear *not*,
17. that it might *not* rain:
1Pet. 1: 8. though now ye see (him) *not*,
14. *not* fashioning yourselves according
2:16. and *not* using (your) liberty for
3: 6. and are *not* afraid with any amazement.
7. that your prayers be *not* hindered.
9. *Not* rendering evil for evil,
10. his lips that they speak *no* guile:
14. be *not* afraid of their terror,
4: 4. think it strange that ye run *not* with
12. think it *not* strange concerning
15. let none (lit. *not* any) of you suffer as
16. let him *not* be ashamed;
5: 2. *not* by constraint, but willingly;
2Pet. 1: 9. he that lacketh these things (lit. to whom these are *not*) is blind,
2:21. *not* to have known the way of
2Pet. 3: 8. be *not* ignorant of this one thing,
9. *not* willing that any should perish,
1Joh. 2: 4. and keepeth *not* his commandments,
15. Love *not* the world, neither the things
28. and *not* be ashamed before him
3:10. whosoever doeth *not* righteousness
— neither he that loveth *not* his brother.
13. Marvel *not*, my brethren,
14. He that loveth *not* (his) brother
18. let us *not* love in word,
21. if our heart condemn us *not*,
4: 1. believe *not* every spirit,
3. every spirit that confesseth *not*
8. He that loveth *not* knoweth not God;
20. for he that loveth *not* his brother
5:10. he that believeth *not* God hath
12. he that hath *not* the Son of God
16. sin a sin (which is) *not* unto death,
— for them that sin *not* unto death.
2Joh. 7. who confess *not* that Jesus Christ is
9. and abideth *not* in the doctrine
10. receive him *not* into (your) house, *neither* bid him God speed:
3Joh. 10. and *not* content therewith,
11. follow *not* that which is evil,
Jude 5. destroyed them that believed *not*.
6. the angels which kept *not* their first
19. having *not* the Spirit.
Rev. 1:17. Fear *not;* I am the first and the last:
3:18. that the shame of thy nakedness do *not*
5: 5. Weep *not:* behold, the Lion of the
6: 6. (see) thou hurt *not* the oil and the wine.
7: 3. Hurt *not* the earth,
16. neither)(‖ shall the sun light on them,
8:12. the day shone *not*[2] for a third part
10: 4. and write them *not*.
11: 2. and measure it *not;*
13:15. that as many as would *not* worship
19:10. See (thou do it) *not:* I am thy
22: 9. See (thou do it) *not:* for I am thy
10. Seal *not* the sayings of the prophecy of this

See also the following compounds: *ἐὰν μή, ἵνα μή, μήγε, μηδαμῶς, μηδέ, μηδείς, μηδέποτε, μηδέπω, μηκέτι, μὴ οὐκ; μήποτε, μήπω, μήπως, μήτε, μήτι, μήτις:* interrogative *οὐ μή*; and refer back to *εἰ μή, εἰ δὲ μή, εἰ δὲ μήγε, εἰ μή τι.*

3362 60 210/240 1437,3361

ἐὰν μή, ean mee.

Mat. 5:20. *except* your righteousness shall exceed
6:15. But *if* ye forgive *not* men
10:13. but *if* it be *not* worthy,
14. who*soever* shall *not* receive you,
11: 6. who*soever* shall *not* be offended in me.
12:29. *except* he first bind the strong man?
18: 3. *Except* ye be converted,
16. But *if* he will *not* hear (thee),
35. *if* ye from your hearts forgive *not*
26:42. *except* I drink it, thy will be done.
Mar 3:27. *except* he will first bind the
4:22. which shall *not* be manifested;
7: 3. *except* they wash (their) hands oft,
4. *except* they wash, they eat not.
10:15. Who*soever* shall *not* receive the kingdom
30. *But* he shall receive an hundredfold
Lu. 7:23. who*soever* shall *not* be offended in me.
13: 3. but, *except* ye repent, ye shall all
5. but, *except* ye repent, ye shall all
18:17. Who*soever* shall *not* receive

Joh 3: 2. *except* God be with him.
3. *Except* a man be born again,
5. *Except* a man be born of water
27. *except* it be given him from heaven.
4:48. *Except* ye see signs and wonders,
5:19. *but* what he seeth the Father do:
6:44. *except* the Father which hath sent me
53. *Except* ye eat the flesh of the Son
65. *except* it were given unto him of
7:51. before it hear (lit. *except* it first have heard) him,
8:24. *if* ye believe *not* that I am (he),
12:24. *Except* a corn of wheat fall into
47. *if* any man hear my words, and believe *not*,
13: 8. *If* I wash thee *not*,
15: 4. *except* it abide in the vine; no more can ye, *except* ye abide in me.
6. *If* a man abide *not* in me,
16: 7. for *if* I go *not* away,
20:25. *Except* I shall see in his hands
Acts 8:31. How can I, *except* some man should
15: 1. *Except* ye be circumcised
27:31. *Except* these abide in the ship,
Ro. 10:15. *except* they be sent?
11:23. *if* they abide *not* in unbelief,
1Co. 8: 8. neither, *if* we eat *not*, are we the worse.
9:16. *if* I preach *not* the gospel!
14: 6. *except* I shall speak to you either
7. *except* they give a distinction in
9. *except* ye utter by the tongue
11. *if* I know *not* the meaning of the
28. But *if* there be *no* interpreter,
15:36. is not quickened, *except* it die:
Gal. 2:16. *but* by the faith of Jesus Christ,
2Th. 2: 3. *except* there come a falling away
2Ti. 2: 5. *except* he strive lawfully.
Jas. 2:17. faith, *if* it hath *not* works, is dead,
1Joh. 3:21. *if* our heart condemn us *not*,
Rev. 2: 5. out of his place, *except* thou repent.
22. *except* they repent of their deeds.
3: 3. *If* therefore thou shalt *not* watch,

3363 97 /494 2443,3361

ἵνα μή, hina mee.

Mat. 7: 1. Judge not, *that* ye be *not* judged.
12:16. *that* they should *not* make him known:
17:27. Notwithstanding, *lest* we should offend
24:20. pray ye *that* your flight be *not* in
26: 5. *lest* there be an uproar
41. *that* ye enter *not* into temptation:
Mar. 3: 9. *lest* they should throng him.
12. *that* they should *not* make him known.
5:10. *that* he would *not* send them away
13:18. pray ye *that* your flight be *not* in
14:38. *lest* ye enter into temptation.
Lu. 8:12. *lest* they should believe and be saved.
31. *that* he would *not* command them
9:45. *that* they perceived it *not*:
16:28. *lest* they also come into this place
18: 5. *lest* by her continual coming she weary
22:32. *that* thy faith fail *not*:
46. *lest* ye enter into temptation.
Joh. 3:15. *That* whosoever believeth in him should *not* perish,
20. *lest* his deeds should be reproved.
4:15. give me this water, *that* I thirst *not*,
5:14. *lest* a worse thing come unto thee.
6:12. *that* nothing be lost.
50. *that* a man may eat thereof, and *not* die.
7:23 *that* the law of Moses should *not* be
Joh. 12:35. *lest* darkness come upon you:
40. *that* they should *not* see with (their)
42. *lest* they should be put out of the
46. *that* whosoever believeth on me should *not* abide in darkness.
16: 1. *that* ye should *not* be offended.
18:28. *lest* they should be defiled;
36. *that* I should *not* be delivered to
19:31. *that* the bodies should *not* remain
Acts 2:25. *that* I should *not* be moved:
4:17. But *that* it spread *no* further
5:26. *lest* they should have been stoned.
24: 4. *that* I be *not* further tedious unto thee,
Ro. 11:25. *lest* ye should be wise in your own
15:20. *lest* I should build upon another
1Co. 1:15. *Lest* any should say that I had
17. *lest* the cross of Christ should be
4: 6. *that no* one of you be puffed up
7: 5. *that* Satan tempt you *not* for your
8:13. *lest* I make my brother to offend.
9:12. *lest* we should hinder the gospel
11:32. *that* we should *not* be condemned
34. *that* ye come *not* together unto
12:25. *That* there should be *no* schism in the
16: 2. *that* there be *no* gatherings when I come.
2Co. 1: 9. *that* we should *not* trust in ourselves,
2: 3. *lest*, when I came, I should have sorrow
5. *that* I may *not* overcharge you all.
11. *Lest* Satan should get an advantage of us
6: 3. *that* the ministry be *not* blamed:
9: 3. *lest* our boasting of you should be
4. *that* we say *not*, ye
10: 9. *That* I may *not* seem as if
12: 7. And *lest* I should be exalted above
— *lest* I should be exalted
Gal. 5:17. so *that* ye can*not* do the things
6:12. only *lest* they should suffer
Eph. 2: 9. *lest* any man should boast.
Phi. 2:27. *lest* I should have sorrow upon
Col. 2: 4. *lest* any man should beguile you
3:21. *lest* they be discouraged.
1Th. 4:13. *that* ye sorrow *not*, even as others
1Ti. 3: 6. *lest* being lifted up with pride
7. *lest* he fall into reproach
6: 1. *that* the name of God and (his) doctrine be *not*
Tit. 2: 5. *that* the word of God be *not* blasphemed.
3:14. *that* they be *not* unfruitful.
Philem. 14. *that* thy benefit should *not* be as it were
19. *albeit* I do *not* say to thee how
Heb 3:13. *lest* any of you be hardened
4:11. *lest* any man fall after the same
6:12. *That* ye be *not* slothful,
11:28. *lest* he that destroyed the firstborn
40. *that* they without us should *not* be
12: 3. *lest* ye be wearied and faint
13. *lest* that which is lame be
Jas. 5: 9. *lest* ye be condemned:
12. *lest* ye fall into condemnation.
2Pet. 3:17. beware *lest* ye also, being led away
1Joh. 2: 1. *that* ye sin *not*.
2Joh. 8. *that* we lose *not* those things
Rev. 7: 1. *that* the wind should *not* blow
9: 4. *that* they should *not* hurt the grass
5. *that* they should *not* kill them,
20. *that* they should *not* worship devils,
11: 6. *that* it rain *not* in the days of
13:17. *that no* man might buy or sell,
16:15. *lest* he walk naked,
18: 4. *that* ye be *not* partakers of her sins, and *that* ye receive *not* of her plagues.
20: 3. *that* he should deceive the nations *no more*,

μήγε see εἰ δὲ μήγε. 1490

3365 2 519/647 3361 amos (somebody)

μηδαμῶς, meedamōs.

Acts10:14. Peter said, *Not so*, Lord; for I
11: 8. But I said, *Not so*, Lord: for nothing

3366 57 519/647 3361,1161

μηδέ, meede.

Mat. 6:25. *nor yet* for your body, what ye shall put
7: 6. *neither* cast ye your pearls before
10: 9. *nor* silver, *nor* brass in your purses,
10. *neither* two coats, *neither* shoes, *nor* yet staves; for the workman
14. receive you, *nor* hear your words,
22:29. the scriptures, *nor* the power of God.
23:10. *Neither* be ye called masters:
24:20. *neither* on the sabbath day:
Mar. 2: 2. *not so much as* about the door:
6:11. *nor* hear you, when ye depart thence,
8:26. *Neither* go into the town, *nor* tell (it) to any in the town.
12:24. *neither* the power of God?
13:11. *neither* do ye premeditate:
15. *neither* enter (therein), to take any thing
Lu. 3:14. *neither* accuse (any) falsely;
10: 4. Carry neither purse, nor scrip, *nor* shoes:
12:22. *neither* for the body, what ye shall
47. *neither* did according to his will,
14:12. *nor* thy brethren, *neither* thy kinsmen, *nor* (thy) rich neighbours;
16:26. *neither* can they pass to us,
17:23. go not after (them), *nor* follow (them).
Joh. 4:15. *neither* come hither to draw.
14:27. *neither* let it be afraid.
Acts 4:18. *nor* teach in the name of Jesus.
21:21. *neither* to walk after the customs.
23: 8. *neither* angel, nor spirit:
Ro. 6:13. *Neither* yield ye your members
9:11. *neither* having done any good or
14:21. *nor* to drink wine, *nor* (any thing) whereby thy brother
1Co. 5: 8. *neither* with the leaven of
11. with such an one *no not* to eat.
10: 7. *Neither* be ye idolaters, as
8. *Neither* let us commit fornication,
9. *Neither* let us tempt Christ,
10. *Neither* murmur ye, as some
2Co. 4: 2. *nor* handling the word of God deceitfully;
Eph. 5: 3. let it *not* be *once* named among you,
Col. 2:21. Touch not; taste *not*; handle *not*;
2Th. 3:10. would not work, *neither* should he eat.
1Ti. 1: 4. *Neither* give heed to fables
5:22. *neither* be partaker of other men's
6:17. *nor* trust in uncertain riches,
2Ti. 1: 8. *nor* of me his prisoner:
Heb 12: 5. *nor* faint when thou art rebuked
1Pet.3:14. of their terror, *neither* be troubled;
5: 2. *not* for filthy lucre, but of a ready mind;
3. *Neither* as being lords over (God's)
1Joh.2:15. *neither* the things (that are) in
3:18. *neither* in tongue; but in deed

3367 92 519/648 3361,1520

μηδείς, μηδεμία, μηδέν, meedis, meedemia, meeden.

|| denotes where the double negative of the Greek is omitted.

Mat. 8: 4. See thou tell *no man*;
9:30. See (that) *no man* know (it).
16:20. that they should tell *no man* that
17: 9. Tell the vision to *no man*, until
27:19. Have thou *nothing* to do with that
Mar. 1:44. See thou say *nothing* to || *any man*
5:26. and was *nothing* bettered,
43. that *no man* should know it;
6: 8. should take *nothing* for (their) journey,
7:36. that they should tell *no man*:
8:30. that they should tell *no man* of him.
9: 9. that they should tell *no man* what
11:14. *No man* eat fruit of thee hereafter
Lu. 3:13. Exact *no* more than that which is
14. Do violence to *no man*,
4:35. he came out of him, and hurt him *not*.
5:14. he charged him to tell *no man*:
6:35. hoping for *nothing* again;
8:56. that they should tell *no man*
9: 3. Take *nothing* for (your) journey,
21. to tell *no man* that thing;
10: 4. and salute *no man* by the way.
Joh. 8:10. and saw *none* but the woman,
Acts 4:17. to *no* man in this name.
21. finding *nothing* how they might
8:24. that *none* of these things which
9: 7. but seeing *no man*.
10:20. doubting *nothing*: for I have sent them.
28. that I should *not* call *any* man common
11:12. go with them, *nothing* doubting.
19. the word to *none* but unto the Jews
13:28. though they found *no* cause of death
15:28. to lay upon you *no* greater burden
16:28. Do thyself *no* harm:
19:36. and to do *nothing* rashly.
40. there being *no* cause whereby
21:25. that they observe *no* such thing,
23:14. that we will eat *nothing* until
22. (See thou) tell *no man* that thou
29. but to have *nothing* laid to his charge
24:23. that he should forbid *none* of his
25:17. without any delay (lit. making *no* delay) on the morrow
25. *nothing* worthy of death,
27:33. continued fasting, having taken *nothing*
28: 6. and saw *no* harm come to him,
18. there was *no* cause of death in me.
Ro. 12:17. Recompense to *no man* evil
13: 8. Owe *no man* || *any thing*,
1Co. 1: 7. So that ye come behind in *no* gift;
3:18. Let *no man* deceive himself.
21. let *no man* glory in men.
10:24. Let *no man* seek his own,
25. asking *no* question for conscience sake:
27. asking *no* question for conscience sake.
2Co. 6: 3. Giving *no* offence in || *any thing*,
10. as having *nothing*, and
7: 9. receive damage by us in *nothing*.
11: 5. I was *not a whit* behind the
13: 7. I pray to God that ye do *no* evil,
Gal. 6: 3. to be something, when he is *nothing*,
17. let *no man* trouble me:
Eph. 5: 6. Let *no man* deceive you
Phi. 1:28. in *nothing* terrified by your
2: 3. (Let) *nothing* (be done) through strife
4: 6. Be careful for *nothing*;
Col. 2:18. Let *no man* beguile you
1Th. 3: 3. That *no man* should be moved
4:12. (that) ye may have lack of *nothing*.
2Th. 2: 3. Let no man deceive you by || *any* means
3:11. working *not at all*,
1Ti. 4:12. Let *no man* despise thy youth;
5:14. give *none* occasion to the adversar
21. doing *nothing* by partiality.

3364, p. 497

5:22. Lay hands suddenly on *no man*,
6: 4. He is proud, knowing *nothing*,
Tit. 2: 8. having *no* evil *thing* to say of you.
15. Let *no man* despise thee.
3: 2. To speak evil of *no man*,
13. that *nothing* be wanting unto them.
Heb 10: 2. should have had *no* more conscience
Jas. 1: 4. perfect and entire, wanting *nothing*.
6. let him ask in faith, *nothing* wavering.
13. Let *no man* say when he is tempted,
1Pet. 3: 6. and are not afraid with)(*any* amazement.
1Joh. 3: 7. let *no man* deceive you:
3Joh. 7. taking *nothing* of the Gentiles.
Rev. 2:10. Fear *none* of those things which
3:11. that *no man* take thy crown.

3368 1 520/648 3366,4218

μηδέποτε, meedepote.

2Ti. 3: 7. and *never* able to come to the knowledge of the truth.

3369 1 520/649 3366,4452

μηδέπω, meedepo.

Heb 11. 7. being warned of God of things *not* seen *as yet*,

3371 21 520/649 3361,2089

μηκέτι, meeketi.

|| denotes where the double negative of the Greek is omitted.

Mat. 21:19. Let *no* fruit grow on thee *henceforward*
Mar 1:45. Jesus could *no more* openly enter
2: 2. that there was *no* room to receive
9:25. and enter *no more* into him.
11:14. No man eat fruit of thee || *hereafter*
Joh. 5:14. sin *no more*, lest a worse thing
8:11. go, and sin *no more*.
Acts 4:17. speak || *henceforth* to no man in
13:34. *no more* to return to corruption,
25:24. he ought not to live || *any longer*.
Ro. 6: 6. that *henceforth* we should *not*
14:13. Let us *not* therefore judge one another *any more*:
15:23. But now having *no more* place
2Co. 5:15. should *not henceforth* live unto
Eph. 4:14. That we (henceforth) be *no more* children,
17. that ye *henceforth* walk *not* as
28. Let him that stole steal *no more*.
1Th. 3: 1. when we could *no longer* forbear,
5. when I could *no longer* forbear,
1Ti. 5:23. Drink *no longer* water,
1Pet. 4: 2. That he *no longer* should live the rest of

3364 5 194/646 3756,3361cf3378
3378 5 521/719 3756,3361cf3378

μὴ οὐκ & οὐ μή, mee ouk & ou mee.

An interrogation put negatively.

Joh. 18:11. shall I *not* drink it?
Ro. 10:18. But I say, Have they *not* heard?
19. Did *not* Israel know?
1Co. 9: 4. Have we *not* power to eat and
5. Have we *not* power to lead about a sister,
11:22. have ye *not* houses to eat and to drink in?

3379 25 521/649 3361,4218

μήποτε or μή ποτε, meepotee or mee potee.

Mat. 4: 6. *lest at any time* thou dash thy
5:25. *lest at any time* the adversary
7: 6. *lest* they trample them under
13:15. *lest at any time* they should se
29. Nay; *lest* while ye gather up
15:32. *lest* they faint in the way.
25: 9. *lest* there be not enough
27:64. *lest* his disciples come by night,
Mar 4:12. *lest at any time* they should be converted,
14: 2. *lest* there be an uproar
Lu. 3:15. *whether* he were the Christ, *or not*:
4:11. *lest at any time* thou dash
12:58. *lest* he hale thee to the judge,
14: 8. *lest* a more honourable man
12. *lest* they also bid thee again,
29. *Lest haply*, after he hath laid
21:34. *lest at any time* your hearts
Joh. 7:26.)(Do the rulers know indeed that this is
Acts 5:39. *lest haply* ye be found even to fight
28:27. *lest* they should see with
2Ti. 2:25. *if* God *peradventure* will give them
Heb 2: 1. *lest at any time* we should let (them) slip.
3:12. *lest* there be in any of you an evil heart of
4: 1. Let us therefore fear, *lest*, a promise
9:17. it is of *no* strength *at all* while

3380 2 521/650 3361,4452

μήπω, meepo.

Ro. 9:11. (the children) being *not yet* born,
Heb 9: 8. was *not yet* made manifest.

3381 12 521/639 3361,4458

μήπως or μή πως, meepōs or mee pōs.

Acts 27:29. fearing *lest* we (lit. they) should have fallen upon rocks,
Ro. 11:21. *lest* he also spare not thee.
1Co. 8: 9. take heed *lest by any means* this
9:27. *lest* that *by any means*, when I have
2Co. 2: 7. *lest perhaps* such a one should be
9: 4. *Lest haply* if they of Macedonia come
11: 3. But I fear, *lest by any means*, as the
12:20. For I fear, *lest*, when I come, I
— *lest* (there be) debates, envyings,
Gal. 2: 2. *lest by any means* I should run,
4:11. *lest* I have bestowed upon you
1Th. 3: 5. *lest by some means* the tempter have

3383 37 527/650 3361,5037

μήτε, meete.

|| marks the omission of a double negative of the Greek.

Mat. 5:34. *neither* by heaven; for it is God's
35. *Nor* by the earth; for it is his footstool. *neither* by Jerusalem;
36. *Neither* shalt thou swear by thy head,
11:18. For John came *neither* eating *nor* drinking,
Mar 3:20. they could not || *so much as* eat
Lu. 7:33. John the Baptist came *neither* eating bread *nor* drinking wine;
9: 3. *neither* staves, *nor* scrip, *neither* bread, *neither* money; *neither* have two coats
Acts 23: 8. neither angel, *nor* spirit:
12. they would *neither* eat *nor* drink
21. they will *neither* eat *nor* drink
27:20. when *neither* sun *nor* stars
Eph. 4:27. *Neither* give place to the devil.
2Th. 2: 2. *or* be troubled, *neither* by spirit, *nor* by word, *nor* by letter as from us.
1Ti. 1: 7. understanding *neither* what they say, *nor* whereof they affirm.

3372-3374, 3376-3377, p. 499

3382, p. 499

Heb 7: 3. having *neither* beginning of days, *nor* end of life;
Jas. 5:12. swear not, *neither* by heaven, *neither* by the earth, *neither* by any other oath:
Rev. 7: 1. should not blow on the earth, *nor* on the sea, *nor* on any tree.
3. Hurt not the earth, *neither* the sea, *nor* the trees, till we have sealed

3385 15 522/651 3361,5100
3386 1 522/651 3361,5100

μήτι, *meeti.* adv. interrog.

Mat. 7:16.)(Do men gather grapes of thorns, or figs of thistles?
12:23. Is *not* this the son of David?
26:22. Lord,)(is it I?
25. Master,)(is it I?
Mar 4:21.)(Is a candle brought to be put under a
14:19.)((Is) it I? and another (said),)((Is) it
Lu. 6:39.)(Can the blind lead the blind?
Joh. 4:29. is *not* this the Christ?
7:31. When Christ cometh,)(will he do
8:22.)(Will he kill himself?
18:35.)(Am I a Jew?
Acts10:47.)(Can any man forbid water,
1Co. 6: 3. *how much more* things that pertain to this
2Co. 1:17.)(did I use lightness?
Jas. 3:11.)(Doth a fountain send forth

3387 4 /639 3361,5100

μήτις or μή τις, *meetis* or *mee tis.* interrog.

Joh. 4:33. Hath *any man* brought him (ought) to
7:48. Have *any* of the rulers or
21: 5. Children, have ye *any* meat?
2Co.12:18.)(Did Titus make a gain of you?

Though μήτις occurs in one word as an indefinite pron. it is better read as μή τις.

3364 94 /646 See also p. 497

οὐ μή, *ou mee.* double negative.

Mat. 5:18. one jot or one tittle shall *in no wise*
20. ye shall *in no case* enter into
26. Thou shalt *by no means* come out
10:23. Ye shall *not* have gone over the
42. he shall *in no wise* lose his reward.
13:14. and shall *not* understand;
— and shall *not* perceive:
15: 6(5). And honour *not* his father or
16:22. this shall *not* be unto thee.
28. which shall *not* taste of death,
18: 3. ye shall *not* enter into the
23:39. Ye shall *not* see me henceforth,
24: 2. There shall *not* be left here one stone upon another, that shall *not* be thrown down.
21. no, *nor ever* shall be.
34. This generation shall *not* pass,
35. but my words shall *not* pass away.
26:29. I will *not* drink henceforth of
35. yet will I *not* deny thee.
Mar 9: 1. which shall *not* taste of death,
41. he shall *not* lose his reward.
10:15. he shall *not* enter therein.
13: 2. there shall *not* be left one stone upon another, that shall *not* be thrown down.
19. unto this time, *neither* shall be.
30. this generation shall *not* pass
Mar13:31. but my words shall *not* pass away.
14:25. I will)(drink no more of the
31. I will *not* deny thee *in any wise.*
16:18. it shall *not* hurt them;
Lu. 1:15. shall drink neither wine nor strong drink; (lit. *not* drink wine or &c.);
6:37. and ye shall *not* be judged: condemn not, and ye shall *not* be condemned:
9:27. which shall *not* taste of death, till
10:19. nothing shall *by any means* hurt you.
12:59. thou shalt *not* depart thence, till
13:35. Ye shall *not* see me, until
18: 7. And shall *not* God avenge his own
17. shall *in no wise* enter therein.
30. Who shall *not* receive manifold
21:18. there shall *not* an hair of your head
32. This generation shall *not* pass
33. but my words shall *not* pass away.
22:16. I will *not* any more eat thereof,
18. I will *not* drink of the fruit
34. the cock shall *not* crow this day,
67. ye will *not* believe:
68. ye will *not* answer me, nor let (me) go.
Joh. 4:14. shall never (lit. *not* ever) thirst;
48. and wonders, ye will *not* believe.
6:35. he that cometh to me shall never (lit. *not*) hunger; and he that believeth on me shall never (lit. *not* ever) thirst.
37. I will *in no wise* cast out.
8:12. shall *not* walk in darkness,
51. he shall never (lit. *not* for ever) see death.
52. he shall never (lit. *not* for ever) taste of
10: 5. a stranger will they *not* follow,
28. and they shall never (lit. *not* for ever) perish,
11:26. and believeth in me shall never (lit. *not*, &c.) die.
56. that he will *not* come to the feast?
13: 8. Thou shalt never (lit. *not*, &c.) wash my
38. The cock shall *not* crow, till
20:25. I will *not* believe.
Acts13:41. which ye shall *in no wise* believe,
28:26. and shall *not* understand; and seeing ye shall see, and *not* perceive:
Ro. 4: 8. to whom the Lord will *not* impute sin.
1Co. 8:13. I will eat *no* flesh while the
Gal. 4:30. shall *not* be heir with the son
5:16. and ye shall *not* fulfil the lust
1Th. 4:15. shall *not* prevent them which
5: 3. and they shall *not* escape.
Heb 8:11. they shall *not* teach every man
12. will I remember *no* more.
10:17. will I remember *no* more.
13: 5. I will *never* leave thee, nor)(forsake thee.
1Pet.2: 6. shall *not* be confounded.
2Pet.1:10. if ye do these things, ye shall never (lit. *not* ever) fall:
Rev. 2:11. shall *not* be hurt of the second death.
3: 3. thou shalt *not* know what hour I will come
5. I will *not* blot out his name
12. and he shall go *no* more out:
15: 4. Who shall *not* fear thee, O Lord,
18: 7. and shall see *no* sorrow.
14. thou shalt find them no more)(*at all.*
21. and shall be found *no* more *at all.*
22. shall be heard *no* more *at all* in thee;
— and no craftsman
— shall be heard *no* more *at all* in thee;
23. shall shine *no* more *at all* in thee;
— shall be heard *no* more *at all* in thee.
21:25. shall *not* be shut *at all* by day:
27. there shall *in no wise* enter into it

3384, p. 499

αηκέτι see after μή. 3361

3372 3 520/649 cf 3173

μῆκος, meekos.

Eph. 3:18. and *length*, and depth, and height;
Rev.21:16. the *length* is as large as the breadth:
— The *length* and the breadth and the height of it are equal.

3373 1 520/649 3372

μηκύνομαι, meekunomai.

Mar 4:27. and the seed should spring and *grow up*,

3374 1 520/649 4:637 mēlon (sheep)

μηλωτή, meelōtee.

Heb 11:37. they wandered about in *sheepskins*

3376 18 520/649 4:638

μήν, meen.

Lu. 1:24. and hid herself five *months*,
26. And in the sixth *month* the angel
36. this is the sixth *month* with her,
56. Mary abode with her about three *months*,
4:25. was shut up three years and six *months*,
Acts 7:20. in his father's house three *months*:
18:11. a year and six *months*,
19: 8. for the space of three *months*,
20: 3. And (there) abode three *months*.
28:11. And after three *months* we departed
Gal. 4:10. Ye observe days, and *months*, and times,
Jas. 5:17. by the space of three years and six *months*.
Rev. 9: 5. should be tormented five *months*:
10. to hurt men five *months*.
15. and a day, and a *month*, and a year,
11: 2. tread under foot forty (and) two *months*.
13: 5. to continue forty (and) two *months*.
22: 2. yielded her fruit every *month*.

3377 7 520/649 maō (to strive)

μηνύω, meenuo.

Lu. 20:37. even Moses *shewed* at the bush,
Joh.11:57. he *should shew* (it), that they might take
Acts23:30. And *when* it *was told* me how that
1Co.10:28. eat not for his sake *that shewed* it,

μὴ οὐκ, μήποτε, μήπω, μήπως,
see after μή. 3361

3382 1 521/650

μηρός, meeros.

Rev.19:16. and on his *thigh* a name written,

1 520/ 3361

μήτε see after μή.

3384 85 521/650 4:642

μήτηρ, meeteer.

Mat. 1:18. When as his *mother* Mary was espoused
2:11. the young child with Mary his *mother*,
13. take the young child and his *mother*,
14. he took the young child and his *mother*
20. take the young child and his *mother*,
21. and took the young child and his *mother*,
10:35. the daughter against her *mother*,
37. He that loveth father or *mother* more
12:46. behold, (his) *mother* and his brethren
47. Behold, thy *mother* and thy brethren
48. Who is my *mother*? and who
49. Behold my *mother* and my brethren!
50. the same is my brother, and sister, and *mother*.
13:55. is not his *mother* called Mary?
14: 8. being before instructed of her *mother*,
11. and she brought (it) to her *mother*.
15: 4. Honour thy father and *mother*: and, He that curseth father or *mother*,
5. shall say to (his) father or (his) *mother*,
6(5). And honour not his father or his *mother*,
19: 5. leave father and *mother*, and shall
12. so born from (their) *mother's* womb:
19. Honour thy father and (thy) *mother*:
29. or *mother*, or wife, or children,
20:20. Then came to him the *mother* of
27:56. and Mary the *mother* of James and Joses, and the *mother* of Zebedee's
Mar 3:31. his brethren and his *mother*,
32. Behold, thy *mother* and thy
33. Who is my *mother*, or my
34. Behold my *mother* and my brethren!
35. and my sister, and *mother*.
5:40. he taketh the father and the *mother*
6:24. and said unto her *mother*,
28. the damsel gave it to her *mother*.
7:10. Honour thy father and thy *mother*; and, Whoso curseth father or *mother*,
11. say to his father or *mother*,
12. for his father or his *mother*;
10: 7. leave his father and *mother*, and cleave
19. Honour thy father and *mother*.
29. or sisters, or father, or *mother*,
30. and sisters, and *mothers*, and
15:40. and Mary the *mother* of James
Lu. 1:15. even from his *mother's* womb.
43. that the *mother* of my Lord should
60. And his *mother* answered and said,
2:33. And Joseph and his *mother*
34. and said unto Mary his *mother*,
43. and Joseph and his *mother* knew not
48. and his *mother* said unto him,
51. but his *mother* kept all these
7:12. the only son of his *mother*,
15. he delivered him to his *mother*.
8:19. Then came to him (his) *mother*
20. Thy *mother* and thy brethren
21. My *mother* and my brethren are these
51. and the *mother* of the maiden.
12:53. the *mother* against the daughter, and the
— daughter against the *mother*;
14:26. hate not his father, and *mother*,
18:20. Honour thy father and thy *mother*.
Joh. 2: 1. and the *mother* of Jesus was there:
3. the *mother* of Jesus saith unto him,
5. His *mother* saith unto the servants,
12. he, and his *mother*, and his brethren,
3: 4. the second time into his *mother's* womb,
6:42. whose father and *mother* we know?

κ κ 2

3375 *men*. eq 3303

3378. See p. 497

Joh. 19:25. stood by the cross of Jesus his *mother*, and his *mother's* sister,
26. When Jesus therefore saw his *mother*,
— he saith unto his *mother*,
27. Behold thy *mother!*
Acts 1:14. and Mary the *mother* of Jesus,
3: 2. lame from his *mother's* womb
12:12. to the house of Mary the *mother*
14: 8. a cripple from his *mother's* womb,
Ro. 16:13. and his *mother* and mine.
Gal. 1:15. separated me from my *mother's* womb,
4:26. which is the *mother* of us all.
Eph 5:31. leave his father and *mother*,
6: 2. Honour thy father and *mother;*
1Ti. 5: 2. The elder women as *mothers;*
2Ti. 1: 5. and thy *mother* Eunice;
Rev. 17: 5. THE *MOTHER* OF HARLOTS AND

μήτι. adv., μήτις. interrog., see after μή. 3361

3388 2 522/651 3384

μήτρα, *meetra.*

Lu. 2:23. Every male that openeth the *womb*
Ro. 4:19. neither yet the deadness of Sarah's *womb:*

3389 1 522/651 3384,rt 257

μητραλῴης, *meetralōees.*

1Ti. 1: 9. and *murderers of mothers*, for

3391 80 229/299 1520

μία, *mia.* fem. to εἷς.

Mat. 5:18. one jot or *one* tittle shall in no wise
19. shall break *one* of these least
36. thou canst not make *one* hair
17: 4. *one* for thee, and *one* for Moses, and *one* for Elias.
19: 5. and they twain shall be *one* flesh?
6. they are no more twain, but *one* flesh.
20:12. These last have wrought (but) *one* hour,
21:19. And when he saw *a* fig tree in the way,
24:41. the *one* shall be taken, and the other (lit. *one*) left.
26:40. could ye not watch with me *one* hour?
69. and *a* damsel came unto him,
28: 1. toward the *first* (day) of the week,
Mar 9: 5. *one* for thee, and *one* for Moses, and *one* for Elias.
10: 8. twain shall be *one* flesh: so then they are no more twain, but *one* flesh.
12:42. there came *a certain* poor widow,
14:37. couldest not thou watch *one* hour?
66. there cometh *one* of the maids of
16: 2. the *first* (day) of the week,
Lu. 5:12. when he was in *a certain* city,
17. it came to pass on *a certain* day,
8:22. it came to pass on *a certain* day,
9:33. *one* for thee, and *one* for Moses, and *one* for Elias:
13:10. he was teaching in *one* of the synagogues
14:18. they all with *one* (consent) began
15: 8. if she lose *one* piece,
16:17. than *one* tittle of the law to fail.
17:22. shall desire to see *one* of the days of
34. there shall be two (men) in *one* bed;
35. the *one* shall be taken, and the other
Lu. 20: 1. on *one* of those days,
22:59. about the space of *one* hour after
24: 1. Now upon the *first* (day) of the week,
Joh. 10:16. and there shall be *one* fold,
20: 1. The *first* (day) of the week cometh
19. being the *first* (day) of the week,
Acts 4:32. were of one heart and of *one* soul:
12:10. and passed on through *one* street;
19:34. all with *one* voice about the space
20: 7. And upon the *first* (day) of the week,
21: 7. and abode with them *one* day.
24:21. Except it be for this *one* voice,
28:13. and after *one* day the south wind
1Co. 6:16. for two, saith he, shall be *one* flesh.
10: 8. fell in *one* day three and twenty thousand.
16: 2. Upon the *first* (day) of the week
2Co. 11:24. received I forty (stripes) save *one*.
Gal. 4:24. the *one* from the mount Sinai,
Eph. 4: 4. ye are called in *one* hope of
5. One Lord, *one* faith, one baptism,
5:31. and they two shall be *one* flesh.
Phi. 1:27. with *one* mind striving together
1Ti. 3: 2. the husband of *one* wife,
12. be the husbands of *one* wife,
Tit. 1: 6. the husband of *one* wife,
3:10. after the *first* and second admonition
Heb 10:12. after he had offered *one* sacrifice
14. For by *one* offering he hath
12:16. who for *one* morsel of meat
2Pet. 3: 8. that *one* day (is) with the Lord
— and a thousand years as *one* day.
Rev. 6: 1. when the Lamb opened *one* of the seals,
9:12. *One* woe is past;
13. I heard *a* voice from the four horns
13: 3. I saw *one* of his heads
17:12. as kings *one* hour with the beast.
13. These have *one* mind,
17. and to agree (lit. to form *one* mind), and give their kingdom
18: 8. shall her plagues come in *one* day,
10. for in *one* hour is thy judgment come.
17(16). For in *one* hour so great riches
19. for in *one* hour is she made desolate.

3392 5 522/651 4:644

μιαίνω, *miaino.*

Joh. 18:28. lest they *should be defiled;*
Tit. 1:15. but unto them *that are defiled*
— their mind and conscience *is defiled.*
Heb 12:15. and thereby many *be defiled;*
Jude 8. these (filthy) dreamers *defile* the flesh,

3393 1 522/651 4:644 3392

μίασμα, *miasma.*

2Pet. 2:20. have escaped the *pollutions* of the world

3394 1 522/651 4:644 3392

μιασμός, *miasmos.*

2Pet. 2:10. in the lust of *uncleanness,*

3395 1 523/651,325 3396

μίγμα, *migma.*

Joh. 19:39. brought a *mixture* of myrrh and aloes,

3396 4 523/651

μίγνυμι, *mignumi.*

Mat. 27:34. vinegar to drink *mingled* with gall:
Lu. 13: 1. whose blood Pilate *had mingled*
Rev. 8: 7. hail and fire *mingled* with blood,
15: 2. a sea of glass *mingled* with fire:

3390 *metropolis* (mother city).
3384, 4172

3397 16 523/651 3398

μικρόν, mikron. adv.

Mat.26:39. And he went *a little* farther, and
73. And after *a while* came unto (him)
Mar 14:35. And he went forward *a little*, and
70. And *a little* after, they that stood by
Joh.13:33. Little children, yet *a little while* I am
14:19. Yet *a little while*, and the world
16:16. *A little while*, and ye shall not see me: and again, *a little while*, and ye
17. *A little while*, and ye shall not see me: and again, *a little while*, and ye
18. What is this that he saith, *A little while*?
19. *A little while*, and ye shall not see me: and again, *a little while*, and ye

3398 30 523/652 4:648

μικρ-ός, -ότερος, mikros, -oteros.

Mat.10:42. unto one of these *little* ones a cup of
11:11. he that is *least* in the kingdom
13:32. is the *least* of all seeds:
18: 6. shall offend one of these *little* ones
10. despise not one of these *little* ones;
14. one of these *little* ones should perish.
Mar 4:31. is *less* than all the seeds
9:42. shall offend one of (these) *little* ones
15:40. Mary the mother of James the *less*
Lu. 7:28. he that is *least* in the kingdom
9:48. he that is *least* among you all,
12:32. Fear not, *little* flock;
17: 2. should offend one of these *little* ones.
19: 3. because he was *little* of stature.
Joh. 7:33. Yet a *little* while am I with you,
12:35. Yet a *little* while is the light
Acts 8:10. from the *least* to the greatest,
26:22. witnessing both to *small* and great,
1Co. 5: 6. Know ye not that a *little* leaven
2Co.11: 1. bear with me a *little* in (my) folly:
16. that I may boast myself a *little*.
Gal. 5: 9. A *little* leaven leaveneth the whole
Heb 8:11. from the *least* to the greatest.
10:37. For yet a *little* while, and he that
Jas. 3: 5. the tongue is a *little* member,
Rev. 3: 8. for thou hast a *little* strength,
6:11. they should rest yet for a *little* season,
11:18. that fear thy name, *small* and great;
13:16. caused all, both *small* and great,
19: 5. that fear him, both *small* and great.
18. both *small* and great.
20: 3. must be loosed a *little* season.
12. I saw the dead, *small* and great,

3400 1 523/652

μίλιον, milion.

Mat. 5:41. shall compel thee to go a *mile*,

3401 4 523/652 4:659 *mimos* (mimic)

μιμέομαι, mimeomai.

2Th. 3: 7. how ye ought *to follow* us:
9. an ensample unto you *to follow* us.
Heb 13: 7. whose faith *follow*, considering
3Joh. 11. *follow* not that which is evil,

3402 7 524/652 4:659 3401

μιμητής, mimeetees.

1Co. 4:16. be ye *followers* of me.
11: 1. Be ye *followers* of me, even as
Eph. 5: 1. Be ye therefore *followers* of God.
1Th. 1: 6. And ye became *followers* of us,
2:14. ye, brethren, became *followers* of the
Heb 6:12. but *followers* of them who through
1Pet. 3:13. if ye be *followers* of that which is good?

3403 2 524/652 4:675 3415

μιμνήσκομαι, mimneeskomai.

Heb 2: 6. that thou *art mindful* of him?
13: 3. *Remember* them that are in bonds,

3404 42 524/652 4:683 *misos* (hatred)

μισέω, miseo.

Mat. 5:43. shalt love thy neighbour, and *hate*
44. do good to them *that hate* you,
6:24. for either he *will hate* the one,
10:22. ye shall be *hated* of all (men)
24: 9. and ye shall be *hated* of all
10. and *shall hate* one another.
Mar 13:13. And ye shall be *hated* of all (men)
Lu. 1:71. from the hand of all *that hate* us;
6:22. when men *shall hate* you,
27. do good to them *which hate* you,
14:26. and *hate* not his father, and mother,
16:13. either he *will hate* the one,
19:14. But his citizens *hated* him,
21:17. ye shall be *hated* of all (men)
Joh. 3:20. *hateth* the light, neither cometh
7: 7. cannot *hate* you; but me it *hateth*,
12:25. he *that hateth* his life in this world
15:18. If the world *hate* you, ye know that it *hated* me before (it hated) you.
19. therefore the world *hateth* you.
23. He *that hateth* me *hateth* my Father also.
24. they both seen and *hated*
25. They *hated* me without a cause.
17:14. the world *hath hated* them,
Ro. 7:15. what I *hate*, that do I.
9:13. Esau *have* I *hated*.
Eph. 5:29. no man ever yet *hated* his own flesh;
Tit. 3: 3. hateful, (and) *hating* one another.
Heb 1: 9. and *hated* iniquity;
1Joh. 2: 9. that saith he is in the light, and *hateth* his brother,
11. But he *that hateth* his brother is in
3:13. if the world *hate* you.
15. *Whosoever hateth* his brother
4:20. and *hateth* his brother,
Jude 23. *hating* even the garment spotted
Rev. 2: 6. that thou *hatest* the deeds of the Nicolaitanes, which I also *hate*.
15. which thing I *hate*.
17:16. these *shall hate* the whore,
18: 2. of every unclean and *hateful* bird.

3405 3 525/653 4:695 3406

μισθαποδοσία, misthapodosia.

Heb 2: 2. received a just *recompence of reward*;
10:35. great *recompence of reward*.
11:26. unto the *recompence of the reward*.

3406 1 525/653 4:695 3409,591

μισθαποδότης, misthapodotees.

Heb 11: 6. he is a *rewarder* of them that

3407 2 525/653 4:695 3408

μίσθιος, misthios.

Lu. 15:17. How many *hired servants* of my father's
19. as one of thy *hired servants*

3409 2 525/653 4:695 3408

μισθόομαι, mistho-omai.

Mat.20: 1. *to hire* labourers into his vineyard.
7. Because no man *hath hired* us.

3408 29 525/653 4:695

μισθός, misthos.

Mat. 5:12. for great (is) your *reward* in heaven:
46. what *reward* have ye?
6: 1. ye have no *reward* of your Father
2. They have their *reward*.
5. They have their *reward*.
16. They have their *reward*.
10:41. shall receive a prophet's *reward*;
— shall receive a righteous man's *reward*
42. shall in no wise lose his *reward*.
20: 8. give them (their) *hire*,
Mar 9:41. he shall not lose his *reward*.
Lu. 6:23. your *reward* (is) great in heaven:
35. your *reward* shall be great,
10: 7. the labourer is worthy of his *hire*.
Joh. 4:36. receiveth *wages*, and gathereth
Acts 1:18. a field with the *reward* of iniquity;
Ro. 4: 4. that worketh is the *reward* not
1Co. 3: 8. shall receive his own *reward*
14. he shall receive a *reward*.
9:17. willingly, I have a *reward*:
18. What is my *reward* then?
1Ti. 5:18. The labourer (is) worthy of his *reward*.
Jas. 5: 4. Behold, the *hire* of the labourers
2Pet. 2:13. receive the *reward* of unrighteousness,
15. who loved the *wages* of unrighteousness;
2Joh. 8. but that we receive a full *reward*.
Jude 11. after the error of Balaam for *reward*,
Rev.11:18. that thou shouldest give *reward*
22:12. and my *reward* (is) with me,

3410 1 525/653 3409

μίσθωμα, misthōma

Acts28:30. two whole years in his own *hired house*.

3411 4 525/653 4:695 3409

μισθωτός, misthōtos.

Mar 1:20. in the ship with the *hired servants*,
Joh.10:12. But he that is an *hireling*,
13. The *hireling* fleeth, because he is an *hireling*, and careth not

3414 9 526/653

μνᾶ, mna.

Lu. 19:13. and delivered them ten *pounds*,
16. saying, Lord, thy *pound* hath gained ten *pounds*.
18. Lord, thy *pound* hath gained five *pounds*.
20. (here is) thy *pound*,
24. Take from him the *pound*, and give (it) to him that hath ten *pounds*.
25. Lord, he hath ten *pounds*.

3415 21 526/652 cf 3403

μνάομαι, mnaomai.

Mat. 5:23. and there *rememberest* that thy brother
26:75. And Peter *remembered* the word
27:63. Sir, we *remember* that that deceiver
Lu. 1:54. in remembrance of (lit. to *remember*) (his) mercy;
72. and *to remember* his holy covenant;
16:25. *remember* that thou in thy lifetime
23:42. Lord, *remember* me when thou
24: 6. *remember* how he spake unto you
8. they *remembered* his words,
Joh. 2:17. And his disciples *remembered* that it
22. his disciples *remembered* that he
12:16. then *remembered* they that these
Acts10:31. thine alms *are had in remembrance*
11:16. Then *remembered* I the word of
1Co.11: 2. that ye *remember* me in all things,
2Ti. 1: 4. *being mindful* of thy tears,
Heb 8:12. their iniquities *will* I *remember* no more.
10:17. and iniquities *will* I *remember* no more.
2Pet.3: 2. That ye may *be mindful* of the words
Jude 17. *remember* ye the words which
Rev.16:19. Babylon *came in remembrance* before God,

3417 7 526/654 4:675 3415,3403

μνεία, mnīa.

Ro. 1: 9. I make *mention* of you always in my
Eph. 1:16. making *mention* of you in my prayers;
Phi. 1: 3. upon every *remembrance* of you,
1Th. 1: 2. making *mention* of you in our prayers;
3: 6. that ye have good *remembrance* of us
2Ti. 1: 3. *remembrance* of thee in my prayers
Philem. 4. making *mention* of thee always

3418 7 526/654 4:675 3415

μνῆμα, mneema.

Mar 5: 5. and in the *tombs*, crying, and
Lu. 8:27. abode in (any) house, but in the *tombs*.
23:53. laid it in a *sepulchre* that was hewn
24: 1. they came unto the *sepulchre*,
Acts 2:29. his *sepulchre* is with us
7:16. laid in the *sepulchre* that Abraham
Rev.11: 9. their dead bodies to be put in *graves*.

3419 42 526/654 4:675 3420

μνημεῖον, mneemīon.

Mat. 8:28. coming out of the *tombs*,
23:29. and garnish the *sepulchres* of
27:52. And the *graves* were opened,
53. And came out of the *graves*
60. laid it in his own new *tomb*,
— great stone to the door of the *sepulchre*,
28: 8. departed quickly from the *sepulchre*
Mar 5: 2. there met him out of the *tombs*
3. had (his) dwelling among the *tombs*;
6:29. and laid it in a *tomb*.
15:46. and laid him in a *sepulchre*
— a stone unto the door of the *sepulchre*.
16: 2. they came unto the *sepulchre* at the
3. from the door of the *sepulchre*?
5. And entering into the *sepulchre*,
8. and fled from the *sepulchre*;
Lu. 11:44. for ye are as *graves* which appear not,
47. for ye build the *sepulchres* of the
48. and ye build their *sepulchres*.
23:55. beheld the *sepulchre*, and how
24: 2. rolled away from the *sepulchre*.
9. returned from the *sepulchre*,
12. and ran unto the *sepulchre*;
22. which were early at the *sepulchre*;
24. were with us went to the *sepulchre*,
Joh. 5:28. all that are in the *graves* shall
11:17. he had (lain) in the *grave* four days
31. She goeth unto the *grave* to weep
38. cometh to the *grave*.

Joh. 12:17. when he called Lazarus out of his *grave*,
19:41. and in the garden a new *sepulchre*,
42. for the *sepulchre* was nigh at hand.
20: 1. unto the *sepulchre*, and seeth the stone taken away from the *sepulchre*.
2. taken away the Lord out of the *sepulchre*,
3. and came to the *sepulchre*.
4. and came first to the *sepulchre*.
6. and went into the *sepulchre*,
8. which came first to the *sepulchre*,
11. Mary stood without at the *sepulchre*
— (and looked) into the *sepulchre*,
Acts13:29. and laid (him) in a *sepulchre*.

3420 1 526/654 4:675 3403

μνήμη, mneemee.

2Pet. 1:15. these things always in *remembrance*.

3421 21 526/654 4:675 3420

μνημονεύω, mneemonũo.

Mat.16: 9. neither *remember* the five loaves of
Mar 8:18. and *do* ye not *remember*?
Lu. 17:32. *Remember* Lot's wife.
Joh. 15:20. *Remember* the word that I said
16: 4. ye *may remember* that I told you of them.
21. she *remembereth* no more the anguish,
Acts20:31. *and remember*, that by the space
35. and *to remember* the words of the Lord
Gal. 2:10. that we *should remember* the poor;
Eph. 2:11. Wherefore *remember*, that ye
Col. 4:18. *Remember* my bonds.
1Th. 1: 3. *Remembering* without ceasing your work
2: 9. For ye *remember*, brethren, our labour
2Th. 2: 5. *Remember* ye not, that,
2Ti. 2: 8. *Remember* that Jesus Christ
Heb 11:15. if they *had been mindful* of that (country)
22. Joseph, when he died, *made mention* of
13: 7. *Remember* them which have the rule
Rev. 2: 5. *Remember* therefore from whence
3: 3. *Remember* therefore how thou hast
18: 5. God *hath remembered* her iniquities.

3422 3 527/655 3421

μνημόσυνον, mneemosunon.

Mat.26:13. be told for a *memorial* of her.
Mar 14: 9. shall be spoken of for a *memorial* of her.
Acts10: 4. thine alms are come up for a *memorial*

3423 3 527/655 3415

μνηστεύομαι, mneestũomai.

Mat. 1:18. *When* as his mother Mary *was espoused* to
Lu. 1:27. To a virgin *espoused* to a man whose
2: 5. To be taxed with Mary his *espoused* wife,

3424 1 527/655 3425,2980

μογιλάλος, mogilalos.

Mar. 7:32. that was deaf, and *had an impediment in his speech*;

3425 1 527/655 4:735 *mogos* (toil)

μόγις, mogis.

Lu. 9:39. *hardly* departeth from him.

3426 3 527/655

μόδιος, modios.

Mat 5:15. a candle, and put it under a *bushel*,
Mar 4:21. to be put under a *bushel*,
Lu. 11:33. neither under a *bushel*,

3427 241 216/252 1698

μοί, moi.

From ἐγώ.

Mat. 2: 8. bring *me* word again,
4: 9. if thou wilt fall down and worship *me*.
7:21. Not every one that saith unto *me*,
22. Many will say to *me* in that day,
8:21. Lord, suffer *me* first to go and bury
22. Follow *me*; and let the dead
9: 9. Follow *me*. And he arose,
11:27. All things are delivered unto *me*
14: 8. Give *me* here John Baptist's head
18. Bring them hither to *me*.
15: 8. draweth nigh unto *me* with their
25. Lord, help *me*.
32. they continue with *me* now three days,
16:24. and take up his cross, and follow *me*.
17:17. bring him hither to *me*.
18:28. Pay *me* that thou owest.
19:21. and come (and) follow *me*.
28. ye which have followed *me*,
20:13. didst not thou agree with *me* for
15. Is it not lawful for *me* to do
21: 2. bring (them) unto *me*.
24. which if ye tell *me*,
22:19. Shew *me* the tribute money.
25:20. Lord, thou deliveredst unto *me* five
22. Lord, thou deliveredst unto *me* two
35. and ye gave *me* meat:
42. and ye gave *me* no meat:
26:15. What will ye give *me*,
53. and he shall presently give *me* more
27:10. as the Lord appointed *me*.
28:18. All power is given unto *me* in heaven and in earth.
Mar 2:14. Follow *me*. And he arose
5: 9. *My* name (is) Legion:
6:25. I will that thou give *me* by and by
8: 2. now been with *me* three days,
34. take up his cross, and follow *me*.
10:21. take up the cross, and follow *me*.
11:29. one question, and answer *me*,
30. or of men? answer *me*.
12:15. bring *me* a penny,
Lu. 1:25. Thus hath the Lord dealt with *me*
38. be it unto *me* according to thy word.
43. And whence (is) this to *me*,
49. hath done to *me* great things;
4:23. Ye will surely say unto *me*
5:27. said unto him, Follow *me*.
7:45. Thou gavest *me* no kiss:
9:23. his cross daily, and follow *me*.
38. for he is *mine* (lit. to *me* an) only child.
59. Follow *me*. But he said, Lord, suffer *me* first to go
61. but let *me* first go bid
10:22. All things are delivered to *me*
40. bid her therefore that she help *me*.
11: 5. lend *me* three loaves;
7. Trouble *me* not: the door is
15: 6. Rejoice with *me*; for I have found
9. Rejoice with *me*; for I have found
12. give *me* the portion of goods
17: 8. gird thyself, and serve *me*,
18: 5. this widow troubleth *me*,
13. God be merciful to *me* a sinner.

Lu. 18:22. and come, follow *me*.
20: 3. ask you one thing; and answer *me:*
24. Shew *me* a penny. Whose
22:29. as my Father hath appointed unto *me;*
68. ye will not answer *me*,
23:14. Ye have brought this man unto *me*,
Joh. 1:33. the same said unto *me*,
43(44). saith unto him, Follow *me*.
3:28. Ye yourselves bear *me* witness,
4: 7. Jesus saith unto her, Give *me* to drink.
10. that saith to thee, Give *me* to drink;
15. give *me* this water,
21. Woman, believe *me*, the hour
29. which told *me* all things
39. He told *me* all that ever I did.
5:11. the same said unto *me*,
36. which the Father hath given *me*
6:37. All that the Father giveth *me*
39. of all which he hath given *me*
8:45. ye believe *me* not.
46. why do ye not believe *me?*
9:11. and said unto *me*, Go
10:27. and they follow *me:*
29. which gave (them) *me*, is greater than
37. works of my Father, believe *me* not.
12:49. he gave *me* a commandment,
50. as the Father said unto *me*,
13:36. canst not follow *me* now; but thou shalt follow *me* afterwards.
14:11. Believe *me* that I (am) in the Father,
— or else believe *me* for the very
31. as the Father gave *me* commandment,
17: 4. which thou gavest *me* to do.
6. which thou gavest *me* out of the world:
7. whatsoever thou hast given *me*
8. the words which thou gavest *me;*
9. but for them which thou hast given *me;*
11. those whom thou hast given *me*,
12. those that thou gavest *me*
22. the glory which thou gavest *me*
24. whom thou hast given *me*, be with
— my glory, which thou hast given *me:*
18: 9. Of them which thou gavest *me* have I
11. the cup which my Father hath given *me*,
20:15. tell *me* where thou hast laid him,
21:19. he saith unto him, Follow *me*.
22. what (is that) to thee? follow thou *me*.
Acts 1: 8. ye shall be witnesses unto *me*
2:28. Thou hast made known to *me* the ways
3: 6. Silver and gold have I none; (lit. is not to *me*)
5: 8. Tell *me* whether ye sold the land
7: 7. and serve *me* in this place.
42. have ye offered to *me* slain beasts
49. Heaven (is) *my* throne, (lit. to *me*)
— what house will ye build *me?*
9:15. he is a chosen vessel unto *me*,
11: 7. a voice saying unto *me*,
9. the voice answered *me* again
12. And the spirit bade *me* go
12: 8. garment about thee, and follow *me*.
13: 2. Separate *me* Barnabas and Saul
18:10. *I* have much people (lit. much people is to *me*)
20:19. which befell *me* by the lying in wait
22. that shall befall *me* there:
21:37. May I (lit. is it allowed to *me* to)
39. suffer *me* to speak unto the people.
22: 5. doth bear *me* witness,
6. it came to pass, that, as *I* made my journey, (lit. to *me* journeying)
7. and heard a voice saying unto *me*,

Acts22: 9. the voice of him that spake to *me*.
11. by the hand of them that were with *me*,
13. and stood, and said unto *me*,
17. it came to pass, that, when *I* was come again (lit. to *me* having returned)
18. saw him saying unto *me*,
27. Tell *me*, art thou a Roman?
23:19. What is that thou hast to tell *me?*
30. And when it was told *me*
24:11. there are yet but twelve days since *I* went (lit. there are not to *me* more days than)
25:24. have dealt with *me*, both at Jerusalem,
27. it seemeth to *me* unreasonable
27:21. ye should have hearkened unto *me*,
23. stood by *me* this night
25. even as it was told *me*.
Ro. 7:10. *I* found (to be) (lit. has been found to *me*)
13. working death in *me* by that which is good;
18. for to will is present with *me;*
9: 1. my conscience also bearing *me* witness
2. *I* have great heaviness
19. Thou wilt say then unto *me*,
12: 3. the grace given unto *me*,
15:15. because of the grace that is given to *me*
30. ye strive together with *me*
1Co. 1:11. For it hath been declared unto *me*
3:10. which is given unto *me*,
5:12. For what have *I* to do to judge them
6:12. All things are lawful unto *me*,
— all things are lawful for *me*,
7: 1. whereof ye wrote unto *me:*
9:15. for (it were) better for *me* to die,
16. *I* have nothing to glory of: for necessity is laid upon *me:* yea, woe is unto *me*, if I preach not
18. What is *my* reward then?
10:23. All things are lawful for *me*,
— all things are lawful for *me*,
15:32. what advantageth it *me*,
16: 9. and effectual is opened unto *me*,
2Co. 2:12. a door was opened unto *me*
6:16. shall be *my* people. (lit. a people to *me*)
18. ye shall be *my* sons
7: 4. Great (is) *my* boldness of speech toward you, great (is) *my* glorying
9: 1. it is superfluous for *me* to write
12: 1. It is not expedient for *me*
7. there was given to *me* a thorn
9. And he said unto *me*, My grace
13. forgive *me* this wrong.
13:10. which the Lord hath given *me*
Gal. 2: 6. it maketh no matter to *me:*
9. the grace that was given unto *me*,
4:15. and have given them to *me*.
21. Tell *me*, ye that desire to be under
6:17. let no man trouble *me:*
Eph. 3: 2. which is given *me* to you-ward:
3. made known unto *me* the mystery;
7. given unto *me* by the effectual
6:19. utterance may be given unto *me*,
Phi. 1:19. this shall turn to *my* salvation
22. this (is) the fruit of my labour: (lit this is to *me* fruit of labour)
2:18. and rejoice with *me*.
3: 7. what things were gain to *me*,
4: 3. laboured with *me* in the gospel,
15. no church communicated with *me*
16. once and again unto *my* necessity.
Col. 1:25. which is given to *me* for you,
4:11. which have been a comfort unto *me*.

2Ti. 3:11. which came unto *me* at Antioch,
4: 8. Henceforth there is laid up for *me*
— the righteous judge, shall give *me*
11. he is profitable to *me* for the ministry.
14. did *me* much evil:
16. no man stood with *me,*
17. the Lord stood with *me,*
Philem.13. he might have ministered unto *me*
19. owest unto *me* even thine own self
22. prepare *me* also a lodging:
Heb 1: 5. he shall be to *me* a Son?
2:13. which God hath given *me.*
8:10. they shall be to *me* a people:
10: 5. a body hast thou prepared *me:*
13: 6. what man shall do unto *me.*
Jas. 2:18. shew *me* thy faith
2Pet. 1:14. Christ hath shewed *me.*
Rev. 1:17. saying unto *me,* Fear not;
5: 5. saith unto *me,* Weep not:
7:13. saying unto *me,* What are these
14. And he said to *me,*
10: 4. saying unto *me,* Seal up
9. Give *me* the little book. And he said unto *me,*
11. And he said unto *me,* Thou must
11: 1. And there was given *me* a reed
14:13. saying unto *me,* Write, Blessed
17: 1. saying unto *me,* Come hither;
7. And the angel said unto *me,*
15. And he saith unto *me,* The waters
19: 9. And he saith unto *me,* Write,
— And he saith unto *me,* These are
10. And he said unto *me,* See
21: 5. And he said unto *me,* Write:
6. And he said unto *me,* It is done.
7. and he shall be *my* son.
10. and shewed *me* that great city,
22: 1. And he shewed *me* a pure river
6. And he said unto *me,* These sayings
8. which shewed *me* these things.
9. Then saith he unto *me,* See
10. And he saith unto *me,* Seal not

3428 7 527/655 4:729 3432

μοιχαλίς, *moikalis.*

Mat.12:39. An evil and *adulterous* generation
16: 4. A wicked and *adulterous* generation
Mar 8:38. in this *adulterous* and sinful generation,
Ro. 7: 3. she shall be called an *adulteress:*
— so that she is no *adulteress,*
Jas. 4: 4. Ye adulterers and *adulteresses,*
2Pet. 2:14. Having eyes full of *adultery,*

3429 6 528/655 4:729 3432

μοιχάομαι, *moikaomai.*

Mat. 5:32. causeth her *to commit adultery:*
— her that is divorced *committeth adultery.*
19: 9. marry another, *committeth adultery:*
— is put away *doth commit adultery.*
Mar 10:11. *committeth adultery* against her.
12. to another, she *committeth adultery.*

3430 4 528/655 4:729 3431

μοιχεία, *moikīa.*

Mat.15:19. murders, *adulteries,* fornications,
Mar 7:21. evil thoughts, *adulteries,* fornications,
Joh. 8: 3. unto him a woman taken in *adultery;*
Gal. 5:19. *Adultery,* fornication, uncleanness,

3431 14 528/655 4:729 3432

μοιχεύω, *moikūo.*

Mat. 5:27. Thou *shalt* not *commit adultery:*
28. *hath committed adultery* with her
19:18. Thou *shalt* not *commit adultery,*
Mar 10:19. *Do* not *commit adultery,*
Lu. 16:18. marrieth another, *committeth adultery:*
— from (her) husband *committeth adultery.*
18:20. *Do* not *commit adultery,*
Joh. 8: 4. was taken *in adultery,*
Ro. 2:22. a man should not *commit adultery,* dost thou *commit adultery?*
13: 9. Thou *shalt* not *commit adultery,*
Jas. 2:11. *Do* not *commit adultery,*
— Now if thou *commit* no *adultery,*
Rev. 2:22. and them *that commit adultery* with her

3432 4 528/655 4:729

μοιχός, *moikos.*

Lu. 18:11. extortioners, unjust, *adulterers,*
1Co. 6: 9. nor idolaters, nor *adulterers,*
Heb 13: 4. whoremongers and *adulterers* God will
Jas. 4: 4. Ye *adulterers* and adulteresses,

3433 6 528/655 4:735 3425

μόλις, *molis.*

Acts14:18. *scarce* restrained they the people,
27: 7. and *scarce* were come over against
8. And, *hardly* passing it, came unto
16. we had much work to come by (lit. we were able *with difficulty* to get) the boat:
Ro. 5: 7. *scarcely* for a righteous man will one die:
1Pet. 4:18. if the righteous *scarcely* be saved,

3435 3 528/655 4:736 3189

μολύνω, *moluno.*

1Co. 8: 7. their conscience being weak *is defiled.*
Rev. 3: 4. which *have* not *defiled* their garments;
14: 4. which *were* not *defiled* with women;

3436 1 528/656 4:736 3435

μολυσμός, *molusmos.*

2Co. 7: 1. from all *filthiness* of the flesh

3437 1 528/656 4:571 3201

μομφή, *momphee.*

Col. 3:13. if any man have a *quarrel* against any:

3438 2 529/656 4:574 3306

μονή, *monee.*

Joh.14: 2. In my Father's house are many *mansions*
23. and make our *abode* with him.

3439 9 529/656 4:737 3441,1096

μονογενής, *monogenees.*

Lu. 7:12. the *only* son of his mother,
8:42. For he had one *only* daughter,
9:38. for he is mine *only child.*
Joh. 1:14. as of the *only begotten* of the Father,
18. the *only begotten* Son, which is
3:16. his *only begotten* Son, that whosoever
18. of the *only begotten* Son of God.
Heb11:17. offered up his *only begotten* (son)
1Joh.4: 9. God sent his *only begotten* Son

3440 66 529/656 3441

μόνον, *monon.*

Mat. 5:47. if ye salute your brethren *only*,
8: 8. but speak the word *only*,
9:21. If I may *but* touch his garment,
10:42. a cup of cold (water) *only*
14:36. that they might *only* touch the
21:19. nothing thereon, but leaves *only*,
21. not *only* do this (which is done) to the
Mar 5:36. Be not afraid, *only* believe.
6: 8. for (their) journey, save a staff *only*,
Lu. 8:50. Fear not: believe *only*,
Joh. 5:18. not *only* had broken the sabbath,
11:52. not for that nation *only*, but that also
12: 9. not for Jesus' sake *only*, but
13: 9. not my feet *only*, but also
17:20. pray I for these *alone*, but for them
Acts 8:16. *only* they were baptized in the
11:19. but unto the Jews *only*.
18:25. knowing *only* the baptism of John.
19:26. not *alone* at Ephesus, but almost
27. So that not *only* this our craft
21:13. not to be bound *only*, but also to die
26:29. not *only* thou, but also all that
27:10. not *only* of the lading and ship,
Ro. 1:32. not *only* do the same, but have pleasure
3:29. the God of the Jews *only*?
4:12. not of the circumcision *only*, but who also
16. not to that *only* which is of the law,
23. for his sake *alone*,
5: 3. And not *only* (so), but we glory in
11. And not *only* (so), but we also joy
8:23. And not *only* (they), but ourselves
9:10. And not *only* (this); but when
24. not of the Jews *only*, but also
13: 5. not *only* for wrath, but also for
1Co. 7.39. to whom she will; *only* in the Lord.
15:19. If in this life *only* we have hope
2Co. 7: 7. And not by his coming *only*, but by
8:10. not *only* to do, but also to be forward
19. And not (that) *only*, but who was also
21. not *only* in the sight of the Lord,
9:12. not *only* supplieth the want of
Gal. 1:23. But they had heard *only*,
2:10. *Only* (they would) that we should
3: 2. This *only* would I learn of you,
4:18. not *only* when I am present with you.
5:13. *only* (use) not liberty for an occasion
6:12. *only* lest they should suffer persecution
Eph. 1:21. not *only* in this world, but also
Phi. 1:27. *Only* let your conversation be
29. not *only* to believe on him, but also
2:12. not as in my presence *only*, but
27. and not on him *only*, but on me also,
1Th. 1: 5. not unto you in word *only*, but also in
8. not *only* in Macedonia and Achaia, but
2: 8. not the gospel of God *only*, but also
2Th. 2: 7. *only* he who now letteth (will let),
1Ti. 5:13. not *only* idle, but tattlers also
2Ti. 2:20. there are not *only* vessels of gold
4: 8. and not to me *only*, but unto all them
Heb 9:10. *only* in meats and drinks, and divers
12:26. I shake not the earth *only*, but also
Jas. 1:22. and not hearers *only*, deceiving
2:24. and not by faith *only*.
1Pet. 2:18. not *only* to the good and gentle,
1Joh. 2: 2. and not for our's *only*, but also for
5: 6. not by water *only*, but by water and blood.

3443 1 530/657 3441

μονόομαι, *monöomai.*

1Ti. 5: 5. that is a widow indeed, and *desolate*,

3441 47 529/657 3306

μόνος, *monos.*

Mat. 4: 4. shall not live by bread *alone*,
10. and him *only* shalt thou serve
12: 4. but *only* for the priests?
14:23. he was there *alone*.
17: 8. saw no man, save Jesus *only*.
18:15. between thee and him *alone*:
24:36. but my Father *only*.
Mar 6:47. and he *alone* on the land.
9: 2. high mountain apart *by themselves*:
8. save Jesus *only* with themselves.
Lu. 4: 4. not live by bread *alone*, but
8. him *only* shalt thou serve.
5:21. can forgive sins, but God *alone*?
6: 4. but for the priests *alone*?
9:36. Jesus was found *alone*.
10:40. hath left me to serve *alone*?
24:12. the linen clothes laid *by themselves*,
18. Art thou *only* a stranger in Jerusalem,
Joh. 5:44. that (cometh) from God *only*?
6:15. into a mountain himself *alone*.
22. his disciples were gone away *alone*;
8: 9. and Jesus was left *alone*,
16. for I am not *alone*,
29. the Father hath not left me *alone*;
12:24. and die, it abideth *alone*:
16:32. and shall leave me *alone*: and yet I am not *alone*,
17: 3. the *only* true God, and Jesus
Ro. 11: 3. and I am left *alone*, and they seek
16: 4. unto whom not *only* I give thanks, but
27. To God *only* wise,
1Co. 9: 6. Or I *only* and Barnabas,
14:36. or came it unto you *only*?
Gal. 6: 4. have rejoicing in himself *alone*,
Phi. 4:15. giving and receiving, but ye *only*.
Col. 4:11. These *only* (are my) fellowworkers
1Th. 3: 1. to be left at Athens *alone*;
1Ti. 1:17. the *only* wise God,
6:15. the blessed and *only* Potentate,
16. Who *only* hath immortality,
2Ti. 4:11. *Only* Luke is with me.
Heb 9: 7. (went) the high priest *alone*
2Joh. 1. and not I *only*, but also all they
Jude 4. and denying the *only* Lord God,
25. To the *only* wise God our Saviour,
Rev. 9: 4. but *only* those men which have not
15: 4. for (thou) *only* (art) holy:

3442 2 530/657 3788,3441

μονόφθαλμος, *monophthalmos.*

Mat. 18: 9. to enter into life *with one eye*,
Mar 9:47. into the kingdom of God *with one eye*,

3444 3 530/657 4:742 rt 3313

μορφή, *morphee.*

Mar 16:12. he appeared in another *form*
Phi. 2: 6. Who, being in the *form* of God,
7. took upon him the *form* of a servant,

3445 1 530/657 4:742 3444

μορφόομαι, *morphöomai.*

Gal. 4:19. until Christ *be formed* in you

3446 2 530/657 4:742 3445

μόρφωσις, *morphōsis.*

Ro. 2:20. which hast the *form* of knowledge
2Ti. 3: 5. Having a *form* of godliness, but

3447 1 530/657 3448,4160

μοσχοποιέω, moskopoyeo.

Acts 7:41. And tney *made a calf* in those days.

3448 6 530/657 4:760 *oschos* (shoot)

μόσχος, moskos.

Lu. 15:23. And bring hither the fatted *calf*,
27. thy father hath killed the fatted *calf*,
30. hast killed for him the fatted *calf*.
Heb 9:12. Neither by the blood of goats and *calves*,
19. the blood of *calves* and of goats,
Rev. 4: 7. the second beast like a *calf*,

3449 3 530/657 rt 3425

μόχθος, mokthos.

2Co.11:27. In weariness and *painfulness*,
1Th. 2: 9. our labour and *travail*:
2Th. 3: 8. wrought with labour and *travail*

3450 586 216/251 1700

μοῦ, mou.

From ἐγώ.

Mat. 2: 6. that shall rule *my* people Israel.
15. Out of Egypt have I called *my* son.
3:11. he that cometh after *me* is mightier than *I*,
17. This is *my* beloved Son,
4:19. saith unto them, Follow *me*,
7:21. the will of *my* Father which is in
24. heareth these sayings of mine, (lit. of *me*)
26. these sayings of mine, (lit. of *me*)
8: 6. *my* servant lieth at home
8. shouldest come under *my* roof:
— and *my* servant shall be healed.
9. and to *my* servant, Do this,
21. to go and bury *my* father.
9:18. *My* daughter is even now dead.
10:22. for *my* name's sake:
32. before *my* Father which is
33. *my* Father which is in heaven.
37. is not worthy of *me*:
— is not worthy of *me*.
38. after *me*, is not worthy of *me*.
11:10. I send *my* messenger before
27. unto me of *my* Father:
29. Take *my* yoke upon you,
30. For *my* yoke (is) easy, and *my* burden is
12:18. Behold *my* servant, whom I have chosen; *my* beloved, in whom *my* soul is well pleased: I will put *my* spirit upon him,
44. into *my* house from whence
48. Who is *my* mother? and who are *my* brethren?
49. Behold *my* mother and *my* brethren!
50. shall do the will of *my* Father
— the same is *my* brother, and sister,
13:30. but gather the wheat into *my* barn.
35. I will open *my* mouth in parables;
15:13. Every plant, which *my* heavenly Father
22. *my* daughter is grievously vexed
16:17. but *my* Father which is in heaven.
18. upon this rock I will build *my* church;
23. Get thee behind *me*, Satan: thou art an offence unto *me*
24. If any (man) will come after *me*,
17: 5. This is *my* beloved Son,
15. Lord, have mercy on *my* son.
18: 5. little child in *my* name
10. the face of *my* Father which is in
Mat.18:19. of *my* Father which is in heaven.
21. how oft shall *my* brother sin agains.
35. So likewise shall *my* heavenly Father
19:20. have I kept from *my* youth up:
29. or lands, for *my* name's sake,
20:21. Grant that these *my* two sons may sit,
23. Ye shall drink indeed of *my* cup
— but to sit on *my* right hand, and on *my* left, is not mine to give, but
— for whom it is prepared of *my* Father.
21:13. *My* house shall be called the house
28. go work to day in *my* vineyard.
37. They will reverence *my* son.
22: 4. I have prepared *my* dinner: *my* oxen and (my) fatlings
44. The Lord said unto *my* Lord, Sit thou on *my* right hand,
24: 5. For many shall come in *my* name,
9. hated of all nations for *my* name's sake.
35. but *my* words shall not pass away.
36. but *my* Father only.
48. *My* Lord delayeth his coming;
25:27. to have put *my* money to
34. Come, ye blessed of *my* Father,
40. of the least of these *my* brethren,
26:12. poured this ointment on *my* body,
18. *My* time is at hand;
— at thy house with *my* disciples.
26. Take, eat; this is *my* body.
28. For this is *my* blood of the new
29. in *my* Father's kingdom.
38. *My* soul is exceeding sorrowful,
39. O *my* Father, if it be possible,
42. O *my* Father, if this cup may not
53. that I cannot now pray to *my* Father,
27:35. They parted *my* garments among them, and upon *my* vesture did they cast lots.
46. *My* God, *my* God, why hast thou
28:10. go tell *my* brethren
Mar 1: 2. Behold, I send *my* messenger
7. There cometh one mightier than *I* after *me*,
11. Thou art *my* beloved Son,
17. Come ye after *me*,
3:33. Who is *my* mother, or *my* brethren?
34. Behold *my* mother and *my* brethren!
35. the same is *my* brother, and *my* sister, and mother.
5:23. *My* little daughter lieth at the
30. Who touched *my* clothes?
31. and sayest thou, Who touched *me*?
6:23. unto the half of *my* kingdom.
7:14. Hearken unto *me* every one
8:33. Get thee behind *me*, Satan:
34. Whosoever will come after *me*,
9: 7. This is *my* beloved Son:
17. I have brought unto thee *my* son,
24. help thou *mine* unbelief.
37. one of such children in *my* name,
39. shall do a miracle in *my* name,
41. of water to drink in *my* name,
10:20. have I observed from *my* youth.
40. But to sit on *my* right hand and on *my* left
11:17. *My* house shall be called
12: 6. They will reverence *my* son.
36. The Lord said to *my* Lord, Sit thou on *my* right hand,
13: 6. many shall come in *my* name,
13. hated of all (men) for *my* name's sake:
31. but *my* words shall not pass
14: 8. to anoint *my* body to the burying.
14. the passover with *my* disciples?

Mar 14:22. Take, eat: this is *my* body.
24. This is *my* blood of the new
34. *My* soul is exceeding sorrowful
15:34. *My* God, *my* God, why hast thou
16:17. In *my* name shall they cast out
Lu. 1:18. and *my* wife well stricken in years.
20. because thou believest not *my* words,
25. to take away *my* reproach
43. that the mother of *my* Lord should
44. salutation sounded in *mine* ears, the babe leaped in *my* womb
46. *My* soul doth magnify the Lord,
47. And *my* spirit hath rejoiced in God *my*
2:30. For *mine* eyes have seen thy
49. must be about *my* Father's business?
3:16. one mightier than *I* cometh,
22. Thou art *my* beloved Son;
4: 7. wilt worship *me*, all shall be
8. Get thee behind *me*, Satan:
6:47. and heareth *my* sayings, and
7: 6. shouldest enter under *my* roof:
7. and *my* servant shall be healed.
8. and to *my* servant, Do this,
27. Behold, I send *my* messenger before
44. thou gavest me no water for *my* feet: but she hath washed *my* feet with tears,
45. hath not ceased to kiss *my* feet.
46. *My* head with oil thou didst not
— hath anointed *my* feet with ointment.
8:21. *My* mother and *my* brethren are these
45. Who touched *me?*
— sayest thou, Who touched *me?*
46. Somebody hath touched *me:*
9:23. If any (man) will come after *me*,
35. This is *my* beloved Son: hear him.
38. I beseech thee, look upon *my* son:
48. shall receive this child in *my* name
59. to go and bury *my* father.
61. which are at home at *my* house.
10:22. are delivered to me of *my* Father:
29. And who is *my* neighbour?
40. dost thou not care that *my* sister
11: 6. For a friend of mine (lit. of *me*)
7. and *my* children are with me
24. I will return unto *my* house
12: 4. I say unto you *my* friends,
13. Master, speak to *my* brother,
17. where to bestow *my* fruits?
18. I will pull down *my* barns, and
— and there will I bestow all *my* fruits and *my* goods.
19. And I will say to *my* soul,
45. *My* lord delayeth his coming;
14:23. that *my* house may be filled.
24. shall taste of *my* supper.
26. he cannot be *my* disciple.
27. and come after *me*, cannot be *my* disciple.
33. he cannot be *my* disciple.
15: 6. I have found *my* sheep which
17. How many hired servants of *my* father's
18. I will arise and go to *my* father,
24. this *my* son was dead,
29. might make merry with *my* friends:
16: 3. *my* lord taketh away from me
5. How much owest thou unto *my* lord?
24. and cool *my* tongue;
27. send him to *my* father's house.
18: 3. Avenge me of *mine* adversary.
21. have I kept from *my* youth up.
19: 8. Lord, the half of *my* goods
23. gavest not thou *my* money
27. But those *mine* enemies,
Lu. 19:27. and slay (them) before *me*.
46. *My* house is the house of prayer.
20:13. I will send *my* beloved son:
42. The Lord said unto *my* Lord, Sit thou on *my* right hand,
21: 8. for many shall come in *my* name,
12. and rulers for *my* name's sake.
17. hated of all (men) for *my* name's sake.
33. but *my* words shall not pass away.
22:11. eat the passover with *my* disciples?
19. This is *my* body which is given
20. the new testament in *my* blood,
28. continued with me in *my* temptations.
29. as *my* Father hath appointed unto me;
30. and drink at *my* table in *my* kingdom,
42. not *my* will, but thine, be done.
53. When *I* was daily with you in
23:42. Lord, remember *me* when thou comest
46. into thy hands I commend *my* spirit:
24:39. Behold *my* hands and *my* feet,
49. I send the promise of *my* Father
Joh. 1:15. He that cometh after *me* is preferred before *me:* for he was before *me*.
27. He it is, who coming after *me* is preferred before *me*,
30. After *me* cometh a man which is preferred before *me:* for he was before *me*.
2: 4. *mine* hour is not yet come.
16. make not *my* Father's house an
4:49. Sir, come down ere *my* child die.
5:17. *My* Father worketh hitherto, and I
24. He that heareth *my* word,
31. of myself, *my* witness is not true.
43. I am come in *my* Father's name,
6:32. but *my* Father giveth you the
51. the bread that I will give is *my* flesh,
54. Whoso eateth *my* flesh, and drinketh *my* blood, hath
55. For *my* flesh is meat indeed, and *my* blood
56. He that eateth *my* flesh, and drinketh *my* blood, dwelleth in me,
65. given unto him of *my* Father.
8:14. *my* record is true:
19. Ye neither know me, nor *my* Father:
— should have known *my* Father also.
28. but as *my* Father hath taught me,
31. (then) are ye *my* disciples indeed;
38. that which I have seen with *my* Father:
49. but I honour *my* Father,
50. I seek not *mine own* glory:
52. If a man keep *my* saying,
54. If I honour myself, *my* honour is nothing: it is *my* Father that
9:11. and anointed *mine* eyes,
15. He put clay upon *mine* eyes,
30. (yet) he hath opened *mine* eyes.
10:15. I lay down *my* life for the sheep.
16. and they shall hear *my* voice:
17. because I lay down *my* life,
18. have I received of *my* Father.
25. the works that I do in *my* Father's name,
27. My sheep hear *my* voice,
28. pluck them out of *my* hand.
29. *My* Father, which gave (them) me,
— to pluck (them) out of *my* Father's hand.
32. have I shewed you from *my* Father;
37. If I do not the works of *my* Father,
11:21. *my* brother had not died.
32. *my* brother had not died.
41. I thank thee that thou hast heard *me*.
42. I knew that thou hearest *me* always:
12: 7. against the day of *my* burying

Joh. 12:27. Now is *my* soul troubled;
47. if any man hear *my* words,
48. and receiveth not *my* words,
13: 6. Lord, dost thou wash *my* feet?
8. Thou shalt never wash *my* feet.
9. Lord, not *my* feet only,
37. I will lay down *my* life for thy sake.
14: 2. In *my* Father's house are many mansions:
7. ye should have known *my* Father
12. because I go unto *my* Father.
13. whatsoever ye shall ask in *my* name,
14. ask any thing in *my* name,
20. ye shall know that I (am) in *my* Father,
21. He that hath *my* commandments,
— loveth me shall be loved of *my* Father,
23. If a man love me, he will keep *my* words: and *my* Father will love him,
24. loveth me not keepeth not *my* sayings:
26. the Father will send in *my* name,
28. for *my* Father is greater than *I*.
15: 1. and *my* Father is the husbandman.
7. and *my* words abide in you,
8. Herein is *my* Father glorified,
10. If ye keep *my* commandments, ye shall abide in *my* love; even as I have kept *my* Father's
14. Ye are *my* friends, if ye do
15. all things that I have heard of *my* Father
16. ye shall ask of the Father in *my* name,
20. if they have kept *my* saying,
21. they do unto you for *my* name's sake,
23. He that hateth me hateth *my* Father
24. and hated both me and *my* Father.
16:10. because I go to *my* Father,
23. ye shall ask the Father in *my* name,
24. have ye asked nothing in *my* name:
26. At that day ye shall ask in *my* name:
18:37. heareth *my* voice.
19:24. They parted *my* raiment among them, and for *my* vesture they did
20:13. Because they have taken away *my* Lord,
17. Touch *me* not; for I am not yet ascended to *my* Father: but go to *my* brethren, and say unto them, I ascend unto *my* Father, and your Father; and (to) *my* God, and your God.
25. put *my* finger into the print of the nails, and thrust *my* hand
27. thy finger, and behold *my* hands; and reach hither thy hand, and thrust (it) into *my* side:
28. *My* Lord and *my* God.
21:15. saith unto him, Feed *my* lambs.
16. saith unto him, Feed *my* sheep.
17. Feed *my* sheep.
Acts 1: 4. which, (saith he), ye have heard of *me*.
2:14. and hearken to *my* words:
17. I will pour out of *my* Spirit upon
18. And on *my* servants and on *my* handmaidens I will pour out in those days of *my* Spirit;
25. the Lord always before *my* face, for he is on *my* right hand,
26. did *my* heart rejoice, and *my* tongue was glad; moreover also *my* flesh
27. thou wilt not leave *my* soul in hell,
34. The Lord said unto *my* Lord, Sit thou on *my* right hand,
7:34. I have seen the affliction of *my* people
49. Heaven (is) my throne, and earth (is) *my*
— or what (is) the place of *my* rest?
50. Hath not *my* hand made all

Acts 7:59. Lord Jesus, receive *my* spirit.
9:15. to bear *my* name before the Gentiles,
16. he must suffer for *my* name's sake.
10:30. at the ninth hour I prayed in *my* house, and, behold, a man stood before *me* in
11: 8. at any time entered into *my* mouth.
13:22. a man after *mine own* heart, which shall fulfil all *my* will.
33. Thou art *my* Son, this day have I
15: 7. that the Gentiles by *my* mouth should
13. brethren, hearken unto *me*:
17. upon whom *my* name is called,
16:15. come into *my* house, and abide
20:24. neither count I *my* life dear unto myself, so that I might finish *my* course with
25. shall see *my* face no more.
29. after *my* departing shall grievous
34. have ministered unto *my* necessities,
21:13. to weep and to break *mine* heart?
22: 1. hear ye *my* defence
17. even while *I* prayed in the temple,
24:13. whereof they now accuse *me*.
17. I came to bring alms to *my* nation,
20. while *I* stood before the council,
25:11. whereof these accuse *me*,
15. when *I* was at Jerusalem,
26: 3. I beseech thee to hear *me* patiently.
4. *My* manner of life from my youth,
— at the first among *mine own* nation
29. but also all that hear *me* this day,
28:19. I had ought to accuse *my* nation of.
Ro. 1: 8. I thank *my* God through Jesus
9. For God is *my* witness, whom I serve with *my* spirit in the gospel
—(10). mention of you always in *my* prayers;
2:16. according to *my* gospel.
7: 4. Wherefore, *my* brethren, ye also
18. that is, in *my* flesh,
23. another law in *my* members, warring against the law of *my* mind,
— the law of sin which is in *my* members.
9: 1. I lie not, *my* conscience also bearing me
2. and continual sorrow in *my* heart.
3. for *my* brethren, *my* kinsmen according to the flesh:
17. that I might shew *my* power in thee, and that *my* name might be declared
25. I will call them *my* people, which were not *my* people;
26. Ye (are) not *my* people;
10:21. I have stretched forth *my* hands
11: 3. and they seek *my* life.
13. I magnify *mine* office:
14. to emulation (them which are) *my* flesh,
15:14. persuaded of you, *my* brethren,
31. that *my* service which (I have)
16: 3. *my* helpers in Christ Jesus:
4. Who have for *my* life laid down
5. Salute *my* wellbeloved Epenetus,
7. Andronicus and Junia, *my* kinsmen, and *my* fellowprisoners,
8. Greet Amplias *my* beloved
9. and Stachys *my* beloved.
11. Salute Herodion *my* kinsman.
21. Timotheus *my* workfellow,
— Jason, and Sosipater, *my* kinsmen,
23. Gaius *mine* host, and of the whole church,
25. according to *my* gospel,
1Co. 1: 4. I thank *my* God always on your
11. declared unto me of you, *my* brethren,
2: 4. And *my* speech and *my* preaching (was) not with enticing words

1Co. 4:14. but as *my* beloved sons I warn
16. be ye followers of *me*.
17. Timotheus, who is *my* beloved son,
— into remembrance of *my* ways
18. as though *I* would not come to you.
8:13. if meat make *my* brother to offend,
— lest I make *my* brother to offend.
9: 1. are not ye *my* work in the Lord?
15. should make *my* glorying void.
18. that I abuse not *my* power in the
27. I keep under *my* body,
10:14. *my* dearly beloved, flee from idolatry.
29. why is *my* liberty judged of another
11: 1. Be ye followers of *me*,
2. that ye remember *me* in all things,
24. Take, eat: this is *my* body,
33. Wherefore, *my* brethren, when ye
13: 3. though I bestow all *my* goods
— though I give *my* body to be burned,
14.14. *my* spirit prayeth, but *my* understanding is unfruitful.
18. I thank *my* God, I speak with
19. five words with *my* understanding,
21. will they not hear *me*, saith the Lord.
15:58. *my* beloved brethren, be ye stedfast,
16:24. *My* love (be) with you all in Christ
2Co. 2:13. I had no rest in *my* spirit, because I found not Titus *my* brother:
11: 1. bear with *me* a little in (my) folly: and indeed bear with *me*.
9. that which was lacking to *me*
28. that which cometh upon *me* daily,
30. which concern *mine* infirmities.
12: 5. but in *mine* infirmities.
9. *My* grace is sufficient for thee: for *my* strength is made perfect
— will I rather glory in *my* infirmities,
21. *my* God will humble me among you,
Gal. 1:14. my equals in *mine own* nation,
— of the traditions of *my* fathers.
15. separated me from *my* mother's womb,
4.14. And *my* temptation which was in *my* flesh
19. *My* little children, of whom I
20. and to change *my* voice;
6:17. I bear in *my* body the marks
Eph 1:16. making mention of you in *my* prayers;
3: 4. ye may understand *my* knowledge
13. at *my* tribulations for you,
14. For this cause I bow *my* knees
6:10. *my* brethren, be strong in the Lord,
19. that I may open *my* mouth boldly,
Phi. 1: 3. I thank *my* God upon every remembrance
4. in every prayer of *mine* for you
7. inasmuch as both in *my* bonds,
— ye all are partakers of *my* grace.
8. For God is *my* record,
13. So that *my* bonds in Christ
14. waxing confident by *my* bonds,
16. to add affliction to *my* bonds:
20. According to *my* earnest expectation
— Christ shall be magnified in *my* body,
2: 2. Fulfil ye *my* joy,
12. Wherefore, *my* beloved, as ye have
— not as in *my* presence only, but now much more in *my* absence,
25. *my* brother, and companion in labour,
— and he that ministered to *my* wants.
3: 1. Finally, *my* brethren, rejoice in
8. the knowledge of Christ Jesus *my* Lord:
17. be followers together of *me*,
4: 1. *my* brethren dearly beloved and longed for, my joy and crown,

Phi. 4: 3. (with) other *my* fellowlabourers,
14. did communicate with *my* affliction.
19. But *my* God shall supply all your need
Col. 1:24. Who now rejoice in *my* sufferings for you,
— in *my* flesh for his body's sake,
2: 1. as have not seen *my* face in the flesh;
4:10. Aristarchus *my* fellowprisoner
18. Remember *my* bonds.
2Ti. 1: 3. in *my* prayers night and day;
6. by the putting on of *my* hands.
12. that which *I* have committed unto him
16. and was not ashamed of *my* chain:
2: 1. *my* son, be strong in the grace
8. according to *my* gospel:
3:10. thou hast fully known *my* doctrine,
4:16. At *my* first answer no man
Philem. 4. I thank *my* God, making mention of thee always in *my* prayers,
10. whom I have begotten in *my* bonds:
20. refresh *my* bowels in the Lord.
23. Epaphras, *my* fellowprisoner
24. Demas, Lucas, *my* fellowlabourers.
Heb 1: 5. Thou art *my* Son, this day have I
13. Sit on *my* right hand,
2:12. declare thy name unto *my* brethren,
3: 9. saw *my* works forty years.
10. have not known *my* ways.
11. So I sware in *my* wrath, They shall not enter into *my* rest.
4: 3. As I have sworn in *my* wrath, if they shall enter into *my* rest:
5. If they shall enter into *my* rest.
5: 5. Thou art *my* Son,
8: 9. when *I* took them by the hand
— they continued not in *my* covenant,
10. I will put *my* laws into their mind,
10:16. put *my* laws into their hearts,
34. compassion of me in *my* bonds,
38. *my* soul shall have no pleasure
12: 5. *My* son, despise not thou the
Jas. 1: 2. *My* brethren, count it all joy
16. Do not err, *my* beloved brethren.
19. Wherefore, *my* beloved brethren, let
2: 1. *My* brethren, have not the faith
3. or sit here under *my* footstool:
5. Hearken, *my* beloved brethren,
14. What (doth it) profit, *my* brethren,
18. I will shew thee *my* faith by *my* works.
3: 1. *My* brethren, be not many masters,
10. *My* brethren, these things ought not
12. Can the fig tree, *my* brethren,
5:10. Take, *my* brethren, the prophets,
12. above all things, *my* brethren,
1Pet. 5:13. and (so doth) Marcus *my* son.
2Pet. 1:14. I must put off (this) *my* tabernacle,
17. This is *my* beloved Son, in whom I am well pleased.
1Joh. 2: 1. *My* little children, these things
3:13. Marvel not, *my* brethren, if the world
18. *My* little children, let us
Rev. 1:10. and heard behind *me* a great voice,
20. which thou sawest in *my* right hand,
2: 3. for *my* name's sake hast laboured,
13. thou holdest fast *my* name, and hast not denied *my* faith,
— Antipas (was) *my* faithful martyr,
16. with the sword of *my* mouth.
26. and keepeth *my* works unto the end,
27. even as I received of *my* Father.
3: 5. I will confess his name before *my* Father.
8. and hast kept *my* word, and hast not denied *my* name.

Rev. 3:10. hast kept the word of *my* patience,
12. a pillar in the temple of *my* God,
— I will write upon him the name of *my* God, and the name of the city of *my* God.
— out of heaven from *my* God: and (I will write upon him) *my* new name.
16. I will spue thee out of *my* mouth.
20. if any man hear *my* voice,
21. to sit with me in *my* throne,
— with *my* Father in his throne.
10:10. in *my* mouth sweet as honey:
— *my* belly was bitter.
11: 3. I will give (power) unto *my* two witnesses,
18: 4. Come out of her, *my* people,
22:12. and *my* reward (is) with me.
16. I Jesus have sent *mine* angel to

3451 1 530/657 Mousa (Muse)

μουσικός, *mousikos.*

Rev.18:22. and *musicians*, and of pipers,

3452 1 530/658

μυελός, *muelos.*

Heb 4:12. and of the joints and *marrow*,

3453 1 530/658 4:802 rt 3466

μυέομαι, *mueomai.*

Phil. 4:12. and in all things I *am instructed* both to be

3454 5 530/658 4:762 rt 3453

μῦθος, *muthos.*

1Ti. 1: 4. Neither give heed to *fables* and
4: 7. refuse profane and old wives' *fables*,
2Ti. 4: 4. and shall be turned unto *fables*.
Tit. 1:14. Not giving heed to Jewish *fables*,
2Pet. 1:16. followed cunningly devised *fables*,

3455 1 531/658 *muzo* (to "moo")

μυκάομαι, *mukaomai.*

Rev.10: 3. as (when) a lion *roareth*:

3456 1 531/658 4:796 cf rt 3455 *mukter* (snout)

μυκτηρίζομαι, *mukteerizomai.*

Gal. 6: 7. God *is* not *mocked*:

3457 1 531/658 3458

μυλικός, *mulikos.*

Mar 9:42. that a *mill*stone were hanged about

3458 4 531/658 rt 3433

μύλος, *mulos.*

Mat.18: 6. that a *millstone* were hanged about
Lu. 17: 2. that a *millstone* were hanged about
Rev.18:21. took up a stone like a great *millstone*,
22. the sound of a *millstone* shall

3459 1 531/658 3458

μύλων, *mulōn.*

Mat.24:41. grinding at the *mill*; the one shall

3461 9 531/658 3463

μυριάς, *murias.*

Lu. 12: 1. an *innumerable multitude* of people,
Acts19:19. fifty thousand (lit. five *ten-thousands*) (pieces) of silver.
21:20. how many thousands (lit. *myriads*) of Jews there are
Heb 12:22. to an *innumerable company* of angels,
Jude 14. the Lord cometh with *ten thousands* of his saints, (lit. with holy *myriads*)
Rev. 5:11. *ten thousand* times *ten thousand* (Elz.)
9:16. two hundred thousand thousand

3462 1 531/658 4:800 3464

μυρίζω, *murizo.*

Mar 14: 8. *to anoint* my body to the burying.

3463 3 531/658

μύριοι, *murioi.*

Mat.18:24. which owed him *ten thousand* talents.
1Co. 4:15. though ye have *ten thousand* instructers
14:19. than *ten thousand* words in an (unknown) tongue.

3464 14 531/658 4:800 cf[4753] cf 4666

μύρον, *muron.*

Mat.26: 7. of very precious *ointment*,
9. For this *ointment* might have
12. hath poured this *ointment* on my body,
Mar 14: 3. an alabaster box of *ointment*
4. this waste of the *ointment* made?
Lu. 7:37. an alabaster box of *ointment*,
38. anointed (them) with the *ointment*.
46. anointed my feet with *ointment*.
23:56. and prepared spices and *ointments*;
Joh. 11: 2. anointed the Lord with *ointment*,
12: 3. took Mary a pound of *ointment*
— filled with the odour of the *ointment*.
5. Why was not this *ointment* sold
Rev.18:13. and odours, and *ointments*,

3466 27 531/658 4:802 *muō* (to shut the mouth)

μυστήριον, *musteerion.*

Mat.13:11. to know the *mysteries* of the kingdom of
Mar 4:11. the *mystery* of the kingdom of God:
Lu. 8:10. the *mysteries* of the kingdom of God
Ro. 11:25. should be ignorant of this *mystery*,
16:25. of the *mystery*, which was kept secret
1Co. 2: 7. the wisdom of God in a *mystery*,
4: 1. stewards of the *mysteries* of God.
13: 2. and understand all *mysteries*,
14: 2. in the spirit he speaketh *mysteries*.
15:51. Behold, I shew you a *mystery*; We
Eph. 1: 9. unto us the *mystery* of his will,
3: 3. made known unto me the *mystery*;
4. knowledge in the *mystery* of Christ
9. the fellowship of the *mystery*,
5:32. This is a great *mystery*: but I speak
6:19. to make known the *mystery* of the gospel,
Col. 1:26. the *mystery* which hath been hid
27. this *mystery* among the Gentiles;
2: 2. *mystery* of God, and of the Father,
4: 3. to speak the *mystery* of Christ,
2Th. 2: 7. For the *mystery* of iniquity doth already
1Ti. 3: 9. Holding the *mystery* of the faith
16. great is the *mystery* of godliness:
Rev. 1:20. The *mystery* of the seven stars
10: 7. the *mystery* of God should be finished,
17: 5. *MYSTERY*, BABYLON THE GREAT,
7. the *mystery* of the woman,

3467 1 532/659 rt 3466, *ops* (face)

μυωπάζω, *muopazo.*

2Pet.1: 9. is blind, *and cannot see afar off,*

3468 1 532/659 4:829 *ops* (face) *molos* ("moil")

μώλωψ, *mōlōps.*

1Pet.2:24. by whose *stripes* ye were healed.

3469 2 532/659 3470

μωμέομαι, *mōmeomai.*

2Co. 6: 3. that the ministry *be not blamed:*
8:20. that no man *should blame* us

3470 1 533/659 4:829 3201

μῶμος, *mōmos.*

2Pet. 2:13. Spots (they are) and *blemishes,*

3471 4 533/659 4:832 3474

μωραίνω, *mōraino.*

Mat. 5:13. but if the salt *have lost* his *savour,*
Lu. 14:34. but if the salt *have lost* his *savour,*
Ro. 1:22. to be wise, they *became fools.*
1Co. 1:20. hath not God *made foolish* the wisdom

3472 5 533/659 4:832 3474

μωρία, *mōria.*

1Co. 1:18. to them that perish *foolishness;*
21. by the *foolishness* of preaching
23. unto the Greeks *foolishness;*
2:14. for they are *foolishness* unto him:
3:19. the wisdom of this world is *foolishness* with God.

3473 1 533/659 4:832 3473,3004

μωρολογία, *mōrologia.* *muō* (to shut the mouth)

Eph. 5: 4. nor *foolish talking*, nor jesting,

3474 13 533/659 4:832

μωρός, *mōros.*

Mat. 5:22. whosoever shall say, Thou *fool,*
7:26. shall be likened unto a *foolish* man,
23:17. (Ye) *fools* and blind: for whether
19. (Ye) *fools* and blind:
25: 2. and five (were) *foolish.*
3. They that (were) *foolish* took
8. the *foolish* said unto the wise,
1Co. 1:25. the *foolish*ness of God is wiser than men;
27. God hath chosen the *foolish* things
3:18. let him become a *fool*, that he may
4:10. We (are) *fools* for Christ's sake,
2Ti. 2:23. *foolish* and unlearned questions avoid,
Tit. 3: 9. But avoid *foolish* questions,

3483 34 534/661

ναί, *nai.*

Mat. 5:37. let your communication be, *Yea, yea:*
9:28. They said unto him, *Yea,* Lord.
11: 9. A prophet? *yea,* I say unto you,
26. *Even so,* Father: for so it seemed good
13:51. They say unto him, *Yea,* Lord.
15:27. And she said, *Truth,* Lord: yet
17:25. He saith, *Yes.*
Mat.21:16. *Yea;* have ye never read, Out of
Mar 7:28. *Yes,* Lord: yet the dogs
Lu. 7:26. A prophet? *Yea,* I say unto you,
10:21. *even so,* Father; for so it seemed good
11:51. *verily* I say unto you, It shall be
12: 5. *yea,* I say unto you, Fear him.
Joh.11:27. *Yea,* Lord: I believe that thou
21:15. He saith unto him, *Yea,* Lord;
16. *Yea,* Lord; thou knowest that I
Acts 5: 8. And she said, *Yea,* for so much.
22:27. art thou a Roman? He said, *Yea.*
Ro. 3:29. *Yes,* of the Gentiles also:
2Co. 1:17. should be *yea yea,* and nay nay?
18. was not *yea* and nay.
19. was not *yea* and nay, but in him was *yea.*
20. all the promises of God in him (are) *yea*
Philem.20. *Yea,* brother, let me have joy of thee
Jas. 5:12. but let your *yea* be *yea;* and
Rev. 1: 7. *Even so,* Amen.
14:13. *Yea,* saith the Spirit,
16: 7. *Even so,* Lord God Almighty,
22:20. *Surely* I come quickly; Amen. *Even so,* come, Lord Jesus.

3485 46 535/661 4:880 *naiō* (to dwell) cf 2411

ναός, *naos.*

Mat.23:16. shall swear by the *temple,*
— shall swear by the gold of the *temple,*
17. or the *temple* that sanctifieth
21. whoso shall swear by the *temple,*
35. between the *temple* and the altar.
26:61. to destroy the *temple* of God, and to
27: 5. the pieces of silver in the *temple,*
40. Thou that destroyest the *temple,*
51. the veil of the *temple* was rent
Mar 14:58. I will destroy this *temple*
15:29. Ah, thou that destroyest the *temple,*
38. the veil of the *temple* was rent
Lu. 1: 9. when he went into the *temple*
21. that he tarried so long in the *temple.*
22. had seen a vision in the *temple:*
23:45. the veil of the *temple* was rent
Joh. 2:19. Destroy this *temple,* and in three days
20. Forty and six years was this *temple*
21. But he spake of the *temple* of his body.
Acts 7:48. the most High dwelleth not in *temples* made with hands;
17:24. dwelleth not in *temples* made
19:24. which made silver *shrines* for Diana,
1Co. 3:16. that ye are the *temple* of God,
17. If any man defile the *temple* of God,
— for the *temple* of God is holy,
6:19. your body is the *temple* of the Holy Ghost
2Co. 6:16. hath the *temple* of God with idols? for ye are the *temple* of the living God;
Eph. 2:21. groweth unto an holy *temple* in the Lord
2Th. 2: 4. sitteth in the *temple* of God,
Rev. 3:12. make a pillar in the *temple* of my God,
7:15. serve him day and night in his *temple:*
11: 1. and measure the *temple* of God,
2. which is without the *temple*
19. the *temple* of God was opened in heaven, and there was seen in his *temple* the ark
14:15. angel came out of the *temple,*
17. another angel came out of the *temple*
15: 5. the *temple* of the tabernacle of
6. seven angels came out of the *temple,*
8. And the *temple* was filled with smoke
— was able to enter into the *temple,*
16: 1. a great voice out of the *temple*
17. voice out of the *temple* of heaven.

Rev.21:22. And I saw no *temple* therein:
— and the Lamb are the *temple* of it.

3487 2 535/662 cf [5373]
νάρδος, nardos.

Mar 14: 3. of ointment of spike*nard*
Joh.12: 3. a pound of ointment of spike*nard*,

3489 2 536/662 4:891 3491,71
ναυαγέω, nauageo.

2Co.11:25. thrice I *suffered shipwreck*,
1Ti. 1:19. concerning faith *have made shipwreck*:

3490 1 536/662 3491,2819
ναύκληρος, naukleeros.

Acts27:11. and the *owner of the ship*, more than

3491 1 536/662 nao (to float)
ναῦς, naus.

Acts27:41. they ran the *ship* aground;

3492 3 536/662 3491
ναύτης, nautees.

Acts27:27. the *shipmen* deemed that they drew near
30. as the *shipmen* were about to flee out
Rev.18:17. *sailors*, and as many as trade by sea,

3494 5 536/662 3501
νεανίας, neanias.

Acts 7:58. their clothes at a *young man's* feet,
20: 9. a certain *young man* named Eutychus,
23:17. Bring this *young man* unto the
18. to bring this *young man* unto thee,
22. captain (then) let the *young man* depart.

3495 10 536/662 3494
νεανίσκος, neaniskos.

Mat.19:20. The *young man* saith unto him,
22. when the *young man* heard that
Mar14:51. followed him a certain *young man*.
— the *young men* laid hold on him.
16: 5. they saw a *young man* sitting
Lu. 7:14. *Young man*, I say unto thee, Arise.
Acts 2:17. your *young men* shall see visions,
5:10. the *young men* came in, and found
1Joh.2:13. I write unto you, *young men*,
14. I have written unto you, *young men*,

3498 132 536/662 4:892 nekus (corpse)
νεκρός, nekros.

Mat. 8:22. Follow me; and let the *dead* bury their *dead*.
10: 8. raise the *dead*, cast out devils:
11: 5. the *dead* are raised up,
14: 2. he is risen from the *dead*;
17: 9. be risen again from the *dead*.
22:31. touching the resurrection of the *dead*,
32. God is not the God of the *dead*,
23:27. within full of *dead* (men's) bones,
27:64. He is risen from the *dead*:
28: 4. and became as *dead* (men)
7. he is risen from the *dead*;
Mar 6:14. the Baptist was risen from the *dead*,
16. he is risen from the *dead*.
Mar 9: 9. Son of man were risen from the *dead*
10. the rising from the *dead* should mean.
26. out of him: and he was as one *dead*.
12:25. when they shall rise from the *dead*,
26. as touching the *dead*, that they rise:
27. He is not the God of the *dead*,
Lu. 7:15. And he that was *dead* sat up,
22. the deaf hear, the *dead* are raised,
9: 7. that John was risen from the *dead*;
60. Jesus said unto him, Let the *dead* bury their *dead*:
15:24. For this my son was *dead*, and is alive
32. for this thy brother was *dead*, and is
16:30. if one went unto them from the *dead*,
31. though one rose from the *dead*.
20:35. and the resurrection from the *dead*,
37. Now that the *dead* are raised,
38. For he is not a God of the *dead*,
24: 5. Why seek ye the living among the *dead*?
46. to rise from the *dead* the third day:
Joh. 2:22. he was risen from the *dead*,
5:21. as the Father raiseth up the *dead*,
25. when the *dead* shall hear the voice
12: 1. whom he raised from the *dead*.
9. whom he had raised from the *dead*.
17. and raised him from the *dead*,
20: 9. that he must rise again from the *dead*.
21:14. after that he was risen from the *dead*.
Acts 3:15. whom God hath raised from the *dead*.
4: 2. the resurrection from the *dead*.
10. whom God raised from the *dead*,
5:10. and found her *dead*,
10:41. after he rose from the *dead*.
42. the Judge of quick and *dead*.
13:30. God raised him from the *dead*:
34. he raised him up from the *dead*,
17: 3. and risen again from the *dead*;
31. he hath raised him from the *dead*.
32. the resurrection of the *dead*,
20: 9. and was taken up *dead*.
23: 6. hope and resurrection of the *dead*
24:15. there shall be a resurrection of the *dead*,
21. Touching the resurrection of the *dead*
26: 8. that God should raise the *dead*?
23. that should rise from the *dead*, and
28: 6. or fallen down *dead* suddenly:
Ro. 1: 4. by the resurrection from the *dead*:
4:17. who quickeneth the *dead*,
24. Jesus our Lord from the *dead*;
6: 4. was raised up from the *dead*
9. Christ being raised from the *dead*
11. to be *dead* indeed unto sin,
13. as those that are alive from the *dead*,
7: 4. be married to another, (even) to him who is raised from the *dead*,
8. without the law sin (was) *dead*.
8:10. the body (is) *dead* because of sin,
11. raised up Jesus from the *dead* dwell in you, he that raised up Christ from the *dead*
10: 7. to bring up Christ again from the *dead*.
9. hath raised him from the *dead*,
11:15. but life from the *dead*?
14: 9. be Lord both of the *dead* and living.
1Co.15:12. that he rose from the *dead*,
— is no resurrection of the *dead*?
13. if there be no resurrection of the *dead*,
15. if so be that the *dead* rise not.
16. For if the *dead* rise not,
20. now is Christ risen from the *dead*,
21. by man (came) also the resurrection of the *dead*.

1Co.15:29. which are baptized for the *dead*, if the *dead* rise not at all? why are they then baptized for the *dead*?
32. if the *dead* rise not?
35. How are the *dead* raised up?
42. So also (is) the resurrection of the *dead*.
52. the *dead* shall be raised incorruptible,
2Co. 1: 9. but in God which raiseth the *dead*:
Gal. 1: 1. who raised him from the *dead*;
Eph. 1:20. when he raised him from the *dead*,
2: 1. who were *dead* in trespasses and
5. when we were *dead* in sins,
5:14. and arise from the *dead*,
Phi. 3:11. unto the resurrection of the *dead*.
Col. 1:18. the firstborn from the *dead*;
2:12. who hath raised him from the *dead*.
13. And you, being *dead* in your sins
1Th. 1:10. whom he raised from the *dead*,
4:16. the *dead* in Christ shall rise first.
2Ti. 2: 8. was raised from the *dead*
4: 1. shall judge the quick and the *dead* at
Heb 6: 1. repentance from *dead* works,
2. resurrection of the *dead*,
9:14. your conscience from *dead* works
17. of force after men are dead: (lit. force upon the basis of *dead ones*)
11:19. to raise (him) up, even from the *dead*;
35. received their *dead* raised to life
13:20. brought again from the *dead* our Lord
Jas. 2:17. hath not works, is *dead*, being alone.
20. faith without works is *dead*?
26. the body without the spirit is *dead*, so faith without works is *dead*
1Pet. 1: 3. of Jesus Christ from the *dead*,
21. that raised him up from the *dead*,
4: 5. judge the quick and the *dead*.
6. preached also to them that are *dead*.
Rev. 1. 5. the first begotten of the *dead*,
17. I fell at his feet as *dead*.
18. he that liveth, and was *dead*;
2: 8. which was *dead*, and is alive;
3: 1. a name that thou livest, and art *dead*.
11:18. the time of the *dead*, that they
14:13. Blessed (are) the *dead* which die in
16: 3. became as the blood of a *dead* (man):
20: 5. the rest of the *dead* lived not again
12. And I saw the *dead*, small and great,
— and the *dead* were judged out of
13. sea gave up the *dead* which were in it; and death and hell delivered up the *dead*

3499 3 537/663 4:892 3498

νεκρόω, nekroō.

Ro. 4:19. considered not his own body now *dead*,
Col. 3: 5. *Mortify* therefore your members
Heb 11.12. even of one, and him as good as *dead*,

3500 2 537/663 4:892 3499

νέκρωσις, nekrōsis.

Ro. 4:19. neither yet the *deadness* of Sarah's womb:
2Co. 4:10. bearing about in the body the *dying* of the Lord Jesus,

3501 24 537/664 4:896

νέος, νεώτερος, neos, neōteros.

Mat. 9:17. Neither do men put *new* wine
— but they put *new* wine into new
Mar 2:22. no man putteth *new* wine into old bottles: else the *new* wine doth burst
Mar 2.22. but *new* wine must be put into new
Lu. 5:37. no man putteth *new* wine into old bottles; else the *new* wine will burst
38. But *new* wine must be put into
39. drunk old (wine) straightway desireth *new*
15:12. the *younger* of them said to (his) father
13. the *younger* son gathered all
22:26. let him be as the *younger*;
Joh.21:18. When thou wast *young*, thou girdedst
Acts 5: 6. And the *young men* arose, wound
1Co. 5: 7. that ye may be a *new* lump,
Col. 3:10. And have put on the *new* (man),
1Ti. 5: 1. the *younger men* as brethren;
2. the *younger* as sisters, with all purity.
11. But the *younger* widows refuse:
14. that the *younger women* marry,
Tit. 2: 4. teach the *young women* to be sober,
6. *Young men* likewise exhort to be
Heb 12:24. mediator of the *new* covenant,
1Pet. 5: 5. Likewise, ye *younger*, submit

3502 1 538/669 3501

νεοσσός, neossos.

Lu. 2:24. or two *young* pigeons.

3503 5 538/664 3501

νεότης, neotees.

Mat.19:20. have I kept from my *youth* up:
Mar10:20. have I observed from my *youth*.
Lu. 18:21. have I kept from my *youth* up.
Acts26: 4. My manner of life from my *youth*,
1Ti. 4:12. Let no man despise thy *youth*;

3504 1 538/664 3501,3453

νεόφυτος, neophutos.

1Ti. 3: 6. Not a *novice*, lest being lifted up

3506 2 538/664

νεύω, nŭo.

Joh.13:24. Peter therefore *beckoned* to him,
Acts24:10. *after that* the governor *had beckoned* unto

3507 26 538/664 4:902 3509

νεφέλη, nephelee.

Mat.17: 5. a bright *cloud* overshadowed them: and behold a voice out of the *cloud*,
24:30. coming in the *clouds* of heaven
26:64. and coming in the *clouds* of heaven.
Mar 9: 7. a *cloud* that overshadowed them: and a voice came out of the *cloud*,
13:26. the Son of man coming in the *clouds*
14:62. and coming in the *clouds* of heaven.
Lu. 9:34. there came a *cloud*, and overshadowed
— as they entered into the *cloud*.
35. came a voice out of the *cloud*,
12:54. When ye see a *cloud* rise out of the west,
21:27. coming in a *cloud* with power
Acts 1: 9. a *cloud* received him out of their sight.
1Co.10: 1. all our fathers were under the *cloud*,
2. unto Moses in the *cloud* and in the sea;
1Th. 4:17. together with them in the *clouds*,
2Pet.2.17. *clouds* that are carried with a tempest;
Jude 12. *clouds* (they are) without water,
Rev. 1: 7. Behold, he cometh with *clouds*,
10: 1. clothed with a *cloud*:
11:12. ascended up to heaven in a *cloud*;
14:14. a white *cloud*, and upon the *cloud* (one) sat like unto the Son of man,

Rev.14:15. to him that sat on the *cloud*,
16. And he that sat on the *cloud* thrust

3509 1 538/664 4:902

νέφος, nephos.

Heb12: 1. with so great a *cloud* of witnesses,

3510 1 539/664 4:911

νεφρός, nephros.

Rev. 2:23. I am he which searcheth the *reins* and hearts:

3511 1 539/664 3485 *koreō* (to sweep)

νεωκόρος, neōkoros.

Acts19:35. is a *worshipper* (lit. *temple-keeper*) of the great goddess

3512 1 539/664 3501

νεωτερικός, neōterikos.

2Ti. 2:22. Flee also *youthful* lusts:

νεώτερος see **νέος.** 3501

3513 1 539/664 3483

νή, nee.

1Co.15:31. *I protest by* your rejoicing which

3514 2 539/664 *neō* (to spin)

νήθω, neetho.

Mat. 6:28. neither do they *spin:*
Lu. 12:27. they toil not, they *spin* not;

3515 1 539/664 4:912 3516

νηπιάζω, neepiazo.

1Co.14:20. howbeit in malice *be ye children*,

3516 14 539/664 4:912 *nē-*, 2031

νήπιος, neepios.

Mat.11:25. hast revealed them unto *babes*.
21:16. Out of the mouth of *babes*
Lu. 10:21. hast revealed them unto *babes:*
Ro. 2:20. a teacher of *babes*,
1Co. 3: 1. as unto *babes* in Christ.
13:11. When I was a *child*, I spake as a *child*, I understood as a *child*, I thought as a *child:*
— I put away childish things. (lit. of a *child*)
Gal. 4: 1. the heir, as long as he is a *child*,
3. when we were *children*, were in
Eph. 4:14. be no more *children*, tossed to and fro,
Heb 5:13. for he is a *babe*.

3519 1 540/665 3520

νησίον, neesion.

Acts27:16. And running under a certain *island*

3520 9 540/665 *neō* (to float)

νῆσος, neesos.

Acts13: 6. had gone through the *isle* unto Paphos,
27:26. be cast upon a certain *island*.
28: 1. that the *island* was called Melita.
7. the chief man of the *island*,
9. in the *island*, came, and were healed:
11. which had wintered in the *isle*,
Rev. 1: 9. was in the *isle* that is called Patmos,
6:14. every mountain and *island* were moved
16:20. And every *island* fled away,

3521 8 540/665 4:924 3522

νηστεία, neestia.

Mat.17:21. not out but by prayer and *fasting*.
Mar 9:29. by nothing, but by prayer and *fasting*.
Lu. 2:37. with *fastings* and prayers night and day.
Acts14:23. and had prayed with *fasting*,
27: 9. because the *fast* was now already past,
1Co. 7: 5. give yourselves to *fasting* and prayer;
2Co. 6: 5. in watchings, in *fastings;*
11:27. in *fastings* often, in cold

3522 21 540/665 4:924 3523

νηστεύω, neestuo.

Mat. 4: 2. *when* he *had fasted* forty days
6:16. Moreover when ye *fast*, be not,
— may appear unto men to *fast*.
17. *when* thou *fastest*, anoint thine head,
18. appear not unto men to *fast*,
9:14. Why *do* we and the Pharisees *fast* oft, but thy disciples *fast* not?
15. and then *shall* they *fast*.
Mar 2:18. the Pharisees used to *fast:*
— Why *do* the disciples of John and of the Pharisees *fast*, but thy disciples *fast* not?
19. children of the bridechamber *fast*,
— bridegroom with them, they cannot *fast*.
20. and then *shall* they *fast* in those days.
Lu. 5:33. Why *do* the disciples of John *fast* often,
34. of the bridechamber *fast*, while the
35. and then *shall* they *fast* in those days.
18:12. I *fast* twice in the week,
Acts10:30. Four days ago I was *fasting* until
13: 2. As they ministered to the Lord, and *fasted*
3. *when* they *had fasted* and prayed,

3523 2 540/665 4:924 2068 *nē-* (not).

νῆστις, neestis.

Mat.15:32. I will not send them away *fasting*,
Mar 8: 3. And if I send them away *fasting*

3524 3 540/665 4:936 3525

νηφάλεος, & νεφάλιος, neephaleos, & nephalios.

1Ti. 3: 2. *vigilant*, sober, of good behaviour,
11. *sober*, faithful in all things.
Tit. 2: 2. That the aged men be *sober*, grave,

3525 6 540/665 4:936

νήφω, neepho.

1Th. 5: 6. but let us watch and *be sober*.
8. *let* us, who are of the day, *be sober*,
2Ti. 4: 5. But *watch* thou in all things,
1Pet. 1:13. *be sober*, and hope to the end
4: 7. be ye therefore sober, and *watch* unto
5: 8. *Be sober*, be vigilant;

3528 28 541/665 4:942 3529

νικάω, nikao.

Lu. 11:22. shall come upon him and *overcome* him,
Joh.16:33. I *have overcome* the world.

Ro. 3: 4. *mightest overcome* when thou art judged.
12:21. *Be* not *overcome* of evil, but *overcome* evil with good.
1Joh.2:13. ye *have overcome* the wicked one.
14. and ye *have overcome* the wicked one.
4: 4. and *have overcome* them:
5: 4. born of God *overcometh* the world:
— the victory *that overcometh* the world,
5. Who is he *that overcometh* the world,
Rev. 2: 7. To him *that overcometh* will I give
11. He *that overcometh* shall not be hurt
17. To him *that overcometh* will I
26. And he *that overcometh*, and keepeth
3: 5. He *that overcometh*, the same
12. Him *that overcometh* will I make
21. To him *that overcometh* will I grant
— even as I also *overcame*, and am set
5: 5. *hath prevailed* to open the book,
6: 2. went forth *conquering*, and to *conquer*.
11: 7. and *shall overcome* them,
12:11. And they *overcame* him by the blood
13: 7. and *to overcome* them:
15: 2. and them *that had gotten the victory* over the beast,
17:14. and the Lamb *shall overcome* them:
21: 7. He *that overcometh* shall inherit all things;

3529 1 541/666 4:942

νίκη, nikee.

1Joh.5: 4. this is the *victory* that overcometh the world, (even) our faith.

3534 4 541/666 4:942 3529

νῖκος, nikos.

Mat.12:20. send forth judgment unto *victory*.
1Co.15:54. Death is swallowed up in *victory*.
55. O grave, where (is) thy *victory?*
57. which giveth us the *victory* through our Lord Jesus Christ.

3537 1 542/666 3538

νιπτήρ, nipteer.

Joh. 13: 5. he poureth water into a *bason*,

3538 17 542/666 4:946 cf 3068

νίπτω, nipto.

Mat. 6:17. and *wash* thy face;
15: 2. for they *wash* not their hands when
Mar 7: 3. except they *wash* (their) hands oft,
Joh. 9: 7. Go, *wash* in the pool of Siloam,
— and *washed*, and came seeing.
11. Go to the pool of Siloam, and *wash*: and I went and *washed*, *and* I received sight.
15. and I *washed*, and do see.
13: 5. and began *to wash* the disciples' feet,
6. Lord, *dost* thou *wash* my feet?
8. Thou *shalt* never *wash* my feet.
— If I *wash* thee not, thou hast no
10. needeth not save *to wash* (his) feet,
12. So after he *had washed* their feet,
14. and Master, *have washed* your feet; ye also ought *to wash* one another's feet.
1Ti. 5:10. if she *have washed* the saints' feet,

3539 14 542/666 4:948 3563

νοέω, noeo.

Mat.15:17. *Do* not ye yet *understand*, that
16: 9. *Do* ye not yet *understand*, neither
Mat.16:11. How is it that ye *do* not *understand*
24:15. whoso readeth, *let* him *understand*:
Mar 7:18. *Do* ye not *perceive*, that whatsoever
8:17. *perceive* ye not yet, neither understand?
13:14. *let* him that readeth *understand*,
Joh.12:40. nor *understand* with (their) heart,
Ro. 1:20. *being understood* by the things that
Eph. 3: 4. ye may *understand* my knowledge in
20. above all that we ask or *think*,
1Ti. 1: 7. *understanding* neither what they say,
2Ti. 2: 7. *Consider* what I say; and the Lord
Heb 11: 3. Through faith we *understand* that

3540 6 542/666 4:948 3539

νόημα, noeema.

2Co. 2:11. we are not ignorant of his *devices*.
3:14. But their *minds* were blinded:
4: 4. hath blinded the *minds* of them
10: 5. bringing into captivity every *thought*
11: 3. so your *minds* should be corrupted
Phi. 4: 7. shall keep your hearts and *minds* through Christ Jesus.

3541 1 543/666

νόθος, nothos.

Heb 12: 8. then are ye *bastards*, and not sons.

3542 2 543/667 rt 3551

νομή, nomee.

Joh.10: 9. go in and out, and find *pasture*.
2Ti. 2:17. their word will eat (lit. will have *pasture*) as doth a canker:

3543 15 543/667 3551

νομίζω, nomizo.

Mat. 5:17. *Think* not that I am come to destroy
10:34. *Think* not that I am come to send peace
20:10. they *supposed* that they should
Lu. 2:44. *supposing* him to have been in the
3:23. being as *was supposed* the son of
Acts 7:25. For he *supposed* his brethren would have
8:20. because thou *hast thought* that the gift
14:19. *supposing* he had been dead.
16:13. where prayer *was wont* to be made;
27. *supposing* that the prisoners had been fled.
17:29. we ought not *to think* that the Godhead
21:29. whom they *supposed* that Paul had
1Co. 7:26. I *suppose* therefore that this is good
36. if any man *think* that he behaveth
1Ti. 6: 5. *supposing* that gain is godliness:

3544 9 543/667 4:1022 3551

νομικός, nomikos.

Mat.22:35. one of them, (which was) a *lawyer*, asked
Lu. 7:30. the Pharisees and *lawyers* rejected
10:25. a certain *lawyer* stood up, and
11:45. Then answered one of the *lawyers*,
46. Woe unto you also, (ye) *lawyers!*
52. Woe unto you, *lawyers!* for ye have
14: 3. spake unto the *lawyers* and Pharisees,
Tit. 3: 9. and strivings *about the law*;
13. Bring Zenas the *lawyer* and Apollos

3545 2 543/667 4:1022 3551

νομίμως, nomimōs.

1Ti. 1: 8. if a man use it *lawfully*;
2Ti. 2: 5. except he strive *lawfully*.

3546 1 543/667 3543

νόμισμα, nomisma.

Mat.22:19. Shew me the tribute *money*.

3547 3 543/667 2:135 3551,1320

νομοδιδάσκαλος, nomodidaskalos.

Lu. 5:17. and *doctors of the law* sitting by,
Acts 5:34. Gamaliel, a *doctor of the law*,
1Ti. 1: 7. Desiring to be *teachers of the law*;

3548 1 543/667 4:1022 3550

νομοθεσία, nomothesia.

Ro. 9: 4. and the *giving of the law*, and

3549 2 544/667 4:1022 3550

νομοθετέω, nomotheteo.

Heb 7:11. for under it the people *received the law*,
8: 6. which *was established* upon better'

3550 1 544/667 4:1022 3551 5087

νομοθέτης, nomothetees.

Jas. 4:12. There is one *lawgiver*, who is able to save and to destroy:

3551 197 544/667 4:1022 nemo (to parcel out)

νόμος, nomos.

' denotes that the article is not in the Greek, though inserted in the English.

Mat. 5:17. that I am come to destroy the *law*,
18. shall in no wise pass from the *law*,
7:12. for this is the *law* and the prophets.
11:13. and the *law* prophesied until John.
12: 5. have ye not read in the *law*,
22:36. the great commandment in the *law*?
40. hang all the *law* and the prophets.
23:23. the weightier (matters) of the *law*,
Lu. 2:22. according to the *law* of Moses
23. As it is written in ' the *law* of the Lord,
24. said in ' the *law* of the Lord,
27. after the custom of the *law*,
39. according to the *law* of the Lord,
10:26. What is written in the *law*?
16:16. The *law* and the prophets (were) until
17. than one tittle of the *law* to fail.
24:44. written in the *law* of Moses,
Joh. 1:17. For the *law* was given by Moses,
45(46). of whom Moses in the *law*, and
7:19. Did not Moses give you the *law*, and (yet) none of you keepeth the *law*?
23. that the *law* of Moses should not
49. who knoweth not the *law* are cursed.
51. Doth our *law* judge (any) man, before
8: 5. Now Moses in the *law* commanded
17. It is also written in your *law*,
10:34. Is it not written in your *law*,
12:34. We have heard out of the *law* that
15:25. that is written in their *law*,
18:31. judge him according to your *law*.
19: 7. We have a *law*, and by our *law* he ought
Acts 6:13. against this holy place, and the *law*:
7:53. Who have received the *law* by
13:15. after the reading of the *law*
39. could not be justified by the *law*
15: 5. to keep the *law* of Moses.
24. be circumcised, and keep the *law*:
18:13. to worship God contrary to the *law*.
15. and (of) your *law*, look ye (to it);
Acts21:20. are all zealous of the *law*:
24. and keepest the *law*.
28. against the people, and the *law*,
22: 3. to the perfect manner of the *law*
12. a devout man according to the *law*,
23: 3. to judge me after the *law*,
29. accused of questions of their *law*,
24: 6. have judged according to our *law*.
14. in the *law* and in the prophets:
25: 8. Neither against the *law* of the Jews,
28:23. both out of the *law* of Moses,
Ro. 2:12. as many as have sinned in ' the *law* shall be judged by the ' *law*;
13. For not the hearers of the *law* (are) just before God, but the doers of the *law*
14. the Gentiles, which have not ' the *law*, do by nature the things contained in the *law*, these, having not ' the *law*, are a *law* unto themselves:
15. the work of the *law* written in their
17. and restest in the *law*,
18. being instructed out of the *law*;
20. and of the truth in the *law*.
23. Thou that makest thy boast of ' the *law*, through breaking the *law* dishonourest thou God?
25. if thou keep ' the *law*: but if thou be a breaker of ' the *law*, thy
26. keep the righteousness of the *law*,
27. if it fulfil the *law*,
— dost transgress ' the *law*?
3:19. soever the *law* saith, it saith to them who are under the *law*:
20. Therefore by the deeds of ' the *law*
— for by ' the *law* (is) the knowledge of sin.
21. of God without ' the *law* is manifested, being witnessed by the *law* and
27. By what *law*? of works? Nay: but by ' the *law* of faith.
28. by faith without the deeds ' of the *law*.
31. make void ' the *law* through faith? God forbid: yea, we establish ' the *law*.
4:13. or to his seed, through ' the *law*,
14. For if they which are of ' the *law*
15. Because the *law* worketh wrath: for where no *law* is, (there is) no
16. which is of the *law*, but
5:13. until ' the *law* sin was in the world:
— not imputed when there is no *law*.
20. Moreover ' the *law* entered, that
6:14. for ye are not under ' the *law*, but
15. because we are not under ' the *law*,
7: 1. for I speak to them that know ' the *law*, how that the *law* hath dominion over
2. is bound by ' the *law* to (her) husband
— is loosed from the *law* of (her) husband.
3. she is free from that *law*;
4. become dead to the *law* by the body of
5. which were by the *law*,
6. now we are delivered from the *law*,
7. (Is) the *law* sin? God forbid. Nay, had not known sin, but by ' the *law*:
— except the *law* had said,
8. For without ' the *law* sin (was) dead.
9. I was alive without ' the *law* once:
12. Wherefore the *law* (is) holy,
14. we know that the *law* is spiritual:
16. I consent unto the *law* that (it is) good.
21. I find then a (lit. the) *law*, that, when I
22. I delight in the *law* of God
23. But I see another *law* in my members, warring against the *law* of my mind.

Ro. 7:23. into captivity to the *law* of sin
25. with the mind I myself serve[1] the *law* of God; but with the flesh[1] the *law* of sin.
8: 2. For the *law* of the Spirit of life
— free from the *law* of sin and death.
3. For what the *law* could not do,
4. the righteousness of the *law*
7. it is not subject to the *law* of God,
9:31. after[1] the *law* of righteousness, hath not attained to[1] the *law* of righteousness.
32. by the works of[1] the *law*.
10: 4. Christ (is) the end of[1] the *law*
5. the righteousness which is of the *law*,
13: 8. hath fulfilled[1] the *law*.
10. love (is) the fulfilling of[1] the *law*.
1Co. 7:39. The wife is bound by[1] the *law*
9: 8. saith not the *law* the same also?
9. it is written in the *law* of Moses,
20. to them that are under [1]the *law*, as under[1] the *law*, that I might gain them that are under[1] the *law*;
14:21. In the *law* it is written, With
34. under obedience, as also saith the *law*.
15:56. the strength of sin (is) the *law*.
Gal. 2:16. not justified by the works of[1] the *law*,
— and not by the works of [1]the *law*: for by the works of [1]the *law* shall no flesh
19. I through [1]the *law* am dead to [1]the *law*,
21. if righteousness (come) by [1]the *law*,
3: 2. the Spirit by the works of [1]the *law*, or
5. by the works of [1]the *law*, or by the hearing
10. as many as are of the works of [1]the *law*
— in the book of the *law* to do them.
11. no man is justified by [1]the *law*
12. And the *law* is not of faith:
13. from the curse of the *law*,
17. the *law*, which was four hundred and
18. if the inheritance (be) of [1]the *law*,
19. Wherefore then (serveth) the *law*?
21. (Is) the *law* then against the promises
— for if there had been a *law* given
— righteousness should have been by [1]the *law*.
23. we were kept under [1]the *law*,
24. Wherefore the *law* was our schoolmaster
4: 4. made under [1]the *law*,
5. To redeem them that were under [1]the *law*,
21. Tell me, ye that desire to be under [1]the *law*, do ye not hear the *law*?
5: 3. is a debtor to do the whole *law*.
4. of you are justified by [1]the *law*;
14. For all the *law* is fulfilled in one
18. ye are not under [1]the *law*.
23. against such there is no *law*.
6: 2. and so fulfil the *law* of Christ.
13. who are circumcised keep [1]the *law*;
Eph. 2:15. enmity, (even) the *law* of commandments
Phi. 3: 5. as touching [1]the *law*, a Pharisee;
6. which is in [1]the *law*, blameless.
9. righteousness, which is of [1]the *law*.
1Ti. 1: 8. we know that the *law* (is) good,
9. that [1]the *law* is not made for a righteous
Heb 7: 5. tithes of the people according to the *law*,
12. a change also of [1]the *law*.
16. after [1]the *law* of a carnal commandment,
19. the *law* made nothing perfect,
28. the *law* maketh men high priests which
— which was since the *law*, (maketh) the
8: 4. that offer gifts according to the *law*:
10. I will put my *laws* into their mind,
9:19. every precept to all the people according to [1]the *law*,
Heb 9:22. things are by the *law* purged with blood;
10: 1. For the *law* having a shadow of
8. which are offered by the *law*;
16. I will put my *laws* into their hearts,
28. He that despised Moses' *law* died
Jas. 1:25. into[1] the perfect *law* of liberty,
2: 8. If ye fulfil[1] the royal *law*
9. and are convinced of the *law*
10. whosoever shall keep the whole *law*,
11. a transgressor of [1]the *law*.
12. be judged by [1]the *law* of liberty.
4:11. speaketh evil of [1]the *law*, and judgeth [1]the *law*: but if thou judge [1]the *law*, thou art not a doer of [1]the *law*, but a judge.

3552 1 545/669 4:1091 3554

νοσέω, noseo.

1Ti. 6: 4. but *doting* about questions and strifes of

3553 1 545/669 4:1091 3552

νόσημα, noseema.

Joh. 5: 4. was made whole of whatsoever *disease*

3554 12 545/669 4:1091

νόσος, nosos.

Mat. 4:23. healing all manner of *sickness*
24. that were taken with divers *diseases*
8:17. and bare (our) *sicknesses*.
9:35. and healing every *sickness* and
10: 1. to heal all manner of *sickness* and
Mar 1:34. many that were sick of divers *diseases*,
3:15. power to heal *sicknesses*,
Lu. 4:40. sick with divers *diseases*
6:17. and to be healed of their *diseases*;
7:21. cured many of (their) *infirmities*
9: 1. over all devils, and to cure *diseases*.
Acts19:12. and the *diseases* departed from them,

3555 1 545/669 3502

νοσσιά, nossia.

Lu. 13.34. as a hen (doth gather) her *brood*

3556 1 545/669 3502

νοσσίον, nossion.

Mat.23:37. as a hen gathereth her *chickens*

3557 3 546/669 *nosphi* (aloof)

νοσφίζομαι, nosphizomai.

Acts 5: 2. *kept back* (part) of the price,
3. to *keep back* (part) of the price
Tit. 2:10. Not *purloining*, but shewing

3558 7 546/669

νότος, notos.

Mat.12:42. The queen of the *south* shall rise up
Lu. 11:31. The queen of the *south* shall rise up
12:55. when (ye see) the *south wind* blow,
13:29. and (from) the *south*, and shall sit down
Acts27:13. And when the *south wind* blew softly,
28:13. the *south wind* blew, and we came
Rev.21:13. on the *south* three gates;

3559 3 546/669 4:948 3563,5087

νουθεσία, nouthesia.

1Co.10:11. they are written for our *admonition*.

Eph. 6: 4. and *admonition* of the Lord.
Tit. 3: 10. after the first and second *admonition* reject;

3560 8 546/669 4:948 rt3559

νουθετέω, noutheteo.

Acts20:31. I ceased not to *warn* every one night and
Ro. 15:14. able also *to admonish* one another.
1Co. 4:14. but as my beloved sons I *warn* (you).
Col. 1:28. *warning* every man, and teaching
3:16. and *admonishing* one another in psalms
1Th. 5:12. over you in the Lord, and *admonish* you;
14. *warn* them that are unruly,
2Th. 3:15. but *admonish* (him) as a brother.

3561 1 546/670 3501,3376

νουμηνία, noumeenia.

Col. 2:16. or of the *new moon*, or of the sabbath

3562 1 546/670 3563,2192

νουνεχῶς, nounekōs.

Mar 12:34. saw that he answered *discreetly*,

3563 24 546/670 4:948 rt 1097 cf 5590

νοῦς, nous.

Lu. 24:45. Then opened he their *understanding*,
Ro. 1:28. God gave them over to a reprobate *mind*,
7:23. warring against the law of my *mind*,
25. with the *mind* I myself serve
11:34. who hath known the *mind* of the Lord?
12: 2. by the renewing of your *mind*,
14: 5. be fully persuaded in his own *mind*.
1Co. 1:10. joined together in the same *mind*
2:16. who hath known the *mind* of the Lord,
— But we have the *mind* of Christ.
14:14. but my *understanding* is unfruitful.
15. I will pray with the *understanding* also:
— I will sing with the *understanding* also.
19. five words with my *understanding*,
Eph. 4:17. in the vanity of their *mind*,
23. be renewed in the spirit of your *mind*;
Phi. 4: 7. which passeth all *understanding*,
Col. 2:18. puffed up by his fleshly *mind*,
2Th. 2: 2. be not soon shaken in *mind*,
1Ti. 6: 5. disputings of men of corrupt *minds*,
2Ti. 3: 8. men of corrupt *minds*, (lit. men corrupt in *mind*)
Tit. 1:15. even their *mind* and conscience is defiled.
Rev.13:18. Let him that hath *understanding*
17: 9. And here (is) the *mind* which hath wisdom.

3565 8 547/670 4:1099 *nuptō* (to veil a bride)

νύμφη, numphee.

Mat.10:35. and the *daughter in law* against
Lu. 12:53. against her *daughter in law*, and the *daughter in law* against her
Joh. 3:29. He that hath the *bride* is the
Rev.18:23. and of the *bride* shall be heard
21: 2. prepared as a *bride* adorned for
9. shew thee the *bride*, the Lamb's wife.
22:17. the Spirit and the *bride* say, Come.

3566 16 547/670 4:1099 3565

νυμφίος, numphios.

Mat. 9:15. as long as the *bridegroom* is with them?
— when the *bridegroom* shall be taken
25: 1. went forth to meet the *bridegroom*.
Mat.25: 5. While the *bridegroom* tarried,
6. Behold, the *bridegroom* cometh;
10. went to buy, the *bridegroom* came;
Mar 2:19. while the *bridegroom* is with them? as long as they have the *bridegroom*
20. when the *bridegroom* shall be taken
Lu. 5:34. while the *bridegroom* is with them?
35. when the *bridegroom* shall be taken
Joh. 2: 9. of the feast called the *bridegroom*,
3:29. that hath the bride is the *bridegroom*: but the friend of the *bridegroom*,
— because of the *bridegroom's* voice:
Rev.18:23. and the voice of the *bridegroom* and

3567 3 547/670 3565

νυμφών, numphōn.

Mat. 9:15. Can the children of the *bridechamber*
Mar 2:19. Can the children of the *bridechamber*
Lu. 5:34. the children of the *bridechamber* fast,

3568 139 547/670 4:1106 cf3569 cf3570

νῦν, nun.

Mat.24:21. since the beginning of the world to *this time*,
26:65. *now* ye have heard his blasphemy.
27:42. let him *now* come down from the cross,
43. let him deliver him *now*, if he will
Mar 10:30. an hundredfold *now* in this time,
13:19. unto *this time*, neither shall be.
15:32. descend *now* from the cross, that we may
Lu. 1:48. from *henceforth* all generations
2:29. Lord, *now* lettest thou thy servant
5:10. from *henceforth* thou shalt catch men.
6:21. Blessed (are ye) that hunger *now*:
— Blessed (are ye) that weep *now*:
25. Woe unto you that laugh *now*!
11:39. *Now* do ye Pharisees make clean
12:52. from *henceforth* there shall be five
16:25. but *now* he is comforted,
19:42. but *now* they are hid from thine eyes.
22:36. But *now*, he that hath a purse,
69. Hereafter shall the Son of man sit (lit. from *now* shall the Son of man be sitting)
Joh. 2: 8. Draw out *now*, and bear unto the governor
4:18. he whom thou *now* hast is not thy
23. But the hour cometh, and *now* is,
5:25. The hour is coming, and *now* is,
8:40. But *now* ye seek to kill me,
52. *Now* we know that thou hast a devil.
9:21. But by what means he *now* seeth,
41. but *now* ye say, We see;
11: 8. Master, the Jews *of late* sought to stone
22. I know, that even *now*, whatsoever
12:27. *Now* is my soul troubled;
31. *Now* is the judgment of this world: *now* shall the prince of this world be cast
13:31. *Now* is the Son of man glorified,
36. thou canst not follow me *now*;
14:29. And *now* I have told you before it
15:22. but *now* they have no cloke for their sin.
24. but *now* have they both seen and
16: 5. But *now* I go my way to him.
22. And ye *now* therefore have sorrow
29. Lo, *now* speakest thou plainly,
30. *Now* are we sure that thou knowest
32. the hour cometh, yea, is *now* come,
17: 5. And *now*, O Father, glorify thou me
7 *Now* they have known that all things

Joh. 17:13. And *now* come I to thee;
18:36. but *now* is my kingdom not from hence.
21:10. fish which ye have *now* caught.
Acts 2:33. this, which ye *now* see and hear.
3:17. And *now*, brethren, I wot that
7: 4. wherein ye *now* dwell.
34. And *now* come, I will send thee
52. of whom ye have been *now* the betrayers
10: 5. And *now* send men to Joppa,
33. *Now* therefore are we all here
12:11. *Now* I know of a surety, that the Lord
13:11. And *now*, behold, the hand of the Lord
15:10. *Now* therefore why tempt ye God,
16:36. *now* therefore depart, and go in
37 and *now* do they thrust us out privily?
18: 6. from *henceforth* I will go unto the
20:22. And *now*, behold, I go bound in the
25. And *now*, behold, I know that ye all,
22: 1. my defence (which I make) *now*
16. And *now* why tarriest thou?
23:15. *Now* therefore ye with the council
21. and *now* are they ready, looking
24:13. things whereof they *now* accuse me.
25. Go thy way for *this time*;
26: 6. And *now* I stand and am judged
17. unto whom *now* I send thee,
Ro. 3:21. But *now* the righteousness of God
26. To declare, (I say), at this time (lit. in the *now* time)
5: 9. being *now* justified by his blood,
11. by whom we have *now* received the
6:19. even so *now* yield your members
21. whereof ye are *now* ashamed?
8: 1. *now* no condemnation to them
18. the sufferings of this *present* time
22. in pain together until *now*.
11: 5. Even so then at this *present* time
30. yet have *now* obtained mercy
31. so have these also *now* not believed,
13:11. for *now* (is) our salvation nearer
16:26. But *now* is made manifest,
1Co. 3: 2. neither yet *now* are ye able.
7:14. but *now* are they holy.
12:20. But *now* (are they) many members,
16:12. was not at all to come *at this time*;
2Co. 5:16. *henceforth* know we no man after
— yet *now* henceforth know we (him) no
6: 2. behold, *now* (is) the accepted time; behold, *now* (is) the day of salvation.
7: 9. *Now* I rejoice, not that ye were
8:14(13). now at this time (lit. in the *now* time) your abundance
13: 2. and being absent *now* I write
Gal. 1:23. *now* preacheth the faith
2:20. life which I *now* live in the flesh
3: 3. are ye *now* made perfect by the flesh?
4: 9. But *now*, after that ye have known
25. to Jerusalem which *now* is,
29. even so (it is) *now*.
Eph. 2: 2. the spirit that *now* worketh in
3: 5. as it is *now* revealed unto his holy
10. To the intent that *now* unto the
5: 8. but *now* (are ye) light in the Lord:
Phi. 1: 5. from the first day until *now*;
20. as always, (so) *now* also Christ
30. (and) *now* hear (to be) in me.
2:12. but *now* much more in my absence,
3:18. and *now* tell you even weeping,
Col. 1:24. Who *now* rejoice in my sufferings
1Th. 3: 8. For *now* we live, if ye stand fast
2Th. 2: 6. And *now* ye know what withholdeth
1Ti. 4: 8. promise of the life that *now* is, and
1Ti. 6:17. Charge them that are rich in *this* world,
2Ti. 1:10. But is *now* made manifest
4:10. having loved this *present* world,
Tit. 2:12. godly, in this *present* world;
Heb 2: 8. But *now* we see not yet all things
9: 5. of which we cannot *now* speak
24. *now* to appear in the presence of God
26. but *now* once in the end of the world
12:26. but *now* he hath promised,
Jas. 4:13. Go to *now*, ye that say,
16. But *now* ye rejoice in your boastings:
5: 1. Go to *now*, (ye) rich men,
1Pet. 1:12. which are *now* reported unto you
2:10. but (are) *now* the people of God:
— but *now* have obtained mercy.
25. but are *now* returned unto the
3:21. baptism doth also *now* save us not the
2Pet. 3: 7. and the earth, which are *now*,
18. To him (be) glory both *now* and for ever.
1Joh. 2:18. even *now* are there many antichrists;
28. And *now*, little children, abide in him;
3: 2. *now* are we the sons of God,
4: 3. even *now* already is it in the world.
2Joh. 5. And *now* I beseech thee, lady,
Jude 25. and power, both *now* and ever. Amen.
See also τὰ νῦν and νυνί.

3569 520 /670 3588,3568

τὰ νῦν or ταvῦν, *ta nun* or *tanun*.

Acts 4:29. And *now*, Lord, behold their threatenings:
5:38. And *now* I say unto you, Refrain
17:30. *but now* commandeth all men
20:32. And *now*, brethren, I commend you
27:22. And *now* I exhort you to be of good

3570 20 548/672 3568

νυνί, *nuni*.

Ro. 6:22. But *now* being made free from sin,
7: 6. But *now* we are delivered from the law,
17. *Now* then it is no more I that do it,
15:23. But *now* having no more place
25. But *now* I go unto Jerusalem
1Co. 5:11. But *now* I have written unto you
12:18. But *now* hath God set the members
13:13. And *now* abideth faith, hope, charity,
14: 6. *Now*, brethren, if I come unto you
15:20. But *now* is Christ risen from the dead,
2Co. 8:11. *Now* therefore perform the doing
22. but *now* much more diligent,
Eph 2:13. But *now* in Christ Jesus ye who
Col. 1:21. yet *now* hath he reconciled
26. but *now* is made manifest to his
3: 8. But *now* ye also put off all these;
Philem. 9. and *now* also a prisoner of Jesus
11. but *now* profitable to thee and to me:
Heb 8: 6. But *now* hath he obtained a more
11:16. But *now* they desire a better (country), that is, an heavenly:

3571 65 548/672 4:1123

νύξ, *nux*.

Mat. 2:14. child and his mother by *night*, and
4: 2. forty days and forty *nights*,
12:40. Jonas was three days and three *nights*
— and three *nights* in the heart of the earth.
14:25. in the fourth watch of the *night*
25: 6. And at mid*night* there was a cry
26:31. be offended because of me this *night*:
34. That this *night*, before the cock crow,
27:64. lest his disciples come by *night*,

Mat.28:13. Say ye, His disciples came by *night*,
Mar 4:27. and rise *night* and day, and the seed
5: 5. And always, *night* and day,
6:48. the fourth watch of the *night*
14:27. offended because of me this *night:*
30. That this day, (even) in this *night*,
Lu. 2: 8. over their flock by *night*.
37. fastings and prayers *night* and day.
5: 5. Master, we have toiled all the *night*,
12:20. this *night* thy soul shall be required
17:34. in that *night* there shall be two
18: 7. which cry day and *night* unto him,
21:37. and at *night* he went out, and abode in the mount
Joh. 3: 2. The same came to Jesus by *night*,
7:50. he that came to Jesus by *night*,
9: 4. the *night* cometh, when no man
11:10. if a man walk in the *night*,
13:30. and it was *night*.
19:39. at the first came to Jesus by *night*,
21: 3. and that *night* they caught nothing.
Acts 5:19. But the angel of the Lord by *night*
9:24. day and *night* to kill him.
25. Then the disciples took him by *night*,
12: 6. the same *night* Peter was sleeping
16: 9. appeared to Paul in the *night;*
33. the same hour of the *night*,
17:10. sent away Paul and Silas by *night*
18: 9. the Lord to Paul in the *night* by a vision,
20:31. to warn every one *night* and day with
23:11. And the *night* following the Lord
23. at the third hour of the *night;*
31. by *night* to Antipatris.
26: 7. serving (God) day and *night*,
27:23. For there stood by me this *night*
27. But when the fourteenth *night* was
— about mid*night* the shipmen
Ro. 13:12. The *night* is far spent,
1Co.11:23. the (same) *night* in which he was
1Th. 2: 9. for labouring *night* and day, because
3:10. *Night* and day praying exceedingly
5: 2. so cometh as a thief in the *night*.
5. we are not of the *night*, nor of darkness.
7. they that sleep sleep in the *night;*
— are drunken in the *night*.
2Th. 3: 8. with labour and travail *night* and day,
1Ti. 5: 5. and prayers *night* and day.
2Ti. 1: 3. in my prayers *night* and day;
2Pet.3:10. will come as a thief in the *night;*
Rev. 4: 8. they rest not day and *night*, saying,
7:15. serve him day and *night* in his temple:
8:12. and the *night* likewise.
12:10. accused them before our God day and *night*.
14:11. they have no rest day nor *night*,
20:10. tormented day and *night* for ever and
21:25. for there shall be no *night* there.
22: 5. And there shall be no *night* there;

3573 2 549/673 3506

νυστάζω, nustazo.

Mat.25: 5. they all *slumbered* and slept.
2Pet. 2: 3. their damnation *slumbereth* not.

3572 2 549/673

νύττω, nutto.

Joh. 19:34. with a spear *pierced* his side,

3574 1 549/673 3571,2250

νυχθήμερον, nuktheemeron.

2Co.11:25. *a night and a day* I have been in the deep;

3576 2 549/673 4:1126 3541

νωθρός, nōthros.

Heb 5:11. seeing ye are *dull* of hearing.
6:12. That ye be not *slothful*, but

3577 1 549/673

νῶτος, nōtos.

Ro. 11:10. and bow down their *back* alway.

3578 2 549/673 5:1 3581

ξενία, xenia.

Acts28:23. came many to him unto (his) *lodging;*
Philem.22. prepare me also a *lodging:*

3579 10 550/673 5:1 3581

ξενίζω, xenizo.

Acts10: 6. He *lodgeth* with one Simon a tanner,
18. whether Simon, which was surnamed Peter, *were lodged* there.
23. called he them in, and *lodged* (them).
32. he *is lodged* in the house of (one) Simon
17:20. thou bringest certain *strange* things
21:16. with whom we *should lodge*.
28: 7. and *lodged* us three days courteously.
Heb 13: 2. some *have entertained* angels unawares.
1Pet. 4: 4. they *think it strange* that ye run not
12. Beloved, *think it* not *strange* concerning the fiery trial

3580 1 550/673 5:1 3581,1209

ξενοδοχέω, xenodokeo.

1Ti. 5:10. if she *have lodged strangers*,

3581 14 550/673 5:1

ξένος, xenos.

Mat.25:35. was a *stranger*, and ye took me in:
38. When saw we thee a *stranger*,
43. I was a *stranger*, and ye took me not in:
44. or a *stranger*, or naked, or sick,
27: 7. the potter's field, to bury *strangers* in.
Acts17:18. a setter forth of *strange* gods:
21. the Athenians and *strangers* which were
Ro. 16:23. Gaius mine *host*, and of the whole church.
Eph. 2:12. and *strangers* from the covenants
19. ye are no more *strangers* and foreigners,
Heb 11:13. confessed that they were *strangers* and
13: 9. with divers and *strange* doctrines.
1Pet. 4:12. as though some *strange* thing happened
3Joh. 5. to the brethren, and to *strangers;*

3582 2 550/673 *xeō* (to smooth producing heat)

ξέστης, xestees.

Mar 7: 4. the washing of cups, and *pots*,
8. the washing of *pots* and cups:

3583 16 550/673 3584

ξηραίνω, xeeraino.

Mat.13: 6. had no root, they *withered away*.
21:19. presently the fig tree *withered away*.
20. How soon *is* the fig tree *withered away*
Mar 3: 1. which had a *withered* hand.
3. which had the *withered* hand.

Mar 4: 6. had no root, it *withered away.*
5:29. the fountain of her blood *was dried up;*
9:18. gnasheth with his teeth, and *pineth away:*
11:20. saw the fig tree *dried up* from the roots.
21. which thou cursedst *is withered away.*
Lu. 8: 6. it *withered away,* because it lacked
Joh. 15: 6. as a branch, and *is withered;*
Jas. 1:11. but it *withereth* the grass, and the
1Pet. 1:24. The grass *withereth,* and the flower
Rev. 14:15. for the harvest of the earth *is ripe.*
16:12. and the water thereof *was dried up,*

3584 7 550/674 rt 3582

ξηρός, *xeeros.*

Mat. 12:10. which had (his) hand *withered.*
23:15. for ye compass sea and *land* to make
Lu. 6: 6. whose right hand was *withered.*
8. which had the *withered* hand,
23:31. what shall be done in the *dry?*
Joh. 5: 3. of blind, halt, *withered,* waiting
Heb 11:29. through the Red sea as by *dry* (land):

3585 2 551/674 3586

ξύλινος, *xulinos.*

2Ti. 2:20. but also *of wood* and of earth;
Rev. 9:20. and *of wood:* which neither can see,

3586 19 551/674 5:37 rt 3582

ξύλον, *xulon.*

Mat. 26:47. with swords and *staves,*
55. with swords and *staves* for to take me?
Mar 14:43. with swords and *staves,*
48. with swords and (with) *staves* to take me?
Lu. 22:52. as against a thief, with swords and *staves?*
23:31. if they do these things in a green *tree,*
Acts 5:30. whom ye slew and hanged on a *tree.*
10:39. whom they slew and hanged on a *tree:*
13:29. they took (him) down from the *tree,*
16:24. and made their feet fast in *the stocks.*
1Co. 3:12. precious stones, *wood,* hay, stubble;
Gal. 3:13. Cursed (is) every one that hangeth on a *tree:*
1Pet. 2:24. bare our sins in his own body on the *tree,*
Rev. 2: 7. will I give to eat of the *tree* of life,
18:12. and all thyine *wood,*
— vessels of most precious *wood,*
22: 2. (was there) the *tree* of life,
— and the leaves of the *tree*
14. may have right to the *tree* of life,

3587 3 551/674 *xuron* (razor)

ξυράω, *xurao.*

Acts 21:24. that they *may shave* (their) heads:
1Co. 11: 5. is even all one as *if* she *were shaven.*
6. for a woman to be shorn or *shaven,*

3588 543 551/674

ὁ, ἡ, τό.

3592 12 555/683 3588,1161

ὅδε, ἥδε, τόδε, *hode, heede, tode.*

Lu. 10:39. And *she* had a sister called Mary.
Lu. 16:25. but now *he* is comforted, and thou
Acts 15:23. they wrote (letters) by them after this manner; (lit. wrote *these* things)
21:11. *Thus* saith the Holy Ghost,
Jas. 4:13. we will go into *such* a city,
Rev. 2: 1. *These* things saith he that holdeth
8. *These* things saith the first and the
12. *These* things saith he which hath
18. *These* things saith the Son of God,
3: 1. *These* things saith he that hath
7. *These* things saith he that is holy,
14. *These* things saith the Amen,

3603 11 3739,1510

ὅ ἐστι, *ho esti.*

(As used in interpretation or specification, like *i. e.* The passages in which the relative pronoun, with ἐστι, forms a clause of a sentence, are classed with ἐστι; and the passages in which it is given at full length with μεθερμηνεύομαι, may be seen under that verb.)

Mar 3:17. Boanerges, *which is,* The sons of thunder:
7:11. Corban, *that is to say,* a gift,
34. Ephphatha, *that is,* Be opened.
12:42. two mites, *which make* a farthing.
15:16. into the hall, *called* Prætorium;
42. *that is,* the day before the sabbath,
Eph. 6:17. the sword of the Spirit, *which is* the word of God:
Col. 1:24. for his body's sake, *which is* the church:
Heb 7: 2. King of Salem, *which is,* King of peace;
Rev. 21: 8. *which is* the second death.
17. the measure of a man, *that is,* of the angel.

3801 15 /281

ὁ ὢν καὶ ὁ ἦν καὶ ὁ ἐρχόμενος, *ho ōn kai ho een kai ho erhomenos.*

(Used as a descriptive title of God.)

Rev. 1: 4. *which is, and which was, and which is to come;*
8. *which is, and which was, and which is to come,*
4: 8. *which was, and is, and is to come.*
11:17. *which art, and wast, and art to come;*
16: 5. *which art, and wast, and shalt be,*

Note. The reading of this last in the most approved modern editions, is ὁ ὢν καὶ ὁ ἦν καὶ ὁ ὅσιος.

3589 2 555/683 3590

ὀγδοήκοντα, *ogdoeekonta.*

Lu. 2:37. a widow of about *fourscore* and four
16: 7. Take thy bill, and write *fourscore.*

3590 5 555/683 3638

ὄγδοος, *ogdoos.*

Lu. 1:59. the *eighth* day they came to circumcise
Acts 7: 8. and circumcised him the *eighth* day;
2Pet. 2: 5. but saved Noah the *eighth* (person),
Rev. 17:11. even he is the *eighth,*
21:20. the *eighth,* beryl;

3591 1 555/683 5:41 rt 43

ὄγκος, *ogkos.*

Heb 12: 1. let us lay aside every *weight,*

3593 1 555/683 3598
ὁδεύω, hodŭo.

Lu. 10:33. a certain Samaritan, *as he journeyed*,

3594 5 555/683 5:42 3595
ὁδηγέω, hodeegeo.

Mat.15:14. if the blind *lead* the blind,
Lu. 6:39. Can the blind *lead* the blind?
Joh.16:13. he *will guide* you into all truth:
Acts 8:31. except some man *should guide* me?
Rev. 7:17. and *shall lead* them unto living

3595 5 556/684 5:42 3598,2233
ὁδηγός, hodeegos.

Mat.15:14. they be blind *leaders* of the blind.
23:16. Woe unto you, (ye) blind *guides*,
24. (Ye) blind *guides*, which strain
Acts 1:16. which was *guide* to them that took Jesus.
Ro. 2:19. art a *guide* of the blind, a light

3596 1 556/684 3598,4198
ὁδοιπορέω, hodoiporeo.

Acts10: 9. *as* they *went on* their *journey*,

3597 2 555/684 3596
ὁδοιπορία, hodoiporia.

Joh. 4: 6. being wearied with (his) *journey*.
2Co.11:26. (In) *journeyings* often, (in) perils

3598 102 556/684 5:42
ὁδός, hodos.

Mat. 2:12. into their own country another *way*
3: 3. Prepare ye the *way* of the Lord,
4:15. (by) the *way* of the sea, beyond Jordan,
5:25. whiles thou art in the *way* with him,
7:13. and broad (is) the *way*,
14. and narrow (is) the *way*,
8:28. so that no man might pass by that *way*.
10: 5. Go not into the *way* of the Gentiles,
10. Nor scrip for (your) *journey*,
11:10. which shall prepare thy *way*
13: 4. some (seeds) fell by the *way* side,
19. received seed by the *way* side.
15:32. lest they faint in the *way*.
20:17. disciples apart in the *way*,
30. sitting by the *way* side,
21: 8. spread their garments in the *way*;
— strawed (them) in the *way*.
19. he saw a fig tree in the *way*,
32. came unto you in the *way* of righteousness,
22: 9. Go ye therefore into the high*ways*,
10. servants went out into the high*ways*
16. and teachest the *way* of God in truth,
Mar 1: 2. which shall prepare thy *way*
3. Prepare ye the *way* of the Lord,
2:23. began, as they went, to pluck (lit. to make *way* plucking) the
4: 4. some fell by the *way* side,
15. these are they by the *way* side,
6: 8. take nothing for (their) *journey*,
8: 3. they will faint by the *way*:
27. by the *way* he asked his disciples,
9:33. disputed among yourselves by the *way*?
34. for by the *way* they had disputed
10:17. when he was gone forth into the *way*,
32. they were in the *way* going up to
46. sat by the *highway* side begging.
52. and followed Jesus in the *way*.
Mar11: 8. spread their garments in the *way*:
— and strawed (them) in the *way*.
12:14. teachest the *way* of God in truth:
Lu. 1:76. to prepare his *ways*;
79. to guide our feet into the *way* of peace.
2:44. went a day's *journey*;
3: 4. Prepare ye the *way* of the Lord,
5. the rough *ways* (shall be) made smooth
7:27. which shall prepare thy *way* before
8: 5. some fell by the *way* side;
12. Those by the *way* side are they
9: 3. nothing for (your) *journey*,
57. as they went in the *way*,
10: 4. and salute no man by the *way*.
31. a certain priest that *way*:
11: 6. in his *journey* is come to me,
12:58. (as thou art) in the *way*, give diligence
14:23. Go out into the *highways*
18:35. sat by the *way* side begging:
19:36. they spread their clothes in the *way*.
20:21. but teachest the *way* of God truly:
24:32. while he talked with us by the *way*,
35. told what things (were done) in the *way*,
Joh. 1:23. Make straight the *way* of the Lord,
14: 4. and the *way* ye know.
5. and how can we know the *way*?
6. I am the *way*, the truth, and the life:
Acts 1:12. a sabbath day's *journey*.
2 28. hast made known to me the *ways* of life.
8:26. unto the *way* that goeth down from
36. And as they went on (their) *way*,
39. he went on his *way* rejoicing.
9 2 that if he found any of this *way*,
17 that appeared unto thee in the *way*
27 had seen the Lord in the *way*,
13:10 cease to pervert the right *ways*
14 16. to walk in their own *ways*.
16 17 shew unto us the *way* of salvation.
18 25 in the *way* of the Lord;
26 the *way* of God more perfectly.
19 9. but spake evil of that *way*
23. no small stir about that *way*.
22 4. And I persecuted this *way* unto
24 14. that after the *way* which they call
22. perfect knowledge of (that) *way*,
25 3. laying wait in the *way* to kill him.
26.13. I saw in the *way* a light from heaven,
Ro. 3:16. and misery (are) in their *ways*:
17. the *way* of peace have they not known:
11:33. and his *ways* past finding out!
1Co. 4:17. of my *ways* which be in Christ,
12:31. a more excellent *way*.
1Th. 3:11. direct our *way* unto you.
Heb 3:10. they have not known my *ways*.
9: 8. the *way* into the holiest of all
10:20. By a new and living *way*,
Jas. 1: 8. (is) unstable in all his *ways*.
2:25. and had sent (them) out another *way*?
5:20. from the error of his *way*
2Pet. 2: 2. the *way* of truth shall be evil spoken of.
15. Which have forsaken the right *way*,
— following the *way* of Balaam
21. not to have known the *way* of
Jude 11. they have gone in the *way* of Cain,
Rev.15: 3. just and true (are) thy *ways*,
16:12. that the *way* of the kings of the east might be prepared.

3599 12 557/685 rt 2068
ὀδούς, odous.

Mat. 5:38. and a *tooth* for a *tooth*

Mat. 8:12. shall be weeping and gnashing of *teeth*.
13:42. shall be wailing and gnashing of *teeth*.
50. shall be wailing and gnashing of *teeth*.
22:13. shall be weeping and gnashing of *teeth*.
24:51. shall be weeping and gnashing of *teeth*.
25:30. shall be weeping and gnashing of *teeth*.
Mar 9:18. and gnasheth with his *teeth*,
Lu. 13:28. shall be weeping and gnashing of *teeth*,
Acts 7:54. they gnashed on him with (their) *teeth*.
Rev. 9: 8. their *teeth* were as (the teeth) of lions.

3600 4 557/685 5:115 3601

ὀδυνάομαι, odunaomai.

Lu. 2:48. and I have sought thee *sorrowing*.
16:24. for I *am tormented* in this flame.
25. and thou *art tormented*.
Acts20:38. *Sorrowing* most of all for the words

3601 2 557/685 5:115 1416

ὀδυνή, odunee.

Ro. 9: 2. and continual *sorrow* in my heart.
1Ti. 6:10. themselves through with many *sorrows*.

3602 2 557/685 5:116

ὀδυρμός, odurmos.

Mat. 2:18. and great *mourning*, Rachel weeping
2Co. 7: 7. your *mourning*, your fervent mind toward

3605 1 557/685

ὄζω, ozo.

Joh. 11:39. by this time he *stinketh*:

3606 15 557/685 3739

ὅθεν, hothen.

Mat12:44. *from whence* I came out;
14: 7. *Whereupon* he promised with an oath
25:24. and gathering *where* thou hast not
26. and gather *where* I have not strawed:
Lu. 11:24. unto my house *whence* I came out.
Acts14:26. *from whence* they had been recommended
26:19. *Whereupon*, O king Agrippa, I was
28:13. And *from thence* we fetched a compass,
Heb 2:17. *Wherefore* in all things it behoved
3: 1. *Wherefore*, holy brethren,
7:25. *Wherefore* he is able also to save
8: 3. *wherefore* (it is) of necessity that
9:18. *Whereupon* neither the first (testament)
11:19. *from whence* also he received him
1Joh. 2:18. *whereby* we know that it is the last time.

3607 2 558/685

ὀθόνη, othonee.

Acts10:11. as it had been a great *sheet*
11: 5. as it had been a great *sheet*,

3608 5 558/685 3607

ὀθόνιον, othonion.

Lu. 24:12. beheld the *linen clothes* laid by
Joh. 19:40. and wound it in *linen clothes*
20: 5. saw the *linen clothes* lying;
6. and seeth the *linen clothes* lie,
7. not lying with the *linen clothes*,

1492 663 219/ 5:116

οἶδα see **εἰδέω.** p. 188

3603, p. 522

3609 3 559/686 5:119 3624

οἰκεῖος, oikīos.

Gal. 6:10. who are *of the houshold* (lit. the *domestics*) of faith.
Eph. 2:19. and *of the houshold* of God;
1Ti. 5: 8. specially for *those of his own house*.

3610 4 559/686 3611

οἰκέτης, oiketees.

Lu. 16:13. No *servant* can serve two masters:
Acts10: 7. he called two of his *houshold servants*,
Ro. 14: 4. that judgest another man's *servant*?
1Pet. 2:18. *Servants*, (be) subject to (your) masters

3611 9 559/686 5:119 cf 3625
3624

οἰκέω, oikeo.

Ro. 7:17. but sin *that dwelleth* in me.
18. *dwelleth* no good thing:
20. but sin *that dwelleth* in me.
8: 9. if so be that the Spirit of God *dwell* in you.
11. if the Spirit of him that raised up Jesus from the dead *dwell* in you,
1Co. 3:16. the Spirit of God *dwelleth* in you?
7:12. and she be pleased *to dwell* with him,
13. if he be pleased *to dwell* with her,
1Ti. 6:16. *dwelling* in the light which no man

3612 1 559/686 3611

οἴκημα, oikeema.

Acts12: 7. a light shined in the *prison*:

3613 2 559/686 5:119 3611

οἰκητήριον, oikeeteerion.

2Co. 5: 2. to be clothed upon with our *house* which is from heaven:
Jude 6. but left their own *habitation*,

3614 95 559/686 5:119 3624

οἰκία, oikia.

Mat. 2:11. were come into the *house*,
5:15. light unto all that are in the *house*.
7:24. which built his *house* upon a rock:
25. and beat upon that *house*;
26. which built his *house* upon the sand:
27. and beat upon that *house*;
8: 6. my servant lieth at *home* sick
14. when Jesus was come into Peter's *house*,
9:10. as Jesus sat at meat in the *house*,
23. Jesus came into the ruler's *house*,
28. when he was come into the *house*,
10:12. come into an *house*, salute it.
13. And if the *house* be worthy,
14. when ye depart out of that *house*
12:25. every city or *house* divided
29. enter into a strong man's *house*,
— and then he will spoil his *house*.
13: 1. went Jesus out of the *house*,
36. and went into the *house*:
57. and in his own *house*.
17:25. when he was come into the *house*,
19:29. that hath forsaken *houses*,
23:14(13). ye devour widows' *houses*.
24:17. to take any thing out of his *house*
43. not have suffered his *house*
26: 6. in the *house* of Simon the leper
Mar 1:29. they entered into the *house* of
2:15. as Jesus sat at meat in his *house*,

Mar 3:25. if a *house* be divided against itself, that *house* cannot stand.
27. into a strong man's *house*,
— and then he will spoil his *house*.
6: 4. and in his own *house*.
10. ye enter into an *house*,
7:24. and entered into an *house*,
9:33. and being in the *house* he asked
10:10. And in the *house* his disciples asked
29. no man that hath left *house*,
30. *houses*, and brethren, and sisters,
12:40. Which devour widows' *houses*,
13:15. not go down into the *house*,
— to take any thing out of his *house*:
34. who left his *house*, and gave authority
35. when the master of the *house* cometh,
14: 3. in the *house* of Simon the leper,
Lu. 4:38. and entered into Simon's *house*.
5:29. a great feast in his own *house*:
6:48. like a man which built an *house*,
— vehemently upon that *house*,
49. built an *house* upon the earth;
— the ruin of that *house* was great.
7: 6. he was now not far from the *house*,
36. he went into the Pharisee's *house*,
37. sat at meat in the Pharisee's *house*,
44. I entered into thine *house*,
8:27. neither abode in (any) *house*,
51. when he came into the *house*,
9: 4. whatsoever *house* ye enter into,
10: 5. into whatsoever *house* ye enter,
7. in the same *house* remain,
— Go not from *house* to *house*.
15: 8. and sweep the *house*, and seek
25. and drew nigh to the *house*,
17:31. and his stuff in the *house*,
18:29. no man that hath left *house*,
20:47. Which devour widows' *houses*,
22:10. follow him into the *house*
11. say unto the goodman of the *house*,
Joh. 4:53. believed, and his whole *house*.
8:35. servant abideth not in the *house* for ever:
11:31. with her in the *house*,
12: 3. and the *house* was filled with the odour
14: 2. In my Father's *house* are many
Acts 4:34. possessors of lands or *houses* sold them,
9:11. and enquire in the *house* of Judas
17. and entered into the *house*;
10: 6. whose *house* is by the sea side:
17. made enquiry for Simon's *house*,
32. in the *house* of (one) Simon
11:11. come unto the *house* where I was,
12:12. he came to the *house* of Mary
16:32. to all that were in his *house*.
17: 5. and assaulted the *house* of Jason,
18: 7. into a certain (man's) *house*,
— whose *house* joined hard to the
1Co.11:22. have ye not *houses* to eat and to
16:15. ye know the *house* of Stephanas,
2Co. 5: 1. For we know that if our earthly *house*
— a building of God, an *house* not made
Phi. 4:22. they that are of Cæsar's *houshold*.
1Ti. 5:13. wandering about from house to house; (lit. going the round of the *houses*)
2Ti. 2:20. But in a great *house* there are
3: 6. are they which creep into *houses*,
2Joh. 10. receive him not into (your) *house*,

3615 2 560/687 3614

οἰκιακός, oikiakos.

Mat.10:25. (shall they call) *them of* his *houshold*?
Mat.10:36. (shall be) *they of* his own *houshold*.

3616 1 560/687 2:44 3617

οἰκοδεσποτέω, oikodespoteo.

1Ti. 5:14. *guide the house*, give none occasion

3617 12 560/687 2:44 3624,1203

οἰκοδεσπότης, oikodespotees.

Mat.10:25. have called the *master of the house*
13:27. servants of the *housholder* came
52. unto a man (that is) an *housholder*,
20: 1. unto a man (that is) an *housholder*,
11. against the *goodman of the house*,
21:33. There was a certain *housholder*,
24:43. if the *goodman of the house* had
Mar 14:14. say ye to the *goodman of the house*,
Lu. 12:39. if the *goodman of the house* had
13:25. When once the *master of the house* is
14:21. Then the *master of the house* being
22:11. shall say unto the *goodman* (lit. *housholder* of the house)

3618 39 560/687 5:119 rt 3619

οἰκοδομέω, oikodomeo.

Mat. 7:24. which *built* his house upon a rock:
26. which *built* his house upon the sand;
16:18. upon this rock I *will build* my church,
21:33. a winepress in it, and *built* a tower,
42. The stone which the *builders* rejected,
23:29. because ye *build* the tombs of the
26:61. and *to build* it in three days.
27:40. and *buildest* (it) in three days,
Mar 12: 1. and *built* a tower, and let it out
10. The stone which the *builders* rejected
14:58. within three days I *will build* another
15:29. and *buildest* (it) in three days,
Lu. 4:29. whereon their city *was built*,
6:48. like a man *which built* an house,
49. like a man *that...built* an house upon the earth;
7: 5. and he *hath built* us a synagogue.
11:47. for ye *build* the sepulchres of
48. and ye *build* their sepulchres.
12:18. I will pull down my barns, and *build*
14:28. intending *to build* a tower,
30. This man began *to build*,
17:28. they planted, they *builded*;
20:17. The stone which the *builders* rejected,
Joh. 2:20. *was* this temple *in building*,
Acts 4:11. was set at nought of you *builders*,
7:47. But Solomon *built* him an house.
49. what house *will* ye *build* me?
9:31. had the churches rest...*and were edified*;
Ro. 15:20. lest I *should build* upon another
1Co. 8: 1. Knowledge puffeth up, but charity *edifieth*.
10. *shall* not the conscience...*be emboldened* to eat those things
10:23. but all things *edify* not.
14: 4. in an (unknown) tongue *edifieth* himself; but he that prophesieth *edifieth* the
17. but the other *is not edified*.
Gal. 2:18. if I *build* again the things which
1Th. 5:11. and *edify* one another,
1Pet. 2: 5. Ye also, as lively stones, *are built up*
7. the stone which the *builders* disallowed,

3619 18 561/688 5:119 rt1430, 3624

οἰκοδομή, oikodomee.

Mat.24: 1. to shew him the *buildings* of the temple

Mar 13: 1. and what *buildings* (are here)!
2. Seest thou these great *buildings?*
Ro 14:19. and things wherewith one may edify (lit. of *edifying*)
15: 2. for (his) good to *edification*.
1Co. 3: 9. (ye are) God's *building*.
14: 3. speaketh unto men (to) *edification*,
5. that the church may receive *edifying*.
12. to the *edifying* of the church.
26. Let all things be done unto *edifying*.
2Co. 5: 1. we have a *building* of God,
10: 8. the Lord hath given us for *edification*,
12:19. beloved, for your *edifying*.
13:10. hath given me to *edification*,
Eph 2:21. In whom all the *building*
4:12. for the *edifying* of the body
16. unto the *edifying* of itself in love.
29. which is good to the use of *edifying*,

3621 1 562/688 3623

οἰκονομέω, *oikonomeo*.

Lu. 16: 2. thou mayest *be* no longer *steward*.

3622 7 562/688 5:119 3623

οἰκονομία, *oikonomia*.

Lu. 16: 2. give an account of thy *stewardship;*
3. taketh away from me the *stewardship:*
4. when I am put out of the *stewardship*,
1Co. 9:17. a *dispensation* (of the gospel) is
Eph 1:10. That in the *dispensation* of the fulness
3: 2. If ye have heard of the *dispensation* of the grace of God
Col. 1:25. according to the *dispensation* of God
1Ti. 1: 4. rather than godly *edifying* which is in faith:

Note. The Translators appear to have read *οἰκοδομήν* in this last passage.

3623 10 562/688 5:119 3624,3551

οἰκονόμος, *oikonomos*.

Lu. 12:42. that faithful and wise *steward*,
16: 1. rich man, which had a *steward;*
3. the *steward* said within himself,
8. commended the unjust *steward*,
Ro. 16:23. Erastus the *chamberlain* of the city
1Co. 4: 1. and *stewards* of the mysteries of God.
2. it is required in *stewards*, that
Gal. 4: 2. But is under tutors and *governors*
Tit. 1: 7. blameless, as the *steward* of God;
1Pet. 4:10. as good *stewards* of the manifold grace of God.

3624 114 562/688 5:119

οἶκος, *oikos*.

Mat. 9: 6. and go unto thine *house*.
7. and departed to his *house*.
10: 6. to the lost sheep of the *house* of Israel.
11: 8. wear soft (clothing) are in kings' *houses*.
12: 4. entered into the *house* of God,
44. I will return into my *house*
15:24. lost sheep of the *house* of Israel.
21:13. My *house* shall be called the *house* of
23:38. your *house* is left unto you desolate.
Mar 2: 1. it was noised that he was in the *house*.
11. go thy way into thine *house*.
26. How he went into the *house* of God
3:19(20). they went into an *house*.

3620 *oikodomia*. rt 3619

Mar 5:19. Go *home* to thy friends, and tell them
38. he cometh to the *house* of the ruler
7:17. when he was entered into the *house*
30. when she was come to her *house*,
8: 3. fasting to their own *houses*,
26. he sent him away to his *house*,
9:28. when he was come into the *house*,
11:17. My *house* shall be called of all nations the *house* of prayer?
Lu. 1:23. he departed to his own *house*.
27. Joseph, of the *house* of David;
33. reign over the *house* of Jacob for ever;
40. entered into the *house* of Zacharias,
56. and returned to her own *house*.
69. in the *house* of his servant David;
2: 4. he was of the *house* and lineage
5:24. and go unto thine *house*.
25. departed to his own *house*,
6: 4. How he went into the *house* of God,
7:10. returning to the *house*, found the
8:39. Return to thine own *house*,
41. that he would come into his *house:*
9:61. which are at home at my *house*.
10: 5. Peace (be) to this *house*.
38. received him into her *house*.
11:17. a *house* (divided) against a *house* falleth.
24. I will return unto my *house*
51. the altar and the *temple:*
12:39. not have suffered his *house* to be
52. five in one *house* divided,
13:35. Behold, your *house* is left unto you
14: 1. as he went into the *house* of one
23. that my *house* may be filled.
15: 6. when he cometh *home*, he calleth
16: 4. may receive me into their *houses*.
27. send him to my father's *house:*
18:14. this man went down to his *house*
19: 5. I must abide at thy *house*.
9. This day is salvation come to this *house*,
46. My *house* is the *house* of prayer:
22:54. into the high priest's *house*.
Joh. 2:16. make not my Father's *house* an *house* of merchandise.
17. The zeal of thine *house* hath eaten me up.
7:53. every man went unto his own *house*.
11:20. but Mary sat (still) in the *house*.
Acts 2: 2. it filled all the *house* where
36. let all the *house* of Israel know
46. breaking bread from house to *house*,
5:42. and in every *house*, they ceased not
7:10. over Egypt and all his *house*.
20. in his father's *house* three months:
42. O ye *house* of Israel, have ye
47. Solomon built him an *house*.
49. what *house* will ye build me?
8: 3. entering into every *house*, and
10: 2. feared God with all his *house*,
22. to send for thee into his *house*,
30. I prayed in my *house*, and, behold,
11:12. we entered into the man's *house:*
13. he had seen an angel in his *house*,
14. whereby thou and all thy *house* shall
16:15. was baptized, and her *houshold*,
— come into my *house*, and abide
31. thou shalt be saved, and thy *house*.
34. brought them into his *house*,
18: 8. believed on the Lord with all his *house;*
19:16. they fled out of that *house* naked
20:20. publickly, and from house to *house*,
21: 8. entered into the *house* of Philip
Ro. 16: 5. the church that is in their *house*.
1Co. 1:16. I baptized also the *houshold* of

1Co.11:34. let him eat at *home;*
14:35. ask their husbands at *home:*
16:19. church that is in their *house.*
Col. 4:15. church which is in his *house.*
1Ti. 3: 4. ruleth well his own *house,*
5. know not how to rule his own *house,*
12. and their own *houses* well.
15. to behave thyself in the *house* of God,
5: 4. first to shew piety at *home,*
2Ti. 1:16. The Lord give mercy unto the *house* of
4:19. and the *houshold* of Onesiphorus.
Tit. 1:11. who subvert whole *houses,*
Philem. 2. and to the church in thy *house:*
Heb 3: 2. Moses (was faithful) in all his *house.*
3. hath more honour than the *house.*
4. every *house* is builded by some
5. (was) faithful in all his *house,*
6. Christ as a son over his own *house;* whose *house* are we,
8: 8. with the *house* of Israel and with the *house* of Judah:
10. I will make with the *house* of Israel
10:21. an high priest over the *house* of God;
11: 7. to the saving of his *house;*
1Pet.2: 5. are built up a spiritual *house,*
4:17. must begin at the *house* of God:

3625 16 563/689 5:119 3611

οἰκουμένη. oikoumenee.

Mat.24:14. shall be preached in all the *world*
Lu. 2: 1. that all the *world* should be taxed.
4: 5. unto him all the kingdoms of the *world*
21:26. which are coming on the *earth:*
Acts11:28. dearth throughout all the *world:*
17: 6. have turned the *world* upside down
31. in the which he will judge the *world*
19:27. whom all Asia and the *world* worshippeth.
24: 5. among all the Jews throughout the *world,*
Ro. 10:18. their words unto the ends of the *world.*
Heb 1: 6. the firstbegotten into the *world,*
2: 5. not put in subjection the *world* to come,
Rev. 3:10. which shall come upon all the *world,*
12: 9. which deceiveth the whole *world:*
16:14. kings of the earth and of the whole *world,*

3626 1 564/690 3624

οἰκουρός, oikouros. *ouros* (guard)

Tit. 2: 5. *keepers at home,* good, obedient

3627 2 564/690 5:159 *oiktos* (pity)

οἰκτείρω, οἰκτειρέω, oiktīro, oiktīreo.

Ro. 9:15. I *will have compassion on* whom I will *have compassion.*

3628 5 564/690 5:159 3627

οἰκτιρμός, oiktirmos.

Ro. 12: 1. by the *mercies* of God, that ye
2Co. 1: 3. the Father of *mercies,*
Phi. 2: 1. if any bowels and *mercies,*
Col. 3:12. bowels of *mercies,* kindness,
Heb10.28. despised Moses' law died without *mercy*

3629 3 564/690 5:159 3627

οἰκτίρμων oiktirmōn.

Lu. 6:36. Be ye therefore *merciful,* as your Father also is *merciful.*
Jas. 5:11. is very pitiful, and *of tender mercy.*

3633 1 565/690

See also below **οἶμαι, oimai.**

Joh.21:25. I *suppose* that even the world

3630 2 564/690 3631

οἰνοπότης, oinopotees. *poō* (4095) (to drink)

Mat.11:19. and a *winebibber,*
Lu. 7:34. a gluttonous man, and a *winebibber,*

3631 33 564/690 5:162 [3196]

οἶνος, oinos.

Mat. 9:17. Neither do men put new *wine*
— and the *wine* runneth out,
— but they put new *wine* into new
Mar 2:22. no man putteth new *wine* into old bottles, else the new *wine* doth burst the bottles, and the *wine* is
— but new *wine* must be put into new
15:23. they gave him to drink *wine*
Lu. 1:15. shall drink neither *wine* nor strong
5:37. no man putteth new *wine* into
— else the new *wine* will burst the
38. But new *wine* must be put into new
7:33. neither eating bread nor drinking *wine;*
10:34. pouring in oil and *wine,*
Joh. 2: 3. And when they wanted *wine,*
— They have no *wine.*
9. tasted the water that was made *wine,*
10. doth set forth good *wine;*
— hast kept the good *wine* until now.
4:46. where he made the water *wine.*
Ro. 14:21. nor to drink *wine,*
Eph. 5:18. be not drunk with *wine,*
1Ti. 3: 8. not given to much *wine,*
5:23. but use a little *wine* for thy
Tit. 2: 3. not given to much *wine,*
Rev. 6: 6. hurt not the oil and the *wine.*
14: 8. drink of the *wine* of the wrath
10. shall drink of the *wine* of the wrath
16:19. unto her the cup of the *wine* of
17: 2. drunk with the *wine* of her
18: 3. have drunk of the *wine* of the wrath
13. and *wine,* and oil,
19:15. he treadeth the *wine*press of

3632 1 565/690 3631,rt 5397

οἰνοφλυγία, oinophlugia.

1Pet.4: 3. *excess of wine,* revellings,

3633 2 565/690 3634

See also above **οἴομαι, oiomai.**

Phi. 1:16. *supposing* to add affliction
Jas. 1: 7. *let* not that man *think* that he

3634 15 565/690 cf 3588etc

οἷος, hoios.

Mat.24:21. tribulation, *such as* was not since
Mar 9: 3. *so as* no fuller on earth can white them.
13:19. affliction, *such as* was not from the
Lu. 9:55. Ye know not *what manner of* spirit
Ro. 9: 6. Not *as* though the word of God
1Co.15:48. *As* (is) the earthy, such (are) they
— *as* (is) the heavenly, such (are) they
2Co.10:11. *such as* we are in word by letters
12:20. I shall not find you *such as* I would,
— unto you *such as* ye would not
Phi 1:30. Having the same conflict *which* ye saw
1Th. 1: 5. ye know *what manner of* men we were

2Ti. 3:11. afflictions, *which* came unto me at
— *what* persecutions I endured:
Rev.16:18. *such as* was not since men were

οἴσει & οἴσουσι see φέρω. 5342

3635 1 565/691 *oknos* (hesitation)

ὀκνέω, *okneo.*

Acts 9:38. that he would not *delay* to come

3636 3 565/691 5:166 3635

ὀκνηρός, *okneeros.*

Mat.25:26. (Thou) wicked and *slothful* servant,
Ro. 12:11. Not *slothful* in business; fervent
Phi. 3: 1. to me indeed (is) not *grievous,*

3637 1 565/691 3638,2250

ὀκταήμερος, *oktaeemeros.*

Phi. 3: 5. Circumcised *the eighth day,*

3638 9 565/691

ὀκτώ, *okto.*

Lu. 2:21. when *eight* days were accomplished
9:28. about an *eight* days after
13: 4. Or those *eight*een, upon whom
11. a spirit of infirmity *eight*een years,
16. lo, these *eight*een years,
Joh. 5: 5. an infirmity thirty and *eight* years.
20:26. after *eight* days again his disciples
Acts 9:33. which had kept his bed *eight* years,
1Pet.3:20. *eight* souls were saved by water.

3639 4 566/691 5:167 *ollumi* (to ruin)

ὄλεθρος, *olethros.*

1Co. 5: 5. for the *destruction* of the flesh,
1Th. 5: 3. then sudden *destruction* cometh
2Th. 1: 9. with everlasting *destruction* from
1Ti. 6: 9. which drown men in *destruction* and

3640 5 566/691 6:174 3641,4102

ὀλιγόπιστος, *oligopistos.*

Mat. 6:30. O ye *of little faith?*
8:26. Why are ye fearful, O ye *of little faith?*
14:31. O thou *of little faith,* wherefore didst
16: 8. O ye *of little faith,* why reason ye
Lu. 12:28. (will he clothe) you, O ye *of little faith?*

3641 43 566/691 5:171

ὀλίγος, *oligos.*

Mat. 7:14. and *few* there be that find it.
9:37. but the labourers (are) *few;*
15:34. and a *few* little fishes.
20:16. for many be called, but *few* chosen.
22:14. but *few* (are) chosen.
25:21. hast been faithful over a *few* things,
23. hast been faithful over a *few* things,
Mar 1:19. when he had gone a *little* farther
6: 5. he laid his hands upon a *few* sick
31. and rest *a while:*
8: 7. And they had a *few* small fishes:
Lu. 5: 3. thrust out *a little* from the land.
7:47. to whom *little* is forgiven, (the same) loveth *little.*
10: 2. but the labourers (are) *few:*
Lu. 12:48. shall be beaten with *few* (stripes).
13:23. Lord, are there *few* that be saved?
Acts12:18. there was no *small* stir among the
14:28. there they abode long (lit. not a *little*) time with
15: 2. no *small* dissension and disputation
17: 4. and of the chief women not a *few.*
12. and of men, not a *few.*
19:23. there arose no *small* stir
24. no *small* gain unto the craftsmen;
26:28. Almost (lit. in a *little*) thou persuadest me
29. were both almost, and altogether (lit. in a *little,* and in much)
27:20. and no *small* tempest lay on (us),
2Co. 8:15. he that (had gathered) *little* had no lack.
Eph. 3: 3. as I wrote afore in *few* words,
1Ti. 4: 8. bodily exercise profiteth *little:*
5:23. but use a *little* wine
Heb 12:10. for a *few* days chastened (us)
Jas. 3: 5. how great a matter a *little* fire
4:14. appeareth for a *little* time,
1Pet.1: 6. though now for a *season,*
3:20. wherein *few,* that is, eight souls
5:10. after that ye have suffered *a while,*
12. I have written *brief*ly,
Rev. 2:14. I have a *few* things against thee,
20. I have a *few* things against thee,
3: 4. Thou hast a *few* names even in Sardis
12:12. that he hath but a *short* time.
17:10. he must continue a *short space.*

3642 1 567/691 9:608 3641,5590

ὀλιγόψυχος, *oligopsukos.*

1Th. 5:14. comfort the *feebleminded,*

3643 1 567/691 3641 *ōra* ("care")

ὀλιγωρέω, *oligōreo.*

Heb 12: 5. *despise* not thou the chastening of the Lord, nor faint

---

3644 1 567/691 5:167 3645

ὀλοθρευτής, *olothrūtees.*

1Co.10:10. were destroyed of the *destroyer.*

3645 1 567/691 3639

ὀλοθρεύω, *olothrūo.*

Heb 11:28. lest he *that destroyed* the firstborn

3646 3 567/692 3650,2545

ὁλοκαύτωμα, *holokautōma.*

Mar 12:33. is more than all *whole burnt offerings*
Heb 10: 6. In *burnt offerings* and (sacrifices) for sin
8. and *burnt offerings* and (offering) for sin thou wouldest not,

---

3647 1 567/692 3:758 3648

ὁλοκληρία, *holokleeria.*

Acts 3:16. hath given him this *perfect soundness*

3648 2 567/692 3:758 3650,2819

ὁλόκληρος, *holokleeros.*

1Th. 5:23. (I pray God) your *whole* spirit and
Jas. 1: 4. that ye may be perfect and *entire,*

3649 1 567/692 5:173
ὀλολύζω, ololuzo.

Jas. 5: 1. weep *and howl* for your miseries

3650 112 567/692 5:174
ὅλος, holos.

Mat. 1:22. Now *all* this was done, that
4:23. Jesus went about *all* Galilee,
24. his fame went throughout *all* Syria:
5:29. and not (that) thy *whole* body should
30. and not (that) thy *whole* body should
6:22. thy *whole* body shall be full of light.
23. thy *whole* body shall be full of darkness.
9:26. fame hereof went abroad into *all* that land.
31. his fame in *all* that country.
13:33. till the *whole* was leavened.
14:35. they sent out into *all* that country
16:26. if he shall gain the *whole* world,
20: 6. Why stand ye here *all* the day idle?
21: 4. *All* this was done, that
22:37. love the Lord thy God with *all* thy heart, and with *all* thy soul, and with *all* thy
40. hang *all* the law and the prophets.
24:14. in *all* the world for a witness
26:13. be preached in the *whole* world,
56. But *all* this was done, that
59. and *all* the council, sought false
27:27. gathered unto him the *whole* band
Mar 1:28. throughout *all* the region round about Galilee.
33. *all* the city was gathered
39. synagogues throughout *all* Galilee,
6:55. ran through that *whole* region
8:36. if he shall gain the *whole* world,
12:30. love the Lord thy God with *all* thy heart, and with *all* thy soul, and with *all* thy mind, and with *all* thy strength:
33. to love him with *all* the heart, and with *all* the understanding, and with *all* the soul, and with *all* the strength,
44. (even) *all* her living.
14: 9. throughout the *whole* world,
55. and *all* the council sought
15: 1. and the *whole* council,
16. they call together the *whole* band.
33. darkness over the *whole* land
Lu. 1:65. throughout *all* the hill country of
4:14. a fame of him through *all* the region
5: 5. we have toiled *all* the night,
7:17. went forth throughout *all* Judæa,
8:39. published throughout the *whole* city
43. had spent *all* her living upon
9:25. if he gain the *whole* world,
10:27. love the Lord thy God with *all* thy heart, and with *all* thy soul, and with *all* thy strength, and with *all* thy mind;
11:34. thy *whole* body also is full of
36. If thy *whole* body therefore (be)
— the *whole* shall be full of light,
13:21. till the *whole* was leavened.
23: 5. teaching throughout *all* Jewry,
44. darkness over *all* the earth until
Joh. 4:53. believed, and his *whole* house.
7:23. I have made a man *every whit* whole on the sabbath
9:34. Thou wast *altogether* born in sins,
11:50. that the *whole* nation perish not,
13:10. but is clean *every whit:*
19:23. woven from the top through*out.*
Acts 2: 2. and it filled *all* the house
47. favour with *all* the people.
Acts 5:11. great fear came upon *all* the church,
7:10. governor over Egypt and *all* his house.
11. a dearth over *all* the land of Egypt
8:37. If thou believest with *all* thine heart,
9:31. churches rest throughout *all* Judæa
42. it was known throughout *all* Joppa;
10:22. among *all* the nation of the Jews,
37. was published throughout *all* Judæa,
11:26. that a *whole* year they assembled
28. throughout *all* the world:
13:49. throughout *all* the region.
15:22. and elders, with the *whole* church,
18: 8. believed on the Lord with *all* his house;
19:27. whom *all* Asia and the world
29. the *whole* city was filled with
21:30. And *all* the city was moved,
31. that *all* Jerusalem was in an uproar.
22:30. And *all* their council to appear,
28:30. Paul dwelt two *whole* years in
Ro. 1: 8. spoken of throughout the *whole* world.
8:36. we are killed *all* the day long;
10:21. *All* day long I have stretched forth
16:23. mine host, and of the *whole* church,
1Co. 5: 6. leaveneth the *whole* lump?
12:17. If the *whole* body (were) an eye,
— If the *whole* (were) hearing,
14:23. If therefore the *whole* church
2Co. 1: 1. which are in *all* Achaia:
Gal. 5: 3. he is a debtor to do the *whole* law.
9. leaveneth the *whole* lump.
Phi. 1:13. are manifest in *all* the palace,
1Th. 4:10. which are in *all* Macedonia:
Tit. 1:11. who subvert *whole* houses,
Heb 3: 2. Moses (was faithful) in *all* his house.
5. verily (was) faithful in *all* his house,
Jas. 2:10. whosoever shall keep the *whole* law,
3: 2. (and) able also to bridle the *whole* body
3. and we turn about their *whole* body.
6. that it defileth the *whole* body,
1Joh. 2: 2. but also for (the sins of) the *whole* world.
5:19. the *whole* world lieth in wickedness.
Rev. 3:10. which shall come upon *all* the world,
12: 9. which deceiveth the *whole* world:
13: 3. *all* the world wondered after the beast.
16:14. and of the *whole* world, to gather them

3651 1 567/693 5:174 3650,5056
ὁλοτελής, holotelees.

1Th. 5:23. very God of peace sanctify you *wholly;*

3653 1 568/693 7:751
ὄλυνθος, olunthos.

Rev. 6:13. as a fig tree casteth her *untimely figs,*

3654 4 568/693 3650
ὅλως, holōs.

Mat. 5:34. Swear not *at all;*
1Co. 5: 1. It is reported *commonly* (that there is)
6: 7. there is *utterly* a fault among you,
15:29. if the dead rise not *at all?*

3655 1 568/693
ὄμβρος, ombros.

Lu. 12:54. ye say, There cometh a *shower;*

3656 4 568/693 3658
ὁμιλέω, homileo.

Lu. 24:14. they *talked* together of all these

Lu. 24. 15. that, while they *communed* (together)
Acts 20:11. and *talked* a long while,
24:26. and *communed* with him.

3657 1 568/693 3658

ὁμιλία, homilia.

1Co.15:33 evil *communications* corrupt

3658 1 568/ *homos* (same), *hile* (crowd)

ὅμιλος, homilos.

Rev.18:17. and all the *company* in ships,

3659 1 568/693 3700

ὄμμα, omma.

Mar 8:23. and when he had spit on his *eyes*,

3660 27 568/693 5:176 *omō* (to unite)

ὄμνυμι, ὀμνύω, omnumi, omnuo.

With the tenses from ὀμόω.

Mat. 5:34. *Swear* not at all; neither by heaven;
36. Neither *shalt* thou *swear* by thy head,
23:16. Whosoever *shall swear* by the temple, it is nothing; but whosoever *shall swear* by the gold of the temple, he is a debtor!
18. Whosoever *shall swear* by the altar,
— but whosoever *sweareth* by the gift
20. *Whoso* therefore shall *swear* by the altar, *sweareth* by it, and by all
21. And *whoso* shall *swear* by the temple, *sweareth* by it, and by him that
22. he *that* shall *swear* by heaven, *sweareth* by
26:74. Then began he to curse and *to swear*,
Mar 6:23. And he *sware* unto her, Whatsoever
14:71. began to curse and *to swear*, (saying),
Lu. 1:73. which he *sware* to our father Abraham,
Acts 2:30. that God *had sworn* with an oath
7:17. which God *had sworn* to Abraham,
Heb 3:11. So I *sware* in my wrath, They shall not
18. to whom *sware* he that they
4: 3. As I *have sworn* in my wrath,
6:13. because he could *swear* by no greater, he *sware* by himself,
16. For men verily *swear* by the greater:
7:21. The Lord *sware* and will not repent,
Jas. 5:12. above all things, my brethren, *swear* not,
Rev.10: 6. And *sware* by him that liveth for ever

3661 12 569/693 5:185 rt 3674 2372

ὁμοθυμαδόν, homothumadon.

Acts 1:14. continued *with one accord* in prayer and
2: 1. were all *with one accord* in one place.
46. daily *with one accord* in the temple,
4:24. their voice to God *with one accord*,
5:12. they were all *with one accord*
7:57. and ran upon him *with one accord*,
8: 6. the people *with one accord* gave heed
12:20. but they came *with one accord* to him,
15:25. being assembled *with one accord*,
18:12. made insurrection *with one accord*
19:29. rushed *with one accord* into the theatre.
Ro. 15: 6. That ye may *with one mind* (and) one

3662 1 569/694 3664

ὁμοιάζω, homoiazo.

Mar 14:70. and thy speech *agreeth* (thereto).

3663 2 569/694 5:904 3664,3806

ὁμοιοπαθής, homoiopathees.

Acts 14:15. We also are men *of like passions* with you,
Jas. 5:17. a man *subject to like passions* as we are.

3664 47 569/694 5:186 rt 3674

ὅμοιος, homoios.

Mat.11:16. It is *like* unto children sitting
13:31. The kingdom of heaven is *like* to a grain
33. of heaven is *like* unto leaven,
44. is *like* unto treasure hid in a field;
45. is *like* unto a merchant man,
47. kingdom of heaven is *like* unto a net,
52. *like* unto a man (that is) an housholder,
20: 1. is *like* unto a man (that is) an housholder,
22:39. And the second (is) *like* unto it,
Mar 12:31. And the second (is) *like*, (namely)
Lu. 6:47. I will shew you to whom he is *like*:
48. He is *like* a man which built
49. *like* a man that without a foundation
7:31. to what are they *like*?
32. They are *like* unto children sitting
12:36. *like* unto men that wait for their
13:18. Unto what is the kingdom of God *like*?
19. It is *like* a grain of mustard seed,
21. It is *like* leaven, which a woman
Joh. 8:55. I shall be a liar *like* unto you:
9: 9. others (said), He is *like* him:
Acts17:29. that the Godhead is *like* unto gold,
Gal. 5:21. revellings, and such *like*:
1Joh.3: 2. when he shall appear, we shall be *like* him;
Jude 7. in *like* manner, giving themselves
Rev. 1:13. (one) *like* unto the Son of man,
15. his feet *like* unto fine brass,
2:18. feet (are) *like* fine brass;
4: 3. was to look upon *like* a jasper and
— in sight *like* unto an emerald.
6. a sea of glass *like* unto crystal:
7. the first beast (was) *like* a lion, and the second beast *like* a calf, and
— the fourth beast (was) *like* a flying eagle.
9: 7. (were) *like* unto horses prepared
— as it were crowns *like* gold,
10. they had tails *like* unto scorpions,
19. their tails (were) *like* unto serpents,
11: 1. a reed *like* unto a rod:
13: 2. was *like* unto a leopard,
4. Who (is) *like* unto the beast?
11. he had two horns *like* a lamb,
14:14. (one) sat *like* unto the Son of man,
16:13. three unclean spirits *like* frogs
18:18. What (city is) *like* unto this great city!
21:11. her light (was) *like* unto a stone most
18. pure gold, *like* unto clear glass.

3665 2 570/694 5:186 3664

ὁμοιότης, homoiotees.

Heb 4:15. in all points tempted *like as* (we are), (lit. according to *likeness*)
7:15. after the *similitude* of Melchisedec

3666 15 570/694 5:186 3664

ὁμοιόω, homoioō.

Mat 6: 8. *Be* not ye therefore *like* unto them:
7:24. I *will liken* him unto a wise man,
26. *shall be likened* unto a foolish man,
11:16. whereunto *shall* I *liken* this generation?
13:24. *is likened* unto a man which sowed

Mat.18:23. Therefore *is* the kingdom of heaven *likened* unto a certain king,
22: 2. *is like* unto a certain king, which made a
25: 1. Then *shall...be likened* unto ten virgins,
Mar. 4:30. Whereunto *shall* we *liken* the kingdom
Lu. 7:31. *shall* I *liken* the men of this generation?
13:18. whereunto *shall* I *resemble* it?
20. Whereunto *shall* I *liken* the kingdom
Acts14:11. *in the likeness* of men.
Ro. 9:29. and *been made like* unto Gomorrha.
Heb. 2:17. *to be made like* unto (his) brethren,

3667 6 570/694 5:186 3666

ὁμοίωμα, *homoiōma.*

Ro. 1:23. into an image made like to (lit. in the *similitude* of an image of)
5:14. after the *similitude* of Adam's
6: 5. in the *likeness* of his death,
8: 3. in the *likeness* of sinful flesh,
Phi. 2: 7. was made in the *likeness* of men:
Rev. 9: 7. And the *shapes* of the locusts (were)

3668 30 570/695 3664

ὁμοίως, *homoiōs.*

Mat.22:26. *Likewise* the second also,
26:35. *Likewise* also said all the disciples.
27:41. *Likewise* also the chief priests
Mar 4:16. these are they *likewise* which are
15:31. *Likewise* also the chief priests
Lu. 3:11. let him do *likewise.*
5:10. And *so* (was) also James, and John,
33. and *likewise* (the disciples) of the
6:31. do ye also to them *likewise.*
10:32. And *likewise* a Levite,
37. Go, and do thou *likewise.*
13: 5. ye shall all *likewise* perish.
16:25. *likewise* Lazarus evil things:
17:28. *Likewise* also as it was in the days
31. let him *likewise* not return back.
22:36. and *likewise* (his) scrip:
Joh. 5:19. these also doeth the Son *likewise.*
6:11. and *likewise* of the fishes as much
21:13. and giveth them, and fish *likewise.*
Ro. 1:27. *likewise* also the men,
1Co. 7: 3. *likewise* also the wife unto the
4. *likewise* also the husband hath
22. *likewise* also he that is called,
Heb 9:21. he sprinkled (lit. he sprinkled *likewise*) with blood
Jas. 2:25. *Likewise* also was not Rahab
1Pet.3: 1. *Likewise,* ye wives, (be) in
7. *Likewise,* ye husbands, dwell with
5: 5. *Likewise,* ye younger, submit
Jude 8. *Likewise* also these (ο. μεντοι)
Rev. 8:12. and the night *likewise.*

3669 1 571/695 5:186 3666

ὁμοίωσις, *homoiōsis.*

Jas. 3: 9. are made after the *similitude* of God.

3670 23 571/695 5:199 3056 rt 3674

ὁμολογέω, *homologeo.*

Mat. 7:23. then *will* I *profess* unto them,
10:32. *shall confess* me before men, him *will* I *confess* also before my Father
14: 7. he *promised* with an oath
Lu. 12: 8. *shall confess* me before men, him *shall* the Son of man also *confess*
Joh. 1:20. he *confessed,* and denied not; but *confessed,* I am not the Christ.
9:22. that if any man did *confess* that he was Christ,
12:42. because of the Pharisees they *did* no *confess* (him),
Acts23: 8. but the Pharisees *confess* both.
24:14. But this I *confess* unto thee,
Ro. 10: 9. if thou *shalt confess* with thy mouth
10. with the mouth *confession is made*
1Ti. 6:12. and *hast professed* a good profession
Tit. 1:16. They *profess* that they know God;
Heb 11:13. and *confessed* that they were strangers
13:15. of (our) lips *giving thanks* to his name
1Joh.1: 9. If we *confess* our sins,
4: 2. Every spirit that *confesseth*
3. every spirit that *confesseth* not
15. Whosoever *shall confess* that Jesus is
2Joh. 7. *who confess* not that Jesus Christ

3671 6 571/695 5:199 rt 3670

ὁμολογία, *homologia.*

2Co. 9:13. for your *professed* subjection
1Ti. 6:12. hast professed a good *profession*
13. witnessed a good *confession;*
Heb 3: 1. and high priest of our *profession,*
4:14. let us hold fast (our) *profession.*
10:23. Let us hold fast the *profession* of

3672 1 572/695 5:199 3670

ὁμολογουμένως, *homologoumenōs.*

1Ti. 3:16. And *without controversy* great is

3673 1 572/695 rt 3674,5078

ὁμότεχνος, *homoteknos.*

Acts18: 3. because he was *of the same craft,*

3674 3 572/695 *homos* (same)

ὁμοῦ, *homou*

Joh. 4:36. that reapeth may rejoice *together.*
20: 4. So they ran both *together:*
21: 2. There were *together* Simon Peter, and

3675 1 572/695 rt 3674,5424

ὁμόφρων, *homophrōn.*

1Pet.3: 8. Finally, (be ye) all *of one mind,*

ὀμόσαι see ὄμνυμι. 3660

3676 3 572/695 rt 3674

ὅμως, *homōs.*

Joh.12:42. *Nevertheless* among the (ο. μεντοι)
1Co.14: 7. *And even* things without life
Gal. 3:15. *Though* (it be) *but* a man's covenant,

3677 6 572/696 5:220

ὄναρ, *onar.*

Mat. 1:20. appeared unto him in a *dream,*
2:12. being warned of God in a *dream*
13. appeareth to Joseph in a *dream,*
19. appeareth in a *dream* to Joseph
22. being warned of God in a *dream,*
27:19. this day in a *dream* because of him.

3678 1 573/696 5:283 3688

ὀνάριον, *onarion.*

Joh. 12:14. when he had found a *young ass,*

3679 10 573/696 5:238 3681

ὀνειδίζω, *onīdizo.*

Mat. 5:11. when (men) *shall revile* you,
11:20. Then began he *to upbraid* the cities
27:44. *cast* the same *in* his *teeth.*
Mar 15:32. were crucified with him *reviled* him.
16:14. and *upbraided* them with their
Lu. 6:22. and *shall reproach* (you),
Ro. 15: 3. of them *that reproached* thee fell on me.
1Ti. 4:10. we both labour and *suffer reproach,*
Jas. 1: 5. and *upbraideth* not;
1Pet 4:14. If ye *be reproached* for the name

3680 5 573/696 5:238 3679

ὀνειδισμός, *onīdismos.*

Ro. 15: 3. The *reproaches* of them that
1Ti. 3: 7. lest he fall into *reproach*
Heb 10:33. both by *reproaches* and afflictions;
11:26. Esteeming the *reproach* of Christ
13:13. bearing his *reproach.*

3681 1 573/696 5:238 cf 1097

ὄνειδος, *onīdos.*

Lu. 1:25. to take away my *reproach* among men.

3685 1 573/696

ὄνημι, *oneemi.*

Philem. 20. let me *have joy* of thee in the Lord:

3684 2 573/696 3688

ὀνικός, *onikos.*

Mat 18: 6. that a millstone (lit. a mill turned *by an ass*) were hanged
Lu. 17: 2. that a millstone (lit. a mill turned &c.) were

3686 230 573/696 5:242 rt 1097

ὄνομα, *onoma.*

Mat. 1:21. thou shalt call his *name* JESUS:
23. they shall call his *name* Emmanuel,
25. and he called his *name* JESUS.
6: 9. Hallowed be thy *name.*
7:22. have we not prophesied in thy *name?* and in thy *name* have cast out devils? and in thy *name* done
10: 2. Now the *names* of the twelve
22. hated of all (men) for my *name's* sake:
41. in the *name* of a prophet
— in the *name* of a righteous man
42. in the *name* of a disciple,
12:21. And in his *name* shall the Gentiles trust.
18: 5. one such little child in my *name*
20. are gathered together in my *name,*
19:29. for my *name's* sake, shall receive
21: 9. that cometh in the *name* of the Lord;
23:39. he that cometh in the *name* of the Lord.
24: 5. many shall come in my *name,*
9. of all nations for my *name's* sake.
27:32. a man of Cyrene, Simon by *name:*
57. rich man of Arimathæa, *named* Joseph,
28:19. in the *name* of the Father, and
Mar 3:16. Simon he surnamed (lit. added the *name*) Peter;
Mar 3:17. he surnamed (lit. added the *name* to) them Boanerges,
5: 9. What (is) thy *name?*
— My *name* (is) Legion:
22. rulers of the synagogue, Jairus by *name;*
6:14. for his *name* was spread abroad:
9:37. one of such children in my *name,*
38. casting out devils in thy *name,*
39. which shall do a miracle in my *name,*
41. water to drink in my *name,*
11: 9. that cometh in the *name* of the Lord:
10. that cometh in the *name* of the Lord:
13: 6. many shall come in my *name,*
13. for my *name's* sake:
14:32. which was named (lit. of which the *name* was) Gethsemane:
16:17. In my *name* shall they cast out devils;
Lu. 1: 5. a certain priest *named* Zacharias,
— and her *name* (was) Elisabeth.
13. thou shalt call his *name* John.
26. a city of Galilee, *named* Nazareth,
27. to a man whose *name* was Joseph,
— the virgin's *name* (was) Mary.
31. and shalt call his *name* JESUS.
49. and holy (is) his *name.*
59. after the *name* of his father.
61. that is called by this *name.*
63. His *name* is John.
2:21. his *name* was called JESUS,
25. whose *name* (was) Simeon;
5:27. saw a publican, *named* Levi,
6:22. and cast out your *name* as evil.
8:30. What is thy *name?*
41. there came a man *named* Jairus,
9:48. this child in my *name*
49. casting out devils in thy *name;*
10:17. are subject unto us through thy *name.*
20. because your *names* are written in
38. *named* (lit. by *name*) Martha
11: 2. Hallowed be thy *name.*
13:35. that cometh in the *name* of the Lord.
16:20. a certain beggar *named* Lazarus,
19: 2. *named* (lit. by *name* called) Zacchæus,
38. that cometh in the *name* of the Lord:
21: 8. many shall come in my *name,*
12. for my *name's* sake.
17. hated of all (men) for my *name's* sake.
23:50. a man *named* Joseph,
24:13. to a village *called* Emmaus,
18. whose *name* was Cleopas,
47. should be preached in his *name*
Joh. 1: 6. whose *name* (was) John.
12. to them that believe on his *name:*
2:23. many believed in his *name,*
3: 1. *named* Nicodemus, (lit. N. his *name*)
18. hath not believed in the *name* of
5:43. I am come in my Father's *name,*
— if another shall come in his own *name.*
10: 3. he calleth his own sheep by *name,*
25. that I do in my Father's *name,*
12:13. that cometh in the *name* of the Lord.
28. Father, glorify thy *name.*
14:13. whatsoever ye shall ask in my *name,*
14. shall ask any thing in my *name,*
26. the Father will send in my *name,*
15:16. shall ask of the Father in my *name,*
21. do unto you for my *name's* sake,
16:23. ye shall ask the Father in my *name,*
24. have ye asked nothing in my *name:*
26. ye shall ask in my *name:*
17: 6. I have manifested thy *name* unto
11. keep through thine own *name*

Joh. 17:12. I kept them in thy *name:*
26. I have declared unto them thy *name*.
18:10. The servant's *name* was Malchus.
20:31. might have life through his *name*.
Acts 1:15. the number of the *names* together
2:21. shall call on the *name* of the Lord
38. in the *name* of Jesus Christ for
3: 6. In the *name* of Jesus Christ of
16. And his *name* through faith in his *name* hath made this man strong,
4: 7. or by what *name*, have ye done this?
10. that by the *name* of Jesus Christ
12. there is none other *name* under
17. to no man in this *name*.
18. nor teach in the *name* of Jesus.
30. by the *name* of thy holy child Jesus.
5: 1. a certain man *named* Ananias,
28. that ye should not teach in this *name?*
34. a Pharisee, *named* Gamaliel,
40. should not speak in the *name* of Jesus,
41. worthy to suffer shame for his *name*.
8: 9. there was a certain man, *called* Simon,
12. and the *name* of Jesus Christ,
16. baptized in the *name* of the Lord Jesus.
9:10. *named* (lit. by *name*) Ananias;
11. for (one) *called* Saul, (lit. by *name* Saul)
12. a man *named* Ananias coming in,
14. to bind all that call on thy *name*.
15. to bear my *name* before the Gentiles,
16. he must suffer for my *name's* sake.
21. which called on this *name* in Jerusalem,
27. at Damascus in the *name* of Jesus.
29(28) spake boldly in the *name* of the Lord
33. a certain man *named* Æneas,
36. a certain disciple *named* Tabitha,
10: 1. *called* (lit. by *name*) Cornelius,
43. that through his *name* whosoever
48. to be baptized in the *name* of the Lord.
11:28. one of them *named* Agabus,
12:13. came to hearken, *named* Rhoda.
13: 6. a Jew, whose *name* (was) Bar-jesus:
8. for so is his *name* by interpretation
15:14. out of them a people for his *name*.
17. upon whom my *name* is called,
26. for the *name* of our Lord Jesus
16: 1. disciple was there, *named* Timotheus,
14. *named* Lydia, a seller of purple,
18. in the *name* of Jesus Christ
17:34. and a woman *named* Damaris,
18: 2. *named* Aquila, born in Pontus,
7. *named* Justus, (one) that worshipped God,
15. if it be a question of words and *names*,
24. *named* Apollos, born at Alexandria,
19: 5. baptized in the *name* of the Lord Jesus.
13. which had evil spirits the *name* of
17. and the *name* of the Lord Jesus was
24. *named* Demetrius, a silversmith,
20: 9. *named* Eutychus, being fallen into a deep
21:10. a certain prophet, *named* Agabus.
13. for the *name* of the Lord Jesus.
22:16. calling on the *name* of the Lord.
26: 9. contrary to the *name* of Jesus of
27: 1. *named* Julius, a centurion
28: 7. whose *name* was Publius;
Ro. 1: 5. among all nations, for his *name:*
2:24. For the *name* of God is blasphemed
9:17. that my *name* might be declared
10:13. shall call upon the *name* of the Lord
15: 9. and sing unto thy *name*.
1Co. 1: 2. in every place call upon the *name* of
10. by the *name* of our Lord Jesus
13. were ye baptized in the *name* of Paul?
1Co. 1:15. I had baptized in mine own *name*.
5: 4. In the *name* of our Lord Jesus
6:11. in the *name* of the Lord Jesus,
Eph. 1:21. and every *name* that is named,
5:20. in the *name* of our Lord Jesus
Phi. 2: 9. a *name* which is above every *name:*
10. That at the *name* of Jesus every knee
4: 3. whose *names* (are) in the book of life.
Col. 3:17. (do) all in the *name* of the Lord
2Th. 1:12. That the *name* of our Lord Jesus
3: 6. in the *name* of our Lord Jesus
1Ti. 6: 1. that the *name* of God and (his) doctrine
2Ti. 2:19. that nameth the *name* of Christ
Heb 1: 4. a more excellent *name* than they.
2:12. I will declare thy *name* unto
6:10. ye have shewed toward his *name*,
13:15. giving thanks to his *name*.
Jas. 2: 7. that worthy *name* by the which
5:10. who have spoken in the *name* of the Lord,
14. with oil in the *name* of the Lord:
1Pet. 4:14. If ye be reproached for the *name* of Christ,
1Joh. 2:12. forgiven you for his *name's* sake.
3:23. That we should believe on the *name* of
5:13. believe on the *name* of the Son of God;
— may believe on the *name* of the Son of
3Joh. 7. for his *name's* sake they went forth.
14(15). Greet the friends by *name*.
Rev. 2: 3. for my *name's* sake hast laboured,
13. thou holdest fast my *name*,
17. and in the stone a new *name*
3: 1. thou hast a *name* that thou livest,
4. Thou hast a few *names* even in Sardis
5. I will not blot out his *name*
— but I will confess his *name* before
8. and hast not denied my *name*.
12. the *name* of my God, and the *name* of the city of my God,
— my new *name*.
6: 8. his *name* that sat on him was Death,
8:11. the *name* of the star is called
9:11. whose *name* in the Hebrew tongue
— hath (his) *name* Apollyon.
11:13. were slain)(of men seven thousand:
18. and them that fear thy *name*,
13: 1. upon his heads, the *name* of blasphemy.
6. to blaspheme his *name*, and his
8. whose *names* are not written in
17. or the *name* of the beast, or the number of his *name*.
14: 1. having his Father's *name* written in
11. receiveth the mark of his *name*.
15: 2. (and) over the number of his *name*,
4. O Lord, and glorify thy *name?*
16: 9. and blasphemed the *name* of God,
17: 3. full of *names* of blasphemy,
5. upon her forehead (was) a *name*
8. whose *names* were not written in
19:12. he had a *name* written, that no
13. his *name* is called The Word of God.
16. and on his thigh a *name* written,
21:12. and *names* written thereon,
14. in them the *names* of the twelve apostles.
22: 4. his *name* (shall be) in their foreheads.

3687 10 577/699 5:242 3686

ὀνομάζω, *onomazo.*

Lu. 6:13. whom also he *named* apostles;
14. Simon, whom he also *named* Peter,
Acts 19:13. to *call* over them which had evil spirits
Ro. 15:20. not where Christ *was named*, lest

1Co. 5: 1. as *is* not so much as *named* among
11. if any man *that is called* a brother be
Eph 1:21. and every name *that is named*,
3:15. family in heaven and earth *is named*,
5: 3. *let* it not *be* once *named* among you,
2Ti. 2:19. Let every one *that nameth* the name

3688 6 577/699 5:283

ὄνος, onos.

Mat.21: 2. ye shall find an *ass* tied,
5. meek, and sitting upon an *ass*,
7. And brought the *ass*,
Lu. 13:15. loose his ox or (his) *ass* from the stall,
14: 5. Which of you shall have an *ass* or
Joh.12:15. sitting on an *ass's* colt.

ὄντα, ὄντας, &c. see under ὤν. 5607

3689 10 577/699 5607(1510)

ὄντως, ontōs.

Mar 11:32. that he was a prophet *indeed*.
Lu. 23:47. *Certainly* this was a righteous man.
24:34. The Lord is risen *indeed*,
Joh. 8:36. ye shall be free *indeed*.
1Co.14:25. that God is in you *of a truth*.
Gal. 3:21. *verily* righteousness should have
1Ti. 5: 3. Honour widows that are widows *indeed*.
5. Now she that is a widow *indeed*,
16. relieve them that are widows *indeed*.
2Pet. 2:18. those that were *clean* escaped

3690 7 577/699 3691

ὄξος, oxos.

Mat.27:34. gave him *vinegar* to drink mingled
48. and filled (it) with *vinegar*,
Mar 15:36. and filled a spunge full of *vinegar*,
Lu. 23:36. and offering him *vinegar*,
Joh.19:29. a vessel full of *vinegar*: and they filled a spunge with *vinegar*,
30. had received the *vinegar*, he said,

3691 8 578/699 5:288 cf rt 188

ὀξύς, oxus.

Ro. 3:15. Their feet (are) *swift* to shed blood:
Rev. 1:16. went a *sharp* twoedged sword:
2:12. which hath the *sharp* sword
14:14. and in his hand a *sharp* sickle.
17. he also having a *sharp* sickle.
18. to him that had the *sharp* sickle, saying, Thrust in thy *sharp* sickle,
19:15. out of his mouth goeth a *sharp* sword,

3692 2 578/699 3700

ὀπή, opee.

Heb 11:38. and (in) dens and *caves* of the earth.
Jas 3:11. at the same *place* sweet (water) and

3693 7 578/699 5:289 opis (regard)

ὄπισθεν, opisthen.

Mat. 9:20. came *behind* (him), and touched
15:23. for she crieth *after* us.
Mar 5:27. came in the press *behind*, and touched
Lu. 8:44. Came *behind* (him), and touched
23:26. that he might bear (it) *after* Jesus.
Rev. 4: 6. full of eyes before and *behind*.
5: 1. written within and on the *backside*,

3694 36 578/699 5:289 opis (regard)

ὀπίσω, opiso.

Mat. 3:11. but he that cometh *after* me
4:19. Follow me, (lit. come *after* me)
10:38. and followeth *after* me,
16:23. Get thee *behind* me, Satan:
24. If any (man) will come *after* me,
24:18. return *back* to take his clothes.
Mar 1: 7. cometh one mightier than I *after* me,
17. Come ye *after* me,
20. and went *after* him.
8:33. Get thee *behind* me, Satan:
34. Whosoever will come *after* me,
13:16. that is in the field not turn *back*
Lu. 4: 8. Get thee *behind* me, Satan:
7:38. And stood at his feet *behind* (him)
9:23. If any (man) will come *after* me,
62. and looking *back*, is fit for the
14:27. and come *after* me, cannot be
17:31. let him likewise not return *back*.
19:14. and sent a message *after* him,
21: 8. go ye not therefore *after* them.
Joh. 1:15. He that cometh *after* me is
27. He it is, who coming *after* me is
30. *After* me cometh a man which is
6:66. many of his disciples went *back*,
12:19. the world is gone *after* him.
18: 6. they went *backward*, and fell to the
20:14. she turned herself *back*,
Acts 5:37. drew away much people *after* him:
20:30. to draw away disciples *after* them.
Phi. 3:13(14). forgetting those things which are *behind*,
1Ti. 5:15. are already turned aside *after* Satan.
2Pet. 2:10. that walk *after* the flesh in
Jude 7. and going *after* strange flesh,
Rev. 1:10. and heard *behind* me a great voice,
12:15. as a flood *after* the woman,
13: 3. all the world wondered *after* the beast.

3696 5 579/700 5:292 hepō (to be busy about)

ὅπλα, hopla.

Joh.18: 3. and torches and *weapons*.
Ro. 6:13. (as) *instruments* of unrighteousness
— (as) *instruments* of righteousness
13:12. let us put on the *armour* of light.
2Co. 6: 7. by the *armour* of righteousness
10: 4. For the *weapons* of our warfare

3695 1 578/700 5:292 3696

ὁπλίζομαι, hoplizomai.

1Pet.4: 1. *arm yourselves* likewise *with* the same

3697 5 579/700 3739,4169

ὁποῖος, hopoios.

Acts26:29. and altogether such *as* I am,
1Co. 3:13. every man's work *of what sort* it is.
Gal. 2: 6. *whatsoever* they were, it maketh no
1Th. 1: 9. *what manner of* entering in we had
Jas 1:24. forgetteth *what manner of* man he was.

3698 1 579/700 3739,4218

ὁπότε, hopote.

Lu. 6: 3. *when* himself was an hungred.

3699 82 579/700 3739,4225

ὅπου, hopou.

Mat. 6:19. *where* moth and rust doth corrupt, and *where* thieves break through and steal:
20. *where* neither moth nor rust doth corrupt, and *where* thieves do not break
21. For *where* your treasure is, there
8:19. I will follow thee *whither*soever thou
13: 5. *where* they had not much earth:
24:28. *where*soever the carcase is, there
25:24. reaping *where* thou hast not sown,
26. that I reap *where* I sowed not,
26:13. *Where*soever this gospel shall be
57. *where* the scribes and the elders were
28: 6. Come, see the place *where* the Lord lay.
Mar 2: 4. uncovered the roof *where* he was:
4: 5. *where* it had not much earth;
15. *where* the word is sown;
5:40. entereth in *where* the damsel was
6:10. *In what place* soever ye enter
55. *where* they heard he was.
56. And *whither*soever he entered,
9:18. *where*soever he taketh him,
44. *Where* their worm dieth not,
46. *Where* their worm dieth not,
48. *Where* their worm dieth not,
13:14. standing *where* it ought not,
14: 9. *Where*soever this gospel shall be
14. *where*soever he shall go in,
— *where* I shall eat the passover
16: 6. behold the place *where* they laid him.
Lu. 9:57. *whither*soever thou goest.
12:33. *where* no thief approacheth,
34. For *where* your treasure is,
17:37. *Wheresoever* the body (is), thither
22:11. *where* I shall eat the passover
Joh. 1:28. *where* John was baptizing.
3: 8. The wind bloweth *where* it listeth,
4:20. *where* men ought to worship.
46. *where* he made the water wine.
6:23. unto the place *where* they did eat bread,
62. ascend up *where* he was before?
7:34. *where* I am, (thither) ye cannot come.
36. and *where* I am, (thither) ye cannot
42. of Bethlehem, *where* David was?
8:21. *whither* I go, ye cannot come.
22. *Whither* I go, ye cannot come.
10:40. *where* John at first baptized;
11:30. was in that place *where* Martha met him.
32. when Mary was come *where* Jesus
12: 1. *where* Lazarus was which had been
26. *where* I am, there shall also my
13:33. *Whither* I go, ye cannot come;
36. *Whither* I go, thou canst not
14: 3. that *where* I am, (there) ye may be
4. And *whither* I go ye know,
17:24. be with me *where* I am;
18: 1. *where* was a garden,
20. *whither* the Jews always resort;
19:18. *Where* they crucified him, and
20. for the place *where* Jesus was
41. in the place *where* he was
20:12. *where* the body of Jesus had lain.
19. *where* the disciples were assembled
21:18. and walkedst *whither* thou wouldest:
— and carry (thee) *whither* thou wouldest not.
Acts17: 1. *where* was a synagogue of the Jews:
Ro. 15:20. not *where* Christ was named, lest
1Co. 3: 3. for *whereas* (there is) among you
Col. 3:11. *Where* there is neither Greek nor
Heb 6:20. *Whither* the forerunner is for us
Heb 9.16. For *where* a testament (is), there
10:18. Now *where* remission of these (is),
Jas. 3: 4. *whither*soever the governor listeth.
16. For *where* envying and strife (is),
2Pet. 2:11. *Whereas* angels, which are greater
Rev. 2:13. *where* Satan's seat (is):
— *where* Satan dwelleth.
11: 8. *where* also our Lord was crucified.
12 6. *where* she hath a place prepared
14. *where* she is nourished for a time, and
14: 4. follow the Lamb *whither*soever he goeth
17: 9. on which the woman sitteth. (lit. *where* the woman sitteth on them)
20:10. *where* the beast and the false prophet

3700 1 580/701 5:315

ὀπτάνομαι, optanomai.

Acts 1: 3. *being seen* of them forty days,

3701 4 580/701 5:315 3700

ὀπτασία, optasia.

Lu. 1:22. that he had seen a *vision* in the temple
24:23. they had also seen a *vision* of angels,
Acts26:19. disobedient unto the heavenly *vision:*
2Co.12: 1. I will come to *visions* and revelations

3700 58 580/702 (3708),cf 991, cf 1492,cf 2300,cf 2334,cf 4648

ὄπτομαι, optomai.

Mat. 5: 8. for they *shall see* God.
17: 3. there *appeared* unto them Moses and
24:30. they *shall see* the Son of man
26:64. Hereafter *shall* ye *see* the Son of man
27: 4. *see* thou (to that).
24. of this just person: *see* ye (to it).
28: 7. there *shall* ye *see* him:
10. and there *shall* they *see* me.
Mar 9: 4. there *appeared* unto them Elias with
13:26. then *shall* they *see* the Son of man
14:62. ye *shall see* the Son of man sitting on
16: 7. there *shall* ye *see* him,
Lu. 1:11. there *appeared* unto him an angel
3: 6. all flesh *shall see* the salvation
9:31. Who *appeared* in glory, *and* spake
13:28. when ye *shall see* Abraham,
17:22. and ye *shall* not *see* (it).
21:27. then *shall* they *see* the Son of man
22:43. And there *appeared* an angel
24:34. and *hath appeared* to Simon.
Joh. 1:50(51). thou *shalt see* greater things than
51(52). Hereafter ye *shall see* heaven open
3:36. believeth not the Son *shall* not *see* life;
11:40. thou shouldest *see* the glory of God?
16:16. and ye *shall see* me,
17. a little while, and ye *shall see* me:
19. a little while, and ye *shall see* me?
22. but I *will see* you again,
19:37. They *shall look* on him whom they
Acts 2: 3. there *appeared* unto them cloven tongues
17. your young men *shall see* visions,
7: 2. The God of glory *appeared* unto our
26. he *shewed himself* unto them as
30. there *appeared* to him in the
35. of the angel *which appeared* to him in the bush.
9:17. Jesus, *that appeared* unto thee
13:31. he *was seen* many days of them

Acts16: 9. a vision *appeared* to Paul
18:15. *look* ye (to it); for I will be no
20:25. *shall see* my face no more.
26:16. I *have appeared* unto thee for this
— in the which I *will appear* unto thee;
Ro. 15:21. not spoken of, they *shall see:*
1Co.15: 5. And that he *was seen* of Cephas,
6. After that, he *was seen* of above
7. After that, he *was seen* of James;
8. And last of all he *was seen* of me
1Ti. 3:16. *seen* of angels, preached unto the
Heb 9:28. unto them that look for him *shall* he *appear*
12:14. without which no man *shall see* the Lord:
13:23. with whom, if he come shortly, I *will see* you.
1 Joh. 3: 2. for we *shall see* him as he is.
Rev. 1: 7. and every eye *shall see* him,
11:19. there *was seen* in his temple the ark
12: 1. And there *appeared* a great wonder in
3. there *appeared* another wonder
22: 4. And they *shall see* his face;

3702 1 580/701 *hepsō* (to "steep")

ὀπτός, optos.

Lu. 24:42. they gave him a piece of a *broiled* fish,

3703 1 580/701 rt 3796,5610

ὀπώρα, opōra.

Rev.18:14. And the *fruits* that thy soul lusted after

3704 56 580/701 3739,4459

ὅπως, hopōs.

Mat. 2: 8. *that* I may come and worship him
23. *that* it might be fulfilled which
5:16. *that* they may see your good works,
45. *That* ye may be the children of your
6: 2. *that* they may have glory of men.
4. *That* thine alms may be in secret:
5. *that* they may be seen of men.
16. *that* they may appear unto men to fast.
18. *That* thou appear not unto men to
8:17. *That* it might be fulfilled which
34. *that* he would depart out of their
9:38. *that* he will send forth labourers
12:14. *how* they might destroy him.
17. *That* it might be fulfilled which
13:35. *That* it might be fulfilled which
22:15. *how* they might entangle him
23:35. *That* upon you may come all the
26:59. *to* put him to death; (lit. *that* they might &c.)
Mar 3: 6. *how* they might destroy him.
5:23. *that* she may be healed;
Lu. 2:35. *that* the thoughts of many hearts may
7: 3. *that* he would come and heal his
10: 2. *that* he would send forth labourers
11:37. besought him *to* dine with him:
16:26. *so that* they which would pass
28. *that* he may testify unto them,
24:20. And *how* the chief priests and
Joh. 11:57. *that* they might take him.
Acts 3:19. *when* the times of refreshing shall come (lit. *that* the times...may come)
8:15. *that* they might receive the Holy Ghost:
24. *that* none of these things which ye
9: 2. *that* if he found any of this way,
Acts 9:12. *that* he might receive his sight.
17. *that* thou mightest receive thy sight,
24. day and night *to* kill him.
15:17. *That* the residue of men might
20:16. *because* he would not spend the time
23:15. *that* he bring him down unto you
20. *that* thou wouldest bring down Paul
23. *to* go to Cæsarea,
24:26. *that* he might loose him:
25: 3. *that* he would send for him to
26. *that*, after examination had, I might
Ro. 3: 4. *That* thou mightest be justified
9:17. *that* I might shew my power in thee, and *that* my name might be
1Co. 1:29. *That* no flesh should glory in his
2Co. 8:11. *that* as (there was) a readiness
14. *that* there may be equality:
Gal. 1: 4. *that* he might deliver us from
2Th. 1:12. *That* the name of our Lord Jesus
Philem. 6. *That* the communication of thy faith
Heb 2: 9. *that* he by the grace of God should
9:15. *that* by means of death, for the
Jas. 5:16. *that* ye may be healed.
1Pet. 2: 9. *that* ye should shew forth the

3705 12 580/701 5:315 3708

ὅραμα, horama.

Mat.17: 9. Tell the *vision* to no man,
Acts 7:31. he wondered at the *sight:*
9:10. to him said the Lord in a *vision,*
12. And hath seen in a *vision* a man
10: 3. He saw in a *vision* evidently
17. what this *vision* which he had
19. While Peter thought on the *vision,*
11: 5. and in a trance I saw a *vision,*
12: 9. but thought he saw a *vision.*
16: 9. a *vision* appeared to Paul in the night;
10. And after he had seen the *vision,*
18: 9. to Paul in the night by a *vision,*

3706 4 581/702 5:315 3708

ὅρασις, horasis.

Acts 2:17. your young men shall see *visions,*
Rev. 4: 3. was *to look upon* like a jasper and
— *in sight* like unto an emerald.
9:17. I saw the horses in the *vision,*

3707 1 581/702 5:315 3708

ὁρατός, horatos.

Col. 1:16. *visible* and invisible, whether

3708 59 581/702 5:315

ὁράω, horao.

Mat. 8: 4. *See* thou tell no man;
9:30. *See* (that) no man know (it).
16: 6. *Take heed* and beware of the leaven
18:10. *Take heed* that ye despise not one
24: 6. *see* that ye be not troubled:
Mar 1:44. *See* thou say nothing to any man:
8:15. *Take heed,* beware of the leaven
24. I see men as)(trees, walking.
Lu. 1:22. perceived that he *had seen* a vision
9:36. those things which they *had seen.*
12:15. *Take heed,* and beware of covetousness:
16:23. and *seeth* Abraham afar off.

Lu. 23:49. stood afar off, *beholding* these things.
24:23. saying, that they *had* also *seen* a vision
Joh. 1:18. No man *hath seen* God at any time;
34. And I *saw*, and bare record that
3:11. and testify that we *have seen*;
32. what he *hath seen* and heard,
4:45. *having seen* all the things that he did
5:37. nor *seen* his shape.
6: 2. because they *saw* his miracles
36. ye also *have seen* me, and believe not.
46. Not that any man *hath seen* the Father,
— he *hath seen* the Father.
8:38. I speak that which I *have seen*
— ye do that which ye *have seen*
57. and *hast* thou *seen* Abraham?
9:37. Thou *hast* both *seen* him, and it is he
14: 7. ye know him, and *have seen* him.
9. he that *hath seen* me *hath seen* the Father;
15:24. now *have* they both *seen* and hated
19:35. And he *that saw* (it) bare record,
20:18. that she *had seen* the Lord,
25. We *have seen* the Lord.
29. because thou *hast seen* me,
Acts 7:44. to the fashion that he *had seen*.
8:23. I *perceive* that thou art in the
22:15. of what thou *hast seen* and heard.
26. *Take heed* what thou doest:
1Co. 9: 1. *have* I not *seen* Jesus Christ our Lord?
Col. 2: 1. as many as *have* not *seen* my face
18. things which he *hath* not *seen*,
1Th. 5:15. *See* that none render evil for evil
Heb 2: 8. But now we *see* not yet all things put
8: 5. *See*, saith he, (that) thou make
11:27. as *seeing* him who is invisible.
Jas. 2:24. Ye *see* then how that by works
1Pet.1: 8. *though* now ye *see* (him) not,
1Joh 1: 1. which we *have seen* with our eyes,
2. we *have seen* (it), and bear witness,
3. That which we *have seen* and heard
3: 6. *hath* not *seen* him, neither known him.
4:20. his brother whom he *hath seen*, how can he love God whom he *hath* not *seen*?
3Joh. 11. he that doeth evil *hath* not *seen* God.
Rev.18:18. *when* they *saw* the smoke of her
19:10. *See* (thou do it) not: I am thy
22: 9. saith he unto me, *See* (thou do it) not:

3709 36 582/703 5:382 3713

ὀργή, orgee.

Mat. 3: 7. to flee from the *wrath* to come?
Mar 3: 5. round about on them with *anger*,
Lu. 3: 7. to flee from the *wrath* to come?
21:23. and *wrath* upon this people.
Joh. 3:36. but the *wrath* of God abideth on him.
Ro. 1:18. For the *wrath* of God is revealed
2: 5. treasurest up unto thyself *wrath* against the day of *wrath*
8. unrighteousness, indignation and *wrath*,
3: 5. God unrighteous who taketh *vengeance*?
4:15. the law worketh *wrath*:
5: 9. be saved from *wrath* through him.
9:22. if God, willing to shew (his) *wrath*,
— the vessels of *wrath* fitted to destruction:
12:19. but (rather) give place unto *wrath*:
13: 4. to (execute) *wrath* upon him that doeth evil.
5. not only for *wrath*, but also
Eph. 2: 3. by nature the children of *wrath*,
4:31. and wrath, and *anger*, and clamour,
5: 6. because of these things cometh the *wrath*
Col. 3: 6. For which things' sake the *wrath* of God
3: 8. put off all these, *anger*, wrath,
1Th. 1:10. which delivered us from the *wrath*
2:16. for the *wrath* is come upon them
5: 9. God hath not appointed us to *wrath*,
1Ti. 2: 8. without *wrath* and doubting.
Heb 3:11. So I sware in my *wrath*,
4: 3. As I have sworn in my *wrath*,
Jas. 1:19. slow to speak, slow to *wrath*:
20. For the *wrath* of man worketh not
Rev. 6:16. and from the *wrath* of the Lamb:
17. For the great day of his *wrath* is come;
11:18. and thy *wrath* is come,
14:10. into the cup of his *indignation*;
16:19. the wine of the fierceness of his *wrath*
19:15. and *wrath* of Almighty God.

3710 8 583/703 5:382 3709

ὀργίζομαι, orgizomai.

Mat. 5:22. *who*soever *is angry* with his brother
18:34. his lord *was wroth, and* delivered
22: 7. he *was wroth*: and he sent forth
Lu. 14:21. the master of the house *being angry*
15:28. he *was angry*, and would not go in.
Eph. 4:26. *Be* ye *angry*, and sin not:
Rev.11:18. the nations *were angry*,
12:17. the dragon *was wroth* with the woman,

3711 1 583/703 5:382 3709

ὀργίλος, orgilos.

Tit. 1: 7. not *soon angry*, not given to wine,

3712 2 583/703 3713

ὀργυιά, orgwya.

Acts27:28. and found (it) twenty *fathoms*:
— and found (it) fifteen *fathoms*.

3713 3 583/703 5:447

ὀρέγομαι, oregomai.

1Ti. 3: 1. If a man *desire* the office of a bishop,
6:10. which *while* some *coveted after*, they
Heb 11:16. But now they *desire* a better

3714 2 583/704 3735

ὀρεινός, orīnos.

Lu. 1:39. and went into the *hill* country
65. throughout all the *hill* country

3715 1 583/704 5:447 3713

ὄρεξις, orexis.

Ro. 1:27. burned in their *lust* one toward

3716 1 583/704 5:449 3717,4228

ὀρθοποδέω, orthopodeo.

Gal. 2:14. that they *walked* not *uprightly*

3717 2 583/704 5:449 rt 3735

ὀρθός, orthos.

Acts14:10. Stand *upright* on thy feet.
Heb 12:13. make *straight* paths for your feet.

3718 1 584/704 8:106 3717 rt5114

ὀρθοτομέω, orthotomeo.

2Ti. 2:15. *rightly dividing* the word of truth.

3719 1 584/704 3722

ὀρθρίζω, *orthrizo.*

Lu. 21:38. all the people *came early in the morning*

3720 1 584/704 3722

ὀρθρινός, *orthrinos.*

Rev 22:16. the bright and *morning* star.

3721 1 584/704 3722

ὄρθριος, *orthrios.*

Lu. 24:22. which were *early* at the sepulchre;

3722 3 584/704 rt 3735

ὄρθρος, *orthros.*

Lu. 24: 1. very *early in the morning*, they came
Joh. 8: 2. *early in the morning* he came again
Acts 5:21. into the temple *early in the morning*,

3723 4 584/704 3717

ὀρθῶς, *orthōs.*

Mar 7:35. and he spake *plain*.
Lu. 7:43. Thou hast *rightly* judged.
10:28. Thou hast answered *right:*
20:21. thou sayest and teachest *rightly*,

3725 11 584/704 *horos* (limit)

ὅρια, *horia.*

Mat. 2:16. and in all the *coasts* thereof,
4:13. in the *borders* of Zabulon and
8:34. would depart out of their *coasts*.
15:22. out of the same *coasts*, and cried
39. came into the *coasts* of Magdala.
19: 1. and came into the *coasts* of Judæa
Mar 5:17. to depart out of their *coasts*.
7:31. from the *coasts* of Tyre and Sidon,
— the midst of the *coasts* of Decapolis.
10: 1. and cometh into the *coasts* of Judæa
Acts13:50. expelled them out of their *coasts*.

3724 8 584/704 5:452 3725

ὁρίζω, *horizo.*

Lu. 22:22. as it *was determined:*
Acts 2:23. by the *determinate* counsel and
10:42. *which was ordained* of God (to be) the Judge
11:29. *determined* to send relief unto
17:26. *and hath determined* the times
31. by (that) man whom he *hath ordained;*
Ro. 1: 4. And *declared* (to be) the Son of God with power,
Heb 4: 7. he *limiteth* a certain day,

3726 3 584/704,338 5:457 3727

ὁρκίζω, *horkizo.*

Mar 5: 7. I *adjure* thee by God, that thou torment me not.
Acts19:13. We *adjure* you by Jesus whom Paul
1Th. 5:27. I *charge* you by the Lord that this epistle be read

3727 10 584/704 5:457 *herkos* (fence)

ὅρκος, *horkos.*

Mat. 5:33. shalt perform unto the Lord thine *oaths:*
14: 7. promised with an *oath* to give her
Mat.14: 9. for the *oath's* sake,
26:72. again he denied with an *oath*,
Mar 6:26. (yet) for his *oath's* sake,
Lu. 1:73. The *oath* which he sware to our
Acts 2:30. God had sworn with an *oath* to him,
Heb 6:16. an *oath* for confirmation (is)
17. confirmed (it) by an *oath:*
Jas. 5:12. neither by any other *oath*·

3728 4 584/704 5:457 3727,3660

ὁρκωμοσία, *horkōmosia.*

Heb 7:20. inasmuch as not without an *oath*
21(20). For those priests were made without an *oath;* but this with an *oath* by him
28. but the word of the *oath*, which was since the law,

3729 5 585/704 5:467 3730

ὁρμάω, *hormao.*

Mat. 8:32. *ran violently* down a steep place
Mar 5:13. herd *ran violently* down a steep place
Lu. 8:33. herd *ran violently* down a steep place
Acts 7:57. and *ran* upon him with one accord,
19:29. they *rushed* with one accord into

3730 2 585/704 5:467

ὁρμή, *hormee.*

Acts14: 5. when there was an *assault* made
Jas. 3: 4. whithersoever the governor (lit. the *impulse* of the governor) listeth.

3731 1 585/704 5:467 3730

ὅρμημα, *hormeema.*

Rev.18:21. Thus with *violence* shall that great city

3732 3 585/704 3733

ὄρνεον, *orneon.*

Rev 18: 2. a cage of every unclean and hateful *bird*.
19:17. saying to all the *fowls* that fly
21. all the *fowls* were filled with their flesh.

3733 2 585/705 rt 3735

ὄρνις, *ornis.*

Mat 23:37. as a *hen* gathereth her chickens
Lu. 13:34. as a *hen* (doth gather) her brood

3734 1 585/705 rt 3725,5087

ὁροθεσία, *horothesia.*

Acts17:26. and the *bounds* of their habitation;

3735 65 585/705 5:475 *orō* (to rise)

ὄρος, *oros.*

Mat. 4: 8. into an exceeding high *mountain*,
5: 1. he went up into a *mountain:*
14. A city that is set on an *hill* cannot be hid
8: 1. was come down from the *mountain*.
14:23. he went up into a *mountain* apart
15:29. and went up into a *mountain*,
17: 1. into an high *mountain* apart,
9. as they came down from the *mountain*.
20. ye shall say unto this *mountain*,
18:12. and goeth into the *mountains*,
21: 1. unto the *mount* of Olives, then sent
21. if ye shall say unto this *mountain*,

Mat.24: 3. as he sat upon the *mount* of Olives,
16. which be in Judæa flee into the *mountains*:
26:30. they went out into the *mount* of Olives.
28:16. into a *mountain* where Jesus had
Mar 3:13. And he goeth up into a *mountain*,
5: 5. he was in the *mountains*, and in
11. nigh unto the *mountains* a great herd
6:46. he departed into a *mountain* to pray.
9: 2. into an high *mountain* apart
9. as they came down from the *mountain*,
11: 1. at the *mount* of Olives,
23. shall say unto this *mountain*,
13: 3. as he sat upon the *mount* of Olives
14. that be in Judæa flee to the *mountains*:
14:26. they went out into the *mount* of Olives.
Lu. 3: 5. every *mountain* and hill shall be
4: 5. taking him up into an high *mountain*,
29. unto the brow of the *hill*
6:12. he went out into a *mountain* to pray,
8:32. feeding on the *mountain*:
9:28. and went up into a *mountain* to pray.
37. were come down from the *hill*,
19:29. at the *mount* called (the mount) of Olives,
37. at the descent of the *mount* of Olives,
21:21. are in Judæa flee to the *mountains*;
37. and abode in the *mount*
22:39. to the *mount* of Olives;
23:30. to say to the *mountains*, Fall on us;
Joh. 4:20. worshipped in this *mountain*;
21. neither in this *mountain*, nor
6: 3. Jesus went up into a *mountain*,
15. into a *mountain* himself alone.
8: 1. Jesus went unto the *mount* of Olives
Acts 1:12. from the *mount* called Olivet,
7:30. in the wilderness of *mount* Sina
38. spake to him in the *mount* Sina,
1Co.13: 2. so that I could remove *mountains*,
Gal. 4:24. the one from the *mount* Sinai,
25. For this Agar is *mount* Sinai
Heb 8: 5. shewed to thee in the *mount*.
11:38. and (in) *mountains*, and (in) dens
12:18. unto the *mount* that might be touched,
20. as a beast touch the *mountain*,
22. ye are come unto *mount* Sion,
2Pet.1:18. with him in the holy *mount*.
Rev. 6:14. every *mountain* and island were moved
15. in the rocks of the *mountains*;
16. said to the *mountains* and rocks,
8: 8. as it were a great *mountain*
14: 1. a Lamb stood on the *mount* Sion,
16:20. and the *mountains* were not found.
17: 9. seven heads are seven *mountains*,
21:10. to a great and high *mountain*,

3736 3 586/705

ὀρύσσω, orusso.

Mat.21:33. and *digged* a winepress in it,
25:18. and *digged* in the earth, and hid
Mar 12: 1. and *digged* (a place for) the winefat,

3737 2 586/705 5:487

ὀρφανός, orphanos.

Joh.14:18. I will not leave you *comfortless*:
Jas. 1:27. To visit the *fatherless* and widows

3738 4 587/706

orchos (row)

ὀρχέομαι, orkeomai.

Mat.11:17. and ye *have* not *danced*;
14: 6. the daughter of Herodias *danced*
Mar 6:22. came in, and *danced*,
Lu. 7:32. and ye *have* not *danced*;

3739 1393 587/706 3588,cf 3757

ὅς, ἥ, ὅ

3740 3 589/712 3739

ὁσάκις, hosakis.

1Co.11:25. *as oft as* ye drink (it), in remembrance
26. For *as often as* ye eat this bread,
Rev.11: 6. with all plagues, *as often as* they will.

3741 8 589/712 5:489 cf 1342 cf 2413,cf 40

ὅσιος, hosios.

Acts 2:27. thine *Holy* One to see corruption.
13:34. I will give you the sure *mercies* of David.
35. Thou shalt not suffer thine *Holy* One to
1Ti. 2: 8. lifting up *holy* hands, without wrath
Tit. 1: 8. sober, just, *holy*, temperate;
Heb 7:26. (who is) *holy*, harmless, undefiled,
Rev.15: 4. for (thou) only (art) *holy*:
16: 5. which art, and wast, and *shalt be*,

Note.—The reading in Rev. 16:5, appears to have been in some copies ὁ ἐσόμενος.

3742 2 589/712 5:489 3741

ὁσιότης, hosiotees.

Lu. 1:75. In *holiness* and righteousness before
Eph. 4:24. in righteousness and true *holiness*.

3743 1 589/712 5:489 3741

ὁσίως, hosiōs.

1Th. 2:10. how *holily* and justly and

3744 6 590/712 5:493 3605

ὀσμή, osmee.

Joh.12: 3. filled with the *odour* of the ointment
2Co. 2:14. the *savour* of his knowledge by us
16. To the one (we are) the *savour* of death
— to the other the *savour* of life unto
Eph. 5: 2. for a sweetsmelling *savour*.
Phi. 4:18. an *odour* of a sweet smell,

3745 115 590/712 3739

ὅσος, hosos.

² denotes that it is coupled with ἄν.

Mat. 7:12. all things *whatsoever*² ye would that
9:15. *as long as* the bridegroom is with them?
13:44. goeth and selleth all *that* he hath,
46. went and sold all *that* he had,
14:36. *as many as* touched were made perfectly
17:12. done unto him *whatsoever* they listed.
18:18. *Whatsoever* (ὅσα ἐὰν) ye shall bind on
— *whatsoever* (ὅσα ἐὰν) ye shall loose on
25. and all *that* he had, and payment
21:22. *whatsoever*² ye shall ask in prayer
22: 9. *as many as*² ye shall find, bid
10. *as many as* they found, both bad and
23: 3. *whatsoever*² they bid you observe,
25:40. In*asmuch as* ye have done (it) unto
45. In*asmuch as* ye did (it) not to one
28:20. *whatsoever* I have commanded you:
Mar 2:19. *as long as* they have the bridegroom
3: 8. when they had heard *what great* things
10. *as many as* had plagues.

Mar 3:28. *wherewith soever*[2] they shall blaspheme:
5:19. tell them *how great* things the Lord
20. *how great* things Jesus had done for
6:11. And *whosoever*[2] shall not receive you,
30. both *what* they had done, and *what* they
56. *as many as*[2] touched him were
7:36. but *the more* he charged them,
9:13. done unto him *whatsoever* they listed,
10:21. sell *whatsoever* thou hast,
11:24. *What* things *soever*[2] ye desire,
12:44. did cast in all *that* she had,
Lu. 4:23. *whatsoever* we have heard done
40. all they *that* had any sick
8:39. shew *how great* things God hath done
— *how great* things Jesus had done
9: 5. And *whosoever*[2] will not receive you,
10. told him *all that* they had done.
11: 8. *as many as* he needeth.
12: 3. *whatsoever* ye have spoken in darkness
18:12. I give tithes of all *that* I possess.
22. sell all *that* thou hast, and
Joh. 1:12. But *as many as* received him,
4:29. which told me all things *that ever*
39. He told me all *that ever* I did.
6:11. of the fishes *as much as* they would.
10: 8. All *that ever* came before me are
41. but all things *that* John spake of
11:22. *whatsoever*[2] thou wilt ask of God,
15:14. if ye do *whatsoever* I command you.
16:13. *whatsoever*[2] he shall hear, (that)
15. All things *that* the Father hath are mine:
23. *Whatsoever*[2] ye shall ask the Father
17: 7. that all things *whatsoever* thou hast given
21:25. also many other things *which* Jesus did,
Acts 2:39. *as many as*[2] the Lord our God shall call
3:22. in all things *whatsoever*[2] he shall
24. *as many as* have spoken,
4: 6. *as many as* were of the kindred of
23. and reported *all that* the chief priests
28. For to do *whatsoever* thy hand
34. for *as many as* were possessors of
5:36. and all, *as many as* obeyed him,
37. *as many as* obeyed him,
9:13. *how much* evil he hath done
16. *how great* things he must suffer
39. garments *which* Dorcas made,
10:45. *as many as* came with Peter,
13:48. and *as many as* were ordained to
14:27. *all that* God had done with them,
15: 4. declared *all* things *that* God had done
12. declaring *what* miracles and wonders
Ro. 2:12. *as many as* have sinned without
— and *as many as* have sinned in
3:19. that *what* things *soever* the law saith,
6: 3. *so many* of us *as* were baptized into
7: 1. *as long as* he liveth?
8:14. For *as many as* are led
11:13. in*asmuch as* I am the apostle
15: 4. For *whatsoever* things were written
1Co. 7:39. *as long as* her husband liveth;
2Co. 1:20. For *all* the promises of God in him
Gal. 3:10. For *as many as* are of the works of
27. For *as many* of you *as* have been
4: 1. the heir, *as long as* he is a child,
6:12. *As many as* desire to make
16. *as many as* walk according to
Phi. 3:15. *as many as* be perfect,
4: 8. *whatsoever* things are true, *whatsoever*
— *whatsoever* things (are) just, *whatsoever*
— *whatsoever* things (are) lovely, *whatsoever*
Col. 2: 1. and (for) *as many as* have not seen
1Ti. 6: 1. Let *as many* servants *as* are under

2Ti. 1:18. and in *how many* things he ministered
Heb 1: 4. *as* he hath by inheritance obtained
2:15. deliver them *who* through fear of death
3: 3. in*asmuch as* he who hath builded
7:20. And in*asmuch as* not without an oath
8: 6. by *how much* also he is the mediator
9:27. And *as* it is appointed unto men
10:25. so much the more, *as* ye see the day
37. For yet a little while, (lit. *how* little *how!*)
2Pet. 1:13. *as long as* I am in this tabernacle,
Jude 10. of *those things* which they know not: but
what they know naturally,
Rev. 1: 2. and of *all* things *that* he saw.
2:24. *as many as* have not this doctrine,
3:19. *As many as* (ὅσους ἐὰν) I love, I rebuke
and chasten:
13:15. that *as many as*[2] would not worship
18: 7. *How much* she hath glorified herself,
17. *as many as* trade by sea,
21:16. the length is as large *as* the breadth:

3747 5 590/713

ὀστέον, *osteon.*

Mat. 23:27. full of dead (men's) *bones*,
Lu. 24:39. hath not flesh and *bones*, as ye see me
Joh. 19:36. A *bone* of him shall not be broken.
Eph. 5:30. of his flesh, and of his *bones*.
Heb 11:22. commandment concerning his *bones*.

3748 153 590/713 3739,5100cf3754

ὅστις, *hostis.*

[2] denotes that it is coupled with ἄν, [3] that it is coupled with both πᾶς and ἄν,

Mat. 2: 6. a Governor, *that* shall rule my people
5:39. but *whosoever* shall smite thee
41. And *whosoever* shall compel thee
7:15. *which* come to you in sheep's clothing,
24. *whosoever* heareth these sayings
— *which* built his house upon a rock:
26. *which* built his house upon the sand:
10:32. *Whosoever* therefore shall confess me
33. *whosoever*[2] shall deny me
12:50. *whosoever*[2] shall do the will of
13:12. *whosoever* hath, to him shall be
— but *whosoever* hath not, from him
52. *which* bringeth forth out of his
16:28. *which* shall not taste of death,
18: 4. *Whosoever* therefore shall humble
28. Pay me *that* thou owest.
19:12. *which* were so born
— *which* were made eunuchs of men:
— *which* have made themselves eunuchs
20: 1. *which* went out early in the morning
21:33. *which* planted a vineyard,
41. *which* shall render him the fruits
22: 2. *which* made a marriage for his son.
23:12. *whosoever* shall exalt himself
— and *he that* shall humble himself
27. *which* indeed appear beautiful
25: 1. *which* took their lamps, and
3. *They that* (were) foolish took
27:55. *which* followed Jesus from Galilee,
62. *that* followed the day of the
Mar 4:20. *such as* hear the word, and
8:34. *Whosoever* will come after me,
9: 1. *which* shall not taste of death,
12:18. *which* say there is no resurrection;
15: 7. *who* had committed murder
Lu. 1:20. *which* shall be fulfilled in
2: 4. *which* is called Bethlehem;

3746 *hosper* (whomsoever).
3739, 4007

Lu. 2:10. *which* shall be to all people.
7:37. *which* was a sinner.
39. woman (this is) *that* toucheth him:
8: 3. *which* ministered unto him
15. *which* in an honest and good heart,
26. *which* is over against Galilee.
43. *which* had spent all her living
9:30. *which* were Moses and Elias:
10:35. and *whatsoever* [2] thou spendest more,
42. *which* shall not be taken away
12: 1. leaven of the Pharisees, *which* is
14:27. *whosoever* doth not bear his cross,
15: 7. *which* need no repentance.
23:19. *Who* for a certain sedition made in
55. *which* came with him from Galilee,
Joh. 2: 5. *Whatsoever* [2] he saith unto you, do
8:25. even (the same) *that* I said unto you
53. Abraham, *which* is dead?
14:13. *whatsoever* [2] ye shall ask in my name,
15:16. that *whatsoever* [2] ye shall ask of the
21:25. *the which*, if they should be written
Acts 3:23. every soul, *which* [3] will not hear that
5:16. *and they* were healed every one.
7:53. *Who* have received the law by the
8:15. *Who*, when they were come down.
9:35. and (lit. *who*) turned to the Lord.
10:41. to us, *who* did eat and drink with him
47. *which* have received the Holy Ghost
11:20. *which*, when they were come to Antioch,
28. *which* came to pass in the days of
12:10. *which* opened to them of his own
13:31. *who* are his witnesses unto the people.
43. *who*, speaking to them, persuaded
16:12. *which* is the chief city of that
16. *which* brought her masters much
17. *which* shew unto us the way of
17:10. *who* coming (thither) went into
11. *in that they* received the word
21: 4. *who* said to Paul through the Spirit,
23:14. *And they* came to the chief priests
21. *which* have bound themselves
33. *Who*, when they came to Cæsarea,
24: 1. *who* informed the governor against
28:18. *Who*, when they had examined me,
Ro. 1:25. *Who* changed the truth of God into
32. *Who* knowing the judgment of God,
2:15. *Which* shew the work of the law
6: 2. How shall we, *that* are dead to sin,
9: 4. *Who* are Israelites; to whom
11: 4. *who* have not bowed the knee to
16: 4. *Who* have for my life laid down
6. *who* bestowed much labour on us.
7. *who* are of note among the apostles,
12. *which* laboured much in the Lord.
1Co. 3:17. *which* (temple) ye are.
5: 1. such fornication *as* is not so much as
6:20. in your spirit, *which* are God's.
7:13. woman *which* hath an husband that
16: 2. *as* [2] (God) hath prospered him,
2Co. 3:14. *which* (vail) is done away in Christ.
8:10. *who* have begun before, not only to
9:11. *which* causeth through us thanksgiving
Gal. 2: 4. *who* came in privily to spy out
4:24. *Which* things are an allegory:
— gendereth to bondage, *which* is Agar.
26. is free, *which* is the mother of us all.
5: 4. *whosoever* of you are justified by
10. bear his judgment, *whosoever* [2] he be.
19. *which* are (these); Adultery,
Eph. 1:23. *Which* is his body, the fulness of
3:13. *which* is your glory.
4:19. *Who* being past feeling
Eph. 6: 2. *which* is the first commandment with
Phi. 1:28. *which* is to them an evident token
2:20. *who* will naturally care for
3: 7. But *what* things were gain to me,
4: 3. women *which* laboured with me in
Col. 2:23. *Which* things have indeed a shew
3: 5. and covetousness, *which* is idolatry:
14. *which* is the bond of perfectness.
17. And *whatsoever* [3] ye do in word
23. *whatsoever* [3] ye do, do (it) heartily, as
4:11. *which* have been a comfort unto me.
2Th. 1: 9. *Who* shall be punished with
1Ti. 1: 4. *which* minister questions, rather than
3:15. *which* is the church of the living God,
6: 9. *which* drown men in destruction
2Ti. 1: 5. *which* dwelt first in thy grandmother
2: 2. *who* shall be able to teach others
18. *Who* concerning the truth have erred,
Tit. 1:11. *who* subvert whole houses,
Heb 2: 3. *which* at the first began to be spoken
8: 5. *Who* serve unto the example and
6. *which* was established upon better
9: 2. *which* is called the sanctuary.
9. *Which* (was) a figure for the time
10: 8. *which* are offered by the law;
11. *which* can never take away sins:
35. *which* hath great recompence of
12: 5. *which* speaketh unto you as unto
13: 7. *who* have spoken unto you the word
Jas. 2:10. For *whosoever* shall keep the whole law,
4:14. *Whereas ye* know not what (shall be)
1Pet. 2:11. *which* war against the soul;
2Pet. 2: 1. *who* privily shall bring in damnable
1Joh. 1: 2. *which* was with the Father,
Rev. 1: 7. and *they* (also) *which* pierced him:
12. to see the voice *that* spake with me.
2:24. and *which* have not known the
9: 4. *which* have not the seal of God
11: 8. *which* spiritually is called Sodom
12:13. *which* brought forth the man (child).
17: 8. the beast *that* was, and is not, and yet is.
12. *which* have received no kingdom as yet;
19: 2. *which* did corrupt the earth
20: 4. and *which* had not worshipped the beast,

See also ὅτου.

3749 2 591/715 *ostrakon* (tile)

ὀστράκινος, *ostrakinos.*

2Co. 4: 7. this treasure in *earthen* vessels,
2Ti. 2:20. but also of wood and *of earth*;

3750 1 591/715 3605

ὄσφρησις, *osphreesis.*

1Co. 12:17. where (were) the *smelling*?

3751 8 591/715 5:496

ὀσφύς, *osphus.*

Mat. 3: 4. a leathern girdle about his *loins*;
Mar 1: 6. girdle of a skin about his *loins*;
Lu. 12:35. Let your *loins* be girded about,
Acts 2:30. that of the fruit of his *loins*,
Eph. 6:14. having your *loins* girt about
Heb 7: 5. come out of the *loins* of Abraham:
10. he was yet in the *loins* of his father,
1Pet. 1:13. gird up the *loins* of your mind,

3752 122 592/715 3753,302

ὅταν, *hotan.*

Mat. 5:11. *when* (men) shall revile you,

Mat. 6: 2. *when* thou doest (thine) alms,
5. And *when* thou prayest,
6. But thou, *when* thou prayest,
16. *when* ye fast, be not, as the
9:15. *when* the bridegroom shall be taken
10:19. But *when* they deliver you up
23. But *when* they persecute you
12:43. *When* the unclean spirit is gone
13:32. *when* it is grown, it is the greatest
15: 2. *when* they eat bread.
19:28. *when* the Son of man shall sit
21:40. *When* the lord therefore of the
23:15. *when* he is made, ye make him twofold
24:15. *When* ye therefore shall see the
32. *When* his branch is yet tender,
33. *when* ye shall see all these things,
25:31. *When* the Son of man shall come
26:29. until that day *when* I drink it
Mar 2:20. *when* the bridegroom shall be taken
3:11. unclean spirits, *when* they saw him,
4:15. but *when* they have heard, Satan
16. *when* they have heard the word,
29. *when* the fruit is brought forth,
31. *when* it is sown in the earth,
32. But *when* it is sown, it groweth up,
8:38. *when* he cometh in the glory of his
9: 9. till (lit. except *when*) the Son of man
11:25. *when* ye stand praying, forgive,
12:23. *when* they shall rise,
25. For *when* they shall rise from the
13: 4. *when* all these things shall be
7. *when* ye shall hear of wars and
11. But *when* they shall lead (you), and
14. But *when* ye shall see the abomination
28. *When* her branch is yet tender,
29. *when* ye shall see these things
14: 7. *whensoever* ye will ye may do them good:
25. until that day *that* I drink it new
Lu. 5:35. *when* the bridegroom shall be taken
6:22. *when* men shall hate you, and *when* they shall separate you (from their company),
26. Woe unto you, *when* all men shall
8:13. which, *when* they hear, receive the word
9:26. *when* he shall come in his own
11 2. *When* ye pray, say, Our Father
21. *When* a strong man armed keepeth
24. *When* the unclean spirit is gone
34. *when* thine eye is single,
36. as *when* the bright shining of a
1: 11. *when* they bring you unto the synagogues,
54. *When* ye see a cloud rise out of the
55. *when* (ye see) the south wind blow,
1 28. *when* ye shall see Abraham,
1 8. *When* thou art bidden of any (man)
10. But *when* thou art bidden,
— that *when* he that bade thee cometh,
12. *When* thou makest a dinner or a
13. But *when* thou makest a feast,
16: 4. *when* I am put out of the stewardship,
9. that, *when* ye fail, they may
17:10. *when* ye shall have done all those
21: 7. *when* these things shall come to pass?
9. But *when* ye shall hear of wars and
20. And *when* ye shall see Jerusalem
30. *When* they now shoot forth,
31. *when* ye see these things come to pass,
23:42. *when* thou comest into thy kingdom.
Joh. 2:10. and *when* men have well drunk,
4:25. *when* he is come, he will tell us all
5: 7. I have no man, *when* the water is troubled,
7:27. but *when* Christ cometh,
Joh. 7:31. *When* Christ cometh, will he do more
8:28. *When* ye have lifted up the Son
44. *When* he speaketh a lie,
9: 5. *As long as* I am in the world,
10: 4. And *when* he putteth forth his own
13:19. that, *when* it is come to pass,
14:29. that, *when* it is come to pass,
15:26. But *when* the Comforter is come,
16: 4. that *when* the time shall come,
13. *when* he, the Spirit of truth, is come.
21. A woman *when* she is in travail
— but *as soon as* she is delivered
21:18. but *when* thou shalt be old,
Acts23:35. *when* thine accusers are also come
24:22. *When* Lysias the chief captain
Ro. 2:14. For *when* the Gentiles,
11:27. *when* I shall take away their sins.
1Co. 3: 4. For *while* one saith, I am of Paul;
13:10. But *when* that which is perfect is come,
14:26. *when* ye come together,
15:24. *when* he shall have delivered up
— *when* he shall have put down
27. But *when* he saith, All things are
28. And *when* all things shall be subdued
54. So *when* this corruptible shall have
16: 2. that there be no gatherings *when* I come.
3. And *when* I come, whomsoever ye
5. *when* I shall pass through Macedonia:
12. *when* he shall have convenient time.
2Co.10: 6. *when* your obedience is fulfilled.
12:10. for *when* I am weak, then am I strong.
13: 9. we are glad, *when* we are weak,
Col. 3: 4. *When* Christ, (who is) our life, shall
4:16. And *when* this epistle is read
1Th. 5: 3. For *when* they shall say, Peace and safety,
2Th. 1:10. *When* he shall come to be glorified
1Ti. 5:11. for *when* they have begun to wax
Tit. 3:12. *When* I shall send Artemas
Heb 1: 6. *when* he bringeth in the firstbegotten
Jas. 1: 2. *when* ye fall into divers temptations;
1Joh.2:28. that, *when* he shall appear, we may
5: 2. *when* we love God, and keep his
Rev 4: 9. And *when* those beasts give glory
9: 5. of a scorpion, *when* he striketh a man.
10: 7. *when* he shall begin to sound,
11: 7. *when* they shall have finished their
12: 4. to devour her child *as soon as* it was born.
17:10. and *when* he cometh, he must
18: 9. *when* they shall see the smoke
20: 7. *when* the thousand years are expired,

3753 105 592/717 3739,5037

ὅτε, *hote.*

Mat. 7:28. *when* Jesus had ended these sayings,
9:25. But *when* the people were put forth,
11: 1. *when* Jesus had made an end of
12: 3. what David did, *when* he was an hungred,
13:26. But *when* the blade was sprung up,
48. Which, *when* it was full, they drew
53. *when* Jesus had finished these parables,
17:25. And *when* he was come into the house,
19: 1. *when* Jesus had finished these sayings,
21: 1. And *when* they drew nigh unto Jerusalem,
34. And *when* the time of the fruit drew near,
26: 1. *when* Jesus had finished all these
27:31. And *after that* they had mocked him,
Mar 1:32. *when* the sun did set,
2:25. *when* he had need, and was an hungred,
4:10. And *when* he was alone,
6:21. day was come, *that* Herod on his
7:17. And *when* he was entered into the house

Mar 8:19. *When* I brake the five loaves
20. And *when* the seven among
11: 1. And *when* they came nigh to
19. And *when* even was come,
14:12. *when* they killed the passover,
15:20. And *when* they had mocked him,
41. *when* he was in Galilee,
Lu. 2:21. And *when* eight days were accomplished
22. And *when* the days of her purification
42. And *when* he was twelve years old,
4:25. *when* the heaven was shut up
6:13. And *when* it was day, he called
13:35. come *when* ye shall say, Blessed
15:30. But *as soon as* this thy son was come,
17:22. *when* ye shall desire to see one of
22:14. And *when* the hour was come,
35. *When* I sent you without purse, and
23:33. And *when* they were come to the place,
Joh. 1:19. *when* the Jews sent priests and
2:22. *When* therefore he was risen from
4:21. *when* ye shall neither in this
23. *when* the true worshippers shall
45. Then *when* he was come into Galilee,
5:25. *when* the dead shall hear the voice
6:24. *When* the people therefore saw
9: 4. the night cometh, *when* no man can work.
14. *when* Jesus made the clay,
12:16. but *when* Jesus was glorified,
17. *when* he called Lazarus out of his
41. *when* he saw his glory, and
13:12. So *after* he had washed their feet,
31(30). *when* he was gone out,
16:25. the time cometh, *when* I shall
17:12. *While* I was with them in the world,
19: 6. *When* the chief priests therefore
8. *When* Pilate therefore heard that
23. *when* they had crucified Jesus.
30. *When* Jesus therefore had received
20:24. was not with them *when* Jesus came.
21:15. So *when* they had dined,
18. *When* thou wast young,
Acts 1:13. And *when* they were come in,
8:12. But *when* they believed Philip
39. And *when* they were come up out of
11: 2. And *when* Peter was come up to
12: 6. And *when* Herod would have brought
21: 5. And *when* we had accomplished those
35. And *when* he came upon the stairs,
22:20. And *when* the blood of thy martyr
27:39. And *when* it was day, they knew not
28:16. And *when* we came to Rome,
Ro. 2:16. In the day *when* God shall judge
6:20. For *when* ye were the servants of sin,
7: 5. For *when* we were in the flesh,
13:11. nearer than *when* we believed.
1Co. 13:11. *When* I was a child,
— but *when* I became a man,
Gal. 1:15. But *when* it pleased God, who
2:11. But *when* Peter was come to Antioch,
12. *when* they were come, he withdrew
14. But *when* I saw that they walked not
4: 3. *when* we were children, were in
4. But *when* the fulness of the time was
Phi. 4:15. *when* I departed from Macedonia,
Col. 3: 7. *when* ye lived in them.
1Th. 3: 4. *when* we were with you,
2Th. 3:10. For even *when* we were with you,
2Ti. 4: 3. *when* they will not endure sound
Tit. 3: 4. But *after that* the kindness and love
Heb 7:10. *when* Melchisedec met him.
9:17. *while* the testator liveth.
1Pet. 3:20. *when* once the longsuffering of God
Jude 9. *when* contending with the devil
Rev 1:17. And *when* I saw him, I fell at his feet
5: 8. And *when* he had taken the book,
6: 1. And I saw *when* the Lamb opened one
3. And *when* he had opened the second
5. And *when* he had opened the third
7. And *when* he had opened the fourth
9. And *when* he had opened the fifth
12. I beheld *when* he had opened the sixth
8: 1. And *when* he had opened the seventh
10: 3. and *when* he had cried, seven
4. And *when* the seven thunders had
10. and *as soon as* I had eaten it,
12:13. And *when* the dragon saw that he
22: 8. And *when* I had heard and seen, I fell

3754 1293 592/718 3748

ὅτι, *hoti.*

Mat. 2:16. when he saw *that* he was mocked
18. *because* they are not.
22. But when he heard *that* Archelaus
23.)(He shall be called a Nazarene.
3: 9. I say unto you, *that* God is able of
4: 6.)(He shall give his angels charge
12. Now when Jesus had heard *that* John
5: 3. *for* their's is the kingdom of heaven.
4. *for* they shall be comforted.
5. *for* they shall inherit the earth.
6. *for* they shall be filled.
7. *for* they shall obtain mercy.
8. *for* they shall see God.
9. *for* they shall be called the children of
10. *for* their's is the kingdom of heaven.
12. *for* great (is) your reward in heaven:
17. Think not *that* I am come to destroy
20. *That* except your righteousness shall
21. Ye have heard *that* it was said by
22. *That* whosoever is angry with his
23. *that* thy brother hath ought against thee;
27. *that* it was said by them of old time,
28. *That* whosoever looketh on a woman
31. It hath been said,)(Whosoever shall put
32. But I say unto you, *That* whosoever shall
33. ye have heard *that* it hath been said
34. *for* it is God's throne:
35. *for* it is his footstool: neither by Jerusalem; *for* it is the city of the great King.
36. *because* thou canst not make one hair
38. Ye have heard *that* it hath been said,
43. Ye have heard *that* it hath been said,
45. *for* he maketh his sun to rise on
6: 5. *for* they love to pray standing in the
—)(They have their reward.
7. *for* they think that they shall be heard
13. *For* thine is the kingdom,
16.)(They have their reward.
26. *for* they sow not,
29. And yet I say unto you, *That* even
32. knoweth *that* ye have need of all these
7:13. *for* wide (is) the gate,
14. *Because* strait (is) the gate,
23.)(I never knew you:
8:11. *That* many shall come from the east and
27. *that* even the winds and the sea
9: 6. But that ye may know *that* the Son
18.)(My daughter is even now dead:
28. Believe ye *that* I am able to do this?
33.)(It was never so seen in Israel.
36. *because* they fainted, and were scattered
10: 7.)(The kingdom of heaven is at hand.
34. Think not *that* I am come to send

Mat.11:20. *because* they repented not:
21. *for* if the mighty works, which were
23. *for* if the mighty works, which have
24. *That* it shall be more tolerable for
25. *because* thou hast hid these things
26. *for* so it seemed good in thy sight.
29. *for* I am meek and lowly in heart:
12. 5. *how that* on the sabbath days
6. *That* in this place is (one) greater than
36. *That* every idle word that men shall
41. *because* they repented at the
42. *for* she came from the uttermost
13:11. *Because* it is given unto you to know
13. *because* they seeing see not;
16. *for* they see: and your ears, *for* they hear.
17. *That* many prophets and righteous
14: 5. *because* they counted him as a prophet.
26. were troubled, saying,)(It is a spirit;
15:12. Knowest thou *that* the Pharisees
17. *that* whatsoever entereth in at the
23. *for* she crieth after us.
32. *because* they continue with me
16: 7. (It is) *because* we have taken no bread.
8. *because* ye have brought no bread?
11. that ye do not understand *that* I spake
12. Then understood they how *that* he bade (them) not
17. *for* flesh and blood hath not revealed (it)
18. *That* thou art Peter,
20. tell no man *that* he was Jesus
21. *how that* he must go unto Jerusalem,
23. *for* thou savourest not the things
17:10. *that* Elias must first come?
12. *That* Elias is come already,
13. *that* he spake unto them of John
15. *for* he is lunatick, and sore vexed:
18:10. *That* in heaven their angels do
13. I say unto you,)(he rejoiceth more
19. *That* if two of you shall agree
19: 4. *that* he which made (them) at the
8.)(Moses because of the hardness of your
9. I say unto you,)(Whosoever shall
23. *That* a rich man shall hardly
28. *That* ye which have followed me,
20: 7. *Because* no man hath hired us.
10. they supposed *that* they should have received more;
12. Saying,)(These last have wrought
15. *because* I am good?
25. Ye know *that* the princes of the
30. when they heard *that* Jesus
21: 3. ye shall say,)(The Lord hath need of
16. have ye never read,)(Out of the mouth
31. *That* the publicans and the harlots
43. say I unto you,)(The kingdom of God
45. heard his parables, they perceived *that* he
22:16. Master, we know *that* thou art true,
34. Pharisees had heard *that* he had put
23:13(14). *for* ye shut up the kingdom of heaven
14(13). *for* ye devour widows' houses,
15. *for* ye compass sea and land to make
23. *for* ye pay tithe of mint and
25. *for* ye make clean the outside
27. *for* ye are like unto whited
29. *because* ye build the tombs of
31. *that* ye are the children of them
24:32. ye know *that* summer (is) nigh:
33. know *that* it is near, (even) at the doors.
42. *for* ye know not what hour your
43. *that* if the goodman of the house
44. *for* in such an hour as ye think not
47. *That* he shall make him ruler over

Mat.25: 8. *for* our lamps are gone out.
13. *for* ye know neither the day nor
24. Lord, I knew thee *that* thou art an
26. thou knewest *that* I reap where I
26: 2. Ye know *that* after two days is
21. *that* one of you shall betray me.
29. But I say unto you,)(I will not drink
34. *That* this night, before the cock crow,
53. Thinkest thou *that* I cannot now pray
54. *that* thus it must be?
65. saying,)(He hath spoken blasphemy;
72. with an oath,)(I do not know the man.
74. (saying),)(I know not the man.
75. said unto him,)(Before the cock crow,
27: 3. when he saw *that* he was condemned,
18. For he knew *that* for envy they had
24. saw *that* he could prevail nothing,
43. he said,)(I am the Son of God.
47. said,)(This (man) calleth for Elias.
63. Sir, we remember *that* that deceiver
28: 5. for I know *that* ye seek Jesus,
7. *that* he is risen from the dead;
13. Say ye,)(His disciples came by night,
Mar 1:15. And saying,)(The time is fulfilled,
27. *for* with authority commandeth he
34. *because* they knew him.
37.)(All (men) seek for thee.
40.)(If thou wilt, thou canst make me
2: 1. it was noised *that* he was in the house.
8. *that* they so reasoned within themselves,
10. *that* the Son of man hath power
12.)(We never saw it on this fashion.
16. How is it *that* he eateth and drinketh
3:11.)(Thou art the Son of God.
21.)(He is beside himself.
22.)(He hath Beelzebub, and)(by the prince of the devils casteth he
28.)(All sins shall be forgiven
30. *Because* they said, He hath an
4:29. *because* the harvest is come.
38. carest thou not *that* we perish?
41. *that* even the wind and the sea
5: 9. *for* we are many
23.)(My little daughter lieth
28.)(If I may touch but his clothes,
29. *that* she was healed of that plague.
35.)(Thy daughter is dead: why troublest
6: 2. *that* even such mighty works
4.)(A prophet is not without honour,
14. *That* John the Baptist was risen
15. Others said, *That* it is Elias. And others said, *That* it is a prophet,
16.)(It is John, whom I beheaded: he is risen
17. *for* he had married her.
18.)(It is not lawful for thee to
23.)(Whatsoever thou shalt ask of me,
34. *because* they were as sheep not
35.)(This is a desert place, and now
55. where they heard)(he was.
7: 6.)(Well hath Esaias prophesied
18. Do ye not perceive, *that* whatsoever
19. *Because* it entereth not into
20.)(That which cometh out of the man
8: 2. *because* they have now been with
16. (It is) *because* we have no bread.
17. reason ye, *because* ye have no bread?
24. said)(I see men as trees, walking.
31. to teach them, *that* the Son of man
33. *for* thou savourest not the things
9: 1. *That* there be some of them that stand
11. *Why* say the scribes *that* Elias must first

Mar 9:13. I say unto you, *That* Elias is indeed come,
25. saw *that* the people came running
26. many said,)(He is dead.
28. *Why* could not we cast him out?
31.)(The Son of man is delivered into
38. *because* he followeth not us.
41. *because* ye belong to Christ,
10:33.)(Behold, we go up to Jerusalem;
42. Ye know *that* they which are accounted to rule
47. And when he heard *that* it was Jesus
11: 3. say ye *that* the Lord hath need of him;
17. written,)(My house shall be called of all
18. *because* all the people was astonished
23. I say unto you, *That* whosoever
— believe *that* those things which he saith
24. believe *that* ye receive (them),
32. counted John, *that* he was a prophet
12: 6.)(They will reverence my son.
7.)(This is the heir; come, let us
12. *that* he had spoken the parable against
14. we know *that* thou art true,
19.)(If a man's brother die,
26. the dead, *that* they rise:
28. perceiving *that* he had answered them
29.)(The first of all the commandments
32. *for* there is one God; and there is
34. saw *that* he answered discreetly,
35. say the scribes *that* Christ is the son
43. say unto you, *That* this poor widow hath
13: 6. saying,)(I am (Christ); and shall
28. ye know *that* summer is near:
29. *that* it is nigh, (even) at the doors.
30. *that* this generation shall not pass,
14:14.)(The master saith, Where is the
18. I say unto you,)(One of you which
25.)(I will drink no more of the fruit
27.)(All ye shall be offended because of me this night: *for* it is written, I will smite
30. *That* this day, (even) in this night,
58.)(We heard him say,)(I will destroy this temple
69.)(This is (one) of them.
71.)(I know not this man of whom ye
72.)(Before the cock crow twice,
15:10. *that* the chief priests had delivered
39. saw *that* he so cried out, and gave
16: 4. they saw *that* the stone was rolled
7. *that* he goeth before you into
11. heard *that* he was alive,
14. *because* they believed not them
Lu. 1:22. perceived *that* he had seen a vision
25.)(Thus hath the Lord dealt with me
37. *For* with God nothing shall be impossible.
45. *for* there shall be a performance
48. *For* he hath regarded the low
49. *For* he that is mighty hath done
58. *how* the Lord had shewed great
61.)(There is none of thy kindred
68. *for* he hath visited and redeemed
2:11. *For* unto you is born this day
23.)(Every male that openeth
30. *For* mine eyes have seen
49. How is it *that* ye sought me? wist ye not *that* I must be
3: 8. for I say unto you, *That* God is able
4: 4. written, *That* man shall not live by
6. *for* that is delivered unto me;
10.)(He shall give his angels charge
11. And)(in (their) hands they shall
12.)(It is said, Thou shalt not tempt
21.)(This day is this scripture fulfilled

Lu. 4:24.)(No prophet is accepted in his own
32. *for* his word was with power.
36. *for* with authority and power he
41.)(Thou art Christ the Son of God.
— *for* they knew that he was Christ.
43.)(I must preach the kingdom of God
— *for* therefore am I sent.
5: 8. *for* I am a sinful man, O Lord.
24. ye may know *that* the Son of man hath
26.)(We have seen strange things
36.)(No man putteth a piece of
6: 5. *That* the Son of man is Lord also
19. *for* there went virtue out of him,
20. *for* your's is the kingdom of God
21. *for* ye shall be filled.
— *for* ye shall laugh.
24. *for* ye have received your consolation
25. *for* ye shall hunger.
— *for* ye shall mourn.
35. *for* he is kind unto the unthankful
7: 4. *That* he was worthy for whom he
16. *That* a great prophet is risen up among us; and, *That* God hath visited his people.
22. *how that* the blind see, the lame
37. knew *that* (Jesus) sat at meat
39. *for* she is a sinner.
43. I suppose *that* (he), to whom he forgave
47. *for* she loved much:
8:25. *for* he commandeth even the winds
30. *because* many devils were entered into
37. *for* they were taken with great fear:
42. *For* he had one only daughter.
47. saw *that* she was not hid,
49.)(Thy daughter is dead; trouble not
53. knowing *that* she was dead.
9: 7. *that* John was risen from the dead;
8. *that* Elias had appeared; and of others, *that* one of the old prophets
12. *for* we are here in a desert place.
19. others (say), *that* one of the old prophets
22.)(The Son of man must suffer
38. *for* he is mine only child.
49. *because* he followeth not with us.
53. *because* his face was as though
10:11. *that* the kingdom of God is come nigh
12. *that* it shall be more tolerable
13. *for* if the mighty works had been
20. *that* the spirits are subject unto you,
— *because* your names are written
21. *that* thou hast hid these things
— *for* so it seemed good in thy sight.
24. I tell you, *that* many prophets
40. *that* my sister hath left me to serve
11:18. *because* ye say that I cast out
31. *for* she came from the utmost parts
32. *for* they repented at the preaching
38. he marvelled *that* he had not first
42. *for* ye tithe mint and rue and all
43. *for* ye love the uppermost seats
44. *for* ye are as graves which
46. *for* ye lade men with burdens
47. *for* ye build the sepulchres of
48. *for* they indeed killed them,
52. *for* ye have taken away the key of
12:15. *for* a man's life consisteth not
17. *because* I have no room where to
24. *for* they neither sow nor reap;
30. your Father knoweth *that* ye have
32. *for* it is your Father's good pleasure
37. *that* he shall gird himself, and
39. And this know, *that* if the goodman

Lu 12:40. *for* the Son of man cometh at an hour
44. *that* he will make him ruler over all
51. Suppose ye *that* I am come to give
55. ye say,)(There will be heat;
13: 2. Suppose ye *that* these Galilæans
— *because* they suffered such things?
4. think ye *that* they were sinners
14. *because* that Jesus had healed on
24. *for* many, I say unto you, will seek
31. *for* Herod will kill thee.
33. *for* it cannot be that a prophet
35.)(Ye shall not see me, until
14:11. *For* whosoever exalteth himself shall
14. *for* they cannot recompense thee:
17. Come; *for* all things are now ready.
24. *That* none of those men which
30.)(This man began to build,
15: 2.)(This man receiveth sinners, and
6. *for* I have found my sheep which
7. *that* likewise joy shall be in heaven
9. *for* I have found the piece which I
24. *For* this my son was dead,
27. he said unto him,)(Thy brother is come;
— *because* he hath received him safe
32. *for* this thy brother was dead,
16: 3. *for* my lord taketh away from me
8. *because* he had done wisely: *for* the children of this world are
15. *for* that which is highly esteemed
24. *for* I am tormented in this flame.
25. remember *that* thou in thy lifetime
17: 9. *because* he did the things that were
10.)(We are unprofitable servants:)(we have done that which was our
15. when he saw *that* he was healed,
18: 8. I tell you *that* he will avenge them
9. trusted in themselves *that* they
11. I thank thee, *that* I am not as other
14. *for* every one that exalteth himself
29.)(There is no man that hath left house,
37. And they told him, *that* Jesus of
19: 3. *because* he was little of stature.
4. *for* he was to pass that (way).
7. *That* he was gone to be guest with
9.)(This day is salvation come to this
11. *because* they thought that the kingdom
17. *because* thou hast been faithful
21. *because* thou art an austere man.
22. Thou knewest *that* I was an austere man,
26. *That* unto every one which hath
31. *Because* the Lord hath need of him.
40. *that*, if these should hold their peace,
42.)(If thou hadst known, even thou,
43. *For* the days shall come upon thee,
20: 5.)(If we shall say, From heaven;
19. for they perceived *that* he had spoken
21. we know *that* thou sayest and
37. Now *that* the dead are raised,
21: 3. *that* this poor widow hath cast
5. *how* it was adorned with goodly
8. saying,)(I am (Christ);
20. then know *that* the desolation
22. *For* these be the days of vengeance,
30. *that* summer is now nigh at hand.
31. know ye *that* the kingdom of God
32.)(This generation shall not pass away,
22:16.)(I will not any more eat thereof,
18.)(I will not drink of the fruit of the vine,
37. *that* this that is written must yet
61.)(Before the cock crow, thou shalt
70. Ye say *that* I am.
23: 5.)(He stirreth up the people,

Lu. 23: 7. as soon as he knew *that* he belonged
29. *For*, behold, the days are coming,
31. *For* if they do these things in a
40. seeing)(thou art in the same
24: 7.)(The Son of man must be delivered
21. But we trusted *that* it had been
29. *for* it is toward evening,
34.)(The Lord is risen indeed,
39. *that* it is I myself:
— *for* a spirit hath not flesh and
44. *that* all things must be fulfilled,
46.)(Thus it is written, and thus it
Joh. 1:15. *for* he was before me.
17. *For* the law was given by Moses,
20.)(I am not the Christ.
30. *for* he was before me.
32.)(I saw the Spirit descending
34. *that* this is the Son of God.
50(51). *Because* I said unto thee,
2:17. remembered *that* it was written,
18. seeing *that* thou doest these things?
22. remembered *that* he had said
25. and)(needed not that any
3: 2. we know *that* thou art a teacher
7. Marvel not *that* I said unto thee,
11. I say unto thee,)(We speak that
18. *because* he hath not believed in
19. *that* light is come into the world,
21. *that* they are wrought in God.
23. *because* there was much water
28. *that* I said, I am not the Christ, but *that* I am sent before him.
33. hath set to his seal *that* God is true.
4: 1. When therefore the Lord knew *how* the Pharisees had heard *that* Jesus
17. Thou hast well said,)(I have no husband:
19. Sir, I perceive *that* thou art a prophet.
20. and ye say, *that* in Jerusalem
21. believe me,)(the hour cometh,
22. *for* salvation is of the Jews.
25. I know *that* Messias cometh,
27. and marvelled *that* he talked with
35. Say not ye,)(There are yet four months,
— *for* they are white already to harvest.
37.)(One soweth, and another reapeth.
39.)(He told me all that ever I did.
42.)(Now we believe, not because of
— and know *that* this is indeed
44. *that* a prophet hath no honour
47. When he heard *that* Jesus was come
51.)(Thy son liveth.
52.)(Yesterday at the seventh hour the fever
53. So the father knew *that* (it was)
—)(Thy son liveth: and himself believed,
5: 6. and knew *that* he had been now
15. and told the Jews *that* it was Jesus,
16. *because* he had done these things
18. *because* he not only had broken the
24.)(He that heareth my word,
25.)(The hour is coming, and now is,
27. *because* he is the Son of man.
28. *for* the hour is coming,
30. *because* I seek not mine own will,
32. and I know *that* the witness
36. *that* the Father hath sent me.
38. *for* whom he hath sent,
39. *for* in them ye think ye have
42. But I know you, *that* ye have not
45. Do not think *that* I will accuse
6: 2. *because* they saw his miracles
5. and saw)(a great company come
14.)(This is of a truth that prophet

Joh. 6:15. perceived *that* they would come
22. saw *that* there was none other boat
— and *that* Jesus went not with his
24. saw *that* Jesus was not there,
26. not *because* ye saw the miracles, but
because ye did eat of the loaves,
36. unto you, *That* ye also have seen
38. *For* I came down from heaven,
41. *because* he said, I am the bread which
42.)(I came down from heaven?
46. Not *that* any man hath seen the Father,
61. knew in himself *that* his disciples
65. *that* no man can come unto me,
69. *that* thou art that Christ,
7: 1. *because* the Jews sought to kill him.
7. but me it hateth, *because* I testify of it,
that the works thereof are evil.
8. *for* my time is not yet full come.
12. for some said,)(He is a good man:
22. not *because* it is of Moses,
23. are ye angry at me, *because* I have
26. Do the rulers know indeed *that* this
29. But I know him: *for* I am from him,
30. *because* his hour was not yet come.
31.)(When Christ cometh, will he do
35. Whither will he go, *that* we shall not
39. *because* that Jesus was not yet
42. *That* Christ cometh of the seed of
52. Search, and look: *for* out of Galilee
8:14. *for* I know whence I came,
16. *for* I am not alone,
17. *that* the testimony of two men is true.
20. *for* his hour was not yet come.
22. *because* he saith, Whither I go,
24. *that* ye shall die in your sins: for if ye
believe not *that* I am (he),
27. They understood not *that* he spake
28. then shall ye know *that* I am (he),
29. *for* I do always those things that
33. how sayest thou,)(Ye shall be made free?
34.)(Whosoever committeth sin is the
37. I know *that* ye are Abraham's seed;
— *because* my word hath no place in you.
43. *because* ye cannot hear my word.
44. *because* there is no truth in him.
— *for* he is a liar, and the father of it.
45. And *because* I tell (you) the truth,
47. *because* ye are not of God.
48. Say we not well *that* thou art a
52. Now we know *that* thou hast a devil.
54. *that* he is your God:
55. and if I should say,)(I know him not,
9: 8. had seen him *that* he was blind,
9. Some said,)(This is he: others (said),
)(He is like him: (but) he said,)(I
am (he).
16. *because* he keepeth not the sabbath
17. *that* he hath opened thine eyes? He said,
)(He is a prophet.
18. *that* he had been blind,
19. who ye say)(was born blind?
20. We know *that* this is our son, and *that* he
was born blind:
22. *because* they feared the Jews:
23.)(He is of age; ask him.
24. we know *that* this man is a sinner.
25. *that*, whereas I was blind, now I see.
29. We know *that* God spake unto Moses:
30. *that* ye know not from whence he is,
31. Now we know *that* God heareth not
32. *that* any man opened the eyes of
35. Jesus heard *that* they had cast him out:

Joh. 9:41. but now ye say,)(We see:
10: 4. *for* they know his voice.
5. *for* they know not the voice of
7.)(I am the door of the sheep.
13. fleeth, *because* he is an hireling,
17. *because* I lay down my life,
33. and *because* that thou, being a man,
36.)(Thou blasphemest; *because* I said, I am
the Son of God?
38. *that* the Father (is) in me,
41.)(John did no miracle:
11: 6. had heard therefore *that* he was sick,
9. *because* he seeth the light of this world.
10. *because* there is no light in him.
13. they thought *that* he had spoken of
15. for your sakes *that* I was not there,
20. as soon as she heard *that* Jesus
22. But I know, *that* even now,
24. I know *that* he shall rise again
27. I believe *that* thou art the Christ,
31. *that* she rose up hastily and
—)(She goeth unto the grave to weep
40. Said I not unto thee, *that*, if thou
41. I thank thee *that* thou hast heard me.
42. I knew *that* thou hearest me always:
— may believe *that* thou hast sent me.
47. *for* this man doeth many miracles.
50. Nor consider *that* it is expedient
51. he prophesied *that* Jesus should die
56. *that* he will not come to the feast?
12: 6. not *that* he cared for the poor; but *because*
he was a thief,
9. knew *that* he was there:
11. *Because that* by reason of him
12. when they heard *that* Jesus was coming
16. remembered they *that* these things
18. *for that* they heard that he had
19. Perceive ye *how* ye prevail nothing?
34. *that* Christ abideth for ever: and how
sayest thou,)(The Son of man
39. *because* that Esaias said again,
49. *For* I have not spoken of myself;
50. I know *that* his commandment is
13: 1. when Jesus knew *that* his hour was
3. Jesus knowing *that* the Father
— and *that* he was come from God,
19. ye may believe *that* I am (he).
21. *that* one of you shall betray me.
29. *that* Jesus had said unto him, Buy
33.)(Whither I go, ye cannot come;
35. *that* ye are my disciples,
14:10. Believest thou not *that* I am in
11. Believe me *that* I (am) in the Father,
12. *because* I go unto my Father.
17. *because* it seeth him not,
— *for* he dwelleth with you, and
19. *because* I live, ye shall live also.
20. *that* I (am) in my Father,
22. how is it *that* thou wilt manifest
28. Ye have heard *how* I said unto you.
— *because* I said, I go unto the Father: *for*
my Father is greater than I.
31. may know *that* I love the Father;
15: 5. *for* without me ye can do nothing.
15. *for* the servant knoweth not what
— *for* all things that I have heard
18. ye know *that* it hated me before
19. but *because* ye are not of the world,
21. *because* they know not him that sent me.
25.)(They hated me without a cause.
27. *because* ye have been with me from
16: 3. *because* they have not known the Father,

Joh. 16: 4. remember *that* I told you of them.
— *because* I was with you.
6. But *because* I have said these things
9. *because* they believe not on me;
10. *because* I go to my Father,
11. *because* the prince of this world is judged.
14. *for* he shall receive of mine,
15. *that* he shall take of mine,
16. *because* I go to the Father.
17. *Because* I go to the Father?
19. Jesus knew *that* they were desirous
— enquire among yourselves of that)(I said,
20. *That* ye shall weep and lament,
21. *because* her hour is come:
— for joy *that* a man is born
23.)(Whatsoever ye shall ask the Father in
26. *that* I will pray the Father for you:
27. *because* ye have loved me, and have believed *that* I came out from God.
30. Now are we sure *that* thou knowest
— by this we believe *that* thou camest
32. *because* the Father is with me.
17: 7. Now they have known *that* all things
8. *For* I have given unto them the words which
— *that* I came out from thee, and they have believed *that* thou didst send me.
9. *for* they are thine.
14. *because* they are not of the world,
21. that the world may believe *that* thou
23. may know *that* thou hast sent me,
24. *for* thou lovedst me before the foundation
25. and these have known *that* thou hast
18: 2. *for* Jesus ofttimes resorted thither
6. had said unto them,)(I am (he),
8. I have told you *that* I am (he):
9.)(Of them which thou gavest me
14. *that* it was expedient that one man
18. *for* it was cold:
37. Thou sayest *that* I am a king.
19: 4. that ye may know *that* I find no fault
7. *because* he made himself the Son of God.
10. *that* I have power to crucify thee,
20. *for* the place where Jesus was crucified
21. but *that* he said, I am King of the Jews.
28. Jesus knowing *that* all things were now
35. he knoweth *that* he saith true,
42. *for* the sepulchre was nigh
20: 9. *that* he must rise again
13. *Because* they have taken away my Lord,
14. and knew not *that* it was Jesus.
15. She, supposing)(him to be the gardener,
18. *that* she had seen the Lord,
29. Thomas, *because* thou hast seen me,
31. that ye might believe *that* Jesus
21: 4. the disciples knew not *that* it was Jesus.
7. Peter heard *that* it was the Lord,
12. knowing *that* it was the Lord.
15. thou knowest *that* I love thee.
16. thou knowest *that* I love thee.
17. Peter was grieved *because* he said
— thou knowest *that* I love thee.
23. *that* that disciple should not die: yet Jesus said not unto him,)(He shall not die;
24. we know *that* his testimony is true.
Acts 1: 5. *For* John truly baptized with water;
17. *For* he was numbered with us,
2: 6. *because* that every man heard them
13. said,)(These men are full of new wine.
25. *for* he is on my right hand, that
27. *Because* thou wilt not leave my soul
29. *that* he is both dead and buried.
Acts 2: 30. and knowing *that* God had sworn
31. *that* his soul was not left in hell,
36. *that* God hath made that same Jesus,
3: 10. they knew *that* it was he which
17. I wot *that* through ignorance ye did (it)
22.)(A prophet shall the Lord your God
4: 10. *that* by the name of Jesus Christ
13. perceived *that* they were unlearned
— *that* they had been with Jesus.
16. for *that* indeed a notable miracle
21. *for* all (men) glorified God for
5: 4. why)(hast thou conceived this thing
9. How is it *that* ye have agreed
23.)(The prison truly found we shut
25.)(Behold, the men whom ye put in
38. *for* if this counsel or this work
41. rejoicing *that* they were counted worthy
6: 1. *because* their widows were neglected
11.)(We have heard him speak blasphemous
14. *that* this Jesus of Nazareth shall
7: 6. *That* his seed should sojourn in
25. *how that* God by his hand would
8: 14. heard *that* Samaria had received
18. when Simon saw *that* through laying on
20. *because* thou hast thought that the
33. *for* his life is taken from the earth.
9: 15. *for* he is a chosen vessel unto me,
20. *that* he is the Son of God.
22. proving *that* this is very Christ.
26. and believed not *that* he was a disciple.
27. and *that* he had spoken to him,
38. had heard *that* Peter was there,
10: 14. *for* I have never eaten any thing that is
34. I perceive *that* God is no respecter
38. *for* God was with him.
42. and to testify *that* it is he
45. *because that* on the Gentiles also
11: 1. heard *that* the Gentiles had also
3.)(Thou wentest in to men uncircumcised,
8. *for* nothing common or unclean
24. *For* he was a good man,
12: 3. And because he saw)(it pleased the Jews,
9. and wist not *that* it was true
11. *that* the Lord hath sent his angel,
13: 32. glad tidings, *how that* the promise
34. And *as concerning that* he raised
—)(I will give you the sure mercies of David.
38. *that* through this man is preached
41. *for* I work a work in your days,
14: 9. perceiving *that* he had faith to be
22. and *that* we must through much
27. and *how* he had opened the door of faith
15: 1.)(Except ye be circumcised
5. *That* it was needful to circumcise
7. ye know *how that* a good while ago
24. *that* certain which went out from us
16: 3. for they knew all *that* his father
10. assuredly gathering *that* the Lord
19. when her masters saw *that* the hope
36.)(The magistrates have sent to let
38. when they heard *that* they were Romans.
17: 3. *that* Christ must needs have suffered,
— and *that* this Jesus, whom I preach
6.)(These that have turned the world
13. had knowledge *that* the word of God
18. *because* he preached unto them Jesus.
18: 13.)(This (fellow) persuadeth men to
19: 21.)(After I have been there, I must
25. ye know *that* by this craft we have our
26. *that* not alone at Ephesus, but
— saying *that* they be no gods,

Acts 19 34. But when they knew that he was a Jew,
20 23. Save *that* the Holy Ghost witnesseth in every city, saying *that* bonds
25. I know *that* ye all, among whom
26. to record this day, *that* I (am) pure from
29. For I know this, *that* after my
31. remember, *that* by the space of three
34. *that* these hands have ministered
35. *how that* so labouring ye ought
— *how* he said, It is more blessed
38. *that* they should see his face no more.
21:21. *that* thou teachest all the Jews
22. for they will hear *that* thou art come.
24. *that* those things, whereof they
29. whom they supposed *that* Paul had
31. *that* all Jerusalem was in an uproar.
22: 2. when they heard *that* he spake in
15. *For* thou shalt be his witness
19. Lord, they know *that* I imprisoned
21. Depart: *for* I will send thee far hence
29. after he knew *that* he was a Roman, and *because* he had bound him.
23: 5. I wist not, brethren, *that* he was
6. when Paul perceived *that* the one part
20.)(The Jews have agreed to desire thee
22. tell no man *that* thou hast shewed
27. having understood *that* he was a Roman.
34. understood *that* (he was) of Cilicia;
24:11. understand, *that* there are yet
14. *that* after the way which they
21.)(Touching the resurrection
26. He hoped also *that* money should
25: 8.)(Neither against the law of the Jews,
16.)(It is not the manner of the Romans
26: 5. *that* after the most straitest sect
27. I know *that* thou believest.
31.)(This man doeth nothing worthy of death
27:10. I perceive *that* this voyage will
25. *that* it shall be even as
28: 1. then they knew *that* the island
22. *that* every where it is spoken against.
25.)(Well spake the Holy Ghost
28. *that* the salvation of God is sent
Ro 1: 8. *that* your faith is spoken of
13. *that* oftentimes I purposed to
32. *that* they which commit such
2: 2. we are sure *that* the judgment
3. *that* thou shalt escape the judgment
4. not knowing *that* the goodness of God
3: 2. because *that* unto them were
8.)(Let us do evil,
10.)(There is none righteous, no, not one:
19. *that* what things soever the law saith,
4: 9. for we say *that* faith was reckoned
17.)(I have made thee a father of many
21. being fully persuaded *that*, what
23. *that* it was imputed to him;
5: 3. knowing *that* tribulation worketh
5. *because* the love of God is shed
8. *in that*, while we were yet sinners,
6: 3. Know ye not, *that* so many of us
6. Knowing this, *that* our old man
8. believe *that* we shall also live
9. Knowing *that* Christ being raised
15. *because* we are not under the law,
16. Know ye not, *that* to whom ye yield
17. But God be thanked, *that* ye were
7: 1. *how that* the law hath dominion
14. For we know *that* the law is spiritual:
16. I consent unto the law *that* (it is) good.
18. For I know *that* in me

Ro. 7:21. *that*, when I would do good, evil is
8:16. *that* we are the children of God:
18. For I reckon *that* the sufferings
21. *Because* the creature itself also
22. For we know *that* the whole creation
27. *because* he maketh intercession
28. we know *that* all things work
29. *For* whom he did foreknow,
36. *For* thy sake we are killed
38. For I am persuaded, *that* neither
9: 2. *That* I have great heaviness and
6. Not as *though* the word of God
7. Neither, *because* they are the seed
12.)(The elder shall serve the younger.
17.)(Even for this same purpose have I
28. *because* a short work will the Lord
30. *That* the Gentiles, which followed not
32. *Because* (they sought it) not by faith.
10: 2. *that* they have a zeal of God,
5. *That* the man which doeth those things
9. *That* if thou shalt confess with thy
— *that* God hath raised him from the
11:25. *that* blindness in part is happened
36. *For* of him, and through him, and to him
13:11. *that* now (it is) high time to awake
14:11.)(every knee shall bow to me,
14. *that* (there is) nothing unclean of
23. *because* (he eateth) not of faith:
15:14. *that* ye also are full of goodness,
29. And I am sure *that*, when I come
1Co. 1: 5. *That* in every thing ye are enriched
11. *that* there are contentions among you.
12. *that* every one of you saith,
14. *that* I baptized none of you, but
15. Lest any should say *that* I had
25. *Because* the foolishness of God is wise
26. *how that* not many wise men
2:14. *because* they are spiritually
3:13. *because* it shall be revealed by fire;
16. Know ye not *that* ye are the temple
20. thoughts of the wise, *that* they are vain.
4: 9. For I think *that* God hath set forth
— *for* we are made a spectacle unto
5: 6. Know ye not *that* a little leaven
6: 2. Do ye not know *that* the saints
3. Know ye not *that* we shall judge
7. *because* ye go to law one with another.
9. Know ye not *that* the unrighteous
15. Know ye not *that* your bodies
16. know ye not *that* he which is joined
19. know ye not *that* your body is
7:26. *that* (it is) good for a man so to be.
8: 1. we know *that* we all have knowledge.
4. we know *that* an idol (is) nothing
— *that* (there is) none other God but one
9:10. *that* he that ploweth should
13. Do ye not know *that* they which
24. Know ye not *that* they which run
10: 1. be ignorant, *how that* all our fathers
17. *For* we (being) many are one bread,
19. What say I then? *that* the idol is any thing or)(that which is offered
20. But (I say), *that* the things which the
11: 2. *that* ye remember me in all things,
3. *that* the head of every man is Christ;
14. *that*, if a man have long hair,
15. *for* (her) hair is given her for a
17. I praise (you) not, *that* ye come together
23. *That* the Lord Jesus the (same) night
12: 2. Ye know *that* ye were Gentiles,
3. *that* no man speaking by the Spirit
15. *Because* I am not the hand,

1 Co.12:16. *Because* I am not the eye,
14:21.)(With (men of) other tongues
23. will they not say *that* ye are mad?
25. and report *that* God is in you
37. *that* the things that I write
15: 3. *how that* Christ died for our sins
4. And *that* he was buried, and *that* he rose again the third day
5. And *that* he was seen of Cephas,
12. Now if Christ be preached *that* he rose
— *that* there is no resurrection
15. *because* we have testified of God *that* he raised up Christ:
27. But when he saith,)(All things are put under (him, it is) manifest *that* he is
50. *that* flesh and blood cannot inherit
58. ye know *that* your labour is not
16:15. *that* it is the firstfruits of Achaia,
17. *for* that which was lacking
2Co 1: 5. *For* as the sufferings of Christ
7. knowing, *that* as ye are partakers
8. *that* we were pressed out of measure,
10. in whom we trust *that* he will yet
12. *that* in simplicity and godly sincerity,
13. and I trust)(ye shall acknowledge
14. *that* we are your rejoicing,
18. But (as) God (is) true,)(our word toward you
23. *that* to spare you I came not as yet
24. Not *for that* we have dominion over
2: 3. *that* my joy is (the joy) of you all.
15. *For* we are unto God a sweet savour
3: 3. manifestly declared)(to be the epistle
5. Not *that* we are sufficient of ourselves
4: 6. *For* God, who commanded the light
14. Knowing *that* he which raised up
5: 1. For we know *that* if our earthly
6. knowing *that*, whilst we are
14(15). because we thus judge, *that* if one died
19. To wit, *that* God was in Christ,
6:16. as God hath said,)(I will dwell in them,
7: 3. *that* ye are in our hearts to die
8. *For* though I made you sorry with
— for I perceive *that* the same epistle
9. not *that* ye were made sorry, but *that* ye sorrowed to repentance:
13. *because* his spirit was refreshed
14. *For* if I have boasted any thing
16. *that* I have confidence in you in all
8: 2. *How that* in a great trial of affliction
3. *For* to (their) power, I bear record,
9. *that*, though he was rich, yet for
17. *For* indeed he accepted the
9: 2. *that* Achaia was ready a year ago;
12. *For* the administration of this
10: 7. *that*, as he (is) Christ's, even so
10. *For* (his) letters, say they, (are) weighty
11. *that*, such as we are in word by
11: 7. *because* I have preached to you
10.)(no man shall stop me of this
11. Wherefore? *because* I love you not?
21. as *though* we had been weak.
31. knoweth *that* I lie not.
12: 4. *How that* he was caught up into
13. *that* I myself was not burdensome
19. think ye *that* we excuse ourselves
13: 2. *that*, if I come again, I will not spare:
5. *how that* Jesus Christ is in you,
6. But I trust *that* ye shall know *that* we are not reprobates.
Gal. 1: 6. I marvel *that* ye are so soon
11. *that* the gospel which was preached
Gal. 1:13. *how that* beyond measure I persecuted
20. behold, before God,)(I lie not.
23. *That* he which persecuted us
2: 7. when they saw *that* the gospel of the
11. *because* he was to be blamed.
14. But when I saw *that* they walked not
16. Knowing *that* a man is not justified
3: 7. *that* they which are of faith,
8. foreseeing *that* God would justify
—)(In thee shall all nations be blessed.
11. But *that* no man is justified by
— *for*, The just shall live by faith.
4: 6. And *because* ye are sons,
12. *for* I (am) as ye
13. Ye know *how* through infirmity
15. for I bear you record, *that*, if
20. *for* I stand in doubt of you.
22. *that* Abraham had two sons,
27. *for* the desolate hath many more
5: 2. *that* if ye be circumcised,
3. *that* he is a debtor to do
10. *that* ye will be none otherwise minded:
21. *that* they which do such things
6: 8. *For* he that soweth to his flesh
Eph. 2:11. *that* ye (being) in time past Gentiles
12. *That* at that time ye were without Christ,
18. *For* through him we both have access
3: 3. *How that* by revelation
4: 9. what is it but *that* he also descended
25. *for* we are members one of another.
5: 5. *that* no whoremonger, nor unclean person,
16. *because* the days are evil.
23. *For* the husband is the head of
30. *For* we are members of his body,
6: 8. Knowing *that* whatsoever good
9. knowing *that* your Master also
12. *For* we wrestle not against flesh
Phi. 1: 6. *that* he which hath begun a good work
12. *that* the things (which happened)
17. knowing *that* I am set for the
19. For I know *that* this shall turn
20. *that* in nothing I shall be ashamed,
25. know *that* I shall abide
27. *that* ye stand fast in one spirit,
29. *For* unto you it is given
2:11. *that* Jesus Christ (is) Lord,
16. *that* I have not run in vain,
22. *that*, as a son with the father,
24. *that* I also myself shall come shortly.
26. ye had heard *that* he had been sick.
30. *Because* for the work of Christ
3:12. Not *as though* I had already attained,
4:10. *that* now at the last your care of me
11. Not *that* I speak in respect of want:
15. *that* in the beginning of the gospel,
16. *For* even in Thessalonica ye sent
17. Not *because* I desire a gift:
Col. 1:16. *For* by him were all things created,
19. *For* it pleased (the Father) that
2: 9. *For* in him dwelleth all the fulness
3:24. Knowing *that* of the Lord ye shall
4: 1. knowing *that* ye also have a Master
13. *that* he hath a great zeal for you,
1Th. 1: 5. *For* our gospel came not unto you
2: 1. *that* it was not in vain:
13. *because*, when ye received the word
14. *for* ye also have suffered like things
3: 3. know *that* we are appointed thereunto.
4. *that* we should suffer tribulation;
6. and *that* ye have good remembrance
8. *For* now we live, if ye stand fast
4:14. For if we believe *that* Jesus died

1Th. 4:15. *that* we which are alive (and) remain
16. *For* the Lord himself shall descend
5: 2. *that* the day of the Lord so cometh
9. *For* God hath not appointed us to wrath,
2Th. 1: 3. *because that* your faith groweth
10. *because* our testimony among you
2: 2. as *that* the day of Christ is at hand.
3. *for* (that day shall not come), except
4. shewing himself *that* he is God.
5. *that*, when I was yet with you,
13. *because* God hath from the beginning
3: 4. *that* ye both do and will do
7. *for* we behaved not ourselves
9. Not *because* we have not power,
10. *that* if any would not work,
1Ti. 1: 8. But we know *that* the law (is) good,
9. *that* the law is not made for
12. *for that* he counted me faithful,
13. *because* I did (it) ignorantly
15. *that* Christ Jesus came into
4: 1. *that* in the latter times some
4. *For* every creature of God (is) good,
10. *because* we trust in the living God,
5:12. *because* they have cast off their
6: 2. *because* they are brethren;
— *because* they are faithful
7. (it is) certain)(we can carry nothing out.
2Ti. 1: 5. I am persuaded *that* in thee also.
12. persuaded *that* he is able to keep
15. *that* all they which are in Asia
16. *for* he oft refreshed me,
2:23. knowing *that* they do gender strifes.
3: 1. *that* in the last days perilous
15. And *that* from a child
Tit. 3:11. Knowing *that* he that is such
Philem. 7. *because* the bowels of the saints
19. I do not say to thee *how* thou owest
21. knowing *that* thou wilt also do
22. for I trust *that* through your prayers
Heb 2: 6. What is man, *that* thou art mindful
— *that* thou visitest him?
3:19. we see *that* they could not enter
7: 8. of whom it is witnessed *that* he liveth.
14. For (it is) evident *that* our Lord
17.)(Thou (art) a priest for ever
8: 9. *because* they continued not in my
10. *For* this (is) the covenant that I will
11. *for* all shall know me,
12. *For* I will be merciful to their
10: 8.)(Sacrifice and offering and
11: 6. must believe *that* he is,
13. confessed *that* they were strangers
14. declare plainly *that* they seek a
18. *That* in Isaac shall thy seed be called:
19. Accounting *that* God (was) able
12:17. For ye know *how that* afterward,
13.18. for we trust)(we have a good conscience,
Jas. 1: 3. *that* the trying of your faith
7. let not that man think *that* he
10. *because* as the flower of the grass
12. *for* when he is tried,
13.)(I am tempted of God:
23. *For* if any be a hearer of the word,
2:19. Thou believest *that* there is one God;
20. *that* faith without works is dead?
22. Seest thou *how* faith wrought
24. Ye see then *how that* by works
3: 1. knowing *that* we shall receive
4: 4. *that* the friendship of the world
5. Do ye think *that* the scripture
5: 8. *for* the coming of the Lord draweth nigh.
11. *that* the Lord is very pitiful, and of tender
Jas. 5:20. *that* he which converteth the sinner
1Pet. 1:12. *that* not unto themselves, but
16. Be ye holy; *for* I am holy.
18. *that* ye were not redeemed with
2: 3. tasted *that* the Lord (is) gracious.
15. *For* so is the will of God,
21. *because* Christ also suffered
3: 9. knowing *that* ye are thereunto called,
12. *For* the eyes of the Lord (are) over
18. *For* Christ also hath once suffered
4: 1. *for* he that hath suffered in the
8. *for* charity shall cover the
14. *for* the spirit of glory and of God
17. *For* the time (is come) that judgment
5: 5. *for* God resisteth the proud,
7. *for* he careth for you.
8. *because* your adversary the devil,
2Pet. 1:14. Knowing *that* shortly I must put off
20. *that* no prophecy of the scripture
3: 3. *that* there shall come in the last days
5. *that* by the word of God
8. *that* one day (is) with the Lord as
1Joh. 1: 5. *that* God is light,
6. If we say *that* we have fellowship
8. If we say *that* we have no sin,
10. If we say *that* we have not sinned,
2: 3. hereby we do know *that* we know him,
5. hereby know we *that* we are in him.
8. *because* the darkness is past,
11. *because that* darkness hath blinded
12. *because* your sins are forgiven
13. *because* ye have known him
— *because* ye have overcome
— *because* ye have known the Father.
14. *because* ye have known him
— *because* ye are strong,
16. *For* all that (is) in the world,
18. as ye have heard *that* antichrist
— we know *that* it is the last time.
19. *that* they were not all of us.
21. *because* ye know not the truth, but *because* ye know it, and *that* no lie is
22. that denieth *that* Jesus is the Christ?
29. If ye know *that* he is righteous, ye know *that* every one that
3: 1. *because* it knew him not.
2. we know *that*, when he shall appear,
— *for* we shall see him as he is.
5. And ye know *that* he was manifested
8. *for* the devil sinneth from the
9. *for* his seed remaineth in him:
— *because* he is born of God.
11. *For* this is the message that
12. *Because* his own works were evil,
14. We know *that* we have passed from death unto life, *because* we love the
15. and ye know *that* no murderer
16. *because* he laid down his life
19. we know *that* we are of the truth,
20. *For* if our heart condemn us,)(God is greater than
22. *because* we keep his commandments,
24. we know *that* he abideth in us,
4: 1. *because* many false prophets
3. ye have heard *that* it should come;
4. *because* greater is he that is in you,
7. *for* love is of God;
8. *for* God is love.
9. *because that* God sent his only
10. not *that* we loved God but *that* he loved us,
13. know we *that* we dwell in him,

1Joh. 4:13. *because* he hath given us of his Spirit.
14. *that* the Father sent the Son
15. shall confess *that* Jesus is the Son
17. *because* as he is, so are we in
18. *because* fear hath torment.
19. *because* he first loved us.
20. If a man say,)(I love God,
5: 1. Whosoever believeth *that* Jesus
2. By this we know *that* we love
4. *For* whatsoever is born of God
5. but he that believeth *that* Jesus
6. *because* the Spirit is truth.
7. *For* there are three that bear record
9. *for* this is the witness of God
10. *because* he believeth not the
11. *that* God hath given to us eternal life,
13. may know *that* ye have eternal
14. *that*, if we ask any thing according
15. if we know *that* he hear us,
— we know *that* we have the petitions
18. We know *that* whosoever is born of
19. we know *that* we are of God,
20. we know *that* the Son of God is come,
2Joh. 4. *that* I found of thy children
7. *For* many deceivers are entered
3Joh. 12. and ye know *that* our record is true.
Jude 5. *how that* the Lord, having saved
11. *for* they have gone in the way of Cain,
18. *How that* they told you)(there should be mockers in the
Rev. 2: 2. and *how* thou canst not bear
4. *because* thou hast left thy first love.
6. *that* thou hatest the deeds of
14. *because* thou hast there them
20. *because* thou sufferest that woman
23. the churches shall know *that* I am he
3. 1. *that* thou hast a name *that* thou livest, and art dead.
4. *for* they are worthy.
8. *for* thou hast a little strength,
9. and to know *that* I have loved thee.
10. *Because* thou hast kept the word
15. *that* thou art neither cold nor hot:
16. So then *because* thou art lukewarm,
17. *Because* thou sayest,)(I am rich,
— knowest not *that* thou art wretched,
4:11. *for* thou hast created all things,
5: 4. *because* no man was found worthy
9. *for* thou wast slain,
6:17. *For* the great day of his wrath is
7:17. *For* the Lamb which is in the
8:11. *because* they were made bitter.
10: 6. *that* there should be time no longer:
11: 2. *for* it is given unto the Gentiles:
10. *because* these two prophets
17. *because* thou hast taken to thee
12:10. *for* the accuser of our brethren is cast
12. *for* the devil is come down
— knoweth *that* he hath but a short time.
13. when the dragon saw *that* he was cast
14. 7. *for* the hour of his judgment is come:
8. *because* she made all nations drink
15. *for* the time is come for thee to reap; *for* the harvest of the earth is ripe.
18. *for* her grapes are fully ripe.
15: 1. *for* in them is filled up the wrath of God:
4. *for* (thou) only (art) holy: *for* all nations shall come and worship before thee; *for* thy judgments are made
16: 5. *because* thou hast judged thus,
6. *For* they have shed the blood of saints
21. *for* the plague thereof was exceeding

Rev. 17:14. *for* he is Lord of lords, and
18: 3. *For* all nations have drunk
5. *For* her sins have reached unto
7. *for* she saith in her heart,
8. *for* strong (is) the Lord God who
10. *for* in one hour is thy judgment
11. *for* no man buyeth their merchandise
17(16). *For* in one hour so great riches
19. *for* in one hour is she made
20. *for* God hath avenged you on her.
23. *for* thy merchants were the great
— *for* by thy sorceries were all
19: 2. *For* true and righteous (are) his judgments: *for* he hath judged the great
6. *for* the Lord God omnipotent reigneth.
7. *for* the marriage of the Lamb is come,
21: 4. *for* the former things are passed away.
5. *for* these words are true and
22: 5. *for* the Lord God giveth them light:
10. *for* the time is at hand

3755 6 594/713 3748

ὅτου, *hotou*, for οὗτινος, gen. of ὅστις.

It is combined with ἕως, and has χρόνου understood.

Mat. 5:25. *whiles* thou art in the way with
Lu. 13: 8. till)(I shall dig about it, and dung
15: 8. seek diligently till)(she find (it)?
22:16. until)(it be fulfilled in thee
18. until)(the kingdom of God shall come.
Joh. 9:18. until)(they called the parents

3757 27 594/719 3739

οὗ, *hou*. adv. of place.

Mat. 2: 9. and stood over *where* the young child
18:20. For *where* two or three are gathered
28:16. *where* Jesus had appointed them.
Lu. 4:16. *where* he had been brought up:
17. found the place *where* it was written,
10: 1. *whither* he himself would come.
22:10. into the house *where* he entereth in.
23:53. *wherein* never man before was laid.
24:28. unto the village, *whither* they went:
Joh. 11:41. *where* the dead was laid.
Acts 1:13. *where* abode both Peter, and James,
2: 2. it filled all the house *where* they were sitting.
7:29. *where* he begat two sons.
12:12. *where* many were gathered
16:13. *where* prayer was wont to be made;
20: 6. *where* we abode seven days.
8. *where* they were gathered together.
25:10. *where* I ought to be judged:
28:14. *Where* we found brethren, and
Ro. 4:15. for *where* no law is, (there is) no
5:20. But *where* sin abounded, grace did
9:26. in the place *where* it was said
1Co. 16: 6. on my journey *whither*soever I go.
2Co. 3:17. and *where* the Spirit of the Lord (is),
Col. 3: 1. *where* Christ sitteth on the right hand
Heb 3: 9. When (lit. *where*) your fathers tempted
Rev 17:15. *where* the whore sitteth,

3756 1453 594/719 cf 3364 cf 3372

οὐ, οὐκ, οὐχ, *ou*, *ouk*, *ouk*.

Those passages in which it is combined with μη, as a strong double negation, will be found above in the series οὐ μή; and for those in which it is closely combined with ἔτι, see οὐκέτι. || shews that it is combined with another negative in the Greek.

Mat. 1:25. And knew her *not* till she had
2:18. and would *not* be comforted, because they are *not*.
3:11. whose shoes I am *not* worthy to bear:
4: 4. Man shall *not* live by bread alone,
7. Thou shalt *not* tempt the Lord
5:14. A city that is set on an hill can*not* be hid.
17. I am *not* come to destroy, but
21. Thou shalt *not* kill;
27. Thou shalt *not* commit adultery:
33. Thou shalt *not* forswear thyself,
36. because thou canst *not* make one hair
37. Yea, yea; *Nay, nay:*
6: 1. otherwise ye have *no* reward of
5. thou shalt *not* be as the hypocrites
20. where thieves do *not* break through
24. Ye can*not* serve God and
26. for they sow *not*, neither do
— Are ye *not* much better than they?
28. they toil *not*, neither do they spin:
30. (shall he) *not* much more (clothe)
7: 3. considerest *not* the beam
18. A good tree can*not* bring forth
21. *Not* every one that saith unto me,
22. have we *not* prophesied in thy name?
25. and it fell *not:*
29. and *not* as the scribes.
8: 8. I am *not* worthy that thou
20. the Son of man hath *not* where to
9:12. need *not* a physician,
13. and *not* sacrifice: for I am *not* come to
14. but thy disciples fast *not?*
24. for the maid is *not* dead, but sleepeth.
10:20. For it is *not* ye that speak,
24. The disciple is *not* above (his)
26. nothing covered, that shall *not* be revealed; and hid, that shall *not* be known.
29. and one of them shall *not* fall
34. I came *not* to send peace, but
37. is *not* worthy of me:
— is *not* worthy of me.
38. he that taketh *not* his cross,
— is *not* worthy of me.
11:11. there hath *not* risen a greater
17. and ye have *not* danced;
— and ye have *not* lamented.
20. because they repented *not:*
12: 2. do that which is *not* lawful
3. Have ye *not* read what David did,
4. which was *not* lawful for him
5. Or have ye *not* read in the law,
7. I will have mercy, and *not* sacrifice, ye would *not* have condemned
19. He shall *not* strive, nor cry;
20. shall he *not* break, and smoking flax shall he *not* quench,
24. doth *not* cast out devils, but by
25. against itself shall *not* stand:
31. shall *not* be forgiven unto men.
32. it shall *not* be forgiven him,
39. and there shall *no* sign be given
43. seeking rest, and findeth *none*.
13: 5. where they had *not* much earth:
11. but to them it is *not* given.
12. but whosoever hath *not*,
13. because they seeing see *not;* and hearing they hear *not*,
17. and have *not* seen (them),

Mat.13:17. and have *not* heard (them).
21. Yet hath he *not* root in himself,
29. But he said, *Nay;* lest while
34. without a parable spake he *not* unto them:
55. Is *not* this the carpenter's son?
57. A prophet is *not* without honour.
58. And he did *not* many mighty works
14: 4. It is *not* lawful for thee to have her.
16. They need *not* depart;
17. We have here but (lit. we have *not* here except) five loaves,
15: 2. for they wash *not* their hands when
11. *Not* that which goeth into the mouth
13. hath *not* planted, shall be rooted up.
20. defileth *not* a man.
23. he answered her *not* a word.
24. I am *not* sent but unto the lost
26. It is *not* meet to take the children's
32. and have *no*thing to eat (lit. *not* anything): and I will *not* send them away fasting,
16: 3. but can ye *not* (discern) the signs
4. there shall *no* sign be given unto it,
7. because we have taken *no* bread.
8. because ye have brought *no* bread?
11. How is it that ye do *not* understand that I spake (it) *not* to you
12. how that he bade (them) *not* beware
17. flesh and blood hath *not* revealed
18. and the gates of hell shall *not* prevail
23. for thou savourest *not* the things
17:12. and they knew him *not*,
16. and they could *not* cure him.
19. Why could *not* we cast him out?
21. this kind goeth *not* out but by
24. Doth *not* your master pay tribute?
18:14. it is *not* the will of your Father
22. I say *not* unto thee, Until seven times:
30. And he would *not:*
33. Shouldest *not* thou also have had
19: 4. Have ye *not* read, that he which
8. from the beginning it was *not* so.
10. it is *not* good to marry.
11. All (men) can*not* receive this
18. thou shalt do *no* murder, Thou shalt *not* commit adultery, Thou shalt *not* steal, Thou shalt *not* bear false witness,
20:13. I do thee *no* wrong:
15. Is it *not* lawful for me to do
22. Ye know *not* what ye ask.
23. is *not* mine to give,
26. But it shall *not* be so among you:
28. the Son of man came *not* to be
21:21. ye shall *not* only do this
25. Why did ye *not* then believe him?
27. We can*not* tell.
29. and said, I will *not:* but
30. I (go), sir: and went *not*.
32. and ye believed him *not:*
— repented *not* afterward, that ye
22: 3. and they would *not* come.
8. which were bidden were *not* worthy.
11. which had *not* on a wedding
16. *neither* || carest thou for any (man): for thou regardest *not* the person of men.
17. to give tribute unto Cæsar, or *not?*
31. have ye *not* read that which was spoken
32. God is *not* the God of the dead,
23: 3. for they say, and do *not*.
4. will *not* move them with one
13(14). for ye *neither* go in (yourselves),
30. we would *not* have been partakers

Mat.23:37. and ye would *not!*
24: 2. See ye *not* all these things?
21. such as was *not* since the beginning
22. there should *no* flesh be saved:
29. the moon shall *not* give her light,
39. And knew *not* until the flood came,
42. for ye know *not* what hour your Lord
43. would *not* have suffered his house
44. in such an hour as ye think *not*
50. in a day when he looketh *not* for (him), and in an hour that he is *not* aware of,
25 3. and took *no* oil with them:
9. lest there be *not* enough for us
12. I know you *not*.
13. for ye know *neither* the day
24. reaping where thou hast *not* sown, and gathering where thou hast *not* strawed:
26. that I reap where I sowed *not*, and gather where I have *not* strawed:
42. and ye gave me *no* meat: I was thirsty, and ye gave me *no* drink:
43. and ye took me *not* in: naked, and ye clothed me *not:* sick, and in prison, and ye visited me *not*.
44. and did *not* minister unto thee?
45. as ye did (it) *not* to one of the least
26:11. but me ye have *not* always.
24. if he had *not* been born.
39. nevertheless *not* as I will,
40. What, could ye *not* watch with me
42. if this cup may *not* pass away
53. Thinkest thou that I can*not* now
55. and ye laid *no* hold on me.
60. But found *none:*
— (yet) found they *none*.
70. I know *not* what thou sayest.
72. I do *not* know the man.
74. I know *not* the man.
27: 6. It is *not* lawful for to put them into
13. Hearest thou *not* how many things
14. he answered)(‖ him to never a word;
34. he would *not* drink.
42. himself he can*not* save.
28: 6. He is *not* here:
Mar 1: 7. I am *not* worthy to stoop down
22. and *not* as the scribes.
34. and suffered *not* the devils to speak,
2:17. They that are whole have *no* need
— I came *not* to call the righteous.
18. but thy disciples fast *not?*
19. bridegroom with them, they can*not* fast.
24. that which is *not* lawful?
26. which is *not* lawful to eat
27. and *not* man for the sabbath:
3:24. that kingdom can*not* stand.
25. that house can*not* stand.
26. he can*not* stand, but hath an end.
27. No man can)(‖ enter into a strong
29. hath *never* forgiveness, but is in danger
4: 5. where it had *not* much earth;
7. and it yielded *no* fruit.
13. Know ye *not* this parable?
17. have *no* root in themselves,
21. and *not* to be set on a candlestick?
22. For there is *no*thing hid, which
25. and he that hath *not*, from him shall
27. he knoweth *not* how.
34. without a parable spake he *not* unto them:
38. Master, carest thou *not* that we
40. how is it that ye have *no* faith?
5:19. Jesus suffered him *not*,
37. he suffered)(‖ no man to follow him,

Mar 5:39. the damsel is *not* dead, but
6: 3. Is *not* this the carpenter,
— and are *not* his sisters here
4. A prophet is *not* without honour,
5. he could there)(‖ do no mighty work,
18. It is *not* lawful for thee to have
19. but she could *not:*
26. he would *not* reject her.
36. for they have *no*thing to eat.
52. they considered *not* (the miracle)
7: 3. except they wash (their) hands oft, eat *not*,
4. except they wash, they eat *not*.
5. Why walk *not* thy disciples according
18. Do ye *not* perceive,
— (it) can*not* defile him;
19. Because it entereth *not* into
24. but he could *not* be hid.
27. for it is *not* meet to take the
8: 2. and have *no*thing to eat:
14. *neither* had they (lit. and they had *not*) in the ship
16. because we have *no* bread.
17. because ye have *no* bread?
18. Having eyes, see ye *not?* and having ears, hear ye *not?* and do ye *not* remember?
21. How is it that ye do *not* understand?
33. thou savourest *not* the things
9: 3. so as *no* fuller on earth can
6. For he wist *not* what to say;
18. and they could *not*.
28. Why could *not* we cast him out?
30. and he would *not* that any man
37. receiveth *not* me, but him that
38. and he followeth *not* us:
— because he followeth *not* us.
40. For he that is *not* against us
44. Where their worm dieth *not*, and the fire is *not* quenched.
46. Where their worm dieth *not*, and the fire is *not* quenched.
48. Where their worm dieth *not*, and the fire is *not* quenched.
10:27. impossible, but *not* with God:
38. Ye know *not* what ye ask:
40. is *not* mine to give;
43. so shall it *not* be among you:
45. the Son of man came *not* to be
11:13. for the time of figs was *not* (yet).
16. would *not* suffer that any man
17. Is it *not* written, My house
26. if ye do *not* forgive,
31. Why then did ye *not* believe him?
33. We can*not* tell.
12:14. and carest)(‖ for no man: for thou regardest *not* the person of men,
— to give tribute to Cæsar, or *not?*
20. and dying left *no* seed.
22. And the seven had her, and left *no* seed:
24. Do ye *not* therefore err,
26. have ye *not* read in the book of
27. He is *not* the God of the dead,
31. There is *none* other commandment greater
32. and there is *none* other but he:
34. Thou art *not* far from the kingdom
13:11. for it is *not* ye that speak,
14. standing where it ought *not*,
19. such as was *not* from the beginning
20. *no* flesh should be saved:
24. the moon shall *not* give her light,
33. for ye know *not* when the time is.
35. for ye know *not* when the master

Mar14: 7. but me ye have *not* always.
21. if he had *never* been born.
29. be offended, yet (will) *not* I.
36. nevertheless *not* what I will,
37. couldest *not* thou watch one hour?
40. *neither* wist they what to answer
49. and ye took me *not:*
55. to put him to death; and found *none.*
56. but their witness agreed *not*
60. Answerest)(‖ thou nothing?
68. I know *not*, neither understand
71. I know *not* this man of whom
15: 4. Answerest)(‖ thou nothing?
23. but he received (it) *not.*
31. himself he can*not* save.
16: 6. he is risen; he is *not* here:
14. because they believed *not*
Lu. 1: 7. And they had *no* child,
20. because thou believest *not* my words,
22. he could *not* speak unto them:
33. of his kingdom there shall be *no* end.
34. seeing I know *not* a man?
37. with God *no*thing shall be impossible.
2: 7. there was *no* room for them in the inn.
37. which departed *not* from the temple,
43. Joseph and his mother knew *not* (of it).
49. wist ye *not* that I must be
50. they understood *not* the saying
3:16. I am *not* worthy to unloose:
4: 2. in those days he did)(‖ eat nothing:
4. shall *not* live by bread alone,
12. Thou shalt *not* tempt the Lord
22. Is *not* this Joseph's son?
41. suffered them *not* to speak:
5:31. need *not* a physician;
32. I came *not* to call the righteous,
36. agreeth *not* with the old.
6: 2. that which is *not* lawful to do on
4. which it is *not* lawful to eat
40. The disciple is *not* above his master:
41. but perceivest *not* the beam that is
42. when thou thyself beholdest *not*
43. good tree bringeth *not* forth
44. of thorns men do *not* gather figs,
46. and do *not* the things which I say?
48. and could *not* shake it:
7: 6. he was now *not* far from the house,
— for I am *not* worthy that thou
32. and ye have *not* danced;
— and ye have *not* wept.
44. thou gavest me *no* water for my feet:
45. Thou gavest me *no* kiss:
— hath *not* ceased to kiss my feet.
46. thou didst *not* anoint:
8:13. and these have *no* root,
14. and bring *no* fruit to perfection.
17. For *nothing* is secret, that shall *not* be made manifest;
— that shall *not* be known
19. and could *not* come at him
27. and ware *no* clothes, *neither* abode in (any) house,
43. *neither* ‖ could be healed of any,
47. that she was *not* hid,
51. he suffered)(‖ no man to go in,
52. she is *not* dead, but sleepeth.
9:13. We have *no* more but five loaves
40. and they could *not.*
49. because he followeth *not* with us.
50. he that is *not* against us
53. And they did *not* receive him,
55. Ye know *not* what manner of spirit

Lu. 9:56. is *not* come to destroy men's lives,
58. hath *not* where to lay (his) head.
10:24. and have *not* seen (them);
— and have *not* heard (them).
40. dost thou *not* care that my sister
42. which shall *not* be taken away
11: 6. and I have *no*thing to set before him?
7. I can*not* rise and give thee.
8. Though he will *not* rise and give him,
29. there shall *no* sign be given
38. marvelled that he had *not* first washed
40. did *not* he that made that which
44. are *not* aware (of them).
46. yourselves touch *not* the burdens
52. ye entered *not* in yourselves,
12: 2. that shall *not* be revealed; neither hid, that shall *not* be known.
6. and *not* one of them is forgotten
10. it shall *not* be forgiven.
15. consisteth *not* in the abundance
17. because I have *no* room where
24. for they *neither* sow nor reap; which *neither* have storehouse
27. they toil *not*, they spin not;
33. where *no* thief approacheth,
39. and *not* have suffered his house
40. at an hour when ye think *not.*
46. when he looketh *not* for (him), and at an hour when he is *not* aware,
56. how is it that ye do *not* discern
57. judge ye *not* what is right?
13: 6. sought fruit thereon, and found *none.*
7. on this fig tree, and find *none:*
15. doth *not* each one of you on the
16. And ought *not* this woman,
24. and shall *not* be able.
25. I know you *not* whence ye are:
27. I know you *not* whence ye are;
33. for it can*not* be that
34. and ye would *not!*
14: 5. and will *not* straightway pull
6. And they could *not* answer
14. for they can*not* recompense
20. and therefore I can*not* come.
26. and hate *not* his father, and
— he can*not* be my disciple.
27. whosoever doth *not* bear his
— can*not* be my disciple.
30. and was *not* able to finish.
33. that forsaketh *not* all that he hath, he can*not* be my disciple.
15: 4. doth *not* leave the ninety and nine
7. which need *no* repentance.
13. And *not* many days after
28. and would *not* go in:
16: 2. for thou mayest be *no* longer steward.
3. I can*not* dig; to beg I am ashamed.
11. ye have *not* been faithful
12. if ye have *not* been faithful in that
13. Ye can*not* serve God and mammon.
31. If they hear *not* Moses and the
17: 9. that were commanded him? I trow *not.*
18. There are *not* found that returned
20. The kingdom of God cometh *not* with
22. and ye shall *not* see (it).
18: 4. And he would *not* for a while:
— Though I fear *not* God, *nor* regard man;
11. that I am *not* as other men
13. would *not* ‖ lift up so much
34. *neither* knew they the things which
19: 3. and could *not* for the press,
14. We will *not* have this (man) to reign

Lu. 19:21. that thou layedst *not* down, and reapest that thou didst *not* sow.
22. that I laid *not* down, and reaping that I did *not* sow:
23. Wherefore then gavest *not* thou
44. they shall *not* leave in thee one
— thou knewest *not* the time of thy
48. And could *not* find what they
20: 5. Why then believed ye him *not?*
21. *neither* acceptest thou the person
22. to give tribute unto Cæsar, or *no?*
26. And they could *not* take hold
31. and they left *no* children,
38. For he is *not* a God of the dead,
21: 6. shall *not* be left one stone upon another, that shall *not* be thrown down.
9. but the end (is) *not* by and by.
15. shall *not* be able to gainsay
22:26. But ye (shall) *not* (be) so:
53. ye stretched forth *no* hands
57. Woman, I know him *not*.
58. And Peter said, Man, I am *not*.
60. Man, I know *not* what thou sayest.
23:29. and the wombs that *never* bare, and the paps which *never* gave suck.
34. for they know *not* what they do.
51. The same had *not* consented to the
53. wherein)(‖ never man before was laid.
24: 3. and found *not* the body of the Lord
6. He is *not* here, but is risen:
18. and hast *not* known the things
24. but him they saw *not*.
39. for a spirit hath *not* flesh and bones,
Joh. 1: 5. the darkness comprehended it *not*.
8. He was *not* that Light,
10. and the world knew him *not*.
11. and his own received him *not*.
13. Which were born, *not* of blood,
20. he confessed, and denied *not;* but confessed, I am *not* the Christ.
21. I am *not*. Art thou that prophet? And he answered, *No*.
25. if thou be *not* that Christ,
26. whom ye know *not;*
27. I am *not* worthy to unloose.
31. And I knew him *not:*
33. And I knew him *not:*
47(48). in whom is *no* guile!
2: 3. They have *no* wine.
9. and knew *not* whence it was:
12. they continued there *not* many days.
24. Jesus did *not* commit himself
25. And needed *not* that any should
3: 3. he can*not* see the kingdom of God.
5. he can*not* enter into the kingdom
8. but canst *not* tell whence it cometh,
10. and knowest *not* these things?
11. and ye receive *not* our witness.
12. and ye believe *not*,
17. For God sent *not* his Son into the
18. is *not* condemned:
20. *neither* cometh to the light,
27. A man can)(‖ receive nothing, except it be given him
28. that I said, I am *not* the Christ,
34. God giveth *not* the Spirit by measure
36. shall *not* see life;
4: 2. Jesus himself baptized *not*, but
9. for the Jews have *no* dealings with
17. I have *no* husband.
— Thou hast well said, I have *no* husband:
18. is *not* thy husband:

Joh. 4:22. Ye worship ye know *not* what:
32. I have meat to eat that ye know *not* of
35. Say *not* ye, There are yet four months,
38. whereon ye bestowed *no* labour.
44. that a prophet hath *no* honour in
5: 7. Sir, I have *no* man, when the
10. it is *not* lawful for thee to
13. he that was healed wist *not* who
18. because he *not* only had broken the
19. The Son can)(‖ do nothing of himself, but what he
23. honoureth *not* the Father
24. and shall *not* come into condemnation;
30. I can)(‖ of mine own self do nothing.
— I seek *not* mine own will,
31. of myself, my witness is *not* true.
34. I receive *not* testimony from man.
38. ye have *not* his word abiding
— him ye believe *not*.
40. And ye will *not* come to me,
41. I receive *not* honour from men.
42. ye have *not* the love of God in you.
43. and ye receive me *not:*
44. and seek *not* the honour that
47. But if ye believe *not* his writings,
6: 7. of bread is *not* sufficient for them,
17. and Jesus was *not* come to them.
22. that there was *none* other boat
— and that Jesus went *not* with
24. saw that Jesus was *not* there,
26. *not* because ye saw the miracles,
32. Moses gave you *not* that bread
36. have seen me, and believe *not*.
38. *not* to do mine own will,
42. Is *not* this Jesus, the son of
46. *Not* that any man hath seen
53. ye have *no* life in you.
58. *not* as your fathers did eat
63. the flesh)(‖ profiteth nothing:
64. some of you that believe *not*.
70. Have *not* I chosen you twelve,
7. 1. for he would *not* walk in Jewry,
7. The world can*not* hate you; but
10. *not* openly, but as it were in secret.
12. *Nay;* but he deceiveth the people.
16. My doctrine is *not* mine,
18. and *no* unrighteousness is in him.
19. Did *not* Moses give you the law,
22. *not* because it is of Moses,
25. Is *not* this he, whom they seek
28. I am *not* come of myself,
— whom ye know *not*.
34. and shall *not* find (me): and where I am, (thither) ye can*not* come.
35. that we shall *not* find him?
36. and shall *not* find (me): and where I am, (thither) ye can*not* come?
45. Why have ye *not* brought him?
52. out of Galilee ariseth *no* prophet.
8:13. thy record is *not* true.
14. but ye can*not* tell whence I come,
15. I judge)(‖ no man.
16. for I am *not* alone,
21. whither I go, ye can*not* come.
22. Whither I go, ye can*not* come.
23. I am *not* of this world.
27. They understood *not* that he spake
29. hath *not* left me alone;
35. abideth *not* in the house for ever:
37. hath *no* place in you.
40. this did *not* Abraham.
41. We be *not* born of fornication;

Joh. 8:43. Why do ye *not* understand my speech? (even) because ye can*not* hear my word.
44. and abode *not* in the truth, because there is *no* truth in him.
45. ye believe me *not*.
46. why do ye *not* believe me?
47. ye therefore hear (them) *not*, because ye are *not* of God.
48. Say we *not* well that thou art
49. I have *not* a devil;
50. I seek *not* mine own glory:
55. Yet ye have *not* known him;
— if I should say, I know him *not*,
9: 8. Is *not* this he that sat and begged?
12. He said, I know *not*.
16. This man is *not* of God, because he keepeth *not* the sabbath
18. But the Jews did *not* believe
21. we know *not*; or who hath opened his eyes, we know *not*:
25. I know *not*: one thing I know,
27. and ye did *not* hear:
29. we know *not* from whence he is.
30. that ye know *not* from whence he is,
31. God heareth *not* sinners:
32. Since the world began was it *not* heard
33. he could)(‖ do nothing.
41. ye should have *no* sin:
10: 5. they know *not* the voice of strangers.
6. they understood *not* what things
8. but the sheep did *not* hear them.
10. The thief cometh *not*, but for
12. and *not* the shepherd, whose own the sheep are *not*,
13. and careth *not* for the sheep.
16. which are *not* of this fold:
21. These are *not* the words of him that
25. I told you, and ye believed *not*:
26. But ye believe *not*, because ye are *not* of my sheep,
28. *neither* shall any (man) pluck them
33. For a good work we stone thee *not*;
34. Is it *not* written in your law,
35. and the scripture can*not* be broken;
37. If I do *not* the works of my Father,
11: 4. This sickness is *not* unto death,
9. he stumbleth *not*,
10. because there is *no* light in him.
15. that I was *not* there,
21. my brother had *not* died.
32. my brother had *not* died.
37. Could *not* this man, which opened
40. Said I *not* unto thee,
49. Ye know)(‖ nothing at all,
51. this spake he *not* of himself:
52. And *not* for that nation only,
12: 5. Why was *not* this ointment sold
6. *not* that he cared for the poor;
8. but me ye have *not* always.
9. came *not* for Jesus' sake only,
16. These things understood *not* his
19. Perceive ye how ye prevail)(‖ nothing?
30. This voice came *not* because
35. knoweth *not* whither he goeth.
37. yet they believed *not* on him:
39. Therefore they could *not* believe,
42. they did *not* confess (him),
44. believeth *not* on me, but on him
47. I judge him *not*: for I came *not* to judge the world,
49. For I have *not* spoken of myself,
13: 7. What I do thou knowest *not* now,

Joh. 13. 8. thou hast *no* part with me.
10. He that is washed needeth *not*
16. The servant is *not* greater than
18. I speak *not* of you all:
33. Whither I go, ye can*not* come;
36. thou canst *not* follow me now;
37. why can*not* I follow thee now?
14: 5. Lord, we know *not* whither thou
9. and yet hast thou *not* known me,
10. Believest thou *not* that I am in
— I speak *not* of myself: but
17. whom the world can*not* receive, because it seeth him *not*,
18. I will *not* leave you comfortless:
22. Judas saith unto him, *not* Iscariot,
24. keepeth *not* my sayings: and the word which ye hear is *not* mine,
27. *not* as the world giveth, give I
30. and hath)(‖ nothing in me.
15: 4. As the branch can*not* bear fruit
5. for without me ye can)(‖ do nothing.
15. for the servant knoweth *not* what
16. Ye have *not* chosen me, but
19. but because ye are *not* of the world,
20. The servant is *not* greater than
21. because they know *not* him that
22. they had *not* had sin: but now they have *no* cloke for their sin.
24. they had *not* had sin:
16: 3. because they have *not* known the Father,
4. these things I said *not* unto you at
7. the Comforter will *not* come unto you;
9. because they believe *not* on me;
12. but ye can*not* bear them now.
13. for he shall *not* speak of himself;
16. and ye shall *not* see me:
17. A little while, and ye shall *not* see me:
18. we can*not* tell what he saith.
19. and ye shall *not* see me:
23. in that day ye shall)(‖ ask me nothing
24. Hitherto have ye)(‖ asked nothing in
26. and I say *not* unto you,
30. and needest *not* that any man
32. and yet I am *not* alone,
17: 9. I pray *not* for the world,
14. they are *not* of the world, even as I am *not* of the world.
15. I pray *not* that thou shouldest
16. They are *not* of the world, even as I am *not* of the world.
20. *Neither* pray I for these alone,
25. the world hath *not* known thee:
18: 9. which thou gavest me have I)(‖ lost none.
17. He saith, I am *not*.
25. He denied (it), and said, I am *not*.
26. Did *not* I see thee in the garden with
28. went *not* into the judgment hall,
30. we would *not* have delivered him up
31. It is *not* lawful for us to put any
36. My kingdom is *not* of this world:
— but now is my kingdom *not* from hence.
19: 6. for I find *no* fault in him.
9. But Jesus gave him *no* answer.
10. Speakest thou *not* unto me? knowest thou *not* that I
11. Thou couldest)(‖ have no power (at all)
12. thou art *not* Cæsar's friend:
15. We have *no* king but Cæsar.
33. they brake *not* his legs:
36. A bone of him shall *not* be broken.
20: 2. and we know *not* where they have
5. yet went he *not* in.

Joh.20: 7. *not* lying with the linen clothes,
13. and I know *not* where they have laid him.
14. and knew *not* that it was Jesus.
24. was *not* with them when Jesus came.
30. which are *not* written in this book:
21: 4. but the disciples knew *not* that it
5. They answered him, *No.*
8. for they were *not* far from land,
11. yet was *not* the net broken.
18. carry (thee) whither thou wouldest *not.*
23. that that disciple should *not* die: yet Jesus said *not* unto him, He shall *not* die;
Acts 1: 5. *not* many days hence.
7. It is *not* for you to know
2: 7. Behold, are *not* all these which
15. For these are *not* drunken, as
24. because it was *not* possible
27. Because thou wilt *not* leave
31. his soul was *not* left in hell,
34. For David is *not* ascended
3: 6. Silver and gold have I *none;*
4:12. *Neither* is there salvation in any other:
16. and we can*not* deny (it).
20. For we can*not* but speak the things
5: 4. thou hast *not* lied unto men,
22. and found them *not* in the prison,
26. without violence: (lit. *not* with violence)
28. Did *not* we straitly command
39. ye can*not* overthrow it;
42. they ceased *not* to teach
6: 2. It is *not* reason that we should
10. And they were *not* able to resist
13. This man ceaseth *not* to speak
7: 5. And he gave him *none* inheritance
— when (as yet) he had *no* child.
11. and our fathers found *no* sustenance.
18. which knew *not* Joseph.
25. but they understood *not.*
32. and durst *not* behold.
39. our fathers would *not* obey,
40. we wot *not* what is become of him.
48. dwelleth *not* in temples made
52. have *not* your fathers persecuted?
53. and have *not* kept (it).
8:21. Thou hast *neither* part nor lot
— is *not* right in the sight of God.
32. so opened he *not* his mouth:
39. that the eunuch saw)(‖ him no more:
9: 9. and *neither* did eat nor drink.
21. Is *not* this he that destroyed
10:34. that God is *no* respecter of persons:
41. *Not* to all the people,
12: 9. and wist *not* that it was true
14. she opened *not* the gate
18. there was *no* small stir
22. the voice of a god, and *not* of a man.
23. because he gave *not* God the glory:
13:10. wilt thou *not* cease to pervert
25. I am *not* (he). But, behold,
— I am *not* worthy to loose.
35. Thou shalt *not* suffer thine Holy One
37. whom God raised again, saw *no* corruption.
39. from which ye could *not* be justified
46. and judge yourselves *un*worthy
14:17. he left *not* himself without witness,
28. they abode long time (lit. *no* small time)
15: 1. ye can*not* be saved.
2. had *no* small dissension
24. whom we gave *no* (such) commandment:
16: 7. but the Spirit suffered them *not.*
21. which are *not* lawful for us to
37. *nay* verily; but let them come

Acts17: 4. and of the chief women *not* a few.
12. and of men, *not* a few.
24. dwelleth *not* in temples made with hands;
27. though he be *not* far from every one
29. we ought *not* to think that the
18:15. I will be *no* judge of such (matters).
20. with them, he consented *not;*
19:11. God wrought special miracles (lit. *no* common miracles)
23. there arose *no* small stir
24. *no* small gain unto the craftsmen;
26. that *not* alone at Ephesus, but
— that they be *no* gods, which are made
27. *not* only this our craft
30. the disciples suffered him *not.*
32. the more part knew *not* wherefore
35. that knoweth *not* how that the city
20:12. and were *not* a little comforted.
27. I have *not* shunned to declare
31. I ceased *not* to warn every one
21:13. I am ready *not* to be bound only,
38. Art *not* thou that Egyptian,
39. a citizen of *no* mean city:
22: 9. but they heard *not* the voice
11. And when I could *not* see for
18. for they will *not* receive thy
22. for it is *not* fit that he should live.
23: 5. I wist *not,* brethren, that he
— Thou shalt *not* speak evil of
24:11. that there are yet but (lit. *not* more than) twelve days
18. *neither* with multitude, nor
25: 7. which they could *not* prove.
11. I refuse *not* to die:
16. It is *not* the manner of the Romans
26. I have *no* certain thing to write
26:19. I was *not* disobedient
25. I am *not* mad,
26. I am)(‖ persuaded that none of these
— was *not* done in a corner.
29. that *not* only thou, but also all
27:10. *not* only of the lading and ship,
14. But *not* long after there arose
20. and *no* small tempest lay
31. ye can*not* be saved.
39. they knew *not* the land:
28: 2. shewed us *no* little kindness:
4. vengeance suffereth *not* to live.
19. *not* that I had ought to accuse
Ro. 1:13. I would *not* have you ignorant,
16. For I am *not* ashamed
21. glorified (him) *not* as God,
28. even as they did *not* like
32. *not* only do the same, but
2:11. For there is *no* respect of persons
13. For *not* the hearers of the law
21. teachest thou *not* thyself?
28. For he is *not* a Jew which is
29. in the spirit, (and) *not* in the letter; whose praise (is) *not* of men,
3: 9. *No,* in no wise: for we have before
10. There is *none* righteous,
11. There is *none* that understandeth, there is *none* that seeketh after God.
12. there is *none* that doeth good, *no,* not one.
17. the way of peace have they *not* known:
18. There is *no* fear of God before
20. there shall *no* flesh be justified
22. for there is *no* difference:
4: 2. but *not* before God.
4. is the reward *not* reckoned of grace,
10. *Not* in circumcision, but in

Ro. 4:12. to them who are *not* of the circumcision
13. (was) *not* to Abraham, or to his seed, through the law,
15. for where *no* law is,
16. *not* to that only which is of the law,
19. he considered *not* his own body
20. He staggered *not* at the promise
23. it was *not* written for his sake
5: 3. *not* only (so), but we glory
5. hope maketh *not* ashamed;
11. *not* only (so), but we also joy
13. is *not* imputed when there is no
15. But *not* as the offence, so also (is)
16. And *not* as (it was) by one that
6: 14. For sin shall *not* have dominion over you: for ye are *not* under the law,
15. because we are *not* under the law,
16. Know ye *not*, that to whom ye
7: 6. and *not* (in) the oldness of the letter.
7. Nay, I had *not* known sin, but by the law: for I had *not* known lust, except the law had said, Thou shalt *not* covet.
15. For that which I do I allow *not:* for what I would, that do I *not*,
16. If then I do that which I would *not*,
18. dwelleth *no* good thing:
— to perform that which is good I find *not*.
19. the good that I would I do *not:* but the evil which I would *not*,
20. if I do that I would *not*,
8: 7. for it is *not* subject to the law of God,
8. they that are in the flesh can*not* please God.
9. But ye are *not* in the flesh,
— if any man have *not* the Spirit of Christ, he is *none* of his.
12. we are debtors, *not* to the flesh,
15. ye have *not* received the spirit of
18. (are) *not* worthy (to be compared)
20. *not* willingly, but by reason of
23. And *not* only (they), but
24. hope that is seen is *not* hope:
25. if we hope for that we see *not*,
26. we know *not* what we should
32. He that spared *not* his own Son,
9: 1. I say the truth in Christ, I lie *not*,
6. *Not* as though the word of God
— For they (are) *not* all Israel, which
8. these (are) *not* the children of God:
10. And *not* only (this); but when
11. *not* of works, but of him that calleth;
16. *not* of him that willeth,
21. Hath *not* the potter power over
24. *not* of the Jews only,
25. *not* my people; and her beloved, which was *not* beloved.
26. Ye (are) *not* my people;
31. hath *not* attained to the law of
32. (they sought it) *not* by faith,
33. believeth on him shall *not* be ashamed.
10: 2. *not* according to knowledge.
3. have *not* submitted themselves
11. shall *not* be ashamed.
12. For there is *no* difference
14. in whom they have *not* believed?
— of whom they have *not* heard?
16. they have *not* all obeyed
19. (them that are) *no* people,
11: 2. God hath *not* cast away his people
— Wot ye *not* what the scripture
4. who have *not* bowed the knee
7. Israel hath *not* obtained that which
18. thou bearest *not* the root,

Ro. 11:21. if God spared *not* the natural branches,
25. I would *not*, brethren, that ye
12: 4. all members have *not* the same
13: 1. there is *no* power but of God:
3. rulers are *not* a terror to good
4. for he beareth *not* the sword in vain:
5. *not* only for wrath, but
9. Thou shalt *not* commit adultery, Thou shalt *not* kill, Thou shalt *not* steal, Thou shalt *not* bear false witness, Thou shalt *not* covet;
10. Love worketh *no* ill
14: 6. to the Lord he doth *not* regard (it).
— to the Lord he eateth *not*,
17. the kingdom of God is *not* meat and
23. (he eateth) *not* of faith: for whatsoever (is) *not* of faith is sin.
15: 3. even Christ pleased *not* himself;
18. I will *not* dare to speak of any
— which Christ hath *not* wrought by me,
20. *not* where Christ was named,
21. To whom he was *not* spoken of, they
— they that have *not* heard shall
16: 4. unto whom *not* only I give thanks,
18. serve *not* our Lord Jesus Christ,
1Co. 1:16. I know *not* whether I baptized
17. Christ sent me *not* to baptize,
— *not* with wisdom of words,
21. the world by wisdom knew *not* God,
26. *not* many wise men after the flesh, *not* many mighty, *not* many noble, (are called):
2: 1. *not* with excellency of speech
2. *not* to know any thing among you,
4. *not* with enticing words of man's
6. *not* the wisdom of this world,
8. they would *not* have crucified
9. Eye hath *not* seen, *nor* ear heard, *neither* have entered into the heart of man,
12. *not* the spirit of the world,
13. *not* in the words which man's wisdom
14. the natural man receiveth *not*
— *neither* can he know (them),
3: 1. could *not* speak unto you as
2. with milk, and *not* with meat:
16. Know ye *not* that ye are the temple
4: 4. yet am I *not* hereby justified:
7. that thou didst *not* receive?
14. I write *not* these things to shame
15. yet (have ye) *not* many fathers:
19. *not* the speech of them which are
20. the kingdom of God (is) *not* in word,
5: 6. Your glorying (is) *not* good. Know ye *not* that a little leaven
10. Yet *not* altogether with the
6: 2. Do ye *not* know that the saints
3. Know ye *not* that we shall judge
5. that there is *not* a wise man among
9. Know ye *not* that the unrighteous shall *not* inherit the kingdom of God?
10. *nor* revilers, *nor* extortioners, shall)(|| inherit the kingdom of God.
12. but all things are *not* expedient:
— but I will *not* be brought under
13. Now the body (is) *not* for fornication,
15. Know ye *not* that your bodies
16. know ye *not* that he which is
19. know ye *not* that your body is
— and ye are *not* your own?
7: 4. The wife hath *not* power of her own body
— husband hath *not* power of his own body.
6. (and) *not* of commandment.

1Co. 7: 9. But if they can*not* contain,
10. (yet) *not* I, but the Lord,
12. But to the rest speak I, *not* the Lord:
15. or a sister is *not* under bondage
25. I have *no* commandment of the Lord:
28. thou hast *not* sinned; and if a virgin marry, she hath *not* sinned.
35. *not* that I may cast a snare upon you,
36. he sinneth *not*: let them marry.
8: 7. *not* in every man that knowledge:
8. meat commendeth us *not* to God:
9: 1. Am I *not* an apostle? am I *not* free?
— are *not* ye my work in the Lord?
2. If I be *not* an apostle unto others,
6. have *not* we power to forbear working?
7. and eateth *not* of the fruit thereof?
— eateth *not* of the milk of the flock?
9. Thou shalt *not* muzzle the mouth
12. (are) *not* we rather? Nevertheless we have *not* used this power;
3. Do ye *not* know that they which
5. *neither* have I written these things,
6. I have *nothing* to glory of:
24. Know ye *not* that they which run
26. *not* as uncertainly; so fight I, *not* as one that beateth the air:
10: 1. I would *not* that ye should be
5. God was *not* well pleased:
13. There hath *no* temptation taken you
— who will *not* suffer you to be tempted
20. and *not* to God: and I would *not* that ye should have
21. Ye can*not* drink the cup of the Lord, and
— ye can*not* be partakers of the
23. but all things are *not* expedient:
— all things edify *not*.
11: 6. if the woman be *not* covered,
7. ought *not* to cover (his) head,
8. the man is *not* of the woman;
9. *Neither* was the man created for
16. we have *no* such custom,
17. I praise (you) *not*, that ye come together *not* for the better, but
20. (this) is *not* to eat the Lord's supper.
22. I praise (you) *not*.
31. we should *not* be judged.
12: 1. I would *not* have you ignorant.
14. the body is *not* one member,
15. Because I am *not* the hand, I am *not* of the body; is it therefore *not* of the
16. Because I am *not* the eye, I am *not* of the body; is it therefore *not* of the body?
21. the eye can*not* say unto the hand, I have *no* need of thee:
— I have *no* need of you.
24. For our comely (parts) have *no* need:
13: 4. charity envieth *not*; charity vaunteth *not* itself, is *not* puffed up,
5. Doth *not* behave itself unseemly, seeketh *not* her own, is *not* easily provoked thinketh *no* evil;
6. Rejoiceth *not* in iniquity,
14: 2. speaketh *not* unto men, but
16. seeing he understandeth *not* what
17. the other is *not* edified.
22. *not* to them that believe, but
— *not* for them that believe not, but
23. will they *not* say that ye are mad?
33. God is *not* (the author) of confusion,
34. it is *not* permitted unto them
15: 9. that am *not* meet to be called
10. was *not* in vain;

1Co.15: 10. yet *not* I, but the grace of God
12. that there is *no* resurrection of the dead?
13. if there be *no* resurrection of the dead,
14. And if Christ be *not* risen,
15. whom he raised *not* up, if so be that the dead rise *not*.
16. For if the dead rise *not*,
17. And if Christ be *not* raised,
29. if the dead rise *not* at all?
32. if the dead rise *not*?
36. is *not* quickened, except
37. thou sowest *not* that body that shall be,
39. All flesh (is) *not* the same flesh:
46. that (was) *not* first which is spiritual.
50. can*not* inherit the kingdom
51. We shall *not* all sleep,
58. is *not* in vain in the Lord.
16: 7. I will *not* see you now by the way;
12. but his will was *not* at all to come
22. If any man love *not* the Lord Jesus Christ
2Co. 1: 8. For we would *not*, brethren, have you
12. *not* with fleshly wisdom,
13. For we write *none* other things
17. be yea yea, and *nay nay*?
18. was *not* yea and *nay*.
19. was *not* yea and *nay*,
24. *Not* for that we have dominion
2: 4. *not* that ye should be grieved,
5. he hath *not* grieved me,
11. we are *not* ignorant of his
13. I had *no* rest in my spirit,
17. For we are *not* as many,
3: 3. written *not* with ink,
— *not* in tables of stone, but in fleshy
5. *Not* that we are sufficient of
6. *not* of the letter, but of the spirit:
13. And *not* as Moses, (which) put a vail
4: 1. received mercy, we faint *not*;
5. For we preach *not* ourselves,
8. yet *not* distressed; (we are) perplexed but *not* in despair;
9 Persecuted, but *not* forsaken; cast down, but *not* destroyed;
6. For which cause we faint *not*;
5: 3. we shall *not* be found naked.
4. *not* for that we would be unclothed,
7. we walk by faith, *not* by sight:
12. we commend *not* ourselves
— in appearance, and *not* in heart.
6: 12. Ye are *not* straitened in us,
7: 3. I speak *not* (this) to condemn (you):
7. And *not* by his coming only,
8. I do *not* repent,
9. *not* that ye were made sorry,
12. *not* for his cause that had done
14. I am *not* ashamed;
8: 5. *not* as we hoped,
8. I speak *not* by commandment,
10 *not* only to do, but also
12. *not* according to that he hath *not*.
13. *not* that other men be eased,
15. much had *nothing* over; and he that (had gathered) little had *no* lack.
19. And *not* (that) only, but who was
21. *not* only in the sight of the Lord,
9: 12. *not* only supplieth the want of
10: 3. we do *not* war after the flesh:
4. of our warfare (are) *not* carnal,
8. and *not* for your destruction, I should *not* be ashamed:
12. For we dare *not* make ourselves of the among themselves, are *not* wise.

2Co.10:14. For we stretch *not* ourselves
15. *Not* boasting of things without
16. *not* to boast in another man's
18. For *not* he that commendeth himself
11: 4. whom we have *not* preached,
— which ye have *not* received, or another gospel, which ye have *not* accepted,
6. yet *not* in knowledge;
9(8). I was)(‖ chargeable to no man:
10. no man shall stop me of this boasting (lit. this boasting shall *not* be stopped to me)
11. because I love you *not?*
14. And *no* marvel; for Satan himself
15. Therefore (it is) *no* great thing if
17. I speak (it) *not* after the Lord,
29. am *not* weak? who is offended, and I burn *not?*
31. knoweth that I lie *not*.
12: 1. It is *not* expedient for me
2. I can*not* tell; or whether out of the body, I can*not* tell:
3. or out of the body, I can*not* tell:
4. which it is *not* lawful for a man
5. yet of myself I will *not* glory,
6. I shall *not* be a fool;
13. that I myself was *not* burdensome
14. I will *not* be burdensome to you: for I seek *not* your's, but you: for the children ought *not* to lay up
16. I did *not* burden you:
18. walked we *not* in the same spirit? (walked we) *not* in the same steps?
20. I shall *not* find you such as I would,
— such as ye would *not*:
13: 2. if I come again, I will *not* spare:
3. which to you-ward is *not* weak,
5. Know ye *not* your own selves,
6. that we are *not* reprobates.
7. *not* that we should appear approved,
8. For we can do *no*thing against
10. and *not* to destruction.
Gal. 1: 1. Paul, an apostle, *not* of men,
7. Which is *not* another;
10. I should *not* be the servant of Christ.
11. is *not* after man.
16. I conferred *not* with flesh and blood:
19. other of the apostles saw I *none*, save
20. behold, before God, I lie *not*.
2: 6. God accepteth *no* man's person:
14. I saw that they walked *not* uprightly
— and *not* as do the Jews,
15. and *not* sinners of the Gentiles,
16. a man is *not* justified by the
— and *not* by the works of the law: for by the works of the law shall *no* flesh
21. I do *not* frustrate the grace of God:
3:10. that continueth *not* in all things
12. the law is *not* of faith:
16. He saith *not*, And to seeds,
17. can*not* disannul, that it should
20. Now a mediator is *not* (a mediator)
28. There is *neither* Jew nor Greek, there is *neither* bond nor free, there is *neither*
4: 8. when ye knew *not* God,
14. in my flesh ye despised *not*,
17. affect you, (but) *not* well;
21. do ye *not* hear the law?
27. barren that bearest *not*;
— thou that travailest *not*:
31. we are *not* children of the
5: 8. This persuasion (cometh) *not* of him that
18. ye are *not* under the law.

Gal. 5:21. shall *not* inherit the kingdom
23. against such there is *no* law.
6: 4. and *not* in another.
7. God is *not* mocked:
Eph 1:16. Cease *not* to give thanks for you
21. *not* only in this world, but also
2: 8. and that *not* of yourselves:
9. *Not* of works, lest any
3: 5. was *not* made known unto the sons
4:20. But ye have *not* so learned Christ,
5: 4. which are *not* convenient:
5. that *no* whoremonger, nor...hath any
6: 7. as to the Lord, and *not* to men:
9. *neither* is there respect of persons
12. For we wrestle *not* against flesh
Phi. 1:16. *not* sincerely, supposing to add
22. what I shall choose I wot *not*.
29. *not* only to believe on him,
2: 6. thought it *not* robbery to be
16. that I have *not* run in vain,
21. *not* the things which are Jesus Christ's
27. and *not* on him only,
3: 1. to me indeed (is) *not* grievous,
3. and have *no* confidence in the
12. *Not* as though I had already
13. I count *not* myself to have
4:11. *Not* that I speak in respect of
17. *Not* because I desire a gift:
Col. 1: 9. do *not* cease to pray for you,
2: 1. as have *not* seen my face in
8. and *not* after Christ.
19. And *not* holding the Head,
23. *not* in any honour to the
3:11. Where there is *neither* Greek
23. and *not* unto men;
25. and there is *no* respect of persons.
1Th. 1: 5. our gospel came *not* unto you in
8. *not* only in Macedonia and
2: 1. that it was *not* in vain:
3. (was) *not* of deceit,
4. *not* as pleasing men,
8. *not* the gospel of God only,
13. ye received (it) *not* (as) the word of
17. in presence, *not* in heart,
4: 7. God hath *not* called us unto
8. despiseth *not* man, but God,
9. ye need *not* that I write unto you:
13. I would *not* have you to be
5: 1. ye have *no* need that I write
4. are *not* in darkness,
5. we are *not* of the night,
9. God hath *not* appointed us to wrath,
2Th. 2: 5. Remember ye *not*, that, when I
10. received *not* the love of the truth,
3: 2. for all (men) have *not* faith.
7. we behaved *not* ourselves disorderly
9. *Not* because we have *not* power,
10. if any would *not* work,
14. if any man obey *not* our word
1Ti. 1: 9. the law is *not* made for a
2: 7. truth in Christ, (and) lie *not*;
12. I suffer *not* a woman to teach,
14. Adam was *not* deceived,
3: 5. if a man know *not* how to rule
5: 8. if any provide *not* for his own,
13. and *not* only idle,
18. Thou shalt *not* muzzle the ox that
25. that are otherwise can*not* be hid.
2Ti. 1: 7. For God hath *not* given us the
9. *not* according to our works
12. I am *not* ashamed:
16. was *not* ashamed of my chain:

2Ti. 2: 5. (yet) is he *not* crowned, except
9. the word of God is *not* bound.
13. he can*not* deny himself.
20. there are *not* only vessels of gold
24. the servant of the Lord must *not* strive;
3: 9. they shall proceed *no* further:
4: 3. will *not* endure sound doctrine;
8. and *not* to me only,
Tit. 3: 5. *Not* by works of righteousness
Heb 1:12. and thy years shall *not* fail.
2: 5. hath he *not* put in subjection
11. he is *not* ashamed to call them
16. he took *not* on (him the nature of)
3:10. they have *not* known my ways.
16. *not* all that came out of Egypt
19. they could *not* enter in because
4: 2. the word preached did *not* profit
6. entered *not* in because of
8. then would he *not* afterward
13. *Neither* is there (lit. and there is *not*) any creature that
15. For we have *not* an high priest
5: 4. *no* man taketh this honour unto
5. Christ glorified *not* himself
12. and *not* of strong meat.
6:10. God (is) *not* unrighteous to forget
7:11. and *not* be called after the order
16. *not* after the law of a carnal
20. as *not* without an oath
21. and will *not* repent,
27. Who needeth *not* daily, as
8: 2. which the Lord pitched, and *not* man.
7. then should *no* place have been
9. *Not* according to the covenant
— because they continued *not* in
9: 5. of which we can*not* now speak
7. once every year, *not* without blood,
11. *not* made with hands, that is to say, *not* of this building;
22. without shedding of blood is *no* remission.
24. Christ is *not* entered into the holy
10: 1. *not* the very image of the things,
2. would they *not* have ceased to be
5. and offering thou wouldest *not*,
6. thou hast had *no* pleasure.
8. for sin thou wouldest *not*,
37. and will *not* tarry.
38. my soul shall have *no* pleasure
39. we are *not* of them who draw back
11: 1. the evidence of things *not* seen.
5. and was *not* found,
16. God is *not* ashamed to be called their
23. they were *not* afraid of the kings
31. Rahab perished *not* with them
35. were tortured, *not* accepting deliverance;
38. Of whom the world was *not* worthy:
39. received *not* the promise:
12: 7. whom the father chasteneth *not*?
8. are ye bastards, and *not* sons.
9. shall we *not* much rather be
11. *no* chastening for the present
17. he found *no* place of repentance,
18. For ye are *not* come unto the mount
20. they could *not* endure that which
25. if they escaped *not* who
26. I shake *not* the earth only, but
13: 6. I will *not* fear what man
9. *not* with meats, which have *not* profited
10. they have *no* right to eat which
14. here have we *no* continuing city,
Jas 1:17. with whom is *no* variableness,
20. the wrath of man worketh *not* the

Jas. 1:23. and *not* a doer,
25. being *not* a forgetful hearer
2: 4. Are ye *not* then partial in
5. Hath *not* God chosen the poor
6. Do *not* rich men oppress you,
7. Do *not* they blaspheme that worthy
11. Now if thou commit *no* adultery.
21. Was *not* Abraham our father justified
24. and *not* by faith only.
25. was *not* Rahab the harlot justified
3: 2. If any man offend *not* in word,
10. these things ought *not* so to be.
15. descendeth *not* from above,
4: 1. (come they) *not* hence,
2. Ye lust, and have *not*:
— and can*not* obtain: ye fight and war, yet ye have *not*,
3. Ye ask, and receive *not*, because
4. know ye *not* that the friendship
11. thou art *not* a doer of the law,
14. ye know *not* what (shall be) on
5: 6. (and) he doth *not* resist you.
12. and (your) *nay, nay;*
17. and it rained *not* on the earth
1Pet. 1: 8. Whom having *not* seen, ye love;
12. that *not* unto themselves,
18. *not* redeemed with corruptible
23. *not* of corruptible seed, but
2:10. in time past (were) *not* a people,
— had *not* obtained mercy, but
18. *not* only to the good and gentle,
22. Who did *no* sin,
23. reviled *not* again; when he suffered, he threatened *not;*
3: 3. let it *not* be that outward
21. *not* the putting away of the filth of
2Pet. 1: 8. *neither* (be) barren nor unfruitful
12. I will *not* be negligent to put
16. we have *not* followed cunningly
20. *no* prophecy of the scripture is of
21. came *not* in old time by the will of
2: 3. now of a long time lingereth *not* and their damnation slumbereth *not*.
4. if God spared *not* the angels
5. And spared *not* the old world,
10. *not* afraid to speak evil of
11. bring *not* railing accusation
3: 9. The Lord is *not* slack
1Joh. 1: 5. and in him is)(‖ no darkness
6. and do *not* the truth:
8. If we say that we have *no* sin,
— and the truth is *not* in us.
10. If we say that we have *not* sinned,
— and his word is *not* in us.
2: 2. and *not* for our's only,
4. the truth is *not* in him.
7. I write *no* new commandment
10. there is *none* occasion of stumbling
11. knoweth *not* whither he goeth,
15. the love of the Father is *not* in him.
16. is *not* of the Father, but
19. but they were *not* of us;
— that they were *not* all of us.
21. I have *not* written unto you because ye know *not* the truth,
— and that *no* lie is of the truth.
22. but he that denieth that Jesus is)(the Christ?
27. and ye need *not* that any man
— and is *no* lie,
3: 1. the world knoweth us *not*, because it knew him *not*.

1Joh.3: 5. and in him is *no* sin.
6. abideth in him sinneth *not:* whosoever sinneth hath *not* seen him,
9. doth *not* commit sin;
— and he can*not* sin,
10. doeth not righteousness is *not* of God,
12. *Not* as Cain, (who) was of that
15. that *no* murderer hath eternal life
4: 3. is *not* of God:
6. he that is *not* of God heareth *not* us.
8. knoweth *not* God; for God is love.
10. *not* that we loved God,
18. There is *no* fear in love;
— is *not* made perfect in love.
20. whom he hath *not* seen?
5: 3. his commandments are *not* grievous.
6. *not* by water only,
10. because he believeth *not* the record
12. not the Son of God hath *not* life.
16. I do *not* say that he shall pray for it.
17. there is a sin *not* unto death.
18. is born of God sinneth *not;*
— that wicked one toucheth him *not.*
2Joh. 1 and *not* I only,
5. *not* as though I wrote a new
9. doctrine of Christ, hath *not* God.
10. and bring *not* this doctrine,
12. I would *not* (write) with paper and
3Joh. 4. I have *no* greater joy than
9. preeminence among them, receiveth us *not.*
11. he that doeth evil hath *not* seen God.
13. but I will *not* with ink and pen
Jude 9. durst *not* bring against him
10. of those things which they know *not*
Rev. 2: 2. how thou canst *not* bear them
— say they are apostles, and are *not,*
3. and hast *not* fainted.
9. say they are Jews, and are *not,*
13. and hast *not* denied my faith,
21. and she repented *not.*
24. as many as have *not* this doctrine, and which have *not* known the depths
— I will put upon you *none* other
3: 2. I have *not* found thy works
4. which have *not* defiled their
8. and hast *not* denied my name.
9. say they are Jews, and are *not,*
17. and knowest *not* that thou art
4: 8. they rest *not* day and night, saying,
6: 10. dost thou *not* judge and avenge
7: 16. They shall hunger *no* more,
9: 4. which have *not* the seal of God
6. and shall *not* find it;
20. which were *not* killed by these
21. *Neither* repented (lit. and they repented *not*) they of their
10: 6. that there should be time *no* longer:
11: 9. shall *not* suffer their dead bodies
12: 8. And prevailed *not;*
11. they loved *not* their lives
13: 8. whose names are *not* written
14: 4. which were *not* defiled with
5. And in their mouth was found *no* guile:
11. and they have *no* rest day nor
16: 9. and they repented *not*
11. and repented *not* of their deeds.
18. such as was *not* since men
20. and the mountains were *not* found.
17: 8. that thou sawest was, and is *not;*
— were *not* written in the book of
— that was, and is *not*, and yet is.

Rev.17: 11. the beast that was, and is *not,*
18: 7. I sit a queen, and am *no* widow,
20: 4. had *not* worshipped the beast,
— *neither* had received (his) mark
5. the rest of the dead lived *not* again until
6. the second death hath *no* power,
11. there was found *no* place for them.
15. was *not* found written in
21: 1. and there was *no* more sea.
4. there shall be *no* more death,
— neither shall there)(‖ be any more pain.
22. I saw *no* temple therein;
23. the city had *no* need of the sun,
25. for there shall be *no* night there.
22: 3. And there shall be *no* more curse:
5. And there shall be *no* night there; and they need *no* candle, neither

See also οὐ and οὐκ in the compounds *μὴ οὐκ*, *οὐ μή*, and *οὐκέτι*.

3758 1 595/720

οὐά or οὐαί, *oua* or *ouai.*

Mar 15:29. *Ah,* thou that destroyest the

3759 47 595/721

οὐαί, *ouai.*

Mat.11:21. *Woe* unto thee, Chorazin! *woe* unto thee,
18: 7. *Woe* unto the world
— but *woe* to that man by whom
23:13(14). *woe* unto you, scribes and
14(13). *Woe* unto you, scribes and
15. *Woe* unto you, scribes and Pharisees,
16. *Woe* unto you, (ye) blind guides,
23. *Woe* unto you, scribes and
25. *Woe* unto you, scribes and
27. *Woe* unto you, scribes and
29. *Woe* unto you, scribes and
24:19. *woe* unto them that are with child,
26:24. but *woe* unto that man by
Mar 13:17. *woe* to them that are with child,
14:21. *woe* to that man by whom
Lu. 6:24. *woe* unto you that are rich!
25. *Woe* unto you that are full!
— *Woe* unto you that laugh now!
26. *Woe* unto you, when all men
10:13. *Woe* unto thee, Chorazin! *woe* unto thee,
11:42. *woe* unto you, Pharisees!
43. *Woe* unto you, Pharisees!
44. *Woe* unto you, scribes and
46. *Woe* unto you also, (ye) lawyers!
47. *Woe* unto you! for ye build
52. *Woe* unto you, lawyers!
17: 1. *woe* (unto him), through whom they
21:23. But *woe* unto them that are
22:22. *woe* unto that man by whom
1Co. 9:16. *woe* is unto me, if I preach not
Jude 11. *Woe* unto them! for they have
Rev. 8:13. *Woe, woe, woe,* to the inhabiters
9:12. One *woe* is past; (and), behold, there come two *woes* more
11:14. The second *woe* is past; (and), behold, the third *woe* cometh
12:12. *Woe* to the inhabiters of the
18:10. *Alas, alas* that great city Babylon,
16. *Alas, alas* that great city, that
19. *Alas, alas* that great city, wherein

3760 1 595/721 3762

οὐδαμῶς, *oudamōs.*

Mat. 2: 6. art *not* the least among the

3757, p. 552

3761 137 595/721 3756,1161

οὐδέ, oude.

|| is placed where the Greek has two or more negatives.

Mat. 5:15. *Neither* do men light a candle, and
6:15. *neither* will your Father forgive
20. do not break through *nor* steal:
26. they sow not, *neither* do they reap, *nor* gather into barns;
28. *neither* do they spin:
29. That *even* Solomon in all his glory was *not* arrayed
7:18. *neither* (can) a corrupt tree
8:10. so great faith, *no, not* in Israel.
9:17. *Neither* do men put new wine
24. *nor* the servant above his lord.
11:27. *neither* knoweth any man the Father,
12: 4. *neither* for them which were with him,
19. He shall not strive, *nor* cry; *neither* shall any man hear his
13:13. *neither* do they understand.
16: 9. *neither* remember the five loaves
10. *Neither* the seven loaves
21:27. *Neither* tell I you by what authority
22:46. *neither* durst any (man) from that day
23:13(14). *neither* suffer ye them that
24:21. no, *nor* || ever shall be.
36. *no, not* the angels of heaven,
25:13. *nor* the hour wherein the Son of man
45. ye did (it) *not* to me.
27:14. he answered him to || *never* a word;

Mar. 4:22. *neither* was any thing kept secret,
6:31. they had *no* leisure *so much as* to eat.
8:17. perceive ye not yet, *neither* understand?
11:26. *neither* will your Father which
33. *Neither* do I tell you by what
12:10. have ye *not* read this scripture;
21. *neither* left he any seed:
13:32. *no, not* the angels which are in heaven, *neither* the Son,
14:59. *neither* so did their witness
68. *neither* understand I what thou sayest.
16:13. *neither* believed they them.

Lu. 6: 3. Have ye *not* read *so much as* this,
43. *neither* doth a corrupt tree
44. *nor* of a bramble bush gather
7: 7. *neither* thought I myself worthy
9. so great faith, *no, not* in Israel.
8:17. *neither* (any thing) hid, that shall
11:33. *neither* under a bushel,
12:24. they neither sow *nor* reap; which neither have storehouse *nor* barn;
27. they toil not, they spin *not*;
— that Solomon in all his glory was *not*
33. *neither* moth corrupteth.
16 31. *neither* will they be persuaded,
17:21. *Neither* shall they say, Lo here!
18:13. would not lift up || *so much as* (his) eyes unto heaven,
20: 8. *Neither* tell I you by what
21:15. not be able to gainsay *nor* resist.
23:15. *No, nor* yet Herod: for I sent you
40. Dost *not* thou fear God,

Joh. 1: 3. without him was *not* any thing made
13. *nor* of the will of the flesh, *nor* of the will of man,
5:22. For)(|| the Father judgeth no man,
6:24. *neither* his disciples,
7: 5. *neither* did his brethren believe
8:11. *Neither* do I condemn thee:
42. *neither* came I of myself,
11:50. *Nor* consider that it is expedient
13:16. *neither* he that is sent greater
14:17. seeth him not, *neither* knoweth him:
15: 4. *no more* (lit. so *neither*) can ye, except ye
16: 3. not known the Father, *nor* me.
21:25. *even* the world itself could *not*

Acts 2:27. *neither* wilt thou suffer thine
31. *neither* his flesh did see corruption.
4:32. *neither* said any (of them) that
34. *Neither* was there any among
7: 5. *no, not* (so much as) to set his
8:21. Thou hast neither part *nor* lot
9: 9. and neither did eat *nor* drink.
16:21. *neither* to observe, being Romans.
17:25. *Neither* is worshipped with
19: 2. We have *not so much as* (αλλ' o.)
20:24. *neither* count I my life dear
24:18. with multitude, *nor* with tumult.

Ro. 2:28. *neither* (is that) circumcision,
3:10. There is none righteous, *no, not* one:
4:15. (there is) *no* transgression.
8: 7. *neither* indeed can be.
9: 7. *Neither*, because they are the seed
16. *nor* of him that runneth,
11:21. lest he *also* spare *not* thee.

1Co. 2: 6. *nor* of the princes of this world,
4: 3. yea, I judge *not* mine own self.
5: 1. as is *not so much as* named
6: 5. *no, not* one that shall be able
11:14. Doth *not even* nature itself
16. *neither* the churches of God.
14:21. yet for all that will they *not* hear me,
15:13. *then* is Christ *not* risen:
16. *then* is *not* Christ raised:
50. *neither* doth corruption inherit

2Co. 3:10. even that which was made glorious had *no*
7:12. *nor* for his cause that suffered

Gal. 1: 1. not of men, *neither* by man,
12. For I *neither* received it of man,
17. *Neither* went I up to Jerusalem
2: 3. But *neither* Titus, who was with me,
5. *no, not* for an hour;
3:28. There is neither Jew *nor* Greek, there is neither bond *nor* free,
4:14. ye despised not, *nor* rejected;
6:13. For *neither* they themselves who

Phi. 2:16. *neither* laboured in vain.

1Th. 2: 3. *nor* of uncleanness, nor in guile:
5: 5. we are not of the night, *nor* of darkness.

2Th. 3: 8. *Neither* did we eat any man's

1Ti. 2:12. *nor* to usurp authority over
6: 7. (and it is) certain we can carry nothing out. (lit. certain that *neither* can we carry any thing out)
16. no man hath seen, *nor* can see:

Heb 8: 4. he should *not* be a priest,
9:12. *Neither* by the blood of goats and
18. *neither* the first (testament) was
25. *Nor yet* that he should offer himself
10: 8. *neither* hadst pleasure (therein);
13: 5. I will never leave thee, *nor* || forsake

1Pet. 2:22. *neither* was guile found in his

2Pet. 1: 8. *nor* unfruitful in the knowledge

1Joh. 2:23. the same hath *not* the Father:
3: 6. not seen him, *neither* known him.

Rev 5: 3. no man in heaven, *nor* in earth, *neither* under the earth, was able
— *neither* to look thereon.
7:16. *neither* thirst any more; *neither* || shall the sun light on them, *nor* any heat.
9: 4. *neither* any green thing, *neither* any tree;
21:23. *neither* of the moon, to shine in it:

3763 16 596/725 3761,4218

οὐδέποτε, *oudepote.*

Mat. 7:23. I *never* knew you:
9:33. It was *never* so seen in Israel.
21:16. have ye *never* read, Out of the
42. Did ye *never* read in the scriptures,
26:33. (yet) will I *never* be offended.
Mar 2:12. We *never* saw it on this fashion.
25. Have ye *never* read what David
Lu. 15:29. *neither* transgressed I *at any time*
— and yet thou *never* gavest me a kid,
Joh. 7:46. *Never* man spake like this man.
Acts10:14. I have *never* eaten any thing that is
11: 8. *no*thing common or unclean hath *at any time*
14: 8. who *never* had walked:
1Co.13: 8. Charity *never* faileth:
Heb10: 1. can *never* with those sacrifices
11. which can *never* take away sins:

3764 5 596/725 3761,4452

οὐδέπω, *oudepo.*

‖ denotes where there is a double negative in the Greek.

Lu. 23:53. wherein *never* ‖ man *before* was laid.
Joh. 7:39. Jesus was *not yet* glorified.
19:41. wherein was *never* ‖ man *yet* laid.
20: 9. For *as yet* they knew *not* the
1Co. 8: 2. he knoweth nothing ‖ *yet* as he ought

3762 235 596/723 3761,1520

οὐδείς, *oudīs.*

‖ denotes where there is a double negative in the Greek.

'*No one*,' is the literal rendering of the passages translated '*no man*.'

Mat. 5:13. it is thenceforth good for *nothing*,
6:24. *No man* can serve two masters:
9:16. *No man* putteth a piece of new
10:26. for there is *nothing* covered, that
11:27. and *no man* knoweth the Son,
17: 8. they saw *no man*, save Jesus
20. and *nothing* shall be impossible
19:17. (there is) *none* good but one,
20: 7. Because *no man* hath hired us.
21:19. and found *nothing* thereon,
22:16. neither carest thou for ‖ *any* (man):
46. *no man* was able to answer him
23:16. swear by the temple, it is *nothing*;
18. swear by the altar, it is *nothing*;
24:36. and hour knoweth *no* (man),
26:62. Answerest thou *nothing*?
27:12. he answered *nothing*.
24. saw that he could prevail *nothing*,
Mar 2:21. *No man* also seweth a piece
22. *no man* putteth new wine
3:27. ‖ *No man* can enter into a strong
5: 3. *no man* could bind him,
4. neither could any (man) tame him. (lit. and *no one* could, &c.)
37. he suffered ‖ *no man* to follow him,
6: 5. he could there do ‖ *no* mighty work,
7:12. ye suffer him no more to do ‖ *ought* for
15. There is *nothing* from without
24. would have *no man* know (it):
9: 8. they saw ‖ *no man* any more, save
29. can come forth by *nothing*, but
39. for there is *no man* which shall
10:18. (there is) *none* good but one,
29. There is *no man* that hath left
11: 2. whereon never man sat; (lit. *no one* of men)
13. he found *nothing* but leave-
Mar 12:14. and carest ‖ for *no man*:
34. And *no man* ‖ after that durst
13:32. and (that) hour knoweth *no man*,
14:60. Answerest ‖ thou *nothing*?
61. held his peace, and answered *nothing*.
15: 4. Answerest thou *nothing*?
5. Jesus yet answered ‖ *nothing*;
16: 8. *neither* said they *any thing* to ‖ *any*
Lu. 1:61. There is *none* of thy kindred
4: 2. in those days he did eat ‖ *nothing*:
24. *No* prophet is accepted in his own
26. But unto *none* of them was Elias
27. and *none* of them was cleansed, saving
5: 5. and have taken *nothing*:
36. *No man* putteth a piece of a new
37. *no man* putteth new wine
39. *No man* also having drunk old
7:28. there is *not a* greater prophet
8:16. *No man*, when he hath lighted a
43. neither could be healed of ‖ *any*,
51. he suffered ‖ *no man* to go in, save
9:36. and told *no man* in those days ‖ *any* of
62. *No man*, having put his hand to
10:19. and *nothing* ‖ shall by any means
22. *no man* knoweth who the Son is,
11:33. *No man*, when he hath lighted
12: 2. For there is *nothing* covered,
14:24. That *none* of those men which
15:16. *no man* gave unto him.
16:13. *No* servant can serve two
18:19. *none* (is) good, save one,
29. There is *no man* that hath left
34. they understood *none* of these
19:30. whereon yet never man sat: (lit. *no man* ever sat)
20:40. they durst not ask him ‖ *any*
22:35. And they said, *Nothing*.
23: 4. I find *no* fault in this man.
9. but he answered him *nothing*.
14. have found *no* fault in this man
15. *nothing* worthy of death is done
22. I have found *no* cause of death in him:
41. this man hath done *nothing* amiss.
53. wherein never ‖ *man* before was laid.
Joh 1:18. *No man* hath seen God at any time;
3: 2. for *no man* can do these miracles
13. And *no man* hath ascended up to
27. A man can receive *nothing*, except
32. and *no man* receiveth his
4:27. yet *no man* said, What seekest
5:19. The Son can do ‖ *nothing* of himself,
22. For the Father judgeth *no man*,
30. I can of mine own self do *nothing*:
6:44. *No man* can come to me, except
63. the flesh profiteth ‖ *nothing*:
65. *no man* can come unto me,
7: 4. *no man* (that) doeth any thing in
13. *no man* spake openly of him
19. and (yet) *none* of you keepeth the law?
26. and they say *nothing* unto him.
27. *no man* knoweth whence he is.
30. *no man* laid hands on him,
44. but *no man* laid hands on him.
8:10. hath *no man* condemned thee?
11. She said, *No man*, Lord.
15. I judge ‖ *no man*.
20. *no man* laid hands on him;
28. and (that) I do *nothing* of myself;
33. and were never in bondage to any man (lit. were in bondage to *none* ever)
54. my honour is *nothing*:
9: 4. when *no man* can work.

Joh. 9:33. he could do || *nothing*.
10:18. *No man* taketh it from me,
29. and *no* (man) is able to pluck
41. John did *no* miracle:
11:49. Ye know || *nothing* at all,
12:19. how ye prevail || *nothing?*
13:28. Now *no man* at the table knew
14: 6. *no man* cometh unto the Father, but
30. and hath || *nothing* in me.
15: 5. without me ye can do || *nothing*.
13. Greater love hath *no man* than this,
24. which *none* other man did,
16: 5. and *none* of you asketh me,
22. your joy *no man* taketh from you.
23. in that day ye shall ask me || *nothing*.
24. Hitherto have ye asked || *nothing* in
29. and speakest *no* proverb.
17:12. and *none* of them is lost, but
18: 9. have I lost || *none*.
20. and in secret have I said *nothing*.
31. It is not lawful for us to put || *any man*
38. I find in him *no* fault (at all).
19: 4. that I find *no* fault in him
11. Thou couldest have *no* power (at all)
41. wherein was never || *man* yet laid.
21: 3. that night they caught *nothing*.
12. And *none* of the disciples durst
Acts 4:12. Neither is there salvation in || *any* other:
14. they could say *nothing* against it.
5:13. of the rest durst *no man* join himself
23. we found *no man* within.
36. and brought to *nought*.
8:16. he was fallen upon *none* of them:
9: 8. he saw *no* man:
15: 9. And put *no* difference between us
17:21. spent their time in *nothing* else,
18:10. *no man* shall set on thee to hurt
17. Gallio cared for *none* of those things.
19:27. Diana should be despised, (lit. be counted for *nothing*)
20:20. how I kept back *nothing* that
24. But *none* of these things move me,
33. I have coveted *no man's* silver,
21:24. concerning thee, are *nothing;*
23: 9. We find *no* evil in this man.
25:10. to the Jews have I done *no* wrong,
11. but if there be *none* of these things
— *no man* may deliver me unto them.
18. they brought *none* accusation
26:22. saying *none* other things than
26. that *none* of these things are
31. This man doeth *nothing* worthy
27:22. *no* loss of (any man's) life
34. there shall *not* an hair fall from the head of *any* of you.
28: 5. and felt *no* harm.
17. I have committed *nothing* against
Ro. 8: 1. now *no* condemnation to them
14: 7. For *none* of us liveth to himself, and *no man* dieth to himself.
14. that (there is) *nothing* unclean of
1Co. 1:14. that I baptized *none* of you, but
2: 8. Which *none* of the princes of
11. the things of God knoweth *no man*,
15. he himself is judged of *no man*.
3:11. can *no man* lay than that is laid,
4: 4. I know *nothing* by myself;
7:19. Circumcision is *nothing*, and uncircumcision is *nothing*,
8: 2. he knoweth *nothing* || yet as he ought
4. an idol (is) *nothing* in the world, and that (there is) *none* other

1Co. 9:15. I have used *none* of these things:
12: 3. that *no man* speaking by the Spirit
— *no man* can say that Jesus is
13: 2. and have not charity, I am *nothing*.
3. it profiteth me *nothing*.
14: 2. for *no man* understandeth (him);
10. *none* of them (is) without signification.
2Co. 5:16. know we *no man* after the flesh:
7: 2. have wronged *no man*, we have corrupted *no man*, we have defrauded *no man*
5. our flesh had *no* rest,
11: 9. I was chargeable || to *no man:*
12:11. for in *nothing* am I behind the
— though I be *nothing*.
Gal. 2: 6. it maketh *no* matter to me:
— in conference added *nothing* to me:
3:11. But that *no man* is justified by
15. *no man* disannulleth, or
4: 1. differeth *nothing* from a servant,
12. ye have *not* injured me *at all*.
5: 2. Christ shall profit you *nothing*.
10. that ye will be *none* otherwise minded
Eph. 5:29. For *no man* ever yet hated his own
Phi. 1:20. that in *nothing* I shall be ashamed,
2:20. I have *no man* likeminded,
4:15. *no* church communicated with me
1Ti. 4: 4. and *nothing* to be refused,
6: 7. For we brought *nothing* into (this)
16. whom *no* man hath seen,
2Ti. 2: 4. *No man* that warreth
14. about words to *no* profit,
4:16. *no man* stood with me,
Tit. 1:15. unbelieving (is) *nothing* pure;
Philem. 14. would I do *nothing;*
Heb 2: 8. he left *nothing* (that is) not put
6:13. because he could swear by *no* greater,
7:13. of which *no man* gave attendance
14. Moses spake *nothing* concerning
19. the law made *nothing* perfect,
12:14. without which *no man* shall see
Jas. 1:13. *neither* tempteth he *any* man:
3: 8. the tongue can *no* man tame;
12. so (can) *no* fountain both yield
1Joh. 1: 5. and in him is || *no* darkness at all.
4:12. *No man* hath seen God at any time.
Rev. 2:17. which *no man* knoweth saving
3: 7. and *no man* shutteth; and shutteth, and *no man* openeth;
8. and *no man* can shut it:
17. and have need of *nothing;*
5: 3. And *no man* in heaven, nor
4. because *no man* was found worthy
7: 9. which *no man* could number,
14: 3. and *no man* could learn that song
15: 8. and *no man* was able to enter
18:11. for *no man* || buyeth their merchandise
19:12. that *no man* knew, but he himself.

οὐθέν, see under οὐδείς. 3762

1 Cor. 13:2. in some copies.

3765 48 596/725 3756,2089

οὐκέτι or οὐκ ἔτι, *ouketi* or *ouk eti*.

² is placed where the words are printed apart, οὐκ ἔτι; and || shews where either form is combined with an additional negative in the Greek.

Mat. 19: 6. they are *no more* twain,
22:46. from that day forth ask him || *any more*
Mar 7:12. *no more* to do || ought for his father
9: 8. they saw no man || *any more*,

Mar 10: 8. they are *no more* twain,
12:34. no man || *after that* durst ask him
14:25. I will || drink *no more* of the fruit
15: 5. Jesus || *yet* answered nothing;
Lu. 15:19. And am *no more* worthy to be called
21. and am *no more* worthy to be called
20:40. *after that*[2] they durst *not* || ask him any
22:16. I will *not any more* || eat thereof,
Joh. 4:42. *Now* we believe, *not* because of thy
6:66. and walked *no more* with him.
11:54. Jesus therefore walked *no more*[2] openly
14:19. and the world seeth me *no more;*[2]
30. *Hereafter* I will *not*[2] talk much
15:15. *Henceforth* I call you *not* servants;
16:10. and ye see me *no more;*[2]
21. she remembereth *no more*[2] the
25. when I shall *no more*[2] speak unto
17:11. And *now* I am *no more*[2] in the world,
21: 6. and *now* they were *not*[2] able to draw it
Acts 8:39. the eunuch saw him || *no more:*
20:25. shall see my face *no more.*
38. they should see his face *no more.*
Ro 6: 9. dieth *no more;*[2] death hath *no more*[2] dominion over him.
7:17. Now then it is *no more*[2] I that do it,
20. it is *no more*[2] I that do it, but
11: 6. then (is it) *no more*[2] of works: otherwise grace is *no more*[2] grace. But if (it be) of works, then is it *no more*[2] grace: otherwise work is *no more*[2] work.
14:15. *now* walkest thou *not*[2] charitably.
2Co. 1:23. I came *not as yet* unto Corinth.
5:16. now henceforth know we (him) *no more.*[2]
Gal. 2:20. *yet not*[2] I, but Christ liveth in me:
3:18. (it is) *no more*[2] of promise:
25. we are *no longer*[2] under a schoolmaster.
4: 7. thou art *no more*[2] a servant, but
Eph 2:19. ye are *no more* strangers and
Philem.16. *Not now* as a servant, but above
Heb10:18. (there is) *no more*[2] offering for sin.
26. *no more*[2] sacrifice for sins,
Rev.18:11. for no man buyeth their merchandise || *any more:*
14. shalt find them *no more* || at all.

Those passages in which ἐτι is combined with ου, ουκ, ουδε, ουτε, but with the intervention of words between them, will be found under ἐτι.

3766 1 597/726 3756,3767

οὐκοῦν, oukoun.

Joh. 18:37. ? Art thou a king *then?*

3364 **οὐ μή see after μή.** p. 498

3767 526 597/726

οὖν, oun.

[1] is affixed to those passages where it is combined with μέν.

Mat. 1:17. *So* all the generations from Abraham
3: 8. Bring forth *therefore* fruits meet
10. *therefore* every tree which
5:19. Whosoever *therefore* shall break one
23. *Therefore* if thou bring thy gift
48. Be ye *therefore* perfect,
6: 2. *Therefore* when thou doest (thine) alms,
8. Be not ye *therefore* like unto them:
9. After this manner *therefore* pray ye:
22. if *therefore* thine eye be single,
23. If *therefore* the light that is in thee
31. *Therefore* take no thought,
Mat. 6:34. Take *therefore* no thought for
7:11. If ye *then*, being evil, know
12. *Therefore* all things whatsoever
24. *Therefore* whosoever heareth these
9:38. Pray ye *therefore* the Lord of the
10:16. be ye *therefore* wise as serpents,
26. Fear them not *therefore:*
31. Fear ye not *therefore,*
32. Whosoever *therefore* shall confess
12:12. How much *then* is a man better
26. how shall *then* his kingdom
13:18. Hear ye *therefore* the parable
27. from whence *then* hath it tares?
28. Wilt thou *then* that we go and
40. As *therefore* the tares are gathered
56. Whence *then* hath this (man) all
17:10. Why *then* say the scribes
18: 4. Whosoever *therefore* shall humble
26. The servant *therefore* fell down,
29. *And* his fellowservant fell down
19: 6. What *therefore* God hath joined
7. Why did Moses *then* command
21:25. Why did ye not *then* believe
40. When the lord *therefore* of the
22: 9. Go ye *therefore* into the highways,
17. Tell us *therefore*, What thinkest thou
21. Render *therefore* unto Cæsar
28. *Therefore* in the resurrection
43. How *then* doth David in spirit call
45. If David *then* call him Lord,
23: 3. All *therefore* whatsoever they bid
20. Whoso *therefore* shall swear
24:15. When ye *therefore* shall see the
26. *Wherefore* if they shall say unto you,
42. Watch *therefore:* for ye know not what
25:13. Watch *therefore*, for ye know neither
27. Thou oughtest *therefore* to have
28. Take *therefore* the talent from
26:54. But how *then* shall the scriptures
27:17. *Therefore* when they were gathered
22. What shall I do *then* with Jesus
64. Command *therefore* that the sepulchre
28:19. Go ye *therefore*, and teach all
Mar 3:31. There came *then* his brethren and
10: 9. What *therefore* God hath joined
11:31. Why *then* did ye not believe him?
12: 6. Having yet *therefore* one son,
9. What shall *therefore* the lord of
23. In the resurrection *therefore,*
27. ye *therefore* do greatly err.
37. David *therefore* himself calleth him
13:35. Watch ye *therefore:* for ye know not
15:12. What will ye *then* that I shall do
16:19. *So then*[1] after the Lord had spok
Lu. 3: 7. *Then* said he to the multitude
8. Bring forth *therefore* fruits
9. every tree *therefore* which
10. What shall we do *then?*
18. *And*[1] many other things in his
4: 7. If thou *therefore* wilt worship me,
6: 9. *Then* said Jesus unto them,
36. Be ye *therefore* merciful, as your
7:31. Whereunto *then* shall I liken
42. Tell me *therefore*, which of them
8:18. Take heed *therefore* how ye hear:
10: 2. *Therefore* said he unto them,
— pray ye *therefore* the Lord of the
36. Which *now* of these three,
37. *Then* said Jesus unto him, Go, and do
40. bid her *therefore* that she help me.
11:13. If ye *then*, being evil, know how
34. *therefore* when thine eye is single,

Lu. 11:35. Take heed *therefore* that the light
36. If thy whole body *therefore*
12: 7. Fear not *therefore*: ye are of more value
26. If ye *then* be not able to do that
40. Be ye *therefore* ready also:
13:14. in them *therefore* come and be
15. The Lord *then* answered him,
14:33. So *likewise*, whosoever he be
15:28. *therefore* came his father out,
16:11. If *therefore* ye have not been
27. I pray thee *therefore*, father,
19:12. He said *therefore*, A certain
20: 5. Why *then* believed ye him not?
15. What *therefore* shall the lord
17. What is this *then* that is written,
29. There were *therefore* seven
33. *Therefore* in the resurrection
44. David *therefore* calleth him Lord,
21: 7. *but* when shall these things be?
8. go ye not *therefore* after them.
14. Settle (it) *therefore* in your hearts,
36. Watch ye *therefore*, and pray always,
22:36. *Then* said he unto them,
70. Art thou *then* the Son of God?
23:16. I will *therefore* chastise him, and
20. Pilate *therefore*, willing to
22. I will *therefore* chastise him, and let
Joh. 1:21. What *then?* Art thou Elias?
22. *Then* said they unto him,
25. Why baptizest thou *then*,
2:18. *Then* answered the Jews
20. *Then* said the Jews, Forty and six
22. When *therefore* he was risen
3:25. *Then* there arose a question
29. this my joy *therefore* is fulfilled.
4: 1. When *therefore* the Lord knew
5. *Then* cometh he to a city of
6. Jesus *therefore*, being wearied with
9. *Then* saith the woman of Samaria
11. from whence *then* hast thou that
28. The woman *then* left her waterpot,
30. *Then* they went out of the city,
33. *Therefore* said the disciples
40. *So* when the Samaritans were
45. *Then* when he was come into Galilee,
46. *So* Jesus came again into Cana
48. *Then* said Jesus unto him,
52. *Then* enquired he of them the hour
53. *So* the father knew that (it was)
5: 4. whosoever *then* first after the
10. The Jews *therefore* said unto him
12. *Then* asked they him, What man
18. Therefore)(the Jews sought the more
19. *Then* answered Jesus and said
6: 5. When Jesus *then* lifted up (his) eyes,
10. *So* the men sat down,
13. *Therefore* they gathered (them) together,
14. *Then* those men, when they had seen
15. When Jesus *therefore* perceived
19. *So* when they had rowed about
21. *Then* they willingly received him
24. When the people *therefore* saw
28. *Then* said they unto him,
30. They said *therefore* unto him, What sign shewest thou *then*,
32. *Then* Jesus said unto them,
34. *Then* said they unto him, Lord,
41. The Jews *then* murmured at him,
42. how is it *then* that he saith,
43. Jesus *therefore* answered and said
45. Every man *therefore* that hath heard,
52. The Jews *therefore* strove among

Joh 6:53. *Then* Jesus said unto them,
60. Many *therefore* of his disciples,
62. (What) and if)(ye shall see the Son
67. *Then* said Jesus unto the twelve,
68. *Then* Simon Peter answered him,
7: 3. His brethren *therefore* said unto him,
6. *Then* Jesus said unto them,
11. *Then* the Jews sought him
25. *Then* said some of them
28. *Then* cried Jesus in the temple
30. *Then* they sought to take him:
33. *Then* said Jesus unto them,
35. *Then* said the Jews among themselves,
40. Many of the people *therefore*,
43. *So* there was a division among
45. *Then* came the officers
47. *Then* answered them the Pharisees,
8: 5. *but* what sayest thou?
12. *Then* spake Jesus again unto them,
13. The Pharisees *therefore* said unto
19. *Then* said they unto him,
21. *Then* said Jesus again unto
22. *Then* said the Jews, Will he kill
24. I said *therefore* unto you,
25. *Then* said they unto him,
28. *Then* said Jesus unto them,
31. *Then* said Jesus to those
36. If the Son *therefore* shall make
38. and ye)(do that which ye have seen
41. *Then* said they to him, We be not
42. Jesus)(said unto them, If God
48. *Then* answered the Jews, and
52. *Then* said the Jews unto him,
57. *Then* said the Jews unto him,
59. *Then* took they up stones
9: 7. He went his way *therefore*, and washed,
8. The neighbours *therefore*, and they
10. *Therefore* said they unto him,
12. *Then* said they unto him,
15. *Then* again the Pharisees also
16. *Therefore* said some of the Pharisees,
18. *But* the Jews did not believe
19. how *then* doth he now see?
24. *Then* again called they the man
25. He)(answered and said, Whether he
28. *Then* they reviled him,
41. *therefore* your sin remaineth.
10: 7. *Then* said Jesus unto them
19. There was a division *therefore* again
24. *Then* came the Jews round about him,
31. *Then* the Jews took up stones again
39. *Therefore* they sought again to take him
11: 3. *Therefore* his sisters sent unto him,
6. When he had heard *therefore* that he
12. *Then* said his disciples, Lord, if he
14. *Then* said Jesus unto them plainly,
16. *Then* said Thomas, which is called
17. *Then* when Jesus came, he found
20. *Then* Martha, as soon as she heard
21. *Then* said Martha unto Jesus,
31. The Jews *then* which were with her
32. *Then* when Mary was come
33. When Jesus *therefore* saw her weeping,
36. *Then* said the Jews, Behold how
38. Jesus *therefore* again groaning
41. *Then* they took away the stone
45. *Then* many of the Jews which came
47. *Then* gathered the chief priests and
53. *Then* from that day forth
54. Jesus *therefore* walked no more
56. *Then* sought they for Jesus,
12: 1. *Then* Jesus six days before the

Joh. 12: 2. There)(they made him a supper;
3. *Then* took Mary a pound of ointment
4. *Then* saith one of his disciples,
7. *Then* said Jesus, Let her alone:
9. Much people of the Jews *therefore* knew
17. The people *therefore* that was with
19. The Pharisees *therefore* said
21. The same came *therefore* to Philip,
28. *Then* came there a voice from
29. The people *therefore*, that stood by,
35. *Then* Jesus said unto them,
50. whatsoever I speak *therefore*,
13: 6. *Then* cometh he to Simon Peter:
12. *So* after he had washed their feet,
14. If I *then*, (your) Lord and Master,
22. *Then* the disciples looked one on
24. Simon Peter *therefore* beckoned
27. *Then* said Jesus unto him,
30. He *then* having received the sop
31(30). *Therefore*, when he was gone out,
16:17. *Then* said (some) of his disciples
18. They said *therefore*, What is this
19. *Now* Jesus knew that they were desirous to ask him,
22. And ye now *therefore* have sorrow:
18: 3. Judas *then*, having received a band
4. Jesus *therefore*, knowing all things
6. As soon *then* as he had said
7. *Then* asked he them again, Whom
8. if *therefore* ye seek me, let these
10. *Then* Simon Peter having a sword
11. *Then* said Jesus unto Peter,
12. *Then* the band and the captain
16. *Then* went out that other disciple,
17. *Then* saith the damsel that kept
19. The high priest *then* asked Jesus
25. They said *therefore* unto him,
27. Peter *then* denied again:
28. *Then* led they Jesus from Caiaphas
29. Pilate *then* went out unto them,
31. *Then* said Pilate unto them,
— The Jews *therefore* said unto him,
33. *Then* Pilate entered into the judgment
37. Pilate *therefore* said unto him,
39. will ye *therefore* that I release
40. *Then* cried they all again,
19: 1. Then Pilate *therefore* took Jesus,
4. Pilate *therefore* went forth again,
5. *Then* came Jesus forth, wearing
6. When the chief priests *therefore*
8. When Pilate *therefore* heard that
10. *Then* saith Pilate unto him,
13. When Pilate *therefore* heard that
16. Then delivered he him *therefore*
20. This title *then* read many of the
21. *Then* said the chief priests
23. *Then* the soldiers, when they had
24. They said *therefore* among themselves,
— These things *therefore*[1] the soldiers
26. When Jesus *therefore* saw his mother,
29. *Now* there was set a vessel full of
30. When Jesus *therefore* had received
31. The Jews *therefore*, because it was
32. *Then* came the soldiers, and brake the
38. He came *therefore*, and took the body
40. *Then* took they the body of Jesus,
42. There laid they Jesus *therefore*
20: 2. *Then* she runneth, and cometh to
3. Peter *therefore* went forth,
6. *Then* cometh Simon Peter
8. Then)(went in also that other
10. *Then* the disciples went away
Joh. 20:11. *and* as she wept, she stooped
19. *Then* the same day at evening,
20. *Then* were the disciples glad, when
21. *Then* said Jesus to them again,
25. The other disciples *therefore* said
30. And many other signs *truly*[1] did Jesus
21: 5. *Then* Jesus saith unto them,
6. They cast *therefore*, and now they
7. *Therefore* that disciple whom
— *Now* when Simon Peter heard
9. As soon *then* as they were come
13. Jesus *then* cometh, and taketh
15. *So* when they had dined,
23. *Then* went this saying abroad
Acts 1: 6. When they *therefore*[1] were come
18. *Now*[1] this man purchased a field
21. *Wherefore* of these men which
2:30. *Therefore* being a prophet,
33. *Therefore* being by the right hand
36. *Therefore* let all the house of
41. *Then*[1] they that gladly received
3:19. Repent ye *therefore*, and be
5:41. *And*[1] they departed from the
6: 3. *Wherefore*, brethren, look ye out
8: 4. *Therefore*[1] they that were scattered
22. Repent *therefore* of this thy
25. *And*[1] they, when they had testified and
9:31. *Then*[1] had the churches rest
10:23. *Then* called he them in,
29. I ask *therefore* for what
32. Send *therefore* to Joppa,
33. Immediately *therefore* I sent to
— Now *therefore* are we all here
11:17. Forasmuch *then* as God gave them
19. *Now*[1] they which were scattered
12: 5. Peter *therefore*[1] was kept in prison:
13: 4. *So*[1] they, being sent forth by the
38. Be it known unto you *therefore*,
40. Beware *therefore*, lest that come
14: 3. Long time *therefore*[1] abode they
15: 2. When *therefore* Paul and Barnabas had
3. *And*[1] being brought on their way
10. Now *therefore* why tempt ye God,
27. We have sent *therefore* Judas and
30. *So*[1] when they were dismissed,
39. *And* the contention was so sharp
16: 5. *And so*[1] were the churches established
11. *Therefore* loosing from Troas,
36. *therefore* depart, and go in peace.
17:12. *Therefore*[1] many of them believed;
17. *Therefore*[1] disputed he in the
20. we would know *therefore* what
23. Whom *therefore* ye ignorantly
29. Forasmuch *then* as we are
30. *And*[1] the times of this ignorance
18:14. If)([1] it were a matter of wrong or
19: 3. Unto what *then* were ye baptized?
32. Some *therefore*[1] cried one thing,
36. Seeing *then* that these things
38. *Wherefore*[1] if Demetrius, and
20:28. Take heed *therefore* unto yourselves,
21:22. What is it *therefore*?
23. Do *therefore* this that we say
22:29. *Then* straightway they departed
23:15. Now *therefore* ye with the
18. *So*[1] he took him, and brought
21. *But* do not thou yield unto them:
22. *So*[1] the chief captain (then)
31. *Then*[1] the soldiers, as it was
25: 1. *Now* when Festus was come
4. *But*[1] Festus answered, that Paul
5. Let them *therefore*, said he,

Acts25:17. *Therefore*, when they were come
23. *And* on the morrow, when Agrippa
26: 4. My)([1] manner of life from my youth,
9. I *verily*[1] thought with myself,
22. Having *therefore* obtained help
28: 5. *And*[1] he shook off the beast into
9. *So* when this was done,
20. For this cause *therefore* have I
28. Be it known *therefore* unto you,
Ro 2:21. Thou *therefore* which teachest
26. *Therefore* if the uncircumcision
3: 1. What advantage *then* hath the Jew ?
9. What *then?* are we better (than)
27. Where (is) boasting *then?*
28. *Therefore* we conclude that
31. Do we *then* make void the law
4: 1. What shall we *then* say
9. (Cometh) this blessedness *then*
10. How was it *then* reckoned ?
5: 1. *Therefore* being justified by faith,
9. Much more *then*, being now
18. *Therefore* (ἀρα οὐν) as by the offence of
6: 1. What shall we say *then?*
4. *Therefore* we are buried with him
12. Let not sin *therefore* reign in
15. What *then?* shall we sin,
21. What fruit had ye *then* in
7: 3. *So* then (ἀρα οὐν) if, while (her) husband
7. What shall we say *then?*
13. Was *then* that which is good
25. *So* then (ἀρα οὐν) with the mind I myself
8:12. *Therefore* (ἀρα οὐν), brethren, we are
31. What shall we *then* say to these
9:14. What shall we say *then?*
16. *So* then (ἀρα οὐν) (it is) not of him that
18. *Therefore* (ἀρα οὐν) hath he mercy on
19. Thou wilt say *then* unto me,
30. What shall we say *then?*
10:14. How *then* shall they call on
11: 1. I say *then*, Hath God cast away
5. Even so *then* at this present
7. What *then?* Israel hath not
11. I say *then*, Have they stumbled
19. Thou wilt say *then*,
22. Behold *therefore* the goodness
12: 1. I beseech you *therefore*, brethren,
20. *Therefore* if thine enemy hunger,
13: 7. Render *therefore* to all their dues:
10. *therefore* love (is) the fulfilling
12. let us *therefore* cast off the
14: 8. whether we live *therefore*, or
12. *So* then (ἀρα οὐν) every one of us shall
13. Let us not *therefore* judge
16. Let not *then* your good be evil
19. Let us *therefore* (ἀρα οὐν) follow after
15:17. I have *therefore* whereof I may glory
28. When *therefore* I have performed
16:19. I am glad *therefore* on your
1Co. 3: 5. Who *then* is Paul, and who
4:16. *Wherefore* I beseech you,
5: 7. Purge out *therefore* the old leaven,
6: 4. If *then*[1] ye have judgments of things
7. Now *therefore*[1] there is utterly
15. shall I *then* take the members of Christ,
7:26. I suppose *therefore* that this is
8: 4. As concerning *therefore* the eating
9:18. What is my reward *then?*
25. *Now*[1] they (do it) to obtain a corruptible
10:19. What say I *then?*
31. Whether *therefore* ye eat, or drink,
11:20. When ye come together *therefore*
14:11. *Therefore* if I know not the meaning

1Co.14:15. What is it *then?*
23. If *therefore* the whole church
26. How is it *then*, brethren ?
15:11. *Therefore* whether (it were) I
16:11. Let no man *therefore* despise him:
18. *therefore* acknowledge ye them that
2Co. 1:17. When I *therefore* was thus minded,
3:12. Seeing *then* that we have such hope,
5: 6. *Therefore* (we are) always confident,
11. Knowing *therefore* the terror of
20. *Now then* we are ambassadors
7: 1. Having *therefore* these promises,
8:24. *Wherefore* shew ye to them, and
9: 5. *Therefore* I thought it necessary
11:15. *Therefore* (it is) no great thing
12: 9. Most gladly *therefore* will I
Gal. 3: 5. He *therefore* that ministereth
19. Wherefore *then* (serveth) the law?
21. (Is) the law *then* against the promises
4:15. Where is *then* the blessedness
5: 1. Stand fast *therefore* in the liberty
6:10. we have *therefore* (ἀρα οὐν) opportunity
Eph. 2:19. *Now* therefore (ἀρα οὐν) ye are no more
4: 1. I *therefore*, the prisoner of the Lord,
17. This I say *therefore*, and testify
5: 1. Be ye *therefore* followers of God,
7. Be not ye *therefore* partakers
15. See *then* that ye walk circumspectly,
6:14. Stand *therefore*, having your loins
Phi. 2: 1. If (there be) *therefore* any consolation
23. Him *therefore*[1] I hope to send
28. I sent him *therefore* the more
29. Receive him *therefore* in the Lord
3:15. Let us *therefore*, as many as be
Col. 2: 6. As ye have *therefore* received Christ
16. Let no man *therefore* judge you
20. *Wherefore* if ye be dead with Christ
3: 1. If ye *then* be risen with Christ,
5. Mortify *therefore* your members
12. Put on *therefore*, as the elect
1Th. 4: 1. Furthermore *then* we beseech you,
5: 6. *Therefore* (ἀρα οὐν) let us not sleep, as
2Th. 2:15. *Therefore* (ἀρα οὐν), brethren, stand fast,
1Ti. 2: 1. I exhort *therefore*, that, first
8. I will *therefore* that men pray
3: 2. A bishop *then* must be blameless,
5:14. I will *therefore* that the younger
2Ti. 1: 8. Be not thou *therefore* ashamed
2: 1. Thou *therefore*, my son, be strong
3. Thou *therefore* endure hardness,
21. If a man *therefore* purge himself
4: 1. I charge (thee) *therefore* before God,
Philem 17. If thou count me *therefore* a
Heb 2:14. Forasmuch *then* as the children
4: 1. Let us *therefore* fear, lest,
6. Seeing *therefore* it remaineth
11. Let us labour *therefore* to enter
14. Seeing *then* that we have a great
16. Let us *therefore* come boldly
7:11. If *therefore*[1] perfection were by
9: 1. *Then*[1] verily the first (covenant)
23. (It was) *therefore* necessary
10:19. Having *therefore*, brethren, boldness
35. Cast not away *therefore* your
13:15. By him *therefore* let us offer
Jas. 4: 4. whosoever *therefore* will be a friend
7. Submit yourselves *therefore* to God.
17. *Therefore* to him that knoweth
5: 7. Be patient *therefore*, brethren,
1Pet. 2: 1. *Wherefore* laying aside all malice,
7. Unto you *therefore* which believe (he is)
13. Submit yourselves)(to every ordinance

Pet.4: 1. Forasmuch *then* as Christ hath
7. be ye *therefore* sober,
5: 6. Humble yourselves *therefore*
2Pet. 3:11. (Seeing) *then* (that) all these things
17. Ye *therefore*, beloved, seeing ye
1Joh. 2:24. Let that *therefore* abide in you, which
3Joh. 8. We *therefore* ought to receive such,
Rev. 2: 5. Remember *therefore* from whence
3: 3. Remember *therefore* how thou hast
— If *therefore* thou shalt not watch,
19. be zealous *therefore*, and repent.

3768 23 597/726 3756,4452

οὔπω, oupo.

Mat. 15:17. Do *not* ye *yet* understand,
16: 9. Do ye *not yet* understand,
24: 6. but the end is *not yet*.
Mar 8:17. perceive ye *not yet*,
13: 7. but the end (shall) *not* (be) *yet*.
Joh. 2: 4. mine hour is *not yet* come.
3:24. John was *not yet* cast into prison.
7: 6. My time is *not yet* come:
8. I go *not* up *yet* unto this feast; for my time is *not yet* full come.
30. his hour was *not yet* come.
39. the Holy Ghost was *not yet* (given);
8:20. his hour was *not yet* come.
57. Thou art *not yet* fifty years old,
11:30. Jesus was *not yet* come into the
20:17. for I am *not yet* ascended to my
Acts 8:16. For|| *as yet* he was fallen upon none
1Co. 3: 2. for *hitherto* ye were *not* able
Heb 2: 8. now we see *not yet* all things put
12: 4. Ye have *not yet* resisted unto
1Joh. 3: 2. it doth *not yet* appear what we
Rev. 17:10. the other is *not yet* come;
12. have received *no* kingdom *as yet*;

3769 5 598/726

οὐρά, oura.

Rev. 9:10. And they had *tails* like unto scorpions, and there were stings in their *tails*:
19. and in their *tails*: for their *tails* (were) like unto serpents,
12: 4. And his *tail* drew the third part

3770 8 596/727 5:497 3772

οὐράνιος, ouranios.

Mat. 6:14. your *heavenly* Father will also forgive
26. yet your *heavenly* Father feedeth
32. for your *heavenly* Father knoweth
15:13. my *heavenly* Father hath not planted,
Lu. 2:13. a multitude of the *heavenly* host
Acts 26:19. I was not disobedient unto the *heavenly* vision:

3771 2 598/727 5:497 3772

οὐρανόθεν, ouranothen.

Acts 14:17. gave us rain *from heaven*,
26:13. in the way a light *from heaven*,

3772 284 598/727 5:497 rt 3735

οὐρανός, ouranos.

[2] denotes the word in Greek to be plural.

Mat. 3: 2. the kingdom of *heaven*[2] is at hand.
16. and, lo, the *heavens*[2] were opened
17. And lo a voice from *heaven*,[2]
4:17. the kingdom of *heaven*[2] is at hand.
5: 3. for their's is the kingdom of *heaven*.[2]
10. for their's is the kingdom of *heaven*.[2]
12. great (is) your reward in *heaven*:[2]
16. your Father which is in *heaven*.[2]
18. Till *heaven* and earth pass,
19. least in the kingdom of *heaven*:[2]
— great in the kingdom of *heaven*.[2]
20. into the kingdom of *heaven*.[2]
34. neither by *heaven*; for it is God's
45. of your Father which is in *heaven*:[2]
48. even as your Father which is in *heaven*[2]
6: 1. of your Father which is in *heaven*.[2]
9. Our Father which art in *heaven*,[2]
10. as (it is) in *heaven*.
20. treasures in *heaven*,
26. Behold the fowls of the *air*:
7:11. your Father which is in *heaven*[2]
21. the kingdom of *heaven*;[2]
— which is in *heaven*.[2]
8:11. and Jacob, in the kingdom of *heaven*.[2]
20. the birds of the *air* (have) nests;
10: 7. The kingdom of *heaven*[2] is at hand.
32. my Father which is in *heaven*.[2]
33. before my Father which is in *heaven*.[2]
11:11. that is least in the kingdom of *heaven*[2]
12. the kingdom of *heaven*[2] suffereth
23. art exalted unto *heaven*,
25. Lord of *heaven* and earth,
12:50. my Father which is in *heaven*,[2]
13:11. mysteries of the kingdom of *heaven*,[2]
24. The kingdom of *heaven*[2] is likened unto
31. The kingdom of *heaven*[2] is like to
32. the birds of the *air* come and lodge
33. The kingdom of *heaven*[2] is like unto
44. Again, the kingdom of *heaven*[2] is like
45. the kingdom of *heaven*[2] is like
47. the kingdom of *heaven*[2] is like unto a net,
52. instructed unto the kingdom of *heaven*[2]
14:19. looking up to *heaven*,
16: 1. a sign from *heaven*.
2. for the *sky* is red.
3. for the *sky* is red and lowring.
— ye can discern the face of the *sky*;
17. my Father which is in *heaven*.[2]
19. the keys of the kingdom of *heaven*:[2]
— shall be bound in *heaven*:[2]
— shall be loosed in *heaven*.[2]
18: 1. the greatest in the kingdom of *heaven*?[2]
3. not enter into the kingdom of *heaven*.[2]
4. is greatest in the kingdom of *heaven*.[2]
10. That in *heaven*[2] their angels
— my Father which is in *heaven*.[2]
14. your Father which is in *heaven*,[2]
18. shall be bound in *heaven*:
— shall be loosed in *heaven*.
19. my Father which is in *heaven*.[2]
23. the kingdom of *heaven*[2]
19:12. the kingdom of *heaven's*[2] sake.
14. of such is the kingdom of *heaven*.[2]
21. shalt have treasure in *heaven*:
23. enter into the kingdom of *heaven*.[2]
20: 1. For the kingdom of *heaven*[2] is like
21:25. from *heaven*, or of men?
— From *heaven*; he will say unto us,
22: 2. The kingdom of *heaven*[2] is like
30. as the angels of God in *heaven*.
23: 9. which is in *heaven*.[2]
13(14). shut up the kingdom of *heaven*[2]
22. that shall swear by *heaven*,
24:29. the stars shall fall from *heaven*, and the powers of the *heavens*[2] shall
30. sign of the Son of man in *heaven*:

Mat.24:30. coming in the clouds of *heaven*
31. from one end of *heaven*[2] to
35. *Heaven* and earth shall pass
36. not the angels of *heaven*,[2]
25: 1. the kingdom of *heaven*[2]
26:64. coming in the clouds of *heaven*.
28: 2. descended from *heaven*, and came
18. is given unto me in *heaven* and in earth.
Mar 1:10. he saw the *heavens*[2] opened,
11. there came a voice from *heaven*,[2]
4: 4. the fowls of the *air* came and
32. the fowls of the *air* may lodge
6:41. he looked up to *heaven*,
7:34. And looking up to *heaven*,
8:11. seeking of him a sign from *heaven*,
10:21. thou shalt have treasure in *heaven*:
11:25. your Father also which is in *heaven*[2]
26. your Father which is in *heaven*[2]
30. from *heaven*, or of men?
31. If we shall say, From *heaven*;
12:25. as the angels which are in *heaven*.[2]
13:25. the stars of *heaven* shall fall, and the powers that are in *heaven*[2]
27. to the uttermost part of *heaven*.
31. *Heaven* and earth shall pass away:
32. not the angels which are in *heaven*,
14:62. and coming in the clouds of *heaven*.
16:19. he was received up into *heaven*,
Lu. 2:15. gone away from them into *heaven*,
3:21. the *heaven* was opened,
22. and a voice came from *heaven*,
4:25. when the *heaven* was shut up
6:23. your reward (is) great in *heaven*:
8: 5. the fowls of the *air* devoured it.
9:16. and looking up to *heaven*,
54. fire to come down from *heaven*,
58. and birds of the *air* (have) nests;
10:15. which art exalted to *heaven*,
18. Satan as lightning fall from *heaven*.
20. your names are written in *heaven*.[2]
21. Lord of *heaven* and earth,
11: 2. Our Father which art in *heaven*,[2]
— as in *heaven*, so in earth.
13. shall (your) *heaven*ly Father give
16. sought of him a sign from *heaven*.
12:33. a treasure in the *heavens*[2]
56. ye can discern the face of the *sky*
13:19. the fowls of the *air* lodged in the
15: 7. joy shall be in *heaven* over one
18. I have sinned against *heaven*,
21. Father, I have sinned against *heaven*,
16:17. it is easier for *heaven* and earth to
17:24. out of the one (part) under *heaven*, shineth unto the other (part) under *heaven*;
29. and brimstone from *heaven*,
18:13. so much as (his) eyes unto *heaven*,
22. thou shalt have treasure in *heaven*:
19:38. peace in *heaven*, and glory in
20: 4. was it from *heaven*, or of men?
5. If we shall say, From *heaven*;
21:11. great signs shall there be from *heaven*.
26. the powers of *heaven*[2] shall be shaken.
33. *Heaven* and earth shall pass away:
22:43. an angel unto him from *heaven*,
24:51. and carried up into *heaven*.
Joh. 1:32. from *heaven* like a dove,
51(52). ye shall see *heaven* open,
3:13. no man hath ascended up to *heaven*, but he that came down from *heaven*, (even) the Son of man which is in *heaven*.
27. except it be given him from *heaven*.
31. he that cometh from *heaven* is

Joh. 6:31. He gave them bread from *heaven*
32. not that bread from *heaven*;
— the true bread from *heaven*.
33. is he which cometh down from *heaven*,
38. I came down from *heaven*,
41. which came down from *heaven*.
42. I came down from *heaven*?
50. which cometh down from *heaven*,
51. which came down from *heaven*:
58. that bread which came down from *heaven*
12:28. Then came there a voice from *heaven*,
17: 1. lifted up his eyes to *heaven*,
Acts 1:10. looked stedfastly toward *heaven*
11. gazing up into *heaven*?
— taken up from you into *heaven*,
— as ye have seen him go into *heaven*.
2: 2. there came a sound from *heaven*
5. of every nation under *heaven*.
19. shew wonders in *heaven*
34. not ascended into the *heavens*:[2]
3:21. Whom the *heaven* must receive
4:12. none other name under *heaven*
24. which hast made *heaven*, and
7:42. to worship the host of *heaven*;
49. *Heaven* (is) my throne,
55. looked up stedfastly into *heaven*.
56. Behold, I see the *heavens*[2] opened.
9: 3. a light from *heaven*:
10:11. And saw *heaven* opened,
12. and fowls of the *air*.
16. received up again into *heaven*.
11: 5. let down from *heaven*
6. and fowls of the *air*.
9. answered me again from *heaven*,
10. drawn up again into *heaven*.
14:15. which made *heaven*, and earth,
17:24. Lord of *heaven* and earth,
22: 6. there shone from *heaven* a great
Ro. 1:18. is revealed from *heaven*
10: 6. Who shall ascend into *heaven*?
1Co. 8: 5. whether in *heaven* or in earth,
15:47. (is) the Lord from *heaven*.
2Co. 5: 1. eternal in the *heavens*.[2]
2. our house which is from *heaven*.
12: 2. caught up to the third *heaven*.
Gal. 1: 8. or an angel from *heaven*,
Eph. 1:10. both which are in *heaven*,[2]
3:15. in *heaven*[2] and earth is named,
4:10. far above all *heavens*,[2]
6: 9. your Master also is in *heaven*;[2]
Phi. 3:20. our conversation is in *heaven*;[2]
Col. 1: 5. laid up for you in *heaven*,[2]
16. that are in *heaven*,[2] and that are
20. or things in *heaven*.[2]
23. which is under *heaven*;
4: 1. ye also have a Master in *heaven*.[2]
1Th. 1:10. to wait for his Son from *heaven*,[2]
4:16. shall descend from *heaven*
2Th. 1: 7. be revealed from *heaven*
Heb 1:10. and the *heavens*[2] are the works of
4:14. that is passed into the *heavens*,[2]
7:26. made higher than the *heavens*;[2]
8: 1. the Majesty in the *heavens*;[2]
9:23. patterns of things in the *heavens*[2]
24. but into *heaven* itself,
10:34. that ye have in *heaven*[2] a better
11:12. as the stars of the *sky*
12:23. written in *heaven*,[2]
25. that (speaketh) from *heaven*:[2]
26. not the earth only, but also *heaven*.
Jas. 5:12. neither by *heaven*,
18. and the *heaven* gave rain,

1Pet. 1: 4. reserved in *heaven*[2] for you,
12. Holy Ghost sent down from *heaven;*
3:22. Who is gone into *heaven,*
2Pet. 1:18. this voice which came from *heaven*
3: 5. the *heavens*[2] were of old,
7. But the *heavens*[2] and the earth,
10. the *heavens*[2] shall pass away
12. the *heavens*[2] being on fire
13. for new *heavens*[2] and a new earth,
1Joh.5: 7. three that bear record in *heaven,*
Rev. 3:12. out of *heaven* from my God:
4: 1. a door (was) opened in *heaven:*
2. a throne was set in *heaven,*
5: 3. no man in *heaven,* nor in earth,
13. every creature which is in *heaven,*
6:13. And the stars of *heaven* fell
14. And the *heaven* departed
8: 1. there was silence in *heaven*
10. there fell a great star from *heaven.*
9: 1. I saw a star fall from *heaven*
10: 1. angel come down from *heaven,*
4. I heard a voice from *heaven*
5. lifted up his hand to *heaven,*
6. who created *heaven,* and the things
8. which I heard from *heaven*
11: 6. have power to shut *heaven,*
12. a great voice from *heaven*
— they ascended up to *heaven*
13. gave glory to the God of *heaven.*
15. great voices in *heaven,*
19. was opened in *heaven,*
12: 1. a great wonder in *heaven;*
3. another wonder in *heaven,*
4. third part of the stars of *heaven,*
7. And there was war in *heaven:*
8. found any more in *heaven.*
10. a loud voice saying in *heaven,*
12. Therefore rejoice, (ye) *heavens,*[2]
13: 6. them that dwell in *heaven.*
13. fire come down from *heaven*
14: 2. I heard a voice from *heaven,*
7. that made *heaven,* and earth,
13. I heard a voice from *heaven*
17. the temple which is in *heaven,*
15: 1. I saw another sign in *heaven,*
5. the tabernacle of the testimony in *heaven* was opened:
16:11. blasphemed the God of *heaven*
17. out of the temple of *heaven,*
21. a great hail out of *heaven,*
18: 1. down from *heaven,* having
4. another voice from *heaven,*
5. have reached unto *heaven,*
20. Rejoice over her, (thou) *heaven,*
19: 1. of much people in *heaven,*
11. And I saw *heaven* opened,
14. (which were) in *heaven* followed him
20: 1. down from *heaven,* having
9. from God out of *heaven,*
11. the earth and the *heaven* fled away;
21: 1. I saw a new *heaven* and a new earth: for the first *heaven* and
2. from God out of *heaven,*
3. a great voice out of *heaven*
10. descending out of *heaven* from God,

3775 37 600/730 5:543

οὖς, *ous.*

Mat.10:27. what ye hear in the *ear,*
11:15. He that hath *ears* to hear.
13: 9. Who hath *ears* to hear.
Mat.13:15. and (their) *ears* are dull of
— and hear with (their) *ears,*
16. and your *ears,* for they hear.
43. Who hath *ears* to hear,
Mar 4: 9. He that hath *ears* to hear,
23. If any man have *ears* to hear,
7:16. If any man have *ears* to hear,
33. and put his fingers into his *ears,*
8:18. and having *ears,* hear ye not?
Lu. 1:44. thy salutation sounded in mine *ears,*
4:21. fulfilled in your *ears.*
8: 8. He that hath *ears* to hear,
9:44. sink down into your *ears:*
12: 3. which ye have spoken in the *ear*
14:35. He that hath *ears* to hear,
22:50. and cut off his right *ear.*
Acts 7:51. uncircumcised in heart and *ears,*
57. and stopped their *ears,* and
11:22. came unto the *ears* of the church
28:27. and their *ears* are dull of hearing,
— and hear with (their) *ears,*
Ro. 11: 8. and *ears* that they should not hear;
1Co. 2: 9. nor *ear* heard, neither have entered
12:16. And if the *ear* shall say,
Jas. 5: 4. are entered into the *ears* of the Lord
1Pet. 3:12. and his *ears* (are open) unto their
Rev. 2: 7. He that hath an *ear,* let him hear
11. He that hath an *ear,* let him hear
17. He that hath an *ear,* let him hear
29. He that hath an *ear,* let him hear
3: 6. He that hath an *ear,* let him hear
13. He that hath an *ear,* let him hear
22. He that hath an *ear,* let him hear
13: 9 If any man have an *ear,*

οὖσα, οὔση, &c., see ὤν. 5607

3776 2 600/731 5607

οὐσία, *ousia.*

Lu. 15:12. give me the portion of *goods*
13. wasted his *substance* with

3777 94 600/731 3756,5037

οὔτε, *oute.*

Mat. 6:20. where *neither* moth *nor* rust doth
12:32. *neither* in this world, *neither* in the (world) to come.
22:30. they *neither* marry, *nor* are given
Mar 5: 3. ‖*no, not* with chains:
12:25. *neither* marry, *nor* are given in
Lu. 12:26. If ye then be *not* able to do that thing which is least,
14:35. It is *neither* fit for the land, *nor yet*
20:35. *neither* marry, *nor* are given in
36. *Neither* can they die any more:
Joh. 1:25. *nor* Elias, *neither* that prophet?
4:11. thou hast *nothing* to draw with,
21. *neither* in this mountain, *nor yet* at
5:37. Ye have *neither* heard his voice at any time, *nor* seen his shape.
8:19. Ye *neither* know me, *nor* my Father:
9: 3. *Neither* hath this man sinned, *nor* his parents:
Acts 4:12. for there is *none* other name
15:10. which *neither* our fathers *nor* we were
19:37. *neither* robbers of churches, *nor yet*
24:12. they *neither* found me in the temple
— *neither* in the synagogues, *nor* in the city
13. *Neither* can they prove the things

Acts25: 8. *Neither* against the law of the Jews, *neither* against the temple, *nor yet* against
28:21. We *neither* received letters
— *neither* any of the brethren
Ro. 8:38. For I am persuaded, that *neither* death, *nor* life, *nor* angels, *nor* principalities, *nor* powers, *nor* things present, *nor* things to come,
39. *Nor* height, *nor* depth, *nor* any other
1Co. 3: 2. *neither* yet now are ye able.
7. *neither* is he that planteth any thing, *neither* he that watereth;
6: 9. *neither* fornicators, *nor* idolaters, *nor* adulterers, *nor* effeminate, *nor* abusers of themselves with
10. *Nor* thieves, *nor* covetous, *nor* drunkards,
8: 8. for *neither*, if we eat, are we the better; *neither*, if we eat not, are
11:11. *neither* is the man without the woman, *neither* the woman without the
Gal. 1:12. *neither* was I taught (it),
5: 6. Jesus Christ *neither* circumcision availeth any thing, *nor* uncircumcision;
6:15. *neither* circumcision availeth any thing, *nor*
1Th. 2: 3. nor of uncleanness, *nor* in guile.
5. For *neither* at any time used we
— *nor* a cloke of covetousness;
6. *Nor* of men sought we glory, *neither* of you, *nor* (yet) of others,
3Joh. 10. *neither* doth he himself receive
Rev. 3:15. that thou art *neither* cold *nor* hot:
16. and *neither* cold *nor* hot,
5: 4. *neither* to look thereon.
9:20. *yet* repented *not* of the works
— which *neither* can see, *nor* hear, *nor* walk:
21. *nor* of their sorceries, *nor* of their fornication, *nor* of their thefts.
12: 8. *neither* was their place found
20: 4. worshipped the beast, *neither* his image,
21: 4. *neither* sorrow, *nor* crying, *neither* shall there be any more pain:

3778a 192 600/731 3588,846

οὗτος, houtos.

Mat. 3: 3. For *this* is he that was spoken of
17. *This* is my beloved Son,
5:19. *the same* shall be called great
7:12. for *this* is the law and the prophets.
8:27. What manner of man is *this*,
9: 3. *This* (man) blasphemeth.
10:22. endureth to the end)(shall be saved.
11:10. For *this* is (he), of whom it is written,
12:23. Is not *this* the son of David?
24. *This* (fellow) doth not cast out
13:19. *This* is he which received seed by
20. *the same* is he that heareth the
22. is *he* that heareth the word;
23. is *he* that heareth the word,
55. Is not *this* the carpenter's son?
14: 2. *This* is John the Baptist;
15: 8. *This* people draweth nigh unto me
17: 5. *This* is my beloved Son,
18: 4. *the same* is greatest in the kingdom
21:10. city was moved, saying, Who is *this?*
11. *This* is Jesus the prophet
38. *This* is the heir; come, let us kill him,
42. *the same* is become the head of the
24:13. *the same* shall be saved.
26:23. *the same* shall betray me.
6.. *This* (fellow) said, I am able
71. *This* (fellow) was also with Jesus

Mat.27:37. *THIS* IS JESUS THE KING OF THE JEWS.
47. *This* (man) calleth for Elias.
54. Truly *this* was the Son of God.
58. *He* went to Pilate, and begged the body
28:15. *this* saying is commonly reported
Mar 2: 7. Why doth *this* (man) thus speak
3:35. *the same* is my brother,
4:41. What manner of man is *this*, that
6: 3. Is not *this* the carpenter,
16. *It* (lit. *this*) is John, whom I beheaded:
7: 6. *This* people honoureth me with (their)
8:35. *the same* shall save it.
9: 7. *This* is my beloved Son: hear him.
12: 7. *This* is the heir; come, let us
10. which the builders rejected)(is become
13:13. *the same* shall be saved.
14:69. *This* is (one) of them.
15:39. Truly *this* man was the Son of God.
Lu. 1:29. what manner of salutation *this* should be
32. *He* shall be great, and
36. *this* is the sixth month with her,
2:25. *the same* man (was) just and
34. *this* (child) is set for the fall and
4:22. Is not *this* Joseph's son?
36. What a word (is) *this!*
5:21. Who is *this* which speaketh
7:17. *this* rumour of him went forth
27. *This* is (he), of whom it is written,
39. *This man*, if he were a prophet,
49. Who is *this* that forgiveth sins
8:25. What manner of man is *this!*
9:24. *the same* shall save it.
35. *This* is my beloved Son: hear him
48. *the same* shall be great.
14:30. *This* man began to build,
15: 2. *This man* receiveth sinners,
24. For *this* my son was dead,
30. But as soon as *this* thy son
32. for *this* thy brother was dead,
16: 1. *the same* was accused unto him
17:18. glory to God, save *this* stranger.
18:11. or even as *this* publican.
14. *this man* went down to his house
19: 2. and *he* was rich.
20:14. *This* is the heir: come, let us kill him,
17. *the same* is become the head
28. and *he* die without children,
30. and *he* died childless.
22:56. *This man* was also with him.
59. Of a truth *this* (fellow) also
23:22. Why, what evil hath *he* done?
35. if *he* be Christ, the chosen of God.
38. *THIS* IS THE KING OF THE JEWS.
41. *this man* hath done nothing amiss.
47. Certainly *this* was a righteous man.
51. *The same* had not consented to
52. *This* (man) went unto Pilate, and
Joh. 1: 2. *The same* was in the beginning
7. *The same* came for a witness,
15. *This* was he of whom I spake,
30. *This* is he of whom I said,
33. *the same* is he which baptizeth
34. that *this* is the Son of God.
41(42). *He* first findeth his own brother
2:20. Forty and six years was *this* temple in
3: 2. *The same* came to Jesus by night,
26. behold, *the same* baptizeth,
4:29. is not *this* the Christ?
42. *this* is indeed the Christ, the
47. When *he* heard that Jesus
6:14. *This* is of a truth that prophet

Joh. **6:42.** Is not *this* Jesus,
— how is it then that *he* saith,
46. *he* hath seen the Father.
50. *This* is the bread which cometh down
52. How can *this man* give us (his) flesh
58. *This* is that bread which came
60. *This* is an hard saying;
71. for *he it was that* should betray
7:15. How knoweth *this man* letters,
18. *the same* is true,
25. Is not *this* he, whom they seek
26. that *this* is the very Christ?
31. which *this* (man) hath done?
35. Whither will *he* go,
36. What (manner of) saying is *this*
40. Of a truth *this* is the prophet.
41. *This* is the Christ.
46. Never man spake like *this* man.
49. But *this* people who knoweth not
9: 2. who did sin, *this man*, or his
3. Neither hath *this man* sinned,
8. Is not *this* he that sat and begged?
9. Some said, *This* is he:
16. *This* man is not of God,
19. Is *this* your son,
20. We know that *this* is our son,
24. we know that *this* man is a sinner.
33. If *this man* were not of God,
11:37. Could not *this man*, which
— that even *this man* should not
47. for *this* man doeth many miracles
12:34. who is *this* Son of man?
15: 5. *the same* bringeth forth much fruit.
18:30. If *he* were not a malefactor,
21:21. what (shall) *this man* (do)?
23. Then went *this* saying abroad
24. *This* is the disciple which
Acts **1:11.** *this same* Jesus, which is taken up
18. Now *this man* purchased a field
3:10. they knew that it was *he* which sat
4: 9. by what means *he* is made whole;
10. (even) by him doth *this man* stand
11. *This* is the stone which was set
6:13. *This* man ceaseth not to speak
14. that *this* Jesus of Nazareth shall
7:19. *The same* dealt subtilly with our
36. *He* brought them out, after
37. *This* is that Moses, which said
38. *This* is he, that was in the church
40. for (as for) *this* Moses, which brought us
8:10. *This man* is the great power of God.
9:15. for *he* is a chosen vessel unto me,
20. that *he* is the Son of God.
21. Is not *this* he that destroyed them
22. proving that *this* is very Christ.
10: 6. *He* lodgeth with one Simon a tanner,
— *he* shall tell thee what thou
32. *he* is lodged in the house of (one)
36. *he* is Lord of all:
13: 7. *who* called for Barnabas and Saul,
14: 9. *The same* heard Paul speak:
17: 3. and that *this* Jesus, whom I preach
18. What will *this* babbler say?
24. seeing that *he* is Lord of heaven
18:13. *This* (fellow) persuadeth men to
25. *This man* was instructed in the
26. And *he* began to speak boldly
19:26. *this* Paul hath persuaded and
21:28. *This* is the man, that teacheth
22:26. for *this* man is a Roman.
26:31. *This* man doeth nothing worthy of death
32. *This* man might have been set

Acts28: 4. No doubt *this* man is a murderer,
Ro. 4: 9. (Cometh) *this* blessedness then
8: 9. *he* is none of his.
9: 9. For *this* (is) the word of promise,
1Co. 8: 3. *the same* is known of him.
Heb 3: 3. For *this* (man) was counted worthy
7: 1. For *this* Melchisedec, king of Salem,
4. consider how great *this man* (was),
Jas. 1:23. *he* is like unto a man beholding
25. *he* being not a forgetful hearer,
— *this man* shall be blessed
3: 2. *the same* (is) a perfect man,
1Pet.2: 7. *the same* is made the head of the
2Pet.1:17. *This* is my beloved Son,
1Joh.2:22. *He* is antichrist, that denieth
5: 6. *This* is he that came by water and
20. *This* is the true God,
2Joh. 7. *This* is a deceiver and an antichrist.
9. *he* hath both the Father and the Son.
Rev. 3: 5. *the same* shall be clothed in white
20:14. *This* is the second death.

3778b 80 600/736 3588,846

οὗτοι, *houtoi*. from **οὗτος**.

denotes it to be compounded with **αὐτός**.

Mat. 4: 3. command that *these* stones be made
13:38. the good seed)(are the children of the
20:12. *These* last have wrought (but)
21. Grant that *these* my two sons
21:16. Hearest thou what *these* say?
25:46. And *these* shall go away into
26:62. what (is it which) *these* witness
Mar 4:15. And *these* are they by the way side,
16. And *these* are they likewise
18. And *these* are they which are
such as hear the word,
20. And *these* are they which are sown
12:40. *these* shall receive greater damnation.
14:60. what (is it which) *these* witness
Lu. 8:13. and *these* have no root,
14. are *they*, which, when they have heard,
15. are *they*, which in an honest and
21. are *these* which hear the word
9: 9. but who is *this*, of whom I hear
13: 2. Suppose ye that *these* Galilæans
4. think ye that *they* were sinners above
19:40. I tell you that, if *these* should hold
20:47. *the same* shall receive greater damnation.
21: 4. For all *these* have of their abundance
24:17. communications (are) *these* that ye
44. *These* (are) the words which I
Joh. 6: 5. that *these* may eat?
12:21. *The same* came therefore to Philip,
17:11. but *these* are in the world,
25. and *these* have known that thou
18:21. *they* know what I said.
Acts 1:14. *These* all continued with one accord
2: 7. are not all *these* which speak Galilæans?
15. For *these* are not drunken,
11:12. *these* six brethren accompanied me,
13: 4. So *they*, being sent forth by the Holy
16:17. *These* men are the servants of
20. *These* men, being Jews,
17: 6. *These* that have turned the world upside
7. and *these* all do contrary to
11. *These* were more noble than those
20: 5. *These* going before tarried for us
24:15. which *they*[2] themselves also allow
20. Or else let *these*[2] same (here) say
25:11. whereof *these* accuse me,

Acts27:31. Except *these* abide in the ship,
Ro. 2:14. *these*, having not the law,
8:14. *they* are the sons of God.
9: 6. For *they* (are) not all Israel, which
11:24. how much more shall *these*, which be the
31. Even so have *these* also now
1Co.16:17. on your part *they* have supplied.
Gal. 3: 7. *the same* are the children of
6:12. *they* constrain you to be circumcised;
Col. 4:11. *These* only (are my) fellowworkers
1Ti. 3:10. let *these* also first be proved;
2Ti. 3: 8. so do *these* also resist
Heb11:13. *These* all died in faith,
39. And *these* all, having obtained a
2Pet. 2:12. But *these*, as natural brute
17. *These* are wells without water,
1Joh.5: 7. and *these* three are one.
Jude 8. Likewise also *these* (filthy) dreamers
10. But *these* speak evil of those things
12. *These* are spots in your feasts
16. *These* are murmurers, complainers,
19. *These* be they who separate
Rev. 7:13. What are *these* which are arrayed
14. *These* are they which came out
11: 4. *These* are the two olive trees,
6. *These* have power to shut heaven,
10. because *these* two prophets
14: 4. *These* are they which were not defiled
— *These* are they which follow
— *These* were redeemed from
17:13. *These* have one mind,
14. *These* shall make war with
16. *these* shall hate the whore,
19: 9. *These* are the true sayings of God.
21: 5. *these* words are true and faithful.
22: 6. *These* sayings (are) faithful and true:

3778c 81 600/733 3588,846

αὕτη, *hautee.* fem. sing. of **οὗτος.**

Mat. 9:26. the fame *hereof* went abroad
13:54. Whence hath this (man) *this* wisdom,
21:42. *this* is the Lord's doing, and it is
22:20. unto them, Whose (is) *this* image
38. *This* is the first and great commandment.
24:34. *This* generation shall not pass,
26: 8. To what purpose (is) *this* waste?
12. in that *she* hath poured this ointment on
13. that *this woman* hath done, be
Mar 1:27. what new doctrine (is) *this?*
8:12. Why doth *this* generation seek
12:11. *This* was the Lord's doing, and it is
16. Whose (is) *this* image and superscription?
30. *this* (is) the first commandment.
31. second (is) like, (namely) *this*,
43. *this* poor widow hath cast more
44. *she* of her want did cast in
13:30. *this* generation shall not pass,
14: 4. Why was *this* waste of the ointment
8. She hath done what *she* could:
9. that *she* hath done shall be
Lu. 2: 2. *this* taxing was first made
36. *she* was of a great age, and had
37. *she* (was) a widow of about
38. *she* coming in that instant
4:21. *this* scripture fulfilled in your ears.
7:44. *she* hath washed my feet with tears,
45. *this woman* since the time
46. *this woman* hath anointed my
8: 9. What might *this* parable be?
11. Now the parable is *this:*
42. of age, and *she* lay a dying.
Lu. 11:29. *This* is an evil generation: they
21: 3. that *this* poor widow hath cast
4. *she* of her penury hath cast in
32. *This* generation shall not pass
22:53. *this* is your hour, and the power
Joh. 1:19. *this* is the record of John, when
3:19. And *this* is the condemnation,
29. *this* my joy therefore is fulfilled.
8: 4. *this* woman was taken in
11: 4. *This* sickness is not unto death,
12:30. *This* voice came not because of me,
15:12. *This* is my commandment, That
17: 3. *this* is life eternal, that they might
Acts 5:38. for if *this* counsel or this work
8:26. Jerusalem unto Gaza, *which* is desert.
32. scripture which he read was *this*,
9:36. *this woman* was full of good works
16:17. *The same* followed Paul and us,
17:19. we know what *this* new doctrine,
21:11. the man that owneth *this* girdle,
Ro. 7:10. the commandment,...I found)((to be) unto death.
11:27. For *this* (is) my covenant unto them,
16: 2. for *she* hath been a succourer of many,
1Co. 8: 9. by any means *this* liberty of your's
9: 3. Mine answer to them that do examine me is *this*,
2Co. 1:12. For our rejoicing is *this*, the
2: 6. to such a man (is) *this* punishment,
11:10. shall stop me of *this* boasting
Eph. 3: 8. is *this* grace given, that I should
Tit. 1:13. *This* witness is true. Wherefore
Heb. 8:10. For *this* (is) the covenant that I
10:16. *This* (is) the covenant that I will
Jas. 1:27. before God and the Father is *this*, To visit
3:15. *This* wisdom descendeth not from
1Joh.1: 5. *This* then is the message which
2:25. *this* is the promise that he
3:11. For *this* is the message that ye
23. *this* is his commandment,
5: 3. For *this* is the love of God, that
4. *this* is the victory that overcometh
9. for *this* is the witness of God
11 *this* is the record, that God
— *this* life is in his Son.
14. *this* is the confidence that we
2Joh. 6. *this* is love, that we walk after
— *This* is the commandment,
Rev.20: 5. *This* (is) the first resurrection.

3778d 3 600/736 3588,846

αὗται, *hautai.* fem. plur. of **οὗτος.**

Lu. 21:22. For *these* be the days of vengeance,
Acts20:34. that *these* hands have ministered
Gal. 4:24. for *these* are the two covenants;

The other cases of this pronoun, viz: *ταῦτα, ταύτῃ, τοῦτο, τούτων*, &c., will be found severally in their alphabetical places.

3779 213 602/737 3778

οὕτω, οὕτως, *houto, houtōs.*

[2] denotes where the force of *καὶ* is blended into that of *οὕτω.*

Mat. 1:18. the birth of Jesus Christ was *on this wise.*
2: 5. for *thus* it is written by the prophet,
3:15. for *thus* it becometh us to fulfil
5:12. for *so* persecuted they the prophets
16. Let your light *so* shine before men,
19. and shall teach men *so*,
47. do not even the publicans *so?*
6: 9. *After this manner* therefore pray ye:

Mat. 6:30. if God *so* clothe the grass
7:12. do ye *even so*[2] to them:
17. *Even so* every good tree
9:33. It was never *so* seen in Israel.
11:26. for *so* it seemed good in thy sight.
12:40. *so* shall the Son of man be three days
45. *Even so* shall it be also unto this
13:40. *so* shall it be in the end of this
49. *So* shall it be at the end of the
17:12. *Likewise* shall also the Son of man
18:14. *Even so* it is not the will of your
35. *So* likewise shall my heavenly
19: 8. but from the beginning it was not *so*.
10. If the case of the man be *so* with
12. which were *so* born from (their)
20:16 *So* the last shall be first,
26. But it shall not be *so* among you:
23:28. *Even so* ye also outwardly
24:27. *so* shall also the coming of the
33. *So* likewise ye, when ye shall see
37. *so* shall also the coming of
39. *so* shall also the coming of the Son of
46. shall find *so* doing.
26:40. *What*, could ye not watch with me
54. that *thus* it must be?
Mar 2: 7. Why doth this (man) *thus* speak
8. that they *so* reasoned within
12. We never saw it *on this fashion*.
4.26. *So* is the kingdom of God
40. Why are ye *so* fearful?.
7:18. Are ye *so* without understanding also?
10:43. But *so* shall it not be among you:
13:29. *So* ye *in like manner*,[2] when ye
14:59. But neither *so* did their witness
15:39. saw that he *so* cried out,
Lu. 1:25. *Thus* hath the Lord dealt with me
2:48. why hast thou *thus* dealt with us?
6.10. And he did *so*: and his hand
9:15. And they did *so*, and made them
10:21. for *so* it seemed good in thy sight.
11:30. *so* shall also the Son of man
12:21. *So* (is) he that layeth up treasure
28. If then God *so* clothe the grass,
38. and find (them) *so*, blessed are
43. shall find *so* doing.
54. and *so* it is.
14:33. *So* likewise, whosoever he be of you
15: 7. that *likewise* joy shall be in
10. *Likewise*, I say unto you, there is joy
17:10. *So* likewise ye, when ye shall
24. *so* shall also the Son of man be
26. *so* shall it be also in the days
19:31. *thus* shall ye say unto him,
21:31. *So* likewise ye, when ye see
22:26. But ye (shall) not (be) *so*:
24:24. and found (it) even *so* as the women
46. *Thus* it is written, and *thus* it behoved Christ to suffer,
Joh. 3: 8. *so* is every one that is born of the Spirit.
14. *even so* must the Son of Man be
16. For God *so* loved the world,
4: 6. sat *thus* on the well:
5:21. *even so*[2] the Son quickeneth whom
26. *so* hath he given to the Son to
7:46. Never man spake *like* (lit. *so* spake as) this man.
8:59. and *so* passed by.
11:48. If we let him *thus* alone,
12:50. said unto me, *so* I speak.
14:31. gave me commandment, *even so* I do.
15: 4. *no more* (lit. *so* neither) can ye,
18:22. Answerest thou the high priest *so*?

Joh.21: 1. and *on this wise* shewed he (himself.)
Acts 1:11. shall *so* come in like manner as
3:18. he hath *so* fulfilled.
7: 1. Are these things *so*?
6. And God spake *on this wise*,
8. and *so* (Abraham) begat Isaac,
8:32. *so* opened he not his mouth:
12: 8. And *so* he did.
15. affirmed that it was *even so*.
13: 8. for *so* is his name by interpretation
34. he said *on this wise*, I will give
47. For *so* hath the Lord commanded
14: 1. and *so* spake, that a great multitude
17:11. whether those things were *so*.
33. *So* Paul departed from among them.
19:20. *So* mightily grew the word of God
20:11. till break of day, *so* he departed.
13. for *so* had he appointed,
35. how that *so* labouring ye ought
21:11. *So* shall the Jews at Jerusalem bind
22:24. wherefore they cried *so* against him.
23:11. *so* must thou bear witness also at Rome.
24: 9. saying that these things were *so*.
14. *so* worship I the God of my fathers,
27:17. and *so* were driven.
25. it shall be *even* as it was told me.
44. And *so* it came to pass, that
28:14. and *so* we went toward Rome.
Ro. 1:15. *So*, as much as in me is, I am ready
4:18. *So* shall thy seed be.
5:12. and *so* death passed upon all
15. *so* also (is) the free gift.
18. *even so*[2] by the righteousness of one
19. *so*[2] by the obedience of one
21. *even so* might grace reign
6: 4. *even so* we also should walk
11. *Likewise* reckon ye also yourselves
19. *even so* now yield your members
9:20. Why hast thou made me *thus*?
10: 6. speaketh *on this wise*, Say not
11: 5. *Even so*[2] then at this present
26. And *so* all Israel shall be saved:
31. *Even so* have these also now not
12 5. *So* we, (being) many, are one
15:20. Yea, *so* have I strived to preach
1Co. 2:11. *even so*[2] the things of God
3:15. yet *so* as by fire.
4: 1. Let a man *so* account of us,
5: 3. that hath *so* done this deed,
6: 5. Is it *so*, that there is not a
7: 7. one *after this manner*, and another *after that*.
17. *so* let him walk. And *so* ordain I in all churches.
26. good for a man *so* to be.
36. and need *so* require,
40. But she is happier if she *so* abide,
8:12. when ye sin *so* against the brethren,
9:14. *Even so*[2] hath the Lord ordained
15. that it should be *so* done unto me:
24. *So* run, that ye may obtain.
26. I therefore *so* run, not as uncertainly; *so* fight I, not as
11:12. *even so* (is) the man also by the
28. and *so* let him eat of (that)
12:12. *so* also (is) Christ.
14: 9. *So* likewise ye, except ye utter
12. *Even so*[2] ye, forasmuch as ye are
21. and yet *for all that* (lit. and neither *thus*) will they not hear me,
25. And *thus* are the secrets of his heart made manifest; and *so* falling down

F F

1Co.15:11. *so* we preach, and *so* ye believed
22. *even so*[2] in Christ shall all
42. *So* also (is) the resurrection of
45. And *so* it is written,
16: 1. *even so*[2] do ye.
2Co. 1: 5. *so* our consolation also aboundeth
7. *so* (shall ye be) also of the consolation.
7:14. *even so*[2] our boasting,
8: 6. *so* he would also finish
11. *so* (there may be) a performance also
9: 5. might be ready, as (a matter of) bounty, (lit. ready *thus*, as, &c.)
10: 7. *even so*[2] (are) we Christ's.
11: 3. *so* your minds should be corrupted
Gal. 1: 6. I marvel that ye are *so* soon removed
3: 3. Are ye *so* foolish?
4: 3. *Even so*[2] we, when we were children,
29. *even so*[2] (it is) now.
6: 2. and *so* fulfil the law of Christ.
Eph 4:20. But ye have not *so* learned Christ;
5:24. *so*[2] (let) the wives (be) to their own
28. *So* ought men to love their wives
28. *so* love his wife even as himself;
Phi. 3:17. and mark them which walk *so*
4: 1. *so* stand fast in the Lord,
Col. 3:13. *so* also (do) ye.
1Th. 2: 4. *even so* we speak;
8. *So* being affectionately desirous
4:14. *even so* them also which sleep
17. and *so* shall we ever be with the Lord.
5: 2. the day of the Lord *so* cometh
2Th. 3:17. token in every epistle: *so* I write.
2Ti. 3: 8. *so* do these also resist the truth:
Heb 4: 4. of the seventh (day) *on this wise*,
5: 3. *so* also for himself,
5. *So* also Christ glorified not himself
6: 9. though we *thus* speak.
15. And *so*, after he had patiently
9: 6. when these things were *thus* ordained,
28. *So* Christ was once offered
10:33. companions of them that were *so* used.
12:21. And *so* terrible was the sight,
Jas. 1:11. *so* also shall the rich man fade
2:12. *So* speak ye, and *so* do,
17. *Even so*[2] faith, if it hath not works,
26. *so* faith without works is dead also.
3: 5. *Even so*[2] the tongue is a little
6. *so* is the tongue among our
10. these things ought not *so* to be.
12. *so* (can) no fountain both yield
1Pet. 2:15. For *so* is the will of God,
3: 5. For *after this manner* in the old time the holy women also,
2Pet. 1:11. For *so* an entrance shall be
3: 4. all things continue *as* (they were)
1Joh. 2: 6. ought himself also *so* to walk, even as he
4:11. Beloved, if God *so* loved us,
Rev. 2:15. *So* hast thou also them that
3:16. *So* then because thou art lukewarm,
9:17. And *thus* I saw the horses in the
11: 5. he must *in this manner* be killed.
16:18. so mighty an earthquake, (and) *so* great.
18:21. *Thus* with violence shall that great city

οὐχ see οὐ. 3756

3780 56 602/740 3756

οὐχί, *ouki.*

Mat. 5:46. do *not* even the publicans the same?
47. do *not* even the publicans so?
Mat. 6:25. Is *not* the life more than meat,
10:29. Are *not* two sparrows sold for
12:11. will he *not* lay hold on it, and
13:27. Sir, didst *not* thou sow good seed
55. is *not* his mother called Mary?
56. are they *not* all with us?
18:12. doth he *not* leave the ninety and
20:13. didst *not* thou agree with me
Lu. 1:60. *Not* (so); but he shall be called John.
6:39. shall they *not* both fall into
12: 6. Are *not* five sparrows sold for
51. I tell you, *Nay*; but rather division:
13: 3. I tell you, *Nay*: but, except ye
5. *Nay*: but, except ye repent, ye
14:28. sitteth *not* down first, and counteth
31. sitteth *not* down first, and consulteth
15: 8. doth *not* light a candle, and
16:30. And he said, *Nay*, father Abraham:
17: 8. And will *not* rather say unto him,
17. Were there *not* ten cleansed?
22:27. (is) *not* he that sitteth at meat?
24:26. Ought *not* Christ to have suffered
32. Did *not* our heart burn within us,
Joh. 7:42. Hath *not* the scripture said,
11: 9. Are there *not* twelve hours in
13:10. and ye are clean, but *not* all.
11. Ye are *not* all clean.
14:22. and *not* unto the world?
Acts 5: 4. was it *not* thine own?
7:50. Hath *not* my hand made all
Ro. 2:26. shall *not* his uncircumcision
3:27. *Nay*: but by the law of faith.
29. (is he) *not* also of the Gentiles?
8:32. how shall he *not* with him also
1Co. 1:20. hath *not* God made foolish the
3: 3. are ye *not* carnal, and walk as men?
4. are ye *not* carnal?
5: 2. and have *not* rather mourned,
12. do *not* ye judge them that are
6: 1. and *not* before the saints?
7. Why do ye *not* rather take wrong? why do ye *not* rather (suffer)
8:10. shall *not* the conscience of him
9: 1. have I *not* seen Jesus Christ
8. or saith *not* the law the same
10:16. is it *not* the communion of the blood
— is it *not* the communion of the body
18. are *not* they which eat of the
29. Conscience, I say, *not* thine own.
2Co. 3: 8. How shall *not* the ministration
10:13. we will *not* boast of things without
1Th. 2:19. (Are) *not* even ye in the presence
Heb 1:14. Are they *not* all ministering
3:17. (was it) *not* with them that had sinned,

3781 7 603/740 5:559 3784

ὀφειλέτης, *ophīletees.*

Mat. 6:12. as we forgive our *debtors*.
18:24. *which owed* him ten thousand
Lu. 13: 4. think ye that they were *sinners* above
Ro. 1:14. I am *debtor* both to the Greeks, and
8:12. we are *debtors*, not to the flesh,
15:27. and their *debtors* they are.
Gal. 5: 3. he is a *debtor* to do the whole law.

3782 2 603/740 5:559 3784

ὀφειλή, *ophīlee.*

Mat.18:32. I forgave thee all that *debt*.
Ro 13: 7. Render therefore to all their *dues*.

3783 2 603/740 5:559 3784

ὀφείλημα, ophĭleema.

Mat. 6:12. And forgive us our *debts*,
Ro. 4: 4. not reckoned of grace, but of *debt*.

3784 36 603/740 5:559 rt 3786 cf 3785

ὀφείλω, ophĭlo.

Mat. 18:28. which *owed* him an hundred pence:
— Pay me that thou *owest*.
30. till he should pay the *debt*.
34. till he should pay all *that was due*
23:16. he *is a debtor!* (lit. *oweth*, or *is bound*)
18. he is *guilty*. (lit. *oweth*, or *is bound*)
Lu. 7:41. the one *owed* five hundred pence,
11: 4. every one *that is indebted* to us.
16: 5. How much *owest* thou unto my lord?
7. And how much *owest* thou?
17:10. we have done that which *was* our *duty* to
Joh. 13:14. ye also *ought* to wash one another's feet.
19: 7. by our law he *ought* to die.
Acts 17:29. we *ought* not to think that
Ro 13: 8. *Owe* no man any thing,
15: 1. that are strong *ought* to bear the
27. their *duty is* also to minister unto
1Co. 5:10. then *must* ye *needs* go out of the
7: 3. unto the wife *due* benevolence:
36. and *need* so require, (lit. it *needs* so to be)
9:10. he that ploweth *should* plow (lit. *ought* to plough) in hope;
11: 7. a man indeed *ought* not to cover
10. For this cause *ought* the woman
2Co. 12:11. for I *ought* to have been commended
14. the children *ought* not to lay up for
Eph 5:28. So *ought* men to love their wives
2Th. 1: 3. We *are bound* to thank God
2:13. we *are bound* to give thanks
Philem 18. or *oweth* (thee) ought,
Heb 2:17. in all things it *behoved* him
5: 3. by reason hereof he *ought*, as for
12. *when* for the time ye *ought* to be
1Joh. 2: 6. *ought* himself also so to walk,
3:16. we *ought* to lay down (our) lives
4:11. we *ought* also to love one another.
3Joh. 8. We therefore *ought* to receive such,

3785 4 603/741 3784

ὄφελον, ophelon.

1Co. 4: 8. and I *would to God* (lit. I *would*) ye did reign,
2Co. 11: 1. *Would to God* (lit., &c.) ye could bear
Gal. 5:12. I *would* they were even cut off
Rev. 3:15. I *would* thou wert cold or hot.

3786 3 604/741 ophellō (to heap up)

ὄφελος, ophelos.

1Co. 15:32. what *advantageth* it me, (lit. what the *profit* to me)
Jas. 2:14. What (doth it) *profit*, my brethren,
16. what (doth it) *profit?*

3787 2 604/741 2:261 3788,1397

ὀφθαλμοδουλεία, ophthalmodoulīa.

Eph 6: 6. Not with *eyeservice*, as menpleasers;
Col. 3:22. not with *eyeservice*, as menpleasers;

3788 102 604/741 5:315 3700

ὀφθαλμός, ophthalmos.

Mat. 5:29. if thy right *eye* offend thee
38. An *eye* for an *eye*.
6:22. The light of the body is the *eye*: if therefore thine *eye* be single,
23. But if thine *eye* be evil,
7: 3. that is in thy brother's *eye*,
— that is in thine own *eye?*
4. the mote out of thine *eye*; and, behold, a beam (is) in thine own *eye?*
5. out of thine own *eye*;
— out of thy brother's *eye*.
9:29. Then touched he their *eyes*,
30. And their *eyes* were opened;
13:15. their *eyes* they have closed;
— they should see with (their) *eyes*,
16. But blessed (are) your *eyes*,
17: 8. when they had lifted up their *eyes*,
18: 9. And if thine *eye* offend thee,
— rather than having two *eyes*
20:15. Is thine *eye* evil, because
33. Lord, that our *eyes* may be opened.
34. and touched their *eyes*:
— their *eyes* received sight,
21:42. and it is marvellous in our *eyes?*
26:43. for their *eyes* were heavy.
Mar 7:22. an evil *eye*, blasphemy, pride,
8:18. Having *eyes*, see ye not?
25. hands again upon his *eyes*,
9:47. And if thine *eye* offend thee,
— than having two *eyes*
12:11. it is marvellous in our *eyes?*
14:40. for their *eyes* were heavy,
Lu 2:30. For mine *eyes* have seen thy
4:20. And the *eyes* of all them that wer
6:20. lifted up his *eyes* on his disciples,
41. that is in thy brother's *eye*,
— that is in thine own *eye?*
42. the mote that is in thine *eye*,
— the beam that is in thine own *eye?*
— the beam out of thine own *eye*,
— the mote that is in thy brother's *eye*.
10:23. Blessed (are) the *eyes* which see the
11:34. The light of the body is the *eye*: therefore when thine *eye* is single,
16:23. in hell he lift up his *eyes*,
18:13. so much as (his) *eyes* unto heaven,
19:42. they are hid from thine *eyes*.
24:16. But their *eyes* were holden
31. And their *eyes* were opened,
Joh. 4:35. Lift up your *eyes*, and look on the
6: 5. Jesus then lifted up (his) *eyes*,
9: 6. he anointed the *eyes* of the blind
10. How were thine *eyes* opened?
11. and anointed mine *eyes*,
14. and opened his *eyes*.
15. He put clay upon mine *eyes*,
17. that he hath opened thine *eyes?*
21. who hath opened his *eyes*,
26. how opened he thine *eyes?*
30. he hath opened mine *eyes*.
32. that any man opened the *eyes*
10:21. Can a devil open the *eyes* of the
11:37. which opened the *eyes* of the blind,
41. Jesus lifted up (his) *eyes*,
12:40. He hath blinded their *eyes*,
— should not see with (their) *eyes*,
17: 1. and lifted up his *eyes*
Acts 1: 9. received him out of their *sight*.
9: 8. when his *eyes* were opened.
18. there fell from his *eyes*
40. And she opened her *eyes*:
26:18. To open their *eyes*, (and) to turn
28:27. their *eyes* have they closed; lest they should see with (their) *eyes*,

Ro. 3:18. no fear of God before their *eyes*.
11: 8. *eyes* that they should not see,
10. Let their *eyes* be darkened,
1Co. 2: 9. *Eye* hath not seen, nor ear
12:16. Because I am not the *eye*,
17. If the whole body (were) an *eye*,
21. And the *eye* cannot say unto
15:52. in the twinkling of an *eye*,
Gal. 3: 1. before whose *eyes* Jesus Christ
4:15. have plucked out your own *eyes*,
Eph. 1:18. The *eyes* of your understanding
Heb 4:13. opened unto the *eyes* of him
1Pet.3:12. For the *eyes* of the Lord (are) over
2Pet.2:14. Having *eyes* full of adultery,
1Joh.1: 1. which we have seen with our *eyes*,
2:11. darkness hath blinded his *eyes*.
16. and the lust of the *eyes*,
Rev. 1: 7. and every *eye* shall see him,
14. his *eyes* (were) as a flame of fire;
2:18. who hath his *eyes* like unto
3:18. anoint thine *eyes* with eyesalve,
4. 6. four beasts full of *eyes*
8. and (they were) full of *eyes* within:
5. 6. and seven *eyes*, which are the
7:17. wipe away all tears from their *eyes*.
19:12. His *eyes* (were) as a flame of fire,
21: 4. wipe away all tears from their *eyes*;

3789 14 604/742 5:566 3700

ὄφις, ophis.

Mat. 7:10. will he give him a *serpent?*
10:16. be ye therefore wise as *serpents*,
23:33. (Ye) *serpents*, (ye) generation of vipers,
Mar 16:18. They shall take up *serpents*;
Lu. 10:19. power to tread on *serpents*
11:11. will he for a fish give him a *serpent?*
Joh. 3:14. And as Moses lifted up the *serpent* in
1Co.10: 9. and were destroyed of *serpents*.
2Co.11: 3. as the *serpent* beguiled Eve
Rev. 9:19. their tails (were) like unto *serpents*,
12: 9. that old *serpent*, called the Devil,
14. from the face of the *serpent*.
15. And the *serpent* cast out of his
20: 2. that old *serpent*, which is the devil,

3790 1 605/742 3700

ὀφρύς, ophrus.

Lu. 4:29. and led him unto the *brow* of the hill

3791 2 605/ 3793

ὀχλέομαι, okleomai.

Lu. 6:18. And they *that were vexed* with
Acts 5:16. and them *which were vexed* with unclean spirits:

3792 1 605/742 3793,4160

ὀχλοποιέω, oklopoyeo.

Acts17. 5. *gathered a company, and* set all the city on an uproar,

---

3793 175 605/742 5:582 2192

ὄχλος, oklos.

Mat. 4:25. there followed him great *multitudes*
5: 1. And seeing the *multitudes*,
7.28. the *people* were astonished at his
8:1. great *multitudes* followed him.
18. when Jesus saw great *multitudes*
Mat. 9 8. But when the *multitudes* saw (it),
23. and the *people* making a noise,
25. But when the *people* were put forth
33. and the *multitudes* marvelled,
36. when he saw the *multitudes*,
11: 7. began to say unto the *multitudes*
12:15. and great *multitudes* followed him,
23. And all the *people* were amazed,
46. While he yet talked to the *people*,
13: 2. And great *multitudes* were gathered
— and the whole *multitude* stood on
34. spake Jesus unto the *multitude*
36. Then Jesus sent the *multitude*
14: 5. he feared the *multitude*,
13. and when the *people* had heard
14. and saw a great *multitude*,
15. send the *multitude* away,
19. he commanded the *multitude*
— and the disciples to the *multitude*.
22. while he sent the *multitudes*
23. sent the *multitudes* away,
15:10. he called the *multitude*,
30. And great *multitudes* came
31. Insomuch that the *multitude*
32. compassion on the *multitude*,
33. as to fill so great a *multitude?*
35. he commanded the *multitude*
36. and the disciples to the *multitude*.
39. And he sent away the *multitude*,
17:14. were come to the *multitude*,
19: 2. And great *multitudes* followed
20:29. a great *multitude* followed him.
31. And the *multitude* rebuked
21: 8. And a very great *multitude*
9. And the *multitudes* that went before,
11. And the *multitude* said, This is
26. we fear the *people*;
46. they feared the *multitude*,
22:33. And when the *multitude* heard
23: 1. Then spake Jesus to the *multitude*,
26:47. with him a great *multitude*
55. said Jesus to the *multitudes*,
27:15. to release unto the *people* a
20. persuaded the *multitude* that they
24. hands before the *multitude*,
Mar 2: 4. nigh unto him for the *press*,
13. and all the *multitude* resorted
3: 9. because of the *multitude*, lest
20. And the *multitude* cometh
32. And the *multitude* sat about him,
4: 1. unto him a great *multitude*,
— and the whole *multitude* was by
36. sent away the *multitude*,
5:21. much *people* gathered unto him:
24. much *people* followed him,
27. came in the *press* behind,
30. turned him about in the *press*,
31. Thou seest the *multitude* thronging
6:33. And the *people* saw them
34. saw much *people*, and was moved
45. while he sent away the *people*.
7:14. when he had called all the *people*
17. into the house from the *people*,
33. aside from the *multitude*,
8: 1. the *multitude* being very great,
2. compassion on the *multitude*,
6. he commanded the *people* to
— set (them) before the *people*.
34. when he had called the *people*
9:14. he saw a great *multitude*
15. straightway all the *people*, when
17. And one of the *multitude* answered

Mar 9:25. When Jesus saw that the *people* came
10: 1. and the *people* resort unto him again
46. and a great *number of people*,
11:18. because all the *people* was astonished
12:12. but feared the *people* :
37. the common *people* heard him gladly.
41. and beheld how the *people* cast
14:43. with him a great *multitude* with
15: 8. And the *multitude* crying aloud
11. the chief priests moved the *people*,
15. willing to content the *people*,
Lu 3: 7. Then said he to the *multitude*
10. And the *people* asked him,
4:42. and the *people* sought him,
5: 1. as the *people* pressed upon him
3. and taught the *people*
15. and great *multitudes* came
19. because of the *multitude*,
29. a great *company* of publicans and
6:17. and the *company* of his disciples,
19. And the whole *multitude* sought
7: 9. and said unto the *people* that followed
11. went with him, and much *people*.
12. much *people* of the city was with her.
24. he began to speak unto the *people*
8: 4. And when much *people* were
19. could not come at him for the *press*.
40. the *people* (gladly) received him:
42. the *people* thronged him.
45. the *multitude* throng thee
9:11. And the *people*, when they knew
12. Send the *multitude* away,
16. to set before the *multitude*.
18. Whom say the *people* that I am?
37. much *people* met him.
38. a man of the *company* cried out,
11:14. and the *people* wondered.
27. a certain woman of the *company*
29. And when the *people* were gathered
12: 1. innumerable multitude of *people*,
13. one of the *company* said unto him,
54. And he said also to the *people*,
13:14. and said unto the *people*,
17. and all the *people* rejoiced
14:25. there went great *multitudes* with him:
18:36. hearing the *multitude* pass by,
19: 3. and could not for the *press*,
39. from among the *multitude*
22: 6. in the absence of the *multitude*.
47. yet spake, behold a *multitude*,
23: 4. to the chief priests and (to) the *people*,
48. And all the *people* that came together
Joh. 5:13. a *multitude* being in (that) place.
6: 2. And a great *multitude* followed him,
5. saw a great *company* come
22. when the *people* which stood
24. When the *people* therefore saw
7:12. among the *people* concerning him:
— he deceiveth the *people*.
20. The *people* answered and said,
31. And many of the *people* believed
32. heard that the *people* murmured such
40. Many of the *people* therefore,
43. was a division among the *people*
49. But this *people* who knoweth not
11:42. because of the *people* which
12: 9. Much *people* of the Jews therefore
12. On the next day much *people*
17. The *people* therefore that was
18. For this cause the *people* also met him,
29. The *people* therefore, that stood by,
34. The *people* answered him,

Acts 1:15. the *number* of the names together
6: 7. and a great *company* of the priests
8: 6. And the *people* with one accord
11:24. and much *people* was added unto
26. and taught much *people*.
13:45. when the Jews saw the *multitudes*.
14:11. when the *people* saw what Paul
13. would have done sacrifice with the *people*.
14. and ran in among the *people*,
18. restrained they the *people*,
19. who persuaded the *people*,
16:22. And the *multitude* rose up together
17: 8. And they troubled the *people* and the
13. and stirred up the *people*.
19:26. and turned away much *people*,
33. drew Alexander out of the *multitude*,
35. had appeased the *people*,
21:27. stirred up all the *people*,
34. some another, among the *multitude* :
35. for the violence of the *people*.
24:12. neither raising up the *people*,
18. neither with *multitude*, nor with tumult.
Rev. 7: 9. and, lo, a great *multitude*,
17:15. peoples, and *multitudes*, and nations,
19: 1. a great voice of much *people*
6. the voice of a great *multitude*,

3794 1 606/744 5:590 cf 2192

ὀχύρωμα, okurōma.

2Co.10: 4. the pulling down of *strong holds* ;

3795 5 606/744 rt 3702

ὀψάριον, opsarion.

Joh. 6: 9. loaves, and two *small fishes* :
11. and likewise of the *fishes*
21: 9. and *fish* laid thereon,
10. Bring of the *fish* which ye have now
13. giveth them, and *fish* likewise.

3796 3 606/744 rt 3694

ὀψέ, opse.

Mat.28: 1. *In the end* of the sabbath,
Mar 11:19. And when *even* was come,
13:35. *at even*, or at midnight,

3798 15 606/744 3796

ὀψία, opsia.

Mat. 8:16. When the *even* was come,
14:15. And when it was *evening*,
23. and when the *evening* was come,
16: 2. When it is *evening*, ye say,
20: 8. So when *even* was come, the lord of
26:20. Now when the *even* was come,
27:57. When the *even* was come, there came
Mar 1:32. And at *even*, when the sun did set,
4:35. when the *even* was come, he saith
6:47. And when *even* was come, the ship
11:11. and now the *eventide* was come,
14:17. in the *evening* he cometh with the twelve
15:42. And now when the *even* was come,
Joh. 6:16. And when *even* was (now) come,
20:19. the same day at *evening*, being the

3797 1 606/745 3796

ὄψιμος, opsimos.

Jas. 5: 7. the early and *latter* rain.

3799 3 606/745 3700
ὄψις, opsis.

Joh. 7:24. Judge not according to the *appearance*,
11:44. and his *face* was bound about with a
Rev. 1:16. his *countenance* (was) as the sun

3800 4 606/745 5:591 rt 3795
ὀψώνιον, opsōnion.

Lu. 3:14. and be content with your *wages*.
Ro. 6:23. For the *wages* of sin (is) death;
1Co. 9: 7. warfare any time at his own *charges?*
2Co.11: 8. taking *wages* (of them), to do you service.

3802 1 607/745 5:593 3803
παγιδεύω, pagidūo.

Mat.22:15. how they *might entangle* him in (his) talk.

3803 5 607/745 5:593 4078
παγίς, pagis.

Lu. 21:35. as a *snare* shall it come
Ro 11: 9. Let their table be made a *snare*,
1Ti. 3: 7. and the *snare* of the devil.
6: 9. fall into temptation and a *snare*,
2Ti. 2:26. out of the *snare* of the devil,

3804 16 607/745 5:904 3806
πάθημα, patheema.

Ro. 7: 5. the *motions* of sins, which were by
8:18. I reckon that the *sufferings* of this
2Co. 1: 5. For as the *sufferings* of Christ abound
6. in the enduring of the same *sufferings*
7. as ye are partakers of the *sufferings*, so
Gal. 5:24. have crucified the flesh with the *affections*
Phi. 3:10. the fellowship of his *sufferings*,
Col. 1:24. Who now rejoice in my *sufferings*
2Ti. 3:11. Persecutions, *afflictions*, which came
Heb 2: 9. for the *suffering* of death, crowned
10. perfect through *sufferings*.
10:32. endured a great fight of *afflictions*;
1Pet. 1:11. the *sufferings* of Christ, and the
4:13. ye are partakers of Christ's *sufferings*;
5: 1. a witness of the *sufferings* of Christ,
9. the same *afflictions* are accomplished

3805 1 607/745 5:904 rt 3804
παθητός, patheetos.

Acts26:23. That Christ should *suffer*,

3806 3 607/745 5:904 *pathō* (3958)
πάθος, pathos.

Ro. 1:26. gave them up unto vile *affections:*
Col. 3: 5. uncleanness, *inordinate affection*,
1Th. 4: 5. Not in the *lust* of concupiscence,

3807 3 608/745 5:596 3816,71
παιδαγωγός, paidagōgos.

1Co. 4:15. ten thousand *instructers* in Christ, yet
Gal. 3:24. the law was our *schoolmaster*
25. no longer under a *schoolmaster*.

3808 2 608/745 5:626 3816
παιδάριον, paidarion.

Mat.11:16. It is like unto *children* sitting in the
Joh. 6: 9. There is a *lad* here,

3801 p. 522

3809 6 608/745 5:596 3811
παιδεία, paidīa.

Eph 6: 4. in the *nurture* and admonition
2Ti. 3:16. for *instruction* in righteousness:
Heb 12: 5. despise not thou the *chastening* of
7. If ye endure *chastening*, God
8. But if ye be without *chastisement*,
11. Now no *chastening* for the present

3810 2 608/745 5:596 3811
παιδευτής, paidūtees.

Ro. 2:20. An *instructor* of the foolish,
Heb 12: 9. fathers of our flesh *which corrected* (us)

3811 13 608/745 5:596 3816
παιδεύω, paidūo.

Lu. 23:16. I will therefore *chastise* him, *and*
22: I will therefore *chastise* him, *and*
Acts 7:22. And Moses *was learned* in all
22: 3. *taught* according to the perfect manner
1Co.11:32. we *are chastened* of the Lord,
2Co. 6: 9. as *chastened*, and not killed;
1Ti. 1:20. that they *may learn* not to blaspheme.
2Ti. 2:25. In meekness *instructing* those that,
Tit. 2:12. *Teaching* us that, denying ungodliness
Heb 12: 6. whom the Lord loveth he *chasteneth*,
7. whom the father *chasteneth* not?
10. for a few days *chastened* (us)
Rev. 3:19. As many as I love, I rebuke and *chasten*:

3812 1 609/746 3813
παιδιόθεν, paidiothen.

Mar 9:21. And he said, *Of a child*.

3813 51 609/746 5:636 3816
παιδίον, paidion.

Mat. 2: 8. search diligently for the *young child*;
9. over where the *young child* was.
11. they saw the *young child* with Mary
13. Arise, and take the *young child* and his
— Herod will seek the *young child* to
14. he took the *young child* and his mother
20. Arise, and take the *young child* and his
— which sought the *young child's* life.
21. and took the *young child* and his mother,
14:21. beside women and *children*.
15:38. beside women and *children*.
18: 2. And Jesus called a *little child* unto
3. and become as *little children*,
4. humble himself as this *little child*,
5. receive one such *little child* in
19:13. brought unto him *little children*,
14. Jesus said, Suffer *little children*,
Mar 5:39. the *damsel* is not dead, but sleepeth
40. father and the mother of the *damsel*,
— and entereth in where the *damsel* was
41. he took the *damsel* by the hand,
7:28. eat of the *children's* crumbs.
9:24. And straightway the father of the *child*
36. And he took a *child*, and set him
37. receive one of such *children* in my
10:13. brought *young children* to him,
14. Suffer the *little children* to come
15. kingdom of God as a *little child*,
Lu. 1:59. to circumcise the *child*;
66. What manner of *child* shall this be!
76. And thou, *child*, shalt be called
80. And the *child* grew, and waxed strong
2:17. was told them concerning this *child*.

Lu 2:21. for the circumcising of the *child*,
27. the parents brought in the *child* Jesus,
40. And the *child* grew, and waxed strong in
7:32. unto *children* sitting in the marketplace,
9:47. took a *child*, and set him by him,
48. Whosoever shall receive this *child* in my
11: 7. my *children* are with me in bed;
18:16. Suffer *little children* to come unto me,
17. receive the kingdom of God as a *little child*
Joh. 4:49. Sir, come down ere my *child* die.
16:21. as soon as she is delivered of the *child*.
21: 5. *Children*, have ye any meat?
1Co.14:20. be not *children* in understanding:
Heb 2:13. Behold I and the *children* which
14. Forasmuch then as the *children* are
11:23. they saw (he was) a proper *child*;
1Joh.2:13. I write unto you, *little children*,
18. *Little children*, it is the last time:

3814 13 609/746 3816

παιδίσκη, *paidiskee.*

Mat.26:69. and a *damsel* came unto him,
Mar 14:66. there cometh one of the *maids* of the
69. And a *maid* saw him again,
Lu. 12:45. to beat the menservants and *maidens*,
22:56. But a certain *maid* beheld him as
Joh.18:17. Then saith the *damsel* that kept the door
Acts12:13. a *damsel* came to hearken, named Rhoda.
16:16. a certain *damsel* possessed with a spirit
Gal. 4:22. two sons, the one by a *bondmaid*,
23. But he (who was) of the *bondwoman*
30. Cast out the *bondwoman* and her son: for the son of the *bondwoman* shall not
31. we are not children of the *bondwoman*,

3815 1 609/747 5:625 3816

παίζω, *paizo.*

1Co.10: 7. and rose up *to play*.

3816 24 609/747 5:636,654 3817

παῖς, *pais.*

Mat. 2:16. and slew all the *children* that were
8: 6. Lord, my *servant* lieth at home
8. and my *servant* shall be healed.
13. And his *servant* was healed
12:18. Behold my *servant*, whom I have
14: 2. And said unto his *servants*, This is
17:18. and the *child* was cured from
21:15. and the *children* crying in the temple,
Lu. 1:54. He hath holpen his *servant* Israel,
69. in the house of his *servant* David;
2:43. the *child* Jesus tarried behind in
7: 7. and my *servant* shall be healed.
8:51. and the mother of the *maiden*.
54. and called, saying, *Maid*, arise.
9:42. and healed the *child*, and delivered
12:45. to beat the *menservants* and
15:26. and he called one of the *servants*,
Joh. 4:51. Thy *son* liveth.
Acts 3:13. hath glorified his *Son* Jesus;
26. God, having raised up his *Son* Jesus,
4:25. Who by the mouth of thy *servant* David
27. against thy holy *child* Jesus, whom
30. name of thy holy *child* Jesus.
20:12. And they brought the *young man* alive,

3817 5 610/747 cf 5180

παίω, *paio.*

Mat.26:68 Who is he *that smote* thee?
Mar 14:47. and *smote* a servant of the high priest,
Lu. 22:64. who is it *that smote* thee?
Joh.18:10. and *smote* the high priest's servant,
Rev. 9: 5. a scorpion, when he *striketh* a man.

3819 6 610/747 5:717 3825

πάλαι, *palai.*

Mat.11:21. they would have repented *long ago* in
Mar 15:44. whether he had been *any while* dead.
Lu. 10:13. they had *a great while ago* repented,
Heb 1: 1. spake *in time past* unto the fathers by
2Pet. 1: 9. purged from his *old* sins.
Jude 4. were before *of old* ordained to this

3820 19 610/747 5:717 3819

παλαιός, *palaios.*

Mat. 9:16. new cloth unto an *old* garment,
17. new wine into *old* bottles:
13:52. out of his treasure (things) new and *old*.
Mar 2:21. a piece of new cloth on an *old* garment:
— taketh away from the *old*,
22. putteth new wine into *old* bottles:
Lu. 5.36. of a new garment upon an *old*;
— agreeth not with the *old*.
37. putteth new wine into *old* bottles;
39. No man also having drunk *old* (wine)
— for he saith, The *old* is better,
Ro. 6: 6. our *old* man is crucified with
1Co. 5: 7. Purge out therefore the *old* leaven
8. not with *old* leaven,
2Co. 3:14. in the reading of the *old* testament;
Eph. 4:22. the *old* man, which is corrupt
Col. 3: 9. ye have put off the *old* man with
1Joh.2: 7. but an *old* commandment which ye
— The *old* commandment is the word which

3821 1 610/747 5:717 3820

παλαιότης, *palaiotees.*

Ro. 7: 6. and not (in) the *oldness* of the letter.

3822 4 610/747 5:717 3820

παλαιόω, *palaioō.*

Lu. 12:33. bags *which wax* not *old*,
Heb 1:11. they all *shall wax old* as doth a
8:13. he *hath made* the first *old*. Now that *which decayeth*

3823 1 610/747 5:721 *pallo* (to vibrate)

πάλη, *palee.*

Eph. 6:12. we wrestle not against flesh and blood, (lit. the *wrestling* is not to us &c.)

3824 2 611/749 1:681 3825,1078

παλιγγενεσία, *palingenesia.*

Mat.19:28. in the *regeneration* when the Son of man
Tit. 3: 5. by the washing of *regeneration*,

3825 142 611/747 *pallō* (to vibrate)

πάλιν, *palin.*

Mat. 4: 7. It is written *again*, Thou shalt not
8. *Again*, the devil taketh him up
5:33. *Again*, ye have heard that it hath
13:44. *Again*, the kingdom of heaven is like
45. *Again*, the kingdom of heaven is
47. *Again*, the kingdom of heaven is

Mat.18:19. *Again* I say unto you, That if two
19:24. And *again* I say unto you, It is easier
20: 5. *Again* he went out about the sixth
21:36. *Again*, he sent other servants more
22: 1. and spake unto them *again* by parables,
4. *Again*, he sent forth other servants,
26:42. He went away *again* the second time,
43. came and found them asleep *again:*
44. and went away *again*, and prayed
72. And *again* he denied with an oath,
27:50. Jesus, when he had cried *again*
Mar 2: 1. And *again* he entered into Capernaum
13. And he went forth *again* by the sea
3: 1. And he entered *again* into the synagogue;
20. the multitude cometh together *again*,
4: 1. And he began *again* to teach by the
5:21. when Jesus was passed over *again* by ship
7:31. and *again*, departing from the coasts
8:13. and entering into the ship *again*
25. he put (his) hands *again* upon his eyes,
10: 1. resort unto him *again*, and, as he was wont, he taught them *again*.
10. his disciples asked him *again* of the
24. But Jesus answereth *again*, and saith
32. And he took *again* the twelve, and
11:27. And they come *again* to Jerusalem:
12: 4. And *again* he sent unto them another
5. And *again* he sent another; and him
14:39. And *again* he went away, and prayed,
40. he found them asleep *again*,
61. *Again* the high priest asked him,
69. And a maid saw him *again*,
70. he denied it *again*. And a little after, they that stood by said *again* to Peter,
15: 4. And Pilate asked him *again*, saying,
12. Pilate answered and said *again* unto
13. And they cried out *again*, Crucify him.
Lu. 13:20. And *again* he said, Whereunto shall
23:20. willing to release Jesus, spake *again*
Joh 1:35. *Again* the next day after John stood, and
4: 3. and departed *again* into Galilee.
13. of this water shall thirst *again:*
46. So Jesus came *again* into Cana of Galilee,
54. This (is) *again* the second miracle
6:15. he departed *again* into a mountain
8: 2. he came *again* into the temple,
8. And *again* he stooped down, and
12. Then spake Jesus *again* unto them,
21. Then said Jesus *again* unto them,
9:15. Then *again* the Pharisees also asked
17. They say unto the blind man *again*,
26. Then said they to him *again*,
27. wherefore would ye hear (it) *again?*
0: 7. Then said Jesus unto them *again*,
17. my life, that I might take it *again*.
18. and I have power to take it *again*.
19. There was a division therefore *again*
31. the Jews took up stones *again* to
39. Therefore they sought *again* to take
40. And went away *again* beyond Jordan
1: 7. Let us go into Judæa *again*.
8. and goest thou thither *again?*
38. *again* groaning in himself
12:22. and *again* Andrew and Philip
28. and will glorify (it) *again*.
39. because that Esaias said *again*,
13:12. and was set down *again*, he said
14: 3. I will come *again*, and receive you
16:16. and *again*, a little while, and ye
17. and *again*, a little while, and
19. and *again*, a little while, and
22. but I will see you *again*,
Joh.16:28. *again*, I leave the world, and go to
18: 7. Then asked he them *again*, Whom seek
27. Peter then denied *again:*
33. into the judgment hall *again*,
38. he went out *again* unto the Jews,
40. Then cried they all *again*, saying,
19: 4. Pilate therefore went forth *again*,
9. And went *again* into the judgment hall
37. And *again* another scripture saith,
20:10. the disciples went away *again*
21. said Jesus to them *again*,
26. And after eight days *again* his disciples
21: 1. Jesus shewed himself *again* to the
16. He saith to him *again* the second time
Acts10:15. the voice (spake) unto him *again*
16. the vessel was received up *again*
11:10. all were drawn up *again* into heaven
17:32. We will hear thee *again* of this
18:21. I will return *again* unto you,
27:28. they sounded *again*, and found
Ro. 8:15. the spirit of bondage *again* to fear;
11:23. is able to graff them in *again*.
15:10. And *again* he saith, Rejoice, ye Gentiles.
11. And *again*, Praise the Lord, all ye
12. And *again*, Esaias saith,
1Co. 3:20. And *again*, The Lord knoweth the
7: 5. and come together *again*, that Satan
12:21. nor *again* the head to the feet, I have
2Co. 1:16. and to come *again* out of Macedonia
2: 1. not come *again* to you in heaviness.
3: 1. begin *again* to commend ourselves?
5:12. we commend not ourselves *again* unt
10: 7. let him of himself think this *again*,
11:16. I say *again*, Let no man think me
12:19. *Again*, think ye that we excuse
21. (And) lest, when I come *again*,
13: 2. that, if I come *again*, I will not spare:
Gal. 1: 9. so say I now *again*,
17. returned *again* unto Damascus.
2: 1. I went up *again* to Jerusalem
18. For if I build *again* the things
4: 9. how turn ye *again* to the weak
— ye desire *again* (πάλιν ἄνωθεν lit. *again*, anew) to be in bondage?
19. of whom I travail in birth *again*
5: 1. be not entangled *again* with the yoke
3. For I testify *again* to every man
Phi. 1:26. by my coming to you *again*.
2:28. that, when ye see him *again*, ye may
4: 4. (and) *again* I say, Rejoice.
Heb 1: 5. And *again*, I will be to him a Father,
6. And *again*, when (lit. and when *again* he bringeth in the firstbegotten
2:13. And *again*, I will put my trust in him. And *again*, Behold I and the
4: 5. And in this (place) *again*, If they shall
7. *Again*, he limiteth a certain day,
5:12. ye have need that one teach you *again* (lit. ye have need *again*, &c.)
6: 1. not laying *again* the foundation of
6. to renew them *again* unto repentance;
10:30. And *again*, The Lord shall judge his
Jas. 5:18. And he prayed *again*, and the heaven
2Pet. 2:20. they are *again* entangled therein,
1Joh. 2: 8. *Again*, a new commandment I write
Rev.10: 8. from heaven spake unto me *again*,
11. Thou must prophesy *again* before

3826 1 612/749 3956,4128

παμπληθεί, pampleethī.

Lu. 23:18. they cried out *all at once*, saying,

3827 1 612/835 3956,4183

πάμπολυς, pampolus.

Mar 8: 1. the multitude being *very great.*

3829 1 612/749 3956,1209

πανδοχεῖον, pandokīon.

Lu. 10:34. brought him to an *inn,*

3830 1 612/749 rt 3829

πανδοχεύς, pandokūs.

Lu. 10:35. two pence, and gave (them) to the *host,*

3831 1 612/749 5:722 3956,58

πανήγυρις, paneeguris.

Heb 12:23. To the *general assembly* and church of

3832 1 612/749 3956,3624

πανοικί, panoiki.

Acts16:34. believing in God *with all* his *house.*

3833 3 612/749 5:292 3956,3696

πανοπλία, panoplia.

Lu. 11:22. taketh from him *all* his *armour*
Eph. 6:11. Put on the *whole armour* of God,
13. take unto you the *whole armour* of God,

3834 5 612/749 5:722 3835

πανουργία, panourgia.

Lu. 20:23. perceived their *craftiness,* and said
1Co. 3:19. the wise in their own *craftiness.*
2Co. 4: 2. not walking in *craftiness,*
11: 3. beguiled Eve through his *subtilty,*
Eph. 4:14. sleight of men, (and) *cunning craftiness,*

3835 1 613/749 5:722 3956,2041

πανοῦργος, panourgos.

2Co.12:16. nevertheless, being *crafty,* I caught you

3836 1 613/749 3837

πανταχόθεν, pantakothen.

Mar 1:45. they came to him *from every quarter.*

3837 7 613/749 3956

πανταχοῦ, pantakou.

Mar 16:20. went forth, and preached *every where,*
Lu. 9: 6. and healing *every where.*
Acts17:30. commandeth all men *every where*
21:28. that teacheth all (men) *every where*
24: 3. always, and *in all places,* most noble Felix,
28:22. that *every where* it is spoken against.
1Co. 4:17. as I teach *every where* in every church.

3838 2 613/749 8:49 3956,5056

παντελές, panteles.

(εἰς τὸ παντελές).

Lu. 13:11. could in no wise (lit. not *altogether*) lift up (herself).
Heb 7:25. to save them to the *uttermost*

3839 1 613/749 3956

πάντῃ, pantee.

Acts24: 3. We accept (it) *always,* and in

3840 3 613/749 3956

πάντοθεν, pantothen.

Lu. 19:43. and keep thee in *on every side,*
Joh.18:20. whither the Jews *always* resort; [Some copies read πάντοτε]
Heb 9: 4. overlaid *round about* with gold,

3841 10 613/749 3:905 3956,2904

παντοκράτωρ, pantokratōr.

2Co. 6:18. saith the Lord *Almighty.*
Rev. 1: 8. and which is to come, the *Almighty.*
4: 8. Holy, holy, holy, Lord God *Almighty,*
11:17. O Lord God *Almighty,* which
15: 3. thy works, Lord God *Almighty;*
16: 7. Lord God *Almighty,* true and
14. that great day of God *Almighty.*
19: 6. the Lord God *omnipotent* reigneth
15. and wrath of *Almighty* God.
21:22. the Lord God *Almighty* and the Lamb

3842 42 614/750 3956,3753

πάντοτε, pantote.

Mat.26:11. ye have the poor *always* with you; but me ye have not *always.*
Mar 14: 7. ye have the poor with you *always,*
— but me ye have not *always*
Lu. 15:31. Son, thou art *ever* with me,
18: 1. that men ought *always* (to) pray,
Joh. 6:34. Lord, *evermore* give us this bread.
7: 6. but your time is *alway* ready.
8:29. for I do *always* those things that
11:42. I knew that thou hearest me *always:*
12: 8. the poor *always* ye have with you; but me ye have not *always.*
18:20. I *ever* taught in the synagogue,
— whither the Jews *always* resort;
Ro. 1: 9(10). *always* in my prayers;
1Co. 1: 4. thank my God *always* on your behalf,
15:58. *always* abounding in the work of the
2Co. 2:14. which *always* causeth us to triumph
4:10. *Always* bearing about in the body
5: 6. Therefore (we are) *always* confident,
9: 8. that ye, *always* having all sufficiency
Gal. 4:18. good to be zealously affected *always* in
Eph 5:20. Giving thanks *always* for all things
Phi. 1: 4. *Always* in every prayer of mine
20. with all boldness, as *always,* (so) now
2:12. my beloved, as ye have *always* obeyed,
4: 4. Rejoice in the Lord *alway:*
Col. 1: 3. praying *always* for you,
4: 6. Let your speech (be) *alway* with grace,
12. *always* labouring fervently for you
1Th. 1: 2. We give thanks to God *always* for you all.
2:16. to fill up their sins *alway:*
3: 6. ye have good remembrance of us *always,*
4:17. and so shall we *ever* be with the Lord.
5:15. *ever* follow that which is good,
16. Rejoice *evermore.*
2Th. 1: 3. We are bound to thank God *always* for
11. Wherefore also we pray *always* for you,
2:13. bound to give thanks *alway* to God
2Ti. 3: 7. *Ever* learning, and never able
Philem. 4. mention of thee *always* in my prayers,
Heb 7:25. he *ever* liveth to make intercession

3843 9 614/750 3956

πάντως, pantōs.

Lu. 4:23. Ye will *surely* say unto me this
Acts18:21. I must *by all means* keep this feast
21:22. the multitude must *needs* (lit. *by all means* must) come together:
28: 4. *No doubt* this man is a murderer,

Ro. 3: 9. No, *in no wise:* (lit. not *at all*)
1Co. 5:10. Yet not *altogether* with the
9:10. Or saith he (it) *altogether* for our
22. that I might *by all means* save some.
16:12. his will was not *at all* to come

3844 200 614/750 5:727

παρά, para.

The cases governed are respectively marked by [g], [d], [a].

Mat. 2: 4. demanded *of*[g] them where Christ
7. enquired *of*[g] them diligently
16. enquired *of*[g] the wise men.
4:18. walking *by*[a] the sea of Galilee,
6: 1. no reward *of*[d] your Father which
13: 1. and sat *by*[a] the sea *side.*
4. fell *by*[a] the way *side,*
19. received seed *by*[a] the way *side.*
15:29. and came *nigh unto*[a] the sea of
30. and cast them down *at*[a] Jesus' feet;
18:19. it shall be done for them *of*[g] my Father
19:26. *With*[d] men this is impossible; but *with*[d] God all things are possible.
20:20. a certain thing *of*[g] him.
30. sitting *by*[a] the way *side,*
1:25. reasoned *with*[d] themselves,
42. this is the Lord's doing, (lit. *from*[g] the Lord)
22:25. there were *with*[d] us seven brethren·
28:15. reported *among*[d] the Jews until
Mar 1:16. as he walked *by*[a] the sea of
2:13. went forth again *by*[a] the sea *side;*
3:21. when *his* friends (lit. they *of*[g] him) heard (of it),
4: 1. to teach *by*[a] the sea *side:*
4. some fell *by*[a] the way *side,*
15. these are they *by*[a] the way *side,*
5:21. he was *nigh unto*[a] the sea.
26. spent all that she had, (lit. *all* things *of*[g] herself)
8:11. seeking *of*[g] him a sign
10:27. *With*[d] men (it is) impossible, but not *with*[d] God: for *with*[d] God all things are possible.
46. sat *by*[a] the highway *side*
12: 2. might receive *from*[g] the husbandmen
11. This was the Lord's doing, (lit. *from*[g] the Lord)
14:43. *from*[g] the chief priests and
Lu 1:30. thou hast found favour *with*[d] God.
37. For *with*[d] God nothing shall be
45. which were told her *from*[g] the Lord.
2: 1. there went out a decree *from*[g] Cæsar
52. and in favour *with*[d] God and man.
3:13. no more *than*[a] that which is appointed
5: 1. he stood *by*[a] the lake of Gennesaret,
2. two ships standing *by*[a] the lake:
6:19. there went virtue out *of*[g] him,
34. ye lend (to them) *of*[g] whom ye hope to
7:38. And stood *at*[a] his feet behind (him)
8: 5. some fell *by*[a] the way *side;*
12. Those *by*[a] the way *side* are they
35. sitting *at*[a] the feet of Jesus,
41. and he fell down *at*[a] Jesus' feet,
49 *from*[g] the ruler of the synagogue's (house),
9:47. and set him *by*[d] him,
10: 7. such things as they give: (lit. the things *of*[g] them)
39. which also sat *at*[a] Jesus' feet,
11:16 sought *of*[g] him a sign

Lu. 11:37. besought him to dine *with*[d] him:
12:48. *of*[g] him shall be much required:
13: 2. sinners *above*[a] all the Galilæans,
4. that they were sinners *above*[a] all
17:16. fell down on (his) face *at*[a] his feet,
18:27. things which are impossible *with*[d] men are possible *with*[d] God.
35. blind man sat *by*[a] the way *side*
19: 7. guest *with*[d] a man that is a sinner.
Joh. 1: 6. a man sent *from*[g] God,
14. the only begotten *of*[g] the Father,
39(40). and abode *with*[d] him that day:
40(41). One of the two which heard John (speak), (lit. heard *of*[g] John)
4: 9. askest drink *of*[g] me,
40. that he would tarry *with*[d] them:
52. Then enquired he *of*[g] them the hour
5:34. I receive not testimony *from*[g] man:
41. I receive not honour *from*[g] men.
44. which receive honour one *of*[g] another,
— not the honour that (cometh) *from*[g] God
6:45. and hath learned *of*[g] the Father,
46. save he which is *of*[g] God,
7:29. I am *from*[g] him,
51. before it hear)([g] him,
8:26. which I have heard *of*[g] him.
38. which I have seen *with*[d] my Father:
— which ye have seen *with*[d] your father.
40. which I have heard *of*[g] God:
9:16. This man is not *of*[g] God,
33. If this man were not *of*[g] God,
10:18. have I received *of*[g] my Father.
14:17. for he dwelleth *with*[d] you,
23. and make our abode *with*[d] him.
25. being (yet) present *with*[d] you.
15:15. that I have heard *of*[g] my Father
26. send unto you *from*[g] the Father,
— which proceedeth *from*[g] the Father.
16:27. that I came out *from*[g] God.
28. I came forth *from*[g] the Father,
17: 5. *with*[d] thine own self with the glory which I had *with*[d] thee
7. thou hast given me are *of*[g] thee.
8. that I came out *from*[g] thee,
19:25. Now there stood *by*[d] the cross
Acts 2:33. having received *of*[g] the Father
3: 2. to ask alms *of*[g] them that
5. to receive something *of*[g] them.
4:35. laid (them) down *at*[a] the apostles' feet:
37. and laid (it) *at*[a] the apostles' feet.
5: 2. and laid (it) *at*[a] the apostles' feet.
10. *at*[a] his feet, and yielded up the
7:16. money *of*[g] the sons of Emmor
58. *at*[a] a young man's feet,
9: 2. And desired *of*[g] him letters
14. authority *from*[g] the chief priests
43. *with*[d] one Simon a tanner.
10: 6. *with*[d] one Simon a tanner, whose house is *by*[a] the sea *side:*
22. to hear words *of*[g] thee.
32. (one) Simon a tanner *by*[a] the sea *side:*
16:13. we went out of the city *by*[a] a river *side,*
17: 9. they had taken security *of*[g] Jason,
18: 3. he abode *with*[d] them,
13. *contrary to*[a] the law.
20. to tarry longer time *with*[d] them,
20:24. I have received *of*[g] the Lord Jesus,
21: 7. and abode *with*[d] them one day.
8. and abode *with*[d] him.
16. *with*[d] whom we should lodge.
22: 3. *at*[a] the feet of Gamaliel,
5. *from*[g] whom also I received letters

Acts22:30. he was accused *of*[g] the Jews,
24: 8. by examining of whom thyself (lit. *of*[g] whom thyself examining) mayest take knowledge
26 8. a thing incredible *with*[d] you,
10. authority *from*[g] the chief priests;
12. commission *from*[g] the chief priests,
22. obtained help *of*[g] God,
28:22. we desire to hear *of*[g] thee what thou
Ro. 1:25. the creature *more than*[a] the Creator,
26. which is *against*[a] nature:
2:11. no respect of persons *with*[d] God.
13. (are) just *before*[d] God, but
4:18. Who *against*[a] hope believed
9:14. (Is there) unrighteousness *with*[d] God?
11:24. graffed *contrary to*[a] nature
25. be wise *in*[d] your own conceits;
27. this (is) my covenant (lit. the covenant *from*[g] me) unto them,
12: 3. more highly *than*[a] he ought
16. Be not wise *in*[d] your own conceits.
14: 5. one day *above*[a] another:
16:17. *contrary to*[a] the doctrine which
1Co. 3:11. *than*[a] that is laid,
19. is foolishness *with*[d] God.
7:24. therein abide *with*[d] God.
12:15. is it there*fore*[a] (lit. *notwithstanding* this) not of the body?
16. is it there*fore*[a] (lit. *&c.*) not of the body?
16: 2. every one of you lay *by*[d] him in store,
2Co. 1:17. that *with*[d] me there should be yea
11:24. forty (stripes) *save*[a] one.
Gal. 1: 8. *than*[a] that which we have preached
9. *than*[a] that ye have received,
12. I neither received it *of*[g] man,
3:11. by the law *in the sight of*[d] God,
Eph 6: 8. the same shall he receive *of*[g] the Lord,
9. respect of persons *with*[d] him.
Phi. 4:18. received *of*[g] Epaphroditus the things (which were sent) *from*[g] you,
Col. 4:16. when this epistle is read *among*[d] you,
1Th. 2:13. which ye heard *of*[g] us,
4: 1. as ye have received *of*[g] us,
2Th. 1: 6. a righteous thing *with*[d] God
3: 6. which he received *of*[g] us.
8. any man's bread for nought; (lit. bread *of*[g] any)
2Ti. 1:18. which thou hast heard *of*[g] me,
18. may find mercy *of*[g] the Lord
2: 2. that thou hast heard *of*[g] me
3:14. knowing *of*[g] whom thou hast learned
4:13. that I left at Troas *with*[d] Carpus,
Heb 1: 4. a more excellent name *than*[a] they.
9. *above*[a] thy fellows.
2: 7. a little lower *than*[a] the angels;
9. made a little lower *than*[a] the angels
3: 3. worthy of more glory *than*[a] Moses,
9:23. with better sacrifices *than*[a] these.
11: 4. a more excellent sacrifice *than*[a] Cain,
11. when she was *past*[a] age,
12. which is *by*[a] the sea shore
12:24. better things *than*[a] (that of) Abel.
Jas. 1: 5. let him ask *of*[g] God,
7. receive any thing *of*[g] the Lord.
17. *with*[d] whom is no variableness,
27. *before*[d] God and the Father
1Pet. 2: 4. chosen *of*[d] God, (lit. *before* or *with* God)
20. this (is) acceptable *with*[d] God.
2Pet. 1:17. he received *from*[g] God the Father
2:11. against them *before*[d] the Lord.
3: 8. one day (is) *with*[d] the Lord
Joh. 3:22. we ask, we receive *of*[g] him,
1Joh. 5:15. that we desired *of*[g] him.
2Joh. 3. *from*[g] God the Father, and *from*[g] the Lord Jesus Christ,
4. commandment *from*[g] the Father.
Rev. 2:13. who was slain *among*[d] you,
27. as I received *of*[g] my Father.
3:18. to buy *of*[g] me gold tried in the fire,

3845 4 616/752 5:736 3844rt939

παραβαίνω, *parabaino.*

Mat.15: 2. Why *do* thy disciples *transgress* the
3. Why *do* ye also *transgress* the
Acts 1:25. from which Judas *by transgression fell*,
2Joh. 9. *Whosoever transgresseth*, and abideth

3846 2 616/752 3844,906

παραβάλλω, *paraballo.*

Mar 4:30. with what comparison shall we *compare*
Acts20:15. and the next (day) we *arrived* at Samos,

3847 7 617/752 5:736 3845

παράβασις, *parabasis.*

Ro. 2:23. through *breaking* the law dishonourest
4:15. where no law is, (there is) no *transgression*.
5:14. not sinned after the similitude of Adam's *transgression*,
Gal. 3:19. It was added because of *transgressions*,
1Ti. 2:14. was in the *transgression*.
Heb 2: 2. and every *transgression* and disobedience
9:15. for the redemption of the *transgressions* (that)

3848 5 617/752 5:736 3845

παραβατης, *parabatees.*

Ro. 2:25. but if thou be a *breaker* of the law,
27. judge thee, *who...dost transgress* the law?
Gal. 2:18. I make myself a *transgressor*.
Jas. 2: 9. are convinced of the law as *transgressors*.
11. art become a *trangressor* of the law.

3849 2 617/752 3844,971

παραβιάζομαι, *parabiazomai.*

Lu. 24:29. But they *constrained* him, saying,
Acts16:15. And she *constrained* us.

3850 50 617/752 5:744 3846

παραβολή, *parabolee.*

Mat.13: 3. many things unto them in *parables*,
10. Why speakest thou unto them in *parables*?
13. Therefore speak I to them in *parables*:
18. Hear ye therefore the *parable* of the
24. Another *parable* put he forth
31. Another *parable* put he forth unto
33. Another *parable* spake he unto them;
34. spake Jesus unto the multitude in *parables* and without a *parable* spake he not
35. I will open my mouth in *parables*;
36. Declare unto us the *parable* of the tares
53. when Jesus had finished these *parables*,
15:15. Declare unto us this *parable*.
21:33. Hear another *parable*: There was
45. and Pharisees had heard his *parables*,
22: 1. spake unto them again by *parables*,
24:32. Now learn a *parable* of the fig tree;
Mar 3:23. and said unto them in *parables*,
4: 2. taught them many things by *parables*,
10. the twelve asked of him the *parable*.

Mar 4:11. all (these) things are done in *parables:*
13. Know ye not this *parable?* and how then will ye know all *parables?*
30. or with what *comparison* shall we compare
33. And with many such *parables* spake
34. But without a *parable* spake he not
7:17. asked him concerning the *parable.*
12: 1. began to speak unto them by *parables.*
12. had spoken the *parable* against them:
13:28. Now learn a *parable* of the fig tree;
Lu. 4:23. say unto me this *proverb,* Physician,
5:36. And he spake also a *parable* unto them;
6:39. And he spake a *parable* unto them,
8: 4. he spake by a *parable:*
9. What might this *parable* be?
10. but to others in *parables;* that
11. Now the *parable* is this: The seed is
12:16. And he spake a *parable* unto them,
41. Lord, speakest thou this *parable* unto us,
13: 6. He spake also this *parable;*
14: 7. And he put forth a *parable* to those
15: 3. And he spake this *parable* unto them,
18: 1. And he spake a *parable* unto them
9. And he spake this *parable* unto
19:11. he added and spake a *parable,*
20: 9. to speak to the people this *parable;*
19. had spoken this *parable* against them.
21:29. And he spake to them a *parable;*
Heb 9: 9. Which (was) a *figure* for the time then
11:19. whence also he received him in a *figure.*

3851 1 618/752 3844,1011

παραβουλεύομαι, *paraboulĕuomai.*

Phi. 2:30. *not regarding* his life, to supply your

3852 5 618/753 5:761 3853

παραγγελία, *parangelia.*

Acts 5:28. Did not we straitly command you (lit. with *commandment* command)
16:24. Who, having received such a *charge,* thrust
1Th. 4: 2. ye know what *commandments* we gave
1Ti. 1: 5. Now the end of the *commandment* is
18. This *charge* I commit unto thee, son

3853 30 618/753 5:761 3844,rt32

παραγγέλλω, *parangello.*

Mat. 10: 5. *and commanded* them, saying, Go not
Mar 6: 8. And *commanded* them that they should
8: 6. And he *commanded* the people to sit down
Lu. 5:14. And he *charged* him to tell no man:
8:29. For he had *commanded* the unclean spirit
56. but he *charged* them that they should
9:21. he straitly charged them, and *commanded*
Acts 1: 4. *commanded* them that they should not
4:18. and *commanded* them not to speak at all
5:28. *Did* not we straitly *command* you that ye
40. they *commanded* that they should not
10:42. he *commanded* us to preach unto
15: 5. and *to command* (them) to keep the law
16:18. I *command* thee in the name of Jesus Christ
23. *charging* the jailor to keep them safely:
17:30. but now *commandeth* all men every
23:22. *and charged* (him, See thou) tell no man
30. *and gave commandment* to his accusers
1Co. 7:10. unto the married I *command,*
11:17. in this *that* I *declare* (unto you) (lit. *declaring* this) I praise (you) not.
1Th. 4:11. as we *commanded* you;
2Th. 3: 4. do the things which we *command*
6. Now we *command* you, brethren.
10. this we *commanded* you, that if
12. that are such we *command*
1Ti. 1: 3. that thou *mightest charge* some that
4:11. These things *command* and teach.
5: 7. And these things *give in charge,*
6:13. I *give* thee *charge* in the sight of
17. *Charge* them that are rich

3854 37 618/753 3844,1096

παραγίνομαι, *paragĭnomai.*

Mat. 2: 1. behold, there *came* wise men from
3: 1. In those days *came* John the Baptist,
13. Then *cometh* Jesus from Galilee
Mar 14:43. while he yet spake, *cometh* Judas,
Lu. 7: 4. And *when* they *came* to Jesus,
20. *When* the men *were come* unto him,
8:19. Then *came* to him (his) mother and
11: 6. in his journey *is come* to me, and
12:51. Suppose ye that I *am come* to give
14:21. So that servant *came, and* shewed
19:16. Then *came* the first, saying, Lord,
22:52. and the elders, *which were come* to him,
Joh. 3:23. and they *came,* and were baptized.
8: 2. in the morning he *came* again into
Acts 5:21. But the high priest *came,* and they that
22. But when the officers *came, and*
25. Then *came* one *and* told them,
9:26. And *when* Saul *was come* to Jerusalem,
39. *When* he *was come,* they brought him
10:32. who, *when* he *cometh,* shall speak
33. well done *that* thou *art come.*
11:23. Who, *when* he *came,* and had seen
13:14. they *came* to Antioch in Pisidia,
14:27. And *when* they *were come,* and
15: 4. And *when* they *were come* to Jerusalem,
17:10. who *coming* (thither) went into the
18:27. who, *when* he *was come,* helped them
20:18. And when they *were come* to him, he said
21:18. and all the elders *were present.*
23:16. he *went* and entered into the castle,
35. when thine accusers *are* also *come.*
24:17. I *came* to bring alms to my nation,
24. *when* Felix *came* with his wife
25: 7. And *when* he *was come,* the Jews which
28:21. neither any of the brethren *that came*
1Co. 16: 3. And when I *come,* whomsoever
Heb 9:11. But Christ *being come* an high priest

3855 10 619/754 1:128 3844,71

παράγω, *parago.*

Mat. 9: 9. And *as* Jesus *passed forth* from thence
27. And *when* Jesus *departed* thence, two
20:30. when they heard that Jesus *passed by,* cried
Mar 2:14. And *as* he *passed by,* he saw Levi
15:21. Simon a Cyrenian, *who passed by,*
Joh. 8:59. midst of them, and so *passed by.*
9: 1. And *as* (Jesus) *passed by,* he saw
1Co. 7:31. the fashion of this world *passeth away.*
1Joh. 2: 8. because the darkness *is past,* and
17. And the world *passeth away,*

3856 2 619/754 2:25 3844,1165

παραδειγματίζω, *paradĭgmatizo.*

Mat. 1:19. *to make* her *a publick example,* was
Heb 6: 6. and *put* (him) *to an open shame.*

3857 3 619/754 5:765 [6508]

παράδεισος, paradīsos.

Lu. 23:43. shalt thou be with me in *paradise*.
2Co.12: 4. he was caught up into *paradise*,
Rev. 2: 7. in the midst of the *paradise* of God.

3858 5 619/754 3844,1209

παραδέχομαι, paradekomai.

Mar 4:20. such as hear the word, and *receive* (it),
Acts16:21. which are not lawful for us *to receive*,
22:18. for they *will* not *receive* thy testimony
1Ti. 5:19. Against an elder *receive* not an
Heb 12: 6. scourgeth every son whom he *receiveth*.

3859 1 619/205 3844,1304

παραδιατριβή, paradiatribee.

1Ti. 6: 5. *Perverse disputings* of men of

3860 121 619/754 2:166 3844,1325

παραδίδωμι, paradidōmi.

Mat. 4:12. heard that John *was cast into prison*,
5:25. adversary *deliver* thee to the judge, and the judge *deliver* thee
10: 4. Iscariot, *who* also *betrayed* him.
17. will *deliver* you *up* to the councils,
19. But when they *deliver* you *up*,
21. the brother *shall deliver up* the
11:27. All things *are delivered* unto me of
17:22. The Son of man shall *be betrayed*
18:34. and *delivered* him to the tormentors,
20:18. the Son of man *shall be betrayed*
19. And *shall deliver* him to the Gentiles
24: 9. Then *shall* they *deliver* you *up* to be
10. and *shall betray* one another,
25:14. and *delivered* unto them his goods.
20. Lord, thou *deliveredst* unto me five
22. Lord, thou *deliveredst* unto me two talents:
26: 2. Son of man *is betrayed* to be crucified.
15. and I *will deliver* him unto you?
16. he sought opportunity to *betray* him.
21. one of you *shall betray* me.
23. dish, the same *shall betray* me.
24. by whom the Son of man *is betrayed!*
25. Then Judas, *which betrayed* him,
45. *is betrayed* into the hands of sinners.
46. he is at hand *that doth betray* me.
48. Now he *that betrayed* him gave
27: 2. and *delivered* him to Pontius Pilate
3. Then Judas, *which had betrayed* him,
4. have sinned *in that* I have *betrayed*
18. for envy they *had delivered* him.
26. he *delivered* (him) to be crucified.
Mar. 1:14. after that John *was put in prison*,
3: 19. Judas Iscariot, which also *betrayed* him:
4:29. when the fruit *is brought forth*.
7:13. your tradition, which ye *have delivered:*
9:31. *is delivered* into the hands of men,
10:33. the Son of man *shall be delivered*
— and *shall deliver* him to the Gentiles:
13: 9. they *shall deliver* you *up* to
11. *and deliver* you *up*, take no thought
12. the brother *shall betray* the brother
14:10. priests, to *betray* him unto them.
11. how he *might* conveniently *betray* him.
18. eateth with me *shall betray* me.
21. by whom the Son of man *is betrayed!*
41. the Son of man *is betrayed* into the
42. he *that betrayeth* me is at hand.
44. And he *that betrayed* him had given
Mar 15: 1. and *delivered* (him) to Pilate.
10. priests *had delivered* him for envy.
15. and *delivered* Jesus, when he had
Lu. 1: 2. Even as they *delivered* them unto us,
4: 6. the glory of them: for that *is delivered* unto me;
9:44. the Son of man shall *be delivered* into
10:22. All things *are delivered* to me of
12:58. and the judge *deliver* thee to
18:32. For he *shall be delivered* unto the
20:20. that so they might *deliver* him unto
21:12. *delivering* (you) *up* to the synagogues,
16. And ye *shall be betrayed* both by
22: 4. how he *might betray* him unto
6. sought opportunity *to betray* him
21. the hand of him *that betrayeth* me
22. unto that man by whom he *is betrayed!*
48. Judas, *betrayest* thou the Son of man
23:25. but he *delivered* Jesus to their will.
24: 7. must *be delivered* into the hands of
20. and our rulers *delivered* him to be
Joh. 6:64. and who should *betray* him.
71. he it was that should *betray* him,
12: 4. Simon's (son), which should *betray* him
13: 2. Simon's (son), to *betray* him;
11. For he knew *who* should *betray* him;
21. that one of you *shall betray* me.
18: 2. And Judas also, *which betrayed* him,
5. *which betrayed* him, stood with them.
30. we would not *have delivered* him
35. the chief priests *have delivered* thee
36. that I *should* not *be delivered* to the
19:11. therefore he *that delivered* me unto
16. Then *delivered* he him therefore
30. and *gave up* the ghost.
21:20. Lord, which is he *that betrayeth* thee?
Acts 3:13. whom ye *delivered up*, and
6:14. the customs which Moses *delivered* us.
7:42. and *gave* them *up* to worship the
8: 3. men and women *committed* (them) to
12: 4. *and delivered* (him) to four quaternions
14:26. they had been *recommended* to the grace
15:26. Men *that have hazarded* their lives
40. *being recommended* by the brethren
16: 4. they *delivered* them the decrees for
21:11. and *shall deliver* (him) into the hands
22: 4. and *delivering* into prisons both men
27: 1. they *delivered* Paul and certain
28:16. the centurion *delivered* the prisoners
17. yet *was* I *delivered* prisoner from
Ro. 1:24. Wherefore God also *gave* them *up* to
26. God *gave* them *up* unto vile affections:
28. God *gave* them *over* to a reprobate
4:25. Who *was delivered* for our offences,
6:17. form of doctrine which was delivered you. (lit. into which ye *were delivered*)
8:32. but *delivered* him *up* for us all,
1Co. 5: 5. *To deliver* such an one unto Satan
11: 2. ordinances, as I *delivered* (them) to you.
23. which also I *delivered* unto you,
— night in which he *was betrayed* took bread:
13: 3. though I *give* my body to be burned,
15: 3. For I *delivered* unto you first of
24. when he shall *have delivered up*
2Co. 4:11. *are* alway *delivered* unto death for
Gal. 2:20. who loved me, and *gave* himself for me.
Eph 4:19. past feeling *have given* themselves over
5: 2. and *hath given* himself for us
25. the church, and *gave* himself for it;
1Ti. 1:20. whom I *have delivered* unto Satan,
1Pet. 2:23. but *committed* (himself) to him
2Pet. 2: 4. and *delivered* (them) into chains

2Pet.2:21. holy commandment *delivered* unto
Jude 3. the faith *which was* once *delivered* unto the

3861 1 621/756 2:232 3844,1391

παράδοξος, paradoxos.

Lu. 5:26. We have seen *strange* things to day.

3862 13 621/756 2:166 3860

παράδοσις, paradosis.

Mat.15: 2. transgress the *tradition* of the elders?
3. commandment of God by your *tradition*?
6. of none effect by your *tradition*.
Mar 7: 3. not, holding the *tradition* of the elders.
5. according to the *tradition* of the elders,
8. ye hold the *tradition* of men,
9. that ye may keep your own *tradition*.
13. of none effect through your *tradition*,
1Co.11: 2. and keep the *ordinances*, as I delivered
Gal. 1:14. zealous of the *traditions* of my fathers.
Col. 2: 8. after the *tradition* of men, after
2Th. 2:15. stand fast, and hold the *traditions* which
3: 6. and not after the *tradition* which he

3863 4 621/756 2:877 3844,2206

παραζηλόω, parazeeloō.

Ro. 10:19. I *will provoke* you *to jealousy*
11:11. for *to provoke* them *to jealousy*.
14. I *may provoke to emulation*
1Co.10.22. *Do* we *provoke* the Lord *to jealousy*?

3864 1 621/756 3844,2281

παραθαλάσσιος, parathalassios.

Mat. 4:13. in Capernaum, *which is upon the sea coast*,

3865 1 621/756 3844,2334

παραθεωρέω, paratheōreo.

Acts 6: 1. their widows *were neglected* in

3866 1 621/756 8:152 3908

παραθήκη, paratheekee.

2Ti. 1:12. is able to keep *that which* I have *committed unto* him

3867 2 621/756 3844,134

παραινέω, paraineo.

Acts27: 9. Paul *admonished* (them),
22. And now I *exhort* you to be of

3868 11 621/756 1:191 3844,154

παραιτέομαι, paraiteomai.

Lu. 14:18. with one (consent) began *to make excuse*.
— I pray thee have me *excused*.
19. I pray thee have me *excused*.
Acts25:11. I *refuse* not to die:
1Ti. 4: 7. *refuse* profane and old wives' fables,
5:11. But the younger widows *refuse*:
2Ti. 2:23. foolish and unlearned questions *avoid*,
Tit. 3:10. and second admonition *reject*;
Heb 12:19. *intreated* that the word should not
25. See that ye *refuse* not him that
— *who refused* him that spake on earth,

3869 1 622/756 3844,2523

παρακαθίζω, parakathizo.

Lu. 10:39. which also *sat* at Jesus' feet, *and*

3870 108 622/756 5:773 3844,2564

παρακαλέω, parakaleo.

Mat. 2:18. would not *be comforted*, because
5: 4. for they *shall be comforted*.
8: 5. a centurion, *beseeching* him,
31. the devils *besought* him, saying,
34. they *besought* (him) that he would
14:36. And *besought* him that they
18:29. and *besought* him, saying,
32. because thou *desiredst* me:
26:53. I cannot now *pray* to my
Mar 1:40. a leper to him, *beseeching* him,
5:10. And he *besought* him much
12. And all the devils *besought* him,
17. And they began *to pray* him to
18. *prayed* him that he might be
23. And *besought* him greatly,
6:56. and *besought* him that they
7:32. and they *beseech* him to put his
8:22. and *besought* him to touch him.
Lu. 3:18. *in* his *exhortation* preached he
7: 4. they *besought* him instantly,
8:31. And they *besought* him that
32. and they *besought* him that
41. and *besought* him that he would
15:28. his father out, and *intreated* him.
16:25. but now he *is comforted*, and thou
Acts 2:40. did he testify and *exhort*, saying,
8:31. And he *desired* Philip that
9:38. *desiring* (him) that he would not
11:23. and *exhorted* them all, that with
13:42. the Gentiles *besought* that these words
14:22. *exhorting* them to continue in
15:32. *exhorted* the brethren with many
16: 9. *and prayed* him, saying, Come
15. she *besought* (us), saying, If ye
39. And they came and *besought* them,
40. the brethren, they *comforted* them,
19:31. *desiring* (him) that he would not
20: 2. and *had given* them much *exhortation*,
12. and *were* not a little *comforted*.
21:12. *besought* him not to go up to Jerusalem.
24: 4. I *pray* thee that thou wouldest
25: 2. against Paul, and *besought* him,
27:33. Paul *besought* (them) all to take
34. I *pray* you to take (some) meat:
28:14. and *were desired* to tarry with them
20. have I *called for* you, to see (you),
Ro. 12: 1. I *beseech* you therefore, brethren,
8. Or he *that exhorteth*, on exhortation:
15:30. Now I *beseech* you, brethren, for
16:17. Now I *beseech* you, brethren, mark
1Co. 1:10. Now I *beseech* you, brethren, by
4:13. Being defamed, we *intreat*:
16. Wherefore I *beseech* you, be ye
14:31. and all *may be comforted*.
16:12. Apollos, I greatly *desired* him to come
15. I *beseech* you, brethren,
2Co. 1: 4. *Who comforteth* us in all our tribulation, that we may be able *to comfort*
— wherewith we ourselves *are comforted* of
6. or whether we *be comforted*,
2: 7. to forgive (him), and *comfort* (him),
8. Wherefore I *beseech* you that
5:20. as *though* God *did beseech* (you)
6: 1. *beseech* (you) also that ye receive
7: 6. God, *that comforteth* those that are cast down, *comforted* us by
7. wherewith he *was comforted* in you,
13. we *were comforted* in your comfort:
8: 6. Insomuch that we *desired* Titus,
9: 5. I thought it necessary *to exhort* the

2Co.10: 1. I Paul myself *beseech* you by
12: 8. I *besought* the Lord thrice,
18. I *desired* Titus, and with
13:11. Be perfect, *be of good comfort*,
Eph. 4: 1. *beseech* you that ye walk
6:22. and (that) he *might comfort* your
Phi. 4: 2. I *beseech* Euodias, and *beseech* Syntyche,
Col. 2: 2. That their hearts *might be comforted*,
4: 8. and *comfort* your hearts;
1Th. 2:11. ye know how we *exhorted*
3: 2. and *to comfort* you concerning
7. we *were comforted* over you
4: 1. and *exhort* (you) by the Lord
10. but we *beseech* you, brethren,
18. Wherefore *comfort* one another
5:11. Wherefore *comfort* yourselves together,
14. Now we *exhort* you, brethren,
2Th. 2:17. *Comfort* your hearts, and stablish
3:12. and *exhort* by our Lord Jesus,
1Ti. 1: 3. As I *besought* thee to abide
2: 1. I *exhort* therefore, that, first
5: 1. but *intreat* (him) as a father;
6: 2. These things teach and *exhort*.
2Ti. 4: 2. rebuke, *exhort* with all
Tit. 1: 9. both *to exhort* and to convince the
2: 6. *exhort* to be sober minded.
15. speak, and *exhort*, and rebuke
Philem 9. Yet for love's sake I rather *beseech*
10. I *beseech* thee for my son Onesimus,
Heb 3:13. But *exhort* one another daily,
10:25. but *exhorting* (one another): and
13:19. But I *beseech* (you) the rather
22. I *beseech* you, brethren, suffer
1Pet. 2:11. Dearly beloved, I *beseech* (you) as
5: 1. I *exhort*, who am also an elder,
12. I have written briefly, *exhorting*, and
Jude 3. for me to write unto you, *and exhort*

3871 1 623/757 3844,2572

παρακαλύπτω, *parakalupto*.

Lu. 9:45. and it was *hid* from them, that they

3872 2 623/756 8:152 3844,2698

παρακαταθήκη, *parakatatheekee*.

1Ti. 6:20. keep *that which is committed to* thy *trust*,
2Ti. 1:14. *That* good *thing which was committed unto* thee keep

---

3873 2 623/757 3:654 3844,2749

παράκειμαι, *parakīmai*.

Ro. 7:18. for to will *is present* with me;
21. evil *is present* with me.

3874 29 623/758 5:773 3870

παράκλησις, *parakleesis*.

Lu. 2:25. waiting for the *consolation* of Israel:
6:24. ye have received your *consolation*.
Acts 4:36. The son of *consolation*,
9:31. and in the *comfort* of the Holy Ghost,
13:15. any word of *exhortation* for the people,
15:31. they rejoiced for the *consolation*.
Ro. 12: 8. Or he that exhorteth, on *exhortation*:
15: 4. and *comfort* of the scriptures
5. the God of patience and *consolation*
1Co.14: 3. and *exhortation*, and comfort.
2Co. 1: 3. and the God of all *comfort*;
4. by the *comfort*, wherewith we
5. so our *consolation* also aboundeth
2Co. 1: 6. (it is) for your *consolation* and
— for your *consolation* and salvation.
7. also of the *consolation*.
7: 4. I am filled with *comfort*,
7. but by the *consolation* wherewith
13. we were comforted in your *comfort*
8: 4. Praying us with much *intreaty* that
17. he accepted the *exhortation*;
Phi. 2: 1. any *consolation* in Christ, if
1Th. 2: 3. For our *exhortation* (was) not
2Th. 2:16. given (us) everlasting *consolation*
1Ti. 4:13. to *exhortation*, to doctrine.
Philem. 7. joy and *consolation* in thy love,
Heb 6:18. we might have a strong *consolation*,
12: 5. forgotten the *exhortation* which
13:22. suffer the word of *exhortation*:

3875 5 623/758 5:800

παράκλητος, *parakleetos*.

Joh.14:16. give you another *Comforter*,
26. the *Comforter*, (which is) the Holy Ghost,
15:26. But when the *Comforter* is come,
16: 7. the *Comforter* will not come unto
1Joh.2: 1. an *advocate* with the Father, Jesus

3876 3 624/758 1:216 3878

παρακοή, *parakoee*.

Ro. 5:19. by one man's *disobedience*
2Co.10: 6. to revenge all *disobedience*,
Heb 2: 2. every transgression and *disobedience*

3877 4 624/758 1:210 3844,190

παρακολουθέω, *parakoloutheo*.

Mar16:17. And these signs *shall follow*
Lu. 1: 3. *having had* perfect *understanding* of all
1Ti. 4: 6. whereunto thou *hast attained*.
2Ti. 3:10. But thou *hast fully known* my doctrine,

3878 2 624/758 1:216 3844,191

παρακούω, *parakouo*.

Mat.18:17. And if he *shall neglect to hear* them,
— but if he *neglect to hear* the church,

3879 5 624/758 5:814 3844,2955

παρακύπτω, *parakupto*.

Lu. 24:12. and *stooping down*, he beheld the
Joh.20: 5. And he *stooping down*,
11. she *stooped down*, (and looked) into
Jas. 1:25. But *whoso looketh* into the
1Pet. 1:12. angels desire *to look* into.

3880 50 624/758 4:5 3844,2983

παραλαμβάνω, *paralambano*.

Mat. 1:20. fear not *to take unto* thee Mary
24. and *took unto* him his wife:
2:13. Arise, and *take* the young child
14. When he arose, he *took* the
20. Saying, Arise, and *take* the
21. And he arose, and *took*
4: 5. Then the devil *taketh* him *up*
8. Again, the devil *taketh* him *up*
12:45. Then goeth he, and *taketh* with himself
17: 1. Jesus *taketh* Peter, James, and
18. 16. *take* with thee one or two
20:17. *took* the twelve disciples apart
24:40. the one shall *be taken*, and

Mat.24:41. the one shall *be taken*, and the
26:37. And he *took with* him Peter and
27:27. *took* Jesus into the common hall, *and*
Mar 4:36. they *took* him even as he was
5:40. he *taketh* the father and the mother
7: 4. which they *have received* to hold,
9: 2. Jesus *taketh* (with him) Peter,
10:32. he *took* again the twelve, *and*
14:33. And he *taketh* with him Peter
Lu. 9:10. And he *took* them, *and* went aside
28. he *took* Peter and John and James, *and*
11:26. and *taketh* (to him) seven other
17:34. the one *shall be taken*, and
35. the one *shall be taken*, and (& 36, Elz.)
18:31. he *took* (unto him) the twelve, *and*
Joh. 1:11. his own *received* him not.
14: 3. I will come again, and *receive* you unto myself;
19:16. And they *took* Jesus, and led
Acts15:39. so Barnabas *took* Mark, *and*
16:33. And he *took* them the same hour
21:24. Them *take, and* purify thyself
26. Then Paul *took* the men, *and*
32. Who immediately *took* soldiers
23:18. So he *took* him, *and* brought
1Co.11:23. For I *have received* of the Lord
15: 1. which also ye *have received*,
3. that which I also *received*,
Gal. 1: 9. than that ye *have received*,
12. For I neither *received* it of man,
Phi. 4: 9. ye have both learned, and *received*,
Col. 2: 6. As ye *have* therefore *received* Christ Jesus
4:17. ministry which thou *hast received* in the
1Th. 2:13. *when* ye *received* the word of God
4: 1. that as ye *have received* of us
2Th. 3: 6. which he *received* of us.
Heb 12:28. Wherefore we *receiving* a kingdom

3881 2 625/759 3844,3004

παραλέγομαι, *paralegomai.*

Acts27: 8. And, hardly *passing* it, came
13. they *sailed* close *by* Crete.

3882 1 625/759 3844,251

παράλιος, *paralios.*

Lu. 6:17. from the *sea coast* of Tyre (lit. *maritime* Tyre) and Sidon,

3883 1 625/759 3844,236

παραλλαγή, *parallagee.*

Jas. 1:17. with whom is no *variableness*, neither

3884 2 625/759 3844,3049

παραλογίζομαι, *paralogizomai.*

Col 2: 4. lest any man *should beguile* you
Jas. 1:22. *deceiving* your own selves.

3886 5 625/759 3844,3089

παραλύομαι, *paraluomai.*

Lu. 5:18. a man which was taken with a palsy: (lit. *palsied*)
24. he said unto the *sick of the palsy*,
Acts 8: 7. and many *taken with palsies*,
9:33. and was *sick of the palsy*.
Heb 12:12. which hang down, and the *feeble* knees;

3885 10 625/759 3886

παραλυτικός, *paralutikos.*

and those *that had the palsy;*
Mat. 8: 6. lieth at home *sick of the palsy*,
9: 2. brought to him a man *sick of the palsy*,
— said unto the *sick of the palsy*; Son,
6. then saith he to the *sick of the palsy*,
Mar 2: 3. bringing one *sick of the palsy*, which
4. bed wherein the *sick of the palsy* lay.
5. he said unto the *sick of the palsy*, Son,
9. easier to say to the *sick of the palsy*,
10. he saith to the *sick of the palsy*,

3887 3 625/759 4:574 3844,3306

παραμένω, *parameno.*

1Co.16: 6. And it may be that I *will abide*, yea,
Heb 7:23. they were not suffered *to continue*
Jas. 1:25. law of liberty, and *continueth* (therein),

3888 4 626/759 5:816 3844,3454

παραμυθέομαι, *paramutheomai*

Joh.11:19. came to Martha and Mary, to *comfort* them
31. in the house, and *comforted* her,
1Th. 2:11. ye know how we exhorted and *comforted*
5:14. *comfort* the feebleminded,

3889 1 626/759 5:816 3888

παραμυθία, *paramuthia.*

1Co.14: 3. and exhortation, and *comfort.*

3890 1 626/759 5:816 3889

παραμύθιον, *paramuthion.*

Phi. 2: 1. if any *comfort* of love,

3891 1 626/759 4:1022 3844

παρανομέω, *paranomeo.* 3551

Acts23: 3. commandest me to be smitten *contrary to the law?* (lit. *transgressing law*)

3892 1 626/759 4:1022 rt 3891

παρανομία, *paranomia.*

2Pet. 2:16. But was rebuked for his *iniquity:*

3893 1 626/759 6:122 3844,4087

παραπικραίνω, *parapikraino.*

Heb 3:16. when they had heard, *did provoke:*

3894 2 626/759 6:122 3893

παραπικρασμός, *parapikrasmos.*

Heb 3: 8. your hearts, as in the *provocation*,
15. not your hearts, as in the *provocation.*

3895 1 626/760 6:161 3844,4098

παραπίπτω, *parapipto.*

Heb 6: 6. *If* they shall *fall away*, to renew

3896 1 626/760 3844,4126

παραπλέω, *parapleo.*

Acts20:16. Paul had determined *to sail by* Ephesus,

3897 1 626/760 3844 rt 4139

παραπλήσιον, *parapleesion.*

Phi. 2:27. he was sick *nigh*

3898 1 627/760 rt 3897

παραπλησίως, *parapleesiōs.*

Heb 2.14. he also himself *likewise* took part

3899 5 627/760 3844,4198

παραπορεύομαι, *paraporūomai.*

Mat.27:39. And they *that passed by* reviled
Mar 2:23. came to pass, that he *went* through the
9:30. and *passed* through Galilee;
11:20. *as* they *passed by*, they saw the fig tree
15:29. And they *that passed by* railed on him,

3900 23 627/760 6:161 3895

παράπτωμα, *paraptōma.*

Mat. 6:14. if ye forgive men their *trespasses*,
15. not men their *trespasses*, neither will your Father forgive your *trespasses*.
18:35. every one his brother their *trespasses*.
Mar 11:25. may forgive you your *trespasses*.
26. in heaven forgive your *trespasses*.
Ro. 4:25. Who was delivered for our *offences*,
5:15. But not as the *offence*, so also (is) the
— For if through the *offence* of one
16. free gift (is) of many *offences* unto
17. For if by one man's *offence* death
18. Therefore as by the *offence* of one
20. the law entered, that the *offence* might
11:11. through their *fall* salvation (is come)
12. Now if the *fall* of them (be) the
2Co. 5:19. not imputing their *trespasses*
Gal. 6: 1. if a man be overtaken in a *fault*,
Eph. 1: 7. the forgiveness of *sins*,
2: 1. dead in *trespasses* and sins;
5. when we were dead in *sins*,
Col. 2:13. you, being dead in your *sins*
— having forgiven you all *trespasses*
Jas. 5:16. Confess (your) *faults* one to another,

3901 1 627/760 3844,4482

παραῤῥυέω, *pararrueo.*

Heb 2: 1. lest at any time we *should let* (them) *slip*.

3902 1 627/760 3844,rt 4591

παράσημος, *paraseemos.*

Acts28:11. *whose sign was* Castor and Pollux.

3903 4 627/760 3844,4632

παρασκευάζω, *paraskūazo.*

Acts10:10. but *while* they *made ready*, he fell
1Co.14: 8. who *shall prepare himself* to the battle?
2Co. 9: 2. Achaia *was ready* a year ago;
3. ye may be *ready*:

3904 6 627/760 7:1 3903

παρασκευή, *paraskūee.*

Mat.27:62. followed the day of the *preparation*,
Mar 15:42. because it was the *preparation*,
Lu. 23:54. that day was the *preparation*, and
Joh.19:14. it was the *preparation* of the passover,
31. because it was the *preparation*,
42. because of the Jews' *preparation* (day);

3905 1 627/760 3844 *teinō* (to stretch)

παρατείνω, *paratīno.*

Acts 20:7. and *continued* his speech until midnight.

3906 6 627/760 8:140 3844,5083

παρατηρέω, *parateereo.*

Mar 3: 2. And they *watched* him,
Lu. 6: 7. *watched* him, whether he would heal
14: 1. that they *watched* him.
20:20. And they *watched* (him), *and*
Acts 9:24. And they *watched* the gates day and
Gal. 4:10. Ye *observe* days, and months, and

3907 1 628/760 8:140 3906

παρατήρησις, *parateereesis.*

Lu. 17:20. The kingdom of God cometh not with *observation*.

3908 19 628/760 8:152 3844,5087

παρατίθημι, *paratitheemi.*

Mat.13:24. Another parable *put* he *forth* unto
31. Another parable *put* he *forth* unto
Mar 6:41. to his disciples to *set before* them;
8: 6. to his disciples to *set before* (them); and they *did set* (them) *before* the people.
7. to *set* them also *before* (them).
Lu. 9:16. to *set before* the multitude.
10: 8. eat such things *as are set before* you:
11: 6. I have nothing to *set before* him?
12:48. to whom men *have committed* much,
23:46. into thy hands I *commend* my spirit:
Acts14:23. they *commended* them to the Lord,
16:34. he *set* meat *before* them,
17: 3. Opening and *alledging*, that Christ
20:32. brethren, I *commend* you to God,
1Co.10:27. *what*soever is *set before* you,
1Ti. 1:18. This charge I *commit* unto thee,
2Ti. 2: 2. the same *commit* thou to faithful
1Pet.4:19. *let* them that...*commit the keeping of* their souls

3909 1 628/761 3844,5177

παρατυγχάνω, *paratunkano.*

Acts17:17. daily with them *that met with* him.

3910 1 628/761 3844,846

παραυτίκα, *parautika.*

2Co. 4:17. affliction, which is *but for a moment*,

3911 2 628/761 3844,5342

παραφέρω *paraphero.*

Mar 14:36. *take away* this cup from me:
Lu. 22:42. *remove* this cup from me:

3912 1 628/761 3844,5426

παραφρονέω, *paraphroneo.*

2Co.11:23. I speak *as a fool*

3913 1 628/761 3912

παραφρονία, *paraphronia.*

2Pet. 2:16. forbad the *madness* of the prophet.

3914 4 629/761 3844,5492

παραχειμάζω, *parakīmazo.*

Acts27:12. to Phenice, (and there) *to winter*;
28:11. *which had wintered* in the isle,
1Co.16: 6. yea, and *winter* with you, that
Tit. 3:12. I have determined there *to winter*

3915 1 629/761 3914

παραχειμασία, parakīmasia.

Acts27:12. haven was not commodious *to winter in,*

3916 19 629/761 3844,5536

παραχρῆμα, parakreema.

Mat.21:19. And *presently* the fig tree withered
20. How *soon* is the fig tree withered
Lu. 1:64. mouth was opened *immediately,*
4:39. and *immediately* she arose and
5:25. And *immediately* he rose up
8:44. and *immediately* her issue of blood
47. how she was healed *immediately.*
55. and she arose *straightway:*
13:13. and *immediately* she was made straight,
18:43. And *immediately* he received his sight,
19:11. of God should *immediately* appear.
22:60. And *immediately,* while he yet spake,
Acts 3: 7. and *immediately* his feet and ancle
5:10. Then fell she down *straightway* at
9:18. and he received sight *forthwith,*
12:23. And *immediately* the angel of the
13:11. And *immediately* there fell on
16:26. and *immediately* all the doors were
33. he and all his, *straightway.*

3917 1 629/761 *pardos* (panther)

πάρδαλις, pardalis.

Rev.13: 2. which I saw was like unto a *leopard,*

3918 23 629/761 5:858 3844,1510

πάρειμι, parīmi.

Mat.26:50. Friend, wherefore *art* thou *come?*
Lu. 13: 1. There *were present* at that season
Joh. 7: 6. My time *is* not yet *come:*
11:28. The Master *is come,* and
Acts10:21. the cause wherefore ye *are come?*
33. Now therefore *are* we all *here present*
12:20. they *came* with one accord to him,
17: 6. *are come* hither also;
24:19. ought *to have been here* before thee,
1Co. 5: 3. but *present* in spirit, have judged already, as *though* I *were present,*
2Co.10: 2. may not be bold *when* I *am present*
11. also in deed *when* we *are present.*
11: 9(8). And *when* I *was present* with you,
13: 2. as *if* I *were present,*
10. lest *being present* I should use
Gal. 4:18. when I *am present* with you.
20. I desire *to be present* with you
Col. 1: 6. *Which is come* unto you,
Heb 12:11. no chastening for the *present*
13: 5. content with such things as ye have: (lit. things *that are present*)
2Pet. 1: 9. But he that lacketh (lit. to whom *are* not *present*) these things is blind,
12. established in the *present* truth.

3919 1 630/761 5:824 3844,1521

παρεισάγω, parīsago.

2Pet. 2: 1. who *privily shall bring in* damnable

3920 1 630/761 5:824 3919

παρείσακτος, parīsaktos.

Gal. 2: 4. because of false brethren *unawares brought in.*

3921 1 630/761 3844,1519,1416

παρεισδύνω, parīsduno.

Jude 4. For there *are* certain men *crept in unawares,*

3922 2 630/761 2:666 3844,1525

παρεισέρχομαι, parīserkomai.

Ro. 5:20. Moreover the law *entered,* that the
Gal. 2: 4. who *came in privily* to spy out our

3923 1 630/762 3844,1533

παρεισφέρω, parīsphero.

2Pet. 1: 5. *giving* all diligence, add to

3924 3 630/762 3844,1622

παρεκτός, parektos.

Mat. 5:32. *saving* for the cause of fornication.
Acts26:29. such as I am, *except* these bonds.
2Co.11:28. Beside those things that are *without,*

3925 10 630/762 3844,1685

παρεμβολή, parembolee.

Acts21:34. to be carried into the *castle.*
37. Paul was to be led into the *castle,*
22:24. to be brought into the *castle,*
23:10. to bring (him) into the *castle.*
16. entered into the *castle,* and told Paul.
32. and returned to the *castle:*
Heb 11:34. turned to flight the *armies* of the aliens.
13:11. are burned without the *camp.*
13. unto him without the *camp,*
Rev.20: 9. and compassed the *camp* of the saints

3926 1 631/762 3844,1776

παρενοχλέω, parenokleo.

Acts15:19. that we *trouble* not them, which

3927 3 631/762 2:63 3844rt1927

παρεπίδημος, parepideemos.

Heb 11:13. confessed that they were strangers and *pilgrims*
1Pet. 1: 1. to the *strangers* scattered throughout
2:11. as strangers and *pilgrims,* abstain

3928 31 631/762 2:666 3844,2064

παρέρχομαι, parerkomai.

Mat. 5:18. Till heaven and earth *pass,*
— one tittle shall in no wise *pass* from
8:28. that no man might *pass* by that way.
14:15. and the time *is* now *past;*
24:34. This generation shall not *pass,* till
35. Heaven and earth *shall pass away,* but my words shall not *pass away.*
26:39. *let* this cup *pass* from me:
42. if this cup may not *pass away*
Mar 6:48. and would have *passed by* them.
13:30. this generation shall not *pass,* till
31. Heaven and earth *shall pass away.* but my words shall not *pass away.*
14:35. the hour *might pass* from him.
Lu. 11:42. and *pass over* judgment and
12:37. and will *come forth and* serve them.
15:29. neither *transgressed* I at any time
16:17. it is easier for heaven and earth *to pass,*
17: 7. *Go and* sit down to meat?
18:37. that Jesus of Nazareth *passeth by*

Lu. 21:32. This generation shall not *pass away*,
33. Heaven and earth *shall pass away*: but my words shall not *pass away*.
Acts16: 8. And they *passing by* Mysia
24: 7. the chief captain Lysias *came* (upon us), *and*
27: 9. because the fast *was* now already *past*,
2Co. 5:17. old things *are passed away*;
Jas. 1:10. of the grass he *shall pass away*.
1Pet. 4: 3. For the time *past* of (our) life
2Pet. 3:10. the heavens *shall pass away*
Rev.21: 1. first earth *were passed away*;

3929 1 631/762 1:509 2935

πάρεσις, paresis.

Ro. 3:25. for the *remission* of sins that are past,

3930 16 631/762 3844,2192

παρέχω, pareko.

Mat.26:10. Why trouble ye (lit. *give* ye trouble to) the woman?
Mar14: 6. why trouble ye her? (lit. *give* &c.)
Lu. 6:29. (one) cheek *offer* also the other;
7: 4. worthy for whom he should *do* this:
11: 7. Trouble me not: (lit. *give* me not &c.)
18: 5. because this widow troubleth me, (lit. *giveth* &c.)
Acts16:16. which *brought* her masters much
17:31. (whereof) he hath *given* assurance
19:24. *brought* no small gain unto the
22: 2. they *kept* the more silence:
28: 2. *shewed* us no little kindness:
Gal. 6:17 let no man trouble me: (lit. *let* none *give* &c.)
Col. 4: 1. *give* unto (your) servants that
1Ti. 1: 4. which *minister* questions,
6:17. *who giveth* us richly all things to
Tit. 2: 7. *shewing* thyself a pattern of good works:

3931 1 632/762 3844,58

παρηγορία, pareegoria.

Col. 4:11. which have been a *comfort* unto me.

3932 1 632/762 3933

παρθενία, parthenia.

Lu. 2:36. seven years from her *virginity*;

3933 14 632/762 5:826

παρθένος, parthenos.

Mat. 1:23. Behold, a *virgin* shall be with child
25: 1. ten *virgins*, which took their
7. Then all those *virgins* arose
11. came also the other *virgins*
Lu. 1:27. To a *virgin* espoused to a
— and the *virgin's* name (was) Mary.
Acts21: 9. had four daughters, *virgins*,
1Co. 7:25. Now concerning *virgins* I have no
28. and if a *virgin* marry,
34. between a wife and a *virgin*.
36. uncomely toward his *virgin*,
37. keep his *virgin*, doeth well.
2Co.11: 2: a chaste *virgin* to Christ.
Rev.14: 4. for they are *virgins*.

3936 2 633/763 5:837 3844,2476

παριστάνω, paristano.

Ro. 6:13. Neither *yield* ye your members
16. that to whom ye *yield* yourselves

3936 39 633/763 5:837 3844,2476

παρίστημι, paristeemi.

Mat.26:53. and he *shall presently give* me more
Mar 4:29. because the harvest *is come*,
14:47. one of them *that stood by* drew
69. began to say to them *that stood by*.
70. they *that stood by* said again
15:35. some of them *that stood by*, when
39. centurion, *which stood* over against him,
Lu. 1:19. Gabriel, *that stand* in the presence
2:22. *to present* (him) to the Lord;
19:24. he said unto them *that stood by*,
Joh. 18:22. one of the officers *which stood by*
19:26. and the disciple *standing by*,
Acts 1: 3. To whom also he *shewed* himself
10. two men *stood by* them in white
4:10. *doth* this man *stand here* before you
26. The kings of the earth *stood up*,
9:39. and all the widows *stood by* him weeping
41. *presented* her alive.
23: 2. them *that stood by* him to smite
4. they *that stood by* said,
24. And *provide* (them) beasts,
33. *presented* Paul also before him.
24:13. Neither can they *prove* the things
27:23. For there *stood by* me this night
24. thou must *be brought before* (lit. *stand before*) Cæsar:
Ro. 6:13. but *yield* yourselves unto God,
19. as ye *have yielded* your members
— so now *yield* your members
12: 1. that ye *present* your bodies a
14:10. we *shall* all *stand before* the
16: 2. and that ye *assist* her in whatsoever
1Co. 8: 8. But meat *commendeth* us not to God:
2Co. 4:14. and *shall present* (us) with you.
11: 2. that I may *present* (you as) a chaste
Eph. 5:27. That he *might present* it to himself
Col. 1:22. *to present* you holy and unblameable
28. that we *may present* every man
2Ti. 2:15. Study *to shew* thyself approved
4:17. the Lord *stood with* me, and

3935 1 636/763 3844 hiēmi(to send)

παρίεμαι, pariemai.

Heb 12:12. lift up the hands *which hang down*,

3938 1 634/763 3844,3598

πάροδος, parodos.

1Co.16: 7. For I will not see you now by the *way*;

3939 2 634/763 5:841 3844,3611

παροικέω, paroikeo.

Lu. 24:18. *Art* thou only *a stranger* in Jerusalem,
Heb 11: 9. he *sojourned in* the land of promise, as (in) a strange country,

3940 2 634/763 5:841 3941

παροικία, paroikia.

Acts13:17. when they dwelt as strangers (lit. in the *sojourning*)
1Pet. 1:17. pass the time of your *sojourning* (here)

3941 4 634/763 5:841 3844,3624

πάροικος, paroikos.

Acts 7: 6. his seed should *sojourn* in a strange land
29. and was a *stranger* in the land of
Eph 2:19. no more strangers and *foreigners*.
1Pet. 2:11. as *strangers* and pilgrims,

3942 5 634/764 5:854 3844,3633

παροιμία, paroimia.

Joh.10: 6. This *parable* spake Jesus
16:25. have I spoken unto you in *proverbs*:
— no more speak unto you in *proverbs*,
29. and speakest no *proverb*.
2Pet. 2:22. according to the true *proverb*,

3945 1 634/764 5:186 3946

παρομοιάζω, paromoiazo.

Mat.23.27. for ye *are like unto* whited sepulchres,

3946 2 634/764 5:186 3844,3664

παρόμοιος, paromoios.

Mar 7: 8. and many other such *like* things ye
13. and many such *like* things do ye.

3943 2 634/764 3844,3631

πάροινος, paroinos.

1Ti. 3: 3. Not *given to wine*, no striker,
Tit. 1: 7. not soon angry, not *given to wine*,

3944 1 634/764 3844 . oichomai (to depart)

παροίχομαι, paroikomai.

Acts14 16. Who in times *past* suffered all

3947 2 634/764 3844,3691

παροξύνομαι, paroxunomai.

Acts17:16. his spirit *was stirred* in him,
1Co.13: 5. *is* not *easily provoked*,

3948 2 634/764 5:857 3947

παροξυσμός, paroxusmos.

Acts15:39. And the *contention* was *so sharp*
Heb 10:24. *to provoke unto* love and to

3949 2 635/764 5:382 3844,3710

παροργίζω, parorgizo.

Ro. 10:19. by a foolish nation I *will anger* you.
Eph 6: 4. ye fathers, *provoke* not your children *to wrath*:

3950 1 635/764 5:382 3949

παροργισμός, parorgismos.

Eph 4:26. let not the sun go down upon your *wrath*:

3951 1 635/764 5:857 3844 otrunō (to spur)

παροτρύνω, parotruno.

Acts13:50. But the Jews *stirred up* the devout

3952 24 635/764 5:858 3918

παρουσία, parousia.

Mat.24: 3. what (shall be) the sign of thy *coming*,
27. so shall also the *coming* of the Son of
37. so shall also the *coming* of the Son
39. so shall also the *coming* of the Son
1Co.15:23. they that are Christ's at his *coming*.
16:17. glad of the *coming* of Stephanas
2Co. 7: 6. by the *coming* of Titus;
7. And not by his *coming* only,
10:10. but (his) bodily *presence* (is) weak,
Phi. 1:26. by my *coming* to you again.
Phi. 2:12. not as in my *presence* only,
1Th. 2:19. Christ at his *coming*?
3:13. at the *coming* of our Lord Jesus
4:15. (and) remain unto the *coming* of
5:23. unto the *coming* of our Lord
2Th. 2: 1. by the *coming* of our Lord
8. the brightness of his *coming*:
9. (Even him), whose *coming* is after
Jas. 5: 7. unto the *coming* of the Lord.
8. for the *coming* of the Lord draweth nigh.
2Pet. 1:16. the power and *coming* of our Lord
3: 4. Where is the promise of his *coming*?
12. and hasting unto the *coming* of the day
1Joh. 2:28. before him at his *coming*.

3953 2 635/764 3844,rt 3795

παροψίς, paropsis.

Mat.23:25. the outside of the cup and of the *platter*,
26. that (which is) within the cup and *platter*

3954 51 635/764 5:871 3956,4483

παῤῥησία, parreesia.

Note.—The dative case is used adverbially.

Mar 8:32. And he spake that saying *openly*.
Joh. 7: 4. seeketh to be known *openly*.
13. no man spake *openly* of him
26. But, lo, he speaketh *boldly*,
10:24. If thou be the Christ, tell us *plainly*.
11:14. Then said Jesus unto them *plainly*
54. walked no more *openly*
16:25. but I shall shew you *plainly*
29. Lo, now speakest thou *plainly*,
18:20. I spake *openly* to the world;
Acts 2:29. let me *freely* speak unto you
4:13. when they saw the *boldness* of
29. with all *boldness* they may speak
31. and they spake the word of God with *boldness*.
28:31. with all *confidence*, no man forbidding
2Co. 3:12. we use great *plainness* of speech:
7: 4. Great (is) my *boldness of speech*
Eph 3:12. In whom we have *boldness*
6:19. may open my mouth *boldly*,
Phi. 1:20. but (that) with all *boldness*,
Col. 2:15. he made a shew of them *openly*,
1Ti. 3:13. and great *boldness* in the faith
Philem. 8. though I might be much *bold* in
Heb 3: 6. if we hold fast the *confidence*
4:16. Let us therefore come *boldly*
10:19. *boldness* to enter into the holiest
35. your *confidence*, which hath
1Joh. 2:28. we may have *confidence*,
3:21. (then) have we *confidence* toward
4:17. that we may have *boldness* in
5:14. this is the *confidence* that

3955 9 636/765 5:871 3954

παῤῥησιάζομαι, parreesiazomai.

Acts 9:27. how he had *preached boldly* at Damascus
29(28). And he spake *boldly* (lit. *having boldness*) in the name
13:46. Paul and Barnabas *waxed bold*, and
14: 3. *speaking boldly* in the Lord,
18:26. he began *to speak boldly* in the
19: 8. and *spake boldly* for the space of
26:26. before whom also I speak *freely*:
Eph 6:20. I *may speak boldly*, as I ought
1Th. 2: 2. we *were bold* in our God to speak

3956 1243 636/765 5:886
πᾶς, πᾶσα, πᾶν, pas, pasa, pan.

denotes it to be used with ὅστις: [3] with ὅσος: and one of the two words is frequently omitted in the rendering.

Mat. 1:17. So *all* the generations from Abraham
2: 3. and *all* Jerusalem with him.
4. had gathered *all* the chief priests
16. and slew *all* the children that
— and in *all* the coasts thereof,
3: 5. and *all* Judæa, and *all* the region round about Jordan,
10. therefore *every* tree which
15. us to fulfil *all* righteousness.
4: 4. but by *every* word that proceedeth
8. and sheweth him *all* the kingdoms
9. *All* these things will I give thee,
23. healing *all manner of* sickness and *all manner of* disease among the
24. brought unto him *all* sick people
5:11. and shall say *all manner of* evil
15. giveth light unto *all* that are in
18. till *all* be fulfilled.
22. That *whosoever* is angry with his brother
28. *whosoever* looketh on a woman
6:29. Solomon in *all* his glory was not
32. For after *all* these things do the
33. and *all* these things shall be added
7: 8. For *every one* that asketh receiveth;
12. Therefore *all*[3] things whatsoever
17. Even so *every* good tree bringeth
19. *Every* tree that bringeth not forth
21. Not *every one* that saith unto me,
24. Therefore *whosoever*[2] heareth
26. And *every one* that heareth
8:16. and healed *all* that were sick:
32. and, behold, the *whole* herd of swine
33. and told *every* thing,
34. *the whole* city came out to meet
9:35. Jesus went about *all* the cities
— healing *every* sickness and *every* disease among the people.
10: 1. and to heal *all manner of* sickness and *all manner of* disease.
22. ye shall be hated of *all* (men) for
30. hairs of your head are *all* numbered.
32. *Whosoever*[2] therefore shall confess
11:13. For *all* the prophets and the law
27. *All* things are delivered unto me
28. Come unto me, *all* (ye) that labour
12:15. and he healed them *all*;
23. And *all* the people were amazed,
25. *Every* kingdom divided against
— and *every* city or house divided
31. *All manner of* sin and blasphemy
36. That *every* idle word that men
13: 2. and *the whole* multitude stood
19. When *any one* heareth the word
32. is the least of *all* seeds:
34. *All* these things spake Jesus
41. out of his kingdom *all* things that
44. and selleth *all*[3] that he hath,
46. went and sold *all*[3] that he had,
47. and gathered of *every* kind:
51. Have ye understood *all* these things?
52. Therefore *every* scribe (which is)
56. sisters, are they not *all* with us?
— this (man) *all* these things?
14:20. And they did *all* eat, and
35. and brought unto him *all* that were

Mat.15:13. *Every* plant, which my heavenly
17. *whatsoever* entereth in at the mouth
37. And they did *all* eat, and were filled:
17:11. first come, and restore *all* things.
18:10. angels do *always* (διὰ παντὸς) behold
16. *every* word may be established.
19. as touching *any* thing that they
25. and *all*[3] that he had,
26. and I will pay thee *all*.
29. and I will pay thee *all*.
31. told unto their lord *all* that was done.
32. I forgave thee *all* that debt,
34. till he should pay *all* that was due
19: 3. put away his wife for *every* cause?
11. *All* (men) cannot receive this saying,
20. *All* these things have I kept from
26. with God *all* things are possible.
27. we have forsaken *all*, and followed thee
29. And *every one* that hath forsaken
21:10. *all* the city was moved, saying, Who
12. and cast out *all* them that sold
22. *all*[3] things, whatsoever ye shall ask
26. for *all* hold John as a prophet.
22: 4. and *all* things (are) ready: come
10. and gathered together *all*[3] as many
27. And last of *all* the woman died also
28. for they *all* had her.
23: 3. *All*[3] therefore whatsoever they bid
5. But *all* their works they do for
8. and *all* ye are brethren.
20. and by *all* things thereon.
27. bones, and of *all* uncleanness.
35. may come *all* the righteous blood
36. *All* these things shall come
24: 2. See ye not *all* these things?
6. for *all* (these things) must come to pass,
8. *All* these (are) the beginning of sorrows.
9. ye shall be hated of *all* nations for
14. for a witness unto *all* nations;
22. there should no (lit. not *any*) flesh be saved:
30. then shall *all* the tribes of the earth
33. when ye shall see *all* these things,
34. till *all* these things be fulfilled.
47. ruler over *all* his goods.
25: 5. they *all* slumbered and slept.
7. Then *all* those virgins arose,
29. For unto *every one* that hath
31. and *all* the holy angels with
32. before him shall be gathered *all* nations:
26: 1. when Jesus had finished *all* these sayings
27. saying, Drink ye *all* of it;
31. *All* ye shall be offended because
33. Though *all* (men) shall be offended
35. Likewise also said *all* the disciples.
52. for *all* they that take the sword
56. Then *all* the disciples forsook him,
70. But he denied before (them) *all*, saying
27: 1. morning was come, *all* the chief priests
22. (They) *all* say unto him, Let him
25. Then answered *all* the people,
45. there was darkness over *all* the lan
28:18. *All* power is given unto me in
19. and teach *all* nations,
20. to observe *all*[3] things whatsoever
— lo, I am with you *alway*, (πάσας τὸς ἡμέρας)
Mar 1: 5. went out unto him *all* the land of
— and were *all* baptized of him in
27. And they were *all* amazed,
32. brought unto him *all* that were diseased.
37. *All* (men) seek for thee.

Mar 2:12. went forth before them *all;* insomuch that they were *all* amazed,
13. and *all* the multitude resorted
3:28. *All* sins shall be forgiven
4: 1. and the *whole* multitude was
11. *all* (these) things are done in parables:
13. how then will ye know *all* parables?
31. is less than *all* the seeds that be
32. becometh greater than *all* herbs,
34. he expounded *all* things to his disciples.
5:12. And *all* the devils besought
20. and *all* (men) did marvel.
26. and had spent *all* that she had,
33. and told him *all* the truth.
6:30. and told him *all* things, both
33. ran afoot thither out of *all* cities,
39. to make *all* sit down by
41. fishes divided he among them *all.*
42. And they did *all* eat,
50. For they *all* saw him, and were troubled.
7: 3. and *all* the Jews, except they wash
14. when he had called *all* the people
— Hearken unto me *every one* (of you),
18. that *whatsoever* thing from without
19. purging *all* meats?
23. *All* these evil things come from
37. He hath done *all* things well:
9:12. and restoreth *all* things;
15. And straightway *all* the people,
23. *all* things (are) possible to him that
35. (the same) shall be last of *all*, and servant of *all.*
49. *every one* shall be salted with fire, and *every* sacrifice
10:20. *all* these have I observed from
27. with God *all* things are possible.
28. Lo, we have left *all*, and have
44. chiefest, shall be servant of *all.*
11:11. looked round about upon *all* things,
17. called of *all* nations the house of prayer?
18. *all* the people was astonished at
24. *What* things *soever*[3] ye desire, when ye
12:22. last of *all* the woman died also.
28. Which is the first commandment of *all?*
29. The first of *all* the commandments (is),
33. is more than *all* whole burnt offerings
43. hath cast more in, than *all* they
44. For *all* (they) did cast in of their
— did cast in *all*[3] that she had,
13: 4. when *all* these things shall be
10. be published among *all* nations.
13. hated of *all* (men) for my name's
20. no (lit. not *any*) flesh should be saved:
23. behold, I have foretold you *all* things.
30. till *all* these things be done.
37. I say unto *all*, Watch.
14:23. and they *all* drank of it.
27. *All* ye shall be offended because
29. Although *all* shall be offended,
31. Likewise also said they *all.*
36. *all* things (are) possible unto thee;
50. And they *all* forsook him, and fled.
53. were assembled *all* the chief priests
64. And they *all* condemned him to
16:15. and preach the gospel to *every* creature.
Lu. 1: 3. perfect understanding of *all* things
6. walking in *all* the commandments
10. And the *whole* multitude of the
37. with God nothing (lit. not *any* thing) shall be impossible.
48. from henceforth *all* generations shall
63. And they marvelled *all.*

Lu. 1:65. And fear came on *all* that dwelt
— and *all* these sayings were noised
66. And *all* they that heard (them)
71. and from the hand of *all* that hate us:
75. before him, *all* the days of our life.
2: 1. that *all* the world should be taxed.
3. And *all* went to be taxed, every
10. which shall be to *all* people.
18. And *all* they that heard (it) wondered
19. But Mary kept *all* these things.
20. praising God for *all* the things
23. *Every* male that openeth the
31. before the face of *all* people;
38. and spake of him to *all* them that
47. And *all* that heard him were astonished
51. his mother kept *all* these sayings
3: 3. he came into *all* the country about
5. *Every* valley shall be filled, and *every* mountain and hill
6. And *all* flesh shall see the
9. *every* tree therefore which
15. and *all* men mused in their hearts
19. and for *all* the evils which Herod
20. Added yet this above *all*, that he
4: 4. but by *every* word of God.
5. shewed unto him *all* the kingdoms
7. worship me, *all* shall be thine.
13. the devil had ended *all* the temptation,
15. being glorified of *all.*
20. And the eyes of *all* them that
22. And *all* bare him witness,
25. famine was throughout *all* the land;
28. And *all* they in the synagogue,
36. And they were *all* amazed,
37. of him went out into *every* place
40. *all*[3] they that had any sick
5: 9. and *all* that were with him,
17. out of *every* town of Galilee,
6:10. round about upon them *all*,
17. people out of *all* Judæa and
19. And the *whole* multitude sought
— and healed (them) *all.*
26. when *all* men shall speak well
30. Give to *every* man that asketh
40. but *every one* that is perfect
47. *Whosoever* cometh to me, and
7: 1. when he had ended *all* his sayings
17. throughout *all* the region round about.
18. shewed him of *all* these things.
29. And *all* the people that heard (him),
35. wisdom is justified of *all* her children.
8:40. for they were *all* waiting for him.
45. When *all* denied, Peter and they that
47. declared unto him before *all* the people
52. And *all* wept, and bewailed
54. And he put them *all* out, and took
9: 1. and authority over *all* devils, and to
7. heard of *all* that was done by him:
13. buy meat for *all* this people.
17. and were *all* filled:
23. he said to (them) *all*, If any (man) will
43. And they were *all* amazed at the
— while they wondered *every one* at *all* things which Jesus did,
48. that is least among you *all*, the same
10: 1. into *every* city and place, whither he
19. and over *all* the power of the enemy:
22. *All* things are delivered to me of
4. for we also forgive *every one* that
10. For *every one* that asketh receiveth;
17. *Every* kingdom divided against
41. and, behold, *all* things are clean

Lu. 11:42. rue and *all manner of* herbs,
50. That the blood of *all* the prophets,
12:7. hairs of your head are *all* numbered.
8. *Whosoever* shall confess me before
10. And *whosoever* shall speak a word
18. there will I bestow *all* my fruits
27. Solomon in *all* his glory was not
30. For *all* these things do the nations
31. and *all* these things shall be added
41. this parable unto us, or even to *all?*
44. make him ruler over *all* that he hath.
48. For unto *whomsoever* much is
13: 2. were sinners above *all* the Galilæans,
3. ye shall *all* likewise perish.
4. sinners above *all* men that
5. ye shall *all* likewise perish.
17. *all* his adversaries were ashamed: and *all* the people rejoiced for *all* the glorious
27. depart from me, *all* (ye) workers
28. and *all* the prophets, in the kingdom
14:11. For *whosoever* exalteth himself
17. Come; for *all* things are now ready.
18. And they *all* with one (consent)
29. *all* that behold (it) begin to
33. *whosoever* he be of you that forsaketh not *all* that he hath,
15: 1. *all* the publicans and sinners
14. And when he had spent *all*,
31. and *all* that I have is thine.
16:14. covetous, heard *all* these things:
16. and *every* man presseth into it.
18. *Whosoever* putteth away his wife,
— and *whosoever* marrieth her
26. And beside *all* this, between us
17:10. when ye shall have done *all*
18:12. I give tithes of *all*³ that I possess.
14. *every one* that exalteth himself
21. *All* these have I kept from
22. sell *all*³ that thou hast, and
28. Lo, we have left *all*, and followed
31. and *all* things that are written
43. and *all* the people, when they saw
19:26. That unto *every one* which hath
37. with a loud voice for *all* the mighty
20: 6. *all* the people will stone us:
18. *Whosoever* shall fall upon that
32. Last of *all* the woman died also.
38. for *all* live unto him.
45. Then in the audience of *all* the people
21: 3. cast in more than they *all:*
15. which *all* your adversaries
17. be hated of *all* (men) for my
22. that *all* things which are written
24. captive into *all* nations:
29. Behold the fig tree, and *all* the trees;
32. shall not pass away, till *all* be fulfilled.
35. shall it come on *all* them that dwell on the face of the *whole* earth.
36. and pray *always*, (ἐν παντὶ καιρῷ)
— to escape *all* these things
38. And *all* the people came early
22:70. Then said they *all*, Art thou then
23:48. And *all* the people that came
49. And *all* his acquaintance,
24: 9. told *all* these things unto the eleven, and to *all* the rest.
14. talked together of *all* these things
19. before God and *all* the people:
21. and beside *all* this, to day is
25. slow of heart to believe *all* that
27. at Moses and *all* the prophets, he expounded unto them in *all* the scriptures

Lu. 24:44. that *all* things must be fulfilled,
47. among *all* nations, beginning at
Joh. 1: 3. *All* things were made by him;
7. that *all* (men) through him
9. which lighteth *every* man that
16. fulness have *all* we received,
2:10. *Every* man at the beginning
15. he drove them *all* out of the temple,
24. because he knew *all* (men),
3: 8. so is *every one* that is born of
15. That *whosoever* believeth in him
16. that *whosoever* believeth in him
20. For *every one* that doeth evil
26. and *all* (men) come to him.
31. that cometh from above is above *all:*
— that cometh from heaven is above *all.*
35. given *all* things into his hand.
4:13. *Whosoever* drinketh of this water
25. he will tell us *all* things.
29. which told me *all*³ things that
39. He told me *all*³ that ever I did.
45. having seen *all* the things that he
5:20. and sheweth him *all* things
22. hath committed *all* judgment unto
23. That *all* (men) should honour the
28. *all* that are in the graves shall
6:37. *All* that the Father giveth me
39. of *all* which he hath given me
40. *every one* which seeth the Son,
45. they shall be *all* taught of God.
— *Every* man therefore that
7:21. I have done one work, and ye *all* marvel.
8: 2. and *all* the people came unto
34. *Whosoever* committeth sin is
10: 8. *All*³ that ever came before me
29. gave (them) me, is greater than *all;*
41. but *all*³ things that John spake
11:26. And *whosoever* liveth and believeth
48. *all* (men) will believe on him:
12:32. will draw *all* (men) unto me.
46. that *whosoever* believeth on me
13: 3. Father had given *all* things
10. ye are clean, but not *all.*
11. Ye are not *all* clean.
18. I speak not of you *all:*
35. By this shall *all* (men) know
14:26. he shall teach you *all* things, and bring *all* things to your remembrance, whatsoever
15: 2. *Every* branch in me that
— and *every* (branch) that beareth
15. for *all* things that I have heard
21. But *all* these things will the
16: 2. that *whosoever* killeth you will
13. he will guide you into *all* truth:
15. *All*³ things that the Father hath
30. that thou knowest *all* things, and
17: 2. given him power over *all* flesh,
— eternal life to *as many as* (πᾶν ὃ) thou hast given him.
7. known that *all*³ things whatsoever
10. And *all* mine are thine,
21. That they *all* may be one;
18: 4. knowing *all* things that should come upon
37. *Every one* that is of the truth
40. Then cried they *all* again, saying,
19:12. *whosoever* maketh himself a king
28. that *all* things were now accomplished,
21:17. Lord, thou knowest *all* things;
Acts 1: 1. of *all* that Jesus began both to do
8. and in *all* Judæa, and in Samaria,
14. These *all* continued with one accord
18. and *all* his bowels gushed out.

Acts 1:19. It was known unto *all* the dwellers
21. companied with us *all* the time that
24. which knowest the hearts of *all* (men,
2: 5. out of *every* nation under heaven.
7. And they were *all* amazed and
— are not *all* these which speak
12. And they were *all* amazed,
17. out of my Spirit upon *all* flesh:
21. *whosoever* shall call on the name
25. I foresaw the Lord *always* (διὰ παντὸς)
32. whereof we *all* are witnesses.
36. Therefore let *all* the house of Israel
39. and to *all* that are afar off,
43. And fear came upon *every* soul:
44. *all* that believed were together,
45. and parted them to *all* (men), as
3: 9. And *all* the people saw him walking
11. *all* the people ran together
16. in the presence of you *all*.
18. by the mouth of *all* his prophets,
21. of restitution of *all* things, which
— by the mouth of *all* his holy prophets
22. hear in *all*[3] things whatsoever
23. come to pass, (that) *every*[2] soul, which
24. Yea, and *all* the prophets from
25. in thy seed shall *all* the kindreds
4:10. Be it known unto you *all*, and to *all* the people of Israel,
16. (is) manifest to *all* them that dwell
21. for *all* (men) glorified God for
24. sea, and *all* that in them is:
29. that with *all* boldness they
33. and great grace was upon them *all*.
5: 5. and great fear came on *all*
11. upon *as many as* heard
17. and *all* they that were with him,
20. *all* the words of this life.
21. and *all* the senate of the
23. found we shut with *all* safety,
34. in reputation among *all* the people,
36. and *all*,[3] as many as obeyed him,
37. and *all*,[3] (even) as many as obeyed
42. And daily (lit. *every* day) in the temple,
6: 5. pleased the *whole* multitude:
7:10. And delivered him out of *all* his afflictions,
14. and *all* his kindred, threescore and
22. learned in *all* the wisdom of the
50. my hand made *all* these things?
8: 1. and they were *all* scattered abroad
10. To whom they *all* gave heed,
27. the charge of *all* her treasure,
40. he preached in *all* the cities,
9:14. to bind *all* that call on thy name.
21. But *all* that heard (him)
26. but they were *all* afraid of him
32. throughout *all* (quarters),
35. And *all* that dwelt at Lydda
39. and *all* the widows stood by
40. But Peter put them *all* forth, and
10: 2. feared God with *all* his house,
12. Wherein were *all manner of* fourfooted
14. I have never eaten *any* thing that is
33. Now therefore are we *all* here
— to hear *all* things that
35. But in *every* nation he that
36. he is Lord of *all*:
38. healing *all* that were oppressed of
39. we are witnesses of *all* things which
41. Not to *all* the people, but unto
43. To him give *all* the prophets witness,
— *whosoever* believeth in him
44. the Holy Ghost fell on *all* them

Acts 11: 8. for nothing (lit. not *any* thing) common
14. whereby thou and *all* thy house
23. and exhorted them *all*, that with
12:11. and (from) *all* the expectation of
13:10. O full of *all* subtilty and *all* mischief,
— (thou) enemy of *all* righteousness,
22. which shall fulfil *all* my will. [plural]
24. repentance to *all* the people of Israel.
27. which are read *every* sabbath day,
39. And by him *all* that believe are justified from *all* things, from
44. came almost the *whole* city
14:15. and *all* things that are therein:
16. in times past suffered *all* nations
15: 3. caused great joy unto *all* the brethren.
12. Then *all* the multitude kept silence,
17. and *all* the Gentiles, upon whom
— who doeth *all* these things.
18. Known unto God are *all* his works
21. read in the synagogues *every* sabbath day
36. visit our brethren in *every* city
16:26. immediately *all* the doors were opened, and *every one's* bands
32. to *all* that were in his house.
33. and was baptized, he and *all* his,
17: 7. and these *all* do contrary to
11. received the word with *all* readiness
17. in the market daily (lit. on *every* day)
21. For *all* the Athenians and
22. I perceive that in *all* things ye
24. made the world and *all* things
25. he giveth to *all* life, and breath, and *all* things;
26. made of one blood *all* nations of men for to dwell on *all* the face of
30. now commandeth *all* men every where
31. hath given assurance unto *all*
18: 2. Claudius had commanded *all* Jews
4. reasoned in the synagogue *every* sabbath,
17. Then *all* the Greeks took Sosthenes,
23. strengthening *all* the disciples.
19: 7. And *all* the men were about twelve.
10. so that *all* they which dwelt in Asia
17. this was known to *all* the Jews
— and fear fell on them *all*,
19. and burned them before *all* (men).
26. almost throughout *all* Asia, this Paul
34. *all* with one voice about the
20:18. been with you at *all* seasons,
19. with *all* humility of mind,
25. I know that ye *all*, among whom
26. pure from the blood of *all*
27. *all* the counsel of God.
28. and to *all* the flock, over the which
32. among *all* them which are sanctified
35. I have shewed you *all* things,
36. and prayed with them *all*.
37. And they *all* wept sore, and
21: 5. and they *all* brought us on our way,
18. and *all* the elders were present.
20. and they are *all* zealous of the law:
21. that thou teachest *all* the Jews which
24. and *all* may know that those things,
27. stirred up *all* the people, and laid
28. that teacheth *all* (men) every where
22: 3. as ye *all* are this day.
5. and *all* the estate of the elders:
10. it shall be told thee of *all* things
12. having a good report of *all* the Jews
15. shalt be his witness unto *all* men of
23: 1. I have lived in *all* good conscience
24: 3. most noble Felix, with *all* thankfulness

Acts24: 5. a mover of sedition among *all* the Jews
8. mayest take knowledge of *all* these things,
14. believing *all* things which are written
25:24. King Agrippa, and *all* men which
-- about whom *all* the multitude of
26: 2. touching *all* the things whereof
3. to be expert in *all* customs and
4. know *all* the Jews;
11. I punished them oft in *every* synagogue,
14. when we were *all* fallen to the earth,
20. and throughout *all* the coasts of Judæa,
29. but also *all* that hear me this day,
27:20. *all* hope that we should be saved
24. God hath given thee *all* them
35. in presence of them *all*:
36. Then were they *all* of good cheer,
37. we were in *all* in the ship (lit. *all* the souls)
44. they escaped *all* safe to land.
28: 2. and received us *every one*, because
30. and received *all* that came in unto him,
31. with *all* confidence, no man
Ro. 1: 5. faith among *all* nations, for
7. To *all* that be in Rome,
8. through Jesus Christ for you *all*,
16. salvation to *every one* that believeth;
18. against *all* ungodliness and
29. Being filled with *all* unrighteousness,
2: 1. O man, *whosoever* thou art that
9. upon *every* soul of man that
10. to *every* man that worketh good,
3: 2. Much *every* way: chiefly, because
4. but *every* man a liar; as it is
9. that they are *all* under sin;
12. They are *all* gone out of the way,
19. that *every* mouth may be stopped, and *all* the world may
20. there shall no (lit. not *any*) flesh be
22. unto *all* and upon *all* them that believe:
23. For *all* have sinned, and come
4:11. might be the father of *all* them that
16. might be sure to *all* the seed;
— who is the father of us *all*,
5:12. and so death passed upon *all* men, for that *all* have sinned:
18. upon *all* men to condemnation;
— upon *all* men unto justification;
7: 8. in me *all manner of* concupiscence.
8:22. the *whole* creation groaneth
28. *all* things work together for
32. delivered him up for us *all*,
— also freely give us *all* things?
37. Nay, in *all* these things we
9: 5. who is over *all*, God blessed for ever.
6. For they (are) not *all* Israel,
7. Neither,...(are they) *all* children:
17. declared throughout *all* the earth.
33. *whosoever* believeth on him
10: 4. for righteousness to *every one* that
11. *Whosoever* believeth on him
12. the same Lord over *all* is rich unto *all* that call upon him.
13. For *whosoever* shall call upon
16. But they have not *all* obeyed
18. their sound went into *all* the earth,
11:26. And so *all* Israel shall be
32. concluded them *all* in unbelief, that he might have mercy upon *all*.
36. and to him, (are) *all* things:
12: 3. God hath dealt to *every* man
4. and *all* members have not the
17. honest in the sight of *all* men.
18. live peaceably with *all* men

Ro. 13: 1. Let *every* soul be subject unto
7. Render therefore to *all* their dues:
14: 2. that he may eat *all* things:
5. another esteemeth *every* day
10. for we shall *all* stand before
11. *every* knee shall bow to me, and *every* tongue shall confess to God.
20. *All* things indeed (are) pure; but
23. *whatsoever* (is) not of faith is sin.
15:11. Praise the Lord, *all* ye Gentiles; and laud him, *all* ye people.
13. fill you with *all* joy and peace
14. filled with *all* knowledge,
33. the God of peace (be) with you *all*.
16: 4. but also *all* the churches of
15. and *all* the saints which are
19. is come abroad unto *all* (men).
24. (be) with you *all*. Amen.
26. made known to *all* nations
1Co. 1: 2. with *all* that in *every* place
5. That in *every* thing ye are enriched by him, in *all* utterance, and (in) *all* knowledge;
10. that ye *all* speak the same thing,
29. That no (lit. not *any*) flesh should glory
2:10. the Spirit searcheth *all* things,
15. is spiritual judgeth *all* things,
3:21. For *all* things are your's;
22. or things to come; *all* are your's;
4:13. the offscouring of *all* things
17. I teach every where in *every* church.
6:12. *All* things are lawful unto me, but *all* things are not expedient: *all* things are lawful for me,
18. *Every* sin that a man doeth is
7: 7. For I would that *all* men were
17. And so ordain I in *all* churches.
8: 1. we know that we *all* have knowledge,
6. of whom (are) *all* things, and we in him;
— by whom (are) *all* things, and we by him.
7. Howbeit (there is) not in *every* man
9:12. but suffer *all* things, lest we should
19. though I be free from *all* (men), yet have I made myself servant unto *all*,
22. I am made *all* things to *all* (men), that I
24. run in a race run *all*, but one
25. And *every* man that striveth for the mastery is temperate in *all* things.
10: 1. how that *all* our fathers were
— and *all* passed through the sea;
2. And were *all* baptized unto Moses
3. And did *all* eat the same
4. And did *all* drink the same
11. Now *all* these things happened
17. for we are *all* partakers of that
23. *All* things are lawful for me, but *all* things are not expedient: *all* things are lawful for me, but *all* things edify not.
25. *Whatsoever* is sold in the
27. *whatsoever* is set before you,
31. do *all* to the glory of God.
33. I please *all* (men) in *all* (things),
11: 2. that ye remember me in *all* things,
3. the head of *every* man is Christ;
4. *Every* man praying or
5. But *every* woman that
12. but *all* things of God.
12: 6. same God which worketh *all* in *all*
11. But *all* these worketh that one
12. and *all* the members of that one
13. are we *all* baptized into one
— and have been *all* made to drink

1Co.12: 19. And if they were *all* one member,
26. *all* the members suffer with it;
— *all* the members rejoice with it.
29. (Are) *all* apostles? (are) *all* prophets? (are) *all* teachers? (are) *all* workers of miracles?
30. Have *all* the gifts of healing? do *all* speak with tongues? do *all* interpret?
13: 2. and understand *all* mysteries, and *all* knowledge; and though I have *all* faith,
3. though I bestow *all* my goods to feed
7. Beareth *all* things, believeth *all* things, hopeth *all* things, endureth *all* things.
14: 5. I would that ye *all* spake with
18. with tongues more than ye *all*:
23. and *all* speak with tongues, and
24. But if *all* prophesy, and there come
— he is convinced of *all*, he is judged of *all*:
26. Let *all* things be done unto
31. For ye may *all* prophesy one by one, that *all* may learn, and *all* may be
33. as in *all* churches of the saints.
40. Let *all* things be done decently and
15: 7. then of *all* the apostles.
8. And last of *all* he was seen of
10. more abundantly than they *all*:
19. we are of *all* men most miserable.
22. For as in Adam *all* die, even so in Christ shall *all* be made alive.
24. when he shall have put down *all* rule and *all* authority
25. till he hath put *all* enemies
27. hath put *all* things under his feet. But when he saith, *All* things
— which did put *all* things under him.
28. And when *all* things shall be
— unto him that put *all* things under him, that God may be *all* in *all*.
30. why stand we in jeopardy *every* hour?
39. *All* flesh (is) not the same flesh:
51. We shall not *all* sleep, but we shall *all* be changed,
16:14. Let *all* your things be done with charity.
16. and to *every one* that helpeth with
20. *All* the brethren greet you.
24. My love (be) with you *all* in
2Co. 1: 1. with *all* the saints which are in
3. the God of *all* comfort;
4. in *all* our tribulation,
— them which are in *any* trouble
2: 3. having confidence in you *all*, that my joy is (the joy) of you *all*.
5. I may not overcharge you *all*.
9. whether ye be obedient in *all* things.
14. his knowledge by us in *every* place.
3: 2. known and read of *all* men:
18. But we *all*, with open face
4: 2. to *every* man's conscience (lit. to *all* conscience of men)
8. (We are) troubled on *every* side, (lit. in *all*.)
15. For *all* things (are) for your sakes.
5: 10. For we must *all* appear before
14(15). if one died for *all*, then were *all* dead:
15. And (that) he died for *all*, that
17. behold, *all* things are become new.
18. And *all* things (are) of God,
6: 4. But in *all* (things) approving
10. and (yet) possessing *all* things.
7: 1. from *all* filthiness of the
4. joyful in *all* our tribulation.
5. we were troubled on *every* side; (lit. in *all*)
11. In *all* (things) ye have approved

2Co. 7: 13. was refreshed by you *all*.
14. but as we spake *all* things to you in
15. remembereth the obedience of you *all*,
16. I have confidence in you in *all* (things).
8: 7. as ye abound in *every* (thing),
— and (in) *all* diligence,
18. throughout *all* the churches;
9: 8. God (is) able to make *all* grace
— having *all* sufficiency in *all* (things), may abound to *every* good work:
11. in *every* thing to *all* bountifulness,
13. unto them, and unto *all* (men);
10: 5. and *every* high thing that exalteth
— into captivity *every* thought
6. a readiness to revenge *all* disobedience,
11: 6. have been *throughly* made manifest among you in *all* things.
9. and in *all* (things) I have kept
28. daily, the care of *all* the churches.
12: 12. wrought among you in *all* patience.
19. but (we do) *all* things, dearly beloved,
13: 1. three witnesses shall *every* word be
2. and to *all* other, that, if I come again,
13(12). *All* the saints salute you.
14(13). (be) with you *all*. Amen.
Gal. 1: 2. And *all* the brethren which are
2: 14. I said unto Peter before (them) *all*,
16. shall no (lit. not *any*) flesh be justified.
3: 8. In thee shall *all* nations be blessed.
10. *every one* that continueth not in *all* things which
13. Cursed (is) *every one* that hangeth
22. hath concluded *all* under sin,
26. For ye are *all* the children of God
28. for ye are *all* one in Christ Jesus.
4: 1. though he be lord of *all*;
26. which is the mother of us *all*.
5: 3. For I testify again to *every* man that
14. For *all* the law is fulfilled in
6: 6. him that teacheth in *all* good things.
10. let us do good unto *all* (men),
Eph 1: 3. hath blessed us with *all* spiritual
8. abounded toward us in *all* wisdom
10. gather together in one *all* things
11. who worketh *all* things
15. and love unto *all* the saints,
21. Far above *all* principality,
— and *every* name that is named,
22. put *all* (things) under his feet, and gave him (to be) the head over *all* (things)
23. of him that filleth *all* in *all*.
2: 3. Among whom also we *all* had our
21. In whom *all* the building
3: 8. less than the least of *all* saints,
9. And to make *all* (men) see
— who created *all* things by Jesus
15. Of whom the *whole* family in
18. to comprehend with *all* saints
19. with *all* the fulness of God.
20. above *all* that we ask or
21. throughout *all* ages, world
4: 2. With *all* lowliness and
6. One God and Father of *all*, who (is) above *all*, and through *all*, and in you *all*.
10. up far above *all* heavens, that he might fill *all* things.
13. Till we *all* come in the
14. and carried about with *every* wind
15. grow up into him in *all* things,
16. From whom the *whole* body fitly
— by that which *every* joint supplieth
19. to work *all* uncleanness with

Eph. 4:29. no (lit. not *any*) corrupt communication
31. Let *all* bitterness, and wrath,
— with *all* malice:
5: 3. and *all* uncleanness,
5. that no (lit. not *any*) whoremonger.
9. (is) in *all* goodness
13. *all* things that are reproved
— for *whatsoever* doth make
20. thanks always for *all* things unto God
24. to their own husbands in *every* thing.
6:16. Above *all* taking the shield
— to quench *all* the fiery darts
18. Praying *always* (ἐν. π. κ.) with *all* prayer
— thereunto with *all* perseverance and supplication for *all* saints;
21. make known to you *all* things:
24. Grace (be) with *all* them that love
Phi. 1: 1. to *all* the saints in Christ
3. upon *every* remembrance of you,
4. in *every* prayer of mine for you *all* making request with joy,
7. to think this of you *all*,
— ye *all* are partakers of my grace.
8. I long after you *all* in
9. and (in) *all* judgment;
13. in all the palace, and in *all* other (places);
18. notwithstanding, *every* way, whether
20. with *all* boldness, as always,
25. with you *all* for your furtherance
2: 9. a name which is above *every* name:
10. *every* knee should bow,
11. And (that) *every* tongue should
14. Do *all* things without murmurings
17. and rejoice with you *all*.
21. For *all* seek their own,
26. longed after you *all*,
29. with *all* gladness; and hold such
3: 8. I count *all* things (but) loss
— suffered the loss of *all* things,
21. to subdue *all* things unto himself.
4: 5. be known unto *all* men.
6. but in *every* thing by prayer
7. passeth *all* understanding,
12. *every* where and in *all* things I am
13. I can do *all* things through
18. But I have *all*, and abound
19. shall supply *all* your need
21. Salute *every* saint in Christ Jesus.
22. *All* the saints salute you,
23. (be) with you *all*. Amen.
Col. 1: 4. to *all* the saints,
6. in *all* the world;
9. of his will in *all* wisdom
10. unto *all* pleasing, being fruitful in *every* good work,
11. Strengthened with *all* might,
— unto *all* patience
15. the firstborn of *every* creature:
16. were *all* things created,
— *all* things were created by him,
17. he is before *all* things, and by him *all* things consist.
18. that in *all* (things) he might
19. should *all* fulness dwell;
20. to reconcile *all* things unto himself;
23. to *every* creature which is under
28. warning *every* man, and teaching *every* man in *all* wisdom; that we may present *every* man
2: 2. and unto *all* riches of the
3. are hid *all* the treasures of
9. dwelleth *all* the fulness of

Col. 2:10. the head of *all* principality
13. forgiven you *all* trespasses;
19. from which *all* the body
22. Which *all* are to perish
3: 8. put off *all* these; anger, wrath,
11. but Christ (is) *all*, and in *all*
14. And above *all* these things
16. richly in *all* wisdom;
17. *whatsoever*[2] ye do in word
— (do) *all* in the name of
20. in *all* things: for this is
22. obey in *all* things (your)
23. And *whatsoever*[2] ye do,
4: 7. *All* my state shall Tychicus
9. make known unto you *all* things
12. complete in *all* the will of God.
1Th. 1: 2. to God always for you *all*,
7. ensamples to *all* that believe
8. in *every* place your faith
2:15. and are contrary to *all* men:
3: 7. in *all* our affliction
9. for *all* the joy wherewith we
12. and toward *all* (men),
13. Jesus Christ with *all* his saints.
4: 6. the avenger of *all* such,
10. toward *all* the brethren which are
5: 5. Ye are *all* the children of light.
14. be patient toward *all* (men).
15. among yourselves, and to *all* (men).
18. In *every* thing give thanks:
21. Prove *all* things; hold fast that
22. Abstain from *all* appearance
26. Greet *all* the brethren
27. be read unto *all* the holy brethren.
2Th. 1: 3. charity of every one of you *all*
4. in *all* your persecutions
10. admired in *all* them that
11. and fulfil *all* the good pleasure
2: 4. above *all* that is called God,
9. with *all* power and signs
10. And with *all* deceivableness
12. That they *all* might be damned
17. in *every* good word and work.
3: 2. for *all* (men) have not faith.
6. from *every* brother that
16. peace *always* (διὰ παντὸς) by *all* means The Lord (be) with you *all*.
17. the token in *every* epistle:
18. (be) with you *all*. Amen.
1Ti. 1:15. worthy of *all* acceptation,
16. shew forth *all* longsuffering,
2: 1. that, first of *all*, supplications,
— be made for *all* men;
2. (for) *all* that are in authority;
— peaceable life in *all* godliness
4. Who will have *all* men to be
6. a ransom for *all*,
8. that men pray *every* where,
11. learn in silence with *all* subjection.
3: 4. in subjection with *all* gravity;
11. faithful in *all* things.
4: 4. For *every* creature of God (is)
8. profitable unto *all* things,
9. worthy of *all* acceptation.
10. the saviour of *all* men, specially
15. may appear to *all*.
5: 2. younger as sisters, with *all* purity
10. followed *every* good work.
20. rebuke before *all*, that others
6: 1. worthy of *all* honour,
10. the root of *all* evil:
13. who quickeneth *all* things,

1Ti. 6:17. richly *all* things to enjoy;
2Ti. 1:15. *all* they which are in Asia be turned
2: 7. give thee understanding in *all* things.
10. I endure *all* things for the
19. Let *every one* that nameth
21. prepared unto *every* good work.
24. gentle unto *all* (men),
3: 9. shall be manifest unto *all*
11. out of (them) *all* the Lord delivered
12. Yea, and *all* that will live
16. *All* scripture (is) given
17. unto *all* good works.
4: 2. exhort with *all* longsuffering
5. watch thou in *all* things,
8. but unto *all* them also that love
16. but *all* (men) forsook me:
17. and (that) *all* the Gentiles
18. from *every* evil work,
21. and *all* the brethren.
Tit. 1:15. Unto the pure *all* things (are)
16. unto *every* good work reprobate.
2: 7. In *all* things shewing thyself
9. to please (them) well in *all* (things);
10. shewing *all* good fidelity;
— of God our Saviour in *all* things.
11. hath appeared to *all* men,
14. might redeem us from *all* iniquity,
15. rebuke with *all* authority
3: 1. to *every* good work,
2. shewing *all* meekness unto *all* men.
15. *All* that are with me
— Grace (be) with you *all*.
Philem. 5. and toward *all* saints;
6. acknowledging of *every* good thing
Heb 1: 2. appointed heir of *all* things,
3. upholding *all* things by the word
6. And let *all* the angels of God
11. and they *all* shall wax old
14. Are they not *all* ministering
2: 2. and *every* transgression
8. Thou hast put *all* things in
— in that he put *all* in subjection under
— we see not yet *all* things put under him.
9. should taste death for *every* man.
10. for whom (are) *all* things, and by whom (are) *all* things,
11. (are) *all* of one:
15. were *all* their lifetime subject
17. Wherefore in *all* things
3: 4. For *every* house is builded by some (man); but he that built *all* things (is) God.
16. not *all* that came out of Egypt
4: 4. the seventh day from *all* his works.
12. sharper than *any* twoedged sword,
13. but *all* things (are) naked
15. was in *all* points tempted
5: 1. For *every* high priest
9. unto *all* them that obey him;
13. For *every one* that useth milk
6:16. an end of *all* strife.
7: 2. gave a tenth part of *all*;
7. And without *all* contradiction
8: 3. For *every* high priest
5. make *all* things according to
11. for *all* shall know me,
9:19. spoken *every* precept to *all* the people
— both the book, and *all* the people,
21. and *all* the vessels of the ministry.
22. And almost *all* things are by
10:11. And *every* priest standeth
11:13. These *all* died in faith, not having
39. And these *all*, having obtained a

Heb 12: 1. let us lay aside *every* weight,
6. and scourgeth *every* son whom
8. whereof *all* are partakers,
11. Now no (lit. not *any*) chastening
14. Follow peace with *all* (men),
23. to God the Judge of *all*,
13: 4. honourable in *all*,
18. in *all* things willing to live
21. in *every* good work to do his will,
24. Salute *all* them that have
— and *all* the saints.
25. Grace (be) with you *all*. Amen.
Jas. 1: 2. count it *all* joy when ye fall
5. that giveth to *all* (men) liberally,
8. in *all* his ways.
17. *Every* good gift and *every* perfect gift
19. let *every* man be swift to hear,
21. lay apart *all* filthiness
2:10. he is guilty of *all*.
3: 7. For *every* kind of beasts,
16. and *every* evil work.
4:16. *all* such rejoicing is evil.
5:12. above *all* things, my brethren,
1Pet. 1:15. holy in *all manner of* conversation;
24. For *all* flesh (is) as grass, and *all* the glory of man
2: 1. laying aside *all* malice, and *all* guile,
— and *all* evil speakings,
13. to *every* ordinance of man
17. Honour *all* (men). Love the brotherhood.
18. masters with *all* fear;
3: 8. (be ye) *all* of one mind,
15. an answer to *every* man that
4: 7. the end of *all* things is at hand:
8. And above *all* things have
11. that God in *all* things may be
5: 5. Yea, *all* (of you) be subject one to
7. Casting *all* your care upon
10. But the God of *all* grace,
14. Peace (be) with you *all* that are in
2Pet. 1: 3. given unto us *all* things that
5. giving *all* diligence, add to your
20. that no (lit. not *any*) prophecy of the
3: 4. *all* things continue as
9. but that *all* should come to
11. (that) *all* these things shall be dissolved
16. As also in *all* (his) epistles,
1Joh. 1: 7. cleanseth us from *all* sin.
9. cleanse us from *all* unrighteousness.
2:16. For *all* that (is) in the world,
19. that they were not *all* of us.
20. and ye know *all* things.
21. that no (lit. not *any*) lie is of the truth.
23. *Whosoever* denieth the Son,
27. teacheth you of *all* things,
29. *every one* that doeth righteousness
3: 3. And *every* man that hath this
4. *Whosoever* committeth sin
6. *Whosoever* abideth in him
— *whosoever* sinneth hath not seen
9. *Whosoever* is born of God
10. *whosoever* doeth not righteousness
15. *Whosoever* hateth his brother
— that no (lit. not *any*) murderer hath
20. and knoweth *all* things.
4: 1. believe not *every* spirit,
2. *Every* spirit that confesseth
3. And *every* spirit that
7. and *every* one that loveth
5: 1. *Whosoever* believeth that Jesus
— and *every one* that loveth
4. For *whatsoever* is born of

1Joh 5: 17. *All* unrighteousness is sin:
18. *whosoever* is born of God
2Joh 1. but also *all* they that have known
9. *Whosoever* transgresseth, and
3Joh 2. I wish above *all* things
12. hath good report of *all*
Jude 3. when I gave *all* diligence
15. judgment upon *all*, and to convince *all*
— of *all* their ungodly deeds...and of *all* their hard (speeches) which
25. both now and ever. (lit. to *all* ages)
Rev. 1: 7. and *every* eye shall see him,
— and *all* kindreds of the earth shall
2:23. and *all* the churches shall know
4:11. for thou hast created *all* things,
5: 6. sent forth into *all* the earth.
9. out of *every* kindred, and tongue,
13. And *every* creature which is
— sea, and *all* that are in them,
6:14. *every* mountain and island were
15. *every* bondman, and *every* free man,
7: 1. nor on *any* tree.
4. of *all* the tribes of the children of
9. of *all* nations, and kindreds,
11. And *all* the angels stood round
16. sun light on them, nor *any* heat.
17. wipe away *all* tears from their eyes.
8: 3. with the prayers of *all* saints
7. and *all* green grass was burnt
9: 4. neither *any* green thing, neither *any* tree;
11: 6. to smite the earth with *all* plagues,
12: 5. who was to rule *all* nations with
13: 7. over *all* kindreds, and tongues,
8. And *all* that dwell upon the
12. And he exerciseth *all* the power of
16. And he caused *all*, both small
14: 6. and to *every* nation, and kindred,
8. because she made *all* nations drink
15: 4. for *all* nations shall come and
16: 3. and *every* living soul died in the
20. And *every* island fled away,
18: 2. the hold of *every* foul spirit, and a cage of *every* unclean
3. For *all* nations have drunk
12. and *all* thyine wood,
— and *all manner* vessels of ivory, and *all manner* vessels of most
14. and *all* things which were dainty
17. And *every* shipmaster, and *all* the company
19. were made rich *all* that had ships
22. and no (lit. not *any*) craftsman, of *whatsoever* craft (he be),
23. were *all* nations deceived.
24. and of *all* that were slain upon
19: 5. Praise our God, *all* ye his servants,
17. saying to *all* the fowls that fly in
18. and the flesh of *all* (men, both) free
21. and *all* the fowls were filled with
21: 4. God shall wipe away *all* tears from
5. Behold, I make *all* things new.
7. shall inherit *all* things;
8. and *all* liars, shall have their part
19. with *all manner of* precious stones.
27. into it *any* thing that defileth,
22: 3. And there shall be no more)(curse:
15. and *whosoever* loveth and maketh
18. I testify unto *every* man that heareth
21. (be) with you *all*. Amen.

3957 29 638/778 5:896 [6453]

πασχα, paska.

Mat.26: 2. two days is (the feast of) the *passover*,
17. prepare for thee to eat the *passover?*
18. I will keep the *passover* at thy house
19. and they made ready the *passover*.
Mar 14: 1. was (the feast of) the *passover*,
12. when they killed the *passover*,
— that thou mayest eat the *passover?*
14. where I shall eat the *passover* with
16. and they made ready the *passover*.
Lu. 2:41. every year at the feast of the *passover*.
22: 1. which is called the *passover*.
7. when the *passover* must be killed.
8. Go and prepare us the *passover*,
11. where I shall eat the *passover*
13. and they made ready the *passover*.
15. desired to eat this *passover* with you
Joh. 2:13. And the Jews' *passover* was at hand.
23. when he was in Jerusalem at the *passover*, in the feast
6: 4. And the *passover*, a feast of the Jews,
11:55. And the Jews' *passover* was nigh at
— before the *passover*, to purify themselves.
12: 1. Jesus six days before the *passover*
13: 1. Now before the feast of the *passover*,
18:28. but that they might eat the *passover*.
39. release unto you one at the *passover*:
19:14. it was the preparation of the *passover*
Acts12: 4. intending after *Easter* to bring him forth
1Co. 5: 7. Christ our *passover* is sacrificed for us:
Heb 11:28. Through faith he kept the *passover*,

3958 42 637/778 5:904

πάσχω, pasko.

Mat.16:21. and *suffer* many things of the elders
17:12. shall also the Son of man *suffer* of them.
15. he is lunatick, and sore *vexed*:
27:19. for I *have suffered* many things this
Mar 5:26. And *had suffered* many things of
8:31. the Son of man must *suffer* many
9:12. that he *must suffer* many things,
Lu. 9:22. The Son of man must *suffer* many
13: 2. because they *suffered* such things?
17:25. But first must he *suffer* many
22:15. this passover with you before I *suffer*:
24:26. Ought not Christ *to have suffered*
46. it behoved Christ *to suffer*, and to
Acts 1: 3. he shewed himself alive after his *passion*
3:18. that Christ should *suffer*, he hath so
9:16. how great things he must *suffer* for
17: 3. Christ must needs *have suffered*,
28: 5. beast into the fire, and *felt* no harm.
1Co.12:26. one member *suffer*, all the members
2Co. 1: 6. same sufferings which we also *suffer*:
Gal. 3: 4. *Have* ye *suffered* so many things in vain?
Phi. 1:29. but also *to suffer* for his sake;
1Th. 2:14. for ye also *have suffered* like things
2Th. 1: 5. for which ye also *suffer*:
2Ti. 1:12. For the which cause I also *suffer* these things:
Heb 2:18. he himself *hath suffered* being tempted,
5: 8. by the things which he *suffered*;
9:26. For then must he often *have suffered*
13:12. *suffered* without the gate.
1Pet.2:19. endure grief, *suffering* wrongfully.
20. when ye do well, and *suffer* (for it),
21. Christ also *suffered* for us, leaving
23. *when* he *suffered*, he threatened not;
3:14. But and if ye *suffer* for righteousness'
17. that ye *suffer* for well doing,
18. Christ also *hath* once *suffered* for
4: 1. *Forasmuch* then *as* Christ *hath suffered* for us

1Pet.4: 1. for he *that hath suffered* in the flesh
15. But *let* none of you *suffer* as a
19. Wherefore let them *that suffer*
5:10. *after that* ye *have suffered* a while,
Rev. 2:10. of those things which thou shalt *suffer:*

3960 10 640/778 5:939 cf 5180
πατάσσω, patasso. 3817

Mat.26:31. I *will smite* the shepherd, and
51. *struck* a servant of the high priest's, *and*
Mar 14:27. I *will smite* the shepherd,
Lu. 22:49. Lord, *shall* we *smite* with the sword?
50. *smote* the servant of the high priest,
Acts 7:24. *and smote* the Egyptian:
12: 7. he *smote* Peter on the side, *and*
23. the angel of the Lord *smote* him,
Rev.11: 6. and *to smite* the earth with
19:15. that with it he *should smite* the nations:

3961 5 640/779 5:940 3817
πατέω, pateo.

Lu. 10:19. power *to tread* on serpents
21:24. Jerusalem shall be *trodden down*
Rev.11: 2. holy city *shall* they *tread under foot*
14:20. And the winepress *was trodden*
19:15. and he *treadeth* the winepress of

3962 418 640/779 5:945
πατήρ, pateer.

Mat. 2:22. in the room of his *father* Herod,
3: 9. We have Abraham to (our) *father:*
4:21. in a ship with Zebedee their *father,*
22. left the ship and their *father,*
5:16. and glorify your *Father* which is
45. That ye may be the children of your *Father*
48. perfect, even as your *Father* which is
6: 1. of your *Father* which is in heaven.
4. and thy *Father* which seeth in secret
6. pray to thy *Father* which is in secret; and thy *Father* which seeth in
8. your *Father* knoweth what things
9. Our *Father* which art in heaven,
14. your heavenly *Father* will also
15. neither will your *Father* forgive
18. but unto thy *Father* which is in secret: and thy *Father,* which seeth
26. yet your heavenly *Father* feedeth
32. for your heavenly *Father* knoweth
7:11. how much more shall your *Father*
21. he that doeth the will of my *Father*
8:21. first to go and bury my *father.*
10:20. but the Spirit of your *Father* which
21. and the *father* the child:
29. fall on the ground without your *Father.*
32. before my *Father* which is in heaven.
33. before my *Father* which is in heaven.
35. a man at variance against his *father,*
37. He that loveth *father* or mother
11:25. I thank thee, O *Father,* Lord of
26. Even so, *Father:* for so it seemed good
27. delivered unto me of my *Father:* and no man knoweth the Son, but the *Father;* neither knoweth any man the *Father,*
12:50. shall do the will of my *Father*
13:43. in the kingdom of their *Father.*
15: 4. Honour thy *father* and mother: and, He that curseth *father* or mother,
5. Whosoever shall say to (his) *father*
Mat.15: 6(5). And honour not his *father* or his
13. which my heavenly *Father* hath not
16:17. but my *Father* which is in heaven.
27. come in the glory of his *Father*
18:10. always behold the face of my *Father*
14. it is not the will of your *Father* which
19. be done for them of my *Father* which
35. shall my heavenly *Father* do also
19: 5. shall a man leave *father* and mother,
19. Honour thy *father* and (thy) mother:
29. or brethren, or sisters, or *father,* or
20:23. for whom it is prepared of my *Father.*
21:31. twain did the will of (his) *father?*
23: 9. And call no (man) your *father*
— for one is your *Father,* which is
30. If we had been in the days of our *fathers,*
32. the measure of your *fathers.*
24:36. but my *Father* only.
25:34. Come, ye blessed of my *Father,*
26:29. with you in my *Father's* kingdom.
39. O my *Father,* if it be possible,
42. O my *Father,* if this cup may not
53. that I cannot now pray to my *Father,*
28:19. in the name of the *Father,* and of
Mar 1:20. they left their *father* Zebedee in
5:40. he taketh the *father* and the
7:10. Honour thy *father* and thy mother; and, Whoso curseth *father* or mother,
11. If a man shall say to his *father*
12. no more to do ought for his *father*
8:38. the glory of his *Father* with the
9:21. And he asked his *father,* How long
24. And straightway the *father* of the
10: 7. shall a man leave his *father*
19. Honour thy *father* and mother.
29. or brethren, or sisters, or *father,* or
11:10. the kingdom of our *father* David,
25. that your *Father* also which is
26. neither will your *Father* which
13:12. and the *father* the son;
32. neither the Son, but the *Father.*
14:36. And he said, Abba, *Father,* all
15:21. the *father* of Alexander and Rufus.
Lu. 1:17. to turn the hearts of the *fathers*
32. the throne of his *father* David:
55. As he spake to our *fathers,*
59. Zacharias, after the name of his *father.*
62. made signs to his *father,* how
67. And his *father* Zacharias was
72. the mercy (promised) to our *fathers,*
73. sware to our *father* Abraham,
2:48. behold, thy *father* and I have sought
49. must be about my *Father's* business?
3: 8. We have Abraham to (our) *father:*
6:23. did their *fathers* unto the prophets.
26. did their *fathers* to the false prophets.
36. as your *Father* also is merciful.
8:51. and the *father* and the mother of
9:26. and (in his) *Father's,* and of the holy
42. and delivered him again to his *father.*
59. to go and bury my *father.*
10:21. I thank thee, O *Father,* Lord of
— even so, *Father;* for so it
22. delivered to me of my *Father:*
— but the *Father;* and who the *Father* is,
11: 2. Our *Father* which art in
11. of any of you that is a *father,*
13. much more shall (your) heavenly *Father*
47. and your *fathers* killed them.
48. allow the deeds of your *fathers:*
12:30. and your *Father* knoweth
32. it is your *Father's* good pleasure

Lu. 12:53. The *father* shall be divided against the son, and the son against the *father;*
14:26. and hate not his *father*, and
15:12. said to (his) *father*, *Father*, give me
17. servants of my *father's* have
18. arise and go to my *father*, and will say unto him, *Father*, I have sinned
20. he arose, and came to his *father*.
— his *father* saw him, and had compassion,
21. *Father*, I have sinned against
22. But the *father* said to his servants,
27. and thy *father* hath killed the fatted
28. therefore came his *father* out,
29. said to (his) *father*, Lo, these many years
16:24. *Father* Abraham, have mercy on me,
27. I pray thee therefore, *father*, that thou wouldest send him to my *father's* house:
30. And he said, Nay, *father* Abraham:
18:20. Honour thy *father* and thy
22:29. as my *Father* hath appointed unto me;
42. Saying, *Father*, if thou be willing,
23:34. *Father*, forgive them;
46. *Father*, into thy hands I commend
24:49. I send the promise of my *Father* upon
Joh. 1:14. as of the only begotten of the *Father*,
18. in the bosom of the *Father*, he
2:16. make not my *Father's* house an
3:35. The *Father* loveth the Son, and
4:12. greater than our *father* Jacob,
20. Our *fathers* worshipped in this
21. nor yet at Jerusalem, worship the *Father*.
23. shall worship the *Father* in spirit and in truth: for the *Father* seeketh such
53. So the *father* knew that
5:17. My *Father* worketh hitherto,
18. said also that God was his *Father*,
19. but what he seeth the *Father* do:
20. For the *Father* loveth the Son,
21. For as the *Father* raiseth up
22. For the *Father* judgeth no man,
23. as they honour the *Father*.
— honoureth not the *Father*
26. For as the *Father* hath life
30. but the will of the *Father* which
36. which the *Father* hath given me
— that the *Father* hath sent me.
37. And the *Father* himself, which
43. I am come in my *Father's* name,
45. that I will accuse you to the *Father:*
6:27. for him hath God the *Father* sealed.
31. Our *fathers* did eat manna in
32. but my *Father* giveth you
37. All that the *Father* giveth
39. And this is the *Father's* will
42. whose *father* and mother we
44. except the *Father* which
45. hath learned of the *Father*,
46. that any man hath seen the *Father*,
— he hath seen the *Father*.
49. Your *fathers* did eat manna
57. the living *Father* .... by the *Father:*
58. not as your *fathers* did eat
65. given unto him of my *Father*.
7:22. of Moses, but of the *fathers;*
8:16. the *Father* that sent me.
18. the *Father* that sent me
19. Where is thy *Father?*
— know me, nor my *Father*.
— ye should have known my *Father* also.
27. he spake to them of the *Father*.
28. as my *Father* hath taught me,
29. the *Father* hath not left me alone;

Joh. 8:38. I have seen with my *Father:*
— which ye have seen with your *father*
39. Abraham is our *father*.
41. Ye do the deeds of your *father*.
— we have one *Father*, (even) God.
42. If God were your *Father*,
44. Ye are of (your) *father* the devil, and the lusts of your *father* ye will do.
— for he is a liar, and the *father* of it.
49. but I honour my *Father*,
53. greater than our *father* Abraham,
54. it is my *Father* that honoureth
56. Your *father* Abraham rejoiced
10:15. As the *Father* knoweth me, even so know I the *Father:*
17. Therefore doth my *Father* love me,
18. have I received of my *Father*.
25. that I do in my *Father's* name, they
29. My *Father*, which gave (them) me,
— out of my *Father's* hand.
30. I and (my) *Father* are one.
32. I shewed you from my *Father;*
36. whom the *Father* hath sanctified,
37. the works of my *Father*, believe me not.
38. that the *Father* (is) in me, and I in him.
11:41. *Father*, I thank thee that thou hast
12:26. him will (my) *Father* honour.
27. *Father*, save me from this hour:
28. *Father*, glorify thy name.
49. but the *Father* which sent me,
50. even as the *Father* said unto me,
13: 1. this world unto the *Father*,
3. that the *Father* had given all things into
14: 2. In my *Father's* house are many
6. unto the *Father*, but by me.
7. have known my *Father* also:
8. Lord, shew us the *Father*, and it
9. hath seen the *Father;* and how sayest thou (then), Shew us the *Father?*
10. that I am in the *Father*, and the *Father* in me?
— but the *Father* that dwelleth in me,
11. that I (am) in the *Father*, and the *Father* in me:
12. because I go unto my *Father*.
13. that the *Father* may be glorified
16. And I will pray the *Father*,
20. I (am) in my *Father*,
21. shall be loved of my *Father*,
23. and my *Father* will love him,
24. but the *Father's* which sent me.
26. whom the *Father* will send in my
28. because I said, I go unto the *Father*. for my *Father* is greater than I.
31. that I love the *Father;* and as the *Father* gave me commandment,
15: 1. and my *Father* is the husbandman.
8. Herein is my *Father* glorified,
9. As the *Father* hath loved me,
10. I have kept my *Father's*
15. that I have heard of my *Father*
16. ask of the *Father* in my
23. hateth my *Father* also.
24. hated both me and my *Father*.
26. send unto you from the *Father*,
— which proceedeth from the *Father*,
16: 3. not known the *Father*, nor me.
10. because I go to my *Father*,
15. All things that the *Father* hath
16. because I go to the *Father*.
17. Because I go to the *Father?*
23. ye shall ask the *Father* in my

Joh.16: 25. shew you plainly of the *Father*.
26. will pray the *Father* for you:
27. For the *Father* himself loveth
28. I came forth from the *Father*,
— and go to the *Father*.
32. because the *Father* is with me.
17: 1. *Father*, the hour is come;
5. And now, O *Father*, glorify thou
11. Holy *Father*, keep through
21. as thou, *Father*, (art) in me,
24. *Father*, I will that they also,
25. O righteous *Father*, the world
18:11. the cup which my *Father* hath
20:17. not yet ascended to my *Father*:
— I ascend unto my *Father*, and your *Father*;
21. as (my) *Father* hath sent me,
Acts 1: 4. the promise of the *Father*,
7. which the *Father* hath put in his
2:33. having received of the *Father*
3:13. the God of our *fathers*, hath glorified
22. Moses truly said unto the *fathers*,
25. which God made with our *fathers*,
5:30. The God of our *fathers* raised up
7: 2. Men, brethren, and *fathers*, hearken;
— appeared unto our *father* Abraham,
4. when his *father* was dead,
11. and our *fathers* found no sustenance.
12. sent out our *fathers* first.
14. and called his *father* Jacob to (him),
15. he, and our *fathers*,
19. and evil entreated our *fathers*,
20. nourished up in his *father*'s house
32. I (am) the God of thy *fathers*,
38. and (with) our *fathers*:
39. To whom our *fathers* would not
44. Our *fathers* had the tabernacle
45. Which also our *fathers* that came after
— before the face of our *fathers*,
51. as your *fathers* (did), so (do) ye
52. have not your *fathers* persecuted?
13:17. chose our *fathers*, and exalted the people
32. promise which was made unto the *fathers*,
36. and was laid unto his *fathers*,
15:10. which neither our *fathers* nor we
16: 1. but his *father* (was) a Greek:
3. that his *father* was a Greek.
22: 1. Men, brethren, and *fathers*, hear ye
14. The God of our *fathers* hath chosen
26: 6. made of God unto our *fathers*:
28: 8. that the *father* of Publius lay sick
25. the prophet unto our *fathers*,
Ro. 1: 7. from God our *Father*,
4: 1. our *father* as pertaining to the flesh,
11. the *father* of all them that believe,
12. And the *father* of circumcision
— faith of our *father* Abraham,
16. who is the *father* of us all,
17. I have made thee a *father* of many
18. become the *father* of many nations,
6: 4. by the glory of the *Father*,
8:15. we cry, Abba, *Father*.
9: 5. Whose (are) the *fathers*, and of whom
10. (even) by our *father* Isaac;
11:28. beloved for the *fathers*' sakes.
15: 6. God, even the *Father* of our Lord
8. promises (made) unto the *fathers*
1Co. 1: 3. and peace, from God our *Father*
4:15. yet (have ye) not many *fathers*:
5: 1. one should have his *father*'s wife.
8: 6. one God, the *Father*, of whom (are)
10: 1. all our *fathers* were under the cloud,
15:24. the kingdom to God, even the *Father*;
2Co. 1: 2. from God our *Father*, and (from)
3. even the *Father* of our Lord
— the *Father* of mercies, and the God of
6:18. And will be a *Father* unto you,
11:31. The God and *Father* of our Lord Jesus Christ,
Gal. 1: 1. and God the *Father*, who raised
3. peace from God the *Father*, and (from)
4. the will of God and our *Father*:
4: 2. the time appointed of the *father*.
6. your hearts, crying, Abba, *Father*.
Eph. 1: 2. from God our *Father*,
3. the God and *Father* of our Lord
17. the *Father* of glory, may give
2:18. by one Spirit unto the *Father*.
3:14. my knees unto the *Father* of our Lord
4: 6. One God and *Father* of all,
5:20. unto God and the *Father*
31. leave his *father* and mother,
6: 2. Honour thy *father* and mother;
4. And, ye *fathers*, provoke not
23. from God the *Father* and the Lord
Phi. 1: 2. from God our *Father*, and (from) the
2:11. to the glory of God the *Father*.
22. as a son with the *father*, he hath served
4:20. unto God and our *Father* (be) glory
Col. 1: 2. from God our *Father*
3. to God and the *Father* of our Lord Jesus
12. Giving thanks unto the *Father*,
2: 2. and of the *Father*, and of Christ;
3:17. to God and the *Father* by him.
21. *Fathers*, provoke not your children
1Th. 1: 1. in God the *Father* and (in) the Lord
— from God our *Father*, and the Lord Jesus Christ.
3. in the sight of God and our *Father*,
2:11. as a *father* (doth) his children,
3:11. Now God himself and our *Father*,
13. before God, even our *Father*,
2Th. 1: 1. in God our *Father* and the Lord
2. from God our *Father* and the Lord
2:16. and God, even our *Father*, which
1Ti. 1: 2. from God our *Father* and Jesus Christ
5: 1. but intreat (him) as a *father*;
2Ti. 1: 2. from God the *Father* and Christ Jesus our Lord.
Tit. 1: 4. from God the *Father* and the Lord Jesus
Philem. 3. from God our *Father* and the Lord Jesus
Heb 1: 1. spake in time past unto the *fathers*
5. I will be to him a *Father*,
3: 9. When your *fathers* tempted me,
7:10. in the loins of his *father*,
8: 9. that I made with their *fathers* in the day
11:23. was hid three months of his *parents*,
12: 7. what son is he whom the *father*
9. Furthermore we have had *fathers*
— unto the *Father* of spirits, and live?
Jas. 1:17. from the *Father* of lights,
27. before God and the *Father*
2:21. Was not Abraham our *father* justified
3: 9. bless we God, even the *Father*;
1Pet. 1: 2. the foreknowledge of God the *Father*,
3. Blessed (be) the God and *Father* of our
17. And if ye call on the *Father*,
2Pet. 1:17. For he received from God the *Father*
3: 4. since the *fathers* fell asleep, all things
1Joh. 1: 2. life, which was with the *Father*,
3. with the *Father*, and with his Son Jesus
2: 1. an advocate with the *Father*, Jesus
13. I write unto you, *fathers*,
— ye have known the *Father*.
14. I have written unto you, *fathers*,

1Joh.2:15. the love of the *Father* is not in him.
16. is not of the *Father*, but is of the world.
22. that denieth the *Father* and the Son.
23. the same hath not the *Father:*
24. continue in the Son, and in the *Father.*
3: 1. love the *Father* hath bestowed
4:14. that the *Father* sent the Son
5: 7. the *Father*, the Word, and the Holy Ghost:
2Joh. 3. from God the *Father*, and from the Lord
— the Son of the *Father*, in truth and love.
4. received a commandment from the *Father.*
9. hath both the *Father* and the Son.
Jude 1. sanctified by God the *Father*,
Rev. 1: 6. priests unto God and his *Father;*
2:27. as I received of my *Father.*
3: 5. before my *Father*, and before his angels.
21. set down with my *Father* in his throne.
14: 1. having his *Father's* name written

3964 1 642/784 3962,3389

πατραλῴης, patralōees.

1Ti. 1: 9. for *murderers of fathers* and

3965 3 643/783 5:945 3962

πατρία, patria.

Lu. 2: 4. of the house and *lineage* of David:
Acts 3:25. in thy seed shall all the *kindreds* of the
Eph. 3:15. Of whom the whole *family* in heaven and

3966 4 642/783 3965,757

πατριάρχης, patriarkees.

Acts 2:29. speak unto you of the *patriarch* David,
7: 8. Jacob (begat) the twelve *patriarchs.*
9. the *patriarchs*, moved with envy, sold
Heb 7: 4. the *patriarch* Abraham gave

3967 1 642/783 5:945 3962

πατρικός, patrikos.

Gal. 1:14. zealous of the traditions *of* my *fathers.*

3968 8 642/783 3962

πατρίς, patris.

Mat.13:54. he was come into his *own country*,
57. save in his *own country*,
Mar 6: 1. and came into his *own country;*
4. without honour, but in his *own country*,
Lu. 4:23. do also here in thy *country.*
24. accepted in his *own country.*
Joh. 4:44. hath no honour in his own *country.*
Heb 11:14. that they seek a *country.*

3970 1 642/784 3962,3860

πατροπαράδοτος, patroparadotos.

1Pet. 1:18. conversation (*received*) *by tradition from* your *fathers;*

3971 3 642/784 5:945 3962

πατρῷος, patrōos.

Acts22: 3. manner of the law *of* the *fathers*,
24:14. so worship I the God *of* my *fathers*,
28:17. against the people, or customs *of* our *fathers.*

3973 15 643/785

παύομαι, pauomai.

Lu. 5: 4. Now when he *had left* speaking,
8:24. and they *ceased*, and there was a calm.
11: 1. when he *ceased*, one of his disciples said
Acts 5:42. they *ceased* not to teach and preach
6:13. This man *ceaseth* not to speak blasphemous
13:10. *wilt* thou not *cease* to pervert
20: 1. And after the uproar *was ceased*,
31. I *ceased* not to warn every one
21:32. they *left* beating of Paul.
1Co.13: 8. whether (there be) tongues, they *shal cease;*
Eph. 1:16. *Cease* not to give thanks for you,
Col. 1: 9. *do* not *cease* to pray for you,
Heb 10: 2. would they not *have ceased* to be offered ?
1Pet. 3:10. *let* him *refrain* his tongue from evil,
4: 1. suffered in the flesh *hath ceased* from sin;

3975 2 644/786 5:1022 4078

παχύνομαι, pakunomai.

Mat.13:15. For this people's heart *is waxed gross*,
Acts28:27. For the heart of this people *is waxed gross*,

3976 3 644/786 4228

πέδη, pedee.

Mar 5: 4. often bound with *fetters* and chains,
— and the *fetters* broken in pieces:
Lu. 8:29. bound with chains and in *fetters;*

3977 1 644/786 4228

πεδινός, pedinos.

Lu. 6:17. and stood in the *plain*,

3978 1 644/786 3979

πεζεύω, pezūo.

Acts20:13. minding himself *to go afoot.*

3979 2 644/786 4228

πεζῇ, pezee.

Mat.14:13. followed him *on foot* out of the cities.
Mar 6:33. and ran *afoot* thither out of all

3980 4 644/786 6:1 3982,757

πειθαρχέω, pītharkeo.

Acts 5:29. We ought *to obey* God rather than
32. hath given to them *that obey* him.
27:21. ye should *have hearkened* unto me, *and*
Tit. 3: 1. *to obey magistrates*, to be ready to

3981 1 644/786 6:1 3982

πειθός, pīthos.

1Co. 2: 4. not with *enticing* words of man's wisdom,

3982 55 644/786 6:1

πείθω πέποιθα, pītho, pepoitha.

Mat.27:20. priests and elders *persuaded* the multitude
43. He *trusted* in God; let him deliver
28:14. we *will persuade* him, and secure you
Mar 10:24. for them *that trust* in riches to
Lu. 11:22. his armour wherein he *trusted*,
16:31. neither *will* they *be persuaded*,
18: 9. certain *which trusted* in themselves
20: 6. for they be *persuaded* that John

Acts 5:36. and all, as many as *obeyed* him,
37. and all, (even) as many as *obeyed* him,
40. And to him they *agreed*:
12:20. and, *having made* Blastus...their *friend*,
13:43. *persuaded* them to continue
14:19. who *persuaded* the people, and, having
17: 4. And some of them *believed*,
18: 4. and *persuaded* the Jews and the
19: 8. and *persuading* the things concerning
26. this Paul *hath persuaded and* turned
21:14. And *when* he *would* not *be persuaded*,
23:21. *do* not thou *yield* unto them:
26:26. for I *am persuaded* that none
28. Almost thou *persuadest* me to be
27:11. the centurion *believed* the master
28:23. *persuading* them concerning Jesus,
24. And some *believed* the things which
Ro. 2: 8. but *obey* unrighteousness,
19. And *art confident* that thou thyself
8:38. For I *am persuaded*, that neither
14:14. and *am persuaded* by the Lord Jesus,
15:14. also *am persuaded* of you, my brethren,
2Co. 1: 9. that we should not *trust* in ourselves,
2: 3. *having confidence* in you all,
5:11. we *persuade* men; but we are made
10: 7. If any man *trust* to himself that
Gal. 1:10. For *do* I now *persuade* men, or God?
3: 1. that ye should not *obey* the truth,
5: 7. that ye should not *obey* the truth?
10. I *have confidence* in you through the Lord,
Phi. 1: 6. *Being confident* of this very thing,
14. *waxing confident* by my bonds,
25. And *having* this *confidence*, I know
2:24. But I *trust* in the Lord that I
3: 3. and *have* no *confidence* in the flesh.
4. thinketh that he hath whereof he might trust (lit. thinketh *to trust*)
2Th. 3: 4. we *have confidence* in the Lord
2Ti. 1: 5. and I *am persuaded* that in thee also.
12. and *am persuaded* that he is able
Philem 21. *Having confidence* in thy obedience
Heb 2:13. I will put my trust (lit. I will be *having trusted*) in him.
6: 9. we *are persuaded* better things of you,
11:13. and *were persuaded* of (them), and
13:17. *Obey* them that have the rule over you,
18. for we *trust* we have a good conscience,
Jas. 3: 3. that they may *obey* us;
1Joh. 3:19. and *shall assure* our hearts before him.

3983 23 645/787 6:12 rt 3993

πεινάω, pīnao.

Mat. 4: 2. he *was* afterward *an hungred*.
5: 6. Blessed (are) they *which do hunger*
12: 1. his disciples *were an hungred*,
3. when he *was an hungred*,
21:18. into the city, *he hungered*.
25:35. I *was an hungred*, and ye gave me
37. when saw we thee *an hungred*,
42. For I *was an hungred*, and ye
44. when saw we thee *an hungred*,
Mar 2:25. he had need, and *was an hungred*,
11:12. come from Bethany, he *was hungry*:
Lu. 1:53. He hath filled the *hungry* with
4: 2. he afterward *hungered*.
6: 3. when himself *was an hungred*,
21. Blessed (are ye) *that hunger* now.
25. that are full! for ye *shall hunger*.
Joh. 6:35. *shall* never *hunger*; and he that
Ro. 12:20. Therefore if thine enemy *hunger*,
1Co. 4:11. we both *hunger*, and thirst, and
11:21. one *is hungry*, and another
34. And if any man *hunger*,
Phi. 4:12. to be full and *to be hungry*,
Rev. 7:16. They *shall hunger* no more,

3984 2 645/787 6:23 rt 4008

πεῖρα, pīra.

Heb 11:29. which the Egyptians *assaying* to do (lit. of which the Egyptians taking the *trial*)
36. had *trial* of (cruel) mockings and

3985 39 646/787 6:23 3984

πειράζω, pīrazo.

Mat. 4: 1. wilderness *to be tempted* of the devil.
3. And when the *tempter* came to him,
16: 1. and *tempting* desired him that he
19: 3. came unto him, *tempting* him,
22:18. Why *tempt* ye me, (ye) hypocrites?
35. *tempting* him, and saying,
Mar 1:13. forty days, *tempted* of Satan;
8:11. a sign from heaven, *tempting* him.
10: 2. to put away (his) wife? *tempting* him.
12:15. Why *tempt* ye me? bring me
Lu. 4: 2. *Being* forty days *tempted* of the devil.
11:16. And others, *tempting* (him), sought of
20:23. said unto them, Why *tempt* ye me?
Joh. 6: 6. And this he said to *prove* him:
8: 6. This they said, *tempting* him,
Acts 5: 9. agreed together *to tempt* the Spirit of
15:10. Now therefore why *tempt* ye God,
16: 7. they *assayed* to go into Bithynia:
24: 6. † Who also *hath gone about* to profane
1Co. 7: 5. that Satan *tempt* you not for
10: 9. † as some of them also *tempted*.
13. will not suffer you *to be tempted* above
2Co. 13: 5. *Examine* yourselves, whether ye be in
Gal. 6: 1. lest thou also *be tempted*.
1Th. 3: 5. † lest by some means the *tempter have tempted* you,
Heb 2:18. hath suffered *being tempted*, he is able to succour them *that are tempted*.
3: 9. † When your fathers *tempted* me,
4:15. but *was* in all points *tempted* like as
11:17. *when* he *was tried*, offered up Isaac:
37. sawn asunder, *were tempted*,
Jas. 1:13. say *when* he *is tempted*, I *am tempted* of God:
— neither *tempteth* he any man:
14. But every man *is tempted*, when
Rev. 2: 2. † and thou *hast tried* them which say
10. into prison, that ye *may be tried*;
3:10. *to try* them that dwell upon the earth.

Note.—"Those marked † may be formed also from πειράω."—*Schmid.*

3986 21 646/788 6:23 3985

πειρασμός, pīrasmos.

Mat. 6:13. And lead us not into *temptation*,
26:41. that ye enter not into *temptation*.
Mar 14:38. lest ye enter into *temptation*.
Lu. 4:13. the devil had ended all the *temptation*.
8:13. and in time of *temptation* fall away.
11: 4. lead us not into *temptation*;
22:28. continued with me in my *temptations*.
40. that ye enter not into *temptation*.
46. lest ye enter into *temptation*.
Acts 20:19. and *temptations*, which befell me by
1Co. 10:13. There hath no *temptation* taken you

1Co.10:13. will with the *temptation* also make
Gal. 4:14. And my *temptation* which was in my
1Ti. 6: 9. fall into *temptation* and a snare,
Heb 3: 8. in the day of *temptation* in the wilderness:
Jas. 1: 2. when ye fall into divers *temptations;*
12. Blessed (is) the man that endureth *temptation:*
1Pet. 1: 6. heaviness through manifold *temptations:*
4:12. the fiery trial which is to try you, (lit. the fiery proof for *trial* to you)
2Pet. 2: 9. deliver the godly out of *temptations,* [sing.]
Rev. 3:10. from the hour of *temptation,* which

3987 2 646/788 6:23 3984

πειράω, pīrao.

Acts 9:26. he *assayed* to join himself to the
26:21. and *went about* to kill (me).

See also those in πειράζω which have the mark † affixed.

3988 1 647/788 6:1 3982

πεισμονή, pīsmonee.

Gal. 5: 8. This *persuasion* (cometh) not of him

3989 2 647/788

πέλαγος, pelagos.

Mat.18: 6. drowned in the *depth* of the sea.
Acts27: 5. sailed over the *sea* of Cilicia

3990 1 647/788 4141

πελεκίζομαι, pelekizomai.

Rev.20: 4. the souls of them *that were beheaded*

3991 4 647/788 4002

πέμπτος, pemptos.

Rev. 6: 9. when he had opened the *fifth* seal,
9: 1. And tne *fifth* angel sounded,
16:10. the *fifth* angel poured out his vial
21:20. The *fifth,* sardonyx;

3992 81 647/788 1:398 cf 4724 cf hiēmi (to send)

πέμπω, pempo.

Mat. 2: 8. And he *sent* them to Bethlehem, *and*
11: 2. he *sent* two of his disciples,
14:10. he *sent, and* beheaded John
22: 7. he *sent* forth his armies, *and* destroyed
Mar 5:12. *Send* us into the swine,
Lu. 4:26. *was* Elias *sent,* save unto Sarepta,
7: 6. the centurion *sent* friends to him,
10. And they *that were sent,* returning
19. *sent* (them) to Jesus, saying,
15:15. and he *sent* him into his fields
16:24. and *send* Lazarus, that he may
27. that thou *wouldest send* him to
20:11. again he sent (lit. added *to send*) another servant:
12. And again he sent (lit. he added *to send*) a third:
13. I *will send* my beloved son:
Joh. 1:22. give an answer to them *that sent* us.
33. but he *that sent* me to baptize
4:34. the will of him *that sent* me,
5:23. the Father *which hath sent* him.
24. on him *that sent* me,
30. of the Father *which hath sent* me.
37. the Father himself, *which hath sent* me,
6:38. the will of him *that sent* me.
Joh. 6:39. the Father's will *which hath sent* me,
40. the will of him *that sent* me,
44. the Father *which hath sent* me
7:16. but his *that sent* me.
18. his glory *that sent* him,
28. but he *that sent* me is true,
33. I go unto him *that sent* me.
8:16. but I and the Father *that sent* me.
18. and the Father *that sent* me beareth
26. but he *that sent* me is true;
29. And he *that sent* me is with me:
9: 4. the works of him *that sent* me,
12:44. on him *that sent* me.
45. seeth him *that sent* me.
49. but the Father *which sent* me,
13:16. greater than he *that sent* him.
20. whomsoever I *send* receiveth me;
— receiveth him *that sent* me.
14:24. but the Father's *which sent* me.
26. whom the Father *will send* in my name,
15:21. they know not him *that sent* me.
26. whom I *will send* unto you from
16: 5. I go my way to him *that sent* me;
7. I *will send* him unto you.
20:21. even so *send* I you.
Acts10: 5. now *send* men to Joppa,
32. *Send* therefore to Joppa, and
33. therefore I *sent* to thee;
11:29. determined *to send* relief unto
15:22. *to send* chosen men of their own
25. *to send* chosen men unto you
19:31. *sent* unto him, desiring (him)
20:17. he *sent* to Ephesus, *and* called
23:30. I *sent* straightway to thee,
25:21. till I *might send* him to Cæsar.
25. I have determined *to send* him.
27. to *send* a prisoner, *and* not withal
Ro. 8: 3. God *sending* his own Son
1Co. 4:17. *have* I *sent* unto you Timotheus,
16: 3. them *will* I *send* to bring your
2Co. 9: 3. Yet *have* I *sent* the brethren, lest
Eph. 6:22. Whom I *have sent* unto you
Phi. 2:19. *to send* Timotheus shortly
23. I hope *to send* presently,
25. necessary *to send* to you Epaphroditus.
28. I *sent* him therefore
4:16. ye *sent* once and again
Col. 4: 8. Whom I *have sent* unto you
1Th. 3: 2. And *sent* Timotheus, our brother,
5. I *sent* to know your faith,
2Th. 2:11. God *shall send* them strong delusion,
Tit. 3:12. When I *shall send* Artemas
1Pet. 2:14. as unto them *that are sent* by him
Rev. 1:11. and *send* (it) unto the seven churches
11:10. and *shall send* gifts one to another;
14:15. *Thrust in* thy sickle, and reap:
18. *Thrust in* thy sharp sickle,
22:16. I Jesus *have sent* mine angel

3993 1 648/789 6:37 cf 4434 penō (to toil)

πένης, penees.

2Co. 9: 9. he hath given to the *poor:*

3994 6 648/789 3995

πενθερά, penthera.

Mat. 8:14. he saw his *wife's mother* laid, and
10:35. against her *mother in law.*
Mar 1:30. Simon's *wife's mother* lay sick
Lu. 4:38. And Simon's *wife's mother* was taken with
12:53. the *mother in law* against her
— against her *mother in law.*

3995 1 648/789

πενθερός, pentheros.

Joh.18:13. for he was *father in law* to Caiaphas,

3996 10 648/789 6:40 3997

πενθέω, pentheo.

Mat. 5: 4. Blessed (are) they *that mourn*.
9:15. Can the children of the bridechamber *mourn*,
Mar 16:10. *as* they *mourned* and wept.
Lu. 6:25. for ye *shall mourn* and weep.
1Co. 5: 2. and *have* not rather *mourned*,
2Co.12:21. and (that) I *shall bewail* many
Jas. 4: 9. and *mourn*, and weep: let
Rev.18:11. shall weep and *mourn* over her;
15. weeping and *wailing*,
19. and cried, weeping and *wailing*,

3997 5 648/789 6:40 3958

πένθος, penthos.

Jas. 4: 9. laughter be turned to *mourning*,
Rev.18: 7. so much torment and *sorrow* give her:
— and shall see no *sorrow*.
8. death, and *mourning*, and famine;
21: 4. neither *sorrow*, nor crying,

3998 1 648/789 6:37 rt 3993

πενιχρός, penikros.

Lu. 21: 2. a certain *poor* widow casting in

3999 1 648/789 4002

πεντάκις, pentakis.

2Co.11:24. *five times* received I forty (stripes) save one.

4000 6 648/789 3999,5507

πεντακισχίλιοι, pentakiskilioi.

Mat.14:21. were about *five thousand* men,
16: 9. the five loaves of the *five thousand*,
Mar 6:44. were about *five thousand* men.
8:19. the five loaves among *five thousand*,
Lu. 9:14. they were about *five thousand* men.
Joh. 6:10. in number about *five thousand*.

4001 2 648/790 4002,1540

πεντακόσιοι, pentakosioi.

Lu. 7:41. the one owed *five hundred* pence,
1Co.15: 6. seen of above *five hundred* brethren

4002 38 648/790

πέντε, pente.

Mat.14:17. but *five* loaves, and two fishes.
19. and took the *five* loaves,
16: 9. neither remember the *five* loaves
25: 2. And *five* of them were wise, and *five* (were) foolish.
15. unto one he gave *five* talents,
16. he that had received the *five* talents
— and made (them) other *five* talents.
20. And so he that had received *five* talents came and brought other *five*
— thou deliveredst unto me *five* talents:
— beside them *five* talents more.
Mar 6:38. they say, *Five*, and two fishes.
41. when he had taken the *five* loaves
8:19. When I brake the *five* loaves
Lu. 1:24. and hid herself *five* months,
9:13. no more but *five* loaves
16. he took the *five* loaves
12: 6. Are not *five* sparrows sold
52. there shall be *five* in one house
14:19. I have bought *five* yoke of oxen,
16:28. For I have *five* brethren;
19:18. thy pound hath gained *five* pounds.
19. Be thou also over *five* cities.
Joh. 4:18. For thou hast had *five* husbands;
5: 2. Bethesda, having *five* porches.
6: 9. which hath *five* barley loaves,
13. of the *five* barley loaves,
19. had rowed about *five* and twenty
Acts 4: 4. of the men was about *five* thousand.
7:14. his kindred, threescore and fifteen (lit. seventy *five*) souls
19:19. and found (it) fifty thousand (pieces) (lit. *five* ten thousands) of silver.
20: 6. came unto them to Troas in *five* days;
24: 1. And after *five* days
1Co.14:19. I had rather speak *five* words
Rev. 9: 5. be tormented *five* months:
10. to hurt men *five* months.
17:10. *five* are fallen, and one is,

4003 1 648/790 4002,2532,1182

πεντεκαιδέκατος, pentekaidekatos.

Lu. 3: 1. Now in the *fifteenth* year

4004 7 648/790 4002

πεντήκοντα, penteekonta.

Mar 6:40. by hundreds, and by *fifties*.
Lu. 7:41. and the other *fifty*.
9:14. by *fifties* in a company.
16: 6. quickly, and write *fifty*.
Joh. 8:57. Thou art not yet *fifty* years old,
21:11. an hundred and *fifty* and three:
Acts13:20. four hundred and *fifty* years,

4005 3 648/790 6:44 4004

πεντηκοστή, penteekostee.

Acts 2: 1. And when the day of *Pentecost*
20:16. at Jerusalem the day of *Pentecost*.
1Co.16: 8. at Ephesus until *Pentecost*.

πέποιθα see **πείθω**. 3982

4006 6 649/790 6:1 3982

πεποίθησις, pepoitheesis.

2Co. 1:15. And in this *confidence* I was minded
3: 4. And such *trust* have we
8:22. the great *confidence* which (I have) in
10: 2. with that *confidence*, wherewith
Eph. 3:12. access with *confidence* by the faith
Phi. 3: 4. might also have *confidence* in the flesh.

4007 4 649/ rt 4008

περ, per.

Mar 15: 6. whom*soever* they desired.
Heb 3: 6. if)(we hold fast the confidence
14. if)(we hold the beginning of our
6: 3. if)(God permit.

See the compound forms of this word in εἴπερ, ἐπείπερ, ἐπειδήπερ, ἤπερ, καθάπερ, καίπερ, ὥσπερ. Its force is perhaps limitation, e. g. ἐάνπερ, that is to say if.

4008 23 649/790 peirō (to pierce)

πέραν, peran.

Mat. 4:15. the way of the sea, *beyond* Jordan,
25. and (from) *beyond* Jordan.
8:18. commandment to depart unto the *other side*.
28. when he was come to the *other side*
14:22. before him unto the *other side*,
16: 5. disciples were come to the *other side*,
19: 1. coasts of Judæa *beyond* Jordan;
Mar 3: 8. and (from) *beyond* Jordan;
4:35. pass over unto the *other side*.
5: 1. unto the *other side* of the sea,
21. by ship unto the *other side*,
6:45. to go to the *other side* before
8:13. departed to the *other side*.
10: 1. by the *farther side* of Jordan:
Lu. 8:22. unto the *other side* of the lake.
Joh. 1.28. in Bethabara *beyond* Jordan,
3:26. he that was with thee *beyond* Jordan,
6: 1. went *over* the sea of Galilee,
17. went *over* the sea toward Capernaum.
22. stood *on the other side* of the sea
25. found him *on the other side* of the sea,
10:40. went away again *beyond* Jordan
18: 1. *over* the brook Cedron.

4009 4 649/791 rt 4008

πέρας, peras.

Mat.12:42. from the *uttermost parts* of the earth
Lu. 11:31. from the *utmost parts* of the earth
Ro. 10:18. their words unto the *ends* of the world.
Heb 6:16. (is) to them an *end* of all strife.

4012 331 650/791 6:53 rt 4008

περί, peri.

Governs a genitive and an accusative. ª denotes the latter.

Mat. 2: 8. search diligently *for* the young child;
3: 4. girdle *about*ª his loins;
4: 6. his angels charge *concerning* thee:
6:28. why take ye thought *for* raiment?
8:18. great multitudes *about*ª him,
9:36. moved with compassion *on* them,
11: 7. unto the multitudes *concerning* John,
10. is (he), *of* whom it is written,
12:36. shall give account there*of*
15: 7. did Esaias prophesy *of* you,
16:11. spake (it) not to you *concerning* bread,
17:13. spake unto them *of* John the
18:19. agree on earth *as touching* any thing
20: 3. went out *about*ª the third hour,
5. *about*ª the sixth and ninth hour,
6. And *about*ª the eleventh hour
9. (hired) *about*ª the eleventh hour,
24. indignation *against* the two brethren.
21:45. perceived that he spake *of* them.
22:16. neither carest thou *for* any (man):
31. But *as touching* the resurrection of
42. What think ye *of* Christ?
24:36. But *of* that day and hour knoweth
26:24. as it is written *of* him:
28. which is shed *for* many
27:46. And *about*ª the ninth hour
Mar 1: 6. girdle of a skin *about*ª his loins;
30. they tell him *of* her.
44. offer *for* thy cleansing
3: 8. and they *about*ª Tyre and Sidon,
32. And the multitude sat *about*ª him.
Mar 3:34. on them which sat *about*ª him,
4:10. they that were *about*ª him
19. and the lusts *of*ª other things
5:16. and (also) *concerning* the swine.
27. When she had heard *of* Jesus,
6:48. and *about*ª the fourth watch of the night
7: 6. prophesied *of* you hypocrites,
17. asked him *concerning* the parable.
25. heard *of* him, and came and fell
8:30. tell no man *of* him.
9:14. a great multitude *about*ª them,
42. were hanged *about*ª his neck,
10:10. asked him again *of* the same (matter).
41. much displeased *with* James and John.
12:14. and carest *for* no man:
26. And *as touching* the dead, that they
13:32. But *of* that day and (that) hour knoweth
14:21. as it is written *of* him:
24. which is shed *for* many.
Lu. 1: 1. a declaration *of* those things which are
4. where*in* thou hast been instructed.
2:17. they made known abroad)(the saying
— told them *concerning* this child.
18. wondered *at* those things which were
27. to do *for* him after the custom
33. things which were spoken *of* him.
38. spake *of* him to all them
3:15. mused in their hearts *of* John,
19. reproved by him *for* Herodias
— and *for* all the evils which Herod
4:10. angels charge *over* thee,
14. fame *of* him through all the region
37. the fame *of* him went out into every
38. besought him *for* her.
5:14. offer *for* thy cleansing,
15. a fame abroad *of* him:
7: 3. when he heard *of* Jesus, he sent
17. And this rumour *of* him went forth
18. shewed him *of* all these things.
24. unto the people *concerning* John,
27. *of* whom it is written,
9: 9. *of* whom I hear such things?
11. spake unto them *of* the kingdom of God,
45. to ask him *of* that saying.
10:40. was cumbered *about*ª much serving,
41. and troubled *about*ª many things:
11:53. provoke him to speak *of* many things:
12:26. why take ye thought *for* the rest?
13: 1. told him *of* the Galilæans,
8. till I shall dig *about*ª it,
16: 2. How is it that I hear this *of* thee?
17: 2. hanged *about*ª his neck,
19:37. *for* all the mighty works that
21: 5. And as some spake *of* the temple,
22:32. I have prayed *for* thee,
37. the things *concerning* me have an end.
49. When they which were *about*ª him
23: 8. he had heard many things *of* him;
24: 4. as they were much perplexed there*about*,
14. talked together *of* all these things
19. *Concerning* Jesus of Nazareth.
27. the things *concerning* himself.
44. and (in) the psalms, *concerning* me.
Joh. 1: 7. to bear witness *of* the Light,
8. to bear witness *of* that Light.
15. bare witness *of* him,
22. What sayest thou *of* thyself?
30. This is he *of* whom I said,
47(48). and saith *of* him, Behold an Israelite
2:21. he spake *of* the temple of his body.
25. should testify *of* man: for he knew
3:25. and the Jews *about* purifying.

4012

Joh. 5:31. If I bear witness *of* myself,
32. another that beareth witness *of* me ;
— which he witnesseth *of* me
36. bear witness *of* me,
37. hath borne witness *of* me.
39. which testify *of* me.
46. for he wrote *of* me.
6:41. The Jews then murmured *at* him,
61. disciples murmured *at* it,
7: 7. I testify *of* it, that the works
12. murmuring among the people *concerning* him:
13. no man spake openly *of* him
17. he shall know *of* the doctrine,
32. murmured such things *concerning* him;
39. this spake he *of* the Spirit,
8:13. Thou bearest record *of* thyself;
14. Though I bear record *of* myself,
18. I am one that bear witness *of* myself,
— that sent me beareth witness *of* me.
26. to say and to judge *of* you:
46. convinceth me *of* sin?
9.17. What sayest thou *of* him,
18. believe *concerning* him, that he had
21. he shall speak *for* (lit. *about*) himself.
10:13. and careth not *for* the sheep.
25. they bear witness *of* me.
33. *For* a good work we stone thee not; but *for* blasphemy;
41. that John spake *of* this man
11:13. Jesus spake *of* his death:
— spoken *of* taking of rest in sleep.
19. came to Martha and Mary, (lit. to those *around*[a] Martha and Mary)
— *concerning* their brother.
12: 6. not that he cared *for* the poor;
41. and spake *of* him.
13.18. I speak not *of* you all:
22. doubting *of* whom he spake.
24. who it should be *of* whom he spake.
15.22. no cloke *for* their sin.
26. he shall testify *of* me:
16: 8. he will reprove the world *of* sin, and *of* righteousness, and *of* judgment:
9. *Of* sin, because they believe not
10. *Of* righteousness, because I go
11. *Of* judgment, because the prince
19. enquire among yourselves *of* that I said,
25. I shall shew you plainly *of* the Father.
26. pray the Father *for* you:
17: 9. I pray *for* them: I pray not *for* the world, but *for* them which thou hast given me;
20. Neither pray I *for* these alone, but *for* them also which shall
18:19. asked Jesus *of* his disciples, and *of* his doctrine.
23. bear witness *of* the evil:
34. did others tell it thee *of* me?
19:24. but cast lots *for* it, whose
21:24. which testifieth *of* these things,
Acts 1: 1. have I made, O Theophilus, *of* all that
3. the things *pertaining to* the kingdom
16. *concerning* Judas, which was guide
2:29. unto you *of* the patriarch David,
31. spake *of* the resurrection of Christ,
5:24. they doubted *of* them
7:52. shewed before *of* the coming of the
8:12. things *concerning* the kingdom of God,
15. prayed *for* them, that they
34. *of* whom speaketh the prophet this? *of* himself, or *of* some other
9:13. heard by many *of* this man, how

Acts10: 9. *about*[a] the sixth hour:
19. thought *on* the vision,
11:22. Then tidings *of* these things came
13:13. when Paul and his company (lit. when they *about*[a] Paul)
29. all that was written *of* him,
15: 2. apostles and elders *about* this question.
6. to consider *of* this matter.
17:32. hear thee again *of* this (matter).
18:15. a question *of* words and names,
25. diligently the things *of* the Lord,
19: 8. the things *concerning* the kingdom
23. no small stir *about* that way.
25. the workmen of like occupation, (lit. the workmen *about*[a] such things)
39. enquire any thing *concerning* other
40. *for* this day's uproar, there being no cause where*by* we may give
21. 8. we that were of Paul's company (lit. those *about*[a] Paul)
21. And they are informed *of* thee,
24. informed *concerning* thee,
25. *As touching* the Gentiles which believe,
22: 6. *about*[a] noon, suddenly there shone
— light round *about*[a] me.
10. told thee *of* all things which are
18. thy testimony *concerning* me.
23: 6. *of* the hope and resurrection of the dead
11. as thou hast testified *of* me in Jerusalem,
15. more perfectly *concerning* him:
20. enquire somewhat *of* him more
29. accused *of* questions of their law,
24: 8. take knowledge *of* all these things,
10. cheerfully answer *for* myself:
13. the things where*of* they now accuse
21. Except it be *for* this one voice,
— *Touching* the resurrection of the dead
22. having more perfect knowledge *of* (that) way,
24. *concerning* the faith in Christ.
25. reasoned *of* righteousness, temperance,
25: 9. and there be judged *of* these things
15. *About* whom, when I was at
16. *concerning* the crime laid against him.
18. *Against* whom when the accusers
19. questions against him *of* their own superstition, and *of* one Jesus,
20. I doubted of such manner of questions, (lit. as to the question *about* this)
— and there be judged *of* these matters.
24. *about* whom all the multitude
26. *Of* whom I have no certain thing to
26: 2. *touching* all the things whereof
7. *For* which hope's *sake*, king Agrippa,
26. knoweth *of* these things,
28: 7. In the same quarters were (lit. in the (quarters) *about*[a] the place)
15. the brethren heard *of* us, they came
21. letters out of Judæa *concerning* thee,
— or spake any harm *of* thee.
22. *as concerning* this sect, we know
23. persuading them *concerning* Jesus,
31. those things *which concern* the Lord Jesus
Ro. 1: 3. *Concerning* his Son Jesus Christ
8: 3. likeness of sinful flesh, and *for* sin,
14:12. shall give account *of* himself to God.
15:14. am persuaded *of* you, my brethren,
21. To whom he was not spoken of, (lit. to whom it was not announced *concerning* him)
1Co. 1: 4. I thank my God always *on* your *behalf*,
11. [illegible] clared unto me *of* you.

1Co. 7: 1. whereof ye wrote unto me:
25. Now *concerning* virgins I have
37. but hath power *over* his own will,
8: 1. *as touching* things offered unto idols,
4. *As concerning* therefore the eating
12: 1. Now *concerning* spiritual (gifts),
16: 1. *concerning* the collection for the saints,
12. *As touching* (our) brother Apollos,
2Co. 9: 1. *as touching* the ministering
10: 8. boast somewhat more *of* our authority,
Eph. 6:18. and supplication *for* all saints;
22. ye might know our affairs, (lit. the things *concerning* us)
Phi. 1:27. I may hear of your affairs, (lit. the things *concerning* you)
2:19. when I know your state. (lit. the things *concerning* you)
20. care for your state. (lit. the things *concerning* you)
23. I shall see how it will go with me. (lit. the things *about*[a] me)
Col. 1: 3. praying always *for* you,
2: 1. great conflict I have *for* you,
4: 3. praying also *for* us,
8. he might know your estate, (lit. the things *concerning* you)
10. *touching* whom ye received
1Th. 1: 2. to God always *for* you all,
9. themselves shew *of* us
3: 2. comfort you *concerning* your faith:
9. render to God again *for* you,
4: 6. the avenger *of* all such,
9. *as touching* brotherly love
13. *concerning* them which are asleep,
5: 1. But *of* the times and the seasons,
25. Brethren, pray *for* us.
2Th. 1: 3. thank God always *for* you,
11. pray always *for* you,
2:13. thanks alway to God *for* you,
3: 1. Finally, brethren, pray *for* us,
1Ti. 1: 7. nor where*of* they affirm.
19. *concerning*[a] faith have made shipwreck:
6: 4. but doting *about*[a] questions
21. have erred *concerning*[a] the faith.
2Ti. 1: 3. I have remembrance *of* thee
2:18. *concerning*[a] the truth have erred,
3: 8. reprobate *concerning*[a] the faith.
Tit. 2: 7. *In*[a] all things shewing thyself
8. having no evil thing to say *of* you.
3: 8.)(these things I will that thou affirm
Philem.10. I beseech thee *for* my son Onesimus,
Heb 2: 5. the world to come, where*of* we speak.
4: 4. spake in a certain place *of* the seventh (day)
8. have spoken *of* another day.
5: 3. he ought, as *for* the people, so also *for* himself, to offer for sins.
11. *Of* whom we have many things to say,
6: 9. persuaded better things *of* you,
7:14. spake nothing *concerning* priesthood.
9: 5. *of* which we cannot now speak
10: 6. In burnt offerings and (sacrifices) *for* sin
7. it is written *of* me,
8. and (offering) *for* sin thou wouldest not,
18. no more offering *for* sin.
26. no more sacrifice *for* sins,
11: 7. warned of God *of* things not seen as yet,
20. *concerning* things to come.
22. mention *of* the departing of the children
— commandment *concerning* his bones.
32. would fail me to tell *of* Gedeon,
40. some better thing *for* us,
Heb 13:11. by the high priest *for* sin,
18. Pray *for* us: for we trust we
1Pet. 1:10. *Of* which salvation the prophets
— prophesied *of* the grace (that should)
3:15. a reason *of* the hope that is in you
18. hath once suffered *for* sins,
5: 7. for he careth *for* you.
2Pet. 1:12. in remembrance *of* these things,
3:16. speaking in them *of* these things;
1Joh. 1: 1. have handled, *of* the Word of life;
2: 2. the propitiation *for* our sins: and not *for* our's only, but also *for* (the sins of) the
26. *concerning* them that seduce you.
27. teacheth you *of* all things,
4:10. the propitiation *for* our sins.
5: 9. he hath testified *of* his Son.
10. that God gave *of* his Son.
16. say that he shall pray *for* it.
3Joh. 2. I wish *above* all things that
Jude 3. to write unto you *of* the common
7. and the cities *about*[a] them
9. disputed *about* the body of Moses,
15. *of* all their ungodly deeds
— and *of* all their hard (speeches)
Rev.15: 6. having their breasts girded with golden (lit. girded *about*[a] their breasts with)

4013 6 651/795 4012,71

περιάγω, periago.

Mat. 4:23. And Jesus *went about* all Galilee,
9:35. And Jesus *went about* all the cities
23:15. for ye *compass* sea and land
Mar 6: 6. And he *went* round *about* the villages,
Acts13:11. and he *went about* seeking some
1Co. 9: 5. power *to lead about* a sister, a wife,

4014 4 651/795 4012,138

περιαιρέω, periaireo.

Acts27:20. all hope that we should be saved *was* then *taken away*.
40. And *when* they *had taken up* the anchors, they committed (themselves) unto the sea, (lit. *having unfastened* the anchors they let go into the sea)
2Co. 3:16. the vail shall *be taken away*.
Heb 10:11. which can never *take away* sins:

4015 2 651/795 4012,797

περιαστράπτω, periastrapto.

Acts 9: 3. there *shined round about* him
22: 6. there *shone* from heaven a great light *round* about me.

4016 24 651/795 4012,906

περιβάλλω, periballo.

Mat. 6:29. *was* not *arrayed* like one of these.
31. Wherewithal shall we *be clothed*?
25:36. Naked, and ye *clothed* me:
38. or naked, and *clothed* (thee)?
43. naked, and ye *clothed* me not.
Mar 14:51. having a linen cloth cast about (lit. *clothed about* with a linen)
16: 5. *clothed* in a long white garment;
Lu. 12:27. *was* not *arrayed* like one of these.
19:43. thine enemies *shall cast* a trench *about* thee.
23:11. *arrayed* him in a gorgeous robe, *and*
Joh. 19: 2. and they *put on* him a purple robe,
Acts12: 8. *Cast* thy garment *about* thee,
Rev. 3: 5. the same *shall be clothed* in white raiment;

Rev. 3:18. raiment, that thou *mayest be clothed*,
4: 4. *clothed* in white raiment;
7: 9. *clothed* with white robes,
13. these *which are arrayed* in white robes?
10: 1. from heaven, *clothed* with a cloud:
11: 3. *clothed* in sackcloth.
12: 1. a woman *clothed* with the sun,
17: 4. And the woman was *arrayed* in purple
18:16. city, *that was clothed* in fine linen,
19: 8. that she *should be arrayed* in fine linen,
13. And he (was) *clothed* with a vesture

4017 7 652/795 4012,991

περιβλέπω, periblepo.

Mar 3: 5. And *when* he *had looked round about on*
34. he *looked* round *about on* them
5:32. And he *looked round about* to see
9: 8. *when* they *had looked round about*,
10:23. Jesus *looked round about, and*
11:11. and *when* he *had looked round about upon* all
Lu. 6:10. And *looking round about upon* them

4018 2 652/795 4016

περιβόλαιον, peribolaion.

1Co.11:15. hair is given her for a *covering*.
Heb 1:12. And as a *vesture* shalt thou fold

4019 1 652/795 4012,1210

περιδέομαι, perideomai.

Joh.11:44. his face *was bound about* with a napkin.

περιδρέμω see **περιτρέχω**. 4063

περιελών see **περιαιρέω**. 4022

4020 1 652/795 4012,2038

περιεργάζομαι, periergazomai.

2Th. 3:11. working not at all, but *are busybodies*.

4021 2 652/795 4012,2041

περίεργος, periergos.

Acts19:19. which used *curious* arts
1Ti 5:13. but tattlers also and *busy*bodies,

4022 4 652/795 2:666 4012,2064

περιέρχομαι, perierkomai.

Acts19:13. certain of the *vagabond* Jews,
28:13. thence we *fetched a compass, and* came
1Ti. 5:13. *wandering about* from house to house;
Heb 11:37. they *wandered about* in sheepskins

4023 3 652/795 4012,2192

περιέχω, perieko.

Lu. 5: 9. For he was astonished, and all (lit. astonishment *involved* him and all)
Acts23:25. a letter after this manner: (lit. *having* this form)
1Pet. 2. 6. also it *is contained* in the scripture,

4024 7 652/795 5:292 4012,2224

περιζώννυμι, perizōnnumi.

Lu. 12:35. Let your loins be *girded about*,
37. that he *shall gird* himself.
Lu. 17: 8. and *gird* thy*self, and* serve me,
Acts12: 8. *Gird* thy*self*, and bind on thy sandals.
Eph. 6:14. having your loins girt about with (lit. *girt about* your loins with)
Rev. 1:13. *girt* about the paps with a golden
15: 6. having their breasts girded (lit. *girded* about the breasts) with golden girdles

4025 1 653/795 4060

περίθεσις, perithesis.

1Pet. 3: 3. of plaiting the hair, and of *wearing* of gold,

4026 4 653/795 4012,2476

περιΐστημι, periisteemi.

Joh.11:42. because of the people *which stand by*
Acts25: 7. from Jerusalem *stood round about*,
2Ti. 2:16. *shun* profane (and) vain babblings:
Tit. 3: 9. But *avoid* foolish questions,

4027 1 653/796 3:413 4012,2508

περικάθαρμα, perikatharma.

1Co. 4:13. we are made as the *filth* of the world,

4028 3 653/796 4012,2572

περικαλύπτω, perikalupto.

Mar 14:65. to spit on him, and *to cover* his face,
Lu. 22:64. And *when* they *had blindfolded* him,
Heb 9: 4. *overlaid* round about with gold,

4029 5 653/796 3:654 4012,2749

περίκειμαι, perikīmai.

Mar 9:42. that a millstone were *hanged about*
Lu. 17: 2. were *hanged about*
Acts28:20. of Israel I *am bound with* this chain.
Heb 5: 2. himself also *is compassed with* infirmity.
12: 1. we also are compassed about with so great a cloud (lit. having so great... *encompassing* us)

4030 2 653/796 5:292 4012,2776

περικεφαλαία, perikephalaia.

Eph. 6:17. And take the *helmet* of salvation,
1Th. 5: 8. and for an *helmet*, the hope of

4031 1 654/796 4012,2904

περικρατής, perikratees.

Acts27:16. we had much work *to come by* the boat: (lit. to become *masters* of the boat)

4032 1 654/796 4012,2928

περικρύπτω, perikrupto.

Lu. 1:24. and *hid* herself five months,

4033 1 654/796 4012,2944

περικυκλόω, perikukloō.

Lu. 19:43. shall cast a trench about thee, and *compass* thee *round*,

4034 2 654/796 4:16 4012,2989

περιλάμπω, perilampo.

Lu. 2: 9. glory of the Lord *shone round about* them;
Acts26:13. *shining round about* me and them

4035 2 645/796 4:194 4012,3007

περιλείπομαι, *perilipomai.*

1Th. 4:15. (and) *remain* unto the coming of the Lord
17. which are alive (and) *remain* shall be

4036 5 654/796 4:313 4012,3077

περίλυπος, *perilupos.*

Mat.26:38. My soul is *exceeding sorrowful,*
Mar 6:26. And the king was *exceeding sorry;*
14:34. My soul is *exceeding sorrowful*
Lu. 18:23. heard this, he was *very sorrowful:*
24. Jesus saw that he was *very sorrowful,*

4037 1 654/796 4:574 4012,3306

περιμένω, *perimeno.*

Acts 1: 4. but *wait for* the promise of the Father,

4038 1 654/796 4012

πέριξ, *perix.*

Acts 5:16. (out) of the cities *round about*

4039 1 654/796 4012,3611

περιοικέω, *perioikeo.*

Lu. 1:65. on all *that dwelt round about* them:

4040 1 654/796 4012,3624

περίοικος, *perioikos.*

Lu. 1:58. And her *neighbours* and her cousins

4041 1 654/796 6:57 4012,1510

περιούσιος, *periousios.*

Tit. 2:14. unto himself a *peculiar* people,

4042 1 654/796 4023

περιοχή, *periokee.*

Acts 8:32. The *place* (lit. the *period* or *context*) of the scripture which he read

4043 96 654/796 5:490 4012,3961

περιπατέω, *peripateo.*

Mat. 4:18. *walking* by the sea of Galilee,
9: 5. or to say, Arise, and *walk?*
11: 5. and the lame *walk,*
14:25. *walking* on the sea.
26. disciples saw him *walking* on the sea,
29. he *walked* on the water, to go to
15:31. the lame to *walk,*
Mar 1:16. Now *as* he *walked* by the sea
2: 9. take up thy bed, and *walk?*
5:42. the damsel arose, and *walked;*
6:48. *walking* upon the sea,
49. But when they saw him *walking*
7: 5. Why *walk* not thy disciples
8:24. I see men as trees, *walking.*
11:27. and *as* he *was walking* in the temple,
12:38. which love *to go* in long clothing,
16:12. unto two of them, *as* they *walked,*
Lu. 5:23. or to say, Rise up and *walk?*
7:22. the blind see, the lame *walk,*
11:44. the men *that walk* over (them)
20:46. which desire *to walk* in long robes,
24:17. *as* ye *walk,* and are sad?
Joh. 1:36. looking upon Jesus *as* he *walked,*
5: 8. Rise, take up thy bed, and *walk.*
9. took up his bed, and *walked:*
11. Take up thy bed, and *walk.*
Joh. 5:12. Take up thy bed, and *walk?*
6:19. they see Jesus *walking* on the sea,
66. and *walked* no more with him.
7: 1. Jesus *walked* in Galilee: for he would not *walk* in Jewry,
8:12. *shall* not *walk* in darkness,
10:23. Jesus *walked* in the temple in
11: 9. If any man *walk* in the day,
10. But if a man *walk* in the night,
54. *walked* no more openly among
12:35. *Walk* while ye have the light,
— for he *that walketh* in darkness
21:18. and *walkedst* whither thou wouldest:
Acts 3: 6. rise up and *walk.*
8. he leaping up stood, and *walked,*
— into the temple, *walking,* and leaping,
9. saw him *walking* and praising God:
12. we had made this man *to walk?*
14: 8. who never *had walked:*
10. And he leaped and *walked.*
21:21 neither *to walk* after the customs.
Ro. 6: 4. we also *should walk* in newness of life
8: 1. *who walk* not after the flesh,
4. in us, *who walk* not after the flesh,
13:13. *Let* us *walk* honestly, as in
14:15. now *walkest* thou not charitably.
1Co. 3: 3. are ye not carnal, and *walk* as men?
7:17. so *let* him *walk.*
2Co. 4: 2. not *walking* in craftiness,
5: 7. we *walk* by faith, not by sight:
10: 2. as if we walked (lit. as *walking*) according to the flesh.
3. For *though* we *walk* in the flesh,
12:18. *walked* we not in the same spirit?
Gal. 5:16. *Walk* in the Spirit,
Eph. 2: 2. in time past ye *walked*
10. that we *should walk* in them.
4: 1. that ye *walk* worthy of the vocation
17. that ye henceforth *walk* not as other Gentiles *walk,*
5: 2. And *walk* in love,
8. *walk* as children of light:
15. See then that ye *walk* circumspectly,
Phi. 3:17. mark them *which walk* so as
18. For many *walk,* of whom I
Col. 1:10. That ye might *walk* worthy of the Lord
2: 6. (so) *walk* ye in him:
3: 7. In the which ye also *walked*
4: 5. *Walk* in wisdom toward them
1Th. 2:12. That ye would *walk* worthy of God,
4: 1. how ye ought *to walk*
12. That ye *may walk* honestly toward
2Th. 3: 6. from every brother *that walketh* disorderly,
11. some *which walk* among you disorderly,
Heb 13: 9. profited them *that have been occupied* therein.
1Pet.5: 8. *walketh about,* seeking whom
1Joh.1: 6. and *walk* in darkness, we lie,
7. But if we *walk* in the light,
2: 6. ought himself also so *to walk,* even as he *walked.*
11. and *walketh* in darkness,
2Joh. 4. I found of thy children *walking* in truth,
6. that we *walk* after his commandments.
— ye *should walk* in it.
3Joh. 3. thou *walkest* in the truth.
4. that my children *walk* in truth.
Rev. 2: 1. *who walketh* in the midst of the
3: 4. they *shall walk* with me in white:
9:20. neither can see, nor hear, nor *walk:*
16:15. lest he *walk* naked,
21:24. *shall walk* in the light of it:

4044 1 655/797 4012,rt 4008

περιπείρω, peripiro.

1Ti. 6:10. and *pierced* themselves *through* with

4045 3 655/797 6:161 4012,4098

περιπίπτω, peripipto.

Lu. 10:30. and *fell among* thieves,
Acts27:41. And *falling into* a place where two seas
Jas. 1: 2. when ye *fall into* divers temptations;

4046 2 655/797 4012,4160

περιποιέομαι, peripoyeomai.

Acts20:28. he *hath purchased* with his own blood.
1Ti. 3:13. *purchase* to themselves a good degree,

4047 5 655/797 4046

περιποίησις, peripoyeesis.

Eph 1:14. the redemption of the *purchased possession*,
1Th. 5: 9. but *to obtain* salvation
2Th. 2:14. to the *obtaining* of the glory of our Lord
Heb 10:39. to the *saving* of the soul.
1Pet. 2: 9. a *peculiar* people; (lit. a people of *acquirement* to himself)

4048 1 656/797 4012,4486

περιῤῥήγνυμι, perirreegnumi.

Acts16:22. the magistrates *rent off* their clothes, *and*

4049 1 656/797 4012,4685

περισπάομαι, perispaomai.

Lu. 10:40. Martha *was cumbered* about much

4050 4 656/798 6:51 4052

περισσεία, perissīa.

Ro. 5:17. they which receive *abundance* of grace
2Co. 8: 2. the *abundance* of their joy
10:15. according to our rule *abundantly*,
Jas. 1:21. and *superfluity* of naughtiness,

4051 5 656/798 6:58 4052

περίσσευμα, perissūma.

Mat.12:34. out of the *abundance* of the heart
Mar 8: 8. took up of the broken (meat) *that was left* (lit. the *remnants over and above*)
Lu. 6:45. for of the *abundance* of the heart
2Co. 8:14(13). your *abundance* (may be a supply)
— that their *abundance* also may be

4052 39 656/798 6:58 4053

περισσεύω, perissūo.

Mat. 5:20. except your righteousness *shall exceed*
13:12. and he *shall have more abundance:*
14:20. of the fragments *that remained* (lit. that *which was over* of the fragments)
15:37. of the broken (meat) *that was left*
25:29. and he *shall have abundance:*
Mar 12:44. did cast in of their *abundance;*
Lu. 9:17. of fragments *that remained* to them
12:15. consisteth not in the *abundance* of the
15:17. *have* bread *enough and to spare*,
21: 4. these have of their *abundance* cast in
Joh. 6:12. Gather up the fragments *that remain*,
13. which *remained over and above* unto them
Acts16: 5. and *increased* in number daily.
Ro. 3: 7. hath *more abounded* through my lie
5:15. *hath abounded* unto many.
15:13. that ye may *abound* in hope,
1Co. 8: 8. neither, if we eat, *are we the better;*
14:12. that ye *may excel* to the edifying
15:58. always *abounding* in the work
2Co. 1: 5. sufferings of Christ *abound* in us, so our consolation also *aboundeth* by Christ
3: 9. of righteousness *exceed* in glory.
4:15. abundant grace *might...redound* to
8: 2. *abounded* unto the riches of their
7. as ye *abound* in every (thing, in) faith,
— that ye *abound* in this grace also.
9: 8. *to make* all grace *abound* toward you;
— *may abound* to every good work:
12. is *abundant* also by many thanksgivings
Eph 1: 8. Wherein he *hath abounded* toward us
Phi. 1: 9. that your love *may abound* yet more
26. rejoicing *may be more abundant* in
4:12. and I know how *to abound:*
— both *to abound* and to suffer need.
18. I have all, and *abound:*
Col. 2: 7. *abounding* therein with thanksgiving.
1Th. 3:12. make you to increase and *abound*
4: 1. (so) ye *would abound* more and more.
10. that ye *increase* more and more;

4053 22 657/798 4012

περισσός & περισσότερος, perissos & perissoteros.

Mat. 5:37. for whatsoever is *more* than these
47. what do ye *more* (than others)?
11: 9. and *more* than a prophet.
23:14. ye shall receive the *greater* damnation.
Mar 6:51. sore amazed in themselves *beyond measure*,
12:40. shall receive *greater* damnation.
14:31. spake the more *vehemently*,
Lu. 7:26. and *much more* than a prophet.
12: 4. have no *more* that they can do.
48. of him they will ask the *more*.
20:47. shall receive *greater* damnation.
Joh.10:10. might have (it) *more abundantly*.
Ro. 3: 1. What *advantage* then hath the Jew?
1Co.12:23. we bestow *more abundant* honour;
— have *more abundant* comeliness.
24. given *more abundant* honour
2Co. 2: 7. swallowed up with *overmuch* sorrow.
9: 1. it is *superfluous* for me to write to you:
10: 8. I should boast somewhat *more* of
Eph 3:20. able to do *exceeding abundantly* above
1Th. 3:10. Night and day praying *exceedingly*
5:13. And to esteem them *very highly*

Note.—These three last passages are the rendering of the compound form, ὑπὲρ ἐκ περισσοῦ.

4054 4 657/798 4055

περισσότερον, perissoteron. adv.

Mar 7:36. so much the more *a great deal*
1Co.15:10. I laboured *more abundantly* than they all
Heb 6:17. willing *more abundantly* to shew (lit. *extremely* desirous to shew)
7:15. it is yet *far more* evident.

4044-4056 13 657/799 4053

περισσοτέρως, perissoteros.

Mar 15:14. they cried out *the more exceedingly*,
2Co. 1:12. and *more abundantly* to you-ward.
2: 4. I have *more abundantly* unto you.

2Co. 7:13. *exceedingly* the more joyed we
15. his inward affection is *more abundant* toward you,
11:23. in labours *more abundant*,
— in prisons *more frequent*,
12:15. *the more abundantly* I love you,
Gal. 1:14. being *more exceedingly* zealous
Phi. 1:14. are *much more* bold to speak
1Th. 2:17. endeavoured *the more abundantly*
Heb 2: 1. we ought to give the more earnest heed (lit. we ought *much more* to attend)
13:19. I beseech (you) *the rather* to do this, that

4059 18 658/799 6:72 4012rt5114

περισσῶς, perissōs.

Mat.27:23. they cried out *the more*, saying,
Mar 10:26. they were astonished *out of measure*,
Acts26:11. being *exceedingly* mad against them,

4057 3 657/799 4053

περιστερά, peristera.

Mat. 3:16. descending like a *dove*,
10:16. and harmless as *doves*.
21:12. the seats of them that sold *doves*,
Mar 1:10. and the Spirit like a *dove* descending
11:15. the seats of them that sold *doves;*
Lu. 2:24. A pair of turtledoves, or two young *pigeons*.
3:22. in a bodily shape like a *dove*
Joh. 1:32. descending from heaven like a *dove*,
2:14. that sold oxen and sheep and *doves*,
16. said unto them that sold *doves*,

4058 10 657/799 6:63

περιτέμνω, peritemno.

Lu. 1:59. they came *to circumcise* the child;
2:21. accomplished for the *circumcising* of the child,
Joh. 7:22. ye on the sabbath day *circumcise* a man.
Acts 7: 8. and *circumcised* him the eighth day;
15: 1. Except ye *be circumcised*
5. That it was needful *to circumcise* them,
24. saying, (Ye must) *be circumcised*,
16: 3. and took and *circumcised* him
21:21. saying that they ought not *to circumcise*
1Co. 7:18. Is any man called *being circumcised?*
— *let* him not *be circumcised.*
Gal. 2: 3. was compelled *to be circumcised:*
5: 2. that if ye *be circumcised*,
3. to every man *that is circumcised*,
6:12. they constrain you *to be circumcised;*
13. they themselves *who are circumcised*
— desire *to have* you *circumcised*, (lit. you *to be circumcised*)
Col 2:11. In whom also ye *are circumcised* with the

4060 8 658/799 4012,5087

περιτίθημι, perititheemi.

Mat.21:33. and hedged it round about, (lit. *placed about* it a hedge)
27:28. and *put on* him a scarlet robe.
48. *put* (it) *on* a reed, *and* gave
Mar 12: 1. *set* an hedge *about* (it),
15:17. *put* it *about* his (head),
36. and *put* (it) *on* a reed, *and* gave
Joh. 19:29. and *put* (it) *upon* hyssop, *and*
1Co.12:23 *upon* these we *bestow* more abundant

4061 36 658/799 6:72 4059

περιτομή, peritomee.

Joh. 7:22. gave unto you *circumcision;*
23. on the sabbath day receive *circumcision*,
Acts 7: 8. gave him the covenant of *circumcision:*
10:45. they of the *circumcision*
11: 2. they that were of the *circumcision*
Ro. 2:25. For *circumcision* verily profiteth, if
— thy *circumcision* is made
26. be counted for *circumcision?*
27. by the letter and *circumcision*
28. (is that) *circumcision*, which is outward
29. and *circumcision* (is that) of the heart,
3: 1. what profit (is there) of *circumcision?*
30. shall justify the *circumcision* by
4: 9. upon the *circumcision* (only),
10. when he was in *circumcision*,
— Not in *circumcision*, but
11. received the sign of *circumcision*,
12. the father of *circumcision* to them who are not of the *circumcision* only,
15: 8. was a minister of the *circumcision*
1Co. 7:19. *Circumcision* is nothing, and
Gal. 2: 7. (the gospel) of the *circumcision* (was)
8. to the apostleship of the *circumcision*,
9. and they unto the *circumcision*.
12. them which were of the *circumcision*.
5: 6. neither *circumcision* availeth any thing,
11. if I yet preach *circumcision*,
6:15. neither *circumcision* availeth any thing,
Eph. 2:11. called the *Circumcision* in the flesh
Phi. 3: 3. For we are the *circumcision*,
5. Circumcised the eighth day, (lit. of the eighth day in *circumcision*) [The best copies read π. in the dative.]
Col. 2:11. with the *circumcision* made without hands,
— by the *circumcision* of Christ:
3:11. *circumcision* nor uncircumcision,
4:11. who are of the *circumcision*.
Tit. 1:10. specially they of the *circumcision:*

4062 1 658/800 4012,rt 5157

περιτρέπω, peritrepo.

Acts26:24. much learning doth make thee mad. (lit. *perverts* thee to madness)

4063 1 659/800 4012,5143

περιτρέχω, peritreko.

Mar 6:55. *And ran through* that whole region

4064 5 659/800 4012,5342

περιφέρω, periphero.

Mar 6:55. *to carry about* in beds those that were sick
2Co. 4:10. Always *bearing about* in the body
Eph. 4:14. and *carried about* with every wind
Heb 13: 9. *Be* not *carried about* with divers
Jude 12. *carried about* of winds;

4065 1 659/800 3:631 4012,5426

περιφρονέω, periphroneo.

Tit. 2:15. *Let* no man *despise* thee.

4066 10 659/800 4012,5561

περίχωρος, perikōros.

Mat. 3: 5. all the *region round about* Jordan,
14:35. all that *country round about*,
Mar 1:28. all the *region round about* Galilee.
6:55. through that whole *region round about*,

Lu. 3: 3. into all the *country about* Jordan,
4:14. through all the *region round about.*
37. every place of the *country round about.*
7:17. throughout all the *region round about.*
8:37. of *the country* of the Gadarenes *round about*
Acts14: 6. and unto *the region that lieth round about:*

4067 1 659/800 6:84 4012 psaō (to rub)

περίψημα, peripseema.

1Co. 4:13. the *offscouring* of all things unto this day.

4068 1 659/800 6:93 perperos (braggart)

περπερεύομαι, perperūomai.

1Co. 13: 4. charity *vaunteth* not *itself,*

4070 2 659/800 4009

πέρυσι, perusi.

2Co. 8:10. to be forward *a year ago.*
9: 2. was ready *a year ago;*

4072 4 659/800
(see below) πετάομαι, petaomai.

Rev. 4: 7. (was) like a *flying* eagle.
8:13. an angel *flying* through the midst
14: 6. saw another angel *fly*
19:17. saying to all the fowls *that fly* in

4071 14 659/800 4072

πετεινόν, petinon.

Mat. 6:26. Behold the *fowls* of the air.
8:20. and the *birds* of the air (have) nests;
13: 4. the *fowls* came and devoured
32. the *birds* of the air come and lodge
Mar 4: 4. and the *fowls* of the air came
32. the *fowls* of the air may lodge
Lu. 8: 5. the *fowls* of the air devoured it.
9:58. *birds* of the air (have) nests;
12:24. are ye better than the *fowls?*
13:19. the *fowls* of the air lodged in
Acts10:12. and *fowls* of the air.
11: 6. and *fowls* of the air.
Ro. 1:23. to corruptible man, and to *birds,*
Jas. 3: 7. every kind of beasts, and of *birds,*

4072 1 660/800
(see above) πέτομαι, petomai.

Rev.12:14. that she *might fly* into the wilderness,

4073 16 660/800 6:95 cf 4074 cf 2786,[3710]

πέτρα, petra.

Mat. 7:24. built his house upon a *rock:*
25. for it was founded upon a *rock.*
16:18. upon this *rock* I will build
27:51. and the *rocks* rent;
60. which he had hewn out in the *rock:*
Mar 15:46. which was hewn out of a *rock,*
Lu. 6:48. laid the foundation on a *rock:*
— for it was founded upon a *rock.*
8: 6. And some fell upon a *rock;*
13. They on the *rock* (are they), which,
Ro. 9:33. a stumblingstone and *rock* of offence
1Co.10: 4. drank of that spiritual *Rock* that followed them: and that *Rock* was Christ.
1Pet.2: 8(7). and a *rock* of offence,
Rev. 6:15. in the dens and in the *rocks* of the
16. And said to the mountains and *rocks.*

4074 1 660/800 cf 2786

πέτρος, petros.

Joh. 1:42(43). by interpretation, A *stone.*

4075 4 661/802 4073,1491

πετρώδης, petrōdees.

Mat.13: 5. Some fell upon *stony* places,
20. received the seed into *stony* places,
Mar 4: 5. And some fell on *stony* ground,
16. which are sown on *stony* ground;

4076 1 661/802 4078

πήγανον, peeganon.

Lu. 11:42. for ye tithe mint and *rue*

4077 12 661/802 6:112 4078

πηγή, peegee.

Mar 5:29. the *fountain* of her blood was dried up;
Joh. 4: 6. Now Jacob's *well* was there.
— sat thus on the *well:*
14. shall be in him a *well* of water
Jas. 3:11. Doth a *fountain* send forth
12. so (can) no *fountain* both yield
2Pet. 2:17. These are *wells* without water,
Rev. 7:17. unto living *fountains* of waters:
8:10. and upon the *fountains* of waters;
14: 7. and the *fountains* of waters.
16: 4. upon the rivers and *fountains*
21: 6. of the *fountain* of the water of life

4078 1 661/802

πήγνυμι, peegnumi

Heb 8: 2. which the Lord *pitched,* and not man.

4079 2 661/802 pēdon (blade)

πηδάλιον, peedalion.

Acts27:40. and loosed the *rudder* bands,
Jas. 3: 4. turned about with a very small *helm,*

4080 2 662/802 rt 4225

πηλίκος, peelikos.

Gal. 6:11. Ye see *how large* a letter I have written (lit. in *how large* letters)
Heb 7: 4. Now consider *how great* this man (was),

4081 6 662/802 6:118

πηλός, peelos.

Joh. 9: 6. and made *clay* of the spittle, and he anointed the eyes of the blind man with the *clay,*
11. A man that is called Jesus made *clay,*
14. when Jesus made the *clay,*
15. He put *clay* upon mine eyes,
Ro. 9:21. Hath not the potter power over the *clay*

4082 6 662/802 6:119

πήρα, peera.

Mat.10:10. Nor *scrip* for (your) journey,
Mar 6: 8. no *scrip,* no bread, no money
Lu. 9: 3. neither staves, nor *scrip,*
10: 4. Carry neither purse, nor *scrip.*

Lu. 22:35. and *scrip*, and shoes, lacked ye
36. let him take (it), and likewise (his) *scrip:*

4083 4 662/802

πῆχυς, *peekus.*

Mat. 6:27. one *cubit* unto his stature?
Lu. 12:25. can add to his stature one *cubit?*
Joh. 21: 8. as it were two hundred *cubits,*
Rev. 21:17. an hundred (and) forty (and) four *cubits,*

4084 12 662/803 cf 971

πιάζω, *piazo.*

Joh. 7:30. Then they sought *to take* him:
32. sent officers to *take* him.
44. some of them would *have taken* him;
8:20. and no man *laid hands on* him;
10:39. they sought again *to take* him:
11:57. that they *might take* him.
21: 3. that night they *caught* nothing.
10. which ye *have* now *caught.*
Acts 3: 7. he *took* him by the right hand, *and*
12: 4. *when* he *had apprehended* him,
2Co. 11:32. desirous *to apprehend* me:
Rev. 19:20. And the beast *was taken,*

4085 1 662/803 eq 4084

πιέζω, *piezo.*

Lu. 6:38. good measure, *pressed down,* and shaken together,

4086 1 663/803 3982,3056

πιθανολογία, *pithanologia.*

Col. 2: 4. beguile you with *enticing words.*

4087 4 663/803 6:122 4089

πικραίνω, *pikraino.*

Col. 3:19. and *be* not *bitter* against them.
Rev. 8:11. because they *were made bitter.*
10: 9. it *shall make* thy belly *bitter,*
10. my belly *was bitter.*

4088 4 663/803 6:122 4089

πικρία, *pikria.*

Acts 8:23. thou art in the gall of *bitterness,*
Ro. 3:14. full of cursing and *bitterness:*
Eph. 4:31. Let all *bitterness,* and wrath,
Heb 12:15. lest any root of *bitterness*

4089 2 663/803 6:122 4078

πικρός, *pikros.*

Jas. 3:11. sweet (water) and *bitter?*
14. if ye have *bitter* envying

4090 2 663/803 4089

πικρῶς, *pikrōs.*

Mat. 26:75. And he went out, and wept *bitterly.*
Lu. 22:62. Peter went out, and wept *bitterly.*

4092 1 664/803 *preō* (to burn)

πίμπραμαι, *pimpramai.*

Acts 28: 6. when he should have *swollen.*

4093 1 664/803 4094

πινακίδιον, *pinakidion.*

Lu. 1:63. he asked for a *writing table,* (lit. *tablet*)

4094 5 664/803 4109

πίναξ, *pinax.*

Mat. 14: 8. John Baptist's head in a *charger.*
11. was brought in a *charger,*
Mar 6:25. by and by in a *charger*
28. brought his head in a *charger,*
Lu. 11:39. outside of the cup and the *platter;*

4095 75 664/803 6:135

πίνω, πίω, πίομαι, *pino, pio, piomai.*

Mat. 6:25. or what ye shall *drink;*
31. What shall we *drink?*
11:18. came neither eating nor *drinking,*
19. came eating and *drinking,*
20:22. Are ye able *to drink* of the cup that I shall *drink* of,
23. Ye *shall drink* indeed of my cup,
24:38. they were eating and *drinking,*
49. to eat and *drink* with the drunken;
26:27. *Drink* ye all of it;
29. I will not *drink* henceforth
— when I *drink* it new with you
42. except I *drink* it,
27:34. They gave him vinegar *to drink*
— he would not *drink.*
Mar 2:16. eateth and *drinketh* with publicans
10:38. can ye *drink* of the cup that I *drink* of?
39. Ye *shall* indeed *drink* of the cup that I *drink* of;
14:23. and they all *drank* of it.
25. I will *drink* no more of the fruit of the vine, until that day that I *drink* it
15:23. they gave him *to drink* wine
16:18. and if they *drink* any deadly
Lu. 1:15. and shall *drink* neither wine
5:30. Why do ye eat and *drink* with
33. but thine eat and *drink?*
39. No man also *having drunk* old (wine)
7:33. nor *drinking* wine;
34. is come eating and *drinking;*
10: 7. eating and *drinking* such things
12:19. take thine ease, eat, *drink,* (and) be
29. or what ye shall *drink,*
45. to eat and *drink,* and to be drunken;
13:26. We have eaten and *drunk* in thy
17: 8. till I have eaten and *drunken;* and afterward thou shalt eat and *drink?*
27. They did eat, they *drank,* they
28. they did eat, they *drank,* they bought,
22:18. I will not *drink* of the fruit of
30. That ye may eat and *drink* at my
Joh. 4: 7. Give me *to drink.*
9. askest *drink* of me, which am a woman
10. Give me *to drink;*
12. and *drank* thereof himself,
13. Whosoever *drinketh* of this water
14. But whosoever *drinketh* of the
6:53. and *drink* his blood,
54. and *drinketh* my blood,
56. He that eateth my flesh, and *drinketh*
7:37. let him come unto me, and *drink.*
18:11. shall I not *drink* it?
Acts 9: 9. and neither did eat nor *drink.*
23:12. they would neither eat nor *drink*
21. they will neither eat nor *drink*
Ro. 14:21. nor *to drink* wine, nor
1Co. 9: 4. power to eat and *to drink?*
10: 4. *did* all *drink* the same spiritual drink: for they *drank* of that spiritual
7. sat down to eat and *drink,*
21. Ye cannot *drink* the cup of the Lord,

1Co.10:31. Whether therefore ye eat, or *drink*,
11:22. houses to eat and *to drink* in?
25. as oft as ye *drink* (it),
26. as ye eat this bread, and *drink*
27. and *drink* (this) cup of the Lord,
28. let him eat of (that) bread, and *drink*
29. For he that eateth and *drinketh* unworthily, eateth and *drinketh*
15:32. let us eat and *drink;*
Heb 6: 7. the earth *which drinketh* in the rain
Rev.14:10. The same *shall drink* of the wine
16: 6. thou hast given them blood *to drink;*
18: 3. all nations *have drunk* of the wine

4096 1 664/804 piōn (fat)

πιότης, *piotees.*

Ro. 11:17. and *fatness* of the olive tree;

4097 9 664/804 6:160 *perao* (to traverse)

πιπράσκω, *piprasko.*

Mat.13:46. went and *sold* all that he had, and
18:25. his lord commanded him *to be sold,*
26: 9. might *have been sold* for much,
Mar 14: 5. might *have been sold* for more
Joh.12: 5. Why *was* not this ointment *sold*
Acts 2:45. And *sold* their possessions and goods,
4:34. prices of the things *that were sold,*
5: 4. and *after* it *was sold*, was it not
Ro. 7:14. but I am carnal, *sold* under sin.

4098 90 664/804 6:161 *peto* cf 4072

πίπτω, ἔπεσον, *pipto, epeson.*

Mat. 2:11. and *fell down, and* worshipped him:
4: 9. if thou wilt *fall down and* worship me.
7:25. and it *fell* not: for it was founded
27. and it *fell:* and great was the fall of it.
10:29. *shall* not *fall* on the ground
13: 4. some (seeds) *fell* by the way side,
5. Some *fell* upon stony places,
7. And some *fell* among thorns;
8. other *fell* into good ground,
15:14. both *shall fall* into the ditch.
27. crumbs *which fall* from their masters'
17: 6. they *fell* on their face,
15. ofttimes he *falleth* into the fire,
18:26. *fell down, and* worshipped him,
29. *fell down* at his feet, *and*
21:44. *whosoever shall fall* on this stone
— on whomsoever it shall *fall,*
24:29. the stars *shall fall* from heaven,
26:39. and *fell* on his face, and prayed,
Mar 4: 4. some *fell* by the way side,
5. some *fell* on stony ground,
7. some *fell* among thorns,
8. other *fell* on good ground,
5:22. when he saw him, he *fell* at his feet,
9:20. he *fell* on the ground, *and* wallowed
14:35. and *fell* on the ground, and prayed
Lu. 5:12. *fell* on (his) face, *and* besought
6:39. *shall* they not both *fall* into the
49. and immediately it *fell;*
8: 5. some *fell* by the way side;
6. And some *fell* upon a rock;
7. some *fell* among thorns;
8. other *fell* on good ground,
14. that *which fell* among thorns
41. he *fell down* at Jesus' feet, *and*

Lu. 10:18. Satan as lightning *fall* from heaven
11:17. a house (divided) against a house *falleth*
13: 4. upon whom the tower in Siloam *fell,*
16:17. than one tittle of the law *to fail.*
21. with the crumbs *which fell* from the
17:16. And *fell down* on (his) face
20:18. *Whosoever* shall *fall* upon that stone shall be broken; but on whomsoever it shall *fall,*
21:24. And they *shall fall* by the edge of
23:30. *Fall* on us; and to the hills, Cover us.
Joh.11:32. she *fell down* at his feet,
12:24. *fall* into the ground *and* die,
18: 6. and *fell* to the ground.
Acts 1:26. and the lot *fell* upon Matthias;
5: 5. *fell down, and* gave up the ghost:
10. Then *fell* she *down* straightway
9: 4. he *fell* to the earth, *and* heard
10:25. and *fell down* at his feet, *and*
15:16. tabernacle of David, *which is fallen down;*
20: 9. and *fell down* from the third loft,
22: 7. And I *fell* unto the ground,
27:34. there *shall* not an hair *fall* from the head
Ro. 11:11. Have they stumbled that they *should fall?*
22. on them *which fell*, severity;
14: 4. to his own master he standeth or *falleth.*
1Co.10: 8. and *fell* in one day
12. thinketh he standeth take heed lest he *fall.*
14:25. and so *falling down* on (his) face
Heb 3:17. whose carcases *fell* in the wilderness?
4:11. lest any man *fall* after the same
11:30. the walls of Jericho *fell down,*
Jas. 5:12. lest ye *fall* into condemnation.
Rev. 1:17. I *fell* at his feet as dead.
4:10. elders *fall down* (lit. *shall f. d.*) before him
5: 8. *fell down* before the Lamb,
14. *fell down* and worshipped him
6:13. the stars of heaven *fell* unto the earth,
16. and rocks, *Fall* on us,
7:11. and *fell* before the throne on their
16. neither shall the sun *light* on them,
8:10. and there *fell* a great star from
— and it *fell* upon the third part
9: 1. and I saw a star *fall* from heaven
11:11. and great fear *fell* upon them
13. and the tenth part of the city *fell,*
16. *fell* upon their faces, and worshipped God,
14: 8. Babylon *is fallen, is fallen,*
16:19. and the cities of the nations *fell:*
17:10. five *are fallen*, and one is,
18: 2. Babylon the great *is fallen, is fallen,*
19: 4. and the four beasts *fell down* and
10. And I *fell* at his feet to worship
22: 8. I *fell down* to worship before

4100 248 665/805 6:174 4102

πιστεύω, *pistūo.*

Mat. 8:13. and as thou *hast believed,*
9:28. *Believe* ye that I am able to do
18: 6. little ones *which believe* in me,
21:22. ye shall ask in prayer *believing,*
25. Why *did* ye not then *believe* him?
32. and ye *believed* him not: but the publicans and the harlots *believed* him:
— that ye might *believe* him.
24:23. *believe* (it) not.
26. *believe* (it) not.
27:42. and we *will believe* him.
Mar 1:15. and *believe* the gospel.
5:36. Be not afraid, only *believe*

Mar 9:23. If thou canst *believe*, all things (are) possible to him *that believeth*.
24. Lord, I *believe;* help thou mine unbelief.
42. little ones *that believe* in me,
11:23. but *shall believe* that those things
24. *believe* that ye receive (them),
31. Why then *did* ye not *believe* him?
13:21. *believe* (him) not:
15:32. that we may see and *believe*.
16:13. neither *believed* they them.
14. because they *believed* not them
16. He *that believeth* and is baptized
17. these signs shall follow them *that believe;*
Lu. 1:20. because thou *believest* not my words,
45. blessed (is) she *that believed:*
8:12. lest they should *believe and* be saved.
13. which for a while *believe*,
50. *believe* only, and she shall be made whole.
16:11. who *will commit* to your *trust*
20: 5. Why then *believed* ye him not?
22:67. ye will not *believe:*
24:25. O fools, and slow of heart *to believe*
Joh. 1: 7. all (men) through him *might believe*.
12. to them *that believe* on his name:
50(51). Because I said unto thee,...*believest* thou?
2:11. his disciples *believed* on him.
22. and they *believed* the scripture,
23. many *believed* in his name,
24. Jesus *did* not *commit* himself unto them,
3:12. and ye *believe* not, how *shall* ye *believe*, if I tell you (of) heavenly things?
15. *who*soever *believeth* in him should not
16. *who*soever *believeth* in him should not
18. He *that believeth* on him is not condemned: but he *that believeth* not is condemned already, because he *hath* not *believed*
36. He *that believeth* on the Son hath
4:21. Woman, *believe* me, the hour cometh,
39. of the Samaritans of that city *believed*
41. many more *believed* because of his
42. Now we *believe*, not because
48. ye will not *believe*.
50. the man *believed* the word
53. himself *believed*, and his whole house.
5:24. and *believeth* on him that sent me,
38. him ye *believe* not.
44. How can ye *believe*,
46. For *had* ye *believed* Moses, ye would *have believed* me:
47. But if ye *believe* not his writings, how *shall* ye *believe* my words?
6:29. that ye *believe* on him whom he hath
30. that we may see, and *believe* thee?
35. he *that believeth* on me shall never thirst.
36. ye also have seen me, and *believe* not.
40. and *believeth* on him, may have
47. He *that believeth* on me hath
64. some of you that *believe* not.
— who they were *that believed* not,
69. And we *believe* and are sure that thou art
7: 5. neither *did* his brethren *believe* in him.
31. many of the people *believed* on him,
38. He *that believeth* on me, as the
39. which they *that believe* on him should
48. or of the Pharisees *believed* on him?
8:24. if ye *believe* not that I am (he),
30. many *believed* on him.
31. to those Jews *which believed* on him,
45 ye *believe* me not.
46. why *do* ye not *believe* me?
9:18. the Jews *did* not *believe*

Joh. 9:35. *Dost* thou *believe* on the Son of God?
36. that I *might believe* on him?
38. Lord, I *believe*.
10:25. and ye *believed* not:
26. But ye *believe* not,
37. *believe* me not.
38. though ye *believe* not me, *believe* the works: that ye may know, and *believe* that the Father
42. many *believed* on him there
11:15. to the intent ye *may believe;*
25. he *that believeth* in me,
26. and *believeth* in me shall never die. *Believest* thou this?
27. I *believe* that thou art the Christ,
40. if thou *wouldest believe*,
42. that they *may believe* that
45. *believed* on him.
48. all (men) *will believe* on him:
12:11. and *believed* on Jesus.
36. *believe* in the light,
37. yet they *believed* not on him.
38. who *hath believed* our report?
39. Therefore they could not *believe*,
42. many *believed* on him;
44. He *that believeth* on me, *believeth* not on
46. that *who*soever *believeth* on me
47. and *believe* not,
13:19. ye *may believe* that I am (he).
14: 1. ye *believe* in God, *believe* also in me.
10. *Believest* thou not that I am in
11. *Believe* me that I (am) in the Father,
— or else *believe* me for the very works'
12. He *that believeth* on me, the works
29. when it is come to pass, ye *might believe*
16: 9. because they *believe* not on me;
27. and *have believed* that I came out
30. by this we *believe* that thou camest
31. *Do* ye now *believe?*
17: 8. and they *have believed* that thou didst
20. for them also *which shall believe*
21. that the world *may believe* that thou
19:35. he saith true, that ye *might believe*.
20: 8. and he saw, and *believed*.
25. I *will* not *believe*.
29. thou *hast believed:*
— and (yet) *have believed*.
31. that ye *might believe* that Jesus
— and that *believing* ye might have life
Acts 2:44. And all *that believed* were together,
4: 4. which heard the word *believed;*
32. of them *that believed* were of one heart
5:14. And *believers* were the more added
8:12. But when they *believed* Philip
13. Then Simon himself *believed* also:
37. If thou *believest* with all thine heart,
— I *believe* that Jesus Christ is the Son of
9:26. *and believed* not that he was a disciple.
42. and many *believed* in the Lord.
10:43. *who*soever *believeth* in him shall
11:17. *who believed* on the Lord Jesus Christ;
21. a great number *believed*, *and* turned
13:12. when he saw what was done, *believed*,
39. by him all *that believe* are justified
41. which ye shall in no wise *believe*,
48. were ordained to eternal life *believed*.
14: 1. and also of the Greeks *believed*.
23. on whom they *believed*.
15: 5. certain...of the Pharisees *which believed*,
7. hear the word of the gospel, and *believe*.
11. But we *believe* that through the grace
16:31. *Believe* on the Lord Jesus Christ.

Acts 16:34. *believing* in God with all his house.
17:12. Therefore many of them *believed;*
34. clave unto him, and *believed:*
18: 8. *believed* on the Lord with all his house;
— many of the Corinthians hearing *believed,*
27. helped them much *which had believed*
19: 2. received the Holy Ghost *since* ye *believed?*
4. that they *should believe* on him
18. And many *that believed* came,
21:20. of Jews there are *which believe;*
25. touching the Gentiles *which believe,*
22:19. them *that believed* on thee:
24:14. *believing* all things which are
26:27. King Agrippa, *believest* thou the prophets? I know that thou *believest.*
27:25. for I *believe* God, that it shall
Ro. 1:16. to every one *that believeth;*
3: 2. unto them *were committed* (lit. they *were intrusted with*) the oracles of God.
22. unto all and upon all them *that believe:*
4: 3. Abraham *believed* God, and it was
5. but *believeth* on him that
11. the father of all them *that believe,*
17. before him whom he *believed,*
18. against hope *believed* in hope,
24. *if* we *believe* on him that raised
6: 8. we *believe* that we shall also (live)
9:33. *who*soever *believeth* on him
10: 4. to every one *that believeth.*
9. and shalt *believe* in thine heart
10. with the heart man believeth (lit. *is it believed*)
11. *Who*soever *believeth* on him
14. in whom they *have* not *believed?* and how *shall* they *believe*
16. who *hath believed* our report?
13:11. nearer than when we *believed.*
14: 2. For one *believeth* that he may
15:13. with all joy and peace in *believing,*
1Co. 1:21. to save them *that believe.*
3: 5. ministers by whom ye *believed,*
9:17. a dispensation (of the gospel) *is committed* unto me. (lit. I *am intrusted* with a dispensation)
11:18. and I partly *believe* it.
13: 7. *believeth* all things, hopeth all
14:22. not to them *that believe,* but
— but for them *which believe.*
15: 2. unless ye *have believed* in vain.
11. so we preach, and so ye *believed.*
2Co. 4:13. I *believed,* and therefore have I spoken; we also *believe,* and therefore speak;
Gal. 2: 7. *was committed* unto me, (lit. I *was intrusted with* the gospel)
16. even we *have believed* in Jesus Christ,
3: 6. as Abraham *believed* God,
22. might be given to them *that believe.*
Eph. 1:13. in whom also *after that* ye *believed,*
19. to us-ward *who believe,*
Phi. 1:29. not only *to believe* on him,
1Th. 1: 7. ensamples to all *that believe*
2: 4. *to be put in trust with* the gospel,
10. among you *that believe:*
13. also in you *that believe.*
4:14. For if we *believe* that Jesus died and
2Th. 1:10. admired in all them *that believe*
— our testimony among you *was believed*
2:11. that they should *believe* a lie:
12. *who believed* not the truth,
1Ti. 1:11. which *was committed* to my trust. (lit. *with* which I *was intrusted*)
16. should hereafter *believe* on him.
1Ti. 3:16. *believed on* in the world,
2Ti. 1:12. I know whom I *have believed.*
Tit. 1: 3. which *is committed* unto me (lit. *with* which I *have been intrusted*)
3: 8. that they *which have believed*
Heb 4: 3. we *which have believed* do enter
11: 6. must *believe* that he is, and
Jas. 2:19. Thou *believest* that there is one God;
— the devils also *believe,* and tremble.
23. Abraham *believed* God,
1Pet. 1: 8. yet *believing,* ye rejoice
21. *Who* by him *do believe* in God,
2: 6. and he *that believeth* on him
7. Unto you therefore *which believe*
1Joh. 3:23. That we *should believe* on the
4: 1. Beloved, *believe* not every spirit,
16. we have known and *believed*
5: 1. *Who*soever *believeth* that Jesus
5. he *that believeth* that Jesus is
10. He *that believeth* on the Son
— he *that believeth* not God
— because he *believeth* not the
13. unto you *that believe* on the name
— that ye *may believe* on the name
Jude 5. destroyed them *that believed* not.

4101 2 668/808 4102

πιστικός, pistikos.

Mar 14: 3. of *spike*nard very precious;
Joh. 12: 3. of ointment of *spike*nard, very costly,

4102 244 668/808 6:174 3982

πίστις, pistis.

[1] indicates that there is no article before π. in the Greek, though one is inserted in the English, [2] that there is an article in the Greek, though omitted in the English. When a pronoun, pers. or poss., or an adj. accompanies πίστις, the article is mostly blended with it in the rendering.

Mat. 8:10. I have not found so great *faith,*
9: 2. Jesus seeing their *faith*
22. thy *faith* hath made thee whole.
29. According to your *faith* be it
15:28. O woman, great (is) thy *faith:*
17:20. If ye have *faith* as a grain of
21:21. If ye have *faith,* and doubt not,
23:23. judgment, mercy, and [2]*faith:*
Mar 2: 5. When Jesus saw their *faith,*
4:40. how is it that ye have no *faith?*
5:34. Daughter, thy *faith* hath made
10:52. thy *faith* hath made thee whole.
11:22. Have *faith* in God.
Lu. 5:20. when he saw their *faith,*
7: 9. I have not found so great *faith,*
50. Thy *faith* hath saved thee;
8:25. Where is your *faith?*
48. thy *faith* hath made thee whole;
17: 5. Increase our *faith.*
6. If ye had *faith* as a grain of
19. thy *faith* hath made thee whole.
18: 8. shall he find [2]*faith* on the earth?
42. thy *faith* hath saved thee.
22:32. that thy *faith* fail not:
Acts 3:16. through [2]*faith* in his name
— yea, the *faith* which is by him
6: 5. a man full of *faith*
7. of the priests were obedient to the *faith.*
8. Stephen, full of *faith* and power.
11:24. full of the Holy Ghost and of *faith.*
13: 8. to turn away the deputy from the *faith.*
14: 9. that he had *faith* to be healed.

Acts14:22. to continue in the *faith*,
27. how he had opened the door of *faith*
15: 9. purifying their hearts by [2]*faith*.
16: 5. established in the *faith*,
17:31. he hath given *assurance* unto all
20:21. and *faith* toward our Lord Jesus
24:24. concerning the *faith* in Christ.
26:18. sanctified by *faith* that is in me.
Ro. 1: 5. for obedience to the [1]*faith* (lit. of *faith*)
8. that your *faith* is spoken of
12. by the mutual *faith* both of you and
17. revealed from *faith* to *faith* :
— The just shall live by *faith*.
3: 3. make the *faith* of God without effect ?
22. (which is) by *faith* of Jesus Christ
25. a propitiation through [2]*faith*
26. of him which believeth (lit. of *faith*) in Jesus.
27. but by the law of *faith*.
28. a man is justified by *faith*
30. justify the circumcision by *faith*. and uncircumcision through [2]*faith*.
31. make void the law through [2]*faith* ?
4: 5. his *faith* is counted for righteousness.
9. for we say that [2]*faith* was reckoned
11. a seal of the righteousness of the *faith*
12. walk in the steps of that *faith* of our
13. through the righteousness of *faith*.
14. [2]*faith* is made void, and the promise
16. Therefore (it is) of *faith*,
— which is of the [1]*faith* of Abraham ;
19. being not weak in [2]*faith*,
20. but was strong in [2]*faith*,
5: 1. being justified by *faith*,
2. we have access by [2]*faith* into
9:30. righteousness which is of *faith*.
32. Because (they sought it) not by *faith*,
10: 6. righteousness which is of *faith*
8. that is, the word of [2]*faith*,
17. So then [2]*faith* (cometh) by hearing,
11:20. and thou standest by [2]*faith*.
12: 3. to every man the measure of *faith*.
6. the proportion of [2]*faith* ;
14: 1. Him that is weak in the *faith*
22. Hast thou *faith*?
23. because (he eateth) not of *faith* : for whatsoever (is) not of *faith* is
16:26. to all nations for the obedience of *faith* :
1Co. 2: 5. That your *faith* should not stand in
12: 9. To another *faith* by the same
13: 2. though I have all *faith*,
13. And now abideth *faith*, hope,
15.14. and your *faith* (is) also vain.
17. your *faith* (is) vain ;
16:13. stand fast in the *faith*,
2Co. 1:24. have dominion over your *faith*,
— for by [2]*faith* ye stand.
4:13. having the same spirit of [2]*faith*,
5: 7. For we walk by *faith*,
8: 7. (in) *faith*, and utterance, and knowledge,
10:15. when your *faith* is increased,
13: 5. whether ye be in the *faith* ;
Gal. 1:23. now preacheth the *faith* which
2:16. but by the [1]*faith* of Jesus Christ,
— justified by the [1]*faith* of Christ,
20. I live by the [1]*faith* of the Son
3: 2. or by the hearing of *faith*?
5. or by the hearing of *faith* ?
7. they which are of *faith*,
8. justify the heathen through *faith*.
9. they which be of *faith* are blessed
11. The just shall live by *faith*.

Gal. 3:12. the law is not of *faith* :
14. promise of the Spirit through *faith*.
22. the promise by *faith* of Jesus Christ
23. But before [2]*faith* came,
— shut up unto the *faith*
24. that we might be justified by *faith*.
25. But after that [2]*faith* is come,
26. children of God by [2]*faith* in Christ
5: 5. the hope of righteousness by *faith*.
6. but *faith* which worketh by love.
22. gentleness, goodness, *faith*,
6:10. who are of the houshold of [2]*faith*.
Eph 1:15. after I heard of your *faith* in the Lord
2: 8. are ye saved through [2]*faith* ;
3:12. with confidence by the *faith* of him.
17. dwell in your hearts by [2]*faith* ;
4: 5. One Lord, one *faith*, one baptism,
13. in the unity of the *faith*
6:16. taking the shield of [2]*faith*,
23. and love with *faith*,
Phi. 1:25. your furtherance and joy of [2]*faith* ;
27. for the *faith* (τῇ πίστει) of the gospel ;
2:17. sacrifice and service of your *faith*,
3: 9. which is through the [1]*faith* of Christ,
— which is of God by [2]*faith* :
Col. 1: 4. Since we heard of your *faith* in Christ
23. If ye continue in the *faith* grounded
2: 5. and the stedfastness of your *faith* in
7. and stablished in the *faith*,
12. through the *faith* of the operation of God.
1Th. 1: 3. your work of *faith*, and labour of love,
8. your *faith* to God-ward is spread abroad;
3: 2. to comfort you concerning your *faith* :
5. I sent to know your *faith*,
6. good tidings of your *faith* and charity,
7. our affliction and distress by your *faith*
10. which is lacking in your *faith* ?
5: 8. the breastplate of *faith* and love ;
2Th. 1: 3. your *faith* groweth exceedingly,
4. for your patience and *faith* in all
11. and the work of *faith* with power:
2:13. and *belief* of the truth:
3: 2. for all (men) have not [2]*faith*.
1Ti. 1: 2. (my) own son in the [1]*faith* :
4. godly edifying which is in *faith* :
5. and (of) *faith* unfeigned:
14. with *faith* and love which is in
19. Holding *faith*, and a good conscience;
— concerning [2]*faith* have made shipwreck:
2: 7. of the Gentiles in *faith* and verity.
15. if they continue in *faith*
3: 9. Holding the mystery of the *faith* in a
13. great boldness in the [1]*faith* which is
4: 1. some shall depart from the *faith*,
6. in the words of [2]*faith* and of good
12. in spirit, in *faith*, in purity.
5: 8. he hath denied the *faith*, and is
12. they have cast off their first *faith*.
6:10. they have erred from the *faith*,
11. godliness, *faith*, love, patience,
12. Fight the good fight of [2]*faith*,
21. have erred concerning the *faith*.
2Ti. 1: 5. the unfeigned *faith* that is in thee,
13. in *faith* and love which is in Christ
2:18. and overthrow the *faith* of some.
22. follow righteousness, *faith*,
3: 8. reprobate concerning the *faith*.
10. [2]*faith*, longsuffering, charity,
15. through *faith* which is in Christ
4: 7. I have kept the *faith* :
Ti 1: 1. according to the [1]*faith* of God's elect,
4. (mi e) own son after the common

Tit. 1:13. may be sound in the *faith;*
2: 2. sound in [2]*faith,* in charity, in patience,
10. but shewing all good *fidelity;*
3:15. that love us in the [1]*faith.*
Philem. 5. of thy love and *faith,*
6. the communication of thy *faith*
Heb 4: 2. not being mixed with [2]*faith* in them
6: 1. and of *faith* toward God,
12. who through *faith* and patience
10:22. in full assurance of *faith,*
38. the just shall live by *faith:*
39. but of them that believe (lit. of *faith*) to the saving of
11: 1. Now *faith* is the substance of things
3. Through *faith* we understand that
4. By *faith* Abel offered unto God a more excellent
5. By *faith* Enoch was translated
6. But without *faith* (it is) impossible to
7. By *faith* Noah, being warned of God
— righteousness which is by *faith.*
8. By *faith* Abraham, when he was
9. By *faith* he sojourned in the land
11. Through *faith* also Sara herself
13. These all died in *faith,* not having
17. By *faith* Abraham, when he was tried,
20. By *faith* Isaac blessed Jacob and Esau
21. By *faith* Jacob, when he was a dying,
22. By *faith* Joseph, when he died,
23. By *faith* Moses, when he was born,
24. By *faith* Moses, when he was come to
27. By *faith* he forsook Egypt,
28. Through *faith* he kept the passover,
29. By *faith* they passed through the Red sea
30. By *faith* the walls of Jericho fell
31. By *faith* the harlot Rahab
33. Who through *faith* subdued kingdoms,
39. a good report through [2]*faith,*
12: 2. and finisher of (our) *faith;*
13: 7. whose *faith* follow,
Jas. 1: 3. the trying of your *faith* worketh
6. But let him ask in *faith,*
2: 1. brethren, have not the *faith* of our Lord
5. rich in *faith,* and heirs of the kingdom
14. though a man say he hath *faith,* and have not works? can [2]*faith* save him?
17. Even so [2]*faith,* if it hath not works,
18. Thou hast *faith,* and I have works: shew me thy *faith* without thy works, and I will shew thee my *faith* by my works.
20. that [2]*faith* without works is dead?
22. Seest thou how [2]*faith* wrought, with his works, and by works was [2]*faith*
24. and not by *faith* only.
26. so [2]*faith* without works is dead
5: 15. the prayer of [2]*faith* shall save
Pet. 1: 5. through *faith* unto salvation
7. That the trial of your *faith,*
9. Receiving the end of your *faith,*
21. that your *faith* and hope might
5: 9. stedfast in the *faith,*
2Pet. 1: 1. obtained like precious *faith* with us
5. add to your *faith* virtue;
1Joh. 5: 4. that overcometh the world, (even) our *faith.*
Jude 3. contend for the *faith* which was once
20. on your most holy *faith,*
Rev. 2:13. and hast not denied my *faith,*
19. thy works, and charity, and service, and *faith,*
13:10. the patience and the *faith* of the saints.
14:12. and the *faith* of Jesus

4103 66 670/811 6:174 3982

πιστός, *pistos*

Mat.24:45. Who then is a *faithful* and wise servant,
25:21. Well done, (thou) good and *faithful* servant: thou hast been *faithful* over a few
23. Well done, good and *faithful* servant; thou hast been *faithful* over a few
Lu. 12:42. Who then is that *faithful* and wise steward,
16:10. He that is *faithful* in that which is least is *faithful* also in much:
11. ye have not been *faithful* in the
12. And if ye have not been *faithful*
19:17. thou hast been *faithful* in
Joh. 20:27. be not faithless, but *believing.*
Acts 10:45. they of the circumcision *which believed* were astonished,
13:34. the *sure* mercies of David.
16: 1. which was a Jewess, *and believed;* (lit. a *believing* Jewess)
15. If ye have judged me to be *faithful* to the Lord,
1Co. 1: 9. God (is) *faithful,* by whom ye were
4: 2. that a man be found *faithful.*
17. and *faithful* in the Lord,
7:25. mercy of the Lord to be *faithful.*
10:13. but God (is) *faithful,* who will not
2Co. 1:18. But (as) God (is) *true,* our word
6:15. he *that believeth* with an infidel?
Gal. 3: 9. are blessed with *faithful* Abraham.
Eph. 1: 1. and to the *faithful* in Christ Jesus:
6:21. and *faithful* minister in the Lord,
Col. 1: 2. To the saints and *faithful* brethren
7. a *faithful* minister of Christ;
4: 7. and a *faithful* minister
9. a *faithful* and beloved brother,
1Th. 5:24. *Faithful* (is) he that calleth you,
2Th. 3: 3. But the Lord is *faithful,*
1Ti. 1:12. that he counted me *faithful,*
15. This (is) a *faithful* saying, and worthy
3: 1. This (is) a *true* saying, If a man
11. *faithful* in all things.
4: 3. them *which believe* and know the truth.
9. This (is) a *faithful* saying and
10. specially of those *that believe.*
12. be thou an example of the *believers,*
5:16. If any man or woman *that believeth* (lit. if any *believing* (man) or *believing* (woman))
6: 2. they that have *believing* masters,
— because they are *faithful*
2Ti. 2: 2. commit thou to *faithful* men,
11. (It is) a *faithful* saying: For if we
13. he abideth *faithful:*
Tit. 1: 6. having *faithful* children,
9. Holding fast the *faithful* word
3: 8. (This is) a *faithful* saying, and these
Heb 2:17. a merciful and *faithful* high priest
3: 2. Who was *faithful* to him that
5. Moses verily (was) *faithful* in all his
10:23. he (is) *faithful* that promised;
11:11. she judged him *faithful* who had
1Pet. 4:19. as unto a *faithful* Creator.
5:12. By Silvanus, a *faithful* brother
1Joh. 1: 9. he is *faithful* and just to forgive
3Joh. 5. thou doest *faithfully* whatsoever
Rev. 1: 5. (who is) the *faithful* witness,
2:10. be thou *faithful* unto death,
13. Antipas (was) my *faithful* martyr,
3:14. the *faithful* and true witness,
17:14. called, and chosen, and *faithful.*
19:11. (was) called *Faithful* and True,

Rev.21: 5. these words are true and *faithful*.
22: 6. These sayings (are) *faithful* and true:

4104 1 671/811 6:174 4103

πιστόω, *pistoō.*

2Ti. 3:14. and *hast been assured of*,

4105 39 671/812 6:228 4106

πλανάω, *planao.*

Mat.18:12. and one of them *be gone astray*,
— and seeketh that *which is gone astray?*
13. which *went* not *astray*.
22:29. Ye *do err*, not knowing
24: 4. Take heed that no man *deceive* you.
5. and *shall deceive* many.
11. and *shall deceive* many.
24. they shall *deceive* the very elect.
Mar 12:24. *Do* ye not therefore *err*,
27. ye therefore *do* greatly *err*.
13: 5. Take heed lest any (man) *deceive* you:
6. and *shall deceive* many.
Lu. 21: 8. Take heed that ye *be* not *deceived*:
Joh. 7:12. Nay; but he *deceiveth* the people.
47. *Are* ye also *deceived?*
1Co. 6: 9. *Be* not *deceived*: neither fornicators,
15:33. *Be* not *deceived*: evil communications
Gal. 6: 7. *Be* not *deceived*; God is not mocked:
2Ti. 3:13. *deceiving*, and *being deceived*.
Tit. 3: 3. *deceived*, serving divers lusts
Heb 3:10. They *do* alway *err* in (their) heart:
5: 2. and on them *that are out of the way*;
11:38. they *wandered* in deserts,
Jas. 1:16. *Do* not *err*, my beloved brethren.
5:19. Brethren, if any of you *do err* from
1Pet. 2:25. ye were as sheep *going astray*;
2Pet. 2:15. and *are gone astray*, following
1Joh. 1: 8. we *deceive* ourselves, and the
2:26. concerning them *that seduce* you.
3: 7. *let* no man *deceive* you:
Rev. 2:20. to teach and *to seduce* my servants
12: 9. and Satan, *which deceiveth* the whole
13:14. And *deceiveth* them that dwell on
18:23. *were* all nations *deceived*.
19:20. with which he *deceived* them
20: 3. that he *should deceive* the nations no more,
8. go out *to deceive* the nations
10. the devil *that deceived* them

4106 10 671/812 6:228 4108

πλάνη, *planee.*

Mat.27:64. so the last *error* shall be worse than
Ro. 1:27. that recompence of their *error* which
Eph. 4:14. whereby they lie in wait *to deceive*; (lit. unto circumvention of *deception*)
1Th. 2: 3. our exhortation (was) not of *deceit*,
2Th. 2:11. God shall send them strong *delusion*,
Jas. 5:20. from the *error* of his way
2Pet. 2:18. from them who live in *error*.
3:17. being led away with the *error* of the
1Joh. 4: 6. and the spirit of *error*.
Jude 11. ran greedily after the *error* of Balaam

4107 1 672/812 6:228 4108

πλανήτης, *planeetees.*

Jude 13. *wandering* stars, to whom is reserved

4108 5 672/812 6:228

πλάνος, *planos.*

Mat.27:63. we remember that that *deceiver* said,
2Co. 6: 8. as *deceivers*, and (yet) true;
1 Ti. 4: 1. giving heed to *seducing* spirits,
2Joh. 7. For many *deceivers* are entered
— This is a *deceiver* and an antichrist.

4109 3 672/812 4111

πλάξ, *plax.*

2Co. 3: 8. not in *tables* of stone, but in fleshy *tables* of the heart.
Heb 9: 4. and the *tables* of the covenant;

4110 1 672/812 6:254 4111

πλάσμα, *plasma.*

Ro. 9:20. Shall the *thing formed* say to him

4111 2 672/812 6:254

πλάσσω, *plasso.*

Ro. 9:20. say to him *that formed* (it),
1Ti. 2:13. For Adam *was* first *formed*,

4112 1 672/812 6:254 4111

πλαστός, *plastos.*

2Pet. 2: 3. with *feigned* words make merchandise

4113 9 672/812 4116

πλατεῖα, *platīa.*

Mat. 6: 5. and in the corners of the *streets*,
12:19. hear his voice in the *streets*.
Lu. 10:10. out into the *streets* of the same,
13:26. and thou hast taught in our *streets*.
14:21. Go out quickly into the *streets* and
Acts 5:15. the sick into the *streets*, and
Rev.11: 8. their dead bodies (shall lie) in the *street*
21:21. and the *street* of the city (was)
22: 2. In the midst of the *street* of it,

4114 4 672/813 4116

πλάτος, *platos.*

Eph. 3:18. what (is) the *breadth*, and length,
Rev.20: 9. they went up on the *breadth* of the earth,
21:16. the length is as large as the *breadth*:
— and the *breadth* and the height of it

4115 3 672/813 4116

πλατύνω, *platuno.*

Mat.23: 5. they *make broad* their phylacteries,
2Co. 6:11. our heart *is enlarged*.
13. *be* ye also *enlarged*.

4116 1 673/813 4111

πλατύς, *platus.*

Mat. 7:13. for *wide* (is) the gate, and broad (is) the

4117 1 673/813 4120

πλέγμα, *plegma.*

1Ti. 2: 9. not with *broidered hair*,

4118-4119 59 673/813 4183

πλείων, πλεῖον or πλέον, πλεῖστος,

plīōn, plīon or *pleon, plīstos.*

Mat. 5:20. shall exceed (the righteousness) of the scribes (lit. shall abound *more* than, &c.

Mat. 6:25. Is not the life *more* than meat,
11:20. wherein *most* of his mighty works
12:41. a *greater* than Jonas (is) here.
42. a *greater* than Solomon (is) here.
20:10. that they should have received *more;*
21: 8. And a *very great* multitude spread
36. other servants *more* than the first:
26:53. *more* than twelve legions of angels?
Mar 12:33. is *more* than all whole burnt offerings
43. hath cast *more* in, than all they
Lu. 3:13. Exact no *more* than that which is
7:42. which of them will love him *most?*
43. that (he), to whom he forgave *most.*
9:13. We have no *more* but five loaves and
11:31. a *greater* than Solomon (is) here.
32. a *greater* than Jonas (is) here.
53. to speak of *many* things:
12:23. The life is *more* than meat,
21: 3. hath cast in *more* than they all:
Joh. 4: 1. baptized *more* disciples than John,
41. And many *more* believed
7:31. will he do *more* miracles than
15: 2. may bring forth *more* fruit.
21:15. lovest thou me *more* than these?
Acts 2:40. And with *many* other words
4:17. that it spread no *further* among
22. For the man was *above* (lit. of *more* than) forty years
13:31. he was seen *many* days of them
15:28. to lay upon you no *greater* burden
18:20. to tarry *longer* time with them,
19:32. and the *more part* knew not
20: 9. and as Paul was *long* preaching,
21:10. as we tarried (there) *many* days,
23:13. they were *more* than forty
21. *more* than forty men, which have
24: 4. that I be not *further* tedious
11. there are yet but twelve days (lit. not *more* than, &c.)
17. Now after *many* years I came
25: 6. among them *more* than ten days,
14. when they had been there *many* days,
27:12. the *more part* advised to depart
20. nor stars in *many* days appeared,
28:23. there came *many* to him into
1Co. 9:19. that I might gain the *more.*
10: 5. But with *many* of them God was
14:27. by two, or at the *most* (by) three,
15: 6. the *greater part* remain unto
2Co. 2: 6. which (was inflicted) of *many.*
4:15. through the thanksgiving of *many*
9: 2. your zeal hath provoked *very many.*
Phi. 1:14. And *many* of the brethren in the Lord,
2Ti. 2:16. they will increase unto *more* ungodliness.
3: 9. they shall proceed no *further:*
Heb 3: 3. counted worthy of *more* glory
— hath *more* honour than the house.
7:23. they truly were *many* priests,
11: 4. a *more excellent* sacrifice than
Rev. 2:19. and the last (to be) *more* than the first.

4120 3 673/813

πλέκω, *pleko*

Mat. 27:29. *when* they *had platted* a crown of thorns,
Mar 15:17. and *platted* a crown of thorns, *and*
Joh. 19: 2. the soldiers *platted* a crown of thorns, *and*

4121 9 673/814 6:263 4119

πλεονάζω, *pleonazo.*

Ro. 5:20. that the offence *might abound.* But where sin *abounded,*
6: 1. that grace *may abound?*
2Co. 4:15. that the *abundant* grace might
8:15. (gathered) much *had* nothing *over;*
Phi. 4:17. that may abound (lit. *abounding*) to your account.
1Th. 3:12. the Lord *make* you *to increase* and abound
2Th. 1: 3. toward each other *aboundeth;*
2Pet. 1: 8. these things be in you, and *abound,*

4122 5 673/814 6:266 4123

πλεονεκτέω, *pleonekteo.*

2Co. 2:11. Lest Satan *should get an advantage of* us: (lit. lest we *should be overreached* by Satan)
7: 2. we *have defrauded* no man.
12:17. *Did* I *make* a *gain of* you
18. *Did* Titus *make* a *gain of* you?
1Th. 4: 6. and *defraud* his brother in (any) matter:

4123 4 673/814 6:266 4119,2192

πλεονέκτης, *pleonektees.*

1Co. 5:10. or with the *covetous,*
11. or *covetous,* or an idolater,
6:10. nor *covetous,* nor drunkards,
Eph. 5: 5. nor *covetous* man, who is an idolater,

4124 10 673/814 6:266 4123

πλεονεξία, *pleonexia.*

Mar 7:22. *covetousness* [plural], wickedness,
Lu. 12:15. and beware of *covetousness:*
Ro. 1:29. wickedness, *covetousness,* maliciousness;
2Co. 9: 5. and not as (of) *covetousness.*
Eph 4:19. to work all uncleanness with *greediness.*
5: 3. all uncleanness, or *covetousness,*
Col. 3: 5. and *covetousness,* which is idolatry:
1Th. 2: 5. nor a cloke of *covetousness;*
2Pet. 2: 3. through *covetousness* shall they
14. exercised with *covetous practices;*

4125 5 673/814

πλευρά, *plūra.*

Joh. 19:34. with a spear pierced his *side,*
20:20. (his) hands and his *side.*
25. and thrust my hand into his *side,*
27. and thrust (it) into my *side:*
Acts 12: 7. and he smote Peter on the *side,*

4126 5 673/814 4150,cf 4130

πλέω, *pleo.*

Lu. 8:23. But *as* they *sailed* he fell asleep:
Acts 21: 3. we left it on the left hand, and *sailed*
27: 2. meaning *to sail* by the coasts
6. a ship of Alexandria *sailing* into Italy,
24. all them *that sail* with thee.

4127 21 674/814 4141

πληγή, *pleegee.*

Lu. 10:30. *wounded* (him), *and* departed, (lit. having laid on *wounds*)
12:48. things worthy of *stripes,*
Acts 16:23. when they had laid many *stripes* upon
33. and washed (their) *stripes;*
2Co. 6: 5. In *stripes,* in imprisonments,
11:23. in *stripes* above measure,
Rev. 9:20. were not killed by these *plagues*
11: 6. and to smite the earth with all *plagues,*

Rev.13: 3. and his deadly *wound* was healed:
12. whose deadly *wound* was healed.
14. which had the *wound* by a sword,
15: 1. having the seven last *plagues;*
6. having the seven *plagues,*
8. till the seven *plagues* of the seven
16: 9. hath power over these *plagues:*
21. because of the *plague* of the hail; for the *plague* thereof was exceeding great.
18: 4. that ye receive not of her *plagues.*
8. shall her *plagues* come in one day,
21: 9. full of the seven last *plagues,*
22:18. God shall add unto him the *plagues* that

4128 32 674/814 6:274 4130

πλῆθος, pleethos.

Mar 3: 7. and a great *multitude* from Galilee
8. a great *multitude,* when they had heard
Lu. 1:10. And the whole *multitude* of the people
2:13. a *multitude* of the heavenly host
5: 6. a great *multitude* of fishes:
6:17. and a great *multitude* of people
8:37. Then the whole *multitude* of the country
19:37. the whole *multitude* of the disciples
23: 1. the whole *multitude* of them arose,
27. a great *company* of people,
Joh. 5: 3. In these lay a great *multitude*
21: 6. for the *multitude* of fishes.
Acts 2: 6. the *multitude* came together,
4:32. And the *multitude* of them that
5:14. *multitudes* both of men and women.
16. There came also a *multitude* (out)
6: 2. the twelve called the *multitude* of the disciples
5. pleased the whole *multitude:*
14: 1. a great *multitude* both of the Jews
4. But the *multitude* of the city was
15:12. Then all the *multitude* kept silence,
30. gathered the *multitude* together,
17: 4. devout Greeks a great *multitude,*
19: 9. evil of that way before the *multitude,*
21:22. the *multitude* must needs come
36. the *multitude* of the people followed
23: 7. and the *multitude* was divided.
25:24. all the *multitude* of the Jews
28: 3. gathered a *bundle* of sticks,
Heb 11:12. the stars of the sky in *multitude,*
Jas. 5:20. shall hide a *multitude* of sins.
1Pet.4: 8. shall cover the *multitude* of sins.

4129 12 674/815 6:274 eq 4128

πληθύνω, pleethuno.

Mat.24:12. because iniquity shall *abound,*
Acts 6: 1. *when* the number of the disciples *was multiplied,*
7. the number of the disciples *multiplied*
7:17. people grew and *multiplied*
9:31. in the comfort of the Holy Ghost, *were multiplied.*
12:24. the word of God grew and *multiplied.*
2Co. 9:10. and *multiply* your seed sown,
Heb 6:14. and *multiplying* I *will multiply* thee.
1Pet.1: 2. and peace, *be multiplied.*
2Pet.1: 2. Grace and peace *be multiplied* unto
Jude 2. and love, *be multiplied.*

4130 24 663/815 4126

πλήθω, pleetho.

Mat.22:10. the wedding *was furnished* with guests.
Mat.27:48. and *filled* (it) with vinegar,
Lu. 1:15. he *shall be filled* with the Holy Ghost,
23. the days of...*were accomplished,*
41. *was filled* with the Holy Ghost:
57. Elisabeth's *full* time *came*
67. Zacharias *was filled* with the
2: 6. the days *were accomplished* that
21. eight days *were accomplished*
22. when the days...*were accomplished,*
4:28. heard these things, *were filled* with wrath,
5: 7. and *filled* both the ships,
26. and *were filled* with fear,
6:11. they *were filled* with madness;
Joh.19:29. and they *filled* a spunge with vinegar,
Acts 2: 4. they *were* all *filled* with the Holy Ghost.
3:10. and they *were filled* with wonder and
4: 8. Then Peter, *filled* with the Holy Ghost,
31. they *were* all *filled* with the Holy Ghost,
5:17. and *were filled* with indignation,
9:17. and *be filled* with the Holy Ghost.
13: 9. Paul, *filled* with the Holy Ghost,
45. they *were filled* with envy,
19:29. the whole city *was filled* with confusion:

4131 2 675/815 4141

πλήκτης, pleektees.

1Ti. 3: 3. Not given to wine, no *striker,*
Tit. 1: 7. no *striker,* not given to filthy lucre;

4132 1 675/815 4130

πλημμύρα, pleemmura.

Lu. 6:48. and when the *flood* arose,

4133 31 675/815 4119

πλήν, pleen.

Mat.11:22. *But* I say unto you, It shall be
24. *But* I say unto you, That it shall
18: 7. *but* woe to that man by whom
26:39. *nevertheless* not as I will, but
64. *nevertheless* I say unto you,
Mar 12:32. and there is none other *but* he:
Lu. 6:24. *But* woe unto you that are rich
35. *But* love ye your enemies,
10:11. *notwithstanding* be ye sure of this,
14. *But* it shall be more tolerable for
20. *Notwithstanding* in this rejoice not,
11:41. *But rather* give alms of such things
12:31. *But rather* seek ye the kingdom
13:33. *Nevertheless* I must walk to day,
18: 8. *Nevertheless* when the Son of man
19:27. *But* those mine enemies, which
22:21. *But,* behold, the hand of him that
22. *but* woe unto that man by
42. *nevertheless* not my will, but
23:28. *but* weep for yourselves, and
Joh. 8:10. and saw none *but* the woman,
Acts 8: 1. *except* the apostles.
15:28. *than* these necessary things;
20:23. *Save* that the Holy Ghost witnesseth
27:22. life among you, *but* of the ship.
1Co.11:11. *Nevertheless* neither is the man
Eph. 5:33. *Nevertheless* let every one of
Phi. 1:18. What then? *notwithstanding,* every
3:16. *Nevertheless,* whereto we have
4:14. *Notwithstanding* ye have well
Rev. 2:25. *But* that which ye have (already)

4134 17 675/815 6:283 4130

πλήρης, pleerees.

Mat.14:20. that remained twelve baskets *full.*

Mat.15:37. left seven baskets *full*.
Mar 4:28. the *full* corn in the ear.
6:43. twelve baskets *full* of the fragments,
8:19. how many baskets *full* of
Lu. 4: 1. Jesus being *full* of the Holy Ghost
5:12. behold a man *full* of leprosy:
Joh. 1:14. *full* of grace and truth.
Acts 6: 3. *full* of the Holy Ghost
5. a man *full* of faith and of
8. Stephen, *full* of faith and power,
7:55. he, being *full* of the Holy Ghost,
9:36. this woman was *full* of good works
11:24. and *full* of the Holy Ghost
13:10. O *full* of all subtilty
19:28. they were *full* of wrath,
2Joh. 8. that we receive a *full* reward.

4135 5 676/816 6:283 4134,5409

πληροφορέω, *pleerophoreo.*

Lu. 1: 1. of those things *which are most surely believed* among us, (lit. *which have full course*)
Ro. 4:21. And *being fully persuaded* that,
14: 5. *Let* every man *be fully persuaded*
2Ti. 4: 5. *make full proof of* thy ministry.
17. the preaching *might be fully known*,

4136 4 676/816 6:283 4135

πληροφορία, *pleerophoria.*

Col. 2: 2. of the *full assurance* of understanding,
1Th. 1: 5. and in much *assurance*;
Heb 6:11. to the *full assurance* of hope
10:22. in *full assurance*(lit. in *full bearing*) of faith,

4137 90 676/816 6:283 4134

πληρόω, *pleeroō.*

Mat. 1:22. that it *might be fulfilled*
2:15. that it *might be fulfilled* which was
17. Then *was fulfilled* that which was
23. that it *might be fulfilled*
3:15. *to fulfil* all righteousness.
4:14. That *it might be fulfilled*
5:17. not come to destroy, but *to fulfil*
8:17. That it *might be fulfilled*
12:17. That it *might be fulfilled* which
13:35. That it *might be fulfilled* which
48. Which, when it *was full*, they drew
21: 4. that it *might be fulfilled*
23:32. *Fill* ye *up* then the measure of
26:54. shall the scriptures *be fulfilled*,
56. that the scriptures of the prophets *might be fulfilled*.
27: 9. Then *was fulfilled* that which
35. that it *might be fulfilled* which
Mar 1:15. The time *is fulfilled*, and the kingdom
14:49. but the scriptures must be fulfilled. (lit. but that the scriptures *be fulfilled*)
15:28. And the scripture *was fulfilled*,
Lu. 1:20. which *shall be fulfilled* in their season.
2:40. strong in spirit, *filled* with wisdom:
3: 5. Every valley *shall be filled*,
4:21. This day *is* this scripture *fulfilled*
7: 1. when he *had ended* all his sayings
9:31. which he should *accomplish* at
21:22. are written may *be fulfilled*.
24. until the times of the Gentiles *be fulfilled*.
22:16. until it *be fulfilled* in the kingdom
24:44. that all things must *be fulfilled*,
Joh. 3:29. this my joy therefore *is fulfilled*.
Joh. 7: 8. my time *is* not yet *full come*.
12: 3. the house *was filled* with the
38. *might be fulfilled*, which he spake,
13:18. that the scripture *may be fulfilled*,
15:11. (that) your joy *might be full*.
25. that the word *might be fulfilled*
16: 6. sorrow *hath filled* your heart.
24. that your joy may be *full*.
17:12. the scripture *might be fulfilled*.
13. might have my joy *fulfilled*
18: 9. the saying *might be fulfilled*,
32. saying of Jesus *might be fulfilled*,
19:24. the scripture *might be fulfilled*,
36. the scripture *should be fulfilled*,
Acts 1:16. must needs *have been fulfilled*,
2: 2. and it *filled* all the house
28. thou *shalt make* me *full* of joy
3:18. he hath so *fulfilled*.
5: 3. why *hath* Satan *filled* thine heart
28. and, behold, ye *have filled* Jerusalem
7:23. when he was full forty years old, (lit. when the space of...*was fulfilled*)
30. *when* forty years *were expired*,
9:23. after that many days *were fulfilled*,
12:25. *when* they *had fulfilled* (their) ministry,
13:25. as John *fulfilled* his course,
27. they *have fulfilled* (them) in condemning
52. the disciples *were filled* with joy,
14:26. for the work which they *fulfilled*.
19:21. After these things *were ended*,
24:27. But *after* two years (lit. two years *having been fulfilled*)
Ro. 1:29. *Being filled* with all unrighteousness,
8: 4. the law *might be fulfilled* in us,
13: 8. *hath fulfilled* the law.
15:13. *fill* you with all joy and peace in
14. *filled* with all knowledge,
19. I *have fully preached* the gospel of
2Co. 7: 4. I *am filled* with comfort,
10: 6. when your obedience *is fulfilled*.
Gal. 5:14. all the law *is fulfilled* in one word,
Eph. 1:23. of him *that filleth* (lit. that *is filled*) all in all.
3:19. *might be filled* with all the fulness of God.
4:10. that he *might fill* all things.
5:18. but *be filled* with the Spirit;
Phi. 1:11. *Being filled* with the fruits of
2: 2. *Fulfil* ye my joy, that ye be
4:18. I *am full*, having received
19. my God *shall supply* all your need
Col. 1: 9. that ye *might be filled* with the
25. *to fulfil* the word of God;
2:10. And ye are *complete* in him,
4:12. perfect and *complete* in all the will
17. that thou *fulfil* it.
2Th. 1:11. and *fulfil* all the good pleasure
2 Ti. 1: 4. that I *may be filled* with joy;
Jas. 2:23. the scripture *was fulfilled*
1Joh.1: 4. that your joy may be *full*.
2Joh. 12. that our joy may be *full*.
Rev. 3: 2. I have not found thy works *perfect*
6:11. their brethren, that should be killed as they (were), should *be fulfilled*.

4138 17 678/817 6:283 4137

πλήρωμα, *pleerōma.*

Mat. 9:16. that *which is put in to fill* it *up* taketh
Mar 2:21. the new *piece that filled* it *up*
8:20. how many baskets *full* of fragments
Joh. 1:16. of his *fulness* have all we received,

Ro. 11:12. how much more their *fulness?*
25. until the *fulness* of the Gentiles
13:10. love (is) the *fulfilling* of the law.
15:29. come in the *fulness* of the blessing
1Co.10:26. (is) the Lord's, and the *fulness* thereof.
28. the Lord's, and the *fulness* thereof:
Gal. 4: 4. when the *fulness* of the time was come,
Eph. 1:10. dispensation of the *fulness* of times
23. the *fulness* of him that filleth
3:19. with all the *fulness* of God.
4:13. stature of the *fulness* of Christ:
Col. 1:19. in him should all *fulness* dwell;
2: 9. all the *fulness* of the Godhead bodily.

4139 1 678/817 *pelas* (near)

πλησίον, *pleesion.* adv.

Joh. 4: 5. *near* to the parcel of ground

4139 17 678/817 6:311 *pelas* (near)

ὁ πλησίον, *ho pleesion.*

The adv. used as an adj.

Mat. 5:43. shalt love thy *neighbour*, (lit. the one *near*)
19:19. Thou shalt love thy *neighbour* as thyself.
22:39. Thou shalt love thy *neighbour* as
Mar 12:31. Thou shalt love thy *neighbour* as
33. and to love (his) *neighbour* as himself,
Lu. 10:27. and thy *neighbour* as thyself.
29. And who is my *neighbour?*
36. was *neighbour* unto him that
Acts 7:27. But he that did his *neighbour* wrong
Ro. 13: 9. Thou shalt love thy *neighbour* as
10. Love worketh no ill to his *neighbour:*
15: 2. please (his) *neighbour* for (his) good
Gal. 5:14. Thou shalt love thy *neighbour* as
Eph. 4:25. truth with his *neighbour:*
Heb 8:11. not teach every man his *neighbour*,
Jas. 2: 8. Thou shalt love thy *neighbour* as

4140 1 678/817 6:128 4130

πλησμονή, *pleesmonee.*

Col. 2:23. to the *satisfying* of the flesh.

4141 1 679/817 4111,cf 5180

πλήσσω, *pleesso.*

Rev. 8:12. part of the sun *was smitten*,

4142 6 679/817 4143

πλοιάριον, *ploiarion.*

Mar 3: 9. that a *small ship* should wait on him
4:36. also with him other *little ships.*
Joh. 6:22. there was none other *boat* there,
— went not with his disciples into the *boat*,
23. there came other *boats* from Tiberias
21: 8. the other disciples came in a *little ship;*

4143 67 679/817 4126

πλοῖον, *ploion.*

Mat. 4:21. In a *ship* with Zebedee their father,
22. they immediately left the *ship* and
8:23. when he was entered into a *ship*,
24. insomuch that the *ship* was covered
9: 1. And he entered into a *ship*,
13: 2. so that he went into a *ship*,
14:13. he departed thence by *ship*
22. constrained his disciples to get into a *ship*,
24. But the *ship* was now in the midst of
29. when Peter was come down out of the *ship*,
32. when they were come into the *ship*,
33. Then they that were in the *ship* came
15:39. and took *ship*, and came into
Mar 1:19. in the *ship* mending their nets.
20. left their father Zebedee in the *ship*
4: 1. so that he entered into a *ship*,
36. even as he was in the *ship*.
37. the waves beat into the *ship*,
5: 2. when he was come out of the *ship*,
18. when he was come into the *ship*,
21. by *ship* unto the other side,
6:32. into a desert place by *ship* privately.
45. to get into the *ship*, and to go
47. the *ship* was in the midst of the sea,
51. he went up unto them into the *ship;*
54. when they were come out of the *ship*,
8:10. straightway he entered into a *ship*
13. and entering into the *ship* again
14. neither had they in the *ship*
Lu. 5: 2. And saw two *ships* standing by
3. he entered into one of the *ships*,
— taught the people out of the *ship.*
7. which were in the other *ship*,
— they came, and filled both the *ships*,
11. when they had brought their *ships* to
8:22. that he went into a *ship* with
37. he went up into the *ship*,
Joh. 6:17. And entered into a *ship*,
19. and drawing nigh unto the *ship:*
21. received him into the *ship:*
— and immediately the *ship* was
24. they also took *shipping*, (lit. entered into *ships*)
21: 3. and entered into a *ship*
6. Cast the net on the right side of the *ship*,
Acts20:13. And we went before to *ship*,
38. they accompanied him unto the *ship*.
21: 2. And finding a *ship* sailing
3. for there the *ship* was to unlade
6. we took *ship;* and they
27: 2. And entering into a *ship* of
6. there the centurion found a *ship* of
10. not only of the lading and *ship*,
15. And when the *ship* was caught,
17. undergirding the *ship;*
19. the tackling of the *ship*.
22. but of the *ship*.
30. about to flee out of the *ship*,
31. Except these abide in the *ship*,
37. we were in all in the *ship*
38. they lightened the *ship*,
39. to thrust in the *ship*.
44. some on (broken pieces) of the *ship*.
28:11. we departed in a *ship* of
Jas. 3: 4. Behold also the *ships*,
Rev. 8: 9. the third part of the *ships* were
18:17. all the company in *ships*,
19. all that had *ships* in the sea

4144 3 679/818 4126

πλόος, *ploös.*

Acts21: 7. finished (our) *course* from Tyre,
27: 9. when *sailing* was now dangerous,
10. I perceive that this *voyage* will be

4145 28 679/818 6:318 4149

πλούσιος, *plousios.*

Mat.19:23. That a *rich* man shall hardly ... ter

Mat.19:24. than for a *rich* man to enter
27:57. there came a *rich* man of Arimathæa,
Mar 10:25. than for a *rich* man to enter into the
12:41. and many that were *rich* cast in
Lu. 6:24. woe unto you that are *rich!*
12:16. The ground of a certain *rich* man
14:12. nor (thy) *rich* neighbours;
16: 1. There was a certain *rich* man,
19. There was a certain *rich* man,
21. which fell from the *rich* man's table:
22. the *rich* man also died,
18:23. for he was very *rich*.
25. than for a *rich* man to enter into
19: 2. and he was *rich*.
21: 1. and saw the *rich* men casting their
2Co. 8: 9. though he was *rich*, yet for your
Eph. 2: 4. God, who is *rich* in mercy,
1Ti. 6:17. Charge them that are *rich* in this world,
Jas. 1:10. But the *rich*, in that he is made low:
11. so also shall the *rich* man fade away
2: 5. *rich* in faith, and heirs of
6. Do not *rich* men oppress you,
5: 1. Go to now, (ye) *rich* men,
Rev. 2: 9. but thou art *rich*
3:17. Because thou sayest, I am *rich*,
6:15. and the *rich* men, and the chief
13:16. *rich* and poor, free and bond,

4146 4 679/818 4145

πλουσίως, *plousiōs*.

Col. 3:16. word of Christ dwell in you *richly*
1Ti. 6:17. who giveth us *richly* all things
Tit. 3: 6. Which he shed on us *abundantly*
2Pet. 1:11. shall be ministered unto you *abundantly*

4147 12 679/818 6:318 4148

πλουτέω, *plouteo*.

Lu. 1:53. the *rich* he hath sent empty away.
12:21. and *is* not *rich* toward God.
Ro. 10:12. *is rich* unto all that call
1Co. 4: 8. now ye *are rich*,
2Co. 8: 9. ye through his poverty *might be rich*.
1Ti. 6: 9. they that will *be rich* fall
18. that they *be rich* in good works,
Rev. 3:17. I am rich, and *increased with goods*,
18. that thou *mayest be rich*;
18: 3. *are waxed rich* through the abundance
15. *which were made rich* by her, shall
19. wherein *were made rich* all that

4148 3 686/819 6:318 4149

πλουτίζω, *ploutizo*.

1Co. 1: 5. ye *are enriched* by him,
2Co. 6:10. as poor, yet *making* many *rich*;
9:11. *Being enriched* in every thing

4149 1 680/819 6:318 rt 4130

πλοῦτος, *ploutos*.

Mat.13:22. the deceitfulness of *riches*,
Mar 4:19. and the deceitfulness of *riches*,
Lu. 8:14. choked with cares and *riches*
Ro. 2: 4. Or despisest thou the *riches* of his
9:23. make known the *riches* of his glory
11:12. if the fall of them (be) the *riches* of the world, and the diminishing of them the *riches* of the Gentiles;
33. O the depth of the *riches* both of
2Co. 8: 2. unto the *riches* of their liberality.
Eph 1: 7. according to the *riches* of his grace;
18. what the *riches* of the glory of
2: 7. the exceeding *riches* of his grace
3: 8. the unsearchable *riches* of Christ;
16. according to the *riches* of his glory,
Phi. 4:19. according to his *riches* in glory
Col. 1:27. what (is) the *riches* of the glory
2: 2. unto all *riches* of the full assurance of
1Ti. 6:17. nor trust in uncertain *riches*,
Heb 11:26. greater *riches* than the treasures in
Jas. 5: 2. Your *riches* are corrupted,
Rev. 5:12. to receive power, and *riches*, and wisdom
18:17(16). so great *riches* is come to nought.

4150 1 680/819 *pluō* (to flow) cf 3068

πλύνω, *pluno*. cf 3538

Rev. 7:14. and *have washed* their robes, and

4151 385 680/819 6:332 cf 5590

πνεῦμα, *pnūma*.

Note.—[1]. πνεῦμα. [2]. τὸ πνεῦμα. [3]. πνεῦμα ἅγιον. [4]. τὸ ἅγιον πνεῦμα. [5]. τὸ πνεῦμα τὸ ἅγιον. The passages not marked are defined by some genitive or other adjunct.

Mat. 1:18. she was found with child of the Holy *Ghost*.[3]
20. is of the Holy *Ghost*.[3]
3:11. with the Holy *Ghost*,[3] and (with) fire:
16. he saw the *Spirit* of God descending
4: 1. led up of the *spirit*[2] into the wilderness
5: 3. Blessed (are) the poor in *spirit*:[2]
8:16. he cast out the *spirits* with (his) word
10: 1. power (against) unclean *spirits*,
20. but the *Spirit* of your Father
12:18. I will put my *spirit* upon him,
28. if I cast out devils by the *Spirit* of God,
31. blasphemy (against) the (Holy) *Ghost*[2]
32. speaketh against the Holy *Ghost*,[5]
43. When the unclean *spirit* is gone out
45. seven other *spirits* more wicked
22:43. How then doth David in *spirit*[1] call
26:41. the *spirit*[2] indeed (is) willing,
27:50. yielded up the *ghost*.[2]
28:19. and of the Son, and of the Holy *Ghost*:[4]
Mar 1: 8. shall baptize you with the Holy *Ghost*.[3]
10. and the *Spirit*[2] like a dove
12. immediately the *spirit*[2] driveth him
23. a man with an unclean *spirit*;
26. when the unclean *spirit* had torn
27. even the unclean *spirits*,
2: 8. perceived in his *spirit* that they
3:11. And unclean *spirits*, when they saw
29. blaspheme against the Holy *Ghost*[5]
30. they said, He hath an unclean *spirit*.
5: 2. a man with an unclean *spirit*,
8. out of the man, (thou) unclean *spirit*.
13. And the unclean *spirits* went out,
6: 7. power over unclean *spirits*;
7:25. had an unclean *spirit*,
8:12. he sighed deeply in his *spirit*,
9:17. which hath a dumb *spirit*,
20. the *spirit*[2] tare him;
25. he rebuked the foul *spirit*,
— (Thou) dumb and deaf *spirit*,
12:36. David himself said by the Holy *Ghost*,[5]
13:11. not ye that speak, but the Holy *Ghost*.[5]
14:38. The *spirit*[2] truly (is) ready,
Lu. 1:15. shall be filled with the Holy *Ghost*[3]
17. in the *spirit* and power of Elias.

Lu 1:35. The Holy *Ghost*[3] shall come upon thee,
41. was filled with the Holy *Ghost:*[3]
47. my *spirit* hath rejoiced in God
67. was filled with the Holy *Ghost,*[3]
80. and waxed strong in *spirit,*[1]
2:25. and the Holy *Ghost*[3] was upon him.
26. unto him by the Holy *Ghost,*[5]
27. he came by the *Spirit*[2] into
40. and waxed strong in *spirit,*[1]
3:16. baptize you with the Holy *Ghost*[3] and
22. And the Holy *Ghost*[5] descended
4: 1. being full of the Holy *Ghost*[3]
— was led by the *Spirit*[2] into
14. in the power of the *Spirit*[2]
18. The *Spirit* of the Lord (is) upon me,
33. which had a *spirit* of an unclean devil,
36. he commandeth the unclean *spirits,*
6:18. vexed with unclean *spirits:*
7:21. and of evil *spirits;*
8: 2. had been healed of evil *spirits*
29. commanded the unclean *spirit* to
55. And her *spirit* came again,
9:39. lo, a *spirit*[1] taketh him,
42. Jesus rebuked the unclean *spirit,*
55. what manner of *spirit* ye are of.
10:20. that the *spirits* are subject unto you;
21. Jesus rejoiced in *spirit,*[2]
11:13. give the Holy *Spirit*[3] to them that ask him?
24. When the unclean *spirit* is gone out
26. seven other *spirits* more wicked than
12:10. against the Holy *Ghost*[4]
12. For the Holy *Ghost*[4] shall teach you
13:11. which had a *spirit* of infirmity
23:46. into thy hands I commend my *spirit:*
24:37. that they had seen a *spirit.*[1]
39. a *spirit*[1] hath not flesh and bones,
Joh. 1:32. I saw the *Spirit*[2] descending from heaven like a dove,
33. thou shalt see the *Spirit*[2] descending,
— baptizeth with the Holy *Ghost.*[3]
3: 5. of water and (of) the *Spirit,*[1]
6. that which is born of the *Spirit*[2] is *spirit.*[1]
8. The *wind*[2] bloweth where it listeth,
— so is every one that is born of the *Spirit.*[2]
34. for God giveth not the *Spirit*[2] by measure
4:23. worship the Father in *spirit*[1] and
24. God (is) a *Spirit.*[1] and they that worship him must worship (him) in *spirit*[1] and
6:63. It is the *spirit*[2] that quickeneth;
— (they) are *spirit,*[1] and (they) are life.
7:39. this spake he of the *Spirit,*[2]
— for the Holy *Ghost*[3] was not yet (given);
11:33. he groaned in the *spirit,*[2]
13:21. he was troubled in *spirit,*[2]
14:17. the *Spirit* of truth; whom the world
26. the Holy *Ghost,*[5] whom the Father
15:26. the *Spirit* of truth, which
16:13. when he, the *Spirit* of truth, is come,
19:30. and gave up the *ghost.*[2]
20:22. Receive ye the Holy *Ghost:*[3]
Acts 1: 2. he through the Holy *Ghost*[3] had given
5. be baptized with the Holy *Ghost*[3]
8. after that the Holy *Ghost*[4] is come
16. which the Holy *Ghost*[5] by the mouth of
2: 4. all filled with the Holy *Ghost,*[3]
— as the *Spirit*[2] gave them utterance.
17. I will pour out of my *Spirit* upon
18. pour out in those days of my *Spirit;*
33. the promise of the Holy *Ghost,*[4]
38. receive the gift of the Holy *Ghost.*[4]
4: 8. Peter filled with the Holy *Ghost*[3]

Acts 4:31. filled with the Holy *Ghost,*[3]
5: 3. to lie to the Holy *Ghost,*[5]
9. to tempt the *Spirit* of the Lord?
16. vexed with unclean *spirits:*
32. and (so is) also the Holy *Ghost,*[5]
6: 3. full of the Holy *Ghost*[3] and
5. full of faith and of the Holy *Ghost,*[3]
10. the wisdom and the *spirit*[2] by which
7:51. ye do always resist the Holy *Ghost:*[5]
55. being full of the Holy *Ghost,*[3]
59. Lord Jesus, receive my *spirit.*
8: 7. For unclean *spirits,* crying
15. might receive the Holy *Ghost:*[3]
17. they received the Holy *Ghost.*[3]
18. the Holy *Ghost*[5] was given,
19. he may receive the Holy *Ghost.*[3]
29. Then the *Spirit*[2] said unto Philip,
39. the *Spirit* of the Lord caught away
9:17. and be filled with the Holy *Ghost.*[3]
31. and in the comfort of the Holy *Ghost,*[4]
10:19. the *Spirit*[2] said unto him,
38. with the Holy *Ghost*[3] and with power.
44. the Holy *Ghost*[5] fell on all them
45. the gift of the Holy *Ghost.*[4]
47. have received the Holy *Ghost*[5] as well
11:12. And the *spirit*[2] bade me go
15. the Holy *Ghost*[5] fell on them,
16. be baptized with the Holy *Ghost.*[3]
24. and full of the Holy *Ghost*[3]
28. signified by the *spirit*[2] that
13: 2. the Holy *Ghost*[5] said, Separate me
4. being sent forth by the Holy *Ghost,*[5]
9. Paul, filled with the Holy *Ghost,*[3]
52. and with the Holy *Ghost.*[3]
15: 8. giving them the Holy *Ghost,*[5]
28. it seemed good to the Holy *Ghost,*[4]
16: 6. were forbidden of the Holy *Ghost*[4]
7. but the *Spirit*[2] suffered them not.
16. possessed with a *spirit* of divination (lit. *spirit* of Python)
18. turned and said to the *spirit,*[2]
17:16. his *spirit* was stirred in him,
18: 5. Paul was pressed in the *spirit,*[2]
25. being fervent in the *spirit,*[2]
19: 2. Have ye received the Holy *Ghost*[3]
— whether there be any Holy *Ghost.*[3]
6. the Holy *Ghost*[5] came on them;
12. the evil *spirits* went out of them.
13. which had evil *spirits*
15. And the evil *spirit* answered
16. the man in whom the evil *spirit* was
21. Paul purposed in the *spirit,*[2]
20:22. I go bound in the *spirit*[2] unto Jerusalem,
23. Save that the Holy *Ghost*[5] witnesseth
28. the Holy *Ghost*[5] made you overseers,
21: 4. who said to Paul through the *Spirit,*[2]
11. Thus saith the Holy *Ghost,*[5]
23: 8. neither angel, nor *spirit:*[1]
9. but if a *spirit*[1] or an angel
28:25. Well spake the Holy *Ghost*[5] by
Ro. 1: 4. according to the *spirit* of holiness,
9. whom I serve with my *spirit*
2:29. In the *spirit,*[1] (and) not in the letter;
5: 5. by the Holy *Ghost*[3] which is given
7: 6. in newness of *spirit,*[1] and not
8: 1. not after the flesh, but after the *Spirit.*[1]
2. For the law of the *Spirit* of life
4. not after the flesh, but after the *Spirit.*[1]
5. but they that are after the *Spirit*[1] the things of the *Spirit.*[2]
6. but to be *spiritually* minded (lit. the mind of the *Spirit*[2]) (is) life and peace:

Ro. 8: 9. but in the Spirit.[1] if so be that the Spirit of God dwell in you.
— have not the *Spirit* of Christ,
10. but the *Spirit*[2] (is) life because
11. But if the *Spirit* of him that
— by his *Spirit* that dwelleth in you.
13. if ye through the *Spirit*[1] do mortify
14. as are led by the *Spirit* of God,
15. received the *spirit* of bondage
— received the *Spirit* of adoption,
16. The *Spirit*[2] itself beareth witness with our *spirit*,
23. the firstfruits of the *Spirit*,[2]
26. Likewise the *Spirit*[2] also helpeth
— but the *Spirit* itself maketh
27. what (is) the mind of the *Spirit*,[2]
9: 1. bearing me witness in the Holy *Ghost*,[3]
11: 8. hath given them the *spirit* of slumber,
12:11. fervent in *spirit*;[2] serving the Lord;
14:17. and joy in the Holy *Ghost*.[3]
15:13. the power of the Holy *Ghost*.[3]
16. sanctified by the Holy *Ghost*.[3]
19. by the power of the *Spirit* of God; (πνεύματος Θεοῦ)
30. for the love of the *Spirit*,[2]
1Co. 2: 4. in demonstration of the *Spirit*[1]
10. unto us by his *Spirit*: for the *Spirit*[2] searcheth all things,
11. save the *spirit* of man which
— but the *Spirit* of God.
12. Now we have received, not the *spirit* of the world, but the *spirit* which is of God;
13. but which the Holy *Ghost*[3] teacheth
14. the things of the *Spirit* of God:
3:16. and (that) the *Spirit* of God dwelleth
4:21. and (in) the *spirit* of meekness?
5: 3. but present in *spirit*,[2]
4. and my *spirit*, with the power of
5. that the *spirit*[2] may be saved
6:11. and by the *Spirit* of our God.
17. he that is joined unto the Lord is one *spirit*.
19. the temple of the Holy *Ghost*[4] (which is) in you,
20. and in your *spirit*, which are God's.
7:34. both in body and in *spirit*:[1]
40. also that I have the *Spirit* of God.
12: 3. no man speaking by the *Spirit* of God
— but by the Holy *Ghost*.[3]
4. but the same *Spirit*.
7. the manifestation of the *Spirit*[2]
8. to one is given by the *Spirit*[2]
— knowledge by the same *Spirit*;
9. faith by the same *Spirit*;
— of healing by the same *Spirit*;
10. to another discerning of *spirits*,
11. that one and the selfsame *Spirit*,
13. For by one *Spirit* are we all baptized
— all made to drink into one *Spirit*.
14: 2. howbeit in the *spirit*[1] he speaketh
12. zealous of *spiritual* (gifts), (lit. of *spirits*)
14. my *spirit* prayeth,
15. I will pray with the *spirit*,[2]
— I will sing with the *spirit*,[2]
16. when thou shalt bless with the *spirit*,[2]
32. the *spirits* of the prophets are
15:45. a quickening *spirit*.
16:18. they have refreshed my *spirit*
2Co. 1:22. given the earnest of the *Spirit*[2]
2:13. I had no rest in my *spirit*,
3: 3. but with the *Spirit* of the living God;
6. not of the letter, but of the *spirit*:[1]
— but the *spirit*[2] giveth life.

2Co. 3: 8. the ministration of the *spirit*[2]
17. Now the Lord is that *Spirit*:[2] and where the *Spirit* of the Lord (is),
18. as by the *Spirit* of the Lord. (ἀπὸ Κυρίου πνεύματος)
4:13. We having the same *spirit* of faith,
5: 5. the earnest of the *Spirit*.[2]
6: 6. by the Holy *Ghost*,[3] by love
7: 1. filthiness of the flesh and *spirit*,[1]
13. because his *spirit* was refreshed
11: 4. or (if) ye receive another *spirit*,
12:18. walked we not in the same *spirit*?
13:14(13). the communion of the Holy *Ghost*,[4]
Gal. 3: 2. Received ye the *Spirit*[2] by the works
3. having begun in the *Spirit*,[1]
5. that ministereth to you the *Spirit*,[2]
14. the promise of the *Spirit*[2]
4: 6. sent forth the *Spirit* of his Son
29. (that was born) after the *Spirit*,[1]
5: 5. For we through the *Spirit*[1] wait
16. Walk in the *Spirit*,[1]
17. For the flesh lusteth against the *Spirit*,[2] and the *Spirit*[2] against the flesh:
18. if ye be led of the *Spirit*,[1]
22. the fruit of the *Spirit*[2] is love,
25. If we live in the *Spirit*,[1] let us also walk in the *Spirit*.[1]
6: 1. restore such an one in the *spirit* of meekness;
8. he that soweth to the *Spirit*[2] shall of the *Spirit*[2] reap life
18. (be) with your *spirit*.
Eph. 1:13. sealed with that holy *Spirit*[5] of promise,
17. give unto you the *spirit* of wisdom
2: 2. the *spirit* that now worketh
18. access by one *Spirit* unto the Father.
22. habitation of God through the *Spirit*.
3: 5. and prophets by the *Spirit*;[1]
16. by his *Spirit* in the inner man;
4: 3. the unity of the *Spirit*[2] in the
4. one body, and one *Spirit*, even
23. be renewed in the *spirit* of your mind;
30. grieve not the Holy *Spirit*[5] of God,
5: 9. For the fruit of the *Spirit*[2] (is)
18. be filled with the *Spirit*;[1]
6:17. the sword of the *Spirit*,[2]
18. prayer and supplication in the *Spirit*,[1]
Phi. 1:19. supply of the *Spirit* of Jesus Christ,
27. that ye stand fast in one *spirit*,
2: 1. if any fellowship of the *Spirit*,[1]
3: 3. which worship God in the *spirit*,[1]
Col. 1: 8. your love in the *Spirit*.[1]
2: 5. yet am I with you in the *spirit*,[2]
1Th. 1: 5. in power, and in the Holy *Ghost*,[3]
6. with joy of the Holy *Ghost*:[3]
4: 8. also given unto us his holy *Spirit*.
5:19. Quench not the *Spirit*.[2]
23. your whole *spirit* and soul and body
2Th. 2: 2. neither by *spirit*,[1] nor by word,
8. with the *spirit* of his mouth,
13. through sanctification of the *Spirit*[1]
1Ti. 3:16. justified in the *Spirit*,[1]
4: 1. Now the *Spirit*[2] speaketh expressly,
— giving heed to seducing *spirits*,
12. in charity, in *spirit*,[1] in faith,
2Ti. 1: 7. God hath not given us the *spirit* of fear;
14. keep by the Holy *Ghost*[3] which dwelleth in us.
4:22. (be) with thy *spirit*.
Tit. 3: 5. and renewing of the Holy *Ghost*;[3]
Philem 25. (be) with your *spirit*.
Heb 1: 7. Who maketh his angels *spirits*,

Heb 1:14. Are they not all ministering *spirits*,
2: 4. and gifts of the Holy *Ghost*,[3]
3: 7. as the Holy *Ghost*[5] saith,
4:12. dividing asunder of soul and *spirit*,[1]
6: 4. made partakers of the Holy *Ghost*,[3]
9: 8. The Holy *Ghost*[5] this signifying,
14. who through the eternal *Spirit*
10:15. the Holy *Ghost*[5] also is a witness to us:
29. despite unto the *Spirit* of grace?
12: 9. unto the Father of *spirits*,
23. and to the *spirits* of just men
Jas. 2:26. as the body without the *spirit*[1] is dead,
4: 5. The *spirit* that dwelleth in us
1Pet. 1: 2. through sanctification of the *Spirit*,[1]
11. the *Spirit* of Christ which was in them
12. with the Holy *Ghost*[3] sent down
22. obeying the truth through the *Spirit*[1] unto
3: 4. of a meek and quiet *spirit*,
18. quickened by the *Spirit*:[2]
19. preached unto the *spirits* in prison;
4: 6. according to God in the *spirit*.[1]
14. for the *spirit* of glory and of God
2Pet. 1:21. moved by the Holy *Ghost*.[3]
1Joh. 3:24. by the *Spirit*[2] which he hath given us.
4: 1. believe not every *spirit*, but try the *spirits* whether
2. Hereby know ye the *Spirit* of God: Every *spirit* that confesseth
3. every *spirit* that confesseth not
6. the *spirit* of truth, and the *spirit* of error.
13. he hath given us of his *Spirit*.
5: 6. it is the *Spirit*[2] that beareth witness, because the *Spirit*[2] is truth.
7. and the Holy *Ghost*:[4] and these three
8. the *spirit*,[2] and the water, and the blood:
Jude 19. having not the *Spirit*.[1]
20. praying in the Holy *Ghost*,[3]
Rev. 1: 4. from the seven *spirits* which are
10. I was in the *Spirit*[1] on the Lord's
2: 7. let him hear what the *Spirit*[2] saith
11. let him hear what the *Spirit*[2] saith
17. let him hear what the *Spirit*[2] saith
29. let him hear what the *Spirit*[2] saith
3: 1. that hath the seven *Spirits* of God,
6. let him hear what the *Spirit*[2] saith
13. let him hear what the *Spirit*[2] saith
22. let him hear what the *Spirit*[2] saith
4: 2. immediately I was in the *spirit*:[1]
5. which are the seven *Spirits* of God.
5: 6. which are the seven *Spirits* of God
11:11. the *Spirit* of life from God entered into
13:15. he had power to give *life*[1] unto the image
14:13. Yea, saith the *Spirit*,[2] that they may rest
16:13. I saw three unclean *spirits* like frogs
14. For they are the *spirits* of devils,
17: 3. So he carried me away in the *spirit*[1]
18: 2. and the hold of every foul *spirit*,
19:10. of Jesus is the *spirit* of prophecy.
21:10. he carried me away in the *spirit*[1] to
22:17. And the *Spirit*[2] and the bride say, Come.

4152 26 685/824 6:332 4151 cf 5591

πνευματικός, pnūmatikos.

Ro. 1:11. unto you some *spiritual* gift, to the end
7:14. that the law is *spiritual*:
15:27. partakers of their *spiritual* things,
1Co. 2:13. comparing *spiritual* things with *spiritual*.
15. But he that is *spiritual* judgeth all
3: 1. as unto *spiritual*, but as unto carnal,
9:11. have sown unto you *spiritual* things,
10: 3. did all eat the same *spiritual* meat;
4. the same *spiritual* drink: for they drank of that *spiritual* Rock
12: 1. Now concerning *spiritual* (gifts),
14: 1. and desire *spiritual* (gifts),
37. to be a prophet, or *spiritual*,
15:44. it is raised a *spiritual* body.
— and there is a *spiritual* body.
46. not first which is *spiritual*,
— afterward that which is *spiritual*.
Gal. 6: 1. ye which are *spiritual*, restore
Eph. 1: 3. with all *spiritual* blessings
5:19. and hymns and *spiritual* songs,
6:12. against *spiritual* wickedness in
Col. 1: 9. wisdom and *spiritual* understanding;
3:16. psalms and hymns and *spiritual* songs,
1Pet. 2: 5. are built up a *spiritual* house, an holy priesthood, to offer up *spiritual* sacrifices,

4153 2 685/824 4152

πνευματικῶς, pnūmatikōs.

1Co. 2:14. because they are *spiritually* discerned.
Rev. 11: 8. which *spiritually* is called Sodom and

4154 7 685/824 6:332 cf 5594

πνέω, pneo.

Mat. 7:25. and the winds *blew*,
27. the winds *blew*, and beat upon that house;
Lu. 12:55. when (ye see) the south wind *blow*,
Joh. 3: 8. The wind *bloweth* where it listeth,
6:18. by reason of a great wind *that blew*.
Acts 27:40. the mainsail to the *wind*,
Rev. 7: 1. that the wind *should* not *blow*

4155 2 686/824 6:455 4154

πνίγω, pnigo.

Mat. 18:28. and *took* (him) *by the throat*, saying,
Mar 5:13. and *were choked* in the sea.

4156 3 686/824 6:455 4155

πνικτός, pniktos.

Acts 15:20. and (from) things *strangled*,
29. from things *strangled*, and from
21:25. from blood, and from *strangled*,

4157 2 686/824 4154

πνοή, pnoee.

Acts 2: 2. as of a rushing mighty *wind*,
17:25. he giveth to all life, and *breath*,

4158 1 686/824 4228

ποδήρης, podeerees.

Rev. 1.13. clothed with a *garment down to the foot*,

4159 28 686/824 rt 4213

πόθεν, pothen.

Mat. 13:27. *from whence* then hath it tares?
54. *Whence* hath this (man) this wisdom,
56. *Whence* then hath this (man) all these things?
15:33. *Whence* should we have so much bread in
21:25. *whence* was it? from heaven, or of men?
Mar 6: 2. *From whence* hath this (man) these
8: 4. *From whence* can a man satisfy these
12:37. and *whence* is he (then) his son?
Lu. 1:43. And *whence* (is) this to me,
13:25. I know you not *whence* ye are:
27. I know you not *whence* ye are;

Lu. 20: 7. that they could not tell *whence* (it was)
Joh. 1:48,(49) *Whence* knowest thou me?
2: 9. knew not *whence* it was:
3: 8. but canst not tell *whence* it cometh,
4:11. *from whence* then hast thou that living water?
6: 5. *Whence* shall we buy bread, that
7:27. we know this man *whence* he is.
— no man knoweth *whence* he is.
28. and ye know *whence* I am:
8:14. for I know *whence* I came, and whither I go; but ye cannot tell *whence* I come,
9:29. we know not *from whence* he is.
30. that ye know not *from whence* he is,
19: 9. *Whence* art thou? But Jesus
Jas. 4: 1. *From whence* (come) wars and
Rev. 2: 5. *from whence* thou art fallen,
7:13. and *whence* came they?

4160 576 687/824 6:458 cf 4238

ποιέω, poyeo.

Mat. 1:24. *did* as the angel of the Lord had bidden
3: 3. *make* his paths straight.
8. *Bring forth* therefore fruits meet for
10. every tree *which bringeth* not *forth* good
4:19. and I *will make* you fishers of men.
5:19. but whosoever *shall do* and teach (them),
32. *causeth* her to commit adultery:
36. thou canst not *make* one hair
44. *do* good to them that hate you,
46. *do* not even the publicans the same?
47. what *do* ye more (than others)? *do* not even the publicans so?
6: 1. Take heed that ye *do* not your
2. when thou *doest* (thine) alms,
— as the hypocrites *do* in the synagogues
3. But *when* thou *doest* alms,
— what thy right hand *doeth*:
7:12. that men *should do* to you, *do* ye even so
17. good tree *bringeth forth* good fruit; but a corrupt tree *bringeth forth* evil
18. A good tree cannot *bring forth* evil
— a corrupt tree *bring forth* good
19. Every tree *that bringeth* not *forth*
21. but he *that doeth* the will of
22. and in thy name *done* many wonderful
24. heareth these sayings of mine, and *doeth* them,
26. and *doeth* them not,
8: 9. *Do* this, and he *doeth* (it).
9:28. Believe ye that I am able *to do* this?
12: 2. thy disciples *do* that which is not lawful *to do* upon
3. Have ye not read what David *did*,
12. it is lawful *to do* well on the
16. that they *should* not *make* him known:
33. Either *make* the tree good,
— or else *make* the tree corrupt,
50. whosoever shall *do* the will of my
13:23. and *bringeth forth*, some an
26. and *brought forth* fruit,
28. An enemy *hath done* this.
41. and them *which do* iniquity;
58. And he *did* not many mighty works
17: 4. *let* us *make* here three tabernacles;
12. but *have done* unto him
18:35. *shall* my heavenly Father *do* also
19: 4. that he *which made* (them) at
— *made* them male and female,
16. what good thing *shall* I *do*, that
20: 5. ninth hour, and *did* likewise.

Mat.20:12. These last *have wrought* (but) one hour and thou *hast made* them equal unto us,
15. Is it not lawful for me *to do* what I will
32. that I *shall do* unto you?
21: 6. and *did* as Jesus commanded them,
13. but ye *have made* it a den of thieves.
15. the wonderful things that he *did*,
21. ye *shall* not only *do* this
23. By what authority *doest* thou these
24. by what authority I *do* these things.
27. by what authority I *do* these things.
31. Whether of them twain *did* the will of
36. and they *did* unto them likewise.
40. what *will* he *do* unto those husbandmen?
43. and given to a nation *bringing forth* the fruits thereof.
22: 2. which *made* a marriage for his son,
23: 3. Observe and *do*; but *do* not ye after their works: for they say, and *do* not.
5. they *do* for to be seen of men:
15. compass sea and land *to make* one
— ye *make* him twofold more the child
23. these ought ye *to have done*,
24:46. when he cometh shall find so *doing*.
25:16. and *made* (them) other five talents.
40. Inasmuch as ye *have done* (it) unto one
— ye *have done* (it) unto me.
45. Inasmuch as ye *did* (it) not to one
— ye *did* (it) not to me.
26:12. she *did* (it) for my burial.
13. that this woman *hath done*,
18. I will *keep* the passover at thy house
19. the disciples *did* as Jesus had
73. for thy speech bewrayeth thee. (lit. *maketh* thee manifest)
27:22. What *shall* I *do* then with Jesus
23. Why, what evil *hath* he *done*?
28:14. and secure you. (lit. *make* you without care)
15. and *did* as they were taught:
Mar 1: 3. *make* his paths straight.
17. I *will make* you to become fishers of
2:23. began, as they went, to pluck (lit. *to make* their way plucking)
24. why *do* they on the sabbath day
25. Have ye never read what David *did*,
3: 6. *took* counsel with the Herodians against him,
8. they had heard what great things he *did*,
12. they *should* not *make* him known.
14. And he *ordained* twelve, that they
35. whosoever shall *do* the will of God,
4:32. and *shooteth out* great branches;
5:19. how great things the Lord *hath done* for thee,
20. how great things Jesus *had done* for him:
32. to see her *that had done* this thing.
6: 5. he could there *do* no mighty work,
20. he *did* many things, and heard
21. *made* a supper to his lords,
30. both what they *had done*,
7: 8. other such like things ye *do*.
12. ye suffer him no more *to do* ought
13. many such like things *do* ye.
37. He *hath done* all things well: he *maketh* both the deaf to hear,
8:25. upon his eyes, and *made* him look up:
9: 5. *let* us *make* three tabernacles;
13. they *have done* unto him whatsoever
39. no man which *shall do* a miracle
10: 6. God *made* them male and female.
17. what *shall* I *do* that I may

Mar 10:35. that thou *shouldest do* for us
36. What would ye that I should *do* for you?
51. What wilt thou that I *should do*
11: 3. Why *do* ye this?
5. What *do* ye, loosing the colt?
17. ye *have made* it a den of thieves.
28. By what authority *doest* thou
— authority to *do* these things?
29. by what authority I *do* these things.
33. by what authority I *do* these things.
12: 9. What *shall* therefore the lord of the vineyard *do?*
14: 7. whensoever ye will ye may *do* them good:
8. She *hath done* what she could:
9. (this) also that she *hath done*
15: 1. the chief priests *held* a consultation
7. who *had committed* murder in the
8. as he *had* ever *done* unto them.
12. What will ye then that I *shall do* (unto him)
14. Why, what evil *hath* he *done?*
15. willing to content the people, (lit. *to do* that which suited)

Lu. 1:25. Thus *hath* the Lord *dealt* with me
49. *hath done* to me great things;
51. He *hath shewed* strength with his arm;
68. for he hath visited and redeemed his people, (lit. *made* redemption for his people)
72. To *perform* the mercy (promised) to
2:27. *to do* for him after the custom of
48. why *hast* thou thus *dealt* with us?
3: 4. *make* his paths straight.
8. *Bring forth* therefore fruits worthy of
9. *which bringeth* not *forth* good fruit
10. What *shall* we *do* then?
11. he that hath meat, *let* him *do* likewise.
12. Master, what *shall* we *do?*
14. And what *shall* we *do?*
19. all the evils which Herod *had done*,
4:23. *do* also here in thy country.
5: 6. *when* they *had* this *done*,
29. Levi *made* him a great feast
33. fast often, and *make* prayers,
34. Can ye *make* the children of the
6: 2. Why *do* ye that which is not lawful *to do* on the sabbath days?
3. what David *did*, when himself was an
10. And he *did* so: and his hand
11. what they *might do* to Jesus.
23. in the like manner *did* their fathers unto
26. for so *did* their fathers to the false
27. *do* good to them which hate you,
31. as ye would that men *should do* to you, *do* ye also to them likewise.
33. for sinners also *do* even the same.
43. *bringeth* not *forth* (lit. is not *bringing forth*) corrupt fruit; neither *doth* a corrupt tree *bring forth* good fruit.
46. and *do* not the things which I say?
47. and heareth my sayings, and *doeth* them,
49. But he that heareth, and *doeth* not,
7: 8. *Do* this, and he *doeth* (it).
8: 8. and *bare* fruit an hundredfold.
21. hear the word of God, and *do* it.
39. great things God *hath done* unto thee.
— Jesus *had done* unto him.
9:10. told him all that they *had done*.
15. And they *did* so, and made them
33. *let* us *make* three tabernacles;
43. at all things which Jesus *did*,
54. even as Elias *did?*

Lu. 10:25. what shall I *do* to inherit (lit. *having done* what shall I inherit)
28. this *do*, and thou shalt live.
37. He *that shewed* mercy on him.
— Go, and *do* thou likewise.
11:40. *did* not he *that made* that which is without *make* that which is within also?
42. these ought ye *to have done*,
12: 4. no more that they can *do*.
17. What *shall* I *do*, because I have no
18. And he said, This *will* I *do:*
33. *provide* yourselves bags which
43. when he cometh shall find so *doing*.
47. neither *did* according to his will,
48. and *did commit* things worthy of stripes,
13: 9. And if it *bear* fruit, (well):
22. and journeying (lit. *making* a journey) toward Jerusalem.
14:12. When thou *makest* a dinner or a
13. when thou *makest* a feast,
16. A certain man *made* a great supper,
15:19. *make* me as one of thy hired servants.
16: 3. What *shall* I *do?* for my lord
4. I am resolved what to *do*, that, when
8. because he *had done* wisely:
9. *Make* to yourselves friends of the
17: 9. because he *did* the things that were
10. when ye *shall have done* all those
— we *have done* that which was our duty *to do*.
18: 7. shall not God avenge his own elect, (lit. *shall* not God *make* the avenging of)
8. that he will avenge them speedily. (lit. he *will make* the avenging of them)
18. what shall I *do* to inherit eternal life? (lit. *having done* what shall I inherit, &c.)
41. that I *shall do* unto thee?
19:18. thy pound *hath gained* five pounds.
46. but ye *have made* it a den of thieves.
48. could not find what they *might do:*
20: 2. by what authority *doest* thou these things?
8. by what authority I *do* these things.
13. What *shall* I *do?* I will send
15. *shall* the lord of the vineyard *do* unto them?
22:19. this *do* in remembrance of me.
23:22. Why, what evil *hath* he *done?*
31. if they *do* these things in a green tree,
34. for they know not what they *do*.

Joh. 2: 5. Whatsoever he saith unto you, *do*
11. This beginning of miracles *did* Jesus
15. *when* he *had made* a scourge
16. *make* not my Father's house an
18. seeing that thou *doest* these things?
23. the miracles which he *did*.
3: 2. can *do* these miracles that thou *doest*,
21. But he *that doeth* truth cometh to the
4: 1. that Jesus *made* and baptized more
29. told me all things that ever I *did:*
34. My meat is to *do* the will of him that
39. He told me all that ever I *did*.
45. all the things that he *did* at
46. where he *made* the water wine.
54. the second miracle (that) Jesus *did*,
5:11. He *that made* me whole,
15. *which had made* him whole.
16. because he *had done* these things on
18. *making* himself equal with God.
19. The Son can *do* nothing of himself, but what he seeth the Father *do:* for what things soever he *doeth*, these also *doeth* the Son likewise.

Joh. 5:20. all things that himself *doeth*:
27. authority *to execute* judgment also,
29. they *that have done* good,
30. I can of mine own self *do* nothing:
36. the same works that I *do*,
6: 2. which he *did* on them that were
6. he himself knew what he would *do*.
10. *Make* the men sit down.
14. the miracle that Jesus *did*,
15. take him by force to *make* him a king,
28. What shall we *do*, that we
30. What sign *shewest* thou then,
38. not to *do* mine own will,
7: 3. see the works that thou *doest*.
4. (that) *doeth* any thing in secret,
— If thou *do* these things, shew
17. If any man will *do* his will,
19. (yet) none of you *keepeth* the law?
21. I *have done* one work,
23. because I *have made* a man every
31. When Christ cometh, *will* he *do*
— which this (man) *hath done*?
51. and know what he *doeth*?
8:28. I *do* nothing of myself;
29. for I *do* always those things
34. *Whosoever committeth* sin is
38. ye *do* that which ye have seen
39. ye would *do* the works of
40. this *did* not Abraham.
41. Ye *do* the deeds of your father.
44. the lusts of your father ye will *do*.
53. whom *makest* thou thyself?
9: 6. and *made* clay of the spittle,
11. A man that is called Jesus *made* clay,
14. when Jesus *made* the clay,
16. How can a man that is a sinner *do* such
26. What *did* he to thee?
31. and *doeth* his will, him he heareth.
33. he could *do* nothing.
10:25. the works that I *do* in my Father's name,
33. being a man, *makest* thyself God.
37. If I *do* not the works of my Father,
38. But if I *do*, though ye believe
41. John *did* no miracle: but
11:37. *have caused* that even this man
45. had seen the things which Jesus *did*,
46. what things Jesus *had done*.
47. What *do* we? for this man *doeth* many miracles.
12: 2. There they *made* him a supper;
16. (that) they *had done* these things
18. that he *had done* this miracle.
37. *though* he *had done* so many miracles
13: 7. What I *do* thou knowest not now;
12. Know ye what I *have done* to you?
15. that ye *should do* as I *have done* to you.
17. happy are ye if ye *do* them.
27. That thou *doest*, *do* quickly.
14:10. he *doeth* the works.
12. the works that I *do shall* he *do* also; and greater (works) than these *shall* he *do*; because
13. that *will* I *do*, that the Father may
14. I *will do* (it).
23. will come unto him, and *make* our abode
31. even so I *do*.
15: 5. without me ye can *do* nothing.
14. if ye *do* whatsoever I command
15. knoweth not what his lord *doeth*:
21. all these things *will* they *do* unto you
24. If I *had* not *done* among them the works which none other man *did*,

Joh. 16: 2. They shall put you out of the synagogues: (lit. they *shall make* you put out &c.)
3. these things *will* they *do* unto you,
17: 4. which thou gavest me to *do*.
18:18. *who had made* a fire of coals;
35. what *hast* thou *done*?
19: 7. because he *made* himself the Son
12. *whosoever maketh* himself a king
23. and *made* four parts,
24. These things therefore the soldiers *did*.
20:30. many other signs truly *did* Jesus
21:25. many other things which Jesus *did*,
Acts 1: 1. The former treatise *have* I *made*,...of all that Jesus began both *to do* and teach,
2:22. which God *did* by him in the midst
36. God *hath made* that same Jesus,
37. what *shall* we *do*?
3:12. we *had made* this man to walk?
4: 7. by what name, *have* ye *done* this?
16. What *shall* we *do* to these men?
24. *which hast made* heaven, and earth,
28. For *to do* whatsoever thy hand
5:34. *to put* the apostles forth a little
6: 8. *did* great wonders and miracles
7:19. so that they *cast out* (lit. *made* cast out) their young
24. and avenged (lit. *made* avenging of) him that was
36. *after* that he *had shewed* wonders
40. *Make* us gods to go before us:
43. which ye *made* to worship them:
44. that he should *make* it
50. *Hath* not my hand *made* all these
8: 2. and *made* great lamentation
6. seeing the miracles which he *did*.
9: 6. what wilt thou have me *to do*?
— be told thee what thou must *do*.
13. how much evil he *hath done*
36. and almsdeeds which she *did*.
39. garments which Dorcas *made*,
10: 2. *which gave* much alms
6. tell thee what thou oughtest *to do*.
33. thou *hast* well *done* that thou art
39. which he *did* both in the land of
11:30. Which also they *did*, and sent it
12: 8. bind on thy sandals. And so he *did*.
13:22. which *shall fulfil* all my will.
14:11. saw what Paul *had done*,
15. why *do* ye these things?
— the living God, which *made* heaven, and earth,
27. all that God *had done* with them,
15: 3. they *caused* great joy unto all the
4. all things that God *had done* with
12. God *had wrought* among the Gentiles
17. the Lord, *who doeth* all these things.
33. *after* they *had tarried* (there) a space
16:18. And this *did* she many days.
21. neither to *observe*, being Romans.
30. Sirs, what must I *do* to be saved?
17:24. God *that made* the world
26. And *hath made* of one blood
18:21. I must by all means *keep* this feast
23. *after* he *had spent* some time (there),
19:11. God *wrought* special miracles by
14. seven sons of...*which did* so.
24. *which made* silver shrines for Diana,
20: 3. And (there) *abode* three months.
24. But none of these things move me, (lit. I *make* account of none)
21:13. What mean ye to weep and to break (lit. What *do* ye weeping &c.)

Acts21: 19. God *had wrought* among the Gentiles
23. *Do* therefore this that we say to thee:
33. who he was, and what he *had done.*
22: 10. What *shall* I *do,* Lord?
— which are appointed for thee *to do.*
26. Take heed what thou *doest:* (lit. art about *to do*)
23: 12. certain of the Jews banded together, (lit. *having made* a confederation)
13. *which had made* this conspiracy.
24: 12. neither raising up the people, (lit. *making* an insurrection)
17. I came to *bring* alms to my nation,
25: 3. laying wait in the way to kill him. (lit. *making* a lying in wait)
17. without any delay (lit. *having made* no delay) on the morrow I sat
26: 10. Which thing I also *did* in Jerusalem:
27: 18. the next (day) they lightened the ship; (lit. they *made* a casting out)
28: 17. *though* I *have committed* nothing against
Ro. 1: 9. I *make* mention of you always in
28. *to do* those things which are not
32. not only *do* the same, but have
2: 3. and *doest* the same,
14. *do* by nature the things contained
3: 8. *Let* us *do* evil, that good may come?
12. there is none *that doeth* good,
4: 21. he was able also *to perform.*
7: 15. but what I hate, that *do* I.
16. If then I *do* that which I would not,
19. the good that I would I *do* not:
20. Now if I *do* that I would not,
21. that, when I would *do* good,
9: 20. Why *hast* thou *made* me thus?
21. *to make* one vessel unto honour,
28. a short work *will* the Lord *make*
10: 5. the man *which doeth* those things
12: 20. for in so *doing* thou shalt heap
13: 3. *do* that which is good, and
4. But if thou *do* that which is evil,
14. and *make* not provision for the flesh,
15: 26. *to make* a certain contribution
16: 17. mark them *which cause* divisions
1Co. 5: 2. he *that hath done* this deed
6: 15. and *make* (them) the members
18. Every sin that a man *doeth* is
7: 36. *let* him *do* what he will,
37. will keep his virgin, *doeth* well.
38. that giveth (her) in marriage *doeth* well;
— not in marriage *doeth* better.
9: 23. And this I *do* for the gospel's sake,
10: 13. *will* with the temptation also *make* a way
31. or whatsoever ye *do, do* all to the glory of God.
11: 24. this *do* in remembrance of me.
25 this *do* ye, as oft as ye drink (it),
15: 29. Else what *shall* they *do* which are
16: 1. even so *do* ye.
2Co. 5: 21. he *hath made* him (to be) sin for us,
8: 10. not only *to do,* but also
11. Now therefore perform the *doing*
11: 7. *Have* I *committed* an offence in
12. But what I *do,* that I *will do,*
25. a night and a day I *have been* in the deep
13: 7. I pray to God that ye *do* no evil;
— but that ye *should do* that which is
Gal. 2: 10. which I also was forward *to do.*
3: 10. the book of the law *to do* them.
12. The man *that doeth* them shall live
5: 3 a debtor *to do* the whole law.
17. so that ye cannot *do* the things

Gal. 6: 9. let us not be weary in well *doing*
Eph 1: 16. *making* mention of you in my prayers;
2: 3. *fulfilling* the desires of the flesh
14. *who hath made* both one,
15. one new man, (so) *making* peace;
3: 11. purpose which he *purposed* (lit. *made*) in Christ Jesus
20. that is able *to do* exceeding
4: 16. *maketh* increase of the body unto
6: 6. *doing* the will of God from the heart;
8. whatsoever good thing any man *doeth,*
9. *do* the same things unto them,
Phi. 1: 4. *making* request with joy,
2: 14. *Do* all things without murmurings
4: 14. ye *have* well *done,* that ye did
Col. 3: 17. whatsoever ye *do* in word or
23. whatsoever ye *do,* do (it) heartily
4: 16. *cause* that it be read also in
1Th. 1: 2. *making* mention of you in our prayers;
4: 10. And indeed ye *do* it toward all the
5: 11. even as also ye *do.*
24. who also *will do* (it).
2Th. 3: 4. that ye both *do* and *will do* the things
1Ti. 1: 13. I *did* (it) ignorantly in unbelief.
2: 1. giving of thanks, *be made* for all men;
4: 16. for in *doing* this thou shalt
5: 21. *doing* nothing by partiality.
2Ti. 4: 5. *do* the work of an evangelist,
Tit. 3: 5. Not by works of righteousness which we *have done,*
Philem. 4. *making* mention of thee always
14. would I *do* nothing;
21. that thou *wilt* also *do* more than
Heb 1: 2. by whom also he *made* the worlds;
3. when he had by himself purged (lit. *having made* purgation of, &c.)
7. *Who maketh* his angels spirits,
3: 2. faithful to him *that appointed* him,
6: 3. And this *will* we *do,* if God permit.
7: 27. for this he *did* once, when he
8: 5. See,..thou *make* all things according
9. that I *made* with their fathers
10: 7. I come...*to do* thy will, O God.
9. Lo, I come *to do* thy will, O God.
36. *after* ye *have done* the will of God,
11: 28. Through faith he *kept* the passover,
12: 13. *make* straight paths for your feet,
27. as of things *that are made,*
13: 6. what man *shall do* unto me.
17. that they *may do* it with joy,
19. I beseech (you) the rather *to do* this,
21. *to do* his will, *working* in you that which
Jas. 2: 8. ye *do* well:
12. So speak ye, and so *do,* as they
13. *that hath shewed* no mercy;
19. thou *doest* well:
3: 12. Can the fig tree,...*bear* olive berries?
— no fountain both *yield* salt
18. of them *that make* peace.
4: 13. and *continue* there a year,
15. and *do* this, or that.
17. to him that knoweth *to do* good, and *doeth* (it) not,
5: 15. if he *have committed* sins.
1Pet. 2: 22. Who *did* no sin, neither was guile
3: 11. Let him eschew evil, and *do* good;
12. (is) against them *that do* evil.
2Pet. 1: 10. *to make* your calling and election sure: for *if* ye do these things,
15. *to have* these things always in remembrance.
19. ye *do* well that ye take heed.

1Joh. 1: 6. we lie, and *do* not the truth:
10. we *make* him a liar,
2:17. but he *that doeth* the will of God
29. that every one *that doeth* righteousness
3: 4. *Whosoever committeth* sin transgresseth also the law: (lit. *doeth* also lawlessness)
7. he *that doeth* righteousness is
8. He *that committeth* sin is of the devil;
9. *doth* not *commit* sin;
10. *whosoever doeth* not righteousness
22. and *do* those things that are
5:10. *hath made* him a liar;
3Joh. 5. thou *dost* faithfully whatsoever
6. thou *shalt do* well:
10. his deeds which he *doeth,*
Jude 3. *when* I *gave* all diligence to write
15. To *execute* judgment upon all,
Rev. 1: 6. And *hath made* us kings and priests
2: 5. and *do* the first works;
3: 9. I *will make* them to come and worship
12. Him that overcometh *will* I *make* a
5:10. And *hast made* us unto our God kings
11: 7. *shall make* war against them,
12:15. that he *might cause* her to be carried
17. and went *to make* war with the
13: 5. *to continue* forty (and) two months.
7. *to make* war with the saints,
12. he *exerciseth* all the power of the first beast before him, and *causeth* the earth
13. And he *doeth* great wonders, so that he *maketh* fire come down from
14. which he had power *to do* in the sight
— that they should *make* an image
15. and *cause* that as many as
16. And he *causeth* all, both small
14: 7. worship him *that made* heaven,
16:14. spirits of devils, *working* miracles,
17:16. and *shall make* her desolate and
17. to *fulfil* his will, and to agree, (lit. *to make* one mind)
19:19. *to make* war against him that
20. false prophet *that wrought* miracles
21: 5. Behold, I *make* all things new.
27. (whatsoever) *worketh* abomination,
22: 2. *which bare* twelve (manner of)
14. Blessed (are) they *that do* his
15. whosoever loveth and *maketh* a lie.

4161 2 689/831 6:458 4160

ποίημα, poyeema.

Ro. 1:20. by the *things that are made,*
Eph. 2:10. For we are his *workmanship,*

4162 1 689/831 6:458 4160

ποίησις, poyeesis.

Jas. 1:25. shall be blessed in his *deed.* (lit. *doing*)

4163 6 689/831 6:458 4160

ποιητής, poyeetees.

Acts17:28. of your own *poets* have said,
Ro. 2:13. but the *doers* of the law
Jas. 1:22. be ye *doers* of the word,
23. and not a *doer,*
25. but a *doer* of the work,
4:11. art not a *doer* of the law, but a judge

4164 10 690/831 6:484

ποικίλος, poikilos.

Mat. 4:24 with *divers* diseases and
Mar 1:34. sick of *divers* diseases,
Lu. 4:40. sick with *divers* diseases
2Ti. 3: 6. led away with *divers* lusts,
Tit. 3: 3. serving *divers* lusts and pleasures,
Heb 2: 4. and with *divers* miracles, and gifts
13: 9. with *divers* and strange doctrines.
Jas. 1: 2. when ye fall into *divers* temptations;
1Pet. 1: 6. through *manifold* temptations:
4:10. stewards of the *manifold* grace of God.

4165 11 690/831 6:485 4166

ποιμαίνω, poimaino.

Mat. 2: 6. *shall rule* (lit. *shall tend*) my people Israel.
Lu. 17: 7. a servant plowing or *feeding cattle,*
Joh.21:16. He saith unto him, *Feed* my sheep.
Acts20:28. *to feed* the church of God,
1Co. 9: 7. who *feedeth* a flock, and eateth not
1Pet.5: 2. *Feed* the flock of God which is
Jude 12. *feeding* themselves without fear:
Rev. 2:27. he *shall rule* them with a rod of iron;
7:17. midst of the throne *shall feed* them,
12: 5. who was *to rule* all nations with
19:15. he *shall rule* them with a rod of iron:

4166 18 690/831 6:485

ποιμήν, poimeen.

Mat. 9:36. as sheep having no *shepherd.*
25:32. as a *shepherd* divideth (his) sheep
26:31. I will smite the *shepherd,*
Mar 6:34. as sheep not having a *shepherd:*
14:27. I will smite the *shepherd,*
Lu. 2: 8. *shepherds* abiding in the field,
15. the *shepherds* said one to another,
18. told them by the *shepherds.*
20. And the *shepherds* returned,
Joh.10: 2. is the *shepherd* of the sheep.
11. I am the good *shepherd:* the good *shepherd* giveth his life
12. and not the *shepherd,*
14. I am the good *shepherd,*
16. one fold, (and) one *shepherd.*
Eph. 4:11. and some, *pastors* and teachers;
Heb 13:20. that great *Shepherd* of the sheep,
1Pet. 2:25. returned unto the *Shepherd* and Bishop of your souls.

4167 5 691/831 6:485 4165

ποίμνη, poimnee.

Mat.26:31. and the sheep of the *flock* shall
Lu. 2: 8. over their *flock* by night.
Joh.10:16. one *fold,* (and) one shepherd.
1Co. 9: 7. who feedeth a *flock,* and eateth not of the milk of the *flock?*

4168 5 691/831 6:485 4167

ποιμνίον, poimnion.

Lu. 12:32. Fear not, little *flock;*
Acts20:28. and to all the *flock,*
29. not sparing the *flock.*
1Pet. 5: 2. Feed the *flock* of God which
3. being ensamples to the *flock.*

4169 34 691/831 rt 4226,3634

ποῖος, poios.

Mat.19:18. He saith unto him, *Which?*
21:23. By *what* authority doest thou
24. by *what* authority I do these things.
27. by *what* authority I do these things.

Mat.22:36. *which* (is) the great commandment
24:42. for ye know not *what* hour
43. known in *what* watch the thief
Mar. 4:30. or with *what* comparison shall we
11:28. By *what* authority doest thou these things?
29. by *what* authority I do these things.
33. by *what* authority I do these things.
12:28. *Which* is the first commandment of all?
Lu. 5:19. by *what* (way) they might bring
6:32. *what* thank have ye? for sinners
33. *what* thank have ye? for sinners
34. *what* thank have ye? for sinners
12:39. *what* hour the thief would come,
20: 2. by *what* authority doest thou these things?
8. Neither tell I you by *what* authority
24:19. he said unto them, *What* things?
Joh.10:32. for *which* of those works do ye
12:33. signifying *what* death he should die.
18:32. signifying *what* death he should die.
21:19. by *what* death he should glorify
Acts 4: 7. they asked, By *what* power, or by *what* name,
7:49. *what* house will ye build me?
23:34. he asked of *what* province he was.
Ro. 3:27. By *what* law? of works? Nay:
1Co.15:35. and with *what* body do they come?
Jas. 4:14. For *what* (is) your life?
1Pet. 1:11. Searching what, or *what manner of* time
2:20. For *what* glory (is it),
Rev. 3: 3. thou shalt not know *what* hour

4170 7 691/832 6:502 4171

πολεμέω, *polemeo.*

Jas 4: 2. ye fight and *war*, yet ye have not,
Rev. 2:16. and *will fight* against them with
12: 7. Michael and his angels *fought* against the dragon; and the dragon *fought* and his angels,
13: 4. who is able *to make war* with him?
17:14. These *shall make war* with the Lamb,
19:11. he doth judge and *make war*.

4171 18 691/832 6:502 pelomai (to bustle)

πόλεμος, *polemos.*

Mat.24: 6. shall hear of *wars* and rumours of *wars*:
Mar13: 7. of *wars* and rumours of *wars*, be ye not
Lu. 14:31. going to make *war* against another
21: 9. shall hear of *wars* and commotions,
1Co.14: 8. prepare himself to the *battle*?
Heb 11:34. waxed valiant in *fight*,
Jas. 4: 1. From whence (come) *wars* and fightings
Rev. 9: 7. horses prepared unto *battle*;
9. many horses running to *battle*.
11: 7. shall make *war* against them,
12: 7. And there was *war* in heaven:
17. and went to make *war* with the remnant
13: 7. to make *war* with the saints,
16:14. to the *battle* of that great day of
19:19. to make *war* against him that sat on the horse,
20: 8. to gather them together to *battle*:

4172 164 691/832 6:516 rt 4171

πόλις, *polis.*

Mat. 2:23. and dwelt in a *city* called Nazareth:
4: 5. taketh him up into the holy *city*,
5:14. A *city* that is set on an hill cannot
35. for it is the *city* of the great King.
8:33. and went their ways into the *city*,
Mat. 8:34. behold, the whole *city* came out to
9: 1. and came into his own *city*.
35. went about all the *cities* and villages,
10: 5. and into (any) *city* of the Samaritans
11. into whatsoever *city* or town ye shall enter,
14. when ye depart out of that house or *city*,
15. in the day of judgment, than for that *city*.
23. when they persecute you in this *city*,
— over the *cities* of Israel, till
11: 1. to teach and to preach in their *cities*.
20. Then began he to upbraid the *cities*
12:25. and every *city* or house divided
14:13. they followed him on foot out of the *cities*.
21:10. all the *city* was moved, saying,
17. and went out of the *city* into
18. as he returned into the *city*,
22: 7. and burned up their *city*.
23:34. persecute (them) from *city* to *city*:
26:18. Go into the *city* to such a man,
27:53. and went into the holy *city*,
28:11. some of the watch came into the *city*,
Mar 1:33. And all the *city* was gathered together
45. openly enter into the *city*,
5:14. and told (it) in the *city*,
6:11. day of judgment, than for that *city*.
33. ran afoot thither out of all *cities*,
56. into villages, or *cities*, or country,
11:19. he went out of the *city*.
14:13. Go ye into the *city*,
16. and came into the *city*,
Lu. 1:26. unto a *city* of Galilee,
39. with haste, into a *city* of Juda;
2: 3. every one into his own *city*.
4. out of the *city* of Nazareth, into Judæa, unto the *city* of David,
11. in the *city* of David a Saviour,
39. to their own *city* Nazareth.
4:29. and thrust him out of the *city*,
— the hill whereon their *city* was built,
31. Capernaum, a *city* of Galilee,
43. the kingdom of God to other *cities* also:
5:12. when he was in a certain *city*,
7:11. he went into a *city* called Nain;
12. he came nigh to the gate of the *city*,
— much people of the *city* was with her.
37. And, behold, a woman in the *city*,
8: 1. throughout every *city* and village,
4. were come to him out of every *city*,
27. there met him out of the *city*
34. went and told (it) in the *city*
39. published throughout the whole *city*
9: 5. when ye go out of that *city*,
10. belonging to the *city* called Bethsaida.
10: 1. into every *city* and place,
8. into whatsoever *city* ye enter,
10. into whatsoever *city* ye enter,
11. Even the very dust of your *city*.
12. for Sodom, than for that *city*.
13:22. he went through the *cities* and villages
14:21. into the streets and lanes of the *city*,
18: 2. There was in a *city* a judge,
3. there was a widow in that *city*;
19:17. have thou authority over ten *cities*.
19. Be thou also over five *cities*.
41. he beheld the *city*, and wept over it,
22:10. when ye are entered into the *city*,
23:19. for a certain sedition made in the *city*,
51. of Arimathæa, a *city* of the Jews:
24:49. tarry ye in the *city* of Jerusalem,
Joh. 1:44(45). Bethsaida, the *city* of Andrew and Peter.

Jon. 4: 5. Then cometh he to a *city* of Samaria,
8. unto the *city* to buy meat.
28. and went her way into the *city*,
30. Then they went out of the *city*,
39. the Samaritans of that *city* believed
11: 54. into a *city* called Ephraim,
19: 20. was nigh to the *city*:
Acts 5: 16. (out) of the *cities* round about
7: 58. And cast (him) out of the *city*,
8: 5. went down to the *city* of Samaria,
8. there was great joy in that *city*.
9. in the same *city* used sorcery,
40. he preached in all the *cities*,
9: 6. Arise, and go into the *city*,
10: 9. and drew nigh unto the *city*,
11: 5. I was in the *city* of Joppa praying:
12: 10. that leadeth unto the *city*;
13: 44. came almost the whole *city* together
50. and the chief men of the *city*,
14: 4. But the multitude of the *city* was
6. Lystra and Derbe, *cities* of Lycaonia,
13. which was before their *city*,
19. drew (him) out of the *city*,
20. he rose up, and came into the *city*:
21. preached the gospel to that *city*,
15: 21. in every *city* them that preach him,
36. visit our brethren in every *city*
16: 4. they went through the *cities*,
12. the chief *city* of that part of
— we were in that *city* abiding
13. we went out of the *city* by a river
14. of the *city* of Thyatira,
20. exceedingly trouble our *city*,
39. depart out of the *city*.
17: 5. set all the *city* on an uproar,
16. when he saw the *city* wholly given
18: 10. I have much people in this *city*.
19: 29. And the whole *city* was filled
35. how that the *city* of the Ephesians
20: 23. witnesseth in every *city*,
21: 5. till (we were) out of the *city*:
29. with him in the *city* Trophimus an Ephesian,
30. And all the *city* was moved,
39. a citizen of no mean *city*:
22: 3. brought up in this *city*
24: 12. neither in the synagogues, nor in the *city*.
25: 23. principal men of the *city*,
26: 11. persecuted (them) even unto strange *cities*.
27: 8. whereunto was the *city* (of) Lasea.
Ro. 16: 23. Erastus the chamberlain of the *city*
2Co. 11: 26. (in) perils in the *city*,
32. kept the *city* of the Damascenes
Tit. 1: 5. ordain elders in every *city*,
Heb 11: 10. For he looked for a *city* which
16. he hath prepared for them a *city*.
12: 22. unto the *city* of the living God,
13: 14. here have we no continuing *city*,
Jas. 4: 13. we will go into such a *city*,
2Pet. 2: 6. turning the *cities* of Sodom an'
Jude 7. and the *cities* about them
Rev. 3: 12. the name of the *city* of my God,
11: 2. and the holy *city* shall they tread
8. the street of the great *city*,
13. and the tenth part of the *city* fell,
14: 8. is fallen, that great *city*,
20. trodden without the *city*,
16: 19. And the great *city* was divided into three parts, and the *cities* of the nations fell:
17: 18. that great *city*, which reigneth
18: 10. Alas, alas that great *city* Babylon that mighty *city*
Rev. 18: 16. Alas, alas that great *city*,
18. What (city is) like unto this great *city*!
19. Alas, alas that great *city*,
21. that great *city* Babylon be thrown down.
20: 9. and the beloved *city*:
21: 2. I John saw the holy *city*,
10. and shewed me that great *city*,
14. And the wall of the *city*
15. had a golden reed to measure the *city*,
16. And the *city* lieth foursquare,
— he measured the *city* with the reed,
18. the *city* (was) pure gold,
19. the foundations of the wall of the *city*
21. and the street of the *city* (was) pure gold,
23. the *city* had no need of the sun,
22: 14. through the gates into the *city*.
19. and out of the holy *city*,

4173 2 692/834 4172,757

πολιτάρχης, politarkees.

Acts17: 6. unto the *rulers of the city*,
8. and the *rulers of the city*, when

4174 2 692/834 6:516 4177

πολιτεία, politīa.

Acts22: 28. With a great sum obtained I this *freedom*. (lit. *citizenship*)
Eph 2: 12. aliens from the *commonwealth* (lit. *polity*) of Israel,

---

4175 1 692/834 6:516 4176

πολίτευμα, politūma.

Phi. 3: 20. For our *conversation* (lit. *enfranchisement* or *community*) is in heaven;

4176 2 693/834 6:516 4177

πολιτεύομαι, politūomai.

Acts23: 1. I *have lived* in all good conscience before God
Phi. 1: 27. *let* your *conversation be* (lit. *be regulated*) as it becometh

---

4177 3 693/834 6:516 4172

πολίτης, politees.

Lu. 15: 15. joined himself to a *citizen* of that
19: 14. But his *citizens* hated him,
Acts21: 39. a *citizen* of no mean city:

πολλά see πολύς. 4183

4178 18 693/834 4183

πολλάκις, pollakis.

Mat. 17: 15. for *ofttimes* he falleth into the fire, and *oft* into the water.
Mar 5: 4. had been *often* bound with fetters
9: 22. And *ofttimes* it hath cast him
Joh. 18: 2. for Jesus *ofttimes* resorted thither
Acts26: 11. I punished them *oft* in every synagogue,
Ro. 1: 13. that *oftentimes* I purposed to come
2Co. 8: 22. whom we have *oftentimes* proved
11: 23. in prisons more frequent, in deaths *oft*.
26. (In) journeyings *often*,
27. in watchings *often*,
— in fastings *often*,
Phi. 3: 18. of whom I have told you *often*,
2Ti. 1: 16. for he *oft* refreshed me,
Heb. 6: 7. the rain that cometh *oft* upon it,
9: 25. that he should offer himself *often*

Heb 9:26. For then must he *often* have suffered
10:11. offering *oftentimes* the same

4179 1 693/834 4183,4120
πολλαπλασίων, pollaplasiōn.

Lu. 18:30. shall not receive *manifold more* in this

4180 1 693/834 6:545 4183,3056
πολυλογία, polulogia.

Mat. 6: 7. be heard for their *much speaking.*

4181 1 693/834 4183,3313
πολυμερῶς, polumerōs.

Heb 1: 1. God, who *at sundry times* (lit. *by many portions*) and in divers manners

4182 1 694/834 6:484 4183,4164
πολυποίκιλος, polupoikilos.

Eph 3:10. the *manifold* wisdom of God,

4183 365 694/834 cf 4118, cf 4119
πολύς, polus. *pollos* (much)

[1] indicates the use of the neut. sing. πολὺ, as an adv. [2] the same use of the neut. plur. πολλά.
† denotes the article to be combined with the plural.

Mat. 2:18. and *great* mourning, Rachel weeping
3: 7. when he saw *many* of the Pharisees
4:25. *great* multitudes of people from
5:12. for *great* (is) your reward
6:30. (shall he) not *much* more (clothe) you,
7:13. and *many* there be which go in thereat:
22. *Many* will say to me in that day,
— done *many* wonderful works?
8: 1. *great* multitudes followed him.
11. *many* shall come from the east
16. unto him *many* that were possessed
18. when Jesus saw *great* multitudes
30. an herd of *many* swine feeding.
9:10. *many* publicans and sinners came
14. Why do we and the Pharisees fast *oft,*[2]
37. The harvest truly (is) *plenteous,*
10:31. of more value than *many* sparrows.
12:15. and *great* multitudes followed
13: 2. And *great* multitudes were
3. he spake *many* things unto them
5. where they had not *much* earth:
17. That *many* prophets and righteous
58. did not *many* mighty works there
14:14. and saw a *great* multitude,
15:30. And *great* multitudes came unto
— dumb, maimed, and *many* others,
16:21. and suffer *many* things of the
19: 2. And *great* multitudes followed him;
22. for he had *great* possessions.
30. But *many* (that are) first
20:16. for *many* be called, but few chosen.
28. and to give his life a ransom for *many.*
29. a *great* multitude followed him.
22:14. For *many* are called, but few (are) chosen.
24: 5. For *many* shall come in my name,
— and shall deceive *many.*
10. And then shall *many* be offended,
11. And *many* false prophets shall rise, and shall deceive *many.*
12. the love of † *many* shall wax cold.
30. with power and *great* glory.

Mat.25:19. After a *long* time the lord
21. make thee ruler over *many* things:
23. make thee ruler over *many* things:
26: 9. might have been sold for *much,*
28. which is shed for *many* for the remission
47. and with him a *great* multitude
60. though *many* false witnesses came,
27:19. for I have suffered *many* things this day
52. and *many* bodies of the saints
53. and appeared unto *many.*
55. And *many* women were there
Mar 1:34. healed *many* that were sick of divers diseases, and cast out *many* devils;
45. and began to publish (it) *much,*[2]
2: 2. *many* were gathered together,
15. *many* publicans and sinners sat
— for there were *many,* and they
3: 7. a *great* multitude from Galilee
8. a *great* multitude, when they had heard
10. For he had healed *many;*
12. And he *straitly*[2] charged them
4: 1. gathered unto him a *great* multitude,
2. he taught them *many* things
5. where it had not *much* earth;
33. And with *many* such parables
5: 9. My name (is) Legion: for we are *many.*
10. And he besought him *much*[2]
21. *much* people gathered unto him:
23. And besought him *greatly,*[2]
24. and *much* people followed him,
26. And had suffered *many* things of *many* physicians,
38. that wept and wailed *greatly.*
43. he charged them *straitly*[2] that
6: 2. and *many* hearing (him) were astonished,
13. they cast out *many* devils, and anointed with oil *many* that were sick,
20. he did *many* things, and heard him gladly
31. there were *many* coming and going,
33. and *many* knew him, and ran afoot
34. saw *much* people, and was moved
— he began to teach them *many* things.
35. when the day was now *far spent,*
— now the time (is) *far passed:*
7: 4. And *many* other things there be,
8. *many* other such like things ye do
13. *many* such like things do ye.
8:31. Son of man must suffer *many* things,
9:12. he must suffer *many* things,
14. he saw a *great* multitude
26. (the spirit) cried, and rent him *sore,*[2]
— that *many* said, He is dead.
10:22. for he had *great* possessions.
31. But *many* (that are) first shall be
45. and to give his life a ranson for *many.*
48. *many* charged him that he
— he cried the more *a great deal,*
11: 8. And *many* spread their garments
12: 5. and him they killed, and *many* others;
27. ye therefore do *greatly*[1] err.
37. And the *common* people heard him gladly.
41. and *many* that were rich cast in *much*[2]
13: 6. For *many* shall come in my name,
— and shall deceive *many.*
26. with *great* power and glory.
14:24. which is shed for *many.*
43. and with him a *great* multitude
56. For *many* bare false witness
15: 3. the chief priests accused him of *many* things:
41. and *many* other women
Lu. 1: 1. Forasmuch as *many* have taken in hand

Lu. 1:14. and *many* shall rejoice at his birth.
16. And *many* of the children of Israel
2:34. and rising again of *many* in Israel;
35. that the thoughts of *many* hearts
36. she was of a *great* age, and had lived
3:18. And *many* other things in his exhortation
4:25. *many* widows were in Israel
27. And *many* lepers were in Israel
41. And devils also came out of *many*,
5: 6. they inclosed a *great* multitude of fishes:
15. and *great* multitudes came together
29. and there was a *great* company
6:17. and a *great* multitude of people
23. your reward (is) *great* in heaven:
35. and your reward shall be *great*,
7:11. went with him, and *much* people.
21. he cured *many* of (their) infirmities
— and unto *many* (that were) blind
47. Her sins, which are † *many*, are forgiven; for she loved *much*:[1]
8: 3. Susanna, and *many* others, which ministered
4. *much* people were gathered together,
29. For *often*times it had caught him:
30. because *many* devils were entered
9:22. The Son of man must suffer *many* things,
37. *much* people met him.
10: 2. The harvest truly (is) *great*,
24. that *many* prophets and kings
40. cumbered about *much* serving,
41. troubled about *many* things:
12: 7. more value than *many* sparrows.
19. thou hast *much* goods laid up for *many* years;
47. shall be beaten with *many* (stripes).
48. unto whomsoever *much* is given, of him shall be *much* required: and to whom men have committed *much*,
13:24. for *many*, I say unto you, will seek
14:16. made a great supper, and bade *many*:
25. there went *great* multitudes
15:13. And not *many* days after
16:10. is faithful also in *much*:
— is unjust also in *much*.
17:25. first must he suffer *many* things,
18:39. but he cried *so much* the more,
21: 8. for *many* shall come in my name,
27. with power and *great* glory.
22:65. *many* other things blasphemously
23: 8. he had heard *many* things of him;
27. a *great* company of people,
Joh. 2:12. continued there not *many* days.
23. *many* believed in his name,
3:23. because there was *much* water there:
4:39. And *many* of the Samaritans
41. And *many* more believed because
5: 3. a *great* multitude of impotent folk,
6. he had been now a *long* time
6: 2. And a *great* multitude followed him,
5. and saw a *great* company come unto him,
10. Now there was *much* grass in the place.
60. *Many* therefore of his disciples,
66. *many* of his disciples went back,
7:12. there was *much* murmuring among
31. And *many* of the people believed
40. *Many* of the people therefore,
8:26. I have *many* things to say
30. *many* believed on him.
10:20. And *many* of them said, He hath
32. *Many* good works have I shewed
41. And *many* resorted unto him,
42. And *many* believed on him there.

Joh. 11:19. And *many* of the Jews came to
45. Then *many* of the Jews which
47. this man doeth *many* miracles.
55. and *many* went out of the country
12: 9. *Much* people of the Jews therefore
11. *many* of the Jews went away,
12. *much* people that were come
24. it bringeth forth *much* fruit.
42. also *many* believed on him;
14: 2. In my Father's house are *many* mansions:
30. I will not talk *much*[2] with you:
15: 5. the same bringeth forth *much* fruit:
8. that ye bear *much* fruit;
16:12. I have yet *many* things to say
19:20. This title then read *many* of the Jews:
20:30. And *many* other signs truly did Jesus
21:25. there are also *many* other things
Acts 1: 3. by *many* infallible proofs,
5. the Holy Ghost not *many* days hence.
2:43. and *many* wonders and signs were done
4: 4. *many* of them which heard the word
5:12. were *many* signs and wonders wrought
6: 7. a *great* company of the priests
8: 7. came out of *many* that were possessed (with them): and *many* taken with palsies,
25. in *many* villages of the Samaritans.
9:13. I have heard by *many* of this man,
42. and *many* believed in the Lord.
10: 2. which gave *much* alms to the people,
27. and found *many* that were come
11:21. and a *great* number believed,
13:43. *many* of the Jews and religious proselytes
14: 1. that a *great* multitude both
22. we must through *much* tribulation
15: 7. when there had been *much* disputing,
32. exhorted the brethren with *many* words,
35. with *many* others also.
16:16. brought her masters *much* gain
18. And this did she *many* days.
23. when they had laid *many* stripes
17: 4. devout Greeks a *great* multitude,
12. Therefore *many* of them believed;
18: 8. and *many* of the Corinthians hearing
10. I have *much* people in this city.
27. helped them *much*[1] which had
19:18. And *many* that believed came,
20: 2. had given them *much* exhortation,
19. and with *many* tears, and temptations,
21:40. there was made a *great* silence,
22:28. With a *great* sum obtained I this
23:10. there arose a *great* dissension,
24: 2. by thee we enjoy *great* quietness,
7. with *great* violence took (him)
10. thou hast been of *many* years a judge
25: 7. laid *many* and grievous complaints
23. and Bernice, with *great* pomp,
26: 9. I ought to do *many* things contrary
10. and *many* of the saints did I shut up
24. † *much* learning doth make thee mad.
29. were both almost, and *altogether* (lit. both in little and in *much*) such as I am,
27:10. will be with hurt and *much* damage,
14. But not *long* after there arose
21. But after *long* abstinence
28: 6. after they had looked *a great while*,
10. honoured us with *many* honours;
29. and had *great* reasoning among themselves.
Ro. 3: 2. *Much* every way: chiefly, because
4:17. a father of *many* nations,
18. the father of *many* nations,
5: 9. *Much* more then, being now justified

Ro 5:10. *much* more, being reconciled,
15. the offence of one † *many* be dead, *much* more the grace of God,
— hath abounded unto † *many*.
16. of *many* offences unto justification.
17. *much* more they which receive
19. † *many* were made sinners,
— shall † *many* be made righteous.
8:29. the firstborn among *many* brethren.
9:22. with *much* longsuffering
12: 4. as we have *many* members in one body,
5. So we, (being) † *many*, are one body
15:22. I have been † *much*[2] hindered
23. these *many* years to come unto you;
16: 2. she hath been a succourer of *many*,
6. who bestowed *much*[2] labour on us.
12. which laboured *much*[2] in the Lord.
1Co. 1:26. how that not *many* wise men after the flesh, not *many* mighty, not *many* noble, (are called):
2: 3. and in fear, and in *much* trembling.
4:15. yet (have ye) not *many* fathers:
8: 5. as there be gods *many*, and lords *many*,
10:17. For we (being) † *many* are one bread,
33. but the (profit) of † *many*,
11:30. For this cause *many* (are) weak
12:12. and hath *many* members,
— being *many*, are one body:
14. the body is not one member, but *many*.
20. But now (are they) *many* members,
22. Nay, *much* more those members
16: 9. and (there are) *many* adversaries.
12. I *greatly*[2] desired him to come unto you
19. salute you *much*[2] in the Lord,
2Co. 1:11. by the means of *many* persons thanks may be given by *many*
2: 4. For out of *much* affliction and anguish
— I wrote unto you with *many* tears;
17. For we are not as † *many*,
3: 9. *much* more doth the ministration
11. *much* more that which remaineth
12. we use *great* plainness of speech:
6: 4. in *much* patience, in afflictions,
10. as poor, yet making *many* rich;
7: 4. *Great* (is) my boldness of speech toward you, *great* (is) my glorying of you:
8: 2. How that in a *great* trial of affliction
4. Praying us with *much* intreaty
15. He that (had gathered) *much*
22. proved diligent in *many* things, but now *much*[1] more diligent, upon the *great* confidence which
9:12. by *many* thanksgivings unto God;
11:18. Seeing that *many* glory after the flesh,
12:21. I shall bewail *many* which have
Gal. 1:14. above *many* my equals
3:16. And to seeds, as of *many*;
4:27. hath many more children than (lit. *many* children rather than)
Eph. 2: 4. for his *great* love wherewith he
Phi. 1:23. which is *far* better: (lit. by *much* more better)
2:12. but now *much* more in my absence,
3:18. For *many* walk, of whom I have told
Col. 4:13. that he hath a *great* zeal for you,
1Th. 1: 5. in the Holy Ghost, and in *much* assurance;
6. received the word in *much* affliction,
2: 2. with *much* contention.
17. to see your face with *great* desire.
1Ti. 3: 8. not given to *much* wine,
13. and *great* boldness in the faith
6: 9. *many* foolish and hurtful lusts,
1Ti. 6:10. pierced themselves through with *many* sorrows.
12. a good profession before *many* witnesses.
2Ti. 2: 2. among *many* witnesses,
4:14. the coppersmith did me *much* evil:
Tit. 1:10. For there are *many* unruly and vain
2: 3. not given to *much* wine,
Philem. 7. For we have *great* joy and consolation
8. I might be *much* bold in Christ
Heb 2:10. in bringing *many* sons unto glory,
5:11. we have *many* things to say,
9:28. once offered to bear the sins of *many*;
10:32. ye endured a *great* fight of afflictions;
12: 9. shall we not *much* rather be in subjection
15. thereby *many* be defiled;
25. *much* more (shall not) we (escape),
Jas. 3: 1. My brethren, be not *many* masters,
2. For in *many*[2] things we offend all.
5:16. of a righteous man availeth *much*.[1]
1Pet. 1: 3. according to his *abundant* mercy
7. being *much*[1] more precious than
2Pet. 2: 2. And *many* shall follow their
1Joh. 2:18. even now are there *many* antichrists;
4: 1. because *many* false prophets are
2Joh. 7. For *many* deceivers are entered
12. Having *many* things to write
3Joh. 13. I had *many* things to write,
Rev. 1:15. as the sound of *many* waters.
5: 4. And I wept *much*,[2] because no man
11. I heard the voice of *many* angels
7: 9. and, lo, a *great* multitude,
8: 3. *much* incense, that he should offer
11. and *many* men died of the waters,
9: 9. of *many* horses running to battle.
10:11. before *many* peoples, and nations,
14: 2. as the voice of *many* waters,
17: 1. that sitteth upon *many* waters:
19: 1. I heard a great voice of *much* people
6. the voice of a *great* multitude, and as the voice of *many* waters,
12. and on his head (were) *many* crowns;

4184 1 696/838 7:548 4183,4698

πολύσπλαγχνος, polusplanknos.

Jas. 5:11. that the Lord is *very pitiful*,

4185 3 696/838 4183,5056

πολυτελής, poluteleės.

Mar 14: 3. of spikenard *very precious*
1Ti. 2: 9. or pearls, or *costly* array;
1Pet. 3: 4. in the sight of God *of great price*.

4186 2 696/838 4183,5092

πολύτιμος, polutimos.

Mat. 13:46. found one pearl *of great price*,
Joh. 12: 3. ointment of spikenard, *very costly*,

4187 1 696/838 4183,5158

πολυτρόπως, polutropōs.

Heb 1: 1. God, who at sundry times and *in divers manners*

4188 2 696/838 6:135 *poō* (4095) (to drink)

πόμα, poma.

1Co. 10: 4. did all drink the same spiritual *drink*:
Heb 9:10. (Which stood) only in meats and *drinks*,

4189 7 697/838 6:546 4190

πονηρία, poneeria.

Mat. 22:18. Jesus perceived their *wickedness*,

Mar 7:22. covetousness, *wickedness*, [plural]
Lu. 11:39. full of ravening and *wickedness.*
Acts 3:26. every one of you from his *iniquities.*
Ro. 1:29. *wickedness*, covetousness,
1Co. 5: 8. leaven of malice and *wickedness*
Eph 6:12. against spiritual *wickedness*

4190-4191 4192,cf 2556
78 697/839 6:546 cf 4550
πονηρός, *poneeros.* cf 4191

Mat. 5:11. shall say all manner of *evil* against
37. whatsoever is more than these cometh of *evil.*
39. That ye resist not *evil:*
45. he maketh his sun to rise on the *evil*
6:13. but deliver us from *evil:*
23. But if thine eye be *evil,*
7:11. If ye then, being *evil*, know
17. a corrupt tree bringeth forth *evil* fruit.
18. cannot bring forth *evil* fruit,
9: 4. Wherefore think ye *evil* in your hearts?
12:34. how can ye, being *evil*, speak good
35. an *evil* man out of the *evil* treasure bringeth forth *evil* things.
39. An *evil* and adulterous generation
45. spirits *more wicked* than himself,
— unto this *wicked* generation.
13:19. then cometh the *wicked* (one),
38. tares are the children of the *wicked* (one);
49. and sever the *wicked* from among
15:19. out of the heart proceed *evil* thoughts,
16: 4. A *wicked* and adulterous generation
18:32. O thou *wicked* servant, I forgave
20:15. Is thine eye *evil*, because I am good?
22:10. as many as they found, both *bad* and good:
25:26. (Thou) *wicked* and slothful servant,
Mar 7:22. lasciviousness, an *evil* eye, blasphemy,
23. All these *evil* things come from within,
Lu. 3:19. for all the *evils* which Herod had done,
6:22. cast out your name as *evil*,
35. unto the unthankful and (to) the *evil.*
45. and an *evil* man out of the *evil* treasure of his heart bringeth forth that which is *evil:*
7:21. and plagues, and of *evil* spirits;
8: 2. healed of *evil* spirits and infirmities,
11: 4. but deliver us from *evil.*
13. If ye then, being *evil*, know how
26. spirits *more wicked* than himself;
29. This is an *evil* generation:
34. but when (thine eye) is *evil*,
19:22. will I judge thee, (thou) *wicked* servant.
Joh. 3:19. because their deeds were *evil.*
7: 7. that the works thereof are *evil.*
17:15. shouldest keep them from the *evil.*
Acts17: 5. *lewd* fellows of the baser sort,
18:14. of wrong or *wicked* lewdness,
19:12. and the *evil* spirits went out of them.
13. call over them which had *evil* spirits the
15. And the *evil* spirit answered
16. the man in whom the *evil* spirit
28:21. or spake any *harm* of thee.
Ro. 12: 9. Abhor that which is *evil*,
1Co. 5:13. put away...that *wicked* person.
Gal. 1: 4. deliver us from this present *evil* world,
Eph 5:16. because the days are *evil.*
6:13. to withstand in the *evil* day,
16. the fiery darts of the *wicked.*
Col. 1:21. in (your) mind by *wicked* works,
1Th. 5:22. Abstain from all appearance of *evil.*
2Th 3: 2. from unreasonable and *wicked* men:
3. and keep (you) from *evil.*
1Ti. 6: 4. railings, *evil* surmisings,
2Ti. 3:13. But *evil* men and seducers shall
4:18. from every *evil* work,
Heb 3:12. an *evil* heart of unbelief,
10:22. sprinkled from an *evil* conscience,
Jas. 2: 4. are become judges of *evil* thoughts?
4:16. all such rejoicing is *evil.*
1Joh. 2:13. ye have overcome the *wicked* one.
14. ye have overcome the *wicked* one.
3:12. (who) was of that *wicked* one,
— Because his own works were *evil*,
5:18. and that *wicked* one toucheth him not.
19. the whole world lieth in wickedness. (lit in the *wicked*)
2Joh. 11. is partaker of his *evil* deeds.
3Joh. 10. prating against us with *malicious* words:
Rev.16: 2. a noisome and *grievous* sore upon

4192 3 698/839 rt 3993
πόνος, *ponos.*

Rev.16:10. they gnawed their tongues for *pain*,
11. because of their *pains* and their sores,
21: 4. neither shall there be any more *pain*

4197 2 698/840 4198
πορεία, *poria.*

Lu. 13:22. and *journey*ing toward Jerusalem.
Jas. 1:11. shall the rich man fade away in his *ways*

4198 154 698/840 6:566 *poros* (passage way)
πορεύομαι, *poruomai.*

Mat. 2: 8. *Go and* search diligently for the
9. they *departed*; and, lo, the star,
20. and *go* into the land of Israel:
8: 9. I say to this (man), *Go*, and he *goeth*;
9:13. But *go* ye *and* learn what (that)
10: 6. But *go* rather to the lost sheep
7. And *as* ye *go*, preach, saying,
11: 4. *Go and* shew John again those things
7. And *as* they *departed*, Jesus began
12: 1. At that time Jesus *went* on the sabbath
45. Then *goeth* he, and taketh with
17:27. *go* thou to the sea, *and* cast
18:12. *goeth* into the mountains, *and*
19:15. and *departed* thence.
21: 2. *Go* into the village over against
6. And the disciples *went*,
22: 9. *Go* ye therefore into the highways,
15. Then *went* the Pharisees, *and*
24: 1. and *departed* from the temple:
25: 9. but *go* ye rather to them that sell,
16. *went and* traded with the same,
41. *Depart* from me, ye cursed,
26:14. *went* unto the chief priests,
27:66. So they *went*, *and* made the sepulchre
28: 7. And *go* quickly, *and* tell his disciples
9. And as they *went* to tell his disciples,
11. Now *when* they *were going*,
16. the eleven disciples *went away* into
19. *Go* ye therefore, *and* teach all nations,
Mar 16:10. she *went and* told them that had been
12. as they walked, and *went* into the country
15. *Go* ye into all the world, *and*
Lu. 1: 6. *walking* in all the commandments
39. and *went* into the hill country
2: 3. And all *went* to be taxed,
41. Now his parents *went* to Jerusalem
4:30. through the midst of them *went* his *way*,
42. he departed and *went* into a desert
— that he should not *depart* from them.

Lu. 5:24. and *go* unto thine house
7: 6. Then Jesus *went* with them.
8. I say unto one, *Go*, and he *goeth;*
11. that he *went* into a city called Nain;
22. *Go* your *way, and* tell John
50. Thy faith hath saved thee; *go* in peace.
8:14. *go forth, and* are choked with cares
48. thy faith hath made thee whole; *go* in peace.
9:13. except we should *go and* buy meat
51. set his face *to go* to Jerusalem,
52. and *they went, and* entered into a
53. *as though* he *would go* to Jerusalem.
56. And they *went* to another village.
57. *as* they *went* in the way,
10:37. *Go*, and do thou likewise.
38. as they *went*, that he entered
11: 5. and *shall go* unto him at midnight,
26. Then *goeth* he, and taketh (to him)
13:31. Get thee out, and *depart* hence: for
32. *Go* ye, *and* tell that fox,
33. I must *walk* to day, and
14:10. *go and* sit down in the lowest room;
19. and I *go* to prove them:
31. *going* to make war against
15: 4. and *go* after that which is lost,
15. And he *went and* joined himself to
18. I will arise and *go* to my father,
16:30. but if one *went* unto them from the
17:11. as he *went* to Jerusalem,
14. *Go* shew yourselves unto the priests.
19. Arise, *go* thy *way:*
19:12. *went* into a far country
28. he *went* before, ascending up to
36. And *as* he *went*, they spread
21: 8. *go* ye not therefore after them.
22: 8. *Go and* prepare us the passover,
22. the Son of man *goeth*, as it
33. I am ready *to go* with thee, both into
39. and *went*, as he was wont,
24:13. two of them went (lit. were *going*) that same day
28. unto the village, whither they *went:* and he made as though he would have gone (lit. *to go*) further.
Joh. 4:50. *Go* thy *way;* thy son liveth.
— and he *went* his *way*.
7:35. Whither will he *go*,
— will he *go* unto the dispersed
53. every man *went* unto his own house.
8: 1. Jesus *went* unto the mount of Olives.
11. *go*, and sin no more.
10: 4. he *goeth* before them,
11:11. but I *go*, that I may awake him
14: 2. I *go* to prepare a place for you.
3. if I *go* and prepare a place for you,
12. because I *go* unto my Father.
28. I *go* unto the Father:
16: 7. but if I *depart*, I will send him
28. I leave the world, and *go* to the Father.
20:17. but *go* to my brethren,
Acts 1:10. *as* he *went up*, behold, two men
11. as ye have seen him *go* into heaven.
25. that he might *go* to his own place.
5:20. *Go*, stand and speak in the temple
41. And they *departed* from the presence
8:26. Arise, and *go* toward the south
27. And he arose and *went:*
36. And as they *went* on (their) way,
39. and he *went* on his way rejoicing.
9: 3. And as he *journeyed*, he came near
11. Arise, and *go* into the street which is

Acts 9:15. *Go* thy *way:* for he is a chosen
31. and *walking* in the fear of the Lord,
10:20. get thee down, and *go* with them,
12:17. and *went* into another place.
14:16. suffered all nations *to walk* in their
16: 7. they assayed *to go* into Bithynia:
16. *as* we *went* to prayer, a certain damsel
36. depart, and *go* in peace.
17:14. *to go* as it were to the sea:
18: 6. I *will go* unto the Gentiles.
19:21. *to go* to Jerusalem, saying,
20: 1. departed for *to go* into Macedonia.
22. behold, I *go* bound in the spirit
21: 5. we departed and *went* our *way;*
22: 5. and *went* to Damascus, to bring
6. that, *as* I *made* my *journey*,
10. Arise, and *go* into Damascus;
21. *Depart:* for I will send thee far
23:23. two hundred soldiers to *go* to Cæsarea,
32. left the horsemen *to go* with him,
24:25. *Go* thy *way* for this time;
25:12. unto Cæsar *shalt* thou *go*.
20. whether he would *go* to Jerusalem,
26:12. *as* I *went* to Damascus
13. them *which journeyed* with me.
27: 3. gave (him) liberty to *go* unto his friends
28:26. *Go* unto this people, and say,
Ro. 15:24. Whensoever I *take* my *journey* into Spain,
25. now I *go* unto Jerusalem
1Co. 10:27. and ye be disposed *to go;*
16: 4. if it be meet that I *go* also, they *shall go* with me.
6. on my journey whithersoever I *go*.
1Ti. 1: 3. *when* I *went* into Macedonia.
2Ti. 4:10. and *is departed* unto Thessalonica;
Jas. 4:13. we will *go* into such a city,
1Pet. 3:19. By which also he *went and* preached
22. Who *is gone* into heaven, *and* is on
4: 3. *when* we *walked* in lasciviousness,
2Pet. 2:10. them *that walk* after the flesh
3: 3. *walking* after their own lusts,
Jude 11. they *have gone* in the way of Cain,
16. *walking* after their own lusts;
18. *who should walk* (lit. *walking*) after their own

4199 3 699/841

perthō (to sack)

πορθέω, *portheo.*

Acts 9:21. Is not this he *that destroyed* them
Gal. 1:13. the church of God, and *wasted* it:
23. the faith which once he *destroyed*.

4200 2 699/841

poros (way, means)

πορισμός, *porismos.*

1Ti. 6: 5. supposing that *gain* is godliness: (lit. that godliness is *gain*)
6. godliness with contentment is great *gain*.

4202 26 699/842 6:579 4203

πορνεία, *pornīa.*

Mat. 5:32. saving for the cause of *fornication*,
15:19. adulteries, *fornications*, thefts,
19: 9. except (it be) for *fornication*,
Mar 7:21. adulteries, *fornications*, murders,
Joh. 8:41. We be not born of *fornication*,
Acts 15:20. and (from) *fornication*, and
29. and from *fornication:*
21:25. from strangled, and from *fornication*.
Ro. 1:29. *fornication*, wickedness, covetousness,

1Co. 5: 1. (that there is) *fornication* among you, and such *fornication* as is not
6:13. Now the body (is) not for *fornication*,
18. Flee *fornication*.
7: 2. (to avoid) *fornication*, let every
2Co.12:21. and *fornication* and lasciviousness
Gal. 5:19. Adultery, *fornication*, uncleanness,
Eph. 5: 3. But *fornication*, and all uncleanness,
Col. 3: 5. *fornication*, uncleanness,
1Th. 4: 3. ye should abstain from *fornication*:
Rev. 2:21. to repent of her *fornication*;
9:21. nor of their *fornication*,
14: 8. the wine of the wrath of her *fornication*.
17: 2. with the wine of her *fornication*.
4. filthiness of her *fornication*:
18: 3. wine of the wrath of her *fornication*,
19: 2. corrupt the earth with her *fornication*,

4203 8 700/842 6:579 4204

πορνεύω, *pornŭo*.

1Co. 6:18. but he *that committeth fornication*
10: 8. Neither *let us commit fornication*, as some of them *committed*,
Rev. 2:14. unto idols, and *to commit fornication*.
20. *to commit fornication*, and to eat
17: 2. the kings of the earth *have committed fornication*,
18: 3. *have committed fornication* with her,
9. *who have committed fornication* and

4204 12 700/842 6:579 4205

πόρνη, *pornee*.

Mat.21:31. and the *harlots* go into the kingdom
32. and the *harlots* believed him:
Lu. 15:30. devoured thy living with *harlots*,
1Co. 6:15. the members of an *harlot*?
16. is joined to an *harlot* is one body?
Heb 11:31. By faith the *harlot* Rahab perished not
Jas. 2:25. was not Rahab the *harlot* justified by
Rev.17: 1. the judgment of the great *whore*
5. THE MOTHER OF *HARLOTS*
15. where the *whore* sitteth,
16. these shall hate the *whore*,
19: 2. he hath judged the great *whore*,

4205 10 700/842 6:579 cf 4097 *pernemi* (to sell)

πόρνος, *pornos*.

1Co. 5: 9. not to company with *fornicators*:
10. with the *fornicators* of this world,
11. is called a brother be a *fornicator*,
6: 9. neither *fornicators*, nor idolaters,
Eph. 5: 5. that no *whoremonger*, nor unclean
1Ti. 1:10. For *whoremongers*, for them that defile
Heb 12:16. Lest there (be) any *fornicator*, or profane
13: 4. but *whoremongers* and adulterers God
Rev.21: 8. and *whoremongers*, and sorcerers,
22:15. *whoremongers*, and murderers,

4206,4208 4 700/842 4253 cf 4207

πόῤῥω, ποῤῥωτέρω, *porro, porrōtero*.

Mat.15: 8. but their heart is *far* from me.
Mar 7: 6. but their heart is *far* from me.
Lu. 14:32. while the other is yet *a great way off*,
24:28. as though he would have gone *further*.

4207 2 700/842 4206

πόῤῥωθεν, *porrōthen*.

Lu. 17:12. which stood *afar off*:
Heb 11:13. but having seen them *afar off*,

4209 5 700/842

πορφύρα, *porphura*.

Mar 15:17. And they clothed him with *purple*,
20. they took off the *purple* from him,
Lu. 16:19. which was clothed in *purple* and
Rev.17: 4. was arrayed in *purple* and scarlet
18:12. and *purple*, and silk, and scarlet,

4210 3 700/842 4209

πορφύρεος, πορφυροῦς, *porphureos, porphurous*.

Joh.19: 2. and they put on him a *purple* robe,
5. crown of thorns, and the *purple* robe.
Rev.18:16. in fine linen, and *purple*, and scarlet,

4211 1 700/842 4209,4453

πορφυρόπωλις, *porphuropōlis*.

Acts16:14. Lydia, a *seller of purple*,

4212 3 701/842 4214

ποσάκις, *posakis*.

Mat.18:21. *how oft* shall my brother sin
23:37. *how often* would I have gathered
Lu. 13:34. *how often* would I have gathered

4213 3 701/843 4095

πόσις, *posis*.

Joh. 6:55. and my blood is *drink* indeed.
Ro. 14:17. the kingdom of God is not meat and *drink*;
Col. 2:16. judge you in meat, or in *drink*,

4214 27 701/843 6:135 3739 *pos* (what)

πόσος, *posos*.

Mat. 6:23. *how great* (is) that darkness!
7:11. *how much* more shall your Father
10:25. *how much* more (shall they call)
12:12. *How much* then is a man better than
15:34. *How many* loaves have ye?
16: 9. and *how many* baskets ye took up?
10. and *how many* baskets ye took up?
27:13. Hearest thou not *how many* things
Mar 6:38. *How many* loaves have ye?
8: 5. *How many* loaves have ye?
19. *how many* baskets full of
20. *how many* baskets full of fragments
9:21. *How long* is it ago since this came
15: 4. *how many* things they witness
Lu. 11:13. *how much* more shall (your)
12:24. *how much* more are ye better than
28. *how much* more (will he clothe) you.
15:17. *How many* hired servants of my
16: 5. *How much* owest thou unto
7. And *how much* owest thou?
Acts21:20. *how many* thousands of Jews
Ro. 11:12. *how much* more their fulness?
24. *how much* more shall these, which be
2Co. 7:11. *what* carefulness it wrought in you,
Philem 16. but *how much* more unto thee,
Heb 9:14. *How much* more shall the blood
10:29. Of *how much* sorer punishment,

4215 16 701/843 6:595 cf 4224

ποταμος, potamos.

. 7:25. and the *floods* came,
27. rain descended, and the *floods* came,
Mar 1: 5. baptized of him in the *river* of Jordan,
Lu. 6:48. when the flood arose, the *stream* beat
49. against which the *stream* did beat
Joh. 7:38. shall flow *rivers* of living water.
Acts16:13. we went out of the city by a *river*
2Co.11:26. (in) perils of *waters*, (in) perils of robbers,
Rev. 8:10. upon the third part of the *rivers*,
9:14. bound in the great *river* Euphrates.
12:15. cast out of his mouth water as a *flood*
16. and swallowed up the *flood*
16: 4. poured out his vial upon the *rivers*
12. upon the great *river* Euphrates;
22: 1. a pure *river* of water of life,
2. and on either side of the *river*,

4216 1 701/843 6:595 4215,5409

ποταμοφόρητος, potamophoreetos.

Rev.12:15. cause her to be *carried away of the flood.*

4217 7 701/843 4219, rt 4226

ποταπός, potapos.

Mat. 8:27. *What manner of* man is this,
Mar 13: 1. Master, see *what manner of* stones and *what* buildings (are here)!
Lu. 1:29. *what manner of* salutation this should be.
7:39. and *what manner of* woman
2Pet.3:11. *what manner* (*of* persons) ought ye to be
1Joh.3: 1. Behold, *what manner of* love the

4218 32 701/843 rt 4225,5037

ποτέ, pote. indefinitely.

Lu. 22:32. and *when* thou art converted,
Joh. 9:13. him that *aforetime* was blind.
Acts28:27. lest)(they should see with (their) eyes,
Ro. 1:10. now *at length* I might have a
7: 9. I was alive without the law *once:*
11:30. For as ye *in times past* have not
1Co. 9: 7. Who goeth a warfare *any time* at his
Gal. 1:13. of my conversation *in time past*
23. which persecuted us *in times past* now preacheth the faith which *once* he
2: 6. whatsoever)(they were, it maketh no matter
Eph. 2: 2. Wherein *in time past* ye walked
3. *in times past* in the lusts of our flesh,
11. that ye (being) *in time past* Gentiles
13. ye who *sometimes* were far off
5: 8. For ye were *sometimes* darkness,
29. no man *ever yet* hated his own flesh;
Phi. 4:10. that now *at the last* your care of me
Col. 1:21. that were *sometime* alienated
3: 7. ye also walked *some time*, when ye
1Th. 2: 5. neither *at any time* used we
Tit. 3: 3. ourselves also were *sometimes* foolish,
Philem 11. Which *in time past* was to thee
Heb 1: 5. unto which of the angels said he *at any time*,
13. to which of the angels said he *at any time*,
2: 1. lest *at any time* we should let
4: 1. Let us therefore fear, lest,)(a promise
1Pet.2:10. Which *in time past* (were) not a
3: 5. after this manner *in the old time*
20. Which *sometime* were disobedient,
2Pet.1:10. if ye do these things, ye shall never (lit. not *ever*) fall:
21. prophecy came not *in old time* by the

4219 19 701/843 rt 4226,5037

πότε, pote. interrog., or definitely.

Mat.17:17. how long (lit. until *when*) shall I be with you? how long (lit. &c.) shall I suffer you?
24: 3. *when* shall these things be?
25:37. *when* saw we thee an hungred, and fed (thee)?
38. *When* saw we thee a stranger,
39. Or *when* saw we thee sick,
44. *when* saw we thee an hungred,
Mar 9:19. how long (lit. until *when*) shall I be with you? how long (lit. &c.) shall I suffer you?
13: 4. *when* shall these things be?
33. for ye know not *when* the time is.
35. for ye know not *when* the master
Lu. 9:41. how long (lit. until *when*) shall I be with you,
12:36. *when* he will return from the wedding;
17:20. *when* the kingdom of God should come,
21: 7. but *when* shall these things be?
Joh. 6:25. Rabbi, *when* camest thou hither?
10:24. How long (lit. &c.) dost thou make us to doubt?
Rev. 6:10. How long (lit. &c.), O Lord, holy

4220 1 702/844 rt 4226

πότερον, poteron.

Joh. 7:17. *whether* it be of God, or (whether

4221 33 702/844 6:135 cf 4224

ποτήριον, poteerion.

Mat.10:42. a *cup* of cold (water) only in the
20:22. Are ye able to drink of the *cup*
23. Ye shall drink indeed of my *cup*,
23:25. ye make clean the outside of the *cup*
26. cleanse first that (which is) within the *cup*
26:27. And he took the *cup*, and gave thanks,
39. let this *cup* pass from me:
42. if this *cup* may not pass away
Mar 7: 4. (as) the washing of *cups*, and pots,
8. (as) the washing of pots and *cups:*
9:41. a *cup* of water to drink
10:38. can ye drink of the *cup* that I
39. Ye shall indeed drink of the *cup*
14:23. And he took the *cup*, and when
36. take away this *cup* from me:
Lu. 11:39. make clean the outside of the *cup* and
22:17. And he took the *cup*, and gave thanks,
20. Likewise also the *cup* after supper, saying, This *cup* (is) the new testament
42. if thou be willing, remove this *cup*
Joh.18:11. the *cup* which my Father hath given
1Co.10:16. The *cup* of blessing which we bless,
21. Ye cannot drink the *cup* of the Lord, and the *cup* of devils:
11:25. After the same manner also (he took) the *cup*,
— This *cup* is the new testament
26. and drink this *cup*, ye do shew
27. and drink (this) *cup* of the Lord,
28. and drink of (that) *cup*.
Rev.14:10. into the *cup* of his indignation;
16:19. the *cup* of the wine of the fierceness
17: 4. having a golden *cup* in her hand
18: 6. in the *cup* which she hath filled

4222 15 702/844 6:135 *poō* (4095) (to drink)

ποτίζω, potizo.

Mat.10:42. whosoever shall *give to drink*

Mat.25:35. and ye *gave* me *drink*.
37. and *gave* (thee) *drink?*
42. and ye *gave* me no *drink:*
27:48. and *gave* him *to drink*.
Mar 9:41. shall *give* you a cup of water *to drink*
15:36. and *gave* him *to drink*, saying,
Lu. 13:15. and lead (him) away to *watering?*
Ro. 12:20. if he thirst, *give* him *drink:*
1Co. 3: 2. I *have fed* you with milk,
6. I have planted, Apollos *watered*
7. neither he *that watereth;*
8. and he *that watereth* are one:
12:13. and *have been* all *made to drink* into
Rev.14: 8. because she *made* all nations *drink*

4224 1 702/844 *poō* (4095) (to drink)

πότος, *potos*.

1Pet.4: 3. *banquetings*, (lit. *drinkings*) and abominable idolatries:

4225 3 703/844 *pos* (some)

που, *pou*. indefinitely.

Ro. 4:19. when he was *about* an hundred
Heb 2: 6. But one *in a certain place* testified,
4: 4. spake *in a certain place* of the seventh

4226 47 702/844 *pos* (what)

ποῦ, *pou*. interrog., or definitely.

Mat. 2: 2. *Where* is he that is born King of
4. *where* Christ should be born.
8:20. the Son of man hath not *where* to lay
26:17. *Where* wilt thou that we prepare
Mar 14:12. *Where* wilt thou that we go and
14. *Where* is the guestchamber,
15:47. beheld *where* he was laid.
Lu. 8:25. *Where* is your faith?
9:58. the Son of man hath not *where* to lay
12:17. *where* to bestow my fruits?
17:17. but *where* (are) the nine?
37. *Where*, Lord? And he said
22: 9. *Where* wilt thou that we prepare?
11. *Where* is the guestchamber,
Joh. 1:38(39). *where* dwellest thou?
39(40). They came and saw *where* he dwelt,
3: 8. and *whither* it goeth:
7:11. at the feast, and said, *Where* is he?
35. *Whither* will he go, that we shall not
8:10. *where* are those thine accusers?
14. whence I came, and *whither* I go;
— whence I come, and *whither* I go.
19. *Where* is thy Father?
9:12. *Where* is he? He said, I know not.
11:34. *Where* have ye laid him?
57. if any man knew *where* he were,
12:35. knoweth not *whither* he goeth.
13:36. Lord, *whither* goest thou?
14: 5. we know not *whither* thou goest;
16: 5. *Whither* goest thou?
20: 2. we know not *where* they have laid
13. I know not *where* they have laid
15. tell me *where* thou hast laid him,
Ro. 3:27. *Where* (is) boasting then?
1Co. 1:20. *Where* (is) the wise? *where* (is) the scribe? *where* is the disputer of this world?
12:17. *where* (were) the hearing?
— *where* (were) the smelling?
19. *where* (were) the body?
1Co.15:55. O death, *where* (is) thy sting? O grave, *where* (is) thy victory?
Heb 11: 8. not knowing *whither* he went.
1Pet.4:18. *where* shall the ungodly and
2Pet.3: 4. *Where* is the promise of his coming?
1Joh.2:11. and knoweth not *whither* he goeth,
Rev. 2:13. and *where* thou dwellest,

4228 93 703/845 6:624

πούς, *pous*.

Mat. 4: 6. lest at any time thou dash thy *foot*
5:35. for it is his *foot*stool: (lit. the footstool of his *feet*)
7: 6. lest they trample them under their *feet*,
10:14. shake off the dust of your *feet*.
15:30. cast them down at Jesus' *feet;*
18. 8. if thy hand or thy *foot* offend thee,
— than having two hands or two *feet*
29. fellowservant fell down at his *feet*,
22:13. Bind him hand and *foot*,
44. till I make thine enemies thy *foot*stool? (lit. &c.)
28: 9. and held him by the *feet*,
Mar 5:22. he fell at his *feet*,
6:11. the dust under your *feet* for a testimony
7:25. and came and fell at his *feet:*
9:45. if thy *foot* offend thee, cut it off:
— than having two *feet* to be cast
12:36. make thine enemies thy *foot*stool. (lit. &c.)
Lu. 1:79. to guide our *feet* into the way of peace.
4:11. thou dash thy *foot* against a stone.
7:38. stood at his *feet* behind (him) weeping, and began to wash his *feet* with tears,
— and kissed his *feet*,
44. thou gavest me no water for my *feet:* but she hath washed my *feet* with
45. hath not ceased to kiss my *feet*.
46. anointed my *feet* with ointment.
8:35. sitting at the *feet* of Jesus, clothed,
41. he fell down at Jesus' *feet*,
9: 5. the very dust from your *feet*
10:39. which also sat at Jesus' *feet*,
15:22. and shoes on (his) *feet:*
17:16. fell down on (his) face at his *feet*,
20:43. thine enemies thy *foot*stool. (lit. &c.)
24:39. Behold my hands and my *feet*,
40. shewed them (his) hands and (his) *feet*.
Joh.11: 2. and wiped his *feet* with her hair,
32. she fell down at his *feet*,
44. bound hand and *foot* with graveclothes:
12: 3. and anointed the *feet* of Jesus, and wiped his *feet* with her hair:
13: 5. to wash the disciples' *feet*,
6. dost thou wash my *feet?*
8. Thou shalt never wash my *feet*.
9. Lord, not my *feet* only, but also
10. save to wash (his) *feet*,
12. after he had washed their *feet*,
14. and Master, have washed your *feet;* ye also ought to wash one anothers' *feet*.
20:12. and the other at the *feet*,
Acts 2:35. Until I make thy foes thy *foot*stool. (lit. &c.)
4:35. laid (them) down at the apostles' *feet:*
37. and laid (it) at the apostles' *feet*.
5: 2. and laid (it) at the apostles' *feet*.
9. behold, the *feet* of them which have
10. fell she down straightway at his *feet*,
7: 5. no, not (so much as) to set his *foot* on:
33. Put off thy shoes from thy *feet:*
49. and earth (is) my *foot*stool: (lit. &c.)
58. at a young man's *feet*,
10:25. and fell down at his *feet*.

Acts13:25. whose shoes (his) *feet* I am not
51. shook off the dust of their *feet*
14: 8. impotent in his *feet*,
10. Stand upright on thy *feet*.
16:24. made their *feet* fast in the stocks.
21:11. bound his own hands and *feet*,
22: 3. at the *feet* of Gamaliel,
26:16. rise, and stand upon thy *feet*:
Ro. 3:15. Their *feet* (are) swift to shed blood:
10:15. How beautiful are the *feet* of them
16:20. shall bruise Satan under your *feet* shortly.
1Co.12:15. If the *foot* shall say, Because
21. nor again the head to the *feet*,
15:25. hath put all enemies under his *feet*.
27. he hath put all things under his *feet*.
Eph. 1:22. hath put all (things) under his *feet*,
6:15. And your *feet* shod with the
1Ti. 5:10. if she have washed the saints' *feet*,
Heb 1:13. thine enemies thy *foot*stool?
2: 8. in subjection under his *feet*.
10:13. till his enemies be made his *foot*stool.
12:13. make straight paths for your *feet*,
Rev. 1:15. And his *feet* like unto fine brass,
17. I fell at his *feet* as dead.
2:18. and his *feet* (are) like fine brass;
3: 9. and worship before thy *feet*,
10: 1. and his *feet* as pillars of fire:
2. and he set his right *foot* upon the sea,
11:11. and they stood upon their *feet*;
12: 1. and the moon under her *feet*,
13: 2. and his *feet* were as (the feet) of
19:10. I fell at his *feet* to worship him.
22: 8. before the *feet* of the angel which

4229 11 703/846 6:632 4238

πρᾶγμα, pragma.

Mat.18:19. touching any *thing* that they shall ask,
Lu. 1: 1. a declaration of those *things*
Acts 5: 4. why hast thou conceived this *thing*
Ro. 16: 2. in whatsoever *business* she hath need
1Co. 6: 1. having a *matter* against another,
2Co. 7:11. to be clear in this *matter*.
1Th. 4: 6. defraud his brother in (any) *matter*:
Heb 6:18. That by two immutable *things*,
10: 1. not the very image of the *things*,
11: 1. is the substance of *things* hoped for,
Jas. 3:16. confusion and every evil *work*.

4230 1 704/846 6:632 4231

πραγματεία, pragmatīa.

2Ti. 2: 4. entangleth himself with the *affairs* (lit. *negotiations*) of (this) life;

4231 1 704/846 6:632 4229

πραγματεύομαι, pragmatūomai.

Lu. 19:13. *Occupy* (lit. *trade*) till I come.

4232 8 704/846

πραιτώριον, praitōrion.

Mat.27:27. took Jesus into the *common hall*,
Mar 15:16. into the hall, called *Prætorium*,
Joh.18:28. unto the *hall of judgment*:
— went not into the *judgment hall*,
33. Pilate entered into the *judgment hall*
19: 9. went again into the *judgment hall*,
Acts23:35. to be kept in Herod's *judgment hall*.
Phi. 1:13. are manifest in all the *palace*,

4233 2 704/846 6:632 4238

πράκτωρ, practōr.

Lu. 12:58. the judge deliver thee to the *officer* and the *officer* cast thee

4234 6 704/846 6:632 4238

πρᾶξις, praxis.

Mat.16:27. according to his *works*. (lit. *acting*)
Lu. 23:51. to the counsel and *deed* of them;
Acts19:18. confessed, and shewed their *deeds*.
Ro. 8:13. do mortify the *deeds* of the body,
12: 4. all members have not the same *office*:
Col. 3: 9. the old man with his *deeds*;

4235 1 705/847 4239

πρᾷος, praos.

Mat.11:29. for I am *meek* and lowly in heart:

4236 9 705/847 4235

πρᾳότης, praotees.

1Co. 4:21. and (in) the spirit of *meekness*?
2Co.10: 1. by the *meekness* and gentleness of Christ,
Gal. 5:23. *Meekness*, temperance:
6: 1. in the spirit of *meekness*,
Eph. 4: 2. With all lowliness and *meekness*,
Col. 3:12. *meekness*, longsuffering;
1Ti. 6:11. patience, *meekness*.
2Ti. 2:25. In *meekness* instructing those
Tit. 3: 2. shewing all *meekness* unto all

4237 1 705/846 *prason* (leak)

πρασιά, prasia.

Mar 6:40. And they sat down *in ranks*, (lit. *range* by *range*)

4238 38 705/846 6:632 cf 4160

πράσσω, πράττω, prasso, pratto.

Lu. 3:13. *Exact* no more than that which is appointed you.
19:23. I might *have required* mine own
22:23. that should *do* this thing.
23:15. nothing worthy of death is *done* unto him
41. we receive the due reward of our *deeds* but this man *hath done* nothing amiss.
Joh. 3:20. every one *that doeth* evil hateth
5:29. and they *that have done* evil,
Acts 3:17. through ignorance ye *did* (it),
5:35. what ye intend *to do* as touching
15:29. ye *shall do* well.
16:28. *Do* thyself no harm:
17: 7. these all *do* contrary to the decrees
19:19. of them also *which used* curious *arts*
36. and *to do* nothing rashly.
25:11. or *have committed* any thing worthy
25. that he *had committed* nothing
26: 9. that I ought *to do* many things
20. *and do* works meet for repentance.
26. this thing was not *done* in a corner.
31. This man *doeth* nothing worthy of
Ro. 1:32. that they *which commit* such
— have pleasure in them *that do* them.
2: 1. *doest* the same things.
2. against them *which commit* such things.
3. judgest them *which do* such things
25. if thou *keep* the law:
7:15. what I would, that *do* I not;
19. which I would not, that I *do*.
9:11. neither *having done* any good or evil,

Ro. 13: 4. upon him *that doeth* evil.
1Co. 9:17. For if I *do* this thing willingly,
2Co. 5:10. according to that he *hath done*,
12:21. which they *have committed*.
Gal. 5:21. that they *which do* such things
Eph. 6:21. (and) how I *do*, Tychicus,
Phi. 4: 9. and seen in me, *do:*
1Th. 4:11. and *to do* your own business,

4239 3 705/847 6:645 cf 4235

πρᾳΰς, praüs.

Mat. 5: 5. Blessed (are) the *meek:* for
21: 5. thy King cometh unto thee, *meek*, and
1Pet. 3: 4. of a *meek* and quiet spirit,

4240 3 705/847 6:645 4239

πρᾳΰτης, praütees.

Jas. 1:21. receive with *meekness* the engrafted
3:13. his works with *meekness* of wisdom.
1Pet. 3:15. with *meekness* and fear:

πράω see πιπράσκω. 4097

4241 7 706/847

πρέπει, prepī.

Mat. 3:15. for thus it *becometh* (lit. is *becoming* for) us to fulfil all
1Co. 11:13. is it *comely* that a woman
Eph. 5: 3. as *becometh* saints;
1Ti. 2:10. which *becometh* women professing
Tit. 2: 1. which *become* sound doctrine:
Heb 2:10. For it *became* him, for whom
7:26. such an high priest *became* us,

4242 2 706/847 4243

πρεσβεία, presbīa.

Lu. 14:32. he sendeth an *ambassage*,
19:14. and sent a *message* after him,

4243 2 706/847 6:651 rt4245

πρεσβεύω, presbūo.

2Co. 5:20. we *are ambassadors* for Christ,
Eph. 6:20. I *am* an *ambassador* in bonds:

4244 3 706/847 6:651 4245

πρεσβυτέριον, presbuterion.

Lu. 22:66. the *elders* of the people and
Acts 22: 5. and all the *estate of* the *elders*.
1Ti. 4:14. of the hands of the *presbytery*.

4245 67 706/847 6:651 presbus (elderly)

πρεσβύτερος, -τέρα, presbuteros, -tera.

Mat. 15: 2. the tradition of the *elders?*
16:21. suffer many things of the *elders*
21:23. and the *elders* of the people
26: 3. and the *elders* of the people,
47. and *elders* of the people.
57. and the *elders* were assembled.
59. the chief priests, and *elders*,
27: 1. and *elders* of the people
3. to the chief priests and *elders*,
12. accused of the chief priests and *elders*,
20. the chief priests and *elders* persuaded
41. with the scribes and *elders*,
28:12. were assembled with the *elders*,
Mar 7: 3. holding the tradition of the *elders*.
5. according to the tradition of the *elders*,
8:31. and be rejected of the *elders*,
11:27. and the scribes, and the *elders*,
14:43. priests and the scribes and the *elders*.
53. and the *elders* and the scribes.
15: 1. with the *elders* and scribes
Lu. 7: 3. he sent unto him the *elders* of the Jews,
9:22. and be rejected of the *elders*
15:25. Now his *elder* son was in the field:
20: 1. came upon (him) with the *elders*,
22:52. and captains of the temple, and the *elders*,
Joh. 8: 9. beginning at the *eldest*, [plural]
Acts 2:17. and your *old men* shall dream dreams:
4: 5. that their rulers, and *elders*,
8. Ye rulers of the people, and *elders* of Israel,
23. and *elders* had said unto them.
6:12. and the *elders*, and the scribes,
11:30. and sent it to the *elders* by
14:23. ordained them *elders* in every church,
15: 2. unto the apostles and *elders* about this
4. and (of) the apostles and *elders*,
6. And the apostles and *elders*
22. pleased it the apostles and *elders*,
23. The apostles and *elders* and brethren
16: 4. that were ordained of the apostles and *elders*
20:17. and called the *elders* of the church.
21:18. and all the *elders* were present.
23:14. the chief priests and *elders*,
24: 1. high priest descended with the *elders*,
25:15. the chief priests and the *elders* of the Jew
1Ti. 5: 1. Rebuke not an *elder*, but intreat
2. The *elder women* as mothers;
17. Let the *elders* that rule well
19. Against an *elder* receive not an accusation, but before two
Tit. 1: 5. ordain *elders* in every city,
Heb 11: 2. For by it the *elders* obtained a good report.
Jas. 5:14. let him call for the *elders* of the church;
1Pet. 5: 1. The *elders* which are among you
5. submit yourselves unto the *elder*. [plural]
2Joh. 1. The *elder* unto the elect lady
3Joh. 1. The *elder* unto the wellbeloved Gaius,
Rev. 4: 4. I saw four and twenty *elders* sitting,
10. The four and twenty *elders*
5: 5. And one of the *elders* saith unto me,
6. and in the midst of the *elders*,
8. four (and) twenty *elders* fell down
11. and the beasts and the *elders:*
14. the four (and) twenty *elders* fell down
7:11. and (about) the *elders* and the four
13. And one of the *elders* answered,
11:16. the four and twenty *elders*, which sat
14: 3. before the four beasts, and the *elders:*
19: 4. the four and twenty *elders* and the four

4246 3 707/848 6:651 rt 4245

πρεσβύτης, presbutees.

Lu. 1:18. for I am an *old man*, and my wife
Tit. 2: 2. That the *aged men* be sober,
Philem. 9. being such an one as Paul the *aged*,

4247 1 707/848 4246

πρεσβῦτις, presbutis.

Tit. 2: 3. The *aged women* likewise,

4248 1 707/848 4253

πρηνής, preenees.

Acts 1:18 and falling *headlong*, he burst

4249 1 707/848

πρίζω, *prizo.* *prio* (to saw)

Heb 11:37. they *were sawn asunder,*

4250 14 707/849 4253

πρίν, πρὶν ἤ, *prin,* & *prin ee.*

Mat. 1:18. *before* they came together,
26:34. *before* the cock crow,
75. *Before* the cock crow, thou shalt
Mar 14:30. *before* the cock crow twice,
72. *Before* the cock crow twice,
Lu. 2:26. *before* he had seen the Lord's Christ.
22:34. *before that* thou shalt thrice deny
61. *Before* the cock crow,
Joh. 4:49. Sir, come down *ere* my child die.
8:58. *Before* Abraham was, I am.
14:29. I have told you *before* it come to pass,
Acts 2:20. *before* that great and notable day
7: 2. *before* he dwelt in Charran,
25:16. *before that* he which is accused

πρίω see πρίζω. 4249

4253 49 708/849 6:683

πρό, *pro.*

Note.—It governs the genitive.

Mat. 5:12. the prophets which were *before* you.
6: 8. ye have need of, *before* ye ask him.
8:29. to torment us *before* the time?
11:10. I send my messenger *before* thy face,
24:38. in the days that were *before* the flood
Mar 1: 2. I send my messenger *before* thy face,
Lu. 1:76. thou shalt go *before* the face of the Lord
2:21. *before* he was conceived in the womb.
7:27. I send my messenger *before* thy face,
9:52. And sent messengers *before* his face:
10: 1. two and two *before* his face into every
11:38. he had not first washed *before* dinner.
21:12. But *before* all these, they shall
22:15. this passover with you *before* I suffer:
Joh. 1:48(49). *Before* that Philip called thee,
5: 7. another steppeth down *before* me.
10: 8. All that ever came *before* me are thieves
11:55. up to Jerusalem *before* the passover,
12: 1. Then Jesus six days *before* the passover (πρὸ ἓξ ἡμερῶν τοῦ πάσχα)
13: 1. Now *before* the feast of the passover,
19. Now I tell you *before* it come,
17: 5. which I had with thee *before* the world
24. *before* the foundation of the world.
Acts 5:23. standing without *before* the doors:
36. For *before* these days rose up Theudas,
12: 6. and the keepers *before* the door kept
14. told how Peter stood *before* the gate.
13:24. *before* (lit. *before* the face of) his coming
14:13. which was *before* their city,
21:38. which *before* these days madest
23:15. and we, *or ever* he come near, are ready
Ro. 16: 7. who also were in Christ *before* me.
1Co. 2: 7. God ordained *before* the world
4: 5. judge nothing *before* the time,
2Co.12: 2. *above* fourteen years *ago,*
Gal. 1:17. which were apostles *before* me;
2:12. For *before* that certain came from James,
3:23. But *before* faith came,
Eph. 1: 4. *before* the foundation of the world,
Col. 1:17. And he is *before* all things, and
2Ti. 1: 9. *before* the world began;
4:21. Do thy diligence to come *before* winter.
Tit. 1: 2. promised *before* the world began,
Heb 11: 5. for *before* his translation he had
Jas. 5: 9. the judge standeth *before* the door.
12. But *above* all things, my brethren,
1Pet. 1:20. foreordained *before* the foundation of
4: 8. *above* all things have fervent charity

4254 18 708/849 1:128 4253,71

προάγω, *proago.*

Mat. 2: 9. *went before* them, till it came and
14:22. *to go before* him unto the other side,
21: 9. the multitudes *that went before,*
31. *go* into the kingdom of God *before* you.
26:32. I *will go before* you into Galilee.
28: 7. he *goeth before* you into Galilee;
Mar 6:45. *to go* to the other side *before* unto
10:32. and Jesus *went before* them:
11: 9. And they *that went before,*
14:28. I *will go before* you into Galilee.
16: 7. that he *goeth before* you into Galilee:
Lu. 18:39. they *which went before* rebuked him,
Acts 12: 6. when Herod would have *brought* him *forth,*
16:30. And *brought* them out, *and* said,
25:26. I *have brought* him *forth* before you,
1Ti. 1:18. according to the prophecies *which went before* on thee,
5:24. *going before* to judgment;
Heb 7:18. of the commandment *going before*

4255 1 709/850 4253,138

προαιρέομαι, *proaireomai.*

2Co. 9: 7. according as he *purposeth* in his heart,

4256 1 709/850 4253,156

προαιτιάομαι, *proaitiaomai.*

Ro. 3: 9. for we *have before proved* both Jews and Gentiles,

4257 1 709/850 4253,191

προακούω, *proakouo.*

Col. 1: 5. whereof ye *heard before* in the word

4258 2 709/850 4253,264

προαμαρτάνω, *proamartano.*

2Co.12:21. bewail many *which have sinned already,*
13: 2. write to them *which heretofore have sinned,*

4259 1 709/850 4253,833

προαύλιον, *proaulion.*

Mar 14:68. And he went out into the *porch;*

4260 5 709/850 4253,rt 939

προβαίνω, *probaino.*

Mat. 4:21. And *going on* from thence,
Mar 1:19. *when* he *had gone* a little *farther* thence,
Lu. 1: 7. both were (now) *well stricken* in years.
18. and my wife *well stricken* in years.
2:36. she was of a great age, (lit. *advanced* in days)

4261 2 709/850 4253,906

προβάλλω, *proballo.*

Lu. 21:30. When they now *shoot forth,*
Acts 19:33. the Jews *putting* him *forward.*

4262 1 709/850 4263

τροβατικός, probatikos.

Joh. 5: 2. by the *sheep* (market) a pool,

4263 41 709/850 6:689 4260

πρόβατον, probaton.

Mat. 7:15. come to you in *sheep's* clothing,
9:36. as *sheep* having no shepherd.
10: 6. go rather to the lost *sheep* of the
16. I send you forth as *sheep* in the
12:11. that shall have one *sheep*,
12. is a man better than a *sheep*?
15:24. but unto the lost *sheep* of the
18:12. have an hundred *sheep*,
25:32. divideth (his) *sheep* from the goats:
33. he shall set the *sheep* on his
26:31. the *sheep* of the flock shall be scattered
Mar 6:34. they were as *sheep* not having a
14:27. and the *sheep* shall be scattered.
Lu. 15: 4. having an hundred *sheep*,
6. for I have found my *sheep* which
Joh. 2:14. that sold oxen and *sheep* and doves,
15. and the *sheep*, and the oxen;
10: 1. by the door into the *sheep*fold,
2. is the shepherd of the *sheep*.
3. and the *sheep* hear his voice: and he calleth his own *sheep* by name,
4. he putteth forth his own *sheep*, he goeth before them, and the *sheep* follow him:
7. I am the door of the *sheep*.
8. but the *sheep* did not hear them.
11. giveth his life for the *sheep*.
12. whose own the *sheep* are not,
— leaveth the *sheep*, and fleeth:
— and scattereth the *sheep*.
13. and careth not for the *sheep*.
15. I lay down my life for the *sheep*.
16. And other *sheep* I have,
26. ye are not of my *sheep*,
27. My *sheep* hear my voice,
21:16. He saith unto him, Feed my *sheep*.
17. Jesus saith unto him, Feed my *sheep*.
Acts 8:32. He was led as a *sheep* to the slaughter;
Ro. 8:36. accounted as *sheep* for the slaughter.
Heb 13:20. that great Shepherd of the *sheep*,
1Pet. 2:25. For ye were as *sheep* going astray;
Rev. 18:13. beasts, and *sheep*, and horses,

4264 2 710/850 4253,971

προβιβάζω, probibazo.

Mat. 14: 8. *being before instructed* of her mother,
Acts 19:33. they *drew* Alexander out of the multitude,

4265 1 710/850 4253,991

προβλέπω, problepo.

Heb 11:40. God *having provided* some better thing for us,

4266 1 710/850 4253,1096

προγίνομαι, proginomai.

Ro. 3:25. for the remission of sins *that are past*,

4267 5 710/851 1:689 4253,1097

προγινώσκω, proginōsko.

Acts 26: 5. *Which knew* me from the beginning,
Ro. 8:29. For whom he *did foreknow*,
11: 2. his people which he *foreknew*.
1Pet. 1:20. *Who* verily *was foreordained* before
2Pet. 3:17. *seeing* ye *know* (these things) *before*,

4268 2 710/851 1:689 4267

πρόγνωσις, prognōsis.

Acts 2:23. and *foreknowledge* of God,
1Pet. 1: 2. according to the *foreknowledge* of

4269 2 710/851 4266

πρόγονοι, progonoi.

1Ti. 5: 4. and to requite their *parents*:
2Ti. 1: 3. whom I serve from (my) *forefathers*

4270 5 710/851 1:742 4253,1125

προγράφω, prographo.

Ro. 15: 4. whatsoever things *were written aforetime were written* for our learning,
Gal. 3: 1. Jesus Christ *hath been evidently set forth*,
Eph. 3: 3. as I *wrote afore* in few words,
Jude 4. *who were before* of old *ordained* to this

4271 3 711/851 4253,1212

πρόδηλος, prodeelos.

1Ti. 5:24. Some men's sins are *open beforehand*,
25. the good works (of some) are *manifest beforehand*;
Heb 7:14. For (it is) *evident* that our Lord

4272 1 711/851 4253,1325

προδίδωμι, prodidōmi.

Ro. 11:35. Or who *hath first given* to him,

4273 3 711/851 4272

προδότης, prodotees.

Lu. 6:16. which also was the *traitor*.
Acts 7:52. ye have been now the *betrayers* and
2Ti. 3: 4. *Traitors*, heady, highminded,

προδρέμω see προτρέχω. 4390

4274 1 711/851 8:226 4253,1408

πρόδρομος, prodromos.

Heb 6:20. Whither the *forerunner* is for us

4275 2 711/851 5:315 4253,1492

προειδέω, proïdeo.

Acts 2:31. He *seeing* this *before* spake of
Gal. 3: 8. And the scripture, *foreseeing* that

4276 1 711/851 2:517 4253,1679

προελπίζω, proelpizo.

Eph. 1:12. *who first trusted* in Christ.

4277 3 711/851 4253,2036

προέπω, proëpo. cf 4280

Acts 1:16. the Holy Ghost by the mouth of David *spake before* concerning Judas,
Gal. 5:21. as I *have* also *told* (you) *in time past*,
1Th. 4: 6. as we also *have forewarned* you

4278 2 712/851 4253,1728

προενάρχομαι, proenarkomai.

2Co. 8: 6. that as he *had begun*, so he would also finish in you
10. who *have begun before*, not only to do,

4279 1 712/851 2:576 4253,1861
προεπαγγέλλομαι, proepangellomai.

Ro. 1: 2. Which he *had promised afore* by his

4280 (4277) 9 711/851 4253,2046
προερέω, proereo.

Mat 24:25. I *have told* you *before*.
Mar 13:23. I *have foretold* you all things.
Ro. 9:29. as Esaias *said before*, Except
2Co. 7: 3. I *have said before*, that ye are
13: 2. I *told* you *before*, and foretell
Gal. 1: 9. As we *said before*, so say I now
Heb 10:15. after that he *had said before*,
2Pet. 3: 2. of the words *which were spoken before*
Jude 17. the words *which were spoken before*

4281 9 712/851 4253,2064
προέρχομαι, proerkomai.

Mat 26:39. he *went* a little *farther*, *and*
Mar 6:33. out of all cities, and *outwent* them,
14:35. And he *went forward* a little, *and*
Lu. 1:17. he *shall go before* him in the
22:47. one of the twelve, *went before* them,
Acts 12:10. and *passed on through* one street;
20: 5. These *going before* tarried for us
13. And we *went before* to ship, *and*
2Co. 9. 5. that they *would go before* unto you,

4282 2 712/851 2:704 4253,2090
προετοιμάζω, proetoimazo.

Ro. 9:23. which he *had afore prepared*
Eph. 2:10. which God *hath before ordained* that

4283 1 712/851 2:707 4253,2097
προευαγγελίζομαι, proüangelizomai.

Gal. 3: 8. *preached before the gospel* unto Abraham,

4284 1 712/851 6:692 4253,2192
προέχομαι, proëkomai.

Ro. 3: 9. What then? *are we better* (than they)?

4285 1 712/851 2:907 4253, 2233
προηγέομαι, proeegeomai.

Ro. 12:10. in honour *preferring* one another;

4286 12 713/851 8:152 4388
πρόθεσις, prothesis.

Mat 12: 4. and did eat the *shew*bread, (lit. the bread of *setting before*)
Mar 2:26. did eat the *shew*bread, (lit. the bread &c.)
Lu. 6: 4. did take and eat the *shew*bread, (lit. &c.)
Acts 11:23. that with *purpose* of heart
27:13. that they had obtained (their) *purpose*,
Ro. 8:28. the called according to (his) *purpose*.
9:11. that the *purpose* of God according to election
Eph. 1:11. according to the *purpose* of him
3:11. According to the eternal *purpose*
2Ti. 1: 9. according to his own *purpose*
3:10. manner of life, *purpose*, faith,
Heb 9: 2. and the *shew*bread; (lit. the *setting before* of bread)

4287 1 713/852 6:694 4253,5087
προθεσμία, prothesmia.

Gal 4: 2. until the *time appointed* of the father.

4288 5 713/852 4289
προθυμία, prothumia.

Acts 17:11. with all *readiness of mind*,
2Co. 8:11. as (there was) a *readiness* to will,
12. if there be first a *willing mind*,
19. and (declaration of) your *ready mind*:
9: 2. I know the *forwardness of* your *mind*,

4289 3 713/852 6:694 4253,2372
πρόθυμος, prothumos.

Mat. 26:41. the spirit indeed (is) *willing*,
Mar 14:38. The spirit truly (is) *ready*,
Ro. 1:15. So, as much as in me is, I am *ready* to preach the gospel to

4290 1 713/852 6:700 4289
προθύμως, prothumōs.

1Pet. 5: 2. but *of a ready mind*

4291 8 713/852 4253,2476
προΐστημι, proïsteemi.

Ro. 12: 8. he *that ruleth*, with diligence;
1Th. 5:12. and *are over* you in the Lord,
1Ti. 3: 4. One *that ruleth* well his own house,
5. if a man know not how *to rule* his
12. *ruling* their children and their own
5:17. Let the elders *that rule* well be
Tit. 3: 8. be careful *to maintain* good works.
14. learn *to maintain* good works

4292 1 714/852 3:487 4253,2564
προκαλέομαι, prokaleomai.

Gal. 5:26. *provoking* one another, envying

4293 4 714/852 1:56 4253,2605
προκαταγγέλλω, prokatangello.

Acts 3:18. which God *before had shewed* by
24. *have* likewise *foretold of* these days.
7:52. slain them *which shewed before* of
2Co. 9: 5. your bounty, whereof ye *had notice before*, (lit. your *previously notified* bounty)

4294 1 714/852 4253,2675
προκαταρτίζω, prokatartizo.

2Co. 9: 5. and *make up beforehand* your bounty,

4295 5 714/852 3:654 4253,2749
πρόκειμαι, prokīmai.

2Co. 8:12. if there *be first* a willing mind,
Heb. 6:18. to lay hold upon the hope *set before* us:
12: 1. the race *that is set before* us,
2. for the joy *that was set before* him
Jude 7. *are set forth* for an example,

4296 2 714/852 3:683 4253,2784
προκηρύσσω, prokeerusso.

Acts 3:20. Jesus Christ, *which before was preached* unto you:
13:24. *When* John *had first preached* before his coming the baptism of

4297 3 714/852 6:703 4298
προκοπή, prokopee.

Phi. 1:12. unto the *furtherance* of the gospel;

Phi. 1:25. for your *furtherance* and joy of faith;
1Ti. 4:15. that thy *profiting* may appear to all.

4298 6 714/852 6:703 4253,2875

προκόπτω, prokopto.

Lu. 2:52. Jesus *increased* in wisdom and
Ro. 13:12. The night *is far spent*,
Gal. 1:14. And *profited* in the Jews' religion
2Ti. 2:16. for they *will increase* unto more
3: 9. But they *shall proceed* no further:
13. *shall wax* worse and worse, deceiving,

4299 1 715/852 3:921 4253,2919

πρόκριμα, prokrima.

1Ti. 5:21. without *preferring one before another*,

4300 1 715/852 4253,2964

προκυρόομαι, prokuroömai.

Gal. 3:17. the covenant, *that was confirmed before* of God in Christ,

4301 3 715/852 4:5 4253,2983

προλαμβάνω, prolambano.

Mar 14: 8. she *is come aforehand* (lit. *hath anticipated*) to anoint
1Co.11:21. every one *taketh before* (other) his
Gal. 6: 1. if a man *be overtaken* in a fault,

4302 3 715/852 4253,3004

προλέγω, prolego.

2Co.13: 2. and *foretell* (you), as if I were present,
Gal. 5:21. of the which I *tell* you *before*,
1Th. 3: 4. we *told* you *before* that we should

4303 1 715/852 4:474 4253,3143

προμαρτύρομαι, promarturomai.

1Pet.1:11. *when it testified beforehand* the sufferings of Christ, and the glory

4304 1 715/852 4253,3191

προμελετάω, promeletao.

Lu. 21:14. not *to meditate before* what ye shall

4305 1 715/853 4:589 4253,3309

προμεριμνάω, promerimnao.

Mar13:11. *take* no *thought beforehand* what

4306 3 715/853 4:948 4253,3539

προνοέω, pronoeo.

Ro. 12:17. *Provide* things honest in the sight
2Co. 8:21. *Providing for* honest things,
1Ti. 5: 8. But if any *provide* not *for* his own,

4307 2 715/853 4:948 4306

πρόνοια, pronoya.

Acts24: 2. unto this nation by thy *providence*,
Ro. 13:14. and make not *provision for* the

4308 2 716/853 5:315 4253,3708

προοράω, proörao.

Acts 2:25. I *foresaw* the Lord always before my face,
21:29. For they had *seen before* with him

4309 6 716/853 5:452 4253,3724

προορίζω, proörizo.

Acts 4:28. *determined before* to be done.
Ro. 8:29. *did predestinate* (to be) conformed
30. whom he *did predestinate*, them he also
1Co. 2: 7. which God *ordained* (lit. *pre-ordained*) before the world
Eph 1: 5. *Having predestinated* us unto the adoption
11. *being predestinated* according to the purpose of him

4310 1 716/853 5:904 4253,3958

προπάσχω, propasko.

1Th. 2: 2. *after that* we *had suffered before*,

4311 9 716/853 4253,3992

προπέμπω, propempo.

Acts15: 3. And *being brought on* their *way* by the church,
20:38. And they *accompanied* him unto the ship.
21: 5. *and* they all *brought* us *on* our *way*,
Ro. 15:24. and *to be brought on* my *way* thitherward
1Co.16: 6. that ye *may bring* me *on* my *journey*
11. but *conduct* him *forth* in peace,
2Co. 1:16. of you *to be brought on* my *way*
Tit. 3:13. *Bring* Zenas the lawyer and Apollos *on* their *journey* diligently,
3Joh 6. *if* thou *bring forward on* their *journey*

4312 2 716/853 4253,4098

προπετής, propetees.

Acts19:36. and to do nothing *rash*ly.
2Ti. 3: 4. Traitors, *heady*, highminded,

4313 2 716/853 4253,4198

προπορεύομαι, proporuomai.

Lu. 1:76. thou *shalt go before* the face of the Lord
Acts 7:40. Make us gods to *go before* us:

4314 711 716/853 6:720 4253

πρός, pros.

Note.—It governs the accusative case with these few exceptions: In five places it is found with a dative, marked [d]; in one passage, Acts. 27:34, it has a genitive, marked [g].

Mat. 2:12. they should not return *to* Herod,
3: 5. Then went out *to* him Jerusalem,
10. the ax is laid *unto* the root
13. to Jordan *unto* John,
14. and comest thou *to* me?
15. Jesus answering said *unto* him,
4: 6. thou dash thy foot *against* a stone.
5:28. on a woman *to* lust after her
6: 1. *to* be seen of them:
7:15. which come *to* you in sheep's
10: 6. But go rather *to* the lost sheep of
13. let your peace return *to* you.
11:28. Come *unto* me, all (ye) that labour
13: 2. were gathered together *unto* him,
30. bind them in bundles *to* burn them.
56. are they not all *with* us?
14:25. Jesus went *unto* them,
28. bid me come *unto* thee on the water.
29. on the water, to go *to* Jesus.
17:14. when they were come *to* the multitude,
19: 8. *because of* the hardness of your hearts
14. and forbid them not, to come *unto* me:

Mat.21: 1. *unto* the mount of Olives,
32. For John came *unto* you
34. sent his servants *to* the husbandmen,
37. he sent *unto* them his son,
23: 5. *for* to be seen of men:
34. I send *unto* you prophets,
37. which are sent *unto* thee,
25: 9. but go ye rather *to* them that sell,
36. and ye came *unto* me.
39. and came *unto* thee?
26:12. she did (it) *for* my burial.
14. went *unto* the chief priests,
18. Go into the city *to* such a man,
— keep the passover *at* thy house (πρὸς σὲ)
40. he cometh *unto* the disciples,
45. Then cometh he *to* his disciples,
55. I sat daily *with* you teaching
57. led (him) away *to* Caiaphas
27: 4. What (is that) *to* us?
14. he answered him *to* never a word;
19. his wife sent *unto* him,
62. Pharisees came together *unto* Pilate,
Mar 1: 5. And there went out *unto* him all
27. they questioned *among* themselves,
32. they brought *unto* him all that
33. was gathered together *at* the door.
40. And there came a leper *to* him,
45. and they came *to* him from
2: 2. not so much as *about* the door:
3. And they come *unto* him,
13. the multitude resorted *unto* him,
3: 7. with his disciples *to* the sea:
8. came *unto* him.
13. and they came *unto* him.
31. sent *unto* him, calling him.
4: 1. there was gathered *unto* him
— was *by* the sea on the land.
41. and said one *to* another,
5:11. *nigh unto* the mountains
15. And they come *to* Jesus,
19. Go home *to* thy friends,
22. he fell *at* his feet,
6: 3. are not his sisters here *with* us?
25. with haste *unto* the king,
30. themselves together *unto* Jesus,
33. and came together *unto* him.
45. *unto* Bethsaida, while he
48. he cometh *unto* them,
51. he went up *unto* them into the ship;
7: 1. Then came together *unto* him
25. and came and fell *at* his feet:
31. he came *unto* the sea of Galilee,
8:16. they reasoned *among* themselves,
9:10. they kept that saying *with* themselves,
14. And when he came *to* (his) disciples,
16. What question ye *with* them?
17. I have brought *unto* thee my son,
19. how long shall I be *with* you?
— bring him *unto* me.
20. And they brought him *unto* him:
33. that ye disputed *among* yourselves
34. they had disputed *among* themselves,
10: 1. the people resort *unto* him again;
5. *For* the hardness of your heart he wrote
7. and cleave *to* his wife;
14. the little children to come *unto* me,
26. saying *among* themselves,
50. and came *to* Jesus.
11: 1. *at* the mount of Olives,
4. and found the colt tied *by* the door
7. And they brought the colt *to* Jesus,
27. there come *to* him the chief priests,
Mar 11:31. they reasoned *with* themselves,
12: 2. he sent *to* the husbandmen
4. he sent *unto* them another
6. he sent him also last *unto* them,
7. said *among* themselves,
12. had spoken the parable *against* them:
13. And they send *unto* him
18. Then come *unto* him the Sadducees,
13:22. *to* seduce, if (it were) possible,
14: 4. that had indignation *within* themselves.
10. went *unto* the chief priests,
49. I was daily *with* you in the temple
53. they led Jesus away *to* the high priest:
54. and warmed himself *at* the fire.
15:31. said *among* themselves
43. went in boldly *unto* Pilate,
16: 3. they said *among* themselves,
Lu. 1:13. But the angel said *unto* him,
18. Zacharias said *unto* the angel,
19. and am sent to speak *unto* thee,
27. *To* a virgin espoused to a man
28. the angel came in *unto* her,
34. Then said Mary *unto* the angel,
43. of my Lord should come *to* me?
55. As he spake *to* our fathers,
61. And they said *unto* her,
73. which he sware *to* our father
80. till the day of his shewing *unto* Israel.
2:15. the shepherds said one *to* another.
18. which were told)(them by the shepherds.
20. as it was told *unto* them.
34. and said *unto* Mary his mother,
48. and his mother said *unto* him,
49. And he said *unto* them,
3: 9. the axe is laid *unto* the root
12. and said *unto* him, Master,
13. And he said *unto* them, Exact no
14. And he said *unto* them, Do
4: 4. And Jesus answered)(him, saying,
11. thou dash thy foot *against* a stone.
21. And he began to say *unto* them,
23. And he said *unto* them, Ye will
26. But *unto* none of them was Elias
— *unto* a woman (that was) a widow.
36. and spake *among* themselves,
40. brought them *unto* him;
43. And he said *unto* them, I must
5: 4. he said *unto* Simon, Launch
10. And Jesus said *unto* Simon, Fear not;
22. he answering said *unto* them;
30. murmured *against* his disciples,
31. Jesus answering said *unto* them,
33. And they said *unto* him, Why do
34. And he said *unto* them, Can ye
36. spake also a parable *unto* them
6: 3. Jesus answering)(them said,
9. Then said Jesus *unto* them,
11. and communed one *with* another
47. Whosoever cometh *to* me,
7: 3. he sent *unto* him the elders
4. And when they came *to* Jesus,
6. the centurion sent friends *to* him,
7. worthy to come *unto* thee:
19. sent (them) *to* Jesus, saying,
20. When the men were come *unto* him,
— John Baptist hath sent us *unto* thee,
24. he began to speak *unto* the people
40. said *unto* him, Simon,
44. he turned *to* the woman,
50. And he said *to* the woman,
8: 4. and were come *to* him out of
13. which *for* a while believe.

Lu. 8:19. Then came *to* him (his) mother
21. and said *unto* them, My mother
22. and he said *unto* them, Let us go
25. saying one *to* another,
35. and came *to* Jesus,
9: 3. And he said *unto* them, Take nothing
13. But he said *unto* them, Give ye
14. he said *to* his disciples,
23. And he said *to* (them) all, If any
33. Peter said *unto* Jesus,
41. how long shall I be *with* you,
43. he said *unto* his disciples,
50. And Jesus said *unto* him, Forbid (him)
57. a certain (man) said *unto* him,
59. And he said *unto* another, Follow
62. And Jesus said *unto* him,
10: 2. Therefore said he *unto* them,
23. he turned him *unto* (his) disciples,
26. He said *unto* him, What is written
29. said *unto* Jesus, And who is
11: 1. one of his disciples said *unto* him,
5. And he said *unto* them, Which of you shall have a friend, and shall go *unto* him
6. in his journey is come *to* me,
39. And the Lord said *unto* him,
53. as he said these things *unto* them,
12: 1. he began to say *unto* his disciples
3. which ye have spoken *in* the ear
15. And he said *unto* them, Take heed,
16. he spake a parable *unto* them, saying,
22. And he said *unto* his disciples,
41. speakest thou this parable *unto* us or even *to* all?
47. neither did *according to* his will,
58. lest he hale thee *to* the judge,
13: 7. Then said he *unto* the dresser of
23. And he said *unto* them,
34. stonest them that are sent *unto* thee;
14: 3. spake *unto* the lawyers and Pharisees,
5. And answered)(them, saying,
6. could not answer him again *to* these things.
7. a parable *to* those which were bidden,
— saying *unto* them,
23. the lord said *unto* the servant,
25. he turned, and said *unto* them,
26. If any (man) come *to* me, and hate not
28. whether he have (sufficient) *to* finish (it)? (lit. the things *unto* completion)
32. and desireth conditions of peace. (lit. the things *unto* peace)
15: 3. he spake this parable *unto* them,
18. I will arise and go *to* my father,
20. and came *to* his father.
22. But the father said *to* his servants,
16: 1. And he said also *unto* his disciples,
20. which was laid *at* his gate,
26. which would pass from hence *to* you cannot; neither can they pass *to* us,
30. but if one went *unto* them from the
17: 1. Then said he *unto* the disciples,
22. And he said *unto* the disciples,
18: 1. a parable unto them (*to this end*), *that* men ought always
3. and she came *unto* him, saying,
7. which cry day and night *unto* him,
9. he spake this parable *unto* certain
11. and prayed thus *with* himself,
16. Suffer little children to come *unto* me,
31. and said *unto* them, Behold, we go
40. to be brought *unto* him:
19: 5. and said *unto* him, Zacchæus,
8. and said *unto* the Lord; Behold,

Lu. 19: 9. Jesus said *unto* him, This day
13. and said *unto* them, Occupy till I come.
29. *at* the mount called (the mount) of Olives,
33. the owners thereof said *unto* them,
35. And they brought him *to* Jesus:
37. *at*[d] the descent of the mount of Olives,
39. the multitude said *unto* him,
42. the things (which belong) *unto* thy peace
20: 2. And spake *unto* him, saying,
3. and said *unto* them, I will also
5. they reasoned *with* themselves,
9. Then began he to speak *to* the people
10. he sent a servant *to* the husbandmen,
14. they reasoned *among* themselves,
19. he had spoken this parable *against* them.
23. and said *unto* them, Why tempt ye me?
41. And he said *unto* them, How say
21:38. came early in the morning *to* him
22:15. And he said *unto* them,
23. began to enquire *among* themselves,
45. and was come *to* his disciples,
52. Then Jesus said *unto* the chief priests,
56. as he sat *by* the fire,
70. And he said *unto* them,
23: 4. Then said Pilate *to* the chief priests
7. he sent him *to* Herod,
12. they were at enmity *between* themselves.
14. Said *unto* them, Ye have brought
15. for I sent you *to* him;
22. And he said *unto* them
28. But Jesus turning *unto* them
24: 5. they said *unto* them,
10. told these things *unto* the apostles.
12. wondering *in* himself at that
14. And they talked together (lit. one *to* another) of all
17. And he said *unto* them,
— that ye have one *to* another,
18. answering said *unto* him,
25. Then he said *unto* them,
29. for it is *toward* evening,
32. And they said one *to* another,
44. which I spake *unto* you,
Joh. 1: 1. and the Word was *with* God,
2. The same was in the beginning *with* God.
29. John seeth Jesus coming *unto* him,
42(43). And he brought him *to* Jesus.
47(48). saw Nathanael coming *to* him,
2: 3. the mother of Jesus saith *unto* him,
3: 2. The same came *to* Jesus by night,
4. Nicodemus saith *unto* him,
20. neither cometh *to* the light,
21. doeth truth cometh *to* the light,
26. And they came *unto* John,
— and all (men) come *to* him.
4:15. The woman saith *unto* him,
30. and came *unto* him.
33. the disciples one *to* another,
35. are white already *to* harvest.
40. were come *unto* him,
47. he went *unto* him,
48. Then said Jesus *unto* him,
49. The nobleman saith *unto* him,
5:33. Ye sent *unto* John,
35. ye were willing *for* a season
40. And ye will not come *to* me,
45. that I will accuse you *to* the Father:
6: 5. a great company come *unto* him, he saith *unto* Philip,
17. Jesus was not come *to* them.
28. Then said they *unto* him, What
34. Then said they *unto* him, Lord,

Joh. 6:35. he that cometh *to* me shall never
37. shall come *to* me; and him that cometh *to* me I will
44. No man can come *to* me, except
45. cometh *unto* me.
52. strove *among* themselves,
65. no man can come *unto* me, except
68. *to* whom shall we go?
7: 3. said *unto* him, Depart hence,
33. I go *unto* him that sent me.
35. Then said the Jews *among* themselves,
37. let him come *unto* me, and drink.
45. Then came the officers *to* the chief
50. Nicodemus saith *unto* them, he that came *to* Jesus by night,
8: 2. all the people came *unto* him ;
3. brought *unto* him a woman taken
7. and said *unto* them,
31. Then said Jesus *to* those Jews which
57. Then said the Jews *unto* him,
9:13. They brought *to* the Pharisees him
10:35. *unto* whom the word of God came,
41. many resorted *unto* him,
11: 3. his sisters sent *unto* him,
4. This sickness is not *unto* death,
15. let us go *unto* him.
19. many of the Jews came *to* Martha and
21. Then said Martha *unto* Jesus,
29. and came *unto* him.
45. which came *to* Mary,
46. went their ways *to* the Pharisees.
12:19. said *among* themselves,
32. will draw all (men) *unto* me.
13: 1. out of this world *unto* the Father,
3. and went *to* God ;
6. Then cometh he *to* Simon Peter:
28. *for* what *intent* he spake this unto him.
14: 3. and receive you *unto* myself;
6. no man cometh *unto* the Father, but
12. because I go *unto* my Father.
18. I will come *to* you.
23. we will come *unto* him,
28. and come (again) *unto* you.
— I go *unto* the Father:
16: 5. I go my way *to* him that sent me ;
7. the Comforter will not come *unto* you ;
— I will send him *unto* you.
10. because I go *to* my Father,
16. because I go *to* the Father.
17. of his disciples *among* themselves,
— Because I go *to* the Father ?
28. and go *to* the Father.
17:11. and I come *to* thee.
13. And now come I *to* thee ;
18:13. And led him away *to* Annas first ;
16. But Peter stood *at*[d] the door
24. had sent him bound *unto* Caiaphas
29. Pilate then went out *unto* them,
38. he went out again *unto* the Jews,
19:24. said therefore *among* themselves,
39. at the first came *to* Jesus by night,
20: 2. and cometh *to* Simon Peter, and *to* the other disciple,
10. *unto* their own home. (πρὸς ἑαυτοὺς)
11. without *at* the sepulchre
12. the one *at*[d] the head, and the other *at*[d] the feet,
17. I am not yet ascended *to* my Father: but go *to* my brethren, and say unto them, I ascend *unto* my Father, and
21:22. what (is that) *to* thee? follow thou me.
23. what (is that) *to* thee ?

Acts 1: 7. And he said *unto* them,
2: 7. saying one *to* another, Behold,
12. saying one *to* another, What
29. let me freely speak *unto* you of the
37. and said *unto* Peter
38. Then Peter said *unto* them,
47. having favour *with* all the people.
3: 2. daily *at* the gate of the temple
10. which sat *for* alms at the Beautiful
11. the people ran together *unto* them
12. he answered *unto* the people,
22. Moses truly said *unto* the fathers,
— whatsoever he shall say *unto* you.
25. which God made *with* our fathers, saying *unto* Abraham,
4: 1. And as they spake *unto* the people,
8. said *unto* them, Ye rulers of
15. they conferred *among* themselves,
19. and said *unto* them,
23. they went *to* their own company,
— priests and elders had said *unto* them.
24. lifted up their voice *to* God
5: 9. Then Peter said *unto* her,
10. buried (her) *by* her husband.
35. And said *unto* them,
6: 1. of the Grecians *against* the Hebrews,
7: 3. And said *unto* him, Get thee
31. the voice of the Lord came *unto* him,
8:14. sent *unto* them Peter and John:
20. But Peter said *unto* him,
24. Pray ye *to* the Lord for me,
26. spake *unto* Philip, saying,
9: 2. letters to Damascus *to* the synagogues,
5. to kick *against* the pricks.
6. And the Lord (said) *unto* him,
10. *to* him said the Lord in a vision,
11. And the Lord (said) *unto* him,
15. But the Lord said *unto* him,
27. and brought (him) *to* the apostles,
29. and disputed *against* the Grecians:
32. he came down also *to* the saints which
38. they sent *unto* him two men,
40. and turning (him) *to* the body
10: 3. coming in *to* him,
13. And there came a voice *to* him,
15. the voice (spake) *unto* him again
21. Peter went down *to* the men which were sent *unto* him from Cornelius;
28. And he said *unto* them,
33. therefore I sent *to* thee ;
11: 2. contended *with* him,
3. Thou wentest in *to* men uncircumcised,
11. sent from Cæsarea *unto* me.
14. Who shall tell)(thee words,
20. spake *unto* the Grecians,
30. and sent it *to* the elders
12: 5. prayer was made...*unto* God for him.
8. And the angel said *unto* him,
15. And they said *unto* her,
20. they came with one accord *to* him,
21. and made an oration *unto* them.
13:15. sent *unto* them, saying,
— of exhortation *for* the people,
31. his witnesses *unto* the people.
32. which was made *unto* the fathers,
36. and was laid *unto* his fathers,
14:11. The gods are come down *to* us
15: 2. and disputation *with* them,
— *unto* the apostles and elders
7. and said *unto* them,
25. to send chosen men *unto* you
33. from the brethren *unto* the apostles.

Acts15:36. Paul said *unto* Barnabas
16:36. told this saying *to* Paul,
37. But Paul said *unto* them,
17: 2. went in *unto* them,
15. a commandment *unto* Silas and Timotheus for to come *to* him
17. *with* them that met with him.
18: 6. and said *unto* them,
14. Gallio said *unto* the Jews,
21. I will return again *unto* you, if
19: 2. He said *unto* them,
— And they said *unto* him,
3. And he said *unto* them,
31. his friends, sent *unto* him,
38. have a matter *against* any man,
20: 6. came *unto* them to Troas
18. when they were come *to* him,
21:11. when he was come *unto* us,
18. Paul went in with us *unto* James;
37. May I speak *unto* thee?
39. suffer me to speak *unto* the people.
22: 1. (which I make) now *unto* you.
5. I received letters *unto* the brethren,
8. And he said *unto* me,
10. And the Lord said *unto* me,
13. Came *unto* me, and stood, and said
15. thou shalt be his witness *unto* all
21. And he said *unto* me, Depart
25. Paul said *unto* the centurion
23: 3. Then said Paul *unto* him,
15. that he bring him down *unto* you
17. Bring this young man *unto* the chief
18. and brought (him) *to* the chief captain,
— to bring this young man *unto* thee,
22. thou hast shewed these things *to* me.
24. bring (him) safe *unto* Felix
30. I sent straightway *to* thee,
— what (they had) *against* him.
24:12. disputing *with* any man,
16. void of offence *toward* God, and
19. if they had ought *against* me.
25:16. *To* whom I answered,
19. certain questions *against* him of
21. till I might send him *to* Cæsar.
22. Then Agrippa said *unto* Festus,
26: 1. Then Agrippa said *unto* Paul,
6. made of God *unto* our fathers:
9. contrary *to* the name of Jesus
14. I heard a voice speaking *unto* me,
— for thee to kick *against* the pricks.
26. *before* whom also I speak freely:
28. Then Agrippa said *unto* Paul,
31. they talked *between* themselves,
27: 3. liberty to go *unto* his friends
12. was not commodious *to* winter in,
34. for this is *for*g your health:
28: 4. they said *among* themselves,
8. *to* whom Paul entered in,
10. with such things as were necessary. (lit. *for* need)
17. he said *unto* them,
21. And they said *unto* him,
23. there came many *to* him
25. when they agreed not *among* themselves,
— the prophet *unto* our fathers,
26. Go *unto* this people, and say,
30. and received all that came in *unto* him,
Ro 1:10. by the will of God to come *unto* you.
13. I purposed to come *unto* you,
3:26. *To* declare, (I say), at this time
4: 2. but not *before* God.
5: 1. we have peace *with* God through

Ro. 8:18. not worthy (to be compared) *with* the glory
31. What shall we then say *to* these things?
10: 1. and prayer *to* God for Israel is,
21. But *to* Israel he saith,
— *unto* a disobedient and gainsaying people.
15: 2. for (his) good *to* edification.
17. in those things *which pertain to* God.
22. hindered from coming *to* you.
23. these many years to come *unto* you;
24. I will come *to* you:
29. I am sure that, when I come *unto* you,
30. in (your) prayers *to* God for me;
32. That I may come *unto* you with joy
1Co. 2: 1. when I came *to* you,
3. And I was *with* you in weakness,
4:18. as though I would not come *to* you.
19. But I will come *to* you shortly, if
21. shall I come *unto* you with a rod,
6: 1. having a matter *against* another,
5. I speak *to* your shame.
7: 5. except (it be) with consent *for* a time,
35. this I speak *for* your own profit;
— but *for* that which is comely,
10:11. they are written *for* our admonition,
12: 2. carried away *unto* these dumb idols,
7. to every man *to* profit withal.
13:12. but then face *to* face:
14: 6. if I come *unto* you speaking with
12. *to* the edifying of the church.
26. Let all things be done *unto* edifying.
15:34. I speak (this) *to* your shame.
16: 5. Now I will come *unto* you,
6. I will abide, yea, and winter *with* you,
7. I trust to tarry a while *with* you,
10. that he may be *with* you without fear:
11. that he may come *unto* me:
12. to come *unto* you with the brethren:
2Co. 1:12. and more abundantly *to* you-*ward*.
15. I was minded to come *unto* you before,
16. out of Macedonia *unto* you,
18. our word *toward* you was not yea and nay.
20. *unto* the glory of God by us.
2: 1. not come again *to* you in heaviness.
16. who (is) sufficient *for* these things?
3: 1. epistles of commendation *to* you,
4. have we through Christ *to* God-*ward*:
13. *that* the children of Israel could not
16. when it shall turn *to* the Lord,
4: 2. commending ourselves *to* every man's conscience
6. *to* (give) the light of the knowledge
5: 8. and to be present *with* the Lord.
10. *according to* that he hath done,
12. somewhat *to* (answer) them which glory in
6:11. our mouth is open *unto* you,
14. hath light *with* darkness?
15. what concord hath Christ *with* Belial?
7: 3. I speak not (this) *to* condemn (you):
4. my boldness of speech *toward* you,
8. though (it were) but *for* a season.
12. might appear *unto* you.
8:17. of his own accord he went *unto* you.
19. administered by us *to* the glory of the
10: 4. mighty through God *to* the pulling down
11: 8. *to* do you service.
9(8). And when I was present *with* you,
12:14. I am ready to come *to* you;
17. whom I sent *unto* you?
21. my God will humble me *among* you,
13: 1. I am coming *to* you.
7. Now I pray *to* God that ye do no evil;

Gal 1:17. *to* them which were apostles
18. and abode *with* him fifteen days.
2: 5. no, not *for* an hour;
— might continue *with* you.
14. *according to* the truth of the gospel,
4:18. not only when I am present *with* you.
20. I desire to be present *with* you now,
6:10. let us do good *unto* all (men), especially *unto* them who are of
Eph 2:18. by one Spirit *unto* the Father.
3: 4. Where*by*, when ye read,
14. I bow my knees *unto* the Father
4:12. *For* the perfecting of the saints,
14. whereby they lie in wait to deceive; (lit. *unto* circumvention of deception)
29. good *to* the use of edifying,
5:31. shall be joined *unto* his wife,
6: 9. do the same things *unto* them,
11. *that* ye may be able to stand *against* the wiles of the devil.
12. we wrestle not *against* flesh and blood, but *against* principalities, *against* powers, *against* the rulers of the darkness of this world, *against* spiritual wickedness in high (places).
22. Whom I have sent *unto* you
Phi. 1:26. by my coming *to* you again.
2:25. supposed it necessary to send *to* you
30. your lack of service *toward* me.
4: 6. let your requests be made known *unto*
Col. 2:23. *to* the satisfying of the flesh.
3:13. if any man have a quarrel *against* any:
19. be not bitter *against* them.
4: 5. Walk in wisdom *toward* them that
8. Whom I have sent *unto* you,
10. if he come *unto* you,
1Th. 1: 8. your faith *to* God-*ward*
9. entering in we had *unto* you, and how ye turned *to* God from idols
2: 1. our entrance in *unto* you,
2. to speak *unto* you the gospel
9. because we would not (lit. *in order* not to) be chargeable unto any of you,
17. *for* a short time
18. we would have come *unto* you,
3: 4. when we were *with* you,
6. came from you *unto* us,
11. direct our way *unto* you.
4:12. *toward* them that are without,
5:14. be patient *toward* all (men).
2Th. 2: 5. when I was yet *with* you,
3: 1. even as (it is) *with* you:
8. *that* we might (lit. *in order*) not be chargeable to any of you:
10. For even when we were *with* you,
1Ti. 1:16. *for* a pattern to them which should
3:14. hoping to come *unto* thee shortly:
4: 7. exercise thyself (rather) *unto* godliness.
8. bodily exercise profiteth)(little: but godliness is profitable *unto* all things,
2Ti. 2:24. but be gentle *unto* all
3:16. and (is) profitable *for* doctrine, *for* reproof, *for* correction, *for* instruction in righteousness:
17. furnished *unto* all good works.
4: 9. to come shortly *unto* me:
Tit. 1:16. and *unto* every good work reprobate,
3: 1. to be ready *to* every good work,
2. all meekness *unto* all men.
12. When I shall send Artemas *unto* thee,
— be diligent to come *unto* me
Philem. 5. *toward* the Lord Jesus,
Philem. 13. I would have retained *with* me,
15. he therefore departed *for* a season,
Heb 1: 7. And *of* the angels he saith,
8. But *unto* the Son (he saith),
13. But *to* which of the angels said he
2:17. in things (pertaining) *to* God,
4:13. *with* whom we have to do.
5: 1. in things (pertaining) *to* God,
5. but he that said *unto* him,
7. *unto* him that was able to save him
14. exercised *to* discern both good and evil.
6:11. the same diligence *to* the full assurance of hope
7:21. by him that said *unto* him,
9:13. sanctifieth *to* the purifying of the flesh·
20. which God hath injoined *unto* you.
10:16. that I will make *with* them
11:18. *Of* whom it was said, That in Isaac
12: 4. striving *against* sin.
10. they verily *for* a few days
11. no chastening *for* the present
13:13. Let us go forth therefore *unto* him without the camp,
Jas. 3: 3. *that* they may obey us,
4: 5. lusteth *to* envy?
14. that appeareth *for* a little time,
1Pet. 2: 4. *To* whom coming,
3:15. ready always *to* (give) an answer
4:12. which is to try you, (lit. *for* trial to you)
2Pet. 1: 3. all things that (pertain) *unto* life and godliness,
3:16. *unto* their own destruction.
1Joh. 1: 2. which was *with* the Father,
2: 1. we have an advocate *with* the Father,
3:21. have we confidence *toward* God.
5:14. the confidence that we have *in* him,
16. a sin (which is) not *unto* death,
— for them that sin not *unto* death. There is a sin *unto* death:
17. and there is a sin not *unto* death.
2Joh. 10. If there come any *unto* you,
12. but I trust to come *unto* you, and speak face *to* face,
3Joh. 14. we shall speak face *to* face.
Rev. 1:13. girt *about*[d] the paps with
17. I fell *at* his feet as dead.
3:20. I will come in *to* him, and
10: 9. And I went *unto* the angel,
12: 5. her child was caught up *unto* God,
12. the devil is come down *unto* you,
13: 6. in blasphemy *against* God,
21: 9. And there came *unto* me
22:18. If any man shall add *unto* these

4315 1 718/860 4253,4521,cf3904

προσάββατον, *prosabbaton*.

Mar 15:42. that is, *the day before the sabbath*,

4316 1 718/860 4314,58

προσαγορεύομαι, *prosagorŭomai*.

Heb 5:10. *Called* of God an high priest

4317 4 718/860 1:128 4314,71

προσάγω, *prosago*.

Lu. 9:41. *Bring* thy son hither.
Acts 16:20. And *brought* them to the magistrates,
27:27. that they *drew near* to some country; (lit some country *drew near* them)
1Pet 3:18. that he *might bring* us to God.

4318 3 718/860 1:128 4317
προσαγωγή, prosagōgee.

Ro. 5: 2. we have *access* by faith into this
Eph. 2:18. we both have an *access* by one Spirit
3:12. and *access* with confidence by the faith of him.

4319 3 718/861 4314,154
προσαιτέω, prosaiteo.

Mar 10:46. sat by the highway side *begging.*
Lu. 18:35. sat by the way side *begging:*
Joh. 9: 8. Is not this he that sat and *begged?*

4320 1 718/861 4314,305
προσαναβαίνω, prosanabaino.

Lu. 14:10. Friend, *go up* higher:

4321 1 718/861 4314,355
προσαναλίσκω, prosanalisko.

Lu. 8:43. which *had spent* all her living upon

4322 2 718/861 4314,378
προσαναπληρόω, prosanapleeroō.

2Co. 9:12. not only *supplieth* the want of the saints,
11: 9. the brethren which came from Macedonia *supplied:*

4323 2 718/861 1:353 4314,394
προσανατίθημι, prosanatitheemi.

Gal. 1:16. I *conferred* not with flesh and blood:
2: 6. *in conference added* nothing to me:

4324 1 718/861 4314,546
προσαπειλέομαι, prosapīleomai.

Acts 4:21. *when* they *had further threatened*

4325 1 719/861 4314,1159
προσδαπανάω, prosdapanao.

Lu. 10:35. whatsoever thou *spendest more,*

4326 1 719/861 2:40 4314,1189
προσδέομαι, prosdeomai.

Acts17:25. *as though* he *needed* any thing,

4327 14 719/861 2:50 4314,1209
προσδέχομαι, prosdekomai.

Mar 15:43. which also *waited for* the kingdom
Lu. 2:25. *waiting for* the consolation of Israel:
38. to all them *that looked for* redemption
12:36. like unto men *that wait for* their lord,
15: 2. This man *receiveth* sinners, and
23:51. *waited for* the kingdom of God.
Acts23:21. *looking for* a promise from thee.
24:15. which they themselves also *allow,*
Ro. 16: 2. That ye *receive* her in the Lord,
Phi 2:29. *Receive* him therefore in the Lord
Tit. 2:13. *Looking for* that blessed hope,
Heb 10:34. and *took* joyfully the spoiling of
11:35. not *accepting* deliverance; that
Jude 21 *looking for* the mercy of our Lord

4328 16 719/861 6:725 4314 dokeuō (to watch)
προσδοκάω, prosdokao.

Mat.11: 3. or do we *look for* another?
24:50. when he *looketh* not *for* (him),
Lu. 1:21. the people *waited for* Zacharias,
3:15. *as* the people *were in expectation*
7:19. or *look* we *for* another?
20. or *look* we *for* another?
8:40. for they were all *waiting for* him
12:46. when he *looketh* not *for* (him),
Acts 3: 5. *expecting* to receive something
10:24. And Cornelius *waited for* them,
27:33. the fourteenth day that ye have *tarried and* continued
28: 6. they *looked when* he should have
— but *after* they *had looked* a great while,
2Pet. 3:12. *Looking for* and hasting unto the
13. *look for* new heavens and a new earth,
14. *seeing that* ye *look for* such things,

4329 2 719/861 6:725 4328
προσδοκία, prosdokia.

Lu. 21:26. and for *looking after* those things
Acts12:11. and (from) all the *expectation* **of the** people of the Jews.

προσδρέμω see προστρέχω. 4370

4330 1 719/861 4314,1439
προσεάω, proseao.

Acts27: 7. the wind not *suffering* us,

4331 1 719/861 2:330 4314,1448
προσεγγίζω, prosengizo.

Mar 2: 4. they could not *come nigh unto* him

4332 1 719/761 4314,rt 1476
προσεδρεύω, prosedrūo.

1Co. 9:13. and they *which wait at* the altar are

4333 1 720/861 4314,2038
προσεργάζομαι, prosergazomai.

Lu. 19:16. thy pound *hath gained* ten pounds.

4334 86 720/861 2:666 4314,2064
προσέρχομαι, proserkomai.

Mat. 4: 3. *when* the tempter *came to* him,
11. angels *came* and ministered unto him.
5: 1. his disciples *came unto* him:
8: 5. there *came unto* him a centurion,
19. And a certain scribe *came, and*
25. And his disciples *came to* (him), *and*
9:14. Then *came to* him the disciples of
20. *came* behind (him), *and* touched
28. the blind men *came to* him:
13:10. And the disciples *came, and* said
27. *came and* said unto him, Sir,
36. and his disciples *came unto* him,
14:12. And his disciples *came, and* took up
15. his disciples *came to* him,
15: 1. Then *came to* Jesus scribes and
12. Then *came* his disciples, *and*
23. And his disciples *came and*
30. And great multitudes *came unto* him.

Mat.16: 1. with the Sadducees *came, and* tempting
17: 7. Jesus *came and* touched them,
14. there *came to* him a (certain) man,
19. *came* the disciples *to* Jesus apart, *and*
24. *came to* Peter, and said, Doth not
18: 1. *came* the disciples *unto* Jesus,
21. Then *came* Peter *to* him, *and* said,
19: 3. The Pharisees also *came unto* him,
16. And, behold, one *came and* said
20:20. Then *came to* him the mother of
21:14. the blind and the lame *came to* him
23. the elders of the people *came unto* him
28. and he *came to* the first, *and* said,
30. And he *came to* the second, *and* said
22:23. The same day *came to* him the Sadducees,
24: 1. and his disciples *came to* (him)
3. the disciples *came unto* him
25:20. *came and* brought other five talents,
22. *came and* said, Lord, thou
24. *came and* said, Lord, I knew thee
26: 7. There *came unto* him a woman
17. the disciples *came to* Jesus,
49. he *came to* Jesus, *and* said, Hail, master;
50. Then *came* they, *and* laid hands on Jesus,
60. *though* many false witnesses *came*,
— At the last *came* two false witnesses,
69. a damsel *came unto* him,
73. *came unto* (him) they that stood by, *and*
27:58. He *went to* Pilate, *and* begged the body
28: 2. and *came and* rolled back the stone
9. they *came and* held him by the feet,
18. And Jesus *came and* spake unto them,
Mar 1:31. And he *came and* took her by the hand,
6:35. his disciples *came unto* him, *and*
10: 2. the Pharisees *came to* him, *and*
12:28. And one of the scribes *came, and*
14:45. he *goeth* straightway *to* him,
7:14. And he *came and* touched the bier:
8:24. And they *came to* him, and awoke
44. *Came* behind (him), *and* touched
9:12. then *came* the twelve, *and* said
42. And *as* he was yet *a coming*,
10:34. And *went to* (him), *and* bound up
13:31. The same day there *came* certain of
20:27. Then *came to* (him) certain of the
23:36. *coming to* him, and offering him
52. This (man) *went unto* Pilate, *and*
Joh. 12:21. The same *came* therefore to Philip,
Acts 7:31. and *as he drew near* to behold (it),
8:29. *Go near*, and join thyself to this
9: 1. *went unto* the high priest,
10:28. or *come unto* one of another nation;
12:13. a damsel *came* to hearken,
18: 2. and *came unto* them.
22:26. he *went and* told the chief captain,
27. Then the chief captain *came, and*
23:14. And they *came to* the chief priests
24:23. to minister or *come unto* him.
28: 9. *came*, and were healed:
1Ti. 6: 3. and *consent* not to wholesome words,
Heb 4:16. *Let* us therefore *come* boldly *unto*
7:25. *that come unto* God by him,
10: 1. the *comers thereunto* perfect.
22. *Let* us *draw near* with a true
11: 6. for he *that cometh to* God
12:18. For ye *are* not *come unto* the mount
22. But ye *are come unto* mount Sion,
1Pet. 2: 4. To whom *coming*, (as unto) a living stone,

4335 37 720/863 2:775 4336

προσευχή, prosūkee.

Mat. 17:21. but by *prayer* and fasting.
Mat. 21:13. shall be called the house of *prayer*,
22. whatsoever ye shall ask in *prayer*
Mar 9:29. but by *prayer* and fasting.
11:17. called of all nations the house of *prayer*?
Lu. 6:12. continued all night in *prayer* to God.
19:46. My house is the house of *prayer*:
22:45. when he rose up from *prayer*,
Acts 1:14. continued with one accord in *prayer* and supplication,
2:42. in breaking of bread, and in *prayers*.
3: 1. at the hour of *prayer*, (being) the ninth (hour).
6: 4. continually to *prayer*, and to the ministry of the word.
10: 4. Thy *prayers* and thine alms are come up
31. Cornelius, thy *prayer* is heard, and
12: 5. but *prayer* was made without ceasing
16:13. where *prayer* was wont to be made;
16. as we went to *prayer*, a certain damsel
Ro. 1: 9(10). mention of you always in my *prayers*;
12:12. continuing instant in *prayer*;
15:30. in (your) *prayers* to God for me;
1Co. 7: 5. give yourselves to fasting and *prayer*;
Eph. 1:16. making mention of you in my *prayers*;
6:18. Praying always with all *prayer* and supplication in
Phi. 4: 6. but in every thing by *prayer* and supplication with
Col. 4: 2. Continue in *prayer*, and watch
12. fervently for you in *prayers*,
1Th. 1: 2. making mention of you in our *prayers*;
1Ti. 2: 1. supplications, *prayers*, intercessions,
5: 5. in supplications and *prayers* night and day.
Philem. 4. mention of thee always in my *prayers*,
22. I trust that through your *prayers*
Jas. 5:17. and he prayed earnestly (lit. prayed with *prayer*)
1Pet. 3: 7. that your *prayers* be not hindered.
4: 7. and watch unto *prayer*.
Rev. 5: 8. which are the *prayers* of saints.
8: 3. with the *prayers* of all saints upon the
4. with the *prayers* of the saints,

4336 87 720/863 2:775 4314,2172

προσεύχομαι, prosūkomai.

Mat. 5:44. *pray* for them which despitefully
6: 5. And when thou *prayest*, thou shalt not
— for they love *to pray* standing in
6. when thou *prayest*, enter into
— *pray* to thy Father which is in secret;
7. But *when* ye *pray*, use not vain
9. After this manner therefore *pray* ye:
14:23. into a mountain apart *to pray*:
19:13. put (his) hands on them, and *pray*:
23:14(13). for a pretence *make* long *prayer*:
24:20. But *pray* ye that your flight
26:36. while I go and *pray* yonder.
39. and fell on his face, *and prayed*,
41. Watch and *pray*, that ye enter not into
42. and *prayed*, saying, O my Father,
44. and *prayed* the third time,
Mar 1:35. solitary place, and there *prayed*.
6:46. into a mountain *to pray*.
11:24. ye desire, *when* ye *pray*, believe
25. And when ye stand *praying*,
12:40. for a pretence *make* long *prayers*:
13:18. And *pray* ye that your flight
33. watch and *pray*: for ye know not
14:32. Sit ye here, while I shall *pray*.
35. and *prayed* that, if it were
38. Watch ye and *pray*, lest ye enter

Mar 14:39. and *prayed*, and spake the same
Lu. 1:10. the people were *praying* without
3:21. Jesus also being baptized, and *praying*,
5:16. into the wilderness, and *prayed*.
6:12. went out into a mountain *to pray*,
28. and *pray* for them which
9:18. as he was alone *praying*,
28. into a mountain *to pray*.
29. And as he *prayed*,
11: 1. as he was *praying* in a certain
— Lord, teach us *to pray*,
2. When ye *pray*, say, Our Father
18: 1. men ought always *to pray*,
10. into the temple *to pray*;
11. and *prayed* thus with himself,
20:47. *make* long *prayers*:
22:40. *Pray* that ye enter not into
41. and kneeled down, and *prayed*,
44. he *prayed* more earnestly.
46. rise and *pray*, lest ye enter into
Acts 1:24. And they *prayed*, *and* said,
6: 6. and *when* they *had prayed*, they
8:15. *prayed* for them, that they
9:11. for, behold, he *prayeth*,
40. and kneeled down, and *prayed*;
10: 9. upon the housetop *to pray*
30. I *prayed* in my house,
11: 5. I was in the city of Joppa *praying*:
12:12. many were gathered together *praying*.
13: 3. when they had fasted and *prayed*,
14:23. *and had prayed* with fasting,
16:25. Paul and Silas *prayed*, *and* sang praises
20:36. and *prayed* with them all.
21: 5. we kneeled down on the shore, and *prayed*.
22:17. *while* I *prayed* in the temple,
28: 8. and *prayed*, *and* laid his hands on him,
Ro. 8:26. what we *should pray for* as we
1Co.11: 4. Every man *praying* or prophesying,
5. But every woman *that prayeth*
13. is it comely that a woman *pray*
14:13. *let* him...*pray* that he may interpret.
14. For if I *pray* in an (unknown) tongue, my spirit *prayeth*, but
15. I *will pray* with the spirit, and I *will pray* with the understanding
Eph. 6:18. *Praying* always with all prayer
Phi. 1: 9. And this I *pray*, that your love
Col. 1: 3. *praying* always for you,
9. do not cease to *pray* for you,
4: 3. Withal *praying* also for us,
1Th. 5:17. *Pray* without ceasing.
25. Brethren, *pray* for us.
2Th. 1:11. we *pray* always for you,
3: 1. Finally, brethren, *pray* for us,
1Ti. 2: 8. that men *pray* every where,
Heb 13:18. *Pray* for us: for we trust
Jas. 5:13. afflicted? *let* him *pray*.
14. *let* them *pray* over him,
17. and he *prayed* earnestly that it
18. And he *prayed* again, and the heaven
Jude 20. *praying* in the Holy Ghost,

4337 24 721/864 4314,2192

προσέχω, proseko.

Mat 6: 1. *Take heed* that ye do not your alms
7:15. *Beware* of false prophets,
10:17. But *beware* of men:
16: 6. Take heed and *beware* of the leaven
11. that ye should *beware* of the leaven
12. not *beware* of the leaven of bread, but
Lu. 12: 1. *Beware* ye of the leaven of the
17: 3. *Take heed to* yourselves:
20:46. *Beware* of the scribes,
21:34. *take heed to* yourselves, lest
Acts 5:35. *take heed to* yourselves what ye intend
8: 6. *gave heed unto* those things
10. *To* whom they all *gave heed*,
11. And *to* him they *had regard*,
16:14. that she *attended unto* the things
20:28. *Take heed* therefore *unto* yourselves,
1Ti. 1: 4. Neither *give heed to* fables and
3: 8. not *given to* much wine,
4: 1. *giving heed to* seducing spirits,
13. *give attendance to* reading,
Tit. 1:14. Not *giving heed to* Jewish fables,
Heb 2: 1. *to give* the more earnest *heed to* the
7:13. no man *gave attendance at* the altar.
2Pet. 1:19. whereunto ye do well *that* ye *take heed*,

4338 1 722/864 4314,2247

προσηλόω, proseeloō.

Col. 2:14. *nailing* it *to* his cross;

4339 4 722/864 6:727

προσήλυτος, proseelutos.

Mat.23:15. to make one *proselyte*,
Acts 2:10. Jews and *proselytes*,
6: 5. Nicolas a *proselyte* of Antioch:
13:43. many of the Jews and religious *proselytes* followed Paul.

4340 4 722/864 4314,2540

πρόσκαιρος, proskairos.

Mat.13:21. but *dureth for a while*: (lit. is *temporary*,
Mar 4:17. and so *endure but for a time*:
2Co. 4:18. the things which are seen (are) *temporal*;
Heb 11:25. to enjoy the pleasures of sin *for a season*; (lit. to have *temporary* enjoyment of sin)

4341 30 722/864 3:487 4314,2564

προσκαλέομαι, proskaleomai.

Mat.10: 1. And *when* he *had called unto* (him) his
15:10. And he *called* the multitude, *and*
32. Then Jesus *called* his disciples (*unto* him), *and*
18: 2. And Jesus *called* a little child *unto* him, *and*
32. *after that* he *had called* him,
20:25. But Jesus *called* them (*unto* him), *and*
Mar 3:13. and *calleth* (*unto* him) whom he
23. And he *called* them (*unto* him), *and*
6: 7. And he *called* (*unto* him) the twelve,
7:14. *when* he *had called* all the people (*unto*)
8: 1. Jesus *called* his disciples (*unto* him), *and*
34. *when* he *had called* the people (*unto* him)
10:42. But Jesus *called* them (*to* him), *and*
12:43. he *called* (*unto* him) his disciples, *and*
15:44. and *calling* (*unto* him) the centurion,
Lu. 7:19(18)And John *calling* (*unto* him) two
15:26. he *called* one of the servants, *and*
16: 5. So he *called* every one of his lord's debtors (*unto* him), *and*
18:16. But Jesus *called* them (*unto* him), *and*
Acts 2:39. as the Lord our God *shall call*.
5:40. *when* they *had called* the apostles,
6: 2. Then the twelve *called* the...(*unto* them), *and*
13: 2. whereunto I *have called* them.
7. who *called for* Barnabas and Saul, *and*
16:10. that the Lord *had called* us

Acts20: 1. Paul *called unto* (him) the disciples, and
23:17. *called* one of the centurions *unto* (him), *and*
18. Paul the prisoner *called* me *unto* (him), *and*
23. And he *called unto* (him) two
Jas. 5:14. *let* him *call for* the elders

4342 10 722/865 3:617 4314,2594
προσκαρτερέω, *proskartereo.*

Mar 3: 9. a small ship *should wait on* him
Acts 1:14. These all *continued* with one accord
2:42. And they *continued stedfastly* in
46. And they, *continuing* daily with one accord
6: 4. we *will give* ourselves *continually to* prayer, and to
8:13. he *continued with* Philip,
10: 7. of them *that waited on* him *continually;*
Ro. 12:12. *continuing instant in* prayer;
13: 6. *attending continually upon* this very thing.
Col 4: 2. *Continue in* prayer,

4343 1 723/865 3:617 4342
προσκαρτέρησις, *proskartereesis.*

Eph. 6:18. with all *perseverance* and supplication

4344 1 723/865 4314,2776
προσκεφάλαιον, *proskephalaion.*

Mar 4:38. asleep on a *pillow:*

4345 1 723/865 3:758 4314,2820
προσκληρόομαι, *proskleeröomai.*

Acts17: 4. and *consorted with* Paul and Silas;

4346 1 723/865 4314,2827
πρόσκλισις, *prosklisis.*

1Ti. 5:21. doing nothing by *partiality.*

4347 4 723/865 4314,2853
προσκολλάομαι, *proskollaomai.*

Mat 19: 5. and *shall cleave to* his wife:
Mar 10: 7. and *cleave to* his wife;
Acts 5:36. about four hundred, *joined themselves:*
Eph. 5:31. and *shall be joined* unto his wife,

4348 6 723/865 6:745 4350
πρόσκομμα, *proskomma.*

Ro. 9:32. they stumbled at that *stumbling*stone;
33. I lay in Sion a *stumbling*stone and rock
14:13. that no man put a *stumblingblock*
20. for that man who eateth with *offence.*
1Co. 8: 9. become a *stumblingblock* to them that
1Pet. 2: 8(7). And a stone of *stumbling,*

4349 1 723/865 6:745 4350
προσκοπή, *proskopee.*

2Co. 6: 3. Giving no *offence* in any thing,

4350 8 723/865 6:745 4314,2875
προσκόπτω, *proskopto.*

Mat 4: 6. lest at any time thou *dash* thy foot against a stone.
7:27. and *beat upon* that house;
Lu. 4:11. lest at any time thou *dash* thy foot against a stone.
Joh. 11: 9. walk in the day, he *stumbleth* not.
10. walk in the night, he *stumbleth.*
Ro. 9:32. they *stumbled at* that stumblingstone;
14:21. whereby thy brother *stumbleth,*
1Pet. 2: 8. which *stumble at* the word,

4351 2 723/865 4314,2947
προσκυλίω, *proskulio.*

Mat 27:60. and he *rolled* a great stone *to* the door
Mar 15:46. and *rolled* a stone unto the

4352 60 723/865 6:758 4314,2965
προσκυνέω, *proskuneo.*

Mat. 2: 2. and are come *to worship* him.
8. that I may come and *worship* him
11. fell down, and *worshipped* him:
4: 9. if thou wilt fall down and *worship* me.
10. Thou *shalt worship* the Lord
8: 2. a leper and *worshipped* him,
9:18. came a certain ruler, and *worshipped* him,
14:33. came and *worshipped* him,
15:25. came she and *worshipped* him, saying,
18:26. fell down, and *worshipped* him,
20:20. with her sons, *worshipping* (him),
28: 9. by the feet, and *worshipped* him.
17. they *worshipped* him: but some doubted.
Mar 5: 6. he ran and *worshipped* him,
15:19. bowing (their) knees *worshipped* him.
Lu. 4: 7. If thou therefore wilt *worship* me,
8. Thou *shalt worship* the Lord
24:52. And they *worshipped* him, *and*
Joh. 4:20. Our fathers *worshipped* in this mountain;
— where men ought *to worship.*
21. when ye *shall* neither in this...*worship* the Father.
22. Ye *worship* ye know not what: we know what we *worship:*
23. *shall worship* the Father in spirit
— seeketh such to *worship* him.
24. they *that worship* him must *worship* (him) in spirit and in
9:38. I believe. And he *worshipped* him.
12:20. that came up to *worship* at the feast:
Acts 7:43. which ye made *to worship* them:
8:27. to Jerusalem for to *worship,*
10:25. at his feet, and *worshipped* (him).
24:11. to Jerusalem for to *worship.*
1Co. 14:25. falling down on (his) face he *will worship* God,
Heb 1: 6(7). *let* all the angels of God *worship* him.
11:21. and *worshipped,* (leaning) upon
Rev. 3: 9. to come and *worship* before thy feet,
4:10. and *worship* him that liveth
5:14. and *worshipped* him that liveth
7:11. on their faces, and *worshipped* God,
9:20. that they *should* not *worship* devils,
11: 1. and them *that worship* therein.
16. upon their faces, and *worshipped* God,
13: 4. they *worshipped* the dragon
— and they *worshipped* the beast,
8. *shall worship* him, whose names
12. to *worship* the first beast,
15. as many as *would* not *worship*
14: 7. *worship* him that made heaven, and
9. If any man *worship* the beast
11. *who worship* the beast and his image,
15: 4. shall come and *worship* before thee;
16: 2. them *which worshipped* his image.
19: 4. fell down and *worshipped* God
10. I fell at his feet *to worship* him.

Rev.19:10. *worship* God:
20. and them *that worshipped* his image.
20: 4. which *had* not *worshipped* the beast,
22: 8. fell down *to worship* before the feet
9. *worship* God.

4353 1 724/866 6:758 4352

προσκυνητής, proskuneetees.

Joh. 4:23. when the true *worshippers* shall

4354 2 724/866 4314,2980

προσλαλέω, proslaleo.

Acts13:43. who, *speaking to* them, persuaded
28:20. to see (you), and *to speak with* (you):

4355 14 724/866 4:5 4314,2983

προσλαμβάνω, proslambano.

Mat.16:22. Then Peter *took* him, *and* began
Mar 8:32. Peter *took* him, *and* began to rebuke him.
Acts17: 5. *took unto* them certain lewd fellows
18:26. they *took* him *unto* (them),
27:33. fasting, *having taken* nothing.
34. I pray you *to take* (some) meat:
36. and they also *took* (some) meat.
28: 2. and *received* us every one,
Ro. 14: 1. weak in the faith *receive* ye,
3. for God *hath received* him.
15: 7. *receive* ye one another, as Christ also *received* us
Philem 12. thou therefore *receive* him, that is,
17. *receive* him as myself.

4356 1 724/866 4:5 4355

πρόσληψις, prosleepsis.

Ro. 11:15. what (shall) the *receiving* (of them be),

4357 6 724/866 4:574 4314,3306

προσμένω, prosmeno.

Mat.15:32. because they *continue with* me
Mar 8: 2. they *have* now *been with* me
Acts11:23. they would *cleave unto* the Lord.
18:18. Paul (after this) *tarried* (there) yet
1Ti. 1: 3. *to abide still* at Ephesus,
5: 5. *continueth in* supplications and prayers

4358 1 724/866 4314,rt 3730

προσορμίζομαι, prosormizomai.

Mar 6:53. and *drew to the shore.*

4359 1 725/866 4314,3784

προσοφείλω, prosophīlo.

Philem.19. thou *owest* unto me even thine own self *besides.*

4360 2 725/867 4314 *ochteō* (to be vexed)

προσοχθίζω, prosokthizo.

Heb 3:10. I *was grieved with* that generation,
17. *with* whom *was* he *grieved* forty years?

4361 1 725/867 4314,3983

πρόσπεινος, prospīnos.

Acts10:10. And he became *very hungry*

4362 1 725/867 4314,4078

προσπήγνυμι, prospeegnumi.

Acts 2:23. by wicked hands *have crucified and* slain:

4363 8 725/867 4314,4098

προσπίπτω, prospipto.

Mat. 7:25. and *beat upon* that house;
Mar 3:11. when they saw him, *fell down before* him,
5:33. came and *fell down before* him,
7:25. and came and *fell* at his feet:
Lu. 5: 8. he *fell down at* Jesus' knees,
8:28. and *fell down before* him,
47. and *falling down before* him, she
Acts16:29. and *fell down before* Paul and

4364 1 725/867 4314,4160

προσποιέομαι, prospoyeomai.

Lu. 24:28. he *made as though* he would have gone further.

4365 1 725/867 4314,4198

προσπορεύομαι, prosporūomai.

Mar 10:35. the sons of Zebedee, *come unto* him,

4366 2 725/867 4314,4486

προσρήγνυμι, prosreegnumi.

Lu. 6:48. stream *beat vehemently upon* that
49. *against* which the stream *did beat vehemently,*

4367 7 725/867 8:27 4314,5021

προστάσσω, prostasso.

Mat. 1:24. as the angel of the Lord *had bidden* him
8: 4. offer the gift that Moses *commanded,*
21: 6. and did as Jesus *commanded* them,
Mar 1:44. those things which Moses *commanded,*
Lu. 5:14. according as Moses *commanded,*
Acts10:33. *that are commanded* thee of God.
48. he *commanded* them to be baptized

4368 1 726/867 4291

προστάτις, prostatis.

Ro. 16: 2. she hath been a *succourer* of many,

4369 18 726/867 8:152 4314,5087

προστίθημι, prostitheemi.

Mat. 6:27. can *add* one cubit unto his stature?
33. all these things *shall be added* unto you.
Mar 4:24. *unto* you that hear *shall more be given.*
Lu. 3:20. *Added* yet this above all,
12:25. can *add* to his stature one cubit?
31. all these things *shall be added* unto you.
17: 5. Lord, *Increase* our faith.
19:11. he *added and* spake a parable,
20:11. And again he sent (lit. he *added* to send) another servant:
12. again he sent (lit. he *added* &c.) a third:
Acts 2:41. there *were added* (unto them)
47. And the Lord *added* to the church daily
5:14. believers *were* the more *added* to the Lord,
11:24. and much people was *added* unto the Lord.
12: 3. he *proceeded further* to take Peter
13:36. *was laid* unto his fathers, and saw
Gal. 3:19. It *was added* because of transgressions,
Heb 12:19. that the word should not *be spoken to* them *any more*

4370 3 726/867 4314,5143
προστρέχω, prostreko.

Mar 9:15. and *running to* (him) saluted him.
10:17. there came one *running*, and
Acts 8:30. Philip *ran thither to* (him), *and* heard

4371 1 726/867 4314,5315
προσφάγιον, prosphagion.

Joh. 21: 5. Children, have ye any *meat?*

4372 1 726/867 6:766 4253,4969
πρόσφατος, prosphatos.

Heb 10:20. By a *new* and living way,

4373 1 726/867 6:766 4372
προσφάτως, prosphatōs.

Acts 18: 2. *lately* come from Italy,

4374 48 726/867 9:56 4314,5342
προσφέρω, προσήνεγκα, prosphero, proseenenka.

Mat. 2:11. they *presented unto* him gifts;
4:24. they *brought unto* him all sick
5:23. if thou *bring* thy gift to the altar,
24. then come and *offer* thy gift.
8: 4. and *offer* the gift that Moses
16. they *brought unto* him many that
9: 2. they *brought to* him a man
32. they *brought to* him a dumb
12:22. Then *was brought unto* him one
14:35. and *brought unto* him all that
17:16. And I *brought* him *to* thy
18:24. one *was brought unto* him,
19:13. Then *were* there *brought unto* him
22:19. they *brought unto* him a penny.
25:20. came and *brought* other five talents,
Mar 1:44. and *offer* for thy cleansing
10:13. they *brought* young children *to* him,
— disciples rebuked those *that brought*
Lu. 5:14. and *offer* for thy cleansing,
12:11. when they *bring* you *unto* the
18:15. And they *brought unto* him also
23:14. Ye *have brought* this man *unto* me,
36. and *offering* him vinegar,
Joh. 16: 2. will think that he *doeth* God service.
19:29. and *put* (it) *to* his mouth.
Acts 7:42. *have* ye *offered to* me slain beasts
8:18. he *offered* them money,
21:26. until that an offering should *be offered*
Heb 5: 1. that he *may offer* both gifts and
3. so also for himself, *to offer* for sins.
7. *when* he *had offered up* prayers
8: 3. *to offer* gifts and sacrifices:
— that this man have somewhat also to *offer*.
4. priests *that offer* gifts according to
9: 7. which he *offered* for himself,
9. in which were *offered* both gifts and
14. *offered* himself without spot
25. Nor yet that he *should offer* himself
28. So Christ was once *offered* to bear the
10: 1. which they *offered* year by year
2. would they not have ceased to be *offered?*
8. which *are offered* by the law;
11. and *offering* oftentimes the same
12. *after* he *had offered* one sacrifice for sins,
11: 4. By faith Abel *offered unto* God
17. when he was tried, *offered up* Isaac:
— *offered up* his only begotten (son),
12: 7. God *dealeth with* you as with sons;

4375 1 727/868 4314,5368
προσφιλής, prosphilees. 4253, *teinō* (to stretch)

Phi. 4: 8. whatsoever things (are) *lovely*,

4376 9 727/868 9:56 4374
προσφορά, prosphora.

Acts 21:26. until that an *offering* should be
24:17. alms to my nation, and *offerings*.
Ro 15:16. that the *offering up* of the Gentiles
Eph. 5: 2. an *offering* and a sacrifice to God
Heb 10: 5. Sacrifice and *offering* thou wouldest not,
8. Sacrifice and *offering* and burnt offerings
10. through the *offering* of the body
14. For by one *offering* he hath
18. (there is) no more *offering* for sin.

4377 7 727/868 4314,5455
προσφωνέω, prosphōneo.

Mat. 11:16. and *calling unto* their fellows,
Lu. 6:13. he *called* (*unto* him) his disciples:
7:32. *calling* one *to* another, and saying,
13:12. he *called* (her *to* him),
23:20. to release Jesus, *spake* again *to* them.
Acts 21:40. he *spake unto* (them) in the Hebrew
22: 2. he *spake* in the Hebrew tongue *to* them,

4378 1 727/868 4314 *cheō* (to pour)
πρόσχυσις, proskusis.

Heb 11:28. the passover, and the *sprinkling* of blood,

4379 1 727/868 4314 *psauō* (to touch)
προσψαύω, prospsauo.

Lu. 11:46. ye yourselves *touch* not the burdens

4380 1 728/868 6:768 4381
προσωποληπτέω, prosōpoleepteo.

Jas. 2: 9. But if ye *have respect to persons*,

4381 1 728/868 6:768 4383,2983
προσωπολήπτης, prosōpoleeptees.

Acts 10.34. God is no *respecter of persons:*

4382 4 728/868 6:768 4381
προσωποληψία, prosōpoleepsia.

Ro. 2:11. there is no *respect of persons* with God.
Eph. 6: 9. neither is there *respect of persons*
Col. 3:25. and there is no *respect of persons*.
Jas. 2: 1. have not the faith...with *respect of persons*

4383 78 728/868 6:768 4314 *ōps* (face)
πρόσωπον, prosōpon.

Mat. 6:16. for they disfigure their *faces*,
17. anoint thine head, and wash thy *face*
11:10. I send my messenger before thy *face*,
16: 3. ye can discern the *face* of the sky;
17: 2. and his *face* did shine as the sun,
6. they fell on their *face*, and were
18:10. do always behold the *face* of my Father
22:16. thou regardest not the *person* of men
26:39. and fell on his *face*, and prayed,
67. Then did they spit in his *face*,
Mar 1: 2. I send my messenger before thy *face*,
12:14. thou regardest not the *person* of men
14:65. and to cover his *face*, and to buffet him,

Lu 1:76. thou shalt go before the *face* of the Lord
2:31. prepared before the *face* of all people;
5:12. who seeing Jesus fell on (his) *face*,
7:27. I send my messenger before thy *face*,
9:29. the fashion of his *countenance* was
51. he stedfastly set his *face* to go to
52. And sent messengers before his *face*:
53. because his *face* was as though he
10: 1. and sent them two and two before his *face*
12:56. ye can discern the *face* of the sky
17:16. And fell down on (his) *face* at his feet,
20:21. neither acceptest thou the *person* (of any),
21:35. on the *face* of the whole earth.
22:64. they struck him on the *face*,
24: 5. bowed down (their) *faces* to the earth,
Acts 2:28. full of joy with thy *countenance*.
3:13. and denied him in the *presence* of Pilate,
19. shall come from the *presence* of the Lord;
5:41. from the *presence* of the council,
6:15. looking stedfastly on him, saw his *face* as it had been the *face* of an angel.
7:45. before the *face* of our fathers,
13:24. had first preached *before* his coming (πρὸ προσώπου τῆς εἰσόδου)
17:26. to dwell on all the *face* of the earth,
20:25. shall see my *face* no more.
38. should see his *face* no more.
25:16. have the accusers face to *face*,
1Co. 13:12. but then *face* to *face*:
14:25. and so falling down on (his) *face*
2Co. 1:11. by the means of many *persons*
2:10. (forgave I it) in the *person* of Christ;
3: 7. Israel could not stedfastly behold the *face* of Moses for the glory of his *countenance*;
13. (which) put a vail over his *face*,
18. with open *face* beholding as in
4: 6. glory of God in the *face* of Jesus Christ.
5:12. which glory in *appearance*,
8:24. and *before* (εἰς πρόσωπον) the churches,
10: 1. who in *presence* (am) base among you,
7. after the *outward appearance*?
11:20. if a man smite you on the *face*.
Gal. 1:22. And was unknown by *face*
2: 6. God accepteth no man's *person*:
11. I withstood him to the *face*,
Col. 2: 1. as have not seen my *face*
1Th. 2:17. for a short time in *presence*,
— to see your *face* with great
3:10. that we might see your *face*,
2Th. 1: 9. from the *presence* of the Lord,
Heb 9:24. in the *presence* of God for us:
Jas. 1:11. the grace of the *fashion* of it
23. beholding his natural *face* in
1Pet. 3:12. the *face* of the Lord (is) against
Jude 16. having *men's persons* in admiration
Rev. 4: 7. third beast had a *face* as a man,
6:16. hide us from the *face* of him that
7:11. fell before the throne on their *faces*,
9: 7. and their *faces* (were) as the *faces* of men.
10: 1. and his *face* (was) as it were the sun,
11:16. fell upon their *faces*, and worshipped God,
12:14. from the *face* of the serpent.
20:11. from whose *face* the earth and the
22: 4. And they shall see his *face*;

4384 1 729/867 4253,5021

προτάσσομαι, protassomai.

Acts17:26. determined the times *before appointed*,

4385 1 729/869 *teinō* (to stretch)

προτείνω, protīno.

Acts22:25. And as they *bound* him (lit. as he *bound* him)

4386 10 729/870 4387

πρότερον, τὸ πρότερον, proteron, & to proteron.

Joh. 6:62. ascend up where he was *before*?
7:51. judge (any) man, *before* (lit. unless *previously*) it hear him,
9: 8. they which *before* had seen him
2Co. 1:15. minded to come unto you *before*,
Gal. 4:13. I preached the gospel unto you *at the first*.
1Ti. 1:13. Who was *before* a blasphemer,
Heb 4: 6. to whom it was *first* preached
7:27. *first* for his own sins,
10:32. call to remembrance the *former* days,
1Pet. 1:14. according to the *former* lusts

4387 1 729/870 4253

πρότερος, proteros.

Eph. 4:22. concerning the *former* conversation

4388 3 729/870 8:152 4253,5087

προτίθημι, protitheemi.

Ro. 1:13. I *purposed* to come unto you,
3:25. Whom God *hath set forth* (to be)
Eph. 1: 9. which he *hath purposed* in himself:

4389 1 729/870 4253,rt 5157

προτρέπομαι, protrepomai.

Acts18:27. the brethren wrote, *exhorting* the disciple to receive him:

4390 2 729/870 4253,5143

προτρέχω, protreko.

Lu. 19: 4. And he *ran before, and* climbed
Joh.20: 4. the other disciple *did outrun* (lit. *ran before* more quickly than) Peter,

4391 2 729/870 4253,5225

προϋπάρχω, proüparko.

Lu. 23:12. for *before* they *were* at enmity
Acts 8: 9. there *was* a certain man...which *beforetime* in the same city

4392 7 729/870 4253,5316

πρόφασις, prophasis.

Mat. 23:14. for a *pretence* make long prayer:
Mar 12:40. for a *pretence* make long prayers:
Lu. 20:47. and for a *shew* make long prayers:
Joh. 15:22. they have no *cloke* for their sin.
Acts27:30. under *colour* as though they would
Phi. 1:18. whether in *pretence*, or in truth,
1Th. 2: 5. nor a *cloke* of covetousness;

4393 2 730/870 4253,5342

προφέρω, prophero.

Lu. 6:45. *bringeth forth* that which is good;
— *bringeth forth* that which is evil:

4394 19 730/870 6:781 4396

προφητεία, propheetīa.

Mat. 13:14. is fulfilled the *prophecy* of Esaias,
Ro. 12: 6. whether *prophecy*, (let us prophesy)

1Co.12:10. to another *prophecy;*
13: 2. And though I have (the gift of) *prophecy,*
8. whether (there be) *prophecies,* they shall
14: 6. or by *prophesying,* or by doctrine?
22. but *prophesying* (serveth) not for
1Th. 5:20. Despise not *prophesyings.*
1Ti. 1:18. according to the *prophecies* which went before on thee,
4:14. which was given thee by *prophecy,* with
2Pet. 1:20. that no *prophecy* of the scripture
21. For the *prophecy* came not in old
Rev. 1: 3. that hear the words of this *prophecy,*
11: 6. in the days of their *prophecy:*
19:10. of Jesus is the spirit of *prophecy.*
22: 7. the sayings of the *prophecy* of this
10. Seal not the sayings of the *prophecy* of
18. heareth the words of the *prophecy* of
19. of the book of this *prophecy,*

4395 28 730/870 6:781 4396

προφητεύω, *propheetĕuo.*

Mat. 7:22. *have* we not *prophesied* in thy name?
11:13. prophets and the law *prophesied* until John.
15: 7. well *did* Esaias *prophesy* of you,
26:68. Saying, *Prophesy* unto us,
Mar 7: 6. Well *hath* Esaias *prophesied* of you
14:65. buffet him, and to say unto him, *Prophesy:*
Lu. 1:67. and *prophesied,* saying,
22:64. saying, *Prophesy,* who is it that smote
Joh. 11:51. he *prophesied* that Jesus should die
Acts 2:17. your daughters *shall prophesy,*
18. of my Spirit; and they *shall prophesy:*
19: 6. they spake with tongues, and *prophesied.*
21: 9. virgins, *which did prophesy.*
1Co. 11: 4. Every man praying or *prophesying,*
5. that prayeth or *prophesieth* with (her)
13: 9. know in part, and we *prophesy* in part.
14: 1. but rather that ye *may prophesy.*
3. But he *that prophesieth* speaketh
4. he *that prophesieth* edifieth the church.
5. but rather that ye *prophesied:* for greater (is) he *that prophesieth*
24. But if all *prophesy,* and there come
31. For ye may all *prophesy* one by one,
39. covet *to prophesy,* and forbid not to
1Pet. 1:10. *who prophesied* of the grace
Jude 14. *prophesied* of these, saying, Behold,
Rev. 10:11. Thou must *prophesy* again before
11: 3. two witnesses, and they *shall prophesy*

4396 149 730/871 6:781 4253,5346

προφήτης, *propheetees.*

Mat. 1:22. spoken of the Lord by the *prophet,*
2: 5. thus it is written by the *prophet,*
15. spoken of the Lord by the *prophet,*
17. by Jeremy the *prophet,*
23. which was spoken by the *prophets,*
3: 3. spoken of by the *prophet* Esaias,
4:14. spoken by Esaias the *prophet,* saying,
5:12. so persecuted they the *prophets*
17. to destroy the law, or the *prophets:*
7:12. this is the law and the *prophets.*
8:17. spoken by Esaias the *prophet,*
10:41. He that receiveth a *prophet* in the name of a *prophet* shall receive a *prophet's* reward;
11: 9. A *prophet?* yea, I say unto you, and more than a *prophet.*
13. For all the *prophets* and the law
12:17. spoken by Esaias the *prophet,*
Mat. 12:39. the sign of the *prophet* Jonas:
13:17. That many *prophets* and righteous
35. spoken by the *prophet,* saying, I will
57. A *prophet* is not without honour,
14: 5. they counted him as a *prophet.*
16: 4. the sign of the *prophet* Jonas.
14. Jeremias, or one of the *prophets.*
21: 4. spoken by the *prophet,* saying,
11. This is Jesus the *prophet* of Nazareth
26. for all hold John as a *prophet.*
46. because they took him for a *prophet.*
22:40. hang all the law and the *prophets.*
23:29. ye build the tombs of the *prophets,*
30. in the blood of the *prophets.*
31. of them which killed the *prophets.*
34. I send unto you *prophets,* and wise
37. (thou) that killest the *prophets,*
24:15. spoken of by Daniel the *prophet,*
26:56. that the scriptures of the *prophets* might
27: 9. was spoken by Jeremy the *prophet,*
35. which was spoken by the *prophet,*
Mar 1: 2. As it is written in the *prophets,*
6: 4. A *prophet* is not without honour,
15. others said, That it is a *prophet,* or as one of the *prophets.*
8:28. and others, One of the *prophets.*
11:32. that he was a *prophet* indeed.
13:14. spoken of by Daniel the *prophet,*
Lu. 1:70. by the mouth of his holy *prophets,*
76. be called the *prophet* of the Highest:
3: 4. the words of Esaias the *prophet,*
4:17. the book of the *prophet* Esaias.
24. No *prophet* is accepted in his own
27. in the time of Eliseus the *prophet;*
6:23. did their fathers unto the *prophets.*
7:16. That a great *prophet* is risen up
26. A *prophet?* Yea, I say unto you, and much more than a *prophet.*
28. there is not a greater *prophet* than John
39. This man, if he were a *prophet,*
9: 8. that one of the old *prophets* was risen
19. that one of the old *prophets* is risen
10:24. that many *prophets* and kings
11:29. but the sign of Jonas the *prophet.*
47. ye build the sepulchres of the *prophets,*
49. I will send them *prophets* and apostles,
50. That the blood of all the *prophets,*
13:28. and all the *prophets,* in the kingdom
33. that a *prophet* perish out of Jerusalem.
34. Jerusalem, which killest the *prophets,*
16:16. The law and the *prophets* (were) until John:
29. They have Moses and the *prophets;*
31. If they hear not Moses and the *prophets,*
18:31. that are written by the *prophets*
20: 6. persuaded that John was a *prophet.*
24:19. which was a *prophet* mighty in deed
25. all that the *prophets* have spoken:
27. at Moses and all the *prophets,*
44. in the law of Moses, and (in) the *prophets,* and (in) the psalms,
Joh. 1:21. Art thou that *prophet?*
23. as said the *prophet* Esaias.
25. nor Elias, neither that *prophet?*
45(46). and the *prophets,* did write
4:19. I perceive that thou art a *prophet.*
44. that a *prophet* hath no honour in
6:14. that *prophet* that should come
45. It is written in the *prophets,*
7:40. said, Of a truth this is the *prophet.*
52. for out of Galilee ariseth no *prophet.*
8:52. Abraham is dead, and the *prophets:*

Joh. 8:53. and the *prophets* are dead:
9:17. He said, He is a *prophet*.
12:38. That the saying of Esaias the *prophet*
Acts 2:16. spoken by the *prophet* Joel;
30. Therefore being a *prophet*, and
3:18. by the mouth of all his *prophets*,
21. the mouth of all his holy *prophets*
22. A *prophet* shall the Lord your
23. which will not hear that *prophet*,
24. Yea, and all the *prophets* from
25. the children of the *prophets*,
7:37. A *prophet* shall the Lord your God
42. written in the book of the *prophets*,
48. made with hands; as saith the *prophet*,
52. Which of the *prophets* have not
8:28. in his chariot read Esaias the *prophet*.
30. heard him read the *prophet* Esaias,
34. of whom speaketh the *prophet* this?
10:43. To him give all the *prophets* witness,
11:27. came *prophets* from Jerusalem
13: 1. certain *prophets* and teachers;
15. after the reading of the law and the *prophets*
20. until Samuel the *prophet*.
27. because they knew him not, nor yet the voices of the *prophets* which
40. spoken of in the *prophets*;
15:15. agree the words of the *prophets*;
32. being *prophets* also themselves,
21:10. a certain *prophet*, named Agabus.
24:14. written in the law and in the *prophets*:
26:22. which the *prophets* and Moses did say
27. believest thou the *prophets*?
28:23. and (out of) the *prophets*, from morning till evening.
25. the Holy Ghost by Esaias the *prophet*
Ro. 1: 2. by his *prophets* in the holy scriptures,
3:21. witnessed by the law and the *prophets*,
11: 3. Lord, they have killed thy *prophets*,
1Co.12:28. first apostles, secondarily *prophets*,
29. (are) all *prophets*? (are) all teachers?
14:29. Let the *prophets* speak two or three,
32. And the spirits of the *prophets* are subject to the *prophets*.
37. think himself to be a *prophet*,
Eph 2:20. of the apostles and *prophets*,
3: 5. unto his holy apostles and *prophets*
4:11. some, *prophets*; and some, evangelists;
1Th. 2:15. both killed the Lord Jesus, and their own *prophets*,
Tit. 1:12. (even) a *prophet* of their own, said, The Cretians
Heb 1: 1. unto the fathers by the *prophets*,
11:32. and Samuel, and (of) the *prophets*:
Jas. 5:10. the *prophets*, who have spoken in the name of the Lord,
1Pet. 1:10. Of which salvation the *prophets*
2Pet. 2:16. forbad the madness of the *prophet*.
3: 2. before by the holy *prophets*,
Rev.10: 7. hath declared to his servants the *prophets*.
11:10. because these two *prophets* tormented
18. unto thy servants the *prophets*,
16: 6. the blood of saints and *prophets*,
18:20. (ye) holy apostles and *prophets*; for God
24. the blood of *prophets*, and of saints,
22: 6. the Lord God of the holy *prophets*
9. and of thy brethren the *prophets*,

4397 2 731/872 6:781 4396
προφητικός, propheetikos.

Ro 16:26. by the scriptures *of the prophets*,
2Pet. 1:19. a more sure word *of prophecy*;

4398 2 731/872 6:781 4396
προφῆτις, propheetis.

Lu. 2:36. Anna, a *prophetess*, the daughter of
Rev. 2:20. which calleth herself a *prophetess*,

4399 1 731/872 9:88 4253,5348
προφθάνω, prophthano.

Mat.17:25. Jesus *prevented* (lit. *forestalled*) him,

4400 2 731/872 6:862 4253,5495
προχειρίζομαι, prokīrizomai.

Acts22:14. *hath chosen* thee, that thou shouldest
26:16. *to make* thee a minister and a witness

4401 1 732/872 4253,5500
προχειροτονέομαι, prokīrotoneomai.

Acts10:41. unto witnesses *chosen before* of God,

4403 3 732/873 *prumnus* (hindmost)
πρύμνα, prumna.

Mar 4:38. he was in the *hinder part of the ship*,
Acts27:29. they cast four anchors out of the *stern*,
41. but the *hinder part* was broken

4404 10 732/873 4253
πρωΐ, prōi.

Mat.16: 3. And *in the morning*, (It will be) foul
20: 1. went out *early in the morning*
Mar 1:35. *in the morning*, rising up a great while
11:20. And *in the morning*, as they passed
13:35. at the cockcrowing, or *in the morning*:
15: 1. And straightway in *the morning*
16: 2. And very *early in the morning*
9. was risen *early* the first (day) of
Joh.20: 1. cometh Mary Magdalene *early*,
Acts28:23. from *morning* till evening.

4405 4 732/873 4404
πρωΐα, prōia.

Mat.21:18. Now in the *morning* as he returned
27: 1. When the *morning* was come, all the
Joh.18:28. and it was *early*; and they themselves
21: 4. But when the *morning* was now come.

4406 10 732/852 4404
πρώϊμος, prōimos.

Jas. 5: 7. he receive the *early* and latter rain.

4407 1 732/873 4404
πρωϊνός, prōinos.

Rev. 2:28. I will give him the *morning* star.

4408 2 732/873 4253
πρώρα, prōra.

Acts27:30. cast anchors out of the *foreship*,
41. and the *forepart* stuck fast,

4409 1 732/873 6:865 4413
πρωτεύω, protuo.

Col. 1:18. he might *have the preeminence*.

4410 4 732/873 6:865 4413,2515

πρωτοκαθεδρία, prōtokathedria.

Mat.23: 6. the *chief seats* in the synagogues,
Mar 12:39. the *chief seats* in the synagogues,
Lu. 11:43. love the *uppermost seats* in the synagogues,
20:46. and the *highest seats* in the synagogues,

4411 5 732/873 6:865 4413,2828

πρωτοκλισία, prōtoklisia.

Mat.23: 6. love the *uppermost rooms* (lit. the *first place*) at feasts,
Mar 12:39. the *uppermost rooms* (lit. *first places*) at
Lu. 14: 7. how they chose out the *chief rooms*;
8. sit not down in the *highest room*,
20:46. and the *chief rooms* at feasts;

4412 60 732/873 6:865 4413

πρῶτον & τὸ πρῶτον, prōton & to prōton.

Mat. 5:24. *first* be reconciled to thy brother,
6:33. But seek ye *first* the kingdom of God,
7: 5. *first* cast out the beam out of
8:21. suffer me *first* to go and bury my
12:29. except he *first* bind the strong
13:30. Gather ye together *first* the tares,
17:10. that Elias must *first* come?
11. Elias truly shall *first* come,
23:26. cleanse *first* that (which is) within
Mar. 3:27. he will *first* bind the strong man;
4:28. *first* the blade, then the ear,
7:27. Let the children *first* be filled:
9:11. that Elias must *first* come?
12. Elias verily cometh *first*,
13:10. the gospel must *first* be published
16: 9. he appeared *first* to Mary
Lu. 6:42. cast out *first* the beam
9:59. suffer me *first* to go and bury my
61. let me *first* go bid them farewell,
10: 5. *first* say, Peace (be) to this house.
11:38. that he had not *first* washed
12: 1. to say unto his disciples *first of all*,
14:28. sitteth not down *first*, and counteth
31. sitteth not down *first*, and consulteth
17:25. But *first* must he suffer
21: 9. these things must *first* come
Joh. 2:10. Every man *at the beginning*
10:40. where John *at first* baptized;
12:16. understood not his disciples *at the first*:
15:18. *before* (it hated) you.
18:13. to Annas *first*; for he was
19:39. which *at the first* came to Jesus by
Acts 3:26. Unto you *first* God, having raised up
7:12. he sent out our fathers *first*.
11:26. called Christians *first* in Antioch.
13:46. should *first* have been spoken to you:
15:14. how God *at the first* did visit
26:20. But shewed *first* unto them of Damascus,
Ro. 1: 8. *First*, I thank my God through
16. to the Jew *first*, and also to the Greek.
2: 9. of the Jew *first*, and also of the Gentile;
10. to the Jew *first*, and also to the Gentile:
3: 2. *chiefly*, because that unto them
15:24. if *first* I be somewhat filled
1Co.11:18. For *first of all*, when ye come
12:28. *first* apostles, secondarily prophets,
15:46. that (was) not *first* which is spiritual,
2Co. 8: 5. but *first* gave their own selves
Eph. 4: 9. he also descended *first* into the lower
1Th. 4:16. the dead in Christ shall rise *first*:
2Th. 2: 3. except there come a falling away *first*,
1Ti. 2: 1. that, *first* of all, supplications,
3:10. let these also *first* be proved;
5: 4. let them learn *first* to shew piety
2Ti. 1: 5. which dwelt *first* in thy grandmother
Heb. 7: 2. *first* being by interpretation
Jas. 3:17. is *first* pure, then peaceable,
1Pet.4:17. if (it) *first* (begin) at us,
2Pet.1:20. Knowing this *first*, that
3: 3. Knowing this *first*, that there shall

4413 100 732/874 6:865 4253

πρῶτος, prōtos.

Mat.10: 2. The *first*, Simon, who is called Peter,
12:45. of that man is worse than the *first*.
17:27. the fish that *first* cometh up;
19:30. many (that are) *first* shall be last; and the last (shall be) *first*.
20: 8. beginning from the last unto the *first*.
10. But when the *first* came,
16. So the last shall be *first*, and the *first* last:
27. whosoever will be *chief* among you,
21:28. and he came to the *first*,
31. They say unto him, The *first*.
36. servants more than the *first*:
22:25. and the *first*, when he had married
38. This is the *first* and great commandment.
26:17. Now the *first* (day) of the (feast of)
27:64. last error shall be worse than the *first*.
Mar 6:21. and *chief* (estates) of Galilee;
9:35. If any man desire to be *first*,
10:31. But many (that are) *first* shall be last and the last *first*.
44. will be the *chiefest*, shall be
12:20. and the *first* took a wife,
28. Which is the *first* commandment
29. The *first* of all the commandments
30. this (is) the *first* commandment.
14:12. And the *first* day of unleavened
16: 9. early the *first* (day) of the week,
Lu. 2: 2. this taxing was *first* made
11:26. worse than the *first*.
13:30. shall be *first*, and there are *first*
14:18. The *first* said unto him,
15:22. Bring forth the *best* robe,
16: 5. and said unto the *first*, How much
19:16. Then came the *first*, saying, Lord,
47. and the *chief* of the people
20:29. and the *first* took a wife,
Joh. 1:15. for he was *before* me.
30. for he was *before* me.
41(42). He *first* findeth his own brother
5: 4. whosoever then *first* after the
8: 7. let him *first* cast a stone at her.
19:32. and brake the legs of the *first*,
20: 4. and came *first* to the sepulchre.
8. which came *first* to the sepulchre,
Acts 1: 1. The *former* treatise have I made,
12:10. When they were past the *first* and the second ward,
13:50. and the *chief* men of the city,
16:12. which is the *chief* city of that part of
17: 4. and of the *chief* women not a few.
20:18. Ye know, from the *first* day
25: 2. and the *chief* of the Jews
26:23. he should be the *first* that should rise
27:43. should cast (themselves) *first* (into the sea),
28: 7. of the *chief* man of the island,
17. Paul called the *chief* of the Jews
Ro. 10:19. *First* Moses saith, I will provoke
1Co.14:30. let the *first* hold his peace.

1Co.15: 3. I delivered unto you *first* of all
45. The *first* man Adam was made a
47. The *first* man (is) of the earth,
Eph 6: 2. which is the *first* commandment with
Phi. 1: 5. from the *first* day until now;
1Ti. 1:15. of whom I am *chief*.
16. that in me *first* Jesus Christ might
2:13. For Adam was *first* formed,
5:12. cast off their *first* faith.
2Ti. 2: 6. must be *first* partaker of the fruits.
4:16. At my *first* answer no man
Heb 8: 7. For if that *first* (covenant)
13. he hath made the *first* old.
9: 1. Then verily the *first* (covenant)
2. the *first*, wherein (was) the candlestick,
6. went always into the *first* tabernacle,
8. while as the *first* tabernacle was yet
15. under the *first* testament,
18. neither the *first* (testament) was
10: 9. He taketh away the *first*, that he may
2Pet. 2:20. is worse with them than the *beginning*.
1Joh. 4:19. because he *first* loved us.
Rev. 1:11. I am Alpha and Omega, the *first* and the last:
17. I am the *first* and the last:
2: 4. thou hast left thy *first* love.
5. and do the *first* works; or else
8. the *first* and the last, which was
19. the last (to be) more than the *first*.
4: 1. and the *first* voice which I heard
7. And the *first* beast (was) like
8: 7. The *first* angel sounded,
13:12. all the power of the *first* beast
— to worship the *first* beast,
16: 2. And the *first* went, and poured out
20: 5. This (is) the *first* resurrection.
6. part in the *first* resurrection:
21: 1. the *first* heaven and the *first* earth were passed away;
4. the *former* things are passed away.
19. The *first* foundation (was) jasper;
22:13. the *first* and the last.

4414 1 734/875 4413,2476

πρωτοστάτης, prōtostatees.

Acts24: 5. a *ringleader* of the sect of the

4415 1 734/875 6:865 4416

πρωτοτόκια, prōtotokia.

(substantive plural.)

Heb 12:16. for one morsel of meat sold his *birthright*.

4416 9 734/875 6:865 4413 teko (to produce)

πρωτότοκος, prōtotokos.

Mat. 1:25. had brought forth her *firstborn* son:
Lu. 2: 7. she brought forth her *firstborn* son,
Ro. 8:29. the *firstborn* among many brethren.
Col. 1:15. the *firstborn* of every creature: (or it may be,—*born before* all creation)
18. the *firstborn* from the dead;
Heb 1: 6. bringeth in the *firstbegotten* into the world,
11:28. he that destroyed the *firstborn* [neut. plur.]
12:23. and church of the *firstborn*, [plur.]
Rev. 1: 5. the *first begotten* of the dead,

4417 5 734/875 6:883 eq 4098

πταίω, ptaio.

Ro. 11:11. *Have* they *stumbled* that they should fall?
Jas. 2:10. shall keep the whole law, and yet *offend* in one (point),
Jas. 3: 2. For in many things we *offend* all. If any man *offend* not in word,
2Pet. 1:10. if ye do these things, ye shall never *fall*.

4418 1 734/875

πτέρνα, pterna.

Joh. 13:18. hath lifted up his *heel* against me.

4419 2 734/875 4420

πτερύγιον, pterugion.

Mat. 4: 5. on a *pinnacle* of the temple,
Lu. 4: 9. set him on a *pinnacle* of the temple,

4420 5 734/875 4072

πτέρυξ, pterux.

Mat.23:37. her chickens under (her) *wings*,
Lu. 13:34. her brood under (her) *wings*,
Rev. 4: 8. four beasts had each of them six *wings*
9: 9. the sound of their *wings* (was) as
12:14. two *wings* of a great eagle,

4421 1 734/875 4071

πτηνόν, pteenon.

1Co.15:39. (and) another of *birds*.

4422 2 734/875 cf 4098 cf 4072

πτοέομαι, ptoèomai.

Lu. 21: 9. *be* not *terrified*: for these things
24:37. But they were *terrified* and

4423 1 735/875 4422

πτόησις, ptoeesis.

1Pet. 3: 6. and are not afraid with any *amazement*.

4425 2 735/875 4429

πτύον, ptuon.

Mat. 3:12. Whose *fan* (is) in his hand, and
Lu. 3:17. Whose *fan* (is) in his hand, and he

4426 1 735/875 4429 cf 4422

πτύρομαι, pturomai.

Phi. 1:28. in nothing *terrified* by your adversaries:

4427 1 735/875 4429

πτύσμα, ptusma.

Joh. 9: 6. and made clay of the *spittle*,

4428 1 735/875 *petannumi* (to spread)

πτύσσω, ptusso.

Lu. 4:20. And he *closed* the book, and

4429 3 735/875

πτύω, ptuo.

Mar. 7:33. and he *spit*, *and* touched his tongue;
8:23. *when* he *had spit* on his eyes.
Joh. 9: 6. he *spat* on the ground,

4430 5 735/875 6:161 *petō* (4098) (to fall)

πτῶμα, ptōma.

Mat.24:28. For wheresoever the *carcase* is.
Mar. 6:29. they came and took up his *corpse*.

Rev.11: 8. And their *dead bodies* (shall lie) in the
9. shall see their *dead bodies* three days
— shall not suffer their *dead bodies* to

4431 2 735/876 6:161 petō (4098) (to fall)

πτῶσις, ptōsis.

Mat. 7:27. and great was the *fall* of it.
Lu. 2:34. this (child) is set for the *fall* and rising again of many in Israel;

4432 3 735/876 6:885 4433

πτωχεία, ptōkia.

2Co. 8. 2. their deep *poverty* abounded
9. ye through his *poverty* might be rich.
Rev. 2: 9. works, and tribulation, and *poverty*,

4433 1 735/876 6:885 4434

πτωχεύω, ptōkūo.

2Co. 8: 9. yet for your sakes he *became poor*,

4434 34 735/876 6:885 cf 3993 ptosso (to crouch)

πτωχός, ptōkos.

Mat. 5: 3. Blessed (are) the *poor* in spirit.
11: 5. the *poor* have the gospel
19:21. sell that thou hast, and give to the *poor*,
26. 9. and given to the *poor*.
11. For ye have the *poor* always
Mar.10:21. sell whatsoever thou hast, and give to the *poor*,
12:42. a certain *poor* widow,
43. That this *poor* widow hath
14: 5. and have been given to the *poor*.
7. ye have the *poor* with you always,
Lu. 4:18. preach the gospel to the *poor*;
6:20. Blessed (be ye) *poor*: for your's is
7:22. to the *poor* the gospel is preached.
14:13. when thou makest a feast, call the *poor*,
21. bring in hither the *poor*, and the maimed,
16:20. there was a certain *beggar*
22. that the *beggar* died,
18:22. and distribute unto the *poor*,
19: 8. half of my goods I give to the *poor*;
21: 3. that this *poor* widow hath cast in more
Joh.12: 5. and given to the *poor*?
6. not that he cared for the *poor*;
8. For the *poor* always ye have with you;
13:29. should give something to the *poor*.
Ro. 15:26. contribution for the *poor* saints
2Co. 6:10. as *poor*, yet making many rich;
Gal. 2:10. should remember the *poor*;
4: 9. and *beggarly* elements,
Jas. 2: 2. there come in also a *poor* man
3. and say to the *poor*, Stand thou
5. Hath not God chosen the *poor* of this
6. But ye have despised the *poor*.
Rev. 3:17. and *poor*, and blind, and naked:
13:16. rich and *poor*, free and bond,

4435 1 736/876 6:915 pux (fist)

πυγμῇ, pugmee.

Mar. 7: 3. except they wash (their) hands *oft* (lit. to the *wrist*, or, the *fist*)

4437 3 736/876 rt 4635

πυκνός, puknos.

Note.—The neut. of this, as of many other adjectives, is used adverbially.

Lu. 5:33. the disciples of John fast *often*,
Acts24:26. he sent for him *the oftener*,
1Ti. 5:23. and thine *often* infirmities.

4438 1 736/876 6:915 rt 4435

πυκτεύω, puktūo.

1Co. 9:26. so *fight* I, not as one that beateth

4439 10 736/876 6:921

πύλη, pulee.

Mat. 7:13. Enter ye in at the strait *gate*: for wide (is) the *gate*,
14. Because strait (is) the *gate*,
16:18. the *gates* of hell shall not prevail
Lu. 7:12. when he came nigh to the *gate* of
13:24. Strive to enter in at the strait *gate*:
Acts 3:10. at the Beautiful *gate* of the temple:
9:24. And they watched the *gates* day and
12:10. they came unto the iron *gate*
Heb 13:12. suffered without the *gate*.

4440 18 736/876 6:921 4439

πυλών, pulōn.

Mat.26:71. out into the *porch*, another (maid)
Lu. 16:20. which was laid at his *gate*,
Acts10:17. and stood before the *gate*,
12:13. knocked at the door of the *gate*,
14. she opened not the *gate* for gladness,
— told how Peter stood before the *gate*.
14:13. oxen and garlands unto the *gates*,
Rev.21:12. (and) had twelve *gates*, and at the *gates* twelve angels,
13. On the east three *gates*; on the north three *gates*; on the south three *gates*; and on the west three *gates*.
15. and the *gates* thereof, and the wall
21. And the twelve *gates* (were) twelve pearls; every several *gate* was
25. And the *gates* of it shall not be shut
22:14. enter in through the *gates* into the city.

4441 12 737/876 cf 2065, cf 154 cf 2212, cf 1189

πυνθάνομαι, punthanomai.

Mat. 2: 4. he *demanded* of them where Christ
Lu. 15:26. and *asked* what these things meant.
18:36. pass by, he *asked* what it meant.
Joh. 4:52. Then *enquired* he of them the hour
13:24. that he should *ask* who it should be
Acts 4: 7. they *asked*, By what power, or by what
10:18. and *asked* whether Simon,
29. I *ask* therefore for what intent
21:33. and *demanded* who he was, and what
23:19. aside privately, and *asked* (him), What
20. as though they would *enquire*
34. And *when* he *understood* that (he was) of

4442 74 737/876 6:928

πῦρ, pur.

Mat. 3:10. hewn down, and cast into the *fire*.
11. with the Holy Ghost, and (with) *fire*:
12. the chaff with unquenchable *fire*.
5:22. shall be in danger of hell *fire*. (lit. gehenna of *fire*)
7:19. hewn down, and cast into the *fire*.
13:40. are gathered and burned in the *fire*;
42. into a furnace of *fire*: there shall be
50. shall cast them into the furnace of *fire*:

Mat.17:15. ofttimes he falleth into the *fire*,
18: 8. to be cast into everlasting *fire*.
9. to be cast into hell *fire*. (lit. gehenna of *fire*)
25:41. ye cursed, into everlasting *fire*, prepared
Mar 9:22. it hath cast him into the *fire*,
43. into the *fire* that never shall be
44. and the *fire* is not quenched.
45. into the *fire* that never shall be
46. and the *fire* is not quenched.
47. to be cast into hell *fire*: (lit. gehenna of *fire*)
48. and the *fire* is not quenched.
49. every one shall be salted with *fire*,
Lu. 3: 9. is hewn down, and cast into the *fire*.
16. with the Holy Ghost and with *fire*:
17. he will burn with *fire* unquenchable.
9:54. that we command *fire* to come
12:49. I am come to send *fire* on the earth;
17:29. it rained *fire* and brimstone
22:55. when they had kindled a *fire*
Joh. 15: 6. and cast (them) into the *fire*,
Acts 2: 3. cloven tongues like as of *fire*,
19. blood, and *fire*, and vapour of smoke:
7:30. in a flame of *fire* in a bush.
28: 5. he shook off the beast into the *fire*,
Ro. 12:20. heap coals of *fire* on his head.
1Co. 3:13. it shall be revealed by *fire*; and the *fire* shall try every
15. shall be saved; yet so as by *fire*.
2Th. 1: 8. In flaming *fire* taking vengeance on
Heb 1: 7. his ministers a flame of *fire*.
10:27. and *fiery* indignation,
11:34. Quenched the violence of *fire*,
12:18. and that burned with *fire*,
29. our God (is) a consuming *fire*.
Jas. 3: 5. a little *fire* kindleth!
6. And the tongue (is) a *fire*,
5: 3. shall eat your flesh as it were *fire*.
1Pet. 1: 7. though it be tried with *fire*,
2Pet. 3: 7. reserved unto *fire* against
Jude 7. the vengeance of eternal *fire*.
23. pulling (them) out of the *fire*;
Rev. 1:14. his eyes (were) as a flame of *fire*;
2:18. his eyes like unto a flame of *fire*,
3:18. gold tried in the *fire*,
4: 5. seven lamps of *fire* burning
8: 5. and filled it with *fire* of the altar,
7. hail and *fire* mingled with blood,
8. mountain burning with *fire*
9:17. out of their mouths issued *fire* and
18. by the *fire*, and by the smoke,
10: 1. his feet as pillars of *fire*:
11: 5. *fire* proceedeth out of their mouth,
13:13. he maketh *fire* come down from
14:10. with *fire* and brimstone
18. which had power over *fire*;
15: 2. a sea of glass mingled with *fire*:
16: 8. to scorch men with *fire*.
17:16. and burn her with *fire*.
18: 8. she shall be utterly burned with *fire*
19:12. His eyes (were) as a flame of *fire*,
20. into a lake of *fire* burning with
20: 9. and *fire* came down from God
10. into the lake of *fire* and brimstone,
14. cast into the lake of *fire*.
15. was cast into the lake of *fire*.
21: 8. which burneth with *fire* and brimstone:

4443 2 738/877 4442
πυρά, pura.

Acts28: 2. they kindled a *fire*, and received us
3. of sticks, and laid (them) on the *fire*,

4444 4 738/878 6:953
πύργος, purgos.

Mat.21:33. a winepress in it, and built a *tower*,
Mar 12: 1. winefat and built a *tower*,
Lu. 13: 4. upon whom the *tower* in Siloam fell,
14:28. intending to build a *tower*, sitteth not

4445 2 738/878 6:956 4443
πυρέσσω, puresso.

Mat. 8:14. and *sick of a fever*.
Mar 1:30. wife's mother lay *sick of a fever*.

4446 6 738/878 6:956 4445
πυρετός, puretos.

Mat. 8:15. and the *fever* left her:
Mar 1:31. and immediately the *fever* left her,
Lu. 4:38. was taken with a great *fever*;
39. rebuked the *fever*; and it left her:
Joh. 4:52. at the seventh hour the *fever* left him.
Acts28: 8. lay sick of a *fever* and of a

4447 1 738/878 6:928 4443
πυρινός, purinos.

Rev. 9:17. having breastplates *of fire*,

4448 6 738/878 6:928 4442
πυρόομαι, puröomai.

1Co. 7: 9. better to marry than *to burn*.
2Co.11:29. and I *burn* not?
Eph 6:16. all the *fiery* darts of the wicked.
2Pet. 3:12. the heavens *being on fire* shall
Rev. 1:15. as *if* they *burned* in a furnace;
3:18. gold *tried* in the fire,

4449 2 738/878 4450
πυῤῥάζω, purrazo.

Mat.16: 2. for the sky *is red*.
3. for the sky *is red* and lowring.

4450 2 738/878 6:928 4442
πυῤῥός, purros.

Rev. 6: 4. another horse (that was) *red*:
12: 3. a great *red* dragon,

4451 3 738/878 6:928 4448
πύρωσις, purōsis.

1Pet. 4:12. concerning the *fiery trial*
Rev.18: 9. the smoke of her *burning*,
18. saw the smoke of her *burning*,

4452 4458
πω see μήπω, μηδέπω, οὔπω, & οὐδέπω.

4453 22 738/878 pelomai (to be busy)
πωλέω, pōleo.

Mat.10:29. *Are* not two sparrows *sold* for a
13:44. and *selleth* all that he hath,
19:21. go (and) *sell* that thou hast.
21:12. cast out all them *that sold* and
— and the seats of them *that sold* doves.

Mat.25: 9. go ye rather to them *that sell*,
Mar 10:21. *sell* whatsoever thou hast,
11:15. to cast out them *that sold* and
— the seats of them *that sold* doves;
Lu. 12: 6. *Are* not five sparrows *sold* for
33. *Sell* that ye have, and give alms;
17:28. they bought, they *sold*, they planted,
18:22. *sell* all that thou hast, and distribute
19:45. to cast out them *that sold* therein,
22:36. *let* him *sell* his garment, and buy one.
Joh. 2:14. those *that sold* oxen and sheep
16. said unto them *that sold* doves,
Acts 4:34. *sold* them, *and* brought the prices
37. Having land, *sold* (it), *and* brought
5: 1. *sold* a possession,
1Co. 10:25. *Whatsoever is sold* in the shambles,
Rev. 13:17. that no man might buy or *sell*,

4454 12 739/878 6:959

πῶλος, pōlos.

Mat.21: 2. and a *colt* with her:
5. and a *colt* the foal of an ass.
7. and the *colt*, and put on them their
Mar 11: 2. ye shall find a *colt* tied,
4. and found the *colt* tied by the door
5. What do ye, loosing the *colt?*
7. they brought the *colt* to Jesus,
Lu. 19:30. ye shall find a *colt* tied,
33. as they were loosing the *colt*,
— Why loose ye the *colt?*
35. cast their garments upon the *colt*,
Joh. 12:15. sitting on an ass's *colt*.

4455 6 739/878 4452,4218

πώποτε, pōpote.

Lu. 19:30. whereon yet never man sat: (lit. none *ever*)
Joh. 1:18. No man hath seen God *at any time;*
5:37. neither heard his voice *at any time*,
6:35. shall never (lit. not *ever*) thirst.
8:33. were never (lit. to none *ever*) in bondage to any man:
1Joh. 4:12. No man hath seen God *at any time*.

4456 5 739/878 5:1022 *poros* (a kind of stone)

πωρόω, pōroō.

Mar 6:52. for their heart was *hardened*.
8:17. have ye your heart yet *hardened?*
Joh. 12:40. He hath blinded their eyes, and *hardened* their heart;
Ro. 11: 7. and the rest *were blinded*
2Co. 3:14. But their minds *were blinded:*

4457 3 739/878 5:1022 4456

πώρωσις, pōrōsis.

Mar 3: 5. for the *hardness* of their hearts,
Ro. 11:25. that *blindness* in part is happened to
Eph 4:18. because of the *blindness* of their heart:

4458 16 740/258 rt 4225, cf 4459

πώς, pōs. indefinitely.

Acts 27:12. if *by any means* they might
29. Then fearing lest)(we should have
Ro. 1:10. If *by any means* now at length
11:14. If *by any means* I may provoke
21. lest)(he also spare not thee.
1Co. 8: 9. lest *by any means* this liberty
1Co. 9:27. lest that *by any means*, when I have
2Co. 2: 7. lest *perhaps* such a one should
9: 4. Lest *haply* if they of Macedonia
11: 3. lest *by any means*, as the serpent
12:20. For I fear, lest,)(when I come,
— lest)((there be) debates,
Gal. 2: 2. lest *by any means* I should run,
4:11. lest)(I have bestowed upon you
Phi. 3:11. If *by any means* I might attain
1Th. 3: 5. lest *by some means* the tempter

4459 103 739/879 rt 4226

πῶς, pōs. interrog. or definitely.

Mat. 6:28. *how* they grow; they toil not,
7: 4. Or *how* wilt thou say to thy brother,
10:19. *how* or what ye shall speak:
12: 4. *How* he entered into the house of God,
26. *how* shall then his kingdom stand?
29. *how* can one enter into a strong man's
34. *how* can ye, being evil, speak good
16:11. *How* is it that ye do not understand
21:20. *How* soon is the fig tree withered
22:12. *how* camest thou in hither
43. *How* then doth David in spirit call
45. *how* is he his son?
23:33. *how* can ye escape the damnation of hell?
26:54. *how* then shall the scriptures be fulfilled,
Mar 2:26. *How* he went into the house of God
3:23. *How* can Satan cast out Satan?
4:13. *how* then will ye know all parables?
40. *how* is it that ye have no faith?
5:16. told them *how* it befell to him that was
8:21. *How* is it that ye do not understand?
9:12. and *how* it is written of the Son of man,
10:23. *How* hardly shall they that have riches
24. *how* hard is it for them that trust in
11:18. sought *how* they might destroy him:
12:35. *How* say the scribes that Christ is the
41. beheld *how* the people cast money into
14: 1. sought *how* they might take him
11. sought *how* he might conveniently betray
Lu. 1:34. *How* shall this be, seeing
6:42. *how* canst thou say to thy brother,
8:18. Take heed therefore *how* ye hear:
36. told them *by what means* he that was
10:26. *how* readest thou?
11:18. *how* shall his kingdom stand?
12:11. take ye no thought *how* or what
27. Consider the lilies *how* they grow.
50. and *how* am I straitened till it
56. *how* is it that ye do not discern
14: 7. *how* they chose out the chief rooms;
18:24. *How* hardly shall they that have
20:41. *How* say they that Christ is
44. *how* is he then his son?
22: 2. sought *how* they might kill him;
4. *how* he might betray him
Joh. 3: 4. *How* can a man be born when he is
9. *How* can these things be?
12. *how* shall ye believe, if I tell you
4: 9. *How* is it that thou, being a Jew,
5:44. *How* can ye believe, which
47. *how* shall ye believe my words?
6:42. *how* is it then that he saith, I came
52. *How* can this man give us (his)
7:15. *How* knoweth this man letters,
8:33. *how* sayest thou, Ye shall be
9:10. *How* were thine eyes opened?
15. *how* he had received his sight.
16. *How* can a man that is a sinner
19. *how* then doth he now see?

Joh 9:21. But *by what means* he now seeth,
26. *how* opened he thine eyes?
11:36. Behold *how* he loved him!
12:34. and *how* sayest thou,
14: 5. *how* can we know the way?
9. *how* sayest thou (then), Shew us
Acts 2: 8. And *how* hear we every man in
4:21. *how* they might punish them,
8:31 *How* can I, except some man
9:27. *how* he had seen the Lord in the way,
— and *how* he had preached boldly at
11:13. *how* he had seen an angel
12:17. *how* the Lord had brought him out
15:36. (and see) *how* they do.
20:18. *after what manner* I have been with
Ro. 3: 6. for then *how* shall God judge the world?
4:10. *How* was it then reckoned?
6: 2. *How* shall we, that are dead to sin,
8:32. *how* shall he not with him also freely
10:14. *How* then shall they call on him
— and *how* shall they believe in him
— and *how* shall they hear without a
15. And *how* shall they preach, except
1Co. 3:10. take heed *how* he buildeth thereupon.
7:32. *how* he may please the Lord:
33. *how* he may please (his) wife.
34. *how* she may please (her) husband.
14: 7. *how* shall it be known what is piped
9. *how* shall it be known what
16. *how* shall he that occupieth the room of
15:12. *how* say some among you that
35. *How* are the dead raised up?
2Co. 3: 8. *How* shall not the ministration of the
Gal. 4: 9. *how* turn ye again to the weak and
Eph. 5:15. See then *that* ye walk circumspectly,
Col. 4: 6. *how* ye ought to answer every man.
1Th. 1: 9. *how* ye turned to God from idols
4: 1. *how* ye ought to walk and
2Th. 3: 7. *how* ye ought to follow us:
1Ti. 3: 5. *how* shall he take care of the church
15. *how* thou oughtest to behave thyself
Heb 2: 3. *How* shall we escape, if we neglect
1Joh. 3:17. *how* dwelleth the love of God in him?
4:20. *how* can he love God whom he hath not seen?
Rev. 3: 3. Remember therefore *how* thou hast received and heard,

4461 17 740/880 6:961 [7227]

ῥαββί, *rabbi.*

Mat. 23: 7. to be called of men, *Rabbi, Rabbi.*
8. But be not ye called *Rabbi:*
26:25. *Master*, is it I?
49. Hail, *master;* and kissed him.
Mar 9: 5. *Master*, it is good for us to be here:
11:21. *Master*, behold, the fig tree
14:45. *Master, master;* and kissed him.
Joh. 1:38(39). They said unto him, *Rabbi,*
49(50). *Rabbi*, thou art the Son of God;
3: 2. *Rabbi*, we know that thou art a
26. *Rabbi*, he that was with thee
4:31. saying, *Master*, eat.
6:25. *Rabbi*, when camest thou hither?
9: 2. *Master*, who did sin, this man, or
11: 8. *Master*, the Jews of late sought to

4462 2 740/880 6:961 4461

ῥαββονί, ῥαββουνί, *rabboni, rabbouni.*

Mar 10:51. *Lord*, that I might receive my sight.
Joh. 20:16. *Rabboni;* which is to say, Master.

4463 2 740/880 6:966 4464

ῥαβδίζω, *rabdizo.*

Acts 16:22. and commanded *to beat* (them).
2Co. 11:25. Thrice *was I beaten with rods,*

4464 12 740/880 6:966 rt 4474

ῥάβδος, *rabdos.*

Mat. 10:10. nor yet *staves:*
Mar 6: 8. save a *staff* only;
Lu. 9: 3. neither *staves*, nor scrip,
1Co. 4:21. shall I come unto you with a *rod,*
Heb. 1: 8. a *sceptre* of righteousness (is) the *sceptre* of thy kingdom.
9: 4. and Aaron's *rod* that budded,
11:21. (leaning) upon the top of his *staff.*
Rev. 2:27. rule them with a *rod* of iron,
11: 1. a reed like unto a *rod:*
12: 5. to rule all nations with a *rod* of iron:
19:15. shall rule them with a *rod* of iron:

4465 2 740/880 6:966 4464,2192

ῥαβδοῦχος, *rabdoukos.*

Acts 16:35. the magistrates sent the *serjeants,*
38. And the *serjeants* told these words

4467 1 741/880 6:972

ῥᾳδιούργημα, *radiourgeema.*

Acts 18:14. matter of wrong or wicked *lewdness,*

4468 1 741/880 6:972

ῥᾳδιουργία, *radiourgia.*

Acts 13:10. full of all subtilty and all *mischief,*

4469 1 741/880 6:973 cf [7386]

ῥακά, *raka.*

Mat. 5:22. shall say to his brother, *Raca,*

4470 2 741/880 4486

ῥάκος, *rakos.*

Mat. 9:16. a piece of new *cloth* unto an old garment,
Mar 2:21. a piece of new *cloth* on an old garment:

4472 4 741/880 6:976 *rhainō* (to sprinkle)

ῥαντίζω, *rantizo.*

Heb 9:13. *sprinkling* the unclean,
19. and *sprinkled* both the book,
21. Moreover he *sprinkled* with blood
10:22. having our hearts *sprinkled* from an evil conscience,

4473 2 741/880 6:976 4472

ῥαντισμός, *rantismos.*

Heb 12:24. to the blood of *sprinkling,*
1Pet. 1: 2. unto obedience and *sprinkling* of the blood of Jesus Christ:

4474 2 741/881 cf 5180 *rhepō* (to let fall)

ῥαπίζω, *rapizo.*

Mat. 5:39. whosoever *shall smite* thee on thy right cheek,
26:67. others *smote* (him) *with the palms of their hands*

4475 3 741/881 4474

ῥάπισμα, rapisma.

Mar 14:65. did strike him with the *palms of* their *hands*.
Joh. 18:22. *struck* Jesus *with the palm of* his *hand*, (lit. gave a *slap* to Jesus)
19: 3. they smote him with their hands. (lit. they gave him *smitings*)

4476 3 742/881 *rhaptō* (to sew)

ῥαφίς, raphis.

Mat. 19:24. to go through the eye of a *needle*,
Mar 10:25. to go through the eye of a *needle*,
Lu. 18:25. to go through a *needle's* eye,

4480 1 742/881

ῥέδα, reda.

Rev. 18:13. and horses, and *chariots*,

4482 1 742/881

ῥέω, reo.

Joh. 7·38. out of his belly *shall flow* rivers of living water.

4483,(2036) 26 cf 4482,cf 3004

ῥέω, reo.

Note.—It is only used in the passive: Some trace to this root several of the words given in the series ἐρέω.

Mat. 1:22. *which was spoken* of the Lord by
2:15. *which was spoken* of the Lord by
17. *which was spoken* by Jeremy
23. *which was spoken* by the prophets,
3: 3. is he *that was spoken of* by the prophet
4:14. *which was spoken* by Esaias
5:21. it *was said* by them of old time,
27. it *was said* by them of old time,
31. It *hath been said*, Whosoever
33. it *hath been said* by them of old time,
38. that it *hath been said*, An eye
43. it *hath been said*, Thou shalt
8:17. *which was spoken* by Esaias
12:17. *which was spoken* by Esaias
13:35. *which was spoken* by the prophet,
21: 4. *which was spoken* by the prophet,
22·31. *which was spoken* unto you by God,
24:15. *spoken of* by Daniel the prophet,
27: 9. *which was spoken* by Jeremy
35. *which was spoken* by the prophet,
Mar 13:14. *spoken of* by Daniel the prophet,
Ro. 9:12. It *was said* unto her, The elder
26. where it *was said* unto them,
Gal. 3:16. *were* the promises *made*.
Rev. 6:11. and it *was said* unto them,
9: 4. And it *was commanded* them that

4485 1 742/881 4486

ῥῆγμα, reegma.

Lu. 6:49. and the *ruin* of that house was great.

4486 7 742/881 *rhekō* (*agnumi*) (to break)

ῥήγνυμι, ῥήσσω, reegnumi, & reesso.

Mat. 7: 6. lest they...and turn again and *rend* you.
9:17. else the bottles *break*,
Mar 2:22. *doth burst* the bottles,
9:18. he *teareth* him :
Lu. 5:37. new wine *will burst* the bottles,
9:42. the devil *threw* him *down*, and tare (him).
Gal. 4:27. *break forth* and cry, thou that

4487 70 742/881 4:69 4483

ῥῆμα, reema.

Mat. 4: 4. but by every *word* that proceedeth
5:11. shall say all manner of evil (lit. every evil *word*) against you falsely,
12:36. That every idle *word* that men
18:16. every *word* may be established.
26:75. Peter remembered the *word* of Jesus,
27:14. answered him to never a *word*;
Mar 9:32. understood not that *saying*,
14:72. the *word* that Jesus said unto him,
Lu. 1:37. with God no*thing* shall be impossible.
38. be it unto me according to thy *word*.
65. and all these *sayings* were noised
2:15. and see this *thing* which is come
17. made known abroad the *saying*
19. But Mary kept all these *things*,
29. depart in peace, according to thy *word*:
50. understood not the *saying* which
51. his mother kept all these *sayings* in her heart.
3: 2. the *word* of God came unto John
4: 4. but by every *word* of God.
5: 5. at thy *word* I will let down the net.
7: 1. when he had ended all his *sayings*
9:45. they understood not this *saying*,
— they feared to ask him of that *saying*,
18:34. and this *saying* was hid from them,
20:26. they could not take hold of his *words*
24. 8. And they remembered his *words*,
11. their *words* seemed to them as idle
Joh. 3:34. speaketh the *words* of God:
5:47. how shall ye believe my *words*?
6:63. the *words* that I speak unto you,
68. thou hast the *words* of eternal life.
8:20. These *words* spake Jesus in the
47. He that is of God heareth God's *words*.
10:21. These are not the *words* of him that
12:47. if any man hear my *words*,
48. and receiveth not my *words*,
14:10. the *words* that I speak unto you
15: 7. and my *words* abide in you,
17: 8. I have given unto them the *words* which
Acts 2.14. and hearken to my *words*:
5:20. all the *words* of this life.
32. we are his witnesses of these *things*;
6.11. blasphemous *words* against Moses,
13. blasphemous *words* against this holy
10·22. and to hear *words* of thee.
37. That *word*, (I say), ye know, which
44. While Peter yet spake these *words*,
11 14. Who shall tell thee *words*,
16. remembered I the *word* of the Lord,
13.42. besought that these *words* might
16:38. the serjeants told these *words*
26:25. but speak forth the *words* of truth and
28:25. after that Paul had spoken one *word*,
Ro. 10: 8. The *word* is nigh thee,
— the *word* of faith, which we preach;
17. and hearing by the *word* of God.
18. and their *words* unto the ends of
2Co. 12: 4. and heard unspeakable *words*,
13: 1. shall every *word* be established.
Eph 5:26. the washing of water by the *word*,
6:17. the sword of the Spirit, which is the *word* of God:
Heb 1: 3. all things by the *word* of his power,
6: 5. have tasted the good *word* of God,
11: 3. were framed by the *word* of God,
12:19. and the voice of *words*;
1Pet. 1:25. But the *word* of the Lord endureth for ever. And this is the *word* which by

2Pet. 3: 2. That ye may be mindful of the *words*
Jude 17. remember ye the *words* which were spoken before of the apostles
Rev. 17: 17. until the *words* of God shall be fulfilled.

ῥήσσω see ῥήγνυμι· 4486

4489 1 743/882 4483
ῥήτωρ, reetōr.

Acts24: 1. (with) a certain *orator* (named)

4490 1 743/882 4483
ῥητῶς, reetōs.

1Ti. 4: 1. the Spirit speaketh *expressly*,

4491 17 743/882 6:985
ῥίζα, riza.

Mat. 3: 10. the ax is laid unto the *root* of the
13: 6. because they had no *root*,
21. Yet hath he not *root* in himself,
Mar 4: 6. because it had no *root*,
17. And have no *root* in themselves,
11: 20. dried up from the *roots*.
Lu. 3: 9. the axe is laid unto the *root* of the
8: 13. and these have no *root*,
Ro. 11: 16. and if the *root* (be) holy, so (are)
17. partakest of the *root* and fatness of
18. thou bearest not the *root*, but the *root* tnee
15: 12. There shall be a *root* of Jesse,
1Ti. 6: 10. the love of money is the *root* of all evil:
Heb 12: 15. lest any *root* of bitterness springing up
Rev. 5: 5. the *Root* of David, hath prevailed
22: 16. I am the *root* and the offspring of David,

4492 2 743/882 4491
ῥιζόομαι, rizoömai.

Eph. 3: 17(18). *being rooted* and grounded in love,
Col. 2: 7. *Rooted* and built up in him,

4493 1 743/882 4496
ῥιπή, ripee.

1Co. 15: 52. in the *twinkling* of an eye,

4494 1 743/882 4496
ῥιπίζομαι, ripizomai.

Jas. 1: 6. driven with the wind and *tossed*.

4495-4496 cf rt4474cf906
8 743/882 6:991
ῥίπτω, ripto.

Mat. 9: 36. and were *scattered abroad*, as sheep
15: 30. and *cast* them *down* at Jesus' feet;
27: 5. And he *cast down* the pieces of silver
Lu. 4: 35. *when* the devil *had thrown* him
17: 2. and he *cast* into the sea,
Acts22: 23. And as they cried out, and *cast off* (their) clothes,
27: 19. we *cast out* with our own hands
29. they *cast* four anchors out of the stern, *and*

4500 1 744/882 *rhoizos* (whir)
ῥοιζηδόν, roizeedon.

2Pet. 3: 10. shall pass away *with* a *great noise*,

4501 7 744/882 6:998
ῥομφαία, romphaia.

Lu. 2: 35. Yea, a *sword* shall pierce through
Rev. 1: 16. a sharp twoedged *sword*:
2: 12. which hath the sharp *sword*
16. with the *sword* of my mouth.
6: 8. to kill with *sword*,
19: 15. out of his mouth goeth a sharp *sword*,
21. slain with the *sword* of him that sat

4505 4 744/883 4506
ῥύμη, rumee.

Mat. 6: 2. and in the *streets*, that they may
Lu. 14: 21. into the streets and *lanes* of the city,
Acts 9: 11. Arise, and go into the *street* which is called Straight,
12: 10. passed on through one *street*;

4507 1 745/883 4508
ῥυπαρία, ruparia.

Jas. 1: 21. lay apart all *filthiness* and superfluity of

4508 1 745/883 4509
ῥυπαρός, ruparos.

Jas. 2: 2. a poor man in *vile* raiment;

4509 1 745/883
ῥύπος, rupos.

1Pet. 3: 21. the putting away of the *filth* of the flesh,

4510 2 745/883 4509
ῥυπόω, rupoō.

Rev. 22: 11. he *which is filthy*, *let* him *be filthy* still:

4511 3 745/883 4506
ῥύσις, rusis.

Mar 5: 25. which had an *issue* of blood
Lu. 8: 43. having an *issue* of blood
44. her *issue* of blood stanched.

4512 1 745/883 4506
ῥυτίς, rutis.

Eph 5: 27. or *wrinkle*, or any such thing;

4506 18 744/883 6:998 cf 4482
ῥύομαι, ruomai.

Mat. 6: 13. but *deliver* us from evil:
27: 43. *let* him *deliver* him now,
Lu. 1: 74. that we *being delivered* out of
11: 4. but *deliver* us from evil.
Ro. 7: 24. who *shall deliver* me from the body of this death?
11: 26. out of Sion the *Deliverer*,
15: 31. That I *may be delivered* from
2Co. 1: 10. Who *delivered* us from so great a death, and *doth deliver*: in whom we trust that he *will* yet *deliver* (us);
Col. 1: 13. *hath delivered* us from the power
1Th. 1: 10. Jesus, *which delivered* us from the wrath
2Th. 3: 2. that we *may be delivered* from
2Ti. 3: 11. the Lord *delivered* me.
4: 17. and I *was delivered* out of the mouth of the lion.
18. the Lord *shall deliver* me
2Pet. 2: 7. And *delivered* just Lot,
9. The Lord knoweth how *to deliver*

4517 2 745/883 *rhōomai* (to dart)
ῥώννυμαι, rōnnumai.

Acts15:29. *Fare ye well.*
23:30. to say before thee what (they had) against him. *Farewell.*

4518 2 746/884 [7662]
σαβαχθανί, sabakthani.

Mat.27:46. Eli, Eli, lama *sabacthani?* that is to say, My God, my God, why hast thou forsaken me?
Mar 15:34. Eloi, Eloi, lama *sabacthani?* which is,... why hast thou forsaken me?

4519 2 746/884 [6635]
σαβαώθ, sabaōth.

Ro. 9:29. Except the Lord of *Sabaoth* had left
Jas. 5: 4. are entered into the ears of the Lord of *sabaoth* (i. e. of *hosts*)

4520 1 746/884 7:1 4521
σαββατισμός, sabbatismos.

Heb 4: 9. There remaineth therefore a *rest* to the

4521 68 746/884 7:1 [7676]
σάββατον, σάββατα, sabbaton, & sabbata.

Note.—Those which are the cases of σάββατον, a noun of the second declension, and in the singular, have the figure [2]. Those which are of the third declension, and are neut. plur., are marked [3].

Mat.12: 1. Jesus went on the *sabbath day*[3] through
2. lawful to do upon the *sabbath day.*[2]
5. on the *sabbath days*[3] the priests in the temple profane the *sabbath,*[2]
8. is Lord even of the *sabbath day.*[2]
10. lawful to heal on the *sabbath days?*[3]
11. if it fall into a pit on the *sabbath day,*[3]
12. is lawful to do well on the *sabbath days.*[3]
24:20. neither on the *sabbath day:*[2]
28: 1. In the end of the *sabbath,*[3] as it began to dawn toward the first (day) of the *week,*[3]
Mar 1:21. on the *sabbath day*[3] he entered into
2:23. the corn fields on the *sabbath day;*[3]
24. why do they on the *sabbath day*[3]
27. The *sabbath*[2] was made for man, and not man for the *sabbath:*[2]
28. is Lord also of the *sabbath.*[2]
3: 2. heal him on the *sabbath day;*[3]
4. to do good on the *sabbath days,*[3]
6: 2. And when the *sabbath day*[2] was come,
16: 1. And when the *sabbath*[2] was past,
2. in the morning the first (day) of the *week,*[3]
9. risen early the first (day) of the *week,*[2]
Lu. 4:16. the synagogue on the *sabbath*[3] day,
31. taught them on the *sabbath days.*[3]
6: 1. on the second *sabbath*[2] after the first,
2. lawful to do on the *sabbath days?*[3]
5. Lord also of the *sabbath.*[2]
6. to pass also on another *sabbath,*[2]
7. whether he would heal on the *sabbath day;*[2]
9. lawful on the *sabbath days*[3] to do good,
13:10. in one of the synagogues on the *sabbath.*[3]
14. had healed on the *sabbath day,*[2]
— and not on the *sabbath*[2] day.
15. doth not each one of you on the *sabbath*[2]
16. be loosed from this bond on the *sabbath*[2] day?
Lu. 14: 1. to eat bread on the *sabbath day,*[2]
3. Is it lawful to heal on the *sabbath day?*[2]
5. pull him out on the *sabbath*[2] day?
18:12. I fast twice in the *week,*[2]
23:54. and the *sabbath*[2] drew on.
56. and rested the *sabbath day*[2]
24: 1. upon the first (day) of the *week,*[3]
Joh. 5: 9. the same day was the *sabbath.*[2]
10. It is the *sabbath day:*[2]
16. done these things on the *sabbath day.*[2]
18. he not only had broken the *sabbath,*[2]
7:22. ye on the *sabbath day*[2] circumcise
23. If a man on the *sabbath day*[2]
— whole on the *sabbath day?*[2]
9:14. And it was the *sabbath day*[2] when
16. he keepeth not the *sabbath day.*[2]
19:31. upon the cross on the *sabbath day,*[2] for that *sabbath*[2] *day* was an high day,
20: 1. The first (day) of the *week*[3]
19. the first (day) of the *week,*[3]
Acts 1:12. a *sabbath day's*[2] journey.
13:14. into the synagogue on the *sabbath*[3] day,
27. which are read every *sabbath day,*[2]
42. preached to them the next *sabbath.*[2]
44. And the next *sabbath*[2] *day* came
15:21. read in the synagogues every *sabbath day.*[2]
16:13. And on the *sabbath*[3] (lit. the day of the *sabbath*) we went out
17: 2. three *sabbath days*[3] reasoned
18: 4. in the synagogue every *sabbath,*[2]
20: 7. the first (day) of the *week,*[3]
1Co.16: 2. Upon the first (day) of the *week*[3] let
Col. 2:16. new moon, or of the *sabbath*[3] (days):

4522 1 746/885 *sattō* (to equip)
σαγήνη, sageenee.

Mat.13:47. kingdom of heaven is like unto a *net,*

4525 1 747/885 7:54 cf 4579
σαίνω, saino.

1Th. 3: 3. That no man should *be moved* by these

4526 4 747/885 7:56 [8242]
σάκκος, sakkos.

Mat.11:21. long ago in *sackcloth* and ashes.
Lu. 10:13. sitting in *sackcloth* and ashes.
Rev. 6:12. black as *sackcloth* of hair.
11: 3. clothed in *sackcloth.*

4531 15 747/885 7:65 4535
σαλεύω, salūo.

Mat.11: 7. A reed *shaken* with the wind?
24:29. the powers of the heavens *shall be shaken:*
Mar 13:25. powers that are in heaven *shall be shaken.*
Lu. 6:38. pressed down, and *shaken together,*
48. and could not *shake* it:
7:24. A reed *shaken* with the wind?
21:26. the powers of heaven *shall be shaken.*
Acts 2:25. that I *should* not *be moved:*
4:31. the place *was shaken* where they
16:26. foundations of the prison *were shaken:*
17:13. *and stirred up* the people.
2Th. 2: 2. That ye *be* not soon *shaken* in mind,
Heb 12:26. Whose voice then *shook* the earth:
27. of those things *that are shaken,*
— that those things *which cannot be shaken* (lit. the things not *shaken*) may remain.

4535 1 748/885 7:65 rt 4525
σάλος, salos.

Lu. 21:25. the sea and the *waves* roaring;

4536 11 748/885 7:71 4535
σάλπιγξ, salpinx.

Mat.24:31. with a great sound of a *trumpet*,
1Co.14: 8. if the *trumpet* give an uncertain
15:52. at the last *trump*:
1Th. 4:16. and with the *trump* of God:
Heb 12:19. And the sound of a *trumpet*, and
Rev. 1:10. a great voice, as of a *trumpet*,
4: 1. as it were of a *trumpet*
8: 2. to them were given seven *trumpets*.
6. which had the seven *trumpets*
13. the other voices of the *trumpet*
9:14. the sixth angel which had the *trumpet*,

4537 12 748/885 7:71 4536
σαλπίζω, salpizo.

Mat. 6: 2. do not *sound a trumpet* before thee,
1Co.15:52. for the *trumpet shall sound*,
Rev. 8: 6. prepared themselves to *sound*.
7. The first angel *sounded*,
8. the second angel *sounded*,
10. And the third angel *sounded*,
12. And the fourth angel *sounded*,
13. angels, which are yet *to sound*!
9: 1. And the fifth angel *sounded*,
13. And the sixth angel *sounded*,
10: 7. when he shall begin *to sound*,
11:15. And the seventh angel *sounded*;

4538 1 748/886 7:71 4537
σαλπιστής, salpistees.

Rev.18:22. and of pipers, and *trumpeters*,

4547 2 749/886 5:292 *sandalon* (sandal)
σανδάλιον, sandalion.

Mar 6: 9. But (be) shod with *sandals*;
Acts12: 8. and bind on thy *sandals*.

4548 1 749/886
σανίς, sanis.

Acts27.44. And the rest, some on *boards*, and some

4550 8 749/886 7:94 4595cf4190
σαπρός, sapros.

Mat. 7:17. but a *corrupt* tree bringeth forth
18. neither (can) a *corrupt* tree
12:33. or else make the tree *corrupt*, and his fruit *corrupt*:
13:48. but cast the *bad* away.
Lu. 6:43. a good tree bringeth not forth *corrupt* fruit; neither doth a *corrupt* tree bring
Eph. 4:29. Let no *corrupt* communication

4552 1 749/886 [5601]
σάπφειρος, sapphīros.

Rev.21:19. the second, *sapphire*;

4553 1 749/886 [8276]
σαργάνη, sarganee.

2Co.11:33. in a *basket* was I let down

4555 1 750/886 rt 4556
σάρδινος, sardinos.

Rev. 4: 3. like a jasper and a *sardine* stone.

4556 1 750/886
σάρδιος, sardios.

Rev.21:20. the sixth, *sardius*;

4557 1 750/886 *onux* (nail of the finger) rt 4556
σαρδόνυξ, sardonux.

Rev.21:20. The fifth, *sardonyx*;

4559 11 750/886 7:98 4561
σαρκικός, sarkikos.

Ro. 7:14. but I am *carnal*, sold under sin.
15:27. to minister unto them in *carnal* things.
1Co. 3: 1. but as unto *carnal*,
3. For ye are yet *carnal*:
— are ye not *carnal*, and walk as men?
4. are ye not *carnal*?
9:11. if we shall reap your *carnal* things?
2Co. 1:12. not with *fleshly* wisdom, but
10: 4. the weapons of our warfare (are) not *carnal*,
Heb 7:16. not after the law of a *carnal* commandment,
1Pet. 2:11. abstain from *fleshly* lusts,

4560 1 750/887 7:98 4561
σάρκινος, sarkinos.

2Co. 3: 3. but in *fleshy* tables of the heart.

4561 151 750/887 7:98 rt 4563
σάρξ, sarx.

Mat.16:17. *flesh* and blood hath not revealed (it)
19: 5. and they twain shall be one *flesh*?
6. are no more twain, but one *flesh*.
24:22. there should no *flesh* be saved:
26:41. willing, but the *flesh* (is) weak.
Mar 10: 8. shall be one *flesh*: so then they are no more twain, but one *flesh*.
13:20. no *flesh* should be saved:
14:38. but the *flesh* (is) weak.
Lu. 3: 6. And all *flesh* shall see the salvation
24:39. a spirit hath not *flesh* and bones,
Joh. 1:13. nor of the will of the *flesh*,
14. And the Word was made *flesh*,
3: 6. That which is born of the *flesh* is *flesh*;
6:51. and the bread that I will give is my *flesh*,
52. give us (his) *flesh* to eat?
53. Except ye eat the *flesh* of the Son
54. Whoso eateth my *flesh*,
55. For my *flesh* is meat indeed,
56. He that eateth my *flesh*,
63. the *flesh* profiteth nothing·
8.15. Ye judge after the *flesh*;
17: 2. given him power over all *flesh*,
Acts 2:17. pour out of my Spirit upon all *flesh*:
26. also my *flesh* shall rest in hope:
30. of his loins, according to the *flesh*, he
31. neither his *flesh* did see corruption.
Ro. 1: 3. the seed of David according to the *flesh*;
2:28. which is outward in the *flesh*:
3:20. there shall no *flesh* be justified
4: 1. our father as pertaining to the *flesh*, hath found?
6:19. because of the infirmity of your *flesh*:
7: 5. For when we were in the *flesh*,
18. in me, that is, in my *flesh*,
25. but with the *flesh* the law of sin.
8: 1. who walk not after the *flesh*,
3. it was weak through the *flesh*,

Ro. 8: 3. in the likeness of sinful *flesh*, and for sin, condemned sin in the *flesh*:
4. who walk not after the *flesh*,
5. they that are after the *flesh* do mind the things of the *flesh*;
6. to be *carnally* minded (is) death; (lit. the minding of the *flesh*)
7. the *carnal* mind (is) (lit. the minding of the *flesh*) enmity against God:
8. they that are in the *flesh* cannot
9. ye are not in the *flesh*, but in the
12. we are debtors, not to the *flesh*, to live after the *flesh*.
13. For if ye live after the *flesh*, ye
9: 3. my kinsmen according to the *flesh*:
5. of whom as concerning the *flesh* Christ
8. They which are the children of the *flesh*,
11:14. emulation (them which are) my *flesh*,
13:14. make not provision for the *flesh*, to
1Co. 1:26. not many wise men after the *flesh*,
29. That no *flesh* should glory
5: 5. unto Satan for the destruction of the *flesh*,
6:16. two, saith he, shall be one *flesh*.
7:28. such shall have trouble in the *flesh*:
10:18. Behold Israel after the *flesh*:
15:39. All *flesh* (is) not the same *flesh*: but (there is) one (kind of) *flesh* of men, another *flesh* of beasts,
50. *flesh* and blood cannot inherit the
2Co. 1:17. do I purpose according to the *flesh*,
4:11. be made manifest in our mortal *flesh*.
5:16. no man after the *flesh*: yea, though we have known Christ after the *flesh*,
7: 1. from all filthiness of the *flesh* and spirit,
5. our *flesh* had no rest, but we were
10: 2. as if we walked according to the *flesh*.
3. in the *flesh*, we do not war after the *flesh*:
11:18. that many glory after the *flesh*,
12: 7. a thorn in the *flesh*, the messenger of
Gal. 1:16. I conferred not with *flesh* and blood:
2:16. shall no *flesh* be justified.
20. the life which I now live in the *flesh*
3: 3. are ye now made perfect by the *flesh*?
4:13. through infirmity of the *flesh* I
14. temptation which was in my *flesh*
23. was born after the *flesh*;
29. he that was born after the *flesh*
5:13. liberty for an occasion to the *flesh*, but
16. ye shall not fulfil the lust of the *flesh*.
17. the *flesh* lusteth against the Spirit, and the Spirit against the *flesh*:
19. the works of the *flesh* are manifest,
24. have crucified the *flesh* with the
6: 8. he that soweth to his *flesh* shall of the *flesh* reap corruption.
12. to make a fair shew in the *flesh*,
13. that they may glory in your *flesh*.
Eph. 2: 3. in the lusts of our *flesh*, fulfilling the desires of the *flesh* and of the mind;
11. in time past Gentiles in the *flesh*,
— called the Circumcision in the *flesh*
15. Having abolished in his *flesh* the enmity,
5:29. no man ever yet hated his own *flesh*;
30. of his *flesh*, and of his bones.
31. they two shall be one *flesh*.
6: 5. masters according to the *flesh*,
12. we wrestle not against *flesh* and blood,
Phi. 1:22. But if I live in the *flesh*, this
24. Nevertheless to abide in the *flesh*
3 3. and have no confidence in the *flesh*.
4. might also have confidence in the *flesh*.
— whereof he might trust in the *flesh*,
Col 1:22. In the body of his *flesh* through death,
24. in my *flesh* for his body's sake,
2: 1. as have not seen my face in the *flesh*;
5. absent in the *flesh*, yet am I
11. putting off the body of the sins of the *flesh*
13. the uncircumcision of your *flesh*,
18. puffed up by his *flesh*ly mind,
23. to the satisfying of the *flesh*.
3:22. masters according to the *flesh*;
1Ti. 3:16. God was manifest in the *flesh*,
Philem. 16. both in the *flesh*, and in the Lord?
Heb. 2:14. children are partakers of *flesh* and blood,
5: 7. Who in the days of his *flesh*,
9:10. and *carnal* ordinances,
13. to the purifying of the *flesh*:
10:20. through the veil, that is to say, his *flesh*;
12: 9. we have had fathers of our *flesh*
Jas. 5: 3. shall eat your *flesh* as it were fire.
1Pet. 1:24. For all *flesh* (is) as grass,
3:18. put to death in the *flesh*, but
21. putting away of the filth of the *flesh*,
4: 1. hath suffered for us in the *flesh*,
— he that hath suffered in the *flesh*
2. live the rest of (his) time in the *flesh*
6. judged according to men in the *flesh*,
2Pet. 2:10. that walk after the *flesh* in the lust
18. they allure through the lusts of the *flesh*,
1Joh. 2:16. the lust of the *flesh*, and the lust
4: 2. Jesus Christ is come in the *flesh*
3. Jesus Christ is come in the *flesh*
2Joh. 7. Jesus Christ is come in the *flesh*.
Jude 7. going after strange *flesh*,
8. dreamers defile the *flesh*, despise
23. even the garment spotted by the *flesh*.
Rev. 17:16. and shall eat her *flesh*, and burn her
19:18. *flesh* of kings, and the *flesh* of captains, and the *flesh* of mighty men, and the *flesh*,
— and the *flesh* of all (men, both)
21. fowls were filled with their *flesh*.

4563 3 752/888 sairo (to brush off)

σαρόω, saroō.

Mat. 12:44. *swept*, and garnished.
Lu. 11:25. he findeth (it) *swept* and garnished.
15: 8. doth not light a candle, and *sweep* the

4568 2 752/889 4568 [5429]

σάτον, saton.

Mat. 13:33. hid in three *measures* of meal,
Lu. 13:21. hid in three *measures* of meal,

σαυτοῦ, ῷ, όν see σεαυτοῦ. 4572

4570 8 752/889 7:165

σβέννυμι, sbennumi.

Mat. 12:20. smoking flax *shall* he not *quench*,
25: 8. for our lamps *are gone out*.
Mar 9:44. and the fire *is* not *quenched*.
46. and the fire *is* not *quenched*.
48. and the fire *is* not *quenched*.
Eph. 6:16. able *to quench* all the fiery darts
1Th. 5:19. *Quench* not the Spirit.
Heb 11:34. *Quenched* the violence of fire,

4571 196 779/910 4771

σέ, se.

From σύ.

Mat. 4: 6. they shall bear *thee* up,

Mat. 5:25. deliver *thee* to the judge, and the judge deliver *thee*
29. thy right eye offend *thee*,
30. thy right hand offend *thee*,
39. whosoever shall smite *thee*
41. shall compel *thee* to go a mile,
42. Give to him that asketh *thee*,
9:22. thy faith hath made *thee* whole.
14:28. bid me come unto *thee*
18: 8. if thy hand or thy foot offend *thee*,
9. And if thine eye offend *thee*,
15. thy brother shall trespass against *thee*,
33. Shouldest not *thou* also have had
— even as I had pity on *thee*?
20:13. I do *thee* no wrong:
25:21. I will make *thee* ruler
23. I will make *thee* ruler
24. I knew *thee* that thou art
27. *Thou* oughtest (lit. it behoved *thee*)
37. when saw we *thee* an hungred,
38. When saw we *thee* a stranger,
39. Or when saw we *thee* sick, or in prison, and came unto *thee*?
44. when saw we *thee* an hungred,
26:18. keep the passover at *thy house* (πρός σε)
35. yet will I not deny *thee*.
63. I adjure *thee* by the living God,
68. Who is he that smote *thee*?
73. thy speech bewrayeth *thee*.

Mar 1:24. I know *thee* who thou art,
3:32. thy brethren without seek for *thee*.
5: 7. I adjure *thee* by God,
19. hath had compassion on *thee*.
31. the multitude thronging *thee*,
34. thy faith hath made *thee* whole;
9:17. I have brought unto *thee* my son,
43. And if thy hand offend *thee*,
45. And if thy foot offend *thee*,
47. And if thine eye offend *thee*,
10:49. rise; he calleth *thee*.
52. thy faith hath made *thee* whole.
14:31. I will not deny *thee*

Lu. 1:19. and am sent to speak unto *thee*,
35. The Holy Ghost shall come upon *thee*,
2:48. have sought *thee* sorrowing.
4:10. charge over thee, to keep *thee*:
11. they shall bear *thee* up,
34. I know *thee* who thou art;
6:29. And unto him that smiteth *thee*
30. Give to every man that asketh of *thee*;
7: 7. myself worthy to come unto *thee*:
20. John Baptist hath sent us unto *thee*,
50. Thy faith hath saved *thee*;
8:20. desiring to see *thee*.
45. the multitude throng *thee* and press
48. thy faith hath made *thee* whole;
11:27. Blessed (is) the womb that bare *thee*,
36. shining of a candle doth give *thee* light.
12:58. lest he hale *thee* to the judge, and the judge deliver *thee* to the officer, and the officer cast *thee* into prison.
13:31. for Herod will kill *thee*.
14: 9. And he that bade *thee* and him
10. he that bade *thee* cometh,
12. lest they also bid *thee* again,
18. I pray *thee* have me excused.
19. I pray *thee* have me excused.
16.27. I pray *thee* therefore, father,
17: 3. thy brother trespass against *thee*,
4. against *thee* seven times in a day, and even times in a day turn again to *thee*,
19. thy faith hath made *thee* whole.

Lu. 18:42. thy faith hath saved *thee*.
19:21. For I feared *thee*,
22. Out of thine own mouth will I judge *thee*,
43. For the days shall come upon *thee*,
— and compass *thee* round, and keep *thee* in on every side,
44. And shall lay *thee* even with the ground,
22:64. Prophesy, who is it that smote *thee*?

Joh. 1:48(49). Before that Philip called *thee*, when thou wast under the fig tree, I saw *thee*.
50(51). I saw *thee* under the fig tree,
7:20. who goeth about to kill *thee*?
8:10. hath no man condemned *thee*?
11. Neither do I condemn *thee*:
10:33. For a good work we stone *thee* not,
11: 8. Jews of late sought to stone *thee*;
28. and calleth for *thee*.
13: 8. If I wash *thee* not,
16:30. that any man should ask *thee*:
17: 1. that thy Son also may glorify *thee*:
3. that they might know *thee*
4. I have glorified *thee* on the earth:
11. and I come to *thee*.
13. And now come I to *thee*;
25. the world hath not known *thee*: but I have known *thee*,
18:26. Did not I see *thee* in the garden with him?
35. priests have delivered *thee* unto me:
19:10. to crucify *thee*, and have power to release *thee*?
21:15. Lord; thou knowest that I love *thee*.
16. thou knowest that I love *thee*.
17. thou knowest that I love *thee*.
18. another shall gird *thee*,
20. which is he that betrayeth *thee*?
22. what (is that) to *thee*?
23. what (is that) to *thee*?

Acts 4:30. By)(stretching forth thine hand to heal;
5: 3. filled thine heart)(to lie to the Holy
9. and shall carry *thee* out.
7:27. Who made *thee* a ruler and a
34. I will send *thee* into Egypt.
35. saying, Who made *thee* a ruler
8:23. I perceive that *thou* art in the gall of
9: 6. it shall be told thee what *thou* must do.
34. Jesus Christ maketh *thee* whole:
10: 6. shall tell thee what *thou* oughtest to do.
19. Behold, three men seek *thee*.
22. to send for *thee* into his house,
33. therefore I sent to *thee*;
11:14. Who shall tell *thee* words,
13:11. the hand of the Lord (is) upon *thee*,
33. this day have I begotten *thee*.
47. I have set *thee* to be a light of the Gentiles, that *thou* shouldest be for
18:10. no man shall set on thee to hurt *thee*.
21:37. May I speak unto *thee*?
22:14. hath chosen *thee*, that thou shouldest know (lit. hath chosen *thee* to know)
19. them that believed on *thee*:
21. I will send *thee* far hence unto
23: 3. God shall smite *thee*,
11. so must *thou* bear witness also at Rome.
18. to bring this young man unto *thee*,
20. have agreed to desire *thee* that
30. I sent straightway to *thee*,
24: 4. that I be not further tedious unto *thee*, I pray thee that *thou* wouldest hear us
8. accusers to come unto *thee*:
10. that *thou* hast been of many years
25. I will call for *thee*.
26: 3. *thee* to be expert in all customs

Acts26:16. to make *thee* a minister and a witness
17. Delivering *thee* from the people,
— unto whom now I send *thee*,
24. much learning doth make *thee* mad.
29. that not only *thou*, but also all
27:24. *thou* must be brought before Cæsar:
Ro. 2: 4. goodness of God leadeth *thee* to
27. judge *thee*, who by the letter
3: 4. overcome when *thou* art judged.
4:17. I have made *thee* a father of many
9:17. have I raised *thee* up,
11:18. bearest not the root, but the root *thee*.
22. but toward *thee*, goodness,
15: 3. of them that reproached *thee*
1Co. 4: 7. For who maketh *thee* to differ
8:10. For if any man see *thee*
Phi. 4: 3. And I intreat *thee* also,
1Ti. 1: 3. As I besought *thee* to abide still
18. prophecies which went before on *thee*.
3:14. hoping to come unto *thee* shortly:
6:14. That *thou* keep (this) commandment
2Ti. 1: 4. Greatly desiring to see *thee*,
6. Wherefore I put *thee* in remembrance
3:15. which are able to make *thee* wise unto
4:21. Eubulus greeteth *thee*,
Tit. 1: 5. For this cause left I *thee* in Crete,
3: 8. I will that *thou* affirm constantly,
12. I shall send Artemas unto *thee*,
15. All that are with me salute *thee*.
Philem.10. I beseech *thee* for my son
18. If he hath wronged *thee*,
23. There salute *thee* Epaphras,
Heb. 1: 5. this day have I begotten *thee?*
9. thy God, hath anointed *thee*
2:12. will I sing praise unto *thee*.
5: 5. to day have I begotten *thee*.
6:14. blessing I will bless *thee*, and multiplying I will multiply *thee*.
13: 5. I will never leave *thee*, nor forsake *thee*.
2Joh. 5. And now I beseech *thee*, lady,
13. The children of thy elect sister greet *thee*.
3Joh. 2. that *thou* mayest prosper
14. I shall shortly see *thee*,
— (Our) friends salute *thee*.
Rev. 3: 3. I will come on *thee* as a thief,
— what hour I will come upon *thee*.
9. and to know that I have loved *thee*.
10. I also will keep *thee* from the hour
16. I will spue *thee* out of my mouth.
10:11. *Thou* must prophesy again before
15: 4. Who shall not fear *thee*, O Lord,

4572 40 753/889 4571,846

σεαυτοῦ, τῷ, τόν, *seautou, to, ton*, also σαυτοῦ, τῷ, τόν.

Mat. 4: 6. cast *thyself* down:
8: 4. shew *thyself* to the priest,
19:19. love thy neighbour as *thyself*.
22:39. love thy neighbour as *thyself*.
27:40. save *thyself*.
Mar 1:44. shew *thyself* to the priest,
12:31. love thy neighbour as *thyself*.
15:30. Save *thyself*, and come down
Lu. 4: 9. cast *thyself* down from hence:
23. Physician, heal *thyself*:
5:14. shew *thyself* to the priest,
10:27. and thy neighbour as *thyself*.
23:37. the king of the Jews, save *thyself*.
39. save *thyself* and us.
Joh. 1:22. What sayest thou of *thyself?*
7: 4. shew *thyself* to the world.
8:13. Thou bearest record of *thyself*;
53. whom makest thou *thyself?*
10:33. makest *thyself* God.
14:22. manifest *thyself* unto us,
17: 5. glorify thou me with *thine own self* with
21:18. thou girdedst *thyself*,
Acts 9:34. make *thy* bed. (lit. for *thyself*)
16:28. Do *thyself* no harm:
26: 1. permitted to speak for *thyself*.
Ro. 2: 1. thou condemnest *thyself*;
5. treasurest up unto *thyself*
19. that *thou thyself* art a guide
21. teachest thou not *thyself?*
14:22. have (it) to *thyself*
Gal. 6: 1. considering *thyself*, lest thou also
1Ti. 4: 7. exercise *thyself* (rather) unto godliness.
16. Take heed unto *thyself*,
— thou shalt both save *thyself*, and
5:22. keep *thyself* pure.
2Ti. 2:15. Study to shew *thyself* approved
4:11. bring him with *thee*:
Tit. 2: 7. In all things shewing *thyself* a pattern
Philem.19. owest unto me even *thine own self*
Jas. 2: 8. thy neighbour as *thyself*,

4573 1 753/889 7:168 4576

σεβάζομαι, *sebazomai*.

Ro. 1:25. and *worshipped* and served the creature

4574 2 753/889 7:168 4573

σέβασμα, *sebasma*.

Acts17:23. and beheld your *devotions*,
2Th. 2: 4. that is called God, or *that is worshipped*;

4575 3 753/889 4573

σεβαστός, *sebastos*, adj.

Acts27: 1. a centurion of *Augustus'* band. (or it may be rendered, of the *imperial* guard)

4576 10 753/890 7:168

σέβομαι, *sebomai*.

Mat.15: 9. in vain they *do worship* me,
Mar 7: 7. in vain *do* they *worship* me,
Acts13:43. many of the Jews and *religious* proselytes
50. the *devout* and honourable women,
16:14. *which worshipped* God, heard (us);
17: 4. of the *devout* Greeks a great multitude,
17. and with the *devout* persons,
18: 7. Justus, (one) *that worshipped* God,
13. persuadeth men *to worship* God contrary
19:27. Asia and the world *worshippeth*.

4577 1 753/890 4951

σειρά, *sira*.

2Pet. 2: 4. into *chains* of darkness,

4578 14 753/890 7:196 4579

σεισμός, *sismos*.

Mat. 8:24. there arose a great *tempest* in the sea,
24: 7. and *earthquakes*, in divers places.
27:54. saw the *earthquake*, and those things
28: 2. behold, there was a great *earthquake*.
Mar13: 8. there shall be *earthquakes* in divers
Lu. 21:11. great *earthquakes* shall be in
Acts16:26. there was a great *earthquake*, so that
Rev. 6:12. lo, there was a great *earthquake*;
8: 5. lightnings, and an *earthquake*.
11:13. was there a great *earthquake*,

Rev.11:13. and in the *earthquake* were slain
19. and an *earthquake*, and great hail.
16:18. and there was a great *earthquake*,
— so mighty an *earthquake*,

4579 5 753/890 7:196
σείω, sīo.

Mat.21:10. all the city *was moved*, saying,
27:51. and the earth *did quake*, and the rocks
28: 4. the keepers *did shake*, and became as dead
Heb12:26. I *shake* not the earth only,
Rev. 6:13. *when she is shaken* of a mighty wind.

4582 9 754/890 *selas* (brilliancy)
σελήνη, seleenee.

Mat.24:29. the *moon* shall not give her light,
Mar13:24. the *moon* shall not give her light,
Lu. 21:25. signs in the sun, and in the *moon*,
Acts 2:20. and the *moon* into blood,
1Co.15:41. and another glory of the *moon*,
Rev. 6:12. and the *moon* became as blood;
8:12. and the third part of the *moon*,
12: 1. and the *moon* under her feet,
21:23. no need of the sun, neither of the *moon*,

4583 2 754/890 4582
σεληνιάζομαι, seleeniazomai.

Mat. 4:24. and those *which were lunatick*,
17:15. for he *is lunatick*,

4585 1 754/890
σεμίδαλις, semidalis.

Rev.18:13. and *fine flour*, and wheat,

4586 4 754/890 7:168 4576
σεμνός, semnos.

Phi. 4: 8. whatsoever things (are) *honest*.
1Ti. 3: 8. Likewise (must) the deacons (be) *grave*,
11. Even so (must their) wives (be) *grave*,
Tit. 2: 2. the aged men be sober, *grave*,

4587 3 754/890 7:168 4586
σεμνότης, semnotees.

1Ti. 2: 2. in all godliness and *honesty*.
3: 4. children in subjection with all *gravity*;
Tit. 2: 7. uncorruptness, *gravity*, sincerity,

4591 6 755/890 7:200 *sēma* (mark)
σημαίνω, seemaino.

Joh.12:33. *signifying* what death he should die.
18:32. *signifying* what death he
21:19. *signifying* by what death he should
Acts11:28. and *signified* by the spirit that
25:27. *to signify* the crimes (laid) against him.
Rev. 1: 1. and *signified* (it) by his angel unto

4592 77 755/890 7:200 rt 4591
σημεῖον, seemīon.

Mat.12:38. we would see a *sign* from thee.
39. seeketh after a *sign*; and there shall no *sign* be given to it, but the *sign* of the prophet Jonas:
16: 1. would shew them a *sign*
3. (discern) the *signs* of the times?
4. seeketh after a *sign*; and there shall no *sign* be given unto it. but the *sign* of the prophet Jonas.
Mat.24: 3. and what (shall be) the *sign* of thy
24. and shall shew great *signs*
30. shall appear the *sign* of the Son of man
26:48. gave them a *sign*, saying,
Mar 8:11. seeking of him a *sign* from heaven,
12. this generation seek after a *sign*?
— no *sign* be given unto this generation.
13: 4. and what (shall be) the *sign* when all
22. and shall shew *signs* and wonders,
16:17. And these *signs* shall follow them
20. confirming the word with *signs* following.
Lu. 2:12. And this (shall be) a *sign* unto you;
34. and for a *sign* which shall be spoken
11:16. sought of him a *sign* from heaven.
29. they seek a *sign*; and there shall no *sign* be given it, but the *sign* of Jonas the prophet.
30. For as Jonas was a *sign* unto the
21: 7. what *sign* (will there be) when
11. and great *signs* shall there be
25. And there shall be *signs* in the sun,
23: 8. to have seen some *miracle*
Joh. 2:11. This beginning of *miracles*
18. What *sign* shewest thou unto us,
23. saw the *miracles* which he did.
3: 2. can do these *miracles*
4:48. Except ye see *signs* and wonders,
54. This (is) again the second *miracle*
6: 2. because they saw his *miracles*
14. they had seen the *miracle* that
26. not because ye saw the *miracles*,
30. What *sign* shewest thou then,
7:31. will he do more *miracles*
9:16. that is a sinner do such *miracles*?
10:41. John did no *miracle*:
11:47. this man doeth many *miracles*.
12:18. he had done this *miracle*.
37. he had done so many *miracles*
20:30. And many other *signs* truly did Jesus
Acts 2:19. and *signs* in the earth beneath;
22. by miracles and wonders and *signs*,
43. many wonders and *signs* were done
4:16. a notable *miracle* hath been done
22. on whom this *miracle* of healing
30. that *signs* and wonders may be done
5:12. were many *signs* and wonders wrought
6: 8. did great wonders and *miracles*
7:36. had shewed wonders and *signs* in the
8: 6. seeing the *miracles* which he did.
13. beholding the miracles and *signs* which
14: 3. and granted *signs* and wonders to be done
15:12. declaring what *miracles* and wonders
Ro. 4:11. And he received the *sign* of circumcision,
15:19. Through mighty *signs* and wonders,
1Co. 1:22. For the Jews require a *sign*, and the
14:22. Wherefore tongues are for a *sign*, not
2Co.12:12. Truly the *signs* of an apostle were
— in *signs*, and wonders, and mighty deeds
2Th. 2: 9. all power and *signs* and lying wonders,
3:17. which is the *token* in every epistle:
Heb 2: 4. witness, both with *signs* and wonders,
Rev.12: 1. appeared a great *wonder* in heaven;
3. appeared another *wonder* in heaven;
13:13. And he doeth great *wonders*,
14. those *miracles* which he had power to do
15: 1. And I saw another *sign* in heaven,
16:14. the spirits of devils, working *miracles*,
19:20. the false prophet that wrought *miracles*

Note.—In Acts 8:13 some copies read *δυνάμεις καὶ σημεῖα μεγάλα γινόμενα*, with which the order of words in the English Translation agrees.

4593 1 756/891 7:200 4592
σημειόομαι, seemīöömai.

2Th. 3:14. *note* that man, and have no company

4594 41 756/891 7:269 2250 cf 3588
σήμερον, seemeron.

Mat. 6:11. Give us *this day* our daily bread.
30. which *to day* is, and to morrow
11:23. it would have remained until *this day*.
16: 3. (It will be) foul weather *to day*:
21:28. go work *to day* in my vineyard.
27: 8. called, The field of blood, unto *this day*.
19. suffered many things *this day* in a dream
28:15. reported among the Jews until *this day*.
Mar 14:30. That *this day*, (even) in this night,
Lu. 2:11. For unto you is born *this day*
4:21. *This day* is this scripture fulfilled
5:26. We have seen strange things *to day*.
12:28. which is *to day* in the field,
13:32. and I do cures *to day* and to morrow,
33. I must walk *to day*, and to morrow,
19: 5. for *to day* I must abide at thy house.
9. *This day* is salvation come
22:34. the cock shall not crow *this day*,
23:43. *To day* shalt thou be with me
24:21. *to day* is the third day since
Acts 4: 9. If we *this day* be examined
13:33. *this day* have I begotten thee.
19:40. called in question for *this day's* uproar,
20:26. I take you to record *this day*,
22: 3. as ye all are *this day*.
24:21. I am called in question by you *this day*.
26: 2. I shall answer for myself *this day*
29. but also all that hear me *this day*,
27:33. *This day* is the fourteenth day
Ro. 11: 8. unto this day. (lit. unto the *to day* day)
2Co. 3:14. for until *this day* remaineth
15. But even unto *this day*, when Moses
Heb 1: 5. *this day* have I begotten thee?
3: 7. *To day* if ye will hear his voice,
13. while it is called *To day*;
15. *To day* if ye will hear his voice,
4: 7. *To day*, after so long a time;
— *To day* if ye will hear his voice,
5: 5. *to day* have I begotten thee.
13: 8. the same yesterday, and *to day*, and for ever.
Jas. 4:13. *To day* or to morrow we will go

4595 1 756/892 7:94
σήπω, seepo.

Jas. 5: 2. Your riches *are corrupted*,

4596 1 756/894
σηρικόν, seerikon.

Rev.18:12. and purple, and *silk*, and scarlet,

4597 3 756/892 7:275 [5580]
σής, sees.

Mat. 6:19. where *moth* and rust doth corrupt,
20. where neither *moth* nor rust
Lu. 12:33. neither *moth* corrupteth.

4598 1 758/892 7:275 4597,977
σητόβρωτος, seetobrōtos.

Jas. 5: 2. and your garments are *motheaten*.

4599 1 756/892 *sthenos* (vigor)
σθενόω, sthenoō.

1Pet.5:10. stablish, *strengthen*, settle (you).

4600 2 756/892
σιαγών, siagōn.

Mat. 5:39. smite thee on thy right *cheek*,
Lu. 6:29. smiteth thee on the (one) *cheek*

4601 9 757/892 4602
σιγάω, sigao.

Lu. 9:36. And they *kept* (it) *close*,
20:26. and *held* their *peace*.
Acts12:17 beckoning unto...*to hold* their *peace*,
15:12. Then all the multitude *kept silence*,
13. after they *had held* their *peace*,
Ro. 16:25. of the mystery, *which was kept secret*
1Co.14:28. *let* him *keep silence* in the church;
30. *let* the first *hold* his *peace*.
34. *Let* your women *keep silence* in the

4602 2 757/892 cf 4623 *sizō* (to hiss)
σιγή, sigee.

Acts21:40. And when there was made a great *silence*,
Rev. 8: 1. there was *silence* in heaven

4603 5 757/892 4604
σιδήρεος, sidereos.

Acts12:10. they came unto the *iron* gate
Rev. 2:27. And he shall rule them with a rod *of iron*:
9: 9. as it were breastplates *of iron*;
12: 5. to rule all nations with a rod *of iron*:
19:15. he shall rule them with a rod *of iron*:

4604 1 757/892
σίδηρος, sideeros.

Rev.18:12. and of brass, and *iron*, and marble,

4607 1 757/892 7:278 cf 5406
σικάριος, sikarios.

Acts21:38. men that were *murderers*?

4608 1 757/892 [7941]
σίκερα, sikera.

Lu. 1:15. neither wine nor *strong drink*,

4612 1 758/893
σιμικίνθιον, simikinthion.

Acts19:12. handkerchiefs or *aprons*, and the

4615 5 759/893 7:287 *sinomai* (to hurt)
σίναπι, sinapi.

Mat.13:31. is like to a grain of *mustard seed*,
17:20. faith as a grain of *mustard seed*,
Mar 4:31. (It is) like a grain of *mustard seed*,
Lu. 13:19. It is like a grain of *mustard seed*,
17: 6. faith as a grain of *mustard seed*,

4616 6 759/894
σινδών, sindōn.

Mat.27:59. wrapped it in a clean *linen cloth*,
Mar 14:51. having a *linen cloth* cast about
52. And he left the *linen cloth*,
15:46. And he bought *fine linen*,
— and wrapped him in the *linen*,
Lu. 23:53. and wrapped it in *linen*, and laid

4617 1 759/894 7:291 *sinion* (sieve)
σινιάζω, siniazo.

Lu. 22:31. that he may *sift* (you) as wheat:

4618 3 759/894 4621

σιτευτός, sitūtos.

Lu. 15:23. And bring hither the *fatted* calf,
27. hath killed the *fatted* calf,
30. killed for him the *fatted* calf.

4619 1 759/894 4621

σιτιστός, sitistos.

Mat.22: 4. and (my) *fatlings* (are) killed,

4620 1 759/894 4621,3358

σιτομέτριον, sitometrion.

Lu. 12:42. to give (them their) *portion of meat* in due season?

4621 14 759/894

σῖτος, sitos.

Mat. 3:12. and gather his *wheat* into the garner;
13:25. and sowed tares among the *wheat,*
29. ye root up also the *wheat* with them.
30. but gather the *wheat* into my barn.
Mar 4:28. after that the full *corn* in the ear.
Lu. 3:17. will gather the *wheat* into his garner;
16: 7. An hundred measures of *wheat.*
22:31. that he may sift (you) as *wheat:*
Joh. 12:24. Except a corn of *wheat* fall into
Acts 7:12. heard that there was *corn* in Egypt,
27:38. and cast out the *wheat* into the sea.
1Co.15:37. it may chance of *wheat,*
Rev. 6: 6. A measure of *wheat* for a penny,
18:13. and fine flour, and *wheat,*

4623 11 760/894 cf 4602 cf 2974
siōpē (silence)

σιωπάω, siōpao.

Mat.20:31. because they *should hold* their *peace:*
26:63. But Jesus *held* his *peace.*
Mar 3: 4. But they *held* their *peace.*
4:39. *Peace,* be still.
9:34. But they *held* their *peace.*
10:48. that he *should hold* his *peace*
14:61. But he *held* his *peace,*
Lu. 1:20. *dumb,* and not able to speak,
18:39. rebuked him, that he *should hold* his *peace:*
19:40. if these *should hold* their *peace,*
Acts18: 9. speak, and *hold* not thy *peace:*

4624 30 760/894 7:339 4625

σκανδαλίζω, scandalizo.

Mat. 5:29. if thy right eye *offend* thee,
30. if thy right hand *offend* thee,
11: 6. whosoever shall not *be offended* in me.
13:21. by and by he *is offended.*
57. And they *were offended* in him.
15:12. that the Pharisees *were offended,* after
17:27. lest we *should offend* them, go thou
18: 6. whoso shall *offend* one of these little
8. if thy hand or thy foot *offend* thee,
9. And if thine eye *offend* thee,
24:10. And then *shall* many *be offended,*
26:31. All ye *shall be offended* because of me
33. Though all (men) *shall be offended* because of thee, (yet) *will* I never *be offended.*
Mar 4:17. immediately they *are offended.*
6: 3. And they *were offended* at him.
9:42. whosoever shall *offend* one of (these)
43. And if thy hand *offend* thee,
45. And if thy foot *offend* thee,
47. And if thine eye *offend* thee,
Mar 14:27. All ye *shall be offended* because of me
29. Although all *shall be offended,*
Lu. 7:23. whosoever *shall* not *be offended* in me.
17: 2. than that he *should offend* one of these
Joh. 6:61. *Doth* this *offend* you?
16: 1. that ye *should* not *be offended.*
Ro. 14:21. stumbleth, or *is offended,*
1Co. 8:13. if meat *make* my brother *to offend,*
— lest I *make* my brother *to offend.*
2Co.11:29. who *is offended,* and I burn not?

4625 15 760/894 7:339 2578

σκάνδαλον, scandalon.

Mat.13:41. all *things that offend,*
16:23. thou art an *offence* unto me:
18: 7. Woe unto the world because of *offences!* for it must needs be that *offences* come;
— by whom the *offence* cometh!
Lu. 17: 1. but that *offences* will come:
Ro. 9:33. and rock of *offence:*
11: 9. a *stumblingblock,* and a recompence
14:13. or an *occasion to fall* in (his) brother's way.
16:17. which cause divisions and *offences*
1Co. 1:23. unto the Jews a *stumblingblock,* and unto
Gal. 5:11. then is the *offence* of the cross ceased.
1Pet.2: 8(7). a stone of stumbling, and a rock of *offence,*
1Joh. 2:10. there is none *occasion of stumbling* in him.
Rev. 2:14. to cast a *stumblingblock* before the

4626 3 760/895

σκάπτω, skapto.

Lu. 6:48. and *digged* deep, (lit. who *digged* and deepened)
13: 8. till I *shall dig* about it,
16: 3. I cannot *dig;* to beg

4627 3 761/895

σκάφη, skaphee.

Acts27:16. much work to come by the *boat:*
30. when they had let down the *boat*
32. cut off the ropes of the *boat,* and let

4628 3 761/895 *skellō* (to parch)

σκέλος, skelos.

Joh.19:31. that their *legs* might be broken,
32. brake the *legs* of the first, and of
33. they brake not his *legs:*

4629 1 761/895 *skepas* (covering)

σκέπασμα, skepasma.

1Ti. 6: 8. having food and *raiment* (lit. *coverings*)

4631 1 761/895 4632

σκευή, skūee.

Acts27:19. we cast out...the *tackling* of the ship.

4632 23 761/895 7:358

σκεῦος, skūos.

Mat.12:29. and spoil his *goods,* except
Mar 3:27. and spoil his *goods,* except
11:16. carry (any) *vessel* through the temple.
Lu. 8:16. a candle, covereth it with a *vessel,*
17:31. and his *stuff* in the house.

Joh. 19:29. there was set a *vessel* full of vinegar:
Acts 9:15. he is a chosen *vessel* unto me,
10:11. and a certain *vessel* descending
16. and the *vessel* was received up again
11: 5. A certain *vessel* descend,
27:17. strake *sail*, and so were driven.
Ro. 9:21. to make one *vessel* unto honour,
22. the *vessels* of wrath fitted to
23. on the *vessels* of mercy, which he
2Co. 4: 7. have this treasure in earthen *vessels*,
1Th. 4: 4. possess his *vessel* in sanctification
2Ti. 2:20. not only *vessels* of gold and of silver,
21. he shall be a *vessel* unto honour,
Heb 9:21. and all the *vessels* of the ministry.
1Pet.3: 7. as unto the weaker *vessel*,
Rev. 2:27. as the *vessels* of a potter shall they
18:12. all manner *vessels* of ivory, and all manner *vessels* of most precious wood,

4633 20 762/895 7:368 cf 4632 4639

σκηνή, *skeenee.*

Mat.17: 4. make here three *tabernacles;*
Mar 9: 5. make three *tabernacles;* one for thee,
Lu. 9:33. let us make three *tabernacles;* one
16: 9. receive you into everlasting *habitations.*
Acts 7:43. took up the *tabernacle* of Moloch,
44. Our fathers had the *tabernacle* of witness in the wilderness,
15:16. build again the *tabernacle* of David,
Heb 8: 2. of the true *tabernacle*, which the Lord
5. when he was about to make the *tabernacle:*
9: 1. Then verily the first (covenant) had (some copies read ἡ πρώτη σκηνή)
2. there was a *tabernacle* made; the first,
3. after the second veil, the *tabernacle* which is called the Holiest of all;
6. went always into the first *tabernacle*,
8. as the first *tabernacle* was yet standing:
11. by a greater and more perfect *tabernacle*,
21. with blood both the *tabernacle*, and
11: 9. dwelling in *tabernacles* with Isaac
13:10. which serve the *tabernacle.*
Rev.13: 6. blaspheme his name, and his *tabernacle*,
15: 5. the temple of the *tabernacle* of the testimony in heaven
21: 3. the *tabernacle* of God (is) with men,

4634 1 762/895 7:368 4636,4078

σκηνοπηγία, *skeenopeegia.*

Joh. 7: 2. the Jews' feast of *tabernacles* (lit. the *tabernacle-fixing*)

4635 1 762/895 7:368 4633,4160

σκηνοποιός, *skeenopoyos.*

Acts18: 3. they were *tentmakers.*

4636 2 762/895 7:368 4633

σκῆνος, *skeenos.*

2Co. 5: 1. our earthly house of (this) *tabernacle*
4. we that are in (this) *tabernacle* do groan,

4637 5 762/896 4636

σκηνόω, *skeenoō.*

Joh. 1:14. and *dwelt* among us, (lit. *tabernacled*)
Rev. 7:15. *shall dwell* among them. (lit. *shall tab.*)
12:12. heavens, and ye *that dwell* in them.
13: 6. and them *that dwell* in heaven.
21: 3. and he *will dwell* with them,

4638 3 763/896 7:368 4637

σκήνωμα, *skeenōma.*

Acts 7:46. to find a *tabernacle* for the God of Jacob.
2Pet. 1:13. as long as I am in this *tabernacle*,
14. I must put off (this) my *tabernacle*,

4639 7 763/896 7:394

σκιά, *skia.*

Mat. 4:16. sat in the region and *shadow* of death
Mar 4:32. may lodge under the *shadow* of it.
Lu. 1:79. and (in) the *shadow* of death,
Acts 5:15. the *shadow* of Peter passing by
Col. 2:17. Which are a *shadow* of things to come;
Heb 8: 5. the example and *shadow* of heavenly things,
10: 1. the law having a *shadow* of good things to come,

4640 3 763/896 7:401 *skairō* (to skip)

σκιρτάω, *skirtao.*

Lu. 1:41. the babe *leaped* in her womb;
44. the babe *leaped* in my womb for joy.
6:23. *leap for joy:* for, behold, your reward

4641 3 763/896 3:605 4642,2588

σκληροκαρδία, *skleerokardia.*

Mat.19: 8. because of the *hardness of* your *hearts*
Mar 10: 5. For the *hardness of* your *heart*
16:14. their unbelief and *hardness of heart*,

4642 6 763/896 5:1022 rt 4628

σκληρός, *skleeros.*

Mat.25:24. that thou art an *hard* man,
Joh. 6:60. This is an *hard* saying; who
Acts 9: 5. *hard* for thee to kick against
26:14. *hard* for thee to kick against
Jas. 3: 4. driven of *fierce* winds,
Jude 15. and of all their *hard* (speeches) which

4643 1 763/896 5:1022 4642

σκληρότης, *skleerotees.*

Ro. 2: 5. thy *hardness* and impenitent heart

4644 1 763/896 5:1022 4642 5137

σκληροτράχηλος, *skleerotrakeelos.*

Acts 7:51. Ye *stiffnecked* and uncircumcised

4645 6 763/896 5:1022 4642

σκληρύνω, *skleeruno.*

Acts19: 9. But when divers *were hardened*,
Ro. 9:18. and whom he will he *hardeneth.*
Heb 3: 8. *Harden* not your hearts, as in
13. lest any of you *be hardened*
15. *harden* not your hearts, as in
4: 7. *harden* not your hearts.

4646 4 763/896 7:403 rt 4628

σκολιός, *skolios.*

Lu. 3: 5. and the *crooked* shall be made straight,
Acts 2:40. from this *untoward* generation.
Phi. 2:15. in the midst of a *crooked* and perverse nation,
1Pet 2:18. but also to the *froward.*

4647 1 763/896 7:409 rt 4628 3700
σκόλοψ, skọlops.

2Co.12: 7. was given to me a *thorn* in the flesh,

4648 6 764/896 7:413 4649 cf 3700
σκοπέω, skopeo.

Lu. 11:35. *Take heed* therefore that the light
Ro. 16:17. *mark* them which cause divisions
2Co. 4:18. *While* we *look* not *at* the things which
Gal. 6: 1. *considering* thyself, lest thou also
Phi. 2: 4. *Look* not every man *on* his own
3:17. *mark* them which walk so as

4649 1 764/896 7:413 *skeptomai* (to peer about)
σκοπός, skopos.

Phi. 3:14. I press toward the *mark*

4650 5 764/896 7:418 rt 4651
σκορπίζω, skorpizo.

Mat.12:30. gathereth not with me *scattereth abroad.*
Lu. 11:23. he that gathereth not with me *scattereth.*
Joh.10:12. the wolf catcheth them, and *scattereth*
16:32. is now come, that ye shall *be scattered,*
2Co. 9: 9. He *hath dispersed abroad;* he hath

4651 5 764/896 *skerpō* (to pierce)
σκορπίος, skorpios.

Lu. 10:19. to tread on serpents and *scorpions,*
11:12. will he offer him a *scorpion?*
Rev. 9: 3. as the *scorpions* of the earth have power.
5. as the torment of a *scorpion,*
10. tails like unto *scorpions,*

4652 3 764/896 7:423 4655
σκοτεινός, skotīnos.

Mat. 6:23. body shall be *full of darkness.*
Lu. 11:34. thy body also (is) *full of darkness.*
36. having no part *dark,*

4653 16 764/896 7:423 4655
σκοτία, skotia.

Mat.10:27. What I tell you in *darkness,*
Lu. 12: 3. whatsoever ye have spoken in *darkness*
Joh. 1: 5. the light shineth in *darkness;* and the *darkness* comprehended it not.
6:17. And it was now *dark,*
8:12. shall not walk in *darkness,*
12:35. lest *darkness* come upon you: for he that walketh in *darkness*
46. should not abide in *darkness.*
20: 1. when it was yet *dark,*
1Joh.1: 5. in him is no *darkness* at all.
2: 8. because the *darkness* is past,
9. is in *darkness* even until now.
11. is in *darkness,* and walketh in *darkness,*
— because that *darkness* hath blinded

4654 8 764/896 7:423 4655
σκοτίζομαι, skotizomai.

Mat.24:29. *shall* the sun *be darkened,*
Mar.13:24. the sun *shall be darkened,* and the
Lu. 23:45. the sun *was darkened,* and the veil
Ro. 1:21. their foolish heart *was darkened.*
11:10. *Let* their eyes *be darkened,*
Eph 4:18. Having the understanding *darkened,*
Rev. 8:12. so as the third part of them *was darkened,*
9: 2. the sun and the air *were darkened*

4656 1 765/897 7:423 4655
σκοτόομαι, skotŏŏmai.

Rev.16:10. his kingdom was *full of darkness;* (lit. *darkened*)

4655 32 764/897 7:423 rt 4639
σκότος, skotos.

Mat. 4:16. The people which sat in *darkness.*
6:23. be *darkness,* how great (is) that *darkness*
8:12. be cast out into outer *darkness:*
22:13. cast (him) into outer *darkness;*
25:30. unprofitable servant into outer *darkness:*
27:45. there was *darkness* over all the land
Mar 15:33. there was *darkness* over the whole land
Lu. 1:79. light to them that sit in *darkness*
11:35. the light which is in thee be not *darkness.*
22:53. your hour, and the power of *darkness.*
23:44. there was a *darkness* over all the earth
Joh. 3:19. men loved *darkness* rather than light,
Acts 2:20. The sun shall be turned into *darkness,*
13:11. fell on him a mist and a *darkness;*
26:18. to turn (them) from *darkness* to light,
Ro. 2:19. a light of them which are in *darkness*
13:12. cast off the works of *darkness,*
1Co. 4: 5. the hidden things of *darkness,*
2Co. 4: 6. the light to shine out of *darkness,*
6:14. what communion hath light with *darkness?*
Eph 5: 8. ye were sometimes *darkness,*
11. the unfruitful works of *darkness,*
6:12. the rulers of the *darkness* of this world,
Col. 1:13. delivered us from the power of *darkness*
1Th. 5: 4. ye, brethren, are not in *darkness,*
5. we are not of the night, nor of *darkness.*
Heb 12:18. nor unto blackness, and *darkness,* and
1Pet.2: 9. called you out of *darkness* into his
2Pet.2:17. mist of *darkness* is reserved for ever.
1Joh.1: 6. and walk in *darkness,* we lie,
Jude 13. the blackness of *darkness* for ever.

Note.—It occurs in Heb. 12:18 as the dat. sing. of the second declension.

4657 1 765/897 7:445 1519,2965 906
σκύβαλον, skubalon.

Phi. 3: 8. and do count them (but) *dung,*

4659 2 765/897 7:450 3700 *skuthros* (sullen)
σκυθρωπός, skuthrōpos.

Mat. 6:16. as the hypocrites, *of a sad countenance:*
Lu. 24:17. as ye walk, and are *sad?*

4660 3 765/897
σκυλλω, skullo.

Mar 5:35. why *troublest* thou the Master
Lu. 7: 6. Lord, *trouble* not thy*self:* for I
8:49. *trouble* not the Master.

4661 1 765/897 4660
σκῦλον, skulon.

Lu. 11.22 and divideth his *spoils.*

4662 1 765/897 4663,977

σκωληκόϐρωτος, skōleekobrōtos.

Acts12:23. and he was *eaten of worms*,

4663 3 765/897 7:452

σκώληξ, skōleex.

Mar 9:44. Where their *worm* dieth not,
46. Where their *worm* dieth not,
48. Where their *worm* dieth not,

4664 1 765/897 4665

σμαράγδινος, smaragdinos.

Rev. 4: 3. in sight like unto an *emerald*.

4665 1 765/897

σμάραγδος, smaragdos.

Rev.21:19. the fourth, an *emerald* ;

4666 2 766/897 7:457 3464

σμύρνα, smurna.

Mat. 2:11. gold, and frankincense, and *myrrh*.
Joh. 19:39. a mixture of *myrrh* and aloes,

4669 1 766/897 7:457 4667

σμυρνίζομαι, smurnizomai.

Mar 15:23. wine *mingled with myrrh* : but he

4671 221 779/910 4771

σοί, soi.

From συ.

Mat. 2:13. until I bring *thee* word:
4: 9. All these things will I give *thee*,
5:26. Verily I say unto *thee*,
29. for it is profitable for *thee*
30. for it is profitable for *thee*
40. if any man will sue *thee* at the law,
6: 4. himself shall reward *thee* openly.
6. shall reward *thee* openly.
18. shall reward *thee* openly.
23. the light that is in *thee* be darkness,
8:13. (so) be it done unto *thee*.
19. Master, I will follow *thee*
29. What have we to do with *thee*, Jesus,
9: 2. thy sins be forgiven *thee*.
5. (Thy) sins be forgiven *thee* ;
11:21. woe unto *thee*, Chorazin! woe unto *thee*, Bethsaida!
23. works, which have been done in *thee*,
24. in the day of judgment, than for *thee*.
25. I thank *thee*, O Father, Lord of heaven
12:47. desiring to speak with *thee*.
14: 4. It is not lawful for *thee* to have
15:28. be it unto *thee* even as thou wilt.
16:17. hath not revealed (it) unto *thee*,
18. And I say also unto *thee*, That thou art
19. And I will give unto *thee* the keys
22. Be it far from *thee*, Lord: this shall not be unto *thee*.
17: 4. three tabernacles; one for *thee*,
25. What thinkest *thou*, Simon?
18: 8. it is better for *thee* to enter into life
9. it is better for *thee* to enter into life
17. let him be unto *thee* as an heathen man
22. I say not unto *thee*, Until seven times:
26. and I will pay *thee* all.
29. and I will pay *thee* all.

Mat.18:32. I forgave *thee* all that debt,
19:27. have forsaken all, and followed *thee*
20:14. unto this last, even as unto *thee*
21: 5. thy King cometh unto *thee*,
23. and who gave *thee* this authority?
22:16. neither carest *thou* for any (man):
17. What thinkest *thou*?
25:44. and did not minister unto *thee*?
26:17. that we prepare for *thee* to eat
33. shall be offended because of *thee*,
34. Verily I say unto *thee*,
35. Though I should die with *thee*,
27:19. Have *thou* nothing to do with that just man:
Mar 1:24. what have we to do with *thee*,
2: 5. thy sins be forgiven *thee*.
9. (Thy) sins be forgiven *thee* ;
11. I say unto *thee*, Arise,
4:38. Master, carest *thou* not that we
5: 7. What have I to do with *thee*, Jesus,
9. What (is) *thy* name?
19. how great things the Lord hath done for *thee*,
41. Damsel, I say unto *thee*, arise.
6:18. It is not lawful for *thee*
22. and I will give (it) *thee*.
23. I will give (it) *thee*,
9: 5. three tabernacles; one for *thee*,
25. (Thou) dumb and deaf spirit, I charge *thee*,
43. better for *thee* to enter into life maimed,
45. better for *thee* to enter halt into life,
47. better for *thee* to enter into the kingdom
10:21. One thing *thou* lackest:
28. and have followed *thee*.
51. that I should do unto *thee*?
11:28. and who gave *thee* this authority
12:14. and)(carest for no man:
14:30. Verily I say unto *thee*,
31. If I should die with *thee*,
36. all things (are) possible unto *thee* ;
Lu. 1: 3. to write unto *thee* in order,
13. Elisabeth shall bear *thee* a son,
14. And *thou* shalt have joy and gladness;
19. and to shew *thee* these glad tidings.
35. the power of the Highest shall overshadow *thee*:
3:22. in *thee* I am well pleased.
4: 6. All this power will I give *thee*,
34. what have we to do with *thee*,
5:20. thy sins are forgiven *thee*.
23. Thy sins be forgiven *thee* ;
24. I say unto *thee*, Arise,
7:14. Young man, I say unto *thee*, Arise.
40. I have somewhat to say unto *thee*.
47. Wherefore I say unto *thee*,
8:28. What have I to do with *thee*, Jesus,
30. saying, What is *thy* name?
39. how great things God hath done unto *thee*.
9:33. three tabernacles; one for *thee*,
57. I will follow *thee* whithersoever thou
61. Lord, I will follow *thee* ;
10:13. Woe unto *thee*, Chorazin! woe unto *thee* Bethsaida!
21. I thank *thee*, O Father, Lord of heaven
35. when I come again, I will repay *thee*.
36. Which now of these three, thinkest *thou*,
40. Lord, dost *thou* not care that my sister
11: 7. I cannot rise and give *thee*.
35. that the light which is in *thee* be not
12:59. I tell *thee*, thou shalt not depart thence,
14: 9. and say to *thee*, Give this man place,

Lu. 14:10. say unto *thee*, Friend, go up higher: then shalt *thou* have worship in the presence of them that sit at meat with *thee*.
12. and a recompence be made *thee*.
14. for they cannot recompense *thee*: for *thou* shalt be recompensed at
15:29. these many years do I serve *thee*,
18:11. God, I thank *thee*, that I am not as other men
22. Yet lackest *thou* one thing:
28. we have left all, and followed *thee*.
41. What wilt thou that I shall do unto *thee*?
19:43. shall cast a trench about *thee*,
44. and thy children within *thee*;
— leave in *thee* one stone upon another;
20: 2. who is he that gave *thee* this authority?
22:11. The Master saith unto *thee*,
34. And he said, I tell *thee*, Peter,
23:43. Verily I say unto *thee*,
Joh. 1:50(51). Because I said unto *thee*, I saw thee
2: 4. what have I to do with *thee*?
3: 3. Verily, verily, I say unto *thee*,
5. Verily, verily, I say unto *thee*,
7. Marvel not that I said unto *thee*,
11. Verily, verily, I say unto *thee*
4:10. who it is that saith to *thee*,
— he would have given *thee* living water.
26. I that speak unto *thee* am (he).
5:10. it is not lawful for *thee* to carry (thy) bed.
12. What man is that which said unto *thee*,
14. lest a worse thing come unto *thee*.
6:30. that we may see, and believe *thee*?
9:26. What did he to *thee*?
11:22. God will give (it) *thee*.
40. Said I not unto *thee*, that, if thou
41. Father, I thank *thee* that thou hast heard
13:37. Lord, why cannot I follow *thee* now?
38. Verily, verily, I say unto *thee*,
17: 5. which I had with *thee* before the world
21. as thou, Father, (art) in me, and I in *thee*,
18:30. have delivered him up unto *thee*.
34. or did others tell it *thee* of me?
19:11. except it were given *thee* from above: therefore he that delivered me unto *thee*
21: 3. We also go with *thee*.
18. Verily, verily, I say unto *thee*,
Acts 3: 6. but such as I have give I *thee*:
5: 4. Whiles it remained, was it not *thine own*?
7: 3. into the land which I shall shew *thee*.
8:20. Thy money perish with *thee*,
21. *Thou* hast neither part nor lot
22. thought of thine heart may be forgiven *thee*.
9: 5. hard for *thee* to kick against the pricks.
6. and it shall be told *thee*
17. Jesus, that appeared unto *thee*
10: 6. he shall tell *thee* what thou oughtest to do.
32. when he cometh, shall speak unto *thee*.
33. all things that are commanded *thee*
16:18. I command *thee* in the name of
18:10. and no man shall set on *thee*
21:23. this that we say to *thee*:
22:10. there it shall be told *thee* of all things which are appointed for *thee* to do.
23:18. who hath something to say unto *thee*.
24:14. But this I confess unto *thee*,
26: 1. *Thou* art permitted to speak for thyself.
14. hard for *thee* to kick against the pricks.
16. I have appeared unto *thee* for this purpose,
— in the which I will appear unto *thee*;
27:24. lo, God hath given *thee* all them

Ro. 9: 7. In Isaac shall *thy* seed be called.
17. that I might shew my power in *thee*,
13: 4. the minister of God to *thee* for good.
15: 9. I will confess to *thee* among the Gentiles
1Co. 7:21. care)(not for it:
2Co. 6: 2. have I succoured *thee*:
12: 9. My grace is sufficient for *thee*:
Gal. 3: 8. In *thee* shall all nations be blessed.
Eph. 5:14. and Christ shall give *thee* light.
6: 3. That it may be well with *thee*,
1Ti. 1:18. This charge I commit unto *thee*.
3:14. These things write I unto *thee*,
4:14. Neglect not the gift that is in *thee*, which was given *thee*
6:13. I give *thee* charge in the sight of
2Ti. 1: 5. the unfeigned faith that is in *thee*,
— and I am persuaded that in *thee* also.
6. the gift of God, which is in *thee*
2: 7. and the Lord give *thee* understanding
Tit. 1: 5. in every city, as I had appointed *thee*:
Philem 8. to injoin *thee* that which is convenient,
11. was to *thee* unprofitable, but now profitable to *thee* and to me;
16. but how much more unto *thee*,
19. albeit I do not say to *thee* how thou
21. I wrote unto *thee*, knowing that
Heb. 8: 5. the pattern shewed to *thee* in the mount.
11:18. in Isaac shall *thy* seed be called:
Jas. 2:18. I will shew *thee* my faith by my works.
2Joh. 5. I wrote a new commandment unto *thee*,
3Joh. 13. with ink and pen write unto *thee*:
14. Peace (be) to *thee*.
Jude 9. but said, The Lord rebuke *thee*.
Rev. 2: 5. I will come unto *thee* quickly,
10. and I will give *thee* a crown of life.
16. I will come unto *thee* quickly,
3:18. I counsel *thee* to buy of me
4: 1. and I will shew *thee* things
11:17. We give *thee* thanks, O Lord
14:15. for the time is come for *thee* to reap;
17: 1. I will shew unto *thee* the judgment
7. I will tell *thee* the mystery
18:22. shall be heard no more at all in *thee*,
— shall be found any more in *thee*;
— shall be heard no more at all in *thee*;
23. shall shine no more at all in *thee*;
— shall be heard no more at all in *thee*:
21: 9. Come hither, I will shew *thee* the bride,

4673 1 766/898 cf rt 4987

σορός, *soros.*

Lu. 7:14. And he came and touched the *bier*:

4674 27 766/898 4771

σός, *sos.*

Mat. 7: 3. the beam that is in *thine own* eye?
22. prophesied in *thy* name? and in *thy* name have cast out devils? and in *thy* name
13:27. sow good seed in *thy* field?
20:14. Take (that) *thine* (is), and go thy way:
24: 3. and what (shall be) the sign of *thy* coming,
25:25. lo, (there) thou hast (that is) *thine*
Mar 2:18. but *thy* disciples fast not?
5:19. Go home to *thy friends*,
Lu. 5:33. but *thine* eat and drink?
6:30. of him that taketh away *thy goods*
15:31. and all that I have is *thine*.
22:42. not my will, but *thine*, be done.
Joh. 4:42. we believe, not because of *thy* saying.

Joh. 17: 6. *thine* they were, and thou gavest them me;
9. for they are *thine*.
10. And all mine are *thine*, and *thine* are mine;
17. *thy* word is truth.
18:35. *Thine own* nation and the chief priests
Acts 5: 4. was it not in *thine own* power?
24: 2. done unto this nation by *thy* providence,
4. hear us of *thy* clemency a few words.
1Co. 8:11. And through *thy* knowledge shall the weak
14:16. at *thy* giving of thanks,
Philem. 14. But without *thy* mind would I do nothing;

4675 498 779/909 4771

σοῦ, *sou*.

From σύ.

Mat. 1:20. to take unto thee Mary *thy* wife:
2: 6. for out of *thee* shall come a Governor,
3:14. I have need to be baptized of *thee*,
4: 6. give his angels charge concerning *thee*:
— thou dash *thy* foot against a stone.
7. Thou shalt not tempt the Lord *thy* God.
10. Thou shalt worship the Lord *thy* God,
5:23. bring *thy* gift to the altar, and there rememberest that *thy* brother hath ought against *thee*;
24. Leave there *thy* gift
— first be reconciled to *thy* brother, and then come and offer *thy* gift.
25. Agree with *thine* adversary quickly,
29. if *thy* right eye offend thee, pluck it out, and cast (it) from *thee*:
— that one of *thy* members should perish, and not (that) *thy* whole body
30. And if *thy* right hand offend thee, cut it off, and cast (it) from *thee*:
— that one of *thy* members should perish, and not (that) *thy* whole body
33. perform unto the Lord *thine* oaths:
36. Neither shalt thou swear by *thy* head,
39. smite thee on *thy* right cheek,
40. and take away *thy* coat,
42. that would borrow of *thee*
43. Thou shalt love *thy* neighbour, and hate *thine* enemy.
6: 2. do not sound a trumpet before *thee*,
3. But when *thou* doest alms, let not *thy* left hand know what *thy* right hand doeth:
4. That *thine* alms may be in secret: and *thy* Father which seeth in secret
6. enter into *thy* closet, and when thou hast shut *thy* door, pray to *thy* Father which is in secret; and *thy* Father which seeth in secret
9. Hallowed be *thy* name.
10. *Thy* kingdom come. *Thy* will be done
13. For *thine* is the kingdom,
17. anoint *thine* head, and wash *thy* face;
18. but unto *thy* Father which is in secret: and *thy* Father, which
22. if therefore *thine* eye be single, *thy* whole body shall be full of light.
23. But if *thine* eye be evil, *thy* whole body shall be full of darkness.
7: 3. the mote that is in *thy* brother's eye,
4. Or how wilt thou say to *thy* brother, Let me pull out the mote out of *thine* eye; and, behold, a beam (is) in *thine own* eye?
5. cast out the beam out of *thine own* eye;
— to cast out the mote out of *thy* brother's eye.
9: 2. *thy* sins be forgiven thee.
6. take up *thy* bed, and go unto *thine* house.

Mat. 9:14. but *thy* disciples fast not?
18. lay *thy* hand upon her,
22. *thy* faith hath made thee whole.
11:10. my messenger before *thy* face, which shall prepare *thy* way before *thee*.
26. so it seemed good in *thy* sight.
12: 2. *thy* disciples do that which
13. Stretch forth *thine* hand.
37. by *thy* words thou shalt be justified, and by *thy* words thou shalt
38. we would see a sign from *thee*.
47. *thy* mother and *thy* brethren stand
15: 2. Why do *thy* disciples transgress
4. Honour *thy* father and mother:
28. O woman, great (is) *thy* faith:
17:16. And I brought him to *thy* disciples,
27. and give unto them for me and *thee*.
18: 8. if *thy* hand or *thy* foot offend thee, cut them off, and cast (them) from *thee*:
9. And if *thine* eye offend thee,
— cast (it) from *thee*:
15. if *thy* brother shall trespass against
— between *thee* and him alone: if he shall hear *thee*, thou hast gained *thy* brother.
16. take with *thee* one or two more,
33. have had compassion on *thy* fellowservant,
19:19. Honour *thy* father and (thy) mother:
— love *thy* neighbour as thyself.
21. (and) sell that *thou* hast,
20:15. Is *thine* eye evil, because I am good?
21. the one on *thy* right hand,
— in *thy* kingdom.
21: 5. Behold, *thy* King cometh unto thee,
19. Let no fruit grow on *thee* henceforward
22:37. Thou shalt love the Lord *thy* God with all *thy* heart, and with all *thy* soul, and with all *thy* mind.
39. love *thy* neighbour as thyself.
44. till I make *thine* enemies *thy* footstool?
23:37. have gathered *thy* children together,
25:21. into the joy of *thy* lord.
23. into the joy of *thy* lord.
25. and hid *thy* talent in the earth:
26:42. except I drink it, *thy* will be done.
52. Put up again *thy* sword into
62. (which) these witness against *thee*?
73. for *thy* speech bewrayeth thee.
27:13. they witness against *thee*?
Mar 1: 2. I send my messenger before *thy* face, which shall prepare *thy* way before *thee*.
44. and offer for *thy* cleansing
2: 5. *thy* sins be forgiven thee.
9. take up *thy* bed, and walk?
11. Arise, and take up *thy* bed, and go thy way into *thine* house.
3: 5. Stretch forth *thine* hand.
32. Behold, *thy* mother and *thy* brethren without seek for thee.
5:19. Go home (lit. to *thy* house) to thy friends,
34. *thy* faith hath made thee whole;
— and be whole of *thy* plague.
35. *Thy* daughter is dead: why
6:18. to have *thy* brother's wife.
7: 5. Why walk not *thy* disciples
10. Honour *thy* father and *thy* mother;
29. the devil is gone out of *thy* daughter
9:18. I spake to *thy* disciples
38. casting out devils in *thy* name,
43. And if *thy* hand offend thee,
45. And if *thy* foot offend thee,
47. And if *thine* eye offend thee,
10:19. Honour *thy* father and mother.

Mar 10:37. we may sit, one on *thy* right hand, and the other on *thy* left hand, in *thy* glory.
52. *thy* faith hath made thee whole.
11:14. eat fruit of *thee* hereafter
12:30. love the Lord *thy* God with all *thy* heart, and with all *thy* soul, and with all *thy* mind, and with all *thy* strength:
31. love *thy* neighbour as thyself.
36. till I make *thine* enemies *thy* footstool.
14:60. (which) these witness against *thee?*
70. and *thy* speech agreeth (thereto).
15: 4. they witness against *thee.*
Lu. 1:13. *thy* prayer is heard; and *thy* wife Elisabeth
28. the Lord (is) with *thee :*
35. which shall be born of *thee*
36. And, behold, *thy* cousin Elisabeth,
38. according to *thy* word. And
42. blessed (is) the fruit of *thy* womb.
44. the voice of *thy* salutation
61. There is none of *thy* kindred
2:29. now lettest thou *thy* servant depart in peace, according to *thy* word:
30. have seen *thy* salvation,
32. and the glory of *thy* people Israel.
35. shall pierce through *thy* own soul
48. *thy* father and I have sought thee
4: 7. all shall be *thine.*
8. shalt worship the Lord *thy* God,
10. He shall give his angels charge over *thee,*
11. thou dash *thy* foot against a stone.
12. Thou shalt not tempt the Lord *thy* God.
23. do also here in *thy* country.
5: 5. nevertheless at *thy* word
14. and offer for *thy* cleansing,
20. *thy* sins are forgiven thee.
23. *Thy* sins be forgiven thee;
24. take up *thy* couch, and go unto *thine* house.
6:10. Stretch forth *thy* hand.
29. him that taketh away *thy* cloke
41. the mote that is in *thy* brother's eye,
42. how canst thou say to *thy* brother, Brother,
— the mote that is in *thine* eye,
— the beam that is in *thine own* eye?
— first the beam out of *thine own* eye,
— the mote that is in *thy* brother's eye.
7:27. messenger before *thy* face, which shall prepare *thy* way before *thee.*
44. I entered into *thine* house,
48. *Thy* sins are forgiven.
50. *Thy* faith hath saved thee;
8:20. *Thy* mother and *thy* brethren
28. I beseech *thee,* torment me not.
39. Return to *thine own* house,
48. *thy* faith hath made thee whole;
49. *Thy* daughter is dead;
9:38. Master, I beseech *thee,* look upon
40. And I besought *thy* disciples to cast
41. Bring *thy* son hither.
49. casting out devils in *thy* name;
10:17. subject unto us through *thy* name.
21. it seemed good in *thy* sight.
27. Thou shalt love the Lord *thy* God with all *thy* heart, and with all *thy* soul, and with all *thy* strength, and with all *thy* mind; and *thy* neighbour as thyself.
11: 2. Hallowed be *thy* name. *Thy* kingdom come. *Thy* will be done,
34. when *thine* eye is single, *thy* whole body also is full of light;
— *thy* body also (is) full of darkness.
36. If *thy* whole body therefore
12:20. *thy* soul shall be required *of thee*

Lu. 12:58. goest with *thine* adversary
13:12. thou art loosed from *thine* infirmity.
26. eaten and drunk in *thy* presence.
34. gathered *thy* children together,
14: 8. a more honourable man than *thou*
12. call not *thy* friends, nor *thy* brethren, neither *thy* kinsmen,
15:18. sinned against heaven, and before *thee,*
19. no more worthy to be called *thy* son: make me as one of *thy* hired servants.
21. and in *thy* sight, and am no more worthy to be called *thy* son.
27. *Thy* brother is come; and *thy* father hath killed
29. transgressed I at any time *thy* commandment:
30. But as soon as this *thy* son was come, which hath devoured *thy* living
32. for this *thy* brother was dead, and is alive
16: 2. How is it that I hear this of *thee?* give an account of *thy* stewardship;
6. Take *thy* bill, and sit down quickly,
7. Take *thy* bill, and write fourscore.
25. thou in *thy* lifetime receivedst *thy* good
17: 3. If *thy* brother trespass against thee,
19. *thy* faith hath made thee whole.
18:20. Honour *thy* father and *thy* mother.
42. *thy* faith hath saved thee.
19: 5. I must abide at *thy* house.
16. Lord, *thy* pound hath gained ten
18. Lord, *thy* pound hath gained five
20. Lord, behold, (here is) *thy* pound,
22. Out of *thine own* mouth will I judge thee,
39. Master, rebuke *thy* disciples.
42. even thou, at least in this *thy* day, the things (which belong) unto *thy* peace but now they are hid from *thine* eyes.
43. *thine* enemies shall cast a trench about
44. and *thy* children within thee;
— the time of *thy* visitation.
20:43. Till I make *thine* enemies *thy* footstool.
22:32. But I have prayed for *thee,* that *thy* faith fail not:
— strengthen *thy* brethren.
33. I am ready to go with *thee,*
23:42. when thou comest into *thy* kingdom.
46. Father, into *thy* hands I commend
Joh. 2:17. The zeal of *thine* house hath
3:26. he that was with *thee* beyond Jordan,
4:16. Go, call *thy* husband, and come
18. whom thou now hast is not *thy* husband
50. Go thy way; *thy* son liveth.
51. saying, *Thy* son liveth.
53. *Thy* son liveth:
5: 8. Rise, take up *thy* bed, and walk.
11. Take up *thy* bed, and walk.
12. Take up *thy* bed, and walk?
7: 3. that *thy* disciples also may see the works that *thou* doest.
8:10. where are those *thine* accusers?
13. *thy* record is not true.
19. Where is *thy* Father?
9:10. How were *thine* eyes opened?
17. that he hath opened *thine* eyes?
26. how opened he *thine* eyes?
37. it is he that talketh with *thee.*
11:23. *Thy* brother shall rise again.
12:15. behold, *thy* King cometh,
28. Father, glorify *thy* name.
13:37. I will lay down my life for *thy* sake.
38. Wilt thou lay down *thy* life for my sake?
17: 1. glorify *thy* Son, that *thy* Son also may

Joh. 17: 6. I have manifested *thy* name unto the
— and they have kept *thy* word.
7. whatsoever thou hast given me are of *thee*.
8. that I came out from *thee*,
11. keep through *thine own* name those
12. I kept them in *thy* name:
14. I have given them *thy* word;
17. Sanctify them through *thy* truth.
26. declared unto them *thy* name,
18:11. Put up *thy* sword into the sheath:
19:26. Woman, behold *thy* son!
27. Behold *thy* mother!
20:27. Reach hither *thy* finger,
— and reach hither *thy* hand,
21:18. thou shalt stretch forth *thy* hands,
Acts 2:27. wilt thou suffer *thine* Holy One
28. full of joy with *thy* countenance.
35. Until I make *thy* foes *thy* footstool.
3:25. And in *thy* seed shall all the kindreds
4:25. by the mouth of *thy* servant David
27. against *thy* holy child Jesus,
28. whatsoever *thy* hand and *thy* counsel
29. and grant unto *thy* servants,
— they may speak *thy* word,
30. By stretching forth *thine* hand
— by the name of *thy* holy child Jesus.
5: 3. why hath Satan filled *thine* heart
4. conceived this thing in *thine* heart?
9. them which have buried *thy* husband
7: 3. Get thee out of *thy* country, and from *thy* kindred,
32. I (am) the God of *thy* fathers,
33. Put off thy shoes from *thy* feet:
8:20. *Thy* money perish with thee,
21. for *thy* heart is not right
22. Repent therefore of this *thy* wickedness,
— the thought of *thine* heart may
34. I pray *thee*, of whom speaketh the prophet
9:13. he hath done to *thy* saints
14. to bind all that call on *thy* name.
10: 4. *Thy* prayers and *thine* alms are come up
22. and to hear words of *thee*.
31. *thy* prayer is heard, and *thine* alms are
11:14. whereby thou and all *thy* house
12: 8. and bind on *thy* sandals.
— Cast *thy* garment about thee,
13:35. Thou shalt not suffer *thine* Holy One
14:10. Stand upright on *thy* feet.
16:31. thou shalt be saved, and *thy* house.
17:19. new doctrine, whereof *thou* speakest,
32. We will hear *thee* again of this (matter).
18:10. For I am with *thee*,
21:21. And they are informed of *thee*,
24. whereof they were informed concerning *thee*,
39. and I beseech *thee*, suffer me to speak
22:16. and wash away *thy* sins,
18. they will not receive *thy* testimony
20. the blood of *thy* martyr Stephen
23: 5. evil of the ruler of *thy* people.
21. looking for a promise from *thee*.
30. to say before *thee* what (they had) against him.
35. I will hear *thee*, said he, when *thine* accusers are also come.
24: 2. by *thee* we enjoy great quietness,
11. Because that *thou* mayest understand,
19. Who ought to have been here before *thee*,
25:26. specially before *thee*, O king Agrippa,
26: 2. answer for myself this day before *thee*
3. I beseech *thee* to hear me patiently.
16. and stand upon *thy* feet:

Acts27:24. given thee all them that sail with *thee*.
28:21. letters out of Judæa concerning *thee*.
— spake any harm of *thee*.
22. But we desire to hear of *thee*
Ro. 2: 5. But after *thy* hardness and
25. *thy* circumcision is made
3: 4. be justified in *thy* sayings,
4:18. So shall *thy* seed be.
8:36. For *thy* sake we are killed
10: 6. Say not in *thine* heart,
8. The word is nigh *thee*, (even) in *thy* mouth, and in *thy* heart:
9. confess with *thy* mouth the Lord Jesus, and shalt believe in *thine* heart
11: 3. Lord, they have killed *thy* prophets, and digged down *thine* altars:
21. lest he also spare not *thee*.
12:20. if *thine* enemy hunger,
13: 9. love *thy* neighbour as thyself.
14:10. why dost thou judge *thy* brother? or why dost thou set at nought *thy* brother?
15. But if *thy* brother be grieved
— Destroy not him with *thy* meat,
21. whereby *thy* brother stumbleth,
15: 9. and sing unto *thy* name.
1Co.12:21. I have no need of *thee*:
15:55. O death, where (is) *thy* sting? O grave, where (is) *thy* victory?
2Co. 6: 2. I have heard *thee* in a time accepted,
Gal. 3:16. And to *thy* seed, which is Christ.
5:14. Thou shalt love *thy* neighbour as thyself.
Eph 6: 2. Honour *thy* father and mother;
1Ti. 4:12. Let no man despise *thy* youth;
15. that *thy* profiting may appear to all.
16. and them that hear *thee*.
5:23. for *thy* stomach's sake and *thine* often infirmities.
6:21. Grace (be) with *thee*. Amen.
2Ti. 1: 3. I have remembrance of *thee*
4. being mindful of *thy* tears,
5. which dwelt first in *thy* grandmother Lois, and *thy* mother Eunice;
4: 5. make full proof of *thy* ministry.
22. The Lord Jesus Christ (be) with *thy* spirit.
Tit. 2:15. Let no man despise *thee*.
Philem. 2. and to the church in *thy* house:
4. making mention of *thee* always
5. Hearing of *thy* love and faith,
6. That the communication of *thy* faith
7. consolation in *thy* love,
— the saints are refreshed by *thee*,
13. in *thy* stead he might have ministered unto me
14. that *thy* benefit should not be as it were of necessity,
20. let me have joy of *thee* in the Lord:
21. Having confidence in *thy* obedience
Heb 1: 8. *Thy* throne, O God, (is) for ever and ever
— the sceptre of *thy* kingdom.
9. *thy* God, hath anointed thee with the oil of gladness above *thy* fellows.
10. the heavens are the works of *thine* hands:
12. and *thy* years shall not fail.
13. until I make *thine* enemies *thy* footstool?
2: 7. over the works of *thy* hands:
12. I will declare *thy* name unto my
10: 7. to do *thy* will, O God.
9. I come to do *thy* will, O God.
Jas. 2: 8. Thou shalt love *thy* neighbour as thyself.
18. shew me *thy* faith without *thy* works,
2Joh. 4. I found of *thy* children walking in

2Joh. 13. The children of *thy* elect sister
3Joh. 2. even as *thy* soul prospereth.
3. testified of the truth that is in *thee,*
6. borne witness of *thy* charity
Rev. 2: 2. I know *thy* works, and *thy* labour, and *thy* patience,
4. I have (somewhat) against *thee*, because thou hast left *thy* first love.
5. and will remove *thy* candlestick
9. I know *thy* works, and
13. I know *thy* works, and where
14. I have a few things against *thee,*
19. I know *thy* works,
— and *thy* patience, and *thy* works;
20. I have a few things against *thee,*
3: 1. I know *thy* works,
2. I have not found *thy* works perfect
8. I know *thy* works: behold, I have set before *thee* an open door,
9. and worship before *thy* feet,
11. that no man take *thy* crown.
15. I know *thy* works,
18. (that) the shame of *thy* nakedness
— and anoint *thine* eyes with eyesalve,
4:11. and for *thy* pleasure they are
5: 9. redeemed us to God by *thy* blood
10: 9. it shall make *thy* belly bitter, but it shall be in *thy* mouth sweet
11:17. taken to thee *thy* great power,
18. and *thy* wrath is come,
— give reward unto *thy* servants the prophets,
— and them that fear *thy* name,
14:15. Thrust in *thy* sickle, and reap:
18. Thrust in *thy* sharp sickle,
15: 3. marvellous (are) *thy* works,
— just and true (are) *thy* ways,
4. and glorify *thy* name?
— shall come and worship before *thee;* for *thy* judgments are made manifest.
16: 7. righteous (are) *thy* judgments.
18:10. in one hour is *thy* judgment come.
14. And the fruits that *thy* soul lusted after are departed from *thee,*
— are departed from *thee,*
23. for *thy* merchants were the great men of the earth; for by *thy* sorceries
19:10. I am *thy* fellowservant, and of *thy* brethren that
22: 9. for I am *thy* fellowservant, and of *thy* brethren the prophets,

4676 4 766/898

σουδάριον, *soudarion.*

Lu. 19:20. kept laid up in a *napkin:*
Joh. 11:44. bound about with a *napkin.*
20: 7. the *napkin*, that was about his head,
Acts 19:12. brought unto the sick *handkerchiefs*

4678 51 766/898 7:465 4680

σοφία, *sophia.*

Mat. 11:19. But *wisdom* is justified of her children.
12:42. to hear the *wisdom* of Solomon;
13:54. Whence hath this (man) this *wisdom,*
Mar 6: 2. what *wisdom* (is) this which is given unto him,
Lu. 2:40. filled with *wisdom:* and the grace of God
52. Jesus increased in *wisdom* and stature,
7:35. *wisdom* is justified of all her children.
11:31. to hear the *wisdom* of Solomon;
49. Therefore also said the *wisdom* of God,
Lu. 21:15. I will give you a mouth and *wisdom,*
Acts 6: 3. full of the Holy Ghost and *wisdom,*
10. they were not able to resist the *wisdom*
7:10. and gave him favour and *wisdom*
22. in all the *wisdom* of the Egyptians,
Ro. 11:33. the depth of the riches both of the *wisdom* and knowledge of God!
1Co. 1:17. not with *wisdom* of words, lest
19. I will destroy the *wisdom* of the wise,
20. made foolish the *wisdom* of this world?
21. For after that in the *wisdom* of God the world by *wisdom* knew not God,
22. the Greeks seek after *wisdom:*
24. the power of God, and the *wisdom* of God.
30. who of God is made unto us *wisdom,*
2: 1. with excellency of speech or of *wisdom,*
4. with enticing words of man's *wisdom,*
5. not stand in the *wisdom* of men,
6. Howbeit we speak *wisdom* among
— yet not the *wisdom* of this world,
7. we speak the *wisdom* of God in a mystery,
13. words which man's *wisdom* teacheth,
3:19. the *wisdom* of this world is foolishness
12: 8. by the Spirit the word of *wisdom;*
2Co. 1:12. not with fleshly *wisdom*, but by
Eph. 1: 8. abounded toward us in all *wisdom*
17. the spirit of *wisdom* and revelation in
3:10. the manifold *wisdom* of God,
Col. 1: 9. in all *wisdom* and spiritual understanding;
28. teaching every man in all *wisdom;*
2: 3. treasures of *wisdom* and knowledge.
23. a shew of *wisdom* in will worship,
3:16. dwell in you richly in all *wisdom;*
4: 5. Walk in *wisdom* toward them that
Jas. 1: 5. If any of you lack *wisdom*, let him
3:13. his works with meekness of *wisdom.*
15. This *wisdom* descendeth not from above,
17. But the *wisdom* that is from above
2Pet. 3:15. according to the *wisdom* given unto him
Rev. 5:12. and *wisdom*, and strength, and honour,
7:12. Blessing, and glory, and *wisdom,*
13:18. Here is *wisdom.* Let him that hath
17: 9. here (is) the mind which hath *wisdom.*

4679 2 767/899 7:465 4680

σοφίζω, *sophizo.*

2Ti. 3:15. which are able *to make* thee *wise* unto salvation
2Pet. 1:16. not followed *cunningly devised* fables,

4680 22 767/899 7:465 cf 5429 cf *saphēs* (clear)

σοφός, *sophos.*

Mat. 11:25. hid these things from the *wise* and prudent,
23:34. I send unto you prophets, and *wise* men,
Lu. 10:21. these things from the *wise* and prudent,
Ro. 1:14. both to the *wise*, and to the unwise.
22. Professing themselves to be *wise*, they
16:19. *wise* unto that which is good, and
27. To God only *wise*, (be) glory
1Co. 1:19. I will destroy the wisdom of the *wise,*
20. Where (is) the *wise?* where (is) the scribe
25. the foolishness of God is *wiser* than men
26. not many *wise* men after the flesh,
27. of the world to confound the *wise;*
3:10. as a *wise* masterbuilder, I have laid
18. seemeth to be *wise* in this world, let him become a fool, that he may be *wise.*
19. He taketh the *wise* in their own craftiness.
20. The Lord knoweth the thoughts of the *wise,*

1Co. 6: 5. It is so, that there is not a *wise* man among you?
Eph. 5:15. not as fools, but as *wise*,
1Ti. 1:17. the only *wise* God, (be) honour
Jas. 3:13. Who (is) a *wise* man and endued with
Jude 25. To the only *wise* God our Saviour,

4682 4 768/899 spairō (to gasp)

σπαράσσω, sparasso.

Mar 1:26. *when* the unclean spirit *had torn* him,
9:20. straightway the spirit *tare* him;
26. (the spirit) cried, and *rent* him sore, *and*
Lu. 9:39. it *teareth* him that he foameth again,

4683 2 768/899 sparganon (strip)

σπαργανόω, sparganoo.

Lu. 2: 7. and *wrapped* him *in swaddling clothes*,
12. the babe *wrapped in swaddling clothes*,

4685 2 768/899

σπάομαι, spaomai.

Mar 14:47. them that stood by *drew* a sword, *and*
Acts 16:27. he *drew out* his sword, *and* would

4684 2 768/899 spatalē (luxury)

σπαταλάω, spatalao.

1Ti. 5: 6. But she *that liveth in pleasure* is
Jas. 5: 5. and *been wanton*;

4686 7 768/899 4696

σπεῖρα, spīra.

Mat. 27:27. gathered unto him the whole *band*
Mar 15:16. and they call together the whole *band*.
Joh. 18: 3. having received a *band* (of men) and
12. Then the *band* and the captain and
Acts 10: 1. a centurion of the *band* called the
21:31. unto the chief captain of the *band*.
27: 1. Julius, a centurion of Augustus' *band*.

4687 53 768/899 7:536 4685

σπείρω, spīro.

Mat. 6:26. Behold the fowls of the air: for they *sow* not,
13: 3. a *sower* went forth *to sow*;
4. And when he *sowed*, some (seeds) fell
18. Hear ye therefore the parable of the *sower*.
19. that *which was sown* in his heart. This is he *which received seed* by the way side.
20. But he *that received* the *seed* into stony places,
22. He also *that received seed* among the thorns
23. But he *that received seed* into the good ground
24. is likened unto a man *which sowed* good
25. and *sowed* tares among the wheat,
27. *didst* not thou *sow* good seed in thy field?
31. a man took, and *sowed* in his field:
37. He *that soweth* the good seed is
39. The enemy *that sowed* them is the
25:24. reaping where thou *hast* not *sown*,
26. I reap where I *sowed* not,
Mar 4: 3. there went out a *sower to sow*:
4. And it came to pass, as he *sowed*,
14. The *sower soweth* the word.
15. where the word *is sown*;
— taketh away the word *that was sown*
Mar 4:16. *which are sown* on stony ground,
18. they *which are sown* among thorns;
20. they *which are sown* on good ground;
31. when it *is sown* in the earth,
32. But when it *is sown*, it groweth up,
Lu. 8: 5. A *sower* went out *to sow* his seed: and as he *sowed*, some fell by
12:24. for they neither *sow* nor reap;
19:21. and reapest that thou *didst* not *sow*.
22. and reaping that I *did* not *sow*:
Joh. 4:36. that both he *that soweth* and he that
37. One *soweth*, and another reapeth.
1Co. 9:11. If we *have sown* unto you spiritual
15:36. that which thou *sowest* is not quickened,
37. And that which thou *sowest*, thou *sowest* not that body that shall be,
42. It *is sown* in corruption;
43. It *is sown* in dishonour;
— it *is sown* in weakness;
44. It *is sown* a natural body;
2Co. 9: 6. He *which soweth* sparingly shall reap
— and he *which soweth* bountifully shall
10. he that ministereth seed to the *sower*
Gal. 6: 7. for whatsoever a man *soweth*,
8. For he *that soweth* to his flesh
— but he *that soweth* to the Spirit
Jas. 3:18. the fruit of righteousness *is sown* in peace

4688 1 769/900

σπεκουλάτωρ, spekoulator.

Mar 6:27. the king sent an *executioner*, and

4689 2 769/900 7:528

σπένδομαι, spendomai.

Phi. 2:17. Yea, and if I *be offered* upon
2Ti. 4: 6. For I *am* now *ready to be offered*,

4690 44 769/900 7:536 4687

σπέρμα, sperma.

Mat. 13:24. unto a man which sowed good *seed*
27. Sir, didst not thou sow good *seed*
32. is the least of all *seeds*:
37. He that soweth the good *seed* is the
38. the good *seed* are the children of the kingdom;
22:24. and raise up *seed* unto his brother.
25. and, having no *issue*, left his wife
Mar 4:31. is less than all the *seeds* that be
12:19. and raise up *seed* unto his brother.
20. and dying left no *seed*.
21. neither left he any *seed*:
22. seven had her, and left no *seed*:
Lu. 1:55. to Abraham, and to his *seed* for ever.
20:28. and raise up *seed* unto his brother.
Joh. 7:42. That Christ cometh of the *seed* of David,
8:33. We be Abraham's *seed*, and were
37. I know that ye are Abraham's *seed*;
Acts 3:25. And in thy *seed* shall all the kindreds
7: 5. and to his *seed* after him,
6. That his *seed* should sojourn in a
13:23. Of this man's *seed* hath God
Ro. 1: 3. which was made of the *seed* of David
4:13. (was) not to Abraham, or to his *seed*,
16. promise might be sure to all the *seed*
18. was spoken, So shall thy *seed* be.
9: 7. because they are the *seed* of Abraham
— In Isaac shall thy *seed* be called.
8. are counted for the *seed*.
29. the Lord of Sabaoth had left us a *seed*,

Ro. 11: 1. an Israelite, of the *seed* of Abraham,
1Co.15:38. and to every *seed* his own body.
2Co. 9:10. Now he that ministereth *seed* to the sower
11:22. Are they the *seed* of Abraham? so (am) I.
Gal. 3:16. Now to Abraham and his *seed* were the promises made. He saith not, And to *seeds*, as of many; but as of one, And to thy *seed*, which
19. till the *seed* should come to whom
29. then are ye Abraham's *seed*,
2Ti. 2: 8. Jesus Christ of the *seed* of David
Heb 2:16. but he took on (him) the *seed* of Abraham.
11:11. received strength to conceive *seed*,
18. That in Isaac shall thy *seed* be called:
1Joh.3: 9. for his *seed* remaineth in him:
Rev.12:17. to make war with the remnant of her *seed*,

4691 1 769/901 4690,3004

σπερμολόγος, *spermologos.*

Acts17:18. What will this *babbler* say?

4692 6 769/901 4228

σπεύδω, *spūdo.*

Lu. 2:16. And they came *with haste*,
19: 5. Zacchæus, *make haste, and* come down;
6. And he *made haste, and* came down,
Acts20:16. for he *hasted*, if it were possible
22:18. *Make haste*, and get thee quickly out
2Pet.3:12. and *hasting unto* the coming of the day

4693 6 769/901 *speos* (grotto)

σπήλαιον, *speelaion.*

Mat.21:13. but ye have made it a *den* of thieves.
Mar11:17. but ye have made it a *den* of thieves.
Lu. 19:46. but ye have made it a *den* of thieves.
Joh. 11:38. It was a *cave*, and a stone lay upon it.
Heb11:38. and (in) *dens* and caves of the earth.
Rev. 6:15. hid themselves in the *dens*

4694 1 770/901

σπιλάς, *spilas.*

Jude 12. These are *spots* in your feasts of

4695 2 770/901

σπῖλος, *spilos.*

Eph. 5:27. not having *spot*, or wrinkle,
2Pet.2:13. *Spots* (they are) and blemishes,

4696 2 770/901

σπιλόω, *spiloō.*

Jas. 3: 6. *that* it *defileth* the whole body,
Jude 23. the garment *spotted* by the flesh.

4698 11 770/901 7:548 *splēn*

σπλάγχνα, *splankna.* ("spleen")

(neut. plur.)

Lu. 1:78. Through the tender mercy (lit. *bowels* of mercy) of our God;
Acts 1:18. and all his *bowels* gushed out.
2Co. 6:12. ye are straitened in your own *bowels*.
7:15. And his *inward affection* is more
Phi. 1: 8. how greatly I long after you all in the *bowels* of Jesus Christ.
2: 1. if any *bowels* and mercies,
Col. 3:12. *bowels* of mercies, kindness,
Philem. 7. the *bowels* of the saints are refreshed
Philem.12. receive him, that is, mine own *bowels*
20. refresh my *bowels* in the Lord.
1Joh.3:17. shutteth up his *bowels* (of compassion)

4697 12 770/901 7:548 4698

σπλαγχνίζομαι, *splanknizomai.*

Mat. 9:36. he *was moved with compassion* on them,
14:14. *was moved with compassion* toward
15:32. I *have compassion* on the multitude,
18:27. *was moved with compassion, and* loosed
20:34. Jesus *had compassion* (on them), *and*
Mar 1:41. Jesus, *moved with compassion*, put forth
6:34. *was moved with compassion* toward
8: 2. I *have compassion* on the multitude,
9:22. *have compassion* on us, *and* help us.
Lu. 7:13. he *had compassion* on her,
10:33. he *had compassion* (on him),
15:20. saw him, and *had compassion*, and ran,

4699 3 770/901

σπόγγος, *spongos.*

Mat.27:48. took a *spunge*, and filled (it)
Mar 15:36. And one ran and filled a *spunge*
Joh.19:29. and they filled a *spunge* with vinegar,

4700 3 770/901

σποδός, *spodos.*

Mat.11:21. repented long ago in sackcloth and *ashes*
Lu. 10:13. sitting in sackcloth and *ashes*.
Heb 9:13. the *ashes* of an heifer sprinkling the

4701 1 770/901 7:536 4687

σπορά, *spora.*

1Pet.1:23. not of corruptible *seed*, but of

4702 3 770/901 7:536 4703

σπόριμα, *sporima.*

(neut. plur.)

Mat.12: 1. went on the sabbath day through the *corn*;
Mar 2:23. that he went through the *corn fields*
Lu. 6: 1. that he went through the *corn fields*;

4703 5 770/901 7:536 4687

σπόρος, *sporos.*

Mar 4:26. as if a man should cast *seed* into the ground;
27. and the *seed* should spring and grow up,
Lu. 8: 5. A sower went out to sow his *seed*:
11. The *seed* is the word of God.
2Co. 9:10. and multiply your *seed sown*,

4704 11 771/901 7:559 4710

σπουδάζω, *spoudazo.*

Gal. 2:10. the same which I also *was forward* to do.
Eph 4: 3. *Endeavouring* to keep the unity of the Spirit
1Th. 2:17. *endeavoured* the more abundantly
2Ti. 2:15. *Study* to shew thyself approved
4: 9. *Do* thy *diligence* to come shortly unto me
21. *Do* thy *diligence* to come before winter.
Tit. 3:12. *be diligent* to come unto me to
Heb 4:11. *Let us labour* therefore to enter into
2Pet.1:10. *give diligence* to make your calling
15. I *will endeavour* that ye may be able
3:14. *be diligent* that ye may be found of him

4705,4707 3 771/902 7:559 4710

σπουδαῖος, spoudaios.

2Co. 8:17. but being *more forward*,
22. proved *diligent* in many things, but now much *more diligent*,

4706 1 771/902 4707

σπουδαιότερον, spoudaioteron.

2Ti. 1:17. he sought me out *very diligently*,

4708,4709 3 771/902 7:559 4705

σπουδαίως, -οτέρως, spoudaiōs, spoudaioterōs.

Lu. 7: 4. they besought him *instantly*, saying,
Phi. 2:28. I sent him therefore *the more carefully*,
Tit. 3:13. and Apollos on their journey *diligently*,

4710 12 771/902 4692

σπουδή, spoudee.

Mar 6:25. she came in straightway with *haste*
Lu. 1:39. went into the hill country with *haste*,
Ro. 12: 8. he that ruleth, with *diligence*;
11. Not slothful in *business*;
2Co. 7:11. what *carefulness* it wrought in you,
12. our *care* for you in the sight of God
8: 7. and knowledge, and (in) all *diligence*,
8. by occasion of the *forwardness* of others,
16. put the same *earnest care* into the heart
Heb. 6:11. do shew the same *diligence*
2Pet. 1: 5. giving all *diligence*, add to your faith
Jude 3. when I gave all *diligence* to write

4711 5 771/902 4687

σπυρίς, spuris.

Mat.15:37. (meat) that was left seven *baskets* full.
16:10. and how many *baskets* ye took up?
Mar 8: 8. the broken (meat) that was left seven *baskets*.
20. how many *baskets* full of fragments
Acts 9:25. down by the wall in a *basket*.

4712 6 771/902 rt 2476

στάδιος, στάδιον, stadios, stadion.

Lu. 24:13. (about) threescore *furlongs*.
Joh. 6:19. five and twenty or thirty *furlongs*,
11:18. about fifteen *furlongs* off.
1Co. 9:24. they which run in a *race* run all,
Rev.14:20. a thousand (and) six hundred *furlongs*.
21:16. the reed, twelve thousand *furlongs*.

4713 1 771/902 rt 2476

στάμνος, stamnos.

Heb. 9: 4. wherein (was) the golden *pot* that had manna,

4714 9 771/902 7:568 rt 2476

στάσις, stasis.

Mar15: 7. committed murder in the *insurrection*.
Lu. 23:19. for a certain *sedition* made in the city,
25. him that for *sedition* and murder
Acts15: 2. had no small *dissension* and
19:40. called in question for this day's *uproar*,
23: 7. there arose a *dissension* between the
10. when there arose a great *dissension*,
Acts24: 5. and a mover of *sedition* among
Heb 9: 8. the first tabernacle was yet standing: (lit yet having a *standing*)

4715 1 772/902 rt 2746

στατήρ, stateer.

Mat.17:27. thou shalt find a *piece of money*:

4716 28 772/902 7:572 rt 2476

σταυρός, stauros.

Mat.10:38. And he that taketh not his *cross*,
16:24. deny himself, and take up his *cross*,
27:32. him they compelled to bear his *cross*.
40. Son of God, come down from the *cross*.
42. let him now come down from the *cross*,
Mar 8:34. deny himself, and take up his *cross*,
10:21. and come, take up the *cross*,
15:21. Rufus, to bear his *cross*.
30. and come down from the *cross*.
32. descend now from the *cross*,
Lu. 9:23. deny himself, and take up his *cross* daily,
14:27. And whosoever doth not bear his *cross*,
23:26. and on him they laid the *cross*,
Joh.19:17. And he bearing his *cross*
19. and put (it) on the *cross*.
25. Now there stood by the *cross* of Jesus
31. the bodies should not remain upon the *cross*
1Co. 1:17. lest the *cross* of Christ should be made
18. For the preaching of the *cross* is to
Gal. 5:11. then is the offence of the *cross* ceased.
6:12. persecution for the *cross* of Christ.
14. save in the *cross* of our Lord Jesus
Eph. 2:16. both unto God in one body by the *cross*,
Phi. 2: 8. even the death of the *cross*.
3:18. the enemies of the *cross* of Christ.
Col. 1:20. peace through the blood of his *cross*,
2:14. nailing it to his *cross*;
Heb12: 2. endured the *cross*, despising the shame,

4717 46 772/902 7:572 4716

σταυρόω, stauroō.

Mat.20:19. and to scourge, and *to crucify* (him):
23:34. (some) of them ye shall kill and *crucify*,
26: 2. Son of man is betrayed *to be crucified*.
27:22. *Let* him *be crucified*.
23. *Let* him *be crucified*.
26. he delivered (him) to *be crucified*.
31. and led him away *to crucify* (him).
35. they *crucified* him, *and* parted
38. Then *were* there two thieves *crucified*
28: 5. ye seek Jesus, *which was crucified*.
Mar15:13. they cried out again, *Crucify* him.
14. out the more exceedingly, *Crucify* him.
15. delivered Jesus,...to *be crucified*.
20. and led him out to *crucify* him.
24. And *when* they *had crucified* him,
25. and they *crucified* him.
27. And with him they *crucify* two thieves;
16: 6. Jesus of Nazareth, *which was crucified*:
Lu. 23:21. saying, *Crucify* (him), *crucify* him.
23. requiring that he might *be crucified*.
33. there they *crucified* him,
24: 7. and *be crucified*, and the third day
20. and *have crucified* him.
Joh.19: 6. saying, *Crucify* (him), *crucify* (him).
— Take ye him, and *crucify* (him).
10. I have power *to crucify* thee.
15. away with (him), *crucify* him.

Joh. 19:15. *Shall* I *crucify* your King?
16. unto them to *be crucified.*
18. Where they *crucified* him, and two other
20. for the place where Jesus *was crucified*
23. when they *had crucified* Jesus,
41. Now in the place where he *was crucified*
Acts 2:36. Jesus, whom ye *have crucified,*
4:10. of Nazareth, whom ye *crucified,*
1Co. 1:13. *was* Paul *crucified* for you?
23. But we preach Christ *crucified,*
2: 2. save Jesus Christ, and him *crucified.*
8. would not *have crucified* the Lord of
2Co. 13: 4. he *was crucified* through weakness,
Gal. 3: 1. set forth, *crucified* among you?
5:24. *have crucified* the flesh with the
6:14. by whom the world *is crucified* unto me,
Rev. 11: 8. where also our Lord *was crucified.*

4718 3 773/903 rt 4735
σταφυλή, staphulee.

Mat. 7:16. Do men gather *grapes* of thorns,
Lu. 6:44. nor of a bramble bush gather they *grapes.*
Rev. 14:18. for her *grapes* are fully ripe.

4719 5 773/903 rt 2476
στάχυς, stakus.

Mat. 12: 1. and began to pluck the *ears of corn,*
Mar 2:23. to pluck the *ears of corn.*
4:28. first the blade, then the *ear,*
— after that the full corn in the *ear.*
Lu. 6: 1. his disciples plucked the *ears of corn,*

4721 3 773/903 *tegos* ("thatch")
στέγη, stegee.

Mat. 8: 8. shouldest come under my *roof:*
Mar 2: 4. they uncovered the *roof* where he was:
Lu. 7: 6. that thou shouldest enter under my *roof:*

4722 4 773/903 7:585 4721
στέγω, stego.

1Co. 9:12. but *suffer* all things, lest we
13: 7. *Beareth* all things, believeth all things,
1Th. 3: 1. *when* we *could* no longer *forbear,*
5. *when* I *could* no longer *forbear,* I sent

4723 4 773/903 4731
στεῖρα, stīra.

Lu. 1: 7. because that Elisabeth was *barren,*
36. month with her, who was called *barren.*
23:29. Blessed (are) the *barren,* and the wombs
Gal. 4:27. Rejoice, (thou) *barren* that bearest not;

4724 2 773/903 7:588 rt 2476
στέλλομαι, stellomai.

2Co. 8:20. *Avoiding* this, that no man should
2Th. 3: 6. that ye *withdraw* yourselves from every

4725 1 773/903 rt 4735
στέμμα, stemma.

Acts 14:13. brought oxen and *garlands* unto the gates,

4726 2 773/903 7:600 4727
στεναγμός, stenagmos.

Acts 7:34. and I have heard their *groaning,*
Ro. 8:26 with *groanings* which cannot be uttered.

4727 6 773/903 7:600 4728
στενάζω, stenazo.

Mar 7:34. he *sighed,* and saith unto him,
Ro. 8:23. even we ourselves *groan* within ourselves,
2Co. 5: 2. For in this we *groan,* earnestly desiring
4. For we that are in (this) tabernacle *do groan,*
Heb 13:17. do it with joy, and not *with grief:* (lit not *groaning*)
Jas. 5: 9. *Grudge* not one against another

4728 3 773/903 7:604 rt 2476
στενός, stenos.

Mat. 7:13. Enter ye in at the *strait* gate:
14. Because *strait* (is) the gate, and narrow
Lu. 13:24. Strive to enter in at the *strait* gate:

4729 3 774/904 7:604 rt 4730
στενοχωρέομαι, stenokōreomai.

2Co. 4: 8. troubled on every side, yet not *distressed;*
6:12. Ye *are* not *straitened* in us, but ye *are straitened* in your own bowels.

4730 4 774/904 7:604 4728,5561
στενοχωρία, stenokōria.

Ro. 2: 9. Tribulation and *anguish,* upon every soul
8:35. (shall) tribulation, or *distress,*
2Co. 6: 4. in necessities, in *distresses,*
12:10. in *distresses* for Christ's sake:

4731 4 774/904 7:609 2476
στερεός, stereos.

2Ti. 2:19. the foundation of God standeth *sure,*
Heb 5:12. and not of *strong* meat. (lit. *solid* food)
14. But *strong* meat (lit. *solid* food) belongeth to them that
1Pet. 5: 9. Whom resist *stedfast* in the faith,

4732 3 774/904 7:609 4731
στερεόω, stereoō.

Acts 3: 7. his feet and ancle bones *received strength.*
16. *hath made* this man *strong,*
16: 5. And so *were* the churches *established* in the faith,

4733 1 774/904 7:609 4732
στερέωμα, stereōma.

Col. 2: 5. and the *stedfastness* of your faith in Christ.

4735 8 774/904 7:615 *stephō* (to wreathe)
στέφανος, stephanos.

Mat. 27:29. when they had platted a *crown* of thorns,
Mar 15:17. and platted a *crown* of thorns,
Joh. 19: 2. the soldiers platted a *crown* of thorns,
5. wearing the *crown* of thorns,
1Co. 9:25. to obtain a corruptible *crown;*
Phi. 4: 1. my joy and *crown,* so stand fast
1Th. 2:19. our hope, or joy, or *crown* of rejoicing?
2Ti. 4: 8. for me a *crown* of righteousness,
Jas. 1:12. he shall receive the *crown* of life,
1Pet. 5: 4. a *crown* of glory that fadeth not away.
Rev. 2:10. I will give thee a *crown* of life.
3:11. that no man take thy *crown.*
4: 4. on their heads *crowns* of gold.
10. cast their *crowns* before the throne
6: 2. and a *crown* was given unto him:

Rev. 9: 7. as it were *crowns* like gold,
12: 1. upon her head a *crown* of twelve stars:
14:14. having on his head a golden *crown*,

4737 3 775/904 7:615 4735

στεφανόω, stephanoō.

2Ti. 2: 5. (yet) *is* he not *crowned*, except
Heb 2: 7. thou *crownedst* him with glory and honour,
9. *crowned* with glory and honour;

4738 5 775/904 2476

στῆθος, steethos.

Lu. 18:13. but smote upon his *breast*,
23:48. smote their *breasts*, and returned.
Joh. 13:25. He then lying on Jesus' *breast*
21:20. which also leaned on his *breast*
Rev. 15: 6. their *breasts* girded with golden girdles.

4739 8 775/904 7:636 2476

στήκω, steeko.

Mar 11:25. And when ye *stand* praying,
Ro. 14: 4. to his own master he *standeth* or falleth.
1Co. 16:13. *stand fast* in the faith,
Gal. 5: 1. *Stand fast* therefore in the liberty
Phi. 1:27. that ye *stand fast* in one spirit,
4: 1. so *stand fast* in the Lord,
1Th. 3: 8. if ye *stand fast* in the Lord.
2Th. 2:15. brethren, *stand fast*, and hold

4740 1 775/904 7:653 4741

στηριγμός, steerigmos.

2Pet 3:17. fall from your own *stedfastness*.

4741 13 775/904 7:653 2476

στηρίζω, steerizo.

Lu. 9:51. he *stedfastly set* his face to go to Jerusalem,
16:26. there *is* a great gulf *fixed*:
22:32. when thou art converted, *strengthen* thy brethren.
Ro. 1:11. to the end ye may *be established*;
16:25. *to stablish* you according to my gospel,
1Th. 3: 2. *to establish* you, and to comfort you
13. To the end he may *stablish* your hearts
2Th. 2:17. and *stablish* you in every good word
3: 3. who *shall stablish* you, and keep (you)
Jas. 5: 8. Be ye also patient; *stablish* your hearts:
1Pet. 5:10. make you perfect, *stablish*,
2Pet. 1:12. and be *established* in the present truth.
Rev. 3: 2. *strengthen* the things which remain, that

4742 1 776/905 7:567 stizō (to prick)

στίγμα, stigma.

Gal. 6:17. the *marks* of the Lord Jesus.

4743 1 776/905 4742

στιγμή, stigmee.

Lu. 4: 5. in a *moment* of time.

4744 1 776/905 7:665

στίλβω, stilbo.

Mar 9: 3. And his raiment became *shining*,

4745 4 776/905 2476

στόα, stoa.

Joh. 5: 2. having five *porches*.
10:23. walked in the temple in Solomon's *porch*.
Acts 3:11. in the *porch* that is called Solomon's,
5:12. with one accord in Solomon's *porch*.

4746 1 776/905 steibō (to tramp)

στοιβάς, stoibas.

Mar 11: 8. and others cut down *branches*

4747 7 776/905 7:666 rt 4748

στοιχεῖον, stoikīon.

Gal. 4: 3. were in bondage under the *elements* of the world:
9. to the weak and beggarly *elements*,
Col. 2: 8. after the *rudiments* of the world, and not
20. dead with Christ from the *rudiments* of the world,
Heb 5:12. the first *principles* of the oracles of God;
2Pet. 3:10. the *elements* shall melt with fervent
12. the *elements* shall melt with fervent

4748 5 777/905 7:666 steichō (to line up)

στοιχέω, stoikeo.

Acts 21:24. *walkest orderly*, and keepest the law.
Ro. 4:12. but *who* also *walk* in the steps of that
Gal. 5:25. *let* us also *walk* in the Spirit.
6:16. as many as *walk* (lit. in rec. text, *shall walk*) according to this rule,
Phi. 3:16. let us *walk* by the same rule,

4749 9 777/905 7:687 4724

στολή, stolee.

Mar 12:38. which love to go in *long clothing*,
16: 5. clothed in a *long* white *garment*;
Lu. 15:22. Bring forth the best *robe*,
20:46. which desire to walk in *long robes*,
Rev. 6:11. white *robes* were given unto every one
7: 9. clothed with white *robes*,
13. What are these which are arrayed in white *robes*?
14. have washed their *robes*, and made them (lit. their *robes*) white in the blood of the Lamb

4750 78 777/905 7:692 rt 5114

στόμα, stoma.

Mat. 4: 4. that proceedeth out of the *mouth* of God.
5: 2. And he opened his *mouth*, and taught them,
12:34. abundance of the heart the *mouth* speaketh.
13:35. I will open my *mouth* in parables;
15: 8. draweth nigh unto me with their *mouth*,
11. Not that which goeth into the *mouth*
— but that which cometh out of the *mouth*,
17. whatsoever entereth in at the *mouth*
18. which proceed out of the *mouth*
17:27. when thou hast opened his *mouth*,
18:16. that in the *mouth* of two or three
21:16. Out of the *mouth* of babes and sucklings
Lu. 1:64. And his *mouth* was opened immediately,
70. by the *mouth* of his holy prophets,
4:22. which proceeded out of his *mouth*.
6:45. of the abundance of the heart his *mouth* speaketh.
11:54. to catch something out of his *mouth*,

Lu. 19.22. Out of thine own *mouth* will I judge thee,
21:15. For I will give you a *mouth* and wisdom,
24. fall by the *edge* of the sword,
22:71. have heard of his own *mouth*.
Joh.19:29. and put (it) to his *mouth*.
Acts 1:16. by the *mouth* of David spake before
3:18. had shewed by the *mouth* of all his prophets,
21. by the *mouth* of all his holy prophets
4:25. by the *mouth* of thy servant David
8:32. so opened he not his *mouth*:
35. Then Philip opened his *mouth*, and
10:34. Then Peter opened (his) *mouth*, and
11: 8. at any time entered into my *mouth*.
15: 7. that the Gentiles by my *mouth*
18:14. Paul was now about to open (his) *mouth*,
22:14. shouldest hear the voice of his *mouth*.
23: 2. to smite him on the *mouth*.
Ro. 3:14. Whose *mouth* (is) full of cursing and
19. that every *mouth* may be stopped,
10: 8. The word is nigh thee, (even) in thy *mouth*,
9. confess with thy *mouth* the Lord Jesus,
10. and with the *mouth* confession is made
15: 6. with one mind (and) one *mouth*
2Co. 6:11. our *mouth* is open unto you, our
13: 1. In the *mouth* of two or three witnesses
Eph. 4:29. proceed out of your *mouth*, but
6:19. that I may open my *mouth* boldly,
Col. 3: 8. filthy communication out of your *mouth*.
2Th. 2: 8. consume with the spirit of his *mouth*,
2Ti. 4:17. delivered out of the *mouth* of the lion.
Heb 11:33. stopped the *mouths* of lions,
34. escaped the *edge* of the sword,
Jas. 3: 3. we put bits in the horses' *mouths*,
10. Out of the same *mouth* proceedeth
1Pet. 2:22. neither was guile found in his *mouth*:
2Joh. 12. and speak *face* to *face*,
3Joh. 14. and we shall speak *face* to *face*.
Jude 16. and their *mouth* speaketh great swelling
Rev. 1:16. and out of his *mouth* went a sharp
2:16. against them with the sword of my *mouth*.
3:16. I will spue thee out of my *mouth*.
9:17. and out of their *mouths* issued fire
18. which issued out of their *mouths*.
19. For their power is in their *mouth*,
10: 9. it shall be in thy *mouth* sweet as honey.
10. it was in my *mouth* sweet as honey:
11: 5. fire proceedeth out of their *mouth*,
12:15. cast out of his *mouth* water as a
16. and the earth opened her *mouth*,
— which the dragon cast out of his *mouth*.
13: 2. and his *mouth* as the *mouth* of a lion:
5. a *mouth* speaking great things and
6. And he opened his *mouth* in blasphemy
14: 5. And in their *mouth* was found no guile:
16:13. (come) out of the *mouth* of the dragon, and out of the *mouth* of the beast, and out of the *mouth* of the false prophet.
19:15. out of his *mouth* goeth a sharp sword,
21. which (sword) proceeded out of his *mouth*:

4751 1 777/906 4750

στόμαχος, stomakos.

1Ti. 5:23. a little wine for thy *stomach*'s sake

4752 2 777/906 7:701 4754

στρατεία, stratīa.

2Co.10: 4. the weapons of our *warfare* (are) not carnal,
1Ti. 1:18. that thou by them mightest war a good *warfare*;

4753 8 778/906 7:701 4754

στράτευμα, stratūma.

Mat.22: 7. and he sent forth his *armies*,
Lu. 23:11. And Herod with his *men of war*
Acts23:10. commanded the *soldiers* to go down,
27. then came I with an *army*,
Rev. 9:16. the number of the *army* of the horsemen
19:14. And the *armies* (which were) in heaven
19. and their *armies*, gathered together
— and against his *army*.

4754 7 778/906 7:701 rt 4756

στρατεύομαι, stratūomai.

Lu. 3:14. the *soldiers* likewise demanded of him,
1Co. 9: 7. Who *goeth a warfare* any time at
2Co.10: 3. we *do* not *war* after the flesh:
1Ti. 1:18. that thou by them *mightest war* a good warfare;
2Ti. 2: 4. No man *that warreth* entangleth himself
Jas. 4: 1. of your lusts *that war* in your members?
1Pet.2:11. lusts, which *war* against the soul;

4755 10 778/906 7:701 rt 4756
71 or 2233

στρατηγός, strateegos.

Lu. 22: 4. with the chief priests and *captains*,
52. and *captains* of the temple,
Acts 4: 1. and the *captain* of the temple,
5:24. and the *captain* of the temple
26. Then went the *captain* with the
16:20. And brought them to the *magistrates*,
22. and the *magistrates* rent off their clothes,
35. the *magistrates* sent the serjeants,
36. The *magistrates* have sent to let you go:
38. told these words unto the *magistrates*:

4756 2 778/906 7:701 *stratos* (army)

στρατία, stratia.

Lu. 2:13. a multitude of the heavenly *host*
Acts 7:42. to worship the *host* of heaven;

4757 26 778/907 7:701 rt 4756

στρατιώτης, stratiōtees.

Mat. 8: 9. having *soldiers* under me:
27:27. Then the *soldiers* of the governor
28:12. they gave large money unto the *soldiers*.
Mar 15:16. And the *soldiers* led him away
Lu. 7: 8. having under me *soldiers*,
23:36. And the *soldiers* also mocked him,
Joh.19: 2. And the *soldiers* platted a crown
23. Then the *soldiers*, when they had crucified Jesus,
— to every *soldier* a part;
24. These things therefore the *soldiers* did.
32. Then came the *soldiers*, and brake
34. But one of the *soldiers* with a spear
Acts10: 7. and a devout *soldier* of them that
12: 4. (him) to four quaternions of *soldiers*
6. Peter was sleeping between two *soldiers*,
18. there was no small stir among the *soldiers*
21:32. Who immediately took *soldiers*
— saw the chief captain and the *soldiers*,
35. he was borne of the *soldiers*

Acts23:23. Make ready two hundred *soldiers*
31. Then the *soldiers*, as it was commanded
27:31. said to the centurion and to the *soldiers*,
32. Then the *soldiers* cut off the ropes
42. And the *soldiers'* counsel was to kill
28:16. by himself with a *soldier* that kept him.
2Ti. 2: 3. endure hardness, as a good *soldier* of

4758 1 778/907 7:701 rt 4756 3004

στρατολογέω, stratologeo.

2Ti. 2: 4. that he may please him *who hath chosen* him *to be a soldier*.

4759 1 778/907 4760,757

στρατοπεδάρχης, stratopedarkees.

Acts28:16. delivered the prisoners *to the captain of the guard*:

4760 1 778/907 7:701 rt 4756 rt 3977

στρατόπεδον, stratopedon.

Lu. 21:20. Jerusalem compassed with *armies*,

4761 1 778/907 4762

στρεβλόω, strebloō.

2Pet.3:16. unlearned and unstable *wrest*, as

4762 18 778/907 7:714 rt 5157

στρέφω, strepho.

Mat. 5:39. *turn* to him the other also.
7: 6. and *turn again and* rend you.
16:23. But he *turned, and* said unto Peter,
18: 3. Except ye *be converted*, and become as
Lu. 7: 9. and *turned him about, and* said
44. And he *turned* to the woman, *and* said unto Simon,
9:55. But he *turned, and* rebuked them,
10:23. And he *turned him* unto (his) disciples, *and* said privately,
14:25. and he *turned, and* said unto them,
22:61. And the Lord *turned, and* looked
23:28. But Jesus *turning* unto them said,
Joh. 1:38. Then Jesus *turned*, and saw them
20:14. she *turned* herself back, and saw Jesus
16. She *turned* herself, *and* saith unto him,
Acts 7:39. and in their hearts *turned back again* into Egypt,
42. Then God *turned*, and gave them up
13:46. lo, we *turn* to the Gentiles.
Rev.11: 6. power over waters *to turn* them to blood,

4763 2 779/907 4764

στρηνιάω, streeniao.

Rev.18: 7. she hath glorified herself, and *lived deliciously*,
9. and *lived deliciously* with her,

4764 1 779/907 cf 4731

στρῆνος, streenos.

Rev.18: 3. through the abundance of her *delicacies*.

4765 4 779/907 7:730 *strouthos* (sparrow)

στρουθίον, strouthion.

Mat.10:29. Are not two *sparrows* sold for a farthing?
Mat.10:31. ye are of more value than many *sparrows*.
Lu. 12: 6. not five *sparrows* sold for two farthings,
7. ye are of more value than many *sparrows*

4766 7 779/907 *stroō* (to spread)

στρώννυμι, στρωννύω, strōnnumi, strōnnuo.

Mat.21: 8. *spread* their garments in the way;
— from the trees, and *strawed* (them) in
Mar 11: 8. And many *spread* their garments
— off the trees, and *strawed* (them) in
14:15. a large upper room *furnished*
Lu. 22:12. a large upper room *furnished*:
Acts 9:34. arise, and *make* thy *bed*.

4767 1 779/907 *stugo* (to hate)

στυγητός, stugeetos.

Tit. 3: 3. *hateful*, (and) hating one another.

4768 2 779/907 rt 4767

στυγνάζω, stugnazo.

Mat.16: 3. for the sky is red and *lowring*.
Mar 10:22. And he *was sad* at that saying, *and*

4769 4 779/907 7:732 *stuo* (to stiffen)

στῦλος, stulos.

Gal. 2: 9. who seemed to be *pillars*,
1Ti. 3:15. the *pillar* and ground of the truth.
Rev. 3:12. a *pillar* in the temple of my God,
10: 1. and his feet as *pillars* of fire:

4771 178 779/908 (4571,4671,4675 5209,5210,5213,5216)

σύ, su.

Mat. 2: 6. And *thou* Bethlehem, (in) the land of Juda.
3:14. and comest *thou* to me?
6: 6. But *thou*, when thou prayest,
17. But *thou*, when thou fastest,
11: 3. Art *thou* he that should come,
23. And *thou*, Capernaum, which art exalted
14:28. Lord, if it be *thou*, bid me come
16:16. *Thou* art the Christ, the Son of the living God.
18. I say also unto thee, That *thou* art Peter,
26:25. He said unto him, *Thou* hast said.
39. not as I will, but as *thou* (wilt).
63. that thou tell us whether *thou* be the Christ,
64. Jesus saith unto him, *Thou* hast said:
69. *Thou* also wast with Jesus
73. Surely *thou* also art (one) of them;
27: 4. What (is that) to us? see *thou* (to that).
11. Art *thou* the King of the Jews? And Jesus said unto him, *Thou* sayest.
Mar 1:11. *Thou* art my beloved Son,
3:11. saying, *Thou* art the Son of God.
8:29. *Thou* art the Christ.
14:36. not what I will, but what *thou* wilt.
61. Art *thou* the Christ, the Son of the Blessed?
67. And *thou* also wast with Jesus
68. neither understand I what *thou* sayest.
15: 2. Art *thou* the King of the Jews? And he answering said unto him, *Thou* sayest (it).
Lu. 1:28. blessed (art) *thou* among women.
42. Blessed (art) *thou* among women,
76. And *thou*, child, shalt be called the prophet
3:22. *Thou* art my beloved Son;

Lu. 4: 7. If *thou* therefore wilt worship me,
41. *Thou* art Christ the Son of God.
7:19. Art *thou* he that should come?
20. Art *thou* he that should come?
9:60. but go *thou* and preach the kingdom of God.
10:15. And *thou*, Capernaum, which art exalted
37. Go, and do *thou* likewise.
15:31. Son, *thou* art ever with me,
16: 7. And how much owest *thou?*
25. remember that *thou* in thy lifetime
— and *thou* art tormented.
17: 8. afterward *thou* shalt eat and drink?
19:19. Be *thou* also over five cities.
42. If thou hadst known, even *thou*,
22:32. and when *thou* art converted,
58. *Thou* art also of them. And
67. Art *thou* the Christ? tell us.
70. Art *thou* then the Son of God?
23: 3. Art *thou* the King of the Jews? And he answered him and said, *Thou* sayest (it).
37. If *thou* be the king of the Jews,
39. If *thou* be Christ, save thyself and us.
40. Dost not *thou* fear God,
24:18. Art *thou* only a stranger in Jerusalem,
Joh. 1:19. to ask him, Who art *thou?*
21. What then? Art *thou* Elias?
— Art *thou* that prophet?
25. if *thou* be not that Christ, nor Elias,
42(43). *Thou* art Simon the son of Jona. *thou* shalt be called Cephas,
49(50). *thou* art the Son of God; *thou* art the King of Israel.
2:10. *thou* hast kept the good wine until now.
20. and wilt *thou* rear it up in three days?
3: 2. can do these miracles that *thou* doest,
10. Art *thou* a master of Israel, and
26. to whom *thou* barest witness,
4: 9. How is it that *thou*, being a Jew,
10. *thou* wouldest have asked of him,
12. Art *thou* greater than our father Jacob,
19. I perceive that *thou* art a prophet.
6:30. What sign shewest *thou* then, that we
69. and are sure that *thou* art that Christ,
7:52. Art *thou* also of Galilee?
8: 5. should be stoned: but what sayest *thou?*
13. *Thou* bearest record of thyself;
25. Then said they unto him, Who art *thou?*
33. how sayest *thou*, Ye shall be made free?
48. Say we not well that *thou* art a Samaritan,
52. and *thou* sayest, If a man keep my
53. Art *thou* greater than our father
— whom makest *thou* thyself?
9:17. What sayest *thou* of him,
28. and said, *Thou* art his disciple;
34. *Thou* wast altogether born in sins, and dost *thou* teach us?
35. Dost *thou* believe on the Son of God?
10:24. If *thou* be the Christ, tell us plainly.
33. *thou*, being a man, makest thyself God.
11:27. I believe that *thou* art the Christ,
42. they may believe that *thou* hast sent me.
12:34. and how sayest *thou*, The Son of man must be
13: 6. Lord, dost *thou* wash my feet?
7. What I do *thou* knowest not now;
14: 9. and how sayest *thou* (then), Shew us
17: 5. And now, O Father, glorify *thou* me
8. have believed that *thou* didst send me.
21. as *thou*, Father, (art) in me, and I in thee,
— may believe that *thou* hast sent me.
23. I in them, and *thou* in me,
Joh.17:23. may know that *thou* hast sent me,
25. these have known that *thou* hast sent me.
18:17. Art not *thou* also (one) of this man's
25. Art not *thou* also (one) of his disciples?
33. Art *thou* the King of the Jews?
34. Sayest *thou* this thing of thyself,
37. Art *thou* a king then? Jesus answered, *Thou* sayest that I am a king.
19: 9. and saith unto Jesus, Whence art *thou?*
20:15. Sir, if *thou* have borne him hence,
21:12. durst ask him, Who art *thou?*
15. Yea, Lord; *thou* knowest that I love thee.
16. Yea, Lord; *thou* knowest that I love thee.
17. Lord, *thou* knowest all things; *thou* knowest that I love thee.
22. what (is that) to thee? follow *thou* me.
Acts 1:24. *Thou*, Lord, which knowest the hearts
4:24. Lord, *thou* (art) God, which hast made
7:28. Wilt *thou* kill me, as thou diddest the
9: 5. I am Jesus whom *thou* persecutest:
10:15. (that) call not *thou* common.
33. and *thou* hast well done that thou art come.
11: 9. (that) call not *thou* common.
14. whereby *thou* and all thy house
13:33. *Thou* art my Son, this day have I begotten thee.
16:31. and *thou* shalt be saved, and thy house.
21:38. Art not *thou* that Egyptian,
22: 8. Jesus of Nazareth, whom *thou* persecutest.
27. Tell me, art *thou* a Roman?
23: 3. for sittest *thou* to judge me after the law,
21. But do not *thou* yield unto them:
25:10. done no wrong, as *thou* very well knowest.
26:15. I am Jesus whom *thou* persecutest.
Ro. 2: 3. that *thou* shalt escape the judgment of
17. Behold, *thou* art called a Jew,
9:20. who art *thou* that repliest against God?
11:17. and *thou*, being a wild olive tree,
18. *thou* bearest not the root, but the root thee.
20. and *thou* standest by faith.
22. otherwise *thou* also shalt be cut off.
24. For if *thou* wert cut out of the olive
14: 4. Who art *thou* that judgest another man's
10. But why dost *thou* judge thy brother? or why dost *thou* set at nought
32. Hast *thou* faith? have (it) to thyself
1Co.14:17. For *thou* verily givest thanks well,
15:36. that which *thou* sowest is not quickened,
Gal. 2:14. If *thou*, being a Jew, livest after the
6: 1. lest *thou* also be tempted.
1Ti. 6:11. But *thou*, O man of God, flee these
2Ti. 1:18. at Ephesus, *thou* knowest very well.
2: 1. *Thou* therefore, my son, be strong in
3. *Thou* therefore endure hardness,
3:10. But *thou* hast fully known my
14. But continue *thou* in the things
4: 5. But watch *thou* in all things,
15. Of whom be *thou* ware also;
Tit. 2: 1. But speak *thou* the things which become sound doctrine:
Philem 12. *thou* therefore receive him,
Heb. 1: 5. *Thou* art my Son, this day have I begotten thee?
10. And, *Thou*, Lord, in the beginning
11. They shall perish; but *thou* remainest;
12. but *thou* art the same, and thy years
5: 5. *Thou* art my Son, to day have I begotten thee.
6. *Thou* (art) a priest for ever
7:17. *Thou* (art) a priest for ever
21. *Thou* (art) a priest for ever

Jas. 2: 3. Sit *thou* here in a good place;
— Stand *thou* there, or sit here under
18. *Thou* hast faith, and I have works:
19. *Thou* believest that there is one God;
4:12. who art *thou* that judgest another?
3Joh. 3. even as *thou* walkest in the truth.
Rev. 2:15. So hast *thou* also them that hold the
3:17. knowest not that *thou* art wretched,
4:11. for *thou* hast created all things,
7:14. and I said unto him, Sir, *thou* knowest.

4772 3 780/914 7:736 4773
συγγένεια, sungenīa.

Lu. 1:61. There is none of thy *kindred* that is
Acts 7: 3. out of thy country, and from thy *kindred*,
14. and all his *kindred*, threescore and fifteen souls.

4773 12 780/914 7:736 4862,1085
συγγενής, sungenees.

Mar 6: 4. among his own *kin*, and in his own house.
Lu. 1:36. And, behold, thy *cousin* Elisabeth,
58. And her neighbours and her *cousins*
2:44. and they sought him among (their) *kinsfolk*
14:12. thy *kinsmen*, nor (thy) rich neighbours;
21:16. brethren, and *kinsfolks*, and friends;
Joh. 18:26. being (his) *kinsman* whose ear Peter
Acts10:24. and had called together his *kinsmen*
Ro. 9: 3. for my brethren, my *kinsmen* according to the flesh:
16: 7. Salute Andronicus and Junia, my *kinsmen*,
11. Salute Herodion my *kinsman*.
21. Lucius, and Jason, and Sosipater, my *kinsmen*,

4774 1 780/915 1:689 4862,1097
συγγνώμη, sungnōmee.

1Co. 7: 6. But I speak this by *permission*,

4775 2 780/923 4862,2521
συγκάθημαι, sunkatheemai.

Mar 14:54. and he *sat with* the servants,
Acts26:30. and Bernice, and they *that sat with* them:

4776 2 780/923 7:766 4862,2523
συγκαθίζω, sunkathizo.

Lu. 22:55. and *were set down together*,
Eph. 2: 6. and *made* (us) *sit together* in heavenly (places) in Christ Jesus:

4777 1 780/923 5:904 4862,2553
συγκακοπαθέω, sunkakopatheo.

2Ti. 1: 8. but *be* thou *partaker of the afflictions* of the gospel

4778 1 780/923 4862,2558
συγκακουχέομαι, sunkakoukeomai.

Heb 11:25. Choosing rather *to suffer affliction with* the people of God,

4779 8 780/923 3:487 4862,2564
συγκαλέω, sunkaleo.

Mar 15:16. and they *call together* the whole band.
Lu. 9: 1. *called* his twelve disciples *together, and*
15: 6. he *calleth together* (his) friends
9. *calleth* (her) friends and (her) neighbours *together*,
23:13. *when* he *had called together* the chief
Acts 5:21. and *called* the council *together*,
10:24. *and had called together* his kinsmen
28:17. Paul *called* the chief of the Jews *together*

4780 1 781/923 7:743 4862,2572
συγκαλύπτομαι, sunkaluptomai.

Lu. 12: 2. there is nothing *covered*, that shall not

4781 1 781/923 4862,2578
συγκάμπτω, sunkampto.

Ro. 11:10. and *bow down* their back alway.

4782 1 781/923 4862,2597
συγκαταβαίνω, sunkatabaino.

Acts25: 5. *go down with* (me), *and* accuse

4783 1 780/923 4784
συγκατατίθεμαι, sunkatatithemai.

Lu. 23:51. had not *consented* to the counsel and

4784 1 781/923 4862,2698
συγκατάθεσις, sunkatathesis.

2Co. 6:16. what *agreement* hath the temple of God with idols?

4785 1 781/923 9:604 4862,2596 5585
συγκαταψηφίζομαι, sunkatapseephizomai.

Acts 1:26. and he *was numbered with* the eleven apostles.

4786 2 781/923 4862,2767
συγκεράννυμι, sunkerannumi.

1Co.12:24. God *hath tempered* the body *together*,
Heb 4: 2. not *being mixed with* faith in them

4787 1 781/923 4682,2795
συγκινέω, sunkineo.

Acts 6:12. they *stirred up* the people, and the

4788 4 781/923 7:744 4862,2808
συγκλείω, sunklīo.

Lu. 5: 6. they *inclosed* a great multitude of fishes:
Ro. 11:32. For God *hath concluded* them all in unbelief,
Gal. 3:22. But the scripture *hath concluded* all under sin,
23. *shut up* unto the faith which should

4789 4 781/923 3:758,7:766 4862,2818
συγκληρονόμος, sunkleeronomos.

Ro. 8:17. heirs of God, and *joint-heirs* with Christ;
Eph. 3: 6. That the Gentiles should be *fellowheirs*,
Heb 11: 9. *the heirs with* him of the same promise.
1Pet.3: 7. *heirs together* of the grace of life;

4790 3 781/924 3:789 4862,2841
συγκοινωνέω, *sunkoinōneo.*

Eph. 5:11. And *have* no *fellowship with* the unfruitful works of darkness,
Phi. 4:14. ye have well done, *that* ye *did communicate with* my affliction.
Rev.18: 4. that ye *be* not *partakers of* her sins,

4791 4 782/924 3:789 4862,2844
συγκοινωνός, *sunkoinōnos.*

Ro. 11:17. and *with* them *partakest* of the root
1Co. 9:23. I might be *partaker* thereof *with* (you).
Phi. 1: 7. ye all are *partakers* of my grace.
Rev. 1: 9. and *companion* in tribulation,

4792 1 782/924 4862,2865
συγκομίζω, *sunkomizo.*

Acts 8: 2. And devout men *carried* Stephen (to his burial),

4793 3 782/924 3:921 4862,2919
συγκρίνω, *sunkrino.*

1Co. 2:13. *comparing* spiritual things *with* spiritual.
2Co.10:12. or *compare* ourselves *with* some that
— *comparing* themselves *among* themselves,

4794 1 782/924 4862,2955
συγκύπτω, *sunkupto.*

Lu. 13:11. and was *bowed together*, and could in no wise

4795 1 782/915 4862 *kureo* (to happen)
συγκυρία, *sunkuria.*

Lu. 10:31. by *chance* (lit. *coincidence*) there came down a certain

4796 7 782/926 9:359 4862,5463
συγχαίρω, *sunkairo.*

Lu. 1:58. and they *rejoiced with* her.
15: 6. *Rejoice with* me; for I have found my sheep
9. *Rejoice with* me; for I have found the piece
1Co.12:26. all the members *rejoice with* it.
13: 6. but *rejoiceth in* the truth;
Phi. 2:17. I joy, and *rejoice with* you all.
18. also do ye joy, and *rejoice with* me.

4797 1 782/926 4862 *cheo* (to pour)
See also below **συγχέω, *sunkeo.***

Acts21:27. *stirred up* all the people, and laid hands

4798 1 783/926 4862,5530
συγχράομαι, *sunkraomai.*

Joh. 4: 9. for the Jews *have* no *dealings with* the Samaritans.

4797 4 783/926 4797
See also above **συγχύνω, *sunkuno.***

Acts 2: 6. the multitude came together, and *were confounded*, because
9:22. and *confounded* the Jews which dwelt at
19:32. for the assembly was *confused*;
21:31. that all Jerusalem *was in an uproar*.

4799 1 783/915 4797
σύγχυσις, *sunkusis.*

Acts19:29. whole city was filled with *confusion*:

4800 3 783/922 7:766 4862,2198
συζάω, *suzao.*

Ro. 6: 8. we believe that we *shall* also *live with* him:
2Co. 7: 3. ye are in our hearts to die and *live with* (you).
2Ti. 2:11. we *shall* also *live with* (him):

4801 2 783/922 4862,rt 2201
συζευγνύω, *suzūgnuo.*

Mat.19: 6. What therefore God *hath joined together*,
Mar10: 9. What therefore God *hath joined together*,

4802 10 783/922 7:747 4862,2212
συζητέω, *suzeeteo.*

Mar 1:27. they *questioned* among themselves,
8:11. and began to *question with* him,
9:10. *questioning one with another*
14. and the scribes *questioning with* them.
16. What *question* ye with them?
12:28. and having heard them *reasoning together*,
Lu. 22:23. they began to *enquire* among themselves,
24:15. while they communed (together) and *reasoned*,
Acts 6: 9. and of Asia, *disputing with* Stephen.
9:29. and *disputed* against the Grecians:

4803 3 783/922 7:747 4802
συζήτησις, *suzeeteesis.*

Acts15: 2. no small dissension and *disputation*
7. when there had been much *disputing*,
28:29. had great *reasoning* among themselves.

4804 1 783/922 7:747 4802
συζητητής, *suzeeteetees.*

1Co. 1:20. where (is) the *disputer* of this world?

4805 1 783/922 7:748 4801
σύζυγος, *suzugos.*

Phi. 4: 3. I intreat thee also, true *yokefellow*,

4806 2 783/922 7:766 4862,2227
συζωοποιέω, *suzōöpoyeo.*

Eph 2: 5. *hath quickened* us *together with* Christ,
Col. 2:13. *hath* he *quickened together with* him,

4807 1 783/915 7:751 cf 4809 [8256]
συκάμινος, *sukaminos.*

Lu. 17: 6. ye might say unto this *sycamine tree*,

4808 16 783/915 7:751 4810
συκῆ, *sukee.*

Mat.21:19. And when he saw a *fig tree* in the way,
— And presently the *fig tree* withered away.
20. How soon is the *fig tree* withered away!
21. not only do this (which is done) to the *fig tree*,
24:32. Now learn a parable of the *fig tree*;
Mar11:13. And seeing a *fig tree* afar off having
20. they saw the *fig tree* dried up
21. behold, the *fig tree* which thou cursedst

Mar 13:28. Now learn a parable of the *fig tree*;
Lu. 13: 6 A certain (man) had a *fig tree* planted
7. I come seeking fruit on this *fig tree*,
21:29. Behold the *fig tree*, and all the trees;
Joh. 1:48(49). when thou wast under the *fig tree*,
50(51). I saw thee under the *fig tree*,
Jas. 3:12. Can the *fig tree*, my brethren, bear olive berries?
Rev. 6:13. as a *fig tree* casteth her untimely figs,

4809 1 784/915 7:751 4810 *moron* (mulberry) cf 4807

συκομωραία, sukomōraia.

Lu. 19: 4. and climbed up into a *sycomore tree*

4810 4 784/915 7:751

σῦκον, sukon.

Mat. 7:16. grapes of thorns, or *figs* of thistles?
Mar 11:13. the time of *figs* was not (yet).
Lu. 6:44. of thorns men do not gather *figs*,
Jas. 3:12. either a vine, *figs*? so (can)

4811 2 784/915 7:751 4810,5316

συκοφαντέω, sukophanteo.

Lu. 3:14. neither *accuse* (any) *falsely*;
19: 8. if I *have taken* any thing from any man *by false accusation*,

4812 1 784/915 rt 4813,71

συλαγωγέω, sulagōgeo.

Col. 2: 8. Beware lest any man *spoil* you

4813 1 784/915 *sullo* (to strip)

συλάω, sulao.

2Co. 11: 8. I *robbed* other churches, taking wages

4814 6 784/924 4862,2980

συλλαλέω, sullaleo.

Mat. 17: 3. Moses and Elias *talking* with him.
Mar 9: 4. and they were *talking with* Jesus.
Lu. 4:36. and *spake* among themselves,
9:30. there *talked with* him two men,
22: 4. and *communed with* the chief priests
Acts 25:12. Then Festus, *when* he *had conferred* with the council,

4815 16 784/915 7:759 4862,2983

συλλαμβάνω, sullambano.

Mat. 26:55. with swords and staves for *to take* me?
Mar 14:48. with swords and (with) staves *to take* me?
Lu. 1:24. his wife Elisabeth *conceived*, and
31. thou *shalt conceive* in thy womb,
36. she *hath* also *conceived* a son
2:21. before he *was conceived* in the womb.
5: 7. that they should come and *help* them.
9. at the draught of the fishes which they *had taken*:
22:54. Then *took* they him, *and* led (him),
Joh. 18:12. and officers of the Jews *took* Jesus,
Acts 1:16. guide to them *that took* Jesus.
12: 3. he proceeded further *to take* Peter
23:27. This man was *taken* of the Jews,
26:21. the Jews *caught* me in the temple, *and*
Phi. 4: 3. *help* those women which laboured with me
Jas. 1:15. Then *when* lust *hath conceived*,

4816 8 784/915 4862,3004

συλλέγω, sullego.

Mat. 7:16. *Do* men *gather* grapes of thorns
13:28. that we go and *gather* them *up*?
29. Nay; lest *while* ye *gather up* the tares
30. *Gather* ye *together* first the tares,
40. As therefore the tares *are gathered*
41. and they *shall gather* out of his kingdom
48. and *gathered* the good into vessels,
Lu. 6:44. of thorns men *do* not *gather* figs,

4817 1 784/915 4862,3049

συλλογίζομαι, sullogizomai.

Lu. 20: 5. And they *reasoned with* themselves,

4818 1 784/924 4:313 4862,3076

συλλυπέομαι, sullupeomai.

Mar 3: 5. *being grieved* for the hardness of their hearts,

4819 8 784/915 4862,rt 939

συμβαίνω, sumbaino.

Mar 10:32. what things should *happen unto* him,
Lu. 24:14. of all these things *which had happened*.
Acts 3:10. at that *which had happened unto* him.
20:19. and temptations, *which befell* me by
21:35. *so* it *was*, that he was borne of the soldiers
1Co 10:11. all these things *happened unto* them for
1Pet. 4:12. as though some strange thing *happened unto* you:
2Pet. 2:22. But it *is happened* unto them

4820 6 785/919 4862,906

συμβάλλω, sumballo.

Lu. 2:19. *and pondered* (them) in her heart.
14:31. *to make* war (lit. *to encounter* in war) against another king,
Acts 4:15. they *conferred* among themselves,
17:18. and of the Stoicks, *encountered* him.
18:27. *helped* them much which had believed
20:14. And when he *met with* us at Assos,

4821 2 785/919 1:564,7:766 4862,936

συμβασιλεύω, sumbasilūo.

1Co. 4: 8. that we also *might reign with* you.
2Ti. 2:12. we *shall* also *reign with* (him):

4822 6 785/919 7:763 4862 *bibazo* (to force)

συμβιβάζω, sumbibazo.

Acts 9:22. *proving* that this is very Christ.
16:10. *assuredly gathering* that the Lord had
1Co. 2:16. mind of the Lord, that he may *instruct* him?
Eph. 4:16. and *compacted* by that which every joint
Col. 2: 2. *being knit together* in love,
19. and *knit together*, increaseth with the increase of God.

4823 5 785/916 4862,1011

συμβουλεύω, sumboulūo.

Mat. 26: 4. *consulted* that they might take
Joh. 11:53. they *took counsel together* for to put
18:14. Caiaphas was he, *which gave counsel*

Acts 9:23. the Jews *took counsel* to kill him:
Rev. 3:18. I *counsel* thee to buy of me gold

4824 8 785/916 4825

συμβούλιον, *sumboulion.*

Mat 12:14. and held a *council* against him,
22:15. and took *counsel* how they might entangle
27: 1. and elders of the people took *counsel*
7. And they took *counsel*, and bought
28:12. and had taken *counsel*, they gave
Mar 3: 6. and straightway took *counsel*
15: 1. the chief priests held a *consultation*
Acts25:12. when he had conferred with the *council*,

4825 1 785/916 4862,1012

σύμβουλος, *sumboulos.*

Ro. 11:34. or who hath been his *counsellor?*

4827 1 786/924 4:390 4862,3129

συμμαθητής, *summatheetees.*

Joh. 11:16. unto his *fellowdisciples*, Let us

4828 4 786/924 4:474 4862,3140

συμμαρτυρέω, *summartureo.*

Ro. 2:15. their conscience *also bearing witness*,
8:16. The Spirit itself *beareth witness with*
9: 1. my conscience *also bearing* me *witness*
Rev. 22:18. For I *testify unto* every man that

4829 1 786/924 4862,3307

συμμερίζομαι, *summerizomai.*

1Co. 9:13. are *partakers with* the altar?

4830 2 786/924 4862,3353

συμμέτοχος, *summetokos.*

Eph. 3: 6. and *partakers* (lit. *co-partakers*) of his promise in Christ
5: 7. Be not ye therefore *partakers* with them.

4831 1 786/924 4:659 4862,3401

συμμιμητής, *summimeetees.*

Phi. 3:17. be *followers together* of me,

4832 2 786/916 4:766 4862,3444

συμμορφόομαι, *summorphŏomai.*

Phi. 3:10. *being made conformable unto* his death;

4833 1 786/916 7:766 4832

σύμμορφος, *summorphos.*

Ro. 8:29. (to be) *conformed to* the image of his Son,
Phi. 3:21. *fashioned like unto* his glorious body,

4834 2 786/924 5:904 4835

συμπαθέω, *sumpatheo.*

Heb. 4:15. which cannot *be touched with the feeling of* our infirmities;
10:34. *had compassion of* me in my bonds,

4835 1 786/916 5:905 4841

συμπαθής, *sumpathees.*

1Pet. 3: 8. *having compassion one of another.*

4836 2 786/924 4862,3854

συμπαραγίνομαι, *sumparaginomai.*

Lu. 23:48. And all the people *that came together*
2Ti. 4:16. no man *stood with* me.

4837 1 786/924 4862,3870

συμπαρακαλέομαι, *sumparakaleomai.*

Ro. 1:12. that I may *be comforted together* with you

4838 4 786/924 4862,3880

συμπαραλαμβάνω, *sumparalambano.*

Acts12:25. and *took with* them John,
15:37. determined *to take with* them John,
38. thought not good *to take* him *with* them,
Gal. 2: 1. *and took* Titus *with* (me) also.

4839 1 786/759 4862,3887

συμπαραμένω, *sumparameno.*

Phi. 1:25. that I shall abide and *continue with* you all

4840 1 786/924 4862,3918

συμπάρειμι, *sumparīmi.*

Acts25:24. and all men *which are here present with* us,

4841 2 786/924 5:904,7:766 4862,3958

συμπάσχω, *sumpasko.*

Ro. 8:17. if so be that we *suffer with* (him),
1Co.12:26. all the members *suffer with* it:

4842 2 787/924 4862,3992

συμπέμπω, *sumpempo.*

2Co. 8:18. And we *have sent with* him the brother,
22. And we *have sent with* them our brother,

4843 1 787/925 4862,4012,2983

συμπεριλαμβάνω, *sumperilambano.*

Acts20:10. and fell on him, and *embracing* (him)

4844 1 787/925 4862,4095

συμπίνω, *sumpino.*

Acts10:41. who did eat and *drink with* him

4845 3 787/925 6:283 4862,4137

συμπληρόω, *sumpleeroō.*

Lu. 8:23. and they *were filled* (with water),
9:51. when the time *was come*
Acts 2: 1. the day of Pentecost *was fully come*,

4846 5 787/925 6:455 4862,4155

συμπνίγω, *sumpnigo.*

Mat.13:22. and the deceitfulness of riches, *choke* the word,
Mar 4: 7. and *choked* it, and it yielded no
19. entering in, *choke* the word,
Lu. 8:14. go forth, and *are choked* with cares
42. But as he went the people *thronged* him.

4847 1 787/925 4862,4177

συμπολίτης, *sumpolitees.*

Eph 2:19. but *fellowcitizens* with the saints,

4848 4 787/925 4862,4198

συμπορεύομαι, *sumporuomai.*

Mar10: 1. and the people *resort* unto him again;
Lu. 7:11. and many of his disciples *went with* him,
14:25. And there *went* great multitudes *with*
24:15. drew near, and *went with* them.

4849 1 787/916 4844

συμπόσιον, *sumposion.*

Mar 6:39. to make all sit down by *companies* (lit. *company* by *company*)

4850 1 787/925 6:651 4862,4245

συμπρεσβύτερος, *sumpresbuteros.*

1Pet.5: 1. who am *also* an *elder*, (lit. a *co-elder*)

συμφαγεῖν see συνεσθίω. 4906

4851 17 787/916 9:56 4862,5342

συμφέρω, *sumphero.*

Mat. 5:29. for it *is profitable for* thee that one
30. for it *is profitable for* thee that one
18: 6. t were *better for* him that a millstone
19:10. it *is* not *good* to marry.
Joh.11:50. Nor consider that it *is expedient for* us,
16: 7. It *is expedient for* you that I go away:
18:14. that it *was expedient* that one man
Acts19:19. *brought* their books *together, and*
20:20. nothing *that was profitable* (unto you),
1Co. 6:12. but all things *are* not *expedient:*
7:35. And this I speak for your own *profit;*
10:23. but all things *are* not *expedient:*
33. not seeking mine own *profit,*
12: 7. given to every man to *profit* withal.
2Co. 8:10. for this *is expedient for* you,
12: 1. It *is* not *expedient for* me doubtless to glory.
Heb12:10. but he for (our) *profit,*

Note. That the verb is used transitively in Acts 19: 19, whereas in all the other passages it is intransitive, and in most of them impersonal.

4852 1 788/926 4862,5346

σύμφημι, *sumpheemi.*

Ro. 7:16 I *consent unto* the law that (it is) good.

4853 1 788/916 4862,5443

συμφυλέτης, *sumphuletees.*

1Th. 2:14. suffered like things of your own *countrymen,*

4855 1 788/926 4862,5453

συμφύομαι, *sumphuomai.*

Lu. 8: 7. the thorns *sprang up with it, and*

4854 1 788/916 7:766 4862,5453

σύμφυτος, *sumphutos.*

Ro. 6: 5. if we have been *planted together* in

4856 6 788/916 4859

συμφωνέω, *sumphōneo.*

Mat.18:19. That if two of you *shall agree* on earth
20: 2. And *when* he *had agreed* with the labourers
13. *didst* not thou *agree with* me for
Lu. 5:36. *agreeth* not *with* the old.
Acts 5: 9. ye *have agreed together* to tempt
15:15. to this *agree* the words of the prophets;

4857 1 788/916 9:278 4856

συμφώνησις, *sumpnōneesis.*

2Co. 6:15. And what *concord* hath Christ with Belial?

4858 1 788/916 9:278 4859

συμφωνία, *sumphōnia.*

Lu. 15:25. he heard *musick* and dancing.

4859 1 788/916 9:278 4862,5456

σύμφωνος, *sumphōnos.*

1Co. 7: 5. except (it be) with *consent* for a time,

4860 1 789/916 9:604 4862,5585

συμψηφίζω, *sumpseephizo.*

Acts19:19. and they *counted* the price of them,

4861 1 789/916 4862,5590

σύμψυχος, *sumpsukos.*

Phi. 2: 2. (being) *of one accord*, of one mind.

4862 125 789/916 7:766 cf 3844
cf 3326

σύν, *sun.*

prep. governing the dative case.

Mat.25:27. have received mine own *with* usury.
26:35. Though I should die *with* thee, yet
27:38. Then were there two thieves crucified *with* him,
Mar 2:26. gave also to them which were *with* him?
4:10. they that were about him *with* the twelve
8:34. called the people (unto him) *with* his disciples
9: 4. appeared unto them Elias *with* Moses:
15:27. And *with* him they crucify two thieves;
Lu. 1:56. And Mary abode *with* her about
2: 5. To be taxed *with* Mary his espoused wife,
13. And suddenly there was *with* the angel
5: 9. and all that were *with* him,
19. *with* (his) couch into the midst
7: 6. Then Jesus went *with* them.
12. much people of the city was *with* her.
8: 1. and the twelve (were) *with* him,
38. besought him that he might be *with* him:
9:32. Peter and they that were *with* him
19:23. required mine own *with* usury?
20: 1. the scribes came upon (him) *with* the elders,
22:14. and the twelve apostles *with* him.
56. This man was also *with* him.
23:11. And Herod *with* his men of war
32. led *with* him to be put to death.
35. And the rulers also *with* them
24: 1. and certain (others) *with* them.
10. and other (women that were) *with* them
21. and *beside* all this, to day
24. certain of them which were *with* us
29. to tarry *with* them.

Lu. 24:33. and them that were *with* them,
44. while I was yet *with* you,
Joh.18: 1. he went forth *with* his disciples
21: 3. We also go *with* thee. They went
Acts 1:14. *with* the women, and Mary the mother of Jesus, and *with* his brethren.
17. For he was numbered *with* us,
22. ordained to be a witness *with* us
2:14. But Peter, standing up *with* the eleven,
3: 4. fastening his eyes upon him *with* John,
8. and entered *with* them into the temple,
4:13. that they had been *with* Jesus.
14. the man which was healed standing *with*
27. and Pontius Pilate, *with* the Gentiles,
5: 1. Ananias, *with* Sapphira his wife,
17. and all they that were *with* him,
21. and they that were *with* him,
26. Then went the captain *with* the officers,
8:20. Thy money perish *with* thee,
31. he would come up and sit *with* him.
10: 2. one that feared God *with* all his house,
20. get thee down, and go *with* them,
23. Peter went away *with* them,
11:12. accompanied me, (lit. came *with* me)
13: 7. Which was *with* the deputy
14: 4. and part held *with* the Jews, and part *with* the apostles.
5. and also of the Jews *with* their rulers,
13. done sacrifice *with* the people.
20. he departed *with* Barnabas to Derbe.
28. they abode long time *with* the disciples.
15:22. and elders, *with* the whole church,
— *with* Paul and Barnabas;
25. *with* our beloved Barnabas and Paul,
16: 3. Him would Paul have to go forth *with* him;
17:34. Damaris, and others *with* them.
18: 8. believed on the Lord *with* all his house;
18. and *with* him Priscilla and Aquila;
19:38. and the craftsmen which are *with* him,
20:36. and prayed *with* them all.
21: 5. *with* wives and children,
16. There went *with* us also (certain) of the disciples
18. Paul went in *with* us unto James;
24. and purify thyself *with* them,
26. purifying himself *with* them
29. they had seen before *with* him in the city
22: 9. And they that were *with* me saw
23:15. Now therefore ye *with* the council
27. then came I *with* an army,
32. they left the horsemen to go *with* him,
24:24. when Felix came *with* his wife
25:23. *with* the chief captains, and
26:13. and them which journeyed *with* me.
27: 2. a Macedonian of Thessalonica, being *with* us.
28:16. *with* a soldier that kept him.
Ro. 6: 8. Now if we be dead *with* Christ,
8:32. *with* him also freely give us all things?
16:14. and the brethren which are *with* them.
15. all the saints which are *with* them.
1Co. 1: 2. *with* all that in every place
5: 4. *with* the power of our Lord Jesus Christ,
10:13. *with* the temptation also make a way
11:32. not be condemned *with* the world.
15:10. the grace of God which was *with* me.
16: 4. they shall go *with* me.
19. *with* the church that is in their house.
2Co. 1: 1. *with* all the saints which are in all
21. he which stablisheth us *with* you
4:14. and shall present (us) *with* you.
2Co. 8:19. to travel with us *with* this gra
9: 4. if they of Macedonia come *with* me
13: 4. but we shall live *with* him
Gal. 1: 2. And all the brethren which are *with* me,
2: 3. neither Titus, who was *with* me,
3: 9. are blessed *with* faithful Abraham.
5:24. have crucified the flesh *with* the affections
Eph. 3:18. to comprehend *with* all saints
4:31. be put away from you, *with* all malice:
Phi. 1: 1. *with* the bishops and deacons:
23. to depart, and to be *with* Christ;
2:22. he hath served *with* me in the gospel.
4:21. The brethren which are *with* me
Col. 2: 5. yet am I *with* you in the spirit,
13. hath he quickened together *with* him,
20. Wherefore if ye be dead *with* Christ
3: 3. your life is hid *with* Christ in God.
4. ye also shall appear *with* him in glory.
9. ye have put off the old man *with* his deeds;
4: 9. *With* Onesimus, a faithful and
1Th. 4:14. will God bring *with* him.
17. shall be caught up together *with* them
— so shall we ever be *with* the Lord.
5:10. we should live together *with* him.
Jas. 1:11. is no sooner risen *with* a burning heat,
2Pet. 1:18. when we were *with* him in the holy mount

4863 62 789/917 4862,71

συνάγω, *sunago*.

Mat. 2: 4. *when* he *had gathered. . . . together*
3:12. and *gather* his wheat into the garner;
6:26. nor *gather* into barns;
12:30. and he *that gathereth* not with me
13: 2. And great multitudes *were gathered together*
30. but *gather* the wheat into my barn.
47. and *gathered* of every kind:
18:20. are *gathered together* in my name,
22:10. and *gathered together* all
34. they were *gathered* together.
41. *While* the Pharisees *were gathered together*,
24:28. there *will* the eagles *be gathered together*.
25:24. and *gathering* where thou hast not strawed:
26. and *gather* where I have not strawed:
32. And before him *shall be gathered* all nations:
35. a stranger, and ye *took* me *in*:
38. a stranger, and *took* (thee) *in*?
43. a stranger, and ye *took* me not *in*:
26: 3. Then *assembled together* the chief priests,
57. scribes and the elders *were assembled*.
27:17. *when* they *were gathered together*,
27. and *gathered* unto him the whole band
62. priests and Pharisees *came together*
28:12. And *when* they *were assembled* with
Mar 2: 2. many *were gathered together*,
4: 1. and there *was gathered* unto him
5:21. much people *gathered* unto him:
6:30. the apostles *gathered* themselves *together*
7: 1. *came together* unto him the Pharisees,
Lu. 3:17. and *will gather* the wheat into his
11:23. and he *that gathereth* not with me
12:17. no room where to *bestow* my fruits?
18. there *will* I *bestow* all my fruits
15:13. younger son *gathered* all *together*, *and*
17:37. *will* the eagles *be gathered together*.
22:66. priests and the scribes *came together*,
Joh. 4:36. and *gathereth* fruit unto life eternal:
6:12. *Gather up* the fragments that remain,
13. Therefore they *gathered* (them) *together*,
11:47. Then *gathered* the chief priests and

Joh. 11:52. but that also he *should gather together* in one the children of God
15: 6. and men *gather* them, and cast
18: 2. for Jesus ofttimes *resorted* thither with
20:19. where the disciples were *assembled*
Acts 4: 6(5). *were gathered together* at Jerusalem.
26. and the rulers were *gathered* together
27. and the people of Israel, *were gathered together*,
31. where they were *assembled together*;
11:26. they *assembled* themselves with the church,
13:44. *came* almost the whole city *together*
14:27. and *had gathered* the church *together*,
15: 6. the apostles and elders *came together*
30. and *when* they *had gathered* the multitude *together*,
20: 7. *when* the disciples *came together*
8. where they were *gathered together*.
1Co. 5: 4. *when* ye *are gathered together*,
Rev.13:10. He that *leadeth into* captivity
16:14. *to gather* them to the battle
16. And he *gathered* them *together*
19:17. Come and *gather* yourselves *together*
19. and their armies, *gathered together*
20: 8. *to gather* them *together* to battle:

4864 57 790/917 7:798 4863

συναγωγή, sunagōgee.

Mat. 4:23. teaching in their *synagogues*,
6: 2. as the hypocrites do in the *synagogues*
5. love to pray standing in the *synagogues*
9:35. teaching in their *synagogues*,
10:17. they will scourge you in their *synagogues*;
12: 9. he went into their *synagogue*:
13:54. he taught them in their *synagogue*,
23: 6. chief seats in the *synagogues*,
34. shall ye scourge in your *synagogues*,
Mar 1:21. he entered into the *synagogue*,
23. And there was in their *synagogue*
29. they were come out of the *synagogue*,
39. And he preached in their *synagogues*
3: 1. he entered again into the *synagogue*;
6: 2. he began to teach in the *synagogue*:
12:39. And the chief seats in the *synagogues*,
13: 9. in the *synagogues* ye shall be beaten:
Lu. 4:15. And he taught in their *synagogues*,
16. he went into the *synagogue*
20. all them that were in the *synagogue*
28. And all they in the *synagogue*,
33. in the *synagogue* there was a man,
38. And he arose out of the *synagogue*,
44. And he preached in the *synagogues*
6: 6. he entered into the *synagogue* and
7: 5. and he hath built us a *synagogue*.
8:41. he was a ruler of the *synagogue*:
11:43. the uppermost seats in the *synagogues*,
12:11. when they bring you unto the *synagogues*,
13:10. he was teaching in one of the *synagogues*
20:46. the highest seats in the *synagogues*,
21:12. delivering (you) up to the *synagogues*,
Joh. 6:59. These things said he in the *synagogue*,
18:20. I ever taught in the *synagogue*,
Acts 6: 9. certain of the *synagogue*, which is called
9: 2. letters to Damascus to the *synagogues*,
20. he preached Christ in the *synagogues*,
13: 5. preached the word of God in the *synagogues*
14. and went into the *synagogue*
42. the Jews were gone out of the *synagogue*,
43. when the *congregation* was broken up,
14: 1. went both together into the *synagogue*
Acts15:21. being read in the *synagogues*
17: 1. where was a *synagogue* of the Jews:
10. went into the *synagogue* of the Jews.
17. disputed he in the *synagogue*
18: 4. And he reasoned in the *synagogue*
7. whose house joined hard to the *synagogue*
19. he himself entered into the *synagogue*,
26. to speak boldly in the *synagogue*:
19: 8. And he went into the *synagogue*,
22:19. and beat in every *synagogue*
24:12. neither in the *synagogues*, nor in
26:11. punished them oft in every *synagogue*,
Jas. 2: 2. if there come unto your *assembly*
Rev. 2: 9. but (are) the *synagogue* of Satan.
3: 9. them of the *synagogue* of Satan,

4865 1 791/918 4862,75

συναγωνίζομαι, sunagōnizomai.

Ro. 15:30. that ye *strive together with* me

4866 2 791/918 1:167 4862,118

συναθλέω, sunathleo.

Phi. 1:27. *striving together for* the faith of the gospel;
4: 3. which *laboured with* me in the gospel,

4867 3 791/918 4862 *athroizō* (to hoard)

συναθροίζω, sunathroizo.

Lu. 24:33. and found the eleven *gathered together*,
Acts12:12. where many were *gathered together*
19:25. Whom he *called together* with the

4868 3 791/918 4862,142

συναίρω, sunairo.

Mat.18:23. which would *take* account of his servants.
24. And when he had begun *to reckon*,
25:19. cometh, and *reckoneth* (lit. *taketh* account) with them.

4869 3 791/918 1:195 4862,164

συναιχμάλωτος, sunaikmalōtos.

Ro. 16: 7. my kinsmen, and my *fellowprisoners*,
Col. 4:10. Aristarchus my *fellowprisoner*
Philem 23. Epaphras, my *fellowprisoner* in Christ Jesus;

4870 2 791/918 1:210 4862,190

συνακολουθέω, sunakoloutheo.

Mar 5:37. And he suffered no man *to follow* him,
Lu. 23:49. and the women *that followed* him from Galilee,

4871 1 791/918 4862 *halizō* (to throng)

συναλίζομαι, sunalizomai.

Acts 1: 4. And *being assembled together* with (them), commanded them that

---

4872 2 791/918 4862,305

συναναβαίνω, sunanabaino.

Mar15:41. many other women *which came up with* him unto Jerusalem.
Acts13:31. of them *which came up with* him

4873 9 792/918 3:654 4862,345

συνανάκειμαι, sunanakīmai.

Mat. 9:10. came and *sat down with* him and his
14: 9. and them *which sat with* him *at meat,*
Mar 2:15. sinners *sat* also *together with* Jesus
6:22. pleased Herod and them *that sat with* him,
26. and for their sakes *which sat with* him,
Lu. 7:49. And they *that sat at meat with* him
14:10. of them *that sit at meat with* thee.
15. one of them *that sat at meat with* him
Joh.12: 2. of them *that sat at the table with* him.

4874 3 792/918 7:852 4862,303 3396

συναναμίγνυμι, sunanamignumi.

1Co. 5: 9. not *to company with* fornicators:
11. written unto you not *to keep company,*
2Th. 3:14. and *have* no *company with* him,

4875 1 792/919 4862,373

συναναπαύομαι, sunanapauomai.

Ro. 15:32. and may *with* you *be refreshed.*

4876 6 792/919 4862, 473

συναντάω, sunantao.

Lu. 9:37. much people *met* him.
22:10. there *shall* a man *meet* you, bearing
Acts10:25. Cornelius *met* him, and fell down at
20:22. not knowing the things *that shall befall* me
Heb 7: 1. *who met* Abraham returning
10. when Melchisedec *met* him.

4877 1 792/972 4876

συνάντησις, sunanteesis.

Mat. 8:34. the whole city came out to *meet* Jesus:

4878 2 792/919 1:375 4862,482

συναντιλαμβάνομαι, sunantilambanomai.

Lu. 10:40. bid her therefore that she *help* me.
Ro. 8:26. the Spirit also *helpeth* our infirmities:

4879 3 792/919 4862,520

συναπάγομαι, sunapagomai.

Ro. 12:16. but *condescend* to men of low estate.
Gal. 2:13. Barnabas also *was carried away with*
2Pet.3:17. *being led away with* the error of the

4880 3 792/919 3:766 4862,599

συναποθνήσκω, sunapothneesko.

Mar 14:31. If I should *die with* thee, I will
2Co. 7: 3. ye are in our hearts *to die* and live *with* (you).
2Ti. 2:11. For if we *be dead with* (him),

4881 1 792/919 4862,622

συναπόλλυμαι, sunapollumai.

Heb 11:31. Rahab *perished* not *with* them that believed not,

4882 1 792/919 4862,649

συναποστέλλω, sunapostello.

2Co.12:18. and *with* (him) I *sent* a brother

4883 2 792/919 7:855 4862,719 3004

συναρμολογέομαι, sunarmologeomai.

Eph 2:21. In whom all the building *fitly framed together*
4:16. From whom the whole body *fitly joined together*

4884 4 792/919 4862,726

συναρπάζω, sunarpazo.

Lu. 8:29. For oftentimes it *had caught* him:
Acts 6:12. *caught* him, and brought (him)
19:29. and *having caught* Gaius and
27:15. And *when* the ship *was caught,* and could not bear up

4885 1 793/919 4862,837

συναυξάνομαι, sunauxanomai.

Mat.13:30. Let both *grow together* until the harvest:

4887 1 793/919 4862,1210

συνδέομαι, sundeomai.

Heb13: 3. that are in bonds, as *bound with* them;

4886 4 793/919 7:856 4862,1199

σύνδεσμος, sundesmos.

Acts 8:23. and (in) the *bond* of iniquity.
Eph 4: 3. unity of the Spirit in the *bond* of peace.
Col. 2:19. the body by joints and *bands* having nourishment ministered,
3:14. which is the *bond* of perfectness.

4888 1 793/919 2:232,7:766 4862,1392

συνδοξάζομαι, sundoxazomai.

Ro. 8:17. that we *may be* also *glorified together.*

4889 10 793/919 2:261 4862,1401

σύνδουλος, sundoulos.

Mat.18:28. and found one of his *fellowservants,*
29. And his *fellowservant* fell down
31. So when his *fellowservants* saw what was
33. have had compassion on thy *fellowservant,*
24:49. shall begin to smite (his) *fellowservants,*
Col. 1: 7. Epaphras our dear *fellowservant,*
4: 7. and *fellowservant* in the Lord:
Rev. 6:11. until their *fellowservants* also
19:10. I am thy *fellowservant,* and of thy
22: 9. I am thy *fellowservant,* and of thy

4890 1 793/920 4936

συνδρομή, sundromee.

Acts21:30. and the people *ran together:* (lit. there was a *concourse* &c. of)

4891 1 793/920 7:766 4862,1453

συνεγείρω, sunegīro.

Eph 2: 6. And *hath raised* (us) *up together,*
Col. 2:12. wherein also ye *are risen with* (him)
3: 1. If ye then *be risen with* Christ,

4892 22 793/920 7:860 4862 rt 1476

συνέδριον, sunedrion.

Mat. 5:22. shall be in danger of the *council:*

Mat.10:17. they will deliver you up to the *councils*,
26:59. and elders, and all the *council*,
Mar 13: 9. for they shall deliver you up to *councils*;
14:55. the chief priests and all the *council*
15: 1. and scribes and the whole *council*,
Lu. 22:66. and led him into their *council*, saying,
Joh.11:47. Then gathered the chief priests and the Pharisees a *council*,
Acts 4:15. to go aside out of the *council*,
5:21. and called the *council* together,
27. they set (them) before the *council*:
34. Then stood there up one in the *council*,
41. from the presence of the *council*,
6:12. and brought (him) to the *council*,
15. And all that sat in the *council*,
22:30. and all their *council* to appear,
23: 1. Paul, earnestly beholding the *council*,
6. he cried out in the *council*,
15. Now therefore ye with the *council*
20. bring down Paul to morrow into the *council*,
28. brought him forth into their *council*:
24:20. while I stood before the *council*,

4894 4 /920 7:899 4862,1492
συνειδέω, sunīdeo.

Acts 5: 2. his wife also *being privy* (to it),
12:12. And *when* he *had considered* (the thing),
14: 6. They *were ware* of (it), *and* fled unto Lystra
1Co. 4: 4. For I *know* nothing *by* myself; (lit. *am conscious* of nought)

4893 32 794/920 7:899 4894
συνείδησις, sunīdeesis.

Joh. 8: 9. being convicted by (their own) *conscience*,
Acts23: 1. I have lived in all good *conscience*
24:16. to have always a *conscience* void of
Ro. 2:15. their *conscience* also bearing witness,
9: 1. my *conscience* also bearing me witness
13: 5. but also for *conscience* sake.
1Co. 8: 7. for some with *conscience* of the idol
— and their *conscience* being weak is defiled.
10. shall not the *conscience* of him which is weak
12. and wound their weak *conscience*,
10:25. asking no question for *conscience* sake:
27. asking no question for *conscience* sake.
28. and for *conscience* sake: for the earth
29. *Conscience*, I say, not thine own,
— judged of another (man's) *conscience*?
2Co. 1:12. the testimony of our *conscience*,
4: 2. commending ourselves to every man's *conscience*
5:11. are made manifest in your *consciences*.
1Ti. 1: 5. and (of) a good *conscience*, and
19. Holding faith, and a good *conscience*;
3: 9. the mystery of the faith in a pure *conscience*.
4: 2. having their *conscience* seared
2Ti. 1: 3. with pure *conscience*, that without
Tit. 1:15. their mind and *conscience* is defiled.
Heb 9: 9. perfect, as pertaining to the *conscience*;
14. purge your *conscience* from dead works
10: 2. no more *conscience* of sins.
22. sprinkled from an evil *conscience*,
13:18. we trust we have a good *conscience*,
1Pet.2:19. if a man for *conscience* toward God
3:16. Having a good *conscience*;
21. but the answer of a good *conscience*

4895 2 794/920 4862,1510
σύνειμι, sunīmi.

Lu. 9:18. his disciples *were with* him:
Acts22:11. led by the hand of them *that were with* me

4896 1 794/920 4862 *eimi* (to go)
σύνειμι, sunīmi.

Lu. 8: 4. when much people *were gathered together*,

4897 2 794/920 4862,1525
συνεισέρχομαι, sunīserkomai.

Joh. 6:22. Jesus *went* not *with* his disciples *into* the boat,
18:15. *went in with* Jesus into the palace of

4898 2 794/920 4862,rt 1553
συνέκδημος, sunekdeemos.

Acts19:29. Paul's *companions in travel*,
2Co. 8:19. chosen of the churches to *travel with* us

4899 1 794/920 4862,1586
συνεκλεκτός, suneklektos.

1Pet. 5:13. *elected together with* (you), saluteth you;

4900 1 794/918 4862,1643
συνελαύνω, sunelauno.

Acts 7:26. and would have set them at one again, (lit. *drew* them *together* to peace)

4901 1 795/920 4:474 4862,1957
συνεπιμαρτυρέω, sunepimartureo.

Heb 2: 4. God *also bearing* (them) *witness*,

4902 1 795/921 4862 *hepo* (to follow)
συνέπομαι, sunepomai.

Acts20: 4. there *accompanied* him into Asia

4903 5 795/921 7:871 4904
συνεργέω, sunergeo.

Mar16:20. the Lord *working with* (them),
Ro. 8:28. all things *work together* for good to them
1Co.16:16. and to every one *that helpeth with* (us),
2Co. 6: 1. We then, (as) *workers together* (with him),
Jas. 2:22. how faith *wrought with* his works,

4904 13 795/921 7:871 4862 rt 2041
συνεργός, sunergos.

Ro. 16: 3. Priscilla and Aquila my *helpers* in Christ Jesus:
9. Salute Urbane, our *helper* in Christ,
21. Timotheus my *workfellow*, and
1Co. 3: 9. For we are *labourers together with* God:
2Co. 1:24. but are *helpers* of your joy:
8:23. my partner and *fellowhelper* concerning you:
Phi. 2:25. my brother, and *companion in labour*,
4: 3. (with) other my *fellowlabourers*,
Col. 4:11. These only (are my) *fellowworkers* unto
1Th. 3: 2. our *fellowlabourer* in the gospel
Philem. 1. our dearly beloved, and *fellowlabourer*,
24. Demas, Lucas, my *fellowlabourers*.
3Joh. 8. might be *fellowhelpers* to the truth.

4905 32 795/921 2:666 4862,2064

συνέρχομαι, sunerkomai.

Mat. 1:18. before they *came together*, she
Mar 3:20. the multitude *cometh together* again,
6:33. and *came together* unto him.
14:53. and *with* him *were assembled*
Lu. 5:15. great multitudes *came together* to hear,
23:55. the women also, *which came with* him from
Joh. 11:33. the Jews also weeping *which came with* her,
18:20. whither the Jews always *resort*; and
Acts 1: 6. *When* they therefore *were come together*,
21. of these men *which have companied with* us
2: 6. the multitude *came together*,
5:16. There *came* also a multitude (out) of
9:39. Then Peter arose and *went with* them.
10:23. brethren from Joppa *accompanied* him.
27. and found many *that were come together*.
45. as many as *came with* Peter, because
11:12. the spirit bade me *go with* them,
15:38. and *went* not *with* them to the work.
16:13. unto the women *which resorted* (thither).
19:32. knew not wherefore they *were come together*.
21:16. There *went with* us also (certain) of the
22. the multitude must needs *come together*:
25:17. *when* they *were come* hither.
28:17. and *when* they *were come together*, he
1Co. 7: 5. and *come together* again,
11:17. that ye *come together* not for the better,
18. *when* ye *come together* in the church,
20. *When* ye *come together* therefore
33. *when* ye *come together* to eat,
34. that ye *come* not *together* unto condemnation.
14:23. the whole church *be come together*
26. when ye *come together*, every one of you

4906 5 796/921 4862,2068

συνεσθίω, sunesthio.

Lu. 15: 2. receiveth sinners, and *eateth with* them.
Acts 10:41. who *did eat* and drink *with* him
11: 3. and *didst eat with* them.
1Co. 5:11. *with* such an one no not *to eat*.
Gal. 2:12. he *did eat with* the Gentiles:

4907 7 796/921 7:888 4920

σύνεσις, sunesis.

Mar 12:33. and with all the *understanding*,
Lu. 2:47. were astonished at his *understanding*
1Co. 1:19. bring to nothing the *understanding* of the prudent.
Eph. 3: 4. my *knowledge* in the mystery of Christ
Col. 1: 9. in all wisdom and spiritual *understanding*;
2: 2. unto all riches of the full assurance of *understanding*,
2Ti. 2: 7. and the Lord give thee *understanding* in all things.

4908 4 921 7:888 4920

συνετός, sunetos. cf 5429

Mat. 11:25. from the wise and *prudent*,
Lu. 10:21. from the wise and *prudent*,
Acts 13: 7. Sergius Paulus, a *prudent* man;
1Co. 1:19. will bring to nothing the understanding of the *prudent*.

4909 6 796/921 4862,2106

συνευδοκέω, sunūdokeo.

Lu. 11:48. that ye *allow* the deeds of your fathers.
Acts 8: 1. And Saul was *consenting* unto his death
22:20. and *consenting* unto his death,
Ro. 1:32. but *have pleasure* in them that do them.
1Co. 7:12. and she *be pleased* to dwell with him,
13. and if he *be pleased* to dwell with her,

4910 2 796/921 4862,2095,2192

συνευωχέομαι, sunūōkeomai.

2Pet. 2:13. *while* they *feast with* you;
Jude 12. *when* they *feast with* you,

4911 1 796/922 4862,2186

συνεφίστημι, sunephisteemi.

Acts 16:22. And the multitude *rose up together* against them:

4912 12 796/922 7:877 4862,2192

συνέχω, suneko.

Mat. 4:24. sick people *that were taken with* divers diseases
Lu. 4:38. Simon's wife's mother was *taken with* a great fever;
8:37. for they *were taken with* great fear:
45. Master, the multitude *throng* thee and
12:50. how *am* I *straitened* till it be accomplished!
19:43. and *keep* thee *in* on every side,
22:63. the men *that held* Jesus mocked him,
Acts 7:57. *stopped* their ears, and ran upon him
18: 5. Paul *was pressed* in the spirit,
28: 8. the father of Publius lay *sick of* a fever and of
2Co. 5:14. the love of Christ *constraineth* us; because
Phi. 1:23. For I *am in a strait* betwixt two,

4913 1 797/922 4862,rt 2237

συνήδομαι, suneedomai.

Ro. 7:22. For I *delight* in the law of God

4914 2 797/922 4862,2239

συνήθεια, suneethīa.

Joh. 18:39. But ye have a *custom*,
1Co. 11:16. we have no such *custom*,

4915 1 797/922 4862,2244

συνηλικιώτης, suneelikiōtees.

Gal. 1:14. above many my *equals* in mine own nation

4916 2 797/922 7:766 4862,2290

συνθάπτομαι, sunthaptomai.

Ro. 6: 4. we *are buried with* (lit. *have been buried with*) him by baptism into death:
Col. 2:12. *Buried with* him in baptism,

4917 2 797/922 4862 *thlaō* (to crush)

συνθλάομαι, sunthlaomai.

Mat. 21:44. fall on this stone *shall be broken*:
Lu. 20:18. fall upon that stone *shall be broken*;

4918 2 797/922 4862,2346

συνθλίβω, sunthlibo.

Mar 5:24. people followed him, and *thronged* him
31. Thou seest the multitude *thronging* thee

4919 1 797/922 4862 *thruptō* (to crumble)

συνθρύπτω, sunthrupto

Acts21:13. What mean ye to weep and to *break* mine heart?

4920 26 797/922 7:888 4862 *hiemi* (to send)

συνίημι, sunieemi.

Mat.13:13. neither *do* they *understand.*
14. ye shall hear, and shall not *understand:*
15. and *should understand* with (their) heart,
19. and *understandeth* (it) not, then
23. heareth the word, and *understandeth*
51. *Have* ye *understood* all these things?
15:10. Hear, and *understand:*
16:12. Then *understood* they how that he
17:13. Then the disciples *understood*
Mar 4:12. they may hear, and not *understand;*
6:52. For they *considered* not
7:14. Hearken unto me every one (of you), and *understand:*
8:17. perceive ye not yet, neither *understand?*
21. How is it that ye *do* not *understand?*
Lu. 2:50. And they *understood* not the saying which
8:10. and hearing they *might* not *understand.*
18:34. And they *understood* none of these things:
24:45. they might *understand* the scriptures,
Acts 7:25. his brethren would have *understood*
— but they *understood* not.
28:26. ye shall hear, and shall not *understand;*
27. and *understand* with (their) heart,
Ro. 3:11. There is none *that understandeth,*
15:21. that have not heard *shall understand.*
2Co.10:12. comparing themselves among themselves, *are* not *wise.*
Eph. 5:17. but *understanding* what the will of the

4921 3 798/923 7:896 4862,2476

συνιστάνω, sunistano.

2Co. 3: 1. Do we begin again *to commend* ourselves?
5:12. we *commend* not ourselves again unto you,
10:12. with some *that commend* themselves:

4921 13 798/923 7:896 4862,2476

συνιστάω, συνίστημι, sunistao, sunisteemi.

Lu. 9:32. and the two men *that stood with* him.
Ro. 3: 5. But if our unrighteousness *commend* the
5: 8. But God *commendeth* his love toward us,
16: 1. I *commend* unto you Phebe our sister,
2Co. 4: 2. *commending* ourselves to every man's conscience
6: 4. But in all (things) *approving* ourselves
7:11. In all (things) ye *have approved* yourselves
10:18. For not he *that commendeth* himself
— but whom the Lord *commendeth.*
12:11. I ought *to have been commended* of you:
Gal. 2:18. I *make* myself a transgressor.
Col. 1:17. and by him all things *consist,*
2Pet.3: 5. *standing* out of the water and in the water:

4922 1 798/924 4862,3593

συνοδεύω, sunodūo.

Acts 9: 7. And the men *which journeyed with* him

4923 1 798/924 4862,3598

συνοδία, sunodia.

Lu. 2:44. supposing him to have been in the *company,*

4924 1 799/924 4862,3611

συνοικέω, sunoikeo.

1Pet. 3: 7. *dwell with* (them) according to knowledge,

4925 1 799/924 5:119 4862,3618

συνοικοδομέομαι, sunoikodomeomai.

Eph 2:22. In whom ye also *are builded together*

4926 1 799/924 4862,3656

συνομιλέω, sunomileo.

Acts10:27. And *as* he *talked with* him, he went

4927 1 799/924 4862,rt 3674 rt 3725

συνομορέω, sunomoreo.

Acts18: 7. whose house *joined hard* to the synagogue

4928 2 799/924 7:877 4912

συνοχή, sunokee.

Lu. 21:25. upon the earth *distress* of nations,
2Co. 2: 4. out of much affliction and *anguish* of heart I wrote unto you

4929 2 799/925 4862,5021

συντάσσω, suntasso.

Mat.26:19. And the disciples did as Jesus *had appointed* them;
27:10. as the Lord *appointed* me.

4930 6 799/925 8:49 4931

συντέλεια, suntelīa.

Mat.13:39. the harvest is the *end* of the world; (συντέλεια τοῦ αἰῶνός)
40. so shall it be in the *end* of this world. (συντ. τ. αἰ.)
49. So shall it be at the *end* of the world: (σ. τ. αἰ.)
24: 3. and of the *end* of the world? (σ. τ. αἰ.)
28:20. unto the *end* of the world. (σ. τ. αἰ.)
Heb 9:26. once in the *end* of the world hath he (σ. τ. αἰ.)

4931 7 799/925 8:49 4862,5055

συντελέω, sunteleo.

Mat. 7:28. when Jesus *had ended* these sayings,
Mar13: 4. when all these things shall *be fulfilled?*
Lu. 4: 2. and *when* they *were ended,* he
13. And *when* the devil *had ended* all the
Acts21:27. when the seven days were almost *ended,*
Ro. 9:28. he will *finish* the work, and cut (it) short
Heb 8: 8. I *will make* a new covenant with the

4932 2 800/925 4862,rt 5114

συντέμνω, suntemno.

Ro. 9:28. and *cut* (it) *short* in righteousness: because a *short* work will the Lord make

4933 4 800/925 8:140 4862,5083

συντηρέω, sunteereo.

Mat. 9:17. and both *are preserved.*
Mar 6:20. and *observed* him; and when he heard him,

Lu. 2:19. Mary *kept* all these things, and pondered
5:38. and both *are preserved.*

4934 4 800/925 4862,5087

συντίθημι, *suntitheemi.*

Lu. 22: 5. and *covenanted* to give him money.
Joh. 9:22. for the Jews *had agreed* already, that if
Acts23:20. The Jews *have agreed* to desire thee that
24: 9. And the Jews also *assented,* saying

4935 1 800/925 4932

συντόμως, *suntomōs.*

Acts24: 4. hear us of thy clemency *a few words.* (lit. *concisely*)

4936 3 800/926 4862,5143

συντρέχω, *suntreko.*

Mar. 6:33. and *ran* afoot thither out of all cities,
Acts 3:11. all the people *ran together* unto them
1Pet. 4: 4. *that* ye *run* not *with* (them) to the same excess

4937 8 801/926 7:919 4862

συντρίβω, *suntribo.* rt 5147

Mat.12:20. A *bruised* reed shall he not break,
Mar 5: 4. and the fetters *broken in pieces:*
14: 3. and she *brake* the box, and poured
Lu. 4:18. he hath sent me to heal the *broken*hearted,
9:39. *bruising* him hardly departeth from him.
Joh. 19:36. A bone of him *shall* not *be broken.*
Ro. 16:20. *shall bruise* Satan under your feet
Rev. 2:27. as the vessels of a potter *shall* they *be broken to shivers:* (lit. *are broken,* &c.)

Note.—Some copies here read συντριβήσεται.

4938 1 801/926 7:919 4937

σύντριμμα, *suntrimma.*

Ro. 3:16. *Destruction* and misery (are) in their ways:

4939 1 801/926 4862,5162

σύντροφος, *suntrophos.*

Acts13: 1. *which had been brought up with* Herod

4940 1 801/926 4862,5177

συντυγχάνω, *suntunkano.*

Lu. 8:19. and could not *come at* him for the press.

4942 1 801/926 8:559 4862,5271

συνυποκρίνομαι, *sunupokrinomai.*

Gal. 2:13. And the other Jews *dissembled* likewise *with* him;

4943 1 801/926 4862,5259rt2041

συνυπουργέω, *sunupourgeo.*

2Co. 1:11. Ye also *helping together* by prayer

4944 1 801/926 4862,5605

συνωδίνω, *sunōdino.*

8:22. *travaileth in pain together* until now.

4945 1 801/926 4862,3660

συνωμοσία, *sunōmosia.*

Acts23:13. which had made this *conspiracy.*

4950 1 802/926 4951

σύρτις, *surtis.*

Acts27:17. lest they should fall into the *quicksands,*

4951 5 802/926 cf 138

σύρω, *suro.*

Joh.21: 8. *dragging* the net with fishes.
Acts 8: 3. and *haling* men and women
14:19. having stoned Paul, *drew* (him) out of
17: 6. *drew* Jason and certain brethren unto
Rev 12: 4. his tail *drew* the third part of the stars

4952 1 802/926 4862,4682

συσπαράσσω, *susparasso.*

Lu. 9:42. the devil threw him down, and *tare* (him)

4953 1 802/927 7:200 4862

σύσσημον, *susseemon.* rt 4591

Mar14:44. had given them a *token,* saying,

4954 1 802/925 7:1024 4862 4983

σύσσωμα, *sussōma.*

Eph 3: 6. fellowheirs, and *of the same body,*

4955 1 802/902 4862,4714

συστασιαστής, *sustasiastees.*

Mar 15: 7. bound with them *that had made insurrection with* him,

4956 2 802/927 4921

συστατικός, *sustatikos.*

2Co. 3: 1. epistles *of commendation* to you, or (letters) *of commendation* from you?

4957 5 802/925 7:766 4862,4717

συσταυρόω, *sustauroō.*

Mat.27:44. The thieves also, *which were crucified with* him,
Mar 15:32. they *that were crucified with* him
Joh.19:32. and of the other *which was crucified with* him.
Ro. 6: 6. our old man *is crucified with* (him), (lit. *has been crucified with*)
Gal. 2:20. I *am crucified with* Christ: (lit. I *have been crucified with*)

4958 2 802/925 7:588 4862,4724

συστέλλω, *sustello.*

Acts 5: 6. And the young men arose, *wound* him *up,*
1Co. 7:29. But this I say, brethren, the time (is) *short:*

4959 1 802/925 7:600 4862,4727

συστενάζω, *sustenazo.*

Ro. 8:22. *groaneth* and travaileth in pain *together*

4960 1 803/925 7:666 4862,4748

συστοιχέω, sustoikeo.

Gal. 4:25. and *answereth to* Jerusalem which now is,

4961 2 803/925 7:701 4862,4757

συστρατιώτης, sustratiōtees.

Phi. 2:25. companion in labour, and *fellowsoldier*,
Philem 2. and Archippus our *fellowsoldier*,

4962 1 803/927 4862,4762

συστρέφω, sustrepho.

Acts28: 3. And *when* Paul *had gathered* a bundle of

4963 2 803/927 4962

συστροφή, sustrophee.

Acts19:40. may give an account of this *concourse*.
23:12. certain of the Jews banded together, (lit. having made a *combination*)

4964 2 803/925 4862,4976

συσχηματίζομαι, suskeematizomai.

Ro. 12: 2. And *be* not *conformed to* this world:
1Pet. 1:14. not *fashioning* yourselves *according to* the former lusts

4967 3 803/927 7:925 4969

σφαγή, sphagee.

Acts 8:32. He was led as a sheep to the *slaughter*;
Ro. 8:36. accounted as sheep for the *slaughter*.
Jas. 5: 5. as in a day of *slaughter*.

4968 1 803/927 4967

σφάγιον, sphagion.

Acts 7:42. have ye offered to me *slain beasts*

4969 10 803/927 7:925

σφάττω, sphatto.

1Joh.3:12. and *slew* his brother. And wherefore *slew* he him?
Rev. 5: 6. stood a Lamb as it *had been slain*,
9. for thou *wast slain*, and hast redeemed us
12. Worthy is the Lamb *that was slain*
6: 4. that they *should kill* one another:
9. the souls of them *that were slain*
13: 3. one of his heads as it were *wounded* to death;
8. written in the book of life of the Lamb *slain* from the foundation of the world.
18:24. and of all *that were slain* upon the earth.

4970 11 803/927 *sphodros* (violent)

σφόδρα, sphodra.

Mat. 2:10. they rejoiced with *exceeding* great joy.
17: 6. and were *sore* afraid.
23. And they were *exceeding* sorry.
18:31. they were *very* sorry, and came
19:25. they were *exceedingly* amazed,
26:22. And they were *exceeding* sorrowful,
27:54. they feared *greatly*, saying,
Mar 16: 4. for it was *very* great.
Lu. 18:23. for he was *very* rich.
Acts 6: 7. the number of the disciples multiplied in Jerusalem *greatly*;
Rev.16:21. the plague thereof was *exceeding* great.

4971 1 803/927 rt 4970

σφοδρῶς, sphodrōs.

Acts27:18. And we being *exceedingly* tossed

4972 26 803/927 7:939 4973

σφραγίζω, sphragizo.

Mat.27:66. *sealing* the stone, and setting a watch.
Joh. 3:33. *hath set to* his *seal* that God is true.
6:27. for him *hath* God the Father *sealed*,
Ro. 15:28. and *have sealed* to them this fruit,
2Co. 1:22. *Who hath* also *sealed* us, and given
11:10. no man shall stop me of this boasting (lit. this boasting *shall* not *be sealed* to me)
Eph. 1:13. ye *were sealed* with that holy Spirit
4:30. whereby ye *are sealed* unto the day
Rev. 7: 3. till we have *sealed* the servants of our God
4. the number of them *which were sealed*. (and there were) *sealed* an hundred (and) forty
5. of Juda (were) *sealed* twelve thousand.
— of Reuben (were) *sealed* twelve thousand.
— of Gad (were) *sealed* twelve thousand.
6. of Aser (were) *sealed* twelve thousand.
— of Nepthalim (were) *sealed* twelve thousand.
— of Manasses (were) *sealed* twelve thousand.
7. of Simeon (were) *sealed* twelve thousand.
— of Levi (were) *sealed* twelve thousand.
— of Issachar (were) *sealed* twelve thousand.
8. of Zabulon (were) *sealed* twelve thousand.
— of Joseph (were) *sealed* twelve thousand.
— of Benjamin (were) *sealed* twelve thousand.
10: 4. *Seal up* those things which the seven
20: 3. and shut him up, and *set a seal* upon him,
22:10. *Seal* not the sayings of the prophecy of this book:

Note.—In 2Co.11:10, the received text reads φραγήσεται, and so also the best MSS. and all the versions.

4973 16 804/927 7:939 5420

σφραγίς, sphragis.

Ro. 4:11. a *seal* of the righteousness of the faith
1Co. 9: 2. the *seal* of mine apostleship are ye
2Ti. 2:19. having this *seal*, The Lord knoweth...his.
Rev. 5: 1. sealed with seven *seals*.
2. and to loose the *seals* thereof?
5. and to loose the seven *seals* thereof.
9. and to open the *seals* thereof:
6: 1. the Lamb opened one of the *seals*,
3. when he had opened the second *seal*,
5. when he had opened the third *seal*,
7. when he had opened the fourth *seal*,
9. when he had opened the fifth *seal*,
12. when he had opened the sixth *seal*,
7: 2. having the *seal* of the living God:
8: 1. when he had opened the seventh *seal*,
9: 4. have not the *seal* of God in their foreheads.

4974 1 804/927 *sphaira* (ball)

σφυρόν, sphuron.

Acts 3: 7. his feet and *ancle bones* received strength

4975 3 804/928 *scheō* (2192) (to hold)

σχεδόν, skedon.

Acts13:44. came *almost* the whole city together
19:26. but *almost* throughout all Asia,
Heb 9:22. And *almost* all things are by the law

4976 2 804/928 7:954 *scheo* (2192) (to hold)

σχῆμα, *skeema.*

1Co. 7:31. for the *fashion* of this world passetn
Phi. 2: 8. And being found in *fashion* as a man,

4977 10 805/928 7:959

σχίζω, *skizo.*

Mat.27:51. the veil of the temple *was rent* in twain
— the earth did quake, and the rocks *rent;*
Mar 1:10. he saw the heavens *opened,*
15:38. the veil of the temple *was rent* in twain
Lu. 5:36. then both the new *maketh a rent,*
23:45. veil of the temple *was rent* in the midst.
Joh. 19:24. *Let* us not *rend* it, but cast lots for it,
21:11. yet *was* not the net *broken.*
Acts14: 4. the multitude of the city *was divided:*
23: 7. and the multitude *was divided.*

4978 8 805/928 7:959 4977

σχίσμα, *skisma.*

Mat. 9:16. and the *rent* is made worse.
Mar 2:21. and the *rent* is made worse.
Joh. 7:43. there was a *division* among the people
9:16. there was a *division* among them.
10:19. There was a *division* therefore
1Co. 1:10. (that) there be no *divisions* among you;
11:18. I hear that there be *divisions* among you;
12:25. That there should be no *schism* in the

4979 1 805/928 *schoinos* (rush)

σχοινίον, *skoinion.*

Joh. 2:15. made a scourge of *small cords,*
Acts27:32. soldiers cut off the *ropes* of the boat,

4980 2 805/928 4981

σχολάζω, *skolazo.*

Mat.12:44. he findeth (it) *empty,* swept,
1Co. 7: 5. that ye *may give* yourselves *to* fasting

4981 2 805/928 *scheo* (2192) (to hold)

σχολή, *skolee.*

Acts19: 9. daily in the *school* of one Tyrannus.

4982 111 805/928 *sos* (*saos*) (safe)

σώζω, *sōzo.*

Mat. 1:21. for he *shall save* his people from their sins.
8:25. saying, Lord, *save* us: we perish.
9:21. but touch his garment, I *shall be whole.*
22. thy faith *hath made* thee *whole.* And the woman *was made whole* from that hour.
10:22. he that endureth to the end *shall be saved.*
14:30. he cried, saying, Lord, *save* me.
16:25. whosoever will *save* his life shall lose it:
18:11. is come *to save* that which was lost.
19:25. saying, Who then can *be saved?*
24:13. endure unto the end, the same *shall be saved.*
22. there should no flesh *be saved:*
27:40. buildest (it) in three days, *save* thyself.
42. He *saved* others; himself he cannot *save.*
49. whether Elias will come to *save* him.
Mar 3: 4. to *save* life, or to kill?
5:23. hands on her, that she *may be healed,*
28. may touch but his clothes, I *shall be whole.*
34. thy faith *hath made* thee *whole;*
Mar 6:56. as many as touched him *were made whole.*
8:35. whosoever will *save* his life shall lose it;
— the same *shall save* it.
10:26. Who then can *be saved?*
52. thy faith *hath made* thee *whole.*
13:13. unto the end, the same *shall be saved.*
20. no flesh should *be saved:*
15:30. *Save* thyself, and come down
31. He *saved* others; himself he cannot *save.*
16:16. and is baptized *shall be saved;*
Lu. 6: 9. *to save* life, or to destroy (it)?
7:50. Thy faith *hath saved* thee; go in peace.
8:12. lest they should believe and *be saved.*
36. was possessed of the devils *was healed.*
48. thy faith *hath made* thee *whole;*
50. and she *shall be made whole.*
9:24. whosoever will *save* his life shall lose it:
— the same *shall save* it.
56. to destroy men's lives, but *to save*
13:23. Lord, are there few *that be saved?*
17:19. thy faith *hath made* thee *whole.*
33. seek *to save* his life shall lose it;
18:26. Who then can *be saved?*
42. thy faith *hath saved* thee.
19:10. and *to save* that which was lost.
23:35. He *saved* others; *let* him *save* himself,
37. If thou be the king of the Jews, *save* thyself.
39. If thou be Christ, *save* thyself and us.
Joh. 3:17. that the world through him *might be saved.*
5:34. these things I say, that ye *might be saved.*
10: 9. he *shall be saved,* and shall go in and out,
11:12. Lord, if he sleep, he *shall do well.*
12:27. Father, *save* me from this hour:
47. to judge the world, but to *save* the world.
Acts 2:21. on the name of the Lord *shall be saved.*
40. *Save* yourselves (lit. *be saved*) from this untoward generation.
47. the Lord added to the church daily such as should be saved. (lit. the *saved*)
4: 9. by what means he *is made whole;*
12. whereby we must *be saved.*
11:14. thou and all thy house *shall be saved.*
14: 9. he had faith *to be healed,*
15: 1. after the manner of Moses, ye cannot *be saved.*
11. we shall *be saved,* even as they.
16:30. what must I do to *be saved?*
31. and thou *shalt be saved,* and thy house.
27:20. all hope that we should *be saved*
31. Except these abide in the ship, ye cannot *be saved.*
Ro. 5: 9. we *shall be saved* from wrath through him.
10. we *shall be saved* by his life.
8:24. For we *are saved* by hope:
9:27. a remnant *shall be saved:*
10: 9. that God hath raised him from the dead, thou *shalt be saved.*
13. upon the name of the Lord *shall be saved.*
11:14. and might *save* some of them.
26. And so all Israel *shall be saved:*
1Co. 1:18. unto us *which are saved* it is the power of God.
21. *to save* them that believe.
3:15. but he himself *shall be saved;* yet so as by fire.
5: 5. that the spirit *may be saved* in the day
7:16. whether thou *shalt save* (thy) husband?
— whether thou *shalt save* (thy) wife?
9:22. that I might by all means *save* some.
10:33. but the (profit) of many, that they *may be saved*

1Co.15: 2. By which also ye *are saved*,
2Co. 2:15. a sweet savour of Christ, in them *that are saved*.
Eph 2: 5. by grace ye are *saved*;
8. For by grace are ye *saved* through faith;
1Th. 2:16. that they *might be saved*,
2Th. 2:10. the love of the truth, that they might *be saved*.
1Ti. 1:15. Christ Jesus came into the world *to save* sinners;
2: 4. Who will have all men *to be saved*,
15. Notwithstanding she *shall be saved* in childbearing,
4:16. thou *shalt* both *save* thyself, and them that
2Ti. 1: 9. *Who hath saved* us, and called (us)
4:18. and *will preserve* (me) unto his heavenly kingdom:
Tit. 3: 5. but according to his mercy he *saved* us,
Heb 5: 7. unto him that was able *to save* him
7:25. able also *to save* them to the uttermost
Jas. 1:21. the engrafted word, which is able *to save* your souls.
2:14. and have not works? can faith *save* him?
4:12. who is able *to save* and to destroy:
5:15. And the prayer of faith *shall save* the sick,
20. *shall save* a soul from death,
1Pet. 3:21. (even) baptism *doth* also now *save* us
4:18. And if the righteous scarcely *be saved*,
Jude 5. *having saved* the people out of the land of
23. And others *save* with fear, pulling (them) out
Rev.21:24. And the nations of them *which are saved*

4983 146 806/929 7:1024 4982

σῶμα, sōma.

Mat. 5:29. not (that) thy whole *body* should be
30. thy whole *body* should be cast into hell.
6:22. The light of the *body* is the eye:
— thy whole *body* shall be full of light.
23. thy whole *body* shall be full of darkness.
25. for your *body*, what ye shall put on.
— and the *body* than raiment?
10:28. And fear not them which kill the *body*,
— to destroy both soul and *body* in hell.
14:12. came, and took up the *body*, and
26:12. she hath poured this ointment on my *body*,
26. Take, eat; this is my *body*.
27:52. and many *bodies* of the saints which slept
58. begged the *body* of Jesus. Then Pilate commanded the *body* to be delivered.
59. when Joseph had taken the *body*,
Mar 5:29. and she felt in (her) *body* that she
14: 8. to anoint my *body* to the burying.
22. Take, eat: this is my *body*.
15:43. and craved the *body* of Jesus.
45. he gave the *body* to Joseph.
Lu. 11:34. The light of the *body* is the eye:
— thy whole *body* also is full of light;
— thy *body* also (is) full of darkness.
36. If thy whole *body* therefore (be) full of light,
12: 4. Be not afraid of them that kill the *body*,
22. for the *body*, what ye shall put on.
23. and the *body* (is more) than raiment.
17:37. Wheresoever the *body* (is), thither will
22:19. This is my *body* which is given for you:
23:52. unto Pilate, and begged the *body* of Jesus.
55. and how his *body* was laid.
24: 3. found not the *body* of the Lord Jesus.
23. when they found not his *body*, they came,
Joh. 2:21. he spake of the temple of his *body*.
Joh. 19:31. the *bodies* should not remain upon the cross
38. that he might take away the *body* of Jesus:
— and took the *body* of Jesus.
40. Then took they the *body* of Jesus,
20:12. where the *body* of Jesus had lain.
Acts 9:40. and turning (him) to the *body* said,
Ro. 1:24. to dishonour their own *bodies*
4:19. he considered not his own *body* now dead.
6: 6. that the *body* of sin might be destroyed,
12. reign in your mortal *body*,
7: 4. dead to the law by the *body* of Christ;
24. deliver me from the *body* of this death?
8:10. the *body* (is) dead because of sin;
11. shall also quicken your mortal *bodies*
13. do mortify the deeds of the *body*,
23. (to wit), the redemption of our *body*.
12: 1. that ye present your *bodies* a living
4. as we have many members in one *body*,
5. we, (being) many, are one *body* in Christ,
1Co. 5: 3. For I verily, as absent in *body*,
6:13. Now the *body* (is) not for fornication,
— and the Lord for the *body*.
15. your *bodies* are the members of Christ?
16. joined to an harlot is one *body*?
18. that a man doeth is without the *body*;
— sinneth against his own *body*.
19. your *body* is the temple of the Holy Ghost
20. therefore glorify God in your *body*,
7: 4. The wife hath not power of her own *body*,
— the husband hath not power of his own *body*,
34. she may be holy both in *body* and in spirit
9:27. But I keep under my *body*,
10:16. the communion of the *body* of Christ?
17. (being) many are one bread, (and) one *body*:
11:24. Take, eat: this is my *body*,
27. shall be guilty of the *body* and blood of
29. not discerning the Lord's *body*.
12:12. For as the *body* is one, and hath
— the members of that one *body*, being many, are one *body*: so also (is) Christ.
13. are we all baptized into one *body*,
14. For the *body* is not one member, but
15. I am not of the *body*; is it therefore not of the *body*?
16. I am not of the *body*; is it therefore not of the *body*?
17. If the whole *body* (were) an eye,
18. every one of them in the *body*,
19. all one member, where (were) the *body*?
20. many members, yet but one *body*.
22. those members of the *body*,
23. And those (members) of the *body*,
24. but God hath tempered the *body* together,
25. should be no schism in the *body*;
27. Now ye are the *body* of Christ,
13: 3. though I give my *body* to be burned,
15:35. and with what *body* do they come?
37. thou sowest not that *body* that shall be,
38. But God giveth it a *body* as it hath pleased him, and to every seed his own *body*.
40. also celestial *bodies*, and *bodies* terrestrial·
44. It is sown a natural *body*; it is raised a spiritual *body*. There is a natural *body*, and there is a spiritual *body*.
2Co. 4:10. bearing about in the *body* the dying of
— might be made manifest in our *body*.
5: 6. whilst we are at home in the *body*,
8. rather to be absent from the *body*,
10. receive the things (done) in (his) *body*
10:10. but (his) *bodily* presence (is) weak,

2Co.12: 2. the *body*, I cannot tell; or whether out of the *body*,
3. in the *body*, or out of the *body*, I cannot tell:
Gal. 6:17. I bear in my *body* the marks of the Lord
Eph. 1:23. Which is his *body*, the fulness of him
2:16. unto God in one *body* by the cross,
4: 4. (There is) one *body*, and one Spirit,
12. for the edifying of the *body* of Christ:
16. From whom the whole *body* fitly joined
— maketh increase of the *body* unto
5:23. and he is the saviour of the *body*.
28. to love their wives as their own *bodies*.
30. For we are members of his *body*,
Phi. 1:20. Christ shall be magnified in my *body*,
3:21. Who shall change our vile *body*,
— like unto his glorious *body*,
Col. 1:18. And he is the head of the *body*,
22. In the *body* of his flesh through death,
24. in my flesh for his *body's* sake,
2:11. putting off the *body* of the sins of the flesh
17. but the *body* (is) of Christ.
19. from which all the *body* by joints and
23. humility, and neglecting of the *body*;
3:15. to the which also ye are called in one *body*;
1Th. 5:23. and *body* be preserved blameless unto
Heb 10: 5. but a *body* hast thou prepared me:
10. through the offering of the *body* of Jesus
22. our *bodies* washed with pure water.
13: 3. as being yourselves also in the *body*.
11. For the *bodies* of those beasts,
Jas. 2:16. things which are needful to the *body*;
26. as the *body* without the spirit is dead,
3: 2. able also to bridle the whole *body*.
3. and we turn about their whole *body*.
6. that it defileth the whole *body*,
1Pet. 2:24. bare our sins in his own *body* on the tree,
Jude 9. he disputed about the *body* of Moses,
Rev. 18:13. *slaves*, (lit. *bodies*) and souls of men.

4984 2 807/931 7:1024 4983

σωματικός, sōmatikos.

Lu. 3:22. the Holy Ghost descended in a *bodily* shape
1Ti. 4: 8. For *bodily* exercise profiteth little: but

4985 1 807/931 4984

σωματικῶς, sōmatikōs.

Col. 2: 9. all the fulness of the Godhead *bodily*.

4987 2 808/931 7:1094 4673

σωρεύω, sōrūo.

Ro. 12:20. thou *shalt heap* coals of fire on his head.
2Ti. 3: 6. and lead captive silly women *laden* with

4990 24 808/931 7:965 4982

σωτήρ, soteer.

Lu. 1:47. hath rejoiced in God my *Saviour*.
2:11. a *Saviour*, which is Christ the Lord.
Joh. 4:42. the Christ, the *Saviour* of the world.
Acts 5:31. (to be) a Prince and a *Saviour*, for to
13:23. raised unto Israel a *Saviour*, Jesus:
Eph 5:23. and he is the *saviour* of the body.
Phi. 3:20. we look for the *Saviour*, the Lord Jesus
1 Ti. 1: 1. by the commandment of God *our Saviour*, and Lord Jesus Christ.
1Ti. 2: 3. in the sight of God our *Saviour*;
4:10. who is the *saviour* of all men, specially
2Ti. 1:10. by the appearing of our *Saviour* Jesus
Tit. 1: 3. the commandment of God our *Saviour*;
4. and the Lord Jesus Christ our *Saviour*.
2:10. adorn the doctrine of God our *Saviour*
13. of the great God and our *Saviour* Jesus
3: 4. and love of God our *Saviour* toward
6. through Jesus Christ our *Saviour*;
2Pet. 1: 1. of God and our *Saviour* Jesus Christ:
11. kingdom of our Lord and *Saviour* Jesus
2:20. the knowledge of the Lord and *Saviour* Jesus Christ,
3: 2. of us the apostles of the Lord and *Saviour*:
18. our Lord and *Saviour* Jesus Christ.
1Joh. 4:14. the Father sent the Son (to be) the *Saviour* of the world.
Jude 25. To the only wise God our *Saviour*,

4991 45 808/931 7:965 4990

σωτηρία, soteeria.

Lu. 1:69. hath raised up an horn of *salvation* for us
71. *That* we *should be saved* (lit. *salvation*) from our enemies,
77. To give knowledge of *salvation* unto his people
19: 9. This day is *salvation* come to this house,
Joh. 4:22. for *salvation* is of the Jews.
Acts 4:12. Neither is there *salvation* in any other:
7:25. by his hand would *deliver* them:
13:26. to you is the word of this *salvation* sent.
47. for *salvation* unto the ends of the earth.
16:17. shew unto us the way of *salvation*.
27:34. for this is for your *health*:
Ro. 1:16. is the power of God unto *salvation*
10: 1. that they *might be saved*.
10. confession is made unto *salvation*.
11:11. *salvation* (is come) unto the Gentiles,
13:11. for now (is) our *salvation* nearer than
2Co. 1: 6. (it is) for your consolation and *salvation*,
— (it is) for your consolation and *salvation*.
6: 2. in the day of *salvation* have I succoured
— behold, now (is) the day of *salvation*.
7:10. worketh repentance to *salvation*
Eph 1:13. the gospel of your *salvation*:
Phi. 1:19. this shall turn to my *salvation*
28. but to you of *salvation*, and that of God.
2:12. work out your own *salvation* with fear
1Th. 5: 8. for an helmet, the hope of *salvation*.
9. to obtain *salvation* by our Lord Jesus
2Th. 2:13. chosen you to *salvation* through
2Ti. 2:10. that they may also obtain the *salvation*
3:15. able to make thee wise unto *salvation*
Heb 1:14. who shall be heirs of *salvation*?
2: 3. if we neglect so great *salvation*;
10. make the captain of their *salvation* perfect
5: 9. the author of eternal *salvation*
6: 9. and things that accompany *salvation*,
9:28. second time without sin unto *salvation*.
11: 7. prepared an ark to the *saving* of his house;
1Pet. 1: 5. by the power of God through faith unto *salvation*
9. (even) the *salvation* of (your) souls.
10. Of which *salvation* the prophets
2Pet. 3:15. longsuffering of our Lord (is) *salvation*;
Jude 3. unto you of the common *salvation*,
Rev 7:10. *Salvation* to our God which sitteth upon the throne,
12:10. Now is come *salvation*, and strength,
19: 1. *Salvation*, and glory, and honour and

4992 4 809/932 rt 4991
σωτήριον, sōteerion.

Lu 2:30. For mine eyes have seen thy *salvation*,
3: 6. all flesh shall see the *salvation* of God.
Acts28:28. that the *salvation* of God is sent unto the Gentiles,
Eph. 6:17. And take the helmet of *salvation*,

4992 1 809/932 7:965 rt 4991
σωτήριος, sōteerios.

Tit. 2:11. the grace of God *that bringeth salvation*

4993 6 809/932 7:1097 4998
σωφρονέω, sōphroneo.

Mar 5:15. and clothed, and *in* his *right mind*:
Lu. 8:35. clothed, and *in* his *right mind*:
Ro. 12: 3. but to think *soberly*, according as God
2Co. 5:13. or whether we *be sober*,
Tit. 2: 6. likewise exhort *to be sober minded*.
1Pet.4: 7. *be* ye therefore *sober*, and watch unto

4994 1 809/932 7:1097 4998
σωφρονίζω, sōphronizo.

Tit. 2: 4. That they *may teach* the young women *to be sober*,

4995 1 809/932 7:1097 4994
σωφρονισμός, sōphronismos.

2Ti. 1: 7. and of love, and of a *sound mind*.

4996 1 809/932 4998
σωφρόνως, sōphronōs.

Tit. 2.12. we should live *soberly*, righteously, and godly,

4997 3 809/932 7:1097 4998
σωφροσύνη, sōphrosunee.

Acts26:25. the words of truth and *soberness*.
1Ti. 2: 9. with shamefacedness and *sobriety*;
15. and charity and holiness with *sobriety*.

4998 4 810/932 7:1097 rt 4982 rt 5424
σώφρων, sōphrōn.

1Ti. 3: 2. vigilant, *sober*, of good behaviour,
Tit. 1: 8. *sober*, just, holy, temperate;
2: 2. *temperate*, sound in faith,
5. *discreet*, chaste, keepers at home,

5001 1 810/932 8:27 5021
τάγμα, tagma.

1Co.15:23. But every man in his own *order*

5002 1 810/932 5021
τακτός, taktos.

Acts12:21. And upon a *set* day Herod, arrayed

5003 1 810/932 5005
ταλαιπωρέω, talaipōreo.

Jas. 4: 9. *Be afflicted*, and mourn, and weep:

5004 2 810/932 5005
ταλαιπωρία, talaipōria.

Ro. 3:16. Destruction and *misery* (are) in their ways.
Jas. 5: 1. weep and howl for your *miseries*

5005 2 811/932 rt 5007, rt 3984
ταλαίπωρος, talaipōros.

Ro. 7:24. O *wretched* man that I am!
Rev. 3:17. and knowest not that thou art *wretched*,

5006 1 811/932 5007
ταλαντιαῖος, talantiaios.

Rev.16:21. (every stone) about *the weight of a talent*:

5007 15 811/932 *tlaō* (to bear)
τάλαντον, talanton.

Mat.18:24. which owed him ten thousand *talents*.
25:15. And unto one he gave five *talents*,
16. he that had received the five *talents*
— and made (them) other five *talents*.
20. he that had received five *talents* came and brought other five *talents*,
— thou deliveredst unto me five *talents*: behold, I have gained beside them five *talents* more.
22. He also that had received two *talents* came and said, Lord, thou deliveredst unto me two *talents*:
— gained two other *talents* beside them.
24. he which had received the one *talent*
25. and hid thy *talent* in the earth:
28. Take therefore the *talent* from him, and give (it) unto him which hath ten *talents*.

5008 1 811/933 cf [2924]
ταλιθά, talitha.

Mar 5:41. *Talitha* cumi; which is, being interpreted, Damsel, I say unto thee, arise.

5009 4 811/933 *tamias* (distributor)
ταμεῖον, tamīon.

Mat. 6: 6. when thou prayest, enter into thy *closet*.
24:26. behold, (he is) in the *secret chambers*;
Lu. 12: 3. that which ye have spoken in the ear in *closets*
24. which neither have *storehouse* nor barn;

ταννῦν see after νῦν. 3568

5010 10 811/933 5021
τάξις, taxis.

Lu. 1: 8. before God in the *order* of his course.
1Co.14:40. be done decently and in *order*.
Col. 2: 5. joying and beholding your *order*,
Heb 5: 6. for ever after the *order* of Melchisedec.
10. high priest after the *order* of Melchisedec
6:20. after the *order* of Melchisedec.
7:11. after the *order* of Melchisedec, and not be called after the *order* of Aaron?
17. for ever after the *order* of Melchisedec.
21. after the *order* of Melchisedec

5011 8 811/933 8:1
ταπεινός, *tapīnos.*

Mat.11:29. for I am meek and *lowly* in heart:
Lu. 1:52. and exalted them *of low degree.*
Ro. 12:16. condescend to men *of low estate.*
2Co. 7: 6. comforteth those that are *cast down,*
10: 1. who in presence (am) *base* among you,
Jas. 1: 9. Let the brother *of low degree* rejoice
4: 6. but giveth grace unto the *humble.*
1Pet.5: 5. and giveth grace to the *humble.*

5012 7 812/933 8:1 5011,rt5424
ταπεινοφροσύνη, *tapīnophrosunee.*

Acts20:19. Serving the Lord with all *humility of mind,*
Eph. 4: 2. With all *lowliness* and meekness,
Phi. 2: 3. but in *lowliness of mind* let each esteem
Col. 2:18. in a voluntary *humility*
23. and *humility,* and neglecting of the body;
3:12. *humbleness of mind,* meekness,
1Pet.5: 5. and be clothed with *humility :*

5013 14 812/933 8:1 5011
ταπεινόω, *tapīnoō.*

Mat.18: 4. Whosoever therefore *shall humble* himself
23:12. whosoever shall exalt himself *shall be abased;* and he that *shall humble* himself
Lu. 3: 5. mountain and hill *shall be brought low ;*
14:11. whosoever exalteth himself *shall be abased;* and he *that humbleth* himself
18:14. *shall be abased;* and he *that humbleth* himself shall
2Co.11: 7. in *abasing* myself that ye might
12:21. my God *will humble* me among you,
Phi. 2: 8. he *humbled* himself, and became obedient
4:12. I know both how *to be abased,* and
Jas. 4:10. *Humble yourselves* in the sight of the Lord,
1Pet.5: 6. *Humble yourselves* therefore under the

5014 4 812/933 8:1 5013
ταπείνωσις, *tapīnōsis.*

Lu. 1:48. For he hath regarded the *low estate* of his handmaiden:
Acts 8:33. In his *humiliation* his judgment was taken away:
Phi. 3:21. Who shall change our *vile* body, (lit. body of *humiliation*)
Jas. 1:10. But the rich, in *that* he *is made low :*

5015 17 812/933
ταράσσω, *tarasso.*

Mat. 2: 3. he *was troubled,* and all Jerusalem
14:26. they *were troubled,* saying, It is a spirit ;
Mar 6:50. For they all saw him, and *were troubled.*
Lu. 1:12. when Zacharias saw (him), he *was troubled,*
24:38. Why are ye *troubled ?* and why do thoughts
Joh. 5: 4. into the pool, and *troubled* the water:
7. no man, when the water *is troubled,*
11:33. he groaned in the spirit, and was *troubled,*
12:27. Now *is* my soul *troubled ;*
13:21. he *was troubled* in spirit, and testified,
14: 1. *Let* not your heart *be troubled :*
27. *Let* not your heart *be troubled,*
Acts15:24. which went out from us *have troubled* you
17: 8. And they *troubled* the people
Gal. 1: 7. but there be some *that trouble* you,
5:10. he *that troubleth* you shall bear his judgment,
1Pet.3:14. be not afraid of their terror, neither *be troubled;*

5016 2 813/934 5015
ταραχή, *tarakee.*

Mar 13: 8. there shall be famines and *troubles*
Joh. 5: 4. after the *troubling* of the water

5017 2 813/934 5015
τάραχος, *tarakos.*

Acts12:18. no small *stir* among the soldiers,
19:23. there arose no small *stir* about that way.

5020 1 813/934 *Tartaros* (abyss of Hades)
ταρταρόω, *tartaroō.*

2Pet. 2: 4. but *cast* (them) *down to hell,* and

5021 8 813/934 8:27
τάσσω, *tasso.*

Mat.28:16. where Jesus *had appointed* them.
Lu. 7: 8. am a man *set* under authority,
Acts13:48. as were *ordained* to eternal life believed.
15: 2. they *determined* that Paul and Barnabas,
22:10. which *are appointed* for thee to do.
28:23. And *when* they *had appointed* him a day,
Ro. 13: 1. the powers that be are *ordained* of God.
1Co.16:15. they *have addicted* themselves to the ministry

5022 4 813/934 [cf 8450]
ταῦρος, *tauros.*

Mat.22: 4. my *oxen* and (my) fatlings (are) killed,
Acts14.13. brought *oxen* and garlands unto the gates,
Heb 9:13. if the blood of *bulls* and of goats,
10: 4. not possible that the blood of *bulls* and

5023 4 813/ 3778
ταὐτά, *tauta,* from ὁ αὐτος.

Lu. 6:23. for in the *like manner* (κατὰ ταὐτὰ) did their fathers
26. *so* (κ. τ.) did their fathers to the false
17:30. *Even thus* (κ. τ.) shall it be in the day when
1Th. 2:14. have suffered *like* things of your own countrymen, even as they

Note.—In all of the above passages many copies read ταῦτα, and some of the best MSS. read in all of them τὰ αὐτά.

5024 247 600/737 3588,846
ταῦτα, *tauta.* from οὗτος.

Mat. 1:20. But while he thought on *these* things,
4: 9. All *these* things will I give thee,
6:32. after all *these* things do the Gentiles
33. and all *these* things shall be added
9:18. While he spake *these* things unto them,
10: 2. the names of the twelve apostles are *these*
11:25. hast hid *these* things from the wise
13:34. All *these* things spake Jesus unto
51. Have ye understood all *these* things?
56. hath this (man) all *these* things?
15:20. *These* are (the things) which defile
19:20. All *these* things have I kept from
21:23. By what authority doest thou *these* things?
24. by what authority I do *these* things.
27. by what authority I do *these* things.
23:23. *these* ought ye to have done,
36. All *these* things shall come upon this
24: 2. See ye not all *these* things?
3. Tell us, when shall *these* things be?

Mat.24 8. *these* (are) the beginning of sorrows.
33. when ye shall see all *these* things,
34. till all *these* things be fulfilled.
Mar 2: 8. Why reason ye *these* things in your hearts?
6: 2. whence hath this (man) *these* things?
7:23. *these* evil things come from within,
10:20. all *these* have I observed from
11:28. authority doest thou *these* things?
— this authority to do *these* things?
29. by what authority I do *these* things.
33. by what authority I do *these* things.
13: 4. Tell us, when shall *these* things be?
— all *these* things shall be fulfilled?
8(9). *these* (are) the beginnings of sorrows.
29. shall see *these* things come to pass,
30. shall not pass, till all *these* things be done.
16:12. After *that* he appeared in another
17. And *these* signs shall follow
Lu. 1:19. to shew thee *these* glad tidings.
20. that *these* things shall be performed,
65. all *these* sayings were noised abroad
2:19. But Mary kept all *these* things,
51. his mother kept all *these* sayings
4:28. when they heard *these* things,
5:27. And after *these* things he went forth,
7: 9. When Jesus heard *these* things,
8: 8. when he had said *these* things,
9:34. While he *thus* spake, (lit. *these things*)
10: 1. After *these* things the Lord appointed
21. that thou hast hid *these* things
11:27. as he spake *these* things,
42. *these* ought ye to have done,
45. *thus* saying thou reproachest us also.
53. And as he said *these* things unto
12: 4. and after *that* have no more
30. For all *these* things do the nations
31. all *these* things shall be added
13:17. when he had said *these* things,
14: 6. answer him again to *these* things.
15. heard *these* things, he said unto him,
21. and shewed his lord *these* things.
15:26. asked what *these* things meant.
16:14. covetous, heard all *these* things:
17: 8. and after*ward* thou shalt eat and drink?
18: 4. but after*ward* he said within himself,
11. prayed *thus* with himself, (lit. *these things*)
21. All *these* have I kept from my youth up.
22. Now when Jesus heard *these* things
23. when he heard *this*, (lit. *these things*)
19:11. And as they heard *these* things,
28. when he had *thus* spoken,
20: 2. authority doest thou *these* things?
8. by what authority I do *these* things.
21: 6. (As for) *these* things which ye behold,
7. but when shall *these* things be?
— when *these* things shall come to pass?
9. *these* things must first come to pass;
31. when ye see *these* things come to pass,
36. worthy to escape all *these* things
23:31. if they do *these* things in a green tree,
46. having said *thus*,
49. stood afar off, beholding *these* things.
24: 9. told all *these* things unto the eleven,
10. told *these* things unto the apostles.
21. third day since *these* things were done.
26. Christ to have suffered *these* things,
36. And as they *thus* spake,
Joh. 1:28. *These* things were done in Bethabara
2:16. Take *these* things hence;
18. that thou doest *these* things?
3: 2. no man can do *these* miracles
9. How can *these* things be?

Joh. 3:10. and knowest not *these* things?
22. After *these* things came Jesus and
5: 1. After *this* there was a feast
14. After*ward* Jesus findeth him
16. because he had done *these* things
19. *these* also doeth the Son likewise.
34. *these* things I say, that ye might be saved.
6: 1. After *these* things Jesus went over
9. but what are *they* among so many?
59. *These* things said he in the synagogue,
7: 1. After *these* things Jesus walked in
4. If thou do *these* things, shew thyself
9. When he had said *these* words
32. the people murmured *such* things
8:20. *These* words spake Jesus in the treasury,
26. *those* things which I have heard of him.
28. hath taught me, I speak *these* things.
30. As he spake *these* words, many believed
9: 6. When he had *thus* spoken, he spat on
22. *These* (words) spake his parents,
40. heard *these* words, and said unto him,
10:21. *These* are not the words of him that
25. *they* (lit. *these*) bear witness of me.
11:11. *These* things said he: and after that
28. And when she had *so* said,
43. And when he *thus* had spoken,
12:16. *These* things understood not his
— that *these* things were written of him,
— they had done *these* things unto him.
36. *These* things spake Jesus, and
41. *These* things said Esaias, when he
13: 7. but thou shalt know *here*after (lit. after *these*)
17. If ye know *these* things,
21. When Jesus had *thus* said,
14:25. *These* things have I spoken unto you,
15:11. *These* things have I spoken unto you,
17. *These* things I command you,
21. But all *these* things will they do
16: 1. *These* things have I spoken unto you,
3. And *these* things will they do
4. But *these* things have I told you,
— And *these* things I said not unto you
6. because I have said *these* things
25. *These* things have I spoken unto you in
33. *These* things I have spoken unto you,
17: 1. *These* words spake Jesus, and lifted
13. and *these* things I speak in the world,
18: 1. When Jesus had spoken *these* words,
22. when he had *thus* spoken,
19:24. *These* things therefore the soldiers did.
36. For *these* things were done, that
38. And after *this* Joseph
20:14. And when she had *thus* said,
18. he had spoken *these* things unto her.
31. *these* are written, that ye might believe
21: 1. After *these* things Jesus shewed himself again
24. and wrote *these* things: and we know
Acts 1: 9. And when he had spoken *these* things,
5: 5. on all them that heard *these* things.
11. upon as many as heard *these* things.
7: 1. the high priest, Are *these* things so?
7. and after *that* shall they come forth,
50. Hath not my hand made all *these* things?
54. When they heard *these* things,
10:44. While Peter yet spake *these* words,
11:18. When they heard *these* things,
12:17. Go shew *these* things unto James,
13:20. after *that* he gave (unto them) judges
42. the Gentiles besought that *these* words
14:15. Sirs, why do ye *these* things?

3 A

Acts14:18. with *these* sayings scarce restrained they
15:16. After *this* I will return,
17. the Lord, who doeth all *these* things.
16:38. And the serjeants told *these* words
17: 8. when they heard *these* things.
11. daily, whether *those* things were so.
20. therefore what *these* things mean.
18: 1. After *these* things Paul departed
19:21. After *these* things were ended,
41. And when he had *thus* spoken,
20:36. And when he had *thus* spoken,
21:12. And when we heard *these* things,
23:22. thou hast shewed *these* things to me.
24: 9. saying that *these* things were so.
22. when Felix heard *these* things,
26:24. And as he *thus* spake for himself,
30. And when he had *thus* spoken,
27:35. And when he had *thus* spoken,
28:29. And when he had said *these* words,
Ro. 8:31. What shall we then say to *these* things?
9: 8. *these* (are) not the children of God:
1Co 4: 6. And *these* things, brethren, I have
14. I write not *these* things to shame you,
6: 8. ye do wrong, and defraud, and *that* (your) brethren.
11. And *such* were some of you:
13. God shall destroy both it and *them*.
9: 8. Say I *these* things as a man? or saith not the law *the same* also?
15. neither have I written *these* things,
10: 6. *these* things were our examples,
11. Now all *these* things happened
12:11. But all *these* worketh that one and
13:13. faith, hope, charity, *these* three; but
2Co. 2:16. who (is) sufficient for *these* things?
13:10. I write *these* things being absent,
Gal. 2:18. For if I build again *the* (lit. *those*) things which I
5:17. *these* are contrary the one to the other: so that ye cannot do *the* (lit. *those*) things
Eph 5: 6. because of *these* things cometh the wrath
Phi. 3: 7. *those* I counted loss for Christ.
4: 8. think on *these* things.
9. *Those* things, which ye have both learned,
2Th. 2: 5. yet with you, I told you *these* things?
1Ti. 3:14. *These* things write I unto thee,
4: 6. in remembrance of *these* things,
11. *These* things command and teach.
15. Meditate upon *these* things;
5: 7. And *these* things give in charge,
21. that thou observe *these* things
6: 2. *These* things teach and exhort.
11. O man of God, flee *these* things;
2Ti. 1:12. I also suffer *these* things:
2: 2. the *same* commit thou to faithful men,
14. Of *these* things put (them) in remembrance,
Tit. 2:15. *These* things speak, and exhort,
3: 8. *These* things are good and profitable
Heb 4: 8. would he not after*ward* have spoken of
7:13. he of whom *these* things are spoken
11:12. of one, and him as good as dead, (lit. of one, and *that*, of one dead)
Jas. 3:10. *these* things ought not so to be.
1Pet. 1:11. and the glory that should follow. (lit. the glories after *these*)
2Pet. 1: 8. For if *these* things be in you,
9. But he that lacketh *these* things
10. for if ye do *these* things,
3:14. seeing that ye look for *such* things,
1Joh. 1: 4. And *these* things write we unto you,
2: 1. *these* things write I unto you.
1Joh. 2:26. *These* (things have I written unto you
5:13. *These* things have I written unto you
Rev. 1:19. the things which shall be *here*after; (lit. after *these*)
4: 1. After *this* I looked, and, behold,
— things which must be *here*after. (lit. after *these*)
7: 1. after *these* things I saw four angels
9. After *this* I beheld, and, lo,
9:12. two woes more *here*after. (lit. after *these*)
10: 4. and write *them* not. (lit. *these*)
15: 5. And after *that* I looked, and, behold,
16: 5. because thou hast judged *thus*.
18: 1. And after *these* things I saw another
19: 1. And after *these* things I heard a
20: 3. and after *that* he must be loosed
22: 8. And I John saw *these* things,
— which shewed me *these* things.
16. to testify unto you *these* things
18. If any man shall add unto *these* things,
20. He which testifieth *these* things

5025a 12 600/737 3778

ταύταις, *tautais*, from οὗτος.

Mat.22:40. On *these* two commandments hang all
Lu. 1:39. And Mary arose in *those* days,
6:12. And it came to pass in *those* days,
13:14. in *them* therefore come and be healed,
23: 7. was at Jerusalem at *that* time. (lit. in *those* days)
24:18. are come to pass there in *these* days?
Joh. 5: 3. In *these* lay a great multitude of
Acts 1:15. And in *those* days Peter stood up
6: 1. And in *those* days, when the number
11:27. And in *these* days came prophets
1Th. 3: 3. should be moved by *these* afflictions:
Rev. 9:20. which were not killed by *these* plagues

5025b 9 600/737 3778

ταύτας, *tautas*, from οὗτος.

Mat.13:53. when Jesus had finished *these* parables,
Mar 13: 2. Seest thou *these* great buildings?
Lu. 1:24. And after *those* days his wife Elisabeth
Acts 1: 5. with the Holy Ghost not many days *hence*.
3:24. likewise foretold of *these* days.
21:15. And after *those* days we took up our
2Co. 7: 1. Having therefore *these* promises,
Heb 9:23. with better sacrifices than *these*.
Rev.16: 9. which hath power over *these* plagues:

5026a 31 600/735 3778

ταύτῃ, *tautee*, from οὗτος.

Mat.10:23. they persecute you in *this* city,
12:45. be also unto *this* wicked generation.
16:18. and upon *this* rock I will build
26:31. offended because of me *this* night:
34. That *this* night, before the cock crow,
Mar 8:12. no sign be given unto *this* generation.
38. in *this* adulterous and sinful
14:27. offended because of me *this* night:
30. That this day, (even) in *this* night,
Lu. 11:30. the Son of man be to *this* generation.
12:20. *this* night thy soul shall be required
13: 7. seeking fruit on *this* fig tree,
32. Go ye, and tell *that* fox, Behold,
16:24. I am tormented in *this* flame.
17: 6. say unto *this* sycamine tree.
34. I tell you, in *that* night there shall be
19:42. even thou, at least in *this* thy day,

Acts16:12. and we were in *that* city abiding
18:10. I have much people in *this* city.
22: 3. yet brought up in *this* city at the feet
27:23. For there stood by me *this* night
1Co. 7:20. abide in *the same* calling wherein he was
9:12. we have not used *this* power;
15:19. If in *this* life only we have hope in
2Co. 1:15. And in *this* confidence I was minded
8: 7. that ye abound in *this* grace also.
19. to travel with us with *this* grace,
20. in *this* abundance which is administered
9: 4. ashamed in *this same* confident boasting.
11:17. in *this* confidence of boasting.
Heb 11: 2. by *it* the elders obtained a good report.

5026b 57 600/736 3778

ταύτην, *tauteen*, from οὗτος.

Mat.11:16. whereunto shall I liken *this* generation?
15:15. Declare unto us *this* parable.
21:23. and who gave thee *this* authority?
23:36. shall come upon *this* generation.
Mar 4:13. Know ye not *this* parable?
10: 5. he wrote you *this* precept.
11:28. and who gave thee *this* authority
12:10. have ye not read *this* scripture;
Lu. 4: 6. All *this* power will I give thee,
23. Ye will surely say unto me *this* proverb,
7:44. unto Simon, Seest thou *this* woman?
12:41. speakest thou *this* parable unto us,
13: 6. He spake also *this* parable;
16. And ought not *this* woman, being a
15: 3. And he spake *this* parable unto them,
18: 5. Yet because *this* widow troubleth me,
9. And he spake *this* parable unto certain
20: 2. who is he that gave thee *this* authority?
9. to speak to the people *this* parable;
19. he had spoken *this* parable against them.
23:48. came together to *that* sight,
24:21. to day is *the* third day (lit. *this*)
Joh. 2:11. *This* beginning of miracles did Jesus
7: 8. Go ye up unto *this* feast: I go not up yet unto *this* feast;
10: 6. *This* parable spake Jesus unto them:
18. *This* commandment have I received
12:27. for this cause came I unto *this* hour.
Acts 1:16. *this* scripture must needs have been fulfilled,
3:16. hath given him *this* perfect soundness
7: 4. he removed him into *this* land,
60. lay not *this* sin to their charge.
8:19. Give me also *this* power,
13:33. God hath fulfilled *the same*
22: 4. persecuted *this* way unto the death,
28. With a great sum obtained I *this* freedom.
23:13. which had made *this* conspiracy.
27:21. to have gained *this* harm and loss.
28:20. For *this* cause therefore have I
— I am bound with *this* chain.
Ro. 5: 2. into *this* grace wherein we stand,
1Co. 6:13. God shall destroy both *it* and them.
2Co. 4: 1. Therefore seeing we have *this* ministry,
8: 6. finish in you *the same* grace also.
9: 5. that *the same* might be ready,
12:13. forgive me *this* wrong.
1Ti. 1:18. *This* charge I commit unto thee,
2Ti. 2:19. standeth sure, having *this* seal,
Heb 5: 3. And by reason *hereof* (lit. of *this*) he ought,
1Pet.5:12. that *this* is the true grace of God
2Pet.1:18. *this* voice which came from heaven
3: 1. This second epistle, beloved,
1Joh.3: 3. every man that hath *this* hope in him
4:21. And *this* commandment have we
2Joh. 10. and bring not *this* doctrine,
Rev. 2:24. as many as have not *this* doctrine,
12:15. might cause *her* to be carried away

5026c 34 600/735 3778

ταύτης, *tautees*, from οὗτος.

Mat.12:41. in judgment with *this* generation,
42. in the judgment with *this* generation,
Lu. 7:31. shall I liken the men of *this* generation?
11:31. with the men of *this* generation,
32. in the judgment with *this* generation,
50. may be required of *this* generation;
51. It shall be required of *this* generation
17:25. and be rejected of *this* generation.
Joh.10:16. which are not of *this* fold:
12:27. Father, save me from *this* hour
15:13. Greater love hath no man than *this*,
Acts 1:17. had obtained part of *this* ministry.
25. That he may take part of *this* ministry
2: 6. Now when *this* was noised abroad,
29. his sepulchre is with us unto *this* day.
40. Save yourselves from *this* untoward
5:20. to the people all the words of *this* life.
6: 3. we may appoint over *this* business.
8:22. Repent therefore of *this* thy wickedness,
35. began at the *same* scripture, and
10:30. I was fasting until *this* hour;
13:26. is the word of *this* salvation sent.
19:25. by *this* craft we have our wealth.
40. may give an account of *this* concourse.
23: 1. conscience before God until *this* day.
24:21. Except it be for *this* one voice,
26:22. I continue unto *this* day,
28:22. for as concerning *this* sect,
2Co. 9:12. For the administration of *this* service
13. by the experiment of *this* ministration
Heb. 9:11. that is to say, not of *this* building;
12:15. *thereby* (lit. by *this*) many be defiled;
13: 2. *thereby* (lit. &c.) some have entertained
Rev.22:19. words of the book of *this* prophecy,

Note.—For the other cases, see οὗτος, τοῦτο, &c.

5027 1 813/934 2290

ταφή, *taphee*.

Mat.27: 7. to bury strangers in. (lit. for the *burial* of strangers)

5028 7 814/934 2290

τάφος, *taphos*.

Mat.23:27. ye are like unto whited *sepulchres*,
29. ye build the *tombs* of the prophets,
27:61. sitting over against the *sepulchre*.
64. that the *sepulchre* be made sure
66. went, and made the *sepulchre* sure,
28: 1. and the other Mary to see the *sepulchre*.
Ro. 3:13. Their throat (is) an open *sepulchre*;

5029 2 814/934 5036

τάχα, *taka*.

Ro. 5: 7. yet *peradventure* for a good man
Philem 15. For *perhaps* he therefore departed

5030 10 814/934 5036

ταχέως, *takeōs*.

Lu. 14:21. Go out *quickly* into the streets
16: 6. sit down *quickly*, and write fifty.

3 A 2

Joh. 11:31. that she rose up *hastily* and went out,
1Co. 4:19. But I will come to you *shortly*,
Gal. 1: 6. that ye are so *soon* removed from
Phi. 2:19. to send Timotheus *shortly* unto you,
24. that I also myself shall come *shortly*.
2Th. 2: 2. That ye be not *soon* shaken in mind,
1Ti. 5:22. Lay hands *suddenly* on no man,
2Ti. 4: 9. Do thy diligence to come *shortly*

5031 2 814/934 5034

ταχινός, *takinos.*

2Pet. 1:14. that *shortly* I must put off
2: 1. bring upon themselves *swift* destruction.

5032 5 814/934 5036

τάχιον, *takion.*

Joh. 13. 27. That thou doest, do *quickly*.
20: 4. the other disciple did *out*run Peter,
1Ti. 3:14. hoping to come unto thee *shortly*:
Heb 13:19. that I may be restored to you *the sooner*.
23. with whom, if he come *shortly*,

5033 1 814/934 5036

τάχιστα, *takista.*

Acts17:15. to come to him *with all speed*, (ὡς τ.)

5034 7 814/934 rt 5036

τάχος, *takos.*

Lu. 18: 8. he will avenge them speedily. (lit. with *speed*)
Acts12: 7. saying, Arise up *quick*ly. (lit. in *speed*)
22:18. get thee *quick*ly out of Jerusalem:
25: 4. would depart *short*ly (thither).
Ro. 16:20. bruise Satan under your feet *short*ly.
Rev. 1: 1. things which must *short*ly come to pass
22: 6. things which must *short*ly be done.

5035 13 814/935 5036

ταχύ, *taku.*

Mat. 5:25. Agree with thine adversary *quickly*,
28: 7. And go *quickly*, and tell his disciples
8. And they departed *quickly* from the
Mar 9:39. that can *lightly* speak evil of me.
16: 8. And they went out *quickly*,
Joh. 11:29. she arose *quickly*, and came unto him.
Rev. 2: 5. else I will come unto thee *quickly*,
16. else I will come unto thee *quickly*,
3:11. Behold, I come *quickly*:
11:14. the third woe cometh *quickly*.
22: 7. Behold, I come *quickly*:
12. And, behold, I come *quickly*;
20. Surely I come *quickly*; Amen

5036 1 814/935

ταχύς, *takus.*

Jas. 1:19. let every man be *swift* to hear,

5037 204 815/935

τε, *te.*

² shews where the two particles τε καί are in correlative connection, in a more forcible way than being mere copulatives. τε is sometimes followed by καί twice repeated, as Heb. 11:32.

Mat. 22:10. many as they found, *both*² bad and good.
Mat. 23: 6. *And* love the uppermost rooms
27:48. *and* filled (it) with vinegar,
28:12. *and* had taken counsel,
Mar 15:36. full of vinegar, *and* put (it) on a reed,
Lu. 2:16. *and*² found Mary and Joseph,
12:45. *and*² to eat and drink, and
21:11. *And* great earthquakes shall be
— *and* fearful sights and great signs
22:66. *and*² the chief priests and the scribes
23:12. And the same day)(² Pilate and Herod
24:20. *And* how the chief priests and
Joh. 2:15. *and*² the sheep, and the oxen;
4:42. *And* said unto the woman,
6:18. *And* the sea arose by reason of
Acts 1: 1. Jesus began *both*² to do and teach,
8. *both* in Jerusalem, and in all Judæa,
13. *both* Peter, and James, and
15.)(the number of the names together were
2: 3. *and* it sat upon each of them.
9. *and* in Judæa, and Cappadocia,
10.)(Phrygia, *and* Pamphylia, in Egypt,
—)(² Jews *and* proselytes,
33. *and* having received of the Father
37. *and* said unto Peter and to the rest
40. *And* with many other words did he
43. *and* many wonders and signs were done
46. *And* they, continuing daily with one
— *and* breaking bread from house to
3:10. *And* they knew that it was he
4:13. *and* they took knowledge of them,
27. *both*² Herod, and Pontius Pilate,
33. *and* great grace was upon them all.
5:14. to the Lord, multitudes *both*² of men and
19. *and* brought them forth, and said,
24. Now when)(² the high priest and the captain of the temple
35. *And* said unto them, Ye men of
42. *And* daily in the temple, and in
6: 7. *and* a great company of the priests
12. *And* they stirred up the people,
13. *And* set up false witnesses, which
7:26. *And* the next day he shewed himself
8: 1. *and* they were all scattered abroad
3. *and* haling men and women
6. *And* the people with one accord gave
12. they were baptized, *both*² men and
13. *and* wondered, beholding the miracles and signs
25. *and* preached the gospel in many
28.)(Was returning, and sitting in his
31. *And* he desired Philip that he would
38. *both*² Philip and the eunuch;
9: 2. *whether*² they were men or women,
6. *And* he trembling and astonished said,
15. and kings, *and* the children of Israel:
18. *and* he received sight forthwith,
24. *And* they watched the gates)(² day and night to kill him.
29. And he)(² spake boldly in...and
10: 2.)(which gave much alms to the people
22. *and* of good report among all
28. *And* he said unto them, Ye know
33. *and* thou hast well done that thou
39. *both*² in the land of the Jews, and in
48. *And* he commanded them to be baptized
11:13. *And* he shewed us how he had
21. *and* a great number believed,
26. *And* the disciples were called Christians
12: 6. *and* the keepers before the door
8. *And* the angel said unto him, Gird
12. *And* when he had considered (the thing).
13. 1. as)(Barnabas, and Simeon that was

Acts 13: 1. *and* Manaen, which had been brought up
2. Separate me)(Barnabas and Saul
4. *and* from thence they sailed to Cyprus.
14: 1. *both*[2] of the Jews and also of the Greeks
5. *both*[2] of the Gentiles, and also of the Jews
12. *And* they called Barnabas, Jupiter;
21. *And* when they had preached the gospel
15: 4. *and* they declared all things that God
5. *and* to command (them) to keep the law
9. no difference between)([2] us and them,
39. *and* so Barnabas took Mark,
16: 11. *and* the next (day) to Neapolis;
12. *And* from thence to Philippi,
13. *And* on the sabbath we went out
23. *And* when they had laid many stripes
26. *and* immediately all the doors
34. *And* when he had brought them into his
17: 4. *and* of the devout Greeks a great multitude, *and* of the chief women not a few.
5. *and* assaulted the house of Jason,
10. sent away)([2] Paul and Silas by night
14. but)([2] Silas and Timotheus abode
19. *And* they took him, and brought
26. *And* hath made of one blood all nations
18: 4. *and* persuaded the Jews and the Greeks.
5. when)([2] Silas and Timotheus were come
11. *And* he continued (there) a year
26. *And* he began to speak boldly in
19: 3. *And* he said unto them, Unto what
6. *and* they spake with tongues, and
10. *both*[2] Jews and Greeks.
11. *And* God wrought special miracles
12. *and* the evil spirits went out of them.
17. known)([2] to all the Jews and Greeks also
18. *And* many that believed came,
29. *and* having caught Gaius and
20: 3. *And* (there) abode three months.
7. *and* continued his speech until
11. *and* talked a long while, even
21. *both*[2] to the Jews, and also to the Greeks,
35. *and* to remember the words of the Lord
21: 11. *and* bound his own hands and feet,
12. *both*[2] we, and they of that place,
18. *and* all the elders were present.
20. *and* said unto him, Thou seest, brother,
25.)(from (things) offered to idols, and
28. *and* further brought Greeks also
30. *And* all the city was moved, and
37. *And* as Paul was to be led into the
22: 4. into prisons *both*[2] men and women.
7. *And* I fell unto the ground, and
8. *And* he said unto me, I am Jesus
28. *And* the chief captain answered,
23: 5. *Then* said Paul, I wist not, (lit. *and*)
10. *and* to bring (him) into the castle.
24. *And* provide (them) beasts, that they
35. *And* he commanded him to be kept
24: 3. We accept (it))([2] always, and in all places,
5. *and* a ringleader of the sect of the Nazarenes:
15. *both*[2] of the just and unjust.
23. *And* he commanded a centurion to keep Paul, *and* to let (him) have liberty,
27. *and* Felix, willing to shew the Jews a
25: 23. with)([2] the chief captains, and principal
24. *both*[2] at Jerusalem, and (also) here,
26: 3. expert)([2]in all customs and questions
10. *and* when they were put to death,
11. *and* being exceedingly mad against
16. a witness *both* of these things which thou hast seen, *and* of those things in

Acts 26: 20. *and*[2] throughout all the coasts of Judæa, and
22. witnessing *both*[2] to small and great,
— which)([2] the prophets and Moses did
30. *and* Bernice, and they that sat with them:
27: 1. delivered)([2] Paul and certain other
3. *And* the next (day) we touched at
5. *And* when we had sailed over the sea of
8. *And*, hardly passing it, came unto a place
17. *and*, fearing lest they should fall
20. *and* no small tempest lay on (us),
21. *and* to have gained this harm and loss.
29. *Then* fearing lest we should (lit. *and*)
43. *and* commanded that they which
28: 23.)(persuading them concerning Jesus, *both*[2] out of the law of Moses, and (out of) the prophets,

Ro. 1: 12. the mutual faith *both*[2] of you and me.
14. *both*[2] to the Greeks, and to the Barbarians; *both*[2] to the wise, and to the unwise.
16.)([2] to the Jew first, and also to the Greek.
20. (even))([2] his eternal power and Godhead;
26. for *even* (lit. *both*) their women did change
27. *And* likewise also the men,
2: 9.)([2] of the Jew first, and also of
10.)([2] to the Jew first, and also to
19. *And* art confident that thou thyself
3: 9. *both*[2] Jews and Gentiles, that they are all
7: 7. for)(I had not known lust, except
10: 12. difference between)([2] the Jew and the
14: 8. whether (lit. if *either*) we live
— *and* whether we die, we die unto
— whether (lit. if *either*) we live therefore, or (lit. if *either*) die, we are the Lord's.
16: 26. *and* by the scriptures of the prophets,

1Co. 1: 2. Jesus Christ our Lord, *both*[2] their's and our's:
24. *both*[2] Jews and Greeks, Christ the power
30. of God is made unto us wisdom, *and* righteousness
4: 21. *and* (in) the spirit of meekness?

2Co. 10: 8. For)(though I should boast

Eph. 1: 10. *both*[2] which are in heaven, and which are on earth;
3: 19. *And* to know the love of Christ,

Phi. 1: 7. inasmuch as *both* in my bonds, and

Heb 1: 3. *and* upholding all things by the word
2: 4. *both* with signs and wonders, and with
11. For *both*[2] he that sanctifieth and they
4: 12. dividing asunder)([2] of soul and spirit, *and*[2] of the joints and marrow,
5: 1. that he may offer *both*[2] gifts and sacrifices
7. offered up)([2] prayers and supplications
14. to discern *both*[2] good and evil.
6: 2. *and* of laying on of hands, *and* of resurrection of the dead,
4. *and* have tasted of the heavenly gift,
5. *and* the powers of the world to come,
19. an anchor of the soul, *both*[2] sure and stedfast,
8: 3. to offer)([2] gifts and sacrifices:
9: 1. *and* a worldly sanctuary.
2.)(the candlestick, and the table,
9. were offered *both*[2] gifts and sacrifices,
19. sprinkled *both*[2] the book, and all the
10: 33. *both*[2] by reproaches and afflictions;
11: 32. *and* (of) Barak, and (of) Samson, and
— (of) David *also*, and Samuel, and
12: 2. *and* is set down at the right hand

Jas. 3: 7. every kind)([2] of beasts, and of birds, *and*[3] of serpents, and of things in the sea,

Jude 6. *And* the angels which kept not
Rev. 1: 2. *and* of all things that he saw.
21:12. *And* had a wall great and high,

5038 9 815/935 cf rt 5088
τεῖχος, *tikos*

Acts 9:25. down by the *wall* in a basket.
2Co. 11:33. was I let down by the *wall*,
Heb 11:30. By faith the *walls* of Jericho fell
Rev. 21:12. And had a *wall* great and high,
14. And the *wall* of the city had twelve
15. the gates thereof, and the *wall* thereof.
17. And he measured the *wall* thereof,
18. And the building of the *wall* of it
19. And the foundations of the *wall* of

5039 1 815/935 *tekmar* (limit)
τεκμήριον, *tekmeerion.*

Acts 1: 3. by many *infallible proofs*,

5040 9 815/935 5:636 5043
τεκνίον, *teknion.*

Joh. 13:33. *Little children*, yet a little while I am
Gal. 4:19. My *little children*, of whom I travail
1Joh. 2: 1. My *little children*, these things write I
12. I write unto you, *little children*,
28. And now, *little children*, abide in him;
3: 7. *Little children*, let no man deceive you:
18. My *little children*, let us not love in word,
4: 4. Ye are of God, *little children*, and
5:21. *Little children*, keep yourselves from idols.

5041 1 815/935 5043,rt 1096
τεκνογονέω, *teknogoneo.*

1Ti. 5:14. that the younger women marry, *bear children*,

5042 1 815/935 5041
τεκνογονία, *teknogonia.*

1Ti. 2:15. she shall be saved in *childbearing*,

5043 99 815/935 5:636 rt 5098
τέκνον, *teknon.*

Mat. 2:18. Rachel weeping (for) her *children*,
3: 9. to raise up *children* unto Abraham.
7:11. to give good gifts unto your *children*,
9: 2. *Son*, be of good cheer; thy sins
10:21. and the father the *child*: and the *children* shall rise up
11:19. But wisdom is justified of her *children*.
15:26. not meet to take the *children's* bread,
18:25. to be sold, and his wife, and *children*,
19:29. or *children*, or lands, for my name's sake,
21:28. A (certain) man had two *sons*;
— *Son*, go work to day in my vineyard.
22:24. If a man die, having no *children*,
23:37. have gathered thy *children* together,
27:25. His blood (be) on us, and on our *children*.
Mar 2: 5. *Son*, thy sins be forgiven thee.
7:27. Let the *children* first be filled:
— not meet to take the *children's* bread,
10:24. *Children*, how hard is it for them that
29. or *children*, or lands, for my sake,
30. and *children*, and lands, with persecutions;
12:19. and leave no *children*, that his brother
13:12. to death, and the father the *son* (lit. the *child*); and *children* shall rise up against (their)
Lu. 1: 7. And they had no *child*, because that
17. the hearts of the fathers to the *children*,
2:48. *Son*, why hast thou thus dealt
3: 8. to raise up *children* unto Abraham.
7:35. wisdom is justified of all her *children*.
11:13. to give good gifts unto your *children*:
13:34. have gathered thy *children* together,
14:26. *children*, and brethren, and sisters
15:31. *Son*, thou art ever with me,
16:25. *Son*, remember that thou in thy lifetime,
18:29. or *children*, for the kingdom of God's sake,
19:44. and thy *children* within thee;
20:31. and they left no *children*, and died.
23:28. for yourselves, and for your *children*.
Joh. 1:12. power to become the *sons* of God, (lit. *children*)
8:39. If ye were Abraham's *children*,
11:52. in one the *children* of God that were scattered abroad.
Acts 2:39. is unto you, and to your *children*,
7: 5. when (as yet) he had no *child*.
13:33(32). God hath fulfilled the same unto us their *children*,
21: 5. all brought us on our way, with wives and *children*,
21. not to circumcise (their) *children*,
Ro. 8:16. that we are the *children* of God:
17. And if *children*, then heirs;
21. into the glorious liberty of the *children* of God.
9: 7. the seed of Abraham, (are they) all *children*:
8. They which are the *children* of the flesh, these (are) not the *children* of God: but the *children* of the promise
1Co. 4:14. but as my beloved *sons* I warn (you). (lit *children*)
17. Timotheus, who is my beloved *son*,
7:14. else were your *children* unclean;
2Co. 6:13. I speak as unto (my) *children*,
12:14. the *children* ought not to lay up for the parents, but the parents for the *children*.
Gal. 4:25. and is in bondage with her *children*.
27. the desolate hath many more *children*
28. as Isaac was, are the *children* of promise.
31. we are not *children* of the bondwoman,
Eph. 2: 3. were by nature the *children* of wrath,
5: 1. followers of God, as dear *children*;
8. walk as *children* of light:
6: 1. *Children*, obey your parents in the Lord·
4. provoke not your *children* to wrath:
Phi. 2:15. the *sons* of God, without rebuke, (lit. *children*)
22. that, as a *son* with the father,
Col. 3:20. *Children*, obey (your) parents in all things
21. Fathers, provoke not your *children*
1Th. 2: 7. even as a nurse cherisheth her *children*:
11. as a father (doth) his *children*,
1Ti. 1: 2. Unto Timothy, (my) own *son*
18. I commit unto thee, *son* Timothy,
3: 4. having his *children* in subjection
12. ruling their *children* and their own houses
5: 4. But if any widow have *children*
2Ti. 1: 2. To Timothy, (my) dearly beloved *son*
2: 1. Thou therefore, my *son*, be strong
Tit. 1: 4. To Titus, (mine) own *son* after
6. having faithful *children*, not accused
Philem 10. I beseech thee for my *son* Onesimus.
1Pet. 1:14. As obedient *children*, not fashioning
3: 6. whose *daughters* ye are, (lit. *children*)
2Pet. 2:14. exercised with covetous practises; cursed *children*:

1Joh. 3: 1. that we should be called the *sons* of God: (lit. *children*)
2. now are we the *sons* of God, (lit. *children*)
10. In this the *children* of God are manifest, and the *children* of the devil;
5: 2. we know that we love the *children* of God,
2Joh. 1. unto the elect lady and her *children*,
4. that I found of thy *children* walking in truth,
13. The *children* of thy elect sister greet
3Joh. 4. to hear that my *children* walk in truth.
Rev. 2:23. And I will kill her *children*
12: 4. to devour her *child* as soon as
5. her *child* was caught up unto God, and (to) his throne.

5044 1 816/936 5043,5142

τεκνοτροφέω, *teknotropheo*.

1Ti. 5:10. if she *have brought up children*,

5045 2 816/936 rt 5098

τέκτων, *tektōn*.

Mat.13:55. Is not this the *carpenter's* son?
Mar 6: 3. Is not this the *carpenter*,

5046 19 816/936 8:49 5056

τέλειος, *telīos*.

Mat. 5:48. Be ye therefore *perfect*, even as your Father which is in heaven is *perfect*.
19:21. If thou wilt be *perfect*, go (and)
Ro. 12: 2. and acceptable, and *perfect*, will of God.
1Co. 2: 6. wisdom among them that are *perfect*:
13:10. when that which is *perfect* is come,
14:20. but in understanding be *men*.
Eph 4.13. unto a *perfect* man, unto the measure of
Phi. 3:15. Let us therefore, as many as be *perfect*,
Col. 1:28. that we may present every man *perfect* in Christ Jesus:
4:12. that ye may stand *perfect* and complete
Heb 5:14. belongeth to them that are *of full age*,
9:11. greater and more *perfect* tabernacle,
Jas. 1: 4. let patience have (her) *perfect* work, that ye may be *perfect* and entire,
17. and every *perfect* gift is from above,
25. looketh into the *perfect* law of liberty,
3: 2. the same (is) a *perfect* man, (and)
1Joh.4:18. but *perfect* love casteth out fear:

5047 2 817/936 8:49 5046

τελειότης, *telīotees*.

Col. 3:14. which is the bond of *perfectness*.
Heb 6: 1. let us go on unto *perfection*;

5048 24 817/936 8:49 5046

τελειόω, *telīoō*.

Lu. 2:43. And *when* they *had fulfilled* the days,
13:32. the third (day) I shall be *perfected*.
Joh. 4:34. and to *finish* his work.
5:36. the Father hath given me to *finish*,
17: 4. I *have finished* the work which
23. that they may be *made perfect* in one;
19:28. that the scripture *might be fulfilled*,
Acts20:24. that I might *finish* my course with joy,
2Co.12: 9. my strength *is made perfect* in weakness.
Phi. 3:12. either *were* already *perfect*:
Heb. 2:10. *to make* the captain of their salvation *perfect*.
Heb 5: 9. And *being made perfect*, he became
7:19. For the law *made* nothing *perfect*.
28. the Son, *who is consecrated* for evermore.
9: 9. that could not *make* him that did the service *perfect*,
10: 1. *make* the comers thereunto *perfect*.
14. For by one offering he *hath perfected* for ever
11:40. that they without us *should* not *be made perfect*.
12:23. to the spirits of just men *made perfect*,
Jas. 2:22. by works *was* faith *made perfect*?
1Joh.2: 5. in him verily *is* the love of God *perfected*:
4:12. and his love is *perfected* in us.
17. Herein *is* our love *made perfect*, that
18. He that feareth *is* not *made perfect* in love

5049 1 818/937 5046

τελείως, *telīōs*.

1Pet.1:13. and hope *to the end* (lit. trust *perfectly*) for the grace

---

5050 2 818/937 8:49 5448

τελείωσις, *telīōsis*.

Lu. 1:45. there shall be a *performance* of those
Heb 7:11. If therefore *perfection* were by the Levitical priesthood,

---

5051 1 818/937 8:49 5048

τελειωτής, *telīōtees*.

Heb 12: 2. Jesus the author and *finisher* of (our)

5052 1 818/937 5056,5342

τελεσφορέω, *telesphoreo*.

Lu. 8:14. and bring no *fruit to perfection*.

5053 12 818/937 5055

τελευτάω, *telūtao*.

Mat. 2:19. But *when* Herod *was dead*,
9:18. My daughter *is* even now *dead*:
15: 4. *let* him *die* the death.
22:25. the first, when he had married a wife, *deceased*,
Mar 7:10. *let* him *die* the death:
9:44. Where their worm *dieth* not,
46. Where their worm *dieth* not,
48. Where their worm *dieth* not,
Lu. 7: 2. was sick, and ready *to die*.
Acts 2:29. David, that he *is* both *dead* and buried,
7:15. So Jacob went down into Egypt, and *died*,
Heb 11:22. By faith Joseph, *when* he *died*, (lit. *dying*)

5054 1 818/937 5053

τελευτή, *telutee*.

Mat. 2:15. And was there until the *death* of Herod:

5055 26 818/937 8:49 5056

τελέω, *teleo*.

Mat.10:23. Ye *shall* not *have gone over* the cities
11: 1. when Jesus *had made an end* of commanding his
13:53. when Jesus *had finished* these parables,
17:24. *Doth* not your master *pay* tribute?
19: 1. when Jesus *had finished* these sayings,

Mat.26: 1. *had finished* all these sayings,
Lu. 2:39. when they *had performed* all things
12:50. straitened till it be *accomplished!*
18:31. concerning the Son of man *shall be accomplished.*
22:37. must yet *be accomplished* in me,
Joh. 19:28. all things *were* now *accomplished,*
30. he said, It *is finished:* and he bowed
Acts13:29. when they *had fulfilled* all that
Ro. 2:27. if it *fulfil* the law, judge thee,
13: 6. for this cause *pay* ye tribute also:
Gal. 5:16. ye *shall* not *fulfil* the lust of the flesh.
2Ti. 4: 7. I *have finished* (my) course,
Jas. 2: 8. If ye *fulfil* the royal law according to
Rev.10: 7. the mystery of God *should be finished,*
11: 7. And when they *shall have finished* their
15: 1. for in them *is filled up* the wrath of God.
8. till the seven plagues of the seven angels *were fulfilled.*
17:17. until the words of God *shall be fulfilled.*
20: 3. till the thousand years *should be fulfilled:*
5. until the thousand years were (lit. *should be*) *finished.*
7. when the thousand years are (lit. *should be*) *expired*

5056 42 818/937 8:49 cf 5411

τέλος, *telos.* *tellō* (to set out)

Mat.10:22. but he that endureth to the *end* shall be
17:25. of whom do the kings of the earth take *custom*
24: 6. but the *end* is not yet.
13. But he that shall endure unto the *end,*
14. and then shall the *end* come.
26:58. with the servants, to see the *end.*
Mar 3:26. he cannot stand, but hath an *end.*
13: 7. but the *end* (shall) not (be) yet.
13. but he that shall endure unto the *end,*
Lu. 1:33. of his kingdom there shall be no *end.*
18: 5. lest by her continual coming (lit. unto the *end*)
21: 9. but the *end* (is) not by and by.
22:37. the things concerning me have an *end.*
Joh. 13: 1. he loved them unto the *end.*
Ro. 6:21. for the *end* of those things (is) death.
22. and the *end* everlasting life.
10: 4. For Christ (is) the *end* of the law
13: 7. *custom* to whom *custom;*
1Co. 1: 8. Who shall also confirm you unto the *end,*
10:11. upon whom the *ends* of the world are come.
15:24. Then (cometh) the *end,* when he shall have
2Co. 1:13. ye shall acknowledge even to the *end;*
3:13. to the *end* of that which is abolished:
11:15. whose *end* shall be according to
Phi. 3:19. Whose *end* (is) destruction,
1Th. 2:16. wrath is come upon them to the *uttermost.*
1Ti. 1: 5. Now the *end* of the commandment
Heb 3: 6. the rejoicing of the hope firm unto the *end.*
14. our confidence stedfast unto the *end,*
6: 8. whose *end* (is) to be burned.
11. assurance of hope unto the *end:*
7: 3. beginning of days, nor *end* of life;
Jas. 5:11. and have seen the *end* of the Lord;
1Pet. 1: 9. Receiving the *end* of your faith,
3: 8. *Finally,* (be ye) all of one mind,
4: 7. But the *end* of all things is at hand:
17. what shall the *end* (be) of them that obey not
Rev. 1: 8. the beginning and the *ending,*
2:26. and keepeth my works unto the *end,*
Rev.21: 6. the beginning and the *end.*
22:13. Alpha and Omega, the beginning an the *end,*

5057 22 820/938 8:88 5056,5608

τελώνης, *telōnees*

Mat. 5:46. do not even the *publicans* the same?
47. do not even the *publicans* so?
9:10. many *publicans* and sinners came
11. Why eateth your Master with *publicans*
10: 3. Thomas, and Matthew the *publican;*
11:19. a friend of *publicans* and sinners.
18:17. as an heathen man and a *publican.*
21:31. That the *publicans* and the harlots go into
32. the *publicans* and the harlots believed him:
Mar 2:15. many *publicans* and sinners sat also
16. *publicans* ... drinketh with *publicans*
Lu. 3:12. Then came also *publicans* to be baptized,
5:27. and saw a *publican,* named Levi,
29. there was a great company of *publicans*
30. drink with *publicans* and sinners?
7:29. and the *publicans,* justified God,
34. a friend of *publicans* and sinners!
15: 1. all the *publicans* and sinners for to hear him.
18:10. the one a Pharisee, and the other a *publican.*
11. adulterers, or even as this *publican.*
13. And the *publican,* standing afar off,

5058 3 820/938 5057

τελώνιον, *telōnion.*

Mat. 9: 9. sitting at the *receipt of custom:*
Mar 2:14. sitting at the *receipt of custom,*
Lu. 5:27. sitting at the *receipt of custom:*

5059 16 820/938 8:113

τέρας, *teras.*

Mat.24:24. and shall shew great signs and *wonders;*
Mar 13:22. and shall shew signs and *wonders,*
Joh. 4:48. Except ye see signs and *wonders,*
Acts 2:19. And I will shew *wonders* in heaven above,
22. by miracles and *wonders* and signs,
43. and many *wonders* and signs were done
4:30. that signs and *wonders* may be done
5:12. were many signs and *wonders* wrought
6: 8. did great *wonders* and miracles among
7:36. after that he had shewed *wonders*
14: 3. granted signs and *wonders* to be done
15:12. declaring what miracles and *wonders*
Ro. 15:19. Through mighty signs and *wonders,*
2Co.12:12. in signs, and *wonders,* and mighty deeds.
2Th. 2: 9. with all power and signs and lying *wonders,*
Heb 2: 4. both with signs and *wonders,*

5062 22 820/939 8:127 5064

τεσσαράκοντα, *tessarakonta.*

Mat. 4: 2. he had fasted *forty* days and *forty* nights,
Mar 1:13. was there in the wilderness *forty* days,
Lu. 4: 2. Being *forty* days tempted of the devil.
Joh. 2:20. *Forty* and six years was this temple
Acts 1: 3. being seen of them *forty* days,
4:22. the man was above *forty* years old,
7:30. And when *forty* years were expired,
36. and in the wilderness *forty* years.
42. *forty* years in the wilderness?
13:21. by the space of *forty* years.

Acts23:13 And they were more than *forty* which had made
21. of them more than *forty* men,
2Co.11:24. received I *forty* (stripes) save one.
Heb 3: 9. and saw my works *forty* years.
17. with whom was he grieved *forty* years?
Rev. 7: 4. an hundred (and) *forty* (and) four thousand
11: 2. tread under foot *forty* (and) two months.
13: 5. to continue *forty* (and) two months.
14: 1. with him an hundred *forty* (and) four thousand,
3. but the hundred (and) *forty* (and) four thousand,
21:17. an hundred (and) *forty* (and) four cubits,

5063 2 820/939 8:127 5062,2094

τεσσαρακονταετής, tessarakontaetees.

Acts 7:23. when he was full *forty years old*, (lit. when the time *of forty years* was completed to him)
13:18. And about the time *of forty years*

5064 42 820/938 8:127

τέσσαρες, -ρα, tessares, -ra.

Mat.24:31. his elect from the *four* winds,
Mar 2: 3. sick of the palsy, which was borne of *four*.
13:27. his elect from the *four* winds,
Lu. 2:37. of about fourscore and *four* years,
Joh. 11:17. (lain) in the grave *four* days already.
19:23. *four* parts, to every soldier a part;
Acts10:11. sheet knit at the *four* corners,
11: 5. let down from heaven by *four* corners;
12: 4. and delivered (him) to *four* quaternions
21: 9. the same man had *four* daughters,
23. We have *four* men which have a vow
27:29. cast *four* anchors out of the stern,
Rev. 4: 4. (were) *four* and twenty seats:
— I saw *four* and twenty elders sitting,
6. *four* beasts full of eyes before and
8. And the *four* beasts had each of them
10. The *four* and twenty elders fall down
5: 6. of the throne and of the *four* beasts,
8. the *four* beasts and *four* (and) twenty elders fell down before the Lamb,
14. And the *four* beasts said, Amen. And the *four* (and) twenty elders fell down
6: 1. one of the *four* beasts saying, Come
6. in the midst of the *four* beasts say,
7: 1. after these things I saw *four* angels standing on the *four* corners of the earth, holding the *four* winds of the earth,
2. he cried with a loud voice to the *four* angels,
4. an hundred (and) forty (and) *four* thousand
11. (about) the elders and the *four* beasts,
9:13. I heard a voice from the *four* horns
14. Loose the *four* angels which are bound
15. And the *four* angels were loosed,
11:16. And the *four* and twenty elders, which
14: 1. an hundred forty (and) *four* thousand,
3. and before the *four* beasts,
— but the hundred (and) forty (and) *four* thousand,
15: 7. And one of the *four* beasts gave
19: 4. the *four* and twenty elders and the *four* beasts
20: 8. are in the *four* quarters of the earth,
1:17. an hundred (and) forty (and) *four* cubits,

5065 2 821/939 5064,2532,1182

τεσσαρεσκαιδέκατος, tessareskaidekatos.

Acts27:27. when the *fourteenth* night was come,
33. This day is the *fourteenth* day that ye

5066 1 821/939 8:27 5064

τεταρταῖος, tetartaios.

Joh. 11:39. for he hath been (dead) four days. (lit. he is *of the fourth day*)

5067 10 821/939 8:127 5064

τέταρτος, tetartos.

Mat.14:25. And in the *fourth* watch of the night
Mar. 6:48. about the *fourth* watch of the night
Acts10:30. *Four* days ago I was fasting until
Rev. 4: 7. *fourth* beast (was) like a flying eagle.
6: 7. opened the *fourth* seal, I heard the voice of the *fourth* beast
8. over the *fourth* part of the earth,
8:12. And the *fourth* angel sounded,
16: 8. the *fourth* angel poured out his vial
21:19. the *fourth*, an emerald;

5068 1 821/939 5064,1137

τετράγωνος, tetragōnos.

Rev.21:16. And the city lieth *foursquare*,

5069 1 821/940 *tetras* (group of four)

τετράδιον, tetradion.

Acts12: 4. to four *quaternions* of soldiers

5070 5 821/940 5064,5507

τετρακισχίλιοι, tetrakiskilioi.

Mat.15:38. *four thousand* men, beside women and
16:10. the seven loaves of the *four thousand*,
Mar 8: 9. were about *four thousand*: and he
20. And when the seven among *four thousand*,
Acts21:38. *four thousand* men that were murderers?

5071 4 821/940 5064,1540

τετρακόσιοι, -σια, tetrakosioi, -sia.

Acts 5:36. a number of men, about *four hundred*,
7: 6. entreat (them) evil *four hundred* years.
13:20. space of *four hundred* and fifty years,
Gal. 3:17. *four hundred* and thirty years after,

5072 1 821/940 5064,3376

τετράμηνον, tetrameenon.

Joh. 4:35. Say not ye, There are yet *four months*,

5073 1 821/940 5064,rt 4118

τετραπλόος, tetraploos.

Lu. 19: 8. I restore (him) *fourfold*.

5074 3 821/940 5064,4228

τετράπους, tetrapous.

Acts10:12. all manner of *fourfooted beasts* of the earth
11: 6. and saw *fourfooted beasts* of the earth,
Ro. 1:23. *fourfooted beasts*, and creeping things

5076 4 821/939 5064,757

τετράρχης, tetrarkees.

Mat.14: 1. At that time Herod the *tetrarch* heard
Lu. 3:19. But Herod the *tetrarch*, being reproved
9: 7. Now Herod the *tetrarch* heard of all
Acts13: 1. brought up with Herod the *tetrarch*,

5075 3 821/939 5076

τετραρχέω, tetrarkeo.

Lu. 3: 1. Herod *being tetrarch* of Galilee, and his brother Philip *tetrarch* of Ituræa
— Lysanias the *tetrarch* (lit. being *tetrarch*) of Abilene,

5077 1 821/940 *tephra* (ashes)

τεφρόω, tephroō.

2Pet 2: 6. *turning* the cities of Sodom and Gomorrha *into ashes*

5078 3 821/940 rt 5088

τέχνη, teknee.

Acts17:29. stone, graven by *art* and man's device.
18: 3. by their *occupation* they were tentmakers.
Rev.18:22. craftsman, of whatsoever *craft* (he be),

5079 4 821/940 5078

τεχνίτης, teknitees.

Acts19:24. no small gain unto the *craftsmen*;
38. and the *craftsmen* which are with him,
Heb 11:10. whose *builder* and maker (is) God.
Rev.18:22. no *craftsman*, of whatsoever craft

5080 1 822/940

τήκομαι, teekomai.

2Pet. 3:12. elements shall *melt* with fervent heat?

5081 1 822/940 5056,827

τηλαυγῶς, teelaugōs.

Mar 8:25. and saw every man *clearly*.

5082 4 822/940 3588,2245,3778

τηλικοῦτος, teelikoutos.

2Co. 1:10. Who delivered us from *so great* a death,
Heb 2: 3. if we neglect *so great* salvation;
Jas. 3: 4. which though (they be) *so great*,
Rev.16:18. *so mighty* an earthquake, (and) so great.

5083 75 822/940 8:140 cf 5442, cf 2892 *teros* (watch)

τηρέω, teereo.

Mat.19:17. *keep* the commandments.
23: 3. whatsoever they bid you *observe*, (that) *observe*
27:36. they *watched* him there;
54. they that were with him, *watching* Jesus,
28: 4. for fear of him the *keepers* did shake,
20. Teaching them *to observe* all things
Mar 7: 9. that ye *may keep* your own tradition.
Joh. 2:10. thou *hast kept* the good wine until now.
8:51. If a man *keep* my saying,
52. thou sayest, If a man *keep* my saying,
55. but I know him, and *keep* his saying.
9:16. because he *keepeth* not the sabbath day.
12: 7. of my burying *hath* she *kept* this.
Joh.14:15. If ye love me, *keep* my commandments.
21. and *keepeth* them, he it is that loveth me:
23. If a man love me, he *will keep* my words:
24. loveth me not *keepeth* not my sayings:
15:10. If ye *keep* my commandments,
— even as I *have kept* my Father's
20. if they *have kept* my saying, they *will keep* your's also.
17: 6. and they *have kept* thy word.
11. Holy Father, *keep* through thine own
12. I *kept* them in thy name:
15. *shouldest keep* them from the evil.
Acts12: 5. Peter therefore *was kept* in prison:
6. the keepers before the door *kept* the
15: 5. to command (them) *to keep* the law of
24. (Ye must) be circumcised, and *keep* the law:
16:23. charging the jailor *to keep* them safely:
21:25. that they *observe* no such thing,
24:23. he commanded a centurion *to keep* Paul (lit. that Paul *be kept*)
25: 4. that Paul should *be kept* at Cæsarea,
21. when Paul had appealed *to be reserved*
— I commanded him *to be kept* till
1Co. 7:37. that he will *keep* his virgin, doeth well.
2Co.11: 9. in all (things) I *have kept* myself from
— and (so) *will I keep* (myself).
Eph 4: 3. Endeavouring *to keep* the unity of the
1Th. 5:23. *be preserved* blameless unto the coming
1Ti. 5:22. *keep* thyself pure.
6:14. That thou *keep* (this) commandment
2Ti. 4: 7. I *have kept* the faith:
Jas. 1:27. (and) *to keep* himself unspotted from the world.
2:10. whosoever *shall keep* the whole law,
1Pet. 1: 4. *reserved* in heaven for you,
2Pet. 2: 4. to be *reserved* unto judgment;
9. and *to reserve* the unjust unto the day
17. to whom the mist of darkness *is reserved* for ever.
3: 7. *reserved* unto fire against the day of
1Joh 2: 3. if we *keep* his commandments.
4. and *keepeth* not his commandments,
5. But whoso *keepeth* his word, in him
3:22. because we *keep* his commandments,
24. And he *that keepeth* his commandments
5: 2. and *keep* his commandments.
3. that we *keep* his commandments:
18. begotten of God *keepeth* himself, and
Jude 1. and *preserved* in Jesus Christ,
6. And the angels *which kept* not their
— he *hath reserved* in everlasting chains
13. to whom *is reserved* the blackness
21. *Keep* yourselves in the love of God,
Rev. 1: 3. and *keep* those things which are written
2:26. and *keepeth* my works unto the end,
3: 3. and *hold fast*, and repent.
8. and *hast kept* my word, and hast not
10. thou *hast kept* the word of my patience, I also *will keep* thee
12:17. *which keep* the commandments of God,
14:12. they *that keep* the commandments of
16:15. that watcheth, and *keepeth* his garments,
22: 7. blessed (is) he *that keepeth* the sayings
9. and of them *which keep* the sayings of this book:

5084 3 823/941 8:140 5083

τήρησις, teeresis.

Acts 4: 3. and put (them) in *hold* unto the next

Acts 5:18. put them in the common *prison*.
1 Co. 7:19. but the *keeping* of the commandments

5087 96 823/941 8:152 cf 2476 cf 2749

τίθημι, ἔθηκα, ἐθέμην, θῶ, &c. *titheemi, etheeka, ethemeen, tho,* &c.

Mat. 5:15. and *put* it under a bushel,
12:18. I *will put* my spirit upon him,
14: 3. *put* (him) in prison for Herodias' sake,
22:44. till I *make* thine enemies thy footstool?
24:51. shall cut him asunder, and *appoint* (him) his portion with
27:60. And *laid* it in his own new tomb,
Mar 4:21. Is a candle brought to *be put* under a
6:29. and *laid* it in a tomb.
56. they *laid* the sick in the streets,
10:16. *put* (his) hands upon them, *and*
12:36. till I *make* thine enemies thy footstool.
15:19. *bowing* (their) knees worshipped him.
47. beheld where he was *laid*.
16: 6. behold the place where they *laid* him.
Lu. 1:66. *laid* (them) *up* in their hearts,
5:18. and *to lay* (him) before him.
6:48. and *laid* the foundation on a rock:
8:16. or *putteth* (it) under a bed;
9:44. *Let* these sayings *sink down* into your ears: (lit. *put* ye these &c.)
11:33. *putteth* (it) in a secret place,
12:46. and *will appoint* him his portion with
14:29. *after* he *hath laid* the foundation,
19:21. takest up that thou *layedst* not *down*,
22. taking up that I *laid* not *down*,
20:43. Till I *make* thine enemies thy footstool.
21:14. *Settle* (it) therefore in your hearts,
22:41. kneeled down, and (lit. *having placed* his knees) prayed,
23:53. and *laid* it in a sepulchre
55. and how his body *was laid*.
Joh. 2:10. at the beginning *doth set forth* good
10:11. the good shepherd *giveth* his life for
15. I *lay down* my life for the sheep.
17. because I *lay down* my life,
18. but I *lay* it *down* of myself. I have power *to lay* it *down*,
11:34. Where *have* ye *laid* him?
13: 4. and *laid aside* his garments;
37. I *will lay down* my life for thy sake.
38. *Wilt* thou *lay down* thy life for
15:13. that a man *lay down* his life for his
16. I have chosen you, and *ordained* you, that ye should go
19:19. wrote a title, and *put* (it) on the cross.
41. wherein *was* never man yet *laid*.
42. There *laid* they Jesus therefore
20: 2. we know not where they *have laid* him.
13. I know not where they *have laid* him.
15. tell me where thou *hast laid* him,
Acts 1: 7. which the Father *hath put* in his own power.
2:35. Until I *make* thy foes thy footstool.
3: 2. whom they *laid* daily at the gate of the
4: 3. and *put* (them) in hold unto the next day:
35. And *laid* (them) *down* at the apostles' feet:
37. and *laid* (it) at the apostles' feet.
5: 2. and *laid* (it) at the apostles' feet.
4. why *hast* thou *conceived* this thing in thine heart?
15. and *laid* (them) on beds and couches,
18. and *put* them in the common prison.
Acts 5:25. the men whom ye *put* in prison
7:16. were carried over into Sychem, and *laid* in the sepulchre that
60. And he kneeled down, and cried (lit. *having placed* his knees)
9:37. they *laid* (her) in an upper chamber.
40. kneeled down, and (lit. *having &c.*) prayed;
12: 4. he *put* (him) in prison, and
13:29. and *laid* (him) in a sepulchre.
47. I *have set* thee to be a light of the
19:21. Paul *purposed* in the spirit,
20:28. the Holy Ghost *hath made* you overseers,
36. he kneeled down, and (lit. *having &c.*) prayed
21: 5. and we kneeled down (lit. *having &c.*)
27:12. the more part advised (lit. *formed* the counsel) to depart thence also,
Ro. 4:17. I *have made* thee a father of
9:33. I *lay* in Sion a stumblingstone
14:13. that no man *put* a stumblingblock
1Co. 3:10. I *have laid* the foundation, and another
11. For other foundation can no man *lay*
9:18. I may *make* the gospel of Christ without charge,
12:18. But now *hath* God *set* the members
28. And God *hath set* some in the church,
15:25. till he *hath put* all enemies under his feet.
16: 2. *let* every one of you *lay* by him in store,
2Co. 3:13. *put* a vail over his face,
5:19. and *hath committed* unto us the word of reconciliation.
1Th. 5: 9. God *hath* not *appointed* us to wrath,
1Ti. 1:12. *putting* me into the ministry;
2: 7. Whereunto I *am ordained* a preacher,
2Ti. 1:11. Whereunto I *am appointed* a preacher,
Heb 1: 2. whom he *hath appointed* heir of all
13. until I *make* thine enemies thy footstool?
10:13. till his enemies be *made* his footstool.
1Pet. 2: 6. I *lay* in Sion a chief corner stone,
8. whereunto also they *were appointed*.
2Pet. 2: 6. *making* (them) an ensample unto those
1Joh. 3:16. because he *laid down* his life for us:
— and we ought *to lay down* (our) lives
Rev. 10: 2. he *set* his right foot upon the sea,
11: 9. and shall not suffer their dead bodies *to be put* in graves.

5088 19 824/942 teko (to produce)

τίκτω, ἔτεκον, *tikto, etekon.*

Mat. 1:21. And she *shall bring forth* a son,
23. and *shall bring forth* a son,
25. till she *had brought forth* her firstborn son.
2: 2. Where is he *that is born* King of the Jews?
Lu. 1:31. and *bring forth* a son, and shalt call
57. time came that she should *be delivered*;
2: 6. that she should *be delivered*.
7. she *brought forth* her firstborn son,
11. For unto you *is born* this day in the
Joh. 16:21. A woman when she *is in travail*
Gal. 4:27. Rejoice, (thou) barren *that bearest* not;
Heb 6: 7. and *bringeth forth* herbs meet for them
11:11. and *was delivered of a child* when
Jas. 1:15. Then when lust hath conceived, it *bringeth forth* sin:
Rev. 12: 2. and pained *to be delivered*.
4. the woman which was ready *to be delivered*, for to devour her child as soon as it was *born*. (lit. when she *should have brought forth*)
5. And she *brought forth* a man child,
13. the woman which *brought forth* the man

5089 3 824/942 cf *hellomai*

τίλλω, *tillo.*

Mat.12: 1. and began *to pluck* the ears of corn,
Mar 2:23. began, as they went, to *pluck* the ears of corn.
Lu. 6: 1. his disciples *plucked* the ears of corn,

5091 21 824/942 8:169 5093

τιμάω, *timao.*

Mat.15: 4. *Honour* thy father and mother:
6(5). And *honour* not his father or his mother,
8. and *honoureth* me with (their) lips;
19:19. *Honour* thy father and (thy) mother:
27: 9. price of him *that was valued*, whom they of the children of Israel *did value;*
Mar 7: 6. This people *honoureth* me with (their) lips,
10. *Honour* thy father and thy mother;
10:19. *Honour* thy father and mother.
Lu. 18:20. *Honour* thy father and thy mother.
Joh. 5:23. That all (men) *should honour* the Son, even as they *honour* the Father. He *that honoureth* not the Son *honoureth* not the Father which
8:49. but I *honour* my Father, and ye
12:26. him *will* (my) Father *honour*.
Acts28:10. Who also *honoured* us with many honours;
Eph. 6: 2. *Honour* thy father and mother;
1Ti. 5: 3. *Honour* widows that are widows indeed.
1Pet.2:17. *Honour* all (men). Love the brotherhood. Fear God. *Honour* the king.

5092 43 825/943 8:169 5099

τιμή, *timee.*

Mat.27: 6. because it is the *price* of blood.
9. the *price* of him that was valued,
Joh. 4:44. hath no *honour* in his own country.
Acts 4:34. and brought the *prices* of the things that were sold,
5: 2. kept back (part) of the *price*, his wife also being privy (to it),
3. (part) of the *price* of the land?
7:16. Abraham bought for a *sum* of money
19:19. and they counted the *price* of them,
28:10. honoured us with many *honours*,
Ro. 2: 7. seek for glory and *honour*
10. But glory, *honour*, and peace,
9:21. to make one vessel unto *honour*,
12:10. in *honour* preferring one another;
13: 7. *honour* to whom *honour*.
1Co. 6:20. For ye are bought with a *price:*
7:23. Ye are bought with a *price;*
12:23. we bestow more abundant *honour;*
24. having given more abundant *honour*
Col. 2:23. not in any *honour* to the satisfying
1Th. 4: 4. vessel in sanctification and *honour;*
1Ti. 1:17. (be) *honour* and glory for ever and ever.
5:17. be counted worthy of double *honour*,
6: 1. their own masters worthy of all *honour*,
16. to whom (be) *honour* and power
2Ti. 2:20. some to *honour*, and some to dishonour.
21. he shall be a vessel unto *honour*,
Heb 2: 7. crownedst him with glory and *honour*,
9. crowned with glory and *honour;*
3: 3. hath more *honour* than the house.
5: 4. taketh this *honour* unto himself,
1Pet.1: 7. be found unto praise and *honour*
2: 7. Unto you therefore which believe (he is) *precious:* (lit. the *preciousness*)
3: 7. giving *honour* unto the wife, as unto
2Pet.1:17. from God the Father *honour* and glory,
Rev. 4: 9. those beasts give glory and *honour*
11. to receive glory and *honour* and
5:12. and *honour*, and glory, and blessing.
13. Blessing, and *honour*, and glory,
7:12. and *honour*, and power, and might,
19: 1. Salvation, and glory, and *honour*,
21:24. bring their glory and *honour* into it.
26. glory and *honour* of the nations into it.

5093 14 825/943 5092

τίμιος, *timios.*

Acts 5:34. *had in reputation* among all the people,
20:24. neither count I my life *dear*
1Co. 3:12. *precious* stones, wood, hay, stubble;
Heb13: 4. Marriage (is) *honourable* in all,
Jas. 5: 7. waiteth for the *precious* fruit
1Pet.1: 7. being much *more precious* than of gold
19. But with the *precious* blood of Christ,
2Pet.1: 4. exceeding great and *precious* promises:
Rev.17: 4. decked with gold and *precious* stones
18:12. of gold, and silver, and *precious* stones, vessels of *most precious* wood,
16. decked with gold, and *precious* stones,
21:11. like unto a stone *most precious*,
19. with all manner of *precious* stones.

5094 1 825/943 5093

τιμιότης, *timiotees.*

Rev.18:19. by reason of her *costliness!*

5097 2 826/944 5092 *ouros* (guard)

τιμωρέω, *timōreo.*

Acts22: 5. unto Jerusalem, for to *be punished*.
26:11. And I *punished* them oft in every synagogue, *and*

5098 1 826/944 5097

τιμωρία, *timōria.*

Heb10:29. Of how much sorer *punishment*,

5100 452 827/949

τις, *tis.* indefinite.

Note.—It is frequently rendered 'a man,' 'any man, —the literal in such cases is simply 'any' or 'any one.'

Mat. 5:23. thy brother hath *ought* against thee;
8:28. that no *man* (lit. not *any*) might pass by that
9: 3. *certain* of the scribes said within
11:27. neither knoweth *any man* the Father,
12:19. neither shall *any man* hear his voice
29. how can *one* enter into a strong man's
38. Then *certain* of the scribes and of the
47. Then *one* said unto him, Behold,
16:28. There be *some* standing here,
18:12. if *a man* have an hundred sheep,
20:20. and desiring a *certain thing* of him.
21: 3. And if *any* (man) say *ought* unto you,
33. There was a *certain* housholder,
22:24. If a *man* die, having no children,
46. neither durst *any* (man) from that day
24: 4. Take heed that no *man* (lit. lest *any*) deceive you.
17. to take *any thing* out of his house:
23. Then if *any man* shall say unto you,
27:47. *Some* of them that stood there,
28:11. *some* of the watch came into the city,

5099, p. 740

Mar 2: 6. But there were *certain* of the scribes
4:22. there is nothing hid, (lit. not *any thing*)
5:25. a *certain* woman, which had an issue
7: 1. and *certain* of the scribes,
2. when they saw *some* of his disciples
8: 2. have nothing to eat: (lit. not *any* thing)
3. for *divers* of them came from far.
4. whence can a *man* satisfy
26. nor tell (it) to *any* in the town.
9: 1. there be *some* of them that stand here,
30. that *any man* should know (it).
38. we saw *one* casting out devils in
11: 3. And if *any man* say unto you,
5. And *certain* of them that stood there
13. he might find *any thing* thereon:
16. that *any man* should carry (any) vessel
25. if ye have *ought* against *any*:
12:13. send unto him *certain* of the Pharisees
19. If a *man's* brother die,
13: 5. Take heed lest *any* (man) deceive
15. to take *any thing* out of his house:
21. And then if *any man* shall say
14: 4. were *some* that had indignation
47. And one)(of them that stood by
51. followed him a *certain* young man,
57. And there arose *certain*, and bare
65. And *some* began to spit on him,
15:21. And they compel *one* Simon
35. And *some* of them that stood by,
16:18. and if they drink *any* deadly thing,
Lu. 1: 5. a *certain* priest named Zacharias,
6: 2. And *certain* of the Pharisees said
7: 2. And a *certain* centurion's servant,
19(18). calling (unto him) two)(of his
36. *one* of the Pharisees desired him
40. I have *somewhat* to say unto thee.
41. a *certain* creditor which had
8: 2. *certain* women, which had been healed
27. a *certain* man, which had devils
46. *Somebody* hath touched me:
49. there cometh *one* from the ruler
9: 7. because that it was said of *some*,
8. And of *some*, that Elias
19. *one* of the old prophets is risen
23. If *any* (man) will come after me,
27. there be *some* standing here,
49. we saw *one* casting out devils
57. a *certain* (man) said unto him,
10:25. a *certain* lawyer stood up, and
30. A *certain* (man) went down from
31. there came down a *certain* priest
33. But a *certain* Samaritan,
38. he entered into a *certain* village: and a *certain* woman named Martha
11. 1. as he was praying in a *certain* place, when he ceased, *one* of his
15. But *some* of them said, He casteth
27. a *certain* woman of the company
36. having no (lit. not having *any*) part dark,
37. a *certain* Pharisee besought
45. Then answered *one* of the lawyers,
54. seeking to catch *something* out of his
12: 4. after that have no (lit. not *any*) more
13. And *one* of the company said
15. a *man's* life consisteth not (lit. not in abundance to *any* is his life)
16 The ground of a *certain* rich man
13: 1. *some* that told him of the Galilæans,
6. A *certain* (man) had a fig tree
23. Then said *one* unto him, Lord,
31. there came *certain* of the Pharisees,
14: 1. house of *one* of the chief Pharisees

Lu. 14: 2. there was a *certain* man before him
8. When thou art bidden of *any* (man)
15. And when *one* of them that sat at
16. A *certain* man made a great supper
15:11. A *certain* man had two sons:
16: 1. There was a *certain* rich man,
19. There was a *certain* rich man,
20. And there was a *certain* beggar
30. if *one* went unto them from the dead,
31. though *one* rose from the dead.
17:12. he entered into a *certain* village,
18: 2. There was in a)(city a)(judge,
9. this parable unto *certain* which
18. And a *certain* ruler asked him,
35. a *certain* blind man sat by the way
19: 8. if I have taken *any thing* from *any man*
12. A *certain* nobleman went into
31. And if *any man* ask you,
39. And *some* of the Pharisees
20: 9. A *certain* man planted a vineyard,
27. *certain* of the Sadducees,
28. If *any man's* brother die,
39. Then *certain* of the scribes
21: 2. he saw also a *certain* poor widow
5. And as *some* spake of the temple,
22:35. lacked ye *any thing*?
50. one)(of them smote the servant
56. But a *certain* maid beheld him
59. another)(confidently affirmed,
23: 8. to have seen *some* miracle done
19. Who for a *certain* sedition made
26. laid hold upon *one* Simon, a Cyrenian,
24: 1. and *certain* (others) with them.
22. Yea, and *certain* women also
24. And *certain* of them which were
41. Have ye here *any* meat?
Joh. 1:46(47). Can there *any* good thing come
2:25. that *any* should testify of man:
3: 3. Except a *man* be born again,
5. Except a *man* be born of water
4:33. Hath *any man* brought him (ought)
46. there was a *certain* nobleman,
5: 5. And a *certain* man was there,
14. lest a worse *thing* (lit. *something* worse) come unto thee.
19. but *what* he seeth the Father do:
6: 7. every one of them may take a)(little.
12. that nothing (lit. lest *ought*) be lost.
46. Not that *any man* hath seen the
50. that a *man* may eat thereof, and not die.
51. if *any man* eat of this bread,
64. But there are *some* of you that
7: 4. (that) doeth *any thing* in secret,
17. If *any man* will do his will,
25. Then said *some* of them of Jerusalem,
37. If *any man* thirst, let him come unto me
44. *some* of them would have taken him;
48. Have *any* of the rulers or of the
8:51. If a *man* keep my saying,
52. If a *man* keep my saying,
9:16. said *some* of the Pharisees,
22. if *any man* did confess that he
31. if *any man* be a worshipper of God,
32. that *any man* opened the eyes
10: 9. by me if *any man* enter in,
28. neither shall *any* (man) pluck them
11: 1. Now a *certain* (man) was sick,
9. If *any man* walk in the day,
10. But if a *man* walk in the night,
37. And *some* of them said,
46. *some* of them went their ways
49. one)(of them, (named) Caiaphas,

Joh. 11:57. that, if *any man* knew where he were.
12:20. And there were *certain* Greeks
26. If *any man* serve me, let him
— if *any man* serve me, him will
47. And if *any man* hear my words,
13:20. He that receiveth *whom*soever I send
29. For *some* (of them) thought, because
— he should give *something* to the poor.
14:14. If ye shall ask *any thing* in my name,
23. If a *man* love me, he will
15: 6. If a *man* (lit. *any*) abide not in me,
13. that a *man* lay down his life
16:30. that *any man* should ask thee:
20:23. *Whose* soever sins ye remit,
— (and) *whose* soever (sins) ye retain,
Acts 2:45. as *every man* had need.
3: 2. And a *certain* man lame from
5. to receive *something* of them.
4:32. neither said any (of them) that *ought*
34. Neither was there *any* among them
35. according as *he* (lit. *any*) had need.
5: 1. But a *certain* man named Ananias,
2. and brought a *certain* part,
15. might overshadow *some* of them.
25. Then came *one* and told them,
34. Then stood there up *one* in the council,
— put the apostles forth a)(little space;
36. boasting himself to be *somebody;*
6: 9. arose *certain* of the synagogue,
7:24. seeing *one* (of them) suffer wrong,
8: 9. But there was a *certain* man,
— that himself was *some* great one:
31. except *some man* should guide me?
34. of himself, or of *some* other man?
36. they came unto a *certain* water:
9: 2. that if he found *any* of this way,
10. And there was a *certain* disciple
19. Then was Saul *certain* days
33. And there he found a *certain* man
36. at Joppa a *certain* disciple
43. with *one* Simon a tanner.
10: 1. a *certain* man in Cæsarea
6. lodgeth with *one* Simon a tanner,
11. and a *certain* vessel descending
23. and *certain* brethren from Joppa
47. Can *any man* forbid water,
48. Then prayed they him to tarry *certain* days.
11: 5. A *certain* vessel descend, as
20. And *some* of them were men of
29. every man according to his ability, (lit. each of them according as *any* abounded)
12: 1. to vex *certain* of the church.
13: 1. *certain* prophets and teachers;
6. they found a *certain* sorcerer,
41. though a *man* declare it unto you.
14: 8. there sat a *certain* man at Lystra,
15: 1. And *certain* men which came down
2. Barnabas, and *certain* other of them,
5. *certain* of the sect of the Pharisees
24. that *certain* which went out from us
36. And *some* days after Paul said
16: 1. a *certain* disciple was there, named Timotheus, the son of a *certain* woman,
9. There stood a)(man of Macedonia,
12. In that city abiding *certain* days.
14. a *certain* woman named Lydia,
16. a *certain* damsel possessed with a
17: 4. And *some* of them believed,
5. took unto them *certain* lewd fellows
6. they drew Jason and *certain* brethren
8. Then *certain* philosophers of the
— *some* said, What will this babbler say?

Acts 17:20. thou bringest *certain* strange things
21. or to hear *some* new thing.
25. as though he needed *any thing,*
28. as *certain* also of your own poets
34. *certain* men clave unto him,
18: 2. a *certain* Jew named Aquila,
7. entered into a *certain* (man's) house,
14. If it were *a* (lit. *any*) matter of wrong
23. after he had spent *some* time (there),
24. And a *certain* Jew named Apollos,
19: 1. and finding *certain* disciples,
9. But when *divers* were hardened,
— daily in the school of *one* Tyrannus.
13. Then *certain* of the vagabond Jews,
14. there were seven sons of (one) Sceva, (lit *certain* sons of Sceva seven)
24. a *certain* (man) named Demetrius,
31. And *certain* of the chief of Asia,
32. Some therefore cried)(one thing,
38. have a matter against *any* man,
39. if ye enquire *any thing* concerning
20: 9. a *certain* young man named
21:10. a *certain* prophet, named Agabus.
16. with them *one* Mnason of Cyprus,
34. And some cried)(one thing,
37. May I speak)(unto thee?
22:12. *one* Ananias, a devout man
23:12. *certain* of the Jews banded together,
17. hath a *certain thing* to tell him.
18. hath *something* to say unto thee.
20. would enquire *somewhat* of him
23. unto (him))(two centurions,
24: 1. a *certain* orator (named) Tertullus,
12. in the temple disputing with *any man,*
18. Whereupon *certain* Jews from Asia
20. have found *any* evil doing in me,
24. And after *certain* days, when Felix
25: 5. if there be *any* wickedness in him.
8. have I offended *any thing at all.*
11. committed *any thing* worthy of death,
13. after *certain* days king Agrippa
14. There is a *certain* man left in bonds
16. to deliver *any* man to die.
19. had *certain* questions against him
— of *one* Jesus, which was dead, whom
26. Of whom I have no certain *thing* to write
— I might have *somewhat* to write.
26:26. I am persuaded that none (lit. not *any*) of these things are hidden from him;
27: 1. Paul and *certain* other prisoners
8. came unto a)(place which is called
16. running under a *certain* island
26. be cast upon a *certain* island.
27. they drew near to *some* country;
39. they discovered a *certain* creek
42. lest *any* of them should swim out,
44. on (broken pieces) of the ship. (lit. upon *some* of the things from the ship)
28:19. not that I had *ought* to accuse
21. neither *any* of the brethren that came shewed or spake *any* harm of thee.
Ro. 1:11. impart unto you *some* spiritual gift,
13. that I might have *some* fruit among you
3: 3. For what if *some* did not believe?
8. and as *some* affirm that we say,
5: 7. scarcely for a righteous man will *one* die
— *some* would even dare to die.
8: 9. if *any man* have not the Spirit of Christ.
24. for what a *man* seeth, why doth.
39. nor depth, nor *any* other creature.
9:11. having done *any* good or evil,
11:14. and might save *some* of them.

Ro 11:17. if *some* of the branches be broken off,
14:14. esteemeth *any thing* to be unclean,
15:18. dare to speak of *any* of those things
26. to make a *certain* contribution
1Co. 1:15. Lest *any* should say that I had baptized
2: 2. not to know *any thing* among you,
3: 4. For while *one* saith, I am of Paul;
7. neither is he that planteth *any thing*,
12. Now if *any man* build upon this
14. If *any man's* work abide which he
17. If *any man* defile the temple of
4: 2. that a *man* be found faithful.
5. judge nothing (lit. not *ought*) before the
18. Now *some* are puffed up, as though
5: 1. that *one* should have his father's wife.
11. if *any man* that is called a brother
6: 1. Dare *any* of you, having a matter
11. And such were *some* of you:
12. be brought under the power of *any*.
7: 5. except (it be))(with consent for a time,
12. If *any* brother hath a wife that
18. Is *any man* called being circumcised?
— Is *any* called in uncircumcision?
36. But if *any man* think that he
8: 2. And if *any man* think that he knoweth *any thing*,
3. But if *any man* love God, the
7. for *some* with conscience of the idol
10. For if *any man* see thee which hast
9:12. lest we should hinder the gospel (lit. should give *any* hindrance to)
15. than that *any man* should make my
22. that I might by all means save *some*.
10: 7. be ye idolaters, as (were) *some* of them;
8. as *some* of them committed,
9. as *some* of them also tempted,
10. as *some* of them also murmured,
19. that the idol is *any thing*, or that which is offered in sacrifice to idols is *any thing?*
27. If *any* of them that believe not
28. But if *any man* say unto you,
31. or *whatsoever* ye do, do all to the
11:16. But if *any man* seem to be contentious,
18. and I partly believe it. (lit. in *some* part)
34. And if *any man* hunger, let him
14:24. there come in *one* that believeth not,
27. If *any man* speak in an (unknown) tongue,
35. And if they will learn *any thing*,
38. But if *any man* be ignorant,
15: 6. but *some* are fallen asleep.
12. how say *some* among you that there is no
34. for *some* have not the knowledge of God:
35. But *some* (man) will say, How are the dead
37. chance of wheat, or of *some* other (grain):
16: 7. I trust to tarry *a* while (lit. *some* time) with you,
11. Let no man (lit. not *any*) therefore despise
22. If *any man* love not the Lord Jesus Christ,
2Co. 2: 5. But if *any* have caused grief,
10. To whom ye forgive *any thing*, I (forgive) also: for if I forgave *any thing*,
3: 1. or need we, as *some* (others), epistles of
5. to think *any thing* as of ourselves;
8:12. according to that a *man* hath,
20. that no man (lit. lest *any*) should blame
10: 2. against *some*, which think of us
7. If *any man* trust to himself that he
8. For though I should boast *somewhat*
12. with *some* that commend themselves:
11:16. Let no man (lit. not *any*) think me a fool;
— that I may boast myself a little. (lit. *some* little)

2Co.11:20. if a *man* bring you into bondage, if a *man* devour (you), if a *man* take (of you), if a *man* exalt himself, if a *man* smite you on the face.
21. whereinsoever *any* is bold,
12: 6. lest *any man* should think of me
— or (that) he heareth)(of me.
17. by *any* of them whom I sent unto you?
13: 5. except ye be)(reprobates?
8. can do nothing (lit. not *any* thing) against
Gal. 1: 7. but there be *some* that trouble you,
2: 6. who seemed to be *somewhat*,
12. before that *certain* came from James,
5: 6. neither circumcision availeth *any thing*,
6: 1. if a man be overtaken in a)(fault,
3. For if a *man* think himself to be *something*,
15. neither circumcision availeth *any thing*,
Eph. 2: 9. Not of works, lest *any man* should boast.
5:27. spot, or wrinkle, or *any* such thing;
6: 8. *what*soever good thing any man doeth,
Phi. 1:15. *Some* indeed preach Christ even of envy and strife; and *some* also of good will:
2: 1. If (there be) therefore *any* consolation in Christ, if *any* comfort of love, if *any* fellowship of the Spirit, if *any* bowels and mercies,
3:15. if in *any thing* ye be otherwise minded,
4: 8. *any* virtue, and if (there be) *any* praise,
Col. 2: 4. lest *any man* should beguile you
8. Beware lest *any man* spoil you
16. Let no man (lit. not *any*) therefore judge
23. not in *any* honour to the satisfying
3:13. if *any man* have a quarrel against *any*:
1Th. 1: 8. so that we need not to speak *any thing*.
2: 9. not be chargeable unto *any* of you,
5:15. See that none (lit. not *any*) render evil for evil unto *any*
2Th. 2: 3. Let no man (lit. not *any*) deceive you
3: 8. did we eat *any man's* bread for nought;
— not be chargeable to *any* of you:
11. For we hear that there are *some* which
14. And if *any man* obey not our word
1Ti. 1: 3. that thou mightest charge *some* that
6. From which *some* having swerved
8. if a *man* use it lawfully;
19. which *some* having put away
3: 1. If a *man* desire the office of a bishop,
5. if a *man* know not how to rule
4: 1. *some* shall depart from the faith,
5: 4. But if *any* widow have children
8. But if *any* provide not for his own,
15. For *some* are already turned aside
24. *Some* men's sins are open beforehand,
— and *some* (men) they follow after.
6: 7. we can carry nothing (lit. not *ought*) out.
10. which while *some* coveted after
21. Which *some* professing have erred
2Ti. 2: 5. if a *man* also strive for masteries,
18. and overthrow the faith of *some*.
21. If a *man* therefore purge himself from these,
Tit. 1:12. *One* of themselves, (even) a prophet of
Philem 18. hath wronged thee, or oweth (thee) *ought*,
Heb 2: 6. But *one* in a certain place testified,
7. Thou madest him *a* (lit. *some*) little lower than
9. who was made *a* (lit. &c.) little lower than
3: 4. every house is builded by *some* (*man*);
12. lest there be in *any* of you an evil heart
13. lest *any* of you be hardened
16. For *some*, when they had heard
4: 1. *any* of you should seem to come short

Heb. 4: 6. it remaineth that *some* must enter
7. Again, he limiteth a *certain* day,
11. lest *any man* fall after the same example
5: 4. no man (lit. not *any*) taketh this honour
8: 3. that this man have *somewhat* also
10:25. as the manner of *some* (is);
27. But a *certain* fearful looking for
28. He (lit. *any*) that despised Moses' law died
11:40. having provided *some* better thing for us,
12:15. lest *any man* fail of the grace of God; lest *any* root of bitterness
16. Lest there (be) *any* fornicator, or profane
13: 2. for thereby *some* have entertained angels
Jas. 1: 5. If *any* of you lack wisdom,
7. that he shall receive *any thing* of the Lord.
18. *a kind of* firstfruits of his creatures.
26. If *any man* among you seem to be religious,
2:14. though a *man* say he hath faith,
16. And *one* of you say unto them,
18. Yea, a *man* may say, Thou hast faith,
5:12. neither by *any* other oath:
13. Is *any* among you afflicted? let him pray. Is *any* merry? let
14. Is *any* sick among you? let him
19. if *any* of you do err from the truth, and *one* convert him;
Pet. 2:19. if a *man* for conscience toward
3: 1. that, if *any* obey not the word, they
4:11. If *any man* speak, (let him speak) as the
— if *any man* minister, (let him do it) as
15. But let none (lit. not *any*) of you suffer as a
Pet. 2:19. of whom a *man* is overcome,
3: 9. as *some* men count slackness;
— not willing that *any* should perish,
16. *some* things hard to be understood,
1Joh. 2: 1. And if *any man* sin, we have an advocate
15. If *any man* love the world, the love of
27. and ye need not that *any man* teach you:
4:20. If a *man* say, I love God, and hateth
5:14. if we ask *any thing* according to his will,
16. If *any man* see his brother sin a sin
2Joh. 10. If there come *any* unto you,
Jude 4. For there are *certain* men crept in
Rev. 3:20. if *any man* hear my voice,
11: 5. and if *any man* will hurt them, he
13: 9. If *any man* have an ear, let him hear.
10. He that (lit. if *any*) leadeth into captivity
— he that (lit. if *any*) killeth with the sword
17. that no man (lit. that not *any*) might buy or sell,
14: 9. If *any man* worship the beast
11. and *who*soever receiveth the mark of his
22:18. If *any man* shall add unto these things,
19. And if *any man* shall take away

see also εἴτις, μήτις, ὅστις.

5101 538 826/944 5100

τίς, *tis*.

Interrogative or definite.

Mat. 3: 7. *who* hath warned you to flee
5:13. *where*with shall it be salted?
46. *what* reward have ye? do not even
47. *what* do ye more (than others)?
6: 3. *what* thy right hand doeth:
25. *what* ye shall eat, or *what* ye shall drink;
— *what* ye shall put on.
27. *Which* of you by taking thought
28. *why* take ye thought for raiment?
Mat. 6:31. *What* shall we eat? or, *What* shall we drink? or, *Where*withal shall we be clothed?
7: 3. And *why* beholdest thou the mote
9. Or *what* man is there of you,
8:26. *Why* are ye fearful, O ye of little faith?
29. *What* have we to do with thee, Jesus,
9: 5. For *whether* is easier, to say,
13. go ye and learn *what* (that) meaneth,
10:11. enquire *who* in it is worthy; and
19. take no thought how or *what* ye shall speak.
— in that same hour *what* ye shall speak.
11: 7. *What* went ye out into the wilderness to
8. But *what* went ye out for to see?
9. But *what* went ye out for to see?
16. But *where*unto shall I liken this
12: 3. Have ye not read *what* David did,
7. But if ye had known *what* (this) meaneth,
11. *What* man shall there be among you,
27. by *whom* do your children cast
48. *Who* is my mother? and *who* are my brethren?
14:31. O thou of little faith, *where*fore didst thou doubt?
15:32. and have nothing (lit. not *what*) to eat:
16: 8. *why* reason ye among yourselves,
13. *Whom* do men say that I the Son of man
15. But *whom* say ye that I am?
26. For *what* is a man profited, if
— or *what* shall a man give in exchange
17:10. *Why* then say the scribes that Elias
25. saying, *What* thinkest thou, Simon? of *whom* do the kings of the earth
18: 1. *Who* is the greatest in the kingdom
12. *How* think ye? if a man have
19: 7. *Why* did Moses then command to give
16. *what* good thing shall I do, that
17. *Why* callest thou me good?
20. from my youth up: *what* lack I yet?
25. *Who* then can be saved?
27. *what* shall we have therefore?
20: 6. *Why* stand ye here all the day idle?
21. And he said unto her, *What* wilt thou?
22. Ye know not *what* ye ask.
32. *What* will ye that I shall do unto you?
21:10. the city was moved, saying, *Who* is this?
16. Hearest thou *what* these say?
23. and *who* gave thee this authority?
28. But *what* think ye? A (certain)
31. *Whether* of them twain did the will
40. *what* will he do unto those husbandmen?
22:17. Tell us therefore, *What* thinkest thou?
18. *Why* tempt ye me, (ye) hypocrites?
20. *Whose* (is) this image and superscription?
28. *whose* wife shall she be of the seven?
42. *What* think ye of Christ? *whose* son is he?
23:17. for *whether* is greater, the gold,
19. for *whether* (is) greater, the gift,
24: 3. and *what* (shall be) the sign of thy
45. *Who* then is a faithful and wise servant,
26: 8. To *what* purpose (is) this waste?
10. *Why* trouble ye the woman?
15. *What* will ye give me, and I will deliver
62. *what* (is it which) these witness against thee?
65. *what* further need have we of witnesses?
66. *What* think ye? They answered and said,
68. *Who* is he that smote thee?
70. I know not *what* thou sayest.
27: 4. *What* (is that) to us? see thou (to that).
17. *Whom* will ye that I release unto you?
21. *Whether* of the twain will ye that I release
22. *What* shall I do then with Jesus

Mat.27:23. Why, *what* evil hath he done?
Mar 1:24. *what* have we to do with thee,
— I know thee *who* thou art, the Holy
27. *What* thing is this? *what* new doctrine (is) this?
2: 7. *Why* doth this (man) thus speak blasphemies? *who* can forgive sins but
8. *Why* reason ye these things in
9. *Whether* is it easier to say
16. *How* is it that he eateth and drinketh
24. *why* do they on the sabbath day that
25. Have ye never read *what* David did,
3:33. *Who* is my mother, or my brethren?
4:24. Take heed *what* ye hear:
30. *Where*unto (lit. to *what*) shall we liken the
40. *Why* are ye so fearful? how is it that ye
41. *What* manner of man is this, that even
5: 7. *What* have I to do with thee, Jesus,
9. And he asked him, *What* (is) thy name?
14. they went out to see *what* it was that
30. and said, *Who* touched my clothes?
31. and sayest thou, *Who* touched me?
35. *why* troublest thou the Master any
39. *Why* make ye this ado, and weep?
6: 2. and *what* wisdom (is) this which is given
24. *What* shall I ask? And she said,
36. for they have nothing (lit. have not *what*) to eat.
8: 1. having nothing (lit. not having *what*) to eat,
12. *Why* doth this generation seek after
17. *Why* reason ye, because ye have no bread?
27. *Whom* do men say that I am?
29. But *whom* say ye that I am?
36. For *what* shall it profit a man,
37. Or *what* shall a man give in exchange
9: 6. For he wist not *what* to say;
10. *what* the rising from the dead should
16. *What* question ye with them?
33. *What* was it that ye disputed
34. *who* (should be) the greatest.
50. *where*with will ye season it?
10: 3. *What* did Moses command you?
17. *what* shall I do that I may inherit
18. *Why* callest thou me good?
26. *Who* then can be saved?
36. *What* would ye that I should do
38. Ye know not *what* ye ask:
51. *What* wilt thou that I should do
11: 3. *Why* do ye this? say ye that
5. *What* do ye, loosing the colt?
28. and *who* gave thee this authority
12: 9. *What* shall therefore the lord of the
15. *Why* tempt ye me? bring me a penny,
16. *Whose* (is) this image and superscription?
23. *whose* wife shall she be of them?
13: 4. and *what* (shall be) the sign when
11. beforehand *what* ye shall speak,
14: 4. *Why* was this waste of the ointment
6. Let her alone; *why* trouble ye her?
36. not *what* I will, but *what* thou wilt.
40. neither wist they *what* to answer him.
60. *what* (is it which) these witness against
63. *What* need we any further witnesses?
64. Ye have heard the blasphemy: *what* think ye?
68. neither understand I *what* thou sayest.
15:12. *What* will ye then that I shall do
14. Why, *what* evil hath he done?
24. *what* every man should take.
34. *why* hast thou forsaken me?
16: 3. *Who* shall roll us away the stone

Lu. 1:18. *Where*by shall I know this?
62. *how* he would have him called.
66. *What* manner of child shall this be!
2:48. *why* hast thou thus dealt with us?
49. *How* is it that ye sought me?
3: 7. *who* hath warned you to flee
10. saying, *What* shall we do then?
12. Master, *what* shall we do?
14. And *what* shall we do?
4:34. *what* have we to do with thee,
— I know thee *who* thou art; the Holy
36. saying, *What* a word (is) this!
5:21. *Who* is this which speaketh blasphemies? *Who* can forgive sins, but
22. *What* reason ye in your hearts?
23. *Whether* is easier, to say, Thy
6: 2. *Why* do ye that which is not lawful
9. ask you one thing; Is it lawful on (lit. I will ask you: *Whether* is it lawful on, &c.)
11. *what* they might do to Jesus.
41. And *why* beholdest thou the mote
46. And *why* call ye me, Lord,
47. I will shew you to *whom* he is like:
7:24. *What* went ye out into the wilderness
25. But *what* went ye out for to see?
26. But *what* went ye out for to see?
31. *Where*unto then shall I liken the men
— and to *what* are they like?
39. *who* and what manner of woman (this is)
42. *which* of them will love him most?
49. *Who* is this that forgiveth sins also?
8: 9. *What* might this parable be?
25. *What* manner of man is this!
28. *What* have I to do with thee, Jesus,
30. asked him, saying, *What* is thy name?
45. And Jesus said, *Who* touched me?
— and sayest thou, *Who* touched me?
9: 9. but *who* is this, of whom I hear such
18. *Whom* say the people that I am?
20. But *whom* say ye that I am?
25. For *what* is a man advantaged,
46. *which* of them should be greatest.
10:22. no man knoweth *who* the Son is, but the Father; and *who* the Father is, but the Son, and (he) to
25. *what* shall I do to inherit eternal
26. *What* is written in the law?
29. And *who* is my neighbour?
36. *Which* now of these three, thinkest thou,
11: 5. *Which* of you shall have a friend,
11. If a son shall ask bread of any of you that is a father, (lit. *Which* of you, a father, if his son ask bread, will)
19. by *whom* do your sons cast (them) out?
12: 5. I will forewarn you *whom* ye shall fear:
11. how or *what thing* ye shall answer, or *what* ye shall say:
14. Man, *who* made me a judge or
17. *What* shall I do, because I have no room
20. then *whose* shall those things be,
22. thought for your life, *what* ye shall eat; neither for the body, *what* ye shall put
25. *which* of you with taking thought
26. *why* take ye thought for the rest?
29. *what* ye shall eat, or *what* ye shall drink,
42. *Who* then is that faithful and wise
49. *what* will I, if it be already kindled?
57. Yea, and *why* even of yourselves
13:18. Unto *what* is the kingdom of God like? and *where*unto shall I resemble it?

Lu 13:20. *Whereunto* shall I liken the kingdom
14: 5. *Which* of you shall have an ass
28. For *which* of you, intending to build
31. Or *what* king, going to make war
34. *where*with shall it be seasoned?
15: 4. *What* man of you, having an hundred
8. Either *what* woman having ten pieces
26. and asked *what* these things meant.
16: 2. *How* is it that I hear this of thee?
3. *What* shall I do? for my lord
4. I am resolved *what* to do, that,
11. *who* will commit to your trust the true
12. *who* shall give you that which is your
17: 7. But *which* of you, having a servant
8. Make ready *where*with I may sup,
18: 6. Hear *what* the unjust judge saith.
18. *what* shall I do to inherit eternal life?
19. *Why* callest thou me good? none
26. *Who* then can be saved?
36. he asked *what* it meant.
41. *What* wilt thou that I shall do unto thee?
19: 3. he sought to see Jesus *who* he was;
15. that he might know *how much every* man had gained by trading.
33. *Why* loose ye the colt?
48. And could not find *what* they might do:
20: 2. or *who* is he that gave thee this
13. *What* shall I do? I will send my beloved son:
15. *What* therefore shall the lord of the
17. *What* is this then that is written,
23. said unto them, *Why* tempt ye me?
24. *Whose* image and superscription
33. *whose* wife of them is she?
21: 7. and *what* sign (will there be) when
22:23. *which* of them it was that should
24. *which* of them should be accounted
27. For *whether* (is) greater, he that sitteth
46. *Why* sleep ye? rise and pray,
64. Prophesy, *who* is it that smote thee?
71. *What* need we any further witness?
23:22. Why, *what* evil hath he done?
31. *what* shall be done in the dry?
34. for they know not *what* they do.
24: 5. *Why* seek ye the living among the dead?
17. *What manner of* communications
38. *Why* are ye troubled?
Joh. 1:19. to ask him, *Who* art thou?
21. *What* then? Art thou Elias?
22. Then said they unto him, *Who* art thou?
— *What* sayest thou of thyself?
25. *Why* baptizest thou then, if thou be not
38(39). and saith unto them, *What* seek ye?
2: 4. Woman, *what* have I to do with thee?
18. *What* sign shewest thou unto us,
25. for he knew *what* was in man.
4:10. and *who* it is that saith to thee,
27. *What* seekest thou? or, *Why* talkest thou with her?
5:12. *What* man is that which said unto thee,
13. wist not *who* it was: for Jesus had
6: 6. he himself knew *what* he would do.
9. but *what* are they among so many?
28. *What* shall we do, that we might work
30. *What* sign shewest thou then,
— *what* dost thou work?
60. an hard saying; *who* can hear it?
64. *who* they were that believed not, and *who* should betray him.
68. Lord, to *whom* shall we go?
7:19. *Why* go ye about to kill me?
20. *who* goeth about to kill thee?

Joh. 7:36. *What* (manner of) saying is this that he
51. and know *what* he doeth?
8: 5. but *what* sayest thou?
25. Then said they unto him, *Who* art thou?
46. *Which* of you convinceth me of sin?
53. *whom* makest thou thyself?
9: 2. *who* did sin, this man, or his parents,
17. *What* sayest thou of him, that he hath
21. or *who* hath opened his eyes, we know not:
26. to him again, *What* did he to thee?
27. *wherefore* would ye hear (it) again?
36. *Who* is he, Lord, that I might believe on him?
10: 6. they understood not *what* things they were
20. and is mad; *why* hear ye him?
11:47. *What* do we? for this man doeth
56. *What* think ye, that he will not come
12:27. and *what* shall I say? Father, save
34. *who* is this Son of man?
38. Lord *who* hath believed our report? and to *whom* hath the arm of the Lord
49. *what* I should say, and *what* I should speak.
13:12. Know ye *what* I have done to you?
22. doubting of *whom* he spake.
24. *who* it should be of whom he spake.
25. saith unto him, Lord, *who* is it?
28. no man at the table knew for *what* intent
14:22. Lord, *how* is it that thou wilt manifest
15:15. knoweth not *what* his lord doeth:
16:17. *What* is this that he saith unto us,
18. *What* is this that he saith, A little while? we cannot tell *what* he saith.
18: 4. and said unto them, *Whom* seek ye?
7. Then asked he them again, *Whom* seek
21. *Why* askest thou me? ask them
— *what* I have said unto them:
23. but if well, *why* smitest thou me?
29. *What* accusation bring ye against
35. *what* hast thou done?
38. Pilate saith unto him, *What* is truth?
19:24. but cast lots for it, *whose* it shall be:
20:13. Woman, *why* weepest thou?
15. *why* weepest thou? *whom* seekest thou?
21:12. durst ask him, *Who* art thou?
20. Lord, *which* is he that betrayeth thee?
21. Lord, and *what* (shall) this man (do)?
22. *what* (is that) to thee?
23. *what* (is that) to thee?
Acts 1:11. *why* stand ye gazing up into heaven?
2:12. saying one to another, *What* meaneth this?
37. Men (and) brethren, *what* shall we do?
3:12. *why* marvel ye at this? or *why* look ye so earnestly on us,
4: 9. by *what* means he is made whole;
16. *What* shall we do to these men?
5: 4. *why* hast thou conceived this thing
9. *How* is it that ye have agreed
24. *whereunto* this would grow. (lit. *what* this might be)
35. *what* ye intend to do as touching
7:27. *Who* made thee a ruler and a judge over
35. *Who* made thee a ruler and a judge?
40. we wot not *what* is become of him.
49. or, *what* (is) the place of my rest?
52. *Which* of the prophets have not your
8:33. and *who* shall declare his generation?
34. of *whom* speaketh the prophet this?
36. *what* doth hinder me to be baptized?
9: 4. Saul, Saul, *why* persecutest thou me?
5. And he said, *Who* art thou, Lord?

Acts 9: 6. Lord, *what* wilt thou have me to do?
— it shall be told thee *what* thou must do.
10: 4. and said, *What* is it, Lord?
6. tell thee *what* thou oughtest to do.
17. *what* this vision which he had seen
21. *what* (is) the cause wherefore ye are come?
29. for *what* intent ye have sent for me?
11:17. *what* was I, that I could withstand God?
12:18. *what* was become of Peter.
13:25. *Whom* think ye that I am?
14:15. Sirs, *why* do ye these things?
15:10. Now therefore *why* tempt ye God,
16:30. Sirs, *what* must I do to be saved?
17:18. *What* will this babbler say?
19. May we know *what* this new doctrine,
20. *what* these things mean.
19: 3. Unto *what* then were ye baptized?
15. and Paul I know; but *who* are ye?
32. knew not *where*fore they were come
35. *what* man is there that knoweth not
21:13. *What* mean ye to weep and to break
22. *What* is it therefore? the multitude
33. and demanded *who* he was, and *what* he had done.
22. 7. Saul, Saul, *why* persecutest thou me?
8. And I answered, *Who* art thou, Lord?
10. And I said, *What* shall I do, Lord?
16. And now *why* tarriest thou?
26. Take heed *what* thou doest:
30. *wherefore* he was accused of the Jews,
23:19. *What* is that thou hast to tell me?
26: 8. *Why* should it be thought a thing
14. Saul, Saul, *why* persecutest thou me?
15. And I said, *Who* art thou, Lord?
Ro. 3: 1. *What* advantage then hath the Jew? or *what* profit (is there) of
3. For *what* if some did not believe?
5. *what* shall we say? (Is) God unrighteous
7. *why* yet am I also judged as a sinner?
9. *What* then? are we better (than they)?
4: 1. *What* shall we then say that Abraham,
3. For *what* saith the scripture?
6: 1. *What* shall we say then? Shall we
15. *What* then? shall we sin, because
21. *What* fruit had ye then in those
7: 7. *What* shall we say then? (Is) the law
24. *who* shall deliver me from the body
8:24. for what a man seeth, *why* doth he
26. for we know not *what* we should pray for
27. *what* (is) the mind of the Spirit,
31. *What* shall we then say to these things?
— *who* (can be) against us?
33. *Who* shall lay any thing to the charge of
34. *Who* (is) he that condemneth?
35. *Who* shall separate us from the love of
9:14. *What* shall we say then? (Is there)
19. *Why* doth he yet find fault? For *who* hath resisted his will?
20. *who* art thou that repliest against
— *Why* hast thou made me thus?
30. *What* shall we say then?
10: 6. *Who* shall ascend into heaven?
7. Or, *Who* shall descend into the deep?
8. But *what* saith it? The word is nigh thee,
16. *who* hath believed our report?
11: 2. *what* the scripture saith of Elias?
4. But *what* saith the answer of God
7. *What* then? Israel hath not obtained
15. *what* (shall) the receiving (of them be),
34. For *who* hath known the mind of the Lord? or *who* hath been his counsellor?
35. Or *who* hath first given to him,

Ro. 12: 2. that ye may prove *what* (is) that good,
14: 4. *Who* art thou that judgest another man's
10. *why* dost thou judge thy brother? or *why* dost thou set at nought thy
1Co. 2:11. For *what* man knoweth the things of a man,
16. For *who* hath known the mind of the Lord,
3: 5. *Who* then is Paul, and *who* (is) Apollos,
4: 7. For *who* maketh thee to differ
— and *what* hast thou that thou
— *why* dost thou glory, as if thou hadst
21. *What* will ye? shall I come unto you
5:12. For *what* have I to do to judge them
7:16. For *what* knowest thou, O wife,
— or *how* knowest thou, O man,
9: 7. *Who* goeth a warfare any time at
— *who* planteth a vineyard, and
— or *who* feedeth a flock, and eateth not
18. *What* is my reward then?
10:19. *What* say I then? that the idol
29. for *why* is my liberty judged
30. *why* am I evil spoken of for that
11:22. *What* shall I say to you?
14: 6. *what* shall I profit you, except
8. *who* shall prepare himself to the battle?
15. *What* is it then? I will pray with the
16. he understandeth not *what* thou sayest?
26. *How* is it then, brethren?
15: 2. saved, if ye keep in memory what I preached (lit. saved, with *what* word I preached, if ye, &c.)
29. Else *what* shall they do which are
— *why* are they then baptized for the dead?
30. And *why* stand we in jeopardy every
32. *what* advantageth it me, if the dead
2Co. 2: 2. *who* is he then that maketh me glad,
16. And *who* (is) sufficient for these things?
6:14. for *what* fellowship hath righteousness
— and *what* communion hath light
15. *what* concord hath Christ with Belial? or *what* part hath he that believeth
16. *what* agreement hath the temple of God
11:29. *Who* is weak, and I am not weak? *who* is offended, and I burn not?
12:13. For *what* is it wherein you were inferior
Gal. 2:14. *why* compellest thou the Gentiles to live
3: 1. *who* hath bewitched you, that ye
19. *Where*fore then (serveth) the law?
4:15. *Where* is then the blessedness ye spake of? (lit. *what* then was your blessedness? —some copies read ποῦ)
30. Nevertheless *what* saith the scripture?
5: 7. *who* did hinder you that ye should not
11. *why* do I yet suffer persecution?
Eph. 1:18. *what* is the hope of his calling, and *what* the riches of the glory of
19. And *what* (is) the exceeding greatness of
3: 9. *what* (is) the fellowship of the mystery,
18. *what* (is) the breadth, and length, and
4: 9. *what* is it but that he also descended
5:10. Proving *what* is acceptable unto the Lord.
17. *what* the will of the Lord (is).
6:21. may know my affairs, (and) *how* I do,
Phi. 1:18. *What* then? notwithstanding, every way,
22. yet *what* I shall choose I wot not.
Col. 1:27. *what* (is) the riches of the glory of
2:20. *why*, as though living in the world,
1Th. 2:19. For *what* (is) our hope, or joy, or
3: 9. For *what* thanks can we render to God
4: 2. For ye know *what* commandments
1Ti. 1: 7. nor *where*of they affirm.
2Ti. 3:14. knowing of *whom* thou hast learned (them);
Heb. 1: 5. For unto *which* of the angels said he at

3 B 2

Heb. 1:13. But to *which* of the angels said he at
2: 6. *What* is man, that thou art mindful
3:17. But with *whom* was he grieved
18. And to *whom* sware he that they
5:12. *which* (be) the first principles of
7:11. *what* further need (was there) that
11:32. And *what* shall I more say? for the
12: 7. for *what* son is he whom the father
13: 6. fear *what* man shall do unto me.
Jas. 2:14. *What* (doth it) profit, my brethren,
16. *what* (doth it) profit?
3:13. *Who* (is) a wise man and endued
4:12. *who* art thou that judgest another?
1Pet. 1:11. Searching *what*, or what manner of time
3:13. And *who* (is) he that will harm you,
4:17. *what* shall the end (be) of them that
5: 8. seeking *whom* he may devour:
1Joh. 2:22. *Who* is a liar but he that denieth
3: 2. not yet appear *what* we shall be:
12. And *where*fore slew he him?
5: 5. *Who* is he that overcometh the world,
Rev. 2: 7. *what* the Spirit saith unto the churches;
11. *what* the Spirit saith unto the churches;
17. *what* the Spirit saith unto the churches;
29. *what* the Spirit saith unto the churches.
3: 6. *what* the Spirit saith unto the churches.
13. *what* the Spirit saith unto the churches.
22. *what* the Spirit saith unto the churches.
5: 2. *Who* is worthy to open the book,
6:17. and *who* shall be able to stand?
7:13. *What* are these which are arrayed in white
13: 4. *Who* (is) like unto the beast? *who* is able to make war with him?
15: 4. *Who* shall not fear thee, O Lord,
18:18. *What* (city is) like unto this great city

See also *διατί*.

5102 2 828/954

τίτλος, titlos.

Joh. 19:19. And Pilate wrote a *title*, and put
20. This *title* then read many of the Jews:

5099 1 826/944

τίω, tio.

2Th. 1: 9. Who shall be punished with (lit. *shall suffer* (as) punishment) everlasting destruction from

5104 1 828/628 3588

τοι, toi.

2Ti. 2:19. Nevertheless (lit. *but* indeed) the foundation

5105 2 828/954 5104,1063,3767

τοιγαροῦν, toigaroun.

1Th. 4: 8. He *therefore* that despiseth,
Heb 12: 1. *Wherefore* seeing we also are compassed

5106 4 828/954 5104,3568

τοίνυν, toinun.

Lu. 20:25. Render *therefore* unto Cæsar the
1Co. 9:26. I *therefore* so run, not as uncertainly;
Heb 13:13. Let us go forth *therefore* unto him without the camp,
Jas. 2:24. Ye see *then* how that by works a man

5107 1 828/954 5104,1161

τοιόσδε, toiosde.

2Pet 1:17. when there came *such* a voice to him

5108 61 828/954 5104,3778

τοιοῦτος, toioutos.

Mat. 9: 8. which had given *such* power unto men.
18: 5. shall receive one *such* little child
19:14. for of *such* is the kingdom of heaven.
Mar 4:33. And with many *such* parables
6: 2. that even *such* mighty works are
7: 8. and many other *such* like things ye do.
13. and many *such* like things do ye.
9:37. one of *such* children in my name,
10:14. for of *such* is the kingdom of God.
13:19. *such* as was not from the beginning
Lu. 9: 9. of whom I hear *such* things?
13: 2. because they suffered *such* things?
18:16. for of *such* is the kingdom of God.
Joh. 4:23. the Father seeketh *such* to worship him.
8: 5. that *such* should be stoned:
9:16. a man that is a sinner do *such* miracles?
Acts 16:24. Who, having received *such* a charge,
19:25. the workmen of *like* occupation,
21:25. that they observe no *such* thing,
22:22. Away with *such* a (fellow) from
26:29. and altogether *such* as I am,
Ro. 1:32. they which commit *such* things
2: 2. against them which commit *such* things.
3. them which do *such* things,
16:18. For they that are *such* serve not
1Co. 5: 1. and *such* fornication as is not
5. To deliver *such* an *one* unto Satan
11. with *such* an *one* no not to eat.
7:15. is not under bondage in *such* (cases):
28. *such* shall have trouble in the flesh:
11:16. we have no *such* custom,
15:48. *such* (are) they also that are earthy:
— *such* (are) they also that are heavenly.
16:16. submit yourselves unto *such*,
18. acknowledge ye them that are *such*.
2Co. 2: 6. Sufficient to *such* a man (is) this
7. *such* a *one* should be swallowed up
3: 4. And *such* trust have we through
12. Seeing then that we have *such* hope,
10:11. Let *such* an *one* think this,
— *such* (will we be) also in deed when
11:13. For *such* (are) false apostles,
12: 2. *such* an *one* caught up to the third
3. And I knew *such* a man, whether
5. Of *such* an *one* will I glory:
Gal. 5:21. that they which do *such* things shall
23. against *such* there is no law.
6: 1. restore *such* an *one* in the spirit of
Eph 5:27. or wrinkle, or any *such* thing;
Phi. 2:29. and hold *such* in reputation:
2Th. 3:12. Now them that are *such* we command
1Ti. 6: 5. from *such* withdraw thyself.
Tit. 3:11. he that is *such* is subverted,
Philem. 9. being *such* an *one* as Paul the aged,
Heb 7:26. For *such* an high priest became us, (who)
8: 1. We have *such* an high priest, who is set
11:14. For they that say *such* things declare
12: 3. him that endured *such* contradiction
13:16. with *such* sacrifices God is well pleased.
Jas. 4:16. all *such* rejoicing is evil.
3Joh. 8. We therefore ought to receive *such*,

5109 1 829/955 eq 5038

τοῖχος, toikos.

Acts 23: 3. shall smite thee, (thou) whited *wall:*

5110 2 829/955 rt 5088

τόκος, tokos.

Mat. 25:27. received mine own with *usury*.
Lu. 19:23. required mine own with *usury*?

5111 16 829/955 8:181 *tolma* (boldness)
τολμάω, tolmao.

Mat.22:46. neither *durst* any (man) from
Mar 12:34. no man after that *durst* ask him
15:43. and went in *boldly* unto Pilate,
Lu. 20:40. they *durst* not ask him any
Joh.21:12. none of the disciples *durst* ask him,
Acts 5:13. And of the rest *durst* no man join
7:32. Moses trembled, and *durst* not behold.
Ro. 5: 7. some would even *dare* to die.
15:18. For I *will* not *dare* to speak of
1Co. 6: 1. *Dare* any of you, having a matter
2Co.10: 2. wherewith I think *to be bold* against
12. For we *dare* not make ourselves
11:21. whereinsoever any *is bold*,
— I *am bold* also.
Phi. 1:14. *are* much more *bold* to speak
Jude 9. *durst* not bring against him

5112 1 829/955 8:181 rt 5111
τολμηρότερον, tolmeeroteron.

Ro. 15:15. I have written *the more boldly* unto

5113 1 829/955 8:181 5111
τολμητής, tolmeetees.

2Pet.2:10. *Presumptuous* (are they), selfwilled,

5114 1 829/955 cf 2875 *temnō* (to cut)
τομώτερος, tomōteros.

Heb 4:12. and *sharper* than any twoedged sword,

5115 1 829/955 rt 5088
τόξον, toxon.

Rev. 6: 2. he that sat on him had a *bow*;

5116 1 829/955
τοπάζιον, topazion.

Rev.21:20. the ninth, a *topaz*;

5117 92 830/955 8:187 cf 5561
τόπος, topos.

Mat.12:43. he walketh through dry *places*,
14:13. by ship into a desert *place* apart:
15. saying, This is a desert *place*,
35. And when the men of that *place*
24: 7. and earthquakes, in divers *places*.
15. stand in the holy *place*,
26:52. again thy sword into his *place*:
27:33. unto a *place* called Golgotha, that is to say, a *place* of a skull,
28: 6. see the *place* where the Lord lay.
Mar 1:35. departed into a solitary *place*,
45. but was without in desert *places*:
6:31. apart into a desert *place*, and
32. they departed into a desert *place* by
35. This is a desert *place*, and now
13: 8. earthquakes in divers *places*,
15:22. unto the *place* Golgotha, which is, being interpreted, The *place* of a skull.
16: 6. behold the *place* where they laid him.
Lu. 2: 7. no *room* for them in the inn.
4:17. found the *place* where it was written,
37. went out into every *place* of the
42. and went into a desert *place*:
6:17. and stood in the plain, (lit. plain *place*)
9:10. privately into a desert *place*
12. we are here in a desert *place*.
10: 1. before his face into every city and *place*,
Lu. 10:32. a Levite, when he was at the *place*,
11: 1. as he was praying in a certain *place*,
24. he walketh through dry *places*,
14: 9. Give this man *place*; and thou begin with shame to take the lowest *room*. (lit. *place*)
10. sit down in the lowest *room*;
22. and yet there is *room*.
16:28. come into this *place* of torment.
19: 5. And when Jesus came to the *place*,
21:11. earthquakes shall be in divers *places*,
22:40. And when he was at the *place*,
23:33. And when they were come to the *place*,
Joh. 4:20. that in Jerusalem is the *place* where
5:13. a multitude being in (that) *place*.
6:10. there was much grass in the *place*.
23. nigh unto the *place* where they did eat
10:40. into the *place* where John at first
11: 6. in the same *place* where he was.
30. was in that *place* where Martha met him.
48. take away both our *place* and nation.
14: 2. I go to prepare a *place* for you.
3. And if I go and prepare a *place* for you,
18: 2. which betrayed him, knew the *place*:
19:13. in a *place* that is called the Pavement
17. forth into a *place* called (the place) of
20. for the *place* where Jesus was crucified
41. Now in the *place* where he was crucified
20: 7. but wrapped together in a *place* by itself.
Acts 1:25. that he might go to his own *place*.
4:31. the *place* was shaken where they were
6:13. against this holy *place*, and the law:
14. Jesus of Nazareth shall destroy this *place*,
7: 7. and serve me in this *place*.
33. for the *place* where thou standest
49. or what (is) the *place* of my rest?
12:17. and went into another *place*.
16: 3. of the Jews which were in those *quarters*:
21:28. against the people, and the law, and this *place*:
— and hath polluted this holy *place*.
25:16. and have *licence* to answer for
27: 2. to sail by the *coasts* of Asia; (lit. the *places* along Asia)
8. came unto a *place* which is called
29. we should have fallen upon rocks, (lit. rough *places*)
41. And falling into a *place* where two
28: 7. In the same *quarters* were possessions (lit. in the (parts) about that *place*)
Ro. 9:26. in the *place* where it was said
12:19. (rather) give *place* unto wrath:
15:23. having no more *place* in these parts,
1Co. 1: 2. with all that in every *place*
14:16. that occupieth the *room* of the unlearned
2Co. 2:14. of his knowledge by us in every *place*.
Eph. 4:27. Neither give *place* to the devil.
1Th. 1: 8. but also in every *place* your faith
1Ti. 2: 8. that men pray every *where*,
Heb. 8: 7. then should no *place* have been sought for the second.
11: 8. when he was called to go out into a *place*
12:17. for he found no *place* of repentance,
2Pet. 1:19. that shineth in a dark *place*,
Rev. 2: 5. remove thy candlestick out of his *place*,
6:14. island were moved out of their *places*.
12: 6. where she hath a *place* prepared of
8. neither was their *place* found any more
14. into her *place*, where she is nourished for
16:16. together into a *place* called in the Hebrew tongue Armageddon.
20:11. and there was found no *place* for them.

5118 21 831/956 3778
τοσοῦτος, tosoutos. *tosoutos*
tosos (so much)

Mat. 8:10. I have not found *so great* faith, no, not in
15:33. *so much* bread in the wilderness, as to fill *so great* a multitude?
Lu. 7: 9. I have not found *so great* faith, no, not
15:29. Lo, *these many* years do I serve thee, neither
Joh. 6: 9. but what are they among *so many?*
12:37. had done *so many* miracles before them,
14: 9. Have I been *so long* time with you, and
21:11. and for all there were *so many*,
Acts 5: 8. whether ye sold the land for *so much*? And she said, Yea, for *so much*.
1Co.14:10. *so many* kinds of voices in the world,
Gal. 3: 4. Have ye suffered *so many* things in vain?
Heb. 1: 4. made *so much* better than the angels,
4: 7. To day, after *so long* a time; as it is said,
7:22. By *so much* was Jesus made a surety of a better
10:25. and *so much* the more, as ye see the day
12: 1. with *so great* a cloud of witnesses,
Rev.18: 7. *so much* torment and sorrow give her:
17. *so great* riches is come to nought.
21:16. the length is *as large* as the breadth:

5119 159 831/957 3588,3753
τότε, tote.

Mat. 2: 7. *Then* Herod, when he had privily
16. *Then* Herod, when he saw that
17. *Then* was fulfilled that which was
3: 5. *Then* went out to him Jerusalem,
13. *Then* cometh Jesus from Galilee
15. *Then* he suffered him.
4: 1. *Then* was Jesus led up of the spirit
5. *Then* the devil taketh him up
10. *Then* saith Jesus unto him, Get
11. *Then* the devil leaveth him, and,
17. From *that time* Jesus began to preach,
5:24. and *then* come and offer thy gift.
7: 5. and *then* shalt thou see clearly
23. And *then* will I profess unto them,
8:26. *Then* he arose, and rebuked the winds
9: 6. *then* saith he to the sick of the palsy,
14. *Then* came to him the disciples of John,
15. and *then* shall they fast.
29. *Then* touched he their eyes, saying,
37. *Then* saith he unto his disciples,
11:20. *Then* began he to upbraid the
12:13. *Then* saith he to the man, Stretch forth
22. *Then* was brought unto him one
29. and *then* he will spoil his house.
38. *Then* certain of the scribes and of
44. *Then* he saith, I will return into my house
45. *Then* goeth he, and taketh with himself
13:26. *then* appeared the tares also.
36. *Then* Jesus sent the multitude away,
43. *Then* shall the righteous shine forth as
15: 1. *Then* came to Jesus scribes and
12. *Then* came his disciples, and said
28. *Then* Jesus answered and said unto
16:12. *Then* understood they how that he bade
20. *Then* charged he his disciples that
21. From *that time* forth began Jesus to
24. *Then* said Jesus unto his disciples,
27. and *then* he shall reward every man
17:13. *Then* the disciples understood that
19. *Then* came the disciples to Jesus
18:21. *Then* came Peter to him, and said,
32. *Then* his lord, after that he had called
19:13. *Then* were there brought unto him
27. *Then* answered Peter and said unto him,
Mat.20:20. *Then* came to him the mother of Zebedee's
21: 1. *then* sent Jesus two disciples,
22: 8. *Then* saith he to his servants,
13. *Then* said the king to the servants,
15. *Then* went the Pharisees, and took counsel
21. *Then* saith he unto them,
23: 1. *Then* spake Jesus to the multitude,
24: 9. *Then* shall they deliver you up
10. And *then* shall many be offended,
14. and *then* shall the end come.
16. *Then* let them which be in Judæa
21. For *then* shall be great tribulation,
23. *Then* if any man shall say unto you,
30. And *then* shall appear the sign
— and *then* shall all the tribes of the
40. *Then* shall two be in the field;
25: 1. *Then* shall the kingdom of heaven
7. *Then* all those virgins arose, and
31. *then* shall he sit upon the throne
34. *Then* shall the King say unto them
37. *Then* shall the righteous answer
41. *Then* shall he say also unto them
44. *Then* shall they also answer him,
45. *Then* shall he answer them, saying,
26: 3. *Then* assembled together the chief
14. *Then* one of the twelve, called
16. And from *that time* he sought
31. *Then* saith Jesus unto them, All ye
36. *Then* cometh Jesus with them unto
38. *Then* saith he unto them, My soul
45. *Then* cometh he to his disciples,
50. *Then* came they, and laid hands
52. *Then* said Jesus unto him, Put up
56. *Then* all the disciples forsook him,
65. *Then* the high priest rent his clothes,
67. *Then* did they spit in his face,
74. *Then* began he to curse and to swear,
27: 3. *Then* Judas, which had betrayed him,
9. *Then* was fulfilled that which was
13. *Then* said Pilate unto him, Hearest
16. And they had *then* a notable prisoner,
26. *Then* released he Barabbas unto them:
27. *Then* the soldiers of the governor
38. *Then* were there two thieves crucified
58. *Then* Pilate commanded the body to be
28:10. *Then* said Jesus unto them, Be not
Mar 2:20. and *then* shall they fast in those days.
3:27. and *then* he will spoil his house.
13:14. *then* let them that be in Judæa flee
21. And *then* if any man shall say to you,
26. And *then* shall they see the Son of man
27. And *then* shall he send his angels,
Lu. 5:35. *then* shall they fast in those days.
6:42. and *then* shalt thou see clearly to
11:26. *Then* goeth he, and taketh (to him) seven
13:26. *Then* shall ye begin to say, We have eaten
14: 9. and)(thou begin with shame to take
10. *then* shalt thou have worship in the
21. *Then* the master of the house being angry
16:16. since *that time* the kingdom of God is
21:10. *Then* said he unto them, Nation
20. *then* know that the desolation thereof
21. *Then* let them which are in Judæa
27. And *then* shall they see the Son of man
23:30. *Then* shall they begin to say to the
24:45. *Then* opened he their understanding,
Joh. 2:10. *then* that which is worse: (but) thou
7:10. *then* went he also up unto the feast,
8:28. *then* shall ye know that I am (he),
11: 6.)(he abode two days still in the same
14. *Then* said Jesus unto them plainly,
12:16. *then* remembered they that these

Joh. 13:27. And after the sop)(Satan entered into
9: 1. *Then* Pilate therefore took Jesus,
16. *Then* delivered he him therefore
20: 8. *Then* went in also that other disciple,
Acts 1:12. *Then* returned they unto Jerusalem
4: 8. *Then* Peter, filled with the Holy Ghost,
5:26. *Then* went the captain with the
6:11. *Then* they suborned men, which said,
7: 4. *Then* came he out of the land of
8:17. *Then* laid they (their) hands on them,
10:46. *Then* answered Peter,
48. *Then* prayed they him to tarry
13: 3. And when they had fasted (lit. *then* having fasted)
12. *Then* the deputy, when he saw
15:22. *Then* pleased it the apostles and
17:14. And *then* immediately the brethren
21:26. *Then* Paul took the men, and the next
33. *Then* the chief captain came near,
23: 3. *Then* said Paul unto him, God shall
25:12. *Then* Festus, when he had conferred
26: 1. *Then* Paul stretched forth the hand, and
27:21.)(Paul stood forth in the midst of them,
32. *Then* the soldiers cut off the ropes
28: 1. *then* they knew that the island was
Ro. 6:21. What fruit had ye *then* in those things
1Co. 4: 5. and *then* shall every man have praise
13:10. *then* that which is in part shall
12. but *then* face to face:
— but *then* shall I know even as
15:28. *then* shall the Son also himself
54. *then* shall be brought to pass the
16: 2. that there be no gatherings)(when I come.
2Co.12:10. when I am weak, *then* am I strong.
Gal. 4: 8. Howbeit *then*, when ye knew not God,
29. But as *then* he that was born after the
6: 4. *then* shall he have rejoicing in himself
Col. 3: 4. *then* shall ye also appear with him in glory.
1Th. 5: 3. *then* sudden destruction cometh
2Th. 2: 8. And *then* shall that Wicked be revealed,
Heb 10: 7. *Then* said I, Lo, I come
9. *Then* said he, Lo, I come to do thy will,
12:26. Whose voice *then* shook the earth:
2Pet. 3: 6. Whereby the world that *then* was,

5120 1 3588

τοῦ, *tou*, for τούτου.

Acts17:28. we are also *his* offspring.

5120

τοῦ &c. see Appendix.

5121 3 831/958 3588,1726

τοὐναντίον, *tounantion*.

2Co. 2: 7. So that *contrariwise* ye (ought)
Gal. 2: 7. But *contrariwise*, when they saw
1Pet.3: 9. but *contrariwise* blessing;

5122 1 831/958 3588,3686

τοὔνομα, *tounoma*.

Mat.27:57. a rich man of Arimathæa, named Joseph, (lit. the *name* Joseph)
See also ὄνομα.

5123 17 831/735 5124,2076

τουτέστι or τοῦτ' ἔστι, *toutesti* or *tout' esti*.

Mat.27:46. *that is to say*, My God, my God,
Mar 7: 2. *that is to say*, with unwashen, hands,
Acts 1:19. *that is to say*, The field of blood.
19: 4. *that is*, on Christ Jesus.
Ro. 7:18. *that is*, in my flesh,
9: 8. *That is*, They which are the children
10: 6. *that is*, to bring Christ down
7. *that is*, to bring up Christ again
8. *that is*, the word of faith, which
Philem 12. receive him, *that is*, mine own bowels:
Heb 2:14. him that had the power of death, *that is*, the devil;
7: 5. *that is*, of their brethren, though they
9:11. *that is to say*, not of this building;
10:20. through the veil, *that is to say*, his flesh;
11:16. a better (country), *that is*, an heavenly:
13:15. *that is*, the fruit of (our) lips giving
1Pet.3:20. wherein few, *that is*, eight souls were saved by water.

5124 320 /734 3778

τοῦτο, *touto*.

From οὗτος.

Obs. The words 'therefore' and 'wherefore,' when partly in italics in this series, are the rendering of διὰ τοῦτο, excepting in three cases for εἰς τοῦτο, and in two cases for παρὰ τοῦτο, which are noted. ² denotes its being compounded with αὐτός.

Mat. 1:22. Now all *this* was done, that it
6:25. *There*fore I say unto you,
8: 9. and to my servant, Do *this*, and he
9:28. Believe ye that I am able to do *this*?
12:11. and if *it* fall into a pit on the sabbath
27. *there*fore they shall be your judges.
31. *Where*fore I say unto you, All manner
13:13. *There*fore speak I to them in parables:
28. An enemy hath done *this*.
52. *There*fore every scribe (which is)
14: 2. and *there*fore mighty works do shew
15:11. *this* defileth a man.
16:22. *this* shall not be unto thee.
17:21. Howbeit *this* kind goeth not out
18: 4. humble himself as *this* little child,
23. *There*fore is the kingdom of heaven
19:26. With men *this* is impossible;
21: 4. All *this* was done, that it might be
43. *There*fore say I unto you,
23:14. *there*fore ye shall receive the greater
34. *Where*fore, behold, I send unto you
24:14. And *this* gospel of the kingdom
44. *There*fore be ye also ready:
26: 9. For *this* ointment might have been
12. she hath poured *this* ointment
13. Wheresoever *this* gospel shall be
26. Take, eat; *this* is my body.
28. For *this* is my blood of the new
39. let *this* cup pass from me:
42. if *this* cup may not pass away
56. But all *this* was done, that the
28.14. if *this* come to the governor's ears.
Mar 1:27. saying, What thing is *this*?
38. for *there*fore (εἰς τοῦτο) came I forth.
5:32. her that had done *this* thing.
43. that no man should know *it*;
• 6:14. and *there*fore mighty works
9:21. since *this* came unto him?
29. *This* kind can come forth by nothing.
11: 3. Why do ye *this*? say ye that
24. *There*fore I say unto you,
12:24. Do ye not *there*fore err,
13:11. in that hour, *that* speak ye·

Mar 14: 5. For *it* might have been sold
9. Wheresoever *this* gospel shall be
22. Take, eat: *this* is my body.
24. *This* is my blood of the new testament,
36. take away *this* cup from me:
1:18. Whereby shall I know *this?*
34. How shall *this* be, seeing I know not a man?
43. And whence (is) *this* to me,
66. What manner of child shall *this* be!
2:12. And *this* (shall be) a sign unto you;
15. and see *this* thing which is come to pass,
3:20. Added yet *this* above all,
4:43. for *there*fore (εἰς τοῦτο) am I sent.
5: 6. And when they had *this* done,
6: 3. Have ye not read so much as *this*,
7: 4. for whom he should do *this:*
8. to my servant, Do *this*, and he doeth (it).
9:21. to tell no man *that* thing;
45. But they understood not *this* saying,
48. Whosoever shall receive *this* child
10:11. notwithstanding be ye sure of *this*,
28. *this* do, and thou shalt live.
11:19. *there*fore shall they be your judges.
49. *There*fore also said the wisdom of God,
12:18. And he said, *This* will I do:
22. *There*fore I say unto you,
39. And *this* know, that if the goodman
13: 8. let it alone *this* year also,
14:20. and *there*fore I cannot come.
16: 2. How is it that I hear *this* of thee?
18:34. and *this* saying was hid from them,
36. he asked what *it* meant.
20:17. What is *this* then that is written,
22:15. I have desired to eat *this* passover
17. Take *this*, and divide (it) among yourselves:
19. *This* is my body which is given for you: *this* do in remembrance of me.
20. *This* cup (is) the new testament in my
23. that should do *this* thing.
37. that *this* that is written must
42. remove *this* cup from me:
24:40. And when he had *thus* spoken,

Joh. 1:31. *there*fore am I come baptizing
2:12. After *this* he went down to Capernaum,
22. he had said *this* unto them;
3:32. and heard, *that* he testifieth;
4:15. Sir, give me *this* water,
18. in *that* saidst thou truly.
54. *This* (is) again the second miracle
5:16. And *there*fore did the Jews persecute
18. *There*fore the Jews sought the more
28. Marvel not at *this:* for the hour
6: 6. And *this* he said to prove him.
29. *This* is the work of God, that ye
39. And *this* is the Father's will
40. And *this* is the will of him
61. he said unto them, Doth *this* offend you?
65. *There*fore said I unto you,
7:22. Moses *there*fore gave unto you circumcision;
39. But *this* spake he of the Spirit.
8: 6. *This* they said, tempting him,
40. *this* did not Abraham.
47. ye *there*fore hear (them) not,
9:23. *There*fore said his parents, He is of age;
10:17. *There*fore doth my Father love me,
11: 7. after *that* saith he to (his) disciples,
11. and after *that* he saith unto them,
26. Believest thou *this?*
51. And *this* spake he not of himself:

Joh. 12: 5. Why was not *this* ointment sold
6. *This* he said, not that he cared for
18. For *this* cause the people also met him,
— that he had done *this* miracle.
27. for *this* cause came I unto this hour.
33. *This* he said, signifying what death
39. *There*fore they could not believe,
13:11. *there*fore said he, Ye are not all clean.
28. for what intent he spake *this* unto him.
14:13. *that* will I do, that the Father may be
15:19. *there*fore the world hateth you.
16:15. *there*fore said I, that he shall take of
17. What is *this* that he saith unto us,
18. What is *this* that he saith,
18:34. Sayest thou *this* thing of thyself,
37. To *this* end was I born, and for *this* cause came I into the world,
38. And when he had said *this*, he went
19:11. *there*fore he that delivered me
28. After *this*, Jesus knowing that all
20:20. And when he had *so* said,
22 And when he had said *this*,
21:14. *This* is now the third time that
19. *This* spake he, signifying by what
— And when he had spoken *this*,

Acts 2:12. one to another, What meaneth *this?*
14. be *this* known unto you, and
16. But *this* is that which was spoken
26. *There*fore did my heart rejoice,
33. he hath shed forth *this*, which ye now
3: 6. but such as I have give)(I thee: In the name of
4: 7. by what name, have ye done *this?*
22. on whom *this* miracle of healing
5: 4. conceived *this* thing in thine heart?
24. whereunto *this* would grow.
38. or *this* work be of men,
7:60. when he had said *this*, he fell asleep.
8:34. of whom speaketh the prophet *this?*
9:21. which called on *this* name in Jerusalem, and came hither for *that* intent,
10:16. *This* was done thrice:
11:10. And *this* was done three times
16:18. And *this* did she many days.
19:10. And *this* continued by the space of
14. seven sons of (one) Sceva,...which did so.
17. And *this* was known to all the Jews
27. So that not only *this* our craft is
20:29. For I know *this*, that after my
21:23. Do therefore *this* that we say to thee:
23: 7. And when he had *so* said,
24:14. But *this* I confess unto thee, that
26:16. appeared unto thee for *this* purpose,
26. for *this* thing was not done in a corner
27:34. for *this* is for your health:

Ro. 1:12. *That* is, that I may be comforted
26. For *this* cause God gave them up unto
2: 3. And thinkest thou *this*, O man,
4:16. *There*fore (it is) of faith,
5:12. *Where*fore, as by one man sin entered
6: 6. Knowing *this*, that our old man is
7:15. for what I would, *that* do I not; but what I hate, *that* do I.
16. If then I do *that* which I would not,
19. the evil which I would not, *that* I do.
20. Now if I do *that* I would not,
9:17. Even for *this*[2] same purpose have I raised
10: 6. *that* is, to bring Christ down (from above)
7. *that* is, to bring up Christ again
8. *that* is, the word of faith, which
11:25. should be ignorant of *this* mystery,
12:20. for in *so* doing thou shalt heap

Ro. 13: 6. for *this* cause pay ye tribute also:
— continually upon *this*² very thing.
11. And *that*, knowing the time,
14: 9. For to *this* end Christ both died,
13. but judge *this* rather, that no man
15: 9. For *this* cause I will confess to thee
28. When therefore I have performed *this*,
1Co. 1:12. Now *this* I say, that every one of
4:17. For *this* cause have I sent unto you
5: 2. he that hath done *this* deed
3. him that hath so done *this* deed,
6: 6. and *that* before the unbelievers.
7: 6. But I speak *this* by permission,
26. that *this* is good for the present
29. But *this* I say, brethren, the time
35. And *this* I speak for your own profit;
37. and hath *so* decreed in his heart
9:17. For if I do *this* thing willingly,
23. And *this* I do for the gospel's sake,
10:28. *This* is offered in sacrifice unto idols,
11:10. For *this* cause ought the woman
17. Now in *this* that I declare (unto you)
24. Take, eat: *this* is my body,
— *this* do in remembrance of me.
25. *This* cup is the new testament in my blood: *this* do ye, as oft as
26. and drink *this* cup, ye do shew
30. For *this* cause many (are) weak
12:15. is it *there*fore (παρὰ τοῦτο) not of the body?
16. is it *there*fore (παρὰ τοῦτο) not of the
15:50. Now *this* I say, brethren, that flesh
53. For *this* corruptible must put on
— and *this* mortal (must) put on
54. when *this* corruptible shall have
— and *this* mortal shall have put on
2Co. 1:17. When I therefore was *thus* minded,
2: 1. I determined *this* with myself,
3. And I wrote *this*² same unto you,
9. For to *this* end also did I write,
4: 1. *There*fore seeing we have this ministry,
5: 5. wrought us for the *self*same² thing
14. because we *thus* judge,
7:11. For behold *this*² selfsame thing, that ye
13. *There*fore we were comforted in your
8:10. for *this* is expedient for you,
20. Avoiding *this*, that no man should
9: 6. But *this* (I say), He which soweth
10: 7. let him of himself think *this* again,
11. Let such an one think *this*,
13: 1. *This* (is) the third (time) I am coming
9. and *this* also we wish, (even) your perfection.
10. *There*fore I write these things being absent,
Gal. 2:10. the same)(² which I also was forward to
3: 2. *This* only would I learn of you,
17. And *this* I say, (that) the covenant,
6: 7. man soweth, *that* shall he also reap.
Eph 1:15. *Where*fore I also, after I heard
2: 8. and *that* not of yourselves: (it is)
4:17. *This* I say therefore, and testify
5: 5. *this* ye know, that no whoremonger,
17. *Where*fore be ye not unwise,
32. *This* is a great mystery:
6: 1. parents in the Lord: for *this* is right.
8. *the same* shall he receive of the Lord,
13. *Where*fore take unto you the whole
18. watching thereunto (lit. unto *this*² same) with all
22. sent unto you for the (lit. for *this*² same) same purpose,
Phi. 1: 6. Being confident of *this*² very thing,
Phi. 1: 7. meet for me to think *this* of you all
9. And *this* I pray, that your love
19. that *this* shall turn to my salvation
22. *this* (is) the fruit of my labour:
25. And having *this* confidence,
28. to you of salvation, and *that* of God.
2: 5. Let *this* mind be in you,
3:15. as many as be perfect, be *thus* minded·
— God shall reveal even *this* unto you.
Col. 1: 9. For *this* cause we also, since the
2: 4. And *this* I say, lest any man should
3:20. *this* is well pleasing unto the Lord.
4: 8. unto you for the same (lit. for *this*² same) purpose,
1Th. 2:13. For *this* cause also thank we God
3: 3. that we are appointed *there*unto.
5. For *this* cause, when I could no longer
7. *There*fore, brethren, we were comforted
4: 3. For *this* is the will of God,
15. For *this* we say unto you by the word
5:18. for *this* is the will of God in Christ
2Th. 2:11. And for *this* cause God shall send
3:10. *this* we commanded you, that if any
1Ti. 1: 9. Knowing *this*, that the law is not
16. for *this* cause I obtained mercy,
2: 3. For *this* (is) good and acceptable
4:10. *there*fore (εἰς τοῦτο) we both labour and
16. doing *this* thou shalt both save thyself,
5: 4. for *that* is good and acceptable
2Ti. 1:15. *This* thou knowest, that all they which
2:10. *There*fore I endure all things for
3: 1. *This* know also, that in the last days
Philem 15. he *there*fore departed for a season,
18. put *that* on mine account;
Heb 1: 9. *there*fore God, (even) thy God,
2: 1. *There*fore we ought to give the more
6: 3. And *this* will we do, if God permit.
7:27. for *this* he did once, when he offered
9: 8. The Holy Ghost *this* signifying,
15. And for *this* cause he is the mediator
20. *This* (is) the blood of the testament
27. but after *this* the judgment:
10:33. *Partly*, whilst ye were made a
— and *partly*, whilst ye became
13:17. they may do *it* with joy, and not with grief: for *that* (is) unprofitable for you.
19. the rather to do *this*, that I may
Jas. 4:15. we shall live, and do *this*, or that.
1Pet. 1:25. And *this* is the word which by
2:19. For *this* (is) thankworthy, if a man
20. *this* (is) acceptable with God.
21. For even *here*unto were ye called:
3: 9. that ye are *there*unto called,
4: 6. For for *this* cause was the gospel preached
2Pet. 1: 5. And beside *this*, (lit. *this*² same) giving all diligence,
20. Knowing *this* first, that no prophecy
3: 3. Knowing *this* first, that there shall
5. For *this* they willingly are ignorant of
8. be not ignorant of *this* one thing,
1Joh. 3: 1. *there*fore the world knoweth us not,
8. For *this* purpose the Son of God was
4: 3. and *this* is that (spirit) of antichrist,
5. *there*fore speak they of the world,
3Joh. 10. *Where*fore, if I come, I will
Jude 4. ordained to *this* condemnation,
5. though ye once knew *this*,
Rev. 2: 6. But *this* thou hast, that thou
7:15. *There*fore are they before the throne
12:12. *There*fore rejoice, (ye) heavens.
18: 8. *There*fore shall her plagues come in

See also τουτέστι.

5125 19 /737 3778

τούτοις, *toutois.*

From οὗτος.

Lu 16:26. And beside all *this*, between us
24:21. and beside all *this*, to day is the third
Acts 4:16. What shall we do to *these* men?
5:35. intend to do as touching *these* men.
Ro. 8:37. in all *these* things we are more
14:18. For he that in *these* things serveth
15:23. no more place in *these* parts,
1Co.12:23. upon *these* we bestow more abundant
Gal. 5:21. revellings, and *such* like: of the which
Col. 3:14. And above all *these* things (put on)
1Th. 4:18. comfort one another with *these* words.
1Ti. 4:15. give thyself wholly to *them*;
6: 8. let us be *there*with content.
Heb 9:23. should be purified with *these*;
2Pet.2:20. they are again entangled *there*in,
3Joh. 10. and not content *there*with,
Jude 7. in like manner, (lit. in like manner to *these*) giving themselves over
10. in *those* things they corrupt themselves.
14. prophesied of *these*, saying, Behold,

5126 64 /735 3778

τοῦτον, *touton.*

From οὗτος.

Mat.19:11. All (men) cannot receive *this* saying,
21:44. shall fall on *this* stone shall be
27:32. *him* they compelled to bear his cross.
Mar 7:29. For *this* saying go thy way;
14:58. I will destroy *this* temple that is
71. I know not *this* man of whom ye
Lu. 9:13. and buy meat for all *this* people.
26. of *him* shall the Son of man be
12: 5. yea, I say unto you, Fear *him*.
56. that ye do not discern *this* time?
16:28. come into *this* place of torment.
19:14. not have *this* (man) to reign over us.
20:12. and they wounded *him* also,
13. reverence (him) when they see *him*.
23: 2. We found *this* (fellow) perverting
14. Ye have brought *this* man unto me,
18. Away with *this* (man), and release
Joh. 2:19. Destroy *this* temple, and in three days
5: 6. When Jesus saw *him* lie,
6:27. for *him* hath God the Father sealed.
34. Lord, evermore give us *this* bread.
58. he that eateth of *this* bread shall live
7:27 we know *this* man whence he is:
9:29. *this* (fellow), we know not from whence he is.
39. I am come into *this* world, that
18:40. Not *this* man, but Barabbas.
19: 8. When Pilate therefore heard *that* saying,
12. If thou let *this* man go, thou art not
13. Pilate therefore heard *that* saying,
20. *This* title then read many of the Jews:
21:21. Peter seeing *him* saith to Jesus,
Acts 2:23. *Him*, being delivered by the determinate
32. *This* Jesus hath God raised up,
36. *that* same Jesus, whom ye have crucified,
3:16. made *this* man strong, whom ye see
5:31. *Him* hath God exalted with his right hand
37. After *this* man rose up Judas of
6:14. shall destroy *this* place,
7:35. *This* Moses whom they refused,
— *the same* did God send (to be) a ruler
10:40. *Him* God raised up the third day,
13:27. because they knew *him* not,
15:38. not good to take *him* with them.
Acts16: 3. *Him* would Paul have to go forth
17:23. *him* declare I unto you.
21:28. and hath polluted *this* holy place.
23:17. Bring *this* young man unto the chief
18. to bring *this* young man unto thee,
25. a letter after *this* manner:
27. *This* man was taken of the Jews,
24: 5. For we have found *this* man
25:24. ye see *this* man, about whom
28:26. Go unto *this* people, and say,
Ro. 9: 9. At *this* time will I come,
15:28. have sealed to them *this* fruit,
1Co. 2: 2. Jesus Christ, and *him* crucified.
3:12. if any man build upon *this* foundation
17. *him* shall God destroy;
11:26. as often as ye eat *this* bread,
27. whosoever shall eat *this* bread,
2Co. 4: 7. But we have *this* treasure
Phi. 2:23. *Him* therefore I hope to send
2Th. 3:14. note *that* man, and have no company
Heb 8: 3. that *this* man have somewhat also to offer

5127 77 /735 3778

τούτου, *toutou.*

From οὗτος.

Note.—[2] denotes it to be compounded with αὐτός.

Mat.13:15. For *this* people's heart is waxed gross,
22. and the care of *this* world,
40. in the end of *this* world.
19: 5. For *this* cause shall a man leave
26:29. henceforth of *this* fruit of the vine,
27:24. of the blood of *this* just person:
Mar 4:19. And the cares of *this* world,
10: 7. For *this* cause shall a man leave
Lu. 2:17. told them concerning *this* child.
9:45. to ask him of *that* saying.
13:16. be loosed from *this* bond
16: 8. for the children of *this* world
20:34. The children of *this* world marry,
22:51. Suffer ye *thus* far.
24: 4. as they were much perplexed *there*about,
Joh. 4:13. Whosoever drinketh of *this* water
6:51. if any man eat of *this* bread,
61. his disciples murmured at *it*,
66. From *that* (time) many of his disciples
8:23. ye are of *this* world; I am not of *this*
9:31. and doeth his will, *him* he heareth.
10:41. that John spake of *this* man
11: 9. he seeth the light of *this* world.
12:31. Now is the judgment of *this* world: now shall the prince of *this* world be cast out.
13: 1. he should depart out of *this* world
14:30. for the prince of *this* world cometh,
16:11. the prince of *this* world is judged.
19. among yourselves of *that* I said,
18:17. also (one) of *this* man's disciples?
29. What accusation bring ye against *this* man?
36. My kingdom is not of *this* world: if my kingdom were of *this* world,
19:12. And from *thence*forth Pilate sought
Acts 5:28. to bring *this* man's blood upon us.
6:13. words against *this* holy place,
9:13. I have heard by many of *this* man,
13:17. The God of *this* people of Israel
23. Of *this* man's seed hath God
38. through *this* man is preached unto you
15: 2. and elders about *this* question.
6. for to consider of *this* matter.
17:32. We will hear thee again of *this*
21:28. and the law, and *this* place:
22:22. him audience unto *this* word

Acts25:20. because I doubted of such manner of questions, (lit. I was at a loss about enquiry intc *this*)
25. that he himself hath appealed (lit. that *this*[2] man, himself &c.)
28: 9. So when *this* was done, others
27. For the heart of *this* people is waxed
Ro. 7:24. from the body of *this* death?
11: 7. Israel hath not obtained *that* which
1Co. 1:20. the disputer of *this* world?
— foolish the wisdom of *this* world?
2: 6. not the wisdom of *this* world, nor of the princes of *this* world,
8. none of the princes of *this* world knew·
3:19. For the wisdom of *this* world
5:10. the fornicators of *this* world,
7:31. the fashion of *this* world passeth
2Co. 4: 4. In whom the god of *this* world
12: 8. For *this* thing I besought the Lord
Eph. 2: 2. according to the course of *this* world,
3: 1. For *this* cause I Paul,
14. For *this* cause I bow my knees
5:31. For *this* cause shall a man leave
6:12. the rulers of the darkness of *this* world,
Col. 1:27. the riches of the glory of *this* mystery
Tit. 1: 5. For *this* cause left I thee in Crete
Jas. 1:26. *this* man's religion (is) vain.
2: 5. chosen the poor of *this* world
1Joh.4: 6. *Here*by know we the spirit of truth,
Rev.19:20. and with *him* the false prophet
22: 7. of the prophecy of *this* book.
9. which keep the sayings of *this* book:
10. the sayings of the prophecy of *this* book:
18. words of the prophecy of *this* book,

5128 27 /737 3778

τούτους, toutous.

From οὗτος.

Mat. 7:24. whosoever heareth *these* sayings of mine,
26. that heareth *these* sayings of mine,
28. Jesus had ended *these* sayings,
10: 5. *These* twelve Jesus sent forth,
19: 1. when Jesus had finished *these* sayings,
26: 1. when Jesus had finished all *these* sayings,
Mar 8: 4. whence can a man satisfy *these* (men)
Lu. 9:28. eight days after *these* sayings,
44. Let *these* sayings sink down into
19:15. then he commanded *these* servants
20:16. and destroy *these* husbandmen,
Joh.10:19. among the Jews for *these* sayings.
18: 8. let *these* go their way:
Acts 2:22. Ye men of Israel, hear *these* words;
5: 5. And Ananias hearing *these* words
24. and the chief priests heard *these* things,
10:47. that *these* should not be baptized,
16:36. told *this* saying to Paul,
19:37. ye have brought hither *these* men,
21:24. *Them* take, and purify thyself with them,
Ro. 8:30. *them* he also called:
— *them* he also justified:
— *them* he also glorified.
1Co. 6: 4. set *them* to judge who are least
16: 3. *them* will I send to bring your
2Ti. 3: 5. from *such* turn away.
Heb. 2:15. And deliver *them* who through fear

5129 89 /735 3778

τούτῳ, toutō.

From οὗτος.

Mat. 8: 9. and I say to *this* (man), Go, and he
12:32. forgiven him, neither in *this* world,
13:54. Whence hath *this* (man) this wisdom
56. Whence then hath *this* (man) all these
17:20. ye shall say unto *this* mountain,
20:14. I will give unto *this* last,
21:21. if ye shall say unto *this* mountain,
Mar 6: 2. whence hath *this* (man) these things?
10:30. an hundredfold now in *this* time,
11:23. shall say unto *this* mountain,
Lu. 1:61. that is called by *this* name.
4: 3. command *this* stone that it be made bread
7: 8. and I say unto *one*, Go, and he goeth;
10: 5. first say, Peace (be) to *this* house.
20. Notwithstanding in *this* rejoice not,
14: 9. Give *this* man place; and thou
18:30. manifold more in *this* present time,
19: 9. salvation come to *this* house,
19. And he said likewise to *him*,
21:23. and wrath upon *this* people.
23: 4. I find no fault in *this* man.
14. have found no fault in *this* man
Joh. 4:20. worshipped in *this* mountain;
21. ye shall neither in *this* mountain,
27. And upon *this* came his disciples.
37. And *here*in is that saying true,
5:38. *him* ye believe not.
9:30. Why *here*in is a marvellous thing,
10: 3. To *him* the porter openeth;
12:25. hateth his life in *this* world
13:24. Simon Peter therefore beckoned to *him*,
35. By *this* shall all (men) know
15: 8. *Here*in is my Father glorified,
16:30. by *this* we believe that thou camest
20:30. which are not written in *this* book:
Acts 1: 6. Lord, wilt thou at *this* time restore
3:12. why marvel ye at *this*? or why
4:10. by *him* doth this man stand here
17. henceforth to no man in *this* name.
5:28. ye should not teach in *this* name?
7: 7. and serve me in *this* place.
29. Then fled Moses at *this* saying,
8:21. part nor lot in *this* matter:
29. and join thyself to *this* chariot.
10:43. To *him* give all the prophets witness,
13:39. And by *him* all that believe are
15:15. And to *this* agree the words of
21: 9. And *the same* man had four daughters,
23: 9. We find no evil in *this* man:
24: 2(3). worthy deeds are done unto *this* nation
10. a judge unto *this* nation,
16. And *here*in do I exercise myself,
25: 5. if there be any wickedness in *him*.
Ro. 12: 2. And be not conformed to *this* world:
13: 9. comprehended in *this* saying,
1Co. 3:18. to be wise in *this* world,
4: 4. yet am I not *here*by justified.
7:24. *there*in abide with God.
31. And they that use *this* world,
11:22. shall I praise you in *this*?
14:21. will I speak unto *this* people;
2Co. 3:10. had no glory in *this* respect,
5: 2. For in *this* we groan, earnestly desiring
8:10. And *here*in I give (my) advice:
9: 3. should be in vain in *this* behalf;
Gal. 6:16. as walk according to *this* rule,
Eph 1:21. not only in *this* world, but also in that
Phi. 1:18. and I *there*in do rejoice, yea, and will
Heb 4: 5. And in *this* (place) again, If they
1Pet.4:16. let him glorify God on *this* behalf.
2Pet.1:13. as long as I am in *this* tabernacle,
2:19. of the same (lit. to *the same*) is he brought in bondage.

1Joh.2: 3. And *here*by we do know that we
4. and the truth is not in *him*.
5. in *him* verily is the love of God perfected: *here*by know we that we are in him.
3:10. In *this* the children of God are manifest,
16. *Here*by perceive we the love (of God),
19. And *here*by we know that we are
24. And *here*by we know that he abideth
4: 2. *Here*by know ye the Spirit of God:
9. In *this* was manifested the love of
10. *Here*in is love, not that we loved God,
13. *Here*by know we that we dwell in him,
17. *Here*in is our love made perfect,
— so are we in *this* world.
5: 2. By *this* we know that we love the children
Rev.22:18. plagues that are written in *this* book:
19. things which are written in *this* book.

5130 69 /737 3778

τούτων, toutōn.

From οὗτος.

Mat. 3: 9. God is able of *these* stones to raise up
5:19. one of *these* least commandments,
37. for whatsoever is more than *these*
6:29. was not arrayed like one of *these*.
32. ye have need of all *these* things.
10:42. unto one of *these* little ones a cup
11: 7. And as *they* departed, Jesus
18: 6. shall offend one of *these* little ones
10. ye despise not one of *these* little ones;
14. that one of *these* little ones should
25:40. of the least of *these* my brethren,
45. not to one of the least of *these*,
Mar 12:31. commandment greater than *these*.
Lu. 3: 8. is able of *these* stones to raise up
7:18. shewed him of all *these* things.
10:36. Which now of *these* three,
12:27. arrayed like one of *these*.
30. that ye have need of *these* things.
17: 2. offend one of *these* little ones.
18:34. they understood none of *these* things:
21:12. But before all *these*, they shall
28. And when *these* things begin to
24:14. they talked together of all *these* things
48. And ye are witnesses of *these* things.
Joh. 1:50(51). thou shalt see greater things than *these*.
5:20. shew him greater works than *these*,
7:31. will he do more miracles than *these*
14:12. greater (works) than *these* shall he do;
17:20. Neither pray I for *these* alone, but for
21:15. lovest thou me more than *these*?
24. which testifieth of *these* things,
Acts 1:21(22). Wherefore of *these* men which...must one be ordained to be a witness
24. whether of *these* two thou hast chosen,
5:32. we are his witnesses of *these* things;
36. For before *these* days rose up Theudas,
38. Refrain from *these* men, and let them
14:15. should turn from *these* vanities
15:28. than *these* necessary things;
18:15. for I will be no judge of *such* (matters).
17. And Gallio cared for none of *those* things.
19:36. Seeing then that *these* things cannot be
21:38. that Egyptian, which before *these* days
24: 8. take knowledge of all *these* things,
25: 9. be judged of *these* things before me?
20. and there be judged of *these* matters.
26:21. For *these* causes the Jews caught me
26. the king knoweth of *these* things,
— that none of *these* things are hidden
29. such as I am, except *these* bonds.
Ro. 11:30. obtained mercy through *their* unbelief:
1Co. 9:15. But I have used none of *these* things:
13:13. but the greatest of *these* (is) charity.
1Th. 4: 6. the Lord (is) the avenger of all *such*,
2Ti. 2:21. therefore purge himself from *these*,
3: 6. For of *this sort* are they which creep
Tit. 3: 8. *these* things I will that thou affirm
Heb 1: 2(1). Hath in *these* last days spoken unto
9: 6. Now when *these* things were thus
10:18. Now where remission of *these* (is),
13:11. For the bodies of *those* beasts,
2Pet. 1: 4. that by *these* ye might be partakers
12. always in remembrance of *these* things,
15. to have *these* things always in remembrance.
3:11. all *these* things shall be dissolved,
16. speaking in them of *these* things;
3Joh. 4. I have no greater joy (lit. greater than *these*)
Rev. 9:18. By *these* three was the third part of
18:15. The merchants of *these* things,
20: 6. on *such* the second death hath no power,

Note.—οὗτος, αὕτη, ταῦτα, &c. are arranged severally.

5131 4 831/958 rt 5176

τράγος, tragos.

Heb. 9:12. Neither by the blood of *goats* and
13. if the blood of bulls and of *goats*,
19. the blood of calves and of *goats*,
10: 4. the blood of bulls and of *goats*

5132 15 832/958 8:209 5064,3979

τράπεζα, trapeza.

Mat.15:27. which fall from their masters' *table*.
21:12. the *tables* of the moneychangers,
Mar 7:28. yet the dogs under the *table* eat of
11:15. the *tables* of the moneychangers,
Lu. 16:21. which fell from the rich man's *table*:
19:23. thou my money into the *bank*,
22:21. (is) with me on the *table*.
30. at my *table* in my kingdom,
Joh. 2:15. and overthrew the *tables*;
Acts 6: 2. leave the word of God, and serve *tables*.
16:34. he set *meat* before them,
Ro. 11: 9. Let their *table* be made a snare,
1Co.10:21. ye cannot be partakers of the Lord's *table*, and of the *table* of devils.
Heb 9: 2. and the *table*, and the shewbread;

5133 1 832/958 5132

τραπεζίτης, trapezitees.

Mat.25:27. to have put my money to the *exchangers*,

5134 1 832/959 cf 5149 titrōskō (to wound)

τραῦμα, trauma.

Lu. 10:34. and bound up his *wounds*,

5135 2 832/959 5134

τραυματίζω, traumatizo.

Lu. 20:12. they *wounded* him also, *and* cast
Acts19:16. out of that house naked and *wounded*.

5136 1 832/959 5137

τραχηλίζομαι, trakeelizomai.

Heb 4:13. naked and *opened* unto the eyes of him with

5137 7 832/959 5143

γράχηλος, trakeelos.

Mat.18: 6 were hanged about his *neck*,
Mar 9:42. were hanged about his *neck*,
Lu. 15:20. fell on his *neck*, and kissed him.
17: 2. millstone were hanged about his *neck*,
Acts15:10. a yoke upon the *neck* of the disciples,
20:37. and fell on Paul's *neck*, and kissed him,
Ro. 16: 4. laid down their own *necks*:

5138 2 832/959 rt 4486

τραχύς, trakus.

Lu. 3: 5. *rough* ways (shall be) made smooth;
Acts27:29. lest we should have fallen upon rocks, (lit. upon *rough* places)

5140a 68 833/959 8:216

τρεῖς, τρία, trīs, tria.

Mat.12:40. as Jonas was *three* days and *three* nights
— be *three* days and *three* nights in
13:33. and hid in *three* measures of meal,
15:32. with me now *three* days,
17: 4. make here *three* tabernacles;
18:16. of two or *three* witnesses every word
20. where two or *three* are gathered
26:61. and to build it in *three* days.
27:40. and buildest (it) in *three* days,
63. After *three* days I will rise again.
Mar 8: 2. have now been with me *three* days,
31. and after *three* days rise again.
9: 5. let us make *three* tabernacles;
14:58. and within *three* days I will build
15:29. and buildest (it) in *three* days,
Lu. 1:56. abode with her about *three* months,
2:46. after *three* days they found him
4:25. was shut up *three* years and six months.
9:33. let us make *three* tabernacles;
10:36. Which now of these *three*,
11: 5. Friend, lend me *three* loaves;
12.52. *three* against two, and two against *three*.
13: 7. these *three* years I come seeking fruit
21 and hid in *three* measures of meal,
Joh. 2: 6. two or *three* firkins apiece.
19. in *three* days I will raise it up.
20. thou rear it up in *three* days?
21:11. an hundred and fifty and *three*:
Acts 5: 7. the space of *three* hours after,
7:20. in his father's house *three* months:
9. 9. And he was *three* days without sight,
10:19. Behold, *three* men seek thee.
11:11. there were *three* men already come
17. 2. and *three* sabbath days reasoned
19: 8. for the space of *three* months,
20: 3. And (there) abode *three* months.
25: 1. after *three* days he ascended from Cæsarea
28: 7. lodged us *three* days courteously.
11. And after *three* months we departed
12. we tarried (there) *three* days.
17. that after *three* days Paul called
1Co.10: 8. in one day *three* and twenty thousand.
13:13. faith, hope, charity, these *three*;
14:27. or at the most (by) *three*,
29. Let the prophets speak two or *three*,
2Co.13: 1. In the mouth of two or *three* witnesses
Gal. 1:18. Then after *three* years I went up
1Ti. 5:19. but before two or *three* witnesses.
Heb 10:28. under two or *three* witnesses:
Jas. 5:17. by the space of *three* years and six months.
1Joh.5: 7. For there are *three* that bear record in
— and these *three* are one.
1Joh.5: 8. are *three* that bear witness in earth,
— and these *three* agree in one.
Rev. 6: 6. *three* measures of barley for a penny;
8:13. of the trumpet of the *three* angels,
9:18. By these *three* was the third part
11: 9. their dead bodies *three* days and an half,
11. And after *three* days and an half
16:13. And I saw *three* unclean spirits
19. the great city was divided into *three* parts,
21:13. On the east *three* gates; on the north *three* gates; on the south *three* gates; and on the west *three* gates.

5141 4 833/960 *treō* (to dread)

τρέμω, tremo.

Mar 5:33. the woman fearing and *trembling*,
Lu. 8:47. she came *trembling*, and falling down
Acts 9. 6. And he *trembling* and astonished
2Pet.2:10. they *are* not *afraid* to speak evil of

5142 8 833/960 rt 5157

τρέφω, trepho.

Mat. 6:26. yet your heavenly Father *feedeth* them.
25:37. an hungred, and *fed* (thee)?
Lu. 4:16. where he had been *brought up*:
12:24. and God *feedeth* them:
Acts12:20. because their country *was nourished* by
Jas. 5: 5. ye *have nourished* your hearts, as in
Rev.12: 6. that they *should feed* her there
14. where she *is nourished* for a time,

5143 20 833/960 8:226

τρέχω, treko.

Mat.27:48. straightway one of them *ran, and*
28: 8. *did run* to bring his disciples word.
Mar 5: 6. he *ran* and worshipped him,
15:36. And one *ran* and filled a spunge
Lu. 15:20. and *ran, and* fell on his neck,
24:12. Then arose Peter, and *ran* unto the
Joh.20: 2. Then she *runneth*, and cometh
4. So they *ran* both together:
Ro. 9:16. nor of him *that runneth*, but of
1Co. 9:24. they *which run* in a race *run* all,
— So *run*, that ye may obtain.
26. I therefore so *run*, not as
Gal. 2: 2. lest by any means I should *run*, or *had run*, in vain.
5: 7. Ye *did run* well; who
Phi. 2:16. that I *have* not *run* in vain,
2Th. 3: 1. that the word of the Lord *may have* (free) *course*, and be glorified,
Heb 12: 1. and *let* us *run* with patience the
Rev. 9: 9. of many horses *running* to battle.

τρία see τρεῖς. 5140a

5144 11 833/960 5140

τριάκοντα, triakonta.

Mat.13: 8. some sixtyfold, some *thirtyfold*.
23. some sixty, some *thirty*.
26:15. with him for *thirty* pieces of silver.
27: 3. brought again the *thirty* pieces of silver
9. they took the *thirty* pieces of silver,
Mar 4: 8. some *thirty*, and some sixty, and
20. some *thirtyfold*, some sixty, and
Lu. 3:23. to be about *thirty* years of age,
Joh. 5: 5. an infirmity *thirty* and eight years.

Joh. 6:19. five and twenty or *thirty* furlongs,
Gal. 3:17. four hundred and *thirty* years after,

5145 2 833/960 5140,1540
τριακόσιοι, triakosioi.

Mar 14: 5. for more than *three hundred* pence,
Joh. 12: 5. sold for *three hundred* pence,

5146 2 833/960 5140.956
τρίβολος, tribolos.

Mat. 7:16. or figs of *thistles?*
Heb 6: 8. that which beareth thorns and *briers*

5147 4 834/960 tribō (to rub)
τρίβος, tribos.

Mat. 3: 3. make his *paths* straight.
Mar 1: 3. make his *paths* straight.
Lu. 3: 4. make his *paths* straight.

5148 1 834/960 5140,2094
τριετία, trietia

Acts20:31. by the *space of three years* I ceased not

5149 1 834/960
τρίζω, trizo.

Mar 9:18. and *gnasheth* with his teeth,

5150 1 834/960 5140,3376
τρίμηνον, trimeenon.

Heb 11:23. was hid *three months* of his parents.

5151 12 834/960 8:216 5140
τρίς, tris.

Mat.26:34. thou shalt deny me *thrice*.
75. thou shalt deny me *thrice*.
Mar 14:30. thou shalt deny me *thrice*.
72. thou shalt deny me *thrice*.
Lu. 22:34. before that thou shalt *thrice* deny
61. thou shalt deny me *thrice*.
Joh. 13:38. till thou hast denied me *thrice*.
Acts10:16. This was done *thrice:* and the
11:10. And this was done *three times:*
2Co.11:25. *Thrice* was I beaten with rods,
— *thrice* I suffered shipwreck,
12: 8. I besought the Lord *thrice*, that it

5152 1 834/960 5140,4721
τρίστεγον, tristegon.

Acts20: 9. and fell down from the *third loft*,

5153 1 834/961 5151,5507
τρισχίλιοι, triskilioi.

Acts 2:41. about *three thousand* souls.

5154 57 834/961 8:216 5140
τρίτος, tritos.

Mat.16:21. and be raised again the *third* day.
17:23. and the *third* day he shall be raised
20: 3. he went out about the *third* hour,
19. and the *third* day he shall rise again.
22:26. also, and the *third*. unto the seventh.
26:44. and prayed the *third* time,
Mat.27:64. be made sure until the *third* day,
Mar 9:31. he shall rise the *third* day.
10:34. and the *third* day he shall rise again.
12:21. and the *third* likewise.
14:41. And he cometh the *third* time, and
15:25. And it was the *third* hour,
Lu. 9:22. and be raised the *third* day.
12:38. or come in the *third* watch,
13:32. and the *third* (day) I shall be perfected.
18:33. and the *third* day he shall rise again.
20:12. And again he sent a *third:* and they
31. And the *third* took her;
23:22. he said unto them the *third* time,
24: 7. and the *third* day rise again.
21. to day is the *third* day
46. to rise from the dead the *third* day:
Joh. 2: 1. And the *third* day there was
21:14. This is now the *third* time that Jesus
17. He saith unto him the *third* time, Simon,
— because he said unto him the *third* time,
Acts 2:15. it is (but) the *third* hour of the day.
10:40. Him God raised up the *third* day,
23:23. at the *third* hour of the night;
27:19. And the *third* (day) we cast out
1Co.12:28. *third*ly teachers, after that miracles,
15: 4. he rose again the *third* day
2Co.12: 2. caught up to the *third* heaven.
14. Behold, the *third* time I am ready to come
13: 1. This (is) the *third* (time) I am coming to you.
Rev. 4: 7. and the *third* beast had a face as
6: 5. when he had opened the *third* seal, I heard the *third* beast say,
8: 7. the *third* part of trees was burnt up,
8. the *third* part of the sea became blood,
9. the *third* part of the creatures
— and the *third* part of the ships
10. And the *third* angel sounded,
— upon the *third* part of the rivers, and
11. the *third* part of the waters became
12. the *third* part of the sun was smitten, and the *third* part of the moon, and the *third* part of the stars; so as the *third* part of them was darkened, and the day shone not for a *third* part of it,
9:15. for to slay the *third* part of men.
18. was the *third* part of men killed,
11:14. the *third* woe cometh quickly.
12: 4. drew the *third* part of the stars of
14: 9. And the *third* angel followed them,
16: 4. And the *third* angel poured out
21:19. the *third*, a chalcedony;

Note.—In 1 Co.12:28, and other places, the neuter is used as an adverb.

τρίχες see θρίξ. 2359

5155 1 834/961 2359
τρίχινος, trikinos.

Rev. 6:12. black as sackcloth *of hair*,

5156 5 834/961 5141
τρόμος, tromos.

Mar 16 8. for they trembled and were amazed· (lit. *trembling* and amazement held them)
1Co. 2: 3. in fear, and in much *trembling*.
2Co. 7:15. how with fear and *trembling* ye received

Eph 6: 5. be obedient to...with fear and *trembling*,
Phi. 2:12. work out your own salvation with fear and *trembling*.

5157 1 834/961 *trepō* (to turn)

τροπή, *tropee.*

Jas. 1:17. neither shadow of *turning*.

5158 13 835/961 rt 5157

τρόπος, *tropos.*

Mat.23:37. even as (lit. what *manner*) a hen gathereth her chickens
Lu. 13:34. as (lit. &c.) a hen (doth gather) her brood
Acts 1:11. shall so come in like *manner* as
7:28. as (lit. &c.) thou diddest the Egyptian
15:11. we shall be saved, even as (lit. &c.) they.
27:25. it shall be even as (lit. &c.) it was told me.
Ro. 3: 2. Much every *way*: chiefly, because
Phi. 1:18. every *way*, whether in pretence, or in
2Th. 2: 3. Let no man deceive you by any *means*:
3:16. give you peace always by all *means*.
2Ti. 3: 8. Now as (lit. what *manner*) Jannes and Jambres
Heb 13: 5. (Let your) *conversation* (be) without covetousness;
Jude 7. in like *manner*, giving themselves

5159 1 835/961 5158,5409

τροποφορέω, *tropophoreo.*

Acts13:18. *suffered* he their *manners* in the wilderness.

5160 16 835/961 5142

τροφή, *trophee.*

Mat. 3: 4. his *meat* was locusts and wild honey.
6:25. Is not the life more than *meat*,
10:10. the workman is worthy of his *meat*.
24:45. to give them *meat* in due season?
Lu. 12:23. The life is more than *meat*,
Joh. 4: 8. unto the city to buy *meat*.
Acts 2:46. did eat their *meat* (lit. *food*) with gladness
9:19. And when he had received *meat*,
14:17. filling our hearts with *food* and
27:33. Paul besought (them) all to take *meat*, (lit. *food*)
34. I pray you to take (some) *meat*:
36. they also took (some) *meat*. (lit. *food*)
38. when they had eaten enough, (lit. being satisfied with *food*)
Heb 5:12. and not of strong *meat*. (lit. solid *food*)
14. But strong *meat* belongeth to them
Jas. 2:15. and destitute of daily *food*,

5162 1 835/962 5142

τροφός, *trophos.*

1Th 2: 7. as a *nurse* cherisheth her children:

5163 1 835/962 5164

τροχία, *trokia.*

Heb 12:13. And make straight *paths* for your feet,

5164 1 835/962 5143

τροχός, *trokos.*

Jas. 3: 6. setteth on fire the *course* of nature;

5165 2 836/962

τρυβλίον *trublion.*

Mat.26:23. (his) hand with me in the *dish*,
Mar 14:20. that dippeth with me in the *dish*.

5166 3 836/962 *trugō* (to dry)

τρυγάω, *trugao.*

Lu. 6:44. nor of a bramble bush *gather* they grapes.
Rev.14:18. *gather* the clusters of the vine
19. and *gathered* the vine of the earth,

5167 1 836/962 6:63 *truzō* (to murmur)

τρυγών, *trugōn.*

Lu. 2:24. A pair of *turtledoves*,

5168 2 836/962 cf 5169 *truō* (to wear away)

τρυμαλιά, *trumalia.*

Mar 10:25. to go through the *eye* of a needle,
Lu. 18:25. camel to go through a needle's *eye*,

5169 1 836/962 rt 5168

τρύπημα, *trupeema.*

Mat.19:24. to go through the *eye* of a needle.

5171 1 836/962 5172

τρυφάω, *truphao.*

Jas. 5: 5. Ye *have lived in pleasure* on the earth,

5172 2 836/962 *thrupto* (to make feeble)

τρυφή, *truphee.*

Lu. 7:25. and live *delicately*, are in kings' courts.
2Pet.2:13. that count it pleasure *to riot* in the day time.

5176 6 836/962 8:236

τρώγω, *trōgo.*

Mat.24:38. they were *eating* and drinking,
Joh. 6:54. *Whoso eateth* my flesh, and drinketh
56. He *that eateth* my flesh, and drinketh
57. so he *that eateth* me, even he shall live
58. he *that eateth* of this bread shall live
13:18. He *that eateth* bread with me hath lifted

5177 13 837/962 8:238 cf 5180 *tuchō* (to make ready)

τυγχάνω, *tunkano.*

Lu. 10:30. leaving (him) half dead. (lit. *being* half dead)
20:35. worthy *to obtain* that world,
Acts19:11. And God wrought special miracles (lit. no *common* miracles)
24: 2(3). *Seeing that* by thee we *enjoy* great quietness,
26:22. *Having* therefore *obtained* help of God,
27: 3. to go unto his friends to refresh himself. (lit. to *meet with* care)
28: 2. shewed us no *little* kindness: (lit. no *common* k.)
1Co.14:10. There are, it *may be*, so many kinds
15:37. bare grain, it *may chance* of wheat,
2Ti. 2:10. they *may* also *obtain* the salvation
Heb 8: 6. But now *hath* he *obtained* a more excellent
11:35. that they *might obtain* a better resurrection.

See also τυχόν.

5178 1 837/962 5180

τυμπανίζομαι, tumpanizomai.

Heb 11:35. and others *were tortured*,

5179 16 837/963 8:246 5180

τύπος, tupos.

Joh. 20:25. in his hands the *print* of the nails, and put my finger into the *print* of the nails,
Acts 7:43. *figures* which ye made to worship
44. make it according to the *fashion* that he had seen.
23:25. he wrote a letter after this *manner:*
Ro. 5:14. who is the *figure* of him that was to come.
6:17. that *form* of doctrine which was
1Co. 10: 6. Now these things were our *examples*,
11. happened unto them for *ensamples:*
Phi. 3:17. as ye have us for an *ensample*.
1Th. 1: 7. So that ye were *ensamples* to all
2Th. 3: 9. but to make ourselves an *ensample*
1Ti. 4:12. be thou an *example* of the believers,
Tit. 2: 7. shewing thyself a *pattern* of good works:
Heb 8: 5. according to the *pattern* shewed to thee
1Pet. 5: 3. but being *ensamples* to the flock.

5180 14 838/963 8:260 cf 3817 cf 3960, cf 4141, cf 4474, cf 5177

τύπτω, tupto.

Mat. 24:49. And shall begin *to smite* (his)
27:30. and *smote* him on the head.
Mar 15:19. And they *smote* him on the head
Lu. 6:29. And unto him *that smiteth* thee on
12:45. and shall begin *to beat* the menservants
18:13. but *smote* upon his breast, saying,
22:64. they *struck* him on the face,
23:48. *smote* their breasts, *and* returned.
Acts 18:17. and *beat* (him) before the judgment seat.
21:32. they left *beating* of Paul.
23: 2. *to smite* him on the mouth.
3. God shall *smite* thee, (thou) whited wall:
— commandest me *to be smitten* contrary
1Co. 8:12. and *wound* their weak conscience,

5182 1 838/461 cf 2351

τυρβάζομαι, turbazomai.

Lu. 10:41. thou art careful and *troubled* about many things:

5185 53 838/963 8:270 5187

τυφλός, tuphlos.

Mat. 9:27. two *blind* men followed him,
28. the *blind* men came to him:
11: 5. The *blind* receive their sight,
12:22. one possessed with a devil, *blind*,
— insomuch that the *blind* and dumb
15:14. they be *blind* leaders of the *blind*. And if the *blind* lead the *blind*,
30. lame, *blind*, dumb, maimed,
31. and the *blind* to see:
20:30. And, behold, two *blind* men
21:14. And the *blind* and the lame came
23:16. Woe unto you, (ye) *blind* guides,
17. (Ye) fools and *blind:* for whether is
19. (Ye) fools and *blind:* for whether
24. (Ye) *blind* guides, which strain at a gnat,
26. (Thou) *blind* Pharisee, cleanse first that
Mar 8:22. they bring a *blind* man unto him,
23. he took the *blind* man by the hand.
10:46. *blind* Bartimæus, the son of Timæus,
Mar 10:49. And they call the *blind* man,
51. The *blind* man said unto him,
Lu. 4:18. and recovering of sight to the *blind*,
6:39. Can the *blind* lead the *blind?*
7:21. unto many (that were) *blind* he gave sight.
22. how that the *blind* see,
14:13. the maimed, the lame, the *blind:*
21. the maimed, and the halt, and the *blind*.
18:35. a certain *blind* man sat by the way side
Joh. 5: 3. of *blind*, halt, withered, waiting for
9: 1. which was *blind* from (his) birth.
2. that he was born *blind?*
6. anointed the eyes of the *blind* man
8. had seen him that he was *blind*,
13. him that aforetime was *blind*.
17. They say unto the *blind* man again,
18. that he had been *blind*, and received
19. who ye say was born *blind?*
20. and that he was born *blind:*
24. called they the man that was *blind*,
25. whereas I was *blind*, now I see.
32. the eyes of one that was born *blind*.
39. they which see might be made *blind*.
40. Are we *blind* also?
41. If ye were *blind*, ye should have no sin:
10:21. open the eyes of the *blind?*
11:37. which opened the eyes of the *blind*,
Acts 13:11. and thou shalt be *blind*,
Ro. 2:19. thyself art a guide of the *blind*,
2Pet. 1: 9. he that lacketh these things is *blind*, and
Rev. 3:17. and poor, and *blind*, and naked:

5186 3 838/964 8:270 5185

τυφλόω, tuphloō.

Joh. 12:40. He *hath blinded* their eyes,
2Co. 4: 4. In whom the god of this world *hath blinded* the minds
1Joh. 2:11. darkness *hath blinded* his eyes.

5188 1 839/964

τύφομαι, tuphomai.

Mat. 12:20. and *smoking* flax shall he not quench,

5187 3 838/964 5188

τυφόομαι, tuphöomai.

1Ti. 3: 6. lest *being lifted up with pride* he fall
6: 4. He *is proud*, knowing nothing,
2Ti. 3: 4. heady, *highminded*, (lit. *puffed up*)

5189 1 839/964 5188

τυφωνικός, tuphōnikos.

Acts 27:14. a *tempestuous* wind, called Euroclydon.

5177 See also p. 751

τυχόν, tukon.

1Co. 16: 6. And it *may be* that I will abide,

5191 1 839/964 5192

ὑακίνθινος, huakinthinos.

Rev. 9:17. breastplates of fire, and *of jacinth*,

5192 1 839/964

ὑάκινθος, *huakinthos.*

Rev.21:20. the eleventh, a *jacinth;*

5193 3 839/964 5194

ὑάλινος, *hualinos.*

Rev. 4: 6. a sea *of glass* like unto crystal:
15: 2. as it were a sea *of glass* mingled with fire:
— stand on the sea *of glass*, having the harps of God.

5194 2 839/964 rt 5205

ὕαλος, *hualos.*

Rev.21:18. city (was) pure gold, like unto clear *glass.*
21. pure gold, as it were transparent *glass.*

5195 5 839/964 8:295 5196

ὑβρίζω, *hubrizo.*

Mat.22: 6. and *entreated* (them) *spitefully,*
Lu. 11:45. thus saying thou *reproachest* us also.
18:32. shall be mocked, and *spitefully entreated,*
Acts14: 5. to *use* (them) *despitefully,* and to stone
1Th. 2: 2. after that we had suffered before, and *were shamefully entreated,*

5196 3 839/964 8:295 5228

ὕβρις, *hubris.*

Acts27:10. will be with *hurt* and much damage,
21. to have gained this *harm* and loss.
2Co.12:10. I take pleasure in infirmities, in *reproaches,*

5197 2 839/964 8:295 5195

ὑβριστής, *hubristees.*

Ro. 1:30. haters of God, *despiteful,*
1Ti. 1:13. and a persecutor, and *injurious:*

5198 12 839/964 8:308 5199

ὑγιαίνω, *hugiaino.*

Lu. 5:31. They *that are whole* need not a physician;
7:10. found the servant *whole* that had been sick
15:27. he hath received him *safe and sound.*
1Ti. 1:10. that is contrary to *sound* doctrine;
6: 3. and consent not to *wholesome* words,
2Ti. 1:13. Hold fast the form of *sound* words,
4: 3. when they will not endure *sound* doctrine;
Tit. 1: 9. he may be able by *sound* doctrine
13. that they *may be sound* in the faith;
2: 1. things which become *sound* doctrine:
2. *sound* (lit. *being sound*) in faith, in
3Joh. 2. mayest prosper and *be in health,*

5199 14 840/964 8:308 rt 837

ὑγιής, *hugiees.*

Mat.12:13. it was restored *whole,* like as the other.
15:31. the maimed to be *whole,*
Mar 3: 5. was restored *whole* as the other.
5:34. and be *whole* of thy plague.
Lu. 6:10. hand was restored *whole* as the other.
Joh. 5: 4. was made *whole* of whatsoever disease
6. Wilt thou be made *whole?*
9. was made *whole,* and took up his bed,
11. He that made me *whole,*
14. thou art made *whole:* sin no more,
15. it was Jesus, which had made him *whole.*

Joh. 7:23. every whit *whole* on the sabbath day?
Acts 4:10. this man stand here before you *whole.*
Tit. 2: 8. *Sound* speech, that cannot be condemned

5200 1 840/964 rt 5205

ὑγρός, *hugros.*

Lu. 23:31. they do these things in a *green* tree,

5201 3 840/965 5204

ὑδρία, *hudria.*

Joh. 2: 6. And there were set there six *waterpots* of
7. Fill the *waterpots* with water.
4:28. The woman then left her *waterpot,*

5202 1 840/965 5204,4095

ὑδροποτέω, *hudropoteo.*

1Ti. 5:23. *Drink* no longer *water,* but use a

5203 1 840/965 5204,3700

ὑδρωπικός, *hudrōpikos.*

Lu. 14: 2. man before him *which had the dropsy.*

5204 79 840/965 8:314 rt 5205

ὕδωρ, *hudōr.*

Mat. 3:11. I indeed baptize you with *water*
16. went up straightway out of the *water:*
8:32. and perished in the *waters.*
14:28. come unto thee on the *water.*
29. he walked on the *water,* to go to
17:15. and oft into the *water.*
27:24. he took *water,* and washed (his) hands
Mar 1: 8. I indeed have baptized you with *water:*
10. coming up out of the *water,* he saw
9:22. into the fire, and into the *waters,*
41. a cup of *water* to drink in my name,
14:13. a man bearing a pitcher of *water:*
Lu. 3:16. I indeed baptize you with *water;*
7:44. thou gavest me no *water* for my feet:
8:24. and the raging of the *water:*
25. he commandeth even the winds and *water,*
16:24. dip the tip of his finger in *water,*
22:10. bearing a pitcher of *water;*
Joh. 1:26. I baptize with *water:*
31. am I come baptizing with *water.*
33. that sent me to baptize with *water,*
2: 7. Fill the waterpots with *water.*
9. tasted the *water* that was made wine,
— the servants which drew the *water* knew;
3: 5. Except a man be born of *water* and
23. there was much *water* there:
4: 7. a woman of Samaria to draw *water:*
10. he would have given thee living *water*
11. whence then hast thou that living *water?*
13. Whosoever drinketh of this *water*
14. whosoever drinketh of the *water* that
— but the *water* that I shall give him shall be in him a well of *water*
15. Sir, give me this *water,* that I
46. where he made the *water* wine.
5: 3. waiting for the moving of the *water.*
4. and troubled the *water:* whosoever then first after the troubling of the *water*
7. when the *water* is troubled,
7:38. shall flow rivers of living *water.*
13: 5. After that he poureth *water* into a bason
19:34. came thereout blood and *water.*
Acts 1: 5. For John truly baptized with *water;*

3 C

Acts 8:36. they came unto a certain *water:*
— See, (here is) *water;* what doth hinder
38. they went down both into the *water,*
39. they were come up out of the *water,*
10:47. Can any man forbid *water,* that
11:16. John indeed baptized with *water;*
Eph 5:26. with the washing of *water* by the word,
Heb 9:19. with *water,* and scarlet wool, and
10:22(23). our bodies washed with pure *water.*
Jas 3:12. both yield salt *water* and fresh.
1Pet.3:20. eight souls were saved by *water.*
2Pet.3: 5. and the earth standing out of the *water* and in the *water*
6. being overflowed with *water,* perished:
1Joh.5: 6. that came by *water* and blood, (even) Jesus Christ; not by *water* only, but by *water* and blood.
8. the spirit, and the *water,* and the blood:
Rev. 1:15. his voice as the sound of many *waters.*
7:17. unto living fountains of *waters:* and God
8:10. and upon the fountains of *waters;*
11. and the third part of the *waters* became wormwood; and many men died of the *waters,*
11: 6. and have power over *waters* to turn
12:15. out of his mouth *water* as a flood
14: 2. as the voice of many *waters,*
7. and the fountains of *waters.*
16: 4. upon the rivers and fountains of *waters;*
5. I heard the angel of the *waters* say,
12. and the *water* thereof was dried up,
17: 1. whore that sitteth upon many *waters:*
15. The *waters* which thou sawest, where
19: 6. and as the voice of many *waters,*
21: 6. of the fountain of the *water* of life freely.
22: 1. a pure river of *water* of life, clear
17. let him take the *water* of life freely.

5205 6 841/965 *huo* (to rain)

ὑετός, *huetos.*

Acts14:17. and gave us *rain* from heaven,
28: 2. because of the present *rain,*
Heb 6: 7. the earth which drinketh in the *rain*
Jas. 5: 7. he receive the early and latter *rain.*
18. prayed again, and the heaven gave *rain,*
Rev.11: 6. to shut heaven, that it rain not (lit. that the *rain* wet not) in the days

---

5206 5 841/966 8:334 5207,5087

υἱοθεσία, *whyothesia.*

Ro. 8:15. ye have received the Spirit of *adoption,*
23. waiting for the *adoption,* (to wit), the
9: 4. to whom (pertaineth) the *adoption,* and
Gal. 4: 5. we might receive the *adoption of sons.*
Eph 1: 5. us unto the *adoption of children* by Jesus Christ to himself,

---

5207 381 841/966 8:334,400,478

υἱός, *whyos.*

Mat. 1: 1. of Jesus Christ, the *son* of David, the *son* of Abraham.
20. Joseph, thou *son* of David, fear not to
21. she shall bring forth a *son,* and thou
23. and shall bring forth a *son,*
25. had brought forth her firstborn *son:*
2:15. Out of Egypt have I called my *son.*
3:17. This is my beloved *Son,* in whom I am well pleased.
4: 3. If thou be the *Son* of God, command
Mat. 4 6. If thou be the *Son* of God, cast
5: 9. for they shall be called the *children* of God.
45. That ye may be the *children* of your Father which is in heaven:
7: 9. if his *son* ask bread, will he give him
8:12. But the *children* of the kingdom shall be cast out
20. but the *Son* of man hath not where
29. with thee, Jesus, thou *Son* of God?
9: 6. may know that the *Son* of man hath
15. Can the *children* of the bridechamber
27. (Thou) *son* of David, have mercy on us.
10:23. till the *Son* of man be come.
37. he that loveth *son* or daughter more
11:19. The *Son* of man came eating and
27. and no man knoweth the *Son,* but the Father;
— save the *Son,* and (he) to whomsoever the *Son* will reveal (him).
12: 8. For the *Son* of man is Lord even of
23. Is not this the *son* of David?
27. by whom do your *children* cast (them)
32. a word against the *Son* of man,
40. so shall the *Son* of man be three days
13:37. He that soweth the good seed is the *Son* of man;
38. the good seed are the *children* of the kingdom; but the tares are the *children* of the wicked (one);
41. The *Son* of man shall send forth
55. Is not this the carpenter's *son?*
14:33. Of a truth thou art the *Son* of God.
15:22. on me, O Lord, (thou) *son* of David;
16:13. that I the *Son* of man am?
16. Thou art the Christ, the *Son* of the living God.
27. For the *Son* of man shall come in the glory of his Father
28. till they see the *Son* of man coming
17: 5. This is my beloved *Son,* in whom I am well pleased; hear ye him.
9. until the *Son* of man be risen
12. Likewise shall also the *Son* of man suffer
15. Lord, have mercy on my *son:*
22. The *Son* of man shall be betrayed
25. of their own *children,* or of strangers?
26. Then are the *children* free.
18:11. For the *Son* of man is come to save
19:28. when the *Son* of man shall sit in the throne of his glory,
20:18. and the *Son* of man shall be betrayed
20. came to him the mother of Zebedee's *children* with her *sons,* worshipping
21. Grant that these my two *sons* may sit,
28. Even as the *Son* of man came not to
30. on us, O Lord, (thou) *son* of David.
31. O Lord, (thou) *son* of David.
21: 5. and a colt the *foal* of an ass.
9. Hosanna to the *son* of David:
15. Hosanna to the *son* of David;
37. he sent unto them his *son,* saying, They will reverence my *son.*
38. when the husbandmen saw the *son,*
22: 2. which made a marriage for his *son,*
42. What think ye of Christ? whose *son* is he?
45. call him Lord, how is he his *son?*
23:15. twofold more the *child* of hell than
31. that ye are the *children* of them which
35. blood of Zacharias *son* of Barachias,
24:27. so shall also the coming of the *Son* of man be.
30. the sign of the *Son* of man in heaven:

Mat.24:30. and they shall see the *Son* of man coming
37. so shall also the coming of the *Son* of man be.
39. the coming of the *Son* of man be.
44. the *Son* of man cometh.
25:13. the hour wherein the *Son* of man cometh.
31. When the *Son* of man shall come in his
26: 2. and the *Son* of man is betrayed
24. The *Son* of man goeth as it is written
— by whom the *Son* of man is betrayed !
37. Peter and the two *sons* of Zebedee,
45. and the *Son* of man is betrayed
63. whether thou be the Christ, the *Son* of God.
64. Hereafter shall ye see the *Son* of man
27. 9. they of the *children* of Israel did value ;
40. If thou be the *Son* of God, come down
43. for he said, I am the *Son* of God.
54. Truly this was the *Son* of God.
56. and the mother of Zebedee's *children*.
28:19. in the name of the Father, and of the *Son*, and of the Holy Ghost:
Mar 1: 1. of Jesus Christ, the *Son* of God;
11. Thou art my beloved *Son*, in whom
2:10. that the *Son* of man hath power
19. Can the *children* of the bridechamber
28. the *Son* of man is Lord also of the sabbath.
3:11. Thou art the *Son* of God.
17. Boanerges, which is, The *sons* of thunder:
28. forgiven unto the *sons* of men,
5: 7. Jesus, (thou) *Son* of the most high God?
6: 3. the carpenter, the *son* of Mary, the
8:31. the *Son* of man must suffer many
38. of him also shall the *Son* of man be ashamed,
9. 7. This is my beloved *Son*: hear him.
9. till the *Son* of man were risen
12. it is written of the *Son* of man,
17. I have brought unto thee my *son*,
31. The *Son* of man is delivered into
10:33. the *Son* of man shall be delivered unto
35. James and John, the *sons* of Zebedee,
45. For even the *Son* of man came not to
46. Bartimæus, the *son* of Timæus,
47. Jesus, (thou) *son* of David, have
48. *son* of David, have mercy on me.
12: 6. Having yet therefore one *son*, his wellbeloved,
— They will reverence my *son*.
35. that Christ is the *son* of David?
37. and whence is he (then) his *son?*
13:26. shall they see the *Son* of man coming in
32. neither the *Son*, but the Father.
14:21. The *Son* of man indeed goeth,
— by whom the *Son* of man is betrayed!
41. the *Son* of man is betrayed into
61. Art thou the Christ, the *Son* of the Blessed?
62. Jesus said, I am: and ye shall see the *Son* of man sitting on
15:39. Truly this man was the *Son* of God.
Lu. 1:13. Elisabeth shall bear thee a *son*,
16. many of the *children* of Israel shall he
31. and bring forth a *son*, and shalt
32. and shall be called the *Son* of the Highest:
35. shall be called the *Son* of God.
36. she hath also conceived a *son*
57. and she brought forth a *son*.
2: 7. she brought forth her firstborn *son*,
3: 2. came unto John the *son* of Zacharias
22. Thou art my beloved *Son*; in thee I am
23. being, as was supposed, the *son* of Joseph,
Lu. 4: 3. If thou be the *Son* of God, command
9. If thou be the *Son* of God, cast
22. Is not this Joseph's *son?*
41. Thou art Christ the *Son* of God.
5:10. James, and John, the *sons* of Zebedee,
24. that the *Son* of man hath power
34. Can ye make the *children* of the
6: 5. That the *Son* of man is Lord also of
22. for the *Son* of man's sake.
35. ye shall be the *children* of the Highest:
7:12. the only *son* of his mother, and she
34. The *Son* of man is come eating
8:28. Jesus, (thou) *Son* of God most high?
9:22. The *Son* of man must suffer
26. of him shall the *Son* of man be ashamed,
35. This is my beloved *Son*: hear him.
38. I beseech thee, look upon my *son*:
41. Bring thy *son* hither.
44. the *Son* of man shall be delivered
56. For the *Son* of man is not come to
58. but the *Son* of man hath not where
10: 6. And if the *son* of peace be there,
22. no man knoweth who the *Son* is, but the Father; and who the Father is, but the *Son*, and (he) to whom the *Son* will reveal (him).
11:11. If a *son* shall ask bread of any
19. by whom do your *sons* cast (them) out?
30. so shall also the *Son* of man be to this
12: 8. him shall the *Son* of man also confess
10. a word against the *Son* of man,
40. for the *Son* of man cometh at an hour
53. The father shall be divided against the *son* and the *son* against the father;
15:11. A certain man had two *sons*:
13. the younger *son* gathered all together,
19. no more worthy to be called thy *son*:
21. And the *son* said unto him, Father,
— am no more worthy to be called thy *son*.
24. For this my *son* was dead, and is alive
25. Now his elder *son* was in the field:
30. But as soon as this thy *son* was come,
16: 8. for the *children* of this world are
— wiser than the *children* of light.
17:22. one of the days of the *Son* of man,
24. so shall also the *Son* of man be in his day.
26. be also in the days of the *Son* of man.
30. in the day when the *Son* of man is revealed.
18: 8. Nevertheless when the *Son* of man cometh,
31. concerning the *Son* of man
38. Jesus, (thou) *son* of David, have mercy
39. *son* of David, have mercy on me.
19: 9. as he also is a *son* of Abraham.
10. For the *Son* of man is come to seek
20:13. I will send my beloved *son*:
34. The *children* of this world marry,
36. and are the *children* of God, being the *children* of the resurrection.
41. How say they that Christ is David's *son?*
44. how is he then his *son?*
21:27. shall they see the *Son* of man coming
36. and to stand before the *Son* of man.
22:22. And truly the *Son* of man goeth,
48. betrayest thou the *Son* of man with a kiss?
69. Hereafter shall the *Son* of man sit on
70. Art thou then the *Son* of God?
24: 7. The *Son* of man must be delivered
Joh. 1:18. the only begotten *Son*, which is in the bosom of the Father,
34. that this is the *Son* of God.
42(43). Thou art Simon the *son* of Jona:

3 c 2

Joh. 1:45(46). Jesus of Nazareth, the *son* of Joseph.
49(50). thou art the *Son* of God; thou art
51(52). and descending upon the *Son* of man.
3:13. the *Son* of man which is in heaven.
14. must the *Son* of man be lifted up:
16. he gave his only begotten *Son*, that
17. God sent not his *Son* into the world to
18. name of the only begotten *Son* of God.
35. The Father loveth the *Son*, and hath
36. He that believeth on the *Son* hath
— he that believeth not the *Son* shall not
4: 5. ground that Jacob gave to his *son* Joseph.
12. and his *children*, and his cattle?
46. whose *son* was sick at Capernaum.
47. come down, and heal his *son*:
50. Go thy way; thy *son* liveth.
53. Jesus said unto him, Thy *son* liveth:
5:19. The *Son* can do nothing of himself, but
— these also doeth the *Son* likewise.
20. For the Father loveth the *Son*, and
21. even so the *Son* quickeneth whom he will.
22. hath committed all judgment unto the *Son*:
23. That all (men) should honour the *Son*, even
— He that honoureth not the *Son*
25. shall hear the voice of the *Son* of God·
26. hath he given to the *Son* to have life in himself;
27. because he is the *Son* of man.
6:27. which the *Son* of man shall give
40. that every one which seeth the *Son*,
42. Is not this Jesus, the *son* of Joseph,
53. ye eat the flesh of the *Son* of man,
62. if ye shall see the *Son* of man ascend
69. thou art that Christ, the *Son* of the living God.
8:28. When ye have lifted up the *Son* of man,
35. (but) the *Son* abideth ever.
36. If the *Son* therefore shall make you free,
9:19. Is this your *son*, who ye say was born blind?
20. We know that this is our *son*, and that
35. Dost thou believe on the *Son* of God?
10:36. because I said, I am the *Son* of God?
11: 4. that the *Son* of God might be glorified
27. that thou art the Christ, the *Son* of God,
12:23. that the *Son* of man should be glorified.
34. The *Son* of man must be lifted up? who is this *Son* of man?
36. that ye may be the *children* of light.
13:31. Now is the *Son* of man glorified,
14:13. the Father may be glorified in the *Son*.
17: 1. the hour is come; glorify thy *Son*, that thy *Son* also may glorify thee:
12. is lost, but the *son* of perdition;
19: 7. because he made himself the *Son* of God.
26. Woman, behold thy *son*!
20:31. that Jesus is the Christ, the *Son* of God;
Acts 2:17. your *sons* and your daughters shall
3:25. Ye are the *children* of the prophets,
4:36. interpreted, The *son* of consolation,
5:21. the senate of the *children* of Israel,
7:16. for a sum of money of the *sons* of Emmor
21. nourished him for her own *son*.
23. visit his brethren the *children* of Israel.
29. Madian, where he begat two *sons*.
37. which said unto the *children* of Israel,
56. heavens opened, and the *Son* of man
8:37. I believe that Jesus Christ is the *Son* of God.
9:15. and the *children* of Israel:
20. that he is the *Son* of God.

Acts 10:36. sent unto the *children* of Israel,
13:10. (thou) *child* of the devil, (thou) enemy
21. gave unto them Saul the *son* of Cis,
26. *children* of the stock of Abraham,
33. Thou art my *Son*, this day have I begotten thee.
16: 1. Timotheus, the *son* of a certain woman,
19:14. there were seven *sons* of (one) Sceva,
23: 6. I am a Pharisee, the *son* of a Pharisee
16. And when Paul's sister's *son* heard of
Ro. 1: 3. Concerning his *Son* Jesus Christ our Lord,
4. declared (to be) the *Son* of God with
9. serve with my spirit in the gospel of his *Son*,
5:10. reconciled to God by the death of his *Son*,
8: 3. God sending his own *Son* in the likeness
14. as many as are led by the Spirit of God, they are the *sons* of God.
19. for the manifestation of the *sons* of God.
29. conformed to the image of his *Son*,
32. He that spared not his own *Son*, but
9: 9. and Sarah shall have a *son*.
26. be called the *children* of the living God.
27. Though the number of the *children* of
1Co. 1: 9. called unto the fellowship of his *Son* Jesus Christ our Lord.
15:28. then shall the *Son* also himself be subject
2Co. 1:19. For the *Son* of God, Jesus Christ, who
3: 7. so that the *children* of Israel could not
13. that the *children* of Israel could not
6:18. and ye shall be my *sons* and daughters,
Gal. 1:16. To reveal his *Son* in me, that
2:20. I live by the faith of the *Son* of God, who
3: 7. the same are the *children* of Abraham.
26. ye are all the *children* of God by faith in Christ Jesus.
4: 4. God sent forth his *Son*,
6. because ye are *sons*, God hath sent forth the Spirit of his *Son* into
7. no more a servant, but a *son*; and if a *son*, then an heir of God through Christ
22. that Abraham had two *sons*,
30. Cast out the bondwoman and her *son*. for the *son* of the bondwoman shall not be heir with the *son* of the freewoman.
Eph. 2: 2. worketh in the *children* of disobedience:
3: 5. not made known unto the *sons* of men,
4:13. and of the knowledge of the *Son* of God,
5: 6. upon the *children* of disobedience.
Col. 1:13. into the kingdom of his dear *Son*:
3: 6. on the *children* of disobedience:
1Th. 1:10. And to wait for his *Son* from heaven,
5: 5. Ye are all the *children* of light, and the *children* of the day:
2Th. 2: 3. that man of sin be revealed, the *son* of perdition;
Heb 1: 2(1). spoken unto us by (his) *Son*,
5. Thou art my *Son*, this day have I begotten thee?
— and he shall be to me a *Son*?
8. But unto the *Son* (he saith), Thy throne,
2: 6. or the *son* of man, that thou visitest him?
10. in bringing many *sons* unto glory,
3: 6. But Christ as a *son* over his own house
4:14. Jesus the *Son* of God, let us hold fast
5: 5. Thou art my *Son*, to day have I begotten thee.
8. Though he were a *Son*, yet learned he
6: 6. crucify to themselves the *Son* of God afresh,
7: 3. but made like unto the *Son* of God;
5. that are of the *sons* of Levi,

Heb 7:28. the *Son*, who is consecrated for evermore.
10:29. hath trodden under foot the *Son* of God,
11:21. blessed both the *sons* of Joseph ;
22. the departing of the *children* of Israel ;
24. to be called the *son* of Pharaoh's daughter;
12: 5. speaketh unto you as unto *children*, My *son*, despise not thou the chastening
6. scourgeth every *son* whom he receiveth.
7. God dealeth with you as with *sons* ; for what *son* is he whom the father
8. then are ye bastards, and not *sons*.
Jas. 2:21. offered Isaac his *son* upon the altar ?
1Pet.5:13. and (so doth) Marcus my *son*.
2Pet.1:17. This is my beloved *Son*, in whom I am well pleased.
1Joh.1: 3. and with his *Son* Jesus Christ.
7. the blood of Jesus Christ his *Son* cleanseth
2:22. that denieth the Father and the *Son*.
23. Whosoever denieth the *Son*, the same hath not the Father:
24. shall continue in the *Son*, and in the Father.
3: 8. For this purpose the *Son* of God was
23. That we should believe on the name of his *Son* Jesus Christ,
4: 9. God sent his only begotten *Son* into
10. sent his *Son* (to be) the propitiation
14. the Father sent the *Son* (to be) the Saviour of the world.
15. shall confess that Jesus is the *Son* of God,
5: 5. believeth that Jesus is the *Son* of God?
9. which he hath testified of his *Son*.
10. He that believeth on the *Son* of God hath
— the record that God gave of his *Son*.
11. and this life is in his *Son*.
12. He that hath the *Son* hath life ; (and) he that hath not the *Son* of God hath not life.
13. believe on the name of the *Son* of God ;
— believe on the name of the *Son* of God.
20. we know that the *Son* of God is come,
— we are in him that is true, (even) in his *Son* Jesus Christ.
2Joh. 3. and from the Lord Jesus Christ, the *Son* of the Father,
9. he hath both the Father and the *Son*.
Rev. 1:13. like unto the *Son* of man,
2:14. before the *children* of Israel, to eat
18. These things saith the *Son* of God,
7: 4. of all the tribes of the *children* of Israel.
12: 5. she brought forth a man *child*, who was to rule all nations
14:14. like unto the *Son* of man, having on
21: 7. I will be his God, and he shall be my *son*.
12. the twelve tribes of the *children* of Israel:

5208 1 843/970 cf 3586

ὕλη, *hulee.*

Jas. 3: 5. how great a *matter* a little fire kindleth! (lit. how much *material*)

5209 437 /914 5210

ὑμᾶς, *humas.*

From σύ.

Mat. 3:11. I indeed baptize *you* with water
— he shall baptize *you* with the Holy Ghost,
4:19. and I will make *you* fishers of men.
5:11. when (men) shall revile *you*, and
44. bless them that curse *you*, do good to them that hate *you*, and pray for them which despitefully use *you*, and persecute *you* ;
46. if ye love them which love *you*,
6: 8. things ye have need of, before *ye* ask him.
30. (shall he) not much more (clothe) *you*,
7: 6. and turn again and rend *you*.
15. which come to *you* in sheep's clothing,
23. I never knew *you*: depart from me,
10:13. let your peace return to *you*.
14. And whosoever shall not receive *you*,
16. Behold, I send *you* forth as sheep in
17. they will deliver *you* up to the councils, and they will scourge *you* in
19. But when they deliver *you* up,
23. But when they persecute *you* in this
40. He that receiveth *you* receiveth me,
11:28. and I will give *you* rest.
29. Take my yoke upon *you*, and
12:28. the kingdom of God is come unto *you*.
21:24. I also will ask *you* one thing,
31. into the kingdom of God before *you*.
32. For John came unto *you* in the way of
23:34. I send unto *you* prophets,
35. That upon *you* may come all
24: 4. Take heed that no man deceive *you*.
9. Then shall they deliver *you* up to be afflicted, and shall kill *you*:
25:12. I say unto you, I know *you* not.
26:32. I will go before *you* into Galilee.
55. I sat daily with *you* teaching in
28: 7. he goeth before *you* into Galilee ;
14. persuade him, and secure *you*.
Mar 1: 8. I indeed have baptized *you* with water: but he shall baptize *you* with
17. and I will make *you* to become
6:11. whosoever shall not receive *you*,
9:19. how long shall I be with *you* ?
41. whosoever shall give *you* a cup of water
11:29. I will also ask of *you* one question,
13: 5. lest any (man) deceive *you* :
9. for they shall deliver *you* up to
11. shall lead (you), and deliver *you* up,
36. Lest coming suddenly he find *you* sleeping.
14:28. I will go before *you* into Galilee.
49. I was daily with *you* in the temple
16: 7. he goeth before *you* into Galilee:
Lu. 3:16. I indeed baptize *you* with water ;
— he shall baptize *you* with the Holy Ghost and
6: 9. I will ask *you* one thing ;
22. when men shall hate *you*, and when they shall separate *you*
26. all men shall speak well of *you* !
27. do good to them which hate *you*,
28. for them which despitefully use *you*.
32. if ye love them which love *you*,
33. to them which do good to *you*,
9: 5. whosoever will not receive *you*,
41. how long shall I be with *you*,
10: 3. I send *you* forth as lambs among
6. if not, it shall turn to *you* again.
8. ye enter, and they receive *you*,
9. The kingdom of God is come nigh unto *you*.
10. and they receive *you* not, go your ways
11. the kingdom of God is come nigh unto *you*.
16. he that despiseth *you* despiseth me ;
19. shall by any means hurt *you*.
11:20. the kingdom of God is come upon *you*.
12:11. when they bring *you* unto the synagogues,
12. For the Holy Ghost shall teach *you*
14. a judge or a divider over *you* ?

Lu. 12:28. how much more (will he clothe) *you*,
13:25. I know *you* not whence ye are:
27. I know *you* not whence ye are;
28. and *you* (yourselves) thrust out.
16: 9. receive *you* into everlasting habitations.
26. from hence to *you* cannot;
19:31. if any man ask *you*, Why do ye
20: 3. I will also ask *you* one thing;
21:12. they shall lay their hands on *you*,
34. that day come upon *you* unawares.
22:31. Satan hath desired (to have) *you*, that he
35. When I sent *you* without purse,
23:15. nor yet Herod: for I sent *you* to him;
24:44. the words which I spake unto *you*, while
49. the promise of my Father upon *you*:
Joh. 3: 7. *Ye* must be born again.
4:38. I sent *you* to reap that whereon
5:42. But I know *you*, that ye have not the love
6:61. he said unto them, Doth this offend *you*?
70. Have not I chosen *you* twelve,
7: 7. The world cannot hate *you*;
8:32. the truth shall make *you* free.
36. If the Son therefore shall make *you* free,
11:15. And I am glad for *your* sakes (lit. on account of *you*) that
12:30. but for *your* sakes.
35. lest darkness come upon *you*:
13:34. love one another; as I have loved *you*,
14: 3. and receive *you* unto myself;
18. I will not leave *you* comfortless: I will come to *you*.
26. he shall teach *you* all things, and bring all things to *your* remembrance,
28. I go away, and come (again) unto *you*.
15: 9. As the Father hath loved me, so have I loved *you*:
12. love one another, as I have loved *you*.
15. Henceforth I call *you* not servants;
— but I have called *you* friends;
16. but I have chosen *you*, and ordained *you*, that ye should
18. If the world hate *you*, ye know
19. but I have chosen *you* out of the world, therefore the world hateth *you*.
20. they will also persecute *you*;
16: 2. They shall put *you* out of the synagogues·
— that whosoever killeth *you* will think
7. the Comforter will not come unto *you*;
— I will send him unto *you*.
13. he will guide *you* into all truth:
22. but I will see *you* again, and your heart
27. For the Father himself loveth *you*,
20:21. hath sent me, even so send I *you*.
Acts 1: 8. the Holy Ghost is come upon *you*:
2:22. a man approved of God among *you*
29. speak unto *you* of the patriarch David,
3:22. whatsoever he shall say unto *you*.
26. sent him to bless *you*, in turning
7:43. I will carry *you* away beyond Babylon.
13:32. And we declare unto *you* glad tidings,
40. lest that come upon *you*, which is
14:15. preach unto you that *ye* should turn
15:24. have troubled *you* with words,
25. to send chosen men unto *you*
17:22. in all things *ye* are too superstitious.
28. as certain also of your own poets (lit. of poets among *you*)
18:15. and (of) your law, (lit. the law which is among *you*)
21. but I will return again unto *you*,
19:13. saying, We adjure *you* by Jesus
36. *ye* ought to be quiet and to do

Acts 20:20. and have taught *you* publickly,
28. the Holy Ghost hath made *you* overseers,
29. shall grievous wolves enter in among *you*,
32. I commend *you* to God, and to the word
22: 1. defence (which I make) now unto *you*.
23:15. that he bring him down unto *you*
24:22. I will know the uttermost of *your* matter (lit. the things among *you*)
27:22. I exhort *you* to be of good cheer:
34. Wherefore I pray *you* to take (some) meat:
28:20. have I called for *you*, to see (you),
Ro. 1:10. by the will of God to come unto *you*.
11. For I long to see *you*, that I may
— to the end *ye* may be established;
13. Now I would not have *you* ignorant,
— I purposed to come unto *you*,
2:24. blasphemed among the Gentiles through *you*,
7: 4. that *ye* should be married to another,
10:19. I will provoke *you* to jealousy by
— by a foolish nation I will anger *you*.
11:25. that *ye* should be ignorant of
28. (they are) enemies for *your* sakes.
12: 1. I beseech *you* therefore, brethren,
2. that *ye* may prove what (is) that good,
14. Bless them which persecute *you*:
15:13. Now the God of hope fill *you* with all joy
— that *ye* may abound in hope, through the
15. as putting *you* in mind, because of the grace
22. much hindered from coming to *you*.
23. these many years to come unto *you*;
24. into Spain, I will come to *you*: for I trust to see *you* in my journey,
29. that, when I come unto *you*, I shall
30. Now I beseech *you*, brethren, for the Lor
32. That I may come unto *you* with joy by
16:16. The churches of Christ salute *you*.
17. Now I beseech *you*, brethren, mark
19. but yet I would have *you* wise unto
21. and Sosipater, my kinsmen, salute *you*.
22. who wrote (this) epistle, salute *you* in the
23. saluteth *you*. Erastus the chamberlain of the city saluteth *you*,
25. that is of power to stablish *you*
1Co. 1: 7. So that *ye* come behind in no gift;
8. Who shall also confirm *you* unto
10. Now I beseech *you*, brethren, by
2: 1. brethren, when I came to *you*,
3. And I was with *you* in weakness,
3: 2. I have fed *you* with milk, and not
4: 6. to myself and (to) Apollos for *your* sakes;
14. write not these things to shame *you*,
15. in Christ Jesus I have begotten *you*
16. Wherefore I beseech *you*, be ye
17. who shall bring *you* into remembrance of my ways which be in Christ,
18. as though I would not come to *you*.
19. But I will come to *you* shortly,
21. shall I come unto *you* with a rod,
7: 5. that Satan tempt *you* not for your
32. I would have *you* without carefulness.
10: 1. I would not that *ye* should be ignorant,
13. There hath no temptation taken *you* but
— will not suffer *you* to be tempted above
— that *ye* may be able to bear (it).
20. that *ye* should have fellowship with devils.
27. If any of them that believe not bid *you*
11: 2. Now I praise *you*, brethren, that ye
3. But I would have *you* know, that
14. Doth not even nature itself teach *you*,

1Co.11:22. shall I praise *you* in this
12: 1. I would not have *you* ignorant.
14: 5. I would that *ye* all spake with tongues,
6. if I come unto *you* speaking with tongues, what shall I profit *you*, except
36. or came it unto *you* only?
16: 5. Now I will come unto *you*, when
6. that I will abide, yea, and winter with *you*,
7. I will not see *you* now by the way; but I trust to tarry a while with *you*,
10. he may be with *you* without fear:
12. him to come unto *you* with the brethren:
15. I beseech *you*, brethren, ye know
19. The churches of Asia salute *you*. Aquila and Priscilla salute *you* much
20. All the brethren greet *you*.
2Co. 1: 8. have *you* ignorant of our trouble
12. and more abundantly to *you*-ward.
15. I was minded to come unto *you* before,
16. to come again out of Macedonia unto *you*,
18. our word toward *you* was not yea and nay.
2: 1. come again to *you* in heaviness.
2. For if I make *you* sorry, who is he then
3. having confidence in *you* all,
4. which I have more abundantly unto *you*.
5. that I may not overcharge *you* all.
7. *ye* (ought) rather to forgive (him),
8. Wherefore I beseech *you* that ye
10. for *your* sakes (forgave I it) in the person of Christ;
3: 1. epistles of commendation to *you*,
4:15. For all things (are) for *your* sakes,
6: 1. that *ye* receive not the grace of God in vain.
11. our mouth is open unto *you*,
17. and I will receive *you*,
7: 4. Great (is) my boldness of speech toward *you*,
8. For though I made *you* sorry with a letter,
— the same epistle hath made *you* sorry,
11. that *ye* sorrowed after a godly sort,
12. in the sight of God might appear unto *you*.
15. is more abundant toward *you*,
8: 6. he would also finish in *you* the same
9. yet for *your* sakes he became poor,
17. of his own accord he went unto *you*.
22. the great confidence which (I have) in *you*.
23. and fellowhelper concerning *you*:
9: 4. and find *you* unprepared,
5. that they would go before unto *you*,
8. to make all grace abound toward *you*,
14. which long after *you* for the exceeding
10: 1. Now I Paul myself beseech *you*
— being absent am bold toward *you*:
9. as if I would terrify *you* by letters.
14. as though we reached not unto *you*:
11: 2. For I am jealous over *you* with
— I have espoused *you* to one husband,
6. made manifest among *you* in all things.
9(8). And when I was present with *you*,
11. because I love *you* not?
20. if a man bring *you* into bondage,
— if a man smite *you* on the face.
12:14. I am ready to come to *you*;
— for I seek not your's, but *you*:
15. though the more abundantly I love *you*,
16. But be it so, I did not burden *you*:
— being crafty, I caught *you* with guile.
17. Did I make a gain of *you* by any of them whom I sent unto *you*?
18. Did Titus make a gain of *you*?
20. I shall not find *you* such as I would,
21. my God will humble me among *you*

2Co.13: 1. I am coming to *you*.
3. which to *you*-ward is not weak,
4. by the power of God toward *you*.
7. I pray to God that *ye* do no evil;
13(12). All the saints salute *you*.
Gal. 1: 6. removed from him that called *you*
7. there be some that trouble *you*,
9. preach any other gospel unto *you*
2: 5. of the gospel might continue with *you*.
3: 1. who hath bewitched *you*,
4:11. I am afraid of *you*, lest I have bestowed upon *you* labour in vain.
17. They zealously affect *you*, (but) not well; yea, they would exclude *you*,
18. when I am present with *you*.
20. to be present with *you* now,
5: 2. Christ shall profit *you* nothing.
7. who did hinder *you* that ye should not
8. (cometh) not of him that calleth *you*.
10. I have confidence in *you* through the Lord,
— but he that troubleth *you* shall bear
12. were even cut off which trouble *you*.
6:12. they constrain *you* to be circumcised;
13. but desire to have *you* circumcised,
Eph 1:15. after I heard of *your* faith
18. that *ye* may know what is the hope
2: 1. And *you* (hath he quickened), who were dead
3: 2. which is given me to *you*-ward:
4: 1. beseech *you* that ye walk worthy
17. that *ye* henceforth walk not
22. That *ye* put off concerning the former
5: 6. Let no man deceive *you* with vain
6:11. that *ye* may be able to stand
22. Whom I have sent unto *you*
Phi. 1: 7. because I have *you* in my heart;
— *ye* all are partakers of my grace.
8. how greatly I long after *you* all
10. That *ye* may approve things that
12. But I would *ye* should understand,
24. in the flesh (is) more needful for *you*
26. by my coming to *you* again.
27. that whether I come and see *you*,
2:25. to send to *you* Epaphroditus,
26. For he longed after *you* all,
4:21. which are with me greet *you*.
22. All the saints salute *you*,
Col. 1: 6. Which is come unto *you*,...and bringeth
10. That *ye* might walk worthy of the Lord
21. And *you*, that were sometime alienated
22. to present *you* holy and unblameable,
25. which is given to me for *you*, to fulfil
2: 1. For I would that *ye* knew what
4. beguile *you* with enticing words.
8. Beware lest any man spoil *you*
13. And *you*, being dead in your sins
16. Let no man therefore judge *you*
18. Let no man beguile *you* of your reward
4: 6. how *ye* ought to answer every man.
8. Whom I have sent unto *you*
10. my fellowprisoner saluteth *you*,
— if he come unto *you*, receive him;
12. a servant of Christ, saluteth *you*,
14. the beloved physician, and Demas, greet *you*.
1 Th. 1: 5. came not unto *you* in word only,
— we were among you for *your* sake.
7. So that *ye* were ensamples
9. manner of entering in we had unto *you*,
2: 1. know our entrance in unto *you*,
2. to speak unto *you* the gospel of God
9. we preached unto *you* the gospel

1Th. 2:11. and charged every one of *you*,
12. That *ye* would walk worthy of God, who hath called *you* unto his kingdom
18. we would have come unto *you*,
3: 2. to establish *you*, and to comfort *you* concerning your faith:
4. verily, when we were with *you*,
5. the tempter have tempted *you*,
6. as we also (to see) *you*:
9. wherewith we joy for *your* sakes
11. direct our way unto *you*.
12. the Lord make *you* to increase and
— even as we (do) toward *you*:
4: 1. we beseech *you*, brethren, and exhort
— how *ye* ought to walk
3. that *ye* should abstain from
10. but we beseech *you*, brethren, that ye
13. I would not have *you* to be ignorant,
5: 4. should overtake *you* as a thief.
12. And we beseech *you*, brethren, to know
— over you in the Lord, and admonish *you*;
14. Now we exhort *you*, brethren, warn
18. will of God in Christ Jesus concerning *you*.
23. God of peace sanctify *you* wholly;
24. Faithful (is) he that calleth *you*,
27. I charge *you* by the Lord that this
2Th. 1: 5. that *ye* may be counted worthy
6. to them that trouble *you*;
10. because our testimony among *you* was
11. that our God would count *you* worthy
2. 1. Now we beseech *you*, brethren, by the
2. That *ye* be not soon shaken in mind,
3. Let no man deceive *you*
5. when I was yet with *you*, I told
13. God hath from the beginning chosen *you*
14. Whereunto he called *you* by our gospel,
17. and stablish *you* in every good word
3: 1. and be glorified, even as (it is) with *you*:
3. is faithful, who shall stablish *you*,
4. have confidence in the Lord touching *you*,
6. that *ye* withdraw yourselves from every
10. For even when we were with *you*,
Heb 5:12. ye have need that one teach *you* again
9:20. which God hath injoined unto *you*.
13:21. Make *you* perfect in every good work
22. And I beseech *you*, brethren, suffer
23. if he come shortly, I will see *you*.
24. They of Italy salute *you*.
Jas. 2: 6. and draw *you* before the judgment seats?
7. by the which *ye* are called?
4: 2. ye have not, because *ye* ask not.
10. and he shall lift *you* up.
15. For that *ye* (ought) to say,
1Pet. 1: 4. reserved in heaven for *you*,
10. of the grace (that should come) unto *you*:
12. that have preached the gospel unto *you*
15. as he which hath called *you* is holy,
20. manifest in these last times for *you*,
25. by the gospel is preached unto *you*.
2: 9. who hath called *you* out of darkness
3:13. who (is) he that will harm *you*,
15. to every man that asketh *you*
4:14. of glory and of God resteth upon *you*:
— but on *your* part he is glorified.
5: 6. that he may exalt *you* in due time:
10. make *you* perfect, stablish, strengthen,
13. elected together with (you), saluteth *you*;
2Pet. 1:12. to put *you* always in remembrance
13. to stir *you* up by putting (you)
15. I will endeavour that *ye* may be able
2: 3. make merchandise of *you*
2Pet. 3: 8. But, beloved, be not)(ignorant of
11. what manner (of persons) ought *ye* to be
1Joh. 2:26. concerning them that seduce *you*.
27. ye need not that any man teach *you*: but as the same anointing teacheth *you*
— and even as it hath taught *you*,
3: 7. Little children, let no man deceive *you*:
13. if the world hate *you*.
2Joh. 10. If there come any unto *you*,
12. but I trust to come unto *you*,
Jude 5. I will therefore put *you* in remembrance, though *ye* once knew this,
24. able to keep *you* from falling,
Rev. 2:24. I will put upon *you* none other burden.
12:12. the devil is come down unto *you*, having great wrath, because

Note.—Some editions have given ἡμᾶς as in Gal. 4:17, 1 Pet. 1:4, &c. Some copies read αὐτούς.

5210 243 843/910 4771

ὑμεῖς, humīs.

From σύ.

Mat. 5:13. *Ye* are the salt of the earth:
14. *Ye* are the light of the world.
48. Be *ye* therefore perfect,
6: 9. After this manner therefore pray *ye*
26. Are *ye* not much better than they?
7:11. If *ye* then, being evil, know how
12. do *ye* even so to them:
9: 4. Wherefore think *ye* evil in your hearts?
10:20. For it is not *ye* that speak,
31. *ye* are of more value than many
13:18. Hear *ye* therefore the parable
14:16. They need not depart; give *ye* them to eat.
15: 3. do *ye* also transgress the commandment
5. But *ye* say, Whosoever shall say to
16. Are *ye* also yet without understanding?
16:15. But whom say *ye* that I am?
19:28. That *ye* which have followed me,
— *ye* also shall sit upon twelve thrones,
20: 4. Go *ye* also into the vineyard, and
7. Go *ye* also into the vineyard; and
21:13. but *ye* have made it a den of thieves.
32. and *ye*, when ye had seen (it),
23: 8. But be not *ye* called Rabbi: for one
— and all *ye* are brethren.
13. for *ye* neither go in (yourselves),
28. Even so *ye* also outwardly appear
32. Fill *ye* up then the measure of your
24:33. So likewise *ye*, when ye shall see all
44. Therefore be *ye* also ready:
26:31. All *ye* shall be offended because of me
27:24. of this just person: see *ye* (to it).
28: 5. Fear not *ye*: for I know that ye seek
Mar 6:31. Come *ye* yourselves apart into a
37. and said unto them, Give *ye* them to eat
7:11. But *ye* say, If a man shall say to
18. Are *ye* so without understanding also?
8:29. But whom say *ye* that I am?
11:17. but *ye* have made it a den of thieves.
26. But if *ye* do not forgive, neither
12:27. *ye* therefore do greatly err.
13: 9. But take)(heed to yourselves:
11. for it is not *ye* that speak,
23. But take *ye* heed: behold, I have
29. So *ye* in like manner, when ye
Lu. 6:31. do to you, do *ye* also to them likewise.
9:13. said unto them, Give *ye* them to eat.
20. But whom say *ye* that I am?

Lu. 9:44. Let these sayings sink down (lit. put *ye* these sayings) into your ears:
55. what manner of spirit *ye* are of.
10:23. which see the things that *ye* see:
24. to see those things which *ye* see,
11:13. If *ye* then, being evil, know how to
39. Now do *ye* Pharisees make clean
48. and *ye* build their sepulchres.
12:24. much more are *ye* better than the fowls?
29. And seek not *ye* what ye shall eat,
36. And *ye yourselves* like unto men
40. Be *ye* therefore ready also:
16:15. *Ye* are they which justify yourselves
17:10. So likewise *ye*, when ye shall have done
19:46. but *ye* have made it a den of thieves.
21:31. So likewise *ye*, when ye see these
22:26. But *ye* (shall) not (be) so: but he that
28. *Ye* are they which have continued
70. *Ye* say that I am.
24:48. And *ye* are witnesses of these things.
49. but tarry *ye* in the city of Jerusalem,
Joh. 1:26. one among you, whom *ye* know not;
3:28. *Ye* yourselves bear me witness,
4:20. and *ye* say, that in Jerusalem
22. *Ye* worship ye know not what:
32. meat to eat that *ye* know not of.
35. Say not *ye*, There are yet four months,
38. whereon *ye* bestowed no labour:
— and *ye* are entered into their labours.
5:20. than these, that *ye* may marvel.
33. *Ye* sent unto John, and he bare
34. that *ye* might be saved.
35. and *ye* were willing for a season
38. him *ye* believe not.
39. for in them *ye* think ye have eternal life:
44. How can *ye* believe, which receive
45. Moses, in whom *ye* trust.
6:67. Will *ye* also go away?
7: 8. Go *ye* up unto this feast:
28. is true, whom *ye* know not.
34. where I am, (thither) *ye* cannot come.
36. where I am, (thither) *ye* cannot come?
47. Are *ye* also deceived?
8:14. but *ye* cannot tell whence I come,
15. *Ye* judge after the flesh; I judge
21. whither I go, *ye* cannot come.
22. Whither I go, *ye* cannot come.
23. *Ye* are from beneath; I am from
— *ye* are of this world; I am not of this
31. If *ye* continue in my word,
38. and *ye* do that which ye have seen
41. *Ye* do the deeds of your father.
44. *Ye* are of (your) father the devil,
46. why do *ye* not believe me?
47. *ye* therefore hear (them) not,
49. and *ye* do dishonour me.
54. of whom *ye* say, that he is your God:
9:19. who *ye* say was born blind?
27. will *ye* also be his disciples?
30. that *ye* know not from whence he is,
10:26. But *ye* believe not, because ye are not
36. Say *ye* of him, whom the Father
11:49. *Ye* know nothing at all,
13:10. and *ye* are clean, but not all.
13. *Ye* call me Master and Lord:
14. *ye* also ought to wash one another's
15. that *ye* should do as I have done
33. Whither I go, *ye* cannot come;
34. that *ye* also love one another.
14: 3. where I am, (there) *ye* may be also.
17. but *ye* know him; for he dwelleth
19. but *ye* see me: because I live, *ye* shall
Joh. 14:20. At that day *ye* shall know that I (am) in my Father, and *ye* in me, and I in you.
15: 3. Now *ye* are clean through the word
4. no more can *ye*, except ye abide in me.
5. I am the vine, *ye* (are) the branches:
14. *Ye* are my friends, if ye do whatsoever
16. *Ye* have not chosen me, but I have
— that *ye* should go and bring forth fruit.
27. And *ye* also shall bear witness,
16:20. That *ye* shall weep and lament, but
— and *ye* shall be sorrowful, but
22. And *ye* now therefore have sorrow:
27. because *ye* have loved me, and have
18:31. Take *ye* him, and judge him
19: 6. Take *ye* him, and crucify (him):
35. he saith true, that *ye* might believe.
Acts 1: 5. but *ye* shall be baptized with the
2:15. not drunken, as *ye* suppose, seeing it is
33. which *ye* now see and hear.
36. that same Jesus, whom *ye* have crucified,
3:13. whom *ye* delivered up, and denied
14. But *ye* denied the Holy One
25. *Ye* are the children of the prophets,
4: 7. by what name, have *ye* done this?
10. whom *ye* crucified, whom God raised
5:30. whom *ye* slew and hanged on a
7: 4. into this land, wherein *ye* now dwell.
26. Sirs, *ye* are brethren; why do
51. *ye* do always resist the Holy Ghost: as your fathers (did), so (do) *ye*.
52. of whom *ye* have been now the betrayers
8:24. Pray *ye* to the Lord for me,
10:28. *Ye* know how that it is an unlawful
37. That word, (I say), *ye* know, which was
11:16. but *ye* shall be baptized with the Holy
15: 7. *ye* know how that a good while ago
19:15. and Paul I know; but who are *ye*?
20:18. *Ye* know, from the first day that I came
25. I know that *ye* all, among whom I
22: 3. zealous toward God, as *ye* all are this day.
23:15. Now therefore *ye* with the council
27:31. abide in the ship, *ye* cannot be saved.
Ro. 1: 6. Among whom are *ye* also the called of
6:11. Likewise reckon *ye* also yourselves to
7: 4. *ye* also are become dead to the law
8: 9. But *ye* are not in the flesh,
9:26. *Ye* (are) not my people;
11:30. For as *ye* in times past have not
16:17. the doctrine which *ye* have learned;
1Co. 1:30. But of him are *ye* in Christ Jesus,
3:17. the temple of God is holy, which (temple) *ye* are.
23. And *ye* are Christ's; and Christ (is)
4:10. but *ye* (are) wise in Christ; we (are) weak, but *ye* (are) strong; *ye* (are) honourable, but we (are) despised.
5: 2. And *ye* are puffed up, and have not
12. do not *ye* judge them that are within?
6: 8. Nay, *ye* do wrong, and defraud,
9: 1. are not *ye* my work in the Lord?
2. the seal of mine apostleship are *ye*
10:15. judge *ye* what I say.
12:27. Now *ye* are the body of Christ, and
14: 9. So likewise *ye*, except ye utter by
12. Even so *ye*, forasmuch as ye are zealous
16: 1. to the churches of Galatia, even so do *ye*.
6. that *ye* may bring me on my journey
16. That *ye* submit yourselves unto such,
2Co. 1:14. even as *ye* also (are) our s in the day
3: 2. *Ye* are our epistle written in our hearts,
6:13. be *ye* also enlarged.
16. for *ye* are the temple of the living God;

2Co 6:18. and *ye* shall be my sons and daughters,
8: 9. that *ye* through his poverty
9: 4. that we say not, *ye*
11: 7. abasing myself that *ye* might be exalted,
12:11. *ye* have compelled me:
13: 7. but that *ye* should do that which
9. when we are weak, and *ye* are strong:
Gal. 3:28. for *ye* are all one in Christ Jesus.
29. And if *ye* (be) Christ's, then are ye
4:12. be as I (am); for I (am) as *ye* (are):
5:13. *ye* have been called unto liberty;
6: 1. *ye* which are spiritual, restore such
Eph. 1:13. In whom *ye* also (trusted), after that
2:11. that *ye* (being) in time past Gentiles
13. *ye* who sometimes were far off
22. In whom *ye* also are builded together
4:20. But *ye* have not so learned Christ;
5:33. let every one of *you* in particular
6:21. But that *ye* also may know my
Phi. 2:18. For the same cause also do *ye* joy,
4:15. Now *ye* Philippians know also,
— concerning giving and receiving, but *ye* only.
Col. 3: 4. then shall *ye* also appear with him
7. In the which *ye* also walked some time,
8. But now *ye* also put off all these;
13. as Christ forgave you, so also (do) *ye*.
4: 1. knowing that *ye* also have a Master
16. and that *ye* likewise read the (epistle)
1Th. 1: 6. And *ye* became followers of us,
2:10. *Ye* (are) witnesses, and God (also),
14. For *ye*, brethren, became followers
— for *ye* also have suffered like things
19. (Are) not even *ye* in the presence of our
20. For *ye* are our glory and joy.
3: 8. if *ye* stand fast in the Lord.
4: 9. for *ye* yourselves are taught of God
5: 4. But *ye*, brethren, are not in darkness,
5. *Ye* are all the children of light,
2Th. 1:12. be glorified in you, and *ye* in him,
3:13. But *ye*, brethren, be not weary
Jas. 2: 6. But *ye* have despised the poor.
5: 8. Be *ye* also patient; stablish your hearts:
1Pet.2: 9. But *ye* (are) a chosen generation,
4: 1. arm)(yourselves likewise with the same mind:
2Pet.3:17. *Ye* therefore, beloved, seeing ye know
1Joh.1: 3. that *ye* also may have fellowship with us:
2:20. But *ye* have an unction from the Holy One,
24. Let that therefore abide in you, (lit. *ye* therefore let abide in you that which)
— *ye* also shall continue in the Son,
27. But the anointing which ye have received (lit. And *ye*, the anointing which, &c.)
4: 4. *Ye* are of God, little children, and
Jude 17. beloved, remember *ye* the words which
20. But *ye*, beloved, building up yourselves

5212 10 843/970 5210

ὑμέτερος, *humeteros.*

Lu. 6:20. for *your's* is the kingdom of God.
16:12. who shall give you that which is *your own?*
Joh. 7: 6. but *your* time is alway ready.
8:17. It is also written in *your* law,
15:20. kept my saying, they will keep *your's* also.
Acts27:34. meat: for this is for *your* health:
Ro. 11:31. not believed, that through *your* mercy they also (lit. have not believed *your* mercy, i. e. the mercy *to you*,)
1Co.15:31. I protest by *your* rejoicing which
2Co. 8: 8. to prove the sincerity of *your* love.
Gal. 6:13. that they may glory in *your* flesh.

5213 621 /913 5210

ὑμῖν, *humin.*

From σύ.

Mat. 3: 7. who hath warned *you* to flee
9. for I say unto *you*, that God is able
5:18. For verily I say unto *you*, Till heaven
20. For I say unto *you*, That except your
22. But I say unto *you*, That whosoever
28. But I say unto *you*, That whosoever
32. But I say unto *you*, That whosoever
34. But I say unto *you*, Swear not
39. But I say unto *you*, That ye
44. But I say unto *you*, Love your
6: 2. Verily I say unto *you*, They have their
5. Verily I say unto *you*, They have their
14. your heavenly Father will also forgive *you*:
16. Verily I say unto *you*, They have their
19. Lay not up for *yourselves* treasures
20. But lay up for *yourselves* treasures in
25. Therefore I say unto *you*, Take no thought
29. And yet I say unto *you*, That even
33. all these things shall be added unto *you*.
7: 2. it shall be measured to *you* again.
7. Ask, and it shall be given *you*; seek,
— knock, and it shall be opened unto *you*.
12. ye would that men should do to *you*,
8:10. Verily I say unto *you*, I have not found
11. And I say unto *you*, That many shall come
9:29. According to your faith be it unto *you*.
10:15. Verily I say unto *you*, It shall be
19. for it shall be given *you* in that same
20. of your Father which speaketh in *you*.
23. for verily I say unto *you*,
27. What I tell *you* in darkness,
42. verily I say unto *you*,
11: 9. I say unto *you*, and more than a prophet.
11. Verily I say unto *you*,
17. We have piped unto *you*,
— we have mourned unto *you*,
21. which were done in *you*, had been
22. But I say unto *you*, It shall be
— at the day of judgment, than for *you*.
24. But I say unto *you*, That it shall be
12: 6. But I say unto *you*, That in this place
31. Wherefore I say unto *you*.
36. But I say unto *you*, That every
13:11. Because it is given unto *you* to know
17. For verily I say unto *you*,
16:11. I spake (it) not to *you* concerning bread,
28. Verily I say unto *you*, There be some
17:12. But I say unto *you*, That Elias is
20. for verily I say unto *you*,
— nothing shall be impossible unto *you*.
18: 3. And said, Verily I say unto *you*,
10. for I say unto *you*, That in heaven
12. How think *ye*? if a man have an hundred
13. verily I say unto *you*, he rejoiceth
18. Verily I say unto *you*, Whatsoever
19. Again I say unto *you*, That if two
35. my heavenly Father do also unto *you*,
19: 8. suffered *you* to put away your wives·
9. And I say unto *you*, Whosoever shall
23. Verily I say unto *you*, That a rich man
24. And again I say unto *you*, It is easier
28. Verily I say unto *you*, That ye which
20: 4. whatsoever is right I will give *you*.
26. it shall not be so among *you*: but whosoever will be great among *you*.

Mat.20 27. whosoever will be chief among *you*,
32. What will ye that I shall do unto *you?*
21: 3. And if any (man) say ought unto *you*,
21. Verily I say unto *you*, If ye have faith,
24. I in like wise will tell *you*
27. Neither tell I *you* by what authority
28. But what think *ye?* A (certain) man
31. Verily I say unto *you*, That the publicans
43. Therefore say I unto *you*, The kingdom
22:31. which was spoken unto *you* by God,
42. What think *ye* of Christ?
23: 3. whatsoever they bid *you* observe,
13. But woe unto *you*, scribes and Pharisees,
14. Woe unto *you*, scribes and Pharisees,
15. Woe unto *you*, scribes and Pharisees,
16. Woe unto *you*, (ye) blind guides,
23. Woe unto *you*, scribes and
25. Woe unto *you*, scribes and
27. Woe unto *you*, scribes and
29. Woe unto *you*, scribes and
36. Verily I say unto *you*, All these things
38. your house is left unto *you* desolate.
39. For I say unto *you*, Ye shall not see
24: 2. verily I say unto *you*, There shall
23. if any man shall say unto *you*,
25. Behold, I have told *you* before.
26. if they shall say unto *you*,
34. Verily I say unto *you*, This generation
47. Verily I say unto *you*, That he shall
25: 9. there be not enough for us and *you:*
12. Verily I say unto *you*, I know you not.
34. inherit the kingdom prepared for *you*
40. Verily I say unto *you*, Inasmuch as
45. Verily I say unto *you*, Inasmuch as
26:13. Verily I say unto *you*, Wheresoever
15. and I will deliver him unto *you?*
21. Verily I say unto *you*, that one of you
29. But I say unto *you*, I will not drink
64. nevertheless I say unto *you*,
66. What think *ye?* They answered and
27:17. Whom will ye that I release unto *you?*
21. will ye that I release unto *you?*
28: 7. there shall ye see him: lo, I have told *you*.
20. whatsoever I have commanded *you:*
Mar 3:28. Verily I say unto *you*, All sins shall be
4:11. Unto *you* it is given to know the mystery
24. it shall be measured to *you:* and unto *you* that hear shall more be given.
6:11. Verily I say unto *you*, It shall be
8:12. verily I say unto *you*, There shall no
9: 1. Verily I say unto *you*, That there
13. But I say unto *you*, That Elias is indeed
41. verily I say unto *you*, he shall not lose
10: 3. What did Moses command *you?*
5. he wrote *you* this precept.
15. Verily I say unto *you*, Whosoever
29. Verily I say unto *you*, There is no man
36. What would ye that I should do for *you?*
43. But so shall it not be among *you:* but whosoever will be great among *you*,
11: 3. And if any man say unto *you*,
23. For verily I say unto *you*, That
24. Therefore I say unto *you*, What things
— receive (them), and *ye* shall have (them).
25. may forgive *you* your trespasses.
29. and I will tell *you* by what authority
33. Neither do I tell *you* by what authority
12:43. Verily I say unto *you*, That this poor widow
13:11. whatsoever shall be given *you* in that hour,
21. if any man shall say to *you*, Lo,
23. I have foretold *you* all things.

Mar 13:30. Verily I say unto *you*, that this generation
37. And what I say unto *you* I say unto all,
14: 9. Verily I say unto *you*, Wheresoever
13. and there shall meet *you* a man
15. And he will shew *you* a large upper room
18. Verily I say unto *you*, One of you
25. Verily I say unto *you*, I will drink
64. have heard the blasphemy: what think *ye?*
15: 9. Will ye that I release unto *you*
16: 7. there shall ye see him, as he said unto *you*.
Lu. 2:10. I bring *you* good tidings of great joy,
11. For unto *you* is born this day in
12. And this (shall be) a sign unto *you;*
3: 7. who hath warned *you* to flee from the
8. for I say unto *you*, That God is able
13. than that which is appointed *you*.
4:24. Verily I say unto *you*, No prophet
25. But I tell *you* of a truth, many
6:24. But woe unto *you* that are rich!
25. Woe unto *you* that are full!
— Woe unto *you* that laugh now!
26. Woe unto *you*, when all men shall
27. But I say unto *you* which hear,
28. Bless them that curse *you*,
31. that men should do to *you*,
32. what thank have *ye?*
33. what thank have *ye?*
34. what thank have *ye?*
38. and it shall be given unto *you;*
— it shall be measured to *you* again.
47. I will shew *you* to whom he is like·
7: 9. I say unto *you*, I have not found
26. Yea, I say unto *you*, and much more
28. For I say unto *you*, Among those that
32. We have piped unto *you*,
— we have mourned to *you*,
8:10. Unto *you* it is given to know the mysteries
9:27. But I tell *you* of a truth,
48. for he that is least among *you* all,
10: 8. eat such things as are set before *you*.
11. we do wipe off against *you:*
12. But I say unto *you*, that it shall be
13. which have been done in *you*,
14. at the judgment, than for *you*.
19. Behold, I give unto *you* power
20. that the spirits are subject unto *you;*
24. For I tell *you*, that many prophets
11: 8. I say unto *you*, Though he will not rise
9. And I say unto *you*, Ask, and it shall be given *you;*
— knock, and it shall be opened unto *you*.
41. all things are clean unto *you*.
42. But woe unto *you*, Pharisees!
43. Woe unto *you*, Pharisees! for ye
44. Woe unto *you*, scribes and Pharisees,
46. Woe unto *you* also, (ye) lawyers!
47. Woe unto *you!* for ye build the sepulchres
51. verily I say unto *you*, It shall be required
52. Woe unto *you*, lawyers! for ye have taken away
12: 4. And I say unto *you* my friends,
5. But I will forewarn *you* whom ye shall fear:
— yea, I say unto *you*, Fear him.
8. Also I say unto *you*, Whosoever
22. Therefore I say unto *you*, Take no thought
27. and yet I say unto *you*, that Solomon
31. these things shall be added unto *you*.
32. pleasure to give *you* the kingdom.
37. verily I say unto *you*, that he shall gird
44. Of a truth I say unto *you*,
51. I tell *you*, Nay; but rather division:

Lu. 13: 3. I tell *you*, Nay: but, except
5. I tell *you*, Nay: but, except
24. for many, I say unto *you*, will seek
25. he shall answer and say unto *you*,
27. I tell *you*, I know you not whence ye are;
35. your house is left unto *you* desolate: and verily I say unto *you*,
14:24. For I say unto *you*, That none of those men
15: 7. I say unto *you*, that likewise joy shall be
10. Likewise, I say unto *you*, there is joy
16: 9. And I say unto *you*, Make to yourselves
11. who will commit to *your* trust the true
12. who shall give *you* that which is your own?
17: 6 and it should obey *you*.
10. those things which are commanded *you*,
23. And they shall say to *you*, See here;
34. I tell *you*, in that night there shall be
18: 8. I tell *you* that he will avenge them
14. I tell *you*, this man went down to his
17. Verily I say unto *you*, Whosoever
29. Verily I say unto *you*, There is no man
19:26. For I say unto *you*, That unto every one
40. I tell *you* that, if these should hold
20: 8. Neither tell I *you* by what authority
21: 3. Of a truth I say unto *you*, that this poor widow hath cast in more
13. And it shall turn to *you* for a testimony.
15. For I will give *you* a mouth and wisdom, which all *your* adversaries shall not
32. Verily I say unto *you*, This generation
22:10. there shall a man meet *you*,
12. And he shall shew *you* a large upper room
16. For I say unto *you*, I will not any more
18. For I say unto *you*, I will not drink
26. but he that is greatest among *you*,
29. And I appoint unto *you* a kingdom,
37. I say unto *you*, that this that is written
67. If I tell *you*, ye will not believe:
24: 6. remember how he spake unto *you*
36. saith unto them, Peace (be) unto *you*.
44. while I was yet with *you*,

Joh. 1:51(52). Verily, verily, I say unto *you*,
2: 5. Whatsoever he saith unto *you*, do (it).
3.12. If I have told *you* earthly things,
— if I tell *you* (of) heavenly things?
4:35. behold, I say unto *you*, Lift up
5:19. Verily, verily, I say unto *you*,
24. Verily, verily, I say unto *you*,
25. Verily, verily, I say unto *you*,
38. ye have not his word abiding in *you*:
6:26. Verily, verily, I say unto *you*,
27. which the Son of man shall give unto *you*:
32. Verily, verily, I say unto *you*, Moses gave *you* not that bread from heaven; but my Father giveth *you* the true bread
36. But I said unto *you*, That ye also
47. Verily, verily, I say unto *you*,
53. Verily, verily, I say unto *you*,
63. the words that I speak unto *you*,
65. Therefore said I unto *you*,
7:19. Did not Moses give *you* the law,
22. Moses therefore gave unto *you* circumcision;
8:24. I said therefore unto *you*,
25. that I said unto *you* from the beginning.
34. Verily, verily, I say unto *you*,
37. because my word hath no place in *you*.
40. a man that hath told *you* the truth,
51. Verily, verily, I say unto *you*,
58. Verily, verily, I say unto *you*,

Joh. 9:27. I have told *you* already,
10: 1. Verily, verily, I say unto *you*,
7. Verily, verily, I say unto *you*.
25. I told *you*, and ye believed not:
26. ye are not of my sheep, as I said unto *you*.
32. works have I shewed *you* from my Father
11:56. What think *ye*, that he will not come
12:24. Verily, verily, I say unto *you*,
13:12. Know ye what I have done to *you*?
15. For I have given *you* an example, that ye should do as I have done to *you*.
16. Verily, verily, I say unto *you*,
19. Now I tell *you* before it come,
20. Verily, verily, I say unto *you*,
21. Verily, verily, I say unto *you*,
33. so now I say to *you*.
34. A new commandment I give unto *you*,
14: 2. if (it were) not (so), I would have told *you*. I go to prepare a place for *you*.
3. and prepare a place for *you*,
10. the words that I speak unto *you*
12. Verily, verily, I say unto *you*,
16. and he shall give *you* another Comforter,
17. for he dwelleth with *you*, and shall be in *you*.
20. and ye in me, and I in *you*.
25. spoken unto *you*, being (yet) present with *you*.
26. whatsoever I have said unto *you*.
27. Peace I leave with *you*, my peace I give unto *you*: not as the world giveth, give I unto *you*.
28. Ye have heard how I said unto *you*,
29. And now I have told *you* before
15: 3. which I have spoken unto *you*.
4. Abide in me, and I in *you*.
7. and my words abide in *you*,
— and it shall be done unto *you*.
11. These things have I spoken unto *you*, that my joy might remain in *you*, (lit. that my joy in *you* might remain)
14. whatsoever I command *you*.
15. I have made known unto *you*.
16. the Father in my name, he may give it *you*.
17. These things I command *you*,
20. the word that I said unto *you*,
21. But all these things will they do unto *you*
26. whom I will send unto *you* from
16: 1. These things have I spoken unto *you*,
3. these things will they do unto *you*,
4. But these things have I told *you*,
— ye may remember that I told *you* of them. And these things I said not unto *you* at
6. because I have said these things unto *you*,
7. Nevertheless I tell *you* the truth; It is expedient for *you* that I go away:
12. I have yet many things to say unto *you*,
13. he will shew *you* things to come.
14. and shall shew (it) unto *you*.
15. and shall shew (it) unto *you*.
20. Verily, verily, I say unto *you*,
23. verily, I say unto *you*, Whatsoever ye shall ask the Father in my name, he will give (it) *you*.
25. have I spoken unto *you* in proverbs:
— no more speak unto *you* in proverbs, but I shall shew *you* plainly of the Father.
26. and I say not unto *you*, that I
33. These things I have spoken unto *you*,
18: 8. I have told *you* that I am (he):
39. But *ye* have a custom, that I should release unto *you* one

Joh. 18:39. that I release unto *you*
19: 4. Behold, I bring him forth to *you*,
20:19. Peace (be) unto *you*.
21. Peace (be) unto *you*:
26. Peace (be) unto *you*.
Acts 2:14. be this known unto *you*,
39. For the promise is unto *you*,
3:14. a murderer to be granted unto *you*;
20. which before was preached unto *you*:
22. the Lord your God raise up unto *you*
26. Unto *you* first God, having raised up
4:10. Be it known unto *you* all, and to
5: 9. that ye have agreed together (lit. that it hath been agreed together by *you*)
28. Did not we straitly command *you*
38. And now I say unto *you*,
7:37. the Lord your God raise up unto *you*
13:15. if *ye* have any word of exhortation
26. whosoever among *you* feareth God, to *you* is the word of this salvation sent.
34. I will give *you* the sure mercies
38. Be it known unto *you* therefore,
— that through this man is preached unto *you*
41. though a man declare it unto *you*
46. first have been spoken to *you*:
14:15. men of like passions with *you*,
15:28. to lay upon *you* no greater burden
17: 3. whom I preach unto *you*, is Christ.
23. him declare I unto *you*.
20:20. but have shewed *you*, and have taught
26. Wherefore I take *you* to record
27. I have not shunned to declare unto *you*
32. and to give *you* an inheritance
35. I have shewed *you* all things,
22:25. Is it lawful for *you* to scourge a man
25: 5. which among *you* are able,
26: 8. be thought a thing incredible with *you*
28:28. Be it known therefore unto *you*,
Ro. 1: 7. Grace to *you* and peace from God
11. that I may impart unto *you* some
12. be comforted together with *you* by
13. I might have some fruit among *you* also.
15. am ready to preach the gospel to *you*
8: 9. that the Spirit of God dwell in *you*.
10. And if Christ (be) in *you*,
11. if the Spirit of him that raised up Jesus from the dead dwell in *you*,
— by his Spirit that dwelleth in *you*.
11:13. For I speak to *you* Gentiles, inasmuch
12: 3. to every man that is among *you*,
15: 5. grant *you* to be likeminded
15. I have written the more boldly unto *you*
32. and may with *you* be refreshed.
16: 1. I commend unto *you* Phebe our sister,
19. I am glad therefore on *your* behalf:
1Co. 1: 3. Grace (be) unto *you*, and peace,
4. which is given *you* by Jesus Christ;
6. the testimony of Christ was confirmed in *you*:
10. and (that) there be no divisions among *you*;
11. that there are contentions among *you*.
2: 1. declaring unto *you* the testimony of God.
2. to know any thing among *you*,
3: 1. speak unto *you* as unto spiritual,
3. for whereas (there is) among *you* envying,
16. the Spirit of God dwelleth in *you*?
18. If any man among *you* seemeth to be
4: 8. that we also might reign with *you*.
17. have I sent unto *you* Timotheus,
5: 1. (that there is) fornication among *you*,

1Co. 5: 9. I wrote unto *you* in an epistle
11. But now I have written unto *you*
6: 2. and if the world shall be judged by *you*,
5. I speak to *your* shame. Is it so, that there is not a wise man among *you*?
7. there is utterly a fault among *you*,
19. temple of the Holy Ghost (which is) in *you*,
7:35. may cast a snare upon *you*,
9: 2. yet doubtless I am to *you*:
11. If we have sown unto *you* spiritual
10:27. whatsoever is set before *you*,
28. But if any man say unto *you*,
11: 2. as I delivered (them) to *you*.
13. Judge in *your*selves: Is it comely
18. there be divisions among *you*;
19. there must be also heresies among *you*,
— be made manifest among *you*.
22. What shall I say to *you*?
23. which also I delivered unto *you*,
30. many (are) weak and sickly among *you*,
12: 3. Wherefore I give *you* to understand,
31. and yet shew I unto *you*
14: 6. except I shall speak to *you* either by
25. that God is in *you* of a truth.
37. the things that I write unto *you*
15: 1. I declare unto *you* the gospel which I preached unto *you*,
2. what I preached unto *you*,
3. For I delivered unto *you* first of all
12. how say some among *you* that
34. I speak (this) to *your* shame.
51. Behold, I shew *you* a mystery;
2Co. 1: 2. Grace (be) to *you* and peace
13. we write none other things unto *you*,
19. who was preached among *you* by us,
21. which stablisheth us with *you* in Christ,
2: 3. And I wrote this same unto *you*,
4. I wrote unto *you* with many tears;
4:12. death worketh in us, but life in *you*.
14. and shall present (us) with *you*.
5:12. we commend not ourselves again unto *you*, but give *you* occasion to glory on our behalf,
13. whether we be sober, (it is) for *your* cause.
6:18. And will be a Father unto *you*,
7: 7. wherewith he was comforted in *you*,
11. what carefulness it wrought in *you*,
12. Wherefore, though I wrote unto *you*,
14. we spake all things to *you* in truth,
16. that I have confidence in *you* in all (things).
8: 1. we do *you* to wit of the grace of God
10. for this is expedient for *you*,
13. other men be eased, and ye burdened: (lit. burden to *you*)
9: 1. superfluous for me to write to *you*:
14. the exceeding grace of God in *you*.
10: 1. in presence (am) base among *you*,
15. that we shall be enlarged by *you* (lit. magnified in *you*)
11: 7. because I have preached to *you* the
9. from being burdensome unto *you*,
12:12. wrought among *you* in all patience,
19. that we excuse ourselves unto *you*?
20. I shall be found unto *you* such
13: 3. but is mighty in *you*.
5. how that Jesus Christ is in *you*,
Gal. 1: 3. Grace (be) to *you* and peace from
8. preach any other gospel unto *you* than that which we have preached unto *you*,
11. But I certify *you*, brethren,

Gal. 1:20. the things which I write unto *you*,
3: 1. evidently set forth, crucified among *you*?
5. that ministereth to *you* the Spirit, and worketh miracles among *you*,
4:13. I preached the gospel unto *you*
15. for I bear *you* record, that, if
16. because I tell *you* the truth?
19. again until Christ be formed in *you*,
20. for I stand in doubt of *you*.
5: 2. Behold, I Paul say unto *you*,
21. of the which I tell *you* before,
6:11. I have written unto *you* with mine own hand.
Eph 1: 2. Grace (be) to *you*, and peace, from
17. may give unto *you* the spirit of wisdom
2:17. and preached peace to *you* which were
3:16. That he would grant *you*, according
4: 6. and through all, and in *you* all.
32. for Christ's sake hath forgiven *you*.
5: 3. not be once named among *you*,
6:21. shall make known to *you* all things:
Phi. 1: 2. Grace (be) unto *you*, and peace,
6. hath begun a good work in *you*
25. and continue with *you* all
28. but to *you* of salvation, and that of God.
29. For unto *you* it is given in the behalf
2: 5. Let this mind be in *you*, which was also
13. which worketh in *you* both to will
17. I joy, and rejoice with *you* all.
19. to send Timotheus shortly unto *you*,
3: 1. To write the same things to *you*, to me indeed (is) not grievous, but for *you* (it is) safe.
15. God shall reveal even this unto *you*.
18. of whom I have told *you* often,
Col. 1: 2. Grace (be) unto *you*, and peace, from
5. For the hope which is laid up for *you*
6. as (it doth) also in *you*, since the day
27. which is Christ in *you*, the hope of glory:
2: 5. yet am I with *you* in the spirit,
13. having forgiven *you* all trespasses,
3:13. even as Christ forgave *you*, so also (do)
16. dwell in *you* richly in all wisdom;
4: 7. shall Tychicus declare unto *you*,
9. They shall make known unto *you*
16. And when this epistle is read among *you*,
1Th. 1: 1. Grace (be) unto *you*, and peace,
5. we were among *you* for your sake.
2: 8. willing to have imparted unto *you*,
10. we behaved ourselves among *you* that
13. worketh also in *you* that believe.
3: 4. we told *you* before that we should
7. we were comforted over *you* in all
4: 2. what commandments we gave *you*
6. as we also have forewarned *you*
9. ye need not that I write unto *you*
11. as we commanded *you*;
15. For this we say unto *you* by the word
5: 1. ye have no need that I write unto *you*.
12. them which labour among *you*,
2Th. 1: 2. Grace unto *you*, and peace,
4. So that we ourselves glory in *you*
7. And to *you* who are troubled rest with us,
12. may be glorified in *you*,
2: 5. I told *you* these things?
3: 4. the things which we command *you*.
6. Now we command *you*, brethren,
7. ourselves disorderly among *you*;
9. an ensample unto *you* to follow us.
10. this we commanded *you*, that if any
11. which walk among *you* disorderly,
16. give *you* peace always by all means

Philem 3. Grace to *you*, and peace, from God
6. which is in *you* in Christ Jesus.
22. I shall be given unto *you*.
Heb 12: 5. which speaketh unto *you* as unto children,
7. God dealeth with *you* as with sons;
13: 7. who have spoken unto *you* the word of God:
17. for that (is) unprofitable for *you*.
19. that I may be restored to *you* the sooner.
21. working in *you* that which is wellpleasing
22. written a letter unto *you* in few words.
Jas. 1:26. If any man among *you* seem to be
3:13. and endued with knowledge among *you*?
4: 1. wars and fightings among *you*?
8. and he will draw nigh to *you*.
5: 3. shall be a witness against *you*,
6. (and) he doth not resist *you*.
13. Is any among *you* afflicted?
14. Is any sick among *you*?
19. if any of *you* do err from the truth,
1Pet. 1: 2. Grace unto *you*, and peace,
12. which are now reported unto *you* by
13. the grace that is to be brought unto *you*
2: 7. Unto *you* therefore which believe (he is)
3:15. a reason of the hope that is in *you*
4:12. think it not strange concerning the fiery trial which is to try *you* (lit. among *you* for trial to *you*), as though some strange thing happened unto *you*:
5: 1. The elders which are among *you*
2. the flock of God which is among *you*,
12. By Sylvanus, a faithful brother unto *you*,
14. Peace (be) with *you* all that are in Christ Jesus.
2Pet. 1: 2. Grace and peace be multiplied unto *you*
8. For if these things be in *you*,
11. an entrance shall be ministered unto *you* abundantly into
16. when we made known unto *you*
2: 1. there shall be false teachers among *you*,
13. while they feast with *you*;
3: 1. beloved, I now write unto *you*;
15. hath written unto *you*;
1Joh. 1: 2. and shew unto *you* that eternal life,
3. and heard declare we unto *you*,
4. And these things write we unto *you*,
5. and declare unto *you*, that God is light,
2: 1. these things write I unto *you*,
7. I write no new commandment unto *you*,
8. a new commandment I write unto *you*, which thing is true in him and in *you*:
12. I write unto *you*, little children, because your sins are forgiven *you*
13. I write unto *you*, fathers, because
— I write unto *you*, young men, because
— I write unto *you*, little children,
14. I have written unto *you*, fathers,
— I have written unto *you*, young men,
— and the word of God abideth in *you*,
21. I have not written unto *you* because
24. Let that therefore abide in *you*,
— from the beginning shall remain in *you*,
26. These (things) have I written unto *you*
27. received of him abideth in *you*,
4: 4. greater is he that is in *you*, than he that is in
5:13. These things have I written unto *you*
2Joh. 12. Having many things to write unto *you*,
Jude 2. Mercy unto *you*, and peace, and love.
3. diligence to write unto *you* of the common salvation, it was needful for me to write unto *you*,

Jude 16. How that they told *you* there should be
Rev. 1: 4. Grace (be) unto *you*, and peace,
2:13. martyr, who was slain among *you*,
23. and I will give unto every one of *you*
24. But unto *you* I say, and unto the rest in
18: 6. Reward her even as she rewarded *you*,
22:16. I Jesus have sent mine angel to testify
unto *you* these things

5214 4 844/970 8:489 5215
ὑμνέω, *humneo*.

Mat 26:30. And *when* they *had sung an hymn*,
Mar 14:26. And *when* they *had sung an hymn*,
Acts 16:25. and *sang praises unto* God:
Heb 2:12. *will* I *sing praise unto* thee.

5215 2 844/970 8:489 *hudeō* (to celebrate)
ὕμνος, *humnos*.

Eph. 5:19. in psalms and *hymns* and spiritual
Col. 3:16. in psalms and *hymns* and spiritual

5216 583 /913 5210
ὑμῶν, *humōn*.

From σύ.

Note.—"Of you" is the literal rendering of this word, instead of "your," and is frequently more strict to the point.

Mat. 5:11. say all manner of evil against *you*
12. for great (is) *your* reward in heaven:
— the prophets which were before *you*.
16. Let *your* light so shine before men, that
they may see *your* good works, and glorify *your* Father which is
20. That except *your* righteousness
37. But let *your* communication be,
44. Love *your* enemies, bless them
45. be the children of *your* Father
47. And if ye salute *your* brethren only,
48. even as *your* Father which is in heaven
6: 1. ye do not *your* alms before men,
— otherwise ye have no reward of *your* Father
8. for *your* Father knoweth what things
14. *your* heavenly Father will also forgive
you:
15. neither will *your* Father forgive *your* trespasses.
21. For where *your* treasure is, there will *your*
heart be also.
25. Take no thought for *your* life,
— nor yet for *your* body,
26. yet *your* heavenly Father feedeth them.
27. Which of *you* by taking thought
32. for *your* heavenly Father knoweth
7: 6. neither cast ye *your* pearls before swine,
9. Or what man is there of *you*, whom if his
11. to give good gifts unto *your* children,
— how much more shall *your* Father
9: 4. Wherefore think ye evil in *your* hearts?
11. Why eateth *your* Master with publicans
29. According to *your* faith be it unto you.
10: 9. nor silver, nor brass in *your* purses,
13. let *your* peace come upon it:
— let *your* peace return to you.
14. receive you, nor hear *your* words,
— shake off the dust of *your* feet.
20. but the Spirit of *your* Father which
speaketh

Mat. 10:29. fall on the ground without *your* Father.
30. But the very hairs of *your* head are
11:29. and ye shall find rest unto *your* souls.
12:11. What man shall there be among *you*,
27. by whom do *your* children cast
— therefore they shall be *your* judges.
13:16. But blessed (are) *your* eyes, for they see:
and *your* ears, for they hear.
15: 3. the commandment of God by *your* tradition?
6. of none effect by *your* tradition.
7. well did Esaias prophesy of *you*,
17:17. how long shall I be with *you?* how long
shall I suffer *you?*
20. Because of *your* unbelief:
24. Doth not *your* master pay tribute?
18:14. it is not the will of *your* Father
19. That if two of *you* shall agree
35. if ye from *your* hearts forgive not
19: 8. because of the hardness of *your* hearts
suffered you to put away *your* wives:
20:26. let him be *your* minister;
27. let him be *your* servant:
21: 2. into the village over against *you*,
43. shall be taken from *you*,
23. 8. for one is *your* Master, (even) Christ;
9. And call no (man) *your* father upon the
earth: for one is *your* Father,
10. for one is *your* Master, (even) Christ.
11. But he that is greatest among *you* shall
be *your* servant.
15. more the child of hell than *yourselves*.
32. Fill ye up then the measure of *your* fathers
34. shall ye scourge in *your* synagogues,
38. *your* house is left unto you desolate.
24:20. But pray ye that *your* flight be not
42. what hour *your* Lord doth come.
25: 8. Give us of *your* oil; for our lamps
26:21. that one of *you* shall betray me.
29. when I drink it new with *you* in
28:20. and, lo, I am with *you* alway,
Mar 2: 8. Why reason ye these things in *your* hearts?
6:11. shall not receive you, nor hear *you*,
— shake off the dust under *your* feet for
7: 6. Esaias prophesied of *you* hypocrites,
9. that ye may keep *your own* tradition.
13. of none effect through *your* tradition,
8:17. have ye *your* heart yet hardened?
9:19. how long shall I suffer *you?*
10: 5. For the hardness of *your* heart he wrote
43. shall be *your* minister:
44. And whosoever of *you* will be the chiefest,
11: 2. into the village over against *you*.
25. that *your* Father also which is in heaven
may forgive you *your* trespasses.
26. neither will *your* Father which is in heaven
forgive *your* trespasses.
13:18. And pray ye that *your* flight be not
14:18. One of *you* which eateth with me
Lu. 3:14. and be content with *your* wages.
4:21. is this scripture fulfilled in *your* ears.
5: 4. and let down *your* nets for a draught.
22. What reason ye in *your* hearts?
6:22. and cast out *your* name as evil,
23. *your* reward (is) great in heaven:
24. ye have received *your* consolation.
27. Love *your* enemies, do good to them
35. But love ye *your* enemies,
— and *your* reward shall be great,
36. as *your* Father also is merciful.
38. shall men give into *your* bosom.
8:25. Where is *your* faith? And they

Lu. 9: 5. shake off the very dust from *your* feet
41. shall I be with you, and suffer *you?*
44. Let these sayings sink down into *your* ears:
10: 6. *your* peace shall rest upon it:
11. Even the very dust of *your* city, which
16. He that heareth *you* heareth me;
20. because *your* names are written in heaven.
11. 5. Which of *you* shall have a friend,
11. of any of *you* that is a father,
13. to give good gifts unto *your* children:
19. by whom do *your* sons cast (them) out?
— therefore shall they be *your* judges.
39. but *your* inward part is full of ravening
46. the burdens with one of *your* fingers.
47. and *your* fathers killed them.
48. that ye allow the deeds of *your* fathers:
12: 7. hairs of *your* head are all numbered.
22. Take no thought for *your* life,
25. And which of *you* with taking thought
30. and *your* Father knoweth that ye have need
32. for it is *your* Father's good pleasure
33. Sell that *ye* have, and give alms;
34. For where *your* treasure is, there will *your* heart be also.
35. Let *your* loins be girded about,
13:15. doth not each one of *you* on the sabbath
35. *your* house is left unto you desolate:
14: 5. Which of *you* shall have an ass
28. For which of *you*, intending to build
33. whosoever he be of *you* that forsaketh not
15: 4. What man of *you*, having an hundred
16:15. but God knoweth *your* hearts:
26. between us and *you* there is a great gulf
17: 7. But which of *you*, having a servant
21. the kingdom of God is within *you*.
21:14. Settle (it) therefore in *your* hearts,
16. and (some) of *you* shall they cause
18. there shall not an hair of *your* head perish.
19. In *your* patience possess ye *your* souls.
28. lift up *your* heads; for *your* redemption draweth nigh.
34. *your* hearts be overcharged with surfeiting,
22:10. when *ye* are entered into the city,
15. to eat this passover with *you* before
19. my body which is given for *you:*
20. in my blood, which is shed for *you*.
27. I am among *you* as he that serveth.
53. When I was daily with *you* in the temple,
— but this is *your* hour, and the power
23:14. I, having examined (him) before *you*,
28. for yourselves, and for *your* children.
24:38. why do thoughts arise in *your* hearts?
Joh. 1:26. there standeth one among *you*,
4:35. Lift up *your* eyes, and look on
5:45. that I will accuse *you* to the Father: there is (one) that accuseth *you*,
6:49. *Your* fathers did eat manna
58. not as *your* fathers did eat manna,
64. there are some of *you* that believe not.
70. and one of *you* is a devil?
7:19. and (yet) none of *you* keepeth the law?
33. Yet a little while am I with *you*,
8: 7. He that is without sin among *you*,
21. and shall die in *your* sins:
24. that ye shall die in *your* sins:
— ye shall die in *your* sins.
26. many things to say, and to judge of *you:*
38. which ye have seen with *your* father.
41. Ye do the deeds of *your* father.
42. If God were *your* Father, ye would love me:

Joh. 8:44. and the lusts of *your* father ye will do.
46. Which of *you* convinceth me of sin?
54. of whom ye say, that he is *your* God:
55. I shall be a liar like unto *you:*
56. *Your* Father Abraham rejoiced to see
9:19. Is this *your* son, who ye say was
41. therefore *your* sin remaineth.
10:34. Is it not written in *your* law,
12:35. little while is the light with *you*.
13:14. have washed *your* feet; ye also ought
18. I speak not of *you* all: I know whom
21. that one of *you* shall betray me.
33. yet a little while I am with *you*.
14: 1. Let not *your* heart be troubled:
9. Have I been so long time with *you*,
16. that he may abide with *you* for ever;
27. Let not *your* heart be troubled,
30. I will not talk much with *you:*
15:11. and (that) *your* joy might be full.
16. and (that) *your* fruit should remain:
18. it hated me before (it hated) *you*.
16: 4. because I was with *you*.
5. and none of *you* asketh me,
6. sorrow hath filled *your* heart.
20. but *your* sorrow shall be turned into joy.
22. and *your* heart shall rejoice, and *your* joy no man taketh from *you*.
24. that *your* joy may be full.
26. that I will pray the Father for *you:*
18:31. and judge him according to *your* law.
19:14. he saith unto the Jews, Behold *your* King!
15. Shall I crucify *your* King?
20:17. I ascend unto my Father, and *your* Father; and (to) my God, and *your* God.
Acts 1: 7. It is not for *you* to know the times
11. which is taken up from *you* into
2:17. and *your* sons and *your* daughters shall prophesy, and *your* young men shall see visions, and *your* old men shall
22. God did by him in the midst of *you*,
38. and be baptized every one of *you*
39. is unto you, and to *your* children,
3:16. in the presence of *you* all.
17. ye did (it), as (did) also *your* rulers.
19. that *your* sins may be blotted out,
22. A prophet shall the Lord *your* God raise up unto you of *your* brethren,
26. in turning away every one of you from his iniquities. (lit. from *your* iniquities)
4:10. stand here before *you* whole.
11. set at nought of *you* builders,
19. to hearken unto *you* more than
5:28. filled Jerusalem with *your* doctrine,
6: 3. among *you* seven men of honest report,
7:37. shall the Lord *your* God raise up unto you of *your* brethren,
43. and the star of *your* god Remphan,
51. as *your* fathers (did), so (do) ye.
52. have not *your* fathers persecuted?
13:41. for I work a work in *your* days,
15:24. subverting *your* souls, saying,
17:23. and beheld *your* devotions,
18: 6. *Your* blood (be) upon *your* own heads;
14. that I should bear with *you:*
19:37. nor yet blasphemers of *your* goddess.
20:18. I have been with *you* at all seasons.
30. Also of *your* own selves shall men arise,
24:21. I am called in question by *you* this day.
25:26. I have brought him forth before *you*.
27:22. no loss of (any man's) life among *you*,
34. fall from the head of any of *you*.

Ro. 1: 8. through Jesus Christ for *you* all, that *your* faith is spoken of throughout
9. without ceasing I make mention of *you*
12. the mutual faith both of *you* and me.
6: 12. reign in *your* mortal body,
13. Neither yield ye *your* members
— and *your* members (as) instruments
14. For sin shall not have dominion over *you*:
19. because of the infirmity of *your* flesh: for as ye have yielded *your* members
— even so now yield *your* members
22. ye have *your* fruit unto holiness,
8: 11. shall also quicken *your* mortal bodies
12: 1. that ye present *your* bodies a living sacrifice,
— (which is) *your* reasonable service.
2. by the renewing of *your* mind,
18. as much as lieth in *you*,
14: 16. Let not then *your* good be evil spoken of.
15: 14. I myself also am persuaded of *you*,
24. brought on my way thitherward by *you*, if first I be somewhat filled with *your* (company).
28. I will come by *you* into Spain.
33. Now the God of peace (be) with *you* all.
16: 2. in whatsoever business she hath need of *you*;
19. For *your* obedience is come abroad
20. bruise Satan under *your* feet shortly. The grace of our Lord Jesus Christ (be) with *you*.
24. The grace of our Lord Jesus Christ (be) with *you* all.
1Co. 1: 4. I thank my God always on *your* behalf,
11. it hath been declared unto me of *you*,
12. that every one of *you* saith, I am of
13. was Paul crucified for *you*?
14. I baptized none of *you*, but Crispus and
26. For ye see *your* calling, brethren,
2: 5. That *your* faith should not stand
3: 21. For all things are *your's*;
22. or things to come; all are *your's*;
4: 3. that I should be judged of *you*,
5: 2. might be taken away from among *you*.
4. when *ye* are gathered together,
6. *Your* glorying (is) not good.
13. Therefore put away from among *yourselves*
6: 1. Dare any of *you*, having a matter
15. that *your* bodies are the members of Christ?
19. that *your* body is the temple of the
20. therefore glorify God in *your* body, and in *your* spirit, which are God's.
7: 5. tempt you not for *your* incontinency.
14. else were *your* children unclean;
28. but I spare *you*.
35. And this I speak for *your* own profit;
8: 9. liberty of *your's* become a stumblingblock
9: 11. if we shall reap *your* carnal things?
12. be partakers of (this) power over *you*,
11: 18. when *ye* come together in the church,
20. When *ye* come together therefore
24. my body, which is broken for *you*:
12: 21. to the feet, I have no need of *you*.
14: 18. I speak with tongues more than *ye* all:
26. every one of *you* hath a psalm,
34. Let *your* women keep silence in the
36. came the word of God out from *you*?
15: 14. and *your* faith (is) also vain.
17. *your* faith (is) vain: ye are yet in *your* sins.

1Co. 15. 58. that *your* labour is not in vain in the Lord.
16: 2. let every one of *you* lay by him in store,
3. them will I send to bring *your* liberality
14. Let all *your* things be done with charity.
17. for that which was lacking on *your* part
18. they have refreshed my spirit and *your's*.
23. The grace of our Lord Jesus Christ (be) with *you*.
24. My love (be) with *you* all in Christ Jesus.
2Co. 1: 6. (it is) for *your* consolation and salvation,
— (it is) for *your* consolation and
7(6). And our hope of *you* (is) stedfast,
11. *Ye* also helping together by prayer
14. that we are *your* rejoicing, even as ye
16. And to pass by *you* into Macedonia,
— and of *you* to be brought on my way
23. that to spare *you* I came not as yet
24. that we have dominion over *your* faith, but are helpers of *your* joy:
2: 3. that my joy is (the joy) of *you* all.
9. that I might know the proof of *you*,
3: 1. or (letters) of commendation from *you*?
4: 5. ourselves *your* servants for Jesus' sake.
5: 11. are made manifest in *your* consciences.
6: 12. but ye are straitened in *your own* bowels.
7: 4. great (is) my glorying of *you*:
7. *your* earnest desire, *your* mourning, *your* fervent mind toward me;
12. but that our care for *you* [many copies read, "*your* care for us"]
13. we were comforted in *your* comfort:
— his spirit was refreshed by *you* all.
14. if I have boasted any thing to him of *you*,
15. he remembereth the obedience of *you* all,
8: 7. and (in) *your* love to us, (see) that
14(13). now at this time *your* abundance
— may be (a supply) for *your* want:
16. care into the heart of Titus for *you*.
19. and (declaration of) *your* ready mind:
24. the proof of *your* love, and of our boasting on *your* behalf.
9: 2. For I know the forwardness of *your* mind, for which I boast of *you* to them of
— and *your* zeal hath provoked very many.
3. lest our boasting of *you* should be in vain
5. and make up beforehand *your* bounty,
10. and multiply *your* seed sown, and increase the fruits of *your* righteousness;
13. for *your* professed subjection unto
14. And by their prayer for *you*,
10: 6. when *your* obedience is fulfilled.
8. and not for *your* destruction,
13. a measure to reach even unto *you*.
14. for we are come as far as to *you* also
15. when *your* faith is increased,
16. the gospel in the (regions) beyond *you*,
11: 3. so *your* minds should be corrupted
8. taking wages (of them), to do *you* service.
12: 11. for I ought to have been commended of *you*:
13. was not burdensome to *you*?
14. and I will not be burdensome to *you*: for I seek not *your's*, but you:
15. gladly spend and be spent for *you*; (lit. for *your* souls)
19. dearly beloved, for *your* edifying.
13: 9. this also we wish, (even) *your* perfection.
11. the God of love and peace shall be with *you*.
14(13). (be) with *you* all. Amen
Gal. 3: 2. This only would I learn of *you*.
4: 6. the Spirit of his Son into your hearts

Gal. 4:12. Brethren, I beseech *you*, be as I (am);
15. Where is then the blessedness *ye* spake of? (lit. *your* blessedness)
— would have plucked out *your* own eyes,
16. Am I therefore become *your* enemy,
6:18. (be) with *your* spirit. Amen.
Eph. 1:13. the gospel of *your* salvation:
16. Cease not to give thanks for *you*, making mention of *you* in my prayers;
18. The eyes of *your* understanding being
2: 8. and that not of *yourselves*: (it is) the gift
3: 1. the prisoner of Jesus Christ for *you* Gentiles,
13. faint not at my tribulations for *you*, which is *your* glory.
17. That Christ may dwell in *your* hearts
4: 4. ye are called in one hope of *your* calling;
23. And be renewed in the spirit of *your* mind;
26. sun go down upon *your* wrath:
29. proceed out of *your* mouth,
31. be put away from *you*, with all malice:
5:19. and making melody in *your* heart to
6: 1. Children, obey *your* parents in the Lord:
4. provoke not *your* children to wrath:
5. in singleness of *your* heart, as unto Christ;
9. knowing that *your* Master also is in heaven;
14. having *your* loins girt about with truth,
22. and (that) he might comfort *your* hearts.
Phi. 1: 3. upon every remembrance of *you*,
4. in every prayer of mine for *you* all
5. For *your* fellowship in the gospel
7. meet for me to think this of *you* all,
9. that *your* love may abound yet more
19. to my salvation through *your* prayer,
25. for *your* furtherance and joy of faith;
26. That *your* rejoicing may be more abundant
27. I may hear of *your* affairs,
2:17. and service of *your* faith,
19. of good comfort, when I know *your* state.
20. who will naturally care for *your* state.
25. and fellowsoldier, but *your* messenger,
30. to supply *your* lack of service toward me.
4: 5. Let *your* moderation be known unto all men.
6. let *your* requests be made known unto God.
7. shall keep *your* hearts and minds through Christ Jesus.
9. and the God of peace shall be with *you*.
17. fruit that may abound to *your* account.
18. the things (which were sent) from *you*,
19. my God shall supply all *your* need
23. The grace of our Lord Jesus Christ (be) with *you* all.
Col. 1: 3. praying always for *you*,
4. Since we heard of *your* faith
7. who is for *you* a faithful minister
8. unto us *your* love in the Spirit.
9. do not cease to pray for *you*,
24. Who now rejoice in my sufferings for *you*,
2: 1. what great conflict I have for *you*,
5. joying and beholding *your* order, and the stedfastness of *your* faith
13. and the uncircumcision of *your* flesh,
3: 3. and *your* life is hid with Christ in God.
5. Mortify therefore *your* members
8. filthy communication out of *your* mouth.
15. let the peace of God rule in *your* hearts,
16. singing with grace in *your* hearts
21. Fathers, provoke not *your* children
4: 6. Let *your* speech (be) alway with grace,
8. that he might know *your* estate, and comfort *your* hearts;

Col. 4: 9. and beloved brother, who is (one) of *you*.
12. Epaphras, who is (one) of *you*, a servant of
— always labouring fervently for *you* in
13. that he hath a great zeal for *you*,
18. Grace (be) with *you*. Amen.
1Th. 1: 2. We give thanks to God always for *you* all, making mention of *you* in our prayers;
3. *your* work of faith, and labour of love,
4. Knowing, brethren beloved, *your* election
8. For from *you* sounded out the word
— *your* faith to God-ward is spread abroad;
2: 6. glory, neither of *you*, nor (yet) of others,
7. But we were gentle among *you*,
8. So being affectionately desirous of *you*,
9. be chargeable unto any of *you*,
11. and charged every one of *you*,
17. being taken from *you* for a short time
— to see *your* face with great desire.
3: 2. to comfort you concerning *your* faith:
5. I sent to know *your* faith,
6. when Timotheus came from *you* unto us, and brought us good tidings of *your* faith and charity,
7. in all our affliction and distress by *your* faith:
9. can we render to God again for *you*,
10. that we might see *your* face,
— that which is lacking in *your* faith?
13. he may stablish *your* hearts unblameable
4: 3. is the will of God, (even) *your* sanctification,
4. That every one of *you* should know how
11. and to work with *your* own hands,
5:12. and are over *you* in the Lord,
23. the very God of peace sanctify *you* wholly;
28. The grace of our Lord Jesus Christ (be) with *you*.
2Th. 1: 3. to thank God always for *you*,
— that *your* faith groweth exceedingly, and the charity of every one of *you* all
4. for *your* patience and faith in all *your* persecutions and tribulations
11. also we pray always for *you*,
2:13. to give thanks alway to God for *you*,
17. Comfort *your* hearts, and stablish
3: 5. And the Lord direct *your* hearts
8. not be chargeable to any of *you*:
16. The Lord (be) with *you* all.
18. The grace of our Lord Jesus Christ (be) with *you* all.
2Ti. 4:22. Grace (be) with *you*. Amen.
Tit. 2: 8. having no evil thing to say of *you*.
3:15. Grace (be) with *you* all. Amen.
Philem 22. I trust that through *your* prayers
25. (be) with *your* spirit. Amen.
Heb 3: 8. Harden not *your* hearts, as in
9. When *your* fathers tempted me,
12. lest there be in any of *you*
13. lest any of *you* be hardened
15. harden not *your* hearts, as in
4: 1. any of *you* should seem to come short of it.
7. harden not *your* hearts.
6: 9. persuaded better things of *you*,
10. unrighteous to forget *your* work
11. we desire that every one of *you* do shew
9:14. purge *your* conscience from dead works
10:34. the spoiling of *your* goods.
35. Cast not away therefore *your* confidence,
12: 3. and faint in *your* minds.
13. And make straight paths for *your* feet,
13: 7. which have the rule over *you*,

Heb 13:17. Obey them that have the rule over *you*,
— for they watch for *your* souls,
24. all them that have the rule over *you*,
25. Grace (be) with *you* all. Amen.
Jas 1: 3. that the trying of *your* faith worketh
5. If any of *you* lack wisdom,
21. which is able to save *your* souls.
2: 2. if there come unto *your* assembly
6. Do not rich men oppress *you*, and
16. And one of *you* say unto them,
3:14. envying and strife in *your* hearts,
4: 1. of *your* lusts that war in *your* members?
3. ye may consume (it) upon *your* lusts.
7. and he will flee from *you*.
9. let *your* laughter be turned to mourning,
14. For what (is) *your* life? It is even a vapour,
16. now ye rejoice in *your* boastings:
5: 1. for *your* miseries that shall come
2. *Your* riches are corrupted, and *your* garments are motheaten.
3. *Your* gold and silver is cankered;
— and shall eat *your* flesh as it were fire.
4. who have reaped down *your* fields, which is of *you* kept back by fraud,
5. ye have nourished *your* hearts, as in
8. stablish *your* hearts: for the coming
12. but let *your* yea be yea;
1Pet. 1: 7. That the trial of *your* faith,
9. Receiving the end of *your* faith,
13. gird up the loins of *your* mind,
14. to the former lusts in *your* ignorance:
17. pass the time of *your* sojourning (here)
18. from *your* vain conversation
21. that *your* faith and hope might be in God.
22. Seeing ye have purified *your* souls
2:12. Having *your* conversation honest among
— whereas they speak against *you*
25. unto the Shepherd and Bishop of *your*
3: 2. While they behold *your* chaste conversation
7. that *your* prayers be not hindered.
15. sanctify the Lord God in *your* hearts:
16. whereas they speak evil of *you*,
— *your* good conversation in Christ.
4: 4. that *ye* run not with (them) to
15. But let none of *you* suffer as
5: 7. Casting all *your* care upon him; for he careth for *you*.
8. because *your* adversary the devil,
9. are accomplished in *your* brethren
2Pet. 1: 5. add to *your* faith virtue;
10. to make *your* calling and election
19. the day star arise in *your* hearts:
3: 1. I stir up *your* pure minds by way of
1Joh. 1: 4. that *your* joy may be full. [some copies, "*our* joy"]
2Joh. 3. Grace be with *you*, [some copies "with *us*"]
Jude 12. These are spots in *your* feasts of charity,
20. building up yourselves on *your* most holy faith,
Rev. 1: 9. I John, who also am *your* brother,
2:10. shall cast (some) of *you* into prison,
23. unto every one of you according to *your* works.
18:20. for God hath avenged *you* (lit. judged *your* judgment)
22:21. The grace of our Lord Jesus Christ (be) with *you* all.

5217 81 844/970 8:504 5259,71

ὑπάγω, *hupago*.

Mat. 4:10. *Get* thee *hence*, Satan: for it is written,
5:24. thy gift before the altar, and *go* thy *way*,
41. to go a mile, *go* with him twain.
8: 4. but *go* thy *way*, shew thyself to the priest,
13. *Go* thy *way*; and as thou hast believed,
32. And he said unto them, *Go*. And
9: 6. thy bed, and *go* unto thine house.
13:44. and for joy thereof *goeth* and selleth
16:23. unto Peter, *Get* thee behind me, Satan:
18:15. *go* and tell him his fault between thee
19:21. *go* (and) sell that thou hast, and give
20: 4. *Go* ye also into the vineyard,
7. *Go* ye also into the vineyard;
14. Take (that) thine (is), and *go* thy *way*:
21:28. Son, *go* work to day in my vineyard.
26:18. *Go* into the city to such a man,
24. The Son of man *goeth* as it is written
27:65. Ye have a watch: *go* your *way*,
28:10. Be not afraid: *go* tell my brethren
Mar 1:44. but *go* thy *way*, shew thyself to the priest,
2:11. and *go* thy *way* into thine house.
5:19. *Go* home to thy friends, and tell them
34. *go* in peace, and be whole of thy plague.
6:31. there were many coming and *going*,
33. And the people saw them *departing*,
38. How many loaves have ye? *go* and see.
7:29. For this saying *go* thy *way*; the devil
8:33. *Get* thee behind me, Satan: for thou
10:21. *go* thy *way*, sell whatsoever thou hast,
52. *Go* thy *way*; thy faith hath made thee whole.
11: 2. *Go* your *way* into the village over
14:13. *Go* ye into the city, and there shall meet
21. The Son of man indeed *goeth*,
16: 7. But *go* your *way*, tell his disciples
Lu. 4: 8. *Get* thee behind me, Satan: for it is written,
8:42. But as he *went* the people thronged him.
10: 3. *Go* your *ways*: behold, I send you
12:58. When thou *goest* with thine adversary
17:14. as they *went*, they were cleansed.
19:30. *Go* ye into the village over against (you),
Joh. 3: 8. tell whence it cometh, and whither it *goeth*:
4:16. *Go*, call thy husband, and come hither.
6:21. was at the land whither they *went*.
67. Will ye also *go away*?
7: 3. Depart hence, and *go* into Judæa.
33. and (then) I *go* unto him that sent me.
8:14. whence I came, and whither I *go*;
— whence I come, and whither I *go*.
21. I *go* my *way*, and ye shall seek me,
— whither I *go*, ye cannot come.
22. Whither I *go*, ye cannot come.
9: 7. *Go*, wash in the pool of Siloam,
11. *Go* to the pool of Siloam, and wash:
11: 8. and *goest* thou thither again?
31. She *goeth* unto the grave to weep there.
44. Loose him, and let him *go*.
12:11. by reason of him many of the Jews *went away*, and believed on Jesus.
35. knoweth not whither he *goeth*.
13: 3. that he was come from God, and *went* to God;
33. Whither I *go*, ye cannot come;
36. Lord, whither *goest* thou?
— Whither I *go*, thou canst not follow me now;
14: 4. And whither I *go* ye know, and the way
5. Lord, we know not whither thou *goest*;
28. I *go away*, and come (again) unto you.
15:16. that ye should *go* and bring forth fruit,

3 D 2

Joh.16: 5. I go my way to him that sent me; and none of you asketh me, Whither *goest* thou?
10. because I *go* to my Father,
16. because I *go* to the Father.
17. and, Because I *go* to the Father?
18: 8. if therefore ye seek me, let these *go* their *way*.
21: 3. Simon Peter saith unto them, I *go* a fishing.
Jas. 2:16. say unto them, *Depart* in peace,
1Joh 2:11. and knoweth not whither he *goeth*,
Rev.10: 8. *Go* (and) take the little book which
13:10. into captivity shall *go* into captivity:
14: 4. follow the Lamb whithersoever he *goeth*.
16: 1. *Go* your *ways*, and pour out the vials
17: 8. shall ascend out of the bottomless pit, and *go* into perdition:
11. and *goeth* into perdition.

5218 15 844/971 1:216 5219

ὑπακοή, *hupakoee*.

Ro. 1: 5. for *obedience* to the faith among all nations,
5:19. so by the *obedience* of one shall many
6:16. ye yield yourselves servants to *obey*,
— or of *obedience* unto righteousness?
15:18. to make the Gentiles obedient, (lit. for *obedience* of the Gentiles)
16:19. For your *obedience* is come abroad
26. to all nations for the *obedience* of faith:
2Co. 7:15. whilst he remembereth the *obedience* of you all, how with fear
10: 5. every thought to the *obedience* of Christ;
6. to revenge all disobedience, when your *obedience* is fulfilled.
Philem 21. Having confidence in thy *obedience*
Heb. 5: 8. yet learned he *obedience* by the things which
1Pet. 1: 2. unto *obedience* and sprinkling of the blood of Jesus Christ:
14. As *obedient* children, not fashioning
22. Seeing ye have purified your souls in *obeying* the truth (lit. through *obedience* of the truth)

5219 21 845/971 1:216 5259,191

ὑπακούω, *hupakouo*.

Mat. 8:27. the winds and the sea *obey* him!
Mar 1:27. and they do *obey* him.
4:41. the wind and the sea *obey* him?
Lu. 8:25. and water, and they *obey* him.
17: 6. planted in the sea; and it should *obey* you.
Acts 6: 7. a great company of the priests *were obedient to* the faith.
12:13. a damsel came *to hearken*, (lit. *to answer*)
Ro. 6:12. that ye should *obey* it in the lusts
16. his servants ye are to whom ye *obey*;
17. but ye have *obeyed* from the heart that form of doctrine
10:16. But they *have* not all *obeyed* the gospel.
Eph. 6: 1. Children, *obey* your parents in the Lord:
5. Servants, *be obedient to* them that are
Phi. 2:12. my beloved, as ye *have* always *obeyed*,
Col. 3:20. Children, *obey* (your) parents in all things:
22. Servants, *obey* in all things (your) masters
2Th. 1: 8. on them that know not God, and *that obey* not the gospel of
3:14. And if any man *obey* not our word
Heb 5: 9. salvation unto all them *that obey* him;
11: 8. *obeyed*; and he went out, not knowing

1Pet. 3: 6. Even as Sara *obeyed* Abraham, calling him lord:

5220 1 845/971 5259,473

ὕπανδρος, *hupandros*.

Ro. 7: 2. For the woman *which hath an husband*

5221 5 845/972 3:623 5257,473

ὑπαντάω, *hupantao*.

Mat. 8:28. there *met* him two possessed with
Lu. 8:27. there *met* him out of the city a
Joh.11:20. *went and met* him: but Mary sat (still)
30. was in that place where Martha *met* him.
12:18. For this cause the people also *met* him,

5222 1 845/972 3:623 5221

ὑπάντησις, *hupanteesis*.

Joh.12:13. and went forth to *meet* him,

5223 2 845/972 5225

ὕπαρξις, *huparxis*.

Acts 2:45. sold their possessions and *goods*, and parted them to all
Heb 10:34. ye have in heaven a better and an enduring *substance*.

5224 14 845/972 5225

ὑπάρχοντα, *huparkonta*.

The participle used as a substantive.

Mat.19:21. go (and) sell *that* thou *hast*,
24:47. make him ruler over all his *goods*.
25:14. and delivered unto them his *goods*.
Lu. 8: 3. ministered unto him of their *substance*.
11:21. his *goods* are in peace:
12:15. in the abundance of the *things which* he *possesseth*.
33. Sell *that* ye *have*, and give alms;
44. make him ruler over all *that* he *hath*.
14:33. that forsaketh not all *that* he *hath*,
16: 1. that he had wasted his *goods*.
19: 8. Lord, the half of my *goods* I give to the poor;
Acts 4:32. that ought of the *things* which he *possessed*
1Co.13: 3. though I bestow all my *goods* to feed
Heb 10:34. took joyfully the spoiling of your *goods*,

5225 48 845/972 5259,756

ὑπάρχω, *huparko*.

Lu. 7:25. and *live* delicately, are in kings' courts.
8:41. and he *was* a ruler of the synagogue:
9:48. for he *that is* least among you all,
11:13. If ye then, *being* evil, know how to give
16:14. the Pharisees also, *who were* covetous,
23. he lift up his eyes, *being* in torments,
23:50. a man named Joseph,)(a counsellor;
Acts 2:30. Therefore *being* a prophet, and knowing
3: 2. And a certain man)(lame from his
6. Silver and gold *have* I none; (lit. *is* not to me)
4:34. Neither *was* there any among them that lacked: for as many as *were* possessors of lands
37. *Having* land (lit. land *being* to him), sold (it),
5: 4. *was* it not in thine own power?
7:55. But he, *being* full of the Holy Ghost,

Acts 8:16. only they *were* baptized in the name of
10:12. Wherein *were* all manner of fourfooted
14: 8. *being* a cripple from his mother's womb,
16: 3. that his father *was* a Greek
20. These men, *being* Jews, do exceedingly trouble
37. us openly uncondemned, *being* Romans,
17:24. *seeing that* he *is* Lord of heaven and
27. though he *be* not far from every one of us:
29. *Forasmuch* then *as* we *are* the offspring of God, we ought not
19:36. ye ought *to be* quiet, and to do nothing
40. there *being* no cause whereby we may give
21:20. and they *are* all zealous of the law:
22: 3. *and was* zealous toward God, as ye
27:12. And *because* the haven *was* not commodious
21. But after (lit. but there *being*) long abstinence
34. for this *is* for your health:
28: 7. In the same quarters *were* possessions
18. because there *was* no cause of death in me.
Ro. 4:19. when he *was* about an hundred years old,
1 Co. 7:26. that this *is* good for the present distress,
11: 7. *forasmuch as* he *is* the image and
18. I hear that there *be* divisions among you;
12:22. which seem *to be* more feeble,
2Co. 8:17. but *being* more forward, of his own accord
12:16. *being* crafty, I caught you with guile.
Gal. 1:14. *being* more exceedingly zealous
2:14. If thou, *being* a Jew, livest after the
Phi. 2: 6. Who, *being* in the form of God,
3:20. For our conversation *is* in heaven;
Jas. 2:15. If a brother or sister *be* naked,
2Pet 1: 8. For *if* these things *be* in you, and abound,
2:19. themselves *are* the servants of corruption:
3:11. what manner (of persons) ought ye *to be*

See also ὑπάρχοντα.

5226 1 846/972 5259
eikō (to yield)

ὑπείκω, hupīko.

Heb 13:17. and *submit* your*selves*: for they watch

5227 2 846/972 5259,1727

ὑπεναντίος, hupenantios.

Col. 2:14. which was *contrary* to us,
Heb10:27. which shall devour the *adversaries*.

5228 160 846/972 8:507

ὑπέρ, huper.

Governing a genitive case, except where ᵃ is placed to mark the accusative: and six elliptical passages, marked †.

Mat. 5:44. and pray *for* them which despitefully
10:24. The disciple is not *above*ᵃ (his) master, nor the servant *above*ᵃ his lord.
37. loveth father or mother *more than*ᵃ me
— loveth son or daughter *more than*ᵃ me
Mar 9:40. that is not against us is *on* our *part*.
Lu. 6:28. and pray *for* them which despitefully
40. The disciple is not *above*ᵃ his master:
9:50. that is not against us is *for* us.
16: 8. wiser *than*ᵃ the children of light.
22:19. my body which is given *for* you:
20. my blood, which is shed *for* you.
Joh. 6:51. I will give *for* the life of the world.
10:11. giveth his life *for* the sheep.
15. I lay down my life *for* the sheep.
11: 4. but *for* the glory of God, that the Son
50. that one man should die *for* the people,
51. that Jesus should die *for* that nation;
Joh. 11:52. And not *for* that nation only, but that
13:37. I will lay down my life *for* thy *sake*.
38. thou lay down thy life *for* my *sake*?
15:13. lay down his life *for* his friends.
17:19. And *for* their *sakes* I sanctify myself,
18:14. one man should die *for* the people.
Acts 5:41. worthy to suffer shame *for* his name.
8:24. Pray ye to the Lord *for* me,
9:16. he must suffer *for* my name's *sake*.
12: 5. of the church unto God *for* him.
15:26. *for* the name of our Lord Jesus Christ.
21:13. *for* the name of the Lord Jesus.
26. should be offered *for* every one of them.
26: 1. Thou art permitted to speak *for* thyself.
13. *above*ᵃ the brightness of the sun,
Ro. 1: 5. among all nations, *for* his name.
8. through Jesus Christ *for* you all,
5: 6. Christ died *for* the ungodly.
7. For scarcely *for* a righteous man will one die: yet peradventure *for* a good man some
8. we were yet sinners, Christ died *for* us.
8:26. the Spirit itself maketh intercession *for*
27. he maketh intercession *for* the saints
31. If God (be) *for* us, who (can be) against us?
32. but delivered him up *for* us all,
34. who also maketh intercession *for* us.
9: 3. accursed from Christ *for* my brethren,
27. Esaias also crieth *concerning* Israel,
10: 1. and prayer to God *for* Israel is,
14:15. with thy meat, *for* whom Christ died.
15: 8. of the circumcision *for* the truth of God,
9. the Gentiles might glorify God *for* (his) mercy;
30. in (your) prayers to God *for* me;
16: 4. Who have *for* my life laid down their
1Co. 1:13. was Paul crucified *for* you?
4: 6. not to think (of men) *above*ᵃ that which is written,
— be puffed up *for* one against another.
5: 7. Christ our passover is sacrificed *for* us:
10:13. to be tempted *above*ᵃ that ye are able;
30. *for* which I give thanks?
11:24. my body, which is broken *for* you:
12:25. have the same care one *for* another.
15: 3. how that Christ died *for* our sins
29. which are baptized *for* the dead,
— why are they then baptized *for* the dead?
2Co. 1: 6. *for* your consolation and
— *for* your consolation and
7(6). And our hope *of* you (is) stedfast,
8. have you ignorant *of* our trouble
— pressed out of measure, *above*ᵃ strength,
11. helping together by prayer *for* us,
— may be given by many *on* our *behalf*.
5:12. occasion to glory *on* our *behalf*,
14(15). that if one died *for* all, then were all dead:
15. And (that) he died *for* all, that they
— but unto him which died *for* them,
20. we are ambassadors *for* Christ, as
— we pray (you) *in* Christ's *stead*, be ye
21. made him (to be) sin *for* us, who knew no sin;
7: 4. great (is) my glorying *of* you:
7. your fervent mind *toward* me;
12. but that our care *for* you [many copies read, "your care *for* us"]
14. boasted any thing to him *of* you,
8: 3. yea, and *beyond*ᵃ (their) power
16. care into the heart of Titus *for* you.

2Co. 8:23. Whether (any do enquire) *of* Titus,
24. and of our boasting *on* your *behalf.*
9: 2. for which I boast *of* you to them
3. lest our boasting *of* you should be in vain
14. And by their prayer *for* you,
11: 5. a whit behind the very chiefest apostles. (lit. those *above*† very apostles)
23. I speak as a fool I (am) *more;*†
12: 5. *Of* such an one will I glory: yet *of* myself I will not glory, but in
6. *above*[a] that which he seeth me (to be),
8. *For* this thing I besought the Lord thrice,
10. in distresses *for* Christ's *sake:*
11. behind the very chiefest apostles, (lit. those *above,*† &c.)
13. you were inferior *to*[a] other churches,
15. gladly spend and be spent *for* you; (lit. *for* the souls of you)
19. all things, dearly beloved, *for* your edifying.
13: 8. against the truth, but *for* the truth.
Gal. 1: 4. Who gave himself *for* our sins,
14. *above*[a] many my equals in mine own nation,
2:20. and gave himself *for* me.
3:13. being made a curse *for* us:
Eph 1:16. Cease not to give thanks *for* you,
22. the head *over*[a] all (things) to the church,
3: 1. prisoner of Jesus Christ *for* you Gentiles,
13. at my tribulations *for* you,
20. to do *exceeding*† abundantly *above*[a] all that we ask or think,
5: 2. and hath given himself *for* us
20. thanks always *for* all things unto God
25. loved the church, and gave himself *for* it;
6:19. And *for* me, that utterance may be given
20. *For* which I am an ambassador in bonds:
Phi. 1: 4. in every prayer of mine *for* you all
7. to think this *of* you all,
29. it is given *in the behalf of* Christ,
— but also to suffer *for* his *sake;*
2: 9. a name which is *above*[a] every name:
13. and to do *of* (his) good pleasure.
4:10. your care *of* me hath flourished again;
Col. 1: 7. who is *for* you a faithful minister
9. do not cease to pray *for* you,
24. rejoice in my sufferings *for* you,
— in my flesh *for* his body's *sake,*
4:12. labouring fervently *for* you in prayers,
13. that he hath a great zeal *for* you,
1Th. 3:10. Night and day praying *exceedingly*† (ὑπὲρ ἐκπερισσοῦ)
5:10. Who died *for* us, that, whether we wake
13. esteem them *very*† highly in love
2Th. 1: 4. *for* your patience and faith in all
5. kingdom of God, *for* which ye also suffer:
2: 1. we beseech you, brethren, *by* the coming of our Lord
1Ti. 2: 1. be made *for* all men;
2. *For* kings, and (for) all that are in
6. Who gave himself a ransom *for* all,
Tit. 2:14. Who gave himself *for* us, that he
Philem 13. that *in* thy *stead* he might have ministered
16. Not now as a servant, but *above*[a] a servant,
21. thou wilt also do *more than*[a] I say.
Heb 2: 9. should taste death *for* every man.
4:12. and sharper *than*[a] any twoedged sword,
5: 1. is ordained *for* men in things (pertaining) to God, that he may offer both gifts and sacrifices *for* sins:
3. so also for himself, to offer *for* sins.
6:20. the forerunner is *for* us entered,
7:25. liveth to make intercession *for* them.
Heb 7:27. first *for* his own sins, and then
9: 7. which he offered *for* himself, and (for) the errors
24. to appear in the presence of God *for* us:
10:12. after he had offered one sacrifice *for* sins,
13:17. for they watch *for* your souls,
Jas. 5:16. and pray one *for* another,
1Pet. 2:21. because Christ also suffered *for* us,
3:18. the just *for* the unjust, that he might bring
4: 1. as Christ hath suffered *for* us in the flesh,
1Joh. 3:16. because he laid down his life *for* us:
— to lay down (our) lives *for* the brethren.
3Joh. 7. Because that *for* his name's *sake* they went forth,

---

5229 3 847/974 5228,142
ὑπεραίρομαι, *huperairomai.*

2Co.12: 7. lest I *should be exalted above measure*
— lest I *should be exalted above measure.*
2Th. 2: 4. Who opposeth and *exalteth* him*self* above all

5230 1 847/974 5228,rt 188
ὑπέρακμος, *huperakmos.*

1Co. 7:36. if she pass the flower of (her) age, (lit. be *past prime*)

5231 3 847/974 5228,507
ὑπεράνω, *huperano.*

Eph. 1:21. *Far above* all principality, and
4:10. that ascended up *far above* all heavens,
Heb 9: 5. And *over* it the cherubims of glory

5232 1 847/974 8:517 5228,837
ὑπεραυξάνω, *huperauxano.*

2Th. 1: 3. that your faith *groweth exceedingly,*

5233 1 848/974 5:736 5228
ὑπερβαίνω, *huperbaino.* rt 939

1Th. 4: 6. That no (man) *go beyond* and defraud

5234 1 848/974 8:520 5235
ὑπερβαλλόντως, *huperballontōs.*

2Co.11:23. in stripes *above measure,*

5235 5 848/974 8:520 5228,906
ὑπερβάλλω, *huperballo.*

2Co. 3:10. by reason of the glory *that excelleth.*
9:14. for the *exceeding* grace of God in you.
Eph. 1:19. And what (is) the *exceeding* greatness of his power to us-ward
2: 7. shew the *exceeding* riches of his grace
3:19. the love of Christ, *which passeth* knowledge,

5236 8 848/975 8:520 5235
ὑπερβολή, *huperbolee.*

Ro. 7:13. might become *exceeding* (καθ' ὑπ. lit. of *excess*) sinful.
1Co.12:31. shew I unto you a *more excellent* way. (κ.ὑ.)
2Co. 1: 8. we were pressed *out of measure,* (κ. ὑ.)
4: 7. that the *excellency* of the power may be
17. worketh for us a *far more exceeding* (κ. ὑ. εἰς ὑ.)
12: 7. through the *abundance* of the revelations,
Gal. 1:13. *beyond measure* (κ. ὑ.) I persecuted the church

5237 1 848/975 5228,1492
ὑπερείδω, *huperīdo.*

Acts17:30. the times of this ignorance God *winked at*; but

5238 1 848/975 2:460 5228,1565
ὑπερέκεινα, *huperekīna.*

2Co.10:16. the gospel in the (regions) *beyond* you,

5239 1 848/975 5228,1614
ὑπερεκτείνω, *huperektīno.*

2Co.10:14. For we *stretch* not ourselves *beyond* (our measure),

5240 1 848/975 5228,1632
ὑπερεκχύνομαι, *huperekkunomai.*

Lu. 6:38 and *running over*, shall men give

5241 1 848/975 8:238 5228,1793
ὑπερεντυγχανω, *huperentunkano.*

Ro. 8:26. the Spirit itself *maketh intercession for* us with groanings which

5242 5 848/975 8:523 5228,2192
ὑπερέχω, *hupereko.*

Ro. 13: 1. be subject unto the *higher* powers.
Phi. 2: 3. each esteem other *better* than themselves.
3: 8. for the *excellency* of the knowledge of Christ Jesus my Lord:
4: 7. the peace of God, *which passeth* all understanding,
1Pet.2:13. whether it be to the king, as *supreme*;

5243 1 849/975 8:525 5244
ὑπερηφανία, *hupereephania.*

Mar 7:22. blasphemy, *pride*, foolishness:

5244 5 849/975 8:525 5228,5316
ὑπερήφανος, *hupereephanos.*

Lu. 1:51. scattered the *proud* in the imagination of their hearts.
Ro. 1:30. *proud*, boasters, inventors of evil things,
2Ti. 3: 2. boasters, *proud*, blasphemers,
Jas. 4: 6. he saith, God resisteth the *proud*, but
1Pet.5: 5. for God resisteth the *proud*, and giveth

5245 1 849/975 4:942 5228,3528
ὑπερνικάω, *hupernikao.*

Ro. 8:37. we *are more than conquerors* through him

5246 2 849/975 5228,3591
ὑπέρογκος, *huperonkos.*

2Pet.2:18. they speak *great swelling* (words) of vanity,
Jude 16. mouth speaketh *great swelling* (words),

5247 2 849/975 8:528 5242
ὑπεροχή, *huperokee.*

1Co. 2: 1. came not with *excellency* of speech
1Ti. 2: 2. and (for) all that are in *authority*;

5248 2 849/975 6:58 5228,4052
ὑπερπερισσεύω, *huperperissuo.*

Ro. 5:20. grace *did much more abound*:
2Co. 7: 4. I *am exceeding* joyful in all our

5249 1 849/975 5228,4057
ὑπερπερισσῶς, *huperperissōs.*

Mar 7:37. And were *beyond measure* astonished.

5250 1 849/975 6:263 5228,4121
ὑπερπλεονάζω, *huperpleonazo.*

1Ti. 1:14. And the grace of our Lord *was exceeding abundant* with faith and

5251 1 849/975 8:602 5228,5312
ὑπερυψόω, *huperupsoō.*

Phi. 2: 9. God also *hath highly exalted* him,

5252 1 850/975 5228,5426
ὑπερφρονέω, *huperphroneo.*

Ro. 12: 3. not *to think* (of himself) *more highly*

5253 4 850/975 5228
ὑπερῷον, *huperōon.*

Acts 1:13. went up into an *upper room*, where abode
9:37. they laid (her) in an *upper chamber*.
39. they brought him into the *upper chamber*.
20: 8. there were many lights in the *upper chamber*,

5254 1 850/975 5259,2192
ὑπέχω, *hupeko.*

Jude 7. *suffering* the vengeance of eternal fire.

5255 3 850/975 1:216 5219
ὑπήκοος, *hupeekoös.*

Acts 7:39. To whom our fathers would not *obey*, (lit. *be obedient*)
2Co. 2: 9. whether ye be *obedient* in all things.
Phi. 2: 8. and became *obedient* unto death,

5256 3 850/975 8:530 5257
ὑπηρετέω, *hupeereteo.*

Acts13:36. David, *after* he *had served* his own generation
20:34. these hands *have ministered unto* my
24:23. *to minister* or come unto him.

5257 20 850/976 8:530 5259 *eressō* (to row)
ὑπηρέτης, *hupeeretees.*

Mat. 5:25. the judge deliver thee to the *officer*,
26:58. and sat with the *servants*, (lit. (court *officers*) to see the end.
Mar 14:54. and he sat with the *servants*,
65. and the *servants* did strike him
Lu. 1: 2. eyewitnesses, and *ministers* of the word;
4:20. and he gave (it) again to the *minister*,
Joh. 7:32. and the chief priests sent *officers*
45. Then came the *officers* to the chief priests
46. The *officers* answered, Never man spake
18: 3. received a band (of men) and *officers* from the chief priests and Pharisees,
12. the band and the captain and *officers* of the Jews took Jesus,
18. And the servants and *officers* stood there,
22. one of the *officers* which stood by struck
36. then would my *servants* fight,
19: 6. chief priests therefore and *officers* saw him, they cried out,
Acts 5:22. But when the *officers* came, and found them not

Acts 5:26. Then went the captain with the *officers*,
13: 5. and they had also John to (their) *minister*.
26:16. to make thee a *minister* and a witness
1Co. 4: 1. Let a man so account of us, as of the *ministers* of Christ,

5258 6 850/976 8:545 cf 5259

ὕπνος, hupnos.

Mat. 1:24. Joseph being raised from *sleep*
Lu. 9:32. that were with him were heavy with *sleep*.
Joh. 11:13. he had spoken of taking of rest in *sleep*.
Acts 20: 9. Eutychus, being fallen into a deep *sleep*:
— he sunk down with *sleep*, and fell
Ro. 13:11. high time to awake out of *sleep*:

5259 230 850/978,976

ὑπό, hupo.

Governing a genitive case, with the exception of the passages marked [a].

Mat. 1:22. spoken *of* the Lord by the prophet,
2:15. spoken *of* the Lord by the prophet,
16. that he was mocked *of* the wise men,
17. spoken *by* Jeremy the prophet,
3: 3. that was spoken of *by* the prophet Esaias,
6. And were baptized *of* him in Jordan,
13. unto John, to be baptized *of* him.
14. I have need to be baptized *of* thee,
4: 1. led up *of* the spirit into the wilderness to be tempted *of* the devil.
5:13. and to be trodden under foot *of* men.
15. and put it *under*[a] a bushel,
6: 2. that they may have glory *of* men.
8: 8. that thou shouldest come *under*[a] my roof:
9. a man *under*[a] authority, having soldiers *under*[a] me:
24. that the ship was covered *with* the waves:
10:22. And ye shall be hated *of* all (men)
11: 7. A reed shaken *with* the wind?
27. are delivered unto me *of* my Father:
14: 8. being before instructed *of* her mother,
24. in the midst of the sea, tossed *with* waves:
17:12. shall also the Son of man suffer *of* them.
19:12. which were made eunuchs *of* men:
20:23. for whom it is prepared *of* my Father.
22:31. that which was spoken unto you *by* God,
23: 7. and to be called *of* men, Rabbi, Rabbi.
37. as a hen gathereth her chickens *under*[a] (her) wings,
24: 9. and ye shall be hated *of* all nations for
27:12. And when he was accused *of* the chief priests
35. which was spoken *by* the prophet,
Mar 1: 5. baptized *of* him in the river of Jordan,
9. and was baptized *of* John in Jordan.
13. forty days, tempted *of* Satan;
2: 3. which was borne *of* four.
4:21. Is a candle brought to be put *under*[a] a bushel, or *under*[a] a bed?
32. may lodge *under*[a] the shadow of it.
5: 4. chains had been plucked asunder *by* him,
26. suffered many things *of* many physicians,
13:13. And ye shall be hated *of* all (men)
14. spoken of *by* Daniel the prophet,
16:11. and had been seen *of* her, believed not.
Lu. 1:26. the angel Gabriel was sent *from* God
2:18. which were told them *by* the shepherds.
21. which was so named *of* the angel
26. revealed unto him *by* the Holy Ghost,
3: 7. that came forth to be baptized *of* him,
19. being reproved *by* him for Herodias

Lu. 4: 2. forty days tempted *of* the devil.
15. in their synagogues, being glorified *of* all
5:15. to be healed *by* him of their infirmities.
6:18. they that were vexed *with* unclean spirits
7: 6. thou shouldest enter *under*[a] my roof:
8. I also am a man set *under*[a] authority having *under*[a] me soldiers,
24. A reed shaken *with* the wind.
30. being not baptized *of* him.
8:14. are choked *with* cares and riches
29. and was driven *of* the devil into the wilderness.
43. neither could be healed *of* any,
9: 7. heard of all that was done *by* him:
— it was said *of* some, that John was
8. And *of* some, that Elias had appeared,
10:22. are delivered to me *of* my Father:
11:33. neither *under*[a] a bushel,
13:17. the glorious things that were done *by* him.
34. (doth gather) her brood *under*[a] (her)
14: 8. art bidden *of* any (man) to a wedding,
— than thou be bidden *of* him;
16:22. carried *by* the angels into Abraham's bosom:
17:20. when he was demanded *of* the Pharisees,
24. out of the one (part) *under*[a] heaven, shineth unto the other (part) *under*[a] heaven;
21:16. ye shall be betrayed both *by* parents,
17. And ye shall be hated *of* all (men)
20. Jerusalem compassed *with* armies,
24. be trodden down *of* the Gentiles,
23: 8. to have seen some miracle done *by* him.
Joh. 1:48(49). when thou wast *under*[a] the fig tree,
8: 9. being convicted *by* (their own) conscience,
10:14. and am known *of* mine.
14:21. shall be loved *of* my Father,
Acts 2: 5. devout men, out of every nation *under*[a] heaven.
24. not possible that he should be holden *of* it.
4:11. which was set at nought *of* you builders,
12. none other name *under*[a] heaven given
36. who *by* the apostles was surnamed Barnabas,
5:16. vexed *with* unclean spirits:
21. into the temple early *in* the morning, (lit. *on*[a] the dawn)
8: 6. those things which Philip spake, (lit. spoken *by* Philip)
10:22. of good report *among* all the nation of the Jews, was warned from God *by* an holy angel
33. all things that are commanded thee *of* God.
38. all that were oppressed *of* the devil;
41. unto witnesses chosen before *of* God,
42. that it is he which was ordained *of* God (to be) the Judge of quick and dead.
12: 5. without ceasing *of* the church unto God
13: 4. being sent forth *by* the Holy Ghost,
45. those things which were spoken *by* Paul,
15: 3. brought on their way *by* the church,
4. they were received *of* the church,
40. being recommended *by* the brethren
16: 2. well reported of *by* the brethren
4. that were ordained *of* the apostles and elders
6. and were forbidden *of* the Holy Ghost
14. unto the things which were spoken *of* Paul.
17:13. the word of God was preached *of* Paul
19. this new doctrine, whereof thou speakest, (lit. spoken *by* thee)

Acts17:25. Neither is worshipped *with* men's hands,
20: 3. when the Jews laid wait for him, (lit. there being a design against him *by* the Jews)
21:35. that he was borne *of* the soldiers
22 11. led by the hand *of* them that were with me,
12. having a good report *of* all the Jews
23:10. Paul should have been pulled in pieces *of*
27. This man was taken *of* the Jews,
— and should have been killed *of* them:
30. how that the Jews laid wait for the man, (lit. an enterprise against him *by* the Jews)
24:21. I am called in question *by* you this day.
26. money should have been given him *of* Paul,
25.14. There is a certain man left in bonds *by* Felix:
26: 2. whereof I am accused *of* the Jews:
6. of the promise made *of* God unto our fathers:
7. king Agrippa, I am accused *of* the Jews.
27:11. than those things which were spoken *by* Paul.
41. broken *with* the violence of the waves.
Ro. 3: 9. that they are all *under*ᵃ sin;
13. the poison of asps (is) *under*ᵃ their lips:
21. witnessed *by* the law and the prophets;
6:14. ye are not *under*ᵃ the law, but *under*ᵃ grace.
15. we are not *under*ᵃ the law, but *under*ᵃ grace?
7:14. but I am carnal, sold *under*ᵃ sin.
12:21. Be not overcome *of* evil, but overcome
13: 1. the powers that be are ordained *of* God.
15:15. the grace that is given to me *of* God,
24. to be brought on my way thitherward *by* you,
16:20. shall bruise Satan *under*ᵃ your feet shortly.
1Co. 1:11. *by* them (which are of the house) of Chloe,
2:12. that are freely given to us *of* God.
15. yet he himself is judged *of* no man.
4: 3. that I should be judged *of* you, or *of* man's judgment:
6:12. not be brought under the power *of* any.
7:25. as one that hath obtained mercy *of* the Lord
8: 3. the same is known *of* him.
9:20. to them that are *under*ᵃ the law, as *under*ᵃ the law, that I might gain them that are *under*ᵃ the law;
10: 1. all our fathers were *under*ᵃ the cloud,
9. and were destroyed *of* serpents.
10. and were destroyed *of* the destroyer.
29. judged *of* another (man's) conscience?
11:32. we are chastened *of* the Lord,
14:24. he is convinced *of* all, he is judged *of* all:
15:25. he hath put all enemies *under*ᵃ his feet.
27. he hath put all things *under*ᵃ his feet.
2Co. 1: 4. we ourselves are comforted *of* God.
16. and *of* you to be brought on my way
2: 6. which (was inflicted) *of* many.
11. Lest Satan should get an advantage of us: (lit. lest we should be taken advantage of *by* Satan)
3: 2. known and read *of* all men:
3. ministered *by* us, written not with
5: 4. might be swallowed up *of* life.
8:19. who was also chosen *of* the churches
— grace, which is administered *by* us
20. abundance which is administered *by* us:
11:24. *Of* the Jews five times received I

2Co.12:11. to have been commended *of* you:
Gal. 1:11. the gospel which was preached *of* me
3:10. are *under*ᵃ the curse: for it is written,
17. confirmed before *of* God in Christ,
22. hath concluded all *under*ᵃ sin,
23. we were kept *under*ᵃ the law,
25. no longer *under*ᵃ a schoolmaster.
4: 2. But is *under*ᵃ tutors and governors
3. *under*ᵃ the elements of the world:
4. of a woman, made *under*ᵃ the law,
5. them that were *under*ᵃ the law,
9. or rather are known *of* God,
21. that desire to be *under*ᵃ the law,
5:15. that ye be not consumed one *of* another.
18. ye are not *under*ᵃ the law.
Eph. 1:22. And hath put all (things) *under*ᵃ his feet
2:11. *by* that which is called the Circumcision
5:12. which are done *of* them in secret.
13. are made manifest *by* the light:
Phi. 1:28. in nothing terrified *by* your adversaries
3:12. I am apprehended *of* Christ Jesus.
Col. 1:23. to every creature which is *under*ᵃ heaven
2:18. vainly puffed up *by* his fleshly mind,
1Th. 1: 4. Knowing, brethren beloved, your election *of* God. [or, beloved *by* God, your election]
2: 4. But as we were allowed *of* God
14. like things *of* your own countrymen, even as they (have) *of* the Jews:
2Th. 2:13. brethren beloved *of* the Lord,
1Ti. 6: 1. servants as are *under*ᵃ the yoke
2Ti. 2:26. who are taken captive *by* him at
Heb 2: 3. confirmed unto us *by* them that heard (him);
3: 4. For every house is builded *by* some (man);
5: 4. but he that is called *of* God,
10. Called *of* God an high priest
7: 7. the less is blessed *of* the better.
9:19. when Moses had spoken every precept (lit. every precept having been spoken *by* Moses)
11:23. hid three months *of* his parents,
12: 3. endured such contradiction *of* sinners
5. when thou art rebuked *of* him:
Jas. 1:14. he is drawn away *of* his own lust,
2: 3. or sit here *under*ᵃ my footstool:
9. and are convinced *of* the law
3: 4. and (are) driven *of* fierce winds,
— turned about *with* a very small helm,
6. and it is set on fire *of* hell.
1Pet.2: 4. disallowed indeed *of* men,
5: 6. *under*ᵃ the mighty hand of God,
2Pet.1:17. to him *from* the excellent glory,
21. spake (as they were) moved *by* the Holy Ghost.
2: 7. vexed *with* the filthy conversation of the wicked:
17. clouds that are carried *with* a tempest;
3: 2. were spoken before *by* the holy prophets,
3Joh. 12. Demetrius hath good report *of* all (men), and *of* the truth itself:
Jude 6. in everlasting chains *under*ᵃ darkness unto
12. carried about *of* winds;
17. which were spoken before *of* the apostles
Rev. 6: 8. with death, and *with* the beasts of the
13. when she is shaken *of* a mighty wind.
9:18. *By* these three was the third part of men

5260 1 851/978 5259,906

ὑποβάλλω, *hupoballo.*

Acts 6:11. Then they *suborned* men, which said,

5261 1 851/978 1:742 5259,1125

ὑπογραμμός, hupogrammos.

1Pet.2:21. leaving us an *example*, that ye should

5262 6 851/978 2:25 5263

ὑπόδειγμα, hupodigma.

Joh.13:15. For I have given you an *example*, that ye
Heb 4:11. after the same *example* of unbelief.
8: 5. Who serve unto the *example* and shadow
9:23. that the *patterns* of things in the heavens
Jas. 5:10. for an *example* of suffering affliction,
2Pet.2: 6. making (them) an *ensample* unto those that after should live ungodly;

5263 6 851/978 5259,1166

ὑποδείκνυμι, hupodiknumi.

Mat. 3: 7. who *hath warned* you to flee
Lu. 3: 7. who *hath warned* you to flee
6:47. I *will shew* you to whom he is like.
12: 5. But I *will forewarn* you whom
Acts 9:16. For I *will shew* him how great things
20:35. I *have shewed* you all things,

5265 3 852/978 5:292 5259,1210

ὑποδέομαι, hupodeomai.

Mar 6: 9. But (be) *shod* with sandals;
Acts12: 8. Gird thyself, and *bind on* thy sandals.
Eph. 6:15. your feet *shod* with the preparation

5264 4 852/978 5259,1209

ὑποδέχομαι, hupodekomai.

Lu. 10:38. Martha *received* him into her house.
19: 6. and *received* him joyfully.
Acts17: 7. Whom Jason *hath received*:
Jas. 2:25. *when* she *had received* the messengers,

5266 10 852/978 5:292 5265

ὑπόδημα, hupodeema.

Mat. 3:11. whose *shoes* I am not worthy to bear:
10:10. neither two coats, neither *shoes*,
Mar 1: 7. the latchet of whose *shoes* I am not worthy
Lu. 3:16. the latchet of whose *shoes* I am not worthy
10: 4. neither purse, nor scrip, nor *shoes*:
15:22. and put a ring on his hand, and *shoes* on (his) feet:
22:35. without purse, and scrip, and *shoes*,
Joh. 1:27. whose *shoe's* latchet I am not worthy
Acts 7:33. Put off thy *shoes* from thy feet·
13:25. whose *shoes* of (his) feet I am not

5267 1 852/979 8:557 5259,1349

ὑπόδικος, hupodikos.

Ro. 3:19. all the world may become *guilty* before God.

5268 2 852/979 5259,2218

ὑποζύγιον, hupozugion.

Mat.21: 5. and a colt the foal of an *ass*.
2Pet. 2:16. the dumb *ass* speaking with man's voice

5269 1 852/979 5259,2224

ὑποζώννυμι, hupozonnumi.

Acts27:17 they used helps, *undergirding* the ship;

5270 9 852/979 5259,2736

ὑποκάτω, hupokato.

Mar 6:11. shake off the dust *under* your feet
7:28. yet the dogs *under* the table eat of
Lu. 8:16. or putteth (it) *under* a bed;
Joh. 1:50(51). I saw thee *under* the fig tree,
Heb 2: 8. all things in subjection *under* his feet.
Rev. 5: 3. nor in earth, neither *under* the earth,
13. and on the earth, and *under* the earth,
6: 9. I saw *under* the altar the souls
12: 1. and the moon *under* her feet,

5271 1 852/979 8:559 5259,2919

ὑποκρίνομαι, hupokrinomai.

Lu. 20:20. sent forth spies, *which should feign* (lit. *feigning*) themselves just men,

5272 7 852/979 8:559 5271

ὑπόκρισις, hupokrisis.

Mat.23:28. within ye are full of *hypocrisy*
Mar12:15. But he, knowing their *hypocrisy*,
Lu. 12: 1. the leaven of the Pharisees, which is *hypocrisy*.
Gal. 2:13. was carried away with their *dissimulation*.
1Ti. 4: 2. Speaking lies in *hypocrisy*;
Jas. 5:12. lest ye fall into *condemnation*.
1Pet.2: 1. and all guile, and *hypocrisies*,

Note.—The rendering of Jas.5:12 has arisen from a different reading, ὑπὸ κρίσιν.

5273 20 853/979 8:559 5271

ὑποκριτής, hupokritees.

Mat. 6: 2. as the *hypocrites* do in the synagogues
5. thou shalt not be as the *hypocrites*
16. when ye fast, be not, as the *hypocrites*, of
7: 5. Thou *hypocrite*, first cast out the beam
15: 7. (Ye) *hypocrites*, well did Esaias prophesy
16: 3. O (ye) *hypocrites*, ye can discern
22:18. Why tempt ye me, (ye) *hypocrites*?
23:13. scribes and Pharisees, *hypocrites*!
14. scribes and Pharisees, *hypocrites*!
15. scribes and Pharisees, *hypocrites*!
23. scribes and Pharisees, *hypocrites*!
25. scribes and Pharisees, *hypocrites*!
27. scribes and Pharisees, *hypocrites*!
29. scribes and Pharisees, *hypocrites*!
24:51. and appoint (him) his portion with the *hypocrites*:
Mar 7: 6. Esaias prophesied of you *hypocrites*,
Lu. 6:42. Thou *hypocrite*, cast out first the beam
11:44. scribes and Pharisees, *hypocrites*! for ye are
12:56. (Ye) *hypocrites*, ye can discern the face
13:15. (Thou) *hypocrite*, doth not each one of

5274 4 853/979 4:5 5259,2983

ὑπολαμβάνω, hupolambano.

Lu. 7:43. I *suppose* that (he), to whom he forgave most.
10:30. And Jesus *answering* said, A certain
Acts 1: 9. a cloud *received* him out of their sight.
2:15. these are not drunken, as ye *suppose*,

5275 1 853/979 5295,3007

ὑπολείπομαι, hupolipomai.

Ro. 11: 3. and I *am left* alone, and they seek

5276 1 853/979 4:254 5259,3025
ὑπολήνιον, hupoleenion.

Mar 12: 1. and digged (a place for) the *winefat*,

5277 1 853/979 5275
ὑπολιμπάνω, hupolimpano.

1Pet. 2:21. suffered for us, *leaving* us an example,

5278 17 853/979 4:574 5259,3306
ὑπομένω, hupomeno.

Mat. 10:22. but he *that endureth* to the end
24:13. But he *that shall endure* unto the end,
Mar 13:13. but he *that shall endure* unto the end,
Lu. 2:43. the child Jesus *tarried behind* in
Acts 17:14. Silas and Timotheus *abode* there still.
Ro. 12:12. *patient* in tribulation;
1Co. 13: 7. hopeth all things, *endureth* all things.
2Ti. 2:10. Therefore I *endure* all things for the
12. If we *suffer*, we shall also reign with (him):
Heb 10:32. ye *endured* a great fight of afflictions;
12: 2. *endured* the cross, despising the shame,
3. him *that endured* such contradiction
7. If ye *endure* chastening, God dealeth
Jas. 1:12. Blessed (is) the man that *endureth* temptation:
5:11. we count them happy *which endure*.
1Pet. 2:20. for your faults, ye shall *take it patiently*?
— ye *take it patiently*, this (is) acceptable

5279 7 853/980 5259,3403
ὑπομιμνήσκω, hupomimneesko.

Lu. 22:61. Peter *remembered* the word of the Lord,
Joh. 14:26. shall teach you all things, and *bring* all things *to your remembrance*,
2Ti. 2:14. Of these things *put* (them) *in remembrance*,
Tit. 3: 1. *Put* them *in mind* to be subject
2Pet. 1:12. *to put* you always *in remembrance*
3Joh. 10. I *will remember* his deeds which he doeth,
Jude 5. I will therefore *put* you *in remembrance*,

5280 3 854/980 1:348 5279
ὑπόμνησις, hupomneesis.

2Ti. 1: 5. When I call to *remembrance* the unfeigned
2Pet. 1:13. *by putting* (you) *in remembrance*;
3: 1. your pure minds by way of *remembrance*:

5281 32 854/980 4:574 5278
ὑπομονή, hupomonee.

Lu. 8:15. and bring forth fruit with *patience*.
21:19. In your *patience* possess ye your souls.
Ro. 2: 7. by *patient continuance* in well doing
5: 3. that tribulation worketh *patience*;
4. And *patience*, experience;
8:25. do we with *patience* wait for (it).
15: 4. through *patience* and comfort of the
5. Now the God of *patience* and consolation
2Co. 1: 6. which is effectual in the *enduring* of the same sufferings
6: 4. in much *patience*, in afflictions,
12:12. wrought among you in all *patience*,
Col. 1:11. unto all *patience* and longsuffering
1Th. 1: 3. and *patience* of hope in our Lord
2Th. 1: 4. for your *patience* and faith
3: 5. and into the *patient waiting* for Christ. (lit. the *patience* of Christ)
1Ti. 6:11. faith, love, *patience*, meekness.
2Ti. 3:10. faith, longsuffering, charity, *patience*.
Tit. 2: 2. sound in faith, in charity, in *patience*.
Heb 10:36. For ye have need of *patience*,
12: 1. and let us run with *patience* the race
Jas. 1: 3. the trying of your faith worketh *patience*.
4. But let *patience* have (her) perfect work,
5:11. Ye have heard of the *patience* of Job,
2Pet. 1: 6. and to temperance *patience*; and to *patience* godliness;
Rev. 1: 9. in the kingdom and *patience* of Jesus Christ,
2: 2. and thy labour, and thy *patience*,
3. And hast borne, and hast *patience*,
19. and thy *patience*, and thy works;
3:10. thou hast kept the word of my *patience*,
13:10. Here is the *patience* and the faith of
14:12. Here is the *patience* of the saints:

5282 3 854/980 4:948 5259,3539
ὑπονοέω, huponoeo.

Acts 13:25. Whom *think* ye that I am?
25:18. of such things as I *supposed*:
27:27. the shipmen *deemed* that they drew near

5283 1 854/980 4:948 5282
ὑπόνοια, huponoya.

1Ti. 6: 4. strife, railings, evil *surmisings*,

5284 2 854/980 5259,4126
ὑποπλέω, hupopleo.

Acts 27: 4. we *sailed under* Cyprus,
7. we *sailed under* Crete,

5285 1 854/980 5259,4154
ὑποπνέω, hupopneo.

Acts 27:13. And *when* the south wind *blew softly*,

5286 9 854/980 5259.4228
ὑποπόδιον, hupopodion.

Mat. 5:35. by the earth; for it is his *footstool*:
22:44. till I make thine enemies thy *footstool*?
Mar 12:36. till I make thine enemies thy *footstool*.
Lu. 20:43. Till I make thine enemies thy *footstool*.
Acts 2:35. Until I make thy foes thy *footstool*.
7:49. and earth (is) my *footstool*:
Heb 1:13. until I make thine enemies thy *footstool*?
10:13. till his enemies be made his *footstool*.
Jas. 2: 3. or sit here under my *footstool*:

5287 5 854/980 8:572 5259,2476
ὑπόστασις, hupostasis.

2Co. 9: 4. in this same *confident* boasting. (lit. *confidence* of boasting)
11:17. in this *confidence* of boasting.
Heb 1: 3. and the express image of his *person*,
3:14. if we hold the beginning of our *confidence*
11: 1. faith is the *substance* of things hoped for,

5288 4 855/980 7:588 5259,4724
ὑποστέλλω, hupostello.

Acts 20:20. (And) how I *kept back* nothing
27. For I *have* not *shunned* to declare
Gal. 2:12. he *withdrew* and separated himself,
Heb 10:38. but if (any man) *draw back*

5289 1 855/981 7:588 5288

ὑποστολή, hupostolee.

Heb 10:39. we are not of them who *draw back* (lit. of the *drawing back*) unto perdition;

5290 35 855/981 5259,4762

ὑποστρέφω, hupostrepho.

Mar 14:40. And *when* he *returned*, he found them
Lu. 1:56. and *returned* to her own house.
2:39. they *returned* into Galilee,
43. as they *returned*, the child Jesus
45. they *turned back again* to Jerusalem,
4: 1. *returned* from Jordan, and was led
14. And Jesus *returned* in the power
7:10. *returning* to the house, found the servant
8:37. into the ship, and *returned back again*.
39. *Return* to thine own house,
40. that, when Jesus *was returned*,
9:10. the apostles, *when* they *were returned*, told
10:17. the seventy *returned again* with joy,
11:24. I *will return* unto my house
17:15. *turned back*, and with a loud voice
18. *that returned* to give glory to God, save
19:12. for himself a kingdom, and *to return*.
23:48. smote their breasts, and *returned*.
56. they *returned, and* prepared spices
24: 9. *returned* from the sepulchre, and told
33. and *returned* to Jerusalem,
52. *returned* to Jerusalem with great joy:
Acts 1:12. Then *returned* they unto Jerusalem
8:25. *returned* to Jerusalem, and
28. Was *returning*, and sitting in his chariot
12:25. Barnabas and Saul *returned* from Jerusalem,
13:13. John departing from them *returned* to
34. no more *to return* to corruption,
14:21. they *returned again* to Lystra,
20: 3. *to return* through Macedonia.
21: 6. and they *returned* home *again*.
22:17. *when* I *was come again* to Jerusalem,
23:32. and *returned* to the castle:
Gal. 1:17. and *returned* again unto Damascus.
Heb. 7: 1. met Abraham *returning* from the slaughter of the kings,

5291 1 855/981 5259,4766

ὑποστρώννυμι, hupostrōnnumi.

Lu. 19:36. they *spread* their clothes in the way.

5292 4 855/981 8:27 5293

ὑποταγή, hupotagee.

2Co. 9:13. for your professed *subjection* unto the gospel
Gal. 2: 5. we gave place by *subjection*, no, not for an hour;
1Ti. 2:11. learn in silence with all *subjection*.
3: 4. having his children in *subjection*

5293 40 855/981 8:27 5259,5021

ὑποτάσσω, hupotasso.

Lu. 2:51. and was *subject unto* them.
10:17. even the devils *are subject unto* us
20. that the spirits *are subject unto* you;
Ro. 8: 7. for it *is* not *subject to* the law of God,
20. the creature *was made subject to* vanity,
— by reason of him who *hath subjected*
10: 3. *have* not *submitted* themselves *unto* the
13: 1. *Let* every soul *be subject unto* the higher
Ro. 13: 5. Wherefore (ye) must needs *be subject*
1Co.14:32. *are subject to* the prophets.
34. *to be under obedience*, as also saith
15:27. For he *hath put* all things *under* his feet.
— All things *are put under* (him, it is)
— *which did put* all things *under* him.
28. when all things shall *be subdued unto* him, then *shall* the Son also himself *be subject unto* him *that put* all things *under* him,
16:16. That ye *submit* yourselves *unto* such,
Eph. 1:22. And *hath put* all (things) *under* his feet,
5:21. *Submitting* yourselves one *to* another
22. Wives, *submit* yourselves *unto* your
24. as the church *is subject unto* Christ,
Phi. 3:21. *to subdue* all things *unto* himself.
Col. 3:18. Wives, *submit* yourselves *unto* your
Tit. 2: 5. *obedient to* their own husbands,
9. servants *to be obedient unto* their own
3: 1. *to be subject to* principalities and
Heb. 2: 5. *hath* he not *put in subjection* the world
8. Thou *hast put* all things *in subjection*
— For in that he *put* all *in subjection under*
— we see not yet all things *put under* him.
12: 9. *shall* we not much rather *be in subjection unto* the Father of spirits,
Jas. 4: 7. *Submit* yourselves therefore *to* God.
1Pet. 2:13. *Submit* yourselves *to* every ordinance of man
18. Servants, (be) *subject to* (your) masters
3: 1. *in subjection to* your own husbands;
5. *being in subjection unto* their own husbands:
22. angels and authorities and powers *being made subject unto* him.
5: 5. ye younger, *submit* yourselves *unto* the elder. Yea, all (of you) *be subject* one *to* another, *and*

5294 2 856/982 5259,5087

ὑποτίθημι, hupotitheemi.

Ro 16: 4. Who *have* for my life *laid down* their own necks:
1Ti. 4: 6. *If* thou *put* the brethren *in remembrance* of these things,

5295 1 856/982 5259,5143

ὑποτρέχω, hupotreko.

Acts27:16. And *running under* a certain island

5296 2 856/982 8:246 5259,5179

ὑποτύπωσις, hupotupōsis.

1Ti. 1:16. for a *pattern* to them (lit. *pattern* of them) which should hereafter believe
2Ti. 1:13. Hold fast the *form* of sound words,

5297 3 856/982 5259,5342

ὑποφέρω, hupophero.

1Co.10:13. that ye may be able *to bear* (it).
2Ti. 3:11. what persecutions I *endured*:
1Pet. 2:19. if a man for conscience toward God *endure* grief,

5298 2 856/982 5259,5562

ὑποχωρέω, hupokōreo.

Lu. 5:16. *withdrew* himself into the wilderness,
9:10. and *went aside* privately into a desert place belonging to

5299 2 856/982 8:590 5259,3700
ὑπωπιάζω, hupōpiazo.

Lu. 18: 5. lest by her continual coming she *weary* me.
1Co. 9:27. But I *keep under* my body, and bring

5300 1 856/982
ὗς, hus.

2Pet. 2:22. and the *sow* that was washed to her

5301 2 856/982 [231]
ὕσσωπος, hussōpos.

Joh. 19:29. and put (it) upon *hyssop*, and
Heb 9:19. with water, and scarlet wool, and *hyssop*,

5302 16 856/982 8:592 5306
ὑστερέω, hustereo.

Mat. 19:20. from my youth up: what *lack* I yet?
Mar 10:21. One thing thou *lackest*: go thy way,
Lu. 15:14. and he began *to be in want*.
22:35. *lacked* ye any thing? And they said,
Joh. 2: 3. when they wanted wine, (lit. the wine *having failed*)
Ro. 3:23. and *come short* of the glory of God;
1Co. 1: 7. So that ye *come behind* in no gift;
8: 8. neither, if we eat not, *are we the worse*.
12:24. honour *to that* (part) *which lacked*:
2Co. 11: 5. I suppose I *was* not a whit *behind* the very
9(8). I was present with you, and *wanted*,
12:11. for in nothing *am* I *behind* the very
Phi. 4:12. both to abound and *to suffer need*.
Heb 4: 1. should seem *to come short of* it.
11:37. *being destitute*, afflicted, tormented;
12:15. lest any man *fail* of the grace of God;

5303 9 857/982 8:592 5302
ὑστέρημα, hustereema.

Lu. 21: 4. but she of her *penury* hath cast in
1Co. 16:17. for *that which was lacking* on your part
2Co. 8:14(13). (may be a supply) for their *want*,
— may be (a supply) for your *want*:
9:12. not only supplieth the *want* of the saints,
11: 9. for *that which was lacking* to me
Phi. 2:30. to supply your *lack* of service toward me.
Col. 1:24. and fill up *that which is behind* of the afflictions of Christ
1Th. 3:10. *that which is lacking* in your faith?

5304 2 857/982 8:592 5302
ὑστέρησις, hustereesis.

Mar 12:44. but she of her *want* did cast in
Phi. 4:11. Not that I speak in respect of *want*:

5305 12 857/982 8:592 5306
ὕστερον, husteron. adv.

Mat. 4: 2. he was *afterward* an hungred.
21:29. but *afterward* he repented, and went.
32. when ye had seen (it), repented not *afterward*,
37. But *last of all* he sent unto them his son,
22:27. And *last* of all the woman died also.
25:11. *Afterward* came also the other virgins,
26:60. *At the last* came two false witnesses,
Mar 16:14. *Afterward* he appeared unto the eleven as
Lu. 4: 2. he *afterward* hungered.
20:32. *Last* of all the woman died also.
Joh. 13:36. but thou shalt follow me *afterwards*.
Heb 12:11. *afterward* it yieldeth the peaceable fruit

5306 1 857/982 8:592 5259
ὕστερος, husteros.

1Ti. 4: 1. in the *latter* times some shall depart from the faith,

5307 1 857/982 huphainō (to weave)
ὑφαντός, huphantos.

Joh. 19:23 *woven* from the top throughout.

5308 11 857/982 5311
ὑψηλός, hupseelos.

Mat. 4: 8. him up into an exceeding *high* mountain,
17: 1. bringeth them up into an *high* mountain
Mar 9: 2. leadeth them up into an *high* mountain
Lu. 4: 5. taking him up into an *high* mountain,
16:15. for that which is *highly esteemed* among men
Acts 13:17. and with an *high* arm brought he them out
Ro. 12:16. Mind not *high* things,
Heb 1: 3. the right hand of the Majesty on *high*;
7:26. and made *higher* than the heavens;
Rev. 21:10. in the spirit to a great and *high* mountain,
12. And had a wall great and *high*,

5309 2 857/983 5308,5424
ὑψηλοφρονέω, hupseelophroneo.

Ro. 11:20. *Be* not *highminded*, but fear:
1Ti. 6:17. that they *be* not *highminded*,

5310 13 857/983 8:602 rt 5311
ὕψιστος, hupsistos.

The mark † denotes that the plural is used to supply the word "places."

Mat. 21: 9. Hosanna in the *highest*. †
Mar 5: 7. Jesus, (thou) Son of the *most high* God?
11:10. Hosanna in the *highest*. †
Lu. 1:32. be called the Son of the *Highest*:
35. and the power of the *Highest* shall overshadow thee:
76. be called the prophet of the *Highest*:
2:14. Glory to God in the *highest*,† and on earth peace,
6:35. ye shall be the children of the *Highest*:
8:28. Jesus, (thou) Son of God *most high*?
19:38. peace in heaven, and glory in the *highest*. †
Acts 7:48. Howbeit the *most High* dwelleth not
16:17. the servants of the *most high* God,
Heb 7: 1. priest of the *most high* God, who met

5311 6 858/983 8:602 5228
ὕψος, hupsos.

Lu. 1:78. dayspring from *on high* hath visited us,
24:49. ye be endued with power from *on high*.
Eph. 3:18. and length, and depth, and *height*;
4: 8. When he ascended up on *high*,
Jas. 1: 9. rejoice in that he is exalted: (lit. in his *exaltation*)
Rev. 21:16. and the *height* of it are equal.

5312 20 858/983 8:602 5311
ὑψόω, hupsoō.

Mat. 11:23. Capernaum, *which art exalted* unto
23:12. And whosoever *shall exalt* himself
— shall humble himself *shall be exalted*.
Lu. 1:52. and *exalted* them of low degree.
10:15. *which art exalted* to heaven,
14:11. For whosoever *exalteth* himself
— that humbleth himself *shall be exalted*.

Lu. 18:14. every one *that exalteth* himself
— that humbleth himself *shall be exalted.*
Joh. 3:14. And as Moses *lifted up* the serpent
— so must the Son of man *be lifted up:*
8:28. When ye *have lifted up* the Son of man,
12:32. if I *be lifted up* from the earth,
34. The Son of man must *be lifted up?* who
Acts 2:33. *being* by the right hand of God *exalted,*
5:31. Him *hath* God *exalted* with his right hand
13:17. and *exalted* the people when they dwelt as
2Co.11: 7. abasing myself that ye *might be exalted,*
Jas. 4:10. and he *shall lift* you *up.*
1Pet.5: 6. that he *may exalt* you in due time:

5313 2 858/983 8:602 5312

ὕψωμα, *hupsōma.*

Ro. 8:39. Nor *height*, nor depth, nor any other
2Co.10: 5. and every *high thing* that exalteth itself

5314 2 859/983 5315

φάγος, *phagos.*

Mat.11:19. Behold a man *gluttonous,* and a
Lu. 7:34. Behold a *gluttonous* man, and a

5315 97 312/389 eq 2068

φάγω, *phago.*

Mat. 6:25. what ye shall *eat,* or what ye
31. saying, What shall we *eat?* or,
12: 4. and *did eat* the shewbread, which was not lawful for him *to eat,*
14:16. give ye them *to eat.*
20. And they *did* all *eat,* and were filled:
15:20. but *to eat* with unwashen hands
32. three days, and have nothing to *eat.* (lit. what they *may eat*)
37. And they *did* all *eat,* and were filled:
25:35. and ye gave me *meat:* (lit. *to eat*)
42. an hungred, and ye gave me no *meat:*
26:17. that we prepare for thee *to eat* the
26. Take, *eat;* this is my body.
Mar 2:26. and *did eat* the shewbread, which is not lawful *to eat* but for the priests,
3:20. could not so much as *eat* bread.
5:43. something should be given her *to eat.*
6:31. they had no leisure so much as *to eat.*
36. for they have nothing to *eat.*
37. Give ye them *to eat.*
— of bread, and give them *to eat?*
42. And they *did* all *eat,* and were filled.
44. And they *that did eat* of the loaves
8: 1. and having nothing to *eat,*
2. and have nothing to *eat:*
8. So they *did eat,* and were filled:
9. And they *that had eaten* were
11:14. No man *eat* fruit of thee hereafter
14:12. and prepare that thou *mayest eat* the
14. where I shall *eat* the passover with
22. Take, *eat:* this is my body.
Lu. 4: 2. in those days he *did eat* nothing:
6: 4. and did take and *eat* the shewbread,
— which it is not lawful *to eat* but for
7:36. desired him that he *would eat* with him.
8:55. he commanded to give her *meat.*
9:13. Give ye them *to eat.*
17. And they *did eat,* and were all filled:
12:19. take thine ease, *eat,* drink, (and) be merry.
22. for your life, what ye shall *eat;*
Lu. 12:29. seek not ye what ye shall *eat,*
13:26. We *have eaten* and drunk in thy
14: 1. *to eat* bread on the sabbath day,
15. Blessed (is) he that *shall eat* bread in
15:23. and let us *eat, and* be merry:
17: 8. till I *have eaten* and drunken; and afterward thou *shalt eat* and drink?
22: 8. prepare us the passover, that we *may eat*
11. where I shall *eat* the passover with
15. I have desired *to eat* this passover
16. I will not any more *eat* thereof,
24:43. he took (it), and *did eat* before them.
Joh. 4:31. saying, Master, *eat.*
32. I have meat *to eat* that ye
33. Hath any man brought him (ought) *to eat?*
6: 5. that these *may eat?*
23. where they *did eat* bread,
26. but because ye *did eat* of the loaves,
31. Our fathers *did eat* manna in the
— gave them bread from heaven *to eat.*
49. Your fathers *did eat* manna in the
50. that a man *may eat* thereof, and not die.
51. if any man *eat* of this bread,
52. this man give us (his) flesh *to eat?*
53. Except ye *eat* the flesh of the Son of
58. not as your fathers *did eat* manna,
18:28. but that they *might eat* the passover.
Acts 9: 9. and neither *did eat* nor drink.
10:13. Rise, Peter; kill, and *eat.*
14. for I *have* never *eaten* any thing that
11: 7. Arise, Peter; slay and *eat.*
23:12. saying that they would neither *eat* nor
21. an oath, that they will neither *eat* nor
Ro. 14: 2. believeth that he may *eat* all things:
21. (It is) good neither *to eat* flesh, nor
23. that doubteth is damned if he *eat,*
1Co. 8: 8. neither, if we *eat,* are we the better neither, if we *eat* not, are we the worse
13. I will *eat* no flesh while the world
9: 4. Have we not power *to eat* and to drink?
10: 3. *did* all *eat* the same spiritual meat;
7. The people sat down *to eat* and drink,
11:20. (this) is not *to eat* the Lord's supper.
21. For in *eating* every one taketh before
24. Take, *eat:* this is my body,
33. when ye come together *to eat,*
15:32. *let* us *eat* and drink; for to morrow
2Th. 3: 8. Neither *did* we *eat* any man's bread
Heb 13:10. whereof they have no right *to eat* which
Jas. 5: 3. and *shall eat* your flesh as it were fire.
Rev. 2: 7. will I give *to eat* of the tree of life,
14. *to eat* things sacrificed unto idols,
17. will I give *to eat* of the hidden
20. *to eat* things sacrificed unto idols.
10:10. as soon as I *had eaten* it,
17:16. and *shall eat* her flesh, and burn
19:18. That ye *may eat* the flesh of kings,

5341 1 862/986

φαιλόνης, *phailonees.*

2Ti. 4:13. The *cloke* that I left at Troas

5316 31 859/983 9:1 rt 5457

φαίνω, *phaino.*

Mat. 1:20. the angel of the Lord *appeared* unto
2: 7. what time the star *appeared.*
13. *appeareth* to Joseph in a dream,
19. *appeareth* in a dream to Joseph
6: 5. that they *may be seen* of men.
16. that they *may appear* unto men to fast.

Mat. 6:18. That thou *appear* not unto men to fast,
9:33. It *was* never so *seen* in Israel.
13:26. then *appeared* the tares also.
23:27. which indeed *appear* beautiful outward,
28. ye also outwardly *appear* righteous
24:27. and *shineth* even unto the west;
30. then *shall appear* the sign of the Son
Mar 14:64. what think ye? (lit. *seems* to you)
16: 9. he *appeared* first to Mary Magdalene,
Lu. 9: 8. of some, that Elias *had appeared;*
24:11. their words *seemed* to them as idle tales,
Joh. 1: 5: And the light *shineth* in darkness;
5:35. He was a burning and a *shining* light:
Ro. 7:13. But sin, that it *might appear* sin,
2Co.13: 7. not that we *should appear* approved,
Phi. 2:15. among whom ye *shine* as lights in
Heb 11: 3. not made of things *which do appear.*
Jas. 4:14. a vapour, *that appeareth* for a little
1Pet.4:18. where *shall* the ungodly and the sinner *appear?*
2Pet.1:19. as unto a light *that shineth* in a dark place,
1Joh.2: 8. and the true light now *shineth.*
Rev. 1:16. as the sun *shineth* in his strength.
8:12. and the day *shone* not for a third
18:23. the light of a candle shall *shine* no more
21:23. neither of the moon, to *shine* in it:

5318 21 860/984 9:1 5316

φανερός, phaneros.

Mat. 6: 4. shall reward thee *openly.*
6. shall reward thee *openly.*
18. shall reward thee *openly.*
12:16. they should not make him *known:*
Mar 3:12. they should not make him *known.*
4:22. secret, but that it should come *abroad.*
6:14. for his name was spread *abroad:*
Lu. 8:17. that shall not be made *manifest;*
— be known and come *abroad.*
Acts 4:16. (is) *manifest* to all them that
7:13. Joseph's kindred was made *known* unto
Ro. 1:19. is *manifest* in them; for God
2:28. a Jew, which is one *outwardly;*
— which is *outward* in the flesh:
1Co. 3:13. shall be made *manifest:* for the day
11:19. may be made *manifest* among you.
14:25. the secrets of his heart made *manifest;*
Gal. 5:19. the works of the flesh are *manifest,*
Phi. 1:13. my bonds in Christ are *manifest* in all
1Ti. 4:15. that thy profiting may appear (lit. may be *apparent*) to all.
1Joh.3:10. In this the children of God are *manifest,*

5319 49 860/984 9:1 5318

φανερόω, phaneroō.

Mar 4:22. hid, which *shall* not *be manifested;*
16:12. After that he *appeared* in another form
14. Afterward he *appeared* unto the eleven
Joh. 1:31. that he *should be made manifest* to
2:11. and *manifested forth* his glory;
3:21. that his deeds *may be made manifest,*
7: 4. *shew* thyself to the world.
9: 3. that the works of God *should be made manifest* in him.
17: 6. I *have manifested* thy name
21: 1. Jesus *shewed* himself again to the
— on this wise *shewed* he (himself).
14. third time that Jesus *shewed* himself to
Ro. 1:19. for God *hath shewed* (it) unto them.
3:21. without the law *is manifested,* (lit *has been manifested*)

Ro. 16:26. But now is *made manifest,* and
1Co. 4: 5. and *will make manifest* the counsels of
2Co. 2:14. and *maketh manifest* the savour of
3: 3. *manifestly declared* to be the epistle of
4:10. *might be made manifest* in our body.
11. *might be made manifest* in our
5:10. we must all *appear* before the judgment
11. but we *are made manifest* unto God; and I trust also are *made manifest* in your consciences.
7:12. might *appear* unto you.
11: 6. but we have been throughly *made manifest* among you
Eph 5:13. are *made manifest* by the light: for *whatsoever doth make manifest*
Col. 1:26. but now *is made manifest* to his saints:
3: 4. When Christ, (who is) our life, *shall appear,* then *shall* ye also *appear* with him in glory.
4: 4. That I *may make* it *manifest,*
1Ti. 3:16. God *was manifest* in the flesh,
2Ti. 1:10. But is now *made manifest* by the
Tit. 1: 3. *hath* in due times *manifested* his word
Heb 9: 8. that the way into the holiest of all *was* not yet *made manifest,*
26. *hath* he *appeared* to put away sin by
1Pet.1:20. but *was manifest* in these last times
5: 4. *when* the chief Shepherd *shall appear,*
1Joh.1: 2. the life *was manifested,*
— and *was manifested* unto us;
2:19. that they *might be made manifest* that
28. that, when he *shall appear,* we may
3: 2. it *doth* not yet *appear* what we shall be:
— when he *shall appear,* we shall be
5. that he *was manifested* to take away
8. the Son of God *was manifested,*
4: 9. In this *was manifested* the love of God
Rev. 3:18. (that) the shame of thy nakedness *do not appear;*
15: 4. for thy judgments *are made manifest.*

5320 3 860/984 5318

φανερῶς, phanerōs.

Mar 1:45. could no more *openly* enter
Joh. 7:10. not *openly,* but as it were in secret.
Acts10: 3. He saw in a vision *evidently*

5321 2 861/984 9:1 5319

φανέρωσις, phanerōsis.

1Co.12: 7. the *manifestation* of the Spirit
2Co. 4: 2. but by *manifestation* of the truth

5322 1 861/984 5316

φανός, phanos.

Joh.18: 3. thither with *lanterns* and torches

5324 1 861/984 9:1 5316

φαντάζομαι, phantazomai.

Heb 12:21. And so terrible was the *sight,*

5325 1 861/985 5324

φαντασία, phantasia.

Acts25:23. with great *pomp,* and was entered

5326 2 861/985 9:1 5324

φάντασμα, phantasma.

Mat.14:26. It is a *spirit;* (lit. a *phantom*)
Mar 6:49. they supposed it had been a *spirit,*

5327 1 861/985 rt 4008 or 4486

φάραγξ, *pharanx.*

Lu. 3: 5. Every *valley* shall be filled, and

5331 3 861/986 5332

φαρμακεία, *pharmakīa.*

Gal. 5:20. Idolatry, *witchcraft*, hatred,
Rev. 9:21. nor of their *sorceries*, nor of their
18:23. for by thy *sorceries* were all nations

5332 1 861/986 *pharmakon* (drug)

φαρμακεύς, *pharmakūs.*

Rev.21: 8. whoremongers, and *sorcerers*, and

5333 1 862/986 rt 5332

φαρμακός, *pharmakos.*

Rev.22:15. For without (are) dogs, and *sorcerers*,

5334 1 862/986 5346

φάσις, *phasis.*

Acts21:31. *tidings* came unto the chief captain

5335 4 862/986 rt 5346

φάσκω, *phasko.*

Acts24: 9. *saying* that these things were so.
25:19. whom Paul *affirmed* to be alive.
Ro. 1:22. *Professing* themselves to be wise,
Rev. 2: 2. tried them *which say* they are apostles,

5336 4 862/986 9:49 *pateomai* (to eat)

φάτνη, *phatnee.*

Lu. 2: 7. and laid him in a *manger*;
12. in swaddling clothes, lying in a *manger*.
16. and the babe lying in a *manger*.
13:15. loose his ox or (his) ass from the *stall*,

5337 4 862/986

φαῦλος, *phaulos.*

Joh. 3:20. every one that doeth *evil* hateth the
5:29. and they that have done *evil*, unto the
Tit. 2: 8. having no *evil* thing to say of you.
Jas. 3:16. there (is) confusion and every *evil* work.

5338 3 862/986 cf rt5457

φέγγος, *phengos.*

Mat.24:29. the moon shall not give her *light*,
Mar13:24. moon shall not give her *light*,
Lu. 11:33. they which come in may see the *light*.

5339 10 862/986

φείδομαι, *phīdomai.*

Acts20:29. among you, not *sparing* the flock.
Ro 8:32. He that *spared* not his own Son,
11:21. if God *spared* not the natural branches, (take heed) lest he also *spare* not thee.
1Co. 7:28. trouble in the flesh: but I *spare* you.
2Co. 1:23. to *spare* you I came not as yet
12: 6. I *forbear*, lest any man should think of me
13: 2. if I come again, I *will* not *spare*:
2Pet. 2: 4. if God *spared* not the angels that sinned,
5. And *spared* not the old world, but

5340 2 862/986 5339

φειδομένως, *phīdomenōs.*

2Co. 9: 6. He which soweth *sparingly* shall reap also *sparingly*;

5341 1 862/986

φελονης see φαιλόνης. p. 782

5342 64 862/986 9:56

φέρω, οἴσω, ἤνεγκα, *phero, oiso, eenenka.*

Mat.14:11. his head *was brought* in a charger,
— and she *brought* (it) to her mother.
18. He said, *Bring* them hither to me.
17:17. *bring* him hither to me.
Mar 1:32. they *brought* unto him all that were
2: 3. *bringing* one sick of the palsy,
4: 8. and *brought forth*, some thirty,
6:27. and commanded his head *to be brought*.
28. And *brought* his head in a charger,
7:32. they *bring* unto him one that was deaf,
8:22. and they *bring* a blind man unto him,
9:17. I *have brought* unto thee my son,
19. *bring* him unto me.
20. And they *brought* him unto him.
12:15. *bring* me a penny,
16 And they *brought* (it).
15:22. they *bring* him unto the place Golgotha,
Lu. 5:18. And, behold, men *brought* in a bed
15:23. *bring* hither the fatted calf, *and*
23:26. that he might *bear* (it) after Jesus.
24: 1. *bringing* the spices which they had prepared,
Joh. 2: 8. and *bear* unto the governor of the feast. And they *bare* (it).
4:33. Hath any man *brought* him (ought) to eat?
12:24. it *bringeth forth* much fruit.
15: 2. branch in me *that beareth* not fruit
— every (branch) that *beareth* fruit, he purgeth it, that it *may bring forth* more fruit.
4. As the branch cannot *bear* fruit of itself,
5. the same *bringeth forth* much fruit:
8. that ye *bear* much fruit;
16. that ye should go and *bring forth* fruit,
18:29. What accusation *bring* ye against this man?
19:39. *and brought* a mixture of myrrh
20:27. *Reach* hither thy finger, and behold my hands; and *reach* hither thy hand,
21.10. *Bring* of the fish which ye have now
18. shall gird thee, and *carry* (thee) whither
Acts 2: 2. as of a *rushing* mighty wind,
4:34. and *brought* the prices of the things
37. and *brought* the money, and laid (it) at
5: 2. and *brought* a certain part, and laid
16. unto Jerusalem, *bringing* sick folks,
12:10. the iron gate *that leadeth* unto the city,
14:13. *brought* oxen and garlands unto the gates,
25: 7. *and laid* many and grievous complaints
27:15. we let (her) drive. (lit. giving to it we *were borne along*)
17. strake sail, and so *were driven*.
Ro. 9:22. *endured* with much longsuffering the
2Ti. 4:13. *bring* (with thee), and the books,
Heb 1: 3. *upholding* all things by the word of his power,
6: 1. *let* us *go on* unto perfection; (lit. *be brought* forward)
9:16. there must also of necessity *be* the death of the testator.

Heb 12:20. For they could not *endure* that which was commanded,
13:13. Let us go forth...*bearing* his reproach.
1Pet. 1:13. for the grace that is to be brought (lit. *that is brought*) unto you
2Pet. 1:17. *when* there *came* such a voice to him
18. And this voice *which came* from heaven
21. For the prophecy *came* not in old time by
— spake (as they were) *moved* by the Holy Ghost.
2:11. *bring* not railing accusation against
2Joh. 10. and *bring* not this doctrine,
Rev.21:24. *do bring* their glory and honour into it.
26. *they shall bring* the glory and honour

5343 3 863/987

φεύγω, phūgo.

Mat. 2:13. and *flee* into Egypt,
3: 7. *to flee* from the wrath to come?
8:33. And they that kept them *fled*,
10:23. *flee* ye into another:
23:33. how *can* ye *escape* the damnation of hell?
24:16. Then *let* them which be in Judæa *flee* into
26:56. Then all the disciples forsook him, and *fled*.
Mar 5:14. And they that fed the swine *fled*,
13:14. then *let* them that be in Judæa *flee* to
14:50. And they all forsook him, and *fled*.
52. and *fled* from them naked.
16: 8. and *fled* from the sepulchre;
Lu. 3: 7. *to flee* from the wrath to come?
8:34. they *fled*, and went and told
21:21. Then *let* them which are in Judæa *flee* to the mountains;
Joh. 10: 5. but *will flee* from him:
12. and leaveth the sheep, and *fleeth*:
13. The hireling *fleeth*, because he is an
Acts 7:29. Then *fled* Moses at this saying,
27:30. were about *to flee* out of the ship,
1Co. 6:18. *Flee* fornication. Every sin that a man
10:14. my dearly beloved, *flee* from idolatry.
1Ti. 6:11. O man of God, *flee* these things;
2Ti. 2:22. *Flee* also youthful lusts:
Heb 11:34. *escaped* the edge of the sword,
12:25. For if they *escaped* not who refused
Jas. 4: 7. and he *will flee* from you.
Rev. 9: 6. and death *shall flee* from them.
12: 6. the woman *fled* into the wilderness,
16:20. And every island *fled away*,
20:11. the earth and the heaven *fled away*,

5345 2 864/988 5346

φήμη, pheemee.

Mat. 9:26. And the *fame* hereof went abroad
Lu. 4:14. and there went out a *fame* of him

5346 58 864/988 rt 5457, cf 3004

φημί, pheemi.

Mat. 4: 7. Jesus *said* unto him, It is written
8: 8. The centurion answered and *said*,
13:28. He *said* unto them, An enemy hath
29. But he *said*, Nay; lest while ye
14: 8. *said*, Give me here John Baptist's head
17:26. Jesus *saith* unto him, Then are the children
19:21. Jesus *said* unto him, If thou wilt be
21:27. And he *said* unto them Neither tell I
25:21. His lord *said* unto him, Well done,
23. His lord *said* unto him, Well done,
26:34. Jesus *said* unto him, Verily I say
Mat.26:61. This (fellow) *said*, I am able to
27:11. And Jesus *said* unto him, Thou sayest.
23. the governor *said*, Why, what evil
65. Pilate *said* unto them, Ye have a watch:
Mar 14:29. But Peter *said* unto him, Although all
Lu. 7:40. And he *saith*, Master, say on.
44. *said* unto Simon, Seest thou this woman?
22:58. another saw him, and *said*, Thou art
70. And he *said* unto them, Ye say that I am
23: 3. he answered him and *said*, Thou sayest (it)
Joh. 1:23. He *said*, I (am) the voice of one crying
9:38. And he *said*, Lord, I believe.
Acts 2:38. Peter *said* unto them, Repent, and be
7: 2. And he *said*, Men, brethren, and fathers,
8:36. and the eunuch *said*, See, (here is) water;
10:28. he *said* unto them, Ye know how that
30. And Cornelius *said*, Four days ago
31. And *said*, Cornelius, thy prayer is heard,
16:30. and *said*, Sirs, what must I do to
37. But Paul *said* unto them, They have beaten
17:22. and *said*, (Ye) men of Athens,
19:35. he *said*, (Ye) men of Ephesus,
21:37. Who *said*, Canst thou speak Greek?
22:2(3). they kept the more silence: and he *saith*,
27. art thou a Roman? He *said*, Yea.
28. And Paul *said*, But I was (free) born.
23: 5. Then *said* Paul, I wist not, brethren,
17. and *said*, Bring this young man unto
18. and *said*, Paul the prisoner called me
35. I will hear thee, *said* he, when thine
25: 5. Let them therefore, *said* he, which among
22. Then Agrippa *said* unto Festus, I would
— To morrow, *said* he, thou shalt hear him.
24. And Festus *said*, King Agrippa, and all men
26: 1. Then Agrippa *said* unto Paul, Thou
24. Festus *said* with a loud voice,
25. But he *said*, I am not mad,
28. Then Agrippa *said* unto Paul, Almost
32. Then *said* Agrippa unto Festus, This
Ro. 3: 8. and as some *affirm* that we say,
1Co. 6:16. for two, *saith* he, shall be one flesh.
7:29. But this I *say*, brethren, the time (is) short:
10:15. judge ye what I *say*.
19. What *say* I then? that the idol is any thing,
15:50. Now this I *say*, brethren, that flesh and
2Co.10:10. For (his) letters, *say* they, (lit. *saith* he) (are) weighty
Heb 8: 5. for, See, *saith* he, (that) thou make all

5348 7 864/988 9:88 5338cf5346

φθάνω, phthano

Mat.12:28. then the kingdom of God *is come* unto you
Lu. 11:20. the kingdom of God *is come* upon you.
Ro. 9:31. *hath* not *attained* to the law of
2Co.10:14. for we *are come* as far as to you also
Phi. 3:16. whereto we *have already attained*,
1Th. 2:16. for the wrath *is come* upon them to
4:15. *shall* not *prevent* them which are asleep.

5349 6 864/989 9:93 5351

φθαρτός, phthartos.

Ro. 1:23. an image made like to *corruptible* man,
1Co. 9:25. to obtain a *corruptible* crown;
15:53. this *corruptible* must put on incorruption,
54. So when this *corruptible* shall have put
1Pet. 1:18. ye were not redeemed with *corruptible*
23. not of *corruptible* seed, but of

5350 3 864/989 5338,5346

φθέγγομαι, phthengomai.

Acts 4:18. not *to speak* at all nor teach in the name
2Pet.2:16. the dumb ass *speaking* with man's voice
18. For *when* they *speak* great swelling

5351 8 865/989 9:93 *phthiō* (to waste away)

φθείρω, phthīro.

1Co. 3:17. If any man *defile* the temple of God, him *shall* God *destroy;*
15:33. evil communications *corrupt* good
2Co. 7: 2. we *have corrupted* no man,
11: 3. so your minds *should be corrupted* from
Eph. 4:22. the old man, *which is corrupt* according to the deceitful lusts;
Jude 10. in those things they *corrupt* themselves.
Rev.19: 2. which *did corrupt* the earth with her fornication,

5352 1 865/989 3703 *phthinō* (to wane)

φθινοπωρινός, phthinopōrinos.

Jude 12. trees *whose fruit withereth,*

5353 2 865/989 5350

φθόγγος, phthongos.

Ro. 10:18. Yes verily, their *sound* went into all
1Co.14: 7. except they give a distinction in the *sounds,*

5354 1 865/989 5355

φθονέω, phthoneo.

Gal. 5:26. *envying* one another.

5355 9 865/989 cf rt5351

φθόνος, phthonos.

Mat.27:18. that for *envy* they had delivered him.
Mar 15:10. had delivered him for *envy.*
Ro. 1:29. full of *envy,* murder, debate,
Gal. 5:21. *Envyings,* murders, drunkenness,
Phi. 1:15. preach Christ even of *envy* and strife;
1Ti. 6: 4. whereof cometh *envy,* strife,
Tit. 3: 3. living in malice and *envy,*
Jas. 4: 5. The spirit that dwelleth in us lusteth to *envy?*
1Pet.2: 1. guile, and hypocrisies, and *envies,*

5356 9 865/989 9:93 5351

φθορά, phthora.

Ro. 8:21. delivered from the bondage of *corruption*
1Co.15:42. It is sown in *corruption;* it is raised
50. neither doth *corruption* inherit incorruption.
Gal. 6: 8. shall of the flesh reap *corruption;*
Col. 2:22. Which all are to *perish* with the using;
2Pet.1: 4. having escaped the *corruption* that is
2:12. beasts, made to be taken and *destroyed,*
— shall utterly perish in their own *corruption;*
19. themselves are the servants of *corruption:*

5357 12 866/989

φιάλη, phialee.

Rev. 5: 8. and golden *vials* full of odours,
15: 7. unto the seven angels seven golden *vials*
16: 1. pour out the *vials* of the wrath of God
2. poured out his *vial* upon the earth;
3. poured out his *vial* upon the sea;
Rev.16: 4. poured out his *vial* upon the rivers and
8. poured out his *vial* upon the sun;
10. out his *vial* upon the seat of the beast
12. his *vial* upon the great river Euphrates;
17. poured out his *vial* into the air;
17: 1. angels which had the seven *vials,*
21: 9. which had the seven *vials* full of the

5358 1 866/989 1:10- 5384,18

φιλάγαθος, philagathos.

Tit. 1: 8. But a lover of hospitality, a *lover of good men,*

5360 6 866/989 1:144 5361

φιλαδελφία, philadelphia.

Ro. 12:10. (Be) kindly affectioned one to another with *brotherly love;*
1Th. 4: 9. But as touching *brotherly love*
Heb 13: 1. Let *brotherly love* continue.
1Pet.1:22. unto unfeigned *love of the brethren,*
2Pet.1: 7. And to godliness *brotherly kindness;* and to *brotherly kindness* charity.

5361 1 866/989 1:144 5384,80

φιλάδελφος, philadelphos.

1Pet.3: 8. *love as brethren,* (be) pitiful,

5362 1 866/989 5384,435

φίλανδρος, philandros.

Tit. 2: 4. to *love their husbands,* to love their

5363 2 866/990 9:107 rt 5364

φιλανθρωπία, philanthrōpia.

Acts28: 2. shewed us no little *kindness:*
Tit. 3: 4. after that the kindness and *love* of God our Saviour *toward man* appeared,

5364 1 866/990 9:107 5384,444

φιλανθρώπως, philanthrōpōs.

Acts27: 3. Julius *courteously* entreated Paul,

5365 1 866/990 5366

φιλαργυρία, philarguria.

1Ti. 6:10. For the *love of money* is the root of all evil:

5366 2 866/990 5384,696

φιλάργυρος, philarguros.

Lu. 16:14. the Pharisees also, who were *covetous,*
2Ti. 3: 2. lovers of their own selves, *covetous,*

5367 1 866/990 5384,846

φίλαυτος, philautos.

2Ti. 3: 2. *lovers of their own selves,* covetous,

5368 25 866/990 9:113 5384,cf25

φιλέω, phileo.

Mat. 6: 5. for they *love* to pray standing in the
10:37. He *that loveth* father or mother more than me
— and he *that loveth* son or daughter more
23: 6. And *love* the uppermost rooms at feasts,

Mat.26:48. Whomsoever I *shall kiss*, that same is he:
Mar14:44. Whomsoever I *shall kiss*, that same is he;
Lu. 20:46. and *love* greetings in the markets,
22:47. and drew near unto Jesus *to kiss* him.
Joh. 5:20. For the Father *loveth* the Son,
11: 3. he whom thou *lovest* is sick.
36. Behold how he *loved* him!
12:25. He *that loveth* his life shall lose it;
15:19. the world would *love* his own:
16:27. For the Father himself *loveth* you, because ye *have loved* me,
20: 2. to the other disciple, whom Jesus *loved*,
21:15. thou knowest that I *love* thee.
16. thou knowest that I *love* thee.
17. Simon, (son) of Jonas, *lovest* thou me?
— *Lovest* thou me?
— thou knowest that I *love* thee.
1Co.16:22. If any man *love* not the Lord Jesus Christ,
Tit. 3:15. Greet them *that love* us in the faith.
Rev. 3:19. As many as I *love*, I rebuke and
22:15. and whosoever *loveth* and maketh a lie.

5369 1 867/990 2:909 5384,2237

φιλήδονος, phileedonos.

2Ti. 3: 4. *lovers of pleasures* more than lovers of God;

5370 7 867/990 9:113 5368

φίλημα, phileema.

Lu. 7:45. Thou gavest me no *kiss*:
22:48. betrayest thou the Son of man with a *kiss?*
Ro. 16:16. Salute one another with an holy *kiss*.
1Co.16:20. Greet ye one another with an holy *kiss*.
2Co.13:12. Greet one another with an holy *kiss*.
1Th. 5:26. Greet all the brethren with an holy *kiss*.
1Pet 5:14. one another with a *kiss* of charity.

5373 1 867/990 9:113 5384

φιλία, philia.

Jas. 4: 4. that the *friendship* of the world is enmity with God?

5377 1 868/991 5384,2316

φιλόθεος, philotheos.

2Ti. 3: 4. lovers of pleasures more than *lovers of God;*

5379 1 868/991 5380

φιλονεικία, philonīkia.

Lu. 22:24. there was also a *strife* among them, which

5380 1 868/991 5384 *neikos* (quarrel)

φιλόνεικος, philonīkos.

1Co.11:16. But if any man seem to be *contentious*,

5381 2 868/991 5:1 5382

φιλοξενία, philoxenia.

Ro. 12:13. given to *hospitality*.
Heb13: 2. Be not forgetful to *entertain strangers*:

5382 3 868/991 5:1 5384,3581

φιλόξενος, philoxenos.

1Ti. 3: 2. *given to hospitality*, apt to teach;
Tit. 1: 8. But a *lover of hospitality*, a lover of
1Pet.4: 9. *Use hospitality* one to another without

5383 1 868/991 5384,4413

φιλοπρωτεύω, philoprōtuo.

3Joh. 9. but Diotrephes, *who loveth to have the pre-eminence* among them.

5384 29 868/991 9:113

φίλος, philos.

Mat.11:19. a *friend* of publicans and sinners.
Lu. 7: 6. the centurion sent *friends* to him,
34. a *friend* of publicans and sinners!
11: 5. Which of you shall have a *friend*,
— *Friend*, lend me three loaves;
6. For a *friend* of mine in his journey is
8. and give him, because he is his *friend*,
12: 4. And I say unto you my *friends*,
14:10. *Friend*, go up higher:
12. call not thy *friends*, nor thy brethren,
15: 6. he calleth together (his) *friends* and
9. she calleth (her) *friends* and (her)
29. that I might make merry with my *friends*:
16: 9. Make to yourselves *friends* of the mammon
21:16. brethren, and kinsfolks, and *friends*;
23:12. Pilate and Herod were made *friends*
Joh. 3:29. but the *friend* of the bridegroom,
11:11. Our *friend* Lazarus sleepeth;
15:13. a man lay down his life for his *friends*.
14. Ye are my *friends*, if ye do whatsoever
15. but I have called you *friends*;
19:12. thou art not Cæsar's *friend*:
Acts10:24. his kinsmen and near *friends*.
19:31. the chief of Asia, which were his *friends*,
27: 3. to go unto his *friends* to refresh himself.
Jas. 2:23. and he was called the *Friend* of God.
4: 4. whosoever therefore will be a *friend* of the world is the enemy of God.
3Joh. 14(15). (Our) *friends* salute thee. Greet the *friends* by name.

5385 1 869/991 9:172 5386

φιλοσοφία, philosophia.

Col. 2: 8. spoil you, through *philosophy* and vain deceit, after the tradition of

5386 1 869/991 9:172 5384,4680

φιλόσοφος, philosophos.

Acts17:18. certain *philosophers* of the Epicureans,

5387 1 869/991 5384 *storgē* (fondness)

φιλόστοργος, philostorgos.

Ro. 12:10. (Be) *kindly affectioned* one to another

5388 1 869/991 5384,5043

φιλότεκνος, philoteknos.

Tit. 2: 4. to *love their children*,

5389 3 869/991 5384,5092

φιλοτιμέομαι, philotimeomai.

Ro. 15:20. Yea, so *have I strived* to preach the gospel,
2Co. 5: 9. Wherefore we *labour*, that, whether
1Th. 4:11. And that ye *study* to be quiet, and to do

3 E 2

5390 1 869/991 5391

φιλοφρόνως, philophronōs.

Acts28: 7. and lodged us three days *courteously*.

5391 1 869/989 5384,5424

φιλόφρων, philophrōn.

1Pet.3: 8. (be) pitiful, (be) *courteous:*

phimos (muzzle)

5392 8 869/991

φιμόω, phimoō.

Mat.22:12. And he *was speechless*.
34. that he *had put* the Sadducees *to silence*,
Mar 1:25. *Hold* thy *peace*, and come out of him.
4:39. and said unto the sea, Peace, *be still*.
Lu. 4:35. *Hold* thy *peace*, and come out of him.
1Co. 9: 9. Thou *shalt* not *muzzle* the mouth of the
1Ti. 5:18. Thou *shalt* not *muzzle* the ox that treadeth
1Pet.2:15. may *put to silence* the ignorance of

5394 2 869/991 5395

φλογίζω, phlogizo.

Jas. 3: 6. and *setteth on fire* the course of nature; and it *is set on fire* of hell.

phlegō (to flame)

5395 7 870/991

φλόξ, phlox.

Lu. 16:24. for I am tormented in this *flame*.
Acts 7:30. in a *flame* of fire in a bush.
2Th. 1: 8. In *flaming* fire taking vengeance
Heb 1: 7. and his ministers a *flame* of fire.
Rev. 1:14. his eyes (were) as a *flame* of fire,
2:18. his eyes like unto a *flame* of fire,
19:12. His eyes (were) as a *flame* of fire,

5396 1 870/992 5397

φλυαρέω, phluareo.

3Joh. 10. *prating against* us with malicious words:

phluō (to bubble)

5397 1 870/992

φλύαρος, phluaros.

1Ti. 5:13. but *tattlers* also and busybodies,

5399 93 870/992 9:189 5401

φοβέομαι, phobeomai.

Mat. 1:20. *fear* not to take unto thee Mary
2:22. he *was afraid* to go thither:
10:26. *Fear* them not therefore:
28. And *fear* not them which kill the
— but rather *fear* him which is able to
31. *Fear* ye not therefore, ye are of
14: 5. he *feared* the multitude, because they
27. it is I; *be* not *afraid*.
30. the wind boisterous, he *was afraid*;
17: 6. fell on their face, and *were* sore *afraid*.
7. Arise, and *be* not *afraid*.
21:26. we *fear* the people; for all hold John
46. they *feared* the multitude, because they
25:25. And I was *afraid*, and went and hid thy
27:54. they *feared* greatly, saying, Truly this
28: 5. *Fear* not ye: for I know that ye seek
10. *Be* not *afraid:* go tell my brethren that
4:41. they *feared* exceedingly, and said
5:15. and they *were afraid*.
33. But the woman *fearing* and trembling.
Mar 5:36. *Be* not *afraid*, only believe.
6:20. For Herod *feared* John, knowing
50. it is I; *be* not *afraid*.
9:32. and *were afraid* to ask him.
10:32. and as they followed, they *were afraid*.
11:18. for they *feared* him, because all
32. Of men; they *feared* the people:
12:12. to lay hold on him, but *feared* the people
16: 8. for they *were afraid*.
Lu. 1:13. *Fear* not, Zacharias: for thy prayer
30. *Fear* not, Mary: for thou hast found
50. And his mercy (is) on them *that fear* him
2: 9. and they *were* sore *afraid*.
10. *Fear* not: for, behold, I bring you
5:10. And Jesus said unto Simon, *Fear* not;
8:25. And they *being afraid* wondered
35. and they *were afraid*.
50. *Fear* not: believe only,
9:34. *feared* as they entered into the cloud.
45. they *feared* to ask him of that saying.
12: 4. *Be* not *afraid* of them that kill the
5. whom ye *shall fear: Fear* him, which after he hath killed
— I say unto you, *Fear* him.
7. *Fear* not therefore: ye are of more value
32. *Fear* not, little flock;
18: 2. a judge, *which feared* not God,
4. Though I *fear* not God,
19:21. For I *feared* thee, because thou art
20:19. and they *feared* the people: for they
22: 2. for they *feared* the people.
23:40. *Dost* not thou *fear* God, seeing thou art
Joh. 6:19. unto the ship: and they *were afraid*.
20. It is I; *be* not *afraid*.
9:22. because they *feared* the Jews:
12:15. *Fear* not, daughter of Sion: behold,
19: 8. he *was* the more *afraid*;
Acts 5:26. for they *feared* the people, lest
9:26. but they *were* all *afraid* of him,
10: 2. and one *that feared* God with
22. and one *that feareth* God,
35. But in every nation he *that feareth* him
13:16. and ye *that fear* God, give audience.
26. and *whosoever* among you *feareth* God,
16:38. they *feared*, when they heard that they
18: 9. *Be* not *afraid*, but speak, and hold not
22:29. and the chief captain also *was afraid*,
27:17. and, *fearing* lest they should fall into
24. Saying, *Fear* not, Paul; thou must be
29. *fearing* lest we should have fallen
Ro. 11:20. Be not highminded, but *fear:*
13: 3. Wilt thou then not *be afraid* of the power?
4. if thou do that which is evil, *be afraid*.
2Co.11: 3. But I *fear*, lest by any means, as the
12:20. For I *fear*, lest, when I come, I
Gal 2:12. *fearing* them which were of the
4:11. I *am afraid* of you, lest I have bestowed
Eph 5:33. and the wife (see) that she *reverence* (her)
Col. 3:22. but in singleness of heart, *fearing* God:
Heb 4: 1. *Let* us therefore *fear*, lest, a promise
11:23. and they *were* not *afraid* of the king's
27. not *fearing* the wrath of the king:
13: 6. I *will* not *fear* what man shall do unto
1Pet.2:17. *Fear* God. Honour the king.
3: 6. and *are* not *afraid* with any amazement.
14. and *be* not *afraid* of their terror,
1Joh.4:18. He *that feareth* is not made perfect in
Rev. 1:17. saying unto me, *Fear* not; I am the
2:10. *Fear* none of those things which thou
11:18. to the saints, and them *that fear* thy name,
14: 7. *Fear* God, and give glory to him;

Rev.15: 4. Who *shall* not *fear* thee, O Lord, and
19· 5. and ye *that fear* him, both small and

5398 3 870/993 5401

φοβερός, phoberos.

Heb 10: 27. *fearful* looking for of judgment
31. (It is) a *fearful* thing to fall into the
12: 21. And so *terrible* was the sight,

5400 1 871/993 5399

φόβητρον, phobeetron.

Lu. 21: 11. and *fearful sights* and great signs

5401 47 871/993 9:189 *phebomai* (to be made afraid)

φόβος, phobos.

Mat.14: 26. and they cried out for *fear*.
28: 4. for *fear* of him the keepers did shake,
8. from the sepulchre with *fear* and great joy;
Mar 4: 41. And they feared exceedingly, (lit. f. a great *fear*)
Lu. 1: 12. and *fear* fell upon him.
65. And *fear* came on all that dwelt
2: 9. and they were sore afraid. (lit. feared, &c.)
5: 26. and were filled with *fear*, saying, We
7: 16. And there came a *fear* on all:
8: 37. for they were taken with great *fear:*
21: 26. for *fear*, and for looking after those
Joh. 7: 13. openly of him for *fear* of the Jews.
19: 38. but secretly for *fear* of the Jews,
20: 19. assembled for *fear* of the Jews, came Jesus
Acts 2: 43. And *fear* came upon every soul:
5: 5. great *fear* came on all them that
11. great *fear* came upon all the church,
9: 31. and walking in the *fear* of the Lord,
19: 17. and *fear* fell on them all,
Ro. 3: 18. There is no *fear* of God before
8: 15. the spirit of bondage again to *fear*,
13: 3. rulers are not a *terror* to good works,
7. *fear* to whom *fear;*
1Co. 2: 3. and in *fear*, and in much trembling.
2Co. 5: 11. Knowing therefore the *terror* of the Lord,
7: 1. perfecting holiness in the *fear* of God.
5. within (were) *fears*.
11. (what) indignation, yea, (what) *fear*,
15. how with *fear* and trembling ye received
Eph. 5: 21. one to another in the *fear* of God.
6: 5. with *fear* and trembling, in singleness
Phi. 2: 12. your own salvation with *fear* and
1 Ti. 5: 20. others also may fear. (lit. may have *fear*)
Heb 2: 15. who through *fear* of death were all
1Pet. 1: 17. the time of your sojourning (here) in *fear:*
2: 18. subject to (your) masters with all *fear;*
3: 2. your chaste conversation (coupled) with *fear*.
14. and be not afraid of their *terror*,
15. with meekness and *fear:*
1Joh.4: 18. There is no *fear* in love; but perfect love casteth out *fear:* because *fear* hath torment.
Jude 23. And others save with *fear*, pulling
Rev.11: 11. great *fear* fell upon them which saw them.
18: 10. afar off for the *fear* of her torment,
15. stand afar off for the *fear* of her torment, weeping and wailing.

5404 2 872/993

φοῖνιξ, phoinix.

Joh. 12: 13. Took branches of *palm trees*,
Rev. 7: 9 white robes, and *palms* in their hands;

5406 7 872/993 5408cf443cf4607

φονεύς, phonūs.

Mat.22: 7. and destroyed those *murderers*,
Acts 3: 14. desired a *murderer* to be granted unto you;
7: 52. of whom ye have been now the betrayers and *murderers:*
28: 4. No doubt this man is a *murderer*,
1Pet.4: 15. let none of you suffer as a *murderer*, or
Rev.21: 8. and *murderers*, and whoremongers,
22: 15. and *murderers*, and idolaters, and

5407 12 872/994 5406

φονεύω, phonūo.

Mat. 5: 21. Thou *shalt* not *kill;* and whosoever *shall kill*
19: 18. Thou *shalt do* no *murder*,
23: 31. of them *which killed* the prophets.
35. whom ye *slew* between the temple and
Mar 10: 19. *Do* not *kill*,
Lu. 18: 20. *Do* not *kill*,
Ro. 13: 9. Thou *shalt* not *kill*,
Jas. 2: 11. said also, *Do* not *kill*.
— yet if thou *kill*, thou art become a
4: 2. ye *kill*, and desire to have,
5: 6. Ye have condemned (and) *killed* the just;

5408 10 872/994 *phenō* (to slay)

φόνος, phonos.

Mat.15: 19. proceed evil thoughts, *murders*,
Mar 7: 21. adulteries, fornications, *murders*,
15: 7. committed *murder* in the insurrection
Lu. 23: 19. in the city, and for *murder*,
25. him that for sedition and *murder* was
Acts 9: 1. breathing out threatenings and *slaughter* against the disciples
Ro. 1: 29. full of envy, *murder*, debate,
Gal. 5: 21. Envyings, *murders*, drunkenness,
Heb 11: 37. were slain with the sword: (lit. *slaughter* of the sword)
Rev. 9: 21. Neither repented they of their *murders*,

5409 6 872/994 9:56 5411

φορέω, phoreo.

Mat.11: 8. they *that wear* soft (clothing) are in kings' houses.
Joh.19: 5. *wearing* the crown of thorns,
Ro. 13: 4. for he *beareth* not the sword in vain:
1Co. 15: 49. as we *have borne* the image of the earthy, we *shall* also *bear* the image of
Jas. 2: 3. to him *that weareth* the gay clothing,

5411 5 872/994 9:56 5342cf5056

φόρος, phoros.

Lu. 20: 22. Is it lawful for us to give *tribute* unto Cæsar, or no?
23: 2. and forbidding to give *tribute* to Cæsar,
Ro. 13: 6. For for this cause pay ye *tribute* also:
7. *tribute* to whom *tribute* (is due);

5412 2 872/994 9:56 5414

φορτίζω, phortizo.

Mat.11: 28. Come unto me, all (ye) that labour and are *heavy laden*,
Lu. 11: 46. for ye *lade* men with burdens grievous to

5413 5 873/994 9:56 5414

φορτίον, phortion.

Mat.11: 30. and my *burden* is light.

Mat.23: 4. For they bind heavy *burdens* and
Lu. 11:46. with *burdens* grievous to be borne, and ye yourselves touch not the *burdens* with
Gal. 6: 5. For every man shall bear his own *burden*.

5414 1 873/994 5342
φόρτος, phortos.

Acts27:10 not only of the *lading* and ship, but also

5416 1 873/994 rt 5417
φραγέλλιον, phragellion.

Joh. 2:15. when he had made a *scourge* of small cords,

5417 2 873/994
φραγελλόω, phragelloō.

Mat.27:26. *when* he *had scourged* Jesus,
Mar15:15. delivered Jesus, *when* he *had scourged* (him),

5418 4 873/994 5420
φραγμός, phragmos.

Mat.21:33. and *hedged* it round about,
Mar12: 1. and set an *hedge* about (it),
Lu. 14:23. Go out into the highways and *hedges*,
Eph. 2:14. and hath broken down the middle wall of *partition* (between us);

5419 4 873/994 cf 5420
φράζω, phrazo.

Mat.13:36. *Declare* unto us the parable
15:15. *Declare* unto us this parable.

5420 2 873/994 rt 5424
φράσσω, phrasso.

Ro. 3:19. that every mouth *may be stopped*,
2Co.11:10. no man shall stop me of this boasting (lit. this boasting *shall* not *be stopped* to me)
Heb11:33. *stopped* the mouths of lions,

5421 7 873/994
φρέαρ, phrear.

Lu. 14: 5. have an ass or an ox fallen into a *pit*,
Joh. 4:11. and the *well* is deep:
12. which gave us the *well*,
Rev. 9: 1. was given the key of the bottomless *pit*.
2. And he opened the bottomless *pit*; and there arose a smoke out of the *pit*,
— by reason of the smoke of the *pit*.

5422 1 873/994 5423
φρεναπατάω, phrenapatao.

Gal. 6: 3. when he is nothing, he *deceiveth* himself.

5423 1 873/994 5424,539
φρεναπάτης, phrenapatees.

Tit. 1:10. and vain talkers and *deceivers*,

5424 2 873/994 9:220 phraō (to curb)
φρένες, phrenes.

Plural from φρήν.

1Co.14:20. be not children in *understanding*:
— but in *understanding* be men.

5425 1 873/995
φρίσσω, phrisso.

Jas. 2:19. the devils also believe, and *tremble*. (lit *quiver*)

5426 29 874/995 9:220 5424
φρονέω, phroneo.

Mat.16:23. *savourest* not the things that be of God,
Mar 8:33. thou *savourest* not the things that be
Acts28:22. to hear of thee what thou *thinkest*:
Ro. 8: 5. *do mind* the things of the flesh;
12: 3. more highly than he ought *to think*; but *to think* soberly,
16. (Be) of the same mind (lit. *minding* the same) one toward another. *Mind* not high things,
14: 6. He *that regardeth* the day, *regardeth* (it) unto the Lord; and he *that regardeth* not the day, to the Lord he *doth* not *regard* (it).
15: 5. *to be* like*minded* one toward another
1Co. 4: 6. not *to think* (of men) above that which is
13:11. I *understood* as a child:
2Co.13:11. *be of* one *mind*, (lit. *mind* ye the same)
Gal. 5:10. that ye *will be* none otherwise *minded*:
Phi. 1: 7. meet for me *to think* this of you all,
2: 2. that ye *be* like*minded*,
— (being) of one accord, of one *mind*. (lit. *minding* the one thing)
5. *Let* this *mind be* in you, which was
3:15. *Let* us therefore, as many as be perfect, *be* thus *minded*: and if in any thing ye *be* otherwise *minded*,
16. let us *mind* the same thing.
19. *who mind* earthly things.
4: 2. that they *be* of the same *mind* in the Lord.
10. your *care* of me hath flourished again; wherein ye *were* also *careful*, but
Col. 3: 2. *Set* your *affection on* things above,

5427 4 874/995 9:220 5426
φρόνημα, phroneema.

Ro. 8: 6. *to be* carnally *minded* (is) death; but *to be* spiritually *minded* (is) life and peace.
7. Because the carnal *mind* (is) enmity
27. knoweth what (is) the *mind* of the Spirit,

5428 2 874/995 9:220 5426
φρόνησις, phroneesis.

Lu. 1:17. the disobedient to the *wisdom* of the just;
Eph. 1: 8. in all wisdom and *prudence*;

5429 14 874/995 9:220 cf 4680 5424,cf 4908
φρόνιμος, phronimos.

Mat. 7:24. I will liken him unto a *wise* man,
10:16. be ye therefore *wise* as serpents,
24:45. Who then is a faithful and *wise* servant,
25: 2. And five of them were *wise*,
4. the *wise* took oil in their vessels with
8. And the foolish said unto the *wise*,
9. But the *wise* answered, saying,
Lu. 12:42. Who then is that faithful and *wise* steward,
16: 8. *wiser* than the children of light.
Ro. 11:25. lest ye should be *wise* in your own conceits;
12:16. Be not *wise* in your own conceits.
1Co. 4:10. but ye (are) *wise* in Christ;
10:15. I speak as to *wise* men; judge ye
2Co.11:19. seeing ye (yourselves) are *wise*.

5430 1 874/995 5429

φρονίμως, phronimōs.

Lu. 16: 8. because he had done *wisely:*

5431 1 874/995 5424

φροντίζω, phrontizo.

Tit. 3: 8. *might be careful* to maintain good works.

5432 4 875/995 4253,3708 cf5083

φρουρέω, phroureo.

2Co.11:32. *kept* the city of the Damascenes *with a garrison,*
Gal. 3:23. we *were kept* under the law, shut up unto
Phi. 4: 7. *shall keep* your hearts and minds through
1Pet.1: 5. *Who are kept* by the power of God through faith unto salvation

---

5433 1 875/995 cf 1031

φρυάσσω, phruasso.

Acts 4:25. Why *did* the heathen *rage,* and the

5434 1 875/995 phrugō (to roast)

φρύγανον, phruganon.

Acts28: 3. Paul had gathered a bundle of *sticks,*

5437 2 875/995 5343

φυγή, phugee.

Mat.24:20. that your *flight* be not in the winter,
Mar 13:18. that your *flight* be not in the winter.

5438 47 875/995 9:236 5442

φυλακή, phulakee.

Mat. 5:25. and thou be cast into *prison.*
14: 3. and put (him) in *prison* for Herodias' sake,
10. and beheaded John in the *prison.*
25. And in the fourth *watch* of the night
18:30. went and cast him into *prison,* till he
24:43. in what *watch* the thief would come,
25:36. I was in *prison,* and ye came unto me.
39. when saw we thee sick, or in *prison,*
43. sick, and in *prison,* and ye
44. or sick, or in *prison,* and did not
Mar 6:17. bound him in *prison* for Herodias' sake,
27(28). and beheaded him in the *prison,*
48. about the fourth *watch* of the night
Lu. 2: 8. keeping *watch* over their flock by night.
3:20. that he shut up John in *prison.*
12:38. in the second *watch,* or come in the third *watch,*
58. and the officer cast thee into *prison.*
21:12. to the synagogues, and into *prisons,*
22:33. both into *prison,* and to death.
23:19. and for murder, was cast into *prison.*
25. and murder was cast into *prison,*
Joh. 3:24. For John was not yet cast into *prison.*
Acts 5:19. by night opened the *prison* doors,
22. and found them not in the *prison,*
25. the men whom ye put in *prison*
8: 3. men and women committed (them) to *prison.*
12: 4. he put (him) in *prison,* and delivered
5. Peter therefore was kept in *prison:*
6. keepers before the door kept the *prison.*
10. were past the first and the second *ward,*
17. had brought him out of the *prison.*
16:23. they cast (them) into *prison,*
Acts16:24. thrust them into the inner *prison,*
27. and seeing the *prison* doors open,
37. and have cast (us) into *prison,*
40. And they went out of the *prison,*
22: 4. and delivering into *prisons* both
26:10. of the saints did I shut up in *prison.*
2Co. 6: 5. In stripes, in *imprisonments,*
11:23. in *prisons* more frequent,
Heb 11:36. moreover of bonds and *imprisonment*
1Pet. 3:19. preached unto the spirits in *prison;*
Rev. 2:10. devil shall cast (some) of you into *prison.*
18: 2. and the *hold* of every foul spirit, and a *cage* of every unclean and hateful bird.
20: 7. Satan shall be loosed out of his *prison,*

5439 1 876/996 5441

φυλακίζω, phulakizo.

Acts22:19. that I *imprisoned* and beat in every

5440 1 876/996 5442

φυλακτήριον, phulakteerion.

Mat.23: 5. they make broad their *phylacteries,*

5441 3 876/996 5442

φύλαξ, phulax.

Acts 5:23. and the *keepers* standing without
12: 6. and the *keepers* before the door kept
19. he examined the *keepers,* and commanded

5442 30 876/996 9:236 cf 5083 5443

φυλάσσω, phulasso.

Mat.19:20. All these things *have I kept* from
Mar.10:20. all these *have I observed* from my youth.
Lu. 2: 8. *keeping* watch over their flock
8:29. he was *kept* bound with chains and in
11:21. When a strong man armed *keepeth* his
28. that hear the word of God, and *keep* it.
12:15. and *beware* of covetousness:
18:21. All these *have* I *kept* from my youth up.
Joh.12:25. *shall keep* it unto life eternal.
17:12. that thou gavest me I *have kept,*
Acts 7:53. of angels, and *have* not *kept* (it).
12: 4. to four quaternions of soldiers *to keep* him;
16: 4. delivered them the decrees *for to keep,*
21:24. walkest orderly, and *keepest* the law.
25. only that they *keep* them*selves* from
22:20. *kept* the raiment of them that slew him.
23:35. *to be kept* in Herod's judgment hall.
28:16. with a soldier *that kept* him.
Ro. 2:26. *keep* the righteousness of the law,
Gal. 6:13. who are circumcised *keep* the law;
2Th. 3: 3. shall stablish you, and *keep* (you) from evil.
1Ti. 5:21. that thou *observe* these things
6:20. *keep* that which is committed to thy trust,
2Ti. 1:12. that he is able *to keep* that which I have
14. which was committed unto thee *keep* by the Holy Ghost
4:15. Of whom *be* thou *ware* also;
2Pet. 2: 5. but *saved* Noah the eighth (person),
3:17. ye know (these things) before, *beware* lest
1Joh.5:21. *keep* yourselves from idols.
Jude 24. that is able *to keep* you from falling,

5443 31 876/996 9:236 cf 5444 5453

φυλή, phulee.

Mat.19:28. judging the twelve *tribes* of Israel

Mat.24:30. and then shall all the *tribes* of the earth
Lu. 2:36. daughter of Phanuel, of the *tribe* of Aser.
22:30. judging the twelve *tribes* of Israel.
Acts13:21. son of Cis, a man of the *tribe* of Benjamin,
Ro. 11: 1. (of) the *tribe* of Benjamin.
Phi. 3: 5. (of) the *tribe* of Benjamin, an Hebrew of
Heb 7:13. pertaineth to another *tribe*, of which no
14. of which *tribe* Moses spake nothing
Jas. 1: 1. to the twelve *tribes* which are scattered
Rev. 1: 7. and all *kindreds* of the earth shall wail
5: 5. the Lion of the *tribe* of Juda,
9. out of every *kindred*, and tongue,
7: 4. of all the *tribes* of the children of Israel.
5. Of the *tribe* of Juda (were) sealed twelve
— Of the *tribe* of Reuben (were),
— Of the *tribe* of Gad (were)
6. Of the *tribe* of Aser (were)
— Of the *tribe* of Nepthalim (were)
— Of the *tribe* of Manasses (were)
7. Of the *tribe* of Simeon (were)
— Of the *tribe* of Levi (were)
— Of the *tribe* of Issachar (were)
8. Of the *tribe* of Zabulon (were)
— Of the *tribe* of Joseph (were)
— Of the *tribe* of Benjamin (were)
9. and *kindreds*, and people, and tongues,
11: 9. and *kindreds* and tongues and nations
13: 7. over all *kindreds*, and tongues, and
14: 6. and to every nation, and *kindred*, and
21:12. (the names) of the twelve *tribes* of the children of Israel:

5444 6 877/997 rt 5443

φύλλον, *phullon.*

Mat.21:19. nothing thereon, but *leaves* only,
24:32. tender, and putteth forth *leaves*,
Mar 11:13. seeing a fig tree afar off having *leaves*,
— he found nothing but *leaves*;
13:28. and putteth forth *leaves*, ye know
Rev.22: 2. and the *leaves* of the tree (were) for the healing of the nations.

φῦμι see φύω. 5453

5445 5 877/997 *phurō* (to mix)

[illegible]μα, *phurama.*

Ro. 9:21. of the same *lump* to make one vessel
11:16. firstfruit (be) holy, the *lump* (is) also (holy):
1Co. 5: 6. a little leaven leaveneth the whole *lump*?
7. that ye may be a new *lump*,
Gal. 5: 9. A little leaven leaveneth the whole *lump*.

5446 3 877/997 9:251 5449

φυσικός, *phusikos.* cf 5591

Ro. 1:26. their women did change the *natural* use
27. leaving the *natural* use of the woman,
2Pet. 2:12. But these, as *natural* brute beasts,

5447 1 877/997 9:251 5446

φυσικῶς, *phusikōs.*

Jude 10. but what they know *naturally*, as

5448 7 877/997 5449

φυσιόω, *phusioō.*

1 Co. 4: 6. that no one of you *be puffed up* for one
18. Now some *are puffed up*, as though I
19. not the speech of them *which are puffed up*,
5: 2. And ye are *puffed up*, and have not
8: 1. Knowledge *puffeth up*, but charity
13: 4. *is* not *puffed up*,
Col. 2:18. vainly *puffed up* by his fleshly mind,

5449 14 877/997 9:251 5453

φύσις, *phusis.*

Ro. 1:26. into that which is against *nature*:
2:14. do by *nature* the things contained in the law,
27. uncircumcision which is by *nature*,
11:21. For if God spared not the *natur*al branches,
24. out of the olive tree which is wild by *nature*, and wert graffed contrary to *nature* into
— shall these, which be the *natur*al (branches),
1Co.11:14. Doth not even *nature* itself teach you,
Gal. 2:15. We (who are) Jews by *nature*,
4: 8. which by *nature* are no gods.
Eph. 2: 3. and were by *nature* the children of wrath,
Jas. 3: 7. every *kind* of beasts, and of birds, and
— hath been tamed of man*kind*:
2Pet. 1: 4. ye might be partakers of the divine *nature*,

5450 1 877/997 5448

φυσίωσις, *phusiōsis.*

2Co.12:20. whisperings, *swellings*, tumults.

5451 1 878/997 5452

φυτεία, *phutia.*

Mat.15:13. Every *plant*, which my heavenly Father hath not planted,

5452 11 878/997 5453

φυτεύω, *phutūo.*

Mat.15:13. which my heavenly Father *hath* not *planted*,
21:33. which *planted* a vineyard,
Mar 12: 1. A (certain) man *planted* a vineyard,
Lu. 13: 6. A certain (man) had a fig tree *planted* in
17: 6. and *be* thou *planted* in the sea,
28. they *planted*, they builded;
20: 9. A certain man *planted* a vineyard,
1Co. 3: 6. I *have planted*, Apollos watered;
7. neither is he *that planteth* any thing.
8. Now he *that planteth* and he that
9: 7. who *planteth* a vineyard, and eateth not

5453 3 878/997

φύω, *phuo.*

Lu. 8: 6. *as soon as* it *was sprung up*, it withered away
8. and *sprang up*, *and* bare fruit
Heb 12:15. any root of bitterness *springing* up

5454 2 878/997

φωλεός, *pholeos.*

Mat. 8:20. The foxes have *holes*, and the birds
Lu. 9:58. Foxes have *holes*, and birds of the air

5455 42 878/997 9:278 5456

φωνέω, *phōneo.*

Mat.20:32. Jesus stood still, and *called* them,
26:34. That this night, before the cock *crow*,
74. And immediately the cock *crew*.

Mat.26:75. Before the cock *crow*, thou shalt deny me
27:47. This (man) *calleth for* Elias.
Mar 3:31. standing without, sent unto him, *calling* him.
9:35. and *called* the twelve, and saith
10:49. and commanded him *to be called*. And *they call* the blind man,
— rise; he *calleth* thee.
14:30. before the cock *crow* twice, thou shalt
68. and the cock *crew*.
72. And the second time the cock *crew*.
— Before the cock *crow* twice, thou
15:35. Behold, he *calleth* Elias.
Lu. 8: 8. when he had said these things, he *cried*, He
54. and *called*, saying, Maid, arise.
14:12. *call* not thy friends,
16: 2. And he *called* him, *and* said unto him,
24. And he *cried and* said, Father Abraham,
19:15. these servants *to be called* unto him,
22:34. the cock *shall* not *crow* this day, before
60. while he yet spake, the cock *crew*.
61. Before the cock *crow*, thou shalt
23:46. *when* Jesus *had cried* with a loud voice, he said, Father,
Joh. 1:48(49). Before that Philip *called* thee,
2: 9. of the feast *called* the bridegroom,
4:16. *call* thy husband, and come hither
9:18. until they *called* the parents of him that
24. Then again *called* they the man that
11:28. and *called* Mary her sister secretly,
— The master is come, and *calleth for* thee.
12:17. when he *called* Lazarus out of his grave,
13:13. Ye *call* me Master and Lord:
38. The cock *shall* not *crow*, till thou
18:27. and immediately the cock *crew*.
33. *called* Jesus, and said unto him, Art
Acts 9:41. *when* he *had called* the saints and widows,
10: 7. he *called* two of his houshold servants,
18. And *called*, *and* asked whether Simon,
16:28. Paul *cried* with a loud voice, saying,
Rev.14:18. *cried* with a loud cry to him that had

5456 141 878/998 9:278 cf 5316

φωνή, phōnee.

Mat. 2:18. In Rama was there a *voice* heard,
3: 3. The *voice* of one crying in the wilderness,
17. And lo a *voice* from heaven, saying,
12:19. hear his *voice* in the streets.
17: 5. and behold a *voice* out of the cloud,
24:31. with a great *sound* of a trumpet,
27:46. Jesus cried with a loud *voice*,
50. when he had cried again with a loud *voice*,
Mar 1: 3. The *voice* of one crying in the wilderness,
11. And there came a *voice* from heaven,
26. and cried with a loud *voice*,
5: 7. And cried with a loud *voice*,
9: 7. and a *voice* came out of the cloud,
15:34. Jesus cried with a loud *voice*,
37. Jesus cried with a loud *voice*,
Lu. 1:42. she spake out with a loud *voice*,
44. as soon as the *voice* of thy salutation
3: 4. The *voice* of one crying in the wilderness,
22. and a *voice* came from heaven,
4:33. and cried out with a loud *voice*,
8:28. and with a loud *voice* said,
9:35. And there came a *voice* out of the cloud,
36. And when the *voice* was past,
11:27. a certain woman...lifted up her *voice*,
17:13. And they lifted up (their) *voices*,
15. and with a loud *voice* glorified God,
19:37. and praise God with a loud *voice*
Lu. 23:23. And they were instant with loud *voices*,
— And the *voices* of them and of the chief
46. when Jesus had cried with a loud *voice*,
Joh. 1:23. I (am) the *voice* of one crying in the
3: 8. and thou hearest the *sound* thereof,
29. because of the bridegroom's *voice*:
5:25. shall hear the *voice* of the Son of God:
28. in the graves shall hear his *voice*,
37. Ye have neither heard his *voice*
10: 3. and the sheep hear his *voice*:
4. for they know his *voice*.
5. they know not the *voice* of strangers.
16. and they shall hear my *voice*,
27. My sheep hear my *voice*,
11:43. he cried with a loud *voice*, Lazarus,
12:28. Then came there a *voice* from heaven,
30. This *voice* came not because of me,
18:37. that is of the truth heareth my *voice*.
Acts 2: 6. Now when this was noised (lit. this *voice* went) abroad,
14. lifted up his *voice*, and said
4:24. they lifted up their *voice* to God
7:31. the *voice* of the Lord came unto him,
57. they cried out with a loud *voice*,
60. and cried with a loud *voice*,
8: 7. crying with loud *voice*, came out
9: 4. and heard a *voice* saying unto him,
7. hearing a *voice*, but seeing no man.
10:13. And there came a *voice* to him,
15. And the *voice* (spake) unto him again
11: 7. And I heard a *voice* saying unto me,
9. But the *voice* answered me again
12:14. And when she knew Peter's *voice*,
22. the *voice* of a god, and not of a man.
13:27. nor yet the *voices* of the prophets which
14:10. Said with a loud *voice*, Stand upright
11. they lifted up their *voices*, saying
16:28. Paul cried with a loud *voice*,
19:34. all with one *voice* about the space
22: 7. and heard a *voice* saying unto me,
9. but they heard not the *voice* of him that
14. and shouldest hear the *voice* of his mouth
22. and (then) lifted up their *voices*,
24:21. Except it be for this one *voice*,
26:14. I heard a *voice* speaking unto me,
24. Festus said with a loud *voice*,
1Co.14: 7. even things without life giving *sound*,
8. if the trumpet give an uncertain *sound*,
10. so many kinds of *voices* in the world,
11. if I know not the meaning of the *voice*,
Gal. 4:20. and to change my *voice*;
1Th. 4:16. with the *voice* of the archangel,
Heb 3: 7. To day if ye will hear his *voice*,
15. To day if ye will hear his *voice*,
4: 7. To day if ye will hear his *voice*,
12:19. and the *voice* of words;
26. Whose *voice* then shook the earth:
2Pet.1:17. when there came such a *voice* to him
18. this *voice* which came from heaven we
2:16. the dumb ass speaking with man's *voice*
Rev. 1:10. and heard behind me a great *voice*,
12. And I turned to see the *voice*
15. and his *voice* as the *sound* of many waters.
3:20. if any man hear my *voice*, and open
4: 1. and the first *voice* which I heard
5. and thunderings and *voices*:
5: 2. proclaiming with a loud *voice*,
11. and I heard the *voice* of many angels
12. Saying with a loud *voice*, Worthy is
6: 1. as it were the *noise* of thunder,
6. And I heard a *voice* in the midst of
7. I heard the *voice* of the fourth beast

Rev. 6:10. And they cried with a loud *voice*,
7: 2. and he cried with a loud *voice*
10. And cried with a loud *voice*,
8: 5. there were *voices*, and thunderings,
13. saying with a loud *voice*, Woe,
— by reason of the other *voices* of the
9: 9. and the *sound* of their wings (was) as the *sound* of chariots
13. and I heard a *voice* from the four horns
10: 3. And cried with a loud *voice*, as
— seven thunders uttered their *voices*.
4. seven thunders had uttered their *voices*,
— and I heard *a voice* from heaven
7. But in the days of the *voice* of the seventh
8. And the *voice* which I heard from heaven
11:12. they heard a great *voice* from heaven
15. and there were great *voices* in heaven,
19. and *voices*, and thunderings,
12:10. I heard a loud *voice* saying in heaven,
14: 2. And I heard a *voice* from heaven, as the *voice* of many waters, and as the *voice* of a great thunder: and I heard the *voice* of harpers harping with their harps:
7. Saying with a loud *voice*, Fear God,
9. saying with a loud *voice*, If any
13. And I heard a *voice* from heaven
15. crying with a loud *voice* to him
16: 1. And I heard a great *voice* out of
17. came a great *voice* out of the temple
18. And there were *voices*, and thunders,
18: 2. cried mightily with a strong *voice*,
4. I heard another *voice* from
22. And the *voice* of harpers, and
— and the *sound* of a millstone shall be
23. the *voice* of the bridegroom and of the bride
19: 1. I heard a great *voice* of much people
5. And a *voice* came out of the throne,
6. as it were the *voice* of a great multitude, and as the *voice* of many waters, and as the *voice* of mighty thunderings, saying, Alleluia:
17. and he cried with a loud *voice*,
21: 3. a great *voice* out of heaven saying, Behold,

5457 70 879/999 9:310 *phaō* (to shine)

φῶς, phōs.

Mat. 4:16. which sat in darkness saw great *light*;
— *light* is sprung up.
5:14. Ye are the *light* of the world.
16. Let your *light* so shine before men,
6:23. If therefore the *light* that is in thee
10:27. (that) speak ye in *light*:
17: 2. his raiment was white as the *light*.
Mar 14:54. and warmed himself at the *fire*.
Lu. 2:32. A *light* to lighten the Gentiles, and
8:16. that they which enter in may see the *light*.
11:35. that the *light* which is in thee
12: 3. shall be heard in the *light*;
16: 8. wiser than the children of *light*.
22:56. beheld him as he sat by the *fire*,
Joh. 1: 4. and the life was the *light* of men.
5. And the *light* shineth in darkness;
7. to bear witness of the *Light*,
8. He was not that *Light*, but (was sent) to bear witness of that *Light*.
9. (That) was the true *Light*, which lighteth
3:19. that *light* is come into the world, and men loved darkness rather than *light*,
20. that doeth evil hateth the *light*, neither cometh to the *light*, lest

Joh. 3:21. he that doeth truth cometh to the *light*,
5:35. for a season to rejoice in his *light*.
8:12. I am the *light* of the world:
— but shall have the *light* of life.
9: 5. I am the *light* of the world.
11: 9. because he seeth the *light* of this world.
10. because there is no *light* in him.
12:35. Yet a little while is the *light* with you. Walk while ye have the *light*, lest
36. While ye have *light*, believe in the *light*, that ye may be the children of *light*.
46. I am come a *light* into the world,
Acts 9: 3. round about him a *light* from heaven:
12: 7. and a *light* shined in the prison:
13:47. I have set thee to be a *light* of the Gentiles
16:29. he called for a *light*, and sprang in,
22: 6. a great *light* round about me.
9. saw indeed the *light*, and were afraid;
11. not see for the glory of that *light*,
26:13. I saw in the way a *light* from heaven,
18. to turn (them) from darkness to *light*,
23. should shew *light* unto the people,
Ro. 2:19. a *light* of them which are in darkness,
13:12. and let us put on the armour of *light*.
2Co. 4: 6. who commanded the *light* to shine out of darkness,
6:14. what communion hath *light* with darkness?
11:14. is transformed into an angel of *light*.
Eph. 5: 8. but now (are ye) *light* in the Lord: walk as children of *light*:
13. are made manifest by the *light*: for whatsoever doth make manifest is *light*.
Col. 1:12. of the inheritance of the saints in *light*
1Th. 5: 5. Ye are all the children of *light*,
1Ti. 6:16. dwelling in the *light* which no man can
Jas. 1:17. cometh down from the Father of *lights*,
1Pet.2: 9. out of darkness into his marvellous *light*.
1Joh.1: 5. that God is *light*, and in him is no
7. But if we walk in the *light*, as he is in the *light*, we have fellowship
2: 8. and the true *light* now shineth.
9. He that saith he is in the *light*,
10. abideth in the *light*, and there is none
Rev.18:23. the *light* of a candle shall shine no more
21:24. shall walk in the *light* of it:
22: 5. need no candle, neither *light* of the sun;

5458 2 880/1000 9:310 5457

φωστήρ, phōsteer.

Phi. 2:15. among whom ye shine as *lights* in the world;
Rev.21:11. and her *light* (was) like unto a stone most precious,

5459 1 880/1000 9:310 5457,5342

φωσφόρος, phōsphoros.

2Pet.1:19. and the *day star* arise in your hearts:

5460 5 880/1000 9:310 5457

φωτεινός, phōtinos.

Mat. 6:22. thy whole body shall be *full of light*.
17: 5. a *bright* cloud overshadowed them:
Lu. 11:34. thy whole body also is *full of light*;
36. If thy whole body therefore (be) *full of light*,
— the whole shall be *full of light*, as when

5461 11 880/1000 9:310 5457

φωτίζω, phōtizo.

Lu. 11:36. as when the bright shining of a candle *doth give* thee *light*.

Joh. 1: 9. which *lighteth* every man that cometh
1Co. 4: 5. who both *will bring to light* the hidden
Eph. 1:18. The eyes of your understanding *being enlightened;*
3: 9. And *to make* all (men) *see* what
2Ti. 1:10. and *hath brought* life and immortality *to light*
Heb 6: 4. for those *who were* once *enlightened,*
10:32. in which, *after* ye *were illuminated,*
Rev.18: 1. the earth *was lightened* with his glory.
21:23. for the glory of God *did lighten* it,
22: 5. for the Lord God *giveth* them *light:*

5462 2 881/1000 9:310 5461

φωτισμός, phōtismos.

2Co. 4: 4. lest the *light* of the glorious gospel of
6. to (give) the *light* of the knowledge of the glory of God

5463 74 881/1000 9:359

χαίρω, kairo.

The mark † shews where it is used as a phrase of salutation.

Mat. 2:10. they *rejoiced* with exceeding great joy.
5:12. *Rejoice,* and be exceeding glad:
18:13. he *rejoiceth* more of that (sheep),
26:49. and said, *Hail,*† master;
27:29. *Hail,*† king of the Jews!
28: 9. Jesus met them, saying, *All hail.*†
Mar 14:11. when they heard (it), they *were glad,*
15:18. *Hail,*† King of the Jews!
Lu. 1:14. and many *shall rejoice* at his birth.
28. *Hail,*† (thou that art) highly favoured,
6:23. *Rejoice* ye in that day, and leap for joy:
10:20. Notwithstanding in this *rejoice* not,
— but rather *rejoice,* because your names
13:17. and all the people *rejoiced* for all
15: 5. layeth (it) on his shoulders, *rejoicing.*
32. we should make merry, and *be glad:*
19: 6. and received him *joyfully.*
37. began to *rejoice and* praise God
22: 5. And they *were glad,* and covenanted to
23: 8. Herod saw Jesus, he *was* exceeding *glad:*
Joh. 3:29. *rejoiceth* greatly because of the
4:36. and he that reapeth *may rejoice* together.
8:56. and he saw (it), and *was glad.*
11:15. And I *am glad* for your sakes
14:28. ye *would rejoice,* because I said,
16:20. and lament, but the world *shall rejoice:*
22. and your heart *shall rejoice,*
19: 3. *Hail,*† King of the Jews!
20:20. Then *were* the disciples *glad,* when
Acts 5:41. *rejoicing* that they were counted
8:39. and he went on his way *rejoicing.*
11:23. *was glad,* and exhorted them all,
13:48. Gentiles heard this, they *were glad,*
15:23. (send) *greeting*† unto the brethren
31. they *rejoiced* for the consolation.
23:26. unto...Felix (sendeth) *greeting.*†
Ro. 12:12. *Rejoicing* in hope; patient
15. *Rejoice* with them *that do rejoice,*
16:19. I *am glad* therefore on your behalf:
1Co. 7:30. they *that rejoice,* as though they *rejoiced* not;
13: 6. *Rejoiceth* not in iniquity, but
16:17. I *am glad* of the coming of Stephanas
2Co. 2: 3. of whom I ought *to rejoice;*
6:10. sorrowful, yet alway *rejoicing;*
7: 7. so that I *rejoiced* the more.
2Co. 7: 9. Now I *rejoice,* not that ye were made
13. exceedingly the more *joyed* we for the
16. I *rejoice* therefore that I have
13: 9. For we *are glad,* when we are weak,
11. Finally, brethren, *farewell.*†
Phi. 1:18. and I therein *do rejoice,* yea, and *will rejoice.*
2:17. I *joy,* and rejoice with you all.
18. *do* ye *joy,* and rejoice with me.
28. when ye see him again, ye *may rejoice,*
3: 1. Finally, my brethren, *rejoice* in the Lord.
4: 4. *Rejoice* in the Lord alway: (and) again I say, *Rejoice.*
10. But I *rejoiced* in the Lord greatly,
Col. 1:24. Who now *rejoice* in my sufferings for you,
2: 5. *joying* and beholding your order,
1Th. 3: 9. wherewith we *joy* for your sakes
5:16. *Rejoice* evermore.
Jas. 1: 1. to the twelve tribes which are scattered abroad, *greeting.*†
1Pet.4:13. *rejoice,* inasmuch as ye are partakers
— ye may be *glad* also with exceeding joy.
2Joh. 4. I *rejoiced* greatly that I found of thy
10. neither bid him *God speed:*†
11. For he that biddeth him *God speed*†
3Joh. 3. For I *rejoiced* greatly, when the brethren
Rev.11:10. they that dwell upon the earth *shall rejoice* over them,
19: 7. *Let* us *be glad* and rejoice, and

5464 4 882/1001 5465

χάλαζα, kalaza.

Rev. 8: 7. followed *hail* and fire mingled with
11:19. earthquake, and great *hail.*
16:21. there fell upon men a great *hail* out of
— because of the plague of the *hail;*

5465 7 882/1001 rt 5490

χαλάω, kalao.

Mar 2: 4. they *let down* the bed wherein the sick
Lu. 5: 4. and *let down* your nets for a draught.
5. at thy word I *will let down* the net.
Acts 9:25. and let (him) down by the wall in a basket. (lit. *lowering* him in a basket)
27:17. *strake* sail, and so were driven.
30. *when* they *had let down* the boat into the sea,
2Co.11:33. in a basket *was* I *let down* by the wall,

5467 2 882/1001 5465

χαλεπός, kalepos.

Mat. 8:28. exceeding *fierce,* so that no man
2Ti. 3: 1. last days *perilous* times shall come.

5468 2 882/1001 5469,71

χαλιναγωγέω, kalinagōgeo.

Jas. 1:26. and *bridleth* not his tongue,
3: 2. able also *to bridle* the whole body.

5469 2 882/1001 5465

χαλινός, kalinos.

Jas. 3: 3. we put *bits* in the horses' mouths,
Rev.14:20. even unto the horse *bridles,*

5470 1 883/1001 5475

χάλκεος, kalkeos.

Rev. 9:20. idols of gold, and silver, and *brass,*

5471 1 882/1001 5475
χαλκευς, kalkūs.

2Ti. 4:14. Alexander the *coppersmith* did me much

5472 1 882/1001 5475,1491
χαλκηδών, kalkeedon.

Rev.21:19. the third, a *chalcedony*;

5473 1 883/1001 5475
χαλκίον, kalkion.

Mar 7: 4. the washing of cups, and pots, *brasen vessels*, and of tables.

5474 2 883/1001 5475,3030
χαλκολίβανον, kalkolibanon.

Rev. 1:15. And his feet like unto *fine brass*,
2:18. and his feet (are) like *fine brass*

5475 5 883/1001 5465
χαλκός, kalkos.

Mat.10: 9. gold, nor silver, nor *brass* in your purses,
Mar 6: 8. no bread, no *money* in (their) purse:
12:41. people cast *money* into the treasury:
1Co.13: 1. I am become (as) sounding *brass*,
Rev.18:12. and of *brass*, and iron, and marble,

5476 2 883/1001 rt 5490
χαμαί, kamai.

Joh. 9: 6. he spat *on the ground*, and made clay
18: 6. went backward, and fell *to the ground*.

5479 59 883/1002 9:359 5463
χαρά, kara.

Mat. 2:10. rejoiced with exceeding great *joy*.
13:20. and anon with *joy* receiveth it;
44. and for *joy* thereof goeth and selleth
25:21. enter thou into the *joy* of thy lord.
23. enter thou into the *joy* of thy lord.
28: 8. from the sepulchre with fear and great *joy*;
Mar 4:16. immediately receive it with *gladness*,
Lu. 1:14. And thou shalt have *joy* and gladness;
2:10. bring you good tidings of great *joy*,
8:13. receive the word with *joy*;
10:17. the seventy returned again with *joy*,
15: 7. likewise *joy* shall be in heaven
10. there is *joy* in the presence of the
24:41. while they yet believed not for *joy*,
52. returned to Jerusalem with great *joy*:
Joh. 3:29. rejoiceth greatly (lit. rejoiceth with *joy*) because of the bridegroom's voice: this my *joy* therefore is fulfilled.
15:11. that my *joy* might remain in you (lit. my *joy* in you might remain), and (that) your *joy* might be full.
16:20. your sorrow shall be turned into *joy*.
21. for *joy* that a man is born into the world.
22. your *joy* no man taketh from you.
24. that your *joy* may be full.
17:13. might have my *joy* fulfilled in themselves.
Acts 8: 8. And there was great *joy* in that city.
12:14. opened not the gate for *gladness*,
13:52. the disciples were filled with *joy*,
15: 3. caused great *joy* unto all the brethren.
20:24. might finish my course with *joy*,
Ro. 14:17. and *joy* in the Holy Ghost.
Ro. 15:13. fill you with all *joy* and peace in
32. That I may come unto you with *joy*
2Co. 1:24. but are helpers of your *joy*:
2: 3. that my *joy* is (the joy) of you all.
7: 4. I am exceeding *joy*ful in all our
13. the more joyed we for the *joy* of Titus.
8: 2. the abundance of their *joy* and their
Gal. 5:22. the fruit of the Spirit is love, *joy*,
Phi. 1: 4. for you all making request with *joy*,
25. for your furtherance and *joy* of faith;
2: 2. Fulfil ye my *joy*, that ye be likeminded,
29. Receive him therefore in the Lord with al *gladness*;
4: 1. my *joy* and crown, so stand fast
Col. 1:11. and longsuffering with *joyfulness*,
1Th. 1: 6. with *joy* of the Holy Ghost:
2:19. For what (is) our hope, or *joy*, or
20. For ye are our glory and *joy*.
3: 9. for all the *joy* wherewith we joy for
2Ti. 1: 4. that I may be filled with *joy*;
Heb 10:34. took *joy*fully the spoiling of your goods,
12: 2. who for the *joy* that was set before him
11. seemeth to be joyous, (lit. of *joy*)
13:17. that they may do it with *joy*,
Jas. 1: 2. My brethren, count it all *joy* when
4: 9. and (your) *joy* to heaviness.
1Pet. 1: 8. ye rejoice with *joy* unspeakable and
1Joh. 1: 4. that your *joy* may be full.
2Joh. 12. that our *joy* may be full.
3Joh. 4. I have no greater *joy* than to hear that

5480 9 884/1002 9:416 rt 5482
χάραγμα, karagma.

Acts17:29. or stone, *graven* by art (lit. by the *sculpture* of art) and man's device.
Rev.13:16. to receive a *mark* in their right hand,
17. save he that had the *mark*,
14: 9. and receive (his) *mark* in his forehead,
11. whosoever receiveth the *mark* of his name.
15: 2. and over his image, and over his *mark*,
16: 2. upon the men which had the *mark* of th
19:20. that had received the *mark* of the beast,
20: 4. neither had received (his) *mark* upon

5481 1 884/1002 9:418 rt 5482
χαρακτήρ, karakteer.

Heb 1: 3. and the *express image* of his person,

5482 1 884/1002 charassō (to sharpen to a point)
χάραξ, karax.

Lu. 19:43. thine enemies shall cast a *trench* about thee, and compass thee

5483 23 884/1002 9:359 5485
χαρίζομαι, karizomai.

Lu. 7:21. unto many (that were) blind he *gave* sight.
42. he *frankly forgave* them both.
43. (he), to whom he *forgave* most.
Acts 3:14. desired a murderer *to be granted* unto you:
25:11. no man may *deliver* me unto them.
16. *to deliver* any man to die, before that
27:24. and, lo, God *hath given* thee all them tha sail with thee.
Ro. 8:32. how *shall* he not with him also *freely give* us all things?
1Co. 2:12. that we might know the things *that are freely given* to us of God.

2Co. 2: 7. ye (ought) rather *to forgive* (him),
10. To whom ye *forgive* any thing,
— for if I *forgave* any thing, to whom I *forgave* (it), for
12:13. *forgive* me this wrong.
Gal. 3:18. but God *gave* (it) to Abraham by promise.
Eph 4:32. *forgiving* one another, even as God for Christ's sake *hath forgiven* you.
Phi. 1:29. you it *is given* in the behalf of Christ,
2: 9. and *given* him a name which is above
Col. 2:13. *having forgiven* you all trespasses;
3:13. and *forgiving* one another, if any
— even as Christ *forgave* you, so also (do) ye.
Philem 22. I *shall be given* unto you.

5484 9 885/1003 5485

χάριν, *karin.*

Lu. 7:47. Where*fore* I say unto thee, Her sins,
Gal. 3:19. It was added *because of* transgressions,
Eph 3: 1. *For* this *cause* I Paul, the prisoner of
14. *For* this *cause* I bow my knees unto
1Ti. 5:14. give none occasion to the adversary to speak reproachfully. (lit. to the adversary *for cause of* reproach)
Tit. 1: 5. *For* this *cause* left I thee in Crete,
11. *for* filthy lucre's *sake*.
1Joh. 3:12. And where*fore* slew he him?
Jude 16. having men's persons in admiration *because of* advantage.

5485 156 885/1003 9:359 5463

χάρις, *karis.*

Lu. 1:30. for thou hast found *favour* with God.
2:40. and the *grace* of God was upon him.
52. and in *favour* with God and man.
4:22. wondered at the *gracious* words which
6:32. what *thank* have ye?
33. what *thank* have ye?
34. what *thank* have ye?
17: 9. Doth he *thank* that servant (lit. hath he favor, or *thanks*, to)
Joh. 1:14. full of *grace* and truth.
16. of his fulness have all we received, and *grace* for *grace*.
17. *grace* and truth came by Jesus Christ.
Acts 2:47. and having *favour* with all the people.
4:33. and great *grace* was upon them all.
7:10. gave him *favour* and wisdom in the sight of Pharaoh
46. Who found *favour* before God,
11:23. and had seen the *grace* of God, was glad,
13:43. to continue in the *grace* of God.
14: 3. testimony unto the word of his *grace*,
26. recommended to the *grace* of God for
15:11. through the *grace* of the Lord Jesus
40. being recommended by the brethren unto the *grace* of God.
18:27. which had believed through *grace*:
20:24. to testify the gospel of the *grace* of God.
32. you to God, and to the word of his *grace*,
24:27. willing to shew the Jews a *pleasure*,
25: 3. And desired *favour* against him,
9. willing to do the Jews a *pleasure*,
Ro. 1: 5. By whom we have received *grace* and
7. *Grace* to you and peace from
3:24. Being justified freely by his *grace*
4: 4. is the reward not reckoned of *grace*, but of debt.
16. of faith, that (it might be) by *grace*;
5: 2. by faith into this *grace* wherein we stand,
15. much more the *grace* of God, and the gift by *grace*,
17. they which receive abundance of *grace*
20. *grace* did much more abound:
21. even so might *grace* reign through
6: 1 continue in sin, that *grace* may abound?
14. ye are not under the law, but under *grace*
15. not under the law, but under *grace*?
17. But God be thanked, (lit. *thanks* to God) that ye were
11: 5. remnant according to the election of *grace*.
6. if by *grace*, then (is it) no more of works otherwise *grace* is no more *grace*.
— of works, then is it no more *grace*:
12: 3. through the *grace* given unto me,
6. according to the *grace* that is given to us,
15:15. because of the *grace* that is given to me
16:20. The *grace* of our Lord Jesus Christ (be)
24. The *grace* of our Lord Jesus Christ (be)
1Co. 1: 3. *Grace* (be) unto you, and peace, from
4. for the *grace* of God which is given you
3:10. According to the *grace* of God which
10:30. For if I by *grace* be a partaker,
15:10. But by the *grace* of God I am what I am: and his *grace* which (was bestowed) upon me
— not I, but the *grace* of God which was with me.
57. But *thanks* (be) to God, which giveth us
16: 3. to bring your *liberality* unto Jerusalem.
23. The *grace* of our Lord Jesus Christ (be)
2Co. 1: 2. *Grace* (be) to you and peace from
12. but by the *grace* of God, we have had our
15. that ye might have a second *benefit*;
2:14. Now *thanks* (be) unto God, which
4:15. that the abundant *grace* might through
6: 1. ye receive not the *grace* of God in vain.
8: 1. do you to wit of the *grace* of God bestowed
4. that we would receive the *gift*, and
6. finish in you the same *grace* also.
7. (see) that ye abound in this *grace* also.
9. ye know the *grace* of our Lord Jesus
16. But *thanks* (be) to God, which put
19. to travel with us with this *grace*, which
9: 8. And God (is) able to make all *grace* abound toward you;
14. for the exceeding *grace* of God in you.
15. *Thanks* (be) unto God for his
12: 9. My *grace* is sufficient for thee:
13:14(13). The *grace* of the Lord Jesus Christ,
Gal. 1: 3. *Grace* (be) to you and peace from
6. that called you into the *grace* of Christ
15. and called (me) by his *grace*,
2: 9. perceived the *grace* that was given unto
21. I do not frustrate the *grace* of God:
5: 4. ye are fallen from *grace*.
6:18. the *grace* of our Lord Jesus Christ (be)
Eph. 1: 2. *Grace* (be) to you, and peace, from
6. To the praise of the glory of his *grace*,
7. according to the riches of his *grace*;
2: 5. by *grace* ye are saved;
7. shew the exceeding riches of his *grace*
8. For by *grace* are ye saved through faith;
3: 2. of the dispensation of the *grace* of God which is given me
7. according to the gift of the *grace* of God
8. is this *grace* given, that I should preach
4: 7. unto every one of us is given *grace*
29. it may minister *grace* unto the hearers.
6:24. *Grace* (be) with all them that love our Lord Jesus Christ

Phi. 1: 2. *Grace* (be) unto you, and peace, from
7. ye all are partakers of my *grace*,
4:23. The *grace* of our Lord Jesus Christ (be)
Col. 1: 2. *Grace* (be) unto you, and peace, from
6. and knew the *grace* of God in truth:
3:16. singing with *grace* in your hearts to
4: 6. Let your speech (be) alway with *grace*,
18. *Grace* (be) with you. Amen.
1Th. 1: 1. *Grace* (be) unto you, and peace, from
5:28. The *grace* of our Lord Jesus Christ (be)
2Th. 1: 2. *Grace* unto you, and peace, from
12. according to the *grace* of our God and
2:16. consolation and good hope through *grace*,
3:18. The *grace* of our Lord Jesus Christ (be)
1Ti. 1: 2. *Grace*, mercy, (and) peace, from
12. And I *thank* Christ Jesus our Lord,
14. And the *grace* of our Lord was exceeding abundant
6:21. *Grace* (be) with thee. Amen.
2Ti. 1: 2. *Grace*, mercy, (and) peace from
3. I *thank* God, whom I serve from
9. according to his own purpose and *grace*,
2: 1. be strong in the *grace* that is in Christ
4:22. *Grace* (be) with you. Amen.
Tit. 1: 4. *Grace*, mercy, (and) peace, from
2:11. For the *grace* of God that bringeth
3: 7. That being justified by his *grace*, we
15. *Grace* (be) with you all. Amen.
Philem. 3. *Grace* to you, and peace, from
7. we have great *joy* and consolation
25. The *grace* of our Lord Jesus Christ (be)
Heb 2: 9. that he by the *grace* of God should taste
4:16. come boldly unto the throne of *grace*,
— and find *grace* to help in time of need.
10:29. done despite unto the Spirit of *grace*?
12:15. lest any man fail of the *grace* of God;
28. let us have *grace*, whereby we may serve
13: 9. the heart be established with *grace*;
25. *Grace* (be) with you all. Amen.
Jas. 4: 6. But he giveth more *grace*.
— but giveth *grace* unto the humble.
1Pet. 1: 2. *Grace* unto you, and peace, be multiplied.
10. who prophesied of the *grace* (that should come) unto you:
13. for the *grace* that is to be brought
2:19. For this (is) *thankworthy*, if a man
20. this (is) *acceptable* with God.
3: 7. being heirs together of the *grace* of life;
4:10. stewards of the manifold *grace* of God.
5: 5. and giveth *grace* to the humble.
10. But the God of all *grace*, who hath
12. testifying that this is the true *grace* of God wherein ye stand.
2Pet. 1: 2. *Grace* and peace be multiplied unto you
3:18. But grow in *grace*, and (in) the knowledge
2Joh. 3. *Grace* be with you, mercy, (and) peace,
Jude 4. turning the *grace* of our God into
Rev. 1: 4. *Grace* (be) unto you, and peace, from
22:21. The *grace* of our Lord Jesus Christ (be)

5486 17 887/1005 9:359 5483

χάρισμα, karısma.

Ro. 1:11. impart unto you some spiritual *gift*,
5:15. so also (is) the *free gift*.
16. but the *free gift* (is) of many offences
6:23. the *gift* of God (is) eternal life
11:29. For the *gifts* and calling of God (are)
12: 6. Having then *gifts* differing
1Co. 1: 7. ye come behind in no *gift*;
7: 7. every man hath his proper *gift*
12: 4. there are diversities of *gifts*, but the
9. to another the *gifts* of healing by the
28. then *gifts* of healings, helps,
30. Have all the *gifts* of healing?
31. covet earnestly the best *gifts*: and yet
2Co. 1:11. for the *gift* (bestowed) upon us by the
1Ti. 4:14. Neglect not the *gift* that is in thee,
2Ti. 1: 6. stir up the *gift* of God, which is in thee
1Pet. 4:10. As every man hath received the *gift*,

5487 2 887/1005 9:359 5485

χαριτόω, karitoō.

Lu. 1:28. Hail, (thou that art) *highly favoured*,
Eph 1: 6. of his grace, wherein he hath *made us accepted* (lit. *hath graced* us) in the beloved.

5489 1 887/1005 rt 5482

χάρτης, kartees.

2Joh. 12. I would not (write) with *paper* and ink:

5490 1 887/1005 *chaō* (to yawn)

χάσμα, kasma.

Lu. 16:26. there is a great *gulf* fixed:

5491 7 887/1005 rt 5490

χεῖλος, kīlos.

Mat. 15: 8. and honoureth me with (their) *lips*;
Mar 7: 6. honoureth me with (their) *lips*,
Ro. 3:13. poison of asps (is) under their *lips*:
1Co. 14:21. With (men of) other tongues and other *lips*
Heb 11:12. and as the sand which is by the sea *shore*
13:15. the fruit of (our) *lips* giving thanks to
1Pet. 3:10. and his *lips* that they speak no guile.

5492 1 887/1005 rt 5494

χειμάζομαι, kīmazomai.

Acts 27:18. And we *being* exceedingly *tossed with a tempest*,

---

5493 1 887/1005 rt 5494,4482

χείμαῤῥος, kīmarros.

Joh. 18: 1. over the *brook* Cedron,

5494 6 888/1005 *cheō* (to pour)

χειμών, kīmōn.

Mat. 16: 3. (It will be) *foul weather* to day
24:20. that your flight be not in the *winter*,
Mar 13:18. your flight be not in the *winter*.
Joh. 10:22. dedication, and it was *winter*.
Acts 27:20. no small *tempest* lay on (us),
2Ti. 4:21. Do thy diligence to come before *winter*.

5495 779 888/1005 9:424 rt 5494

χείρ, kīr.

Mat. 3:12. Whose fan (is) in his *hand*,
4: 6. in (their) *hands* they shall bear thee up,
5:30. if thy right *hand* offend thee,
8: 3. Jesus put forth (his) *hand*, and touched him,
15. he touched her *hand*, and the fever left
9:18. lay thy *hand* upon her, and she shall live.
25. took her by the *hand*, and the maid arose.

Mat.12:10 which had (his) *hand* withered.
13. Stretch forth thine *hand*.
49. he stretched forth his *hand* toward his
14:31. stretched forth (his) *hand*, and caught him,
15: 2. for they wash not their *hands* when
20. but to eat with unwashen *hands*
17:22. shall be betrayed into the *hands* of men:
18: 8. if thy *hand* or thy foot offend thee,
— rather than having two *hands* or two feet
19:13. should put (his) *hands* on them, and
15. he laid (his) *hands* on them, and departed
22:13. Bind him *hand* and foot,
26:23. He that dippeth (his) *hand* with me
45. is betrayed into the *hands* of sinners.
50. laid *hands* on Jesus, and took him.
51. stretched out (his) *hand*, and drew his sword,
27:24. washed (his) *hands* before the multitude,
Mar 1:31. and took her by the *hand*,
41. put forth (his) *hand*, and touched
3: 1. which had a withered *hand*.
3. which had the withered *hand*, Stand forth.
5. Stretch forth thine *hand*.
— and his *hand* was restored whole as
5:23. come and lay thy *hands* on her,
41. took the damsel by the *hand*,
6: 2. are wrought by his *hands*?
5. laid his *hands* upon a few sick folk,
7: 2. with unwashen, *hands*, they found fault.
3. except they wash (their) *hands* oft,
5. eat bread with unwashen *hands*?
32. to put his *hand* upon him.
8:23. he took the blind man by the *hand*,
— his eyes, and put his *hands* upon him,
25. he put (his) *hands* again upon his eyes,
9:27. took him by the *hand*, and lifted him up;
31. is delivered into the *hands* of men,
43. if thy *hand* offend thee, cut it
— than having two *hands* to go into hell,
10:16. in his arms, put (his) *hands* upon them, and blessed them.
14:41. is betrayed into the *hands* of sinners.
46. laid their *hands* on him, and took him.
16:18. they shall lay *hands* on the sick, and they
Lu. 1:66. And the *hand* of the Lord was with him.
71. and from the *hand* of all that hate us;
74. delivered out of the *hand* of our enemies
3:17. Whose fan (is) in his *hand*,
4:11. And in (their) *hands* they shall bear
40. laid his *hands* on every one of them,
5:13. he put forth (his) *hand*, and touched him,
6: 1. did eat, rubbing (them) in (their) *hands*.
6. whose right *hand* was withered.
8. which had the withered *hand*,
10. Stretch forth thy *hand*.
— his *hand* was restored whole
8:54. and took her by the *hand*, and called,
9:44. shall be delivered into the *hands* of men.
62. No man, having put his *hand* to the plough,
13:13. And he laid (his) *hands* on her:
15:22. and put a ring on his *hand*, and
20:19. sought to lay *hands* on him;
21:12. they shall lay their *hands* on you,
22:21. the *hand* of him that betrayeth me
53. ye stretched forth no *hands* against me:
23:46. into thy *hands* I commend my spirit:
24: 7. be delivered into the *hands* of sinful men,
39. Behold my *hands* and my feet,
40. he shewed them (his) *hands* and (his) feet.
50. he lifted up his *hands*, and blessed them.

Joh. 3:35. and hath given all things into his *hand*.
7:30. but no man laid *hands* on him, because
44. but no man laid *hands* on him.
10:28. pluck them out of my *hand*.
29. to pluck (them) out of my Father's *hand*.
39. he escaped out of their *hand*,
11:44. bound *hand* and foot with graveclothes:
13: 3. given all things into his *hands*,
9. but also (my) *hands* and (my) head.
20:20. shewed unto them (his) *hands*
25. Except I shall see in his *hands*
— and thrust my *hand* into his side,
27. Reach hither thy finger, and behold my *hands*; and reach hither thy *hand*, and thrust
21:18. thou shalt stretch forth thy *hands*,
Acts 2:23. by wicked *hands* have crucified
3: 7. took him by the right *hand*, and lifted
4: 3. they laid *hands* on them, and put
28. whatsoever thy *hand* and thy counsel
30. stretching forth thine *hand* to heal;
5:12. by the *hands* of the apostles were many
18. laid their *hands* on the apostles, and put
6: 6. prayed, they laid (their) *hands* on them.
7:25. how that God by his *hand* would
35. by the *hand* of the angel which appeared
41. rejoiced in the works of their own *hands*.
50. Hath not my *hand* made
8:17. Then laid they (their) *hands* on them, and they received
18. through laying on of the apostles' *hands*
19. that on whomsoever I lay *hands*,
9:12. coming in, and putting (his) *hand* on him,
17. and putting his *hands* on him said,
41. he gave her (his) *hand*, and lifted
11:21. And the *hand* of the Lord was with them:
30. by the *hands* of Barnabas and Saul.
12: 1. the king stretched forth (his) *hands* to vex
7. chains fell off from (his) *hands*.
11. me out of the *hand* of Herod,
17. beckoning unto them with the *hand* to
13: 3. prayed, and laid (their) *hands* on them,
11. behold, the *hand* of the Lord (is) upon thee,
16. beckoning with (his) *hand* said,
14: 3. and wonders to be done by their *hands*.
15:23. they wrote (letters) by them (lit. by the *hand* of them)
17:25. Neither is worshipped with men's *hands*,
19: 6. when Paul had laid (his) *hands* upon them
11. special miracles by the *hands* of Paul:
26. be no gods, which are made with *hands*:
33. Alexander beckoned with the *hand*,
20:34. these *hands* have ministered unto my
21:11. bound his own *hands* and feet,
— shall deliver (him) into the *hands* of the
27. all the people, and laid *hands* on him,
40. beckoned with the *hand* unto the people.
23:19. captain took him by the *hand*, and went
24: 7. took (him) away out of our *hands*,
26: 1. Paul stretched forth the *hand*,
28: 3. and fastened on his *hand*.
4. beast hang on his *hand*,
8. laid his *hands* on him, and healed him.
17. into the *hands* of the Romans.
Ro. 10:21. I have stretched forth my *hands* unto
1Co. 4:12. labour, working with our own *hands*:
12:15. Because I am not the *hand*, I am not of
21. And the eye cannot say unto the *hand*,
16:21. salutation of (me) Paul with mine own *hand*

2Co.11:33. and escaped his *hands.*
Gal. 3:19. by angels in the *hand* of a mediator.
6:11. written unto you with mine own *hand.*
Eph. 4:28. working with (his) *hands* the thing which
Col. 4:18. The salutation by the *hand* of me Paul.
1Th. 4:11. and to work with your own *hands.*
2Th. 3:17. of Paul with mine own *hand,*
1Ti. 2: 8. lifting up holy *hands*, without wrath
4:14 with the laying on of the *hands* of the presbytery.
5:22. Lay *hands* suddenly on no man,
2Ti. 1: 6. in thee by the putting on of my *hands.*
Philem 19. written (it) with mine own *hand,*
Heb 1:10. the heavens are the works of thine *hands:*
2: 7. set him over the works of thy *hands:*
6: 2. of baptisms, and of laying on of *hands,*
8: 9. when I took them by the *hand* to lead them
10:31. to fall into the *hands* of the living God.
12:12. lift up the *hands* which hang down,
Jas. 4: 8. Cleanse (your) *hands*, (ye) sinners;
1Pet.5: 6. under the mighty *hand* of God, that he
1Joh.1: 1. and our *hands* have handled, of the
Rev. 1:16. he had in his right *hand* seven stars:
17. he laid his right *hand* upon me,
6: 5. pair of balances in his *hand.*
7: 9. and palms in their *hands;*
8: 4. up before God out of the angel's *hand.*
9:20. repented not of the works of their *hands*, that they should not worship
10: 2. he had in his *hand* a little book
5. lifted up his *hand* to heaven,
8. which is open in the *hand* of the angel
10. book out of the angel's *hand,*
13:16. to receive a mark in their right *hand*, or
14: 9. mark in his forehead, or in his *hand,*
14. and in his *hand* a sharp sickle.
17: 4. having a golden cup in her *hand* full of
19: 2. and hath avenged the blood of his servants at her *hand.*
20: 1. and a great chain in his *hand.*
4. upon their foreheads, or in their *hands;*

5496 2 889/1007 9:424 5497

χειραγωγέω, *kīragōgeo.*

Acts 9: 8. they *led* him *by the hand,* and
22:11. *being led by the hand* of them that

5497 1 889/1007 9:424 5495,71

χειραγωγός, *kīragōgos.*

Acts13:11. seeking *some to lead* him *by the hand.*

5498 1 889/1007 9:424 5495,1125

χειρόγραφον, *kīrographon.*

Col. 2:14. Blotting out the *handwriting* of ordinances that was against us,

---

5499 6 889/1007 9:424 5495,4160

χειροποίητος, *kīropoyeetos.*

Mar 14:58. this temple that is *made with hands,*
Acts 7:48. dwelleth not in temples *made with hands;*
17:24. not in temples *made with hands;*
Eph 2:11. Circumcision in the flesh *made by hands;*
Heb 9:11. tabernacle, not *made with hands,*
24. into the holy places *made with hands,*

5500 2 889/1007 9:424 5495 *teinō* (to stretch)

χειροτονέω, *kīrotoneo.*

Acts14:23. *when* they *had ordained* them elders in every church,
2Co. 8:19. *who was* also *chosen* of the churches to travel with us with this grace.

5501 11 889/1007 cf 2556 *cherēs* (an inferior)

χείρων, χεῖρον, *kīrōn, kīron.*

Mat. 9:16. and the rent is made *worse.*
12:45. of that man is *worse* than the first.
27:64. last error shall be *worse* than the first.
Mar 2:21. and the rent is made *worse.*
5:26. but rather grew *worse,*
Lu. 11:26. of that man is *worse* than the first.
Joh. 5:14. lest a *worse* thing come unto thee.
1Ti. 5: 8. and is *worse* than an infidel.
2Ti. 3:13. But evil men and seducers shall wax *worse and worse,*
Heb10:29. Of how much *sorer* punishment,
2Pet.2:20. the latter end is *worse* with them than

5503 26 889/1008 9:440 cf 5490

χήρα, *keera.*

Mat.23:14. for ye devour *widows'* houses,
Mar 12:40. Which devour *widows'* houses,
42. And there came a certain poor *widow,*
43. this poor *widow* hath cast more in,
Lu. 2:37. she (was) a *widow* of about fourscore
4:25. many *widows* were in Israel in
26. unto a woman (that was) a *widow.*
7:12. only son of his mother, and she was a *widow:*
18: 3. And there was a *widow* in that city;
5. Yet because this *widow* troubleth me,
20:47. Which devour *widows'* houses,
21: 2. a certain poor *widow* casting in
3. this poor *widow* hath cast in more than
Acts 6: 1. because their *widows* were neglected in
9:39. all the *widows* stood by him weeping,
41. when he had called the saints and *widows,*
1Co. 7: 8. to the unmarried and *widows,* It is good
1Ti. 5: 3. Honour *widows* that are *widows* indeed.
4. if any *widow* have children or nephews,
5. she that is a *widow* indeed, and desolate, trusteth in God,
9. Let not a *widow* be taken into the number under
11. But the younger *widows* refuse:
16. If any man or woman that believeth have *widows,* let them
— may relieve them that are *widows* indeed.
Jas. 1:27. To visit the fatherless and *widows* in their affliction,
Rev.18: 7. sit a queen, and am no *widow,* and shall see no sorrow.

5504 3 890/407

χθές, *kthes.*

Joh. 4:52. *Yesterday* at the seventh hour the fever
Acts 7:28. as thou diddest the Egyptian *yesterday?*
Heb 13: 8. Jesus Christ the same *yesterday,* and to day, and for ever.

5505 23 890/1008 5507

χιλιάδες, *kiliades.*

Lu. 14:31. able with ten *thousand* to meet him that cometh against him with twenty *thousand?*

Acts 4: 4. of the men was about five *thousand.*
1Co.10: 8. one day three and twenty *thousand.*
Rev. 5:11. and *thousands* of *thousands;*
7: 4. an hundred (and) forty (and) four *thousand* of all the tribes of the
5. of Juda (were) sealed twelve *thousand.*
— of Reuben (were) sealed twelve *thousand.*
— of Gad (were) sealed twelve *thousand.*
6. of Aser (were) sealed twelve *thousand.*
— of Nepthalim (were) sealed twelve *thousand.*
— of Manasses (were) sealed twelve *thousand.*
7. of Simeon (were) sealed twelve *thousand.*
— of Levi (were) sealed twelve *thousand.*
— of Issachar (were) sealed twelve *thousand.*
8. of Zabulon (were) sealed twelve *thousand.*
— of Joseph (were) sealed twelve *thousand.*
— of Benjamin (were) sealed twelve *thousand.*
11:13. slain of men seven *thousand:*
14: 1. an hundred forty (and) four *thousand,* having his Father's name
3. but the hundred (and) forty (and) four *thousand,*
21:16. twelve *thousand* furlongs.

5506 22 890/1008 5507,757

χιλίαρχος, *kiliarkos.*

Mar 6:21. a supper to his lords, *high captains,* and
Joh.18:12. Then the band and the *captain* and
Acts21:31. tidings came unto the *chief captain*
32 they saw the *chief captain* and the
33. Then the *chief captain* came near,
37. he said unto the *chief captain,*
22:24. The *chief captain* commanded him to be brought
26. he went and told the *chief captain,*
27. Then the *chief captain* came, and said
28. And the *chief captain* answered, With
29. the *chief captain* also was afraid,
23:10. the *chief captain,* fearing lest Paul
15. signify to the *chief captain* that he
17. Bring this young man unto the *chief captain:*
18. and brought (him) to the *chief captain,*
19. the *chief captain* took him by the hand,
22. *chief captain* (then) let the young man
24: 7. But the *chief captain* Lysias came
22. When Lysias the *chief captain* shall
25:23. with the *chief captains,* and principal men
Rev. 6:15. the rich men, and the *chief captains,*
19:18. of kings, and the flesh of *captains,*

5507 11 890/1008 9:466

χίλιοι, *kilioi.*

Obs.—This word is only used for 'one thousand,' but χιλιάδες signifies 'thousands.'

2Pet.3: 8. as a *thousand* years, and a *thousand* years as one day.
Rev.11: 3. prophesy a *thousand* two hundred (and) threescore days,
12: 6. feed her there a *thousand* two hundred (and) threescore days.
14:20. a *thousand* (and) six hundred furlongs.
20: 2. and bound him a *thousand* years,
3. till the *thousand* years should be fulfilled:
4. and they lived and reigned with Christ a *thousand* years.
5. until the *thousand* years were finished.
6. shall reign with him a *thousand* years.
7. when the *thousand* years are expired,

5509 11 890/1008 [3801]

χιτών, *kitōn.*

Mat. 5:40. at the law, and take away thy *coat,* let
10:10. neither two *coats,* neither shoes, nor
Mar 6: 9. and not put on two *coats.*
14:63. Then the high priest rent his *clothes,*
Lu. 3:11. He that hath two *coats,* let him impart to
6:29. cloke forbid not (to take thy) *coat* also.
9: 3. neither have two *coats* apiece.
Joh.19:23. and also (his) *coat:* now the *coat* was without seam, woven from
Acts 9:39. shewing the *coats* and garments which
Jude 23. hating even the *garment* spotted by the

5510 3 890/1009 cf rt 5490 or 5495

χιών, *kiōn.*

Mat.28: 3. and his raiment white as *snow:*
Mar 9: 3. became shining, exceeding white as *snow,*
Rev. 1:14. white like wool, as white as *snow;*

5511 2 890/1009

χλαμύς, *klamus.*

Mat.27:28. and put on him a scarlet *robe.*
31. they took the *robe* off from him,

5512 2 890/1009 5491

χλευάζω, *klūazo.*

Acts 2:13. Others *mocking* said, These men
17:32. resurrection of the dead, some *mocked:*

5513 1 890/1009 *chliō* (to warm)

χλιαρός, *kliaros.*

Rev. 3:16. So then because thou art *lukewarm,*

5515 4 890/1009 rt 5514

χλωρός, *klōros.*

Mar 6:39. by companies upon the *green* grass.
Rev. 6: 8. I looked, and behold a *pale* horse:
8: 7. and all *green* grass was burnt up.
9: 4. neither any *green* thing, neither any tree;

5516 1 891/

χξς' (Rev. 13:18), see respectively ἑξακόσιοι, ἑξήκοντα and ἕξ.

5517 4 891/1009 9:472 5522

χοϊκός, *koikos.*

1Co.15:47. The first man (is) of the earth, *earthy:*
48. As (is) the *earthy,* such (are) they also that are *earthy:* and as
49. we have borne the image of the *earthy,* we

5518 2 891/1009

χοῖνιξ, *koinix.*

Rev. 6: 6. A *measure* of wheat for a penny, and three *measures* of barley for a penny;

5519 14 891/1009

χοῖρος, *koiros.*

Mat. 7: 6. neither cast ye your pearls before *swine*
8:30. an herd of many *swine* feeding.

3 F

Mat. 8:31. to go away into the herd of *swine*.
32. went into the herd of *swine*: and behold, the whole herd of *swine* ran
Mar 5:11. great herd of *swine* feeding.
12. Send us into the *swine*, that we may
13. and entered into the *swine*:
14. they that fed the *swine* fled,
16. and (also) concerning the *swine*.
Lu. 8:32. an herd of many *swine* feeding
33. and entered into the *swine*:
15:15. he sent him into his fields to feed *swine*.
16. with the husks that the *swine* did eat:

5520 1 891/1009 5521

χολάω, kolao.

Joh. 7:23. *are* ye *angry* at me, because I

5521 2 891/1009

χολή, kolee.

Mat.27:34. vinegar to drink mingled with *gall*:
Acts 8:23. thou art in the *gall* of bitterness,

5522 2 891/1010 rt 5494

χόος, kŏŏs.

Mar 6:11. shake off the *dust* under your feet for a
Rev.18:19. And they cast *dust* on their heads,

5524 2 892/1009 5525,71

χορηγέω, koreegeo.

2Co. 9:10. both *minister* bread for (your) food,
1Pet.4:11. as of the ability which God *giveth*:

5525 1 892/1009

χορός, koros.

Lu. 15:25. he heard musick and *dancing*.

5526 15 892/1009 5528

χορτάζω, kortazo.

Mat. 5: 6. for they *shall be filled*.
14:20. they did all eat, and *were filled*:
15:33. as *to fill* so great a multitude?
37. they did all eat, and *were filled*:
Mar 6:42. they did all eat, and *were filled*.
7:27. Let the children first *be filled*:
8: 4. whence can a man *satisfy* these
8. they did eat, and *were filled*:
Lu. 6:21. that hunger now: for ye *shall be filled*.
9:17. they did eat, and *were* all *filled*:
16:21. desiring *to be fed* with the crumbs
Joh. 6:26. eat of the loaves, and *were filled*.
Phi. 4:12. both *to be full* and to be hungry,
Jas. 2:16. be (ye) warmed and *filled*;
Rev.19:21. the fowls *were filled* with their flesh.

5527 1 892/1009 5526

χόρτασμα, kortasma.

Acts 7:11. and our fathers found no *sustenance*.

5528 15 892/1009

χόρτος, kortos.

Mat. 6:30. if God so clothe the *grass* of the field,
13:26. But when the *blade* was sprung up,
14:19. to sit down on the *grass*, and took
Mar 4:28. first the *blade*, then the ear,
6:39. by companies upon the green *grass*.
Lu. 12:28. If then God so clothe the *grass*,
Joh. 6:10. there was much *grass* in the place.
1Co. 3:12. precious stones, wood, *hay*, stubble,
Jas. 1:10. as the flower of the *grass* he shall pass
11. but it withereth the *grass*, and the
1Pet. 1:24. For all flesh (is) as *grass*, and all the glory of man as the flower of *grass*. The *grass* withereth, and the flower
Rev. 8: 7. all green *grass* was burnt up.
9: 4. should not hurt the *grass* of the earth,

5530 11 892/1010 cf 5531,cf 5534

χράομαι, kraomai.

Acts27: 3. Julius courteously *entreated* Paul, and
17. they *used* helps, undergirding
1Co. 7:21. if thou mayest be made free, *use* (it) rather
31. And they *that use* this world, as not
9:12. Nevertheless we *have* not *used* this power;
15. But I *have used* none of these things:
2Co. 1:17. thus minded, *did* I *use* lightness?
3:12. we *use* great plainness of speech:
13:10. lest being present I *should use* sharpness,
1Ti. 1: 8. the law (is) good, if a man *use* it lawfully;
5:23. but *use* a little wine for thy

5531 1 893/1010 rt 5530

χράω, krao.

Lu. 11: 5. Friend, *lend* me three loaves;

5532 49 893/1010 rt 5530 or 5534

χρεία, krīa.

Mat. 3:14. I have *need* to be baptized of thee,
6: 8. knoweth what things ye have *need* of,
9:12. They that be whole *need* not a
14:16. They *need* not depart;
21: 3. The Lord hath *need* of them;
26:65. what further *need* have we of witnesses?
Mar 2:17. They that are whole have no *need* of the
25. when he had *need*, and was an hungred,
11: 3. the Lord hath *need* of him;
14:63. What *need* we any further witnesses?
Lu. 5:31. They that are whole *need* not a
9:11. healed them that had *need* of healing.
10:42. But one thing is *needful*: and Mary
15: 7. just persons, which *need* no repentance.
19:31. the Lord hath *need* of him.
34. The Lord hath *need* of him.
22:71. What *need* we any further witness?
Joh. 2:25. needed (lit. had *need*) not that any should testify of man:
13:10. *needeth* not save to wash (his) feet,
29. that we have *need* of against the feast;
16:30. *needest* not that any man should ask thee:
Acts 2:45. to all (men), as every man had *need*.
4:35. unto every man according as he had *need*.
6: 3. whom we may appoint over this *business*.
20:34. that these hands have ministered unto my *necessities*,
28:10. with such things as were *necessary*.
Ro. 12:13. Distributing to the *necessity* of saints;
1Co.12:21. I have no *need* of thee:
— I have no *need* of you.
24. For our comely (parts) have no *need*:
Eph 4:28. to give to him that *needeth*.
29. but that which is good to the *use* of edifying, (lit. to the edifying of *need*)
Phi. 2:25. and he that ministered to my *wants*.
4:16. once and again unto my *necessity*.
19. my God shall supply all your *need*
1Th. 1: 8. we *need* not to speak any thing.
4: 9. ye *need* not that I write unto you:
12. ye may have *lack* of nothing.

1Th. 5: 1. ye have no *need* that I write unto you.
Tit. 3:14. to maintain good works for necessary *uses*,
Heb 5:12. ye have *need* that one teach you again
— are become such as have *need* of milk,
7:11. what further *need* (was there) that another
10:36. For ye have *need* of patience, that,
1Joh. 2:27. ye *need* not that any man teach you:
3:17. seeth his brother have *need*, and shutteth
Rev. 3:17. and have *need* of nothing;
21:23. the city had no *need* of the sun,
22: 5. they *need* no candle, neither light of

5533 2 893/1010 5531,3781

χρεωφειλέτης, kreōphīletees.

Lu. 7:41. a certain creditor which had two *debtors*:
16: 5. called every one of his lord's *debtors*

5534 1 893/1010 rt 5530 or 5531

χρή, kree.

Jas. 3:10. these things *ought* not so to be.

5535 5 893/1010 5532

χρῄζω, kreezo.

Mat. 6:32. that ye *have need* of all these things.
Lu. 11: 8. and give him as many as he *needeth*.
12:30. knoweth that ye *have need* of these things.
Ro. 16: 2. assist her in whatsoever business she *hath need* of you:
2Co. 3: 1. or *need* we, as some (others), epistles of

5536 7 893/1010 9:480

χρῆμα, kreema.

Mar 10:23. shall they that have *riches* enter
24. is it for them that trust in *riches*
Lu. 18:24. How hardly shall they that have *riches*
Acts 4:37. and brought the *money*, and laid (it) at
8:18. he offered them *money*,
20. may be purchased with *money*.
24:26. He hoped also that *money* should

5537 9 893/1011 9:480 5536

χρηματίζω, kreematizo.

Mat. 2:12. *being warned of God* in a dream that they
22. *being warned of God* in a dream, he
Lu. 2:26. it was *revealed* unto him by the Holy Ghost,
Acts10:22. *was warned from God* by an holy angel to
11:26. the disciples *were called* (lit. *to call* the disciples) Christians first in Antioch.
Ro. 7: 3. she *shall be called* an adulteress:
Heb 8: 5. as Moses *was admonished of God* when
11: 7. Noah, *being warned of God* of things not
12:25. who refused him *that spake* on earth,

5538 1 894/1011 9:480 5537

χρηματισμός, kreematismos.

Ro. 11: 4. what saith the *answer of God* unto him?

5539 1 894/1011 5540

χρήσιμος, kreesimos.

2Ti. 2:14. strive not about words to no *profit*, (but)

5540 2 894/1011 5530

χρῆσις, kreesis.

Ro. 1:26. did change the natural *use*
27. leaving the natural *use* of the woman,

5541 1 894/1011 9:483 5543

χρηστεύομαι, kreestŭomai.

1Co.13: 4. suffereth long, (and) *is kind*;

5542 1 894/1011 9:483 5543,3004

χρηστολογία, kreestologia.

Ro. 16:18. by *good words* and fair speeches deceive

5543 7 894/1011 9:483 5530

χρηστός, kreestos.

Mat.11:30. For my yoke (is) *easy*, and my burden is light.
Lu. 5:39. he saith, The old is *better*.
6:35. for he is *kind* unto the unthankful and
Ro. 2: 4. not knowing that the *goodness* of God leadeth thee to
1Co.15:33. evil communications corrupt *good*
Eph 4:32. And be ye *kind* one to another,
1Pet.2: 3. tasted that the Lord (is) *gracious*

5544 10 894/1011 9:483 5543

χρηστότης, kreestotees.

Ro. 2: 4. despisest thou the riches of his *goodness*
3:12. there is none that doeth *good*,
11:22. Behold therefore the *goodness* and
— but toward thee, *goodness*, if thou continue in (his) *goodness*:
2Co. 6: 6. by longsuffering, by *kindness*, by the Holy Ghost,
Gal. 5:22. longsuffering, *gentleness*, goodness,
Eph 2: 7. in (his) *kindness* toward us through Christ
Col. 3:12. *kindness*, humbleness of mind, meekness,
Tit. 3: 4. But after that the *kindness* and love of God our Saviour

5548 5 895/1018 9:493 cf 5530

χρίω, krio.

Lu. 4:18. because he *hath anointed* me to preach
Acts 4:27. against thy holy child Jesus, whom thou *hast anointed*,
10:38. How God *anointed* Jesus of Nazareth with the Holy Ghost and
2Co. 1:21. and *hath anointed* us, (is) God;
Heb 1: 9. *hath anointed* thee with the oil of gladness

5545 3 894/1011 9:493 5548

χρίσμα, krisma.

1Joh. 2:20. ye have an *unction* from the Holy One,
27. But the *anointing* which ye have received of
— but as the same *anointing* teacheth you

5549 5 896/1018 5550

χρονίζω, kronizo.

Mat.24:48. My lord *delayeth* his coming;
25: 5. *While* the bridegroom *tarried*, they
Lu. 1:21. marvelled that he *tarried so long* in
12:45. My lord *delayeth* his coming;
Heb 10:37. he that shall come will come, and *will* not *tarry*.

3 F 2

5550 53 896/1018 9:581 cf 2540

χρόνος, *kronos.* cf 165

Mat. 2: 7. enquired of them diligently what *time*
16. according to the *time* which he had
25:19. After a long *time* the lord of those
Mar 2:19. as long)(as they have the bridegroom
9:21. How long)(is it ago since this came
Lu. 1:57. Now Elisabeth's full *time* came that
4: 5. in a moment of *time*.
8:27. which had devils long *time*,
29. For often*times* it had caught him:
18: 4. And he would not for a *while*:
20: 9. into a far country for a long *time*.
Joh. 5: 6. that he had been now a long *time*
7:33. Yet a little *while* am I with you,
12:35. Yet a little *while* is the light with you.
14: 9. Have I been so long *time* with you,
Acts 1: 6. Lord, wilt thou at this *time* restore
7. to know the *times* or the seasons,
21. have companied with us all the *time*
3:21. must receive until the *times* of restitution
7:17. when the *time* of the promise drew nigh,
23. when he was full forty years old, (lit. when the *time* of forty years was filled to him)
8:11. of long *time* he had bewitched them
13:18. about the *time* of forty years suffered
14: 3. Long *time* therefore abode they
28. they abode long *time* with the disciples.
15:33. after they had tarried (there) a *space*,
17:30. And the *times* of this ignorance God
18:20. to tarry longer *time* with them,
23. after he had spent some *time* (there),
19:22. himself stayed in Asia for a *season*.
20:18. I have been with you at all *seasons*,
27: 9. Now when much *time* was spent,
Ro. 7: 1. as long)(as he liveth?
16:25. kept secret since the world began, (lit. in the *times* of ages)
1Co. 7:39. as long)(as her husband liveth;
16: 7. but I trust to tarry a *while* with you,
Gal. 4: 1. as long)(as he is a child,
4. when the fulness of the *time* was come,
1Th. 5: 1. But of the *times* and the seasons,
2Ti. 1: 9. given us in Christ Jesus before the world began; (lit. before the *times* of ages)
Tit. 1: 2. promised before the world began; (lit. &c.)
Heb 4: 7. To day, after so long a *time*;
5:12. when for the *time* ye ought to be teachers,
11:32. for the *time* would fail me to tell of
1Pet. 1:17. pass the *time* of your sojourning (here)
20. was manifest in these last *times* for you,
4: 2. should live the rest of (his) *time* in
3. For the *time* past of (our) life may
Jude 18. there should be mockers in the last *time*,
Rev. 2:21. And I gave her *space* to repent of
6:11. should rest yet for a little *season*,
10: 6. that there should be *time* no longer:
20: 3. he must be loosed a little *season*.

5551 1 896/1018 5550,rt 5147

χρονοτριβέω, *kronotribeo.*

Acts20:16. he would not *spend* the *time* in Asia:

5552 18 896/1018 5557

χρύσεος, *kruseos.*

2Ti. 2:20. not only vessels *of gold* and of silver,
Heb 9: 4. Which had the *golden* censer,
— the *golden* pot that had manna.
Rev. 1:12. saw seven *golden* candlesticks;
13. about the paps with a *golden* girdle.
20. and the seven *golden* candlesticks.
2: 1. midst of the seven *golden* candlesticks;
4: 4. they had on their heads crowns *of gold*.
5: 8. and *golden* vials full of odours,
8: 3. having a *golden* censer;
— upon the *golden* altar which was before
9:13. from the four horns of the *golden* altar
20. devils, and idols *of gold*, and silver,
14:14. having on his head a *golden* crown,
15: 6. breasts girded with *golden* girdles.
7. seven *golden* vials full of the wrath of God,
17: 4. having a *golden* cup in her hand full
21:15. had a *golden* reed to measure the city.

5553 9 896/1019 5557

χρυσίον, *krusion.*

Acts 3: 6. Silver and *gold* have I none;
20:33. I have coveted no man's silver, or *gold*,
Heb 9: 4. overlaid round about with *gold*,
1Pet. 1: 7. much more precious than of *gold* that
18. not redeemed with corruptible things, (as) silver and *gold*,
3: 3. plaiting the hair, and of wearing of *gold*,
Rev. 3:18. to buy of me *gold* tried in the fire,
21:18. and the city (was) pure *gold*, like unto clear glass.
21. the street of the city (was) pure *gold*, as it were transparent glass.

5554 1 896/1019 5557,1146

χρυσοδακτύλιος, *krusodaktulios.*

Jas. 2: 2. a man *with a gold ring*, in

5555 1 896/1019 5557,3037

χρυσόλιθος, *krusolithos.*

Rev.21:20. the seventh, *chrysolite*;

5556 1 897/1019 5557 *prason* (leek)

χρυσόπρασος, *krusoprasos.*

Rev.21:20. the tenth, a *chrysoprasus*;

5557 13 897/1019 rt 5530

χρυσός, *krusos.*

Mat. 2:11. unto him gifts; *gold*, and frankincense,
10: 9. Provide neither *gold*, nor silver, nor
23:16. shall swear by the *gold* of the temple,
17. whether is greater, the *gold*, or the temple that sanctifieth the *gold*?
Acts17:29. that the Godhead is like unto *gold*, or
1Co. 3:12. upon this foundation *gold*, silver,
1Ti. 2: 9. not with broidered hair, or *gold*, or
Jas. 5: 3. Your *gold* and silver is cankered;
Rev. 9: 7. as it were crowns like *gold*,
17: 4. decked with *gold* and precious stone
18:12. The merchandise of *gold*, and silver,
16. decked with *gold*, and precious stones,

5558 2 897/1019 5557

χρυσόω, *krusoo.*

Rev.17: 4. *decked* with gold (lit. *made golden* with gold)
18:16. *decked* with gold, (lit. *made golden*, &c.)

5559 1 897/1019 cf rt 5530

χρώς, krōs.

Acts19:12. So that from his *body* were brought

5560 15 897/1019

χωλός, kōlos.

Mat.11: 5. the *lame* walk, the lepers are cleansed,
15:30. *lame*, blind, dumb, maimed,
31. the *lame* to walk, and the blind to see:
18: 8. to enter into life *halt* or
21:14. the blind and the *lame* came to him
Mar 9:45. better for thee to enter *halt* into life,
Lu. 7:22. the *lame* walk, the lepers are
14:13. the maimed, the *lame*, the blind:
21. and the *halt*, and the blind.
Joh. 5: 3. of blind, *halt*, withered, waiting for
Acts 3: 2. man *lame* from his mother's womb
11. as the *lame* man which was healed held
8: 7. and that were *lame*, were healed.
14: 8. impotent in his feet, being a *cripple* from his mother's womb,
Heb12:13. lest that which is *lame* be turned out of the way;

5561 27 897/1019 rt 5490,cf 5117

χώρα, kōra.

Mat. 2:12. into their own *country* another way.
4:16. to them which sat in the *region* and
8:28. into the *country* of the Gergesenes,
Mar 1: 5. unto him all the *land* of Judæa,
5: 1. into the *country* of the Gadarenes.
10. away out of the *country*.
Lu. 2: 8. were in the same *country* shepherds
3: 1. and of the *region* of Trachonitis,
8:26. at the *country* of the Gadarenes,
12:16. The *ground* of a certain rich man brought
15:13. took his journey into a far *country*,
14. a mighty famine in that *land*;
15. to a citizen of that *country*;
19:12. went into a far *country* to receive
21:21. let not them that are in the *countries* enter thereinto.
Joh. 4:35. look on the *fields*; for they are white
11:54. unto a *country* near to the wilderness,
55. many went out of the *country* up to
Acts 8: 1. throughout the *regions* of Judæa and
10:39. which he did both in the *land* of the Jews,
12:20. because their *country* was nourished by
13:49. published throughout all the *region*.
16: 6. and the *region* of Galatia,
18:23. went over (all) the *country* of Galatia
26:20. and throughout all the *coasts* of Judæa,
27:27. that they drew near to some *country*;
Jas. 5: 4. who have reaped down your *fields*,

5562 10 897/1020 5561

χωρέω, kōreo.

Mat.15:17. *goeth* into the belly, and is cast
19:11. All (men) *cannot receive* this saying,
12. He that is able *to receive* (it), *let* him *receive* (it).
Mar 2: 2. insomuch that there *was* no *room to receive* (them), no, not
Joh. 2: 6. *containing* two or three firkins apiece.
8:37. because my word *hath* no *place* in you.
21:25. I suppose that even the world itself *could* not *contain* the books
2Co. 7: 2. *Receive* us; we have wronged no man,
2Pet.3: 9. but that all should *come* to repentance.

5563 13 898/1020 5561

χωρίζω, kōrizo.

Mat.19: 6. *let* not man *put asunder*.
Mar 10: 9. *let* not man *put asunder*.
Acts 1: 4. that they should not *depart* from
18: 1. Paul *departed* from Athens, *and*
2. commanded all Jews *to depart* from Rome
Ro. 8:35. Who *shall separate* us from the love of
39. shall be able *to separate* us from the love
1Co. 7:10. Let not the wife *depart* from (her)
11. But and if she *depart*, let her
15. if the unbelieving *depart*, *let* him *depart*.
Philem 15. For perhaps he therefore *departed* for a
Heb 7:26. undefiled, *separate* (lit. *separated*) from sinners,

5564 10 898/1020 5561

χωρίον, kōrion.

Mat.26:36. unto a *place* called Gethsemane,
Mar14:32. a *place* which was named Gethsemane:
Joh. 4: 5. near to the *parcel of ground* that Jacob
Acts 1:18. purchased a *field* with the reward of
19. that *field* is called in their proper tongue, Aceldama, that is to say, The *field* of blood.
4:34. as many as were possessors of *lands* or
5: 3. (part) of the price of the *land*?
8. whether ye sold the *land* for so much?
28: 7. were *possessions* of the chief man of the

5565 39 898/1020 5561

χωρίς, kōris.

Mat.13:34. *without* a parable spake he not unto them:
14:21. *beside* women and children.
15:38. *beside* women and children.
Mar 4:34. *without* a parable spake he not unto them:
Lu. 6:49. a man that *without* a foundation
Joh. 1: 3. *without* him was not any thing made
15: 5. *without* me ye can do nothing.
20: 7. wrapped together in a place *by itself*.
Ro. 3:21. righteousness of God *without* the law
28. by faith *without* the deeds of the law.
4: 6. imputeth righteousness *without* works,
7: 8. For *without* the law sin (was) dead.
9. I was alive *without* the law once:
10:14. how shall they hear *without* a preacher?
1Co. 4: 8. ye have reigned as kings *without* us:
11:11. neither is the man *without* the woman, neither the woman *without* the man, in the Lord.
2Co.11:28. *Beside* those things that are without,
Eph. 2:12. at that time ye were *without* Christ,
Phi. 2:14. Do all things *without* murmurings and
1Ti. 2: 8. *without* wrath and doubting.
5:21. *without* preferring one before another,
Philem 14. *without* thy mind would I do nothing;
Heb 4:15. tempted like as (we are, yet) *without* sin.
7: 7. *without* all contradiction the less
20. inasmuch as not *without* an oath
21(20). those priests were made *without* an oath;
9: 7. not *without* blood, which he offered
18. was dedicated *without* blood.
22. and *without* shedding of blood is no remission.
28. appear the second time *without* sin unto
10:28. died *without* mercy under two or three
11: 6. But *without* faith (it is) impossible
40. that they *without* us should not be
12: 8. But if ye be *without* chastisement,
14. *without* which no man shall see the Lord:

Jas. 2:20. that faith *without* works is dead?
26. as the body *without* the spirit is dead, so faith *without* works

5566 1 899/1020
χῶρος, kōros.

Acts27:12. toward the south west and *north west.*

5567 5 899/1021 8:489 *psaō* (to rub)

ψάλλω, psallo.

Ro. 15: 9. I will confess...and *sing* unto thy name.
1Co.14:15. I *will sing* with the spirit, and I *will sing* with the understanding
Eph. 5:19. singing and *making melody* in your heart to the Lord;
Jas. 5:13. Is any merry? *let* him *sing psalms.*

5568 7 899/1021 8:489 cf 5603 5567
ψαλμός, psalmos.

Lu. 20:42. David himself saith in the book of *Psalms,*
24:44. and (in) the *psalms,* concerning me.
Acts 1:20. it is written in the book of *Psalms,* Let
13:33. it is also written in the second *psalm,*
1Co.14:26. every one of you hath a *psalm,*
Eph. 5:19. Speaking to yourselves in *psalms* and
Col. 3:16. admonishing one another in *psalms*

5569 2 899/1021 1:144 5571,80
ψευδάδελφος, psūdadelphos.

2Co.11:26. (in) perils among *false brethren;*
Gal. 2: 4. And that because of *false brethren*

5570 1 899/1021 1:398 5571,652
ψευδαπόστολος, psūdapostolos.

2Co.11:13. For such (are) *false apostles,*

5571 3 899/1021 9:594 5574
ψευδής, psūdees.

Acts 6:13. And set up *false* witnesses.
Rev. 2: 2. and hast found them *liars:*
21: 8. sorcerers, and idolaters, and all *liars,*

5572 1 899/1021 5571,1320
ψευδοδιδάσκαλος, psūdodidaskalos.

2Pet.2: 1. there shall be *false teachers* among you,

5573 1 899/1021 5571,3004
ψευδολόγος, psūdologos.

1Ti. 4: 2. *Speaking lies* in hypocrisy;

5574 12 899/1021 9:594
ψεύδομαι, psūdomai.

Mat. 5:11. all manner of evil against you *falsely,*
Acts 5: 3. why hath Satan filled thine heart *to lie* to the Holy Ghost,
4. thou *hast* not *lied* unto men, but
Ro. 9: 1. I say the truth in Christ, I *lie* not,
2Co.11:31. knoweth that I *lie* not.
Gal. 1:20. behold, before God, I *lie* not.
Col. 3: 9. *Lie* not one to another, seeing that ye
1Ti. 2: 7. I speak the truth in Christ, (and) *lie* not;
Heb 6:18. in which (it was) impossible for God *to lie,*
Jas. 3:14. glory not, and *lie* not against the truth.
1Joh.1: 6. we *lie,* and do not the truth:
Rev. 3: 9. say they are Jews, and are not, but *do lie*

5575 3 900/1021 4:474 5571,3144
ψευδομάρτυρ, psūdomartur.

Mat.26:60. though many *false witnesses* came,
— At the last came two *false witnesses,*
1Co.15:15. we are found *false witnesses* of God;

5576 6 900/1021 4:474 5575
ψευδομαρτυρέω, psūdomartureo.

Mat.19:18. Thou shalt not *bear false witness,*
Mar 10:19. *Do* not *bear false witness,*
14:56. For many *bare false witness* against him,
57. arose certain, and *bare false witness* against him,
Lu. 18:20. *Do* not *bear false witness,*
Ro. 13: 9. Thou *shalt* not *bear false witness,*

5577 2 900/1021 4:474 5575
ψευδομαρτυρία, psūdomarturia.

Mat.15:19. thefts, *false witness,* blasphemies:
26:59. sought *false witness* against Jesus,

5578 11 900/1021 6:781 5571,4396
ψευδοπροφήτης, psudopropheetees.

Mat. 7:15. Beware of *false prophets,*
24:11. And many *false prophets* shall rise,
24. and *false prophets,* and shall shew
Mar 13:22. For false Christs and *false prophets* shall rise,
Lu. 6:26. so did their fathers to the *false prophets.*
Acts13: 6. sorcerer, a *false prophet,* a Jew,
2Pet.2: 1. But there were *false prophets* also
1Joh.4: 1. because many *false prophets* are gone out into the world.
Rev.16:13. and out of the mouth of the *false prophet.*
19:20. and with him the *false prophet* that
20:10. where the beast and the *false prophet*

5579 9 900/1021 9:594 5574
ψεῦδος, psūdos.

Joh. 8:44. When he speaketh a *lie,* he speaketh
Ro. 1:25. changed the truth of God into a *lie,*
Eph 4:25. Wherefore putting away *lying,*
2Th. 2: 9. all power and signs and *lying* wonders,
11. that they should believe a *lie:*
1Joh.2:21. and that no *lie* is of the truth.
27. and is truth, and is no *lie,*
Rev.21:27. worketh abomination, or (maketh) a *lie.*
22:15. whosoever loveth and maketh a *lie.*

5580 2 900/1021 5571,5547
ψευδόχριστος, psūdokristos.

Mat.24:24. For there shall arise *false Christs,*
Mar 13:22. For *false Christs* and false prophets shall rise,

5581 1 900/1022 5:242 5571,3686
ψευδώνυμος, psūdonumos.

1Ti. 6:20. oppositions of science *falsely so called:*

5582 1 900/1022 9:594 5574

ψεῦσμα, *psusma.*

Ro. 3: 7. abounded through my *lie* unto his glory;

5583 10 900/1022 9:594 5574

ψεύστης, *psustees.*

Joh. 8:44. for he is a *liar*, and the father of it.
55. I shall be a *liar* like unto you:
Ro. 3: 4. let God be true, but every man a *liar*;
1Ti. 1:10. for *liars*, for perjured persons,
Tit. 1:12. said, The Cretians (are) alway *liars*, evil beasts,
1Joh. 1:10. that we have not sinned, we make him a *liar*,
2: 4. keepeth not his commandments, is a *liar*,
22. Who is a *liar* but he that denieth
4:20. and hateth his brother, he is a *liar*:
5:10. believeth not God hath made him a *liar*;

5584 4 900/1022 rt 5567, cf 5586

ψηλαφάω, *pseelaphao.*

Lu. 24:39. *handle* me, and see; for a spirit
Acts17:27. if haply they *might feel after* him,
Heb 12:18. unto the mount *that might be touched*,
1Joh. 1: 1. and our hands *have handled*,

5585 2 900/1022 9:604 5586

ψηφίζω, *pseephizo.*

Lu. 14:28. and *counteth* the cost,
Rev. 13:18. *Let* him that hath understanding *count* the number of the beast:

5586 3 901/1022 9:604 rt 5584

ψῆφος, *pseephos.*

Acts26:10. I gave my *voice* (lit. *pebble of voting*) against (them).
Rev. 2:17. will give him a white *stone*, and in the *stone* a new name written,

5587 1 901/1022 psithos (whisper)

ψιθυρισμός, *psithurismos.*

2Co. 12:20. *whisperings*, swellings, tumults:

5588 1 901/1022 rt 5587

ψιθυριστής, *psithuristees.*

Ro. 1:29(30). full of...deceit, malignity; *whisperers*,

5589 3 901/1022 rt 5567

ψιχίον, *psikion.*

Mat. 15:27. eat of the *crumbs* which fall from
Mar 7:28. eat of the children's *crumbs*.
Lu. 16:21. to be fed with the *crumbs* which fell

5590 105 901/1022 9:608 cf 4151
5594, cf 2222

ψυχή, *psukee.*

Mat. 2:20. which sought the young child's *life*.
6:25. Take no thought for your *life*, what ye
— Is not the *life* more than meat,
10:28. but are not able to kill the *soul*:
— to destroy both *soul* and body in hell.
39. He that findeth his *life* shall lose it: and he that loseth his *life* for my sake
11:29. and ye shall find rest unto your *souls*.
12:18. in whom my *soul* is well pleased.
16:25. whosoever will save his *life* shall lose it. and whosoever will lose his *life* for my
26. the whole world, and lose his own *soul*? or what shall a man give in exchange for his *soul*?
20:28. to give his *life* a ransom for many.
22:37. with all thy heart, and with all thy *soul*,
26:38. My *soul* is exceeding sorrowful,
Mar 3: 4. to save *life*, or to kill?
8:35. whosoever will save his *life* shall lose it; but whosoever shall lose his *life* for my
36. gain the whole world, and lose his own *soul*?
37. give in exchange for his *soul*?
10:45. to give his *life* a ransom for many.
12:30. with all thy heart, and with all thy *soul*,
33. the understanding, and with all the *soul*,
14:34. My *soul* is exceeding sorrowful
Lu. 1:46. My *soul* doth magnify the Lord,
2:35. shall pierce through thy own *soul*
6: 9. to save *life*, or to destroy (it)?
9:24. whosoever will save his *life* shall
— whosoever will lose his *life* for my
56. is not come to destroy men's *lives*, but to
10:27. all thy heart, and with all thy *soul*,
12:19. And I will say to my *soul*, *Soul*, thou hast much goods
20. this night thy *soul* shall be required
22. Take no thought for your *life*, what
23. The *life* is more than meat,
14:26. yea, and his own *life* also, he cannot be
17:33. Whosoever shall seek to save his *life*
21:19. In your patience possess ye your *souls*.
Joh. 10:11. the good shepherd giveth his *life* for
15. I lay down my *life* for the sheep.
17. because I lay down my *life*,
24. How long dost thou make us (lit. our *soul*) to doubt?
12:25. He that loveth his *life* shall lose it; and he that hateth his *life* in this
27. Now is my *soul* troubled;
13:37. I will lay down my *life* for thy sake.
38. Wilt thou lay down thy *life* for my sake?
15:13. that a man lay down his *life* for his
Acts 2:27. thou wilt not leave my *soul* in hell,
31. that his *soul* was not left in hell,
41. about three thousand *souls*.
43. fear came upon every *soul*:
3:23. every *soul*, which will not hear that
4:32. were of one heart and of one *soul*:
7:14. his kindred, threescore and fifteen *souls*.
14: 2. and made their *minds* evil affected
22. Confirming the *souls* of the disciples,
15:24. subverting your *souls*, saying,
26. Men that have hazarded their *lives* for
20:10. for his *life* is in him.
24. neither count I my *life* dear unto myself,
27:10. lading and ship, but also of our *lives*.
22. there shall be no loss of (any man's) *life*
37. we were in all in the ship two hundred threescore and sixteen *souls*.
Ro. 2: 9. upon every *soul* of man that doeth evil,
11: 3. I am left alone, and they seek my *life*.
13: 1. Let every *soul* be subject unto the
16: 4. have for my *life* laid down their own necks:
1Co. 15:45. The first man Adam was made a living *soul*;
2Co. 1:23. I call God for a record upon my *soul*,
12:15. gladly spend and be spent for you: (lit. for your *souls*)
Eph 6: 6. doing the will of God from the *heart*;

Phi. 1:27. with one *mind* striving together for the
2.30. not regarding his *life*, to supply
Col. 3:23. whatsoever ye do, do (it) *heart*ily,
1Th. 2: 8. gospel of God only, but also our own *souls*,
5:23. your whole spirit and *soul* and body
Heb 4:12. the dividing asunder of *soul* and spirit,
6:19. we have as an anchor of the *soul*,
10:38. my *soul* shall have no pleasure in him.
39. that believe to the saving of the *soul*.
12: 3. lest ye be wearied and faint in your *minds*.
13:17. for they watch for your *souls*, as
Jas. 1:21. word, which is able to save your *souls*.
5:20. shall save a *soul* from death,
1Pet. 1: 9. (even) the salvation of (your) *souls*.
22. Seeing ye have purified your *souls* in
2:11. which war against the *soul*;
25. unto the Shepherd and Bishop of your *souls*.
3:20. few, that is, eight *souls* were saved
4:19. commit the keeping of their *souls*
2Pet. 2: 8. vexed (his) righteous *soul* from day to day
14. beguiling unstable *souls*:
1Joh. 3:16. he laid down his *life* for us: and we ought to lay down (our) *lives* for the brethren.
3Joh. 2. even as thy *soul* prospereth.
Rev. 6: 9. I saw under the altar the *souls* of them
8: 9. which were in the sea, and had *life*, died;
12:11. they loved not their *lives* unto the death.
16: 3. every living *soul* died in the sea.
18:13. and slaves, and *souls* of men.
14. the fruits that thy *soul* lusted after
20: 4. the *souls* of them that were beheaded for

5591 6 902/1023 9:608 cf 4152
5590, cf 5446

ψυχικός, psukikos.

14. But the *natural* man receiveth not
15.44. It is sown a *natural* body; it is
— There is a *natural* body, and there
46. but that which is *natural*; and afterward
Jas. 3:15. but (is) earthly, *sensual*, devilish.
Jude 19. *sensual*, having not the Spirit.

5594 1 903/1023 cf 4154
cf rt 109

ψύχομαι, psukomai.

Mat. 24:12. the love of many *shall wax cold*.

5592 3 902/1023 5594

ψῦχος, psukos.

Joh. 18:18. a fire of coals; for it was *cold*:
Acts 28: 2. present rain, and because of the *cold*.
2Co. 11:27. in fastings often, in *cold* and nakedness.

5593 4 902/1023 5592

ψυχρός, psukros.

Mat. 10:42. of these little ones a cup of *cold* (water)
Rev. 3:15. that thou art neither *cold* nor hot: I would thou wert *cold* or hot.
16. and neither *cold* nor hot, I will

5595 2 903/1023 rt 5596

ψωμίζω, psōmizo.

Ro. 12:20. if thine enemy hunger, *feed* him;
1Co. 13: 3. And though I *bestow* all my goods *to feed* (the poor),

5596 4 903/1024 rt 5597

ψωμίον, psōmion.

Joh. 13:26. He it is, to whom I shall give a *sop*, when
— when he had dipped the *sop*, he gave (it
27. after the *sop* Satan entered into him.
30. He then having received the *sop* went

5597 1 903/1024 rt 5567

ψώχω, psōko.

Lu. 6: 1. did eat, *rubbing* (them) in (their) hands.

5598 4 903/1024

Ω, ōmega.

Rev. 1: 8. I am Alpha and *Omega*,
11. Saying, I am Alpha and *Omega*,
21: 6. I am Alpha and *Omega*,
22:13. I am Alpha and *Omega*,

5599 16 903/1024

ὦ, ō.

Mat. 15:28. *O* woman, great (is) thy faith:
17:17. *O* faithless and perverse generation,
Mar 9:19. *O* faithless generation, how long
Lu. 9:41. *O* faithless and perverse generation,
24:25. *O* fools, and slow of heart to believe
Acts 1: 1. treatise have I made, *O* Theophilus, of all
13:10. *O* full of all subtilty and all mischief,
18:14. *O* (ye) Jews, reason would that I should bear
27:21.)(Sirs, ye should have hearkened
Ro. 2: 1. *O* man, whosoever thou art that judgest:
3. And thinkest thou this, *O* man, that
9:20. Nay but, *O* man, who art thou
11:33. *O* the depth of the riches
Gal. 3: 1. *O* foolish Galatians, who hath
1Ti. 6:20. *O* Timothy, keep that which is
Jas. 2:20. But wilt thou know, *O* vain man,

5600 66 221/277 1510

ὦ, ᾖς, ᾖ &c., ō, ees, ee.

From εἰμί.

Mat. 6: 4. That thine alms *may be* in secret:
22. if therefore thine eye *be* single,
23. But if thine eye *be* evil,
10:13. And if the house *be* worthy,
— but if it *be* not worthy, let your
20. 4. and whatsoever *is* right I will give you.
7. whatsoever *is* right, (that) shall ye receive.
24:28. For wheresoever the carcase *is*, there
Mar 3:14. that they *should be* with him,
5:18. prayed him that he *might be* with him.
Lu. 10: 6. And if the son of peace *be* there,
11:34. therefore when thine eye *is* single,
— but when (thine eye) *is* evil, thy
14: 8. lest a more honourable...*be* bidden
Joh. 3: 2. except God *be* with him.
27. except it *be* given him from heaven.
6:65. except it *were* given unto him of my
9: 5. As long as I *am* in the world, I am the
31. but if any man *be* a worshipper of God,
14: 3. that where I am, (there) ye *may be* also.
16:24. shall receive, that your joy *may be* full.
17:11. that they *may be* one, as we (are).
19. that they also *might be* sanctified
21. That they all *may be* one;
— that they also *may be* one in us:

Joh. 17:22. that they *may be* one, even as we are one:
23. that they *may be* made perfect in one;
24. I will that they also, whom thou hast given me, *be* with me where I am;
26. *may be* in them, and I in them.
Acts 5:38. if this counsel or this work *be* of men,
Ro. 2:25. but if thou *be* a breaker of the law,
9:27. Though the number of...*be* as the sand
11:25. lest ye *should be* wise in your own
1Co. 1:10. (that) there *be* no divisions among you; but (that) ye *be* perfectly joined
2: 5. That your faith *should* not *stand* in the wisdom of men,
5: 7. that ye *may be* a new lump,
7:29. *be* as though they had none;
34. that she *may be* holy both in body and
36. if she pass the flower of (her) age, (lit. *be* past-prime)
12:25. That there *should be* no schism in
14:28. But if there *be* no interpreter,
15:28. that God *may be* all in all.
16: 4. And if it *be* meet that I go also,
2Co. 1: 9. that we should not trust in ourselves, (lit. *should* not *be* trusting)
17. that with me there *should be* yea yea, and
4: 7. *may be* of God, and not of us.
9: 3. that, as I said, ye *may be* ready:
13: 7. though we *be* as reprobates.
9. when we are weak, and ye *are* strong:
Gal. 5:10. bear his judgment, whosoever he *be*.
Eph. 4:14. That we (henceforth) *be* no more children,
5:27. but that it *should be* holy and without
Phi. 1:10. that ye *may be* sincere and without
2:28. and that I *may be* the less sorrowful.
1Ti. 4:15. that thy profiting may appear (lit. *may be* apparent) to all.
5: 7. that they *may be* blameless.
2Ti. 3:17. That the man of God *may be* perfect,
Tit. 1: 9. that he *may be* able by sound
3:14. that they *be* not unfruitful.
Philem 14. that thy benefit *should* not *be* as
Jas. 1: 4. that ye *may be* perfect and entire,
2:15. be naked, and)(destitute of daily food,
5:15. and if he have committed sins, (lit. *be* having committed)
1Joh. 1: 4. that your joy *may be* full.
2Joh. 12. that our joy *may be* full.

5602 60 903/1024 3592

ὧδε, hōde.

Mat. 8:29. art thou come *hither* to torment us
12: 6. *in this place* is (one) greater than the temple.
41. a greater than Jonas (is) *here*.
42. a greater than Solomon (is) *here*.
14: 8. Give me *here* John Baptist's head
17. We have *here* but five loaves,
18. Bring them *hither* to me.
16:28. There be some standing *here*,
17: 4. it is good for us to be *here*:
— let us make *here* three tabernacles;
17. bring him *hither* to me,
20: 6. Why stand ye *here* all the day idle?
22:12. Friend, how camest thou in *hither*
24: 2. There shall not be left *here* one stone
23. say unto you, Lo, *here* (is) Christ, or *there*; believe (it) not.
26:38. tarry ye *here*, and watch with me.
28: 6. He is not *here*: for he is risen, as
Mar 6: 3. are not his sisters *here* with us?
8: 4. with bread *here* in the wilderness?
Mar 9: 1. there be some of them that stand *here*,
5. it is good for us to be *here*:
11: 3. straightway he will send him *hither*.
13:21. Lo, *here* (is) Christ; or, lo,
14:32. Sit ye *here*, while I shall pray.
34. tarry ye *here*, and watch.
16: 6. he is not *here*: behold the place
Lu. 4:23. do also *here* in thy country.
9:12. for we are *here* in a desert place.
27. there be some standing *here*, which
33. it is good for us to be *here*:
41. Bring thy son *hither*.
11:31. a greater than Solomon (is) *here*.
32. a greater than Jonas (is) *here*.
14:21. bring in *hither* the poor, and the maimed,
17:21. Neither shall they say, Lo *here*! or,
23. And they shall say to you, See *here*;
19:27. bring *hither*, and slay (them) before me.
22:38. behold, *here* (are) two swords.
23: 5. beginning from Galilee to *this place*.
24: 6. He is not *here*, but is risen:
Joh. 6: 9. There is a lad *here*, which hath
25. Rabbi, when camest thou *hither*?
11:21. Lord, if thou hadst been *here*,
32. if thou hadst been *here*, my brother
20:27. Reach *hither* thy finger, and
Acts 9:14. And *here* he hath authority from
21. and came *hither* for that intent,
Col. 4: 9. unto you all things which (are done) *here*.
Heb 7: 8. And *here* men that die receive tithes;
13:14. For *here* have we no continuing city,
Jas. 2: 3. Sit thou *here* in a good place;
— or sit *here* under my footstool:
Rev. 4: 1. which said, Come up *hither*, and I
11:12. saying unto them, Come up *hither*.
13:10. *Here* is the patience and the faith of the saints.
18. *Here* is wisdom. Let him that hath
14:12. *Here* is the patience of the saints: *here* (are) they that keep the
17: 9. And *here* (is) the mind which hath wisdom.

5603 7 903/1024 1:163 103 cf 5215, cf 5568

ᾠδή, ōdee.

Eph 5:19. hymns and spiritual *songs*,
Col. 3:16. psalms and hymns and spiritual *songs*,
Rev. 5: 9. And they sung a new *song*, saying,
14: 3. they sung as it were a new *song*
— no man could learn that *song*
15: 3. they sing the *song* of Moses the servant of God, and the *song* of the Lamb,

---

5604 4 904/1025 9:667 cf 3601

ὠδίν, ōdin.

Mat. 24: 8. All these (are) the beginning of *sorrows*.
Mar 13: 8. these (are) the beginnings of *sorrows*.
Acts 2:24. having loosed the *pains* of death:
1Th. 5: 3. as *travail* upon a woman with child;

5605 3 905/1025 9:667 5604

ὠδίνω, ōdino.

Gal. 4:19. of whom I *travail in birth* again
27. and cry, thou *that travailest* not:
Rev. 12: 2. cried, *travailing in birth*, and

5606 2 904/1025 5342

ὦμος, ōmos.

Mat. 23: 4. and lay (them) on men's *shoulders*;
Lu. 15: 5. he layeth (it) on his *shoulders*, rejoicing.

5607 154 221/279 1510

ὤν, οὖσα, ὄν, ōn, ousa, on.

From εἰμί.

Mat. 1:19. *being* a just (man),
6:30. grass of the field, *which* to day *is*, and
7:11. If ye then, *being* evil, know how to
12:30. He *that is* not with me is against me;
34. how can ye, *being* evil, speak good things?
Mar 2:26. gave also to them *which were* with him?
5:25. woman, which had an issue of blood (lit. *being* in a flowing of blood) twelve years,
8: 1. the multitude *being* very great,
11:11. *and* now the eventide *was come*,
13:16. And let him *that is* in the field
14: 3. And *being* in Bethany in the house of
43.)(one of the twelve,
66. *as* Peter *was* beneath in the palace,
Lu. 2: 5. *being* great with child.
3:23. *being* as was supposed the son of
6: 3. and they *which were* with him;
8:43. a woman *having* an issue of blood
11:23. He *that is* not with me is against me:
12:28. the grass, *which is* to day in the field,
13:16. *being* a daughter of Abraham,
14:32. *while* the other *is* yet a great way off,
20:36. *being* the children of the resurrection.
22: 3. *being* of the number of the twelve.
53. *When* I *was* daily with you in the temple,
23: 7. to Herod, *who* himself also *was* at Jerusalem
12. for before they were)(at enmity
24: 6. *when* he *was* yet in Galilee,
44. unto you, *while* I *was* yet with you,
Joh. 1:18. *which is* in the bosom of the Father,
48(49). *when* thou *wast* under the fig tree,
3: 4. How can a man be born *when* he *is* old?
13. the Son of man *which is* in heaven.
31. he *that is* of the earth is earthly,
4: 9. How is it that thou, *being* a Jew, askest drink of me, *which am* a woman of
5:13. a multitude *being* in (that) place.
6:46. save he *which is* of God,
71. *being* one of the twelve.
7:50. *being* one of them,
8:47. He *that is* of God heareth God's words:
9:25. that, *whereas* I *was* blind, now I see.
40. (some) of the Pharisees *which were* with him
10:12. he that is an hireling and not)(the shepherd,
33. because that thou, *being* a man, makest thyself God.
11:31. The Jews then *which were* with her
49. *being* the high priest that same year,
51. but *being* high priest that year,
12:17. The people therefore *that was* with him
18:26. *being* (his) kinsman whose ear Peter
37. Every one *that is* of the truth
19:38. *being* a disciple of Jesus, but secretly
20: 1. *when* it *was* yet dark,
19. the same day at evening, (lit. it *being* evening)
21:11. *for all* there *were* so many,
Acts 5:17. *which is* the sect of the Sadducees,
7: 2. *when* he *was* in Mesopotamia,
5. when (as yet) he had no child. (lit. a child not *being* to him)
12. Jacob heard that there *was* corn in
8:23. I perceive that thou *art* in the gall
9: 2. that if he found any)(of this way,
38. *forasmuch as* Lydda *was* nigh to
Acts 9:39. Dorcas made, *while* she *was* with them.
11: 1. and brethren *that were* in Judæa
13: 1. in the church *that was* at Antioch
14:13. of Jupiter, *which was* before their city,
15:32. *being* prophets also themselves,
16: 3. because of the Jews *which were* in those
21. neither to observe, *being* Romans.
17:16. when he saw the city)(wholly given to idolatry.
18:24.)(mighty in the scriptures,
19:31. *which were* his friends, sent unto him,
35. city of the Ephesians *is* a worshipper
36. Seeing then that these things cannot be spoken against, (lit. these things *being* undeniable)
20:34. and to them *that were* with me.
21: 8. *which was* (one) of the seven;
22: 5. to bring them *which were* there bound
9. And they *that were* with me saw
24:10. Forasmuch as I know that thou *hast been*
24. his wife Drusilla, *which was* a Jewess,
25:23. and principal men of the city, (lit. men *being* of eminence)
26: 3. (because I know) thee *to be* expert
27: 2. Aristarchus,...*being* with us.
9. *when* sailing *was* now dangerous,
28:17. Paul called the chief (lit. those *that were* the chief) of the Jews together:
25. when they agreed not (lit. they *being* discordant)
Ro. 1: 7. To all *that be* in Rome, beloved of God,
4:10. *when* he *was* in circumcision, or in
17. calleth those things *which be* not as though they were. (lit. as *being*)
5: 6. *when* we *were* yet without strength,
8. in that, *while* we *were* yet sinners,
10. For if, *when* we *were* enemies, we
13. sin is not imputed *when* there *is* no law.
7:23. to the law of sin *which is* in my members
8: 5. For they *that are* after the flesh do
8. So then they *that are* in the flesh
28. to them *who are* the called according
9: 5. *who is* over all, God blessed for ever.
11:17. and thou, *being* a wild olive tree,
12: 3. to every man *that is* among you,
13: 1. the powers *that be* are ordained of God.
16: 1. Phebe our sister, *which is* a servant of
11. of Narcissus, *which are* in the Lord.
1Co. 1: 2. Unto the church of God *which is* at Corinth,
28. and things *which are* not, to bring to nought things *that are*;
8: 7. their conscience *being* weak is defiled.
10. the conscience of him *which is* weak
9:19. For *though* I *be* free from all
21. *being* not without law to God, but
12:12. *being* many, are one body:
2Co. 1: 1. unto the church of God *which is* at Corinth, with all the saints *which are* in
5: 4. we *that are* in (this) tabernacle
8: 9. that, *though* he *was* rich, yet for
22. have oftentimes proved)(diligent
11:19. *seeing* ye (yourselves) *are* wise.
31. *which is* blessed for evermore,
Gal. 2: 3. Titus, who was with me, *being* a Greek,
4: 1. *though* he *be* lord of all;
8. unto them *which* by nature *are* no gods.
6: 3. to be something, *when* he *is* nothing,
Eph 1: 1. to the saints *which are* at Ephesus,
2: 1. *who were* dead in trespasses and sins:
4. But God, *who is* rich in mercy,
5. Even *when* we *were* dead in sins,

Eph 2:13. ye *who* sometimes *were* far off
20. Jesus Christ himself *being* the chief corner (stone);
4:18. *being* alienated from the life of God through the ignorance *that is* in them,
Phi. 1: 1. saints in Christ Jesus *which are* at Philippi,
7. *inasmuch as*...ye all *are* partakers of my grace.
Col. 1:21. you, *that were* sometime alienated
2:13. And you, *being* dead in your sins
4:11. *who are* of the circumcision.
1Th. 2:14. of the churches of God *which* in Judæa *are* in Christ Jesus:
5: 8. But let us, *who are* of the day,
2Th. 2: 5. that, *when* I *was* yet with you,
1Ti. 1:13. *Who was* before a blasphemer, and
2: 2. and (for) all *that are* in authority;
3:10. *being* (found) blameless.
2Ti. 2:19. The Lord knoweth them *that are* his.
Tit. 1:16. *being* abominable, and disobedient,
3:11. sinneth, *being* condemned of himself.
Philem 9. *being* such an one as Paul the aged,
Heb 1: 3. Who *being* the brightness of (his) glory,
3: 2. *Who was* faithful to him that appointed
5: 8. Though he *were* a Son, yet learned
8: 4. *seeing that there are* priests that
13: 3. as *being* yourselves also in the body.
Jas. 3: 4. Behold also the ships, which *though* (they *be*) so great,
2Pet. 1:18. *when* we *were* with him in the holy mount.
2:11. angels, *which are* greater in power
Rev. 5: 5. behold, the Lion)(of the tribe of Juda,

ὁ ὢν, καὶ ὁ ἦν, καὶ ὁ ἐρχόμενος, see under O. 3801

5608 1 904/1025 *onos* (price)

ὠνέομαι, ōneomai.

Acts 7:16. Abraham *bought* for a sum of

5609 1 904/1025

ᾠόν, ōon.

Lu. 11:12. Or if he shall ask an *egg*, will he

5610 108 904/1025 9:675

ὥρα, hōra.

Mat. 8:13. was healed in the selfsame *hour*.
9:22. was made whole from that *hour*.
10:19. it shall be given you in that same *hour*
14:15. and the *time* is now past;
15:28. And her daughter was made whole from that very *hour*.
17:18. cured from that very *hour*.
18: 1. At the same *time* came the disciples
20: 3. he went out about the third *hour*,
5. about the sixth and ninth *hour*,
6. about the eleventh *hour* he went out, and
9. that (were hired) about the eleventh *hour*,
12. These last have wrought (but) one *hour*,
24:36. But of that day and *hour* knoweth no
42. ye know not what *hour* your Lord
44. in such an *hour* as ye think not
50. in an *hour* that he is not aware of,
Mat. 25:13. ye know neither the day nor the *hour*
26:40. could ye not watch with me one *hour?*
45. the *hour* is at hand, and the Son
55. In that same *hour* said Jesus to the
27:45. from the sixth *hour* there was darkness over all the land unto the ninth *hour*.
46. about the ninth *hour* Jesus cried
Mar 6:35. And when the *day* was now far spent,
— and now the *time* (is) far passed:
11:11. and now the even*tide* was come.
13:11. shall be given you in that *hour*,
32. of that day and (that) *hour* knoweth no
14:35. the *hour* might pass from him.
37. couldest not thou watch one *hour?*
41. it is enough, the *hour* is come;
15:25. And it was the third *hour*, and they
33. And when the sixth *hour* was come,
— whole land until the ninth *hour*.
34. And at the ninth *hour* Jesus cried
Lu. 1:10. praying without at the *time* of incense.
2:38. And she coming in that *instant*
7:21. And in the same *hour* he cured many of (their) infirmities
10:21. In that *hour* Jesus rejoiced
12:12. shall teach you in the same *hour*
39. had known what *hour* the thief
40. Son of man cometh at an *hour*
46. at an *hour* when he is not aware.
14:17. sent his servant at supper *time*
20:19. and the scribes the same *hour* sought
22:14. when the *hour* was come, he sat down,
53. but this is your *hour*, and the
59. And about the space of one *hour* after
23:44. it was about the sixth *hour*,
— over all the earth until the ninth *hour*.
24:33. they rose up the same *hour*, and returned to Jerusalem,
Joh. 1:39(40). for it was about the tenth *hour*
2: 4. mine *hour* is not yet come.
4: 6. it was about the sixth *hour*.
21. the *hour* cometh, when ye shall neither
23. the *hour* cometh, and now is, when the true
52. enquired he of them the *hour* when he
— Yesterday at the seventh *hour*
53. knew that (it was) at the same *hour*, in
5:25. The *hour* is coming, and now is, when the dead
28. the *hour* is coming, in the which all that
35. were willing for a *season* to rejoice in
7:30. because his *hour* was not yet come.
8:20. for his *hour* was not yet come.
11: 9. Are there not twelve *hours* in the day?
12:23. The *hour* is come, that the Son of
27. Father, save me from this *hour:* but for this cause came I unto this *hour*.
13: 1. when Jesus knew that his *hour* was come
16: 2. yea, the *time* cometh, that whosoever
4. that when the *time* shall come, ye
21. because her *hour* is come:
25. the *time* cometh, when I shall no more
32. Behold, the *hour* cometh, yea, is now come,
17: 1. Father, the *hour* is come;
19:14. of the passover, and about the sixth *hour*
27. from that *hour* that disciple took her
Acts 2:15. it is (but) the third *hour* of the day.
3: 1. into the temple at the *hour* of prayer, (being) the ninth (hour).
5: 7. about the space of three *hours* after.
10: 3. about the ninth *hour* of the day
9. to pray about the sixth *hour:*

Acts10:30. I was fasting until this *hour;* and at the ninth *hour* I prayed in
16:18. And he came out the same *hour.*
33. he took them the same *hour* of the night,
19:34. about the space of two *hours* cried out,
22:13. And the same *hour* I looked up upon him.
23:23. at the third *hour* of the night;
Ro. 13:11. that now (it is) *high time* to awake
1Co. 4:11. Even unto this present *hour* we
15:30. why stand we in jeopardy every *hour?*
2Co. 7: 8. sorry, though (it were) but for a *season.*
Gal. 2: 5. by subjection, no, not for an *hour;*
1Th. 2:17. taken from you for a *short* time (lit. for the time of an *hour*)
Philem 15. he therefore departed for a *season,* that
1Joh.2:18. Little children, it is the last *time:*
— whereby we know that it is the last *time.*
Rev. 3: 3. shalt not know what *hour* I will come
10. keep thee from the *hour* of temptation,
9:15. prepared for an *hour,* and a day, and a
11:13. And the same *hour* was there a great
14: 7. for the *hour* of his judgment is come:
15. for the *time* is come for thee to reap;
17:12. as kings one *hour* with the beast.
18:10. for in one *hour* is thy judgment come.
17(16). For in one *hour* so great riches
19. for in one *hour* is she made desolate.

5611 4 905/1026 5610

ὡραῖος, hōraios.

Mat.23:27. which indeed appear *beautiful* outward,
Acts 3: 2. which is called *Beautiful,*
10. sat for alms at the *Beautiful* gate
Ro. 10:15. How *beautiful* are the feet of them

5612 1 905/1026

ὠρύομαι, ōruomai.

1Pet.5: 8. as a *roaring* lion, walketh about,

5613 492 905/1026,1030 3739

ὡς, hōs.

Mat. 1:24. did *as* the angel of the Lord had bidden
6:10. in earth, *as* (it is) in heaven.
12. our debts, *as* we forgive our debtors.
29. was not arrayed *like* one of these.
7:29. taught them *as* (one) having authority, and not *as* the scribes.
8:13. *as* thou hast believed, (so) be it done
10:16. I send you forth *as* sheep in the midst of wolves: be ye therefore wise *as* serpents, and harmless *as* doves.
25. for the disciple that he be *as* his master, and the servant *as* his lord.
12:13. it was restored whole, *like as* the other.
13:43. shine forth *as* the sun in the kingdom of
14: 5. they counted him *as* a prophet.
15:28. be it unto thee *even as* thou wilt.
17: 2. his face did shine *as* the sun, and his raiment was white *as* the light.
20. If ye have faith *as* a grain of
18: 3. and become *as* little children, ye
4. shall humble himself *as* this little child,
33. even *as* I had pity on thee?
19:19. Thou shalt love thy neighbour *as* thyself.
20:14. unto this last, even *as* unto thee.
21:26. all hold John *as* a prophet.
46. they took him *for* a prophet.
Mat.22:30. are *as* the angels of God
39. love thy neighbour *as* thyself.
26:19. disciples did *as* Jesus had appointed them:
39. nevertheless not *as* I will, but *as* thou (wilt).
55. Are ye come out *as* against a thief
27:65. make (it) as sure *as* ye can.
28: 3. His countenance was *like* lightning,
9. And *as* they went to tell his
15. and did *as* they were taught:
Mar 1: 2. *As* it is written in the prophets,
22. *as* one that had authority, and not *as* the scribes.
3: 5. restored whole *as* the other.
4:26. *as* if a man should cast seed
27. grow up, he knoweth not *how.* (lit. *as* he knoweth not)
31. (It is) *like* a grain of mustard seed,
36. took him *even as* he was in the ship.
5:13. they were *about* two thousand;
6:15. or *as* one of the prophets.
34. *as* sheep not having a shepherd:
7: 6. *as* it is written, This people
8: 9. had eaten were *about* four thousand.
24. I see men *as* trees, walking.
9: 3. exceeding white *as* snow;
21. How long is it ago *since* this came unto him?
10: 1. and, *as* he was wont, he taught them
15. the kingdom of God *as* a little child,
12:25. but are *as* the angels which are in
26. *how* in the bush God spake unto him,
31. love thy neighbour *as* thyself.
33. love (his) neighbour *as* himself,
13:34. *as* a man taking a far journey, who
14:48. Are ye come out, *as* against a thief,
Lu. 1:23. *as soon as* the days of his
41. that, *when* Elisabeth heard the
44. *as soon as* the voice of thy salutation
2:15. *as* the angels were gone away
37. a widow of *about* fourscore and
39. And *when* they had performed all
3: 4. *As* it is written in the book
23. being *as* was supposed the son of Joseph,
4:25. *when* great famine was throughout
5: 4. Now *when* he had left speaking,
6: 4. *How* he went into the house of God,
10. restored whole *as* the other.
22. cast out your name *as* evil,
40. that is perfect shall be *as* his master.
7:12. Now *when* he came nigh to the gate of the city,
8:42. *about* twelve years of age,
47. and *how* she was healed immediately.
9:54. consume them, even *as* Elias did?
10: 3. *as* lambs among wolves.
18. I beheld Satan *as* lightning fall from
27. and thy neighbour *as* thyself.
11: 1. *when* he ceased, one of his
2. Thy will be done, *as* in heaven, so in
36. *as* when the bright shining of a candle doth give thee light.
44. ye are *as* graves which appear not,
12:27. not arrayed *like* one of these.
58. *When* thou goest with thine
14:22. it is done *as* thou hast commanded,
15:19. make me *as* one of thy hired
25. and *as* he came and drew nigh
16: 1. accused unto him that he had wasted (lit. *as* wasting) his goods.
17: 6. faith *as* a grain of mustard seed,
28. also *as* it was in the days of Lot:

Lu. 18:11. or even *as* this publican.
17. the kingdom of God *as* a little child
19: 5. And *when* Jesus came to the place,
29. *when* he was come nigh to Bethphage
41. *when* he was come near, he beheld the city,
20:37. *when* he calleth the Lord the God of
21:35. For *as* a snare shall it come
22:26. let him be *as* the younger; and he that is chief, *as* he that doth serve.
27. among you *as* he that serveth.
31. he may sift (you) *as* wheat:
52. Be ye come out, *as* against a thief,
61. *how* he had said unto him, Before
66. And *as soon as* it was day, the elders
23:14. *as* one that perverteth the people:
26. And *as* they led him away, they
55. and *how* his body was laid.
24: 6. remember *how* he spake
32. *while* he talked with us by the way, and *while* he opened to us the
35. and *how* he was known of them in
Joh. 1:14. the glory *as* of the only begotten
39(40). for it was *about* the tenth hour.
2: 9. *When* the ruler of the feast had tasted
23. Now *when* he was in Jerusalem
4: 1. *When* therefore the Lord knew
40. So *when* the Samaritans were come unto him, they
6:12. *When* they were filled, he
16. And *when* even was (now) come,
19. rowed *about* five and twenty or
7:10. But *when* his brethren were gone up,
— but *as it were* in secret.
46. Never man spake *like* this man.
8: 7. So *when* they continued asking
11: 6. *When* he had heard therefore
18. *about* fifteen furlongs off:
20. Then Martha, *as soon as* she heard
29. *As soon as* she heard (that), she arose
32. Then *when* Mary was come where
33. *When* Jesus therefore saw her weeping,
15: 6. he is cast forth *as* a branch,
18: 6. *As soon* then *as* he had said unto them,
19:33. *when* they came to Jesus, and saw that he
20:11. and *as* she wept, she stooped down,
21: 8. *as it were* two hundred cubits,
9. *As soon* then *as* they were come to land,
Acts 1:10. And *while* they looked stedfastly
15. together were *about* an hundred and twenty,
2:15. are not drunken, *as* ye suppose,
3:12. *as* though by our own power
22. *like* unto me; him shall ye hear
5: 7. *about* the space of three hours after,
24. Now *when* the high priest
7:23. And *when* he was full forty years
37. brethren, *like* unto me; him shall
51. *as* your fathers (did), so (do) ye.
8:32. He was led *as* a sheep to the slaughter; and *like* a lamb dumb before
36. And *as* they went on (their) way,
9:23. And *after that* many days were fulfilled,
10: 7. And *when* the angel which spake unto
11. *as it had been* a great sheet knit at
17. Now *while* Peter doubted in himself
25. And *as* Peter was coming in,
28. Ye know *how* that it is an unlawful
38. *How* God anointed Jesus of
11: 5. *as it had been* a great sheet,
16. *how* that he said, John indeed
17. the like gift *as* (he did) unto us,

Acts13:18. And *about* the time of forty years
20. *about* the space of four hundred and
25. And *as* John fulfilled his course,
29. And *when* they had fulfilled all
33. *as* it is also written in the second
14: 5. And *when* there was an assault
16: 4. And *as* they went through the cities,
10. And *after* he had seen the vision,
15. And *when* she was baptized,
17:13. But *when* the Jews of Thessalonica
14. to go *as it were* to the sea:
15. to come to him with all speed, (lit. *as* most quickly)
22. I perceive that in all things ye are too superstitious. (lit. I see you *as* very &c.)
28. *as* certain also of your own poets
18: 5. And *when* Silas and Timotheus were
19: 9. But *when* divers were hardened,
21. *After* these things were ended,
34. *about* the space of two hours cried
20:14. And *when* he met with us at Assos,
18. And *when* they were come to him,
20. (And) *how* I kept back nothing
24. *so that* I might finish my course with
21: 1. it came to pass, that after we were gotten from (lit. *when* it was that we &c.)
12. And *when* we heard these things,
27. And *when* the seven days were
22: 5. *As* also the high priest doth bear me
11. And *when* I could not see for
25. And *as* they bound him with thongs,
23:11. for *as* thou hast testified of me in
15. *as* though ye would enquire something
20. *as* though they would enquire somewhat
25:10. *as* thou very well knowest.
14. And *when* they had been there many days,
27: 1. And *when* it was determined
27. But *when* the fourteenth night
30. under colour *as* though they would
28: 4. And *when* the barbarians saw
19. not *that* I had ought to accuse
Ro. 1: 9. *that* without ceasing I make mention
21. they glorified (him) not *as* God,
3: 7. why yet am I also judged *as* a sinner?
4:17. things which be not *as* though they were.
5:15. But not *as* the offence, so also
16. And not *as* (it was) by one that sinned,
18. Therefore *as* by the offence of one
6:13. *as* those that are alive from the dead,
8:36. accounted *as* sheep for the slaughter.
9:27. Israel be *as* the sand of the sea,
29. we had been *as* Sodoma, and been made like *unto* (lit *as*) Gomorrha.
32. but *as it were* by the works of the law.
10:15. *How* beautiful are the feet of
11: 2. *how* he maketh intercession to God against Israel,
33. *how* unsearchable (are) his judgments.
12: 3. *according as* God hath dealt to every
13: 9. love thy neighbour *as* thyself.
13. Let us walk honestly, *as* in the day;
15:15. *as* putting you in mind,
24. *Whensoever* I take my journey into Spain,
1Co. 3: 1. speak unto you *as* unto spiritual, but *as* unto carnal, (even) *as* unto babes in Christ.
5. *even as* the Lord gave to every man?
10. *as* a wise masterbuilder,
15. shall be saved; yet so *as* by fire.
4: 1. *as* of the ministers of Christ,
7. *as* if thou hadst not received (it)?
9. *as it were* appointed to death:

1Co. 4:13. we are made *as* the filth of the world,
14. but *as* my beloved sons I warn (you).
18. are puffed up, *as* though I would not come
5: 3. *as* absent in body, but present in spirit, have judged already, *as* though I were present,
7: 7. all men were even *as* I myself.
8. if they abide even *as* I.
17. But *as* God hath distributed to every man, *as* the Lord hath called every one, so
25. *as* one that hath obtained mercy of
29. be *as* though they had none;
30. they that weep, *as* though they wept not; and they that rejoice, *as* though they rejoiced not; and they that buy, *as* though they possessed not;
31. they that use this world, *as* not abusing
8: 7. eat (it) *as* a thing offered unto an idol;
9: 5. a wife, as well *as* other apostles,
20. unto the Jews I became *as* a Jew,
— that are under the law, *as* under the law,
21. are without law, *as* without law,
22. To the weak became I *as* weak,
26. run, not *as* uncertainly; so fight I, not *as* one that beateth the air:
10: 7. *as* it is written, The people sat
15. I speak *as* to wise men;
11:34. will I set in order *when* I come.
12: 2. even *as* ye were led.
13:11. a child, I spake *as* a child, I understood *as* a child, I thought *as* a child:
14:33. *as* in all churches of the saints.
16:10. worketh the work of the Lord, *as* I also (do).
2Co. 2:17. For we are not *as* many, which corrupt the word of God: but *as* of sincerity, but *as* of God, in the sight
3: 1. or need we, *as* some (others), epistles of
5. to think any thing *as* of ourselves;
5:19. *To wit*, (lit. *how*) that God was in Christ,
20. *as* though God did beseech (you) by us:
6: 4. ourselves *as* the ministers of God,
8. *as* deceivers, and (yet) true;
9. *As* unknown, and (yet) well known; *as* dying, and, behold, we live; *as* chastened, and not killed;
10. *As* sorrowful, yet alway rejoicing; *as* poor, yet making many rich; *as* having nothing, and (yet)
13. I speak *as* unto (my) children,
7:14. but *as* we spake all things to you
15. *how* with fear and trembling ye
9: 5. *as* (a matter of) bounty, and not
10: 2. *as* if we walked according to
9. *as* if I would terrify you by
14. *as* though we reached not unto you:
11: 3. *as* the serpent beguiled Eve
15. be transformed *as* the ministers of
16. yet *as* a fool receive me,
17. but *as it were* foolishly, in this
21. *as* though we had been weak.
13: 2. *as* if I were present, the second time;
7. though we be *as* reprobates.
Gal. 1: 9. *As* we said before, so say I now
3:16. *as* of many; but *as* of one,
4:12. I beseech you, be *as* I (am); for I (am) *as* ye (are):
14. received me *as* an angel of God, (even) *as* Christ Jesus.
5:14. love thy neighbour *as* thyself.
6:10. *As* we have therefore opportunity,

Eph 2: 3. children of wrath, even *as* others.
3: 5. *as* it is now revealed unto
5: 1. followers of God, *as* dear children;
8. walk *as* children of light:
15. walk circumspectly, not *as* fools, but *as* wise,
22. *as* unto the Lord.
23. even *as* Christ is the head of the
28. to love their wives *as* their own bodies.
33. so love his wife *even as* himself;
6: 5. of your heart, *as* unto Christ;
6. Not with eyeservice, *as* menpleasers; but *as* the servants of Christ,
20. boldly, *as* I ought to speak.
Phi. 1: 8. *how* greatly I long after you all in
20. *as* always, (so) now also Christ shall
2: 8. And being found in fashion *as* a man
12. not *as* in my presence only,
15. shine *as* lights in the world;
22. *as* a son with the father,
23. *as soon as* I shall see how it
Col. 2: 6. *As* ye have therefore received
20. why, *as* though living in the world,
3:12. *as* the elect of God, holy and
18. *as* it is fit in the Lord.
22. not with eyeservice, *as* menpleasers;
23. *as* to the Lord, and not unto men;
: 4. it manifest, *as* I ought to speak.
1Th. 2: 4. not *as* pleasing men, but God,
6(7). *as* the apostles of Christ.
7. even *as* a nurse cherisheth her
10. *how* holily and justly and
11. ye know *how* we exhorted and
— *as* a father (doth) his children,
5: 2. cometh *as* a thief in the
4. overtake you *as* a thief.
6. not sleep, *as* (do) others;
2Th. 2: 2. *as* from us, *as* that the day of Christ is at hand.
4. he *as* God sitteth in the temple
3:15. Yet count (him) not *as* an enemy, but admonish (him) *as* a brother.
1Ti. 5: 1. but intreat (him) *as* a father; (and) the younger men *as* brethren;
2. The elder women *as* mothers; the younger *as* sisters, with all purity.
2Ti. 1. 3. *that* without ceasing I have
2: 3. *as* a good soldier of Jesus Christ.
9. *as* an evil doer, (even) unto bonds:
17. their word will eat *as* doth a canker:
3: 9. *as* their's also was.
Tit. 1: 5. *as* I had appointed thee:
7. *as* the steward of God;
Philem 9. such an one *as* Paul the aged,
14. should not be *as it were* of necessity, but
16. Not now *as* a servant, but
17. receive him *as* myself.
Heb 1:11. shall wax old *as* doth a garment;
3: 2. *as* also Moses (was faithful)
5. *as* a servant, for a testimony of
6. But Christ *as* a son over his own house;
8. your hearts, *as* in the provocation,
11. *So* I sware in my wrath,
15. your hearts, *as* in the provocation.
4: 3. *As* I have sworn in my wrath,
6:19. we have *as* an anchor of
7: 9. And *as* I may so say, Levi
11: 9. *as* (in) a strange country,
27. *as* seeing him who is invisible.
29. Red sea *as* by dry (land):
12: 5. speaketh unto you *as* unto children,
7. dealeth with you *as* with sons:

Heb 12:16. or profane person, *as* Esau,
27. *as* of things that are made,
13: 3. in bonds, *as* bound with them;
— *as* being yourselves also in the body.
17. *as* they that must give account,
Jas. 1:10. because *as* the flower of the
2: 8. love thy neighbour *as* thyself,
9. convinced of the law *as* transgressors.
12. *as* they that shall be judged by
5: 3. shall eat your flesh *as it were* fire.
5. *as* in a day of slaughter.
1Pet. 1:14. *As* obedient children, not
19. *as* of a lamb without blemish
24. For all flesh (is) *as* grass,
— *as* the flower of grass.
2: 2. *As* newborn babes, desire
5. Ye also, *as* lively stones, are
11. I beseech (you) *as* strangers and
12. speak against you *as* evildoers,
13. to the king, *as* supreme;
14. *as* unto them that are sent
16. *As* free, and not using (your) liberty *for* (lit. *as*) a cloke of maliciousness, but *as* the servants of God.
25. ye were *as* sheep going astray;
3: 6. *Even as* Sara obeyed Abraham,
7. *as* unto the weaker vessel, and *as* being heirs together of
16. evil of you, *as* of evildoers,
4:10. *as* good stewards of the manifold
11. (let him speak) *as* the oracles of God;
— *as* of the ability which God giveth:
12. *as* though some strange thing
15. let none of you suffer *as* a murderer,
— or *as* a busybody in other men's matters.
16. if (any man suffer) *as* a Christian,
19. *as* unto a faithful Creator.
5: 3. Neither *as* being lords over
8. *as* a roaring lion, walketh about,
12. a faithful brother unto you, *as* I suppose, I have written briefly,
2Pet. 1: 3. *According as* his divine power
19. *as* unto a light that shineth
2: 1. even *as* there shall be false teachers
12. these, *as* natural brute beasts,
3: 8. with the Lord *as* a thousand years, and a thousand years *as* one day.
9. *as* some men count slackness;
10. will come *as* a thief in the
16. *As* also in all (his) epistles,
— *as* (they do) also the other scriptures,
1Joh. 1: 7. in the light, *as* he is in the light,
2:27. *as* the same anointing teacheth you
2Joh. 5. not *as* though I wrote a new
Jude 7. *Even as* Sodom and Gomorrha.
10. know naturally, *as* brute beasts,
Rev. 1:10. a great voice, *as* of a trumpet,
14. white like wool, as white *as* snow;
— eyes (were) *as* a flame of fire;
15. *as* if they burned in a furnace;
— *as* the sound of many waters.
16. *as* the sun shineth in his strength.
17. I fell at his feet *as* dead.
2:18. his eyes *like unto* a flame
24. the depths of Satan, *as* they speak;
27. *as* the vessels of a potter shall they
— even *as* I received of my Father.
3: 3. will come on thee *as* a thief,
21. *as* I also overcame, and am
4: 1. *as it were* of a trumpet
7. beast had a face *as* a man,
5: 6. a Lamb, *as* it had been slain,
Rev. 6: 1. *as it were* the noise of thunder,
11. that should be killed *as* they (were),
12. black *as* sackcloth of hair,
— the moon became *as* blood,
13. *as* a fig tree casteth her
14. departed *as* a scroll when
8: 1. *about* the space of half an hour.
8. *as it were* a great mountain
10. burning *as it were* a lamp,
9: 2. *as* the smoke of a great furnace;
3. *as* the scorpions of the earth
5. *as* the torment of a scorpion,
7. *as it were* crowns like gold, and their faces (were) *as* the faces of men.
8. hair *as* the hair of women, and their teeth were *as* (the teeth) of lions.
9. *as it were* breastplates of iron;
— *as* the sound of chariots of many horses
17. (were) *as* the heads of lions;
10: 1. his face (was) *as it were* the sun, and his feet *as* pillars of fire:
7. *as* he hath declared to his
9. in thy mouth sweet *as* honey.
10. and it was in my mouth sweet *as* honey:
12:15. water *as* a flood after the woman,
13: 2. his feet were *as* (the feet) of a bear, and his mouth *as* the mouth of a lion:
3. *as it were* wounded to death;
11. he spake *as* a dragon.
14: 2. *as* the voice of many waters, and *as* the voice of a great thunder:
3. they sung *as it were* a new song
15: 2. I saw *as it were* a sea of glass
16: 3. it became *as* the blood of a dead (man):
15. Behold, I come *as* a thief.
21. (every stone) *about* the weight of a talent:
17:12. receive power *as* kings one hour
18: 6. even *as* she rewarded you,
21. a stone *like* a great millstone,
19: 6. heard *as it were* the voice of a great multitude, and *as* the voice of many waters, and *as* the voice of mighty thunderings,
12. His eyes (were) *as* a flame of fire,
20: 8. of whom (is) *as* the sand of the sea.
21: 2. prepared *as* a bride adorned for
11. *even like* a jasper stone,
21. *as it were* transparent glass.
22: 1. water of life, clear *as* crystal,
12. *according as* his work shall be.

5614-5615 p. 817

ὡσαύτως & Ὡσαννά, see after ὥστε.

5616 34 907/1031 5613,1487

ὡσεί, *hosī*.

Mat. 3:16. descending *like* a dove,
9:36. *as* sheep having no shepherd.
14:21. were *about* five thousand men,
28: 3. his raiment white *as* snow:
4. and became *as* dead (men).
Mar 1:10. the Spirit *like* a dove descending
6:44. were *about* five thousand men.
9:26. and he was *as* one dead;
Lu. 1:56. abode with her *about* three months,
3:22. in a bodily shape *like* a dove
23. began to be *about* thirty years of age,
9:14. were *about* five thousand men.
28. *about* an eight days after these
22:41. from them *about* a stone's cast,

Lu. 22:44. was *as it were* great drops of blood
59. *about* the space of one hour after
23:44. And it was *about* the sixth hour,
24:11. seemed to them *as* idle tales,
Joh. 1:32. descending from heaven *like* a dove,
4: 6. it was *about* the sixth hour.
6:10. in number *about* five thousand.
19:14. and *about* the sixth hour:
39. *about* an hundred pound (weight).
Acts 2: 3. cloven tongues *like as* of fire,
41. (unto them) *about* three thousand souls.
4: 4. of the men was *about* five thousand.
5:36. men, *about* four hundred,
6:15. *as it had been* the face of an angel.
9:18. from his eyes *as it had been* scales:
10: 3. *about* the ninth hour of the
19: 7. all the men were *about* twelve.
Heb 1:12. And *as* a vesture shalt thou
11:12. and *as* the sand which is by the sea
Rev. 1:14. white *like* wool, as white as snow;

5618 42 908/1032 5613,4007

ὥσπερ, *hōsper*.

Mat. 5:48. *even as* your Father which is in
6: 2. *as* the hypocrites do in the
5. thou shalt not be *as* the hypocrites
7. use not vain repetitions, *as* the heathen
16. be not, *as* the hypocrites, of a sad
12:40. For *as* Jonas was three days and
13:40. *As* therefore the tares are gathered
18:17. let him be unto thee *as* an heathen
20:28. *Even as* the Son of man came
24:27. For *as* the lightning cometh
37. But *as* the days of Noe (were),
38. For *as* in the days that were
25:14. For (the kingdom of heaven is) *as* a man travelling into a far
32. *as* a shepherd divideth (his) sheep from
Lu. 17:24. For *as* the lightning, that lighteneth
18:11. that I am not *as* other men (are),
Joh. 5:21. For *as* the Father raiseth up
26. For *as* the Father hath life in
Acts 2: 2. *as* of a rushing mighty wind,
3:17. *as* (did) also your rulers.
11:15. *as* on us at the beginning.
Ro. 5:12. Wherefore, *as* by one man
19. For *as* by one man's disobedience
21. That *as* sin hath reigned unto
6: 4. that *like as* Christ was raised
19. for *as* ye have yielded your members
11:30. For *as* ye in times past have
1Co. 8: 5. *as* there be gods many, and lords many,
11:12. For *as* the woman (is) of the man,
15:22. For *as* in Adam all die,
16: 1. *as* I have given order to the
2Co. 1: 7. *as* ye are partakers of the
8: 7. Therefore, *as* ye abound in every
9: 5. and not *as* (of) covetousness.
Gal. 4:29. But *as* then he that was born
Eph. 5:24. Therefore *as* the church is
1Th. 5: 3. *as* travail upon a woman with
Heb 4:10. *as* God (did) from his.
7:27. needeth not daily, *as* those high priests,
9:25. *as* the high priest entereth
Jas. 2:26. For *as* the body without the
Rev. 10: 3. *as* (when) a lion roareth.

5619 1 908/1032 5618,1487

ὡσπερεί, *hōsperī*.

1Co. 15: 8. *as* of one born out of due time.

5620 83 908/1032 5613,5037

ὥστε, *hōste*.

Mat. 8:24. *insomuch that* the ship was covered
28. *so that* no man might pass
10: 1. (against) unclean spirits, *to* cast them out, (lit. *so as to* cast, &c.)
12:12. *Wherefore* (lit. *so that*) it is lawful to do well on the
22. *insomuch that* the blind and dumb
13: 2. *so that* he went into a ship,
32. *so that* the birds of the air
54. *insomuch that* they were astonished
15:31. *Insomuch that* the multitude
33. *as* to fill (lit. *so as* to fill) so great
19: 6. *Wherefore* they are no more twain,
23:31. *Wherefore* ye be witnesses unto
24:24. *insomuch that*, if (it were) possible,
27: 1. against Jesus *to* put him to death:
14. *insomuch that* the governor
Mar 1:27. *insomuch that* they questioned
45. *insomuch that* Jesus could no
2: 2. *insomuch that* there was no room
12. *insomuch that* they were all amazed,
28. *Therefore* the Son of man is Lord
3:10. *insomuch that* they pressed upon him
20. *so that* they could not so much as eat
4: 1. *so that* he entered into a ship,
32. *so that* the fowls of the air
37. *so that* it was now full.
9:26. *insomuch that* many said, He is dead.
10: 8. *so then* they are no more twain.
15: 5. *so that* Pilate marvelled.
Lu. 5: 7. *so that* they began to sink.
9:52. to (lit. *so as* to) make ready for him.
12: 1. *insomuch that* they trode one
Joh. 3:16. *that* he gave his only begotten Son.
Acts 1:19. *insomuch as* that field is called
5:15. *Insomuch that* they brought forth
14: 1. and so spake, *that* a great multitude. believed.
15:39. *that* (lit. *so that*) they departed asunder
16:26. *so that* the foundations of the
19:10. *so that* all they which dwelt
12. *So that* from his body were
16. *so that* they fled out of that house
Ro. 7: 4. *Wherefore*, my brethren, ye also are
6. *that* we should serve in newness
12. *Wherefore* the law (is) holy,
13: 2. Whosoever *therefore* resisteth (lit. *so that* whosoever)
15:19. *so that* from Jerusalem, and
1Co. 1: 7. *So that* ye come behind in no
3: 7. *So then* neither is he that planteth
21. *Therefore* let no man glory in men.
4: 5. *Therefore* judge nothing before the
5: 1. *that* one should have his father's wife.
8. *Therefore* let us keep the feast,
7:38. *So then* he that giveth (her) in
10:12. *Wherefore* let him that thinketh
11:27. *Wherefore* whosoever shall eat
33. *Wherefore*, my brethren, when
13: 2. *so that* I could remove mountains,
14:22. *Wherefore* tongues are for a sign,
39. *Wherefore*, brethren, covet to
15:58. *Therefore*, my beloved brethren, be ye
2Co. 1: 8. *insomuch that* we despaired
2: 7. *So that* contrariwise ye (ought)
3: 7. *so that* the children of Israel could not
4:12. *So then* death worketh in us,
5:16. *Wherefore* henceforth know we no man
17. *Therefore* if any man (be) in Christ,
7: 7 *so that* I rejoiced the more.

Gal. 2:13. *insomuch that* Barnabas
3: 9. *So then* they which be of faith
24. *Wherefore* the law was our
4: 7. *Wherefore* thou art no more a servant,
16. Am I *therefore* become your enemy,
Phi. 1:13. *So that* my bonds in Christ are
2:12. *Wherefore,* my beloved, as ye have
4: 1. *Therefore,* my brethren dearly
1Th. 1: 7. *So that* ye were ensamples
8. *so that* we need not to speak
4:18. *Wherefore* comfort one another
2Th. 1: 4. *So that* we ourselves glory in you
2: 4. *so that* he as God sitteth in the
Heb 13: 6. *So that* we may boldly say,
Jas. 1:19. *Wherefore,* my beloved brethren, let
1Pet. 1:21. *that* your faith and hope might be in God.
4:19. *Wherefore* let them that suffer

5615 17 907/1031 5613,846

ὡσαύτως, hōsautōs.

Mat.20: 5. the ninth hour, and did *likewise.*
21:30. came to the second, and said *likewise.*
36. they did unto them *likewise.*
25:17. And *likewise* he that (had received) two,
Mar 12:21. and the third *likewise.*
14:31. *Likewise* also said they all.
Lu. 13: 3. ye shall all *likewise* perish.
20:31. and *in like manner* the seven also:
22:20. *Likewise* also the cup after
Ro. 8:26. *Likewise* the Spirit also helpeth
1Co.11:25. *After the same manner* also (he took)
1Ti. 2: 9. *In like manner* also, that women
3: 8. *Likewise* (must) the deacons
11. *Even so* (must their) wives (be) grave,
5:25. *Likewise* also the good works (of some)
Tit. 2: 3. The aged women *likewise,* that
6. Young men *likewise* exhort to

5614 6 907/1031 9:682 [3467, 4994]

Ὡσαννά, hosanna.

Mat.21: 9. *Hosanna* to the son of David:
— *Hosanna* in the highest.
15. *Hosanna* to the son of David;
Mar 11: 9. *Hosanna;* Blessed (is) he that cometh in
10. *Hosanna* in the highest.
Joh.12:13. *Hosanna:* Blessed (is) the King of Israel

ὡσεί see after ὡς. p. 815

ὥσπερ, ὥστε see after ὡς. p. 816

5621 5 908/1033 5:543 3775

ὠτίον, ōtion.

Mat.26:51. and smote off his *ear.*
Mar 14:47. and cut off his *ear.*
Lu. 22:51. he touched his *ear,* and healed him.
Joh. 18:10. and cut off his right *ear.*
26. (his) kinsman whose *ear* Peter cut off,

5622 2 908/1033 rt 5624

ὠφέλεια, ōphelīa.

Ro. 3. 1. what *profit* (is there) of circumcision?
Jude 16. having men's persons in admiration because of *advantage.*

5623 15 908/1033 rt 5622

ὠφελέω, ōpheleo.

Mat.15: 5. thou *mightest be profited* by me;
16:26. For what *is* a man *profited,* if he
27:24. Pilate saw that he could *prevail* nothing
Mar 5:26. and was nothing *bettered,* but rather
7:11. thou *mightest be profited* by me;
8:36. For what *shall* it *profit* a man,
Lu. 9:25. For what *is* a man *advantaged,*
Joh. 6:63. the flesh *profiteth* nothing:
12:19. Perceive ye how ye *prevail* nothing?
Ro. 2:25. circumcision verily *profiteth,* if
1Co.13: 3. it *profiteth* me nothing.
14: 6. what *shall* I *profit* you, except I
Gal. 5: 2. Christ *shall profit* you nothing.
Heb 4: 2. the word preached did not *profit* them,
13: 9. which have not *profited* them that (lit. by which they *have* not *been profited*)

5624 4 909/1033 3786

ὠφέλιμος, ōphelimos.

1Ti. 4: 8. For bodily exercise *profiteth* (lit. is *profitable*) little: but godliness is *profitable* unto all things,
2Ti. 3:16. and (is) *profitable* for doctrine, for
Tit. 3: 8. These things are good and *profitable* unto men.

Proper Names Concordance

2 5 1/1 1:3 [175]

Ἀαρών, Aärōn.

Lu. 1: 5. his wife (was) of the daughters of *Aaron*,
Acts 7:40. Saying unto *Aaron*, Make us gods to go
Heb 5: 4. called of God, as (was) *Aaron*.
7:11. and not be called after the order of *Aaron*?
9: 4. that had manna, and *Aaron's* rod

3 1 1/1 1:4 [11]

Ἀβαδδών, Abaddōn.

Rev. 9:11. in the Hebrew tongue (is) *Abaddon*,

6 4 1/1 1:6 [1893]

Ἄβελ, Abel.

Mat.23:35. from the blood of righteous *Abel*
Lu. 11:51. From the blood of *Abel* unto the blood
Heb 11: 4. By faith *Abel* offered unto God
12:24. speaketh better things than (that of) *Abel*.

7 3 1/1 [29]

Ἀβιά, Abia.

Mat. 1: 7. begat *Abia*; and *Abia* begat Asa;
Lu. 1: 5. of the course of *Abia*:

8 1 1/1 [54]

Ἀβιάθαρ, Abiathar.

Mar 2:26. in the days of *Abiathar* the high priest,

9 1 1/1 cf [58]

Ἀβιληνή, Abileenee.

Lu. 3: 1. Lysanias the tetrarch of *Abilene*,

10 2 1/1 [31]

Ἀβιούδ, Abioud.

Mat. 1:13. begat *Abiud*; and *Abiud* begat Eliakim;

11 73 1/1 1:8 [85]

Ἀβραάμ, Abraäm.

Mat. 1: 1. the son of David, the son of *Abraham*.
2. *Abraham* begat Isaac;
17. all the generations from *Abraham*
3: 9. We have *Abraham* to (our) father:
— to raise up children unto *Abraham*.
8:11. shall sit down with *Abraham*,
22:32. I am the God of *Abraham*,
Mar 12:26. I (am) the God of *Abraham*,
Lu. 1:55. As he spake to our fathers, to *Abraham*,
73. he sware to our father *Abraham*,
3: 8. We have *Abraham* to (our) father:
-- to raise up children unto *Abraham*.
Lu. 3:34. which was (the son) of *Abraham*,
13:16. this woman, being a daughter of *Abraham*
28. when ye shall see *Abraham*,
16:22. carried by the angels into *Abraham's* bosom:
23. and seeth *Abraham* afar off,
24. Father *Abraham*, have mercy on me,
25. But *Abraham* said, Son, remember that
29. *Abraham* saith unto him,
30. Nay, father *Abraham*:
19: 9. forsomuch as he also is a son of *Abraham*.
20:37. when he calleth the Lord the God of *Abraham*,
Joh. 8:33. We be *Abraham's* seed,
37. I know that ye are *Abraham's* seed;
39. *Abraham* is our father.
— If ye were *Abraham's* children, ye would do the works of *Abraham*.
40. this did not *Abraham*.
52. *Abraham* is dead, and the prophets;
53. Art thou greater than our father *Abraham*,
56. *Abraham* rejoiced to see my day:
57. and hast thou seen *Abraham*?
58. Before *Abraham* was, I am.
Acts 3:13. The God of *Abraham*,
25. saying unto *Abraham*, And in thy seed
7: 2. appeared unto our father *Abraham*,
16. the sepulchre that *Abraham* bought
17. which God had sworn to *Abraham*,
32. the God of thy fathers, the God of *Abraham*,
13:26. children of the stock of *Abraham*,
Ro. 4: 1. What shall we then say that *Abraham*,
2. if *Abraham* were justified by works,
3. *Abraham* believed God,
9. faith was reckoned to *Abraham*
12. that faith of our father *Abraham*,
13. not to *Abraham*, or to his seed, through the law,
16. which is of the faith of *Abraham*;
9: 7. Neither, because they are the seed of *Abraham*,
11: 1. of the seed of *Abraham*,
2Co.11:22. Are they the seed of *Abraham*? so am I.
Gal. 3: 6. Even as *Abraham* believed God,
7. are the children of *Abraham*.
8. preached before the gospel unto *Abraham*,
9. blessed with faithful *Abraham*.
14. the blessing of *Abraham* might come
16. to *Abraham* and his seed were the promises
18. God gave (it) to *Abraham* by promise.
29. then are ye *Abraham's* seed,
4:22. *Abraham* had two sons, the one by
Heb 2:16. but he took on (him) the seed of *Abraham*.
6:13. when God made promise to *Abraham*,
7: 1. met *Abraham* returning from the
2. To whom also *Abraham* gave a tenth

Heb 7: 4. *Abraham* gave the tenth
5. though they come out of **the loins of** *Abraham:*
6. received tithes of *Abraham,*
9. payed tithes in *Abraham.*
11: 8. By faith *Abraham*, when he was called
17. By faith *Abraham*, when he was tried,
Jas. 2:21. Was not *Abraham* our father justified
23. *Abraham* believed God, and it was imputed
1Pet. 3: 6. Sara obeyed *Abraham*, calling him lord:

13 2 2/2 cf [2285]

Ἄγαβος, *Agabos.*

Acts11:28. one of them named *Agabus,*
21:10. a certain prophet, named *Agabus.*

28 2 6/8 1:55 [1904]

Ἄγαρ, *Agar.*

Gal. 4:24. gendereth to bondage, which is *Agar.*
25. For this *Agar* is mount Sinai

67 12 13/15 66,2462

Ἀγρίππας, *Agrippas.*

Acts25:13. king *Agrippa* and Bernice came
22. Then *Agrippa* said unto Festus,
23. when *Agrippa* was come,
24. And Festus said, King *Agrippa,*
26. before thee, O king *Agrippa,* that,
26: 1. Then *Agrippa* said unto Paul,
2. I think myself happy, king *Agrippa,*
7. For which hope's sake, king *Agrippa,*
19. Whereupon, O king *Agrippa,*
27. King *Agrippa*, believest thou the
28. Then *Agrippa* said unto Paul,
32. Then said *Agrippa* unto Festus,

76 9 15/17 1:141 [121]

Ἀδάμ, *Adam.*

Lu. 3:38. which was (the son) of *Adam,*
Ro. 5:14. death reigned from *Adam* to Moses,
— similitude of *Adam's* transgression,
1Co.15:22. For as in *Adam* all die, even so
45. The first man *Adam* was made a
— the last *Adam* (was made)
1Ti. 2:13. For *Adam* was first formed,
14. And *Adam* was not deceived,
Jude 14. And Enoch also, the seventh from *Adam,*

78 1 15/17 cf [5716]

Ἀδδί, *Addi.*

Lu. 3:28. which was (the son) of *Addi,*

98 1 18/22

Ἀδραμυττηνός, *Adramutteenos.*

Acts27: 2. entering into a ship of *Adramyttium,*

99 1 18/22

Ἀδρίας, *Adrias.*

Acts27:27. driven up and down in *Adria,*

107 2 19/23 cf [5809]

Ἀζώρ, *Azōr.*

Mat. 1:13. and Eliakim begat *Azor;*
14. And *Azor* begat Sadoc;

108 1 19/23 [795]

Ἄζωτος, *Azōtos.*

Acts 8:40. But Philip was found at *Azotus:*

116 4 20/24

Ἀθῆναι, *Atheenai.*

Acts17:15. brought him unto *Athens:*
16. while Paul waited for them at *Athens,*
18: 1. Paul departed from *Athens,*
1Th. 3: 1. left at *Athens* alone;

117 2 20/24 116

Ἀθηναῖος, *Atheenaios.*

Acts17:21. For all the *Athenians* and strangers
22. (Ye) men *of Athens,*

124 5 21/24 125

Αἰγύπτιος, *Aiguptios.*

Acts 7:22. all the wisdom of the *Egyptians,*
24. and smote the *Egyptian:*
28. as thou diddest the *Egyptian* yesterday?
21:38. Art not thou that *Egyptian,*
Heb 11:29. *Egyptians* assaying to do were drowned.

125 24 21/24

Αἴγυπτος, *Aiguptos.*

Mat. 2:13. flee into *Egypt*, and be thou
14. departed into *Egypt:*
15. Out of *Egypt* have I called my son.
19. to Joseph in *Egypt,*
Acts 2:10. in *Egypt*, and in the parts of Libya
7: 9. sold Joseph into *Egypt:*
10. Pharaoh king of *Egypt*; and he made him — governor over *Egypt*
11. dearth over all the land of *Egypt*
12. corn in *Egypt*, he sent out our
15. Jacob went down into *Egypt,*
17. grew and multiplied in *Egypt,*
34. the affliction of my people which is in *Egypt,*
— I will send thee into *Egypt.*
36. wonders and signs in the land of *Egypt,*
39. back again into *Egypt,*
40. out of the land of *Egypt,*
13:17. strangers in the land of *Egypt,*
Heb 3:16. came out of *Egypt* by Moses.
8: 9. to lead them out of the land of *Egypt;*
11:26. than the treasures in *Egypt:*
27. By faith he forsook *Egypt,*
Jude 5. saved the people out of the land of *Egypt,*
Rev.11: 8. spiritually is called Sodom and *Egypt,*

128 2 21/24

Αἰθίοψ, *Aithiops.*

Acts 8:27. and, behold, a man *of Ethiopia,*
— queen of the *Ethiopians,*

132 2 23/26

Αἰνέας, *Aineas.*

Acts 9:33. a certain man named *Æneas,*
34. And Peter said unto him, *Æneas,*

137 1 23/26 [5869]

Αἰνών, *Ainōn.*

Joh. 3:23. baptizing in *Ænon* near to Salim,

184 1 29/135 [2506,1818]

Ακελδαμά, *Akeldama.*

Acts 1:19. *Aceldama*, that is to say, The field of blood.

207 6 133/39

Ἀκύλας, *Akulas.*

Acts18: 2. a certain Jew named *Aquila*,
18. with him Priscilla and *Aquila*;
26. when *Aquila* and Priscilla had heard,
Ro. 16: 3. Greet Priscilla and *Aquila*
1Co.16:19. *Aquila* and Priscilla salute you
2Ti. 4:19. Salute Prisca and *Aquila*,

221 2 34/40 Alexandria

Ἀλεξανδρεύς, *Alexandrūs.*

Acts 6: 9. *Alexandrians*, and of them of Cilicia
18:24. Apollos, born at Alexandria (lit. an *Alexandrian* by birth),

222 2 35/40 rt 221

Ἀλεξανδρῖνος, *Alexandrinos.*

Acts27: 6. a ship *of Alexandria*
28:11. we departed in a ship *of Alexandria*,

223 6 35/40 rt 220,435

Ἀλέξανδρος, *Alexandros.*

Mar 15·21. the father of *Alexander* and
Acts 4: 6. John, and *Alexander*, and as many as were
19:33. they drew *Alexander* out of the multitude,
— *Alexander* beckoned with the hand,
1Ti. 1:20. Of whom is Hymenæus and *Alexander*;
2Ti. 4:14. *Alexander* the coppersmith did

256 5 41/47 cf [2501]

Ἀλφαῖος, *Alphaios.*

Mat.10: 3. James (the son) of *Alphæus*,
Mar 2:14. Levi the (son) of *Alphæus* sitting
3:18. James the (son) of *Alphæus*,
Lu. 6:15. James the (son) of *Alphæus*,
Acts 1:13. James (the son) of *Alphæus*,

284 3 45/52 [5992]

Ἀμιναδάβ, *Aminadab.*

Mat. 1: 4. Aram begat *Aminadab*; and *Aminadab*
Lu. 3:33. Which was (the son) of *Aminadab*,

291 1 46/53

Ἀμπλίας, *Amplias.*

Ro. 16: 8. Greet *Amplias* my beloved

295 1 46/53 rt 297,4172

Ἀμφίπολις, *Amphipolis.*

Acts17: 1. passed through *Amphipolis*

300 2 47/ [526]

Ἀμών, *Amōn.*

Mat. 1:10. Manasses begat *Amon*; and *Amon* begat Josias;

301 1 47/53 [531]

Ἀμώς, *Amōs.*

Lu. 3:25. which was (the son) of *Amos*,

367 11 58/61 [2608]

Ἀνανίας, *Ananias.*

Acts 5: 1. a certain man named *Ananias*,
3. But Peter said, *Ananias*
Acts 5: 5. And *Ananias* hearing these words
9:10. a certain disciple at Damascus, named *Ananias*;
— said the Lord in a vision, *Ananias*.
12. in a vision a man named *Ananias*
13. Then *Ananias* answered, Lord,
17. And *Ananias* went his way,
22:12. one *Ananias*, a devout man
23: 2. the high priest *Ananias* commanded
24: 1. after five days *Ananias* the high priest

406 13 63/64 435

Ἀνδρέας, *Andreas.*

Mat. 4:18. Simon called Peter, and *Andrew*
10: 2. Peter, and *Andrew* his brother;
Mar 1:16. Simon and *Andrew* his brother
29. the house of Simon and *Andrew*,
3:18. And *Andrew*, and Philip,
13: 3. John and *Andrew* asked him privately,
Lu. 6:14. and *Andrew* his brother,
Joh. 1:40(41). *Andrew*, Simon Peter's brother.
44(45). city of *Andrew* and Peter.
6: 8. One of his disciples, *Andrew*,
12:22. Philip cometh and telleth *Andrew*: and again *Andrew* and Philip tell Jesus.
Acts 1:13. *Andrew*, Philip, and Thomas,

408 1 63/64 435,3534

Ἀνδρόνικος, *Andronikos.*

Ro. 16: 7. Salute *Andronicus* and Junia,

451 1 69/77 [2584]

Ἄννα, *Anna.*

Lu. 2:36. one *Anna*, a prophetess,

452 4 69/77 [2608]

Ἄννας, *Annas.*

Lu. 3: 2. *Annas* and Caiaphas being the
Joh.18:13. led him away to *Annas* first;
24. *Annas* had sent him bound unto
Acts 4: 6. *Annas* the high priest, and

490 18 74/80

Ἀντιόχεια, *Antiokīa.*

Acts11:19. Cyprus, and *Antioch*,
20. when they were come to *Antioch*,
22. go as far as *Antioch*.
26(25). brought him unto *Antioch*.
— called Christians first in *Antioch*.
27. from Jerusalem unto *Antioch*.
13: 1. in the church that was at *Antioch*
14. they came to *Antioch* in Pisidia,
14:19. (certain) Jews from *Antioch*
21. Iconium, and *Antioch*,
26. And thence sailed to *Antioch*,
15:22. chosen men of their own company to *Antioch*
23. Gentiles in *Antioch* and Syria
30. they came to *Antioch*:
35. continued in *Antioch*, teaching
18:22. he went down to *Antioch*.
Gal. 2:11. when Peter was come to *Antioch*,
2Ti. 3:11. afflictions, which came unto me at *Antioch*,

491 1 75/80 490

Αντιοχεύς, *Antiokūs.*

Acts 6: 5. a proselyte *of Antioch*:

493 1 75/80 473,3962
Ἀντίπας, *Antipas.*

Rev. 2:13. wherein *Antipas* (was) my faithful **martyr,**

494 1 75/80 rt 493
Ἀντιπατρίς, *Antipatris.*

Acts23:31. by night to *Antipatris.*

500 5 75/ 473,5547
Ἀντίχριστος, see amongst Appellatives.

559 1 83/85
Ἀπελλῆς, *Apellees.*

Ro. 16:10. Salute *Apelles* approved in Christ.

623 1 95/97 1:394 622
Ἀπολλύων, *Apolluōn.*

Rev. 9:11. (his) name *Apollyon.*

624 1 95/97 623
Ἀπολλωνία, *Apollōnia.*

Acts17: 1. Amphipolis and *Apollonia,*

625 10 95/97 rt 624
Ἀπολλώς, *Apollōs.*

Acts18:24. a certain Jew named *Apollos,*
19: 1. while *Apollos* was at Corinth,
1Co. 1:12. and I of *Apollos;*
3: 4. another, I (am) of *Apollos;*
5. and who (is) *Apollos,*
6. *Apollos* watered; but God gave the increase.
22. Whether Paul, or *Apollos,*
4: 6. and (to) *Apollos* for your sakes;
16:12. touching (our) brother *Apollos,*
Tit. 3:13. Zenas the lawyer and *Apollos*

675 1 /103,994
Ἀππίου φόρον, *Appiou phoron.*

Acts28:15. as far as *Appii forum,*

682 1 102/103
Ἀπφία, *Apphia.*

Philem. 2. to (our) beloved *Apphia,*

688 2 103/104 [6152]
Ἀραβία, *Arabia.*

Gal. 1:17. I went into *Arabia,*
4:25. mount Sinai in *Arabia,*

689 3 103/104 [7410]
Ἀράμ, *Aram.*

Mat. 1: 3. Esrom begat *Aram;*
4. *Aram* begat Aminadab;
Lu. 3:33. which was (the son) of *Aram,*

690 1 104/104 688
Ἄραψ, *Araps.*

Acts 2:11. Cretes and *Arabians,*

702 1 105/105
Ἀρέτας, *Aretas.*

2Co.11:32. *Aretas* the king kept the city

697 2 104/105
Ἄρειος Πάγος, *Arīos pagos.*

Acts17:19. brought him unto *Areopagus,*
22. Paul stood in the midst of *Mars' hill,*

698 1 104/105 697
Ἀρεοπαγίτης, *Areopagitees.*

Acts17:34. Dionysius the *Areopagite,*

707 4 106/106 [7414]
Ἀριμαθαία, *Arimathīa.*

Mat.27:57. a rich man of *Arimathæa,*
Mar15:43. Joseph of *Arimathæa,*
Lu. 23:51. *Arimathæa,* a city of the Jews:
Joh.19:38. Joseph of *Arimathæa,*

708 5 106/106 rt 712,757
Ἀρίσταρχος, *Aristarkos.*

Acts19:29. Gaius and *Aristarchus,*
20: 4. *Aristarchus* and Secundus;
27: 2. (one) *Aristarchus,* a Macedonian
Col. 4:10. *Aristarchus* my fellowprisoner
Philem 24(23). Marcus, *Aristarchus,* Demas,

711 1 106/106 rt 712,1012
Ἀριστόβουλος, *Aristoboulos.*

Ro. 16:10. which are of *Aristobulus'* (houshold).

717 1 107/104,106 [4023][2022]
Ἀρμαγεδδών, *Armageddōn.*

Rev.16:16. in the Hebrew tongue *Armageddon.*

734 1 109/108 735,1435
Ἀρτεμᾶς, *Artemas.*

Tit. 3:12. send *Artemas* unto thee,

735 5 109/108 rt 736
Ἄρτεμις, *Artemis.*

Acts19:24. silver shrines for *Diana,*
27. temple of the great goddess *Diana*
28. Great (is) *Diana* of the Ephesians.
34. Great (is) *Diana* of the Ephesians.
35. worshipper of the great goddess *Diana,*

742 1 110/110 [775]
Ἀρφαξάδ, *Arphaxad.*

Lu. 3:36. which was (the son) of *Arphaxad,*

745 1 111/110 757,2994
Ἀρχέλαος, *Arkelaos.*

Mat. 2:22. that *Archelaus* did reign

751 2 112/112 746,2462
Ἄρχιππος, *Arkippos.*

Col. 4:17. say to *Archippus,* Take heed
Philem 2. *Archippus* our fellowsoldier,

760 2 113/114 [609]
Ἀσά, *Asa.*

Mat. 1: 7. and Abia begat *Asa;*
8. And *Asa* begat Josaphat;

768 2 114/115 [836]

'Ασήρ, *Aseer.*

Lu. 2:36. of the tribe of *Aser:*
Rev. 7: 6. Of the tribe of *Aser* (were) sealed

773 19 115/116

'Ασία, *Asia.*

Acts 2: 9. Pontus, and *Asia,*
6: 9. them of Cilicia and of *Asia,*
16: 6. to preach the word in *Asia,*
19:10. all they which dwelt in *Asia*
22. stayed in *Asia* for a season.
26. but almost throughout all *Asia,*
27. all *Asia* and the world worshippeth.
20: 4. accompanied him into *Asia*
16. would not spend the time in *Asia:*
18. that I came into *Asia,*
21:27. the Jews which were of *Asia,*
24:18. certain Jews from *Asia*
27: 2. by the coasts of *Asia;*
1Co.16:19(18). The churches of *Asia* salute you.
2Co. 1: 8. which came to us in *Asia,*
2Ti. 1:15. all they which are in *Asia*
1Pet. 1: 1. *Asia,* and Bithynia,
Rev. 1: 4. seven churches which are in *Asia:*
11. seven churches which are in *Asia;*

774 1 115/116 773

'Ασιανός, *Asianos.*

Acts20: 4. *of Asia,* Tychicus and Trophimus.

775 1 115/116 773,746

'Ασιάρχης, *Asiarkees.*

Acts19:31. certain of the *chief of Asia,*

789 2 117/116

*Ασσος, *Assos.*

Acts20:13. sailed unto *Assos,* there intending
14. he met with us at *Assos,*

N.B. Stephens considers ἄσσον, Acts 27:13, as a proper name.

799 1 118/118 1,4793

'Ασύγκριτος, *Asunkritos.*

Ro. 16:14. Salute *Asyncritus,* Phlegon,

825 1 120/119

'Αττάλεια, *Attalia.*

Acts14:25. they went down into *Attalia:*

828 1 120/119

Αὔγουστος, *Augoustos.*

Lu. 2: 1. a decree from Cæsar *Augustus,*

881 2 127/135 [271]

*Αχαζ, *Akaz.*

Mat. 1: 9. Joatham begat *Achaz;* and *Achaz* begat Ezekias;

882 11 127/135

'Αχαΐα, *Akaïa.*

Acts18:12. Gallio was the deputy of *Achaia,*
27. to pass into *Achaia,*
19:21. Macedonia and *Achaia,*
Ro. 15:26. them of Macedonia and *Achaia*
16: 5. Epenetus, who is the firstfruits of *Achaia*
1Co.16:15. firstfruits of *Achaia,*
2Co. 1: 1. saints which are in all *Achaia:*
9: 2. *Achaia* was ready a year ago;
11:10. the regions of *Achaia.*
1Th. 1: 7. to all that believe in Macedonia and *Achaia.*
8. not only in Macedonia and *Achaia,*

883 1 127/135 882

'Αχαϊκός, *Akaïkos.*

1Co.16:17. Fortunatus and *Achaicus:*

885 1 127/135 cf [3137]

'Αχείμ, *Akīm.*

Mat. 1:14. and Sadoc begat *Achim;* and *Achim*

884 2 127/136 1,5483

*Αψινθος, *Apsinthos.*

Rev. 8:11. the name of the star is called *Wormwood*

896 1 129/136 [1168]

Βάαλ, *Baäl.*

Ro. 11: 4. to (the image of) *Baal.*

897 12 129/136 1:514 [894]

Βαβυλών, *Babulōn.*

Mat. 1:11. carried away to *Babylon:*
12. brought to *Babylon,*
17. the carrying away into *Babylon*
— carrying away into *Babylon*
Acts 7:43. carry you away beyond *Babylon.*
1Pet.5:13. The (church that is) at *Babylon,*
Rev.14: 8. *Babylon* is fallen,
16:19. great *Babylon* came in remembrance
17: 5. *BABYLON* THE GREAT,
18: 2. *Babylon* the great is fallen,
10. that great city *Babylon,*
21. great city *Babylon* be thrown down,

903 3 130/136 1:524 [1109]

Βαλαάμ, *Balaäm.*

2Pet.2:15. following the way of *Balaam*
Jude 11. the error of *Balaam*
Rev. 2:14. the doctrine of *Balaam,*

904 1 130/136 [1111]

Βαλάκ, *Balak.*

Rev. 2:14. who taught *Balac* to cast

910 14 132/ 907

Βαπτιστής, see amongst Appellatives.

912 11 132/139 [1347],[5]

Βαραββᾶς, *Barabbas.*

Mat.27:16. a notable prisoner, called *Barabbas.*
17. *Barabbas,* or Jesus which is called Christ?
20. that they should ask *Barabbas.*
21. They said, *Barabbas.*
26. Then released he *Barabbas*

Mar 15: 7. And there was (one) named *Barabbas*,
11. that he should rather release *Barabbas*
15. released *Barabbas* unto them,
Lu. 23:18. and release unto us *Barabbas*:
Joh. 18:40. Not this man, but *Barabbas*. **Now *Barabbas*** was a robber.

913 1 132/140 [1301]

Βαράκ, *Barak.*

Heb 11:32. to tell of Gedeon, and (of) *Barak*,

914 4 132/140 [1296]

Βαραχίας, *Barakias.*

Mat. 23:35. Zacharias son of *Barachias*,

918 6 133/140 [1247],[8526]

Βαρθολομαῖος, *Bartholomaios.*

Mat. 10: 3. Philip, and *Bartholomew*;
Mar 3:18. and *Bartholomew*, and Matthew,
Lu. 6:14. Philip and *Bartholomew*,
Acts 1:13. Philip, and Thomas, *Bartholomew*,

919 1 133/140 [1247],[3091]

Βαριησοῦς, *Barïeesous.*

Acts 13: 6. a Jew, whose name (was) *Bar-jesus*:

920 1 133/140 [1247],[3124]

Βὰρ-Ἰωνᾶ, *Bar-iōna.*

Mat. 16:17. Blessed art thou, Simon *Bar-jona*:

921 1 133/140 [1247],[5029]

Βαρνάβας, *Barnabas.*

Acts 4:36. And Joses, who by the apostles was surnamed *Barnabas*,
9:27. But *Barnabas* took him,
11:22. and they sent forth *Barnabas*,
25. Then departed *Barnabas* to Tarsus,
30. and sent it to the elders by the hands of *Barnabas*
12:25. And *Barnabas* and Saul returned from Jerusalem,
13: 1. as *Barnabas*, and Simeon
2. Separate me *Barnabas* and Saul for the work
7. who called for *Barnabas* and Saul,
43. followed Paul and *Barnabas*:
46. Then Paul and *Barnabas* waxed bold,
50. and raised persecution against Paul and *Barnabas*,
14:12. And they called *Barnabas*,
14. (Which) when the apostles, *Barnabas* and Paul,
20. and the next day he departed with *Barnabas*
15: 2. When therefore Paul and *Barnabas*
— they determined that Paul and *Barnabas*,
12. and gave audience to *Barnabas* and Paul,
22. to Antioch with Paul and *Barnabas*;
25. with our beloved *Barnabas* and Paul,
35. Paul also and *Barnabas* continued in Antioch,
36. And some days after Paul said unto *Barnabas*,
37. And *Barnabas* determined to take with them
39. and so *Barnabas* took Mark,
1Co. 9: 6. Or I only and *Barnabas*,
Gal. 2: 1. I went up again to Jerusalem with *Barnabas*,
9. they gave to me and *Barnabas*
13. insomuch that *Barnabas* also was carried away
Col. 4:10. and Marcus, sister's son to *Barnabas*,

923 2 133/140 [1247],[6634]

Βαρσαβᾶς, *Barsabas.*

Acts 1:23. *Barsabas*, who was surnamed Justus,
15:22. (namely), Judas surnamed *Barsabas*,

924 1 133/140 [1247],[2931]

Βαρτίμαιος, *Bartimaios.*

Mar 10:46. blind *Bartimæus*, the son of Timæus,

954 7 138/146 1:605 [1176]

Βεελζεβούλ, *Beëlzeboul.*

Mat. 10:25. called the master of the house *Beelzebub*,
12:24. but by *Beelzebub* the prince of the devils.
27. And if I by *Beelzebub* cast out devils,
Mar 3:22. said, He hath *Beelzebub*,
Lu. 11:15. He casteth out devils through *Beelzebub*
18. I cast out devils through *Beelzebub*.
19. And if I by *Beelzebub* cast out devils,

955 1 138/146 1:607 [1100]

Βελίαλ, *Belial.*

2Co. 6:15. And what concord hath Christ with *Belial*?

958 4 139/146 [1144]

Βενιαμίν, *Beniamin.*

Acts 13:21. a man of the tribe of *Benjamin*,
Ro. 11: 1. (of) the tribe of *Benjamin*.
Phi. 3: 5. (of) the tribe of *Benjamin*,
Rev. 7: 8. Of the tribe of *Benjamin*

959 3 139/146 5342,3529

Βερνίκη, *Bernikee*

Acts 25:13. and *Bernice* came unto Cæsarea
23. and *Bernice*, with great pomp,
26:30. and *Bernice*, and they that sat with them·

960 2 139/146 4008

Βέροια, *Beroya.*

Acts 17:10. sent away Paul and Silas by night unto *Berea*:
13. was preached of Paul at *Berea*,

961 1 139/146 960

Βεροιαῖος, *Beroyaios.*

Acts 20: 4. into Asia Sopater *of Berea*;

962 1 139/146 [1004],[5679]

Βηθαβαρά, *Beethabara.*

Joh. 1:28. These things were done in *Bethabara*

963 11 139/146

Βηθανία, *Beethania.*

Mat. 21:17. and went out of the city into *Bethany*;
26: 6. Now when Jesus was in *Bethany*,
Mar 11: 1. unto Bethphage and *Bethany*,
11. he went out unto *Bethany* with the twelve.
12. when they were come from *Bethany*,

Mar 14: 3. And being in *Bethany* in the house of Simon
Lu. 19:29. when he was come nigh to Bethphage and *Bethany,*
24:50. And he led them out as far as to *Bethany,*
Joh. 11: 1. (named) Lazarus, of *Bethany,*
18. Now *Bethany* was nigh unto Jerusalem,
12: 1. before the passover came to *Bethany,*

964 1 139/146 [1004],[2617]

Βηθεσδά, *Beethesda.*

Joh. 5: 2. in the Hebrew tongue *Bethesda,*

965 8 139/146 [1036]

Βηθλεέμ, *Beethleëm.*

Mat. 2: 1. Jesus was born in *Bethlehem*
5. In *Bethlehem* of Judæa:
6. And thou *Bethlehem,* (in) the land of Juda,
8. And he sent them to *Bethlehem,*
16. and slew all the children that were in *Bethlehem,*
Lu. 2: 4. which is called *Bethlehem ;*
15. Let us now go even unto *Bethlehem,*
Joh. 7:42. and out of the town of *Bethlehem,*

966 7 139/146 [1004],[6719]

Βηθσαϊδάν, -δά, *Beethsaïdan, -da.*

Mat. 11:21. woe unto thee, *Bethsaida !*
Mar 6:45. and to go to the other side before unto *Bethsaida,*
8:22. And he cometh to *Bethsaida ;*
Lu. 9:10. belonging to the city called *Bethsaida.*
10:13. woe unto thee, *Bethsaida !*
Joh. 1:44(45). Now Philip was of *Bethsaida,*
12:21. which was of *Bethsaida*

967 3 139/146 [1004],[6719]

Βηθφαγή, *Beethphagee.*

Mat. 21: 1. and were come to *Bethphage,*
Mar 11: 1. unto *Bethphage* and Bethany,
Lu. 19:29. come nigh to *Bethphage* and Bethany,

978 2 141/147

Βιθυνία, *Bithunia.*

Acts 16: 7. they assayed to go into *Bithynia:*
1Pet. 1: 1. Cappadocia, Asia, and *Bithynia,*

986 1 142/148 rt 985

Βλάστος, *Blastos.*

Acts 12:20. and, having made *Blastus*

993 1 143/ [1123],[7266]

Βοανεργές, *Boanerges.*

Mar 3:17. and he surnamed them *Boanerges,*

1003 2 144/151 [1162]

Βοόζ, *Boöz.*

Mat. 1: 5. And Salmon begat *Booz* of Rachab; and *Booz* begat Obed of Ruth;
Lu. 3:32. which was (the son) of *Booz,*

1005 2 144/

Βοῤῥᾶς, see amongst Appellatives.

1007 1 144/146.151 [1160]

Βοσόρ, *Bosor.*

2Pet. 2:15. Balaam (the son) of *Bosor,*

1042 1 148/153 [1355]

Γαββαθᾶ, *Gabbatha.*

Joh. 19:13. but in the Hebrew, *Gabbatha.*

1043 2 148/153 [1403]

Γαβριήλ, *Gabrieel.*

Lu. 1:19. I am *Gabriel,* that stand in the
26. And in the sixth month the angel *Gabriel*

1045 1 148/153 [1410]

Γάδ, *Gad.*

Rev. 7: 5. Of the tribe of *Gad*

1046 3 148/153,160

Γαδαρηνός, *Gadareenos.*

Mar 5: 1. into the country of the *Gadarenes.*
Lu. 8:26. And they arrived at the country of the *Gadarenes,*
37. of the country of the *Gadarenes*

1048 1 148/154 [5804]

Γάζα, *Gaza.*

Acts 8:26. down from Jerusalem unto *Gaza,*

1050 5 149/154

Γάϊος, *Gaïos.*

Acts 19:29. and having caught *Gaius*
20: 4. and *Gaius* of Derbe,
Ro. 16:23. *Gaius* mine host, and of the whole church,
1Co. 1:14. but Crispus and *Gaius ;*
3Joh. 1. The elder unto the wellbeloved *Gaius,*

1052 1 149/154 1053

Γαλάται, *Galatai.*

Gal. 3: 1. O foolish *Galatians,* who hath

1053 4 149/154

Γαλατία, *Galatia.*

1Co. 16: 1. to the churches of *Galatia,*
Gal. 1: 2. unto the churches of *Galatia :*
2Ti. 4:10. Crescens to *Galatia,* Titus unto Dalmatia.
1Pet. 1: 1. throughout Pontus, *Galatia,*

1054 2 149/154 1053

Γαλατικός, *Galatikos.*

Acts 16: 6. and the region *of Galatia,*
18:23. the country *of Galatia*

1056 63 149/154 [1551]

Γαλιλαία, *Galilaia.*

Mat. 2:22. into the parts of *Galilee :*
3:13. Then cometh Jesus from *Galilee*
4:12. he departed into *Galilee ;*
15. *Galilee* of the Gentiles ;
18. walking by the sea of *Galilee,*
23. And Jesus went about all *Galilee,*
25. multitudes of people from *Galilee,*
15:29. unto the sea of *Galilee ;*

Mat.17:22. And while they abode in *Galilee*,
19: 1. he departed from *Galilee*,
21:11. the prophet of Nazareth of *Galilee*.
26:32. I will go before you into *Galilee*.
27:55. which followed Jesus from *Galilee*,
28: 7. he goeth before you into *Galilee*;
10. that they go into *Galilee*,
16. went away into *Galilee*,
Mar 1: 9. came from Nazareth of *Galilee*,
14. Jesus came into *Galilee*,
16. walked by the sea of *Galilee*,
28. all the region round about *Galilee*.
39. throughout all *Galilee*, and cast out
3: 7. and a great multitude from *Galilee*
6:21. and chief (estates) of *Galilee*;
7:31. he came unto the sea of *Galilee*,
9:30. and passed through *Galilee*;
14:28. I will go before you into *Galilee*.
15:41. when he was in *Galilee*,
16: 7. that he goeth before you into *Galilee*:
Lu. 1:26. unto a city of *Galilee*,
2: 4. And Joseph also went up from *Galilee*,
39. they returned into *Galilee*,
3: 1. and Herod being tetrarch of *Galilee*,
4:14. in the power of the Spirit into *Galilee*:
31. a city of *Galilee*, and taught them
44. And he preached in the synagogues of *Galilee*.
5:17. out of every town of *Galilee*,
8:26. which is over against *Galilee*.
17:11. midst of Samaria and *Galilee*.
23: 5. beginning from *Galilee* to this place.
6. When Pilate heard of *Galilee*,
49. that followed him from *Galilee*,
55. which came with him from *Galilee*,
24: 6. when he was yet in *Galilee*,
Joh. 1:43(44). would go forth into *Galilee*,
2: 1. there was a marriage in Cana of *Galilee*;
11. did Jesus in Cana of *Galilee*,
4: 3. and departed again into *Galilee*.
43. and went into *Galilee*.
45. Then when he was come into *Galilee*,
46. So Jesus came again into Cana of *Galilee*,
47. was come out of Judæa into *Galilee*,
54. when he was come out of Judæa into *Galilee*.
6: 1. went over the sea of *Galilee*,
7: 1. After these things Jesus walked in *Galilee*:
9. he abode (still) in *Galilee*.
41. Shall Christ come out of *Galilee*?
52. Art thou also of *Galilee*?
— for out of *Galilee* ariseth no prophet.
12:21. which was of Bethsaida of *Galilee*,
21: 2. and Nathanael of Cana in *Galilee*,
Acts 9:31. throughout all Judæa and *Galilee*
10:37. and began from *Galilee*,
13:31. which came up with him from *Galilee*

1057 11 149/155 1056

Γαλιλαῖος, *Galilaios*.

Mat.26:69. Thou also wast with Jesus *of Galilee*.
Mar 14:70. for thou art a *Galilæan*,
Lu. 13: 1. some that told him of the *Galilæans*,
2. Suppose ye that these *Galilæans* were sinners above all the *Galilæans*,
22:59. for he is a *Galilæan*.
23: 6. asked whether the man were a *Galilæan*.
Joh. 4:45. the *Galilæans* received him,
Acts 1:11. Ye men *of Galilee*, why stand ye
2: 7. are not all these which speak *Galilæans*?
5:37. rose up Judas *of Galilee*

1058 3 149/155

Γαλλίων, *Galliōn*.

Acts18:12. And when *Gallio* was the deputy
14. *Gallio* said unto the Jews,
17. And *Gallio* cared for none of those

1059 2 150/155 [1583]

Γαμαλιήλ, *Gamalieel*.

Acts 5:34. a Pharisee, named *Gamaliel*,
22: 3. at the feet of *Gamaliel*,

1066 1 152/157 [1439]

Γεδεών, *Gedeōn*.

Heb 11:32. would fail me to tell of *Gedeon*,

1068 2 152/157 [1660],[8081]

Γεθσημανῆ, *Gethseemanee*.

Mat.26:36. a place called *Gethsemane*,
Mar 14:32. which was named *Gethsemane*:

1082 3 155/160 cf [3672]

Γεννησαρέτ, *Genneesaret*.

Mat.14:34. into the land of *Gennesaret*.
Mar 6:53. into the land of *Gennesaret*.
Lu. 5: 1. he stood by the lake of *Gennesaret*,

1086 1 155/160 [1622]

Γεργεσηνός, *Gergeseenos*.

Mat. 8:28. the country of the *Gergesenes*,

1115 3 164/174 [1538]

Γολγοθᾶ, *Golgotha*.

Mat.27:33. a place called *Golgotha*,
Mar 15:22. unto the place *Golgotha*,
Joh.19:17. which is called in the Hebrew *Golgotha*:

1116 2 164/174 [6017]

Γόμοῤῥα, τὰ, *Gomorra*.

Mat.10:15. the land of Sodom and *Gomorrha*
Mar 6:11. for Sodom and *Gomorrha*

1116 3 164/174 [6017]

Γόμοῤῥα, ἡ, *Gomorra*.

Ro. 9:29. been made like unto *Gomorrha*.
2Pet.2: 6. the cities of Sodom and *Gomorrha*
Jude 7. Even as Sodom and *Gomorrha*,

1136 1 167/182 1:789 [1463]

Γώγ, *Gōg*.

Rev.20: 8. *Gog* and Magog, to gather them

1138 59 168/184 [1732]

Δαβίδ, *Dabid*.

Mat. 1: 1. the son of *David*, the son of Abraham.
6. And Jesse begat *David* the king; and *David*
17. So all the generations from Abraham to *David*
— from *David* until the carrying away into Babylon

Mat. 1:20. **Joseph, thou son of *David*, fear not to**
9:27. (Thou) son of *David*, have mercy on us.
12: 3. Have ye not read what *David* did, when
23. said, Is not this the son of *David?*
15:22. O Lord, (thou) son of *David;* my daughter
20:30. on us, O Lord, (thou) son of *David.*
31. on us, O Lord, (thou) son of *David.*
21: 9. Hosanna to the son of *David:* Blessed (is)
15. Hosanna to the son of *David;* they were
22:42. They say unto him, (The son) of *David.*
43. How then doth *David* in spirit call him
45. If *David* then call him Lord, how is
Mar 2:25. Have ye never read what *David* did, when
10:47. Jesus, (thou) son of *David*, have mercy on
48. (Thou) son of *David*, have mercy on me.
11:10. of our father *David*, that cometh in the
12:35. that Christ is the son of *David?*
36. For *David* himself said by the Holy Ghost,
37. *David* therefore himself calleth him Lord; and whence
Lu. 1:27. name was Joseph, of the house of *David;*
32. unto him the throne of his father *David:*
69. in the house of his servant *David;*
2: 4. the city of *David*, which is called Bethlehem;
— was of the house and lineage of *David:*
11. is born this day in the city of *David*
3:31. of Nathan, which was (the son) of *David*,
6: 3. what *David* did, when himself was an hungred,
18:38. Jesus, (thou) son of *David*, have mercy on
39. (Thou) son of *David*, have mercy on me.
20:41. How say they that Christ is *David's* son?
42. And *David* himself saith in the book of
44. *David* therefore calleth him Lord, how is he
Joh. 7:42. That Christ cometh of the seed of *David*,
— out of the town of Bethlehem, where *David*
Acts 1:16. which the Holy Ghost by the mouth of *David*
2:25. For *David* speaketh concerning him, I foresaw
29. of the patriarch *David*, that he is both
34. For *David* is not ascended into the heavens:
4:25. Who by the mouth of thy servant *David*
7:45. of our fathers, unto the days of *David;*
13:22. raised up unto them *David* to be
— I have found *David* the (son) of Jesse,
34. will give you the sure mercies of *David*.
36. For *David*, after he had served his own
15:16. will build again the tabernacle of *David*,
Ro. 1: 3. which was made of the seed of *David*
4: 6. Even as *David* also describeth the blessedness
11: 9. And *David* saith, Let their table be made
2Ti. 2: 8. that Jesus Christ of the seed of *David*
Heb 4: 7. he limiteth a certain day, saying in *David*,
11:32. *David* also, and Samuel, and (of) the prophets:
Rev. 3: 7. he that hath the key of *David*, he
5: 5. the Root of *David*, hath prevailed to open
22:16. I am the root and the offspring of *David*,

1148 1 169/183

Δαλμανουθά, *Dalmanoutha.*

Mar 8:10. disciples, and came into the parts of *Dalmanutha.*

1149 1 169/183

Δαλματία, *Dalmatia.*

2Ti. 4:10. unto Thessalonica; Crescens to Galatia, Titus unto *Dalmatia.*

1152 1 169/183 rt 1150

Δάμαρις, *Damaris.*

Acts 17:34. and a woman named *Damaris*, and others with

1153 1 169/184 1154

Δαμασκηνός, *Damaskeenos.*

2Co. 11:32. the king kept the city of the *Damascenes*

1154 15 169/184 [1834]

Δαμασκός, *Damaskos.*

Acts 9: 2. And desired of him letters to *Damascus*
3. as he journeyed, he came near *Damascus:*
8. by the hand, and brought (him) into *Damascus.*
10. there was a certain disciple at *Damascus*,
19. days with the disciples which were at *Damascus.*
22. and confounded the Jews which dwelt at *Damascus*,
27. how he had preached boldly at *Damascus*
22: 5. and went to *Damascus*, to bring them
6. my journey, and was come nigh unto *Damascus*
10. Arise, and go into *Damascus;* and there it
11. that were with me, I came into *Damascus.*
26:12. Whereupon as I went to *Damascus* with authority
20. But shewed first unto them of *Damascus*, and
2Co. 11:32. In *Damascus* the governor under Aretas the king
Gal. 1:17. went into Arabia, and returned again unto *Damascus.*

1158 2 169/184 [1840]

Δανιήλ, *Danieel.*

Mat. 24:15. spoken of by *Daniel* the prophet,
Mar 13:14. spoken of by *Daniel* the prophet, standing

1179 3 173/187 1176,4172

Δεκάπολις, *Dekapolis.*

Mat. 4:25. and (from) *Decapolis*, and (from) Jerusalem, and (from)
Mar 5:20. and began to publish in *Decapolis* how
7:31. through the midst of the coasts of *Decapolis.*

1190 1 174/189 1191

Δερβαῖος, *Derbaios.*

Acts 20: 4. Aristarchus and Secundus; and Gaius *of Derbe*, and

---

1191 3 174/189

Δέρβη, *Derbee.*

Acts 14: 6. and fled unto Lystra and *Derbe*, cities of
20. next day he departed with Barnabas to *Derbe.*
16: 1. Then came he to *Derbe* and Lystra: and,

1214 3 177/192 1216

Δημᾶς, *Deemas.*

Col. 4:14. Luke, the beloved physician, and *Demas* greet you.

2Ti. 4:10. For *Demas* hath forsaken me, having
Philem 24. Marcus, Aristarchus, *Demas*, Lucas, my fellowlabourers.

1216 1 177/192

Δημήτριος, Deemeetrios.

Acts19:24. For a certain (man) named *Demetrius*, a silversmith,
38. Wherefore if *Demetrius*, and the craftsmen which are
3Joh. 12. *Demetrius* hath good report of all (men),

1324 3 191/211 1364

Δίδυμος, Didumos.

Joh. 11:16. Then said Thomas, which is called *Didymus*, unto
20:24. Thomas, one of the twelve, called *Didymus*,
21: 2. were together Simon Peter, and Thomas called *Didymus*,

1354 1 198/220

Διονύσιος, Dionusios.

Acts17:34. and believed: among the which (was) *Dionysius* the

1356 1 198/

Διοπετής.

The neuter of this adjective is placed among the Appellatives.

1359 1 198/220 2203,rt 2877

Διόσκουροι, Dioskouroi.

Acts28:11. a ship...whose sign was *Castor and Pollux*. (lit. the *Dioscuri*)

1361 1 198/221 2203,5142

Διοτρεφής, Diotrephees.

3Joh. 9. I wrote unto the church: but *Diotrephes*, who

1393 2 203/227

Δορκάς, Dorkas.

Acts 9:36. which by interpretation is called *Dorcas*: this woman
39. which *Dorcas* made, while she was with

1409 1 206/229

Δρούσιλλα, Drousilla.

Acts24:24. when Felix came with his wife *Drusilla*, which

1443 1 212/244 [5677]

Ἑβέρ, Heber.

Lu. 3:35. which was (the son) of *Heber*,

1444 1 212/ 3:357 1443

Ἑβραϊκός, Hebraïkos.

Lu. 23:38. letters of Greek, and Latin, and *Hebrew*,

1445 4 212/244 3:357 1443

Ἑβραῖος, Hebraios.

Acts 6: 1. of the Grecians against the *Hebrews*,
2Co.11:22. Are they *Hebrews*? so (am) I.
Phi. 3: 5. an *Hebrew* of the *Hebrews*;

1446 3 212/244 3:357 [5680] 1443

Ἑβραΐς, Hebraïs.

Acts21:40. spake unto (them) in the *Hebrew* tongue,
22: 2. that he spake in the *Hebrew* tongue
26:14. saying in the *Hebrew* tongue, Saul,

1447 6 212/244 3:357 1446

Ἑβραϊστί, Hebraïsti.

Joh. 5: 2. called *in the Hebrew tongue* Bethesda,
19:13. the Pavement, but *in the Hebrew*, Gabbatha.
17. called *in the Hebrew* Golgotha:
20. written *in Hebrew*, (and) Greek, (and) Latin.
Rev. 9:11. name *in the Hebrew tongue* (is) Abaddon,
16:16. called *in the Hebrew tongue* Armageddon.

1478 2 217/255 [2396]

Ἐζεκίας, Ezekias.

Mat. 1: 9. and Achaz begat *Ezekias*;
10. And *Ezekias* begat Manasses;

1639 1 247/323 [5867]

Ἐλαμῖται, Elamitai.

Acts 2: 9. Parthians, and Medes, and *Elamites*,

1648 2 248/323 [499]

Ἐλεάζαρ, Eleazar.

Mat. 1:15. And Eliud begat *Eleazar*; and *Eleazar* begat Matthan;

1662 3 250/325 [471]

Ἐλιακείμ, Eliakīm.

Mat. 1:13. Abiud begat *Eliakim*; and *Eliakim* begat Azor;
Lu. 3:30. which was (the son) of *Eliakim*,

1663 1 250/325 [461]

Ἐλιέζερ, Eliezer.

Lu. 3:29. which was (the son) of *Eliezer*,

1664 2 250/325 [410],[1935]

Ἐλιούδ, Elioud.

Mat. 1:14. and Achim begat *Eliud*;
15. And *Eliud* begat Eleazar;

1665 9 250/324 [472]

Ἐλισάβετ, Elisabet.

Lu. 1: 5. and her name (was) *Elisabeth*.
7. because that *Elisabeth* was barren,
13. and thy wife *Elisabeth* shall bear
24. his wife *Elisabeth* conceived,
36. And, behold, thy cousin *Elisabeth*,
40. into the house of Zacharias, and saluted *Elisabeth*.

Lu. 1:41. when *Elisabeth* heard the salutation
— and *Elisabeth* was filled with the Holy
57. Now *E'lisabeth's* full time came

1666 1 250/325 [477]
'Ελισσαῖος, *Elissaιos.*

Lu. 4:27. in the time of *Eliseus* the prophet;

1671 1 251/326 2:504
'Ελλάς, *Hellas.*

Acts20: 2. exhortation, he came into *Greece,*

1672 27 251/326 2:504 1671
Ἕλλην, *Helleen.*

Joh. 7:35. the dispersed among *the Gentiles,* and teach the *Gentiles?*
12:20. there were certain *Greeks* among
Acts14: 1. the Jews and also of the *Greeks*
16: 1. his father (was) a *Greek:*
3. knew all that his father was a *Greek.*
17: 4. the devout *Greeks* a great multitude,
18: 4. persuaded the Jews and the *Greeks.*
17. all the *Greeks* took Sosthenes,
19:10. Lord Jesus, both Jews and *Greeks.*
17. known to all the Jews and *Greeks*
20:21. to the Jews, and also to the *Greeks,*
21:28. brought *Greeks* also into the temple,
Ro. 1:14. I am debtor both to the *Greeks,*
16. the Jew first, and also to the *Greek.*
2: 9. the Jew first, and also of the *Gentile;*
10. the Jew first, and also to the *Gentile:*
3: 9. proved both Jews and *Gentiles,*
10:12. between the Jew and the *Greek:*
1Co. 1:22. the *Greeks* seek after wisdom:
23. unto the *Greeks* foolishness;
24. are called, both Jews and *Greeks,*
10:32. to the Jews, nor to the *Gentiles,*
12:13. whether (we be) Jews or *Gentiles,*
Gal. 2: 3. who was with me, being a *Greek,*
3:28. There is neither Jew nor *Greek,*
Col. 3:11. there is neither *Greek* nor Jew,

1673 2 251/326 2:504 1672
'Ελληνικός, *Helleenikos.*

Lu. 23:38. in letters *of Greek,* and Latin, and Hebrew,
Rev. 9:11. in the *Greek* tongue hath (his) name

1674 2 251/326 2:504 1672
'Ελληνίς, *Helleenis.*

Mar 7:26. The woman was a *Greek,*
Acts17:12. honourable women which were *Greeks,*

1675 3 251/326 2:504 1672
'Ελληνιστής, *Helleenistees.*

Acts 6: 1. arose a murmuring of the *Grecians*
9:29. disputed against the *Grecians:*
11:20. spake unto the *Grecians,* preaching

1676 2 251/326 2:504 rt 1675
'Ελληνιστί, *Helleenisti.*

Joh. 19:20. written in Hebrew, (and) *Greek,* (and) Latin.
Acts21:37. Who said, Canst thou speak *Greek?*

1678 1 251/326 cf [486]
'Ελμωδάμ, *Elmōdam.*

Lu. 3:28. which was (the son) of *Elmodam,*

1681 1 253/327
'Ελύμας, *Elumas.*

Acts13: 8. But *Elymas* the sorcerer

1694 1 254/328 [6005]
'Εμμανουήλ, *Emmanoueel.*

Mat. 1:23. they shall call his name *Emmanuel,*

1695 1 254/328 cf [3222]
'Εμμαούς, *Emmäous.*

Lu. 24:13. to a village called *Emmaus,*

1697 1 254/328 [2544]
'Εμμόρ, *Emmor.*

Acts 7:16. of the sons of *Emmor* (the father) of Sychem.

1800 1 270/341 [583]
'Ενώς, *Enōs.*

Lu. 3:38. Which was (the son) of *Enos,*

1802 3 270/341 2:556 [2585]
'Ενώχ, *Enōk.*

Lu. 3:37. which was (the son) of *Enoch,*
Heb11: 5. By faith *Enoch* was translated
Jude 14. And *Enoch* also, the seventh from

1866 1 281/351 1867
'Επαινετός, *Epainetos.*

Ro. 16: 5. Salute my wellbeloved *Epenetus,*

1889 3 283/352 1891
'Επαφρᾶς, *Epaphras.*

Col. 1: 7. As ye also learned of *Epaphras*
4:12. *Epaphras,* who is (one) of you,
Philem 23. There salute thee *Epaphras,*

1891 2 283/352 1909 *Aphroditē* (Venus)
'Επαφρόδιτος, *Epaphroditos.*

Phi. 2:25. to send to you *Epaphroditus,*
4:18. having received of *Epaphroditus*

1946 1 296/368 cf [1947]
'Επικούρειος, *Epikourios.*

Acts17:18. certain philosophers of the *Epicureans,*

2037 3 306/376 *eraō* (to love)
Ἔραστος, *Erastos.*

Acts19:22. Timotheus and *Erastus;*
Ro. 16:23. *Erastus* the chamberlain of the city
2Ti. 4:20. *Erastus* abode at Corinth:

2057 1 309/380 2060
'Ερμᾶς, *Hermas.*

Ro. 16:14. Phlegon, *Hermas,* Patrobas, Hermes,

2060 2 310/380 2046
'Ερμῆς, *Hermees.*

Acts14:12. Barnabas, Jupiter; and Paul, *Mercurius,*
Ro. 16:14. *Hermes,* and the brethren which are

2061 1 310/380 2060,1096

Ἑρμογένης, *Hermogenees.*

2Ti. 1:15. of whom are Phygellus and *Hermogenes.*

2063 2 310/380

Ἐρυθρὰ Θάλασσα, *Eruthra Thalassa.*

Acts 7:36. in the land of Egypt, and in the *Red sea,*
Heb 11:29. they passed through the *Red sea*

2069 1 313/391 [454]

Ἐσλί, *Esli.*

Lu. 3:25. which was (the son) of *Esli,*

2074 3 313/391 [2696]

Ἐσρώμ, *Esrōm.*

Mat. 1: 3. and Phares begat *Esrom;* and *Esrom* begat Aram;
Lu. 3:33. which was (the son) of *Esrom,*

2096 2 317/396 [2332]

Εὔα, *Ūa.*

2Co. 11: 3. as the serpent beguiled *Eve*
1Ti. 2:13. For Adam was first formed, then *Eve.*

2103 1 319/398 2095,1014

Εὔβουλος, *Ūboulos.*

2Ti. 4:21. *Eubulus* greeteth thee, and Pudens,

2131 1 323/401 2095,3529

Εὐνείκη, *Ūnīkee.*

2Ti. 1: 5. and thy mother *Eunice;*

2136 1 324/402 rt 2137

Εὐοδία, *Ūodīa.*

Phi. 4: 2. I beseech *Euodias,* and beseech Syntyche,

2148 1 326/402 2830 *Euros.*

Εὐροκλύδων, *Ūrokludōn.*

Acts 27:14. a tempestuous wind, called *Euroclydon.*

2161 1 327/405 2095,5177

Εὔτυχος, *Ūtukos.*

Acts 20: 9. young man named *Eutychus,*

2166 2 328/405 cf [6578]

Εὐφράτης, *Ūphratees.*

Rev. 9:14. in the great river *Euphrates.*
16:12. upon the great river *Euphrates;*

2179 1 /406 2181

Ἐφεσῖνος, *Ephesinos.*

Rev. 2: 1. of the church *of Ephesus* write;

2180 5 330/406 2181

Ἐφέσιος, *Ephesios.*

Acts 19:28. Great (is) Diana of the *Ephesians.*
34. Great (is) Diana of the *Ephesians.*
35 (Ye) men *of Ephesus,* what man is there
Acts 19:35. that the city of the *Ephesians*
21:29. in the city Trophimus an *Ephesian,*

2181 15 330/406

Ἔφεσος, *Ephesos.*

Acts 18:19. And he came to *Ephesus,*
21. And he sailed from *Ephesus.*
24. mighty in the scriptures, came to *Ephesus.*
19: 1. passed through the upper coasts came to *Ephesus:*
17. Greeks also dwelling at *Ephesus;*
26. that not alone at *Ephesus,*
20:16. had determined to sail by *Ephesus,*
17. And from Miletus he sent to *Ephesus,*
1Co. 15:32. I have fought with beasts at *Ephesus,*
16: 8. But I will tarry at *Ephesus*
Eph. 1: 1. to the saints which are at *Ephesus,*
1Ti. 1: 3. As I besought thee to abide still at *Ephesus*
2Ti. 1:18. he ministered unto me at *Ephesus,*
4:12. And Tychicus have I sent to *Ephesus.*
Rev. 1:11. unto *Ephesus,* and unto Smyrna,

2187 1 331/406 [669] or [6085]

Ἐφραΐμ, *Ephraïm.*

Joh. 11:54. into a ity called *Ephraim,*

2194 3 336/416 [2074]

Ζαβουλών, *Zaboulōn.*

Mat. 4:13. in the borders of *Zabulon*
15. The land of *Zabulon,*
Rev. 7: 8. Of the tribe of *Zabulon*

2195 3 336/416 cf [2140]

Ζακχαῖος, *Zakkaios.*

Lu. 19: 2. (there was) a man named *Zacchæus,*
5. and said unto him, *Zacchæus,*
8. And *Zacchæus* stood, and said

2196 1 336/416 [2226]

Ζαρά, *Zara.*

Mat. 1: 3. Judas begat Phares and *Zara*

Ζαρούχ see Σαρούχ. 4562

2197 11 336/417 [2148]

Ζαχαρίας, *Zakarias.*

Mat. 23:35. unto the blood of *Zacharias*
Lu. 1: 5. a certain priest named *Zacharias,*
12. And when *Zacharias* saw (him),
13. said unto him, Fear not, *Zacharias:*
18. And *Zacharias* said unto the angel,
21. And the people waited for *Zacharias,*
40. And entered into the house of *Zacharias,*
59. and they called him *Zacharias,*
67. And his father *Zacharias* was filled
3: 2. the son of *Zacharias* in the wilderness.
11:51. unto the blood of *Zacharias,*

2199 12 337/418 cf [2067]

Ζεβεδαῖος, *Zebedaios.*

Mat. 4:21. James (the son) of *Zebedee,*

Mat. 4:21. in a ship with *Zebedee* their father,
10: 2. James (the son) of *Zebedee*,
20:20. *Zebedee's* children with her sons,
26:37. and the two sons of *Zebedee*,
27:56. and the mother of *Zebedee's* children.
Mar 1:19. James the (son) of *Zebedee*,
20. and they left their father *Zebedee*
3:17. And James the (son) of *Zebedee*,
10:35. James and John, the sons of *Zebedee*,
Lu. 5:10. James, and John, the sons of *Zebedee*,
Joh. 21: 2. and the (sons) of *Zebedee*,

2203 2 338/419

Ζεύς, *Zūs.*

Acts 14:12. And they called Barnabas, *Jupiter*;
13. Then the priest of *Jupiter*,

2208 2 338/419 rt 2207

Ζηλωτής, *Zeelōtees.*

Lu. 6:15. and Simon called *Zelotes*,
Acts 1:13. and Simon *Zelotes*, and Judas

2211 1 339/419 2203,1435

Ζηνᾶς, *Zeenas.*

Tit. 3:13. Bring *Zenas* the lawyer

2216 3 340/421 [2216]

Ζοροβάβελ, *Zorobabel.*

Mat. 1:12. and Salathiel begat *Zorobabel*;
13. And *Zorobabel* begat Abiud;
Lu. 3:27. which was (the son) of *Zorobabel*,

2242 1 345/423 [5941]

Ἡλί, *Heeli.*

Lu. 3:23. which was (the son) of *Heli*,

2243 30 345/423 2:928 [452]

Ἡλίας, *Eelias.*

Mat. 11:14. this is *Elias*, which was for to come.
16:14. some, *Elias*; and others, Jeremias,
17: 3. Moses and *Elias* talking with him.
4. and one for Moses, and one for *Elias*.
10. that *Elias* must first come?
11. *Elias* truly shall first come,
12. That *Elias* is come already,
27:47. This (man) calleth for *Elias*.
49. whether *Elias* will come to save him.
Mar 6:15. Others said, That it is *Elias*.
8:28. but some (say), *Elias*; and others,
9: 4. And there appeared unto them *Elias*
5. and one for Moses, and one for *Elias*.
11. that *Elias* must first come?
12. *Elias* verily cometh first,
13. That *Elias* is indeed come,
15:35. Behold, he calleth *Elias*.
36. whether *Elias* will come to take him
Lu. 1:17. in the spirit and power of *Elias*,
4:25. were in Israel in the days of *Elias*,
26. But unto none of them was *Elias* sent,
9: 8. And of some, that *Elias* had appeared;
19. but some (say), *Elias*;
30. which were Moses and *Elias*:
33. and one for Moses, and one for *Elias*:
Lu. 9:54. and consume them, even as *Elias* did?
Joh. 1:21. What then? Art thou *Elias*?
25. nor *Elias*, neither that prophet?
Ro. 11: 2. Wot ye not what the scripture saith of *Elias*?
Jas. 5:17. *Elias* was a man subject to

2262 1 349/432 [6147]

Ἤρ, *Eer.*

Lu. 3:28. which was (the son) of *Er*,

2267 1 349/433 2264

Ἡρωδίων, *Heerōdiōn.*

Ro. 16:11. Salute *Herodion* my kinsman. Greet them that be

2264 44 349/432 1491 *hērōs* (hero),

Ἡρώδης, *Heerōdees.*

Mat. 2: 1. in the days of *Herod* the king, behold, there
3. When *Herod* the king had heard (these things),
7. Then *Herod*, when he had privily called
12. that they should not return to *Herod*, they
13. for *Herod* will seek the young child to
15. And was there until the death of *Herod*:
16. Then *Herod*, when he saw that he was
19. But when *Herod* was dead, behold, an angel
22. in the room of his father *Herod*, he
14: 1. At that time *Herod* the tetrarch heard of
3. For *Herod* had laid hold on John, and
6. when *Herod's* birthday was kept, the daughter of Herodias danced before them, and pleased *Herod*.
Mar 6:14. king *Herod* heard (of him); for his name
16. But when *Herod* heard (thereof), he said,
17. For *Herod* himself had sent forth and laid
18. For John had said unto *Herod*, It is
20. For *Herod* feared John, knowing that he
21. that *Herod* on his birthday made a
22. came in, and danced, and pleased *Herod*
8:15. the Pharisees, and (of) the leaven of *Herod*.
Lu. 1: 5. There was in the days of *Herod*, the
3: 1. and *Herod* being tetrarch of Galilee, and
19. But *Herod* the tetrarch, being reproved by
— for all the evils which *Herod* had done,
8: 3. And Joanna the wife of Chuza *Herod's* steward,
9: 7. Now *Herod* the tetrarch heard of all that
9. And *Herod* said, John have I beheaded:
13:31. and depart hence: for *Herod* will kill thee.
23: 7. that he belonged unto *Herod's* jurisdiction, he sent him to *Herod*, who himself also
8. And when *Herod* saw Jesus, he was exceeding
11. And *Herod* with his men of war set
12. Pilate and *Herod* were made friends
15. No, nor yet *Herod*: for I sent you to
Acts 4:27. whom thou hast anointed, both *Herod*, and Pontius
12: 1. Now about that time *Herod* the king
6. And when *Herod* would have brought him
11. out of the hand of *Herod*, and (from)
19. And when *Herod* had sought for him,
20. And *Herod* was highly displeased with them of
21. And upon a set day *Herod*, arrayed in
13: 1. brought up with *Herod* the tetrarch, and Saul.
23:35. him to be kept in *Herod's* judgment hall.

2265 3 349/433 2264

Ἡρωδιανοί, Heerōdianoi.

Mat.22:16. their disciples with the *Herodians*, saying,
Mar 3: 6. took counsel with the *Herodians* against
12:13. the Pharisees and of the *Herodians*, to catch

2266 6 349/433 2264

Ἡρωδιάς, Heerōdias.

Mat.14: 3. and put (him) in prison for *Herodias'* sake,
6. daughter of *Herodias* danced before them,
Mar 6:17. for *Herodias'* sake, his brother Philip's wife:
19. Therefore *Herodias* had a quarrel against him,
22. when the daughter of the said *Herodias*
Lu. 3:19. being reproved by him for *Herodias* his brother

2268 21 349/433 [3470]

Ἡσαΐας, Heesaïas.

Mat. 3: 3. spoken of by the prophet *Esaias*, saying,
4:14. which was spoken by *Esaias* the prophet, saying,
8:17. which was spoken by *Esaias* the prophet, saying,
12:17. might be fulfilled which was spoken by *Esaias*
13:14. is fulfilled the prophecy of *Esaias*, which saith,
15: 7. (Ye) hypocrites, well did *Esaias* prophesy
Mar 7: 6. Well hath *Esaias* prophesied of you hypocrites,
Lu. 3: 4. in the book of the words of *Esaias* the
4:17. unto him the book of the prophet *Esaias*.
Joh. 1:23. of the Lord, as said the prophet *Esaias*.
12:38. That the saying of *Esaias* the prophet might
39. could not believe, because that *Esaias* said
41. These things said *Esaias*, when he saw his
Acts 8:28. sitting in his chariot read *Esaias* the prophet.
30. and heard him read the prophet *Esaias*,
28:25. Well spake the Holy Ghost by *Esaias* the
Ro. 9:27. *Esaias* also crieth concerning Israel, Though
29. And as *Esaias* said before, Except the Lord
10:16. For *Esaias* saith, Lord, who hath believed
20. But *Esaias* is very bold, and saith, I
15:12. And again, *Esaias* saith, There shall be a

2269 3 349/433 2:953 [6215]

Ἠσαῦ, Eesau.

Ro. 9:13. Jacob have I loved, but *Esau* have I hated.
Heb 11:20. By faith Isaac blessed Jacob and *Esau*
12:16. (be) any fornicator, or profane person, as *Esau*,

2280 2 350/434

Θαδδαῖος, Thaddaios.

Mat.10: 3. And Lebbæus, whose surname was *Thaddæus*;
Mar 3:18. the (son) of Alphæus, and *Thaddæus*, and Simon

2283 1 351/435 3:1 [8559]

Θάμαρ, Thamar.

Mat. 1: 3. And Judas begat Phares and Zara of *Thamar*;

2291 1 352/437 [8646]

Θάρα, Thara.

Lu. 3:34. which was (the son) of *Thara*, which was

2321 2 359/457 2316,5384

Θεόφιλος, Theophilos.

Lu. 1: 3. most excellent *Theophilus*,
Acts 1: 1. have I made, O *Theophilus*,

2331 4 360/458 2332

Θεσσαλονικεύς, Thessalonikūs.

Acts20: 4. and of the *Thessalonians*, Aristarchus
27: 2. (one) Aristarchus, a Macedonian *of Thessalonica*,
1Th. 1: 1. unto the church of the *Thessalonians*
2Th. 1: 1. unto the church of the *Thessalonians*

2332 5 360/458 3529 *Thessalos*

Θεσσαλονίκη, Thessalonikee.

Acts17: 1. they came to *Thessalonica*,
11. more noble than those in *Thessalonica*,
13. the Jews of *Thessalonica*
Phi. 4:16. For even in *Thessalonica*
2Ti. 4:10. is departed unto *Thessalonica*;

2333 1 360/458

Θευδᾶς, Thūdas.

Acts 5:36. rose up *Theudas*, boasting

2363 4 365/463

Θυάτειρα, τὰ, Thuatīra.

Acts16:14. of the city of *Thyatira*,
Rev. 1:11. and unto *Thyatira*, and unto Sardis,
2:18. of the church in *Thyatira*
24. unto the rest in *Thyatira*,

2381 12 367/465 cf [8380]

Θωμᾶς, Thōmas.

Mat.10: 3. *Thomas*, and Matthew the publican;
Mar 3:18. *Thomas*, and James the (son) of Alphæus,
Lu. 6:15. Matthew and *Thomas*, James
Joh.11:16. *Thomas*, which is called Didymus,
14: 5. *Thomas* saith unto him,
20:24. But *Thomas*, one of the twelve,
26. and *Thomas* with them:
27. Then saith he to *Thomas*,
28. *Thomas* answered and said
29. *Thomas*, because thou hast seen me,
21: 2. Simon Peter, and *Thomas*
Acts 1:13. Philip, and *Thomas*, Bartholomew,

2383 2 368/465 [2971]

Ἰάειρος, Iäīros.

Mar 5:22. of the synagogue, *Jairus* by name;
Lu. 8:41. there came a man named *Jairus*.

2384 27 368/465 3:191 [3290]

Ἰακώβ, Ïakōb.

Mat. 1: 2. begat *Jacob;* and *Jacob* begat
15. and Matthan begat *Jacob;*
16. And *Jacob* begat Joseph
8:11. and Isaac, and *Jacob,*
22:32. and the God of *Jacob?*
Mar 12:26. and the God of *Jacob?*
Lu. 1:33. over the house of *Jacob*
3:34. Which was (the son) of *Jacob*, which was (the son) of Isaac,
13:28. and Isaac, and *Jacob,*
20:37. and the God of *Jacob.*
Joh. 4: 5. that *Jacob* gave to his son Joseph.
6. *Jacob's* well was there.
12. than our father *Jacob,*
Acts 3:13. and of Isaac, and of *Jacob,*
7: 8. (begat) *Jacob;* and *Jacob*
12. But when *Jacob* heard
14. his father *Jacob* to (him),
15. *Jacob* went down into Egypt,
32. and the God of *Jacob.*
46. the God of *Jacob.*
Ro. 9:13. *Jacob* have I loved,
11:26. turn away ungodliness from *Jacob.*
Heb 11: 9. with Isaac and *Jacob,*
20. Isaac blessed *Jacob* and Esau
21. By faith *Jacob,* when he was a dying,

2385 42 368/466 rt 2384

Ἰάκωβος, Ïakōbos.

Mat. 4:21. *James* (the son) of Zebedee,
10: 2(3). *James* (the son) of Zebedee,
3. *James* (the son) of Alphæus,
13:55. *James,* and Joses, and Simon,
17: 1. *James,* and John his brother,
27:56. Mary the mother of *James*
Mar 1:19. *James* the (son) of Zebedee,
29. with *James* and John.
3:17. *James* the (son) of Zebedee, and John the brother of *James;*
18. and *James* the (son) of Alphæus,
5:37. *James,* and John the brother of *James.*
6: 3. the brother of *James,* and
9: 2. *James,* and John, and leadeth
10:35. *James* and John, the sons of
41. with *James* and John.
13: 3. Peter and *James*
14:33. *James* and John, and began to be
15:40. the mother of *James* the less
16: 1. Mary the (mother) of *James,*
Lu 5:10. also *James,* and John,
6:14. *James* and John, Philip and
15. *James* the (son) of Alphæus,
16. And Judas (the brother) of *James,*
8:51. and *James,* and John,
9:28. John and *James,* and went up
54. *James* and John saw (this),
24:10. and Mary (the mother) of *James,*
Acts 1:13. Peter, and *James,* and John,
— *James* (the son) of Alphæus,
— and Judas (the brother) of *James.*
12: 2. And he killed *James* the brother
17. *James,* and to the brethren.
15:13. *James* answered, saying,
21:18. with us unto *James;*
1Co. 15: 7. After that, he was seen of *James;*
Gal. 1:19. save *James* the Lord's brother.
2: 9. *James,* Cephas, and John,
12. that certain came from *James,*

Jas. 1: 1. *James,*...of God and of the Lord Jesus Christ,
Jude 1. and brother of *James,*

2387 1 368/466 3:192

Ἰαμβρῆς, Iambrees.

2Ti. 3: 8. Jannes and *Jambres* withstood Moses,

2388 1 368/466 cf [3238]

Ἰαννά, Ïanna.

Lu. 3:24. which was (the son) of *Janna,* which was (the son) of Joseph,

2389 1 368/466 3:192

Ἰαννῆς, Ïannees.

2Ti. 3: 8. *Jannes* and Jambres withstood Moses,

2391 1 369/467 [3382]

Ἰαρέδ, Ïared.

Lu. 3:37. which was (the son) of *Jared,* which was (the son) of Maleleel,

2394 5 369/467 2390

Ἰάσων, Ïasōn.

Acts 17: 5. the house of *Jason,*
6. they drew *Jason* and certain brethren
7. Whom *Jason* hath received:
9. of *Jason,* and of the other,
Ro. 16:21. Lucius, and *Jason,* and

2401 1 372/471 [123]

Ἰδουμαία, Idoumaia.

Mar 3: 8. from Jerusalem, and from *Idumæa,*

2403 1 372/471 3:217 [348]

Ἰεζαβήλ, Ïezabeel.

Rev. 2:20. thou sufferest that woman *Jezebel,*

2404 1 372/471 2413,4172

Ἱεράπολις, Hïerapolis.

Col. 4:13. and them in *Hierapolis.*

2408 3 372/471 3:218 [3414]

Ἱερεμίας, Hïeremias.

Mat. 2:17. by *Jeremy* the prophet,
16:14. and others, *Jeremias,* or one
27: 9. by *Jeremy* the prophet,

2410 7 372/471 [3405]

Ἱεριχώ, Hïeriko.

Mat. 20:29. as they departed from *Jericho,*
Mar 10:46. they came to *Jericho:* and as he went out of *Jericho*
Lu. 10:30. from Jerusalem to *Jericho,*
18:35. as he was come nigh unto *Jericho,*
19: 1. and passed through *Jericho.*
Heb 11:30. the walls of *Jericho* fell down,

2414 59 373/473 7:292 cf 2419 [3389]

Ἱεροσόλυμα, Hïerosoluma.

Mat. 2: 1. there came...to *Jerusalem,*

Mat. 2: 3. all *Jerusalem* with him.
3: 5. to him *Jerusalem*, and all Judæa,
4:25. and (from) *Jerusalem*, and
5:35. neither by *Jerusalem*; for it is
15: 1. which were of *Jerusalem*,
16:21. go unto *Jerusalem*, and suffer
20:17. Jesus going up to *Jerusalem*
18. we go up to *Jerusalem*;
21: 1. when they drew nigh unto *Jerusalem*,
10. when he was come into *Jerusalem*,
Mar 3: 8. from *Jerusalem*, and from
22. which came down from *Jerusalem*
7: 1. which came from *Jerusalem*.
10:32. going up to *Jerusalem*;
33. we go up to *Jerusalem*;
11:11. entered into *Jerusalem*,
15. they come to *Jerusalem*:
27. they come again to *Jerusalem*:
15:41. came up with him unto *Jerusalem*.
Lu. 2:22. they brought him to *Jerusalem*,
42. they went up to *Jerusalem*
18:31. we go up to *Jerusalem*,
19:28. ascending up to *Jerusalem*.
23: 7. who himself also was at *Jerusalem*
Joh. 1:19. priests and Levites from *Jerusalem*
2:13. went up to *Jerusalem*,
23. he was in *Jerusalem*
4:20. that in *Jerusalem* is the place
21. nor yet at *Jerusalem*,
45. at *Jerusalem* at the feast:
5: 1. Jesus went up to *Jerusalem*.
2. Now there is at *Jerusalem*
10:22. at *Jerusalem* the feast of the dedication,
11:18. Bethany was nigh unto *Jerusalem*,
55. many went...to *Jerusalem*
12:12. Jesus was coming to *Jerusalem*,
Acts 1: 4. not depart from *Jerusalem*,
8: 1. which was at *Jerusalem*;
14. the apostles which were at *Jerusalem*
11: 2. Peter was come up to *Jerusalem*,
22. which was in *Jerusalem*:
27. came prophets from *Jerusalem*
13:13. departing from them returned to *Jerusalem*.
18:21. keep this feast that cometh in *Jerusalem*:
20:16. to be at *Jerusalem*
21:17. we were come to *Jerusalem*,
25: 1. he ascended from Cæsarea to *Jerusalem*.
7. which came down from *Jerusalem*
9. Wilt thou go up to *Jerusalem*,
15. when I was at *Jerusalem*,
24. at *Jerusalem*, and (also) here,
26: 4. mine own nation at *Jerusalem*,
10. I also did in *Jerusalem*:
20. first...and at *Jerusalem*,
28:17. delivered prisoner from *Jerusalem*
Gal. 1:17. Neither went I up to *Jerusalem*
18. I went up to *Jerusalem* to see
2: 1. I went up again to *Jerusalem*

2415 2 374/473 7:292 2414

Ἱεροσολυμῖται, *Hierosolumitai.*

Mar 1: 5. and they *of Jerusalem*,
Joh. 7:25. some of them *of Jerusalem*,

2419 83 374/474 5:292 [3389]
cf 2414

Ἱερουσαλήμ, *Hierousaleem.*

Mat.23:37. O *Jerusalem*, *Jerusalem*, (thou) that killest
Mar 11: 1. they came nigh to *Jerusalem*,
Lu. 2:25. there was a man in *Jerusalem*,

Lu. 2:38. looked for redemption in *Jerusalem*.
41. to *Jerusalem* every year
43. child Jesus tarried behind in *Jerusalem*;
45. they turned back again to *Jerusalem*
4: 9. he brought him to *Jerusalem*,
5:17. and Judæa, and *Jerusalem*:
6:17. of all Judæa and *Jerusalem*,
9:31. which he should accomplish at *Jerusalem*.
51. to go to *Jerusalem*,
53. was as though he would go to *Jerusalem*.
10:30. from *Jerusalem* to Jericho,
13: 4. men that dwelt in *Jerusalem*?
22. journeying toward *Jerusalem*.
33. a prophet perish out of *Jerusalem*.
34. O *Jerusalem*, *Jerusalem*, which killest
17:11. as he went to *Jerusalem*,
19:11. he was nigh to *Jerusalem*,
21:20. *Jerusalem* compassed with armies,
24. and *Jerusalem* shall be trodden down
23:28. Daughters of *Jerusalem*, weep not
24:13. from *Jerusalem* (about) threescore
18. a stranger in *Jerusalem*,
33. and returned to *Jerusalem*,
47. among all nations, beginning at *Jerusalem*.
49. in the city of *Jerusalem*,
52. and returned to *Jerusalem*
Acts 1: 8. witnesses unto me both in *Jerusalem*,
12. returned they unto *Jerusalem*
— from *Jerusalem* a sabbath day's journey.
19. the dwellers at *Jerusalem*;
2: 5. And there were dwelling at *Jerusalem*
14. (ye) that dwell at *Jerusalem*,
4: 6(5). were gathered together at *Jerusalem*.
16. to all them that dwell in *Jerusalem*:
5:16. (out) of the cities round about unto *Jerusalem*,
28. ye have filled *Jerusalem*
6: 7. of the disciples multiplied in *Jerusalem*
8:25. returned to *Jerusalem*, and preached
26. from *Jerusalem* unto Gaza,
27. to *Jerusalem* for to worship,
9: 2. might bring them bound unto *Jerusalem*.
13. to thy saints at *Jerusalem*:
21. that destroyed...in *Jerusalem*,
26. Saul was come to *Jerusalem*,
28. going out at *Jerusalem*.
10:39. the land of the Jews, and in *Jerusalem*;
12:25. And Barnabas and Saul returned from *Jerusalem*,
13:27. For they that dwell at *Jerusalem*, and their
31. came up with him from Galilee to *Jerusalem*,
15: 2. other of them, should go up to *Jerusalem*
4. And when they were come to *Jerusalem*,
16: 4. the apostles and elders which were at *Jerusalem*.
19:21. through Macedonia and Achaia, to go to *Jerusalem*,
20:22. I go bound in the spirit unto *Jerusalem*,
21: 4. that he should not go up to *Jerusalem*.
11. So shall the Jews at *Jerusalem* bind the
12. besought him not to go up to *Jerusalem*.
13. but also to die at *Jerusalem* for the
15. up our carriages, and went up to *Jerusalem*.
31. chief captain of the band, that all *Jerusalem*
22: 5. bring them which were there bound unto *Jerusalem*,
17. that, when I was come again to *Jerusalem*,
18. haste, and get thee quickly out of *Jerusalem*:
23:11. as thou hast testified of me in *Jerusalem*,
24:11. twelve days since I went up to *Jerusalem*

Acts25: 3. that he would send for him to *Jerusalem*,
20. asked (him) whether he would go to *Jerusalem*,
Ro. 15:19. so that from *Jerusalem*, and round
25. But now I go unto *Jerusalem* to minister
26. for the poor saints which are at *Jerusalem*.
31. that my service which (I have) for *Jerusalem*
1Co.16: 3. I send to bring your liberality unto *Jerusalem*.
Gal. 4:25. mount Sinai in Arabia, and answereth to *Jerusalem*
26. But *Jerusalem* which is above is free, which
Heb 12:22. city of the living God, the heavenly *Jerusalem*,
Rev. 3:12. city of my God, (which is) new *Jerusalem*,
21: 2. I John saw the holy city, new *Jerusalem*,
10. shewed me that great city, the holy *Jerusalem*,

2403 1 372/

Ἰεσαβήλ see **Ἰεζαβήλ**. p. 832

2421 5 374/475 [3448]

Ἰεσσαί, *Iessai*.

Mat. 1: 5. begat Obed of Ruth; and Obed begat *Jesse*;
6. And *Jesse* begat David the king; and David
Lu. 3:32. Which was (the son) of *Jesse*, which was
Acts13:22. I have found David the (son) of *Jesse*,
Ro. 15:12. saith, There shall be a root of *Jesse*,

2422 1 374/475 [3316]

Ἰεφθάε, *Iephthae*.

Heb 11:32. (of) Samson, and (of) *Jephthae*; (of) David also,

---

2423 2 374/475 [3204]

Ἰεχονίας, *Iekonias*.

Mat. 1:11. And Josias begat *Jechonias* and his brethren, about
12. And after they were brought to Babylon, *Jechonias*

2424 975 374/475 3:284 [3091]

Ἰησοῦς, *Ieesous*.

Mat. 1: 1. The book of the generation of *Jesus* Christ,
16. whom was born *Jesus*, who is called Christ.
18. Now the birth of *Jesus* Christ was on
21. a son, and thou shalt call his name *JESUS*:
25. firstborn son: and he called his name *JESUS*.
2: 1. when *Jesus* was born in Bethlehem of Judæa
3:13. Then cometh *Jesus* from Galilee to Jordan unto
15. And *Jesus* answering said unto him, Suffer
16. And *Jesus*, when he was baptized, went up
4: 1. Then was *Jesus* led up of the spirit
7. *Jesus* said unto him, It is written again,
10. Then saith *Jesus* unto him, Get thee hence,
12. Now when *Jesus* had heard that John was
17. From that time *Jesus* began to preach, and
18. And *Jesus*, walking by the sea of Galilee,
23. And *Jesus* went about all Galilee, teaching
7:28. And it came to pass, when *Jesus* had
8: 3. And *Jesus* put forth (his) hand, and touched
Mat. 8: 4. And *Jesus* saith unto him, See thou tell
5. And when *Jesus* was entered into Capernaum, there
7. And *Jesus* saith unto him, I will come
10. When *Jesus* heard (it), he marvelled, and
13. And *Jesus* said unto the centurion, Go thy
14. And when *Jesus* was come into Peter's
18. Now when *Jesus* saw great multitudes about him,
20. And *Jesus* saith unto him, The foxes have
22. But *Jesus* said unto him, Follow me; and
29. What have we to do with thee, *Jesus*,
34. the whole city came out to meet *Jesus*:
9: 2. *Jesus* seeing their faith said unto the sick
4. And *Jesus* knowing their thoughts said, Wherefore think
9. And as *Jesus* passed forth from thence, he
10. And it came to pass, as *Jesus* sat
12. when *Jesus* heard (that), he said unto them,
15. And *Jesus* said unto them, Can the children
19. And *Jesus* arose, and followed him, and
22. But *Jesus* turned him about, and when he
23. And when *Jesus* came into the ruler's house,
27. And when *Jesus* departed thence, two blind men
28. the blind men came to him: and *Jesus*
30. And their eyes were opened; and *Jesus*
35. *Jesus* went about all the cities and villages,
10: 5. These twelve *Jesus* sent forth, and commanded them,
11: 1. when *Jesus* had made an end of commanding
4. *Jesus* answered and said unto them, Go and
7. And as they departed, *Jesus* began to say
25. *Jesus* answered and said, I thank thee,
12: 1. At that time *Jesus* went on the sabbath
15. But when *Jesus* knew (it), he withdrew
25. And *Jesus* knew their thoughts, and said
13: 1. The same day went *Jesus* out of the
34. All these things spake *Jesus* unto the
36. Then *Jesus* sent the multitude away, and
51. *Jesus* saith unto them, Have ye understood
53. when *Jesus* had finished these parables, he
57. But *Jesus* said unto them, A prophet is
14: 1. the tetrarch heard of the fame of *Jesus*,
12. and buried it, and went and told *Jesus*.
13. When *Jesus* heard (of it), he departed
14. And *Jesus* went forth, and saw a great
16. But *Jesus* said unto them, They need not
22. And straightway *Jesus* constrained his disciples to get
25. in the fourth watch of the night *Jesus*
27. But straightway *Jesus* spake unto them,
29. walked on the water, to go to *Jesus*.
31. And immediately *Jesus* stretched forth (his) hand,
15: 1. Then came to *Jesus* scribes and Pharisees,
16. And *Jesus* said, Are ye also yet without
21. Then *Jesus* went thence, and departed into
28. *Jesus* answered and said unto her, O woman,
29. And *Jesus* departed from thence, and came nigh
30. and cast them down at *Jesus'* feet; and
32. Then *Jesus* called his disciples (unto him),
34. And *Jesus* saith unto them, How many
16: 6. Then *Jesus* said unto them, Take heed
8. (Which) when *Jesus* perceived, he said unto them,
13. When *Jesus* came into the coasts of Cæsarea
17. And *Jesus* answered and said unto him,

Mat.16:20. should tell no man that he was *Jesus*
21. From that time forth began *Jesus* to shew
24. Then said *Jesus* unto his disciples, If any
17: 1. after six days *Jesus* taketh Peter, James,
4. Then answered Peter, and said unto *Jesus*,
7. *Jesus* came and touched them, and said,
8. their eyes, they saw no man, save *Jesus*
9. as they came down from the mountain, *Jesus*
11. And *Jesus* answered and said unto them,
17. *Jesus* answered and said, O faithless and
18. And *Jesus* rebuked the devil; and he
19. Then came the disciples to *Jesus* apart,
20. *Jesus* said unto them, Because of your
22. while they abode in Galilee, *Jesus* said
25. when he was come into the house, *Jesus*
26. Peter saith unto him, Of strangers. *Jesus*
18: 1. the same time came the disciples unto *Jesus*,
2. And *Jesus* called a little child unto him,
22. *Jesus* saith unto him, I say not unto
19: 1. when *Jesus* had finished these sayings, he
14. But *Jesus* said, Suffer little children, and
18. Which? *Jesus* said, Thou shalt do no murder,
21. *Jesus* said unto him, If thou wilt be perfect,
23. Then said *Jesus* unto his disciples, Verily I
26. But *Jesus* beheld (them), and said unto
28. And *Jesus* said unto them, Verily I say
20:17. And *Jesus* going up to Jerusalem took the
22. But *Jesus* answered and said, Ye know
25. But *Jesus* called them (unto him), and
30. when they heard that *Jesus* passed by,
32. *Jesus* stood still, and called them, and
34. So *Jesus* had compassion (on them), and
21: 1. the mount of Olives, then sent *Jesus* two
6. the disciples went, and did as *Jesus* commanded
11. This is *Jesus* the prophet of Nazareth of Galilee.
12. And *Jesus* went into the temple of God,
16. Hearest thou what these say? And *Jesus*
21. *Jesus* answered and said unto them, Verily
24. *Jesus* answered and said unto them, I
27. they answered *Jesus*, and said, We cannot
31. The first. *Jesus* saith unto them, Verily I
42. *Jesus* saith unto them, Did ye never read
22: 1. And *Jesus* answered and spake unto them
18. *Jesus* perceived their wickedness, and said,
29. *Jesus* answered and said unto them, Ye do
37. *Jesus* said unto him, Thou shalt love the
41. While the Pharisees were gathered together, *Jesus* asked
23: 1. Then spake *Jesus* to the multitude, and to
24: 1. *Jesus* went out, and departed from the
2. And *Jesus* said unto them, See ye not
4. *Jesus* answered and said unto them, Take
26: 1. And it came to pass, when *Jesus* had
4. consulted that they might take *Jesus* by
6. Now when *Jesus* was in Bethany, in the
10. When *Jesus* understood (it), he said unto
17. (of) unleavened bread the disciples came to *Jesus*,
19. the disciples did as *Jesus* had appointed
26. And as they were eating, *Jesus* took bread,
31. Then saith *Jesus* unto them, All ye shall
34. *Jesus* said unto him, Verily I say unto
36. Then cometh *Jesus* with them unto a place
49. he came to *Jesus*, and said, Hail, master;
50. *Jesus* said unto him, Friend, wherefore
— Then came they, and laid hands on *Jesus*,
51. one of them which were with *Jesus*

Mat.26:52. Then said *Jesus* unto him, Put up again
55. In that same hour said *Jesus* to the
57. And they that had laid hold on *Jesus*
59. all the council, sought false witness against *Jesus*,
63. *Jesus* held his peace. And the high priest
64. *Jesus* saith unto him, Thou hast said:
69. saying, Thou also wast with *Jesus* of Galilee.
71. This (fellow) was also with *Jesus* of Nazareth.
75. Peter remembered the word of *Jesus*, which
27: 1. took counsel against *Jesus* to put him to
11. *Jesus* stood before the governor: and the
— And *Jesus* said unto him, Thou sayest.
17. that I release unto you? Barabbas, or *Jesus*
20. that they should ask Barabbas, and destroy *Jesus*.
22. What shall I do then with *Jesus* which
26. when he had scourged *Jesus*, he delivered
27. the soldiers of the governor took *Jesus*
37. THIS IS *JESUS* THE KING OF THE JEWS.
46. about the ninth hour *Jesus* cried with
50. *Jesus*, when he had cried again with a
54. watching *Jesus*, saw the earthquake, and
55. which followed *Jesus* from Galilee, ministering unto him:
57. named Joseph, who also himself was *Jesus*' disciple:
58. went to Pilate, and begged the body of *Jesus*.
28: 5. for I know that ye seek *Jesus*, which
9. *Jesus* met them, saying, All hail. And they
10. Then said *Jesus* unto them, Be not afraid:
16. into a mountain where *Jesus* had appointed
18. *Jesus* came and spake unto them, saying,
Mar 1: 1. The beginning of the gospel of *Jesus* Christ,
9. *Jesus* came from Nazareth of Galilee, and
14. after that John was put in prison, *Jesus*
17. *Jesus* said unto them, Come ye after me,
24. thou *Jesus* of Nazareth? art thou come to
25. *Jesus* rebuked him, saying, Hold thy peace,
41. And *Jesus*, moved with compassion, put forth (his)
2: 5. When *Jesus* saw their faith, he said unto
8. And immediately when *Jesus* perceived in his spirit
15. And it came to pass, that, as *Jesus*
17. When *Jesus* heard (it), he saith unto them,
19. *Jesus* said unto them, Can the children
3: 7. *Jesus* withdrew himself with his disciples to
5: 6. when he saw *Jesus* afar off, he ran
7. What have I to do with thee, *Jesus*,
13. And forthwith *Jesus* gave them leave. And
15. And they come to *Jesus*, and see him
19. Howbeit *Jesus* suffered him not, but saith
20. how great things *Jesus* had done for him:
21. And when *Jesus* was passed over again by
27. When she had heard of *Jesus*, came in
30. *Jesus*, immediately knowing in himself that
36. As soon as *Jesus* heard the word that
6: 4. But *Jesus* said unto them, A prophet is
30. And the apostles gathered themselves together unto *Jesus*,
34. And *Jesus*, when he came out, saw much
7:27. But *Jesus* said unto her, Let the children
8: 1. and having nothing to eat, *Jesus* called his
17. And when *Jesus* knew (it), he saith unto
27. And *Jesus* went out, and his disciples, into

Mar 9. 2. after six days *Jesus* taketh (with him) Peter,
4. with Moses: and they were talking with *Jesus*.
5. Peter answered and said to *Jesus*, Master,
8. they saw no man any more, save *Jesus*
23. *Jesus* said unto him, If thou canst believe,
25. When *Jesus* saw that the people came
27. But *Jesus* took him by the hand, and
39. But *Jesus* said, Forbid him not: for there
10: 5. And *Jesus* answered and said unto them,
14. But when *Jesus* saw (it), he was much
18. *Jesus* said unto him, Why callest thou me
21. Then *Jesus* beholding him loved him, and
23. And *Jesus* looked round about, and saith
24. But *Jesus* answereth again, and saith unto
27. *Jesus* looking upon them saith, With men
29. And *Jesus* answered and said, Verily I say
32. and *Jesus* went before them: and they were
38. But *Jesus* said unto them, Ye know not
39. *Jesus* said unto them, Ye shall indeed drink
42. But *Jesus* called them (to him), and saith
47. When he heard that it was *Jesus* of Nazareth, he began to cry out, and say, *Jesus*,
49. *Jesus* stood still, and commanded him to
50. away his garment, rose, and came to *Jesus*.
51. *Jesus* answered and said unto him, What
52. And *Jesus* said unto him, Go thy way;
— he received his sight, and followed *Jesus*
11: 6. And they said unto them even as *Jesus*
7. And they brought the colt to *Jesus*, and
11. *Jesus* entered into Jerusalem, and into the
14. And *Jesus* answered and said unto it, No
15. And they come to Jerusalem: and *Jesus*
22. *Jesus* answering saith unto them, Have faith
29. And *Jesus* answered and said unto them, I
33. And they answered and said unto *Jesus*,
— *Jesus* answering saith unto them, Neither
12:17. *Jesus* answering said unto them, Render
24. And *Jesus* answering said unto them, Do
29. *Jesus* answered him, The first of all the
34. when *Jesus* saw that he answered discreetly,
35. *Jesus* answered and said, while he taught
41. *Jesus* sat over against the treasury, and
13: 2. *Jesus* answering said unto him, Seest thou
5. *Jesus* answering them began to say, Take
14: 6. *Jesus* said, Let her alone; why trouble
18. And as they sat and did eat, *Jesus*
22. And as they did eat, *Jesus* took bread,
27. And *Jesus* saith unto them, All ye shall
30. And *Jesus* saith unto him, Verily I say
48. *Jesus* answered and said unto them, Are
53. they led *Jesus* away to the high priest:
55. all the council sought for witness against *Jesus*
60. and asked *Jesus*, saying, Answerest thou nothing?
62. And *Jesus* said, I am: and ye shall see
67. And thou also wast with *Jesus* of Nazareth.
72. Peter called to mind the word that *Jesus*
15: 1. and bound *Jesus*, and carried (him) away,
5. *Jesus* yet answered nothing; so that Pilate
15. and delivered *Jesus*, when he had scourged (him),
34. And at the ninth hour *Jesus* cried with
37. And *Jesus* cried with a loud voice,
43. unto Pilate, and craved the body of *Jesus*.
16: 6. Be not affrighted: Ye seek *Jesus* of Nazareth,
Lu. 1:31. a son, and shalt call his name *JESUS*.
2:21. his name was called *JESUS*, which was
27. when the parents brought in the child *Jesus*,

Lu. 2:43. as they returned, the child *Jesus* tarried
52. And *Jesus* increased in wisdom and stature,
3:21. it came to pass, that *Jesus* also being
23. And *Jesus* himself began to be about thirty
4: 1. And *Jesus* being full of the Holy Ghost
4. And *Jesus* answered him, saying, It is written,
8. *Jesus* answered and said unto him, Get
12. *Jesus* answering said unto him, It is said,
14. *Jesus* returned in the power of the Spirit
34. *Jesus* of Nazareth? art thou come to
35. And *Jesus* rebuked him, saying, Hold
5: 8. Peter saw (it), he fell down at *Jesus*'
10. And *Jesus* said unto Simon, Fear not;
12. a man full of leprosy: who seeing *Jesus*
19. with (his) couch into the midst before *Jesus*.
22. But when *Jesus* perceived their thoughts,
31. And *Jesus* answering said unto them,
6: 3. *Jesus* answering them said, Have ye not
9. Then said *Jesus* unto them, I will ask
11. with another what they might do to *Jesus*.
7. 3. And when he heard of *Jesus*, he sent
4. when they came to *Jesus*, they besought
6. Then *Jesus* went with them. And when
9. When *Jesus* heard these things, he
19. two of his disciples sent (them) to *Jesus*,
22. Then *Jesus* answering said unto them,
40. *Jesus* answering said unto him, Simon,
8:28. When he saw *Jesus*, he cried out, and
— What have I to do with thee, *Jesus*,
30. *Jesus* asked him, saying, What is thy
35. see what was done; and came to *Jesus*,
— sitting at the feet of *Jesus*,
38. that he might be with him: but *Jesus*
39. throughout the whole city how great things *Jesus*
40. And it came to pass, that, when *Jesus*
41. and he fell down at *Jesus*' feet, and
45. *Jesus* said, Who touched me? When all
46. And *Jesus* said, Somebody hath touched
50. But when *Jesus* heard (it), he answered
9:33. Peter said unto *Jesus*, Master, it is good
36. And when the voice was past, *Jesus* was
41. And *Jesus* answering said, O faithless
42. And *Jesus* rebuked the unclean spirit,
43. every one at all things which *Jesus* did,
47. And *Jesus*, perceiving the thought of their
50. And *Jesus* said unto him, Forbid (him)
58. And *Jesus* said unto him, Foxes have
60. *Jesus* said unto him, Let the dead bury
62. And *Jesus* said unto him, No man,
10:21. In that hour *Jesus* rejoiced in spirit, and
29. said unto *Jesus*, And who is my neighbour?
30. And *Jesus* answering said, A certain (man) went
37. Then said *Jesus* unto him, Go, and do
39. called Mary, which also sat at *Jesus*' feet,
41. *Jesus* answered and said unto her, Martha,
13: 2. And *Jesus* answering said unto them,
12. And when *Jesus* saw her, he called
14. because that *Jesus* had healed on the
14: 3. And *Jesus* answering spake unto the
17:13. they lifted up (their) voices, and said *Jesus*,
17. *Jesus* answering said, Were there not ten
18:16. But *Jesus* called them (unto him), and
19. *Jesus* said unto him, Why callest thou
22. Now when *Jesus* heard these things, he
24. when *Jesus* saw that he was very sorrowful.
37. And they told him, that *Jesus* of Nazareth
38. he cried, saying, *Jesus*, (thou) son of

Lu. 18:40. *Jesus* stood, and commanded him to be
42. And *Jesus* said unto him, Receive thy
19: 3. And he sought to see *Jesus* who he was;
5. And when *Jesus* came to the place, he
9. *Jesus* said unto him, This day is salvation
35. And they brought him to *Jesus:* and
— upon the colt, and they set *Jesus* thereon.
20: 8. And *Jesus* said unto them, Neither tell I
34. And *Jesus* answering said unto them, The children
22:47. and drew near unto *Jesus* to kiss him.
48. But *Jesus* said unto him, Judas, betrayest thou
51. *Jesus* answered and said, Suffer ye thus
52. Then *Jesus* said unto the chief priests,
63. And the men that held *Jesus* mocked him,
23: 8. And when Herod saw *Jesus*, he was
20. Pilate therefore, willing to release *Jesus*,
25. whom they had desired; but he delivered *Jesus*
26. cross, that he might bear (it) after *Jesus*.
28. But *Jesus* turning unto them said,
34. Then said *Jesus*, Father, forgive them;
42. And he said unto *Jesus*, Lord, remember
43. And *Jesus* said unto him, Verily I say
46. And when *Jesus* had cried with a loud
52. unto Pilate, and begged the body of *Jesus*.
24: 3. found not the body of the Lord *Jesus*.
15. and reasoned, *Jesus* himself drew near,
19. they said unto him, Concerning *Jesus* of
36. And as they thus spake, *Jesus* himself
Joh. 1:17. grace and truth came by *Jesus* Christ.
29. The next day John seeth *Jesus* coming
36. And looking upon *Jesus* as he walked, he
37. disciples heard him speak, and they followed *Jesus*.
38. *Jesus* turned, and saw them following,
42(43). he brought him to *Jesus*. And when *Jesus* beheld
43(44). The day following *Jesus* would go
45(46). and the prophets, did write, *Jesus* of
47(48). *Jesus* saw Nathanael coming to him,
48(49). Whence knowest thou me? *Jesus* answered and said
50(51). *Jesus* answered and said unto him,
2: 1. Cana of Galilee; and the mother of *Jesus*
2. *Jesus* was called, and his disciples, to the
3. they wanted wine, the mother of *Jesus*
4. *Jesus* saith unto her, Woman, what have
7. *Jesus* saith unto them, Fill the waterpots
11. This beginning of miracles did *Jesus* in
13. the Jews' passover was at hand, and *Jesus*
19. *Jesus* answered and said unto them,
22. believed the scripture, and the word which *Jesus*
24. But *Jesus* did not commit himself unto
3: 2. The same came to *Jesus* by night, and
3. *Jesus* answered and said unto him, Verily,
5. *Jesus* answered, Verily, verily, I say unto
10. *Jesus* answered and said unto him, Art
22. After these things came *Jesus* and his
4: 1. that *Jesus* made and baptized more disciples than
2. Though *Jesus* himself baptized not, but his
6. Jacob's well was there. *Jesus* therefore,
7. a woman of Samaria to draw water: *Jesus*
10. *Jesus* answered and said unto her, If thou
13. *Jesus* answered and said unto her,
16. *Jesus* saith unto her, Go, call thy husband,
17. I have no husband. *Jesus* said unto her,
21. *Jesus* saith unto her, Woman, believe me,
26. *Jesus* saith unto her, I that speak unto

Joh. 4:34. *Jesus* saith unto them, My meat is to
44. For *Jesus* himself testified, that a prophet
46. So *Jesus* came again into Cana of Galilee.
47. When he heard that *Jesus* was come out
48. Then said *Jesus* unto him, Except ye see
50. *Jesus* saith unto him, Go thy way;
— And the man believed the word that *Jesus*
53. which *Jesus* said unto him, Thy son liveth:
54. This (is) again the second miracle (that) *Jesus*
5: 1. was a feast of the Jews; and *Jesus*
6. When *Jesus* saw him lie, and knew that
8. *Jesus* saith unto him, Rise, take up thy
13. for *Jesus* had conveyed himself away, a multitude
14. Afterward *Jesus* findeth him in the temple,
15. and told the Jews that it was *Jesus*,
16. And therefore did the Jews persecute *Jesus*,
17. But *Jesus* answered them, My Father worketh hitherto,
19. Then answered *Jesus* and said unto them,
6: 1. *Jesus* went over the sea of Galilee, which
3. And *Jesus* went up into a mountain, and
5. When *Jesus* then lifted up (his) eyes, and
10. And *Jesus* said, Make the men sit down.
11. And *Jesus* took the loaves; and when he
14. the miracle that *Jesus* did, said, This is
15. When *Jesus* therefore perceived that they would come
17. And it was now dark, and *Jesus* was not
19. they see *Jesus* walking on the sea, and
22. and that *Jesus* went not with his disciples
24. *Jesus* was not there, neither his disciples,
— and came to Capernaum, seeking for *Jesus*,
26. *Jesus* answered them and said, Verily,
29. *Jesus* answered and said unto them,
32. Then *Jesus* said unto them, Verily, verily,
35. And *Jesus* said unto them, I am the
42. And they said, Is not this *Jesus*, the
43. *Jesus* therefore answered and said unto them, Murmur
53. Then *Jesus* said unto them, Verily, verily
61. When *Jesus* knew in himself that his
64. For *Jesus* knew from the beginning who
67. Then said *Jesus* unto the twelve, Will ye
70. *Jesus* answered them, Have not I chosen
7: 1. After these things *Jesus* walked in Galilee:
6. Then *Jesus* said unto them, My time is
14. Now about the midst of the feast *Jesus*
16. *Jesus* answered them, and said, My doctrine is
21. *Jesus* answered and said unto them, I have
28. Then cried *Jesus* in the temple as he
33. Then said *Jesus* unto them, Yet a little
37. that great (day) of the feast, *Jesus* stood
39. not yet (given); because that *Jesus* was
8: 1. *Jesus* went unto the mount of Olives.
6. But *Jesus* stooped down, and with (his)
9. and *Jesus* was left alone, and the woman
10. When *Jesus* had lifted up himself,
11. She said, No man, Lord. And *Jesus* said
12. Then spake *Jesus* again unto them, saying,
14. *Jesus* answered and said unto them, Though
19. Where is thy Father? *Jesus* answered, Ye neither know me,
20. These words spake *Jesus* in the treasury,
21. Then said *Jesus* again unto them, I go
25. And *Jesus* saith unto them, Even (the same)
28. Then said *Jesus* unto them, When ye have
31. Then said *Jesus* to those Jews which
34. *Jesus* answered them, Verily, verily, I say
39. Abraham is our father. *Jesus* saith unto

Joh. 8:42. *Jesus* said unto them, If God were your
49. *Jesus* answered, I have not a devil; but
54. *Jesus* answered, If I honour myself, my
58. *Jesus* said unto them, Verily, verily, I say
59. but *Jesus* hid himself, and went out of
9: 3. *Jesus* answered, Neither hath this man
11. A man that is called *Jesus* made clay,
14. the sabbath day when *Jesus* made the clay,
35. *Jesus* heard that they had cast him out;
37. And *Jesus* said unto him, Thou hast both
39. And *Jesus* said, For judgment I am come
41. *Jesus* said unto them, If ye were blind,
10: 6. This parable spake *Jesus* unto them: but
7. Then said *Jesus* unto them again, Verily,
23. *Jesus* walked in the temple in Solomon's
25. *Jesus* answered them, I told you, and ye
32. *Jesus* answered them, Many good works have I
34. *Jesus* answered them, Is it not written in
11: 4. When *Jesus* heard (that), he said, This
5. Now *Jesus* loved Martha, and her sister,
9. *Jesus* answered, Are there not twelve hours
13. Howbeit *Jesus* spake of his death: but they
14. Then said *Jesus* unto them plainly, Lazarus is dead.
17. Then when *Jesus* came, he found that he
20. Martha, as soon as she heard that *Jesus*
21. Then said Martha unto *Jesus*, Lord, if thou
23. *Jesus* saith unto her, Thy brother
25. *Jesus* said unto her, I am the resurrection,
30. Now *Jesus* was not yet come into the town,
32. Then when Mary was come where *Jesus*
33. When *Jesus* therefore saw her weeping,
35. *Jesus* wept.
38. *Jesus* therefore again groaning in himself
39. *Jesus* said, Take ye away the stone. Martha,
40. *Jesus* saith unto her, Said I not unto
41. And *Jesus* lifted up (his) eyes, and said,
44. *Jesus* saith unto them, Loose him, and let
45. and had seen the things which *Jesus* did,
46. and told them what things *Jesus* had done.
51. he prophesied that *Jesus* should die for that
54. *Jesus* therefore walked no more openly among the
56. Then sought they for *Jesus*, and spake
12: 1. Then *Jesus* six days before the passover
3. And anointed the feet of *Jesus*, and wiped
7. Then said *Jesus*, Let her alone: against the
9. and they came not for *Jesus*' sake only,
11. the Jews went away, and believed on *Jesus*.
12. when they heard that *Jesus* was coming to
14. And *Jesus*, when he had found a young
16. but when *Jesus* was glorified, then
21. desired him, saying, Sir, we would see *Jesus*.
22. Andrew: and again Andrew and Philip tell *Jesus*.
23. And *Jesus* answered them, saying, The
30. *Jesus* answered and said, This voice came
35. Then *Jesus* said unto them, Yet a little
36. These things spake *Jesus*, and departed,
44. *Jesus* cried and said, He that believeth on
13: 1. before the feast of the passover, when *Jesus*
3. *Jesus* knowing that the Father had given
7. *Jesus* answered and said unto him, What I
8. Thou shalt never wash my feet. *Jesus*
10. *Jesus* saith to him, He that is washed
21. When *Jesus* had thus said, he was troubled
23. Now there was leaning on *Jesus*' bosom one of his disciples, whom *Jesus* loved.

Joh. 13:25. He then lying on *Jesus*' breast saith unto
26. *Jesus* answered, He it is, to whom I
27. Then said *Jesus* unto him, That thou doest,
29. because Judas had the bag, that *Jesus* had
31. Therefore, when he was gone out, *Jesus*
36. *Jesus* answered him, Whither I go, thou
38. *Jesus* answered him, Wilt thou lay down
14: 6. *Jesus* saith unto him, I am the way,
9. *Jesus* saith unto him, Have I been so
23. *Jesus* answered and said unto him, If a
16:19. Now *Jesus* knew that they were desirous
31. *Jesus* answered them, Do ye now believe?
17: 1. These words spake *Jesus*, and lifted up his
3. the only true God, and *Jesus* Christ,
18: 1. When *Jesus* had spoken these words,
2. which betrayed him, knew the place: for *Jesus*
4. *Jesus* therefore, knowing all things that should come
5. They answered him, *Jesus* of Nazareth *Jesus* saith
7. Whom seek ye? And they said, *Jesus* of
8. *Jesus* answered, I have told you that I
11. Then said *Jesus* unto Peter, Put up thy
12. captain and officers of the Jews took *Jesus*,
15. And Simon Peter followed *Jesus*,
— and went in with *Jesus* into the palace
19. The high priest then asked *Jesus* of his
20. *Jesus* answered him, I spake openly to the
22. which stood by struck *Jesus* with the palm
23. *Jesus* answered him, If I have spoken evil,
28. Then led they *Jesus* from Caiaphas unto
32. That the saying of *Jesus* might be fulfilled,
33. and called *Jesus*, and said unto him, Art
34. *Jesus* answered him, Sayest thou this thing
36. *Jesus* answered, My kingdom is not of this
37. Art thou a king then? *Jesus* answered, Thou
19: 1. Then Pilate therefore took *Jesus*, and scourged (him).
5. Then came *Jesus* forth, wearing the crown
9. and saith unto *Jesus*, Whence art thou? But *Jesus* gave him no answer.
11. *Jesus* answered, Thou couldest have no
13. he brought *Jesus* forth, and sat down in
16. And they took *Jesus*, and led (him) away.
18. on either side one, and *Jesus* in the
19. *JESUS* OF NAZARETH THE KING OF THE JEWS.
20. for the place where *Jesus* was crucified was
23. Then the soldiers, when they had crucified *Jesus*,
25. Now there stood by the cross of *Jesus*
26. When *Jesus* therefore saw his mother, and
28. After this, *Jesus* knowing that all things
30. When *Jesus* therefore had received the vinegar,
33. But when they came to *Jesus*, and saw
38. Joseph of Arimathæa, being a disciple of *Jesus*,
— that he might take away the body of *Jesus*:
— He came therefore, and took the body of *Jesus*.
39. Nicodemus, which at the first came to *Jesus*
40. Then took they the body of *Jesus*, and
42. There laid they *Jesus* therefore because of
20: 2. and to the other disciple, whom *Jesus* loved,
12. at the feet, where the body of *Jesus*
14. she turned herself back, and saw *Jesus* standing, and knew not that it was *Jesus*.
15. *Jesus* saith unto her, Woman, why weepest
16. *Jesus* saith unto her, Mary. She turned
17. *Jesus* saith unto her, Touch me not: for

Joh 20:19. for fear of the Jews, came *Jesus* and
21. Then said *Jesus* to them again, Peace (be)
24. Didymus, was not with them when *Jesus*
26. (then) came *Jesus*, the doors being shut,
29. *Jesus* saith unto him, Thomas, because thou hast
30. And many other signs truly did *Jesus* in
31. believe that *Jesus* is the Christ, the Son
21: 1. After these things *Jesus* shewed himself
4. was now come, *Jesus* stood on the shore: but the disciples knew not that it was *Jesus*.
5. Then *Jesus* saith unto them, Children, have
7. that disciple whom *Jesus* loved saith unto Peter,
10. *Jesus* saith unto them, Bring of the fish
12. *Jesus* saith unto them, Come (and) dine.
13. *Jesus* then cometh, and taketh bread, and
14. This is now the third time that *Jesus*
15. when they had dined, *Jesus* saith to Simon
17. I love thee. *Jesus* saith unto him, Feed
20. Peter, turning about, seeth the disciple whom *Jesus*
21. Peter seeing him saith to *Jesus*, Lord, and
22. *Jesus* saith unto him, If I will that
23. yet *Jesus* said not unto him, He shall
25. which *Jesus* did, the which, if they should
Acts 1: 1. O Theophilus, of all that *Jesus* began both
11. ye gazing up into heaven? this same *Jesus*,
14. and Mary the mother of *Jesus*, and with
16. which was guide to them that took *Jesus*.
21. all the time that the Lord *Jesus* went in
2:22. Ye men of Israel, hear these words; *Jesus*
32. This *Jesus* hath God raised up, whereof we
36. that God hath made that same *Jesus*, whom
38. in the name of *Jesus* Christ for the
3: 6. In the name of *Jesus* Christ of Nazareth
13. of our fathers, hath glorified his Son *Jesus*.
20. he shall send *Jesus* Christ, which before
26. God, having raised up his Son *Jesus*, sent
4: 2. and preached through *Jesus* the resurrection from the
10. by the name of *Jesus* Christ of Nazareth,
13. of them, that they had been with *Jesus*.
18. all nor teach in the name of *Jesus*.
27. of a truth against thy holy child *Jesus*,
30. by the name of thy holy child *Jesus*.
33. witness of the resurrection of the Lord *Jesus*:
5:30. The God of our fathers raised up *Jesus*,
40. should not speak in the name of *Jesus*,
42. ceased not to teach and preach *Jesus* Christ.
6:14. that this *Jesus* of Nazareth shall destroy this
7:55. and saw the glory of God, and *Jesus*
59. Stephen, calling upon (God), and saying, Lord *Jesus*,
8:12. and the name of *Jesus* Christ, they were
16. baptized in the name of the Lord *Jesus*.
35. the same scripture, and preached unto him *Jesus*.
37. I believe that *Jesus* Christ is the Son
9: 5. And the Lord said, I am *Jesus* whom
17. Brother Saul, the Lord, (even) *Jesus*, that
27. boldly at Damascus in the name of *Jesus*.
29(28). boldly in the name of the Lord *Jesus*,
34. Peter said unto him, Æneas, *Jesus* Christ
10:36. preaching peace by *Jesus* Christ:
38. How God anointed *Jesus* of Nazareth with
11:17. who believed on the Lord *Jesus* Christ;
20. spake unto the Grecians, preaching the Lord *Jesus*.
13:23. promise raised unto Israel a Saviour, *Jesus*:

Acts13:33(32). in that he hath raised up *Jesus* again,
15:11. that through the grace of the Lord *Jesus*
26. their lives for the name of our Lord *Jesus*
16:18. I command thee in the name of *Jesus*
31. Believe on the Lord *Jesus* Christ, and thou
17: 3. risen again from the dead; and that this *Jesus*,
7. that there is another king, (one) *Jesus*.
18. he preached unto them *Jesus*, and the
18: 5. and testified to the Jews (that) *Jesus* (was) Christ.
28. shewing by the scriptures that *Jesus* was Christ.
19: 4. come after him, that is, on Christ *Jesus*.
5. baptized in the name of the Lord *Jesus*.
10. Asia heard the word of the Lord *Jesus*,
13. evil spirits the name of the Lord *Jesus*, saying, We adjure you by *Jesus* whom
15. evil spirit answered and said, *Jesus* I know,
17. and the name of the Lord *Jesus* was
20:21. and faith toward our Lord *Jesus* Christ.
24. which I have received of the Lord *Jesus*,
35. to remember the words of the Lord *Jesus*,
21:13. Jerusalem for the name of the Lord *Jesus*.
22: 8. And he said unto me, I am *Jesus*
25:19. and of one *Jesus*, which was dead, whom
26: 9. contrary to the name of *Jesus* of Nazareth.
15. And he said, I am *Jesus* whom thou
28:23. the kingdom of God, persuading them concerning *Jesus*,
31. which concern the Lord *Jesus* Christ, with all confidence,
Ro. 1: 1. Paul, a servant of *Jesus* Christ, called (to be)
3(4). his Son *Jesus* Christ our Lord,
6. are ye also the called of *Jesus* Christ:
7. God our Father, and the Lord *Jesus* Christ.
8. I thank my God through *Jesus* Christ
2:16. secrets of men by *Jesus* Christ according
3:22. (which is) by faith of *Jesus* Christ unto
24. the redemption that is in Christ *Jesus*:
26. the justifier of him which believeth in *Jesus*.
4:24. on him that raised up *Jesus* our Lord
5: 1. peace with God through our Lord *Jesus* Christ:
11. joy in God through our Lord *Jesus* Christ,
15. (which is) by one man, *Jesus* Christ, hath
17. shall reign in life by one, *Jesus* Christ.
21. righteousness unto eternal life by *Jesus* Christ
6: 3. baptized into *Jesus* Christ were baptized
11. unto God through *Jesus* Christ our Lord.
23. God (is) eternal life through *Jesus* Christ
7:25. I thank God through *Jesus* Christ our Lord.
8: 1. which are in Christ *Jesus*, who walk not
2. of the Spirit of life in Christ *Jesus*
11. the Spirit of him that raised up *Jesus*
39. love of God, which is in Christ *Jesus*
10: 9. confess with thy mouth the Lord *Jesus*,
13:14. But put ye on the Lord *Jesus* Christ,
14:14. I know, and am persuaded by the Lord *Jesus*,
15: 5. toward another according to Christ *Jesus*:
6. the Father of our Lord *Jesus* Christ.
8. Now I say that *Jesus* Christ
16. I should be the minister of *Jesus* Christ
17. I may glory through *Jesus* Christ
30. for the Lord *Jesus* Christ's sake
16: 3. my helpers in Christ *Jesus*:
18. serve not our Lord *Jesus* Christ,
20. The grace of our Lord *Jesus* Christ
24. The grace of our Lord *Jesus* Christ

Ro. 16:25. and the preaching of *Jesus* Christ,
27. (be) glory through *Jesus* Christ
1Co. 1: 1. (to be) an apostle of *Jesus* Christ
2. to them that are sanctifed in Christ *Jesus*,
— call upon the name of *Jesus* Christ
3. and (from) the Lord *Jesus* Christ.
4. which is given you by *Jesus* Christ;
7. coming of our Lord *Jesus* Christ:
8. in the day of our Lord *Jesus* Christ.
9. of his Son *Jesus* Christ our Lord.
10. by the name of our Lord *Jesus* Christ,
30. But of him are ye in Christ *Jesus*,
2: 2. save *Jesus* Christ, and him crucified.
3:11. that is laid, which is *Jesus* Christ.
4:15. for in Christ *Jesus* I have begotten you
5: 4. In the name of our Lord *Jesus*
— the power of our Lord *Jesus* Christ,
5. in the day of the Lord *Jesus*.
6:11. in the name of the Lord *Jesus*,
8: 6. and one Lord *Jesus* Christ,
9: 1. have I not seen *Jesus* Christ our Lord?
11:23. That the Lord *Jesus* the (same) night
12: 3. Spirit of God calleth *Jesus* accursed: and (that) no man can say that *Jesus*
15:31. I have in Christ *Jesus* our Lord,
57. through our Lord *Jesus* Christ.
16:22. love not the Lord *Jesus* Christ,
23. The grace of our Lord *Jesus* Christ
24. My love (be) with you all in Christ *Jesus*.
2Co. 1: 1. Paul, an apostle of *Jesus* Christ
2. and (from) the Lord *Jesus* Christ.
3. the Father of our Lord *Jesus* Christ,
14. in the day of the Lord *Jesus*.
19. For the Son of God, *Jesus* Christ,
4: 5. but Christ *Jesus* the Lord;
— your servants for *Jesus*' sake.
6. in the face of *Jesus* Christ.
10. the dying of the Lord *Jesus*, that the life also of *Jesus*
11. delivered unto death for *Jesus*' sake, that the life also of *Jesus*
14. the Lord *Jesus* shall raise up us also by *Jesus*, and shall present (us) with
5:18. reconciled us to himself by *Jesus* Christ,
8: 9. the grace of our Lord *Jesus* Christ,
11: 4. he that cometh preacheth another *Jesus*,
31. and Father of our Lord *Jesus* Christ,
13: 5. how that *Jesus* Christ is in you,
14(13). The grace of the Lord *Jesus* Christ,
Gal. 1: 1. by *Jesus* Christ, and God the Father,
3. and (from) our Lord *Jesus* Christ,
12. by the revelation of *Jesus* Christ.
2: 4. which we have in Christ *Jesus*,
16. but by the faith of *Jesus* Christ, even we have believed in *Jesus* Christ,
3. 1. before whose eyes *Jesus* Christ
14. come on the Gentiles through *Jesus* Christ;
22. that the promise by faith of *Jesus* Christ
26. by faith in Christ *Jesus*.
28. for ye are all one in Christ *Jesus*.
4:14. an angel of God, (even) as Christ *Jesus*.
5: 6. For in *Jesus* Christ neither circumcision
6:14. save in the cross of our Lord *Jesus* Christ,
15. For in Christ *Jesus* neither circumcision
17. the marks of the Lord *Jesus*.
18. the grace of our Lord *Jesus* Christ
Eph. 1: 1 Paul, an apostle of *Jesus* Christ
and to the faithful in Christ *Jesus*:
2. and (from) the Lord *Jesus* Christ.
3. and Father of our Lord *Jesus* Christ,
5. the adoption of children by *Jesus* Christ
Eph. 1:15. I heard of your faith in the Lord *Jesus*,
17. the God of our Lord *Jesus* Christ,
2: 6. in heavenly (places) in Christ *Jesus*:
7. kindness toward us through Christ *Jesus*.
10. created in Christ *Jesus* unto good works,
13. But now in Christ *Jesus*
20. *Jesus* Christ himself being the chief
3: 1. the prisoner of *Jesus* Christ
9. who created all things by *Jesus* Christ:
11. purposed in Christ *Jesus* our Lord:
14. the Father of our Lord *Jesus* Christ,
21. by Christ *Jesus* throughout all ages,
4:21. as the truth is in *Jesus*:
5:20. in the name of our Lord *Jesus* Christ;
6:23. and the Lord *Jesus* Christ.
24. that love our Lord *Jesus* Christ
Phi. 1: 1. the servants of *Jesus* Christ, to all the saints in Christ *Jesus*
2. and (from) the Lord *Jesus* Christ.
6. until the day of *Jesus* Christ:
8. in the bowels of *Jesus* Christ.
11. which are by *Jesus* Christ,
19. of the Spirit of *Jesus* Christ,
26. may be more abundant in *Jesus* Christ
2: 5. which was also in Christ *Jesus*:
10. That at the name of *Jesus*
11. should confess that *Jesus* Christ (is) Lord,
19. But I trust in the Lord *Jesus*
21. not the things which are *Jesus* Christ's.
3: 3. and rejoice in Christ *Jesus*,
8. of the knowledge of Christ *Jesus*
12. I am apprehended of Christ *Jesus*.
14. the high calling of God in Christ *Jesus*.
20. the Saviour, the Lord *Jesus* Christ:
4: 7. hearts and minds through Christ *Jesus*.
19. to his riches in glory by Christ *Jesus*.
21. Salute every saint in Christ *Jesus*.
23. The grace of our Lord *Jesus* Christ
Col. 1: 1. Paul, an apostle of *Jesus* Christ
2. our Father and the Lord *Jesus* Christ.
3. the Father of our Lord *Jesus* Christ,
4. we heard of your faith in Christ *Jesus*,
28. every man perfect in Christ *Jesus*:
2: 6. therefore received Christ *Jesus* the Lord,
3:17. (do) all in the name of the Lord *Jesus*,
1Th. 1: 1. and (in) the Lord *Jesus* Christ:
— and the Lord *Jesus* Christ.
3. patience of hope in our Lord *Jesus* Christ,
10. whom he raised from the dead, (even) *Jesus*,
2:14. which in Judæa are in Christ *Jesus*:
15. Who both killed the Lord *Jesus*,
19. in the presence of our Lord *Jesus* Christ
3:11. and our Lord *Jesus* Christ,
13. at the coming of our Lord *Jesus* Christ
4: 1. exhort (you) by the Lord *Jesus*,
2. we gave you by the Lord *Jesus*.
14. if we believe that *Jesus* died
— them also which sleep in *Jesus*
5: 9. salvation by our Lord *Jesus* Christ,
18. this is the will of God in Christ *Jesus*
23. the coming of our Lord *Jesus* Christ.
28. The grace of our Lord *Jesus* Christ
2Th. 1: 1. and the Lord *Jesus* Christ:
2. and the Lord *Jesus* Christ.
7. the Lord *Jesus* shall be revealed
8. the gospel of our Lord *Jesus* Christ:
12. the name of our Lord *Jesus* Christ
— our God and the Lord *Jesus* Christ.
2: 1. the coming of our Lord *Jesus* Christ,
14. of the glory of our Lord *Jesus* Christ.
16. Now our Lord *Jesus* Christ

2Th 3: 6. in the name of our Lord *Jesus* Christ,
12. and exhort by our Lord *Jesus* Christ,
18. The grace of our Lord *Jesus* Christ
1Ti. 1: 1. Paul, an apostle of *Jesus* Christ
— our Saviour, and Lord *Jesus* Christ,
2. our Father and *Jesus* Christ our Lord.
12. And I thank Christ *Jesus* our Lord,
14. and love which is in Christ *Jesus*.
15. that Christ *Jesus* came into the world
16. that in me first *Jesus* Christ
2: 5. the man Christ *Jesus*;
3:13. in the faith which is in Christ *Jesus*.
4: 6. a good minister of *Jesus* Christ,
5:21. before God, and the Lord *Jesus* Christ,
6: 3. the words of our Lord *Jesus* Christ,
13. and (before) Christ *Jesus*,
14. appearing of our Lord *Jesus* Christ:
2Ti. 1: 1. Paul, an apostle of *Jesus* Christ
— of life which is in Christ *Jesus*,
2. the Father and Christ *Jesus* our Lord.
9. which was given us in Christ *Jesus*
10. appearing of our Saviour *Jesus* Christ,
13. and love which is in Christ *Jesus*.
2: 1. the grace that is in Christ *Jesus*.
3. as a good soldier of *Jesus* Christ.
8. Remember that *Jesus* Christ
10. the salvation which is in Christ *Jesus*
3:12. all that will live godly in Christ *Jesus*
15. through faith which is in Christ *Jesus*.
4: 1. before God, and the Lord *Jesus* Christ,
22. The Lord *Jesus* Christ (be) with thy spirit.
Tit. 1: 1. and an apostle of *Jesus* Christ,
4. and the Lord *Jesus* Christ our Saviour.
2:13. God and our Saviour *Jesus* Christ;
3: 6. through *Jesus* Christ our Saviour;
Philem. 1. Paul, a prisoner of *Jesus* Christ,
3. our Father and the Lord *Jesus* Christ.
5. which thou hast toward the Lord *Jesus*,
6. which is in you in Christ *Jesus*.
9. now also a prisoner of *Jesus* Christ.
23. my fellowprisoner in Christ *Jesus*;
25. The grace of our Lord *Jesus* Christ
Heb 2: 9. But we see *Jesus*, who was made
3: 1. of our profession, Christ *Jesus*;
4:14. *Jesus* the Son of God,
6:20. (even) *Jesus*, made an high priest
7:22. By so much was *Jesus* made
10:10. of the body of *Jesus* Christ once (for all).
19. into the holiest by the blood of *Jesus*,
12: 2. Looking unto *Jesus* the author
24. And to *Jesus* the mediator
13: 8. *Jesus* Christ the same yesterday,
12. Wherefore *Jesus* also, that he might
20. again from the dead our Lord *Jesus*,
21. in his sight, through *Jesus* Christ;
Jas. 1: 1. and of the Lord *Jesus* Christ,
2: 1. the faith of our Lord *Jesus* Christ,
1Pet. 1: 1. Peter, an apostle of *Jesus* Christ,
2. sprinkling of the blood of *Jesus* Christ:
3. and Father of our Lord *Jesus* Christ,
— by the resurrection of *Jesus* Christ
7. at the appearing of *Jesus* Christ:
13. at the revelation of *Jesus* Christ;
2: 5. acceptable to God by *Jesus* Christ.
3:21. by the resurrection of *Jesus* Christ:
4:11. may be glorified through *Jesus* Christ,
5:10. unto his eternal glory by Christ *Jesus*,
14. Peace (be) with you all that are in Christ *Jesus*.
2Pet. 1: 1. and an apostle of *Jesus* Christ,
— of God and our Saviour *Jesus* Christ:
2. and of *Jesus* our Lord,
2Pet. 1: 8. the knowledge of our Lord *Jesus* Christ
11. of our Lord and Saviour *Jesus* Christ.
14. our Lord *Jesus* Christ hath shewed me.
16. and coming of our Lord *Jesus* Christ,
2:20. of the Lord and Saviour *Jesus* Christ,
3:18. of our Lord and Saviour *Jesus* Christ.
1Joh. 1: 3. and with his Son *Jesus* Christ.
7. the blood of *Jesus* Christ his Son
2: 1. *Jesus* Christ the righteous:
22. he that denieth that *Jesus* is the Christ?
3:23. on the name of his Son *Jesus* Christ
4: 2. that *Jesus* Christ is come in the flesh
3. that *Jesus* Christ is come in the flesh
15. Whosoever shall confess that *Jesus*
5: 1. Whosoever believeth that *Jesus*
5. believeth that *Jesus* is the Son of God?
6. by water and blood, (even) *Jesus* Christ;
20. (even) in his Son *Jesus* Christ.
2Joh. 3. and from the Lord *Jesus* Christ,
7. that *Jesus* Christ is come in the flesh.
Jude 1. Jude, the servant of *Jesus* Christ,
— and preserved in *Jesus* Christ,
4. and our Lord *Jesus* Christ.
17. the apostles of our Lord *Jesus* Christ;
21. for the mercy of our Lord *Jesus* Christ
Rev. 1: 1. The Revelation of *Jesus* Christ,
2. and of the testimony of *Jesus* Christ,
5. And from *Jesus* Christ,
9. the kingdom and patience of *Jesus* Christ,
— the testimony of *Jesus* Christ.
12:17. and have the testimony of *Jesus* Christ.
14:12. of God, and the faith of *Jesus*.
17: 6. the blood of the martyrs of *Jesus*:
19:10. that have the testimony of *Jesus*:
— for the testimony of *Jesus*
20: 4. beheaded for the witness of *Jesus*,
22:16. I *Jesus* have sent mine angel
20. Even so, come, Lord *Jesus*.
21. The grace of our Lord *Jesus* Christ

2424 2 /485 [3091]

Ἰησοῦς, *Ieesous*.

(Joshua).

Acts 7:45. that came after brought in with *Jesus*
Heb 4: 8. For if *Jesus* had given them rest,

2424 1 /485 [3091]

Ἰησοῦς, *Ieesous*.

(Justus).

Col. 4:11. And *Jesus*, which is called Justus,

2430 2 376/486 1504

Ἰκόνιον, *Ikonion*.

Acts 13:51. and came unto *Iconium*.
14: 1. And it came to pass in *Iconium*,
19. Jews from Antioch and *Iconium*,
21. and (to) *Iconium*, and Antioch,
16: 2. that were at Lystra and *Iconium*.
2Ti. 3:11. at Antioch, at *Iconium*, at Lystra;

2437 1 376/486

Ἰλλυρικόν, *Illurikon*.

Ro. 15:19. and round about unto *Illyricum*.

2445 10 379/495 [3305]

Ἰόππη, *Ïoppee*.

Acts 9:36. Now there was at *Joppa*
38. forasmuch as Lydda was nigh to *Joppa*,
42. And it was known throughout all *Joppa*,
43. that he tarried many days in *Joppa*

Acts10: 5. And now send men to *Joppa*,
8. he sent them to *Joppa*.
23. and certain brethren from *Joppa*
32. Send therefore to *Joppa*,
11: 5. I was in the city of *Joppa*
13. said unto him, Send men to *Joppa*,

2446 15 379/495 6:595 [3383]

Ἰορδάνης, *Iordanees*.

Mat. 3: 5. and all the region round about *Jordan*,
6. And were baptized of him in *Jordan*,
13. Then cometh Jesus from Galilee to *Jordan*
4:15. (by) the way of the sea, beyond *Jordan*,
25. and (from) beyond *Jordan*.
19: 1. the coasts of Judæa beyond *Jordan*;
Mar 1: 5. baptized of him in the river of *Jordan*,
9. was baptized of John in *Jordan*.
3: 8. and (from) beyond *Jordan*;
10: 1. by the farther side of *Jordan*:
Lu. 3: 3. into all the country about *Jordan*,
4: 1. returned from *Jordan*, and was led
Joh. 1:28. in Bethabara beyond *Jordan*,
3:26. he that was with thee beyond *Jordan*,
10:40. And went away again beyond *Jordan*

2448,2449 45 379/496 3:357 [3063]

Ἰουδαία, *Ïoudaia*.

Mat. 2: 1. in Bethlehem of *Judæa*
5. In Bethlehem of *Judæa*:
22. that Archelaus did reign in *Judæa*
3: 1. preaching in the wilderness of *Judæa*,
5. Jerusalem, and all *Judæa*,
4:25. and (from) Jerusalem, and (from) *Judæa*,
19: 1. the coasts of *Judæa* beyond Jordan;
24:16. Then let them which be in *Judæa*
Mar 1: 5. out unto him all the land of *Judæa*,
3: 7. followed him, and from *Judæa*,
10: 1. cometh into the coasts of *Judæa*
13:14. then let them that be in *Judæa*
Lu. 1: 5. Herod, the king of *Judæa*,
65. all the hill country of *Judæa*.
2: 4. out of the city of Nazareth, into *Judæa*,
3: 1. Pontius Pilate being governor of *Judæa*,
5:17. out of every town of Galilee, and *Judæa*,
6:17. multitude of people out of all *Judæa*
7:17. went forth throughout all *Judæa*,
21:21. Then let them which are in *Judæa*
23: 5. teaching throughout all *Jewry*,
Joh. 3:22. and his disciples into the land of *Judæa*;
[see Ἰουδαῖος]
4: 3. He left *Judæa*, and departed again
47. that Jesus was come out of *Judæa*
54. when he was come out of *Judæa*
7: 1. for he would not walk in *Jewry*,
3. Depart hence, and go into *Judæa*,
11: 7. Let us go into *Judæa* again.
Acts 1: 8. and in all *Judæa*, and in Samaria,
2: 9. dwellers in Mesopotamia, and in *Judæa*,
8: 1. the regions of *Judæa* and Samaria,
9:31. throughout all *Judæa* and Galilee
10:37. was published throughout all *Judæa*,
11: 1. brethren that were in *Judæa*
29. the brethren which dwelt in *Judæa*:
12:19. And he went down from *Judæa*
15: 1. which came down from *Judæa*
21:10. there came down from *Judæa*
26:20. throughout all the coasts of *Judæa*,
28:21. neither received letters out of *Judæa*
Ro. 15:31. them that do not believe in *Judæa*;
2Co. 1:16. brought on my way toward *Judæa*.
Gal. 1:22. unto the churches of *Judæa*
1Th. 2:14. which in *Judæa* are in Christ Jesus

2451 1 380/496 3:357 2453

Ἰουδαϊκός, *Ïoudaïkos*.

Tit. 1:14. Not giving heed to *Jewish* fables,

2452 1 380/496 2451

Ἰουδαϊκῶς, *Ïoudaïkōs*.

Gal. 2:14. after the manner of Gentiles, and not as *do the Jews*,

2453 198 380/496 2448

Ἰουδαῖος, *Ïoudaios*.

Mat. 2: 2. he that is born King of the *Jews*?
27:11. Art thou the King of the *Jews*?
29. saying, Hail, king of the *Jews*!
37. THIS IS JESUS THE KING OF THE *JEWS*.
28:15. is commonly reported among the *Jews*
Mar 1: 5. unto him all the land *of Judæa*,
7: 3. For the Pharisees, and all the *Jews*,
15: 2. Art thou the King of the *Jews*?
9. release unto you the King of the *Jews*?
12. whom ye call the King of the *Jews*?
18. salute him, Hail, King of the *Jews*!
26. THE KING OF THE *JEWS*.
Lu. 7: 3. he sent unto him the elders of the *Jews*,
23: 3. Art thou the King of the *Jews*?
37. If thou be the king of the *Jews*,
38. THIS IS THE KING OF THE *JEWS*.
51. (he was) of Arimathæa, a city of the *Jews*:
Joh. 1:19. when the *Jews* sent priests and Levites
2: 6. manner of the purifying of the *Jews*,
13. And the *Jews*' passover was at hand,
18. Then answered the *Jews* and said
20. Then said the *Jews*, Forty and six years
3: 1. Nicodemus, a ruler of the *Jews*:
22. into the land *of Judæa*;
25. and the *Jews* about purifying.
4: 9. How is it that thou, being a *Jew*,
— for the *Jews* have no dealings with
22. for salvation is of the *Jews*.
5: 1. there was a feast of the *Jews*;
10. The *Jews* therefore said unto him
15. The man departed, and told the *Jews*
16. And therefore did the *Jews* persecute Jesus,
18. Therefore the *Jews* sought the more
6: 4. And the passover, a feast of the *Jews*,
41. The *Jews* then murmured at him,
52. The *Jews* therefore strove among
7: 1. because the *Jews* sought to kill him.
2. Now the *Jews*' feast of tabernacles
11. Then the *Jews* sought him at the feast,
13. openly of him for fear of the *Jews*.
15. And the *Jews* marvelled, saying,
35. Then said the *Jews* among themselves,
8:22. Then said the *Jews*, Will he kill himself?
31. Then said Jesus to those *Jews*
48. Then answered the *Jews*, and said
52. Then said the *Jews* unto him,
57. Then said the *Jews* unto him,
9:18. But the *Jews* did not believe
22. because they feared the *Jews*: for the *Jews* had agreed already,
10:19. among the *Jews* for these sayings.
24. Then came the *Jews* round about him,
31. Then the *Jews* took up stones
33. The *Jews* answered him, saying,
11: 8. the *Jews* of late sought to stone thee;
19. And many of the *Jews* came to Martha
31. The *Jews* then which were with her
33. and the *Jews* also weeping which came
36. said the *Jews*, Behold how he loved him!
45. Then many of the *Jews* which came

Joh. 11:54. walked no more openly among the *Jews;*
55. And the *Jews'* passover was nigh
12: 9. Much people of the *Jews* therefore
11. many of the *Jews* went away,
13:33. and as I said unto the *Jews*,
18:12. the captain and officers of the *Jews*
14. which gave counsel to the *Jews*,
20. whither the *Jews* always resort;
31. The *Jews* therefore said unto him,
33. Art thou the King of the *Jews?*
35. Pilate answered, Am I a *Jew?*
36. I should not be delivered to the *Jews:*
38. he went out again unto the *Jews*,
39. release unto you the King of the *Jews?*
19: 3. And said, Hail, King of the *Jews!*
7. The *Jews* answered him, We have a law,
12. but the *Jews* cried out, saying,
14. saith unto the *Jews*, Behold your King!
19. JESUS OF NAZARETH THE KING OF THE *JEWS*.
20. This title then read many of the *Jews:*
21. Then said the chief priests of the *Jews*
— Write not, The King of the *Jews;* but that he said, I am King of the *Jews*.
31. The *Jews* therefore, because it was
38. but secretly for fear of the *Jews*,
40. as the manner of the *Jews* is to bury.
42. because of the *Jews'* preparation (day);
20:19. were assembled for fear of the *Jews*,
Acts 2: 5. were dwelling at Jerusalem *Jews*,
10. strangers of Rome, *Jews* and proselytes,
14. Ye men *of Judæa* (lit. *Jews*), and all (ye)
9:22. the *Jews* which dwelt at Damascus,
23. the *Jews* took counsel to kill him:
10:22. among all the nation of the *Jews*,
28. a man that is a *Jew* to keep company,
39. in the land of the *Jews*, and in Jerusalem;
11:19. the word to none but unto the *Jews* only.
12: 3. because he saw it pleased the *Jews*.
11. expectation of the people of the *Jews*.
13: 5. in the synagogues of the *Jews:*
6. a *Jew*, whose name (was) Bar-jesus:
42. And when the *Jews* were gone out
43. many of the *Jews* and religious proselytes
45. when the *Jews* saw the multitudes,
50. But the *Jews* stirred up the devout
14: 1. into the synagogue of the *Jews*,
— both of the *Jews* and also of the Greeks
2. unbelieving *Jews* stirred up the Gentiles,
4. and part held with the *Jews*,
5. and also of the *Jews* with their rulers,
19. And there came thither (certain) *Jews*
16: 1. which was a *Jewess*, and believed;
3. circumcised him because of the *Jews*
20. saying, These men, being *Jews*,
17: 1. where was a synagogue of the *Jews:*
5. But the *Jews* which believed not,
10. went into the synagogue of the *Jews*.
13. But when the *Jews* of Thessalonica
17. in the synagogue with the *Jews*.
18: 2. And found a certain *Jew* named Aquila,
— all *Jews* to depart from Rome:
4. persuaded the *Jews* and the Greeks.
5. to the *Jews* (that) Jesus (was) Christ.
12. the *Jews* made insurrection with one accord
14. Gallio said unto the *Jews*,
— O (ye) *Jews*, reason would that I should
19. and reasoned with the *Jews*.
24. And a certain *Jew* named Apollos,
28. For he mightily convinced the *Jews*,
19:10. the Lord Jesus, both *Jews* and Greeks.
13. Then certain of the vagabond *Jews*.

Acts 19:14. Sceva, a *Jew*, (and) chief of the priests,
17. And this was known to all the *Jews*
33. the *Jews* putting him forward.
34. But when they knew that he was a *Jew*,
20: 3. when the *Jews* laid wait for him,
19. by the lying in wait of the *Jews:*
21. Testifying both to the *Jews*.
21:11. So shall the *Jews* at Jerusalem
20. thousands of *Jews* there are which believe
21. that thou teachest all the *Jews*
27. the *Jews* which were of Asia,
39. I am a man (which am) a *Jew*
22: 3. I am verily a man (which am) a *Jew*,
12. having a good report of all the *Jews*
30. wherefore he was accused of the *Jews*,
23:12. certain of the *Jews* banded together,
20. The *Jews* have agreed to desire thee
27. This man was taken of the *Jews*,
30. that the *Jews* laid wait for the man,
24: 5. a mover of sedition among all the *Jews*
9. And the *Jews* also assented,
18. Whereupon certain *Jews* from Asia
24. his wife Drusilla, which was a *Jewess*,
27. willing to shew the *Jews* a pleasure,
25: 2. and the chief of the *Jews* informed him
7. the *Jews* which came down
8. Neither against the law of the *Jews*,
9. willing to do the *Jews* a pleasure,
10. to the *Jews* have I done no wrong,
15. the elders of the *Jews* informed (me),
24. all the multitude of the *Jews*
26: 2. whereof I am accused of the *Jews:*
3. which are among the *Jews:*
4. at Jerusalem, know all the *Jews;*
7. king Agrippa, I am accused of the *Jews*.
21. the *Jews* caught me in the temple,
28:17. Paul called the chief of the *Jews* together
19. But when the *Jews* spake against (it),
29. said these words, the *Jews* departed,
Ro. 1:16. to the *Jew* first, and also to the Greek.
2: 9. of the *Jew* first, and also of the Gentile.
10. to the *Jew* first, and also to the Gentile:
17. Behold, thou art called a *Jew*,
28. he is not a *Jew*, which is one outwardly;
29. he (is) a *Jew*, which is one inwardly;
3: 1. What advantage then hath the *Jew?*
9. proved both *Jews* and Gentiles,
29. (Is he) the God of the *Jews* only?
9:24. *Jews* only, but also of the Gentiles?
10:12. between the *Jew* and the Greek:
1Co. 1:22. For the *Jews* require a sign.
23. unto the *Jews* a stumblingblock,
24. which are called, both *Jews* and Greeks,
9:20. And unto the *Jews* I became as a *Jew*, that I might gain the *Jews;*
10:32. neither to the *Jews*, nor to the Gentiles,
12:13. whether (we be) *Jews* or Gentiles.
2Co. 11:24. Of the *Jews* five times received I
Gal. 2:13. And the other *Jews* dissembled
14. If thou, being a *Jew*,
15. We (who are) *Jews* by nature,
3:28. There is neither *Jew* nor Greek,
Col. 3:11. Where there is neither Greek nor *Jew*
1Th. 2:14. even as they (have) of the *Jews:*
Rev. 2: 9. them which say they are *Jews*,
3: 9. which say they are *Jews*, and are not,

2455 45 380/499 [3063]

Ἰούδας, *Ioudas.*

Mat. 1: 2. and Jacob begat *Judas* and
3. And *Judas* begat Phares and Zara

Mat. 2: 6. Bethlehem, (in) the land of *Juda*, art not the least among the princes of *Juda:*
10: 4. and *Judas* Iscariot, who also betrayed him.
13:55. and Joses, and Simon, and *Judas?*
26:14. Then one of the twelve, called *Judas* Iscariot,
25. Then *Judas*, which betrayed him,
47. And while he yet spake, lo, *Judas*,
27: 3. Then *Judas*, which had betrayed him,
Mar 3:19. And *Judas* Iscariot, which also betrayed him:
6: 3. Joses, and of *Juda*, and Simon?
14:10. And *Judas* Iscariot, one of the twelve,
43. cometh *Judas*, one of the twelve,
Lu. 1:39. with haste, into a city of *Juda;*
3:26. which was (the son) of *Juda*,
30. which was (the son) of *Juda*,
33. which was (the son) of *Juda*,
6:16. And *Judas* (the brother) of James, and *Judas* Iscariot, which also was the traitor.
22: 3. Then entered Satan into *Judas*
47. and he that was called *Judas*,
48. But Jesus said unto him, *Judas*,
Joh. 6:71. He spake of *Judas* Iscariot
12: 4. *Judas* Iscariot, Simon's (son),
13: 2. put into the heart of *Judas* Iscariot,
26. to *Judas* Iscariot, (the son) of Simon.
29. because *Judas* had the bag,
14:22. *Judas* saith unto him, not Iscariot,
18: 2. And *Judas* also, which betrayed him,
3. *Judas* then, having received a band
5. And *Judas* also, which betrayed him,
Acts 1:13. and *Judas* (the brother) of James.
16. spake before concerning *Judas*,
25. from which *Judas* by transgression fell,
5:37. After this man rose up *Judas*
9:11. and enquire in the house of *Judas*
15:22. (namely), *Judas* surnamed Barsabas,
27. We have sent therefore *Judas*
32. And *Judas* and Silas, being prophets
Heb 7:14. that our Lord sprang out of *Juda;*
8: 8. with the house of *Judah:*
Jude 1. *Jude*, the servant of Jesus Christ,
Rev. 5: 5. Lion of the tribe of *Juda*,
7: 5. Of the tribe of *Juda*

2456 1 381/499 rt 2457

'Ιουλία, Ïoulia.

Ro. 16:15. Salute Philologus, and *Julia*,

2457 2 381/499

'Ιούλιος, Ïoulios.

Acts27: 1. unto (one) named *Julius*, a centurion
3. And *Julius* courteously entreated Paul,

2458 1 381/499

'Ιουνίας, Ïounias.

Ro. 16: 7. Salute Andronicus and *Junia*,

2459 3 381/499

'Ιοῦστος, Ïoustos.

Acts 1:23. Barsabas, who was surnamed *Justus*,
18: 7. *Justus*, (one) that worshipped God,
Col. 4:11. And Jesus, which is called *Justus*

2464 20 381/500 [3327]

'Ισαάκ, Isaäk.

Mat. 1: 2. Abraham begat *Isaac;* and *Isaac* begat Jacob;
8:11. shall sit down with Abraham, and *Isaac*
22:32. and the God of *Isaac*,
Mar 12:26. and the God of *Isaac*,
Lu. 3:34. which was (the son) of *Isaac*,
13:28. Abraham, and *Isaac*, and Jacob,
20:37. and the God of *Isaac*,
Acts 3:13. God of Abraham, and of *Isaac*,
7: 8. and so (Abraham) (begat) *Isaac*,
— and *Isaac* (begat) Jacob;
32. and the God of *Isaac*,
Ro. 9: 7. In *Isaac* shall thy seed be called.
10. (even) by our father *Isaac;*
Gal. 4:28. Now we, brethren, as *Isaac* was,
Heb 11: 9. in tabernacles with *Isaac* and Jacob,
17. when he was tried, offered up *Isaac:*
18. That in *Isaac* shall thy seed be called:
20. By faith *Isaac* blessed Jacob
Jas. 2:21. offered *Isaac* his son upon the altar?

2466 1 /501 [3485]

'Ισαχάρ, Isakar.

Rev. 7: 7. Of the tribe of *Issachar*

2469 11 /500

'Ισκαριώτης, Iskariōtees.

Mat.10: 4. *Iscariot*, who also betrayed him.
26:14. one of the twelve, called Judas *Iscariot*.
Mar 3:19. *Iscariot*, which also betrayed him:
14:10. *Iscariot*, one of the twelve,
Lu. 6:16. *Iscariot*, which also was the traitor.
22: 3. into Judas surnamed *Iscariot*,
Joh. 6:71. He spake of Judas *Iscariot*
12: 4. Judas *Iscariot*, Simon's (son),
13: 2. *Iscariot*, Simon's (son), to betray him;
26. he gave (it) to Judas *Iscariot*,
14:22. Judas saith unto him, not *Iscariot*,

2474 70 /500 3:357 [3478]

'Ισραήλ, Israeel.

Mat. 2: 6. that shall rule my people *Israel*.
20. and go into the land of *Israel:*
21. and came into the land of *Israel*.
8:10. found so great faith, no, not in *Israel*.
9:33. It was never so seen in *Israel*.
10: 6. the lost sheep of the house of *Israel*.
23. have gone over the cities of *Israel*,
15:24. the lost sheep of the house of *Israel*.
31. and they glorified the God of *Israel*.
19:28. judging the twelve tribes of *Israel*.
27: 9. the children of *Israel* did value;
42. If he be the King of *Israel*,
Mar12:29. commandments (is), Hear, O *Israel;*
15:32. Let Christ the King of *Israel*
Lu. 1:16. And many of the children of *Israel*
54. He hath holpen his servant Israel,
68. Blessed (be) the Lord God of *Israel;*
80. the day of his shewing unto *Israel*.
2:25. waiting for the consolation of *Israel:*
32. and the glory of thy people *Israel*.
34. and rising again of many in *Israel;*
4:25. many widows were in *Israel*
27. And many lepers were in *Israel*
7: 9. so great faith, no, not in *Israel*.
22:30. judging the twelve tribes of *Israel*.
24:21. which should have redeemed *Israel:*

Joh. 1:31. should be made manifest to *Israel*,
49(50). thou art the King of *Israel*.
3:10. Art thou a master of *Israel*,
12:13. Blessed (is) the King of *Israel*
Acts 1: 6. restore again the kingdom to *Israel*?
2:36. Therefore let all the house of *Israel*
4: 8. rulers of the people, and elders of *Israel*,
10. and to all the people of *Israel*,
27. the Gentiles, and the people of *Israel*,
5:21. senate of the children of *Israel*,
31. for to give repentance to *Israel*,
7:23. his brethren the children of *Israel*.
37. said unto the children of *Israel*,
42. O ye house of *Israel*,
9:15. and kings, and the children of *Israel*:
10:36. sent unto the children of *Israel*,
13:17. The God of this people of *Israel*
23. to (his) promise raised unto *Israel*
24. repentance to all the people of *Israel*.
28:20. for the hope of *Israel* I am bound
Ro. 9: 6. For they (are) not all *Israel*, which are of *Israel*:
27. Esaias also crieth concerning *Israel*,
— of *Israel* be as the sand of the sea,
31. But *Israel*, which followed after
10: 1. and prayer to God for *Israel*
19. But I say, Did not *Israel* know?
21. But to *Israel* he saith,
11: 2. intercession to God against *Israel*,
7. *Israel* hath not obtained
25. in part is happened to *Israel*,
26. And so all *Israel* shall be saved:
1Co.10:18. Behold *Israel* after the flesh:
2Co. 3: 7. so that the children of *Israel*
13. that the children of *Israel*
Gal. 6:16. and upon the *Israel* of God.
Eph. 2:12. from the commonwealth of *Israel*,
Phi. 3: 5. the eighth day, of the stock of *Israel*,
Heb. 8: 8. covenant with the house of *Israel*
10. I will make with the house of *Israel*
11:22. departing of the children of *Israel*;
Rev. 2:14. before the children of *Israel*,
7: 4. tribes of the children of *Israel*.
21: 12. tribes of the children of *Israel*.

2475 9 /501 3:357 2474

Ἰσραηλίτης, *Israeelitees*.

Joh. 1:47(48). Behold an *Israelite* indeed,
Acts 2:22. Ye men of *Israel*, hear these words;
3:12. Ye men of *Israel*, why marvel
5:35. Ye men of *Israel*, take heed
13:16. Men of *Israel*, and ye that fear God,
21:28. Crying out, Men of *Israel*,
Ro. 9: 4. Who are *Israelites*; to whom (pertaineth)
11: 1. For I also am an *Israelite*,
2Co.11:22. Are they *Israelites*? so (am) I.

2482 4 /504

Ἰταλία, *Italia*.

Acts18: 2. lately come from *Italy*,
27: 1. that we should sail into *Italy*,
6. ship of Alexandria sailing into *Italy*;
Heb 13:24. They of *Italy* salute you.

2483 1 384/504 2482

Ἰταλικός, *Italikos*.

Acts10: 1. of the band called the *Italian* (band),

2484 1 /504 [3195]

Ἰτουραία, *Itouraia*.

Lu. 3: 1. Philip tetrarch of *Ituræa*

2488 2 /504 [3147]

Ἰωάθαμ, *Iōatham*.

Mat. 1: 9. And Ozias begat *Joatham*; and *Joatham* begat Achaz;

2489 2 385/504 rt 2491

Ἰωάννα, *Iōanna*.

Lu. 8: 3. And *Joanna* the wife of Chuza
24:10. It was Mary Magdalene, and *Joanna*,

2490 1 385/505 2491

Ἰωαννᾶς, *Iōannas*.

Lu. 3:27. Which was (the son) of *Joanna*,

2491 133 385/506 [3110]

Ἰωάννης, *Iōannees*.

(Apostle).

Mat. 4:21. Zebedee, and *John* his brother,
10: 2(3). Zebedee, and *John* his brother;
17: 1. Peter, James, and *John* his brother,
Mar 1:19. Zebedee, and *John* his brother,
29. and Andrew, with James and *John*.
3:17. and *John* the brother of James;
5:37. and *John* the brother of James.
9: 2. Peter, and James, and *John*,
38. And *John* answered him, saying,
10:35. And James and *John*, the sons of Zebedee
41. much displeased with James and *John*.
13: 3. Peter and James and *John*
14:33. Peter and James and *John*,
Lu. 5:10. James, and *John*, the sons of Zebedee,
6:14. *John*, Philip and Bartholomew,
8:51. save Peter, and James, and *John*,
9:28. he took Peter and *John* and James,
49. And *John* answered and said,
54. when his disciples James and *John*
22: 8. And he sent Peter and *John*,
Acts 1:13. both Peter, and James, and *John*,
3: 1. Now Peter and *John* went up together
3. Who seeing Peter and *John*
4. with *John*, said, Look on us.
11. was healed held Peter and *John*,
4:13. saw the boldness of Peter and *John*,
19. But Peter and *John* answered
8:14. they sent unto them Peter and *John*:
12: 2. the brother of *John* with the sword.
12. of Mary the mother of *John*.
Gal. 2: 9. And when James, Cephas, and *John*,
Rev. 1: 1. unto his servant *John*:
4. *John* to the seven churches
9. I *John*, who also am your brother,
21: 2. And I *John* saw the holy city,
22: 8. And I *John* saw these things,

2491 92 /505 [3110]

Ἰωάννης, *Iōannees*.

(Baptist).

Mat. 3: 1. In those days came *John* the Baptist,
4. the same *John* had his raiment
13. unto *John*, to be baptized of him.
14. But *John* forbad him, saying,
4:12. that *John* was cast into prison,
9:14. came to him the disciples of *John*,
11: 2. Now when *John* had heard in the prison

Mat.11: 4. Go and shew *John* again those things
7. the multitudes concerning *John*,
11. a greater than *John* the Baptist:
12. from the days of *John* the Baptist
13. and the law prophesied until *John*.
18. For *John* came neither eating
14: 2. This is *John* the Baptist;
3. For Herod had laid hold on *John*,
4. For *John* said unto him,
8. *John* Baptist's head in a charger.
10. and beheaded *John* in the prison.
16:14. Some (say that thou art) *John* the Baptist:
17:13. he spake unto them of *John* the Baptist.
21:25. The baptism of *John*, whence was it?
26. for all hold *John* as a prophet.
32. For *John* came unto you
Mar 1: 4. *John* did baptize in the wilderness,
6. And *John* was clothed with camel's hair,
9. was baptized of *John* in Jordan.
14. Now after that *John* was put in prison,
2:18. And the disciples of *John*
— Why do the disciples of *John*
6:14. That *John* the Baptist was risen
16. It is *John*, whom I beheaded:
17. and laid hold upon *John*,
18. For *John* had said unto Herod,
20. For Herod feared *John*,
24. said, The head of *John* the Baptist.
25. in a charger the head of *John* the Baptist.
8:28. And they answered, *John* the Baptist:
11:30. The baptism of *John*, was (it) from heaven,
32. *John*, that he was a prophet indeed.
Lu. 1:13. and thou shalt call his name *John*.
60. Not (so); but he shall be called *John*.
63. and wrote, saying, His name is *John*.
3: 2. came unto *John* the son of Zacharias
15. mused in their hearts of *John*,
16. *John* answered, saying unto (them)
20. that he shut up *John* in prison.
5:33. Why do the disciples of *John* fast
7:18. And the disciples of *John* shewed him
19. And *John* calling (unto him)
20. they said, *John* Baptist hath sent us
22. tell *John* what things ye have seen
24. messengers of *John* were departed,
— unto the people concerning *John*,
28. a greater prophet than *John* the Baptist:
29. baptized with the baptism of *John*.
33. For *John* the Baptist came
9: 7. that *John* was risen from the dead;
9. And Herod said, *John* have I beheaded:
19. They answering said, *John* the Baptist;
11: 1. as *John* also taught his disciples.
16:16. and the prophets (were) until *John*:
20: 4. The baptism of *John*, was it from heaven,
6. persuaded that *John* was a prophet.
Joh. 1: 6. from God, whose name (was) *John*.
15. *John* bare witness of him,
19. And this is the record of *John*,
26. *John* answered them, saying,
28. where *John* was baptizing.
29. The next day *John* seeth Jesus
32. And *John* bare record, saying,
35. *John* stood, and two of his disciples;
40(41). One of the two which heard *John*
3:23. And *John* also was baptizing
24. For *John* was not yet cast into prison.
25. between (some) of *John's* disciples
26. And they came unto *John*, and said
27. *John* answered and said,
4: 1. baptized more disciples than *John*,
5:33. Ye sent unto *John*, and he bare witness
Joh. 5:36. greater witness than (that) of *John*.
10:40. where *John* at first baptized;
41. and said, *John* did no miracle:
— that *John* spake of this man were true.
Acts 1: 5. For *John* truly baptized with water;
22. Beginning from the baptism of *John*,
10:37. the baptism which *John* preached,
11:16. *John* indeed baptized with water;
13:24. When *John* had first preached
25. And as *John* fulfilled his course,
18:25. knowing only the baptism of *John*.
19: 3. And they said, Unto *John's* baptism.
4. Then said Paul, *John* verily baptised

2491 1 /506 [3110]

'Ιωάννης, *Iōannees*.

(Chief priest).

Acts 4: 6. Caiaphas, and *John*, and Alexander

2491 4 /506 [3110]

'Ιωάννης, *Iōannees*.

(Mark)

Acts12:25. *John*, whose surname was Mark.
13: 5. they had also *John* to (their) minister.
13. and *John* departing from them
15:37. *John*, whose surname was Mark.

2492 1 /506 [347]

'Ιώβ, *Iōb*.

Jas. 5:11. Ye have heard of the patience of *Job*,

2493 1 /506 [3100]

'Ιωήλ, *Iōeel*.

Acts 2:16. which was spoken by the prophet *Joel*;

2494 1 386/506 2491 or 2495

'Ιωνάν, *Iōnan*.

Lu. 3:30. which was (the son) of *Jonan*,

2495 9 /506 3:406 [3124]

'Ιωνᾶς, *Iōnas*.

(Prophet).

Mat.12:39. but the sign of the prophet *Jonas*:
40. For as *Jonas* was three days
41. repented at the preaching of *Jonas*; and, behold, a greater than *Jonas* (is) here.
16: 4. but the sign of the prophet *Jonas*.
Lu. 11:29. but the sign of *Jonas* the prophet.
30. *Jonas* was a sign unto the Ninevites,
32. repented at the preaching of *Jonas*;
— a greater than *Jonas* (is) here.

2495 4 /506 [3124]

'Ιωνᾶς, *Iōnas*.

Joh. 1:42. Thou art Simon the son of *Jona*:
21:15. Simon Peter, Simon, (son) of *Jonas*,
16. Simon, (son) of *Jonas*, lovest thou me?
17. Simon, (son) of *Jonas*, lovest thou me?

2496 2 /506 [3141]

'Ιωράμ, *Iōram*.

Mat. 1: 8. and Josaphat begat *Joram*; and *Joram* begat Ozias;

2497 1 386/506 2496

Ἰωρείμ, Iōrim.

Lu 3:29. which was (the son) of *Jorim*,

2498 2 /507 [3092]

Ἰωσαφάτ, Iōsaphat.

Mat. 1: 8. And Asa begat *Josaphat*; and *Josaphat* begat Joram;

2499-2500 7 386/507 2501

Ἰωσῆς, Iōsees.

Mat.13:55. James, and *Joses*, and Simon,
27:56. the mother of James and *Joses*,
Mar 6: 3. the brother of James, and *Joses*,
15:40. mother of James the less and of *Joses*,
47. and Mary (the mother) of *Joses*
Lu. 3:29. Which was (the son) of *Jose*,
Acts 4:36. And *Joses*, who by the apostles

2501 6 /507 [3130]

Ἰωσήφ, Iōseeph.

(Of Arimathæa).

Mat.27:57. man of Arimathæa, named *Joseph*,
59. when *Joseph* had taken the body,
Mar 15:43. *Joseph* of Arimathæa,
45. he gave the body to *Joseph*.
Lu. 23:50. a man named *Joseph*, a counsellor;
Joh. 19:38. after this *Joseph* of Arimathæa,

2501 1 /507 [3130]

Ἰωσήφ, Iōseeph.

(Barsabas).

Acts 1:23. *Joseph* called Barsabas

2501 9 /507 [3130]

Ἰωσήφ, Iōseeph.

(Son of Jacob).

Joh. 4: 5. that Jacob gave to his son *Joseph*.
Acts 7: 9. moved with envy, sold *Joseph*
13. *Joseph* was made known to his brethren; and *Joseph's* kindred was made known
14. Then sent *Joseph*, and called his father
18. another king arose, which knew not *Joseph*.
Heb 11:21. blessed both the sons of *Joseph*;
22. By faith *Joseph*, when he died,
Rev. 7: 8. Of the tribe of *Joseph*

2501 1 /507 [3130]

Ἰωσήφ, Iōseeph.

(Son of Judas).

Lu. 3:26. which was (the son) of *Joseph*,

2501 1 /507 [3130]

Ἰωσήφ, Iōseeph.

(Son of Jonan).

Lu. 3:30. which was (the son) of *Joseph*,

2501 16 /507 [3130]

Ἰωσήφ, Iōseeph.

(Husband of Mary).

Mat. 1:16. And Jacob begat *Joseph*
18. Mary was espoused to *Joseph*,
19. Then *Joseph* her husband,
20. *Joseph*, thou son of David, fear not
24. Then *Joseph* being raised from sleep
2:13. appeareth to *Joseph* in a dream,
19. appeareth in a dream to *Joseph*
Lu. 1:27. a man whose name was *Joseph*,
2: 4. *Joseph* also went up from Galilee,
16. and found Mary, and *Joseph*,
33. And *Joseph* and his mother marvelled
43. *Joseph* and his mother knew not (of it).
3:23. as was supposed the son of *Joseph*,
4:22. they said, Is not this *Joseph's* son?
Joh. 1:45. Jesus of Nazareth, the son of *Joseph*.
6:42. Is not this Jesus, the son of *Joseph*,

2501 1 /507 [3130]

Ἰωσήφ, Iōseeph.

(Son of Mattathias).

Lu. 3:24. which was (the son) of *Joseph*,

2502 2 /507 [2977]

Ἰωσίας, Iōsias.

Mat. 1:10. and Amon begat *Josias*;
11. And *Josias* begat Jechonias

2533 9 /514

Καϊάφας, Kaïaphas.

Mat.26: 3. who was called *Caiaphas*,
57. led (him) away to *Caiaphas*
Lu. 3: 2. and *Caiaphas* being the high priests,
Joh.11:49. And one of them, (named) *Caiaphas*,
18:13. he was father in law to *Caiaphas*,
14. Now *Caiaphas* was he,
24. unto *Caiaphas* the high priest.
28. Then led they Jesus from *Caiaphas*
Acts 4: 6. and *Caiaphas*, and John,

2535 3 /514 1:6 [7014]

Κάϊν, Kaïn.

Heb 11: 4. a more excellent sacrifice than *Cain*,
1 Joh.3:12. Not as *Cain*, (who) was of that
Jude 11. gone in the way of *Cain*,

2536 2 /514 [7018]

Καϊνάν, Kaïnan.

Lu. 3:36. Which was (the son) of *Cainan*,
37. which was (the son) of *Cainan*,

2541 30 /516

Καῖσαρ, Kaisar.

Mat.22:17. to give tribute unto *Cæsar*, or not?
21. They say unto him, *Cæsar's*.
— unto *Cæsar* the things which are *Cæsar's*;
Mar 12:14. to give tribute to *Cæsar*, or not?
16. And they said unto him, *Cæsar's*.
17. to *Cæsar* the things that are *Cæsar's*,
Lu. 2: 1. a decree from *Cæsar* Augustus,
3: 1. the reign of Tiberius *Cæsar*,
20:22. to give tribute unto *Cæsar*, or no?
24. They answered and said, *Cæsar's*.
25. unto *Cæsar* the things which be *Cæsar's*,
23: 2. forbidding to give tribute to *Cæsar*.
Joh.19:12. thou art not *Cæsar's* friend:
— speaketh against *Cæsar*.
15. We have no king but *Cæsar*.
Acts 11:28. in the days of Claudius *Cæsar*.
17: 7. contrary to the decrees of *Cæsar*,
25: 8. nor yet against *Cæsar*,

Acts25:10. I stand at *Cæsar's* judgment seat,
11. I appeal unto *Cæsar*.
12. Hast thou appealed unto *Cæsar?* unto *Cæsar* shalt thou go.
21. till I might send him to *Cæsar*.
26:32. if he had not appealed unto *Cæsar*.
27:24. thou must be brought before *Cæsar:*
28:19. to appeal unto *Cæsar;*
Phi. 4:22. they that are of *Cæsar's* houshold.

2542 2 /516 2541

Καισάρεια, *Kaisaria.*

(ἡ Φιλίππου)

Mat.16:13. the coasts of *Cæsarea* Philippi,
Mar 8:27. into the towns of *Cæsarea* Philippi:

2542 17 396/516 2541

Καισάρεια, *Kaisaria.*

(ἡ Στράτωνος)

Acts 8:40. till he came to *Cæsarea*.
9:30. they brought him down to *Cæsarea,*
10: 1. a certain man in *Cæsarea*
24. they entered into *Cæsarea.*
11:11. sent from *Cæsarea* unto me.
12:19. from Judæa to *Cæsarea,*
18:22. he had landed at *Cæsarea,*
21: 8. and came unto *Cæsarea:*
16. of the disciples of *Cæsarea,*
23:23. soldiers to go to *Cæsarea,*
33. when they came to *Cæsarea,*
25: 1. from *Cæsarea* to Jerusalem.
4. Paul should be kept at *Cæsarea,*
6. he went down unto *Cæsarea;*
13. Bernice came unto *Cæsarea*

2568 1 401/ 2570,3040

Καλοὶ λιμένες see among the **Appellatives.**

2580 4 /522 cf [7071]

Κανᾶ, *Kana.*

Joh. 2: 1. in *Cana* of Galilee;
11. did Jesus in *Cana* of Galilee,
4:46. Jesus came again into *Cana*
21: 2. Nathanael of *Cana* in Galilee,

p. 867, 5477

Χαναάν see Χαναάν.

2581 2 /522 cf [7067]

Κανανίτης, *Kananitees.*

Mat.10: 4. Simon the *Canaanite,* and Judas
Mar 3:18. and Simon the *Canaanite,*

2582 1 /522

Κανδάκη, *Kandakee.*

Acts 8:27. under *Candace* queen of the

2584 16 /543 [3723],[5151]

Καπερναούμ, *Kapernaoum.*

Mat. 4:13. he came and dwelt in *Capernaum,*
8: 5. when Jesus was entered into *Capernaum,*
11:23. And thou, *Capernaum,* which art
17:24. were come to *Capernaum,*
Mar 1:21. they went into *Capernaum;*
2: 1. he entered into *Capernaum*
9:33. And he came to *Capernaum:*
Lu. 4:23. in *Capernaum,* do also here
31. And came down to *Capernaum.*
7. 1. he entered into *Capernaum.*
10:15. And thou, *Capernaum,* which
Joh. 2:12. he went down to *Capernaum,*
4:46. was sick at *Capernaum.*
6:17. over the sea toward *Capernaum.*
24. and came to *Capernaum,*
59. as he taught in *Capernaum.*

2587 2 /523

Καππαδοκία, *Kappadokia.*

Acts 2: 9. and *Cappadocia,* in Pontus,
1Pet.1: 1. Galatia, *Cappadocia,* Asia, and

2591 1 405/525 2590

Κάρπος, *Karpos.*

2Ti. 4:13. cloke that I left at Troas with *Carpus,*

p. 867, 5488

Καῤῥάν see Χαῤῥάν.

2747 2 /544

Κεγχρεαί, *Kenkreai.*

Acts18:18. having shorn (his) head in *Cenchrea:*
Ro. 16: 1. the church which is at *Cenchrea:*

2748 1 /543 [6939]

Κέδρος, or Κεδρών, *Kedros,* or *Kedrōn.*

Joh.18: 1. over the brook *Cedron,*

Note.—Some copies read τῶν Κέδρων, others τοῦ Κεδρών.

2786 6 /547 6:100 cf [3710]

Κηφᾶς, *Keephas.*

Joh. 1:42(43). thou shalt be called *Cephas,*
1Co. 1:12. and I of *Cephas;*
3:22. Whether Paul, or Apollos, or *Cephas,*
9: 5. the brethren of the Lord, and *Cephas?*
15: 5. he was seen of *Cephas,*
Gal. 2: 9. And when James, *Cephas,* and John,

2791 8 /547

Κιλικία, *Kilikia.*

Acts 6: 9. and of them of *Cilicia* and of Asia,
15:23. in Antioch and Syria and *Cilicia:*
41. he went through Syria and *Cilicia,*
21:39. a Jew of Tarsus, (a city) in *Cilicia,*
22: 3. born in Tarsus, (a city) in *Cilicia,*
23:34. when he understood that (he was) of *Cilicia;*
27: 5. we had sailed over the sea of *Cilicia*
Gal. 1:21. into the regions of Syria and *Cilicia;*

2797 1 /543 [7027]

Κίς, *Kis.*

Acts13:21. Saul the son of *Cis,*

2802 1 /549

Κλαύδη, *Klaudee.*

Acts27:16. a certain island which is called *Clauda,*

2803 1 /549

Κλαυδία, Klaudia.

2Ti. 4:21. and *Claudia*, and all the brethren.

2804 3 /549

Κλαύδιος, Klaudios.

Acts11:28. in the days of *Claudius* Cæsar.
18: 2. *Claudius* had commanded all Jews
23:26. *Claudius* Lysias unto the most

2810 1 435/549 2811,3962

Κλεόπας, Kleopas.

Lu. 24:18. one of them, whose name was *Cleopas*,

2815 1 /550

Κλήμης, Kleemees.

Phi. 4: 3. in the gospel, with *Clement* also,

2832 1 /551 cf 256

Κλωπᾶς, Klōpas.

Joh. 19:25. Mary the (wife) of *Cleophas*,

2834 1 /551

Κνίδος, Knidos.

Acts27: 7. scarce were come over against *Cnidus*,

2857 1 /553

Κολασσαί, Kolassai.

Col. 1: 2. in Christ which are at *Colosse:*
NOTE. Some copies read Κολοσσαῖς.

2879 1 /555 [7141]

Κορέ, Kore.

Jude 11. perished in the gainsaying of *Core*.

2881 2 445/555 2882

Κορίνθιος, Korinthios.

Acts18: 8. many of the *Corinthians*
2Co. 6:11. O (ye) *Corinthians;* our mouth is open

2882 6 /555

Κόρινθος, Korinthos.

Acts18: 1. and came to *Corinth;*
19: 1. while Apollos was at *Corinth*,
1Co. 1: 2. the church of God which is at *Corinth*,
2Co. 1: 1. church of God which is at *Corinth*,
23. I came not as yet unto *Corinth*.
2Ti. 4:20. Erastus abode at *Corinth:*

2883 10 /555

Κορνήλιος, Korneelios.

Acts10: 1. *Cornelius*, a centurion of the band
3. saying unto him, *Cornelius*.
7. the angel which spake unto *Cornelius*
17. the men which were sent from *Cornelius*
21. were sent unto him from *Cornelius;*
22. they said, *Cornelius* the centurion,
24. *Cornelius* waited for them,
25. *Cornelius* met him, and fell down
30. *Cornelius* said, Four days ago
31. *Cornelius*, thy prayer is heard,

2890 1 /557

Κούαρτος, Kouartos.

Ro. 16:23. and *Quartus* a brother.

2913 1 /560

Κρήσκης, Kreeskees.

2Ti. 4:10. *Crescens* to Galatia, Titus unto

2912 2 451/560 2914

Κρής, Κρῆτες, Krees, Kreetes.

Acts 2:11. *Cretes* and Arabians, we do hear them
Tit. 1:12. The *Cretians* (are) alway liars,

2914 5 /560

Κρήτη, Kreetee.

Acts27: 7. we sailed under *Crete*, (marg. *Candy*)
12. (which is) an haven of *Crete*,
13. they sailed close by *Crete*.
21. and not have loosed from *Crete*,
Tit. 1: 5. For this cause left I thee in *Crete*,

2921 2 /562

Κρίσπος, Krispos.

Acts18: 8. And *Crispus*, the chief ruler of the
1Co. 1:14. I baptized none of you, but *Crispus*

2953 3 458/565 2954

Κύπριος, Kuprios.

Acts 4:36. of the country of *Cyprus*, (lit. a *Cyprian* by nation)
11:20. some of them were men of *Cyprus*
21:16. with them one Mnason of *Cyprus*,

2954 5 /565

Κύπρος, Kupros.

Acts11:19. and *Cyprus*, and Antioch, preaching
13: 4. from thence they sailed to *Cyprus*.
15:39. took Mark, and sailed unto *Cyprus*
21: 3. when we had discovered *Cyprus*,
27: 4. we sailed under *Cyprus*,

2956 6 459/565 2957

Κυρηναῖος, Kureenaios.

Mat.27:32. a man of *Cyrene*, Simon by name
Mar 15:21. compel one Simon a *Cyrenian*,
Lu. 23:26. upon one Simon, a *Cyrenian*,
Acts 6: 9. of the Libertines, and *Cyrenians*,
11:20. were men of Cyprus and *Cyrene*,
13: 1. and Lucius of *Cyrene*,

2957 1 /565

Κυρήνη, Kureenee.

Acts 2:10. parts of Libya about *Cyrene*,

2958 1 /565

Κυρήνιος, Kureenios.

Lu. 2: 2. when *Cyrenius* was governor of Syria.

2972 1 /575

Κῶς, Kōs.

Acts21: 1. with a straight course unto *Coos*,

2973 1 /575 cf [7081]

Κωσάμ, Kōsam.

Lu. 3:28. Addi, which was (the son) of *Cosam*.

2976 15 /575 [499]

Λάζαρος, Lazaros.

Lu. 16:20. a certain beggar named *Lazarus*,
23. and *Lazarus* in his bosom.
24. mercy on me, and send *Lazarus*,
25. and likewise *Lazarus* evil things:
Joh. 11: 1. (named) *Lazarus*, of Bethany,
2. whose brother *Lazarus* was sick.
5. and her sister, and *Lazarus*.
11. Our friend *Lazarus* sleepeth;
14. them plainly, *Lazarus* is dead.
43. *Lazarus*, come forth.
12: 1. where *Lazarus* was which had been dead,
2. but *Lazarus* was one of them
9. but that they might see *Lazarus*
10. might put *Lazarus* also to death;
17. called *Lazarus* out of his grave,

2984 1 /581 [3929]

Λάμεχ, Lamek.

Lu. 3:36. which was (the son) of *Lamech*,

2993 5 467/582 2992,1349

Λαοδίκεια, Laodikīa.

Col. 2: 1. and (for) them at *Laodicea*,
4:13. and them (that are) in *Laodicea*,
15. the brethren which are in *Laodicea*,
16. the (epistle) from *Laodicea*.
Rev. 1:11. and unto *Laodicea*.

2994 2 467/582 2993

Λαοδικεύς, Laodikūs.

Col. 4:16. in the church of the *Laodiceans*,
Rev. 3:14. church of the *Laodiceans* write;

2996 1 /584

Λασαία, Lasaia.

Acts 27: 8. whereunto was the city (of) *Lasea*.

3002 1 /584

Λεββαῖος, Lebbaios.

Mat. 10: 3. James (the son) of Alphæus, and *Lebbæus*,

3017 5 473/598 4:234 [3878]

Λευΐ, Lūi. cf 3018

(Son of Jacob.)

Heb 7: 5. that are of the sons of *Levi*,
9. as I may so say, *Levi* also,
Rev. 7: 7. Of the tribe of *Levi* (were) sealed

3018 1 /598 4:234 3017

Λευΐ, Lūi.

(Son of Melchi.)

Lu. 3:24. which was (the son) of *Levi*,

3018 1 /598 4:234 3017

Λευΐ, Lūi.

(Son of Simeon.)

Lu. 3:29. which was (the son) of *Levi*,

3018 3 473/598 4:234 3017

Λευΐς, Lūis.

Mar 2:14. as he passed by, he saw *Levi*
Lu. 5:27. saw a publican, named *Levi*,
29. And *Levi* made him a great feast

3019 3 473/598 4:239 3017

Λευΐτης, Lūitees.

Lu. 10:32. And likewise a *Levite*,
Joh. 1:19. when the Jews sent priests and *Levites*
Acts 4:36. The son of consolation, a *Levite*

3020 1 473/598 3019

Λευϊτικός, Lūitikos.

Heb 7:11. were by the *Levitical* priesthood,

3032 1 /599 4:265

Λιβερτῖνοι, Libertinoi.

Acts 6: 9. (the synagogue) of the *Libertines*,

3033 1 474/599 3047

Λιβύα, Libua.

Acts 2:10. and in the parts of *Libya*

3038 1 475/600 3037,4766

Λιθόστρωτος, Lithostrōtos.

Joh. 19:13. the *Pavement*, but in the Hebrew, Gabbatha

3044 1 476/600 3043

Λῖνος, Linos.

2Ti. 4:21. Pudens, and *Linus*, and Claudia,

Λίψ, see among Appellatives. p. 461

3065 3 /606

Λουκᾶς, Loukas.

Col. 4:14. *Luke*, the beloved physician,
2Ti. 4:11. Only *Luke* is with me.
Philem 24(23). Demas, *Lucas*, my fellowlabourers.

3066 2 /606

Λούκιος, Loukios.

Acts 13: 1. and *Lucius* of Cyrene, and Manaen,
Ro. 16:21. and *Lucius*, and Jason, and Sosipater,

3069 3 /606 [3850]

Λύδδα, Ludda.

Acts 9:32. the saints which dwelt at *Lydda*.
35. And all that dwelt at *Lydda*
38. as *Lydda* was nigh to Joppa,

3070 2 /606

Λυδία, Ludia.

Acts 16:14. a certain woman named *Lydia*,
40. entered into (the house of) *Lydia*:

3071 1 /606 cf 3074

Λυκαονία, Lukaonia.

Acts 14: 6. Lystra and Derbe, cities of *Lycaonia*.

3072 1 482/606 3071

Λυκαονιστί, *Lukaonisti.*

Acts14:11. saying in the *speech of Lycaonia,*

3073 1 482/606 3074

Λυκία, *Lukia.*

Acts27: 5. we came to Myra, (a city) of *Lycia.*

3078 1 483/607 3080 *ania* (trouble)

Λυσανίας, *Lusanias.*

Lu. 3: 1. *Lysanias* the tetrarch of Abilene,

3079 3 /607

Λυσίας, *Lusias.*

Acts23:26. Claudius *Lysias* unto the most
24: 7. the chief captain *Lysias* came (upon us),
22. When *Lysias* the chief captain shall come

3082 3 /607

Λύστρα (ἡ), *Lustra.*

Acts14: 6. and fled unto *Lystra* and Derbe,
21. they returned again to *Lystra,*
16: 1. Then came he to Derbe and *Lystra:*

3082 3 /607

Λύστρα (τά), *Lustra.*

Acts14: 8. there sat a certain man at *Lystra,*
16: 2. by the brethren that were at *Lystra*
2Ti. 3:11. at Antioch, at Iconium, at *Lystra;*

3090 1 /608

Λωΐς, *Lōis.*

2Ti. 1: 5. first in thy grandmother *Lois,*

3091 4 /608 [3876]

Λώτ, *Lōt.*

Lu. 17:28. as it was in the days of *Lot;*
29. the same day that *Lot* went out of Sodom
32. Remember *Lot's* wife.
2Pet. 2: 7. And delivered just *Lot,*

3092 1 /608

Μαάθ, *Maäth.*

Lu. 3:26. Which was (the son) of *Maath,*

3093 1 /608 cf [4026]

Μαγδαλά, *Magdala.*

Mat.15:39. and came into the coasts of *Magdala.*

3094 12 485/608 3093

Μαγδαληνή, *Magdaleenee.*

Mat.27:56. Among which was Mary *Magdalene,*
61. And there was Mary *Magdalene,*
28: 1. came Mary *Magdalene* and the other
Mar 15:40. among whom was Mary *Magdalene,*
47. And Mary *Magdalene* and Mary
16: 1. Mary *Magdalene,* and Mary the
9. he appeared first to Mary *Magdalene,*
Lu. 8: 2. Mary called *Magdalene,* out of whom
24:10. It was Mary *Magdalene,* and Joanna,
Joh.19:25. (wife) of Cleophas, and Mary *Magdalen*
20: 1. cometh Mary *Magdalene* early,
18. Mary *Magdalene* came and told

3098 1 /608 [4031]

Μαγώγ, *Magōg.*

Rev.20: 8. Gog and *Magog,* to gather them

3099 1 /608 [4080]

Μαδιάμ, *Madiam.*

Acts 7:29. stranger in the land of *Madian,*

3103 1 /611 [4968]

Μαθουσάλα, *Mathousala.*

Lu. 3:37. Which was (the son) of *Mathusala,*

3104 1 /628

Μαϊνάν, *Maïnan.*

Lu. 3:31. which was (the son) of *Menan,*

3109 22 488/612 3110

Μακεδονία, *Makedonia.*

Acts16: 9. Come over into *Macedonia,*
10. we endeavoured to go into *Macedonia,*
12. of that part of *Macedonia,*
18: 5. were come from *Macedonia,*
19:21. when he had passed through *Macedonia*
22. So he sent into *Macedonia* two of them
20: 1. departed for to go into *Macedonia.*
3. purposed to return through *Macedonia.*
Ro. 15:26. it hath pleased them of *Macedonia*
1Co.16: 5. *Macedonia:* for I do pass through *Macedonia.*
2Co. 1:16. to pass by you into *Macedonia,* and to come again out of *Macedonia*
2:13. I went from thence into *Macedonia.*
7: 5. when we were come into *Macedonia,*
8: 1. bestowed on the churches of *Macedonia;*
11: 9. brethren which came from *Macedonia*
Phi. 4:15. when I departed from *Macedonia,*
1Th. 1: 7. all that believe in *Macedonia*
8. word of the Lord not only in *Macedonia*
4:10. brethren which are in all *Macedonia:*
1Ti. 1: 3. when I went into *Macedonia,*

3110 5 /612

Μακεδών, *Makedōn.*

Acts16: 9. There stood a man of *Macedonia,*
19:29. men of *Macedonia,* Paul's companions
27: 2. a *Macedonian* of Thessalonica,
2Co. 9: 2. I boast of you to them of *Macedonia,*
4. Lest haply if they of *Macedonia*

3121 1 /613 [4111]

Μαλελεήλ or Μαλαλεήλ, *Malelëel* or *Malalëel.*

Lu. 3:37. which was (the son) of *Maleleel,*

3124 1 /614 [4429]

Μάλχυς, *Malkos.*

Joh. 18:10. The servant's name was *Malchus.*

3126 4 /614 4:388
Μαμμωνᾶς & Μαμωνᾶς, *Mammōnas & Mamōnas.*

Mat. 6:24. Ye cannot serve God and *mammon.*
Lu. 16: 9. friends of the *mammon* of unrighteousness;
11. faithful in the unrighteous *mammon,*
13. Ye cannot serve God and *mammon.*

3127 1 /615
Μαναήν, *Manaeen.*

Acts13: 1. Lucius of Cyrene, and *Manaen.*

3128 3 /615 [4519]
Μανασσῆς, *Manassees.*

Mat. 1:10. And Ezekias begat *Manasses;* and *Manasses* begat Amon;
Rev. 7: 6. Of the tribe of *Manasses* (were) sealed

3136 13 /615
Μάρθα, *Martha.*

Lu. 10:38. a certain woman named *Martha*
40. But *Martha* was cumbered about much
41. and said unto her, *Martha, Martha,*
Joh. 11: 1. town of Mary and her sister *Martha.*
5. Now Jesus loved *Martha,*
19. the Jews came to *Martha* and Mary,
20. Then *Martha,* as soon as she heard
21. Then said *Martha* unto Jesus,
24. *Martha* saith unto him,
30. place where *Martha* met him.
39. *Martha,* the sister of him that was dead,
12: 2. made him a supper; and *Martha* served:

3137 54 /615 [4813]
Μαρία, Μαριάμ, *Maria, Mariam.*

Mat. 1:16. begat Joseph the husband of *Mary,*
18. *Mary* was espoused to Joseph,
20. fear not to take unto thee *Mary*
2:11. saw the young child with *Mary*
13:55. is not his mother called *Mary?*
27:56. Among which was *Mary* Magdalene, and *Mary* the mother of James and
61. And there was *Mary* Magdalene, and the other *Mary,* sitting over
28: 1. came *Mary* Magdalene and the other *Mary* to see the sepulchre.
Mar 6: 3. the carpenter, the son of *Mary,*
15:40. among whom was *Mary* Magdalene, and *Mary* the mother of James
47. And *Mary* Magdalene and *Mary* (the mother) of Joses
16: 1. *Mary* Magdalene, and *Mary* the (mother) of James,
9. appeared first to *Mary* Magdalene,
Lu. 1:27. and the virgin's name (was) *Mary.*
30. angel said unto her, Fear not, *Mary.*
34. Then said *Mary* unto the angel,
38. And *Mary* said, Behold the handmaid
39. And *Mary* arose in those days,
41. heard the salutation of *Mary,*
46. *Mary* said, My soul doth magnify the Lord,
56. And *Mary* abode with her about
2: 5. To be taxed with *Mary* his espoused
16. and found *Mary,* and Joseph,
19. But *Mary* kept all these things,
34. and said unto *Mary* his mother,
8: 2. *Mary* called Magdalene, out of
Lu. 10:39. she had a sister called *Mary,*
42. *Mary* hath chosen that good part,
24:10. *Mary* Magdalene, and Joanna, and *Mary* (the mother) of James,
Joh. 11: 1. Lazarus, of Bethany, the town of *Mary*
2. *Mary* which anointed the Lord
19. Jews came to Martha and *Mary,*
20. but *Mary* sat (still) in the house.
28. called *Mary* her sister secretly,
31. when they saw *Mary,*
32. when *Mary* was come where Jesus
45. the Jews which came to *Mary,*
12: 3. took *Mary* a pound of ointment
19:25. *Mary* the (wife) of Cleophas, and *Mary* Magdalene.
20: 1. cometh *Mary* Magdalene early,
11. But *Mary* stood without
16. Jesus saith unto her, *Mary.*
18. *Mary* Magdalene came and told
Acts 1:14. and *Mary* the mother of Jesus,
12:12. he came to the house of *Mary*
Ro. 16: 6. Greet *Mary,* who bestowed much

3138 8 /616
Μάρκος, *Markos.*

Acts12:12. whose surname was *Mark;*
25. whose surname was *Mark.*
15:37. whose surname was *Mark.*
39. and so Barnabas took *Mark,*
Col. 4:10. and *Marcus,* sister's son to Barnabas,
2Ti. 4:11. Take *Mark,* and bring him with thee:
Philem 24. *Marcus,* Aristarchus, Demas,
1Pet. 5:13. and (so doth) *Marcus* my son.

3156 5 497/611 3161
Ματθαῖος, *Matthaios.*

Mat. 9: 9. he saw a man, named *Matthew,*
10: 3. Thomas, and *Matthew* the publican:
Mar 3:18. Bartholomew, and *Matthew,* and Thomas,
Lu. 6:15. *Matthew* and Thomas, James the (son)
Acts 1:13. Thomas, Bartholomew, and *Matthew,*

3157 2 /611 [4977]
Ματθάν, *Matthan.*

Mat. 1:15. and Eleazar begat *Matthan;* and *Matthan* begat Jacob;

3158 2 497/611 3161
Ματθάτ, *Matthat.*

Lu. 3:24. Which was (the son) of *Matthat,*
29. which was (the son) of *Matthat,*

3159 2 497/611 3161
Ματθίας, *Matthias.*

Acts 1:23. who was surnamed Justus, and *Matthias.*
26. the lot fell upon *Matthias;*

3160 1 497/619 3161
Ματταθά, *Mattatha.*

Lu. 3:31. which was (the son) of *Mattatha,*

3161 2 497/619 [4993]
Ματταθίας, *Mattathias.*

Lu. 3:25. Which was (the son) of *Mattathias,*
26. which was (the son) of *Mattathias,*

3190 1 /623

Μελεᾶς, *Meleas.*

Lu. 3:31. Which was (the son) of *Melea,*

3194 1 /623

Μελίτη, *Melitee.*

Acts28: 1. the island was called *Melita.*

3197 2 /625 [4428]

Μελχί, *Melki.*

Lu. 3:24. which was (the son) of *Melchi,*
28. Which was (the son) of *Melchi,*

3198 9 /625 4:568 [4442]

Μελχισεδέκ, *Melkisedek.*

Heb 5: 6. after the order of *Melchisedec.*
10. after the order of *Melchisedec.*
6:20. after the order of *Melchisedec.*
7: 1. For this *Melchisedec,* king of Salem,
10. when *Melchisedec* met him.
11. rise after the order of *Melchisedec,*
15. after the similitude of *Melchisedec*
17. after the order of *Melchisedec.*
21. after the order of *Melchisedec:*

3318 2 508/630 3319,4215

Μεσοποταμία, *Mesopotamia.*

Acts 2: 9. and the dwellers in *Mesopotamia,*
7: 2. when he was in *Mesopotamia,*

3323 2 /631 [4899]

Μεσσίας, *Messias.*

Joh. 1:41(42). We have found the *Messias,*
4:25. I know that *Messias* cometh,

3370 1 /649 cf [4074]

Μῆδος, *Meedos.*

Acts 2: 9. Parthians, and *Medes,* and Elamites,

3399 3 /652

Μίλητος, *Mileetos.*

Acts20:15. the next (day) we came to *Miletus.*
17. from *Miletus* he sent to Ephesus,
2Ti. 4:20. Trophimus have I left at *Miletum*

3412 1 /653

Μιτυλήνη, *Mituleenee.*

Acts20:14. and came to *Mitylene*

3413 2 /653 [4317]

Μιχαήλ, *Mikaeel.*

Jude 9. Yet *Michael* the archangel,
Rev.12: 7. *Michael* and his angels fought

3416 1 /654

Μνάσων, *Mnasōn.*

Acts21:16. brought with them one *Mnason* of Cyprus,

3434 1 /655 [4432]

Μολόχ, *Molok.*

Acts 7:43. took up the tabernacle of *Moloch,*

3460 1 /658

Μύρα, *Mura.*

Acts27: 5. to *Myra,* (a city) of Lycia.

3465 2 /658

Μυσία, *Musia.*

Acts16 7. After they were come to *Mysia,*
8. passing by *Mysia* came down to Troas.

3475 24 /659 [4872]

Μωσεύς, *Mōsūs.*

Mat.23: 2. Pharisees sit in *Moses'* seat:
Mar 9: 4. appeared unto them Elias with *Moses:*
5. one for thee, and one for *Moses,*
12:26. read in the book of *Moses,*
Lu. 2:22. according to the law of *Moses*
9:33. one for *Moses,* and one for Elias:
16:29. They have *Moses* and the prophets;
31. If they hear not *Moses* and the
24:27. And beginning at *Moses* and all
44. written in the law of *Moses,*
Joh. 1:17. For the law was given by *Moses,*
7:22. not because it is of *Moses,*
23. law of *Moses* should not be broken;
9:28. but we are *Moses'* disciples.
Acts13:39. justified by the law of *Moses.*
21:21. among the Gentiles to forsake *Moses,*
28:23. both out of the law of *Moses,*
Ro. 5:14. death reigned from Adam to *Moses,*
1Co. 9: 9. written in the law of *Moses,*
2Co. 3: 7. stedfastly behold the face of *Moses*
Heb 3:16. came out of Egypt by *Moses.*
10:28. He that despised *Moses'* law
Jude 9. disputed about the body of *Moses,*
Rev.15: 3. And they sing the song of *Moses*

See also Μωσῆς, Μωϋσεύς & Μωϋσῆς.

3475 49 /659 [4872]

Μωσῆς, *Mōsees.*

Mat. 8: 4. the gift that *Moses* commanded,
17: 3. appeared unto them *Moses* and
4. one for *Moses,* and one for Elias.
19: 7. Why did *Moses* then command to
8. *Moses* because of the hardness
22:24. Saying, Master, *Moses* said,
Mar 1:44. those things which *Moses* commanded,
7:10. *Moses* said, Honour thy father
10: 3. What did *Moses* command you?
4. And they said, *Moses* suffered to write
12:19. Master, *Moses* wrote unto us,
Lu 5:14. according as *Moses* commanded,
9:30. which were *Moses* and Elias:
20:28. Saying, Master, *Moses* wrote
37. even *Moses* shewed at the bush,
Joh. 1:45(46). of whom *Moses* in the law,
3:14. as *Moses* lifted up the serpent
5:45. (even) *Moses,* in whom ye trust.
46. For had ye believed *Moses,*
6:32. *Moses* gave you not that bread
7:19. Did not *Moses* give you the law,
22. *Moses* therefore gave unto you
8: 5. *Moses* in the law commanded us,
9:29. We know that God spake unto *Moses:*
Acts 3:22. For *Moses* truly said unto the fathers.
6:11. blasphemous words against *Moses,*
7:20. In which time *Moses* was born,
22. *Moses* was learned in all the wisdom
29. Then fled *Moses* at this saying,

Acts 7:31. When *Moses* saw (it), he wondered
32. Then *Moses* trembled, and durst not
40. for (as for) this *Moses*, which brought
44. had appointed, speaking unto *Moses*,
15:21. For *Moses* of old time hath
26:22. the prophets and *Moses* did say
Ro. 9:15. For he saith to *Moses*, I will
10: 5. *Moses* describeth the righteousness
19. First *Moses* saith, I will
1Co.10: 2. And were all baptized unto *Moses*
2Co. 3:13. not as *Moses*, (which) put a vail
15. even unto this day, when *Moses* is read,
Heb 3: 2. as also *Moses* (was faithful) in all
3. worthy of more glory than *Moses*,
5. And *Moses* verily (was) faithful
7:14. of which tribe *Moses* spake nothing
8: 5. as *Moses* was admonished of God
11:23. By faith *Moses*, when he was born,
24. By faith *Moses*, when he was come
12:21. *Moses* said, I exceedingly fear

See also Μωϋσῆς, Μωσεύς & Μωϋσεύς.

3475 4 /659 [4872]

Μωϋσεύς, *Mōüsūs.*

Acts15: 1. circumcised after the manner of *Moses*,
5. to keep the law of *Moses*.
2Ti. 3: 8. as Jannes and Jambres withstood *Moses*,
Heb 9:19. when *Moses* had spoken every precept

See also Μωσεύς, Μωσῆς & Μωϋσῆς.

3475 3 /659 4:848 [4872]

Μωϋσῆς, *Mōüsees.*

Acts 6:14. customs which *Moses* delivered us.
7:35. This *Moses* whom they refused,
37. This is that *Moses*, which said unto

See also Μωσεύς, Μωσῆς & Μωϋσεύς.

3476 3 /660 [5177]

Ναασσών, *Naässōn.*

Mat. 1: 4. Aminadab begat *Naasson*; and *Naasson* begat Salmon;
Lu. 3:32. which was (the son) of *Naassor*

3477 1 /660 cf [5052]

Ναγγαί, *Nangai.*

Lu. 3:25. which was (the son) of *Nagge*,

See below, 3480 See below

Ναζαραῖος, see Ναζωραῖος.

3478 12 /660

Ναζαρέθ, -ρέτ, *Nazareth, -ret.*

Mat. 2:23. dwelt in a city called *Nazareth*:
4:13. And leaving *Nazareth*, he came
21:11. Jesus the prophet of *Nazareth*
Mar 1: 9. that Jesus came from *Nazareth*
Lu. 1:26. a city of Galilee, named *Nazareth*,
2: 4. out of the city of *Nazareth*,
39. to their own city *Nazareth*.
51. with them, and came to *Nazareth*,
4:16. And he came to *Nazareth*,
Joh. 1:45(46). Jesus of *Nazareth*, the son of Joseph.
46(47). good thing come out of *Nazareth*?
Acts10:38. How God anointed Jesus of *Nazareth*

3479 4 /660 4:874

Ναζαρηνός, *Nazareenos.*

Mar 1:24. do with thee, thou Jesus of *Nazareth*?
14:67. thou also wast with Jesus of *Nazareth*.
16: 6. Ye seek Jesus of *Nazareth*,
Lu. 4:34. do with thee, (thou) Jesus of *Nazareth*?

3480 15 534/660 4:874 3478

Ναζωραῖος, *Nazōraios.*

Mat. 2:23. He shall be called a *Nazarene*.
26:71. was also with Jesus of *Nazareth*.
Mar 10:47. heard that it was Jesus of *Nazareth*,
Lu. 18:37. that Jesus of *Nazareth* passeth by.
24:19. Concerning Jesus of *Nazareth*,
Joh. 18: 5. answered him, Jesus of *Nazareth*.
7. And they said, Jesus of *Nazareth*.
19:19. JESUS OF *NAZARETH* THE KING OF THE JEWS.
Acts 2:22. Jesus of *Nazareth*, a man approved of God
3: 6. In the name of Jesus Christ of *Nazareth*
4:10. name of Jesus Christ of *Nazareth*,
6:14. that this Jesus of *Nazareth* shall destroy
22: 8. Jesus of *Nazareth*, whom thou persecutest.
24: 5. ringleader of the sect of the *Nazarenes*:
26: 9. to the name of Jesus of *Nazareth*.

3481 1 /661 [5416]

Ναθάν, *Nathan.*

Lu. 3:31. which was (the son) of *Nathan*,

3482 6 /661 [5417]

Ναθαναήλ, *Nathanaeel.*

Joh. 1:45(46). Philip findeth *Nathanael*, and saith
46(47). And *Nathanael* said unto him,
47(48). Jesus saw *Nathanael* coming to him,
48(49). *Nathanael* saith unto him, Whence
49(50). *Nathanael* answered and saith
21: 2. and *Nathanael* of Cana in Galilee,

3484 1 /661 cf [4999]

Ναΐν, *Naïn.*

Lu. 7:11. he went into a city called *Nain*;

3486 1 /662 [5151]

Ναούμ, *Naoum.*

Lu. 3:25. which was (the son) of *Naum*,

3488 1 /662 *narkē* (stupefaction)

Νάρκισσος, *Narkissos.*

Ro. 16:11. that be of the (houshold) of *Narcissus*,

3493 1 /662 [5152]

Ναχώρ, *Nakōr*

Lu. 3:34. which was (the son) of *Nachor*,

3496 1 536/ 3501,4172

Νεάπολις, *Neapolis.*

Acts16:11. and the next (day) to *Neapolis*

3497 1 /661 [5283]
Νεεμάν, Neëman.
Lu. 4:27. saving *Naaman* the Syrian.

3508 3 /664 [5321]
Νεφθαλείμ, Nephthalīm.
Mat. 4:13. borders of Zabulon and *Nephthalim:*
15. and the land of *Nephthalim,*
Rev. 7: 6. Of the tribe of *Nepthalim* (were) sealed

3517 1 539/665 rt 3491
Νηρεύς, Neerūs.
Ro. 16:15. Salute Philologus, and Julia, *Nereus,*

3518 1 /665 [5374]
Νηρί, Neeri.
Lu. 3:27. which was (the son) of *Neri,*

3526 1 /665
Νίγερ, Niger.
Acts13: 1. and Simeon that was called *Niger,*

3527 1 541/665 3528
Νικάνωρ, Nikanōr.
Acts 6: 5. and Prochorus, and *Nicanor,* and

3530 5 541/666 3534,1218
Νικόδημος, Nikodeemos.
Joh. 3: 1. named *Nicodemus,* a ruler of the Jews:
4. *Nicodemus* saith unto him,
9. *Nicodemus* answered and said unto him,
7:50. *Nicodemus* saith unto them,
19:39. And there came also *Nicodemus,*

3531 2 541/666 3532
Νικολαΐτης, Nikolaïtees.
Rev. 2: 6. the deeds of the *Nicolaitanes,*
15. the doctrine of the *Nicolaitanes,*

3532 1 542/666 3534,2994
Νικόλαος, Nikolaos.
Acts 6: 5. *Nicolas* a proselyte of Antioch:

3533 1 541/666 3534,4172
Νικόπολις, Nikopolis.
Tit. 3:12. to come unto me to *Nicopolis:*

3535 1 /666 [5210]
Νινευΐ, Ninūi.
Lu. 11:32. The men of *Nineve* shall rise

3536 2 542/666 3535
Νινευΐτης, Ninūitees.
Mat.12:41. The men of *Nineveh* shall rise
Lu. 11:30. was a sign unto the *Ninevites,*

3558
Νότος, see among Appellatives.

3564 1 547/670 3565,1435
Νυμφᾶς, Numphas.
Col. 4:15. and *Nymphas,* and the church

3575 8 /673 [5146]
Νῶε, Nōë.
Mat.24:37. But as the days of *Noe* (were),
38. that *Noe* entered into the ark,
Lu. 3:36. which was (the son) of *Noe,*
17:26. as it was in the days of *Noe,*
27. day that *Noe* entered into the ark.
Heb11: 7. By faith *Noah,* being warned of God
1Pet.3:20. of God waited in the days of *Noah,*
2Pet.2: 5. but saved *Noah* the eighth (person),

3604 2 /685 [5818]
Ὀζίας, Ozias.
Mat. 1: 8. and Joram begat *Ozias;*
9. And *Ozias* begat Joatham;

3652 1 /693
Ὀλυμπᾶς, Olumpas.
Ro. 16:15. and *Olympas,* and all the saints

3682 2 573/696 3685
Ὀνήσιμος, Oneesimos.
Col. 4: 9. With *Onesimus,* a faithful and
Philem 10. I beseech thee for my son *Onesimus,*

3683 2 573/696 3685,5411
Ὀνησίφορος, Oneesiphoros.
2Ti. 1:16. unto the house of *Onesiphorus;*
4:19. and the houshold of *Onesiphorus.*

3773 1 /730
Οὐρβανός, Ourbanos.
Ro. 16: 9. Salute *Urbane,* our helper in Christ,

3774 1 /730 [223]
Οὐρίας, Ourias.
Mat. 1: 6. (that had been the wife) of *Urias;*

3828 5 612/749 3956,5443
Παμφυλία, Pamphulia.
Acts 2:10. Phrygia, and *Pamphylia,* in Egypt,
13:13. they came to Perga in *Pamphylia:*
14:24. Pisidia, they came to *Pamphylia.*
15:38. departed from them from *Pamphylia,*
27: 5. sea of Cilicia and *Pamphylia,*

3934 1 /763
Πάρθος, Parthos.
Acts 2: 9. *Parthians,* and Medes, and Elamites,

3937 1 633/763 *Parmenidēs*
Παρμενᾶς, Parmenas.
Acts 6: 5. and Timon, and *Parmenas,* and

3957
Πάσχα, see among Appellatives.

3959 1 640/778
Πάταρα, *Patara.*

Acts21: 1. and from thence unto *Patara:*

3963 1 642/783
Πάτμος, *Patmos.*

Rev. 1: 9. in the isle that is called *Patmos,*

3969 1 642/784 3962,979
Πατρόβας, *Patrobas.*

Ro. 16:14. *Patrobas,* Hermes, and the brethren

3972 1 642/784 cf 3973
Παῦλος, *Paulos.*

(The Deputy.)

Acts13: 7. with the deputy of the country, Sergius *Paulus,*

3972 163 642/784 cf 3973
Παῦλος, *Paulos.*

Acts13: 9. Then Saul, who also (is called) *Paul,*
13. Now when *Paul* and his company (lit. those about *Paul*)
16. Then *Paul* stood up, and beckoning with (his) hand
43. followed *Paul* and Barnabas:
45. which were spoken by *Paul,*
46. Then *Paul* and Barnabas waxed bold,
50. persecution against *Paul* and Barnabas,
14: 9. The same heard *Paul* speak:
11. saw what *Paul* had done,
12. and *Paul,* Mercurius, because he was
14. the apostles, Barnabas and *Paul,* heard (of),
19. and, having stoned *Paul,* drew (him) out
15: 2. When therefore *Paul* and Barnabas had
— they determined that *Paul* and Barnabas,
12. gave audience to Barnabas and *Paul,*
22. to Antioch with *Paul* and Barnabas;
25. with our beloved Barnabas and *Paul,*
35. *Paul* also and Barnabas continued in
36. *Paul* said unto Barnabas,
38. But *Paul* thought not good to take him
40. And *Paul* chose Silas, and departed,
16: 3. Him would *Paul* have to go forth with him;
9. a vision appeared to *Paul* in the night;
14. unto the things which were spoken of *Paul.*
17. The same followed *Paul* and us,
18. But *Paul,* being grieved, turned and
19. they caught *Paul* and Silas, and drew
25. And at midnight *Paul* and Silas prayed,
28. But *Paul* cried with a loud voice,
29. and fell down before *Paul* and Silas,
36. told this saying to *Paul,*
37. But *Paul* said unto them,
17: 2. And *Paul,* as his manner was,
4. and consorted with *Paul* and Silas;
10. sent away *Paul* and Silas by night
13. was preached of *Paul* at Berea,
14. sent away *Paul* to go as it were
15. they that conducted *Paul* brought
16. Now while *Paul* waited for them
22. Then *Paul* stood in the midst of Mars' hill,
33. So *Paul* departed from among them.
18: 1 After these things *Paul* departed
5. *Paul* was pressed in the spirit,
Acts18: 9. spake the Lord to *Paul* in the night
12. with one accord against *Paul,*
14. And when *Paul* was now about
18. And *Paul* (after this) tarried (there)
19: 1. *Paul* having passed through the
4. Then said *Paul,* John verily
6. And when *Paul* had laid (his) hands
11. miracles by the hands of *Paul:*
13. Jesus whom *Paul* preacheth.
15. Jesus I know, and *Paul* I know;
21. *Paul* purposed in the spirit,
26. this *Paul* hath persuaded and turned
29. of Macedonia, *Paul's* companions
30. when *Paul* would have entered in
20: 1. *Paul* called unto (him) the disciples,
7. *Paul* preached unto them,
9. and as *Paul* was long preaching,
10. *Paul* went down, and fell on him,
13. there intending to take in *Paul:*
16. For *Paul* had determined to sail
37. and fell on *Paul's* neck, and kissed him,
21: 4. who said to *Paul* through the Spirit,
8. we that were of *Paul's* company
11. he took *Paul's* girdle, and bound his own hands
13. Then *Paul* answered, What mean ye
18. *Paul* went in with us unto James;
26. Then *Paul* took the men, and the next day
29. they supposed that *Paul* had brought
30. took *Paul,* and drew him out of the temple:
32. they left beating of *Paul.*
37. And as *Paul* was to be led into the castle,
39. But *Paul* said, I am a man (which am)
40. *Paul* stood on the stairs, and beckoned
22:25. *Paul* said unto the centurion
28. And *Paul* said, But I was (free) born.
30. brought *Paul* down, and set him
23: 1. And *Paul,* earnestly beholding the council,
3. Then said *Paul* unto him,
5. said *Paul,* I wist not, brethren,
6. when *Paul* perceived that the one part
10. lest *Paul* should have been pulled in pieces
11. Be of good cheer, *Paul:*
12. till they had killed *Paul.*
14. nothing until we have slain *Paul.*
16. And when *Paul's* sister's son
— the castle, and told *Paul.*
17. *Paul* called one of the centurions
18. and said, *Paul* the prisoner called
20. bring down *Paul* to morrow
24. that they may set *Paul* on, and bring
31. took *Paul,* and brought (him)
33. presented *Paul* also before him.
24: 1. informed the governor against *Paul.*
10. Then *Paul,* after that the governor
23. a centurion to keep *Paul,*
24. he sent for *Paul,* and heard him
26. money should have been given him of *Paul,*
27. left *Paul* bound.
25: 2. informed him against *Paul,*
4. *Paul* should be kept at Cæsarea,
6. commanded *Paul* to be brought.
7. grievous complaints against *Paul.*
9. answered *Paul,* and said,
10. Then said *Paul,* I stand at Cæsar's
14. Festus declared *Paul's* cause
19. *Paul* affirmed to be alive.
21. But when *Paul* had appealed to be
23. *Paul* was brought forth.
26: 1. Agrippa said unto *Paul,*
— *Paul* stretched forth the hand.

Acts26:24. *Paul*, thou art beside thyself,
28. Agrippa said unto *Paul*,
29. *Paul* said, I would to God,
27: 1. delivered *Paul* and certain other
3. Julius courteously entreated *Paul*,
9. *Paul* admonished (them),
11. which were spoken by *Paul*.
21. *Paul* stood forth in the midst of them,
24. Saying, Fear not, *Paul*;
31. *Paul* said to the centurion
33. *Paul* besought (them) all to take meat,
43. willing to save *Paul*, kept them
28: 3. when *Paul* had gathered a bundle
8. *Paul* entered in, and prayed,
15. whom when *Paul* saw, he thanked God,
16. but *Paul* was suffered to dwell
17. *Paul* called the chief of the Jews
25. after that *Paul* had spoken
30. *Paul* dwelt two whole years
Ro. 1: 1. *Paul*, a servant of Jesus Christ,
1Co. 1: 1. *Paul*, called (to be) an apostle of
12. I am of *Paul*; and I of Apollos;
13. was *Paul* crucified for you? or were ye baptized in the name of *Paul*?
3: 4. I am of *Paul*; and another, I (am) of
5. Who then is *Paul*, and who (is) Apollos,
22. Whether *Paul*, or Apollos, or Cephas,
16:21. The salutation of (me) *Paul*
2Co. 1: 1. *Paul*, an apostle of Jesus Christ
10: 1. Now I *Paul* myself beseech you
Gal. 1: 1. *Paul*, an apostle, not of men,
5: 2. Behold, I *Paul* say unto you,
Eph. 1: 1. *Paul*, an apostle of Jesus Christ
3: 1. For this cause I *Paul*, the prisoner
Phi. 1: 1. *Paul* and Timotheus, the servants
Col. 1: 1. *Paul*, an apostle of Jesus Christ
23. whereof I *Paul* am made a minister;
4:18. The salutation by the hand of me *Paul*.
1Th. 1: 1. *Paul*, and Silvanus, and Timotheus,
2:18. even I *Paul*, once and again;
2Th. 1: 1. *Paul*, and Silvanus, and Timotheus,
3:17. The salutation of *Paul* with mine own hand,
1Ti. 1: 1. *Paul*, an apostle of Jesus Christ
2Ti. 1: 1. *Paul*, an apostle of Jesus Christ
Tit. 1: 1. *Paul*, a servant of God, and an apostle of Jesus Christ,
Philem 1. *Paul*, a prisoner of Jesus Christ,
9. being such an one as *Paul* the aged,
19. I *Paul* have written (it) with mine
2Pet. 3:15. as our beloved brother *Paul* also

3974 2 643/785

Πάφος, *Paphos*.

Acts13: 6. gone through the isle unto *Paphos*,
13. and his company loosed from *Paphos*,

4010 2 649/791 4444

Πέργαμος, *Pergamos*.

Rev. 1:11. unto Smyrna, and unto *Pergamos*,
2:12. of the church in *Pergamos* write;

4011 3 650/741 rt 4010

Πέργη, *Pergee*.

Acts13:13. they came to *Perga* in Pamphylia:
14. when they departed from *Perga*,
25. had preached the word in *Perga*,

4069 1 659/

Περσίς, *Persis*.

Ro. 16:12. Salute the beloved *Persis*,

4074 162 660/800 6:150 cf 4073

Πέτρος, *Petros*.

Mat. 4:18. Simon called *Peter*, and Andrew
8:14. was come into *Peter's* house,
10: 2. The first, Simon, who is called *Peter*,
14:28. And *Peter* answered him and said,
29. And when *Peter* was come down out
15:15. Then answered *Peter* and said
16:16. And Simon *Peter* answered and said,
18. unto thee, That thou art *Peter*,
22. Then *Peter* took him, and began
23. turned, and said unto *Peter*,
17: 1. Jesus taketh *Peter*, James, and John
4. Then answered *Peter*, and said
24. tribute (money) came to *Peter*,
26. *Peter* saith unto him,
18:21. Then came *Peter* to him,
19:27. Then answered *Peter* and said unto him
26:33. *Peter* answered and said
35. *Peter* said unto him,
37. took with him *Peter* and the two sons
40. and saith unto *Peter*, What, could
58. But *Peter* followed him afar off
69. Now *Peter* sat without
73. and said to *Peter*, Surely thou also
75. And *Peter* remembered the word
Mar 3:16. And Simon he surnamed *Peter*;
5:37. to follow him, save *Peter*, and James, and John
8:29. And *Peter* answereth and saith
32. And *Peter* took him, and began
33. he rebuked *Peter*, saying,
9: 2. taketh (with him) *Peter*, and James, and John,
5. And *Peter* answered and said
10:28. Then *Peter* began to say unto him, Lo,
11:21. And *Peter* calling to remembrance
13: 3. *Peter* and James and John and Andrew asked
14:29. But *Peter* said unto him,
33. taketh with him *Peter* and James and John,
37. and saith unto *Peter*, Simon, sleepest
54. And *Peter* followed him afar off,
66. And as *Peter* was beneath in
67. when she saw *Peter* warming
70. said again to *Peter*, Surely thou
72. And *Peter* called to mind
16: 7. tell his disciples and *Peter*
Lu. 5: 8. When Simon *Peter* saw (it), he fell
6:14. Simon, whom he also named *Peter*,
8:45. *Peter* and they that were with
51. to go in, save *Peter*, and James, and John
9:20. *Peter* answering said, The Christ of God
28. he took *Peter* and John and James,
32. But *Peter* and they that were with
33. *Peter* said unto Jesus,
12:41. Then *Peter* said unto him,
18:28. Then *Peter* said, Lo, we have left
22: 8. And he sent *Peter* and John, saying,
34. I tell thee, *Peter*, the cock
54. And *Peter* followed afar off.
55. *Peter* sat down among them.
58. *Peter* said, Man, I am not.
60. *Peter* said, Man, I know not
61. and looked upon *Peter*. And *Peter* remembered the word

Lu. 22:62. And *Peter* went out, and wept bitterly.
24:12. Then arose *Peter*, and ran
Joh. 1:40(41). Andrew, Simon *Peter's* brother.
44(45). Bethsaida, the city of Andrew and *Peter*.
6: 8. Simon *Peter's* brother, saith unto him,
68. Simon *Peter* answered him,
13: 6. Then cometh he to Simon *Peter:*
8. *Peter* saith unto him,
9. Simon *Peter* saith unto him,
24. Simon *Peter* therefore beckoned
36. Simon *Peter* said unto him,
37. *Peter* said unto him, Lord, why
18:10. Simon *Peter* having a sword
11. said Jesus unto *Peter*, Put up
15. And Simon *Peter* followed Jesus,
16. *Peter* stood at the door without.
— and brought in *Peter*.
17. that kept the door unto *Peter*,
18. and *Peter* stood with them,
25. Simon *Peter* stood and warmed himself.
26. whose ear *Peter* cut off,
27. *Peter* then denied again:
20: 2. and cometh to Simon *Peter*,
3. *Peter* therefore went forth,
4. the other disciple did outrun *Peter*,
6. Then cometh Simon *Peter*
21: 2. together Simon *Peter*, and Thomas
3. Simon *Peter* saith unto them,
7. saith unto *Peter*, It is the Lord. Now when Simon *Peter* heard that
11. Simon *Peter* went up, and drew the net
15. Jesus saith to Simon *Peter*,
17. *Peter* was grieved because he said
20. Then *Peter*, turning about, seeth
21. *Peter* seeing him saith
Acts 1:13. abode both *Peter*, and James, and John,
15. in those days *Peter* stood up
2:14. But *Peter*, standing up with the eleven,
37. said unto *Peter* and to the rest
38. Then *Peter* said unto them,
3: 1. *Peter* and John went up together
3. Who seeing *Peter* and John
4. *Peter*, fastening his eyes
6. *Peter* said, Silver and gold have I none;
11. held *Peter* and John,
12. when *Peter* saw (it), he answered
4: 8. *Peter*, filled with the Holy Ghost,
13. the boldness of *Peter* and John,
19. *Peter* and John answered and said
5: 3. But *Peter* said, Ananias, why
8. And *Peter* answered unto her,
9. Then *Peter* said unto her,
15. the shadow of *Peter* passing by
29. *Peter* and the (other) apostles
8:14. sent unto them *Peter* and John:
20. But *Peter* said unto him,
9:32. as *Peter* passed throughout all
34. And *Peter* said unto him,
38. heard that *Peter* was there,
39. *Peter* arose and went with them.
40. *Peter* put them all forth,
— saw *Peter*, she sat up.
10: 5. whose surname is *Peter:*
9. *Peter* went up upon the housetop
13. Rise, *Peter;* kill, and eat.
14. *Peter* said, Not so, Lord;
17. while *Peter* doubted in himself
18. which was surnamed *Peter*,
19. While *Peter* thought on the vision,
21. Then *Peter* went down
23. on the morrow *Peter* went away
Acts10:25. as *Peter* was coming in,
26. But *Peter* took him up,
32. Simon, whose surname is *Peter;*
34. Then *Peter* opened (his) mouth,
44. While *Peter* yet spake
45. as many as came with *Peter*,
46. Then answered *Peter*,
11: 2. *Peter* was come up to Jerusalem,
4. *Peter* rehearsed (the matter)
7. Arise, *Peter;* slay and eat.
13. whose surname is *Peter;*
12: 3. proceeded further to take *Peter*
5. *Peter* therefore was kept in prison:
6. the same night *Peter* was sleeping
7. smote *Peter* on the side,
11. *Peter* was come to himself,
13. as *Peter* knocked at the door
14. she knew *Peter's* voice,
— how *Peter* stood before the gate.
16. But *Peter* continued knocking:
18. what was become of *Peter*.
15: 7. *Peter* rose up, and said unto them,
Gal. 1:18. went up to Jerusalem to see *Peter*,
2: 7. of the circumcision (was) unto *Peter;*
8. wrought effectually in *Peter*
11. when *Peter* was come to Antioch,
14. I said unto *Peter* before (them) all,
1Pet.1: 1. *Peter*, an apostle of Jesus Christ,
2Pet.1: 1. Simon *Peter*, a servant and an apostle of Jesus Christ,

---

4091 55 /786

Πιλάτος, *Pilatos.*

Mat.27: 2. and delivered him to Pontius *Pilate*
13. Then said *Pilate* unto him,
17. gathered together, *Pilate* said unto them,
22. *Pilate* saith unto them, What
24. When *Pilate* saw that he could
58. He went to *Pilate*, and begged the body of Jesus. Then *Pilate* commanded the
62. Pharisees came together unto *Pilate*,
65. *Pilate* said unto them, Ye have
Mar15: 1. and delivered (him) to *Pilate*.
2. *Pilate* asked him, Art thou
4. And *Pilate* asked him again,
5. nothing; so that *Pilate* marvelled.
9. But *Pilate* answered them,
12. *Pilate* answered and said again
14. Then *Pilate* said unto them,
15. And (so) *Pilate*, willing to content
43. went in boldly unto *Pilate*, and craved
44. And *Pilate* marvelled if he were
Lu. 3: 1. *Pilate* being governor of Judæa,
13: 1. whose blood *Pilate* had mingled
23: 1. and led him unto *Pilate*.
3. And *Pilate* asked him, saying,
4. Then said *Pilate* to the chief priests
6. When *Pilate* heard of Galilee,
11. and sent him again to *Pilate*.
12 *Pilate* and Herod were made friends
13. And *Pilate*, when he had called
20. *Pilate* therefore, willing to release
24. And *Pilate* gave sentence that it
52. This (man) went unto *Pilate*,
Joh.18:29. *Pilate* then went out unto them,
31. Then said *Pilate* unto them,
33. Then *Pilate* entered into the judgment hall
35. *Pilate* answered, Am I a Jew?
37. *Pilate* therefore said unto him,
38. *Pilate* saith unto him, What is truth?

Joh.19: 1. *Pilate* therefore took Jesus, and scourged (him).
4. *Pilate* therefore went forth again,
6. *Pilate* saith unto them, Take ye him,
8. When *Pilate* therefore heard that saying,
10. Then saith *Pilate* unto him, Speakest
12. thenceforth *Pilate* sought to release him:
13. When *Pilate* therefore heard that saying,
15. *Pilate* saith unto them, Shall I crucify
19. And *Pilate* wrote a title, and put
21. chief priests of the Jews to *Pilate*,
22. *Pilate* answered, What I have written
31. besought *Pilate* that their legs
38. besought *Pilate* that he might take away the body of Jesus: and *Pilate* gave (him) leave.
Acts 3:13. denied him in the presence of *Pilate*,
4:27. both Herod, and Pontius *Pilate*,
13:28. yet desired they *Pilate* that he should
1Ti. 6:13. who before Pontius *Pilate* witnessed

4099 2 /805

Πισιδία, *Pisidia.*

Acts13:14. they came to Antioch in *Pisidia*,
14:24. after they had passed throughout *Pisidia*,

4193 1 698/840 4195

Ποντικός, *Pontikos.*

Acts18: 2. a certain Jew named Aquila, born in *Pontus*,

4194 4 698/840

Πόντιος, *Pontios.*

Mat.27: 2. and delivered him to *Pontius* Pilate
Lu. 3: 1. *Pontius* Pilate being governor of Judæa,
Acts 4:27. both Herod, and *Pontius* Pilate,
1Ti. 6:13. who before *Pontius* Pilate witnessed

4195 2 698/840

Πόντος, *Pontos.*

Acts 2: 9. and Cappadocia, in *Pontus*, and Asia,
1Pet.1: 1. to the strangers scattered throughout *Pontus*,

4196 2 698/840

Πόπλιος, *Poplios.*

Acts28: 7. whose name was *Publius*;
8. the father of *Publius* lay sick of a fever

4201 1 699/842

Πόρκιος, *Porkios.*

Acts24:27. after two years *Porcius* Festus

4223 1 /844

Ποτίολοι, *Potioloi.*

Acts28:13. and we came the next day to *Puteoli*:

4227 1 703/845

Πούδης, *Poudees.*

2Ti. 4:21. Eubulus greeteth thee, and *Pudens*,

4251 1 /849

Πρίσκα, *Priska.*

2Ti. 4:19 Salute *Prisca* and Aquila,

4252 5 /849 4251

Πρίσκιλλα, *Priskilla.*

Acts18: 2. from Italy, with his wife *Priscilla*;
18. and with him *Priscilla* and Aquila;
26. when Aquila and *Priscilla* had heard,
Ro. 16: 3. Greet *Priscilla* and Aquila my helpers
1Co.16:19. Aquila and *Priscilla* salute you

4402 1 732/873 4253,5525

Πρόχορος, *Prokoros.*

Acts 6: 5. and Philip, and *Prochorus*, and Nicanor,

4424 1 /875

Πτολεμαΐς, *Ptolemaïs.*

Acts21: 7. from Tyre, we came to *Ptolemais*,

4436 1 736/876 6:917

Πύθων, *Puthōn.* ×

Acts16:16. possessed with a spirit of *divination* (lit. of *Pytho*)

4460 2 740/880 [7343]

Ῥαάϐ, *Raäb.*

Heb 11:31. By faith the harlot *Rahab* perished not
Jas. 2:25. was not *Rahab* the harlot justified
See also Ῥαχαϐ.

4466 1 741/880 [7466]

Ῥαγαῦ, *Ragau.*

Lu. 3:35. which was (the son) of *Ragau*,

4471 1 741/880 [7414]

Ῥαμά, *Rama.*

Mat. 2:18. In *Rama* was there a voice heard,

4477 1 742/881 3:1 rt 4460

Ῥαχάϐ, *Rakab.*

Mat. 1: 5. Salmon begat Booz of *Rachab*;
See also Ῥααϐ.

4478 1 742/881 [7354]

Ῥαχήλ, *Rakeel.*

Mat. 2:18. *Rachel* weeping (for) her children,

4479 1 742/881 [7259]

Ῥεϐέκκα, *Rebekka.*

Ro. 9:10. but when *Rebecca* also had conceived

4481 1 742/881 [3594]

Ῥεμφάν, *Remphan.*

Acts 7:43. and the star of your god *Remphan*,

4484 1 742/881

Ῥήγιον, *Reegion.*

Acts28:13. fetched a compass, and came to *Rhegium*:

4488 1 743/882 cf [7509]

Ῥησά, *Reesa.*

Lu. 3:27. which was (the son) of *Rhesa*.

4497 2 744/882 [7346]
Ῥοβοάμ, *Roboam.*

Mat. 1: 7. And Solomon begat *Roboam;* and *Roboam* begat Abia;

4498 1 744/882 *rhodē* (rose)
Ῥόδη, *Rodee.*

Acts12:13. a damsel came to hearken, named *Rhoda.*

4499 1 744/882 *rhodon* (rose)
Ῥόδος, *Rodos.*

Acts21: 1. and the (day) following unto *Rhodes,*

4502 1 744/883 [7205]
Ῥουβήν, *Roubeen.*

Rev. 7: 5. Of the tribe of *Reuben* (were) sealed

4503 1 744/883 3:1 [7327]
Ῥούθ, *Routh.*

Mat. 1: 5. Booz begat Obed of *Ruth;*

4504 2 744/883
Ῥοῦφος, *Rouphos.*

Mar 15:21. the father of Alexander and *Rufus,*
Ro. 16:13. Salute *Rufus* chosen in the Lord.

4513 1 745/ 4514
Ῥωμαϊκός, *Rōmaikos.*

Lu. 23:38. letters of Greek, and *Latin,* and Hebrew,

4514 12 745/883 4516
Ῥωμαῖος, *Rōmaios.*

Joh. 11:48. the *Romans* shall come and take away
Acts 2:10. and strangers of *Rome,* Jews
16:21. neither to observe, being *Romans.*
37. openly uncondemned, being *Romans,*
38. when they heard that they were *Romans.*
22:25. to scourge a man that is a *Roman,*
26. for this man is a *Roman.*
27. Tell me, art thou a *Roman?*
29. after he knew that he was a *Roman,*
23:27. understood that he was a *Roman.*
25:16. It is not the manner of the *Romans*
28:17. into the hands of the *Romans.*

4515 1 745/883 4516
Ῥωμαϊστί, *Romaisti.*

Joh. 19:20. in Hebrew, (and) Greek, (and) *Latin.*

4516 8 745/883 rt 4517
Ῥώμη, *Rōmee.*

Acts18: 2. all Jews to depart from *Rome:*
19:21. I must also see *Rome.*
23:11. thou bear witness also at *Rome.*
28:14. and so we went toward *Rome.*
16. And when we came to *Rome,*
Ro. 1: 7. To all that be in *Rome,*
15. gospel to you that are at *Rome* also.
2Ti. 1:17. But, when he was in *Rome,*

4523 14 747/885 7:45 4524
Σαδδουκαῖος, *Saddoukaios.*

Mat. 3: 7. many of the Pharisees and *Sadducees*
Mat.16: 1. The Pharisees also with the *Sadducees*
6. the leaven of the Pharisees and of the *Sadducees.*
11. leaven of the Pharisees and of the *Sadducees?*
12. doctrine of the Pharisees and of the *Sadducees.*
22:23. came to him the *Sadducees,*
34. put the *Sadducees* to silence,
Mar 12:18. Then come unto him the *Sadducees,*
Lu. 20:27. certain of the *Sadducees,*
Acts 4: 1. and the *Sadducees,* came upon them,
5:17. which is the sect of the *Sadducees,*
23: 6. the one part were *Sadducees,*
7. a dissension between the Pharisees and the *Sadducees:*
8. For the *Sadducees* say

4524 2 747/885 [6659]
Σαδώκ, *Sadōk.*

Mat. 1:14. Azor begat *Sadoc;* and *Sadoc* begat

4527 2 747/885 [7974]
Σαλά, *Sala.*

Lu. 3:35. Heber, which was (the son) of *Sala,*

4528 3 747/885 [7597]
Σαλαθιήλ, *Salathieel.*

Mat. 1:12. Jechonias begat *Salathiel;* and *Salathiel*
Lu. 3:27. Zorobabel, which was (the son) of *Salathiel,*

4529 1 747/885 4535
Σαλαμίς, *Salamis.*

Acts13: 5. And when they were at *Salamis,*

4530 1 748/885 rt 4531
Σαλείμ, *Salīm.*

Joh. 3:23. in Ænon near to *Salim,*

4532 2 748/885 [8004]
Σαλήμ, *Saleem.*

Heb 7: 1. this Melchisedec, king of *Salem,*
2. also King of *Salem.*

4533 3 748/885 [8012]
Σαλμών, *Salmōn.*

Mat. 1: 4. Naasson begat *Salmon;*
5. And *Salmon* begat Booz
Lu. 3:32. Booz, which was (the son) of *Salmon,*

4534 1 748/885 rt 4529
Σαλμώνη, *Salmōnee.*

Acts27: 7. under Crete, over against *Salmone,*

4539 2 748/886 [7965]
Σαλώμη, *Salōmee.*

Mar 15:40. and of Joses, and *Salome,*
16: 1. Mary the (mother) of James, and *Salome,*

4540 11 748/886 7:88 [8111]
Σαμάρεια, *Samarīa.*

Lu. 17:11. the midst of *Samaria* and Galilee.

Joh. 4: 4. And he must needs go through *Samaria.*
5. to a city of *Samaria,*
7. a woman of *Samaria* to draw water·
Acts 1: 8. and in *Samaria,* and unto the
8: 1. the regions of Judæa and *Samaria,*
5. Philip went down to the city of *Samaria,*
9. and bewitched the people of *Samaria,*
14. *Samaria* had received the word
9:31. and Galilee and *Samaria,*
15: 3. through Phenice and *Samaria,*

4541 9 748/886 7:88 4540

Σαμαρείτης, *Samaritees.*

Mat.10: 5. into (any) city of the *Samaritans*
Lu. 9:52. into a village of the *Samaritans,*
10:33. But a certain *Samaritan,*
17:16. and he was a *Samaritan.*
Joh. 4: 9. dealings with the *Samaritans.*
39. And many of the *Samaritans* of that city
40. So when the *Samaritans* were come
8:48. thou art a *Samaritan,* and hast a devil?
Acts 8:25. in many villages of the *Samaritans.*

4542 2 749/886 7:88 4541

Σαμαρεῖτις, *Samaritis.*

Joh. 4. 9. Then saith the woman of *Samaria*
— which am a woman of *Samaria?*

4543 1 749/886 Samos of Thrace

Σαμοθράκη, *Samothrakee.*

Acts16:11. with a straight course to *Samothracia,*

4544 1 749/886

Σάμος, *Samos.*

Acts20:15. the next (day) we arrived at *Samos,*

4545 3 749/886 [8050]

Σαμουήλ, *Samoueel.*

Acts 3:24. Yea, and all the prophets from *Samuel*
13:20. until *Samuel* the prophet.
Heb 11:32. David also, and *Samuel,*

4546 1 749/886 [8123]

Σαμψών, *Sampsōn.*

Heb 11:32. and (of) *Samson* and (of) Jephthae;

4549 9 749/886 eq 4569,[7586]

Σαούλ, *Säoul.*

Acts 9: 4. *Saul, Saul,* why persecutest thou me?
17. Brother *Saul,* the Lord, (even) Jesus,
13:21. God gave unto them *Saul* the son of Cis,
22: 7. *Saul, Saul,* why persecutest thou me?
13. Brother *Saul,* receive thy sight.
26:14. *Saul, Saul,* why persecutest thou me?

4551 1 749/886 4552

Σαπφείρη, *Sapphiree.*

Acts 5: 1. Ananias, with *Sapphira* his wife,

4554 3 749/886

Σάρδεις, *Sardis.*

Rev. 1:11. unto Thyatira, and unto *Sardis,*
3: 1. angel of the church in *Sardis* write;
4. Thou hast a few names even in *Sardis*

4558 1 750/886 [6886]

Σάρεπτα, *Sarepta.*

Lu. 4:26. was Elias sent, save unto *Sarepta,*

4562 1 752/890 [8286]

Σαρούχ, *Sarouk.*

Lu. 3:35. Which was (the son) of *Saruch,*

4564 4 752/888 [8283]

Σάῤῥα, *Sarra.*

Ro. 4:19. the deadness of *Sarah's* womb:
9: 9. and *Sarah* shall have a son.
Heb 11:11. *Sara* herself received strength
1Pet. 3: 6. Even as *Sara* obeyed Abraham,

4565 1 752/888 [8289]

Σάρων *Sarōn.*

Acts 9:35. all that dwelt at Lydda and *Saron,*

4566 1 752/888 7:151 [7854]

Σατᾶν, *Satan.* cf 4567

2Co.12: 7. the messenger of *Satan*

4567 36 752/888 7:151 eq 4566

Σατανᾶς, *Satanas.* cf 3972

Mat. 4:10. Get thee hence, *Satan:*
12:26. And if *Satan* cast out *Satan,*
16:23. Get thee behind me, *Satan:*
Mar 1:13. forty days, tempted of *Satan;*
3:23. How can *Satan* cast out *Satan?*
26. And if *Satan* rise up against himself,
4:15. *Satan* cometh immediately, and
8:33. Get thee behind me, *Satan:*
Lu. 4: 8. Get thee behind me, *Satan:*
10:18. I beheld *Satan* as lightning
11:18. If *Satan* also be divided
13:16. whom *Satan* hath bound,
22: 3. Then entered *Satan* into Judas
31. behold, *Satan* hath desired (to have) you,
Joh. 13:27. *Satan* entered into him.
Acts 5: 3. Ananias, why hath *Satan*
26:18. and (from) the power of *Satan*
Ro. 16:20. bruise *Satan* under your feet
1Co. 5: 5. unto *Satan* for the destruction
7: 5. that *Satan* tempt you not
2Co. 2:11. Lest *Satan* should get an advantage
11:14. for *Satan* himself is transformed
1Th. 2:18. but *Satan* hindered us.
2Th. 2: 9. after the working of *Satan*
1Ti. 1:20. whom I have delivered unto *Satan,*
5:15. already turned aside after *Satan.*
Rev. 2: 9. but (are) the synagogue of *Satan.*
13. where *Satan's* seat (is):
— where *Satan* dwelleth.
24. known the depths of *Satan,*
3: 9. them of the synagogue of *Satan.*
12: 9. called the Devil, and *Satan,*
20: 2. which is the devil, and *Satan,*
7. *Satan* shall be loosed

4569 17 752/889 eq 4549,cf 3972

Σαῦλος, *Saulos.*

Acts 7:58. whose name was *Saul.*

Acts 8: 1. And *Saul* was consenting unto his death.
3. As for *Saul*, he made havock
9: 1. And *Saul*, yet breathing out threatenings
8. And *Saul* arose from the earth,
11. for (one) called *Saul*, of Tarsus:
19. Then was *Saul* certain days
22. But *Saul* increased the more in
24. their laying await was known of *Saul*.
26. And when *Saul* was come
11:25. for to seek *Saul*.
30. by the hands of Barnabas and *Saul*.
12:25. And Barnabas and *Saul* returned
13: 1. Herod the tetrarch, and *Saul*.
2. Separate me Barnabas and *Saul*
7. who called for Barnabas and *Saul*,
9. Then *Saul*, who also (is called) Paul,

4575 3 753/889 7:168 4573

Σεβαστός, *Sebastos*.

Acts25:21. reserved unto the hearing of *Augustus*,
25. himself hath appealed to *Augustus*,

4580 1 754/890

Σεκοῦνδος, *Sekoundos*.

Acts20: 4. Aristarchus and *Secundus*;

4581 1 754/890

Σελεύκεια, *Selūkia*.

Acts13: 4. departed unto *Seleucia*;

4584 1 754/890 [8096]

Σεμεΐ, *Semei*.

Lu. 3:26. which was (the son) of *Semei*,

4588 1 754/890

Σέργιος, *Sergios*.

Acts13: 7. *Sergius* Paulus, a prudent man,

4589 1 755/890 [8352]

Σήθ, *Seeth*.

Lu. 3:38. which was (the son) of *Seth*,

4590 1 755/890 [8035]

Σήμ, *Seem*.

Lu. 3:36. which was (the son) of *Sem*,

4605 11 757/892 [6721]

Σιδών, *Sidōn*.

Mat.11:21. had been done in Tyre and *Sidon*,
22. It shall be more tolerable for Tyre and *Sidon*
15:21. into the coasts of Tyre and *Sidon*.
Mar 3: 8. and they about Tyre and *Sidon*,
7:24. into the borders of Tyre and *Sidon*,
31. from the coasts of Tyre and *Sidon*,
Lu. 4:26. Sarepta, (a city) of *Sidon*,
6:17. the sea coast of Tyre and *Sidon*,
10:13. done in Tyre and *Sidon*,
14 more tolerable for Tyre and *Sidon*
Acts27:3. we touched at *Sidon*.

4606 1 757/892 4605

Σιδώνιος, *Sidōnios*.

Acts12:20. with them of Tyre and *Sidon*:

4609 13 758/892 4610

Σίλας, *Silas*.

Acts15:22. Barsabas, and *Silas*, chief men
27. Judas and *Silas*, who shall also
32. Judas and *Silas*, being prophets
34. it pleased *Silas* to abide there
40. And Paul chose *Silas*, and
16:19. they caught Paul and *Silas*,
25. Paul and *Silas* prayed, and sang
29. and fell down before Paul and *Silas*,
17: 4. consorted with Paul and *Silas*;
10. sent away Paul and *Silas*
14. but *Silas* and Timotheus abode there
15. receiving a commandment unto *Silas*
18: 5. when *Silas* and Timotheus were come

4610 4 758/893 cf 4609

Σιλουανός, *Silouanos*.

2Co. 1:19. (even) by me and *Silvanus*
1Th. 1: 1. Paul, and *Silvanus*, and Timotheus,
2Th. 1: 1. Paul, and *Silvanus*, and Timotheus,
1Pet.5:12. By *Silvanus*, a faithful brother

4611 13 758/893 [7975]

Σιλωάμ, *Silōam*.

Lu. 13: 4. upon whom the tower in *Siloam*
Joh. 9: 7. Go, wash in the pool of *Siloam*,
11. Go to the pool of *Siloam*,

4613 76 758/893 cf 4826,[8095]

Σίμων, *Simōn*.

Mat. 4:18. *Simon* called Peter, and Andrew
10: 2. The first, *Simon*, who is called **Peter**,
4. *Simon* the Canaanite, and Judas
13:55. Joses, and *Simon*, and Judas?
16:16. And *Simon* Peter answered
17. Blessed art thou, *Simon* Bar-jona:
17:25. What thinkest thou, *Simon*?
26: 6. in the house of *Simon* the leper.
27:32. a man of Cyrene, *Simon* by name:
Mar 1:16. he saw *Simon* and Andrew
29. entered into the house of *Simon*
30. But *Simon's* wife's mother
36. And *Simon* and they that were
3:16. and *Simon* he surnamed Peter;
18. and *Simon* the Canaanite,
6: 3. of Juda, and *Simon*?
14: 3. the house of *Simon* the leper,
37. *Simon*, sleepest thou?
15:21. they compel one *Simon*
Lu. 4:38. and entered into *Simon's* house. **And** *Simon's* wife's mother was taken
5: 3. of the ships, which was *Simon's*,
4. he said unto *Simon*, Launch out
5. And *Simon* answering said
8. When *Simon* Peter saw (it),
10. which were partners with *Simon*. And Jesus said unto *Simon*, Fear not;
6:14. *Simon*, whom he also named Peter,
15. and *Simon* called Zelotes,
7:40. *Simon*, I have somewhat to say unto thee.
43. *Simon* answered and said,
44. and said unto *Simon*,
22:31. *Simon*, *Simon*, behold, Satan hath desired
23:26. they laid hold upon one *Simon*,
24:34. hath appeared to *Simon*.
Joh. 1:40(41). Andrew, *Simon* Peter's brother.
41(42). his own brother *Simon*,
42(43). Thou art *Simon* the son of Jona

Joh. 6: 8. Andrew, *Simon* Peter's brother,
68. *Simon* Peter answered him,
71. Judas Iscariot (the son) of *Simon:*
12: 4. Judas Iscariot, *Simon's* (son),
13: 2. Judas Iscariot, *Simon's* (son),
6. Then cometh he to *Simon* Peter.
9. *Simon* Peter saith unto him,
24. *Simon* Peter therefore beckoned to him,
26. to Judas Iscariot, (the son) of *Simon.*
36. *Simon* Peter said unto him, Lord,
18:10. *Simon* Peter having a sword
15. And *Simon* Peter followed Jesus,
25. *Simon* Peter stood and warmed himself.
20: 2. Then she runneth, and cometh to *Simon* Peter,
6. Then cometh *Simon* Peter following him,
21: 2. There were together *Simon* Peter, and Thomas
3. *Simon* Peter saith unto them,
7. Now when *Simon* Peter heard
11. *Simon* Peter went up, and drew
15. Jesus saith to *Simon* Peter, *Simon,* (son) of Jonas, lovest thou me
16. *Simon,* (son) of Jonas, lovest thou me?
17. *Simon,* (son) of Jonas, lovest thou me?
Acts 1:13. and *Simon* Zelotes, and Judas
8: 9. a certain man, called *Simon,*
13. Then *Simon* himself believed
18. And when *Simon* saw
24. Then answered *Simon,* and said,
9:43. with one *Simon* a tanner.
10: 5. *Simon,* whose surname is Peter:
6. He lodgeth with one *Simon*
17. had made enquiry for *Simon's* house,
18. *Simon,* which was surnamed Peter,
32. and call hither *Simon,*
— in the house of (one) *Simon* a tanner
11:13. and call for *Simon,*

4614 4 759/893 7:282 [5514]

Σινᾶ, *Sina.*

Acts 7:30. in the wilderness of Mount *Sina*
38. which spake to him in the mount *Sina,*
Gal. 4:24. covenants; the one from the mount *Sinai,*
25. For this Agar is mount *Sinai*

4622 7 759/894 7:292 [6726]

Σιών, *Siōn.*

Mat.21: 5. Tell ye the daughter of *Sion,*
Joh.12:15. Fear not, daughter of *Sion:*
Ro. 9:33. I lay in *Sion* a stumblingstone
11:26. There shall come out of *Sion* the Deliverer,
Heb 12:22. But ye are come unto mount *Sion,*
1Pet.2: 6. I lay in *Sion* a chief corner stone,
Rev.14: 1. a Lamb stood on the mount *Sion,*

4630 1 761/895

Σκευᾶς, *Skūas.*

Acts19:14. there were seven sons of (one) *Sceva,*

4658 1 765/897 7:447

Σκύθης, *Skuthees.*

Col. 3:11. Barbarian, *Scythian,* bond (nor) free:

4667 1 766/897 rt 4666

Σμύρνα, *Smurna.*

Rev. 1:11. and unto *Smyrna,* and unto Pergamos,

4668 1 766/897 4667

Σμυρναῖος, *Smurnaios.*

Rev. 2: 8. the angel of the church in *Smyrna*

4670 10 766/897 [5467]

Σόδομα, (τα), *Sodoma.*

Mat.10:15. tolerable for the land of *Sodom*
11:23. had been done in *Sodom,*
24. tolerable for the land of *Sodom*
Mar 6:11. more tolerable for *Sodom*
Lu. 10:12. tolerable in that day for *Sodom,*
17:29. day that Lot went out of *Sodom*
Ro. 9:29. we had been as *Sodoma,*
2Pet.2: 6. the cities of *Sodom* and Gomorrha
Jude 7. Even as *Sodom* and Gomorrha,
Rev.11: 8. which spiritually is called *Sodom* and Egypt,

4672 12 766/898 7:459 [8010]

Σολομών, -ῶν, *Solomōn.*

Mat. 1: 6. and David the king begat *Solomon*
7. And *Solomon* begat Roboam;
6:29. even *Solomon* in all his glory
12:42. to hear the wisdom of *Solomon,* and, behold, a greater than *Solomon* (is) here.
Lu. 11:31. to hear the wisdom of *Solomon;* and, behold, a greater than *Solomon* (is) here.
12:27. *Solomon* in all his glory
Joh.10:23. in *Solomon's* porch.
Acts 3:11. in the porch that is called *Solomon's,*
5:12. with one accord in *Solomon's* porch.
7:47. But *Solomon* built him an house.

4677 1 766/898 [7799]

Σουσάννα, *Sousanna.*

Lu. 8: 3. Herod's steward, and *Susanna,*

4681 2 768/899

Σπανία, *Spania.*

Ro. 15:24. I take my journey into *Spain,*
28. I will come by you into *Spain.*

4720 1 773/903 rt 4719

Στάχυς, *Stakus.*

Ro. 16: 9. and *Stachys* my beloved.

4734 3 774/904

Στεφανᾶς, *Stephanas.*

1Co. 1:16. also the houshold of *Stephanas:*
16:15. ye know the house of *Stephanas,*
17. I am glad of the coming of *Stephanas*

4736 7 774/904

Στέφανος, *Stephanos.*

Acts 6: 5. and they chose *Stephen,*
8. And *Stephen,* full of faith and power
9. disputing with *Stephen.*
7:59. And they stoned *Stephen,*
8: 2. And devout men carried *Stephen*
11:19. the persecution that arose about *Stephen*
22:20. the blood of thy martyr *Stephen*

4770 1 779/908 4745

Στωϊκός, *Stōikos.*

Acts17:18. of the *Stoicks,* encountered him

4826 7 785/916 rt 4613
Συμεών, Sumeōn.

Lu. 2:25. whose name (was) *Simeon;*
34. And *Simeon* blessed them,
3:30. Which was (the son) of *Simeon,*
Acts13: 1. and *Simeon* that was called Niger,
15:14. *Simeon* hath declared how God
2Pet. 1: 1. *Simon* Peter, a servant and an apostle
Rev. 7: 7. Of the tribe of *Simeon* (were) sealed

4941 1 801/926 4940
Συντύχη, Suntukee.

Phi. 4. 2. I beseech Euodias, and beseech *Syntyche,*

4946 1 801/926
Συράκουσαι, Surakousai.

Acts28:12. And landing at *Syracuse,*

4947 8 801/926 [6865]
Συρία, Suria.

Mat. 4:24. And his fame went throughout all *Syria:*
Lu. 2: 2. when Cyrenius was governor of *Syria.*
Acts15:23. of the Gentiles in Antioch and *Syria*
41. And he went through *Syria*
18:18. and sailed thence into *Syria,*
20: 3. as he was about to sail into *Syria,*
21: 3. and sailed into *Syria,*
Gal. 1.21. I came into the regions of *Syria*

4948 1 801/926 4947
Σύρος, Suros.

Lu. 4:27. saving Naaman the *Syrian.*

4949 1 /926 4948,rt 5403
Συροφοίνισσα, Surophoinissa.

Mar 7:26. a *Syrophenician* by nation;

4965 1 803/927 [7941]
Συχάρ, Sukar.

Joh. 4: 5. of Samaria, which is called *Sychar,*

4966 2 803/927 [7927]
Συχέμ, Sukem.

Acts 7:16. And were carried over into *Sychem,*
— of Emmor (the father) of *Sychem.*

4986 1 807/931 rt 4982,3962
Σώπατρος, Sōpatros.

Acts20: 4. accompanied him into Asia *Sopater*

4988 2 808/931 rt 4982,rt 4599
Σωσθένης, Sōsthenees.

Acts18:17. the Greeks took *Sosthenes,* the chief ruler
1Co. 1: 1. and *Sosthenes* (our) brother,

4989 1 808/931 4986
Σωσίπατρος, Sōsipatros.

Ro. 16:21. and *Sosipater,* my kinsmen, salute you.

4999 1 810/

Ταβέρναι see **Τρεῖς Ταβέρναι.**

5000 2 810/932 cf [6646]
Ταβιθά, Tabitha.

Acts 9:36. certain disciple named *Tabitha,*
40. to the body said, *Tabitha,* arise.

5018 2 813/934 5019
Ταρσεύς, Tarsūs.

Acts 9:11. for (one) called Saul, of *Tarsus:*
21:39. I am a man (which am) a Jew of *Tarsus,* (a city) in Cilicia,

5019 3 813/934 *tarsos* (flat basket)
Ταρσός, Tarsos.

Acts 9:30. and sent him forth to *Tarsus.*
11:25. Then departed Barnabas to *Tarsus,*
22: 3. a man (which am) a Jew, born in *Tarsus,*

5060 1 820/938
Τέρτιος, Tertios.

Ro. 16:22. I *Tertius,* who wrote (this) epistle, salute you

5061 2 820/938
Τέρτυλλος, Tertullos.

Acts24: 1. a certain orator (named) *Tertullus.*
2. *Tertullus* began to accuse (him), saying,

5085 3 823/941 5086
Τιβεριάς, Tiberias.

Joh. 6: 1. which is (the sea) of *Tiberias.*
23. there came other boats from *Tiberias* nigh unto the place
21: 1. to the disciples at the sea of *Tiberias,*

5086 1 823/941
Τιβέριος, Tiberios.

Lu. 3: 1. of the reign of *Tiberius* Cæsar,

5090 1 824/942 cf [2931]
Τίμαιος, Timaios.

Mar 10:46. blind Bartimæus, the son of *Timæus,*

5095 24 826/943 5092,2316
Τιμόθεος, Timotheos.

Acts16: 1. a certain disciple was there, named *Timotheus,*
17:14. but Silas and *Timotheus* abode there still.
15. commandment unto Silas and *Timotheus* for to come to him with all speed,
18: 5. when Silas and *Timotheus* were come
19:22. *Timotheus* and Erastus; but he himself stayed in Asia
20: 4. and Gaius of Derbe, and *Timotheus;*
Ro. 16:21. *Timotheus* my workfellow,
1Co. 4:17. have I sent unto you *Timotheus,*
16:10. Now if *Timotheus* come, see that he may be with you without fear:
2Co. 1: 1. and *Timothy* (our) brother, unto the church
19. by me and Silvanus and *Timotheus,*
Phi. 1: 1. Paul and *Timotheus,* the servants of Jesus Christ,
2:19. to send *Timotheus* shortly unto you,
Col. 1: 1. and *Timotheus* (our) brother,

1 Th. 1: 1. Paul, and Silvanus, and *Timotheus*,
3: 2. And sent *Timotheus*, our brother,
6. But now when *Timotheus* came from you
2 Th. 1: 1. Paul, and Silvanus, and *Timotheus*,
1 Ti. 1: 2. Unto *Timothy*, (my) own son in the faith:
18. This charge I commit unto thee, son *Timothy*,
6:20. O *Timothy*, keep that which is committed
2 Ti. 1: 2. To *Timothy*, (my) dearly beloved son:
Philem. 1. and *Timothy* (our) brother, unto Philemon
Heb. 13:23. brother *Timothy* is set at liberty;

5096 1 826/944 5092

Τίμων, *Timōn.*

Acts 6: 5. and *Timon*, and Parmenas,

5103 13 828/954

Τίτος, *Titos.*

2 Co. 2:13(12). I found not *Titus* my brother:
7: 6. comforted us by the coming of *Titus*;
13. joyed we for the joy of *Titus*,
14. which (I made) before *Titus*,
8: 6. Insomuch that we desired *Titus*,
16. into the heart of *Titus* for you.
23. Whether (any do enquire) of *Titus*,
12:18. I desired *Titus*, and with (him) I sent
— Did *Titus* make a gain of you?
Gal. 2: 1. and took *Titus* with (me) also.
3. But neither *Titus*, who was with me,
2 Ti. 4:10. *Titus* unto Dalmatia.
Tit. 1: 4. To *Titus*, (mine) own son after the common faith:

5139 1 832/959 5138

Τραχωνῖτις, *Trakōnitis.*

Lu. 3: 1. of the region of *Trachonitis*,

5140b 1 810/932

Τρεῖς Ταβέρναι, *Trīs Tabernai.*

Acts 28:15. as far as Apii forum, and *The three taverns*:

5161 3 835/962 5160

Τρόφιμος, *Trophimos.*

Acts 20: 4. of Asia, Tychicus and *Trophimus*.
21:29. with him in the city *Trophimus*
2 Ti. 4:20. but *Trophimus* have I left at Miletum

5170 1 836/962 5172

Τρύφαινα, *Truphaina.*

Ro. 16:12. Salute *Tryphena* and Tryphosa,

5173 1 836/962 5172

Τρυφῶσα, *Truphōsa.*

Ro. 16:12. Salute Tryphena and *Tryphosa*,

5174 6 836/962

Τρωάς, *Trōas.*

Acts 16: 8. came down to *Troas*.
11. Therefore loosing from *Troas*,
20: 5. tarried for us at *Troas*.
and came unto them to *Troas*
2 Co. 2:12. Furthermore, when I came to *Troas*
2 Ti. 4:13. The cloke that I left at *Troas*

5175 1 836/962

Τρωγύλλιον, *Trōgullion.*

Acts 20:15. and tarried at *Trogyllium*;

5181 1 838/963 rt 2962

Τύραννος, *Turannos.*

Acts 19: 9. in the school of one *Tyrannus*.

5183 1 838/963 5184

Τύριος, *Turios.*

Acts 12:20. was highly displeased with them *of Tyre*

5184 11 838/963 [6865]

Τύρος, *Turos.*

Mat. 11:21. had been done in *Tyre* and Sidon,
22. It shall be more tolerable for *Tyre*
15:21. departed into the coasts of *Tyre*
Mar. 3: 8. and they about *Tyre* and Sidon,
7:24. into the borders of *Tyre* and Sidon,
31. departing from the coasts of *Tyre*
Lu. 6:17. and from the sea coast of *Tyre*
10:13. had been done in *Tyre* and Sidon,
14. it shall be more tolerable for *Tyre*
Acts 21: 3. and landed at *Tyre*: for there
7. we had finished (our) course from *Tyre*,

5190 5 839/964 5177

Τυχικός, *Tukikos.*

Acts 20: 4. *Tychicus* and Trophimus.
Eph. 6:21. *Tychicus*, a beloved brother
Col. 4: 7. All my state shall *Tychicus* declare
2 Ti. 4:12. And *Tychicus* have I sent to Ephesus.
Tit. 3:12. or *Tychicus*, be diligent to come unto me

5211 2 843/970 Ὑmēn (god of weddings)

Ὑμέναιος, *Humenaios.*

1 Ti. 1:20. Of whom is *Hymenæus* and Alexander
2 Ti. 2:17. of whom is *Hymenæus* and Philetus;

5317 1 860/984 [6389]

Φαλέκ, *Phalek.*

Lu. 3:35. which was (the son) of *Phalec*,

5323 1 861/984 [6439]

Φανουήλ, *Phanoueel.*

Lu. 2:36. the daughter of *Phanuel*,

5328 5 861/985 [6547]

Φαραώ, *Pharaō.*

Acts 7:10. wisdom in the sight of *Pharaoh*
13. kindred was made known unto *Pharaoh*.
21. *Pharaoh's* daughter took him up,
Ro. 9:17. the scripture saith unto *Pharaoh*,
Heb. 11:24. called the son of *Pharaoh's* daughter;

5329 3 861/985 [6557]

Φαρές, *Phares.*

Mat. 1: 3. Judas begat *Phares*...and *Phares* begat Esrom;
Lu. 3:33. which was (the son) of *Phares*,

5330 100 861/985 9:11 cf [6567]

Φαρισαῖος, *Pharisaios.*

Mat. 3: 7. when he saw many of the *Pharisees*
5:20. of the scribes and *Pharisees*,
• 9:11. And when the *Pharisees* saw (it),
14. we and the *Pharisees* fast oft,
34. the *Pharisees* said, He casteth
12: 2. But when the *Pharisees* saw (it),
14. Then the *Pharisees* went out,
24. But when the *Pharisees* heard (it),
38. scribes and of the *Pharisees* answered,
15: 1. came to Jesus scribes and *Pharisees*,
12. that the *Pharisees* were offended,
16: 1. *Pharisees* also with the Sadducees came,
6. beware of the leaven of the *Pharisees*
11. beware of the leaven of the *Pharisees*
12. but of the doctrine of the *Pharisees*
19: 3. The *Pharisees* also came unto him,
21:45. *Pharisees* had heard his parables,
22:15. Then went the *Pharisees*, and took counsel
34. But when the *Pharisees* had heard
41. While the *Pharisees* were gathered
23: 2. The scribes and the *Pharisees* sit in
13. woe unto you, scribes and *Pharisees*,
14. Woe unto you, scribes and *Pharisees*,
15. Woe unto you, scribes and *Pharisees*,
23. Woe unto you, scribes and *Pharisees*,
25. Woe unto you, scribes and *Pharisees*,
26. (Thou) blind *Pharisee*, cleanse first
27. Woe unto you, scribes and *Pharisees*,
29. Woe unto you, scribes and *Pharisees*,
27:62. chief priests and *Pharisees* came together
Mar. 2:16. when the scribes and *Pharisees* saw
18. of the *Pharisees* used to fast:
— of John and of the *Pharisees* fast,
24. And the *Pharisees* said unto him,
3: 6. And the *Pharisees* went forth,
7: 1. came together unto him the *Pharisees*,
3. For the *Pharisees*, and all the Jews,
5. the *Pharisees* and scribes asked him,
8:11. And the *Pharisees* came forth,
15. beware of the leaven of the *Pharisees*,
10: 2. And the *Pharisees* came to him,
12:13. unto him certain of the *Pharisees*
Lu. 5:17. there were *Pharisees* and doctors
21. and the *Pharisees* began to reason,
30. their scribes and *Pharisees* murmured
33. likewise (the disciples) of the *Pharisees*;
6: 2. certain of the *Pharisees* said
7. the scribes and *Pharisees* watched him,
:30. But the *Pharisees* and lawyers
36. one of the *Pharisees* desired him
— he went into the *Pharisee's* house,
37. at meat in the *Pharisee's* house,
39. *Pharisee* which had bidden him saw
11:37. a certain *Pharisee* besought him to dine
38. And when the *Pharisee* saw (it),
39. ye *Pharisees* make clean the outside
42. But woe unto you, *Pharisees*!
43. Woe unto you, *Pharisees*!
44. Woe unto you, scribes and *Pharisees*,
53. the *Pharisees* began to urge (him)
12: 1. Beware ye of the leaven of the *Pharisees*,
13:31. came certain of the *Pharisees*,
14: 1. one of the chief *Pharisees* to eat
3. spake unto the lawyers and *Pharisees*,
15: 2. the *Pharisees* and scribes murmured,
16:14. *Pharisees* also, who were covetous,
17:20. of the *Pharisees*, when the kingdom
18:10. the one a *Pharisee*, and the other
11. The *Pharisee* stood and prayed
19:39. some of the *Pharisees* from among
Joh. 1:24. were sent were of the *Pharisees*.
3: 1. of the *Pharisees*, named Nicodemus.
4: 1. the *Pharisees* had heard that Jesus
7:32. The *Pharisees* heard that the people
— *Pharisees* and the chief priests sent officers
45. to the chief priests and *Pharisees*;
47. answered them the *Pharisees*,
48. or of the *Pharisees* believed on him?
8: 3. *Pharisees* brought unto him a woman
13. The *Pharisees* therefore said unto him,
9:13. They brought to the *Pharisees*
15. again the *Pharisees* also asked him
16. said some of the *Pharisees*, This man
40. of the *Pharisees* which were with him
11:46. went their ways to the *Pharisees*,
47. gathered the chief priests and the *Pharisees*
57. both the chief priests and the *Pharisees*
12:19. The *Pharisees* therefore said
42. *Pharisees* they did not confess (him),
18: 3. and *Pharisees*, cometh thither with lanterns
Acts 5:34. a *Pharisee*, named Gamaliel,
15: 5. sect of the *Pharisees* which believed,
23: 6. were Sadducees, and the other *Pharisees*
— I am a *Pharisee*, the son of a *Pharisee*:
7. dissension between the *Pharisees* and,
8. but the *Pharisees* confess both.
9. of the *Pharisees'* part arose,
26: 5. our religion I lived a *Pharisee*.
Phi. 3: 5. as touching the law, a *Pharisee*;

5344 9 863/988

Φῆλιξ, *Pheelix.*

Acts 23:24. safe unto *Felix* the governor.
26. unto the most excellent governor *Felix*
24: 3. and in all places, most noble *Felix*,
22. And when *Felix* heard these things,
24. when *Felix* came with his wife
25. *Felix* trembled, and answered,
27. Porcius Festus came into *Felix'* room: and *Felix*, willing to shew the Jews
25:14. left in bonds by *Felix*:

5347 13 864/988

Φῆστος, *Pheestos.*

Acts 24:27. Porcius *Festus* came into Felix' room:
25: 1. Now when *Festus* was come into the province,
4. But *Festus* answered, that Paul
9. But *Festus*, willing to do the Jews
12. Then *Festus* when he had conferred
13. unto Cæsarea to salute *Festus*.
14. *Festus* declared Paul's cause unto the king,
22. Then Agrippa said unto *Festus*,
23. at *Festus'* commandment Paul was brought
24. And *Festus* said, King Agrippa,
26:24. *Festus* said with a loud voice,
25. I am not mad, most noble *Festus*;
32. Then said Agrippa unto *Festus*,

5359 2 866/989 5361

Φιλαδέλφια, *Philadelphia.*

Rev. 1:11. unto Sardis, and unto *Philadelphia*,
3: 7. the church in *Philadelphia* write;

5371 1 867/990 5368

Φιλήμων, *Phileemōn.*

Philem. 1. unto *Philemon* our dearly beloved,

5372 1 867/990 5368

Φιλητός, *Phileetos.*

2 Ti. 2:17. of whom is Hymenæus and *Philetus;*

5374 1 867/990 5375

Φιλιππήσιοι, *Philippeesioi.*

Phi. 4:15. Now ye *Philippians* know also,

5375 4 867/990 5376

Φίλιπποι, *Philippoi.*

Acts 16:12. And from thence to *Philippi,*
20: 6. And we sailed away from *Philippi*
Phi. 1: 1. which are at *Philippi*
1 Th. 2: 2. as ye know, at *Philippi,*

5376 38 867/990 5384,2462

Φίλιππος, *Philippos.*

Mat. 10: 3. *Philip,* and Bartholomew;
14: 3. his brother *Philip's* wife.
16:13. into the coasts of Cæsarea *Philippi,* (lit. of *Philip*)
Mar. 3:18. And Andrew, and *Philip,*
6:17. his brother *Philip's* wife:
8:27. into the towns of Cæsarea *Philippi:* (lit. of *Philip*)
Lu. 3: 1. his brother *Philip* tetrarch of Ituræa
19. his brother *Philip's* wife,
6:14. *Philip* and Bartholomew,
Joh. 1:43(44). and findeth *Philip,* and saith
44(45). Now *Philip* was of Bethsaida,
45(46). *Philip* findeth Nathanael,
46(47). *Philip* saith unto him, Come and see.
48(49). Before that *Philip* called thee,
6: 5. he saith unto *Philip,* Whence shall
7. *Philip* answered him, Two hundred
12:21. The same came therefore to *Philip,*
22. *Philip* cometh and telleth Andrew:
— Andrew and *Philip* tell Jesus.
14: 8. *Philip* saith unto him, Lord, shew
9. and yet hast thou not known me, *Philip?*
Acts 1:13. and Andrew, *Philip,* and Thomas,
6: 5. and *Philip,* and Prochorus,
8: 5. Then *Philip* went down to the city
6. unto those things which *Philip* spake,
12. But when they believed *Philip*
13. he continued with *Philip,*
26. And the angel of the Lord spake unto *Philip,*
29. Then the Spirit said unto *Philip,*
30. And *Philip* ran thither to (him),
31. And he desired *Philip* that he would
34. And the eunuch answered *Philip,*
35. Then *Philip* opened his mouth,
37. And *Philip* said, If thou believest
38. into the water, both *Philip* and the eunuch;
39. the Spirit of the Lord caught away *Philip,*
40. But *Philip* was found at Azotus:
21: 8. into the house of *Philip* the evangelist,

5378 1 868/991

Φιλόλογος, *Philologos.*

Ro. 16:15. Salute *Philologus,* and Julia,

5393 1 869/991 rt 5395

Φλέγων, *Phlegōn.*

Ro. 16:14. Salute Asyncritus, *Phlegon,*

5402 1 872/993 *phoibos* (bright)

Φοίβη, *Phoibee.*

Ro. 16: 1. I commend unto you *Phebe* our sister,

5403 3 872/993 5404

Φοινίκη, *Phoinikee.*

Acts 11:19. travelled as far as *Phenice,*
15: 3. they passed through *Phenice* and Samaria,
21: 2. a ship sailing over unto *Phenicia,*

5405 1 872/993 rt 5404

Φοίνιξ, *Phoinix.*

Acts 27:12. they might attain to *Phenice,* (and there) to winter;

5410 1 872/994

Φόρον Ἀππίου see Ἀππίου Φόρον.

675, p. 821

5415 1 873/994

Φορτουνάτος, *Phortounatos.*

1 Co. 16:17. coming of Stephanas and *Fortunatus*

5435 3 875/995

Φρυγία, *Phrugia.*

Acts 2:10. *Phrygia,* and Pamphylia,
16: 6. Now when they had gone throughout *Phrygia*
18:23. over (all) the country of Galatia and *Phrygia*

5436 1 876/995 5343

Φύγελλος, *Phugellos.*

2 Ti. 1:15. of whom are *Phygellus* and Hermogenes.

5466 1 882/1001 [3778]

Χαλδαῖος, *Kaldaios.*

Acts 7: 4. out of the land of the *Chaldæans,*

5477 2 883/1002 [3667]

Χαναάν, *Kanaăn.*

Acts 7:11. over all the land of Egypt and *Chanaan,*
13:19. destroyed seven nations in the land of *Chanaan,*

5478 1 883/1002 5477

Χαναναῖος, *Kananaios.*

Mat. 15:22. And, behold, a woman of *Canaan* came

5488 2 887/1005 [2771]

Χαῤῥάν, *Karran.*

Acts 7: 2. before he dwelt in *Charran,*
4. and dwelt in *Charran:*

5502 1 889/1007 9:438 [3742]

Χερουβίμ, *Keroubim.*

Heb. 9: 5. *cherubims* of glory shadowing the mercy-seat:

5508 1 890/1008

Χίος, Kios.

Acts 20:15. came the next (day) over against *Chios;*

5514 1 890/1009

Χλόη, Kloee.

1 Co. 1:11. (which are of the house) of *Chloe,*

5523 2 891/1009

Χοραζίν, Korazin.

Mat. 11:21. Woe unto thee, *Chorazin!*
Lu. 10·13. Woe unto thee, *Chorazin!*

5529 1 892/1010

Χουζᾶς, Kouzas.

Lu. 8: 3. Joanna the wife of *Chuza* Herod's steward,

5546 3 895/1011 9:493 5547

Χριστιανός, Kristianos.

Acts 11:26. disciples were called *Christians* first in Antioch.
26:28. persuadest me to be a *Christian.*
1 Pet. 4:16. if (any man suffer) as a *Christian,*

5547 569 895/1011 9·493 5548

Χριστός, Kristos.

Mat. 1: 1. generation of Jesus *Christ,*
16. Jesus, who is called *Christ.*
17. unto *Christ* (are) fourteen generations.
18. the birth of Jesus *Christ* was on
2: 4. where *Christ* should be born.
11: 2. in the prison the works of *Christ,*
16:16. Thou art the *Christ,* the Son of
20. that he was Jesus the *Christ.*
22:42. What think ye of *Christ?*
23: 8. one is your Master, (even) *Christ;*
10. one is your Master, (even) *Christ.*
24: 5. my name, saying, I am *Christ;*
23. Lo, here (is) *Christ,* or there;
26:63. whether thou be the *Christ,*
68. Prophesy unto us, thou *Christ,*
27:17. Jesus which is called *Christ?*
22. Jesus which is called *Christ?*
Mar. 1: 1. beginning of the gospel of Jesus *Christ,*
8:29. Thou art the *Christ.*
9:41. because ye belong to *Christ,*
12:35. How say the scribes that *Christ* is the
13:21. Lo, here (is) *Christ;* or, lo, (he is) there;
14:61. Art thou the *Christ,* the Son of the Blessed?
15:32. Let *Christ* the King of Israel descend
Lu. 2:11. a Saviour, which is *Christ* the Lord.
26. he had seen the Lord's *Christ.*
3:15. whether he were the *Christ,* or not;
4:41. Thou art *Christ* the Son of God.
— they knew that he was *Christ.*
9:20. said, The *Christ* of God.
20:41. *Christ* is David's son?
22:67(66). Art thou the *Christ?*
23: 2. saying that he himself is *Christ*
35. if he be *Christ,* the chosen of God.
39. If thou be *Christ,* save thyself
24:26. Ought not *Christ* to have suffered
46. thus it behoved *Christ* to suffer,
Joh. 1:17. grace and truth came by Jesus *Christ.*
20. confessed, I am not the *Christ.*
25. if thou be not that *Christ,*
Joh. 1:41(42). being interpreted, the *Christ.*
3:28. said, I am not the *Christ,*
4:25. Messias cometh, which is called *Christ*
29. is not this the *Christ?*
42. this is indeed the *Christ,*
6:69. sure that thou art that *Christ,*
7:26. indeed that this is the very *Christ?*
27. when *Christ* cometh, no man
31. When *Christ* cometh, will he do
41. This is the *Christ.*
— Shall *Christ* come out of Galilee?
42. *Christ* cometh of the seed of
9:22. confess that he was *Christ,*
10:24. If thou be the *Christ,* tell us
11:27. I believe that thou art the *Christ,*
12:34. that *Christ* abideth for ever:
17: 3. and Jesus *Christ,* whom thou
20:31. believe that Jesus is the *Christ,*
Acts 2:30. raise up *Christ* to sit on
31. spake of the resurrection of *Christ,*
36. crucified, both Lord and *Christ.*
38. in the name of Jesus *Christ*
3: 6. In the name of Jesus *Christ*
18. prophets, that *Christ* should
20. he shall send Jesus *Christ,*
4:10. by the name of Jesus *Christ*
26. and against his *Christ.*
5:42. to teach and preach Jesus *Christ.*
8: 5. preached *Christ* unto them.
12. and the name of Jesus *Christ,*
37. Jesus *Christ* is the Son of God.
9:20. preached *Christ* in the
22. proving that this is very *Christ.*
34. Jesus *Christ* maketh thee
10:36. peace by Jesus *Christ:*
11:17. believed on the Lord Jesus *Christ;*
15:11. through the grace of the Lord Jesus *Christ*
26. name of our Lord Jesus *Christ.*
16:18. thee in the name of Jesus *Christ*
31. Believe on the Lord Jesus *Christ,*
17: 3. *Christ* must needs have
— preach unto you, is *Christ.*
18: 5. (that) Jesus (was) *Christ.*
28. that Jesus was *Christ.*
19: 4. that is, on *Christ* Jesus.
20:21. faith toward our Lord Jesus *Christ.*
24:24. concerning the faith in *Christ.*
26:23. That *Christ* should suffer,
28:31. which concern the Lord Jesus *Christ,*
Ro. 1: 1. Paul, a servant of Jesus *Christ,*
3(4). Concerning his Son Jesus *Christ*
6. ye also the called of Jesus *Christ:*
7. and the Lord Jesus *Christ.*
8. I thank my God through Jesus *Christ*
16. not ashamed of the gospel of *Christ:*
2:16. secrets of men by Jesus *Christ*
3:22. by faith of Jesus *Christ*
24. redemption that is in *Christ* Jesus:
5: 1. through our Lord Jesus *Christ:*
6. in due time *Christ* died
8. *Christ* died for us.
11. through our Lord Jesus *Christ,*
15. by one man, Jesus *Christ,*
17. life by one, Jesus *Christ.*
21. life by Jesus *Christ* our Lord.
6: 3. were baptized into Jesus *Christ*
4. that like as *Christ* was raised
8. if we be dead with *Christ,*
9. Knowing that *Christ* being raised
11. through Jesus *Christ* our Lord.
23. eternal life through Jesus *Christ*

Ro. 7: 4. law by the body of *Christ;*
25. through Jesus *Christ*
8: 1. them which are in *Christ*
2. Spirit of life in *Christ* Jesus
9. have not the Spirit of *Christ*,
10. if *Christ* (be) in you,
11. he that raised up *Christ*
17. joint-heirs with *Christ;*
34. (It is) *Christ* that died,
35. from the love of *Christ?*
39. which is in *Christ* Jesus
9: 1. say the truth in *Christ*,
3. accursed from *Christ* for my brethren,
5. *Christ* (came), who is over all,
10: 4. *Christ* (is) the end of the law
6. to bring *Christ* down
7. bring up *Christ* again
12: 5. one body in *Christ*,
13:14. on the Lord Jesus *Christ*,
14: 9. *Christ* both died, and rose,
10. judgment seat of *Christ*.
15. for whom *Christ* died.
18. that in these things serveth *Christ*
15: 3. *Christ* pleased not himself;
5. according to *Christ* Jesus:
6. Father of our Lord Jesus *Christ*.
7. as *Christ* also received us
8. Jesus *Christ* was a minister
16. minister of Jesus *Christ*
17. I may glory through Jesus *Christ*
18. which *Christ* hath not
19. fully preached the gospel of *Christ*.
20. where *Christ* was named,
29. blessing of the gospel of *Christ*.
30. for the Lord Jesus *Christ's* sake,
16: 3. helpers in *Christ* Jesus:
5. firstfruits of Achaia unto *Christ*.
7. in *Christ* before me.
9. our helper in *Christ*,
10. Salute Apelles approved in *Christ*.
16. churches of *Christ* salute you.
18. our Lord Jesus *Christ*,
20. grace of our Lord Jesus *Christ*
24. grace of our Lord Jesus *Christ*
25. the preaching of Jesus *Christ*,
27. glory through Jesus *Christ*
1 Co. 1: 1. apostle of Jesus *Christ*
2. sanctified in *Christ* Jesus,
— name of Jesus *Christ*
3. and (from) the Lord Jesus *Christ*.
4. given you by Jesus *Christ;*
6. testimony of *Christ* was confirmed
7. coming of our Lord Jesus *Christ:*
8. day of our Lord Jesus *Christ*.
9. fellowship of his Son Jesus *Christ*
10. beseech you, brethren, by the name of our Lord Jesus *Christ*,
12. and I of *Christ*.
13. Is *Christ* divided?
17. *Christ* sent me not to baptize,
— lest the cross of *Christ* should
23. But we preach *Christ* crucified,
24. *Christ* the power of God,
30. are ye in *Christ* Jesus,
2: 2. save Jesus *Christ*, and him crucified.
16. But we have the mind of *Christ*.
3: 1. as unto babes in *Christ*.
11. which is Jesus *Christ*.
23. ye are *Christ's;* and *Christ* (is) God's.
4: 1. ministers of *Christ*, and stewards
10. for *Christ's* sake, but ye (are) wise in *Christ;*

1 Co. 4:15. instructers in *Christ*, yet (have ye) not many fathers: for in *Christ* Jesus I have
17. which be in *Christ*,
5: 4. In the name of our Lord Jesus *Christ*,
— power of our Lord Jesus *Christ*,
7. *Christ* our passover is sacrificed
6:15. members of *Christ?* shall I then take the members of *Christ*,
7:22. (being) free, is *Christ's* servant.
8: 6. and one Lord Jesus *Christ*,
11. for whom *Christ* died?
12. ye sin against *Christ*.
9: 1. have I not seen Jesus *Christ*
12. hinder the gospel of *Christ*.
18. make the gospel of *Christ*
21. under the law to *Christ*,
10: 4. that Rock was *Christ*.
9. Neither let us tempt *Christ*,
16. the blood of *Christ?*
— of the body of *Christ?*
11: 1. even as I also (am) of *Christ*.
3. of every man is *Christ;*
— head of *Christ* (is) God.
12:12. so also (is) *Christ*.
27. ye are the body of *Christ*,
15: 3. *Christ* died for our sins
12. if *Christ* be preached
13. then is *Christ* not risen:
14. if *Christ* be not risen,
15. he raised up *Christ:*
16. then is not *Christ* raised:
17. if *Christ* be not raised,
18. which are fallen asleep in *Christ*
19. only we have hope in *Christ*,
20. now is *Christ* risen
22. in *Christ* shall all be made alive.
23. *Christ* the firstfruits; afterward they that are *Christ's* at his coming.
31. have in *Christ* Jesus our Lord,
57. through our Lord Jesus *Christ*.
16:22. love not the Lord Jesus *Christ*,
23. grace of our Lord Jesus *Christ*
24. all in *Christ* Jesus.
2 Co. 1: 1. apostle of Jesus *Christ*
2. and (from) the Lord Jesus *Christ*.
3. Father of our Lord Jesus *Christ*,
5. sufferings of *Christ* abound in us, so our consolation also aboundeth by *Christ*.
19. Jesus *Christ*, who was preached
21. with you in *Christ*,
2:10. in the person of *Christ;*
12. *Christ's* gospel, and a door
14. causeth us to triumph in *Christ*,
15. unto God a sweet savour of *Christ*,
17. speak we in *Christ*.
3: 3 epistle of *Christ* ministered by us,
4. we through *Christ* to God-ward:
14 which (vail) is done away in *Christ*.
4: 4. the glorious gospel of *Christ*,
5. but *Christ* Jesus the Lord;
6. face of Jesus *Christ*.
5:10. judgment seat of *Christ;*
14. the love of *Christ* constraineth
16. known *Christ* after the flesh,
17. man (be) in *Christ*,
18. himself by Jesus *Christ*,
19. God was in *Christ*,
20. we are ambassadors for *Christ*,
— in *Christ's* stead, be ye reconciled
6:15. hath *Christ* with Belial?
8: 9. of our Lord Jesus *Christ*.
23. the glory of *Christ*.

2 Co. 9:13. unto the gospel of *Christ*,
10: 1. meekness and gentleness of *Christ*,
5. thought to the obedience of *Christ*;
7. trust to himself that he is *Christ's*,
— he (is) *Christ's*, even so (are) we *Christ's*.
14. (preaching) the gospel of *Christ*:
11: 2. chaste virgin to *Christ*.
3. simplicity that is in *Christ*.
10. truth of *Christ* is in me,
13. into the apostles of *Christ*.
23. Are they ministers of *Christ*?
31. Father of our Lord Jesus *Christ*,
12: 2. a man in *Christ*
9. power of *Christ* may
10. distresses for *Christ's* sake:
19. before God in *Christ*:
13: 3. of *Christ* speaking in me,
5. Jesus *Christ* is in you,
14(13). grace of the Lord Jesus *Christ*,
Gal. 1: 1. but by Jesus *Christ*,
3. (from) our Lord Jesus *Christ*,
6. grace of *Christ* unto another
7. pervert the gospel of *Christ*.
10. the servant of *Christ*.
12. revelation of Jesus *Christ*.
22. which were in *Christ*:
2: 4. have in *Christ* Jesus,
16. by the faith of Jesus *Christ*,
— believed in Jesus *Christ*,
— justified by the faith of *Christ*,
17. we seek to be justified by *Christ*,
— (is) therefore *Christ* the
20. I am crucified with *Christ*:
— *Christ* liveth in me:
21. *Christ* is dead in vain.
3: 1. Jesus *Christ* hath been
13. *Christ* hath redeemed us
14. Gentiles through Jesus *Christ*;
16. seed, which is *Christ*.
17. of God in *Christ*,
22. by faith of Jesus *Christ*
24. (bring us) unto *Christ*,
26. faith in *Christ* Jesus.
27. baptized into *Christ* have put on *Christ*.
28. for ye are all one in *Christ* Jesus.
29. if ye (be) *Christ's*, then
4: 7. heir of God through *Christ*.
14. (even) as *Christ* Jesus.
19. until *Christ* be formed
5: 1. in the liberty wherewith *Christ*
2. *Christ* shall profit you nothing.
4. *Christ* is become of no effect
6. in Jesus *Christ* neither
24. are *Christ's* have crucified
6: 2. fulfil the law of *Christ*.
12. for the cross of *Christ*.
14. cross of our Lord Jesus *Christ*,
15. For in *Christ* Jesus
18. grace of our Lord Jesus *Christ*
Eph. 1: 1. Paul, an apostle of Jesus *Christ*
— faithful in *Christ* Jesus:
2. (from) the Lord Jesus *Christ*.
3. Father of our Lord Jesus *Christ*,
— in heavenly (places) in *Christ*:
5. children by Jesus *Christ*
10. all things in *Christ*,
12. first trusted in *Christ*.
17. God of our Lord Jesus *Christ*,
20. Which he wrought in *Christ*,
2: 5. quickened us together with *Christ*,
6. (places) in *Christ* Jesus:
7. toward us through *Christ* Jesus.
Eph. 2:10. created in *Christ* Jesus
12. without *Christ*, being aliens
13. now in *Christ* Jesus
— by the blood of *Christ*.
20. Jesus *Christ* himself
3: 1. prisoner of Jesus *Christ*
4. in the mystery of *Christ*
6. partakers of his promise in *Christ*
8. unsearchable riches of *Christ*;
9. all things by Jesus *Christ*:
11. purposed in *Christ* Jesus
14. Father of our Lord Jesus *Christ*,
17. *Christ* may dwell in your hearts
19. know the love of *Christ*,
21. by *Christ* Jesus throughout all ages,
4: 7. measure of the gift of *Christ*.
12. of the body of *Christ*:
13. of the fulness of *Christ*:
15. which is the head, (even) *Christ*:
20. ye have not so learned *Christ*;
32. God for *Christ's* sake
5: 2. as *Christ* also hath loved us,
5. kingdom of *Christ* and of God.
14. *Christ* shall give thee light.
20. name of our Lord Jesus *Christ*;
23. *Christ* is the head of the church:
24. the church is subject unto *Christ*,
25. even as *Christ* also loved the
32. concerning *Christ* and the church.
6: 5. singleness of your heart, as unto *Christ*;
6. but as the servants of *Christ*,
23. and the Lord Jesus *Christ*.
24. love our Lord Jesus *Christ*
Phi. 1: 1. the servants of Jesus *Christ*, to all the saints in *Christ* Jesus
2. (from) the Lord Jesus *Christ*.
6. until the day of Jesus *Christ*:
8. in the bowels of Jesus *Christ*.
10. offence till the day of *Christ*;
11. which are by Jesus *Christ*,
13. So that my bonds in *Christ*
15. Some indeed preach *Christ*
16. The one preach *Christ*
18. in truth, *Christ* is preached;
19. of the Spirit of Jesus *Christ*,
20. *Christ* shall be magnified
21. For to me to live (is) *Christ*,
23. and to be with *Christ*;
26. more abundant in Jesus *Christ*
27. becometh the gospel of *Christ*:
29. given in the behalf of *Christ*,
2: 1. any consolation in *Christ*,
5. which was also in *Christ* Jesus:
11. that Jesus *Christ* (is) Lord,
16. rejoice in the day of *Christ*,
21. which are Jesus *Christ's*.
30. Because for the work of *Christ*
3: 3. and rejoice in *Christ* Jesus,
7. I counted loss for *Christ*.
8. knowledge of *Christ* Jesus my Lord:
— that I may win *Christ*,
9. which is through the faith of *Christ*,
12. I am apprehended of *Christ* Jesus.
14. calling of God in *Christ* Jesus.
18. enemies of the cross of *Christ*:
20. the Saviour, the Lord Jesus *Christ*:
4: 7. minds through *Christ* Jesus.
13. *Christ* which strengtheneth me.
19. riches in glory by *Christ* Jesus.
21. Salute every saint in *Christ* Jesus.
23. The grace of our Lord Jesus *Christ*
Col. 1: 1. an apostle of Jesus *Christ*

Col. 1: 2. saints and faithful brethren in *Christ*
— and the Lord Jesus *Christ*.
3. of our Lord Jesus *Christ*,
4. of your faith in *Christ* Jesus,
7. faithful minister of *Christ*;
24. the afflictions of *Christ* in
27. *Christ* in you, the hope of glory:
28. perfect in *Christ* Jesus:
2: 2. of the Father, and of *Christ*;
5. stedfastness of your faith in *Christ*.
6. *Christ* Jesus the Lord,
8. world, and not after *Christ*.
11. by the circumcision of *Christ*:
17. but the body (is) of *Christ*.
20. if ye be dead with *Christ*
3: 1. If ye then be risen with *Christ*,
— where *Christ* sitteth on the right
3. hid with *Christ* in God.
4. When *Christ*, (who is) our life,
11. *Christ* (is) all, and in all.
13. even as *Christ* forgave you,
16. Let the word of *Christ* dwell
24. ye serve the Lord *Christ*.
4: 3. to speak the mystery of *Christ*,
12. a servant of *Christ*, saluteth
1 Th. 1: 1. (in) the Lord Jesus *Christ*:
— and the Lord Jesus *Christ*.
3. hope in our Lord Jesus *Christ*,
2: 6. as the apostles of *Christ*.
14. Judæa are in *Christ* Jesus:
19. presence of our Lord Jesus *Christ*
3: 2. labourer in the gospel of *Christ*,
11. and our Lord Jesus *Christ*,
13. coming of our Lord Jesus *Christ*
4:16. the dead in *Christ* shall rise
5: 9. salvation by our Lord Jesus *Christ*,
18. this is the will of God in *Christ* Jesus
23. coming of our Lord Jesus *Christ*.
28. The grace of our Lord Jesus *Christ*
2 Th. 1: 1. and the Lord Jesus *Christ*:
2. and the Lord Jesus *Christ*.
8. gospel of our Lord Jesus *Christ*:
12. name of our Lord Jesus *Christ*
— and the Lord Jesus *Christ*.
2: 1. coming of our Lord Jesus *Christ*,
2. the day of *Christ* is at hand.
14. glory of our Lord Jesus *Christ*.
16. Now our Lord Jesus *Christ*
3: 5. patient waiting for *Christ*.
6. in the name of our Lord Jesus *Christ*,
12. exhort by our Lord Jesus *Christ*,
18. the grace of our Lord Jesus *Christ*
1 Ti. 1: 1. an apostle of Jesus *Christ*
— Saviour, and Lord Jesus *Christ*,
2. and Jesus *Christ* our Lord.
12. I thank *Christ* Jesus our Lord,
14. which is in *Christ* Jesus.
15. that *Christ* Jesus came into
16. in me first Jesus *Christ*
2: 5. the man *Christ* Jesus;
7. I speak the truth in *Christ*,
3:13. which is in *Christ* Jesus.
4: 6. good minister of Jesus *Christ*,
5:11. wax wanton against *Christ*,
21. and the Lord Jesus *Christ*,
6: 3. the words of our Lord Jesus *Christ*,
13. and (before) *Christ* Jesus,
14. appearing of our Lord Jesus *Christ*:
2 Ti. 1: 1. an apostle of Jesus *Christ*
— which is in *Christ* Jesus,
2. and *Christ* Jesus our Lord.
9. given us in *Christ* Jesus

2 Ti. 1:10. appearing of our Saviour Jesus *Christ*,
13. love which is in *Christ* Jesus.
2: 1. grace that is in *Christ* Jesus.
3. good soldier of Jesus *Christ*.
8. Remember that Jesus *Christ*
10. which is in *Christ* Jesus
19. nameth the name of *Christ*
3:12. will live godly in *Christ* Jesus
15. faith which is in *Christ* Jesus.
4: 1. and the Lord Jesus *Christ*,
22. The Lord Jesus *Christ* (be)
Tit. 1: 1. an apostle of Jesus *Christ*,
4. Lord Jesus *Christ* our Saviour.
2:13. our Saviour Jesus *Christ*;
3: 6. through Jesus *Christ* our Saviour;
Philem. 1. a prisoner of Jesus *Christ*,
3. and the Lord Jesus *Christ*.
6. in you in *Christ* Jesus.
8. might be much bold in *Christ*
9. a prisoner of Jesus *Christ*.
23. fellowprisoner in *Christ* Jesus;
25. grace of our Lord Jesus *Christ*
Heb. 3: 1. high priest of our profession, *Christ* Jesus;
6. But *Christ* as a son over his
14. we are made partakers of *Christ*,
5: 5. So also *Christ* glorified not
6: 1. of the doctrine of *Christ*,
9:11. But *Christ* being come an
14. much more shall the blood of *Christ*,
24. For *Christ* is not entered
28. So *Christ* was once offered
10:10. body of Jesus *Christ* once
11:26. Esteeming the reproach of *Christ*
13: 8. Jesus *Christ* the same yesterday,
21. through Jesus *Christ*;
Jas. 1: 1. of the Lord Jesus *Christ*,
2: 1. faith of our Lord Jesus *Christ*,
1 Pet. 1: 1. an apostle of Jesus *Christ*,
2. of the blood of Jesus *Christ*:
3. Father of our Lord Jesus *Christ*,
— resurrection of Jesus *Christ*
7. the appearing of Jesus *Christ*:
11. the Spirit of *Christ* which
— beforehand the sufferings of *Christ*,
13. at the revelation of Jesus *Christ*;
19. with the precious blood of *Christ*,
2: 5. acceptable to God by Jesus *Christ*.
21. because *Christ* also suffered
3:16. your good conversation in *Christ*.
18. For *Christ* also hath once
21. the resurrection of Jesus *Christ*:
4: 1. Forasmuch then as *Christ* hath
11. glorified through Jesus *Christ*,
13. partakers of *Christ's* sufferings;
14. for the name of *Christ*,
5: 1. of the sufferings of *Christ*,
10. eternal glory by *Christ* Jesus,
14. all that are in *Christ* Jesus.
2 Pet. 1: 1. an apostle of Jesus *Christ*,
— our Saviour Jesus *Christ*:
8. knowledge of our Lord Jesus *Christ*.
11. Lord and Saviour Jesus *Christ*.
14. Lord Jesus *Christ* hath shewed
16. coming of our Lord Jesus *Christ*,
2:20. Lord and Saviour Jesus *Christ*,
3:18. our Lord and Saviour Jesus *Christ*.
1 Joh. 1: 3. and with his Son Jesus *Christ*.
7. the blood of Jesus *Christ*
2: 1. Jesus *Christ* the righteous:
22. denieth that Jesus is the *Christ*?
3:23. name of his Son Jesus *Christ*,
4: 2. confesseth that Jesus *Christ* is

1 Joh. 4: 3. confesseth not that Jesus *Christ* is
5: 1. believeth that Jesus is the *Christ*
6. by water and blood, (even) Jesus *Christ*;
20. (even) in his Son Jesus *Christ*.
2 Joh. 3. from the Lord Jesus *Christ*,
7. Jesus *Christ* is come in the flesh.
9. abideth not in the doctrine of *Christ*,
— abideth in the doctrine of *Christ*,
Jude 1. the servant of Jesus *Christ*,
— preserved in Jesus *Christ*,
4. and our Lord Jesus *Christ*.
17. apostles of our Lord Jesus *Christ*;
21. the mercy of our Lord Jesus *Christ*
Rev. 1: 1. The Revelation of Jesus *Christ*,
2. the testimony of Jesus *Christ*,
5. And from Jesus *Christ*, (who is)
9. and patience of Jesus *Christ*,
— and for the testimony of Jesus *Christ*.
11:15. our Lord, and of his *Christ*;
12:10. and the power of his *Christ*:
17. have the testimony of Jesus *Christ*.
20: 4. lived and reigned with *Christ*
Rev. 20: 6. priests of God and of *Christ*,
22:21. The grace of our Lord Jesus *Christ*

---

p. 868, 5523 •

Χωραζίν see **Χοραζίν**. p.868

5566

Χῶρος see among Appellatives.

5601 3 903/506,1024 [5744]

Ὠβήδ, *Ōbeed.*

Mat. 1: 5. Booz begat *Obed* of Ruth; and *Obed* begat Jesse;
Lu. 3:32. which was (the son) of *Obed*,

5617 1 908/1032 [1954]

Ὠσηέ, *Ōseeĕ.*

Ro. 9:25. As he saith also in *Osee*,

Greek-English Index

A few of the Proper Names are here given in one Alphabet with the Appellatives; those being inserted which might occasion some difficulty from their form being very different in the Greek and in the English.

measure, put up, raise, raise to life, remembrance, restore, return, rise, rising, send set, that, turn, word.
against, εις ... 197
εμπροσθεν ... 239
εν ... 240
επι ... 275
κατα ... 406
μετα ... 484
παρα ... 586
περι ... 613
προς ... 656
against, εναντιος ... 259

against, see beat, boast, bring, crime, cry, mad, murmur, over, prate, prevail, quarrel, rejoice, rise up, say, speak, spoken, strive, war, will.
age, ἡλικια ... 344
ἡμερα ... 347
age, see flower, great, old, pass.
age (of full), τελειος ... 727
aged, πρεσβυτης ... 652
aged man, πρεσβυτης ... —
aged woman, πρεσβυτις ... —
ages, αιων ... 19
γενεα ... 113
ago, απο ... 63
προ ... 653
ago, see year.
agony, αγωνια ... 11
agree, εισι ... 218
ευνοεω ... 324
{ην ... 354
{ισος ... 390
ὁμοιαζω ... 530
πειθω ... 609
(Rev. 17:17) {ποιεω 636 {μια .. 500 {γνωμη 124
συμφωνεω ... 707
συντιθημι ... 714
agree with, συμφωνεω ... 707
agree together, συμφωνεω .. —
agreed (Mar. 14:56), ισος .. 390
agreeing (not), ασυμφωνος 89
agreement, συγκαταθεσις .. 703
aground, see run.
ah, ουα, or ουαι ... 563
air, αηρ ... 15
ουρανος ... 571
alabaster box, αλαβαστρον 26
alas, ουαι ... 563
albeit, ἱνα ... 385
albeit.. not, ἱνα μη ... 495
alien, αλλοτριος ... 31
alienate, απαλλοτριοω ... 59
aliens (be), απαλλοτριοω .. —
alive (be), ζαω ... 335
alive again, αναζαω ... 41
alive (make), ζωοποιεω ... 340
all, ἁπας ... 60
ὁλος ... 529
all, ὁσος ... 539
πας ... 597
all, see any, at, first, house, most, no, places, speed.
all (at), παντως ... 585
all at once, παμπληθει ... 584
all (for), see once.
all manner, πας ... 597
all night, see continue.
all one's, see armour.
all that, ὁσος ... 539
all that, see for.
all things, ἁπας ... 60
alledge, παρατιθημι ... 593
allegory, αλληγορεω ... 29
Alleluia, αλληλουια ... —
allow, γινωσκω ... 122
δοκιμαζω ... 160
προσδεχομαι ... 662
συνευδοκεω ... 712
allure, δελεαζω ... 134
Almighty, παντοκρατωρ ... 585
almost {ολιγος ... 528 {εν ... 240
σχεδον ... 715
almost (be), μελλω ... 478
alms, ελεημοσυνη ... 233
almsdeeds, ελεημοσυνη ... —
aloes, αλοη ... 32
alone, ἑαυτου ... 172
κατ' ιδιαν ... {380 {406
καταμονας ... 413
μονον ... 506
μονος ... —
alone (when they were) ... {ιδιος ... 380 {κατα ... 406
alone, see let.
aloud, see cry.
Alpha, A ... 1
already, ηδη ... 343
already, see attain, now, sin.
also, ἁμα ... 32
δη ... 138
ετι ... 318
μεντοι ... 481
τε ... 724
also, see me, there.
also if, καν ... 403
also.. not, ουδε ... 564
altar, βωμος ... 112
θυσιαστηριον ... 379
altered, ἑτερος ... 318
although, ει ... 183
καιτοι ... 399
altogether, ὁλος ... 529
παντως ... 585
(Acts 26:29) {πολυς 643 {εν ... 240
alway, διαπαντος ... 147
{ἡμερα ... 347
{πας ... 597
παντοτε ... 585
always, αει ... 15
δια ... 139
διαπαντος ... 147
ἑκαστοτε ... 222
always, {καιρος ... 398 {πας ... 597
παντη ... 585
παντοτε ... —
{πας ... 597
{δια ... 138
amazed (Lu. 4:36), θαμβος 359
amazed (be), εκπλησσω ... 229
{εκστασις ... 230
{λαμβανω ... 445
εξιστημι ... 269
θαμβεομαι ... 359
amazed (be greatly), εκθαμβεω ... 226
amazed (be sore), εκθαμβεω —
amazement, εκστασις ... 230
πτοησις ... 672
ambassador (be an), πρεσβευω ... 652
ambassage, πρεσβεια ... —
amen, αμην ... 35
amend (began to) {κομψοτερον ... 428 {εχω ... 329
amethyst, αμεθυστος ... 34
amiss, ατοπος ... 90
κακως ... 401
among, δια ... 142
εις ... 197
εκ ... 215
εν ... 240
επι ... 275
κατα ... 406
μεσος ... 483
μετα ... 484
παρα ... 586
προς ... 656
ὑπο ... 776
among, see compare, dwell, fall, from, in, out, speak.
anathema, αναθεμα ... 41
anchor, αγκυρα ... 8
ancle bone, σφυρον ... 715
and, αλλα ... 29
ἁμα ... 32
γαρ ... 112
δη ... 133
η ... 340
κατα ... 406
(Joh. 3:25), μετα ... 484
ὁστις ... 540
ουν ... 567
τε ... 724
and afterward, κακειθεν ... 399
and even, ὁμως ... 531
and from thence, κακειθεν .. 399
and he, see he also, him also.
and his, see company.
and I, καγω ... 393
and if, καν ... 403
and if, see if.
and if so much, καν ... 403
and so, ουν ... 567
and they, ὁστις ... 540
and there, κακει ... 399
...truly, ουν ... 567
and [two and two], ανα ... 39
and yet, καιπερ ... 398

blame, καταγινωσκω 410
μωμεομαι 512
blame (without), αμωμος 37
blameless, αμεμπτος 34
αμωμητος 37
αναιτιος 42
ανεγκλητος 46
ανεπιληπτος 47
blameless, *adv.* αμεμπτως 35
blaspheme, βλασφημεω 107
blasphemer, βλασφημεω —
βλασφημος 108
blasphemous, βλασφημος —
blasphemously, βλασφημεω 107
blasphemy, βλασφημια 108
blasphemy, *see* speak.
blaze abroad, διαφημιζω 149
blemish, μωμος 512
blemish (without), αμωμος 37
bless, ευλογεω 324
blessed, ευλογητος —
μακαριος 468
blessed (be), ενευλογεομαι 261
blessed (call), μακαριζω 468
blessedness, μακαρισμος 469
blessing, ευλογια 324
blind, τυφλος 752
blind, τυφλοω —
blinded (be), πωροω 675
blindfold, περικαλυπτω 616
blindness, πωρωσις 675
blood, αἱμα 16
blood, *see* issue, shedding.
bloody flux, δυσεντερια 168
blot out, εξαλειφω 266
blow, επιγινομαι 282
πνεω 635
blow softly, ὑποπνεω 779
board, σανις 680
boast, κατακαυχαομαι 411
καυχαομαι 419
λεγω 449
boast against, κατακαυχαομαι 411
boast great things, μεγαλαυχεω 475
boast (make), καυχαομαι 419
boaster, αλαζων 27
boasting, αλαζονεια 26
καυχημα 419
καυχησις —
boat, πλοιαριον 631
σκαφη 686
bodily (2 Co. 10:10), σωμα 717
σωματικος 718
bodily, σωματικως —
body, σωμα 717
χρως 805
body, *see* dead.
body (of the same), συσσωμα 714
boisterous, ισχυρος 392
bold (Philem 8), παρρησια 596
bold (be), Joh. 8:57), εχω 329
θαρρεω 360
παρρησιαζομαι 596
τολμαω 741
bold (be very), αποτολμαω 78
bold (wax), παρρησιαζομαι 596
boldly (Heb. 13:6), θαρρεω 360
παρρησια 596
(Acts 9:28), παρρησιαζομαι —
(Mar.15:43), τολμαω 741
boldly, *see* preach, speak.
boldly (the more), τολμηροτερον 741
boldness, παρρησια 596
boldness, *see* speech.
bond, δεσμος 136
bond, δουλος 163
bond, συνδεσμος 710
bondage, δουλεια 163
bondage (be in), δουλευω —
bondage (be under), δουλοω 164
bondage (bring into), δουλοω —
καταδουλοω 411
bondmaid, παιδισκη 583
bondman, δουλος 163
bonds, ἁλυσις 32
bonds (be in), δεω 137
bonds (that are in), δεσμιος 136
bondwoman, παιδισκη 583
bone, οστεον 540
bone, *see* ancle.
book, βιβλιον 107
βιβλος —
book (little), βιβλαριδιον —
border, κρασπεδον 431
border, μεθορια 478
ὁρια 538
born, γενος 115
born (be), γενναω 114
τικτω 731
born again (be), αναγενναω 40
born out of due time εκτρωμα 231
born (they that are), γεννητος 115
borne, *see* grievous.
borrow, δανειζω 132
bosom, κολπος 428
both, αμφοτερος 37
δυο 167
ἑκαστος 221
τε 724
both me, καμε 393
bottles, ασκος 87
bottom, κατω 418
bottomless, αβυσσος 1
bottomless pit, αβυσσος —
bought, *see* buy.
bound, ὁροθεσια 538
bound about (be), περιδεομαι 616
bound (be), δεσμεω 136
οφειλω 579
bound with (be), περικειμαι —
συνδεομαι 710
bountifully, ευλογια 324
bountifulness, ἁπλοτης 63
bounty, ευλογια 324
bow, τοξον 741
bow, καμπτω 403
κλινω 426
bow, τιθημι 731
bow down, κλινω 426
συγκαμπτω 703
bow the knee, γονυπετεω 126
bow together, συγκυπτω 704
bowels, σπλαγχνα 696
box, αλαβαστρον 26
box, *see* alabaster.
bramble bush, ἡ βατος 106
branch, βαιον 100
κλαδος 423
κλημα 424
στοιβας 699
brasen vessel, χαλκιον 796
brass, χαλκεος 795
brass, χαλκος 796
brass (fine), χαλκολιβανον —
brawler (not a), αμαχος 34
bread, αρτος 83
bread, *see* unleavened.
breadth, πλατος 627
break, διαρρηγνυμι 148
καταγνυμι 411
κατακλαω —
κλαζω 423
λυω 466
ῥηγνυμι 677
συνθρυπτω 713
συντριβω 714
σχιζω 716
break forth, ρηγνυμι 677
break in pieces, συντριβω 714
break of day, αυγη 90
break off, εκκλαζω 227
break through, διορυσσω 158
break to shivers, συντριβω 714
break up, εξορυττω 269
λυω, break down 466
breaker, παραβατης 587
breakers, *see* covenant.
breaking, κλασις 424
(Ro. 2:23), παραβασις 587
breast, στηθος 699
breastplate, θωραξ 379
breath, πνοη 635
breathe, εμπνεω 239
breathe on, εμφυσαω 240
brethren, αδελφοτης 13
brethren, *see* brother.
brethren, *see* love as, love of the.
brethren (false), ψευδαδελφος 806
bride, νυμφη 519
bridechamber, νυμφων —
bridegroom, νυμφιος —
bridle, χαλινος 795
bridle, χαλιναγωγεω —
briefly, { δια 138
{ ολιγος 528
briefly, *see* comprehend.
brier, τριβολος 750
bright, λαμπρος 447
φωτεινος 794
bright, *see* shine.
brightness, απαυγασμα 60

eunuch (make), ευνουχιζω 324
evangelist, ευαγγελιστης 321
even, οψε 581
οψια —
even, γαρ 112
ετι 318
ἑως 334
μεν 480
οὑτω 576
τε 724
even, *see* and, not.
even as, καθαπερ 394
καθως 397
κατα 406
τροπος 751
ὡς 812
ὡσπερ 816
even he, *see* he also.
even I, καγω 393
even I also, καγω —
even like, ὡς 812
even (not), ουδε 564
even now, αρτι 82
ηδη 343
even so, ναι 512
ουτω 576
ωσαυτως 817
even so I, καγω 393
even so I also, καγω —
even thus, ταυτα 720
even to, αχρι 99
even unto, & until, ἑως 334
evening, ἑσπερα 309
οψια 581
eventide, ἑσπερα 309
{οψια 581
{ὡρα 811
ever, αει 15
αιων 19
(Jude 25) {αιων 19
{πας 597
παντοτε 585
ποτε 649
ever, *see* nor, that.
ever (for), αιωνιος 20
διηνεκες 155
{ἡμερα 347
{αιων 19
ever (or), προ 653
everlasting, αιδιος 16
αιωνιος 20
evermore, αιων 19
παντοτε 585
every,
απας 60
πας 597
every, κατα 406
every, *see* day, in, out, quarter, side, throughout.
every man, ανα 39
ἑκαστος 221
τις 732
τίς 736
every one, ἁπας 60
ἑκαστος 221
καθεις or καθ' είς 395
every where, πανταχου 585
every where, *see* go.
every whit, ὁλος 529
every woman, ἑκαστος 221
evidence, ελεγχος 232
evident, δηλος 138
προδηλος 654
evident, *see* token.
evident, καταδηλος 411
evidently, φανερως 783
evidently, *see* set forth.
evil, κακια 400
evil, κακος —
πονηρος 646
φαυλος 784
evil, κακως 401
evil (Mat. 5:11), {ῥημα 677
{πονηρος 646
evil, *see* affected, report, speak, speaking.
evil (do), κακοποιεω 400
evil doing, αδικημα 14
κακοποιεω 400
evil (entreat), κακοω —
evil speaking, βλασφημια 108
evildoer, κακοποιος 400
κακουργος —
exact, πρασσω 651
exalt, ὑψοω 781
exalt highly, ὑπερυψοω 775
exalt...self, επαιρω 272
ὑπεραιρομαι 774
exalted above measure (be), ὑπεραιρομαι —
exalted (be) (James 1:9), ὑψος 781
examination, ανακρισις 43
examine, ανακρινω —
ανεταζω 47
δοκιμαζω 160
πειραζω 610
example, δειγμα 133
τυπος 752
ὑπογραμμος 778
ὑποδειγμα —
example (make a publick), παραδειγματιζω 588
exceed (Mat. 5:20), {περισσευω 618
{πλειων 627
περισσευω 618
exceeding (Acts7:20), θεος 364
λιαν 460
σφοδρα 715
ὑπερ 773
ὑπερβαλλω 774
(Ro. 7:13), {ὑπερβολη 774
{κατα 406
exceeding, *see* abundant, abundantly, glad, great, joy, sorrowful, sorry.
exceeding (far more) (2Co. 4:17), {ὑπερβολη 774
{κατα 406
{εις 197
exceeding joyful (be), {ὑπερπερισσευω 775
{χαρα 796
exceedingly, {μεγας 470
{φοβος 789
(1Th. 3:10), {ὑπερ 773
{εκ 215
{περισσος 618
περισσοτερως 618
περισσως 619
σφοδρα 715
σφοδρως —
exceedingly, *see* fear, grow, trouble.
exceedingly (more), περισσοτερως 618
excel, περισσευω —
ὑπερβαλλω 774
excellency, ὑπερβολη —
(Phi.3:8), ὑπερεχω 775
ὑπεροχη —
excellent, μεγαλοπρεπης 476
excellent, *see* more.
excellent (be), διαφερω 149
excellent (be more), διαφερω —
excellent (more), διαφορος —
πλειων 627
(1Co. 12:31), {ὑπερβολη 774
{κατα 406
excellent (most), κρατιστος 432
except, εαν 170
ει μη 186
ει μη τι 187
εκτος 231
εαν μη 494
παρεκτος 594
πλην 629
except it be, η 340
except that, ει μη 186
excepted, εκτος 231
excess, ακρασια 26
αναχυσις 46
ασωτια 89
excess of wine, οινοφλυγια 527
exchange in, ανταλλαγμα 55
exchanger, τραπεζιτης 748
exclude, εκκλειω 227
excuse, απολογεομαι 74
παραιτεομαι 590
excuse (make), παραιτεομαι —
excuse...self, απολογεομαι 74
excuse (without), αναπολογητος 44
execute, ποιεω 636
execute office, *see* Priest.
executioner, σπεκουλατωρ 695
exercise, γυμνασια 129
exercise, ασκεω 87
γυμναζω 129
ποιεω 636
exercise, *see* authority, dominion.
exercise over, *see* lordship.
exhort, παραινεω 590
παρακαλεω —
προτρεπομαι 668
exhortation (Lu.3:18), παρακαλεω 590
παρακλησις 591

forgetful (Jas. 1:25), επιλησμονη 285
forgetful (be), επιλανθανομαι —
forgive, απολυω 75
αφιημι 97
forgive frankly, & forgive, χαριζομαι 796
forgiveness, αφεσις 97
form, μορφη 506
μορφωσις —
τυπος 752
ὑποτυπωσις 780
form, πλασσω 627
formed (be), μορφοομαι 506
formed (thing), πλασμα 627
former, προτερον 668
προτερος —
πρωτος 671
fornication, πορνεια 647
fornication (commit), πορνευω 648
fornication (give self over to), εκπορνευω 230
fornicator, πορνος 648
forsake, αποστασια 76
αποτασσομαι 78
αφιημι 97
εγκαταλειπω 177
καταλειπω 413
forswear self, επιορκεω 285
forth, εξω 270
(Mar. 3:3) { μεσος 483
εις 197
..forth, απο 63
forth, *see* break, bring, brought, call, carry, cast, come, conduct, from, go, hold, launch, let, minister, pass, proceed, put, reach, send, set, setter, shed, shew, shine, shoot, speak, stand, stretch.
forth at, εκ 215
forth fruit, *see* bring.
forthwith, ευθεως 322
ευθυς 323
παραχρημα 594
forty, τεσσαρακοντα 728
forty years (of), τεσσαρακονταετης 729
forty years old, τεσσαρακονταετης —
forward, *see* go, put.
forward (be), θελω 362
σπουδαζω 696
forward (more), σπουδαιος 697
forward on journey, *see* bring.
forwardness, σπουδη 697
forwardness of mind, προθυμια 655
foul, ακαθαρτος 21
foul, *see* weather.
found, θεμελιοω 363
found (be), γινομαι 117
foundation, θεμελιος 363
καταβολη 410
foundation (lay the), θεμελιοω 363
fountain, πηγη 620
four, τεσσαρες 729
τεταρτος —
four days, τεταρταιος —
four hundred, τετρακοσιοι —
four months, τετραμηνον —
four thousand, τετρακισχιλιοι —
fourfold, τετραπλοος —
fourfooted beasts, τετραπους —
fourscore, ογδοηκοντα 522
foursquare, τετραγωνος 729
fourteen, δεκατεσσαρες 134
fourteenth, τεσσαρεσκαιδεκατος 729
fourth, τεταρτος —
fowl, ορνεον 538
πετεινον 620
fox, αλωπηξ 32
fragments, κλασμα 424
frame, καταρτιζω 415
framed fitly together (be), συναρμολογεομαι 710
frankincense, λιβανος 460
frankly, *see* forgive.
fraud (kept back by), αποστερεω 77
free, ελευθερος 233
free, *see* gift.
free (make), ελευθεροω 234
free man, ελευθερος 233
freed (be), δικαιοω 157
freedom, πολιτεια 642
freely, δωρεαν 170
παρρησια 596
(Acts 26:26), παρρησιαζομαι —
freely, *see* give.
freeman, απελευθερος 61
freewoman, ελευθερος 233
frequent (more), περισσοτερως 618
fresh, γλυκυς 124
friend, ἑταιρος 317
φιλος 787
friend, *see* thy.
friend (make any one a), πειθω 609
friends(his), (Mar.3:21) { παρα 586
with αὐτου
friendship, φιλια 787
frog, βατραχος 106
from, απο 63
δια 142
εγγυς 176
εκ 215
παρα 586
ὑπο 776
from, *see* fall, heaven, off, out, put, thrust, turn, whence.
from above, *see* above.
from among, εκ 215
from being, *see* burdensome.
from far, μακροθεν 469
from..forth, εκ 215
from hence, εντευθεν 263
from [house] to [house], κατα 406
from that place, εκειθεν 224
from the, *see* beginning.
from thence, *see* and.
from thence, εκειθεν 224
ὁθεν 524
from up, εκ 215
from whence, ποθεν 635
from within, εσωθεν 317
from without, εξωθεν 271
froward, σκολιος 687
fruit, γεννημα 114
καρπος 405
οπωρα 536
fruit, *see* bear, bring, perfection.
fruit ..withereth (whose), φθινοπωρινος 786
fruit (without), ακαρπος 21
fruitful, καρποφορος 406
fruitful (be), καρποφορεω 405
frustrate, αθετεω 15
fulfil, αναπληροω 44
εκπληροω 229
πληροω 630
ποιεω 636
συντελεω 713
τελειοω 727
τελεω —
fulfilled (be), γινομαι 117
fulfilling, πληρωμα 630
full, γεμω 113
μεστος 484
πληρης 629
(1 Joh. 1:4, 2 Joh.12) } πληροω 630
(Mar. 8:20), πληρωμα —
full, *see* age, assurance, glory, heaviness, light, make, sores.
full (be), γεμιζω 113
γεμω —
εμπληθω 239
κορεννυμι 429
full come (be), πληροω 630
full (make), πληροω —
full of, *see* darkness.
full [time], came (Lu. 1:57), πληθω 629
full well, καλως 403
fuller, γναφευς 124
fulness, πληρωμα 630
fully, *see* come, know, known, preach, ripe.
furlong, σταδιος 697
furnace, καμινος 403
furnish, πληθω 629
στρωννυμι 701
furnish throughly, εξαρτιζω 266
further, πλειων 627
further, ετι 318
πορρω 648
further, *see* any, proceed, threaten.
further (go), διιστημι 155

glorified together (be), συνδοξαζομαι 710
glorify, δοξαζω 162
glorious, δοξα 161
ενδοξος 260
glorious, *see* make.
glory, δοξα 161
καυχημα 419
κλεος 424
glory, κατακαυχαομαι 411
καυχαομαι 419
glory, *see* have, vain.
glory (desirous of vain), κενοδοξος 420
glory (full of), δοξαζω 162
glory of, καυχημα 419
glory (whereof I may), καυχησις ...... —
glorying, καυχημα ...... —
καυχησις ...... —
gluttonous, φαγος 782
gnash, βρυχω 111
τριζω 750
gnashing, βρυγμος 111
gnat, κωνωψ 442
gnaw, μασσαομαι 472
go, αγω 10
απειμι 61
απερχομαι ...... —
διερχομαι 155
εκπορευομαι 229
εξερχομαι 266
ερχομαι 301
μεταβαινω 487
παραγινομαι 588
παραπορευομαι 593
παρερχομαι 594
περιπατεω 617
πορευομαι 646
προσερχομαι 662
ὑπαγω 771
χωρεω 805
go, *see* aside, compel, country, further, law, let, warfare.
go aboard, επιβαινω 281
go about, διερχομαι 155
επιχειρεω 289
ζητεω 337
πειραζω 610
πειραω 611
περιαγω 615
go abroad, διερχομαι 155
εξερχομαι 266
go again, επιστρεφω 287
go and meet, ὑπανταω 772
go aside, απερχομαι 61
ὑποχωρεω 780
go astray, πλαναω 627
go away, απερχομαι 61
εξερχομαι 266
πορευομαι 646
ὑπαγω 771
go back, απερχομαι 61
go before, προαγω 653
προερχομαι 655
go before, προπορευομαι 656
go beyond, ὑπερβαινω 774
go down, επιδυω 283
go down, καταβαινω 409
κατερχομαι 417
go down with, συγκαταβαινω 703
go every where, διερχομαι 155
go farther, προβαινω 653
προερχομαι 655
go forth, εκπορευομαι 229
εξερχομαι 266
πορευομαι 646
go forward, προερχομαι 655
go in..into, εισειμι 211
εισερχομαι ...... —
εισπορευομαι 214
εμβαινω 235
go into with, & go in with, συνεισερχομαι 711
go (let), απολυω 75
go near, προσερχομαι 662
go on, προβαινω 653
φερω 784
go on a journey, ὁδοιπορεω 523
go one's way, πορευομαι 646
go out, απερχομαι 61
αποβαινω 68
εκπορευομαι 229
εξειμι 266
εξερχομαι ...... —
go out, σβεννυμι 681
go out of the way, εκκλινω. 228
go over, διαπεραω 147
διερχομαι 155
τελεω 727
go ...... about, περιαγω 615
go through, διαπορευομαι 147
διερχομαι 155
εισερχομαι 211
go throughout, διερχομαι 155
διοδευω 158
go to, προσερχομαι 662
go to, αγε 6
go unto, προσερχομαι 662
go up, αναβαινω 39
ανερχομαι 47
πορευομαι 646
προσαναβαινω 662
go up into, εμβαινω 235
go ... way, ὑπαγω 771
go .... ways, απερχομαι 61
go with, συμπορευομαι 707
συνερχομαι 712
goat, εριφιον 301
εριφος ...... —
τραγος 748
goat [skins], αιγειος 15
God, Θεος 364
(Acts19:20), κυριος 436
δαιμονιον 131
God, *see* admonished, answer, lover, ward, would.
God (fight against), θεομαχεω 364
God forbid, { γινομαι ...... 117 / μη ...... 490 }
God (given by inspiration of, θεοπνευστος 364
God (hater of), θεοστυγης 373
God speed, χαιρω 795
God (taught of), θεοδιδακτος 364
God (to fight against) (Acts 5:39), θεομαχος ...... —
God (without), αθεος 15
God (worshipper of), θεοσεβης 373
goddess, Θεα 361
Godhead, θειος ...... —
θειοτης ...... —
θεοτης 373
godliness, ευσεβεια 326
θεοσεβεια 373
godly, ευσεβης 326
{ Θεος ...... 364 / κατα ...... 406 }
godly, ευσεβως 327
godly (after a), *see* sort.
godly fear, ευλαβεια 323
gold, χρυσιον 804
χρυσος ...... —
gold (of), χρυσεος ...... —
gold ring (with a), χρυσοδακτυλος ...... —
golden, χρυσεος ...... —
good, βιος 107
good, χρηστοτης 803
good, αγαθος 1
καλος 402
χρηστος 803
good, ευ 320
καλως 403
good, *see* behaviour, cheer, comfort, deed, increased, olive tree, pleasure, report, seem, think, way.
good (be), ισχυω 392
good (be), συμφερω 707
good (do), αγαθοεργεω 1
αγαθοποιεω ...... —
ευεργετεω 322
ευποια 325
good men, *see* lover.
good place (in a), καλως 403
good things, αγαθος 1
good things, *see* teachers.
good (think), αξιοω 58
good (those that are), *see* despisers.
good tidings (bring), ευαγγελιζω 320
good [while], ἱκανος 384
good will, ευδοκια 322
ευνοια 324
good words, χρηστολογια 803
goodly, καλος 402
λαμπρος 447
goodman, οικοδεσποτης 525
goodness, αγαθωσυνη 2
χρηστος 803
χρηστοτης ...... —
goods, αγαθος 1
ουσια 573
σκευος 686

goods ὑπαρξις 772
ὑπαρχοντα .... —
gorgeous, ενδοξος 260
λαμπρος.......... 447
gospel, ευαγγελιον 321
gospel, *see* preach, preach before.
gospel preached (unto us was the), (Heb. 4:2) } ευαγγελιζω.. 320
εσμεν.. 307
gotten (from), αποσπαω.... 76
government, κυβερνησις.... 436
κυριοτης...... 442
governor, εθναρχης 181
ἡγεμων 343
(Mat.2:6), ἡγεομαι 343
οικονομος 526
governor (be), ἡγεμονευω.. 342
governor of the feast, αρχιτρικλινος 85
grace, ευπρεπεια 325
grace, χαρις 797
gracious, χαρις............ —
χρηστος 803
graff in..or into, εγκεντριζω 177
grain, κοκκος.............. 427
grandmother, μαμμη........ 470
grant, διδωμι............... 151
επω 291
χαριζομαι........... 796
grapes, σταφυλη 698
grass, χορτος 802
grave, ᾅδης................ 13
μνημα.............. 502
μνημειον .... —
grave, σεμνος............... 684
grave (Acts 17:29), χαραγμα 796
graveclothes, κειριαι 420
gravity, σεμνοτης 684
great, ἱκανος 384
λιαν 460
μεγας 476
πολυς 643
great, *see* authority, deal, desire, drops, how, noise, price, shew, so, swelling, very, way, what, while.
great age (be of a), (Lu. 2:36) { προβαινω 654
ἡμερα ... 347
πολυς ... 643
great [curse], αναθεμα 41
great deal, πολυς........... 643
great (exceeding), μεγιστος 477
great (how), ἡλικος 344
great men, μεγιστανες...... 477
great (so), τηλικουτος...... 730
great things, μεγαλεια...... 475
great things, *see* boast.
great (very), παμπολυς 585
great (what), ἡλικος........ 344
great while, πολυς......... 643
great with child, εγκυος 178
greater, μειζοτερος.......... 478
μειζων .... —
περισσοτερος 618
πλειων 627
greater part, πλειων .... —
greatest, μεγας............. 476
μειζων 478
greatly, λιαν 460
μεγαλως........... 476
πολυς 643
σφοδρα 715
χαρα 796
greatly, *see* amazed, desire, long, rejoice, wonder.
greatness, μεγεθος 477
Grecian, Ἑλληνιστης 828
Greece, Ἑλλας............. —
greedily, *see* run.
greediness, πλεονεξια 628
greedy, *see* filthy lucre.
Greek, Ἑλλην 828
Greek, Ἑλληνις .... —
Greek, Ἑλληνικος .... —
Greek, Ἑλληνιστι .... —
green, ὑγρος 753
χλωρος 801
greet, ασπαζομαι........... 88
greeting, χαιρω 795
greetings, ασπασμος....... 88
grief, λυπη 465
grief (cause), λυπεω .... —
grief (with), (Heb. 13:17), στεναζω 698
grieve, λυπεω.............. 465
grieved (be), διαπονεομαι.. 147
συλλυπεομαι 705
grieved with (be), προσοχθιζω 666
grievous, βαρυς 102
(Heb.12:11), λυπη 465
οκνηρος 528
πονηρος 646
grievous to be borne, δυσβαστακτος 168
grievously, δεινως 133
κακως 401
grind, αληθω.............. 28
grind to powder, λικμαω.... 460
groan, εμβριμαομαι......... 235
στεναζω............ 698
groan together, συστεναζω 714
groaning, στεναγμος....... 698
gross (wax), παχυνομαι.... 609
ground, γη 115
εδαφος 181
ἑδραιωμα .... —
χωρα 805
ground, θεμελιοω.......... 363
ground, *see* parcel.
ground (even with), *see* lay.
ground (on the), χαμαι 796
ground (piece of), αγρος.... 10
ground (to the), χαμαι..... 796
grow, αυξανω 91
γινομαι.............. 117
ερχομαι 301
grow exceedingly, ὑπεραυξανω 774
grow together, συναυξανομαι 710
grow up, αναβαινω 39
μηκυνομαι 499
grudge, στεναζω 698
grudging, γογγυσμος....... 125
grudgingly, (2Co. 9:7) { λυπη 465
εκ......... 215
guard, *see* captain.
guest (be), καταλυω 413
guestchamber, καταλυμα .. —
guests, ανακειμαι.......... 42
guide, ὁδηγος.............. 523
guide, κατευθυνω........... 417
ὁδηγεω............. 523
guide, *see* house.
guile, δολος 161
guiltless, αναιτιος 42
guilty, ὑποδικος 778
guilty (be), οφειλω 579
guilty of, ενοχος 262
gulf, χασμα................ 798
gush out, εκχυνω........... 231

habitation, επαυλις......... 273
κατοικητηριον .. 418
κατοικια .... —
οικητηριον 524
σκηνη 687
had (that she), { ἑαυτου 172
παρα 586
hail, χαιρω 795
hail, χαλαζα .... —
hair, θριξ.................. 377
κομη 428
hair (broidered), πλεγμα.... 627
hair (have long), κομαω 428
hair (of), τριχινος 750
hale, κατασυρω............. 416
συρω 714
half, ἡμισυ 351
half, *see* hour.
half dead, ἡμιθανης 350
hall, αυλη.................. 90
hall, *see* judgment.
hall (common), πραιτωριον 651
hall of judgment, πραιτωριον —
hallow, ἁγιαζω 6
halt, χωλος............... 805
hand, χειρ 798
hand, *see* nigh, palm, smite, strike.
hand (at), εγγυς........... 176
hand (be at), εγγιζω....... 175
ενιστημι...... 262
εφιστημι...... 328
hand (right), δεξιος......... 135
hand (some to lead him by the), (Acts 13:11) } χειραγωγος 800
hand (take in), επιχειρεω.. 289
handkerchief, σουδαριον, .. 694
handle, θιγω 376
ψηλαφαω.......... 806
handle deceitfully, δολοω.... 161
handle, *see* shamefully.
handmaid,-en, δουλη 163
hand on (lay), κρατεω 431
πιαζω . . . 621
hand (lead by the), χειραγωγεω 800

hands (made with), } χειρο-
hands (made by), } ποιητος 800
hands (made without), αχειροποιητος 99
hands (with own), αυτοχειρ 96
handwriting, χειρογραφον .. 800
hang, κρεμαμαι............. 432
hang about, περικειμαι...... 616
hang down, παριεμαι....... 595
hang.. self, απαγχομαι...... 59
haply, αρα 79
πως 675
haply, *see* lest.
happen, γινομαι 117
συμβαινω 705
happier, μακαριος........... 468
happy, μακαριος .... —
happy (count), μακαριζω .. —
hard, δυσκολος 169
σκληρος 687
hard, *see* join, understood, uttered.
harden, πωροω 675
σκληρυνω 687
hardly, δυσκολως........... 169
μογις............. 503
μολις............. 505
hardness, πωρωσις 675
σκληροτης 687
hardness (endure), κακοπαθεω 400
hardness of heart, σκληροκαρδια 687
harlot, πορνη............... 648
harm, ατοπος.............. 90
κακος 400
(Acts 28:21), πονηρος 646
υβρις............... 753
harm, κακοω 400
harmless, ακακος........... 21
ακεραιος......... —
harp, κιθαρα 423
harp, κιθαριζω .... —
harper, κιθαρωδος .... —
harvest, θερισμος 374
haste, σπουδη 697
haste
haste unto
haste (with) } σπευδω 696
Lu. 2:16)
haste (make), σπευδω ...... —
hastily, ταχεως............. 723
hate, μισεω................. 501
hateful (Rev. 18:2), μισεω —
στυγητος 701
hater, *see* God.
hatred, εχθρα 329
have, αντιβαλλω............ 56
απεχω 62
γινομαι 117
have (Rev. 22:14), εσομαι 308
εστι 310
εχω 329
ην 354
(Joh. 5:4) κατεχω.... 417
λαμβανω.............. 445
have, μεταλαμβανω 488
(Heb. 13:5), παρειμι 594
ποιεω 636
υπαρχω 772
ων 810
have, *see* admiration, care, company, compassion, confidence, convenient, conversation, course, devil, dominion, enough, hope, indignation, journey, knowledge, lack, leisure, let, need, nourishment, palsy, patience, peace, pity, place, pleasure, power, preeminence, regard, reputation, respect, rule over, testimony, understanding, will.
have abundance, *see* abundance.
have against, *see* quarrel.
have charge of { ην 354
(Acts 8:27) { επι 275
have glory, δοξαζω.......... 162
have in, *see* remembrance.
have long, *see* hair.
have mercy on, *see* mercy.
have on, ενδυω............. 260
have our, *see* being.
have over, πλεοναζω 628
have respect, *see* persons.
have to do (Heb. 4:13) } λογος 462
have vith, *see* fellowship.
haven, λιμην.................. 461
having, *see* compassion, dropsy.
havock (make), λυμαινομαι 465
hay, χορτος 802
hazard, παραδιδωμι 589
he, οδε,.................. 522
ουτος 574
τις 732
he also.. and he.. even he } κακεινος 399
he, him & his, αυτος........ 91
εκεινος 225
he himself, εαυτου.......... 172
he it was that (Joh. 6:71), ουτος 574
he that, ει τις 187
οστις 540
head, κεφαλη............... 421
head (wound in the), κεφαλαιοω .... —
headlong, πρηνης 652
headlong, *see* cast.
heady, προπετης........... 656
heal, διασωζω 148
θεραπευω............. 373
(Acts 4:30), ιασις..... 379
σωζω 716
healed (be), ιαομαι 379
healing, θεραπεια 373
ιαμα..... 379
ιασις.. .. .. —
health, σωτηρια 718
health (be in), υγιαινω 753
heap, επισωρευω 288
σωρευω............ . 718
heap treasure together, θησαυριζω 375
hear, ακουω 22
διακουομαι 145
εισακουω 211
επακουω 272
επακροαομαι .... —
hear, *see* neglect.
hear before, προακουω...... 653
heard [i. q. of hearing], ακοη 22
hearer, ακουω .... —
ακροατης........... 26
hearing, ακοη............... 22
διαγνωσις 144
hearing, *see* audience.
hearing (place of), ακροατηριον 26
hearken, ακουω.............. 22
πειθαρχεω 609
υπακουω 772
hearken to, ενωτιζομαι 265
heart, καρδια...... 404
ψυχη 807
heart, *see* cut, hardness.
hearted, καρδια. 404
hearted, *see* tender.
heartily (Col. 3:23) { ψυχη 807
{ εκ 215
hearts failing, αποψυχω 78
hearts (which knoweth the), καρδιογνωστης 405
heat, θερμη............ . .. 374
καυμα 419
καυσων..... .... —
heat (burning), καυσων .... —
heat (fervent), καυσοω...... —
heathen, εθνος 181
εθνικος........... —
heathen man, εθνικος ...... —
heaven, ουρανος 571
heaven (from), ουρανοθεν. —
heaven (in), επουρανιος.... 290
heaven (midst of), μεσουρανημα 484
heavenly, επουρανιος 290
ουρανιος.......... 571
heavenly (Lu. 11:13) { ουρανος.... —
{ εκ......... 215
heaviness, κατηφεια 418
λυπη 465
heaviness (be full of), αδημονεω 13
heaviness (be in), λυπεω .. 465
heavy, βαρεω.............. 102
βαρυς.......... —
heavy, *see* lade.
heavy (be very), αδημονεω 13
Hebrew, Ἑβραικος......... 82
Hebrew, Ἑβραιος .... —
Hebrew, Ἑβραις .... —
Hebrew (in the), Ἑβραιστι -
Hebrew tongue (in the), Ἑβραιστι................. —
hedge, φραγμος 790

if not, ει μη 186
εαν μη 494
if otherwise, ει δε μη 186
if ought, ει τις 187
if.. peradventure, μηποτε 497
if so, εαν 170
if so be, ει περ | if...that 187
if so be that, ειγε 185
ει περ 187
if yet, ειγε 185
ignorance, αγνοια 9
αγνωσια —
ignorant, ιδιωτης 381
ignorant (be), αγνοεω 8
ignorant of (be), λανθανω 447
ignorantly, αγνοεω 8
ill, κακος 400
illuminate, φωτιζω 794
image, εικων 193
image (express), χαρακτηρ 796
imagination, διαλογισμος 146
διανοια 147
λογισμος 461
imagine, μελεταω 478
immediately, εξαυτης 266
ευθεως 322
ευθυς 323
παραχρημα 594
immortal, αφθαρτος 97
immortality, αθανασια 15
αφθαρσια 97
immutability, αμεταθετος 35
immutable, αμεταθετος —
impart, μεταδιδωμι 487
impediment in his speech (having an), μογιλαλος 503
impenitent, αμετανοητος 35
implacable, ασπονδος 88
implead, εγκαλεω 177
importunity, αναιδεια 42
impose, επικειμαι 284
impossible, αδυνατος 15
ανενδεκτον 47
impossible (be), αδυνατεω 14
impotent, αδυνατος 15
ασθενης 87
impotent folk, ασθενεω —
impotent man, ασθενεω —
imprison, φυλακιζω 791
imprisonment, φυλακη —
impute, ελλογεω 234
λογιζομαι 461
in, ανα 39
απο 63
αχρι 99
δια 139
εις 197
εκ 215
εν 240
επι 275
κατα 406
μετα 484
παρα 586
περι 613
προς 656
(Acts 5:21) ὑπο 776

in, εσω 317
in, *see* abide, act, admiration, adultery, arms, behalf, bondage, bonds, bring, bringing, brought, call, charge, clothed, come, conference, continue, danger, end, entangle, enter, entrance, go, graff, no, order, pour, put, rejoice, run, spring, step, take, thrust, walk, wrap, write.
in a, *see* behold.
in a place, επι 275
in among, εις 197
in at, εις —
in every, κατα 406
in labour, *see* companion.
in law, *see* daughter, mother.
in one's teeth, *see* cast.
in other men's matters, *see* busybody.
in pieces, *see* break.
in respect of, κατα 406
in right, *see* mind.
in sight of, εμπροσθεν 239
in..stead ὑπερ 773
in sunder, *see* cut.
in that, ὁτι 543
in that they, ὁστις 540
in the, *see* audience, morning.
in the absence of, *see* absence.
in the days of, επι 275
in the mind, *see* cast.
in the time of, επι 275
in unawares, *see* creep.
in unto, εις 197
in [where-], περι 613
in with, *see* go.
inasmuch, κατα 406
inasmuch as, { επι 275 | ὁσος 539 }
καθο 396
incense, θυμιαμα 378
incense (burn), θυμιαω —
inclose, συγκλειω 703
incontinency, ακρασια 26
incontinent, ακρατης —
incorruptible, αφθαρτος 97
incorruption, αφθαρσια —
increase, αυξησις 91
increase, αυξανω —
περισσευω 618
προκοπτω 656
προστιθημι 666
increase (give the), αυξανω 91
increase in strength, ενδυναμοω 260
increase (make to), πλεοναζω 628
increased with goods (be), πλουτεω 632
incredible (thing), απιστος 63
indebted (be), οφειλω 579
indeed, αληθως 28
αλλα 29
γαρ 112

indeed, μεν 480
οντως 534

indignation, αγανακτησις 2
ζηλος 337
θυμος 378
οργη 537
indignation (be moved with) αγανακτεω 2
indignation (have), αγανακτεω —
indignation (with), αγανακτεω —
inexcusable, αναπολογητος 44
infallible, *see* proof.
infant, βρεφος 111
inferior (be), ἡτταομαι 358
infidel, απιστος 63
infirmities, ασθενημα 87
infirmity, ασθενεια —
νοσος 518
inform, εμφανιζω 240
κατηχεω 418
inhabitants, κατοικεω —
inhabiters, κατοικεω —
inherit, κληρονομεω 425
inheritance, κληρονομια —
κληρος —
inheritance, *see* obtain.
iniquity, αδικημα 14
αδικια —
ανομια 55
παρανομια 592
πονηρια 645
injoin, εντελλομαι 263
επιτασσω 288
injure, αδικεω 14
injurious, ὑβριστης 753
ink, μελαν 478
inn, καταλυμα 413
πανδοχειον 585
inner, εσω 317
εσωτερος —
innocent, αθωος 15
innumerable, αναριθμητος 44
innumerable, *see* company, multitude.
inordinate affection, παθος 582
inscription, επιγραφω 283
insomuch as, ὡστε 816
insomuch that, εις 197
ὡστε 816
inspiration, *see* God.
instant, ὡρα 811
instant (be), επικειμαι 284
εφιστημι 328
instant in, *see* continue.
instantly, εκτενεια 230
σπουδαιως 697
instruct, κατηχεω 418
μαθητευω 466
παιδευω 582
συμβιβαζω 705
instruct before, προβιβαζω 654
instructed (be), μυεομαι 511
instructer, παιδαγωγος 582
παιδευτης —

look on, θεωρεω 374
look out, επισκεπτομαι 286
look round about on, & look round about, περιβλεπω 616
look stedfastly, ατενιζω 90
look to, βλεπω 108
look..up, αναβλεπω 40
ανακυπτω 43
look upon (to) (Rev. 4:3), ὁρασις 536
look upon, εμβλεπω 235
επιβλεπω 282
εφοραω 329
θεαομαι 361
looking after, προσδοκια 662
looking for, εκδοχη 224
loose, απολυω 75
καταργεω 415
λυω 466
ανιημι 53
loose [a ship], αιρω 17
loose [i. e. depart], αναγω 41
loosed (be), (1 Co. 7:27) λυσις 465
Lord, δεσποτης 136
κυριος 436
ῥαββονι 676
lord of (be), κυριευω 436
lord over (be), κατακυριευω 412
Lord's (the), κυριακος 436
lords, (1 Ti. 6:15) κυριευω —
μεγιστανες 477
lordship over (exercise), κατακυριευω 412
κυριευω 436
lose, απολλυμι 74
ζημιοω 337
lose, *see* savour.
loss, αποβολη 68
ζημια 337
loss, *see* suffer.
lost, *see* saltness.
lost (be), απολλυμι 74
lot, κληρος 425
lot (be his), λαγχανω 442
lots, *see* cast.
loud, μεγας 476
love, αγαπη 3
love, αγαπαω 2
θελω 362
φιλεω 786
love as brethren (1 Pet. 3:8), φιλαδελφος —
love (brotherly), φιλαδελφια —
love of money, φιλαργυρια —
love of the brethren, φιλαδελφια —
love one's children (Tit. 2:4) φιλοτεκνος 787
love their husband (Tit. 2:4) φιλανδρος 786
love to have, *see* preeminence.
love toward man, φιλανθρωπια 786
lovely, προσφιλης 667
lover of God, φιλοθεος 787
lover of good men, φιλαγαθος 786
lover of hospitality, φιλοξενος 787
lover of..own self, φιλαυτος 786
lover of pleasure, φιληδονος 787
low, *see* bring, degree, estate.
low (be made), (Jas. 1:10) ταπεινωσις 720
low estate, ταπεινωσις —
lower, κατωτερος 419
lower [as the sky], στυγναζω 701
lower (make), ελαττοω 232
lowest, εσχατος 317
lowliness, ταπεινοφροσυνη 720
lowliness of mind, ταπεινοφροσυνη —
lowly, ταπεινος —
lucre, κερδος 421
lucre, *see* filthy.
lucre (not greedy of filthy)
Luke, Λουκας 850
lukewarm, χλιαρος 801
lump, φυραμα 792
lunatick (be), σεληνιαζομαι 684
lust, επιθυμια 283
ἡδονη 343
ορεξις 537
παθος 582
lust, επιθυμεω 283
επιποθεω 286
lust after, επιθυμεω 283
(1 Co. 10:6) { επιθυμητης —
ειναι 195 }
επιθυμια 283
...ly (as a termination of adverbs, the other part of the word being some noun or adjective), εκ 215
εν 240
κατα 406
μετα 484
lying, ψευδος 806
lying in wait, ενεδρα 261
επιβουλη 282

mad (Acts 26:24), μανια 471
mad, *see* make.
mad against (be), εμμαινομαι 236
mad (be), μαινομαι 458
made, *see* confession, conformable, gazingstock, low.
made (be), γινομαι 117
(Acts 16:13), ειναι 195
κειμαι 419
made ready to hand, ἑτοιμος 320
made (thing that is), ποιημα 640
made with, *see* hands.
made with hands (not), αχειροποιητος 99
made without, *see* hands.
madness, ανοια 54
παραφρονια 593
magistrate, αρχη 84
αρχων 86
magistrate, στρατηγος 700
magistrates (obey), πειθαρχεω 601
magnificence, μεγαλειοτης 475
magnify, δοξαζω 162
μεγαλυνω 476
maid, κορασιον 429
παιδισκη 583
παις —
maiden, παιδισκη —
παις —
maimed, αναπηρος 44
κυλλος 436
mainsail, αρτεμων 82
maintain, προιστημι 655
majesty, μεγαλειοτης 475
μεγαλωσυνη 476
make, γενναω 114
διατιθεμαι 149
επιτελεω 288
εστι 310
καθιστημι 396
κατασκευαζω 415
κτιζω 435
ποιεω 636
προχειριζομαι 670
(Gal. 3:16), ῥεω 677
συνισταω 713
συντελεω —
τιθημι 731
make, *see* ado, affected, alive, ashamed, astonished, bed, bitter, broad, clean, defence, desolate, differ, difference, distribution, doubt, drink, drunk, end, enquiry, eunuch, excuse, fast, free, friend, full, gain, glad, haste, increase, intercession, journey, known, light, like, lower, matter, meet, melody, mention, merry, noise, obedient, offend, oration, payment, perfect, prayer, promise, reconciliation, rent, request, rich, see, servants, shew, shipwreck, signs, sit down, sit together, sorry straight, strong, subject, sure, uproar, void, war, weak, which, white, whole, wise.
make a, *see* calf.
make a public, *see* example.
make able, *see* able.
make abound, *see* abound.
make accepted, *see* accepted.
make....against, *see* insurrection.
make as though, προσποιεομαι 666
make choice, εκλεγομαι 228
make (ensample), διδωμι 151
make full proof of, πληροφορεω 630
make glorious, δοξαζω 162
make mad, (Acts 26:24) { περιτρεπω 619
μανια 471 }
make merchandise, εμπορευομαι 239

number.
make of no, *see* reputation.
make of none, *see* effect.
make peace, ειρηνοποιεω.... 197
make perfect, επιτελεω...... 288
make ready, ἑτοιμαζω 319
make to rise, ανατελλω 45
make towards, κατεχω...... 417
make up, *see* beforehand.
make [war], (Lu. 14:31), συμβαλλω 705
make with, *see* insurrection.
make without, *see* effect.
maker, δημιουργος......... 138
male, αρσην 82
malefactor, κακοποιος 400
κακουργος ...... —
malice, κακια.............. —
malicious, πονηρος......... 646
maliciousness, κακια 400
malignity, κακοηθεια........ —
mammon, μαμμωνας 470
man, ανηρ 47
ανθρωπινος 49
ανθρωπος .... —
ἀρῤην............ 82
εἰς............... 209
ουδεις............. 565
(1Co.14:20), τελειος . 727
τις 732
man, *see* aged, another, any, every, forbidding, free, heathen, if, impotent, love toward, manner, never, no, not, old, other, some, such, this, wise, yet, young.
man (common to), ανθρωπινος.................. 49
man of war, (Lu. 23:11), στρατευμα 700
man (strong), ισχυρος...... 392
man (young), νεανιας...... 513
νεανισκος.... —
manger, φατνη............. 784
manifest, δηλος 138
εκδηλος.......... 223
εμφανης 240
φανερος 783
manifest, φανεροω .... —
εμφανιζω......... 240
manifest, *see* token.
manifest beforehand, προδηλος 654
manifest forth, φανεροω 783
manifest (make), φανεροω.. —
manifest (not), αφανης 97
manifestation, αποκαλυψις . 70
φανερωσις .. 783
manifestly, *see* declare.
manifold, ποικιλος 640
πολυποικιλος 643
manifold more, πολλαπλασιων .... —
man[kind], ανθρωπινος.... 49
mankind, *see* abusers, defile.
manna, μαννα 471
manner, αρα, 79 | εθος 182
τυπος 752
manner, *see* after, all, like, perfect, this, what.
manner (after the), *see* Gentiles.
manner (after this), (Acts 15:23), ὁδε 522
manner (after this), οὑτω .. 576
manner (after what), πως.. 675
manner[like](Acts 1:11), {τροπος 751 / with ος}
(Jude 7), {τροπος 751 / ὁμοιος. 530}
manner of, *see* men.
manner of life, αγωγη 10
βιωσις 107
manner of man, αρα....... 79
manner of (such), {περι .. 613 / τουτου 746}
manner was, εθω.......... 182
manners, ηθος 344
manners, *see* divers.
manners (suffer the), τροποφορεω 751
manservant, παις 583
mansion, μονη 505
manslayer, ανδροφονος 46
many, ἱκανος.............. 384
πλειων 627
πολυς............. 643
many, *see* how, so, these, very.
many as, *see* as.
maran-atha, μαραν αθα 471
marble, μαρμαρον .... —
mark, σκοπος.............. 688
mark, στιγμα.............. 699
χαραγμα 796
mark, επεχω 275
σκοπεω 688
market, & market-place, αγορα 9
marred (be), απολλυμι 74
marriage, γαμος 112
marriage, *see* given.
marriage (be given in), εκγαμισκομαι 223
marriage (give in), εκγαμιζω —
married (be), γινομαι 117
marrow, μυελος 511
marry, γαμεω 112
επιγαμβρευω 282
marry a wife, γαμεω 112
Mars' hill, Αρειος Παγος .. 821
martyr, μαρτυρ 471
marvel, θαυμαστος......... 361
marvel, θαυμαζω 360
marvellous, θαυμαστος 361
master, δεσποτης 136
διδασκαλος 150
επιστατης......... 287
καθηγητης 395
κυριος............ 436
ῥαββι 676
master [of a ship], κυβερνητης 436
master, *see* house.
masterbuilder, αρχιτεκτων.. 85
matter, λογος 462
πραγμα 651
ὑλη.............. 757
matter, *see* wrong.
matter (make), διαφερω 149
matters, *see* busybody.
may & might, δυναμαι...... 164
may & mayest, εξεστι........ 268
may, ισχυω............... 392
may be (it), ισως 393
me, εγω 178
εμαυτου 235
εμε 236
εμοι .... —
εμου 238
με 473
μοι.................. 503
μου 507
me also, καμοι 393
me (of), εμος 237
meal, αλευρον 27
mean, ασημος 87
mean, ειην 193
εστι 310
θελω............... 362
μελλω 478
(Acts 21:13), ποιεω 636
mean while, μεταξυ 488
meaning, δυναμις 166
means, *see* by, no, seek.
means (by all), παντως 585
(2 Th. 3:16) {τροπος 751 / εν...... 240 / πας.... 597}
means (by any), πως 675
(2 Th. 2:3) {τροπος 751 / κατα .. 406}
means (by some), πως...... 675
means (by what), πως...... —
means of, *see* by.
measure, βατος (ὁ) 106
κορος............ 429
μετρον 489
σατον 68
χοινιξ 807
measure, μετρεω 481
measure (above), ὑπερβαλλοντως................ 774
measure (above), *see* exalted.
measure again, αντιμετρεω 57
measure (beyond), περισσος 618
{κατα .... 406 / ὑπερβολη 774}
ὑπερπερισσως 775
measure (out of), περισσως 619
(2 Co. 1:8) {κατα .... 406 / ὑπερβολη 774}
measure (without), αμετρος 35
meat, βρωμα............... 111
βρωσιμος .... —
βρωσις.............. —
προσφαγιον 667
(Acts 16: 34), τραπεζα 748
τροφη 751
φαγω............... 782

napkin, σουδαριον 694
narrow (Mat. 7:14), θλιβω 376
nation, γενεα 113
γενος 115
εθνος 181
nation *see* another.
natural, γενεσις 114
{φυσις 792
{κατα 406
φυσικος 792
ψυχικος 808
natural, *see* affection.
naturally, γνησιως 124
φυσικως 792
nature, γενεσις 114
φυσις 792
naughtiness, κακια 400
nay, αλλα 29
ου 552
ουχι 578
nay but, μενουνγε 481
near [i. e. intimate], αναγκαιος 41
near, εγγυς 176
πλησιον 631
near, *see* come, draw, go.
nearer, εγγυτερον 176
necessary, αναγκαιος 41
αναγκη —
επαναγκες 273
χρεια 802
necessity, αναγκαιος 41
αναγκη —
χρεια 802
necessity (of), {εχω 329
{αναγκη 41
neck, τραχηλος 749
need, αναγκη 41
χρεια 802
need, δει 132
οφειλω 579
προσδεομαι 662
{χρεια 802
{εχω 329
need & have need, χρηζω 803
need, *see* suffer, time.
needeth not to be, *see* ashamed.
needful, αναγκη 41
χρεια 802
needful (be), δει 132
needful (more), αναγκαιος 41
needful (things which are) (Jas. 2:16), επιτηδειος 288
needle, ῥαφις 677
needs, *see* must.
needs (must), {αναγκη 41
{εστι 310
δει 132
(Acts 21:22) {δει 132
{παντως 585
neglect, αμελεω 34
παραθεωρεω 590
neglect to hear, παρακουω 591
neglecting, αφειδια 97
negligent (be), αμελεω 34
neighbour, γειτων 113
neighbour, περιοικος 617
ὁ πλησιον 631
neither, η 340
μη 490
μηδε 496
μητε 497
ου μη 498
ου 552
ουδε 564
ουτε 573
neither..any (man), ουδεις 565
neither..any thing, ουδεις —
neither..at any time, ουδεποτε 565
neither ουδε 564
neither..nor, ου μη 498
nephews, εκγονα 223
nest, κατασκηνωσις 415
net, αμφιβληστρον 36
δικτυον 157
σαγηνη 679
never, μη 490
μηδεποτε 497
ου μη 498
{ου μη —
{εις 197
{αιων 19
(Joh. 6:35) {ου μη 498
{πωποτε 675
ου 552
ουδε 564
ουδεις 565
ουδεποτε —
(2Pet. 1:10) {ποτε 649
{ου μη 498
never, *see* ever.
never..before, ουδεπω 565
never man, *see* yet.
never..to any man {ουδεις 565
{πωποτε 675
never..yet, ουδεπω 565
nevertheless, αλλα 29
και-τοιγε 399
ὁμως 531
πλην 629
τοι 740
new, αγναφος 8
καινος 398
νεος 514
προσφατος 667
new, *see* moon, wine.
newborn, αρτιγεννητος 83
newness, καινοτης 398
next, ἑξης 268
επιουσα 285
(Acts 13:44), ερχομαι 301
εχω 329
μεταξυ 488
next day, αυριον 91
δευτεραιος 136
ἑτερος 318
next day..after, επαυριον 273
nigh, εγγυς 176
nigh, *see* come, draw.
nigh at hand, εγγυς 176
nigh (be), εγγιζω 175
nigh unto, εγγυς 176
nigh unto, παρα 586
παραπλησιον 592
προς 656
night, νυξ 520
night, *see* continue.
night and a day, νυχθημερον 521
nine, εννεα 262
ninety nine, εννενηκονταεννεα —
ninth, εννατος —
no, αλλα 29
μη 490
{μη —
{τις 732
μηδεις 496
ου μη 498
ου 552
{ουκ —
{πας 597
ουδε 564
ουδεις 565
no, *see* doubt, if, more, wise.
no..as yet, ουπω 571
no..at all, μηποτε 497
ου μη 498
no case (in), ου μη —
no doubt, αρα 79
γαρ 112
no..henceforward, μηκετι 497
no longer, μηκετι —
ουκ ετι 566
no man, μηδεις 496
(2Co.11:10), ου..ουδεις 552
565
no man, *see* forbidding.
no means (by), ου μη 498
no more, μηκετι 497
(Joh. 15:4), {ουδε 564
{οὑτω 576
ουκετι 566
no more, *see* now.
no nor, ουδε 564
no not, μηδε 496
ουδε 564
ουτε 573
no..so much as, ουδε 564
no wise (in), ου μη 498
noble, ευγενης 322
noble (most), κρατιστος 432
nobleman, βασιλικος 105
ευγενης 322
noise, φωνη 793
noise (Acts 2:6), φωνη —
noise (make a), θορυβεομαι 376
noise (with great), ῥοιζηδον 678
noised abroad (be), διαλαλεω 146
noised (be), ακουω 22
noisome, κακος 400
none, μη 490
μηδεις 496
ου 552
ουδεις 565
ουτε 573
{τις 732
{μη 490

receive, *see* damage, law, mercy, seed, sight, strength, tithe

receive (be room to), χωρεω 805

receive by tradition, *see* father.

received (1Ti.4:3), μεταληψις 488

received up, αναλαμβανω .. 43

αναληψις ..... —

receiving, ληψις 460

προσληψις 666

reckon, λογιζομαι 461

(Mat. 25:19), { λογος .... 462 / συναιρω .. 709 }

συναιρω .... —

recommend, παραδιδωμι.... 589

recompence, ανταποδομα .. 56

αντιμισθια 57

recompence of reward, μισθαποδοσια 501

recompense, αποδιδωμι 68

ανταποδιδωμι . 56

reconcile, αποκαταλλαττω.. 70

καταλλασσω 413

reconciled (be), διαλλαττομαι 146

reconciliation, reconciling, } καταλλαγη 413

reconciliation for (make), ἱλασκομαι 384

record, μαρτυρ 471

μαρτυρια 472

record (bear), μαρτυρεω.... 471

record (take to), μαρτυρομαι 472

recover, { εχω .... 329 / καλως .... 403 }

recover ... self, ανανηφω.... 43

recovering, *see* sight.

red, πυρρος.................. 674

red (be), πυρραζω .... —

Red Sea, Ερυθρα Θαλασσα . 829

redeem, αγοραζω............ 9

εξαγοραζω......... 265

λυτροω 465

redeemed (Lu. 1:68), { λυτρωσις 465 / οιεω .... 636 }

redemption, απολυτρωσις .. 74

λυτρωσις 465

redound, περισσευω 618

reed, καλαμος 401

reformation, διορθωσις...... 158

refrain, αφιστημι 98

πανομαι 609

refresh, αναπαυω........... 44

αναψυχω............ 46

refresh..self,(Acts 27:3), { επιμελεια 285 / τυγχανω 751 }

refreshed with (be), συναναπαυομαι 710

refreshing, αναψυξις........ 46

refuse, αρνεομαι 81

παραιτεομαι 590

refused (be), αποβλητος ... 68

regard, βλεπω 108

εντρεπω 264

regard, επιβλεπω 282

φρονεω 790

regard (have), προσεχω 664

regard not, αμελεω 34

regard (not to), παραβουλευομαι.................. 588

regeneration, παλιγγενεσια 583

region, κλιμα 425

χωρα 805

region round about, & region that lieth round about (Acts 14:6), περιχωρος .. 619

rehearse, αναγγελλω........ 40

rehearse from the beginning, αρχομαι 85

reign (Rev. 17:18), { βασιλεια ...... 103 / εχω........... 329 }

reign, ἡγεμονια 342

reign, βασιλευω............. 105

reign over, αρχω 86

reign with, συμβασιλευω.... 705

reins, νεφρος 515

reject, αθετεω............... 15

αποδοκιμαζω 69

εκπτυω 230

παραιτεομαι......... 590

rejected, αδοκιμος 14

rejoice, αγαλλιαω........... 2

ευφραινω 327

καυχαομαι 419

(Phi. 2:16), καυχημα .... —

χαιρω 795

rejoice against, κατακαυχαομαι 411

rejoice (greatly), αγαλλιαω . 2

rejoice with, rejoice in, } συγχαιρω.... 704

rejoicing, καυχημα 419

καυχησις......... —

release, απολυω 75

relief, διακονια 145

relieve, επαρκεω 273

religion, θρησκεια 377

religion, *see* Jews.

religious, θρησκος 377

(Acts 13:43), σεβομαι 683

remain, απολειπω 73

διαμενω 146

μενω............... 481

περιλειπομαι 617

remain, remain over, remain above, } περισσευω.. 618

remain (which) (Rev. 3:2), λοιπος 464

remaineth (it), { το λοιπον.. — / εστι .... 310 }

remember, αναμιμνησκω.... 43

μιμνησκομαι 501

μναομαι 502

μνημονευω 503

ὑπομιμνησκω.... 779

remembrance, αναμνησις .. 43

(Lu. 1:54), μναομαι .. 502

μνεια ...... —

μνημη 503

remembrance, ὑπομνησις . 779

remembrance, again, αναμνησις....................... 43

remembrance (bring to), αναμιμνησκω .... —

ὑπομιμνησκω 779

remembrance (call to), αναμιμνησκω 43

remembrance (come in), μναομαι 502

remembrance (have in), μναομαι .... —

remembrance (put in), αναμιμνησκω................ 43

remembrance (put in), ὑπομνησις, ὑπομιμνησκω 779

ὑποτιθημι 780

remission, αφεσις........... 97

παρεσις......... 595

remit, αφιημι............... 97

remnant, καταλειμμα 412

λειμμα 458

λοιπος 464

remove, κινεω 423

μεθιστανω 477

μεταβαινω 487

μετατιθημι 489

παραφ ω 593

remove into, μετοικιζω 489

removed (be), αιρω 17

removing, μεταθεσις 487

rend, διαρρησσω 148

ῥηγνυμι............. 677

σπαρασσω 695

σχιζω.............. 716

rend off, περιρρηγνυμι...... 618

render, ανταποδιδωμι 56

αποδιδωμι 68

renew, ανακαινιζω......... 42

renewed (be), ανακαινοω .. —

ανανεοω 43

renewing, ανακαινωσις 42

renounce, απειπειν 61

rent, σχισμα 716

rent (make a), σχιζω ...... —

repay, ανταποδιδωμι....... 56

αποδιδωμι 68

αποτιω 78

repent, μεταμελομαι 488

μετανοεω .... —

repent..self, μεταμελομαι .. —

repentance, μετανοια ...... —

repentance (without), αμεταμελητος 35

repented of (not to be), αμεταμελητος .... —

repetitions (use vain), βαττολογεω 106

reply against, ανταποκρινομαι. 56

report, ακοη 22

μαρτυρια 472

report, αναγγελλω 40

απαγγελλω........ 58

report (evil), δυσφημια 169

report (good), ευφημια 327

report (have good), μαρτυρεω 471

report (obtain good), *μαρτυρεω* 471
report (of good), *ευφημος* .. 327
μαρτυρεω 471
report (of honest), (Acts 6:3), *μαρτυρεω* .... —
report (slanderously), *βλασφημεω* 107
reported, *see* commonly.
reported (be), *ακουω* 22
reported of (be well), *μαρτυρεω* 471
reproach, *ατιμια* 90
ονειδισμος 532
ονειδος .... —
ὑβρις 753
reproach, *ονειδιζω* 532
reproach, *ὑβριζω* 753
reproach (suffer), *ονειδιζω* 532
reproachfully, { *λοιδορια* .. 464
{ *χαριν* 797
reprobate, *αδοκιμος* 14
reproof, *ελεγχος* 232
reprove, *ελεγχω* .... —
reputation (be of), *δοκεω* .. 160
reputation (had in), *τιμιος* 732
reputation (in), *εντιμος* 263
reputation(make of no) *κενοω* 420
request, *αιτημα* 18
δεησις 132
request (make), *δεομαι* 135
require, *αιτεω* 18
αιτημα .... —
απαιτεω 59
γινομαι 117
ζητεω 337
πρασσω 651
required (be), *εκζητεω* 226
requite, *αμοιβη* 36
αποδιδωμι 68
rescue, *εξαιρεω* 265
resemble, *ὁμοιοω* 530
reserve, *τηρεω* 730
καταλειπω 413
residue, *καταλοιπος* .... —
λοιπος 464
resist, *ανθιστημι* 49
αντικαθιστημι 56
αντιπιπτω 57
αντιτασσομαι .... —
resolved (be), *γινωσκω* 122
resort, *ερχομαι* 301
συμπορευομαι 707
συναγω 708
συνερχομαι 712
respect, *μερος* 483
respect, *see* persons.
respect (have), *αποβλεπω* 68
respect of, *see* in.
respect of persons, *προσωποληψια* 667
respect to (have), *επιβλεπω* 282
respecter of persons, *προσωποληπτης* 667
rest [i.q. remainder,] *επιλοιπος* .. 285
λοιπος 464

rest, *αναπαυσις* 44
ανεσις 47
ειρηνη 196
καταπαυσις 414
σαββατισμος 679
rest (Rev. 4:8), { *αναπαυσις* 44
{ *εχω* 329
αναπαυω 44
ἡσυχαζω 358
καταπαυω 414
κατασκηνοω 415
rest (give), *αναπαυω* 44
καταπαυω 414
rest in, *επαναπαυομαι* 273
rest (take), *αναπαυω* 44
rest (taking of) *κοιμησι* 426
rest upon, *επαναπαυομαι* .. 273
επισκηνοω 286
restitution, *αποκαταστασις* . 70
restore, *αποδιδωμι* 68
αποκαθισταω 70
καταρτιζω 415
restore again, *αποκαθισταω* 70
restrain, *καταπαυω* 414
resurrection, *αναστασις* 44
εγερσις 177
εξαναστασις .. 266
retain, *εχω* 329
κατεχω 417
κρατεω 431
return, *ανακαμπτω* 42
αναλυω 43
αναστρεφω 45
επαναγω 273
επανερχομαι .... —
επιστρεφω 287
(Acts 13:34), { *μελλω* 478
{ *ὑποστρεφω* 780
ὑποστρεφω .... —
return back again, *ὑποστρεφω* —
reveal, *αποκαλυπτω* 70
χρηματιζω 803
revealed (be), *αποκαλυψις* .. 70
revelation, *αποκαλυψις* .... —
revelling, *κωμος* 442
revenge, *εκδικησις* 223
revenge, *εκδικεω* .... —
revenger, *εκδικος* .... —
reverence, *αιδως* 16
reverence, *φοβεομαι* 788
εντρεπω 264
reverence, *see* give.
revile, *βλασφημεω* 107
λοιδορεω 464
ονειδιζω 532
revile again, *αντιλοιδορεω* .. 57
reviler, *λοιδορος* 464
revive, *αναζαω* 41
reward, *ανταποδοσις* 56
μισθος 502
reward, *αποδιδωμι* 68
reward, *see* beguile, due.
rewarder *μισθαποδοτης* 501
rich, *πλουσιος* 631
rich (Lu. 1:53), }
rich (be), } *πλουτεω* .. 632
rich (be made), }

rich (make), *πλουτιζω* 632
rich (wax), *πλουτεω* .... —
riches, *πλουτος* .... —
χρημα 803
richly, *πλουσιως* 632
right, *δεξιος* 135
right, *δικαιος* 155
ευθυς 323
right, *εξουσια* 269
right, *ορθως* 538
right, *see* hand, mind, side.
righteous, *δικαιος* 155
righteous (be), *δικαιοω* 157
righteous judgment, *δικαιοκρισια* 155
righteously, *δικαιως* 157
righteousness, *δικαιοσυνη* .. 156
δικαιωμα 157
ευθυτης 323
righteousness (to), *δικαιως* .. 157
rightly, *ορθως* 538
rightly, *see* divide.
ring, *δακτυλιος* 132
ring, *see* gold.
ringleader, *πρωτοστατης* 672
riot, *ασωτια* 89
riot, *τρυφη* 751
rioting, *κωμος* 442
riotous, *ασωτως* 90
ripe (be fully), *ακμαζω* 22
ripen, *ξηραινω* 521
rise, *ανατελλω* 45
ανιστημι 53
rise, *εγειρω* 176
rise, *see* make.
rise again, *ανιστημι* 53
εγειρω 176
rise (from the dead), *αναστασις* 44
rise up, *αναβαινω* 39
ανιστημι 53
εγειρω 176
εξανιστημι 266
rise up against, *επανισταμαι* 273
rise up together, *συνεφιστημι* 712
rise with, *συνεγειρω* 710
rising again, *αναστασις* 44
river, *ποταμος* 649
roar, *ηχεω* 358
μυκαομαι 511
ωρυομαι 812
rob *συλαω* 705
robber, *λῃστης* 459
robber of, *see* church.
robbery, *ἁρπαγμος* 82
robe, *εσθης* 306
ἱματιον 384
στολη 699
χλαμυς 801
robe (long), *στολη* 699
rock, *πετρα* 620
(Acts 27:29), { *τοπος* 741
{ *τραχυς* 749
rod, *ῥαβδος* 676
rods, *see* beat.
roll away, *αποκυλιζω* 73

roll back, αποκυλιζω 73
roll to, } roll, } προσκυλιω 665
roll together, ειλισσω 193
roof, στεγη 698
room, τοπος 741
room, *see* receive, upper.
room (chief), πρωτοκλισια . 671
room [" Felix' *room*"], διαδοχος..................... 144
room (highest), πρωτοκλισια 671
room of (in the), αντι 56
room (upper), ὑπερῳον 775
room (uppermost), πρωτοκλισια 671
root, ῥιζα.... 678
root, *see* pluck up.
root up, εκριζοω 230
rooted (be), ῥιζοομαι........ 678
rope, σχοινιον 716
rough, τραχυς 749
round, *see* compass, shine.
round about, κυκλοθεν..... 436
κυκλῳ .... —
παντοθεν 585
περιξ.......... 617
round about, *see* come, country, dwell, go, hedge, region, stand.
round about on, *see* look.
row, ελαυνω 232
royal, βασιλειος 104
βασιλικος 105
rub [as ears of corn], ψωχω 808
rudder, πηδαλιον........... 620
rude, ιδιωτης............... 381
rudiment, στοιχειον 699
rue, πηγανον................ 620
ruin, ῥηγμα.................. 677
ruins (Acts 15:16), κατασκαπτω 415
rule, αρχη 84
rule, κανων................. 404
rule, βραβευω 110
ποιμαινω 640
προιστημι 655
rule over, αρχω 86
rule over (have the), ἡγεομαι 343
ruler, αρχων 86
ἡγεμων 343
κοσμοχρατωρ........ 429
ruler, to make, καθίστημι.. 396
ruler, *see* synagogue.
ruler (chief), αρχων........ 86
ruler of the, *see* city.
ruler of the feast, αρχιτρικλινος 85
rumour, ακοη............... 22
λογος 462
run, ὁρμαω 538
προστρεχω 667
συντρεχω 714
τρεχω 749
run aground, εποκελλω 290
run before, προτρεχω 668
run down, καταTρεχω 416
run greedily, εκχυνω........ 231
run in, εισπηδαω........... 214
εισπρεχω .... —
run out, εκχεω 231
run over, ὑπερεκχυνομαι .. 775
run thither to, προστρεχω.. 667
run through, περιτρεχω 619
run to, προστρεχω......... 667
run together (Acts 21:30), συνδρομη.... 710
συντρεχω.... 714
run under, ὑποτρεχω....... 780
run violently, ὁρμαω 538
run with, συντρεχω 714
running together, *see* come.
rush, ὁρμαω 538
rushing (Acts 2:2), φερω .. 784
rust, βρωσις 111
ιος 390

sabacthani, σαβαχθανι...... 679
sabaoth, σαβαωθ .... —
sabbath-day, } σαββατον .... —
sabbath, } σαββατα .... —
sabbath (day before the), προσαββατον............. 661
sackcloth, σακκος........... 679
sacrifice, θυω 379
θυσια .... —
sacrifice (do), θυω .... —
sacrifice to idols (offered in), sacrificed to idols, } ειδωλοθυτον .. 192
sacrilege, (commit), ἱεροσυλεω 383
sad, σκυθρωπος 688
sad, *see* countenance.
sad (be), στυγναζω 701
safe, ασφαλης 89
safe, *see* bring, escape.
safe and sound, ὑγιαινω 753
safely, ασφαλως 89
safety, ασφαλεια .... —
said, αυτος 91
sail, σκευος 686
sail, αναγω 41
αποπλεω 75
εκπλεω 229
πλεω 628
sail away, εκπλεω 229
sail by, παραλεγομαι...... 592
παραπλεω .... —
sail over, διαπεραω........ 147
διαπλεω .... —
sail slowly, βραδυπλοεω 110
sail thence, εκπλεω......... 229
sail under, ὑποπλεω 779
sailing, πλοος.............. 631
sailor, ναυτης 513
saint, ἁγιος 7
sake, *see* for.
sake of (for), χαριν 797
ὑπερ 773
sake of lucre, *see* filthy.
salt, ἁλας.................. 27
ἁλς 32
salt, ἁλυκος.................. 32
salt, ἁλιζω 29
saltness (lost), αναλος...... 43
salutation, ασπασμος........ 88
salute, ασπαζομαι .... —
salvation, σωτηρια 718
σωτηριον 719
salvation (bringing), σωτηριος........................ —
same, αυτος................. 91
same, *see* body, craft, mind, that, the.
same manner, *see* after.
same (the), εκεινος.......... 225
οὑτος 574
αὑτη............ 576
ταυτα.......... 720
ταυτῃ 722
ταυτην 723
ταυτης .... —
{ τουτο 743
{ with αυτο.... 91
τουτον 746
τουτῳ 747
sanctification, ἁγιασμος 6
sanctify, ἁγιαζω .... —
sanctuary, ἁγιον .... —
sand, αμμος................. 36
sandal, σανδαλιον 680
sapphire, σαπφειρος .... —
sardine, σαρδινος........... —
sardius, σαρδιος ... . —
sardonyx, σαρδονυξ .... —
satisfy, χορταζω 802
satisfying, πλησμονη 631
save, αλλα 29
ει μη 186
η 340
παρα 586
πλην 629
save, διασωζω 148
σωζω 716
σωτηρια 718
φυλασσω 791
save only that, ει μη........ 186
save..self, σωζω 716
save that, ει μη............. 186
saving, ει μη .... —
παρεκτος............ 594
saving, περιποιησις 618
σωτηρια 718
saviour, σωτηρ .... —
savour, οσμη 539
savour, φρονεω.............. 790
savour (lose its), μωραινω.. 512
savour (sweet), ευωδια 328
saw asunder, πριζω 653
say, αποφθεγγομαι......... 78
(Heb. 7:9) { επος 290
{ επω.......... 291
επω .... —
ερεω 300
λαλεω 443
λεγω................ 449
ῥεω 677

some, αλλος 30
εἱς 209
ἑτερος 318
μεν 480
τις 732
some, *see* sort.
some man, τις 732
some means, *see* lest.
some time, ποτε 649
somebody, τις 732
something, τις .... —
sometimes, ποτε 649
somewhat, μερος 483
τις 732
son, παις 583
τεκνον 726
υἱος 754
son, *see* bear, sister's.
song, ᾠδη 809
sons (adoption of), υἱοθεσια 754
soon, παραχρημα 594
soon, ταχεως 723
soon, *see* angry, as.
" soon as it was," γινομαι.. 117
sooner, ταχιον 724
soothsaying (Acts 16 : 16), μαντευομαι 471
sop, ψωμιον 808
sorcerer, μαγος 466
φαρμακευς 784
φαρμακος .... —
sorcery, μαγεια 466
φαρμακεια 784
sorcery (use), μαγευω 466
sore, ἱκανος 384
κακως 401
λιαν 460
{ μεγας 476
{ with φοβος 789
πολυς 643
σφοδρα 715
sore, *see* afraid, amazed, displeased.
sorer, χειρων 800
sores, ἑλκος 234
sores (full of), ἑλκοομαι .... —
sorrow, λυπη 465
οδυνη 524
πενθος 612
ωδιν 809
sorrow, λυπεω 465
οδυναομαι 524
sorrowful (be), λυπεω 465
sorrowful (exceeding), περιλυπος 617
sorrowful (less), αλυποτερος 32
sorrowful (very), } περιλυ-
sorry (exceeding), } πος .. 617
sorry (make), λυπεω 465
sort, *see* baser, this, what.
sort (after a godly), αξιως .. 58
sort (some), μερος 483
soul, ψυχη 807
sound, ἠχος 358
φθογγος 786
φωνη 793
sound, ὑγιης 753
sound, ὑγιαινω 753
sound, βολιζω 109
sound, γινομαι 117
sound, ηχεω 358
σαλπιζω 680
sound, *see* safe.
sound a trumpet, σαλπιζω .. 680
sound (be), ὑγιαινω 753
sound mind, σωφρονισμος .. 719
sound out, εξηχεομαι 269
soundness (perfect), ὁλοκληρια 528
south, μεσημβρια 483
νοτος 518
south west, λιψ 461
south wind, νοτος 518
sow, ὑς 781
sow, σπειρω 695
sower, σπειρω .... —
sown, *see* seed.
space, διαστημα 148
χρονος 804
space, *see* little, three years.
space of, *see* by, for, the.
space of—after (the), διαστημι 155
spare, φειδομαι 784
spare, *see* enough.
sparingly, φειδομενως 784
sparrow, στρουθιον 701
speak, διαλεγομαι 146
επω 291
ερεω 300
λαλεω 443
λεγω 449
ῥεω 677
φθεγγομαι 786
χρηματιζω 803
speak, *see* provoke, truth.
speak against, αντιλεγω 56
καταλαλεω .. 412
speak among, συλλαλεω 705
speak before, προεπω 654
προερεω 655
speak blasphemy, βλασφημεω 107
speak boldly, παρρησιαζομαι 596
speak (can), γινωσκω 122
speak evil, βλασφημεω 107
κακολογεω 400
καταλαλεω 412
speak for self, απολογεομαι . 74
speak forth, αποφθεγγομαι .. 78
speak of, ερεω 300
καταγγελλω 410
speak out, αναφωνεω 46
speak to, } προσλαλεω .. 666
speak with, }
speak to, } προσφωνεω .. 667
speak unto, }
speak to any more, προστιθημι 666
speaker (Acts 14:12), λογος. 462
speaking, *see* evil.
speaking lies, ψευδολογος .. 806
speaking (much), πολυλογια 643
speakings (evil), καταλαλια 412
spear, λογχη 464
spearman, δεξιολαβος 135
special (Acts { τυγχανω .. 75.
19:11), { ου 552
specially, μαλιστα 470
spectacle, θεατρον 361
speech, λαλια 445
λογος 462
speech, *see* impediment.
speech (boldness of), παρρησια 596
speech (fair), ευλογια 324
speech of Lycaonia, Λυκαονιστι 851
speechless, εννεος 262
κωφος 442
speechless (be), φιμοω 788
speed, *see* God.
speed (with all), { ταχιστα . 724
{ ὡς 812
speedily, ταχος 724
spend, δαπαναω 132
ποιεω 636
προσαναλισκω 662
spend more, προσδαπαναω . —
spend time, ευκαιρεω 323
χρονοτριβεω .. 804
spent, *see* far.
spent (be), διαγινομαι 143
εκδαπαναω 223
spent (be far), κλινω 426
προκοπτω .. 656
spices, αρωμα 86
spices (sweet), αρωμα .... —
spikenard, { ναρδος 513
{ πιστικος 624
spilled (be), εκχεω 231
εκχυνω .... —
spin, νηθω 515
spirit, πνευμα 632
φαντασμα 783
spiritual (1 Co. 14 : 12), πνευμα 632
πνευματικος 635
spiritually (Ro. 8:6), πνευμα 632
πνευματικως 635
spiritually, *see* minded.
spit, spit upon, εμπτυω 239
spit, πτυω 672
spitefully, *see* entreat.
spittle, πτυσμα 672
spoil, απεκδυομαι 61
διαρπαζω 147
συλαγωγεω 705
spoiling, ἁρπαγη 82
spoils, ακροθινιον 26
σκυλον 688
spoken against (not to be), αναντιρρητος 43
spoken (be), αναγγελλω 40
sport selves, εντρυφαω 264
spot, σπιλας 696
σπιλος .... —
spot, σπιλοω .... —
spot (without), αμωμος 37
ασπιλος 88
spread, διανεμομαι 147
στρωννυμι 701

spread, ὑποστρωννυμι 780
spread abroad, εξερχομαι ... 266
spread abroad..fame, διαφημιζω 149
spring, ανατελλω........... 45
γενναω 114
spring, see day.
spring in, εισπηδαω 214
spring up, ἀλλομαι......... 30
αναβαινω 39
ανατελλω 45
βλαστανω 107
εξανατελλω...... 266
φυω 792
spring up with, συμφυομαι . 707
sprinkle, ῥαντιζω.......... 676
sprinkling, προσχυσις 667
ῥαντισμος 676
spue, εμεω 236
spunge, σπογγος 696
spy, εγκαθετος 177
κατασκοπος 415
spy out, κατασκοπεω....... —
stablish, βεβαιοω.......... 106
στηριζω 699
staff. ξυλον........... 522
ῥαβδος 676
stagger, διακρινω.......... 145
stairs, αναβαθμος 39
stall, φατνη............ 784
stanch, ἱστημι 391
stand, εγειρω........... 176
εφιστημι 328
ἱστημι........... 391
μενω 481
παριστημι 595
στηκω........... 699
συνισταω 713
(1 Co. 2:5), ω 808
stand, see jeopardy, world.
stand before, εφιστημι 328
παριστημι 595
stand by, εφιστημι 328
ἱστημι 391
παριστημι 595
περιιστημι....... ·6
stand fast, στηκω.......... 699
stand forth, ἱστημι......... 391
stand here, παριστημι 595
stand in doubt, απορεομαι.. 75
stand over, εφιστημι 328
stand round about, κυκλοω 436
περιιστημι 616
stand still, ἱστημι 391
stand up, ἱστημι .... —
παριστημι....... 595
stand up & upright, ανιστημι 53
stand with, παριστημι 595
συμπαραγινομαι 706
συνισταω 713
standing (Heb. 9:8), στασις 697
star, αστηρ 89
αστρον .... —
star, see day.
state (Phi. 2:19, 20), { περι.......... 613 / with τα }
stature, ἡλικια 344

stay, επεχω............. 275
κατεχω 417
stead, see in.
steal, κλεπτω.......... 424
stedfast, βεβαιος 106
ἑδραιος 181
στερεος 698
stedfastly, see behold, continue, look, set.
stedfastness, στερεωμα...... 698
στηριγμος 699
steep place, κρημνος 432
step, ιχνος 393
step down, καταβαινω 409
step in, εμβαινω 235
stern (of a ship), πρυμνα .. 670
steward, επιτροπος......... 289
οικονομος......... 526
steward (be), οικονομεω.... —
stewardship, οικονομια...... —
stick, φρυγανον 791
stick fast, ερειδω 300
stiffnecked, σκληροτραχηλος 687
still, ετι............ 318
still, see abide still, stand.
still (be), φιμοω 788
sting, κεντρον 420
stink, οζω............ 524
stir, ταραχος 720
stir up, αναζωπυρεω....... 41
ανασειω 44
διεγειρω 154
επεγειρω.......... 273
παροτρυνω 596
σαλευω 679
συγκινεω.......... 703
συγχεω 704
stirred (be), παροξυνομαι . 596
stock, γενος 115
stocks, ξυλον............ 522
stomach, στομαχος 700
stone, λιθος 460
πετρος 620
ψηφος......... 807
stone, καταλιθαζω 413
λιθαζω 460
λιθοβολεω......... —
stone, see hewn.
stone(mill-) { μυλικος ...... 511 / λιθος .... 460 }
stone (of), λιθινος .... —
stone (stumbling), { λιθος....... — / προσκομμα.. 665 }
stones, see cast.
stony, πετρωδης 620
stoop, κυπτω.......... 436
stoop down, κυπτω .... —
παρακυπτω .. 591
stop, συνεχω 712
(2 Co. 11:10) { σφραγιζω .... 715 / otherwise / φρασσω ...... 790 }
φρασσω.......... —
stop the, see mouth.
store (in), (1 Co. 16:2), θησαυριζω 375
store, see keep, lay.

storehouse, ταμειον 719
storm, λαιλαψ 443
straight, ευθυς 323
ορθος 537
straight course, ευθυδρομεω 325
straight (make), ανορθοω .. 55
ευθυνω.... 323
straightway, εξαυτης....... 266
ευθεως 322
ευθυς 323
παραχρημα .. 594
strain at, διυλιζω......... 159
strait, στενος.......... 698
strait (be in a), συνεχω 712
straiten, συνεχω .... —
straitened (be), στενοχωρεομαι 698
straitest (most), ακριβεστατος 26
straitly, απειλη 61
πολυς 643
straitly, see charge.
strange, αλλοτριος 31
εξω 270
ἑτερος 318
(Acts17:20), ξενιζω 521
ξενος .... —
παραδοξος......... 590
strange (think it), ξενιζω .. 521
stranger, αλλογενης 30
αλλοτριος 31
ξενος.......... 521
παρεπιδημος...... 594
παροικος 595
stranger (be a), παροικεω .. —
strangers, επιδημεω 283
strangers (as), (Acts13:17), παροικια........... 595
strangers (entertain),φιλοξενια........... 787
strangers (lodge), ξενοδοχεω 521
strangled, πνικτος 635
stream, ποταμος 649
street, αγορα 9
πλατεια.......... 627
ῥυμη 678
strength, δυναμις 166
εξουσια........ 269
ισχυς 392
κρατος 432
strength, see increase.
strength (be of), ισχυω 392
strength (receive), στερεοω 698
strength (without), ασθενης 87
strengthen, δυναμοω....... 167
ενδυναμοω...... 260
ενισχυω 262
επιστηριζω 287
σθενοω......... 685
στηριζω 699
strengthened (be), κραταιοω 431
stretch beyond, ὑπερεκτεινω 775
stretch forth. εκπεταννυμι 229
εκτεινω 230
επιβαλλω ... 281
strew, διασκορπιζω 148
στρωννυμι 701

then, τε 724
τοινυν 740
τοτε 742
then, *see* for, now, so.
then [after that], ειτα 214
then .... not, ουδε 564
thence, εκειθεν 224
thence, *see* and, from, go, sail.
thence also..and thence, κᾳκειθεν 399
thenceforth (Joh19:12), τουτου 746
εκ 215
ετι 318
Theophilus, Θεοφιλος 831
there [in composition], αυτος 91
there, αυτου 92
εκει & εκειθεν 224
εκεισε 226
(Acts 9:38), εν 240
ενθαδε 261
ωδε, 809
there, *see* and.
there [about], τουτου 746
there also, κᾳκει 399
there dwelling, (be), επιδημεω 283
thereabout, *see* about.
thereby, ταυτης 723
δια 138
therefore, αλλα 29
ἄρα 79
ἆρα 80
γαρ 112
δη 138
διο 158
διοτι —
ουν 567
τοιγαρουν 740
τοινυν —
τουτο 743
δια 138
τουτο 743
εις 197
ὡστε 816
therefore, *see* ..fore.
therein, τουτοις 746
τουτῳ 747
εν 240
thereon, *see* build, laid.
thereunto, *see* comers.
thereunto, τουτο 743
εις 197
thereupon, *see* build.
therewith, τουτοις 746
these, ὁδε 522
ουτοι 575
αὑται 576
ταυτα 720
ταυταις 722
ταυτας —
τουτοις 746
τουτους 747
τουτων 748
these, *see* move, things.
these many, τοσουτος 742
these things, τουτων 748
Thessalonian, Θεσσαλονικευς 831
Thessalonica, Θεσσαλονικη 831
Theudas, Θευδας —
they, αυτος 91
αὑτου 92
ἑαυτου 172
εκεινος 225
κᾳκεινος 399
οὑτοι 575
ταυτα 720
τουτων 748
they, *see* and.
they also, κᾳκεινος 399
they that, ὁστις 540
they that are, *see* born.
they were, *see* alone.
they which, ὁστις 540
thick together, *see* gathered.
thief, κλεπτης 424
λῃστης 459
thigh, μηρος 499
thine, σος 690
σου 691
thine own, ἑαυτου 172
ιδιος 380
(Acts 5:4), σοι 689
μενω 481
σος 690
σου 691
thine own self, σεαυτου 683
thing, λογος 462
πραγμα 651
ῥημα 677
thing, *see* any, certain, committed, creeping, draw, formed, high, holy, incredible, one, what.
thing (no-), (Lu. 1:37), πας 597
ουκ 552
ῥημα 677
τις 732
things, these things, αυτος 91
things, *see* all, base, boast, come, good, great, hoped, move, those, weak.
things that (we) have, ενειμι 261
things which are, *see* needful.
think, διαλογιζομαι 146
δοκεω 160
ενθυμεομαι 261
ἡγεομαι 343
κρινω 433
λογιζομαι 461
νοεω 516
νομιζω —
οιομαι 527
ὑπονοεω 779
(Mar.14:64), φαινω 782
φρονεω 790
think, *see* good, strange, worthy.
think good, ευδοκεω 322
think more highly, ὑπερφρονεω 775
think upon, επιβαλλω 281
third, τριτος 750
third loft, τριστεγον —
thirdly, τριτος —
thirst, διψος 159
thirst
thirsty (be), διψαω 158
thirty, τριακοντα 749
thirtyfold, τριακοντα —
this, αυτος 91
εκεινος 225
οὑτος 574
οὑτοι 575
αὑτη 576
ταυτα 720
ταυτῃ 722
ταυτην 723
ταυτης —
τουτο 743
τουτοις 746
τουτον —
τουτου —
τουτους 747
τουτῳ —
this, νυν 519
this, *see* day, hour, place, wise.
this man, αυτος 91
οὑτος 574
this manner (in), οὑτω 576
this place, ὡδε 809
this sort, τουτων 748
this time, νυν 519
this time, *see* by.
this wise (on), οὑτω 576
this woman, αὑτη —
thistle, τριβολος 756
thither, εκει 224
thither also, κᾳκει 399
thitherto, *see* run.
thitherward, εκει 224
Thomas, Θωμας 831
thong, ἱμας 384
thorn, σκολοψ 688
thorns, ακανθα 21
thorns (of), ακανθινος —
those, αυτος 91
εκεινος 225
ταυτα 720
ταυταις 722
ταυτας —
τουτοις 746
τουτων 748
those things (Jude 10), ὁσος 539
thou, σε 681
σοι 689
σου 691
συ 701
thou thyself, σεαυτου 683
though, δια 140
though, εαν 170
ει 183
ει και 186
ει περ 187
καιπερ 398
και-τοιγε 399
καν 403
ὁτι 543
though, *see* as.
though..but, ὁμως 531
thought, διαλογισμος 146
διανοημα 147

tumult, θορυβος 376
turn, ανακαμπτω (t. again) 42
αποβαινω 68
εκτρεπομαι 231
επιστρεφω............. 287
μεταστρεφω 489
μετατιθημι .... —
στρεφω 701
turn, *see* way.
turn about, επιστρεφω 287
μεταγω 487
turn again, επιστρεφω 287
στρεφω 701
turn aside, αναχωρεω 46
εκτρεπομαι 231
turn away, αποστρεφω 77
αποτρεπομαι ... 78
διαστρεφω 148
μεθιστανω 477
turn back, ὑποστρεφω 780
turn back again, στρεφω ... 701
ὑποστρεφω 780
turn from αποστρεφω 77
turn into, *see* ashes.
turn..self about, turn..self, } στρεφω ... 701
turn to flight, κλινω 426
turn upside down, αναστατοω 45
turned (be), γινομαι 117
turning, τροπη 751
turtledove, τρυγων .... —
tutor, επιτροπος 289
twain, δυο 167
twelfth, δωδεκατος........... 169
twelve, δεκαδυο 134
δωδεκα 169
twelve, *see* tribes.
twenty, εικοσι.................. 193
twice, δις 158
twinkling, ῥιπη................ 678
two, δυο 167
two, *see* years.
two and two, *see* and.
two hundred, διακοσιοι...... 145
two thousand, δισχιλιοι ... 159
two ways, *see* meeting.
two (with), *see* edges.
twoedged, διστομος 158
twofold more, διπλους ...... —

unawares, αιφνιδιος 19
λανθανω 447
unawares, *see* brought, creep.
unbelief, απειθεια 60
απιστια 63
unbeliever, απιστος .... —
unbelieving, απειθεω 60
απιστος 63
unblameable, αμεμπτος ... 34
αμωμος 37
unblameably, αμεμπτως ... 35
uncertain, αδηλος 13
uncertain, αδηλοτης .... —
uncertainly, αδηλως .... —
unchangeable, απαραβατος. 59
uncircumcised (Acts 11:3), { ακροβυστια 26, εχω .. 329 }
απεριτμητος . 61
uncircumcised (become), } επισπαομαι 286
uncircumcision, ακροβυστια 26
unclean, ακαθαρτος 21
unclean, κοινος 426
(Heb. 9:11), κοινοω —
uncleanness, ακαθαρσια...... 20
μιασμος......... 500
unclothe, εκδυω............... 224
uncomely, ασχημων 89
uncomely, *see* behave.
uncondemned, ακατακριτος. 21
uncorruptible, αφθαρτος ... 97
uncorruptness, αδιαφθορια.. 14
uncover, αποστεγαζω 76
uncovered, ακατακαλυπτος. 21
unction, χρισμα 803
undefiled, αμιαντος 36
under, ελασσων 232
under, εν 240
επι 275
κατωτερω 418
ὑπο................ 776
under, ὑποκατω.............. 778
under, *see* bondage, curse, earth, keep, obedience, put, run, sail.
under law, εννομος 262
undergird [as a ship], ὑποζωννυμι 778
understand, ακουω 22
γινωσκω 122
ειδεω 188
επισταμαι...... 286
μανθανω 470
νοεω 516
πυνθανομαι .. 673
συνιημι 713
φρονεω 790
understand (give to), γνωριζω............................ 125
understand not, αγνοεω ... 8
understanding, διανοια...... 147
νους.......... 519
συνεσις...... 712
φρενες 790
understanding (have), παρακολουθεω 591
understanding (without), ασυνετος 89
understood (easy to be), ευσημος 327
understood (hard to be), δυσνοητος 169
unequally, *see* yoked together.
unfeigned, ανυποκριτος ... 57
unfruitful, ακαρπος 21
ungodliness, ασεβεια 86
ungodly, ασεβεια .... —
ασεβης .... —
ungodly committed, ασεβεω —
ungodly (live), ασεβεω ...... —
ungodly men, ασεβης ...... —
unholy, ανοσιος 55
κοινος 426
unity, ἑνοτης.................. 262
unjust, αδικια.................. 14
αδικος .... —
unjust (be), αδικεω .... —
unknown, αγνωστος 9
unknown, αγνοεω 8
unlade, αποφορτιζομαι 78
unlawful, ανομος 55
unlawful thing, αθεμιτος ... 15
unlearned, αγραμματος ... 9
αμαθης 32
απαιδευτος 59
ιδιωτης 381
unleavened bread, αζυμος.. 15
unless, εκτος 231
unloose, λυω 466
unmarried, αγαμος 2
unmerciful, ανελεημων...... 46
unmoveable, αμετακινητος. 35
ασαλευτος .. 86
unprepared, απαρασκευαστος 59
unprofitable, αλυσιτελης ... 32
ανωφελης ... 58
αχρειος 99
αχρηστος...... —
unprofitable (become), αχρειοομαι .... —
unprofitableness, ανωφελης 58
unquenchable, ασβεστος ... 86
unreasonable, αλογος 32
ατοπος 90
unrebukable, ανεπιληπτος. 47
unreprovable, ανεγκλητος.. 46
unrighteous, αδικος 14
unrighteousness, αδικια ... —
ανομια ... 55
unruly, ακατασχετος......... 21
ανυποτακτος 57
ατακτος 90
unsearchable, ανεξερευνητος 47
ανεξιχνιαστος —
unseemly, *see* behave.
unseemly (that which is), ασχημοσυνη 89
unskilful, απειρος............ 61
unspeakable, ανεκδιηγητος. 46
ανεκλαλητος.. —
αρρητος 82
unspotted, ασπιλος 88
unstable, ακαταστατος 21
αστηρικτος......... 89
untaken away, { ανακαλυπτω ...... 42, μη .... 490 }
unthankful, αχαριστος...... 99
until, αχρι .... —
εις 197
ἑως 334
μεχρι 490
until, *see* even.
untimely, *see* figs.
unto, αχρι 98
εις...................... 197
εκ 215
εν 240
επι 275
ἑως 334

whither, ὁπου 535
οὑ 552
που 650
whithersoever, { οὑ 552
{ εαν 170
{ ὁπου 535
{ αν 37
{ ὁπου 535
{ εαν 170
who, ὁσος 539
ὁστις 540
ουτος 574
τίς 736
whole, ἁπας 60
ὁλοκληρος 528
ὁλος 529
πας 597
whole, ὑγιαινω 753
whole, ὑγιης .... —
whole, *see* armour, burnt offering.
whole (be), ισχυω 392
σωζω 716
ὑγιαινω 753
whole (be made perfectly), διασωζω 148
whole (make), ιαομαι 379
σωζω 716
wholesome, ὑγιαινω 753
wholly, ὁλοτελης 529
wholly, *see* give.
wholly given, *see* idolatry.
whom, τίς 736
whom[soever], { τις 732
{ εαν 170
whore, πορνη 648
whoremonger, πορνος .... —
whose, τις 732
τίς 736
whosoever, ειτις 187
ὁσος 539
ὁστις 540
πας 597
why, γαρ 112
διατι 149
ἱνατι 390
ὁτι 543
τίς 736
wicked, αθεσμος 15
ανομος 55
κακος 400
πονηρος 646
wicked (more), πονηρος ... —
wickedness, κακια 400
πονηρια 645
(1 Joh. 5:19), πονηρος 646
wide, πλατυς 627
widow, χηρα 800
wife, γυναικειος 129
γυνη .... —
wife, *see* marry.
wife's mother, πενθερα 611
wild, αγριος 10
wild, *see* beast, olive tree.
wilderness, ερημια 300
ερημος (ἡ) .... —

wile, μεθοδεια 477
wilfully, ἑκουσιως 229
will, βουλη 110
βουλημα .... —
γνωμη 124
θελημα 361
θελησις 362
will, βουλομαι 110
will, γινομαι 117
ευχομαι 328
θελω 362
will, *see* good.
will (against the), ακων ... 26
will go (Joh. 7:35), { μελλω 478
{ πορευομαι ... 646
will have, θελω 362
will judge, { μελλω 478
{ κρινω 433
will manifest (Joh. 14:22), { μελλω 478
{ εμφανιζω ... 240
will (of his own), βουλομαι 110
will seek (Mat. 2:13), { μελλω ... 478
{ ζητεω 337
will spue (Rev. 3:16), { μελλω ... 478
{ εμεω 236
will-worship, εθελοθρησκεια 181
willing, προθυμος 655
willing (be), βουλομαι 110
ευδοκεω 322
θελω 362
willing mind, προθυμια ... 655
willing of...selves, αυθαιρετος 90
willing to, *see* communicate.
willingly, ἑκουσιος 229
ἑκουσιως .... —
ἑκων 232
willingly, θελω 362

win, κερδαινω 421
wind, ανεμος 46
πνευμα 632
(Acts 27:40), πνεω ... 635
πνοη .... —
wind, *see* south.
wind, δεω 137
wind (driven with the), ανεμιζομαι 46
wind up [for burial], συστελλω 714
window, θυρις 378
wine, οινος 527
wine, *see* excess of.
wine (given to), παροινος ... 596
wine (new), γλευκος 124
winebibber, οινοποτης 527
winefat, ὑποληνιον 779
winepress, ληνος 459
{ οινος 527
{ ληνος 459
wing, πτερυξ 672
wink at, ὑπερειδω 775
winter, χειμων 798
winter, παραχειμαζω 593
winter in (Acts 27:12), παραχειμασια 594
wipe, εκμασσω 229
wipe away, εξαλειφω 266

wipe off, απομασσομαι 75
wisdom, σοφια 694
φρονησις 790
wise, σοφος 694
φρονιμος 790
wise, *see* no, this.
wise (be), συνιημι 713
wise (in no), (Lu. 13:11), { παντελες ... 585
{ μη 490
παντως 585
wise (make), σοφιζω 694
wise man, μαγος 466
wise (on this), οὑτω 576
wisely, φρονιμως 791
wish, ευχομαι 328
wist, ειδεω 188
wit, *see* to.
wit (do to), γνωριζω 125
witchcraft, φαρμακεια 784
with, ἁμα 32
with, απο 63
δια 139
εις 197
εκ 215
εν 240
επι 275
κατα 406
μετα 484
παρα 586
περι 613
προς 656
συν 707
ὑπο 776
with, *see* accord, affliction, agree, away, be, bear, beasts, bound, brought, buried, clothe, clothed, come, commune, communicate, company, compare, compassed, compassion, confer, consort, continue, crucify, dwellers, entangle, feast, go, indignation, labour, meet, mixed, reason, rejoice, rise, run, send, sit, sit at meat, speak, spring up, stand, suffer, take, talk, travel, work.
with child, { εν 240
{ γαστηρ 113
with fear, *see* move.
with one, *see* mind.
with rods, *see* beat.
withal, ἁμα 32
withdraw, αποσπαω 76
ὑποστελλω 779
withdraw..self, στελλομαι ... 698
αναχωρεω .. 46
αφιστημι ... 98
ὑποχωρεω .. 780
wither, ξηραινω 521
wither away, ξηραινω .... —
withered, ξηρος 522
withereth (whose fruit), φθινοπωρινος 786
withhold, κατεχω 417
within, δια 139
εν 240

wrap, *see* swaddling clothes.
wrap in, ενειλεω ... 261
εντυλιττω ... 264
wrap together, εντυλιττω ... —
wrath, θυμος ... 378
οργη ... 537
παροργισμος ... 596
wrath (provoke to), παροργιζω ... —
wrest, στρεβλοω ... 701
wrestle (Eph. 6:12), { παλη ... 583 / εστι ... 310 }
wretched, ταλαιπωρος ... 719
wrinkle, ρυτις ... 678
write, γραφω ... 127
εγγραφω ... 176
επιστελλω ... 287
write (Ro. 15:4), write aforetime, write afore, } προγραφω 654
write a letter unto, επιστελλω ... 287
write in & on, επιγραφω ... 283
write over, επιγραφω ... —
write unto, επιστελλω ... 287
writing, βιβλιον ... 107
γραφω ... 127
writing, *see* divorcement.
writing table, πινακιδιον ... 621
writings, γραμμα ... 126
written, γραμμα ... —
γραπτος ... —
γραφω ... 127
written (be), απογραφω ... 68
written in, εγγραφω ... 176
wrong & do wrong, αδικεω 14
wrong, αδικια ... —
wrong (matter of), αδικημα —
wrong (suffer), wrong (take), } αδικεω ... —
wrongfully, αδικως ... —
wroth (be), θυμοομαι ... 378
οργιζομαι ... 537
wrought (be), γινομαι ... 117

ye, ὑμας ... 757
ὑμεις ... 760
ὑμιν ... 762
ὑμων ... 767
ye, *see* whereas.
ye yourselves, ὑμεις ... 760
yea, αλλα ... 29
η ... 340
ναι ... 512
yea doubtless, μενουνγε ... 481
yea rather, μενουνγε ... —
year, ενιαυτος ... 262
ετος ... 320
year ago (a), περυσι ... 620
years, ἡμερα ... 347
years, *see* forty, three.
years old, *see* hundred.
years old (two), διετης ... 155
years (to), (Heb. 11:24), μεγας ... 476
years (two) διετια ... 155
yes, ναι ... 512
yes verily, μενουνγε ... 481
yesterday, χθες ... 800
yet, ακμην ... 22
αλλα ... 29
γαρ ... 112
γε ... 113
ετι ... 318
ηδη ... 343
καν ... 403
μεντοι ... 481
(1 Co. 8:2), ουδεπω ... 565
ουκετι ... 566
yet, *see* and, as, if, never, no, nor.
yet, but, { πλειων ... 627 / ου ... 554 }
yet never man (Lu. 19:30), { ουδεις ... 565 / πωποτε ... 675 }
yet not, ουκ ετι ... 566
ουτε ... 573
yet to sound (which are) (Rev. 8:13), } μελλω ... 478 / σαλπιζω ... 680
yield, αποδιδωμι ... 68
διδωμι ... 151
παριστανω ... 595
παριστημι ... —
πειθω ... 609
ποιεω ... 636
yield up, αφιημι ... 97
yield up, *see* ghost.
yoke, ζευγος ... 337
ζυγος ... 338
yoke together unequally, ἑτεροζυγεω ... 318
yokefellow, συζυγος ... 704
yonder, εκει ... 224
yonder place (to), εκει ... —
you, ἑαυτου ... 172
ὑμας ... 757
ὑμεις ... 760
ὑμιν ... 762
ὑμων ... 767
(2 Co. 12:15), { ψυχη ... 807 / ὑμων ... 767 }
young, νεος ... νεοσσος ... 514
young, *see* ass, child, daughter, man.
young children, βρεφος ... 111
young man, woman, νεος ... 514
young man, παις ... 583
younger, ελασσων ... 232
your, ἑαυτου ... 172
(in some copies), ἡμετερος ... 349
ὑμας ... 757
ὑμετερος ... 762
ὑμιν ... —
ὑμων ... 767
your, *see* conversation.
your own, ἑαυτου ... 172
ιδιος ... 380
{ κατα ... 406 / ὑμας ... 757 }
ὑμετερος ... 762
ὑμων ... 767
your own, *see* conceits.
your own business, ιδιος ... 380
your own selves, ἑαυτου ... 172
yourselves, ἑαυτου ... —
ὑμιν ... 762
ὑμων ... 767
yourselves, *see* ye.
youth, νεοτης ... 514
youthful, νεωτερικος ... 515

zeal, ζηλος ... 337
zealous, ζηλωτης ... —
zealous (be), ζηλοω ... ...
zealously, *see* affect.

English-Greek Index

ἅλλομαι . . . 30
leap
spring up

ἄλλος 30
another
more
one
one another
other
otherwise
some
some another
some others

ἀλλοτριοεπίσκοπος 31
busybody in other men's matters

ἀλλότριος . . . 31
alien
another man's
other
other men's
strange
stranger

ἀλλόφυλος . . 32
one of another nation

ἄλλως . . . 32
otherwise

ἀλοάω 32
thresh
tread out the corn

ἄλογος . . . 32
brute
unreasonable

ἀλόη 32
aloes

ἅλς 32
salt

ἁλυκός 32
salt

ἀλυπότερος . . 32
sorrowful, less

ἅλυσις 32
bonds
chain

ἀλυσιτελής. . . 32
unprofitable

ἅλων 32
floor

ἀλώπηξ . . . 32
fox

ἅλωσις 32
taken, be [*see* lit.]

ἅμα 32
also
and
together
with
withal

ἀμαθής . . . 32
unlearned

ἀμαράντινος . . 32
fadeth not away, that

ἀμάραντος . . 32
fadeth not away, that

ἁμαρτάνω . . . 32
faults, for your
offend
sin
trespass

ἁμάρτημα . . . 33
sin

ἁμαρτία . . . 33
offence
sin
sinful

ἀμάρτυρος . . . 34
witness, without

ἁμαρτωλός . . 34
sinful
sinner

ἄμαχος . . . 34
brawler, not a

ἀμάω 34
reap down

ἀμέθυστος . . . 34
amethyst

ἀμελέω . . . 34
light of, make
neglect
negligent, be
regard not

ἄμεμπτος . . . 34
blameless
faultless
unblameable

ἀμέμπτως . . . 35
blameless
unblameably

ἀμέριμνος . . . 35
care, without
carefulness, without
secure, [*see* lit.]

ἀμετάθετος . . 35
immutability
immutable

ἀμετακίνητος . . 35
unmoveable

ἀμεταμέλητος . 35
repentance, without
repented of, not to be

ἀμετανόητος . . 35
impenitent

ἄμετρος . . . 35
measure, things without
measure, without

ἀμήν 35
Amen
verily

ἀμήτωρ . . . 36
mother, without

ἀμίαντος . . . 36
undefiled

ἄμμος 36
sand

ἀμνός 36
Lamb

ἀμοιβή . . . 36
requite

ἄμπελος . . . 36
vine

ἀμπελουργός . . 36
dresser of his vineyard

ἀμπελών . . . 36
vineyard

ἀμύνομαι . . . 36
defend

ἀμφίβληστρον. . 36
net

ἀμφιέννυμι . . 37
clothe

ἄμφοδον . . . 37
where two ways met

ἀμφότερος . . . 37
both

ἀμώμητος . . . 37
blameless
rebuke, without

ἄμωμος . . . 37
blame, without
blemish, without
fault, without
faultless
spot, without
unblameable

ἄν 37
wheresoever
whithersoever

ἀνά 39
and
apiece
by
each
several
every man

ἀνά 39
by
in
through

ἀναβαθμός . . 39
stairs

ἀναβαίνω . . . 39
arise
ascend
ascend, shall (with μελλω, Rev. 17:8)
ascend up
climb up
come
come up
enter
go up
grow up
rise up
spring up

ἀναβάλλομαι . . 40
defer

ἀναβιβάζω . . 40
draw

ἀναβλέπω . 40
look
look up
see
sight, receive

ἀνάβλεψις. . . 40
sight, recovering of

ἀναβοάω . . . 40
cry
cry aloud
cry out

ἀναβολή . . . 40
delay
delay, without any (with ποιεω, μηδεις, Acts 25:17)

ἀναγγέλλω . . 40
declare
rehearse
report
shew
spoken, be
tell

ἀναγεννάω. . . 40
again
beget
born again, be

ἀναγινώσκω . . 40
read

ἀναγκάζω . . . 40
compel
constrain

ἀναγκαῖος . . . 41
more needful
near
necessary
necessity

ἀναγκαστῶς . . 41
constraint, by

ἀνάγκη . . . 41
distress
must needs
must needs (with ἐχω)
necessary
necessity

necessity, of (with εχω)
needeth
needful

ἀναγνωρίζομαι . 41
known, be made

ἀνάγνωσις . . 41
reading

ἀνάγω . . . 41
bring
bring again
bring forth
bring up again
depart
launch
launch forth
lead
lead up
loose
offer
sail
set forth
take up

ἀναδείκνυμι . . 41
appoint
shew

ἀνάδειξις . . . 41
shewing

ἀναδέχομαι . . 41
receive

ἀναδίδωμι . . . 41
deliver

ἀναζάω . . . 41
alive again, be
lived again
revive

ἀναζητέω . . . 41
seek

ἀναζώννυμι . . 41
gird up

ἀναζωπυρέω . . 41
stir up

ἀναθάλλω . . . 41
flourish again

ἀνάθεμα . . . 41
accursed
Anathema
curse
great [see lit.]

ἀναθεματίζω . . 42
curse
curse, bind under a
oath, bind with an

ἀναθεωρέω . . 42
behold
consider

ἀνάθημα . . . 42
gift

ἀναίδεια . . . 42
importunity

ἀναίρεσις . . . 42
death

ἀναιρέω . . . 42
death, be put to
kill
killed, would have (Acts 16:27)
slay
take away
take up

ἀναίτιος . . . 42
blameless
guiltless

ἀνακαθίζω . . . 42
sit up

ἀνακαινίζω . . 42
renew

ἀνακαινόω . . . 42
renewed, be

ἀνακαίνωσις . 42
renewing

ἀνάκειμαι . . 42
guests
lean
lie
meat, sit at
sit
sit down
table, at the

ἀνακαλύπτω . . 42
open
taken away, be
untaken away (with μη)

ἀνακάμπτω . . 42
return
turn (t. again)

ἀνακεφαλαιόομαι . 42
comprehended, be briefly
gather together in one

ἀνακλίνω . . . 42
lay
sit down
sit down, make

ἀνακόπτω . . . 42
hinder

ἀνακράζω . . . 42
cry out

ἀνακρίνω . . . 43
ask question
discern
examine
judge
search

ἀνάκρισις . . . 43
examination

ἀνακύπτω . . . 43
lift up
look up

ἀναλαμβάνω . . 43
receive up
take
take in
take unto
take up

ἀνάληψις . . . 43
received up, that should be

ἀναλίσκω . . . 43
consume

ἀναλογία . . . 43
proportion

ἀναλογίζομαι . 43
consider

ἄναλος . . . 43
saltness, lost

ἀνάλυσις . . . 43
departure

ἀναλύω . . . 43
depart
return

ἀναμάρτητος . . 43
sin, that is without

ἀναμένω . . . 43
wait for

ἀναμιμνήσκω . . 43
mind, call to
remember
remembrance, bring to
remembrance, call to
remembrance, put in

ἀνάμνησις . . . 43
remembrance
remembrance again

ἀνανεόω . . . 43
renewed, be

ἀνανήφω . . . 43
recover selves

ἀναντίῤῥητος . . 43
spoken against, cannot be

ἀναντιῤῥήτως . . 44
gainsaying, without

ἀνάξιος . . . 44
unworthy

ἀναξίως . . . 44
unworthily

ἀνάπαυσις . . . 44
rest
rest (with εχω, Rev. 4:8)

ἀναπαύω . . . 44
ease, take
refresh
rest
rest, give
rest, take

ἀναπείθω . . . 44
persuade

ἀναπέμπω . . . 44
send
send again

ἀνάπηρος . . . 44
maimed

ἀναπίπτω . . . 44
lean
sit down
sit down to meat

ἀναπληρόω . . 44
fill up
fulfil
occupy
supply

ἀναπολόγητος . 44
excuse, without
inexcusable

ἀναπτύσσω . . 44
open

ἀνάπτω . . . 44
kindle

ἀναρίθμητος . . 44
innumerable

ἀνασείω . . . 44
move
stir up

ἀνασκευάζω . . 44
subvert

ἀνασπάω . . . 44
draw up
pull out

ἀνάστασις . . . 44
raised to life again
resurrection
rise from the dead
rise, that should
rising again

ἀναστατόω . . . 45
trouble
turn upside down
uproar, make an

ἀνασταυρόω . . 45
crucify afresh

ἀναστενάζω . . 45
sigh deeply

ἀναστρέφω . . 45
abide
behave self
conversation, have
live
overthrow
pass
return
used, be

ἀναστροφή . . 45
conversation

ἀπολείπω . . . 73
leave
remain

ἀπολείχω . . . 74
lick

ἀπόλλυμι . . . 74
destroy
die
lose
lost, be
marred, be
perish

ἀπολογέομαι . . 74
answer
answer for self
answer, shall (with μελλω, Acts 26:2)
defence, make
excuse
excuse self
speak for self

ἀπολογία . . . 74
answer
answer for self
clearing of self
defence

ἀπολούω . . . 74
wash
wash away

ἀπολύτρωσις . . 74
deliverance
redemption

ἀπολύω . . . 75
depart
dismiss
divorce
forgive
let depart
let go
loose
put away
release
send away
set at liberty

ἀπομάσσομαι . . 75
wipe off

ἀπονέμω . . . 75
give

ἀπονίπτω . . . 75
wash

ἀποπίπτω . . . 75
fall from

ἀποπλανάω . . 75
err
seduce

ἀποπλέω . . . 75
sail

ἀποπλύνω . . . 75
wash

ἀποπνίγω . . . 75
choke

ἀπορέομαι . . 75
doubt
doubt, stand in
perplexed

ἀπορία . . 75
perplexity

ἀποῤῥίπτω . . . 75
cast

ἀπορφανίζομαι . 75
taken, be

ἀποσκευάζομαι . 76
take up our carriages

ἀποσκίασμα . . 76
shadow

ἀποσπάω . . . 76
draw
draw away
gotten from, after were
withdraw

ἀποστασία . . . 76
falling away
forsake

ἀποστάσιον . . 76
divorcement
divorcement, writing of

ἀποστεγάζω . . 76
uncover

ἀποστέλλω . . 76
put in
send
send away
send forth
send out
set [at liberty]

ἀποστολή . . . 77
apostleship

ἀπόστολος . . . 77
apostle
messenger
sent, he that is

ἀποστερέω . . . 77
defraud
destitute
fraud, kept back by

ἀποστοματίζω . . 77
provoke to speak

ἀποστρέφω . . . 77
bring again
pervert
put up again
turn away
turn away from
turn from

ἀποστυγέω . . 78
abhor

ἀποσυνάγωγος . 78
synagogue, put out of the
synagogues, out of the

ἀποτάσσομαι . . 78
farewell, bid
forsake
leave, take
send away

ἀποτελέω . . . 78
finish

ἀποτίθημι . . . 78
cast off
lay apart
lay aside
lay down
put away
put off

ἀποτινάσσω . . 78
shake off

ἀποτίω 78
repay

ἀποτολμάω . . 78
bold, be very

ἀποτομία . . . 78
severity

ἀποτόμως . . 78
sharply
sharpness

ἀποτρέπομαι . . 78
turn away

ἀπουσία . . . 78
absence

ἀποφέρω . . . 78
bring
carry
carry away

ἀποφεύγω . . . 78
escape

ἀποφθέγγομαι . 78
say
speak forth
utterance

ἀποφορτίζομαι . 78
unlade

ἀπόχρησις . . . 78
using

ἀποχωρέω . . . 78
depart

ἀποχωρίζομαι . 78
depart
depart asunder

ἀποψύχω . . . 78
hearts failing

ἀπρόσιτος . . . 78
approach, which no man can

ἀπρόσκοπος . 78
offence, none
offence, void of
offence, without

ἀπροσωπολήπτως . 79
respect of persons, without

ἄπταιστος . . . 79
falling, from

ἅπτομαι . . 79
touch

ἅπτω . . . 79
kindle
light

ἀπωθέομαι . . 79
put from

ἀπώθομαι . . . 79
cast away
put away
thrust away
thrust from

ἀπώλεια . . . 79
damnable
damnation
destruction
die
perdition
perish (with ειην and εις, Acts 8:20)
pernicious ways
waste

ἀρά 79
cursing

ἄρα 79
haply
manner of man
manner
no doubt
perhaps
so be
then
therefore
truly
wherefore

ἆρα 80
therefore

ἀργέω . . . 80
linger

ἀργός 80
barren
idle
slow

ἀργύριον . . . 80
money
silver
silver pieces
silver, pieces of

ἀργυροκόπος . 80
silversmith

3 Q

3 Q 2

it. of
thee
their
their own
them
themselves
they

αὐτόχειρ . . . 96
hands, with own

αὐχμηρός . . . 96
dark

ἀφαιρέω . . . 96
cut off
smite off
take away

ἀφανής . . . 97
manifest, that is not

ἀφανίζω . . . 97
corrupt
disfigure
perish
vanish away

ἀφανισμός . . 97
vanish away

ἄφαντος . . . 97
vanish out of sight

ἀφεδρών . . . 97
draught

ἀφειδία . . 97
neglecting

ἀφελότης . . 97
singleness

ἄφεσις 97
deliverance
forgiveness
liberty
remission

ἁφή 97
joint

ἀφθαρσία . . . 97
immortality
incorruption
sincerity

ἄφθαρτος . . . 97
corruptible, not
immortal
incorruptible
uncorruptible

ἀφίημι 97
cry
forgive
forsake
lay aside
leave
let
let alone
let be
let go
let have
omit
put away
remit
send away
suffer
yield up

ἀφικνέομαι . . 98
come abroad

ἀφιλάγαθος . . 98
despisers of those that are good

ἀφιλάργυρος . . 98
covetousness, without
covetous, not

ἄφιξις 98
departing

ἀφίστημι . . . 98
depart
draw away
fall away
refrain
withdraw self

ἄφνω 98
suddenly

ἀφόβως . . . 99
fear, without

ἀφομοιόω . . . 99
made like

ἀφοράω . . . 99
look
see

ἀφορίζω . . . 99
divide
separate
sever

ἀφορμή . . . 99
occasion

ἀφρίζω . . . 99
foam

ἀφρός 99
[*with*] foaming

ἀφροσύνη . . . 99
folly
foolishly
foolishness

ἄφρων 99
fool
foolish
unwise

ἀφυπνόω . . . 99
fall asleep

ἄφωνος . . . 99
dumb
signification, without

ἀχάριστος . . . 99
unthankful

ἀχειροποίητος . 99
hands, made without
hands, not made with

ἀχλύς 99
mist

ἀχρειόομαι . . 99
unprofitable, be become

ἀχρεῖος . . . 99
unprofitable

ἄχρηστος . . . 99
unprofitable

ἄχρι & ἄχρις 99
as far as
even to
for
in
into
till
to
until
unto
while

ἄχυρον . . . 100
chaff

ἀψευδής . . . 100
lie, that cannot

ἄψινθος . . . 100
wormwood

ἄψυχος . . . 100
life, without

βαθμός . . . 100
degree

βάθος 100
deep
deep things
deepness
depth

βαθύνω . . . 100
deep

βαθύς . . . 100
deep
early, very

βαΐον 100
branch

βαλάντιον . . 100
bag
purse

βάλλω . . . 100
arise
cast
cast out
dung
lay
lie
pour
put
put up
send
strike
throw
throw down
thrust

βαπτίζω . . 101
baptist
baptize
wash

βάπτισμα . . 102
baptism

βαπτισμός . . 102
baptism
washing

βαπτιστής . . 102
baptist

βάπτω . . . 102
dip

βάρβαρος . . 102
barbarian
barbarous

βαρέω . . . 102
burdened, be
charged, be
heavy
pressed, be

βαρέως . . . 102
dull

βάρος 102
burden
burdensome
weight

βαρύνω . . . 102
overcharged, be

βαρύς 102
grievous
heavy
weightier

βαρύτιμος . . 103
precious, very

βασανίζω . . 103
pain
toil
torment
toss
vexed

βασανισμός . . 103
torment

βασανιστής . . 103
tormentor

βάσανος . . 103
torment

βασιλεία . . . 103
kingdom
reign (with εχω Rev. 17:18)

βασίλειον . 104
king's court

δερμάτινος . . 135
leathern
skin, of a

δέρω 135
beat
smite

δεσμεύω 136
bind

δεσμέω . . . 136
bind
bound, be

δέσμη 136
bundle

δέσμιος . . . 136
bonds, in
prisoner

ὁ δεσμὸς & τὰ δεσμά . . . 136
bands
bond
chain
string

δεσμοφύλαξ . . 136
jailor
prison, keeper of the

δεσμωτήριον . . 136
prison

δεσμώτης . . . 136
prisoner

δεσπότης . . . 136
Lord
master

δεῦρο 136
come
come hither
hither*to*

δεῦτε 136
come
follow (with οπισω)

δευτεραῖος . . 136
next day

δευτερόπρωτος 136
second after the first

δεύτερος . 137
afterward
again
second
second time
secondarily

δέχομαι . 137
accept
receive
take

δέω 137
bind
bonds, be in
knit
tie
wind

δή 138
also
and
doubtless
now
therefore

δῆλος 138
bewray (with ποιεω Matt. 26:73)
certain
evident
manifest

δηλόω . . . 138
declare
shew
signify

δημηγορέω . . 138
oration, make an

δημιουργός . . 138
maker

δῆμος 138
people

δημόσιος . . . 138
common
openly
publickly

δηνάριον . . 138
pence
penny*worth*

δήποτε . . . 138
soever
whatsoever

δήπου 138
verily

διά 138
after
always
always (with πας)
among
at
avoid, to
because of
because that
briefly
by
cause, for
for
...fore
from
in
occasion of, by
of
reason of, by
sake, for
that
thereby
*there*by
therefore
*there*fore
though
though [lit. through]
through
throughout
through*out*
throughout (with ὅλος Joh. 19:23)
to
wherefore
*where*fore
with
within

διαβαίνω . . . 143
come over
pass
pass through

διαβάλλομαι . 143
accused

διαβεβαιόομαι . 143
affirm
affirm constantly

διαβλέπω . . . 143
see clearly

διάβολος . . . 143
accuser, false
devil
slanderer

διαγγέλλω . . 143
declared, be
preach
signify

διαγίνομαι . . 143
after
past, be
spent, be

διαγινώσκω . . 143
enquire
enquire, would (Acts 23:15)
know the uttermost

διαγνωρίζω . . 144
known, make

διάγνωσις . . 144
hearing

διαγογγύζω . . 144
murmur

διαγρηγορέω . . 144
awake, be

διάγω 144
lead
living

διαδέχομαι . . 144
come after

διάδημα . . . 144
crown

διαδίδωμι . . . 144
distribute
distribution make
divide
give

διάδοχος . . . 144
room (lit. successor)

διαζώννυμι . 144
gird

διαθήκη . . 144
covenant
testament

διαίρεσις . . . 144
difference
diversities

διαιρέω . . . 144
divide

διακαθαρίζω . . 144
purge, throughly

διακατελέγχομαι. 144
convince

διακονέω . . . 144
administered, be
deacon, use the office of a
minister
minister unto
serve

διακονία . . 145
administration
minister
ministering
ministration
ministry
office
relief
service
serving

διάκονος . . . 145
deacon
minister
servant

διακόσιοι . . . 145
two hundred

διακούομαι . . 145
hear

διακρίνω . . . 145
contend
differ, maketh to
difference, make
difference, put
discern
doubt
judge
partial
stagger
waver

διάκρισις . . . 145
discern
discerning
disputation

διακωλύω . . . 146
forbid

διαλαλέω . . . 146
commune
noised abroad, be

διαλέγομαι . . 146
dispute
preach
preach unto
reason
reason with
speak

διαλείπω . . . 146
cease

διάλεκτος . . . 146
language
tongue

διαλλάττομαι . 146
reconciled, be

διαλογίζομαι . 146
cast in mind
consider
dispute
muse
reason
think

διαλογισμός . . 146
disputing
doubtful
doubting
imagination
reasoning
thought

διαλύομαι. . . 146
scattered, be

διαμαρτύρομαι . 146
charge
testify
testify unto
witness

διαμάχομαι . . 146
strive

διαμένω . . . 146
continue
remain

διαμερίζω . . 146
cloven
divide
part

διαμερισμός . . 147
division

διανέμομαι . . 147
spread

διανεύω . . . 147
beckon

διανόημα . . . 147
thought

διάνοια . . . 147
imagination
mind
understanding

διανοίγω . . . 147
open

διανυκτερεύω . . 147
continue all night

διανύω . . . 147
finish

διαπαντός . . 147
alway
always
continually

διαπεράω . . . 147
go over
pass
pass, can
pass over
sail over

διαπλέω . . . 147
sail over

διαπονέομαι . . 147
grieved, be

διαπορεύομαι . . 147
journey, in
pass by
through, go

διαπορέω . . . 147
doubt
doubt, be in
perplexed, be
perplexed, be much

διαπραγματεύομαι 147
gain by trading

διαπρίομαι . . 147
cut to the heart, be

διαρπάζω . . . 147
spoil

διαῤῥήσσω & διαῤῥήγνυμι . . 148
break
rend

διασαφέω . . . 148
tell unto

διασείω . . . 148
violence to, do

διασκορπίζω . . 148
dispersed, be
scatter
scattered abroad, be
strew
waste

διασπάω . . . 148
pluck asunder
pulled in pieces, be

διασπείρω . . 148
scattered abroad, be

διασπορά . . . 148
dispersed [lit. dispersion]
scattered
scattered abroad, which are

διαστέλλομαι . 148
charge
commanded, that which was
commandment, give

διάστημα . . 148
space

διαστολή . . . 148
difference
distinction

διαστρέφω . . 148
perverse
pervert
turn away

διασώζω . . . 148
bring safe
escape
escape safe
heal
perfectly whole, make,
save

διαταγή . . 148
disposition
ordinance

διάταγμα . . . 148
commandment

διαταράττω . . 148
troubled, be

διατάσσω . . . 148
appoint
commanding
give order
ordain
set in order

διατελέω . . . 149
continue

διατηρέω . . . 149
keep

διατί 149
wherefore
why

διατίθεμαι . . 149
appoint
make
testator

διατρίβω . . 149
abide
be
continue
tarry

διατροφή . . . 149
food

διαυγάζω . . 149
dawn

διαφανής . . . 149
transparent

διαφέρω . . . 149
better, be
carry
differeth from
driven up and down, be
excellent, be
excellent, be more
matter, make
published, be
value, be of more

διαφεύγω . . . 149
escape

διάφορος . . . 149
differing
divers
excellent, more

διαφημίζω . . 149
blaze abroad
reported, be commonly
spread abroad fame

διαφθείρω . . 149
corrupt
destroy
perish

διαφθορά . . . 149
corruption

διαφυλάττω . . 149
keep

διαχειρίζομαι . 150
kill
slay

διαχωρίζομαι . 150
depart

διδακτικός . . 150
apt to teach

διδακτός . . . 150
taught
teacheth, which

διδασκαλία . 150
doctrine
learning
teaching

διδάσκαλος . . 150
doctor
master
teacher

διδάσκω . . . 150
teach

διδαχή . . . 151
doctrine
taught, hath been

δίδραχμον . . 151
tribute

δίδωμι 151
adventure

bestow
bring forth
commit
deliver
deliver up
give
grant
hinder
make
minister
number
offer
power, have
put
receive
set
shew
smite
smite with the hand (with ῥαπισμα)
strike
strike with the palm of the hand (Joh. 18:22)
suffer
take
utter
yield

διεγείρω . . . 154
arise
awake
raised, be
stir up

διέξοδος . . . 154
highway [*see* lit.]

διερμηνευτής . 154
interpreter

διερμηνεύω . . 154
expound
interpret
interpretation, by

διέρχομαι . . 155
come
depart
go
go about
go abroad
go every where
go over
go through
go throughout
pass
pass by
pass over
pass through
pass throughout
pass, was to (with μελλω, Lu. 19:4)
pierce through
travel
walk through

διερωτάω . . . 155
enquiry for, make

διετής 155
two years

διετία 155
two years

διηγέομαι . . 155
declare
shew
tell

διήγησις . . . 155
declaration

(εἰς το) διηνεκής. 155
continually
ever, for

διθάλασσος . . 155
where two seas meet

διϊκνέομαι . . 155
pierce

διΐστημι . . . 155
go further
parted, be
space of, after the

διϊσχυρίζομαι . 155
affirm, confidently
affirm, constantly

δικαιοκρισία . . 155
righteous judgment

δίκαιος . . . 155
just
meet
right
righteous

δικαιοσύνη . . 156
righteousness

δικαιόω . . . 157
freed, be [lit. is justified]
justifier
justify
righteous, be

δικαίωμα . . 157
judgment
justification
ordinance
righteousness

δικαίως . . . 157
justly
righteously
righteousness, to

δικαίωσις . . 157
justification

δικαστής . . . 157
judge

δίκη 157
judgment
punish
vengeance

δίκτυον . . 157
net

δίλογος . . . 157
double tongued

διό 158
cause, for which
therefore
wherefore

διοδεύω . . . 158
go throughout
pass through

διόπερ . . 158
wherefore

διοπετής . . . 158
which fell down from Jupiter

διόρθωσις . . . 158
reformation

διορύσσω . . . 158
break through
broken up, be

διότι 158
because
because that
for
therefore

διπλοῦς . . . 158
double
twofold more

διπλόω . . . 158
double

δίς 158
again
twice

διστάζω . . . 158
doubt

δίστομος . . . 158
edges, with two
two-edged

δισχίλιοι . . . 159
two thousand

διϋλίζω . . . 159
strain at

διχάζω . . . 159
set at variance

διχοστασία . . 159
division
sedition

διχοτομέω . . 159
cut asunder
cut in sunder

διψάω 159
athirst, be
thirst
thirsty, be

δίψος 159
thirst

δίψυχος . . . 159
double minded

διωγμός . . . 159
persecution

διώκτης . . 159
persecutor

διώκω 159
ensue
follow
follow after
given to
persecute
press
suffer persecution

δόγμα 159
decree
ordinance

δογματίζομαι . 160
subject to ordinances, be

δοκέω 160
accounted, be
good, seem
please
pleasure, of own
reputation, be of
seem
suppose
think
trow

δοκιμάζω . . . 160
alloweth
approve
discern
examine
like
prove
try

δοκιμή . 160
experience
experiment
proof
trial

δοκίμιον . . . 160
trial
trying

δόκιμος . . . 160
approved
tried

δοκός . . . 160
beam

δόλιος 161
deceitful

δολιόω . . . 161
use deceit

δόλος . . . 161
craft
deceit
guile
subtilty

δολόω 161
handle deceitfully

δόμα 161
gift

δόξα 161
dignities
glorious
glory
honour
praise
worship

δοξάζω . . 162
glorify
glorious, make
glory, full of
glory, have
honour
magnify

δόσις . . . 163
gift
giving

δότης 163
giver

δουλαγωγέω . . 163
subjection, bring into

δουλεία . . . 163
bondage

δουλεύω . . . 163
bondage, be in
serve
service, do

δούλη 163
handmaid
handmaiden

δοῦλον . . . 163
servant

δοῦλος . . 163
bond
bondman
servant

δουλόω . . . 164
bondage, bring into
bondage, be under
given
servant, became
servants, make

δοχή 164
feast

δράκων . . . 164
dragon

δράσσομαι . . 164
take

δραχμή . . 164
piece
piece of silver

δρέπανον . . . 164
sickle

δρόμος . . 164
course

δύναμαι . . . 164
able, be
can
can do
cannot (with μη)
cannot (with ου)
could
may
might
possible, be
power, be of

δύναμις . . . 166
ability
abundance
deeds, mighty
meaning
might
mightily
mighty
miracle
miracles, workers of
power
strength
violence
virtue
works, mighty
works, wonderful

δυναμόω . . . 167
strengthen

δυνάστης . . . 167
authority, of great
mighty
potentate

δυνατέω . . . 167
mighty, be

δυνατός . . . 167
able
could
mighty
mighty men
mighty, that is
possible
power
strong

δύνω & δῦμι . . 167
set

δύο 167
both
twain
two

δυσβάστακτος . 168
grievous to be borne

δυσεντερία . . 168
bloody flux

δυσερμήνευτος . 168
uttered, hard to be

δύσκολος . . . 169
hard

δυσκόλως . 169
hardly

δυσμή . . . 169
west

δυσνόητος . . 169
understood, hard to be

δυσφημία . . . 169
report, evil

δώδεκα . . . 169
twelve

δωδέκατος . 169
twelfth

δωδεκάφυλον . . 169
twelve tribes

δῶμα 169
housetops

δωρεά 169
gift

δωρεάν . . . 170
cause, without a
freely
nought, for
vain, in

δωρέω 170
give

δώρημα . . . 170
gift

δῶρον 170
gift
offering

ἔα 170
alone, let

ἐάν 170
and if
before
but
except
if
if so
so
though
to whom
whatsoever (with τις Eph. 6:8.)
when
whensoever
wheresoever
whether
whether or
whithersoever
*who*so
*who*soever

ἑαυτ-οῦ,-ῷ,-όν . 172
alone
he himself
her
her own
herself
him
himself
his
his own
itself
one another
one to another
our own
ourselves
that she had (with πασα)
their
their own
their own selves
them
them, of
themselves
they
thine own
thyself
you
your
your own
your own conceits
your own selves
yourselves

ἐάω 175
alone, let
commit
leave
let
suffer

ἑβδομήκοντα . 175
seventy
threescore and ten

ἑβδομηκοντάκις . 175
seventy times

ἕβδομος . . . 175
seventh

ἐγγίζω . . . 175
approach
come near
draw nigh
hand, be at
near, draw
nigh, be
nigh, come

ἐγγράφω . . . 176
write
written in

ἔγγυος . . . 176
surety

ἐγγύς 176
from
hand, at
hand, nigh at
near
nigh
nigh unto
ready

ἐγγύτερον . . 176
nearer

ἐγείρω . . . 176
arise

awake
lift
lift up
raise
raise again
raise up
rear up
rise
rise again
rise up
stand
take up

ἔγερσις . . . 177
resurrection

ἐγκάθετος . . 177
spy

ἐγκαίνια . . . 177
feast of the dedication

ἐγκαινίζω . . 177
consecrate
dedicate

ἐγκαλέω . . 177
accuse
call in question
implead
lay to the charge

ἐγκαταλείπω . . 177
forsake
leave

ἐγκατοικέω . . 177
dwell among

ἐγκεντρίζω . . 177
graff in, *or*, into

ἔγκλημα . . . 178
crime laid against
laid to charge

ἐγκομβόομαι . . 178
clothed with, be

ἐγκοπή . . . 178
hinder

ἐγκόπτω . . . 178
hinder
tedious unto, be

ἐγκράτεια . . . 178
temperance

ἐγκρατεύομαι . 178
cannot contain (with ουκ)
contain, can
temperate, be

ἐγκρατής . . . 178
temperate

ἐγκρίνω . . 178
number, make of the

ἐγκρύπτω . . . 178
hide in

ἔγκυος . . . 178
great with child

ἐγχρίω . . . 178
anoint

ἐγώ 178
I
me

ἐδαφίζω . . . 181
lay even with the ground

ἔδαφος . . . 181
ground

ἑδραῖος . . . 181
settled
stedfast

ἑδραίωμα . . . 181
ground

ἐθελοθρησκεία . 181
will worship

ἐθίζω 181
custom

ἐθνάρχης . . . 181
governor

ἐθνικός . . . 181
heathen
heathen man

ἐθνικῶς . . 181
manner of Gentiles, after the

ἔθνος . . . 181
Gentile
heathen
nation
people

ἔθος 182
custom
manner
wont, be

ἔθω, εἴωθα . 182
custom, be
manner, be
wont, be

εἶ, from εἰμί . . 182
art
be

εἰ 183
*al*though
forasmuch as
if
that
though
whether

εἴγε 185
if
if so be that
if yet

εἰ δὲ μή & εἰ δὲ μήγε . . . 186
else
if not
if otherwise
or else
otherwise

εἰ καὶ 186
if
if that
though

εἰ μὴ . . . 186
but
except
except that
if not
more than
save
save only that
save that
saving
till
till (with ὅταν Mark 9:9)

εἰ μή τι . . . 187
except

εἴ περ 187
if so be
if so be that| if that
seeing
though

εἴ πως . . . 187
if by any means

εἴτε 187
if
or
whether

εἴ τις 187
he that
if a man
if any ...man
if any man's
if any thing
if from any
if ought
whether any
whosoever

εἰδέω, εἴδω, οἶδα . 188
aware, be
behold
can
can (Mat. 27:65)
cannot tell (with ου)
consider
know
knowledge, have
look
look on
perceive
see
sure, be
tell
understand
wist
wot

εἶδος . . . 192
appearance
fashion
shape
sight

εἰδωλεῖον . . 192
idol's temple

εἰδωλόθυτον . . 192
idols, meats offered to
idols, offered in sacrifice to
idols, offered to
idols, sacrificed to
idols, things that are offered in sacrifice unto

εἰδωλολατρεία . 192
idolatry

εἰδωλολάτρης . 193
idolater

εἴδωλον . . . 193
idol

εἴην, εἴης, εἴη, &c. from εἰμί . . 193
mean
perish (with απωλεια, εις, Acts 8:20)
should be
was
were

εἰκῆ 193
cause, without a
vain, in
vainly

εἴκοσι . . . 193
twenty

εἴκω 193
place, give

εἴκω 193
like, be

εἰκών 193
image

εἰλικρίνεια . . 193
sincerity

εἰλικρινής . . 193
pure
sincere

εἱλίσσω . . . 193
roll together

εἰμί 194
am
have been
it is
was

εἶναι, from εἰμί . 195
am
are

come
is
lust after (with επιθυμητης, 1 Cor. 10:6)
made, to be
please ... well (with ευαρεστος, Hb. 2:9)
there is
to be
was

εἰρηνεύω . . . 196
peace, be at
peace, have
peace, live in
peaceably, live

εἰρήνη . . . 196
one
peace
quietness
rest
set at one again (with συνελαυνω, εις, Acts 7:26)

εἰρηνικός . . . 197
peaceable

εἰρηνοποιέω . . 197
peace, make

εἰρηνοποιός . . 197
peacemaker

εἰς 197
abundantly
against
among
as
at
*back*ward
before
before (with προσωπον, 2 Cor. 8:24)
by
concerning
continual (with τελος, Lu. 13:5)
far more exceeding (with κατα, 2 Cor. 4:17)
for
for intent
for purpose
...fore
forth (with μεσος, Mark 3:3)
hereunto (1 Pet. 2:21)
in
in among
in at
in unto
insomuch that
intent, to the
into
mind, of one (with φρονεω, Phi. 2:2)
never (with ου μη, αιων)
of
on
perish (with απωλεια, εις, Acts 8:20)
set at one again (with συνελαυνω, ειρηνη, Acts 7:26)
so that
that
therefore
*there*fore
thereunto
throughout
till
to
to be (Acts 13:22)
to the end
toward
until
unto
upon
...ward
*where*fore
with

εἷς, ἕν . . . 209
a
abundantly (with περισσεια, 2 Cor. 10:15)
an
any
certain, a
man
one
one another
only
other
some

εἷς καθ' εἷς . 211
one by one

εἰσάγω . . . 211
bring in
bring into
lead into
led into, be
led into, was to be (with μελλω, Acts 21:37)

εἰσακούω . . . 211
hear

εἰσδέχομαι . 211
receive

εἴσειμι . . . 211
enter into
go into

εἰσέρχομαι . . 211
arise
come
come in
come into
enter in
enter into
go in
go through

εἰσί, from εἰμί . 213
agree
are
be
dure
is
were

εἰσκαλέω . . . 214
call in

εἴσοδος . . . 214
coming
enter into
entering in

εἰσπηδάω . . . 214
run in
spring in

εἰσπορεύομαι . 214
come in
enter in
go into

εἰστρέχω . . . 214
run in

εἰσφέρω . . 214
bring
bring in
lead into

εἶτα . . . 214
after that
afterward
furthermore
then

ἐκ, ἐξ 215
after
among
are
at
because of
betwixt
beyond
by
by the means of
exceeding abundantly above (with υπερ, Eph. 3:20)
exceedingly (1 Th. 3:10)
for
forth at
from
from among
from forth
from up
grudgingly (with λυπη, 2 Cor. 9:7)
heartily (with ψυχη, Col. 3:23)
heavenly (Lu. 11:13)
hereby (1 Joh. 4:6)
highly, very (with υπερ, 1 Th. 5:13)
in
...ly
of
off
off from
on
out among
out from
out of
over
reason of, by
since
thenceforth (Joh. 19:12)
through
unto
vehemently (Mar. 14:31)
with
without

ἕκαστος . . . 221
any
both
each
each one
every
every man
every one
every woman
particularly

ἑκάστοτε . . . 222
always

ἑκατόν . . . 222
hundred (h. fold)

ἑκατονταέτης . 222
hundred years old

ἑκατονταπλασίων 222
hundredfold

ἑκατοντάρχης . 222
centurion

ἑκατόνταρχος . 222
centurion

ἐκβάλλω . . . 222
bring forth
cast
cast forth
cast out
drive
drive out
expel
leave
pluck out
pull out
put forth, be
put out
send away
send forth
send out
take out | thrust
thrust out

ἔκβασις . . . 223
end
way to escape

ἐκβολή . . . 223
lighten the ship (with ποιεω. Acts 27: 18)

ἐκγαμίζω . . . 223
marriage, give in

ἐκγαμίσκομαι . 223
marriage, be given in

ἔκγονα . . . 223
nephews

ἐκδαπανάω . 223
spent, be

ἐκδέχομαι . . 223
expect
look for
tarry for
wait
wait for

ἔκδηλος . . . 223
manifest

ἐκδημέω . . . 223
absent, be

ἐκδίδωμι . . . 223
let forth
let out

ἐκδιηγέομαι . . 223
declare

ἐκδικέω . . . 223
avenge
revenge

ἐκδίκησις . . . 223
avenge
punishment
revenge
vengeance

ἔκδικος . . . 223
avenger
revenger

ἐκδιώκω . . . 223
persecute

ἔκδοτος . . . 224
delivered

ἐκδοχή . . . 224
looking for

ἐκδύω 224
strip
take off from
unclothe

ἐκεῖ 224
there
thither
thitherward
yonder
yonder place, to

ἐκεῖθεν . . . 224
from that place
from thence
thence
there

ἐκεῖνος . . . 225
he
it
other, the
same, the
selfsame
she
that
that same
that very
their
them
they
this
those

ἐκεῖσε 226
there

ἐκζητέω . . . 226
enquire
required, be
seek after
seek carefully
seek, diligently

ἐκθαμβέω . . 226
affrighted, be
amazed, be greatly
amazed, be sore

ἔκθαμβος . . . 227
greatly wondering

ἔκθετος . . . 227
cast out (Acts 7:19)

ἐκκαθαίρω . . 227
purge
purge out

ἐκκαίομαι . . 227
burn

ἐκκακέω . . . 227
faint, to
weary, be

ἐκκεντέω . . . 227
pierce

ἐκκλάζω . . . 227
break off

ἐκκλείω . . . 227
exclude

ἐκκλησία . . . 227
assembly
church

ἐκκλίνω . . . 228
avoid
eschew
go out of the way

ἐκκολυμβάω . . 228
swim out

ἐκκομίζομαι . . 228
carried out, be

ἐκκόπτω . . . 228
cut down
cut off
cut out
hew down
hinder

ἐκκρέμαμαι . . 228
attentive, be very

ἐκλαλέω . . . 228
tell

ἐκλάμπω . . . 228
shine forth

ἐκλανθάνομαι . 228
forget

ἐκλέγομαι . . 228
choice, made
choose
choose out
chosen

ἐκλείπω . . . 228
fail

ἐκλέκτος . . . 228
chosen
elect

ἐκλογή . . 228
chosen
election

ἐκλύω 229
faint

ἐκμάσσω . . . 229
wipe

ἐκμυκτηοίζω . . 229
deride

ἐκνεύω . . . 229
convey self away

ἐκνήφω . . . 229
awake

ἑκούσιος . . . 229
willingly

ἑκούσιως . . . 229
wilfully
willingly

ἔκπαλαι . . . 229
long time, of a
of old

ἐκπειράζω . . 229
tempt

ἐκπέμπω . . . 229
send away
send forth

ἐκπετάννυμι . . 229
stretch forth

ἐκπίπτω . . . 229
cast, be
fail
fall
fall away
fall off
take none effect

ἐκπλέω . . . 229
sail
sail away
sail thence

ἐκπληρόω . . . 229
fulfil

ἐκπλήρωσις . . 229
accomplishment

ἐκπλήσσω . . 229
amazed, be
astonished, be

ἐκπνέω . . . 229
give up the ghost

ἐκπορεύομαι . . 229
come
come forth
come out of
depart
go
go forth
go out
issue
proceed
proceed out of
would depart (Acts 25:4)

ἐκπορνεύω . . 230
fornication, give self over to

ἐκπτύω . . . 230
reject

ἐκριζόω . . . 230
pluck up by the root
root up

ἔκστασις . . . 230
amazed, be (with λαμβανω)
amazement
astonishment
trance

ἐκστρέφομαι . . 230
subvert

ἐκταράσσω . . 230
trouble, exceedingly

ἐκτείνω . . . 230
cast
cast, would have (Acts 27.30)
put forth
stretch forth
stretch out

ἐκτελέω . . . 230
finish

ἐκτένεια . . . 230
instantly

ἐκτενέστερον . . 230
earnestly, more

ἐκτενής . . . 230
ceasing, without
fervent

ἐκτενῶς . . . 230
fervently

ἐκτίθημι . . . 230
cast out
expound

ἐκτινάσσω . . 230
shake
shake off

ἕκτος 231
sixth

ἐκτός 231
but
except
excepted
other than
out of
outside
unless
without

ἐκτρέπομαι . . 231
avoid
turn
turn aside
turn out of the way

ἐκτρέφω . . . 231
bring up
nourish

ἔκτρωμα . . . 231
born out of due time

ἐκφέρω . . . 231
bear
bring forth
carry forth
carry out

ἐκφεύγω . . . 231
escape
flee

ἐκφοβέω . . . 231
terrify

ἔκφοβος . . . 231
fear exceedingly
sore afraid

ἐκφύω . . . 231
put forth

ἐκχέω . . . 231
pour out
run out
shed
shed forth
spilled, be

ἐκχύνω . . . 231
gush out
pour out
run greedily
shed
shed abroad
spilled, be

ἐκχωρέω . . . 231
depart out

ἐκψύχω . . . 232
ghost, give up the
ghost, yield up the

ἑκών 232
willingly

ἐλαία 232
olive
olive berries
olive tree

ἔλαιον . . . 232
oil

ἐλαιών . . . 232
Olivet

ἐλάσσων & ἐλάττων . . . 232
less
under
worse
younger

ἐλαττονέω . 232
lack, have

ἐλαττόω . . . 232
decrease
lower, make

ἐλαύνω . . . 232
carry
driven, be
row

ἐλαφρία . . . 232
lightness

ἐλαφρός . . . 232
light

ἐλάχιστος . . 232
least
little, very
small, very
smallest

ἐλαχιστότερος . 232
least, less than the

ἔλεγξις . . . 232
rebuke

ἔλεγχος . . . 232
evidence
reproof

ἐλέγχω . . . 232
convicted, be
convince
fault tell a
rebuke
reprove

ἐλεεινός . . . 233
miserable

ἐλεέω 233
compassion, have
mercy, obtain
mercy on, have
mercy, receive
mercy, shew
pity on, have

ἐλεημοσύνη . . 233
alms
almsdeeds

ἐλεήμων . . . 233
merciful

ἔλεος 233
mercy
mercy, tender (with σπλαγχνα, Lu. 1:78)

ἐλευθερία . . . 233
liberty

ἐλεύθερος . . . 233
free
free man
free woman
liberty, at

ἐλευθερόω . . 234
deliver
free, make

ἔλευσις . . . 234
coming

ἐλεφάντινος . . 234
ivory, of

ἑλίσσω . . . 234
fold up

ἑλκόομαι . . . 234
sores, full of

ἕλκος 234
sores

ἑλκύω 234
draw

ἕλκω 234
draw

ἐλλογέω . . . 234
impute
put on account

ἐλπίζω . . . 234
hope
hope for
hope, have
hope, have (with εσμεν, 1 Co. 15:19)
hoped for, things
trust

ἐλπίς 234
faith
hope

Ἐλωΐ 235
Eloi

ἐμαυτοῦ, -τῷ, -τὸν 235
me
mine own
mine own self
myself

ἐμβαίνω . . . 235
come into
enter
enter into
get into
go into
go up into
step in
take ship

ἐμβάλλω . . 235
cast into

ἐμβάπτω . . . 235
dip

ἐμβατεύω . . 235
intrude into

ἐμβιβάζω . . 235
put in

ἐμβλέπω . . 235
behold
could see
gaze up
look upon
see

ἐμβριμάομαι . . 235
groan
murmur against
straitly charge

ἐμέ, from ἐγώ 236
I
me
my
myself

ἐμέω 236
spue
spue, will (Rev. 3:16)

ἐμμαίνομαι . . 236
mad against, be

ἐμμένω . . . 236
continue

ἐμοί, from ἐγώ . 236
I
me
mine
my

ἐμός 237
me, of
mine
mine own
my

ἐμοῦ, from ἐγώ . 235
me
mine
my

3 R

ἐπιούσιος . . 285
daily

ἐπιπίπτω . . 285
fall into (Acts 10: 10)
fall upon
fell on
lie on
press upon

ἐπιπλήττω . . 286
rebuke

ἐπιπνίγω . . . 286
choke

ἐπιποθέω . . . 286
desire
desiring greatly
earnestly desire
long
long after
long after, greatly
lust

ἐπιπόθησις . . 286
desire, earnest
desire, vehement

ἐπιπόθητος . . 286
longed for

ἐπιποθία . . . 286
desire, great

ἐπιπορεύομαι . 286
come

ἐπιῤῥάπτω . . 286
sew on

ἐπιῤῥίπτω . . 286
cast upon

ἐπίσημος . . . 286
notable
note, of

ἐπισιτισμός . . 286
victuals

ἐπισκέπτομαι . 286
look out
visit

ἐπισκηνόω . . 286
rest upon

ἐπισκιάζω . . 286
overshadow

ἐπισκοπέω . . 286
look diligently
take the oversight

ἐπισκοπή . . . 286
bishop, the office of a
bishoprick
visitation

ἐπίσκοπος . . 286
bishop
overseer

ἐπισπάομαι . . 286
become uncircumcised

ἐπίσταμαι . . 286
know
understand

ἐπιστάτης . . 287
master

ἐπιστέλλω . . 287
write
write a letter unto
write unto

ἐπιστήμων . . 287
endued with knowledge

ἐπιστηρίζω . . 287
confirming
strengthening

ἐπιστολή . . . 287
epistle
letter

ἐπιστομίζω . . 287
mouths be stopped

ἐπιστρέφω . . 287
come again
convert
go again
return
turn
turn about
turn again

ἐπιστροφή . . 287
conversion

ἐπισυνάγω . . 287
gather
gather together

ἐπισυναγωγή . 287
assembling together
gathering together

ἐπισυντρέχω . . 287
come running together

ἐπισύστασις . . 288
cometh upon, that which
raising up (with ποιεω, Acts 24:12)

ἐπισφαλής . . 288
dangerous

ἐπισχύω . . . 288
fierce, be the more

ἐπισωρεύω . . 288
heap

ἐπιταγή . . . 288
authority
commandment

ἐπιτάσσω . . . 288
charge
command
injoin

ἐπιτελέω . . 288
accomplish
do
finish
make
perfect
perfect, make
perform
performance (2 Cor. 8: 11)

ἐπιτήδειος . . 288
needful, things which are

ἐπιτίθημι . . 288
add unto
lade
lay upon
put on
put upon
set on, be
set up
surname (with ονομα, Mar. 3:16, 17)
wound (Lu. 10:30)

ἐπιτιμάω . . . 288
charge
rebuke
straitly charge

ἐπιτιμία . . . 289
punishment

ἐπιτρέπω . . . 289
leave, give
let
liberty, give
licence, give
permit
suffer

ἐπιτροπή . . . 289
commission

ἐπίτροπος . . 289
steward
tutor

ἐπιτυγχάνω . . 289
obtain

ἐπιφαίνω . . . 289
appear
light, give

ἐπιφάνεια . . 289
appearing
brightness

ἐπιφανής . . . 289
notable

ἐπιφαύω . . . 289
light, give

ἐπιφέρω . . 289
add
bring
bring against
take

ἐπιφωνεω . . 289
cry
cry against
shout, give a

ἐπιφώσκω . . 289
begin to dawn
draw on

ἐπιχειρέω . . 289
go about
take in hand
take upon

ἐπιχέω . . . 289
pour in

ἐπιχορηγέω . . 289
add
minister
minister unto
nourishment, minister

ἐπιχορηγία . . 289
supply
supply (Eph. 4:16)

ἐπιχρίω . . 290
anoint

ἐποικοδομέω . . 290
build thereon
build thereupon
build up
build upon

ἐποκέλλω . . 290
run aground

ἐπονομάζομαι . 290
called, be

ἐπόπτης . . . 290
eyewitness

ἐποπτεύω . . . 290
behold

ἔπος 290
say (with επω, Heb. 7. 9)

ἐπουράνιος . . 290
celestial
heaven, in
heavenly
high

ἑπτά 290
seven
seventh

ἑπτάκις . 291
seven times

ἑπτακισχίλιοι . 291
seven thousand

ἔπω . . . 291
answer
bid
bring word
call
command

any further
any longer
any more
even
further
henceforth
henceforth more
hereafter
longer
more
moreover
now
still
thenceforth
yet

ἑτοιμάζω . . . 319
prepare
provide
ready, make

ἑτοιμασία . . 320
preparation

ἕτοιμος . . . 320
prepared
readiness
ready
ready to our hand, made

ἑτοίμως . . . 320
ready

ἔτος 320
year

εὖ 320
good
well
well done

εὐαγγελίζω, -ομαι 320
declare
glad tidings, bring
glad tidings, declare
glad tidings, shew
good tidings, bring
gospel, preach the
gospel preached, have the
gospel to be preached, which by the
preach

εὐαγγέλιον . . 321
gospel

εὐαγγελιστής . 321
evangelist

εὐαρεστέω . . 321
please
pleased, be well

εὐάρεστος . . 321
acceptable
accepted
wellpleasing

εὐαρέστως . . 322
acceptably
please...well (with εἶναι, Tit. 2:9)

εὐγενής . . . 322
noble, more
nobleman

εὐδία 322
fair weather

εὐδοκέω . . . 322
good, think
please
pleased, be well
pleasure, be the good
pleasure, have
pleasure, take
willing, be

εὐδοκία . . . 322
desire
good pleasure
good will
seem good

εὐεργεσία . . 322
benefit
good deed done

εὐεργετέω . . 322
do good

εὐεργέτης . . 322
benefactor

εὔθετος . . . 322
fit
meet

εὐθέως . . . 322
anon
as soon as
by and by
forthwith
immediately
shortly
straightway

εὐθυδρομέω . . 323
straight course, come with a
straight course, with a

εὐθυμέω . . . 323
good cheer, be of
merry, be

εὔθυμος . . . 323
good cheer, of

εὐθυμότερον . . 323
cheerfully, more

εὐθύνω . . . 323
list (Jas. 3:4)
straight, make

εὐθύς 323
right
straight

εὐθύς 323
anon
by and by
forthwith
immediately
straightway

εὐθύτης . . . 323
righteousness

εὐκαιρέω . . . 323
convenient time, have
leisure, have
spend time

εὐκαιρία . . . 323
opportunity

εὔκαιρος . . . 323
convenient
time of need, in

εὐκαίρως . . . 323
conveniently
season, in

εὐκοπώτερος . . 323
easier

εὐλάβεια . . . 323
fear, godly
fear ['in that he feared']

εὐλαβέομαι . . 323
fear
fear, moved with

εὐλαβής . . . 324
devout

εὐλογέω . . . 324
bless
praise

εὐλογητός . . 324
blessed

εὐλογία . . . 324
blessing
bountifully
bounty
bounty, (a matter of)
speech, fair

εὐμετάδοτος . . 324
distribute, ready to

εὐνοέω . . . 324
agree

εὔνοια . . . 324
benevolence
good will

εὐνουχίζω . . 324
eunuchs, make

εὐνοῦχος . . . 324
eunuch

εὐοδοῦμαι . . 324
prosper
prosperous journey, have a

εὐπειθής . . . 324
intreated, easy to be

εὐπερίστατος . 324
beset, which doth so easily

εὐποιΐα . . . 325
good, to do

εὐπορέομαι . . 325
ability

εὐπορία . . . 325
wealth

εὐπρέπεια . . 325
grace

εὐπρόσδεκτος . 325
acceptable
accepted

εὐπρόσεδρος . . 325
attend upon (1 Co.7:35)

εὐπροσωπέω . . 325
fair shew, make a

εὑρίσκω . . . 325
find
get
obtain
perceive
see

εὐρύχωρος . . 326
broad

εὐσέβεια . . . 326
godliness
holiness

εὐσεβέω . . 326
piety, shew
worship

εὐσεβής . . . 326
devout
godly

εὐσεβῶς . . . 327
godly

εὔσημος . . . 327
understood, easy to be

εὔσπλαγχνος . 327
pitiful
tenderhearted

εὐσχημόνως . . 327
decently
honestly

εὐσχημοσύνη . 327
comeliness

εὐσχήμων . . 327
comely
honourable

εὐτόνως . . . 327
mightily
vehemently

εὐτραπελία . . 327
jesting

ζωογονέω . . 340
live
preserve

ζῶον . . 340
beast

ζωοποιέω . . . 340
alive, make
life, give
quicken

ἤ 340
and
but
but either
either
except it be
neither
nor
or
or else
rather
save
than
that
what
yea

ἦ μήν 342
surely

ἤπερ 342
than

ἤτοι 342
whether

ἡγεμονία . . . 342
reign

ἡγεμονεύω . . 342
governor, be

ἡγεμών . . 343
governor
prince
ruler

ἡγέομαι . . . 343
account
chief
chief(Acts 14:12; 15:22)
chief, be
count
esteem
governor
judge
rule over, have the
suppose
think

ἡδέως, ἥδιστα . 343
gladly
gladly, most
gladly, very

ἤδη . . . 343
already
even now
now
now already
time, by this
yet

ἡδονή 343
lust
pleasure

ἡδύοσμον . . . 344
mint

ἦθος 344
manners

ἥκω 344
come

Ἠλί 344
Eli

ἡλικία 344
age
stature

ἡλίκος . . . 344
great, how
great, what

ἥλιος 344
east (with ανατολη)
sun

ἧλος 344
nail

ἡμᾶς, from ἐγώ. 344
our
us
we

ἡμεῖς . . . 346
us
we
we ourselves

ἡμέρα 347
age
age, be of a great (with προβαινω, πολυς, Lu. 2:36)
alway (with πας)
daily
day
day by day
day time
ever, for (with αιων)
judgment
mid-day
mid-day
time
while
years

ἡμέτερος . . . 349
our
your [in some copies]

ἤμην 350
be

ἡμιθανής . . . 350
half dead

ἡμῖν 350
our
us
us, for
we

ἥμισυ 351
half

ἡμιώριον . . 351
half an hour

ἡμῶν 351
our
our (with μετα, 1 Joh. 4:17)
our company
us
us (with ψυχη, Joh. 10:24)
we

ἦν, ἦς, ἦσθα . 354
agree (with ισος)
be
charge of, have (with επι, Acts 8:27)
have
hold
use

ἡνίκα 357
when

ἤπιος 357
gentle

ἤρεμος . . . 358
quiet

ἡσυχάζω . . . 358
cease
peace, hold
quiet, be
rest

ἡσυχία . . . 358
quietness
silence

ἡσύχιος . . . 358
peaceable
quiet

ἡττάομαι . . . 358
inferior, be
overcome

ἥττημα . . . 358
diminishing
fault

ἧττον 358
less
worse

ἤτω 358
be

ἠχέω 358
roar
sound

ἦχος 358
fame
sound

θάλασσα . . . 358
sea

θάλπω . . . 358
cherish

θαμβέομαι . . 359
amazed, be
astonished, be

θάμβος . . . 359
amazed (Lu. 4:36)
astonished (with περιεχω, Lu. 5:9)
wonder

θανάσιμος . . 359
deadly

θανατηφόρος . . 359
deadly

θάνατος . . . 359
deadly (Rev. 13:3, 12)
death
death, be—

θανατόω . . . 360
dead, become
death, cause to be put to
death, put to
killed, be
mortify

θάπτω . . . 360
bury

θαῤῥέω . . . 360
bold, be
boldly
confidence, have
confident, be

θαρσέω . . . 360
good cheer, be of
good comfort, be of

θάρσος . . . 360
courage

θαῦμα . . . 360
admiration

θαυμάζω . . . 360
admiration, have in
admired, be
marvel
wonder

θαυμάσιος . . 361
wonderful

θαυμαστός . . 361
marvel
marvellous

Θεά . . . 361
goddess

sacrifice, do
slay

θώραξ 379
breastplate

ἴαμα 379
healing

ἰάομαι . . . 379
healed, be
whole, make

ἴασις 379
cure
heal
healing

ἴασπις . . . 380
jasper

ἰατρός . . . 380
physician

ἴδε 380
behold
lo
see

ἰδέα 380
countenance

ἴδιος 380
acquaintance, his
alone, when they were
apart
aside
due
her own
his
his own
his proper
his several
home
our own
own
private
privately
proper
severally
their
their own
thine own
your own
your own business

ἰδιώτης . . . 381
ignorant
rude
unlearned

ἰδού 381
behold
lo
see

ἱδρώς 382
sweat

ἱερατεία . . . 382
priesthood, office of the priest's office

ἱεράτευμα . . 382
priesthood

ἱερατεύω . . 383
priest's office, execute the

ἱερεύς 383
high priest
priest

ἱερόν 383
temple

ἱεροπρεπής . . 383
holiness, as becometh

ἱερός 383
holy

ἱεροσυλέω . . 383
sacrilege, commit

ἱερόσυλος . . . 383
church, robber of

ἱερουργέω . . 383
minister

ἱερωσύνη . . . 384
priesthood

ἱκανός . . . 384
able
content (with ποιεω, Lu. 15:15)
enough
good
great
large
long
long while
many
meet
much
security
sore
sufficient
worthy

ἱκανότης . . . 384
sufficiency

ἱκανόω . . . 384
make able
make meet

ἱκετηρία . . . 384
supplication

ἰκμάς 384
moisture

ἱλαρός . . . 384
cheerful

ἱλαρότης . . . 384
cheerfulness

ἱλάσκομαι . 384
merciful, be
reconciliation for, make

ἱλασμός . . . 384
propitiation

ἱλαστήριον . . 384
mercy-seat
propitiation

ἵλεως 384
be it far
merciful

ἱμάς 384
latchet
thong

ἱματίζομαι . . 384
clothe

ἱμάτιον . . . 384
apparel
cloke
clothes
garment
raiment
robe
vesture

ἱματισμός . . 385
apparel
apparelled
apparel*led*
array
raiment
vesture

ἱμείρομαι . . 385
affectionately desirous, be

ἵνα 385
albeit
because
for to
intent, to the
intent that, to the
lest
so as
so that
that
to

ἱνατί or **ἵνα τί** . 390
wherefore
why

ἰός 390
poison
rust

ἰουδαΐζω . . . 390
Jews, live as the,—do

ἰουδαϊσμός . . 390
Jews' religion

ἱππεύς . . . 390
horseman

ἱππικόν . . . 390
horse*men*

ἵππος 390
horse

ἶρις 390
rainbow

ἰσάγγελος . . 390
angels, equal unto the

ἴσημι 390
know

ἴσθι 390
be
give self wholly to (with εν, 1 Ti. 4:15)

ἴσος or **ἶσος** . . 390
agree (with ην)
agree (Mark 14:56)
as much
equal
like

ἰσότης . . . 391
equal
equality

ἰσότιμος . . . 391
precious, like

ἰσόψυχος . . . 391
likeminded

ἵστημι . . . 391
abide
appoint
bring
continue
covenant
establish
hold up
lay
present
set
set up
stanch
stand
stand by
stand forth
stand still
stand up

ἱστορέω . . . 392
see

ἰσχυρός . . . 392
boisterous
mightier
mighty
powerful
strong
strong man
stronger
valiant

ἰσχύς 392
ability
might
might*ily*
power
strength

ἰσχύω 392
able, be
avail
can do
cannot
cannot (with ουκ, Lu. 16:3)
could
good, be
might
prevail
strength, be of
whole, be
work, much (with μολις, Acts 27:16)

ἴσως 393
be, it may

ἰχθύδιον . . . 393
fish, little
fish, small

ἰχθύς 393
fish

ἴχνος 393
step

ἰῶτα 393
jot

κἀγώ, κἀμοί, κἀμέ 393
and I
both me
even I
even I also
even so I
even so I also
I
I also
I in like wise
me also
so I

καθά 393
as

καθαίρεσις . . 394
destruction
pulling down

καθαιρέω . . . 394
cast down
destroy
destroyed, should be
pull down
put down
take down

καθαίρω . . . 394
purge

καθάπερ . . . 394
as
as well as
even as

καθάπτω . . . 394
fasten on

καθαρίζω . . . 394
clean
clean, make
cleanse
purge
purify

καθαρισμος . . 394
cleansing
purged, have (with ποιεω, Heb. 1:3)
purification
purifying

κάθαρμα . . . 394
filth

καθαρός . . . 394
clean
clear
pure

καθαρότης . . 394
purifying

καθέδρα . . . 394
seat

καθέζομαι . . 395
sit

καθεῖς or καθ' εἷς 395
every one

καθεξῆς . . . 395
after
afterward
order, by
order, in

καθεύδω . . . 395
asleep, be
sleep

καθηγητής . . 395
master

καθῆκον . . . 395
convenient
fit

κάθημαι . . . 395
dwell
sit
sit by
sit down

καθ' ἡμέραν . . 396
daily
day by day
every day

καθημερινός . 396
daily

καθίζω . . . 396
continue
set
sit
sit down
tarry

καθίημι . . 396
let down

καθίστημι . . 396
appoint
be
conduct
make | make ruler
ordain
set

καθό 396
according to that
as
inasmuch as

καθόλου . . . 396
at all

καθοπλίζομαι . 397
armed, be

καθοράω . . . 397
clearly see

καθότι . . . 397
according as
as
because
because that
forsomuch as

καθώς . . . 397
according as
according to
as
even as
how
when

καινός . . 398
new

καινότης . . . 398
newness

καίπερ . . . 398
and yet
though

καιρός . . 398
always
convenient season
due season
due time
opportunity
season
short time
time
while, a
while time

καίτοι, καί-τοιγε. 399
although
nevertheless
though

καίω 399
burn
light

κἀκεῖ 399
and there
there also
thither also

κἀκεῖθεν . . 399
and afterward
and from thence
and thence
thence also

κἀκεῖνος . . . 399
and him
and other
and they
even he
him also
them
them also
them also; and them
they

κακία 400
evil
malice
maliciousness
naughtiness
wickedness

κακοήθεια . . 400
malignity

κακολογέω . . 400
curse
speak evil

κακοπάθεια . . 400
suffering affliction

κακοπαθέω . . 400
afflicted, be
endure afflictions
endure hardness
suffer trouble

κακοποιέω . . 400
evil, do
evil doing

κακοποιός . 400
evildoer
malefactor

κακὸς & τὸ κακὸν 400
bad
evil
harm
ill
noisome
wicked

κακοῦργος . . 400
evil doer
malefactor

κακουχούμενος . 400
adversity, which suffer
tormented

κακόω . . . 400
affected, make evil
entreat evil
harm
hurt
vex

κακῶς . . . 401
amiss

diseased
evil
grievously
miserably
sick
sore

κάκωσις . . . 401
affliction

κάλαμη . . . 401
stubble

κάλαμος . . . 401
pen
reed

καλέω . . . 401
bid
call
call forth
name was [called], whose
named, be
surname was, whose

καλλιέλαιος . . 402
olive tree, good

καλοδιδάσκαλος . 402
teacher of good things

καλοποιῶν . . 402
well doing

καλός 402
better
better (with μαλλον, 1 Cor. 9:15)
fair
good
goodly
honest
meet
well
worthy

κάλυμμα . . . 403
vail

καλύπτω . . . 403
cover
hide

καλῶς & κάλλιον 403
full well
good
good place, in a
honestly
recover (with εχω)
well
well, very

κάμηλος . . . 403
camel

κάμινος . . 403
furnace

καμμύω . . . 403
close

κάμνω . . . 403
faint
sick
wearied, be

κάμπτω . . . 403
bow

κἄν . . . 403
also if
and if
and if so much as
at the least
if but
though
yet

κανών . . . 404
line
rule

καπηλεύω . . 404
corrupt

καπνός . . . 404
smoke

καρδία . . . 404
brokenhearted (with συντριβω, Lu. 4:18)
heart
hearted

καρδιογνώστης . 405
hearts, which knowest the

καρπός . . . 405
fruit

καρποφορέω . . 405
fruit, bear
fruit, bring forth
fruitful, be

καρποφόρος . . 406
fruitful

καρτερέω . . . 406
endure

κάρφος . . . 406
mote

κατά 406
about
according as
according to
after
against
alone [*see* lit.]
alone, when they were
among
and
apart [*see* lit.]
as
as concerning
as pertaining to
as touching
aside [*see* lit.]
at
before
beyond (Gal. 1:13)
by
*charitab*ly
concerning
covered (1 Cor. 11:4)
*dai*ly
down
even as
every
exceeding (Ro. 7:13)
exceeding, far more (with εις, 2 Co. 4:17)
excellent, more (1 Co. 12:31)
for
from...to [by]
godly
in
in divers
in every
inasmuch
into
like as
like as (Heb. 4:15)
...ly
manner of, after the
means, by any (with τροπος, 2 Th. 2:3)
measure, beyond
measure, out of
mightily (Acts 19:20)
more
natural
of
on
out...out of every
over against
own [poets]
part, on
particularly (with μερος, Heb. 9:5)
*private*ly
respect of, in
so
through
throughout

thus
to
together
toward
unto
upon
uttermost (Acts 24:22)
where
*where*by
with
your own (with υμας)

καταβαίνω . . 409
come down
descend
fall
fall down
get down
go down
step down

καταβάλλω . . 410
cast down

καταβαρέω . 410
burden

κατάβασις . . 410
descent

καταβιβάζομαι . 410
brought down, be
thrust down, be

καταβολή . . . 410
conceive
foundation

καταβραβεύω . 410
beguile of reward

καταγγελεύς . 410
setter forth

καταγγέλλω . . 410
declare
preach
shew
should shew (Acts 26:23)
speak of
teach

καταγελάω . . 410
laugh to scorn

καταγινώσκω . 411
blame
condemn

κατάγνυμι . . 411
break

κατάγω . . . 411
bring
bring down
bring forth
bring to land
land
touch

καταγωνίζομαι . 411
subdue

καταδέω . 411
bind up

κατάδηλος . . 411
evident,

καταδικάζω . . 411
condemn

καταδιώκω . . 411
follow after

καταδουλόω . . 411
bondage, bring into

καταδυναστεύω . 411
oppress

καταισχύνω . 411
ashamed, be
ashamed, make
confound
dishonour
shame

κατακαίω . . . 411
burn
burn up
burn, utterly

κατακαλύπτομαι . 411
cover

κατακαυχάομαι . 411
boast
boast against
glory
rejoice against

κατάκειμαι . . 411
keep
lie
sit at meat
sit down

κατακλάω or κατακλάζω . . 411
break

κατακλείω . . 412
shut up

κατακληροδοτέω . 412
divided by lot

κατακλίνω . . 412
sit at meat
sit down
sit down, make

κατακλύζομαι . 412
overflowed, be

κατακλυσμός . . 412
flood

κατακολουθέω . 412
follow
follow after

κατακοπτω . . 412
cut

κατακρημνίζω . 412
cast down headlong

κατάκριμα . . 412
condemnation

κατακρίνω . . 412
condemn
damned, be

κατάκρισις . . 412
condemn
condemnation

κατακυριεύω . . 412
dominion over, exercise
lords over, be
lordship, exercise
overcame

καταλαλέω . . 412
speak against
speak evil of

καταλαλία . . 412
backbitings
speakings, evil

κατάλαλος . . 412
backbiter

καταλαμβάνω . 412
apprehend
attain
come upon
comprehend
find
obtain
overtake
perceive
take

καταλέγομαι . 412
number, take into the

κατάλειμμα . . 412
remnant

καταλείπω . . 413
forsake
leave
reserve

καταλιθάζω . . 413
stone

καταλλαγή . . 413
atonement
reconciliation
reconciling

καταλλάσσω . . 413
reconcile

κατάλοιπος . . 413
residue

κατάλυμα . . 413
guestchamber
inn

καταλύω . . . 413
come to nought
destroy
dissolve
guest, be
lodge
overthrow
throw down

καταμανθάνω . 413
consider

καταμαρτυρέω . 413
witness against

καταμένω . . 413
abide

καταμόνας . . 413
alone

κατανάθεμα . . 413
curse

καταναθεματίζω 413
curse

καταναλίσκω . 413
consuming

καταναρκέω . . 413
burdensome, be
chargeable, be

κατανεύω . . 413
beckon

κατανοέω . . . 414
behold
consider
discover
perceive

καταντάω . . 414
attain
come

κατάνυξις . . . 414
slumber

κατανύσσω . . 414
prick

καταξιόομαι . . 414
worthy, account
worthy, count

καταπατέω . 414
trample
tread
tread down
tread underfoot

κατάπαυσις . . 414
rest

καταπαύω . . 414
cease
give rest
rest
restrain

καταπέτασμα . 414
veil

καταπίνω . . . 414
devour
drowned, be
swallow
swallow up

καταπίπτω . . 414
fall
fall down

καταπλέω . . . 414
arrive

καταπονέομαι . 414
oppressed, be
vexed, be

καταποντίζομαι 414
drowned, be
sink

κατάρα . . . 414
curse
cursed
cursing

καταράομαι . 414
curse

καταργέω . . 415
abolish
cease
cumber
deliver
destroy
done away, be
effect, become of no
effect, make of none
effect, make without
fail
loose
nought, bring to
nought, come to
put away
put down
vanish away
void, make

καταριθμέομαι . 415
numbered with, be

καταρτίζω . . 415
fit
frame
join together, perfectly
mend
perfect
perfect, make
prepare
restore

κατάρτισις . . 415
perfection

καταρτισμός . . 415
perfecting

κατασείω . . . 415
beckon

κατασκάπτω . . 415
dig down
ruins

κατασκευάζω . . 415
build
make
ordain
prepare

κατασκηνόω . . 415
lodge
rest

κατασκήνωσις . 415
nest

κατασκιάζω . . 415
shadow

κατασκοπέω . 415
spy out

κατάσκοπος . . 415
spy

κατασοφίζομαι 415
deal subtilly with

καταστέλλω . 415
appease
quiet

κατάστημα . . 416
behaviour

κέραμος . . . 421
tiling

κεράννυμι, κεράω 421
fill
pour out

κέρας 421
horn

κεράτιον . . . 421
husk

κερδαίνω . . . 421
gain
gain, get
win

κέρδος 421
gain
lucre

κέρμα . . . 421
money

κερματιστής . . 421
changer of money

κεφάλαιον . . 421
sum

κεφαλαιόω . . 421
wound in the head

κεφαλή . . . 421
head

κεφαλίς . . . 422
volume

κῆνσος . . . 422
tribute

κῆπος 422
garden

κηπουρός . . . 422
gardener

κηρίον . . . 422
honeycomb

κήρυγμα . . . 422
preaching

κήρυξ 422
preacher

κηρύσσω . . . 422
preach
preacher
proclaim
publish

κῆτος 423
whale

κιβωτός . . . 423
ark

κιθάρα . . . 423
harp

κιθαρίζω . . . 423
harp

κιθαρῳδός . . . 423
harper

κινάμωμον . . 423
cinnamon

κινδυνεύω . . 423
danger, be in
jeopardy, be in
jeopardy, stand in

κίνδυνος . . . 423
peril

κινέω 423
move
mover (Acts 24:5)
remove
wag

κίνησις . . . 423
moving

κλάδος . . . 423
branch

κλάζω, κλάω . 423
break

κλαίω 423
bewail
weep

κλάσις . . . 424
breaking

κλάσμα . . . 424
broken
fragments

κλαυθμός . . . 424
wailing
weeping
wept (Acts 20:37)

κλείς 424
key

κλείω 424
shut
shut up

κλέμμα . . . 424
theft

κλέος 424
glory

κλέπτης . . . 424
thief

κλέπτω . . . 424
steal

κλῆμα . . . 424
branch

κληρονομέω . . 425
heir, be
heirs of, shall be (with μελλω, Heb. 1:14)
inherit
inheritance, obtain by

κληρονομία . 425
inheritance

κληρονόμος . . 425
heir

κληρόομαι . . 425
inheritance, obtain an

κλῆρος . . . 425
heritage
inheritance
lot
part

κλῆσις . . . 425
calling
vocation

κλητός . . . 425
called

κλίβανος . . . 425
oven

κλῖμα 425
part
regions

κλίνη 425
bed
table

κλινίδιον . . . 426
couch

κλίνω 426
bow
bow down
far spent, be
lay
turn to flight
wear away

κλισία . . . 426
company

κλοπή 426
theft

κλύδων . . . 426
raging
wave

κλυδωνίζομαι . 426
toss to and fro

κνήθω 426
itching

κοδράντης . . 426
farthing

κοιλία 426
belly
womb

κοιμάομαι . . 426
asleep, be
asleep, fall
dead, be
sleep
sleep, fall on

κοίμησις . . . 426
rest, taking of

κοινός 426
common
defiled
unclean
unholy

κοινόω . . . 426
common, call
defile
pollute
unclean

κοινωνέω . . . 426
communicate
distribute
partaker, be

κοινωνία . . . 427
communicate, to
communication
communion
contribution
distribution
fellowship

κοινωνικός . . 427
communicate, willing to

κοινωνός . . . 427
companion
fellowship
partaker
partner

κοίτη 427
bed
chambering
conceive

κοιτών . . . 427
chamberlain

κόκκινος & τὸ κόκκινον . . . 427
scarlet
scarlet colour
scarlet coloured

κόκκος . . . 427
corn
grain

κολάζομαι . . . 427
punish

κολακεία . . . 427
flattering

κόλασις . . . 427
punishment
torment

κολαφίζω . . . 427
buffet

κολλάω . . . 427
cleave
join
join self
keep company

κολλούριον . . 427
eyesalve

κολλυβιστής . 427
changer
moneychanger

κολοβόω . . . 427
shorten

3 s

λίαν 460
chiefest, very (with ὑπερ, 2 Cor. 11:5)
exceeding
great
greatly
sore
very

λίβανος . . . 460
frankincense

λιβανωτόν . . 460
censer

λιθάζω . . . 460
stone

λίθινος . . . 460
stone, of

λιθοβολέω . . 460
stone
stones, cast

λίθος 460
millstone
stone
stumblingstone
stumblingstone (with προσκομμα)

λικμάω . . . 460
grind to powder

λιμήν 461
haven

λίμνη 461
lake

λιμός 461
dearth
famine
hunger

λίνον 461
flax
linen

λιπαρός . . . 461
dainty

λίτρα 461
pound

λίψ 461
south west

λογία 461
collection
gathering

λογίζομαι . . 461
account
account of
conclude
count
despise (with ουδεν, Acts 19:27)
esteem
impute
imputed, shall be (with μελλω, Ro. 4:24)
lay
number
reason
reckon
suppose
think
think on

λογικός . . . 461
reasonable
word, of the

λόγιον . 461
oracle

λόγιος . 461
eloquent

λογισμός . . . 461
imagination
thought

λογομαχέω . . 461
strive about words

λογομαχία . . 461
strife of words

λόγος . . . 462
account
cause
communication
concerning (Phi. 4:15)
doctrine
fame
have to do (Heb. 4:13)
intent
matter
mouth
none of these things move me (with ποιεω, ουδεις, Acts 20:24)
preaching
question
reason
reckon (with συναιρω, Mat. 25:19)
rumour
saying
shew
speaker (Acts 14:12)
speech
talk
thing
tidings
treatise
utterance
word
work

λόγχη . . . 464
spear

λοιδορέω . . 464
revile

λοιδορία . . . 464
railing
reproach*fully*

λοίδορος . . . 464
railer
reviler

λοιμός . . . 464
pestilence
pestilent

το λοιπόν, ὁ λοιπόν, & λοιπόν 464
besides
finally
from henceforth
furthermore
henceforth
moreover
now
remaineth, it (with εστι)
then

λοιπός . . . 464
other
remain, which
remnant
residue
rest

τοῦ λοιποῦ . . 465
from henceforth

λουτρόν . . . 465
washing

λούω 465
wash

λύκος . . . 465
wolf

λυμαίνομαι . . 465
havock, make

λυπέω . . . 465
grief, cause
grieve
heaviness, be in
sorrow
sorrowful, be
sorry, be
sorry, make

λύπη 465
grief
grievous (Heb. 12:11)
grudgingly (with εκ, 2 Cor. 9:7)
heaviness
sorrow

λύσις 465
loosed, to be

λυσιτελεῖ . . 465
better, be

λύτρον . . . 465
ransom

λυτρόω . . . 465
redeem
redeemed, should have (Lu. 24:31)

λύτρωσις . . 465
redeemed (with οιεω Lu. 1:68)
redemption

λυτρωτής . . . 465
deliverer

λυχνία . . . 465
candlestick

λύχνος . . . 466
candle
light

λύω 466
break, break down
break up
destroy
dissolve
loose
melt
put off
unloose

μαγεία . . . 466
sorcery

μαγεύω . . . 466
sorcery, use

μάγος . . . 466
sorcerer
wise man

μαθητεύω . . . 466
disciple, be
instruct
teach

μαθητής . 466
disciple

μαθήτρια . . . 468
disciple

μαίνομαι . . . 468
beside self, be
mad, be

μακαρίζω . . . 468
blessed, call
happy, count

μακάριος . . . 468
blessed
happier
happy

μακαρισμός . . 469
blessedness

μάκελλον . . . 469
shambles

μακράν . . . 469
afar off
far
far off
good way off
great way off

μακρόθεν . . . 469
afar off
from far

μακροθυμέω . . 469
bear long
long suffering, be
patience, have
patience, have long
patient, be
patiently endure
suffer long

μακροθυμία . . 469
longsuffering
patience

μακροθύμως . . 469
patiently

μακρός . . . 469
far
long

μακροχρόνιος . 469
live long

μαλακία . . . 469
disease

μαλακός . . . 469
effeminate
soft

μάλιστα . . . 470
chiefly
especially
most of all
specially

μᾶλλον . . . 470
better (with καλος, Mark 9:42)
far (Phi. 1:23)
more
more and more
more, the
much
rather
rather, the
so much the more

μάμμη . . . 470
grandmother

μαμμωνᾶς & μαμωνᾶς . . . 470
mammon

μανθάνω . . . 470
learn
understand

μανία 471
mad (Acts 26:24)
make mad (with περιτρεπω, Acts 26:24)

μάννα . . . 471
manna

μαντεύομαι . . 471
soothsaying, by

μαραίνομαι . . 471
fade away

μαρὰν ἀθά . . 471
Maran-atha

μαργαρίτης . . 471
pearl

μάρμαρον . . 471
marble

μάρτυρ & μάρτυς 471
martyr
record
witness

μαρτυρέω -έομαι . 471
charge
give [testify]
record, bear
report, have good
report, obtain good
report, of good
report, of honest
reported of, be well
testify
testimony, give
testimony, have
witness
witness, be
witness, bear
witness, give
witness, obtain

μαρτυρία . . . 472
record
report
testimony
witness

μαρτύριον . . 472
testified, to be
testimony
witness

μαρτύρομαι . . 472
record, take to
testify

μασσάομαι . . 472
gnaw

μαστιγόω . . 472
scourge

μαστίζω . . . 472
scourge

μάστιξ . . . 472
plague
scourging

μαστός . . . 473
paps

ματαιολογία . . 473
vain jangling

ματαιολόγος . . 473
vain talker

ματαιόομαι . . 473
vain, become

μάταιος . . . 473
vain
vanities

ματαιότης . . 473
vanity

μάτην . . 473
vain, in

μάχαιρα . . 473
sword

μάχη 473
fighting
strife
striving

μάχομαι . . . 473
fight
strive

μέ 473
I
me
my

μεγαλαυχέω . . 475
great things, boast

μεγαλεῖα . . 475
great things
wonderful works

μεγαλειότης . . 475
magnificence
majesty
mighty power

μεγαλοπρεπής . 476
excellent

μεγαλύνω . . 476
enlarge
magnify
shew great

μεγάλως . . . 476
greatly

μεγαλωσύνη . . 476
majesty

μέγας . . . 476
afraid, be sore (with φοβεομαι, φοβος, Lu. 2:9)
exceedingly (with φοβος)
fear exceedingly (with φοβος)
great
greatest
high
large
loud
mighty
sore (with φοβος)
strong
years, to

μέγεθος . . . 477
greatness

μεγιστᾶνες . . 477
great men
lord

μέγιστος . . 477
exceeding great

μεθερμηνεύομαι . 477
interpretation, be by
interpreted, be

μέθη 477
drunkenness

μεθιστάνω, μεθίστημι . . . 477
put out
remove
translate
turn away

μεθοδεία . . . 477
wile

μεθόρια . . . 478
border

μεθύσκομαι . . 478
drunk, be
drunken, be

μέθυσος . . . 478
drunkard

μεθύω 478
drink, well
drunk, make
drunken, be

μεῖζον . . 478
more, the

μειζότερος . . 478
greater

μείζων, μεῖζον . 478
elder
greater
greatest
more

μέλαν 478
ink

μέλας 478
black

μέλει 478
care
care, take

μελετάω . . . 478
imagine
meditate
premeditate

μέλι 478
honey

μελίσσιος . . 478
honeycomb
honeycomb

μέλλω . . . 478
about
after should, that
after that
afterwards, which should
almost be
answer, shall (with ἀπολογεομαι, Acts 26:2)

ascend, shall (with αναβαινω, Rev. 17:8)
be
begin, shall
betrayed, shall be, and should betray (with παραδιδωμι, Joh. 6:71)
come, to
come, shall (with ερχομαι)
come, that which is to
come, things to
come, which was for to (with ερχομαι, Mat. 11:14)
delivered, shall be (with παραδιδωμι, Lu. 9:44)
devour, shall (with εσθιω, Heb. 10:27)
drink, shall (with πινω, Mat. 20:22)
fulfilled, shall be (with συντελεω, Mar. 13:4)
hear, shall (with ακουω, Mat. 24:6)
heirs of, shall be (with κληρονομεω, Heb. 1.14)
hereafter, which should
imputed, shall be (with λογιζομαι, Ro. 4:24)
intend
led into, was to be (with εισαγω, Acts 21:37)
mean
mind
pass, shall come to (with γινομαι)
pass, was to (with διερχομαι, Lu. 19:4)
point, be at the
ready
ready, be
return (with ὑποστρεφω, Acts 13:34)
revealed, shall be (with αποκαλυπτω, Ro. 8:18; 1 Pet. 5:1)
shall
should
smite, shall (with τυπτω, Acts 23:3)
suffer shall (with πασχω, Rev. 2:10)
tarry
time to come
which was for
will
would
yet, be

μέλος . . . 479
member

μεμβράνα . . 480
parchment

μέμφομαι . . 480
find fault

μεμψίμοιρος . . 480
complainer

μέν 480
even
indeed
so
some
truly
verily

μενοῦνγε . . . 481
nay but
yea doubtless
yea rather
yes verily

μέντοι . . . 481
but | howbeit
likewise
nevertheless
yet

μένω 481
abide
continue
dwell
endure
present, be
remain
stand
tarry
tarry for
thine own (Acts 5:4)

μέριμνα . . 482
care

μεριμνάω . . 482
care
care, have
careful, be
take thought

μερίζω . . 482
deal
difference between, be
distribute
divide
give part

μερίς . . . 482
part
partakers (Col. 1:12)

μερισμός . . . 483
dividing asunder
gift

μεριστής . . . 483
divider

μέρος . . . 483
behalf
coast
course
craft
particular
particularly (with κατα, Heb. 9:5)
partly (with τις, 1 Cor. 11:18)
parts
piece
portion
respect
side
some sort
somewhat

μεσημβρία . . 483
noon
south

μεσιτεύω . . . 483
confirm

μεσίτης . . . 483
mediator

μεσονύκτιον . . 483
midnight

μέσος 483
among
before them (Mat 14:6)
between
forth (with εις, Mar. 3:3)
mid*day*
mid*night*
midst
way

μεσότοιχον . . 484
middle wall

μεσουράνημα . 484
midst of heaven

μεσόω . . . 484
about midst, be

μεστός . . . 484
full

μεστόω . . . 484
fill

μετά 484
after
afterward
afterward (with ταυτα)
again, that he (Lu. 9:39)
against
among
and (John 3:25)
follow (with εστι, Mat. 27:62)
follow (with ταυτα, 1 Pet. 1:11)
followed (with εστι, Mat. 27:62)
hence
hereafter
*here*after (with ταυτα)
in
joyfully (with χαρα, Heb. 10:34)
...ly
of
on
our (with ἡμων, 1 Joh. 4:17)
setting, and (Mat. 27:66)
since
to
together (with αλληλων, Lu. 23:12)
unto
upon
when
with
without (with ου, Acts 5:26)

μεταβαίνω . . 487
depart
go
pass
remove

μεταβάλλομαι . 487
change mind

μετάγω . . . 487
turn about

μεταδίδωμι . . 487
give
impart

μετάθεσις . . . 487
change
removing
translation

μεταίρω . . . 488
departed

μετακαλέομαι . 488
call
call for
call hither

μετακινέω . . 488
move away

μεταλαμβάνω . 488
eat
have
partaker, be
receive
take

μετάληψις . . 488
received (1 Ti. 4:3)

μεταλλάττω . . 488
change

μεταμέλομαι . . 488
repent
repent self

μεταμορφόομαι . 488
changed, be
transfigured, be
transformed, be

μετανοέω . . 488
repent

little while, a
while, a

μικρ-ός, -ότερος . 501
least
less
little
small

μίλιον . . 501
mile

μιμέομαι . . . 501
follow

μιμητής . . . 501
follower

μιμνήσκομαι . . 501
mindful, be
remember

μισέω 501
hate
hateful

μισθαποδοσία . 501
recompence of reward

μισθαποδότης . 501
rewarder

μίσθιος . . . 501
servant, hired

μισθόομαι . . 502
hire

μισθός . . . 502
hire
reward
wages

μίσθωμα . . . 502
hired house

μισθωτός . . . 502
hired servant
hireling

μνᾶ 502
pound

μνάομαι . . . 502
mindful, be
remember
remembrance (Lu. 1:54)
remembrance, come in
remembrance, have in

μνεία 502
mention
remembrance

μνῆμα . . . 502
grave
sepulchre
tomb

μνημεῖον . . . 502
grave
sepulchre
tomb

μνημη . 503
remembrance

μνημονεύω . . 503
mention, make
mindful, be
remember

μνημόσυνον . 503
memorial

μνηστεύομαι . . 503
espouse

μογιλάλος . . 503
impediment in his speech, having an

μόγις 503
hardly

μόδιος . . . 503
bushel

μοί 503
I
me
mine
my

μοιχαλίς . . 505
adulteress
adulterous
adultery

μοιχάομαι . . 505
adultery, commit

μοιχεία . . 505
adultery

μοιχεύω . . . 505
adultery, commit
adultery, in

μοιχός . . . 505
adulterer

μόλις 505
hardly
scarce
scarcely
work, much (with ισχυω, Acts 27:16)

μολύνω . . . 505
defile

μολυσμός . . 505
filthiness

μομφή . . . 505
quarrel

μονή 505
abode
mansion

μονογενής . . 505
only
only begotten
only child

μόνον . . . 506
alone
but
only

μονόομαι . . . 506
desolate, be

μόνος . . . 506
alone
only
themselves, by

μονόφθαλμος . 506
eye, with one

μορφή 506
form

μορφόομαι . . 506
formed, be

μόρφωσις . . . 506
form

μοσχοποιέω . . 507
calf, make a

μόσχος . . . 507
calf

μόχθος . . . 507
painfulness
travail

μοῦ 507
I
me
mine
mine own
my

μουσικός . . . 511
musician

μυελός . . . 511
marrow

μυέομαι . . . 511
instructed, be

μῦθος 511
fable

μυκάομαι . . . 511
roar

μυκτηρίζομαι . 511
mocked, be

μυλικός . . . 511
millstone

μύλος 511
millstone

μύλων . . . 511
mill

μυριάς . . . 511
hundred thousand thousand (Rev. 9:16)
innumerable company
multitude, innumerable
ten thousand
thousand, fifty (with πεντε)
thousands

μυρίζω . . . 511
anoint

μύριοι 511
ten thousand

μύρον 511
ointment

μυστήριον . . 511
mystery

μυωπάζω . . . 512
see afar off, cannot

μώλωψ . . . 512
stripe

μωμέομαι . . . 512
blame

μῶμος . . . 512
blemish

μωραίνω . . . 512
fool, become
foolish, make
savour, lose

μωρία 512
foolishness

μωρολογία . . 512
foolish talking

μωρός 512
fool
foolish
foolishness (with ὁ, 1 Cor. 1:25)

ναί 512
even so
surely
truth
verily
yea
yes

ναός 512
shrine
temple

νάρδος . . . 513
spikenard

ναυαγέω . . . 513
shipwreck, make
shipwreck, suffer

ναύκληρος . . 513
ship, owner of a

ναῦς 513
ship

ναύτης . . . 513
sailor
shipman

νεανίας . . 513
young man

νεανίσκος . . 513
young man

νεκρός . 513
dead

which is, and which was, and which is to come
which was, and is, and is to come

ὀγδοήκοντα . . 522
fourscore

ογδοος . . . 522
eighth

ὄγκος 522
weight

ὁδεύω . . . 523
journey

ὁδηγέω . . . 523
guide
lead

ὁδηγός . . . 523
guide
leader

ὁδοιπορέω . . . 523
go on a journey

ὁδοιπορία . . . 523
journey
journeying

ὁδός 523
highway
highway (Mat. 22:9)
journey
way

ὀδούς . . . 523
tooth

ὀδυνάομαι . . 524
sorrow
tormented, be

ὀδύνη 524
sorrow

ὀδυρμός . . . 524
mourning

ὄζω 524
stink

ὅθεν 524
thence, from
whence
whence, from
where
whereby
wherefore
whereupon

ὀθόνη 524
sheet

ὀθόνιον . . . 524
linen clothes

οἰκεῖος . . . 524
house, those of his own
houshold, of the

οικετης . . . 524
servant
servant, houshold

οἰκέω 524
dwell

οἴκημα . . . 524
prison

οἰκητήριον . . 524
habitation
house

οἰκία 524
home
house
houshold

οἰκιακός . . . 525
houshold, them of
houshold, they of [his own]

οἰκοδεσποτέω . . 525
house, guide the

οἰκοδεσπότης . 525
goodman
house, goodman of the
house, master of the
housholder

οἰκοδομέω . . 525
build
build up
builder
building, be in
edify
embolden

οἰκοδομή . . . 525
building
edification
edify, wherewith one may (Ro. 14:19)
edifying

οἰκονομέω . . 526
steward, be

οἰκονομία . . 526
dispensation
edifying
stewardship

οἰκονόμος . . 526
chamberlain
governor
steward

οἶκος 526
home
house
household
temple

οἰκουμένη . . . 527
earth
world

οἰκουρός . . . 527
home, keeper at

οἰκτείρω, οἰκτειρέω 527
compassion on, have

οἰκτιρμός . . 527
mercy

οἰκτίρμων . . 527
merciful
mercy, of tender

οἶμαι 527
suppose

οἰνοπότης . . 527
winebibber

οἶνος 527
wine
winepress (with ληνος)

οἰνοφλυγία . . 527
wine, excess of

οἴομαι 527
suppose
think

οἷος 527
as
manner of, what
so as
such as
what
which

ὀκνέω 528
delay

οκνηρός . . . 528
grievous
slothful

ὀκταήμερος . . 528
eighth day

ὀκτώ 528
eight
eighteen (with δεκα)

ὄλεθρος . . . 528
destruction

ὀλιγόπιστος . . 528
little faith, of

ὀλίγος . . . 528
almost (with εν)
brief*ly*
few
little
little, a
long (with ουκ)
season, a
short (s. space)
small
while, a

ὀλιγόψυχος . . 528
feebleminded

ὀλιγωρέω . . 528
despise

ὀλοθρευτής . 528
destroyer

ὀλοθρεύω . . . 528
destroy

ὁλοκαύτωμα . . 528
burnt offering
burnt offering, whole

ὁλοκληρία . . 528
soundness, perfect

ὁλόκληρος . . 528
entire
whole

ὀλολύζω . . . 529
howl

ὅλος 529
all
altogether
every whit
throughout
throughout (with δια, Joh. 19:23)
whole

ὁλοτελής . . . 529
wholly

ὄλυνθος . . . 529
untimely fig

ὅλως 529
at all
commonly
utterly

ὄμβρος . . . 529
shower

ὁμιλέω . . . 529
commune
talk

ὁμιλία . . . 530
communication

ὅμιλος . . . 530
company

ὄμμα 530
eye

ὄμνυμι, ὀμνύω . 530
swear

ὁμοθυμαδόν . . 530
accord, with one
mind, with one

ὁμοιάζω . . 530
agree

ὁμοιοπαθής . . 530
passions, of like
passions, subject to like

ὅμοιος 530
like
like manner (with τροπος, Jude 7)

ὁμοιότης . . 530
like as
similitude

ὁμοιόω . . . 530
like, be
like, make
liken
likeness, in the
resemble

ὁμοίωμα . . . 531
like to, made (Ro. 1:23)
likeness
shape
similitude

ὁμοίως . . . 531
likewise
so

ὁμοίωσις . . . 531
similitude

ὁμολογέω . . . 531
confess
confession is made
give thanks
profess
promise

ὁμολογία . . . 531
confession
professed
profession

ὁμολογουμένως . 531
controversy, without

μότεχνος . . 531
craft, of the same

ὁμοῦ 531
together

ὁμόφρων . . . 531
mind, of one

ὅμως 531
and even
nevertheless
though but

ὄναρ 531
dream

ὀνάριον . . . 532
ass, young

ὀνειδίζω . . . 532
cast in teeth
reproach
reproach, suffer
revile
upbraid

ὀνειδισμός . . 532
reproach

ὄνειδος . . . 532
reproach

ὀνημι 532
joy, have

ὀνικός 532
millstone

ὄνομα 532
called
name
named
surname (with ἐπιτίθημι, Mar. 3:16, 17)

ὀνομάζω . . . 533
call
name

ὄνος 534
ass

ὄντως 534
certainly
clean
indeed
truth, of a
verily

ὄξος 534
vinegar

ὀξύς 534
sharp
swift

ὀπή 534
cave
place

ὄπισθεν . . . 534
after
backside
behind

ὀπίσω 534
after
back
backward
behind
behind, get
follow (with δευτε)

ὅπλα 534
armour
instruments
weapon

ὁπλίζομαι . . 534
arm self

ὁποῖος 534
manner of, what
sort, of what
as
whatsoever

ὁπότε 534
when

ὅπου 535
place, in what
where
whereas
wheresoever
where*soever*
whither
whither*soever*

ὀπτάνομαι . . 535
seen, be

ὀπτασία . . . 535
vision

ὄπτομαι . . . 535
appear
look
see
shew himself

ὀπτός 536
broiled

ὀπώρα 536
fruit

ὅπως 536
because
how
so that
that
to
when

ὅραμα 536
sight
vision

ὅρασις 536
look upon
sight; in
vision

ὁρατός 536
visible

ὁράω 536
behold
perceive
see
take heed

ὀργή 537
anger
indignation
vengeance
wrath

ὀργίζομαι . . . 537
angry, be
wroth, be

ὀργίλος . . . 537
angry, soon

ὀργυιά . . . 537
fathom

ὀρέγομαι . . . 537
covet after
desire

ὀρεινός . . . 537
hill

ὄρεξις 537
lust

ὀρθοποδέω . . 537
uprightly, walk

ὀρθός 537
straight
upright

ὀρθοτομέω . . 537
divide, rightly

ὀρθρίζω . . . 538
morning, come early in the

ὀρθρινός . . . 538
morning

ὄρθριος . . . 538
early

ὄρθρος 538
morning, early in the

ὀρθῶς 538
plain
right
rightly

ὅρια 538
border
coast

ὁρίζω 538
declare
determinate (Acts 2:23)
determine
limit
ordain

ὁρκίζω 538
adjure
charge

ὅρκος 538
oath

ὁρκωμοσία . . 538
oath

ὁρμάω 538
run
run violently
rush

ὁρμή 538
assault

ὅρμημα . . . 538
violence

ὄρνεον 538
bird
fowl

ὄρνις 538
hen

ὁροθεσία . . . 538
bound

ὄρος 538
hill
mount
mountain

ὀρύσσω . . . 539
dig

ὀρφανός . . . 539
comfortless
fatherless

ὀρχέομαι . . . 539
dance

ὁσάκις . . . 539
as oft as
as often as

ὅσιος 539
holy
mercies
shalt be

οὗτος 574
be
he it was that
it (Mat. 6:16)
the same
this
this man
this same
who

οὗτοι, from οὗτος 575
such as
the same
these
they
this

αὕτη, fem. sing. of οὗτος . . . 576
hereof
she
the same
this
this woman
which

αὗται, fem. plur. of οὗτος . . . 576
these

οὕτω, οὕτως . . 576
after that
after this manner
as
even
even so
for all that
like [so]
likewise
manner, in this
no more
no more [so]
on this fashion
on this wise
so
so in like manner
thus
what

οὐχί 578
nay
not

ὀφειλέτης . . . 578
debtor
owed, which
sinner

ὀφειλή . . . 578
debt
due

ὀφείλημα . . . 579
debt

ὀφείλω . . . 579
behove
bound, be
debt
debtor, be
due
duty, be
guilty, be
indebted, be
must needs
need
ought
owe
should

ὄφελον . . 579
God, would to
would

ὄφελος . . . 579
advantageth
profit

ὀφθαλμοδουλεία . 579
eyeservice

ὀφθαλμός . . 579
eye
sight

ὄφις 580
serpent

ὀφρύς 580
brow

ὀχλέομαι . . . 580
vexed, be

ὀχλοποιέω . . 580
gather a company

ὄχλος 580
company
multitude
number
number of people
people
press

ὀχύρωμα . . . 581
strong hold

ὀψάριον . . . 581
fish
small fish

ὀψέ 581
at even
even
in the end

ὀψία 581
even
evening
eventide

ὄψιμος . . . 581
latter

ὄψις 582
appearance
countenance
face

ὀψώνιον . . . 582
charges
wages

παγιδεύω . . 582
entangle

παγίς 582
snare

πάθημα . . . 582
affections
affliction
motion
suffering

παθητός . . . 582
suffer

πάθος 582
affection
inordinate affection
lust

παιδαγωγός . . 582
instructer
schoolmaster

παιδάριον . . 582
child
lad

παιδεία . . . 582
chastening
chastisement
instruction
nurture

παιδευτής . . 582
corrected, which
instructor

παιδεύω . . . 582
chasten
chastise
instruct
learn
teach

παιδιόθεν . . . 582
child, of a

παιδίον . . . 582
child
child, little
child, young
damsel

παιδίσκη . . . 583
bondmaid
bondwoman
damsel
maid
maiden

παίζω 583
play

παῖς 583
child
maid
maiden
manservant
servant
son
young man

παίω 583
smite
strike

πάλαι 583
any while
great while ago, a
long ago
old
old, of
time past, in

παλαιός . . 583
old

παλαιότης . . 583
oldness

παλαιόω . . 583
decay
old, make
wax old

πάλη 583
wrestle (with εστι, Eph. 6:12)

παλιγγενεσία . 583
regeneration

πάλιν . . . 583
again

παμπληθεί . . 584
all at once

πάμπολυς . . 585
very great

πανδοχεῖον . . 585
inn

πανδοχεύς . . 585
host

πανήγυρις . . 585
general assembly

πανοικί . . . 585
with all house

πανοπλία . . . 585
armour, all
armour, whole

πανουργία . . 585
craftiness
craftiness, cunning
subtilty

πανοῦργος . . 585
crafty

πανταχόθεν . . 585
every quarter, from

πανταχοῦ . . 585
places, in all
where, every

παντελές . . 585
in *no* wise [altogether]
uttermost

πάντη . . . 585
always

πάντοθεν . . . 585
round about
side, on every

πατριά . . . 609
family
kindred
lineage

πατριάρχης . . 609
patriarch

πατοικός . . . 609
fathers, of

πατρίς . . . 609
country
own country

πατροπαράδοτος . 609
received by tradition from father

πατρῷος . . . 609
father, of

παύομαι . . 609
cease
leave
refrain

παχύνομαι . . 609
wax gross

πέδη 609
fetter

πεδινός . . . 609
plain

πεζεύω . . 609
go afoot

πεζῇ 609
afoot
foot, on

πειθαρχέω . . 609
hearken
obey
obey magistrates

πειθός . . . 609
enticing

πείθω πέποιθα . 609
agree
assume
believe
confidence, have
confident, be
confident, wax
friend, make
obey
persuade
trust
yield

πεινάω . . . 610
hungred, be an
(hungry, hunger)

πεῖρα 610
assaying
trial

πειράζω . . . 610
assay
examine
go about
prove
tempt
tempter
try

πειρασμός . . 610
temptation
try (1 Pet. 4:12)

πειράω . . . 611
assay
go about

πεισμονή . . . 611
persuasion

πέλαγος . . . 611
depth
sea

πελεκίζομαι . . 611
beheaded, be

πέμπτος . . . 611
fifth

πέμπω . . . 611
send
send again (with προστιθημι, Lu. 20:11, 12)
thrust in

πένης 611
poor

πενθερά . . . 611
mother in law
wife's mother

πενθερός . . . 612
father in law

πενθέω . . . 612
bewail
mourn
wail

πένθος . . . 612
mourning
sorrow

πενιχρός . . . 612
poor

πεντάκις . . . 612
five times

πεντακισχίλιοι . 612
five thousand

πεντακόσιοι . . 612
five hundred

πέντε 612
fifty thousand (with μυριας)
five

πεντεκαιδέκατος . 612
fifteenth

πεντήκοντα . . 612
fifty

πεντηκοστη . . 612
Pentecost

πεποίθησις . . 612
confidence
trust

πέρ . . 612
*whom*soever
whomsoever (with ὁς, Mark 15:6)

πέραν 613
beyond
farther side
other side
over

πέρας 613
end
utmost part
uttermost part

περί 613
about
above
against
as touching
at
behalf, on
company, and his (with οἱ, Acts 13:13&21:8)
concern, which
concerning
concerning, as
estate (with τα, Col. 4:8)
for
how it will go with (with τα, Phi. 2:23)
in
manner of, such (with τουτου)
of
on
over
pertaining
pertaining to
sake, for
state (with τα, Phi. 2:19, 20)
thereabout (with τουτου, Lu. 24:4)
*there*of (Mat. 12:36)
touching
*where*by (with ὁς, Acts 19:40)
*where*in
*where*of (with ἡς, Heb. 2:5)
*where*of (with τις, 1 Tim. 1:7)
with

περιάγω . . . 615
compass
go about
lead about

περιαιρέω . . . 615
take away
take up

περιαστράπτω . 615
shine round
shine round about

περιβάλλω . . . 615
array
cast about
clothe
clothed me
put on

περιβλέπω . . 616
look about on
look round about
look round about on

περιβόλαιον . . 616
covering
vesture

περιδέομαι . . 616
bound about, be

περιεργάζομαι . 616
busybody, be a

περίεργος . . . 616
busybody
curious

περιέρχομαι . . 616
fetch a compass
vagabond
wandering about

περιέχω . . . 616
astonished (with θαμβος, Lu. 5:9)
contain
manner, after this (lit. having this form)

περιζώννυμι . 616
gird
gird about
gird self

περίθεσις . . 616
wearing

περιΐστημι . . 616
avoid
shun
stand by
stand round about

περικάθαρμα . . 616
filth

περικαλύπτω . . 616
blindfold
cover
overlay

περίκειμαι . . 616
bound with, be
compassed with, be
hang about

περικεφαλαία . 616
helmet

πιστις 624
assurance
belief
believe
faith
fidelity

πιστός . . . 626
believe
believer
believing
faithful
faithfully
sure
true

πιστόω . . . 627
assured of, be

πλανάω . . . 627
astray, go
deceive
err
out of the way, be
seduce
wander

πλάνη . . . 627
deceit
deceive, to
delusion
error

πλανήτης . . 627
wandering

πλάνος . . . 627
deceiver
seducing

πλάξ 627
table

πλάσμα . . . 627
thing formed

πλάσσω . . . 627
form

πλαστός . . . 627
feigned

πλατεῖα . . . 627
street

πλάτος . . . 627
breadth

πλατύνω . . . 627
broad, make
enlarge

πλατύς . . . 627
wide

πλέγμα . . . 627
broidered hair

πλείων, πλεῖον or **πλέον, πλεῖστος** 627
above (lit. of more than)
exceed (with *περισσευω*, Mat. 5:20)
excellent more
further
great, very
greater
greater part
long
longer
many
many, very
more
most
part, more
yet but (with *ου*)

πλέκω 628
plait

πλεονάζω . . 628
abound
abundant
increase, make to
over, have

πλεονεκτέω . . 628
advantage of, get an
defraud
gain, make a

πλεονέκτης . . 628
covetous

πλεονεξία . 628
covetous practices
covetousness
greediness

πλευρά . 628
side

πλέω . . . 628
sail

πληγή . . . 628
plague
stripe
wound
wounded

πλῆθος . . 629
bundle
company
multitude

πληθύνω . . . 629
abound
multiply

πλήθω . . . 629
accomplish
fill
full...came
furnish

πλήκτης . . . 629
striker

πλημμύρα . 629
flood

πλήν . . 629
but
but rather
except
nevertheless
notwithstanding
save
than

πλήρης . . . 629
full

πληροφορέω . . 630
believed, be most surely
known, be fully
persuaded, be fully
proof of, make full

πληροφορία . . 630
assurance
assurance, full

πληρόω . . . 630
accomplish
accomplish, should (Lu. 9:31)
after (Acts 24:27)
complete
complete, be
end
expire
fill
fill up
fulfil
full
full come, be
full forty years old (with *χρονος, τεσσαρακονταετης*, Acts 7:23)
full make
fully preach
perfect
supply

πλήρωμα . . . 630
fill up, which is put in to
filled up, piece that
fulfilling
full
fulness

πλησίον . . . 631
near

ὁ πλησίον . . 631
neighbour

πλησμονή . . 631
satisfying

πλήσσω . . . 631
smite

πλοιάριον . . 631
boat
ship, little
ship, small

πλοῖον . . . 631
ship
shipping

πλόος 631
course
sailing
voyage

πλούσιος . . . 631
rich

πλουσίως . . 632
abundantly
richly

πλουτέω . . . 632
increased with goods, be
rich
rich, be made
rich, wax

πλουτίζω . . . 632
enrich
rich, make

πλοῦτος . . . 632
riches

πλύνω . . . 632
wash

πνεῦμα . . . 632
ghost
Holy Ghost (with *αγιος*)
life
spirit
spiritual
spiritually
spiritually minded, be (with *φρονημα*. Ro. 8:6)
wind

πνευματικός . . 635
spiritual

πνευματικῶς . . 635
spiritually

πνέω 635
blow
wind

πνίγω 635
choke
throat, take by the

πνικτός . . . 635
strangled

πνοή 635
breath
wind

ποδήρης . . . 635
garment down to the foot

πόθεν 635
whence
whence, from

ποιέω 636
abide
agree (with *μια, γνωμη*, Rev. 17:17)
appoint
avenge
band together (with *συστροφη*, Acts 23:12)

be
bear
bewray (with δηλος, Mat. 26:73)
bring
bring forth
cast out (lit. made cast out)
cause
commit
content (with ἱκανος, Lu. 15:15)
continue
deal
delay, without any (with αναβολη, μηδεις, Acts 25:17)
do
do, would (Joh. 6:6)
doing
execute
exercise
fulfil
gain
give
have
hold
journeying (Lu. 13:22)
keep
lay wait (with ενεδρα, Acts 25:3)
lighten the ship (with εκβολη, Acts 27:18)
make
mean (Acts 21:13)
none of these things move me (with λογος, ουδεις, Acts 20:24)
observe
ordain
perform
provide
purged, have (with καθαρισμος, Heb. 1:3)
purpose
put
raising up (with επισυστασις, Acts 24:12)
secure (Mat. 28:14)
shew
shoot out
spend
take
tarry
transgress the law (with ανομια, 1 Joh. 3:4)
work
yield

ποίημα . . . 640
thing that is made
workmanship

ποίησις . . . 640
deed

ποιητής . . . 640
doer
poet

ποικίλος . . . 640
divers
manifold

ποιμαίνω . . . 640
feed
feed cattle
rule

ποιμήν . . . 640
pastor
shepherd

ποίμνη . . . 640
flock
fold

ποιμνίον . . . 640
flock

ποῖος 640
what
what manner of
which

πολεμέω . . . 641
fight
make war
war

πόλεμος . . . 641
battle
fight
war

πόλις 641
city

πολιτάρχης . . 642
rulers of the city

πολιτεία . . . 642
commonwealth
freedom

πολίτευμα . . 642
conversation

πολιτεύομαι . . 642
conversation be, let
live

πολίτης . . . 642
citizen

πολλάκις . . 642
oft
often
oftentimes
ofttimes

πολλαπλασίων . 643
manifold more

πολυλογία . . 643
much speaking

πολυμερῶς . . 643
at sundry times

πολυποίκιλος . . 643
manifold

πολύς 643
abundant
altogether (lit. in much)
common
far (lit. by much)
far passed
far spent
great
great age, be of a (with προβαινω, ἡμερα, Lu. 2:36)
great deal
great while
greatly
long
many
much
oft
oftentimes
plenteous
sore
straitly

πολύσπλαγχνος . 645
pitiful, very

πολυτελής . . 645
costly
great price, of
precious, very

πολύτιμος . . 645
costly, very
great price, of

πολυτρόπως . . 645
in divers manners

πόμα . . . 645
drink

πονηρία . . . 645
iniquity
wickedness

πονηρός . . . 646
bad
evil
evil (with ῥημα, Mat. 5:11)
grievous
harm
lewd
malicious
wicked
wicked, more
wickedness (1 Joh. 5:19)

πόνος 646
pain

πορεία 646
journeying
way

πορεύομαι . . . 646
depart
go
go away
go forth
go one's way
go up
go, will (Joh. 7:35)
journey
journey, make a
journey, take a
walk

πορθέω . . . 647
destroy
waste

πορισμός . . . 647
gain

πορνεία . . . 647
fornication

πορνεύω . . . 648
commit
fornication, commit

πόρνη 648
harlot
whore

πόρνος . . . 648
fornicator
whoremonger

πόῤῥω, πορρωτέρω 648
far
further
great way off, a

πόῤῥωθεν . . . 648
afar off

πορφύρα . . . 648
purple

πορφύρεος, πορφυροῦς . . . 648
purple

πορφυρόπωλις . 648
seller of purple, a

ποσάκις . . . 648
how oft
how often

πόσις . . . 648
drink

πόσος . . . 648
how great
how long
how many
how much
what

ποταμός . . . 649
flood
river
stream
water

ποταμοφόρητος . 649
carried away of the flood

ποταπός . . . 649
what
what manner of

ποτέ 649
aforetime

any time
at length
at the last
ever
how long (with ἑως)
in the old time
in time past
once
sometime
when

ποτε 649
at any time
never (with ου μη, 2 Pet. 1:10)
sometimes
when

πότερον . . 649
whether

ποτηριον . . . 649
cup

ποτίζω . . . 649
drink, give to
drink, make to
feed
water

πότος 650
banqueting

που 650
about
certain place, a—in

ποῦ 650
where
whither

πούς 650
foot
footstool

πρᾶγμα . . . 651
business
matter
thing
work

πραγματεία . . 651
affair

πραγματεύομαι . 651
occupy

πραιτώριον . . 651
hall, common
hall, judgment
hall of judgment
palace
prætorium

πράκτωρ . . . 651
officer

πραξις . . . 651
deed
office
work

πρᾶος 651
meek

πρᾳότης . . . 651
meekness

πρασιά . . . 651
ranks, in

πράσσω, πράττω 651
commit
deeds
do
exact
keep
require
should do (Lu. 22:23)
use arts

πραΰς 652
meek

πραΰτης . . . 652
meekness

πρέπει 652
become
comely

πρεσβεία . . . 652
ambassage
message

πρεσβεύω . . . 652
ambassador, be an

πρεσβυτέριον . . 652
elder
elders, estate of
presbytery

πρεσβύτερος, -τέρα 652
elder | elder women
eldest
old men

πρεσβύτης . . 652
aged
aged man
old man

πρεσβῦτις . . 652
aged women

πρηνής . . . 652
headlong

πρίζω 653
saw asunder

πρίν, πρὶν . . 653
before
before that
ere

πρό 653
above
ago
before
before (Acts 13:24)
ever, or

προάγω . . . 653
bring forth
bring
brought, would have (Acts 12:6)
go before

προαιρέομαι . . 653
purpose

προαιτιάομαι . 653
prove, before

προακούω . . . 653
hear before

προαμαρτάνω . 653
sin already
sinned, heretofore

προαύλιον . . 653
porch

προβαίνω . . 653
age, be of a great (with ἡμερα, πολυς, Lu. 2:36)
go farther
go on
stricken, be well

προβάλλω . . 653
put forward
shoot forth

προβατικός . . 654
sheep
sheep [market]

πρόβατον . . . 654
sheep
sheepfold (with αυλη, Joh. 10:1)

προβιβάζω . 654
draw
instruct, before

προβλέπω . . 654
provide

προγίνομαι . . 654
past, be

προγινώσκω . . 654
foreknow
foreordain
know
know before

πρόγνωσις . . 654
foreknowledge

πρόγονοι . . . 654
forefathers
parent

προγράφω . . 654
ordain, before
set forth, evidently
write
write afore
write aforetime

πρόδηλος . . . 654
evident
manifest beforehand
open beforehand

προδίδωμι . . 654
give, first

προδότης . . . 654
betrayer
traitor

πρόδρομος . . 654
forerunner

προειδέω . . . 654
foresee
see before

προελπίζω . . 654
trust, first

προέπω . . . 654
forewarn
speak before
tell in time past

προενάρχομαι . 654
begin
begin before

προεπαγγέλλομαι 655
promise afore

προερέω . . . 655
foretel
say before
speak before
tell before

προέρχομαι . . 655
go before
go farther
go forward
outgo
pass on

προετοιμάζω . . 655
ordain, before
prepare, afore

προευαγγελίζομαι 655
preach before the gospel

προέχομαι . . 655
better, be

προηγέομαι . . 655
prefer

πρόθεσις . . . 655
purpose
shewbread

προθεσμία . . 655
time appointed

προθυμία . . . 655
forwardness of mind
readiness
readiness of mind
ready mind
willing mind

πρόθυμος . . . 655
ready
willing

προθύμως . . 655
of a ready mind

προΐστημι . . 655
maintain

over, be
rule

προκαλέομαι . . 655
provoke

προκαταγγέλλω . 655
foretell
notice before, have
shew, before

προκαταρτίζω . 655
beforehand, make up

πρόκειμαι . . 655
first, be
set before
set forth

προκηρύσσω . . 655
preach, before
preach, first

προκοπή . . . 655
furtherance
profiting

προκόπτω . . . 656
increase
proceed, shall
profit
spent, be far
wax

πρόκριμα . . . 656
prefer one before another

προκυρόομαι . . 656
confirm before

προλαμβάνω . . 656
come aforehand
overtake
take before

προλέγω . . . 656
foretell
tell before

προμαρτύρομαι . 656
testify beforehand

προμελετάω . . 656
meditate before

προμεριμνάω . 656
thought beforehand, take

προνοέω . . . 656
provide
provide for

πρόνοια . . . 656
providence
provision

προοράω . . . 656
foresee
see before

προορίζω . . . 656
determine before
ordain
predestinate

προπάσχω . . 656
suffer before

προπέμπω . . 656
accompany
bring forward on journey
bring on journey
bring on way
conduct forth

προπετής . . . 656
heady
rash*ly*

προπορεύομαι . 656
go before

πρός 656
about
according to
against
among
at
because of
before
between
by
for
house, at thy (Mat. 26:18)
in
intent, for
nigh unto
of
pertain to, which
that
this end that, to
to
together (with αλληλων, Lu. 24:14)
toward
unto
*where*by (with ο)
with
within
you-ward, to
you-ward, to (with ὑμας)

προσάββατον . 661
day before the sabbath, the

προσαγορεύομαι . 661
call

προσάγω . . . 661
bring
draw near

προσαγωγή . . 662
access

προσαιτέω . . 662
beg

προσαναβαίνω 662
go up

προσαναλίσκω 662
spend

προσαναπληρόω . 662
supply

προσανατίθημι . 662
add, in conference
confer

προσαπειλέομαι . 662
threaten, further

προσδαπανάω . 662
spend more

προσδέομαι . . 662
need

προσδέχομαι . . 662
accept
allow
look for
receive
take
wait for

προσδοκάω . . 662
expect
expectation, be in
look
look for
looked when
tarry
wait for

προσδοκία . 662
expectation
looking after

προσεάω . . . 662
suffer

προσεγγίζω . . 662
come nigh

προσεδρεύω . . 662
wait at

προσεργάζομαι . 662
gain

προσέρχομαι . . 662
as soon as come
come
come unto
comers thereunto (Heb. 10:1)
consent
draw near
go
go near
go to
go unto

προσευχή . . 663
pray earnestly (with προσευχομαι, Jas. 5:17)
prayer

προσεύχομαι . . 663
pray
pray earnestly (with προσευχη, Jas. 5:17)
pray for
prayer, make

προσέχω . . . 664
attend unto
attendance at, give
attendance to, give
beware
given to, be
heed, give
heed, take
heed, to give
heed to, take
heed unto, give
regard, to have

προσηλόω . . 664
nail to

προσήλυτος . . 664
proselyte

πρόσκαιρος . . 664
dur*eth* for a while
endure but for a time
season, for a
temporal

προσκαλέομαι . 664
call
call to
call unto
called for

προσκαρτερέω . 665
attend continually upon
continue
continue in
continue instant in
continue stedfastly
continue with
give selves continually
wait on
wait on continually

προσκαρτέρησις . 665
perseverance

προσκεφάλαιον . 665
pillow

προσκληρόομαι . 665
consort with

πρόσκλισις . . 665
partiality

προσκολλάομαι . 665
cleave to
join self
joined, be

πρόσκομμα . . 665
offence
stumbling
stumblingblock
stumbling*stone*
stumblingstone (with λιθος)

προσκοπή . . 665
offence

προσκόπτω . . 665
beat upon
dash

πτηνόν . . . 672
bird

πτοέομαι . . . 672
terrify

πτόησις . . . 672
amazement

πτύον 672
fan

πτύρομαι . . . 672
terrify

πτύσμα . . . 672
spittle

πτύσσω . . . 672
close

πτύω . . . 672
spit

πτῶμα . . . 672
body, dead
carcase
corpse

πτῶσις . . . 673
fall

πτωχεία . . . 673
poverty

πτωχεύω . . . 673
poor, become

πτωχός . . . 673
beggar
beggarly
poor

πυγμῇ . . . 673
oft

πυκνός . . . 673
often
oftener

πυκτεύω . . . 673
fight

πύλη 673
gate

πυλών . . . 673
gate
porch

πυνθάνομαι . . 673
ask
demand
enquire
enquire, would (Acts 23:20)
understand

πῦρ 673
fiery
fire

πυρά 674
fire

πύργος . . . 674
tower

πυρέσσω . . . 674
fever, be sick of a

πυρετός . . . 674
fever

πυρινός . . . 674
fire, of

πυρόομαι . . . 674
burn
fiery
fire, be on
try

πυῤῥάζω . . . 674
red, be

πυῤῥός . . . 674
red

πύρωσις . . . 674
burning
fiery trial

πωλέω . . . 674
sell
sold, whatsoever is

πῶλος 675
colt

πώποτε . . . 675
at any time
never (with *ου μη*, Joh. 6:35)
never...to any man (with *ουδεις*)
yet never man (with *ουδεις*, Lu. 19:30)

πωρόω . . . 675
blinded, be
harden

πώρωσις . . . 675
blindness
hardness

πώς 675
haply
means, by any
means, by some
perhaps

πῶς 675
how
manner, after what
means, by what
that

ῥαββί 676
Master
Rabbi

ῥαββονί, ῥαββουνί 676
Lord
Rabboni

ῥαβδίζω . . . 676
beat
beat with rods

ῥάβδος . . . 676
rod
sceptre
staff

ῥαβδοῦχος . . 676
serjeant

ῥᾳδιούργημα . . 676
lewdness

ῥᾳδιουργία . . 676
mischief

ῥακά 676
Raca

ῥάκος 676
cloth

ῥαντίζω . . . 676
sprinkle

ῥαντισμός . . 676
sprinkling

ῥαπίζω . . . 676
smite
smite with the palm of the hand

ῥάπισμα . . . 677
palm of the hand
smite with the hand (with *διδωμι*)
strike with the palm of hand [*see* lit.]

ῥαφίς 677
needle

ῥέδα 677
chariot

ῥέω 677
flow

ῥέω 677
command
make
say
speak
speak of

ῥῆγμα 677
ruin

ῥήγνυμι, ῥήσσω 677
break
break forth
burst
rend
tear | throw down

ῥῆμα 677
evil (with *πονηρος*, Mat. 5:11)
nothing
nothing (with *πας*, *ουκ*, Lu. 1:37)
saying
word

ῥήτωρ 678
orator

ῥητῶς 678
expressly

ῥίζα . . . 678
root

ῥιζόομαι . 678
rooted, be

ῥιπή 678
twinkling

ῥιπίζομαι . . . 678
tossed, be

ῥίπτω . . . 678
cast
cast down
cast off
cast out
scatter abroad
throw

ῥοιζηδόν . . . 678
noise, with great

ῥομφαία . . . 678
sword

ῥύμη 678
lane
street

ῥυπαρία . . . 678
filthiness

ῥυπαρός . . . 678
vile

ῥύπος 678
filth

ῥυπόω 678
filthy, be

ῥύσις 678
issue

ῥυτίς 678
wrinkle

ῥύομαι . . . 678
deliver
deliverer

ῥώννυμαι . . 679
farewell

σαβαχθανί . . 679
sabacthani

σαβαώθ . . . 679
sabaoth

σαββατισμός . 679
rest

σάββατον, σάββατα . . . 679
sabbath
sabbath day
week

σαγήνη . . . 679
net

σαίνω . . . 679
move

σάκκος . 679
sackcloth

heed, take
look at
look on
mark

σκοπός . . 688
mark

σκορπίζω . . 688
disperse abroad
scatter
scatter abroad

σκορπίος . . 688
scorpion

σκοτεινός . . 688
dark
darkness, full of

σκοτία . . . 688
dark
darkness

σκοτίζομαι . . 688
darkened, be

σκοτόομαι . . . 688
darkness, be full of

σκότος 688
darkness

σκύβαλον . . . 688
dung

σκυθρωπός . . 688
sad
sad countenance, of a

σκύλλω . . . 688
trouble
trouble self

σκῦλον . . . 688
spoils

σκωληκόβρωτος . 689
eaten of worms

σκώληξ . . . 689
worm

σμαράγδινος . 689
emerald

σμάραγδος . 689
emerald

σμύρνα . . . 689
myrrh

σμυρνίζομαι . . 689
myrrh, be mingled with

σόι 689
thee
thine own
thou
thy

σορός 690
bier

σός 690
thine
thine own
thy
thy friends

σοῦ 691
home (Mark 5:19)
thee
thine
thine own
thou
thy

σουδάριον . . 694
handkerchiefs
napkin

σοφία 694
wisdom

σοφίζω 694
cunningly devised
make wise

σοφός . . 694
wise

σπαράσσω . . 695
rend
tear

σπαργανόω . . 695
swaddling clothes, wrap in

σπάομαι . . . 695
draw
draw out

σπαταλάω . . 695
pleasure, live in wanton, be

σπεῖρα . . . 695
band

σπείρω . . . 695
seed, receive
sow
sower

σπεκουλάτωρ . . 695
executioner

σπένδομαι . . 695
offered, be
offered, be ready to be

σπέρμα . . . 695
issue
seed

σπερμολόγος . 696
babbler

σπεύδω . . . 696
haste, make
haste unto
haste, with

σπήλαιον . . . 696
cave
den

σπιλάς . . . 696
spot

σπιλόω . 696
defile
spot

σπῖλος . . . 696
spot

σπλάγχνα . . 696
bowels
inward affection
mercy, tender (with ελεος, Lu. 1:78)

σπλαγχνίζομαι . 696
compassion, have
compassion, be moved with

σπόγγος . . . 696
spunge

σποδός . . . 696
ashes

σπορά 696
seed

σπόριμα . . 696
corn
corn field

σπόρος . . . 696
seed
seed sown

σπουδάζω . . 696
diligence, do
diligence, give
diligent, be
endeavour
forward, be
labour
study

σπουδαῖος . . 697
diligent
diligent, more
forward, more

σπουδαιότερον . 697
diligently, very

σπουδαίως,-οτέρως 697
carefully, the more
diligently
instantly

σπουδή . . . 697
business
care
carefulness
diligence
earnest care
forwardness
haste

σπυρίς 697
basket

στάδιος, στάδιον . 697
furlong
race

στάμνος . . 697
pot

στάσις. . . . 697
dissension
insurrection
sedition
standing (Heb. 9:8)
uproar

στατήρ . . . 697
money, piece of

σταυρός . . . 697
cross

σταυρόω . . . 697
crucify

σταφυλή . . 698
grapes

στάχυς . . . 698
corn, ear of
ear

στέγη 698
roof

στέγω 698
bear
forbear
suffer

στεῖρα 698
barren

στέλλομαι . . 698
avoid
withdraw self

στέμμα . . . 698
garland

στεναγμός . . 698
groaning

στενάζω . . . 698
grief, with
groan
grudge
sigh

στενός . . . 698
strait

στενοχωρέομαι . 698
distressed, be
straitened, be

στενοχωρία . . 698
anguish
distress

στερεός . . . 698
stedfast
strong
sure

στερεόω . . . 698
establish
strength, receive
strong, make

στερέωμα . . . 698
stedfastness

στέφανος . . 698
crown

στεφανόω . . . 699
crown

στῆθος . . . 699
breast
στήκω 699
stand
stand fast
στηριγμός . . 699
stedfastness
στηρίζω . . . 699
established
fix
stablish
stedfastly set
strengthen
στίγμα . . . 699
mark
στιγμή . . . 699
moment
στίλβω . . . 699
shining
στόα 699
porch
στοιβάς . . . 699
branch
στοιχεῖον . . . 699
element
principle
rudiment
στοιχέω . . . 699
walk
walk orderly
στολή 699
clothing, long
garment, long
robe
robe, long
στόμα 699
edge
face
mouth
στόμαχος . . 700
stomach
στρατεία . . . 700
warfare
στράτευμα . . 700
army
soldier
war, man of
στρατεύομαι . . 700
soldiers
war
warfare, go a
στρατηγός . . 700
captain
magistrate
στρατιά . . . 700
host
στρατιώτης . . 700
soldier

στρατολογέω . 701
soldier, choose to be a
στρατοπεδάρχης . 701
captain of the guard
στρατόπεδον . 701
army
στρεβλόω . . 701
wrest
στρέφω . . . 701
convert
turn
turn again
turn back again
turn self
turn self about
στρηνιάω . . . 701
live deliciously
στρῆνος . . . 701
delicacy
στρουθίον . . 701
sparrow
στρώννυμι, στρωννύω . . . 701
bed, make
furnish
spread
strew
στυγητός . . . 701
hateful
στυγνάζω . . 701
lower
sad, be
στύλος 701
pillar
σύ 701
thou
συγγένεια . . 703
kindred
συγγενής . . . 703
cousin
kin
kinsfolk
kinsman
συγγνώμη . . 703
permission
συγκάθημαι . . 703
sit with
συγκαθίζω . . 703
sit down together
sit together, make
συγκακοπαθέω . 703
afflictions, be partaker of
συγκακουχέομαι . 703
affliction with, suffer
συγκαλέω . . 703
call together

συγκαλύπτομαι . 703
cover
συγκάμπτω . . 703
bow down
συγκαταβαίνω . 703
go down with
συγκατατίθεμαι . 703
consent
συγκατάθεσις . 703
agreement
συγκαταψηφίζομαι 703
numbered with, be
συγκεράννυμι . 703
mixed with, be
temper together
συγκινέω . . . 703
stir up
συγκλείω . . . 703
conclude
inclose
shut up
συγκληρονόμος . 703
fellowheir
heir together
heir with
joint-heir
συγκοινωνέω . . 704
communicate with
fellowship with, have
partaker of, be
συγκοινωνός . . 704
companion
partake
partaker
partaker with
συγκομίζω . . 704
carry
συγκρίνω . . . 704
compare among
compare with
συγκύπτω . . 704
bow together
συγκυρία . . . 704
chance
συγχαίρω . . 704
rejoice in
rejoice with
συγχέω . . . 704
stir up
συγχράομαι . . 704
dealings with, have
συγχύνω . . . 704
confound
confuse
uproar, be in an
σύγχυσις . . . 704
confusion

συζάω . . . 704
live with
συζευγνύω . . 704
join together
συζητέω . . . 704
dispute
dispute with
enquire
question
question with
reason
reason together
συζήτησις . . 704
disputation
disputing
reasoning
συζητητής . . 704
disputer
σύζυγος . . . 704
yokefellow
συζωοποιέω . . 704
quicken together with
συκάμινος . . 704
sycamine tree
συκῆ 704
fig tree
συκομωραία . . 705
sycomore tree
σῦκον 705
fig
συκοφαντέω . . 705
accusation, take by false
accuse falsely
συλαγωγέω . . 705
spoil
συλάω . . . 705
rob
συλλαλέω . . 705
commune with
confer with
speak among
talk with
συλλαμβάνω . 705
catch
conceive
help
take
συλλέγω . . . 705
gather
gather together
gather up
συλλογίζομαι 705
reason with
συλλυπέομαι . 705
grieved, be
συμβαίνω . . 705
be

befall
happen
happen, should (Mark 10:32)
happen unto

συμβάλλω . . 705
confer
encounter
help
make
meet with
ponder

συμβασιλεύω . 705
reign with

συμβιβάζω . . 705
compact
gather, assuredly
instruct
knit together
prove

συμβουλεύω . . 705
consult
counsel
counsel, give
counsel, take
counsel together, take

συμβούλιον . . 706
consultation
council
counsel

σύμβουλος . . 706
counsellor

συμμαθητής . . 706
fellowdisciple

συμμαρτυρέω 706
testify unto
witness, also bear
witness with, bear

συμμερίζομαι . 706
partaker with, be

συμμέτοχος . . 706
partaker

συμμιμητής . . 706
follower together

συμμορφόομαι . 706
conformable unto, be made

σύμμορφος . . 706
conformed to
fashioned like unto

συμπαθέω . . 706
compassion, have
touched with a feeling of, be

συμπαθής . . 706
compassion one of another, having

συμπαραγίνομαι 706
come together
stand with

συμπαρακαλέομαι 706
comforted together, be

συμπαραλαμβάνω 706
take with

συμπαραμένω . 706
continue with

συμπάρειμι . . 706
present with, be here

συμπάσχω . . 706
suffer with

συμπέμπω . . 706
send with

συμπεριλαμβάνω 706
embrace

συμπίνω . . . 706
drink with

συμπληρόω . . 706
come
fill up
fully come

συμπνίγω . . 706
choke
throng

συμπολίτης . . 706
fellowcitizen

συμπορεύομαι . 707
go with
resort

συμπόσιον . . 707
company

συμπρεσβύτερος . 707
elder, also an

συμφέρω . . . 707
better for, be
bring together
expedient, be
expedient for, be
good, be
profit
profitable for, be

σύμφημι . . . 707
consent unto

συμφυλέτης . . 707
countryman

συμφύομαι . . 707
spring up with

σύμφυτος . . . 707
planted together

συμφωνέω . . 707
agree
agree together
agree with

συμφώνησις . 707
concord

συμφωνία . . 707
musick

σύμφωνος . . 707
consent

συμψηφίζω . . 707
count

σύμψυχος . . 707
of one accord

σύν 707
beside
with

συνάγω . . . 708
accompany (with ερχομαι, Acts 11:12)
assemble
assemble selves
assemble together
bestow
come together
gather
gather selves together
gather up
gathered together
lead into
resort
take in

συναγωγή . . 709
assembly
congregation
synagogue

συναγωνίζομαι . 709
strive together with

συναθλέω . . . 709
labour with
strive together for

συναθροίζω . . 709
call together
gather together

συναίρω . . . 709
reckon
reckon (with λογος, Mat. 25:19)
take

συναιχμάλωτος . 709
fellowprisoner

συνακολουθέω . 709
follow

συναλίζομαι . . 709
assembled together, be

συναναβαίνω . 709
come up with

συνανάκειμαι . 710
sit at the table with
sit down with
sit together with
sit with
sit with at meat

συναναμίγνυμι . 710
company, keep
company with
company with, have

συναναπαύομαι . 710
refreshed with, be

συναντάω . . 710
befall
meet

συνάντησις . . 710
meet

συναντιλαμβάνομαι 710
help

συναπάγομαι . 710
carried away with, be
condescend
led away with, be

συναποθνήσκω . 710
dead with, be
die with

συναπόλλυμαι . 71
perish with

συναποστέλλω . 710
send, with

συναρμολογέομαι 710
framed together, be fitly
joined together, be fitly

συναρπάζω . . 710
catch

συναυξάνομαι . 710
grow together

συνδέομαι . . 710
bound with, be

σύνδεσμος . . 710
band
bond

συνδοξάζομαι . 710
glorified together, be

σύνδουλος . . 710
fellowservant

συνδρομή . . . 710
run together

συνεγείρω . . 710
raise up together
rise with

συνέδριον . . . 710
council

συνειδέω . . . 711
consider
know by
privy, be
ware of, be

συνείδησις . 711
conscience

σύνειμι . . . 711
with, be

συνείμι . . 711
gathered together be

συνεισέρχομαι . 711
go in with
go with into

συνέκδημος . . 711
companion in travel
travel with

συνεκλεκτός . . 711
elected together with

συνελαύνω . . 711
set at one again (with ειϛ, ειρηνη, Acts 7:26)

συνεπιμαρτυρέω . 711
witness, also bear

συνέπομαι . . 711
accompany

συνεργέω . . . 711
help with
work together
work with
workers together

συνεργός . . . 711
companion in labour
fellowhelper
fellowlabourer
fellowworker
helper
labourer together with
workfellow

συνέρχομαι . . 712
accompany
assemble
assembled with, be
come
come together
come with
company with
go with
resort

συνεσθίω . . . 712
eat with

σύνεσις . . . 712
knowledge
understanding

συνετός . . . 712
prudent

συνευδοκέω . 712
allow
consent
pleased, be
pleasure, have

συνευωχεομαι . 712
feast with

συνεφίστημι . . 712
rise up together

συνέχω . . . 712
constrain
hold
keep in
sick of
press
stop
strait, be in a
straiten
taken with, be
throng

συνήδομαι . . 712
delight

συνήθεια . . . 712
custom

συνηλικιώτης . 712
equal

συνθάπτομαι . . 712
buried with, be

συνθλάομαι . . 712
broken, be

συνθλίβω . . 712
throng

συνθρύπτω . . 713
break

συνίημι . . . 713
consider
understand
wise, be

συνιστάνω . . 713
commend

συνιστάω, συνίστημι . . . 713
approve
commend
consist
make
stand
stand with

συνοδεύω . . . 713
journey with

συνοδία . . . 713
company

συνοικέω . . . 713
dwell with

συνοικοδομέομαι . 713
builded together, be

συνομιλέω . . 713
talk with

συνομορέω . . 713
join hard

συνοχή . . . 713
anguish
distress

συντάσσω . . 713
appoint

συντέλεια . . 713
end

συντελέω . . . 713
end
finish
fulfil
fulfilled, shall be (with μελλω, Mark 13:4)
make

συντέμνω . . . 713
cut short
short (Ro. 9:28)

συντηρέω . . . 713
keep
observe
preserve

συντίθημι . . 714
agree
assent
covenant

συντόμως . . 714
words, a few

συντρέχω . . . 714
run
run together
run with

συντρίβω . . . 714
break
break in pieces
broken to shivers, be
brokenhearted (with καρδια, Lu. 4:18)
bruise

σύντριμμα . . 714
destruction

σύντροφος . . 714
brought up with

συντυγχάνω . . 714
come at

συνυποκρίνομαι . 714
dissemble with

συνυπουργέω . 714
help together

συνωδίνω . . . 714
travail in pain together

συνωμοσία . . 714
conspiracy

σύρτις 714
quicksands

σύρω 714
drag
draw
hale

συσπαράσσω . 714
tear

σύσσημον . . . 714
token

σύσσωμα . . . 714
of the same body

συστασιαστής . 714
insurrection with, make

συστατικός . . 714
commendation, of

συσταυρόω . . 714
crucified with

συστέλλω . . 714
short
wind up [for burial]
wound up

συστενάζω . . 714
groan together

συστοιχέω . . 715
answer to

συστρατιώτης . 715
fellowsoldier

συστρέφω . . . 715
gather

συστροφή . . . 715
band together (with ποιεω Acts 23:12)
concourse

συσχηματίζομαι . 715
conformed to
fashion self according to

σφαγή . . . 715
slaughter

σφάγιον . . . 715
slain beast

σφάττω . . . 715
kill
slay
wound

σφόδρα . . . 715
exceeding
exceedingly
greatly
sore
very

σφοδρῶς . . . 715
exceedingly

σφραγίζω . . 715
seal
seal up
set a seal
set to seal
stop (2 Cor. 11:10)

σφραγίς . . . 715
seal

σφυρόν . . . 715
ancle bone

σχεδόν . . . 715
almost

σχῆμα . . . 716
fashion

σχίζω 716
break

divide
open
rend
rent, make a

σχίσμα . . . 716
division
rent
schism

σχοινίον . . . 716
cord, small
rope

σχολάζω . . . 716
empty
give self

σχολή . . . 716
school

σώζω 716
heal
preserve
save
save self
well, do
whole, be
whole, make

σῶμα 717
bodily
body
slave

σωματικός . . 718
bodily

σωματικῶς . . 718
bodily

σωρεύω . . . 718
heap
load

σωτήρ 718
saviour

σωτηρία . . . 718
deliver
health
salvation
save
saving

σωτήριον . . . 719
salvation

σωτήριος . . . 719
salvation, that bringeth

σωφρονέω . . 719
mind, be in right
sober, be
sober minded, be
soberly

σωφρονίζω . . 719
sober, teach to be

σωφρονισμός . . 719
sound mind

σωφρόνως . . 719
soberly

σωφροσύνη . . 719
soberness
sobriety

σώφρων . . 719
discreet
sober
temperate

τάγμα . . . 719
order

τακτός . . . 719
set

ταλαιπωρέω . . 719
afflicted, be

ταλαιπωρία . . 719
misery

ταλαίπωρος . . 719
wretched

ταλαντιαῖος . . 719
talent, weight of a

τάλαντον . . . 719
talent

ταλιθά . . . 719
Talitha

ταμεῖον . . . 719
chamber, secret
closet
storehouse

τάξις 719
order

ταπεινός . . . 720
base
cast down
degree, of low
estate, of low
humble
lowly

ταπεινοφροσύνη . 720
humbleness of mind
humility
humility of mind
lowliness
lowliness of mind

ταπεινόω . . . 720
abase
bring low
humble
humble self

ταπείνωσις . . 720
estate, low
humiliation
made low, be
vile

ταράσσω . . . 720
trouble

ταραχή . . . 720
trouble
troubling

τάραχος . . . 720
stir

ταρταρόω . . 720
hell, cast down to

τάσσω . . . 720
addict
appoint
determined
ordained
set

ταῦρος . . . 720
bull
ox

ταὐτά, from ὁ αὐτος 720
even thus
like
manner, like
so

ταῦτα, from οὗτος 720
*after*ward
afterward (with μετα)
follow (with μετα, 1Pet. 1:11)
here*after*
*here*after (with μετα)
him (Heb. 11:12)
so
such
that
the
the same
them
these
they
this
those
thus

ταύταις, from οὗτος 722
that
them
these
those

ταύτας, from οὗτος 722
hence
these
those

ταύτῃ, from οὗτος 722
it
same, the
that
this
this same

ταύτην, from οὗτος 723
her
here*of*
it
same, the
that
the
this

ταύτης, from οὗτος 723
same, the
there*by*
this

ταφή 723
bury (Mat. 27:7)

τάφος 723
sepulchre
tomb

τάχα 723
peradventure
perhaps

ταχέως . . . 723
hastily
quickly
shortly
soon
suddenly

ταχινός . . . 724
shortly
swift

τάχιον . 724
out*run*
quickly
shortly
sooner

τάχιστα . . . 724
speed, with all

τάχος 724
quick*ly*
short*ly*
speedily

ταχύ 724
lightly
quickly

ταχύς 724
swift

τε 724
also
and
both
even
then
whether

τεῖχος . . . 726
wall

τεκμήριον . 726
infallible proof

τεκνίον . . . 726
child, little

τεκνογονέω . . 726
children, bear

τεκνογονία . . 726
childbearing

τέκνον . . . 726
child
daughter
son

τοιγαροῦν . . 740
therefore
wherefore

τοίνυν . . . 740
then
therefore

τοιόσδε . . . 740
such

τοιοῦτος . . . 740
like
such
such an one

τοῖχος . . . 740
wall

τόκος 740
usury

τολμαω . . . 741
bold, be
boldly
dare
durst

τολμηρότερον . 741
boldly, the more

τολμητής . . . 741
presumptuous

τομώτερος . . 741
sharper

τόξον 741
bow

τοπάζιον . . . 741
topaz

τόπος 741
coasts
licence
place
plain (Lu. 6:17)
quarter
rock (with τραχυς, Acts 27:29)
room
where

τοσοῦτος . . . 742
as large
so great
so long
so many
so much
these many

τότε 742
that time
then

τοῦ, for **τούτου** . 743
his

τοὐναντίον . . 743
contrariwise

τοὔνομα . . . 743
named (Mat. 27:57)

τουτέστι, or **τουτ' ἔστι** . . . 743
that is
that is to say

τοῦτο 743
here*unto*
it
mind, let this [be in you] (with φρονεω, Phi. 2:5)
partly
self*same*
so
that

the same
there*fore*
there*unto*
this
thus
where*fore*

τούτοις . . . 746
such
them
there*in*
there*with*
these
this
those

τοῦτον . . . 746
him
that
the same
this

τούτου . . . 746
here*by*
him
it
such manner of (with περι)
that
thence*forth*
thereabout
thereabout (with περι, Lu. 24:4)
this
thus

τούτους . . . 747
such
them
these
this

τούτῳ 747
here*by*
here*in*
him
one
the same
there*in*
this

τούτων . . . 748
such
their
these
these things
they
this sort
those

τράγος . . . 748
goat

τράπεζα . . . 748
bank
meat
table

τραπεζίτης . . 748
exchanger

τραῦμα . . . 748
wound

τραυματίζω . . 748
wound

τραχηλίζομαι . 748
opened, be

τράχηλος . . 749
neck

τραχύς . . . 749
rock (with τοπος, Acts 27:29)
rough

τρεῖς, τρία . . 749
three

τρέμω 749
afraid, be
trembling

τρέφω . . . 749
bring up
feed
nourish

τρέχω . . . 749
course, have
run

τριάκοντα . . . 749
thirty
thirty fold

τριακόσιοι . . . 750
three hundred

τρίβολος . . . 750
brier
thistle

τρίβος . . . 750
paths

τριετία . . . 750
three years, space of

τρίζω 750
gnash

τρίμηνον . . . 750
three months

τρίς 750
three times
thrice

τρίστεγον . . 750
third loft

τρισχίλιοι . . 750
three thousand

τρίτος 750
third
thirdly

τρίχινος . . . 750
hair, of

τρόμος . . . 750
tremble (with εχω, Mark 16:8)
trembling

τροπή 751
turning

τρόπος . . . 751
as
conversation
even as
manner, *like* (with ὡς, Acts 1:11)
manner, *like* (with ὁμοιος, Jude 7)
means
means, by any (with κατα, 2 Th. 2:3)
way

τροποφορέω . . 751
manners, suffer the

τροφή 751
food
meat

τροφός . . . 751
nurse

τροχιά . . . 751
path

τροχός . . . 751
course

τρυβλίον . . . 751
dish

τρυγάω . . . 751
gather

τρυγών . . . 751
turtledove

τρυμαλιά . . 751
eye

τρύπημα . . . 751
eye

τρυφάω . . . 751
pleasure, live in

τρυφή 751
delicately
riot

τρώγω . . 751
eat

fear
fear exceedingly (Mar. 4:41)
reverence

φοβερός . 789
fearful
terrible

φόβητρον . . 789
fearful sight

φόβος 789
afraid, be sore (with φοβεομαι, μεγας, Lu. 2:9)
exceedingly (with μεγας)
fear
fear (with εχω, 1 Ti. 5:20)
fear exceedingly (with μεγας)
terror

φοῖνιξ 789
palm
palm tree

φονεύς . . 789
murderer

φονεύω . . . 789
kill
murder do
slay

φόνος 789
murder
slain with, be (with αποθνησκω, Heb. 11:37)
slaughter

φορέω 789
bear
wear

φόρος 789
tribute

φορτίζω . . . 789
lade
laden, be heavy

φορτίον . . . 789
burden

φόρτος . . . 790
lading

φραγέλλιον . . 790
scourge

φραγελλόω . . 790
scourge

φραγμός . . . 790
hedge
hedge round about (with περιτιθημι)
hedged
partition

φράζω . . . 790
declare

φράσσω . . . 790
sto,

φρέαρ 790
pit
well

φρεναπατάω . . 790
deceive

φρεναπάτης . . 790
deceiver

φρένες 790
understanding

φρίσσω . . . 790
tremble

φρονέω . . . 790
affection on, set the
care
careful, be
likeminded, be (with αυτο)
mind
mind, be of one or the same (with αυτος)
mind, let this [be in you] (with τουτο, Phi. 2:5)
mind, of one (with εις, Phi. 2:2)
regardeth
savour
think
understand

φρόνημα . . . 790
mind
minded, to be
minded, be carnally (with σαρξ, Ro. 8:6)
minded, be spiritually (with πνευμα, Ro. 8:6)

φρόνησις . . . 790
prudence
wisdom

φρόνιμος . . . 790
wise
wiser

φρονίμως . . . 791
wisely

φροντίζω . . . 791
careful, be

φρουρέω . . . 791
garrison, keep with a
keep

φρυάσσω . . . 791
rage

φρύγανον . . . 791
stick

φυγή 791
flight

φυλακή . . . 791
cage
hold
imprisonment
prison
ward
watch

φυλακίζω . . . 791
imprison

φυλακτήριον . . 791
phylactery

φύλαξ 791
keeper

φυλάσσω . . . 791
beware
keep
keep self
observe
save

φυλή 791
kindred
tribe

φύλλον . . . 792
leaf

φύραμα . . . 792
lump

φυσικός . . . 792
natural

φυσικῶς . . . 792
naturally

φυσιόω . . . 792
puff up

φύσις 792
kind
*man*kind (with ανθρωπινος)
natur*al*
nature

φυσίωσις . . . 792
swellings

φυτεία . . . 792
plant

φυτεύω . . . 792
plant

φύω . . . 792
spring
spring up

φωλεός . . . 792
hole

φωνέω . 792
call
call for
crow
cry

φωνή 793
noise
noise (Acts 2:6)
sound
voice

φῶς 794
fire
light

φωστήρ . . . 794
light

φωσφόρος . . . 794
star, day

φωτεινός . . . 794
bright
light, full of

φωτίζω . . . 794
enlighten
illuminate
light
light, bring to
light, give (–lighten)
see, to make

φωτισμός . . . 795
light

χαίρω 795
farewell
glad, be
God speed
greeting
hail
joy
joyfully
rejoice

χάλαζα . . . 795
hail

χαλάω . . . 795
let down
strike

χαλεπός . . . 795
fierce
perilous

χαλιναγωγέω . 795
bridle

χαλινός . . . 795
bit
bridle

χάλκεος . . . 795
brass

χαλκεύς . . . 796
coppersmith

χαλκηδών . . 796
chalcedony

χαλκίον . . . 796
brasen vessel

χαλκολίβανον . 796
brass, fine

3 U

χαλκός . . . 796
brass
money

χαμαί . . . 796
ground, on the
ground, to the

χαρά 796
gladness
greatly
joy
joy*ful*
joyful, be exceeding
joyfully (with *μετα*, Heb. 10:34)
joyfulness
joyous (Heb. 12:11)

χάραγμα . . . 796
grave
mark

χαρακτήρ . . 796
express image

χάραξ . . . 796
trench

χαρίζομαι . . 796
deliver
forgive
frankly forgive
give
give, freely
grant

χάριν 797
because of
cause of, for
for sake of
... fore (Lu. 7:47)
reproachfully
*where*fore

χάρις 797
acceptable
benefit
favour
gift
grace
gracious
joy
liberality
pleasure
thank
thanks
thankworthy

χάρισμα . . . 798
free gift
gift

χαριτόω . . . 798
accepted, make
favoured, be highly

χάρτης . . . 798
paper

χάσμα . . . 798
gulf

χεῖλος . . . 798
lip
shore

χειμάζομαι . . 798
tempest, be tossed with a

χείμαῤῥος . 798
brook

χειμών . . . 798
tempest
weather, foul
winter

χείρ 798
hand

χειραγωγέω . . 800
hand, lead by the

χειραγωγός . . 800
hand, some to lead by the

χειρόγραφον . . 800
handwriting

χειροποίητος . . 800
hands, made by
hands, make with

χειροτονέω . . 800
choose
ordain

χείρων, χεῖρον . 800
sorer
worse (and worse)

χήρα 800
widow

χθές 800
yesterday

χιλιάδες . . . 800
thousand

χιλίαρχος . . 801
captain
captain, chief
captain, high

χίλιοι 801
thousand

χιτών 801
clothes
coat
garment

χιών . . . 801
snow

χλαμύς . . . 801
robe

χλευάζω . . . 801
mock

χλιαρός . . . 801
lukewarm

χλωρός . . . 801
green
pale

χοϊκός . . . 801
earthy

χοῖνιξ 801
measure

χοῖρος 801
swine

χολάω . . . 802
angry, be

χολή 802
gall

χόος 802
dust

χορηγεω . . . 802
give
minister

χορός . . . 802
dancing

χορτάζω . . . 802
feed
fill
satisfy

χόρτασμα . . 802
sustenance

χόρτος . . . 802
blade
grass
hay

χράομαι . . . 802
entreat
use

χραω . . . 802
lend

χρεία 802
business
lack
necessary
necessity
need
need (with *εχω*)
needful
use
want

χρεωφειλέτης . 803
debtor

χρή 803
ought

χρῄζω 803
need
need, have

χρῆμα . . . 803
money
riches

χρηματίζω . . 803
called, be
God, be admonished of
God, be warned of
reveal
speak

χρηματισμός . . 803
God, answer of

χρήσιμος . . 803
profit

χρῆσις . . . 803
use

χρηστεύομαι . . 803
kind, be

χρηστολογία . 803
good words

χρηστός . . 803
better
easy
good
goodness
gracious
kind

χρηστότης . . 803
gentleness
good
goodness
kindness

χρίω 803
anoint

χρίσμα . . 803
anointing
unction

χρονίζω . . . 803
delay
tarry (t. so long)

χρόνος . . . 804
oftentimes (Lu. 8:29)
old, full forty years (with *πληροω*, *τεσσαρακονταετης*, Acts 7:23)
season
space
time
while
while, a

χρονοτριβέω . . 804
spend time

χρύσεος . . . 804
gold, of
golden

χρυσίον . . . 804
gold

χρυσοδακτύλιος . 804
gold ring, with a

χρυσολιθος . . 804
chrysolite

χρυσόπρασος . . 804
chrysoprasus

χρυσός . . . 804
gold

χρυσόω . . 804
deck

likewise
manner, after the same
manner, in like

Ὡσαννά . . . 817
hosanna

ὠτίον 817
ear

ὠφέλεια . . . 817
advantage
profit

ὠφελέω . . . 817
advantage
better
prevail
profit

ὠφέλιμος . . . 817
profit
profit (with εστι, 1 Tim. 4:8)
profitable

Comparative Concordance of Various Readings

occuring in

THE GREEK NEW TESTAMENT

as adopted by

GRIESBACH, LACHMANN, TISCHENDORF, TREGELLES, ALFORD, WORDSWORTH, WESTCOTT AND HORT, AND "THE REVISERS"

compared
with the text of Stephens 1550
and the
Authorized Version of 1611

INTRODUCTION.

THIS Concordance of Various Readings is intended mainly as an Appendix to the ENGLISHMAN'S GREEK CONCORDANCE, but it can be used with any Greek Concordance, and is therefore sold separately. To this end the actual Greek words introduced by the various Editors are given, together with the change in English where needed.

It is imperative that every careful student of scripture should give attention to the various readings introduced by Editors of the Greek text. It is a matter of great thankfulness that these various readings do not touch any one of the fundamental doctrines of Christianity; but we want to know the actual words God caused to be written. For instance, all who have studied the subject acknowledge that there are words, &c., in the Authorised Version of 1611 that cannot be maintained, apart altogether from the question of translation. *What* is to be translated is the question raised where the Greek manuscripts differ. "Editors" are those who have devoted their time and energies to discover what the text was originally. We give the readings of several Editors, from Griesbach to the "Revisers" of 1881, and where they *all* agree, or all except Griesbach (seeing there has been so much additional valuable evidence since his day), we judge the reader will be safe in adopting that reading in preference to the one found in the Authorised Version, though of course some of the other well-accredited readings may be the true ones.

The following will explain the way in which the work has been carried out. Every person is supposed to have before him a copy of the Authorised English Version, and, if he wishes to refer to the Greek, a copy of the common Greek text.

Punctuation.—As the oldest Greek MSS have few or no points, Editors were compelled to punctuate for themselves: where they differ in this is more a matter of interpretation than a different reading. We therefore give only those where the Greek text is also altered.

Omissions.—Single words are recorded only under the word omitted. They are given in English where they affect the sense to an English reader. Where the word is required in English the omission is given in Greek.

Omissions of more than one word are recorded under every word omitted, *except* δέ, καί, τε, and ὁ, ἡ, τό, except Mark xvi. 9–20, and John vii. 53–viii. 11; these are recorded on the first page only, as "Lengthy Omissions."

Additions.—Single words are recorded only under the added word, English being given where needed.

Additions of more than one word are recorded under every word except δέ, καί, τε.

In all additions, the inflection used, and the place where the words are added, are pointed out.

New occurrences of words already in the common text are marked with a *.

New words introduced by the Editors are marked with a * in the heading.

Transpositions.—Transpositions which obviously affect the sense, or seem to give precedence to one word over another, are recorded under the words transposed—the new reading being given thus:

Luke 8: 51 *trs* John and James
1 Co. 1: 1 *trs* Christ Jesus

Transpositions which do not obviously affect the sense are given in Greek under one of the principal words. Passages where an alteration occurs as well as the transposition are marked with a †.

Inflections.—These are marked under their respective roots. The actual word adopted by the Editors is given, and English added where, but only where, the sense is materially affected by the alteration.

Substitution.—Where one word is substituted for another, it is given under both headings, thus:

δεύτερος.

Mat. 21:30 second—other, ἕτερος GTAW

ἕτερος.

Mat. 21:30* *ἑτέρῳ for δευτέρῳ (-ρος)* GTAW

Where δέ, καί, τε are interchanged, they are given only under the word that stands in the common text.

Where a pronoun is arranged under separate headings, immediately following one another, as αὐτά, αὐταῖς, αὐτή, &c., the interchange of such words is recorded only under the word in the common text.

The Article.—Changes in the article are recorded under the nouns, adjectives, infinitives and participles, with which they are connected. Other changes are under the heading ὁ, ἡ, τό.

Greek Text.—The Greek Text followed is that of Stephens 1550, but the differences between this and Elzevir 1624, are recorded.

Authorised Version.—The text of 1611 (but as at present printed) is taken, and where this differs materially from the text of Stephens 1550, it is recorded, and a text named which the Editors *probably* followed: in a few places a [?] is added where *no* authority can be traced. A † is added in a few cases where the A.V. as now printed differs from the version of 1611. Words in ( ) are those in italics in the A.V.

Editors.—The readings given (being variations from Stephens 1550) are those adopted by

Griesbach	G	1805
Lachmann	L	1842–50
Tischendorf	T	1865–72
Tregelles	Tr	1857–72
Alford	A	1862–71
Wordsworth	W	1870
Westcott & Hort	WH	1881
"The Revisers"	R	1881
Complutensian	C	1514
Erasmus	Er	1527
Beza	B	1598
Vulgate	Vul	592
Stephens	S	1550
Elzevir	E	1624

The marks [ ] imply that one or more Editors regard the reading as doubtful.

Readings marked doubtful by only *one* Editor are not recorded.

Readings adopted by G and L, unsupported by any of the more modern Editors, are not recorded.

Where all the Editors (except G) agree as to reading, it is marked Eds.

June, 1883.

VARIOUS READINGS.

LENGTHY OMISSIONS.

Mar. 16: 9-20 *omit the verses* T[A] [[WH]]
Joh. 7:53 *to* **8:11** placed by [A] at foot of page, by [[WH]] at end of Gospel; *omit* [G]LTTr[R]

1 A, ἄλφα LTTrAWWH.
Rev. 1:11 *omit* I am Alpha and Omega, the first and the last: and GEds

2 Ἀαρών.
Heb. 5: 4 ὁ Ἀ.—*omit* ὁ GEds

5 ἀββᾶ, ἀββα WH

6 Ἄβελ, Ἅ— WH.

9 Ἀβιληνή, Ἀβει— WH.

11 Ἀβραάμ, Ἁ— R.
Lu. 16:22 τοῦ Ἀ.—*omit* τοῦ GLTTrAWWH
23 τὸν Ἀ.—*omit* τὸν LTTrAWH
Heb. 7: 6 τὸν Ἀ.—*omit* τὸν LTTrAWHR

14* ἀγαθοεργέω, ἀγαθουργέω.
Acts 14:17*ἀγαθουργῶν *for* ἀγαθοποιῶν (-ιέω) Eds

15 ἀγαθοποιέω.
Mar. 3: 4 ἀγαθὸν ποιῆσαι T
Acts 14:17 ἀγαθουργέω Eds

16 ἀγαθοποιΐα.
1 Pet. 4:19 ἀγαθοποιΐαις LW

18 ἀγαθός.
Mat. 12:35 τὰ ἀ.—*omit* τὰ LTrWWHR
19:16 *omit* good[1] LTTrAWHR
17 τί με ἐρωτᾷς περὶ τοῦ ἀγαθοῦ; εἷς ἐστὶν ὁ ἀγαθός (ὁ θεός God W), *read* Why askest thou me concerning the good? One is good GEds
Mar. 3: 4*see* ἀγαθοποιέω
Ro. 10:15 τὰ ἀ.—*omit* τὰ LTrAWWHR
13: 3 τῷ ἀγαθῷ ἔργῳ to the good work Eds

See 14
ἀγαθουργέω, *see* ἀγαθοεργεω.

21 ἀγαλλιάω.
Joh. 5:35 ἀγαλλιαθῆναι GLTTrAWWH
Acts 16:34 ἠγαλλιᾶτο A
1 Pet. 1: 8 ἀγαλλιᾶτε WH
Rev. 19: 7 ἀγαλλιῶμεν LTTrAWHR

22 ἄγαμος.
1 Co. 7:34 *see* γυνή

25 ἀγαπάω.
Lu. 7:42 *trs* ἀγαπήσει αὐτόν LTTrAWH
Joh. 15: 9 *trs* ὑμᾶς ἠγάπησα LTrAWH
Ro. 13: 8 *trs* ἀλλήλους ἀ GLTTrAWWH
2 Co. 12:15 ἀ.[1]—ἀγαπῶ TWHR
1 Joh. 4:10 ἀ.[1]—ἠγαπήκαμεν WH
Jude 1*ἠγαπημένοις *for* ἡγιασμένοις (ἁγιάζω) Eds
Rev. 1: 5 ἀγαπῶντι loveth GEds

26 ἀγάπη.
Joh. 5:42 *trs* οὐκ ἔχετε τὴν ἀ. τοῦ θεοῦ T
1 Co. 13: 4 *omit* charity[3] [LTrA]WH
Eph. 1:15 *omit* love L[A]WHR
Phil. 1:17 *trs verses* 16 *and* 17 *except* οἱ μὲν *and* οἱ δὲ GEds
1 Pet. 4: 8 ἀ.[2] ἡ ἀγάπη EG
2 Pet. 2:13*ἀγάπαις *for* ἀπάταις (-τη) LTrR
Rev. 2:19 *trs* faith, and charity, and service Tr

27 ἀγαπητός.
Lu. 9:35 beloved—chosen, ἐκλέγω TTrAWHR
Philem. 2 beloved—sister, ἀδελφῇ LTTrAWHR
1 Joh. 2: 7*ἀγαπητοί *for* ἀδελφοί (-ός) GEds

28 Ἄγαρ, Ἅ— WH
Gal. 4:25 *omit* Agar LT[Tr]

30 ἀγγεῖον.
Mat. 13:48 ἄγγος TTrAWH

31 ἀγγελία.
1 Joh. 1: 5*ἀγγελία *for* ἐπαγγελία A.V.Vul GEds

* ἀγγέλλω, bring word.
Joh. 4:51 ἤγγειλαν *for* ἀπήγγειλαν (ἀπαγγέλλω) T
20:18 ἀγγέλλουσα *for* ἀπαγγέλλουσα (-λω) LTTrAWHR

32 ἄγγελος.
Mar. 13:32 οἱ ἄ.—ἄγγελος an angel A
Lu. 1:28 *omit* the angel [T]AWHR: *trs* πρὸς αὐτὴν ὁ ἄ. T
22:43, 44 *the verses* [L] [[WH]]
Joh. 5: 4 *omit* waiting for (*ver.* 3) *to end of verse* 4 [G]TTrAWHR
Acts 27:23 *trs* ἄγγελος *after* λατρεύω Eds
Rev. 8: 7 *omit* angel GEds
13 angel—eagle, ἀετός GEds
9:11 τὸν ἄ.—*omit* τὸν A
10: 8 τοῦ ἀγγέλου A.V.C GEds
11: 1 ῥάβδῳ—*add* καὶ ὁ ἄγγελος εἱστήκει and the angel stood A.V.B E
14: 9 *trs* ἄγγελος τρίτος GEds
16: 3 *omit* angel Eds
4, 8, 10, 12, 17 *omit* angel GEds

* ἄγγος, vessel, of various sorts.
Mat. 13:48 ἄγγη *for* ἀγγεῖα (-ῖον) TTrAWH

34 ἀγέλη.
Mat. 8:32 *omit* herd of[1] GLTTrWHR

37 ἁγιάζω.
Mat. 23:17 ἁγιάσας sanctified LTTrAWHR
1 Co. 1: 2 *trs* ἡγιασμένοις ἐν χριστῷ Ἰησοῦ τῇ οὔσῃ ἐν Κορίνθῳ LTrA
Jude 1 sanctified—beloved, ἀγαπάω Eds

40 ἅγιος, ἅγιον.
Mat. 25:31 *omit* holy GLTTrAWHR
Mar. 12:36 τῷ ἁ.—*omit* τῷ GW
Lu. 2:25 *trs* ἦν ἅγιον GEds
10:21*πνεύματι—*add* τῷ ἁγίῳ, *read* the Holy Spirit LTTrAWHR
Joh. 6:69*ὁ ἅγιος *for* ὁ χριστὸς ὁ υἱὸς GLTTrAWHR
7:39 *omit* Holy LT[TrA]WHR
Acts 3:21 τῶν ἁγίων GEds
4:25*add* ἁ. LTTrAWHR, *see* πατήρ
31†*trs* τοῦ ἁ. πνεύματος Eds
6: 3 *omit* Holy GLTTrAWHR
8:18 *omit* Holy T[Tr]AWH
9:13 *trs* τοῖς ἁ. σου ἐποίησεν LTTrAWH
Ro. 15:19*ἁγίου *for* θεοῦ (-ός) GLTr[A]W[WH]R
31 *trs* τοῖς ἁ. γένηται LTTrAWHR
1 Co. 2:13 *omit* Holy GEds
Eph. 3: 8 τῶν ἁ.—*omit* τῶν GEds
1 Th. 5:27 *omit* holy LTTrAWHR
Heb. 9: 2 ἁγία s—ἅγια A.V.B EGEds: ἅγια. ἁγίων. L (*sic*)
3 τὰ ἅγια τῶν ἁγίων Tr
24 *trs* εἰσῆλθεν ἅγια TTrAWH
2 Pet. 1:21 οἱ ἅ.—*omit* οἱ A.V.C GEds: holy men—*omit* holy TAWHR
1 Joh. 5: 7 *omit* in heaven *to* in earth (*ver.* 8) GEds
Jude 14 *trs* ἁγίαις μυριάσιν GEds
20 *trs* ἐποικοδομοῦντες ἑαυτοὺς τῇ ἁγιωτάτῃ ὑμῶν πίστει Eds
Rev. 3: 7 *trs* he that is true, he that is holy A
13: 7 *omit* And it was *to* overcome them L[WH]
14:10†*trs* ἀγγέλων (*omit* τῶν) ἁγίων LTTrWHR: *omit* holy A
15: 3 saints—nations ἐθνῶν GLTTrAW —ages, αἰών WHR
19: 8 *trs* τῶν ἁ. ἐστίν LTTrAWHR
22: 6 holy—spirits of the, πνεῦμα GEds
21*with (all GW)-*add* τῶν ἁγίων the saints GTrAWWHR

41 ἁγιότης.
2 Co. 1:12*ἁγιότητι *for* ἁπλότητι (-ης) LTTrAWHR

45 ἄγκυρα.
Acts 27:30 *trs* ἀγκύρας μελλόντων LTTrAWH

47 ἁγνεία, —νία WH.

50 ἀγνοέω.
1 Co. 14:38 ἀ.[2]—ἀγνοεῖται he is ignored LTWH

54 ἀγνότης.
2 Co. 11: 3*simplicity—*add* καὶ τῆς ἁγνότητος and purity LTrAW[WH]R

58 ἀγορά.
Mat. 11:16†*trs* καθημένοις ἐν ταῖς ἀ. TTrAWH

59 ἀγοράζω.
Mar. 11:15 τοὺς ἀγοράζοντας Eds
Lu. 19:45 *omit* therein and them that bought TTrAWHR
Joh. 6: 5 ἀγοράσωμεν Eds

67 Ἀγρίππας.
Acts 26: 7 *omit* Agrippa Eds

68 ἀγρός.
Mar. 11: 8*ἀγρῶν *for* δένδρων (-ρον) TTrAWHR
Lu. 9:12 τοὺς ἀ.—*omit* τοὺς T[Tr]AWHR
12:28†*trs* (*omit* τῷ) ἐν ἀ. τὸν χόρτον ὄντα σήμερον TAWHR: τὸν χ. σ ἐν ἀ. ὄντα LTr
17:31 τῷ ἀ.—*omit* τῷ TTrAWH
36 *add the verse* A.V.B E, *see* ἀφίημι

71 ἄγω.
Mat. 14: 6 γίνομαι LTTrAWHR
21: 2 ἄγετε LTrA
Mar. 11: 2, 7 φέρω TTrAWHR
13: 9 ἀχθήσεσθε *for* σταθήσεσθε (ἵστημι) A.V. Er
11 ἄγωσιν GEds
Lu. 21:12 ἀπάγω TTrAWHR
23: 1 ἤγαγον GEds
Joh. 18:13*ἤγαγον LTTrWHR *for* ἀπήγαγον (ἀπάγω), [ἀπ]ήγαγον A
Acts 5:26 ἦγεν TWH
13:23*ἤγαγεν *for* ἤγειρεν (ἐγείρω) GEds
17: 5 προάγω LTTrAWHR
22:24 εἰσάγω GLTTrAWWH

73 ἀγών.
2 Ti. 4: 7†*trs* τὸν καλὸν ἀγῶνα LTTrWH

74 ἀγωνία.
Lu. 22:43, 44 *the verses* [L] [[WH]]

75 ἀγωνίζομαι.
Joh. 18:36 *trs* οἱ ἐμοὶ ἠγωνίζοντο ἂν TrWH
1 Ti. 4:10*ἀγωνιζόμεθα *for* ὀνειδιζόμεθα (-ζω) LTTrWHR

78 Ἀδδί, Ἀδδεί TTrAWH.

79 ἀδελφή.
Mar. 3:32*σου[2]—*add* καὶ αἱ (*omit* αἱ W) ἀδελφαί σου and thy sisters LT[A]W
Philem. 2*ἀδελφῇ *for* ἀγαπητῇ (-τός) LTTrAWHR

80 ἀδελφός.
Mat. 12:47 *omit the verse* [T]WH

Mar. 3:31 *trs* his mother and his brethren GLTTrWWHR
Lu. 18:29 *trs* wife, or brethren, or parents TAWHR
Acts 1:15*ἀδελφῶν *for* μαθητῶν (-τής) Eds
15:23 *omit* καὶ οἱ, *read* elder brethren LTTrAWHR
20:32 *omit* brethren LTTrAWHR
28:17 *trs* ἐγώ, ἄνδρες ἀδελ. LTTrAWHR
Ro. 15:15 *omit* brethren LTTr[A]WHR
30 [brethren] AWH
1 Co. 7:14*ἀδελφῷ *for* ἀνδρί (ἀνήρ) Eds
8:11†*trs* ἐν τῇ σῇ γνώσει, ὁ ἀ. Eds
11: 2 *omit* brethren Eds
15:31*rejoicing—*add* ἀδελφοί brethren LTTrAWHR
2 Co. 8:18 *trs* τὸν ἀδελφὸν μετ' αὐτοῦ TR
Eph. 6:10 *omit* my brethren LTTrAWHR
Jas. 5: 9 *trs* ἀδελ. κατ' ἀλλήλων LTrAWHR
10†*trs* ἀ. (*omit* μου Eds) τῆς κακοπαθείας GEds
1 Joh. 2: 7 Brethren—Beloved, ἀγαπητός GEds
3:14 *omit* (his) brother Eds

86 ᾅδης.

Lu. 10:15 τοῦ ᾅδου TrAWH
Acts 2:27 ᾅδην LTTrAWWH
31 ᾅδην TWH
1 Co. 15:55 O grave—O death, θανατός LTTrAWHR
Rev. 1:18 *trs* of death and of hell GEds

90 ἀδιαφθορία.

Tit. 2: 7 ἀφθορία Eds

91 ἀδικέω.

Lu. 10:19 ἀδικήσῃ S—ἀδικήσει ELTTrAWH
Acts 25:10 ἠδίκηκα TTrWH
2 Pet. 2:13*ἀδικούμενοι *for* κομιούμενοι (κομίζω) WHR
Rev. 9: 4 ἀδικήσουσιν LTAWH

93 ἀδικία.

Mat. 23:25*ἀδικίας *for* ἀκρασίας (-ία) GW
Lu. 13:27 τῆς ἀ.—*omit* τῆς LTTrAWHR
2 Th. 2:10 τῆς ἀ.—*omit* τῆς Eds
Heb. 1: 9*ἀδικίαν *for* ἀνομίαν (-ία) T

98 * Ἀδμείν, *see* Ἀράμ.

Ἀδραμυντηνός, Ἁδραμυντηνός WH.

99 Ἀδρίας, Ἁ— WH.

102 ἀδύνατος.

Acts 14: 8 *trs* ἀδύνατος ἐν Λύστροις TWH

104 ἀεί.

Mar. 15: 8 *omit* ever TWHR
2 Pet. 1:12 *trs* ἀεὶ ὑμᾶς GTTrAWWHR

105 ἀετός.

Rev. 8:13*ἀετοῦ *for* ἀγγέλου (-ος) GEds

114 ἀθετέω.

Mar. 6:26 *trs* ἀθετῆσαι αὐτήν TTrAWH

* ἀθροίζω, to gather together.

Lu. 24:33 ἠθροισμένους *for* συνηθροισμένους (συναθροίζω) LTTrAWHR

121 ἀθῷος, ἀθῷος LTAWH.

Mat. 27: 4 innocent—just, δίκαιος WH

122 αἴγειος, —γιος WH.

125 Αἴγυπτος.

Acts 7:11 γῆν Α.—Αἴγυπτον LTTrAWHR
12 Αἴγυπτον Eds
18*ἕτερος—*add* ἐπ' Αἴγυπτον, *read* arose over Egypt LTTrWHR
36 (τῇ LTrWHR) Αἰγύπτῳ GLTTrAWH (R
13:17 Αἰγύπτου LTrWHR
Heb. 11:26 Αἰγύπτου GEds

127 αἰδώς.

Heb. 12:28 *omit* α. *see* δέος

129 αἷμα.

Mat. 23:35 τοῦ α.[1]—*omit* τοῦ W
Lu. 11:51 τοῦ α. *bis*—*omit* τοῦ LTTrAWH
22:43, 44 *the verses* [L] [[WH]]
Acts 17:26 *omit* blood LTTr[A]WHR
20:28†*trs* τοῦ αἵματος τοῦ ἰδίου GEds
21:25 τὸ α.—*omit* τὸ LTTr[A]WWHR

1 Co. 10:16 *trs* ἐστὶν τοῦ α. τοῦ χρ. TrWH
11:27 τοῦ αἵματος GEds
Col. 1:14 *omit* through his blood GEds
Heb. 2:14 *trs* of blood and flesh Eds
Rev. 16: 6 α.[1]—αἵματα T
18:24 αἵματα GTWR

134 αἰνέω.

Lu. 24:53 *omit* praising and [TrA]WHR

138 αἱρέομαι.

2 Th. 2:13 εἵλατο GLTTrAWWH

140 αἱρετίζω.

Mat. 12:18 ἡρέτισα Tr

142 αἴρω.

Mat. 22:13 *omit* take him away, and LTTrAWHR
Mar. 10:21 *omit* take up the cross [L]TTrWHR
13:15 *trs* τι ἆραι TrAWH
Joh. 10:18 ἦρεν took WH
16:22 ἀρεῖ shall take LTrAWH
19:38 ἦρεν—ἦραν T
1 Co. 5: 2*ἀρθῇ *for* ἐξαρθῇ (ἐξαίρω) GEds

146 αἰσχροκερδής.

1 Ti. 3: 3 *omit* not greedy of filthy lucre GEds

154 αἰτέω.

Mat. 7: 9 ἐὰν α.—αἰτήσει, of *read* whom his son shall ask LTTrAWHR
10 αἰτήσει LTTrAWHR
Mar. 6:24 αἰτήσωμαι Eds
15: 6 παραιτέομαι TWHR
Lu. 6:30 τῷ α.—*omit* τῷ [L]TWHR
11:12 αἰτήσῃ S—αἰτήσει ƎTTrAWHR
12:20*αἰτοῦσιν *for* ἀπαιτοῦσιν (-τέω) TrAWH
Joh. 15: 7 αἰτήσασθε ask Eds

157 αἰτίαμα, αἰτίωμα GEds

160 αἰφνίδιος.

Lu. 21:34 *trs* ἐπιστῇ ἐφ' ὑμᾶς αἰφ. (ἐφ—WH) TTrAWH

161 αἰχμαλωσία.

Rev. 13:10 *omit* leadeth into captivity Tr

162 αἰχμαλωτεύω.

2 Ti. 3: 6 αἰχμαλωτίζω GEds

163 αἰχμαλωτίζω.

2 Ti. 3: 6*αἰχμαλωτίζοντες *for* αἰχμαλωτεύοντες (-ύω) GEds

165 αἰών.

Mat. 6:13 *omit* For thine is *to end of verse* GEds
13:39 τοῦ α.—*omit* τοῦ LTTrAWHR
Mar. 11:14 *trs* εἰς τὸν αἰῶνα ἐκ σοῦ LTTrAWH
Lu. 1:70 τῶν ἀπ' α.—*omit* τῶν TTrAWHR
Ro. 16:27*αἰῶνας—*add* τῶν αἰώνων, *read* ever and ever LT
Gal. 1: 4†*trs* τοῦ αἰῶνος τοῦ ἐνεστῶτος LTTrAWHR
Eph. 6:12 *omit* world, *read* this darkness GEds
Heb. 1: 2 *trs* ἐποίησεν τοὺς αἰῶνας Eds
1 Pet. 1:23 *omit* for ever GEds
5:11 *omit* and ever (τῶν α.) WH
2 Pet. 2:17 *omit* for ever LTTrAWHR
Jude 13 τὸν α.—*omit* τὸν GEds
25*power—*add* πρὸ παντὸς τοῦ αἰῶνος before all time Eds
Rev. 1: 6 *omit* and ever (τῶν α.) AWH
5:14 *omit* him that liveth for ever and ever GEds
14:11 *trs* εἰς αἰῶνας αἰώνων ἀναβαίνει GEds
15: 3*αἰώνων *for* ἁγίων (ἅγιος) WHR

166 αἰώνιος.

1 Ti. 6:19 eternal—truly, ὄντως GEds

167 ἀκαθαρσία.

Eph. 5: 3 *trs* ἀκαθαρσία πᾶσα LTTrAWHR

168 ἀκαθάρτης.

Rev. 17: 4 filthiness—unclean things, ἀκάθαρτος GEds

169 ἀκάθαρτος.

Rev. 17: 4*τὰ ἀκάθαρτα *for* ἀκαθάρτητος (-θαρτης) GEds

180* ἀκατάπαυστος, insatiable.

2 Pet. 2:14 ἀκαταπάστους *for* ἀκαταπαύστους (ος) LWH

180 ἀκατάπαυστος.

2 Pet. 2:14 cannot cease—insatiable, ἀκατάπαστος LWH

182 ἀκατάστατος.

Jas. 3: 8*ἀκατάστατον *for* ἀκατάσχετον (-ος) Eds

183 ἀκατάσχετος.

Jas. 3: 8 unruly—restless, ἀκατάστατος Eds

184 Ἀκελδαμά, —άχ LA, Ἁκ—άχ WH, Ἀχ—άχ TTr.

190 ἀκολουθέω.

Mat. 9: 9 ἀ.[2]—ἠκολούθει T
19 ἠκολούθει LTTrAWH
Mar. 2:15 ἠκολούθουν TTrAWHR
3: 7 *trs* ἠ. *after* Ἰουδαίας T: ἠκολούθησεν LTrAWH
8:34*ἀκολουθεῖν *for* ἐλθεῖν (ἔρχομαι) GTTrAW
9:38 *omit* and he followeth not us GWHR
38 ἀ.[2]—ἠκολούθει followed TWHR
10:28 ἠκολουθήκαμεν Eds
32 καὶ ἀ.—οἱ δὲ ἀ. TTrWHR
14:51 followed—followed with, συνακολουθέω LTTrAWHR: ἠκολούθησεν W
16:17*τrs ἀκολουθήσει (*for* παρακολουθήσει, -θέω) ταῦτα TrWH
Lu. 5:28 ἠκολούθει LTTrAWHR
Joh. 10: 5 ἀκολουθήσουσιν Eds
13:36 *trs* ἀ.[2] δὲ ὕστερον LTTrAWHR
37 ἀκολουθεῖν TrWH
21:22 *trs* μοι ἀκολούθει LTTrAWWH
Rev. 6: 8 ἠκολούθει GEds
18: 5 followed—have reached, κολλάω A.V.C GEds

191 ἀκούω.

Mat. 11:15 *omit* to hear T[Tr]AWH
13: 9 *omit* to hear T[Tr]AWHR
16 ἀκούουσιν LTTrAWH
43 *omit* to hear [L]T[Tr]AWHR
17: 5 *trs* ἀκούετε αὐτοῦ LTTrAWH
22: 7 *omit* ἀ. *read* But the king was wroth TTrAWHR
Mar. 3: 8 ἀκούοντες hearing LTTrAWHR
4:18 ἀκούσαντες heard TTrAWHR
24 *omit* that hear GLTTrAWHR
5:36 heard—disregarded, παρακούω TTrAWHR
7:14 ἀκούσατε LTTrAWH
16 *omit the verse* T[TrA]WHR
9: 7 *trs* ἀκούετε αὐτοῦ LTTrAWH
13: 7 ἀκούετε ye hear Tr
Lu. 5: 1 τοῦ ἀ.—*omit* τοῦ TTrAWHR
8:12 ἀκούσαντες heard TTrAWHR
14:35 *omit* to hear T
Joh. 5:25[1] 28 ἀκούσουσιν TTrWH
37 *trs* πώποτε ἀκηκόατε Eds
8:38*ἠκούσατε *for* ἑωράκατε (ὁράω) LTTrAWHR
10:27 ἀκούουσιν TrAWH
12:18 ἤκουσαν GEds
16:13 ἀκούσει TrAR: ἀκούει TWH
Acts 2: 6 ἤκουσεν WH
7:37 *omit* him shall ye hear LTTrA (WHR
9:13 ἤκουσα LTTrAWHR
14: 9 ἤκουσεν LTTr
24:22 *omit* when heard these things GEds
Ro. 10:14 ἀ.[2]—ἀκούσονται T: ἀκούσωσιν LTrAWWHR
Phil. 1:27 ἀκούω LTTrWH
2 Ti. 4:17 ἀκούσωσιν LTTrAWWH
Rev. 22: 8 *trs* ἀκούων καὶ βλέπων ταῦτα GLTrAWWHR: βλ. καὶ ἀ. ταῦ. T
18 τῷ ἀκούοντι GEds

192 ἀκρασία.

Mat. 23:25 excess—unrighteousness, ἀδικία GW

199 ἀκριβῶς.

Eph. 5:15 *trs* ἀκριβῶς πῶς TWHR

202 ἀκροατής.

Jas. 1:22 *trs* ἀκροαταὶ μόνον LTrAWWH

203 ἀκροβυστία.
Ro. 4:12 τῇ ἀ.—*omit* τῇ GEds

206 ἄκρον.
Mat. 24:31 τῶν ἄκρων Tr, [τῶν] ἀ. WH

207 Ἀκύλας.
Acts 18:26 *trs* Priscilla and Aquila LTTrAWHR

* ἅλα, salt.
Mat. 5:13 ἅλα *for* ἅλας *bis* T (*sic*)
Mar. 9:50 ἅλα *for* ἅλας *ter* T
Lu. 14:34 ἅλα *for* ἅλας *bis* T

211 ἀλάβαστρον.
Mar. 14: 3 τὸν ἀ.[2] LTW, τὴν ἀ. TrAWH

212 ἀλαζονεία, –νία TWH

216 ἅλαλος.
Mar. 7:37 τοὺς ἀ.—*omit* τοὺς TTrAWHR

217 ἅλας.
Mat. 5:13 ἅλα *bis* T (*sic*)
Mar. 9:50 ἅλα *ter* T: ἅ.[3]—ἅλς LTrAWH
Lu. 14:34 ἅλα *bis* T

See 231
ἀλεεύς, *see* ἁλιεύς.

220 ἀλέκτωρ.
Mar. 14:68 *omit* and the cock crew [L]WH
Lu. 22:60 ὁ ἀ.—*omit* ὁ GEds

223 Ἀλέξανδρος.
Acts 4: 6 Ἀλέξανδρος LTTrAWHR

225 ἀλήθεια.
Joh. 16:13†*trs* εἰς τὴν ἀλήθειαν πᾶσαν LTrAWH, ἐν τῇ ἀληθείᾳ πάσῃ T
Gal. 3: 1 *omit* that ye should not obey the truth GEds
5: 7 τῇ ἀ.—*omit* τῇ TTr[A]WH
Jas. 3:14†*trs* glory not against the truth and lie T
3 Joh. 4 τῇ ἀληθείᾳ Eds

227 ἀληθής.
Joh. 6:55*ἀληθής *for* ἀληθῶς *bis* LTTrAWHR
8:16 ἀληθινός LTTrAWH

228 ἀληθινός.
Joh. 4:37 ὁ ἀ.—*omit* ὁ TTr[A]WHR
8:16*ἀληθινή *for* ἀληθής LTTrAWH
Rev. 3: 7 *trs* he that is true, he that is holy A
6:10 ὁ ἀ.—*omit* ὁ GEds
19: 9 οἱ ἀληθινοί LAW
21: 5 *trs* faithful and true GEds

230 ἀληθῶς.
Joh. 6:55 ἀληθής *bis* LTTrAWHR
7:26 *omit* very GEds
1 Th. 2:13 *trs* ἀληθῶς ἐστὶν WH

231 ἁλιεύς.
Mat. 4:18, 19 ἁλεεῖς WH
Mar. 1:16, 17 ἁλεεῖς TAWH
Lu. 5: 2 ἁλεεῖς TWH

233 ἁλίζω.
Mar. 9:49 *omit* and every sacrifice shall be salted with salt T[Tr]WHR

235 ἀλλά.
Mar. 2:22 *omit* but new *to end of verse* T[Tr]A[WH], *see* βλητέος
3:27*add *at commencement* ἀ. but TTrAWHR
6:52*ἦν γὰρ—ἀ. ἦν TTrWHR
7:25*ἀκούσασα γὰρ—ἀλλ' εὐθὺς ἀκ. TTrAWHR
9: 8 εἰ μὴ LWHR
Lu. 4: 4 *omit* but by every word of God T[Tr]AWHR
9:56 *omit* For the Son *to* save (them) GLTTrAWHR
11: 4 *omit* but deliver us from evil GTTrAWHR
Joh. 3:15 *omit* should not perish, but [L]TTrAWHR
6:23**for* ἄλλα δὲ WHR
9: 9*add ἀ. [L]TTrAWHR, *see* λέγω
11:22 *omit* But [L]TTrAWHR
Joh. 16:25 *omit* but[1] G[L]TTrAWWHR A.V.†Er
Acts 9: 6*ἀλλὰ ἀνάστηθι but arise GEds
10:20 *itaque* A.V. Vul
Ro. 8: 1 *omit* who walk *to end of ver.* GEds
12:20*ἀ. ἐὰν *for* ἐὰν οὖν LTTrAWHR
1 Co. 3: 5 *omit* but GEds
8: 6 [but] LWH
Phi. 3: 7 *omit* but [L]T[A]
1 Pet. 3:15*ἀλλὰ μετὰ but with Eds
Rev. 2: 9 πλούσιος δὲ—ἀ. πλ. GEds
3: 4*add at commencement ἀ. But GEds

236 ἀλλάττω, –άσσω.
Heb. 1:12*ἀλλάξεις *for* ἑλίξεις (–ίσσω) T

* ἀλλαχοῦ, elsewhere.
Mar. 1:38 let us go—*add* ἀλλαχοῦ elsewhere TTrAWHR

239 ἀλληλούϊα, ἀλληλουιά WH

240 ἀλλήλων.
Lu. 20:14*ἀλλήλους *for* ἑαυτούς TTrAWHR
Acts 2: 7 *omit* one to another LTTrAWHR
28: 4 *trs* πρὸς ἀ. ἔλεγον LTTrAWH
Gal. 5:17 *trs* ἀλλήλοις ἀντίκειται GEds

242 ἅλλομαι.
Acts 14:10 ἥλατο GEds

243 ἄλλος.
Mat. 10:23 another—the next, ἕτερος GLTTrWHR
Mar. 3: 5 *omit* whole as the other GEds
4: 8 ἄλλα others TAWHR
18*ἄλλοι *for* οὗτοι GEds
7: 8 *omit* (as) the washing *to end of verse* T[TrA]WHR
10:12 γαμήσῃ ἄλλον LTTrAWHR
14:19 *omit* and another (said, Is) it I? TTrWHR
Lu. 6:10 *om.* as the other [L]T[Tr]AWHR
7:19 ἕτερος TrWH
Joh. 6:23 ἄλλα δὲ—ἀλλά (*om.* other) WHR
7:41 some (ἄ.[2])—they, οἱ LTrAWHR
18:15 ὁ ἄ.—*om.* ὁ A.V.Er LT[Tr A]WHR
21:25 *omit the verse* T
Rev. 14: 9*καὶ—*add* ἄλλος, *read* another a third angel GEds
16: 7 *omit* another out of GEds
18: 1*I saw—*add* ἄλλον another A.V.C GEds

244 ἀλλοτριοεπίσκοπος, ἀλλοτριε– LTTrWH.

251 ἅλς.
Mar. 9:49 *omit* and every sacrifice shall be salted with salt T[Tr]WHR
50*ἅλα *for* ἅλας[3] LTrAWH

254 ἅλυσις.
Mar. 5: 3 ἁλύσει a chain LTTrAWHR

See 1
ἄλφα, *see* A.

256 Ἀλφαῖος, Ἁλφαῖος WH.
Lu. 6:15 τὸν τοῦ Ἀ.—*omit* τὸν τοῦ TTrAWHR

264 ἁμαρτάνω.
Lu. 17: 4 ἁμαρτήσῃ LTTrAWWH
Ro. 6:15 ἁμαρτήσωμεν Eds

265 ἁμάρτημα.
Mar. 3:28 *trs* τοῖς υἱοῖς τῶν ἀνθ. τὰ ἁ. GEds
29*ἁμαρτήματος *for* κρίσεως (–σις) LTTrAWHR
4:12 *omit* (their) sins, *read* it [L]TTrAWHR
2 Pet. 1: 9*ἁμαρτημάτων *for* ἁμαρτιῶν (–ία) GTTr

266 ἁμαρτία.
Mat. 9: 2 *trs* σου αἱ ἁμαρτίαι LTTrAWHR
Mar. 2: 5 *trs* σου αἱ ἁμαρτίαι GTTrAWHR
10 *trs* ἁμαρτίας ἐπὶ τῆς γῆς WH
Lu. 5:21 *trs* ἁμαρτίας ἀφεῖναι LTTrAWH
7:47†*trs* αὐτῇ (αὐτῆς T) αἱ ἁμαρτίαι LT
Acts 2:38 τῶν ἁμαρτιῶν ὑμῶν LTTrWHR
7:60 *trs* ταύτην τὴν ἁ. LTrAWWH
Col. 2:11 *omit* of the sins GEds
2 Th. 2: 3 sin—lawlessness, ἀνομία TTrWH
Heb. 1: 3 *trs* τῶν ἁ. ποιησ. LTTrAWHR
9:26 τῆς ἁμαρτίας LTTrWH
13:11 *omit* for sin LA
Jas. 5:16*τὰς ἁμαρτίας *for* τὰ παραπτώματα (–μα) LTTrWHR
1 Pet. 4: 1 ἁμαρτίαις WH
2 Pet. 1: 9 ἁμάρτημα GTTr

268 ἁμαρτωλός.
Mar. 2:16 *trs* sinners and publicans[1] LTrAWHR
16†*trs* (*add* τῶν) sinners and publicans[2] LTr
Lu. 5:30 *omit* and sinners A
6:34 οἱ ἁ.—*omit* οἱ LTTrAWHR
Joh. 9:31 *trs* ὁ θεὸς ἁμαρτωλῶν LTrAWH
1 Pet. 4:18 ὁ ἁμαρτωλὸς T
Rev. 21: 8*unbelieving—*add* καὶ ἁμαρτωλοῖς and sinners W

272 ἀμελέω.
2 Pet. 1:12 I will not be negligent—I will take care, μελλήσω Eds

281 ἀμήν.
Mat. 6:13 *omit* For thine *to end of verse* GEds
18:19*ἀμὴν ([ἀ.]WH) λέγω verily I say LTrAWH
28:20 *omit* Amen GLTTrAWHR
Mar. 6:11 *omit* verily *to end of verse* G[L]TTrAWHR
16:20 *omit* Amen EGLTrAWWH
Lu. 13:35 *omit* Verily GEds
24:53 *omit* Amen G[L]TTrAWHR
Joh. 21:25 *omit the verse* T: *omit* Amen GLTTrAWHR
Ro. 15:33 [Amen] LTr
16:20 *add* Amen A.V.B E
24 *omit the verse* LTTr[A]WHR
1 Co. 16:24 *omit* Amen [L]TTr[A]WH
2 Co. 13:14(13) *omit* Amen GEds
Eph. 6:24 *om.* Amen A.V.†LatGLTTrAWHR
Phi. 4:23 *omit* Amen [L]TTr[A]WHR
Col. 4:18 *omit* Amen GEds
1 Th. 3:13*add at end Amen [L]T
5:28 *omit* Amen GEds
2 Th. 3:18 *omit* Amen TTrAWHR
1 Ti. 6:21 *omit* Amen GEds
2 Ti. 4:22 *omit* Amen GEds
Tit. 3:15 *omit* Amen G[L]TTrAWWHR
Philem. 25 *omit* Amen GLTTrAWWH
Heb. 13:25 *omit* Amen TWH
1 Pet. 5:14 *omit* Amen GLTTrAWHR
2 Pet. 3:18 *omit* Amen T[TrA]WH
1 Joh. 5:21 *omit* Amen GEds
2 Joh. 13 *omit* Amen GEds
Rev. 1:18 *omit* Amen GEds
5:14 τὸ ἀμήν W
7:12 *omit* Amen[2] L[WH]
22:21 *omit* Amen GLTTrAWH

284 Ἀμιναδάβ, Ἀμει– A.
Lu. 3:33 *omit* of Aminadab WH

285 ἄμμος.
Heb. 11:12 ἡ ἄμμος GEds

288 ἄμπελος.
Rev. 14:18*clusters—*add* τῆς ἀμπέλου of the vine A.V.B EGEds

290 ἀμπελών.
Lu. 13: 6 *trs* πεφ. ἐν τῷ ἀ. αὐτοῦ LTTrAWHR

291 Ἀμπλίας, –ιᾶτος TTrA, –ιᾶτος WHR.

* ἀμφιάζω, –έζω TTrA, to put on, clothe.
Lu. 12:28 ἀμφιά(έ)ζει *for* ἀμφιέννυσιν (–νυμι) LTTrAWH

* ἀμφιβάλλω, to cast around.
Mar. 1:16 ἀμφιβάλλοντας *for* βάλλοντας (–λω) GEds

293 ἀμφίβληστρον.
Mar. 1:16 *omit* a net TTrAWHR

294 ἀμφιέννυμι.
Lu. 12:28 ἀμφιά(έ)ζω LTTrAWH

297 ἀμφότεροι.
Mat. 9:17 ἀμφότεροι GLTTrAWWH

297

Lu. 5:38 *omit* and both are preserved T[Tr]AWHR
Acts 19:16*ἀμφοτέρων *for* αὐτῶν Eds

298 ἀμώμητος.
Phi. 2:15 ἄμωμος LTTrAWHR

* ἄμωμον, an Indian spice plant.
Rev. 18:13 cinnamon—*add* καὶ ἄμωμον and amomum GEds

299 ἄμωμος.
Phi. 2:15*ἄμωμα *for* ἀμώμητα (–τος) LTTrAWHR

300 Ἀμών, Ἀμώς LTTrAWHR.

302 ἄν.
(for ὃς ἄν see ὅς.)
Mat. 6: 5*omit ἄν LTTrAWWH
7:12 ἐάν TWH
10:23 *omit* ἄν TAWH
33 *omit* ἄν LTrAWH
12:32 ἄν[1]—ἐάν LTTrAWWH
16:25 ἄν[1]—ἐάν LTTrAWH
21:22 ἐάν Tr
44 *omit the verse* [L]T[WH]
22: 9 ἐάν LTTrAWWH
23: 3 ἐάν TWWH
26:48 ἐάν TA
Mar. 3:28 ἐάν TrAWH
4:25 ἄν ἔχῃ—ἔχει LTTrAWHR
6:56 ἄν[1]—ἐάν T
8:35 ἄν[1]—ἐάν TTrAWH
38 ἐάν LTTrAWH
9:18 ἐάν LTTrAWH
10:44 ἐάν GTrA
11:24 *omit* ἄν Eds
14: 9 ἐάν TAWH
Lu. 2:26*ἢ—ἢ ἄν T, ἄν Tr, [ἢ] ἄν WH
9:24 ἄν[1]—ἐάν T
57 ἐάν LTrA
12:39 *omit* he would have watched, and T: *omit* ἄν[2] TrAWHR
13:35 *omit* ἄν TTrAWHR
15:26*ἄν εἴη TrWHR, [ἄν] εἴη LA
18:36*[ἄν] εἴη LTr
Joh. 8:39 *omit* ἄν GTTrAWHR
13:24 *see* λέγω
14: 7 *omit* ἄν T
16:13 *omit* ἄν LTTrAWHR
Acts 2:12 *omit* ἄν LTTrWHR
21 ἐάν TrAWH
3:23 ἐάν TA
8:19 ἐάν EGLTTrAWWH
17:20 *omit* ἄν LTTrWHR
21:33 *omit* ἄν LTTr[A]WWHR
1 Co. 11:25 ἐάν LTTrAWH
26 ἄν[1]—ἐάν LTTrAWH: *omit* ἄν[2] GLTTrAWH
15:25 *omit* ἄν Eds
16: 2 ἐάν TrWH
2 Co. 3:15*ἄν ἀναγινώσκηται LTTrAWHR
16 ἐάν TWH
Gal. 3:19*for οὗ (ὅς) WH
4:15 *omit* ἄν Eds
5:10 ἐάν TTrAWH
17 ἐάν [L]TTrAWH
Col. 3:17 ἐάν LTrWH
1 Th. 2: 7 ἐάν LTTrAWH
Jas. 3: 4 *omit* ἄν TTrWHR
4: 4 ἐάν LTWH
5: 7 *omit* ἄν TTrAWHR
1 Joh. 4:15 ἐάν WH
5:15 ἐάν TWH
Rev. 13:15 ἐάν LTTrAWHR
See also ἐάν.

303 ἀνά, apiece.
Mat. 20:10†*trs* τὸ ([τὸ]AWH) ἀ. δηνάριον καὶ αὐτοί TTrAWH
Mar. 6:40 κατά *bis* LTTrAWH
Lu. 9: 3 *omit* apiece [TrA]WHR

305 ἀναβαίνω.
Mat. 14:32*ἀναβάντων *for* ἐμβάντων (–αίνω) LTTrAWHR
15:39*ἀνέβη *f.* ἐνέβη (ἐμβαίνω) GTrAW
20:17 καὶ ἀ.—μέλλων δὲ ἀναβαίνειν, *read* Jesus being about to go up WH
Mar. 15: 8*ἀναβὰς *for* ἀναβοήσας (–οάω) LTTrAWHR
Lu. 2:42 ἀναβαινόντων LTTrAWHR
Joh. 7:10 *trs* εἰς τὴν ἑορτήν, τότε καὶ αὐτὸς ἀ. LTTrAWHR
21: 3 ἐμβαίνω GEds
Acts 1:13 *trs* εἰς τὸ ὑπερῷον ἀνέβησαν LTTrAWHR
21: 4 ἐπιβαίνω LTTrAWHR
6*ἀνέβημεν *for* ἐπέβημεν (ἐπιβαίνω) TAW
Rev. 7: 2 ἀναβαίνοντα A.V.C GEds
11:12 ἀ.[1]—ἀνάβατε Eds

306 ἀναβάλλομαι.
Acts 24:22†*trs* ἀ. δὲ αὐτοὺς ὁ Φῆλιξ GEds

308 ἀναβλέπω.
Mar. 8:25 *see* διαβλέπω

310 ἀναβοάω.
Mat. 27:46 βοάω TrWH
Mar. 15: 8 crying aloud—coming up, ἀναβαίνω LTTrAWHR
Lu. 9:38 βοάω LTTrAWHR

*ἀνάγαιον, *see* ἀνώγεον.

312 ἀναγγέλλω.
Mat. 28:11*ἀνήγγειλαν *for* ἀπήγγειλαν (ἀπαγγέλλω) T
Mar. 5:14 ἀπαγγέλλω GEds
19 ἀπαγγέλλω Eds
Joh. 5:15 εἶπον TWH
16:25 ἀπαγγέλλω Eds
Acts 14:27 ἀνήγγελλον LTTrAWHR
16:38 ἀπαγγέλλω Eds

314 ἀναγινώσκω.
2 Co. 3:15 ἂν ἀναγινώσκηται LTTrAWHR
Rev. 5: 4 *omit* and to read GEds

318 ἀνάγκη.
Lu. 23:17 *omit the verse* [L]TTr[A]WHR
1 Th. 3: 7 *trs* distress and affliction Eds

319 ἀναγνωρίζομαι.
Acts 7:13 γνωρίζω TrWH

321 ἀνάγω.
Lu. 22:66 led—led away, ἀπάγω TTrAWHR

326 ἀναζάω.
Lu. 15:32 is alive again—is alive, ζάω, TTrAWHR
Ro. 14: 9 revived—lived, ζάω GEds
Rev. 20: 5 lived again—lived, ζάω GEds

327 ἀναζητέω.
Lu. 2:45*ἀναζητοῦντες *for* ζητοῦντες (ζητέω) LTTrAWHR

331 ἀνάθεμα.
Lu. 21: 5*ἀναθέμασιν *for* ἀναθήμασιν (–μα) LT
Ro. 9: 3 *trs* ἀνάθεμα εἶναι αὐτὸς ἐγὼ Eds

334 ἀνάθημα.
Lu. 21: 5 ἀνάθεμα LT

335 ἀναίδεια, –δία TWH.

336 ἀναίρεσις.
Acts 22:20 *omit* unto his death GEds

337 ἀναιρέω.
Acts 2:23 ἀνείλατε GLTTrAWWH
7:21 ἀνείλατο GLTTrAWWH
9:29 *trs* ἀνελεῖν αὐτόν LTTrAWWH
10:39 ἀνεῖλαν LTTrAWH
2 Th. 2: 8*ἀνελεῖ *for* ἀναλώσει (–λίσκω) LTTrAWHR

345 ἀνάκειμαι.
Mar. 5:40 *omit* lying G[L]TTrAWHR
6:26*ἀνακειμένους *for* συνανακειμένους (–μαι) TTrAWHR
Lu. 7:37 κατάκειμαι LTTrAWHR
Joh. 12: 2*ἀνακειμένων σὺν *for* συνανακειμένων (–μαι) GEds

347 ἀνακλίνω.
Mar. 6:39 ἀνακλιθῆναι LWHR
Lu. 7:36 κατακλίνω LTTrAWHR
9:15 κατακλίνω TTrWHR

348 ἀνακόπτω.
Gal. 5: 7 ἐγκόπτω GEds

349 ἀνακράζω.
Lu. 23:18 ἀνέκραγον TTrAWH

350 ἀνακρίνω.
Acts 17:11 *omit* τὸ LTTr[WH]

* ἀνακυλίω, to roll up or away.
Mar. 16: 4 ἀνακεκύλισται *for* ἀποκεκύλισται (ἀποκυλίω) TTrAWHR

352 ἀνακύπτω.
Joh. 8: 7 ἀνέκυψεν καὶ WH

353 ἀναλαμβάνω.
ἀνελήμφθη *for* –λήφθη LTTrAWH
ἀναλημφθεὶς *for* –ηφθεὶς LTTrAWH

354 ἀνάληψις, –λημψις LTTrAWH.

355 ἀναλίσκω.
2 Th. 2: 8 shall consume—will slay, ἀναιρέω LTTrAWHR

360 ἀναλύω.
Lu. 12:36 ἀναλύσῃ LTTrAWHR

367 Ἀνανίας, Ἀ– WH.
Acts 5: 5 ὁ Ἀνανίας GLTTrAWWH
9:12 *trs* Ἀνανίαν ὀνόματι LTTrAWHR
13 ὁ Ἀ.—*omit* ὁ GLTTrAWWH

368 ἀναντιρρήτως, –τιρήτως WH.

370 ἀναξίως.
1 Co. 11:29 *omit* unworthily LTTrAWHR

373 ἀναπαύω.
Mar. 6:31 ἀναπαύσασθε TTrAWHR
Rev. 6:11 ἀναπαύσονται WH
14:13 ἀναπαήσονται LTTrAWHR, ἀναπαύσονται W

374 ἀναπείθω.
Acts 18:13 *trs* ἀναπείθει οὗτος Eds

ἀνάπειρος, *see* ἀνάπηρος. See 376

375 ἀναπέμπω.
Lu. 23:15†*trs* ἀνέπεμψεν γαρ αὐτὸν πρὸς ἡμᾶς, for he sent him back to us TWHR
Acts 25:21*ἀναπέμψω *for* πέμψω (–μπω) Eds

* ἀναπηδάω, to leap, spring up.
Mar. 10:50 ἀναπηδήσας *for* ἀναστὰς (ἀνίστημι) Eds

376 ἀνάπηρος, ἀνάπειρος LTrAWH

377 ἀναπίπτω.
Mar. 6:40 ἀνέπεσαν TTrAWH
Lu. 14:10 ἀνάπεσε LTTrAWWH
17: 7 ἀνάπεσε Eds
Joh. 6:10 ἀ.[2]—ἀνέπεσαν LTTrAWH
13:12 ἀνέπεσεν TTrAWHR
25*ἀναπεσὼν *for* ἐπιπεσὼν (–πιπτω) LTrAWHR

378 ἀναπληρόω.
Gal. 6: 2 ἀναπληρώσετε ye shall fulfil LT

380 ἀναπτύσσω.
Lu. 4:17 ἀνοίγω LTrWHR

381 ἀνάπτω.
Acts 28: 2 ἅπτω LTTrAWWH

385 ἀνασπάω.
Acts 11:10 *trs* ἀνεσπάσθη πάλιν LTTrAWH

386 ἀνάστασις.
Mat. 22:28 *trs* ἀναστάσει οὖν LTTrAWHR
2 Ti. 2:18 τὴν ἀ. —*omit* τὴν TTr[A]WH

390 ἀναστρέφω.
Mat. 17:22 they abode—they abode together, συστρέφω LTTrWH
Joh. 2:15 ἀνατρέπω WH

393 ἀνατέλλω.
Mar. 4: 6 ἡλίου δὲ ἀνατείλαντος—καὶ ὅτε ἀνέτειλεν ὁ ἥλιος LTTrAWHR

395 ἀνατολή.

Rev. 16:12 ἀνατολῆς TTrAWH
21:13 ἀνατολῶν GW

396 ἀνατρέπω.

Joh. 2:15*ἀνέτρεψεν for ἀνέστρεψεν (ἀναστρέφω) WH

397 ἀνατρέφω.

Lu. 4:16*ἀνατεθραμμένος for τεθραμμένος (τρέφω) T

398 ἀναφαίνομαι.

Acts 21: 3 ἀναφάναντες S—ἀναφανέντες EGLTrAW

399 ἀναφέρω.

Lu. 24:51 omit and carried up into heaven T[[WH]]
Heb. 7:27 offered up-offered, προσφέρω T

402 ἀναχωρέω.

Joh. 6:15 departed—escapeth, φεύγω T

414 ἀνεκτός, ἀνεκτότερος.

Mar. 6:11 omit Verily to end of verse G[L]TTrAWHR

ἀνέλεος, see ἀνίλεως.

417 ἄνεμος. See 448

Jas. 3: 4 trs ἀνέμων σκληρῶν LTTrAWWH
Rev. 6:13 trs ἀνέμου μεγάλου GLTTrAWWH

419
ανεξερεύνητος, —ραύνητος TTrAWH.

423
ἀνεπίληπτος, —λημπτος LTTrAWH.

424 ἀνέρχομαι.

Gal. 1:17 went I up—went I, ἀπέρχομαι LA

429 ἀνευρίσκω.

Lu. 2:16 ανεῦραν TTrWH

430 ἀνέχομαι.

Acts 18:14 ἀνεσχόμην LTTrWH
2 Co. 11: 1 ἀνείχεσθε S—ἠνείχεσθε E
4 ἀνείχεσθε GTTrW, ἀνέχεσθε LAWHR

433 ἀνήκω.

Eph. 5: 4 τὰ οὐκ ἀ.—ἃ οὐκ ἀνῆκεν LTTrAWH

435 ἀνήρ.

Lu. 2:36 trs μετὰ ἀνδρὸς ἔτη LTTrWH
6: 8*ἀνδρὶ for ἀνθρώπῳ (—πος) TTrAWH
24: 4 trs ἄνδρες δύο GLTTrAWWH
Joh. 4:16 trs σου τὸν ἄνδρα AWH
17 trs ἄνδρα οὐκ ἔχω[1] T
Acts 10: 5 trs ἄνδρας εἰς Ἰόππην Eds
11:13 omit men GEds
13: 6*found—add ἄνδρα a man Eds
17: 5 trs ἄνδρας τινὰς LTrAWWH
1 Co. 7:13*τὸν ἄνδρα for αὐτόν Eds
14 husband[2]—brother, ἀδελφός Eds
11:11 trs the woman without the man, neither the man without the woman GEds
Eph. 5:23 ὁ ἀ.—omit ὁ GEds
28 trs οἱ ἄνδρες ὀφείλουσιν LW

436 ἀνθίστημι.

Lu. 21:15†trs LTTrAWHR, see ἀντέπω
2 Ti. 4:15 ἀντέστη Eds

442 ἀνθρώπινος.

Acts 17:25*ἀνθρωπίνων for ἀνθρώπων (—πος) LTTrAWHR
1 Co. 2: 4 omit man's GEds

444 ἄνθρωπος.

Mat. 4: 4 ὁ ἄνθρωπος Eds
9:32 omit ἄνθρωπον L[TrA]WHR
12:31 omit unto men[2] LTTr[A]WHR
13:45 omit man WH
18:11 omit the verse LTTr[A]WHR
19: 3 omit for a man LTAWHR
25:13 omit wherein the Son of man cometh GLTTrAWHR
Mar. 7:15*trs ἐκ τοῦ ἀνθρώπου (for ἀπ' αὐτοῦ) ἐκπορευόμενα LTTrAWHR
8:36 τὸν ἄνθρωπον LTr[A]W
12: 1 trs ἄνθρωπος ἐφύτευσεν TWH
15:39 trs οὗτος ὁ ἄνθρωπος LTTrAWH
Lu. 2:15 omit καὶ οἱ ἄνθ. [L]T[TrA]WHR
25 trs ἄνθρωπος ἦν TWH
6: 6 trs ἄνθρωπος ἐκεῖ TTrAWHR
8 ἀνήρ TTrAWH
10 unto the man—unto him, αὐτῷ GEds
45 omit man[2] [L]TTrAWHR
9:56 omit For the Son to save (them) GLTTrAWHR
13: 4 τοὺς ἀνθρώπους LTTrAWHR
Joh. 7:46 om. like this man (read thus) L[TrA]WHR
9:11 ὁ ἄνθρωπος TTrWHR, [ὁ] ἄ. A
16 trs οὐκ ἔστιν οὗτος παρὰ θεοῦ ὁ ἄ. LTTrAWHR
24 trs τὸν ἄ. ἐκ δευτέρου LTTrAWHR
24 trs οὗτος ὁ ἄνθρωπος LWH
35*ἀνθρώπου for θεοῦ (—ός) TWH
Acts 5:34*ἀνθρώπους for ἀποστόλους (—λος) LTTrAWHR
17:25 men's—human, ἀνθρώπινος LTTrAWHR
19:16 trs ὁ ἄνθ. ἐπ' αὐτούς LTTrAWH
35 ἀνθρώπων, read who of men LTTrAWHR
1 Co. 3: 4*ἄνθρωποι for σαρκικοί (—ός) Eds
11:28 trs ἑαυτὸν ἄνθρωπος W
Gal. 3:12 omit the man, read he GEds
Jas. 3: 8 trs δαμάσαι δύναται ἀ. LTrAWH
1 Pet. 1:24 of man—of it, αὐτῆς GEds
Rev. 4: 7 ἀνθρώπου of a man GEds
8:11 τῶν ἀνθρώπων GEds
16:18 ἄνθρωπος ἐγένετο man was LTTrAW: omit οἱ Eds

445 ἀνθυπατεύω.

Acts 18:12 ἀνθυπάτου (-ος) ὄντος LTTrAWH

446 ἀνθύπατος.

Acts 18:12*see ἀνθυπατεύω

448
ἀνίλεως, ἀνέλεος LTTrAWWH.

449 ἄνιπτος.

Mar. 7: 5 unwashen—defiled, κοινός GEds

450 ἀνίστημι.

Mat. 17: 9 ἐγείρω LTTrAWH
20:19 ἐγείρω TTrAWHR
Mar. 6:14*ἀνέστη for ἠγέρθη (ἐγείρω) A
10:50 rose—leaped up, ἀναπηδάω Eds
12:23 omit when they shall rise [L]TrWHR
Lu. 6: 8 ὁ δὲ ἀ.—καὶ ἀ. LTTrAWHR
9:22*ἀναστῆναι for ἐγερθῆναι (ἐγείρω) LA
17:12*ἀνέστησαν for ἔστησαν (ἵστημι) WH
24:12 omit the verse [L]T[Tr][[WH]]
Acts 2:30 omit according to to Christ GLTTrAWHR
3:26 trs ἀναστήσας ὁ θεὸς TAWH
9:11 ἀνάστα LWH
10:23*ἀναστὰς ἐξῆλθεν having arisen he went away GEds
Ro. 14: 9 omit rose and GEds

451 Ἄννα, Ἅ— WH.

452 Ἄννας, Ἅ— WH.

Acts 4:6 Ἅννας LTTrAWHR

455 ἀνοίγω.

Mat. 3:16 ἠνεῴχθησαν LWH
7: 8 ἀνοιγεται it is opened LTr
9:30 ἠνεῴχθησαν LTrA
20:33 ἀνοιγῶσιν LTTrAWH
Mar. 7:35*ἠνοίγησαν for διηνοίχθησαν (διανοίγω) LTTrAWH
Lu. 4:17*ἀνοίξας for ἀναπτύξας (—ύσσω) LTrWHR
11: 9 ἀνοιχθήσεται TA
10 ἀνοιχθήσεται LTAW
Joh. 9:10 ἠνεῴχθησαν LTTrAWH
17 ἠνέῳξεν TrAWH
30 ἤνοιξεν LTTrWH
32 ἠνέῳξεν TrWH
10:21 ἀνοῖξαι TTrAWH
Acts 5:19 ἀνοίξας T
7:56 διανοίγω Eds
9: 8 ἠνεῳγμένων LA, ἠνοιγ— T
12:10 ἠνοίγη LTTrAWH
16:26 ἠνεῴχθησαν LTrAWH, ἠνοίχ— T
Rev. 3: 7 ἀ.[2]—ἀνοίξει shall open TTrAW
3: 8 ἠνεῳγμένην TWH
4: 1 ἀνεῳγμένη GLW
10: 2 | 19:11 ἠνεῳγμένον LTTrAWH
20:12 ἀ.[1]—ἠνοίχθησαν GEds
ἀ.[2]—ἠνοίχθη Eds

458 ἀνομία.

2 Th. 2: 3*ἀνομίας f. ἁμαρτίας (—ία) TTrWH
Heb. 1: 9 iniquity—unrighteousness, ἀδικία T
8:12 omit and their iniquities TTrAWHR

459 ἄνομος.

Mar. 15:28 omit the verse T[Tr]AWHF
1 Co. 9:21 ἀ.[3]—τοὺς ἀνόμους Eds

461 ἀνορθόω.

Lu. 13:13 ἀνορθώθη LTTrA

468 ἀνταπόδομα.

Lu. 14:12 trs ἀνταπόδομά σοι TTrAWHR

471 ἀντέπω, ἀντεῖπον.

Lu. 21:15†trs to resist or (nor L) gainsay ([ἢ ἀ.] Tr) LTTrAWHR

479 ἀντικαλέω.

Lu. 14:12 trs ἀντικαλέσωσίν σε LTTrAWH

481 ἀντικρύ, ἄντικρυς LTTrAWH.

483 ἀντιλέγω.

Lu. 20:27 λέγω, read which say there is no resurrection TrWHR
Acts 13:45 omit contradicting and LTr[A]WHR

484
ἀντίληψις, —λημψις LTTrAWH.

488 ἀντιμετρέω.

Mat. 7: 2 μετρέω (omit again) GEds

493 Ἀντίπας, Ἀντεί— T.

495 ἀντιπέραν.

Lu. 8:26 ἀντιπέρα LTrAW, ἀντίπερα TWH

500 ἀντίχριστος.

1 Joh. 2:18 ὁ ἀ.—omit ὁ Eds

508
ανώγεον, ἀνάγαιον GLTTrAWWH.

514 ἄξιος.

Mat. 3: 8 καρπὸν ἄξιον fruit worthy GEds
Acts 26:31 trs ἢ δεσμῶν ἄξιον LTTrWH
1 Co. 16: 4 trs ἄξιον ᾖ LTrAWHR
Rev. 5:12 ἄξιος T

518 ἀπαγγέλλω.

Mat. 28: 9 omit and as they went to tell his disciples LTTrAWHR
11 ἀναγγέλλω T
Mar. 5:14*ἀπήγγειλαν for ἀνήγγειλαν (ἀναγγέλλω) GEds
19*ἀπάγγειλον for ἀνάγγειλον (—έλλω) Eds
Joh. 4:51 ἀγγέλλω T: omit and told (him) [TrA]WHR
16:25*ἀπαγγελῶ for ἀναγγελῶ (—λλω) Eds
20:18 ἀγγέλλω LTTrAWHR
Acts 16:38*ἀπήγγειλαν for ἀνήγγειλαν (ἀναγγέλλω) Eds
17:30*ἀπαγγέλλει for παραγγέλλει (—λλω) TWH
22:26 trs τῷ χιλιάρχῳ ἀπήγγειλεν GLTTrAWHR
23:17 trs ἀπαγγεῖλαί τι LTrAWWH
26:20 ἀπαγγέλλων S—ἀπήγγελλον A.V.C EGEds

520 ἀπάγω.

Mar. 14:44 ἀπάγετε LTTrAWH
Lu. 13:15 ἀπάγων WH
21:12*ἀπαγομένους for ἀγομένους (ἄγω) TTrAWHR
22:66*ἀπήγαγον for ἀνήγαγον (ἀνάγω) TTrAWHR
Joh. 18:13 ἄγω LTTrWHR, [ἀπ]άγω A
19:16 omit and led (him) away LTTrAWHR
Acts 23:17 ἄπαγε TTrWH
24: 7 omit and would (ver. 6) to come unto thee (ver. 8) LTTr[A]WHR

523 ἀπαιτέω.

Lu. 12:20 αἰτέω TrAWH

528 ἀπαντάω.

Mat. 28: 9 ὑπαντάω TTrWH
Mar. 5: 2 ὑπαντάω LTTrWH
Lu. 14:31 ὑπαντάω Eds
17:12 ὑπαντάω T
Joh. 4:51 ὑπαντάω LTTrAWH
Acts 16:16 ὑπαντάω TTrAWHR

529 ἀπάντησις.

Mat. 25: 1 ὑπάντησις LTTrAWH

530 ἅπαξ.

1 Pet. 3:20 *omit* once GEds
See also ἐφάπαξ.

533 ἀπαρνέομαι.

Mar. 14:30 *trs* με ἀπαρνήσῃ LTTrAWWH
31 ἀπαρνήσωμαι T
72 *trs* τρίς με ἀπαρνήσῃ LTTrAWHR
Lu. 9:23 ἀρνέομαι GLTTrAWHR
22:34†*trs* με ἀπαρνήσῃ εἰδέναι LTrWHR
Joh. 13:38 ἀρνέομαι LTTrAWHR

534 ἀπάρτι.

Joh. 13:19**for* ἀπ' ἄρτι T
14: 7**for* ἀπ' ἄρτι T
Rev. 14:13 ἀπ' ἄρτι GLAWHR

537 ἅπας.

Mar. 1:27*ἅπαντες *for* πάντες (πᾶς) TTrAWH
5:40 πᾶς GEds
8:25 ἅπαντα all things Eds
Lu. 2:39 πᾶς TTrWHR
3:16 πᾶς TWH
4:40*ἅπαντες *for* πάντες (πᾶς) WH
5:11 πᾶς LTTrWH
28 πᾶς LTTrAWHR
7:16 πᾶς GTrAWH
15:13 πᾶς LTrAWH
17:27, 29 πᾶς LTrAWH
19: 7 πᾶς Eds
20: 6*ὁ λαὸς ἅπας *for* πᾶς ὁ λαὸς TTrAWHR
21: 4 ἅ.[1]—πᾶς LWHR: ἅ.[2]—πᾶς LTrWHR
12 πᾶς GEds
15*ἅπαντες *f.* πάντες (πᾶς) TTrAWH
Joh. 4:25*ἅπαντα *for* πάντα (πᾶς) TTrAWH
Acts 2: 1 πᾶς LTTrAWHR
4 πᾶς LTTrWHR
7*ἅπαντες *for* πάντες[2] (πᾶς) LTAR
14 πᾶς LTTrWHR
4:32 πᾶς LWH
5:12 πᾶς LTrWH
6:15 πᾶς LTTrWHR
10: 8 *trs* ἅπαντα αὐτοῖς LTTrAWH
13:29 πᾶς GEds
16:33*ἅπαντες *for* πάντες (πᾶς) TWH
25:24*ἅπαν *for* πᾶν (πᾶς) Eds
Gal. 3:28*ἅπαντες *for* πάντες (πᾶς) TTrA
2 Th. 2:12*ἅπαντες *for* πάντες (πᾶς) TTrA
1 Ti. 1:16*ἅπασαν *for* πᾶσαν (πᾶς) Eds

* ἀπασπάζομαι, to take leave of.

Acts 21: 6 ἀπησπασάμεθα *for* ἀσπασάμενοι (ἀσπάζομαι) Eds

538 ἀπατάω.

1 Ti. 2:14 ἀ.[2]—ἐξαπατάω Eds

539 ἀπάτη.

2 Pet. 2:13 deceivings—love feasts, ἀγάπη LTrR

See 872

ἀπεῖδον, *see* ἀφοράω.

543 ἀπείθεια, –θία WH.

Col. 3: 6 *omit* on the children of disobedience [L]TTrAWH

544 ἀπειθέω.

Acts 14: 2 ἀπειθήσαντες LTTrAWHR
17: 5 *omit* which believed not GEds
1 Pet. 2: 7 unto them which be disobedient—unto the unbelieving, ἀπιστέω TTrWHR

547 ἀπειλή.

Acts 4:17 *omit* straitly LTTr[A]WHR

553 ἀπεκδέχομαι.

Pet. 3:20*ἀπεξεδέχετο *for* ἅπαξ ἐξεδέχετο (ἐκδέχομαι) GEds

561 ἀπέναντι.

Mat. 21: 2 κατέναντι LTTrWH
27:24 κατέναντι LTrWH
Mar. 12:41*ἀπέναντι *for* κατέναντι Tr

565 ἀπέρχομαι.

Mat. 5:30*εἰς γέενναν ἀπέλθῃ *for* βληθῇ (βάλλω) εἰς γ. LTTrAWHR
8:31 suffer us to go away—send us away, ἀποστέλλω GLTTrAWHR
32 ἀπῆλθαν LTrWH
14:25 ἔρχομαι LTTrWHR
21:29, 30†I will not: afterward he repented and went *trs with* I (go) sir: and went not WH
22:22 ἀπῆλθαν LTTrAWH
26:44 *trs* πάλιν ἀπελθών LTTrAWHR
28: 8*ἀπελθοῦσαι *for* ἐξελθοῦσαι (ἐξέρχομαι) TTrAWHR
Mar. 6:27 (28) ὁ δὲ ἀ.—καὶ ἀ. LTTrAWHR
12:12 ἀπῆλθαν WH
Lu. 8:34 *omit* went and GEds
9:12 πορεύομαι GLTTrAWHR
59 *trs* πρῶτον ἀπελθόντι (–θεῖν L) LTTrWH
23:33 ἔρχομαι LTrAWHR
24:12 *omit the verse* [L]T[Tr][[WH]]
24 ἀπῆλθαν WH
Joh. 4:43 *omit* and went [L]TTrAWHR
18: 6 ἀπῆλθαν LTTrAWH
Acts 16:39*ἀπελθεῖν ἀπὸ *for* ἐξελθεῖν (ἐξέρχομαι) LTTrAWHR
23:32*ἀπέρχεσθαι *for* πορεύεσθαι (–όμαι) LTTrAWHR
28:29 *omit the verse* LTTrAWHR
Gal. 1:17*ἀπῆλθον *for* ἀνῆλθον (ἀνέρχομαι) LA
Rev. 10: 9 ἀπῆλθα LTWH
18:14 are departed[1]—are destroyed, ἀπόλλυμι W
14 are departed[2]—are destroyed, ἀπόλλυμι GEds
21: 1*ἀπῆλθον GWR, –θαν LTTrAWH *for* παρῆλθεν (παρέρχομαι)
4 ἀπῆλθαν LTTrAWH, –θεν W

568 ἀπέχω.

Mat. 14:24**add* ἀ. TrWH, *see* στάδιον

569 ἀπιστέω.

1 Pet. 2: 7*ἀπιστοῦσιν *for* ἀπειθοῦσιν (–θέω) TTrWHR

570 ἀπιστία.

Mat. 17:20 unbelief—little faith, ὀλιγοπιστία LTTrAWHR

572 ἁπλότης.

2 Co. 1:12 simplicity—holiness, ἁγιότης LTTrAWHR

575 ἀπό.

Mat. 7: 4 ἐκ LTTrWHR
13: 1 ἐκ LT: *omit* ἀ. TrWH
14:24**add* ἀ. TrWH, *see* στάδιον
17: 9 ἐκ GEds
20:20**for* παρά LTrAWH
24:29 ἐκ T
25:29 ἀ. δὲ τοῦ—τοῦ δέ LTTrAWHR
26:42 *omit* from me [L]TTrAWHR
58 *omit* ἀ. T[WH]
27:51 *omit* ἀ. T[WH]
28: 2 *omit* from the door LTTrAWHR
Mar. 1:10 ἐκ LTTrAWHR
2:21**trs* ἀπ' αὐτοῦ τὸ πλήρωμα A: τὸ πλ. ἀπ' αὐ. LTWHR
7:15 ἐκ LTTrAWHR, *see* ἄνθρωπος
8: 3*ἀ. μακρόθεν TTrAWHR
31 of—by, ὑπό Eds
9: 9 ἐκ LWH
11:13*ἀ. μακρόθεν Eds
14:52 *omit* from them [L]TTrWHR
16: 3**for* ἐκ LTr
9 παρά LTrWHR
Lu. 1:26**for* ὑπό TTrAWHR
2:37 *omit* ἀ. TTrAWH
4:35**for* ἐκ LTTrAWHR
38**for* ἐκ TTrAWHR
5:36*piece[1]—*add* ἀ. from [L]TTrAWH(R
6:18**for* ὑπό GEds
7: 6 *omit* ἀ. T
8: 3 ἐκ LTTrAWHR
29**for* ὑπό WH
43**for* ὑπό LTTrAWHR
10:42 *omit* ἀ. [L]T[TrA]WH
11: 4 *omit* but deliver us from evil GTTrAWHR
12:54 out of—at, ἐπί TWHR
Lu. 13: 7*ἔτη—*add* ἀφ' οὗ TTrAWHR
12*ἀπολέλυσαι—*add* ἀ. LT
29 *omit* ἀ.[2] [L]T[TrA]
15:16 ἐκ WHR
19:26 *omit* from him[2] [L]TAWH
22:18**add* ἀ. T[TrA]WHR, *see* νῦν
43, 44 *the verses* [L][[WH]]
23:49*ἀ. μακρόθεν LTWHR
24:42 *omit* and of an honeycomb LT[TrA]WHR
Joh. 1:51 (52) *omit* hereafter LTTrAWHR
6:38**for* ἐκ LTTrAWHR
8:11*ἀπὸ τοῦ νῦν *for* καί WHR
Acts 1:25**for* ἐκ Eds
4:36**for* ὑπό Eds
9: 3 ἐκ LTTrWWHR
10:17 from—by, ὑπό TWHR
21 *omit* which were sent unto him from Cornelius GEds
33**for* ὑπό LA
15: 4**for* ὑπό TrWH
20 *omit* ἀ. LTTr[A]WH
16:39**add* ἀ. LTTrAWHR, *see* ἀπέρχομαι
40**for* ἐκ TWH
18: 2**for* ἐκ Eds
19:12 *omit* of them GEds
13 καί, *read* certain also LTTrAWHR
21:23**for* ἐπί WH
22:30 *omit* from (his) bands GEds
26:22**for* παρά Eds
27:34**for* ἐκ LTTrAWHR
28: 3**for* ἐκ Eds
Ro. 13: 1 ὑπό LTTrWHR
15:15**for* ὑπό TTrWHR
24**for* ὑπό LA
2 Co. 10: 7 ἐπί TTrWHR
1 Th. 1: 1 *omit* from God *to end of verse* [L]TTrAWHR
10 ἐκ TTrWHR
1 Ti. 6: 5 *omit* from such withdraw thyself Eds
Jas. 1:14**for* ὑπό A
2 Pet. 1:21*ἀπὸ θεοῦ from God TAWHR
1 Joh. 2: 7 *omit* from the beginning[3] LTTrAWHR
3:22**for* παρά LTTrAWHR
5:15**for* παρά LTTrWH
Rev. 1: 5 ἀ.[2]—ἐκ LTTrAWHR
2:17 *omit* to eat of GEds
6: 4 ἐκ GLTTrAW[WH]R
10 ἐκ Eds
7:17 ἐκ GEds
9:18**for* ὑπό GEds
16:17 ἀ.[1]—ἐκ LTTrAWHR
19: 5**for* ἐκ LTrAWWHR
20: 9 *omit* from God LTAWWHR
21: 4 ἐκ LTTrAWHR
See also ἀπάρτι

576 ἀποβαίνω.

Lu. 5: 2 *trs* ἀπ' αὐτῶν ἀποβάντες TTrAWH

582 ἀπογραφή.

Lu. 2: 2 ἡ ἀ.—*omit* ἡ LTTrAWHR

584 ἀποδείκνυμι.

Acts 2:22 *approbatum* A.V. Vul: *trs* ἀποδ. ἀπὸ τοῦ θεοῦ TTrWHR

* ἀποδεκατεύω, to tithe.

Lu. 18:12 ἀποδεκατεύω *for* ἀποδεκατῶ (–τόω) TWH

586 ἀποδεκατόω.

Lu. 18:12 ἀποδεκατεύω TWH
Heb. 7: 5 ἀποδεκατοῖν TTrAWH

588 ἀποδέχομαι.

Lu. 9:11*ἀποδεξάμενος *for* δεξάμενος (δέχομαι) LTTrAWHR
Acts 15: 4 παραδέχομαι Eds
21:17*ἀπεδέξαντο *for* ἐδέξαντο (δέχομαι) Eds

591 ἀποδίδωμι.

Mat. 18:26 *trs* ἀποδώσω σοι ([σοί] A) LTTrAWH
Lu. 20:25 *trs* τοίνυν ἀπόδοτε TTrAWHR
Ro. 14:12*ἀποδώσει *for* δώσει (δίδωμι) LTr, [ἀπο]δώσει A
1 Th. 5:15 ἀποδοῖ T
2 Ti. 4:14 ἀποδώσει shall reward Eds
Heb. 12:16 ἀπέδετο LAWH
Rev. 22: 2 ἀποδιδοὺς TTrA

599 **ἀποθνήσκω.**

Lu. 20:28 die—be, ᾖ (ὦ) LTTrAWHR
30 *omit* took her to wife, and he died childless TTrAWHR
Joh. 11:21* *trs* οὐκ ἂν (ἀπέθανεν *for* ἐτεθνήκει, θνήσκω LTTrWHR) ὁ ἀδελφός μου LTTrAWHR
32 *trs* μου ἀπέθανεν TTrAWH
18:14*ἀποθανεῖν *for* ἀπολέσθαι (ἀπόλλυμι) LTTrAWHR
Ro. 7: 6 ἀποθανόντος that being dead A.V.B E—ἀποθανόντες having died (in that) SGEds
1 Pet. 3:18*ἀπέθανεν *for* ἔπαθεν (πάσχω) LTTrWH

600
ἀποκαθιστάω, –άνω, –ημι.

Mat. 12:13 ἀπεκατεστάθη LTTrAWWH
Mar. 3: 5 ἀπεκατεστάθη GLTTrAWWH
8:25 ἀπεκατέστη TTrAWH
9:12 ἀποκαθιστάνει LTTrA, ἀποκατ- WH
Lu. 6:10 ἀπεκατεστάθη GLTTrAWH

601 **ἀποκαλύπτω.**

1 Co. 2:10 *trs* ἀπεκάλυψεν ὁ θεὸς **Eds**

602 **ἀποκάλυψις.**

1 Co. 14:26 *trs* hath a revelation, hath a tongue **Eds**

609 **ἀποκόπτω.**

Acts 27:32 *trs* ἀπέκοψαν οἱ στρατιῶται LTTrAWH

611 **ἀποκρίνομαι.**

Mat. 22:46 *trs* ἀποκριθῆναι αὐτῷ LTTrAWH
24: 2*And—*add* ἀποκριθεὶς answering (*omit* Jesus) LTTrAWHR
26:63 *omit* answered and TrWHR
Mar. 3:33 ἀποκριθεὶς αὐτοῖς λέγει TTrAWHR
5: 9 *omit* answered GEds, *see* λέγω
7: 6 *omit* answered and TTrAWHR
8:28 answered-spake, εἶπον TAWHR
9: 6*ἀποκριθῇ *for* λαλήσῃ (-λέω) TTrAWHR
12 *omit* answered and TTrAWHR
17 ἀπεκρίθη αὐτῷ answered him LTTrAWHR
38 answered—spake, φημί TTrAWHR
10: 5 καὶ ἀ. ὁ—ὁ δέ (*omit* answered and) TTrAWHR
20 *omit* answered and TWHR
29 *omit* answered and TAWHR
11:29 *omit* answered and TTrAWHR
33 *omit* answering [L]TTrAWHR
12:17 *omit* answering LTTrAWHR
24 *omit* answering TTrAWHR
28 *trs* ἀπεκρίθη αὐτοῖς TTrAWH
13: 2, 5 *omit* answering TTrAWHR
14:20 *omit* answered and LTTrAWHR
40 *trs* ἀποκ. αὐτῷ LTTrAWWH
61†*trs* οὐκ ἀπεκ. οὐδέν TTrWHR
15: 3 *add* but he answered nothing A.V.C
12 *trs* πάλιν ἀποκριθεὶς LTTrAWHR
Lu. 5:22 *omit* answering L[Tr]
14: 5 *omit* answered, *read* he said to them LTr[A]WHR
20:24 *omit* answered and TWHR
34 *omit* answering LTTrAWHR
Joh. 6: 7 ἀποκρίνεται answereth T
12:23 ἀποκρίνεται answereth TTrWHR
13:38 ἀποκρίνεται answereth **Eds**
Acts 8:37 *omit the verse* GLTTrAWHR

613 **ἀποκρύπτω.**

Mat. 11:25 κρύπτω LTTrAWH
615 **25:18** κρύπτω LTTrAWH
ἀποκτείνω, –ταίνω, –τέννω.

Mat. 10:28 ἀποκτεννόντων LTTrA
Mar. 12: 5 ἀποκτέννοντες GLTTrA, -ννυντες WH
8 *trs* ἀπέκτειναν αὐτόν TTrAWHR
Lu. 6: 9*ἀποκτεῖναι *for* ἀπολέσαι (ἀπόλλυμι) GW
12: 4 ἀποκτεννόντων LTTrA
Joh. 5:16 *omit* and sought to slay him G[L]TTrAWHR
2 Co. 3: 6 ἀποκτέννει TTrA
Rev. 6: 8 *trs* ἐπὶ τὸ τέτ. τῆς γῆς, ἀ. GEds
11 ἀποκτέννεσθαι GLTTrAWH
13:10 ἀποκτανθῆναι (is) to be killed A

ἀποκυλίω.

Mar. 16: 4 ἀνακυλίω TTrAWHR

618 **ἀπολαμβάνω.**

Lu. 6:34 α[1].—λαμβάνω TTrAWHR
18:30 λαμβάνω LWH
Col. 3:24 ἀπολήμψεσθε LTTrAWH
2 Joh. 8 ἀπολάβητε ye receive **Eds**
3 Joh. 8 to receive—to sustain, ὑπολαμβάνω **Eds**

620 **ἀπολείπω.**

2 Ti. 4:13, 20 ἀπέλειπον WH
Tit. 1: 5*ἀπέλιπον (-λειπον WH) *for* κατέλιπον (καταλείπω) **Eds**

621 **ἀπολείχω.**

Lu. 16:21 ἐπιλείχω LTTrAWHR

622 **ἀπόλλυμι, –ολλύω.**

Mat. 9:17 ἀπόλλυνται LTTrWHR
18:11 *omit the verse* LTTr[A]WHR
Mar. 2:22†*trs* ἀπόλλυται καὶ οἱ ἀσκοί. *read* the wine perisheth and the bottles. TTrAWHR
8:35 ἀ.[2]—ἀπολέσει TTrAWH
9:41 ἀπολέσει LTr
11:18 ἀπολέσωσιν LTTrAWWH
Lu. 6: 9 destroy—kill, ἀποκτείνω GW
9:56 *omit* for the Son of *to* save (them) GLTTrAWHR
15: 4 ἀ.[1]—ἀπολέσῃ Tr
24 *trs* ἦν ἀπολωλὼς LTTrAWHR
17:33 ἀ.[2]—ἀπολέσει TWH
Joh. 3:15 *om.* not perish, but [L]TTrAWHR
12:25 ἀπολλύει loseth TTrWHR
18:14 ἀποθνήσκω LTTrAWHR
Acts 27:34*ἀπολεῖται *for* πεσεῖται (πίπτω) GEds
1 Co. 8:11 ἀπόλλυται perisheth **Eds**
10: 9 ἀπώλλυντο TTrWHR
2 Joh. 8 ἀπολέσητε ye lose **Eds**
Rev. 18:14*ἀπώλετο *for* ἀπῆλθεν[1] (ἀπέρχομαι) W
14*ἀπώλετο (-λοντο T) *for* ἀπῆλθεν[2] GEds

624 **Ἀπολλωνία.**

Acts 17: 1 τὴν Ἀπολλωνίαν LTTrWH

625 **Ἀπολλώς.**

1 Co. 3: 5 *trs* Apollos *and* Paul **Eds**
4: 6 Ἀπολλῶν TTrWH
Tit. 3:13 Ἀπολλῶν TWH

626 **ἀπολογέομαι.**

Acts 26: 1 *trs* ἀπελογεῖτο *after* χεῖρα **Eds**
2 *trs* ἐπὶ σοῦ μέλλων σήμερον ἀ. GLTTrAWHR

630 **ἀπολύω.**

Mat. 5:32 ἀ.[1]—ὁ ἀπολύων that putteth away LTTrAWHR
19: 9 *omit* and whoso *to end of verse* T[Tr]WH
Mar. 6:45 ἀπολύει sendeth away LTTrAWHR
10:12 γυνὴ ἀ.—αὐτὴ ἀπολύσασα she shall put away TTrAWHR
Lu. 22:68 *om.* nor let (me) go T[TrA]WHR
23:17 *omit the verse* [L]TTr[A]WHR
Joh. 18:39 *trs* ἀπολύσω ὑμῖν[1] LTTrWH
39 *trs* ἀπολύσω ὑμῖν[2] LTTrWWH
19:10 *trs* to release thee, and I have power to crucify thee LTTrAWHR

634 **ἀποπίπτω.**

Acts 9:18 ἀπέπεσαν LTTrAWH

637 **ἀποπλύνω.**

Lu. 5: 2 πλύνω LTTrAWHR

638 **ἀποπνίγω.**

Mat. 13: 7 πνίγω T

639 **ἀπορέομαι, –ρέω.**

Mar. 6:20*ἠπόρει *for* ἐποίει (ποιέω) TWHR
Lu. 24: 4*ἀπορεῖσθαι *for* διαπορεῖσθαι (-ρέω) LTTrAWHR

641 **ἀπορρίπτω.**

Acts 27:43 ἀπορίψαντας TWH

643 **ἀποσκευάζομαι.**

Acts 21:15 ἐπισκευάζομαι **Eds**

649 **ἀποστέλλω.**

Mat. 8:31*ἐπίτρεψον ἡμῖν ἀπελθεῖν—ἀπόστειλον ἡμᾶς GLTTrAWHR, *see* ἀπέρχομαι
Mar. 11: 3 ἀποστέλλει he sendeth GEds
12: 4 *om.* sent (him) away LTTrAWHR
Lu. 4:43 ἀπεστάλην was I sent LTTrAWHR
7:20 ἀπέστειλεν WH
24:49 send—send out, ἐξαποστέλλω TTrAWHR
Joh. 1:24 οἱ ἀ.—*omit* οἱ TTrAWHR
4:38 ἀπέσταλκα T
7:29 ἀπέσταλκεν T
Acts 7:34 ἀποστείλω **Eds**
35 ἀπέσταλκεν **Eds**
10:21 *omit* which were sent unto him from Cornelius GEds
13:26 sent—sent forth, ἐξαποστέλλω **Eds**
15:33*ἀποστείλαντας αὐτούς *for* ἀποστόλους (-λος) GEds
16:36 ἀπέσταλκαν LTTrAWH
21:25*ἀπεστείλαμεν *for* ἐπεστείλαμεν (ἐπιστέλλω) LTrWH
26:17 *trs* ἀποστέλλω σε LTTrAWHR
Rev. 5: 6 *omit* τά LTTrAWHR: ἀπεσταλμένοι LTrWHR, ἀποστελλόμενα W

650 **ἀποστερέω.**

Jas. 5: 4 ἀφυστερέω TTrWH

652 **ἀπόστολος.**

Mar. 3:14*twelve—*add* οὓς καὶ ἀποστόλους ὠνόμασεν whom also he called apostles WH
Acts 5:34 apostles—men, ἄνθρωπος LTTrAWHR
15:33 the apostles—those who sent (ἀποστέλλω) them GEds
1 Co. 9: 1 *trs* am I not free? am I not an apostle? GEds
Rev. 2: 2 *trs* ἀποστόλους εἶναι GW
18:20 καὶ οἱ ἀ. *read* ye saints and ye apostles GEds

654 **ἀποστρέφω.**

Mat. 27: 3 στρέφω TTrAWHR

657 **ἀποτάσσομαι.**

Acts 18:21 ἀποταξάμενος καί taking leave and LTTrAWHR

658 **ἀποτελέω.**

Lu. 13:32*ἀποτελῶ *for* ἐπιτελῶ (-λέω) LTTrAWHR

659 **ἀποτίθημι.**

Mat. 14: 3†*trs* ἐν (*add* τῇ LTrA) φυλακῇ (ἀπέθετο *for* ἔθετο, τίθημι) LTTrAWH

660 **ἀποτινάσσω.**

Lu. 9: 5 ἀποτινάσσετε TAWH
Acts 28: 5 ἀποτιναξάμενος W

663 **ἀποτομια.**

Ro. 11:22 ἀ.[2]—ἀποτομία LTTrAWHR

667 **ἀποφέρω.**

Acts 19:12*ἀποφέρεσθαι *for* ἐπιφέρεσθαι (-ρω) LTTrAWHR

668 **ἀποφεύγω.**

2 Pet. 2:18 ἀποφεύγοντας are escaping from **Eds**

669 **ἀποφθέγγομαι.**

Acts 2: 4 *trs* ἀποφθέγγεσθαι αὐτοῖς **Eds**

ἀπροσωπολήπτως, -ήμπ- LTTrAWH

680 **ἅπτομαι, ἅπτω.**

Mat. 17: 7 ἁψάμενος touching LTWH
Mar. 1:41 *trs* αὐτοῦ ἥψατο LTTrAWH
5:28 *trs* ἅψωμαι *before* κἂν TAWHR
6:56 ἅ.[2]—ἥψαντο LTTrWHR
10:13 *trs* αὐτῶν ἅψηται WH
Lu. 8:45 *omit* and sayest thou, Who touched me? T[TrA]WHR
22:55 περιάπτω TTrAWHR
Acts 28: 2*ἅψαντες *for* ἀνάψαντες (ἀνάπτω) LTTrAWWH

684 **ἀπώλεια.**

Acts 25:16 *omit* to die GEds

2 Pet. 2: 2 pernicious ways—licentiousness, ἀσέλγεια GEds

686 ἄρα ἄραγε, ἄρα γε.

Acts 7: 1 omit ἄρα LTTr[A]WHR
11:18 ἄρα LTTrWHR, ἄρα [γε] A
Gal. 4:31 so then—wherefore, διό LTTrAWHR

See 728
ἀραβών, see ἀρραβών.

689 Ἀράμ.

Lu. 3:33 Ἀράμ—Ἀρνεί R: Ἀδμείν τοῦ Ἀρνεί TAWH

See 729
ἄραφος, see ἄρραφος.

692 ἀργός.

Mat. 20: 6 omit idle[1] GLTTrAWHR
Jas. 2:20* ἀργή for νεκρά (-ρός) LTTrAWHR

694 ἀργύριον.

Mat. 25:27 τὰ ἀργύρια TWH
28:15 τὰ ἀ.—omit τὰ WH
Lu. 19:23 trs μου τὸ ἀργύριον LTTrAWH
1 Co. 3:12* ἀργύριον for ἄργυρον (-ος) TTrWHR

696 ἄργυρος.

1 Co. 3:12 ἀργύριον TTrWHR

698 Ἄρειος, Ἄριος T.
Ἀρεοπαγίτης, —γείτης T, Ἀρειο—W

Acts 17:34 ὁ Ἀ.—omit ὁ L[TrWH]

699 ἀρέσκεια, ἀρεσκία TWH.

700 ἀρέσκω.

Mar. 6:22 καὶ ἀ.—ἤρεσεν LTTrAWHR
1 Co. 7:32, 33, 34 ἀρέσῃ LTTrAWHR

702 Ἀρέτας, Ἁ— WH.

703 ἀρετή.

2 Pet. 1: 3 ἀρετῇ LTTrAWR, see ἴδιος

706 ἀριθμός.

Acts 4: 4 ὁ ἀ.—omit ὁ LT[Tr]AWHR
5:36 trs ἀνδρῶν ἀριθμὸς Eds
Rev. 5:11 elders—add καὶ ἦν ὁ ἀριθμὸς αὐτῶν μυριάδες μυριάδων and the number of them was ten thousand times ten thousand A.V.B EGEds

707 Ἀριμαθαία. Ἁ— WH.

Mat. 27:57 Ἀριμαθαίας W

710 ἀριστερός.

Mar. 10:37* ἀριστερῶν for εὐωνύμων (-μος) TTrAWH

715 ἄρκτος, ἄρκος GEds.

717 Ἀρμαγεδδών, Ἁρμαγεδών (Ἁρ Μ. WH) GEds.

See 689
* Ἀρνεί, see Ἀράμ.

720 ἀρνέομαι.

Lu. 9:23* ἀρνησάσθω for ἀπαρνησάσθω (-νέομαι) GLTTrAWHR
Joh. 13:38* ἀρνήσῃ for ἀπαρνήσῃ (-νέομαι) LTTrAWHR
Acts 4:16 ἀρνεῖσθαι LTTrAWHR
2 Ti. 2:12 ἀρνησόμεθα we shall deny LTTrAWHR

721 ἀρνίον.

Rev. 14: 1 τὸ ἀ. the Lamb GEds
21: 9 trs τὴν γυναῖκα τοῦ ἀ. Eds

726 ἁρπάζω.

Mat. 12:29* ἁρπάσαι for διαρπάσαι (-άζω) LTTrAWH

728 ἀρραβών.

2 Co. 1:22 ἀραβῶνα LT
5: 5 ἀραβῶνα T

729 ἄρραφος, ἄραφος TTrAWH.

730 ἄρρην.

Ro. 1:27 οἱ ἄρρενες S — οἱ ἄρσενες ELTrAWWH
27* ἄρρενες for ἄρσενες (-σην) T
27* ἄρρεσιν for ἄρσεσιν (-σην) T
Rev. 12: 5 ἄρσην Eds
13 ἄρσην LTTrAWH

730 ἄρσην.

Ro. 1:27 see ἄρρην
Rev. 12: 5* ἄρσεν for ἄρρενα (-ρην) Eds
13* ἄρσενα(ν L) for ἄρρενα (-ρην) LTTrAWH

736 ἀρτέμων.

Acts 27:40 ἀρτέμωνα LTTrAWWH

737 ἄρτι.

Mat. 26:53 trs ἄρτι after μοι, read now give TTrWHR
Joh. 1:51(52) omit hereafter LTTrAWHR
See also ἀπάρτι.

740 ἄρτος.

Mat. 16:11 ἄρτων loaves Eds
12 τοῦ ἄ.—τῶν ἄρτων of the loaves LTrA[WH]R: τῶν Φαρισαίων καὶ Σαδδουκαίων of the Pharisees and Sadducees T
26:26 τὸν ἄ.—omit τὸν LTTr[A]WHR
Mar. 6: 8 trs no bread, no scrip TTrAWHR
36 omit ἄ. et γὰρ et οὐκ ἔχουσιν, read buy themselves somewhat to eat [L]TTrAWHR
38 trs ἔχετε ἄρτους WH
7: 2 τοὺς ἄρτους LTTrAWHR
Lu. 9:13 trs ἄρτοι πέντε TWH
11:11 omit bread, will he give him a stone? or if (he ask) WH
Acts 20:11 τὸν ἄρτον Eds

744 ἀρχαῖος.

Mat. 5:27 omit by them of old time GEds
Rev. 20: 2 ὁ ὄφις ὁ ἀρχαῖος LTTrAWH

746 ἀρχή.

Mar. 13: 8(9) ἀρχὴ a beginning LTTrWHR
Joh. 2:11 τὴν ἀ.—omit τὴν LTTrAWHR
1 Joh. 2: 7 omit from the beginning[2] LTTrAWHR
Rev. 1: 8 omit the beginning and the ending GEds
22:13 ἡ ἀ. GLTAWHR: trs the first and the last, the beginning and the end GLTTrAWHR

749 ἀρχιερεύς

Mar. 2:26 τοῦ ἀ.—omit τοῦ Eds
8:31 τῶν ἀρχιερέων GEds
11:18 trs chief priests and scribes Eds
Lu. 3: 2 ἀρχιερέως GEds
20: 1 chief priests—priests, ἱερεύς TA
19 trs the scribes and the chief priests LTTrAWHR
22:50 trs τοῦ ἀρχιερέως τὸν δοῦλον TTrAWH
23:23 omit and of the chief priests [L]T[TrA]WHR
Joh. 7:32 trs the chief priests and the Pharisees Eds: ὑπηρέτας before οἱ ἀ. T
18:16 τοῦ ἀρχιερέως TTrAWH
Acts 4: 1* ἀρχιερεῖς for ἱερεῖς (-εύς) WH
6 ὁ ἀρχιερεὺς LTTrAWHR
25: 2 οἱ ἀρχιερεῖς the chief priests LTTrAWHR
Heb. 10:11* ἀρχιερεὺς for ἱερεύς LA

756 ἄρχομαι, ἄρχω.

Mat. 16:22 omit began A, see λέγω
Mar. 14:69 trs and began again TWHR
Lu. 3:23 trs ἀρ. ὡσεὶ ἐτῶν τριάκ. TTrWHR
24:47 ἀρξάμενοι TTrAWHR
Acts 10:37 ἀρξάμενος TTrAWHR

758 ἄρχων.

Lu. 11:15 τῷ ἄρχοντι Eds

760 Ἀσά, Ἀσάφ LTTrAWHR.

762 ἄσβεστος.

Mar. 9:45 omit into the fire to end of verse [L]TTr[A]WHR

764 ἀσεβέω.

2 Pet. 2: 6 ἀσεβής WH

765 ἀσεβής.

Ro. 4: 5 ἀσεβήν T
2 Pet. 2: 6* ἀσεβέσιν for ἀσεβεῖν (-βέω) WH

766 ἀσέλγεια.

2 Pet. 2: 2* ἀσελγείαις for ἀπωλείαις (-εια) GEds

769 ἀσθένεια.

Acts 28: 9 trs ἐν τῇ νήσῳ ἔχοντες ἀ. LTTrAWHR
Ro. 8:26 τῇ ἀσθενείᾳ infirmity Eds

770 ἀσθενέω.

Mat. 25:39* ἀσθενοῦντα for ἀσθενῆ (-νής) LTTrAWH
Lu. 7:10 omit that had been sick LTTr[A]WHR
9: 2 ἀσθενῆς L[Tr]: omit the sick TAWH
Joh. 5:13* ἀσθενῶν for ἰαθεὶς (ἰάομαι) T
Ro. 14:21 omit or is offended, or is made weak TWHR
1 Co. 8: 9 ἀσθενής Eds
2 Co. 11:21 ἠσθενήκαμεν LTTrWHR

772 ἀσθενής.

Mat. 25:39 ἀσθενέω LTTrAWH
Lu. 9: 2* ἀσθενεῖς for ἀσθενοῦντας (-ενέω) L[Tr]
1 Co. 8: 9* ἀσθενέσιν for ἀσθενοῦσιν (-ενέω) Eds

773 Ἀσία.

Acts 19:27 [ἡ] Ἀ. TrWH
20: 4 omit into Asia T[Tr]WH
Ro. 16: 5* Ἀσίας for Ἀχαΐας (-ΐα) GEds
Rev. 1:11 omit which are in Asia GEds

779 ἀσκός.

Mar. 2:22 omit but new to end of verse T[Tr]A[WH], see βλητέος

780 ἀσμένως.

Acts 2:41 omit gladly LTTrAWHR

782 ἀσπάζομαι.

Acts 21: 6 καὶ ἀσπ.—ἀπασπάζομαι, read having prayed (ver. 5) we took leave Eds
25:13 ἀσπασάμενοι TTrAWHR
Ro. 16:21 ἀσπάζεται Eds
1 Co. 16:19 ἀ.[2]—ἀσπάζεται TAWHR
Philem. 23 ἀσπάζεται GEds

783 ἀσπασμός.

Lu. 1:41 trs τὸν ἀ. τῆς Μαρίας ἡ Ἐ. LTTrAWH

786 ἄσπονδος.

Ro. 1:31 omit implacable Eds

789 Ἄσσος.

Acts 27:13 Ἄσσον S, ἆ—A.V.Er GEds, ἀ—B

796 ἀστραπή

Rev. 16:18 trs lightnings, and voices, and thunders GEds

797 ἀστράπτω.

Lu. 17:24 ἡ ἀ.—omit ἡ T[TrA]WHR
24: 4 ἀστραπτούσῃ LTTrAWHR

799 Ἀσύγκριτος, Ἀσύν— TWH.

804 ἀσφαλής.

Heb. 6:19 ἀσφαλήν LTr

805 ἀσφαλίζω.

Acts 16:24 trs ἠσφ. αὐτῶν LTTrAWH

815 ἄτεκνος.

Lu. 20:30 omit took her to wife, and he died childless TTrAWHR

* ἀτιμάω.

Mar. 12: 4 ἠτίμησαν LTr, ἠτίμασαν TAWHR, for ἠτιμωμένον (ἀτιμόω)

820 ἄτιμος.

1 Co. 12:23 ἀτιμότερα S—ἀτιμώτερα E

821 ἀτιμόω.

Mar. 12: 4 ἀτιμάω LTTrAWHR

824 ἄτοπος.

Acts 25: 5*ἄτοπον *for* τουτῳ LTTrAWHR

825 Ἀττάλεια, –λία TAWH.

837 αὐξάνω, αὔξω.

Mat. 6:28 αὐξάνουσιν LTTrAWH
Mar. 4: 8 αὐξανόμενον LTTrAW, –μενα WHR
Lu. 12:27 *omit* they grow TA
2 Co. 9:10 αὐξήσει will increase GEds
Col. 1: 6*fruit—*add* καὶ αὐξανόμενον and groweth GEds

839 αὔριον.

Acts 23:15 *omit* to-morrow GEds

846 αὐτός.

(αὑτοῦ, αὑτῆς, etc., are not distinguished from αὐτοῦ, αὐτῆς, etc.)

ὁ αὐτός, *etc.*

Mat. 5:46 the same—so, οὕτως LTrA
47*το αὐτό *for* οὕτως Eds
Mar. 10:10 the same—this, τούτου LTTrAWHR
Lu. 6:23, 26*τὰ αὐτά *f.* ταῦτα LTTrAWHR
38 *omit* same LTTrWHR
17:30*τὰ αὐτά (ταὐτά GLW) *for* ταῦτα GEds
Acts 3: 1 *trs* ἐπὶ τὸ αὐτό *after* ἡμέραν (2:47) *read* added together daily LTTrAWHR
1 Co. 12: 9 same[2]—one, εἷς LTTrAWHR
Phil. 3:16 *omit* rule, let us mind the same thing GLTTrAWHR
1 Th. 2:14*τὰ αὐτά *for* ταὐτά GEds
2 Pet. 3: 7 αὐτοῦ S—τῷ αὐτῷ A.V.B ELTWHR: τῷ αὐτοῦ GTrAW
1 Joh. 2:27 the same—his, αὐτοῦ TTrAWHR

αὐτά.

Mat. 18: 8 them[1]—it, αὐτόν LTTrAWHR
Mar. 10:16 *omit* α.[3] TTrAWHR
Joh. 15: 6 them[1]—it, αὐτό T
Ro. 10: 5 *omit* those things [L]TWHR
Rev. 10: 4*for ταῦτα Eds
22:18*for ταῦτα GEds

αὗται, *see under* οὗτος.
See 3778

αὐταῖς.

Lu. 13:14*for ταύταις LTTrAWHR
24: 1 *omit* and certain (others) with them LTTrAWHR
Rev. 9: 3, 4 αὐτοῖς T
5 αὐτοῖς LT

αὐτή.

Mar. 10:12*for γυνή LTTrWHR, *see* ἀπολύω
Lu. 2:37*for αὕτη TTrAWHR
38*for αὕτη W
7:12*for αὕτη WWHR
8:42*for αὕτη WH
Ro. 7:10*for αὕτη GW
16: 2*for αὕτη GLTAWWHR
1 Co. 7:12 αὕτη LTAWWH

αὐτῇ.

Mat. 22:39 αὕτη WHR
Mar. 12:31*for αὕτη LTr
Lu. 7:13 α.[1]—αὐτήν T
21 ἐκεῖνος TTrAWHR
19:41 αὐτήν LTTrAWWH
Joh. 8: 7†*trs* ἐπ' αὐτὴν βαλέτω λίθον WH
11 *omit* unto her WHR
Acts 5: 8 πρὸς αὐτήν LTTrAWHR
Ro. 6:12 *omit* it in GEds
Col. 2: 7 *omit* therein TTr[AWH]R
Heb. 7:11 αὐτῆς, *read* on the ground of it Eds
Rev. 10: 6 α.[2]—*see* θάλασσα
18: 6 *omit* unto her (α.[2]) Eds
9 αὐτήν TTrAWWHR
11 αὐτήν TTrAWHR

αὕτη, *see under* οὗτος.
See 3778

αὐτήν.

Mat. 13:48*they drew—*add* α. it L[A]
19: 7 *omit* her LTTrWH
Mar. 12:22 *omit* had her [L]TTrAWHR
Lu. 6:48*add α. TTrAWHR, *see* θεμελιόω
17:33 *omit* α.[2] [L]TTrAWHR
Acts 7: 5 *trs* αὐτήν *and* αὐτῷ W
9:37 *omit* α.[2] WH
Eph. 5:27 αὐτός (*omit* it) GEds
Heb. 5: 3*for ταύτην Eds
Rev. 2:20*for ἑαυτήν T
12:15*for ταύτην GEds
18: 7*for ἑαυτήν Eds
9 bewail her—*omit* her GEds
20 αὐτῇ GEds

αὐτῆς.

Mat. 1:25 *omit* her firstborn LTTrAWHR
5:28 *omit* α. T: αὐτήν LTrAW[WH]
6:34*for ἑαυτῆς AWH
23:37*for ἑαυτῆς T[Tr]AW[WH]
Mar. 1:31 *omit* α. LT[Tr]AWH
5:26*for ἑαυτῆς GLTrAWWH
6:22 αὐτοῦ WH
Lu. 2:22 αὐτῶν S—αὐτῆς her A.V.B E
10:38 *om.* α. *read* the house T[Tr]WH
12:53 *om.* her[1] T: *om.* her[2] TTrAWHR
Joh. 8: 5*sayest thou—*add* περὶ α. concerning her WR
1 Co. 7:39 *omit* α.[2] LTTrAWHR
10:28 *omit* GEds, *see* γῆ
11: 5*for ἑαυτῆς LTTrAWHR
Heb. 12:15*for ταύτης LWH
1 Pet. 1:24*for ἀνθρώπου (-ος) GEds

αὐτό.

Mat. 14:12 it—him, αὐτόν TTrAWHR
Mar. 4:37 *omit* α. LTTrAWHR, *see* πλοῖον
6:29 it—him, αὐτόν T
Lu. 11:14 *omit* and it was [TrA]WHR
23:53 *omit* α.[1] LTTrAWHR
53 it[3]—him, αὐτόν LTTrAWHR
Joh. 14:17 *omit* α.[2] [L]WH
Acts 5:39 it[2]—them, αὐτούς GLTTrAWHR
1 Co. 3:13*fire[2]—*add* α. itself Eds
4:17*this—*add* α. very T
Phil. 3:21 *omit* that it may be GEds
Rev. 8: 5 αὐτόν EGLTTrAWWH

αὐτοί.

Mat. 5: 9 *omit* α. [L]T[TrAWH]
19:28*for ὑμεῖς[2] TTr
23: 4*τῷ δὲ—αὐτοὶ δὲ τῷ but they themselves LTTrAWHR
Mar. 2: 8*οὕτως—*add* α. G[A]W
7:36*αὐτοὶ μᾶλλον LTTrAWH
Lu. 13: 4*for οὗτοι LTTrAWHR
Joh. 17:11*for οὗτοι TWH
Acts 13: 4*for οὗτοι LTTrAWHR
1 Co. 16:17*for οὗτοι LAW

αὐτοῖς.

Mat. 8:15 unto them—unto him, αὐτῷ Eds
9:12, 24 *omit* unto them LTTrAWHR
13:11 *omit* unto them TWH
37 *omit* unto them LTTrAWHR
51 *omit* Jesus saith unto them LTTrAWHR
16: 8 *omit* unto them GLTTrAWHR
17:11 *omit* unto them LTTr[A]WHR
19: 4 *omit* unto them LTTrAWHR
14*said—*add* α. unto them T
20: 8 *omit* them T[TrA]WH
25:20, 22 *omit* beside them LTTrWHR
26:71*for τοῖς AW
Mar. 4: 9 *omit* unto them GEds
15**see* καρδία
6:34 αὐτούς LTTrAWHR
8:29 αὐτούς LTTrAWHR, *see* ἐπερωτάω
9:14 πρὸς αὐτούς TTrWHR
10:13*for τοῖς προσφέρουσιν (ρω) WHR
11:17 *omit* unto them [L]AWH
12:17 *omit* unto them AWH
38 *omit* unto them TTrAWHR
Lu. 6: 2 *omit* unto them [L]TTrAWHR
19:40 *omit* unto them T[Tr]AWHR
20:25 πρὸς αὐτούς TTrAWHR
23:17 *omit the verse* [L]TTr[A]WHR
20*προσεφώνησεν—*add* α. LWHR
25 *om.* unto them G[L]TTrAWWHR
34 *see* λέγω
35 *omit* with them [L]TTrAWHR
24:36 *omit* and saith *to end of verse* T[[WH]]
40 *omit the verse* T[Tr][[WH]]
44 πρὸς αὐτούς TTrAWHR
Joh. 2:22 *omit* unto them GEds
7: 9 *omit* unto them T
33 *omit* unto them GEds
47 [them] TrWH
8:28 *omit* unto them LTTrAWHR
9:20 *omit* them [L]TTrAWHR
10: 7 *omit* unto them TAWH
25 *omit* them T
17:13 ἑαυτοῖς TTrAWHR
20:20 *trs* α. *after* πλευρὰν LTTrAWHR
Acts 4:18 *omit* α. LTTrAWHR
12:17 *omit* unto them[2] T[Tr]
13:19 *omit* to them TTr[A]WHR
15: 8 *omit* them[2] TTrAWHR
17:18 *omit* unto them TTr[A]WHR
18:20 *omit* with them LTTrAWHR
21 *omit* them LTTrAWHR
19:15*said—*add* α. unto them Eds
Ro. 1:24*for ἑαυτοῖς LTTrAWHR
27*for ἑαυτοῖς WH
9:26 *omit* unto them [L]Tr[WH]
10: 5 them—it, αὐτῇ LTTrAWHR
2 Co. 4: 4 *omit* unto them GEds
Col. 3: 7 them—these things, τούτοις Eds
1 Th. 5:13*for ἑαυτοῖς TTr
Heb. 8: 8 αὐτούς LTWH
Rev. 6:11*given—*add* α. unto them GEds
21:14 αὐτῶν GEds. *see* δώδεκα

αὐτόν.

Mat. 3:15 πρὸς α.—αὐτῷ LWH
7:24 *omit* α. LTTrWHR, *see* ὁμοιόω
14: 3 *omit* α. TWHR
17: 8*for τὸν WH
21: 9*before—*add* α. him LTTrAWHR
44 *omit the verse* [L]T[WH]
22:13 *omit* take him away and LTTrAWHR
13*cast—*add* α. him LTTrAWHR
26:61 *omit* α. TrAWH
71 *omit* α.[1] [L]TrWH
27: 2 *omit* α.[2] LTTrAWHR
43 *omit* him[1] T[Tr]WH
28:14 *omit* α. T[Tr]WH
Mar. 1:40 *omit* and kneeling down to him L[TrA]: *omit* to him[2] TWH
2:16 *omit* him LTTrWHR, *see* ἐσθίω
6:33 *omit* him[1] GLTrAWHR: them αὐτούς T
33 *omit* and came together unto him GEds
8:25 *omit* α. TTrAWHR, *see* διαβλέπω
9:18 *omit* α.[2] T
26 *omit* α. G[L]TTrAWHR
27 *omit* him[1] LTTrWHR
28 εἰσελθόντος αὐτοῦ LTTrWHR
10:26*for ἑαυτούς WHR
34 *omit* α.[2] [L]T[Tr]WHR
12: 8*cast—*add* α. him Eds
14:46 ἐπ' α. τὰς χεῖρας αὐτῶν—τὰς χ. αὐτῷ TTrAWH
15:20 *omit* α.[4] T
Lu. 1:62 him—it, αὐτό LTTrAWH
2:21*for τὸ παιδίον GEds
45 *omit* α.[1] G[L]TTrAWHR
4: 9 *omit* α.[2] T[Tr]AWH
5:18*to lay—*add* α. him A[WH]
6: 7 *omit* him[1] LTTrAW
12*ἐξῆλθεν—ἐξελθεῖν α. TTrAWHR
7: 6 *omit* to him (πρὸς α.) TWH
8:21 *omit* α. GLTTrAWHR
9:62 *omit* unto him A[WH]
10:33 *omit* α.[2] [L]T[Tr]AWHR
11:28 *omit* α. GLTTrAWHR
54 *omit* α. T
17:11 *omit* α. T[TrA]WHR
18: 7 πρὸς α.—αὐτῷ TTrAWHR
19: 5 *omit* saw him and TTr[A]WHR
22:43, 44 *the verses* [L] [[WH]]
54 *omit* α.[2] LTTrAWHR
57 *omit* him[1] LTr[A]WHR
63*for τὸν Ἰησοῦν LTTrAWHR
64 *omit* α.[2] TTrAWH
23:11 *omit* α.[2] [L]T[Tr]AWHR
15 *see* ἀναπέμπω
24:12*for ἑαυτόν Tr: *omit the verse* [L]T[Tr] [[WH]]
52 *omit* worshipped him and T[[WH]]
Joh. 1:19*sent—*add* πρὸς α. unto him LTrAWHR
2:24*for ἑαυτόν LTTrAWHR
3: 2*for τὸν Ἰησοῦν GEds
15 εἰς α.—ἐν αὐτῷ TTrAWHR
4:24 *omit* him[1] T
47 *omit* him[2] [L]TTrAWHR
5:16 *omit* and sought to slay him G[L]TTrAWHR
6:15 *omit* α.[2] LTTrAWH
7:50 *omit* T, *see* ἔρχομαι
8: 3 *omit* unto him WHR
11:44*ἄφετε—*add* α. T[Tr]AWHR
14: 7 *omit* him[2] [LTrA]WH
18:13 *omit* α. [L]TTrWHR
31 *omit* him[2] T
19: 3*add α. LTTrAWHR, *see* ἔρχομαι
6*crucify[2]—*add* α. him GLW
12 α.[2]—ἑαυτόν GEds
38*for τὸ σῶμα τοῦ Ἰησοῦ[2] T
39*for τὸν Ἰησοῦν Eds

Joh. 21:25 omit the verse T
Acts 3: 7*lifted up—add α. him LTTrAWHR
13 omit him¹ LT[TrA]WHR
7:21 α.¹—αὐτοῦ LTTrAWHR
31 omit unto him LTTrAWHR
9: 6 omit GEds, see κέντρον
25 omit α. LTTrAWHR
25*add α. LTTrAWHR, see καθίημι
43 omit α. TWH
10:11 omit unto him GEds
21 omit which were sent unto him from Cornelius GEds
11:26(25) omit α. bis LTTrAWHR
14:17*for ἑαυτόν LTTrWH
17:15 omit α.¹ LTTrAWHR
23:27 omit α. LTTr[A]WWHR
28 omit α. T[Tr]WH
30 omit against him LT
35 trs α. to end of verse LTTrAWHR
24:23*for τὸν Παῦλον GEds
26 omit that he might loose him Eds
25: 7*round about—add α. him Eds
25 omit α.² LTTrAWHR
28:17*for τὸν Παῦλον GEds
1 Co. 7:13 him—the husband, ἀνήρ Eds
Eph. 1:20*ἐκάθισεν—καθίσας α. set him T
1 Ti. 3: 7 omit α. LTTrAWHR
Heb. 2: 6 αὐτοῦ W
7 omit α.³ G[L]T[Tr]A[WH], see χείρ
12: 3 ἑαυτόν LTTrA, ἑαυτούς WHR
Jas. 5:14 omit α.² TWH
1 Joh. 4:19 omit him Eds
5:18*for ἑαυτόν TTrAWHR
Rev. 20: 3 omit him² GEds

αὐτός.

Mat. 6: 4 omit himself LTTrAWHR
12: 3 omit α. GEds
25:17 omit he also LTTr[A]WHR
Mar. 2:25 omit α.¹ [L]TTrWHR
4:38 trs αὐτὸς ἦν WHR
5:40*for ὁ LTTrWHR
6:16 omit ἐστιν· α. G[L]TTrAWHR
7:36 omit α. LTTrAWWH
12:21 om. α. TTrAWHR, see καταλείπω
15: 3 add α. A.V.C, see ἀποκρίνομαι
Lu. 8:41 οὗτος LTrWH
19: 2*for οὗτος LTrAWHR
23:51 omit also himself LTTrAWHR
Joh. 1:27 omit he it is G[L]TTrAWHR
5:37 ἐκεῖνος TTrAWHR
7: 9*α. ἔμεινεν T
9:21 omit α.¹ TTrAWHR see ἐρωτάω
14:10 omit α. TTrAWHR
Acts 3:10*for οὗτος LT
10:42 οὗτος LTrWHR
1 Co. 7:13 οὗτος Eds
9:20*add α. GEds, see νόμος
Heb. 10:12 οὗτος Eds
Rev. 17:11 οὗτος Tr

αὐτοῦ.

Mat. 3: 7 omit α. read the baptism LT[TrA]WH
12*ἀποθήκην α. his garner LTrW
8: 5*for τῷ Ἰησοῦ LTTrAWHR
13 omit α. read the servant LTTr[A]WHR
21 omit α. read the disciples LTTrWHR
25 omit α. GEds
12:46 omit α.² [L]R
49 omit α.¹ T[WH]
13:57 omit α.¹ LTTrAWH, see ἴδιος
14:15 omit α. read the disciples LTTrAWHR
22 omit α. read the disciples GTTrAWWHR
15: 6(5) om. or his mother L[A]WHR
12 omit α. read the disciples LTAWHR
30*for τοῦ Ἰησοῦ LTTrAWHR
33, 36 omit α. read the disciples [L]T[Tr]AWHR
16: 5, 20 omit α read the disciples LTTrAWHR
17:10 omit α. read the disciples LTTrWH
18:25 om. α.² TTrAWH: om. α.³ T[A]WH
29 omit at his feet GLTTr[A]WHR
19:10 omit α. read the disciples T[A]WHR
25 om. α. read the disciples GEds
24:45 omit α.¹ LTTrAWHR
49*συνδούλους α. his fellow-servants Eds
25: 6 omit α. TAWH
Mat. 26: 8, 45 omit α. read the disciples LTTrAWHR
36*μαθηταῖς α. his disciples LR
65 omit α.² read the blasphemy [L]TTrAWHR
27:64 om. α. read the disciples TWH
28: 9 omit And as they went to tell his disciples LTTrAWHR
Mar. 1:16 his—Simon's, Σίμωνος Eds
42 omit as soon as he had spoken LTTrWHR
3:31*ἀδελφοὶ α. GEds
4:34 μαθηταῖς α.—ἰδίοις μ. TAWHR
5:18 trs μετ' αὐτοῦ ᾖ LTTrAWWH
6: 4 α.¹—ἑαυτοῦ T
4*συγγενέσιν α. [L]TTrAWHR
41 omit α. read the disciples TTrAWHR
7:12 omit α. bis LTTrAWH
15 him³—the man, ἄνθρωπος LTTrAWHR
33 omit α.¹ T
8: 1 omit α. read the disciples TTrWH
35 ψυχὴν α.¹—ἑαυτοῦ ψ. WH
35 ψυχὴν α.²—ἑαυτοῦ ψ. GTrW
9:18 omit α. [L]TTrAWHR
27*χειρὸς α. his hand LTTrWHR
10: 7*μητέρα α. his mother T
7 omit and cleave to his wife TWH
10 omit α.¹ read the disciples [L]TTr[A]WHR
12: 6 omit his LTTrAWHR
19 omit α.² read the wife TTrAWH
13:27 omit α. read the angels [L]TTrAWHR
27 om. α. read the elect TTrA[WH]
14:16 omit α. read the disciples T[Tr]WHR
33*for ἑαυτοῦ LTTrAWH
15:20*add α. LTWHR, see ἴδιος
Lu. 1: 5 αὐτῷ LTTrAWHR
29 omit α. read the saying GTTrAWHR
2:28 omit α. [L]T[TrA]WH
33*add α. GTTrAWHR, see πατήρ
33 omit α.¹ GTrAWH
4:24 ἑαυτοῦ T
5:15 omit by him LTTrAWHR
6:40 omit α.¹ read the master LTTrAWHR
45 omit α.¹ read the heart TWH
45 omit treasure of his heart² [L]TTrAWHR
8:19*μήτηρ α. his mother T
45 μετ' α.—σὺν αὐτῷ GLTTrAR: omit and they that were with him WH
9: 1 omit his disciples (read the twelve) GTTrAWWHR
7 omit by him [L]TTrAWHR
51 omit α.² [LTrA]WH
54 omit α. read the disciples T[TrA]WH
62 omit α. [Tr]WH
11:54 omit that they might accuse him T[Tr]AWHR
12:15 α.²—αὐτῷ LTTrAWH
22 [αὐτοῦ] LWH
31*for τοῦ θεοῦ (-ός) LTTrAWHR
47*for ἑαυτοῦ LTTrAWHR
14:26*for ἑαυτοῦ¹ LTTrA
27 ἑαυτοῦ LTAWHR
15: 5*for ἑαυτοῦ TTrAWHR
16 omit his belly WHR
20*for ἑαυτοῦ LTTr
26 omit α. read the servant A.V.B EGEds
29*πατρὶ α. his father LTrAWHR
16: 1 omit α. read the disciples TTrAWHR
17: 1*μαθητὰς α. his disciples Eds
24 omit in his day LWH
18:13 ἑαυτοῦ TrAWH
19:26 omit from him² (α.¹) [L]TAWH
29 omit α. read the disciples T[Tr]AWHR
20:26 α.¹—τοῦ AWHR
45 omit α. read the disciples TTrWH, see μαθητής
22:16 thereof—it, αὐτό LTTrAWHR
39 omit α. read the disciples TTrAWHR
43, 44 the verses [L] [[WH]]
45 μαθητὰς α. A.V.Br E
51 omit α. TTrAWHR
64 omit they struck him on the face, and [L]TTrAWHR
23:49 αὐτῷ LTTrAWHR
24:27*for ἑαυτοῦ EGLTTr
Joh. 2:12 omit α.² [L]Tr[A]WHR
Joh. 3:16 om. α. read the only begotten TWH
17 om. α. read the Son T[TrA]WHR
4:51 omit α. read the servants T
51*for σοῦ LTTrAWHR
5: 5*ἀσθενείᾳ α. his infirmity [L]TTrAWHR
6: 2 omit α. read the miracles GEds
22 omit α.¹ GLTTrAWHR, see ἐκεῖνος
52*σάρκα α. his flesh L[WH]
9: 6*τὸν—α. τὸν (read his eyes) LTTrAWHR
21 α.²—ἑαυτοῦ TTrWHR
11:12 omit α. read the disciples LTTrAWHR
54 omit α. read the disciples TTrAWHR
14:10*add at end α. read his works [L]TTrAWHR
19:17 τὸν σταυρὸν α.—αὐτῷ (ἑαυτῷ TR) τὸν στ. for himself the cross LTTrAWHR
26 omit α. [L]TTr[A]WHR
38*for τοῦ Ἰησοῦ³ LTrAWHR
20:20 omit α. LTTrAWHR
30 omit α. read the disciples LTTrAWHR
21:14 omit α. read the disciples Eds
Acts 2:31 omit his soul GLTTrAWHR
3:11*see ἰάομαι
18 omit α. read the prophets LTTrAWHR
18*χριστὸν α. his Christ Eds
5: 2 omit α. LTTrAWHR
32 omit his TTrWHR
41 omit α. read the name GEds
7:13*for Ἰωσήφ² T
14 omit α.² GLTTrAWHR
20 omit α. GEds
22*ἔργοις α. his deeds GEds
25 omit α.¹ TTr[A]WHR
37 omit him shall ye hear LTTrAWHR
8:33 omit α.¹ read the humiliation LTTrWHR
9:25*οἱ μαθηταὶ α. his disciples LTTrAWHR
10: 7 omit α. read the household servants Eds
12:13*for τοῦ Πέτρου GEds
15:18 omit unto God are all his works GTTrAWHR
16:34 omit α. read the house LT[Tr]AWHR
21:11 ἑαυτοῦ Eds
34*δέ²—add α. LTTrAWWH
22:16*for τοῦ κυρίου (-ος) GEds
20 omit unto his death GEds
24: 8 omit LTTr[A]WHR, see κρίνω
24 omit α.¹ GLTTrAWHR
25: 8 omit α. LTTrAWHR, see Παῦλος
26:30 omit and when he had thus spoken GEds
28:29 omit the verse LTTrAWHR
Ro. 14:14*for ἑαυτοῦ GLTrW
16: 2 trs ἐμοῦ αὐτοῦ LTTrAWHR
1 Co. 1:29 his—God's, θεός GEds
2:10 omit α. read the Spirit LTTr[A]WHR
7:37*καρδίᾳ¹ α. LTTrAWHR
37 omit α. LTTrAWHR, see ἴδιος
9:10 omit of his hope GEds
2 Co. 3:13*for ἑαυτοῦ LTrAWWHR
8:19 omit same LTrAWWHR
Eph. 3: 6 omit α. read the promise LTTrAWHR
4:16*for ἑαυτοῦ T
5:30 omit LTTr[A]WHR, see σάρξ
31 his father—omit his LTTrAWHR
31 his wife—omit α. T
Col. 1:14 omit through his blood GEds
20 omit by him² LTr[WH]
4:15 his—her, αὐτῆς LWH: their αὐτῶν TTrAR
2 Th. 2: 6*for ἑαυτοῦ TTrWHR
Heb. 1: 8*for σοῦ² WH
11: 5 omit α. read the translation LTTrAWHR
12:16 ἑαυτοῦ LTTrAWHR
Jas. 1:26 α.¹—ἑαυτοῦ WH: α.² ἑαυτοῦ LWH
5:20*ψυχὴν α. his soul LTWH
1 Pet. 1:24 omit thereof LTTr[A]WWHR
2:24 omit α.² LTr[A]WHR
3:10 omit α. bis LTTrAWHR
2 Pet. 3: 7 α. S—τῷ α. GTrAW: τῷ αὐτῷ A.V.B ELTWHR
3 Joh. 7 ὀνόματος S— ὀνό. α. A.V.B E
Rev. 2:18 omit his¹ L[WH]
6:17 his—their, αὐτῶν TTrWHR
10: 1*τὴν κεφαλὴν—add α. GEds

Rev. 13: 8*add α. LTTrAWHR, see ὄνομα
14: 1*add α. GEds, see ὄνομα
15: 2 omit over his mark (and) GEds
19:20*for τούτου GEds: trs ὁ μετ' α. (GW
20:11 αὐτόν GT
22:14 αὐτῶν LTTrAWHR, see στολή

αὐτούς.

Mat. 14:14 αὐτοῖς GLTTrAWWH
20:12 trs αὐτοὺς ἡμῖν LTWH
Mar. 1:27 ἑαυτούς LTrAWR
4:15*see καρδία
5:10 αὐτά TTrWH
14*for τοὺς χοίρους (-ρος) GEds
9:16*for τοὺς γραμματεῖς (-τεύς) GLTTrAWHR
14: 7 αὐτοῖς LTrAWH: omit α. T
Lu. 3:14 πρὸς α.—αὐτοῖς LTrAWH
5:17 αὐτόν, read with him to heal TAWHR
9:34*ἐκείνους εἰσελθεῖν—εἰσ. αὐτούς TTrAWHR
11:53 omit α. TTrAWHR, see ἐξέρχομαι
18: 1*προσεύχεσθαι—add α. Eds
19:27*slay—add α. them TTrAWHR
20:45*see μαθητής
23:12*for ἑαυτούς TTrAWH
Joh. 6:17*add α. T, see ἤδη
18: 7 αὐτός W
20:10*for ἑαυτούς TTrWH
Acts 2:40*exhort—add α. them Eds
4: 3*put—add α. them W
5:40 omit α. TTrAWHR
10:48 αὐτοῖς T
11:26 αὐτοῖς καί LTTrAWHR
15:33*add α. GEds, see ἀποστέλλω
16:40 omit α. LTTrAWHR
19: 3 omit unto them Eds
21:25 omit LTTrWHR, see μηδείς
23:30*λέγειν α. LT
2 Th. 1: 4 trs αὐτοὺς ἡμᾶς TTrAWH
Jas. 3: 3 trs ἡμῖν αὐτούς A
1 Pet. 4:14 omit on their part to end of verse LTTrAWHR
Jude 24 them—you, ὑμᾶς A.V.B EGLTTrWWHR
Rev. 5:10*for ἡμᾶς GEds
8: 6*for ἑαυτούς LTTrWHR
11:11 ἐπ' α.—ἐν αὐτοῖς GEds
13: 7 omit L[WH], see δίδωμι

αὐτῷ.

Mat. 3:16 omit unto him [L]TWH
4: 3 omit to him TTrAWHR
3*said—add α. to him Eds
5: 1 omit unto him L[WH]
8: 1 α.[1]—αὐτοῦ LTrWH
5*for τῷ Ἰησοῦ GW
28 α.[1]—αὐτοῦ LTTrWH, see ἔρχομαι
9:27 omit him L[Tr]WH
12:38*answered—add α. him LTTrAWHR
47 omit the verse [T]WH
15:22 omit unto him LTTrAWHR
17:14 α.[2]—αὐτόν GEds
26 omit unto him[1] LTTrWHR
18:34 omit unto him LTrAWHR
19: 3 omit unto him[2] LTTrAWHR
18 omit unto him T
21:23 α.[1]—αὐτοῦ LTTrWHR, see ἔρχομαι
31 omit unto him LTTrAWHR
22:21 omit unto him T[A]WH
25:44 omit him GEds
26:17 omit unto him Eds
75 omit unto him [L]TTrAWHR
27:11 omit unto him TWH
22 omit unto him LTTrAWHR
42 ἐπ' αὐτόν TTrWHR
44 α.[2]—αὐτόν GLTTrAWWH
28:17 omit him[2] LTTrAWHR
Mar. 1:41 omit unto him T
3: 7 omit him [L]TTrAWHR
5: 2 α.[1]—αὐτοῦ LTTrWHR, see ἐξέρχομαι
6 αὐτόν AWH
9*add α. GEds, see λέγω
07 him—with him, μετ' αὐτοῦ TTrAWHR
6: 2 unto him—to this one, τούτῳ TTrAWHR
35 omit unto him T
8:20*add α. AWHR, see λέγω
28*add α. LTTrAWHR, see λέγω
9:17*answered—add α. him LTTrAWHR
19 him[1]—them, αὐτοῖς GEds
10:35*saying—add α. to him [L]TTrAWHR
52*for τῷ Ἰησοῦ GEds
11: 7 α.[2]—αὐτόν LTTrAWHR
12:29 omit him T[Tr]AWHR

Mar. 14:53 omit with him TWH
Lu. 5: 5 omit unto him TWHR
20 omit unto him GLTTrAWHR
6:10*for τῷ ἀνθρώπῳ (-πος) GEds
7: 6 omit unto him T
8: 3 unto him—unto them, αὐτοῖς TTrAWHR
27 omit α.[2] T[TrA]WHR
47 omit unto him LTTrAWHR
49 omit to him T[Tr]WHR
51*add α. LTTrAWHR, see οὐδείς
10:35 omit unto him [L]TTr[A]WHR
11:11 omit α.[1] WH, see ἄρτος
12:17*for ἑαυτῷ WH
21*for ἑαυτῷ TWH
41 omit unto him LTr[A]WHR
14: 6 omit him TTrAWHR
16:29 omit unto him T[TrA]WHR
17: 7*ἐρεῖ—add α. [L]TTrAWHR
9 omit him GEds
12 omit α. L[TrA]WH
19:31 omit unto him [L]TTr[A]WHR
45 omit therein, and them that bought TTrAWHR
22:43, 44 the verses [L][(WH]]
49 omit unto him TTrAWHR
Joh. 1:49(50) trs αὐτῷ after ἀπεκρίθη, answered him TTrAWHR: ἀπ. [α.] L
4:17*said[1]—add α. unto him [L]A[WH]R
8:33 α.—πρὸς αὐτόν LTTrAWHR
9:35 omit unto him T[TrA]WHR
10:38 him—the Father, πατήρ LTTrAWHR
11:12*add α. after οὖν LTR, after μαθηταί TrAWH, read said unto him
12:13 him—them, αὐτῶν W
13:24*add α. LTTrAWHR, see λέγω
26*add α. TTrAWHR, see δίδωμι
32 omit [LTrA]WHR, see θεός
32*for ἑαυτῷ TTrWHR
36 omit him[2] LTTrAWHR
38 omit him Eds
16:29 omit unto him [L]TTrAWHR
18:34 omit him Eds
19: 4 omit in him T
7 omit him T
11*answered—add α. him [L]Tr[A]WHR
Acts 7: 5†trs δοῦναι α. (αὐτήν W) LTTrAWWH
10: 7*for τῷ Κορνηλίῳ GEds
19 omit unto him WH
11:13 omit unto him LTTrWHR
12: 9 omit him LTTrAWHR
2 Co. 1:20 αὐτοῦ Eds, see ἐν
Eph. 2:15*for ἑαυτῷ LTTrAWHR
Phi. 3:21*for ἑαυτῷ LTTrAWHR
Heb. 2: 8 [under him[1]] LWH
Jas. 2: 3 omit unto him GLTTrAWHR
1 Joh. 3:15 ἑαυτῷ LT
5:10*for ἑαυτῷ TTrAWHR
Rev. 6: 2 α.[1], 4 α.[1], 5 αὐτόν GEds
4 [αὐτῷ][2] LWH
13: 7 omit L[WH], see δίδωμι
8 αὐτόν GEds
15 αὐτῇ LWHR
21: 6*δώσω—add α. T[A]W

αὐτῶν.

Mat. 6:15 omit their trespasses T[WH]
7:29*γραμματεῖς α. their scribes LTTrAWHR
11:16 omit α. LTTr[A]WHR
15: 2 omit α. T[Tr]WHR
8 omit GLTTrAWHR, see ἐγγίζω
17:14 omit α. LTTrAWHR
18:31 ἑαυτῶν LTTrAWH
35 omit their trespasses GLTTrAWHR
20:34 omit their eyes[2] LTTrAWHR
21: 7 omit their [L]TTrAWHR
23: 5 omit of their garments LTTrAWHR
26 of them—of it, αὐτοῦ LTTrAWHR
25: 1 ἑαυτῶν LTrAWH
3*for ἑαυτῶν[1] GLTrAW[WH]
4 omit α.[1] read the vessels LTTrAWH
4 α.[2]—ἑαυτῶν LTWH
7 ἑαυτῶν LTTrAWH
26:22 omit of them LTTrAWHR, see εἷς
Mar. 1:18 omit α. read the nets LTTr[A]WHR
2:19*for ἑαυτῶν TTrAWH, see ἔχω
4:15 omit TTrAWHR, see καρδία
9:44, 46 omit the verses T[Tr]WHR
14:46 omit α. L: αὐτῷ TTrAWH

Mar. 14:52 omit from them [L]TTrWHR
Lu. 2:22 α. their—her, αὐτῆς A.V.B. E
39 ἑαυτῶν LTTrAWWH
11:48 omit their sepulchres [L]TTrAWHR
15: 4 trs ἐξ αὐτῶν ἓν TTrAWHR
16: 4 ἑαυτῶν TTrAWHR
19:35*for ἑαυτῶν LTTrAWHR
36 ἑαυτῶν TrWH
22:47 αὐτούς GLTTrAWWH
55 omit α.[1] LTTrAWHR
66*for ἑαυτῶν TTrAWWHR
24:11 their—these, ταῦτα LTTrAWHR
Joh. 6: 7 omit of them LTTrAWHR
8:59 omit going through to end of verse GLTTrAWHR
11:19 omit α. TTrAWHR
16: 4*ὥρα α. their time LTrAWHR
Acts 1:26 their lots—lots for them, αὐτοῖς LTTrAWHR
5:18 omit their Eds
7:34 αὐτοῦ LTrWH
9:38 them—us, ἡμῶν Eds
10: 9*for ἐκείνων (-νος) T
10*for ἐκείνων (-νος) Eds
13:33(32) us their—our, ἡμῶν LTTrWHR
42*for τῶν Ἰουδαίων GEds
51 omit α. LTTrAWHR
14:13 omit α. read the city GEds
14 ἑαυτῶν WH
19:12 omit of them GEds
16 them[2]—both, ἀμφότεροι LTTrAWHR
20:30 α.[2]—ἑαυτῶν TTrAWH
22:30 omit α. read the council GEds
23:30*ἐξ α. for ἐξαυτῆς LTTr, see Ἰουδαῖος
25:17 omit α. [A]WH
Ro. 10: 1*for τοῦ Ἰσραήλ GEds
15:27 trs εἰσὶν αὐτῶν Eds
1 Co. 14:10 omit of them A.V.†Vul Eds
15:29*for τῶν νεκρῶν[2] (-ρός) GEds
2 Co. 3: 5*for ἑαυτῶν[2] LTrWH
Eph. 6: 9†trs καὶ α. καὶ ὑμῶν, read both their Master and yours Eds
Heb. 8:11 omit α.[1] LTTrAWHR
12 omit and their iniquities TTrAWHR
1 Pet. 4:19*for ἑαυτῶν LTTrAWR
Jude 15 omit among them LTTrAWHR
Rev. 2:22 their—her, αὐτῆς GEds
4: 8*for ἑαυτό GLTTrAWHR, see κατά
5:11 add A.V.B EGEds, see ἀριθμός
7:14 see στολή
9: 4 omit α. LTTr[A]WHR
19 see ἐξουσία
19*add A.V.C GEds, see ἐξουσία
11: 8*for ἡμῶν GEds
12:10 αὐτούς LTAWH
17:13*for ἑαυτῶν Eds
19:18 αὐτούς LTrAWHR
20: 4 omit α.[1] GEds
8*ἀριθμὸς—add α. GEds
21: 3 omit (and be) their God TTrWH

847 αὐτοῦ, adv.

Lu. 9:27*for ὧδε TTrAWH
Acts 15:34 omit the verse Eds

***αὐτόφωρος, see ἐπαυτοφώρῳ.**

***αὐχέω, see μεγαλαυχέω.**

851 ἀφαιρέω.

Rev. 22:19 ἀ.[1]—ἀφέλῃ GEds
ἀ.[2]—ἀφελεῖ GEds

861 ἀφθαρσία.

1 Co. 15:54 omit WH, see φθαρτός
Tit. 2: 7 omit sincerity EGEds

862 ἄφθαρτος

1 Ti. 1:17 immortali A.V. Vul

***ἀφθορία, incorruption.**

Tit. 2: 7 ἀφθορίαν for ἀδιαφθορίαν (-ία) Eds

863 ἀφίημι, ἀφέω, ἀφίω.

Mat. 6:12 ἀφήκαμεν have forgiven LTTrAWHR
9: 2, 5 ἀφίενται LTTrWH
18:12 ἀφήσει, read will he not leave LTrWH
23:23 ἀ.[2]—ἀφεῖναι LTTrAWHR
Mar. 2: 5, 9 ἀφίενται LTTrWH
10 trs ἐπὶ τῆς γῆς ἀ. GLTTrWR
11:26 omit the verse TTrWHR
12:21 see καταλείπω

Lu. 11: 4 α.²—ἀφίομεν LTTrAWH
42 to leave undone—to pass by πάρειμι LTTrAWH
17:36 *add* δύο ἔσονται ἐν τῷ ἀγρῷ· ὁ εἷς παραληφθήσεται, καὶ ὁ ἕτερος ἀφεθήσεται A.V.B E
18:28 ἀφέντες τὰ ἴδια, having left our own LTTrAWHR
23:34 [Then said *to* what they do] L[[WH]]
Joh. 20:23 ἀφέωνται LTTrWH
Acts 5:38*ἄφετε *for* ἐάσατε (ἐάω) LTTrAWHR
Rev. 2: 4 ἀφῆκες TTrWH
20*ἀφεῖς *for* ἐᾷς (ἐάω) GEds
11: 9 ἀφίουσιν suffer LTTrAWHR : ἀφιοῦσιν W

868 *ἀφίστημι.*
1 Ti. 6: 5 *omit* from such withdraw thyself Eds

872 **ἀφοράω, ἀπεῖδον.**
Phil. 2:23 ἀφίδω LTTrAWH

873 **ἀφορίζω.**
Mat. 25:32 ἀ.¹—ἀφορίσει TWH

877 *ἀφροσύνη.*
2 Co. 11: 1 τῇ ἀφροσύνῃ S—(τῆς E, *omit* τῇ Eds) ἀφροσύνης EEds

878 *ἄφρων.*
Lu. 12.20 ἄφρον GW
1 Co. 15:36 ἄφρων LTTrAWHR

*ἀφυστερέω, to come too late.
Jas. 5: 4 ἀφυστερημένος *for* ἀπεστερημένος (ἀποστερέω) TTrWH

882 Ἀχαΐα.
Ro. 16: 5 Achaia—Asia, Ἀσία GEds

881 Ἄχαζ, Ἄχας WH.

889 *ἀχρειόομαι.*
Ro. 3:12 ἠχρεώθησαν TTrWH

891 *ἄχρι, ἄχρις.*
Acts 1:22*for ἕως T
20: 4 *omit* into Asia T[Tr]WH
Gal. 4:19 μέχρις TTrWH
Rev. 20: 5*for ἕως GEds

894 Ἄψινθος.
Rev. 8:11 Ἀ.¹—ὁ Ἄψινθος GLTAWWHR

**βαθέως*, deeply.
Lu. 24: 1 *for* βαθέος (-θύς) LTTrAWWH

899 *βάθος.*
Eph. 3:18 *trs* height and depth LTrAWHR
Rev. 2:24 βαθύς GEds

901 *βαθύς.*
Lu. 24: 1 βαθέως LTTrAWWH
Rev. 2:24*βαθέα *for* βάθη (-θος) GEds

904 Βαλάκ.
Rev. 2:14 ἐν τῷ Β.—τὸν Β. A.V.B E

905 *βαλάντιον, βαλλ—* LTTrAWWH.

906 *βάλλω.*
Mat. 5:13 βληθέν LTTrAWHR
30 should be cast (β.²)—go, ἀπέρχομαι LTTrAWHR
27:35 βαλόντες LTA
35 *omit* that it might *to end of verse* GLTTrAWHR
Mar. 1:16 ἀμφιβάλλω GEds
7:27 *trs* τοῖς κυναρίοις βαλεῖν TTrAWH
30 βεβλημένον LTTrAWHR, *see* παιδίον
12:43 β.¹—ἔβαλεν did cast LTrWHR
43 β.²—βαλλόντων Eds
14:65 ἔβαλον W: λαμβάνω, *read* received him with blows of their hands LTTrAWHR
Lu. 12:58 βάλῃ GW, βαλεῖ LTTrAWHR
23:19 βληθεὶς TTr[A]WHR
Joh. 5: 7 βάλῃ GEds
7:44*ἔβαλεν *for* ἐπέβαλεν (ἐπιβάλλω) LTTrAWH
Acts 16:37 ἔβαλαν LTTrAWH

Rev. 2:10 βάλλειν LTrAWHR
24 βάλλω I put Eds
4:10 βάλλουσιν S—βαλοῦσιν shall cast EGEds
6:13 βάλλουσα casting T
12:10*ἐβλήθη *for* κατεβλήθη (καταβάλλω) LTTrAWHR

907 *βαπτίζω.*
Mat. 3:11 β.¹—*trs* ὑμᾶς βαπτίζω LTTrWWH
20:22, 23 *omit* and be baptised *to* baptised with GLTTrAWHR
28:19 βαπτίσαντες having baptised
Mar. 1: 4 ὁ βαπτίζων TTrAWHR (Tr
5 *trs* πάντες, καὶ ἐβ. GLTTrAWHR *read* all they of Jerusalem
6:24*βαπτίζοντος *for* βαπτιστοῦ (-τής) TTrAWHR
7: 4 β.¹—ῥαντίζω WH
1 Co. 1:15 ἐβαπτίσθητε ye were baptised Eds
10: 2 ἐβαπτίσθησαν LT

908 *βάπτισμα.*
Mat. 20:22, 23 *omit* GLTTrAWHR, *see* βαπτίζω
Col. 2:12 βαπτισμός TrA

909 *βαπτισμός.*
Mar. 7: 8 *omit* (as) the washing *to end of verse* T[TrA]WHR
Col. 2:12*βαπτισμῷ *for* βαπτίσματι (-μα) TrA

910 *βαπτιστής.*
Mar. 6:24 βαπτίζω TTrAWHR
Lu. 7:28 *omit* the Baptist TTrAWHR

911 *βάπτω.*
Joh. 13:26 βάψω shall dip TTrAWHR
26*βάψας οὖν *for* καὶ ἐμβάψας (-βάπτω) TTrAWHR
Rev. 19:13 dipped in—sprinkled with, περιρραίνω T, ῥαντίζω WHR

912 **Βαραββᾶς.**
Mat. 27:21 τὸν Βαραββᾶν TTrWH

916 *βαρέω.*
Mar. 14:40 καταβαρύνω Eds
Lu. 21:34*βαρηθῶσιν *for* βαρυνθῶσιν (-νομαι) GEds
2 Co. 1: 8 *trs* ὑπὲρ δύναμιν ἐβαρήθημεν LTTrAWHR

919 **Βαριησοῦς.**
Acts 13: 6 Βαριησοῦ T

920 **Βὰρ Ἰωνᾶ, Βαριωνᾶ** LTAWH.

921 **Βαρνάβας.**
Acts 11:25 *omit* ὁ Β. *read* he LTTrAWHR
13:50 τὸν Β.—*omit* τὸν LTTrAWH
Col. 4:10 Βαρνάβᾳ A.V.B

923 Βαρσαβᾶς, —ββᾶς LTTrAWHR.

925 *βαρύνω.*
Lu. 21:34 βαρέω GEds

927 *βαρύτιμος.*
Mat. 26: 7 πολύτιμος LT

928 *βασανίζω.*
Rev. 9: 5 βασανισθήσονται LTTrAWHR

932 *βασιλεία.*
Mat. 6:13 *omit* For thine *to end of verse* GEds
13:52 τῇ βασιλείᾳ GLTTrAWHR
Mar. 1:14 *omit* of the kingdom [L]TTrAWHR
Lu. 9:62 εἰς τὴν β.—τῇ βασιλείᾳ LTTrAWH
23:42 εἰς τὴν βασιλείαν WH
1 Co. 6: 9 *trs* θεοῦ βασιλείαν GEds
Rev. 1: 6*βασιλείαν *for* βασιλεῖς (-εύς) καί GEds
9 τῇ β.—*omit* τῇ GEds
5:10*βασιλείαν *for* βασιλεῖς (εύς) LTTrAWHR
11:15 ἡ βασιλεία the kingdom GEds

935 *βασιλεύς.*
Mat. 1: 6 *omit* the king² LTTrAWHR
2: 3 *trs* ὁ βασιλεὺς Ἡρώδης LTTrAWH
22: 7 *trs* ὁ δὲ βασιλεὺς LTTrAWHR

Mat. 22:13 *trs* ὁ βασιλεὺς εἶπεν LTTrAWHR
27:29 ὁ β.—βασιλεῦ LTrWH
Mar. 6:22†*trs* ὁ δὲ βασιλεὺς εἶπεν TTrAWHR
15:12 τὸν βασιλέα Eds
18 ὁ βασιλεὺς GAW
Lu. 1: 5 τοῦ β.—*omit* τοῦ TTr[A]WHR
14:31 *trs* ἑτέρῳ β. συμβ. LTTrAWH
19:38 ὁ βασιλεύς WH
23:38†*trs* ὁ β. τῶν Ἰουδαίων οὗτος ([οὗτος]L) LTTrAWHR
Joh. 1:50(49)†*trs* ὁ (*om.* ὁ TTrAWHR) β. εἶ LTTrAWHR
Acts 12: 1 *trs* ὁ βασιλεὺς Ἡρώδης T
26: 7 *trs* βασιλεῦ *after* Ἰουδαίων LTTrAWHR
Rev. 1: 6 kings and—a kingdom, βασιλεία GEds
5:10 kings—a kingdom, βασιλεία LTTrAWHR

936 *βασιλεύω.*
Rev. 5:10 βασιλεύσουσιν they shall reign GT, βασιλεύουσιν they reign LTrAWWHR

938 *βασίλισσα.*
Acts 8:27 τῆς β.—*omit* τῆς Eds

939 *βάσις.*
Acts 3: 7 *trs* αἱ βάσεις αὐτοῦ LTTrAWH

941 *βαστάζω.*
Rev. 2: 3 *trs* hast patience, and hast borne GEds

942 *βάτος.*
Mar. 12:26 τῆς β.—τοῦ β. GLTTrAWWH

944 *βάτραχος.*
Rev. 16:13 βάτραχοι GEds

945 *βαττολογέω, βαττα—* TAWH.

949 *βέβαιος.*
Heb. 3: 6 *omit* firm unto the end A[WH]

954 Βεελζεβούλ, —ύβ A.V.Vul, Βεεζ—WH

955 **Βελίαρ, —αλ** A.V.B ELR

Βενιαμίν, —μείν LTTrWH, at times A

958 **βελόνη*, a needle.
Lu. 18:25 βελόνης *for* ῥαφίδος (-ις) LTTrAWHR

*Βεώρ.
2 Pet. 2:15 *for* Βοσόρ WHR

962 **Βηθαβαρά, —ρᾷ** B
Joh. 1:28 Βηθανίᾳ GEds

963 Βηθανία.
Lu. 19:29 Βηθανιά AWH
Joh. 1:28*Βηθανίᾳ *for* Βηθαβαρᾶ GEds
11:18 ἡ Β.—*omit* ἡ TWH

964 Βηθεσδά, Βηθζαθά, TWH

966 Βηθσαϊδά.
Mat. 11:21 Βηθσαϊδά LTr

967 Βηθφαγή, —ῆ.
Mar. 11: 1 *omit* Bethphage LT

968 *βῆμα.*
Joh. 19:13 τοῦ β.—*omit* τοῦ Eds

970 *βια.*
Acts 24: 7 *omit* LTTr[A]WHR, *see* κρίνω

974 *βιβλαρίδιον.*
Rev. 10: 8 little book—book, βιβλίον LTrAWHR

975 *βιβλίον.*
Joh. 21:25 *omit the verse* T
Rev. 5: 7 *omit* the book LTTrAWHR
10: 8*βιβλίον *for* βιβλαρίδιον LTrAWHR
13: 8*τῷ βιβλίῳ *for* τῇ βίβλῳ (-λος) GEds
20:12 *trs* ἄλλο βιβλίον GEds
22:18 β.²—τῷ βιβλίῳ GEds
19*τοῦ βιβλίου *for* βίβλου¹ (-ος) GEds
19 τῷ βιβλίῳ GEds

976 βίβλος.
Rev. 13: 8 βιβλίον GEds
22:19 β.[1]—βιβλίον GEds
19 book[2]—tree, ξύλον GEds

978 Βιθυνία.
Acts 16: 7 τὴν Β.—*omit* τὴν W

979 βίος.
Lu. 8:43 *omit* WH, *see* ἰατρός
1 Pet. 4: 3 *omit* of (our) life Eds

984 βλάπτω.
Mar. 16:18 βλάψῃ GLTTrAWWH

985 βλαστάνω.
Mar. 4:27 βλαστᾷ LTTrAWH

987 βλασφημέω.
Mar. 2: 7*; βλασφημεῖ· *for* βλασφημίας; (-μία) LTTrAWH
1 Cor. 4:13 δυσφημέω TAWH
1 Pet. 4:14 *omit* on their part *to end of verse* LTTrAWH

988 βλασφημία.
Mar. 2: 7 *read* thus speak? he blasphemeth, βλασφημέω LTTrAWH
3:28 αἱ βλασφημίαι GEds
Rev. 13: 5 *read* great and blasphemous (βλάσφημος) things LA
6 βλασφημίας blasphemies Eds

989 βλάσφημος.
Acts 6:13 *omit* blasphemous GEds: *trs* λαλῶν ῥήματα TTrWH
Rev. 13: 5*βλάσφημα *for* βλασφημίας (-ία) (LA

991 βλέπω.
Mar. 8:23 βλέπεις thou seest AWH
Lu. 7:21 τὸ β.—*omit* τὸ Eds
24:12 *omit the verse* [L]T[Tr] [[WH]]
Joh. 9:19 *trs* βλέπει ἄρτι LTTrAWH
Acts 1:11*βλέποντες *for* ἐμβλέποντες (-πω) TTrWH
Heb. 11: 3 τὸ βλεπόμενον that which is seen LTTrAWH
Rev. 6: 1 ἴδε GW: *omit* and see LTTrAWH
3 *omit* and see GEds
5,7 ἴδε GW: *om.* and see LTTrAWH
11: 9 βλέπουσιν see GEds
17: 8 βλεπόντων GEds
18:18*βλέποντες *for* ὁρῶντες (ὁράω) GEds
22: 8 β.[2]—ἔβλεπον W

992 βλητέος.
Mar. 2:22 *omit* but new wine *to end of verse* T[Tr]A[WH]: *omit* must be put WH

993
Βοανεργές, Βοανη— LTTrAWH.

994 βοάω.
Mat. 27:46*ἐβόησεν *for* ἀνεβόησεν (ἀναβοάω) TrWH
Lu. 9:38*ἐβόησεν *for* ἀνεβόησεν (ἀναβοάω) LTTrAWH
Acts 21:34 ἐπιφωνέω Eds
25:24*βοῶντες *for* ἐπιβοῶντες (-οάω) LTTrWH: [ἐπι]β. A

1002 βολίς.
Heb. 12:20 *omit* or thrust through with a dart GEds

1003 Βοόζ.
Mat. 1: 5 *bis* Βοόζ LTr: Βοές TAWH
Lu. 3:32 Βοός LTTrAWH

1006 βόσκω.
Lu. 8:32 βοσκομένη LWH

1007 Βοσόρ.
2 Pet. 2:15 Βεώρ WH

1011 βουλεύομαι.
Lu. 14:31 βουλεύσεται will consult TWH
Joh. 11:53*ἐβουλεύσαντο *for* συνεβουλεύσαντο (συμβουλεύω) LTTrWH
Acts 5:33 took counsel—resolved, βούλομαι LTrWH
15:37 determined—was minded, βούλομαι Eds
27:39 ἐβουλεύοντο Eds
2 Co. 1:17 β.[1]—βούλομαι Eds

1013 βούλημα.
1 Pet. 4: 3*βούλημα *for* θέλημα Eds

1014 βούλομαι.
Acts 5:33*ἐβούλοντο *for* ἐβουλεύοντο (βουλεύομαι) LTrWH
15:37*ἐβούλετο *for* ἐβουλεύσατο (βουλεύομαι) Eds
2 Co. 1:17*βουλόμενος *for* βουλευόμενος (-μαι) Eds
Jas. 3: 4 βούλεται TTrWH
2 Joh. 12 ἐβουλήθην LTTrAWWH

1025 βρέφος.
Lu. 1:44 *trs* τὸ β. ἐν ἀγαλλιάσει GW
Acts 7:19 *trs* τὰ βρέφη ἔκθετα LTTrAWH

1027 βροντή.
Rev. 4: 5 *trs* voices and thunderings GEds
8: 5 *trs* thunderings and voices TTrAWH
16:18 *trs* lightnings, and voices, and thunders GEds

1039 βύσσινος.
Rev. 18:12*βυσσίνου *for* βύσσου (-ος) GEds

1040 βύσσος.
Rev. 18:12 βύσσινος GEds

1046 Γαδαρηνός.
Mat. 8:28*Γαδαρηνῶν *for* Γεργεσηνῶν TTrAWH
Mar. 5: 1 Γερασηνός LTTrWH: Γεργεσηνός A
Lu. 8:26, 37 Γερασηνός LTrAWH: Γεργεσηνός T

1049 γαζοφυλάκιον.
Lu. 21: 1 *trs* εἰς τὸ γ. τὰ δῶρα αὐτῶν TTrAWH

1050
Γάϊος, Γαῖος (except 3 John 1) WH

1053 Γαλατία.
2 Ti. 4:10 Γαλλία T

1054 Γαλατικός.
Acts 16: 6 τὴν Γ.—*omit* τὴν LTTrAWH

1056 Γαλιλαία.
Mat. 4:23 Γαλιλαίᾳ LTTrAWH, *see* ὅλος
19: 1 τῆς Γ.—*omit* τῆς E
Lu. 4:44 Galilee—Judæa, Ἰουδαία AWH
23: 6 *omit* of Galilee T[A]WH
55 *trs* ἐκ τῆς Γ. αὐτῷ TAWH

*** Γαλλία.**
2 Ti. 4:10 Γαλλίαν *for* Γαλατίαν T

1060 γαμέω, γάμω.
Mat. 19: 9 *omit* T[Tr]WH, *see* ἀπολύω
22:25 γήμας LTTrAWH
Mar. 10:12 γαμήσῃ ἄλλον marry another LTTrAWH
1 Co. 7: 9 γ.[2]—γαμεῖν TWH
28 γ.[1]—γαμήσῃς LTTrAWH

*** γαμίζω,** to marry, to give in marriage.
Mat. 22:30 γαμίζονται *for* ἐκγαμίζονται (-ζω) LTTrAWH
24:38 γαμίζοντες *for* ἐκγαμίζοντες (-ζω) TWH
Mar. 12:25 γαμίζονται *for* γαμίσκονται (-κομαι) LTTrAWWH
Lu. 17:27 ἐγαμίζοντο *for* ἐξεγαμίζοντο (ἐκγαμίζω) LTTrAWH
20:35 γαμίζονται *for* ἐκγαμίσκονται (-κομαι) LTTrWH
1 Co. 7:38 *see* ἐκγαμίζω[1]
38 γαμίζων *for* ἐκγαμίζων[2] (-ζω) GLTTrWH: [ἐκ]γ. A

1061 γαμίσκομαι.
Mar. 12:25 γαμίζω LTTrAWWH
Lu. 20:34*γαμίσκονται *for* ἐκγαμίσκονται (-κομαι) LTTrAWH
35*γαμίσκονται *for* ἐκγαμίσκονται (-κομαι) A

1062 γάμος.
Mat. 22:10 wedding — bride-chamber, νυμφών TWH
Joh. 2: 3*add γ. T, *see* οἶνος

1063 γάρ.
Mat. 1:18 *omit* γ. LTTr[A]WH
11:10 *omit* for [L]T[TrA]WH
13:17 *omit* for T
16: 2 *see* λέγω
18:11 *omit the verse* LTTr[A]WH
20:16 *omit* T[TrA]WH, *see* πολύς
23: 4 for—but, δέ LTTrAWH
5*for δέ[2] LTTrAWH
10 ὅτι LTTrAWH, *see* καθηγητής
24:28 *omit* for LTTrAWH
37*for δέ LTrWH
25: 3*αἱ γ. Tr, αἱ γ. TAWH, *for* αἵτινες (ὅστις)
Mar. 3:35 *omit* for LT[Tr]AWH
4:28 *omit* for LTTrAWH
6:36 *omit* γ. [L]TTrAWH, *see* ἄρτος
52 for[2]—but, *see* ἀλλά TTrWH
7: 8 *omit* for LTTrAWH
25 for—but, *see* ἀλλά TTrAWH
28 *omit* γ. [L]TTrWH
8: 3 for—and, *see* καί LTTrAWH
37*τί γ. *for* ἢ τί TTrAWH
11:18*πᾶς γ. *for* ὅτι πᾶς TTrAWH
23 *omit* for LT[Tr]AWH
12:36 *omit* for [L]T[Tr]AWH
13: 6 *omit* for TAWH
7 *omit* for T[Tr]AWH
9 *omit* for[1] T[Tr]AWH
22 for—and, δέ T
14: 2*for δέ LTTrAWH
16: 8*for δέ LTTrWH
Lu. 1:66*and[2]—καὶ γ. for also LTTrAWH
4: 8 *omit* for GEds
6:33*καί[1]—*add* γ. *read* for also T[WH]
33 *omit* for TWH
34 *omit* for T[Tr]AWH
48 *see* θεμελιόω
7:28 *omit* for TTrAWH
8:52*οὐκ—οὐ γ. *read* for she LTrAWH
9:14 for—and, δέ T
56 *omit* GLTTrAWH, *see* σώζω
10:42*for δέ TWH
12:23*ἡ—*add* γ. *read* for the life [LTrA]WH
14:14 for[2]—but, δέ T
18:14*ἢ—*add* γ. GTW
19:26 *omit* for [L]T[Tr]AWH
20:40*for δέ TTrAWH
42*αὐτὸς γ. *for* καὶ α. TWH
22:37 [for[2]] LTr
23:34 *see* λέγω
Joh. 4: 9 *omit* T[WH], *see* συγχράομαι
5: 4 *omit* [G]TTrAWH, *see* ὕδωρ
6:40*for δέ GEds
10:26 οὐ γ.—ὅτι οὐκ TTrWH
Acts 3:22 *omit* for GEds
18:15 *omit* for Eds
20:29 *omit* for Eds
21:22 *omit* γ. TrWH, *see* δεῖ
25:11 for—therefore, οὖν Eds
Ro. 2: 2*for δέ T
3: 2 *omit* γ. LTr[AWH]
7 for—but, δέ TWH
28*for οὖν GLTTrAWWH
4:15 for (γ.[2])—but, δέ Eds
5: 6 ἔτι γ.—εἴ γε AWH
9:19 *omit* for E
32 *omit* for LTTrAWH
11:13 for—and, δέ LTTrAWH
14: 2 μὲν—*add enim* A.V. Vul
5*μὲν—*add* γ. *read* For one [L]T[WH]
15*for δὲ Eds
15: 2 *omit* γ. GEds
8*for δὲ Eds
1 Co. 2:10*for δέ WH
7: 7 for—but, δέ Eds
40*for δέ[2] WH
8: 8 *omit* for LTTrAWH
11*ἀπόλλυται γ. *for* καὶ ἀπολεῖται LTTrWH
9:16*for δέ GEds
10: 1*for δέ GEds
28 *omit* for the earth *to end of verse* GEds
11:31 for—but, δέ Eds
14: 5 for—and, δέ LTTrAWH
14 [for] LTrWH
16: 7*for δέ GEds
2 Co. 2: 1*for δέ WH
5:12, 21 *omit* for Eds
7: 8 for I—*omit* for [L]TrWH
8:21*add γ. GLTTrAWH, *see* προνοέω
12: 1 for—but, δέ LTTrWH
Gal. 1:10 *omit* for[2] Eds
11*for δέ TrAWH
3:13 γέγραπται γ.—ὅτι γέγ. Eds
4:25 for—now, δέ WH
25*for δέ[2] GEds

Gal. 5:17*for δὲ³ Eds
Phil. 1:23 for—but, δέ GEds
23 πολλῷ—add γ. read for it is far EGEds
2: 5 omit γ. LTTrAWHR
Col. 3:24 omit for Eds
25*for δέ Eds
1 Th. 2: 9 omit for² GEds
5: 3 omit for GTTrAWHR
5*πάντες γ. for ye are all GEds
1 Ti. 2: 3 omit for LTTrWHR
2 Ti. 2:13*γ. ἑαυτὸν, read for he Eds
Heb. 2: 8 trs τῷ γὰρ Eds
8: 4 for if—if then, οὖν Eds
11:32 trs με γὰρ LTTrAWHR
13: 4*for δέ LTTrAWHR
Jas. 2:26 omit for WH
4:14 omit for¹ [Tr]WHR
1 Pet. 2:20*τοῦτο γ. for this LA
3 Joh. 3 omit for T[Tr]
Rev. 14: 5 omit for LAWHR
13*for δέ LTTrAWHR
16: 6 omit for² GEds
22: 9 omit for GEds
10*καιρὸς γ. Eds: omit ὅτι GEds
18 omit for GEds

1065 γέ.

Lu. 19:42 omit at least [L]Tr[A]WHR

See also εἴγε, ἄραγε, καίγε and καίτογε.

1068 Γεθσημανῆ, –νεῖ LTrAW –νεί TWH.

1067 γέεννα.

Mar. 9:47 τὴν γ.—omit τὴν WH

1069 γείτων.

Lu. 15: 9 τὰς γ.—omit τὰς LTTrAWHR

1072 γεμίζω.

Lu. 15:16 χορτάζω WHR

1073 γέμω.

Rev. 4: 8 γέμουσιν are full GEds
17: 3 γέμοντα LTAWHR
4 γέμων T
21: 9 τῶν γεμόντων, read who were full LTTrAWHR: omit τὰς W

1074 γενεά.

Lu. 1:50*γ.²—καὶ γενεὰς, read generations and generations TTrAWHR
11:29*this—add γενεὰ generation LTTrAWHR

1077 γενέσια.

Mat. 14: 6 γενεσίοις LTTrAWHR

1078 γένεσις.

Mat. 1:18*γένεσις for γέννησις GEds
Lu. 1:14*γενέσει for γεννήσει (–σις) GEds

1081 * γένημα, see γέννημα.

1080 γεννάω.

Mat. 1:12 bis, 13¹ γεννᾷ begetteth A
Lu. 1:35 nascetur A.V. Vul
Joh. 3: 6 γεγεννημένον S, γεγενη- bis E
8:41 ἐγεννήθημεν LTrAWHR
Gal. 4:23 γεγέννηται W
Heb.11:12 ἐγενήθησαν LA
2 Pet. 2:12 γεγεννημένα EGLTrAWWHR for γεγενημένα (γίνομαι) ST: trs γ. φυσικὰ Eds
1 Joh. 2:29 γεγέννηται S—γεγέννηται EGEds

1081 γέννημα.

Mat. 26:29 γενήματος LTTrAWWH
Mar. 14:25 γενήματος TTrAWWH
Lu. 12:18 my fruits—the wheat, σῖτος TrWHR: γενήματα S, γεννή- E
22:18 γενήματος LTTrAWWH
2 Co. 9:10 γενήματα GLTTrAWWH

1082 Γεννησαρέτ, Γενησαρέτ.

Mat. 14:34 Γεννησαρέθ LW

1083 γέννησις.

Mat. 1:18 γένεσις GEds
Lu. 1:14 γένεσις GEds

1085 γένος.

Mat. 17:21 omit the verse T[TrA]WHR

* Γερασηνός.

Mar. 5: 1 Γερασηνῶν for Γαδαρηνῶν LTTrWHR
Lu. 8:26, 37 Γερασηνῶν for Γαδαρηνῶν LTrAWHR

1086 Γεργεσηνός.

Mat. 8:28 Γαδαρηνός TTrAWHR
Mat. 5: 1*Γεργεσηνῶν for Γαδαρηνῶν A
Lu. 8:26, 37*Γεργεσηνῶν f. Γαδαρηνῶν T

1089 γεύομαι.

Lu. 9:27 γεύσωνται GLTTrAWWH
Joh. 8:52 γεύσηται GEds

1093 γῆ.

Mat. 6:10 τῆς γ.—omit τῆς Eds
13:23 trs τὴν καλὴν γῆν LTTrAWH
14:24*add γ. TrWH, see στάδιον
25:18 ἐν τῇ γῇ—γῆν TTrAWHR
28:18 τῆς γῆς LTrA: [τῆς] γ. WH
Lu. 11: 2 omit as in heaven, so in earth G[L]TTrAWHR
12:56 trs of the sky and of the earth A.V.C
22:43, 44 the verses [L] [[WH]]
Joh. 6:21 τὴν γῆν T
21:11 εἰς τὴν γῆν LTTrAWHR
Acts 7: 3 γ.²—τὴν γῆν Eds
11 omit the land of LTTrAWHR
36 omit the land of LTrWHR
10:12 see ἑρπετόν
1 Co. 8: 5 τῆς γ.—omit τῆς GEds
10:28 omit for the earth to end of verse GEds
Heb. 11: 9 τὴν γ.—omit τὴν LTTrAWHR
29*dry—add γῆς land Eds
12:25 τῆς γ.—omit τῆς GEds
2 Pet. 3:13 trs καινὴν γῆν T
1 Joh. 5: 8 omit in heaven (ver. 7) to in earth (ver. 8) GEds
Rev. 5:13 ἐπὶ τῆς γῆς GEds
8: 7*earth—add καὶ τὸ τρίτον τῆς γῆς κατεκάη and the third part of the earth was burnt up GEds
10: 2 τῆς γῆς GEds
12:12 τῇ γῇ GW
13: 3 ἡ γῆ EGLTAWWHR, see θαυμάζω
16:14 omit of the earth and GEds
17: 2 trs οἱ κατοικοῦντες τὴν γῆν ἐκ τοῦ οἴνου τῆς πορν. αὐτῆς GEds

1094 γῆρας.

Lu. 1:36 γήρει (–ρος) GLTTrAWWH

* γῆρος, see γῆρας.

1096 γίνομαι.

Mat. 11:23 ἐγενήθησαν LTTrAWH
14: 6*γενομένοις for ἀγομένων (ἄγω) LTTrAWHR
16: 2 When it is to end of verse 3 [TA][[WH]]
18:31 γ.¹—γινόμενα T
24:21 γ.¹—ἐγένετο T
27:54 γινόμενα were happening LTTrAWH
28: 4 ἐγενήθησαν LTTrAWH
Mar. 1:11 omit γ. T[WH]
2:15 γίνεται it cometh to pass TTrAWH
6: 2 γ.²—γινόμεναι TrWHR
35 γινομένης T
9: 3 ἐγένοντο LTrAW
6*trs ἔκφοβοι γὰρ (ἐγένοντο for ἦσαν) LTTrAWHR
7*ἐγένετο f. ἦλθεν (ἔρχομαι) TWHR
10:44 εἶναι LTrWHR
Lu. 2: 2 trs ἐγένετο πρώτη T
8:34 γεγονὸς GEds
40 omit it came to pass, that TrWHR
9:57 omit it came to pass, that TTrAWHR
10:13 γ.¹—ἐγενήθησαν LTTrAWHR
32 omit when he was TrWHR
38 omit it came to pass TrWHR
11: 2 omit Thy will be done GTTrAWHR
18:23 ἐγενήθη TTrAWHR
24 omit that he was very sorrowful (read saw him) T[Tr]AWHR
20:33 is she—shall she be, ἔσται R
21: 9 trs γενέσθαι ταῦτα A
22:26 γινέσθω TTrAWHR
42 γινέσθω TTrAWWHR
43, 44 the verses [L] [[WH]]

Lu. 24:12 omit the verse [L]T[Tr][[WH]]
Joh. 1:27 omit is preferred before me G[L]TTrAWHR
5: 4 omit waiting for (ver. 3) to end of verse 4 [G]TTrAWHR
6:17 omit T, see ἤδη
7:43 trs ἐγ. ἐν τῷ ὄχλῳ LTTrAWHR
10:16 γενήσονται TrAWHR
35 trs ἐγένετο τοῦ θεοῦ T
13: 2 γινομένου TTrWHR
15: 8 γένησθε LTrAWH
21: 4 γινομένης coming TTrWWHR
Acts 1:22 trs σὺν ἡμῖν γενέσθαι Eds
2:43 ἐγίνετο LTTrAWHR
4:22 γεγόνει LTTrAWH
5:12 ἐγένετο S—ἐγίνετο A.V.B EGEds
7:40 ἐγένετο LTTrAWHR
52 ἐγένεσθε Eds
8:13 γινόμενα GW
10:10*ἐγένετο for ἐπέπεσεν (ἐπιπίπτω) Eds
12:11 trs ἐν ἑαυτῷ γ. LTTrAWWH
20:37 trs κλαυθμὸς ἐγέ. LTTrAWWH
21:14 γινέσθω LTTrAWWH
22: 9 omit and were afraid LTTr[A]WHR
23:10 γινομένης LTWHR
24:25 see ἔμφοβος
26:28 to be—to make, ποιέω LTTrAWHR, see πείθω
Ro. 7:13 γ.¹—ἐγένετο Eds
15: 8 γενέσθαι LTr
16: 7 γέγοναν LTTrAWH
1 Co. 10:32 trs καὶ Ἰουδαίοις γ. LTTrAWHR
14:26 γινέσθω GEds
15:20 omit (and) become GEds
2 Co. 1:18 was—is, ἐστίν Eds
5:21 γενώμεθα Eds
Eph. 2:13 trs ἐγενήθητε ἐγγὺς LTTrAWHR
3: 7 ἐγενήθην Eds
Phil. 3:21 omit that it may be GEds
1 Th. 2: 8 ἐγενήθητε Eds
Tit. 3: 7 γενηθῶμεν Eds
Heb. 3:14 trs τοῦ χριστοῦ γεγόναμεν GEds
7:23 trs ἱερεῖς γεγονότες LAW
9:11*γενομένων for μελλόντων (–ω) LWH
1 Pet. 1:16 be ye—ye shall be, ἔσεσθε Eds
2 Pet. 2:12 γεννάω EGLTrAWWHR, read brute beasts, naturally born
2 Joh. 12*γενέσθαι for ἐλθεῖν (ἔρχομαι) Eds
Rev. 1:19 γενέσθαι TA
6:12 trs μέλας ἐγένετο GT
8:11 ἐγένετο Eds
11:15 γ.²—ἐγένετο GEds
16:18 ἄνθρωπος ἐγένετο a man was LTTrAW
21: 6 γέγοναν they are done LTTrWWHR: γέγονα[ν] ἐγώ A

1097 γινώσκω.

Mat. 16: 3 When it is (ver. 2) to end of ver. 3 [TA][[WH]]
Mar. 4:11 om. to know LTTrAWHR: trs τὸ μυστήριον δέδοται TTrAWHR
5:43 γνοῖ LTTrAWH
6:33*ἔγνωσαν for ἐπέγνωσαν (ἐπιγινώσκω) LTrAWH
9:30 γνοῖ LTTrAWH
13:28 γινώσκεται it is known A
Lu. 2:43 ἔγνωσαν LTTrAWHR, see γονεύς
8:17 γνωσθῇ LTTrAWHR
19:15 γνοῖ LTTrAWH
Joh. 10:14 γινώσκομαι ὑπὸ τῶν ἐμῶν—γινώσκουσίν με τὰ ἐμά mine own know me LTTrAWHR
38*γινώσκητε for πιστεύσητε² (–ύω) LTTrAWHR
14: 7 γ.¹—ἐγνώκατε ye have known T
7 γ.²—γνώσεσθε ye will know T: εἴδω TrAWHR
17: 3 γινώσκουσιν they know TTr
Acts 21:24 γνώσονται will know GEds
23:28 ἐπιγινώσκω Eds
24:11 ἐπιγινώσκω LTTrAWHR
Ro. 10:19 trs Ἰσραὴλ οὐκ ἔγνω GEds
1 Co. 2:11*ἔγνωκεν for οἶδεν³ (εἴδω) Eds
8: 2*ἐγνωκέναι for εἰδέναι (εἴδω) Eds
2 γ.¹—ἔγνω LTTrAWHR
Col. 4: 8 γνῶτε, read ye may know our LTTrWHR
Jas. 5:20 γινώσκετε know ye AWH
1 Joh. 3:19 γνωσόμεθα we shall know Eds
5:20 γινώσκομεν we know TTrAWHR
Rev. 2:17 εἴδω GEds
3: 3 γνώσῃ TTr

1100 γλῶσσα.

1 Co. 14:18 γλώσσῃ a tongue LTTrA

1 Co. 14:23 *trs* λαλῶσιν γλ. LTTrAWHR
26 *trs* hath a revelation, hath tongue Eds
39†*trs* μὴ κωλύετε (*add* ἐν [L]A) γλώσσαις LTTrAWHR
1 Joh. 3:18 τῇ γλώσσῃ with the tongue GEds

1103 γνήσιος.

Phil. 4: 3 *trs* γνήσιε σύνζυγε LTTrAWHR

1106 γνώμη.

Acts 20: 3 γνώμης TTrAWHR
Rev. 17:17 *trs* γνώμην μίαν G[A]

1107 γνωρίζω.

Lu. 2:17*ἐγνώρισαν *for* διεγνώρισαν (διαγνωρίζω) LTTrAWHR
Acts 7:13*ἐγνωρίσθη *for* ἀνεγνωρίσθη (ἀναγνωρίζομαι) TrWH
Eph. 3: 3 ἐγνωρίσθη was made known GEds
6:21 *trs* γνωρίσει ὑμῖν LTTrWHR
Col. 4: 9 γνωρίσουσιν LWH

1108 γνῶσις.

Ro. 15:14 τῆς γνώσεως TWH, [τῆς] γ. A
Col. 2: 3 τῆς γ.—*omit* τῆς LTTrAWHR

1110 γνωστός.

Joh. 18:16 ὃς ἦν γ.—ὁ γ. TTrAWH
Acts 15:18 γ. (γνωστὸν LW) *joined to verse* 17 GTTrAWHR

1112 γογγυσμός.

1 Pet. 4: 9 γογγυσμοῦ Eds

1115 Γολγοθᾶ, –ά TrWH.

Mar. 15:22 τὸν (*omit* τὸν A[Tr]) Γολγοθᾶν TAWH

1116 Γόμορρα.

Mat. 10:15 Γομόρρας TrA
Mar. 6:11 *omit* verily *to end of verse* G[L]TTrAWHR

1118 γονεύς.

Lu. 2:43*ἔγνω Ἰωσὴφ καὶ ἡ μήτηρ—ἔγνωσαν οἱ γονεῖς, *read* his parents knew it not LTTrAWHR
18:29 *trs* wife, or brethren, or parents TAWHR

1120 γονυπετέω.

Mar. 1:40 *omit* and kneeling down L[TrAWH]

1121 γράμμα.

Lu. 16: 6, 7 τὰ γράμματα bills LTTrAWHR
23:38 *omit* in letters of Greek, and Latin, and Hebrew [L]TTr[A] (WHR
2 Co. 3: 7 γράμματι LTrA
2 Ti. 3:15 τὰ ἱερὰ γ. — *omit* τὰ [L]T[TrA]WHR

1122 γραμματεύς.

Mat. 15: 1 *trs* Pharisees and scribes TTrWHR: *omit* οἱ LTTrWHR
23:14(13) *omit the verse* LTTrAWHR, *see* κρίμα
26: 3 *om.* and the scribes LTTrAWHR
Mar. 2:16 οἱ γ.—*omit* οἱ T
8:31 τῶν γραμματέων GEds
9:16 the scribes—them, αὐτούς GLTTrAWHR
11:18 *trs* chief priests and scribes Eds
15: 1 τῶν γραμματέων T
Lu. 5:30†*trs* Pharisees and their ([their] Tr) scribes Eds
11:44 *omit* scribes and Pharisees, hypocrites G[L]TTrAWHR
20:19 *trs* scribes and the chief priests LTTrAWHR
Acts 4: 5 τοὺς γραμματεῖς LTTrAWHR
23: 9 τινὲς τῶν γραμματέων some of the scribes TTrAWHR

1124 γραφή.

Mar. 15:28 *omit the verse* T[Tr]AWHR
1 Pet. 2: 6 τῇ γ.—*omit* τῇ TTrAWHR

1125 γράφω.

Lu. 10:20 ἐγγράφω TTrAWHR
23:38 ἐπιγράφω L[Tr]: *omit* written TAWHR

Joh. 8: 6 καταγράφω WHR
17 γεγραμμένον ἐστίν T
15:25 *trs* ἐν τῷ νόμῳ αὐτῶν γ. LTTrAWH
21:24 ὁ γράψας LTrWH, [ὁ] γ. A
25 *omit the verse* T
Acts 24:14 καὶ—*add* τοῖς ἐν GTTr[A]WHR
25:26 γ.[2]—γράψω Eds
Ro. 15: 4*ἐγράφη *for* προεγράφη[3] (προγράφω) Eds
2 Co. 13: 2 *omit* I write GEds
1 Joh. 2:13 γ.[3]—ἔγραψα I have written Eds
2 Joh. 5 γράφω σ—γράφων A.V.B EGEds: *trs* καινὴν γ. σοι LTTr
3 Joh. 13 γ.[1]—γράψαι σοι to write to thee Eds
13 γ.[2]—γράφειν Eds

1127 γρηγορέω.

Lu. 12:39 *om.* would have watched and T

1130 γυμνητεύω, γυμνι– LTTrAWWH.

1133 γυναικάριον.

2 Ti. 3: 6 τὰ γ.—*omit* τὰ GEds

1135 γυνή.

Mat. 15:38 *trs* children and women T
19:29 *omit* or wife LTTrAWHR
Mar. 7:26 *trs* ἡ δὲ γ. ἦν LTAWH, ἡ γ. δὲ ἦν Tr
10: 7 *omit* and cleave to his wife TWH
12 a woman—she, αὐτή TTrAWHR
29 *omit* or wife LTTrAWHR
12:22 *trs* καὶ ἡ γ. ἀπέθανεν LTTrAWHR
Lu. 1: 5 ἡ γ. αὐτοῦ—γ. αὐτῷ LTTrAWHR
28 *omit* blessed (art) thou among women T[Tr]AWHR
2: 5 *omit* wife LTTrAWHR
11:27 *trs* φωνὴν γυνὴ LTAWHR
18:29 *trs* wife, or brethren, or parents TAWHR
20:30 *omit* took her *to end of verse* TTrAWHR
32 *trs* καὶ ἡ γ. ἀπέθανεν TTrAWH
33*add *at commencement* ἡ γυνὴ the woman TAWH
23:55 αἱ γυναῖκες LTrWHR
Joh. 4: 9 *trs* γ. Σαμαρείτιδος οὔσης LTTrAWH
11 *omit* ἡ γ. *read* she [A]WH
8:10 *omit* and saw none but the woman WHR
10 *omit* woman[2] W, γύναι WH
1 Co. 7:33, 34 γυναικί, καὶ μεμέρισται. καὶ ἡ γυνὴ ἡ ἄγαμος καὶ ἡ παρθένος ἡ ἄγαμος (*omit* ἡ ἄγ. TrWH) μεριμνᾷ LTr, (his) wife, and is divided. And the woman that is unmarried and the (unmarried L) virgin careth for LTrWH
11: 7 ἡ γυνὴ Eds
11 *see* ἀνήρ
14:35 γυναικὶ a woman LTTrAWHR
Eph. 5:31 τῇ γυναικὶ LTTr
1 Ti. 2: 9 τὰς γ.—*omit* τὰς Eds
12 *trs* διδάσκειν δὲ γ. LTTrAWHR
1 Pet. 3: 1 αἱ γ.—*omit* αἱ LTTr[A]WHR
Rev. 12:15 *trs* ἐκ τοῦ στόματος αὐτοῦ ὀπίσω τῆς γ. GEds

1138 Δαβίδ, Δαυίδ GW, Δαυείδ LTTrAWH.

Mar. 12:35 *trs* Δαυεὶδ ἐστιν TTrAWH
Lu. 20:41 *trs* εἶναι Δαυεὶδ υἱόν TAWH
Acts 13:22 *trs* τὸν Δ. αὐτοῖς LTTrAWHR
Rev. 3: 7 τοῦ Δ.—*omit* τοῦ LTr[A]WHR
22:16 τοῦ Δ.—*omit* τοῦ GEds

1139 δαιμονίζομαι.

Mat. 12:22 δαιμονιζόμενον LWH

1140 δαιμόνιον.

Mar. 7:29 *trs* ἐκ τῆς θυγατρός σου τὸ δ. TAWH
Lu. 8:29*δαιμονίου *for* δαίμονος (-μων) LTTrAWHR
30 *trs* εἰσῆλθεν δα. πολλὰ LTWH
9:49 τὰ δ.—*omit* τὰ Eds
Rev. 16:14*δαιμονίων *for* δαιμόνων (-μων) GEds
18: 2*δαιμονίων *for* δαιμόνων (-μων) LTTrAWHR

1142 δαίμων.

Mar. 5:12 *omit* all the devils TTrAWHR
Lu. 8:29 δαιμόνιον LTTrAWHR
Rev. 16:14 δαιμόνιον GEds
18: 2 δαιμόνιον LTTrAWHR

1144 δάκρυ, δάκρυον.

Mar. 9:24 *omit* with tears LTTrAWHR
Lu. 7:38 *trs* τοῖς δ. *before* ἤρξατο LTTrAWH

1147 δάκτυλος.

Joh. 8: 8*κύψας—*add* τῷ δακτύλῳ, *read* with his finger wrote R
20:25 *trs* μου τὸν δάκτυλον T

1155 δανείζω, δανιζω TWH.

Lu. 6:34 δ.[1]—δανίσητε TWH: δανείζετε TrA

1156 δάνειον, δάνιον WH.

1157 δανειστής, δανιστής TWH.

1158 Δανιήλ.

Mar. 13:14 *omit* spoken of by Daniel the prophet G[L]TTrAWHR

1161 δέ.

Mat. 6: 1*προσέχετε δέ but take heed T, π. [δέ] AWH
7:15 *omit* δέ[1] LT[TrA]WHR
12:46 ǀ 13:1 *omit* δέ LTTrAWHR
13:46*εὑρὼν δέ and having found GLTTrAWHR
14: 9 *omit* nevertheless LTTrAWH
16:11*add δέ LTTrAWHR, *see* προσέχω
16 ἀποκριθεὶς δέ—καὶ ἀ. W
17:26*add δέ LTTrWHR, *see* λέγω
18:31 so—therefore, οὖν LTTrAWHR
20: 5*πάλιν δέ and again TTrA, [δέ] WH
10 ἐλθόντες δέ—καὶ ἐ. TrAWHR
14 *omit* δέ W
26 *omit* but[1] GLTTrAWHR
21:24 *omit* and[1] L[WH]
29 *omit* but [L]TWH
22: 7 ἀκούσας δέ—καὶ ἀ. W
37 *omit* δέ W
39 *omit* and TWH
23: 4*for γάρ LTTrAWHR
5 δέ[2]—γάρ, *read* for they make LTTrAWHR
23*ταῦτα δέ but these GLTrAW (WHR
24:37 but—for, γάρ LTrWH
25: 9 *omit* but[2] GEds
16 *omit* then [L]T[Tr]WHR
21 *omit* δέ GEds
22 *omit* δέ TWH
26:35*ὁμοίως δέ and likewise W
27:41 *omit* δέ [L]T[TrA]WHR
65 *omit* δέ GEds
Mar. 1: 6 ἦν δέ—καὶ ἦν LTTrAWH
14 μετὰ δέ—καὶ μ. LTrAWH
28 ἐξῆλθεν δέ—καὶ ἐ. LTTrAWH
2: 5 ἰδὼν δέ—καὶ ἰ. TWHR
4: 5 ἄλλο δέ—καὶ ἄ. LTTrAWHR
10 ὅτε δέ—καὶ ὅ. LTTrAWHR
36 *omit* and[2] LTr[A]WHR
37 τὰ δέ—καὶ τὰ LTTrAWHR
5: 6 ἰδὼν δέ—καὶ ἰ. TTrAWHR
13 *omit* δέ [L]TTrAWHR
14 οἱ δέ—καὶ οἱ LTTrAWHR
19 howbeit—and, καὶ GEds
6: 3 ἀδελφὸς δέ—καὶ ἀ. Eds
4 ἔλεγεν δέ—καὶ ἔ. LTTrAWHR
15*ἄλλοι[1] δέ but others Eds
22*add δέ LTTrAWHR, *see* βασιλεύς
24 ἡ δέ[1]—καί TTrAWHR
27(28) ὁ δέ—καί LTTrAWHR
7:27 καί LTTrAWHR
8: 8 ἔφαγον δέ—καὶ ἔ. LTTrWHR
20 *omit* and[1] [TrA]WH: καί T
20 οἱ δέ—καί TAWHR
29 *omit* and[2] LTTrAWHR
9: 9 καταβαινόντων δέ—καί κ. LTTrWHR
38 *omit* and[1] [L]TTrAWHR
10:27 *omit* and TTrAWHR
29 *omit* and[1] GEds
42 καί LTTrAWHR, *see* Ἰησοῦς
52 ὁ δέ—καὶ ὁ WH
11: 4 ἀπῆλθον δέ—καὶ ἀ. LTTrAWHR
8 πολλοὶ δέ—καὶ π. TTrAWH
12: 3, 14 οἱ δέ—καί LTTrAWHR
29 *omit* and TTrAWHR, *see* Ἰησοῦς
13:11 ὅταν δέ—καὶ ὅ. LTTrAWHR
12 παραδώσει δέ—καὶ π. LTTrAWHR
15 *omit* and L[Tr]WH
22*for γάρ T
14: 2 but—for, γάρ LTTrAWHR
9*ἀμὴν δέ and verily [L]TTrAWHR
19 *omit* and οἱ δέ TAWHR
15:31 *omit* δέ GEds
33 γενομένης δέ—καὶ γ. LTTrAWHR
16: 8 γάρ LTTrWHR

Mar. 16:14*ὕστερον δέ and afterward LTrB, [δέ] WH
Lu. 1:76*σὺ δέ thou also TTrAWHR
2:35 omit also [LTr]WH
6: 8 ὁ δέ—καί LTTrAWHR
9*for οὖν LTTrWHR
30 omit δέ [L]T[Tr]WHR
7: 1 ἐπειδή (omit now) LTTrAWHR
21 omit and[1] LTTrAWHR
42 omit and [L]TTrAWHR
43 omit δέ [L]TTrAWHR
9:14*for γάρ T
57 καί TTrAWHR
10: 2*for οὖν LTTrAWHR
8 omit δέ LTTrAWHR
12 omit but G[L]TTrAWWHR
30 omit and[1] TWHR
37*for οὖν GLTTrAWHR
42 and—for, γάρ TWHR, [δέ] A
11:33 omit δέ TTrAWHR
42*ταῦτα δέ now these [L]TrWHR
47 οἱ δέ—καὶ οἱ T
12:42 εἶπεν δέ—καὶ ε. TTrAWHR
13:15*for οὖν LTTrAWHR
18 then—therefore, οὖν TTrAWHR
35 omit and T[WH]: trs λέγω δέ GLTrAWWHR
14:14*for γάρ T
26 τε LTrAWH
15:28*for οὖν LTTrAWHR
16:29*λέγει—add δέ, read but Abraham Eds
17: 1 οὐαὶ δέ—πλὴν ο. LTrWHR
3 omit δέ LTTrAWHR
17 omit but LT[TrWH]
19:22 omit and[1] TTrAWHR
20:32 omit δέ A.V. Br LTTrAWHR
40 and—for, γάρ TTrAWHR
21:13 omit and T[TrA]WHR
23 omit but LTTrAWHR
36*for οὖν LTTrAWHR
22:36*ὁ δὲ εἶπεν TR, ε. δὲ TrWH, for ε. οὖν
44 ἐγένετο δέ—καὶ ἐ. TAWH
47 omit and[1] Eds
69*νῦν—add δέ read but hereafter LTTrAWHR
23:20*for οὖν LTTrAWHR
24 καί LTTrAWHR
44 ἦν δέ—καὶ ἦν LTTrAWHR
24:48 omit and TTrAWHR
Joh. 1:26 omit but TTrAWHR
38 omit then T
39(40) omit for GEds
42(43) omit and[2] GTTrAWWHR
2:17 omit and [L]TTrAWHR
3:18 omit but [L]T[Tr]AWHR
36 omit and T
4:31 omit δέ [L]TTrAWHR
54*τοῦτο δέ now this Tr, [δέ] AWH
5:11*add δέ LTrWHR, see ὅς
29 omit and[2] [L]T[Tr]AWH
6:10 omit and [L]TTrAWHR
11 and[1]—therefore, οὖν LTTrAWHR
23 omit howbeit TTr[A]WHR
35 omit and[1] [L]TrAWHR, οὖν T
40 and[1]—for, γάρ GEds
7: 9 omit δέ A.V. Vul GTTr
12 omit δέ GTW[WH]
29 omit but GEds
41 omit but T
8:14 omit but T
46 omit and GLTTrAWHR
9: 9 omit δέ [L]TTrAWHR
11 and[2]—therefore, οὖν LTTrAWHR
16*ἄλλοι δέ but others R, [δέ] WH
26 οὖν LTTrAWHR
28*οἱ δὲ ἐλοιδόρησαν but they railed Tr
31 omit now LTTrAWHR
37 omit and[1] LTTrAWHR
10:12 omit but T[Tr]WHR
20 and[1]—then, οὖν T
22 τότε WH
11:29*δὲ ὡς and as soon TrWHR, [δέ] A
12: 4*for οὖν T[WH]R
16 omit δέ [L]TTrAWHR
13:23 omit now TTrAWHR
25 omit then TrAWHR, οὖν T
14:17 omit but [L]T[Tr]AWHR
15:26 omit but T[TrA]WH
16:20 omit and[2] LTTrAWHR
18: 4*for οὖν Tr
19:14 omit and[2] Eds
15 omit οἱ δέ TTrAWHR, see ἐκεῖνος
16 and[1]—therefore, οὖν LTTrAWHR
29 omit δέ LTTrAWHR, see πλήθω
21: 6 omit and[1] T
12 omit δέ [Tr]AWH
20 omit then Eds
Acts 1: 7 omit and TTrWH
4:14 τε LTTrAWHR
5:32 omit also LTTr[A]WHR
6: 3*for οὖν TWH
7:15 κατέβη δέ—καὶ κ. LTTrAW
26 τε s—δέ EGW
49 ἡ δέ—καὶ ἡ WH
8:33 omit and LTTr[A]WHR
11:17 omit δέ LTTr[A]WHR
12:17 δέ[2]—τε LTTrAWHR
13:11 τε T
44 τε GA
46 δέ[1]—τε LTTrAWHR
46 omit but LTTrWHR
52 τε LTrAWH
14:11 τε LTAWHR
13 ὁ δέ—ὅ τε LTTrAWHR
15: 2*for οὖν TTrWHR
6 τε TrAWH
32 τε s—δέ E
39*for οὖν LTTrAWHR
16: 7*ἐλθόντες δέ read and after Eds
11*for οὖν TA
38 τε T
17:14 δέ[2]—τε LTTrAWHR
18: 1 omit δέ LTTr[A]WHR
21 omit but[2] LTTrAWHR
19:27 δέ[2] s—τε A.V.B EGLTTrAWHR
20: 5*οὗτοι δέ and these LTTr[A]WHR
15*τῇ[3]—add δέ LTTrWHR
34 omit yea GEds
21:13 ἀπεκρίθη δέ—τότε ἀ. Eds
18 τε T
31 τε LTTrAWHR
22:23 τε LTrAWWH
23:28 τε LTTrAWHR
24:10 τε LTTrAWHR
16 καί Eds
18 omit δέ A.V.B E
26 omit δέ GEds
25: 2 τε LTTrAWHR
22 omit ὁ δέ LTTrAWHR
26:14 | 27:21 | 28: 2 τε Eds
28: 9*for οὖν LTTrAWHR
16 omit but LTTrAWHR
25 τε T
Ro. 2: 2 but—for, γάρ T
17*εἰ δέ for ἴδε GEds
3: 7*for γάρ TWHR
29 omit δέ GLTTrAWHR
4:15*for γάρ[2] Eds
11:13*for γάρ LTTrAWHR
14:15 but—for, γάρ Eds
15: 8 now—for, γάρ Eds
1 Co. 2:10 γάρ WH
4: 2 ὁ δέ—ὧδε here LTTrAWHR
7: 7*for γάρ Eds
38 ὁ δέ—καὶ ὁ GEds
40 and—for, γάρ WH
8: 2 omit and Eds
9:16 yea—for, γάρ GEds
10: 1 moreover—for, γάρ GEds
27 omit δέ Eds
30 omit for[1] GEds
11:31*for γάρ Eds
34 omit and[1] GEds
12: 6 ὁ δέ—καὶ ὁ AWH
9 omit δέ[1] [L]TTr[A]WHR
10 omit δέ[2] et δέ[3] LTr[WH]
10 omit δέ[4] LTTrWHR
21 omit and G[LWH]
13:11 omit but LTTrAWHR
14: 5*for γάρ LTTrAWHR
15 omit and[2] L[TrWH]
40*πάντα δέ read but let all GEds
15:14 omit and[2] Eds
16: 7 but—for, γάρ GEds
2 Co. 2: 1 but—for, γάρ WH
5:16 omit δέ LTTrAWHR
6:14 τίς δέ—ἢ τίς, or what Eds
7:13 trs δέ after ἐπί[1] (commencing a sentence at ἐπί) Eds
8:13 omit and LTTr[A]WHR
9:15 omit δέ LTTrAWHR
12: 1*for γάρ LTTrWHR
13: 9 omit and[2] Eds
Gal. 1:11 but—for, γάρ TrAWHR
2:16*εἰδότες δέ but knowing GEds
4:25*for γάρ WHR
25 and[2]—for, γάρ GEds
5:17 and[2]—for, γάρ Eds
Eph. 4:32 omit and L[WH]
Phil. 1:23*for γάρ GEds
4:12 καί A.V.C GEds
Col. 2: 4 omit and T[TrA]WHR
3:25 but—for, γάρ Eds
1 Th. 2:16 enim A.V. Vul
5:21*πάντα δέ, read but prove GLTTrAW, [δέ] WH
1 Ti. 5:20*τοὺς δέ but them L, [δέ] AWH
25*ὡσαύτως δέ but likewise LW
Philem. 12 omit therefore LTTrAWHR
Heb. 12:11 now—indeed, μέν TWHR
13: 4 but—for, γάρ LTTrAWHR
Jas. 1:19*ἔστω—add δέ LTTrAWHR, read but let, see ὥστε
2:15 omit δέ TTrWHR
3: 3*εἰ δέ for ἰδού Eds
4: 2 omit yet GLTTrAWHR
7*ἀντίστητε δέ but resist LTTrAWHR
12*σὺ δέ, read but who GLTTrAWHR
14 καί LTTrAWHR: omit and W
1 Pet. 3:11*ἐκκλινάτω δέ and let him eschew LTrAWHR
15 omit and[1] LTTr[A]WHR
4: 8 omit and TTrAWHR
2 Pet. 2:22 omit but LTTrAWHR
1 Joh. 3: 2 omit but Eds
5: 5*add δέ after τίς [Tr]R, after ἐστίν [WH], read and who
3 Joh. 11 omit but[2] GEds
Rev. 2: 9 πλούσιος δέ—ἀλλὰ π. GEds
14:13 and[2]—for, γάρ LTTrAWHR
20: 5 omit but LTAWWHR: καὶ οἱ Tr
22:15 omit for GEds

1162 δέησις.

Acts 1:14 omit and supplication GEds

1163 δεῖ.

Mar. 14:31 trs δέῃ με LTrWH
Lu. 24:46 omit and thus it behoved [L]TTrAWHR
Joh. 10:16 trs δεῖ με LTTrAWHR
Acts 10: 6 omit he shall tell to end of verse GEds
18:21 omit I must to Jerusalem LTTrAWHR
21:22 omit the multitude must come together TrWHR: trs δεῖ συνελθεῖν πλῆθος LTA
24:19 δεῖ s—ἔδει A.V.B EGEds
2 Co. 12: 1*for δή LTTrWHR, see συμφέρω
Rev. 13:10 omit must A

1165 δειγματίζω.

Mat. 1:19*δειγματίσαι for παραδειγματίσαι (-τίζω) LTTrAWH

1166 δεικνύω, -υμι.

Lu. 20:24*δείξατε for ἐπιδείξατε (-είκνυμι) GEds
24:40*ἔδειξεν for ἐπέδειξεν (ἐπιδείκνυμι) LTrWHR, [ἐπ]έ. A
Jas. 2:18 trs σοι δείξω TTrWH
Rev. 22: 8 δεικνύντος T

1169 δειλός.

Rev. 21: 8 τοῖς δὲ δ. A.V.C GEds

1177 δεκαδύο.

Acts 19: 7 δώδεκα LTTrAWWH
24:11 δώδεκα LTTrAWH

* δεκαοκτώ, eighteen.

Lu. 13: 4, 11 for δέκα καὶ ὀκτώ T, omit καί [LTrA]WH

1186 δένδρον.

Mar. 11: 8 trees—fields, ἀγρός TTrAWHR

1188 δεξιός.

Mat. 27:29 ἐν τῇ δεξιᾷ LTTrAWHR
Mar. 10:37 trs σου ἐκ δεξιῶν TTrAWH
14:62 trs ἐκ δ. καθήμενον GLTTrAWWH
Rev. 10: 5*αὐτοῦ—add τὴν δεξιάν, read his right hand GEds

1189 δέομαι.

Lu. 8:38 ἐδεεῖτο L, ἐδεῖτο TrAWH

* δέος, fear.

Heb. 12:28 reverence and godly fear—εὐλαβείας καὶ δέους godly fear and awe LTTrAWHR

1196 δεσμέω.

Lu. 8:29 ἐδεσμεύετο TTrWHR

1198 δέσμιος.

Acts 28:16 omit the centurion to the guard: but LTTrAWHR
Heb. 10:34*δεσμίοις for δεσμοῖς μου GEds

1199 δεσμός.

Acts 22:30 omit from (his) bands GEds
Heb. 10:34 me in my bonds—the prisoners, δεσμίοις GEds

1205 δεῦτε.

Lu. 20:14 *omit* come LTTrAWHR

1207 δευτερόπρωτος.

Lu. 6: 1 *omit* second after the first [L]T[A]WHR

1208 δεύτερος.

Mat. 21:30 second—other, ἕτερος GTAW
Acts 13:33 second—first, *see* πρῶτος GLTTr
Rev. 6: 3†*trs* σφραγῖδα τὴν δ. GEds
11:14 ἡ δ.—*omit* ἡ W
14: 8*δεύτερος ἄγγελος ([ἄ.] WH) a second angel LTrAWWHR: ἄγ. δ. T.
21: 8†*trs* ὁ θάνατος ὁ δ. GEds

1209 δέχομαι.

Mar. 6:11 ὃς ἂν τόπος μὴ δέξηται whatsoever place will not receive TTrAWHR
9:37 δ.[3]—δέχηται TTrAWHR
Lu. 9: 5 δέχωνται LTTrAWHR
11 received—welcomed, ἀποδέχομαι LTTrAWHR
Acts 21:17 received—welcomed, ἀποδέχομαι Eds
Co. 8: 4 *omit* that we would receive GEds

1210 δέω.

Acts 10:11 *omit* δ. καί, *read* let down by four corners LTTr[A]WHR
20:22 *trs* δεδεμένος ἐγὼ GLTTrAWWH

1211 δή.

2 Co. 12: 1 δεῖ LTTrWHR, *see* συμφέρω
Rev. 2:10*ἰδού—*add* δή [A]W

* δηλαυγῶς, clearly.

Mar. 8:25 *for* τηλαυγῶς T

1212 δῆλος.

1 Ti. 6: 7 *omit* (it is) certain LTTrAWHR

1220 δηνάριον.

Mar. 6:37 *trs* δην. διακοσίων GLTTrAWWH
14: 5 *trs* δην. τριακοσίων LTTrAWWH

1221 δήποτε.

Joh. 5: 4 *omit* waiting for (*ver.* 3) *to end of verse* 4 [G]TTrAWHR

1222 δήπου, δή που WH.

1223 διά.

Mat. 2:17* ׀ 3:3**for* ὑπό Eds
11: 2**for* δύο Eds
23:14(13) *omit the verse* LTTrAWHR, *see* κρίμα
Mar. 7:31**for* καί[2] LTTrAWHR, *see* ἔρχομαι
10: 1 by—and, καί LTTrAWHR
Lu. 5:19 *omit* by GEds
6:48**add* δ. TTrAWHR, *see* θεμελιόω
19: 4 *omit* δ. GEds
Joh. 7:22 *omit* therefore T
8:59 *omit* going through *to end of verse* GLTTrAWHR
Acts 13:49 κατά T
Ro. 15: 4*and—*add* δ. through Eds
1 Co. 14:19 *omit* δ. Eds, *see* νοῦς
2 Co. 1:20*ἐν αὐτῷ[2]—δι' αὐτοῦ Eds
4:14 by—with, σύν Eds
Eph. 3: 9 *omit* by Jesus Christ GEds
Col. 1:14 *omit* through his blood GEds
20 *omit* by him (I say) LTr[WH]
2 Th. 3:12 ἐν LTTrAWHR, *see* κύριος
Heb. 1: 3 *omit* by himself LTTrAWHR
1 Pet. 1:22 *omit* through the Spirit Eds
2 Pet. 1: 3 *omit* δ.[2] LTTrAWR, *see* ἴδιος
3: 9**for* εἰς[1] LT
Jude 25**add* δ. GEds, *see* κύριος
Rev. 1: 9 *omit* for[2] LTr[A]WHR
6: 9 *omit* for[2] L[A]
21:24**for* ἐν GEds
See also διαπαντός

1227 διαβλέπω.

Mar. 8:25*ἐποίησεν αὐτὸν ἀναβλε. made him look up—διέβλεψεν, he saw distinctly TTrAWHR

1228 διάβολος.

Lu. 4: 5 *omit* the devil TTrAWHR
Rev. 2:10 *trs* ὁ δ. ἐξ ὑμῶν GEds
20: 2 ὁ διάβολος T

1232 διαγνωρίζω.

Lu. 2:17 made known abroad—made known, γνωρίζω LTTrAWHR

1238 διάδημα.

Rev. 12: 3 *trs* ἑπτὰ διαδήματα GEds

1239 διαδίδωμι.

Joh. 6:11 δίδωμι T
Acts 4:35 διεδίδετο LTTrAWH
Rev. 17:13 shall give—give, δίδωμι GEds

1245 διακαθαρίζω.

Lu. 3:17 καὶ δ.–διακαθᾶραι to throughly purge TWHR

1247 διακονέω.

Joh. 12:26 *trs* τις διακονῇ[1] LTTrAWWH
Philem. 13 *trs* μοι διακονῇ GEds

1248 διακονία.

2 Co. 3: 9 ἡ δ.[1]—τῇ διακονίᾳ with the ministration LTTr
Rev. 2:19 *trs* GLTTrAWHR, *see* πίστις

1249 διάκονος.

Mar. 10:43 *trs* ὑμῶν διάκονος GLTTrAWWH
1 Th. 3: 2 minister of—fellow labourer with, συνεργός GLAW

1250 διακόσιοι.

Acts 27:37 *omit* two hundred WH.

1252 διακρίνω.

Mat. 16: 3 When it is (*ver.* 2) *to end of verse* 3 [TA][[WH]]
Acts 11:12 *omit* nothing doubting A: διακρίναντα LTTrWHR
Jude 22 διακρινομένους Eds, *see* ἐλεέω

1253 διάκρισις.

1 Co. 12:10 διάκρισις T

1256 διαλέγομαι.

Acts 17: 2 διελέξατο LTTrWHR
18:19 διελέξατο LTTrWH

1257 διαλείπω.

Lu. 7:45 διέλειπεν T

1260 διαλογίζομαι.

Mar. 11:31*διελογίζοντο *for* ἐλογίζοντο (λογίζομαι) Eds
Joh. 11:50 λογίζομαι Eds

1261 διαλογισμός.

1 Ti. 2: 8 διαλογισμῶν WH

1263 διαμαρτύρομαι.

Acts 2:40 διεμαρτύρατο Eds

1266 διαμερίζω.

Mat. 27:35 *omit* that it might *to end of verse* GLTTrAWHR
Mar. 15:24 διαμερίζονται they part GEds
Lu. 11:17 *trs* δ. ἐφ' ἑαυτὴν T
12:53 διαμερισθήσονται LTTrAWHR: τρισίν (52) δ.' LTTrA

1271 διάνοια.

Lu. 10:27 τῇ διανοίᾳ LTTrWHR, *see* ψυχή
Eph. 1:18 understanding—heart, καρδία GEds
Heb. 10:16 τὴν διάνοιαν mind Eds

1272 διανοίγω.

Mar. 7:35 ἀνοίγω LTTrAWH
Acts 7:56*διηνοιγμένους *for* ἀνεῳγμένους (ἀνοίγω) Eds

1275 διαπαντός.

(*often* διὰ παντός *by* LTrAWH)
Acts 2:25**for* διὰ παντός GT

* διαπαρατριβή, violent contention.

1 Ti. 6: 5 διαπαρατριβαὶ *for* παραδιατριβαὶ (-βή) GEds

1279 διαπορεύομαι.

Mar. 2:23**trs* αὐτὸν ἐν τοῖς σάββασιν (διαπορεύεσθαι *f.* παραπορεύεσθαι, -εύομαι LTrWHR) LTTrAWHR

1280 διαπορέω.

Lu. 24: 4 ἀπορέω LTTrAWHR
Acts 2:12 διηποροῦντο TTrAWHR

1281 διαπραγματεύομαι.

Lu. 19:15 διεπραγματεύσαντο TrAWHR, *see* τίς

1283 διαρπάζω.

Mat. 12:29 δ.[1]—ἁρπάζω LTTrAWH
29 δ.[2]—διαρπάσῃ T

1284 διαρρήσσω, διαρρήγνυμι.

Mat. 26:65 διέρηξεν WH
Mar. 14:63 διαρήξας WH
Lu. 5: 6 διερήσσετο TTrAWH
8:29 διαρήσσων LTTrAWH

1285 διασαφέω.

Mat. 13:36*διασάφησον *for* φράσον (-άζω) LTrWHR

1287 διασκορπίζω.

Mat. 26:31 διασκορπισθήσονται LTTrAWH
Mar. 14:27 διασκορπισθήσονται LTTrAWH: *trs* τὰ πρόβατα δ. TTrAWH

1291 διαστέλλομαι.

Mat. 16:20 ἐπιτιμάω LWH

1299 διατάσσω.

Acts 18: 2 τάσσω T
20:13 *trs* διατεταγμένος ἦν LTTrAWH

1302 διατί, διὰ τί LTrAWH.

Lu. 5:33 *omit* why do TAWHR

1304 διατρίβω.

Joh. 11:54 μένω TrAWHR

* διαυγής, transparent.

Rev. 21:21 διαυγής *for* διαφανής GEds

1307 διαφανής.

Rev. 21:21 διαυγής GEds

1309 διαφεύγω.

Acts 27:42 διαφύγῃ GLTTrAWWH

1310 διαφημίζω.

Mat. 28:15 is commonly reported—is reported, φημίζω T

1311 διαφθείρω.

Rev. 8: 9 διεφθάρησαν LTTrAWHR

* διαχλευάζω, to scoff utterly.

Acts 2:13 διαχλευάζοντες *for* χλευάζοντες (-ζω) GEds

1320 διδάσκαλος.

Mat. 23: 8*διδάσκαλος *for* καθηγητής Eds
Lu. 7:40 *trs* δ. εἰπέ, φησίν TTrAWH

1321 διδάσκω.

Mar. 1:21 *trs* ἐδ. εἰς τὴν συναγωγήν TA
6: 2 *trs* δ. ἐν τῇ συναγωγῇ TTrWH
Lu. 21:37 *trs* δ. ἐν τῷ ἱερῷ Tr
Rev. 2:20 καὶ διδάσκει and she teacheth GEds, see πλανάω

1322 διδαχή.

Mar. 1:27 *omit* ἡ LTTrAWHR, see καινός
12:38†*trs* ἐν τῇ δ. αὐτοῦ ἔλεγεν TTrAWHR
Heb. 6: 2 διδαχὴν LWH

1323 δίδραχμον.

Mat. 17:24 τὰ δ.[2]—*omit* τὰ T

1325 δίδωμι.

Mat. 5:42 δός LTTrAWH
15:36 ἐδίδου TTrWHR
24:45 δοῦναι GLTTrAWH
26:26 δοὺς having given LTTrWHR
Mar. 3: 6*ἐδίδουν *for* ἐποίουν (ποιέω) TrAWH
6:25 *trs* ἐξαυτῆς δῷς μοι LTTrAWHR
37 δ.[2]—δώσομεν LTrAWHR, δώσωμεν T
8:37 [δώσει] A, δοῖ TTrWHR
11:28 *trs* ἐδ. τὴν ἐξουσίαν ταύ. LTrWH
12:14 *trs* δ. κῆνσον Καίσαρι LTrWH

Mar. 13:22 shall shew—shall do, ποιέω TA
Lu. 10:19 δέδωκα I have given TTrAWHR
12:42 τοῦ δ.—*omit* τοῦ L[TrA]
16:12 *trs* δώσει ὑμῖν TTrWHR
19:15 δεδώκει LTTrAWHR
20:10 δώσουσιν LTTrAWHR
Joh. 5:26 *trs* καὶ τῷ υἱῷ ἔδωκεν TTrAWHR
36 δέδωκεν TTrAWHR
6:11*ἔδωκεν *f.* διέδωκεν (διαδίδωμι) T
27†*trs* δίδωσιν ὑμῖν giveth you T
32 δ.[1]—ἔδωκεν LTrAWHR
51 *omit* which I will give LTTrAWHR
7:19 ἔδωκεν LTrAWHR
10:28 *trs* δ. αὐτοῖς ζωὴν αἰώ. TTrAWH
12:49 δέδωκεν Eds
13: 3 ἔδωκεν TTrWHR
15 δέδωκα TR
26*καὶ δώσω αὐτῷ and shall give to him *for* ἐπιδώσω (–δίδωμι) TTrAWHR
14:31**add* δ. LTrWH, *see* ἐντολή
16:23 *trs* the Father, he will give you in my name TTrAWHR
17: 2 δ.[3]—δώσει AWH
6 ἔδωκας *bis* LTTrWHR
7 ἔδωκας LWH
8 δ.[1]—ἔδωκας LTTrAWHR
24 δ.[2]—δέδωκας Eds
19: 3 ἐδίδοσαν LTTrAWH
11 *trs* δεδομένον σοι LTTrAWH
Acts 5:31 τοῦ δοῦναι TR, [τοῦ] δ. WH
11:18 *trs* εἰς ζωὴν ἔδωκεν Eds
14: 3 διδόντος T
20:35 *trs* μᾶλλον διδόναι GEds
Ro. 14:12 ἀποδίδωμι LTr, [ἀπο]δ. A
1 Co. 15:38 *trs* δίδωσιν αὐτῷ Eds
2 Co. 8:16 δόντι W
13:10 *trs* ὁ κύριος ἔδωκέν μοι LTTrAWHR
Eph. 3: 7 τῆς δοθείσης GLTTrAWHR
16 δῷ LTTrAWHR
6:19 δοθῇ GEds
1 Th. 4: 8 διδόντα giveth LTTrWHR
2 Ti. 2: 7 δώσει will give Eds
25 δῴη Eds
Jas. 5:18 *trs* ἔδωκεν ὑετὸν LTTr
2 Pet. 3:15 *trs* δοθεῖσαν αὐτῷ LTTrAWWH
Rev. 3: 9 διδῶ LTAWHR, δίδω Tr
6:11 ἐδόθη was given GEds
8: 3 δ.[2]—δώσει LTTrAWHR
10: 9 δοῦναι to give GEds
13: 7 *omit* and it was given unto *to* overcome them L[WH]
15 *trs* πνεῦμα δοῦναι W
16 δῶσιν they should give GEds
16: 6 δέδωκας LTrAWWHR
17:13*διδόασιν *for* διαδιδώσουσιν (–δίδωμι) GEds
19: 7 δώσομεν we will give LAWH

1326 διεγείρω.

Mat. 1:24 ἐγείρω LTTrAWHR
Mar. 4:38 ἐγείρω TTrAWHR
Lu. 8:24*διεγερθεὶς *for* ἐγερθεὶς (ἐγείρω) TTrWHR
Joh. 6:18 διεγείρετο TrAWH

* διενθυμέομαι, to consider, reflect.

Acts 10:19 διενθυμουμένου *for* ἐνθυμουμένου (ἐνθυμέομαι) GEds

* διεξέρχομαι, to go through.

Acts 28: 3 διεξελθοῦσα *for* ἐξελθοῦσα (ἐξέρχομαι) AW

1328 διερμηνευτής.

1 Co. 14:28 ἑρμηνευτής LTr

1329 διερμηνεύω.

Lu. 24:27 διερμήνευσεν TTrAWHR

1330 διέρχομαι.

Mat. 19:24 to go through—to enter, εἰσέρχομαι) GTTrAWH
Mar. 10:25 διελθεῖν *for* εἰσελθεῖν[1] (εἰσέρχομαι) A.V.B EGEds
Joh. 4:15*διέρχωμαι *for* ἔρχωμαι TAWHR
8:59 *omit* going through *to end of verse* GLTTrAWHR
Acts 11:22 *om.* that he should go LTTrWHR
16: 6 διῆλθον Eds

1342 δίκαιος.

Mat. 20: 7 *omit* and whatsoever is right, (that) shall ye receive LTTrAWHR
27: 4*δίκαιον *for* ἀθῶον (ἀθῷος) WH
24 *omit* just [L]T[Tr]AWH
2 Pet. 2: 8 ὁ δ.—*omit* ὁ LWH

1343 δικαιοσύνη.

Mat. 5:20 *trs* ὑμῶν ἡ δικαιοσύνη TAWH
6: 1*δικαιοσύνην *for* ἐλεημοσύνην (–νη) GEds
Ro. 4:11 τὴν δ.—*omit* τὴν T[WH]
9:28 *om.* in righteousness: because a short work LTTr[A]WHR
31 *omit* of righteousness[2] Eds
10: 3 *omit* righteousness[2] GLTr[A]WWHR
Jas. 3:18 τῆς δ.—*omit* τῆς GLTTrAWWH
Rev. 22:11*δικαιοσύνην ποιησάτω *for* δικαιωθήτω (–αιόω) GEds

1344 δικαιόω.

Lu. 10:29 δικαιῶσαι LTTrAWHR
Ro. 3:28 *trs* δ. πίστει GLTTrAWHR
Gal. 2:16 δ.[3]—*trs* ἐξ ἔργων νόμου οὐ δ. GLTTrAWWH
Rev. 22:11 let him be righteous—let him do righteousness, δικαιοσύνη *et* ποιέω GEds

1345 δικαίωμα.

Heb. 9:10 δικαιώματα Eds

1348 δικαστής.

Lu. 12:14 κριτής LTTrAWHR

1349 δίκη.

Acts 25:15 καταδίκη Eds

1350 δίκτυον.

Lu. 5: 5 τὰ δίκτυα the nets TTrWHR
6 τὰ δίκτυα the nets TTrAWHR

1352 διό.

Acts 13:35 διότι LTTrAWHR
20:26 διότι TAWHR
1 Co. 14:13**for* διόπερ LTTrAWHR
2 Co. 1:20**add* δ. Eds, *see* ἐν
12: 7*revelations—*add* δ. therefore LTr[A]WHR
Gal. 4:31**for* ἄρα LTTrAWHR
1 Th. 2:18 διότι Eds
1 Pet. 2: 6 wherefore — because, διότι GEds

1355 διόπερ.

1 Co. 8:13 διό περ Tr
14:13 διό LTTrAWHR

* διόρθωμα, a making straight.

Acts 24: 2(3) διορθωμάτων *for* κατορθωμάτων (–μα) LTTrAWHR

1358 διορύσσω.

Mat. 24:43 διορυχθῆναι TTrWH
Lu. 12:39 διορυχθῆναι TAWH

1360 διότι.

Acts 10:20 ὅτι GEds
13:35**for* διό LTTrAWHR
17:31 καθότι Eds
20:26**for* διό TAWHR
Ro. 8:21**for* ὅτι T
Gal. 2:16 ὅτι LTTrAWH
1 Th. 2:18**for* διό Eds
1 Pet. 1:16**for* ὅτι T
2: 6**for* διό GEds

1361 Διοτρεφής, –έφης LAWH.

1362 διπλοῦς.

Rev. 18: 6 δ.[1]—τὰ διπλᾶ TTrR, [τὰ] δ. AWH

1364 δίς.

Rev. 9:16**for* δύο WH

* δισμυριάδες, *see* μυριάς.

See 3461

1368 διϋλίζω.

Mat. 23:24 οἱ δ.—*omit* οἱ LTrAWH

1370 διχοστασία.

1 Co. 3: 3 *omit* and divisions LTTrAWHR

1372 διψάω.

Joh. 4:14 । 6:35 διψήσει LTTrAWHR

1377 διώκω.

Lu. 11:49*διώξουσιν *for* ἐκδιώξουσιν (–ώκω) WHR, [ἐκ]δ. TrA
Ro. 14:19 διώκομεν we follow after T
Gal. 6:12 διώκονται T

1380 δοκέω.

Mat. 24:44 *trs* οὐ δοκεῖτε ὥρᾳ LTTrAWH
Lu. 17: 9 *omit* I trow not [L]TTrAWHR
Joh. 11:31*δόξαντες *for* λέγοντες (–γω) TTrAWHR
Acts 15:34 *omit the verse* Eds

1381 δοκιμάζω.

Lu. 12:56 οὐ δ.—οὐκ οἴδατε δοκιμάζειν ye know not how to discern TrWHR
Heb. 3: 9 proved—by proving, δοκιμασία (Eds

* δοκιμασία, proof, trial.

Heb. 3: 9 ἐν δοκιμασίᾳ *for* ἐδοκίμασαν (δοκιμάζω) Eds

1388 δόλος.

Mat. 26: 4 *trs* δ. κρατήσωσιν GLTTrAWWH
Rev. 14: 5 guile—falsehood, ψεῦδος GEds

1390 δόμα.

Lu. 11:13 *trs* δόματα ἀγαθὰ GLTTrAWWH

1391 δόξα.

Mat. 6:13 *omit* for thine *to end of verse* GEds
2 Co. 4: 4 τῆς δ. S—τὸν δ. E
Eph. 1:12 τῆς δ.—*omit* τῆς Eds
Heb. 3: 3 *trs* οὗτος δόξης GEds
1 Pet. 1: 7 *trs* glory and honour Eds
5:11 *omit* glory and LTTrAWHR
2 Pet. 1: 3 δόξῃ LTTrAWR, *see* ἴδιος

1392 δοξάζω.

Mat. 15:31 ἐδόξαζον T
Lu. 23:47 ἐδόξαζεν LTTrAWHR
Joh. 8:54 δ.[1]—δοξάσω LTTrAWH
13:32 *omit* if God be glorified in him [LTrA]WHR
Acts 11:18 ἐδόξασαν LTTrWHR
1 Pet. 4:14 *omit* on their part *to end of verse* LTTrAWHR
Rev. 15: 4 δοξάσει Eds

1397 δουλεία, δουλία T.

1398 δουλεύω.

Acts 7: 7 δουλεύσουσιν TTrAWHR
Gal. 4: 9 δουλεῦσαι TTrWH

1401 δοῦλος.

Mat. 13:28 *omit* servants AWH
Lu. 12:38 *omit* servants T[TrA]WHR
1 Pet. 2:16 *trs* θεοῦ δοῦλοι TTrAWH
Rev. 2:20 τοὺς ἐμοὺς δούλους GEds
10: 7 τοὺς ἑαυτοῦ δούλους GEds
15: 3 τοῦ δούλου A.V.C LTTrAWHR

1404 δράκων.

Rev. 13: 4 τῷ δράκοντι GEds

1410 δύναμαι.

Mat. 16: 3 When it is (*ver.* 2) *to end of verse* 3 [TA][[WH]]
26: 9 ἐδύνατο TAWH
Mar. 3:25 δυνήσεται, *read* will not be able to TTrAWHR
27 *trs* οὐδεὶς δύναται GLTrW
4:33 ἐδύναντο LTr
5: 3 ἐδύνατο LTTrAWH
6: 5 ἐδύνατο TTrAWH
7:24 ἠδυνάσθη TWH
9:22, 23 δύνῃ LTTrAWH
Lu. 1:22 ἐδύνατο LTTrAWH
16: 2 δύνῃ TTrAWHR
Joh. 3: 2 *trs* δ. ταῦτα τὰ σημεῖα LTTrAWH
11:37 ἐδύνατο LTTrAWH
14: 5 *omit* δ. *read* how know we LTTrAWHR
Acts 5:39 οὐ δυνήσεσθε ye will not be able to LTTrWHR
10:47 *trs* δύναται κωλῦσαι LTTrAWH
21:34 δυναμένου LTTrAWWH
26:32 ἠδύνατο LW
1 Co. 3: 2 ἐδύνασθε GLTTrAWH
15:50 δύναται TTrWH
1 Ti. 5:25 δύνανται LTTrAWWH
Heb. 10: 1 δύνανται LTrWHR
Rev. 5: 3 ἐδύνατο TWH
7: 9 ἐδύνατο LTTrAWWH
9:20 δύνανται LTTrAWHR
14: 3 । 15:8 ἐδύνατο LTTrAWH

1411 δύναμις.

Mat. 6:13 *omit* for thine *to end of verse* GEds

Mar. 6: 2 αἱ δυνάμεις WHR
5 *trs* ποιῆσαι οὐδ. δ. LTTrAWH
Lu. 24:49 *trs* ἐξ ὕψους δύναμιν TTrAWHR
Acts 4:33 *trs* δυνάμει μεγάλῃ LTTrAWH
8:13 *trs* miracles and signs A.V.C GW
Ro. 8:38 *trs* nor powers *to end of verse* GEds

1412 δυναμόω.

Heb.11:34*ἐδυναμώθησαν *for* ἐνεδυναμώθησαν (ἐνδυναμόω) LTTrWHR

1414 δυνατέω.

Ro. 14: 4*δ. γάρ ἐστιν—δυνατεῖ γ. Eds
2 Co. 9: 8*δυνατεῖ *for* δυνατός LTTrAWHR

1415 δυνατός.

Mat. 19:26 *trs* δυνατὰ πάντα T
Acts 25: 5 *trs* ἐν ὑμῖν, φησίν, δ. GEds
Ro. 14: 4 δυνατέω Eds
2 Co. 9: 8 δυνατέω LTTrAWHR
Rev. 6:15 mighty men—strong, ἰσχυρός GEds

1416 δύνω.

Mar. 1:32 ἔδυσεν LTrAWH

1417 δύο.

Mat. 11: 2 two of—by, διά Eds
27:51 *trs* εἰς δ. *after* κάτω TTrAWH.
Lu. 10: 1, 17*seventy—*add* [δ. two] LWH
17:35 *trs* ἔσονται δύο LTTrAWHR
36 *add the verse* A.V.B E, *see* ἀφίημι
21: 2 *trs* λεπτὰ δύο TrWH
Acts 10:19*for τρεῖς WH
23:23 *trs* τινας δύο TTrWH
Gal. 4:24 αἱ δ.—*omit* αι GEds
Rev. 9:16 δίς WH: *see* μυριάς
11: 4 δ.²—αἱ δύο A.V.C GEds
12:14 αἱ δύο LTTrWWHR, [αἱ] δ. A

1419 δυσβάστακτος.

Mat. 23: 4 *omit* and grievous to be borne T[Tr]AWH

1420 δυσεντεριά, –ίον LTTrAWWH.

* δυσφημέω, to defame.

1 Co. 4:13 δυσφημούμενοι *for* βλασφημούμενοι (-φημέω) TAWHR

1427 δώδεκα.

Mar. 3:16*add *at commencement* καὶ ἐποίησεν τοὺς δώδεκα and he appointed the twelve TWH.
5:25 *trs* δώδεκα ἔτη TWH
Lu. 22:14 *omit* twelve LTTrAWHR
Acts 19: 7*δώδεκα *for* δεκαδύο LTTrAWWH
24:11*δώδεκα *for* δεκαδύο LTTrAWH
Rev. 7: 5, 6, 7, 8*δώδεκα *for* ιβ' LTTrAWWH
21:14*in them—on them twelve, ἐπ' αὐτῶν δώδεκα GEds

1431 δωρεά.

Ro. 5:17 [of the gift] LWH

1436 ἔα.

Mar. 1:24 *omit* let us alone LTTrAWHR

1437 ἐάν.

Mat. 7: 9, 10 *omit* ἐ. LTTrAWHR
10:14 ἄν LTTrAWH
42 ἄν LTrWH
11: 6 ἄν LTrWH
12:36 *omit* ἐ. LTTrAWH
14: 7 ἄν LTrA
16:19 ἐ.¹—ἄν LTrA: ἐ.² ἄν Tr
18: 5 ἄν LTr
18 ἐ.¹—ἄν LTrA
20: 7 *omit* LTTrAWHR, *see* δίκαιος
26 ἄν LTrWH
27 ἄν LTTrAWH
23:18 ἄν LTTrAWH
Mar. 4:26 *omit* ἐ. TTrAWHR
5:28*ὅτι—*add* ἐ. TAWHR
6:10 ἄν LTr
8:36 *omit* ἐ. TAWHR, *see* κερδαίνω
9:37 ἄν *bis* LTTrAWH
10:11, 15 ἄν LTTrAWH
43 ἄν LTTrWH
11:23 *omit* whatsoever he saith TTr[A]WHR
32 *omit* ἐ. *read* shall we say Eds
14:14 ἄν LTrA
Lu. 4: 6 ἄν LTrAWH
9:48 ἐ.¹—ἄν LWH: ἐ.²—ἄν TWH
10:22 ἄν LTrAWH

Lu. 11:12 *omit* ἐ. TTr[A]WHR
12:38 καὶ ἐ.—κἄν TTrAWHR
17:33 ἐ.²—ἄν TrAWHR
18:17 ἄν LTTrAWH
Joh. 5:19 ἄν TWH
8:55 καὶ ἐ.—κἄν LTTrWH
12:32 ἄν WH
13:20 ἄν LTTrAWH
21:25 *omit the verse* T
Acts 7: 7 ἄν LTrWH
9: 2 ἄν T
Ro. 15:24 ἐ.¹—ἄν Eds
1 Co. 13: 2 καὶ ἐ.¹—κἄν LAWH: κ. ἐ.²—κἄν TrAWH
3 καὶ ἐ.¹—κἄν LTrAWH: κ. ἐ.²—κἄν LAWH
16: 3 ἄν LTr
2 Co. 8:12 ἄν T
Gal. 6: 7 ἄν LTr
Eph. 6: 8 ἄν Tr
Heb. 3: 6*for ἐάνπερ TTrAWHR, ἐάν[περ] L
1 Joh. 2:28*for ὅταν LTTrAWHR
3:22 ἄν WH

See also ἄν.

ἐάνπερ. See 1437

Heb. 3: 6 ἐάν TTrAWHR
14 ἐάν περ LTr
6: 3 ἐάν περ LTrW

1438 ἑαυτοῦ, –ῷ, –όν.

Mat. 6:34 αὐτῆς AWH
18:31*ἑαυτῶν *for* αὐτῶν LTTrAWH
23:37 αὐτῆς T[Tr]AW[WH]
25: 1*ἑαυτῶν *for* αὐτῶν LTrAWH
3 ἐ.¹—αὐτῶν GLTrAW[WH]: *omit* their T
4*ἑαυτῶν *for* αὐτῶν² LTWH
7*ἑαυτῶν *for* αὐτῶν LTTrAWH
27:35 *omit* that it might *to end of verse* GLTTrAWHR
Mar. 1:27*ἑαυτούς *for* αὐτούς LTrAWHR
2:19 αὐτῶν TTrAWH, *see* ἔχω
5:26 αὐτῆς GLTrAWWH
6: 4*ἑαυτοῦ *for* αὐτοῦ¹ T
8:35*ψυχὴν αὐτοῦ¹—ἑαυτοῦ ψ. WH
*ψυχὴν αὐτοῦ²—ἑαυτοῦ ψ. GTrW
9:33 *omit* among yourselves LTTrAWHR
10:26 αὐτόν WHR
14:33 αὐτοῦ LTTrAWH
Lu. 2: 3*ἑαυτοῦ *for* ἰδίαν (-ιος) LTTrWHR
39*ἑαυτῶν *for* αὐτῶν LTTrAWWH
4:24*ἑαυτοῦ *for* αὐτοῦ T
12:17 αὐτῷ WH
21 αὐτῷ TWH
47 αὐτοῦ LTTrAWHR
14:26 ἐ.¹—αὐτοῦ LTTrA
27*ἑαυτοῦ *for* αὐτοῦ LTAWHR
15: 5 αὐτοῦ TTrAWHR
20 αὐτοῦ LTTr
16: 4*ἑαυτῶν *for* αὐτῶν TTrAWHR
18:11 *trs* ταῦτα πρὸς ἐ. TrWHR: *omit* with himself T
13*ἑαυτοῦ *for* αὐτοῦ TrAWH
19:35 αὐτῶν LTTrAWHR
36*ἑαυτῶν *for* αὐτῶν TrWH
20:14 themselves—one another, ἀλλήλων TTrAWHR
22:17 εἰς ἑαυτούς LTTrAWHR
66 αὐτῶν TTrAWWHR
23:12 αὐτούς TTrAWH
48 *omit* ἐ. TTrAWHR
24:12 αὐτόν Tr: *omit the verse* [L]T[Tr][[WH]]
27 ἑαυτοῦ S—αὐτοῦ EGLTr
Joh. 2:24 αὐτόν LTTrAWHR
9:21*ἑαυτοῦ *for* αὐτοῦ TTrWHR
13:32 αὐτῷ TTrWHR
17:13*ἑαυτοῖς *for* αὐτοῖς TTrAWHR
18:34 σεαυτοῦ LTrAWH
19:12*ἑαυτόν *for* αὐτόν² GEds
17*see αὐτοῦ
20:10 αὐτούς TTrWH
Acts 14:14*ἑαυτῶν *for* αὐτῶν WH
17 αὐτόν LTTrWH
20:30*ἑαυτῶν *for* αὐτῶν² TTrAWH
21:11*ἑαυτοῦ *for* αὐτοῦ Eds
28:29 *omit the verse* LTTrAWHR
Ro. 1:24 αὐτοῖς LTTrAWHR
27 αὐτοῖς WH
13: 9 σεαυτόν LTTrAWH
14:14 αὐτοῦ GLTrW
1 Co. 7:38*add ἐ. *see* ἐκγαμίζω
11: 5 αὐτῆς LTTrAWHR
2 Co. 3: 5 ἐ.²—αὐτῶν LTrWH
13 αὐτοῦ TTrAWWHR
Gal. 5:14 σεαυτόν GEds
Eph. 2:15 αὐτῷ LTTrAWHR
4:16 αὐτοῦ T
5:25 *omit* ἐ.¹ LTTrAWHR

Phil. 3:21 αὐτῷ LTTrAWHR
1 Th. 5:13 αὐτοῖς TTr
2 Th. 2: 6 αὐτοῦ TTrWHR
Heb. 1: 3 *omit* by himself LTTrAWHR
10:34 ἑαυτοὺς LTTrWHR
12: 3*αὐτὸν—ἑαυτόν LTTrA, ἑαυτούς WHR
16*ἑαυτοῦ *for* αὐτοῦ LTTrAWHR
Jas. 1:26*ἑαυτοῦ *f.* αὐτοῦ¹ WH: *for* α.² LWH
1 Pet. 4:19 αὐτῶν LTTrAWR: *omit* ἐ. WH
1 Joh. 3:15*ἑαυτῷ *for* αὐτῷ LT
5:10 αὐτῷ TTrAWHR
18 αὐτόν TTrAWHR
21 ἑαυτά LTTrWHR
Jude 19 separate—*add* ἑαυτοὺς themselves A.V.B EG
Rev. 2: 2*add ἐ. GEds, *see* λέγω
20 αὐτήν T
4: 8 αὐτῶν GLTTrAWHR, *see* κατά
8: 6 αὐτούς LTTrWHR
10: 4 *omit* their voices GEds
17:13 αὐτῶν Eds
18: 7 αὐτήν Eds

1439 ἐάω.

Acts 5:38 ἀφίημι LTTrAWHR
Rev. 2:20 ἀφίημι GEds

1443 ἑβδομηκονταέξ, –τα ἕξ GLTTrWWHR.

Ἔβερ, Ἔβερ, Ἔβερ A.V.Vul TrL.

1444 Ἑβραϊκός.

Lu. 23:38 *omit* in letters of Greek, and Latin, and Hebrew [L]TTr[A]WHR

1445 Ἑβραῖος *et* Ἑβραΐς, Ἑ– WH

1447 Ἑβραϊστί, Ἑ– WH.

Joh. 20:16*him—*add* Ἑβραϊστί in Hebrew [L]TTrAWHR

1448 ἐγγίζω.

Mat. 15: 8 *omit* draweth nigh unto me with their mouth, and GLTTrAWHR
Mar. 14:42 ἤγγισεν T
Lu. 15: 1 *trs* αὐτῷ ἐγγίζοντες LTTrAWWH
Jas. 4: 8 ἐ.²—ἐγγίσει WH

1449 ἐγγράφω, ἐνγ– TWH.

Lu. 10:20*ἐγγέγραπται *f.* ἐγράφη (γράφω) TTrAWHR

1453 ἐγείρω.

Mat. 1:24*ἐγερθεὶς *for* διεγερθεὶς (–γείρω) LTTrAWHR
9: 5 ἔγειρε LTTrAWWH
6 ἔγειρε LTrWH
10: 8 *trs* raise the dead, cleanse the lepers GEds
17: 9*ἐγερθῇ *for* ἀναστῇ (ἀνίστημι) LTTrAWH
20:19*ἐγερθήσεται *for* ἀναστήσεται (ἀνίστημι) TTrAWHR
27:52 ἠγέρθησαν LTTrAWH
Mar. 2: 9 ἔγειρε GLTW, ἐγείρου TrAWH
11 ἔγειρε GLTTrAWWH
3: 3 ἔγειρε GLTTrAWH
4:38*ἐγείρουσιν *for* διεγείρουσιν (-ρω) TTrAWHR
5:41 ἔγειρε GLTTrAWWH
6:14†*trs* ἐγήγερται ἐκ νεκ. LTTrWHR: ἀνίστημι A
10:49 ἔγειρε GLTTrAWWH
Lu. 5:23, 24 ἔγειρε GLTTrAWWH
6: 8 ἔγειρε GLTTrAWWH
7:16 ἠγέρθη LTTrAWHR
8:24 arose—awoke διεγείρω TTrWHR
54 ἔγειρε LTrAWH
9: 7 ἠγέρθη LTTrWHR
22 ἀνίστημι LA
Joh. 5: 8 ἔγειρε LTTrAWWH
7:52 ἐγείρεται LTTrAWHR
11:29 ἠγέρθη LTrAWHR
Acts 3: 6 ἔγειρε καὶ L[Tr]: *omit* rise up and T[A]WHR
10:26 *trs* ἤγειρεν αὐτὸν LTTrAWWH
13:23 raised—brought, ἄγω GEds
Eph. 5:14 ἔγειρε GLTTrAWWH
Phil. 1:16*ἐγείρειν *for* ἐπιφέρειν (–ρω) Eds
Rev. 11: 1 ἔγειρε LTTrAWWH

1455 ἐγκάθετος, ἐνκ– TWH.

1456 ἐγκαίνια, ἐνκ– TWH.

1457 ἐγκαινίζω, ἐνκ– TWH.

* ἐγκακέω, see ἐκκακέω
See 1573

1459 ἐγκαταλείπω.
Mar. 15:34 trs ἐγκατέλιπές με LTTrAWH
Acts 2:27 ἐνκ- TWH
31*ἐγκατελείφθη (ἐνκ- TWH) for κατελείφθη (καταλείπω) LTTrAWHR
Ro. 9:29 ἐνκ- T
2 Ti. 4:10 ἐγκατέλειπεν WH
16 ἐγκατέλειπον WH
Heb. 13: 5 ἐγκαταλείπω TA

1460 ἐγκατοικέω, ἐνκ— TWH.

* ἐγκαυχάομαι, to pride oneself in.
2 Th. 1: 4 ἐγκαυχᾶσθαι (ἐνκ- TWH) for καυχᾶσθαι (-χάομαι) LTTrAWHR

1461 ἐγκεντρίζω, ἐνκ— TWH.

1464 ἐγκοπή, ἐκκ- T, ἐνκ— WH.
1 Co. 9:12 trs τινα ἐ. Eds

1465 ἐγκόπτω, ἐνκ— TWH.
Gal. 5: 7*ἐνέκοψεν for ἀνέκοψεν (ἀνακόπτω) GEds
1 Pet. 3: 7*ἐγκόπτεσθαι for ἐκκόπτεσθαι (-τω) Eds

1467 ἐγκρίνω, ἐνκ— TWH.

1470 ἐγκρύπτω.
Lu. 13:21 κρύπτω TTrAWHR

1471 ἔγκυος, ἐνκ— WH.

1472 ἐγχρίω.
Rev. 3:18 ἐγχρίσαι GW, -ῖσαι to anoint LAWHR, ἔγχρισαι TTr

1473 ἐγώ.
Mat. 12:28 trs ἐγὼ after θεοῦ GLTTrAWWH
20:22, 23 omit GLTTrAWHR, see βαπτίζω
Mar. 1: 2 omit ἐ. LTrAWH
14:19 omit and another (said, Is) it I? TTrWHR
Lu. 7:27 omit ἐ. LTTrAWH
9: 9 omit ἐ.² T[Tr]WHR
10: 3 omit ἐ. LTTrAWH
11:20*ἐ. ἐκβάλλω B, [ἐ.] ἐκ. TrWH
24:39 trs ἐγώ εἰμι αὐτός LTTrAWHR
Joh. 1:20 trs ἐγὼ οὐκ εἰμὶ LTTrAWH
27†trs οὐκ εἰμὶ ἐ. ([ἐ.] LTrWH) TTrAWH
3:28*εἶπον [ἐ.] WH, trs ἐ. οὐκ εἰμὶ L
4:14*ἐ. δώσω ² TR
5:36 omit ἐ.² LTTrAWHR
6:51 omit which I will give LTTrAWHR
13:36*ἐ. ὑπάγω T
14:14 ἐ.—τοῦτο, read that I will do WHR
26*add at end ἐ. WH
15:10 I—I also, κἀγώ T
16: 7*γὰρ—add ἐ. L[A]W
16 om. because I go to the Father TTrAWHR : omit ἐ. G[L]W
17 omit ἐ. Eds
17:19 omit ἐ. [L]T[WH]
18:37 omit ἐ.¹ TTr[A]WH
Acts 20:26 I (am)—I am, εἰμί LTTrAWHR
23: 6 omit ἐ.² WH
26:17*οὓς—add ἐ. GEds
27:23*εἰμι—add ἐ. LT[A]
Ro. 7:20 omit ἐ.¹ LTr[A]WWHR
2 Ti. 4: 1 omit ἐ. GEds
Rev. 1:11 omit GEds, see ἄλφα
2:22 omit ἐ. GEds
5: 4 omit ἐ. T[TrWH]
21: 2 omit I John GEds
22:18*add ἐ. GEds, see μαρτυρέω
See also κἀγώ.

1478 Ἐζεκίας, Ἑ— WH.

1479 ἐθελοθρησκεία, -κία TWH.

ἐθέλω, see θέλω.
See 2309

1482 ἐθνικός.
Mat. 5:47*ἐθνικοὶ for τελῶναι (-νης) GEds
3 Joh. 7*ἐθνικῶν for ἐθνῶν (-νος) Eds

1484 ἔθνος.
Mat. 24: 9 τῶν ἐ.—omit τῶν B
Lu. 21:24 trs τὰ ἔθνη πάντα LTTrAWH
Acts 9:15 τῶν ἐθνῶν LR, [τῶν] ἐ. WH
13:42 omit the Gentiles GEds
Ro. 15:11 trs πάντα τὰ ἔθνη τὸν κύριον LTTrAWHR
1 Co. 1:23*ἔθνεσιν for Ἕλλησιν (-ην) GEds
10:20 omit the Gentiles LTA[WH]
2 Ti. 1:11 omit of the Gentiles TWHR
3 Joh. 7 ἐθνικός Eds
Rev. 14: 8 τὰ ἔθνη Eds
15: 3*ἐθνῶν f. ἁγίων (-ιος) GLTTrAW
20: 3 trs ἔτι τὰ ἔθνη GLTTrAWHR

1488 εἰ.
Mat. 20:15 εἰ ὅ—ἢ A.V.B EGEds
27:42 omit if TTrAWHR
Mar. 11:26 omit the verse TTrWHR
14:29 trs εἰ καὶ TTrAWHR
Lu. 6: 9*for τί (τίς) LTTrAWHR
11:11 ἢ GLTTrAWR: omit WH, see ἄρτος
14: 3 omit εἰ TTrAWHR
23:39 οὐχί, read Art not thou the Christ? TTrAWHR
Joh. 13:32 omit [LTrA]WHR, see δοξάζω
Acts 8:37 omit the verse GLTTrAWHR
22:27 omit εἰ GEds
Ro. 2:17*εἰ δέ for ἴδε GEds
11: 6 omit But if to end of verse GLTTr[A]WHR
1 Co. 15:44*εἰ ἔστιν¹, read If there is Eds
2 Co. 5:14 omit if Eds
13: 4 omit though [L]TTrAWHR
Heb. 6:14*εἰ μὴν for ἦ μὴν LTTrAWHR
12: 7 εἰς (omit if) LTTrAWHR
Jas. 3: 3*εἰ δέ for ἰδού Eds
1 Pet. 2: 3*for εἴπερ LTTrWHR

1489 εἴ γε, εἴ γε.
Ro. 5: 6*εἴ γε for ἔτι γάρ AWH
2 Co. 5: 3 εἰ περ LTr

1499 εἰ καί.
Mat. 26:33 omit καί GEds
2 Co. 12:15 omit καί LTTrAWHR

1508 εἰ μή.
Mat. 17:21 omit the verse T[TrA]WHR
19: 9 omit εἰ GLTTrAWWH
17 omit GEds, see ἀγαθός
Mar. 9: 8*for ἀλλά LWHR
Joh. 13:10*for ἢ LTrA[WH]R
Acts 21:25 omit LTTrWHR, see μηδείς
2 Co. 3: 1 ἢ μή A.V.B GLTTrAWHR

1512 εἴ περ, εἴπερ.
Ro. 3:30*for ἐπείπερ LTTrAWHR
2 Co. 5: 3*for εἴ γε LTr
1 Pet. 2: 3 εἰ LTTrWHR

1535 εἴτε.
1 Co. 12:26 whether—if anything, εἴ τι LTr

1536 εἴ τις, εἴ τι.
Mat. 18:28*εἴ τι for ὅ τι (ὅστις) GEds
Mar. 7:16 omit the verse T[TrA]WHR
8:34*for ὅστις LTrWHR
Acts 24:20 omit εἰ, read what evil GEds
1 Co. 7:13*for ἥτις (ὅστις) T
12:26*for εἴτε LTr
Rev. 13:10 qui in A.V. Vul

1492 εἰδέω, εἴδω, οἶδα.
Mat. 2:11*εἶδον for εὗρον (εὑρίσκω) A.V.C GEds
9: 4 εἰδὼς LTrWHR
11: 9†trs ἐξήλ.; προφήτην ἰδεῖν; (i. πρ. B) read why went ye out? to see a prophet? TAWHR
13:17 εἶδον—εἶδαν LTrWH, ἴδαν T
25:37 εἴδαμεν TrWH
38 εἴδαμεν WH
Mar. 1:24 οἴδαμεν we know T
2:12 εἴδαμεν LTTrAWH
6:33 εἶδαν WH
48 ἰδὼν seeing LTTrAWHR
50 εἶδαν TTrWH
9: 9 trs ἃ εἶδ. διηγήσωνται LTTrAWH
14 εἶδον they saw TTrR, εἶδαν WH
15 ἰδόντες LTTrAWH
38 εἴδαμεν WH
12:15 εἰδὼς—ἰδὼν having known T
28 ἰδὼν having perceived LTTr
13:29 trs ἴδητε ταῦτα LTTrWH
Lu. 1:29 omit when she saw (him) GTTrAWHR
2:20 ἴδον T
5: 2 ἴδεν T
26 εἴδαμεν WH
9:32 εἶδαν TWH
47 εἰδὼς TWH
49 εἴδαμεν WH
55 omit and said to end of verse LTTrAWHR
10:24 εἶδον—ἴδαν T, εἶδαν TrAWH
12:56*add ο. TrWHR, see δοκιμάζω
13:35 trs ἴδητέ με LTTrAWH
19: 5 omit saw him, and TTr[A]WHR
20:13 om. when they see LTTr[A]WHR
22:57 trs οὐκ ο. αὐτὸν, γύναι TTrAWHR
23:34 see λέγω
Joh. 1:39(40) see—ye shall see, ὄψεσθε TTrAWHR: ε.² εἶδαν LTTrAWH
5:32 οἴδατε ye know T
6:22 εἶδον LTTrAWHR
8:19 trs ἂν ᾔδειτε LTTrAWH
56 ἴδῃ—εἴδῃ T
14: 4 omit ye know² [L]TTrAWHR
5†trs οἴδαμεν τὴν ὁδόν LTTrAWHR
7*ἂν ᾔδειτε for ἐγνώκειτε (γινώσκω) ἂν TrAWHR
19: 6 ἴδον T
Acts 4:20 εἴδαμεν LTTrAWH
6:15 εἶδαν TrWH
8:18*ἰδὼν for θεασάμενος (θεάομαι) GEds
9:35 | 12:16 εἶδαν LTTrAWH
22:18 ἴδον T
28: 4 εἶδαν TrWH
1 Co. 2: 2 trs (om. τοῦ GEds) τι εἰδέναι GLTrAWWH
11 οἶδεν²—γινώσκω Eds
8: 2 γινώσκω Eds
2 Co. 12: 3 omit I cannot tell L[WH]
Eph. 5: 5*ἴστε for ἐστέ GEds
6:21 trs καὶ ὑμεῖς εἰδῆτε LTTr
Phil. 1:30 εἴδετε A.V. CEds
2:26*ὑμᾶς—add [ἰδεῖν], read to see you LWH
Jas. 1:19*ἴστε for ὥστε LTTrAWHR
5:11 ἴδετε see A
1 Pet. 1: 8 ἰδόντες A.V.B Eds
3: 9 omit knowing (read because ye are) LTTrAWHR
3 Joh. 12 οἶδας thou knowest LTTrAWHR
14 trs σε ἰδεῖν LTTrAWWH
Rev. 1: 2 ἴδεν T
20 om. which thou sawest² GEds
2:17*οἶδεν for ἔγνω (γινώσκω) GEds
4: 1 ἴδον T
4 omit I saw GEds
6: 1, 2, 5, 8, 9, 12 ἴδον T
7: 1, 2, 9 | 8:2, 13 | 9:1, 17 ἴδον T
13: 3 omit I saw GEds
14: 1, 14 | 15:1, 5 | 16:13 ἴδον T
17: 6 εἶδον—εἶδα LTTrA
19:19 | 20:1, 4 ἴδον T
21: 2 trs εἶδον after ἁγίαν A, after καινὴν GLTTrWWHR

1493 εἰδωλεῖον, -λιον TWH.

1494 εἰδωλόθυτον.
1 Co. 10:19 trs that which is offered in sacrifice to idols is anything, or that the idol Eds
28 offered in sacrifice unto idols —offered in sacrifice, ἱερόθυτος LTTrAWHR
Rev. 2:20 trs φαγεῖν εἰδωλόθυτα GEds

1495 εἰδωλολατρεία, -ρία WH

1497 εἴδωλον.
1 Co. 8: 7 trs ἕως ἄρτι τοῦ ε. Eds
10:19 trs Eds, see εἰδωλόθυτον
Rev. 9:20 τὰ εἴδωλα A.V.C GEds

1498 εἴην, εἴης, εἴη, &c.
Joh. 13:24 see λέγω
Acts 20:16*εἴη for ἦν LTTrAWHR
Rev. 3:15 εἴης—ῆς GEds

1500 εἰκῆ, εἰκῇ LWH.
Mat. 5:22 omit without a cause LT[TrA]WHR

1501 εἴκοσι.
Acts 1:15 εἴκοσι LTAWH
Rev. 4: 4 τοὺς ε.—omit τοὺς GTTrWHR
trs ε. τέσσαρας θρόνους LA
5:14 omit four (and) twenty GEds
11:16 οἱ ε.—omit οἱ L[A]

εἰκοσιτρεῖς, —τέσσαρες, —πέντε s. *(in two words by most Editors)*

1504 **εἰκών**

Rev. 13:15 τὴν ε.—τῇ εἰκόνι GTTrWWHR
16: 2 *trs* προσκυ. τῇ ε. αὐτοῦ GEds
20: 4 τῇ εἰκόνι EG

1505 **εἰλικρίνεια, —νία** TWH.

1507 **εἰλίσσω, ἑλίσσω** LTTrAWWH.

1510 **εἰμί.**

Acts 20:26**for* ἐγώ LTTrAWHR
1 Pet. 1:16 *omit* ε. Eds
Rev. 1:11 *omit* GEds, *see* ἄλφα
21: 6 *omit* ε. T[A]WHR
22:13 *omit* ε. GEds

1511 **εἶναι.**

Mar. 6:49 ἐστίν TWHR
10:44**for* γενέσθαι (γίνομαι) LTrWHR
Lu. 14:27 *trs* εἶναί μου TTrAWH
33 *trs* εἶναί μου LTTrWH
Acts 8:37 *omit the verse* GLTTrAWHR
18: 5*Ἰουδαίοις—*add* ε. *read* Jesus was LTTrWHR
28: 6 *trs* αὐτὸν εἶναι θεόν LTTrAWWH
Ro. 6:11 *omit* to be GL[Tr]AW: *trs* εἶναι νεκροὺς μὲν TTrWH
Phil. 3: 8 *omit* ε² LTTrWHR
Rev. 2: 2 *omit* ε. LTTrAWHR

εἵνεκεν, *see* **ἕνεκα.** See 1752

1512 **εἴπερ**, *see under* **εἰ.** See 1488

See 2036 **εἶπον.**

(LTTrAWH *at times read* εἶπαν *for* εἶπον.)

Mat. 4: 3 ε.²—εἰπόν WH
9*εἶπεν *for* λέγει (-γω) LTTrAWHR
8:22 said—saith, λέγω Eds
9:11 λέγω LTTrWH
12:47 *omit the verse* T[WH]
48 ε.²—λέγω LTTrAWH
13:28 said²—say, λέγω LTTrAWHR
15: 4*εἶπεν *f.* ἐνετείλατο (ἐντέλλομαι) λέγων (-γω) LTrWHR
12 said—say, λέγω LTTrAWH
17:20 said—saith, λέγω LTTrAWHR
26**see* λέγω
18:17 | 22:17 εἰπόν TWH
19:16 *trs* αὐτῷ εἶπεν LTTrAWHR
18 φημί WH
20:13 *trs* ἑνὶ αὐτῶν εἶπεν TWH
22:37 φημί GLTTrAWWH
24: 3 εἰπόν WH
27:49*εἶπαν *for* ἔλεγον (λέγω) LTrWH
Mar. 1:42 *omit* as soon as he had spoken LTTrWHR
2: 8 said—saith, λέγω TTrAWHR
3:32 said—say, λέγω Eds
5: 7 said—saith, λέγω Eds
6:16 λέγω TTrAWHR
31 said—saith, λέγω TTrAWWHR
7:27 λέγω LTTrAWHR
36 λέγω TTrAWI
8: 7 *omit* ε. TA, *see* παρατίθημι
20 said—say, λέγω TAWHR
26 *omit* nor tell it to any in the town TWHR
28*εἶπον *for* ἀπεκρίθησαν (ἀποκρίνομαι) TAWHR, *see* λέγω
9:12 φημί TTrAWHR
17 *omit* and said LTTrAWHR
18 εἶπα TTrAWH
10:20 φημί TTrAWHR
29 φημί TAWHR
51**trs* αὐτῷ ὁ Ἰησοῦς (εἶπεν *for* λέγει, -γω) TTrAWHR
11: 6*εἶπεν *f.* ἐνετείλατο (ἐντέλλομαι) LTTrAWHR
23 *omit* whatsoever he saith TTr[A]WHR
12: 7 *trs* πρὸς ἑαυτοὺς εἶπαν TTrAWH
24 φημί TTrAWHR
32 ε.²—εἶπες TWH
36 said¹—saith, λέγω W
36 said²—saith, λέγω GTr
43*εἶπεν *f.* λέγει (-γω) GLTTrWHR
13: 4 εἰπόν LTTrAWH
15: 2 said—saith, λέγω TTrAWHR
12 λέγω TTrAWH
Lu. 2:15 λαλέω TWH
5:13 λέγω LTrWHR
6:26 *trs* εἴπωσιν ὑμᾶς T
7:31 *omit* and the Lord said GEds
42 *omit* tell me LTTr[A]WHR
9:21 λέγω GLTTrAWHR
Lu. 9:55 *omit* and said *to end of verse* LTTrAWHR
10:22 *omit* A.V.B EGTr[A]WHR, *see* μαθητής
40 ε.²—εἰπόν TWH
14:10 ἐρέω TTrWHR
15:17 φημί TWHR
18:16 λέγω TTrAWHR
19:30 λέγω LTrWH
20: 2 ε.²—εἰπόν TTrAWH
22:31 *omit* and the Lord said T[Tr]AWHR
58 φημί TTrAWHR
67 ε.¹—εἰπόν TTrAWH
24:40 *omit the verse* T[Tr][[WH]]
Joh. 1:15 ὃν ε.—ὁ εἰπών WH
4:17 ε.²—εἶπες TWH
5:15*εἶπεν *for* ἀνήγγειλεν (ἀναγγέλλω) TWH
19 λέγω TWH
7:20 *omit* and said LTTrAWHR
8:23 λέγω LTTrAWHR
9:11 *omit* and said¹ [L]TTrAWHR
25 *omit* and said Eds
36 *omit* and said L[AWH]
10:24 εἰπόν TWH
26 *omit* as I said unto you [L]TTr[A]WHR
11:28 ε.²—εἶπασα TrWH
12:30 *trs* καὶ εἶπεν Ἰησοῦς WH
13:24**see* λέγω
14:28 *omit* I said² GEds
18: 4 said—saith, λέγω LTTrAWHR
29 said—saith, φημί TTrAWHR
34 *trs* εἰπόν σοι TrAWH
21: 6 said—saith, λέγω T
17 said²—saith, λέγω T
Acts 4:19 *trs* εἶπον πρὸς αὐτοὺς LTTrAWWH
5: 9 *omit* ε. LTTrAWHR
7: 7 *trs* ὁ θεὸς εἶπεν LTTrAWWH
37 εἶπας LTTrAWH
8:37 *omit the verse* GLTTrAWHR
9: 5 *omit* κύριος ε. Eds
6 *omit* GEds, *see* κέντρον
19: 2 *omit* ε.² Eds
21:13*Παῦλος—*add* καὶ εἶπεν, *read* answered and said T
22:24 εἴπας LTTrAWWH
23: 7*εἰπόντος *for* λαλήσαντος (λαλέω) LTrWR
24:22 εἴπας LTTrAWWH
26:15 ε.¹—εἶπα LTTrAWH
29 *omit* ε. LTTrAWHR
30 *omit* and when he had thus spoken GEds
27:35 εἴπας LTTrAWH
28:26 εἰπόν GLTTrAWWH
29 *omit the verse* LTTrAWHR
1 Co. 11:22 *trs* εἴπω ὑμῖν Eds

1513 **εἴπως**, *see under* **εἰ.** See 1488

1515 **εἰρήνη.**

Lu. 19:38 *trs* ἐν οὐρανῷ ε. TTrAWH
24:36 *omit* and saith *to end of ver.* T[[WH]]
Ro. 10:15 *omit* that preach the gospel of peace, and LTTr[A]WHR
Eph. 2:17*and³—*add* εἰρήνην peace Eds

εἴρω, *see* **ἐρέω.** See 2046

1519 **εἰς.**

Mat. 5:39**for* ἐπί LTTrAWHR
6:13 *omit* ε.² GEds, *see* αἰών
9:13 *omit* to repentance GEds
12:18 ἐν Tr: *omit* ε. LAWH
13:30 *omit* ε.¹ [Tr]A[WH]
52 *omit* ε. GTTrAWHR, *see* βασιλεία
14:34 ἐπί TTrWHR
34*land—*add* ε. unto TTrWHR
18: 6**for* ἐπί A
15 *omit* against thee LT[A]WH
29 *omit* at his feet GLTTr[A]WHR
20:18**add* ε. T, *see* θάνατος
21: 1**for* πρός LTTrAWHR
46**for* ὡς LTTrAWHR
22: 5 ε.²—ἐπί LTTrAWHR
24:16**for* ἐπί LTrWH
27: 5**for* ἐν TTrWHR
Mar. 1:10**for* ἐπί LTTrAWH
39**for* ἐν GEds
2: 1 ἐν οἴκῳ LTTrWH
13**for* παρά T
17 *omit* to repentance GEds
22 *omit* ε.²—T[Tr]A[WH], *see* νέος
3: 7**for* πρός GLT
4: 8**for* ἐν¹ (εἰς) TTrWHR: *for* ἐν²³ TTrR
15**for* ἐν TrAWHR, *see* καρδία
Mar. 4:18 ἐπί T
6:53*ε. Γεννησαρέτ unto Gennesaret TWHR
56*or *bis*—*add* ε. into [L]TTrAWHR
7:31**for* πρός GLTTrAWHR
8:13 *omit* T[Tr]AWHR, *see* πλοῖον
9:42 *omit* in me TAWH
45 *omit* ε.³—[L]TTr[A]WHR, *see* πῦρ
10:10**for* ἐν LTTrAWHR
11: 8 *omit* and strawed (them) in the way TTrAWHR
13:15 *omit* into the house [L]TWHR
14: 6 εἰς ἐμέ—ἐν ἐμοί GEds
Lu. 2:42 *omit* to Jerusalem T[Tr]AWHR
4: 1 into—in ἐν LTTrAWHR
5 *omit* into an high mountain [L]TTrAWHR
23**for* ἐν¹ GLTTrAWHR
29 ε. τὸ—ὥστε GLTTrAWHR
43 ἐπί LTTrAWHR
44**for* ἐν TTrAWHR
6:29**for* ἐπί T
8: 8**for* ἐπί GEds
43 *omit* ε. GEds, *see* ἰατρός
9:62 *omit* ε.² LTTrAWH, *see* βασιλεία
10:11**add* ε. LTTrAWHR, *see* πούς
12:49 ἐπί Eds
14:28**for* πρός GEds
17: 3 *omit* against thee LTTrAWHR
18:13 *omit* upon LTTr[A]WHR
19: 4*ε. τὸ ἔμπροσθεν T[A]WHR
20:20 ε. τὸ—ὥστε LTTrAWHR
21:14 ἐν LTTrAWHR
22:10*οὗ—ε. ἣν LTTrAWHR
17*ἑαυτοῖς—ε. ἑαυτούς LTTrAWHR
23:19 ἐν TTrAWHR
42**for* ἐν WH
24:47**for* καί² TWH
50 πρός LTTrAWHR
51 *omit* and carried up into heaven T[[WH]]
Joh. 3:15 ε. αὐτὸν—ἐν αὐτῷ TTrAWHR
6:22 *omit* ε.¹—GLTTrAWHR, *see* ἐκεῖνος
47 *omit* on me T[TrA]WHR
11:32 πρός TTrAWH
15:21*ὑμῖν—ε. ὑμᾶς LTTrAWHR
16:13 ἐν T
21: 4 ἐπί LT
11**for* ἐπί LTTrAWHR
Acts 2: 5**for* ἐν T
3:19 πρός TWH
4: 6 (5) ἐν LTrAWWHR
5:15*καὶ ε. *for* κατά LTTrWHR
16 *omit* unto LTTrAWHR
7:12**for* ἐν Eds
9:21**for* ἐν T
28**for* ἐν¹ Eds
12:25**for* ἐξ WH
14:21*and³—*add* ε. to LTTrAWHR
21*and⁴—*add* ε. to LTTrA[WH]R
25**for* ἐν T, *see* Πέργη
16: 1*and¹—*add* ε. to LTTrWHR
7**for* κατά² GEds
40 πρός GEds
18:21 *omit* LTTrAWHR, *see* δεῖ
20:13 ἐπί LTTrAWHR
23:15**for* πρός Eds
24:11**for* ἐν Eds
15 πρός T
25: 4**for* ἐν¹ Eds
16 *omit* to die GEds
20 *omit* ε.¹ TTr[A]WHR
26: 6**for* πρός Eds
20 *omit* throughout LTTr[A]WHR
27: 2*πλεῖν—*add* ε. LTTr[A]WHR
29 upon—against, κατά Eds
1 Co. 12:13 *omit* ε.² *read* of one Spirit Eds
2 Co. 9: 5 πρός LTrW
13: 4 [toward you] AWH
Gal. 3:17 *omit* in Christ LTTrAWHR
Eph. 5:32 [εἰς²] LAWH
Phil. 3:14**for* ἐπί LTTrAWHR
21 *omit* that it may be GEds
Col. 1:10 *omit* ε.² GEds, *see* ἐπίγνωσις
2 Ti. 2:14 ἐπί LTTrAWHR
Philem. 5**for* πρός LTrAWH
Heb. 12: 7**for* εἰ LTTrAWHR
Jas. 3: 3**for* πρός LTTrAWHR
5:12 *omit* ε. A.V.B EGEds, *see* ὑπόκρισις
1 Pet. 1:23 *omit* for ever GEds
2: 2**add* ε. GEds, *see* σωτηρία
5*πνευματικός—*add* ε. *read* for an holy LTTrAWHR
3: 5**for* ἐπί Eds
2 Pet. 2:17 *omit* for ever LTTrAWHR
3: 9 to us-ward—because of you, δι' ὑμᾶς LT
1 Joh. 5:13 *omit* ε.¹ GEds, *see* ὄνομα
3 Joh. 5 to²—that, τοῦτο Eds
Rev. 5:14 *omit* GEds, *see* ζάω
13:10*τις¹—*add* ε. LTAWWHR

Rev. 16: 2 *trs* εἰς *and* ἐπί Eds
4 *omit* ε.² LTTrAWHR
17 into—upon, ἐπί GEds

1520 εἷς, ἕν.

Mat. 9:18*ἄρχων—*add* εἷς A.V.C GLTr[WH]R
18:14 ἓν LTTrWH
24 *trs* εἷς αὐτῷ TWH
19:17 *see* ἀγαθός
24:40 *omit* ὁ *bis, read* one is taken, and one LTTrAWHR
26:22*εἷς ἕκαστος LTTrAWHR
Mar. 4: 8 some ἓν—εἰς *ter* A, unto εἰς *ter* TTrR: ἓν¹—εἰς WH: ἓν²³—ἐν WH
20 some¹—in, ἐν TTrWHR
20 some²³—in, ἐν TTr[WH]R
8:28 ἕνα—ὅτι εἷς LTTrAWHR
14:10 ὁ εἷς the one TTrAWHR
51 *omit* ε. LTrWHR
15:36 τις TTrAWHR
Lu. 9: 8 τις TAWHR, τίς Tr
12:25 *om.* ἕ. *read* a cubit T[Tr]AWHR
17:34 [one]¹ LWH
34 ὁ ε.—*omit* ὁ GLTTrAW
35 ἡ μία A.V.Er EGLT[Tr]AWHR
36 *add the verse* A.V.B E, *see* ἀφίημι
18:10 ὁ ε.—*omit* ὁ LTrAWH
20: 3 *omit* ἕ LTTrAWHR
23:17 *omit the verse* [L]TTr[A]WHR
24:18 ὁ ε.—*omit* ὁ LTTrAWHR
Joh. 6: 9 *omit* ἓν [L]TTr[A]WHR
17:21 *omit* one³ [L]TTrAWHR
21:25 *omit the verse* T
Acts 4:32 καρδία—*add unum* A.V. Vul
1 Co. 6: 5 *omit* ε. LTTrAWHR, *see* οὐδέ
12: 9*ἑνὶ *for* αὐτῷ² LTTrAWHR
12 *omit* one² (τοῦ ἑνός) Eds
26 *omit* ἓν³ *read* a member TTr[A]WHR
Jas. 4:13 *omit* ἕ. LTTrWHR
1 Joh. 5: 7 *omit* GEds, *see* λόγος
Rev. 4: 8*add ἓν GLTAWHR, *see* κατά
22: 2 *omit* ἕ. GEds

1521 εἰσάγω.

Acts 22:24*trs ὁ χιλίαρχος (εἰσάγεσθαι *for* ἄγεσθαι, ἄγω) αὐτὸν GLTTrAWWH

1525 εἰσέρχομαι.

Mat. 2:21*εἰσῆλθεν *for* ἦλθεν (ἔρχομαι) LTTrAWH
7:13 ε.¹—εἰσέλθατε LTTrAWH
8: 5 εἰσελθόντος LTTrAWHR
9:18*εἰσελθών *for* ἐλθών (ἔρχομαι) TAW
17:25 εἰσελθόντα LT, ἔρχομαι TrAWH
19:24*εἰσελθεῖν *for* διελθεῖν (διέρχομαι) GTTrAWH
24 *omit* to enter T[Tr]AWH: *trs* ε. *after* πλούσιον LTr
Mar. 1:21 *omit* ε. *read* he taught in the synagogue T[Tr]A
2: 1†*trs* ε. πάλιν LW: εἰσελθὼν π. TTrAWHR
7:25*εἰσελθοῦσα *for* ἐλθοῦσα (ἔρχομαι) T
9:28 εἰσελθόντος αὐτοῦ LTTrWHR
10:25 ε.¹—διέρχομαι A.V.B EGEds
13:15 εἰσελθάτω LTTrWH
14:38 ἔρχομαι TAWH
16: 5 ἔρχομαι A
Lu. 8:33 εἰσῆλθον LTTrAWWH
51 ε.¹—ἔρχομαι GLTTrWWHR
10: 5†*trs* εἰσέλθητε οἰκίαν TTrAWHR: οἰ. εἰσέλ. L
10 εἰσέλθητε LTTrAWHR
11:52 ε.¹—εἰσήλθατε GLTTrAWH
18:24 εἰσπορεύομαι TTrAWH
Acts 10:24 εἰσῆλθεν he entered LTrWH, εἰσῆλθαν T
25 τοῦ εἰσελθεῖν GEds
11: 3†*trs* ε. (εἰσῆλθεν he went in TrWH) *before* πρὸς LTTrAWWH
20 ἔρχομαι GEds
13:14 ἔρχομαι TTrWHR
18: 7*εἰσῆλθεν *for* ἦλθεν (ἔρχομαι) LT
28:16*εἰσήλθομεν LTAR, -θαμεν TrWH, *for* ἤλθομεν (ἔρχομαι)
Jas. 5: 4 εἰσελήλυθαν LTTrAWWH
2 Joh. 7 are entered—are gone forth, ἐξέρχομαι Eds

1526 εἰσίν.

Mat. 11: 8 *omit* ε. T[A]WH
20:16 *omit* T[TrA]WHR, *see* πόλυς
Mar. 4:18 *omit* οὗτοί ε.² A.V.C
8: 3**for* ἥκασιν (ἥκω) AWH
Lu. 14:17**for* ἐστίν T
Joh. 10:12 ἐστίν LTTrAWH
17: 7**for* ἐστίν LTTrAWH
Acts 23:21 *trs* εἰσὶν ἕτοιμοι LTTrAWWH
1 Co. 14:10**for* ἐστίν Eds
37 ἐστίν Eds
Gal. 3: 7 *trs* υἱοί εἰσιν LTTrWH
1 Ti. 5:25**for* ἐστίν W
1 Joh. 5: 7, 8 *omit* in heaven *to* in earth (*ver.* 8) GEds
Rev. 4:11 they are—they were, ἦσαν (ἦν) GEds
9:19 ἐστίν A.V.C GEds, *see* ἐξουσία
14: 4 *omit* ε.³ LTTrAWHR
17: 9 *trs* ἑπτὰ ὄρη ε. GLTTrAWHR
19: 9 *trs* τοῦ θεοῦ ε. LTTrAWHR

1530 εἰσπηδάω.

Acts 14:14 ran in—sprang forth, ἐκπηδάω GEds

1531 εἰσπορεύομαι.

Lu. 18:24**trs* εἰσπορεύονται *for* εἰσελεύσονται (εἰσέρχομαι) *after* θεοῦ TTrAWH

1533 εἰσφέρω.

Lu. 12:11*εἰσφέρωσιν *for* προσφέρωσιν (-ρω) TTrAWHR

1534 εἶτα.

Mar. 4:28 εἶτεν *bis* TWH
Joh. 2: 3**add* ε. T, *see* οἶνος
1 Co. 12:28 ἔπειτα LTTrAWHR
15: 5 ἔπειτα T
7 ἔπειτα TA

1535 εἴτε *see under* εἰ. See 1488

1537 ἐκ, ἐξ.

Mat. 7: 4**for* ἀπό LTTrWHR
10:14*dust—*add* ἐκ, *read* from your feet LT
13: 1**for* ἀπό LT
17: 9**for* ἀπό GEds
18:19**add* ἐξ LTTrAWH, *see* συμφωνέω
19:20 *om.* from my youth up LTTrA (WHR
23:25 *omit* ἐξ L[Tr]
24:29**for* ἀπό T
26:44 *omit* the third time [L]A
Mar. 1:10**for* ἀπό LTTrAWHR
6:16 *omit* from the dead T[Tr]AWHR
51 *omit* beyond measure [Tr]WHR
7:15**for* ἀπό LTTrAWHR, *see* ἄνθρωπος
9: 9**for* ἀπό LWH
21*ἐκ παιδιόθεν from a child Eds
12:33 *omit* and with all the soul [L]TWHR
13: 1*εἷς—*add* ἐκ Tr[A]
25**see* ἐκπίπτω
14:20 *omit* ἐκ T[Tr]WH
31**see* ἐκπερισσῶς
16: 3 ἀπό LTr
14**add* ἐκ L[WH], *see* νεκρός
Lu. 1:35*born,—*add* ἐκ σοῦ A.V.B[L]
61**for* ἐν LTTrAWHR
4:35 ἀπό LTTrAWHR
38 out of—from, ἀπό TTrAWHR
5: 3 out of—in, ἐν T
8: 3**for* ἀπό LTTrAWHR
27 *omit* ἐκ² TTrWH, *see* χρόνος
10:27 ἐξ²³⁴—ἐν LTTrWHR, *see* ψυχή
11:11*δέ—*add* ἐξ Eds
15:16**for* ἀπό WHR
16: 4*μετασταθῶ—*add* ἐκ[L]TTrAWHR
22:16 thereof—it, αὐτό LTTrAWHR
Joh. 6:38 ἀπό LTTrAWHR
66*πολλοὶ—*add* ἐκ [L]TTr[A]WH
12: 2*ἦν—*add* ἐκ TAWHR
4 *omit* ἐκ TrWHR
13:23*εἷς—*add* ἐκ GEds
16:28**for* παρά LTTrAWHR
18: 3*ἐκ ([ἐκ]WH) τῶν Φαρισαίων from the Pharisees TWH
Acts 1:25 ἀπό Eds
7: 3 *omit* ἐκ² [L]Tr[A]WH
8:37 *omit the verse* GLTTrAWHR
9: 3**for* ἀπό LTTrWWHR
12:25 from—to, εἰς WH
13:42 *om.* out of the synagogue GEds
16:40 ἀπό TWH
18: 2 ἀπό Eds
23:30*ἐξ αὐτῆς straightway—ἐξ αὐτῶν by them LTTr: ἐξ αὐτῆς A
24: 7 *omit* LTTr[A]WHR, *see* κρίνω
26:17*ἐκ τῶν ἐθνῶν from the Gentiles LTTrAWHR
27:34 ἀπό LTTrAWHR
28: 3 ἀπό Eds
Ro. 8:34**add* ἐκ [WH]R, *see* νεκρός
11: 6 *omit* But if (it be) *to end of verse* GLTTr[A]WHR
1 Co. 9: 7 *omit* of¹ Eds
2 Co. 2:16*ὀσμὴ *bis*—*add* ἐκ, *read* from death, from life LTTrAWHR
9: 2 *omit* ἐξ LTTr[A]WHR
Gal. 3:21 ἐν WH, *see* νόμος
Eph. 5:30 *omit* ἐκ *bis* LTTr[A]WHR, *see* σάρξ
Phil. 3:11*τὴν ἐκ νεκρῶν from the dead Eds
1 Th. 1:10**for* ἀπό TTrWHR
Jas. 2:18 ἐκ¹ by—χωρίς without A.V.B GEds
3 Joh. 10 *omit* ἐκ T
Rev. 1: 5 *omit* ἐκ GEds
5**for* ἀπό² LTTrAWHR
2: 9*βλασφημίαν—*add* ἐκ GEds
6: 4**for* ἀπό GLTTrAW[WH]R
10**for* ἀπό Eds
7:17**for* ἀπό GEds
9:18 *omit* ἐκ²³ GEds
13: 3*μίαν—*add* ἐκ GEds
15: 2 *om.* over his mark (and) GEds
16: 7 *omit* another out of GEds
11 *omit* ἐκ² A.V. Vul
17**for* ἀπό¹ LTTrAWHR
19: 5 out of—from, ἀπό LTrAWWHR
21: 4**for* ἀπό LTTrAWHR
9*εἷς—*add* ἐκ LTTrAWHR
22:19 *omit* out of² L[TrA]
See also ἑαυτῆς.

1538 ἕκαστος.

1 Co. 10:24 *omit* every man GEds
Eph. 6: 8†*trs* ἕκαστος ὃ (*omit* ὃ TAWH) ἐάν (ἄν Tr) τι (*om.* τι LTrR) Eds
Phil. 2: 4 ἕ.¹—ἕκαστοι LTTrAWHR: ἕ.²—ἕκαστοι GEds
Rev. 4: 8**see* κατά
6:11 *omit* every one of GW: ἑκάστῳ LTTr[A]WHR

1540 ἑκατόν.

Rev. 7: 4 *see* ρμδ'

1542 ἑκατονταπλασίων.

Mat. 19:29 an hundredfold—many times more πολλαπλασίων LTTrAWH

1543 ἑκατοντάρχης, *see* ἑκατόνταρχος.

1543 ἑκατόνταρχος.

Mat. 8: 5, 8 ἑκατοντάρχης T
13 -χῃ GLTTrAWWH
27:54 -χης T
Lu. 7: 6 -χης TWH: *trs* φίλους ὁ ἑ. TTrAWH
23:47 -χης TTrWH
Acts 21:32 -χας LTTrAWWH
22:26 -χης LTWH
23:23 -χῶν WH | 27: 6 -χης LTTrAWH
27:11 -χης GLTTrAWH
43 -χης LTTrAWH
28:16 *omit* the centurion *to* of the guard: but LTTrAWHR

* ἐκβαίνω, to go out.

Heb. 11:15 ἐξέβησαν *for* ἐξῆλθον (ἐξέρχομαι) Eds

1544 ἐκβάλλω.

Mat. 8:12 shall be cast out—shall go forth, ἐξέρχομαι T
25:30 ἐκβάλετε GLTTrAWWH
Mar. 5:40 ὁ δὲ ἐ.—αὐτὸς δὲ ἐ. LTTrWHR
7:26 ἐκβάλῃ GLTTrAWWH
Lu. 6:42 *trs* ἐκβαλεῖν *to end of verse* TAWH
8:54 *omit* put them all out, and LTTrAWHR
9:40 ἐκβάλωσιν GEds
10: 2†*trs* ἐργάτας ἐκβάλῃ TTrAWH, ἐκβάλῃ ἐρ. GLW

1547 ἐκγαμίζω.

Mat. 22:30 γαμίζω LTTrAWH
24:38 γαμίζω TWH
Lu. 17:27 γαμίζω LTTrAWHR
1 Co. 7:38 ἐ.¹—γαμίζων τὴν παρθένον ἑαυτοῦ (ἑα. πα. TWH) giveth his own virgin in marriage LTTr[A]WHR
38 ἐ.²—γαμίζω GLTTrWHR, [ἐκ]γ. A

1548 ἐκγαμίσκομαι.

Lu. 20:34 γαμίσκομαι LTTrAWHR
35 γαμίζω LTTrWHR, γαμίσκομαι A

1551 ἐκδέχομαι.

Joh. 5: 3 *omit* waiting for *to end of verse* 4 [G]TTrAWHR
1 Pet. 3:20 ἀπεκδέχομαι GEds

1554 ἐκδίδωμι.
Mat.21:33 ἐξέδετο TAWH
41 ἐκδώσεται GLTTrAWWH
Mar.12: 1 ἐξέδετο TAWH
Lu. 20: 9 ἐξέδετο TAWH

1559 ἐκδιώκω.
Lu. 11:49 διώκω WHR: [ἐκ]διώξουσιν TrA

1562 ἐκδύω.
Mat.27:31 ἐκδύσαντες T

1563 ἐκεῖ.
Mar. 1:13 *omit* there GEds
6:55 *omit* ἐ. LT[Tr]WHR
14:15 κἀκεῖ T, καὶ ἐ. TrAWHR and there
Lu. 10: 6 *trs* ἐκεῖ ᾖ WH
17:23†*trs* see there; or (*omit* or TTrR) see here TTrAWHR
Acts 14:28 *omit* there GEds
2 Co. 3:17 *omit* there Eds
Rev. 12: 6*ἔχει—*add* ἐ. GTAWWHR
22: 5 there—longer, ἔτι GEds
See also κἀκεῖ.

1564 ἐκεῖθεν.
Mar. 1:19 *omit* thence [L]TTrAWHR
9:30 καὶ ἐ.—κἀκεῖθεν LTTrAWH
10: 1*καὶ ἐ. *for* κἀκεῖθεν LTTrAWWH
Acts 16:12 ἐ. τε—κἀκεῖθεν Eds
27:12**for* κἀκεῖθεν LTTrAWHR
Rev. 22: 2**for* ἐντεῦθεν² Eds

1565 ἐκεῖνος.
Mat. 18: 7 *omit* ἐ. *read* the man LTTrWH
26*δοῦλος ἐκεῖνος that servant T
27 *om.* ἐ. *read* the servant L[WH]
24:38*ἡμέραις—*add* ἐκείναις, *read* those days L[TrWH]R
48 *om.* ἐ. *read* the evil servant T
Mar. 2:20 ἐκείνῃ GEds, *see* ἡμέρα
4:20*ἐκεῖνοι *for* οὗτοι TTrAWHR
6:11 *omit* verily *to end of verse* G[L]TTrAWHR
7:15 *omit* those T[Tr]WHR
Lu. 7:21*ἐκείνῃ *for* αὐτῇ TTrAWHR
9:34 ἐ. εἰσελθεῖν —εἰσ. αὐτούς TTrAWHR
12:38 *omit* those servants T
14:21 | 17: 9 *omit* ἐ. *read* the servant LTTrAWHR
18:14 ἢ ἐ.—παρ' ἐκεῖνον LTrAWH
19:27 those—these, τούτους TTrAWHR
20: 1 *om.* ἐ. *read* the days LTTrAWHR
Joh. 5:37*ἐκεῖνος *for* αὐτός TTrAWHR
6:22 *omit* that whereinto his disciples were entered GLTTrAWHR
8:10 *omit* those thine accusers WHR
13: 6 *omit* ἐκεῖνος LT[Tr]AWHR
19:15*ἐκραύγασαν (*om.* οἱ δὲ)—*add* οὖν ἐκεῖνοι, *read* they therefore cried out TTrAWHR
31 ἐκείνου S—ἐκείνη B
Acts 10: 9 αὐτῶν T
10 αὐτῶν Eds
Ro. 11:23 καὶ ἐ.—κἀκεῖνος GLTTrAWWH
Heb. 3:10 that—this, ταύτῃ Eds
Rev. 16:14 *omit* ἐ. *read* the great LTTrAWHR
See also κἀκεῖνος.

1567 ἐκζητέω.
Ro. 3:11 ὁ ἐ.—*omit* ὁ [L]WH

* ἐκζήτησις a seeking out.
1 Ti. 1: 4 ἐκζητήσεις *for* ζητήσεις (-ησις) TTrWHR

1568 ἐκθαμβέω.
Mar. 9:15 ἐξεθαμβήθησαν LTTrAWH

* ἐκθαυμάζω, to marvel greatly.
Mar. 12:17 ἐξεθαύμαζον *for* ἐθαύμασαν (θαυμάζω) TWHR

1573 ἐκκακέω.
ἐγκακέω LTrAWR, ἐγκ- *or* ἐνκ- TWH

1575 ἐκκλάζω, ἐκκλάω.
Ro. 11:20 κλάζω LTr

1579 ἐκκλησία.
Acts 2:47 *omit* to the church LTTrAWHR
9:31 ἡ μὲν οὖν ἐκκλησία the church Eds
Ro. 16:23 *trs* ὅλης τῆς ἐ. LTTrAWHR
1 Co. 11:18 the church—*omit* τῇ, *read* in assembly GEds
14:35 *trs* λαλεῖν ἐν ἐ. LTTrAWHR
Rev. 2: 1 τῷ ἐν Ἐφέσῳ ἐ. LTrWHR
8 τῆς—τῷ LWHR: *trs* ἐν Σμύρνῃ (Ζμ- T) ἐ. GEds
18 τῷ ἐν Θ. ἐ. LWH

1578 ἐκκλίνω.
Ro. 16:17 ἐκκλίνετε TTrWH

1581 ἐκκόπτω.
1 Pet. 3: 7 ἐγκόπτω GEds

* ἐκκράζω, to cry out.
Acts 24:21 ἐκέκραξα *for* ἔκραξα (κράζω) TTrAWH

1582 ἐκκρέμαμαι.
Lu. 19:48 ἐξεκρέμετο TWH

1586 ἐκλέγω.
Lu. 9:35*ἐκλελεγμένος *for* ἀγαπητός TTrAWHR
Acts 1:24 *trs* ὃν ἐ. ἐκ τούτων τῶν δύο ἕνα GEds
15: 7†*trs* ἐν ὑμῖν (ἡμῖν W) ἐ. ὁ θεὸς Eds
25 ἐκλεξαμένοις, *read* having chosen, to send men LTrWWH

1587 ἐκλείπω.
Lu. 16: 9 ἐκλίπῃ it shall fail LTTrAWHR
22:32 ἐκλίπῃ LTTrAWHR
23:45**for* σκοτίζομαι TWHR, *see* ἥλιος

1588 ἐκλεκτός.
Mat. 20:16 *omit* T[TrA]WHR, *see* πολύς
1 Pet. 2: 6 *trs* ἐκλεκτὸν ἀκρογωνιαῖον WH
2 Joh. 1, 13 Ἐκλέκτος (*as a proper name*) S

1590 ἐκλύω.
Mat. 9:36 fainted—were harassed, σκύλλω GEds

1591 ἐκμάσσω.
Lu. 7:38 ἐξέμαξεν TR

1598 ἐκπειράζω.
1 Co. 10: 9*ἐξεπείρασαν *for* ἐπείρασαν (πειράζω) T

* ἐκπερισσῶς, exceedingly.
Mar. 14:31 *for* ἐκ περισσοῦ LTTrAWHR

* ἐκπηδάω, to leap forth.
Acts 14:14 ἐξεπήδησαν *for* εἰσεπήδησαν (εἰσπηδάω) GEds

1601 ἐκπίπτω.
Mar. 13:25†*trs* ἔσονται ἐκ τοῦ οὐρανοῦ πίπτοντες (*read* from heaven) LTTrAWHR
Acts 12: 7 ἐξέπεσαν LTTrAWH
27:29 ἐκπέσωμεν A.V.C GEds
1 Co. 13: 8 πίπτω LTTrAWHR
Rev. 2: 5 πίπτω GEds

1605 ἐκπλήσσω, -ττω.
Mar. 11:18 ἐξεπλήσσοντο T

1607 ἐκπορεύομαι.
Mat. 17:21 *omit the verse* T[TrA]WHR
Mar. 11:19 ἐξεπορεύοντο they went LTrWH
Acts 19:12*ἐκπορεύεσθαι *for* ἐξέρχεσθαι (ἐξέρχομαι) GEds
Rev. 16:14 ἐκπορεύεσθαι S—ἃ (*omit* ἃ L) ἐκπορεύεται A.V.B EGEds
19:21 ἐξέρχομαι GEds

* ἐκσώζω, to preserve from danger.
Acts 27:39*ἐκσῶσαι *for* ἐξῶσαι (-ωθέω) WH

1617 ἐκτενέστερον.
Lu. 22:43, 44 *the verses* [L][[WH]]

1618 ἐκτενής.
Acts 12: 5 ἐκτενῶς LTTrAWHR

1619 ἐκτενῶς.
Acts 12: 5**for* ἐκτενής LTTrAWHR

1620 ἐκτίθημι.
Acts 7:21 ἐκτεθέντος LTTrAWHR

1623 ἐκτός.
2 Co. 12: 3 out of—apart from, χωρὶς LTTrAWHR

1625 ἐκτρέφω.
Rev. 12: 6*ἐκτρέφωσιν *for* τρέφωσιν (-ω) W

1627 ἐκφέρω.
Mar. 8:23*ἐξήνεγκεν *for* ἐξήγαγεν (ἐξάγω) TTrAWHR

1628 ἐκφεύγω.
Heb. 12:25*ἐξέφυγον *for* ἔφυγον (φεύγω) LTTrAWHR

1631 ἐκφύω.
Mat. 24:32 ἐκφυῇ LTrA
Mar. 13:28 ἐκφυῇ S—ἐκφύῃ EGTWHR

1632 ἐκχέω.
Mar. 2:22 *omit* ἐ. *read* the wine perisheth, and the bottles TTrAWHR
Lu. 11:50*ἐκκεχυμένον *for* ἐκχυνόμενον (ἐκχύνω) TrWH
Acts 22:20 ἐκχύνω LTTrAWH
Rev. 16: 1 ἐκχέετε LTAWH

1632 ἐκχύνω.
Mat. 23:35 | 26:28 ἐκχυννόμενον LTTrAWH
Mar. 14:24 ἐκχυννόμενον LTTrAWH: †*trs* ἐ. ὑπὲρ πολλῶν TTrAWH
Lu. 11:50 ἐκχυννόμενον LTA: ἐκχέω TrWH
22:20 ἐκχυννόμενον LTTrAWH
Acts 22:20*ἐξεχύννετο *for* ἐξεχεῖτο (ἐκχέω) LTTrAWH

1639 Ἐλαμίτης, –μείτης TWH.

ἐλεάω, *see* ἐλεέω. See 1653

* ἐλεγμός, a refuting, reproving.
2 Ti. 3:16 ἐλεγμόν *for* ἔλεγχον (-χος) LTTrAWHR

1650 ἔλεγχος.
2 Ti. 3:16 ἐλεγμός LTTrAWHR

1651 ἐλέγχω.
Joh. 8: 9 *omit* being convicted by (their own) conscience WHR
Jude 15*ἐλέγξαι *for* ἐξελέγξαι (-γχω) LTTrAWHR
22*ἐλέγχετε *for* ἐλεεῖτε (ἐλεέω) LTTrAW

1652 ἐλεεινός.
Rev. 3:17 ὁ ἐ. GL, [ὁ] ἐλεινός A

1653 ἐλεέω, ἐλεάω.
Ro. 9:16 ἐλεῶντος LTTrAWH
Phil. 2:27 *trs* ἠλέησεν αὐτόν LTTrAWWH
Jude 22 ἐλέγχετε (-χω) διακρινομένους, *read* and some convict, when contending LTTrAW: ἐλεᾶτε δ. WHR
23**add* ἐ. Eds, *see* φόβος

1654 ἐλεημοσύνη.
Mat. 6: 1 alms—righteousness, δικαιοσύνη GEds
4 *trs* ἡ σοῦ ἐ. ᾖ T

1656 ἔλεος.
Mat. 9:13 | 12:7 ἔλεος LTTrAWH
23:23 τὸ ἔλεος LTTrAWH
Tit. 1: 4 *omit* mercy TTrAWWHR
3: 5 τὸ αὐτοῦ ἔλεος Eds
Heb. 4:16 ἔλεος Eds

1658 ἐλεύθερος.
1 Co. 9: 1 *trs* Am I not free? am I not an apostle? GEds

* ἕλιγμα, anything tangled.
Joh. 19:39 *for* μίγμα WH

1665 Ἐλισάβετ, Ἐλει- WH.
Lu. 1: 7 *trs* ἦν ἡ (*omit* ἡ L[TrWH]) Ἐ. LTTrAWH

1666 Ἐλισσαῖος, Ἐ- LT, -ισα- LTTrAWHR
Lu. 4:27 *trs* ἐν τῷ Ἰσραὴλ ἐπὶ Ἐ. τοῦ προφήτου LTTrAWHR

1667 ἑλίσσω.
Heb. 1:12 shalt thou fold up—shalt thou change, ἀλλάσσω T

1669 ἑλκόομαι.
Lu. 16:20 εἱλκωμένος LTTrAWH

1670 ἑλκύω.
Joh. 21: 6 ἑλκύσαι WH

1672 Ἕλλην.
Joh. 12:20 *trs* Ἕλληνές τινες LTTrAWH
Acts 11:20* Ἕλληνας *for* Ἑλληνιστάς GLTTrAR
18:17 *omit* the Greeks Eds
1 Co. 1:23 Greeks—Gentiles ἔθνος GEds

1673 Ἑλληνικός
Lu. 23:38 *omit* in letters of Greek, and Latin, and Hebrew [L]TTr[A]WH

1675 Ἑλληνιστής.
Acts 11:20 Grecians—Greeks, Ἕλλην GLTTrAR

1676 Ἑλληνιστί.
Joh. 19:20 *trs* Latin (and) Greek TTrAWH

1677 ἐλλογέω, –άω.
Ro. 5:13 ἐλλογᾶται WH
Philem. 18 ἐλλόγα LTTrAWH

1678
Ἐλμωδάμ, Ἐ– L, –μαδάμ LTTrWH.

1679 ἐλπίζω.
1 Co. 15:19 *trs* ἐν χριστῷ ἠλ. ἐσμὲν Eds

1680 ἐλπίς.
Acts 27:20 *trs* ἐλπὶς πᾶσα LTTrAWH
1 Co. 9:10 *trs* ὀφείλει ἐπ' ἐ. LTTrAWH
10 *omit* of his hope GEds
10† *trs* ἐπ' ἐ. τοῦ μετέχειν in hope of partaking GEds

1682
Ἐλωΐ, –ί WH, Ἐλωΐ LTA.
Mat. 27:46* Ἐλωΐ *for* Ἠλί *bis* WH

1683 ἐμαυτοῦ.
2 Co. 11: 9 *trs* ἐμαυτὸν ὑμῖν LTTrAWH

1684 ἐμβαίνω.
Mat. 14:32 ἀναβαίνω LTTrAWH
15:39 ἀναβαίνω GTrAW
Mar. 5:18 ἐμβαίνοντος, as he was coming Eds
8:13 *trs* πάλιν ἐμβὰς LTTrAWH
Joh. 5: 4 *omit* waiting for (*ver.* 3) *to end of verse* 4 [G]TTrAWH
6:22 *omit* that whereinto his disciples were entered GLTTrAWH
21: 3* ἐνέβησαν *for* ἀνέβησαν (ἀναβαίνω) GEds
Acts 21: 6* ἐνέβημεν *for* ἐπέβημεν (ἐπιβαίνω) LTrWH

1686 ἐμβάπτω.
Joh. 13:26 βάπτω TTrAWH

1689 ἐμβλέπω.
Mar. 8:25 ἐνέβλεπεν LTTrAWH
Acts 1:11 βλέπω TTrWH

1690 ἐμβριμάομαι.
Mat. 9:30 ἐνεβριμήθη LTTrAWH
Mar. 14: 5 ἐνεβριμοῦντο T
Joh. 11:38 ἐμβριμούμενος T

1691 ἐμέ.
Mar. 9:42 *omit* in me TAWH
14: 6 εἰς ἐ.—ἐν ἐμοί GEds
Joh. 6:47 *omit* on me T[TrA]WH
9: 4 I—we, ἡμᾶς TTrWH
Philem. 17 ἐ.[1]—μέ GEds
See also ἐμοι *and* μέ.

1696 ἐμμένω.
Acts 28:30* ἐνέμεινεν *for* ἔμεινεν (μένω) TTrAWH

1697
Ἐμμόρ, Ἐ– WH, –μώρ LTTrAWH.
Ἐμόρ A.V.†Br

1698 ἐμοί.
Mat. 18:26 ἐμέ Tr
29 ἐμέ LTrA
Mar. 14:27 *omit* because of me TTrAWH

Joh. 8:12 μοι LTrWH
Acts 24:20 *omit* in me LT[TrA]WH
See also ἐμέ *and* μοι.

ἐμός.
Joh. 10:14 ἐμῶν—ἐμά LTTrAWH, *see* γινώσκω
1 Co. 9: 2 τῆς ἐμῆς—μοῦ τῆς LTTrAWH
2 Ti. 4: 6 ἐμῆς ἀναλύσεως—ἀ. μοῦ LTTrWH

1700 ἐμοῦ.
Mat. 26:42 *omit* from me [L]TTrAWH
Joh. 6:51* τοῦ ἐ. *for* τούτου τοῦ T
10: 8 *trs* ἦλθον πρὸ ἐ. GLTrAWH: *omit* before me T
13:18 μετ' ἐ.—μοῦ, *read* my bread TrAWH
See also μοῦ.

* ἐμπαιγμονή, mockery.
2 Pet. 3: 3 ἡμερῶν—*add* ἐν ἐμπαιγμονῇ, *read* scoffers with scoffing GEds

1702 ἐμπαίζω.
Mat. 27:29 ἐνέπαιξαν TWH
Lu. 14:29 *trs* αὐτῷ ἐμπαίζειν LTTrAWH
23:36 ἐνέπαιξαν TAWH

1704 ἐμπεριπατέω, ἐνπ– TWH.

* ἐμπιπράω, to kindle.
Acts 28: 6 ἐμπιπρᾶσθαι *for* πίμπρασθαι (πίμπραμαι) T

1706 ἐμπίπτω.
Lu. 6:39* ἐμπεσοῦνται *for* πεσοῦνται (πίπτω) LTTrAWH
14: 5 πίπτω LTTrAWH

1709 ἐμπνέω, ἐνπ– TWH.

1710 ἐμπορεύομαι.
Jas. 4:13 ἐμπορευσώμεθα S — ἐμπορευσόμεθα A.V.B EEds

1713 ἔμπορος.
Rev. 18:23 οἱ ἐ.—*omit* οἱ L[WH]

1715 ἔμπροσθεν.
Mar. 1: 2 *omit* before thee GEds
2:12* *for* ἐναντίον TWH
Lu. 19: 4 εἰς τὸ ἔμπροσθεν T[A]WH
Joh. 1:27 *omit* is preferred before me G[L]TTrAWH
Acts 10: 4* *for* ἐνώπιον LTTrAWH
Rev. 4: 6 ἔνπροσθεν T

1716 ἐμπτύω.
Mar. 10:34 *trs* shall spit upon him, and shall scourge him LTTrAWH

1719 ἔμφοβος.
Acts 22: 9 *omit* and were afraid LTTr[A]WH
24:25 *tremefactus* A.V. Vul

1722 ἐν.
Mat. 4: 4* *for* ἐπί[2] LTrA
23* *add* ἐν TTrAWH, *see* ὅλος
5:48 *omit* ἐν LTTrAWH, *see* οὐρανός
6: 4 *omit* openly Eds
6 *omit* openly LTTrAWH
18 *omit* openly GEds
9:35 *omit* among the people GEds
12:18* *for* εἰς Tr
21 *om.* ἐν *read* on his name GEds
17:21 *omit the verse* T[TrA]WH
20:26 ἐν ὑμῖν[2]—ὑμῶν A
21:25* *for* παρά LTrWH
23: 9 *omit* ἐν LTTrAWH, *see* οὐρανός
24:20 *omit* on GEds
25:13 *omit* wherein the Son of man cometh GLTTrAWH
18 *omit* ἐν TTrAWH, *see* γῆ
27: 5 in—into, εἰς TTrWH, *see* ναός
29* *for* ἐπί[2] LTTrAWH, *see* δεξιός
59* ἐν σινδόνι TrA, [ἐν] σ. WH
Mar. 1: 8 *omit* ἐν[1] T[Tr]AWH
8 *omit* ἐν[2] [LTr]AWH
39 εἰς GEds, *see* συναγωγή
45 ἐπί TTrAWH
2: 1* *for* εἰς[2] LTTrWH, *see* οἶκος
15 *omit* ἐν τῷ T[Tr]WH
24 *omit* ἐν LTTrAWH
3: 2* εἰ—*add* ἐν T
4: 8* *for* ἐν [23] WH
15 εἰς TrAWH, *see* καρδία

Mar. 4:20* *for* ἐν[1] TTrWH
20* *for* ἐν[23] TTr[WH]R
38* *for* ἐπί[1] GEds
6:11 *omit* G[L]TTrAWH, *see* κρίσις
32* ἀπῆλθον—*add* ἐν LWH, *see* ἔρημος
8:26 *omit* nor tell (it) to any in the town TWH
9:38 τινα—*add* ἐν A V.B EEds
10:10 εἰς LTrAWH, *see* οἰκία
44* ἐν ὑμῖν *for* ὑμῶν LWH
11:10 *omit* in the name of the Lord GEds
26 *omit the verse* TTrWH
14: 6* ἐν ἐμοί *for* εἰς ἐμέ GEds
27 *omit* because of me TTrAWH
27 *omit* this night [L]TTrAWWH
30 *omit* in LTTrAWH
15:29 *omit* ἐν LTTrA[WH]
16:18* *add* ἐν Tr[WH], *see* χείρ
Lu. 1:28 *omit* blessed (art) thou among women T[Tr]AWH
61 ἐκ LTTrAWH
2:38 *omit* ἐν LTTr[A]WH
44 *omit* ἐν[3] GEds
52 ἐν τῇ σοφίᾳ T
4: 1* *for* εἰς LTTrAWH
23 ἐν[1]—εἰς GLTTrAWH
44 εἰς TTrAWH
5: 3* *for* ἐκ T
6: 2 *omit* ἐν LTTrAWH
7:17 *om.* throughout[2] [L]T[Tr]AWH
8:40 *trs* ἐν δὲ TrWH
9:37 *omit* ἐν T[Tr]AWH
49* *for* ἐπί WH
10:21 ἐν τῷ πνεύματι T
27* *for* ἐκ[234] LTTrWH, *see* ψυχή
38 *trs* ἐν δὲ TrWH
11: 2 *omit* which art in heaven GTTrAWH
2 *omit* as in heaven, so in earth G[L]TTrAWH
13: 4 *omit* ἐν[2] TrAWH
14: 5 *omit* ἐν [L]Tr
16:26* *for* ἐπί TWH
17:24 *omit* in his day LWH
36 *add the verse* A.V.B E, *see* ἀφίημι
19:13* ἐν ᾧ *for* ἕως LTTrAWH
45 *omit* therein, and them that bought TTrAWH
20:10 *omit* ἐν LTTrAWH
21:14* *for* εἰς LTTrAWH
23 *omit* ἐν[2], *read* to this people GEds
22: 7 *omit* ἐν TrA
55 *omit* ἐν[2] TTrAWH
23:19* *for* εἰς TTrAWH
42 εἰς WH
24:18 *omit* ἐν[1] GTTrAWWH
32 *omit* within us [TrA]WH
Joh. 2:19 [ἐν] TrWH
23 [ἐν][2] LTr
3:13 *omit* which is in heaven WH
15* *for* εἰς TTrAWH
4:53 *omit* ἐν[1] T[Tr]WH
5: 4 *omit* waiting for (*verse* 3) *to end of verse* 4 [G]TTrAWH
6:39 *omit* ἐν TrAWH
40* ἐγώ—*add* ἐν LT
44* αὐτόν[2]—*add* ἐν GEds
7:22 [ἐν] LWH
8: 3 ἐν[1]—ἐπί WH
9:14* *add* ἐν LTTrAWH, *see* ὅτε
12:35* with you—among you, ἐν ὑμῖν GLTTrAWH
13:32 *omit* If God be glorified in him [LTrA]WH
16:13* *for* εἰς T, *see* ἀλήθεια
29* ἐν παρησίᾳ LTTrAWH
17:12 *omit* in the world LTTrAWH
19: 4 *omit* in him T
40* αὐτό—*add* ἐν W
Acts 1: 8 *omit* ἐν[2] L[TrAWH]
17* *for* σύν GEds
21 *omit* ἐν[2] LTTrAWH
2: 5 [ἐν] WH: εἰς T
38* *for* ἐπί LTrWH
41* ἐν τῇ ἡμέρᾳ, *read* in the same day LTTr[A]WH
43* *add* ἐν T, *see* φόβος
3:25* καί[2]—*add* ἐν GEds
4:6(5)* *for* εἰς LTrAWWH
27* *add* ἐν GEds, *see* πόλις
7:12 εἰς Eds
16* Συχέμ[2]—ἐν Σ. in Sychem LTTrWH
22* Μωσῆς—*add* ἐν TTrAW
22 *omit* in[2] LTTrAWH
33 ἐπί LTTrAWH
35 by—with, σύν Eds
39* ἐν ταῖς καρδίαις LTTrAWH
44 *omit* ἐν[1] A.V.Br LTTrAWH

Acts 9:12 *omit* in a vision LT[Tr]A[WH]R
21 εἰς T
28 ε.[1]—εἰς Eds
10:39 *omit* ἐν[2] [L]TrWH
40*ἐν τῇ τρίτῃ T
14:25 εἰς T, *see* Πέργη
20:15 *omit* LTTrWHR, *see* μένω
21:20*εἰσίν—*add* ἐν τοῖς, *read* among the Jews LTrAWWHR
24:11 εἰς Eds
14 καί—*add* ἐν ELW, *add* τοῖς ἐν GTTr[A]WHR
20 *omit* in me LT[TrA]WHR
25: 4 ἐν[1]—εἰς Eds
26:10*ἐγώ—*add* ἐν GEds
28:29 *omit the verse* LTTrAWHR
Ro. 6:12 *omit* it in GEds
7:23*με—*add* ἐν TTr[AWH]R
9:28 *omit* LTTr[A]WHR, *see* λόγος
10:20*εὑρέθην—*add* [ἐν], *read* amongst them LTrA
20*ἐγενόμην—*add* [ἐν], *read* amongst them LTr
11:25*for παρά TrAWH
13: 9 [ἐν τῷ] LTrAWH
1Co. 6: 7 *omit* ἐν GEds
20 *omit* and in your spirit, which are God's GEds
8:11*for ἐπί Eds
10: 8 *omit* ἐν LTTr[A]WH
14: 6 *omit* by[4] T[Tr]
39*add ἐν [L]A, *see* γλῶσσα
2Co. 1:20 καὶ ἐν αὐτῷ—διὸ καὶ δι' αὐτοῦ wherefore also through him Eds
3: 7 *omit* ἐν[2] Eds
9 *omit* ἐν LTTrAWHR
5:12*μὴ ἐν *for* οὐ[2] LTTrWHR
7:11 *omit* ἐν[2] [L]TTrAWWHR
8:19*for σύν LTrAWWHR
11:27 *omit* ἐν[1] Eds
12:10 in[5]—and, καί TWH
12 in signs—*omit* in Eds
Gal. 3: 1 *omit* among you LTTrAWHR
10 *omit* ἐν[1] TTrWH
21*for ἐκ WH, *see* νόμος
6:15 *omit* in Christ Jesus TTrAWHR
Eph. 1: 1 [in Ephesus] TAWH
3 ἐν χριστῷ A.V.B EGEds
6 ἐν ᾗ—ἧς, *read* grace which he freely bestowed on us LTTrA (WHR
10 ἐν[2]—ἐπί LTTrAWHR
2:12 *omit* ἐν[1] Eds
3: 5 *omit* ἐν[1] GEds
8 *omit* ἐν, *read* to the Gentiles LTTrAWHR
5:19*ἑαυτοῖς—*add* [ἐν] LA
19 *omit* ἐν T[TrA]WHR
6: 1 *omit* in the Lord L[TrAWH]
16*for ἐπί LTTrWHR
Phil. 1: 7*καί[1]—*add* ἐν [L]TTrAWWHR
24 *omit* ἐν TWHR
2:15 *omit* ἐν[1] Eds
Col. 2: 7 *omit* ἐν[2] LTTr[A]WHR
7 *omit* therein TTr[AWH]R
13 *omit* ἐν TTrWHR
3:20*add ἐν GEds, *see* κύριος
1Th. 1: 5 *omit* ἐν[4] T[Tr]WHR
5 *omit* ἐν[5] [Tr]WHR
7*and—*add* ἐν in Ed
8*and—*add* ἐν in LT
2: 5 *omit* ἐν[2] WH
2Th. 2:10 *omit* ἐν[2] *read* to them Eds
12 *omit* ἐν [L]TTr[A]WHR
3:12*for διά LTTrAWHR, *see* κύριος
1Ti. 2: 7 *omit* in Christ GEds
3:14*τάχιον—ἐν τάχει LTrWHR
4:12 *omit* in spirit GEds
15 *omit* ἐν[2] A.V.Vul Eds
6:17 ἐν[2]—ἐπί LTTrWHR
Heb. 3: 9*add ἐν Eds, *see* δοκιμασία
10:34 *omit* ἐν[1] GEds
34 *omit* in heaven Eds
11:26 *omit* ἐν, *read* of Egypt GTTrAWWHR
38 ἐπί LTTrAWHR
Jas. 1:26 *omit* among you GEds
5:10*ἐλάλησαν—*add* ἐν LTTrWHR
1Pet. 1:12 *omit* ἐν LTrAWH
4: 1 *omit* ἐν LTTrAWHR
2Pet. 2:18 ἐν ἀσελγείαις B
3: 3*add ἐν GEds, *see* ἐμπαιγμονή
10 *omit* in the night GEds
1Joh. 2:24 *omit* in[4] L[WH]
3:18*ἐν ἔργῳ GEds
4: 3 *omit* that Christ is come in the flesh GLTTrAWHR
5: 6*ἐν τῷ αἵματι by blood Eds
7, 8 *omit* in heaven (*verse* 7) *to* in earth (*verse* 8) GEds
Jude 18 ἐπί Eds, *see* χρόνος
Rev. 1: 9 *omit* in the[1] [illegible] GEds
9*patience—*add* ἐν in Eds

Rev. 1:11 *omit* which are in Asia GEds
2: 1*add ἐν GEds, *see* Ἔφεσος
8*add ἐν GEds, *see* ἐκκλησία
13 *omit* ἐν[2] Eds
14 *omit* ἐν EGEds
3:14*add ἐν GEds, *see* Λαοδικεύς
4: 4 *omit* ἐν LWH
5: 2*ἐν φωνῇ GEds
13 ἐν[2]—ἐπί GEds
8: 7*ἐν αἵματι GEds
9:19*add A.V.C GEds, *see* ἐξουσία
11: 6 *omit* ἐν GEds
6*ἐν πάσῃ GEds
11*for ἐπί[1] GLT[A]W[WH]R
13: 3 *omit* ἐν, *see* θαυμάζω
10 *qui in* A.V.Vul
17:16 *omit* ἐν T[AWH]
18:10 *omit* ἐν GEds
16 *omit* ἐν LTr[AWH]R
23 *omit* ἐν[1] L[A]
19:17*ἐν φωνῇ T[AWH]
21:14 ἐπί GEds, *see* δώδεκα
23 *om.* ἐν, *read* shine for it GEds
24 in—by, διά GEds

1725 **ἔναντι.**

Acts 7:10*for ἐναντίον T
8:21*for ἐνώπιον GEds

1726 **ἐναντίον.**

Mar. 2:12 ἔμπροσθεν TWH
Lu. 1: 6*for ἐνώπιον TTrAWHR
Acts 7:10 ἔναντι T

ἔνατος, *see* **ἔννατος.** See 1766

1731 **ἐνδείκνυμι.**

2Co. 8:24 ἐνδεικνύμενοι LTTrA

1732 **ἔνδειξις.**

Ro. 3:26 τὴν ἔνδειξιν LTTrAWHR

1737 **ἐνδιδύσκω, -ομαι.**

Mar. 15:17*ἐνδιδύσκουσιν *for* ἐνδύουσιν (ἐνδύω) LTTrAWH
Lu. 8:27 ἐνδύω TTrWHR, *see* χρόνος

ἐνδόμησις, ἐνδώμησις TTrWHR.

1743 **ἐνδυναμόω.**

Heb. 11:34 δυναμόω LTTrWHR

1746 **ἐνδύω.**

Mar. 6: 9 ἐνδύσησθε S—ἐνδύσασθαι A.V.B EWH
15:17 ἐνδιδύσκω LTTrAWH
Lu. 8:27*ἐνεδύσατο *for* ἐνεδιδύσκετο (ἐνδιδύσκω) TTrWHR, *see* χρόνος
1Co. 15:54 *omit* ε.[1] WH, *see* φθαρτός

ἐνέγκω, *see* **φέρω.** See 5342

1747 **ἐνέδρα.**

Acts 23:16 τὴν ἐνέδραν *for* τὸ ἔνεδρον EGLTTrAWH

1749 **ἔνεδρον.**

Acts 23:16 ἐνέδρα EGLTTrAWH

1752 **ἕνεκα, ἕνεκεν, εἵνεκεν.**

Mat. 19: 5 ἕνεκα LTTrAWH
29 ἕνεκα T
Mar. 10:29*καί—*add* ἕνεκεν, *read* sake of the gospel G[L]TTrAW[WH]R
Lu. 4:18 εἵνεκεν GLTTrAWWH
18:29 εἵνεκεν TWH
Acts 19:32 ἕνεκα LTTrAWH
28:20 εἵνεκεν TWH
Ro. 8:36 ἕνεκεν GLTTrAWWH
2Co. 3:10 εἵνεκεν LTTrAWH
7:12 ἕνεκεν *ter* LTTrAWH

ἐνενήκοντα, *see* **ἐννενηκονταεννέα.** See 1768

ἐνεός, *see* **ἐννεός.** See 1769

1754 **ἐνεργέω.**

2Co. 1: 6 *trs* τῆς ἐνεργουμένης *to* πάσχομεν *after* παρακλήσεως GTWHR
Eph. 1:20 ἐνήργηκεν LTAWH

1757 **ἐνευλογέομαι.**

Acts 3:25 εὐλογέω WH
Gal. 3: 8 εὐλογέω B

* **ἔνθεν**, thence.

Mat. 17:20 *for* ἐντεῦθεν LTTrAWH
Lu. 16:26 *for* ἐντεῦθεν GEds

1760 **ἐνθυμέομαι.**

Acts 10:19 διενθυμέομαι GEds

1762 **ἔνι** *for* **ἔνεστι.**

1Co. 6: 5*for ἐστίν GEds

1764 **ἐνίστημι.**

Ro. 8:38 *trs* GEds, *see* δύναμις

1765 **ἐνισχύω.**

Lu. 22:43, 44 *the verses* [L][[WH]]
Acts 9:19 ἐνισχύθη WH

ἐνκακέω, *see* **ἐκκακέω.** See 1573

ἐνκόπτω, *see* **ἐγκόπτω.** See 1465

1766 **ἔννατος, ἔνατος.**

Mar. 15:34 τῇ ἐνάτῃ ὥρᾳ LTTrAWH

1768 **ἐννενηκονταεννέα.**

ἐνενήκοντα ἐννέα LTTrWH.

1769 **ἐννεός, ἐνεός** LTTrAWWH.

1773 **ἔννυχον, ἔννυχα** LTTrAWHR.

1774 **ἐνοικέω.**

Ro. 7:17*ἐνοικοῦσα *for* οἰκοῦσα (-κέω) TWH
8:11 διὰ τὸ ἐνοικοῦν αὐτοῦ πνεῦμα because of his Spirit that dwelleth S—διὰ τοῦ ἐνοικοῦντος αὐτοῦ πνεύματος by his Spirit, &c. A.V.B ETWHR

* **ἐνορκίζω**, to adjure.

1Th. 5:27 ἐνορκίζω *for* ὁρκίζω Eds

1776 **ἐνοχλέω.**

Lu. 6:18*ἐνοχλούμενοι *for* ὀχλούμενοι (-λέω) TTrAWHR

1777 **ἔνοχος.**

Mar. 14:64 *trs* ἔνοχον εἶναι TTrAWH

ἔνπροσθεν, *see* **ἔμπροσθεν.** See 1715

1781 **ἐντέλλομαι.**

Mat. 15: 4 commanded, saying—said, εἶπον LTrWHR
Mar. 11: 6 had commanded—said, εἶπον LTTrAWHR
Joh. 14:31 *see* ἐντολή

1782 **ἐντεῦθεν.**

Mat. 17:20 ἔνθεν LTTrAWH
Lu. 16:26 ἔνθεν GEds
Rev. 22: 2 ἐ.[2]—ἐκεῖθεν Eds

1785 **ἐντολή.**

Mat. 15: 6 commandment—word, λόγος LTrWHR: law, νόμος TA
Mar. 12:29 τῶν ἐ.—ἐντολή *read* commandment of all G[L]W: *omit* of all the commandments TTrAWHR
30 *omit* this (is) the first commandment TAWHR
Joh. 11:57 ἐντολάς, commandments TTrAWHR
14:31*ἐντολὴν ἔδωκεν *for* ἐνετείλατο (ἐντέλλομαι) LTrWH
1Co. 14:37 *omit* the commandments T: ἐντολή commandment LTr[A]WWHR
2Joh. 6 *trs* ἡ ἐντολή ἐστιν Eds
Rev. 22:14 *omit* ἐ. LTTrAWHR, *see* στολή

1788 **ἐντρέπομαι.**

Heb. 12: 9 ἐνετρεπόμεθα S—ἐντρεπόμεθα B

1793 **ἐντυγχάνω.**

Acts 25:24 ἐνέτυχέν WH

1798 **ἐνύπνιον.**

Acts 2:17 ἐνυπνίοις with dreams GEds

1799 **ἐνώπιον.**

Lu. 1: 6 ἐναντίον TTrAWHR
76*ἐ. *for* πρὸ προσώπου (-ον) WH
Acts 8:21 ἔναντι GEds
10: 4 ἔμπροσθεν LTTrAWHR
Rev. 14: 5 *omit* before the throne of God GEds

1802 Ἐνώχ, Ἑ– WH.

1803 ἕξ.

Rev. 13:18 *see* χξς´

1806 ἐξάγω.

Mar. 8:23 led out—brought out, ἐκφέρω TTrAWHR

1807 ἐξαιρέω.

Acts 7:10 | 12:11 ἐξείλατο GLTTrAWWH
23:27 ἐξειλάμην LTTrAWWH

1808 ἐξαίρω.

1 Co. 5: 2 αἴρω GEds
13 ἐξάρατε GEds

1810 ἐξαίφνης.

ἐξέφνης (*except* Acts 22:6) WH

1812 ἑξακόσιοι.

Rev. 13:18 *see* χξς´

1813 ἐξαλείφω.

Acts 3:19 ἐξαλιφθῆναι WH

1818 ἐξαπατάω.

2 Co. 11: 3 *trs* ἐξηπάτησεν Εὔαν Eds
1 Ti. 2:14*ἐξαπατηθεῖσα *for* ἀπατηθεῖσα (–τάω) Eds

1821 ἐξαποστέλλω.

Lu. 20:10 *trs* ἐξαπέστειλαν αὐτὸν δείραντες TAWH
24:49*ἐξαποστέλλω *for* ἀποστέλλω TTrAWHR
Acts 13:26*ἐξαπεστάλη *for* ἀπεστάλη (ἀποστέλλω) Eds

1822 ἐξαρτίζω.

Acts 21: 5 *trs* ἐξαρτίσαι ἡμᾶς LTrAWWH

1824 ἐξαυτῆς.

Acts 10:33 | 11:11 | 21:32 ἐξ αὐτῆς A
23:30 straightway—by them, ἐξ αὐτῶν LTTr, ἐξ αὐτῆς A

1827 ἐξελέγχω.

Jude 15 ἐλέγχω LTTrAWHR

1830 ἐξερευνάω, ἐξεραυνάω TTrAWH.

1831 ἐξέρχομαι.

Mat. 8:12*ἐξελεύσονται *for* ἐκβληθήσονται (–βάλλω) T
11: 7, 8, 9 ἐξήλθατε LTTrAWH
12:14 *trs* ἐξελθ. δὲ οἱ Φαρ. συμβ. ἔλαβον κατ᾽ αὐτοῦ LTTrWWHR
26:55 ἐξήλθατε LTTrAWH
28: 8 ἀπέρχομαι TTrAWHR
Mar. 1:29 ἐξελθών, he was come out LTr
38 ἐξῆλθον TTrAWHR
5: 2 ἐξελθόντος αὐτοῦ LTTrWHR
14 went out—went, ἔρχομαι Eds
14:48 ἐξήλθατε LTTrAWWH
Lu. 4:41 ἐξήρχοντο T
6:12 ἐξελθεῖν αὐτόν TTrAWHR
7:24, 25, 26 ἐξήλθατε LTrWH, –θετε R
8:35 ἐ.²—ἐξῆλθεν TWHR
46 ἐξεληλυθυῖαν TTrAWHR
10:35 *omit* when he departed LTTr[A]WHR
11:53*and as he said these things unto them—and as he went out thence, κἀκεῖθεν ἐξελθόντος αὐτοῦ TTrAWHR
14:18 ἐξελθών having gone TTrAWHR
22:52 ἐξήλθατε LTWH, –θετε R
Joh. 13:30 *trs* ἐξῆλθεν εὐθύς LTTrAWHR
18: 4 ἐξῆλθεν LTTrAWHR
19:34 *trs* ἐξῆλθεν εὐθὺς TTrAWHR
21: 3 ἐξῆλθαν WH
Acts 8: 7†*trs* φωνῇ μεγάλῃ ἐξήρχοντο Eds
15:24 *omit* which went out WH
16:39 ἀπέρχομαι LTTrAWHR
40 ἐ.²—ἐξῆλθαν TTrWH
19:12 ἐκπορεύομαι GEds
28: 3 διεξέρχομαι AW
15 ἔρχομαι LTTrAWHR
2 Co. 6:17 ἐξέλθατε LTTrAWH
Heb. 11:15 came out—went out, ἐκβαίνω Eds
1 Joh. 2:19 ἐξῆλθαν LTTrAWWH
2 Joh. 7*ἐξῆλθαν LTrWH, –θον TAWR, *for* εἰσῆλθον (εἰσέρχομαι)
3 Joh. 7 ἐξῆλθαν LTTrWH
Rev. 14:18 *omit* came L[WH]
15: 6 ἐξῆλθαν WH
18: 4 ἐξέλθατε TTrAWWH
19:21*ἐξελθούσῃ *for* ἐκπορευομένῃ (–μαι) GEds

1832 ἔξεστιν.

Mat. 15:26**for* ἔστιν καλόν (–ός) LTA
Acts 8:37 *omit the verse* GLTTrAWHR

1833 ἐξετάζω.

Mat. 2: 8 *trs* ἐξετάσατε ἀκριβῶς LTTrAWH

1835 ἑξήκοντα.

Rev. 13:18 *see* χξς´

1836 ἑξῆς.

Lu. 7:11 τῇ ἑ.—τῷ ἑ. TrWHR

1839 ἐξίστημι, –τάω, –τάνω.

Acts 8: 9 ἐξιστάνων LTTrAWH

1842 ἐξολοθρεύομαι, ἐξολε– LTTrAWH.

1843 ἐξομολογέομαι.

Ro. 14:11 *trs* ἐξομολογήσεται πᾶσα γλῶσσα LTr
Phil. 2:11 ἐξομολογήσεται TAW
Rev. 3: 5 ὁμολογέω GEds

* ἐξουδενέω, to set at nought.

Mar. 9:12 ἐξουδενηθῇ *for* ἐξουδενωθῇ (–νόω) LTrAWH

1847 ἐξουδενόω.

Mar. 9:12 ἐξουδενέω LTrAWH, ἐξουθενόω T

* ἐξουθενόω, to set at nought.

Mar. 9:12 ἐξουθενωθῇ *for* ἐξουδενωθῇ (–νόω) T

1849 ἐξουσία.

Lu. 5:24 *trs* ὁ υἱὸς τοῦ ἀνθ. ἐ. ἔχει TTrAWH
12: 5 *trs* ἔχοντα ἐξουσίαν LTTrAWH
Ro. 13: 1 *omit* ἐ.³ *read* those that be GEds
1 Co. 9:12 *trs* ὑμῶν ἐξουσίας GEds
Rev. 9:19 ἡ γὰρ ἐξουσία τῶν ἵππων (τῶν ἵ. *for* αὐτῶν GLTTrAWHR) ἐν τῷ στόματι αὐτῶν ἐστιν καὶ ἐν ταῖς οὐραῖς αὐτῶν· For the power of the horses (of them A.V. W) is in their mouth and in their tails A.V.C GEds
11: 6 ἐ.¹—τὴν ἐξουσίαν LTr[A]WWHR
13: 4 τὴν ἐξουσίαν GEds
16: 9 τὴν ἐξουσίαν LTTrWWHR
17:13 τὴν ἐ.—*omit* τὴν LTrAWHR

1854 ἔξω.

Mat. 10:14*ἐξερχόμενοι—*add* ἔ. LTTrAWHR
12:47 *omit the verse* [T]WH
Lu. 8:54 *omit* put them all out, and LTTrAWHR
24:50 *omit* ἔξω [L]TTr[A]WHR
Joh. 18:29*Πιλάτος—*add* ἔ. LTTrAWHR
Acts 5:23 *omit* without GEds
16:13 *omit* ἔ. W
Rev. 11: 2 ἔξωθεν A.V.C LTTrWHR
14:20 ἔξωθεν GEds

1855 ἔξωθεν.

Rev. 11: 2 ἔσωθεν within S—ἔ. without A.V.B EGEds
2**for* ἔξω A.V.C LTTrWHR
14:20**for* ἔξω GEds

1856 ἐξωθέω.

Acts 7:45 ἐξέωσεν T
27:39 ἐκσώζω WH

1859 ἑορτή.

Lu. 23:17 *omit the verse* [L]TTr[A]WHR
Joh. 5: 1 ἡ ἑορτή T
Acts 18:21 *omit* LTTrAWHR, *see* δεῖ

1860 ἐπαγγελία.

Gal. 4:23 τῆς ἐ.—*omit* τῆς TrWHR
1 Joh. 1: 5 ἀγγελία A.V.Vul GEds

1862 ἐπάγγελμα.

2 Pet. 3:13 τὰ ἐπαγγέλματα promises LT

1867 ἐπαινέω.

Ro. 15:11 ἐπαινεσάτωσαν LTTrAWHR
1 Co. 11:17 ἐπαινῶν LTrAW

1869 ἐπαίρω.

Joh. 13:18 ἐπῆρκεν T
17: 1 ἐπάρας LTTrAWHR

1870 ἐπαισχύνομαι.

2 Ti. 1:16 ἐπαισχύνθη LTTrAWH

1871 ἐπαιτέω.

Lu. 18:35*ἐπαιτῶν *for* προσαιτῶν (–τέω) LTTrAWH

1876 ἐπάναγκες.

Acts 15:28 *trs* τούτων τῶν ἐπάναγκες LTTrWH

1877 ἐπανάγω.

Mat. 21:18 ἐπαναγαγών LTAWH

1879 ἐπαναπαύομαι.

Lu. 10: 6 ἐπαναπαήσεται TWH

1883 ἐπάνω.

Mat. 21: 7 ἐ.¹—ἐπί LTTrAWH
Lu. 19:19 *trs* ἐπάνω γίνου TAWH
Joh. 3:31 *omit* is above all³ T
Rev. 20:11**for* ἐπί Tr

* ἐπάρατος, accursed.

Joh. 7:49 ἐπάρατοι *for* ἐπικατάρατοι (–τος) LTTrAWHR

1884 ἐπαρκέω.

1 Ti. 5:16 ἐ.¹—ἐπαρκείσθω LTTr

1885 ἐπαρχία –χεία TWH.

Acts 25: 1 ἐπαρχείῳ T

1888 ἐπαυτοφώρῳ.

Joh. 8: 4 ἐπ᾽ αὐτοφώρῳ WWH

1893 ἐπεί.

Mat. 21:46**for* ἐπειδή TTrAWH
Lu. 7: 1 ἐπειδή LTTrAWHR
Ro. 11: 6 *omit* but if (it be) *to end of verse* GLTTr[A]WHR

1894 ἐπειδή.

Mat. 21:46 ἐπεί TTrAWH
Lu. 7: 1**for* ἐπεὶ δέ LTTrAWHR
2 Co. 5: 4 ἐ. S—ἐφ᾽ ᾧ A.V.B EGEds

1897 ἐπείπερ.

Ro. 3:30 seeing—if indeed εἴ περ LTTrAWHR

* ἐπεισέρχομαι, to come in upon.

Lu. 21:34, 35 ἐκείνη ὡς παγίς· ἐπεισελεύσεται (ἐ. *for* ἐπελεύσεται, ἐπέρχομαι) γὰρ ἐπί, *read* unawares as a snare: for it shall come in upon LTTrAWHR

1899 ἔπειτα.

Mar. 7: 5 then—and, καί LTTrAWHR
1 Co. 12:28**for* εἶτα LTTrAWHR
15: 5**for* εἶτα T
7**for* εἶτα TA

1904 ἐπέρχομαι.

Lu. 21:35 *see* ἐπεισέρχομαι
Acts 14:19 ἐπῆλθαν LTTrAWH

1905 ἐπερωτάω.

Mat. 16: 1 ἐπηρώτων T
Mar. 8: 5 ἐρωτάω TTrAWH
29*ἐπηρώτα αὐτούς *for* λέγει (–γω) αὐτοῖς LTTrAWHR
9:28 *trs* κατ᾽ ἰδίαν ἐπηρώτων αὐτόν LTTrAWHR
10: 2 | 12:18 ἐπηρώτων LTTrAWHR
13: 3 ἐπηρώτα TTrAWHR
15: 4 ἐπηρώτα TTrAWH
Lu. 6: 9 ἐπερωτῶ I ask TTrAWHR
23: 3 ἐρωτάω TTrAWHR
Joh. 9:23*ἐπερωτήσατε *for* ἐρωτήσατε (–τάω) TWH
18: 7 *trs* ἐπηρώτησεν αὐτούς LTrAWH

Joh. 18:21 ἐ.[1]—ἐρωτάω Eds
21 ἐ.[2]—ἐρωτάω LTTrAWH
Acts 1: 6 ἐρωτάω LTTrAWH

1908 ἐπηρεάζω.

Mat. 5:44 *omit* despitefully use you, and LTTrAWH

1909 ἐπί.

Mat. 2:22 *omit* ἐ. LT[TrA]WH
4: 4 ἐ.[2]—ἐν LTrA
5:39 εἰς LTTrAWH
10:13**for* πρός WH
13:14 *omit* ἐ. GEds
14:34**for* εἰς TTrWH
18: 6 περί LTTrWH: εἰς to A
21: 5*ἐ. πῶλον upon a colt LTTrAWH
7**for* ἐπάνω[1] LTTrAWH
44 *omit the verse* [L]T[WH]
22: 5**for* εἰς[2] LTTrAWH
24:16 εἰς LTrWH
25:20, 22 *omit* beside them LTTrWH
27:29 ἐ.[2]—ἐν LTTrAWH, *see* δεξιός
35 *omit* that it might *to end of verse* GLTTrAWH
42*αὐτῷ—ἐ. αὐτόν TTrWH, ἐ. αὐτῷ (W
28:14 ὑπό LTr
Mar. 1:10 εἰς LTTrAWH
45**for* ἐν TTrAWH
2: 4 ἐφ' ᾧ wherein—where, ὅπου LTTrAWH
4:18**for* εἰς T
38 ἐ.[1]—ἐν GEds
5:33 *omit* ἐ. *read* done to her [L]TTrAWH
10:24 *omit* for them that trust in riches TWH
14:46 *omit* ἐ. TTrAWH, *see* αὐτόν
15: 1 *omit* ἐ. τὸ LTTr[A]WH
Lu. 4: 4 *omit* but by every word of God T[Tr]AWH
25 *omit* ἐ.[2] LTr[A]WH
43**for* εἰς LTTrAWH
6:29 εἰς T
48 *omit* ἐ.[2] TTrAWH, *see* θεμελιόω
8: 8 on—into, εἰς GEds
9:49 ἐν WH
10:11 *omit* unto you GLTTrAWH
11: 2 *omit* as in heaven so in earth G[L]TTrAWH
12:49**for* εἰς Eds
54**for* ἀπό TWH
16:26 beside—before, ἐν TWH
17: 4 πρός Eds
22:52 ἐ.[1]—πρός T
24:12 *omit the verse* [L]T[Tr][[WH]]
Joh. 8: 3**for* ἐν[1] WH
21: 4**for* εἰς LT
11 εἰς LTTrAWH, *see* γῆ
Acts 2:38 ἐν LTrWH
43**add* ἐ. T, *see* φόβος
3:16 *omit* ἐ. WH
5:23**for* πρό LTTrAWH
7:10*ἐ. ὅλον over all T
18*ἕτερος—*add* ἐπ' Αἴγυπτον, *read* arose over Egypt LTTrWH
33**for* ἐν LTTrAWH
10:11 *omit* unto him GEds
13:40 *omit* upon you LTTr[A]WH
14: 3*μαρτυροῦντι—*add* ἐ. T
15:14 *omit* ἐ. Eds
20:13**for* εἰς LTTrAWH
21:23 ἀπό WH
24: 8 πρός A: *omit* LTTrWH, *see* κρίνω
21**for* ὑπό Eds
28:14 παρά LTTrAWH
Ro. 3:22 *omit* and upon all LTTr[A]WH
1 Co. 8:11 ἐν Eds
2 Co. 5: 4 ἐφ' ᾧ *for* ἐπειδή A.V.B EGEds
10: 7**for* ἀπό TTrWH
Eph. 1:10**for* ἐν[2] LTTrAWH
6:16 above—in, ἐν LTTrWH
Phi. 3:14 εἰς LTTrAWH
Col. 3: 6 *omit* on the children of disobedience [L]TTrAWH
1 Ti. 6:17**for* ἐν[2] LTTrWH
2 Ti. 2:14**for* εἰς LTTrAWH
Heb. 2: 7 *omit* and didst set *to end of verse* G[L]T[Tr]A[WH]
11:38**for* ἐν LTTrAWH
1 Pet. 3: 5 εἰς Eds
Jude 18**for* ἐν Eds, *see* χρόνος
Rev. 3: 3 *omit* on thee, ἐ. σέ[1] LTTrAWH
5:13**for* ἐν[3] GEds
10:11*and[2]—*add* ἐ. before T
11:11 ἐ.[1]—ἐν GLT[A]W[WH]R: *om.* Tr
14: 6*εὐαγγελίσαι—*add* ἐ. Eds
6*καί[2]—*add* ἐ. GEds
16: 2 *trs* εἰς *and* ἐπί Eds
17**for* εἰς GEds
Rev. 17:16 upon—and, καί GEds
20:11 ἐπάνω Tr
21:14**for* ἐν GEds, *see* δώδεκα
22: 5*ἐπ' αὐτούς GLTTrAWH: [ἐπ'] A.
16 *omit* ἐ. W (WH
18**for* πρός GEds
See also ἐφάπαξ.

1910 ἐπιβαίνω.

Acts 21: 4*ἐπιβαίνειν *for* ἀναβαίνειν (-βαίνω) LTTrAWH
6 ἐμβαίνω LTrWH, ἀναβαίνω TAW

1911 ἐπιβάλλω.

Mar. 11: 7 ἐπιβάλλουσιν GEds
14:46 ἐπέβαλαν TWH
Joh. 7:44 βάλλω LTTrAWH
Acts 21:27 ἐπέβαλαν TTrWH

1914 ἐπιβλέπω.

Lu. 9:38 ἐπιβλέψαι GTTrAWWH

1915 ἐπίβλημα.

Lu. 5:36 ἐ.[2]—τὸ ἐπίβλημα TTrAWH

1916 ἐπιβοάω.

Acts 25:24 βοάω LTTrWH, [ἐπι]β. A

1917 ἐπιβουλή.

Acts 20: 3 *trs* ἐπιβουλῆς αὐτῷ LTTrWH

1921 ἐπιγινωσκω.

Mar. 6:33 γινώσκω LTrAWH
Acts 19:34 ἐπιγνόντες GLTTrAWWH
23:28*ἐπιγνῶναι *for* γνῶναι (γινώσκω) Eds
24:11*ἐπιγνῶναι *for* γνῶναι (γινώσκω) LTTrAWH
28: 1 ἐπέγνωμεν we knew Eds

1922 ἐπιγνωσις.

Col. 1:10 τῇ ἐπιγνώσει by the knowledge GEds

1924 ἐπιγράφω.

Lu. 23:38*ἐπιγεγραμμένη *for* γεγραμμένη (γράφω) L[Tr]

1925 ἐπιδείκνυμι.

Lu. 20:24 δείκνυμι GEds
24:40 δείκνυμι LTr[A]WH: *omit the verse* T[Tr][[WH]]

1929 ἐπιδιδωμι.

Lu. 11:11 *omit* ε.[1] WH, *see* ἄρτος
11 *trs* αὐτῷ ἐπιδώσει[2] TTrAWH
Joh. 13:26 δίδωμι TTrAWH

1932 ἐπιεικεια, –κια WH.

1934 ἐπιζητέω.

Mat. 6:32 ἐπιζητοῦσιν LTTrAWH
Mar. 8:12 ζητέω LTTrAWH
Lu. 4:42*ἐπεζήτουν *for* ἐζήτουν (ζητέω) GEds
11:29 ζητεω TTrAWH
12:30 ἐπιζητοῦσιν TTrAWH

1939 ἐπιθυμία.

2 Ti. 4: 3 *omit* τάς, *see* ἴδιος
2 Pet. 3: 3 *trs* ἐπιθυμίας αὐτῶν GLTrAWH
Rev. 18:14 *trs* σου τῆς ἐ. τῆς ψυχῆς Eds

1940 ἐπικαθίζω.

Mat. 21: 7 ἐπεκάθισεν he sat s—ἐπεκάθισαν A.V.BE

1941 ἐπικαλεω, –ομαι.

Mat. 10: 3 *omit* Lebbæus, whose surname was LTrWH: *omit* whose surname was Thaddæus TA
25*ἐπεκάλεσαν *or* ἐκάλεσαν (καλέω) GEds
Lu. 22: 3 surnamed—called, καλέω TTrAWH
Acts 15:22 surnamed—called, καλέω Eds
Ro. 10:14 ἐπικαλέσωνται Eds

1944 ἐπικαταρατος.

Joh. 7:49 ἐπάρατος LTTrAWH

* ἐπικέλλω, to run aground.

Acts 27:41 ἐπέκειλαν *for* ἐπώκειλαν (ἐποκέλλω) LTTrAWH

1946 Ἐπικούρειος, –ριος WH.

1951 ἐπιλέγω, –ομαι.

Joh. 5: 2 λέγω T

* ἐπιλείχω, to lick over.

Lu. 16:21 ἐπέλειχον *for* ἀπέλειχον (ἀπολείχω) LTTrAWH

1961 ἐπιμένω.

Acts 13:43 προσμένω GEds
15:34 *omit the verse* Eds
Ro. 6: 1 ἐπιμένωμεν GEds
11:22 ἐπιμένῃς TTrWH
23 ἐπιμένωσιν TTrWH

1968 ἐπιπιπτω.

Joh. 13:25 ἀναπίπτω LTrAWH
Acts 10:10 γίνομαι Eds
13:11 πίπτω LTTrWH
19:17 πίπτω LTr
Ro. 15: 3 ἐπέπεσαν LTTrAWH
Rev. 11:11*ἐπέπεσεν *for* ἔπεσεν (πίπτω) Eds

1974 ἐπιποθία, –πόθεια WH.

1976 ἐπιρράπτω.

Mar. 2:21 ἐπιράπτει TTrAWH

1977 ἐπιρρίπτω.

Lu. 19:35 ἐπιρίψαντες LTTrAWH
1 Pet. 5: 7 ἐπιρίψαντες LTTrAWH

1980 ἐπισκέπτομαι.

Lu. 1:78 ἐπισκέψεται WH

* ἐπισκευάζομαι, to get ready.

Acts 21:15 ἐπισκευασάμενοι *for* ἀποσκευασάμενοι (-σκευάζομαι) Eds

1982 ἐπισκιάζω.

Lu. 9:34 ἐπεσκίαζεν TTrAWH
Acts 5:15 ἐπισκιάσει TrWH

1983 ἐπισκοπέω.

1 Pet. 5: 2 *omit* taking the oversight (thereof) T[A]WH

* ἐπισπείρω, to sow upon.

Mat. 13:25 ἐπέσπειρεν *for* ἔσπειρεν (σπείρω) LTTrAWH

1987 ἐπίσταμαι.

1 Th. 5: 3*ἐπίσταται *for* ἐφίσταται (-στημι) TTrWH

* ἐπιστασις, a stopping, checking.

Acts 24:12 ἐπίστασιν *for* ἐπισύστασιν (-σις) LTTrAWH
2 Co. 11:28 ἐπίστασις *for* ἐπισύστασις Eds

1989 ἐπιστέλλω.

Acts 21:25 have written—have sent, ἀποστέλλω LTrWH

1991 ἐπιστηρίζω.

Acts 18:23 στηρίζω LTTrAWH

1992 ἐπιστολή.

2 Co. 10:10 *trs* ἐπιστολαὶ μέν LTTrWH
2 Pet. 3:16 ταῖς ἐ.—*omit* ταῖς LTrAWWH

1994 ἐπιστρέφω.

Mat. 9:22 στρέφω LTTrAWH
Lu. 2:20 ὑποστρέφω GEds
39*ἐπέστρεψαν *for* ὑπέστρεψαν (ὑποστρέφω) TWH
Joh. 12:40 στρέφω LTTrAWH
Acts 26:18 τοῦ ε.—καὶ ἐ. A.V.†B
2 Pet. 2:21 to turn—to turn back, ὑποστρέψαι LTTrAWH

1996 ἐπισυνάγω.

Mar. 1:33 *trs* ἦν ολη η πόλις ἐ. LTTrAWH
Lu. 17:37**trs* οι ἀετοὶ ἐπισυναχθήσονται (ἐ. *for* συναχθήσονται, συνάγω) TTrAWH

1999 ἐπισυστασις.

Acts 24:12 ἐπίστασις LTTrAWH
2 Co. 11:28 cometh upon—presseth upon, ἐπίστασις Eds

2004 ἐπιτάσσω.

Mar. 9:25 *trs* ἐπιτάσσω σοι TTrAWH

2005 ἐπιτελέω.

Lu. 13:32 ἀποτελέω LTTrAWHR

2007 ἐπιτίθημι.

Mar. 4:21 τίθημι Eds
8:25 τίθημι TrAWH
Lu. 4:40 ἐπιτιθείς LTTrAWH
8:16 τίθημι LTTrAWHR
Joh. 9: 6*ἐπέθηκεν *for* ἐπέχρισεν (ἐπιχρίω) WH
Acts 8:17 ἐπετίθεσαν LTTrAWH
Rev. 1:17 τίθημι GEds
22:18 ἐ.[1]—ἐπιθῇ GEds

2008 ἐπιτιμάω.

Mat. 16:20*ἐπετίμησεν *for* διεστείλατο (διαστέλλομαι) LWH
22 ἐπιτιμῶν A, *see* λέγω
Mar. 10:13 ἐπετίμησαν WH
Lu. 18:15 ἐπετίμων LTTrAWHR
23:40 ἐπιτιμῶν TTrAWHR
2 Ti. 4: 2 *trs* exhort, rebuke T

2010 ἐπιτρέπω.

Mat. 8:31 *see* ἀποστέλλω
Acts 28:16†*trs* ἐ. τῷ Παύλῳ LTTrAWHR
1 Co. 14:34 ἐπιτρέπεται Eds
16: 7 ἐπιτρέψῃ Eds

2016 ἐπιφανής.

Acts 2:20 *omit* and notable T

2018 ἐπιφέρω.

Acts 19:12 ἀποφέρω LTTrAWHR
25:18 φέρω Eds
Phil. 1:16 to add—to raise up, ἐγείρω Eds (*verse* 17 GEds)

2019 ἐπιφωνέω.

Acts 21:34*ἐπεφώνουν *for* ἐβόων (βοάω) Eds

2025 ἐπιχρίω.

Joh. 9: 6 ἐπετίθημι WH

2026 ἐποικοδομέω.

Acts 20:32 οἰκοδομέω Eds
1 Co. 3:14 ἐποικοδόμησεν TTrAWH
1 Pet. 2: 5*ἐποικοδομεῖσθε *for* οἰκοδομεῖσθε (-μέω) T

2027 ἐποκέλλω.

Acts 27:41 ἐπικέλλω LTTrAWHR

2029 ἐποπτεύω.

1 Pet. 2:12 ἐποπτεύοντες behold Eds

2032 ἐπουράνιος.

Mat. 18:35 οὐράνιος LTTrWH, [ἐπ]ο. A

2033 ἑπτά.

Lu. 11:26 *trs* ἑπτά *after* ἑαυτοῦ TTrAWH
Rev. 1:11*ἑ. ἐκκλησίαις A.V.C GEds
13 *omit* seven LT[TrA]WHR
3: 1 ἑ. πνεύματα A.V.B EGEds
5: 6 *omit* seven[3] L[WH]
6: 1*ἑ. σφραγίδων seven seals GEds
16: 1*ἑ. φιάλας seven vials GEds

2036 ἔπω, *see* εἶπον.

ἐραυνάω, *see* ἐρευνάω.
See 2045

2038 ἐργάζομαι.

Mat. 25:16 ἠργάσατο TAWH
26:10 ἠργάσατο TWH
Mar. 14: 6 ἠργάσατο TWH
Acts 13:41 *trs* ἐργάζομαι ἐγώ Eds
18: 3 ἠργάζετο LTrA, ἠργάζοντο they wrought TWHR
1 Co. 9: 6 τοῦ μὴ ἐ.—*om.* τοῦ LTTr[A]WHR
2 Co. 7:10*ἐργάζεται *for* κατεργάζεται (-ζομαι) Eds
Heb. 11:33 ἠργάσαντο TTrWH
Jas. 1:20*ἐργάζεται *for* κατεργάζεται (-ζομαι) LTTrAWHR
2 Joh. 8 εἰργάσασθε ye have wrought LTTrW: ἠργασάμεθα WH

2040 ἐργάτης.

Lu. 13:27 οἱ ἐ.—*omit* οἱ TTrAWHR

2041 ἔργον.

Mat. 11:19*ἔργων *for* τέκνων (-νον) TTrWHR
Joh. 7: 3 *trs* σου τὰ ἔργα LWH
Acts 9:36 *trs* ἔργων ἀγαθῶν LTrWWH
15:18 *omit* unto God are all his works GTTrAWHR, *see* γνωστός
Ro. 11: 6 *omit* but if (it be) *to end of verse* GLTTr[A]WHR
13: 3 τῷ ἀγαθῷ ἔργῳ the good work Eds
2 Th. 2:17 *trs* work and word Eds
1 Ti. 5:25†*trs* τὰ ἔργα τὰ καλὰ Eds
Heb. 2: 7 *omit* and didst set *to end of verse* G[L]T[Tr]A[WH]
13:21 *omit* work TWHR
Jas. 2:17 *trs* ἔχῃ ἔργα GEds
26 τῶν ἐ.—*omit* τῶν T[Tr]WHR
Rev. 2: 9 *omit* works, and LTTrAWHR
13 *om.* thy works, and LTTrAWHR
3: 2 τὰ ἐ.—*omit* τὰ L[TrA]WHR

2045 ἐρευνάω, ἐραυνάω TTrWH, *at times* A.

2046 ἐρέω, *see* ἐρῶ.

2048 ἔρημος, subst.

Lu. 4: 1 ἐν τῇ ἐρήμῳ LTTrAWHR

2048 ἔρημος, adj.

Mat. 23:38 *omit* desolate LWH
Mar. 6:32†*trs* ἐν τῷ πλοίῳ εἰς ἐ. τόπ. LWHR
Lu. 9:10 *omit* desert place belonging to TTrAWHR
13:35 *omit* desolate GEds

2052 ἐριθεια, –θια WH.

Phil. 1:16 *trs verses* 16 *and* 17 *except* οἱ μὲν *and* οἱ δὲ GEds

2054 ἔρις.

2 Co. 12:20 ἔρις debate LTWHR
Gal. 5:20 ἔρις Eds
Tit. 3: 9 ἔριν contention TWH

2057 Ἑρμᾶς.

Ro. 16:14 *trs* Hermes, Patrobas, Hermas Eds

ἑρμηνεία, –νία WH.

* ἑρμηνευτής, interpreter.

1 Co. 14:28 ἑρμηνευτής *for* διερμηνευτής LTr

ἑρμηνεύω.

Joh. 1:38(39) μεθερμηνεύω LTrAWHR

2060 Ἑρμῆς.

Ro. 16:14 *trs* Eds, *see* Ἑρμᾶς

2061 Ἑρμογένης, Ἑ– T.

2062 ἑρπετόν.

Acts 10:12†*trs* καὶ τὰ (*om.* τὰ LTTrAWHR) ἑ. τῆς γῆς and creeping things of the earth Eds

2064 ἔρχομαι.

Mat. 2:21 came—entered, εἰσέρχομαι LTTrAWH
6:10 ἐλθάτω TWH
7:25 ἦλθαν TrWH
27 ἦλθαν WH
8: 2 προσέρχομαι Eds
28 ἐλθόντος αὐτοῦ LTTrWH
9:18 came—entered, εἰσέρχομαι TAW: προσέρχομαι LWH
10:13 ἐλθάτω TTrWH
13: 4 ἦλθον LTr, ἐλθόντα AWH
14:25*ἦλθεν *for* ἀπῆλθεν (ἀπέρχομαι) LTTrWHR
28 *trs* ἐλθεῖν πρὸς σε LTTrAWH
29 to go—καὶ ἦλθεν and went TWH
33 *omit* came and T[A]WHR
34 ἦλθαν WH
17:25*ἐλθόντα *for* ὅτε εἰσῆλθεν (εἰσέρχομαι) TrAWH
18:11 *omit the verse* LTTr[A]WHR
21:23 ἐλθόντος αὐτοῦ LTTrWHR
24:48 *omit* his coming LTTrWHR
25: 6 *omit* cometh LTTrAWHR
13 *omit* wherein the Son of man cometh GLTTrAWHR
36 ἤλθατε LTTrAWH
Mar. 1:29 ἦλθεν he entered LTr: ἦλθαν WH
39*ἦλθεν *for* ἦν TTrWHR
2: 8 ἦλθαν WH
3:19 they went—ἔρχεται he cometh TWHR
31 ἐ. οὖν—καὶ ἔρχονται LTTrAWWHR, καὶ ἔρχεται T
4:21 *trs* ἔρχεται ὁ λύχνος LTTrAWH
5:14*ἦλθον *for* ἐξῆλθον (ἐξέρχομαι) Eds
38 ἔρχονται they come Eds
6: 1 ἔρχεται cometh TTrAWWHR
29 ἦλθαν TTrAWH
53 *trs* ἐπὶ τὴν γῆν ἦλθον TWHR
7:25 εἰσέρχομαι T
31†*trs* ἦλθεν διὰ Σιδῶνος he came through Sidon LTTrAWHR
8:22 ἔρχονται they come LTTrAWHR
34 come—follow, ἀκολουθέω GTTrAW
9: 7 γίνομαι TWHR
14 ἐλθόντες they came TTrWHR
33 ἦλθον they came LTTrAWHR
12:14 οἱ δὲ ἐ.—καὶ ἐ. LTTrAWHR
14:38*ἔλθητε *for* εἰσέλθητε (-έρχομαι) TAWH
40*ἐλθὼν *for* ὑποστρέψας (-στρέφω) LTrAWHR
15:43 ἐλθὼν Eds
16: 5*ἐλθοῦσαι *for* εἰσελθοῦσαι (-έρχομαι) A
Lu. 1:59 ἦλθαν WH
2:16 ἦλθαν TTrAWH
5: 7 ἐ.[2]—ἦλθαν TWH
6:17 ἦλθαν WH
8:35 ἦλθαν TrWH
51*ἐλθὼν *for* εἰσελθὼν (-έρχομαι) GLTTrWWHR
9:23 ἔρχεσθαι GLTTrAWHR
56 *omit* For the Son *to* to save (them) GLTTrAWHR
11: 2 ἐλθάτω TTrWH
12:38 *om.* he shall come, ἐ.[1] TTrAWHR
17: 1 τοῦ μὴ ἐ.—*omit* τοῦ E: *trs* τὰ σκάνδαλα μὴ ἐλθεῖν TTrAWHR
19:38 *omit* that cometh T
23:26 *omit* τοῦ GEds: ἐρχόμενον LTTrAWHR
33*ἦλθον (-θαν WH) *for* ἀπῆλθον (ἀπέρχομαι) LTrAWHR
24: 1 *trs* ἐπὶ τὸ μνῆμα ἦλθον (-θαν WH) TWH
23 ἦλθαν WH
Joh. 1:27 ὁ ὀπ. μου ἐ.—*omit* ὁ [TrA]WH
39(40) ἦλθαν TTrAWH
3:26 ἐ.[1]—ἦλθαν TrAWH
4:15 ἔρχομαι Tr: διέρχομαι TAWHR
27 ἦλθαν TTrWH
6:14 *trs* εἰς τὸν κόσμον ἐρχόμενος T
23 ἦλθον T
7:27 ἔρχηται S—ἔρχεται E
50 *omit* he that came to Jesus by night T
11:29 ἤρχετο TrAWHR
12: 9 ἦλθαν WH
22*ἔρχεται *f.* καὶ πάλιν LTTrAWHR
13: 1 ἦλθεν LTTrAWHR
16: 7 ἔλθῃ TrWH
19: 3**add at commencement* καὶ ἤρχοντο πρὸς αὐτόν and came to him LTTrAWHR
38 ἦλθον they came T
Acts 11:20*ἐλθόντες *for* εἰσελθόντες (-έρχομαι) GEds
12:10 ἦλθαν LTTrAWH
13:14*ἐλθόντες *for* εἰσελθόντες (-έρχομαι) TTrWHR
44 ἔχω GLAW
14:24 ἦλθαν WH
15:30 κατέρχομαι LTTrAWHR
18: 7 εἰσέρχομαι LT
21 *omit* I must *to* Jerusalem LTTrAWHR
19: 1 κατέρχομαι T
21: 8 ἦλθον they came S—ἤλθομεν (-θαμεν TrWH) A.V.C EGEds
22:30 appear—come together, συνέρχομαι GEds
24: 8 *omit* and would have judged (*ver.* 6) *to* to come unto thee (*ver.* 8) LTTr[A]WHR
28:14 ἤλθαμεν LTTrAWH
15*ἦλθαν (-θον LR) *for* ἐξῆλθον (ἐξέρχομαι) TTrAWHR
16 came—entered, εἰσέρχομαι LTTrAWHR
23*ἦλθον (-θαν WH) *for* ἧκον (ἥκω) LTTrAWH
Ro. 15:24 *omit* I will come to you GEds
32 ἐλθὼν TWHR: *trs* ἐλ. ἐν χαρᾷ T
2 Co. 1:15 *trs* πρότερον πρὸς ὑμᾶς ἐ. (πρότ. ἐ. πρὸς ὑ. W) Eds
2: 1 *trs* ἐν λύπῃ πρὸς ὑμᾶς ἐ. GEds
12:21 ἐλθόντος μου Eds
Gal. 2:12 ἐ.[2]—ἦλθεν he came LTr
Heb. 6: 7 *trs* ἐρχόμενον πολλάκις Eds

1 Joh. 4: 3 *omit* that Christ is come in the flesh GLTTrAWHR
2 Joh. 12 γίνομαι Eds
Rev. 9:12 ἔρχεται LTTrAWHR
11:17 *omit* and art to come GEds
22:17 ἔ.[1] [2]—ἔρχου GEds
17 ἔ.[3]—ἐρχέσθω GEds

ἐρῶ.

Lu. 14:10*ἐρεῖ *for* εἴπῃ (εἶπον) TTrWHR
22:13 εἰρήκει LTTrAWHR
Heb. 4: 7 it is said—it hath been said before, προερέω Eds
10:15*εἰρηκέναι *for* προειρηκέναι (προερέω) Eds
Rev. 17: 7 *trs* ἐρῶ σοι LTrAWHR

2065 ἐρωτάω.

Mat. 15:23 ἠρώτουν LTTrAWH
19:17**for* λέγω GEds, *see* ἀγαθός
Mar. 4:10 ἠρώτων LTrAWHR, ἠρώτουν T
8: 5*ἠρώτα *for* ἐπηρώτα (ἐπερωτάω) TTrAWH
Lu. 7: 4*ἠρώτων *for* παρεκάλουν (παρακαλέω) T
8:37 ἠρώτησεν LTrAWHR
11:37 ἐρωτᾷ beseecheth LTAWHR, ἠρώτα Tr
23: 3*ἠρώτησεν *for* ἐπηρώτησεν (ἐπερωτάω) TTrAWHR
Joh. 9:21†*trs* αὐτὸν ἐ. αὐτὸς (*omit* αὐτὸς TTrAWHR) ἡλικίαν ἔχει LTTrAWHR
23 ἐπερωτάω TWH
18:21*ἐρωτᾷς *for* ἐπερωτᾷς (-τάω) Eds
21*ἐρώτησον *for* ἐπερώτησον (-τάω) LTTrAWHR
Acts 1: 6*ἠρώτων *for* ἐπηρώτων (ἐπερωτάω) LTTrAWH

ἔσεσθαι.

Acts 24:25 *omit* ἔ. GEds See 1510

2066 ἐσθής.

Lu. 24: 4*ἐσθῆτι *for* ἐσθήσεσιν (-θησις) LTTrAWHR
Acts 1:10 ἐσθήσις LTTrAWHR

2067 ἔσθησις.

Lu. 24: 4 ἐσθῆς LTTrAWHR
Acts 1:10*ἐσθήσεσιν *for* ἐσθῆτι (-θής) LTTrAWHR

2068 ἐσθίω, ἔσθω.

Mat. 24:49 ἐσθίῃ shall eat GEds
Mar. 1: 6 ἔσθων TTrAWH
2:16 αὐτὸν ἐ.—ὅτι ἤσθιεν that he did eat TTr: ὅτι ἐσθίει LWHR
7: 2 ἐσθίουσιν TTrWHR
28 ἐσθίουσιν LTTrAWWH
Lu. 6: 1 *trs* and did eat the ears of corn TrAWH
7:33†*trs* ἔσθων ἄρτον LTrAWH, ἐσθίων ἄ. T
10. 7 ἔσθοντες LTTrAWH
22:30 ἔσθητε LTTrAWH

2069 'Ἐλί, —λει TTrAWH.

2070 ἐσμέν.

Joh. 17:22 *omit* ἐ. TTrAWHR
Acts 10:39 *omit* ἐ. GEds
2 Co. 6:16**for* ἐστέ LTTrWHR
Gal. 4:28 ἐστέ LTTrA
1 Joh. 3: 1*κληθῶμεν—*add* καὶ ἐ. *read* sons of God, and we are (such) LTTrAWHR

2071 ἔσομαι, ἔσῃ, ἔσται, ἐσόμεθα, ἔσεσθε, ἔσονται.

Mat. 5:37*ἔσται *for* ἔστω LA
6: 5 ἔσῃ—ἔσεσθε LTTrAWHR, *see* προσεύχομαι
12:11 *omit* shall there be TrA[WH]
17:17 *trs* μεθ' ὑμῶν ἔσομαι LTTrAWH
20:26 it shall be—it is, ἐστίν LTrWH
26*ἔσται *for* ἔστω LTTrAWHR
27*ἔσται *for* ἔστω LTTrWHR
24:40 *trs* ἔσονται δύο LTWH
Mar. 3:29*ἔσται *for* ἐστίν T
6:11 *omit* verily *to end of verse* G[L]TTrAWHR
10:43 shall it be—it is, ἐστίν LTTrAWHR
Lu. 9:48 shall be—is, ἐστίν LTTrAWHR
17:36 *add the verse* A.V.B E, *see* ἀφίημι

Lu. 19:46*καὶ ἔσται (*before* ὁ οἶκος) *for* ἐστίν TTrAWHR, *read* and my house shall be a house
20:33*ἔσται *for* γίνεται (γίνομαι) R
21:25 ἔσονται LTTrAWHR
Joh. 14:17 shall be—is, ἐστίν LTrAWH
1 Pet. 1:16*ἔσεσθε *for* γένεσθε (γίνομαι) Eds
2 Joh. 3 ἔσται—*sit* A.V.Vul
Rev. 10: 6 *trs* οὐκέτι ἔσται GEds
21: 3 *trs* μετ' αὐτῶν ἐ. GLTTrAWWHR
22:12 shall be—is, ἐστίν LTTrAWHR

2071 ἐσόμενος.

Rev. 16: 5 ὅσιος holy one—ἐ. shalt be A.V.B

2074 'Ἐσρώμ, 'Ε— WH.

Lu. 3:33 'Ἐσρών ELWHR

2075 ἐστέ.

Mat. 23:28 *trs* ἐστε μεστοὶ LTTrAWH
Lu. 9:55 *omit* and said *to end of verse* LTTrAWHR
11:48**add* ἐ. TTrAWHR, *see* μάρτυς
24:17 *omit* ἐ. TTrAWHR, *see* ἵστημι
48 *omit* ἐ. T[Tr]AWH
Joh. 8:39**for* ἦτε GLTTrAWHR
2 Co. 6:16 ἐσμέν LTTrWHR
Gal. 4:28**for* ἐσμέν LTTrA
Eph. 2:19*but—*add* ἐ. ye are LTTrAWHR
5: 5 οἶδα GEds
Heb. 12: 8 *trs* καὶ οὐχ υἱοί ἐ. LTTrAWHR
Jas. 4:14**for* ἐστίν Eds

2076 ἐστίν.

Mat. 6:13 *omit* GEds, *see* αἰών
7: 9 *omit* ἐ. LTr[A]WH
10:10 *omit* ἐ. LTTrAWH
11:11 *trs* ἐστιν αὐτοῦ A
15:26 ἐ. καλόν—ἔξεστιν, *read* it is not allowed LTA
18: 7 *omit* ἐ. LTrAWH
19:17**add* ἐ. GEds, *see* ἀγαθός
26 *omit* ἐ.[2] GLTTrAWWH
20:26**for* ἔσται LTrWH
Mar. 3:29 is—will be, ἔσται T
4:31 *omit* ἐ. LTTrAWHR, *see* μικρός
6:15 *omit* ἐ.[2] [L]TTrAWHR
16 *omit* ἐ. αὐτός G[L]TTrAWHR
49**for* εἶναι TWHR
10:27 *omit* ἐ. TTrWH
43**for* ἔσται[1] LTTrAWHR
12:29*first—*add* ἐ. is [L]TTrAWHR, *see* ἐντολή
Lu. 8:25 *omit* ἐ.[1] Eds
9:48**for* ἔσται LTTrAWHR
10: 7 *omit* ἐ. LTTrAWHR
14:17 εἰσίν T
16:15 *omit* ἐ. GEds
19: 9 *omit* ἐ. T[WH]
46 *see* ἔσται
23:38 *omit* ἐ. LTTrAWHR
Joh. 1: 4**for* ἦν LT
27 *omit* he it is G[L]TTrAWHR
2: 3**for* ἔχουσιν (ἔχω) T
3:31 *omit* is above all[2] T
8:17**add* ἐ. T, *see* γράφω
10:12**for* εἰσίν LTTrAWH
13:24*see λέγω
14:11 ἐμοί ἐ. B
17**for* ἔσται LTrAWH
17: 7 εἰσίν TTrAWH
21:25 *omit the verse* T
Acts 12:15 *trs* ἐστιν αὐτοῦ LTTrAWH
15:18 *omit* GLTTrAWHR, *see* ἔργον
28:22 *trs* ἡμῖν ἐστιν LTTrAWHR
Ro. 10: 1 *omit* ἐ. GEds
11: 6 *omit* ἐ.[1] A: *omit* but if (it be) *to end of verse* GLTTr[A]WHR
14: 4 *omit* ἐ. Eds, *see* δυνατέω
1 Co. 1:25 *omit* ἐ.[2] TTrWH
3: 5*δὲ—*add* ἐ. LTTrAWHR
22 *omit* ἐ. LTTrAWHR
6: 5 ἔνι GEds
20 *omit* GEds, *see* θεός
7: 8 *omit* ἐ. GEds
9 *omit* ἐ. W
29†*trs* ἐστίν ('ELTWHR) τὸ λοιπόν Eds
9: 3 *trs* ἐστιν αὕτη LTTrAWHR
12: 6 *omit* it is GEds
14:10 εἰσίν Eds
37**for* εἰσίν Eds
15:17*ὑμῶν—*add* [ἐ.] LWH
44 and there is—*trs* there is also Eds
2 Co. 1:18**for* ἐγένετο (γίνομαι) Eds
2: 2 *omit* ἐ. Eds
13: 5 *omit* ἐ. [L]TTr[A]WH

Gal. 6:15**for* ἰσχύει (-χύω) GEds
Eph. 5:23 *omit* ἐ.[2] Eds
Phil. 1: 8 *omit* ἐ. [L]TTrAWHR
28†*trs* ἐστὶν αὐτοῖς GEds
Col. 3:20 *trs* εὐάρεστόν ἐστιν LTTrAWHR
1 Ti. 5:25 *omit* ἐ. LTTrAWHR, εἰσίν W
Heb. 12: 7 *omit* ἐ. LTTr[A]WHR
Jas. 4:14 it is—ye are, ἐστέ Eds
1 Pet. 1: 6 *omit* ἐ. TTrWH
1 Joh. 1: 5 *trs* ἔστιν αὕτη TTrAWWH
5 *trs* οὐκ ἔστιν ἐν αὐτῷ TrWH
8 *trs* ἐν ἡμῖν οὐκ ἔστιν LTrW
2:10 *trs* οὐκ ἔστιν ἐν αὐτῷ LTA
4:12 *trs* ἐν ἡμῖν ἐστίν TTrAWH
Rev. 1: 4 *omit* ἐ. Eds
5: 2 *omit* ἐ. Eds
13 *omit* ἐ.[1] Eds
13 *omit* such as are TTr, [ἐ.] WH
9:19**for* εἰσίν A.V.C GEds, *see* ἐξουσία
13:18*αὐτοῦ—*add* ἐ. Tr
17: 8 *omit* ἐ.[3] GEds, *see* καίπερ
21:16 *omit* τοσοῦτόν ἐ. GEds
22:12*ἐ. αὐτοῦ *for* α. ἔσται LTTrAWHR

2077 ἔστω, ἔστωσαν.

Mat. 5:37 ἔσται, *read* your communication shall be LA
20:26 let him be—shall be, ἔσται LTTrAWHR
27 let him be—shall be, ἔσται LTTrWHR
Acts 28:28 *trs* ὑμῖν ἔστω AWH

2078 ἔσχατος.

Mar. 10:31 οἱ ἐ.—*omit* οἱ GLW[WH]
12: 6 *trs* ἐ. πρὸς αὐτούς LTTrAWHR
22 ἔσχατον LTTrAWHR
Joh. 8: 9 *omit* (even) unto the last WH
Heb. 1: 2(1) ἐσχάτου, *read* at the end of these days GEds
1 Pet. 1:20 ἐσχάτου, *read* the end of the times Eds
2 Pet. 3: 3 ἐσχάτων Eds
Jude 18 ἐσχάτου Eds, *see* χρόνος
Rev. 1:11 *omit* GEds, *see* ἄλφα
22:13 ὁ ἐ.—*omit* ὁ L[A]: *trs see* ἀρχή

2080 ἔσω.

2 Co. 4:16**for* ἔσωθεν LTTrAWHR

2081 ἔσωθεν.

2 Co. 4:16 ἔσω ἡμῶν our inward LTTrWHR, ἔσω[θεν] ἡ. A
Rev. 11: 2 ἐ. within S—ἔξωθεν without A.V.B EGEds

2083 ἑταῖρος.

Mat. 11:16 their fellows—the others, ἑτέρος TTrWH

2087 ἕτερος.

Mat. 10:23*ἑτέραν *f.* ἄλλην(-λος) GLTTrWHR
11:16*ἑτέροις *for* ἑταίροις(-ρος) TTrWH
21:30*ἑτέρῳ *for* δευτέρῳ (-ρος) GTAW
Lu. 7:19*ἕτερον *for* ἄλλον (-λος) TrWH
17:36 *add the verse* A.V.B E, *see* ἀφίημι
19:20 another—the other, ὁ ἕ. LTTrAWHR
Acts 19:39 περὶ ἑ. concerning other matters—περαιτέρω further LTrWH
1 Co. 8: 4 *omit* ἕ. *read* no God LTTrAWHR
14:21 ἑτέρων, *read* lips of others LTTrAWHR
Jas. 4:12 another — (thy) neighbour, πλησίον LTTrAWHR

2089 ἔτι.

Mar. 8:17 *omit* yet[2] LTTrAWHR
Lu. 22:37 *omit* yet LTTrAWHR
Joh. 11:30*was[2]—*add* ἔ. still LTr[A]WHR
Ro. 5: 6 ἔ. γάρ—εἴ γε AWH
6*ἀσθενῶν—*add* ἔ. GEds
1 Co. 3: 2 [yet] LWH
Rev. 10: 6 οὐκ ἔσται ἔ.—οὐκέτι ἔσ. GEds
22: 5**for* ἐκεῖ GEds

ἑτοιμάζω.

Mat. 22: 4 ἡτοίμακα LTTrAWHR
Mar. 15: 1*ἑτοιμάσαντες *for* ποιήσαντες (ποιέω) T

2094 ἔτος.

Acts 13:19, 20 *trs* by lot about the space of four hundred and fifty years. And after these things he gave LTTrWWHR

Gal. 1:18 *trs* τρία ἔτη TWH
3:17 *trs* τετρακόσια καὶ τριάκοντα ἔτη GEds

2095 **εὖ.**

Lu. 19:17 well—well done, εὖγε LTTrAWH

Εὖα, Εὖα, Εὔα—Εὕα WH.

2097 **εὐαγγελίζω.**

Lu. 4:18 εὐαγγελίσασθαι GEds
Acts 8:25 εὐηγγελίζοντο Eds
14: 7 *trs* εὐαγ. ἦσαν LTTrAWH
21 εὐαγγελιζόμενοι preaching the gospel LT
17:18 *trs* εὐηγ. αὐτοῖς ([α.]A) LA
Ro. 10:15 *omit* preach the gospel of peace and LTTr[A]WHR
1 Co. 9:16 ε.² εὐαγγελίσωμαι LTrAWWH
Gal. 1: 8 ε.¹—εὐαγγελίσηται TWHR

2098 **εὐαγγέλιον.**

Ro. 15:29 *omit* of the gospel GEds
Eph. 6:19 [of the gospel] LWH

2100 **εὐαρεστέω.**

Heb.11: 5 εὐαρεστηκέναι LAWH

* **εὖγε**, well done!

Lu. 19:17 *for* εὖ LTTrAWH

2105 **εὐδία.**

Mat. 16: 2 when it is evening *to end of verse* 3 [TA] [[WH]]

2106 **εὐδοκέω.**

Mat. 3:17 ηὐδόκησα T
12:18 ηὐδόκησεν TTr
17: 5 ηὐδόκησα LTr
Lu. 3:22 εὐδόκησα LTTrAWH
Ro. 15:26, 27 ηὐδόκησαν TTrWH
1 Co. 10: 5 ηὐδόκησεν LTrAWWH
1 Th. 2: 8 ηὐδοκοῦμεν WH
3: 1 ηὐδοκήσαμεν TTrWH
Heb.10: 6 ηὐδόκησας LTTrA
8 ηὐδόκησας LTTr

2107 **εὐδοκία.**

Mat. 11:26 *trs* εὐδοκία ἐγένετο LTWH
Lu. 2:14 εὐδοκίας, *read* among men of good pleasure LTTrAWH
10:21 *trs* εὐδοκία ἐγένετο LTrAWH

2112 **εὐθέως.**

(*Throughout Mark* εὐθύς *is read for* ε. *by most modern Editors.*)

Mat. 14:22 *omit* straightway T[WH]
27 εὐθύς LTTrWH
21: 2 εὐθύς TWH
3 εὐθύς TTrWH
26:74 εὐθύς TrWH
Mar. 1:31 *omit* immediately TTrWHR
2: 2 *omit* straightway [L]T[Tr]WHR
12 *trs* καὶ ε. *read* he arose, and immediately TTrAWHR
5: 2 *omit* immediately L[WH]
13 *omit* forthwith Jesus (*read* he gave) [L]TTr[A]WHR
36 *omit* as soon as [L]TTr[A]WHR
7:35 *omit* straightway [L]TTrAWHR
Lu. 5:39 *omit* straightway TTrAWHR
6:49 εὐθύς TTrAWH
Joh. 5: 9 *omit* immediately T
13:30 εὐθύς LTTrAWHR

See also εὐθύς.

2115 **εὐθυμότερον.**

Acts 24:10 more cheerfully—cheerfully, εὐθύμως LTTrAWHR

* **εὐθύμως**, cheerfully. See 2115

Acts 24:10 *for* εὐθυμότερον LTTrAWHR

εὐθύς, adj.

Lu. 3: 5 εὐθείας LTTrAWHR

2117 **εὐθύς**, adv.

Mat. 3:16 *trs* εὐθὺς ἀνέβη LTTrWWH
Mar. 1:12 εὐθέως LW
23*and¹—*add* ε. straightway TAWHR
5:42*astonished—*add* ε. straightway T[Tr]AWHR
7:25**add* ε. straightway TTrAWHR, *see* ἀλλά
35*and²—*add* ε. straightway T
Mar. 14:72*and¹—*add* ε. straightway LTTrWHR
Joh. 21: 3 *omit* immediately LTTrAWHR
Acts 10:16**for* πάλιν Eds

See also εὐθέως.

2118 **εὐθύτης.**

Heb. 1: 8 τῆς εὐθύτητος LTTrWHR

2119 **εὐκαιρέω.**

Mar. 6:31 εὐκαίρουν LTTrAWH
Acts 17:21 ηὐκαίρουν LTTrAWH

2125 **εὐλαβέομαι.**

Acts 23:10 φοβέομαι LTTrAWHR

2126 **εὐλαβής.**

Acts 22:12*εὐλαβὴς *for* εὐσεβὴς LTTrAWHR

2127 **εὐλογέω.**

Mat. 5:44 *omit* bless them *to* hate you LTTrAWHR
14:19 ηὐλόγησεν LTrA
Mar. 10:16 εὐλόγει blesseth LW: *omit* η. αὐτά, *see* κατευλογέω TTrAWHR
Lu. 1:28 *om.* blessed (art) thou among women T[Tr]AWHR
24:53 *omit* and blessing T
Acts 3:25*εὐλογηθήσονται *for* ἐνευλογηθήσονται (-γέομαι) WH
1 Co. 14:16 εὐλογῇς LTTrAWHR
Gal. 3: 8*εὐλογηθήσονται *for* ἐνευλογηθήσονται (-γέομαι)
Heb.11:20, 21 ηὐλόγησεν LA

2131 **Εὐνείκη, Εὐνί-** BGEds.

2133 **εὔνοια.**

1 Co. 7: 3 *omit* benevolence, *read* (her) due GEds

* **εὐπάρεδρος**, assiduous.

1 Co. 7:35 εὐπάρεδρον *for* εὐπρόσεδρον (-δρος) GEds

2141 **εὐπορέομαι.**

Acts 11:29 εὐπορεῖτο LTTrAWH

2145 **εὐπρόσεδρος.**

1 Co. 7:35 εὐπάρεδρος GEds

2147 **εὑρίσκω.**

Mat. 2:11 found—saw, εἰδέω A.V.C GEds
26:43†*trs* πάλιν εὗρεν αὐτούς, *read* came again and found them LTTrAWHR
60 *omit* (yet) found they none G[L]TTrAWHR
Mar. 1:37 καὶ εὗρον αὐτὸν καὶ and they found him and TTrAWHR
11:13 *trs* τι εὑρήσει LTTrAWWH
14:55 ηὕρισκον LTrAWH
Lu. 8:35 εὗραν TrWH
19:48 ηὕρισκον LTrWH
23: 2 εὕραμεν TTrAWH
Joh. 18:38 *trs* εὑ. ἐν αὐτῷ αἰτίαν LTTrAWH
19: 4†*trs* οὐδεμίαν αἰτίαν εὑρίσκω ἐν αὐτῷ LTrWH, αἰτ. ἐν αὐ. οὐ. εὑ. A, αἰτ. οὐχ εὑ. T
Acts 5:10 εὗραν Tr
7:11 ηὕρισκον TrAWH
19: 1 εὑρεῖν found LTTrAWHR
Ro. 4: 1 *trs* εὑρηκέναι *before* Ἀβραάμ LTTrAR: *omit* hath found [A]WH
7:18 *omit* I find LTTrAWHR
Heb. 9:12 εὑράμενος S—εὑρόμενος B
11: 5 ηὑρίσκετο LTTrAWWH
2 Pet. 3:10*εὑρεθήσεται *for* κατακαήσεται (-καίω) TrWH
Rev. 9: 6 εὕρωσιν LR
18:14†*trs* αὐτὰ οὐ μὴ (οὐ μὴ αὐτὰ TTrWH) εὑρήσουσιν (they shall find) (εὕρῃς W) Eds

2148 **Εὐροκλύδων, Εὐρακύλων** Eds.

2152 **εὐσεβής.**

Acts 22:12 εὐλαβὴς LTTrAWHR

2165 **εὐφραίνω, -ομαι.**

Acts 2:26 ηὐφράνθη LTTrAWWH
Rev. 11:10 εὐφραίνονται Eds

2166 **Εὐφράτης.**

Rev. 16:12 τὸν Ε.—*omit* τὸν GNTrWH]

2168 **εὐχαριστέω.**

Joh. 6:11 εὐχαρίστησεν καί gave thanks and T
Ro. 1:21 ηὐχαρίστησαν GLTTrAWH
7:25 χάρις, *read* thanks (be) to God LTTrAWH

2172 **εὔχομαι.**

Acts 26:29 εὐξάμην T
27:29 ηὔχοντο TTrA
2 Co. 13: 7 εὐχόμεθα we pray Eds
Jas. 5:16 προσεύχομαι LWH

2176 **εὐώνυμος.**

Mar. 10:37 ἀριστερός TTrAWH

2177 **ἐφάλλομαι.**

Acts 19:16 ἐφαλόμενος LTTrAWHR

2178 **ἐφάπαξ.**

Heb. 7:27 | 9:12 | 10:10 ἐφ' ἅπαξ Tr

2179 **Ἐφεσῖνος.**

Rev. 2: 1 in Ephesus, Ἐφεσος GEds

2181 **Ἔφεσος.**

Eph. 1: 1 [at Ephesus] TAWH
Rev. 2: 1*ἐν Ἐφέσῳ *for* Ἐφεσίνης GEds

2186 **ἐφίστημι.**

1 Th. 5: 3 ἐπίσταμαι TTrWH

* **ἐφνίδιος**, *see* **αἰφνίδιος.** See 160

2187 **Ἐφραΐμ, -ίμ** LTWH.

* **ἐχθές** *for* **χθές** Eds.

2190 **ἐχθρός.**

Lu. 1:74 τῶν ἐ.—*omit* τῶν LTTrAWH

2192 **ἔχω.**

Mat. 16: 8*ἔχετε *for* ἐλάβετε (λαμβάνω) LWHR
17:15*ἔχει *for* πάσχει (-χω) LTrWH
18:25 εἶχεν—ἔχει he hath LTrAWH
19:16 σχῶ LTTrAWH
21:38*σχῶμεν *for* κατάσχωμεν (κατέχω) LTTrAWHR
26: 7 *trs* ἐ. ἀλάβαστρον μύρου LTTrWH
Mar. 2:19†*trs* ἐ. τὸν νυμφίον μετ' αὐτῶν (μεθ' ἑαυτῶν L) LTTrAWH
4: 9 ὁ ἔχων—ὃς ἔχει Eds
25 ἂν ἔχῃ—ἔχει LTTrAWHR
6:36 *omit* ἐ. [L]TTrAWHR, *see* ἄρτος
7:16 *omit the verse* T[TrA]WHR
8: 7 εἶχαν LTTrAWH
16 ἔχουσιν they have LTrAWH
9:42**add* ἐχόντων A, *see* πίστις
12: 6†*trs* εἶχεν υἱὸν TTrAWHR
14: 8 ἔσχεν GEds
Lu. 8:27 ὃς εἶχεν—ἔχων TWHR
17: 6 ἔχετε ye have TTrAWHR
23:17 *omit the verse* [L]TTr[A]WHR
Joh. 2: 3**add* εἶχον T, *see* οἶνος
8 they have—there is, ἐστίν T
12: 6 ἔχων TTrAWHR
15:22, 24 εἶχον—εἴχοσαν LTTrAWH
16:33 ἔχετε ye have S—ἕξετε ye shall have A.V.B EL
19:11 couldest have—hast, ἔχεις T
Acts 7: 1 *omit* ἔχει W
9:31 εἶχεν Eds
13:44*ἐχομένῳ *for* ἐρχομένῳ (-μαι) GLAW
20:24 *omit* οὐδὲ ἔχω TTrAWHR
23:25*ἔχουσαν *for* περιέχουσαν (-χω) LTTrWHR, [περι]ἔ. A
29 *trs* ἐ. ἔγκλημα LTTrAWWH
28:29 *omit the verse* LTTrAWHR
Ro. 5: 1 ἔχωμεν let us have TTrAWHR
1 Co. 7: 7 *trs* ἔχει χάρισμα GEds
29 οἱ ἐ.—*omit* οἱ B
12:12 *trs* πολλὰ ἔχει LTTrAWHR
2 Co. 1:15 σχῆτε TTrAWHR
2: 3 σχῶ TTrAWHR
7: 5 ἔσχεν LTr
Gal. 6:10 ἔχωμεν TWH
Col. 1: 4*ἣν ἔχετε [WH] *for* τὴν², *rd.* love which ye have A.V.†Vul Eds
1 Th. 1: 8 *trs* ἔχειν ἡμᾶς Eds
9 ἔσχομεν A.V.C GEds
Philem. 7†*trs* πολλὴν ἔσχον I had great Eds
Heb. 9: 1 εἶχε TWH
1 Pet. 4: 5 *omit* ἔχοντι WH, *see* κρίνω

1 Joh. 2:23* add ἔ. A.V.B GEds, see ὁμολογέω
28 σχῶμεν LTTrAWHR
2 Joh. 5 εἴχαμεν TTrWH
Rev. 2:10 ἔχητε LWH
3: 4 trs ὀλίγα ἔχεις T
4: 4 omit they had GEds
7 ἔχων TTrAWHR
8 εἶχον—ἔχον GLW, ἔχων TTrAWHR
5: 6 ἔχων TTrAWHR
8: 6 οἱ ἔχοντες A.V.C GEds
9: 8 εἶχαν LTTrAWH
9 εἶχαν WH
14 ὁ ἔχων GEds
10: 2 ἔχων GEds
14:18 ἔ.[1]—ὁ ἔχων LAWR, [ὁ] ἔ. WH
15: 6 οἱ ἔχοντες GLTTrWR, [οἱ] ἔ. AWH
17: 3 ἔχοντα TA, ἔχων WH
21:12 ἔ.[1]—ἔχουσα GEds
12 ἔ.[2]—ἔχουσα GLTTrAWHR
14 ἔχων TTrAWHR
22: 5†trs οὐχ ἕξουσιν (οὐκ ἔχουσιν TTrWH) χρείαν LTTrAWWH

2193 ἕως.

Mat. 13:30* for μέχρι LTrAWH
Lu. 2:37* for ὡς LTTrAWHR
16:16 μέχρι TTrAWHR
19:13 ἐν ᾧ LTTrAWH
22:34* for πρὶν ἤ LTTrAWHR
Joh. 8: 9 omit (even) unto the last WH
12:35, 36 ὡς LTTrAWHR
Acts 1:22 ἄχρι T
17:14* for ὡς LTTrWHR
Rev. 20: 5 ἄχρι GEds

2195 Ζαχαρίας.

Lu. 3: 2 τοῦ Ζ.—omit τοῦ GLTTrAWWH

2198 ζάω.

Mar. 5:23 ζήσῃ LTTrAWHR
Lu. 15:32* ἔζησεν for ἀνέζησεν (ἀναζάω) TTrAWHR
Joh. 5:25 ζήσουσιν LTTrAWH
6:51 ζ.[2]—ζήσει TWH
57 ζ.[3]—ζήσει LTTrAWWH
58 ζήσει TTrAWH
69 omit the living GLTTrAWHR
14:19 ζ.[2]—ζήσετε TTrA
Acts 14:15 τὸν ζ.—omit τὸν Eds
25:24 trs αὐτὸν ζῆν LTTrAWWH
Ro. 14: 9* ἔζησεν for ἀνέζησεν (ἀναζάω) GEds
2 Co. 13: 4 ζ.[2]—ζήσομεν Eds
Gal. 2:14 trs καὶ οὐχ (οὐκ TrAWH) Ἰουδαϊκῶς ζῇς LTTrAWH
1 Ti. 6:17 omit the living LTTrAWHR
2 Ti. 3:12 trs ζῆν εὐσεβῶς TTrWH
Jas. 4:15 ζήσομεν A.V.S 1549 Eds
Rev. 5:14 omit him that liveth for ever and ever GEds
7:17 ζωή, read fountains of waters of life GEds
16: 3 ζωή GLTTrAWHR
20: 5* ἔζησαν for ἀνέζησαν (ἀναζάω) GEds

ζβέννυμι, see σβέννυμι. See 4570

2200 ζεστός.

Rev. 3:16 trs hot nor cold GTTrAWWHR

* ζηλεύω, to be zealous.

Rev. 3:19 ζήλευε for ζήλωσον (-λόω) Eds

2205 ζῆλος.

2 Co. 9: 2 ὁ . . . ζ.—τὸ . . . ζ. TTrWH
12:20 ζῆλος envying Eds
Gal. 5:20 ζῆλος emulation LTTrAWWH
Phil. 3: 6 ζῆλος Eds
Col. 4:13 zeal—labour, πόνος GEds

2206 ζηλόω.

Gal. 4:18 τὸ ζ.—omit τὸ LTTrAWHR
Rev. 3:19 ζηλεύω Eds

2207 ζηλωτής.

1 Pet. 3:13* ζηλωταί for μιμηταί (-τής) Eds

2210 ζημιόω.

Mar. 8:36 ζημιωθῆναι to lose TAWHR, see κερδαίνω

2212 ζητέω.

Mat. 12:47 omit the verse [T]WH
Mar. 1:37 trs σε ζητοῦσιν LW
8:12* ζητεῖ σημεῖον for σ. ἐπιζητεῖ (-τέω) LTTrAWHR
Lu. 2:45 ἀναζητέω LTTrAWHR
4:42 ἐπιζητέω GEds
6:19 ἐζήτουν TTrAWH
11:29* ζητεῖ for ἐπιζητεῖ (-τέω) TTrA (WHR
54 omit seeking T[Tr]AWHR
Joh. 5:16 omit and sought to slay him G[L]TTrAWHR
19:12 trs ὁ Πιλάτος ἐζήτει LTTrAWH
Acts 10:19 ζητοῦντες TAWH

2213 ζήτημα.

Acts 18:15 ζητήματα questions LTTrAWHR

2214 ζήτησις.

Acts 15: 2* ζητήσεως for συζητήσεως (-τησις) GEds
7* ζητήσεως for συζητήσεως (-τησις) TTrWHR
1 Ti. 1: 4 ἐκζήτησις TTrWHR

2215 ζιζάνια.

Mat. 13:27 τὰ ζ.—omit τὰ GEds

* Ζμύρνα, see Σμύρνα.

2217 ζόφος.

Heb. 12:18* ζόφῳ for σκότῳ (-τος) Eds

2222 ζωή.

Mat. 19:17 trs εἰς τὴν ζ. εἰσελθ. LTTrAWWH
Mar. 9:43 trs εἰσελθ. εἰς τὴν ζ. LTTrAWWH
Lu. 1:75 omit τῆς ζ. read all our days GEds
1 Joh. 5:20 ἡ ζ.—omit ἡ LTTrAWHR
Rev. 7:17* ζωῆς for ζώσας (ζάω) GEds
16: 3* ζωῆς for ζῶσα (ζάω) GLTTrAWHR

2224 ζωννύω, ζώννυμι.

Joh. 21:18 trs ζώσει σε TrAWH
Acts 12: 8* ζῶσαι for περίζωσαι (-ώννυμι) LTTrAWHR

2225 ζωογονέω.

1 Ti. 6:13* ζωογονοῦντος for ζωοποιοῦντος (-ποιέω) LTTrAWHR

2226 ζῶον, ζῷον LWH.

2227 ζωοποιέω.

1 Ti. 6:13 quickeneth—preserveth alive ζωογονέω LTTrAWHR

2228 ἤ.

Mat. 6:25* for καί[1] LTr[WH]R
7:10* καὶ ἐάν—ἢ καί LTTrAWHR
15: 6(5) om. or his mother L[A]WHR
19:29 omit or wife LTTrAWHR
20:15 omit ἤ LTr[A]WHR
15 for εἰ A.V.B EGEds
26:53 omit ἤ[2] [L]TTrAWH
Mar. 3:33 or—and, καί LTTrWHR
6:11 omit G[L]TTrAWHR, see ἀμήν
15 omit or GEds
8:37 ἢ τί—τί γάρ for what TTrAWHR
10:29 omit or wife LTTrAWHR
38*, 40* for καί LTTrAWHR
11:28* for καί[3] TAWHR
13:21 omit or TAWH
32* for καί GEds
35* ἢ ὀψέ either at even TTrAWHR
Lu. 2:26 omit ἤ Tr[WH]
6:42 omit either T[Tr]AWH
10:42* add ἤ WH, see ὀλίγος
11:11* for εἰ GLTTrAWR
12:11 [or what thing] TrAWH
29 or—and, καί TTrWHR
47* for μηδέ TWHR
14: 3* add at end ἢ οὔ or not? [L]TTrAWHR
17:23 omit or TTrR
18:14 παρά LTrAWH
21:15* for οὐδέ GT[Tr]AWHR
22:34 see πρίν
68 omit me, nor let me go T[TrA]WHR
Joh. 8:14* for καί[3] GTTrAWWHR
18:10 εἰ μή LTrA[WH]R, omit ἤ T
Acts 2:20 omit ἤ LTTrWHR
10:14 or—and, καί LTTrAWHR
17:21* for καί[2] LTTrAWHR
24:11 omit ἤ GEds
23 omit or come Eds
Ro. 14:21 omit TWHR, see ἀσθενέω
1 Co. 3: 5 omit ἀλλ' ἤ GEds
5:10 or[2]—and, καί Eds
11 ἤ[1] either S—ᾖ be A.V.B EGEds
6: 2* add at commencement ἤ or GEds
9: 7 omit or L[Tr]AW[WH]
11:14 omit ἤ Eds
2 Co. 3: 1* ἢ μή for εἰ μή A.V.B GLTTrAWHR
6:14* τίς δέ—ἢ τίς Eds
Eph. 5: 4* for καί[2] LT
Phil. 2: 3 or—nor through, μηδὲ κατά LTTrAWHR
Col. 2:16 or[1]—and, καί AWH
1 Ti. 2: 9 or[1]—and, καί LTTrAWHR
5:16 omit πιστὸς ἤ (omit man or) LTTr[A]WHR
Heb. 12:20 omit or thrust through with a dart GEds
Jas. 4:11* for καί[1] LTTrAWHR
13 καί[1] and—ἤ or A.V.B ELTTrWHR
Rev. 13:17 omit or[2] GEds

2229 ἦ μήν.

Heb. 6:14 εἰ μήν LTTrAWHR

2232 ἡγεμών.

Mat. 27:23 omit ἡ. read he said TTrAWHR
Acts 23:34 omit ὁ ἡ. read he GEds

2235 ἤδη.

Mar. 15:44* for πάλαι LTrWH
Lu. 23:44* ἤδη ὡσεί now about LTWHR, [ἤ.] ὡσεί TrA
24:29* κέκλικεν—add ἤ. read already is far spent [L]TTrAWHR
Joh. 6:17 καὶ σκοτία ἤδη ἐγεγόνει—κατέλαβεν δὲ αὐτοὺς ἡ σκοτία and darkness overtook them T
11:17 omit already T: trs ἤδη ἡμέρας TrAWH
19:28 trs ἤδη πάντα LTTrAWWH
33 trs ἤδη αὐτὸν TTrAWH
Ro. 4:19 omit now [L]T[AWH]

2240 ἥκω.

Mar. 8: 3 came, ἥκασιν S—ἥκουσιν EW: εἰσίν are AWH
Lu. 13:35 ἥξει LT[TrA]: omit (the time) come when WHR
Acts 28:23 ἔρχομαι LTTrAWH
Rev. 3: 9 ἥξουσιν LTTrAWHR

2242 Ἠλί.

Mat. 27:46 Ἠλί bis LA, Ἡλεί T, Ἐλωί WH

2242 Ἠλί, Ἡλεί TTrAWH.

2243 Ἠλίας, Ἡ-, Ἡλείας T, Ἠλείας WH.

Mat. 17: 4 trs Ἡλίᾳ μίαν LTTrAWHR
Lu. 9:54 omit even as Elias did TTr[A]WHR

2244 ἡλικία.

Lu. 2:52 trs in stature and wisdom Tr
12:25 trs ἐπὶ τὴν ἡ. αὐτοῦ προσθ. AWH

2245 ἡλίκος.

Jas. 3: 5* ἡλίκον for ὀλίγον (-γος) Eds

2246 ἥλιος.

Mar. 4: 6 ὁ ἥλιος LTTrAWHR, see ἀνατέλλω
Lu. 23:45 and the sun was darkened—τοῦ ἡλίου ἐκλειπόντες (ἐκλίποντος T), read ninth hour, from the sun failing TWHR
Rev. 22: 5 omit of the sun W

2248 ἡμᾶς.

Mat. 8:25 omit us Eds
Lu. 11: 4 omit but deliver us from evil GTTrAWHR
23:15* for ὑμᾶς TWHR, see ἀναπέμπω
Joh. 9: 4* for ἐμέ TTrWHR: for με T
Acts 7:27 ἡμῶν LTTrWWHR
Ro. 7: 6 [ἡμᾶς] LTrWH
13:11† trs ἤδη ἡ. LTrW: ἤδη ὑμᾶς TAWHR
15: 7 us—you, ὑμᾶς GLTTrAWR
16: 6 us—you, ὑμᾶς LTTrAWHR
1 Co. 6:14 us S—you, ὑμᾶς E
7:15 us—you, ὑμᾶς TWH
2 Co. 8: 4 omit δέξασθαι ἡ. GEds
Gal. 4:17 for ὑμᾶς[2] E
Eph. 5: 2 us[1]—you, ὑμᾶς TTrAWHR
Col. 1:12 us—you, ὑμᾶς TWH
1 Th. 2:15 you ὑμᾶς S—us A.V.B EGEds
4: 8 us—you, ὑμᾶς Eds
1 Pet. 1: 3 us S—you, ὑμᾶς E
4 us—you, ὑμᾶς A.V.B GEds
3:18 us—you, ὑμᾶς WH
21 us—you, ὑμᾶς LTTrAWHR
5:10 us—you, ὑμᾶς Eds
2 Pet. 3: 9 us—you, ὑμᾶς LTTrAWHR
Rev. 1: 6 us—for us, ἡμῖν Tr, ἡμῶν L
5: 9 omit us LTAWWHR
10 us—them, αὐτούς GEds

ἥμεθα, see ἦν.
See 2258

2249 **ἡμεῖς.**

Joh. 7:35 *omit* ἡ. T
Ro. 8:23 *trs* ἡμεῖς καὶ TAR, [ἡ. καὶ] LTrWH
2 Co. 6:16**for* ὑμεῖς LTTrWH
Gal. 4:28 we—you, ὑμεῖς LTTrA
1 Joh.1: 4**for* ὑμῖν TTrAWH

2250 **ἡμέρα.**

Mat. 15:32 ἡμέραι GEds
24:42*ἡμέρᾳ *for* ὥρᾳ LTTrAWH
28:15*σήμερον—*add* ἡμέρας LTrA[WH]
Mar. 1:13†*trs* τεσσεράκοντα ἡ. TTrWH
2:20 ἐκείνῃ τῇ ἡμέρᾳ (ἡ.²) that day GEds
6:11 *omit* verily *to end of verse* G[L]TTrAWH
8: 2 ἡμέραι GEds
9:31 ‖ 10:34 μετὰ τρεῖς ἡμέρας after three days LTTrAWH
Lu. 1:59†*trs* τῇ ἡ. τῇ ὀγδόῃ LTTrAWH
75 πάσαις ταῖς ἡμέραις WH
13:31 day—hour, ὥρα TAWH
14: 5 τῇ ἡ.—*omit* τῇ TWH
17: 4 *omit* in a day² LTTrAWH
24 *omit* in his day LWH
Joh. 2: 1†*trs* τῇ τρίτῃ ἡ. TrA
9:14**add* ἡ. LTTrAWH, *see* ὅτε
Acts 2:20 τὴν ἡ.—*omit* τὴν LTTrAWH
9:43 *trs* αὐτὸν ἡμέρας ἱκανὰς μεῖναι LTr
12: 3 αἱ ἡμέραι GLW, [αἱ] ἡ. A
28: 7 *trs* ἡμέρας τρεῖς AWH
Ro. 14: 6 *omit* and he that regardeth not the day, to the Lord he doth not regard (it) LTTr[A]WH
1 Co. 15: 4†*trs* τῇ ἡμέρᾳ τῇ τρίτῃ Eds
2 Co. 3:14*σήμερον—*add* ἡ. Eds
1 Th. 5: 2 ἡ ἡμέρα—*omit* ἡ LTTr[A]WWH
4 *trs* ὑμᾶς ἡ ἡμέρα LW
2 Th. 3: 8 ἡμέρας LTTrWH
2 Pet. 3:10 ἡ ἡμέρα—*omit* ἡ Eds
Rev. 11: 6 τὰς ἡμέρας GEds

2251 **ἡμέτερος.**

Lu. 16:12**for* ὑμέτερος WH
Acts 24: 6 *omit* and would have judged *to* come unto thee (*ver.* 8) LTTr[A]WH
Ro. 11:31 ὑμετέρῳ S—ἡμετέρῳ E
1 Co. 15:31 our S—your, ὑμετέραν A.V.B EGEds
2 Co. 8: 8 ὑμετέρας S—ἡμετέρας E

2252 ἤμην.

Acts 11:11 I was—we were, ἦμεν LTTrWH

2254 **ἡμῖν.**

Mat. 8:31 ἡμᾶς GLTTrAWH, *see* ἀποστέλλω
Mar. 9:38 *omit* GWH, *see* ἀκολουθέω
Lu. 20:22 ἡμᾶς TTrAWH
24:32 *omit* within us [TrA]WH
Joh. 6:52 *trs* ἡμῖν οὗτος T
11:50 for us—for you, ὑμῖν TTrAWH
Acts 7:38 us—you, ὑμῖν WH
13:26**for* ὑμῖν² TAWH
33(32) to us their—to our, ἡμῶν LTTrWH, αὐτῶν ἡμῶν W
14:17 us—you, ὑμῖν GLT[Tr]AWH
15: 7 us—you, ὑμῖν LTTrAWH
16:17 us² S—you, ὑμῖν ETTrWH
2 Co. 1: 8 *omit* to us Eds
8: 7 ἡμῶν ἐν ὑμῖν, *read* our love to you WH
10: 8 *omit* us LTTrAWH
Eph. 4: 6**for* ὑμῖν GW
Col. 2:13 us S—you, ὑμῖν A.V.BE
Philem. 6**for* ὑμῖν GLTrAWWH
Heb. 13:21**for* ὑμῖν TWH
1 Pet. 1:12 us—you, ὑμῖν GEds
2:21 us² S—you, ὑμῖν EGEds
4: 3 *omit* us LTTrAWH
1 Joh.1: 9 us (our)—our, ἡμῶν W

2255 **ἥμισυ.**

Lu. 19: 8 ἡμίσεια TTrA, -σεα L, -σια WH

ἡμιώριον, -ρον LTTrAWH.

2257 **ἡμῶν.**

Mar. 9:40 you is on your, ὑμῶν *bis* S—us is on our A.V.B ETTrAWWH
Lu. 1:74 *omit* our [L]TTrAWH
9:50 us *bis*—you ὑμῶν GLTTrAWH

Lu. 11: 2 *omit* our GTTrAWH
23: 2*ἔθνος ἡ. our nation LTTr[A]W
Joh. 8:54**for* ὑμῶν TTrAW (WH
19: 7 *om.* ἡ. *read* the law LTTrAWH
Acts 3:22**for* ὑμῶν T
25 our—your, ὑμῶν TrAWH
4:25**add* ἡ. LTTrAWH, *see* πατήρ
7:19 *omit* ἡ. *read* the fathers LTTrAWH
9:38**for* αὐτῶν Eds
13:33(32)**for* αὐτῶν ἡμῖν LTTrWH
14:17 our—your, ὑμῶν GLTTrAWH
15:36 *omit* ἡ. *read* the brethren GEds
19:25 ἡμῖν LTTrAWH
37**for* ὑμῶν LTTrAWH
20: 7**for* τῶν μαθητῶν (-τῆς) GEds
21:10 *omit* ἡ. Eds
24: 7 *omit* LTTr[A]WH, *see* κρίνω
26: 6*πατέρας— *add* ἡ. A.V.Vul. Eds
28:25 our—your, ὑμῶν LTTrAWH
Ro. 6:11 *omit* our Lord GEds
8:26 *omit* for us Eds
16:24 *omit the verse* LTTr[A]WH
1 Co. 5: 4 *om.* ἡ.¹ *read* the Lord [L]T[WH]
5*κυρίου—*add* ἡ. *read* our Lord [L]W
7 *omit* for us Eds
6:11*κυρίου—*add* [ἡ.] LWH
15:14**for* ὑμῶν WH
16:23 κυρίου—*add nostri* A.V.Vul
2 Co. 1:14*κυρίου—*add* ἡ. *read* our Lord [L]TAWH
4:16**add* ἡ. LTTrAWH, *see* ἔσωθεν
17 *omit* our WH
7:12 your care for us S—our care for you A.V.B EG
13**for* ὑμῶν Eds
14 our—your, ὑμῶν LA
8: 7**for* ὑμῶν WH, *see* ἡμῖν
19**for* ὑμῶν GEds
11:31 *omit* ἡ. *read* the Lord Eds
Gal. 4: 6**for* ὑμῶν GEds
Eph. 3:14 *omit* of our Lord Jesus Christ Eds
5: 2 us²—you, ὑμῶν AWH
Phil. 4:23 *omit* ἡ. *read* the Lord Eds
Col. 1: 7**for* ὑμῶν LTrAWH
3: 4 our—your, ὑμῶν TTr
4: 8**for* ὑμῶν¹ LTTrAWH
1 Th. 1: 1 *omit* from God our *to end of verse* [L]TTrAWH
2: 4 our—your, ὑμῶν W
3: 2 *omit* and our fellow-labourer GEds
2 Th. 1: 2 *omit* ἡ. [LTr]AWH
3: 6 *omit* ἡ. *read* the Lord [L]AWH
12 *omit* ἡ. LTTrAWH, *see* κύριος
1 Ti. 1: 2 *omit* ἡ.¹ Eds
Tit. 2: 8**for* ὑμῶν GEds: *trs* λέγειν περὶ ἡ. LTTrAWH
10 *for* ὑμῶν A.V.B EGEds
Philem.25 *omit* ἡ. *read* the Lord TWH
Heb. 1: 3 *omit* our Eds
9:14**for* ὑμῶν LAWWH
13:23*ἀδελφὸν—*add* ἡ. *read* our brother Eds
1 Pet. 2:21 us¹ S—you, ὑμῶν EGLTTrAWH
4: 1 *omit* for us LTTrAWH
2 Pet. 1: 1 σωτῆρος—*add* ἡ. E
2:20*κυρίου ἡ. our Lord LT
3: 2 us the—your, ὑμῶν Eds
1 Joh. 1: 4 our S—your, ὑμῶν A.V.B EGW
3: 5 *omit* our LTTrAWH
21 *om.* our LTr[A]WH: *om.* us WH
2 Joh. 8 us S—you, ὑμῶν A.V.B EGLW
12 our—your, ὑμῶν LTrAWH
Jude 3*κοινῆς—*add* ἡ. *read* our common LTTrAWH
25**add* ἡ. GEds, *see* κύριος
Rev. 1: 5 [ἡμῶν] AWH
4:11**add* ἡ. Eds, *see* κύριος
5:10 *omit* unto our God A
11: 8 our—their, αὐτῶν GEds
19: 6*θεός—*add* ἡ. *read* our God GTTrW[WH]R
22:21 *omit* ἡ. *read* the Lord GEds

2258 **ἦν, ἦς (ἦσθα), ἦν; ἦμεν, ἦτε, ἦσαν.**

Mat. 3: 4 *trs* ἦν αὐτοῦ LTTrAWH
12:10 *omit* there was LTTrAWH
14:24 *omit* ἦν¹ TrWH, *see* στάδιον
23:30 ἦμεν *bis*—ἤμεθα GLTTrAWWH
25: 2 *trs* ἐξ αὐτῶν ἦσαν LTTrAWH
Mar. 1:39 ἔρχομαι, *read* went preaching TTrWH
45 [ἦν] LWH
3: 1 *omit* ἦν L[Tr]
4: 1 ἦσαν TTrAWH
36 ἦν²—ἦσαν T
5:13 *omit* they were [L]TTrAWH

Mar. 9: 6 were—became, *see* γίνομαι LTTrAWH
14:21 *omit* ἦν [L]T[Tr]AWH
15:40 *omit* ἦν T[TrA]WH
Lu. 7:12 *omit* ἦν EGW
12 ἱκανὸς—*add* ἦν EGT[TrA]WH
11:14 *omit* and it was [TrA]WH
13:11 *omit* ἦν¹ LTTrAWH
15:32 *omit* ἦν² LTTrAWH
16:20 *omit* ἦν [L]TTrAWH
19: 2 *omit* ἦν² [L]TrAWH
24:10 [ἦσαν δὲ] TrA
Joh. 1: 4 was¹—is, ἐστίν LT
8:39 were—are, ἐστέ GLTTrAWH
10: 6 ἦ (ὦ) Tr
11:41 *omit* where the dead was laid GLTTrAWH
18:16 ὃς ἦν—ὁ TTrAWH
19:14*δὲ ὡσεί—ἦν ὡς Eds
41*ἐτέθη—ἦν τεθειμένος WH
Acts 2:43**add* ἦν T, *see* φόβος
44 *omit* ἦσαν WH
4:34*ἦν *for* ὑπῆρχεν (ὑπάρχω) LTTrWH
10: 1 *omit* ἦν GEds
11:11*ἦμεν *for* ἤμην LTTrWH
16: 9 *trs* Μακεδών τις ἦν Eds: *omit* ἦν A
20: 8 they were—we were, ἦμεν GEds
16 ἦν—εἴη LTTrAWH
22:29 *trs* αὐτὸν ἦν LTTrAWWH
27:37 ἤμεθα LTTrAWH
Gal. 4: 3 ἦμεν²—ἤμεθα TWH
15 *omit* ἦν Eds
Eph. 2: 3 ἤμεθα TTrAWH
1 Joh.2:19 *trs* ἐξ ἡμῶν ἦσαν² TrWH
Rev. 3:15*ἦς *for* εἴης GEds
4: 3 *omit* ἦν GEds
11*ἦσαν *for* εἰσίν GEds
5:11 *add* ἦν A.V.B EGEds, *see* ἀριθμός
9:10 ἦν—καί, *read* and stings; and in their tails is their power Eds
17: 4*ἦν *for* ἡ² A.V.C GEds
21:18 *omit* ἦν LTAWH

2261 **ἤπιος.**

1 Th. 2: 7 νήπιος LWH

2264 **Ἡρώδης, Ἡρῴδης** WH.

Lu. 9: 9 ὁ Ἡ.—*omit* ὁ GLTTrAW[WH]
23:12 *trs* Herod and Pilate TTrAWH
Acts 12:20 *omit* ὁ Ἡ. *read* he GEds

2265 **Ἡρωδιανοί, Ἡρῳ-** WH.

2266 **Ἡρωδιάς, Ἡρῳ-** WH.

Mar. 6:22 τῆς Ἡ.—*omit* τῆς WH

2268 **Ἡσαΐας, Ἠσαίας** WH.

Mat. 13:35*prophet—*add* Ἡσαΐου Isaiah T
Mar. 1: 2*ἐν—*add* Ἡ. GEds, *see* προφήτης
Lu. 4:17 *trs* τοῦ προφήτου Ἡ. LTTrAWH
Acts 8:28 *trs* Ἡ. τὸν προφήτην W
30 *trs* Ἡ. τὸν προφήτην LTTrAWH

2272 **ἡσύχιος.**

1 Pet. 3: 4 *trs* quiet and meek LWH

2274 **ἡττάομαι.**

2 Co. 12:13 ἡσσώθητε LTTrAWH

2276 **ἧττον, ἥττων, ἧσσον** LTTrAWH.

2278 **ἠχέω.**

Lu. 21:25 ἦχος, *read* in perplexity at the noise of the sea GLTTrAR: ἠχοῦς (ἠχώ) WH

2279 *** ἦχος** (neut.) a sound, noise.

Lu. 21:25 ἤχους *for* ἠχούσης (ἠχέω) GLTTrAR

2278 *** ἠχώ**, an echo, *see* **ἠχέω.**

2280 **Θαδδαῖος.**

Mat. 10: 3 *omit* whose surname was Thaddæus TA

2281 **θάλασσα.**

Mat. 14:24 *omit* θ. TrWH, *see* στάδιον
25 τὴν θάλασσαν LTTrAWH
26 της θαλάσσης LTTrAWH
17:27 τὴν θ.—*omit* τὴν LTTrAWWH
Rev. 10: 2 της θαλάσσης GEds

Rev. 10: 6 [and the sea, and the things which are therein] LWH
12:12 τῇ γῇ καὶ τῇ θαλάσσῃ GW
14: 7 τὴν θάλασσαν GTW

2284 θαμβέω.

Acts 9: 6 *omit* (it is) hard (*ver.* 5) *to* unto him (*ver.* 6) GEds

2288 θάνατος.

Mat. 20:18 εἰς θάνατον T: [θανάτῳ] WH
Acts 25:25 *trs* αὐτὸν θανάτου LTTrAWWH
1 Co. 15:21 ὁ θ.—*omit* ὁ LTTr[A]WWHR
55 θάνατε *for* ᾅδη (ᾅδης) LTTrAWHR
Phil. 2:27 θανάτου WH
Rev. 1:18 *trs* of death and of hell GEds
6: 8 ὁ θ.—*omit* ὁ T[AWH]
20: 6†*trs* ὁ δεύτερος (*omit* ὁ) θάνατος GLTTrAWHR
14†*trs* ὁ θάνατος ο δεύτερός ἐστιν GLTAWWHR, ὁ δεύτ. θ. ἐστιν Tr
21: 4 ὁ θ.—*omit* ὁ T
8†*trs* ὁ θάνατος ὁ δεύτερος GEds

2289 θανατόω.

Mat. 26:59 *trs* θ. αὐτόν W: αὐτὸν θανατώσουσιν LTTrA

2293 θαρσέω.

Lu. 8:48 *omit* be of good comfort LTTrAWHR

2295 θαῦμα.

2 Co. 11:14*θαῦμα *for* θαυμαστόν (-ός) Eds

2296 θαυμάζω.

Mat. 9: 8 marvelled—were afraid, φοβέομαι LTTrAWHR
Mar. 6: 6 ἐθαύμασεν TWH
51 *om.* and wondered [L]TTrAWHR
12:17 ἐθαύμαζον LTrA, ἐκθαυμάζω TWHR
15:44 ἐθαύμαζεν T
Lu. 24:12 *omit the verse* [L]T[Tr][[WH]]
Joh. 4:27 ἐθαύμαζον GEds
5:20 θαυμάζετε T
Acts 7:31 ἐθαύμαζεν GTAW
Rev. 13: 3 ἐθαυμάσθη ἐν ὅλῃ τῇ γῇ there was wonder in all the world S—ἐθαύμασεν (-μάσθη LWH) ὅλη ἡ γῆ all the world wondered A.V.BEGLTAWWHR
17: 8 θαυμασθήσονται LWH

2298 θαυμαστος.

Joh. 9:30 τὸ θαυμαστόν TTrWHR
2 Co. 11:14 θαῦμα Eds

2299 θεά, ἡ θεός.

Acts 19:35 *omit* goddess GEds
37 θεὸν GEds

2300 θεάομαι.

Joh. 8:10 *omit* and saw none but the woman WHR
Acts 8:18 εἰδέω GEds

2303 θεῖον.

Rev. 19:20 τῷ θ.—*omit* τῷ GEds
20:10 τοῦ θείου T

2307 θέλημα.

Mar. 3:35 τὰ θελήματα A
Lu. 11: 2 *omit* thy will be done GTTrAWHR
1 Pet. 4: 3 βούλημα Eds

2309 θέλω.

Mat. 20:15 *trs* ὃ θέλω ποιῆσαι LTTrAWH
21:29 *trs* WH, *see* ἀπέρχομαι
27:34 ἐθέλησεν A, ἠθέλησεν LTTrWH
Mar. 7:24 ἠθέλησεν T
9:13 ἤθελον TTrAWH
10:51 *trs* σοι θέλεις ποιήσω; TWH
15:12 *omit* θ. *read* what then shall I [Tr]WHR
Lu. 8:20 *trs* θέλοντές σε TrWH
18: 4 ἤθελεν Eds
Acts 2:12 θέλει *for* ἂν θέλοι LTTrWHR
9: 6 *omit* it is hard (*ver.* 5) *to* unto him (*ver.* 6) GEds
17:20 τί ἂν θέλοι—τίνα θέλει LTTrWHR
24: 6 *omit* and would have *to* come unto thee (*ver.* 8) LTTr[A]WHR
25: 9 *trs* θέλων τοῖς Ἰουδαίοις LTTrAWWH
2 Co. 11:32 *omit* desirous LTTr[A]WWHR
1 Th. 4:13 θέλομεν we would GEds
Jas. 4:15 θέλῃ WH
1 Pet. 3:17 θέλοι GEds
Rev. 2:21*trs καὶ οὐ (*add* θέλει) μετανοῆσαι ἐκ τῆς πορνείας αὐτῆς, *read* to repent, and she willeth not to repent of her fornication GEds
11: 5 θ.[1]—θέλει GEds
5 θ.[2]—θέλει GLAW, θελήσῃ TTrWHR: *trs* θ. αὐτοὺς LTAWWHR
6†*trs* ὁσάκις ἐὰν θ. ἐν πάσῃ πλ. GW

2311 θεμελιόω.

Lu. 6:48 for it was founded upon a rock—because it was well built, διὰ τὸ καλῶς οἰκοδομεῖσθαι (-μῆσθαι TWHR) αὐτήν TTrAWHR
1 Pet. 5:10 θεμελιώσει will settle GTAW: *omit* settle LTrWHR

2313 θεομαχεω.

Acts 23: 9 *omit* let us not fight against God (*leaving the sentence incomplete*) GEds

2316 θεός.

Mat. 3:16 τοῦ θ.—*omit* τοῦ T[A]WH
6:33 *omit* of God LT[A]WHR
19:17 *omit* GLTTrAWHR, *see* αγαθός
24 God—the heavens, οὐρανός LTTrA
21:12 *omit* of God LTrWH
22:30 *omit* of God LTr[A]WHR: *omit* τοῦ TA
32 ὁ θ.[4] θ.[5]—*omit* θ.[5] *read* he is not LTr[A]WHR, *omit* ὁ θ. T, [ὁ] θ. WH
27:54 *trs* υἱὸς θεοῦ LTrA
Mar. 1: 1 *omit* the Son of God TWH: *omit* τοῦ LTrA
10: 6 *omit* ὁ θ. *read* he [L]TTr[A]WHR
27 τῷ θ.[1]—*omit* τῷ TTrAWWH
12:26 ὁ θ.[3 4]—*omit* ὁ LTrAWWHR
27 ὁ θ.—*omit* ὁ LTrAWWHR
27 *omit* the God[8] GEds
32 *omit* θ. *read* he is one GEds
15:39 *trs* θεοῦ ἦν WH
Lu. 1:37 τοῦ θεοῦ TTrAWHR
2:38*θεῷ *for* κυρίῳ (-ριος) LTTrAWHR
4: 4 *omit* but by every word of God T[Tr]AWHR
12:31 τοῦ θ.—αὐτοῦ, *read* his kingdom LTTrAWHR
18:19 ὁ θ.—*omit* ὁ TA[WH]
27†*trs* παρὰ τῷ (*omit* τῷ L[Tr]) θεῷ ἐστιν LTTrAWH
20:36 τοῦ θ.—*omit* τοῦ TTrAWH
37 τὸν θ.[2 3]—*omit* τὸν LTTrAWHR
21: 4 *omit* of God T[Tr]AWHR
23:35 *trs* τοῦ θεοῦ ο, *read* Christ of God, the chosen TAWHR
Joh. 1:18*θεός *for* υἱός TrWH
3: 5 God—the heavens, οὐρανός T
34 *omit* θ.[3] *read* he [L]T[Tr]AWHR
5:44 [God] LWH
6:45 τοῦ θ.—*omit* τοῦ GLTTrAWWH
46*θεόν *for* πατέρα[2] (-τήρ) T
7:17 τοῦ θ.—*omit* τοῦ T
9:35 of God—of man, ἄνθρωπος TWH
10:36 τοῦ θ.—*omit* τοῦ T
13:32 *omit* if God be glorified in him [LTrA]WHR
16:27 God—the Father, πατήρ TrAWHR
19: 7 θεοῦ S—τοῦ θ. E
Acts 3:13*καί[1 2]—*add* (ὁ T) θεός, *read* God of Isaac and God of Jacob LT
25 *trs* ὁ θεὸς διέθετο LWH
4:24 *omit* ὁ θ. *read* he LTTr[A]WHR
7:32 *omit* the God[3 4] LTTrAWHR
46 God[2]—house, οἶκος LT
8:22 God—the Lord, κύριος Eds
37 *omit the verse* GLTTrAWHR
10:28 *trs* ἔδειξεν ὁ θεὸς T
33 God[2]—the Lord, κύριος LTTrWHR
12:24 of God—of the Lord, κύριος WH
13:44 of God—of the Lord, κύριος LTTr
48*θεοῦ *for* κυρίου (-ος) WHR
14:15 τὸν θ.—*omit* τὸν Eds
15:18 *omit* unto God are all his works GTTrAWHR
40 of God—of the Lord, κύριος Eds
16:10*θεός *for* κύριος LTTrAWHR
32*θεοῦ *for* κυρίου (-ος) WH
17:27*θεόν *f.* κύριον (-ος) GLTTrAWHR
Acts 18:26 *omit* of God A: *trs* ὁδὸν τοῦ θεοῦ LTTrWH
19:11 *trs* ὁ θεὸς ἐποίει LTTrAWWH
20 *Dei for* κυρίου (-ος) A.V. Vul
20:21 τὸν θ.—*omit* τὸν TTrAWH
25 *omit* of God Eds
28 of God—of the Lord, κύριος GLTTr
32 God—the Lord, κύριος WH
21:20*θεόν *for* κύριον (-ος) GEds
Ro. 1:19 *trs* θεὸς γὰρ GEds
2:13 τῷ θ.—*omit* τῷ [L]Tr[WH]
4: 2 τὸν θ.—*omit* τὸν LTTrAWWH
5: 8 *omit* ὁ θ. *read* he A
8:14 *trs* υἱοί εἰσιν θ. LTTrAW, υἱοί θ. εἰσιν WH
28*συνεργεῖ—*add* ὁ θεός, *read* God works together L[WH]
9:11 *trs* πρόθεσις τοῦ θεοῦ GEds
10:17 of God—of Christ, χριστός LTTrAWHR
11:22*add θ. LTTrAWHR, *see* χρηστότης
12: 1 *trs* τῷ θεῷ εὐάρεστον TWH
13: 1 τοῦ θ.—*omit* τοῦ GEds (WHR
14: 4 God—the Lord, κύριος LTTrA
10*θεοῦ *for* χριστοῦ (-τός) Eds
12 [τῳ θεῷ] LWH
15: 7 τοῦ θεοῦ LTTrAWH
17 τὸν θεόν GEds
19 Spirit of God—Holy (ἅγιος) Spirit GLTr[A]W[WH]R
1 Co. 1:14 *omit* τῷ θ. *read* I give thanks that TWH
29*τοῦ θεοῦ *for* αὐτοῦ GEds
2: 7 *trs* θεοῦ σοφίαν GEds
3:19 τῷ θ.—*omit* τῷ L[A]
6:20 *omit* and in your spirit, which are God's GEds
7:17 *trs* the Lord *and* God GEds
24 τῷ θ.—*omit* τῷ GEds
9:21 θεοῦ Eds
14: 2 τῷ θ.—*omit* τῷ LTTr[A]WHR
25†*trs* ὄντως ὁ (*omit* ὁ T) θεὸς Eds
2 Co. 1: 2 *omit* God W
12 θ.[1]—τοῦ θεοῦ LTTrAWWH
19 *trs* τοῦ θεοῦ γὰρ Eds
2:17 τοῦ θ.[2]—*omit* τοῦ LTTr[A]WHR
12:19 τοῦ θ.—*omit* τοῦ LTTrAWWH
Gal. 1:15 *omit* θ. *read* him [L]TA[WH]
2: 6 ὁ θεός T, [ὁ] θ. WH
3:21 [of God] LWH
4: 7 *trs* διὰ θ. through God (*omit* Christ) LTTrAWHR
Eph. 5:21 of God—of Christ, χριστός GEds
Phil. 1:14*word—*add* τοῦ θεοῦ of God LTTrAWHR
2:13 ὁ θ.—*omit* ὁ Eds
3: 3 θεοῦ, *read* by the Spirit of God Eds
Col. 3:15 of God—of Christ, χριστός GEds
16*θεῷ *for* κυρίῳ (-ριος) GEds
22 God—the Lord, κύριος GEds
1 Th. 1: 1 *omit* from God *to end of verse* [L]TTrAWHR
4 τοῦ θεοῦ T, [τοῦ] θ. WH
2: 4 τῷ θ.—*omit* τῷ [L]TTrAWHR
2 Th. 2: 4 *omit* as God GEds
16 ὁ θ.—*omit* ὁ [L]Tr[WH]
1 Ti. 3:16 God—who, ὅς GEds
5: 5 τὸν θ.—*omit* τὸν [L]T[WH]R
6:11 τοῦ θ.—*omit* τοῦ LTTr[A]WHR
13 τοῦ θ.—*omit* τοῦ T
17 τῷ θ.—*omit* τῷ TTrWHR
2 Ti. 2:14*θεοῦ *for* κυρίου (-ριος) TTrWH
Tit. 3: 8 τῷ θ.—*omit* τῷ Eds
Heb. 6:18 τὸν θεόν T
10: 9 *omit* O God GEds
11: 4 τῷ θεῷ, *read* testifying by his gifts to God LTr
6 τῷ θ.—*omit* τῷ T[TrWH]
Jas. 1:13 τοῦ θ.—*omit* τοῦ GLTTrAWWH
27 τῷ θ.—*omit* τῷ TW
2:19†*trs* εἷς ἐστὶν ὁ θ. LTTrR, εἷς ὁ (*omit* ὁ WH) θ. ἐστιν AWWH
3: 9 God[1]—the Lord, κύριος LTTrAWHR
4: 4†θ.[1]—*trs* ἐστὶν τῷ θεῷ T
1 Pet. 2: 5 τῷ θ.—*omit* τῷ LTTrAWHR
3: 5 τὸν θ.—*omit* τὸν Eds
15 God—Christ, χριστός Eds
18 τῷ θ.—*omit* τῷ W
22 τοῦ θ.—*omit* τοῦ TTr[A]WH
5: 2*willingly—*add* κατὰ θεόν according to God LTTrR
1 Joh. 3:16 love—*add* τοῦ θεοῦ of God A.V.†B
5:11 *trs* ὁ θεὸς ἡμῖν WH
13 *om.* that believe on the name of the Son of God[1] GEds
Jude 4 *omit* God[2] GEds

2316

Rev. 1: 8*ὁ κύριος—κ. ὁ θεός (the) Lord God GEds
4:11*add θ. Eds, see κύριος
5: 6 trs πνεύματα τοῦ θ. GLTTrAWHR
10 omit unto our God A
7:10 τῷ καθημένῳ ἐπὶ τοῦ θρόνου τοῦ θεοῦ ἡμῶν S—τῷ θεῷ ἡμῶν τῷ κα. ἐπὶ τῷ θρόνῳ (τοῦ θρόνου BEG) A.V.B EGEds
11: 4 God—Lord, κύριος GEds
14: 5 omit before the throne of God GEds
19: 1 τοῦ θεοῦ GEds
5 τῷ θεῷ Eds
17 τοῦ θ. GEds, see μέγας
20: 9 omit from God LTAWWHR
12 God—the throne, θρόνος GEds
21: 2 trs ἐκ τοῦ οὐρανοῦ ἀπὸ τοῦ θεοῦ GEds
3 omit (and be) their God TTrWH: trs αὐτῶν θ. LAW
4 omit God GTTr[A]WWHR
22:18 trs ἐπ' αὐτὸν ὁ θ. T

2322 θεραπεία.

Mat. 24:45 οἰκετεία LTTrAWHR

2323 θεραπεύω.

Mat. 12:10 θεραπεῦσαι T
Mar. 3: 2 θεραπεύει he healeth T
15 omit to heal sicknesses, and TTrAWHR
Lu. 4:40 ἐθεράπευεν TTrAWH
6: 7 θεραπεύει he healeth LTTrAWH
14: 3 θεραπεῦσαι LTTrAWHR

2325 θερίζω.

Rev. 14:15 τοῦ θ.—omit τοῦ Eds

2334 θεωρέω.

Mar. 3:11 ἐθεώρουν LTTrAWWH
Lu. 23:48 θεωρήσαντες having beheld LTTrAWHR
Joh. 6: 2*ἐθεώρουν for ἑώρων (ὁράω) LTrAWHR
7: 3 θεωρήσουσιν TTrAWH
Acts 17:16 θεωροῦντος Eds

2337 θηλάζω.

Lu. 23:29 gave suck—nourished, τρέφω LTTrAWHR

2342 θηρίον.

Acts 10:12 omit and wild beasts Eds
Rev. 13: 4 τὸ θηρίον—τῷ θηρίῳ GEds
14: 9 trs προσκυνεῖ τὸ θ. GEds
17: 8 θ.[1]—τὸ θηρίον A.V.C GEds
20: 4 τὸ θηρίον GEds

2344 θησαυρός.

Lu. 6:45 omit treasure of his heart[2] [L]TTrAWHR

2347 θλῖψις.

Acts 20:23 trs καὶ θλίψεις με LTTrAWH
1 Th. 3: 7 trs distress and affliction Eds

2348 θνήσκω.

Joh. 11:21 ἀποθνήσκω LTTrWHR
39 τελευτάω Eds
41 omit where the dead was laid GLTTrAWHR
12: 1 omit which had been dead [L]T[TrA]WHR
Acts 14:19 τεθνηκέναι LTTrAWH

* θορυβάζω, to confuse by noise.

Lu. 10:41 θορυβάζῃ for τυρβάζῃ (–ζω) LTTrAWHR

2351 θόρυβος.

Mar. 14: 2 trs ἔσται θόρυβος TTrAWH

2355 θρῆνος.

Mat. 2:18 omit lamentation, and LTTrAWHR

2356 θρησκεία, –κία T.

2357 θρῆσκος, θρησκός TWH.

2361 θρόμβος.

Lu. 22:43, 44 the verses [L][[WH]]

2362 θρόνος.

Acts 2:30 τὸν θρόνον LTTrAWHR
Rev. 4: 2 τοῦ θ.—τὸν θρόνον Eds
4: 4 θ.[2]—θρόνους LT
9 τῷ θρόνῳ LTTrA
5:13 τῷ θρόνῳ LTA
6:16 τῷ θρόνῳ TA
7:10 τῷ θρόνῳ LTTrAWWH, see θεός
15 τοῦ θ.[2]—τῷ θρόνῳ T
14: 5 omit before the throne of God GEds
19: 4 τῷ θρόνῳ Eds
20:12*θρόνου for θεοῦ (–ός) GEds
21: 3*θρόνου for οὐρανοῦ (–νός) LTAWHR
5 τῷ θρόνῳ GEds

2363 Θυάτειρα.

Rev. 1:11 Θυάτειραν LAW

2364 θυγάτηρ.

Mar. 5:34 θυγάτηρ LTrAWH
7:30 her daughter—the child, see παιδίον LTTrAWHR
Lu. 8:48 θυγάτηρ TrWH
12:53 θ.[1]—θυγατέρα LTTrAWHR
Joh. 12:15 θυγάτηρ LTTrAWWH

2372 θυμός.

Ro. 2: 8 trs wrath and indignation GEds

2374 θύρα.

Mat. 28: 2 omit from the door LTTrAWHR
Mar. 11: 4 τὴν θ.—omit τὴν TrAWH
Lu. 13:24*θύρας f. πύλης (–λη) GLTTrAWHR

2378 θυσία.

Mar. 9:49 omit and every sacrifice shall be salted with salt T[Tr]WHR
12:33 τῶν θ.—omit τῶν GLTrAWWH
Heb. 10: 5 trs offering and sacrifice W
8 θυσίας sacrifices Eds

2379 θυσιαστήριον.

Rev. 8: 3 τὸ θ.[1]—τοῦ θυσιαστηρίου TTrAWHR

2380 θύω.

1 Co. 5: 7 ἐτύθη S—ἐθύθη E
10:20 θ.[1]—θύουσιν LTTrAWWH
20 θ.[2]—θύουσιν trs after θεῷ LTTrAWH

2381 Θωμᾶς.

Joh. 20:28 ὁ Θ.—omit ὁ GLTTrAWWH
29 omit Thomas GEds

2384 Ἰακώβ.

Acts 7: 8 ὁ Ἰ.—omit ὁ LTTrAWH

2385 Ἰάκωβος.

Mar. 9: 2 τὸν Ἰ.—omit τὸν W
14:33 τὸν Ἰ.—omit τὸν GLTTrAW
15:40 τοῦ Ἰ—omit τοῦ LTTrAWH
16: 1 τοῦ Ἰ—omit τοῦ T[TrWH]
Lu. 8:51 trs John and James GEds
Acts 1:13 trs John and James Eds

2388 Ἰαννα, –νναί LTTrAWHR.

2390 ἰάομαι.

Mat. 13:15 ἰάσομαι LTTrAWHR
Lu. 4:18 omit to heal the broken-hearted G[L]TTrAWHR
7: 7 ἰαθήτω let be healed TTrAWH
Joh. 5:13 was healed—was impotent, ἀσθενέω T
12:40 ἰάσομαι LTTrAWHR
Acts 3:11 τοῦ ἰ. χωλοῦ the lame man which was healed—αὐτοῦ he GEds
28:27 ἰάσομαι TTrAWHR

2391 Ἰαρέδ, Ἰάρεθ L, –ρετ TWH.

2394 Ἰάσων.

Acts 17: 6 τὸν Ἰ.—omit τὸν LTTr[A]WH

2395 ἰατρός.

Lu. 8:43 εἰς ἰ.—ἰατροῖς GLTTrAWR: omit had spent all her living upon physicians WH

ιβʹ, see δώδεκα. See 1427

2396 ἴδε.

Mar. 13:21*for ἰδού[1] TTrAWH
21*for ἰδού[2] LTTrAWI
15:35*for ἰδού TTrAWH
Joh. 19: 5 ἴδου TTrAWH
26, 27*for ἰδού GLTTrAWH
Ro. 2:17 behold—but if, εἰ δέ GEds
Rev. 6: 1, 5, 7*for βλέπε (–πω) GW

2397 ἰδέα—εἰδέα TTrWH.

2398 ἴδιος.

Mat. 13:57*ἰδίᾳ πατρίδι T
Mar. 4:34*μαθηταῖς αὐτοῦ—ἰδίοις μ. his own disciples TAWHR
15:20 ἱμάτια τὰ ἴ.—ἱμ. αὐτοῦ LWHR: ἴδια ἱμάτια αὐτοῦ T
Lu. 2: 3 ἑαυτοῦ LTTrWHR
18:28*τὰ ἴδια for πάντα (πᾶς) LTTrAWHR
Acts 1:19 omit proper [TrA]WHR
24:24*ἰδίᾳ γυναικί LTTrWHR
1 Co. 7:37*καρδίᾳ αὐτοῦ—ἰδίᾳ κ. his own heart TTrAWHR
15:38 τὸ ἴ.—omit τὸ LTTrAWHR
Eph. 4:28*trs ταῖς (ἰδίαις his own LTTrW) χερσὶν τὸ ἀγαθόν LTTrAWWH
5:24 omit own LTTrAWHR
Col. 3:18 omit own GEds
1 Th. 2:15 om. ἴ. read the prophets GEds
4:11 omit own[2] Eds
2 Ti. 4: 3†trs τὰς ἰ. ἐπιθυμίας GLTTrAWWH
2 Pet. 1: 3*ἰδίᾳ δόξῃ καὶ ἀρετῇ by his own glory and virtue LTTrAWR

2400 ἰδού.

Mat. 12:47 omit the verse [T]WH
Mar. 5:22 omit behold [L]TTrAWHR
13:21 ἰ.[1]—ἴδε TTrAWH
21 ἰ.[2]—ἴδε LTTrAWH
23 omit behold [L]TTrAWH
15:35 ἴδε TTrAWH
Lu. 2: 9 omit lo T[TrA]WHR
17:21 omit lo[2] TAWHR
24:49 omit behold T
Joh. 19: 5*for ἴδε TTrAWH
26, 27 ἴδε GLTTrAWH
Jas. 3: 3 behold—now if, εἰ δέ Eds
Rev. 3:11 omit behold GEds
5: 6 omit lo GEds
6:12 omit lo GEds
15: 5 omit behold GEds

2402 ἱδρώς.

Lu. 22:43, 44 the verses [L][[WH]]

2403 Ἰεζαβήλ, –άβελ GTWHR, –έλ TrAW.

2404 Ἱεράπολις, Ἱερᾷ Πόλει WH.

2405 ἱερατεία, –τια WH.

2409 ἱερεύς.

Mar. 2:26 τοὺς ἱερεῖς TWH
Lu. 20: 1*ἱερεῖς for ἀρχιερεῖς (–ρεύς) TA
Acts 4: 1 priests—high priests, ἀρχιερεύς WH
5:24 omit high priest and the LTTrAWHR
Heb. 7:14*trs περὶ ἱερέων (ἱ. for ἱερωσύνης –νη) οὐδὲν Eds
8: 4 omit τῶν ἱ. read those that offer Eds
10:11 priest—high priest, ἀρχιερεύς LA

2410 Ἱεριχώ, Ἱερει– T, Ἰερει– WH.

* ἱερόθυτος, offered in sacrifice.

1 Co. 10:28 ἱερόθυτον for εἰδωλόθυτον LTTrAWHR

2411 ἱερόν.

Mat. 24: 1†trs ἀπὸ (ἐκ L) τοῦ ἱ. ἐπορεύετο LTTrAWHR
26:55 trs ἐν τῷ ἱ. ἐκα. διδάσ. TTrAWHR
Acts 19:27 trs ἱερὸν Ἀρτέμιδος TA

2413 ἱερος.

2 Ti. 3:15 τὰ ἱ.—omit τὰ [L]T[TrA]WHR

2414 Ἱεροσόλυμα, Ἰ– WH.

Mat. 16:21 trs εἰς Ἱ. ἀπελθεῖν LTTrAWH
Lu. 2:42 omit to Jerusalem T[Tr]AWHR
18:31 Ἱερουσαλήμ TTrAWH
Joh. 2:23 τοῖς Ἱεροσολύμοις GLTTrAWH
10:22 τοῖς Ἱ.—omit τοῖς T
Acts 11: 2 Ἱερουσαλήμ LTTrAWH
22 Ἱερουσαλήμ LTTrAWWH
18:21 omit I must to Jerusalem LTTrAWHR

Acts 20:16 'Ιερουσαλήμ T
2415 *See also* 'Ιερουσαλήμ.

'Ιεροσολυμίτης, 'Ι– WH, –μείτης TWH.

2419 **'Ιερουσαλήμ, 'Ι– WH.**

Mar. 11: 1 'Ιεροσόλυμα LTTrAWWH
Lu. 13:22 'Ιεροσόλυμα TWH
19:11 *trs* εἶναι 'Ι. αὐτόν TTrAWH
21:20 τὴν 'Ι.—*omit* τὴν LTTrAWH
24:49 *omit* of Jerusalem GLTTrAWHR
Acts 2:43**add* 'Ι. T, *see* φόβος
8:25 'Ιεροσόλυμα LTTrAWH
15: 4 'Ιεροσόλυμα TrWH
16: 4 Ιεροσολύμοις (-μα) LTTrAWWH
19:21 'Ιεροσόλυμα LTTrAWWH
21: 4 'Ιεροσόλυμα GLTTrAWWH
15 ǀ 25:20 'Ιεροσόλυμα LTTrAWWH
See also 'Ιεροσόλυμα.

2420 **ἱερωσύνη.**

Heb. 7:14 priesthood — priests, ἱερεύς: *trs* περὶ ἱ. οὐδέν Eds

2424 **'Ιησοῦς.**

Mat. 1:18 *omit* Jesus Tr[WH]
4: 1 ὁ 'Ι.—*omit* ὁ A[WH]
12 *omit* ὁ 'Ι. *read* he TTrAWWHR
18 *omit* ὁ 'Ι. *read* he GEds
23 *omit* Jesus T[Tr]AWH: *trs* ὁ 'Ι. *after* περιῆγεν L[Tr]W
8: 3 *omit* ὁ 'Ι. *read* he LTTrAWHR
5 Jesus—he, αὐτῷ GW, αὐτοῦ LTTrAWHR
7 *omit* ὁ 'Ι. *read* he LT[Tr]AWHR
22 *omit* 'Ι. *read* he T
29 *omit* Jesus GLTTrAWHR
34 τοῦ 'Ιησοῦ T
9:12 *omit* 'Ι. *read* he LT[Tr]AWHR
22 *omit* 'Ι. *read* he T
12:25 ǀ 13:36 *omit* ὁ 'Ι. *read* he LTTrAWHR
31:51 *omit* Jesus saith unto them LTTrAWHR
14:14 *omit* ὁ 'Ι. *read* he LTTrAWHR
16 *omit* 'Ι. *read* he T
22, 25 *omit* ὁ 'Ι. *read* he GEds
27 *omit* ὁ 'Ι. *read* he T[AWH]: *trs* ὁ 'Ι. αὐτοῖς LWH
15:16 *omit* 'Ι. *read* he LTTrAWHR
30 Jesus'—his, αὐτοῦ LTTrAWHR
16:20 *omit* Jesus GEds
21 ὁ 'Ι.—*omit* ὁ L[Tr]AWH
17: 8 τὸν 'Ι.—αὐτὸν 'Ι. WH
11, 20 *omit* 'Ι. *read* he LTTrAWHR
18: 2 *omit* ὁ 'Ι. *read* he TTrAWHR
20:17 ὁ 'Ι.—*omit* ὁ WH
21: 1 ὁ 'Ι.—*omit* ὁ TWH (WHR
11 *trs* the prophet Jesus LTTrA
12 ὁ 'Ι.—*omit* ὁ LTTrAWH
22:20*αὐτοῖς — *add* ὁ 'Ιησοῦς *read* Jesus saith LT
37 *omit* 'Ι. *read* he LTTrAWHR: †*trs* ἔφη αὐτῷ 'Ι. W
24: 2 *omit* 'Ι. *read* he LTTrAWHR
26:38*αὐτοῖς—*add* ὁ 'Ιησοῦς, *read* Jesus saith W
75 τοῦ 'Ι.—*omit* τοῦ LTTrAWH
28: 9 ὁ 'Ι.—*omit* ὁ TAWH
Mar. 1:41 ὁ δὲ 'Ι.—καί, *read* he LTTrWHR
5:13 *omit* forthwith Jesus, *read* he [L]TTr[A]WHR
19 ὁ δὲ 'Ι.—καί, *read* he GEds
6:34 *omit* ὁ 'Ι. *read* he G[L]TTrAWWHR
7:27 ὁ δὲ 'Ι.—καί, *read* he LTTrAWHR
8: 1 *omit* ὁ 'Ι. *read* he GEds
17 *omit* ὁ 'Ι. *read* he T[Tr]AWH
9: 8†*trs* μεθ' ἑαυτῶν εἰ μὴ τὸν 'Ι. μόνον WH
10:42†*trs* καὶ προσκαλεσάμενος αὐτοὺς ὁ 'Ι. LTTrAWHR
52 Jesus[2]—him, αὐτῷ GEds
11:11 *omit* ὁ 'Ι. καί *read* he LTTrAWHR
14, 15 *omit* ὁ 'Ι. *read* he GEds
22 ὁ 'Ιησοῦς GLTTrAWWH
33 *trs* τῷ 'Ι. λέγουσιν TTrAWHR
12:29†*trs* ἀπεκρίθη ὁ 'Ι. TTrAWHR
41 *omit* ὁ 'Ι. *read* he [L]TTrAWHR
14:18 *trs* ὁ 'Ιησοῦς εἶπεν TAWH
22 *om.* ὁ 'Ι. *read* he [L]T[Tr]AWHR
67†*trs* ἦσθα τοῦ 'Ιησοῦ LTTrAWHR
16:19*Lord — *add* 'Ιησοῦς Jesus LTr[WH]R
3:23 ὁ 'Ι.—*omit* ὁ TTrAWH
4: 4†*trs* πρὸς αὐτὸν ὁ 'Ι. LTTrAWH
8 *trs* ὁ 'Ι. εἶπεν αὐτῷ TWH
5: 8 τοῦ 'Ι.—*omit* τοῦ LTTrAWWH

Lu. 5:10 ὁ 'Ι.—*omit* ὁ [Tr]AWH
34*ὁ δέ—*add* 'Ιησοῦς, *read* Jesus said TTrAWHR
6: 3 *trs* ὁ 'Ι. πρὸς αὐτοὺς εἶπεν T
7:19 Jesus—the Lord, κύριος TTrAWHR
22 ǀ 8:38 *omit* ὁ 'Ι. *read* he [L]TTrAWHR
8:41 τοῦ 'Ι.—*omit* τοῦ T[Tr]
9:36 ὁ 'Ι.—*omit* ὁ LTTrAWWH
43 *omit* ὁ 'Ι. *read* he TTrAWHR
50 ὁ 'Ι.—*omit* ὁ T[A]WH
60 *omit* ὁ 'Ι. *read* he [L]TTrAWHR
62 *trs* ὁ 'Ι. πρὸς αὐτόν LTr
10:21 *omit* ὁ 'Ι. *read* he LTTrAWHR
39 Jesus'—the Lord's, κύριος Eds
41 Jesus—the Lord, κύριος TWHR
13: 2 *omit* ὁ 'Ι. *read* he [L]TTrAWHR
18:40 ὁ 'Ι.—*omit* ὁ [Tr]WH
22:48†*trs* 'Ιησοῦς δὲ TTrAWH
52 ὁ 'Ι.—*omit* ὁ LTTrAWH
63 Jesus—him, αὐτόν LTTrAWHR
23:28 ὁ 'Ι.—*omit* ὁ TTrAWH
34 *see* λέγω
42 τῷ 'Ι.—*omit* τῷ (*read* said, Jesus, remember) TTrAWHR
43 *omit* ὁ 'Ι. *read* he T[Tr]AWHR
24:15 ὁ 'Ι.—*omit* ὁ TTrAWH
36 *omit* Jesus GLTTrAWHR
Joh. 1:43(44) *omit* ὁ 'Ι. *read* he GEds
43(44)*αὐτῷ—*add* ὁ 'Ιησοῦς, *read* Jesus findeth Eds
47(48) ὁ 'Ι.—*omit* ὁ LTTrAWWH
48(49) ὁ 'Ι.—*omit* ὁ GLTTrAWWH
2:19 ὁ 'Ι.—*omit* ὁ LTTrAWWH
24 ὁ 'Ι.—*omit* ὁ LTTrAWH
3: 2 Jesus—him, αὐτόν GEds
3 ὁ 'Ι.—*omit* ὁ LTTrAWWH
5 ὁ 'Ι.—*omit* ὁ GLT[TrA]W[WH]
10 ὁ 'Ι.—*omit* ὁ GLTTrAWWH
4: 1*'Ιησοῦς *for* κύριος T
13, 44 ὁ 'Ι.—*omit* ὁ GLTTrAWWH
16 *om.* ὁ 'Ι.—*read* he [L]T[Tr]AWH *omit* ὁ L
46 *om.* ὁ 'Ι.—*read* he GLTTrAWHR: *trs* πάλιν ὁ 'Ι. W
50 'Ι.[2]—ὁ 'Ιησοῦς LTTrAWWH
5: 1 ὁ 'Ι.—*omit* ὁ LTTrAWWH
17 *omit* 'Ι. *read* he TWH
6: 3 ὁ 'Ι.—*omit* ὁ LTTrAWH
5 *trs* τοὺς ὀφθαλμοὺς ὁ 'Ι. LTTrAWWH
14 *omit* ὁ 'Ι.—*read* he TTrAWHR
17†*trs* (*om.* ὁ) 'Ι. πρὸς αὐτούς T
29 ὁ 'Ι.—*omit* ὁ T
43 ὁ 'Ι.—*omit* ὁ TTrWH
7: 1 *trs* μετὰ ταῦτα πε. ὁ ([ὁ]TrWH) 'Ιησοῦς Eds
14 ὁ 'Ι.—*omit* ὁ LTTrAWH
16 ὁ 'Ι.—*omit* ὁ TTrWH
21 ὁ 'Ι.—*omit* ὁ TTrAWH
39 ὁ 'Ι.—*omit* ὁ LTTrAWWH
50 *for* αὐτόν A.V. [?]
8: 9 *omit* ὁ 'Ι. *read* he WH
12 *trs* αὐτοῖς ἐλά. ὁ ([ὁ] TrWH) 'Ι. LTTrAWH
19 ὁ 'Ι.—*omit* ὁ GLTTrAWWH
20 *omit* ὁ 'Ι. *read* he GEds
21 *omit* ὁ 'Ι. *read* he Eds
25, 39 [ὁ] 'Ι. TrWH
34, 42 ὁ 'Ι.—*omit* ὁ L[TrWH]
58 ὁ 'Ι.—*omit* ὁ TTrWH
9: 3 ὁ 'Ι.—*omit* ὁ GLTTrAWWH
35 ὁ 'Ι.—*omit* ὁ T[Tr]WH
10:23, 25, 34 [ὁ] 'Ι. TrWH
11: 9, 20 ὁ 'Ι.—*omit* ὁ GLTTrAWWH
21 τὸν 'Ι.—*omit* τὸν T[Tr]WH
32, 46 ὁ 'Ι.—*omit* ὁ LTTrAWH
39 ὁ 'Ι.—*omit* ὁ L[Tr]
44†*trs* [ὁ] 'Ι. αὐτοῖς WH
45 *omit* ὁ 'Ι.—*read* he GEds
51 ὁ 'Ι.—*omit* ὁ GLTTrAWWH
54†*trs* ὁ οὖν 'Ι. TrAWH
12: 1**add at end* ὁ (*omit* ὁ TWHR) 'Ιησοῦς, *read* Jesus raised Eds
3 [τοῦ] 'Ι. TrWH
12 ὁ 'Ι.—*omit* ὁ GLTTrAWWH
16 ὁ 'Ι.—*omit* ὁ TTrAWWH
30 ὁ 'Ι.—*omit* ὁ TTrAWH
36 ὁ 'Ι.—*omit* ὁ LTTrAWH
13: 3 *omit* ὁ 'Ι. *read* he [L]TTrAWHR
8†*trs* (*omit* ὁ) 'Ιησοῦς αὐτῷ LTTrAWH
10 ὁ 'Ι.—*omit* ὁ T[Tr]WH
21, 27 ὁ 'Ι.—*omit* ὁ TTrAWH
26 [ὁ] 'Ι. TrWH
29 ὁ 'Ι.—*omit* ὁ T[Tr]AWH
31 ὁ 'Ι.—*omit* ὁ TTrAWH
36 ὁ 'Ι.—*omit* ὁ LTTrAWHR
38 ὁ 'Ι.—*omit* ὁ Eds
14: 6 ὁ 'Ι.—*omit* ὁ TWH

Joh. 14:23 ὁ 'Ι.—*omit* ὁ GLTTrAWWH
16:19 ὁ 'Ι.—*omit* ὁ TTrAWHR
31 ὁ 'Ι.—*omit* ὁ TTrAWH
17: 1 ὁ 'Ι.—*omit* ὁ TWH
18: 1, 2 ὁ 'Ι.—*omit* ὁ TTrAWH
5 *om.* ὁ 'Ι. *read* he TrAWH: *om.* ὁ T
8 ὁ 'Ι.—*omit* ὁ GLTTrAWWH
20 ὁ 'Ι.—*omit* ὁ TTrWH
23 ὁ 'Ι.—*omit* ὁ LTTrAWH
34 ὁ 'Ι.—*omit* ὁ LTTrAWHR
36 ὁ 'Ι.—*omit* ὁ GLTTrAWWH
37 ὁ 'Ι.—*omit* ὁ [A]W[WH]
19: 5 [ὁ] 'Ι. TrWH
11 ὁ 'Ι.—*omit* ὁ GLTTrAWWH
30 *om.* ὁ 'Ι. *read* he T: [ὁ] 'Ι. TrWH
38 of Jesus[3] — of him, αὐτοῦ LTrAWHR: him, αὐτόν T
39 Jesus—him, αὐτόν Eds
20:14 ὁ 'Ι.—*omit* ὁ GLTTrAWWH
15 ὁ 'Ι.—*omit* ὁ LTTrAWH
16, 17, 24 ὁ 'Ι.—*omit* ὁ LTTrAWH
21 *omit* ὁ 'Ι. *read* he TTr[AWH]
29 [ὁ] 'Ι. TrWH
31 ὁ 'Ι.—*omit* ὁ GLTTrAWWH
21: 1 *omit* ὁ TTrWH: *omit* ὁ 'Ι. A
4 ὁ 'Ι.—*omit* ὁ LTTrAWH
5 ὁ 'Ι.—*omit* ὁ T[Tr]AWH, [ὁ 'Ι.]L
10, 12 [ὁ] 'Ι. TrWH
13 ὁ 'Ι.—*omit* ὁ LTTrAWHR
14 ὁ 'Ι.—*omit* ὁ LTTrAWH
17 ὁ 'Ι.—*omit* ὁ LTTrAWH: *omit* 'Ι. T[Tr]
25 *omit the verse* T
Acts 1: 1 ὁ 'Ι.—*omit* ὁ LTrAWWH
16 τὸν 'Ι.—*omit* τὸν LTTrAWH
3:20 *trs* Christ Jesus LTTrAWHR
26 *omit* Jesus GLTTrAWHR
5:42 *trs* Christ Jesus LTTrAWHR
8:12 τοῦ 'Ι.—*omit* τοῦ GLTTrAWWH
37 *omit the verse* GLTTrAWHR
9:20*'Ιησοῦν *for* χριστόν GEds
27 τοῦ 'Ι.—*omit* τοῦ LTTrAWH
29(28) *omit* Jesus Eds
10:48*'Ιησοῦ χριστοῦ *for* τοῦ κυρίου (-ος) LTTrWHR
16: 7*Spirit—*add* 'Ιησοῦ of Jesus GEds
17: 3 ὁ 'Ιησοῦς AWHR
18:25*'Ιησοῦ *for* κυρίου[2] (-ος) Eds
19:10 *omit* Jesus GEds
24:24*Christ — *add* 'Ιησοῦν Jesus LTWHR
Ro. 1: 1 *trs* Christ Jesus TTr
2:16 *trs* Christ Jesus TWH
6: 3, 11 *trs* Christ Jesus A.V.[?]
8:11 τὸν 'Ιησοῦν TTr[A]WH
11*Christ — *add* 'Ιησοῦν Jesus [L]TWHR: *trs* ἐκ νεκρῶν χριστὸν 'Ι. TWH
34*Christ—*add* 'Ιησοῦς Jesus [L]T[WH]R
10: 9 κύριος 'Ιησοῦς WH
15: 5 *trs* Jesus Christ Tr
8 *omit* Jesus LTTrAWHR
16 *trs* Christ Jesus Eds
16:18 *omit* Jesus GEds
24 *omit the verse* LTTr[A]WHR
1 Co. 1: 1 *trs* Christ Jesus LTTrAW
4:17*Christ—*add* 'Ιησοῦ Jesus LT[WH]
5: 5 *omit* Jesus AWH
12: 3 'Ιησοῦς *bis* Eds
16:22 *omit* Jesus Christ LTTrAWHR
2 Co. 1: 1 *trs* Christ Jesus TTrAWHR
19 *trs* Christ Jesus TWH
4: 6 *omit* Jesus LTTrAWH
5:18 *omit* Jesus Eds
13: 5 *trs* Christ Jesus TTr
Gal. 2:16 *trs* Christ Jesus[1] TTrWH
16 *trs* Jesus Christ[2] A.V.[?]
3:14 *trs* Jesus Christ A.V.[?]TrWH
5:24*χριστοῦ 'Ιησοῦ, *read* of Christ Jesus [L]TTrAWHR
6:15 *omit* in Christ Jesus TTrAWHR
Eph. 1: 1[1] ǀ 2:20 *trs* Christ Jesus LTTrAWHR
3: 1 *omit* Jesus T[A]
6*Christ—*add* 'Ιησοῦ Jesus LTTrAWHR
9 *omit* by Jesus Christ GEds
14 *omit* of our Lord Jesus Christ Eds
Phil. 1: 1 *trs* Christ Jesus[1] Eds
2 *trs* Christ Jesus W
6 *trs* Christ Jesus LTTrAW
8 *trs* Christ Jesus GEds
2:21 *trs* Jesus Christ A.V.Vul GLTrAWR
3:12 *omit* Jesus GLTrAW[WH]
Col. 1: 1 *trs* Christ Jesus Eds
2 *omit* and the Lord Jesus Christ G[L]TTrAWWHR

Col. 1:28 *omit* Jesus GEds
4:12*Christ—*add* 'Ιησοῦ Jesus LTTrAWHR
1 Th. 1: 1 *omit* from God *to end of verse* [L]TTrAWHR
2 Th. 2: 8*Lord—*add* 'Ιησοῦς Jesus GLTTrAW[WH]R
1 Ti. 1: 1 *trs* Christ Jesus[1] TTrAWWHR
1 *trs* Christ Jesus[2] GEds
2 *trs* Jesus Christ A.V.Er
16 *trs* Christ Jesus LTTrAWH
4: 6 *trs* Christ Jesus Eds
5:21 *trs* Christ Jesus (*omit* Lord) Eds
2 Ti. 1: 1 *trs* Christ Jesus[1] TTrAWWHR
10 *trs* Christ Jesus LTTrWHR
2: 3 *trs* Christ Jesus Eds
4: 1 *trs* Christ Jesus (*omit* Lord) Eds
22 *omit* Jesus Christ TTr[A]WHR
Tit. 1: 4 *trs* Christ Jesus (*omit* Lord) LTTrAWHR
2:13 *trs* Christ Jesus TTrWH
Philem. 6 *omit* Jesus LTTr[A]WHR
9 *trs* Christ Jesus LTTrAWHR
Heb. 10:10 τοῦ 'Ι.—*omit* τοῦ GEds
1 Pet. 5:10 *omit* Jesus T[Tr]WHR
14 *omit* Jesus LTTrAWHR
Jude 5*'Ιησοῦς *for* κύριος LA
25*add 'Ι. GEds, *see* κύριος
Rev. 1: 9 *trs* Christ Jesus[1] W
12:17 τοῦ 'Ι.—*omit* τοῦ GEds
19:10 τοῦ 'Ι. *bis*—*omit* τοῦ Eds

2424* 'Ιησοῦς, son of Eliezer.

Lu. 3:29 'Ιησοῦ *for* 'Ιωσῆ LTTrAWHR

2425 ἱκανός.

Lu. 7: 6 *trs* ἱκανός εἰμι TTrAWH
11 *omit* many of [L]Tr[A]WHR
8:27 ἱκανῷ TTrWHR, *see* χρόνος
23: 8 ἱκανῶν LTTrAWHR, *see* χρόνος
Acts 5:37 *omit* much LTTrAWHR
Ro. 15:23*ἱκανῶν *for* πολλῶν (–λύς) TrAWH

2440 ἱμάτιον.

Mat. 11: 8 *omit* ἱ. [L]TTrAWHR (WHR
23: 5 *omit* of their garments LTTrA
24:18 τὸ ἱμάτιον garment LTTrWHR
27:35 *omit* that it might *to end of verse* GLTTrAWHR
Mar. 2:21 ἱμάτιον παλαιόν LTTrAWHR
Heb. 1:12*αὐτούς—*add* ὡς ἱμάτιον, *read* fold them up, as a garment, L[Tr]WHR

2441 ἱματισμός.

Mat. 27:35 *omit* that it might *to end of verse* GLTTrAWHR

2442 ἱμείρομαι.

1 Th. 2: 8 ὁμείρομαι GEds

2443 ἵνα.

Mat. 12:17*for ὅπως LTTrAWH
20:32*θέλετε—*add* [ἵ.] LA
27:35 *om.* GLTTrAWHR, *see* ἱματισμός
Mar. 4:22*μή—*add* ἵ. LT[A]WHR
5:23**for* ὅπως LTTrAWHR
Lu. 11:54 *omit* that they might accuse him T[Tr]AWHR
Joh. 12: 7*αὐτήν—*add* ἵ. Eds
18:28 *omit* ἵ.[2] LTTrAWHR
Acts 5:26 *omit* ἵ. LTTr[A]WHR
Ro. 15:31 *omit* ἵ.[2] LTTrAWHR
1 Co. 9:15 ἵ. τις—οὐδεὶς LTTrWHR
2 Co. 12: 7 *omit* lest I should be exalted above measure[2] [L]Tr[A]
1 Th. 4: 1*'Ιησοῦ—*add* ἵ. A.V.Vul LTTrA[WH]R
1 Joh. 5:13 *omit* καὶ ἵ. GEds, *see* πιστεύω
2 Joh. 6*ἵ. καθώς T
Rev. 13:15*ποιήσῃ—*add* ἵ. LTr[A]W[WH]R
15 *omit* ἵ.[2] Eds

2445 'Ιόππη.

Acts 9:42 τῆς 'Ι.—*omit* τῆς [Tr]WH
10:23 τῆς 'Ι.—*omit* τῆς GLTTrAWWH

2446 'Ιορδάνης.

Mar. 1: 5 *trs* ὑπ' αὐτοῦ ἐν τῷ 'Ι. ποταμῷ TTrAWH
9 *trs* εἰς τὸν 'Ι. ὑπὸ 'Ιωάννου LTTrAWH

2448 'Ιουδαία.

Lu. 4:44*'Ιουδαίας *for* Γαλιλαίας AWH
Acts 1: 8 τῇ 'Ι.—*omit* τῇ A

2453 'Ιουδαῖος.

Joh. 3:25 'Ιουδαίου a Jew GEds
4: 9 *omit* for the Jews have no dealings with the Samaritans T[WH]
5:16 *trs* οἱ 'Ι. τὸν 'Ιησοῦν LTTrAWHR
19:21 *trs* τῶν 'Ιουδαίων[3] εἰμί TrAWH
Acts 9:22 τοὺς 'Ι.—*omit* τοὺς TWHR
13:42 the Jews—they, αὐτῶν GEds
17:10 *trs* ἀπῄεσαν τῶν 'Ι. A
21:20 *omit* of Jews T: ἐν τοῖς 'Ιουδαίοις among the Jews LTrAWWHR
23:12†*trs* συστροφὴν οἱ 'Ιουδαῖοι GEds
30 *omit* the Jews LTTrAWHR, *see* ἐξαυτῆς
26: 4 οἱ 'Ι.—*omit* οἱ LTrAWHR
7 τῶν 'Ι.—*omit* τῶν GEds
21 οἱ 'Ι.—*omit* οἱ TTrWHR
28:29 *omit the verse* LTTrAWHR

2455 'Ιούδας.

Mar. 14:10 ὁ 'Ι.—*omit* ὁ LTTrAWWH
43 ὁ 'Ιούδας LTrAW, [ὁ] 'Ι. WH
Lu. 3:26 'Ιωδά TTrAWHR
Joh. 13: 2†*trs* ἵνα παραδοῖ αὐτὸν 'Ιούδας Σίμωνος 'Ισκαριώτης TTrAWHR
29 ὁ 'Ι.—*omit* ὁ LTTrAWH

2462 ἵππος.

Rev. 9:19**add* ἵ. GLTTrAWHR, *see* ἐξουσία

2463 ἶρις.

Rev. 10: 1 ἡ ἶρις the rainbow GEds

2464 'Ισαάκ.

Acts 7: 8 ὁ 'Ι.—*omit* ὁ LTTrAWH

2466 'Ισαχάρ, 'Ισασχάρ B, 'Ισσάχαρ T, 'Ισσαχάρ TrAWHR.

2469 'Ισκαριώτης.

Mat. 10: 4 ὁ 'Ισκαριώτης EGLTAWWH
Mar. 3:19 'Ισκαριώθ LTTrAWWH
14:10 'Ισκαριώθ TAWH: *omit* ὁ LTTrAWWH
43*Judas—*add* ὁ 'Ισκαριώτης Iscariot LT[Tr]A
Lu. 6:16 'Ισκαριώθ LTTrAWH
Joh. 6:71 'Ισκαριώτου, *read* Judas (son) of Simon Iscariot LTTrAWHR
12: 4†*trs* 'Ιούδας ὁ 'Ι. εἷς ἐκ (*omit* ἐκ TrWHR) τῶν μαθητῶν αὐτοῦ TTrAWHR
13: 2 'Ισκαριώτης TTrAWHR, *see* 'Ιούδας
26 'Ισκαριώτου, *read* Judas (son) of Simon Iscariot TTrAWHR

2474 'Ισραήλ.

Mat. 10:23 τοῦ 'Ι.—*omit* τοῦ LTrA[WH]
Mar. 15:32 τοῦ 'Ι.—*omit* τοῦ LTTrWH
Acts 4: 8 *omit* of Israel LTTr[A]WHR
Ro. 10: 1 Israel—them, αὐτῶν GEds

'Ισραηλίτης, –λείτης TWH.

2476 ἵστημι, ἱστάω, ἱστάνω.

(*pluperf.* ἱστήκειν WH)

Mat. 2: 9 ἐστάθη LTTrAWH
4: 5 ἔστησεν set LTTrAWHR
12:47 *omit the verse* [T]WH
16:28 ἑστώτων GLTTrAWH: ἑστῶτες (*omit* τῶν) W
24:15 ἑστός S—ἑστώς EG
27:11 ἐστάθη LTTrAWH
47 ἑστηκότων TTrWH
Mar. 3:25†*trs* ἡ οἰκία ἐκείνη σταθῆναι (στῆναι TrAWH) LTTrAWH
26 στῆναι TTrAWH
31 στήκω TTrAWH
13: 9 ἄγω A.V.Br
14 ἑστός S—ἑστώς EG, ἑστηκότα TTrAWHR, ἑστηκός L
Lu. 9:27 ἑστώτων GLTrAW
17:12 ἀνίστημι WH
24:17*; καὶ ἐστάθησαν ([; καὶ ἐ.] A) σκυθρωποί, *read* as ye walk? And they stood sad TTrAWHR
Joh. 1:26 στήκω TTrAWHR
8: 9 standing—being, ὤν WWHR
44 ἔστηκεν WHR
Acts 24:21 *trs* ἐν αὐτοῖς ἑστώς Eds
25:10 *trs* ἑστὼς *before* ἐπί TWH
Ro. 3:31 ἱστάνομεν LTTrAWH
Col. 4:12 σταθῆτε TTrWH
1 Pet. 5:12 στῆτε stand ye LTTrAWHR

Rev. 5: 6 ἑστηκώς TTr
7: 9 ἑστῶτας AW
11 εἱστήκεισαν LTTrA, ἑσ– W
11: 1 *add* ἵ. A.V.B R, *see* ἄγγελος
4 ἑστῶτες GEds
12: 4 ἕστηκεν WHR
13: 1(12:18) ἐστάθη it stood LTrAWHR
14: 1 ἑστός LTTrAWWH

2478 ἰσχυρός.

Mat. 14:30 *omit* boisterous TWHR
Lu. 11:22 ὁ ἰ.—*omit* ὁ LTTrAWHR
15:14 ἰσχυρά LTTrAWWH
Rev. 6:15*ἰσχυροί *for* δυνατοί (–τός) GEds
18: 2*ἰσχυρᾷ *for* ἰσχύϊ (–χύς) GEds

2479 ἰσχύς.

Lu. 10:27 τῇ ἰσχύϊ LTTrWHR, *see* ψυχή
Rev. 18: 2 ἰσχυρός GEds

2480 ἰσχύω.

Mar. 5: 4 *trs* ἴσχυεν αὐτὸν LTTrAWWH
Joh. 21: 6 ἴσχυον LTTrAWHR
Acts 27:16 *trs* ἰσχύσαμεν μόλις Eds
Gal. 6:15 availeth—is, ἐστίν GEds
Rev. 12: 8 ἴσχυσεν he prevailed GWH

2486 ἰχθύς.

Lu. 5: 6 *trs* πλῆθος ἰχθύων GTTrAWWH
9:13 *trs* ἰχθύες δύο GLTTrAWWH
1 Co. 15:39 *trs* of birds, (and) another of fishes Eds

2490 'Ιωαννᾶς.

Lu. 3:27 'Ιωανάν LTTrAWHR

2491 'Ιωάννης, 'Ιωάνης TrWH.

(Apostle.)

Mar. 9: 2 τὸν 'Ι.—*omit* τὸν GLTrAWH
38 ὁ 'Ι.—*omit* ὁ GLW
14:33 τὸν 'Ιωάνην WH
Lu. 8:51 *trs* John and James GEds
9:49 ὁ 'Ι.—*omit* ὁ LTrAWH
Acts 1:13 *trs* John and James Eds
3:11 τὸν 'Ιωάννην LTTrWH
Rev. 1: 1 'Ιωάνει WH
21: 2 *omit* I John GEds

(Baptist.)

Mat. 3:14 *omit* 'Ι. *read* he LT[TrA]WWH
11: 4 'Ιωάνει WH
14: 4†*trs* ὁ (*om.* ὁ T) 'Ι. αὐτῷ LTWH
10 τὸν 'Ι.—*omit* τὸν LTTrAWH
21:32 *trs* 'Ι. πρὸς ὑμᾶς LTTrAWH
Mar. 1: 6 ὁ 'Ιωάννης TTrAWH
Lu. 7:18, 22 'Ιωάννει T, 'Ιωάνει TrWH
Joh. 1:28 ὁ 'Ι. LTTrWH, [ὁ] 'Ι. A
29 *omit* ὁ 'Ι. *read* he GEds
35 ὁ 'Ι.—*omit* ὁ LTrAWH
3:24 ὁ 'Ι.—*omit* ὁ T[TrA]
Acts 13:25 ὁ 'Ι.—*omit* ὁ LTTrAWH

(Chief Priest.)

Acts 4: 6 'Ιωάννης LTTrAWHR

(Mark.)

Acts 15:37 τὸν 'Ι.—*omit* τὸν GLAR

(Father of Peter), *see* 'Ιωνᾶς

* 'Ιωβήδ, *see* 'Ωβήδ.

2493 'Ιωήλ.

Acts 2:16 *omit* Joel A

2494 'Ιωνάν, 'Ιωνάμ TTrAWHR.

2495 'Ιωνᾶς.

Mat. 16:17 *see* Βὰρ 'Ιωνᾶ
Joh. 1:42(43) | 21:15, 16, 17 Jonas—John 'Ιωάνου LTrWHR, 'Ιωάννου TA

2499 'Ιωσῆς.

Mat. 13:55 Joses — Joseph, 'Ιωσήφ LTTrAWHR
27:56 Joses—Joseph, 'Ιωσήφ TWH
Mar. 6: 3 | 15:40 'Ιωσῆτος LTTrAWH
15:47 ἡ 'Ι. R: ἡ 'Ιωσῆτος LTTrAWH
Lu. 3:29 Jose—Jesus, 'Ιησοῦς LTTrAWHR
Acts 4:36 Joses—Joseph, 'Ιωσήφ Eds

2501 'Ιωσήφ.

(*all in one list.*)

Mat. 1:24 ὁ 'Ι.—*omit* ὁ T[WH]
13:55*'Ιωσήφ *for* 'Ιωσῆς LTTrAWHR
27:56*'Ιωσήφ *for* 'Ιωσῆ TWH

Lu. 2:33 **Joseph—his father,** ὁ πατὴρ αὐτοῦ GTTrAWHR
43 **Joseph and his mother—his parents,** γονεῖς LTTrAWHR
3:26 Joseph — Josech, Ἰωσήχ TTrAWHR
Joh. 19:38 ὁ Ἰ.—*omit* ὁ LTTrAWWH
Acts 4:36*Ἰωσήφ *for* Ἰωσῆς Eds
7:13 Joseph's—his, αὐτοῦ T: τοῦ Ἰ. —*omit* τοῦ LTTrAWH

2502
Ἰωσίας, Ἰωσείας LTTrAWH.

2504 **κἀγώ, κἀμοί, κἀμέ.**

Mat. 10:33 ***trs*** κἀγὼ αὐτὸν LTTrAWH
18:33*for καὶ ἐγώ LTTrAWH
26:15 καὶ ἐγώ T
Mar. 11:29 *omit* also, κἀγώ TTrAWHR
Lu. 2:48 καὶ ἐγώ WH
16: 9 καὶ ἐγώ TTrAWH
19:23*for καὶ ἐγώ LTTrAWH
24:49*for καὶ ἰδού ἐγώ T
Joh. 6:44*, 54*for καὶ ἐγώ LTTrAWH
14:16*for καὶ ἐγώ LTTrAWH
21*for καὶ ἐγώ LTTrAWWH
15:10*for ἐγώ T
16:32*for καὶ ἐμέ TTrAWH
17: 6*for καὶ ἐμοί TrWH
11*, 22*for καὶ ἐγώ LTTrAWH
Acts 10:26 καὶ ἐγώ TTrAWH
28*for καὶ ἐμοί LTTrAWH
26:29 καὶ ἐγώ WH
1 Co. 2: 3*for καὶ ἐγώ LTTrAWH
3: 1*for καὶ ἐγώ GLTTrAWWH
16:10*for καὶ ἐγώ LTTrA
2 Co. 2:10*for καὶ ἐγώ LTTrAWWH
Gal. 2: 8*for καὶ ἐμοί LTrW
Rev. 22: 8*for καὶ ἐγώ LTTrAWWH

2508 **καθαίρω.**

Heb. 10: 2 καθαρίζω Eds

2509 **καθάπερ.**

Ro. 3: 4*for καθώς TTrWH
9:13* | 10:15*for καθώς WH
11: 8*for καθώς TTrWH
1 Co. 10:10*for καθώς TTrWHR
Heb. 5: 4 καθώσπερ TTrAWHR

2511 **καθαρίζω.**

Mat. 8: 3 ἐκαθερίσθη TWH
10: 8 ***trs*** raise the dead, cleanse the lepers GEds
Mar. 1:42 ἐκαθερίσθη TAWH
7:19 καθαρίζων LTTrAWHR
Acts 10:15 ἐκαθέρισεν Tr
11: 9 ἐκαθέρισεν Tr
Heb. 10: 2*κεκαθα(ε L)ρισμένους *for* κεκαθαρμένους (καθαίρω) Eds

2513 **καθαρός.**

1 Pet. 1:22 *omit* pure, *read* from the heart LTTrAWHR
Rev. 19: 8 ***trs*** white clean GLTTrAWHR
22: 1 *omit* pure GEds

2516 **καθέζομαι.**

Joh. 6: 3*ἐκαθέζετο *for* ἐκάθητο (κάθημαι) T
Acts 20: 9*καθεζόμενος *for* καθήμενος (-μαι) Eds

2519 **καθηγητής.**

Mat. 23: 8 διδάσκαλος Eds
10†***trs*** ὅτι κ. ὑμῶν ἐστὶν εἷς for your master is one LTTrAWH

καθήκω.

Acts 22:22 καθῆκεν GLTTrAWWH

2521 **κάθημαι.**

Mat. 19:28*καθήσεσθε *for* καθίσεσθε (-ίζω)
26:69 ***trs*** ἐκάθητο ἔξω LTTrAWH (WH
Mar. 12:36 καθίζω TrA
Lu. 10:13 καθήμενοι LTTrAWHR
22:30*καθήσεσθε TTr, κάθησθε A, καθῆσθε WH *for* καθίσησθε (-ίζω)
Joh. 6: 3 καθέζομαι T
Acts 20: 9 καθέζομαι Eds
Jas. 2: 3 ***trs*** ἢ κάθου ἐκεῖ WH
Rev. 11:16 *omit* οἱ² L[AWH]R, οἱ (οἱ *before* ἐνώπιον R) κάθηνται TTrR
14: 6*καθημένους *for* κατοικοῦντας (-κέω) GEds
14 καθήμενον ὅμοιον GEds

2523 **καθίζω.**

Mat. 19:28 κ.²—κάθημαι WH
Mar. 11: 2 ἐκάθισεν WHR
12:36*κάθισον *for* κάθου (-θημαι) TrA
Lu. 22:30 καθίσεσθε GLWR: κάθημαι TTrAWH
Eph. 1:20 καθίσας LTTrAWHR
Heb. 12: 2 κεκάθικεν GEds

2524 **καθίημι.**

Acts 9:25†***trs*** διὰ τοῦ τείχους κ. αὐτόν LTTrAWHR

2525 **καθίστημι.**

Acts 6: 3 καταστήσομεν S—καταστήσωμεν A.V. Vul EW
17:15 καθιστάνοντες LTTrAWH
Heb. 2: 7 *omit* and didst set *to end of verse* G[L]T[Tr]A[WH]

2526 **καθό.**

1 Pet. 4:13 καθό S—καθώς E

2530 **καθότι.**

Acts 17:31*for διότι Eds

2531 **καθώς.**

Mar. 1: 2*for ὡς TTrWHR
Lu. 17:28*for καὶ ὡς TTrAWHR
Joh. 10:26 *omit* as I said unto you [L]TTr[A]WHR
Acts 10:47 ὡς LTTrAWHR
Ro. 3: 4 καθάπερ TTrWH
9:13 | 10:15 καθάπερ WH
11: 8 καθάπερ TTrWH
1 Co. 10:10 καθάπερ TTrWHR
1 Th. 4: 1*add κ. Eds, *see* περιπατέω
1 Pet. 4:13 καθό S—καθώς E

* **καθώσπερ,** even as, καθώς περ Tr.

Heb. 5: 4 *for* καθάπερ TTrAWHR

2532 **καί.**

Mat. 3: 2 *omit* and LT[Tr]AWHR
10 *omit* also Eds
16 κ. βαπτισθείς—β. δέ LTTrAWWH
16 *omit* and² LT[TrA]WH
4:24 *omit* and² LTrAWHR
5:13 *omit* and LTTrAWHR
6:21 *omit* also L[WH]
25 κ.¹—ἤ LTr[WH]R: *omit* κ.¹ T
8: 7 *omit* and¹ LT[Tr]AWH
8 κ. ἀποκριθείς—ἀ. δέ LTTrWH
13 *omit* and² LT[Tr]AWHR
9:10 *omit* κ.² T
10: 2*κ. Ἰάκωβος and James LTWH
11: 5 [and¹] LTr
5*κ. νεκροί and the dead TTrAWHR, [κ.] ν. L
16 and—who, ὃς LTTrAWHR
17 *omit* and¹ LTTrAWHR
12: 8 *omit* even GEds
22 *omit* both LTTrAWHR
44*empty—*add* κ. and [L]T[WH]
13: 4 *omit* and³ AWH
14:13 κ. ἀκούσας—ἀ. δέ LTTrAWHR
19 *omit* and² GLTTrAWWH
26 δέ LTWH, *see* μαθητής
15: 6(5) *omit* and LTTr[A]WHR
31*κ. χωλούς and the lame LTTrA
36 *omit* and¹ LTTrWHR (WHR
36*ἰχθύας—*add* κ. LTWHR
16:17 κ. ἀποκριθείς—ἀ. δέ LTTrAWHR
19 *omit* and¹ T[A]WHR
17: 7*Ἰησοῦς κ. LTTrWH: *omit* κ.² LTWH
18:12*ὄρη—*add* κ. LTrWH
15 *omit* and¹ GLTTrAWHR
20: 9 κ. ἐλθόντες—ἐ. δέ LWH
23 *omit* and¹ LTTrAWHR
24 κ. ἀκούσαντες—ἀ. δέ TA
21: 5 *omit* and¹ A
28 *omit* and¹ TWH
30 κ. προσελθών—π. δέ LTTrAWH
45 κ. ἀκούσαντες—ἀ. δέ T
22:27 *omit* also T[Tr]AWHR
23:34 *omit* and³ LTTrAWHR
24:27 *omit* also Eds
37 *omit* also LTTrAWHR
39 *omit* also LTrAWHR
25:11 *omit* also L[Tr]
17 *omit* and [L]TWH
26:26 *omit* κ.³ LTTrWHR
27 *omit* κ.² L[TrWH]
33 *omit* κ. GEds
60 *omit* yea GLTTrWHR
71 *omit* also TWH
27:31 *omit* and² T
40*κ. κατάβηθι LT
41 *omit* also [L]T[WH]
28: 2*οὐρανοῦ—*add* κ. TTrWHR
Mar. 1: 4 *omit* and [Tr]AWH (A
15 *om.* and saying T[WH], *om.* and
37*add κ. TTrAWHR, *see* εὑρίσκω
40 *omit* and³ T[A]WH
2: 1 *omit* and² [L]TTrAWHR
9 *omit* and¹ G[Tr]AW[WH]
11 *omit* and¹ G[L]TTrAWWHR
21 *omit* also GEds
27*ἐγένετο—*add* κ. TTrAWHR
3:31*for οὖν Eds, *see* ἔρχομαι
33*for ἤ LTTrWHR
4: 5*ground-*add* κ. and [LTr]A[WH]
5:15 *omit* and⁴ LTTrAWHR
38*θόρυβον—*add* κ. A.V.C GEds
6:22 *omit* and³ LTTrAWHR, *see* ἀρέσκω
30 *omit* both Eds
38 *omit* and¹ [L]TTrAWHR
48 *omit* and² LTTrAWHR
50 κ.²—ὁ δέ TWHR
55*ἐκείνην—*add* κ. TTrWHR
7: 5*for ἔπειτα LTTrAWHR
12 *omit* and LTTr[A]WHR
24 κ. ἐκεῖθεν—ἐ. δέ TAWHR
31 διά LTTrAWHR, *see* ἔρχομαι
32*κωφόν—*add* κ. LTTrWHR
8: 3*τινὲς γάρ—κ. τινες LTTrAWHR
19*κ. πόσους T
9:24 *omit* and¹ [L]T[Tr]AWHR
10: 1*for διά LTTrAWHR
5 δέ TTrAWHR, *see* ἀποκρίνομαι
12 *omit* κ.² TTrAWHR
14 *omit* and² GTTrAWWHR
28 *omit* then GEds
32 κ.³—οἱ δέ TTrWHR
38, 40 and—or, ἤ LTTrAWHR
11: 2*add κ. LTTrAWHR, *see* λύω
17*add κ. TTrAWHR, *see* λέγω
24*add κ. LTTrAWHR, *see* προσεύχομαι
28 and²—or, ἤ TAWHR
12: 6 *omit* also [L]TTrAWHR
17 κ. ἀποκ. ὁ—ὁ δέ LTTrAWHR
22 *omit* and² TTrAWHR
31 *omit* and [L]TTrAWHR
32 *omit* and¹ WH
13: 8 *omit* and² TTrAR
8 *omit* and³ T[Tr]AWHR
22 *omit* even T[Tr]AWHR
22 and—or, ἢ GEds
34 *omit* and² LTTrAWHR
14: 3 *omit* and² TAWHR
15*κ. ἐκεῖ and there TrAWHR, κἀκεῖ T
15:24*αὐτόν—*add* κ. TTrAWHR
30 *omit* and LTTrAWHR
36 *omit* and² L[Tr]AWHR
41 *omit* also LT[Tr]WHR
46 *omit* and² Eds
Lu. 1:50*γενεῶν—κ. γενεάς TTrAWHR
2:12*κ. κείμενον and lying [L]TrAWH
3:17 *omit* and¹ TWHR (R
20 *omit* that T[A]WHR
4: 3 κ. εἶπεν—ε. δέ LTTrAWHR
9 κ. ἤγαγεν—ἤ. δέ TTrAWHR
5: 1*him—*add* κ. also TTrAWHR
3 κ. καθίσας—καθίσας δέ TAWHR
12 κ. ἰδών—ἰ. δέ TWHR
39 *omit* κ. WH
6: 4 ἔλαβεν κ.—λαβών LTrAWHR
4 *omit* also LTrAWH
5 *omit* also WHR
6 *omit* also LTTr[A]WHR
8 κ. εἶπεν—ε. δέ TTrAWHR
14*add κ. *bis*, *read* and James . . . and Philip LTTrAWHR
15*add κ. *bis*, *read* and Matthew LTTrAWHR, and JamesT[WH]R
16*add κ. *read* and Judas¹ LTTrAWHR
16 *omit* also LT[Tr]AWHR
18 *omit* and they² LTTrAWHR
28 *omit* and GEds
36 *omit* also [L]T[Tr]WHR
37 *omit* κ.¹ A.V.Er
37*judged—*add* κ. and TAWHR
38 *omit* and¹² LTTrAWHR
39*δέ—*add* κ. *read* spake also LTTrAWHR
7:22*κ. κωφοί and the deaf WHR
32 *omit* and² TTrAWHR
37*sinner—*add* κ. and Eds
8:20 κ. ἀπηγγέλη—ἀ. δέ LTTrAWHR
22 κ. ἐγένετο—ἐ. δέ LTTrAWHR
28 *omit* κ.¹ LTTrAWHR
36 *omit* also LTTr[A]WHR
9: 5 *omit* very [L]TrAWHR
9 κ. εἶπεν—ε. δέ LTTrAWHR
28 *omit* κ.¹ [L]WH
50 κ. εἶπεν—ε. δέ LTTrAWHR
10: 1 *omit* also [TrA]WHR
4 *omit* and T

Lu. 10:25 *omit* κ.^{2} T[Tr]AWHR
38 *omit* that [LTr]WHR
11:54 *omit* and GEds
12:29**for* ἤ TTrWHR
42 *omit* and^{2} LTTrAWHR
13:20 *omit* and W
14:18 *omit* and^{3} TTrAWHR
27 *omit* and^{1} TWHR
34*ἐὰν δὲ κ. but if also LTTrAWHR
15:12 κ.^{2}—ὁ δέ LTrAWHR
19 *omit* and GEds
21 *omit* and^{3} LTTrAWHR
24 *omit* κ.^{2} Eds
32 *omit* and^{3} T
16: 6 κ.^{1}—ὁ δέ LTTrAWHR
7 *omit* and^{3} LTTrAWHR
14 *omit* also TTr[A]WHR
17:24 *omit* also G[L]TTrAWWHR
28 *omit* also TTrAWHR, *see* καθώς
33 κ. ὃς ἐάν—ὃς δ' ἄν WHR
35 κ. ἡ—ἡ δέ TTrAWHR
37*ἐκεῖ κ. thither also TTrAWHR
18: 1 *omit* κ.^{1} LT[TrA]WHR
4 *omit* κ.^{3} LTTrWHR
13 κ. ὁ—ὁ δέ TWHR
28 *omit* and LTTrAWHR, *see* ἀφίημι
19:30*κ. λύσαντες TTrAWH
42 *omit* at least [L]Tr[A]WHR
46**add* κ. TTrAWHR, *see* ἔσται
20:31 ἑπτά—*add* κ. A.V.Er E
42 and—for, *see* γάρ TWHR
21: 2 *omit* also [L]TTr[A]WHR
22:22 and—for, ὅτι TTrAWHR
68 *omit* also LTTrAWHR
23: 2*κ. λεγόντα and saying [L]TTr[A]WHR
5*Jewry—*add* κ. and TTr[A]WHR
11*κ. ὁ 'Ηρώδης Herod also T
27 *omit* also LTTrAWHR
35 *omit* also LT
36 *omit* and^{2} [L]TTrAWHR
45 *omit* κ.^{1} TWHR, *see* ἥλιος
45 κ. ἐσχίσθη—ἐ. δέ TWHR
46 κ. ταῦτα—τοῦτο δέ TTrAWHR
50*ἀνήρ^{2}—κ. ἀνήρ T
51 *omit* also LTTrAWHR
55 *omit* also Eds
24: 3 κ. εἰσελθοῦσαι—ε. δέ LTTrAWHR
21*γε κ. *read* yea and beside LTTrAWHR
24 *omit* even LTrAWHR
32 *omit* and^{2} LTTrAWHR
47 and^{2}—to, εἰς TWH
Joh. 1:16 and^{1}—for, ὅτι GLTTrAWHR
21 *omit* and^{2} T
37 *omit* and^{1} T
42 (43) *omit* and^{1} [L]TTrAWHR
46 (47) *omit* and^{1} T
2: 4*κ. λέγει, *read* and Jesus saith [L]TrAWHR
8 κ.^{3}—οἱ δέ TTrAWHR
3:32 *omit* and^{1} [L]TTrAWHR
4:36 *omit* and^{1} G[L]TTrAWHR
36 *omit* both Tr[A]WHR
46 κ. ἦν—ἦν δέ T
50 *omit* and^{1} [L]T[Tr]AWHR
52 and—therefore, οὖν TTrAWHR
5:10*κ. οὐκ, *read* and it is not [L]T[Tr]AWHR
27 *omit* also LTTrAWHR
6: 2 κ. ἠκολούθει—ἠ. δέ LTTrAWHR
11**add* κ. T, *see* εὐχαριστέω
24 *omit* also Eds
7: 1 *omit* κ. T
15 and—therefore, *see* οὖν Eds
8:11 and^{2}—from henceforth, ἀπὸ τοῦ νῦν WHR
14 and^{3}—or, ἤ GTTrAWWHR
25 *omit* and Eds
9:12**add at commencement* κ. and [Tr]WHR, *see* οὖν
28**add at commencement* κ. and WHR, *see* οὖν
36*κ. τις and who GTTrAWWHR
40 *omit* and^{1} TTrAWHR
10: 4 *omit* and^{1} TTrAWHR
22 *omit* and^{2} TTrAWHR
11:19 κ. πολλοί—π. δέ LTTrAWHR
44 *omit* and^{1} GTTrAWHR
57 *omit* both Eds
12: 6 *omit* and^{2} TTrAWHR
13*κυριου—*add* κ. *read* blessed is he that cometh in the name of the Lord, even the King of Israel TTrAWHR
18 *omit* also Tr
22*Philip^{2}—*add* κ. and LTTrAWHR
26 *omit* κ.^{3} A.V.Vul GLTTrAWHR
29 *omit* and T
13: 6 *omit* and TTrAWHR
12*αὐτοῦ—*add* κ. TTrAWHR
26 *see* βάπτω

Joh. 14: 4 *omit* and^{2} [L]TTrAWHR
5 *omit* and LTrWHR
7 *omit* and^{1} LT[Tr]WHR
9 *omit* and^{2} LT[Tr]WHR
22*κύριε—*add* κ. GT[A]W (Eds
17: 1 *om.* and^{2} LTTrAWHR: *om.* also
11*as—*add* κ. also Tr
12*me—*add* κ. and [L]TTrAWHR
23 *omit* and^{2} LTTrAWHR
18: 4**add* κ. LTTrAWHR, *see* λέγω
18*ἦν δέ—*add* κ. *read* Peter also LTTrAWHR
19: 4**add at commencement* κ. *read* and Pilate LTrAWHR
35*κ. ὑμεῖς ye also GEds
20: 6*κ. Σίμων also Simon TrAWHR
13 *omit* and^{1} TR
14 *omit* and^{1} GLTTrAWWH
20*shewed—*add* κ. both LTrAWH
28 *omit* and^{1} GEds
21:23 κ. οὐκ εἶπεν—ο. ε. δέ TrWHR
Acts 2:17 *omit* and^{1} A
22 *omit* also LTTrAWHR
33*ye—*add* κ. both T[AWH]
36 *omit* both E
42 *omit* and^{3} LTTrAWHR
44*κ. πάντες δέ and all also T
44 *omit* were *and* and^{2} WH
5:15*κ. εἰς *for* κατά LTTrWHR
7:35*θεός—*add* κ. *read* both a ruler LT[Tr]AWHR
8: 8 κ. ἐγένετο—ἐ. δέ LTTrAWHR
28 *omit* κ.^{2} A.V.C LT[Tr]W
9: 3 κ. ἐξαίφνης—ἐ. τε Eds
24*δὲ κ. *for* τε LTTrAWHR
29(28) and he spake—*omit* and LTTrAWHR
40*Πέτρος—*add* κ. Eds
10:14**for* ἤ LTTrAWHR
17 *omit* κ. LTTr[A]WHR
24 κ. τῇ—τῇ δέ Eds
39*whom—*add* κ. also GEds
11: 2 κ. ὅτε—ὅ. δέ LTTrAWHR
7*δέ—*add* κ. *read* heard also LTTrAWHR
20*spake—*add* κ. also LTTrAWHR
26**add* κ. even LTTrAWHR, *see* αὐτούς
28 *omit* κ. LTTrAWHR
12: 3 κ. ἰδών—ἰ. δέ LTTrAWHR
21 *omit* κ. [L]T[Tr]WHR
25 *omit* and^{3} LTTr[A]WHR
13: 9 *omit* κ.^{2} Eds
19 *omit* and WH
39 *omit* and LT[TrA]
50 *omit* and^{1} GEds
14: 3 *omit* and^{1} GEds
15:23 *omit* κ. οἱ^{2}, *read* elder brethren LTTrAWHR
37*with them—*add* κ. also GLTTrAWHR
16: 1*δέ—*add* κ. *read* also to Derbe L[Tr]WHR
9*ἑστώς—*add* κ. LTTrWHR
32 and to all—with (σύν) all GEds
38 κ. ἐφοβήθησαν—ἐ. δέ LTTrAWHR
17:18*τινές δὲ κ. then certain also Eds
21*κ.^{2}—ἤ LTTrAWHR
25 *see* κατά
32**add* κ. LTTrAWHR, *see* πάλιν
33 *omit* κ. LTTrAWHR
18:21**add* κ. LTTrAWHR, *see* ἀποτάσσομαι
21 *omit* and LTTrAWHR
19:13**for* ἀπό LTTrAWHR
16 *omit* κ.^{2} Eds
21: 4 κ. ἀνευρόντες—ἀ. δέ Eds
25:25 *omit* κ. Eds
26:12 *omit* κ.^{1} LTTrAWHR
18 τοῦ ἐπιστρέψαι—κ. ἐ. A.V.†B
Ro. 1:24 *omit* also LTTr[A]WHR
4:11 *omit* also TTr[A]WHR
22 [and] LTrAWH
8:24 *omit* yet LTr[A]WHR
34 *omit* κ.^{1} LTTr[A]WHR
34 *omit* even [L]TWHR
9:23 *omit* and WH
11: 3 *omit* and^{1} Eds
17 *omit* and^{4} T[Tr]AWHR
26 *omit* and^{2}, *read* he shall Eds
30 *omit* κ. GEds
12:15 *omit* and Eds
13:12 κ. ἐνδυσώμεθα—ἐ. ([δέ] WH)Eds
14: 3 κ. ὁ—ὁ δέ LTTrAWHR
6*regard (it)—*add* κ. and GEds
9 *omit* both^{1} Eds
15:32 *omit* and LT[A]WHR
1 Co. 1:28 *omit* and^{3} LTTrA[WH]
3: 2 *omit* and GEds
5:10 *omit* yet Eds: * *for* ἤ^{2} Eds
12 *omit* also LTTrAWHR

1 Co. 5:13 *omit* therefore GEds
7:22 *omit* also Eds
34 [both] LTrWH
8:11 and—for, *see* γάρ LTTrWHR
10: 9, 10 *omit* also Eds
11:19*ἵνα—*add* κ. *read* they also [L]Tr[AWH]
15: 6 *omit* κ. LTTr[A]WHR
14*ἄρα—*add* κ. *read* vain also [L]TAW
28 *omit* also [L]Tr[AWH]
16: 6 *omit* κ. WH
10 *omit* also WH
2 Co. 1:13 *omit* even LTTrAWHR
4:13*therefore—*add* κ. also T
5: 5 *omit* also Eds
8:24 *omit* and^{1} (κ.^{2}) GEds
9: 5 *omit* and^{2} T
10: 8 *omit* κ.^{1} LTTrAWHR
12:10**for* ἐν^{5} TWH
13: 4 γάρ^{2}—*add* κ. E
Gal. 3:29 *omit* and^{2} LTTrAWHR
5:21 *omit* also [L]TTrWHR
Eph. 1:18 *omit* and LTTrAWHR (R
3:21*church—*add* κ. and LTTr[A]WH
4: 8 *omit* κ. LTW[WH]
5: 4 nor^{1} (κ.^{2})—or, ἤ LT
23 *omit* and GEds
28*κ. οἱ, *read* so also LTrAWR, [κ.] οἱ WH
6: 9**add* κ. Eds, *see* αὐτῶν
Phil. 3:12 *omit* that^{1} T
4: 3 and^{1}—yea, ναί GEds
Col. 1: 3 *omit* and LAWHR
6 *omit* and^{1} Eds
7 *omit* also Eds
2:16**for* ἤ^{1} AWH
23 [and^{2}] LWH
3:16 *omit* and^{2} ^{3} Eds
17 *omit* and^{2} Eds
23 *omit* and^{1} Eds
1 Th. 1: 8 *omit* also Eds
2: 2 *omit* even GEds
13*κ. διά, *read* and for this LTTrAWHR
4: 8 *omit* also LTr[A]WHR
5: 6 *omit* κ.^{1} LTTr[A]WHR
15 *omit* both LTTrWHR
25*pray—*add* [κ. also] LWH
2 Th. 2:14*whereunto—*add* κ. also T
16 *omit* even LTTrAWHR
3: 4 *omit* both [L]T[TrWH]
14 *omit* and^{2} LTTrAWHR
1 Ti. 1:12 *omit* and LTTrAWHR
2: 9 *omit* also LT[Tr]WHR
9**for* ἤ^{1} LTTrAWHR
4:10 *omit* both LTTr[A]WHR
6:12 *omit* also GEds
2 Ti. 2:21 *omit* and^{1} LTTrAWHR
4: 1**for* κατά GEds
18 *omit* and^{1} LTTrAWHR
Tit. 1: 4*grace—*add* κ. and TTrAWWHR
10 *omit* κ.^{1} LTTr[A]WHR
3: 1 *omit* and LTTrAWHR
Philem. 1*δέ—*add* κ. *read* but now also T
Heb. 1: 8*ever^{2}—*add* κ. and LTTrAWHR
5:12 *omit* and^{2} T[Tr]WH
7: 4 *omit* even LTrWHR
22*so much—*add* κ. also TAWHR
26*ἡμῖν—*add* κ. *read* high priest also [L]TTrAW[WH]
8: 2 *omit* and^{2} Eds
9: 1 [also] TrWH
10 *omit* and^{3} GLT[Tr]AWWHR
28*so—*add* κ. also GEds
11:20*faith—*add* κ also L[Tr]AWWHR
32*Γεδεών—*add* κ. W
32 *omit* and^{3} LTTrWWHR
32 *omit* and^{4} LTTrWHR
13: 6 *omit* and [L]T[TrA]WHR
Jas. 2: 3 κ. ἐπιβλέψητε—ἐ. δέ AWH
4 *omit* then LTTrAWHR
13 *omit* and GEds
3: 6 *omit* and^{1}, *read* the tongue kindleth T
6**for* ἤ^{3}, *read* both defileth T
12 *omit* κ. GEds, *see* οὐδείς (WHR
17 and without—*omit* and LTTrA
4: 2*πολεμεῖτε—*add* κ. (*om.* δέ) T
9 *omit* and^{2} T
11 and^{1}—or, ἤ LTTrAWHR
13 κ.^{1}—ἤ A.V.B ELTTrWHR
1 Pet. 2: 6 *omit* also GEds
3: 1 *omit* also WH
2 Pet. 2:12**add* κ. Eds, *see* φθείρω
17**add* κ. GEds, *see* νεφέλη
19 *omit* κ. T[Tr]WH
1 Joh. 1: 3*declare we—*add* κ. also Eds
2:20 *omit* and WH
29*κ. πᾶς also everyone TTrAR
3:13**add at commencement* κ. and T
19 *omit* and^{1} L[TrA]WHR

1 Joh. 5: 1 *omit* also [LTr]WH
13 *omit* and GEds
Jude 25 *omit* and[1] Eds
Rev. 1: 6 *omit* and[2] GEds, *see* βασιλεύς
9 *omit* also GEds
2: 3 *omit* and[3] GEds
13 *omit* even T[TrA]
19 *omit* κ.[*] *read* thy last works GEds
20*add κ. GEds, *see* διδάσκω
24 *omit* and *bis* GEds
3: 4 *omit* even GEds
8 and[1]—which, ὅς GEds
20*door[2]—*add* κ. *read* I will both T[A]W
4: 2 *omit* and[1] Eds
4 *omit* κ.[2] GEds
10 *omit* κ.[1] GEds
5: 6 *omit* and, lo GTTrAWWHR
13*κ. ἤκουσα heard I also T
7: 1 *omit* and L[TrA]WHR
9:10 *trs* κ.[3] Eds, *see* ἦν
11 *omit* and GEds
16 *omit* and[2] GEds
10: 7 *omit* κ. A.V.C
11: 2*κ. δύο LAW, [καὶ] δ. WH
14 κ. ἰδού A.V.†B
16 *omit* κ.[2] GEds
17*κ. ὅτι and because T
12: 2*ἔχουσα—*add* κ. *read* was with child, and cried, LT[A]WHR
13: 4*τίς[2]—κ. τίς and who GEds
5*[κ.] δύο LWH
6 *omit* and[3] Eds
17 *omit* and LT[AWH]
15: 6 *omit* and[2] GEds
16: 5 *omit* and[3] GEds
17: 9 ὧδε—*et hic* A.V.Vul
10 *omit* and[2] GEds
16**for* ἐπί GEds
18: 1, 16 *omit* and[1] Eds
20**add* κ. GEds, *see* ἀπόστολος
19: 1 *omit* and[1] GEds
4 *omit* κ.[2] GEds
5 *omit* and[2] T[TrA]WHR
5 *omit* both GEds
8 *omit* and[2] LTTrAWHR
14 *omit* and[2] GLTAWWHR
15 *omit* and[4], *read* fierceness of the wrath GLTTrAWHR
17 *omit* and[3] GEds
20: 3 *omit* and[4] Eds
10*where—*add* κ. both GEds
21:11 *omit* and GEds
13**add* κ. *before* ἀπό[2 3], *read* and on Eds: *before* ἀ.[4] A.V.C Eds
16 *omit* κ.[3] TTr[A]WHR
19 *omit* and LTAWHR
22: 7*κ. ἰδού and behold GEds
12 *omit* and[1] GEds
16 *omit* and[3] (κ.[2]) GTTrAWWHR
17 *omit* and[5] GEds
19 *omit* and[3] GEds

See also κἀγώ, κἀκεῖ, κἀκεῖθεν, κἄν, &c.

2533 Καϊάφας, Καιά– WH.

Acts 4: 6 Καϊάφας LTTrAWHR

καίγε.

Lu. 19:42**for* καί γε GT
Acts 2:18**for* καί γε GT
17:27**for* καίτοιγε TR

2535 Κάϊν, Κάιν WH.

2536 Καϊνάν, Και– WH.

Lu. 3:36 Καϊνάμ TAWH
37 Καϊνάμ TWH

2537 καινός.

Mat. 26:28 *omit* new T[A]WHR
Mar. 1:27 τίς ἡ διδαχὴ ἡ καινὴ αὕτη, ὅτι—διδαχὴ καινή, *read* a new doctrine! with authority he LTrWHR, a new doctrine with authority, he TA
2:22 *omit* T[Tr]A[WH], *see* βλητέος
14:24 *omit* new TTrAWHR
16:17 *omit* new TrWH

2539 καίπερ.

Rev. 17: 8 κ. ἐστίν and yet is—καὶ παρέσται (–ειμι) and shall be present GEds

2540 καιρός.

Mat. 13:30 τῷ κ.—*omit* τῷ GLTTrAWWH
16: 3 when it is (*ver.* 2) *to end of verse* 3 [TA][[WH]]
Mar. 11:13†*trs* ὁ γὰρ κ. οὐκ ἦν TTrAWHR
Lu. 12:56 *trs* καιρὸν δὲ WH
Joh. 5: 4 *omit* waiting for (*ver.* 3) *to end of verse* 4 [G]TTrAWHR
7: 8†*trs* ὁ ἐμὸς κ. LTTrAWH
Ro. 12:11 τῷ καιρῷ in season S—τῷ κυρίῳ (–ριος) the Lord A.V.B EEds

2541 Καῖσαρ.

Mar. 12:17 *trs* τὰ K. ἀπόδοτε TTrAWHR
Lu. 20:25 K. τῷ K. Tr
23: 2 *trs* φόρους Καίσαρι LTTrAWH
Acts 11:28 *omit* Cæsar GEds

2542 Καισάρεια, –ρια TWH.

Acts 12:19 τὴν K.—*omit* τὴν LTTrAWWH
25: 4 εἰς Καισάρειαν Eds

2543 2544 καίτοι, καίτοιγε, καί τοι γε.

Acts 14:17 *omit* γε LTTrWHR
17:27 καὶ γε LTrAWH, καίγε TR

2545 καίω.

Mat. 13:40*καίεται *for* κατακαίεται (–καίω) GTrA
1 Co. 13: 3 καυθήσομαι T: to be burned—that I may boast, καυχάομαι (WH
Rev. 19:20 τῆς καιομένης LTTrAWHR

2546 κἀκεῖ.

Mat. 28:10 καὶ ἐκεῖ T
Mar. 1:38 καὶ ἐκεῖ GWWH
14:15**for* ἐκεῖ T, καὶ ἐκεῖ TrAWHR

2547 κἀκεῖθεν.

Mar. 9:30**for* καὶ ἐκεῖθεν LTTrAWH
10: 1 καὶ ἐκεῖθεν LTTrAWWH
Lu. 11:53**add* κ. TTrAWHR, *see* ἐξέρχομαι
Acts 16:12**for* ἐκεῖθέν τε Eds
27:12 ἐκεῖθεν (*omit* also) LTTrAWHR

2548 κἀκεῖνος.

Mat. 20: 4 καὶ ἐκείνοις TAWH
Joh. 19:35 καὶ ἐκεῖνος LTrWH
Ro. 11:23*κἀκεῖνοι *for* καὶ ἐκεῖνοι (–νος) GLTTrAWWH

2549 κακία.

Ro. 1:29 *trs* maliciousness, covetousness T

2550 κακοήθεια, –θία WH.

2553 κακοπαθέω.

2 Ti. 2: 3 συγκακοπαθέω, *read* endure hardness with (me) Eds

2552 κακοπάθεια, –θια WH.

2555 κακοποιός.

Joh. 18:30 κακὸν ποιῶν TTrAWH
1 Pet. 3:16 *omit* of you as of evildoers TAWHR

2556 κακός, τὸ κακόν.

Joh. 18:30*κακὸν ποιῶν *for* κακοποιός TTrAWH
Ro. 9:11 φαῦλος LTTrAWHR
13: 3 τῷ κακῷ Eds
2 Co. 5:10 φαῦλος TTrWHR

2557 κακοῦργος.

Lu. 23:32 *trs* κακοῦργοι δύο WH

2564 καλέω.

Mat. 10:25 have called—have surnamed ἐπικαλέω GEds
22:43 *trs* κ. αὐτὸν κύριον LTrAWH, κ. κύριον αὐτὸν T
Mar. 3:31*καλοῦντες *for* φωνοῦντες (φωνέω) LTTrAWH
Lu. 9:10 πόλιν καλουμένην TTrAWHR
22: 3*καλούμενον *for* ἐπικαλούμενον (–λέω) TTrAWHR
Joh. 10: 3 φωνέω LTTrAWHR
Acts 8:10*ἡ[2]—*add* καλουμένη, *read* power of God which is called great GEds
15:22*καλούμενον *for* ἐπικαλούμενον (–λέω) Eds
1 Co. 7:18†*trs* κέκληταί τις[2] hath any been called Eds
1 Th. 2:12 *vocavit* A.V.Vul
Heb. 5: 4 ὁ κ.—*omit* ὁ GEds
11: 8 ὁ καλούμενος L, [ὁ] κ. T.
Rev. 19:11†*trs* πιστὸς κ. Tr, π. [κ.] WH, [κ.] π. A
13 κέκληται Eds

5566 κάλλιον, *see* καλῶς.

5570 καλός.

Mat. 15:26 ἔξεστιν LTA, *see* ἐστίν
Mar. 7:27 *trs* ἐστιν καλὸν LTTrAWH
Lu. 3: 9 [good] LWH
Joh. 10:32 *trs* ἔργα καλὰ LT: καλὰ *after* ὑμῖν WH
1 Ti. 5: 4 *omit* good and GEds
Tit. 3: 8 τὰ κ.—*omit* τὰ Eds

5572 καλύπτω.

1 Pet. 4: 8 καλύπτει covereth Eds

5573 καλῶς, κάλλιον.

Mat. 5:44 *omit* LTTrAWHR, *see* μισέω
Lu. 6:48**add* κ. TTrAWHR, *see* θεμελιόω

κἀμέ, κἀμοί, *see* κἀγώ. 2504

2577 κάμνω.

Rev. 2: 3 *omit* κ. GEds, *see* κοπιάω

2579 κἄν.

Lu. 12:38**for* καὶ ἐάν TTrAWHR
38**for* καί[2] TTrAWHR
Joh. 8:55**for* καὶ ἐάν LTTrWH
1 Co. 13: 2**for* καὶ ἐάν[1] LAWH
2**for* καὶ ἐάν[2] TrAWH
3**for* καὶ ἐ.[1] LTrAWH: *for*[2] LAWH

2580 Κανᾶ –ᾷ, –ά WH.

*Καναναῖος, Cananæan, or Zealot, 2581 *see* Κανανίτης.

2581 Κανανίτης.

Mat. 10: 4 Καναναῖος LTTrAWHR
Mar. 3:18 Καναναῖον (–ος) Eds

2583 κανών.

Phi. 3:16 *omit* rule, let us mind the same thing GLTTrAWHR

2584 Καπερναούμ, Καφαρ– LTTrAWWH.

Lu. 4:23 τὴν K. TAWHR, *omit* τῇ GLTr

2588 καρδία.

Mat. 12:35 *omit* of the heart GEds
22:37 τῇ κ.—*omit* τῇ [A]WH
Mar. 4:15 in their hearts—in them, ἐν αὐτοῖς T, εἰς αὐτούς TrAWHR
6:52 *trs* αὐτῶν ἡ κ. LTTrAWWH
12:30, 33 τῆς κ.—*omit* τῆς WH
Lu. 4:18 *omit* to heal the brokenhearted G[L]TTrAWHR
6:45 *omit* treasure of his heart[2] [L]TTrAWHR
45 τῆς κ.[3]—*omit* τῆς LTTrAWHR
10:27 τῆς κ.—*omit* τῆς [Tr]WH
21:14 ἐν ταῖς καρδίαις LTTrAWHR
34 *trs* αἱ καρδίαι ὑμῶν LTrWH
24:38 τῇ καρδίᾳ heart LTTrAWHR
Acts 2:26 *trs* μου ἡ κ. TTrAWH
37 τὴν καρδίαν LTTrAWHR
4:32 ἡ κ.—*omit* ἡ LTTrAWHR
7:51 τῇ κ.—καρδίαις hearts LTTrWHR, ταῖς κ. W
8:37 *omit the verse* GLTTrAWHR
Ro. 10: 6 τῇ κ.—*omit* τῇ B
2 Co. 3: 3 καρδίαις, *read* tables, hearts of flesh LTTrAWHR
Eph. 1:18*καρδίας *for* διανοίας (–ια) GEds
6: 5 τῆς κ.—*omit* τῆς T
Col. 3:16 ταῖς καρδίαις GEds
Heb. 8:10 καρδίαν heart T
Jas. 3:14 *cordibus vestris* A.V.Vul
1 Joh. 3:19 τὴν καρδίαν WHR

2590 καρπός.

Mat. 3: 8 καρπὸν ἄξιον fruit worthy GEds
Mar. 12: 2 τῶν καρπῶν the fruits TTrAWHR
Lu. 13: 6 *trs* ζητῶν καρπὸν GEds
Joh. 15: 2 *trs* καρπὸν πλείονα LTTrAWH
Ro. 1:13 *trs* τινὰ καρπὸν GEds
1 Co. 9: 7 τὸν καρπόν Eds
Phi. 1:11 καρπόν fruit GEds

2596 κατά.

Mar. 6:40**for* ἀνά *bis* LTTrAWH
14: 3 *omit* κ. LTTrAWHR
Lu. 23:17 *omit the verse* [L]TTr[A]WHR
Joh. 5: 4 *omit* [G]TTrAWHR, *see* ὕδωρ
18:29 *omit* κ. TWH

Joh. 21:25 *omit the verse* T
Acts 2:30 *omit* GLTTrAWHR, *see* σάρξ
5:15 into—even into, καὶ εἰς LTTrWHR
13:49**for* διά T
16: 7 κ.[2]—εἰς GEds
17:25 κ. πάντα S—καὶ τὰ π. A.V.B EGEds
24: 6 *omit* LTTr[A]WHR, *see* κρίνω
25: 7 *omit* against Paul LTTrAWHR
27:29**for* εἰς Eds
Ro. 8: 1 *omit* who walk *to end of verse* GEds
1 Co. 7: 7†*trs* ἐν τῇ κ. αὐτοῦ ἑδραῖος LTTrAWHR
Phi. 2: 3*μηδὲ κ. *for* ἤ LTTrAWHR
2 Ti. 4: 1 at—and (by), καί GEds
Heb. 7:21 *omit* after the order of Melchisedec TTrAWHR
Jas. 3:14 *omit* κ. T
1 Pet. 4:14 *omit* on their part *to end of verse* LTTrAWHR
5: 2**add* κ. LTTrR, *see* θεός
Rev. 4: 8 καθ' ἑαυτό—κ. ἐν αὐτῶν GLTAWHR, ἕκαστον αὐτῶν Tr
12: 7 against—with, μετά GEds
See also καταμόνας

2597 καταβαίνω.

Mat. 8: 1 καταβάντος δὲ αὐτοῦ TrWH
11:23*καταβήσῃ *for* καταβιβασθήσῃ (–βιβάζω) LTrAWHR
24:17 καταβάτω LTTrWH
Mar. 15:30 καταβάς LTTrAWHR
Lu. 10:15*καταβήσῃ *for* καταβιβασθήσῃ (–βιβάζω) WH
22:43, 44 *the verses* [L][[WH]]
44 καταβαίνοντος TA
Joh. 5: 4 *omit* waiting for (*ver.* 3) *to end of ver.* 4 [G]TTrAWHR
Rev. 3:12 ἡ καταβαίνουσα S—ἣ καταβαίνει E
13:13†*trs* ἐκ τοῦ οὐρανοῦ καταβαίνειν (–βῇ G, –βαίνῃ W) GLTrAWWHR

2598 καταβάλλω.

Rev. 12:10 βάλλω LTTrAWHR

* καταβαρύνω, to weigh down.

Mar. 14:40 καταβαρυνόμενοι *for* βεβαρημένοι (βαρέω) Eds

2601 καταβιβάζω.

Mat. 11:23 shalt be brought down—shalt descend, καταβαίνω LTrAWHR
Lu. 10:15 shalt be thrust down—shalt descend, καταβαίνω WH

2605 καταγγέλλω.

Acts 3:24*κατήγγειλαν *for* προκατήγγειλαν (–ταγγέλλω) GEds

* καταγράφω, to delineate, write down.

Joh. 8: 6 κατέγραφεν *for* ἔγραφεν (γράφω) WHR

2609 κατάγω.

Acts 21: 3 κατέρχομαι LTTrAWHR
23:15 *trs* καταγάγῃ αὐτόν Eds
20 *trs* τὸν Παῦλον κ. εἰς τὸ συνέδριον LTTrAWWH

* καταδίκη, condemnation.

Acts 25:15 καταδίκην *for* δίκην (–κη) Eds

2614 καταδιώκω.

Mar. 1:36 κατεδίωξεν TWH

2615 καταδουλόω.

Gal. 2: 4 καταδουλώσουσιν Eds

* κατάθεμα, an accursed thing.

Rev. 22: 3 κατάθεμα *for* κατανάθεμα GEds

* καταθεματίζω, to curse.

Mat. 26:74 καταθεματίζειν *for* καταναθεματίζειν (–ζω) GEds

2617 καταισχύνω.

1 Co. 1:27 *trs* κ. τοὺς σοφούς [L]TTrAWHR

2618 κατακαίω.

Mat. 13:40 καίω GTrA
2 Pet. 3:10 shall be burned up—shall be detected, εὑρίσκω TrWH
Rev. 8: 7**add* κ. GEds, *see* γῆ

2621 κατάκειμαι.

Mar. 2:15 ἐν τῷ κ.—*omit* ἐν τῷ T[Tr]WHR
Lu. 7:37*κατάκειται *for* ἀνάκειται (–κειμαι) LTTrAWHR

2624 κατακληροδοτέω.

Acts 13:19 κατακληρονομέω GEds

* κατακληρονομέω, to allot.

Acts 13:19 κατεκληρονόμησεν *for* κατεκληροδότησεν (κατακληροδοτέω) GEds

2625 κατακλίνω.

Lu. 7:36*κατεκλίθη *for* ἀνεκλίθη (ἀνακλίνω) LTTrAWHR
9:15*κατέκλιναν *for* ἀνέκλιναν (ἀνακλίνω) TTrWHR

2628 κατακολουθέω.

Acts 16:17 κατακολουθοῦσα TTrWHR

2630 κατακρημνίζω.

Lu. 4:29 τὸ κ.—*omit* τὸ GLTTrAWHR

2632 κατακρίνω.

Jas. 5: 9 condemned—judged, κρίνω GEds

* κατακύπτω, to bend down.

Joh. 8: 8 κατακύψας *for* κάτω κύψας (κύπτω) WH

2635 καταλαλέω.

1 Pet. 3:16 καταλαλοῦσιν LTrW, –λαλεῖσθε ye are spoken evil of TAWHR

2638 καταλαμβάνω.

Joh. 6:17**add* κ. T, *see* ἤδη
8: 4 κατείληπται WHR
Acts 25:25 κατελαβόμην Eds
Phi. 3:12 κατελήμφθην LTTrAWH

2640 κατάλειμμα.

Ro. 9:27 ὑπόλειμμα LTTrAWHR

2641 καταλείπω.

Mar. 12:21*καὶ οὐδὲ αὐτὸς ἀφῆκεν neither left he any—μὴ καταλιπών leaving no TTrAWHR
Lu. 10:40 κατέλειπεν TrAWHR
Acts 2:31 ἐγκαταλείπω LTTrAWHR
Tit. 1: 5 ἀπολείπω Eds
2 Pet. 2:15 καταλείποντες forsaking TWHR

2649 καταμαρτυρέω.

Mar. 15: 4 witness against—accuse, κατηγορέω LTTrAWHR

2651 καταμόνας, κατὰ μόνας LTTrWH.

2652 κατανάθεμα.

Rev. 22: 3 κατάθεμα GEds

2653 καταναθεματίζω.

Mat. 26:74 καταθεματίζω GEds

2658 καταντάω.

Acts 18:19 κατήντησαν they came LTTrA (WHR
1 Co. 10:11 κατήντηκεν Eds

2661 καταξιόομαι.

Lu. 20:35 *habebuntur* A.V. Vul
21:36 may be accounted worthy—may prevail, κατισχύω TTrAWHR

2662 καταπατέω.

Mat. 7: 6 καταπατήσουσιν LTTrAWH

2663 κατάπαυσις.

Heb. 4: 3 κ.[1]—[τὴν] κ. TrWH

2666 καταπίνω.

1 Pet. 5: 8 καταπιεῖν to devour LTAWHR, καταπίειν Tr

2667 καταπίπτω.

Lu. 8: 6*κατέπεσεν *for* ἔπεσεν (πίπτω) TTrAWHR

2672 καταράομαι.

Mat. 5:44 *omit* bless them *to* hate you LTTrAWHR
25:41 οἱ κ.—*omit* οἱ TWHR

2675 καταρτίζω.

1 Pet. 5:10 καταρτίσει will perfect Eds

2679 κατασκάπτω.

Acts 15:16 καταστρέφω TTrWHR

2681 κατασκηνόω.

Mat. 13:32 κατασκηνοῖν LTTrAWH
Mar. 4:32 κατασκηνοῖν WH

2690 καταστρέφω.

Acts 15:16*κατεστραμμένα TWHR, –ρεμ– Tr *for* κατεσκαμμένα (κατασκάπτω)

2691 καταστρηνιάζω, –άω.

1 Ti. 5:11 καταστρηνιάσουσιν A

2692 καταστροφή.

2 Pet. 2: 6 *omit* with an overthrow WH

2698 κατατίθημι.

Mar. 15:46 τίθημι LTrWHR

2700 κατατοξεύω.

Heb. 12:20 *omit* or thrust through with a dart GEds

2719 καταφάγω.

Joh. 2:17 καταφάγεται shall eat up GEds

2702 καταφέρω.

Acts 25: 7*καταφέροντες *for* φέροντες (–ρω) LTTrAWHR

2704 καταφθείρω.

2 Pet. 2:12 φθείρω Eds

2713 κατέναντι.

Mat. 21: 2**for* ἀπέναντι LTTrWH
27:24**for* ἀπέναντι LTrWH
Mar. 12:41 ἀπέναντι Tr
2 Co. 2:17**for* κατενώπιον LTTrAWHR
12:19**for* κατενώπιον Eds

2714 κατενώπιον.

2 Co. 2:17 κατέναντι LTTrAWHR
12:19 κατέναντι Eds

2716 κατεργάζομαι.

Ro. 7: 8 κατηργάσατο TTrA
2 Co. 7:10 κ.[1]—ἐργάζομαι Eds
11 κατηργάσατο T
12:12 κατηργάσθη T
Jas. 1:20 ἐργάζομαι LTTrAWHR
1 Pet. 4: 3 κατειργάσθαι Eds

2718 κατέρχομαι.

Acts 15:30*κατῆλθον *for* ἦλθον (ἔρχομαι) LTTrAWHR
19: 1*κατελθεῖν *for* ἐλθεῖν (ἔρχομαι) T
21: 3*κατήλθομεν *for* κατήχθημεν (κατάγω) LTTrAWHR
27: 5 κατήλθαμεν TTrWH

2719 κατεσθίω.

Mat. 23:14(13) *omit the verse* LTTrAWHR, *see* κρίμα
Mar. 12:40 κατέσθοντες TrAWH

* κατευλογέω, to bless much.

Mar. 10:16 αὐτά[1]—*add* κατευλόγει TTrAWH, κατηυλόγει R, *see* εὐλογέω

2722 κατέχω.

Mat. 21:38 let us seize on—let us possess, ἔχω LTTrAWHR
Joh. 5: 4 *omit* waiting for (*ver.* 3) *to end of verse* 4 [G]TTrAWHR

2723 κατηγορέω.

Mar. 3: 2 κατηγορήσουσιν LTr
15: 4*κατηγοροῦσιν *for* καταμαρτυροῦσιν (–τυρέω) LTTrAWHR
Lu. 6: 7*κατηγορεῖν *for* κατηγορίαν (–ρία) TTrAWHR
11:54 *omit* that they might accuse him T[Tr]AWHR
Acts 28:19 κατηγορεῖν LTTrAWH

2724 κατηγορία.

Lu. 6: 7 an accusation against—to accuse, κατηγορέω TTrAWHR

2725 κατήγορος.

Joh. 8:10 *omit* those thine accusers WHR
Acts 24: 8 *omit* and would (*ver.* 6) *to* unto thee (*ver.* 8) LTTr[A]WHR
Rev. 12:10 κατήγωρ GLTAWH

* κατήγωρ, an accuser.

Rev. 12:10 κατήγωρ *for* κατήγορος GLTAWH

2729 κατισχύω.

Lu. 21:36*κατισχύσητε *for* καταξιωθῆτε (–ξιόομαι) TTrAWHR

2730 κατοικέω.

Mat. 23:21 κατοικήσαντι dwelt GTrAW
Jas. 4: 5 dwelleth—he made to dwell, κατοικίζω LTTrAWHR
Rev. 2:13 *trs* ὁ σατανᾶς κατοικεῖ GEds
8:13 τοὺς κατοικοῦντας TTrAWHR
12:12 *omit* the inhabiters of GEds
13:12 *trs* ἐν αὐτῇ κ. GTTrAWHR
14: 6 dwell—sit, κάθημαι GEds

* κατοικίζω, to cause to dwell.

Jas. 4: 5 κατῴκισεν *for* κατῴκησεν (κατοικέω) LTTrAWHR

2735 κατόρθωμα.

Acts 24: 2(3) very worthy deeds—reforms, διόρθωμα LTTrAWHR

2736 κάτω, κατωτέρω.

Mar. 14:66 *trs* κάτω ἐν τῇ αὐλῇ TTrAWHR
Joh. 8: 8 κατακύπτω WH

2739 καυματίζω.

Mar. 4: 6 ἐκαυματίσθησαν they were scorched Tr

2743 καυτηριάζομαι, καυστ– TTrWH.

2744 καυχάομαι.

Ro. 5: 3 καυχώμενοι glorying TrA
1 Co. 1:29 καυχήσηται S—καυχήσεται E
13: 3*καυχήσωμαι *for* καυθήσωμαι (καίω) WH
2 Co. 10: 8 καυχήσομαι T
12:11 *omit* in glorying GEds
2 Th. 1: 4 ἐγκαυχάομαι LTTrAWHR

2746 καύχησις.

Ro. 15:17 τὴν ([τὴν] WH) καύχησιν Eds
2 Co. 9: 4 *omit* τῆς κ. *read* same confidence GEds

2747 Κεγχρεαί, Κενχ– TWH.

2748 Κέδρος.

Joh. 18: 1 τοῦ Κεδρών GL, τοῦ κέδρου T

2749 κεῖμαι.

Lu. 2:12 *omit* lying T
24:12 *omit* laid Tr[A]WHR: *omit the verse* [L]T[Tr] [[WH]]
Joh. 2: 6 *trs* κ. *after* Ἰουδαίων TTrAWHR
11:41 *omit* where the dead was laid GLTTrAWHR

2751 κείρω.

Acts 8:32 κείραντος TA

2753 κελεύω.

Mat. 15:35 παραγγέλλω LTTrWHR
Acts 23:35 κελεύσας LTTrAWHR
24: 8 *omit* and would (*ver.* 6) *to* come unto thee (*ver.* 8) LTTr[A]WHR

2758 κενόω.

1 Co. 9:15 κενώσει LTTrAWHR

2759 κέντρον.

Acts 9: 5 *omit* (it is) hard *to* (said) unto him (*ver.* 6) GEds
1 Co. 15:55 *trs* victory *and* sting LTTrWHR

2762 κεραία, κερέα WH.

2768 κέρας.

Rev. 13: 1 *trs* ten horns and seven heads GEds

2770 κερδαίνω.

Mat. 25:16*ἐκέρδησεν *for* ἐποίησεν (ποιέω) LTrWH
Mar. 8:36 ἐὰν κ.—κερδῆσαι to gain TAWHR
1 Co. 9:21 κερδάνω Eds
Jas. 4:13 κερδήσωμεν S—κερδήσομεν A.V.B EEds
1 Pet. 3: 1 κερδηθήσονται LTTrAWHR

2772 κέρμα.

Joh. 2:15 τὰ κέρματα TrAWHR

2775 κεφαλαιόω.

Mar. 12: 4 ἐκεφαλίωσαν TWHR

2776 κεφαλή.

Mat. 26: 7 τῆς κεφαλῆς LTTrWHR
27:29 τῆς κεφαλῆς TTrAWHR
Lu. 7:44 *omit* τῆς κ. *read* with her hairs GEds
Acts 18:18 *trs* ἐν Κεγχρεαῖς τὴν κ. LTTrAWH
Rev. 10: 1 τὴν κεφαλὴν Eds
13: 1 *trs* ten horns and seven heads GEds
14:14 τὴν κεφαλὴν LT

* κημόω, to muzzle.

1 Co. 9: 9 κημώσεις *for* φιμώσεις (–μόω) TTrA

2781 κηρίον.

Lu. 24:42 *omit* and of an honeycomb LT[Tr A]WHR

2783 κήρυξ, κῆρυξ WH.

2784 κηρύσσω.

Mar. 6:12 ἐκήρυξαν TTrAWHR
Ro. 10:15 κηρύξωσιν Eds

2786 Κηφᾶς.

Gal. 1:18*Κηφᾶν *for* Πέτρον Eds
2:11*Κηφᾶς *for* Πέτρος Eds
14*Κηφᾷ *for* Πέτρῳ Eds

2788 κιθάρα.

Rev. 5: 8 κιθάραν a harp Eds

2791 Κιλικία.

Acts 15:41 τὴν Κιλικίαν L, [τὴν] Κ. WH

2792 κιναμωμον, κιννά– LTTrAWHR.

2796 κίνησις.

Joh. 5: 3 *omit* waiting for *to end of verse* 4 GTTrAWHR

2797 Κίς, Κείς LTTrAWH.

2798 κλάδος.

Mar. 13:28 *trs* ἤδη ὁ κλάδος αὐτῆς LTrWH
Ro. 11:19 οἱ κ.—*omit* οἱ GEds

2806 κλάζω, κλάω.

Acts 20: 7 τοῦ κ.—*omit* τοῦ GEds
Ro. 11:20*ἐκλάσθησαν *for* ἐξεκλάσθησαν (ἐκκλάζω) LTr
1 Co. 11:24 *omit* broken LTTrAWHR

2799 κλαίω.

Joh. 20:11 *trs* ἔξω κλαίουσα TTrAWHR
Rev. 18: 9 κλαύσουσιν TTrAWWH

2801 κλάσμα.

Mar. 6:43 κλάσματα AWHR
8:19 *trs* κλασμ. πλήρεις LTTrAWWH

2802 Κλαύδη.

Acts 27:16 Καῦδα LTrWHR, Κλαῦδα T, Κ[λ]αῦδα A

2807 κλείς.

Mat. 16:19 κλεῖδας LTTrAWH
Rev. 3: 7 κλεῖν GEds
20: 1 κλεῖν GEds

2808 κλείω.

Rev. 3: 7 κ.[1]—κλείσει shall shut Eds
7 κ.[2]—κλείων LTTrWHR

2812 κλέπτης.

1 Th. 5: 4 κλέπτας thieves LWH

2816 κληρονομέω.

Gal. 4:30 κληρονομήσει LTTrWH

2817 κληρονομία.

Acts 20:32 τὴν κληρονομίαν TTrAWHR

2819 κλῆρος.

Mat. 27:35 *omit* that it might *to end of verse* GLTTrAWHR
Lu. 23:34 κλήρους TA: *sortes* A.V.Vul
Acts 1:25 part—the place, τόπος LTTrAWHR

2822 κλητός.

Mat. 20:16 *omit* for many be called, but few chosen T[TrA]WHR
1 Co. 1: 1 [called] LA

* κλινάριον, a small bed.

Acts 5:15 κλιναρίων *for* κλινῶν (–νη) LTTrAWHR

2825 κλίνη.

Mar. 7: 4 *omit* and of tables TWHR
30 κλίνην LTTrAWHR, *see* παιδίον
Acts 5:15 κλινάριον LTTrAWHR

2829 κλοπή.

Mar. 7:21, 22 *trs* fornications, thefts, murders, adulteries TTrAWHR

2836 κοιλία.

Lu. 15:16 *omit* his belly WHR
23:29 αἱ κοιλίαι TTrAWHR

2837 κοιμάομαι.

Lu. 22:45 *trs* κοιμωμένους αὐτοὺς TTrAWH
1 Th. 4:13 κοιμωμένων LTTrAWHR

2839 κοινός.

Mar. 7: 5*κοιναῖς *for* ἀνίπτοις (–τος) GEds
Rev. 21:27*κοινόν *for* κοινοῦν (νόω) GEds

2840 κοινόω.

Mar. 7:15 *trs* κοινῶσαι αὐτὸν TWH
Rev. 21:27 that defileth—common, κοινός GEds

2842 κοινωνία.

Eph. 3: 9 fellowship—dispensation, οἰκονομία GEds
Phil. 3:10 τὴν κ.—*omit* τὴν LTTr[A]WHR

2844 κοινωνός.

Mat. 23:30 *trs* αὐτῶν κοινωνοὶ LTrAWH

2847 κόκκινος, τὸ κόκκινον.

Rev. 17: 4 κόκκινον GEds

2848 κόκκος.

Mar. 4:31 κόκκον GLTrAW

2850 κολακεία, –κία TWH.

2857 Κολασσαί S—Κολοσσαί A.V.B EGTAWWHR.

2853 κολλάω.

Mat. 19: 5*κολληθήσεται *for* προσκολληθήσεται (–λάω) LTTrAWWH
Rev. 18: 5*ἐκολλήθησαν *for* ἠκολούθησαν (ἀκολουθέω) A.V.C GEds

2854 κολλούριον, κολλύριον TTrA.

2861 κολυμβήθρα.

Joh. 5: 4 *omit* waiting for (*ver.* 3) *to end of verse* 4 [G]TTrAWHR
9:11 *omit* the pool of GLTTrAWHR

2865 κομίζω.

Eph. 6: 8 κομίσεται LTTrAWH
Col. 3:25 κομίσεται LWH
Heb. 11:13*κομισάμενοι *for* λαβόντες (λαμβάνω) TTrWHR
2 Pet. 2:13 ἀδικέω, *read* suffering wrong as the hire of unrighteousness WHR

2872 κοπιάω.

Mat. 6:28 κοπιῶσιν LTWH, κοπιοῦσιν TrA

2872

Lu. 12:27 οὐ κοπιᾷ, οὐδὲ νήθει they toil not, they spin not—οὔτε νήθει οὔτε ὑφαίνει (-νω) they neither spin nor weave TA

Rev. 2: 3 κ. καὶ οὐ κέκμηκας hast laboured, and hast not fainted —καὶ οὐ κεκοπίακες (-κας R) and hast not grown weary LTTrAWHR, καὶ οὐκ ἐκοπίασας GW

2873 κόπος.

Heb. 6:10 *omit* τοῦ κ. *read* work and love GEds

2874 κοπρία.

Lu. 13: 8 κοπρίαν S-κόπριος EGLTTrAWWH

* κόπριος, full of dung, filthy.

Lu. 13: 8 κόπρια *for* κοπρίαν (-ρία) EGLTTrAWWH

2875 κόπτω.

Mar. 11: 8 κόψαντες TTrAWHR

2883 Κορνήλιος.

Acts 10: 7 Cornelius—him, αὐτῷ GEds
21 *omit* which were sent unto him from Cornelius GEds

2884 κόσμος.

Mat. 13:35 *omit* of the world LTTrAWH
Joh. 8:23 *trs* τούτου τοῦ κόσμου[1] LTrAWH
17:12 *omit* in the world LTTrAWHR
16 *trs* οὐκ εἰμὶ ἐκ τοῦ κόσμου[2] LTTrAWWH
21:25 *omit the verse* T
Ro. 4:13 τοῦ κ.—*omit* τοῦ GEds
1 Co. 7:31 τῷ κ.—τὸν κόσμον LTTrAWHR
Gal. 6:14 τῷ κ.—*omit* τῷ LTTrAWHR
Jas. 2: 5 τῷ κόσμῳ as to the world Eds
1 Pet. 5: 9 τῷ κόσμῳ TTrWH
2 Pet. 1: 4 τῷ κόσμῳ LTTrWHR

2891
κοῦμι, κούμ TWH, κοῦμ TrA.

2894 κόφινος.

Mar. 6:43 κοφίνων TAWHR

2895
κράββατος, κράβαττος LTTrAWWH.

Mar. 2: 9 *trs* τὸν κράβατ. σου LTTrAWWH
Joh. 5:12 *omit* thy bed T[Tr]AWHR
Acts 9:33 κραβάττου Eds

2896 κράζω.

Mat. 15:22*ἔκραζεν LTrWH, ἔκραξεν T *for* ἐκραύγασεν (κραυγάζω)
20:31 ἔκραξαν LTTrAWH
21:15 τοὺς κράζοντας LTTrAWHR
Mar. 1:26 φωνέω TTrAWHR
3:11 ἔκραζον LTTrAWWH
9:26 κράξας GEds
15:39 *om.* cried out, and T[Tr]AWHR
Lu. 4:41 κραυγάζω LT
19:40 κράξουσιν TTrAWHR
Joh. 7:37 ἔκραζεν T
12:13 κραυγάζω LTTrAWHR
19:12 κραυγάζω LTTrWH
Acts 19:34 κράζοντες T
21:36 κράζοντες LTTrAWWH
23: 6 ἔκραζεν TTrAWHR
24:21 ἐκκράζω TTrAWH
Rev. 6:10 ἔκραξαν GEds
7:10 κράζουσιν they cry GEds
18:18 ἔκραξαν LTrAWHR
19 ἔκραξαν LAWHR

2897 κραιπάλη, κρε- WH.

2905 κραυγάζω.

Mat. 15:22 κράζω LTTrWH
Lu. 4:41*κραυγάζοντα *for* κράζοντα (-ζω) LT
Joh. 12:13*ἐκραύγαζον *for* ἔκραζον (κράζω) LTTrAWHR
19:12*ἐκραύγαζον LT, -σαν TrWH *for* ἔκραζον (κράζω)

2906 κραυγή.

Lu. 1:42*κραυγῇ *for* φωνῇ TTrAWHR
Rev. 14:18 cry—voice, φωνῇ LTTrWHR

2909 κρείσσων, κρείττων.

1 Co. 12:31 best—greater, μείζων LTTrAWHR
Heb. 12:24 κρεῖττον a better thing GEds

2910
κρέμαμαι, κρεμάννυμι, κρεμάω.

Mat. 22:40†*trs* κρέμαται καὶ οἱ προφῆται Eds

2915 κριθή.

Rev. 6: 6 κριθῶν Eds

2917 κρίμα, κρῖμα.

Mat. 23:14(13) *omit the verse* LTTrAWHR, (*it is ver.* 13 *in* S, *and* 14 *in* A.V.BE)

2919 κρίνω.

Lu. 22:30 *trs* τὰς δώδεκα φυλὰς κ. WH
Joh. 7:24 κ.[2]—κρίνετε LTrAWH
Acts 20:16 κεκρίκει GEds
24: 6 κρῖναι A: *omit* and would have judged *to* to come unto thee (*ver.* 8) LTTr[A]WHR
25: 9 κριθῆναι LTTrAWWH
1 Co. 5:13 κρινεῖ will judge GLT
Heb. 10:30 *trs* κρινεῖ κύριος Eds
Jas. 4:12 ὃς κ.—ὁ κρίνων LTTrAWHR
5: 9*κριθῆτε *for* κατακριθῆτε (-κρίνω) GEds
1 Pet. 4: 5 ἔχοντι κ.—κρίνοντι WH
Rev. 18: 8 κρίνας judged GEds

2920 κρίσις.

Mar. 3:29 ἁμάρτημα, *read* guilty of eternal sin LTTrAWHR
6:11 *omit* verily *to end of verse* G[L]TTrAWHR
Jas. 5:12 κρίσιν A.V.B EGEds, *see* ὑπόκρισις

2923 κριτής.

Mat. 12:27 *trs* κριταὶ ἔσονται ὑμῶν LTTrAWH
Lu. 11:19 *trs* αὐτοὶ ὑμῶν κ. ἔσονται LAWH, α. κ. ἔσ. ὑ. T, α. κ. ὑ. ἔσ. Tr
12:14*κριτήν *for* δικαστήν (-τής) LTTrAWH
Jas. 4:12*lawgiver—*add* καὶ κριτής and judge GLTTrAWHR
5: 9 ὁ κριτής A.V.C GEds

* κρύπτη, a vault.

Lu. 11:33 κρυπτήν *for* κρυπτόν (-ος) EGEds

2926 κρυπτός.

Mat. 6:18 κρυφαῖος *bis* LTTrAWH
Lu. 11:33 κρυπτὸν S—κρυπτήν (-τη) EGEds
Joh. 7: 4 *trs* τι ἐν κρυπτῷ LTTrAWH

2928 κρύπτω.

Mat. 11:25*ἔκρυψας *for* ἀπέκρυψας (ἀποκρύπτω) LTTrAWH
25:18*ἔκρυψεν *for* ἀπέκρυψεν (ἀποκρύπτω) LTTrAWH
Lu. 13:21*ἔκρυψεν *for* ἐνέκρυψεν (ἐγκρύπτω) TTrAWHR

*κρυφαῖος, secret, hidden.

Mat. 6:18 κρυφαίῳ *bis for* κρυπτῷ (-τός) LTTrAWH

2931 κρυφῇ, -φῆ LWH.

2932 κτάομαι.

Lu. 21:19 κτήσεσθε ye shall possess LTrAWH

2936 κτίζω.

Mat. 19: 4*κτίσας *for* ποιήσας (ποιέω) TrWH

2937 κτίσις.

Col. 1:23 τῇ κ.—*omit* τῇ Eds

2940 κυβεία, κυβίᾳ TWH.

* κυκλεύω, to encircle.

Rev. 20: 9 ἐκύκλευσαν *for* ἐκύκλωσαν (κυκλόω) LTAWWHR

2943 κυκλόθεν.

Rev. 5:11 κύκλῳ GLTTrAWWH

2944 κυκλόω.

Rev. 20: 9 κυκλεύω LTAWWHR

2945 κύκλῳ.

Mar. 3:34 *trs* τοὺς περὶ αὐτὸν κύκλῳ LTTrWHR
Rev. 5:11*κύκλῳ *f.* κυκλόθεν GLTTrAWWH

2946 κύλισμα.

2 Pet. 2:22 κυλισμός TTrAWH

* κυλισμός, a rolling.

2 Pet. 2:22 κυλισμόν *for* κύλισμα TTrAWH

2948 κυλλός.

Mat. 15:30 *trs* κυλλούς, τυφλούς, κωφούς WH
31 *om.* the maimed to be whole WH
18: 8 *trs* maimed or halt LTWHR

2949 κῦμα.

Acts 27:41 *omit* of the waves LT[TrA]WHR

2954 Κύπρος.

Acts 13: 4 τὴν Κ.—*omit* τήν LTTrAWH

2955 κύπτω.

Joh. 8: 8 κατακύπτω WH

2956 Κυρηναῖος.

Lu. 23:26 Κυρηναῖον LTTrAWHR

2959
κυρία—Κυρία (as a proper name) GLT.

2962 κύριος.

Mat. 1:22 ǀ 2:15 τοῦ κ.—*omit* τοῦ LTTrA (WWH
13:51 *omit* Lord LTTrAWHR
18:26 *omit* Lord LTTrAWH
20:30 *omit* O Lord T
30, 31 *trs* κ. ἐλέησον ἡμᾶς LTrAWHR
21:30 *trs* WH, *see* ἀπέρχομαι
22:44 ὁ κ.—*omit* ὁ LTTrAWH
24:48 *trs* μου ὁ κύριος LTTrAWH
28: 6 *omit* ὁ κ. *read* he T[TrA]WH
Mar. 5:19 *trs* ὁ κύριός σοι TTrAWH
9:24 *omit* Lord GEds
11:10 *omit* in the name of the Lord GEds
12:36 ὁ κ.—*omit* ὁ LTrAWH
13:20 *trs* ἐκολόβωσεν κύριος TWH
Lu. 1:15 τοῦ κ.—*omit* τοῦ GT[Tr]WWH
25 ὁ κ.—*omit* ὁ LTTr[A]WH
2:38 the Lord—God, θεός LTTrAWHR
4: 8 *trs* κύριον τὸν θεόν σου προσκυνήσεις LTrWH
7:19*κύριον *for* Ἰησοῦν TTrAWHR
31 *omit* and the Lord said GEds
9:57 *omit* Lord LTTr[A]WHR
59 *omit* Lord TWH
10:39*κυρίου *for* Ἰησοῦ Eds
41*κύριος *for* Ἰησοῦς TWHR
12:37 *trs* ὁ κύριος ἐλθὼν R
13:25 *omit* κ.[2] [L]TTrAWHR
19:18 *trs* ἡ μνᾶ σου, κ. TTrAWHR
20:42 ὁ κ.—*omit* ὁ LTrAWH
44 *trs* αὐτὸν κύριον TrAWH
22:31 *omit* and the Lord said T[Tr]AWHR
23:42 *omit* Lord [L]TTrAWHR
24:34 *trs* ὄντως ἠγέρθη ὁ κ. LTTrAWHR
Joh. 4: 1 the Lord—Jesus, Ἰησοῦς T
Acts 2:34 ὁ κ.—*omit* ὁ TTrAWH
7:30 *omit* of the Lord LTTrAWHR
37 *omit* the Lord LTTrAWHR
8:22*κυρίου *for* θεοῦ (-ός) Eds
9: 5 *omit* κ. εἶπεν Eds
6 *omit* (it is) hard (*ver.* 5) *to* unto him (*ver.* 6) GEds
10 *trs* ἐν ὁράματι ὁ κύριος Eds
10:33*κυρίου *for* θεοῦ[2] LTTrWHR
48†*trs* ἐν τῷ ὀνόματι (τοῦ κυρίου βαπτισθῆναι A) Ἰησοῦ χριστοῦ βαπ. LTTrWHR
11:16 τοῦ κυρίου GLTTrAWWH
12:11 ὁ κύριος WH
24*κυρίου *for* θεοῦ WH
13:10 τοῦ κυρίου WH
11 τοῦ κ.—*omit* τοῦ GLTTrAWWH
44*κυρίου *for* θεοῦ LTTr
48 θεός, *read* word of God WHR
15:11 τοῦ κυρίου GLTTrAWWH
40*κυρίου *for* θεοῦ Eds
16:10 the Lord—God, θεός LTTrAWHR
32 the Lord—God, θεός WH
17:24 *trs* ὑπάρχων κύριος LTTrAWH
27 the Lord — God, θεός GLTTrAWHR
18:25 the Lord[2]—Jesus Ἰησοῦ Eds
19:20 *Dei* A.V.Vul: *trs* τοῦ κ. ὁ λόγος LTTrAWHR
20:28*κυρίου *for* θεοῦ GLTTr
32*κυρίῳ *for* θεῷ WH
21:14 *trs* τοῦ κ. τὸ θέλημα LTTrAWWH
20 the Lord—God, θεός LTTrAWHR
22:16 αὐτοῦ, *read* on his name GEds
26:15*δέ[2]—*add* κύριος *read* and the Lord said Eds

Ro. 6:11 omit our Lord GEds
10: 9 κύριος Ἰησοῦς WH
12:11 τῷ καιρῷ (-ρός) in season s—τῷ κυρίῳ the Lord A.V.B EEds
14: 4*κύριος for θεός LTTrAWHR
6 omit and he that regardeth not to regard (it) LTTr[A]WHR
16:24 omit the verse LTTr[A]WHR
1Co. 7:17 trs as the Lord hath distributed to every man, as God hath called GEds
10: 9*κύριον for χριστόν LTTrAWHR
26 trs κυρίου γὰρ LTTrAWWH
28 omit for the earth to end of verse GEds
11:29 omit Lord's LTTrAWHR
32 τοῦ κυρίου TTr[A]WWH
12: 3 κύριος Ἰησοῦς Eds
14:37 τοῦ κ.—omit τοῦ GEds
15:47 omit the Lord LTTrAWHR
2Co. 4:10 omit the Lord GEds
14 [the Lord] TrAWH
11:17 trs κατὰ κ. λαλῶ Eds
Gal. 1: 3 trs ἡμῶν καὶ κ. WH
6:17 omit the Lord Eds
Eph. 3:14 omit of our Lord Jesus Christ Eds
5:29 the Lord—Christ, χριστός GEds
6: 1 omit in the Lord L[TrAWH]
5 trs κατὰ σάρκα κ. LTTrWHR
8 τοῦ κ.—omit τοῦ GEds
Phil. 2:30*κυρίου for χριστοῦ WH
Col. 1: 2 omit and the Lord Jesus Christ G[L]TTrAWWHR
3:13*κύριος for χριστός LTrAWHR
16 the Lord—God, θεός GEds
17 the Lord Jesus—Jesus Christ, χριστοῦ LW
20 τῷ κ.—ἐν κ. in the Lord GEds
22*κύριον for θεόν GEds
1Th. 1: 1 omit from God our to end of verse [L]TTrAWHR
4: 6 ὁ κ.—omit ὁ LTTrAWHR
2Th. 2: 2*κυρίου for χριστοῦ GEds
3:12 διὰ τοῦ κυρίου ἡμῶν Ἰησοῦ χριστοῦ—ἐν κυρίῳ Ἰησοῦ χριστῷ in the Lord Jesus Christ LTTrAWHR
1Ti. 1: 1 omit Lord GEds
5:21 omit the Lord Eds
2Ti. 2:14 the Lord—God, θεός TTrWH
19*κυρίου for χριστοῦ GEds
4: 1 omit the Lord GEds
Tit. 1: 4 omit the Lord LTTrAWHR
Philem. 20 the Lord[2]—Christ, χριστός GEds
Heb. 10:30 omit saith the Lord TTrWHR
Jas. 1:12 omit the Lord LTTrAWHR
3: 9*κύριον for θεόν LTTrAWHR
4:10 τοῦ κ.—omit τοῦ LTTrAWH
5:14 τοῦ κ.—omit τοῦ L[Tr]A, [τοῦ κ.] WH
2Pet. 2:11 omit before the Lord L[TrWH]
3: 9 ὁ κ.—omit ὁ LTTrAWWH
2Joh. 3 omit the Lord Eds
Jude 5 Ἰησοῦς LA: ὁ κ.—om. ὁ TTrAWH
25*ἡμῶν—add διὰ Ἰησοῦ χριστοῦ τοῦ κυρίου ἡμῶν, read Saviour, through Jesus Christ our Lord GEds
Rev. 1: 8 ὁ κ.—κ. ὁ θεός GEds
4:11 κύριε—ὁ κύριος καὶ ὁ θεὸς ἡμῶν our Lord and our God Eds
11: 4*κυρίου for θεοῦ GEds
16: 5 omit O Lord GEds
18: 8 [the Lord] AWH
19: 1 omit the Lord GEds
22: 6 ὁ κύριος LTTrAWHR

2967 κωλύω.

Mar. 9:38 εκωλύομεν TTrAWHR
Lu. 9:49 ἐκωλύομεν WHR

2968 κώμη.

Mar. 8:26 omit nor tell (it) to any in the town TWHR
Lu. 9:52 village—city, πόλις T

2972 Κῶς.

Acts 21: 1 Κῶ GEds

2974 κωφός.

Mat. 12:22 κ.[1]—κωφόν LWH

2977 λάθρα, —ρᾳ LWH.

2979 λακτίζω.

Acts 9: 5 omit (it is) hard to unto him (ver. 6) GEds

2980 λαλέω.

Mat. 10:19 λ.[2]—λαλήσητε TTrAWH
12:36 λαλήσουσιν TTrAWH
47 omit the verse [T]WH
Mar. 9: 6 say—answer, ἀποκρίνομαι TTrAWHR
11:23*λαλεῖ for λέγει (-γω) LTTrAWHR
12: 1*λαλεῖν f. λέγειν (-γω) LTTrAWHR
14:31*ἐλάλει for ἔλεγεν (λέγω) LTTrAWHR
Lu. 2:15*ἐλάλουν for εἶπον TWH
Joh. 6:63 λελάληκα have spoken Eds
7:46 trs ἐλάλησεν οὕτως LTTrAWHR
46*οὗτος—add λαλεῖ, read this man speaketh T
8:26*λαλῶ for λέγω LTTrAWHR
12:50 trs ἐγὼ λαλῶ LTTrAWHR
14:10 λ.[1]—λέγω TTrAWHR
18:20 λ.[1]—λελάληκα have spoken Eds
Acts 7:44 ὁ λ.—omit ὁ A.V.Vul
10: 6 omit he shall tell thee what thou oughtest to do GEds
32 omit who, when he cometh, shall speak unto thee LTTr[A]WHR
13:45*λαλουμένοις for λεγομένοις (-γω) LTTrWHR
17:19 ἡ ὑπὸ σοῦ λ.—omit ἡ L[TrWH]
23: 7 εἶπον LTrWR, λαλοῦντος WH
26:14 speaking — saying, λέγω LTTrAWHR
Ro. 15:18 trs τι λαλεῖν Eds
1Co. 13:11 trs ἐλάλουν ὡς νήπιος Eds
14:18 λαλῶ LTTrAWHR
15:34*λαλῶ for λέγω LTTrAWHR
Heb. 11: 4 λαλεῖ A.V.Er GEds
Rev. 1:12 ἐλάλει Eds
10: 8 λαλοῦσαν Eds

2981 λαλιά.

Mar. 14:70 omit and thy speech agreeth (thereto) LTTrAWHR

2982 λαμά, λαμμᾶ.

Mat. 27:46 λημά L, λεμά TTrAWH
Mar. 15:34 λεμά LT, λαμά TrAWWHR

2983 λαμβάνω.

(Future λήμψομαι, &c. LTTrAWH)

Mat. 15:36 καὶ λ.—ἔλαβεν LTTrWHR
16: 8 have brought—have, ἔχω LWHR
20: 7 omit and whatsoever is right (that) shall ye receive LTTrAWHR
23:14(13) omit the verse LTTrAWHR, see κρίμα
25:22 omit had received LTTrAWHR
Mar. 11:24 ἐλάβετε have received LTTrAWH (R
12: 3 οἱ δὲ λ.—καὶ λ. LTTrAR
22 omit had her [L]TTrAWHR
14:65*ἔλαβον for ἔβαλλον (βάλλω) LTTrAWHR
Lu. 6: 4 ἔ. καὶ—λαβών LTrAWHR
34*λαβεῖν for ἀπολαβεῖν (-λαμβάνω) TTrAWHR
18:30*λάβῃ for ἀπολάβῃ (-λαμβάνω) LWH
20:30 omit took to end of verse TTrAWHR
Joh. 1:12 ἔλαβαν Tr
13:26*sop[2]—add λαμβάνει καί, read he taketh and giveth TTrAWHR
16:15 λαμβάνει taketh GEds
Acts 1:20 λαβετω Eds (WHR
2:23 omit have taken, and LTTrA
3: 3 omit λαβεῖν A.V.C
16:24 εἰληφώς—λαβών Eds
1Co. 11:24 omit take, eat GEds
2Ti. 1: 5 λαβών LTTrAWHR
Heb. 11:13 κομίζω TTrWHR
Rev. 11:17 εἴληφες WH
18: 4 trs ἐκ τῶν πληγῶν αὐτῆς ἵνα μὴ λ. GEds
22:17 λαβέτω GEds

2986 λαμπρός.

Rev. 19: 8†trs white, clean GLTTrAWHR

2989 λάμπω.

2Co. 4: 6 λ.[1]—λάμψει shall shine LTTrAWHR

2993 Λαοδίκεια, —κια TWH.

Rev. 3:14*ἐν Λαοδικείᾳ ἐκκλησίας GEds

2994 Λαοδικεύς.

Rev. 3:14 of the Laodiceans—in Laodicea, Λαοδίκεια GEds

2992 λαός.

Mat. 9:35 omit among the people GEds
Mar. 11:32 ὄχλος WH
Lu. 1:10 trs ἦν τοῦ λαοῦ GLTTrAWWH
20: 6†trs ὁ λαὸς ἅπας TTrAWHR
Acts 3: 9 trs πᾶς ὁ λ. αὐτόν LTTrAWWH
11 trs πᾶς ὁ λ. πρὸς αὐτ. LTTrAWH
5:12 trs πολλὰ ἐν τῷ λ. LTTrAWWH
Rev. 13: 7*kindreds—add καὶ λαόν and people GEds
18: 4 trs ὁ λ. μου ἐξ αὐτῆς TWHR
21: 3 λαός GW

2996 Λασαία, Λασέα TrAWH, Ἄλασσα L.

3002 Λεββαῖος.

Mat. 10: 3 omit LTrWHR, see ἐπικαλέω

3003 λεγεών.

Mat. 26:53 λεγιώνων T, λεγιῶνας WH
Mar. 5: 9 λεγιών LTTrAWH
15 λεγιῶνα LTTrAWH
Lu. 8:30 λεγιών TTrWH

3004 λέγω.

Mat. 4: 9 saith—said, εἶπον LTTrAWHR
8:22*λέγει for εἶπεν (-πον) Eds
9:11*ἔλεγον for εἶπον LTTrWH
24 ἔλεγεν LTTrAWHR
12:48*λέγοντι for εἰπόντι (-πον) LTTrAWH
13:28*λέγουσιν for εἶπον LTTrAWHR
51 omit Jesus saith unto them LTTrAWHR
15: 4 commanded, saying—said, εἶπον LTrWHR
12*λέγουσιν for εἶπον LTTrAWH
16: 2 when it is evening to end of verse 3 [TA] [[WH]]
22 Πέτρος λέγει αὐτῷ ἐπιτιμῶν Peter saith to him, rebuking A
17:20*λέγει for εἶπεν (-πον) LTTrAWHR
26 λέγει αὐτῷ ὁ Πέτρος—εἰπόντος δέ and when he said LTTrWHR
19:17 ἐρωτάω GEds, see ἀγαθός
18 see φημί
22:16 λέγοντας LTTrWHR
23 οἱ λ.—omit οἱ LTTrAWHR
35 omit and saying LTTrWHR
27:33 trs κρανίου τόπος λ. LTTrAWH
49 εἶπον LTrWH
Mar. 1:15 omit and saying T[WH]
25 omit saying T[WH]
2: 8*λέγει for εἶπεν (-πον) TTrAWHR
12 omit saying [L]A[WH]
25 λέγει saith LTTrWH
3:11 λέγοντες T
32*καὶ λέγουσιν for εἶπον δέ Eds
33 ἀποκριθεὶς αὐτοῖς λέγει TTrAWHR
5: 7*λέγει for εἶπεν (-πον) Eds
9 answered, saying—saith to him, λέγει αὐτῷ GEds
6:11 omit verily to end of verse G[L]TTrAWHR
14 ἔλεγον LWH
16*ἔλεγεν for εἶπεν (-πον) TTrAWHR
31*λέγει f. εἶπεν (-πον) TTrAWWHR
35 ἔλεγον TTrAWHR
7:27*ἔλεγεν f. εἶπεν (-πον) LTTrAWHR
36*λέγωσιν for εἴπωσιν (-πον) TTrAWH
8:16 omit saying LTTrAWH
20*καὶ λέγουσιν αὐτῷ (om. αὐτῷ T) for οἱ δὲ εἶπον TAWHR
28*answered (spake TAWHR)—add αὐτῷ λέγοντες to him saying LTTrAWHR: add ὅτι TAWH
29 saith unto[1]—asked, ἐπερωτάω LTTrAWHR
33 λέγων—καὶ λέγει and saith TTrAWHR
9: 7 omit saying GTTrAWWHR
38 omit saying TWHR
10:51 εἶπον TTrAWHR
11: 9 omit saying [L]TTrAWHR
17 λέγων—καὶ ἔλεγεν and said TTrAWHR
23 λ.[2]—λαλέω LTTrAWHR
28 ἔλεγον said TTrAWHR
12: 1 λαλέω LTTrAWHR
36*λέγει for εἶπεν[1] W, for ε.[2] GTr
43 saith—said, εἶπον GLTTrWHR
13: 5 trs began to say to them LTTrAWH
14: 4 omit and said T[Tr]AWHR

Mar. 14:31 λ.[1]—λαλέω LTTrAWHR
15: 2*αὐτῷ λέγει *for* εἶπεν αὐτῷ TTrAWHR
4 *omit* saying T[WH]
12*ἔλεγεν *for* εἶπεν (–πον) TTrAWH
12 *omit* whom ye call LTr
28 *omit the verse* T[Tr]AWHR
34 *omit* saying TTrAWHR
Lu. 3: 4 *omit* saying LTTrAWHR
11 ἔλεγεν said LTTrAWHR
22 *omit* which said LTTrAWHR
4: 4 *omit* saying TTrAWHR
34 *omit* saying T[Tr]AWHR
5:13*λέγων *for* εἰπών (–πον) LTrWHR
7:32 λέγοντες TTrA, ἃ λέγει WHR
8: 9 *omit* saying LTTr[A]WHR
20 *omit* which said LTTr[A]WHR
30 *omit* saying LWHR
45 *omit* and sayest thou, Who touched me? T[Tr]AWHR
50 *omit* saying LTTr[A]WHR
9:21*λέγειν *for* εἰπεῖν (–πον) GLTTrAWHR
11:53 *omit* λ. TTrAWHR, *see* ἐξέρχομαι
12:22 *trs* λέγω ὑμῖν TrAWHR
13:27 λέγων WH
18:16*λέγων *for* εἶπεν (–πον) TTrAWHR
41 *omit* saying T[Tr]AWHR
19:30*λέγων *for* εἰπών (–πον) LTrWH
20: 2 *omit* saying TrA: *trs* λέγοντες πρὸς αὐτὸν LTWHR
27*λέγοντες *for* ἀντιλέγοντες (–γω) TrWHR
23:34 Then said Jesus *to* what they do [L][[WH]]
39 *omit* saying T[Tr]AWH
40 φημί TTrAWHR
43 *trs* σοι λέγω TTrAWH
24:36 *omit* and saith unto them, Peace (be) unto you T[[WH]]
Joh. 1:49(50) *om.* and saith [L]TTrAWHR
4:51 *omit* saying T
5: 2*τὸ λεγόμενον *for* ἡ ἐπιλεγομένη (–γω) T
19*ἔλεγεν *for* εἶπεν (–πον) TWH
8:23*ἔλεγεν *for* εἶπεν (–πον) LTTrAWHR
26 λαλέω LTTrAWHR
9: 9*δέ, ὅτι—ἔλεγον, Οὐχί, ἀλλά (οὐχί ἀ. L), *read* others said, No, but LTTrAWHR
11 ὁ λεγόμενος TTrWHR, [ὁ] λ. A
10:33 *omit* saying Eds
11:31 saying—thinking, δοκέω TTrA
56 ἔλεγαν T (WHR
12:34 *trs* λέγεις σύ TTrAWH
13:24*πυθέσθαι τίς ἂν εἴη that he should ask who it should be —καὶ λέγει αὐτῷ, Εἰπὲ τίς ἐστιν and saith to him, Say who it is LTTrAWHR
14:10*λέγω *for* λαλῶ[1] (–λέω) TTrAWHR
15:15 *trs* λέγω ὑμᾶς LTTrAWHR
16:12 *trs* ὑμῖν λέγειν TTrAWH
18: 4*καὶ λέγει *for* εἶπεν (–πον) LTTrAWHR
19: 6 *omit* saying T
24 *omit* which saith LTWH
21: 6*λέγει *for* ὁ δὲ εἶπεν (–πον) T
17*λέγει *for* εἶπεν[2] (–πον) T
Acts 5:25 *omit* saying GEds
6: 9 τῶν λεγομένων T
13:45 λαλέω LTTrWHR
15:24 *omit* saying, (Ye must) be circumcised, and keep the law LTTrAWHR
17: 7 *trs* ἕτερον λέγοντες LTTrWH
20:23 λέγων A
26:14*λέγουσαν *for* λαλοῦσαν (–λέω) LTTrAWHR
14 *omit* and saying LTTrAWHR
28:26 λέγων TTrAWH
Ro. 11: 2 *omit* saying GEds
15:11*again—*add* λέγει he saith [L]A
1 Co. 7:12 *trs* λέγω ἐγώ Eds
15:34 λαλέω LTTrAWHR
Heb.10:30 *omit* saith the Lord TTrWHR
2 Joh. 11 *trs* λέγων γὰρ LTTrAWH
Rev. 2: 2*λέγοντας ἑαυτούς *for* φάσκοντας (–κω) GEds
20 ἡ λέγουσα GEds
4: 1 λέγων GEds
8 λέγοντες GEds
6: 7 λέγοντος GEds
9:14 λέγοντα Eds
10: 8 λέγουσαν Eds
11 λέγουσιν they say LTTrAWHR
11:12 λεγούσης TrAWHR
15 λέγοντες GLTAWWHR
12:10 *trs* ἐν τῷ οὐρανῷ λ. GEds
14: 7 λέγων GEds

Rev. 19: 1 λεγόντων Eds
6 λέγοντας S—λέγοντες GA, λεγόντων ELTTrWWHR

3005 λεῖμμα, λίμμα WH.

3007 λείπω.

Tit. 3:13 λίπῃ T

3015 λεπρός.

Mat. 10: 8 *trs* raise the dead, cleanse the lepers GEds

3017 Λευΐ, Λευεί TTrAWH.

Heb. 7: 9 Λευΐς L, Λευείς TTrAWH

3018 Λευΐς, –είς –εΐς TTrAWH.

Lu. 5:29 ὁ Λ.—*omit* ὁ GLTTrAWWH

3019 Λευΐτης, Λευείτης TTrAWH.

3020 Λευϊτικός, Λευει– TAWH.

3022 λευκός.

Acts 1:10 λευκαῖς LTTrAWHR
Rev. 6:11 στολὴ λευκή a white robe GEds
20:11 *trs* μέγαν λευκόν GEds

3023 λέων

Rev. 13: 2 λεόντων of lions T

3028 λῆψις, λῆμψις LTTrAWH.

3031 λιβανωτός.

Rev. 8: 5 τὸ λ. S—τὸν λ. EGLTTrAWWH

3034 λιθάζω.

Joh. 8: 5*λιθάζειν *for* λιθοβολεῖσθαι (–λέω) WWHR
10:32†*trs* ἐμὲ λιθάζετε TTrAWH

3036 λιθοβολέω.

Mar. 12: 4 *omit* cast stones, and LTTrA (WHR
Joh. 8: 5 λιθάζω WWHR

3037 λίθος.

Mat. 21:44 *omit the verse* [L]T[WH]
Mar. 9:42 λίθος μυλικός—μύλος ὀνικός *lit.* a millstone turned by an ass LTTrAWHR
13: 2 λ.[2]—λίθον TTrWHR
Lu. 11:11 *omit* λ. WH, *see* ἄρτος
17: 2*μύλος ὀνικός—λίθος μυλικός LTTrAWHR
19:44†*trs* λίθον ἐπὶ λίθον (λίθῳ L) ἐν σοί LTTrAWHR
Joh. 8: 7 τὸν λ.—*om.* τὸν WHR, *see* αὐτῇ
1 Pet. 2: 7 λίθος LTrAWHR
Rev. 15: 6*λίθον *for* λίνον LTrWHR

3039 λικμάω.

Mat. 21:44 *omit the verse* [L]T[WH]

3041 λίμνη.

Rev. 20:14*add *at end* ἡ λίμνη τοῦ πυρός the lake of fire Eds

3042 λιμός.

Lu. 21:11 *trs* pestilences and famines LTrAWH

3043 λινον.

Rev. 15: 6 linen—stone, λίθος LTrWHR

3044 Λῖνος, Λίνος LTWWH.

3049 λογίζομαι.

Mar. 11:31 διαλογίζομαι Eds
15:28 *omit the verse* T[Tr]AWHR
Joh. 11:50*λογίζεσθε *for* διαλογίζεσθε (–ζομαι) Eds
1 Co. 13:11 *trs* ἐφρόνουν ὡς νήπιος ἐλογιζόμην ὡς νήπιος LTTrAWHR
2 Co. 3: 5†*trs* ἱκανοί ἐσμεν λογίζεσθαί (–σασθαί AW) τι ἀφ' ἑαυτῶν LAW, ἀφ' ἑα. ἱκ. ἐσ. λογίσασθαί τι TTrWHR

3056 λόγος.

Mat. 8: 8 λόγῳ, *read* speak by a word GEds
15: 6*τὸν λόγον *for* τὴν ἐντολήν (–λή) LTrWHR
19:22 *omit* that saying T
25:19 *trs* λόγον μετ' αὐτῶν LTTrAWH
Lu. 1:29†*trs* ἐπὶ τῷ λ. διετα. GTTrAWHR
20:20 λόγον Tr
22:61 ῥῆμα WHR
Joh. 6:60 *trs* ὁ λόγος οὗτος LTTrAWH
7:40 τῶν λόγων τούτων these words (*omit* τούτων W) Eds
8:51 τὸν ἐμὸν λόγον LTTrAWH
19:13 τῶν λόγων τούτων these words Eds
21:23 *trs* οὗτος ὁ λόγος LTTrAWH
Acts 13:15 *trs* ἐν ὑμῖν λόγος LTTrWWH
18: 5*λόγῳ *for* πνεύματι (–μα) GEds
19:38 *trs* ἔχουσιν πρός τινα λ. GLTTr
20:24 λόγου TTrAWHR (AWWH
Ro. 9:28 *om.* in righteousness: because a short work LTTr[A]WHR
13: 9 *trs* τῷ λόγῳ τούτῳ LTTrAWWH
2 Th. 2:17 *trs* work and word Eds
2 Pet. 3: 7 αὐτοῦ λ. S—τῷ αὐτῷ λ. ELTWHR, τῷ αὐτοῦ λ. GTrAW
1 Joh. 5: 7 *omit* in heaven *to* in earth (*ver.* 8) GEds
Jude 15*hard—*add* λόγων speeches T
Rev. 1: 3 τὸν λόγον the word T
17:17*οἱ λόγοι *for* τὰ ῥήματα (–μα) GEds

3061 λοιμός.

Mat. 24: 7 *om.* and pestilences LTTrAWHR
Lu. 21:11 *trs* pestilences and famines LTrAWH

3063 λοιπόν, τὸ λοιπόν.

Mat. 26:45 τὸ λ.—*omit* τὸ [Tr]AWH
Mar. 14:41 τὸ λ.—*omit* τὸ LTrAW[WH]
Eph. 6:10 τοῦ λοιποῦ LTTrAWHR
1 Th. 4: 1 τὸ λ.—*omit* τὸ GEds

3062 λοιπός.

Eph. 4:17 *omit* other LTTrAWHR
Rev. 2:24 τοῖς (*omit* καὶ) λοιποῖς GEds

3064 τοῦ λοιποῦ.

Eph. 6:10 *see* τὸ λοιπόν

3068 λούω.

Heb. 10:22(23) λελουσμένοι TWH (WHR
Rev. 1: 5 washed—freed, λύω LTTr[A]

3069 Λύδδα.

Acts 9:32, 35 Λύδδα LTTrAWH
38 Λύδδας TTrAWH

3076 λυπέω.

Mat. 14: 9 λυπηθείς LTTrAW
Mar. 14:19 οἱ δὲ ἤρξ. λ.—*omit* οἱ δὲ TAWHR

3077 λύπη.

Joh. 16:22 *trs* νῦν μὲν λύπην LTTrAWHR
Phil. 2:27 λύπην GEds

3079 Λυσίας.

Acts 24: 7 *omit* LTTr[A]WHR, *see* κρίνω

3087 λυχνία.

Rev. 1:20†*trs* αἱ (*omit* αἱ W) λυχνίαι αἱ ἑπτὰ GEds

3089 λύω.

Mar. 11: 2 λύσατε αὐτὸν καί LTTrAWHR
Acts 24:26 *omit* that he might loose him Eds
2 Pet. 3:10 λυθήσεται LTTrWHR
Rev. 1: 5*λύσαντι *for* λούσαντι (λούω) LTTrWHR, λ[ο]ύ– A
5: 5 *omit* to loose GEds
20: 3 *trs* λυθῆναι αὐτὸν LAWHR

3090 Λωΐς, Λωίς WH.

* Μαγαδάν.

Mat. 15:39 *for* Μαγδαλά LTTrAWHR

3093 Μαγδαλά.

Mat. 15:39 Μαγαδάν, Magadan LTTrAWHR

3095 μαγεία, –γία TWH.

3098 Μαγώγ.

Rev. 20: 8 τὸν Μ.—*omit* τὸν LT[Tr]AWHR

3100 μαθητεύω.

Mat. 27:57 ἐμαθητεύθη LTTrWH

3101 μαθητής.

Mat. 8:25 *omit* disciples [L]TTrWHR
14:26 *omit* the disciples T: †*trs* οἱ δὲ μ. ἰδόντες αὐτὸν LWH

Mat. 20:17 *omit* disciples TTr[WH]
26:20*twelve—*add* μαθητῶν disciples LT[WH]R
28: 9 *omit* and as they went to tell his disciples LTTrAWHR
Mar. 2:18*οἱ⁴—*add* μαθηταί, *read* the disciples of the Pharisees fast TTrAWHR
23 *trs* οἱ μαθηταὶ αὐτοῦ ἤρξαντο LTTrAWH
3: 7 *trs* μετὰ τῶν μ. αὐτοῦ ἀνεχώρησεν GLTTrAWHR
8:14 *add* οἱ μαθηταί A.V.†B
Lu. 9: 1 *omit* his disciples GTTrAWWHR
10:22 *at commencement* καὶ στραφεὶς πρὸς τοὺς μαθητὰς εἶπεν and having turned to the disciples he said S—*omit* A.V.B EGTr[A]WHR
[illegible] *trs* εἶναί μου μαθητής TTrAWH
20:45 unto his disciples—unto them, πρὸς αὐτούς A
Joh. 1:37 *trs* οἱ δύο μαθηταὶ αὐτοῦ TWHR
6:11 *omit* to the disciples, and the disciples LTTrAWHR
22 *om.* that whereinto his disciples were entered GLTTrAWHR
66 *trs* τῶν μαθητῶν αὐτοῦ ἀπῆλθον LTTrAWH
9:28 *trs* μαθητὴς εἶ LTTrAWH
12:16 *trs* αὐτοῦ οἱ μαθηταὶ TWH
19:27 *trs* ὁ μαθητὴς αὐτὴν GTrAWWH
Acts 1:15 disciples—brethren, ἀδελφός Eds
14:20 *trs* τῶν μαθητῶν αὐτὸν LTTrAWH
20: 7 the disciples—we, ἡμῶν GEds
21: 4 τοὺς μ.—*omit* τοὺς A.V.C

3104 **Μαϊνάν, Μεννά** [L]TTrAWHR, **Μενάμ** A.V.Br.

3107 **μακάριος.**
Mat. 5: 4, 5 *trs the verses* LTTr

3109 **Μακεδονία.**
Acts 16:10 τὴν Μ.—*omit* τὴν LTTrWH
12 τῆς Μ.—*omit* τῆς LTTrWHR
19:22 τὴν Μ.—*omit* τὴν T
20: 1 τὴν Μ.—*omit* τὴν LTTr[A]WH

3114 **μακροθυμέω.**
Lu. 18: 7 μακροθυμεῖ LTTrAWHR

3117 **μακρός.**
Mat. 23:14(13) *omit the verse* LTTrAWHR: *see* κρίμα

3121 **Μαλελεήλ, Με—** T.

3123 **μᾶλλον.**
Mar. 14:31 *omit* the more LTTrAWHR
Lu. 10:20 *omit* rather GEds
2 Co. 2: 7 *omit* rather [TrA]WH

3126 **μαμμωνᾶς.**
Mat. 6:24 μαμωνᾷ GLTTrAWWH

3128 **Μανασσῆς.**
Rev. 7: 6 Μαννασσῆ Tr

3129 **μανθάνω.**
1 Co. 14:35 μανθάνειν WH

3131 **μάννα.**
Joh. 6:49 *trs* ἐν τῇ ἐρήμῳ τὸ μάννα LTTrAWHR
58 *omit* manna GTTrAWHR

3135 **μαργαρίτης.**
Rev. 18:12 μαργαριτῶν TTrAWHR, —τας L
16 μαργαρίτῃ pearl LTTrAWHR
21:21 μ.¹—μαργαρῖται LTAWWHR

3136 **Μάρθα.**
Joh. 11:19 τὰς περὶ Μ.—τὴν Μ. LTrAWHR
24 ἡ Μάρθα LTTrAWH

3137 **Μαρία, Μαριάμ.**
Mat. 1:20 Μαρίαν WH
27:61 Μ.¹—Μαριάμ TWH
28: 1 Μ.¹ Μαριάμ T
Mar. 6: 3 τῆς Μαρίας TTrAWH
15:40 Μ.¹—Μαριάμ WH
Lu. 2:19 Μαρία LTTrAWH
10:39 Μαριάμ TWH
42 Μαριάμ WH
Joh. 11: 1 τῆς Μαρίας T
2 Μαριάμ TrWH
19, 28, 31, 45 Μαριάμ LTTrAWH
20 Μαριάμ WH
32 Μαριάμ TTrAWH
12: 3 Μαριάμ TrWH
19:25 *bis*; 20:1, 11 Μαριάμ T
20:16, 18 Μαριάμ TTrAWH
Acts 1:14 Μαριάμ TTrWH
12:12 τῆς Μαρίας LTTrAWWH
Ro. 16: 6 Μαρίαν LTrAWHR

3144 **μάρτυρ, μάρτυς.**
Lu. 11:48*μάρτυρές ἐστε *for* μαρτυρεῖτε (—ρέω) TTrAWHR

3140 **μαρτυρέω.**
Lu. 11:48 bear witness—are witnesses, μάρτυς TTrAWHR
Acts 26:22 μαρτύρομαι Eds
1 Th. 2:11(12) μαρτύρομαι TTrAWWHR
Heb. 7:17 μαρτυρεῖται it is testified (of him) Eds
1 Joh. 5: 8 *omit* in heaven (*ver.* 7) *to* in earth (*ver.* 8) GEds
Rev. 22:18*μαρτυρῶ ἐγώ *for* συμμαρτυροῦμαι (—τυρέω) γάρ GEds

3141 **μαρτυρία.**
Lu. 22:71 *trs* ἔχομεν μαρτ. χρείαν TTrAWH
Joh. 21:24 *trs* αὐτοῦ ἡ μαρτ. ἐστίν TTrAWH
Acts 22:18 τὴν μ.—*omit* τὴν LTTr[A]WHR

3142 **μαρτύριον.**
1 Co. 2: 1 testimony—mystery, μυστήριον WHR

3143 **μαρτύρομαι.**
Acts 26:22*μαρτυρόμενος *for* μαρτυρούμενος (—τυρέω) Eds
1 Th. 2:11(12)*μαρτυρόμενοι *for* μαρτυρούμενοι (—τυρέω) TTrAWWHR

3144 **μάρτυς,** *see* **μάρτυρ.**

3145 **μασσάομαι.**
Rev. 16:10 ἐμασῶντο LTTrAWWH

3146 **μαστιγόω.**
Mar. 10:34 *trs* shall spit upon him, and shall scourge him LTTrAWHR

3149 **μαστός.**
Rev. 1:13 μαζοῖς L, μασθοῖς T

3156 **Ματθαῖος, Μαθθ—** LTTrAWH.

3157 **Ματθάν, Μαθθ—** LTTrAWH.

3158 **Ματθάτ.**
Lu. 3:24 Μαθθάθ T
29 Μαθθάθ T, Μαθθάτ TrAWH

3161 **Ματταθίας,** Lu. 3:25 **Μαθθ—** Tr.

3162 **μάχαιρα.**
Mat. 26:52 *trs* τὴν μάχαιράν σου LTTrAWH
52 μ.³—μαχαίρῃ LTTrAWH
Lu. 21:24 μαχαίρης TTrWH
22:49 μαχαίρῃ TTrAWH
Acts 12: 2 μαχαίρῃ TTrAWH
16:27 τὴν μάχαιραν LTTrAWHR
Heb. 11:34, 37 μαχαίρης LTTrAWH
Rev. 13:10 μαχαίρῃ *bis* LTTrAWH
14 μαχαίρης LTTrAWH

3165 **μέ.**
Mat. 16:13 *omit* μέ, *read* that the Son of man is [L]TTrAWHR
19:14 ἐμέ T
Mar. 10:36 *omit* με LTrWH, *see* ποιέω
Lu. 1:43 ἐμέ TWH
20:23 *omit* why tempt ye me TTrA (WHR
Joh. 6:35 ἐμέ TTrAWH
36 *omit* me [L]T[WH]
37 ἐμέ T
40 μοῦ LTTrAWHR, *see* πατήρ
44 μέ¹—ἐμέ TrA
45 ἐμέ TTrWWH
65 ἐμέ T
7:34*, 36*find—*add* μέ me LAWHR
37 *omit* unto me T
9: 4 me—us, ἡμᾶς T
10:14*add μέ LTTrAWHR, *see* γινώσκω
32 λιθάζετέ με—ἐμὲ λ. TTrAWH
14: 7 ἐμέ T
14*ask—*add* μέ me [L]T[WH]R
Acts 9: 6 *omit* GEds, *see* κέντρον
13:25 τίνα με—τί ἐμέ LTTrAWHR
18:21 *omit* LTTrAWHR, *see* δεῖ
22: 8, 13 ἐμέ LTTrWH
23:22 ἐμέ TTrWH
24:13 *omit* μέ A.V.B EGEds
19 ἐμέ LTTrAWH
26:16*εἶδές με WHR, *read* wherein thou hast seen me
Ro. 8: 2 me—thee, σέ TWH
1 Co. 16:11 ἐμέ LTr
2 Co. 12:21 ἐλθόντος μου ταπ. με Eds
Heb. 3: 9 *omit* μέ *bis* Eds
Rev. 21: 9 *omit* unto me GEds
See also ἐμέ.

3166 **μεγαλαυχέω.**
Jas. 3: 5 μεγάλα αὐχεῖ LTTrAWHR

3167 **μεγαλεῖα.**
Lu. 1:49 μέγας LTTrWHR

3168 **μεγαλειότης.**
Acts 19:27 τῆς μεγαλειότητος LTTrAWHR

3173 **μέγας.**
Mat. 22:38 ἡ μεγάλη: *trs* the great and first Eds
Mar. 10:43 *trs* μέγας γενέσθαι TTrWH
Lu. 1:49*μεγάλα *for* μεγαλεῖα (—λεῖος) LTTrWHR
13:19 *omit* great [L]T[TrA]WHR
Acts 2:43*add μ. T, *see* φόβος
8: 8 πολὺς LTTrAWHR
13 *omit* μεγάλας A.V.Br
11:28 μεγάλην LTTrAWWH (WHR
26:29*μεγάλῳ *for* πολλῷ (—λύς) LTTrA
Heb. 10:35 *trs* μεγάλην μισθαποδοσίαν Eds
Jas. 3: 5**see* μεγαλαυχέω
Rev. 11:12 φωνῆς μεγάλης TrAWHR
18 τοὺς μεγάλους LTrAWHR
12: 3 *trs* πυρρὸς μέγας LTTrAR
14:15 *trs* φωνῇ μεγάλῃ GLTTrAWWH
19 τὸν μέγαν GLTTrAWH
16: 1 *trs* μεγάλης φωνῆς LTAWWH
17 *omit* great LA
18: 2 *omit* strong GEds, *see* ἰσχύς
19: 1 *trs* μ. ὄχλου πολλοῦ GLTTrAWHR
17 τὸ μέγα τοῦ, *read* great supper of God GEds
20:12 τοὺς μ.: *trs* the great and the small Eds
21:10 *omit* τὴν μ. *read* the holy city GEds

3176 **μέγιστος.**
2 Pet. 1: 4 *trs* precious and exceeding great TWHR

3177 **μεθερμηνεύομαι.**
Mar. 15:22 μεθερμηνευόμενος WH
Joh. 1:38(39)*μεθερμηνευόμενον *for* ἑρμηνευόμενον (—μηνεύω) LTTrAWHR

3179 **μεθιστάνω, —τημι.**
1 Co. 13: 2 μεθιστάναι LTTr

3180 **μεθοδεία, —δία** TWH.

3181 **μεθόρια.**
Mar. 7:24 ὅρια LTTrWH

3185 **μειζων, μεῖζον.**
Mat. 12: 6 μεῖζον Eds
Mar. 4:32 *trs* μείζων (μεῖζον TWHR) πάντων τῶν λαχ. LTTrAWHR
Joh. 5:36 μείζων LTrA
10:29 *trs* πάντων μεῖζον TTrAWH
1 Co. 12:31*μείζονα *for* κρείττονα (—των) LTTrAWHR

3190 **Μελεᾶς, —ᾶς** TTrWH.

3191 **μελετάω.**
Mar. 13:11 *omit* neither do ye premeditate [L]TTr[A]WHR

3193 **μελίσσιος.**
Lu. 24:42 *omit* and of an honeycomb LT[TrA]WHR

3194 **Μελιτη, Μελιτήνη** WH.

3195 **μέλλω.**
Mat. 20:17*add μ. WH, *see* ἀναβαίνω
Lu. 9:31 ἤμελλεν TWH
10: 1 ἤμελλεν LTTrAWWH

Lu. 13: 9 *trs* καρπὸν εἰς τὸ μέλλον· εἰ δὲ μήγε fruit hereafter; but if not TTrAWHR
Joh. 6:71 ἔμελλεν LTTrAWH
7:35 *trs.* μέλλει οὗτος T
39 ἤμελλον T
11:51 ἤμελλεν LTTrAW
Acts 12: 6 ἤμελλεν TTrAWH
16:27 ἤμελλεν LTTrAWH
23:20 they would—thou wouldest, μέλλων Eds
30 *omit* μ. LTTrAWHR
27: 2 μέλλοντι Eds
33†*trs* ἡμέρα ἤμελλεν (ἔμελλεν T) LTTrAWH
Ro. 8:38 *trs* GEds, *see* δύναμις
Heb. 9:11 γίνομαι LWH
11: 8 ἔμελλεν LA
2 Pet. 1:12*μελλήσω *for* οὐκ ἀμελήσω (-λέω) Eds
Rev. 3: 2 are ready—were ready, ἔμελλον GEds
10: 4 ἤμελλον LTrAWWH

3196 μέλος.

Ro. 12: 4 *trs* πολλὰ μέλη Eds

3197 Μελχί, –χεί TTrAWH.

3198 Μελχισεδέκ.

Heb. 7:10 ὁ Μ.—*omit* ὁ LTTrAWHR
21 *omit* after the order of Melchisedec TTrAWHR

3201 μέμφομαι.

Mar. 7: 2 *omit* they found fault GEds

3303 μέν.

Mar. 1: 8 *omit* indeed [L]TTrAWHR
9:12 *omit* verily T[Tr]
10:39 *omit* indeed TTrAWHR
Lu. 10: 6 *omit* μ. GEds
11:28*μ. οὖν *for* μενοῦνγε A
Acts 3:13*ye—*add* μ. indeed GEds
5:23 *omit* truly Eds
14:12 *omit* μ. LTTrAWHR
19: 4 *omit* verily GLTTrAWHR
22: 3 *omit* verily Eds
23: 8 *omit* μ. L[Tr]WH
Ro. 2: 8 *omit* μ. LTTrWHR
6:21*τὸ—*add* μ. *read* for indeed LA
7:25 *omit* μ. T
16:19 *omit* μ. LTTrA[WH]
1 Co. 2:15 *omit* μ. T[TrA]
12:20 *omit* μ. [LTr]WH
15:51 *omit* μ. [L]TTrAWHR
2 Co. 4:12 *omit* μ. GEds
12: 1**for* μοί LTTrWHR, *see* συμφέρω
Gal. 4:23 [μέν] LWH
Phi. 1:28 *omit* μ. GEds
3: 8*μ. οὖν *for* μενοῦνγε GLTrAW
Tit. 1:15 *omit* μ. Eds
Heb. 6:16 *omit* verily LTTr[A]WHR
12:11**for* δέ[1] TWHR
1 Pet. 2:14 *omit* μ. GEds
4:14 *omit* LTTrAWHR. *see* κατά

See 3304

* μενοῦν, *see* μενοῦνγε.

3304 μενοῦνγε.

Lu. 11:28 μενοῦν TTrWHR, μὲν οὖν A
Ro. 9:20 *trs* ὦ ἄνθρωπε μ. (μενοῦν γε LTr) LTTrAWHR
10:18 μενοῦν γε LTrW
Phi. 3: 8 μὲν οὖν GLTrAW, μὲν οὖν γε WH

3305 μέντοι.

2 Ti. 2:19 μέν τοι Tr

3306 μένω.

Mat. 11:23 ἔμεινεν LTTrAWH
Joh. 5:38 *trs* ἐν ὑμῖν μ. TTrAWHR
10:40 ἔμενεν LWH
11:54*ἔμεινεν *for* διέτριβεν (διατρίβω) TrAWHR
14:10 ὁ ἐν ἐμοὶ μ.—*omit* ὁ [LTrA]WHR
16 may abide—may be, ᾖ LTTrA (WHR
15: 4 μ.[2]—μένῃ TWH
4 μ.[3]—μένητε LTTrAWH
6 μένῃ LTTrAWH
11 might remain—might be, ᾖ LTTrAWHR
Acts 16:15 μένετε LTTrWWH
20:15 *omit* and tarried at Trogyllium LTTrWHR
28:30 ἐμμένω TTrAWHR
1 Co. 3:14 μενεῖ shall abide GLTAWWHR
1 Joh. 2:27 *trs* μένει ἐν ὑμῖν LTTrAWHR
27 μ.[2]—μένετε, abide ye Eds
4:16*αὐτῷ—*add* μένει, *read* God abideth in him [L]TA[WH]R

3307 μερίζω.

Mar. 3:26 ἐμερίσθη, καί he is divided, and T, καὶ ἐ. WHR
1 Co. 7:17 μεμέρικεν TTrWHR
34 *see* γυνή

3309 μεριμνάω.

Mat. 6:34 μεριμνήσητε S, -σετε E
Lu. 12:11 μεριμνήσητε TTrWHR

3313 μέρος.

Lu. 11:36 *trs* μέρος τι ([τι] A) TTrAWH
Eph. 4: 9 *omit* μ. W
1 Pet. 4:16 ὄνομα, *read* in this name Eds

3317 μεσονύκτιον.

Mar. 13:35 μεσονύκτιον TTrAWH

3319 μέσος.

Mat. 14:24 *omit* TrWH, *see* στάδιον
Mar. 14:60 τὸ μ.—*omit* τὸ GLTTrAWWH
Lu. 17:11 μέσον LTTrAWHR
22:27 ἐν μέσῳ ὑμῶν εἰμι TTrAWHR
55 ἐν μ.[2]—μέσος TTrAWH
Joh. 8:59 *omit* going through *to end of verse* GLTTrAWHR
Acts 4: 7 τῷ μ.—*omit* τῷ G[A]
Phil. 2:15 ἐν μ.—μέσον Eds
Rev. 2: 7 *omit* the midst of GEds

3324 μεστός.

Joh. 19:29**add* μ. LTTrAWHR, *see* πλήθω

3326 μετά.

Mar. 5:37*αὐτῷ—μετ' αὐτοῦ with him TTrAWHR
9:24 *omit* with tears LTTrAWHR
31* | 10:34* *add* μ. LTTrAWHR, *see* ἡμέρα
15:28 *omit the verse* T[Tr]AWHR
Lu. 8:45 σύν GLTTrAR: *omit* and they that were with him WH
Joh. 5: 4 *omit* [G]TTrAWHR, *see* ὕδωρ
12:35 ἐν ὑμῖν among you GLTTrAWHR
13:18 μετ' ἐμοῦ—μου, *read* my bread TrAWHR
Acts 13:20 *see* ἔτος
20:24 *omit* with joy LTTrAWHR
24: 7 *omit* LTTr[A]WHR, *see* κρίνω
Ro. 16:24 *omit the verse* LTTr[A]WHR
Rev. 12: 7**for* κατά GEds
13: 7 *omit* L[WH], *see* δίδωμι

3327 μεταβαίνω.

Mat. 17:20 μ.[1]—μετάβα LTTrAWH

3328 μεταβάλλομαι.

Acts 28: 6 μεταβαλόμενοι TrAWHR

3335 μεταλαμβάνω.

Acts 27:34*μεταλαβεῖν *for* προσλαβεῖν (-λαμβάνω) GEds

3336 μετάληψις, –λημψις LTTrAWH.

3338 μεταμέλομαι.

Mat. 21:29 *trs* WH, *see* ἀπέρχομαι

3339 μεταμορφόομαι.

Ro. 12: 2 μεταμορφοῦσθαι to be transformed LA

3340 μετανοέω.

Mar. 6:12 μετανοῶσιν LTTrAWH
Lu. 13: 5 μετανοήσητε LTTrAWH
Rev. 2:21 μ.[2]—μετανοῆσαι GEds, *see* θέλω
22 μετανοήσουσιν TTrAWH

3341 μετάνοια.

Mat. 9:13 *omit* to repentance GEds
Mar. 2:17 *omit* to repentance GEds

3343 μεταπέμπω.

Acts 10:29 μ.[2]—μεταπέμψασθε A
20: 1*μεταπεμψάμενος *for* προσκαλεσάμενος (-λέομαι) TTrWHR

3344 μεταστρέφω.

Jas. 4: 9 μετατρέπω WH

* μετατρέπω, to turn back, change.

Jas. 4: 9 μετατραπήτω *for* μεταστραφήτω (-τρέφω) WH

3348 μετέχω.

1 Co. 9:10 τοῦ μετέχειν GEds, *see* ἐλπίς

3354 μετρέω.

Mat. 7: 2*μετρηθήσεται *for* ἀντιμετρηθήσεται (-μετρέω) GEds

3358 μέτρον.

Lu. 6:38 τῷ γὰρ αὐτῷ μ. ᾧ—ᾧ γὰρ μ. LTTrWHR
Rev. 21:15*had—*add* μέτρον a measure GLTTrAWHR

3359 μέτωπον.

Rev. 13:16 τὸ μέτωπον forehead GEds

3360 μέχρι, μέχρις.

Mat. 13:30 ἕως LTrAWH
Lu. 16:16**for* ἕως TTrAWHR
Gal. 4:19**for* ἄχρις TTrWH
Heb. 3: 6 *omit* firm unto the end A[WH]

3361 μή.

Mat. 11:23**for* ἡ LTTrAWHR, *see* ὑψόω
Mar. 8:26**for* μηδέ[1] T
12:21**for* οὐδέ TTrAWHR, *see* καταλείπω
Lu. 7:33**for* μήτε[1] TAWHR
8:49 not—no longer, μηκέτι LTTrWH
10: 4**for* μηδέ TTrAWHR
15**for* ἡ LTTrAWHR, *see* ὑψόω
11:11 *omit* WH, *see* ἄρτος
12 *omit* μή WH
22:34 *omit* μή[2] LTr[A]WHR
Joh. 7:31**for* μήτι LTTrAWHR
8: 6 *add* μή A.V.†C, *see* προσποιέω
Acts 23: 9 *omit* GEds, *see* θεομαχέω
Ro. 8: 1 *omit* who walk *to end of verse* GEds
14: 6 *omit* LTTr[A]WHR, *see* κύριος
1 Co. 9:20**add* μή GEds, *see* νόμος
2 Co. 5:12*μὴ ἐν *for* οὐ[2] LTTrWHR
Gal. 3: 1 *omit* that ye should not obey the truth GEds
Col. 2:18 *omit* not [L]TTrAWHR
1 Ti. 3: 3 *omit* not greedy of filthy lucre GEds
Tit. 2: 3 μή[2]—μηδέ TTrAWHR
Heb. 9:17 μὴ τότε *for* μήποτε WH
12:19 *omit* μή WH
Rev. 2:10**for* μηδέν LTrAWWHR

3363 ἵνα μή.

Joh. 3:15 *omit* not perish, but [L]TTrAWHR
2 Co. 12: 7 *omit* lest I should be exalted above measure[2] [L]Tr[A]
Gal. 6:12 *trs* μή *after* χριστοῦ LTTrAWHR
Col. 2: 4 ἵ. μή τις—ἵνα μηδείς Eds

3366 μηδέ.

Mar. 3:20**for* μήτε LTrAWWHR
8:26 neither—not, μή T
26 *omit* nor tell (it) to any in the town TWHR
13:11 *omit* neither do ye premeditate [L]TTr[A]WHR
Lu. 3:14 neither—no one, μηδείς T
7:33**for* μήτε[2] T
10: 4 μή TTrAWHR
12:47 neither—or, ἤ TWHR
Acts 23: 8 μήτε Eds
Eph. 4:27**for* μήτε Eds
Phil. 2: 3*ἤ—μ. κατά LTTrAWHR
2 Th. 2: 2**for* μήτε[1] Eds
Tit. 2: 3**for* μή[2] TTrAWHR

3367 μηδείς, μηδεμία, μηδέν.

Mar. 1:44 *omit* μηδέν, *read* tell no man L[Tr]
11:14 μηδεὶς S—οὐδεὶς E
Lu. 3:14*μηδένα *for* μηδέ T
6:35 μηδένα T
Joh. 8:10 *omit* and saw none but the woman WHR
Acts 11:12 *omit* nothing doubting A
21:25 *om.* that they observe no such thing, save only LTTrWHR
23:14 μηθέν A
27:33 μηθέν LTTrAWH
Col. 2: 4*μηδεὶς *for* μή τις Eds
Rev. 2:10 none of—not, μή LTrAWWHR

* μηθείς, μηθέν, no one, none.

Acts 23:14 μηθενός *for* μηδενός A
27:33 μηθέν *for* μηδέν LTTrAWH

3371 μηκέτι.

Lu. 8:49**for* μή LTTrWH

3379 *μήποτε, μή ποτε.*

Heb. 9:17 μὴ τότε WH

* *μήπου, μή που*, lest anywhere.

Acts 27:29 *for* μήπως TTrAWHR

3381 *μήπως, μή πως.*

Acts 27:29 μήπω L, μήπου TTrAWHR
Ro. 11:21 *omit* μ. *read* neither will he spare thee LTTr[A]WHR

3383 *μήτε.*

Mar. 3:20 μηδέ LTrAWWHR
Lu. 7:33 μ.[1]—μή TAWHR: μ.[2]—μηδέ T
Acts 23: 8**for* μηδέ Eds
Eph. 4:27 μηδέ Eds
2Th. 2: 2 μ.[1]—μηδέ Eds

3385, 3386 *μήτι, μή τι.*

Mar. 14:19 *omit* and another (said, Is) it I? TTrWHR
Joh. 7:31 μή LTTrAWHR

3364 *οὐ μή.*

Mat. 24: 2 οὐ μή[2]—*omit* μή GEds
25: 9**for* οὐ LTrAWWHR
Mar. 13:31 *omit* μή TrAWH
Lu. 8:17**for* οὐ[3] LTTrAWHR
22:34 *omit* μή[1] TTrAWHR
Joh. 16: 7**for* οὐ TrWH
Rev. 9: 6**for* οὐ GEds

3384 *μήτηρ.*

Mat. 12:47 *omit the verse* [T]WH
15: 6(5) *omit* or his mother L[A]WHR
Mar. 3:31 *trs* his mother and his brethren GLTTrWWHR (WHR
10:29 *trs* or mother or father LTTrA
30 μητέρα mother LTr
Lu. 2:43 *omit* μ. LTTrAWHR, *see* γονεύς
48 *trs* εἶπεν πρὸς αὐτὸν ἡ μ. αὐτοῦ LTTrAWH
12:53 μ.[2]—μητέρα T, τὴν μητέρα LTrAWHR
Eph. 5:31 τὴν μ.—*omit* τὴν LTrA[WH]

3389 *μητραλῴης, μητρο—* LTTrAWH.

3391 *μία* fem. to *εἷς.*

Mar. 16: 2 τῆς μ.—μιᾷ LTr, τῇ ([τῇ] WH) μιᾷ TWHR
Lu. 17:34 [μιᾶς] LWH
35 μία S—ἡ μ. EGLT[Tr]AWHR

3392 *μιαίνω.*

Tit. 1:15 μ.[1]—μεμιαμμένοις LTTrWH, —αμέ— A

3395 *μίγμα.*

Joh. 19:39 ἕλιγμα WH

3396 *μίγνυμι.*

Rev. 8: 7 μεμιγμένον T

3397 *μικρόν.*

Joh. 16:18 τὸ μ.—*omit* τὸ TrAWH
2 Co. 11:16 *trs* κἀγὼ μικρόν τι GEds

3398 *μικρός.*

Mar. 4:31 μικρότερον ὂν LTTrAWHR
Lu. 17: 2 *trs* τῶν μ. τούτων ἕνα TTrAWHR
Rev. 11:18 τοὺς μικρούς LTrAWHR
20:12 τοὺς μ. *trs* the great and the small Eds

3402 *μιμητής.*

1 Pet. 3:13 followers—zealous, ζηλωτής Eds

3403 *μιμνήσκομαι.*

Heb. 10:17 μνησθήσομαι LTTrAWHR

3404 *μισέω.*

Mat. 5:44 τοῖς μισοῦσιν ὑμᾶς GW: *omit* bless *to* hate you LTTrAWHR
Rev. 2:15 which thing I hate—in like manner, ὁμοίως GEds

3408 *μισθός.*

Acts 1:18 τοῦ μ.—*omit* τοῦ GEds

3411 *μισθωτός.*

Joh. 10:13 *omit* the hireling fleeth LTTrAWHR

3415 *μνάομαι, see μιμνήσκομαι.*

3418 *μνῆμα.*

Mar. 5: 3*μνήμασιν *for* μνημείοις(-μεῖον) GEds
5 *trs* tombs, and in the mountains GEds
15:46*μνήματι *for* μνημείῳ (-μεῖον) TWH
16: 2*μνῆμα *for* μνημεῖον T
Rev. 11: 9 μνῆμα a grave GEds

3419 *μνημεῖον.*

Mar. 5: 3 μνῆμα GEds
6:29 τῷ μ.—*omit* τῷ A.V.BE GEds
15:46 μ.[1]—μνῆμα TWH
16: 2 μνῆμα T (WHR
Lu. 11:48 *omit* their sepulchres [L]TTrA
24:12 *omit the verse* [L]T[Tr][[WH]]
Joh. 20:11 τὸ μ.[1]—τῷ μνημείῳ GEds

3421 *μνημονεύω.*

Heb. 11:15 μνημονεύουσιν TTr

3423 *μνηστεύομαι.*

Lu. 1:27 ἐμνηστευμένην LTTrWH
2: 5 ἐμνηστευμένῃ LTTrAWH

* *μογγιλάλος*, speaking with hollow voice.

Mar. 7:32 μογγιλάλον *for* μογιλάλον(-λος) Tr

3424 *μογιλάλος.*

Mar. 7:32 μογγιλάλος Tr

3425 *μόγις.*

Lu. 9:39 μόλις WH

3427 *μοί.*

Mat. 15: 8 *omit* GLTTrAWHR, *see* ἐγγίζω
18:28 *omit* me Eds
Mar. 8: 2 *omit* with me L[Tr]A
Lu. 9:38 *trs* μοι ἐστιν LTTrAWWH
22:68 *omit* me, nor let (me) go T[TrA]WHR
Joh. 13:36 *omit* me[2] LTTrAWHR
14:11 *omit* me[3] T[Tr]WH
Acts 1: 8 μοῦ, *read* my witnesses Eds
9:15 *trs* ἐστίν μοι Eds
11: 9 *omit* me LTTrAWHR
20:22 ἐμοί TWH
23*witnesseth—*add* μ. to me GEds
Ro. 9:19 *trs* μοι οὖν Eds
1 Co. 7: 1 *omit* unto me T[Tr]AWHR
9:18 μοῦ TTrAWH
10:23 *omit* for me *bis* GEds
2 Co. 6:16 μοῦ LTTrWHR
12: 1 μέν LTTrWHR, *see* συμφέρω
2 Ti. 1:18 ministered—*add mihi* A.V.Vul
Rev. 1:17 | 10: 4 *omit* unto me GEds
14:13 | 17: 1 *omit* unto me GEds
21: 5 *omit* unto me LT[TrA]WWHR
See also ἐμοί.

3429 *μοιχάομαι.*

Mat. 5:32 μ.[1]—μοιχεύω LTTrAWHR
19: 9 *omit* T[Tr]WH, *see* ἀπολύω

3430 *μοιχεία.*

Mar. 7:21, 22 *trs* fornications, thefts, murders, adulteries TTrAWHR
Gal. 5:19 *omit* adultery GEds

3431 *μοιχεύω.*

Mat. 5:32*μοιχευθῆναι *for* μοιχᾶσθαι (-χάομαι) LTTrAWHR
Mar. 10:19 *trs* Do not kill, Do not commit adultery LWHR
Jas. 2:11 μ.[2]—μοιχεύεις LTTrAWHR

3432 *μοιχός.*

Jas. 4: 4 *omit* ye adulterers and Eds

3433 *μόλις.*

Lu. 9:39**for* μόγις WH

μόνας, see καταμόνας.

3439 *μονογενής.*

Lu. 7:12 *trs* μονογενὴς υἱὸς TTrAWH
Joh. 1:18 ὁ μ.—*omit* ὁ TrWH

3441 *μόνος.*

Lu. 24:12 [laid by themselves] A: *omit the verse* [L]T[Tr][[WH]]
Rev. 9: 4 *omit* only GEds

3448 *μόσχος.*

Lu. 15:30†*trs* τὸν σιτευτὸν μόσχον TTrAWHR

3450 *μοῦ*

Mat. 4:10**add* μ.—G[L]W, *see* ὀπίσω
16:23 μ. εἶ—εἶ ἐμοῦ LTTrAWHR
18:14**for* ὑμῶν LTrWH
19:20 *omit* from my youth up LTTrAWHR
29 ἐμοῦ ὀνόματος TWH
20:23 *omit* μ.[3] LTTrAWHR
21:28 *omit* μ. TTrAWHR
24:36 *omit* μ. *read* the Father GLTTr
26:39 *omit* my T[Tr] ([A]WHR
27:35 *omit* that it might *to end of verse* GLTTrAWHR
Mar. 3:33 *omit* my[2] Tr[A]WH
35 *omit* my[2] LTTrAWHR
9:41 *omit* μ. GLTrAWHR
10:40 *omit* μ.[2] GEds
14:14*κατάλυμα—*add* μ. *read* my guestchamber [L]TTrAWHR
Lu. 4: 7 ἐμοῦ Eds
8 *omit* get thee behind me, Satan, G[L]TTrAWHR
7: 6 *trs* μου *before* ὑπό W
44 μ.[1]—μοί TrAWH, *see* πούς
8:45 *omit* T[TrA]WHR, *see* λέγω
12:18 *omit* μ [2] Tr[A]WHR
18:21 *omit* my T[Tr]AWH
24:44*λόγοι—*add* μ. *read* my words [L]TTrAWHR
Joh. 1:27 *omit* is preferred before me G[L]TTrAWHR
6:40**see* πατήρ
65 *omit* μ. *read* the Father LTTrAWHR
8:28, 38 *omit* μ. *read* the Father LTTrAWHR
10:29 *omit* μ.[1] *read* the Father's T
29 *omit* μ.[2] *read* the Father T[Tr]AWHR
32 *omit* μ. *read* the Father [L]T[Tr]AWHR
14:12 *omit* μ. *read* the Father LTTrAWHR
28 *omit* μ.[1] *read* the Father [L]TTrAWHR
15:10 *om.* μ.[3] *rd.* the Father's LAWH
16:10 *omit* μ. *read* the Father TTr[A]WHR
20:17 *omit* μ.[2] *read* the Father [L]TTrAWHR
Acts 2:25*κύριον—*add* μ. *read* my Lord T
20:24 *omit* μ.[1] LTTrAWHR
1 Co. 1: 4 *omit* my WH
9: 2*μ. τῆς *for* τῆς ἐμῆς LTTrAWHR
14:18 *omit* my GEds
39*ἀδελφοί—*add* μ. *read* my brethren [L]TTr[A]WHR
2 Co. 11:28 μοί Eds
12: 5 *omit* mine LTr[A]WHR
9 *omit* my[2] LTTrAWHR
9 *omit* my[3] [Tr]WH
Gal. 4:14 my[1]—your, ὑμῶν Eds
Eph. 6:10 *omit* my brethren LTTrAWHR
Col. 1:24 *omit* μ.[1] GEds
Philem. 10 *omit* my[2] LTTrAWHR
Heb. 8: 9 *omit* μ.[1]—E
10:34 *omit* μ. GEds, *see* δεσμός
38*δίκαιος—*add* μ. *read* my just one LTTrA[WH]R
Jas. 2:18 my faith—*omit* my TTrAWWHR
5:10 *omit* my Eds (WHR
19*ἀδελφοί μ. my brethren LTTrA
2 Pet. 1:17**trs* ὁ υἱός μου ὁ ἀγαπητός μου οὗτός ἐστιν AWH
1 Joh. 3:13, 18 *omit* my Eds
Rev. 2: 7*θεοῦ—*add* μ., *read* my God G[A]W
13*πιστος—*add* μ. *read* my faithful one LT[TrA]W[WH]R
3: 2*θεοῦ—*add* μ. *rd.* my God GEds
7:14*κύριε—*add* μ. *read* my lord G[L]TTrAWWHR
See also ἐμοῦ.

3457 *μυλικός.*

Mar. 9:42 *see* λίθος
Lu. 17: 2**see* λίθος

* *μύλινος* of a mill [?]

Rev. 18:21 μύλινον *for* μύλον (-λος) LAWHR

3458 *μύλος.*

Mat. 24:41*μύλῳ *for* μύλωνι (-λών) LTTrAWHR
Mar. 9:42**see* λίθος
Lu. 17: 2 *see* λίθος
Rev. 18:21 μύλινος LAWHR

3459 **μύλων.**
Mat. 24:41 μύλος LTTrAWH

3460 **Μύρα,** Μύρρα LTTrAWH.

3461 **μυριάς.**
Rev. 5:11 *see* ἀριθμός
9:16 δύο μυριάδες—δισμυριάδες LTA, δίς μ. WH

3464 **μύρον.**
Mat. 26: 9 *omit* ointment GEds
Mar. 14: 5*τοῦτο—*add* τὸ μύρον, *read* this ointment GEds

3466 **μυστήριον.**
1 Co. 2: 1*μυστήριον *for* μαρτύριον WH

3474 **μωρός.**
Mat. 23:19 *om.* (ye) fools and [L]TTrAWH
25: 2 *trs* foolish *and* wise LTTrAWH
3 αἱ γὰρ (δὲ L) μ. *for* αἵτινες μ. LTAWH

3475 **Μωσῆς,** Μωϋσῆς LTTrAW, —υ— WH
Mat. 17: 4 Μωϋσεῖ LTTrAWH
Mar. 9: 4, 5 Μωυσῇ TrA
10: 4 *trs* ἐπέτρεψεν M. LTTrAWH
Lu. 9:33 *trs* μίαν M. GLTTrAWWH
Joh. 5:46 Μωϋσεῖ LTTrAWH
7:22 M.¹—ὁ M. T
8: 5†*trs* [ἡμῖν] Μωϋσῆς WH
9:29 Μωϋσεῖ LTTrAWH
Acts 15: 1 τῷ Μωϋσέως LTTrAWH
Ro. 9:15†*trs* M. γὰρ LAW, Μωϋσεῖ γ. TTrWH

3478 **Ναζαρέθ,** —ρέτ.
Mat. 4:13 Ναζαρά TTrAWH
Lu. 4:16 Ναζαρά TWH· *om.* τὴν LTTrAWH

3479 **Ναζαρηνός.**
Mar. 10:47**for* Ναζωραῖος LTTrAWH
Lu. 24:19*Ναζαρηνοῦ *for* Ναζωραίου TTrAWH

3480 **Ναζωραῖος.**
Mar. 10:47 Ναζαρηνός LTTrAWH
Lu. 24:19 Ναζαρηνός TTrAWH
Acts 9: 5*Jesus—*add* ὁ Ναζωραῖος the Nazarene [L]W

3481 **Ναθάν,** Ναθαμ TWH.

3483 **ναί.**
Phil. 4: 3**for* καί GEds
Rev. 22:20 *omit* even so (ν.²) GEds

* **Ναιμάν,** *see* **Νεεμάν.** See 3497

3485 **ναός.**
Mat. 27: 5 εἰς τὸν ναόν TTrWH
Lu. 1:21 *trs* ἐν τῷ ν. αὐτόν WH
Acts 7:48 *omit* temples GEds
Rev. 21:22 ν.²—ὁ ναός LW, [ὁ] ν. A

3494 **νεανίας.**
Acts 23:18 νεανίσκος LTTrA
22 νεανίσκος LTTrAWH

3495 **νεανίσκος.**
Mar. 14:51 *trs* νεανίσκος τις LTrWH
51 *om.* the young men LTTrAWH
Acts 23:18*νεανισκον *for* νεανιαν (-νίας) LTTrA
22*νεανίσκον *for* νεανίαν (-νίας) LTTrAWH

3496 **Νεάπολις.**
Acts 16:11 Νέαν Πόλιν TTrWH

3497 **Νεεμάν,** Ναιμάν LTTrAWH.

3498 **νεκρός.**
Mat. 10: 8 *trs* raise the dead, cleanse the lepers GEds
Mar. 6:16 *om.* from the dead T[Tr]AWH
16:14*ἐγηγερμένον—*add* ἐκ νεκρῶν, *rd.* risen from the dead L[WH]
Acts 24:15 *omit* of the dead LTTrAWH
Ro. 8:34*risen—*add* ἐκ νεκρῶν from the dead [WH]R
1 Co. 15:12 *trs* ἐκ νεκρῶν ὅτι A
29 the dead³—them, αὐτῶν GEds
Eph. 1:20 τῶν νεκρῶν W

Phil. 3:11 τῶν ν.—τὴν ἐκ ν. Eds
Col. 2:12 τῶν ν.—*omit* τῶν GT[A]WWH
1 Th. 1:10 τῶν νεκρῶν GLTTrAR, [τῶν] ν. WH
Jas. 2:20 dead—idle, ἀργός LTTrAWH
Rev. 20:13†*trs* τοὺς ν. τοὺς ἐν αὐτῇ GEds
13†*trs* τοὺς ν. τοὺς ἐν αὐτοῖς GEds

* **νεομηνία,** *see* **νουμηνία.** See 3561

3501 **νέος, νεώτερος.**
Mar. 2:22 *omit* new² LTTrAWH
22 *omit* but new wine *to* bottles T[Tr]A[WH], *see* βλητέος

3502 **νεοσσός,** νοσσός TAWH.

3503 **νεότης.**
Mat. 19:20 *omit* from my youth up LTTrAWH

3507 **νεφέλη.**
Lu. 12:54 τὴν ν.—*omit* τὴν LTTr[A]WH
2 Pet. 2:17 clouds—and mists, καὶ ὁμίχλαι (-λη) GEds
Rev. 14:16 τῆς νεφέλης LTTrAWH

3508 **Νεφθαλείμ,** Rev. 7: 6 λίμ AWH.

3514 **νήθω.**
Mat. 6:28 νήθουσιν LTTrAWH

3516 **νήπιος.**
1 Th. 2: 7*νήπιοι *for* ἤπιοι (-ιος) LWH

3518 **Νηρί,** Νηρεί TTrAWH.

3521 **νηστεία.**
Mat. 17:21 *omit the verse* T[Tr]WH
Mar. 9:29 *omit* and fasting T[A]WH
1 Co. 7: 5 *omit* fasting and GEds

3522 **νηστεύω.**
Lu. 5:34 νηστεῦσαι TTrAWH
Acts 10:30 *omit* fasting LTTr[A]WH

3523 **νῆστις.**
Mar. 8: 3 νήστις T

3524 **νηφάλεος,** —λιος 1 Tim. GEds.

3528 **νικάω.**
Ro. 3: 4 νικήσεις TWH
Rev. 2:17 νικοῦντι LTTr
13: 7 *omit* L[WH], *see* δίδωμι

3530 **Νικόδημος.**
Joh. 3: 4 ὁ N.—*omit* ὁ Tr[WH]

3531 **Νικολαΐτης.**
Rev. 2:15 τῶν N.—*omit* τῶν L[Tr]AWWH

3534 **νῖκος.**
1 Co. 15:55 *trs* victory *and* sting LTTrWH

3535 **Νινευΐ.**
Lu. 11:32 of Nineve—Ninevites, Νινευΐται LTTrWWH, Νινευή A

3536 **Νινευΐτης.**
Mat. 12:41 Νινευεῖται TTrAWH
Lu. 11:30 *trs* τοῖς N. σημεῖον TTrAWH
32*Νινευῖται LTrW, Νινευεῖται TWH *for* Νινευΐ

3543 **νομίζω.**
Acts 14:19 νομίζοντες LTTrAWH
16:13 ἐνομιζομεν προσευχήν, *read* where we supposed was a place for prayer LTTrWH

3549 **νομοθετέω.**
Heb. 7:11 νενομοθέτηται Eds

3550 **νομοθέτης.**
Jas. 4:12 ὁ ν.—*omit* ὁ WH

3551 **νόμος.**
Mat. 15: 6*τὸν νόμον *for* τὴν ἐντολήν TA
Lu. 2:24 τῷ νόμῳ LTTrWH
Acts 13:39 τῷ ν.—*omit* τῷ LTTrAWH
15:24 *omit* saying, (Ye must) be circumcised, and keep the law LTTrAWH
24: 6 *omit* LTTr[A]WH, *see* κρίνω
Ro. 2:13 τοῦ ν.¹—*omit* τοῦ Eds
13 τοῦ ν.²—*omit* τοῦ LTTrAWWH
17 τῷ ν.—*omit* τῷ Eds

Ro. 7: 2 *omit* τοῦ νόμου B
9:32 *omit* of the law LTTr[A]WWH
10: 5 τοῦ ν.—*omit* τοῦ TTrAWH
1 Co. 7:39 *omit* by the law GEds
9:20*νόμον²—*add* μὴ ὢν αὐτὸς ὑπὸ νόμον not being myself under law GEds
Gal. 3:21†*trs* ἐκ νόμου (ἐν νόμῳ WH) ἂν ἦν (ἦν ἂν T) LTTrAWH
Heb. 8: 4 τὸν ν.—*omit* τὸν LTTrAWH
9:19 τὸν νόμον LTrAWWH
10: 8 τὸν ν.—*omit* τὸν LTTr[A]WH

3553 **νόσημα.**
Joh. 5: 4 *omit* waiting for (*ver.* 3) *to end of verse* 4 [G]TTrAWH

3554 **νόσος.**
Mar. 3:15 *omit* to heal sicknesses, and TTrAWH

3560 **νουθετέω.**
1 Co. 4:14 νουθετῶν warning TWH

3561 **νουμηνία,** νεομηνία LTrWH.

3563 **νοῦς.**
1 Co. 14:15 τῷ ν.²—*omit* τῷ B
19 διὰ τοῦ ν.—τῷ νοΐ Eds
Rev. 13:18 τὸν ν.—*omit* τὸν GEds

Νυμφᾶν, Νύμφαν LWH.

3567 **νυμφών.**
Mat. 22:10*νυμφὼν *for* γάμος TWH

3568 **νῦν.**
Lu. 6:25*full—*add* ν. now T[Tr]AWH
22:18*drink—*add* ἀπὸ τοῦ ν. henceforth T[TrA]WH
Joh. 6:42**for* οὖν TTrAWH
8:11*ἀπὸ τοῦ ν. *for* καί WH
16:32 *omit* now LTTrAWH
Acts 2:33 *omit* now GLTTrAWH
13:31*who—*add* ν. now LTTrAW[WH]
32*we—*add* ν. now W (B
22: 1 νυνί GLTTrAWWH
24:13 νυνί LTTrAWH
26:17 *omit* now GEds
Ro. 11:31*they—*add* ν. now [L]TWH
1 Co. 5:11**for* νυνί LTrAWH
12:18**for* νυνί LTrAWH
14: 6**for* νυνί Eds
Col. 1:26**for* νυνί LTTrAWH
Heb. 8: 6**for* νυνί LWH
9:26 νυνί LTTrAWH
11:16**for* νυνί GEds

3570 **νυνί.**
Acts 22: 1**for* νῦν GLTTrAWWH
24:13**for* νῦν LTTrAWH
1 Co. 5:11 νῦν LTrAWH
12:18 νῦν LTrAWH
14: 6 νῦν Eds
Col. 1:26 νῦν LTTrAWH
Heb. 8: 6 νῦν LWH
9:26**for* νῦν LTTrAWH
11:16 νῦν GEds

3571 **νύξ.**
Mat. 27:64 *omit* by night GLTTrAWH
Mar. 14:27 *omit* this night [L]TTrAWWH
30 *trs* ταύτῃ τῇ ν. LTTrAWH
Lu. 5: 5 τῆς ν.—*omit* τῆς LTTrAWH
Joh. 7:50 *omit* by night LTTrAWH
Acts 5:19 τῆς ν.—*omit* τῆς LTTrAWH
16: 9 τῆς ν.—*omit* τῆς LTTr[A]WWH
17:10 τῆς ν.—*omit* τῆς LTTrAWH
18: 9 *trs* ἐν ν. δι' ὁράματος LTTrAWH
23:31 τῆς ν.—*omit* τῆς Eds
27:23 *trs* ταύτῃ τῇ ν. GLTTrAWWH
2 Th. 3: 8 νυκτός LTTrWH
2 Pet. 3:10 *omit* in the night GEds

3575 **Νῶε.**
Lu. 17:26 τοῦ N.—*omit* τοῦ GLTTrAWWH

3581 **ξένος.**
3 Joh. 5 εἰς τοὺς ξ.—τοῦτο ξ. Eds

3582 **ξέστης.**
Mar. 7: 8 *omit* (as) the washing *to end of verse* T[Tr]AWH

3583 **ξηραίνω.**
Mar. 3: 3 ξηρός LTTrAWH

3584 ξηρός.

Mar. 3: 3*trs τὴν χεῖρα ἔχοντι ξηράν (ξ. for ἐξηραμμένην, ξηραίνω) LTrAWHR, τὴν ξηράν χ. ἔχ. T

3586 ξύλον.

Rev. 22:19*τοῦ ξύλου for βίβλου[3] (-λος) GEds

3587 ξυράω.

Acts 21:24 ξυρήσονται TTrAWHR

3588 ὁ, ἡ, τό.

(In addition to those placed with nouns, adjectives, participles, infinitives, and proper names.)

Mat. 6:34 omit the things of Eds
11:23 ἡ ἢ (ὅς) W, μή LTTrAWHR
13:23 ὃ[3]—ὅ (ὅς) LTWH
21:25*βάπτισμα—add τό LTTrAWH
22: 5 ὁ—ὅς bis LTTrAWH
24:17*τά for τι (τις) GEds
38 omit ταῖς πρό, read days of the flood A
26:28 omit τὸ[2]—LTTrAWH
71 τοῖς—αὐτοῖς AW
Mar. 3: 8 omit they[1] [L]TTr[A]WHR
5:27*τὰ περί the things concerning TWHR, [τὰ] π. A
6:24 ἡ δέ[1]—καί TTrAWHR
50*ὁ δέ for καί TWHR
8:20*οἱ δέ—καί TAWHR
11:30*βάπτισμα—add τό Eds
12: 5 τούς—οὕς (ὅς) bis LTTrAWH
25 omit which are GLT[Tr]WWHR
13:32 omit which are TTrAWHR
14:24 omit τό[2] [L]TAWHR
15:23 ὁ—ὅς TTrWH
43 omit ὁ WH
Lu. 1:70 omit τῶν[2] TTrAWHR
2:39 omit τά T
5: 7 omit which were [L]TTrAWHR
6:15 omit τὸν τοῦ TTrAWHR
14:28 omit τά GTTrAWHR
32 omit τά WH
15:12*ὁ δέ for καί[2] LTrAWHR
16: 6*ὁ δέ for καί[1] LTTrAWHR
26 omit οἱ[2] L[A]WHR
20: 4*βάπτισμα—add τό T
24*οἱ δέ TWHR
22:36*εἶπεν οὖν—ὁ δὲ ε. TR
37 τά—τό TTrAWHR
24:10*Μαρία[2]—add ἡ LTTr[A]WWHR
Joh. 2: 8*οἱ δέ for καί[3] TTrAWHR
6:33*ἄρτος—add ὁ T
7:23*νόμος—add ὁ T
41*οἱ for ἄλλοι[2] (-ος) LTrAWHR
9:28*add at commencement οἱ δέ Tr
11:19 τὰς περί—τήν LTrAWHR
19:15 omit οἱ δέ TTrAWHR, see ἐκεῖνος
38 omit ὁ[2] LTrAWH
21: 6 omit ὁ δέ T
Acts 8:12 omit the things Eds
11:23*χάριν—add τήν LTTrAWHR
19: 3*ὁ δὲ εἶπεν for ε. τε T
8 omit the things LTrWH
20:21 omit τήν[2] LTTrAWHR
21: 8 omit τοῦ[2] GEds
23:15 omit τά A.V.Vul
30 omit τά LTTrWHR
24:14*και—add τοῖς ἐν GTTr[A]WHR
25:22 omit ὁ δέ LTTrAWHR
26: 4 omit τήν[2] Tr[A]WH
12 omit της L[Tr]W
28:23 omit τά LTTrAWHR
Ro. 6:10 ὅ s—ὁ E bis
10: 1 omit ἡ[3] Eds
12: 5 ὁ—τὸ Eds
13: 9 [namely] LTrAWH
16.19 omit τό[1] Eds
1 Co. 7: 7*ὁ for ὅς bis Eds
9:13*τὰ ἐκ, read the things of the temple TTrWHR, [τὰ] ἐκ A
21*ἀ.*—τοὺς ἀνόμους Eds
15:10 omit ἡ' LTTrAWHR
2 Co. 7:14 omit which (I made) T[Tr]WH
Gal. 4:14 omit τόν[2] LTTrAWHR
Phil. 1:11 τῶν—τόν G[L]TTrAWWHR
Col. 1: 4 τήν[3]—see ἔχω
16 omit that are[1] LTTrWHR
16 omit that are[2] [L]T[Tr]WHR
1 Th. 4:10 omit which are LT[Tr]WH
Tit. 2:10*διδασκαλίαν—add τήν Eds
Philem. 6 omit which is LTr[WH]
Heb. 10:10 omit οἱ A.V.B EGEds
12:24 τὸ Ἄβελ A.V.†Er
25 trs τόν after παραιτησάμενοι LTTrAWHR
Jas. 4:14 τό—τά L, omit WH
14 omit ἡ[2] WH

1 Pet. 5: 1 omit which are LTrAWHR
Rev. 1: 4 omit τοῦ[1] GEds
4*τῶν for ἃ (ὅς) Tr
11:19*θεοῦ—add ὁ LTTrWHR
16: 3*ἀπέθανεν—add τά LTTrAWWHR
17: 4 ἡ[2]—ἦν A.V.C GEds
19:14 armies—add τά which A.V.†C E ; L[A]WWHR
20:13*add τούς bis GEds, see νεκρός

ὅ, see ὅς. See 3739

3592 ὅδε, ἥδε, τόδε.

Lu. 16:25 ὧδε, read now here Eds (WHR
Acts 15:23 omit after this manner LTTrA

3594 ὁδηγέω.

Acts 8:31 ὁδηγήσει TTrWHR

3598 ὁδός.

Mat. 5:25 trs μετ' αὐτοῦ ἐν τῇ ὁ. Eds
20:17 trs and in the way LTTrAWHR
Mar. 11: 8 omit and strawed (them) in the way TTrAWHR
Acts 9: 2 trs ὄντας τῆς ὁδοῦ T
2 Pet. 2:15 τὴν εὐθεῖαν ὁ —omit τὴν GEds

3604 Ὀζίας, Ὀζείας LTTrAWH.

3608 ὀθόνιον.

Lu. 24:12 omit the verse [L]T[Tr][[WH]]

οἶδα, see εἰδέω. See 1492

3609 οἰκεῖος.

1 Ti. 5: 8 τῶν ο.—omit τῶν LTTr[A]WHR

* οἰκετεία, a household,

Mat. 24:45 οἰκετείας for θεραπείας (-πεία) LTTrAWHR

3611 οἰκέω.

Ro. 7:17 ἐνοικέω TWH
1 Co. 3:16 trs ἐν ὑμῖν οἰκεῖ WH

3614 οἰκία.

Mat. 7:24, 26 trs αὐτοῦ τὴν ο. LTTrAWH
19:29 trs or houses after lands TTrA
23:14(13) omit the verse LTTrAWHR, see κρίμα
Mar. 3:27 trs εἰς τὴν ο. τοῦ ἰσχυροῦ εἰσελθὼν τὰ σκεύη αὐτοῦ TTrWHR
7:24 τὴν ο.—omit τὴν A.V.B Eds
10:10 εἰς τὴν οἰκιαν LTTrAWHR
13:15 omit into the house [L]TWHR
Lu. 7:36 οἶκος LTTrAWH
10:38*τὴν οἰκίαν for τὸν οἶκον (-κος) TWH
22:54*τὴν οἰκίαν for τὸν οἶκον (-κος) TTrAWH

3618 οἰκοδομέω.

Mat. 26:61 trs αὐτὸν οἰκοδομῆσαι T
Mar. 15:29†trs ο. (ἐν[WH]R) τρισὶν ἡμέραις LTTrAWHR
Lu. 4:29 trs ᾠκοδόμητο αὐτῶν TTrAWH
6:48*add ο. TTrAWHR, see θεμελιόω
Joh. 2:20 οἰκοδομήθη TWH
Acts 4:11 οἰκοδόμος LTTrAWH
7:47 οἰκοδόμησεν TrWWH
9:31 οἰκοδομουμενη Eds
20:32*οἰκοδομῆσαι for ἐποικοδομῆσαι (-μέω) Eds
1 Pet. 2: 5 ἐποικοδομέω T

3619 οἰκοδομή.

Eph. 2:21 ἡ ο.—omit ἡ Eds

οἰκοδομία.

1 Ti. 1: 4 οἰκοδομίαν for οἰκονομίαν(-μία) A.V.B E

3623* οἰκοδόμος, a builder.

Acts 4:11 οἰκοδόμων for οἰκοδομούντων (-μέω) LTTrAWH

3622 οἰκονομία.

Eph. 3: 9*οἰκονομία for κοινωνία GEds
1 Ti. 1: 4 οἰκονομίαν dispensation s—οἰκοδομίαν edifying A.V.B E

3624 οἶκος.

Mat. 12:44 trs εἰς τὸν ο. μου ἐπισ. LTTrAWH
Mar. 2: 1 ἐν οἴκῳ LTTrWH
7:17 τὸν οἶκον T
8:26 τὸν ο.—omit τὸν GEds

Lu. 1:69 τῷ ο.—omit τῷ LTTrAWH
7:36*τὸν οἶκον for τὴν οἰκίαν LTTrA (WH
10:38 οἰκία TWH
12:52 trs ἑνὶ οἴκῳ LTTrWHR
14:23 trs μου ὁ οἶκος TTrAWH
22:54 οἰκία TTrAWH
Acts 7:46*οἴκῳ for θεῷ (θεός) LT

* οἰκουργός, a worker at home.

Tit. 2: 5 οἰκουργούς for οἰκουρούς (-ρός) LTTrAWHR

3626 οἰκουρός.

Tit. 2: 5 keepers at home—workers at home, οἰκουργός LTTrAWHR

3628 οἰκτιρμός.

Col 3:12 οἰκτιρμοῦ of mercy GEds

3633 οἶμαι.

Joh. 21:25 omit the verse T

3631 οἶνος.

Mat. 27:34*οἶνον for ὄξος LTTrWHR
Mar. 2:22 omit but new wine to new bottles T[Tr]A[WH]
Lu. 5:37†trs ῥήξει ὁ ο. ὁ νέος LTTrAWWH
7:33 trs πίνων οἶνον LTTrAWH
Joh. 2: 3*ὑστερήσαντος ο. when they wanted wine—οἶνον οὐκ εἶχον, ὅτι συνετελέσθη ὁ οἶνος τοῦ γάμου. εἶτα they had no wine, for the wine of the marriage-feast was finished. Then T
3 ο. οὐκ ἔχουσιν they have no wine—οἶνος οὐκ ἔστιν there is no wine T
Rev. 18: 3 omit the wine L[Tr]A[WH]

3634 οἷος.

Lu. 9:55 omit and said to end of verse LTTrAWHR

3635 ὀκνέω.

Acts 9:38 ὀκνήσῃς, read Delay not Eds

3638 ὀκτώ.

Lu. 13: 4, 11 see δεκαοκτώ
Acts 25: 6*more than—not more than eight or, οὐ πλείους ὀκτὼ ἤ GEds

ὀλεθρεύω, see ὀλοθρεύω. See 3645

* ὀλιγοπιστία, little faith.

Mat. 17:20 ὀλιγοπιστίαν f. ἀπιστίαν (-τία) LTTrAWHR

3641 ὀλίγος.

Mat. 20:16 omit for many be called, but few chosen T[TrA]WHR
Lu. 10:42*commence ὀλίγων δέ ἐστιν χρεία ἢ ἑνός but few things are needful, or one WH
Acts 19:24 trs οὐκ ὀ. ἐργασίαν LTTrAWH
Jas. 3: 5 ἡλίκος Eds
1 Pet. 3:20 ὀλίγοι few (persons) Eds
Rev. 2:20 omit a few things GEds

* ὀλίγως, just.

2 Pet. 2:18 for ὄντως GEds

3645 ὀλοθρεύω, ὀλεθρεύω LA.

3650 ὅλος.

Mat. 4:23 ἐν (om. ἐν L) ὅλῃ τῇ Γαλιλαίᾳ LTTrAWHR
21: 4 omit all LTTrAWHR
Mar. 12:33 omit and with all the soul [L]TWHR
Lu. 8:43 omit WH, see ἰατρός
10:27 ὅλῃ ter LTTrWHR, see ψυχή
Acts 8:37 omit the verse GLTTrAWHR
13: 6*ὅλην τὴν νῆσον the whole island GEds
19:29 omit whole LTTrAWHR
22:30 πᾶς GEds
Rev. 6:12*σελήνη ὅλη whole moon GEds
13: 3 see θαυμάζω

* ὁμείρομαι, to long for.

1 Th. 2: 8 ὁμειρόμενοι for ἱμειρόμενοι (-μαι) GEds

3658 ὅμιλος.

Rev. 18:17 *omit* the company GEds, *see* πλέω

* **ὀμίχλη, ὀ–**, a mist, fog.

2 Pet. 2:17 καὶ ὀμίχλαι *for* νεφέλαι (–λη) GEds

3659 ὄμμα.

Mat. 20:34*ὀμμάτων *for* ὀφθαλμῶν (–μός) LTTrAWH

3660 ὄμνυμι, ὀμνύω.

Mar. 14:71 ὀμνύναι GLTTrAWWH
Acts 7:17 had sworn—vouchsafed, ὁμολογέω Eds

3661 ὁμοθυμαδόν.

Acts 2: 1 with one accord—together, ὁμοῦ LTTrAWHR
18:12 *trs* οἱ Ἰουδαῖοι ὁ. WH

3662 ὁμοιάζω.

Mat. 23:27*ὁμοιάζετε *for* παρομοιάζετε(–ζω) LTr
Mar. 14:70 *omit* and thy speech agreeth (thereto) LTTrAWHR

3664 ὅμοιος.

Mar. 12:31 *omit* (is) like TAWHR
Rev. 4: 3 ὅμοιος² S—ὁμοία E
9: 7 ὁ.¹—ὅμοιοι T
10 ὁμοίοις Tr
14:14 ὅμοιον GEds
16:13 like—as, ὡς GEds
21:18 ὅμοιον Eds

3666 ὁμοιόω.

Mat. 7:24 ὁ. αὐτόν—ὁμοιωθήσεται he shall be likened LTTrWHR

3668 ὁμοίως.

Mar. 4:16 *trs* ὁμοίως εἰσίν T
Lu. 13: 3**for* ὡσαύτως LTTrAWHR
5 ὡσαύτως TTrAWHR
Rev. 2:15**for* ὃ μισῶ (–σέω) GEds

3670 ὁμολογέω.

Lu. 12: 8 ὁ.¹—ὁμολογήσει WH
Acts 7:17*ὡμολόγησεν *for* ὤμοσεν (ὀμνυμι) Eds
1 Joh. 2:23**add at end* ὁ ὁμολογῶν τὸν υἱὸν καὶ τὸν πατέρα ἔχει he that acknowledgeth the Son hath the Father also A.V.B GEds
Rev. 3: 5*ὁμολογήσω *for* ἐξομολογήσομαι (–γέομαι) GEds

3674 ὁμοῦ.

Acts 2: 1**for* ὁμοθυμαδόν LTTrAWHR

3679 ὀνειδίζω.

1 Ti. 4:10 suffer reproach—strive, ἀγωνίζομαι LTTrWHR

3681 ὄνειδος.

Lu. 1:25 τὸ ὄ.—*omit* τὸ TTr[A]WH

3684 ὀνικός.

Mar. 9:42**add* ὀ. LTTrAWHR, *see* λίθος
Lu. 17: 2 *omit* ὀ. LTTrAWHR, *see* λίθος

3686 ὄνομα.

Mar. 3:17 ὄνομα WH
5: 9 *trs* ὄνομά σοι LTTrAWH
9:41 τῷ ὀ.—*omit* τῷ GEds
11:10 *omit* in the name of the Lord GEds
Lu. 1:63 τὸ ὀ.—*omit* τὸ Tr[A]WH
8:30 *trs* ὄνομα ἐστίν LTTrWH
24:18 ᾧ ὀ.—ὀνόματι by name TrAWHR
Joh. 16:23 *trs*, *see* δίδωμι
Acts 5:41 *trs* κατηξιώθησαν ὑπὲρ τοῦ ὀ. LTTrAWHR
9:33 *trs* ὀνόματι Αἰνέαν LTTrAWWH
16:18 τῷ ὀ.—*omit* τῷ LTTrAWH
Phil. 2: 9 τὸ ὄνομα LTTrWWHR, [τὸ] ὀ. A
1 Pet. 4:16*ὀνόματι *for* μέρει (–ρος) Eds
1 Joh. 5:13 *om.* that believe on the name of the Son of God¹ GEds
Rev. 3: 1 τὸ ὀ.—*omit* τὸ GEds
13: 1 ὀνόματα names GLTTrWWHR
8 τὸ ὄνομα the name GW, τὸ ὀ. αὐτοῦ his name LTTrAWHR
14: 1*ὄνομα—*add* αὐτοῦ καὶ τὸ ὄνομα, *read* his name and his Father's name GEds
17: 3 (*add* τὰ Tr) ὀνόματα Eds
8 τὸ ὄνομα the name LTTrAWHR
19:16 τὸ ὀ. - *omit* τὸ A.V.C GEds
21:12*which are—*add* τὰ ὀνόματα the names L[TrA]

3687 ὀνομάζω.

Mar. 3:14**add* ὀ. WH, *see* ἀπόστολος
1 Co. 5: 1 *omit* named GEds

3688 ὄνος.

Lu. 14: 5 an ass—a son, υἱός LTTrAWWH

ὄντα, ὄντας, *etc.*, *see* ὤν.
See 5607

3689 ὄντως.

Mar. 11:32 *trs* ὄντως ὅτι TTrAWHR
1 Ti. 6:19**for* αἰωνίου (–νιος) GEds
2 Pet. 2:18 clean—just, ὀλίγως GEds

3690 ὄξος.

Mat. 27:34 vinegar—wine, οἶνος LTTrWHR
Joh. 19:29 τοῦ ὄξους LTrAWHR, *see* πλήθω

3694 ὀπίσω.

Mat. 4:10*hence—*add* ὀπίσω μου behind me G[L]W
Lu. 4: 8 *omit* get thee behind me, Satan G[L]TTrAWHR

3698 ὁπότε.

Lu. 6: 3 ὅτε LTrWHR

3699 ὅπου.

Mar. 2: 4**for* ἐφ' ᾧ LTTrAWH
9:44, 46 *omit* the verses T[Tr]WHR
Acts 20: 6**for* οὗ T

3700 ὄπτομαι.

Mat. 17: 3 ὤφθη LTTrAWH
27: 4 ὄψη LTTrAWH
Lu. 13:28 ὄψεσθε TTr
22:43, 44 *the verses* [L]{[WH]}
Joh. 1:39(40)*ὄψεσθε *for* ἴδετε (εἰδέω TTrAWHR
1:50(51) ὄψει—ὄψη GLTTrAWWH
11:40 ὄψη LTTrAWWH
Ro. 15:21 *trs.* ὄψονται before οἷς οὐκ WHR

3704 ὅπως.

Mat. 12:17 ἵνα LTTrAWH
Mar. 5:23 ἵνα LTTrAWHR
Acts 24:26 *omit* that he might loose him Eds

3705 ὅραμα.

Acts 9:12 *omit* in a vision LTAR; *trs* ἄνδρα [ἐν ὀ.] TrWH

3708 ὁράω.

Mar. 8:24 *omit* ὅτι *and* ὁρῶ A.V.BG
Lu. 9:36 ἑώρακαν TTrAWH
Joh. 6: 2 θεωρέω LTrAWHR
46 *trs* ἑωρακέν τις LTTrAWWH
8:38 have seen²—have heard, ἀκούω LTTrAWHR
20:18 ἑώρακα I have seen TTrAWHR
Acts 22:26 *omit* take heed, *read* what art thou about to do? GEds
1 Co. 9: 1 ἑόρακα TWH
Col. 2: 1 ἑώρακαν LTrAW, ἑόρακαν TWH
18 ἑόρακεν TAWH
Rev. 18:18 βλέπω GEds

3709 ὀργή.

Ro. 2: 8 *trs* wrath and indignation GEds

3714 **ὀρεινός, ὀρι–** WH.

ὀρθρινός.

Lu. 24:22*ὀρθριναί *for* ὄρθριαι (–ριος) Eds
Rev. 22:16 πρωϊνός GEds

3720 ὄρθριος.

Lu. 24:22 ὀρθρινός Eds

3725 ὅρια.

Mar. 7:24*ὅρια *for* μεθόρια LTTrWH

3726 ὁρκίζω.

Acts 19:13 ὁρκίζω I adjure GEds
1 Th. 5:27 ἐνορκίζω Eds

3733 ὄρνις.

Mat. 23:37 *trs* ὄρνις ἐπισυνάγει LTTrAWH
Lu. 13:34 ὄρνιξ T

3735 ὄρος.

Mar. 5: 5 *trs* tombs *and* mountains GEds
11 τῷ ὄρει the mountain GEds
Lu. 4: 5 *omit* into an high mountain [L]TTrAWHR
Joh. 4:20 *trs* τῷ ὄρει τούτῳ GLTTrAWWH
Heb. 12:18 *omit* the mount LTTrAWHR
2 Pet. 1:18†*trs* τῷ ἁγίῳ ὄρει TrAWH

3739 ὅς, ἥ, ὅ.

Mat. 5:32 ὃς ἄν—πᾶς ὁ LTTrAWHR
11:16*ἃ *for* καί LTTrAWHR
23*ἣ *for* ἡ W
12: 4 οὓς—ὃ LTTrAWH
18 εἰς ὃν—ἐν ᾧ Tr
13:23*ὃ *ter for* ὃ³ ⁴ ⁵ LTWH
46 *omit* who GLTTrAWHR, *see* ὅ
18:30 *omit* οὗ LTTrAWH
34 *omit* οὗ L[WH]
19:29 ὅς—ὅστις LTTrAWWH
20: 7 *omit* LTTrAWHR, *see* δίκαιος
21:44 *omit the verse* [L]T[WH]
22: 5*ὃς *bis for* ὁ LTTrAWH
10*οὓς *for* ὅσους (ὅσος) WH
25: 3*αἳ γάρ *for* αἵτινες (ὅστις) Tr
13 *omit* GLTTrAWHR, *see* υἱός
26:50 ᾧ—ὃ GEds
27:33 ὅς—ὅ GLTTrAWWH (WHR
Mar. 1:11 in whom—in thee, σοί LTTrA
2: 4 ἐφ' ᾧ wherein—ὅπου where LTTrAWH
3:14**add* οὓς WH, *see* ἀπόστολος
4: 9*ὃς *for* ὁ Eds, *see* ἔχω
22 *omit* ὃ LTTrAWHR
6:11*ὃς *for* ὅσοι (–ος) TTrAWHR
23 *omit* ὅ WH
9:38 *omit* GWHR, *see* ἀκολουθέω
11:23 ἃ—ὃ TTrAWHR
23 *omit* whatsoever he saith TTr[A]WHR
12: 5*οὓς *for* τούς *bis* LTTrAWH
13:19 ἧς—ἣν LTTrWH
37 ἃ—ὃ LTTrAWHR, *quod* A.V.Vul
14:72 οὗ—ὃ W, ὡς how LTTrAWHR
15: 6*ὃν *for* ὅνπερ (ὅσπερ) TWHR
12 *omit* whom ye call LTr, [ὃν] W
23*ὃς *for* ὁ TTrWH
Lu. 5: 9 ᾗ—ὧν TrWHR
25 ᾧ—ὃ TTrAWH
7:32**add* ἃ WHR, *see* λέγω
8:18 *trs* ὃς ἂν γάρ TTrAWH
27 *omit* ὃς TWHR, *see* ἔχω
12:50 οὗ—ὅτου Eds
59 *omit* οὗ TTrWH
13: 7*ἔτη—*add* ἀφ' οὗ TTrAWHR
19 ὃν S—ὃ E
14:15 ὅστις TTrAWHR
22*ὃ *for* ὡς TTrAWHR
15: 8*οὗ *for* ὅτου TrWH
16:20 *omit* ὃς [L]TTrAWHR
19:13*ἐν ᾧ *for* ἕως LTTrAWH
21:24*ἄχρι—*add* οὗ LTTrAWH
22:10 οὗ—εἰς ἣν LTTrAWHR
18*οὗ *for* ὅτου TrAWH
24:10 *omit* which LTTr[A]WHR
18 ᾧ ὄνομα—ὀνόματι TrAWHR
Joh. 1:27 *omit* is preferred before me G[L]TTrAWHR
2:22 ᾧ—ὃν LTTrAWH
4:29*ἃ *for* ὅσα (ὅσος) TWHR
39*ἃ *for* ὅσα (ὅσος) TTrAWHR
45 ἃ—ὅσα (ὅσος) LTrAWHR
50 ᾧ—ὃν LTTrAWH
5: 4 *omit* [G]TTrAWHR, *see* ὕδωρ
11*ὃς δὲ ἀπεκρίθη but he answered LTrWHR
6: 9 ὃ—ὃς LTTrAWWH
14 ὃ—ἃ WH
22 *omit* GLTTrAWHR, *see* ἐκεῖνος
51 *omit* which I will give LTTrAWHR
8:38 ἐγὼ ὃ—ἃ ἐγώ LTTrWHR, ἐγὼ ἃ A
38 ὃ²—ἃ LTTrAWHR
9:14**add* ᾗ LTTrAWHR, *see* ὅτε
10:29 ὅς—ὅ TTrAWH
11:45 ἃ—ὃ TrAWHR
13:18 οὓς—τίς TTrAWH (WHR
15:14*ἃ (ὃ WH) *for* ὅσα (ὅσος) LTTrA
17:11 whom—which ᾧ GEds
12 οὓς—ᾧ, *read* in thy name which TTrAWHR
24 οὓς—ὅ, *read* that which thou hast given TTrAWHR
18:16 ὃς ἦν—ὁ TTrAWH
19:17 ὅς—ὅ LTTrAWHR

Joh. 21:25*ἅ *for* ὅσα (ὅσος) LTTrAWHR
Acts 1:19*ὅ καί which also T
7:16 ὅ—ᾧ GLTTrAWWH
8:27 *omit* ὅς² LT[TrWH]
10:32 *omit* LTTr[A]WHR, *see* λαλέω
36 *omit* which L[Tr]WH
45*οἵ *for* ὅσοι (ὅσος) LWH
13:41 ᾧ—ὅ LTTrAWWH
17:23 whom—what, ὅ Eds
20: 6 οὗ—ὅπου T
24:18 οἷς—αἷς LTTrAWHR
Ro. 2:16*ἡμέρα ᾗ LA, ᾗ ἡ. WH (*omit* ὅτε)
4: 8 ᾧ—οὗ, *read* whose sin the Lord will not impute TTrWH
6:10 ὅ s—ὅ *bis* E
14:22*πίστιν—*add* ἣν, *read* the faith which thou hast, have LTTr[A]WHR
16:27 *omit* ᾧ A.V.C [WH] (WHR
1 Co. 2: 9 which—whatsoever, ὅσος LTrA
4: 2 ὃ δέ—ὧδε, *read* here moreover LTTrAWHR
6 ὅ—ἅ Eds
7: 7 ὅς *bis*—ὁ Eds
2 Co. 2:10 ᾧ²—ὅ GEds
5: 4 ἐφ' ᾧ *for* ἐπειδή A.V.B EGEds
Gal. 3:19 οὗ—ἄν WH
5: 1 *omit* ᾗ LTTrAWHR
Eph. 1: 6 ἐν ᾗ—ἧς LTTrAWHR, *see* ἐν
14 ὅς—ὅ LAWHR
5: 4*ἅ *for* τά LTTrAWH
5 ὅς—ὅ LTTrAWHR
6: 8 *omit* ὅ TAWH
Col. 1: 4*see ἔχω
24 ὃς (*qui*) νῦν A.V.Vul
27 ὅς—ὅ LTrAWHR
2:17 ἅ—ὅ LA
3: 6 ἅ—ὅ A
14*ὅ *for* ἥτις (ὅστις) Eds
23*ὅ *for* καὶ πᾶν ὅ τι Eds
1 Ti. 3:16*ὅς *for* θεός GEds
2 Ti. 2: 7 ἅ—ὅ Eds
Tit. 3: 5 ὧν—ἅ LTTrAWHR
Philem. 21 ὅ—ἅ LTTrAWHR
Heb. 7: 1*ὅς *for* ὁ LTrA
9: 9 ὅν—ἥν, *read* according to which Eds
10: 1 ἅς—αἷς TA
Jas. 4:12 ὅς—ὁ LTTrAWHR
1 Pet. 3:21 ὅ s—ᾧ A.V.BE
2 Pet. 3:16 οἷς—αἷς Eds
1 Joh. 5: 9 which—that, ὅτι Eds
Jude 23*add οὓς δέ LTTrAWR, *see* φόβος
Rev. 1: 4 ἅ—τῶν Tr
20 ὧν—οὓς LTTrAWHR
20 *om.* which thou sawest² GEds
2:13 *omit* wherein LTTrWHR, [αἷς] A
15 *see* μισέω
3: 8*ἣν *for* καί¹ GEds
12 ἡ s—ἡ E
4: 5 αἵ—ἅ LTWH
5: 6 οἵ—ἅ W
13 *omit* such as LTTrAWHR
6:11 *omit* οὗ GEds
7: 3 *omit* οὗ LTTrAWHR
9:11*ὄνομα¹—ᾧ ὄνομα T
14 ὅς—ὁ GEds
11:16*οἱ *for* οἱ² R
16*θεοῦ—*add* οἱ TTr
13: 4 ὅς—ὅτι, *read* because he gave GEds
8 ὧν—οὗ LTTrAWHR
14 ὅ—ὅς who Eds
14: 2*add ἣν GEds, *see* φωνή
8*ἣ *for* ὅτι Eds
16:14 *see* ἐκπορεύομαι
20: 2 ὅς—ὅ T
ὅ τι, *see* ὅστις.

3741 ὅσιος.

Rev. 16: 5 ὁ ὅ.—*omit* ὁ LTTrAW[WH]: ἐσόμενος A.V.B

3745 ὅσος.

Mat. 22:10 ὅς WH
Mar. 3:28 ὅσα LTTrAWHR
6:11 ὅς TTrAWHR, *see* δέχομαι
30 *omit* what² T
Joh. 4:29 ὅς TWHR
39 ὅς TTrAWHR
45*ὅσα *for* ἅ (ὅς) LTrAWHR
15:14 whatsoever—what, ὅς LTTrAWHR
16:23 ὅσα ἄν whatsoever—if anything, ἄν τι LTTrAWHR
21:25 ὅς—LTrAWHR: *omit the verse* T
Acts 10:45 as many as—who, οἵ (ὅς) LWH
1 Co. 2: 9*ὅσα *for* ἅ (ὅς) LTrAWHR

3746 ὅσπερ.

Mar. 15: 6 ὅς TWHR

3747 ὀστέον.

Eph. 5:30 *omit* of his flesh, and of his bones LTTr[A]WHR

3748 ὅστις, ἥτις, ὅ τι.

Mat. 18:28 that—if anything, εἴ τι GEds
19:29*ὅστις *for* ὅς LTTrAWWH
25: 3 αἵτινες—αἱ γάρ, *read* for the foolish TAWHR, αἱ γ. Tr, αἱ δέ L
Mar. 8:34 whosoever—if anyone, εἴ τις LTrWHR
9:11*28* ὅ τι *for* ὅτι LW
Lu. 10:35 ὅ τι—ὅτι WH
14:15*ὅστις *for* ὅς TTrAWHR (WH
Joh. 2: 5 | 8:25 | 14:13 | 15:16 ὅ τι—ὅτι
21:25 *omit the verse* T
Acts 9: 6*ὅ τι *for* τί³ LTTrAR
11:28 ἥτις LTTrAWWH
1 Co. 6:20 *omit* GEds, *see* θεός
7:13 which—if any, εἴ τις T
16: 2 ὅ τι—ὅτι WH
2 Co. 3:14 which (veil)—that (it), ὅτι GLTTrAWWH
Col. 3:14, 23 ὅς Eds
17 ὅ τι—ὅτι WH
1 Joh. 3:20*ὅ τι *for* ὅτι LR
Rev. 17: 8 ὅ τι—ὅτι *read* that it was GEds

3752 ὅταν.

Mar. 11:19*for ὅτε TTrWHR
12:23 *omit* when they shall rise L[Tr]WHR
1 Joh. 2:28 when—if, ἐάν LTTrAWHR
Rev. 8: 1*for ὅτε LTTrAWHR

3753 ὅτε.

Mat. 17:25 *omit* ὅ. LTTrAWH, *see* εἰσέρχομαι
Mar. 4: 6*add ὅ LTTrAWHR, *see* ἀνατέλλω
11:19 ὅταν TTrWHR
Lu. 6: 3*for ὁπότε LTrWHR
13:35 *omit* when [TrA]WHR
Joh. 4:45 ὡς T
9:14 when—in the day that, ἐν ᾗ ἡμέρᾳ LTTrAWHR
12:17 when s—because, ὅτι EGLTW
41 when-because, ὅτι GLTTrAWHR
Ro. 2:16 when—in which, ᾗ (ὅς) LAWH
1 Co. 12: 2*that—add ὅ. when [L]TTrAWHR
Rev. 8: 1 ὅταν LTTrAWHR

3754 ὅτι.

Mat. 5:31 *omit* ὅ. LTTrAWH
6: 5 *omit* ὅ.² LTTrAWH
13 *omit* GEds, *see* αἰών
16 *omit* ὅ. LTTrAWH
7:14 because—how, τί GLTr
9:18 *omit* ὅ. T
33 *omit* ὅ. A.V.C GEds
16:28*ὑμῖν—*add* ὅ. LTWH
19: 9 *omit* ὅ. LTrA
24*ὑμῖν—*add* ὅ. T
20:12 *omit* ὅ. LTTr[A]WH
23:10*for γάρ LTTrAWH, *see* καθηγητής
14(13) *omit the verse* LTTrAWHR, *see* κρίμα
36*ὑμῖν—*add* ὅ. G[A]W
24:34*ὑμῖν—*add* ὅ. LTrWH
26:21, 65 *omit* ὅ. LTTrAWH
Mar. 1:27 *omit* ὅ. LTTrAWHR, *see* καινός
2:16*add ὅ. LTTrWHR, *see* ἐσθίω
4:21*αὐτοῖς—*add* ὅ. TAWH
6: 2 *omit* that GEds
16 *omit* ὅ. LTTrAWHR
49*ἔδοξαν—*add* ὅ. TWHR
7: 2*αὐτοῦ—*add* ὅ. TTrWHR
6 *omit* ὅ [L]T[TrA]WH
6*γέγραπται—*add* ὅ. TWH
8: 4*αὐτοῦ—*add* ὅ. TTrAWH
24 *omit* ὅ. *and* ὁρῶ A.V.B G
28*add ὅ. TAWH, *see* λέγω
28*ἕνα—ὅ. εἷς LTTrAWHR
9:11¹, 28 ο τι LW
41*ὑμῖν—*add* ὅ. [L]TTrAWHR
11: 3 *omit* that LTTrAWHR
18 ὅ. πᾶς—πᾶς γάρ TTrAWHR
14:21*add at commencement ὅ. *read* for the Son T[Tr]AWHR
Lu. 4:25*ὑμῖν—*add* ὅ. T
6: 5 *omit* ο. [Tr]WH
7:22 *omit* how that L[Tr]WHR
8:20*ὅ. ἡ μήτηρ T
10:35*for ὅ τι WH
12:54*λέγετε—*add* ὅ. [L]TTrAWHR
13:14*ὄχλῳ—*add* ὅ. TAWH
35 *omit* ὅ. [L]Tr[A]WHR
17:10 *omit* ὅ.² Eds
18:29 *omit* ὅ. T
Lu. 19:34*ὅ. ὁ κύριος LTTrAWHR
40 *omit* ὅ. [Tr]WH
21: 8 *omit* ὅ. [L]T[TrA]WH
22:18 *omit* ὅ. TrAWH
22*for καί TTrAWHR
Joh. 1:16*for καί¹ GLTTrAWHR
50(51)*σοι—*add* ὅ. LTTrAWHR
2: 3*add ὅ. T, *see* οἶνος
5*for ὅ τι WH
4:42 [ὅτι¹] LWH
53 *omit* ὅ.² LTTrAWHR
7:31 *omit* ὅ. LTTrAWHR
40*ἔλεγον—*add* [ὅτι] AWH
8:25*for ὅ τι WH
9: 9 *omit* ὅ.² LTTrAWHR, *see* λέγω
11*μοι—*add* ὅ. TTrWHR
10: 7 *omit* ὅ. [L]Tr[A]WHR
26*οὐ γάρ—ὅ. οὐκ TTrWHR
34*ὑμῶν—*add* ὅ. LTTrAWH
12:17*for ὅτε EGLTW
41*for ὅτε GLTTrAWHR
13:11*εἶπεν—*add* ὅ. LTTrAWHR
14: 2*ὑμῖν¹—*add* ὅ. *read* for I go Eds
13* | 15:16*for ὅ τι WH
16:16 *omit* because I go to the Father TTrAWHR
23 *omit* ὅ. [L]TTrAWHR
18: 6 *omit* ὅ. LTTrWHR
Acts 9: 6*for τί² WH
10:20*for διότι GEds
23: 5*γάρ—*add* ὅ. TTr[A]WH
Ro. 4: 9 *omit* that [L]TTrWHR
8:21 διότι T
9:28 *omit* LTTr[A]WHR, *see* λόγος
10: 5 *trs* ὅ. *after* γράφει TWHR
9*σου¹—*add* ὅ. WH
1 Co. 4: 9 *omit* that Eds
7:29 ἀδελφοί *add* ὅ. B
16: 2*for ὅ τι WH
2 Co. 1:10 [that] LTrWH
3:14*for ὅ τι GLTTrAWWH
Gal. 2:16*for διότι LTTrAWH
3:10*γάρ²—*add* ὅ. GEds
13*ὅ. γέγραπται *for* γ. γάρ Eds
Eph. 3: 3 [ὅτι] LWH
Phil. 1:18*πλήν—*add* ὅ. *read* What then? only that LTTrAWHR
Col. 3:17*for ὅ τι WH
1 Pet. 1:16 διότι T
5: 8 *omit* because GEds
1 Joh. 2: 4*λέγων—*add* ὅ. [L]TTrAWHR
3:20 ὅ.¹—ὅ τι LR: *omit* ὅ.² A.V.Vul
5: 9*for ἣν (ὅς) Eds
Jude 18 *omit* ὅ.² LT[Tr]WHR
Rev. 3:17 *omit* ὅ.² [A]W
13: 4*for ὅς GEds
14: 8 ὅς, *read* which hath made GEds
17: 8*for ὅ τι GEds
18: 7*λέγει—*add* ὅ. LTTrAWHR
21: 4 *omit* for L[TrA]WHR
22:10 ὅ. ὁ καιρός—ὁ κ. γάρ Eds

3755 ὅτου.

Lu. 12:50*for οὗ (ὅς) Eds
15: 8 ὅς TrWH
22:18 ὅς TrAWH

3757 οὗ, adv.

Lu. 22:10 where—in which εἰς ἣν LTTrAWHR
Joh. 11:41 *omit* where the dead was laid GLTTrAWHR
Acts 20: 6 ὅπου T

3756 οὐ, οὐκ, οὐχ.

Mat. 13:34 not—nothing οὐδείς LTTrAWHR
55*for οὐχί LTTrAWH
15:17*for οὔπω LTTrWHR
16: 3 *see* λέγω
17:21 *omit the verse* T[TrA]WHR
21:19*αὐτῇ²—*add* οὐ LT[A]WH
29, 30 *trs* WH, *see* ἀπέρχομαι
32 οὐ²—οὐδέ, *read* did not even repent LTrWHR, οὐ[δέ] A
25: 9 οὐκ—οὐ μή LTrAWWHR
26:60 *omit* (yet) found they none G[L]TTrAWHR
Mar. 3:27 *omit* οὐ GLTrW
4:40 οὕτω; πῶς οὐκ—; οὔπω, *read* why are ye fearful? Have ye not yet faith? LTrWHR
6:36 *omit* [L]TTrAWHR, *see* ἄρτος
8:21 not—not yet, οὔπω LTTrAWHR
9:38 *omit* GWHR, *see* ἀκολουθέω
44, 46 *omit the verses* T[Tr]WHR
11:26 *omit the verse* TTrWHR
14:61*καί¹—*add* οὐκ TTrWHR, *see* ἀποκρίνομαι
68 οὔτε, *read* neither know, nor LTTrAWHR

Lu. 4:22 οὐχί LTTrAWH
8:17 οὐ³—οὐ μή LTTrAWHR
9:55 *omit* and said *to end of verse* LTTrAWHR
56 *omit* for the Son *to* **save** (them) GLTTrAWHR
12:24 οὐ¹—οὔτε TA
27 οὔτε TA, *see* κοπιάω (WHR
14: 3**add at end* ἢ οὔ or not [L]TTrA
17: 9 *omit* I trow not [L]TTrAWHR
17**for* οὐχί LTrWH
18: 4 καὶ ἄνθρωπον οὐκ—οὐδὲ ἄ. LTTrWHR
30 οὐ μή—οὐχὶ μή TAWH
23:34 *see* λέγω
Joh. 2: 3**add* οὐκ T, *see* οἶνος
4: 9 *omit* T[WH], *see* συγχράομαι
6:17 not—not yet, οὔπω LTTrAWHR
42 οὐχί TrWH
7: 8**for* οὔπω¹ GTTrA
42**for* οὐχι LTrAWH
16: 7 οὐ μή TrWH
16 not—no longer, οὐκέτι LTTrA
19: 4**for* οὐδεμίαν (–δείς) T (WHR
Acts 2: 7 οὐχί TrAWH
31 οὔτε, *read* neither . . . nor Eds
5:28 *omit* οὐ, *read* we did straitly LTTrAWHR
19:40*οὐ—*add* οὐ TTr[A]WHR
25: 6**add* οὐ GEds, *see* ὀκτώ
Ro. 3:26**for* οὐχί LTTrWH
4:19 *omit* not² LTTr[A]WHR
13: 9 *omit* thou shalt not bear false witness GEds
14: 6 *omit* LTTr[A]WHR, *see* κύριος
1 Co. 3: 4**for* οὐχί LTTrAWHR
6:10**for* οὔτε³ TAWHR
10 *omit* οὐ³ LTTrAWHR
9: 8*οὐ *after* ταῦτα² *for* οὐχί Eds
15**add* οὐ GEds, *see* χράομαι
10:18**for* οὐχί LTAWWH
2 Co. 3:10**for* οὐδέ GEds
5:12 οὐ²—μή LTTrWHR
10:13**for* οὐχί LTTrAWWH
12: 3 *omit* I cannot tell L[WH]
Phil. 3:13 not—not yet, οὔπω TWHR
Heb. 10: 2 *omit* οὐκ, *read* they would E
Jas. 2: 6 οὐχί LW
2 Pet. 1:12 *omit* οὐκ Eds, *see* ἀμελέω
1 Joh. 4:20**for* πῶς LTTrAWHR
Rev. 7:16*οὐδέ²—οὐδ' οὐ A
9: 6 οὐχ—οὐ μή GEds
20**for* οὔτε¹ A.V.C GWWHR
10: 6 *see* οὐκέτι
See also οὐ μή *after* μή.

3758 **οὐά, οὐᾶ T.**

3759 **οὐαί.**

Mat. 23:14(13) *omit the verse* LTTrAWHR, *see* κριμα

3761 **οὐδέ.**

Mat. 8:10 no, not—with any one, παρ' οὐδενὶ (–δείς) LTrAWH
21:32**for* οὐ² LTrWHR, οὐ[δέ] A
24:36**add* ο. LTWHR, *see* υἱός
Mar. 5: 3**for* οὔτε Eds
11:26 *omit the verse* TTrWHR
12:21 μή TTrAWHR, *see* καταλείπω
14:68 οὔτε Eds
Lu. 12:24 ο.¹—οὔτε TA
26**for* οὔτε LTTrAWHR
27 ο.¹—οὔτε TA, *see* κοπιάω
18: 4*καὶ ἄνθρωπον οὐκ—οὐδὲ ἄνθρωπον LTTrWHR
20:36**for* οὔτε LTrAWHR
21:15 nor—or, ἤ GT[Tr]AWHR
Joh. 1:25**for* οὔτε *bis* LTTrAWHR
21:25 *omit* the verse T
Acts 2:31 οὔτε Eds
4:12**for* οὔτε LTTrWWHR
20:24 *omit* neither count I TTrAWHR
24:13**for* οὔτε LTWHR
1 Co. 3: 2**for* οὔτε GEds
6: 5 σοφος οὐδὲ εἷς—οὐδεὶς σοφός LTTrAWHR
2 Co. 3:10 οὐ Eds
Gal. 1:12**for* οὔτε LTr
1 Th. 2: 3*ο. οὔτε Eds
Rev. 5: 3 ο.¹ ²—οὔτε T: ο.³—οὔτε LTTrWHR
9:20**for* οὔτε¹ TA
12: 8**for* οὔτε GEds
20: 4**for* οὔτε Eds

3762 **οὐδείς, οὐδεμία, οὐδέν.**

Mat. 8:10*οὐδενὶ *for* οὐδέ LTrAWH
13:34*οὐδεν *for* οὐ LTTrAWHR
19:17 *omit* ο. GEds, *see* ἀγαθός
Mar. 11:14 μηδεις S—οὐδεις E
15: 3 *add* A.V.C, *see* ἀποκρίνομαι
Lu. 8:51 οὐδένα no man—τινὰ σὺν αὐτῷ, *read* no man to go in with him LTTrAWHR
22:35 οὐθενός TTrAWH
23:14 οὐθέν TTrWH
Joh. 19: 4 οὐ T
11 *trs* κατ' ἐμοῦ ο. LTTrAWWH
Acts 9: 8 no man—nothing, οὐδέν LTTrWWHR
15: 9 οὐθέν TTrAWH
19:27 οὐθέν LTTrAWH
20:33 οὐθενός T
26:26 οὐθέν T[Tr]AWH, *omit* ο. L
1 Co. 6: 5**see* οὐδέ
8: 2 *omit* LTTrAWHR, *see* οὐδέπω
9:15*οὐδείς *for* ἵνα τις LTTrWHR
13: 2 οὐθέν S—οὐδέν EGW
3 οὐθέν T
2 Co. 11: 9 οὐθενός LTTrAWH
Jas. 3:12 οὐδεμία πηγὴ ἁλυκὸν καί—οὔτε ἁλυκόν, *read* neither (can) salt (water) yield fresh GEds
Rev. 3:17 οὐδέν LTTrAWHR

3764 **οὐδέπω.**

Lu. 23:53 οὔπω LTTrAWHR, *trs* οὐδεὶς ο. T
Joh. 7:39 οὔπω LTTrAWHR
Acts 8:16**for* οὔπω Eds
1 Co. 8: 2 οὐδέπω οὐδέν nothing yet—οὔπω not yet LTTrAWHR

οὐθείς, οὐθέν, *see under* οὐδείς. See 3762

3765 **οὐκέτι, οὐκ ἔτι.**

Mar. 5: 3*οὐκέτι οὐδείς, *read* **bind him** any longer Eds
Lu. 22:16 *omit* any more [LTr]AWHR
Joh. 16:16**for* οὐ LTTrAWHR
Ro. 11: 6 *om.* ο.³ GLTTr[A]WHR, *see* ἔργον
Rev. 10: 6*οὐκ ἔσται ἔτι—οὐκέτι ἔσ. GEds
18:14 *omit* ο. Tr

3767 **οὖν.**

Mat. 6:22 *omit* therefore T
14:15*ἀπόλυσον—*add* ο. *read* **away** therefore T[A]
18:31**for* δέ LTTrAWHR
28:19 *omit* therefore G[L]T[Tr]A
Mar. 3:31 καί Eds, *see* ἔρχομαι
11:31 *omit* then LTrAW[WH]
12: 6 *omit* therefore [L]TTrAWHR
9 *omit* therefore TAWH
20 ἑπτά—*add* ο. A.V.BEW
23 *omit* therefore TTrAWHR
27 *omit* therefore T[Tr]AWHR
37 *omit* therefore [L]TTrAWHR
Lu. 6: 9 then—and, δέ LTTrWHR
36 *omit* therefore LTTrAWHR
10: 2 therefore¹—and, δέ LTTrAWHR
36 *omit* now [L]T[Tr]AWHR
37 then—and, δέ GLTTrAWHR
11:34 *omit* therefore LTTrAWHR
12: 7 *omit* therefore [L]TTrAWHR
40 *omit* therefore LTTrAWHR
13:15 then—but, δέ LTTrAWHR
18**for* δέ TTrAWHR (WHR
14:34*good—*add* ο. therefore T[Tr]A
15:28 therefore—but, δέ LTTrAWHR
16:27 *trs* σε οὖν LTrAWWH
20: 5 *omit* then [L]TTrAWHR
33 *trs* οὖν ἐν τῇ TAWH, *see* γυνή
21: 8 *omit* therefore LTTrAWHR
36 therefore—but, δέ LTTrAWHR
22:36 then—but, δέ TTrWHR
23:20 therefore—and, δέ LTTrAWHR
Joh. 1:39(40)*came—*add* ο. therefore [L]TTrAWHR
4: 9, 11 *omit* then T
30 *omit* then GEds
33 *omit* therefore W
52*καὶ εἶπον—ε. οὖν TTrAWHR
5: 4 *omit* [G]TTrAWHR, *see* ὕδωρ
12 *omit* then [L]T[Tr]AWHR
18 *omit* ο. T
6:11**for* δέ¹ LTTrAWHR
35**for* δέ T
42 then—now, νῦν TTrAWHR
43 *omit* therefore G[L]TTrAWWHR
45 *omit* therefore GLTTrAWHR
66*that (time)-*add* ο. therefore T
68 *omit* then GLTTrAWHR
7: 6 *omit* then T
15*καὶ ἐθαύμαζον—ἐ. οὖν Eds
16*ἀπεκρίθη—*add* ο. *read* **Jesus** therefore Eds
47 *omit* then TA
8:41 *omit* then LTTrAWHR
42 *omit* ο. A.V.Er GLTTrAWHR
48 *omit* then GLTTrAWHR
52 *omit* then LTTrAWHR
Joh. 9:10*how—*add* ο. then [L]T[AWH]R
11**for* δέ LTTrAWHR
12 *omit* then LTTrAWHR, *see* καί
17*say—*add* ο. therefore Eds
20*answered—*add* ο. therefore LTWH
26**for* δέ LTTrAWHR
28 *omit* then GEds, *see* δέ *and* καί
41 *omit* therefore [L]TTrAWHR
10:19 *omit* therefore LTTrAWHR
20**for* δέ T
31 *omit* then T[Tr]WHR
39 *omit* therefore [TrAWH]R
12: 4 then—but, δέ T[WH]R
29 [therefore] LTrWH
34*ἀπεκρίθη—*add* ο. *read* **the** people therefore TAWHR
13:22 *omit* then T[Tr]AWHR
25**for* δέ T
26*answered—*add* ο. therefore [L]AWHR
26**add* ο. TTrAWHR, *see* βάπτω
31 ὅτε—*add* ο. A.V.B ELTTrAWHR
16:19 *omit* now GTTrAWWHR
18: 4 therefore—and, δέ Tr
24 ἀπέστειλεν—*add* ο. A.V.B ELT[Tr]AWHR
31 *omit* therefore (ο.²) LTrAWHR
19: 4 *omit* therefore GLTTrAWHR *see* καί
10 *omit* then T[A]
15**add* ο. TTrAWHR, *see* ἐκεῖνος
16**for* δέ LTTrAWHR
29 *omit* now Eds
29**for* δέ LTTrAWHR, *see* πλήθω
21:11*went up—*add* ο. therefore TrAWHR
13 *omit* then GLTTrAWHR
21*τοῦτον ο. *read* Peter therefore LTTrAWHR
Acts 6: 3 wherefore—but, δέ TWH, δή L
15: 2 therefore—but, δέ TTrWHR
39 δέ LTTrAWHR
16:11 therefore—and, δέ TA
18:14 *omit* ο. LTTr[A]WHR
20:28 *omit* therefore [L]TTrWHR
25:11**for* γάρ Eds
28: 9 so—and, δέ LTTrAWHR
Ro. 3:28 therefore—for, γάρ GLTTrAWWH
9:19*why—*add* ο. then L[A]W
11:13*μέν—*add* ο. *read* inasmuch then LT[Tr]AWWHR
12:20 ἐὰν ο.—ἀλλὰ ἐάν but if LTTrA
13: 7 *omit* therefore Eds (WHR
14:12 *omit* then LTr[AWH]
1 Co. 5: 7 *omit* therefore GEds
6: 7 *omit* therefore T[Tr]
2 Co. 7:16 χαίρω—*add* ο. A.V.B E
Gal. 5: 1 *omit* ο. GEds: στήκετε—*add* ο. Eds
Col. 2:20 *omit* wherefore GEds
1 Th. 4: 1 *omit* then WH
2 Ti. 2: 3 *omit* thou therefore Eds
4: 1 *omit* therefore GEds
Heb. 8: 4**for* γάρ Eds
13:15 *omit* therefore [Tr]WH
Jas. 5:16*confess—*add* ο. therefore LTTrAWHR
1 Pet. 2:13 *omit* ο. A.V.Vul LTTrAWHR
5: 1*elders—*add* ο. therefore LTTrAWHR
2 Pet. 3:11 then—thus, οὕτως AWHR
1 Joh. 2:24 *omit* therefore LTTrAWHR
Rev. 1:19*write—*add* ο. therefore GEds
2:16*repent—*add* ο. therefore GLTr[A]WWHR

3768 **οὔπω.**

Mat. 15:17 not yet—not, οὐ LTTrWHR
Mar. 4:40**add* ο. LTrWHR, *see* οὐ
8:21**for* οὐ LTTrAWHR
11: 2*ο. ἀνθρώπων LTrWHR, ἀνθ. ο. T man yet
Lu. 23:53*οὐδεὶς ο. *for* οὐδέπω οὐδείς LTrAWHR
Joh. 6:17**for* οὐ LTTrAWHR
7: 8 not yet¹—not, οὐ GTTrA
39**for* οὐδέπω LTrAWHR
Acts 8:16 οὐδέπω Eds
1 Co. 8: 2**see* οὐδέπω
Phil. 3:13**for* οὐ TWHR

3769 **οὐρά.**

Rev. 9:19**add* ο. A.V.C GEds, *see* ἐξουσία

3770 **οὐράνιος.**

Mat. 5:48*ὁ οὐράνιος *for* ὁ ἐν τοῖς οὐρανοῖς (–νός) LTTrAWHR
18:35*οὐράνιος *for* ἐπουράνιος LTTrWH, [ἐπ]ο. A

Mat. 23: 9*ὁ οὐράνιος for ὁ ἐν τοῖς οὐρανοῖς (-νός) LTTrAWHR
Lu. 2:13 οὐρανός Tr

3772 οὐρανός.

Mat. 5:48 ἐν τοῖς ο.—οὐράνιος, read your heavenly Father LTTrAWHR
6: 1 τοῖς ο.—omit τοῖς T
7:21 ο.²—τοῖς οὐρανοῖς LTTrAWH
10:32, 33 τοῖς ο. LAWH, [τοῖς] ο. Tr
11:23 τοῦ ο.—omit τοῦ LTTrAWH
16: 2, 3 When it is evening to end of verse 3 [TA][[WH]]
17 τοῖς ο.—omit τοῖς L[TrWH]
18:10 ἐν ο.¹—ἐν τῷ οὐρανῷ [L]A
18 τῷ ο.—omit τῷ bis LT[Tr]AWH
19:21 οὐρανοῖς TrAWH
24*τῶν οὐρανῶν for τοῦ θεοῦ (-ός) LTTrA
22:30 τῷ οὐρανῷ LTTrAWH
23: 9 ἐν τοῖς ο.—οὐράνιος, read your Father, the heavenly LTTrAWHR
24:30 τῷ ο.—omit τῷ LTTrAWH
Mar. 4: 4 omit of the air GEds
11:26 τοῖς ο.—omit τοῖς LA: omit the verse TTrWHR
Lu. 2:13*οὐρανοῦ for οὐρανίου (-νιος) Tr
10:15 τοῦ ο.—omit τοῦ LTTrWH
11: 2 omit which art in heaven GTTrAWHR
2 omit as in heaven, so in earth G[L]TTrAWHR
16 trs ἐξ ο. ἐζήτουν παρ' αὐτοῦ Eds
12:56 trs of the sky, and of the earth A.V.C
15: 7 trs ἐν τῷ ο. ἔσται TAWH
17:24 ο.¹—τὸν οὐρανόν LTTrAWHR
18:13 trs ἐπᾶραι εἰς τὸν ο. TTrAWHR
22 τοῖς (omit τοῖς T[WH]) οὐρανοῖς LTTrAWHR
22:43 τοῦ οὐρανοῦ LTrWH
43, 44 the verses [L][[WH]]
24:51 omit and carried up into heaven T[[WH]]
Joh. 3: 5*τῶν οὐρανῶν for τοῦ θεοῦ (-ός) T
13 omit which is in heaven WH
6:58 τοῦ ο.—omit τοῦ LTTrAWH
Col. 4: 1 οὐρανῷ Eds
Heb.10:34 omit in heaven Eds
12:23 trs ἀπογεγραμμένων ἐν ο. GEds
2 Pet. 3:10 οἱ ο.—omit οἱ TA
1 Joh. 5: 7 omit in heaven to in earth (verse 8) GEds
Rev. 6:14 ὁ οὐρανός A.V.C GEds
12:12 οἱ ο.—omit οἱ TTrAWHR
16:17 omit of heaven Eds
21: 3 heaven—the throne, θρόνος LTAWHR

3775 οὖς.

Mar. 7:16 omit the verse T[TrA]WHR
Lu. 22:50 trs τὸ οὖς αὐτοῦ LTTrAWH

οὖσα, etc., see ὤν. See 5607

3777 οὔτε.

Mar. 5: 3 οὐδέ Eds
14:68*for οὐ LTTrAWHR: for οὐδέ Eds
Lu. 12:24*for οὐ and οὐδέ¹ TA
26 οὐδέ LTTrAWHR
27*see κοπιάω
20:36 οὐδέ LTrAWHR
Joh. 1:25 οὐδέ bis LTTrAWHR
Acts 2:31*for οὐ and οὐδέ Eds
4:12 οὐδέ LTTrWWHR
24:13 οὐδέ LTWHR
1 Co. 3: 2 οὐδέ GEds
6:10 ο.³—οὐ TAWHR
Gal. 1:12 οὐδέ LTr
6:15†trs ο. γάρ¹ TTrAWHR, see ἐν
1 Th. 2: 3 οὐδέ Eds
Jas. 3:12*see οὐδείς
Rev. 5: 3*for οὐδέ¹ ² T: for ο.³ LTTrWHR
9:20 ο.¹—οὐ A.V.C GWWHR, οὐδέ TA
12: 8 οὐδέ GEds
20: 4 οὐδέ Eds

3778 οὗτος.

Mar. 8:35 omit the same GEds
Lu. 8:41*for αὐτός LTrWH
19: 2 αὐτός LTrAWHR, omit ο. T
20:30 omit took her to to end of verse TTrAWHR
Joh. 6:42 omit ο.² [L]TrAWHR
7:46 omit ο. see ἄνθρωπος L[TrA]WHR
Acts 3:10 αὐτός LT
10: 6 omit ο.² GEds, see ποιέω
42*for αὐτός LTrWHR
1 Co. 7:13*for αὐτός Eds
Heb.10:12*for αὐτός Eds
Jas. 1:25 omit he LTTrAWHR
Rev. 3: 5 the same—thus, οὕτως LTTrWH
17:11*for αὐτός Tr (R

3778 οὗτοι.

Mar. 4:18 these—others, ἄλλος GEds
18 omit ο. εἰσίν² A.V.C
20 these—those, ἐκεῖνος TTrAWHR
Lu. 13: 4 αὐτοί LTTrAWHR
Joh. 17:11 αὐτοί TWH
Acts 13: 4 αὐτοί LTTrAWHR
1 Co. 16:17 αὐτοί LAW
1 Joh.5: 7 omit in heaven to in earth (verse 8) GEds
8 hi tres A.V.Vul

3778 αὕτη.

Mat. 22:39*for αὐτῇ WHR
Mar. 1:27 omit α. LTTrAWHR, see καινός
12:30 omit this (is) the first commandment TAWHR
31 αὐτῇ LTr
14: 8 omit α. [L]T[Tr]AWHR
Lu. 2:37 αὐτή TTrAWHR
38 αὐτῇ W, omit α. LTTrAWHR
7:12 αὐτή WWHR
8:42 αὐτή WH
Ro. 7:10 αὐτή GW
16: 2 αὐτή GLTAWWHR
1 Co. 7:12*for αὐτή LTAWWH

3779 οὕτω, οὕτως.

Mat. 5:46*for τὸ αὐτό LTrA
47 so—the same, τὸ αὐτό Eds
24:46 trs οὕτως ποιοῦντα LTTrAWH
Mar. 2: 8 omit so L[WH]
12 trs οὕτως οὐδέποτε TTrAWH
4:40 omit so LTrWHR, see οὐ
9: 3*can—add ο. thus TTrAWHR
Lu. 6:10 omit so GTTrAWWHR
24:46 omit and thus it behoved [L]TTrAWHR
Joh. 8:59 omit going through to end of verse GLTTrAWHR
13:25*ἐκεῖνος—add ο. read lying thus T[Tr]AWWHR
1 Co. 14:25 omit and thus (καὶ ο.¹) GEds
2 Co. 11: 3 omit so LTTrAWHR
Jas. 3: 6, 12 omit so Eds
2 Pet. 3:11*for οὖν AWHR
1 Joh. 2: 6 omit so LTr[A]WHR
Rev. 3: 5*for οὗτος LTTrWHR

οὐχ, see οὐ. See 3756

3780 οὐχί.

Mat. 13:55 οὐ LTTrAWH
Lu. 4:22*for οὐ LTTrAWH
17:17 οὐ LTrWH
18:30*for οὐ TAWH
23:39*for εἰ TTrAWHR
Joh. 6:42*for οὐ TrWH
7:42 οὐ LTrAWH
9: 9*add ο. [L]TTrAWHR, see λέγω
Acts 2: 7*for οὐ TrAWH
Ro. 2:26 οὐ LTTrWH
1 Co. 3: 4 οὐ LTTrAWHR
9: 8 οὐ Eds
10:18 οὐ LTAWWH
2 Co. 10:13 οὐ LTTrWWH
Jas. 2: 6*for οὐ LW

3782 ὀφειλή.

1 Co. 7: 3*ὀφειλήν for ὀφειλομένην (-λω) εὔνοιαν GEds

3783 ὀφείλημα.

Ro. 4: 4 τὸ ὀ.—omit τό GEds

3784 ὀφείλω.

1 Co. 5:10 ὠφείλετε LTTrAWHR
7: 3 due benevolence—(her) due, ὀφειλή GEds

3786 ὄφελος.

Jas. 2:14, 16 τὸ ὄ.—omit τὸ LWH

3787 ὀφθαλμοδουλεία, —λία TWH.

Col. 3:22 ὀφθαλμοδουλείᾳ LW

3788 ὀφθαλμός.

Mat. 6:22 trs ᾖ ὁ ὀφ. σου ἁπλοῦς LTAWH
7: 5 trs ἐκ τοῦ ὀφ. σου τὴν δοκόν LTTrAWH
20:33 trs οἱ ὀφθαλμοὶ ἡμῶν LTTrAWH
34 ὀ.¹—ὄμματα LTTrAWH
34 omit their eyes² LTTrAWHR
Mar. 14:40 trs αὐτῶν οἱ ὀφθαλμοί TWH
Lu. 4:20 trs οἱ ὀφ. ἐν τῇ συναγωγῇ TTrAWHR
Joh. 9:15 trs μου ἐπὶ τοὺς ὀφθ. GEds
Acts 9:18 trs αὐτοῦ ἀπὸ τῶν ὀφθ. LTTrAWH
1 Co. 12:21 ὁ ὀφθαλμός GEds
1 Pet. 3:12 οἱ ὀ.—omit οἱ LTTrAWHR

3789 ὄφις.

Rev. 20: 2 ὁ ὄφις ὁ ἀρχαῖος LTTrAWH

3790 ὀφρύς.

Lu. 4:29 τῆς ὀ.—omit τῆς GTTrAWWHR

3791 ὀχλέω.

Lu. 6:18 ἐνοχλέω TTrAWHR

3793 ὄχλος.

Mat. 8:18 πολλοὺς ὄ.—ὄχλον a crowd LWH
12:15 omit ὄ. read many followed LT[TrA]WHR
15:31 τὸν ὄχλον TAWHR
35 τῷ ὄχλῳ LTTrWHR (R
36 τοῖς ὄχλοις multitudes TTrAWH
Mar. 3:20 ὁ ὄχλος LTrAR, [ὁ] ὄχ. WH
32 trs περὶ αὐτὸν ὄχλος LTTrAWWH
6:33 omit οἱ ὄ. read they saw GEds
9:25 ὁ ὄχλος T
11:32*ὄχλον for λαόν (-ός) WH
Lu. 9:18 trs οἱ ὄχλοι λέγουσιν TTrAWH
12:13 trs ἐκ τοῦ ὄχλου αὐτῷ TWHR
22: 6 trs ἄτερ ὄχλου αὐτοῖς LTTrAWH
Joh. 7:12 ὄ.¹—τῷ ὄχλῳ T
40 trs ἐκ τοῦ ὄχλου οὖν LTTrAWHR
12: 9 ὁ ὄχλος TWHR
12 ὁ ὄχλος WH
Acts 19:35 trs τὸν ὄχλον ὁ γραμματεύς WH

3796 ὀψέ.

Mar. 11:11*for ὀψία TWH

3798 ὄψιος, ὀψία.

Mat. 16: 2 when it is evening to end of verse 3 [TA][[WH]]
Mar. 11:11 ὀψέ TWH

3804 πάθημα.

Phil. 3:10 τῶν π.—omit τῶν TTrWH

3808 παιδάριον.

Mat. 11:16 παιδίον GEds

3809 παιδεία. παιδία (except Eph. 6:4) T.

3813 παιδίον.

Mat. 11:16*παιδίοις for παιδαρίοις (-ριον) GEds
15:38 trs children and women T
Mar. 7:30*trs τὸ παιδίον (π. for θυγατέρα -τηρ) βεβλημένον ἐπὶ τὴν κλίνην καὶ τὸ δαι. ἐξε. LTTrAWHR
Lu. 2:21 the child—him, αὐτόν GEds
9:47 παιδίον TrAWHR

3816 παῖς.

Lu. 1:69 τοῦ π.—omit τοῦ LTTrAWH
Acts 4:25 τοῦ π.—omit τοῦ GEds

3819 πάλαι.

Mar. 15:44 any while—already, ἤδη LTrWH
2 Co. 12:19*for πάλιν LTTrAWHR

3820 παλαιός.

Mar. 2:21 ἱμάτιον παλαιόν LTTrAWHR

3824 παλιγγενεσία, παλινγ— TWH.

3825 πάλιν.

Mat. 13:44 omit again [L]TTrAWHR
26:44*saying—add π. again TWHR
Mar. 7:14*for πάντα (πᾶς) LTTrAWHR
8: 1*add π. LTTrAWHR, see πάμπολυς
11: 3*π. ὧδε again hither TTrWHR
12: 5 omit again GLTTrAWHR
14:40 trs π. after καί¹ LAWHR, omit again Tr
69 omit again A, see ἄρχω
Lu. 6:43*neither—add π. again [L]T[Tr]AWHR
Joh. 9:26 omit again LTTrAWHR
10: 7 omit unto them again T
39 omit again T: trs αὐτὸν π. WH
12:22 and again—cometh, ἔρχομαι LTTrAWHR
18:33 trs π. εἰς τὸ πραιτ. LTrAWWHR

Acts 10:16 again—immediately, εὐθύς Eds
17:32†*trs* περὶ τούτου καὶ π. LTTrAWHR
2 Co. 12:19 again—πάλαι, *read* ye think all this time LTTrAWHR

3826 παμπληθεί, παμπ— TWH.

3827 πάμπολυς.

Mar. 8: 1 very great—again great, πάλιν πολλοῦ LTTrAWHR

3828 Παμφυλία.

Acts 14:24 τὴν Παμφυλίαν TTrWH

3829 πανδοχεῖον.

Lu. 10:34 πανδοκίον T

3830 πανδοχεύς.

Lu. 10:35 πανδοκεί T

3832 πανοικί.

Acts 16:34 πανοικεί TAWH

* πανταχῇ, —χῆ LTrWH, everywhere.

Acts 21:28 *for* πανταχοῦ LTTrAWWH

3836 πανταχόθεν.

Mar. 1:45 πάντοθεν Eds

3837 πανταχοῦ.

Mar. 1:28*εὐθύς—*add* π. *read* abroad everywhere T[Tr]AWHR
Acts 21:28 πανταχῇ LTTrAWWH

3839 πάντη, —η TA.

3840 πάντοθεν.

Mar. 1:45**for* πανταχόθεν Eds
Joh. 18:20 *for* πάντοτε² B

3842 πάντοτε.

Joh. 18:20 always (π.²)—πάντοθεν B: all, πᾶς GEds

3843 πάντως.

Acts 18:21 *omit* LTTrAWHR, *see* δεῖ

3844 παρά.

Mat. 8:10**add* π. LTrAWH, *see* οὐδέ
20:20 ἀπό LTrAWH
21:25 with—among, ἐν LTrWH
Mar. 2:13 by—to, εἰς T
16: 9**for* ἀπό LTrWHR
Lu. 10:39 πρός TTrAWHR
18:14**for* ἤ LTrAWH
Joh. 16:28 ἐκ LTTrAWHR
Acts 4:37 πρός T
5:16 πρός LTTrAWHR
18:20 *omit* with them LTTrAWHR
22:30 ὑπό Eds
26:12 *omit* π. LTTrWHR
22 ἀπό Eds
28:14**for* ἐπί LTTrAWHR
Ro. 11:25 ἐν TrAWH
2 Co. 8: 3**for* ὑπέρ Eds
2 Pet. 2:11 *omit* before the Lord L[TrWH]
1 Joh. 3:22 ἀπό LTTrAWHR
5:15 ἀπό LTTrWH

3845 παραβαίνω.

2 Joh. 9 transgresseth — goeth forward, προάγω Eds

3846 παραβάλλω.

Mar. 4:30 compare—set forth, τίθημι LTTrAWHR

* παραβολεύομαι, to venture.

Phil. 2:30 παραβολευσάμενος *for* παραβουλευσάμενος (-λεύομαι)GEds

3850 παραβολή.

Mat. 22: 1 *trs* ἐν π. αὐτοῖς LTTrAWHR
Mar. 4:10 τὰς παραβολάς the parables TTrAWHR
7:17 τὴν παραβολήν LTTrAWHR
Lu. 8: 9 *trs* αὕτη εἴη ἡ π. TWH
20:19 *trs* εἶπεν τὴν π. ταύτην LTTrAWH

3851 παραβουλεύομαι.

Phil. 2:30 not regarding—hazarding, παραβολεύομαι GEds

3853 παραγγέλλω.

Mat. 15:35*παραγγείλας *for* ἐκέλευσεν (κελεύω) LTTrWHR
Mar. 8: 6 παραγγέλλει commandeth LTTrAWHR
Lu. 8:29 παρήγγελλεν 8 — παρήγγειλεν A.V.BE?
Acts 1: 4 *trs* αὐτοῖς π. AW
17:30 commandeth—sendeth word to, ἀπαγγέλλω TWH
1 Co. 11:17 παραγγέλλω LTrAW

3854 παραγίνομαι.

Lu. 8:19 παρεγένετο TTrWH
Acts 5:22 *trs* π. ὑπηρέται LTTrAWHR
10:32 *omit* who, when he cometh, *to end of verse* LTTr[A]WHR
24:17 *trs* παρεγ. *after* μου LTTrAWHR
2 Ti. 4:16*παρεγένετο *for* συμπαρεγένετο (-ραγίνομαι) LTTrWHR

3855 παράγω.

Mar. 1:16*καὶ παράγων *for* περιπατῶν (—τέω) δέ LTTrAWHR
Joh. 8:59 *omit* going through *to end of verse* GLTTrAWHR

3956 παραδειγματίζω.

Mat. 1:19 δειγματίζω LTTrAWH

3857 παράδεισος.

Rev. 2: 7 τῷ παραδείσῳ GEds

3858 παραδέχομαι.

Acts 15: 4*παρεδέχθησαν *for* ἀπεδέχθησαν (ἀποδέχομαι) Eds

3859 παραδιατριβή.

1 Ti. 6: 5 διαπαρατριβή GEds

3860 παραδίδωμι.

Mat. 5:25 *omit* deliver thee² LT[Tr]WH
10:19 παραδῶσιν LTTrWH
27: 3 παραδούς LTrWH
Mar. 4:29 παραδοῖ LTTrAWH
14:10†*trs* αὐτὸν παραδοῖ TTrAWH, π. α. L
11†*trs* αὐτὸν εὐκαίρως παραδοῖ (-δῷ W) LTTrAWWH
Lu. 10:22 *trs* μοι παρεδόθη LTTrAWWH
12:58 παραδώσει LTTrAWHR
20:20 εἰς τὸ π.—ὥστε π. LTTrAWHR
22: 4 *trs* αὐτοῖς π. αὐτόν LTTrAWH
Joh. 6:71 *trs* παραδιδόναι αὐτόν LTrAWH
13: 2 παραδοῖ LTTrAWHR, *see* Ἰούδας
19:11 παραδούς LTWHR
Acts 16: 4 παρεδίδοσαν LTTrAWWH
28:16 *omit* the centurion *to* the guard: but LTTrAWHR
1 Co. 11:23 π.²— παρεδίδετο LTTrAWH
15:24 παραδιδοῖ LTTrAR, -διδῷ WH

3866 παραθήκη.

1 Ti. 6:20*παραθήκην *for* παρακαταθήκην (-θήκη) GEds
2 Ti. 1:14*παραθήκην *for* παρακαταθήκην (-θήκη) GEds

3868 παραιτέομαι.

Mar. 15: 6*παρῃτοῦντο *for* ᾐτοῦντο (αἰτέω) TWHR
Lu. 14:18 *trs* πάντες π. LTTrAWHR

* παρακαθέζομαι, to sit down near.

Lu. 10:39 παρακαθεσθεῖσα *for* παρακαθίσασα (-θίζω) TTrAWHR

3869 παρακαθίζω.

Lu. 10:39 παρακαθέζομαι TTrAWHR

3870 παρακαλέω.

Mar. 5:23 παρακαλεῖ beseecheth TTrAWH
Lu. 7: 4 besought—asked, ἐρωτάω T (R
8:31 παρεκάλουν A.V.Er LTTrAWHR
32 παρεκάλεσαν LTTrAWH
Acts 16:40 *trs* π. τοὺς ἀδελφούς LTTrAWHR
20: 1*and²—*add* παρακαλέσας exhorted LTTrAWHR
2 Co. 1: 6 *trs* εἴτε παρακαλούμεθα *to* σωτηρίας² *after* ὑπὲρ ὑμῶν LTrAW
2 Ti. 4: 2 *trs* exhort, rebuke T

3872 παρακαταθήκη.

1 Ti. 6:20 παραθήκη GEds
2 Ti. 1:14 παραθήκη GEds

3877 παρακολουθέω.

Mar. 16:17 ἀκολουθέω TrWH
2 Ti. 3:10 παρηκολούθησας didst fully know (*or* follow) LTTrAWHR

3878 παρακούω.

Mar. 5:36*παρακούσας *for* ἀκούσας (ἀκούω) TTrAWHR

3879 παρακύπτω.

Lu. 24:12 *omit the verse* [L]T[Tr][[WH]]

3880 παραλαμβάνω.

Lu. 17:34, 35 παραλημφθήσεται LTTrAWH
36 *add the verse* A.V.BE, *see* ἀφίημι
Joh. 14: 3 παραλήμψομαι LTTrAWH
2 Th. 3: 6 παρελάβοσαν they received GATWR, -βετε ye received LTrWH

3887 παραμένω.

Phil. 1:25*παραμενῶ *for* συμπαραμενῶ LTTrAWHR

3899 παραπορεύομαι.

Mar. 2:23 διαπορεύομαι LTrWHR
9:30 πορεύομαι LTrWH
11:20 *trs* π. πρωΐ LTTrAWHR

3900 παράπτωμα.

Mat. 6:15 *omit* their trespasses T[WH]
18:35 *omit* their trespasses GLTTrA
Mar. 11:26 *omit the verse* TTrWHR (WHR
Jas. 5:16 faults—sins, ἁμαρτία LTTrWHR

3901 παραρρέω.

Heb. 2: 1 παραρυῶμεν LTTrAWH

3904 παρασκευή.

Lu. 23:54 παρασκευῆς LTTrAWHR
Joh. 19:31 *trs* ἐπεὶ π. ἦν *after* Ἰουδαῖοι A.V.Er TTrAWHR

3906 παρατηρέω, —ομαι.

Lu. 6: 7 παρετηροῦντο Eds
Acts 9:24 παρετηροῦντο Eds

3908 παρατίθημι.

Mar. 6:41 παρατιθῶσιν TAWH
8: 6 π.¹—παρατιθῶσιν TTrAWH
7†*trs* αὐτὰ εἶπεν καὶ ταῦτα παρατιθέναι TrWHR: αὐτὰ παρέθηκεν TA
Lu. 9:16 παραθεῖναι TTrAWH
23:46 παρατίθεμαι A.V.Vul Eds

3911 παραφέρω.

Lu. 22:42 παρενέγκαι T, -ένεγκε A.V.Vul LTrWHR
Heb. 13: 9*παραφέρεσθε *for* περιφέρεσθε (-φέρω) GEds
Jude 12*παραφερόμεναι *for* περιφερόμεναι (-φέρω) GEds

3916 παραχρῆμα.

Acts 9:18 *omit* forthwith GLTTrAWHR

* παρεδρεύω, to sit by, serve.

1 Co. 9:13 παρεδρεύοντες *for* προσεδρεύοντες (-δρεύω) Eds

3918 πάρειμι.

Lu. 11:42*παρεῖναι *for* ἀφιέναι (ἀφίημι) LTTrAWH
Rev. 17: 8**for* ἐστίν³ GEds, *see* καίπερ

3921 παρεισδύνω.

Jude 4 παρεισεδύησαν WH

* παρεμβάλλω, to put in beside.

Lu. 19:43 παρεμβαλοῦσιν *for* περιβαλοῦσιν (-βάλλω) TWH

3928 παρέρχομαι.

Mat. 14:15 *trs* παρῆλθεν ἤδη T
24:35 π.¹—παρελεύσεται GLTTrAWH
26:39 παρελθάτω LTTrAWH
Mar. 13:31 π.¹—παρελεύσεται GW
31 π.²—παρελεύσονται TTrAWH
Lu. 21:33 π.²—παρελεύσονται LTTrAWHR
Acts 24: 7 *omit* and would have judged (*verse* 6) *to* to come unto thee (*verse* 8) LTTr[A]WHR
Rev. 21: 1 ἀπέρχομαι GEds

3930 παρέχω.

Lu. 7: 4 παρέξῃ LTTrAWHR
Acts 28: 2 παρεῖχαν LTTrAWH

3932 παρθενία, παρθενεία A.

3933 παρθένος.

Acts 21: 9 *trs* τέσσαρες παρθ. LTTrAWHR
1 Co. 7:28 [ἡ] π. LTrAWH
34 *see* γυνή
38**add* π. LTTr[A]WHR, *see* ἐκγαμίζω

3936 παρίστημι.

Mar. 14:69 παρεστῶσιν TTrAWH
15:35 παρεστώτων T
Joh. 18:22 *trs* π. τῶν ὑπηρετῶν LTTrAWH
Acts 1:10 παριστήκεισαν WH
1 Co. 8: 8 παραστήσει, *read* will not commend us LTTrAWHR

3945 παρομοιάζω.

Mat. 23:27 ὁμοιάζω LTr

3946 παρόμοιος.

Mar. 7: 8 *omit* (as) the washing *to end of verse* T[TrA]WHR

3950 παροργισμός.

Eph. 4:26 τῷ π.—*omit* τῷ LTTr[A]WHR

3953 παροψίς.

Mat. 23:26 *omit* and platter TA[WH]

3956 πᾶς, πᾶσα, πᾶν.

Mat. 5:32*πᾶς ὁ *for* ὃς ἄν LTTrAWHR
13:44 *omit* πάντα WH
18:29 *omit* all [L]TTrAWWHR
19:20 *trs* ταῦτα πάντα LTrWH
23:36 *trs* πάντα ταῦτα LTrA
24: 2 *trs* ταῦτα πάντα LTTrAWH
6 *omit* all LTTr[A]WHR
33 *trs* ταῦτα πάντα TTr
Mar. 1: 5 *trs* all they of Jerusalem, and were baptised GLTTrAWHR
27 ἅπας TTrAWH
4:11 τὰ π.—*omit* τὰ T
5:12 *omit* all G[L]TTrAWWHR
40*πάντας *for* ἅπαντας (ἅπας) GEds
7:14 all—again πάλιν LTTrAWHR
9:49 *omit* π.^{2} T[Tr]WHR, *see* ἅλς
12:28 πάντων GEds, †*trs* ἐντολή πρώτη π. TTrAWHR
29 πάντων GLW: *omit* TTrAWHR, *see* ἐντολή
13:30 *trs* ταῦτα πάντα TTrAWHR
Lu. 1:75 πάσαις ταῖς ἡμέραις WH
2:39*πάντα *for* ἅπαντα (ἅπας) TTrWHR
3:16**trs* λεγων πᾶσιν ὁ Ἰω. TWH
4: 4 *omit* but by every word of God T[Tr]AWHR
7 πᾶσα GEds
40 ἅπας WH
5:11*πάντα *for* ἅπαντα (ἅπας) LTTrWH
28*πάντα *for* ἅπαντα LTTrAWHR
7:16*πάντας *for* ἅπαντες GTrAWH
8:54 *omit* put them all out, and LTTrAWHR
12:15*πάσης *for* τῆς, *read* all covetousness Eds
31 *omit* all [L]TTrAWHR
14:10*ἐνώπιον—*add* πάντων, *read* presence of all LTTrAWHR
17 *omit* π. [L]T[TrA]WHR
15:13*πάντα *for* ἅπαντα (ἅπας) LTTrAWH
16:18 *omit* whosoever,^{2} *read* he that LTTrAWHR
17:27, 29*πάντας *for* ἅπαντας LTrAWH
18:28 all—our own, τὰ ἴδια LTTrAWHR
19: 7*πάντες *for* ἅπαντες Eds
37 πάντων LTr
20: 6 ἅπας TTrAWH
32 *omit* of all LTTrAWHR
21: 4*πάντες *for* ἅπαντες LWHR
4*πάντα *for* ἅπαντα LTTrWHR
12*πάντων *for* ἁπάντων GEds
15 ἅπας TTrAWH
24: 9 *trs* πάντα ταῦτα T
Joh. 3:31 *omit* is above all^{2} T
4:25 ἅπας TTrAWH
10: 4*πάντα *for* πρόβατα^{1} (-τον) LTTrAWHR
16:13 πάσῃ T, *see* ἀλήθεια
18:20*πάντες *for* πάντοτε^{2} GEds
40 *omit* all TWHR
21:17 *trs* πάντα σύ LTTrAWHR
Acts 2: 1*πάντες *for* ἅπαντες LTTrAWHR
4*πάντες *for* ἅπαντες LTTrWHR
2: 7 *omit* all^{1} L[Tr]AWH
7 π.^{2}—ἅπας LTAR
14*πάντες *for* ἅπαντες LTTrWHR
43**add* π. T, *see* φόβος
3:21 *omit* all^{2} GEds
4:32*πάντα *for* ἅπαντα LWH
5:12*πάντες *for* ἅπαντες LTrWH
6:15*πάντες *for* ἅπαντες LTTrWHR
11: 8 *omit* π. GEds
13:29*πάντα *for* ἅπαντα GEds
15:17 *omit* all^{2} GEds
18 *omit* unto God are all his works GTTrAWHR, *om.* all LW
16:33 ἅπας TWH
17:25 κατὰ πάντα S—καὶ τὰ π. A.V.B EGEds
26 παντὸς προσώπου LTTrAWHR
30 πάντας LTTrAWHR
21:21 *omit* all L[Tr]
22:30*πᾶν *for* ὅλον (ὅλος) GEds
25:24 π.^{2}—ἅπας Eds
Ro. 3:22 *omit* and upon all LTTr[A]WHR
9:33 *omit* whosoever, *read* he that Eds
16:16*ἐκκλησίαι—*add* πᾶσαι, *read* all the churches GEds
24 *omit* the verse LTTr[A]WHR
1 Co. 9:22 τὰ π.—*omit* τὰ Eds
23*πάντα *for* τοῦτο Eds
10:11 *omit* all [L]TTr[A]WHR
12:19 [τὰ] π. LTrAWH
15:28 τὰ π.^{3}—*omit* τὰ LTrAWHR
2 Co. 5:17 *omit* all things LTTrAWHR
Gal. 3:28 ἅπας TTrA
4:26 *omit* all G[L]TTrAWHR
Eph. 1:22 π.^{1}—τὰ πάντα W
23 τὰ πάντα GEds
3: 9 *omit* all^{1} [L]TWH
Phil. 4:23 you all—your spirit, τοῦ πνεύματος ὑμῶν Eds
Col. 2: 2 πᾶν Eds
3:11 τὰ π.—*omit* τὰ TWH
23 *omit* π. Eds
2 Th. 2:12 ἅπας TTrA
1 Ti. 1:16 ἅπας Eds
6:17 *trs* π. πλουσίως GEds
Heb. 3: 4 τὰ π.—*omit* τὰ Eds
2 Pet. 1: 3 τὰ πάντα T
1 Joh. 2:20 ye know all things—ye all know, πάντες TWH
Jude 5*πάντα *for* τοῦτο Eds
25**add* π. Eds, *see* αἰών
Rev. 5:13 π.^{2}—πάντας W
6:15 *omit* every^{2} Eds
7: 1 τι (τις) LTr[A]WR
21: 5 *trs* ποιῶ πάντα Eds
7 all things—these things ταῦτα GEds
22:21 *omit* all TrAWHR, *see* ἅγιος

3958 πάσχω.

Mat. 17:15 ἔχω LTrWH
1 Pet. 3:18 suffered—died, ἀποθνήσκω LTTrWH

3960 πατάσσω.

Rev. 19:15 πατάξῃ GEds

3962 πατήρ.

Mat. 2:22 *trs* τοῦ π. αὐτοῦ Ἡ. LTTrAWH
23: 9 *trs* ὑμῶν ὁ πατήρ LTTrWH
Mar. 10:29 *trs* mother or father LTTrA
11:26 *omit the verse* TTrWHR (WHR
Lu. 2:33*ὁ πατὴρ αὐτοῦ his father *for* Joseph GTTrAWHR
23:34 *see* λέγω
Joh. 5:30 \| 6:39 *omit* π. *read* the will of him that GEds
6:40*τοῦ πατρός μου *for* τοῦ πέμψαντός (πέμπω) με LTTrAWHR
46 the Father^{2}—God, θεός T
8:16 *omit* π. *read* he T[WH]
29 *omit* ὁ π. *read* he LTTrAWHR
38 τῷ π. ὑμῶν—τοῦ πατρός LTTrAWHR
44 π.^{1}—τοῦ πατρός GLTTrAWHR
10:17 *trs* με ὁ πατήρ LTTrAWHR
38*τῷ πατρί *for* αὐτῷ LTTrAWHR
15:10†*trs* τοῦ π. (μου T) τὰς ἐντολὰς TAWH
16:16 *omit* because I go to the Father TTrAWHR
27*πατρός *for* θεοῦ (-ός) TrAWHR
17:21 πατήρ TTrAWH
24, 25 πατήρ LTTrAWH
Acts 3:22 *omit* unto the fathers LTTrA
4:25*ὁ διά—ὁ τοῦ πατρὸς ἡμῶν διὰ πνεύματος ἁγίου, *read* who by the Holy Spirit, (by) the mouth of our father LTTrAWHR
7:14 *trs* Ἰακὼβ τὸν π. αὐτοῦ Eds
16: 3†*trs* ὅτι Ἕλλην ὁ π. αὐτοῦ LTrWHR
Ro. 4: 1 father—forefather, προπάτωρ LTTrAWHR
Eph. 5:31 τὸν π.—*omit* τὸν LTrA[WH]
Col. 2: 2 *omit* and of the Father, and of GEds
1 Th. 1: 1 *omit* from God our *to end of verse* [L]TTrAWHR
2 Th. 2:16 ὁ πατήρ LTTrAWHR
1 Joh. 2:23**add* π. *see* ὁμολογέω A.V.B GEds
5: 7 *omit* in heaven *to* in earth (*verse* 8) GEds

3964 πατραλῴης, πατρο— LTTrAWH.

3972 Παῦλος.

Acts 13:13 τὸν Π.—*omit* τὸν LTTrAWWH
45 τοῦ Π.—*omit* τοῦ LTTr[A]WH
14:11 ὁ Π.—*omit* ὁ LTTrAWWH
15:36 *trs* πρὸς Βαρνάβαν Π. LTTrAWH
16: 9 *trs* τῷ Π. ὤφθη TTrAWH
14 τοῦ Π.—*omit* τοῦ TTrWH
18 ὁ Π.—*omit* ὁ TTrWH
28 ὁ Π.—*omit* ὁ LTTrWH: *trs* Π. μεγάλῃ φωνῇ WH, Π. φ. μ. L
17:22 ὁ Π.—*omit* ὁ LTTrWH
18: 1 *omit* ὁ Π. *read* he LTTrAWHR
19:13 ὁ Π.—*omit* ὁ LTTrAWH
29 τοῦ Π.—*omit* τοῦ GLTTrAWWH
30 τοῦ δὲ Π.—Π. δέ LTTrAWWH
21: 8 *omit* that were of Paul's company GEds
23: 1 *trs* τῷ συνε. ὁ Π. LTTr: *omit* ὁ WH
11 *omit* Paul GEds
24:23 Paul—him, αὐτόν GEds
25: 7 *omit* against Paul LTTrAWHR
8*ἀπολ. αὐτοῦ — τοῦ Παύλου ἀπολ. *read* Paul answered LTTrAWHR
26:25*ὁ δέ—*add* Παῦλος, *read* but Paul said LTTrWWHR
27:11 τοῦ Π.—*omit* τοῦ LTTr[A]WWH
28:17 Paul—he, αὐτόν GEds
30 *omit* ὁ Π. *read* he GEds
1 Co. 3: 5 *trs* Apollos *and* Paul Eds

3979 πεζῇ, *see* πεζός.

* πεζός, on foot, walking.

Mat. 14:13 πεζοί *for* πεζῇ T

3981 πειθός, πιθός WH.

3982 πείθω, πέποιθα.

Mar. 10:24 *omit* for them that trust in riches TWH
Acts 26:28 πείθῃ χ. ποιῆσαι, *read* thou persuadest thyself to make me a Christian A
27:11 *trs* μᾶλλον ἐπείθετο LTTrAWHR
Gal. 3: 1 *omit* that ye should not obey the truth GEds
Heb. 11:13 *omit* and were persuaded of (them) GEds
13:18 we trust—πειθόμεθα we are persuaded Eds

3985 πειράζω.

Lu. 20:23 *omit* why tempt ye me? TTrAWHR
Acts 9:26*ἐπείραζεν *for* ἐπειρᾶτο (πειράω) LTTrWHR
1 Co. 10: 9 ἐκπειράζω T
Heb. 4:15 πεπειρασμένον *for* πεπειραμένον (πειράω) A.V.B EGEds
11:37 *trs* were tempted, were sawn asunder TWH
Rev. 2: 2 ἐπείρασας GEds

3986 πειρασμός.

2 Pet. 2: 9 πειρασμῶν A.V.CT

3987 πειράω.

Acts 9:26 πειράζω LTTrWHR
Heb. 4:15 πειράζω A.V.B EGEds

3992 πέμπω.

Lu. 7:10 *trs* εἰς τὸν οἶκον οἱ π. LTTrWHR
20:11 *trs* ἕτερον πέμψαι LTTrAWH
12 *trs* τρίτον πέμψαι LTTrAWH
Joh. 6:40 him that sent me—my Father, πατήρ LTTrAWHR
Acts 25:21 ἀναπέμπω Eds
2 Th. 2:11 πέμπει sendeth Eds
Rev. 11:10 πέμπουσιν send T

3994 πενθερά.

Lu. 4:38 ἡ π.—*omit* ἡ GEds

4002 πέντε.

Mat. 25: 2 αἱ π.—*omit* αἱ EGEds

4004 πεντήκοντα.

Acts 13:20 *see* ἔτος

* περαιτέρω, further, more.

Acts 19:39 περαιτέρω *for* περὶ ἑτέρων (-ρος) LTrWH

4008 πέραν.

Mar. 5:21 *trs* εἰς τὸ πέραν πάλιν T
10: 1 τοῦ π.—*omit* τοῦ LTTrAWHR

4011 Πέργη.

Acts 14:25 εἰς τὴν Πέργην ■

4012 περί.

Mat. 18: 6**for* ἐπί LTTrWHR
19:17**add* π. GEds, *see* ἀγαθός
Mar. 7:17 *omit* concerning LTTrAWHR
14:24 ὑπερ LTTrAWHR, *see* ἐκχύνω
Lu. 6:28**for* ὑπερ TAWH
Joh. 1:30 ὑπέρ LTTrAWHR
8. 5**add* π. WR, *see* αὐτῆς
11:19 τὰς περι—τὴν LTrAWHR
Acts 10: 3*ὡσει—*add* π. Eds
12: 5**for* ὑπέρ LTTrWHR
19:39 concerning other matters—further, περαιτέρω LTrWH
40*λόγον—*add* π. LTTrWHR
21: 8 *omit* that were of Paul's company GEds
26: 1**for* ὑπερ LTTrA
Ro. 1: 8**for* ὑπέρ Eds
2 Co. 1: 8**for* ὑπερ LTTrR
Gal. 1: 4**for* ὑπέρ GLTTrAW
Col. 1: 3 ὑπερ LTr
2: 1 ὑπερ LTTrAWHR
1 Th. 3: 2 ὑπέρ GEds
5:10**for* ὑπερ TTrWH
Heb. 5: 3**for* ὑπερ Eds
13:11 *omit* for sin A

4014 περιαιρέω.

Acts 28:13*περιελόντες *for* περιελθόντες (-έρχομαι) WH

* περιάπτω, to fasten round.

Lu. 22:55 περιαψάντων *for* ἀψάντων (ἅπτω) TTrAWHR

4015 περιαστράπτω.

Acts 9: 3 περιήστραψεν S, περιέσ—B

4016 περιβάλλω.

Lu. 19:43 shall cast about—shall place near, παρεμβάλλω TWH
Rev. 7: 9 περιβ βλημένους GEds
11: 3 περιβεβλημένους TrWH
17: 4 ἡ π.—ἦν π. A.V.C GEds

περιδρέμω, *see* περιτρέχω.

4022 περιέρχομαι.

Acts 28:13 περιαιρέω WH

4023 περιέχω.

Acts 23:25 ἔχω LTTrWHR, [περι]έ. A

4024 περιζώννυμι.

Acts 12: 8 ζώννυμι LTTrAWHR

4036 περίλυπος.

Lu. 18:24 *omit* that he was very sorrowful, *read* saw him T[Tr]AWHR

4043 περιπατέω.

Mar. 1:16 as he walked—as he passed along, παράγω LTTrAWHR
2: 9 walk—go, ὑπαγω T
6:49 *trs* ἐπὶ τῆς θαλάσσης π. TWHR
7: 5 *trs* οὐ π. οἱ μαθη. σου TTrAWH
Lu. 11:44 οἱ π.—*omit* οἱ L[A]W
Joh. 8:12 περιπατήση Eds
Acts 14: 8 περιπεπατήκει S—περιεπ. E, περιεπάτησεν LTTrAWHR
Ro. 8: 1 *omit* who walk *to end of verse* GEds
1 Th. 2:12 περιπατεῖν Eds
1 Th. 4: 1*God—*add* καθὼς καὶ περιπατεῖτε even as ye do walk Eds
Heb. 13: 9 περιπατοῦντες are occupied LTTrWH

4046 περιποιέομαι.

Lu. 17:33*περιποιήσασθαι *for* σῶσαι (σώζω) TTrAWHR

* περιρραίνω, to besprinkle.

Rev. 19:13 περιρεραμμένον *for* βεβαμμένον (βάπτω) T

4048 περιρρήγνυμι.

Acts 16:22 περιρήξαντες LTTrAWH

4051 περίσσευμα.

Lu. 6:45 τοῦ π.—*omit* τοῦ LTTrAWHR

4052 περισσεύω.

Mat. 15:37 *trs* τὸ π. τῶν κλ. ἦραν LTTrAWH
Lu. 15:17 περισσεύονται TrAWHR
Joh. 6:13 ἐπερίσσευσαν LTTrAWH
1 Co. 8: 8†*trs* μὴ φάγωμεν ὑστερούμεθα (περισσευομεν L)· οὔτε ἐὰν φάγωμεν περισσεύομεν (-νόμεθα TrR, ὑστερούμεθα L) LTrAWHR

4053 περισσός, περισσότερος.

Mat. 23:14(13) *omit the verse* LTTrAWHR, *see* κριμα
Mar. 6:51 *omit* beyond measure [Tr]WHR
12:33*περισσότερον *for* πλεῖον TTrWHR
14:31 ἐκ π.—ἐκπερισσῶς LTTrAWHR

4044, 4056 περισσοτέρως.

Mar. 15:14 περισσῶς GEds
2 Co. 11:23 *trs* π. ἐν φυλακαῖς π. ἐν πληγαῖς ὑπερβ. LTrAWHR, π. ἐν πλ. π. ἐν φ. ὑπερβ. T

4057 περισσῶς.

Mar. 15:14**for* περισσοτέρως GEds

4059 περιτέμνω.

Acts 15: 1 περιτμηθῆτε LTTrAWHR
24 *omit* saying, (Ye must) be circumcised, and keep the law LTTrAWHR

4060 περιτίθημι.

Mat. 27:28 *trs* χλαμύδα κοκκίνην π. αὐτῷ LTTrAWH

4061 περιτομή.

Phil. 3: 5 περιτομῇ GEds
Tit. 1:10 τῆς περιτομῆς TTrWH

4063 περιτρέχω.

Mar. 6:55 περιέδραμον TTrWHR

4064 περιφέρω.

Heb. 13: 9 carried about—carried away, παραφέρω GEds
Jude 12 carried about—carried along, παραφέρω GEds

4066 περίχωρος.

Mar. 6:55 region round about—region, χώρα TTrAWHR
Lu. 3: 3 τὴν π.—*omit* τὴν, *read* every country LTrAWH

4072 πετάομαι, πέτομαι GEds.

4071 πετεινόν.

Acts 10:12 τὰ π.—*omit* τὰ LTTrAWHR

4073 πέτρα.

Lu. 6:48 *omit* π.[2] TTrAWHR, *see* θεμελιόω
8:13 τὴν πέτραν T
1 Co. 10: 4 *trs* πέτρα δὲ LTTrAWH

4074 Πέτρος.

Mat. 14:28 *trs* ὁ Π. εἶπεν αὐτῷ LWH
29 ὁ Π.—*omit* ὁ LTTrAWH
17:26 *omit* ὁ Π. LTTrAWHR, *see* λέγω
18:21 *trs* ὁ Π. εἶπεν αὐτῷ LTTrAWHR
Mar. 5:37 τὸν Πέτρον TTrAWH
8:32 *trs* ὁ Πέτρος αὐτὸν LTTrAWH
33 τῷ Π.—*omit* τῷ LTTrAWH
10:28 *trs* λέγειν ὁ Πέτρος TAWH
13: 3 ὁ Πέτρος T
Lu. 9:20†*trs* (*om.* ὁ) Π. δὲ ἀποκριθεὶς TTrAWH
28 τὸν Π.—*omit* τὸν GLTTrAWWH
18:28 ὁ Π.—*omit* ὁ T[A]W
22:62 *omit* ὁ Π. *read* he GTTr[A]WHR
24:12 *omit the verse* [L]T[Tr][[WH]]
Joh. 13:37 ὁ Π.—*omit* ὁ GLTTrAW[WH]
18:17 *trs* τῷ Π. ἡ παιδίσκη ἡ θυρωρός LTTrA
18 *trs* ὁ Π. μετ' αὐτῶν LTTrAWHR
27 ὁ Π.—*omit* ὁ LTTrAWWH
Acts 2:14 ὁ Πέτρος LTTrAWH
3: 1 *trs* Πετρος δὲ LTTrAWHR
12 ὁ Πέτρος LTTrAWH
5: 3 ὁ Πέτρος LTTrAWH
8, 29 ὁ Π.—*omit* ὁ LTTrAWH
8:14 τὸν Π.—*omit* τὸν LTTrAWWH
10:23 *omit* Peter Eds, *see* ἀνίστημι
46 ὁ Π.—*omit* ὁ LTTrAWH
11: 4 ὁ Π.—*omit* ὁ LTTrAWWH
12:13 Peter—he, αὐτοῦ GEds
Gal. 1:18 | 2 11, 14 Peter—Cephas, Κηφᾶς Eds

4077 πηγή.

Jas. 3:12 *omit* π. GEds, *see* οὐδείς

4082 πήρα.

Mar. 6: 8 *trs* no bread, no scrip TTrAWHR

4091 Πιλάτος, -ᾶτος LTTrWH, Πει— TWH.

Mar. 15: 1 τῷ Π.—*omit* τῷ LTTrAWH
43 τὸν Πιλάτον TTrWH
Lu. 23:12 *trs* Herod and Pilate TTrAWH
24 ὁ δὲ Π.—καὶ Π. LTTrAWHR (B
Joh. 18:31 ὁ Π.—*omit* ὁ TrAWH
19: 4 *trs* ὁ Πειλᾶτος ἔχω T

πίμπλημι, *see* πλήθω.

See 4130

4092 πίμπραμαι, -ρημι.

Acts 28: 6 ἐμπιπράω T

4095 πίνω, πίω, πίομαι.

Mat. 6:25 *omit* or what ye shall drink (T[WH]
24:49 πίνῃ GEds
27:34 πεῖν *bis* T
Mar. 2:16 *omit* and drinketh [L]WH
15:23 *omit* to drink TTrAWHR
Joh. 4: 7, 9, 10 πεῖν TTrAWH
Acts 23:12, 21 πεῖν WH
Ro. 14:21 πεῖν WH
1 Co. 9: 4 | 10:7 πεῖν TAWH
10: 4 *trs* πνευματικὸν ἔπιον πόμα LTTrAWWH
Rev. 16: 6 πεῖν TAWH, πῖν L
18: 3 have drunk of—have fallen by, πίπτω TrWHR: πέπωκαν LTW, πεπ[τ]ωκαν A

4098 πίπτω, ἔπεσον.

Mat. 17: 6 ἔπεσαν LTTrAWH
21:44 *omit the verse* [L]T[WH]
Mar. 13:25*πίπτοντες *for* ἐκπίπτοντες (ἐκπίπτω) LTTrAWHR
14:35 ἔπιπτεν TAWHR
Lu. 6:39 ἐμπιπτω LTTrAWHR
49 fell—fell together, συμπίπτω TTrAWHR
8: 6 fell—fell down, καταπίπτω TTrAWHR
14: 5*πεσεῖται *for* ἐμπεσεῖται (ἐμπίπτω) LTTrAWHR
23:30 πέσατε TTrAWH
Joh. 18: 6 ἔπεσαν LTTrAWH
Acts 13:11*ἔπεσεν *for* ἐπέπεσεν (ἐπιπίπτω) LTTrWHR
19:17*ἔπεσεν *for* ἐπέπεσεν (ἐπιπίπτω) LTr
22: 7 ἔπεσα LTTrAWH
27:34 shall fall—shall perish, ἀπόλλυμι GEds
1 Co. 10: 8 ἔπεσαν LTTrAWWH
13: 8*πίπτει *for* ἐκπίπτει (-τω) LTTrAWHR
Heb. 11:30 ἔπεσαν LTTrAWHR
Rev. 2: 5*πέπτωκας (-κες TWH) *for* ἐκπέπτωκας (ἐκπίπτω) GEds
5: 8 | 7:11 ἔπεσαν LTTrAWWH
6:16 πέσατε LAWWH
11:11 ἐπιπίπτω Eds
16:19 ἔπεσαν LTTrAWWH
18: 2 *omit* is fallen[2] Tr[A]
3*πέπτωκαν TrWHR, πέπ[τ]ωκαν A *for* πέπωκεν (πίνω)
19: 4 ἔπεσαν S, ἔπεσον EG
10 ἔπεσα LTTrAWWH
22: 8 ἔπεσα S—ἔπεσον BG

4099 **Πισιδία.**

Acts 13:14 τὴν Πισιδίαν LTTrAWHR

4100 **πιστεύω.**

Mat. 27:42 πιστεύομεν L, πιστεύσωμεν T
Mar. 9:23 *omit* believe TTr[A]WHR
42 believe — have faith, πίστιν ἐχόντων A
11:23 πιστεύῃ TAWHR
13:21 πιστεύετε GLTTrAWWH
Lu. 8:50 πιστευσον TTrAWH
Joh. 4:21†*trs* πίστευέ μοι, γύναι TTrAWHR, πίστευε L
6:29 πιστευητε TTrA R
7:31 *trs* ἐκ τοῦ ὄχλου δὲ πολ. ἐπίσ. LTrAWHR, π. δὲ ἐπ. ἐκ τοῦ ὄχ. T
39 πιστεύσαντες believed LTrAWH
10:38 π.[1]—πιστεύετε T (R
38 π.[2]—πιστεύετε LTTrWHR
38 believe[3] — understand, γινώσκω LTTrAWHR
12:47 believe — keep (them), φυλάσσω Eds
13:19†*trs* πιστευσητε (-εύητε TrWH) ὅταν γένηται TTrAWHR
17:20 πιστευοντων believe GEds
21 πιστεύῃ TTrWH
19:35 | 20:31[1] πιστεύητε TWH
Acts 2:44 πιστεύσαντες TWH
8:37 *omit the verse* GLTTrAWHR
9:42 *trs* ἐπισ. πολλοί LTTrAWWH
11:21 ὁ πιστεύσας LTTrAWHR
Ro. 10:14 π.[2]—πιστεύσωσιν Eds
2 Th. 1:10 π.[1]—πιστεύσασιν believed GEds
1 Pet. 1:21 do believe — are believers, πιστός LTTrAWHR
1 Joh. 3:23 πιστεύωμεν LTTr, -εύ[σ]ωμεν A
5:13 *om.* that believe on the name of the Son of God[1] GEds
13 and that ye may believe — οἱ πιστευοντες who believe GLW, τοῖς πιστεύουσιν unto you that believe TTrAWHR

4102 **πίστις.**

Mar. 9:42*πίστιν ἐχόντων *for* πιστευόντων (-τεύω) A
Acts 6: 8 of faith—of grace, χάριτος GEds
14: 9 *trs* ἔχει πίστιν LTTrAWH
Ro. 3:25 τῆς π.—*omit* τῆς LTTrAWH
5: 2 *omit* by faith [LTr]A[WH]
Eph. 2: 8 τῆς π.—*omit* τῆς LTTr[A]WHR
Tit. 2:10 *trs* πᾶσαν πίστιν LTTrAWHR
Rev. 2:19 *trs* charity, and faith, and service GLTAWHR: faith, and charity, and service Tr

4103 **πιστός.**

1 Ti. 5:16 *omit* πιστὸς ἤ (*omit* man or) LTTr[A]WHR
1 Pet. 1:21*πιστους *for* πιστεύοντας (πιστεύω) LTTrAWHR
Rev. 21: 5 *trs* faithful and true GEds

4105 **πλανάω.**

Mat. 24:24 πλανηθῆναι T, πλανᾶσθαι TrWH
1 Pet. 2:25 πλανώμενοι LTTrAWHR
Rev. 2:20 καὶ διδάσκει καὶ πλανᾷ and she teacheth and seduceth GEds

4118, 4119
πλείων, πλεῖον or πλέον

4118 **πλεῖστος.**

Mat. 20:10 πλεῖον LTrAWH
26:53 πλείω LTTrAWH
Mar. 4: 1*πλεῖστος *for* πολύς TTrAWWHR
12:33 more—much more, περισσότερος TTrWHR
Lu. 21: 3 πλείω LTA
Acts 27:12 πλείονες LTTrAWH
1 Co. 15: 6 πλείονες LTTrAWWH

4124 **πλεονεξία.**

Lu. 12:15 τῆς π.—πάσης π. all covetousness Eds
Ro. 1:29 *trs* maliciousness, covetousness T
2 Pet. 2:14 πλεονεξίας GEds

4126 **πλέω.**

Rev. 18:17*πᾶς ὁ ἐπὶ τόπον πλέων every one that saileth any whither GEds

4127 **πληγή.**

2 Co. 11:23 *trs* in prisons more frequent, in stripes above measure LTrAWH
Rev. 9:18*three—*add* πληγῶν plagues GEds

4128 **πλῆθος.**

Acts 17: 4 *trs* πλῆθος πολύ LTTrAWWH
21:22 *omit* TrWHR, *see* δεῖ

4129 **πληθύνω.**

Acts 9:31 ἐπληθύνετο was multiplied Eds
2 Co. 9:10 πληθυνεῖ shall multiply GLTAWWHR: πληθύνει Tr

4130 **πλήθω.**

Lu. 21:22*πλησθῆναι *for* πληρωθῆναι (-ρόω) Eds
Joh. 19:29 οἱ δὲ πλήσαντες σπόγγον ὄξ. καὶ —σπ. οὖν μεστὸν τοῦ (*om.* τοῦ T) ὄξ. LTTrAWHR

4132 **πλημμύρα.**

Lu. 6:48 πλημμύρης TTrAWH

4133 **πλήν.**

Lu. 17: 1*π. οὐαί *for* οὐαὶ δέ LTrWHR
Joh. 8:10 *omit* WHR, *see* γυνή

4134 **πλήρης.**

Mar. 4:28 πλήρης σῖτος LTTrA
6:43 πληρώματα TTrAWHR

4135 **πληροφορέω.**

Col. 4:12*πεπληροφορημένοι *for* πεπληρωμένοι (πληρόω) Eds

4137 **πληρόω.**

Mat. 27:35 *omit* that it might *to end of verse* GLTTrAWHR
Mar. 15:28 *omit the verse* T[Tr]AWHR
Lu. 21:22 πλήθω GEds
Gal. 5:14 πεπλήρωται Eds
Col. 4:12 complete—fully assured, πληροφορέω Eds
2 Joh. 12 *trs* πεπληρωμένη ᾖ LTWH
Rev. 6:11 πληρωθῶσιν LWWHR, πληρώσωσιν GTTrA

4138 **πλήρωμα.**

Mar. 6:43*πληρώματα *for* πλήρεις (-ρης) TTrAWHR
1 Co. 10:28 *omit* for the earth (is) the Lord's, and the fulness thereof GEds

4139 **ὁ πλησίον.**

Lu. 10:36 *trs* π. δοκεῖ σοι GTTrAWWH
Heb. 8:11 neighbour — fellow citizen, πολίτης GEds
Jas. 4:12*πλησίον *for* ἕτερον (-ρος) LTTrAWHR

4142 **πλοιάριον.**

Mar. 4:36 little ships — ships πλοῖον GLTTrAWHR
Lu. 5: 2*πλοιάρια *for* πλοῖα (-οῖον) TA
Joh. 6:22 boat[2]-ship, πλοῖον GLTTrAWHR
23 boats—ships, πλοῖον LWH
24*πλοιάρια *for* πλοῖα (-οῖον) LTTrAWHR

4143 **πλοῖον.**

Mat. 8:23 τὸ π.—*omit* τὸ LTrAWHR
9: 1 τὸ π.—*omit* τὸ LTTr[A]WHR
13: 2 τὸ π.—*omit* τὸ LTTrAWHR
14:22 τὸ π.—*omit* τὸ TrWH
Mar. 4: 1†*trs* εἰς τὸ (*om.* τὸ TTrWWHR) π. ἐμβάντα LTTrWWHR
36*πλοῖα *for* πλοιάρια (-ριον) GLTTrAWHR
37*ἤδη γεμίζεσθαι τὸ πλοῖον the ship was now filling LTTrAWHR
8:13 *omit* into the ship TAWHR: *omit* τὸ LTrW: [εἰς π.] Tr
Lu. 5: 2 ships—boats, πλοιάριον TA: *trs* πλοῖα δύο WH
3†*trs* ἐκ τοῦ π. ἐδίδασκεν AWH, ἐν τῷ πλοίῳ ἐδί. T
8:37 τὸ π.—*omit* τὸ LTTrAWHR
Joh. 6:17 τὸ π.—*omit* τὸ TTrAWHR
21 *trs* ἐγένετο τὸ πλοῖον LTTrAWH
22*πλοῖον *for* πλοιάριον[2] GLTTrAWHR
23*πλοῖα *for* πλοιάρια (-ριον) LWH
24 πλοιάριον LTTrAWHR
Acts 21: 3 *trs* τὸ πλοῖον ἦν LTTrAWWH
27:37 *trs* αἱ πᾶσαι ψυχαὶ ἐν τῷ π. LTTrAWWH
Rev. 18:17 *omit* π. GEds, *see* πλέω
19 τὰ πλοῖα Eds

4145 **πλούσιος.**

Mat. 19:23 *trs* πλούσιος δυσκόλως LTTrAWH
Rev. 6:15 *trs* chief captains and the rich men GEds

4149 **πλοῦτος.**

2 Co. 8: 2 τὸ πλοῦτος LTTrAWHR
Eph. 1: 7 τὸ πλοῦτος Eds
2: 7 τὸ ὑπερβάλλον πλοῦτος Eds
3: 8 τὸ ἀνεξ. πλοῦτος Eds
16 τὸ πλοῦτος Eds
Phil. 4:19 τὸ πλοῦτος Eds
Col. 1:27 τὸ πλοῦτος Eds
2: 2 πᾶν (τὸ L[Tr]WH) πλοῦτος Eds
Rev. 5:12 τὸν πλοῦτον W

4150 **πλύνω.**

Lu. 5: 2*ἔπλυνον LTTrAWHR, -ναν T *for* ἀπέπλυναν (ἀποπλύνω)
Rev. 22:14*add π. LTTrAWHR, *see* στολή

4151 **πνεῦμα.**

Mat. 3:16 τὸ π.—*omit* τὸ T[A]WH
Mar. 9:20†*trs* τὸ πνεῦμα εὐθὺς LTTrAWHR
25†*trs* ἄλαλον καὶ κωφ. π. LTTrAWH
12:36 τῷ π.—*omit* τῷ TW
Lu. 2:40 *omit* in spirit LTTrAWHR
4: 1 *trs* πλήρης π. ἁγίου LTTrAWH
9:55 *omit* and said *to end of verse* LTTrAWHR
Acts 1: 5 *trs* ἐν π. βαπτισθ. LTTrAWH
2:33†*trs* τοῦ π. τοῦ ἁγίου LTTrAWH
4:25*add π. LTTrAWHR, *see* πατήρ
10:19 *trs* τὸ πνεῦμα αὐτῷ LTTrA
45†*trs* τοῦ π τοῦ ἁγίου LWH
11:12 *trs* τὸ π. μοι LTTrAWH
13: 4†*trs* τοῦ ἁγίου π. LTTrAWH
15:28†*trs* τῷ π. τῷ ἁγίῳ TTrWWH
18: 5 pressed in the spirit—constrained by the word, λόγος GEds
Ro. 8: 1 *omit* who walk *to end of verse* GEds
11 *see* ἐνοικέω
1 Co. 6:20 *omit* and in your spirit, which are God's GEds
7:34 τῷ πνεύματι LTTrAWHR
14:16 τῷ π.—*omit* τῷ LTTrAWHR
Eph. 5: 9 spirit—light, φῶς GEds
Phil. 3: 3 *see* θεός
4:23*add π. Eds, *see* πᾶς
1 Ti. 4:12 *omit* in spirit GEds
1 Pet. 1:22 *omit* through the Spirit Eds
3:18 τῷ π.—*omit* τῷ GEds
1 Joh. 5: 7 *omit* in heaven *to* in earth (*verse* 8) GEds
Rev. 22: 6*πνευμάτων τῶν *for* ἁγίων (ἅγιος) GEds

4152 **πνευματικός.**

1 Co. 10: 3 *trs* π. βρῶμα ἔφαγον TTrWH
Eph. 5:19 [spiritual] LA

4155 **πνίγω.**

Mat. 13: 7*ἔπνιξαν *for* ἀπέπνιξαν (ἀποπνίγω) T

4156 **πνικτός.**

Acts 15:20 τοῦ π.—*omit* τοῦ LTrWH
29 πνικτῶν LTTrAWHR

4159 **πόθεν.**

Jas. 4: 1*π. μάχαι whence fightings Eds

4160 **ποιέω.**

Mat. 5:36 *trs* π. ἢ μέλαιναν LTTrAWH
44 *omit* LTTrAWHR, *see* μισέω
7:18 π.[1]—φέρω TWH: π.[2]—φέρω T
12:50 ποιῇ A
17: 4 ποιήσω I will make LTAWHR
19: 4 made[1]—created, κτίζω TrWH
21:13 ποιεῖτε make LTTrAWHR
23: 3†*trs* do (ποιήσατε) and observe LTTrAWHR
25:16 made (them)—gained, κερδαίνω LTrWH
Mar. 3: 4*ἀγαθὸν ποιῆσαι T
6 took—gave, δίδωμι TrAWH, ἐποίησαν T
8 ποιεῖ is doing TrAWH
12 ποιῶσιν TTrA
16*add π. TWH, *see* δώδεκα
5:19 πεποίηκεν GEds
6:20 did many things—was much perplexed, ἀπορέω TWHR
21 ἐποίησεν LTTrAWHR
7: 8 *omit* (as) the washing *to end of verse* T[TrA]WHR

Mar. 8:25 *omit* TTrAWHR, *see* διαβλέπω
10:36 ποιήσω LTTrWH
11:17 πεποιήκατε TTrAWHR
13:22*ποιήσουσιν *for* δώσουσιν (δίδωμι) TA
15: 1 held—prepared, ἑτοιμάζω T
14 *trs* ἐποίησεν κακόν TTrAWH
15 *trs* π. τὸ ἱκανὸν τῷ ὄχλῳ T
Lu. 3:10, 12 ποιήσωμεν Eds
14†*trs* τί ποιήσομεν (ποιήσωμεν TAWWHR) καὶ ἡμεῖς LTTrAWHR
6: 2 *omit* to do LTrAWH
11 ποιήσαιεν LTTrAWH
8:39 *trs* σοι ἐποίησεν LTTrAWH
9:43 ἐποίει GLTTrAWHR
54 *omit* even as Elias did TTr[A]WHR
14:13 *trs* δοχὴν ποιῇς WH
16 ἐποίει TTrAWHR
16: 9 *trs* ἑαυτοῖς ποιήσατε TAWH
18: 7 ποιήσῃ LTTrAWHR
23:34 *see* λέγω
Joh. 4:34 ποιήσω LTrAWHR
5:19 *trs* ποιεῖ ὁμοίως T
6:28 ποιοῦμεν S—ποιῶμεν A.V.B BGEds
38 ποιήσω T
7:31 π.²—ποιεῖ doeth T
8:39 ποιεῖτε WH
14:23 ποιησόμεθα LTTrAWHR
15:24 π.²—ἐποίησεν LTTrAWHR
18:30*κακὸν ποιῶν TTrAWH
21:25 *omit the verse* T
Acts 2:36 *trs* ἐποίησεν ὁ θεός TWH
37 | 4:16 ποιήσωμεν TTrAWHR
4: 7 *trs* τοῦτο ἐποιήσατε T
8: 2 ἐποίησαν Eds
9: 6 *omit* (it is) hard (*verse* 5) *to* unto him (*verse* 6) GEds
10: 6 *omit* he shall tell *to end of verse* GEds
15:17 ὁ π.—*omit* ὁ LTTrWH
18:21 *om.* I must *to* in Jerusalem LTTrAWHR
19:14 οἱ τοῦτο π.—*om.* οἱ LTTr[A]WHR
23:13 ποιησάμενοι Eds
26:28*ποιῆσαι *for* γενέσθαι (γίνομαι) LTTrAWHR, *see* πείθω
Ro. 2:14 ποιῶσιν LTTrAWHR
3:12 ὁ ποιῶν T
1 Co. 5: 2 πράσσω TWH
7:37, 38² ποιήσει shall do LTTrAWHR
Heb. 8: 5 ποιήσεις thou shalt make Eds
12:13 ποιεῖτε TTrWH
Jas. 4:13 ποιήσωμεν S, ποιήσομεν A.V.B ELTAWWHR
15 ποιήσωμεν S,–σομεν A.V.B EEds
1 Joh. 5: 2*ποιῶμεν *for* τηρῶμεν (τηρέω) Eds
Rev. 13: 7 *trs* π. πόλεμον TTrAWHR: *omit* L[WH], *see* δίδωμι
13 *omit* he maketh GW
21:27 (*add* ὁ TTr[WH]R) ποιῶν Eds
21: 2 ποιῶν T
11*add π. GEds, *see* δικαιοσύνη
14 *omit* π. LTTrAWHR, *see* στολή
15 *trs* maketh and loveth T

4167 ποίμνη.

Joh. 10:16 ovile A.V.Vul

4169 ποῖος.

Mar. 4:30 τίς LTTrAWHR, *see* τίθημι

4170 πολεμέω.

Rev. 12: 7 π.¹—τοῦ (*om.* τοῦ T[A]) πολεμῆσαι GEds

4171 πόλεμος.

Rev. 11: 7 *trs* μετ' αὐτῶν π. GEds
13: 5 to continue, ποιῆσαι S—to make war, πόλεμον ποιῆσαι E
7 *omit* L[WH], *see* δίδωμι
16:14 τὸν πόλεμον A.V.C GEds
19:19 | 20: 8 τὸν πόλεμον Eds

4172 πόλις.

Mar. 1:45 *trs* εἰς π. φανερῶς T
6:11 *omit* verily *to end of verse* G[L]TTrAWHR
Lu. 2:39 τὴν π.—*omit* τὴν LTTrAWH
7:37 *trs* ἥτις ἦν ἐν τῇ π. LTTrAWHR
9:10 πόλιν καλουμένην TTrAWHR
52*πόλιν *for* κώμην (–μη) T
Joh. 19:20 *trs* ὁ τόπος τῆς π. GEds
Acts 4:27*of a truth—*add* ἐν τῇ πόλει ταύτῃ in this city GEds
8: 5 τὴν πόλιν LTWHR
15:36 *trs* πόλιν πᾶσαν LTTrAWH
Acts 16:13 city—gate, πύλη Eds
27: 8 *trs* πόλις ἦν T
2 Co. 11:32 *trs* π. Δαμασκηνῶν LTTrAWH
Rev. 11: 8 τῆς πόλεως A.V.C Eds
14: 8 *omit* ἡ π. *read* Babylon the great is fallen GEds

4177 πολίτης.

Heb. 8:11*πολίτην *for* πλησίον GEds

4179 πολλαπλασίων.

Mat. 19:29*πολλαπλασίονα *for* ἑκατονταπλασίονα (–σίων) LTTrAWH

4183 πολύς.

Mat. 8:18 *omit* great LWH
9:14 *omit* oft LTWH
14:24*add π. TrWH, *see* στάδιον
20:16 *omit* for many be called, but few chosen T[TrA]WHR
25:19 *trs* πολὺν χρόνον LTTrAWH
Mar. 4: 1 great—very great, πλεῖστος TTrAWWHR
6: 2 οἱ πολλοί TWH, [οἱ] π. A
7: 8 *omit* (as) the washing *to end of verse* T[TrA]WHR
8: 1*see* πάμπολυς
9:26 π.²—τοὺς πολλούς LTTrAWHR
14:43 *omit* great [L]TTrAWHR
Lu. 6:17*ὄχλος πολύς a great company TWHR
23: 8 *omit* many things TTrAWHR
Joh. 5: 3 *omit* great [L]TTrAWHR
7:12 *trs* περὶ αὐτοῦ ἦν π. LTrAWHR, ἦν περὶ α. π. T
40 *omit* many, *read* (some) LTTrAWHR
10:42 *trs* π. ἐπίσ. εἰς αὐτὸν ἐκεῖ LTTrAWHR
21:25 *omit the verse* T
Acts 8: 7 π.¹—πολλοί LTTrAWHR
8*χαρὰ μεγάλη (–γας)—πολλὴ χ. LTTrAWHR
20:19 *omit* many GEds
24: 7 *omit* LTTr[A]WHR, *see* κρίνω
26:29 μέγας LTTrAWHR
28:29 *omit the verse* LTTrAWHR
Ro. 15:23 ἱκανός TrAWH
Heb. 12: 9, 25 πολύ LTTrAWHT
15 οἱ πολλοί Eds
1 Pet. 1: 7 *see* πολύτιμος
Rev. 5: 4 πολύ Eds
17: 1 τῶν π.—*omit* τῶν LTTr[A]WHR

4186 πολύτιμος.

Mat. 26: 7*πολυτίμου *for* βαρυτίμου (–μος) LT
1 Pet. 1: 7*πολυτιμότερον *for* πολὺ τιμιώτερον (–μιος) GLTTrAWHR

4190, 4191 πονηρός.

Lu. 11: 4 *omit* but deliver us from evil GTTrAWHR
Joh. 3:19 *trs* αὐτῶν πονηρά LTTrAWH
Acts 25:18*add at end* πονηράν, *read* evil accusation LT[A]W: πονηρῶν accusation of evil things TrWHR

4192 πόνος.

Col. 4:13*ζῆλον πολύν — πολὺν πόνον GLTTrAWHR, π. πολύν W

4194 Πόντιος.

Mat. 27: 2 *omit* Pontius TTrWHR

4198 πορεύομαι.

Mat. 21: 2 πορεύεσθε LTTrAWH
28: 9 *omit* and as they went to tell his disciples LTTrAWHR
Mar. 9:30*ἐπορεύοντο *for* παρεπορεύοντο (παραπορεύομαι) LTrWH
Lu. 7:11 ἐπορεύθη TWHR
9:12*πορευθέντες *for* ἀπελθόντες (ἀπέρχομαι) GLTTrAWHR
22:22 *trs* κατὰ τὸ ὡρισ. π. LTTrAWHR
24:13 *trs* ἐν αὐτῇ τῇ ἡμ. ἦσαν π. TWH
Joh. 7:53 ἐπορεύθησαν WHR (B
Acts 9:31 πορευομένη Eds
16: 7 πορευθῆναι LTTrAWHR
20: 1 πορεύεσθαι LTTrWHR
23:32 ἀπέρχομαι LTTrAWHR
27: 3 πορευθέντι LTTrAWH
Jas. 4:13 πορευσώμεθα S, –σόμεθα A.V.B EEds

4202 πορνεία.

Mar. 7:21, 22 *trs* fornications, thefts, murders, adulteries TTrAWHR
Ro. 1:29 *omit* fornication GEds
Rev. 17: 4 τῆς πορνείας GEds

4204 πόρνη.

Lu. 15:30 τῶν πορνῶν LTrAWHR

4206, 4208 πόρρω, πορρωτέρω, –ρον.

Lu. 14:32 *trs* πόρρω αὐτοῦ W
24:28 πορρώτερον LTrAWH

4209 πορφύρα.

Rev. 17: 4 πορφύρεος GEds

4210 πορφύρεος, –φυροῦς.

Rev. 17: 4*πορφυροῦν *for* πορφύρᾳ GEds

4215 ποταμός.

Mat. 3: 6*Ἰορδάνῃ ποταμῷ the river Jordan LTTrAWHR

4218 ποτέ.

Eph. 2:11 *trs* ποτὲ ὑμεῖς LTTrAWHR

4221 ποτήριον.

Mat. 26:27 τὸ π.—*omit* τὸ, *read* a cup TTrAWHR
42 *omit* cup LTTrAWHR
Mar. 7: 8 *omit* (as) the washing *to end of verse* T[TrA]WHR
14:23 τὸ π.—*omit* τὸ, *read* a cup LTTrAWHR
Lu. 22:20 *trs* καὶ τὸ π. ὡσαύτως TTrAWHR
42 *trs* τοῦτο τὸ ποτήριον TTrAWHR
Rev. 17: 4 *trs* ποτήριον χρυσοῦν Eds

4226 ποῦ.

Gal. 4:15*for τίς A.V.Vul Eds

4228 πούς.

Mat. 18:29 *omit* at his feet GLTTr[A]WHR
Lu. 7:38 *trs* ὀπίσω παρὰ τοὺς π. αὐτοῦ GLTTrAWHR
44†*trs* ὕδωρ μοι ἐπὶ π. TrAWH, ὕ. μοι ἐπὶ τοὺς π. T
46 *trs* τοὺς πόδας μου GLTrAWH
10:11*ὑμῶν—*add* εἰς τοὺς πόδας, *read* on us to the feet LTTrAWHR
24:40 *omit the verse* T[Tr] [[WH]]
Joh. 13: 8 *trs* μου τοὺς πόδας LTTrAWH
10 *omit* save . . . (his) feet T[WH]
Acts 21:11 *trs* feet and hands Eds

4230 πραγματεία, –τία TWH.

4231 πραγματεύομαι.

Lu. 19:13 πραγματεύσασθαι WH

4235 πρᾶος.

Mat. 11:29 πραΰς LTTrAWH

4236 πρᾳότης, by most editors πραΰτης.

1 Ti. 6:11 πραϋπάθεια Eds

4238 πράσσω, πράττω.

Lu. 19:23 *trs* αὐτὸ ἔπραξα LTTrAWH
1 Co. 5: 2*πράξας *for* ποιήσας (–ιέω) TWH

* πραϋπάθεια, –θία TWH, gentleness.

1 Ti. 6:11 πραϋπάθειαν *for* πρᾳότητα (–ότης) Eds

4239 πραΰς.

Mat. 11:29*πραΰς *for* πρᾶος LTTrAWH
1 Pet. 3: 4 πραέως TTrWH, πραέος LA

4245 πρεσβύτερος, –τέρα.

Mat. 26:59 *omit* and elders LTTrAWHR
27: 3 τοῖς π.—*omit* τοῖς LTrAWHR
12 τῶν π.—*omit* τῶν T[A]WHR
Mar. 14:43 τῶν π.—*omit* τῶν T
Acts 4: 5 τοὺς πρεσβυτέρους LTTrAWHR
14:23 *trs* κατ' ἐκκλ. π. LTrAWWH
16: 4 τῶν π.—*omit* τῶν Eds
24: 1 τῶν π.—π. τινῶν certain elders LTTrAWHR

4249 πρίζω, πρίω.

Heb. 11:37 *trs* were tempted, were sawn asunder TWH

4250 πρίν, πρὶν ἤ.

Lu. 22:34 before that—until, ἕως LTTrAWHR

4251 **Πρίσκα.**

Ro. 16: 3*Πρίσκαν *for* Πρίσκιλλαν GEds
1 Co. 16:19*Πρίσκα *for* Πρίσκιλλα TTrWHR

4252 **Πρίσκιλλα.**

Acts 18:26 *trs* Priscilla and Aquila LTTrAWHR
Ro. 16: 3 Priscilla—Prisca, Πρίσκαν GEds
1 Co. 16:19 Priscilla—Prisca, Πρίσκα TTrWHR

4253 **πρό.**

Mat. 24:38 *omit* ταῖς π. *read* days of the flood A
Lu. 1:76 π. προσώπου—ἐνώπιον WH
Joh. 10: 8 *omit* before me T
Acts 5:23 ἐπί LTTrAWHR
Jude 25*add π. Eds, *see* αἰών

4254 **προάγω.**

Acts 12: 6†*trs* π. αὐτὸν Tr, προαγαγεῖν α. LTA, προσαγαγεῖν (–άγω) α. WH
17: 5*προαγαγεῖν *for* ἀγαγειν (ἄγω) LTTrAWHR
2 Joh. 9*προάγων *for* παραβαίνων (–νω) Eds

4255 **προαιρέομαι.**

2 Co. 9: 7 προήρηται hath purposed Eds

4261 **προβάλλω.**

Acts 19:33 προβαλόντων S, –λλόντων EGL

* **προβάτιον**, a little sheep.

Joh. 21:16 προβάτια *f.* πρόβατα (–τον) TWH
17 προβάτια *for* πρόβατα (–τον) TTrAWHR

4263 **πρόβατον.**

Joh. 10: 4 sheep[1]—all, πᾶς, *read* all his own LTTrAWHR
12 *omit* the sheep[3] [L]TTr[A]WHR
21:16 sheep—little sheep, προβάτιον TWH
17 sheep—little sheep, προβάτιον TTrAWHR

4264 **προβιβάζω.**

Acts 19:33 drew—instructed, συμβιβάζω LTTrWHR

4270 **προγράφω.**

Ro. 15: 4 π.[2]—γράφω Eds

4279 **προεπαγγέλλομαι.**

2 Co. 9: 5*προεπηγγελμένην *for* προκατηγγελμένην (–καταγγέλλω) Eds

4280 **προερέω.** (4277)

Heb. 4: 7*προείρηται *for* εἴρηται (ἐρῶ) Eds
10:15 had said before—had said, ἐρῶ Eds

4280 **προέρχομαι.**

Mat. 26:39 προσέρχομαι TTr
Mar. 14:35 προσέρχομαι Tr
Acts 20: 5, 13 προσέρχομαι TrWH

προϊμος, *see* **πρώϊμος.** See 4406

4293 **προκαταγγέλλω.**

Acts 3:24 have foretold—announced, καταγγέλλω GEds
2 Co. 9: 5 whereof ye had notice before—before promised προεπαγγέλλομαι Eds

4296 **προκηρύσσω, –ττω.**

Acts 3:20 before was preached—was foreordained προχειρίζομαι GEds

4301 **προλαμβανω.**

Gal. 6: 1 προλημφθῇ LTTrAWH

4306 **προνοέω.**

2 Co. 8:21 προνοοῦμεν γάρ, for we provide LTTrAWHR
1 Ti. 5: 8 προνοεῖται TTr

4308 **προοράω.**

Acts 2:25 προορώμην LTTrAWH

* **προπάτωρ**, forefather.

Ro. 4: 1 προπάτορα *for* πατέρα (–τήρ) LTTrAWHR

4314 **πρός.**

Mat. 3:15 π. αὐτόν—αὐτῷ LWH
10:13 ἐπί WH
21: 1 εἰς LTTrAWHR
26:55 *omit* with you T[Tr]AWHR
Mar. 1:27 *omit* π. TWH
3: 7 εἰς GLT
6:33 *omit* and came together unto him GEds
7:31 εἰς GLTTrAWHR
9:14*αὐτοῖς—π. αὐτούς TTrWHR
33 *omit* among yourselves LTTrAWHR
10: 7 *om.* and cleave to his wife TWH
15:42*see προσάββατον
Lu. 3:14 π. αὐτούς—αὐτοῖς LTrAWH
7: 6 *omit* to him TWH
9:62 *omit* unto him A[WH]
10:22 *see* μαθητής
39*for παρά TTrAWHR
11:53 *omit* TTrAWHR, *see* ἐξέρχομαι
14:28 εἰς GEds
17: 4*for ἐπί Eds
18: 7 π. αὐτόν—αὐτῷ TTrAWHR
11 *omit* with himself T
20:25*αὐτοῖς—π. αὐτούς TTrAWH
45*see μαθητής
22:52*for ἐπί[1] T
24:12 *omit the verse* [L]T[Tr][[WH]]
44*αὐτοῖς—π. αὐτούς TTrAWHR
50*for εἰς LTTrAWHR
Joh. 1:19*sent—*add* πρὸς αὐτόν unto him LTrAWHR
7:37 *omit* unto me T
50 *omit* π.[2] T, *see* ἔρχομαι
8: 3 *omit* unto him WHR
33*π. αὐτόν *for* αὐτῷ LTTrAWHR
11:32*trs αὐτοῦ εἰς (πρός *for* εἰς TTrAWH) τοὺς πόδας GTTrAWWH
16:16 *omit* because I go to the Father TTrAWHR
19: 3*add π. LTTrAWHR. *see* ἔρχομαι
21:23 *omit* what (is that) to thee T
Acts 2: 7 *omit* one to another LTTrAWHR
3:19*for εἰς TWH
22 *omit* unto the fathers LTTrA (WHR
4:37*for παρά T
5: 8*π. αὐτήν *for* αὐτῇ LTTrAWHR
10*for παρά LTTrAWHR
7:31 *omit* unto him LTTrAWHR
9: 5, 6 *omit* GEds, *see* κέντρον
10:21 *omit* GEds, *see* ἀποστέλλω
16:40*for εἰς GEds
19: 3 *omit* unto them Eds
23:15 εἰς Eds
30 *omit* against him LT
24: 8*for ἐπί A, *see* κρίνω
15*for εἰς T
26: 6 εἰς Eds
Ro. 15:24 *omit* I will come to you GEds
2 Co. 9: 5*for εἰς LTrW
Eph. 5:31 *omit* π. LTTr, *see* γυνή
Philem. 5 εἰς LTrAWH
Jas. 3: 3 εἰς LTTrAWHR
Rev. 12: 5*God and—*add* π. to GEds
21: 9 *omit* unto me GEds
22:18 ἐπί GEds

4315 **προσάββατον, πρὸς σάββ.** LTr.

4317 **προσάγω.**

Mat. 18:24*προσήχθη *for* προσηνέχθη (–σφέρω) LTrAWH
Acts 12: 6*προσαγαγεῖν *for* προάγειν (–άγω) WH

4318 **προσαγωγή.**

Eph. 3:12 τὴν π.—*omit* τὴν LTTr[A]WHR

4319 **προσαιτέω.**

Mar. 10:46 *omit* begging TTrAWHR, *see* προσαίτης
Lu. 18:35 ἐπαιτέω LTTrAWH

* **προσαίτης**, a beggar.

Mar. 10:46 τυφλός—*add* προσαίτης, *read* a blind beggar TTrAWHR
Joh. 9: 8 προσαίτης *for* τυφλός GEds

4321 **προσαναλισκω.**

Lu. 8:43 *omit* π. WH, *see* ἰατρός

4327 **προσδέχομαι.**

Ro. 16: 2 *trs* προσδ. αὐτήν LTrAWH

4331 **προσεγγίζω.**

Mar. 2: 4 come nigh—bring nigh, προσφέρω TWH

4332 **προσεδρεύω.**

1 Co. 9:13 παρεδρεύω Eds

4333 **προσεργάζομαι.**

Lu. 19:16†*trs* δέκα προσηργάσατο LTAWH, δ. προσειρ– Tr

4334 **προσέρχομαι.**

Mat. 5: 1 προσῆλθαν TTrWH
8: 2*προσελθών *for* ἐλθών (ἔρχομαι) Eds
9:18*προσελθών *for* ἐλθών (ἔρχομαι) LWH
28 | 13:36 | 14:15 προσῆλθαν LTr
17: 7 προσῆλθεν LTTrWH (WH
19: 3 | 21:23 προσῆλθαν WH
26:39*προσελθών *for* προελθών (–έρχομαι) TTr
60 *trs* π. ψευδομαρτύρων LTTrAWHR
Mar. 14:35*προσελθών *for* προελθών (–έρχομαι) Tr
Lu. 13:31 προσῆλθαν TTrAWH
Joh. 12:21 προσῆλθαν WH
Acts 20: 5*προσελθόντες *for* προελθόντες (–έρχομαι) TrWH
13*προσελθόντες *for* προελθόντες (–έρχομαι) Tr
24:23 *omit* or come Eds
1 Ti. 6: 3 consent—cleaves, προσέχω T

4335 **προσευχή.**

Mat. 17:21 *omit the verse* T[TrA]WHR
Acts 16:13 προσευχήν LTTrWHR, *see* νομίζω
16 τὴν προσευχήν, *read* the place of prayer Eds
1 Pet. 4: 7 τὰς π.—*omit* τὰς Eds

4336 **προσεύχομαι.**

Mat. 6: 5 προσεύχησθε, οὐκ ἔσεσθε ὡς *read* when ye pray, ye shall not be as LTTrAWHR
23:14(13) *omit the verse* LTTrAWHR, *see* κρίμα
26:36 *trs* ἐκεῖ προσεύξωμαι LTTrAWHR
Mar. 11:24 προσεύχεσθε καί, *read* whatsoever ye pray and ask for LTTrAWHR
13:33 *omit* and pray LT[Tr]AWH
Lu. 22:43, 44 *the verses* [L][[WH]]
Acts 21: 5 προσευξάμενοι Eds, *see* ἀσπάζομαι
Jas. 5:16*προσεύχεσθε *for* εὔχεσθε (–χομαι) LWH

4337 **προσέχω.**

Mat. 16:11 ὑμῖν; προσέχετε δέ (*question ends at* bread) *read* but beware LTTrAWHR
1 Ti. 6: 3*προσέχεται *for* προσέρχεται (–χομαι) T
Heb. 2: 1 *trs* προσέχειν ἡμᾶς Eds

4341 **προσκαλέομαι.**

Lu. 18:16 προσεκαλέσατο TTrAWHR
Acts 20: 1 called unto (him)—sent for μεταπέμπω TTrWHR

* **προσκλίνω**, to incline to.

Acts 5:36 προσεκλίθη *for* προσεκολλήθη (–σκολλάω) Eds

4347 **προσκολλάω.**

Mat. 19: 5 κολλάω LTTrAWWH
Mar. 10: 7 *om.* and cleave to his wife TWH
Acts 5:36 προσκλίνω Eds

4352 **προσκυνέω.**

Lu. 24:52 *omit* worshipped him, and T[[WH]]
Joh. 4:20 *trs* προσκυνεῖν δεῖ LTTrAWWH
24 *trs* προσκυνεῖν δεῖ T
12:20 προσκυνήσουσιν LTrA
Rev. 3: 9 προσκυνήσουσιν LTTrAWHR
4:10 προσκυνοῦσιν S—προσκυνήσουσιν shall worship EGEds
9:20 προσκυνήσουσιν Eds
13:12 προσκυνήσουσιν LTTrAWHR
15 προσκυνήσουσιν T

4353 **προσλαμβάνω.**

Acts 27:34 μεταλαμβάνω GEds
Philem. 12 *omit* thou therefore receive LTTrAWHR

4356 πρόσληψις, –λημψις LTTrAWH.

4357 προσμένω.

Acts 13:43*προσμένειν *for* ἐπιμένειν (–νω) GEds

4363 προσπίπτω.

Mat. 7:25 προσέπεσαν TTrAWH, –παισαν L
Mar. 3:11 προσέπιπτον LTTrAWWH

4364 προσποιέω.

Lu. 24:28 προσεποιήσατο LTTrAWH
Joh. 8: 6 *add at end* μὴ προσποιούμενος A.V.†C

4366 προσρήγνυμι.

Lu. 6:48, 49 προσέρηξεν TTrWH

4367 προστάσσω

Mat.21: 6 συντάσσω LTrAWHR
Acts 17:26*προστεταγμένους (πρὸς τ. L) *for* προτεταγμένους (–τάσσω) GEds

4374 προσφέρω.

Mat. 8: 4 προσένεγκον LTTrAWWH
12:22 προσήνεγκαν LWH
18:24 προσαγω LTrAWH
19:13 προσηνέχθησαν LTTrAWH
Mar. 2: 4*προσενέγκαι *for* προσεγγίσαι (–γίζω) TWH
10:13 those that brought (them)—them, αὐτοῖς WHR
Lu. 12:11 εἰσφέρω TTrAWHR
Heb. 7:27*προσενέγκας *for* ἀνενέγκας (ἀναφέρω) T

4376 προσφορά.

Heb.10: 5 *trs* offering and sacrifice W
8 προσφοράς offerings Eds

4377 προσφωνέω.

Mat.11:16 προσφωνοῦντα LTTrAWHR

4380 προσωποληπτέω, –λημπ– LTTrAWH.

4381 προσωπολήπτης, –λήμπ– LTTrAWH.

4382 προσωποληψία, –λημψ– LTTrAWH.

4383 πρόσωπον.

Mat.16: 3 when it is (*verse* 2) *to end of verse* 3 [TA][[WH]]
Mar.14:65 *trs* αὐτοῦ τὸ π. TTrAWH
Lu. 1:76 πρὸ π.—ἐνώπιον WH
22:64 *omit* struck him on the face, and [L]TTrAWHR
24: 5 τὰ πρόσωπα TTrWHR
Acts 17:26 παντὸς προσώπου LTTrAWHR
2 Co. 11:20 *trs* εἰς πρόσωπον ὑμᾶς Eds
Rev. 7:11 τὰ πρόσωπα GEds
20:11 τοῦ προσώπου Eds

4384 προτάσσω.

Acts 17:26 before appointed—appointed προστάσσω GEds

4385 προτείνω.

Acts 22:25 προέτειναν A.V.B GEds

4386 πρότερον, τὸ πρότερον.

Joh. 7:50*αὐτόν—*add* π. *read* came to him before LTrAWHR
51 πρῶτον LTTrAWHR

4392 πρόφασις.

Mat. 23:14(13) *omit the verse* LTTrAWHR *see* κρίμα

4394 προφητεία.

2 Pet. 1:21 *trs* προφ. ποτέ TrAWHR
Rev. 11: 6 *trs* τῆς π. αὐτῶν GLTTrAWHR

4395 προφητεύω.

Mat. 7:22 ἐπροφητεύσαμεν LTTrAWH
11:13 ἐπροφήτευσαν LTTrAWH
15: 7 ἐπροφήτευσεν LTTrAWH
Mar. 7: 6 ἐπροφήτευσεν LTTrAWH
Lu. 1:67 ἐπροφήτευσεν LTTrAWH
Joh. 11:51 ἐπροφήτευσεν LTTrAWWH
Acts 19: 6 ἐπροφήτευον LTTrAWH
Jude 14 ἐπροφήτευσεν TTrWH

4396 προφήτης.

Mat. 16: 4 *omit* the prophet LTTrAWHR
Mat. 21:11 *trs* ὁ π. 'Ιησοῦς LTTrAWHR
26 *trs* ὡς π. ἔχ. τὸν 'Ιω. LTTrAWH
27:35 *omit* that it might *to end of verse* GLTTrAWHR
Mar. 1: 2 the prophets—τῷ (*omit* τῷ G[Tr]W) 'Ησαΐᾳ τῷ προφήτῃ Isaiah the prophet GEds
13:14 *omit* spoken of by Daniel the prophet G[L]TTrAWHR
Lu. 7:28 *omit* prophet L[TrA]WHR
11:29 *omit* the prophet GLTTrAWHR
24:44 [τοῖς] π. Tr. τοῖς π. WH
Joh. 7:52 *trs* ἐκ τῆς Γαλι. π. LTrAWHR
Acts 3:21 *trs* ἀπ' αἰῶνος αὐ. π. LTTrAWHR
13:20 τοῦ π.—*omit* τοῦ TTr[A]WHR
Rev. 10: 7 τοὺς προφήτας GEds
22: 6 τῶν π. GEds, *see* ἅγιος

4400 προχειρίζομαι.

Acts 3:20*προκεχειρισμένον *for* προκεκηρυγμένον (προκηρύσσω) GEds

4404 πρωΐ, –ί WH.

Mat.16: 3 When it is (*verse* 2) *to end of verse* 3 [TA][[WH]]
21:18*for* πρωΐας TTrWH
Mar. 15: 1 τὸ π.—*omit* τὸ LTTr[A]WHR
Joh. 18:28*for* πρωΐα GLTTrAWWH

4405 πρωΐα.

Mat. 21:18 πρωΐ TTrWH
Joh. 18:28 πρωΐ GLTTrAWWH

4406 πρώϊμος, πρόϊμος TTrWH.

4407 πρωϊνός.

Rev. 22:16*ὁ πρωϊνός *for* ὀρθρινός GEds

4408 πρώρα.

Acts 27:30 πρῴρης LTWH
41 πρῷρα LTWH, πρῶρα Tr

4412 πρῶτον, τὸ πρῶτον.

Mat. 17:11 *omit* first LTTrAWHR
Mar. 13:10 *trs* πρῶτον δεῖ LTTrAWH
Joh. 1:41(42)*for* πρῶτος LTrAWHR
7:51*trs* π. (*for* πρότερον) παρ' αὐτοῦ LTTrAWHR
Acts 11:26 πρώτως TTrAWH
Ro. 1:16 [first] LWH
Eph. 4: 9 *omit* first GEds

4413 πρῶτος.

Mat. 21:31 first—latter, ὕστερος LTrWH (Tr refers 'the latter' to him who 'afterwards' repented: *for* WH *see* ἀπέρχομαι, *verses* 29, 30)
22:38 *trs* great and first Eds
Mar. 12:30 *omit* this (is) the first commandment TAWHR
Joh. 1:41(42) πρῶτον LTrAWHR
5: 4 *omit* waiting for (*verse* 3) *to end of verse* 4 [G]TTrAWHR
Acts 13:33*trs* τῷ πρώτῳ (π. *for* δευτέρῳ, –ρος) ψα. γέγ. GTTr: τῷ ψ. γ. τῷ δ. (πρ. L) LAWWH
Phil. 1: 5 τῆς πρώτης LTTrAWHR
Rev. 1:11 *omit* GEds, *see* ἄλφα
22:13 ὁ π.—*omit* ὁ L[A], *see* ἀρχή

4416 πρωτότοκος.

Mat. 1:25 *omit* her firstborn LTTrAWHR

* πρώτως, *adv.* first.

Acts 11:26 *for* πρῶτον TTrAWH

4417 πταίω.

Jas. 2:10 πταίσῃ Eds

4421 πτηνόν.

1 Co. 15:39 *trs* birds, (and) another of fishes Eds

4430 πτῶμα.

Mat. 14:12*πτῶμα *for* σῶμα LTTrWHR
Mar. 15:45*πτῶμα *for* σῶμα LTTrAWHR
Rev. 11: 8, 9[1] τὸ πτῶμα body GEds

4434 πτωχός.

Mat. 19:21 τοῖς πτωχοῖς LTrAR, [τοῖς] π. WH
26: 9 τοῖς πτωχοῖς LW
Mar. 10:21 τοῖς π.—*omit* τοῖς LTrAW[WH]R
Lu. 19: 8 *trs* τοῖς π. δίδωμι TTrAWH
21: 3 *trs* αὕτη ἡ πτωχὴ LTrWH

4435 πυγμῇ.

Mar. 7: 3 πυκνός T

4436 Πύθων.

Acts 16:16 πύθωνα LTTrAWHR

4437 πυκνός.

Mar. 7: 3*πυκνά *for* πυγμῇ T

4439 πύλη.

Mat. 7:13 *omit* (is) the gate L[T]WH
14 [the gate] LT
Lu. 13:24 gate—door, θύρα GLTTrAWHR
Acts 16:13*πύλης *for* πόλεως (–λις) Eds

4440 πυλών.

Rev. 21:12 τοὺς πυλῶνας Tr

4441 πυνθάνομαι.

Joh. 13:24 *see* λέγω
Acts 10:18 ἐπύθοντο WH

4442 πῦρ.

Mar. 9:22 *trs* καὶ εἰς π. αὐτὸν TAWHR
44 *omit the verse* T[Tr]WHR
45 *omit* into the fire that never shall be quenched [L]TTr[A]
46 *omit the verse* T[Tr]WHR (WHR
47 *omit* fire LTTrAWHR
Joh. 15: 6 τὸ πῦρ TTrAWWHR
2 Th. 1: 8†*trs* φλογὶ πυρός a flame of fire LTrW
Jude 23 τοῦ π.—*omit* τοῦ Eds, *see* φόβος
Rev. 13:13 *trs* καὶ πῦρ ἵνα GW
20:14*add* π. Eds, *see* λίμνη

4448 πυρόω.

Eph. 6:16 τὰ π.—*omit* τὰ L[TrAWH]
Rev. 1:15 πεπυρωμένης (–ένῳ T) it burned LTTrWHR

4449 πυρράζω.

Mat. 16: 2, 3 when it is evening (*ver.* 2) *to end of verse* 3 [TA][[WH]]

* Πύρρος.

Acts 20: 4 Sopater—*add* Πύρρου of Pyrrhus GEds

4453 πωλέω.

Mat. 13:44 *trs* π. πάντα ὅσα ἔχει LTTrA, π. ὅσα ἔχει WH
Lu. 12: 6 πωλοῦνται TTrAWH

4454 πῶλος.

Mar. 11: 4 τὸν π.—*omit* τὸν GLTrAWWHR

4456 πωρόω.

Joh. 12:40 ἐπώρωσεν TTrAWHR

4458 πῶς.

Mar. 2:26 [how] TrAWH
4:30*for* τίνι (τίς) TTrAWHR
40 *omit* LTrWHR, *see* οὐ
8:21 *omit* how is it that TAWHR
12:26*for* ὡς TTrAWHR
Gal. 2:14*for* τί (τίς) GEds
1 Joh. 4:20 οὐ, *read* he cannot love God, LTTrAWHR

4461 ῥαββί, ῥαββεί TWH, in Mark A.

Mat. 23: 7 *omit* Rabbi[2] LTTr[A]WHR
Mar. 14:45 *omit* master[2] LTTr[A]WHR

4462 ῥαββονί –ουνί, –ουνεί WH.

4463 ῥαβδίζω.

2 Co. 11:25 ἐραβδίσθην LTTrAWH

4464 ῥάβδος.

Mat. 10:10 ῥάβδους A.V.C W
Lu. 9: 3 ῥάβδον a staff GLTTrAWHR
Heb. 1: 8 ῥ.[1]—ἡ ῥάβδος TTrAWHR
8 ἡ. ῥ.—*omit* ἡ LTTrWHR

4469 ῥακά, ῥαχά T.

4471 'Ραμᾶ, –ά WH.

4472 ῥαντίζω.

Mar. 7: 4*ῥαντίσωνται *for* βαπτίσωνται (–τίζω) WH
Heb. 9:19, 21 ἐράντισεν LTTrAWH

Heb.10:22 ῥεραντισμένοι LTTrAWH
Rev.19:13*ῥεραντισμένον *for* βεβαμμένον (βάπτω) WHR

4474 ῥαπίζω.

Mat. 5:39 ῥαπίζει smiteth LTTrAWHR
26:67 ἐράπισαν LTTrAWH

4476 ῥαφίς.

Mar.10:25 τῆς ῥ.—*omit* τῆς LTrWWHR
Lu. 18:25 βελόνη LTTrAWHR

4481 Ῥεμφάν.

Acts 7:43 Ῥομφάν T, Ῥεφάν LTrAWR, Ῥομφά WH

4483 ῥέω. (2036)

Mat. 5:21, 27, 31, 33, 38, 43 ἐρρήθη LTrAW
27:35 *omit* that it might *to end of verse* GLTTrAWHR
Mar.13:14 *omit* spoken of by Daniel the prophet G[L]TTrAWHR
Ro. 9:12, 26 ἐρρέθη LTTrAWH
Gal. 3:16 ἐρρέθησαν LTTrAWH

4486 ῥήγνυμι, ῥήσσω.

Mar. 2:22 ῥήξει will burst LTTrAWHR

4487 ῥῆμα.

Mat. 5:11 *omit* ῥ. LTTrAWHR
Mar.14:72 τὸ ῥῆμα Eds
Lu. 4: 4 *omit* but by every word of God T[Tr]AWHR
20:26 αὐτοῦ ῥ.—τοῦ ῥ. AWHR
22:61*ῥήματος *for* λόγου (-γος) WHR
Ro. 10: 9*confess—*add* τὸ ῥῆμα the word WH
Rev.17:17 λόγος GEds

4495, 4496 ῥίπτω.

Mat. 9:36 ἐριμμένοι TTrAWH, ῥεριμ- L
15:30 ἔριψαν TWH
Acts27:19 ἔρριψαν (ἔρι- TWH) they cast out GEds

ῥμδ'.

Rev. 7: 4 ἑκατὸν τεσσεράκοντα (τεσσαρ- GW) τέσσαρες GLTTrAWWH

4506 ῥύομαι.

Lu. 11: 4 *omit* but deliver us from evil GTTrAWHR
2Co. 1:10 ῥ.¹—ἐρύσατο TrWH
10 ῥ.²—ῥύσεται will deliver [L]TTrAWHR
Col. 1:13 ἐρύσατο TTrWH
2Ti. 3:11 ἐρύσατο LTTrWH
4:17 ἐρύσθην LTTrAWH
2Pet. 2: 7 ἐρύσατο TrAWH

* ῥυπαίνω, to make filthy.

Rev.22:11 ῥυπανθήτω *for* ῥυπωσάτω (-πόω) LTTrAWHR

* ῥυπαρεύομαι, to be filthy.

Rev.22:11 ῥυπαρευθήτω *for* ῥυπωσάτω (-πόω) GW

4508 ῥυπαρός.

Rev.22:11*ῥυπαρός *for* ῥυπῶν (-πόω) GEds

4510 ῥυπόω.

Rev.22:11 ῥ.¹—ῥυπαρός GEds
11 ῥ.²—ῥυπαίνω LTTrAWHR, ῥυπαρεύομαι GW

4513 Ῥωμαϊκός.

Lu. 23:38 *omit* in letters of Greek, and Latin, and Hebrew [L]TTr[A]WHR

4515 Ῥωμαϊστί.

Joh. 19:20 *trs* Latin (and) Greek TTrAWHR

4516 Ῥώμη.

Acts 28:16 τὴν Ῥώμην T

4517 ῥώννυμι.

Acts 23:30 *omit* farewell LTTrAWHR

4518 σαβαχθανί, -νεί TTrWH.

4521 σάββατον, σάββατα.

Mar.16: 2 τῶν σαββάτων LTTrWHR
Lu. 6: 5 *trs* τοῦ σ. *after* ἐστιν WH
9 τῷ σαββάτῳ sabbath day LTTrAWHR
Joh. 20:19 τῶν σ.—*omit* τῶν Eds
1Co.16: 2 σαββάτου Eds

4523 Σαδδουκαῖος.

Mat.16:12*add Σ. T, *see* ἄρτος
Acts 23: 7 τῶν Σ.—*omit* τῶν Eds

4525 σαίνω, ἀσαίνω L.

1Th. 3: 3 τῷ μηδ. σ.—τὸ μηδ. σ. Eds

4527 Σαλά.

Lu. 3:32**for* Σαλμών TWH

4531 σαλεύω.

Heb.12:27 *trs* τὴν ([τὴν] WH) τῶν σ. LTTrAWHR

4533 Σαλμών.

Lu. 3:32 Salmon—Sala, Σαλά TWH

4540 Σαμάρεια, -ρία TWH.

4541 Σαμαρείτης, -ρίτης T.

Joh. 4: 9 *omit* for the Jews have no dealings with the Samaritans T[WH]

4442 Σαμαρεῖτις, -ρῖτις T.

4551 Σαπφείρη.

Acts 5: 1 Σαπφείρᾳ LTr

4555 σάρδινος.

Rev. 4: 3 σάρδιος GEds

4556 σάρδιος, -ον.

Rev. 4: 3*σαρδίῳ *for* σαρδίνῳ (-νος) GEds
21:20 σάρδιον Eds

4558 Σάρεπτα, Σάρεφθα W.

4559 σαρκικός.

Ro. 7:14 σάρκινος GEds
1Co. 3: 1 σάρκινος GEds
4 carnal—men, ἄνθρωποι Eds
Heb. 7:16 σάρκινος Eds

4560 σάρκινος.

Ro. 7:14*σάρκινος *for* σαρκικός GEds
1Co. 3: 1*σαρκίνοις *for* σαρκικοῖς (-κός) GEds
Heb. 7:16*σαρκίνης *f.* σαρκικῆς (-κός) Eds

4562 Σαρούχ, Σερούχ GLTTrAWWH.

4561 σάρξ.

Lu. 24:39 σάρκας T
Joh. 6:51 *trs* ὑπὲρ τῆς τοῦ κόσμου ζωῆς, ἡ σ. μου ἐστίν T
Acts 2:30 *omit* according to the flesh, he would raise up Christ GLTTrAWHR
Ro. 8: 1 *omit* who walk *to end of verse* GEds
1Co.15:39 *omit* (kind of) flesh GEds
39*another²—*add* σάρξ flesh [L]TTrAWHR, *see* ἰχθύς
2Co.11:18 τὴν σ.—*omit* τὴν TTr[WH]
Eph. 5:30 *omit* of his flesh, and of his bones LTTr[A]WHR
Heb. 2:14 *trs* of blood and flesh Eds
1Joh.4: 3 *omit* that Christ is come in the flesh GLTTrAWHR

4565 Σαρών.

Acts 9:35 Σαρωνᾶν S, -ῶνα EGLTTrAWWH

4566 Σατᾶν.

2Co.12: 7 Σατανᾶς LTTrAWH

4567 Σατανᾶς.

Lu. 4: 8 *omit* get thee behind me, Satan G[L]TTrAWHR
22: 3 ὁ Σ.—*omit* ὁ GLTTrAWWH
2Co.12: 7*Σατανᾶ *for* Σατᾶν LTTrAWH
Rev.20: 2 ὁ Σατανᾶς Eds

4569 Σαῦλος.

Acts 9: 8 ὁ Σ.—*omit* ὁ LTTrAWWH
19, 26 *omit* ὁ Σ. *read* he GEds
13: 2 τὸν Σ.—*omit* τὸν LTTrAWWH

σαυτοῦ, *see* σεαυτοῦ. See 4572

4570 σβέννυμι.

Mar. 9:44, 46 *omit the verses* T[Tr]WHR
1Th. 5:19 ζβέννυτε T

4571 σέ.

Mat. 5:25 *omit* deliver thee² LT[Tr]WH
18:15 *omit* against thee LT[A]WH
25:27 *trs* σε οὖν TTrAWH
Mar.10:35*desire—*add* σέ of thee Eds
Lu. 17: 3 *omit* against thee LTTrAWHR
Joh. 21:23 *omit* what (is that) to thee? T
Acts 10: 6 *omit* GEds, *see* ποιέω
24: 8 *omit* LTTr[A]WHR, *see* κρίνω
26: 3 *trs* σε ὄντα T
Ro. 8: 2**for* μέ TWH
1Co. 8:10 [thee] LWH
1Ti. 3:15 δεῖ—*add* σε A.V.Vul
Rev. 3: 3 *omit* on thee¹ LTTrAWHR
15: 4 *omit* thee¹ LTTrAWHR

4572 σεαυτοῦ, σαυτοῦ, -τῷ, -τόν.

Mat.18:16*σεαυτοῦ *for* σοῦ T
Joh. 18:34*σεαυτοῦ *for* ἑαυτοῦ LTTrAWH
Ro. 13: 9*σεαυτόν *for* ἑαυτόν LTTrAWH
14:22 σαυτόν—σεαυτόν GLTTrAWWH
Gal. 5:14*σεαυτόν *for* ἑαυτόν GEds

4577 σειρά.

2Pet. 2: 4 chains—dens, σειρός TrAWHR, σιρός LT

* σειρός, pit, cavern.

2Pet. 2: 4 σειροῖς *for* σειραῖς (-ρά) TrAWHR

4579 σείω.

Heb.12:26 σείσω will shake LTTrAWHR

4581 Σελεύκεια, -κια TWH.

Acts 13: 4 τὴν Σ.—*omit* τὴν LTTrAWH

4584 Σεμεΐ, Σεμεείν TTrAWHR.

4591 σημαίνω.

Acts 11:28 ἐσήμαινεν LWH

4592 σημεῖον.

Mat.16: 3 When it is (*verse* 2) *to end of verse* 3 [TA][[WH]]
Lu. 2:12 τὸ σ.—*omit* τὸ WH
21:11 *trs* ἀπ' οὐρανοῦ σ. LWH
Joh. 6:14 σημεῖα WH
11:47 *trs* ποιεῖ σημεῖα LTTrAWWH
Acts 8:13 *trs* miracles and signs A.V.C GW
1Co. 1:22 σημεῖα signs GEds

4594 σήμερον.

Mat.16: 3 When it is (*verse* 2) *to end of verse* 3 [TA][[WH]]
Lu. 22:61*crow—*add* σ. to-day TTrAWHR
24:21 *omit* to-day, *read* it is the third T[TrA]WHR

4596 σηρικόν, σιρικόν LTWHR.

4599 σθενόω.

1Pet. 5:10 σθενώσει will strengthen GEds

4600 σιαγών.

Mat. 5:39 *trs* σ. σου LTrA, σ. [σου] WH

4601 σιγάω.

Lu. 18:39*σιγήσῃ *for* σιωπήσῃ (-πάω) LTTrAWHR

4605 Σιδών.

Mar. 7:24 *omit* and Sidon TA[WH]
Lu. 4:26 Σιδωνίας LTTrAWHR

4606 Σιδώνιος, -νία.

Lu. 4:26*Σιδωνίας *for* Σιδῶνος LTTrAWHR

4609 Σίλας.

Acts 15:34 *omit the verse* Eds
16:19 τὸν Σ.—*omit* τὸν A
29 τῷ Σ.—*omit* τῷ LTrAWH

4611 Σιλωάμ.

Joh. 9:11 τὸν Σ. *read* go to Siloam GLTTrAWHR

4613 **Σίμων.**

Mar. 1:16*(τοῦ LE) Σίμωνος *for* αὐτοῦ Eds
36 ὁ Σ.—*omit* ὁ T[Tr]AWH
3:16 *trs* ὄνομα τῷ Σ. TTrAWH
Lu. 5: 3 τοῦ Σ.—*omit* τοῦ LTTrAWH
5 ὁ Σ.—*omit* ὁ TTrAWH
7:43 ὁ Σ.—*omit* ὁ T[Tr]WH
23:26 Σίμωνα LTTrAWHR
Joh. 12: 4 *omit* Simon's (son) TTrAWHR
Acts 10:17 τοῦ Σίμωνος LTTrAWWH
2 Pet. 1: 1*for* Συμεὼν A.V.C LWH

4614 **Σινᾶ, –ά** WH.

*** σιρός**, pit, cavern.

2 Pet. 2: 4 σιροῖς *for* σειραῖς (-ρά) LT

*** σιτίον**, grain, corn.

Acts 7:12 σιτία *for* σῖτα (-τος) Eds

4620 **σιτομέτριον.**

Lu. 12:42 τὸ σ.—*omit* τὸ TrA[WH]

4621 **σῖτος.**

Mar. 4:28 πλήρης σῖτος LTTrA
Lu. 12:18*τὸν σῖτον *for* τὰ γενήματα (-νημα) TrWHR
Acts 7:12 σιτίον Eds

See 4965
Σιχάρ, see Συχάρ.

4623 **σιωπάω.**

Lu. 18:39 σιγάω LTTrAWHR
19:40 σιωπήσουσιν LTTrAWHR

4624 **σκανδαλίζω.**

Mat. 17:27 σκανδαλίζωμεν T
Mar. 9:43 σκανδαλίσῃ TWHR
Ro. 14:21 *om.* or is offended, or is made weak TWHR

4633 **σκηνή.**

Mar. 9: 5 *trs* τρεῖς σκηνάς LTTrAWH
Heb. 9: 1 *omit* σ. A.V.B GEds

4642 **σκληρός.**

Acts 9: 5 *omit* (it is) hard *to unto* him (*ver.* 6) GEds

4648 **σκοπέω.**

Phil. 2: 4 σκοποῦντες looking GEds

4652 **σκοτεινός, –τινός** WH.

4653 **σκοτία.**

Mat. 4:16*†*trs* σκοτίᾳ (σκότει TW) φῶς εἶδεν LTTrAWWH
Joh. 6:17 ἡ σκοτία T, *see* ἤδη

4654 **σκοτίζομαι.**

Lu. 23:45 ἐκλείπω TWHR, *see* ἥλιος
Eph. 4:18 σκοτόω LTTrAWH
Rev. 9: 2 σκοτόω LTAWH

4655 **σκότος.**

Mat. 4:16 σκοτία LTrAWH
Heb. 12:18 ζόφος Eds

4656 **σκοτόω, –όομαι.**

Eph. 4:18*ἐσκοτωμένοι *for* ἐσκοτισμένοι (σκοτίζομαι) LTTrAWH
Rev. 9: 2*ἐσκοτώθη *for* ἐσκοτίσθη (σκοτίζομαι) LTAWH

4660 **σκύλλω.**

Mat. 9:36*ἐσκυλμένοι *for* ἐκλελυμένοι (ἐκλύω) GEds

4663 **σκώληξ.**

Mar. 9:44, 46 *omit the verses* T[Tr]WHR

4667 **Σμύρνα, Ζμ–** T.

Rev. 2: 8*ἐν Σμύρνῃ *for* Σμυρναίων GEds, *see* ἐκκλησία

4668 **Σμυρναῖος.**

Rev. 2: 8 Σμύρνα GLTrAWWHR, Ζμύρνα T

4670 **Σόδομα.**

Mar. 6:11 *omit* verily *to end of verse* G[L]TTrAWHR

4671 **σοί.**

Mat. 4: 9 *trs* ταῦτά σοι πάντα TTrAWH
9: 2 *omit* thee LTTrAWHR
5 σοῦ (*omit* thee) GEds
12:47 *omit the verse* [T]WH
Mar. 1:11*for* ᾧ (ὅς) LTTrAWHR
2: 5 *omit* thee GTTrAWHR
9 σοῦ (*omit* thee) GTTrAWWHR
9:43 σ. ἐστίν—ἐ. σε LTTrAWHR
45 σέ Eds
47 σέ TTrAWHR
10:21 σέ TAWHR
Joh. 5:14 *trs* σοί τι GEds
9:10 σοῦ S—σοί E
Acts 9: 5 *omit* GEds, *see* κύριος
10: 6 *omit* GEds, *see* ποιέω
32 *omit* LTTr[A]WHR, *see* λαλέω
24:13*δύνανται—*add* σ. *read* prove to thee Eds
1 Ti. 6:13 *omit* σ. T
Philem. 12(11)*sent again—*add* σ. to thee Eds
3 Joh. 13*add* σ. Eds, *see* γράφω
Rev. 14:15 *omit* for thee GEds

4672 **Σολομών, –ῶν.**

Mat. 1: 6 Σολομῶνα GTTrAWWH
12:42 Σολομῶνος *bis* GLTTrAWWH
Lu. 11:31 Σολομῶνος *bis* GLTTrAWWH
Joh. 10:23 (τοῦ TrWH) Σολομῶνος GLTTrA
Acts 3:11 Σολομῶνος GTrW (WWH
5:12 Σολομῶνος GTrAW
7:47 Σαλωμών T

4675 **σοῦ.**

Mat. 5:39 *omit* σ. *read* the right cheek T[WH]
6:13 *omit* GEds, *see* αἰών
21*for* ὑμῶν *bis* LTTrAWHR
9: 5*for* σοί, *read* thy sins GEds
12:47 *omit the verse* [T]WH
15: 4 *omit* thy GEds
18:16 thee—thyself, σεαυτοῦ T, *omit* σ. L
19:19 *omit* thy[1] GLTTrAWWH
20:21 *omit* σ.[1] *read* the right hand LTWH
21*εὐωνύμων σ. thy left GEds
Mar. 1: 2 *omit* before thee GEds
3: 5 *omit* σ. T[Tr]A
32*add σ. LT[A]W, *see* ἀδελφή
10:19*μητέρα σ. thy mother LT
37*εἷς[2]—*add* σ. T
37 *omit* σ.[2] [L]TTrAWHR
14:70 *omit* and thy speech agreeth (thereto) LTTrAWHR
Lu. 1:35*born—*add* ἐκ σ. A.V.B [L]
11: 2 *omit* thy will be done GTTrAWHR
34*ὀφθαλμός[1] σ. thine eye LTTrAWHR
18:20 *omit* σ.[2] LTrAWWHR
19:42 *omit* thy[1] LTr[A]WHR
42 *omit* thy[2] [LTrA]WHR
Joh. 4:51 thy—his, αὐτοῦ LTTrAWHR
5:12 *omit* thy bed T[Tr]AWHR
8:10 *omit* those thine accusers WHR
9:10 σοῦ S—σοί E
17: 1 *omit* σ.[2] *read* the Son TTr[A]WHR
17 *omit* σ. *read* the truth LTTrAWHR
18:11 *omit* σ. *read* the sword GEds
Acts 4:28 *omit* thy[2] L[Tr]WH
30 *omit* σ.[1] LTrWH
26: 3 *omit* σ. LTTrAWHR
1 Ti. 5:23 *omit* σ.[1] LTTrAWHR
6:21 thee—you, ὑμῶν LTTrWHR
Heb. 1: 8 thy[2]—his, αὐτοῦ WH
2: 7 *omit* and didst set *to end of verse* G[L]T[Tr]A[WH]
Jas. 2:18 *omit* thy[2] Eds
Rev. 2: 2 *omit* thy[2] LTTrAWHR
13 *omit* thy works, and LTTrAWHR
19 *omit* thy[2] T
20*γυναῖκα—*add* σ. *read* thy wife GL[A]W

4678 **σοφια.**

Lu. 2:40 σοφίᾳ TrAWH
52 *trs* stature and wisdom Tr: τῇ σοφίᾳ TWH
1 Co. 1:30 *trs* σοφία ἡμῖν LTTrAWHR

4680 **σοφός.**

1 Ti. 1:17 *omit* wise GEds
Jude 25 *omit* wise GEds

4681 **Σπανία.**

Ro. 15:28 τὴν Σ.—*omit* τὴν LTTrAWH

4682 **σπαράσσω, –ττω.**

Mar. 9:20 συσπαράσσω LTWHR
26 σπαράξας GEds

4687 **σπείρω.**

Mat. 13:18 σπείραντος LTTrAWH
24 σπείραντι A.V.C LTTrAWHR
25 ἐπισπείρω LTTrAWHR
27 ἔσπειρες Tr
Mar. 4: 3 τοῦ σ.—*omit* τοῦ LT[Tr]AWH

4688 **σπεκουλάτωρ, –τορ** LTTrAWWH.

4690 **σπέρμα.**

2 Co. 9:10 σπόρος LTr

4694 **σπιλάς.**

Jude 12 εἰσιν—*add* οἱ LTTrAWHR

4696 **σπιλόω.**

Jas. 3: 6 ἡ σ.—καὶ σ. T

4702 **σπόριμα.**

Lu. 6: 1 τῶν σ.—*omit* τῶν LTTrAWHR

4703 **σπόρος.**

2 Co. 9:10*σπόρον *for* σπέρμα LTr

4706 **σπουδαιότερον.**

2 Ti. 1:17 very diligently—diligently, σπουδαίως LTTrWHR

4708, 4709 **σπουδαιως, –οτέρως.**

2 Ti. 1:17*for* σπουδαιότερον LTTrWHR

4711 **σπυρίς, σφυρίς** WH, L at times.

4712 **στάδιος, –ον.**

Mar. 14:24*μέσον τῆς θαλάσσης ἦν was now in the midst of the sea—σταδίους πολλοὺς ἀπὸ τῆς γῆς ἀπεῖχεν was many furlongs distant from the land TrWH
Joh. 6:19 στάδια T
Rev. 21:16 σταδίων S—σταδίους EGLTrA

*** στασιαστής**, an insurgent.

Mar. 15: 7 στασιαστῶν *for* συστασιαστῶν (-τής) LTTrAWHR

4714 **στάσις.**

Acts 24: 5 στάσεις seditions LTTrWWHR

4716 **σταυρός.**

Mar. 10:21 *omit* take up the cross [L]TTrWHR
Gal. 6:12 *trs* τῷ σ. τοῦ χριστοῦ μὴ LTTrAWHR

4717 **σταυρόω.**

Mar. 15:20 σταυρώσουσιν LTTrA
24 σταυροῦσιν TTrAWHR
Lu. 23:21 σταύρου, σταυρου LTTrAWH
Joh. 19:10 *see* ἀπολύω

4718 **σταφυλή.**

Mat. 7:16 σταφυλάς LTTrAWH
Lu. 6:44 *trs* σταφυλὴν τρυγῶσιν TTrAWH

4719 **στάχυς.**

Lu. 6: 1 *trs* and did eat the ears of corn TrAWH

4739 **στήκω.**

Mar. 3:31*στήκοντες *for* ἑστῶτες (ἵστημι) TTrAWH
11:25 στήκετε LTTrAWH
Joh. 1:26*στήκει *for* ἕστηκεν (ἵστημι) TTrAWHR
1 Th. 3: 8 στήκετε TTrAWH

4741 **στηρίζω.**

Lu. 9:51 ἐστήρισεν TTrAWH
22:32 στήρισον LTTrAWH
Acts 18:23*στηρίζων *for* ἐπιστηρίζων (-ζω) LTTrAWHR
1 Pet. 5:10 στηρίξει will stablish GEds
Rev. 3: 2 στήρισον GLTTrAWWH

* **στιβάς**, bed of straw, twigs, &c.

Mar. 11: 8 στιβάδας *for* στοιβάδας (-βάς) LTTrAWHR

4746 **στοιβάς.**

Mar. 11: 8 στιβάς LTTrAWHR

4749 **στολή.**

Lu. 15:22 τὴν σ.—*omit* τὴν LTTrAWHR
Rev. 6:11 στολὴ λευκὴ a white robe GEds
7:14 στολὰς αὐτῶν[2]—αὐτάς ([α.]A) A.V.C GEds
22:14*ποιοῦντες τὰς ἐντολὰς αὐτοῦ do his commandments—πλύνοντες τὰς στολὰς αὐτῶν wash their robes LTTrAWHR

4750 **στόμα.**

Mat. 15: 8 *omit* draweth nigh unto me with their mouth, and GLTTrAWHR

4752 **στρατεία.**

2 Co. 10: 4 στρατιά T

4753 **στράτευμα.**

Rev. 9:16 τῶν στρατευμάτων A.V.C GEds

4754 **στρατεύομαι.**

1 Ti. 1:18 στρατεύσῃ TTr

4755 **στρατηγός.**

Lu. 22: 4 τοῖς σ.—*omit* τοῖς TTrAWHR
Acts 5:24 ὁ σ.—*omit* ὁ LTTrAWHR

4756 **στρατιά.**

2 Co. 10: 4*στρατιᾶς *for* στρατείας (-ία) T

4759 **στρατοπεδάρχης.**

Acts 28:16 *omit* the centurion *to* the guard: but LTTrAWHR

4762 **στρέφω.**

Mat. 9:22*στραφεὶς *for* ἐπιστραφεὶς (-στρέφω) LTTrAWHR
27: 3*ἔστρεψεν *for* ἀπέστρεψεν (ἀποστρέφω) TTrAWHR
Lu. 10:22 *see* μαθητής
Joh. 12:40*στραφῶσιν *for* ἐπιστραφῶσιν (-στρέφω) LTTrAWHR

4766 **στρώννυμι, -ύω.**

Mat. 21: 8 σ.[2]—ἔστρωσαν T
Mar. 11: 8 *omit* and strawed (them) in the way TTrAWHR

4768 **στυγνάζω.**

Mat. 16: 3 When it is (*verse* 2) *to end of verse* 3 [TA] [[WH]]

4770 **Στωϊκός, Στοϊ–** LTA, **Στωι–** WH.

Acts 17:18 τῶν Σ.—*omit* τῶν LTTrAWHR

4771 **σύ.**

Mar. 14:30*that—*add* σύ thou GEds
68 *trs* σὺ τί LTTrAWHR
Lu. 1:28 *om.* blessed (art) thou among women T[Tr]AWHR
16:25 *omit* σύ[1] GTTrAWHR
19:42 *trs* καὶ σύ *after* ταύτῃ WHR
Joh. 1:21 *omit* σύ[1] T: *trs* σὺ ([σὺ]WH) Ἠλίας εἶ TrWH: σὺ οὖν τί; Ἠλ. εἶ A
8:53 *omit* σύ[2] GLTTrAWHR
9:17 *trs* τί σὺ TrAWHR
2 Ti. 2: 3 *omit* thou therefore Eds
Philem. 12 *omit* thou therefore receive LTTrAWHR

4772 **συγγένεια.**

Lu. 1:61 ἐκ τῆς συγγενείας LTTrAWHR

4773 **συγγενής.**

Mar. 6: 4 συγγενεῦσιν TTrWH
Lu. 1:36 συγγενὶς LTWWHR
Ro. 16:11 συγγενῆν Tr

* **συγγενίς**, kinswoman.

Lu. 1:36 συγγενὶς *for* συγγενής LTWWHR

4777 **συγκακοπαθέω.**

2 Ti. 2: 3*συγκακοπάθησον *for* κακοπάθησον (-θέω) Eds

4779 **συγκαλέω.**

Lu. 15: 9 συγκαλεῖ TWHR

4783 **συγκατατίθεμαι.**

Lu. 23:51 συνκατατιθέμενος T

4786 **συγκεράννυμι.**

Heb. 4: 2 συγκεκερασμένους LTrAWHR, -μένος T, συγκεκραμένους W

4788 **συγκλείω.**

Gal. 3:23 συγκλειόμενοι LTTrAWHR

4789 **συγκληρονόμος.**

1 Pet. 3: 7 συγκληρονόμοις TTrA

4798 **συγχράομαι.**

Joh. 4: 9 *omit* for the Jews have no dealings with the Samaritans T[WH]

4797 **συγχύνω.**

Acts 9:22 συνέχυννεν TAWH
21:31 συγχύννεται LTTrAWH, -ύνε- WR

4799 **σύγχυσις.**

Acts 19:29 τῆς συγχύσεως GTTrAWWHR

4803 **συζήτησις.**

Acts 15: 2 ζήτησις GEds
7 ζήτησις TTrWHR
28:29 *omit the verse* LTTrAWHR

4806 **συζωοποιέω.**

Col. 2:13 συνεζωοποίησεν GEds

4809 **συκομωραία** s, **–ρέα** L, **συκομορέα** EGTTrAWWH.

4814 **συλλαλέω.**

Mat. 17: 3 *trs* σ. μετ' αὐτοῦ LTTrWH

4815 **συλλαμβάνω.**

Lu. 1:31 συλλήμψῃ LTTrAWH
36 συνείληφεν TrWHR
2:21 συλλημφθῆναι LTTrAWH
Acts 23:27 συλλημφθέντα LTTrAWH

4819 **συμβαινω.**

1 Co. 10:11 συνέβαινεν TTrWH

4820 **συμβάλλω.**

Acts 4:15 συνέβαλλον LTTrAWH
20:14 συνέβαλλεν LTTrAWHR

4822 **συμβιβάζω.**

Acts 19:33*συνεβίβασαν *for* προεβίβασαν (προβιβάζω) LTTrWHR
Col. 2: 2 συμβιβασθέντες GEds

4823 **συμβουλεύω.**

Joh. 11:53 took counsel together—took counsel, βουλεύομαι LTTrWHR

4826 **Συμεών.**

2 Pet. 1: 1 Σίμων A.V.C LWHR

4828 **συμμαρτυρέω.**

Rev. 22:18 μαρτυρέω GEds

* **συμμορφίζω**, to make conformable.

Phil. 3:10 συμμορφιζόμενος *for* συμμορφούμενος (-φόω) Eds

4832 **συμμορφόω.**

Phil. 3:10 συμμορφίζω Eds

4836 **συμπαραγίνομαι.**

2 Ti. 4:16 stood with—stood by, παραγίνομαι LTTrWHR

4838 **συμπαραλαμβάνω.**

Acts 15:38 συμπαραλαμβάνειν LTTrAWHR

4839 **συμπαραμένω.**

Phil. 1:25 παραμένω LTTrAWHR

* **συμπίπτω**, to fall together.

Lu. 6:49 συνέπεσεν *for* ἔπεσεν (πίπτω) TTrAWHR

συμφάγω, *see* **συνεσθίω.** See 4906

4851 **συμφέρω.**

1 Co. 7:35 σύμφορος LTTrAWHR
10:33 σύμφορος LTTrAWH
2 Co. 12: 1 δεῖ, οὐ συμφέρον μέν, ἐλεύσομαι δέ I must glory, it is not expedient indeed, but I will come LTTrWHR

* **σύμφορος**, profitable.

1 Co. 7:35 σύμφορον *for* συμφέρον (-ρω) LTTrAWHR
10:33 σύμφορον *for* συμφέρον (-ρω) LTTrAWH

4856 **συμφωνέω.**

Mat. 18:19†*trs* συμφωνήσωσιν (-σουσιν TTrA) ἐξ ὑμῶν LTTrAWH
Lu. 5:36 οὐ συμφωνήσει will not agree LTTrAWHR

4862 **σύν.**

Mat. 27:44*συσταυρωθέντες-*ad*.σ. LTTrAWH
Mar. 15:32*συνεσταυρωμένοι-*add* σ. LTWH
Lu. 8:45*σ. αὐτῷ *for* μετ' αὐτοῦ GLTTrAR
51**add* σ. LTTrAWHR, *see* οὐδείς
23:35 *omit* with them [L]TTrAWHR
24: 1 *omit* and certain (others) with them LTTrAWHR
Joh. 12: 2**add* σ. GEds, *see* ἀνάκειμαι
Acts 1:14 *omit* σ.[2] LT[Tr]AW
17 with—among, ἐν GEds
7:35**for* ἐν[1] Eds
16:32**for* καί[2] GEds
2 Co. 4:14**for* διά Eds
8:19 with[2]—in, ἐν LTrAWWHR

4863 **συνάγω.**

Mat. 13:30 συνάγετε LTrWH
25:32 συναχθήσονται LTTrAWH
Mar. 4: 1 συνάγεται is gathered Eds
Lu. 3:17 συναγαγεῖν to gather TWHR
17:37 ἐπισυνάγω TTrAWHR
Joh. 20:19 *omit* assembled LTTrAWHR
Rev. 13:10 *omit* leadeth, *read* (is) for captivity Eds
19:17 συνάχθητε GEds

4864 **συναγωγή.**

Mar. 1:21 τὴν σ.—*omit* τὴν E
39 εἰς τὰς συναγωγάς GEds
3: 1 τὴν σ.—*omit* τὴν T[Tr]AWH
Lu. 4:44 εἰς τὰς συναγωγάς TTrAWHR
21:12 τὰς συναγωγάς TTrWHR, [τὰς] σ. A
Joh. 18:20 τῇ σ.—*omit* τῇ GEds
Acts 13:42 *omit* of the synagogue GEds
17: 1 ἡ σ.—*omit* ἡ LTTr[A]WHR
Jas. 2: 2 τὴν σ.—*omit* τὴν LTTrAWHR

4867 **συναθροίζω.**

Lu. 24:33 ἀθροίζω LTTrAWHR

4870 **συνακολουθέω.**

Mar. 14:51*συνηκολούθει *for* ἠκολούθει (ἀκολουθέω) LTTrAWHR
Lu. 23:49 συνακολουθοῦσαι TTrAWHR

* **συναλλάσσω**, to commune with.

Acts 7:26 συνήλλασσεν *for* συνήλασεν (συνελαύνω) LTTrWWHR

4873 **συνανάκειμαι.**

Mar. 6:26 ἀνάκειμαι (*omit* with him) TTrAWHR
Joh. 12: 2 ἀνάκειμαι σύν GEds

4874 **συναναμίγνυμι.**

2 Th. 3:14 μὴ συναναμίγνυσθαι to have no company LTrAWHR

4875 **συναναπαύομαι.**

Ro. 15:32 *omit* and may with you be refreshed L[A]

4876 **συναντάω.**

Heb. 7: 1 ὁ σ.—ὃς σ. LTrA

4877 **συνάντησις.**

Mat. 8:34 ὑπάντησις LTTrWH

συνβ., συνγ., συνζ., etc.

☞ *In compounds of συν with words commencing with β, γ, ζ, κ, λ, μ, π, σ and ψ, the ν is mostly retained by T and at times by other Editors.*

4894 **συνειδέω, συνεῖδον.**

Acts 5: 2 συνειδυίης LTTrAWH

4893 **συνείδησις.**

Joh. 8: 9 *om.* being convicted by (their own) conscience WHR
1 Co. 8: 7 with conscience of—being used to, συνήθεια LTTrWHR

4900 **συνελαύνω.**

Acts 7:26 συναλλάσσω LTTrWWHR: *reconciliabat* A.V.Vul

* **συνεπιτίθημι** to join in attack.

Acts 24: 9 συνεπέθεντο *for* συνέθεντο (συντίθημι) GEds

4903 **συνεργέω.**

Jas. 2:22 συνεργεῖ worketh with TTr

4904 **συνεργός.**

1 Th. 3: 2*συνεργόν *for* διάκονον (-νος) GLAW
2 *omit* and our fellow-labourer GEds

4905 **συνέρχομαι.**

Mar. 6:33 *omit* and came together unto him GEds
Acts 10:23 συνῆλθαν WH
45 συνῆλθαν TTrWH
21:22 *omit* TrWHR, *see* δεῖ
22:30*συνελθεῖν *for* ἐλθεῖν (ἔρχομαι) GEds
1 Co. 7: 5 come—may be, ἦτε (ὦ) GEds: συνέρχησθε S, συνέρχεσθε E

4906 **συνεσθίω.**

Acts 11: 3 συνέφαγεν did eat TrWH

4914 **συνήθεια.**

1 Co. 8: 7*συνηθείᾳ *for* συνειδήσει (-σις) LTTrWHR

4917 **συνθλάομαι.**

Mat. 21:44 *omit the verse* [L]T[WH]

4920 **συνίημι.**

Mat. 13:23 συνιείς LTTrWH
Mar. 7:14 σύνετε LTTrAWH
Ro. 3:11 ὁ σ.—*omit* ὁ L[TrWH]
2 Co. 10:12 συνιᾶσιν LTTrAWH
Eph. 5:17 συνίετε understand LTTrAWHR

4921 **συνιστάνω, —άω, συνίστημι.**

2 Co. 3: 1 συνιστᾶν LTr
4: 2 | 6: 4 συνιστάντες LTTrAW, —τάνοντες WH
10:18 σ.[1]—συνιστάνων LTTrAWWH
Gal. 2:18 συνιστάνω GLTTrAWWH

4923 **συνοδία.**

Lu. 2:44 *trs* εἶναι ἐν τῇ σ. LTTrAWH

4929 **συντάσσω.**

Mat. 21: 6*συνέταξεν *for* προσέταξεν (προστάσσω) LTrAWHR

4930 **συντέλεια.**

Mat. 24: 3 τῆς σ.—*omit* τῆς LTTrAWH

4931 **συντελέω.**

Mat. 7:28 τελέω LTTrAWHR
Mar. 13: 4 *trs* ταῦτα σ. πάντα TTrAWHR
Joh. 2: 3**add* σ. T, *see* οἶνος

4932 **συντέμνω.**

Ro. 9:28 *omit* σ.[2] LTTr[A]WHR, *see* λόγος

4933 **συντηρέω.**

Lu. 5:38 *omit* and both are preserved T[Tr]AWHR

4934 **συντίθημι.**

Acts 24: 9 assented—joined in the charge, συνεπιτίθημι GEds

4937 **συντρίβω.**

Lu. 4:18 *omit* to heal the broken-hearted G[L]TTrAWHR

4949 **Συροφοίνισσα.**

Mar. 7:26 Σύρα Φ. TrA: Συροφοινίκισσα LTWWH, Συραφ- G

4950 **σύρτις, σῦρτις** L.

Acts 27:17 quicksand—Syrtis (as a proper name) EGTWWHR

4952 **συσπαράσσω.**

Mar. 9:20*συνεσπάραξεν *for* ἐσπάραξεν (σπαράσσω) LTWHR

4955 **συστασιαστής.**

Mar. 15: 7 στασιαστής LTTrAWHR

4956 **συστατικός.**

2 Co. 3: 1 *omit* of commendation[2] Eds

4962 **συστρέφω.**

Mat. 17:22*συστρεφομένων *for* ἀναστρεφομένων (-φω) LTTrWH

4964 **συσχηματίζομαι.**

Ro. 12: 2 μὴ συσχηματίζεσθαι not to be conformed LA

4965 **Συχάρ** S, **Σιχάρ** E.

4966 **Συχέμ.**

Acts 7:16 τοῦ Σ.—*omit* τοῦ TTrWH

4969 **σφάττω.**

Rev. 6: 4 σφάξουσιν LTTrAWHR
13: 8 τοῦ ἐσφαγμένου A.V.C GEds

4972 **σφραγίζω.**

2 Co. 1:22 ὁ καὶ σ.—*omit* ὁ [WH]R
11:10 σφραγίσεται S—φράσσω A.V.B EGEds
Rev. 7: 3 σφραγίζωμεν S—σφραγίσωμεν A.V.B EGEds
5[2,3], 6 *ter*, 7 *ter*, 8[1,2] *omit* (were) sealed Eds

4973 **σφραγίς.**

Rev. 6: 3†*trs* τὴν σ. τὴν δευτέραν GEds
5†*trs* τὴν σ. τὴν τρίτην GEds

* **σφυδρόν**, the ankle.

Acts 3: 7 σφυδρά *for* σφυρά (-ρόν) TWH

σφυρίς, see σπυρίς. See 4711

4974 **σφυρόν.**

Acts 3: 7 σφυδρόν TWH

4977 **σχίζω.**

Lu. 5:36*καινοῦ — *add* σχίσας, *read* rendeth a piece from a new garment TTrAWHR
36 maketh a rent—σχίσει he will rend LTTrAWHR

4978 **σχίσμα.**

1 Co. 12:25 σχίσματα schisms T

4980 **σχολάζω.**

1 Co. 7: 5 σχολάσητε GEds

4982 **σώζω.**

Mat. 18:11 *omit the verse* LTTr[A]WHR
Lu. 9:56 *omit* for the Son *to* to save them GLTTrAWHR
17:33 to save—to gain, περιποιέομαι TTrAWHR
Rev. 21:24 *omit* of them which are saved GEds

4983 **σῶμα.**

Mat. 14:12 body—corpse, πτῶμα LTTrWHR
27:58 *omit* the body[2] T[Tr]WHR
Mar. 14: 8 *trs* τὸ σῶμά μου LTrWH
15:45 body-corpse, πτῶμα LTTrAWHR
Joh. 19:38 *omit* the body[2] T
1 Co. 7:34 τῷ σώματι LTTrAWHR
15:38 τὸ ἴδιον σ.—*omit* τὸ LTTrAWHR
44 *omit* body[4] Eds
2 Co. 4:10 τῷ σ.[2]—τοῖς σώμασιν bodies T

4991 **σωτηρία.**

Acts 7:25 *trs* σωτηρίαν αὐτοῖς Eds
2 Co. 1: 6 *omit* and salvation[2] GTWHR
1 Pet. 2: 2**add at end* εἰς σωτηρίαν unto salvation GEds

4992 **σωτήριος.**

Tit. 2:11 ἡ σ.—*omit* ἡ LTTrAWHR

4994 **σωφρονίζω.**

Tit. 2: 4 σωφρονίζουσιν TTrA

5000 **Ταβιθά, Ταβειθά** WH.

5007 **τάλαντον.**

Mat. 25:16 *omit* talents[2] LTr[A]WH

5008 **ταλιθά, ταλειθά** WH.

5009 **ταμιεῖον.**

Mat. 6: 6 ταμεῖον TAWH

5010 **τάξις.**

Heb. 7:21 *omit* after the order of Melchisedec TTrAWHR

* **ταπεινόφρων**, lowly in mind.

1 Pet. 3: 8 ταπεινόφρονες *for* φιλόφρονες (-φρων) GEds

5013 **ταπεινόω.**

Mat. 18: 4 ταπεινώσει LTTrAWWH
2 Co. 12:21 ταπεινώσει με LTTrA

5015 **ταράσσω.**

Joh. 5: 4 *omit* waiting for (*ver.* 3) *to end of verse* 4 [G]TTrAWHR
Acts 17:13*stirred up—*add* καὶ ταράσσοντες and troubled LTTrAWHR

5016 **ταραχή.**

Mar. 13: 8 *omit* and troubles LTTr[A]WHR
Joh. 5: 4 *omit* waiting for (*ver.* 3) *to end of verse* 4 [G]TTrAWHR

5021 **τάσσω.**

Mat. 8: 9*ἐξουσίαν—*add* τασσόμενος, *read* placed under L[WH]
Acts 18: 2*τεταχέναι *for* διατεταχέναι (διατάσσω) T

5022 **ταῦρος.**

Heb. 9:13 *trs* of goats and of bulls Eds

5023 **ταὐτά, see ὁ αὐτός.**

5024 **ταῦτα from οὗτος.**

Mar. 8: 7**add* τ. TrWHR, *see* παρατίθημι
Lu. 2:51 *omit* these [L]T[A]WHR
6:23, 26 τὰ αὐτά (ὁ αὐτός) LTTrAWHR
11:53 *omit* TTrAWHR, *see* ἐξέρχομαι
13: 2**for* τοιαῦτα (τοιοῦτος) TTrWHR
17:30 ταῦτα—ταὐτά GLW, τὰ αὐτά (ὁ αὐτός) TTrAWHR
18: 4 *trs* ταῦτα δὲ TrAWH
22 *omit* these things LTTrAWHR
23:46 τοῦτο LTTrAWHR
24:11**for* αὐτῶν[2] LTTrAWHR
Joh. 9:40 *omit* these words T
11:28 τοῦτο TTrAWHR
Acts 5: 5 *omit* these things LTTrAWHR
24:22 *omit* when heard these things GEds
26:30 *omit* and when he had thus spoken GEds
28:29 *omit the verse* LTTrAWHR
1 Co. 6: 8 τοῦτο Eds
Rev. 7: 1 these things—this, τοῦτο Eds
10: 4 αὐτά Eds
21: 7**for* πάντα (πᾶς) GEds
22:18 these things—them αὐτά GEds

5025 **ταύταις.**

Lu. 13:14 αὐταῖς LTTrAWHR

5026 **ταύτῃ.**

Mar. 14:27 *omit* this night [L]TTrAWWHR
Acts 4:27**add* τ. GEds, *see* πόλις
Heb. 3:10**for* ἐκείνῃ (-νος) Eds

5026 **ταύτην.**

Mat. 15:15 *omit* τ. *read* the parable LTTr[A]WHR
Joh. 7: 8 *omit* τ.[1] *read* the feast Eds
Acts 1:16 *omit* τ. *read* the scripture LTTr[A]WWHR

Heb. 5: 3 αὐτήν Eds
Rev. 12:15 αὐτήν GEds

5026 ταύτης.

Acts 17:30 *hujus ignorantiæ* A.V.Vul
Heb. 12:15 αὐτῆς LWH

5032 τάχιον, –χειον WH.

1 Ti. 3:14 τάχος LTrWHR

5034 τάχος.

1 Ti. 3:14*ἐν τάχει *for* τάχιον LTrWHR
Rev. 2: 5 τάχει S—ταχύ EGW, *omit* quickly LTTrAWHR

5035 ταχύ.

Mar. 16: 8 *omit* quickly GEds
Lu. 15:22*τ. ἐξενέγκατε bring forth quickly L[Tr]AWHR
Rev. 2: 5 τάχος S—τ. EGW, *omit* quickly LTTrAWHR

5037 τε.

Mat. 23: 6 δέ LTTrAWHR
Mar. 15:36 *omit* and[3] LTTrAWHR
Lu. 15: 2*οἱ[1]—*add* τε, *read* both the Pharisees LTTrAWHR
Acts 2: 3 ἐκάθισέν τε—καὶ ἐ. LTTrWHR
43 δέ TWH
43**add* τε T, *see* φόβος
3:10 δέ LTTrAWHR
7:26 τε S—δέ EGW
8: 1 δέ LTrA[WH]R, *omit* and[3] T
6 δέ LTTrAWWH
28 δέ WH
9: 6 *omit* GEds, *see* σκληρός
15*ἐθνῶν—*add* τε, *read* both Gentiles Eds
24 τε[1]—δὲ καί and also LTTrAWHR
10: 2 *omit* τε Eds
48 δέ TTrWHR
11:13 δέ LTTrWHR
12: 8 δέ LTrWH
13: 2 *omit* τε GEds
15: 3*τήν[1]—*add* τε, *read* both Phenice LTTrAWHR
9 *omit* τε W
32 τε S—δέ E
16:11 δέ LTTrAWHR
12 ἐκεῖθέν τε—κἀκεῖθεν Eds
23 δέ WH
26 δέ LTTrAWHR
17: 5 ἐπιστάντες τε—καὶ ἐ. LTTrAWHR
19 δέ TrWH
18:11 δέ LTTrAWHR
19: 2*εἶπεν—*add* τε, *read* and he said LTTrAWHR
3 εἶπέν τε—ὁ δὲ ε. T
27 *for* δέ[2] EGLTTrAWHR
21:11 *omit* and[2] Eds
22:28 δέ LTTrWHR, *omit* and[1] A
23:10 *omit* τε WH
35 *omit* τε LTTrAWHR
24:23 *omit* and[1] Eds
26: 4*ἐν[2]—*add* τε, *read* and at Jerusalem Eds
10*many—*add* τε also LTTrAWHR
20*πρῶτον—*add* τε, *read* both of Damascus LTTrAWHR
23*τῷ—*add* τε, *read* both unto the people LTTrAWHR
30*ἀνέστη—*add* τε, *read* and the king GEds
1 Co. 1: 2 *omit* both LTTr[A]WHR
2 Co. 10: 8 *omit* τε [L]Tr[A]
12:12*σημείοις—*add* τε, *read* both in signs and TA[WH]R
Eph. 1:10 *omit* both GEds
Heb. 4:12 *omit* τε[1] Eds
5: 1 *omit* both L[TrWH]
6: 2 *omit* and[2] [Tr]WH
11:32 *omit* and[2] LTTrWWHR
Rev. 1: 2 *omit* and[3] GEds
19:18*ἐλευθέρων—*add* τε, *read* both free A.V.†G GEds
18*μικρῶν—*add* τε W, *read* and both small
21:12 *omit* and[1] GEds
See also δέ *and* καί.

5040 τεκνίον.

Gal. 4:19 little children—children, τέκνον LTTr

5043 τέκνον.

Mat. 11:19 children—works, ἔργον TTrWHR
Mar. 12:19†*trs* μὴ ἀφῇ τέκνον leave no child TAWHR
Lu. 7:35 *trs* πάντων τῶν τ. αὐτῆς LTrAWH
1 Co. 4:17 *trs* μου τέκνον LTTrAWHR
Gal. 4:19*τέκνα *for* τεκνία (–νίον) LTTr

5048 τελειόω.

Joh. 17: 4 τελειώσας having finished LTTrAWHR
Acts 20:24 τελειώσω WH
2 Co. 12: 9 τελέω LTTrAWHR

5053 τελευταω.

Mar. 9:44, 46 *omit the verses* T[Tr]WHR
Joh. 11:39*τετελευτηκότος *for* τεθνηκότος (θνήσκω) Eds

5055 τελέω.

Mat. 7:28*ἐτέλεσεν *for* συνετέλεσεν (συντελέω) LTTrAWHR
2 Co. 12: 9*τελεῖται *for* τελειοῦται (όω) LTTrAWHR
Rev. 10: 7 ἐτελέσθη was finished GEds
17:17 τελεσθήσονται GEds

5056 τέλος.

Heb. 3: 6 *omit* firm unto the end A[WH]
Rev. 1: 8 *omit* the beginning and the ending GEds
22:13 τὸ τ. GLTAWHR, *see* ἀρχή

5057 τελώνης.

Mat. 5:47 publicans—heathen, ἐθνικός GEds
Mar. 2:16 *trs* sinners and publicans[1] LTrAWHR
16 *trs* sinners and publicans[2] LTr
Lu. 5:29 *trs* πολὺς τελωνῶν LTTrAWH
30 τῶν τελωνῶν GEds
7:34 *trs* φίλος τελωνῶν GLTTrAWWH

5062 τεσσαράκοντα, τεσσε–

Mat. 4: 2 *trs* τ.[2] νύκτας T
Rev. 7: 4 *see* ρμδ´

5063 τεσσαρακονταετής, τεσσε– TTrAWH.

5064 τέσσαρες –ρα, τέσσε–

Rev. 4: 8 τὰ τ. GEds
5:14 *omit* four (and) twenty GEds
7: 4 *see* ρμδ´
9:13 *omit* four LTr[A]WHR

5071 τετρακόσιοι, –σια

Acts 13:20 *see* ἔτος

5072 τετράμηνος, –νον.

Joh. 4:35 τετράμηνος GEds

5076 τετράρχης, τετραάρχης TWH.

5078 τέχνη.

Acts 18: 3 τῇ τέχνῃ Eds

5081 τηλαυγῶς.

Mar. 8:25 δηλαυγῶς T

5083 τηρέω.

Mat. 19:17 τήρει LTrAWH
23: 3 *omit* observe[1] LTTrAWHR
3 *trs* do and observe LTTrAWHR
Joh. 12: 7 τηρήσῃ she might keep Eds
14:15 τηρήσετε ye will keep TTrWHR
17: 6 τετήρηκαν LTTrAWH
Acts 15:24 *omit* saying (Ye must) be *to* the law LTTrAWHR
21:25 *om.* that they observe no such thing, save only LTTrWHR
1 Co. 7:37 τοῦ τ.—*omit* τοῦ LTTrAWHR
Jas. 2:10 τηρήσῃ Eds
2 Pet. 2: 4 τηρουμένους GTTrAWWHR
1 Joh. 5: 2 keep—do, ποιέω Eds

5087 τίθημι, ἔθηκα, ἐθέμην, θῶ, &c.

Mat. 14: 3 put—put aside, ἀποτίθημι LTTrAWH
Mar. 4:21*τεθῇ *for* ἐπιτεθῇ (–τίθημι) Eds
30*ἐν τίνι αὐτὴν παραβολῇ θῶμεν; (θ. *for* παραβάλωμεν, –βάλλω) with what comparison shall we set it forth? LTTrAWHR
6:56 ἐτίθεσαν TTrAWH
8:25*ἔθηκεν *for* ἐπέθηκεν (ἐπιτίθημι) TrAWH
15:46*ἔθηκεν *for* κατέθηκεν (κατατίθημι) LTrWHR
Mar. 15:47 τέθειται LTTrAWHR
Lu. 8:16*τίθησιν *for* ἐπιτίθησιν (–θημι) LTTrAWHR
21:14 θέτε LTTrAWHR
Joh. 19:41 ἐτέθη—ἦν τεθειμένος WH
20:15 *trs* ἔθηκας αὐτόν GLTTrAWWH
Acts 9:37 *trs* ἔθηκαν αὐτήν TTr
1 Co. 3:10 ἔθηκα I laid LTTrAWHR
1 Joh. 3:16 τιθέναι—θεῖναι Eds
Rev. 1:17*ἔθηκεν *for* ἐπέθηκεν (ἐπιτίθημι) GEds

5088 τίκτω, ἔτεκον.

Heb. 11:11 *omit* was delivered of a child GLTTrAWHR

5091 τιμάω.

Mat. 15: 6(5) τιμήσει, *read* will not honour LTTrAWHR

5092 τιμή.

1 Pet. 1: 7 *trs* glory and honour Eds
Rev. 19: 1 *omit* and honour GEds
21:24 *omit* and honour LTTrAWHR, *omit* τὴν W

5093 τίμιος.

1 Pet. 1: 7 *see* πολύτιμος
2 Pet. 1: 4 *trs* precious and exceeding great TWHR, καὶ τ. ἡμῖν LTrA, τ. ἡ. κ. μ. T, τ. κ. μ. ἡ. WH

5095 Τιμόθεος.

Acts 17:15 τὸν Τιμόθεον TTrWH

5100 τις, τι.

Mat. 12:47 *omit the verse* [T]WH
21:33 *omit* certain GEds
24:17 anything–the things, τά GEds
Mar. 4:22 *omit* τι [L]Tr[A]WH
5:25 *omit* certain LTTr[A]WHR
7:16 *omit the verse* T[TrA]WHR
8:26 *omit* TWHR, *see* εἶπον
14:47 *omit* τις LTrAW[WH]
15:36*τις *for* εἷς TTrAWHR
Lu. 8:51**add* τινά LTTrAWHR, *see* οὐδείς
9: 8*τις *for* εἷς TAWHR, τίς Tr
11:37 *omit* certain TTrAWHR
18: 3*δέ—*add* τις, *read* a certain widow E
20: 9 *omit* certain GEds
21: 2†*trs* τινα [καὶ] A
23:26 τινα LTTrAWHR
24: 1 *omit* and certain (others) with them LTTrAWHR
Joh. 6: 7 *omit* τι [L]Tr[A]WH
15:13 *omit* τις, *read* he lay T
16:23*ἄν τι *for* ὅσα ἄν LTTrAWHR
Acts 5:34 *omit* τι Eds
10: 5*Σίμωνά τινα a certain Simon LTTrAWHR
13: 1 *omit* certain LTTrAWHR
15*εἰ—*add* τις A.V.Vul Eds
16: 1 *omit* certain[2] GEds
17:21*ἀκούειν—*add* τι LT[Tr]WHR
19: 9 *omit* one LTTrAWHR
14 τινος LTrWHR
23: 9**add* τ. LTTrAWHR, *see* γραμματεύς
12 *omit* certain of GEds
24: 1*πρεσβυτέρων τινῶν certain elders LTTrAWHR
25:26 τι[2]—τί (τίς) WHR
26:26 *omit* τι WH
31*τι πράσσει T
28: 3*τι πλῆθος Eds
Ro. 8:24 τις τί—τίς WHR
1 Co. 9:15 ἵνα τις—οὐδεὶς LTTrWHR
2 Co. 8:12 *omit* τις, *read* he hath Eds
11: 1*μικρόν τι some little EEds
12: 6 *omit* τι LTTr[A]WHR
Eph. 6: 8 *omit* τι LTrR
Phil. 2: 1 τινα—τις GLTTrAWHR
Col. 2: 4 μή τις—μηδεὶς Eds
Heb. 3:16 τινές—τίνες, *read* for who, when they heard, did provoke? GEds
1 Pet. 5: 8*τινά *for* τίνα (τίς) LR, *om.* τ. WH
3 Joh. 9*ἔγραψά τι I wrote somewhat Eds
Rev. 7: 1*τι *for* πᾶν LTr[A]WR
See also ὅ τι (ὅστις), εἴ τις, μή τι

5101 τίς, τί.

Mat. 6:25 *omit* or what ye shall drink
7:14*τί *for* ὅτι GLTr (T[WH]
Mar. 1:27 *omit* LTTrAWHR, *see* καινός
2:16 *omit* how is it TTrAWHR (E
4:30 whereunto–how, πῶς TTrAWH

Mar. 4:30*τίνι *for* ποίᾳ LTTrAWHR, *see* τίθημι
Lu. 6: 9 εἰ (*omit* one thing) LTTrAWHR
8:45 *omit* T[TrA]WHR, *see* λέγω
12:11 [or what thing] TrAWH
19:15 *omit* τίς, *read* they had gained TrAWHR
20:23 *omit* why tempt ye me TTrAWHR
Joh. 13:18*τίνας *for* οὓς (ὅς) TTrAWH
21:23 *omit* what (is that) to thee T
Acts 9: 6 *omit* GEds, *see* σκληρός
6 τί²—ὅ τι (ὅστις) LTTrAR, ὅτι WH
10: 6 *omit* GEds, *see* ποιέω
13:25 τίνα με—τί ἐμέ LTTrAWHR
17:20 τί ἄν—τίνα LTTrWHR
25:26*τί *for* τι² (τις) WHR
Ro. 8:24 τις τί—τίς WHR
1 Co. 3: 5 who *bis*—τί what LTTr[A]WHR
Gal. 2:14 why—how, πῶς GEds
4:15 ποῦ Eds, *ubi* A.V.Vul
Col. 1:27 τίς ὁ—τί τό Eds
2 Ti. 3:14 τίνων LTTrAWHR
Heb. 3:16*see τίς
1 Pet. 5: 8 τίνα—τινά (τις) LR, *omit* τ. WH

* Τιτίος.

Acts 18: 7 ὀνόματι—*add* Τιτίου, *read* Titius Justus T[Tr]WH, Τίτου R

5106 τοίνυν.

Jas. 2:24 *omit* then GEds

5108 τοιοῦτος.

Mat. 18: 5†*trs* ἓν παιδίον τοιοῦτον (–το TWH) LTTrAWH
Mar. 7: 8 *omit* (as) the washing *to end of verse* T[TrA]WHR
9:37 such—these, τούτων T
Lu. 13: 2 such—these, ταῦτα TTrWHR
Acts 21:25 *omit* LTTrWHR, *see* μηδέν
1 Ti. 6: 5 *omit* from such withdraw thyself Eds

5112 τολμηρότερον.

Ro. 15:15 τολμηροτερῶς Tr, –έρως WH

* τολμηροτερῶς, more boldly.

Ro. 15:15 *for* τολμηρότερον TrWH

5117 τόπος.

Mar. 6:11*add τ. TTrAWHR, *see* δέχομαι
Lu. 4:17 τὸν τ.—*omit* τὸν T[WH]
9:10 *omit* desert place belonging to the TTrAWHR, *see* πόλις
21:11 *trs* καὶ κατὰ τόπους TTrAWHR
Joh. 14: 3 *trs* τόπον ὑμῖν TTrAWH
20:25*τόπον *for* τύπον² (–πος) LT
Acts 1:25*τόπον *for* κλῆρον (–ρος) LTTrAWHR
Heb. 11: 8 τὸν τ.—*omit* τὸν LTTrAWHR
Rev. 18:17*add τ. GEds, *see* πλέω

5118 τοσοῦτος.

Mat. 8:10 *trs* τ. πίστιν ἐν τῷ 'Ισ. LTrAWH
Joh. 14: 9 τοσούτῳ χρόνῳ LT
Heb. 7:22 τοσοῦτο LTTrAWWH
Rev. 21:16 *omit* τ. ἐστιν GEds

5119 τότε.

Mat. 24:30 *omit* then² T
Lu. 11:24*[τ.] λέγει then he saith LWH
Joh. 2:10 *omit* then [L]T[TrA]WHR
10:22*for δέ WH
Acts 21:13*ἀπεκρίθη δέ—τότε ἀ. Eds
1 Co. 13:10 *omit* then Eds
Heb. 9:17*μὴ τ. *for* μήποτε WH

5124 τοῦτο.

Mat. 17:21 *omit the verse* T[TrA]WHR
20:23*ἐμόν—*add* τ. *read* this is not mine TA
23:14(13) *omit* the verse LTTrAWHR, *see* κρίμα
Mar. 14: 9 *omit* τ. *read* the gospel [L]TTrAWHR
36 *trs* τοῦτο ἀπ' ἐμοῦ LTTrAWWH
Lu. 23:46*for ταῦτα LTTrAWHR
24:40 *omit* the verse T[Tr][[WH]]
Joh. 3:32 *omit* that T
7:22 *omit* therefore T
11:28*for ταῦτα TTrAWHR
14:14*for ἐγώ WHR
16:18 *trs* τί ἐστιν τοῦτο LTrWHR
Acts 20:29 *omit* this Eds
28:28*τ. τὸ σωτήριον this salvation LTTrAWHR
1 Co. 6: 8*for ταῦτα Eds
9:23 this—all things, πάντα Eds
1 Co. 11:26 *omit* τ. *read* the cup Eds
15:54 *omit* WH, *see* φθαρτός
2 Co. 12:14*τρίτον—*add* τ. this third time GLTTr[A]WWHR
Eph. 6:18 *omit* τ. LTTrAWHR
3 Joh. 5*for εἰς² Eds
Jude 5 this—all things, πάντα Eds
Rev. 7: 1*for ταῦτα Eds

5125 τούτοις.

Ro. 14:18 these things—this, τούτῳ GEds
Col. 3: 7*for αὐτοῖς Eds
Jude 7 *trs* τρόπον τούτοις Eds

5126 τοῦτον.

Mat. 19:11 *omit* τ. *read* the saying [L]WH
22*λόγον—*add* [τ.], this saying LAWH
21:44 *omit the verse* [L]T[WH]
Joh. 19:13 τούτων Eds, *see* λόγος
Acts 17:23 him—this, τοῦτο Eds
1 Co. 3:12 *omit* τ. *read* the foundation LTTr[A]WHR
11:27 *omit* τ. *read* the bread GEds

5127 τούτου.

Mat. 13:22 *omit* τ. *read* the world LTTrAWHR
40 *omit* τ. *read* the world LTTr[A]WHR
Mar. 4:19 *omit* τ. *read* the world GLTTrAWHR
10:10*for τοῦ αὐτοῦ LTTrAWHR
Joh. 6:51 this—my, ἐμοῦ T
14:30 *omit* τ. *read* the world GEds
Acts 6:13 *omit* τ. *read* the holy GLTTrAW[WH]
25:20 τούτων Eds
Ro. 11: 7 τοῦτο GEds
1 Co. 1:20 *omit* τ.² *read* the world Eds
Eph. 6:12 *omit* of this world W
Jas. 2: 5 *omit* τ. *read* the world GEds
Rev. 19:20 αὐτοῦ GEds

5128 τούτους.

Mat. 7:24 [these] LTrWH
Lu. 19:27*for ἐκείνους (–νος) TTrAWHR
Acts 16:36 *omit* τ. *read* the saying LTrWHR

5129 τούτῳ.

Mar. 6: 2*for αὐτῷ TTrAWHR
Joh. 9:30 *trs* τ. γάρ TTrAWH
Acts 25: 5 ἄτοπος, *read* anything amiss in the man LTTrAWHR: *omit* τ. G
1 Co. 7:31 *omit* τ. *read* the world LTTrAWHR

5130 τούτων.

Mar. 9:37*παιδίων τ. *for* τοιούτων π. T
42*μικρῶν—*add* τ. *read* these little ones A.V.†C LTTr[A]WHR
Joh. 7:31 *omit* τ. Eds
40*add τ. LTTrAWHR, *see* λόγος
Acts 15:28 *omit* these A

5131 τράγος.

Heb. 9:13 *trs* of goats and of bulls Eds
19 τῶν τράγων Eds

5132 τράπεζα.

Lu. 19:23 τὴν τ.—*omit* τὴν Eds

5133 τραπεζίτης, –ζείτης TWH.

5137 τράχηλος.

Ro. 16: 4 *cervices* A.V.Vul

5140 τρεῖς, τρία.

Mar. 9:31* ׀ 10:34*for τρίτῃ (–τος) LTTrAWHR, *see* ἡμέρα
Acts 10:19 *omit* three TA: two, δύο WH
1 Joh. 5: 7, 8 *omit* in heaven (*verse* 7) *to* in earth (*verse* 8) GEds
8 *hi tres* A.V.Vul

5141 τρέμω.

Acts 9: 6 *omit* (it is) hard (*verse* 5) *to* unto him (*verse* 6) GEds
24:25 *tremefactus* A.V.Vul

5142 τρέφω.

Lu. 4:16 ἀνατρέφω T
23:29*ἔθρεψαν *for* ἐθήλασαν (θηλάζω) LTTrAWHR
Rev. 12: 6 τρέφουσιν they feed TTr: ἐκτρέφω W

5143 τρέχω.

Lu. 24:12 *omit the verse* [L]T[Tr][[WH]]

* τρῆμα, a hole.

Mat. 19:24 τρήματος *for* τρυπήματος (–μα) WH
Lu. 18:25 τρήματος *for* τρυμαλιᾶς (–λιά) LTTrAWHR

τριακονταοκτώ.

Joh. 5: 5 τριακόντα καὶ (*omit* καὶ [L]Tr[WH]) ὀκτώ GLTTrAWWH

5154 τρίτος.

Mat. 20: 3 τὴν τ.—*omit* τὴν GLTTrAWWH
26:44 *omit* the third time [L]A
Mar. 9:31 ׀ 10:34 τρεῖς LTTrAWHR, *see* ἡμέρα
Rev. 8: 7*add τ. GEds, *see* γῆ

5159 τροποφορέω.

Acts 13:18 suffered he their manners—he nourished them, τροφοφορέω GLTAW

* τροφοφορέω, to bring nourishment.

Acts 13:18 ἐτροφοφόρησεν *for* ἐτροποφόρησεν (τροποφορέω) GLTAW

5168 τρυμαλιά.

Mar. 10:25 τῆς τ.—*omit* τῆς LTrWWHR
Lu. 18:25 τρῆμα LTTrAWHR

5169 τρύπημα.

Mat. 19:24 τρῆμα WH

5174 Τρωάς.

(Τρῳάς LTWH, except Acts 16:8, 11.)

Acts 16:11 τῆς τ.—*omit* τῆς LTTrAWH

5175 Τρωγύλλιον.

Acts 20:15 Τρωγυλίῳ A: *omit* and tarried at Trogyllium LTTrWHR

5177 τυγχάνω.

Lu. 10:30 *omit* τ. LTTr[A]WHR
Heb. 8: 6 τέτυχεν LTAWWHR

* τυπικῶς, typically.

1 Co. 10:11 *for* τύποι (–πος) Eds

5179 τύπος.

Joh. 20:25 print²—place, τόπος LT
1 Co. 10:11 for ensamples—typically, τυπικῶς Eds
1 Th. 1: 7 τύπον an ensample Eds

5180 τύπτω.

Lu. 22:64 *omit* they struck him on the face, and [L]TTrAWHR

5182 τυρβάζω.

Lu. 10:41 θορυβάζω LTTrAWHR

5185 τυφλός.

Mat. 12:22 τ.¹—τυφλόν LWH
22 *omit* blind² and LTTrAWHR
15:14 *trs* τυφλοί εἰσιν ὁδηγοὶ LTrWH
14 *omit* of the blind WHR
Mar. 10:46 ὁ τ.—*omit* ὁ LTTrAWHR
Lu. 14:21 *trs* the blind and the halt LTTrAWHR
Joh. 9: 6 *omit* of the blind man [L]TTrAWHR
8 blind—a beggar, προσαίτης GEds
18 *trs* ἦν τυφλὸς TTrAWH

5190 Τυχικός, Τύχικος, WH.

5199 ὑγιής.

Mat. 15:31 *omit* the maimed to be whole WH
Mar. 3: 5 *omit* whole as the other GEds
Lu. 6:10 *omit* whole GEds
Joh. 5: 4 *omit* waiting for (*ver.* 3) *to end of verse* 4 [G]TTrAWHR

5200 ὑγρός.

Lu. 23:31 τῷ ὑ.—*omit* τῷ [Tr]WH

5201 ὑδρία.

Joh. 2: 6 *trs* λίθιναι ὑδρίαι LTTrAWHR

5204 ὕδωρ.

Joh. 1:31 τῷ ὕ.—*omit* τῷ LTTr[A]WHR
5: 3, 4 *omit* waiting for (*ver.* 3) *to end of verse* 4 [G]TTrAWHR
Rev. 8:10 τῶν ὑδάτων GEds
11 τρίτον –*add* τῶν ὑδάτων A.V.B EGEds
17: 1 τῶν ὑ.—*omit* τῶν LTTr[A]WHR
22:17 τὸ ὕ.—*omit* τὸ GEds

5208 ὑετός.

Jas. 5: 7 *omit* ὑ. LTTrAWH
Rev. 11: 6 *trs* ὑετὸς βρέχῃ GEds

5207 υἱός.

Mat. 1:25 τὸν υ.—*omit* τὸν LTTrAWHR
9:27 υἱός LTTrA
15:22 υἱός LTTrAWH
18:11 *omit the verse* LTTr[A]WHR
20:30, 31 υἱέ LT
24:36*heaven—*add* οὐδὲ ὁ υἱός nor the Son LTWHR
25:13 *omit* wherein the Son of man cometh GLTTrAWHR
Mar. 1: 1 *omit* the Son of God TWH
10:35 οἱ υ.—*omit* οἱ A
46 ὁ υἱός Eds
47 ὁ υ.—υἱέ LTTrWH
12:37 *trs* αὐτοῦ ἐστιν υ. TTrAWH
Lu. 3:23 *trs* ὢν υ. ὡς ἐνομίζετο LTTrAWHR
4: 9 ὁ υ.—*omit* ὁ GEds
22†*trs* (*omit* ὁ T[Tr]AWH) υ. ἐστιν Ἰωσὴφ οὗτος TAWH
9:41 *trs* τὸν υἱόν σου ὧδε GW
56 *omit* for the Son *to* save (them) GLTTrAWHR
10: 6 ὁ υἱός A.V.BE
14: 5*υἱός *for* ὄνος LTTrAWWH
15:21 *trs* ὁ υἱὸς αὐτῷ AWH
17:26 τοῦ υ.—*omit* τοῦ E
20:44 *trs* αὐτοῦ υἱός TTrAWH
22:22 *trs* ὁ υἱὸς μέν TTrAWHR
24: 7 *trs* τὸν υ. τοῦ ἀνθρώπου ὅτι δεῖ TTrAWHR
Joh. 1:18 Son—God, θεός TrWH
45(46) τὸν υ.—*om.* τὸν LT[Tr]WHR
6:69 that Christ the Son—the holy one ὁ ἅγιος GLTTrAWHR
19: 7 *trs* υ. θεοῦ ἑαυτὸν LTTrAWH
Acts 8:25 οἱ υἱοί GEds
8:37 *omit the verse* GLTTrAWHR
19:14 *trs* υἱοὶ *after* ἑπτὰ LTTrAWHR
Gal. 2:20 τοῦ υἱοῦ τοῦ θεοῦ—τοῦ θ. καὶ χριστοῦ of God and Christ LTr
Col. 3: 6 *omit* on the children of disobedience [L]TTrAWH
1 Joh.2:23**add* υ. A.V.B GEds, *see* ὁμολογέω
5:13 *omit* that believe on the name of the Son of God GEds
Rev. 1:13 υἱόν TWH
14:14 υἱόν TWHR
21: 7 ὁ υἱός—*omit* ὁ Eds
12 τῶν υ.—*omit* τῶν Eds

5209 ὑμᾶς.

Mat. 5:44 *omit* LTTrAWHR, *see* μισέω
44 *omit* LTTrAWHR, *see* ἐπηρεάζω
26:55 *omit* with you T[Tr]AWHR
Lu. 10:11 *omit* unto you GLTTrAWHR
13:27 *omit* you[2] [L]TrAWHR
23:15 ἡμᾶς TWHR, *see* ἀναπέμπω
Acts 13:40 *omit* upon you LTTr[A]WHR
Ro. 12:14 *omit* you WH
13:11*ἤδη ὑ. *for* ἡμᾶς ἤδη TAWHR
15: 7**for* ἡμᾶς GLTTrAWHR
24 *omit* I will come to you GEds
16: 6**for* ἡμᾶς LTTrAWHR
1 Co. 6:14 *for* ἡμᾶς E
7:15**for* ἡμᾶς TWH
10:13 *omit* ὑ.[3] GEds
2 Co. 7:11 *omit* ὑ. LTTr[A]WHR
13: 4 [toward you] AWH
Gal. 4:17 you[2] S—us, ἡμᾶς E
Eph. 5: 2**for* ἡμᾶς TTrAWHR
Col. 1:10 *omit* ὑ. *read* to walk GLTTrA (WHR
12**for* ἡμᾶς TWH
2:13*συνεζωοποίησεν ὑ. you hath he quickened Eds
1 Th. 2:15 ὑ. S—ἡμᾶς A.V.B EGEds
3: 2 *omit* you[2] Eds
4: 8**for* ἡμᾶς Eds
2 Th. 2:17 *omit* ὑ. Eds
1 Pet. 1: 3 *for* ἡμᾶς E
4 ἡμᾶς S—ὑ. A.V.B GEds
3:18**for* ἡμᾶς WH
21**for* ἡμᾶς LTTrAWHR
4:14 *omit* on their part *to end of verse* LTTrAWHR
1 Pet. 5:10**for* ἡμᾶς Eds
10 *omit* ὑ. Eds, *see* καταρτίζω
2 Pet. 3: 9**for* ἡμᾶς LTTrAWHR
Jude 5 *omit* ὑ.[2] Eds
24 αὐτούς S—ὑμᾶς A.V.B EGLTTrWWHR

5210 ὑμεῖς.

Mat. 9: 4 *omit* ὑ. LTTrAWHR
19:28 ye[2]—yourselves, αὐτοί TTr
Mar. 11:26 *omit the verse* TTrWHR
12:27 *omit* ὑ. οὖν T[Tr]AWHR
Lu. 6:31 *omit* ye also [L]WH
9:55 *omit* and said *to end of verse* LTTrAWHR
Joh. 14:20 *trs* ὑ. γνώσεσθε TrAWH, [ὑ.] γ. L
Acts 7:26 *omit* ὑ. LTTr[A]WWHR
2 Co. 6:16 ye—we, ἡμεῖς LTTrWHR
Gal. 4:28**for* ἡμεῖς LTTrA

5212 ὑμέτερος.

Lu. 16:12 your own—our own, ἡμέτερον (-ρος) WH
Ro. 11:31 your S—our, ἡμέτερος E
1 Co. 15:31 ὑμετέραν *for* ἡμετέραν (-ρος) A.V.B EGEds
16:17*ὑμέτερον *for* ὑμῶν LTTrAWWH
2 Co. 8: 8 your S—our, ἡμέτερος E

5213 ὑμῖν.

Mat. 11:17 *omit* unto you[2] LTTrAWHR
20:26 ἐν ὑ.[2]—ὑμῶν A
23:14(13) *omit the verse* LTTrAWHR, *see* κρίμα
Mar. 6:11 *omit* verily *to end of verse* G[L]TTrAWHR
8:12 *omit* unto you [A]WH
Lu. 6:25 *omit* ὑ.[2] TTrAWHR
26 *omit* ὑ. GEds
28 ὑμᾶς GLTTrA
7:32 *omit* to you (ὑ.[2]) TTrWHR
24:36 *omit* T[[WH]], *see* λέγω
Joh. 10:26 *omit* as I said unto you [L]TTr[A]WHR
11:50**for* ἡμῖν TTrAWHR
15:21 εἰς ὑμᾶς LTTrAWHR
16: 3 *omit* unto you GEds
Acts 7:38**for* ἡμῖν WH
13:26 to you[2]—to us, ἡμῖν TAWHR
14:17**for* ἡμῖν GLT[Tr]AWHR
15: 7**for* ἡμῖν LTTrAWHR
16:17 *for* ἡμῖν[2] ETTrWHR
20:27 *trs* ὑ. *after* θεοῦ LTTrAWH
32 *omit* you[3] LTTrAWHR
Ro. 15:32 *omit* and may with you be refreshed L[A]
1 Co. 15:12 *trs* ἐν ὑμῖν τινὲς Eds
2 Co. 2: 3 *omit* unto you Eds
8: 7**see* ἡμῖν
Gal. 1: 8 *omit* unto you[1] T[WH]
3: 1 *omit* among you LTTrAWHR
Eph. 4: 6 you—us, ἡμῖν GW, *omit* you LTTrAWHR
Phil. 1:28 ὑμῶν, *read* but of your salvation Eds
Col. 2:13 ἡμῖν S—ὑ. A.V.BE
2 Th. 3: 4 *omit* you[2] [L]TTrAWHR
Philem. 6 you—us, ἡμῖν GLTrAWWH
Heb. 13:21 you[2]—us, ἡμῖν TWHR
Jas. 1:26 *omit* among you GEds
1 Pet. 1:12**for* ἡμῖν GEds
2:21 *for* ἡμῖν EGEds
1 Joh. 1: 4 ἡμεῖς (*omit* unto you) TTrAWHR
Jude 12 feast with—*add* ὑ. you A.V.C
Rev. 18: 6 *omit* you GEds

5216 ὑμῶν.

Mat. 6:21 your *bis*—thy, σοῦ LTTrAWHR
13:16 *omit* your[2] L[TrAWH]
18:14 your—my, μοῦ LTrWH
Mar. 9:40 you, your S—us, our ἡμῶν *bis* A.V.B ETTrAWWHR
10:44 ὑ.—ἐν ὑμῖν LWHR
11:26 *omit the verse* TTrWHR
13:18 *omit* your flight, *read* it LTTrAWHR
Lu. 9:50**for* ἡμῶν *bis* GLTTrAWHR
12:22 *omit* ὑ. LTTrAWHR
22*σώματι—*add* ὑ. *read* your body [LWH]R
22:53 *trs* ἐστὶν ὑμῶν LTTrAWH
Joh. 6:58 *omit* ὑ. *read* the fathers LTTrAWHR
8:38 *omit* ὑ. LTTrAWHR, *see* πατήρ
54 your—our, ἡμῶν TTrAW
55 ὑμῖν LTrWH
12:35 μεθ' ὑ.—ἐν ὑμῖν among you GLTTrAWHR
15:18 *omit* (it hated) you T
Acts 2:38*ἁμαρτιῶν—*add* ὑ. *read* your sins LTTrWHR
3:22 your[1]—our ἡμῶν T, *omit* your WHR
25**for* ἡμῶν TrAWHR
26 αὐτῶν L, [ὑμῶν] WH
7:37 *omit* your[1] GLTTrAWHR
43 *omit* ὑ. *read* the God LTTrAWHR
14:17**for* ἡμῶν GLTTrAWHR
19:37 your—our, ἡμῶν LTTrAWHR
28:25**for* ἡμῶν LTTrAWHR
Ro. 12: 2 *omit* ὑ. Eds
16:24 *omit the verse* LTTr[A]WHR
1 Co. 6:20 *omit* and in your spirit which are God's GEds
14:26 *omit* of you LTTr[A]WHR
34 *omit* your LTTrAWHR
15:14 your—our, ἡμῶν WH
16:17 ὑμέτερος LTTrAWWH
2 Co. 7:12 your care for us S—our care for you A.V.BEG
13 your—our, ἡμῶν Eds
14**for* ἡμῶν LA
8: 7 ἡμῶν WH, *see* ἡμῖν
19 your—our, ἡμῶν GEds
12:14 *omit* to you[2] LTTrAWHR
Gal. 4: 6 your—our, ἡμῶν GEds
14**for* μου[1] Eds
Eph. 1:16 *omit* of you LTTrAWHR
2: 1*ἁμαρτίαις—*add* ὑ. *read* your trespasses LTTr[A]WHR
5: 2**for* ἡμῶν AWH
6: 9 *see* αὐτῶν
Col. 1: 7 you—us, ἡμῶν LTrAWHR
3: 4**for* ἡμῶν TTr
5 *omit* ὑ. *read* the members TTrAWHR
4: 8 your[1]—our, ἡμῶν LTTrWHR
1 Th. 1: 2 *omit* of you LTTr[A]WHR
2: 4**for* ἡμῶν W
1 Ti. 6:21**for* σοῦ LTTrWHR
Tit. 2: 8 you—us, ἡμῶν GEds
10 ὑ. S—ἡμῶν A.V.BEGEds
Heb. 3:13 *trs* ἐξ ὑμῶν τις GLAW
9:14 your—our, ἡμῶν LAWWH
Jas. 2: 6 ὑμᾶς T
3:14 *cordibus vestris* A.V.Vul
1 Pet. 1: 9 *omit* your WH
2:21 *for* ἡμῶν EGLTTrAWHR
3:16 *omit* of you, as of evildoers TAWHR
2 Pet. 3: 2**for* ἡμῶν Eds
1 Joh. 1: 4 ἡμῶν S—ὑ. A.V.BEGW
2 Joh. 3 ἡμῶν S—ὑ. A.V.BEGLW
12**for* ἡμῶν LTrAWHR
Rev. 22:21 *omit* you GEds

5217 ὑπάγω.

Mar. 2: 9*ὕπαγε *for* περιπάτει (-τέω) T
Lu. 4: 8 *omit* get thee behind me, Satan G[L]TTrAWHR
Joh. 13:33 *trs* ἐγὼ ὑπάγω GEds
16:16 *omit* because I go to the Father TTrAWHR
Rev. 13:10 *vadet* A.V.Vul
14: 4 ὑπάγει LTrAWH
17: 8 ὑπάγει goeth LAWWH

5219 ὑπακούω.

Mat. 8:27 *trs* αὐτῷ ὑπακ. LTTrAWH
Mar. 4:41 ὑπακούει TTrAWH; αὐτῷ ὑ. T
Heb. 5: 9 *trs* πᾶσιν τοῖς ὑ. αὐτῷ LTTrAWHR
1 Pet. 3: 6 ὑπήκουεν LWH

5221 ὑπαντάω.

Mat. 28: 9*ὑπήντησεν *for* ἀπήντησεν (ἀπαντάω) TTrWH
Mar. 5: 2*ὑπήντησεν *for* ἀπήντησεν (ἀπαντάω) LTTrWH
Lu. 14:31*ὑπαντῆσαι *for* ἀπαντῆσαι (-τάω) Eds
17:12*ὑπήντησαν *for* ἀπήντησαν (ἀπαντάω) T
Joh. 4:51*ὑπήντησαν *for* ἀπήντησαν (ἀπαντάω) LTTrAWHR
Acts 16:16*ὑπαντῆσαι *for* ἀπαντῆσαι (-τάω) TTrAWHR

5222 ὑπάντησις.

Mat. 8:34*ὑπάντησιν *for* συνάντησιν (-σις) LTTrWH
25: 1*ὑπάντησιν *for* ἀπάντησιν (-σις) LTTrAWH

5224 ὑπάρχοντα.

Lu. 19: 8 *trs* μου τῶν ὑ. TTrAWH

5225 ὑπάρχω.

Acts 4:34 ὑ.¹—ἦν LTTrWH
14: 8 *omit* being GEds

5228 ὑπέρ.

Mar. 14:24*for περί LTTrAWH
Lu. 6:28 περί TAWH
Joh. 1:30*for περί LTTrAWH
Acts 12: 5 περί LTTrWH
26: 1 περί LTTrA
Ro. 1: 8 περί Eds
8:26 *omit* for us Eds
1 Co. 5: 7 *omit* for us Eds
2 Co. 1: 8 ὑ.¹—περί LTTrR
8: 3 παρά Eds
11: 5 ı 12:11 *see* ὑπερλίαν
Gal. 1: 4 περί GLTTrAW
Col. 1: 3*for περί LTr
2: 1*for περί LTTrAWH
1 Th. 3: 2*for περί GEds
3:10 ı 5:13 *see* ὑπερεκπερισσοῦ
5:10 περί TTrWH
Heb. 5: 3 περί Eds
1 Pet. 4: 1 *omit* for us LTTrAWH

5229 ὑπεραίρομαι.

2 Co. 12: 7 *omit* lest I should be exalted above measure² [L]Tr[A]

5235 ὑπερβάλλω.

Eph. 2: 7 τὸ ὑπερβάλλον πλοῦτος Eds

* ὑπερεκπερισσοῦ, —σῶς.

Eph. 3:20 ı 1 Th. 3:10 ı 5:13 *for* ὑπὲρ ἐκ περισσοῦ GEds

5240 ὑπερεκχύνομαι.

Lu. 6:38 ὑπερεκχυννόμενον LTTrAWH

* ὑπερλίαν.

2 Co. 11: 5 ı 12:11 *for* ὑπὲρ λίαν GLTAWWH

5257 ὑπηρέτης.

Joh. 7:32 *trs* ὑ. οἱ ἀρχ. καὶ οἱ Φ. T

5259 ὑπό.

Mat. 2:17 ı 3: 3 διά Eds
27:35 *omit* that it might *to end of verse* GLTTrAWH
28:14*for ἐπί LTr
Mar. 8:31*for ἀπό Eds
13:14 *omit* spoken of by Daniel the prophet G[L]TTrAWH
Lu. 1:26 ἀπό TTrAWH
5:15 *omit* by him LTTrAWH
6:18 ἀπό GEds
8:29 ἀπό WH
43 ἀπό LTTrAWH
9: 7 *omit* by him [L]TTrAWH
Joh. 8: 9 *omit* WH, *see* ἐλέγχω
10:14 *omit* ὑ. LTTrAWH, *see* γινώσκω
Acts 4:36 ἀπό Eds
10:17*for ἀπό TWH
33 ἀπό LA
15: 4 ἀπό TrWH
22:30*for παρά Eds
23:30 *omit* ὑ. LTTrAWH
24:21 ἐπί Eds
Ro. 13: 1*for ἀπό LTTrWH
15:15 ἀπό TTrWH
24 ἀπό LA
1 Co. 9:20*add ὑ. GEds, *see* νόμος
Jas. 1:14 ἀπό A
5:12 *for* εἰς A.V.B EGEds, *see* ὑπόκρισις
Rev. 9:18 by¹—from ἀπό GEds

5270 ὑποκάτω.

Mat. 22:44*ὑποκάτω *for* ὑποπόδιον LTTrAWH
Mar. 12:36*ὑποκάτω *for* ὑποπόδιον AWH

5272 ὑπόκρισις.

Lu. 12: 1 *trs* ἥτις ἐστὶν ὑ. τῶν Φα. WH
Jas. 5:12 εἰς ὑπόκρισιν S—ὑπὸ κρίσιν A.V.B EGEds
1 Pet. 2: 1 ὑπόκρισιν WH

5273 ὑποκριτής.

Mat. 16: 3 *omit* O (ye) hypocrites LTTrAWH
23:14(13) *omit the verse* LTTrAWH, *see* κρίμα
Lu. 11:44 *omit* scribes and Pharisees, hypocrites G[L]TTrAWH
13:15 ὑποκριταί ye hypocrites Eds

5274 ὑπολαμβάνω.

3 Joh. 8*ὑπολαμβάνειν *for* ἀπολαμβάνειν (-νω) Eds

* ὑπόλειμμα, remainder.

Ro. 9:27 ὑπόλειμμα (-λιμμα WH) *for* κατάλειμμα LTTrAWH

5278 ὑπομένω.

Acts 17:14 ὑπέμειναν LA, -αν TTrWH
Jas. 5:11 ὑπομείναντας endured LTTrAWH

5281 ὑπομονή.

2 Th. 3: 5 τὴν ὑπομονὴν A.V.C GEds
Rev. 2: 3 *trs* hast patience, and hast borne GEds
14:12 ἡ ὑπομονή Eds

5282 ὑπονοέω.

Acts 25:18 *trs* ἐγὼ ὑπενόουν Eds

5286 ὑποπόδιον.

Mat. 22:44 ὑποκάτω, *read* enemies under thy feet LTTrAWH
Mar. 12:36 ὑποκάτω, *read* enemies under thy feet AWH

5290 ὑποστρέφω.

Mar. 14:40 when he returned—he came, ἔρχομαι LTTrAWH
Lu. 2:20*ὑπέστρεψαν *for* ἐπέστρεψαν (ἐπιστρέφω) GEds
39 ἐπιστρέφω TWH
8:40 ὑποστρέφειν TWH
Acts 8:25 ὑπέστρεφον Eds
2 Pet. 2:21*ὑποστρέψαι *for* ἐπιστρέψαι (-στρέφω) LTTrAWH

5293 ὑποτάσσω.

1 Co. 14:34 ὑποτασσέσθωσαν let them be under obedience LTTrWH
Eph. 5:22 *om* submit yourselves TAWH: ὑποτασσέσθωσαν LTr
1 Pet. 5: 5 *omit* be subject Eds

5302 ὑστερέω.

Joh. 2: 3 *omit* ὑ. T, *see* οἶνος
1 Co. 12:24 ὑστερουμένῳ LTTrAWH

5305 ὕστερον.

Mat. 21:29 *trs* WH, *see* ἀπέρχομαι
Lu. 4: 2 *omit* afterward LTTrAWH

5306 ὕστερος.

Mat. 21:31*for πρῶτος LTrWH

* ὑφαινω, to weave.

Lu. 12:27 ὑφαίνει *for* κοπιᾷ TA, *see* κοπιάω

5308 ὑψηλός.

Lu. 4: 5 *omit* into an high mountain [L]TTrAWH
See also ὑψηλοφρονέω.

5309 ὑψηλοφρονεω.

Ro. 11:20 ὑψηλὰ φρόνει TTrWH
1 Ti. 6:17 ὑψηλὰ φρονεῖν T

5310 ὕψιστος.

Lu. 6:35 τοῦ ὑ.—*omit* τοῦ GLTTrAWWH
Heb. 7: 1 τοῦ ὑ.—*omit* τοῦ A.V.CB

5311 ὕψος.

Eph. 3:18 *trs* height and depth LTrAWH

5312 ὑψόω.

Mat. 11:23 ἡ...ὑ.—μὴ...ὑψωθήσῃ; shalt thou be exalted? LTTrAWH, ἡ (ὅς)...ὑψώθης W
Lu. 10:15 ἡ...ὑ.—μὴ ὑψωθήσῃ; shalt thou be exalted? LTTrAWH

5315 φάγω.

Mat. 12: 4 ἔφαγεν—ἔφαγον LTWH
Mar. 8: 9 *om.* that had eaten T[Tr]AWH (B
14:22 *omit* eat GEds
Lu. 9:13 *trs* φαγεῖν ὑμεῖς LTAWH
1 Co. 11:24 *omit* take, eat GEds
Rev. 2:17 *omit* to eat of GEds

5341 φαιλόνης, φελόνης EGLTTrAWWH.

5316 φαίνω.

Mat. 2:13†*trs* κατ' ὄναρ φ. (ἐφάνη L) LTr
19 *trs* φαίνεται κατ' ὄναρ LTTrAWH
Rev. 8:12 φάνῃ LTWWH, φανῇ TrA
18:23 φάνῃ A.V.Vul LTWH

5317 Φαλέκ, Φάλεκ LTrWH.

νεφάλεος, —λιος, 1 Tim. EGEds.

5318 φανερός.

Mat. 6: 4 *omit* openly Eds
6 *omit* openly LTTrAWH
18 *omit* openly GEds
Mar. 3:12 *trs* φανερὸν αὐτὸν GW
4:22 *trs* ἔλθῃ εἰς φανερόν TTrAWH

5319 φανερόω.

2 Co. 11: 6 φανερώσαντες *read* we have made (it) manifest LTTrAWH

5330 Φαρισαῖος.

Mat. 15: 1 *trs* Pharisees and scribes TTrWH, *omit* οἱ LTTrWH
16:12*add Φ. T, *see* ἄρτος
19: 3 οἱ Φ.—*omit* οἱ LTrAWH
23:14(13) *omit the verse* LTTrAWH, *see* κρίμα
Mar. 2:16 καὶ οἱ Φ.—τῶν Φαρισαίων καί *omit* (καί WH), *read* scribes of the Pharisees TTrWH
18 οἱ τῶν Φ.¹—οἱ Φαρισαῖοι (*omit* of) GEds
9:11*say—*add* οἱ Φαρισαῖοι καί the Pharisees and [L]T
10: 2 οἱ Φ.—*omit* οἱ GLTrAWWH
Lu. 5:30 *trs* Pharisees and their scribes Eds
11:44 *omit* scribes and Pharisees, hypocrites G[L]TTrAWH
14: 1 [τῶν] Φ. AWH
Joh. 7:32 *trs* the chief priests and the Pharisees Eds
18: 3 τῶν Φαρισαίων LTTrWH, [τῶν] Φ. A
Acts 23: 6 Φ.³—Φαρισαίων, *read* son of Pharisees Eds

5331 φαρμακεία.

Gal. 5:20 φαρμακία WH
Rev. 9:21 φαρμακιῶν T, φαρμακός AWH
18:23 φαρμακίᾳ TAWH

5332 φαρμακεύς.

Rev. 21: 8 φαρμακός GEds

5333 φαρμακός.

Rev. 9:21*φαρμάκων *for* φαρμακειῶν (-κεία) AWH
21: 8*φαρμακοῖς *for* φαρμακεῦσιν (-κεύς) GEds

5335 φάσκω.

Rev. 2: 2 λέγω GEds

5336 φάτνη.

Lu. 2: 7 τῇ φ.—*omit* τῇ LTTrAWH
12 τῇ φ.—*omit* τῇ GEds

5337 φαῦλος.

Ro. 9:11*φαῦλον *for* κακόν (-κός) LTTrAWH
2 Co. 5:10*φαῦλον *for* κακόν (-κός) TTrWH

5338 φέγγος.

Lu. 11:33 φῶς LTrAWH

5339 φείδομαι.

Ro. 11:21 φ.²—φείσεται, *read* neither will he spare GEds

φελόνης, *see* φαιλόνης. See 5341

5342 φέρω, οἴσω, ἤνεγκα.

Mat. 7:18*ἐνεγκεῖν *for* ποιεῖν¹ (-έω) TWH *for* π.² T
Mar. 2: 3 *trs* πρὸς αὐτὸν φ. παραλ. LTr φ. πρὸς αὐτὸν παραλ. TAWH
6:27 ἐνέγκαι, *read* (him) to bring his head TTrAWH
11: 2*φέρετε *for* ἀγάγετε (ἄγω) TTrAWH
7*φέρουσιν *for* ἤγαγον (ἄγω) TTrAWH
Lu. 15:23 ἐνέγκαντες—φέρετε TTrAWH
Acts 25: 7 καταφέρω LTTrAWH
18*ἔφερον *for* ἐπέφερον (ἐπιφέρω) Eds

5343 φεύγω.

Mar. 14:50 *trs* ἔφυγον πάντες TTrAWH
Joh. 6:15*φεύγει *for* ἀνεχώρησεν (ἀναχωρέω) T
10:13 *omit* the hireling **fleeth** [L]TTrAWHR
Heb. 12:25 ἐκφεύγω LTTrAWHR
Rev. 9: 6 φεύγει fleeth LTTrAWHR

5346 φημί

Mat. 13:29 φησίν saith LTTrAWHR
19:18*λέγει (ἔφη L) αὐτῷ, ποίας;—ποίας; φησίν, which? saith he T
18*ἔφη *for* εἶπεν (-πον) WH
22:37*ἔφη *for* εἶπεν GLTTrAWWH
Mar. 9:12*ἔφη *for* εἶπεν (-πον) TTrAWHR
38*ἔφη *for* ἀπεκρίθη (ἀποκρίνομαι) TTrAWHR
10:20*ἔφη *for* εἶπεν (-πον) TTrAWHR
29*ἔφη ὁ Ἰησοῦς *for* ὁ Ἰ. εἶπεν TAWHR
12:24*trs ἔφη (ἔ. *for* εἶπεν) αὐτοῖς ὁ Ἰησοῦς TTrAWHR
Lu. 15:17*ἔφη *for* εἶπεν (-πον) TWHR
22:58*ἔφη *for* εἶπεν (-πον) TTrAWHR
23:40*ἔφη *for* λέγων (-γω) TTrAWHR
Joh. 18:29*φησίν *for* εἶπεν(-πον) TTrAWHR
Acts 2:38 *omit* ἔφη LTTrAWHR
38*μετανοήσατε—*add* φησίν T
25:22 *omit* ἔφη LTTrAWHR
26:24 φησίν saith LTTrAWHR
28 *omit* ἔφη Eds

* φημίζω, to speak, report.

Mat. 28:15 ἐφημίσθη *for* διεφημίσθη (διαφημίζω) T

5349 φθαρτός.

1 Co. 15:54 *omit* this corruptible shall have put on incorruption, and WH

5350 φθέγγομαι.

Acts 4:18 τὸ...φ.—*omit* τὸ LTWH

5351 φθείρω.

2 Pet. 2:12*καὶ φθαρήσονται *for* καταφθαρήσονται (-θείρω) Eds

5359 Φιλαδέλφεια, —φία TWH.

φιλέω.

Rev. 22:15 ὁ φ.—*omit* ὁ LTTrAWWH: *trs* maketh and loveth T

5372 Φιλητός, Φίλητος WH.

5376 Φίλιππος.

Mat. 14: 3 *omit* Philip [T]A
Lu. 3:19 *omit* Philip GEds
Joh. 1:46(47) ὁ Φίλιππος LTrAWH
6: 5 τὸν Φ.—*omit* τὸν LTTrAWH
7 ὁ Φίλιππος T
12:22 Φ.[1]—ὁ Φίλιππος TrAWH
Acts 8:37 *omit the verse* GLTTrAWHR

5384 φίλος.

Lu. 11: 8 *trs* φίλον αὐτοῦ TTrAWH
Acts 27: 3 τοὺς φίλους A.V.C GEds

5389 φιλοτιμέομαι.

Ro. 15:20 φιλοτιμοῦμαι LTr

5391 φιλόφρων.

1 Pet. 3: 8 courteous—humble minded, ταπεινόφρων GEds

5392 φιμόω.

1 Co. 9: 9 κημόω TTrA
1 Pet. 2:15 φιμοῖν WH

5395 φλόξ.

2 Th. 1: 8 φλογὶ πυρός a flame of fire LTrW
Rev. 2:18 φλόξ T

5399 φοβέομαι.

Mat. 9: 8*ἐφοβήθησαν *for* ἐθαύμασαν (θαυμάζω) LTTrAWHR
10:28 φ.[1]—φοβεῖσθε GLTTrW
28 φ.[2]—φοβεῖσθε TAWH
31 φοβεῖσθε LTTrAWH
Acts 23:10*φοβηθεὶς *for* εὐλαβηθεὶς (-βέομαι) LTTrAWHR

5400 φόβητρον, —θρον LTrAWH.

5401 φόβος.

Acts 2:43*add at end ἐν Ἰερουσαλήμ, φόβος τε ἦν μέγας ἐπὶ πάντας in Jerusalem, and great fear was upon all T
Jude 23 οὓς δὲ (*omit* οὓς δὲ WH) σώζετε ἐκ πυρὸς ἁρπάζοντες, οὓς δὲ ἐλεᾶτε (ἐλεεῖτε W) ἐν φόβῳ and some save, snatching (them) out of the fire; and on some have mercy with fear Eds

5404 φοῖνιξ.

Rev. 7: 9 φοίνικας T

5407 φονεύω.

Mar. 10:19 *trs* do not kill, do not commit adultery LWHR
Jas. 2:11 φ.[2]—φονεύεις LTTrAWHR

5408 φόνος.

Mar. 7:21, 22 *trs* fornications, thefts, murders, adulteries TTrAWHR
Gal. 5:21 *omit* murders [L]T[TrA]WHR

5409 φορέω.

1 Co. 15:49 φ.[2]—φορέσωμεν let us bear LTTrWH

5413 φορτίον.

Acts 27:10*φορτίου *for* φόρτου (-τος) GEds

5414 φόρτος.

Acts 27:10 φορτίον GEds

5415 Φουρτουνάτος, Φορ— Eds.

5419 φράζω.

Mat. 13:36 declare—explain, διασαφέω LTrWHR

5420 φράσσω.

2 Co. 11:10 *see* σφραγίζω

5422 φρεναπατάω.

Gal. 6: 3 *trs* φ. ἑαυτόν LTTrAWHR

5426 φρονέω.

Ro. 14: 6 *omit* LTTr[A]WHR, *see* κύριος
1 Co. 4: 6 *omit* to think (of men) Eds
Phil. 2: 5 φρονεῖτε LTTrAWHR
3:16 *omit* rule, let us mind the same thing GLTTrAWHR
See also ὑψηλοφρονέω.

5429 φρόνιμος.

Mat. 25: 2 *trs* foolish & wise LTTrAWHR
Lu. 12:42 ὁ φρόνιμος Eds

5436 Φύγελλος, —ελος Eds.

5437 φυγή.

Mar. 13:18 *omit* your flight LTTrAWHR

5438 φυλακή.

Mat. 14: 3 τῇ φυλακῇ LTrA
Mar. 6:17 τῇ φ.—*omit* τῇ GEds
Lu. 3:20 τῇ φ.—*omit* τῇ LTTrAWHR
12:38 *omit* watch[1] TTrAWHR
23:19 εἰς φ.—ἐν τῇ φυλακῇ TTrAWHR
25 τὴν φ.—*omit* τὴν LTTrAWHR
2 Co. 11:23 *trs* in prisons more frequent, in stripes above measure LTrAWHR, *see* περισσοτέρως

5442 φυλάσσω.

Mat. 19:20 ἐφύλαξα LTTrAWH
Lu. 18:21 ἐφύλαξα LTTrAWH
Joh. 12:47*φυλάξῃ *for* πιστεύσῃ (-τεύω) Eds
Acts 21:24 *trs* φ. τὸν νόμον LTTrAWWH

5449 φύσις.

1 Co. 11:14 *trs* ἡ φύσις αὐτὴ Eds
Gal. 4: 8 *trs* φύσει μὴ GEds

5455 φωνέω.

Mar. 1:26*φωνῆσαν *for* κράξαν (κράζω) TTrAWHR
3:31 καλέω LTTrAWH
10:49 εἶπεν, φωνήσατε αὐτόν said, Call ye him TTrAWHR
14:68 *omit* and the cock crew [L]WH
72 *trs* δὶς φωνῆσαι LTrAWH

Joh. 10: 3*φωνεῖ *for* καλεῖ (-λέω) LTTrAWHR
13:38 φωνήσῃ LTTrAWHR

5456 φωνή.

Mat. 24:31 *omit* φ. *read* with a great trumpet TWH
Lu. 1:42 voice—cry, κραυγή TTrAWHR
Joh. 12:30 *trs* ἡ φωνὴ αὕτη LTTrAWWH
Acts 11: 9 *trs* ἐκ δευτέρου φωνή WH
14:10 τῇ φ.—*omit* τῇ LTTrWHR
1 Co. 14: 8 *trs* σάλπιγξ φωνὴν TWH
Rev. 4: 5 *trs* voices and thunderings GEds
6: 1 φωνή GLTTrAWR, φωνῇ WH
7 *omit* the voice of G[Tr]W
8: 5 *trs* thunderings and voices TTrAWHR
10: 4 *omit* their voices GEds
11:12 φωνῆς μεγάλης TrAWHR
14: 2 φ. ἤκουσα—ἡ φωνὴ ἣν ἤκουσα ὡς the voice which I heard (was) as GEds
18*φωνῇ *for* κραυγῇ LTTrWHR
16:18 *trs* lightnings and voices and thunders GEds

5457 φῶς.

Mar. 14:54 τὸ φ.—*omit* τὸ R
Lu. 11:33*φῶς *for* φέγγος LTrAWHR
Eph. 5: 9*φωτὸς *for* πνεύματος(-μα) GEds
Rev. 21:24†*trs* περιπατήσουσιν τὰ ἔθνη διὰ τοῦ φωτὸς αὐτῆς GEds
22: 5*φωτὸς λύχνου light of a candle LTTrAWHR
5 φωτός—φῶς WH

5460 φωτεινός, —τινός WH.

5461 φωτίζω.

Rev. 22: 5 φωτιεῖ (-ίσει LWHR) ἐπ' ([ἐπ'] WH) shall give them light GEds

5463 χαίρω.

Lu. 6:23 χάρητε GEds
Ro. 16:19 *trs* ἐφ' ὑμῖν οὖν χ. Eds
Rev. 11:10 χαίρουσιν rejoice GEds

5472 χαλκηδών, χαλκε— T.

5479 χαρά.

Lu. 15:10 *trs* γίνεται χαρὰ TTrAWHR
Acts 20:24 *omit* with joy LTTrAWHR
2 Co. 1:15*χαράν *for* χάριν (-ρις) WH
Philem. 7 *see* χάρις
3 Joh. 4 joy—thankfulness, χάρις WH

5480 χάραγμα.

Rev. 15: 2 *omit* over his mark (and) GEds

5483 χαρίζομαι.

2 Co. 2:10†*trs* ὃ κεχ. εἴ τι κεχ. GEds

5485 χάρις.

Lu. 17: 9 *trs* ἔχει χάριν LTTrAWH
Acts 6: 8*χάριτος *for* πίστεως (-τις)GEds
24:27 χάριτα Eds
Ro. 7:25*χάρις *for* εὐχαριστῶ (-τέω) LTTrAWH
11: 6 *omit* but if (it be) of works *to end of verse* GLTTr[A]WHR
16:24 *omit the verse* LTTr[A]WHR
2 Co. 1:15 χαρά WH
Eph. 4: 7 ἡ χ.—*omit* ἡ LTr[AWH]
Col. 3:16 τῇ χάριτι LTTrAW
Philem. 7 χάριν S—χαράν (-ρά) A.V.C EGEds
3 Joh. 4*χάριν *for* χαράν (-ρά) WH
Jude 4 χάριτα LTTrAWWH

5494 χειμών.

Mat. 16: 3 When it is (*ver.* 2) *to end of verse* 3 [TA] [[WH]]

5495 χείρ.

Mat. 12:10 τὴν χ.—*omit* τὴν LTTrAWHR
13 *trs* σου τὴν χεῖρα LTTrAWH
19:15 *trs* τὰς χεῖρας αὐτοῖς LTTrAWH
26:23 *trs* τὴν χ. ἐν τῷ τρυ. LTTrAWHR
Mar. 5:23 *trs* τὰς χεῖρας αὐτῇ LTTrAWH
9:27 τῆς χ. αὐτοῦ LTTrWHR
16:18*add at commencement καὶ ἐν ταῖς χερσίν and in (their) hands Tr[WH]
Lu. 24:40 *omit the verse* T[Tr][[WH]]
Joh. 20:25 *trs* μου τὴν χεῖρα TTrAWH

Acts 2:23 χειρός, *read* the hand of lawless (men) LTTrAWHR
9:12 (τὰς L[WH]R) χεῖρας hands LTTrWHR
19: 6 τὰς χ.—*omit* τὰς LTTrAWHR
21:11 *trs* feet and hands Eds
27 *trs* ἐπ' αὐτὸν τὰς χ. GLTTrAWWH
24: 7 *omit* LTTr[A]WHR, *see* κρίνω
Heb. 2: 7 *omit* and didst set *to end of verse* G[L]T[Tr]A[WH]
1 Pet. 5: 6 χεῖραν T
Rev. 1:16 *trs* χειρὶ αὐτοῦ LTTrAWHR
17 *omit* χ. GEds
19: 2 τῆς χ.—*omit* τῆς GEds

5502 Χερουβίμ, –βείν LTTrWH, –βίν A.

5503 χήρα.
Mat. 23:14(13) *omit the verse* LTTrAWHR, *see* κρίμα

5504 χθές, ἐχθές Eds.

5506 χιλίαρχος.
Acts 21:32 τὸν χ.—*omit* τὸν W
24: 7 *omit* LTTr[A]WHR, *see* κρίνω
25:23 τοῖς χ.—*omit* τοῖς LTTrAWHR
Rev. 6:15 *trs* chief captains, and the rich men GEds

5507 χίλιοι.
Rev. 20: 4 τὰ χ.—*omit* τὰ A.V.C Eds
6 τὰ χίλια TTr, [τὰ] χ. AWH

5510 χιών.
Mar. 9: 3 *omit* as snow TTrAWHR

5512 χλευάζω.
Acts 2:13 διαχλευάζω GEds

5516 χξς'.
Rev. 13:18 ἑξακόσιοι ἑξήκοντα ἕξ LAWH

5519 χοῖρος.
Mat. 8:32 τῶν χ.[1]–τοὺς χοίρους GLTTrWHR
32 *omit* of swine[2] GLTTr[A]WHR
Mar. 5:14 the swine—them, αὐτούς GEds

5523 Χοραζίν, –ζείν TTrAWH.
Lu. 10:13 Χωραζίν S, Χο- EGLTTrAWWH

5524 χορηγέω.
2 Co. 9:10 χορηγήσει will minister GEds

5526 χορτάζω.
Lu. 15:16* χορτασθῆναι *for* γεμίσαι (–μίζω) WHR, *see* κοιλία

5528 χόρτος.
Mat. 14:19 τοῦ χόρτου LTTrWH

5530 χράομαι.
1 Co. 9:15 οὐ κέχρημαι οὐδενί GEds

5532 χρεία.
Joh. 13:10 οὐκ ἔχει χ. LTTrAWWH
Acts 28:10 τὴν χ.—τὰς χρείας Eds

5533 χρεωφειλέτης, χρεοφ– LTTrA, χρεοφιλ– WH.

5536 χρῆμα.
Mar. 10:24 τοῖς χ.—*omit* τοῖς LTrAWR, *omit* for them that trust in riches TWH

5543 χρηστός.
Lu. 5:39 better—good χρηστός TTrAWHR
1 Co. 15:33 χρηστά GTTrAWWH

5544 χρηστότης.
Ro. 11:22 goodness[2]—χρηστότης θεοῦ goodness of God LTTrAWHR

5547 Χριστός.
Mat. 16:21* Ἰησοῦς—*add* χριστός WH
23: 8 *omit* (even) Christ GEds
Lu. 4:41 *omit* Christ[1] GLTTrAWHR
23:39† *trs* οὐχὶ (o. *for* εἰ) σὺ εἶ ὁ χ. TTrAWHR
Joh. 1:41(42) ὁ χ.—*omit* ὁ GEds
4:42 *omit* the Christ LTTrAWHR
6:69 *omit* χ. GLTTrAWHR, *see* υἱός
7:42 *trs* ἔρχεται ὁ χριστός LTrAWHR
Acts 2:30 *omit* according to the flesh, he would raise up Christ GLTTrAWHR
36 *trs* αὐτὸν καὶ χ. GEds
3:20 *trs* Christ Jesus LTTrAWHR
4:33* Jesus—*add* χριστοῦ Christ, [L]T, *trs* 'I. χ. τοῦ κυρίου T, τοῦ κυρ. 'I. ([χ.]L) τῆς ἀν. LWH
5:42 *trs* Christ Jesus LTTrAWHR
8:37 *omit the verse* GLTTrAWHR
9:20 Christ—Jesus, Ἰησοῦς GEds
34 ὁ χ.—*omit* ὁ LTTrWWHR
10:48* Ἰησοῦ χριστοῦ *for* τοῦ κυρίου (–ος) LTTrWHR
15:11 *omit* Christ GTTrAWWHR
16:31 *omit* Christ LTTrAWHR
17: 3 ὁ χ.—*omit* ὁ LTTr
19: 4 *omit* Christ GLTTrAWHR
20:21 *omit* Christ L[Tr]AWH
28:31 *omit* Christ T
Ro. 1: 1 *trs* Christ Jesus TTr
16 *omit* of Christ GEds
2:16 *trs* Christ Jesus TWH
6: 3, 11 *trs* Jesus Christ A.V. [?]
8:11 τὸν χ.—*omit* τὸν LTTrAWHR
10:17* χριστοῦ *for* θεοῦ (–ός) LTTrA
14:10 Christ—God, θεός Eds (WHR
18 τῷ χ.—*omit* τῷ L[Tr]
15: 5 *trs* Jesus Christ Tr
16 *trs* Christ Jesus Eds
29 τοῦ χ.—*omit* τοῦ GEds
16:20 *omit* Christ T[Tr]A]WH
24 *omit the verse* LTTr[A]WHR
1 Co. 1: 1 *trs* Christ Jesus LTTrAW
3:11 ὁ χ.—*omit* ὁ GEds
5: 4 *omit* Christ *bis* LTTrAWHR
6:11* Jesus—*add* χριστοῦ Christ LTTrWHR
9: 1 *omit* Christ LTTrAWHR
18 *omit* of Christ Eds
21 χριστοῦ of Christ Eds
10: 9 Christ—the Lord κύριος LTTrAWHR
11: 3 χ.[2]—τοῦ χριστοῦ [L]TTrAWHR
15:23 χ.[2]—τοῦ χριστοῦ GEds
16:22 *omit* Jesus Christ LTTrAWHR
23 *omit* Christ TTrAWH
2 Co. 1: 1 *trs* Christ Jesus TTrAWHR
5 χ.[2]—τοῦ χριστοῦ GEds
19 *trs* Christ Jesus TWH
6:15 χριστοῦ LTTrAWHR
10: 7 *omit* Christ[3] GEds
11: 3 τὸν χ.—*omit* τὸν T
31 *omit* Christ LTTrAWHR
13: 5 *trs* Christ Jesus TTr
Gal. 2:16 χ.[1]—*trs* Christ Jesus TTrWH
16 χ.[2]—*trs* Jesus Christ A.V.[?]
20* *add* χ. LTr, *see* υἱός
3:14 *trs* Jesus Christ A.V.[?] TrWH
17 *omit* in Christ LTTrAWHR
4: 7 *omit* χ. *read* heir through God LTTrAWHR
5: 1 *trs* ἡμᾶς χριστὸς GEds
4 τοῦ χ.—*omit* τοῦ LTTr[A]WH
6:15 *omit* in Christ Jesus TTrAWHR
Eph. 1: 1 *trs* Christ Jesus[1] LTTrAWHR
2:20 *trs* Christ Jesus LTTrAWHR
3: 6 τῷ χ.—*omit* τῷ LTTrAWHR
9 *omit* by Jesus Christ GEds
11 τῷ χριστῷ LTTrAWHR
14 *omit* of our Lord Jesus Christ Eds
4:15 ὁ χ.—*omit* ὁ Eds
5:21* χριστοῦ *for* θεοῦ (–ός) GEds
29* χριστός *for* κύριος GEds
6: 6 τοῦ χ.—*omit* τοῦ LTTrAWWH
Phil. 1: 1 *trs* Christ Jesus[1] Eds
2 *trs* Christ Jesus W
6 *trs* Christ Jesus LTTrAW
8 *trs* Christ Jesus GEds
16 [τὸν] χ. LTrA
2:21 *trs* Jesus Christ A.V.Vul GLTrAWR: *omit* τοῦ GLTTrAWWH
30 *omit* of Christ A: of (the) Lord, κύριος WH: *omit* τοῦ LTTrAWHR
3:12 τοῦ χ.—*omit* τοῦ GEds
4:13 *omit* Christ GEds
Col. 1: 1 *trs* Christ Jesus Eds
2 *omit* and the Lord Jesus Christ G[L]TTrAWWHR
2: 2 *omit* and of Christ GA: *omit* τοῦ GEds
17 τοῦ χ.—*omit* τοῦ GW
20 τῷ χ.—*omit* τῷ GEds
3:13 Christ—the Lord, κύριος LTrAWHR
15* χριστοῦ *for* θεοῦ (–ός) GEds
17* κυρίου Ἰησοῦ—Ἰ. χριστοῦ LW
1 Th. 1. 1 *omit* from God *to end of verse* [L]TTrAWHR
1 Th. 2:19 | 3:11 *omit* Christ LTTrAWHR
3:13 *omit* Christ Eds
2 Th. 1: 8 *omit* Christ [L]TTrAWHR
12 *omit* Christ[1] [L]TTrAWWHR
2: 2 Christ—the Lord, κύριος GEds
3:12 χριστῷ LTTrAWHR, *see* κύριος
1 Ti. 1: 1 *trs* Christ Jesus[1] TTrAWWHR
1 *trs* Christ Jesus[2] GEds
2 *trs* Jesus Christ A.V. Er
16 *trs* Christ Jesus LTrAWH
2: 7 *omit* in Christ GEds
4: 6 *trs* Christ Jesus Eds
5:21 *t.* Christ Jesus(*om.* Lord) Eds
2 Ti. 1: 1 *trs* Christ Jesus[1] TTrAWWHR
10 *trs* Christ Jesus LTTrWHR
2: 3 *trs* Christ Jesus Eds
19 Christ—(the) Lord, κύριος GEds
4: 1 *trs* Christ Jesus (*omit* Lord) Eds
22 *omit* Christ LTTr[A]WHR
Tit. 1: 4 *trs* Christ Jesus (*omit* Lord) LTTrAWHR
2:13 *trs* Christ Jesus TTrWH
Philem. 9 *trs* Christ Jesus LTTrAWHR
20* χριστῷ *for* κυρίῳ[2] (–ριος) GEds
Heb. 3: 1 *omit* Christ GEds
9:24 ὁ χ.—*omit* ὁ Eds
1 Pet. 3:15* χριστόν *for* θεόν (–ός) Eds
1 Joh. 1: 7 *omit* Christ LTTrAWHR
4: 3 *om.* Christ is come in the flesh GLTTrAWHR, *omit* Christ W
5: 6 ὁ χ.—*omit* ὁ TTrAWWHR
2 Joh. 9 *omit* of Christ[2] Eds
Jude 25* *add* χ. GEds, *see* κύριος
Rev. 1: 9 *trs* Christ Jesus[1] W
9 *omit* Christ *bis* LTTrAWHR
12:17 *omit* Christ GLTTrAWWHR
20: 4 χριστοῦ S—τοῦ χ. EGEds
22:21 *omit* Christ LTTrA[WH]R

5549 χρονίζω.
Heb. 10:37 χρονίσει TTrWH

5550 χρόνος.
Lu. 8:27 καὶ χρόνῳ ἱκανῷ οὐκ ἐνεδύσατο ἱμάτιον and for a long time had worn no clothes TTrWHR
23: 8* θέλων ἐξ ἱκανοῦ—ἐξ ἱκανῶν χρόνων θέλων of a long time LTTrAWHR
Joh. 7:33 *trs* χρόνον μικρὸν LTTrAWH
14: 9 τοσούτῳ χρόνῳ LT
Jude 18 ἐπ' ἐσχάτου (*add* τοῦ LT[A]) χρόνου at the end of the time Eds

5552 χρύσεος, –σοῦς.
Rev. 1:13 χρυσᾶν LTTrAWH
2: 1 χρυσέων LTrA
4: 4 χρυσέους Tr
5: 8 χρυσέας Tr

5553 χρυσίον.
1 Co. 3:12* χρυσίον *f.* χρυσόν (ός, TTrWHR
1 Ti. 2: 9* χρυσίῳ *for* χρυσῷ (–σός) LWHR
Rev. 17: 4* χρυσίῳ *for* χρυσῷ (–σός) GLAWWHR
18:16* χρυσίῳ *for* χρυσῷ (–σός) GLTrAWWHR

5557 χρυσός.
1 Co. 3:12 χρυσίον TTrWHR
1 Ti. 2: 9 χρυσίον LWHR
Rev. 17: 4 χρυσίον GLAWWHR
18:16 χρυσίον GLTrAWWHR

5560 χωλός.
Mat. 18: 8 *trs* maimed or halt LTWHR
Lu. 14:21 *trs* the blind and the halt LTTrAWHR
Acts 3:11 *omit* GEds, *see* ἰάομαι

5561 χώρα.
Mat. 6:55* χώραν *for* περίχωρον (–ρος) TTrAWHR

Χωραζίν, *see* Χοραζίν. See 5523

5562 χωρέω.
Joh. 21:25 χωρήσειν TrWHR: *omit the verse* T

5565 χωρίς.
2 Co. 12: 3* *for* ἐκτός LTTrAWHR
Jas. 2:18* *for* ἐκ[1] A.V.B GEds

5568 ψαλμός.

Acts 13:33 *see* πρῶτος

5574 ψεύδομαι.

Jas. 3:14†*trs* glory not against the truth, and lie T

5575 ψευδομάρτυρ.

Mat. 26:60(61) two false witnesses—*omit* false witnesses TTrAWHR

5576 ψευδομαρτυρέω.

Ro. 13: 9 *omit* thou shalt not bear false witness GEds

5579 ψεῦδος.

Rev. 14: 5*ψεῦδος *for* δόλος GEds

5580 ψευδόχριστος.

Mar. 13:22 *omit* false Christs and A

5589 ψιχίον.

Lu. 16:21 *om.* the crumbs [L]T[Tr]AWHR

5590 ψυχή.

Mar. 12:33 *omit* and with all the soul [L]TWHR
Lu. 9:56 *omit* for the Son *to* save (them) GLTTrAWHR
10:27 ἐν ὅλῃ τῇ ψυχῇ σου καὶ ἐν ὅλῃ τῇ ἰσχύϊ σου, καὶ ἐν ὅλῃ τῇ διανοίᾳ LTTrWHR
14:26 *trs* ψυχὴν ἑαυτοῦ WH
Acts 2:31 *omit* his soul GLTTrAWHR
4:32 ἡ ψ.—*omit* ἡ LTTrAWHR

5593 ψυχρός.

Rev. 3:16 *trs* hot nor cold GTTrAWWHR

5595 ψωμίζω.

1 Co. 13: 3 ψωμίσω S—ψωμίζω E

5598 Ω.

Rev. 1: 8 ὦ LAWH
11 *omit* GEds, *see* A
21: 6 ׀ 22:13 ὦ LWH

5600 ᾧ, ἧς, ᾗ, *etc.*

Mat. 20: 7 *omit* LTTrAWHR, *see* δίκαιος
Lu. 20:28*ᾖ *for* ἀποθάνῃ (-θνήσκω) LTTrAWHR
Joh. 10: 6*ᾗ *for* ἦν Tr
14:16*ᾖ (*after* αἰῶνα L, *after* ὑμῶν T) *for* μένῃ (-νω) LTTrAWHR
15:11*ᾖ *for* μείνῃ (μένω) LTTrAWHR
17:19 *trs* ὦσιν καὶ αὐτοὶ Eds
1 Co. 5:11 ᾖ[1] S—ᾖ A.V.B EGEds
7: 5*ἦτε *for* συνέρχησθε (-χομαι) GEds
Jas. 2:15 *omit* ὦσιν TTrAWHR

5601 Ὠβήδ.

Mat. 1: 5 Ἰωβήδ *bis* LTTrAWH
Lu. 3:32 Ἰωβήδ LTTrA, Ἰωβὴλ WH

5602 ὧδε.

Mat. 14:18 *trs* ὧδε αὐτούς LTTrAWH
Mar. 9: 1 *trs* ὧδε τῶν TTrAWHR
13: 2*be left—*add* ὧ. here LTrWHR
Lu. 9:27 αὐτοῦ (*adv.*) TTrAWH
15:17*ὧ. λιμῷ here with famine GTrA, λιμῷ ὧ. LTWHR
16:25*for* ὅδε Eds
17:23 *trs* see there, or see here TTrAWHR
21: 6*stone—*add* ὧ. here LWHR
1 Co 4: 2*for* ὃ δὲ LTTrAWHR
Jas. 2: 3 *omit* here[2] LTTrAWHR
Rev. 14:12 *omit* here (are) GEds

5607 ὤν, οὖσα, ὄν, *etc.*

Mar. 4:31*add* ὄν LTTrAWHR, *see* μικρός
13:16 *omit* ὢν LTTrWHR
14:43 *omit* ὢν A.V.Vul LTTr[A]WHR
Lu. 6: 3 *omit* ὄντες LTrWH
Joh. 3:13 *omit* which is in heaven WH
6:71 *omit* being LTrAWHR
8: 9*οὖσα *for* ἑστῶσα (ἵστημι) WWHR
9:40 *trs* μετ' αὐτοῦ ὄντες LTTrAWHR
Acts 11:22*τῆς[2]—*add* οὔσης TTrWHR
18:12*ἀνθυπάτου ὄντος *for* ἀνθυπατεύοντος (-πατεύω) LTTrAWH
25:23 *omit* οὖσιν Eds
26:21*συλλαβόμενοι—*add* ὄντα T
1 Co. 9:20*add* GEds, *see* νόμος
1 Ti. 1:13 τὸν...ὄντα—τὸ...ὄ. LTTrAWHR
Rev. 5: 5 *omit* ὢν GEds

5609 ᾠόν, ᾠόν WH.

5610 ὥρα.

Mat. 20: 6 *omit* hour LTTrAWHR
24:36 τῆς ὥ.—*omit* τῆς GLTTrAWHR
42 hour—day, ἡμέρα LTTrAWHR
Mar. 15:34†*trs* τῇ ἐνάτῃ ὥρᾳ LTTrAWH
Lu. 13:31*ὥρᾳ *for* ἡμέρᾳ TAWHR
Joh. 4:52 *trs* τὴν ὥ. παρ' αὐτῶν LTTrAWH
11: 9 *trs* ὧραί εἰσιν LTTrAWWH
Acts 10:30 *omit* hour[2] LTTrAWHR

5613 ὡς.

Mat. 5:48* ׀ 6:5*16**for* ὥσπερ LTTrAWHR
9:36**for* ὡσεί Tr
21:46 εἰς LTTrAWHR
24:38*for* ὥσπερ LTAWH, ὧς Tr
28: 3* 4**for* ὡσεί LTTrAWH
9 *omit* LTTrAWHR, *see* μαθητής
Mar. 1: 2 καθώς TTrWHR
10**for* ὡσεί GEds
3: 5 *om.* whole as the other GEds
9: 3 *omit* as snow TTrAWHR
12:26 πῶς TTrAWHR
14:72**for* οὗ LTTrAWHR
Lu. 1:56*for* ὡσεί LTTrWHR
2:37 of about—up to, ἕως LTTrAWHR
3:22**for* ὡσεί LTTrAWHR
6: 4 [how] TrWH, πῶς L
10 *om.* as the other [L]T[Tr]AWHR
9:52**for* ὥστε WH
54 *omit* even as Elias did TTr[A]WHR
11: 2 *omit* as in heaven so in earth G[L]TTrAWHR
14:22 as—which, ὅς TTrAWHR
17:28 also as—even as, καθώς TTrAWHR
18:11*ὧς *for* ὥσπερ LTr
Joh. 1:32*for* ὡσεί GEds
4: 6**for* ὡσεί Eds
45**for* ὅτε T
6:10**for* ὡσεί TTrAWHR
7:10 *omit* as it were T
46 *omit* L[TrA]WHR, *see* ἄνθρωπος
12:35* 36**for* ἕως LTTrAWHR
19:14*δὲ ὡσεί—ἦν ὡς Eds
39**for* ὡσεί GEds
Acts 1:15 ὡσεί T
4: 4**for* ὡσεί [LTrA]WH
5:36**for* ὡσεί Eds
9:18**for* ὡσεί LTTrWH
10:47**for* καθώς LTTrAWHR
17:14 as it were—as far as, ἕως LTTrWHR
19:34 ὡσεί WH
27:37*ship—*add* ὡς about WH
Ro. 6:13 ὡσεί LTTrAWHR
1 Co. 5: 3 *omit* as[1] Eds
9:22 *omit* as [L]TTrAWWHR
10: 7 ὥσπερ LTTrAWHR
13: 1 γέγονα—*add* *velut* A.V.† Vul
2 Co. 1: 7*for* ὥσπερ Eds
2 Co. 9: 5*for* ὥσπερ GEds
Eph. 5:24*for* ὥσπερ LTTrAWHR
6: 7*service—*add* ὡς A.V.B GEds
1 Th. 2:13 οὐ—*add* *ut* A.V.† Vul
2 Th. 2: 4 *omit* as God GEds
Heb. 1:12*add* ὡς L[Tr] · R, *see* ἱμάτιον
11:12*ὡς ἡ *for* ὡσεί GEds
Jas. 5: 5 *omit* as Eds
1 Pet. 3:16 *omit* of you, as of evildoers TAWHR
4:19 *omit* as LTTrAWHR
Rev. 1:14*for* ὡσεί GEds
4: 6*throne[1]—*add* ὡς as GEds
7 *omit* ὡς G[A]W
5:11*I heard—*add* ὡς as TTr[A]
6: 6*I heard—*add* ὡς as LTTrAWHR
14: 2**add* ὡς GEds, *see* φωνή
3 *omit* as it were GT[TrA]
16:13**for* ὅμοια (-ιος) GEds
19: 1*I heard—*add* ὡς as EGEds
12 *omit* as TTr[A]WHR

5614 ὡσαννά, ὡ— LT.

5615 ὡσαύτως.

Lu. 13: 3 ὁμοίως LTTrAWHR
5**for* ὁμοίως TTrAWHR

5616 ὡσεί.

Mat. 9:36 ὡς Tr
28: 3, 4 ὡς LTTrAWH
Mar. 1:10 ὡς GEds
6:44 *omit* about GEds
Lu. 1:56 ὡς LTTrWHR
3:22 ὡς LTTrAWHR
9:14*κλισίας—*add* ὡ. *read* by about [LTr]AWHR
Joh. 1:32 ὡς GEds
4: 6 ὡς Eds
6:10 ὡς TTrAWHR
19:14 δὲ ὡσεί—ἦν ὡς was about Eds
39 ὡς GEds
Acts 1:15*for* ὡς T
4: 4 ὡς [LTrA]WH: *omit* about T
5:36 ὡς Eds
9:18 ὡς LTTrWH
19:34**for* ὡς WH
Ro. 6:13*for* ὡς LTTrAWHR
Heb. 11:12 ὡς ἡ GEds
Rev. 1:14 ὡς GEds

5618 ὥσπερ.

Mat. 5:48 ׀ 6:5, 16 ὡς LTTrAWHR
24:38 ὡς LTTrAWH
Lu. 18:11 ὡς (ὡς) LTr
1 Co. 10: 7*for* ὡς LTTrAWHR
2 Co. 1: 7 ὡς Eds
9: 5 ὡς GEds
Eph. 5:24 ὡς LTTrAWHR

5613 ὥστε.

Lu. 4:29*for* εἰς τό GLTTrAWHR
9:52 ὡς WH
20:20**for* εἰς τό LTTrAWHR
Jas. 1:19 wherefore—ye know (this) εἰδέω LTTrAWHR

* ὠτάριον, a small ear.

Mar. 14:47 ὠτάριον *for* ὠτίον LTTrAWH
Joh. 18:10 ὠτάριον *for* ὠτίον TTrAWHR

5621 ὠτίον.

Mar. 14:47 ὠτάριον LTTrAWH
Joh. 18:10 ὠτάριον TTrAWHR

5622 ὠφέλεια, λία WH.

5623 ὠφελέω.

Mat. 16:26 ὠφεληθήσεται shall be profited LTTrAWHR
Mar. 8:36 ὠφελεῖ doth it profit TAWHR

Alpha-Numeric Index

Normally this index will not be necessary. The best way to find an entry in *The Word Study Concordance* is by its number (which comes either from *The Word Study New Testament* or from Strong's *Exhaustive Concordance of the Bible*). There are, however, some older reference works that will refer to a Greek word without a number. This index will allow the word to be sought alphabetically so that its number can be known. The same thing can be done in the body of the concordance, but this list will make that process more rapid.

For students of Greek, it is important to note that this list of words corresponds to the vocabulary of the Nestle text of the New Testament. *The Word Study Concordance,* on the other hand, is based on the Textus Receptus (which underlies the original text of the King James or Authorized Version of the New Testament and *The Englishman's Greek Concordance*). Because of this fact, there are a few modifications that have been made so that it can still be readily used.

A. *A Word Is Out of Order*

(1) Example: 142 *airein.* Strong alphabetized the vocabulary using verbs in the first person singular. In this list verbs are in their present infinitive form; therefore, some words may be slightly out of numerical sequence. In the example given, #142 follows #137 instead of #141;

(2) Example: 103 *adein* (after #78). In some cases words are more seriously out of numerical sequence. Their placement may be located by referring to the auxiliary list on page 1114, ("Numbers in Different Sequence or Not Included in the Alpha Numeric List"), appended to this list.

(3) Example: 961:5 *Beor* v1007. A word is sometimes out of numerical sequence due to a conflict between the spelling in Strong and the modern texts, or for some other reason. In these cases a new .5 number has been assigned to acknowledge the new alphabetical sequence, but in such cases the original Strong number has been added to the right, usually following a *v* (*vide*), for "see."

B. *Differences in the Vocabulary of the Greek Texts*

(1) Example: 119.5 *athroizo.* Greek words appearing in the Nestle text

but not in the Textus Receptus (nor in Strong) have been given a .2 or .5 number.

(2) Example: *apopluno* M4150, W637. Some words occurring in the *Word Study Concordance* and in Strong do not occur in the Nestle text and are thus not in the main list. These may be found in the Auxiliary List B, ("Auxiliary List of Words Not Included in the Alpha Numeric List"), which is arranged alphabetically.

C. *Numbers to the Right of the Word*

(1) Example: 1078 *genesis* 1083. At times two Strong entries are classified as one word by Moulton and Geden. In such cases both numbers are listed in the index, one to the left and the other to the right of the word.

(2) Example: 961.5 *Beor* v1007. In cases where a word is seriously out of numerical sequence because of a difference in spelling in the Greek texts and a .5 number has been assigned (see A-(3) above), another number preceded by a v is often found to the right of the word. In such a case the *v* refers to the Strong number. If the *v* is followed by an *M* then the number (example: 1125 *graphein* vM2608.5), then the word is to be found in Moulton and Geden under the numerical listing 2608.5. If the *v* is followed by a *W* (example, 1987.5 *epistasis* vW1999) the word is not quite identical in spelling but is the same in meaning and in biblical reference as the W (Strong) word referred to.

D. *Other*

(1) Starred items: example 1944 *epikatarotos.** A star after an entry merely indicates that there was insufficient space on the list proper to give all the additional data. The star refers to a list immediately following the main list where that additional data is given.

(2) Abbreviations:
v (*vide*) = "see"
M - Moulton and Geden's Concordance
W - Wigram and Winter, or the *Word Study Concordance*

2 Ἀαρών
3 Ἀβαδδών
4 ἀβαρής
5 ἀββά
6 Ἅβελ

7 Ἀβιά
8 Ἀβιαθάρ
9 Ἀβιληνή
10 Ἀβιούδ
11 Ἀβραάμ

12 ἄβυσσος
13 Ἅγαβος
14 ἀγαθοεργεῖν
15 ἀγαθοποιεῖν
16 ἀγαθοποιΐα

17 ἀγαθοποιός
18 ἀγαθός
18.5 ἀγαθουργεῖν v15
19 ἀγαθωσύνη
21 ἀγαλλιᾶν

20 ἀγαλλίασις
22 ἄγαμος
23 ἀγανακτεῖν
24 ἀγανάκτησις
25 ἀγαπᾶν

26 ἀγάπη
27 ἀγαπητός
28 Ἅγαρ
29 ἀγγαρεύειν
30 ἀγγεῖον

31 ἀγγελία
31.5 ἀγγέλλειν v518
32 ἄγγελος
32.5 ἄγγος
33 ἄγε

71 ἄγειν
34 ἀγέλη
35 ἀγενεαλόγητος
36 ἀγενής
37 ἁγιάζειν

38 ἁγιασμός
40 ἅγιος 39
41 ἁγιότης
42 ἁγιωσύνη
43 ἀγκάλη

44 ἄγκιστρον
45 ἄγκυρα
46 ἄγναφος
47 ἁγνεία
48 ἁγνίζειν

49 ἁγνισμός
50 ἀγνοεῖν
51 ἀγνόημα
52 ἄγνοια
53 ἁγνός

54 ἁγνότης
55 ἁγνῶς
56 ἀγνωσία
57 ἄγνωστος
58 ἀγορά

59 ἀγοράζειν
60 ἀγοραῖος
61 ἄγρα
62 ἀγράμματος
63 ἀγραυλεῖν

64 ἀγρεύειν
65 ἀγριέλαιος
66 ἄγριος
67 Ἀγρίππας
68 ἀγρός

69 ἀγρυπνεῖν
70 ἀγρυπνία
72 ἀγωγή
73 ἀγών
74 ἀγωνία

75 ἀγωνίζεσθαι
76 Ἀδάμ
77 ἀδάπανος
78 Ἀδδί
103 ᾄδειν

79 ἀδελφή
80 ἀδελφός
81 ἀδελφότης
82 ἄδηλος
83 ἀδηλότης

84 ἀδήλως
85 ἀδημονεῖν
86 ᾅδης
87 ἀδιάκριτος
88 ἀδιάλειπτος

89 ἀδιαλείπτως
91 ἀδικεῖν
92 ἀδίκημα
93 ἀδικία
94 ἄδικος

95 ἀδίκως
95.5 Ἀδμίν
96 ἀδόκιμος
97 ἄδολος
98 Ἀδραμυττηνός

99 Ἀδρίας
100 ἁδρότης
101 ἀδυνατεῖν
102 ἀδύνατος
104 ἀεί

105 ἀετός
106 ἄζυμος
107 Ἀζώρ
108 Ἄζωτος
109 ἀήρ

110 ἀθανασία
111 ἀθέμιτος
112 ἄθεος
113 ἄθεσμος
114 ἀθετεῖν

115 ἀθέτησις
116 Ἀθῆναι
117 Ἀθηναῖος
118 ἀθλεῖν
119 ἄθλησις

119.5 ἀθροίζειν vW4867
120 ἀθυμεῖν
121 ἀθῷος
122 αἴγειος
123 αἰγιαλός

124 Αἰγύπτιος
125 Αἴγυπτος
126 ἀΐδιος
127 αἰδώς
128 Αἰθίοψ

129 αἷμα
130 αἱματεκχυσία
131 αἱμορροεῖν
132 Αἰνέας
134 αἰνεῖν

133 αἴνεσις
135 αἴνιγμα
136 αἶνος
137 Αἰνών
142 αἱρεῖν

138 αἱρεῖσθαι
139 αἵρεσις
140 αἱρετίζειν
141 αἱρετικός
143 αἰσθάνεσθαι

144 αἴσθησις
145 αἰσθητήριον
146 αἰσχροκερδής
147 αἰσχροκερδῶς
148 αἰσχρολογία

149 αἰσχρός v150
151 αἰσχρότης
153 αἰσχύνεσθαι
152 αἰσχύνη
154 αἰτεῖν

155 αἴτημα
156 αἰτία
158 αἴτιον
159 αἴτιος
157 αἰτίωμα

160 αἰφνίδιος
161 αἰχμαλωσία
162 αἰχμαλωτεύειν
163 αἰχμαλωτίζειν
164 αἰχμάλωτος

165 αἰών
166 αἰώνιος
167 ἀκαθαρσία
168 ἀκάθαρτος v169
170 ἀκαιρεῖσθαι

171 ἀκαίρως
172 ἄκακος
173 ἄκανθαι
174 ἀκάνθινος
175 ἄκαρπος

176 ἀκατάγνωστος
177 ἀκατακάλυπτος
178 ἀκατάκριτος
179 ἀκατάλυτος
180 ἀκατάπαυστος *

181 ἀκαταστασία
182 ἀκατάστατος v183
184 Ἁκελδαμάχ
185 ἀκέραιος
186 ἀκλινής

187 ἀκμάζειν
188 ἀκμήν
189 ἀκοή
190 ἀκολουθεῖν
191 ἀκούειν

192 ἀκρασία
193 ἀκρατής
194 ἄκρατος
195 ἀκρίβεια
196 ἀκριβής

198 ἀκριβοῦν
199 ἀκριβῶς v197
200 ἀκρίς
201 ἀκροατήριον
202 ἀκροατής

203 ἀκροβυστία
204 ἀκρογωνιαῖος
205 ἀκροθίνιον
206 ἄκρον
207 Ἀκύλας

208 ἀκυροῦν
209 ἀκωλύτως
210 ἄκων
211 ἀλάβαστρον
212 ἀλαζονεία

213 ἀλαζών
214 ἀλαλάζειν
215 ἀλάλητος
216 ἄλαλος
217 ἅλας

218 ἀλείφειν
219 ἀλεκτοροφωνία
220 ἀλέκτωρ
221 Ἀλεξανδρεύς
222 Ἀλεξανδρῖνος

223 Ἀλέξανδρος
224 ἄλευρον
225 ἀλήθεια
229 ἀλήθειν
226 ἀληθεύειν

227 ἀληθής
228 ἀληθινός
230 ἀληθῶς
232 ἁλιεύειν
231 ἁλιεύς vM217.5

233 ἁλίζειν
234 ἀλίσγημα
235 ἀλλά
236 ἀλλάσσειν
237 ἀλλαχόθεν

237.5 ἀλλαχοῦ
238 ἀλληγορεῖν
239 ἁλληλουϊά
240 ἀλλήλων
241 ἀλλογενής

242 ἅλλομαι
243 ἄλλος [σκοπος
244 ἀλλοτριεπί-
245 ἀλλότριος
246 ἀλλόφυλος

247 ἄλλως
248 ἀλοᾶν
249 ἄλογος
250 ἀλόη
252 ἁλυκός

253 ἄλυπος
254 ἅλυσις
255 ἀλυσιτελής
255.5 ἄλφα v1
256 Ἁλφαῖος

257 ἅλων
258 ἀλώπηξ
259 ἅλωσις
260 ἅμα
261 ἀμαθής

270 ἀμᾶν
262 ἀμαράντινος
263 ἀμάραντος
264 ἁμαρτάνειν
265 ἁμάρτημα

266 ἁμαρτία
267 ἀμάρτυρος
268 ἁμαρτωλός
269 ἄμαχος
271 ἀμέθυστος

272 ἀμελεῖν
273 ἄμεμπτος
274 ἀμέμπτως
275 ἀμέριμνος
276 ἀμετάθετος

277 ἀμετακίνητος
278 ἀμεταμέλητος
279 ἀμετανόητος
280 ἄμετρος
281 ἀμήν

282 ἀμήτωρ
283 ἀμίαντος
284 Ἀμιναδάβ
285 ἄμμος
286 ἀμνός

287 ἀμοιβή
288 ἄμπελος
289 ἀμπελουργός
290 ἀμπελών
291 Ἀμπλιᾶτος

292 ἀμύνεσθαι
292.2 ἀμφιάζειν
292.4 ἀμφιβάλλειν
293 ἀμφίβληστρον
294 ἀμφιεννύναι

295 Ἀμφίπολις
296 ἄμφοδον
297 ἀμφότεροι
298 ἀμώμητος
298.5 ἄμωμον v2368

299 ἄμωμος
300 Ἀμώς v301
302 ἄν
303 ἀνά
304 ἀναβαθμός

305 ἀναβαίνειν
306 ἀναβάλλεσθαι
307 ἀναβιβάζειν
308 ἀναβλέπειν
309 ἀνάβλεψις

310 ἀναβοᾶν
311 ἀναβολή
311.5 ἀνάγαιον vW508
312 ἀναγγέλλειν
321 ἀνάγειν

313 ἀναγεννᾶν
314 ἀναγινώσκειν
315 ἀναγκάζειν
316 ἀναγκαῖος
317 ἀναγκαστῶς

318 ἀνάγκη
319 ἀναγνωρίζεσθαι
320 ἀνάγνωσις
322 ἀναδεικνύναι
323 ἀνάδειξις

324 ἀναδέχεσθαι
325 ἀναδιδόναι
326 ἀναζῆν
327 ἀναζητεῖν
328 ἀναζώννυσθαι

329 ἀναζωπυρεῖν
330 ἀναθάλλειν
331 ἀνάθεμα
332 ἀναθεματίζειν
333 ἀναθεωρεῖν

334 ἀνάθημα
335 ἀναίδεια
337 ἀναιρεῖν
336 ἀναίρεσις
338 ἀναίτιος

339 ἀνακαθίζειν
340 ἀνακαινίζειν
341 ἀνακαινοῦν
342 ἀνακαίνωσις
343 ἀνακαλύπτειν

344 ἀνακάμπτειν
345 ἀνακεῖσθαι [θαι
346 ἀνακεφαλαιοῦσ-
347 ἀνακλίνειν
349 ἀνακράζειν

350 ἀνακρίνειν
351 ἀνάκρισις
351.5 ἀνακυλίειν v617
352 ἀνακύπτειν
353 ἀναλαμβάνειν

354 ἀνάλημψις
355 ἀναλίσκειν
356 ἀναλογία
357 ἀναλογίζεσθαι
358 ἄναλος

359 ἀνάλυσις
360 ἀναλύειν
362 ἀναμένειν
363 ἀναμιμνῄσκειν
364 ἀνάμνησις

365 ἀνανεοῦσθαι
366 ἀνανήφειν
367 Ἁνανίας
368 ἀναντίρρητος
369 ἀναντιρρήτως

370 ἀνάξιος
371 ἀναξίως
373 ἀναπαύειν
372 ἀνάπαυσις
374 ἀναπείθειν

375 ἀναπέμπειν
375.5 ἀναπηδᾶν v450
376 ἀνάπηρος
377 ἀναπίπτειν
378 ἀναπληροῦν

379 ἀναπολόγητος
381 ἀνάπτειν
382 ἀναρίθμητος
383 ἀνασείειν
384 ἀνασκευάζειν

385 ἀνασπᾶν
386 ἀνάστασις
387 ἀναστατοῦν
388 ἀνασταυροῦν
389 ἀναστενάζειν

390 ἀναστρέφειν
391 ἀναστροφή
392 ἀνατάσσεσθαι
393 ἀνατέλλειν
394 ἀνατίθεσθαι

395 ἀνατολή
396 ἀνατρέπειν
397 ἀνατρέφειν
398 ἀναφαίνειν
399 ἀναφέρειν

400 ἀναφωνεῖν
401 ἀνάχυσις
402 ἀναχωρεῖν
403 ἀνάψυξις
404 ἀναψύχειν

405 ἀνδραποδιστής
406 Ἀνδρέας
407 ἀνδρίζεσθαι
408 Ἀνδρόνικος
409 ἀνδροφόνος

410 ἀνέγκλητος
411 ἀνεκδιήγητος
412 ἀνεκλάλητος
413 ἀνέκλειπτος
414 ἀνεκτός

415 ἀνελεήμων
415.5 ἀνέλεος v448
416 ἀνεμίζεσθαι
417 ἄνεμος
418 ἀνένδεκτος

419 ἀνεξερεύνητος
420 ἀνεξίκακος
421 ἀνεξιχνίαστος
422 ἀνεπαίσχυντος
423 ἀνεπίλημπτος

424 ἀνέρχεσθαι
425 ἄνεσις
426 ἀνετάζειν
427 ἄνευ
428 ἀνεύθετος

429 ἀνευρίσκειν
430 ἀνέχεσθαι
431 ἀνεψιός
432 ἄνηθον
433 ἀνήκει

434 ἀνήμερος
435 ἀνήρ
436 ἀνθιστάναι
437 ἀνθομολογεῖσθαι
438 ἄνθος

439 ἀνθρακιά
440 ἄνθραξ [κος
441 ἀνθρωπάρεσ-
442 ἀνθρώπινος
443 ἀνθρωποκτόνος

444 ἄνθρωπος
446 ἀνθύπατος 445
447 ἀνιέναι
449 ἄνιπτος
450 ἀνιστάναι

451 Ἄννα
452 Ἄννας
453 ἀνόητος
454 ἄνοια
455 ἀνοίγειν

456 ἀνοικοδομεῖν
457 ἄνοιξις
458 ἀνομία
459 ἄνομος
460 ἀνόμως

461 ἀνορθοῦν
462 ἀνόσιος
463 ἀνοχή
464 ἀνταγωνίζεσθαι
465 ἀντάλλαγμα

466 ἀνταναπληροῦν
467 ἀνταποδιδόναι
468 ἀνταπόδομα
469 ἀνταπόδοσις
470 ἀνταποκρίνεσθαι†

471 ἀντειπεῖν
472 ἀντέχεσθαι
473 ἀντί
474 ἀντιβάλλειν
475 ἀντιδιατίθεσθαι

476 ἀντίδικος
477 ἀντίθεσις
478 ἀντικαθιστάναι
479 ἀντικαλεῖν
480 ἀντικεῖσθαι

481 ἄντικρυς
482 ἀντιλαμβάνεσθαι
483 ἀντιλέγειν
484 ἀντίλημψις
485 ἀντιλογία

486 ἀντιλοιδορεῖν
487 ἀντίλυτρον
488 ἀντιμετρεῖν
489 ἀντιμισθία
490 Ἀντιόχεια

491 Ἀντιοχεύς
492 ἀντιπαρέρχεσθαι
493 Ἀντίπας
494 Ἀντιπατρίς
495 ἀντιπέρα

496 ἀντιπίπτειν
497 ἀντιστρατεύεσθαι
498 ἀντιτάσσεσθαι
499 ἀντίτυπος
500 ἀντίχριστος

501 ἀντλεῖν
502 ἄντλημα
503 ἀντοφθαλμεῖν
504 ἄνυδρος
505 ἀνυπόκριτος

506 ἀνυπότακτος
507 ἄνω
509 ἄνωθεν
510 ἀνωτερικός
511 ἀνώτερον

512 ἀνωφελής
513 ἀξίνη
514 ἄξιος
515 ἀξιοῦν
516 ἀξίως

517 ἀόρατος
518 ἀπαγγέλλειν v31.5
520 ἀπάγειν
519 ἀπάγχεσθαι
521 ἀπαίδευτος

522 ἀπαίρεσθαι
523 ἀπαιτεῖν
524 ἀπαλγεῖν
525 ἀπαλλάσσειν
526 ἀπαλλοτριοῦσθαι

527 ἁπαλός
528 ἀπαντᾶν
529 ἀπάντησις
530 ἅπαξ
531 ἀπαράβατος

532 ἀπαρασκεύαστος
533 ἀπαρνεῖσθαι
535 ἀπαρτισμός
536 ἀπαρχή
537 ἅπας

537.5 ἀπασπάζεσθαι *
538 ἀπατᾶν
539 ἀπάτη
540 ἀπάτωρ
541 ἀπαύγασμα

543 ἀπείθεια
544 ἀπειθεῖν
545 ἀπειθής
546 ἀπειλεῖν
547 ἀπειλή

548 ἀπεῖναι
550 ἀπειπεῖν
551 ἀπείραστος
552 ἄπειρος
553 ἀπεκδέχεσθαι

554 ἀπεκδύεσθαι
555 ἀπέκδυσις
556 ἀπελαύνειν
557 ἀπελεγμός
558 ἀπελεύθερος

559 Ἀπελλῆς
560 ἀπελπίζειν
561 ἀπέναντι
562 ἀπέραντος
563 ἀπερισπάστως

564 ἀπερίτμητος
565 ἀπέρχεσθαι
566 ἀπέχειν v567,568
549 ἀπιέναι
569 ἀπιστεῖν

570 ἀπιστία v3639.5
571 ἄπιστος
572 ἁπλότης
573 ἁπλοῦς
574 ἁπλῶς

575 ἀπό
576 ἀποβαίνειν
577 ἀποβάλλειν
578 ἀποβλέπειν
579 ἀπόβλητος

580 ἀποβολή
581 ἀπογίνεσθαι
583 ἀπογράφειν
582 ἀπογραφή
584 ἀποδεικνύναι

585 ἀπόδειξις
586 ἀποδεκατεύειν
586.5 ἀποδεκατοῦν v586
587 ἀπόδεκτος
588 ἀποδέχεσθαι

589 ἀποδημεῖν
590 ἀπόδημος
591 ἀποδιδόναι
592 ἀποδιορίζειν
593 ἀποδοκιμάζειν

594 ἀποδοχή
595 ἀπόθεσις
596 ἀποθήκη
597 ἀποθησαυρίζειν
598 ἀποθλίβειν

599 ἀποθνήσκειν
600 ἀποκαθιστάναι
601 ἀποκαλύπτειν
602 ἀποκάλυψις
603 ἀποκαραδοκία

604 ἀποκαταλλάσσειν
605 ἀποκατάστασις
606 ἀποκεῖσθαι
607 ἀποκεφαλίζειν
608 ἀποκλείειν

609 ἀποκόπτειν
610 ἀπόκριμα
611 ἀποκρίνεσθαι
612 ἀπόκρισις
613 ἀποκρύπτειν

614 ἀπόκρυφος
615 ἀποκτείνειν
616 ἀποκυεῖν
617 ἀποκυλίειν v351.5
618 ἀπολαμβάνειν

619 ἀπόλαυσις
620 ἀπολείπειν
622 ἀπολλύναι
623 Ἀπολλύων
624 Ἀπολλωνία

625 Ἀπολλῶς
626 ἀπολογεῖσθαι
627 ἀπολογία
628 ἀπολούειν
630 ἀπολύειν

629 ἀπολύτρωσις
631 ἀπομάσσειν
632 ἀπονέμειν
633 ἀπονίπτειν
634 ἀποπίπτειν

635 ἀποπλανᾶν
636 ἀποπλεῖν
638 ἀποπνίγειν
639 ἀπορεῖν
640 ἀπορία

641 ἀπορίπτειν
642 ἀπορφανίζειν
644 ἀποσκίασμα
645 ἀποσπᾶν
646 ἀποστασία

647 ἀποστάσιον
648 ἀποστεγάζειν
649 ἀποστέλλειν
650 ἀποστερεῖν v879.5
651 ἀποστολή

652 ἀπόστολος
653 ἀποστοματίζειν
654 ἀποστρέφειν
655 ἀποστυγεῖν
656 ἀποσυνάγωγος

657 ἀποτάσσειν
658 ἀποτελεῖν
659 ἀποτιθέναι
660 ἀποτινάσσειν
661 ἀποτίνειν

662 ἀποτολμᾶν
663 ἀποτομία
664 ἀποτόμως
665 ἀποτρέπειν
666 ἀπουσία

667 ἀποφέρειν
668 ἀποφεύγειν
669 ἀποφθέγγεσθαι
670 ἀποφορτίζεσθαι
671 ἀπόχρησις

672 ἀποχωρεῖν
673 ἀποχωρίζειν
674 ἀποψύχειν
675 Ἀππίου φόρον
676 ἀπρόσιτος

677 ἀπρόσκοπος
678 ἀπροσωπολήμ-
679 ἄπταιστος [πτως
680 ἅπτειν 681 v4014.5
682 Ἀπφία

683 ἀπωθεῖν
684 ἀπώλεια
685 ἀρά
686 ἄρα
687 ἆρα

690 Ἄραβες
688 Ἀραβία
689 Ἀράμ
691 ἀργεῖν
692 ἀργός

694 ἀργύριον
695 ἀργυροκόπος
696 ἄργυρος
693 ἀργυροῦς
697 Ἄρειος πάγος

698 Ἀρεοπαγίτης
699 ἀρέσκεια
700 ἀρέσκειν
701 ἀρεστός
702 Ἁρέτας

703 ἀρετή
704 ἀρήν
705 ἀριθμεῖν
706 ἀριθμός
707 Ἁριμαθαία

709 ἀριστᾶν
708 Ἀρίσταρχος
710 ἀριστερός
711 Ἀριστόβουλος
712 ἄριστον

714 ἀρκεῖν
713 ἀρκετός
715 ἄρκος
716 ἅρμα
717 Ἁρμαγεδών

718 ἁρμόζειν
719 ἁρμός
720 ἀρνεῖσθαι
719.5 Ἀρνί
721 ἀρνίον

722 ἀροτριᾶν
723 ἄροτρον
724 ἁρπαγή
725 ἁρπαγμός
726 ἁρπάζειν

727 ἅρπαξ
728 ἀρραβών
729 ἄρραφος
731 ἄρρητος
732 ἄρρωστος

733 ἀρσενοκοίτης
730 ἄρσην
734 Ἀρτεμᾶς
735 Ἄρτεμις
736 ἀρτέμων

737 ἄρτι
738 ἀρτιγέννητος
739 ἄρτιος
740 ἄρτος
741 ἀρτύειν

742 Ἀρφαξάδ
743 ἀρχάγγελος
744 ἀρχαῖος
756 ἄρχειν
745 Ἀρχέλαος

746 ἀρχή
747 ἀρχηγός
748 ἀρχιερατικός
749 ἀρχιερεύς
750 ἀρχιποίμην

751 Ἄρχιππος
752 ἀρχισυνάγωγος
753 ἀρχιτέκτων
754 ἀρχιτελώνης
755 ἀρχιτρίκλινος

758 ἄρχων
759 ἄρωμα
761 ἀσάλευτος
760 Ἀσάφ
762 ἄσβεστος

763 ἀσέβεια
764 ἀσεβεῖν
765 ἀσεβής
766 ἀσέλγεια
767 ἄσημος

768 Ἀσήρ
769 ἀσθένεια
770 ἀσθενεῖν
771 ἀσθένημα
772 ἀσθενής

773 Ἀσία
774 Ἀσιανός
775 Ἀσιάρχαι
776 ἀσιτία
777 ἄσιτος

778 ἀσκεῖν
779 ἀσκός
780 ἀσμένως
781 ἄσοφος
782 ἀσπάζεσθαι *

783 ἀσπασμός
784 ἄσπιλος
785 ἀσπίς
786 ἄσπονδος
787 ἀσσάριον

788 ἆσσον
789 Ἆσσος
790 ἀστατεῖν
791 ἀστεῖος
792 ἀστήρ

793 ἀστήρικτος
794 ἄστοργος
795 ἀστοχεῖν
796 ἀστραπή
797 ἀστράπτειν

798 ἄστρον
799 Ἀσύγκριτος
800 ἀσύμφωνος
801 ἀσύνετος
802 ἀσύνθετος

803 ἀσφάλεια
804 ἀσφαλής
805 ἀσφαλίζειν
806 ἀσφαλῶς
807 ἀσχημονεῖν

808 ἀσχημοσύνη
809 ἀσχήμων
810 ἀσωτία
811 ἀσώτως
812 ἀτακτεῖν

813 ἄτακτος
814 ἀτάκτως
815 ἄτεκνος
816 ἀτενίζειν
817 ἄτερ

818 ἀτιμάζειν 821
819 ἀτιμία
820 ἄτιμος
822 ἀτμίς
823 ἄτομος

824 ἄτοπος
825 Ἀττάλεια
826 αὐγάζειν
827 αὐγή
828 Αὔγουστος

829 αὐθάδης
830 αὐθαίρετος
831 αὐθεντεῖν
832 αὐλεῖν
833 αὐλή

834 αὐλητής
835 αὐλίζεσθαι
836 αὐλός
837 αὐξάνειν
838 αὔξησις

839 αὔριον
840 αὐστηρός
841 αὐτάρκεια
842 αὐτάρκης
843 αὐτοκατάκριτος

844 αὐτόματος
845 αὐτόπτης
846 αὐτός (gr. S)
847 αὐτοῦ Adv.
848 αὐτοῦ

849 αὐτόχειρ
849.5 αὐχεῖν v3166
850 αὐχμηρός
851 ἀφαιρεῖν
852 ἀφανής

853 ἀφανίζειν
854 ἀφανισμός
855 ἄφαντος
856 ἀφεδρών v3790.5
857 ἀφειδία

858 ἀφελότης
859 ἄφεσις
860 ἁφή
861 ἀφθαρσία
862 ἄφθαρτος

862.5 ἀφθορία v90
863 ἀφιέναι
864 ἀφικνεῖσθαι
865 ἀφιλάγαθος
866 ἀφιλάργυρος

867 ἄφιξις
868 ἀφιστάναι
869 ἄφνω
870 ἀφόβως
871 ἀφομοιοῦν

872 ἀφορᾶν
873 ἀφορίζειν
874 ἀφορμή
875 ἀφρίζειν
876 ἀφρός

877 ἀφροσύνη
878 ἄφρων
879 ἀφυπνοῦν
879.5 ἀφυστερεῖν v650
880 ἄφωνος

881 Ἀχάζ
882 Ἀχαΐα
883 Ἀχαϊκός
884 ἀχάριστος
886 ἀχειροποίητος

885 Ἀχίμ
887 ἀχλύς
888 ἀχρεῖος
889 ἀχρειοῦσθαι
890 ἄχρηστος

891 ἄχρι
892 ἄχυρον
893 ἀψευδής
894 Ἄψινθος
895 ἄψυχος

896 Βάαλ
897 Βαβυλών
898 βαθμός
899 βάθος
900 βαθύνειν

901 βαθύς
902 βαΐον
903 Βαλαάμ
904 Βαλάκ
905 βαλλάντιον

906 βάλλειν
911 βάπτειν
907 βαπτίζειν
908 βάπτισμα
909 βαπτισμός

910 βαπτιστής
912 Βαραββᾶς
913 Βαράκ
914 Βαραχίας
915 βάρβαρος

916 βαρεῖσθαι v2599.5
917 βαρέως
918 Βαρθολομαῖος
919 Βαριησοῦς
920 Βαριωνᾶ

921 Βαρναβᾶς
922 βάρος
923 Βαρσαβᾶς
924 Βαρτιμαῖος
926 βαρύς

927 βαρύτιμος
928 βασανίζειν
929 βασανισμός
930 βασανιστής
931 βάσανος

932 βασιλεία
933 βασίλειος 934
936 βασιλεύειν
935 βασιλεύς
937 βασιλικός

938 βασίλισσα
939 βάσις
940 βασκαίνειν
941 βαστάζειν
942 βάτος

943 βάτος
944 βάτραχος
945 βατταλογεῖν
946 βδέλυγμα
947 βδελυκτός

948 βδελύσσεσθαι
949 βέβαιος
950 βεβαιοῦν
951 βεβαίωσις
952 βέβηλος

953 βεβηλοῦν
954 βεεζεβούλ
955 Βελίαρ
955.5 βελόνη v4476
956 βέλος

957 βέλτιον
958 Βενιαμίν
959 Βερνίκη
960 Βέροια
961 Βεροιαῖος

961.5 Βεώρ v1007
963 Βηθανία
964 Βηθζαθά
965 Βηθλέεμ
966 Βηθσαϊδά

967 Βηθφαγή
968 βῆμα
969 βήρυλλος
970 βία
971 βιάζεσθαι

972 βίαιος
973 βιαστής
974 βιβλαρίδιον
975 βιβλίον
976 βίβλος

977 βιβρώσκειν
978 Βιθυνία
979 βίος
980 βιοῦν
981 βίωσις

982 βιωτικός
983 βλαβερός
984 βλάπτειν
985 βλαστάνειν
986 Βλάστος

987 βλασφημεῖν
988 βλασφημία
989 βλάσφημος
990 βλέμμα
991 βλέπειν

992 βλητέον
994 βοᾶν
993 Βοανηργές
995 βοή
996 βοήθεια

997 βοηθεῖν
998 βοηθός
999 βόθυνος
1000 βολή
1001 βολίζειν

1003 Βόος, Βόες
1004 βόρβορος
1005 βορρᾶς
1006 βόσκειν
1008 βοτάνη

1009 βότρυς
1014 βούλεσθαι *
1011 βουλεύεσθαι
1010 βουλευτής
1012 βουλή

1013 βούλημα
1015 βουνός
1016 βοῦς
1017 βραβεῖον
1018 βραβεύειν

1019 βραδύνειν
1020 βραδυπλοεῖν
1021 βραδύς
1022 βραδύτης
1023 βραχίων

1024 βραχύς
1025 βρέφος
1026 βρέχειν
1027 βροντή
1028 βροχή

1029 βρόχος
1030 βρυγμός
1032 βρύειν
1031 βρύχειν
1033 βρῶμα

1034 βρώσιμος
1035 βρῶσις
1036 βυθίζειν
1037 βυθός
1038 βυρσεύς

1039 βύσσινος 1040
1040 βύσσος
1041 βωμός
1042 Γαββαθᾶ
1043 Γαβριήλ

1044 γάγγραινα
1045 Γάδ
1046 Γαδαρηνός *
1048 Γάζα
1047 γάζα

1049 γαζοφυλακεῖον
1050 Γάϊος
1051 γάλα
1052 Γαλάται
1053 Γαλατία vM1057.5

1054 Γαλατικός
1055 γαλήνη
1056 Γαλιλαία
1057 Γαλιλαῖος
1058 Γαλλίων

1059 Γαμαλιήλ
1060 γαμεῖν
1060.2 γαμίζειν *
1060.5 γαμίσκεσθαι v1548
1062 γάμος

1063 γάρ vM2228.5
1064 γαστήρ
1065 γε
1066 Γεδεών
1067 γέεννα

1068 Γεθσημανί
1069 γείτων
1070 γελᾶν
1071 γέλως
1073 γέμειν

1072 γεμίζειν
1074 γενεά
1075 γενεαλογεῖσθαι
1076 γενεαλογία
1077 γενέσια

1078 γένεσις 1083
1079 γενετή
1079.5 γένημα v1081
1080 γεννᾶν
1081 γέννημα

1082 Γεννησαρέτ
1084 γεννητός
1085 γένος
1086 Γερασηνός *
1087 γερουσία

1088 γέρων
1089 γεύεσθαι
1090 γεωργεῖσθαι
1091 γεώργιον
1092 γεωργός

1093 γῆ
1094 γῆρας
1095 γηράσκειν
1096 γίνεσθαι
1097 γινώσκειν

1098 γλεῦκος
1099 γλυκύς
1100 γλῶσσα
1101 γλωσσόκομον
1102 γναφεύς

1103 γνήσιος
1104 γνησίως
1105 γνόφος
1106 γνώμη
1107 γνωρίζειν

1108 γνῶσις
1109 γνώστης
1110 γνωστός
1111 γογγύζειν
1112 γογγυσμός

1113 γογγυστής
1114 γόης
1115 Γολγοθᾶ
1116 Γόμορρα
1117 γόμος

1118 γονεῖς
1119 γόνυ
1120 γονυπετεῖν
1121 γράμμα
1122 γραμματεύς

1123 γραπτός
1125 γράφειν vM2608.5
1124 γραφή
1126 γραφώδης
1127 γρηγορεῖν

1128 γυμνάζειν
1129 γυμνασία
1130 γυμνιτεύειν
1131 γυμνός
1132 γυμνότης

1133 γυναικάριον
1134 γυναικεῖος
1135 γυνή
1136 Γώγ
1137 γωνία

1139 δαιμονίζεσθαι
1140 δαιμόνιον
1141 δαιμονιώδης
1142 δαίμων
1143 δάκνειν

1145 δακρύειν
1144 δάκρυον
1146 δακτύλιος
1147 δάκτυλος
1148 Δαλμανουθά

1149 Δαλματία
1150 δαμάζειν
1151 δάμαλις
1152 Δάμαρις
1153 Δαμασκηνός

1154 Δαμασκός
1155 δανείζειν
1156 δάνειον
1157 δανειστής
1158 Δανιήλ

1159 δαπανᾶν
1160 δαπάνη
1160.5 Δαυίδ vW1138
1161 δέ
1161.5 δέειν (δέω) v1210

1162 δέησις
1164 δεῖγμα
1165 δειγματίζειν
1166 δεικνύναι
1167 δειλία

1168 δειλιᾶν
1169 δειλός
1163 δεῖν (δεῖ)
1170 δεῖνα
1171 δεινῶς

1172 δειπνεῖν
1173 δεῖπνον
1173.5 δεῖσθαι v1189
1175 δεισιδαιμονία
1174 δεισιδαίμων

1176 δέκα
1176.5 δεκαοκτώ v3638
1178 δεκαπέντε
1179 Δεκάπολις
1180 δεκατέσσαρες

1181 δεκάτη
1182 δέκατος
1183 δεκατοῦν
1184 δεκτός
1185 δελεάζειν

1186 δένδρον
1187 δεξιολάβος
1188 δεξιός
1189.5 δέος 127
1190 Δερβαῖος

1191 Δέρβη
1194 δέρειν
1192 δέρμα
1193 δερμάτινος
1195 δεσμεύειν 1196

1197 δέσμη
1198 δέσμιος
1199 δεσμός
1200 δεσμοφύλαξ
1201 δεσμωτήριον

1202 δεσμώτης
1203 δεσπότης
1204 δεῦρο
1205 δεῦτε
1206 δευτεραῖος

1208 δεύτερος
1209 δέχεσθαι
1211 δή
1212 δῆλος
1213 δηλοῦν

1214 Δημᾶς
1215 δημηγορεῖν
1216 Δημήτριος
1217 δημιουργός
1218 δῆμος

1219 δημόσιος
1220 δηνάριον
1222 δήπου
1223 διά (gr. S.)
1224 διαβαίνειν

1225 διαβάλλειν
1226 διαβεβαιοῦσθαι
1227 διαβλέπειν
1228 διάβολος
1229 διαγγέλλειν

1236 διάγειν
1230 διαγίνεσθαι
1231 διαγινώσκειν
1233 διάγνωσις
1234 διαγογγύζειν

1235 διαγρηγορεῖν
1237 διαδέχεσθαι
1238 διάδημα
1239 διαδιδόναι
1240 διάδοχος

1241 διαζωννύναι
1242 διαθήκη
1244 διαιρεῖν
1243 διαίρεσις
1245 διακαθαίρειν

1245.5 διακαθαρίζειν *
1246 διακατελέγχεσ-
1247 διακονεῖν [θαι
1248 διακονία
1249 διάκονος

1250 διακόσιοι
1251 διακούειν
1252 διακρίνειν
1253 διάκρισις
1254 διακωλύειν

1255 διαλαλεῖν
1256 διαλέγεσθαι
1257 διαλείπειν
1258 διάλεκτος
1259 διαλλάσσεσθαι

1260 διαλογίζεσθαι
1261 διαλογισμός
1262 διαλύειν
1263 διαμαρτύρεσθαι
1264 διαμάχεσθαι

1265 διαμένειν
1266 διαμερίζειν
1267 διαμερισμός
1268 διανέμειν
1269 διανεύειν

1270 διανόημα
1271 διάνοια
1272 διανοίγειν
1274 διανύειν
1273 διανυκτερεύειν

1274.5 διαπαρατριβή *
1276 διαπερᾶν
1277 διαπλεῖν
1278 διαπονεῖσθαι
1280 διαπορεῖν

1279 διαπορεύεσθαι
1281 διαπραγματεύε-
1282 διαπρίειν [σθαι
1283 διαρπάζειν
1284 διαρρήσσειν

1285 διασαφεῖν
1286 διασείειν
1287 διασκορπίζειν
1288 διασπᾶν
1289 διασπείρειν

1290 διασπορά
1291 διαστέλλεσθαι
1292 διάστημα
1293 διαστολή
1294 διαστρέφειν

1295 διασῴζειν
1296 διαταγή
1297 διάταγμα
1298 διαταράσσειν
1299 διατάσσειν

1300 διατελεῖν
1301 διατηρεῖν
1303 διατίθεσθαι
1304 διατρίβειν

1305 διατροφή
1306 διαυγάζειν
1307 διαυγής
1308 διαφέρειν
1309 διαφεύγειν

1310 διαφημίζειν *
1311 διαφθείρειν
1312 διαφθορά
1313 διάφορος
1314 διαφυλάσσειν

1315 διαχειρίζεσθαι
1315.5 διαχλευάζειν *
1316 διαχωρίζεσθαι
1317 διδακτικός
1318 διδακτός

1319 διδασκαλία
1320 διδάσκαλος
1321 διδάσκειν
1322 διδαχή
1325 διδόναι

1323 δίδραχμον
1324 Δίδυμος
1326 διεγείρειν
1326.5 διενθυμεῖσθαι *
1327 διέξοδος

1329 διερμηνεύειν
1328 διερμηνευτής
1330 διέρχεσθαι
1331 διερωτᾶν
1332 διετής

1333 διετία
1334 διηγεῖσθαι
1335 διήγησις
1336 διηνεκής
1337 διθάλασσος

1338 διϊκνεῖσθαι
1339 διϊστάναι
1340 διϊσχυρίζεσθαι
1341 δικαιοκρισία
1342 δίκαιος

1343 δικαιοσύνη
1344 δικαιοῦν
1345 δικαίωμα
1346 δικαίως
1347 δικαίωσις

1348 δικαστής
1349 δίκη v2613.5
1350 δίκτυον
1351 δίλογος
1352 διό

1353 διοδεύειν
1354 Διονύσιος
1355 διόπερ
1356 Διοπετής
1356.5 διόρθωμα vW2735

1357 διόρθωσις
1358 διορύσσειν
1359 Διόσκουροι
1360 διότι
1361 Διοτρέφης

1363 διπλοῦν
1362 διπλοῦς
1364 δίς
1364.5 δισμυριάς v1364
1365 διστάζειν

1366 δίστομος
1367 δισχίλιοι
1368 διυλίζειν
1369 διχάζειν
1370 διχοστασία

1371 διχοτομεῖν
1372 διψᾶν
1373 δίψος
1374 δίψυχος
1375 διωγμός

1377 διώκειν
1376 διώκτης
1378 δόγμα
1379 δογματίζεσθαι
1380 δοκεῖν

1381.5 δοκιμάζειν v1381
1381 δοκιμασία
1382 δοκιμή
1383 δοκίμιον
1384 δόκιμος

1385 δοκός
1386 δόλιος
1387 δολιοῦν
1388 δόλος
1389 δολοῦν

1390 δόμα
1391 δόξα
1392 δοξάζειν
1393 Δορκάς
1394 δόσις

1395 δότης
1396 δουλαγωγεῖν
1397 δουλεία
1398 δουλεύειν
1399 δούλη

1401 δοῦλος
1400 δοῦλος -η -ον
1402 δουλοῦν
1403 δοχή
1404 δράκων

1405 δράσσεσθαι
1406 δραχμή
1407 δρέπανον
1408 δρόμος
1409 Δρούσιλλα

1411 δύναμις
1412 δυναμοῦν
1410 δύνασθαι
1413 δυνάστης
1414 δυνατεῖν

1415 δυνατός
1416 δύνειν
1417 δύο
1419 δυσβάστακτος
1420 δυσεντέριον

1421 δυσερμήνευτος
1422 δύσκολος
1423 δυσκόλως
1424 δυσμή
1425 δυσνόητος

1425.5 δυσφημεῖν
1426 δυσφημία
1427 δώδεκα
1428 δωδέκατος
1429 δωδεκάφυλον

1430 δῶμα
1431 δωρεά
1432 δωρεάν
1433 δωρεῖσθαι
1434 δώρημα

1435 δῶρον
1436 ἔα
1437 ἐάν (gr. S.)
1439 ἐᾶν
1437.5 ἐάνπερ v1437

1438 ἑαυτοῦ
1440 ἑβδομήκοντα
1441 ἑβδομηκοντάκις
1442 ἕβδομος
1443 Ἔβερ

1445 Ἑβραῖος
1446 Ἑβραΐς
1447 Ἑβραϊστί
1448 ἐγγίζειν
1449 ἐγγράφειν *

1450 ἔγγυος
1451 ἐγγύς
1453 ἐγείρειν
1454 ἔγερσις
1455 ἐγκάθετος *

1456 ἐγκαίνια *
1457 ἐγκαινίζειν *
1573 ἐγκακεῖν *
1458 ἐγκαλεῖν
1459 ἐγκαταλείπειν

1460 ἐγκατοικεῖν *
2744 ἐγκαυχᾶσθαι *
1461 ἐγκεντρίζειν *
1462 ἔγκλημα
1463 ἐγκομβοῦσθαι

1464 ἐγκοπή *
1465 ἐγκόπτειν *
1466 ἐγκράτεια
1467 ἐγκρατεύεσθαι
1468 ἐγκρατής

1469 ἐγκρίνειν *
1470 ἐγκρύπτειν
1471 ἔγκυος vM1765.94
1472 ἐγχρίειν
1473 ἐγώ (gr. S.)

1474 ἐδαφίζειν
1475 ἔδαφος
1476 ἑδραῖος
1477 ἑδραίωμα
1478 Ἑζεκίας

1486 ἔθειν, εἴωθα *
1479 ἐθελοθρησκία
1480 ἐθίζειν
1481 ἐθνάρχης
1482 ἐθνικός { vW5057, W1484

1483 ἐθνικῶς
1484 ἔθνος
1485 ἔθος
1487 εἰ (gr. S.)
1487.5 εἰδέα vW2397

1492 εἴδον
1492.5 οἶδα vW1492
1491 εἶδος
1493 εἰδωλεῖον
1494 εἰδωλόθυτον *

1496 εἰδωλολάτρης
1495 εἰδωλολατρία
1497 εἴδωλον
1502 εἴκειν
1500 εἰκῇ

1501 εἴκοσι
1504 εἰκών
1505 εἰλικρίνεια
1506 εἰλικρινής
1510 εἶναι (gr. S.)

1511.7 εἰπεῖν vW2036
1512 εἴπερ vM1487.3
1514 εἰρηνεύειν
1515 εἰρήνη
1516 εἰρηνικός

1517 εἰρηνοποιεῖν
1518 εἰρηνοποιός
1519 εἰς
1520 εἷς, μία, ἕν
1521 εἰσάγειν

1522 εἰσακούειν
1523 εἰσδέχεσθαι
1525 εἰσέρχεσθαι
1524 εἰσιέναι
1528 εἰσκαλεῖν

1529 εἴσοδος
1530 εἰσπηδᾶν vM1600.5
1531 εἰσπορεύεσθαι
1532 εἰστρέχειν
1533 εἰσφέρειν

1534 εἶτα
1535 εἶτε
1535.5 εἶτεν vM1534
1537 ἐκ, ἐξ
1538 ἕκαστος

1539 ἑκάστοτε
1540 ἑκατόν
1541 ἑκατονταετής
1542 ἑκατονταπλασίων
1543 ἑκατοντάρχης

1543.5 ἐκβαίνειν v1831
1544 ἐκβάλλειν
1545 ἔκβασις
1546 ἐκβολή
1549 ἔκγονος

1550 ἐκδαπανᾶσθαι
1551 ἐκδέχεσθαι
1552 ἔκδηλος
1553 ἐκδημεῖν
1554 ἐκδιδόναι

1555 ἐκδιηγεῖσθαι
1556 ἐκδικεῖν
1557 ἐκδίκησις
1558 ἔκδικος
1559 ἐκδιώκειν

1560 ἔκδοτος
1561 ἐκδοχή
1562 ἐκδύειν
1563 ἐκεῖ
1564 ἐκεῖθεν

1565 ἐκεῖνος
1566 ἐκεῖσε
1567 ἐκζητεῖν
1567.5 ἐκζήτησις v2214
1568 ἐκθαμβεῖσθαι

1569 ἔκθαμβος
1569.5 ἐκθαυμάζειν *
1570 ἔκθετος
1571 ἐκκαθαίρειν
1572 ἐκκαίειν

1574 ἐκκεντεῖν
1575 ἐκκλᾶν
1576 ἐκκλείειν
1577 ἐκκλησία
1578 ἐκκλίνειν

1579 ἐκκολυμβᾶν
1580 ἐκκομίζειν
1581 ἐκκόπτειν
1582 ἐκκρέμασθαι
1583 ἐκλαλεῖν

1584 ἐκλάμπειν
1585 ἐκλανθάνεσθαι
1586 ἐκλέγεσθαι
1587 ἐκλείπειν
1588 ἐκλεκτός

1589 ἐκλογή
1590 ἐκλύειν
1591 ἐκμάσσειν
1592 ἐκμυκτηρίζειν
1593 ἐκνεύειν

1594 ἐκνήφειν
1595 ἑκούσιος
1596 ἑκουσίως
1597 ἔκπαλαι
1598 ἐκπειράζειν

1599 ἐκπέμπειν
1599.5 ἐκπερισσῶς v4053
1600 ἐκπεταννύναι
1600.5 ἐκπηδᾶν v1530
1601 ἐκπίπτειν

1602 ἐκπλεῖν
1603 ἐκπληροῦν
1604 ἐκπλήρωσις
1605 ἐκπλήσσειν
1606 ἐκπνεῖν

1607 ἐκπορεύεσθαι
1608 ἐκπορνεύειν
1609 ἐκπτύειν
1610 ἐκριζοῦν
1611 ἔκστασις

1612 ἐκστρέφεσθαι
1613 ἐκταράσσειν
1614 ἐκτείνειν
1615 ἐκτελεῖν
1616 ἐκτένεια

1618 ἐκτενής
1619 ἐκτενῶς
1620 ἐκτιθέναι
1621 ἐκτινάσσειν
1622 ἔκτος

1623 ἐκτός
1624 ἐκτρέπεσθαι
1625 ἐκτρέφειν
1626 ἔκτρωμα
1627 ἐκφέρειν

1628 ἐκφεύγειν
1629 ἐκφοβεῖν
1630 ἔκφοβος
1631 ἐκφύειν
1632 ἐκχεῖν

1632 ἐκχύνεσθαι *
1633 ἐκχωρεῖν
1634 ἐκψύχειν
1635 ἑκών
1636 ἐλαία

1637 ἔλαιον
1638 ἐλαιών
1639 Ἐλαμῖται
1640 ἐλάσσων
1641 ἐλαττονεῖν

1642 ἐλαττοῦν
1643 ἐλαύνειν
1644 ἐλαφρία
1645 ἐλαφρός
1646 ἐλάχιστος 1647

1648 Ἐλεάζαρ
1648.5 ἐλεγμός v1650
1649 ἔλεγξις
1651 ἐλέγχειν
1650 ἔλεγχος

1653 ἐλεεῖν
1652 ἐλεεινός
1654 ἐλεημοσύνη
1655 ἐλεήμων
1656 ἔλεος

1657 ἐλευθερία
1658 ἐλεύθερος
1659 ἐλευθεροῦν
1660 ἔλευσις
1661 ἐλεφάντινος

1662 Ἐλιακίμ
1663 Ἐλιέζερ
1664 Ἐλιούδ
1665 Ἐλισάβετ *
1666 Ἐλισαῖος

1667 ἑλίσσειν
1670.5 ἕλκειν v1670
1668 ἕλκος
1669 ἑλκοῦν
1670 ἑλκύειν

1671 Ἑλλάς
1672 Ἕλλην
1673 Ἑλληνικός
1674 Ἑλληνίς
1675 Ἑλληνιστής

1676 Ἑλληνιστί
1677 ἐλλογεῖν
1678 Ἐλμαδάμ
1679 ἐλπίζειν
1680 ἐλπίς

1681 Ἐλύμας
1682 ἐλωΐ
1683 ἐμαυτοῦ
1684 ἐμβαίνειν
1685 ἐμβάλλειν

1686 ἐμβάπτειν
1687 ἐμβατεύειν
1688 ἐμβιβάζειν
1689 ἐμβλέπειν
1690 ἐμβριμᾶσθαι

1692 ἐμεῖν
1693 ἐμμαίνεσθαι
1694 Ἐμμανουήλ
1695 Ἐμμαοῦς
1696 ἐμμένειν

1697 Ἐμμώρ
1699 ἐμός
1699.5 ἐμπαιγμονή *
1701 ἐμπαιγμός
1702 ἐμπαίζειν

1703 ἐμπαίκτης
1704 ἐμπεριπατεῖν *
1705 ἐμπιμπλάναι
1706 ἐμπίπτειν
1707 ἐμπλέκειν

1708 ἐμπλοκή
1709 ἐμπνεῖν vM1777.5
1710 ἐμπορεύεσθαι
1711 ἐμπορία
1712 ἐμπόριον

1713 ἔμπορος
1714 ἐμπρήθειν *
1715 ἔμπροσθεν
1716 ἐμπτύειν
1717 ἐμφανής

1718 ἐμφανίζειν
1719 ἔμφοβος
1720 ἐμφυσᾶν
1721 ἔμφυτος
1722 ἐν

1723 ἐναγκαλίζεσθαι
1724 ἐνάλιος
1725 ἔναντι
1726 ἐναντίον
1727 ἐναντίος

1728 ἐνάρχεσθαι
1728.2 ἔνατος v1766
1729 ἐνδεής
1730 ἔνδειγμα
1731 ἐνδείκνυσθαι

1732 ἔνδειξις
1733 ἕνδεκα
1734 ἑνδέκατος
1735 ἐνδέχεσθαι
1736 ἐνδημεῖν

1737 ἐνδιδύσκειν
1738 ἔνδικος
1740 ἐνδοξάζεσθαι
1741 ἔνδοξος
1746 ἐνδύειν

1742 ἔνδυμα
1743 ἐνδυναμοῦν
1744 ἐνδύνειν
1745 ἔνδυσις
1746.5 ἐνδώμησις v1739

1747 ἐνέδρα 1749
1748 ἐνεδρεύειν
1750 ἐνειλεῖν
1751 ἐνεῖναι
1752 ἕνεκα

1752.2 ἐνενήκοντα v1768
1752.4 ἐνεός v1769
1753 ἐνέργεια
1754 ἐνεργεῖν
1755 ἐνέργημα

1756 ἐνεργής
1757 ἐνευλογεῖσθαι
1758 ἐνέχειν
1759 ἐνθάδε
1759.5 ἔνθεν v1782

1760 ἐνθυμεῖσθαι *
1761 ἐνθύμησις
1762 ἔνι
1763 ἐνιαυτός
1764 ἐνιστάναι

1765 ἐνισχύειν
1768 ἐννέα
1770 ἐννεύειν
1771 ἔννοια
1772 ἔννομος

1773 ἔννυχα
1774 ἐνοικεῖν
1774.5 ἐνορκίζειν v3726
1775 ἑνότης
1776 ἐνοχλεῖν

1777 ἔνοχος
1778 ἔνταλμα
1779 ἐνταφιάζειν
1780 ἐνταφιασμός
1781 ἐντέλλεσθαι

1782 ἐντεῦθεν *
1783 ἔντευξις
1784 ἔντιμος
1785 ἐντολή
1786 ἐντόπιος

1787 ἐντός
1788 ἐντρέπειν
1789 ἐντρέφεσθαι
1790 ἔντρομος *
1791 ἐντροπή

1792 ἐντρυφοῦν
1793 ἐντυγχάνειν
1794 ἐντυλίσσειν
1795 ἐντυποῦν
1796 ἐνυβρίζειν

1797 ἐνυπνιάζεσθαι
1798 ἐνύπνιον
1799 ἐνώπιον
1800 Ἐνώς
1801 ἐνωτίζεσθαι

1802 Ἑνώχ
1803 ἕξ
1804 ἐξαγγέλλειν
1806 ἐξάγειν
1805 ἐξαγοράζειν

1807 ἐξαιρεῖν
1808 ἐξαίρειν
1809 ἐξαιτεῖσθαι
1810 ἐξαίφνης
1811 ἐξακολουθεῖν

1812 ἑξακόσιοι
1813 ἐξαλείφειν
1814 ἐξάλλεσθαι
1815 ἐξανάστασις
1816 ἐξανατέλλειν

1817 ἐξανιστάναι
1818 ἐξαπατᾶν
1819 ἐξάπινα
1820 ἐξαπορεῖσθαι
1821 ἐξαποστέλλειν

1822 ἐξαρτίζειν
1823 ἐξαστράπτειν
1824 ἐξαυτῆς
1825 ἐξεγείρειν
1828 ἐξέλκεσθαι

1829 ἐξέραμα
1830 ἐξερευνᾶν
1831 ἐξέρχεσθαι *
1832 ἔξεστι
1833 ἐξετάζειν

1834 ἐξηγεῖσθαι
1835 ἑξήκοντα
1836 ἑξῆς
1837 ἐξηχεῖσθαι
1826 ἐξιέναι

1838 ἕξις
1839 ἐξιστάναι
1840 ἐξισχύειν
1841 ἔξοδος
1842 ἐξολοθρεύειν

1843 ἐξομολογεῖν
1844 ἐξορκίζειν
1845 ἐξορκιστής
1846 ἐξορύσσειν
1847 ἐξουδενεῖν

1848 ἐξουθενεῖν
1849 ἐξουσία
1850 ἐξουσιάζειν
1851 ἐξοχή
1852 ἐξυπνίζειν

1853 ἔξυπνος
1854 ἔξω
1856 ἐξωθεῖν vM1612.5
1855 ἔξωθεν
1857 ἐξώτερος

1857.5 ἔοικα v1503
1858 ἑορτάζειν
1859 ἑορτή
1860 ἐπαγγελία
1861 ἐπαγγέλλεσθαι

1862 ἐπάγγελμα
1863 ἐπάγειν
1864 ἐπαγωνίζεσθαι
1865 ἐπαθροίζεσθαι
1867 ἐπαινεῖν

1866 Ἐπαίνετος
1868 ἔπαινος
1869 ἐπαίρειν
1870 ἐπαισχύνεσθαι
1871 ἐπαιτεῖν

1872 ἐπακολουθεῖν
1873 ἐπακούειν
1874 ἐπακροᾶσθαι
1875 ἐπάν
1877 ἐπανάγειν

1876 ἐπάναγκες
1878 ἐπαναμιμνήσκειν
1879 ἐπαναπαύεσθαι
1880 ἐπανέρχεσθαι
1881 ἐπανίστασθαι

1882 ἐπανόρθωσις
1883 ἐπάνω
1883.5 ἐπάρατος v1944
1884 ἐπαρκεῖν
1885 ἐπαρχεία

1885.5 ἐπάρχειος v1885
1886 ἔπαυλις
1887 ἐπαύριον
1889 Ἐπαφρᾶς
1890 ἐπαφρίζειν

1891 Ἐπαφρόδιτος
1892 ἐπεγείρειν
1893 ἐπεί
1894 ἐπειδή
1895 ἐπειδήπερ

1898 ἐπεισαγωγή
1898.5 ἐπεισέρχεσθαι *
1899 ἔπειτα
1900 ἐπέκεινα
1901 ἐπεκτείνεσθαι

1902 ἐπενδύεσθαι
1903 ἐπενδύτης
1904 ἐπέρχεσθαι *
1905 ἐπερωτᾶν
1906 ἐπερώτημα

1907 ἐπέχειν
1908 ἐπηρεάζειν
1909 ἐπί (gr. S)
1910 ἐπιβαίνειν
1911 ἐπιβάλλειν

1912 ἐπιβαρεῖν
1913 ἐπιβιβάζειν
1914 ἐπιβλέπειν
1915 ἐπίβλημα
1917 ἐπιβουλή

1918 ἐπιγαμβρεύειν
1919 ἐπίγειος
1920 ἐπιγίνεσθαι
1921 ἐπιγινώσκειν
1922 ἐπίγνωσις

1924 ἐπιγράφειν
1923 ἐπιγραφή
1925 ἐπιδεικνύναι
1896 ἐπιδεῖν
1926 ἐπιδέχεσθαι

1927 ἐπιδημεῖν
1928 ἐπιδιατάσσεσθαι
1929 ἐπιδιδόναι
1930 ἐπιδιορθοῦν
1931 ἐπιδύειν

1932 ἐπιείκεια
1933 ἐπιεικής
1966 ἐπιέναι
1934 ἐπιζητεῖν
1935 ἐπιθανάτιος

1936 ἐπίθεσις
1937 ἐπιθυμεῖν
1938 ἐπιθυμητής
1939 ἐπιθυμία
1940 ἐπικαθίζειν

1941 ἐπικαλεῖν
1942 ἐπικάλυμμα
1943 ἐπικαλύπτειν
1944 ἐπικατάρατος *
1945 ἐπικεῖσθαι

1945.5 ἐπικέλλειν v2027
1946 Ἐπικούρειοι
1947 ἐπικουρία
1948 ἐπικρίνειν
1949 ἐπιλαμβάνεσθαι

1950 ἐπιλανθάνεσθαι
1951 ἐπιλέγειν
1952 ἐπιλείπειν
1952.5 ἐπιλείχειν vW621
1953 ἐπιλησμονή

1954 ἐπίλοιπος
1956 ἐπιλύειν
1955 ἐπίλυσις
1957 ἐπιμαρτυρεῖν
1958 ἐπιμέλεια

1959 ἐπιμελεῖσθαι
1960 ἐπιμελῶς
1961 ἐπιμένειν
1962 ἐπινεύειν
1963 ἐπίνοια

1964 ἐπιορκεῖν
1965 ἐπίορκος
1967 ἐπιούσιος
1968 ἐπιπίπτειν
1969 ἐπιπλήσσειν

1971 ἐπιποθεῖν
1972 ἐπιπόθησις
1973 ἐπιπόθητος
1974 ἐπιποθία
1975 ἐπιπορεύεσθαι

1976 ἐπιράπτειν
1977 ἐπιρίπτειν
1978 ἐπίσημος
1979 ἐπισιτισμός
1980 ἐπισκέπτεσθαι

1980.5 ἐπισκευάζειν *
1981 ἐπισκηνοῦν
1982 ἐπισκιάζειν
1983 ἐπισκοπεῖν
1984 ἐπισκοπή

1985 ἐπίσκοπος
1986 ἐπισπᾶσθαι
1986.5 ἐπισπείρειν v4687
1987 ἐπίστασθαι
1987.5 ἐπίστασις vW1999

1988 ἐπιστάτης
1989 ἐπιστέλλειν
1990 ἐπιστήμων
1991 ἐπιστηρίζειν
1992 ἐπιστολή

1993 ἐπιστομίζειν
1994 ἐπιστρέφειν
1995 ἐπιστροφή
1996 ἐπισυνάγειν
1997 ἐπισυναγωγή

1998 ἐπισυντρέχειν
2000 ἐπισφαλής
2001 ἐπισχύειν
2002 ἐπισωρεύειν
2003 ἐπιταγή

2004 ἐπιτάσσειν
2005 ἐπιτελεῖν
2006 ἐπιτήδειος
2007 ἐπιτιθέναι
2008 ἐπιτιμᾶν

2009 ἐπιτιμία
2010 ἐπιτρέπειν
2011 ἐπιτροπή
2012 ἐπίτροπος
2013 ἐπιτυγχάνειν

2014 ἐπιφαίνειν
2015 ἐπιφάνεια
2016 ἐπιφανής
2017 ἐπιφαύσκειν
2018 ἐπιφέρειν

2019 ἐπιφωνεῖν
2020 ἐπιφώσκειν
2021 ἐπιχειρεῖν
2022 ἐπιχεῖν
2023 ἐπιχορηγεῖν

2024 ἐπιχορηγία
2025 ἐπιχρίειν
2026 ἐποικοδομεῖν
2028 ἐπονομάζεσθαι
2029 ἐποπτεύειν

2030 ἐπόπτης
2031 ἔπος
2032 ἐπουράνιος
2033 ἑπτά
2034 ἑπτάκις

2035 ἑπτακισχίλιοι
2037 Ἔραστος
2038 ἐργάζεσθαι
2039 ἐργασία
2040 ἐργάτης

2041 ἔργον
2042 ἐρεθίζειν
2043 ἐρείδειν
2043.5 ἐρεῖν *
2044 ἐρεύγεσθαι

2045 ἐρευνᾶν vM2037.5
2047 ἐρημία
2048 ἔρημος
2049 ἐρημοῦν
2050 ἐρήμωσις

2051 ἐρίζειν
2052 ἐριθεία
2053 ἔριον
2054 ἔρις
2055 ἐρίφιον

2056 ἔριφος
2057 Ἑρμᾶς
2058 ἑρμηνεία
2059 ἑρμηνεύειν
2060 Ἑρμῆς

2061 Ἑρμογένης
2062 ἑρπετά
2063 ἐρυθρός
2064 ἔρχεσθαι
2065 ἐρωτᾶν

2066 ἐσθής
2067 ἔσθησις
2068 ἐσθίειν *
2069 Ἑσλί
2072 ἔσοπτρον

2073 ἑσπέρα
2074 Ἑσρώμ
2078 ἔσχατος
2079 ἐσχάτως
2080 ἔσω

2081 ἔσωθεν
2082 ἐσώτερος
2083 ἑταῖρος
2084 ἑτερόγλωσσος
2085 ἑτεροδιδασκαλεῖν

2086 ἑτεροζυγεῖν
2087 ἕτερος
2088 ἑτέρως
2089 ἔτι
2090 ἑτοιμάζειν

2091 ἑτοιμασία
2092 ἕτοιμος
2093 ἑτοίμως
2094 ἔτος
2095 εὖ

2096 Εὕα
2097 εὐαγγελίζειν
2098 εὐαγγέλιον
2099 εὐαγγελιστής
2100 εὐαρεστεῖν

2101 εὐάρεστος
2102 εὐαρέστως
2103 Εὔβουλος
2104 εὐγενής
2105 εὐδία

2106 εὐδοκεῖν
2107 εὐδοκία
2108 εὐεργεσία
2109 εὐεργετεῖν
2110 εὐεργέτης

2111 εὔθετος
2112 εὐθέως
2113 εὐθυδρομεῖν
2114 εὐθυμεῖν
2115 εὔθυμος

2115.5 εὐθύμως *
2116 εὐθύνειν
2117 εὐθύς Adj.
2117.5 εὐθύς Adv. *
2118 εὐθύτης

2119 εὐκαιρεῖν
2120 εὐκαιρία
2121 εὔκαιρος
2122 εὐκαίρως
2123 εὔκοπος

2124 εὐλάβεια
2125 εὐλαβεῖσθαι
2126 εὐλαβής
2127 εὐλογεῖν
2128 εὐλογητός

2129 εὐλογία
2130 εὐμετάδοτος
2131 Εὐνίκη
2132 εὐνοεῖν
2133 εὔνοια

2134 εὐνουχίζειν
2135 εὐνοῦχος
2136 Εὐοδία
2137 εὐοδοῦσθαι
2137.5 εὐπάρεδρος *

2138 εὐπειθής
2139 εὐπερίστατος
2140 εὐποιΐα
2141 εὐπορεῖσθαι
2142 εὐπορία

2143 εὐπρέπεια
2144 εὐπρόσδεκτος
2146 εὐπροσωπεῖν
2148 εὐρακύλων
2147 εὑρίσκειν

2149 εὐρύχωρος
2150 εὐσέβεια
2151 εὐσεβεῖν
2152 εὐσεβής
2153 εὐσεβῶς

2154 εὔσημος
2155 εὔσπλαγχνος
2156 εὐσχημόνως
2157 εὐσχημοσύνη
2158 εὐσχήμων

2159 εὐτόνως
2160 εὐτραπελία
2161 Εὔτυχος
2162 εὐφημία
2163 εὔφημος

2164 εὐφορεῖν
2165 εὐφραίνειν
2166 Εὐφράτης
2167 εὐφροσύνη
2168 εὐχαριστεῖν

2169 εὐχαριστία
2170 εὐχάριστος
2172 εὔχεσθαι
2171 εὐχή
2173 εὔχρηστος

2174 εὐψυχεῖν
2175 εὐωδία
2176 εὐώνυμος
2177 ἐφάλλεσθαι
2178 ἐφάπαξ

2180 Ἐφέσιος
2181 Ἔφεσος
2182 ἐφευρετής
2183 ἐφημερία
2184 ἐφήμερος

2185 ἐφικνεῖσθαι
2186 ἐφιστάναι
2187 Ἐφραίμ
2188 ἐφφαθά
2192 ἔχειν

2188.5 ἐχθές vW5504
2189 ἔχθρα
2190 ἐχθρός
2191 ἔχιδνα
2193 ἕως (gr. S.)

2194 Ζαβουλών
2195 Ζακχαῖος
2196 Ζάρα
2197 Ζαχαρίας
2199 Ζεβεδαῖος

2204 ζεῖν
2200 ζεστός
2201 ζεῦγος
2202 ζευκτηρία
2203 Ζεύς

2204.5 ζηλεύειν v2206
2205 ζῆλος
2206 ζηλοῦν
2207 ζηλωτής 2208
2209 ζημία

2210 ζημιοῦν
2198 ζῆν
2211 Ζηνᾶς
2212 ζητεῖν
2213 ζήτημα

2214 ζήτησις vM1567.5
2215 ζιζάνια
2216 Ζοροβαβέλ
2217 ζόφος
2218 ζυγός

2219 ζύμη
2220 ζυμοῦν
2221 ζωγρεῖν
2222 ζωή
2223 ζώνη

2224 ζωννύναι
2225 ζωογονεῖν
2226 ζῷον
2227 ζωοποιεῖν
2228 ἤ (gr. S.)

2233 ἡγεῖσθαι
2230 ἡγεμονεύειν *
2231 ἡγεμονία
2232 ἡγεμών
2234 ἡδέως

2235 ἤδη
2237 ἡδονή
2238 ἡδύοσμον
2239 ἦθος
2240 ἥκειν

2241 ἠλί
2242 Ἠλί
2243 Ἠλίας
2244 ἡλικία
2245 ἡλίκος

2246 ἥλιος
2247 ἧλος
2249 ἡμεῖς (gr. S.) *
2250 ἡμέρα
2251 ἡμέτερος

2253 ἡμιθανής
2255 ἥμισυς
2256 ἡμιώριον
2259 ἡνίκα
2260 ἤπερ

2261 ἤπιος
2262 Ἤρ
2263 ἤρεμος
2264 Ἡρῴδης
2265 Ἡρῳδιανοί

2266 Ἡρῳδιάς
2267 Ἡρῳδίων
2268 Ἠσαΐας
2269 Ἠσαῦ
2276 ἥσσων

- 2270 ἡσυχάζειν
- 2271 ἡσυχία
- 2272 ἡσύχιος
- 2273 ἤτοι
- 2274 ἡττᾶσθαι
- 2275 ἥττημα
- 2278 ἠχεῖν
- 2279 ἦχος
- 2280 Θαδδαῖος
- 2281 θάλασσα
- 2282 θάλπειν
- 2283 Θαμάρ
- 2284 θαμβεῖν
- 2285 θάμβος
- 2286 θανάσιμος
- 2287 θανατηφόρος
- 2288 θάνατος
- 2289 θανατοῦν
- 2290 θάπτειν
- 2291 Θάρα
- 2292 θαρρεῖν
- 2293 θαρσεῖν
- 2294 θάρσος
- 2295 θαῦμα
- 2296 θαυμάζειν *
- 2297 θαυμάσιος
- 2298 θαυμαστός
- 2299 θεά
- 2300 θεᾶσθαι
- 2301 θεατρίζειν
- 2302 θέατρον
- 2303 θεῖον, τό
- 2304 θεῖος, -α, -ον
- 2305 θειότης
- 2306 θειώδης
- 2309 θέλειν
- 2307 θέλημα
- 2308 θέλησις
- 2310 θεμέλιος
- 2311 θεμελιοῦν
- 2312 θεοδίδακτος
- 2314 θεομάχος
- 2315 θεόπνευστος
- 2316 θεός
- 2317 θεοσέβεια
- 2318 θεοσεβής
- 2319 θεοστυγής
- 2320 θεότης
- 2321 Θεόφιλος
- 2322 θεραπεία
- 2323 θεραπεύειν
- 2324 θεράπων
- 2325 θερίζειν
- 2326 θερισμός
- 2327 θεριστής
- 2328 θερμαίνεσθαι
- 2329 θέρμη
- 2330 θέρος
- 2331 Θεσσαλονικεύς
- 2332 Θεσσαλονίκη
- 2333 Θευδᾶς
- 2334 θεωρεῖν
- 2335 θεωρία
- 2336 θήκη
- 2337 θηλάζειν
- 2338 θῆλυς
- 2339 θήρα
- 2340 θηρεύειν
- 2341 θηριομαχεῖν
- 2342 θηρίον
- 2343 θησαυρίζειν
- 2344 θησαυρός
- 2345 θιγγάνειν
- 2346 θλίβειν
- 2347 θλῖψις

- 2348 θνήσκειν
- 2349 θνητός
- 2349.5 θορυβάζειν *
- 2350 θορυβεῖν
- 2351 θόρυβος
- 2352 θραύειν
- 2353 θρέμμα
- 2354 θρηνεῖν
- 2356 θρησκεία
- 2357 θρησκός
- 2358 θριαμβεύειν
- 2359 θρίξ
- 2360 θροεῖσθαι
- 2361 θρόμβος
- 2362 θρόνος
- 2363 Θυάτιρα
- 2364 θυγάτηρ
- 2365 θυγάτριον
- 2380 θύειν
- 2366 θύελλα
- 2367 θύϊνος
- 2368 θυμίαμα
- 2370 θυμιᾶν
- 2369 θυμιατήριον
- 2371 θυμομαχεῖν
- 2372 θυμός
- 2373 θυμοῦσθαι
- 2374 θύρα
- 2375 θυρεός
- 2376 θυρίς
- 2377 θυρωρός
- 2378 θυσία
- 2379 θυσιαστήριον
- 2381 Θωμᾶς
- 2382 θώραξ
- 2383 Ἰάϊρος
- 2384 Ἰακώβ
- 2385 Ἰάκωβος
- 2386 ἴαμα
- 2387 Ἰαμβρῆς
- 2388 Ἰανναί
- 2389 Ἰάννης
- 2391 Ἰάρετ
- 2390 ἰᾶσθαι
- 2392 ἴασις
- 2393 ἴασπις
- 2394 Ἰάσων
- 2395 ἰατρός
- 2396 ἴδε
- 2398 ἴδιος
- 2399 ἰδιώτης
- 2400 ἰδού
- 2401 Ἰδουμαία
- 2402 ἱδρώς
- 2403 Ἰεζάβελ
- 2404 Ἱεράπολις
- 2405 ἱερατεία
- 2407 ἱερατεύειν
- 2406 ἱεράτευμα
- 2408 Ἰερεμίας
- 2409 ἱερεύς
- 2410.5 Ἰεριχώ v1494
- 1494 ἱερόθυτον
- 2411 ἱερόν
- 2412 ἱεροπρεπής
- 2413 ἱερός, -ά, -όν
- 2414 Ἱεροσόλυμα
- 2415 Ἱεροσολυμῖται
- 2416 ἱεροσυλεῖν
- 2417 ἱερόσυλος
- 2418 ἱερουργεῖν
- 2419 Ἰερουσαλήμ
- 2420 ἱερωσύνη
- 2421 Ἰεσσαί
- 2422 Ἰεφθάε

- 2423 Ἰεχονίας
- 2424 Ἰησοῦς
- 2425 ἱκανός
- 2426 ἱκανότης
- 2427 ἱκανοῦν
- 2428 ἱκετηρία
- 2429 ἰκμάς
- 2430 Ἰκόνιον
- 2431 ἱλαρός
- 2432 ἱλαρότης
- 2433 ἱλάσκεσθαι
- 2434 ἱλασμός
- 2435 ἱλαστήριον
- 2436 ἵλεως
- 2437 Ἰλλυρικόν
- 2438 ἱμάς
- 2439 ἱματίζειν
- 2440 ἱμάτιον
- 2441 ἱματισμός
- 2443 ἵνα (gr. S)
- 2444 ἱνατί
- 2445 Ἰόππη
- 2446 Ἰορδάνης
- 2447 ἰός
- 2449 Ἰουδαία 2448*
- 2450 ἰουδαΐζειν
- 2451 Ἰουδαϊκός
- 2452 Ἰουδαϊκῶς
- 2453 Ἰουδαῖος
- 2454 Ἰουδαϊσμός
- 2455 Ἰούδας *
- 2456 Ἰουλία
- 2457 Ἰούλιος
- 2458 Ἰουνίας
- 2459 Ἰοῦστος
- 2460 ἱππεύς
- 2461 ἱππικός
- 2462 ἵππος
- 2463 ἶρις
- 2464 Ἰσαάκ
- 2465 ἰσάγγελος
- 2469 Ἰσκαριώτης *
- 2470 ἴσος
- 2471 ἰσότης
- 2472 ἰσότιμος
- 2473 ἰσόψυχος
- 2474 Ἰσραήλ
- 2475 Ἰσραηλίτης
- 2475.5 Ἰσσαχάρ vW2466
- 2476 ἱστάναι
- 2477 ἱστορεῖν
- 2480 ἰσχύειν
- 2478 ἰσχυρός
- 2479 ἰσχύς
- 2481 ἴσως
- 2482 Ἰταλία
- 2483 Ἰταλικός
- 2484 Ἰτουραία
- 2485 ἰχθύδιον
- 2486 ἰχθύς
- 2487 ἴχνος
- 2488 Ἰωάθαμ
- 2489 Ἰωάννα
- 2490 Ἰωανάν
- 2491 Ἰωάννης *
- 2492 Ἰώβ
- 2492.2 Ἰωβήδ vW5601
- 2492.5 Ἰωδά vW2455
- 2493 Ἰωήλ
- 2494 Ἰωνάμ
- 2495 Ἰωνᾶς
- 2496 Ἰωράμ
- 2497 Ἰωρίμ
- 2498 Ἰωσαφάτ
- 2500 Ἰωσῆς

- 2501 Ἰωσήφ
- 2501.5 Ἰωσήχ *
- 2502 Ἰωσίας vM2498.5
- 2503 ἰῶτα
- 2504 κἀγώ
- 2505 καθά
- 2507 καθαιρεῖν
- 2508 καθαίρειν
- 2506 καθαίρεσις
- 2509 καθάπερ *
- 2510 καθάπτειν
- 2511 καθαρίζειν
- 2512 καθαρισμός
- 2513 καθαρός
- 2514 καθαρότης
- 2515 καθέδρα
- 2516 καθέζεσθαι
- 2517 καθεξῆς
- 2518 καθεύδειν
- 2519 καθηγητής
- 2520 καθήκειν
- 2522 καθημερινός
- 2521 καθῆσθαι
- 2524 καθιέναι
- 2523 καθίζειν
- 2525 καθιστάναι
- 2526 καθό
- 2527 καθόλου
- 2528 καθοτλίζεσθαι
- 2529 καθορᾶν
- 2530 καθότι
- 2531 καθώς
- 2531.5 καθώσπερ v2509
- 2532 καί
- 2533 Καϊάφας
- 2545 καίειν
- 2535 Κάϊν
- 2536 Καϊνάμ
- 2537 καινός
- 2538 καινότης
- 2539 καίπερ
- 2540 καιρός
- 2541 Καῖσαρ
- 2542 Καισάρεια
- 2543 καίτοι
- 2546 κἀκεῖ
- 2547 κἀκεῖθεν
- 2548 κἀκεῖνος
- 2549 κακία
- 2550 κακοήθεια
- 2551 κακολογεῖν
- 2552 κακοπάθεια
- 2553 κακοπαθεῖν
- 2554 κακοποιεῖν
- 2555 κακοποιός
- 2556 κακός
- 2559 κακοῦν
- 2557 κακοῦργος
- 2558 κακουχεῖν
- 2560 κακῶς
- 2561 κάκωσις
- 2562 καλάμη
- 2563 κάλαμος
- 2564 καλεῖν
- 2565 καλλιέλαιος
- 2567 καλοδιδάσκαλος
- 2568 Καλοὶ λιμένες *
- 2569 καλοποιεῖν
- 2570 καλός
- 2571 κάλυμμα
- 2572 καλύπτειν
- 2573 καλῶς
- 2574 κάμηλος
- 2575 κάμινος
- 2576 καμμύειν

- 2577 κάμνειν
- 2578 κάμπτειν
- 2579 κἄν
- 2580 Κανά
- 2581 Καναναῖος
- 2582 Κανδάκη
- 2583 κανών
- 2584 Καπερναούμ *
- 2585 καπηλεύειν
- 2586 καπνός
- 2587 Καππαδοκία
- 2588 καρδία
- 2589 καρδιογνώστης
- 2590 καρπός
- 2591 Κάρπος
- 2592 καρποφορεῖν
- 2593 καρποφόρος
- 2594 καρτερεῖν
- 2595 κάρφος
- 2596 κατά (gr. S.)
- 2597 καταβαίνειν
- 2598 καταβάλλειν
- 2599.5 καταβαρεῖν vW916
- 916 καταβαρύνειν
- 2600 κατάβασις
- 2602 καταβολή
- 2603 καταβραβεύειν
- 2604 καταγγελεύς
- 2605 καταγγέλλειν
- 2609 κατάγειν
- 2606 καταγελᾶν
- 2607 καταγινώσκειν
- 2608 καταγνύναι
- 2610 καταγωνίζεσθαι
- 2611 καταδέειν
- 2612 κατάδηλος
- 2613 καταδικάζειν
- 2613.5 καταδίκη v1349
- 2614 καταδιώκειν
- 2615 καταδουλοῦν
- 2616 καταδυναστεύειν
- 2616.2 κατάθεμα vW2652
- 2616.5 καταθεματίζειν *
- 2617 καταισχύνειν
- 2618 κατακαίειν
- 2619 κατακαλύπτεσθαι
- 2620 κατακαυχᾶσθαι
- 2621 κατακεῖσθαι
- 2622 κατακλᾶν
- 2623 κατακλείειν
- 2624 κατακληρονομεῖν
- 2625 κατακλίνειν
- 2626 κατακλύζειν
- 2627 κατακλυσμός
- 2628 κατακολουθεῖν
- 2629 κατακόπτειν
- 2630 κατακρημνίζειν
- 2631 κατάκριμα
- 2632 κατακρίνειν
- 2633 κατάκρισις
- 2634 κατακυριεύειν
- 2635 καταλαλεῖν
- 2636 καταλαλιά
- 2637 κατάλαλος
- 2638 καταλαμβάνειν
- 2639 καταλέγεσθαι
- 2640 κατάλειμμα *
- 2641 καταλείπειν
- 2642 καταλιθάζειν
- 2643 καταλλαγή
- 2644 καταλλάσσειν
- 2645 κατάλοιπος
- 2647 καταλύειν
- 2646 κατάλυμα
- 2648 καταμανθάνειν

2649 καταμαρτυρεῖν
2650 καταμένειν
2654 καταναλίσκειν
2655 καταναρκεῖν
2656 κατανεύειν

2657 κατανοεῖν
2658 καταντᾶν
2659 κατάνυξις
2660 κατανύσσεσθαι
2661 καταξιοῦν

2662 καταπατεῖν
2664 καταπαύειν
2663 κατάπαυσις
2665 καταπέτασμα
2666 καταπίνειν

2667 καταπίπτειν
2668 καταπλεῖν
2669 καταπονεῖν
2670 καταποντίζεσθαι
2671 κατάρα

2672 καταρᾶσθαι
2673 καταργεῖν
2674 καταριθμεῖν
2675 καταρτίζειν
2676 κατάρτισις

2677 καταρτισμός
2678 κατασείειν
2679 κατασκάπτειν
2680 κατασκευάζειν
2681 κατασκηνοῦν

2682 κατασκήνωσις
2683 κατασκιάζειν
2684 κατασκοπεῖν
2685 κατάσκοπος
2686 κατασοφίζεσθαι

2687 καταστέλλειν
2688 κατάστημα
2689 καταστολή
2690 καταστρέφειν
2691 καταστρηνιᾶν

2692 καταστροφή
2693 καταστρωννύναι
2694 κατασύρειν
2695 κατασφάζειν
2696 κατασφραγίζειν

2697 κατάσχεσις
2698 κατατιθέναι
2699 κατατομή
2701 κατατρέχειν
2719 καταφαγεῖν

2702 καταφέρειν
2703 καταφεύγειν
2704 καταφθείρειν
2705 καταφιλεῖν
2706 καταφρονεῖν

2707 καταφρονητής
2708 καταχεῖν
2709 καταχθόνιος
2710 καταχρᾶσθαι
2711 καταψύχειν

2712 κατείδωλος
2713 κατέναντι
2714 κατενώπιον
2715 κατεξουσιάζειν
2716 κατεργάζεσθαι

2718 κατέρχεσθαι
2719 κατεσθίειν
2720 κατευθύνειν
2720.5 κατευλογεῖν *
2721 κατεφίστασθαι

2722 κατέχειν
2723 κατηγορεῖν
2724 κατηγορία
2725 κατήγορος
2725.5 κατήγωρ v2725

2726 κατήφεια
2727 κατηχεῖν
2728 κατιοῦσθαι
2729 κατισχύειν
2730 κατοικεῖν

2731 κατοίκησις
2732 κατοικητήριον
2733 κατοικία
2733.5 κατοικίζειν v2730
2734 κατοπτρίζεσθαι

2736 κάτω, κατωτέρω
2737 κατώτερος
2738 καῦμα
2739 καυματίζειν
2740 καῦσις

2741 καυσοῦσθαι
2742 καύσων
2743 καυστηριάζεσθαι
2744 καυχᾶσθαι *
2745 καύχημα

2746 καύχησις
2747 Κεγχρεαί *
2748 Κεδρών
2751 κείρειν
2750 κειρία

2749 κεῖσθαι
2753 κελεύειν
2752 κέλευσμα
2754 κενοδοξία
2755 κενόδοξος

2756 κενός
2758 κενοῦν
2757 κενοφωνία
2759 κέντρον
2760 κεντυρίων

2761 κενῶς
2762 κεραία
2763 κεραμεύς
2764 κεραμικός
2765 κεράμιον

2766 κέραμος
2767 κεραννύναι
2768 κέρας
2769 κεράτιον
2770 κερδαίνειν

2771 κέρδος
2772 κέρμα
2773 κερματιστής
2774 κεφάλαιον
2775 κεφαλαιοῦν

2776 κεφαλή
2777 κεφαλίς
2777.5 κημοῦν v5392
2778 κῆνσος
2779 κῆπος

2780 κηπουρός
2782 κήρυγμα
2783 κήρυξ
2784 κηρύσσειν
2785 κῆτος

2786 Κηφᾶς
2787 κιβωτός
2788 κιθάρα
2789 κιθαρίζειν
2790 κιθαρῳδός

2791 Κιλικία
2793 κινδυνεύειν
2794 κίνδυνος
2795 κινεῖν
2792 κιννάμωμον

2797 Κίς
2798 κλάδος
2806 κλάζειν, κλᾶν
2799 κλαίειν
2800 κλάσις

2801 κλάσμα
2802 Κλαύδη *
2803 Κλαυδία
2804 Κλαύδιος
2805 κλαυθμός

2808 κλείειν
2807 κλείς
2809 κλέμμα
2810 Κλεοπᾶς
2811 κλέος

2813 κλέπτειν
2812 κλέπτης
2814 κλῆμα
2815 Κλήμης
2816 κληρονομεῖν

2817 κληρονομία
2818 κληρονόμος
2819 κλῆρος
2820 κληροῦν
2821 κλῆσις

2822 κλητός
2823 κλίβανος
2824 κλίμα
2824.5 κλινάριον v2825
2827 κλίνειν

2825 κλίνη
2826 κλινίδιον
2828 κλισία
2829 κλοπή
2830 κλύδων

2831 κλυδωνίζεσθαι
2832 Κλωπᾶς
2833 κνήθειν
2834 Κνίδος
2835 κοδράντης

2836 κοιλία
2837 κοιμᾶσθαι
2838 κοίμησις
2839 κοινός
2840 κοινοῦν

2841 κοινωνεῖν
2842 κοινωνία
2843 κοινωνικός
2844 κοινωνός
2845 κοίτη

2846 κοιτών
2847 κόκκινος
2848 κόκκος
2849 κολάζειν
2850 κολακεία

2851 κόλασις
2852 κολαφίζειν
2853 κολλᾶσθαι
2854 κολλούριον
2855 κολλυβιστής

2856 κολοβοῦν
2857 Κολοσσαί
2859 κόλπος
2860 κολυμβᾶν
2861 κολυμβήθρα

2862 κολωνία
2863 κομᾶν
2864 κόμη
2865 κομίζειν
2866 κομψότερον

2867 κονιᾶν
2868 κονιορτός
2869 κοπάζειν
2870 κοπετός
2871 κοπή

2872 κοπιᾶν v5306.5
2873 κόπος
2874 κοπρία
2874.5 κόπριον v2874
2875 κόπτειν

2876 κόραξ
2877 κοράσιον
2878 κορβᾶν -νᾶς
2879 Κορέ
2880 κορεννύναι

2881 Κορίνθιος
2882 Κόρινθος
2883 Κορνήλιος
2884 κόρος
2885 κοσμεῖν

2886 κοσμικός
2887 κόσμιος
2888 κοσμοκράτωρ
2889 κόσμος
2890 Κούαρτος

2891 κοῦμ
2892 κουστωδία
2893 κουφίζειν
2894 κόφινος
2895 κράβατος

2896 κράζειν
2897 κραιπάλη
2898 κρανίον
2899 κράσπεδον
2900 κραταιός

2901 κραταιοῦσθαι
2902 κρατεῖν
2903 κράτιστος
2904 κράτος
2905 κραυγάζειν

2906 κραυγή
2907 κρέας
2909 κρείσσων
2910 κρεμαννύναι
2911 κρημνός

2913 Κρήσκης
2912 Κρῆτες
2914 Κρήτη
2915 κριθή
2916 κρίθινος

2917 κρίμα
2919 κρίνειν
2918 κρίνον
2920 κρίσις
2921 Κρίσπος

2922 κριτήριον
2923 κριτής
2924 κριτικός
2925 κρούειν
2928 κρύπτειν

2926 κρύπτη, ἡ v2927
2927 κρυπτός
2929 κρυσταλλίζειν
2930 κρύσταλλος
2930.5 κρυφαῖος v2927

2931 κρυφῇ
2932 κτᾶσθαι
2933 κτῆμα
2934 κτῆνος
2935 κτήτωρ

2936 κτίζειν
2937 κτίσις
2938 κτίσμα
2939 κτίστης
2940 κυβεία

2941 κυβέρνησις
2942 κυβερνήτης
2942.5 κυκλεύειν v2944
2943 κυκλόθεν
2944 κυκλοῦν

2945 κύκλῳ
2947 κυλίεσθαι
2946 κυλισμός
2948 κυλλός
2949 κῦμα

2950 κύμβαλον
2951 κύμινον
2952 κυνάριον
2953 Κύπριος
2954 Κύπρος

2955 κύπτειν v2633.5
2956 Κυρηναῖος
2957 Κυρήνη
2958 Κυρήνιος
2959 κυρία

2960 κυριακός
2961 κυριεύειν
2962 κύριος
2963 κυριότης
2964 κυροῦν

2965 κύων
2966 κῶλον
2967 κωλύειν
2968 κώμη
2969 κωμόπολις

2970 κῶμος
2971 κώνωψ
2972 Κῶς
2973 Κωσάμ
2974 κωφός

2975 λαγχάνειν
2976 Λάζαρος
2977 λάθρα
2978 λαῖλαψ
2978.5 λακᾶν v2997

2979 λακτίζειν
2980 λαλεῖν
2981 λαλιά
2982 λαμά (λεμά) *
2983 λαμβάνειν

2984 Λάμεχ
2985 λαμπάς
2989 λάμπειν
2986 λαμπρός
2987 λαμπρότης

2988 λαμπρῶς
2990 λανθάνειν
2991 λαξευτός
2993 Λαοδικεία
2994 Λαοδικεύς

2992 λαός
2995 λάρυγξ
2996 Λασαία
2998 λατομεῖν
2999 λατρεία

3000 λατρεύειν
3001 λάχανον
3004 λέγειν vM2064.5
3003 λεγιών
3005 λεῖμμα

3006 λεῖος
3007 λείπειν
3008 λειτουργεῖν
3009 λειτουργία
3010 λειτουργικός

3011 λειτουργός
3012 λέντιον
3013 λεπίς
3014 λέπρα
3015 λεπρός

3016 λεπτόν
3017 Λευί 3018
3019 Λευίτης
3020 Λευιτικός
3021 λευκαίνειν

3022 λευκός
3023 λέων
3024 λήθη
3024.5 λῆμψις v3028
3025 ληνός

3026 λῆρος
3027 λῃστής
3029 λίαν
3030 λίβανος
3031 λιβανωτός

3032 Λιβερτῖνοι
3033 Λιβύη
3034 λιθάζειν
3035 λίθινος
3036 λιθοβολεῖν

3037 λίθος
3038 Λιθόστρωτος
3039 λικμᾶν
3040 λιμήν
3041 λίμνη

3042 λιμός
3043 λίνον
3044 Λίνος
3045 λιπαρός
3046 λίτρα

3047 λίψ
3048 λογία
3049 λογίζεσθαι
3050 λογικός
3051 λόγιον

3052 λόγιος
3053 λογισμός
3054 λογομαχεῖν
3055 λογομαχία
3056 λόγος

3057 λόγχη
3058 λοιδορεῖν
3059 λοιδορία
3060 λοίδορος
3061 λοιμός

3062 λοιπός 3063-64
3068 λούειν
3065 Λουκᾶς
3066 Λούκιος
3067 λουτρόν

3069 Λύδδα
3070 Λυδία
3089 λύειν
3071 Λυκαονία
3072 Λυκαονιστί

3073 Λυκία
3074 λύκος
3075 λυμαίνεσθαι
3076 λυπεῖν
3077 λύπη

3078 Λυσανίας
3079 Λυσίας
3080 λύσις
3081 λυσιτελεῖν
3082 Λύστρα

3083 λύτρον
3084 λυτροῦν
3085 λύτρωσις
3086 λυτρωτής
3087 λυχνία

3088 λύχνος
3090 Λωΐς
3091 Λώτ
3092 Μάαθ
3093 Μαγαδάν

3094 Μαγδαληνή
3095 μαγεία
3096 μαγεύειν
3097 μάγος
3098 Μαγώγ

3099 Μαδιάμ
3100 μαθητεύειν
3101 μαθητής
3102 μαθήτρια
3102.2 Μαθθαῖος *

3102.4 Μαθθάν vW3157 *
3102.6 Μαθθάτ, Μαθτάτ
3102.8 Μαθθίας vW3159
3103 Μαθουσάλα
3105 μαίνεσθαι

3106 μακαρίζειν
3107 μακάριος
3108 μακαρισμός
3109 Μακεδονία
3110 Μακεδών

3111 μάκελλον
3112 μακράν
3113 μακρόθεν
3114 μακροθυμεῖν
3115 μακροθυμία

3116 μακροθύμως
3117 μακρός
3118 μακροχρόνιος
3119 μαλακία
3120 μαλακός

3121 Μαλελεήλ
3122 μάλιστα
3123 μᾶλλον
3124 Μάλχος
3125 μάμμη

3126 μαμωνᾶς
3127 Μαναήν
3128 Μανασσῆς
3129 μανθάνειν
3130 μανία

3131 μάννα
3132 μαντεύεσθαι
3133 μαραίνεσθαι
3134 μαρὰν ἀθά
3135 μαργαρίτης

3136 Μάρθα
3137 Μαρία
3138 Μάρκος
3139 μάρμαρος
3140 μαρτυρεῖν

3143 μαρτύρεσθαι
3141 μαρτυρία
3142 μαρτύριον
3144 μάρτυς
3145 μασσᾶσθαι

3146 μαστιγοῦν
3147 μαστίζειν
3148 μάστιξ
3149 μαστός
3150 ματαιολογία

3151 ματαιολόγος
3152 μάταιος
3153 ματαιότης
3154 ματαιοῦσθαι
3155 μάτην

3160 Ματταθά
3161 Ματταθίας
3162 μάχαιρα
3164 μάχεσθαι
3163 μάχη

3167 μεγαλεῖος
3168 μεγαλειότης
3169 μεγαλοπρεπής
3170 μεγαλύνειν
3171 μεγάλως

3172 μεγαλωσύνη
3173 μέγας
3174 μέγεθος
3175 μεγιστάν
3176 μέγιστος

3177 μεθερμηνεύεσθαι
3178 μέθη
3179 μεθιστάνειν
3180 μεθοδεία
3184 μεθύειν

3182 μεθύσκεσθαι
3183 μέθυσος
3187 μείζων *
3188 μέλας 3189
3190 Μελεά

3190.5 μέλει vW3199
3191 μελετᾶν
3192 μέλι
3194 Μελίτη
3195 μέλλειν

3196 μέλος
3197 Μελχί
3198 Μελχισέδεκ
3200 μεμβράνα
3201 μέμφεσθαι

3202 μεμψίμοιρος
3303 μέν
3306 μένειν
3303.5 Μεννά vW3104
3304 μενοῦν

3305 μέντοι
3307 μερίζειν
3308 μέριμνα
3309 μεριμνᾶν
3310 μερίς

3311 μερισμός
3312 μεριστής
3313 μέρος
3314 μεσημβρία
3315 μεσιτεύειν

3316 μεσίτης
3317 μεσονύκτιον
3318 Μεσοποταμία
3319 μέσος
3320 μεσότοιχον

3322 μεσοῦν
3321 μεσουράνημα
3323 Μεσσίας
3324 μεστός
3325 μεστοῦσθαι

3326 μετά (gr. S)
3327 μεταβαίνειν
3328 μεταβάλλεσθαι
3329 μετάγειν
3330 μεταδιδόναι

3331 μετάθεσις
3332 μεταίρειν
3333 μετακαλεῖσθαι
3334 μετακινεῖν
3335 μεταλαμβάνειν

3336 μετάλημψις
3337 μεταλλάσσειν
3338 μεταμέλεσθαι
3339 μεταμορφοῦσθαι
3340 μετανοεῖν

3341 μετάνοια
3342 μεταξύ
3343 μεταπέμπεσθαι
3344 μεταστρέφειν *
3345 μετασχηματίζειν

3346 μετατιθέναι
3346.5 μετατρέπειν v3344
3347 μετέπειτα
3348 μετέχειν
3349 μετεωρίζεσθαι

3350 μετοικεσία
3351 μετοικίζειν
3352 μετοχή
3353 μέτοχος
3354 μετρεῖν

3355 μετρητής
3356 μετριοπαθεῖν
3357 μετρίως
3358 μέτρον
3359 μέτωπον

3360 μέχρι
3361 μή (gr. S.)
3365 μηδαμῶς
3366 μηδέ
3367 μηδείς

3368 μηδέποτε
3369 μηδέπω
3370 Μῆδος
3370.5 μηθέν v3367
3371 μηκέτι

3372 μῆκος
3373 μηκύνεσθαι
3374 μηλωτή
3375 μήν, μηνός
3376 μήν

3377 μηνύειν
3379 μήποτε
3380 μήπω
3382 μηρός
3383 μήτε

3384 μήτηρ
3385 μήτι v3386
3388 μήτρα
3389 μητραλῴης
3392 μιαίνειν

3393 μίασμα
3394 μιασμός
3395 μίγμα vM1662.5
3396 μιγνύναι
3397 μικρόν

3398 μικρός
3399 Μίλητος
3400 μίλιον
3401 μιμεῖσθαι
3402 μιμητής

3403 μιμνήσκεσθαι
3404 μισεῖν
3405 μισθαποδοσία
3406 μισθαποδότης
3407 μίσθιος

3408 μισθός
3409 μισθοῦσθαι
3410 μίσθωμα
3411 μισθωτός
3412 Μιτυλήνη

3413 Μιχαήλ
3414 μνᾶ
3416 Μνάσων
3417 μνεία
3418 μνῆμα

3419 μνημεῖον
3420 μνήμη
3421 μνημονεύειν
3422 μνημόσυνον
3423 μνηστεύεσθαι

3424 μογιλάλος
3426 μόδιος
3428 μοιχαλίς
3429 μοιχᾶσθαι
3430 μοιχεία

3431 μοιχεύειν
3432 μοιχός
3433 μόλις
3434 Μολόχ
3435 μολύνειν

3436 μολυσμός
3437 μομφή
3438 μονή
3439 μονογενής
3440 μόνον

3441 μόνος
3443 μονοῦσθαι
3442 μονόφθαλμος
3444 μορφή
3445 μορφοῦσθαι

3446 μόρφωσις
3447 μοσχοποιεῖν
3448 μόσχος
3451 μουσικός
3449 μόχθος

3453 μυεῖσθαι
3452 μυελός
3454 μῦθος
3455 μυκᾶσθαι
3456 μυκτηρίζεσθαι

3457 μυλικός
3458.5 μύλινος v3458
3458 μύλος
3460 Μύρα
3461 μυριάς

3462 μυρίζειν
3463 μύριοι
3464 μύρον
3465 Μυσία
3466 μυστήριον

3467 μυωπάζειν
3468 μώλωψ
3469 μωμᾶσθαι
3470 μῶμος
3471 μωραίνειν

3472 μωρία
3473 μωρολογία
3474 μωρός
3475 Μωϋσῆς
3476 Ναασσών

3477 Ναγγαί
3478 Ναζαρέτ
3479 Ναζαρηνός
3480 Ναζωραῖος
3481 Ναθάμ

3482 Ναθαναήλ
3483 ναί
3483.5 Ναιμάν vW3497
3484 Ναΐν
3485 ναός

3486 Ναούμ
3487 νάρδος
3488 Νάρκισσος
3489 ναυαγεῖν
3490 ναύκληρος

3491 ναῦς
3492 ναύτης
3493 Ναχώρ
3494 νεανίας
3495 νεανίσκος

3496 Νεὰ πόλις *
3498 νεκρός
3499 νεκροῦν
3500 νέκρωσις
3501 νέος

3503 νεότης
3504 νεόφυτος
3506 νεύειν
3507 νεφέλη
3508 Νεφθαλίμ

3509 νέφος
3510 νεφρός
3511 νεωκόρος
3512 νεωτερικός
3513 νή

3514 νήθειν
3515 νηπιάζειν
3516 νήπιος
3517 Νηρεύς
3518 Νηρί

3519 νησίον
3520 νῆσος
3521 νηστεία
3522 νηστεύειν
3523 νῆστις

3524 νηφάλιος
3525 νήφειν
3526 Νίγερ
3528 νικᾶν
3527 Νικάνωρ

3529 νίκη
3530 Νικόδημος
3531 Νικολαΐται
3532 Νικόλαος
3533 Νικόπολις

3534 νῖκος
3536 Νινευίτης 3535
3538 νίπτειν
3537 νιπτήρ
3539 νοεῖν

3540 νόημα
3541 νόθος
3542 νομή
3543 νομίζειν
3544 νομικός

3545 νομίμως
3546 νόμισμα
3547 νομοδιδάσκαλος
3548 νομοθεσία
3549 νομοθετεῖν

3550 νομοθέτης
3551 νόμος
3552 νοσεῖν
3554 νόσος
3555 νοσσιά

3556 νοσσίον
3556.5 νοσσός vW3502
3557 νοσφίζεσθαι
3558 νότος
3559 νουθεσία

3560 νουθετεῖν
3561 νουμηνία vM3500.5
3562 νουνεχῶς
3563 νοῦς
3564 Νύμφα

3565 νύμφη
3566 νυμφίος
3567 νυμφών
3568 νῦν 3569
3570 νυνί

3571 νύξ
3572 νύσσειν
3573 νυστάζειν
3574 νυχθήμερον
3575 Νῶε

3576 νωθρός
3577 νῶτος
3578 ξενία
3579 ξενίζειν
3580 ξενοδοχεῖν

3581 ξένος
3582 ξέστης
3583 ξηραίνειν
3584 ξηρός
3585 ξύλινος

3586 ξύλον
3587 ξυρᾶσθαι
3588 ὁ, ἡ, τό,
3589 ὀγδοήκοντα
3590 ὄγδοος

3591 ὄγκος
3592 ὅδε, ἥδε, τόδε
3593 ὁδεύειν
3594 ὁδηγεῖν
3595 ὁδηγός

3596 ὁδοιπορεῖν
3597 ὁδοιπορία
3598 ὁδός vM3598.5
3599 ὀδούς
3600 ὀδυνᾶσθαι

3601 ὀδύνη
3602 ὀδυρμός
3605 ὄζειν
3604 Ὀζίας
3606 ὅθεν

3607 ὀθόνη
3608 ὀθόνιον
3633 οἴεσθαι vM3629.5
3611 οἰκεῖν
3609 οἰκεῖος

3609.5 οἰκετεία v2322
3610 οἰκέτης
3612 οἴκημα
3613 οἰκητήριον
3614 οἰκία

3615 οἰκιακός
3616 οἰκοδεσποτεῖν
3617 οἰκοδεσπότης
3618 οἰκοδομεῖν
3619 οἰκοδομή

3619.5 οἰκοδόμος v3618
3621 οἰκονομεῖν
3622 οἰκονομία
3623 οἰκονόμος
3624 οἶκος

3625 οἰκουμένη
3626 οἰκουργός
3627 οἰκτείρειν
3628 οἰκτιρμός
3629 οἰκτίρμων

3630 οἰνοπότης
3631 οἶνος
3632 οἰνοφλυγία
3634 οἷος
3635 ὀκνεῖν

3636 ὀκνηρός
3637 ὀκταήμερος
3638 ὀκτώ
3639 ὄλεθρος
3639.5 ὀλιγοπιστία v570

3640 ὀλιγόπιστος
3641 ὀλίγος
3642 ὀλιγόψυχος
3643 ὀλιγωρεῖν
3643.5 ὀλίγως v3689

3644 ὀλοθρευτής
3645 ὀλοθρεύειν
3646 ὁλοκαύτωμα
3647 ὁλοκληρία
3648 ὁλόκληρος

3649 ὀλολύζειν
3650 ὅλος
3651 ὁλοτελής
3652 Ὀλυμπᾶς
3653 ὄλυνθος

3654 ὅλως
3655 ὄμβρος
3655.5 ὁμείρεσθαι vW2442
3656 ὁμιλεῖν
3657 ὁμιλία

3657.5 ὁμίχλη v3507
3659 ὄμμα
3660 ὀμνύειν
3661 ὁμοθυμαδόν
3663 ὁμοιοπαθής

3664 ὅμοιος
3665 ὁμοιότης
3666 ὁμοιοῦν
3667 ὁμοίωμα
3668 ὁμοίως

3669 ὁμοίωσις
3670 ὁμολογεῖν
3671 ὁμολογία
3672 ὁμολογουμένως
3673 ὁμότεχνος

3674 ὁμοῦ
3675 ὁμόφρων
3676 ὅμως
3677 ὄναρ
3678 ὀνάριον

3679 ὀνειδίζειν
3680 ὀνειδισμός
3681 ὄνειδος
3682 Ὀνήσιμος
3683 Ὀνησίφορος

3684 ὀνικός
3685 ὀνίνασθαι
3686 ὄνομα
3687 ὀνομάζειν
3688 ὄνος

3689 ὄντως v3643.5
3690 ὄξος
3691 ὀξύς
3692 ὀπή
3693 ὄπισθεν

3694 ὀπίσω
3695 ὁπλίζεσθαι
3696 ὅπλον
3697 ὁποῖος
3698 ὁπότε

3699 ὅπου
3700 ὀπτάνεσθαι
3701 ὀπτασία
3702 ὀπτός
3703 ὀπώρα

3704 ὅπως
3705 ὅραμα
3708 ὁρᾶν
3706 ὅρασις
3707 ὁρατός

3709 ὀργή
3710 ὀργίζεσθαι
3711 ὀργίλος
3712 ὀργυιά
3713 ὀρέγεσθαι

3714 ὀρεινός
3715 ὄρεξις
3716 ὀρθοποδεῖν
3717 ὀρθός
3718 ὀρθοτομεῖν

3719 ὀρθρίζειν
3720 ὀρθρινός
3722 ὄρθρος
3723 ὀρθῶς
3724 ὁρίζειν

3725 ὅριον
3726 ὁρκίζειν v1774.5
3727 ὅρκος
3728 ὁρκωμοσία
3729 ὁρμᾶν

3730 ὁρμή
3731 ὅρμημα
3732 ὄρνεον
3733 ὄρνις
3734 ὁροθεσία

3735 ὄρος
3736 ὀρύσσειν
3737 ὀρφανός
3738 ὀρχεῖσθαι
3739 ὅς, ἥ, ὅ (gr. S.)

3740 ὁσάκις
3741 ὅσιος
3742 ὁσιότης
3743 ὁσίως
3744 ὀσμή

3745 ὅσος
3747 ὀστέον -τοῦν
3748 ὅστις, ἥτις, ὅτι
3749 ὀστράκινος
3750 ὄσφρησις

3751 ὀσφύς
3752 ὅταν
3753 ὅτε
3754 ὅτι
3757 οὗ

3756.5 οὔ v3756
3756 οὐ, οὐκ, v3756.5
3758 οὐά † [οὐχ(gr.S.)
3759 οὐαί
3760 οὐδαμῶς

3761 οὐδέ
3762 οὐδείς, -μία,*-έν
3763 οὐδέποτε
3764 οὐδέπω
3764.5 οὐθείς, οὐθέν *

3765 οὐκέτι
3766 οὐκοῦν
3767 οὖν
3768 οὔπω
3769 οὐρά

3770 οὐράνιος
3771 οὐρανόθεν
3772 οὐρανός
3773 Οὐρβανός
3774 Οὐρίας

3775 οὖς
3776 οὐσία
3777 οὔτε
3778 οὗτος (gr. S.) *
3779 οὕτως

3780 οὐχί
3784 ὀφείλειν
3781 ὀφειλέτης
3782 ὀφειλή
3783 ὀφείλημα

3785 ὄφελον
3786 ὄφελος
3787 ὀφθαλμοδουλία
3788 ὀφθαλμός
3789 ὄφις

3790 ὀφρῦς
3791 ὀχλεῖσθαι
3792 ὀχλοποιεῖν
3793 ὄχλος
3794 ὀχύρωμα

3795 ὀψάριον
3796 ὀψέ
3798 ὀψία vM3798.5
3797 ὄψιμος
3799 ὄψις

3800 ὀψώνιον
3802 παγιδεύειν
3803 παγίς
3804 πάθημα
3805 παθητός

3806 πάθος
3807 παιδαγωγός
3808 παιδάριον
3809 παιδεία
3811 παιδεύειν

3810 παιδευτής
3812 παιδιόθεν
3813 παιδίον
3814 παιδίσκη
3817 παίειν

3815 παίζειν
3816 παῖς
3819 πάλαι
3820 παλαιός
3821 παλαιότης

3822 παλαιοῦν
3823 πάλη
3824 παλιγγενεσία
3825 πάλιν
3826 παμπληθεί *

3828 Παμφυλία
3829 πανδοχεῖον
3830 πανδοχεύς
3831 πανήγυρις
3832 πανοικεί

3833 πανοπλία
3834 πανουργία
3835 πανοῦργος
3837.5 πανταχῇ v3837
3837 πανταχοῦ v3837.5

3838 παντελής
3839 πάντη
3840 πάντοθεν
3841 παντοκράτωρ
3842 πάντοτε

3843 πάντως
3844 παρά (gr. S.)
3845 παραβαίνειν
3846 παραβάλλειν
3847 παράβασις

3848 παραβάτης
3849 παραβιάζεσθαι
3851 παραβολεύεσθαι
3850 παραβολή
3852 παραγγελία

3853 παραγγέλλειν
3855 παράγειν
3854 παραγίνεσθαι
3856 παραδειγματίζειν
3857 παράδεισος

3858 παραδέχεσθαι
3860 παραδιδόναι
3861 παράδοξος
3862 παράδοσις
3863 παραζηλοῦν

3864 παραθαλάσσιος
3865 παραθεωρεῖσθαι
3866 παραθήκη
3867 παραινεῖν
3868 παραιτεῖσθαι

3869 παρακαθέζεσθαι
3870 παρακαλεῖν
3871 παρακαλύπτειν
3873 παρακεῖσθαι
3874 παράκλησις

3875 παράκλητος
3876 παρακοή
3877 παρακολουθεῖν
3878 παρακούειν
3879 παρακύπτειν

3880 παραλαμβάνειν
3881 παραλέγεσθαι
3882 παράλιος
3883 παραλλαγή
3884 παραλογίζεσθαι

3886 παραλύεσθαι
3885 παραλυτικός
3887 παραμένειν
3888 παραμυθεῖσθαι
3889 παραμυθία

3890 παραμύθιον
3891 παρανομεῖν
3892 παρανομία
3893 παραπικραίνειν
3894 παραπικρασμός

3895 παραπίπτειν
3896 παραπλεῖν
3897 παραπλήσιον
3898 παραπλησίως
3899 παραπορεύεσθαι

3900 παράπτωμα
3901 παραρεῖν
3902 παράσημος
3903 παρασκευάζειν
3904 παρασκευή

3905 παρατείνειν
3906 παρατηρεῖν
3907 παρατήρησις
3908 παρατιθέναι
3909 παρατυγχάνειν
3910 παραυτίκα
3911 παραφέρειν
3912 παραφρονεῖν
3913 παραφρονία
3914 παραχειμάζειν
3915 παραχειμασία
3916 παραχρῆμα
3917 πάρδαλις
3917.5 παρεδρεύειν *
3918 παρεῖναι
3919 παρεισάγειν
3920 παρείσακτος
3921 παρεισδύειν
3922 παρεισέρχεσθαι
3923 παρεισφέρειν
3924 παρεκτός
3924.5 παρεμβάλλειν *
3925 παρεμβολή
3926 παρενοχλεῖν
3927 παρεπίδημος
3928 παρέρχεσθαι
3929 πάρεσις
3930 παρέχειν
3931 παρηγορία
3932 παρθενία
3933 παρθένος
3934 Πάρθοι
3935 παρίημι
3936 παριστάνειν
3937 Παρμενᾶς
3938 πάροδος
3939 παροικεῖν
3940 παροικία
3941 πάροικος
3942 παροιμία
3943 πάροινος
3944 παροίχεσθαι
3945 παρομοιάζειν
3946 παρόμοιος
3947 παροξύνεσθαι
3948 παροξυσμός
3949 παροργίζειν
3950 παροργισμός
3951 παροτρύνειν
3952 παρουσία
3953 παροψίς
3954 παρρησία
3955 παρρησιάζεσθαι
3956 πᾶς, πᾶσα, πᾶν
3957 πάσχα
3958 πάσχειν
3959 Πάταρα
3960 πατάσσειν
3961 πατεῖν
3962 πατήρ
3963 Πάτμος
3965 πατριά
3966 πατριάρχης
3967 πατρικός
3968 πατρίς
3969 Πατροβᾶς
3969.5 πατρολῴης *
3970 πατροπαράδοτος
3971 πατρῷος
3973 παύειν
3972 Παῦλος
3974 Πάφος
3975 παχύνεσθαι
3976 πέδη
3977 πεδινός

3978 πεζεύειν
3979 πεζῇ vM3979.5
3980 πειθαρχεῖν
3982 πείθειν
3981 πειθός
3983 πεινᾶν
3984 πεῖρα
3985 πειράζειν
3987 πειρᾶσθαι
3986 πειρασμός
3988 πεισμονή
3989 πέλαγος
3990 πελεκίζεσθαι
3992 πέμπειν
3991 πέμπτος
3993 πένης
3996 πενθεῖν
3994 πενθερά
3995 πενθερός
3997 πένθος
3998 πενιχρός
3999 πεντάκις
4000 πεντακισχίλιοι
4001 πεντακόσιοι
4002 πέντε
4003 πεντεκαιδέκατος
4004 πεντήκοντα
4005 πεντηκοστή
4006 πεποίθησις
4006.5 περαιτέρω v2087
4008 πέραν
4009 πέρας
4010 Πέργαμος
4011 Πέργη
4012 περί (gr. S.)
4013 περιάγειν
4014 περιαιρεῖν
4014.5 περιάπτειν v681
4015 περιαστράπτειν
4016 περιβάλλειν
4017 περιβλέπεσθαι
4018 περιβόλαιον
4019 περιδεῖν
4020 περιεργάζεσθαι
4021 περίεργος
4022 περιέρχεσθαι
4023 περιέχειν
4024 περιζωννύναι
4025 περίθεσις
4026 περιϊστάναι
4027 περικάθαρμα
4028 περικαλύπτειν
4029 περικεῖσθαι
4030 περικεφαλαία
4031 περικρατής
4032 περικρύβειν
4033 περικυκλοῦν
4034 περιλάμπειν
4035 περιλείπεσθαι
4036 περίλυπος
4037 περιμένειν
4038 πέριξ
4039 περιοικεῖν
4040 περίοικος
4041 περιούσιος
4042 περιοχή
4043 περιπατεῖν
4044 περιπείρειν
4045 περιπίπτειν
4046 περιποιεῖσθαι
4047 περιποίησις
4048 περιρηγνύναι
4049 περισπᾶσθαι
4050 περισσεία
4052 περισσεύειν

4051 περίσσευμα
4053 περισσός *
4055 περισσότερος *
4056 περισσοτέρως
4057 περισσῶς
4058 περιστερά
4059 περιτέμνειν
4060 περιτιθέναι
4061 περιτομή
4062 περιτρέπειν
4063 περιτρέχειν
4064 περιφέρειν
4065 περιφρονεῖν
4066 περίχωρος
4067 περίψημα
4068 περπερεύεσθαι
4069 Περσίς
4070 πέρυσι
4071 πετεινόν
4072 πέτεσθαι
4073 πέτρα
4074 Πέτρος
4075 πετρώδης
4076 πήγανον
4077 πηγή
4078 πηγνύναι
4079 πηδάλιον
4080 πηλίκος
4081 πηλός
4082 πήρα
4083 πῆχυς
4084 πιάζειν
4085 πιέζειν
4086 πιθανολογία
4087 πικραίνειν
4088 πικρία
4089 πικρός
4090 πικρῶς
4091 Πιλᾶτος *
4092 πίμπρασθαι *
4093 πινακίδιον
4094 πίναξ
4095 πίνειν
4096 πιότης
4097 πιπράσκειν
4098 πίπτειν
4099 Πισιδία
4100 πιστεύειν
4101 πιστικός
4102 πίστις
4103 πιστός
4104 πιστοῦν
4105 πλανᾶν
4106 πλάνη
4107 πλανήτης
4108 πλάνος
4109 πλάξ
4110 πλάσμα
4111 πλάσσειν
4112 πλαστός
4113 πλατεῖα
4114 πλάτος
4115 πλατύνειν
4116 πλατύς
4117 πλέγμα
4126 πλεῖν
4118 πλεῖστος
4119 πλείων, πλεῖον *
4120 πλέκειν
4121 πλεονάζειν
4122 πλεονεκτεῖν
4123 πλεονέκτης
4124 πλεονεξία
4125 πλευρά
4127 πληγή

4130 πλήθειν (πίμ- *
4128 πλῆθος [πλημι)
4129 πληθύνειν
4131 πλήκτης
4132 πλημμύρα
4133 πλήν
4134 πλήρης
4137 πληροῦν
4135 πληροφορεῖν
4136 πληροφορία
4138 πλήρωμα
4139 πλησίον
4140 πλησμονή
4141 πλήσσειν
4142 πλοιάριον
4143 πλοῖον
4144 πλοῦς
4145 πλούσιος
4146 πλουσίως
4147 πλουτεῖν
4148 πλουτίζειν
4149 πλοῦτος
4150 πλύνειν
4154 πνεῖν
4151 πνεῦμα
4152 πνευματικός
4153 πνευματικῶς
4155 πνίγειν
4156 πνικτός
4157 πνοή
4158 ποδήρης
4159 πόθεν
4160 ποιεῖν
4161 ποίημα
4162 ποίησις
4163 ποιητής
4164 ποικίλος
4165 ποιμαίνειν
4166 ποιμήν
4167 ποίμνη
4168 ποίμνιον
4169 ποῖος
4170 πολεμεῖν
4171 πόλεμος
4172 πόλις
4173 πολιτάρχης
4174 πολιτεία
4176 πολιτεύεσθαι
4175 πολίτευμα
4177 πολίτης
4178 πολλάκις
4179 πολλαπλασίων *
4180 πολυλογία
4181 πολυμερῶς
4182 πολυποίκιλος
4183 πολύς
4184 πολύσπλαγχνος
4185 πολυτελής
4186 πολύτιμος
4187 πολυτρόπως
4188 πόμα
4189 πονηρία
4190 πονηρός 4191
4192 πόνος
4193 Ποντικός
4194 Πόντιος
4195 Πόντος
4196 Πόπλιος
4197 πορεία
4198 πορεύεσθαι
4199 πορθεῖν
4200 πορισμός
4201 Πόρκιος
4202 πορνεία
4203 πορνεύειν

4204 πόρνη
4205 πόρνος
4206 πόρρω 4208
4207 πόρρωθεν
4209 πορφύρα
4210 πορφυροῦς
4211 πορφυρόπωλις
4212 ποσάκις
4213 πόσις
4214 πόσος
4215 ποταμός
4216 ποταμοφόρητος
4217 ποταπός
4218 ποτέ
4219 πότε
4220 πότερον
4221 ποτήριον
4222 ποτίζειν
4223 Ποτίολοι
4224 πότος
4225 πού
4226 ποῦ
4227 Πούδης
4228 πούς
4229 πρᾶγμα
4230 πραγματεία
4231 πραγματεύεσθαι
4232 πραιτώριον
4233 πράκτωρ
4234 πρᾶξις
4237 πρασιά
4238 πράσσειν
4236 πραϋπαθία v4240
4239 πραΰς 4235
4240 πραΰτης v4236
4241 πρέπειν
4242 πρεσβεία
4243 πρεσβεύειν
4244 πρεσβυτέριον
4245 πρεσβύτερος
4246 πρεσβύτης
4247 πρεσβῦτις
4248 πρηνής
4249 πρίζειν
4250 πρίν
4251–52 Πρίσκα (-ιλλα)
4253 πρό
4254 προάγειν
4255 προαιρεῖσθαι
4256 προαιτιᾶσθαι
4257 προακούειν
4258 προαμαρτάνειν
4259 προαύλιον
4260 προβαίνειν
4261 προβάλλειν
4262 προβατικός
4263 προβάτιον *
4263.5 πρόβατον v4263
4264 προβιβάζειν
4265 προβλέπεσθαι
4266 προγίνεσθαι
4267 προγινώσκειν
4268 πρόγνωσις
4269 πρόγονος
4270 προγράφειν
4271 πρόδηλος
4272 προδιδόναι
4273 προδότης
4274 πρόδρομος
4277 προειπεῖν
4276 προελπίζειν
4278 προενάρχεσθαι
4279 προεπαγγέλλε-
4280 προερεῖν [σθαι
4281 προέρχεσθαι

4282 προετοιμάζειν
4283 προευαγγελίζε-
4284 προέχεσθαι[σθαι
4285 προηγεῖσθαι
4286 πρόθεσις

4287 προθεσμία
4288 προθυμία
4289 πρόθυμος
4290 προθύμως
4275 προϊδεῖν

4290.5 προΐμος vW4406
4291 προιστάναι
4292 προκαλεῖσθαι
4293 προκαταγγέλλειν
4294 προκαταρτίζειν

4295 πρόκεισθαι
4296 προκηρύσσειν
4297 προκοπή
4298 προκόπτειν
4299 πρόκριμα

4300 προκυροῦν
4301 προλαμβάνειν
4302 προλέγειν
4303 προμαρτύρεσθαι
4304 προμελετᾶν

4305 προμεριμνᾶν
4306 προνοεῖν
4307 πρόνοια
4308 προορᾶν
4309 προορίζειν

4310 προπάσχειν
4310.5 προπάτωρ v3962
4311 προπέμπειν
4312 προπετής
4313 προπορεύεσθαι

4314 πρός (gr. S.)
4315 προσάββατον
4317 προσάγειν *
4316 προσαγορεύειν
4318 προσαγωγή

4319 προσαιτεῖν *
4319.5 προσαίτης v4319
4320 προσαναβαίνειν
4322 προσαναπληροῦν
4323 προσανατίθεσθαι

4324 προσαπειλεῖσθαι
4325 προσδαπανᾶν
4326 προσδεῖσθαι
4327 προσδέχεσθαι
4328 προσδοκᾶν

4329 προσδοκία
4330 προσεᾶν
4333 προσεργάζεσθαι
4334 προσέρχεσθαι
4336 προσεύχεσθαι

4335 προσευχή
4337 προσέχειν
4338 προσηλοῦν
4339 προσήλυτος
4340 πρόσκαιρος

4341 προσκαλεῖσθαι
4342 προσκαρτερεῖν
4343 προσκαρτέρησις
4344 προσκεφάλαιον
4345 προσκληροῦσθαι

4345.5 προσκλίνεσθαι *
4346 πρόσκλισις
4347 προσκολλᾶσθαι *
4348 πρόσκομμα
4349 προσκοπή

4350 προσκόπτειν
4351 προσκυλίειν
4352 προσκυνεῖν
4353 προσκυνητής
4354 προσλαλεῖν

4355 προσλαμβάνεσθαι
4356 πρόσλημψις
4357 προσμένειν
4358 προσορμίζεσθαι
4359 προσοφείλειν

4360 προσοχθίζειν
4361 πρόσπεινος
4362 προσπηγνύναι
4363 προσπίπτειν
4364 προσποιεῖσθαι

4365 προσπορεύεσθαι
4366 προσρηγνύναι
4368 προστάτις
4367 προστάσσειν
4369 προστιθέναι

4370 προστρέχειν
4371 προσφάγιον
4372 πρόσφατος
4373 προσφάτως
4374 προσφέρειν

4375 προσφιλής
4376 προσφορά
4377 προσφωνεῖν
4378 πρόσχυσις
4379 προσψαύειν

4380 προσωπολημπτεῖν
4381 προσωπολήμπτης
4382 προσωπολημψία
4383 πρόσωπον
4385 προτείνειν

4386 πρότερος 4387
4388 προτίθεσθαι
4389 προτρέπειν
4390 προτρέχειν
4391 προϋπάρχειν

4392 πρόφασις
4393 προφέρειν
4394 προφητεία
4395 προφητεύειν
4396 προφήτης

4397 προφητικός
4398 προφῆτις
4399 προφθάνειν
4400 προχειρίζεσθαι
4401 προχειροτονεῖν

4402 Πρόχορος
4403 πρύμνα
4404 πρωΐ
4405 πρωΐα
4407 πρωϊνός

4408 πρῷρα
4409 πρωτεύειν
4410 πρωτοκαθεδρία
4411 πρωτοκλισία
4412 πρῶτον, Adv.

4413 πρῶτος, -τον
4414 πρωτοστάτης
4415 πρωτοτόκια
4416 πρωτότοκος
4416.5 πρώτως v4412

4417 πταίειν
4418 πτέρνα
4419 πτερύγιον
4420 πτέρυξ
4421 πτηνός

4422 πτοεῖσθαι
4423 πτόησις
4424 Πτολεμαΐς
4429 πτύειν
4425 πτύον

4426 πτύρεσθαι
4427 πτύσμα
4428 πτύσσειν
4430 πτῶμα
4431 πτῶσις

4432 πτωχεία
4433 πτωχεύειν
4434 πτωχός
4435 πυγμή
4436 πύθων

4437 πυκνός
4438 πυκτεύειν
4439 πύλη
4440 πυλών
4441 πυνθάνεσθαι

4442 πῦρ
4443 πυρά
4444 πύργος
4445 πυρέσσειν
4446 πυρετός

4447 πύρινος
4448 πυροῦσθαι
4449 πυρράζειν
4450.5 Πύρρος v4450
4450 πυρρός vM4450.5

4451 πύρωσις
4453 πωλεῖν
4454 πῶλος
4455 πώποτε
4456 πωροῦν

4457 πώρωσις
4458 πώς
4459 πῶς
4460 Ῥαάβ
4461 ῥαββί

4462 ῥαββουνί
4463 ῥαβδίζειν
4464 ῥάβδος
4465 ῥαβδοῦχος
4466 Ῥαγαύ

4467 ῥᾳδιούργημα
4468 ῥᾳδιουργία
4469 ῥακά
4470 ῥάκος
4471 Ῥαμά

4472 ῥαντίζειν
4473 ῥαντισμός
4474 ῥαπίζειν
4475 ῥάπισμα
4476 ῥαφίς v955.5

4477 Ῥαχάβ
4478 Ῥαχήλ
4479 Ῥεβέκκα
4480 ῥέδη
4482 ῥεῖν

4484 Ῥήγιον
4485 ῥῆγμα
4487 ῥῆμα
4488 Ῥησά
4486 ῥήσσειν

4489 ῥήτωρ
4490 ῥητῶς
4491 ῥίζα
4492 ῥιζοῦν
4493 ῥιπή

4494 ῥιπίζειν
4495 ῥίπτειν 4496
4497 Ῥοβοάμ
4498 Ῥόδη
4499 Ῥόδος

4500 ῥοιζηδόν
4450.5 Ῥομφά vW4481
4501 ῥομφαία
4502 Ῥουβήν
4503 Ῥούθ

4504 Ῥοῦφος
4506 ῥύεσθαι
4505 ῥύμη
4510 ῥυπαίνεσθαι *
4507 ῥυπαρία

4508 ῥυπαρός
4509 ῥύπος
4511 ῥύσις
4512 ῥυτίς
4514 Ῥωμαῖος

4515 Ῥωμαϊστί
4516 Ῥώμη
4517 ῥώννυσθαι
4518 σαβαχθάνι *
4519 σαβαώθ

4520 σαββατισμός
4521 σάββατον
4522 σαγήνη
4523 Σαδδουκαῖοι
4524 Σαδώκ

4525 σαίνειν
4526 σάκκος
4527 Σαλά
4528 Σαλαθιήλ
4529 Σαλαμίς

4530 Σαλείμ
4531 σαλεύειν
4532 Σαλήμ
4533 Σαλμών
4534 Σαλμώνη

4535 σάλος
4536 σάλπιγξ
4537 σαλπίζειν
4538 σαλπιστής
4539 Σαλώμη

4540 Σαμάρεια *
4541 Σαμαρείτης
4542 Σαμαρῖτις
4543 Σαμοθρᾴκη
4544 Σάμος

4545 Σαμουήλ
4546 Σαμψών
4547 σανδάλιον
4548 σανίς
4549 Σαούλ

4550 σαπρός
4551 Σάπφιρη
4552 σάπφιρος
4553 σαργάνη
4554 Σάρδεις

4555 σάρδιον 4556
4557 σαρδόνυξ
4558 Σάρεπτα
4559 σαρκικός
4560 σάρκινος

4561 σάρξ
4563 σαροῦν
4564 Σάρρα
4565 Σαρών
4567 σατάν, -νᾶς 4566

4568 σάτον
4569 Σαῦλος
4570 σβεννύειν *
4572 σεαυτοῦ
4573 σεβάζεσθαι

4574 σέβασμα
4575 Σεβαστός
4576 σέβεσθαι
4579 σείειν
4578 σεισμός

4580 Σέκουνδος
4581 Σελεύκεια
4582 σελήνη
4583 σεληνιάζεσθαι
4584 Σεμεΐν

4585 σεμίδαλις
4586 σεμνός
4587 σεμνότης
4588 Σέργιος
4588.5 Σερούχ vW4562

4589 Σήθ
4590 Σήμ
4591 σημαίνειν
4592 σημεῖον
4593 σημειοῦσθαι

4594 σήμερον
4595 σήπειν
4596 σηρικός vM4617.2
4597 σής
4598 σητόβρωτος

4599 σθενοῦν
4600 σιαγών
4601 σιγᾶν
4602 σιγή
4603 σιδηροῦς
4604 σίδηρος

4605 Σιδών
4606 Σιδώνιος
4607 σικάριος
4608 σίκερα
4609 Σίλας

4610 Σιλουανός
4611 Σιλωάμ
4612 σιμικίνθιον
4613 Σίμων vM4613.5
4614 Σινᾶ

4615 σίναπι
4616 σινδών
4617 σινιάζειν
4617.5 σιρός vW4577
4618 σιτευτός

4618.5 σιτίον v4621
4619 σιτιστός
4620 σιτομέτριον
4621 σῖτος v4618.5
4622 Σιών

4623 σιωπᾶν
4624 σκανδαλίζειν
4625 σκάνδαλον
4626 σκάπτειν
4627 σκάφη

4628 σκέλος
4629 σκέπασμα
4630 Σκευᾶς
4631 σκευή
4632 σκεῦος

4633 σκηνή
4634 σκηνοπηγία
4635 σκηνοποιός
4636 σκῆνος
4637 σκηνοῦν

4638 σκήνωμα
4639 σκιά
4640 σκιρτᾶν
4641 σκληροκαρδία
4642 σκληρός

4643 σκληρότης
4644 σκληροτράχηλος
4645 σκληρύνειν
4646 σκολιός
4647 σκόλοψ

4648 σκοπεῖν
4649 σκοπός
4650 σκορπίζειν
4651 σκορπίος
4652 σκοτεινός

4653 σκοτία
4654 σκοτίζειν
4655 σκότος
4656 σκοτοῦν
4657 σκύβαλον

4658 Σκύθης
4659 σκυθρωπός
4660 σκύλλειν
4661 σκῦλον
4662 σκωληκόβρωτος

4663 σκώληξ
4664 σμαράγδινος
4665 σμάραγδος
4666 σμύρνα
4667 Σμύρνα 4668

4669 σμυρνίζειν
4670 Σόδομα
4672 Σολομών
4673 σορός
4674 σός

4676 σουδάριον
4677 Σουσάννα
4678 σοφία
4679 σοφίζειν
4680 σοφός

4681 Σπανία
4682 σπαράσσειν
4683 σπαργανοῦν
4685 σπᾶσθαι vM4681.5
4684 σπαταλᾶν

4686 σπεῖρα
4687 σπείρειν v1986.5
4688 σπεκουλάτωρ
4689 σπένδεσθαι
4690 σπέρμα

4691 σπερμολόγος
4692 σπεύδειν
4693 σπήλαιον
4694 σπιλάς
4696 σπίλος

4695 σπιλοῦν
4698 σπλάγχνα
4697 σπλαγχνίζεσθαι
4699 σπόγγος
4700 σποδός

4701 σπορά
4702 σπόριμος
4703 σπόρος
4704 σπουδάζειν
4705 σπουδαῖος 4707

4708 σπουδαίως 4709
4710 σπουδή
4711 σπυρίς
4712 στάδιον
4713 στάμνος

4713.5 στασιαστής *
4714 στάσις
4715 στατήρ
4716 σταυρός
4717 σταυροῦν

4718 σταφυλή
4719 στάχυς
4720 Στάχυς
4722 στέγειν
4721 στέγη

4723 στεῖρος
4724 στέλλεσθαι
4725 στέμμα
4726 στεναγμός
4727 στενάζειν

4728 στενός
4729 στενοχωρεῖσθαι
4730 στενοχωρία
4731 στερεός
4732 στερεοῦν

4733 στερέωμα
4734 Στεφανᾶς
4735 Στέφανος
4736 στέφανος
4737 στεφανοῦν

4738 στῆθος
4739 στήκειν
4740 στηριγμός
4741 στηρίζειν
4741.5 στιβάς vW4746

4742 στίγμα
4743 στιγμή
4744 στίλβειν
4745 στοά
4748 στοιχεῖν

4747 στοιχεῖον
4749 στολή
4750 στόμα
4751 στόμαχος
4752 στρατεία

4754 στρατεύεσθαι
4753 στράτευμα
4755 στρατηγός
4756 στρατιά
4757 στρατιώτης

4758 στρατολογεῖν
4760 στρατόπεδον
4761 στρεβλοῦν
4762 στρέφειν
4763 στρηνιᾶν

4764 στρῆνος
4765 στρουθίον
4766 στρωννύειν
4767 στυγητός
4768 στυγνάζειν

4769 στῦλος
4770 Στωϊκός
4771 σύ (gr. S.)
4772 συγγένεια
4773 συγγενεύς *

4773.2 συγγενής v4773
4773.4 συγγενίς v4773
4774 συγγνώμη *
4775 συγκαθῆσθαι *
4776 συγκαθίζειν *

4777 συγκακοπαθεῖν *
4778 συγκακουχεῖσθαι *
4779 συγκαλεῖν *
4780 συγκαλύπτειν *
4781 συγκάμπτειν *

4782 συγκαταβαίνειν *
4783 συγκατάθεσις *
4784 συγκατατίθεσθαι *
4785 συγκαταψηφίζειν *
4786 συγκεραννύναι *

4787 συγκινεῖν *
4788 συγκλείειν *
4789 συγκληρονόμος *
4790 συγκοινωνεῖν *
4791 συγκοινωνός *

4792 συγκομίζειν *
4793 συγκρίνειν *
4794 συγκύπτειν *
4795 συγκυρία
4796 συγχαίρειν *

4797 συγχεῖν v4797.5 *
4798 συγχρῆσθαι *
4797.5 συγχύνειν v4797 *
4799 σύγχυσις
4801 συζευγνύειν *

4800 συζῆν vM p.922
4802 συζητεῖν vM p.922
4804 συζητητής *
4805 σύζυγος vM p.922
4806 συζωοποιεῖν *

4807 συκάμινος
4808 συκῆ
4809 συκομορέα
4810 σῦκον
4811 συκοφαντεῖν

4812 συλαγωγεῖν
4813 συλᾶν
4814 συλλαλεῖν *
4815 συλλαμβάνειν
4816 συλλέγειν

4817 συλλογίζεσθαι
4818 συλλυπεῖσθαι *
4819 συμβαίνειν
4820 συμβάλλειν *
4821 συμβασιλεύειν *

4822 συμβιβάζειν *
4823 συμβουλεύειν
4824 συμβούλιον
4825 σύμβουλος
4826 Συμεών

4827 συμμαθητής *
4828 συμμαρτυρεῖν *
4829 συμμερίζεσθαι *
4830 συμμέτοχος *
4831 συμμιμητής *

4832 συμμορφίζεσθαι
4833 σύμμορφος
4834 συμπαθεῖν *
4835 συμπαθής *
4836 συμπαραγίνεσθαι *

4837 συμπαρακαλεῖσθαι *
4838 συμπαραλαμβάνειν *
4840 συμπαρεῖναι *
4841 συμπάσχειν *
4842 συμπέμπειν *

4843 συμπεριλαμβάνειν *
4844 συμπίνειν *
4098 συμπίπτειν
4845 συμπληροῦν *
4846 συμπνίγειν *

4847 συμπολίτης *
4848 συμπορεύεσθαι *
4849 συμπόσιον *
4850 συμπρεσβύτερος *
4852 συμφάναι vM4943.2

4851 συμφέρειν v4851.5
" .5 σύμφορος 4851.5*
4855 συμφύεσθαι
4853 συμφυλέτης *
4854 σύμφυτος

4856 συμφωνεῖν
4857 συμφώνησις
4858 συμφωνία
4859 σύμφωνος
4860 συμψηφίζειν

4861 σύμψυχος vM4797.8
4862 σύν
4863 συνάγειν
4864 συναγωγή
4865 συναγωνίζεσθαι

4866 συναθλεῖν
4867 συναθροίζειν *
4868 συναίρειν
4869 συναιχμάλωτος
4870 συνακολουθεῖν

4871 συναλίζεσθαι
4871.5 συναλλάσσειν *
4872 συναναβαίνειν
4873 συνανακεῖσθαι
4874 συναναμίγνυσθαι

4875 συναναπαύεσθαι
4876 συναντᾶν [σθαι
4878 συναντιλαμβάνε-
4879 συναπάγεσθαι
4880 συναποθνήσκειν

4881 συναπόλλυσθαι
4882 συναποστέλλειν
4883 συναρμολογεῖν
4884 συναρπάζειν
4885 συναυξάνεσθαι

4887 συνδεῖν
4886 σύνδεσμος
4888 συνδοξάζειν
4889 σύνδουλος
4890 συνδρομή

4891 συνεγείρειν
4892 συνέδριον
4893 συνείδησις
4895 συνεῖναι
4897 συνεισέρχεσθαι

4898 συνέκδημος
4899 συνεκλεκτός
4902 συνέπεσθαι
4901 συνεπιμαρτυρεῖν
4901.5 συνεπιτίθεσθαι *

4903 συνεργεῖν
4904 συνεργός
4905 συνέρχεσθαι
4906 συνεσθίειν
4907 σύνεσις

4908 συνετός
4909 συνευδοκεῖν
4910 συνευωχεῖσθαι
4911 συνεφιστάναι
4912 συνέχειν

4913 συνήδεσθαι
4914 συνήθεια
4915 συνηλικιώτης
4916 συνθάπτειν
4917 συνθλᾶν

4918 συνθλίβειν
4919 συνθρύπτειν
4894 συνιδεῖν,συνειδέναι
4896 συνιέναι, σύνειμι
4920 συνιέναι, συνίημι

4921 συνιστάνειν
4922 συνοδεύειν
4923 συνοδία
4924 συνοικεῖν
4925 συνοικοδομεῖν

4926 συνομιλεῖν
4927 συνομορεῖν
4928 συνοχή
4929 συντάσσειν M p.926
4930 συντέλεια

4931 συντελεῖν
4932 συντέμνειν
4933 συντηρεῖν
4934 συντιθέναι *
4935 συντόμως

4936 συντρέχειν
4937 συντρίβειν
4938 σύντριμμα
4939 σύντροφος
4940 συντυγχάνειν

4941 Συντύχη
4942 συνυποκρίνεσθαι
4943 συνυπουργεῖν
4944 συνωδίνειν *
4945 συνωμοσία

4946 Συρακοῦσαι
4951 σύρειν
4947 Συρία
4948 Σύρος
4949 Συροφοινίκισσα *

4950 Σύρτις
4952 συσπαράττειν
4953 σύσσημον
4954 σύσσωμος *
4956 συστατικός

4957 συσταυροῦν *
4958 συστέλλειν *
4959 συστενάζειν *
4960 συστοιχεῖν *
4961 συστρατιώτης *

4962 συστρέφειν *
4963 συστροφή vM p.927
4964 συσχηματίζεσθαι *
4965 Συχάρ vM p.927
4966 Συχέμ vM p.927

4967 σφαγή vM p.927
4968 σφάγιον vM p.927
4969 σφάζειν vM p.927
4970 σφόδρα vM p.927
4971 σφοδρῶς vM p.927

4972 σφραγίζειν *
4973 σφραγίς vM p.927
4974 σφυδρόν vM p.927
4975 σχεδόν
4976 σχῆμα

4977 σχίζειν
4978 σχίσμα
4979 σχοινίον
4980 σχολάζειν
4981 σχολή

4982 σῴζειν
4983 σῶμα
4984 σωματικός
4985 σωματικῶς
4986 Σώπατρος

4987 σωρεύειν
4988 Σωσθένης
4989 Σωσίπατρος
4990 σωτήρ
4991 σωτηρία

4992.5 σωτήριον, τό *
4992 σωτήριος v4992.5
4993 σωφρονεῖν
4994 σωφρονίζειν
4995 σωφρονισμός

4996 σωφρόνως
4997 σωφροσύνη
4998 σώφρων
5000 Ταβιθά
5001 τάγμα

5002 τακτός
5003 ταλαιπωρεῖν
5004 ταλαιπωρία
5005 ταλαίπωρος
5006 ταλαντιαῖος

5007 τάλαντον
5008 ταλιθά
5009 ταμιεῖον
5010 τάξις
5011 ταπεινός

5013 ταπεινοῦν
5012 ταπεινοφροσύνη
5012.5 ταπεινόφρων
5014 ταπείνωσις
5015 ταράσσειν

5017 τάραχος
5018 Ταρσεύς
5019 Ταρσός
5020 ταρταροῦν
5021 τάσσειν

5022 ταῦρος
5027 ταφή
5028 τάφος
5029 τάχα
5030 ταχέως

5031 ταχινός
5034 τάχος
5036 ταχύς, -εῖα, -ύ
5035 ταχύ, -ιον, -ιστα
5037 τε

5038 τεῖχος
5039 τεκμήριον
5040 τεκνίον
5041 τεκνογονεῖν
5042 τεκνογονία

5043 τέκνον
5044 τεκνοτροφεῖν
5045 τέκτων
5055 τελεῖν
5046 τέλειος

5047 τελειότης
5048 τελειοῦν
5049 τελείως
5050 τελείωσις
5051 τελειωτής

5052 τελεσφορεῖν
5053 τελευτᾶν
5054 τελευτή
5056 τέλος
5057 τελώνης

5058 τελώνιον
5059 τέρας
5060 Τέρτιος
5061 Τέρτυλλος
5062 τεσσαράκοντα

5063 τεσσαρακονταετής
5064 τέσσαρες vM5061.2
5065 τεσσαρες καιδέ- *
5066 τεταρταῖος [κατος
5067 τέταρτος

5067.2 τετρααρχεῖν vW5075
5067.4 τετραάρχης vW5076
5068 τετράγωνος
5069 τετράδιον
5070 τετρακισχίλιοι

5071 τετρακόσιοι
5072 τετράμηνος
5073 τετραπλοῦς
5074 τετράποδα
5077 τεφροῦν

5078 τέχνη
5079 τεχνίτης
5080 τήκεσθαι
5081 τηλαυγῶς v1211.5
5082 τηλικοῦτος

5083 τηρεῖν
5084 τήρησις
5085 Τιβεριάς
5086 Τιβέριος
5099 τίειν

5087 τιθέναι
5088 τίκτειν
5089 τίλλειν
5090 Τίμαιος
5091 τιμᾶν

5092 τιμή
5093 τίμιος
5094 τιμιότης
5095 Τιμόθεος
5096 Τίμων

5097 τιμωρεῖν
5098 τιμωρία
5100 τις, τι vM p.949
5101 τίς, τί
5103.5 Τίτιος v5103

5102 τίτλος
5103 Τίτος
5105 τοιγαροῦν
5106 τοίνυν
5107 τοιόσδε

5108 τοιοῦτος
5109 τοῖχος
5110 τόκος
5111 τολμᾶν
5112 τολμηροτέρως

5113 τολμητής
5114 τομώτερος
5115 τόξον
5116 τοπάζιον
5117 τόπος

5118 τοσοῦτος
5119 τότε
5121 τοὐναντίον
5122 τοὔνομα
5131 τράγος

5132 τράπεζα
5133 τραπεζίτης
5134 τραῦμα
5135 τραυματίζειν
5136 τραχηλίζεσθαι

5137 τράχηλος
5138 τραχύς
5139 Τραχωνῖτις
5140 τρεῖς, τρία
5140b Τρεῖς ταβέρναι*

5141 τρέμειν
5142 τρέφειν
5143 τρέχειν
5143.5 τρῆμα vW5169
5144 τριάκοντα

5145 τριακόσιοι
5146 τρίβολος
5147 τρίβος
5148 τριετία
5149 τρίζειν

5150 τρίμηνον
5151 τρίς
5152 τρίστεγον
5153 τρισχίλιοι
5154.5 τρίτον Adv. *

5154 τρίτος v5154.5
5155 τρίχινος
5156 τρόμος
5157 τροπή
5158 τρόπος

5159 τροποφορεῖν
5160 τροφή
5161 Τρόφιμος
5162 τροφός
5163 τροχιά

5164 τροχός
5165 τρύβλιον
5166 τρυγᾶν
5167 τρυγών
5168 τρυμαλιά

5170 Τρύφαινα
5171 τρυφᾶν
5172 τρυφή
5173 Τρυφῶσα
5174 Τρῳάς

5176 τρώγειν
5177 τυγχάνειν
5178 τυμπανίζειν
5179.5 τυπικῶς v5179
5179 τύπος v5179.5

5180 τύπτειν
5181 Τύραννος
5183 Τύριος
5184 Τύρος
5188 τύφεσθαι

5185 τυφλός
5186 τυφλοῦν
5187 τυφοῦσθαι
5189 τυφωνικός
5190 Τύχικος

5191 ὑακίνθινος
5192 ὑάκινθος
5193 ὑάλινος
5194 ὕαλος
5195 ὑβρίζειν

5196 ὕβρις
5197 ὑβριστής
5198 ὑγιαίνειν
5199 ὑγιής
5200 ὑγρός

5201 ὑδρία
5202 ὑδροποτεῖν
5203 ὑδρωπικός
5204 ὕδωρ
5205 ὑετός

5206 υἱοθεσία
5207 υἱός
5208 ὕλη
5210 ὑμεῖς (gr. S.)*
5211 Ὑμέναιος

5212 ὑμέτερος
5214 ὑμνεῖν
5215 ὕμνος
5217 ὑπάγειν
5218 ὑπακοή

5219 ὑπακούειν
5220 ὕπανδρος
5221 ὑπαντᾶν
5222 ὑπάντησις
5223 ὕπαρξις

5224 ὑπάρχειν 5225
5226 ὑπείκειν
5227 ὑπεναντίος
5228 ὑπέρ (gr. S.)*
5228.5 ὑπέρ Adv. v5228

5229 ὑπεραίρεσθαι
5230 ὑπέρακμος
5231 ὑπεράνω
5232 ὑπεραυξάνειν
5233 ὑπερβαίνειν

5235 ὑπερβάλλειν
5234 ὑπερβαλλόντως
5236 ὑπερβολή
5238 ὑπερέκεινα
5238.2 ὑπερεκπερισσοῦ*

5238.4 ὑπερεκπερισσῶς*
5239 ὑπερεκτείνειν
5240 ὑπερεκχύνεσθαι
5241 ὑπερεντυγχάνειν
5242 ὑπερέχειν

5243 ὑπερηφανία
5244 ὑπερήφανος
5237 ὑπεριδεῖν
5244.5 ὑπερλίαν *
5245 ὑπερνικᾶν

5246 ὑπέρογκος
5247 ὑπεροχή [σεύειν
5248 ὑπερπερισ-
5249 ὑπερπερισσῶς
5250 ὑπερπλεονάζειν

5251 ὑπερυψοῦν
5252 ὑπερφρονεῖν
5253 ὑπερῷον
5254 ὑπέχειν
5255 ὑπήκοος

5256 ὑπηρετεῖν
5257 ὑπηρέτης
5258 ὕπνος
5259 ὑπό (gr. S.)
5260 ὑποβάλλειν

5261 ὑπογραμμός
5262 ὑπόδειγμα
5263 ὑποδεικνύναι
5265 ὑποδεῖσθαι
5264 ὑποδέχεσθαι

5266 ὑπόδημα
5267 ὑπόδικος
5268 ὑποζύγιον
5269 ὑποζωννύναι
5270 ὑποκάτω

5271 ὑποκρίνεσθαι
5272 ὑπόκρισις
5273 ὑποκριτής
5274 ὑπολαμβάνειν
5274.5 ὑπόλειμμα *

5275 ὑπολείπεσθαι
5276 ὑπολήνιον
5277 ὑπολιμπάνειν
5278 ὑπομένειν
5279 ὑπομιμνήσκειν

5280 ὑπόμνησις
5281 ὑπομονή
5282 ὑπονοεῖν
5283 ὑπόνοια
5284 ὑποπλεῖν

5285 ὑποπνεῖν
5286 ὑποπόδιον
5287 ὑπόστασις
5288 ὑποστέλλειν
5289 ὑποστολή

5290 ὑποστρέφειν
5291 ὑποστρωννύναι
5292 ὑποταγή
5293 ὑποτάσσειν
5294 ὑποτιθέναι

5295 ὑποτρέχειν
5296 ὑποτύπωσις
5297 ὑποφέρειν
5298 ὑποχωρεῖν
5299 ὑπωπιάζειν

5300 ὗς
5301 ὕσσωπος
5302 ὑστερεῖν
5303 ὑστέρημα
5304 ὑστέρησις

5305 ὕστερον Adv.
5306 ὕστερος
5306.5 ὑφαίνειν v2872
5307 ὑφαντός
5308 ὑψηλός

5309 ὑψηλοφρονεῖν
5310 ὕψιστος
5311 ὕψος
5312 ὑψοῦν
5313 ὕψωμα

5315 φαγεῖν vM2068
5314 φάγος
5314.5 φαιλόνης v5341
5316 φαίνειν
5317 Φάλεκ

5317.5 φάναι
5318 φανερός
5319 φανεροῦν
5320 φανερῶς
5321 φανέρωσις

5322 φανός
5323 Φανουήλ
5324 φανταζόμενον
5325 φαντασία
5326 φάντασμα

5327 φάραγξ
5328 Φαραώ
5329 Φάρες
5330 Φαρισαῖος
5331 φαρμακεία

5332 φαρμακός 5333
5334 φάσις
5335 φάσκειν
5336 φάτνη
5337 φαῦλος

5338 φέγγος
5339 φείδεσθαι
5340 φειδομένως
5342 φέρειν
5343 φεύγειν

5344 Φῆλιξ
5345 φήμη
5347 Φῆστος
5348 φθάνειν
5349 φθαρτός

5350 φθέγγεσθαι
5351 φθείρειν
5352 φθινοπωρινός
5353 φθόγγος
5354 φθονεῖν

5355 φθόνος
5356 φθορά
5357 φιάλη
5358 φιλάγαθος
5359 Φιλαδέλφεια

5360 φιλαδελφία
5361 φιλάδελφος
5362 φίλανδρος
5363 φιλανθρωπία
5364 φιλανθρώπως

5365 φιλαργυρία
5366 φιλάργυρος
5367 φίλαυτος
5368 φιλεῖν
5369 φιλήδονος

5370 φίλημα
5371 Φιλήμων
5372 Φίλητος
5373 φιλία
5374 Φιλιππήσιοι

5375 Φίλιπποι
5376 Φίλιππος
5377 φιλόθεος
5378 Φιλόλογος
5379 φιλονεικία

5380 φιλόνεικος
5381 φιλοξενία
5382 φιλόξενος
5383 φιλοπρωτεύειν
5384 φίλος

5385 φιλοσοφία
5386 φιλόσοφος
5387 φιλόστοργος
5388 φιλότεκνος
5389 φιλοτιμεῖσθαι

5390 φιλοφρόνως
5392 φιμοῦν vM2777.5
5393 Φλέγων
5394 φλογίζειν
5395 φλόξ

5396 φλυαρεῖν
5397 φλύαρος
5399 φοβεῖσθαι
5398 φοβερός
5400 φόβητρον

5401 φόβος
5402 Φοίβη
5403 Φοινίκη
5405 Φοῖνιξ
5404 φοῖνιξ

5407 φονεύειν
5406 φονεύς
5408 φόνος
5409 φορεῖν
5411 φόρος

5412 φορτίζειν
5413 φορτίον 5414
5415 Φορτουνάτος
5416 φραγέλλιον
5417 φραγελλοῦν

5418 φραγμός
5419 φράζειν
5420 φράσσειν
5421 φρέαρ
5422 φρεναπατᾶν

5423 φρεναπάτης
5424 φρήν
5425 φρίσσειν
5426 φρονεῖν
5427 φρόνημα

5428 φρόνησις
5429 φρόνιμος
5430 φρονίμως
5431 φροντίζειν
5432 φρουρεῖν

5433 φρυάττειν
5434 φρύγανον
5435 Φρυγία
5436 Φύγελος
5437 φυγή

5453 φύειν
5438 φυλακή
5439 φυλακίζειν
5440 φυλακτήριον
5441 φύλαξ

5442 φυλάσσειν
5443 φυλή
5444 φύλλον
5445 φύραμα
5446 φυσικός

5447 φυσικῶς
5448 φυσιοῦν
5449 φύσις
5450 φυσίωσις
5451 φυτεία

5452 φυτεύειν
5454 φωλεός
5455 φωνεῖν
5456 φωνή
5457 φῶς

5458 φωστήρ
5459 φωσφόρος
5460 φωτεινός
5461 φωτίζειν
5462 φωτισμός

5463 χαίρειν
5464 χάλαζα
5465 χαλᾶν
5466 Χαλδαῖος
5467 χαλεπός

5468 χαλιναγωγεῖν
5469 χαλινός
5471 χαλκεύς
5472 χαλκηδών
5473 χαλκίον

5474 χαλκολίβανον
5475 χαλκός
5470 χαλκοῦς
5476 χαμαί
5477 Χανάαν

5478 Χαναναῖος
5479 χαρά
5480 χάραγμα
5481 χαρακτήρ
5482 χάραξ

5483 χαρίζεσθαι
5484 χάριν Adv.
5485 χάρις
5486 χάρισμα
5487 χαριτοῦν

5488 Χαρράν
5489 χάρτης
5490 χάσμα
5491 χεῖλος
5492 χειμάζεσθαι

5493 χείμαρρος
5494 χειμών
5495 χείρ
5496 χειραγωγεῖν
5497 χειραγωγός

5498 χειρόγραφον
5499 χειροποίητος
5500 χειροτονεῖν
5501 χείρων, -ον
5502 Χερουβίμ

5503 χήρα
5506 χιλίαρχος
5505 χιλιάς
5507 χίλιοι
5508 Χίος

5509 χιτών
5510 χιών
5511 χλαμύς
5512 χλευάζειν*
5513 χλιαρός

5514 Χλόη
5515 χλωρός
5517 χοϊκός
5518 χοῖνιξ
5519 χοῖρος

5520 χολᾶν
5521 χολή
5523 Χοραζίν
5524 χορηγεῖν
5525 χορός

5526 χορτάζειν
5527 χόρτασμα
5528 χόρτος
5529 Χουζᾶς
5529.5 χοῦς vW5522

5531 χρᾶν
5532 χρεία
5533 χρεοφειλέτης
5535 χρῄζειν
5536 χρῆμα

5537 χρηματίζειν
5538 χρηματισμός
5538.2 χρῆναι v5534
5538.4 χρῆσθαι v5530
5539 χρήσιμος

5540 χρῆσις
5541 χρηστεύεσθαι
5542 χρηστολογία
5543 χρηστός
5544 χρηστότης

5548 χρίειν
5545 χρῖσμα
5546 Χριστιανός
5547 Χριστός
5549 χρονίζειν

5550 χρόνος
5551 χρονοτριβεῖν
5553 χρυσίον
5554 χρυσοδακτύλιος
5555 χρυσόλιθος

5556 χρυσόπρασος
5557 χρυσός
5558 χρυσοῦν
5558.5 χρυσοῦς v5552
5559 χρώς

5560 χωλός
5561 χώρα
5562 χωρεῖν
5563 χωρίζειν
5564 χωρίον

5565 χωρίς
5566 χῶρος
5567 ψάλλειν
5568 ψαλμός
5569 ψευδάδελφος

5570 ψευδαπόστολος
5570.5 ψεύδεσθαι v5574
5571 ψευδής
5572 ψευδοδιδάσκαλος
5573 ψευδολόγος

5576 ψευδομαρτυρεῖν
5575 ψευδομάρτυς
5577 ψευδομαρτυρία
5578 ψευδοπροφήτης
5579 ψεῦδος

5580 ψευδόχριστος
5581 ψευδώνυμος
5582 ψεῦσμα
5583 ψεύστης
5584 ψηλαφᾶν

5585 ψηφίζειν
5586 ψῆφος
5587 ψιθυρισμός
5588 ψιθυριστής
5589 ψιχίον

5589.5 ψύχεσθαι v5594
5590 ψυχή
5591 ψυχικός
5592 ψῦχος
5593 ψυχρός

5595 ψωμίζειν
5596 ψωμίον
5597 ψώχειν
5598 Ὦ
5599 ὦ

5601 Ὠβήδ vM2492.2
5602 ὧδε
5603 ᾠδή
5604 ὠδίν
5605 ὠδίνειν

5606 ὦμος
5608 ὠνεῖσθαι
5609 ᾠόν
5610 ὥρα
5611 ὡραῖος

5612 ὠρύεσθαι
5613 ὡς (gr. St.)
5614 ὡσαννά
5615 ὡσαύτως
5616 ὡσεί

5617 Ὡσηέ
5618 ὥσπερ
5619 ὡσπερεί
5620 ὥστε
5621 ὠτάριον vM5621.5

5621.5 ὠτίον vW5621
5622 ὠφέλεια
5623 ὠφελεῖν
5624 ὠφέλιμος

*Items Starred in Main Index

180 v180.5
537.5 v782
782 v537.5
1014 vM4783.5
1046 vM1085.5
1060.2 v1060, 1547
1086 vM1085.5, 1046
1245.5 v1245
1274.5 v3859
1310 vM5346.5
1315.5 v5512
1326.5 v1761
1449 vM1728.4
1455 vM1765.1
1456 vM1765.2
1457 vM1765.3
1460 vM1765.5
1461 vM1765.7
1464 vM1765.8, 1580.5
1465 vM1765.9
1469 vM1765.92
1486 vM1536.5
1494 vM2410.5
1569.5 v2296
1573 vM1765.4
1632 vM1632.5
1665 vM1665.5
1699.5 v1701
1704 vM1777.2
1714 vM1705.5
1760 vM1326.5
1782 v1759.5
1790 vM1625.5
1831 v1543.5
1898.5 v1904
1904 v1898.5
1944 v1883.5
1980.5 vW643
2043.5 v3004, M2064.5
2068 vW5315
2115.5 v2115
2117.5 v2117
2137.5 vW2145
2230 vM2010.5
2249 vM1473.7
2296 v1569.5
2349.5 vW5182
2455 vM2492.5, 2455.2, 2455.5
2469 vM2469.5
2491 vM2491.2 2491.4, 2491.6
2501.5 vW2501, M2501.8
2509 vM2531.5
2568 v3040, 2570
2584 vM2746.5
2616.5 vW2653
2640 v3005
2720.5 v2127
2744 vM1765.6
2747 vM2760.5
2802 vM2737.5
2982 vM3011.5
3102.2 vW3156
3102.6 vW3158
3187 vW3185, 3186
3344 v3346.5
3496 v4172
3762 v3764.5
3764.5 v3762
3778 vM3778.1
3826 vM3835.5
3917.5 vW4332
3924.5 v4016
3969.5 vW3964
4053 vM1599.5
4055 v4054
4091 vM3982.5
4092 vM1705.5
4130 vM4090.5
4179 vM2036.5
4263 v4263.5
4317 v4324.5
4319 v4319.5
4345.5 v4347
4347 vM4345.5
4510 vM4510.5
4518 vM2196.5
4540 vM4542.5
4570 vM2198.5
4713.5 vW4955
4773 v4773.2, 4773.4
4774 vM4885.8
4775-4789, see p. 923 Moulton
4790-4794, see p. 924 Moulton
4822 vM4885.6
4827-4831, see p. 924 Moulton
4834 vM p. 924
4796-4798, see p. 926 Moulton
4801 vM p. 922
4804 vM p. 922
4806 vM p. 922
4814 vM4921.2
4818 vM4921.4
4820 vM4885.2
4821 vM4885.4
4835 vM p. 916
4836-4838, see p. 924 Moulton
4840-4842, see p. 924 Moulton
4843-4848, see p. 925 Moulton
4849 vM p. 916
4850 vM p. 925
4851 vM p. 916
4851.5 v4851
4853 vM p. 916, M4943.5
4867 v119.5
4871.5 vW4900
4901.5 vW4934
4934 vM4901.5
4944 VM p. 926
4949 vM5403.5
4954 vM p. 925
4957-4961, see p. 925 Moulton
4962 vM p. 927
4964 vM p. 925
4972 vM p. 927
4992.5 v4992
5012.5 vW5391
5065 vM5061.4
5140b vW p. 865
5154.5 v5154
5210 vM4771.4
5228 v5228.5
5238.2 v4053
5238.4 v4053
5244.5 vW5228, MW3029, M5244.5
5274.5 vW2640
5512 vM1315.5

Auxiliary List A: Numbers in Different Sequence or Not Included in the Main List

1 See 255.5
20 See after 21
39 See W39, M40
71 See after 33
90 See 862.5
103 See after 78
133 See after 134
142 See after 137
150 See M149; W149,150
157 See after 159
169 See M168; W168,169
183 See M182; W182,183
197 See M199; W197,199
229 See after 225
231 See M217.5
251 hals See M,W251
270 See after 261
301 See M300; W300,301
321 See after 312
337 See after 335
348 anakopto, See W348
361 anamartētos, See M,W361
508 See 311.5
373 See after 371
376 See M374.5
380 anaptusso, See M,W380
445 See M446; W445,446
448 See M415.5; W448
508 See 311.5
519 See after 520
534 aparti See M,W534
549 See after 566
567 See M566, W567
568 See M566, W568
582 See after 583
621 See 1952.5
629 See after 630
637 apopluno, See M4150; W637
643 See M1980.5, W643
681 See 680
690 See after 687
693 See after 696
729 See M689.5
730 See after 733
756 See after 744
757 arko, See M756,757; W757
799 See after 802
821 atimeo, See M818; W821
911 See after 906
925 baruno, See M,W925
962 Beethabara See M,W962
1002 bolis, See W1002
1007 See M,W1007, M961.5
1014 See after 1009
1053 See M1057.5
1083 See 1078
1138 See M1160.5
1158 See after 1155
1163 See after 1169
1189 See 1173.5
1236 See after 1229
1325 See after 1322
1410 See after 1412
1439 See after 1437
1486 See after 1478
1491 See after 1492.5
1498 See M1510.7
1499 i kai, See W1499
1502 See after 1497
1503 īko, See W1503
1507 hīlisso, See W1507
1508 i mee, See W1508; M1487.1
1509 i mee ti, See W1509
1513 i pos, See M1487
1547 ekgamizo, See M1060.2
1548 ekgamiskomai, See M1060.5
1573 See after 1457
1746 See after 1741
1761 See 1326.5
1826 See after 1837
1827 exelenko, See W1827
1888 See M848.5
1896 See after 1925
1897 epiper, See W1897
1916 epiboao, See M994; W1916
1966 See after 1933
1970 epipnigo, See W1970
2027 epokello, See W2027
2046 ereo, See W2046
2077 esto, estosan, See W2077
2179 Ephesinos, See W2179
2192 See after 2188
2198 See after 2210
2204 See after 2199
2229 ee meen, See W2229
2233 See after 2228
2397 See M1487.1
2276 See after 2269
2277 eeto, See W2277
2309 See after 2306
2313 theomakeo, See W2313
2355 threenos, See W2355
2380 See after 2365
2410 See MG after 2407
2442 himiromai, See M3655.5
2448 Ioudaia, See M2445
2449 Ioudaia, See M2445
2467 iseemi, See W2467
2480 See after 2477
2506 See after 2508
2532 kai, See W2532
2534 kaige, See W2534
2545 See after 2533
2544 kai-toige, See W2544
2559 See after 2556
2609 See after 2605
2651 katamonas, See W2651
2652 katanathema, See W2652
2653 katanathematizo, See W2653
2700 katatoxūoma, See W2700
2719 See after 2700
2727 See after 2720
2735 katorthoma, See M1356.5; W2735
2744 See after 1460 (index)
2751 See after 2748
2781 keerion, See M,W2781
2792 See after 2795
2796 kineesis, See M,W2796
2797 Kis, See M,W2797
2806 See after 2798
2827 See after 2824.5
2908 krisson, See W2908
2928 See after 2925
2989 See after 2985
2992 See after 2994
3002 Lebbaios, See M,W3002
3004 See after 3001
3068 See after 3062
3089 See after 3070
3104 See 3303.5
3143 See after 3140
3156 Matthaios, See M3102.2; W3156
3157 Matthan, See M3102.4; W3157
3158 Matthat, See M3102.6; W3158
3159 Matthias, See M3102.8; W3159
3165 me, See M1473.6; W3165
3166 megalaukeo, See M849.5; W3166
3181 methoria, See W3181
3184 See after 3180
3185 mizon, M3187
3186 mizoteros, M3187
3193 melissios, See M,W3193
3199 meli, See M3190.5
3306 See after 3303
3362 ean, mee, M1437.2
3363 hina, M2443.5
3364 ou mee, M,W3364
3378 mee ouk, M,W3364
3378 mee ouk, M,W3364
3381 meepōs, mee pōs, W3381
3386 meeti, M,W3386
3387 meetis, mee tis, W3387
3390 metropolis, W3390
3391 mia, M,W3391
3415 mnaomai, W3415
3425 mogis, M,W3425
3427 moi M1473.4; W342
3450 mou, M1473.2; W3450
3459 mulon, M3458; W3459
3496 Neapolis, W3496
3553 noseema, M,W3553
3603 ho esti, W3603
3611 See before 3609
3633 See after 3608
3620 oikodomia, W3620
3658 homilos, W3658
3662 homoiazo, M,W3662
3708 See after 3705
3721 orthrios, M,W3721
3746 hosper, M3745; W3746
3755 hotou, M3748; W3755
3757 See after 3754
3784 See after 3780
3801 ho, own, kahee, ho, ane, M1511.2; W3801
3817 See after 3814
3827 pampolus, M4183; W3827
3836 pantakothen, W3836
3859 paradiatribee, M1274.5; W3859
3872 parakatatheekee, M3866; W3872
3964 patralōees, M3936.5; W3964
3996 See after 3993
4007 per, W4007
4054 perissoteron, M4055; W4054
4126 See after 4117
4130 See after 4127
4137 See after 4134
4154 See after 4150
4235 praos, M4239; W4235
4236 See after 4238
4275 See after 4290
4321 prosanalisko, M,W4321
4331 prosengizo, M,W4331
4332 prosedruo, M3917.5; W4332
4384 protassomai, W4384
4406 proimos, M4290.5; W4406
4429 See after 4424
4452 po, cf. 4458
4483 reo, M1511.7; W4483
4486 See after 4488
4510 See after 4505
4513 Romaikos, W4513
4562 Sarouk, M4588.5; W4562
4571 se, M4771; W4571
4577 sira, M4617.5; W4577
4579 See after 4576
4671 soi, M4771; W4671
4675 sou, M4771; W4675
4706 spoudaioteron, M4708, 4709; W
4746 stoibas, M4741.5; W4746
4759 stratopedarkees, M,W4759
4803 suzeeteesis, M,W4803
4775 sunkatheemai, M923; W4775
4855 See after 4851.5
4861 sumpsukos, M4797.8; W4861
4877 sunanteesis, M5222, W4877,522
4894 See after 4919
4896 See before 4920
4900 sunelauno, M4871.5; W4900
4902 See after 4899
4951 See after 4946
4955 sustasiastees, M4713.5; W4955
4999 See after 5000 in MG
5013 See after 5011
5016 tarakee, M,W5016
5023 o' autos, M3778.93; W5023
5024 tauta, M3778.93; W5024
5025 tautais, M3779.96; W5025a
5025 tautas, M3778.98; W5025b
5026 tauteen, M3778.9; W5026b
5026 tautees, M3778.5; W5026c
5026 tautee, M3778.7; W5026a
5032 takion, M,W5032

5033 takista, M,W5033
5055 See after 5045
5065 tessares, M5061.2; W5064
5065 tessareskaidekatos, M5061.4; W5065
5075 tetrarkeo, M5067.2; W5075
5076 tephroō, M5067.4; W5076
5099 See after 5086
5100 tis (indefinite) See M after 5100
5104 toi, W5104
5120 toū, W5120, M p.679
5123 toutesti, tout' esti, M3778.3; W5123
5124 touto, M3778.2; W5124
5125 toutois, M3778.95; W5125
5126 touton, M3778.8; W5126
5127 toutou, M3778.4; W5127
5128 toutous, M3778.97; W5128
5129 toutō, M3778.6; W5129
5130 toutōn, M3778.94; W5130
5169 trupeema, M5143.5; W5169
5175 Trōgullion, M,W5175
5182 turbazomai, M2349.5; W5182
5188 See after 5184
5209 humas, M4771.7; W5209
5213 humin, M4771.6; W5213
5216 humōn, M4771.5; W5216
5237 See after 5244
5341 phailonees, W5341
5346 pheemi, M,W5346
5391 philophrōn, M5012.5; W5391
5410 Phoron Appiou, M675; W5410, 675
5453 See after 5437
5470 kalkeos, M,W5470
5504 kthes, W5504
5516 See respectively M,W 1812, 1835, 1803
5548 See after 5544
5600 ō, ees,ee, M1510.6; W5600
5607 ōn, ousa, on, M1511.1; W5607

Auxiliary List B: Aphabetical List of Words Not Included in the Main List

anakopto W348
anamartetos M,W361
anaptusso M,W380
aparti M,W534
apopluno M4150; W637
arko M756,757; W757
atimeo M818, W821
baruno M,W925
Beethabara M,W962
bolis W1002
ean mee M1437.2, W3362
ee meen W2229
ei ou W1487, 1488; M1487.2
ei tis M1487.4, W1536
eemeen, een, ees, eestha M1511.3, W2252, 2258
ees, ee, ō M1510.6, W5600
eeto W2277
ekgamiskomai M1060.5
ekgamizo M1060.2
ekkeo, ekkuno M1632.5, W1632
eme M1473.5, W1691
emoi M1473.3, W1698
emou M1473.1, W1700
epautophōros M848.5
epeimi M1896.5,
Ephesinos W2179
eoubiai M994, W1916
epiper W1897
epipnigo W1970
epokello W2027
ereo W2046
esmen M1510.3, W2070
esomenos M1511.4, 1511.6; W2071
este M1510.4, W2075
esti M1510.2, W2076
esto, estosan W2077
exelenko W1827
ho esti W3603
hals M,W251
heemis M1473.7, W2249
hīlisso W1507
himiromai M3655.5, W2442
hina M2443.5, W3363
ho, own, kahee, ho, ane M1511.2; W3801
homilos W3658
homoiazo M,W3662
hosper M3745, W3746
hotou M3748, W3755
humas M4771.7, W5209
humeteros M4771.4, W5210
humin M4771.6, W5213
humōn M4771.5, W5216
i W1488
i kai W1499
i mee M1487.1, W1508
i mee ti W1509
i pos M1487
idea M1487.5, W2397
ieen, iees, iee M1510.7, W1498
īko W1503
imi M1511.5, W1510
Iōsias M2498.5, W2502
Ioudaia, M2445, W2448,2449
iseemi W2467
isi M1510.5, W1526
kai W2532
kaige W2534
kai-toige W2544
kalkeos M,W5470
katamonas W2651
katanathema W2562
katanathematizo W2653
katatoxuoma W2700
katorthoma M1356.5, W2735
keerion M,W2781
isthi M1510.8, W2468
kineesis M,W2796
Kis M,W2797
krisson W2908
kthes W5504
Lebbaios M,W3002
lūkobussinos M3022.5, W3022
mee ouk M,W3364
Matthaios M3102.2, W3156
Matthan M3102.4, W3157
Matthat M3102.6, W3158
Matthias M3102.8, W3159
meepōs, mee pōs W3381
meeti M,W3386
meetis, mee tis W3387
me M1473.6, W3165
megalaukeo M849.5, W3166
meli M3190.5 W3199
melissios M,W3193
methoria W3181
metropolis W3390
methuo M,W3184
mia M,W3391
mizon M3187, W3185
mizoteros, M3187, W3186
mnaomai W3415
moi M1473.4, W3427
mogis M,W3425
mou M1473.2, W3450
mulon M3458, W3459
Neapolis W3496
noseema M,W3553
o' autos M3778.93, W5023
ou mee M,W3364
oikodomia W3620
on, ousa, M1511.1, W5607
orthrios M,W3721
pampolus M4183, W3827
pantakothen W3836
paradiatribee M1274.5, W3859
parakatatheekee, M3866, W3872
patralōees M3936.5, W3964
per W4007
perissoteron M4055, W4054
phailonees, W5341
pheemi M,W5346
philophrōn M5012.5, W5391
Phoron Appiou M675, W5410
praos M4239, W4235
proimos M4290.5, W4406
prosanalisko M,W4321
prosedruo M3917.5, W4332
prosengizo M,W4331
protassomai, W4384
reo M1511.7, W4483
Romaikos W4513
roū M p. 679, W5120
Sarouk, M4588.5, W4562
se M4771, W4571
seerikos M4617.5, W4596
sira M4617.5, W4577
soi M4771, W4671
soū M4771, W4675
spoudaioteron M4708, W4706
spuris M4974.5, W4711
stoibas M4741.5, W4746
stratopedarkees, M,W4759
sumpsukos M4797.8, W4861
sunanteesis M5222, W4877
sunelauno M4871.5, W4900
sunkataneuo M4783.5, W1014
sunkatheemai M923, W4775
sustasiastees M4713.5, W4955
suzeeteesis M,W4803
takion M,W5032
takista M,W5033
tarakee M,W5016
tauta M3778.93, W5024
tautais M3779.96, W5025
tautas M3778.98, W5025
tautee M3778.7, W5026
tauteen M3778.9, W5026
tautees M3778.5, W5026
tephroō M5067.4, W5076
tessares M5061.2, W5065
tessareskaidekatos M5061.4,W5065
tetrarkeo M5067.2, W5075
threenos W2355
theomakeo W2313
tisti (indefinite) cf. M5100
toi W5104
toutesti, tout' esti M3778.3, W5123
toutō M3778.6, W5129
touto M3778.2, W5124
toutois M3778.95, W5125
touton M3778.8, W5126
toutōn M3778.94, W5130
toutou M3778.4, W5127
toutous M3778.97, W5128
Trōgullion M,W5175
trupeema M5143.5, W5169
turbazomai M2349.5, W5182

This book celebrating
American popular culture is
humbly dedicated to
MARTIN LUTHER KING, JR.,
a champion of peace whose
belief in non-violence
never wavered as he heroically led
the long, tortuous struggle
for racial equality in our iconic
America.

First published in the United States of America in 2007
by UNIVERSE PUBLISHING
A Division of Rizzoli International Publications, Inc.
300 Park Avenue South
New York, NY 10010
www.rizzoliusa.com

Editor and Designer: George Lois
Digital Design and Composition: Luke Lois, Good Karma Creative
Editorial Coordination: Jane Newman
Production Director: Maria Pia Gramaglia
Proofreading: Anna Walker

Special thanks to:
Roberta Greene, Diane Lois, and Elizabeth Wilson for securing rights

2007 2008 2009 2010 / 10 9 8 7 6 5 4 3 2 1
Distributed in the U.S. trade by Random House, New York
Printed in China
ISBN 13: 978-0-7893-1573-1
ISBN 10: 0-7893-1573-4
Library of Congress Catalog Control Number: 2007926565

A ROLLER-COASTER RIDE
THROUGH THE EYE-POPPING
PANORAMA OF AMERICAN
POP CULTURE

BY TOMMY HILFIGER

WITH GEORGE LOIS

MICHAEL ARTS, ORIGINATOR

PREFACE

In a sad time of self-inflicted anti-Americanism, I have endeavored to craft an enlightening book that reminds the world, as well as my fellow citizens, of the variety and magnificence of American pop culture. George Lois, a legendary graphic designer, and I have chosen more than 400 people, places, and things of pivotal import. Some obvious, many surprising, a few shameful, all drawn from the well of American history, celebrating the creativity of a uniquely democratic way of life driven by a multicultural society that continues to influence and inspire friend and foe throughout the world. This bible of quirky American genius is visualized with unexpected juxtaposition of images and penetrating thoughts, saluting—and at times lamenting—breakthrough contributions to the infinitely diverse American experience.

Our iconic and iconoclastic choices are passionately presented in this beautifully produced book dedicated to the intrepid spirit of a people living in freedom, while constantly fighting to keep it so. Since 1776, the very idea of America has been astonishing. Inspired by our passion for the breadth of American creativity, this book, we hope, will dramatize the American ethos more meaningfully (and entertainingly) than any work of art imaginable.

With respect for and in awe of the many dozens of unique cultures throughout world history, America remains alluring, promising, hopeful, and inspiring. With all our faults and bumps on the road in a free society, the *idea* of America continues to be the universal quest of the human spirit, an experience sought after since the beginning of time, because *Iconic America*, most importantly, is not merely about our past, but about our enormously promising future.

Tommy Hilfiger

In CONGRESS, July 4, 1776.

The unanimous Declaration of the thirteen united States of America,

When in the Course of human events, it becomes necessary for one people to dissolve the political bands which have connected them with another, and to assume among the powers of the earth, the separate and equal station to which the Laws of Nature and of Nature's God entitle them, a decent respect to the opinions of mankind requires that they should declare the causes which impel them to the separation. —— We hold these truths to be self-evident, that all men are created equal, that they are endowed by their Creator with certain unalienable Rights, that among these are Life, Liberty and the pursuit of Happiness. — That to secure these rights, Governments are instituted among Men, deriving their just powers from the consent of the governed, — That whenever any Form of Government becomes destructive of these ends, it is the Right of the People to alter or to abolish it, and to institute new Government, laying its foundation on such principles and organizing its powers in such form, as to them shall seem most likely to effect their Safety and Happiness. Prudence, indeed, will dictate that Governments long established should not be changed for light and transient causes; and accordingly all experience hath shewn, that mankind are more disposed to suffer, while evils are sufferable, than to right themselves by abolishing the forms to which they are accustomed. But when a long train of abuses and usurpations, pursuing invariably the same Object evinces a design to reduce them under absolute Despotism, it is their right, it is their duty, to throw off such Government, and to provide new Guards for their future security. — Such has been the patient sufferance of these Colonies; and such is now the necessity which constrains them to alter their former Systems of Government. The history of the present King of Great Britain is a history of repeated injuries and usurpations, all having in direct object the establishment of an absolute Tyranny over these States. To prove this, let Facts be submitted to a candid world. —— He has refused his Assent to Laws, the most wholesome and necessary for the public good. —— He has forbidden his Governors to pass Laws of immediate and pressing importance, unless suspended in their operation till his Assent should be obtained; and when so suspended, he has utterly neglected to attend to them. —— He has refused to pass other Laws for the accommodation of large districts of people, unless those people would relinquish the right of Representation in the Legislature, a right inestimable to them and formidable to tyrants only. —— He has called together legislative bodies at places unusual, uncomfortable, and distant from the depository of their Public Records, for the sole purpose of fatiguing them into compliance with his measures. —— He has dissolved Representative Houses repeatedly, for opposing with manly firmness his invasions on the rights of the people. —— He has refused for a long time, after such dissolutions, to cause others to be elected; whereby the Legislative powers, incapable of Annihilation, have returned to the People at large for their exercise; the State remaining in the mean time exposed to all the dangers of invasion from without, and convulsions within. —— He has endeavoured to prevent the population of these States; for that purpose obstructing the Laws for Naturalization of Foreigners; refusing to pass others to encourage their migrations hither, and raising the conditions of new Appropriations of Lands. —— He has obstructed the Administration of Justice, by refusing his Assent to Laws for establishing Judiciary powers. —— He has made Judges dependent on his Will alone, for the tenure of their offices, and the amount and payment of their salaries. —— He has erected a multitude of New Offices, and sent hither swarms of Officers to harrass our people, and eat out their substance. —— He has kept among us, in times of peace, Standing Armies without the Consent of our legislatures. —— He has affected to render the Military independent of and superior to the Civil power. —— He has combined with others to subject us to a jurisdiction foreign to our constitution, and unacknowledged by our laws; giving his Assent to their Acts of pretended Legislation: — For Quartering large bodies of armed troops among us: — For protecting them, by a mock Trial, from punishment for any Murders which they should commit on the Inhabitants of these States: — For cutting off our Trade with all parts of the world: — For imposing Taxes on us without our Consent: — For depriving us in many cases, of the benefits of Trial by Jury: — For transporting us beyond Seas to be tried for pretended offences — For abolishing the free System of English Laws in a neighbouring Province, establishing therein an Arbitrary government, and enlarging its Boundaries so as to render it at once an example and fit instrument for introducing the same absolute rule into these Colonies: — For taking away our Charters, abolishing our most valuable Laws, and altering fundamentally the Forms of our Governments: — For suspending our own Legislatures, and declaring themselves invested with power to legislate for us in all cases whatsoever. — He has abdicated Government here, by declaring us out of his Protection and waging War against us. —— He has plundered our seas, ravaged our Coasts, burnt our towns, and destroyed the lives of our people. —— He is at this time transporting large Armies of foreign Mercenaries to compleat the works of death, desolation and tyranny, already begun with circumstances of Cruelty & perfidy scarcely paralleled in the most barbarous ages, and totally unworthy the Head of a civilized nation. —— He has constrained our fellow Citizens taken Captive on the high Seas to bear Arms against their Country, to become the executioners of their friends and Brethren, or to fall themselves by their Hands. — He has excited domestic insurrections amongst us, and has endeavoured to bring on the

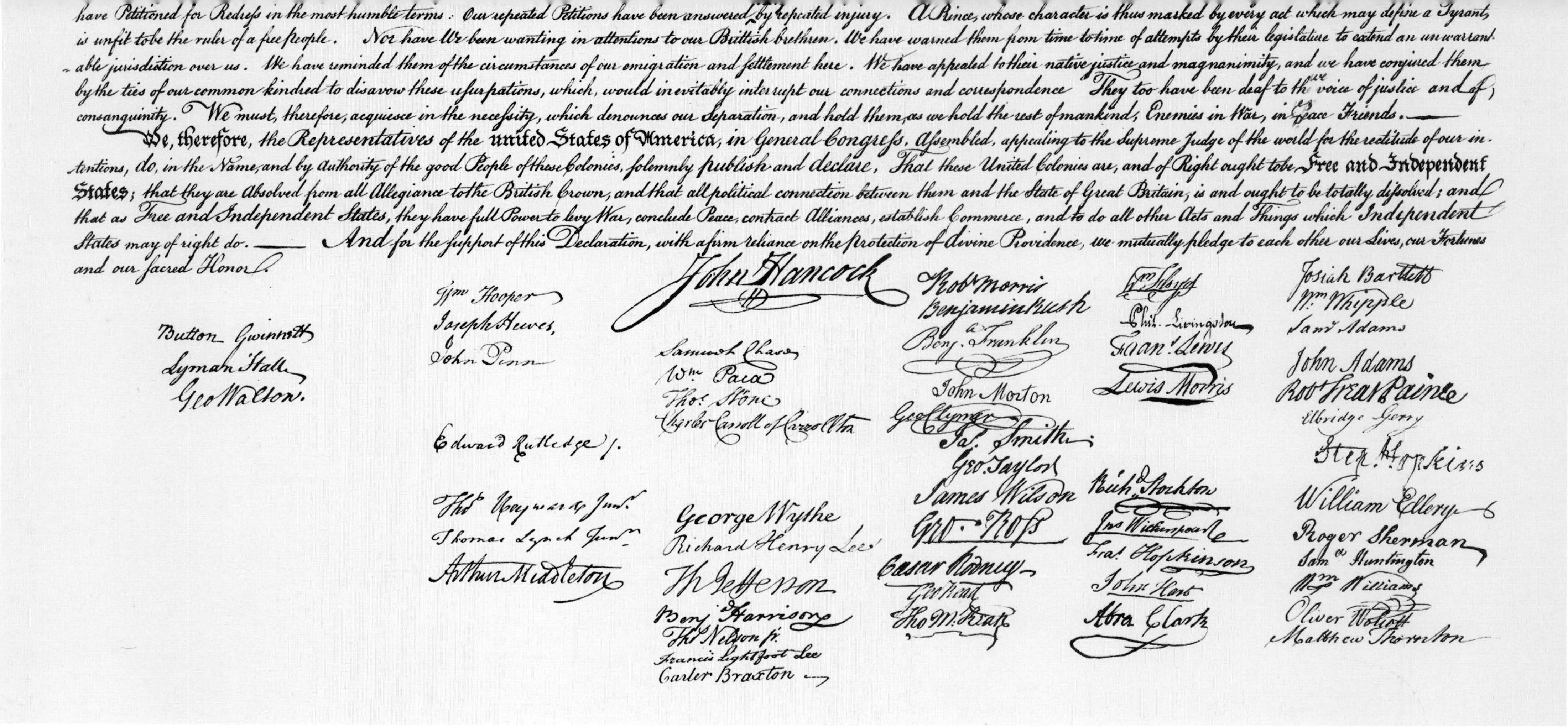

have Petitioned for Redress in the most humble terms: Our repeated Petitions have been answered by repeated injury. A Prince, whose character is thus marked by every act which may define a Tyrant, is unfit to be the ruler of a free people. Nor have We been wanting in attentions to our British brethren. We have warned them from time to time of attempts by their legislature to extend an unwarrantable jurisdiction over us. We have reminded them of the circumstances of our emigration and settlement here. We have appealed to their native justice and magnanimity, and we have conjured them by the ties of our common kindred to disavow these usurpations, which, would inevitably interrupt our connections and correspondence. They too have been deaf to the voice of justice and of consanguinity. We must, therefore, acquiesce in the necessity, which denounces our Separation, and hold them, as we hold the rest of mankind, Enemies in War, in Peace Friends. —

We, therefore, the Representatives of the united States of America, in General Congress, Assembled, appealing to the Supreme Judge of the world for the rectitude of our intentions, do, in the Name, and by Authority of the good People of these Colonies, solemnly publish and declare, That these United Colonies are, and of Right ought to be Free and Independent States; that they are Absolved from all Allegiance to the British Crown, and that all political connection between them and the State of Great Britain, is and ought to be totally dissolved; and that as Free and Independent States, they have full Power to levy War, conclude Peace, contract Alliances, establish Commerce, and to do all other Acts and Things which Independent States may of right do. — And for the support of this Declaration, with a firm reliance on the protection of divine Providence, we mutually pledge to each other our Lives, our Fortunes and our sacred Honor.

John Hancock

Button Gwinnett
Lyman Hall
Geo Walton.

Wm Hooper
Joseph Hewes,
John Penn

Edward Rutledge 1.

Thos Heyward Junr.
Thomas Lynch Junr.
Arthur Middleton

Samuel Chase
Wm. Paca
Thos. Stone
Charles Carroll of Carrollton

George Wythe
Richard Henry Lee
Th Jefferson
Benja Harrison
Thos Nelson jr.
Francis Lightfoot Lee
Carter Braxton

Robt Morris
Benjamin Rush
Benja. Franklin
John Morton
Geo Clymer
Jas. Smith
Geo. Taylor
James Wilson
Geo. Ross
Caesar Rodney
Geo Read
Tho M:Kean

Wm Floyd
Phil. Livingston
Frans. Lewis
Lewis Morris

Richd. Stockton
Jno Witherspoon
Fras. Hopkinson
John Hart
Abra Clark

Josiah Bartlett
Wm. Whipple
Saml Adams
John Adams
Robt Treat Paine
Elbridge Gerry
Step. Hopkins
William Ellery
Roger Sherman
Sam el Huntington
Wm Williams
Oliver Wolcott
Matthew Thornton

ALL MEN ARE CREATED EQUAL

The signing of **THE DECLARATION OF INDEPENDENCE** meant death warrants for the 56 rebellious American delegates to the Continental Congress. If the revolution failed, Benjamin Franklin wryly stated: "We must all hang together, or assuredly we shall all hang separately." Thomas Jefferson powerfully enumerated 27 grievances against the Crown, a stinging indictment of British rule, asserting: "We hold these Truths to be self-evident, that all men are created equal, that they are endowed by their Creator with certain unalienable Rights, that among these are life, liberty, and the pursuit of Happiness."

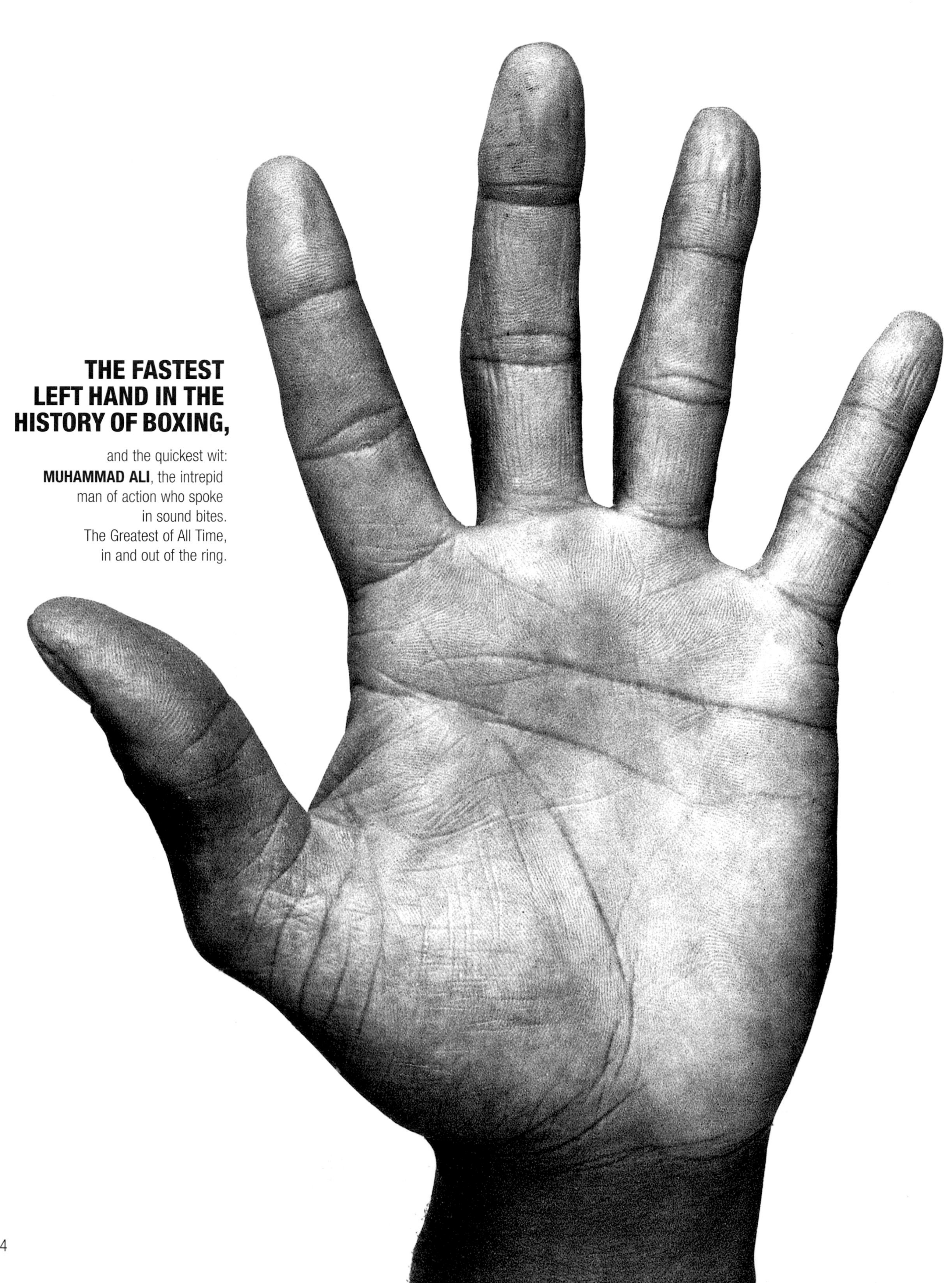

THE FASTEST LEFT HAND IN THE HISTORY OF BOXING,

and the quickest wit: **MUHAMMAD ALI**, the intrepid man of action who spoke in sound bites. The Greatest of All Time, in and out of the ring.

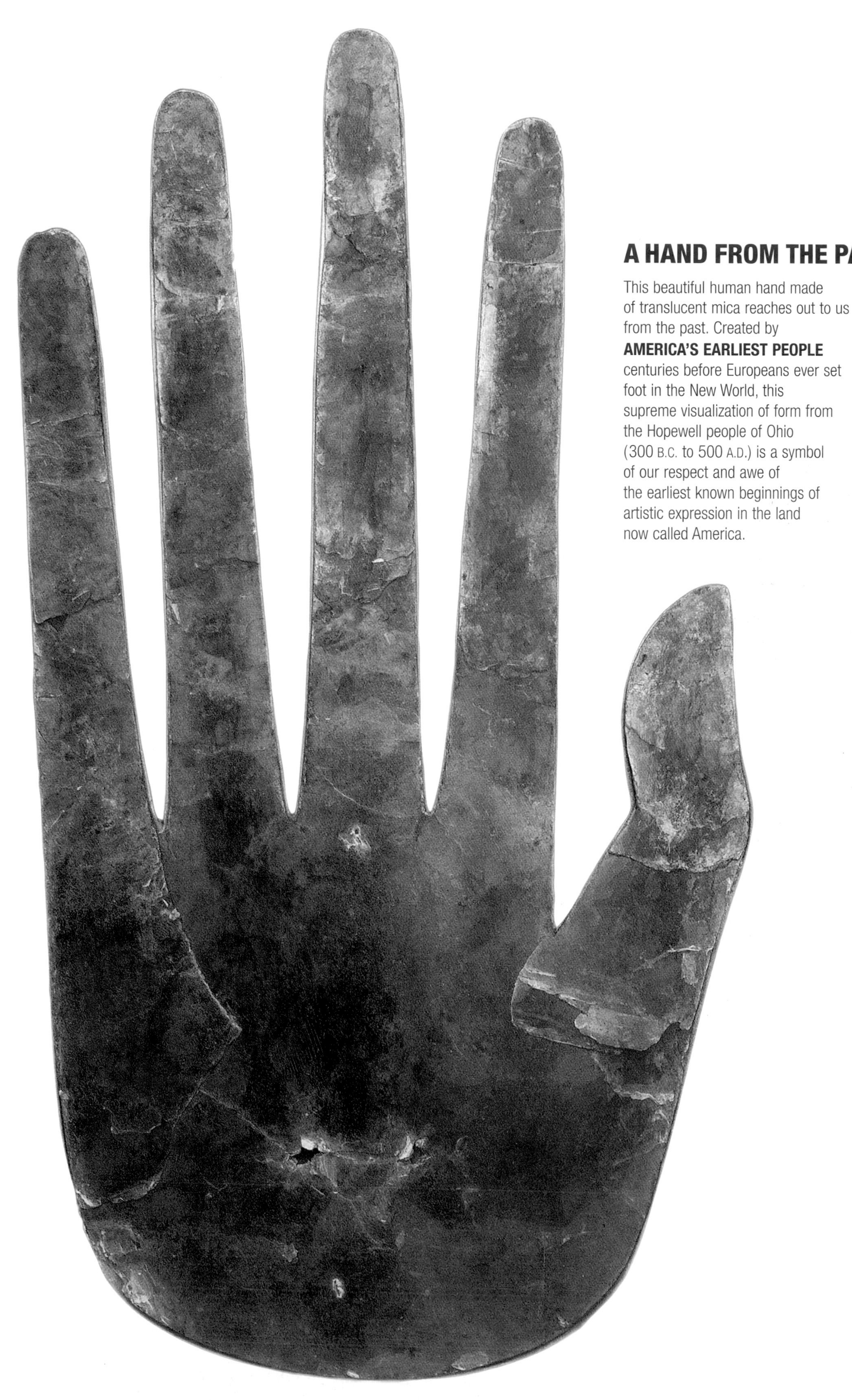

A HAND FROM THE PAST

This beautiful human hand made of translucent mica reaches out to us from the past. Created by **AMERICA'S EARLIEST PEOPLE** centuries before Europeans ever set foot in the New World, this supreme visualization of form from the Hopewell people of Ohio (300 B.C. to 500 A.D.) is a symbol of our respect and awe of the earliest known beginnings of artistic expression in the land now called America.

PORTRAIT OF THE FIRST AMERICANS

"If my life be spared, nothing shall stop me from visiting every nation of Indians on the Continent of North America." From 1830 to 1836, following the trail of the Lewis and Clark expedition, **GEORGE CATLIN** became the first great painter to travel beyond the Mississippi to paint the Indians, and his Indian Gallery, staggering in its ambition, scope, and humanity, is one of the wonders of our nation. His original Indian Gallery came to the Smithsonian Museum seven years after his death in 1872. (Go to Washington, D.C., and pay homage.) This superb 1832 portrait is of Buffalo Bull's Back Fat, a Blackfoot chief.

WAR PAINT FROM TWO PRE-FEMINISTS

Long before the modern feminist movement in America, two whirlwind women, one a young teenage Jewish immigrant born in Poland, the other a horse-set WASP socialite, became American icons who ran competing cosmetic empires. In 1912, in New York, **MADAME HELENA RUBINSTEIN** pioneered the modern-day cosmetics business while constantly feuding with "That Other One" (as she called **ELIZABETH ARDEN**), an equally talented cosmetician and businesswoman. The Madame was a rich, hot-headed, imperious empress, and the blue-blooded Miss Arden was calm, cool, and controlled. (Perhaps the upstart cosmetics entrepreneur Charles Revson, of Revlon, whom both ladies despised, had them in mind when he named his new cologne, Fire and Ice!)

THE WAVING AMERICAN FLAG

The thirteen stripes of our original colonies remain the basis of the symbolism of the American flag. But the star-filled cornerstone has expanded into an ever-more glowing galaxy. Our Grand Old Flag has been a living symbol that has expanded with the nation, a flag continually shaped by the people. Finally, as a provocative and dynamic graphic design, the *waving* American flag transforms even more gloriously into twinkling stars and undulating ripples and waves.

SHE SEWED A MASTERPIECE OF SYMBOLISM

The design of the flag seems to have been the consensus of a flag committee of the Continental Congress. They chose the same colors that they had chosen for the Great Seal of the United States: red stripes for valor, white stripes for purity, and a blue sky with a constellation of stars for justice. A seamstress (whose pew was next to George Washington's in Christ Church in Philadelphia) was given a roughly drawn sketch—and from it she sewed a masterpiece of symbolism. **BETSY ROSS** has become one of the most cherished names in American history.

ADMITTEDLY, AMERICA IS THE CORNIEST COUNTRY IN THE WORLD

CORN is deliciously indigenous to the Americas, spreading to the rest of the world after European contact in the late 15th century. When Columbus discovered America, he also discovered corn.
When the first Thanksgiving was held in 1621, sweet potatoes, cranberry sauce, and pumpkin pie were not on the menu, but Indian corn certainly was. The U.S. produces almost half of the world's harvest; a good crop is predicted if the corn is "knee high by the Fourth of July." In the U.S., the primary products of corn are livestock feed, sweeteners, and grain alcohol. Americans love their corn on the cob, corn bread, corn muffins, corn chips, hominy, grits, succotash, candy corn, and, of course, popcorn.

THE WORLDWIDE DREAM TEAM

The **NATIONAL BASKETBALL ASSOCIATION** was founded in 1946, and in 1950 (three years after Jackie Robinson had broken the color barrier in baseball) three African-American players pioneered the integration of the rising pro basketball league (Earl Lloyd, Sweetwater Clifton, and Chuck Cooper). The early superstars of the NBA were Big George Mikan, Bob Pettit, Elgin Baylor, The Cooze, Bill Russell, The Big O, Hondo Havlicek, The Iceman, Pistol Pete, Dollar Bill, Clyde, Earl the Pearl, The Big Dipper, and the white guy on the NBA logo, Mister Clutch Jerry West. Then came the generation of Dr. J, Magic Johnson, Kareem, The Mailman, Chocolate Thunder, The Admiral, Sir Charles, Larry Bird, Air Jordan, and Shaq. With the inspiration and showmanship of those NBA superstars, in the late 1990s the league underwent a trendsetting globalization with growing numbers of foreign players of superstar status: Hakeem Olajuwon (Nigeria), Dirk Nowitzki (Germany), Steve Nash (Canada), Yao Ming (China), Emanuel Ginobli (Argentina), Pau Gasol (Spain), and Tony Parker (France). Basketball, a homemade, American-played game, has now become a worldwide phenomenon. Vive la différence!

5,600 YEARS OF POP (CORN) CULTURE

Archaeological digs in New Mexico discovered the oldest popped kernels of **POPCORN** ever found, proving that North American Indians were popping corn 5,600 years ago! How American can a food get?! And nothing is more American than watching a good movie while munching popcorn sprinkled with salt and dripping with butter–popcorn has been served in cinemas since 1912.

Address delivered at the dedication of the Cemetery at Gettysburg.

Four score and seven years ago our fathers brought forth on this continent, a new nation, conceived in Liberty, and dedicated to the proposition that all men are created equal.

Now we are engaged in a great civil war, testing whether that nation, or any nation so conceived and so dedicated, can long endure. We are met on a great battle-field of that war. We have come to dedicate a portion of that field, as a final resting place for those who here gave their lives, that that nation might live. It is altogether fitting and proper that we should do this.

But, in a larger sense, we can not dedicate— we can not consecrate— we can not hallow— this ground. The brave men, living and dead, who struggled here, have consecrated it, far above our poor power to add or detract. The world will little note, nor long remember what we say here, but it can never forget what they did here. It is for us the living, rather, to be dedicated here to the unfinished work which they who fought here have thus far so nobly advanced.

It is rather for us to be here dedicated to the great task remaining before us— that from these honored dead we take increased devotion to that cause for which they gave the last full measure of devotion— that we here highly resolve that these dead shall not have died in vain— that this nation, under God, shall have a new birth of freedom— and that government of the people, by the people, for the people, shall not perish from the earth.

Abraham Lincoln.

November 19. 1863.

"PRESIDENT LINCOLN WAS THERE, TOO."

On November 19,1863, President Abraham Lincoln delivered **THE GETTYSBURG ADDRESS**. In ten sentences, 272 words, and about three minutes, the great leader invoked the principles of human equality espoused by the Declaration of Independence, and redefined the catastrophic Civil War as a struggle not merely for the Union, but as "a new birth of freedom" that would bring equality to *all* of its citizens. Some witnesses reported that after his talk the applause was scattered and "barely polite," while others maintained that the multitude standing on the site of the bloody Battle of Gettysburg was stunned in silent awe of Lincoln's magnificent eloquence. Most newspaper accounts gave Lincoln's talk (if they mentioned it at all) second billing to a pompous two-hour speech proceeding his. *The Steubenville Weekly Herald*, an Ohio newspaper, ended its account of the day's proceedings with a one-sentence understatement: "President Lincoln was there, too." (The photograph of the great man was taken by **MATTHEW BRADY** in Washington, D.C., a few months after Lincoln's iconic speech.)

THE BIRTH OF MODERN ADVERTISING

The vast majority of the engaging **SHOP FIGURES** that invited passersby into retail stores were made by ship carpenters—skilled sculptors known for their masterful ship figureheads. These carvers made tens of thousands of shop figures, from fanciful representations of American Indians to baseball players, firemen, and fashionable women. Cigar store Indians were the most common, entering America's emerging popular culture in the 1800s, giving birth to the aggressive modern advertising techniques of today.

THE CUTTING EDGE OF AMERICAN TECHNOLOGY IN THE LATE 19TH CENTURY? THE CAN OPENER!

During the 1820s, when William Parry led expeditions through the frozen wasteland near the North Pole, they survived with the help of a revolutionary new concept: canned food. Tin-coated iron cans allowed the explorers to carry provisions without spoilage. The problem was that the cans of roast veal came with these forbidding instructions: "Cut round the top near the outer edge with a chisel and hammer." Soldiers of the day attacked cans with bayonets. As late as the Civil War, hungry troops resorted to rifle fire to open the cans. In 1858, soon after thinner cans were produced, Ezra Warner patented the first can opener, and the world has never been the same. This classic 1891 can opener could open cans, lift bottle caps, and extract corks–American ingenuity at its best, still widely manufactured today in a form not too unlike the original.

REMEMBER PEARL HARBOR!

The devastating surprise attack on **PEARL HARBOR** shocked a sleeping America. Outraged, President Franklin D. Roosevelt signed a Declaration of War the next day and galvanized a previously divided nation with these historic words: *Yesterday, December 7, 1941–a date which will live in infamy–the United States of America was suddenly and deliberately attacked by naval and air forces of the Empire of Japan.* Within four years, the United States, along with its Allies, overcame the Axis powers of Japan, Nazi Germany, and Fascist Italy. Evoking the heroic leadership of FDR and the intrepid spirit of a people fighting to preserve a democratic way of life, "Remember Pearl Harbor" has assumed mythic status in American history. The painful experience of World War II, with the unspeakable atrocities committed during the fog of war by all adversaries, has alleviated with the passage of time, with ensuing years of growing friendship and respect between our great nations.

REMEMBER THE ALAMO!

The Alamo was a chapel of the San Antonio de Valero Mission, built by the Spanish Empire in the 18th century, abandoned as a church and used as a fortress when it was surrendered to Texan forces in 1836. Two months later it became the scene of the iconic Battle of the Alamo between the forces of the Republic of Texas and Mexico in a 13-day siege by 5,000 Mexican soldiers led by General Santa Anna, resulting in the death of 187 heroic Texans. (The Alamo is often looked at as a relic of Anglo imperialism, with Mexico losing Texas in a land-grab, but for Texan advocates, the Alamo reflects a stubborn Texan drive for independence won from Mexico just as that nation was mired in coups and tyranny.) The anguished mantra "Remember the Alamo" took on symbolic meaning throughout the nation, and was echoed a century later with the cry, "Remember Pearl Harbor."

THE SOARING AMERICAN EAGLE

In 1782, the Continental Congress introduced a powerful emblem into the vocabulary of American design to symbolize the strength and independence of the new republic—the magnificent **BALD EAGLE**. Since that time the eagle has penetrated American life, assuming an aggressive stance on the sterns of our early ships of war, and gracing our public buildings, coins, banknotes—even our furniture and quilts. As a magnificent patriotic motif, it continues to soar and to influence American imagery long after Thomas Jefferson and John Adams persuaded Benjamin Franklin that his recommendation for the national bird, an American Wild Turkey, would have been a national disaster.

THE MASTER OF BIRDIES & EAGLES

TIGER WOODS is the great American melting pot story, an ethnic blending of African-American, Thai, Chinese, Native American, and Dutch (and married to a Swede). A golf prodigy at the age of three, he is on his way to becoming the greatest golfer of all time.

THE WORLD OF TOMORROW

THE 1939 NEW YORK WORLD'S FAIR was a masterpiece of showmanship, a real-life land of Oz, indelibly etched in the annals of pre-World War II America as a brief respite between a decade of economic depression and years of global war. Almost 70 years later, the fair continues to glow in our memory, fascinating students of history, culture, art and design the world over, with the optimistic promise of the dawn of a new day. The graphic imagery of the Trylon and Perisphere was a worldwide symbol of the American Dream.

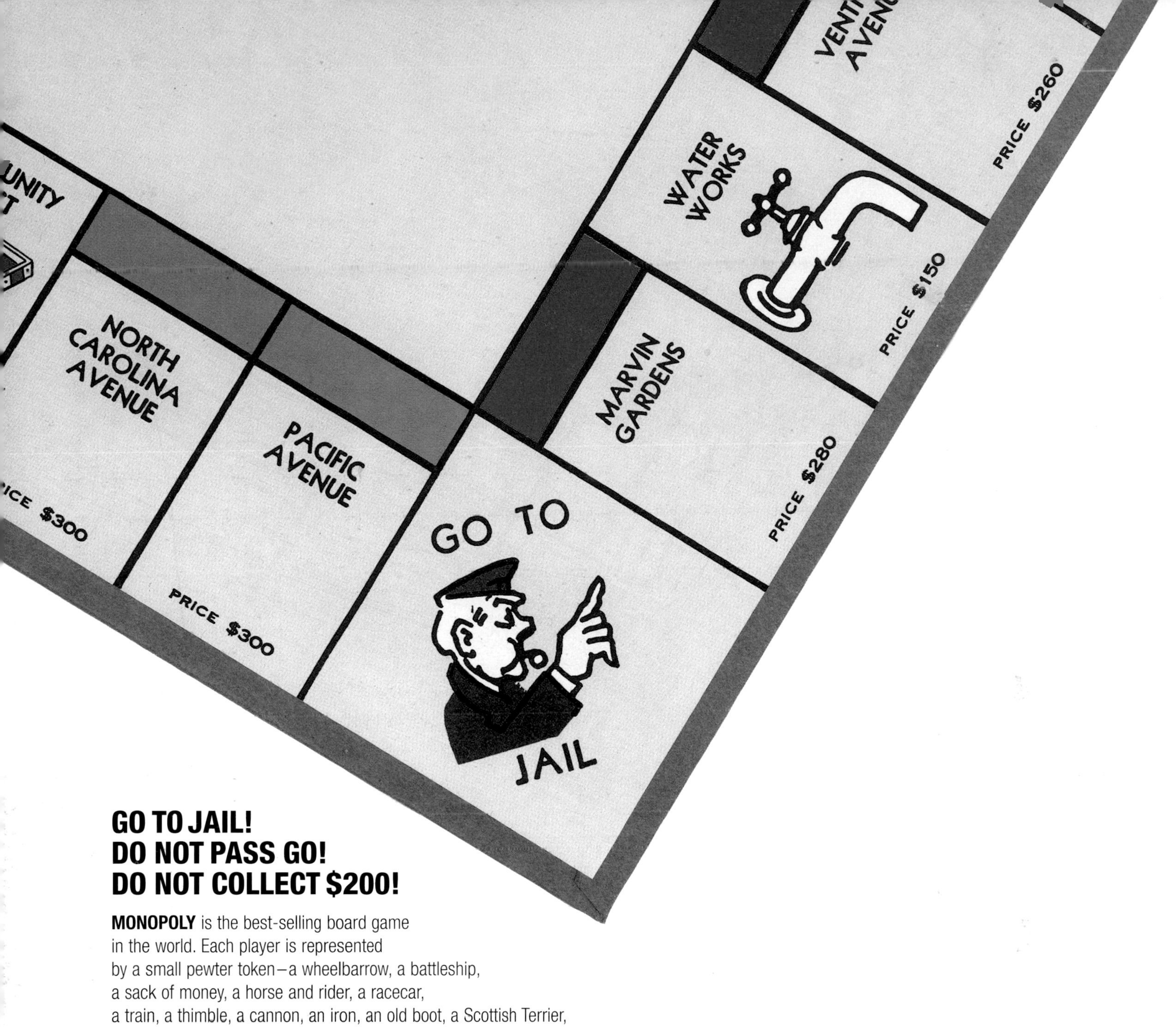

GO TO JAIL!
DO NOT PASS GO!
DO NOT COLLECT $200!

MONOPOLY is the best-selling board game in the world. Each player is represented by a small pewter token—a wheelbarrow, a battleship, a sack of money, a horse and rider, a racecar, a train, a thimble, a cannon, an iron, an old boot, a Scottish Terrier, or a top hat—which is moved around the board on the roll of the dice. If you've never played the game, it involves acquiring wealth by buying, renting, and trading properties using play money. But you probably played when you were a kid—because 500 million people are estimated to have "passed Go," each hoping they don't "Go to Jail."

KING LOUIS

The influence of **LOUIS ARMSTRONG** on the development of jazz is immeasurable: He was a charismatic, innovative talent whose trumpet, voice, and personality transformed jazz from rough regional dance music into America's most unique musical art form. In developing his art, Armstrong invented jazz singing, and "scat" singing, using his voice as creatively as his trumpet. Satchmo's irrepressible personality, both when he was a performer and when he later became a public figure, made him one of the most beloved Americans in history.

THE SHARING OF THE PEACE PIPE

George Washington's administration was a crucial period in America's relations with the Indians, who for the most part had fought for the British during the Revolutionary War. The new nation needed to conciliate them if it was to start its existence in peace. **THE SILVER PEACE MEDAL** became the persuading instrument in its policy! The handsomely hand-engraved medals became marks of rank within the tribes and were highly prized possessions. Years later when an Indian chief or his successor posed for an artist or photographer, he would still wear his medal with great pride.

THE INSTANT ICON

In 2003 the Google search engine became a cultural phenomenon and a verb. To research specific information these days you "google it." Google has sped up information gathering a thousand fold, achieving preeminent status as an augmenter of the human brain, able to direct you to anything you don't know, or have forgotten. (For more info, google Google.)

Google™

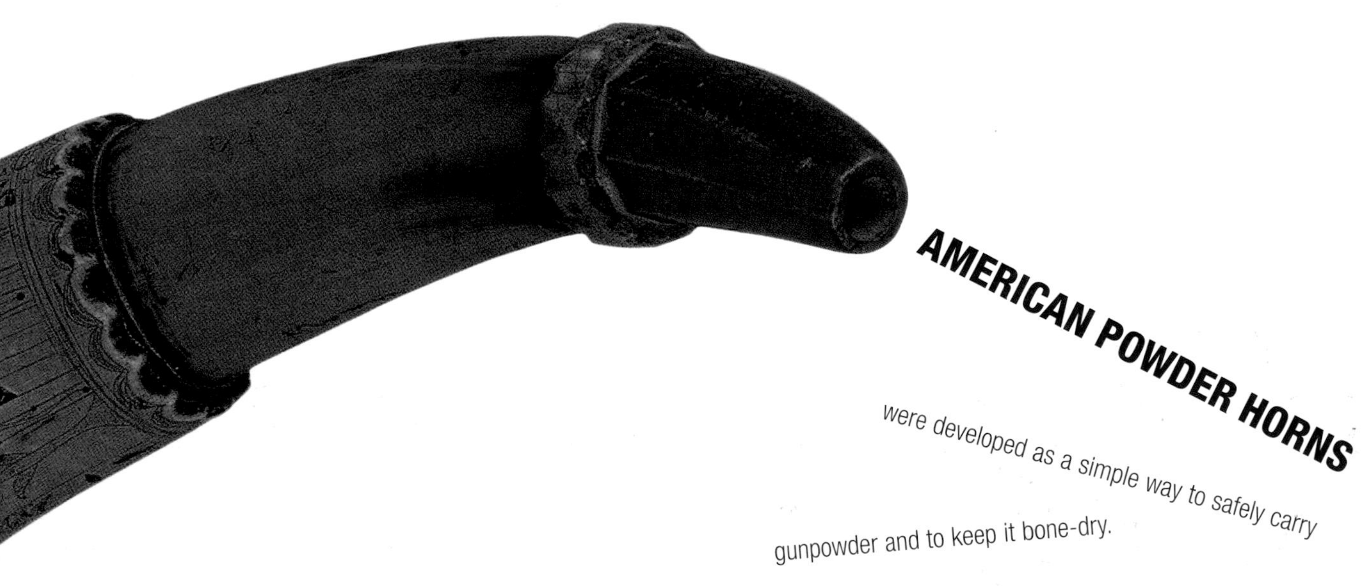

AMERICAN POWDER HORNS

were developed as a simple way to safely carry gunpowder and to keep it bone-dry.

Cow horns did the trick—they were boiled, cleaned, scraped, then plugged on one end for filling and at the other for pouring. Eventually, during the French and Indian War, they became beautiful objects of art, carved with drawings and inscriptions and the name of the owner. During the Revolutionary War, the inscriptions took on a poignant intensity, as on this beauty, with words of yearning for dear Liberty:

"Jabez Gooddel's Horn Made June Y^{e} 7th/A.D. 1776/
To Arms to arms O Free born Sons/Exert the Sword and Spear/
Oppose the Tyrant and his bands./Defend your Rights most Dear."

AH, HA, HA, HA, STAYIN' ALIVE, STAYIN' ALIVE

The 1977 movie **SATURDAY NIGHT FEVER** starred the young John Travolta as Tony Manero, a troubled punk from Brooklyn with a dead-end job and deadbeat friends. But the kid in the flashy white suit was the king of the dance floor, living his weekends in the spotlight, knockin' 'em dead in a local discotheque to the music of the Bee Gees. The John Badham movie popularized disco music around the world and made Travolta, who had been a chorus dancer, a superstar of American culture.

THE ORIGINAL AMERICAN IN PARIS

This painting, popularly referred to as **WHISTLER'S MOTHER**, is the best-known American portrait, a work so famous it is almost regarded as a cliché. In 1871, James Abbott McNeill Whistler portrayed his "mummy" in a handsome *Arrangement in Gray and Black*, sitting in profile with her aged hands in her lap. With Whistler's painting, America ceased to be provincial and came artistically of age. This homespun Yankee mom holds court today in a gallery at the Louvre, an American in Paris.

FREEDOM!

Our American culture is regularly
invigorated by immigrants
seeking a better way of life. That's why
THE STATUE OF LIBERTY,
our welcoming image of freedom,
remains one of America's most
passionate and meaningful symbols.

THE QUILTING OF AMERICA

In a culture of machine-made products,
we remain in awe of this
distinctively feminine art form that still exists today—
not only a popular folk craft, but an
abstract-design tradition that influenced the
abstract art movement.

...AND THE BENEFITS OF FREEDOM!

The good life must include food, shelter, and security for you and your family, all of which we take for granted in America. But freedom is worthless without these necessities. Joining the monumental American inventions of the electric light, the telegraph, the telephone, and the airplane, etc., the development of **REFRIGERATION** changed the world, deliciously.

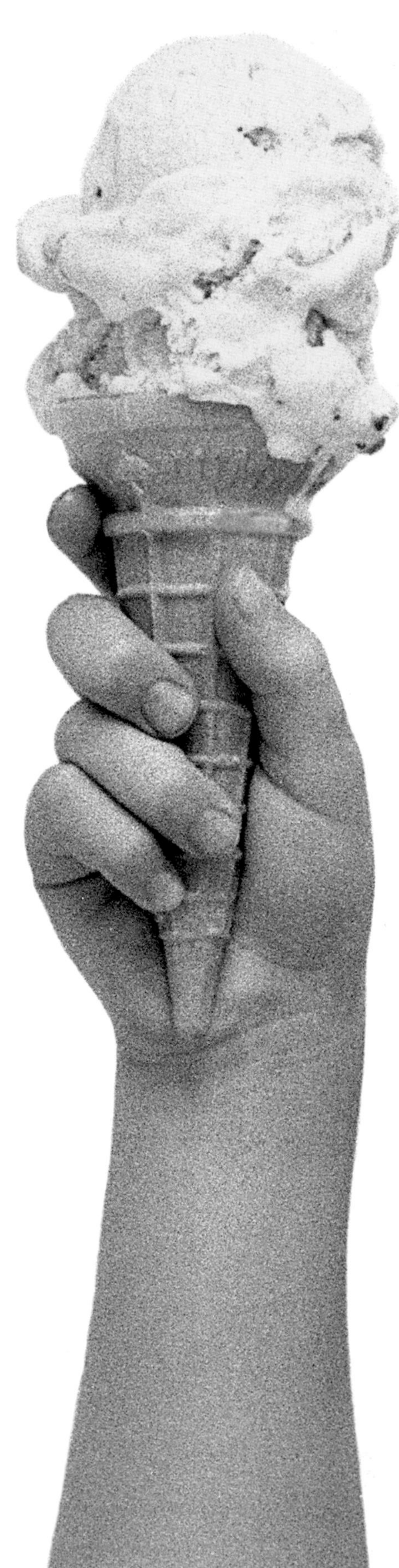

THE SPLASH HEARD 'ROUND THE WORLD

In the early 1920s **JANTZEN** became synonymous with the emancipation of women with a logo of a risqué female diver wearing a stylish Jantzen swimsuit. The Diving Girl in Red (in a modernized version) remains one of the greatest action logos in history!

The first generation of **AMERICAN INDUSTRIAL DESIGNERS** was led by Walter Dorwin Teague, who designed this 1930 Kodak camera incorporating a motif of that new age of Abstract modern painting.

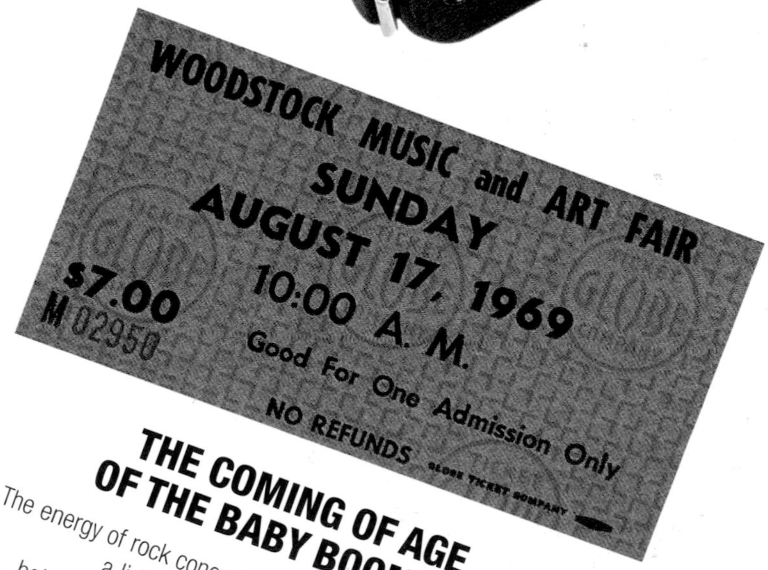

WOODSTOCK MUSIC and ART FAIR
SUNDAY
AUGUST 17, 1969
10:00 A. M.
Good For One Admission Only
NO REFUNDS
$7.00
M 02950

THE COMING OF AGE OF THE BABY BOOMERS

The energy of rock concerts was iconized at **WOODSTOCK**, a living symbol of the constant war between the Establishment and the Counterculture. So-o-o American!

AMERICA LAPPED IT UP

Hard to believe today, but after its first year of operations, **MTV** was an abject failure. But in 1982, after seeing Mick Jagger pick up a phone and bellow "I want my MTV" in television spots, thousands of rock fans mimicked Mick when *they* picked up a phone, called their local cable operator, and screamed for their MTV. Six months later, *Time* magazine called MTV "the most spectacular pop culture phenomenon since the advent of cable television—and, arguably, since the invention of the tube itself."

THE LOWLY LOBSTER

Once, the bottom-feeding lobster was so plentiful it was considered "poverty food." Today, there's no cuisine more American, more upscale, and more finger-lickin' delicious than the Maine lobster.

"I want my

MTV"

MUSIC TELEVISION

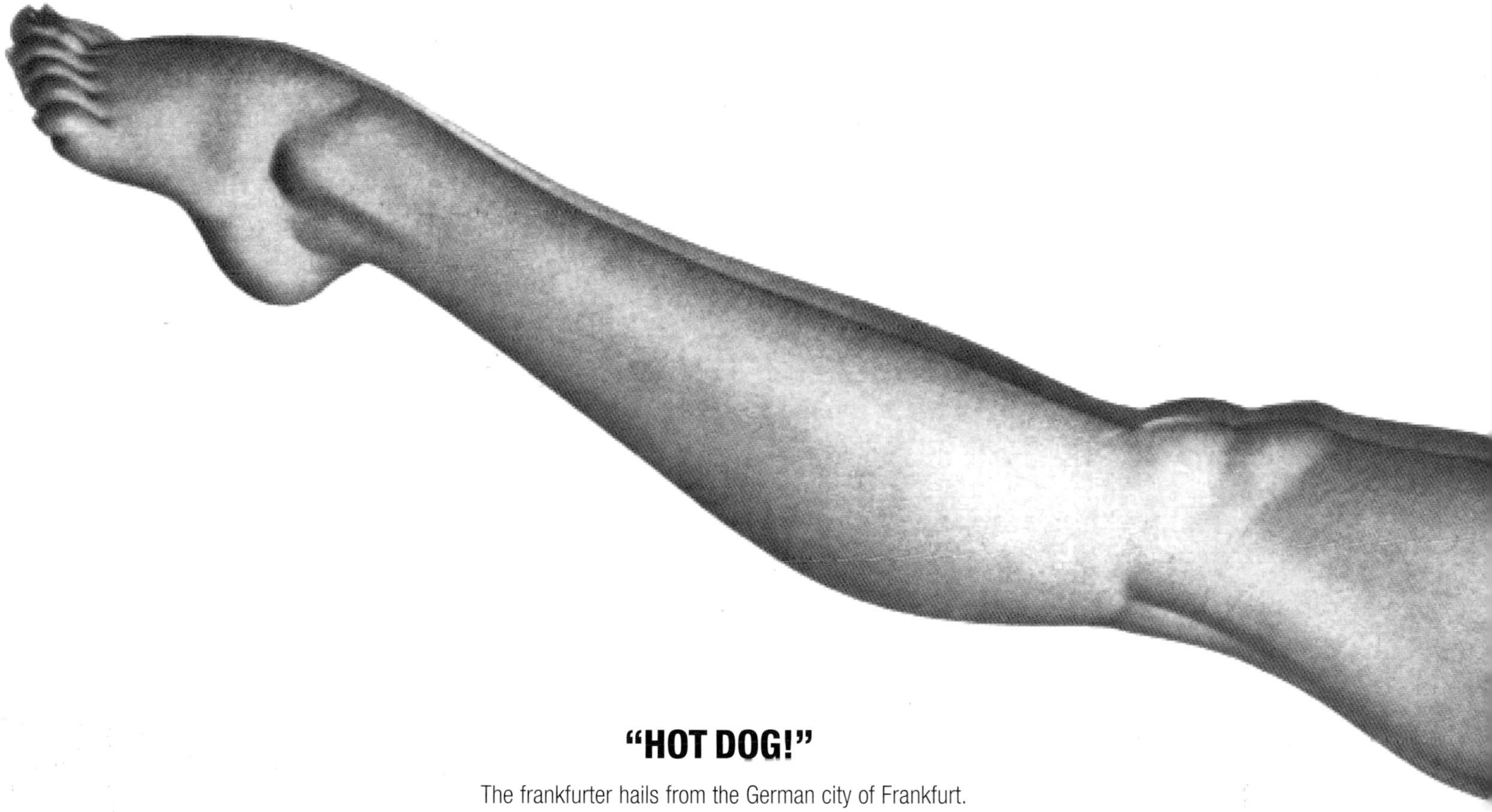

"HOT DOG!"

The frankfurter hails from the German city of Frankfurt. There are many claims to the idea of the frankfurter *bun*, but most likely its use was handed down by German immigrants before becoming widespread in America. But there is serious debate as to the origin of the term "hot dog." Here's the best story: In the press box at a New York Giants baseball game at the Polo Grounds in 1902, Tad Dorgan, the sports cartoonist for the *New York Evening Journal*, was nearing his deadline and desperate for an idea. Hearing the food vendors yelling "Get your Dachshund Sausages while they're red hot!," he hastily drew a cartoon of a frankfurter in a bun with a tail, legs, and a head, so it resembled a Dachshund. Not sure how to spell the word "Dachshund," he simply wrote "Hot Dog!" The cartoon was a sensation and the hot dog was born! Dorgan, a real phrasemaker, also coined these other gems of the American lexicon: *The cat's meow*, *the cat's pajamas*, *hard-boiled* (a tough guy), *cheaters* (eyeglasses), and the exclamation *for crying out loud!*

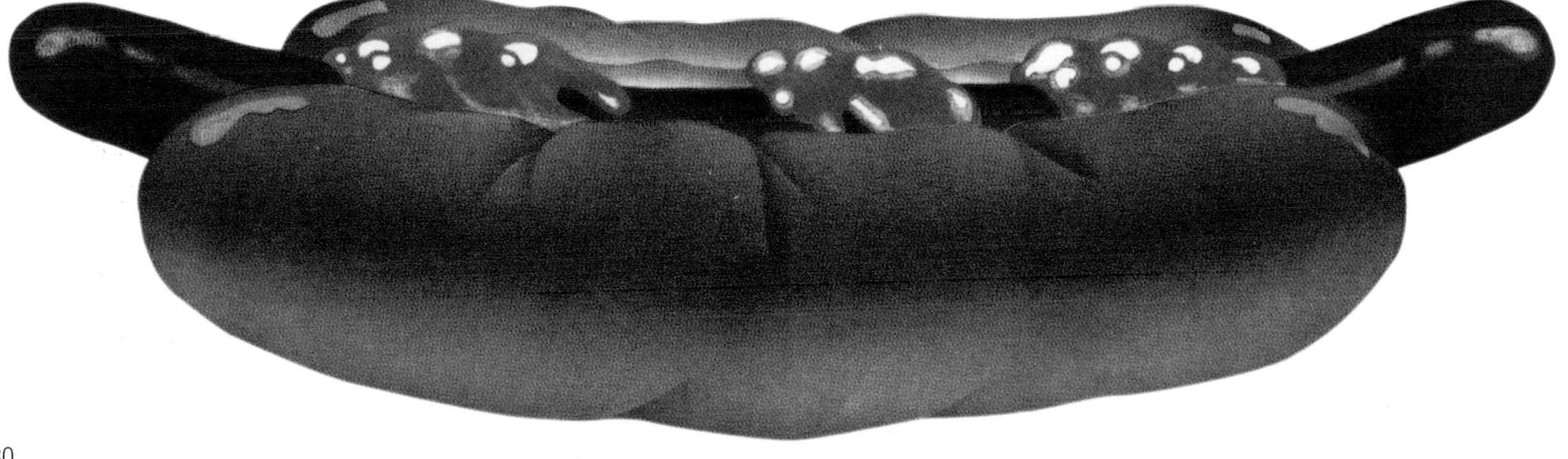

LOOK–AN ICON IN THE SKY!

Since 1925, **THE GOODYEAR BLIMP**, promoting The Goodyear Tire & Rubber Company, has adorned the blue skies of America.

MORE CURVES THAN EVEN GOD ENVISIONED

Just as the cool, unapproachable Gibson Girl was the feminine ideal of young men at the end of the 19th century, the swinging **PETTY GIRL** became the ideal of their wide-eyed sons. In the mid-1930s, George Petty's streamlined, long-legged, air-brushed beauties took the country by storm, later going on to greater heights as nose art on the fuselages of hundreds of World War II bombers. To this day, our favorite American pinup is the Petty Girl of the 1940s.

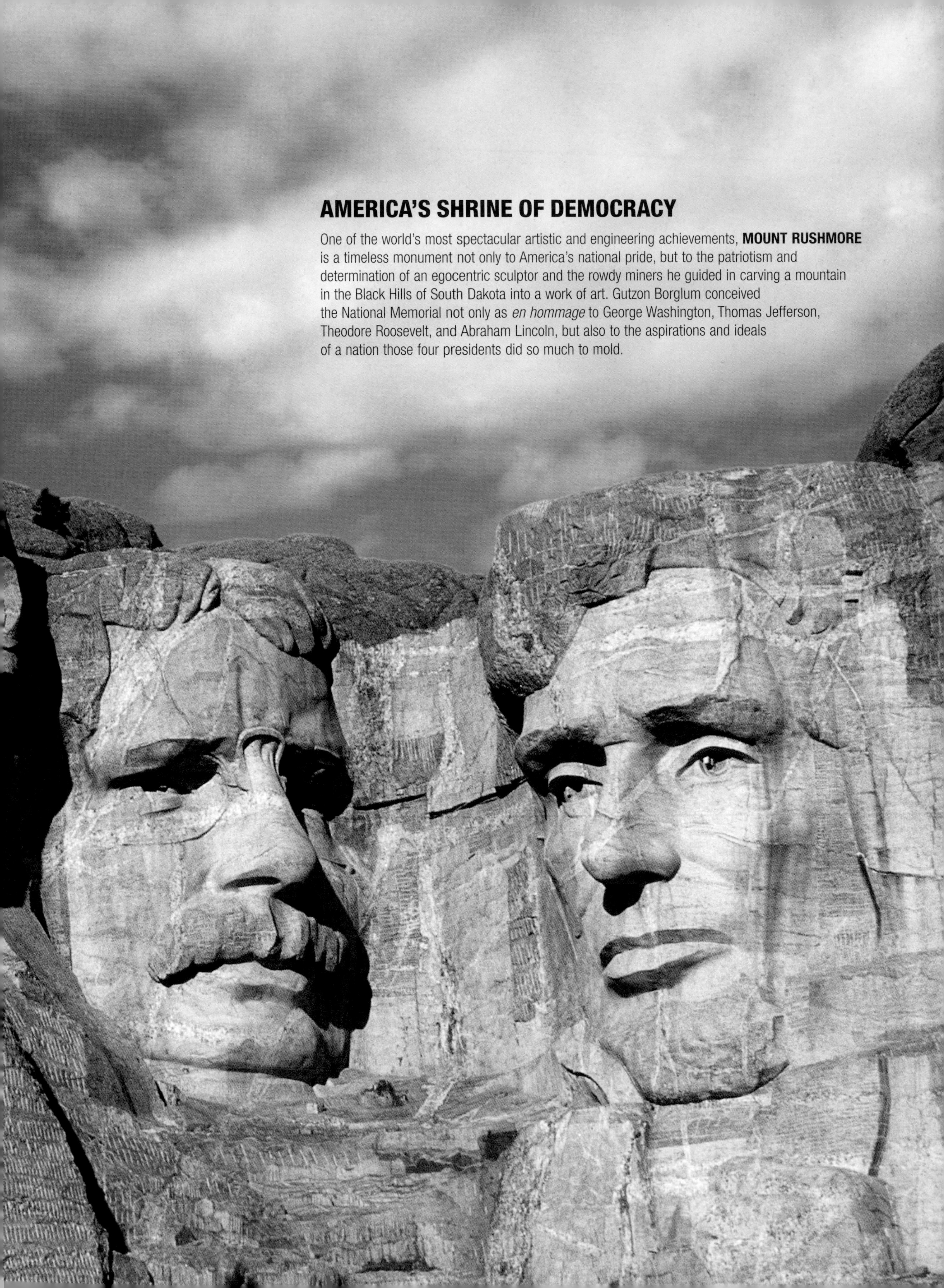

AMERICA'S SHRINE OF DEMOCRACY

One of the world's most spectacular artistic and engineering achievements, **MOUNT RUSHMORE** is a timeless monument not only to America's national pride, but to the patriotism and determination of an egocentric sculptor and the rowdy miners he guided in carving a mountain in the Black Hills of South Dakota into a work of art. Gutzon Borglum conceived the National Memorial not only as *en hommage* to George Washington, Thomas Jefferson, Theodore Roosevelt, and Abraham Lincoln, but also to the aspirations and ideals of a nation those four presidents did so much to mold.

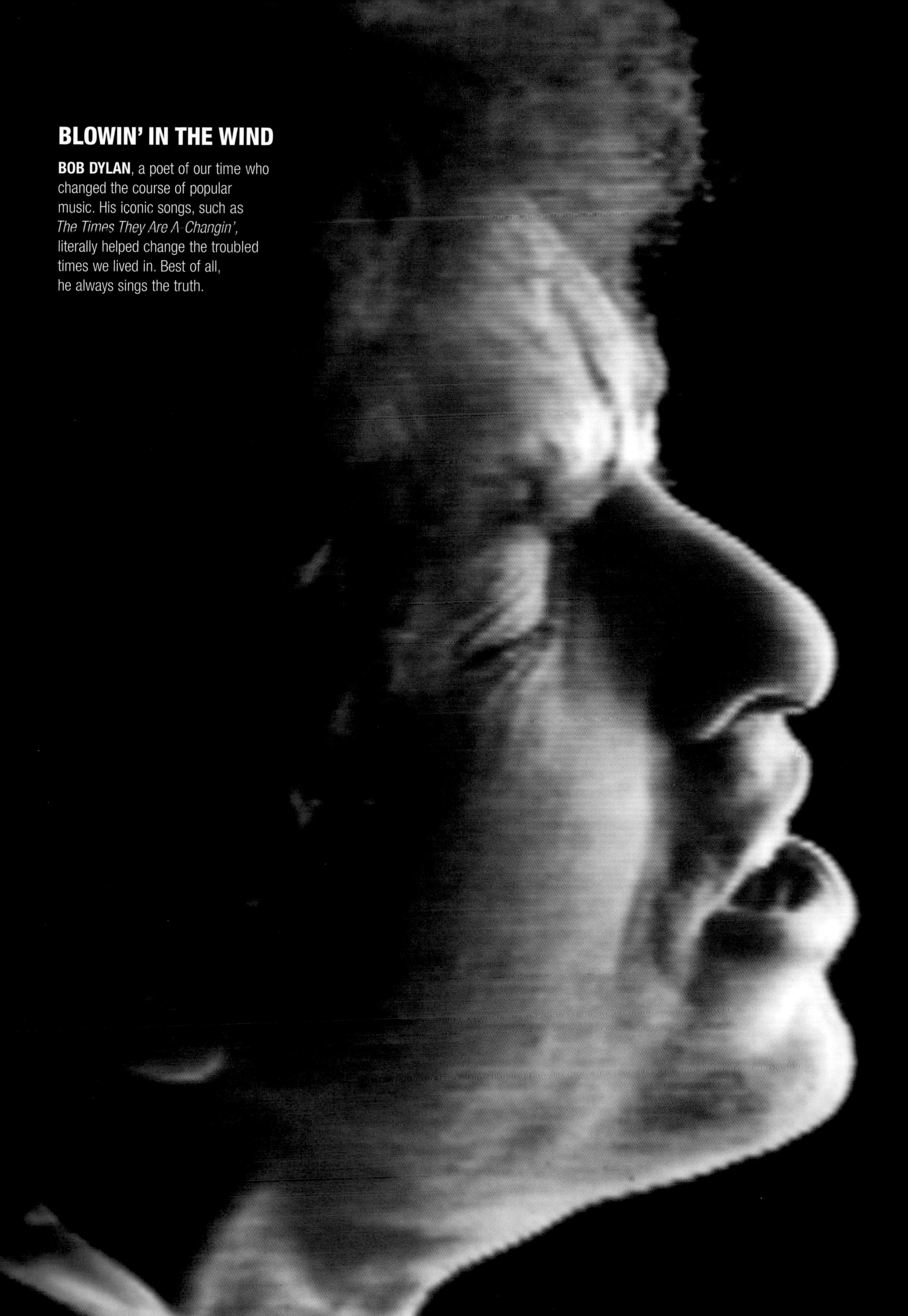

BLOWIN' IN THE WIND

BOB DYLAN, a poet of our time who changed the course of popular music. His iconic songs, such as *The Times They Are A-Changin'*, literally helped change the troubled times we lived in. Best of all, he always sings the truth.

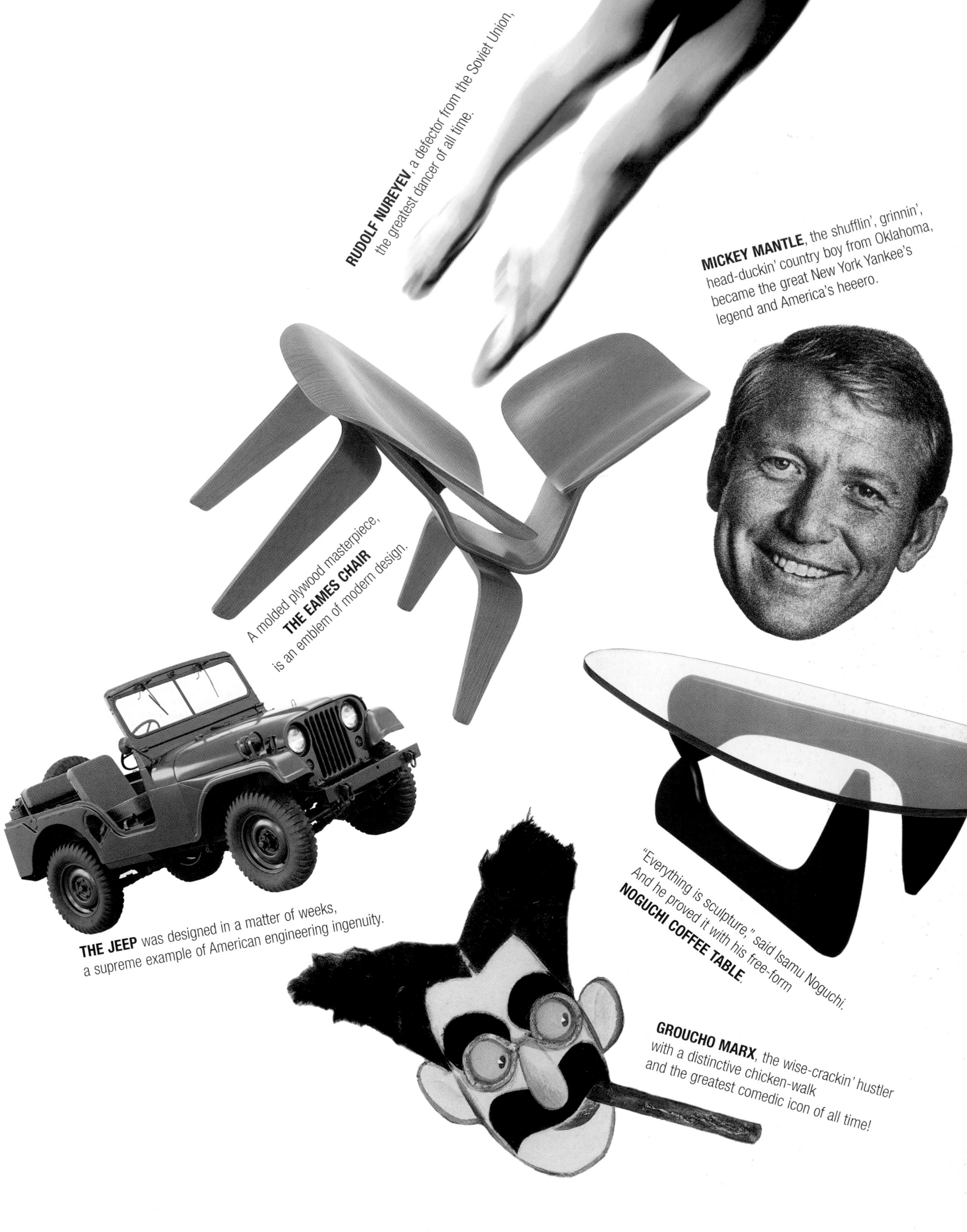

RUDOLF NUREYEV, a defector from the Soviet Union, the greatest dancer of all time.

MICKEY MANTLE, the shufflin', grinnin', head-duckin' country boy from Oklahoma, became the great New York Yankee's legend and America's heeero.

A molded plywood masterpiece, **THE EAMES CHAIR** is an emblem of modern design.

THE JEEP was designed in a matter of weeks, a supreme example of American engineering ingenuity.

"Everything is sculpture," said Isamu Noguchi. And he proved it with his free-form **NOGUCHI COFFEE TABLE**.

GROUCHO MARX, the wise-crackin' hustler with a distinctive chicken-walk and the greatest comedic icon of all time!

THE ICONIC SYMBOL OF VICTORY

On February 19,1945, World War II combat photographer Joe Rosenthal, armed with his trusty Speed Graphic camera, landed with the Marines in an assault on the strategic island of **IWO JIMA**, meeting suicidal resistance from the Japanese. At the conclusion of the five-day battle that claimed 6,821 American lives and left 20,000 wounded, Joe climbed up Iwo Jima's Mount Suribachi and captured the decisive moment when five U.S. Marines and one Navy corpsman were raising the Stars and Stripes. Three of the Marines were killed during the battle. The three remaining men were haunted by the knowledge that they would never be able to live up to the sacrifice their comrades made. The stirring image remains the most powerful symbol of victory since the stalwart scene of General George Washington crossing the Delaware.

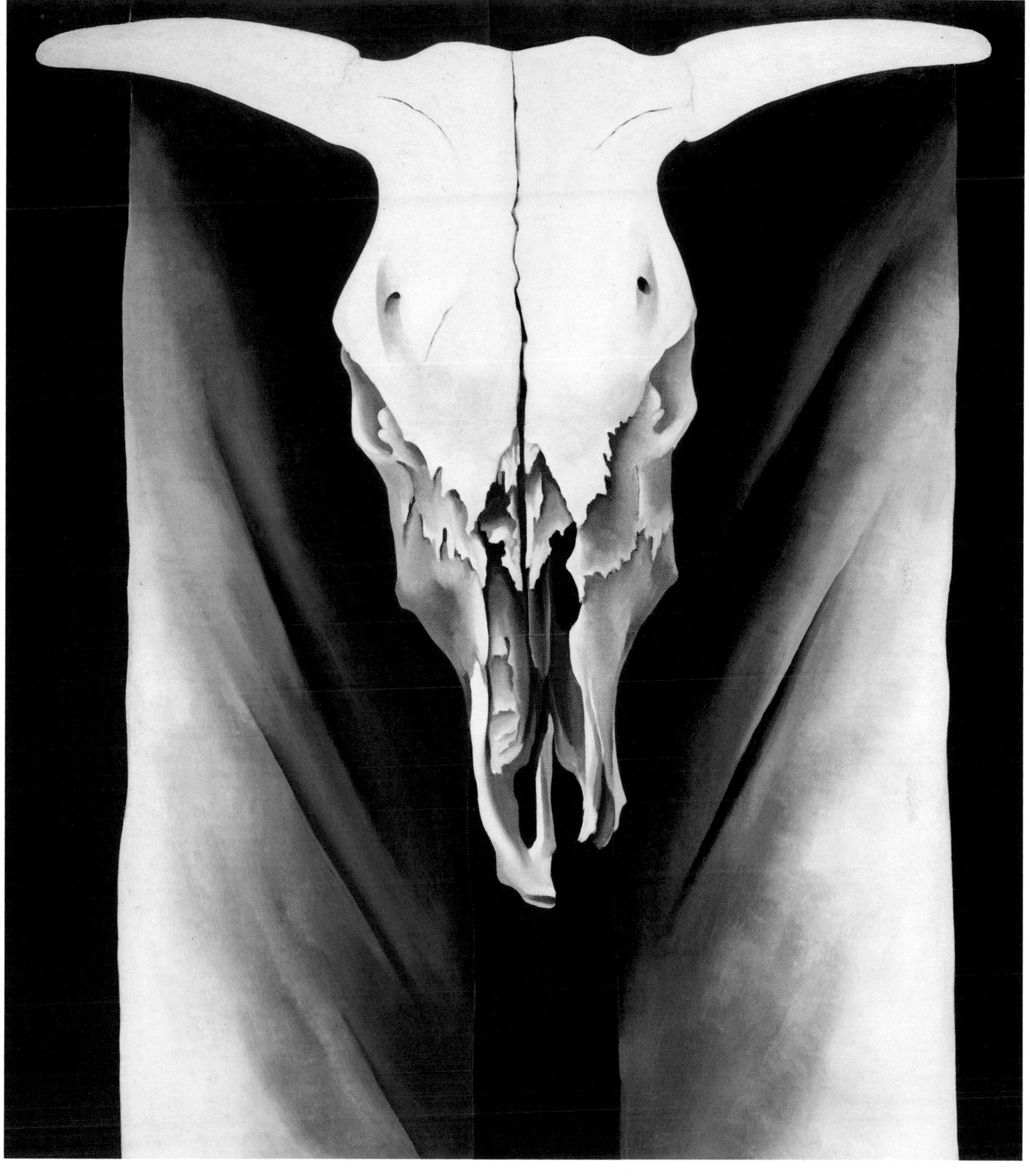

THE GREAT AMERICAN PAINTING

The pioneering modernist painter, **GEORGIA O'KEEFFE**, creator of profound abstract images of the American landscape, wrote this about her iconic painting: "In 1931 I painted a cow's skull on blue. In my Amarillo days cows had been so much a part of the country I couldn't think of it without them. As I was working I thought of the city men I had been seeing in the East. They talked so often about the Great American Novel–The Great American Play–The Great American Poetry. I am not sure they aspired to the Great American *Painting*...how was the Great American *Thing* going to happen? So as I painted along on my *Cow's Skull on Blue* I thought to myself, 'I'll make it an *American* Painting...the red stripes down the sides–Red, White, and Blue!'" The clarity of O'Keeffe's vision and the quintessential American imagery of her paintings ensured her place in the pantheon of great American artists.

THE UNVANQUISHED PUEBLO

This 18th-century **BUFFALO WAR SHIELD** of the Pueblo people was carried on foot by one of their warriors as a defensive device, its effectiveness guaranteed by the supernatural protection afforded by the symbol of a horned apparition painted on it.

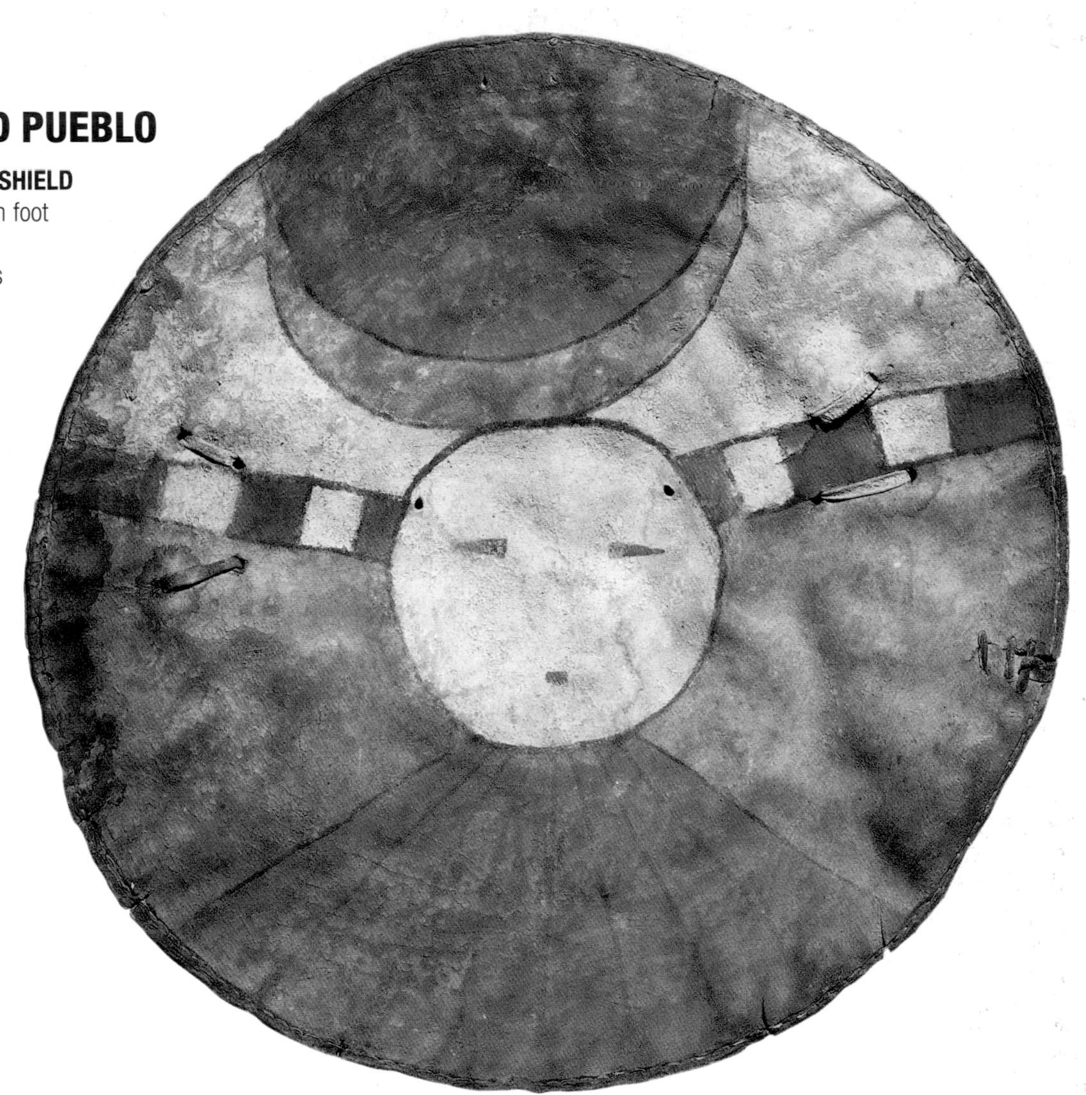

"THERE'S GOLD IN THEM THAR HILLS!"

It was short-lived, but the California Gold Rush was a grand, gaudy adventure for a generation of brash young men, most of them citizens of a brash young nation. They took their nicknames—**THE FORTY-NINERS**—from the year the rush began, 1849, swarming West by the thousands when they heard talk of gold nuggets lying loose on the ground. The lure of gold became the story of America, and the prospect of striking it rich became, and remains, the ultimate "rush" experience in American culture.

American kids made

THE HUNGRY PAC-MAN

the greatest arcade and video game of all time—even their parents ate it up.

THE MARTYRDOM OF MUHAMMAD ALI

In 1967, the world heavyweight champion refused induction into the U.S. Army. He had converted to Islam and had become a Black Muslim minister. When Ali refused military service as a conscientious objector because of his new religion, a federal jury sentenced him to five years in jail for draft evasion. Boxing commissions stripped him of his title and denied him the right to fight, in the prime of his fighting years. He was widely condemned as a draft dodger and even a traitor. When Cassius Clay became Muhammad Ali, he became a martyr. This 1968 *Esquire* cover conceived by George Lois became an iconic symbol of that period of nonviolent protest in those turbulent times, a metaphor for many Americans who took a principled stand against the Vietnam War and paid a heavy price for doing the right thing. Four years passed before the U.S. Supreme Court unanimously threw out Muhammad Ali's conviction. Allah be praised!

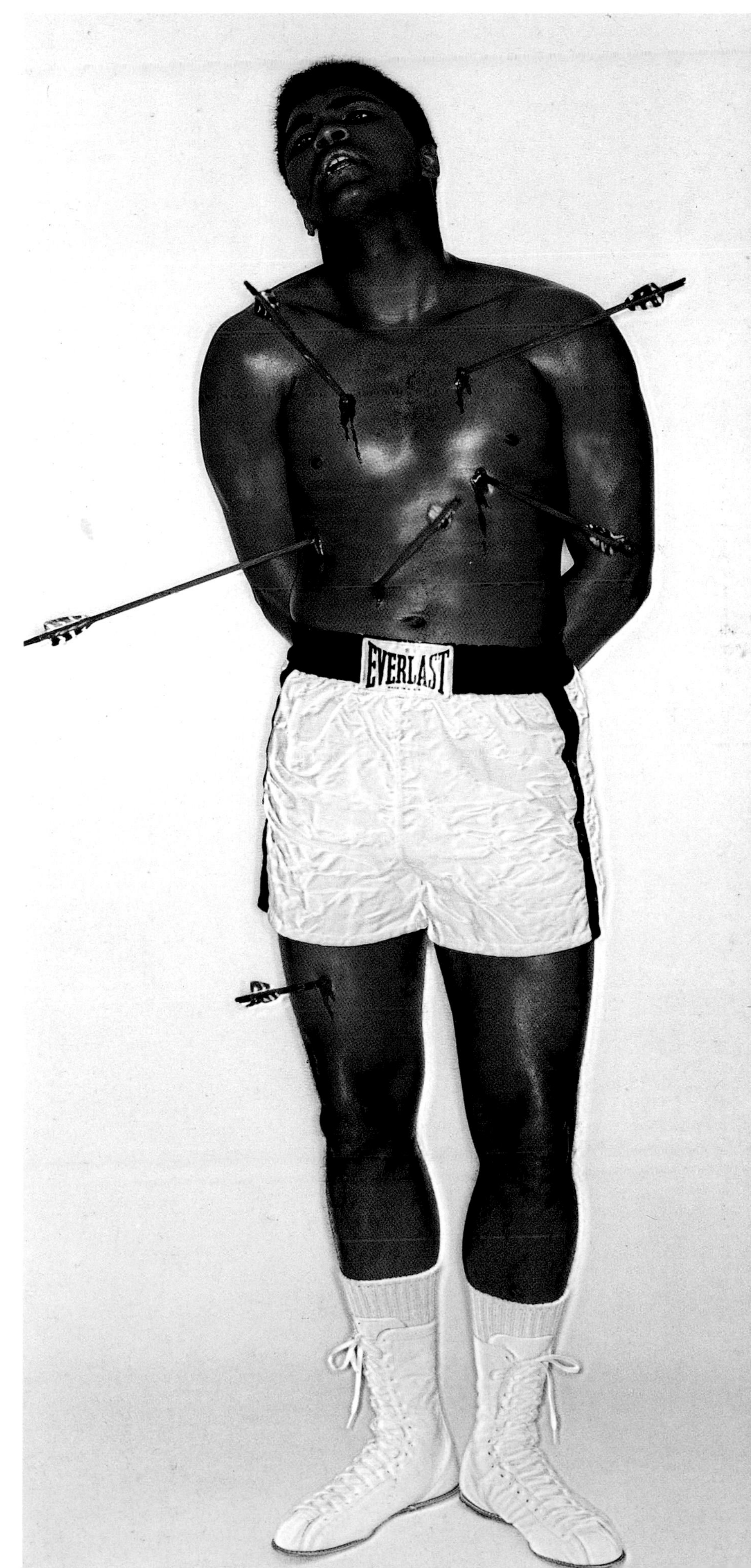

THE WORLD'S MOST COVETED FILM AWARD

THE OSCAR, the most famous and sought-after award in American popular culture, was designed in 1928 by the modern architect and set designer Cedric Gibbons: a gold-plated robot rising out of a film-reel can, a quintessential American Machine Age design. The statuette got its name from a librarian at the Academy of Motion Picture Arts and Sciences, who called it Oscar because it reminded her of her uncle Oscar. After a few years of staff members jokingly referring to the award as "Oscar," the name stuck, and was officially adopted by the Academy in 1939. As to the historical correctness of the awards, unbelievably, the superb actor Cary Grant never received one. (But the Academy made amends when it presented an Honorary Oscar to Grant in 1969.)

P.S. The only Oscar ever to win an Oscar was Oscar Hammerstein II.

LEFTOVERS, SEALED FOR FRESHNESS, STRETCH THE FAMILY BUDGET

TUPPERWARE plastic bowls and containers were developed in 1949 by Earl Tupper to store food and keep it airtight, with a "burping seal" that promised to maintain freshness. Millions of American women, meeting with their new, upwardly mobile postwar neighbors, congregated at Tupperware parties in one anothers' homes to purchase the durable containers (with the reward of free Tupperware for the host). To this day, Tupperware continues to keep America fresh.

THE MOST FRIGHTENING TWO NOTES IN FILM HISTORY

JAWS was a watershed film in motion-picture history, becoming the archetypal summer blockbuster. In 1975, after viewing the great white shark attacks on Amity Island, the fictitious summer resort town, ocean bathers looked far and wide before taking the plunge. Based on Peter Benchley's best-selling thriller and directed by the young Steven Spielberg, the film continues to scare the bejesus out of ocean bathers. The film's Academy Award-winning score, driven by an alternating pattern of two notes, F and F sharp, is a mnemonic soundbite that has become synonymous with approaching danger of any kind.

THE GREAT ALL-AMERICAN COOKOUT

In the backyard and stadium parking lots, Americans love to grill: hamburgers, hot dogs, steaks, ribs, chicken, corn on the cob, (and Heinz ketchup on the burgers).

THE GRAPES OF WRATH

CESAR CHAVEZ, an Arizona-born teenage Mexican-American farm worker, grew to be an iconic labor leader and civil-rights activist, leading the United Farm Workers Union (UFW) in fighting for the rights of migrant workers. From 1965 to 1970 Chavez led a legendary strike of California grape pickers and persuaded millions of Americans to boycott table grapes in an unprecedented show of support for the overworked, underpaid field workers. As the strike gained national attention, a Senate subcommittee stepped in and Senator Robert Kennedy became a champion for the cause of poor migrant workers against the giant farming industry. After five years of struggle, the gallant Chavez was successful in negotiating a new contract, winning the first major victory for U.S. farm workers in America. How sweet it is.

GOURMET AMERICAN FOOD– NO LONGER AN OXYMORON

The 6'4" culinary giant, **JAMES BEARD**, the American Dean of Cuisine, taught America, recipe by recipe, how to eat healthfully, and splendidly. Beard, along with **JULIA CHILD** and **CRAIG CLAIBORNE**, crusaded for great cuisine in America in the mid-20th century. Today they are considered monuments by the dozens of celebrity chefs who strut their stuff in great restaurants all over America.

THE $35 SWOOSH

The legendary Swoosh symbol of the **NIKE** (the brand named for the winged Greek goddess of victory, an appropriate symbol for athletic shoes) was chosen in a 1971 Portland State University contest. The winner, a female student, was awarded 35 big ones (bucks, that is). The "swoosh" is now so recognizable there is no need for the name Nike to appear on the company's products. Nike later made amends by awarding the young lady company stock and a snazzy "swoosh" ring.

BEWARE THE DENIAL OF CHRIST!

The rooster was the earliest **WEATHER VANE** design in America, a biblical reference to Peter's denial of Christ (and served as a warning to the congregation of the town not to do likewise).

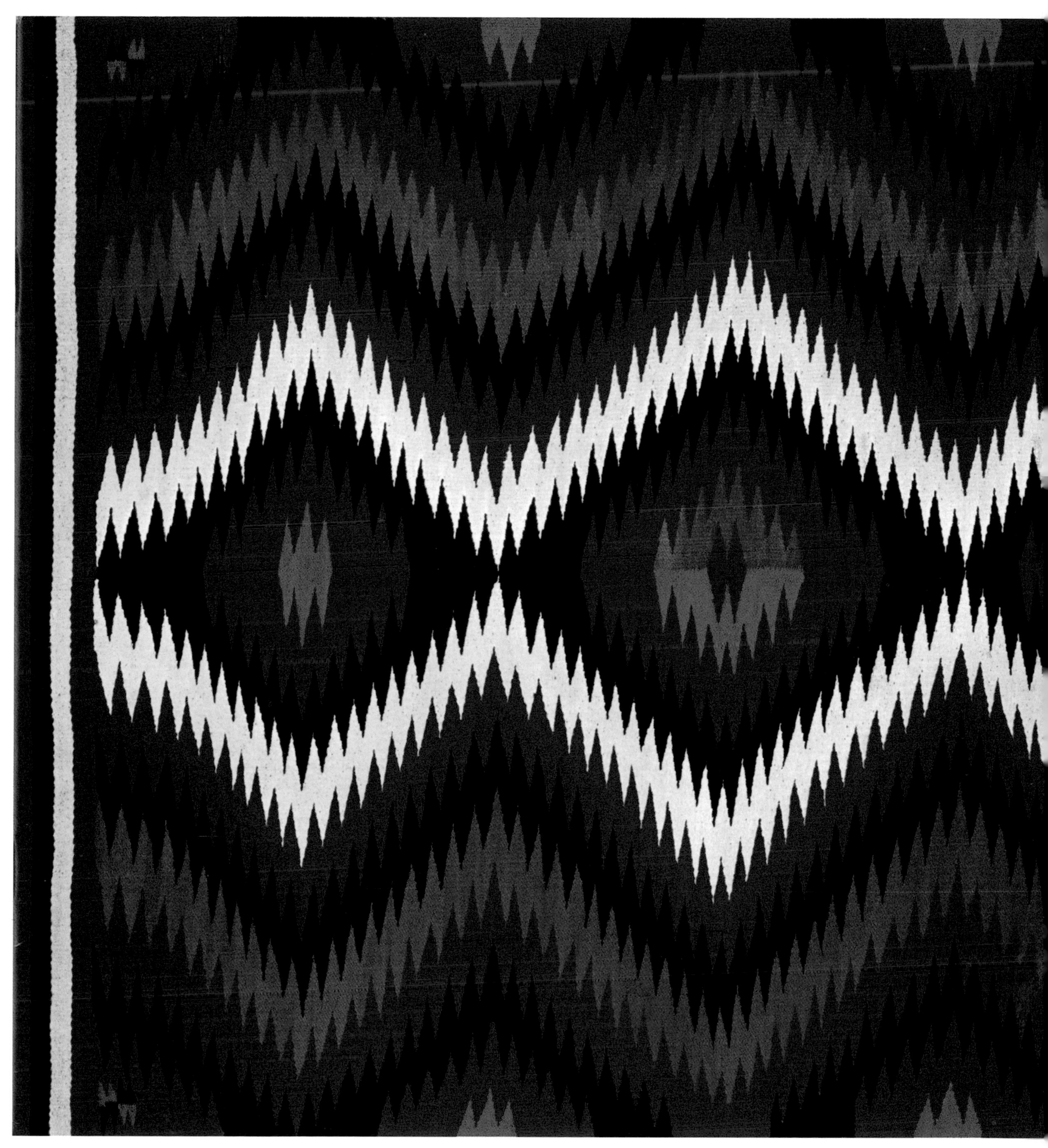

EYEDAZZLER!

The eye-popping art of the **THE NAVAJO BLANKET**, which by tradition is woven only by women, is an abstract art of breathtaking geometric pattern and color. The "Eyedazzler" motif, dating from the late 19th century, anticipates many of the visual ideas we have learned to think of as the special province of so-called "Modern art."

FOREVER 20/20

In 1508 Leonardo da Vinci, while exploring the mechanics of the eye for his *Codex of the Eye*, made discoveries that led to the eye-opening concept of correcting vision with artificial lenses. Glass contact lenses that covered the entire surface of the eye were actually in use in the late 19th century, but they could be tolerated for only an hour of wear. In 1948, American optometrists introduced plastic **CONTACT LENSES**, and in the 1970s a soft contact lens was developed. Even disposable bifocal lenses became available. For the millions who feel that wearing glasses is a stigma, contact lenses are seen not only as a great convenience, but as keeping them forever young.

BRINGING BEAUTY TO THE GARISH LIGHT OF THE ELECTRIC LIGHT BULB

The great American contribution to the lush Art Nouveau style were the stained-glass lamp shades of **LOUIS COMFORT TIFFANY**, who was intent on bringing beauty into the American home.

HE DID IT HIS WAY

In a sycophantic pop culture, **FRANK SINATRA** was the Chairman of the Board. But his unequaled popularity and power in the pop-music world, Hollywood, Las Vegas, and Washington (he was a pal of President John F. Kennedy) were the result of his great style, talent, charisma, acting prowess, and most important, the fact that Ol' Blue Eyes was the greatest crooner in history.

M-I-C-K-E-Y-M-O-U-S-E, MICKEY MOUSE!

Brought to life by Walt Disney, the American entertainment genius, Mickey Mouse is the most beloved cartoon character of all time.
Mickey Mouse is genuine, cheerful, enthusiastic, humble, confident, versatile, adventurous, clever, charismatic, and warm—a glowing symbol of America.

SOREL

AMERICA'S FAVORITE PARADE

Since 1924, rain or shine,
America wakes up every Thanksgiving to the
MACY'S THANKSGIVING DAY PARADE.
From its inception, broadcast on radio, it has
attracted and charmed
millions of kids. Today, 60 million viewers are at
their TV sets every year, along
with more than a million lining the parade route,
to view helium-filled
balloons of Charlie Brown, Bullwinkle, and Kermit the Frog
and the gang float their way
to Macy's flagship store on 34th Street,
getting there just in time for
Americans to prepare to dig into their
Thanksgiving dinners.

AMERICA'S FIRST ENVIRONMENTALIST

No other artist was so sensitively and intimately concerned with the natural wonders of the American scene as **JOHN JAMES AUDUBON**. And certainly he was the greatest painter of birds in the history of the Western world. The Audubon name has become a household word and a rallying cry for wildlife conservation. This magnificent watercolor (1829) shows an osprey carrying its catch of a 5-pound weakfish at Great Egg Harbor, New Jersey.

"HAPPY BIRTH-DAY... MR. PRES-I-DENT..."

There have been hundreds of heart-pounding nights at Madison Square Garden—but May 19, 1962, the night **MARILYN MONROE** sang *Happy Birthday* to President John F. Kennedy, takes the cake. The 15,000 people at Kennedy's 45th birthday tribute were on tenterhooks waiting for the habitually late superstar. There had been persistent rumors that Kennedy and Monroe were having an affair, and when Marilyn finally showed she was emanating sex and wearing a flesh-colored dress with 2,500 rhinestones sewn into it (so perfectly fitting it had to be sewn onto her). The sensuous Monroe breathily began to sing... and the Garden crowd went wild. Her public display of her desire for Kennedy in front of the world (and the First Lady) was a shocker. The President, following a tough act, stepped up to the podium and said, "I can now retire from politics after having had *Happy Birthday* sung to me in such a sweet, wholesome way." (Peter Lawford, Kennedy's brother-in-law, had jokingly introduced Monroe as "the late Marilyn Monroe," to the delight of the audience. Three and a half months later, she was dead.)

"I'VE LOOKED ON MANY WOMEN WITH LUST..."

The first issue of **PLAYBOY**, published in December 1953, did not carry a date because Hugh Hefner wasn't sure there would be a second issue! The rebellious magazine was an immediate sensation and went on to become a worldwide publishing phenomenon (the best-selling issue sold more than seven million copies). The combination of a horny rabbit logo wearing a tuxedo, naked women, and good writing have kept the magazine and brand name relevant for over half a century. The 1976 *Playboy* interview of Jimmy Carter confessing that "I've looked on many women with lust—I've committed adultery in my heart many times," is a legendary example of the *Playboy* interview.

THE REVOLUTIONARY CROWN CAP...

In 1891, William Painter exploded the carbonated beverage business when he invented his ingeniously simple crown cap, a disk of metal with a corrugated flange, and a thin cork lining, economical to produce and absolutely leakproof!

...RESTS ON THE KING OF BEERS!

Since introducing America's first national beer brand in 1867, Anheuser-Busch has formulated the two best-selling beers in the world, **BUDWEISER** and **BUD LIGHT**, with an effervescent 50 percent market share in the U.S. (A generic cap named "Crown," sitting on Budweiser, the "King of Beers," seems to have been ordained in Hops Heaven.)

LOOK–IT'S MOVING! IT'S ALIVE! IT'S ALIVE! IT'S ALIVE!

Directed in 1931 by James Whale, **FRANKENSTEIN** is the most strikingly terrifying movie of all time and one of the greatest of any genre. Based on the Gothic novel written by Mary Shelley (the wife of the great poet Percy Bysshe Shelley), it was a warning against the overreaching of modern man in the Industrial Revolution. The success of the film's moralizing theme and tone was dependent on the brilliant depiction of the man-made creature by the great actor Boris Karloff.

THE WORLDWIDE SYMBOL OF MERCY

Established in 1881 by the legendary Clara Barton, **THE AMERICAN RED CROSS** is a humanitarian organization that provides emergency assistance, disaster relief, services that help the needy, support for military members and their families, blood collection and distribution, first-aid and lifeguard training, and international relief services. But what millions of war-weary veterans remember most about the good work of the Red Cross is that hot cup of coffee and doughnut a good Samaritan dished out to them when they were down and out and homesick.

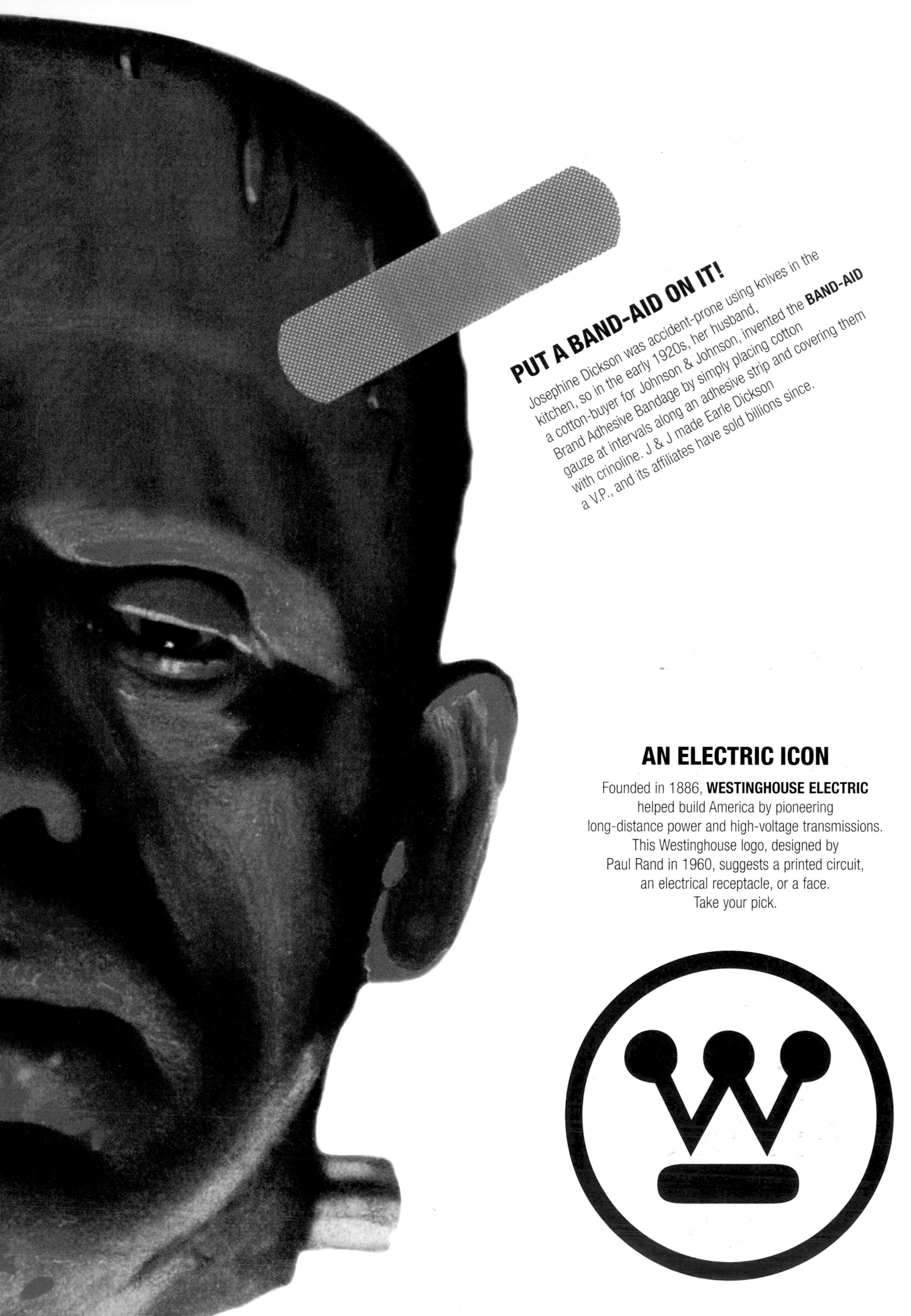

PUT A BAND-AID ON IT!

Josephine Dickson was accident-prone using knives in the kitchen, so in the early 1920s, her husband, a cotton-buyer for Johnson & Johnson, invented the **BAND-AID** Brand Adhesive Bandage by simply placing cotton gauze at intervals along an adhesive strip and covering them with crinoline. J & J made Earle Dickson a V.P., and its affiliates have sold billions since.

AN ELECTRIC ICON

Founded in 1886, **WESTINGHOUSE ELECTRIC** helped build America by pioneering long-distance power and high-voltage transmissions. This Westinghouse logo, designed by Paul Rand in 1960, suggests a printed circuit, an electrical receptacle, or a face. Take your pick.

ONE OF OUR MOST BELOVED AND PERSECUTED HEROES

A giant among men was **PAUL ROBESON**, born to a sixteen-year-old escaped slave who fought for his freedom in the Union Army. Robeson's greatness began with his stardom as a pioneering black athlete and a Phi Beta Kappa at Rutgers University. His reputation grew when he became an interpretive artist in theater, concert stage, and in film (he is shown here as the Emperor Jones, photographed by Edward Steichen in 1933). But his importance expanded in the 1950s with his courageous stand against the evil forces of racism and fascism in America during the McCarthy era. Robeson was regarded as a traitor because of his friendship with the Soviet Union at a time when dissent was not tolerated, but today his name is legendary and the black community, which had regarded him as a pariah in those dark days in America, now reveres him.

THE $20 MASTERPIECE

THE DOUBLE EAGLE, commissioned by President Teddy Roosevelt and designed by Augustus Saint-Gaudens, was an American coin whose artistry rivaled the beauty of the coinage of ancient Greece.

THE 5¢ MASTERPIECE

When it was in circulation, Americans carried a great work of art in their pockets: **THE INDIAN HEAD NICKEL**, designed by James Earle Fraser and posed for by an Onondaga chief in 1913.

SHE PROVED SHE COULD "PLAY LIKE A MAN"

But she accomplished far more than that– when **BILLIE JEAN KING** defeated the arrogant Bobby Riggs in 1973, she single-handedly showed the world that women's tennis was a great spectator sport. Game, Set, and Match!

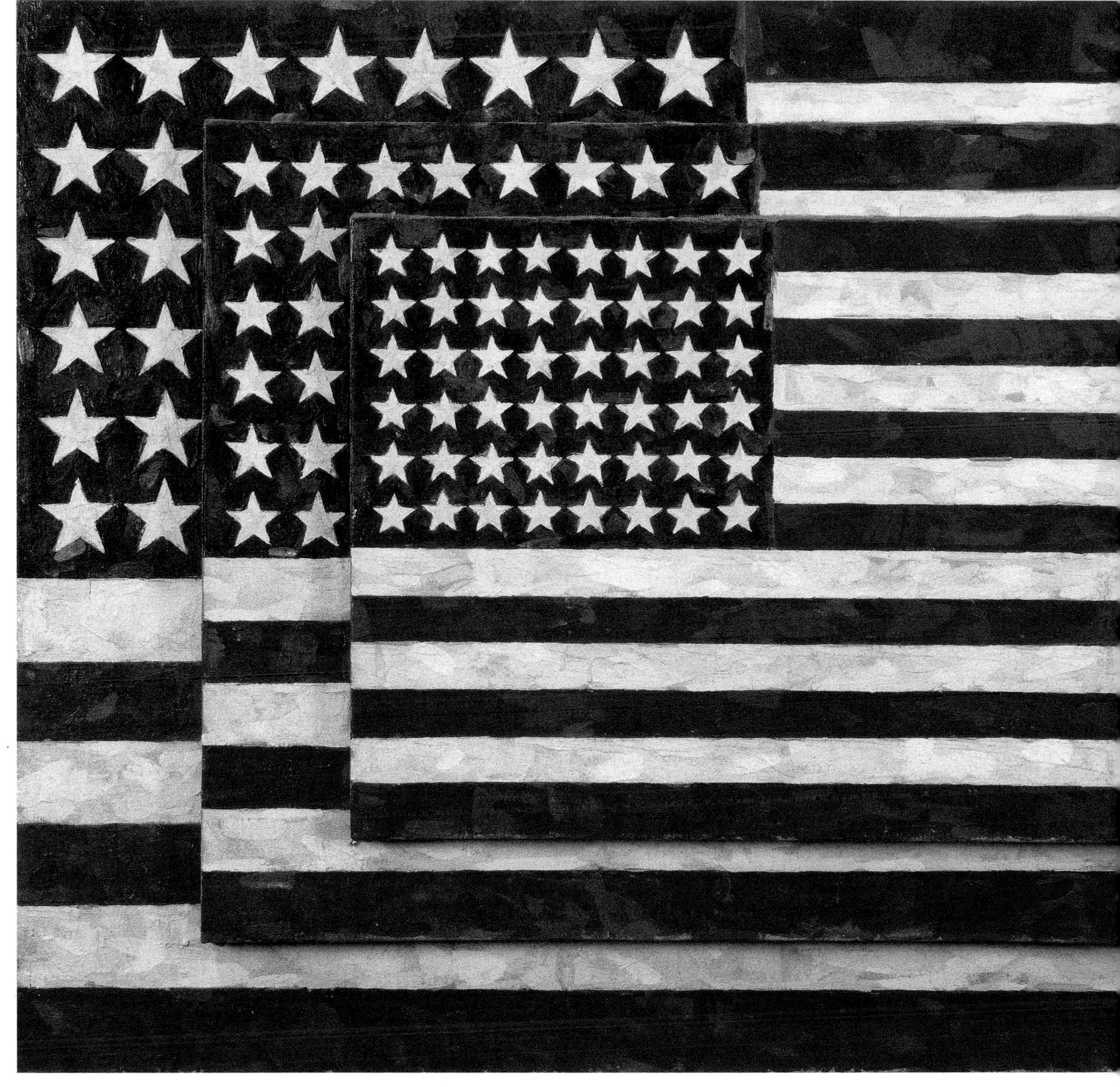

THE GROWING IMAGE OF AMERICA

This conceptual image of **THREE FLAGS**, created by the Pop artist Jasper Johns (before the grand addition of Alaska and Hawaii, our 49th and 50th states) commands a powerful sense of meaning and purpose. Upon first viewing in 1958, most Americans thought, "So what," but through the years a growing love for the painting has made it an iconic work of art.

BEWARE THE LAWMAN IN TOWN

WILD BILL HICKOK was a prototype for the Western lawman, a town constable before he was twenty-one, the most flamboyant and feared of all gunmen, a legend in his own time, earning a reputation as a man it was best not to cross. But Wild Bill didn't stay at it—or any job—for long. As a sheriff, a Union scout, or a professional gambler, he killed for motives that did not always bear close scrutiny.

THE LUCKIEST MAN ON THE FACE OF THE EARTH

The life of **LOU GEHRIG**, The Iron Horse, one of the greatest players in the history of baseball, was tragically cut short by the fatal ALS disease, now known as Lou Gehrig's Disease. On July 4, 1939, New York celebrated "Lou Gehrig Day." After retiring his number 4, and after emotional tributes from VIPs and celebrities (including the retired Babe Ruth) the pride of the Yankees stepped to the microphone and spoke these opening words to his chanting fans, and to all of America: "Fans, for the past two weeks you have been reading about a bad break I got. Yet today, I consider myself the luckiest man on the face of the earth." After a short expression of thank-you's, the dying man concluded with, "So I close by saying that I might have been given a bad break, but I got an awful lot to live for. Thank you." No, thank *you*, Larrupin Lou.

AMERICAN THEATRICAL POSTERS

PAUL DAVIS posters keep alive the spirit of productions long after the run of the show—they themselves are theater! The image on this 1976 *Streamers* poster was a metaphor for the David Rabe play, which dealt with the dehumanizing impact of the Vietnam War on a group of young GI's.

THE NEVERENDING MERRY-GO-ROUND

The concept of the carousel reached its greatest popularity and success through the talent and creativity of American craftsmen during the 19th century. In an energetic period of self-discovery, as the sculptors sought their own direction and freedom of expression, **THE AMERICAN CAROUSEL** became a menagerie of roaring lions, menacing sea serpents, magnificent steeds, treacherous tigers, gangling giraffes, ponderous bison, frogs dressed in pants and bow ties, and decorations galore. To take a whirl on these wondrous rides was the ultimate American entertainment experience, a neverending merry-go-round. The beauty and nostalgia of the carousel are reborn in American hearts as individual figures and whole carousels are lovingly restored and admired. Climb aboard.

SKIING GONE WILD!

Americans have always figured out wacky ways to slide down a hill of snow. They've used sleds, cafeteria trays, skiis tied together—and in 1969, someone figured out that a board based on a surfboard combined its look with the function of skis. Officially, the first **SNOWBOARDING** technology was invented by Jake Burton in 1980, based on evolving designs from the early 1970s. Snowboarding became a worldwide phenomenon, attracting young blood to the slopes—and became a Winter Olympic Sport in 1998. Fundamental freestyle maneuvers include an ollie, a switch, a fakie, a grab, a rotation, a press, suicide runs, and icy kamikaze downhill races. During the early years of the sport, snowboarders were not respected by the ski culture (some still banning the wild ones from their haughty slopes), but today snowboarding has become the elite American-invented acrobatic snow sport. Shown is Ross Powers, an Olympic gold medalist.

A SYMBOL OF A GROWING, HUNGRY NATION

SHOREBIRD DECOYS are a folk art that is singularly American, born out of the unique natural abundance of the North American continent: Every spring and fall there once flew the largest migrations of wildfowl the world has ever known. A flight of geese or ducks could take all day to pass, and darken the moon at night. American Indians were the first to develop decoys to entice succulent, high-flying birds within range of the bow and arrow and into the cooking pot. Newcomers from the old world quickly adapted the Indian ways, carving and hunting with decoys of their own design. (In Europe, game was scarce and hunting restricted to the nobility.) With the advent of the market for commercial food products after the Civil War, decoy making became a test of artistry. We now recognize those decoys as the beginning of a great American art form.

0725
16 29

THE TOMMY GUN AND THE ST. VALENTINE'S DAY MASSACRE

Organized crime loved the Thompson Submachine Gun, and affectionately called it the tommy gun. In 1929 Al Capone's hitmen, wearing cop uniforms, ambushed and cold-bloodedly tommy-gunned to death six hoods in the Bugs Moran gang (and a hapless gofer) in a Chicago garage in 60 seconds flat. No respectable Hollywood gangster film has ever been complete without the blazing rat-a-tat-tat of the tommy gun!

SERPICO, MICHAEL CORLEONE, RICHARD III, TONY MONTANA...

Al Pacino's sunken, coal-black eyes glistening with power and malicious intent, glare at us in theaters and movie houses, giving us the shivers. Growing up in the streets of East Harlem and raised by his Sicilian grandparents, Pacino became the most exciting actor of his generation. His blind, staring eyes in *Scent of a Woman*, his demand for his pound of flesh as Shylock in *The Merchant of Venice*, and his slimy portrayal of the patriotic hypocrisy of Roy Cohn in the TV miniseries *Angels in America*, continue to thrill and chill.

GANGSTA RAP

An icon of the Underworld, the Chicago mobster **AL SCARFACE CAPONE** was notoriously touchy about a broad gash across his left cheek, claiming it was an old World War I wound. (The actual culprit was Frank "Galooch" Galluccio, in retribution for Capone's hitting on his sister.) The megalomaniac mad-dog crime head controlled a 1,000-thug gang with an iron fist. Though safe in Chicago, whose officials he had in his pocket, he was hounded by the Feds in the person of T-man Eliot Ness. What brought him down were bean counters–Capone never paid taxes on his swag, estimated at $20 million a year, and he was nailed for tax evasion in 1931, spending over seven years in the can–four of them in Alcatraz. He died of syphilitic dementia in his Miami mansion.

THE SPLIT PERSONALITY OF DEAN MARTIN & JERRY LEWIS

In the grand American tradition of comedy duos (a straight man and his stooge), Dean Martin, a singer with a ubiquitous glass of booze in his hand, schmoozed with the whacked-out comedian Jerry Lewis, taking the nation by storm. Starting in 1946 they worked in nightclubs, and on radio, television, and film for one hilarious decade, until their personal and professional relationship was acrimoniously severed, and apart from a surprise appearance on one of Jerry's annual telethons for The Muscular Dystrophy Association (orchestrated by mutual pal Frank Sinatra) they never performed together again. What a shame. They were very good separately—but like Laurel & Hardy, Abbott & Costello and Burns & Allen—they were legendary *together*.

THE HUMONGOUS DAGWOOD SANDWICH

The comic strip character Dagwood Bumstead was created in the midst of The Great Depression in 1930. His wealthy family disowned him for insisting on marrying Blondie, a woman "beneath his class." But Blondie and Dagwood were in love and America loved *them*—as she became the most famous homemaker in the world of comics. Dagwood hated door-to-door salesmen and rude salespeople, crashed each morning into the mailman, and got into hot water daily with his boss, Julius C. Dithers. But Dagwood loved Blondie, his kids, and naps on the sofa—and his obsession was making his famous, overabundant Dagwood Sandwich, which grew and grew into the iconic American sandwich.

HIS AIRNESS

The greatest player in the history of basketball (at both ends of the floor), **MICHAEL JORDAN** was the force behind six Chicago Bulls NBA championships. Millions of kids throughout the world aspire to be like Mike, on and off the court. As the most marketed sports figure in history, His Airness continues to make the big bucks with Nike's hugely popular Air Jordan brand, a chain of Michael Jordan Steakhouses, the partial ownership of an NBA team, and as an iconic spokesman for many of the most iconic brands in America.

THE ALL-SEEING EYE

One of the most memorable symbols ever conjured by man is probably in your pocket as you're reading this. On the back of our one-dollar bill are two circular symbols that comprise the Great Seal of the United States. The left-hand symbol incorporates an eye surrounded by a golden aura, at the zenith of an unfinished pyramid. Over the eye are the words *Annuit Coeptis*, meaning, "He has favored our undertakings." On the base of the pyramid are the Roman numerals *MDCCLXXVI* (the date of the Declaration of Independence, 1776), and the Latin phrase *Novus Ordo Seclorum*, "A new order of ages is born," signifies the beginning of the new American Era. The George Washington dollar bill is rife with symbolism reflecting the hubris of a growing nation that believed that God was on its side.

THE COWBOY IN THE OVAL OFFICE

FREDERIC REMINGTON, a painter of the American West, decided to try his hand at sculpture. So in 1895 he conceived and executed a majestic image of a cowboy on a bucking horse. **THE BRONCO BUSTER** was an immediate sensation, winning the hearts of the American people. A bronze cast of the dynamic composition kicks up dust in the Oval Office, usually a must-show when film directors depict the office of the president. The powerful image remains a symbol of the taming of the American West.

THE DUPING OF AMERICA AND THE FALL OF AN ICON
ENRON CORPORATION was an American energy company based in Houston, Texas, employing 21,000 enthusiastic workers and claiming earnings of $111 million in 2000. Fortune magazine named Enron "America's Most Innovative Company" for six straight years. Then the shit hit the (electric) fan—when America found out that the company's superb financial condition was an accounting fraud! Enron went bankrupt, investors rioted, and executives went to jail. The name Enron has become a disgraceful popular symbol of willful corporate greed, fraud, and corruption. The Enron chairman and CEO, Kenneth Lay, who died before he was sentenced, not only screwed investors but 21,000 loyal profit-sharing employees.
ENRON
EEEK–A MOUSE!
In 1963 Douglas Engelbart and a Stanford Research Institute team invented an easy-to-use position indicator for a display system—and called it a "bug." It was soon re-nicknamed a "mouse."

STAGE FLIGHT
THE ALVIN AILEY AMERICAN DANCE THEATER, founded by the legendary Alvin Ailey
and now led by its fearless artistic director, Judith Jamison, continues
to inspire and astound. Cherished as a cultural ambassador to the world, Ailey's choreographic
treasures celebrate the beauty and humanity of African-American
heritage and other cultures with brilliant contributions from a variety of choreographers
and dozens of dancers who shatter the limits of physicality.

"LIKE A BIRD"

The last decades of the 19th century in the United States had been a period of revolutionary progress: The railway, the telegraph, the electric light, the telephone, the bicycle, the electric trolley, the automobile, the radio, photography, and the cinema were transforming the way people lived and the way they perceived the world. Then, on December 17, 1903, came the most extraordinary invention of all, a vehicle that would allow people to fly through the air like birds. In one twelve-second, 120-foot flight at Kitty Hawk, North Carolina, **WILBUR AND ORVILLE WRIGHT** accomplished the impossible: the first flight (piloted by Orville) in a machine that moved through the air under its own power!

THE WICKED WITCH IS DEAD!

The eventual iconic status of **THE WIZARD OF OZ** was only achieved after decades of television airing, beginning in 1956, almost 20 years after its moderate success when it opened in 1939.
Year after year, it has become the most beloved film ever made. A resourceful young American girl (played by the precociously talented Judy Garland) and her dog, Toto, are snatched up by a Kansas tornado and deposited in a fantastic land with a talking Scarecrow, a Tin Man, a Cowardly Lion, a Good Witch, a Bad Witch, and a gaggle of Munchkins. The film's bookend sequences in sepia-toned black and white, with the Land of Oz scenes in full-color, surprise with each viewing.
The movie will delight and inspire young children forever.
Hail to Dorothy! The Wicked Witch is dead!

THE DEVIL'S ROPE

The American invention of **BARBED WIRE** in the 1860s led to the end of the open-range era, making a monumental change in the culture of the Western prairies. When livestock first ran into barbed wire, they were ripped to pieces. Cowboys derisively called it "The Devil's Rope"–but it proved to be a godsend by dramatically ending free-range grazing, so each ranch could control its livestock. In those days, when trail drivers were blocked from access to the Kansas markets by the restricting fences, that meant war–a violent Fence-Cutters War, ended only by laws against wire cutting. Today, "bobwire" is an iconic symbol of the West, but it's a nasty item not easy to love. Remember what it did to your favorite pair of Tommy Jeans?!

"MY NAME IS JOHN L. SULLIVAN, AND I CAN LICK ANY SON-OF-A-BITCH IN THE WORLD."

In the 1880s, a new heavyweight champion toured the country fighting almost every night and offering $50 to anyone who could stay four rounds. No one could. The offer was finally raised to $1,000 by The Great John L., who, when drunk or sober, invariably hammered his man to the floor. He knocked out 59 professionals in a row, most of them in the first round. The public went wild over him. Crowds followed him in the streets. When he wasn't in the ring, he could always be found in the nearest saloon buying drinks for the house. "My name is John L. Sullivan," he'd roar, "And I can lick any son-of-a-bitch in the world."

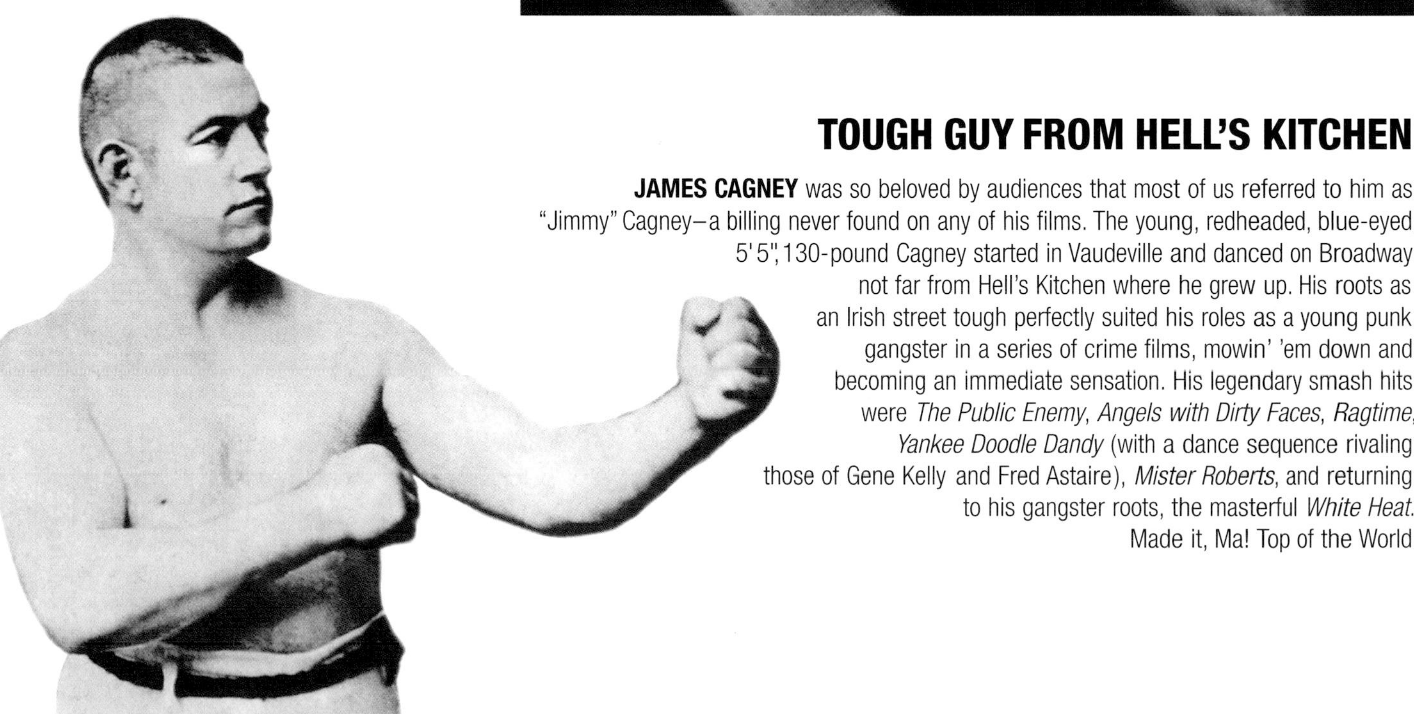

TOUGH GUY FROM HELL'S KITCHEN

JAMES CAGNEY was so beloved by audiences that most of us referred to him as "Jimmy" Cagney—a billing never found on any of his films. The young, redheaded, blue-eyed, 5'5", 130-pound Cagney started in Vaudeville and danced on Broadway not far from Hell's Kitchen where he grew up. His roots as an Irish street tough perfectly suited his roles as a young punk gangster in a series of crime films, mowin' 'em down and becoming an immediate sensation. His legendary smash hits were *The Public Enemy*, *Angels with Dirty Faces*, *Ragtime*, *Yankee Doodle Dandy* (with a dance sequence rivaling those of Gene Kelly and Fred Astaire), *Mister Roberts*, and returning to his gangster roots, the masterful *White Heat*. Made it, Ma! Top of the World.

TOUGH GUY FROM THE POSH UPPER WEST SIDE

Another young actor from New York (but from a privileged background), **HUMPHREY BOGART** began his film career by going to the electric chair 12 times and being sentenced to 800 years of hard labor in a slew of B-movie gangster films. Then came the masterpieces; *The Maltese Falcon*, *Casablanca*, *To Have and Have Not*, *The Big Sleep*, *Dark Passage*, *The Treasure of the Sierra Madre*, *Key Largo*, *Knock on Any Door*, *The African Queen*, *Beat the Devil*, and *The Caine Mutiny*, gaining fame as the greatest male movie star of all time.
Off the set, Bogart was a regular at the Hollywood nightclubs.
The proprietor of Chasen's once said:
"Bogey's a hell of a nice guy until 11:30 p.m.
After that he thinks he's Bogart."

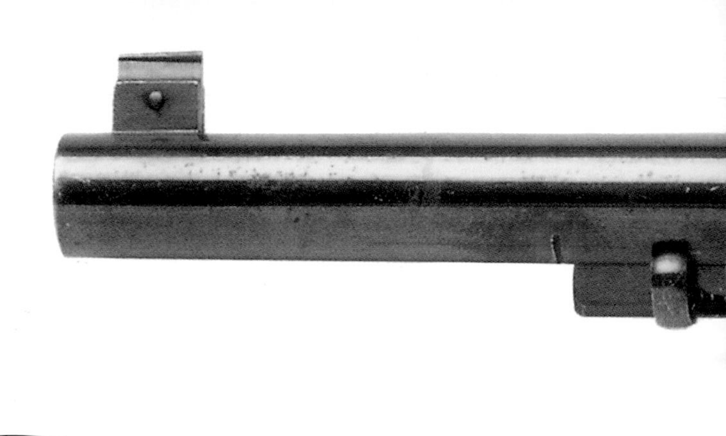

A SHELL OF A LOGO

In 1833, a young man named Marcus Samuel had an import business selling seashells to London collectors. When collecting in the Caspian Sea area in 1892, his son Marcus (Jr.) realized the potential of extracting oil from the region and commissioned the world's first oil tanker—the beginnning of the big idea that became **THE SHELL OIL COMPANY**. The familiar scallop shell logo was first used in 1904, and the famed industrial designer Raymond Loewy spruced it up in 1971.

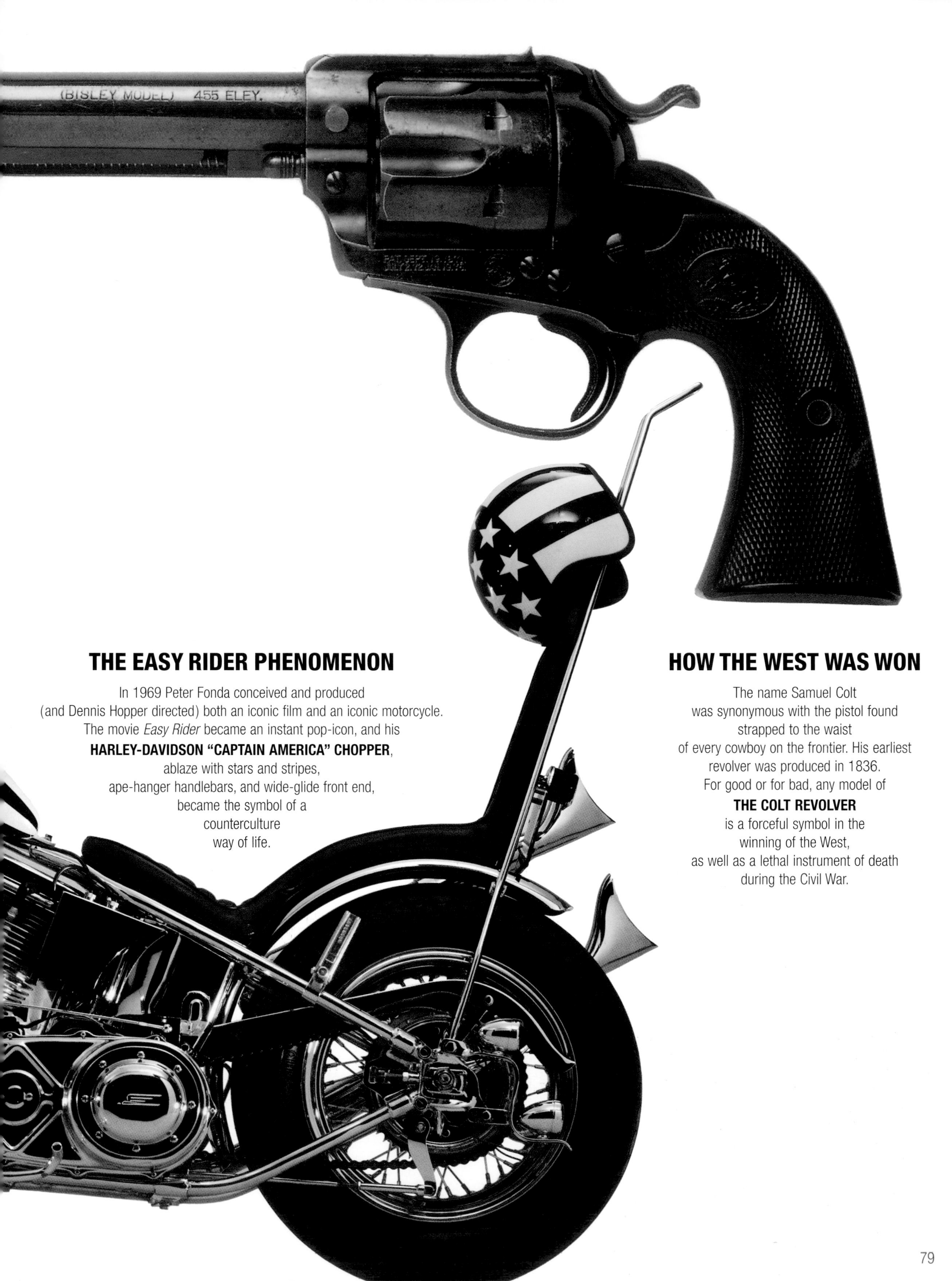

THE EASY RIDER PHENOMENON

In 1969 Peter Fonda conceived and produced (and Dennis Hopper directed) both an iconic film and an iconic motorcycle. The movie *Easy Rider* became an instant pop-icon, and his **HARLEY-DAVIDSON "CAPTAIN AMERICA" CHOPPER**, ablaze with stars and stripes, ape-hanger handlebars, and wide-glide front end, became the symbol of a counterculture way of life.

HOW THE WEST WAS WON

The name Samuel Colt was synonymous with the pistol found strapped to the waist of every cowboy on the frontier. His earliest revolver was produced in 1836. For good or for bad, any model of **THE COLT REVOLVER** is a forceful symbol in the winning of the West, as well as a lethal instrument of death during the Civil War.

THE BITING SATIRE OF *MAD*

In 1952 *Mad*, the madcap magazine with a rollicking, sinister edge to its biting satire, took America by surprise. During the period of Cold War paranoia in a puritan culture of censorship that prevailed in the U.S., Harvey Kurtzman's mad refusal to run advertising enabled his writers and editors to spoof a materialistic culture without fear of reprisal from advertisers. *Mad* spared no one, skewering ongoing ad campaigns, mainstream drugs like tobacco and alcohol, the media, big business, the sexual revolution, hippies, psychoanalysis, the gun lobby, and the Vietnam War. These days, no celebrity on a magazine cover, including Tom Cruise, Julia Roberts or Leonardo DiCaprio, could possibly match the visual punch of **ALFRED E. NEUMAN**, the gap-toothed grinning boy, goofily peeking out at us on the newsstand.

BELA LUGOSI SINKS HIS TEETH INTO HIS ROLE AS DRACULA

Based on an 1897 novel by Irish author Bram Stoker, the 1931 American film version of **DRACULA** starred Bela Lugosi as the legendary vampire Count Dracula, and is considered one of the horror classics of all time. Dozens of other actors sank their teeth into the role (Max Schreck, Christopher Lee, Jack Palance, Frank Langella, Willem Defoe, Gary Oldman, and many more), but Lugosi, a Hungarian immigrant to Hollywood, was the genre-defining Dracula of all time.

THE COURAGEOUS SIGN OF BLACK POWER

Heads down as if in silent prayer.
Arms extended with gloved fists to represent Black Power.
American track and field medal winners
TOMMIE SMITH and **JOHN CARLOS** protested racial inequality
in the U.S. as the National Anthem was played
during the award ceremonies for the 200-meter run
at the Mexico City Olympic Games in 1968.
Smith and Carlos were suspended and disgraced by their
demonstration, but today it is considered an
inspiring historical image for change in the fight for
racial justice in America.

FREE AT LAST! FREE AT LAST!
THANK GOD ALMIGHTY, WE ARE FREE AT LAST!

In the pantheon of heroic Americans, one man stands above all with his inspiring leadership of a mass, non-violent struggle for racial equality, fulfilling, finally, the declaration that we were the land of the free and the home of the brave. **MARTIN LUTHER KING, JR.** energized the nation with his "I Have a Dream" speech on August 28, 1963, motivating his fellow Americans, both black *and* white, to take a public stand for freedom. His iconic speech is now part of the national narrative about the meaning of American democracy. Let us recall the most challenging element of the great leader's thesis:

"I say to you today my friends, so even though we face the difficulties of today and tomorrow, I still have a dream.
It is a dream deeply rooted in the American dream.
I have a dream that one day this nation will rise up and live out the true meaning of its creed:
'We hold these truths to be self-evident; that all men are created equal.'
I have a dream that one day on the red hills of Georgia the sons of former slaves and the sons of former slave owners will be able to sit down together at the table of brotherhood...
I have a dream that my four little children will one day live in a nation where they will not be judged by the color of their skin but by the content of their character...
And when this happens, and when we allow freedom to ring, when we let it ring from every village and every hamlet, from every state and every city, we will be able to speed up that day when all of God's children, black men and white men, Jews and Gentiles, Protestants and Catholics, will be able to join hands and sing in the words of the old Negro spiritual:
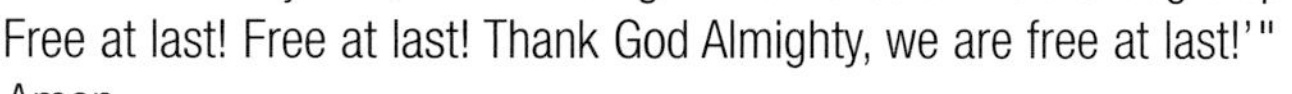
'Free at last! Free at last! Thank God Almighty, we are free at last!'"
Amen.

USA
USA
9
2

"AS AMERICAN AS APPLE PIE"
APPLE CHANGES
THE AMERICAN LIFESTYLE
In 1984 Steve Jobs marketed the
APPLE MACINTOSH HOME COMPUTER,
superb in design as well as revolutionary
in ease of use. There's no place like home.
®

Americans may love their apple pie, but pies are not an American creation.

The ancient Greeks, the Romans, and the English were all pie eaters, but America's Pennsylvania Dutch certainly perfected the apple pie in the 19th century. So where did the famous line "as American as apple pie" come from?

Somehow, through the 19th and early 20th centuries, apple pie became the symbol of an American family's prosperity, especially if the pie was baked with a crust on top. (In poorer homes, to save on lard and flour, only a bottom crust was made—fancy-schmancy households could afford a lower *and* an upper crust, so they became known as "upper crust.")

The actual expression that became famous was "as American as motherhood and apple pie..." during World War II, American GI's asked by journalists what they were fighting for would answer "for mom and apple pie."

Today, moms are left out of the saying, but "as American as apple pie" ain't half bad.

(Shown is a sensational apple pie baked by Rosemary Lois that will now live in posterity in the pages of this book.)

"LUKE, I AM YOUR FATHER"

The fantasy world of the **STAR WARS** saga is a myth of the future dealing with good and evil. The characters, creatures, and droids created by Producer/Director/Writer George Lucas during the 1970s wrought a universe so detailed that it has seemingly become real. The saga began with the film *Star Wars*, which instantly became a worldwide pop-culture phenomenon—spawning five additional films, as well as comics, video games, and tie-ins impossible to count. Luke Skywalker, Princess Leia, Han Solo, Darth Vader, C-3PO, and R2-D2 live in our minds...in a galaxy far, far away. Nothing that exists in the entertainment world has ever approached *Star Wars* as a powerful, metaphorical American phenomenon, and the largest money machine Hollywood has ever generated. *May the Force be with you.*

THE SHADOW KNOWS!

Even after decades, this unmistakable introduction still has a place in the American lexicon: "Who knows what evil lurks in the hearts of men? The Shadow knows!" In the 1930s and '40s radio was king, and the King of Crime on radio was **THE SHADOW**, who supposedly learned "while traveling in the Orient... the mysterious power to cloud men's minds, so they could not see him." Drawn from the pulp magazine of the same name, Lamont Cranston (alias *The Shadow*) skulked in the shadows, always on the side of good—an undercover fighter against crime. For some years, the then-unknown Orson Welles chillingly played The Shadow.

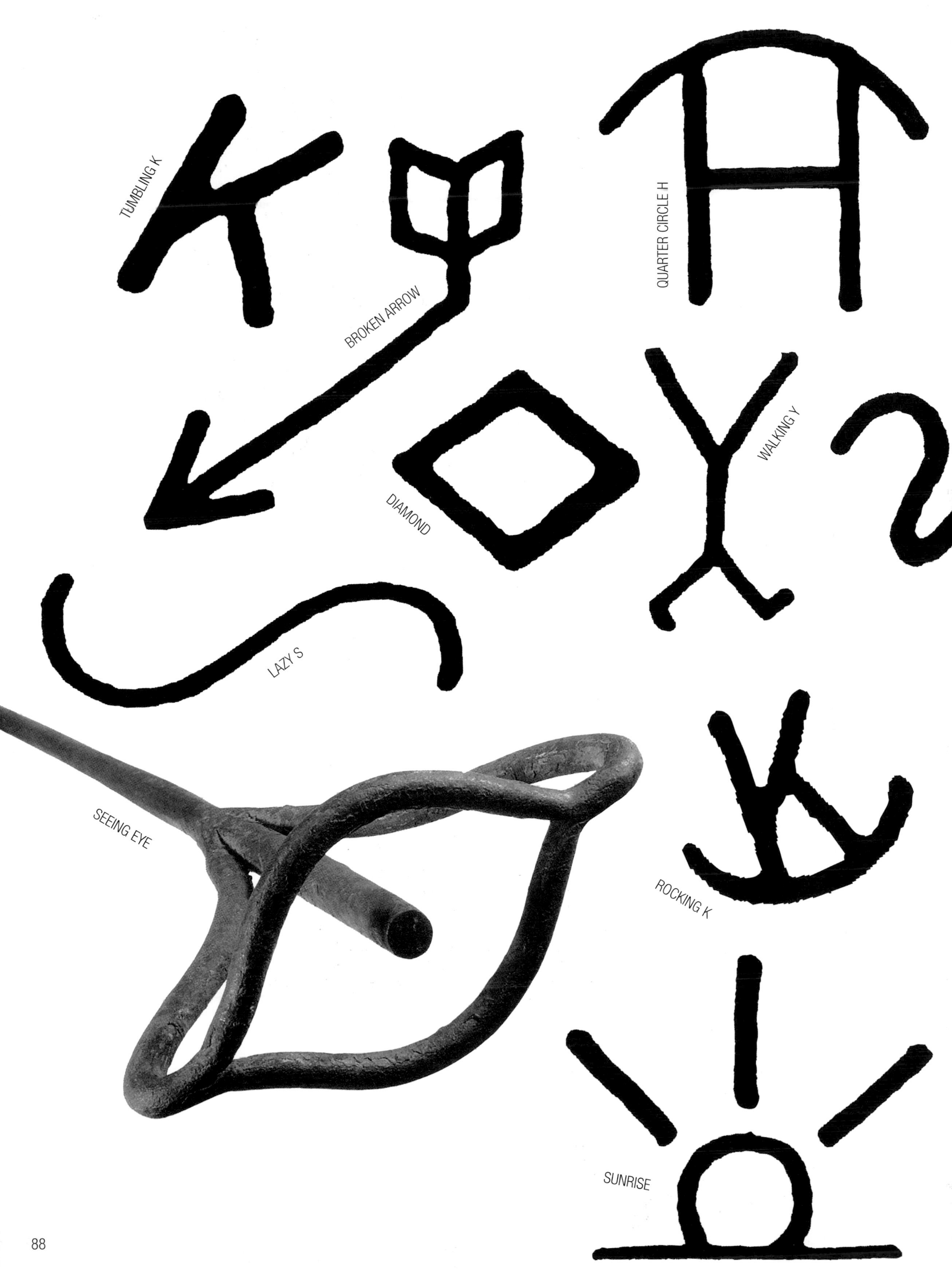
TUMBLING K
BROKEN ARROW
QUARTER CIRCLE H
DIAMOND
WALKING Y
LAZY S
SEEING EYE
ROCKING K
SUNRISE

THE BRANDING OF THE WEST

In the Old West, before barbed wire, horses and cows from different ranches grazed together on the open range. To identify its rightful owner, each animal had a mark called a brand burned into its skin with a hot iron. There were countless brands, usually designed by the ranch owner or top hand, made up of symbols, letters, numbers, and geometric shapes. Brands are the petroglyphs of the American West that kept everybody honest as the animals roamed free.

RIGHT UP AMERICA'S ALLEY

BOWLING became an enormous part of America's recreational and social activity when the boys came home from World War II and took their dates to the bowling alley. Bowling is pure Americana, with its clever team emblems, odd lingo of strikes, spares, and gutterballs, and the camaraderie of the weekly bowling league, when players have a beer in one hand and a ball in the other. With league play, family outings, birthday parties, and big-money professional competition, bowling remains America's most popular participant sport. The sport of bowling—knocking them down and setting them up, is America's favorite game.

THE BIG MAN ON CAMPUS JACKET

THE VARSITY JACKET is worn by American high school and college students to represent their schools and their teams, and most importantly, to identify themselves as a Big Man on Campus. In a school with strong sports teams, you can spot the athletes by his (or her) "letter" jacket, and the swaggering walk. Shown is Tommy Hilfiger's varsity jacket from his Elmira High School days, a fashion item from his youth that he still treasures (along with a photo of Tommy from his senior yearbook).

HO, HO, HO!

As described (and indelibly fixed in the American consciousness) by Clement C. Moore in his 1822 poem *A Visit From Saint Nicholas*, **SANTA CLAUS** is a mirthful, plump, white-bearded old man clad in an ermine-trimmed scarlet suit, wide black belt, heavy black boots, and stocking cap. He carries a huge sack packed with toys for every (good) kid in America. He flies through the air in a sleigh pulled by eight reindeer, delivering gifts to children by squeezing his girth down the chimney and leaving toys to be discovered on Christmas morning (if your home doesn't have a chimney, he finds other ways to get in). Santa Claus has been Americanized to the point that each December 25th is an ode to the children of America, no matter what religion. (For those who believe he exists, he is an American icon. For those who accept him only as a lovable tradition, ditto.)

"SANTA BABY, HURRY DOWN THE CHIMNEY TONIGHT..."

THE ROCKETTES were an instant sensation at Radio City Music Hall's opening night on December 27, 1932. The troupe of "American girls who were taller than the girls in the Ziegfeld Follies and had longer legs and could really do complicated tap routines and eye-high kicks that would knock your socks off" were conceived by choreographer Russell Markert. Originally just 16, the number has grown to 36 in today's Rockette line in the Radio City Christmas Spectacular, their most popular annual show. The Rockettes, a national treasure, have become entwined into the very fabric of Christmas in American culture.

THE SHOCK OF THE NEW

THE GUGGENHEIM MUSEUM was designed as a monument to stand out against the background of the city: a floating, expanding spiral, an erupting conical form within the quadrangular layout of New York City. America's most famous architect, **FRANK LLOYD WRIGHT**, produced a prophetic concept of a museum interior, profoundly influencing modern museum design all over the world. The interior view shown is looking up from the central court at The Guggenheim's six-story spiraling ramp; the museum is a light-flooded cathedral with a roadway to heaven winding round its walls. This 1958 *New Yorker* cartoon by Alan Dunn shows an uptight couple driving down Fifth Avenue, voicing the typical shock of the new upon first sight of the iconoclastic masterpiece.

"Are they allowed to do that on Fifth Avenue?"

"TWOALLBEEFPATTIESSPECIALSAUCELETTUCE

In 1940 Dick and Mac McDonald's Big Idea was "fast food"–as quick as you're in, you're out. But the **McDONALD'S** we know today was formed in 1955 by Ray Kroc's first Golden Arch franchised restaurant.
His empire spread like wildfire, becoming *the* fast-food giant–in 118 countries serving more than 50 million customers a day, selling billions of hamburgers, trillions of french fries, and truckloads of sodas and salads.
McDonald's multinational, multibillion-dollar business and consistent products and procedures have come to symbolize globalization and are part of the the American way of life.

AMERICA LOVED LUCY...

From being a "B-list" movie star and glamour gal of the 1930s and '40s, **LUCILLE BALL**, working with her husband, Desi Arnaz (a Cuban bandleader who spoke English with an accent thicker than the Havana phone book), became *the* archetypal American comedienne, as the star of the landmark sitcom *I Love Lucy* (1951-1960). The domestic comedy about a young married couple setting up house instantly hit home with millions of postwar Americans doing the same and launching the baby boom. The carrot-topped, blue-eyed Lucy Ricardo was an attractive homemaker, unwittingly getting big laughs as she stuffed her face full of chocolates on a production line, getting blotto as the spokeswoman for an alcohol-laced health tonic, or stomping grapes in an Italian vineyard. A 1953 episode heralding the arrival of Little Ricky–and mirroring the real-life birth of Desi, Jr.–drew a prodigious 72 percent of the TV audience. Lucille Ball went on to become a power in Hollywood as president of Desilu Productions, the first woman in television to become a production mogul.

...AND DOES TO THIS DAY

CHEESEPICKLESONIONSONASESAMESEEDBUN"

THE BREAKFAST OF CHAMPIONS

WHEATIES has been fueling elite athletes since 1924. And an athlete being portrayed on the front of a Wheaties box confirms that he or she is a superstar: Lou Gehrig! Babe Ruth! Jackie Robinson! Mary Lou Retton! Walter Payton! Michael Jordan! Tiger Woods! And **JULIUS ERVING**! The gravity-defying Dr. J helped build the ABA into a worthy rival of the NBA, leading to their merger. Erving was the dominant player of his era, an innovator who changed the way the game is played. A gracious, dignified man, Dr. J is the epitome of class, a champion on and off the field.

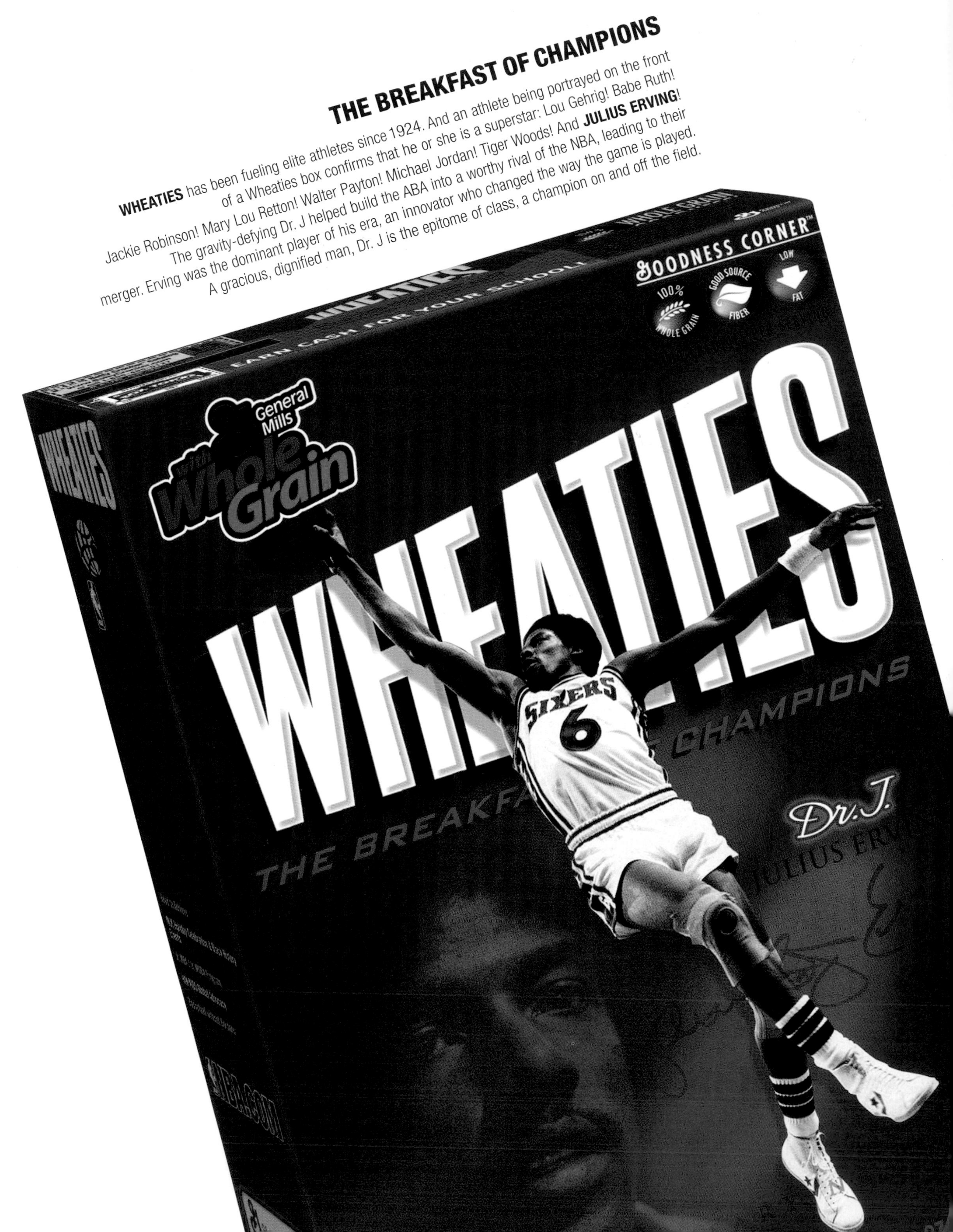

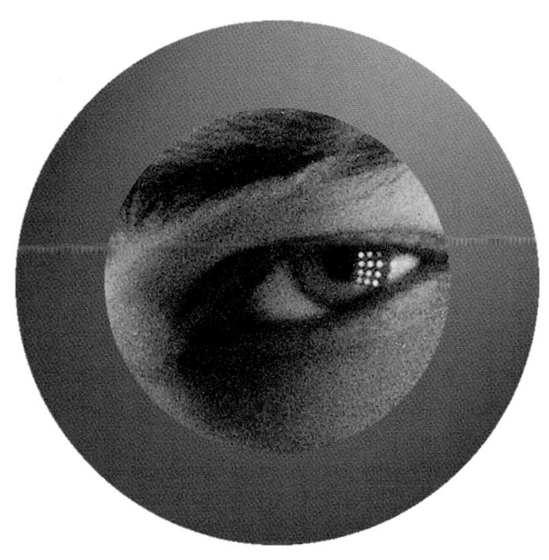

THE SPEAKEASY PEEPHOLE

The dumbest amendment to the U.S. Constitution was the 18th–outlawing alcohol and eliminating saloons, to "morally uplift the people of the United States." In 1919, when Prohibition started, there were 15,000 saloons in New York; within a few years, there were 32,000; all were speakeasies. The illegal saloons gave rise to wise-guy gangsters, the mob, and gangster films. Corruption became a way of life. Courts were overwhelmed with thousands of minor alcohol arrests, and the stupidity of the law became apparent to all. After almost 14 dry years, booze became legal once again. I'll drink to that.

THERE'S A SUCKER BORN EVERY MINUTE

The showmanship and hoaxes of **P.T. BARNUM** made him the master of humbug, as he founded the circus that eventually became the Ringling Brothers and Barnum and Bailey Circus. Among his menagerie were a gnarled, toothless, shrunken "161-year-old African slave," who Barnum claimed had been the nurse of George Washington (she was no older than 80), Tom Thumb (a 25-inch-tall midget), The Feejee Mermaid (a mummified body of *something*), Jumbo (an enormous elephant), Chang and Eng Bunker (the original Siamese twins), Jenny Lind (the Swedish Nightingale), and other assorted circus "freaks." Phineas Taylor Barnum proclaimed the whole shebang was "The Greatest Show on Earth!"

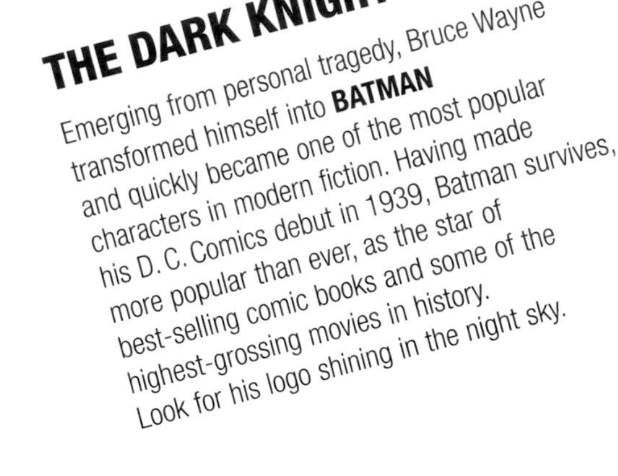

THE DARK KNIGHT

Emerging from personal tragedy, Bruce Wayne transformed himself into **BATMAN** and quickly became one of the most popular characters in modern fiction. Having made his D. C. Comics debut in 1939, Batman survives, more popular than ever, as the star of best-selling comic books and some of the highest-grossing movies in history. Look for his logo shining in the night sky.

THE MAN WHO *WAS* AMERICA

Colonel William F. Cody, aka **BUFFALO BILL**, was the archetypal American folk hero during the era of Western Expansion: A Pony Express rider, a scout for the Indian-fighting U.S. Cavalry, a trapper, a bullwhacker, a wagonmaster, a stagecoach driver, Civil War soldier, buffalo hunter, and the greatest showman of his time. Buffalo Bill was the impresario of a famous Wild West Show with tours at home and abroad, including performances before the crowned heads of Europe. He had a warm friendship with sharpshooter Annie Oakley, was a close pal of Teddy Roosevelt, and was a staunch admirer of an enemy from the past, the great Sitting Bull. During his lifetime, he *was* America–charismatic, courageous, and regaling such feats of mythic grandeur that some called him "Buffalo *Bull*," a fitting metaphor for the part he played in the taming of the West.

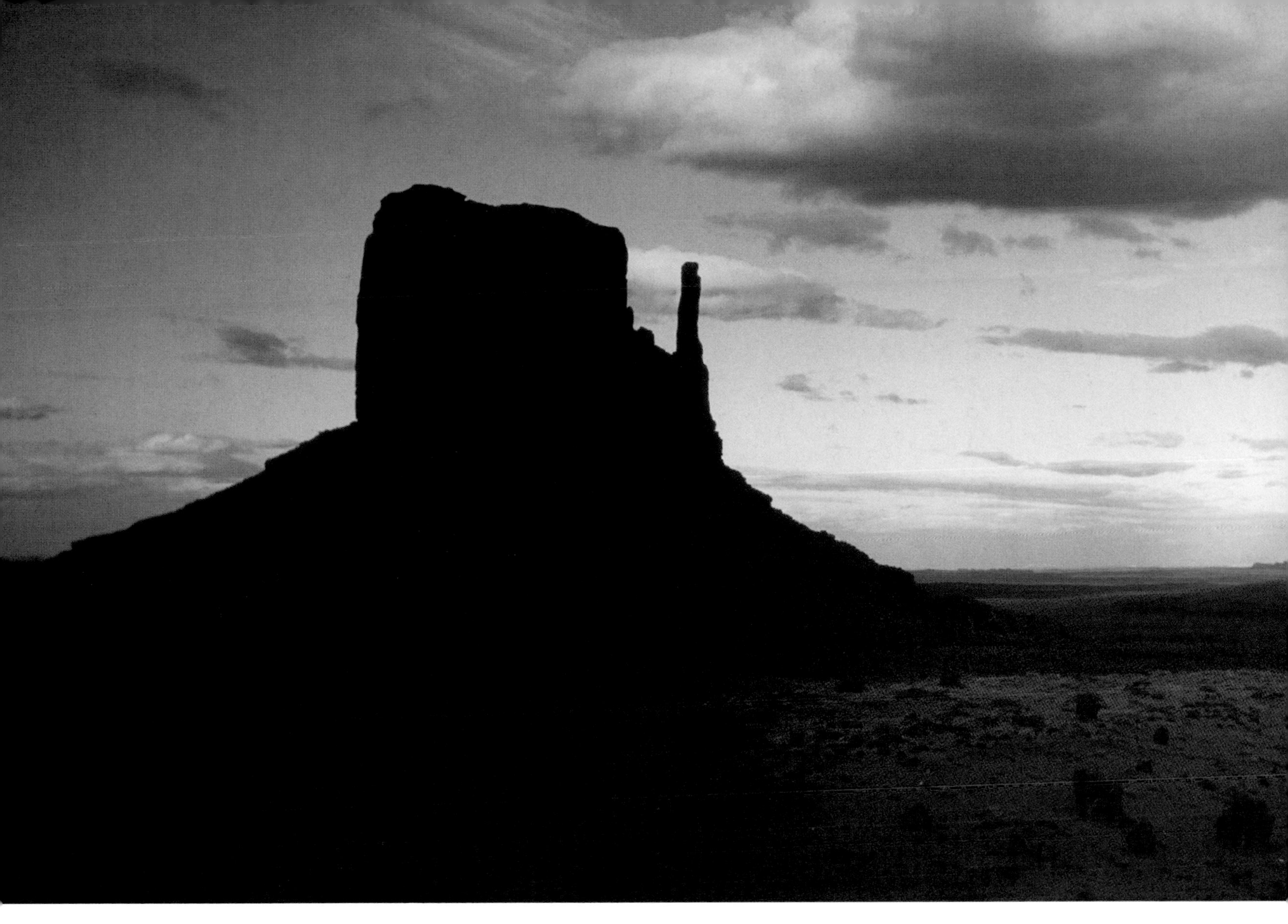

THE MOST SPECTACULAR MOVIE SET EVER CREATED

Between 1931 and 1938, John Wayne appeared in 48 "B" movies, but he became a star when John Ford directed him in the 1939 classic *Stagecoach*.
But the great director introduced another star in that landmark film: **MONUMENT VALLEY**.
Entirely within the Navajo Reservation on the Utah/Arizona border, Monument Valley is, after America viewed it in awe time after time in John Ford's eulogies to the early days of an untamed border, the quintessential western American landscape. Saddle up with DVDs of *My Darling Clementine*, *The Searchers*, *Fort Apache*, or *She Wore a Yellow Ribbon*, and the stark beauty of those red-rock monoliths will take your breath away. The backdrops of John Ford's Westerns are not trickery created on a soundstage, not a composite shot, not computer-generated. The vista of Monument Valley is one of the most enduring and iconic images of the grandeur of America.

THE CAMERA THAT
FILMED EVERY ICONIC
MOVIE SINCE 1973
THE PANAVISION MOVIE CAMERA
is the 35mm reflex camera that has been
used throughout the world.
The Golden Panaflex is the quintessential
movie camera; it can be
converted from a stationary to a handheld
configuration in 60 seconds.
Not available for sale at any price, the Panaflex
can only be rented, so the
maintenance and quality are superbly controlled.
Lights, Camera...Action!
PANAVISION
PANAFLEX
PANAVISION
ELECTRONIC
ZOOM CONTROL
PANAVISION

TEDDY ROOSEVELT

At the start of the 20th century, with bombastic power, Theodore Roosevelt accelerated the ideals and possibilities of America into the future, showing a singular, primitive instinct to *act*. He "land grabbed" Panama and began construction of the Panama Canal. He burnished himself with glory as the champion of individual American enterprise against the "robber barons." He was America's first conservationist president, responsible for preserving untold millions of acres of national parks and forests. And he was the first to protect the American consumer with food and meat-inspection laws. The iconic man they called Teddy was greatly loved by the American people.

TEDDY BEAR!

We can thank the 26th president of the United States, Theodore "Teddy" Roosevelt, for giving the Teddy Bear its name. In 1902 Roosevelt took a break from politics to go on a bear hunt in Mississippi. There were no ferocious bears in sight, and his only chance of a kill was a bear cub that had been cornered and tied to a tree. T.R. refused to shoot it. It became national news, and the little bear came to symbolize the president. Within a year, the cub was transformed into a patriotic toy for children—the Teddy Bear. To this day, millions of American children cannot go to sleep at night without cuddling up with this lovable American icon. *Bully for Teddy.*

THE BODACIOUS MAE WEST

Everything about the legendary Mae West was bodacious, including her suggestive autograph (wink, wink). The unforgettable sexual powerhouse conquered Hollywood with her bawdy double entendres, becoming one of the greatest performers in the history of the motion-picture industry. She was infamous for her battles against censorship, writing most of her own risqué material throughout her long career. In her first movie, in 1932, a hat-check girl said to Mae, "Goodness, what lovely diamonds." Mae's first words on the silver screen became an instant sensation with moviegoers when she replied, "Goodness had nothing to do with it, Dearie!"

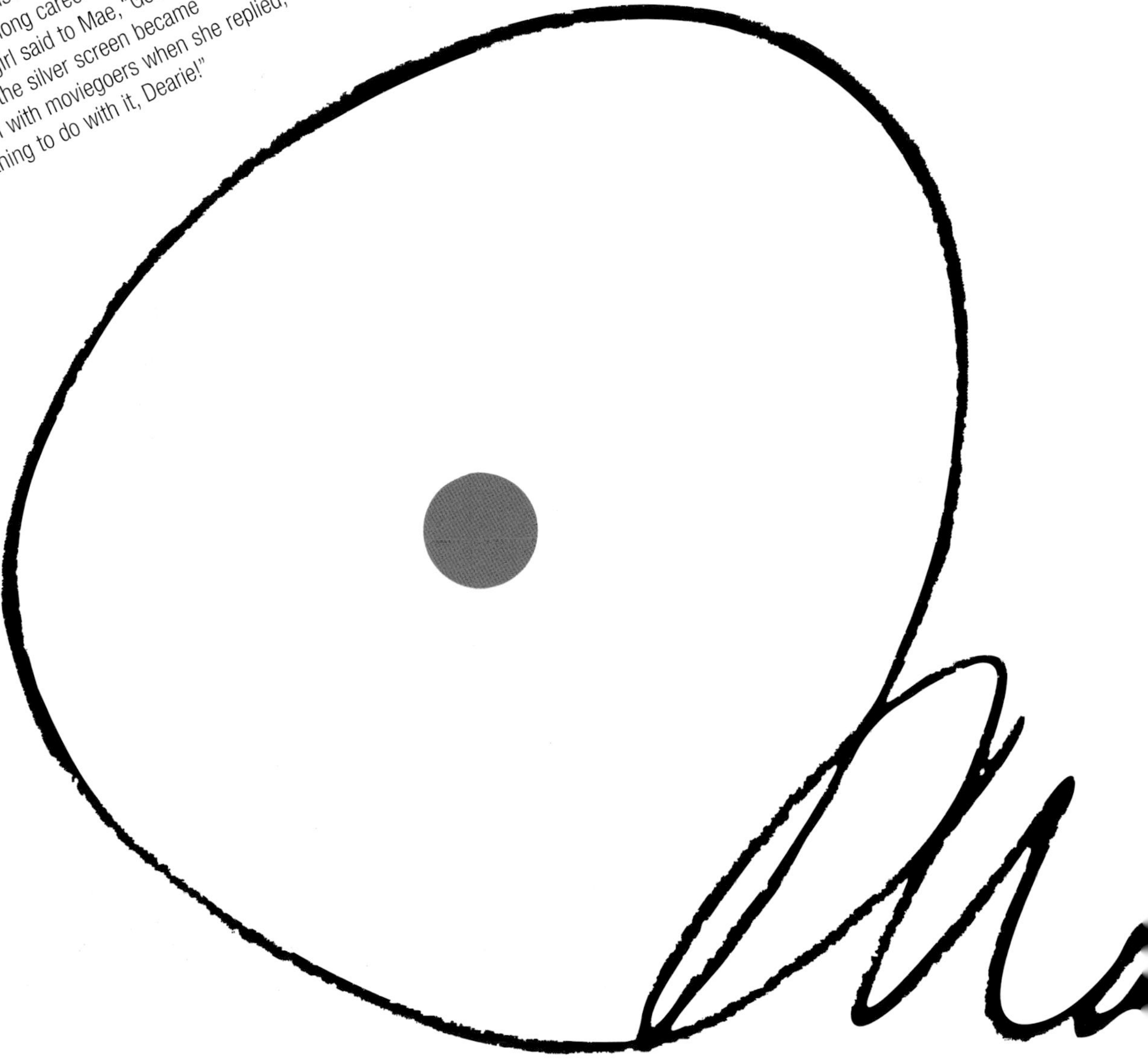

A ROSE IS A ROSE IS A MUSE...

In 1905, when the 24-year-old Pablo Picasso first laid eyes on the American writer **GERTRUDE STEIN**, he met his muse. Stein had moved to Paris to be with her brother Leo, where her extraordinary eye for discovering avant-garde artists and writers led her to purchase paintings by the unknown Gauguin, Renoir, Cézanne, Toulouse-Lautrec, Manet, Degas, Matisse, and, finally, the precocious Picasso. A frequent visitor to the Stein's home at 27, rue de Fleurus, Picasso was stimulated and challenged by the great works of modern art that hung on her walls. The rest is legend–Picasso flourished under her pluperfect eye, becoming the most important and influential artist in the history of art.

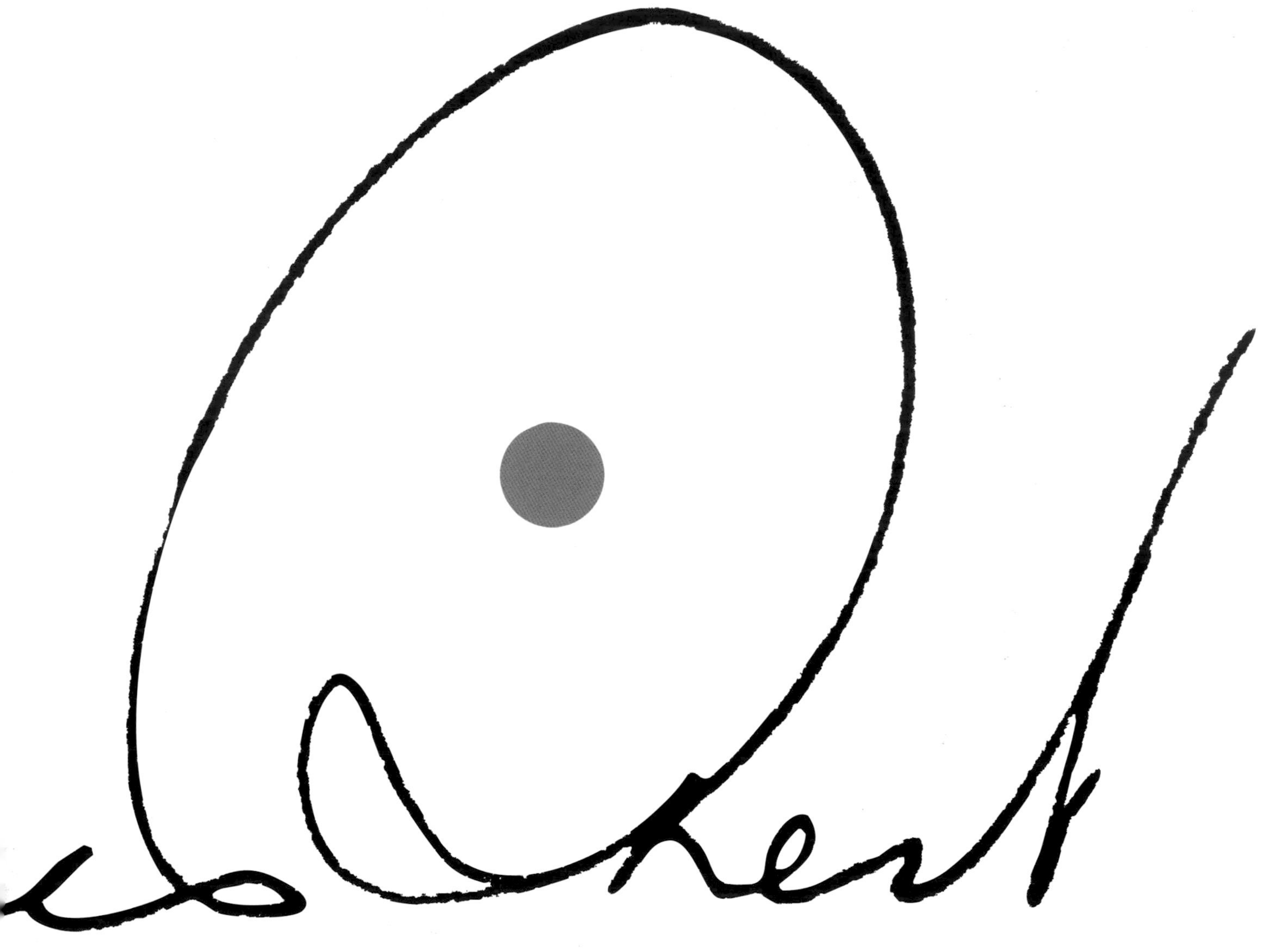

"HELLO? MA BELL? ARE YOU THERE?"

The Bell name and symbol were conceived in 1889, named after **ALEXANDER GRAHAM BELL**, the inventor of the telephone. As the result of an antitrust suit by the U.S. government in 1984, the "Bell System," along with its iconic Bell logo, disappeared from the American landscape. But the company's old nickname, "Ma Bell," still rings true in the American lexicon.

NY
LOUISVILLE SLUGGER
125

WHY NEWSPAPERS WILL NEVER DIE

THE NEW YORK TIMES daily publication has long been the U.S. newspaper of record, avoiding sensationalism and appealing to the cultured readers in America. Sunday offerings include the most respected and influential book review supplement in the nation, as well as the award-winning *New York Times Magazine*, and periodically, the handsomely designed *Play* (sports), *Key* (real estate), and *T* (style) magazines. The old English T logo, shown here, is dramatically transformed by their magazine designers into a modern, cutting-edge symbol of excellence.

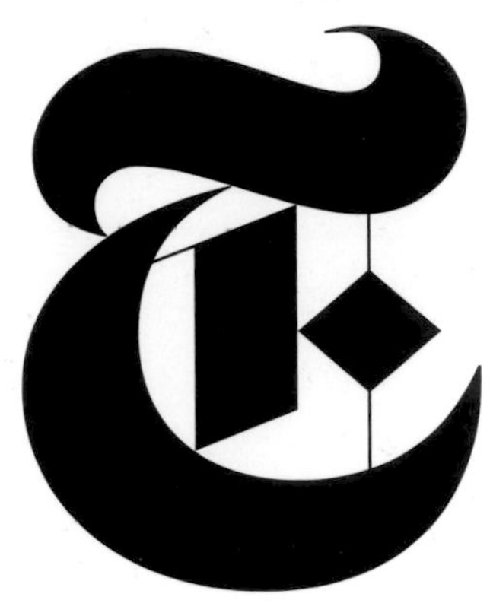

BABE RUTH (WHAT'S IN A NAME?)

In America's Golden Age of Sports, there was **BABE RUTH**—and then there was everyone else. After he became a New York Yankee in 1920 (as a result of the most lopsided trade in the history of baseball), he hit 54 home runs—more than any entire *team* in baseball at that time, changing the character of the game forever. His appetites were as prodigious as his home runs, and his talent and free spirit made him the most beloved sports figure in America. The Sultan of Swat was a national heirloom, a gift from one generation to the next, a treasure from an earlier time. The name Babe Ruth is emblazoned on the psyche of the American experience. We could not imagine an America without the legacy of the great Bambino.

UNWRAP THE NUTTIEST BRAND-NAMING STORY IN HISTORY

BABY RUTH, the luscious candy bar made of chocolate-covered peanuts and nougats, was a smash hit when it appeared in 1920, just as Babe Ruth's fame was rocketing. America assumed the bar was named after the Babe himself! But the Curtiss Candy Company had failed to cut an endorsement deal with the Bambino, so it called its candy *Baby* Ruth, and it claimed for almost 90 years that it was named after ex-president Grover Cleveland's daughter, *Ruth* Cleveland. But Cleveland had left the White House 23 years before—and his daughter had died of diphtheria at the age of 12, in 1904, 16 years before the candy bar was named. Curtiss even went to court and shut down a rival candy that was approved by, and named for, Babe Ruth, on the grounds that the names were too similar!

THE PROTOTYPE FOR THE AMERICAN FEMINIST MOVEMENT

From the populist mind and talented brush of Norman Rockwell, **ROSIE THE RIVETER** appeared on a *Saturday Evening Post* cover in 1943–a hungry, macho gal who was ready, willing, and obviously quite able to fill a man's shoes for the duration of the war. (The pose of Rockwell's gung-ho aircraft factory worker was based on one of Michelangelo's male prophets from the Sistine Chapel!) The National Organization for Women (NOW), in its fight for women's rights, has always recognized the influence of women workers who replaced men during World War II: Rosie was a memorable prototype for the modern feminist movement, gaining some measure of respect, and even awe, from American men (and even a male chauvinist or two).

GOOD GRIEF!

PEANUTS, featuring the perennial eight-year-old Charlie Brown, his dog Snoopy, his sister Sally, and pals Lucy, Linus, Peppermint Patti, Pigpen, Marcie, Franklin, Schroeder, Rerun, and Woodstock, was one of the most popular and influential comic strips in history, running in more than 2,600 newspapers, with a readership of 355 million in 75 countries, and translated into 25 languages. Charles M. Schulz created the strip for 50 years, with no assistants–even in the lettering and coloring process, until his health declined; he died the night before his farewell comic strip was published on February 13, 2000. But it's hard to keep a good man down, Charlie Brown, because Peanuts characters appear regularly in animated specials and TV commercials, and are re-run in newspapers and books to this day.

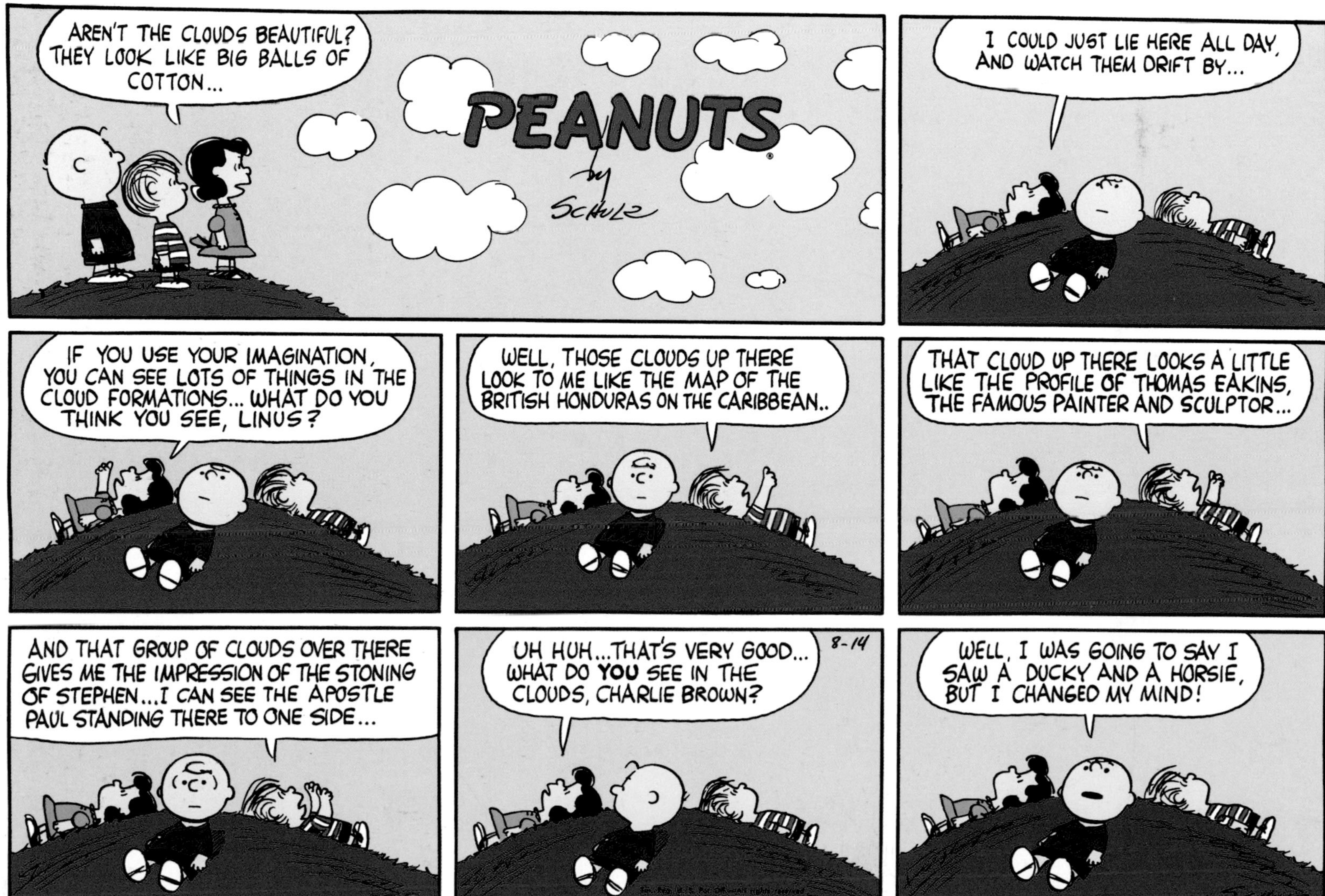

ROSIE

When Howard Hughes, the industrialist and movie producer, rejected the young **CLARK GABLE** for a movie role, he disdainfully said:

"HIS EARS MAKE HIM LOOK LIKE A TAXICAB WITH BOTH DOORS OPEN."

But Gable, big ears and all, went on to earn the indisputable title as "King of Hollywood." Throughout most of the 1930s and '40s, (when he wasn't flying combat missions during World War II with the U.S. Army Air Corps), he was arguably the world's biggest movie star. He is most remembered for his classic 1939 performance as Rhett Butler, saying, *Frankly, my dear, I don't give a damn.* Clark Gable: gone with the wind, but never forgotten.

THE SHIRLEY TEMPLE LOOK-ALIKE CRAZE

In the early 1930s, there was no bigger movie star than **SHIRLEY TEMPLE** (all 37 inches of her). The most famous child actor in history starred—beginning at age three—in films that offered an hour and a half of optimism at the height of the Depression. Shirley Temple lookalikes, with bouncing curls, abounded in every hamlet, city, and town in America. The Little Princess continued acting through her teens, and she went on to represent the United States, first as a delegate to the United Nations and later as an Ambassador to Ghana and then Czechoslovakia, becoming an inspiration for young women to enter public service.

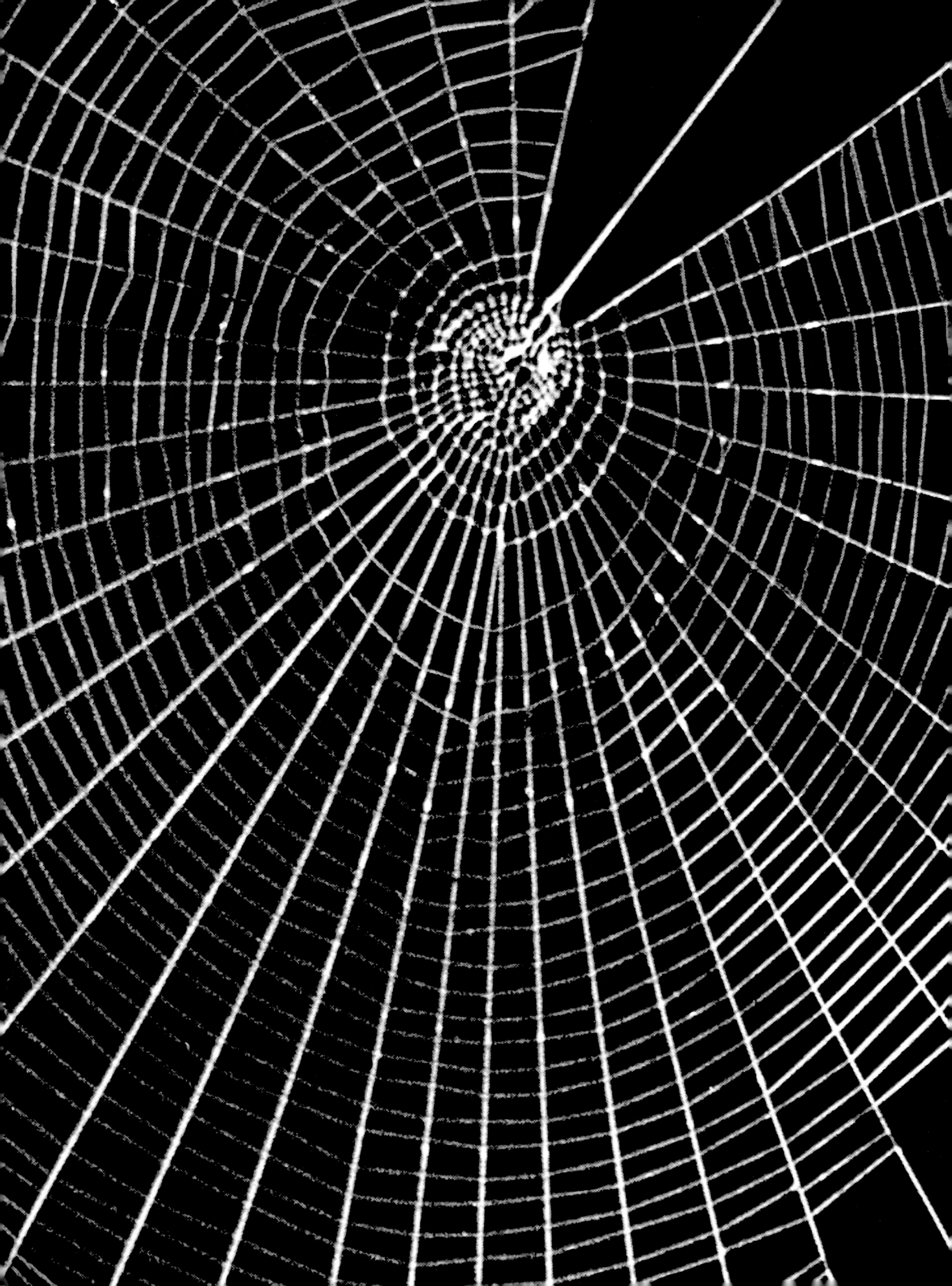

THE WEB OF JUSTICE

Peter Parker was a skinny kid who just didn't know what to do with the extraordinary gift that had unexpectedly come his way. Empowered by the bite of a spider, he became **SPIDER-MAN**, a superhero, but he is spared none of the travails of ordinary people. His powers enabled him to do good for others, but not to improve his own lot in life. Peter Parker remains a nerd, and that makes Spidey a superhero we can all identify with.

THE WEB OF INSTANTANEOUS KNOWLEDGE!

The **INTERNET** is the worldwide, publicly accessible network of interconnected *computer networks* that transmit data, instantaneously. The **WORLD WIDE WEB** is a collection of *interconnected documents* and other resources. The Web is accessible via the Internet, as are many other services including e-mail and file sharing. The Internet has changed the basis for the production, sale, and distribution of office documents, publications, software products, music, photography, video, animation, and graphics, causing seismic shifts in the way the world thinks, communicates, and works. Through keyword-driven search engines like Google, millions worldwide have easy, instant access to a vast and diverse amount of information. Compared to encyclopedias and traditional libraries the World Wide Web has generated a sudden and extreme explosion of information and data. The seeds of the Internet were planted in the 1950s, and its development has been complex, but the technical birth of the Internet was in 1983, through the brilliant work of America's National Science Foundation. For more information, go to Google.

THE MOST POPULAR AMERICAN SONG OF ALL TIME

Israel Isidore Baline, the Jewish kid from Russia who became **IRVING BERLIN**, never learned to read music but in 1940, in 54 words and an unforgettable tune, he wrote **(I'M DREAMING OF) A WHITE CHRISTMAS**, the biggest-selling song in history. After staying up all night conjuring the iconic holiday anthem, he rushed to his office and told his music secretary, "Grab your pen and take down this song. I just wrote the best song I've ever written—hell, I just wrote the best song that *anybody's* ever written!"

SAD, AND YET FANATICAL

In 1930 Grant Wood visited a tiny town in Iowa and came upon a modest five-room house, which had been built in the 1880s in a style known as Carpenter Gothic. The great Regionalist artist depicted a dour, oval-faced, tight-lipped farmer and his equally sourpuss daughter and named his painting **AMERICAN GOTHIC**. Was Wood mocking these country people, or celebrating them? The so-called "Iowa farmer and his wife" (he intended them to be seen as father and daughter) has since been understood as a strong symbol of the pioneering spirit of America. A reviewer in the *New York Saturday Review* wrote that the faces were "sad, and yet fanatical," an indicator of "what is right and what is wrong with America."

FOOD FIGHT! WHO CREATED THE #1 FAST FOOD IN AMERICA?

The American **HAMBURGER**; there is debate about who originally had the big idea of serving a hamburger patty *in* a hamburger bun. Was it Louis' Lunch in New Haven, which served ground steak between sliced bread in the early 1900s? Was it Walter Anderson, a short-order cook who went on to co-found White Castle in 1921? Or Charlie Nagreen of Wisconsin, who tried selling fried meatballs at a county fair but found them too sloppy eat, so he flattened the meatballs and made them into a sandwich he called the "Hamburger"? Or was it Fletcher Davis, who operated a cafe in Athens, Texas, and launched his invention during the 1904 World's Fair, calling his stand "Old Dave's Hamburger Stand"? Whoever It was, by the 1930s, Wimpy, a moocher in the Popeye comics, made hamburgers a famous fast food, with the plea, "I'll gladly pay you Tuesday for a hamburger today." So let's all wolf down our hamburgers, lift our glasses, and drink to Louis, Walter, Charlie, and Old Dave, as well as Wimpy, who lived his life looking forward to his next delicious hamburger.

GRANT
WOOD

IN DREAMS HE WALKED WITH US, IN DREAMS HE TALKED TO US

Hiding behind his sunglasses **ROY ORBISON** was an unlikely looking rock star, a shy songwriter from Texas who scorned onstage ostentation, and a rocker Elvis called "the greatest singer in the world." The great innovator broke all the rules of pop music with a soaring, unearthly tenor voice, singing of his dreams and nightmares, bleeding hearts, and fallen angels crying out from hell. Hearing the words of *Only the Lonely*, *Crying*, *In Dreams*, *Running Scared*, or *It's Over*—as devotional as hymns—brings butterflies to the stomach. His despairing falsetto was regarded with awe by superstars like Bruce Springsteen, the Rolling Stones, and the Beatles. Tom Waits called him "Caruso in sunglasses and a leather jacket."

THE PROPHETIC DREAM OF ABRAHAM LINCOLN

Abraham Lincoln, the 16th president of the United States, was shot at point-blank range by John Wilkes Booth on April 14,1865, during a performance of the play *Our American Cousin* at Ford's Theatre in Washington, D.C., and died the next day, a martyr and national icon. A short time before his tragic assassination, Lincoln described a dream where a funeral was being held in the East Room of the White House:

"*'Who is dead in the White House?'*
I demanded of one of the soldiers.
'The President' was his answer:
'He was killed by an assassin!'
Then came a loud burst of grief from the crowd,
which awoke me from my dream."

(Shown is a life mask taken by Leonard Volk in 1860 of a beardless Lincoln. Oiled paper protected Lincoln's eyes, hence the postmortem gaze.)

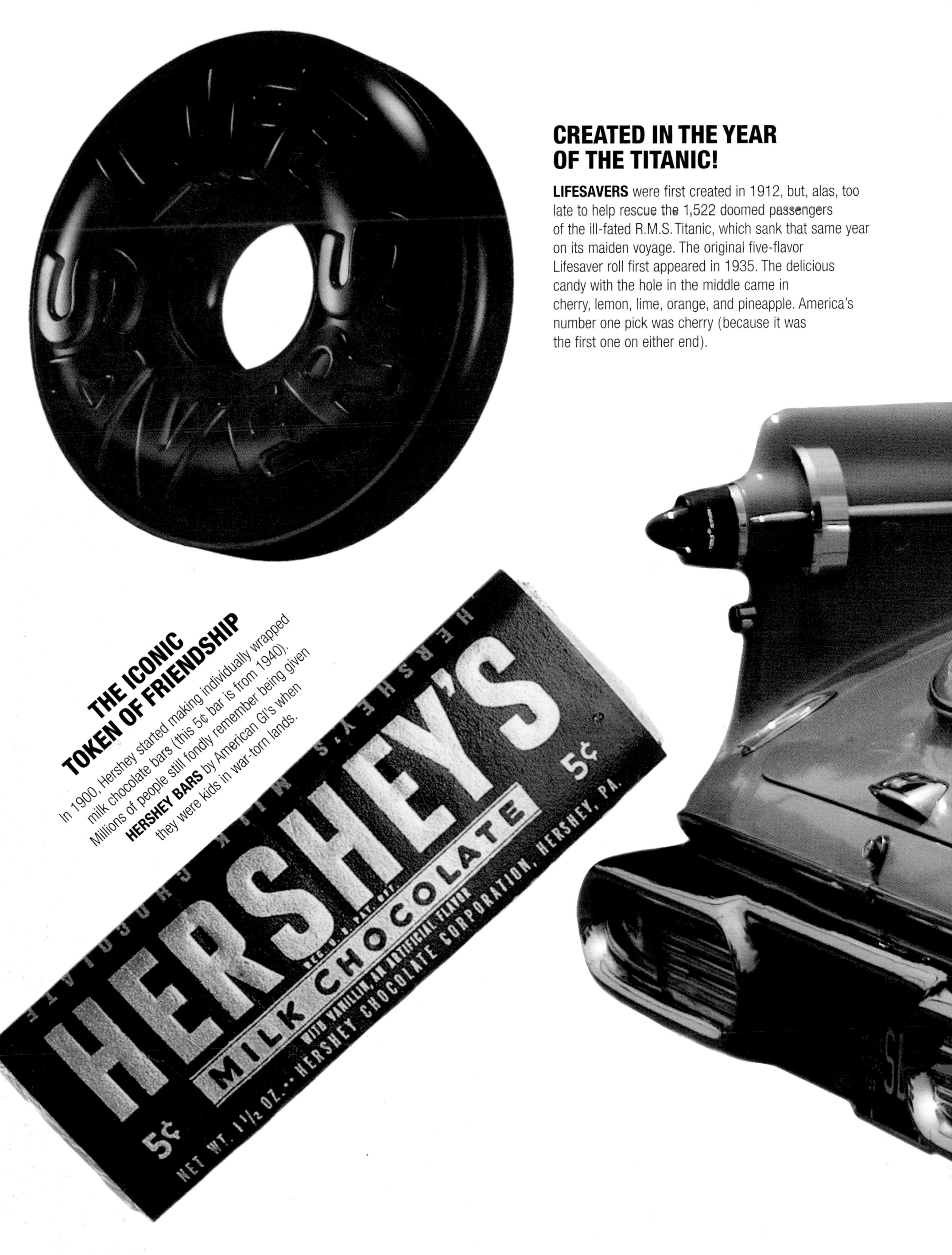

HERSHEY'S
5¢
REG. U.S. PAT. OFF.
MILK CHOCOLATE
WITH VANILLIN, AN ARTIFICIAL FLAVOR
NET WT. 1½ OZ. • • HERSHEY CHOCOLATE CORPORATION, HERSHEY, PA.
5¢

CREATED IN THE YEAR OF THE TITANIC!

LIFESAVERS were first created in 1912, but, alas, too late to help rescue the 1,522 doomed passengers of the ill-fated R.M.S. Titanic, which sank that same year on its maiden voyage. The original five-flavor Lifesaver roll first appeared in 1935. The delicious candy with the hole in the middle came in cherry, lemon, lime, orange, and pineapple. America's number one pick was cherry (because it was the first one on either end).

THE ICONIC TOKEN OF FRIENDSHIP

In 1900, Hershey started making individually wrapped milk chocolate bars (this 5¢ bar is from 1940). Millions of people still fondly remember being given **HERSHEY BARS** by American GI's when they were kids in war-torn lands.

THE OBSESSION OF FLYING FINS

In the 1950s everything was aerodynamic, from Elvis Presley's ducktail to the tail of a Cadillac. Influenced by the twin tail fins of the World War II P-38 Lightning, and the jet magic of the later Sabre Jet, the jazzy styling of automobile **TAIL FINS** caught on, and the shapes and shocking colors continue to exert their influence on fashion and pop culture.
These days, if you own a '58 Chevy Impala, a '56 DeSoto Firedome Convertible, a '55 Buick Century, or a '57 Chrysler Imperial (shown), you're still driving the coolest wheels in town.

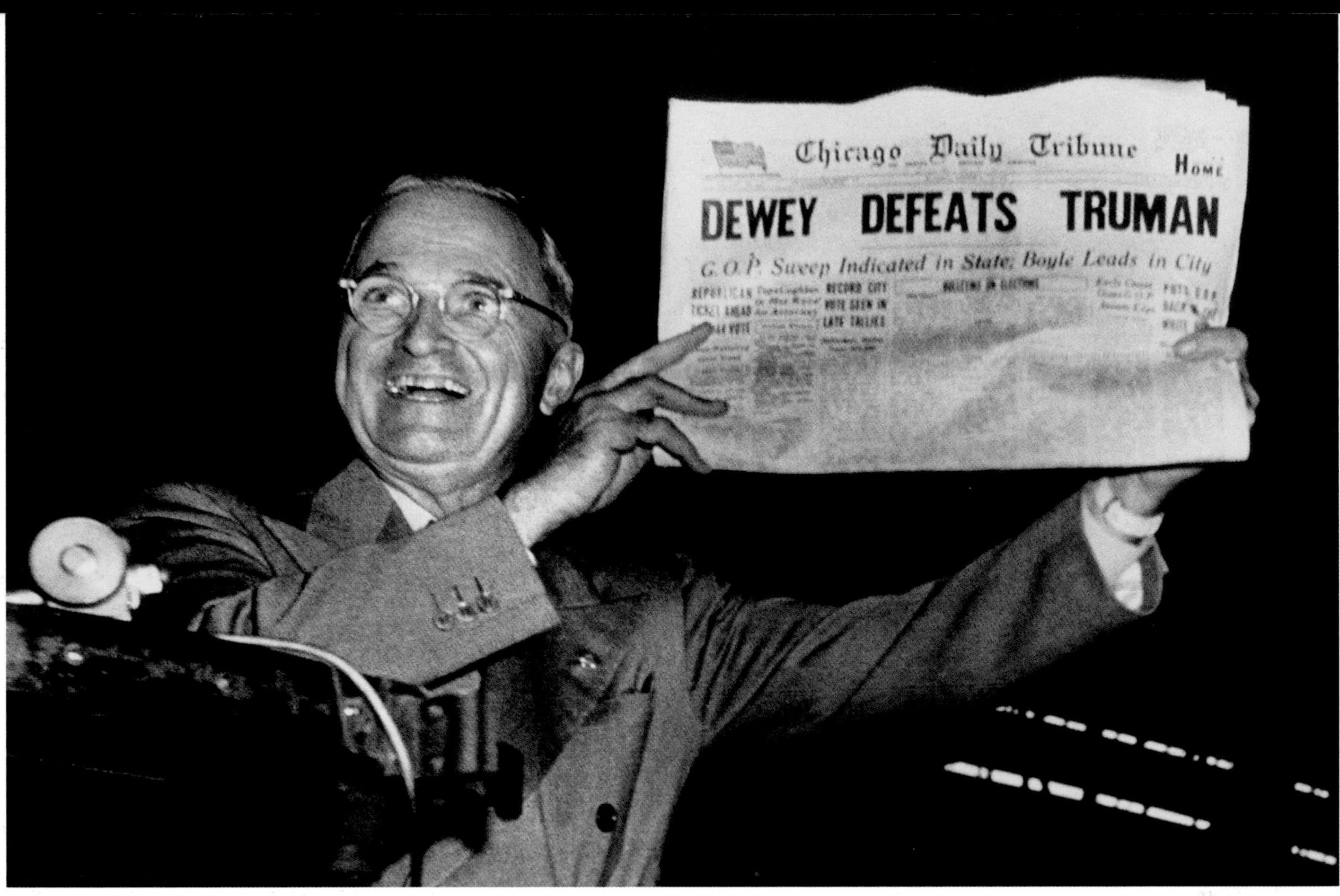

WRONG!

This iconic photo, taken the morning after the 1948 presidential election between President Harry S. Truman and New York Governor Thomas E. Dewey, shows Truman flashing the *Chicago Daily Tribune*, whose front page proclaimed **DEWEY DEFEATS TRUMAN**. Early that morning Truman had a stunning come-from-behind victory—and the erroneous headline became synonymous with counting your chickens before they hatch.

FROM SIX FEET UNDER TO THE ROCK OF GIBRALTAR

Global powerhouse **PRUDENTIAL** was founded in 1875 to sell burial service insurance. Since then the company, with its famous logo of the Rock of Gibraltar and its memorable slogan "Own a piece of the Rock," has become a gigantic financial-services company operating throughout the world.

KILL THE QUARTERBACK

The surest way to outscore your opponent in the National Football League is to obliterate the most important player on the opposing team. This seminal photo, taken in 1964, of New York Giants quarterback **Y.A. TITTLE**, illustrated the brutal nature of professional football in America. A survivor of seventeen years as a pro, Tittle played out the season, then called it quits, leaving us with this indelible image of a heroic, but defeated, warrior.

14

THE NIGHT AFTER ED SULLIVAN INTRODUCED THE BEATLES TO AMERICA, HE FLIPPED HIS WIG

ED SULLIVAN became well known as the gossipy Broadway columnist for the *New York Daily News* and a fierce competitor to the almighty Walter Winchell and his nasty world, as depicted in the movie *Sweet Smell of Success*. Then, in 1955, Sullivan became nationally famous as the stiff who introduced Elvis to America. A decade later, on February 9, 1964, he stunned the nation with another historic introduction. On his Sunday night variety show, this seemingly uncool establishment elder, with his uncanny knack for being on the cutting edge of popular culture (even though he had kept his cameras off the pelvis of Elvis) introduced the Liverpool Fab Four with their outrageous bowl cuts. The next night, after hosting what was then the most watched show in TV history, the "really big" showman posed for an *Esquire* cover for George Lois, wearing a Beatles wig!

AN ICONIC HAIRPIECE QUOTE

"I'm gonna let everybody know that thing you got on your head is a phony, and it comes from the tail of a pony."

MUHAMMAD ALI

TO SPORTS COMMENTATOR HOWARD COSELL

THE ICONIC WIG OF ANDY WARHOL

Strangely enough, the godawful platinum-blonde fright-wig that **ANDY WARHOL** wore about town (usually askew) not only became his visual trademark, but actually seemed to enhance his style and panache.

V-J DAY IN TIMES SQUARE

This enduring photo of a sailor kissing a nurse in New York's Times Square on August 15,1945, celebrated V-J Day (Victory over Japan Day), the joyous end of World War II. This **ALFRED EISENSTAEDT** photo appeared in *Life* magazine and charmed the whole world, instantly becoming the iconic image that symbolized the relief and pure joy of that first day of peace after the end of a morally great but terrible war.

"I YAM WHAT I YAM"

First popping up in the comics in 1929, **POPEYE** was short, odd-looking, belligerent, and his right eye was in a perpetual squint. With his corncob pipe, sailor suit, and bulging forearms (supposedly the result of his timely ingestions of spinach), the irascible Popeye was a precursor to Superman and the many superheros who eventually came to dominate the world of comic books. You'd never guess it, but Popeye is a symbol of the stalwart character of America. He possesses uncompromising moral standards, resorting to force only when threatened, or when he "*can't stands no more.*" Popeye's slogan is "*I yam what I yam, an tha's all I yam, I'm Popeye the Sailor Man,*" an expression of loosey-goosey American individualism. *Toot! Toot!*

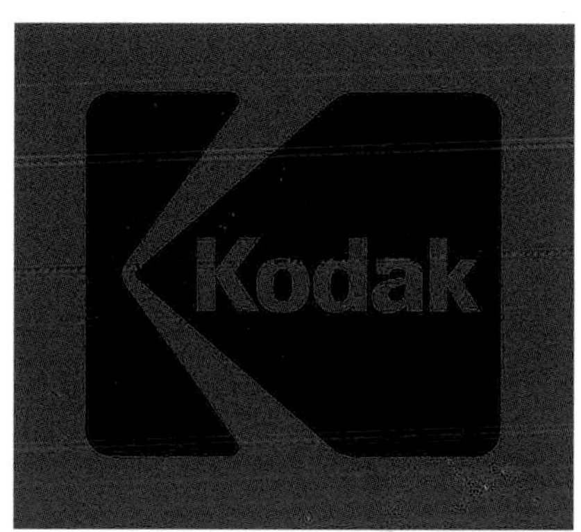

THE KODAK MOMENT

George Eastman put the first simple camera into the hands of a new world of image makers in 1888, making a complicated process simple. For over a century, amateurs and professional photographers have relied on Kodak to capture the decisive moment.

BOND

THE FIRST WHITE ACT AT HARLEM'S APOLLO THEATRE!

BUDDY HOLLY AND THE CRICKETS got the gig because the hip bookers at the Apollo assumed that they were a black group with a phenomenal new sound. With his thick black glasses and boyish face, Buddy Holly seemed an unlikely rock star, but his hiccuping vocal style and ringing electric guitar heard on hits like *Peggy Sue*, *Rave On*, *That'll Be the Day*, *Oh, Boy!*, and *Maybe Baby* are as fresh and exciting today as they were in the 1950s. The sound of Buddy Holly and the Crickets has been a major influence on the rock stars who followed. After Buddy's tragic death in a plane crash at the budding age of 22, a group of young rockers from Liverpool called themselves... the *Beatles*, in homage to Buddy Holly and the *Crickets*.

HALLOWEEN

became a holiday in America in the 19th century, but what we did to the once-holy All Hallow's Eve was downright spooky: festooning it with jack-o'-lanterns, witches, ghosts, tombstones, ghouls, bats, owls, crows, vultures, spiders, goblins, zombies, mummies, skeletons, spooks, aliens, vampires, demons, scary stories, monster movies, and black cats.

BOO!

BUSTER BROWN...STILL AROUND!

The mischievous Buster, with his dog Tige, made every kid in America crave Buster Brown shoes. The Brown Shoe Company sent Buster Brown and Tige to hundreds of towns across the country from 1904 to 1930. Hundreds of children and grownups flocked to see the popular Sunday comic strip character brought to life. Buster and Tige performed tricks, showed movies, gave away souvenirs, and moms responded when their kids walked home in new pairs of Buster Brown shoes.

GERONIMO-O-O-O...

Coney Island, a peninsula in southernmost Brooklyn, with a lush, sandy beach on the Atlantic Ocean, had been a summer resort since the end of the Civil War. At the beginning of the 20th century, it became a cool location for day trippers escaping the summer heat of New York City's tenements. In 1920 new subway lines ushered in a mass of humanity. Coney Island Amusement park featured a sensationally carved carousel, then a huge Ferris Wheel called The Wonder Wheel, the world-famous Cyclone roller coaster, bumper cars (where the idea for the demolition derby originated), and the landmark Nathan's Famous Original hot dog stand. In 1940 **THE CONEY ISLAND PARACHUTE JUMP**, one of the first rides of its kind, where New Yorkers were hoisted 190 feet in the air and then dropped (using guy-wired parachutes), gave thrill seekers the visceral feeling of being a parachutist; riders mimicked U.S. paratroopers by yelling "Geronimo." (Earlier that year, paratroopers at Fort Benning, Georgia, had seen a film about Geronimo the night before their first mass jump. In a tribute to the great Apache's courage, each one shouted "Geronimo-o-o-o!" when leaping out of the airplane. A new expression was added to the American lexicon.)

GERONIMO

In the mid-1870s Geronimo, a medicine man who was destined to become a great warrior, led a band of Apaches and raised terror throughout the Southwest. His forces became the last band of Indian warriors who refused to acknowledge the sovereignty of the American government in their sacred lands. Today, the land of the desert mesas still has the aura of its revered ancestors the Anasazi, "The Ancient Ones."

THE GREAT STONEFACE

Joseph Keaton was given the nickname "Buster" by Harry Houdini, who saw the 18-month-old Keaton tumble down a flight of stairs and pop up unharmed. A few years later, **BUSTER KEATON** starred on the vaudeville stage as a prankster child being disciplined by his actual father and mother, who threw him all over the stage and even into the audience. Buster grew up to be the master of the deadpan, but his body was a mechanical marvel and his face was as expressive as any of the great screen actors. "When he moved his lips," said the critic James Agee, "it was like seeing them move in a statue." (This photo of the actor is from *The Navigator*, 1924.) Buster never mugged at the camera to gain audience sympathy—he made it all look so real, so natural. But his films, many of which he directed, contain astonishing scenes, as when he maintains his serene stillness with his home collapsing around his ears in a hurricane scene in *Steamboat Bill, Jr.* (1928). Keaton's trademark was displaying natural comedic nonchalance in hair-raising situations. His supreme visual economy made him an iconic figure, and his simple style was a refreshing change from the ponderous Germanic manner prevalent in the silent-film era. Buster Keaton displayed even greater talents in the talkies—witness his role as Erronius, alongside Zero Mostel, in *A Funny Thing Happened on the Way to the Forum* (1966), in a performance that can only be described as pure genius.

"LET'S GO FOR A RIDE AND READ THOSE CATCHY BURMA SHAVE SIGNS..."

From 1925 to 1963, 3,000 sets of **BURMA-SHAVE** signs lined the highways of the nation. Each group of five signs created a poem, set in such a way that at 35 mph, it took three seconds to get from one sign to the next—15 seconds total (a lot more time than anyone advertising in magazines or newspapers could hope to hold the reader's attention). It was as hard to read just one Burma-Shave sign as it was to eat just one salted peanut. They became a national phenomenon. Over the course of 38 years, more than 500 poems were plastered all over our U.S. highways. Burma-Shave was owned by the Odell family, and the company's highway ad barrage changed the face of America (and sold carloads of shaving cream). The campaign bit the dust when cars on the new superhighways traveled at speeds that made it impossible to read the words. Turn the next four pages and spend 15 seconds, traveling at 35 mph, and live in the heyday of Burma-Shave!

THE SAD YET GLORIOUS STORY OF LADY DAY

BILLIE HOLIDAY is considered the foremost female singer in jazz history. Contemporary jazz great Wynton Marsalis speaks of Holiday phrasing her performances in the manner of an instrumental soloist, and says she must be seen as a complete jazz musician and not only as a singer. Her voice betrayed a wounded poignancy that was an important part of her attraction to worshipful audiences. She was, above all, a master of singing the blues. Billie Holiday's grandfather was one of 17 children born to a black Virginia slave and a white Irish plantation owner. Her mother was only 13 at the time of Billie's birth, in Philadelphia in 1915; she had moved there to hide her out-of-wedlock pregnancy. Billie had a difficult childhood: she was recruited by a brothel; she worked as a prostitute; and she was even imprisoned for a short time. In the early 1930s, broke and facing eviction, she sang *Body and Soul* in a Harlem club and reduced the audience to tears. She was discovered by talent scout John Hammond, who secured recording sessions with Benny Goodman and booked her in various New York nightclubs. She worked with Lester Young, Count Basie, and Artie Shaw (becoming the first black woman to work with a white orchestra). By the 1950s, Holiday's drug abuse, drinking, relationships with abusive men, and deteriorating health set her life on a steady decline, and she died penniless in 1959, at the age of 44. As is the case with many artists, the true importance of Holiday's music and her tremendous influence were only realized after her death. She struggled against racism and sexism during her entire career but, despite a turbulent life, achieved everlasting fame.

THERE'S A FORD IN YOUR FUTURE

In 1906 Ford's chief engineer and designer, Childe Harold Wills developed the stylized Ford script, adapting a standard typeface. An oval frame was added later, but since 1928 there has been no change in the iconic trademark. It's been a long time since the Model T days (1908-1927) when Henry Ford told us you could choose any color car you wanted, "as long as it's black."

THE FLYING SAUCERS
WARNING! TAKE COVER!

THE FEAR OF FLYING (SAUCERS)

Sightings of aerial phenomena date back to ancient times, when they were usually treated as supernatural portents, angels, or other religious omens, but reports of **UNIDENTIFIED FLYING OBJECTS** (UFO's) became common after the first widely publicized sighting in 1947. A pilot flying his private plane near Mount Rainier in Washington State reported seeing nine objects that "flew like a saucer would if you skipped it across the water"; he estimated they were traveling at 1,200 mph. The Flying Saucer Scare was born! Alien abduction literature abounds, and the motives of the aliens run the gamut from benevolent to hostile—*very* hostile (shown is a movie poster from 1956). Since then there have been thousands of sightings around the world, with Americans reporting more than their share. In a 2006 survey almost 25 percent of Americans said they believed that some UFO's were probably spaceships from other worlds. Be afraid, be very afraid.

THE ICONIC LEMON

The **EDSEL** was the most spectacular failure in the history of the American auto industry. Was its failure the fault of the car's styling, or poor workmanship? Built in 1958, '59, and '60, much of the blame for the fiasco went to Ford honcho Robert McNamara, the "whiz kid" who, a few years later as Secretary of Defense during the Kennedy and Johnson administrations, conceived the strategy for the ill-advised Vietnam War. In 1995 McNamara attempted to apologize for his role in the Vietnam debacle by saying, "We were wrong, terribly wrong." But he never *did* apologize for making the name Edsel synonymous with the proverbial "lemon."

THE FAIRY-TALE LIFE AND DEATH OF PRINCESS GRACE

Born into an Irish Catholic immigrant family of bricklayers, who, after only one generation in America had become prominent figures in Philadelphia society, **GRACE KELLY** made an auspicious film debut starring in *High Noon* (1952) with Gary Cooper, then starred in hit after hit with the drooling Clark Gable, Jimmy Stewart, and Cary Grant, giving every film more than a touch of class. Alfred Hitchcock cast Kelly as his heroine in *Dial M for Murder* (1954), *Rear Window* (1954), and *To Catch a Thief* (1955), for what he described as her "sexual elegance." At the very pinnacle of her explosive career, she left Hollywood to become Her Serene Highness, the Princess of Monaco, as the wife of Prince Rainier. She dutifully bore him three children, Princess Caroline, Princess Stéphanie, and the heir to the throne, Prince Albert, now the reigning prince of Monaco. At the age of 53, Grace Kelly, the fairy-tale princess, died tragically when she suffered a stroke during an automobile accident.

"GO GREYHOUND AND LEAVE THE DRIVING TO US!"

Incorporated in 1926, this racy logo depicting the fastest breed of canine used in racing, helped make Greyhound the largest intercity passenger-bus carrier in the world, ultimately serving 2,200 destinations in America. The 1934 Academy Award-winning movie *It Happened One Night*, starring Clark Gable and Claudette Colbert, prominently featured a Greyhound bus, igniting tremendous interest in bus travel nationwide. After World War II and the building of the interstate highway system in 1956, Americans started their car-buying binge and bus and train use went downhill—but Greyhound's slogan helps the company remain a prominent name as it continues to tour America.

THE SCHNOZZOLA

Known as "the Schnozzola" by his loving fans because of his Cyrano-sized nose, young **JIMMY DURANTE**, the son of an Italian barber, became the piano-playing leader of a ragtime band. He opened his own speakeasy in the 1920s, adopting his lifelong stage character of an aggressive, pugnacious comedian and singer, yelling *Stop the music* at the slightest provocation and behaving as though he had to finish the song before the cops hauled him away for having the nerve to perform. But perform he did! His butchered language delivered in a gravelly voice, along with his schnoz, made him one of America's iconic entertainment personalities from the 1920s to the 1960s. His opening trademark song on radio and TV was *Inka Dinka Doo*, and his ambiguous sign-off that became a national catchphrase was *Good night, Mrs. Calabash, wherever you are.* Among his other famous catchphrases: *It's a catastastroke!*, *Everybody wantsa get into the act!*, *Umbriago*, and *Ha-cha-cha-chaaa!* Dat's my boy!

From the 1920s into the early 1960s, reading Burma-Shave highway signs became an addiction while driving on the roads of America. Read these and you'll understand why:

WITHIN THIS VALE
OF TOIL AND SIN
YOUR HEAD GROWS BALD
BUT NOT YOUR CHIN
BURMA-SHAVE

HE HAD THE RING
HE HAD THE FLAT
BUT SHE FELT HIS CHIN
AND THAT WAS THAT
BURMA-SHAVE

LISTEN BIRDS
THESE SIGNS COST MONEY
SO ROOST AWHILE
BUT DON'T GET FUNNY
BURMA-SHAVE

IF YOUR PEACH
KEEPS OUT OF REACH
BETTER PRACTICE
WHAT WE PREACH
BURMA-SHAVE

SAID FARMER BROWN
WHO'S BALD ON TOP
"WISH I COULD
ROTATE THE CROP"
BURMA-SHAVE

HENRY THE EIGHTH
SURE HAD TROUBLE
SHORT-TERM WIVES
LONG-TERM STUBBLE
BURMA-SHAVE

THIS CREAM MAKES
THE GARDENER'S DAUGHTER
PLANT HER TU-LIPS
WHERE SHE OUGHTER
BURMA-SHAVE

BEN MET ANNA
MADE A HIT
NEGLECTED BEARD
BEN–ANNA SPLIT
BURMA-SHAVE

THE ONE WHO DRIVES
WHEN HE'S BEEN DRINKING
DEPENDS ON YOU
TO DO HIS THINKING
BURMA-SHAVE

IF DAISIES ARE
YOUR FAVORITE FLOWER
KEEP PUSHIN' UP
THOSE MILES-PER-HOUR
BURMA-SHAVE

THE BIG BLUE TUBE'S
JUST LIKE LOUISE
YOU GET A THRILL
FROM EVERY SQUEEZE
BURMA-SHAVE

IF YOU DON'T KNOW
WHOSE SIGNS THESE ARE
YOU CAN'T HAVE
DRIVEN VERY FAR
BURMA-SHAVE

THE 8-FOOT, 2-INCH YELLOW ICON

SESAME STREET, the brainchild of Joan Ganz Cooney, pioneered education and entertainment for America's preschoolers, and became the most highly regarded TV show for children in the world. In the U.S., more than 75 million Americans grew up on *Sesame Street*! The stars on *Sesame Street*, aside from the army who have appeared as guests over the years, are the **MUPPETS**, a motley mob of fuzzy puppets that may represent humans, animals, robots, extraterrestrial creatures, and mythical beings or other unidentified objects. Conceived by Jim Henson, Muppet puppets include Miss Piggy, Oscar the Grouch, Kermit the Frog, Bert & Ernie, Cookie Monster, Count Von Count, The Great Gonzo, Grover, and of course, the full-body muppet, **BIG BIRD**.

1,000 SONGS IN YOUR POCKET

In 2001 CEO Steve Jobs announced the debut of a Mac-compatible product that would put "1,000 songs in your pocket." The pioneering iPod was Apple's high note into the digital-music market, a hard-disk-based digital player that was smaller than the typical portable tape or CD player and was stylishly designed. The bundled software used for transferring, archiving, and managing a comprehensive library of music on the user's computer allowed the user to play, burn, and rip music. The iPod and iTunes have profoundly influenced the way the music industry functions in America. Powerful graphic ads and posters highlighted the iPod's sleek design and distinctive white earphone cords, and its users stood out in a crowd, each a walking advertisement for the product—67 million walking ads in four short years! (Since the introduction of the iPod, the 1,000-song capacity promised by Steve Jobs grows and grows and grows.)

iPod
10,000 songs in your pocket. Mac or PC.

YOU CAN TAKE IT WITH YOU!

Jasper Newton "Jack" Daniel founded his Lynchburg distillery in 1875, producing **JACK DANIEL'S TENNESSEE WHISKEY**, a liquor similar to bourbon and different only because it is filtered through maple charcoal in wooden vats prior to aging. Ironically, while it is legal to distill the product within Moore County, Tennessee, it is illegal to purchase it there! The brand, with its black-and-white label, has become an iconic American whiskey, with a devoted, famous, and fanatic fan base. In the 1978 movie *Animal House*, John Belushi belted down a bottle of Jack in eight seconds; in the 2004 movie *After the Sunset*, Pierce Brosnan's character orders a "Jack on the rocks," stating that if it was good enough for "Frank," it was good enough for him. Jack Daniel's *was* Frank Sinatra's favorite booze—so much so that in accordance with his will (in the tradition of the kings and pharaohs who were interred with the necessities required in the afterlife), a flask of Jack Daniel's Old No. 7 Tennessee Whiskey was buried with him.

"I'D RATHER BE IN PHILADELPHIA"

W. C. FIELDS created one of the most memorable comic personas in film history—a charming drunk, a misanthrope who teetered on the edge of being a buffoon, a man who claimed "anyone who hates children and dogs can't be all bad." Asked if he didn't *really* like children, Fields replied, "Only if they are properly cooked." An accomplished juggler, he developed his unique talents in the days of burlesque and vaudeville. His wild pool skits, playing with bizarrely shaped pool cues, wowed the audiences. As entertaining as his visual antics were, they were greatly enhanced by his raspy voice and verbal pyrotechnics. He drank martinis for breakfast and consumed two quarts of gin a day, paying for it through the nose. When asked by a waiter if he wanted water in the scotch he ordered, he once replied, "Water? I hate water—you know what fish *do in it*, don't ya!" In 1925 *Vanity Fair* asked W.C. what he would like to have engraved on his tombstone, and he replied, "I'd rather be in Philadelphia" (his hometown, which he always knocked). With his bulbous nose, rotund body, blustery nasal voice, and immense talent, he has probably been caricatured more than any other performer in showbiz history.

SEC 11
SEC 9

WE ♥ THIS LOGO

The *I Love New York* logo, created in 1977 by brilliant graphic designer Milton Glaser for the New York State Department of Economic Development, has become a part of the American pop cultural canon (and has "inspired" countless knockoffs, with the state of New York filing an avalanche of trademark oppositions against imitators). Any tourist who doesn't take home a T-shirt with this logo on it doesn't love N.Y.

WHERE HAVE YOU GONE, JOE DIMAGGIO?

After an illustrious baseball career, Joltin' Joe married the ultra-visible Marilyn Monroe, Hollywood's sex goddess, and modestly ducked behind her voluptuous curves and out of the limelight. Because he was too proud, classy, and important to become Mr. Monroe, the two superstars split, and The Yankee Clipper was out of sight again. This July 1966 *Esquire* cover, showing a dreamlike apparition of Joe in one of his tailored civilian suits hitting one into the empty stands of Yankee Stadium, hauntingly reflected on his absence. One year later, *Mrs. Robinson* (by Simon & Garfunkel in 1967), from the hit movie *The Graduate*, sported a lyric evoking all the nostalgia of the time:

Where have you gone, Joe DiMaggio,
Our nation turns its lonely eyes to you.
What's that you say, Mrs. Robinson.
Joltin' Joe has left and gone away,
Hey hey hey.

JOHNNY APPLESEED

John Chapman, popularly known as Johnny Appleseed, was a young nurseryman who planted apple seeds in New York State (some of the orchards there today are said to have originated with his apple trees). In the beginning of the 19th century, Johnny was among the very first to explore the new territories of the West. Moving ahead of the pioneers, he started nurseries, planted apple seeds, and transplanted apple seedlings, and when settlers arrived, they found young trees ready for sale. Apples became a staple of the settlers' diets, and for half a century many homesteaders owed their sustenance to the Apple Tree Man. Chapman's path from east to west is dotted with many sculpted monuments to the memory of a mythic American folk hero.

THE SPELLING BEE originated in America. "AMERICA, A-M-E-R-I-C-A, AMERICA." To be a spelling champion, the contestants, usually children, must study root words and etymologies, and often the foreign languages that English draws upon. Although national spelling bees have been around since 1925, the prestige and rewards of the intellectual competitions has attracted the brightest wunderkinds from the melting pot of American youth.

GOD CREATES DINOSAURS. GOD DESTROYS DINOSAURS.

From an iconic novel written by Michael Crichton, with an iconic book jacket designed by Chip Kidd, evolving into a blockbuster movie directed by Steven Spielberg, **JURASSIC PARK** sparked serious debate on the plausibility of cloning dinosaurs (as if the world didn't have enough problems!).

"OH, BUT MOTHER'S HARMLESS."

One of the most memorable scenes in the history of cinema was Janet Leigh (playing secretary Marion Crane, on the lam after embezzling $40,000 from her employer) taking a quick-cut shower at the dilapidated Bates Motel, in the great horror thriller **PSYCHO** (directed by Alfred Hitchcock in 1960). Shockingly attacked by what seems to be an old woman wielding a brutally long knife, Janet Leigh released the iconic scream heard 'round the world, in the classic Hitchcockian scene driven by music that still scares the hell out of us.

THE MAKING OF McPAPER

THE NATION'S NEWSPAPER
USA TODAY
NO.1 IN THE USA

One of the most important innovations in modern journalism was the creation, in 1982, of the first national newspaper, *USA Today*. Producing a daily early-morning paper would be technically difficult and costly, but Gannett's gutsy chairman, Al Neuharth, made it happen. The paper was derided as "McPaper" for its bold, colorful, and unique graphics as well as for its terse style of reporting the news, but within two years *USA Today* proclaimed to the U.S.A., "First they called us McPaper– Now they call us No. 1!"

GET YOUR KICKS ON ROUTE 66

Our vast nation has a car culture, where Americans hit the road every chance we get. Our highways are the lifelines of commerce and travel, and starting in 1926, Route 66 was on its way to becoming the most memorable stretch of blacktop in the U.S. of A.

"DEEP THROAT– I THOUGHT IT WAS ABOUT A GIRAFFE."

BOB HOPE

DEEP THROAT is the pseudonym of the secret source who leaked the goods about the involvement of President Nixon's gang of thieves in the 1972 Watergate Scandal. *The Washington Post* dubbed the informant "Deep Throat" as a facetious reference to the most successful porno flick of all time. Deep Throat became legendary after the publication of *Post* writers Bob Woodward and Carl Bernstein's book *All the President's Men*, a blow-by-blow account of their investigation. The identity of Deep Throat remained a deep secret until 2005, when William Mark Felt, a career FBI honcho (second only to J. Edgar Hoover) revealed himself as the cloak-and-dagger hero in *Vanity Fair* magazine.

THE LIFE (AND VIOLENT DEATH) OF TUPAC SHAKUR

The legend of Tupac Shakur, the greatest rapper ever, has grown to mythic proportions since he was gunned down in a drive-by shooting in 1996 at the tender age of 25. The killing, presumably by a competing hip-hop faction, mirrors the violent "thug life" of Tupac, whose rap sheet was as long as the row of tattoos on his arm. This modern American folk hero remains the best-selling rap artist ever, as well as the most photographed; images of Shakur include dozens of mug shots posted in police stations all across the U.S.A. Shakur's lyrics spoke with brilliance and insight of the "gangsta" mentality; he was a bad dude who bore witness to his pain as he dealt with the contradictory themes of social inequality and injustice, unbridled aggression, compassion, and hope. The high profile of his killing and the ensuing gang violence have given Tupac Shakur's music (much of it released posthumously on the Death Row record label) an ethereal life force in badass American pop culture.

A WARM AMERICAN ICON

There is nothing more romantic in popular culture than the warm tradition of **TOASTING MARSHMALLOWS** over a toasty fireplace, a roaring fire on a beach, a picnic ground...and especially under a star-filled night sky.

"OH, THE HUMANITY"

One disaster that is permanently etched in the American psyche is forever remembered because of the extraordinary newsreel coverage that was shown continuously in movie theaters, the spectacular photographs, and the most famous news radio broadcast in history. Herbert Morrison frantically and heartbreakingly reported the explosion and slow-motion descent of the German zeppelin, LZ 129 **HINDENBURG**, while attempting to land at Lakehurst Naval Air Station in New Jersey, on May 6, 1937. Starting out in a flat news-reader's drawl as the 804-foot-long hydrogen-filled dirigible began to dock, Morrison became increasingly hysterical until he trailed off in anguished cries of "A mass of humanity" and "Oh, the humanity," as 45 passengers and crew were burned alive. (Though widely seen as a symbol of Nazi power, the Zeppelin company was very openly anti-Nazi. Hitler had wanted the Hindenburg named for him, but Hugo Eckener's Zeppelin company refused. After the conflagration, there were dozens of sabotage hypotheses offered—even one that Adolf Hitler had ordered the Hindenburg destroyed in retaliation for Hugo Eckener's anti-Nazi views.)

A WARM KEEPSAKE

Millions of "windproof" **ZIPPO** lighters went to three wars (World War II, Korea, and Vietnam) in the pockets of American fighting men, taking their place as an inextinguishable American icon. Many thousands have been returned to the loved ones of GI's killed in action, and they are treasured as a symbol of the soldiers' continued presence.

GOING UP!

Who invented **THE ELEVATOR**? Who invented the ship, the automobile, the locomotive, the aircraft? All such complex technology was the brainchild of countless innovators. Elisha Graves Otis didn't actually invent the elevator—but he invented the brilliant *braking* system used in modern elevators. The ability to stop safely made the elevator a practical reality, paving the way for the modern skyscraper and reshaping the landscape of American cities. The human spirit soared.

THE AIRBORNE DANCE STEP

THE LINDY HOP was born in Harlem in the 1920s, an exuberant swing dance based on jazz, tap, the Charleston, and Breakaway. In the 1930s and 1940s, American films, newsreels, and troops stationed overseas made the Lindy Hop popular all over the world. But the Lindy disappeared from popular American dance in the 1950s when rock'n'roll music and dancing replaced swing and all that jazz. Performed by athletic, talented dancers (witness this 1943 photo by *Life* photographer Gjon Mili) there was never a more popular dance in American history.

THE IMMORTAL FLAPPER

In the 1920s America's heroes were sports figures, movie stars, gangsters—and cartoonists. As a consumer of the high life of the Roaring Twenties, a wearer of expensive tweeds and knickers, and owner of a penthouse in the Big Apple, a beach house in Florida, and a farm in Connecticut, **JOHN HELD, JR.**, was a member of the society he caricatured. His obsessions: the fantastic females of his time (and their striking modernity, as expressed in flapper fashions), a fondness for hooch, and the Charleston. Taking the New Woman as a symbol for a restless decade, his derisive pen caricatured and mythologized the Jazz Age as it happened. When Wall Street crashed in 1929, the party was over.

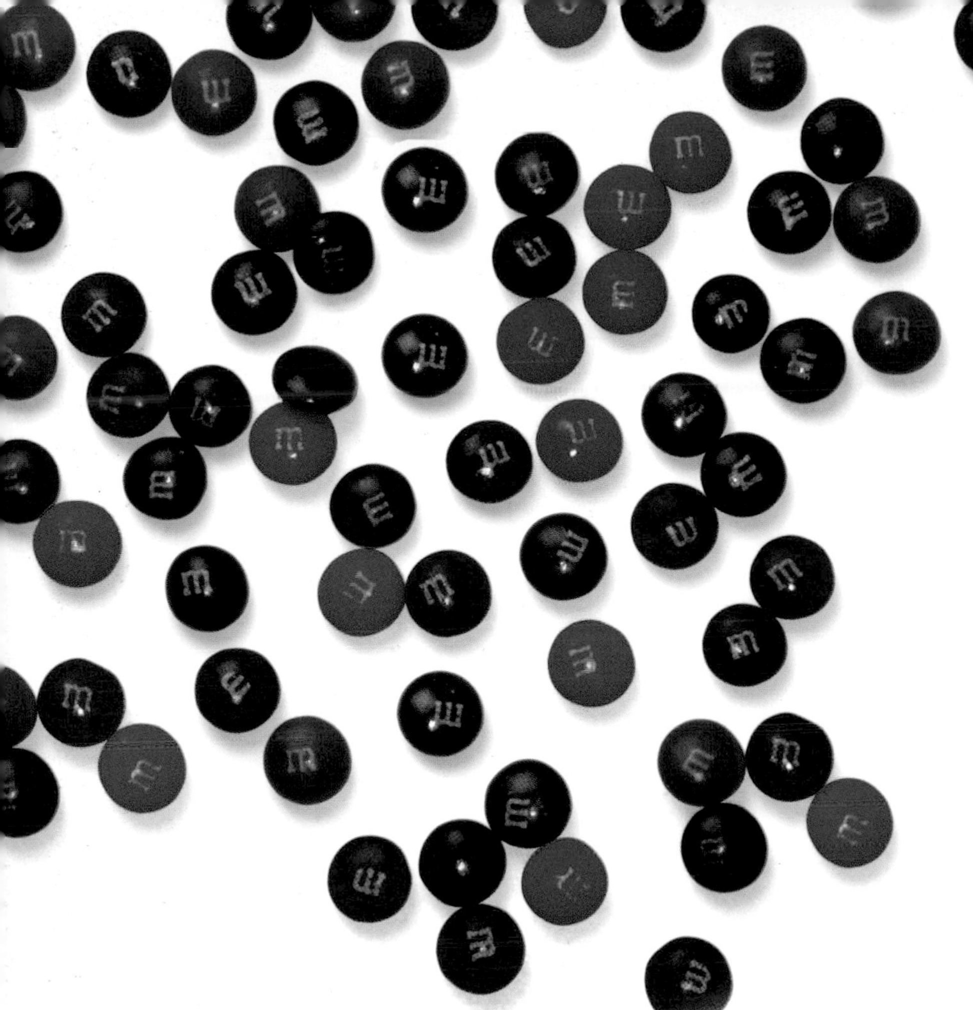

THE MILK CHOCOLATE MELTS IN YOUR MOUTH—NOT IN YOUR HANDS

Watching a flick, multicolored **M&M's** remain the perfect candy. Millions of Americans like to pop one in between mouthfuls of buttered popcorn.

THE STRANGE LOVE AFFAIR OF TRACY & HEPBURN

Reel off the names of the nine movies that starred **SPENCER TRACY** and **KATHARINE HEPBURN** (this movie still is from *Adam's Rib*) and experience one of the strangest, yet romantic, American love affairs:
Woman of the Year,
Keeper of the Flame,
Without Love,
The Sea of Grass,
State of the Union,
Pat and Mike,
Desk Set,
Guess Who's Coming to Dinner.
On film, Spencer Tracy & Katharine Hepburn were great alone, but together they were pure Americana.

AMERICA'S NEW LOVER'S LANE

The advent of the **DRIVE-IN MOVIE** combined the all-American trio of Youth, Freedom, and the Automobile! It began as a gimmick by an auto parts business owner, and spread like wildfire all over America. Watching a movie in the comfort and seclusion of your car (and necking with your date) became the national pastime—it was a magical place where romance, fun, and a sense of community flourished. The phenomenal popularity of the drive-in movie attracted audiences of all ages until the new mega-malls with multiplex cinemas, the rapid growth of multichannel cable television, and rising real estate values, caused its decline in the 1970s. There was nothing more fun than watching the stars under the stars.

THE NOSTALGIC SEXUAL ICON

BETTIE PAGE, the black-banged Queen of Curves, has always been a favorite body type for the American man. In the 1950s, her saucy eye-candy photos in men's magazines like *Wink* rocked America, violating taboos, provoking the wrath of a U.S. Senate committee, and immortalizing her as the consummate sexual icon.

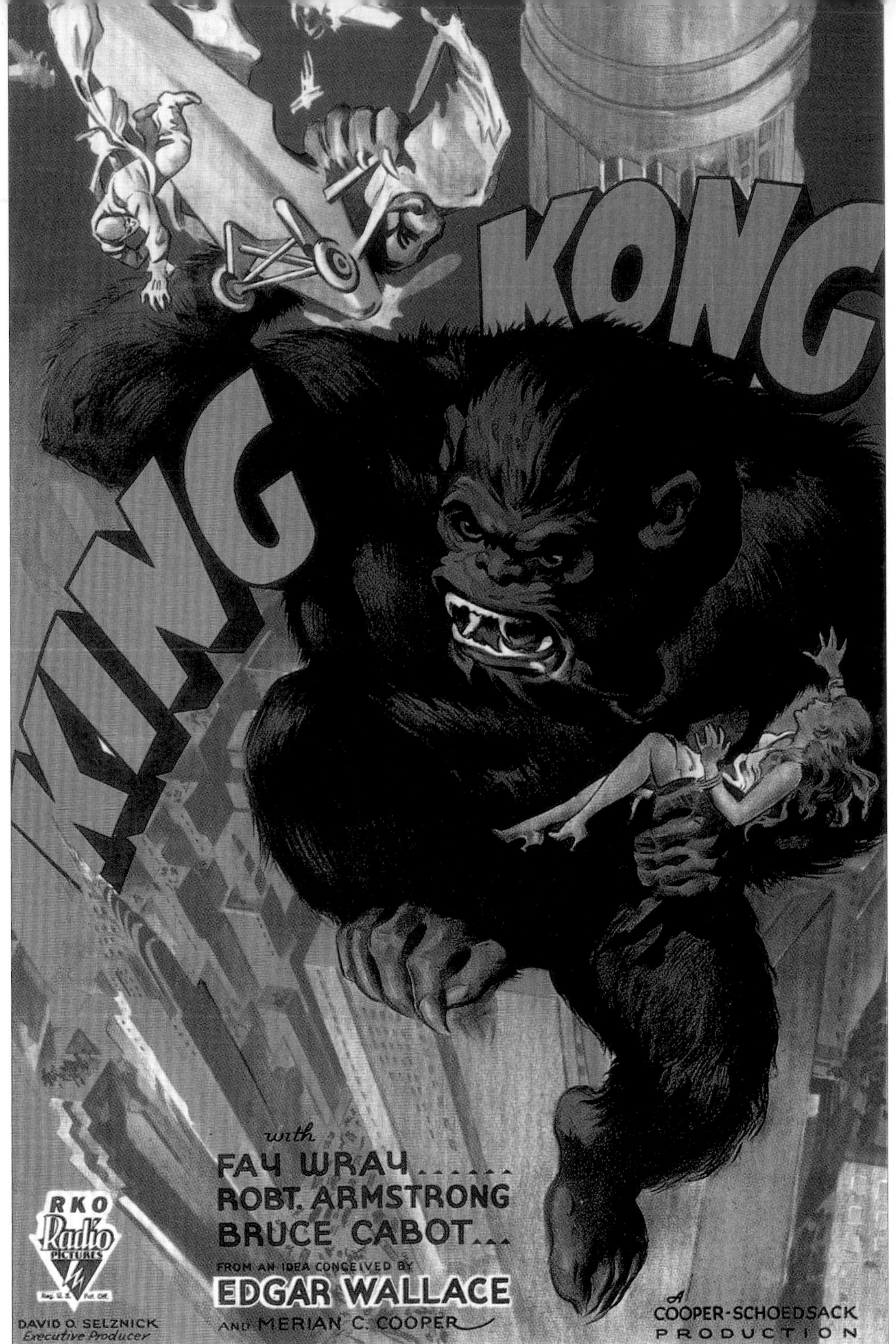

BEAUTY AND THE BEAST

The most famous adventure-fantasy horror film of all time remains **KING KONG**, shot in the midst of the Depression in 1933, starring a beauty and her beast. Fay Wray gets the hots for the big ape, and if they had had their druthers, they would have lived as happily as Tarzan and Jane. Only in America.

July 20, '81

Page 227 RWPI

es for 269 Typed is

hat's supposed to happen He's

turn now He circled

you and you got "

aw he's taking it back

eadily, slowly with Da

the straw

g him

line would take, the

I VANT TO BE ALONE

The camera adored **GRETA GARBO**. The Garbo mystique made leading men John Gilbert, John Barrymore, Frederic March, Robert Taylor, and Clark Gable look like feeble drones worshiping before the Queen Bee. The Great Garbo was one of the few Hollywood stars who ran her own show, picking and choosing her roles. Her most famous line, "I vant to be alone," seemed to be a prediction when she retired at the height of her beauty and power and lived in seclusion. If New Yorkers had sharp eyes, they could spot the iconic Garbo taking long, lonely walks through Manhattan streets, dressed casually and wearing large sunglasses, avoiding prying eyes, the paparazzi, and the world.

MACHO-MAN WRITER

ERNEST HEMINGWAY was *the* all-American journalist, short-story writer, and novelist whose terse, hard-boiled style continues directly to influence American literature. Today, Hemingwayesque writing abounds. Tough, short sentences. Economy and understatement. A brave, romantic macho man in his writing and lifestyle. "Papa" defied death many times as a war journalist, suffered two successive plane crashes on a safari, lived with four wives, and ended his own turbulent life with a shotgun blast to his head. Pick up *A Farewell to Arms*, *The Sun Also Rises*, or *The Old Man and the Sea*, and feel his power.

"MALE CHAUVINIST PIG!"

After taking on feminists Germaine Greer, Kate Millet, Betty Friedan, and Susan Sontag in a retrograde essay entitled *The Prisoner of Sex*, **NORMAN MAILER** debated against an enemies list of feminists at Town Hall in New York. Kate Millet coined the phrase "Male Chauvinist Pig" to describe the pugnacious author—the three most intimidating words one could ever direct at a male chauvinist pig. (Shown is a parody of the rhubarb on a 1971 *Esquire* cover, with Ms. Greer playing Fay Wray in the clutches of King Kong Mailer.)

THE CLEOPATRA AFFAIR

In 1962 *Cleopatra* was a $40 million production–the most expensive movie ever made. During its filming, the affair between **RICHARD BURTON** and the legendary **ELIZABETH TAYLOR** (while hubby **EDDIE FISHER** was growing horns) was a worldwide scandal. There were some hilarious goings-on as the egocentric stars romanced before, during, and after each scene was filmed. The hotter their affair, the better for *Cleopatra*'s box office. The world breathlessly awaited a flamboyant premiere at the Rivoli Theatre in Times Square, where two sign painters touched up Liz's breasts on a giant billboard over the entrance to the baroque movie house. The love affair was the most grotesquely brazen in American history, until 1998, when President Bill Clinton faced impeachment for extracurricular sex in the White House with "that" woman–Monica Lewinsky.

"I'M CHIQUITA BANANA"

The golden age of advertising jingles is long gone, but some keep coming back like a song. One of the most memorable of the golden oldies is the 1944 jingle sung by an animated Miss Chiquita, a Carmen Miranda-look-alike banana, who taught Americans how to ripen and use bananas (preferably the bananas with Chiquita on the label).

I'm Chiquita Banana and I've come to say
Bananas have to ripen in a certain way
When they are fleck'd with brown and have a golden hue
Bananas taste the best and are best for you
You can put them in a salad
You can put them in a pie-aye
Any way you want to eat them
It's impossible to beat them
But, bananas like the climate of the very, very tropical equator
So you should never put bananas in the refrigerator.

The Chiquita jingle is the top banana.

HOW STOUFFER'S GOT FAT ON LEAN CUISINE

Stouffer's had canned the idea of pioneering a frozen gourmet fitness line because it believed a "gourmet" product required expensive ingredients and would eke out low profit margins. But in 1977, when George Lois cooked up the name with the startling promise, **LEAN CUISINE**, the company went whole hog, and its new product became *the* power brand in a revolutionary new food category.

THE WHEELS OF PROGRESS

In 1916 in Memphis, Tennessee, Piggly Wiggly became the very first self-service grocery store. In 1937 Sylvan Goldman, a supermarket owner in Oklahoma City, constructed the first **SHOPPING CART**. As supermarkets grew and grew in America, so did the size of the shopping carts, as store owners found that the larger the vehicle, the more their customers purchased!

ELVIS
LIVES

THE KING OF ROCK 'N' ROLL

was the greatest entertainer of the 20th century and the ultimate icon of American pop culture. **ELVIS PRESLEY** symbolizes the American Dream, rising as he did from humble beginnings to the extreme pinnacle of popular music through charisma with a capital C, unique good looks, raw natural talent, hard work, and oozing sexuality as he shook his Elvis pelvis. Even in the 1950s, an era of blatant racism, Presley publicly spoke of his debt to black performers, pointing to B.B. King, Fats Domino, "Big Boy" Crudup, and Jackie Wilson as influences. His death at 42 shocked the world—but his popularity as a singer of R&B, gospel, country, pop, and rock lives on throughout the world.

In 1946 **LAS VEGAS** was Bugsy Siegel's private territory when the crazy man of the Meyer Lansky crime syndicate built his Flamingo Hotel smack in the middle of the Nevada desert. America thought Bugsy was nuts. Six months later the mobster was bumped off, but his dream of a gambling playland hit the jackpot when the mob took his idea and ran with it, sparking a building boom that started in the 1950s and continues to this day. The list of classic casinos is varied and evocative: The Desert Inn, The Sands, The Dunes, The Riviera, The Tropicana, The Stardust, The Moulin Rouge, The Mirage, The Luxor, The Golden Nugget, Treasure Island, The MGM Grand, and Caesars Palace (to name just a few!). There's no city in the world like it—Vegas is *the* gambling mecca and *the* capital of hedonism (what happens in Vegas stays in Vegas). But Sin City also became an entertainment center, with casino lounges offering showbiz luminaries from dawn to dusk whose names became synonymous with Vegas: Buddy Hackett, Don Rickles, Shecky Greene, Alan King, Liberace, Frank Sinatra (and his Rat Pack pals Dean Martin, Sammy Davis Jr., and Joey Bishop), Shirley MacLaine, and the coup de grâce, the King, Elvis Presley, belting out his knockout rendition of *Viva Las Vegas*.

THE THIRD HANGOUT

STARBUCKS was named after Starbuck, the coffee-loving first mate in Herman Melville's classic American novel, *Moby-Dick*. The long-haired lady in the logo, actually a siren or a two-tailed mermaid, seems to be an enigma, but originally she was a crowned siren, stark naked from the waist up, and a double fishtail below. Today Starbucks is the most recognized coffee brand in America, with an international chain of almost 13,000 stores. The phenomenal success comes in part from its conception of its coffee houses as a third place to hang out, besides home and work. Some characters spend full days there, working their laptop computers to save office rent, sipping lattes, cappuccinos, Frappaccino blended beverages, and nibbling on sandwiches and pastries.

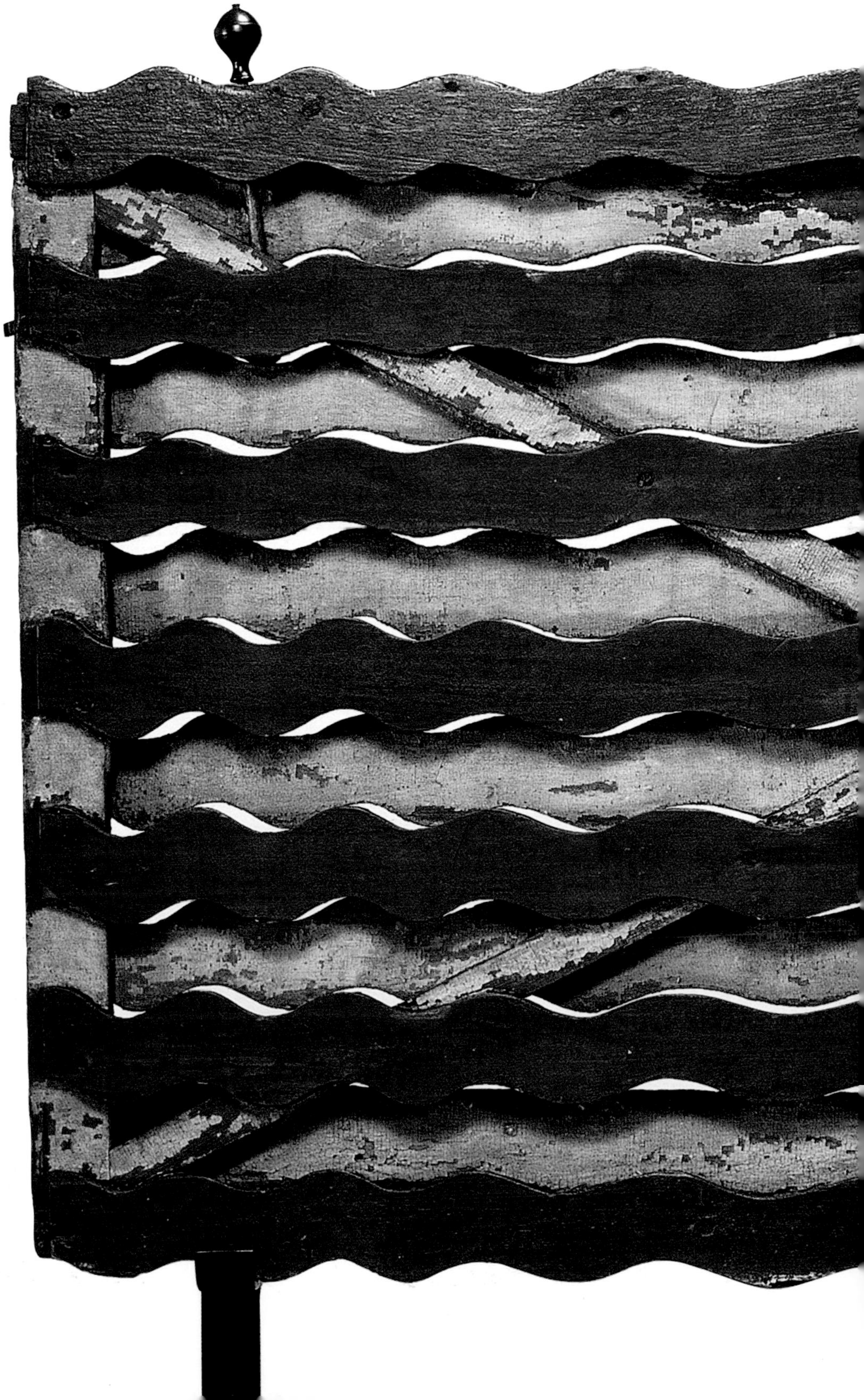

POKE HIS TUMMY AND HE GIGGLES

Poppin' Fresh, aka **THE PILLSBURY DOUGHBOY**, took his soft-sell approach for ready-to-bake dough to TV in 1965. He walked, talked, and bounced right back when a finger poked his tummy, becoming American housewives' In-house chef.

THE AMERICAN GATEWAY

This extraordinary evocation of the American spirit, an **AMERICAN FOLK ART GATE** patterned after a rippling Old Glory, graced the Darling Farm in Jefferson County, New York. The celebration of the centennial of American Independence and the great Centennial Exhibition held at Philadelphia in 1876 heightened the national consciousness of Americans, and inspired an unknown artist to create this grand entranceway into a humble farm. It is considered one of the best known works of 19th-century American folk art.

"GODS DO NOT ANSWER LETTERS"

You're looking at a 1939 photo of rookie **TED WILLIAMS**, who said at the time that he would be "the greatest hitter who ever lived." Mission accomplished. He had a career batting average of .344 and was the last player in Major League Baseball to bat over .400 in a single season. While most professional athletes served in cushy "Special Service" units, Williams fought as a U.S. Marine combat pilot during both World War II (flying a propeller-driven Corsair) and the Korean War (flying a Panther jet), taking five years out of his glorious career. But he never bitched. Ted was on uncomfortable terms with Boston Red Sox fans and Boston media, and stubbornly refused to tip his hat when he circled the bases or to respond to the prolonged cheers of "We want Ted!" After his famous home run in his very last career at bat, Williams characteristically refused to tip his hat one last time. Ted's aloof attitude was defended by author John Updike, who observed, "Gods do not answer letters."

YOU'VE GOT MAIL!

In 1902 the U.S. Postal Service began providing free delivery to the backwoods of America—finally uniting city and country in the U.S. Before 1915, country folk used homemade receptacles (usually leaky) for their precious mail. Then Roy Joroleman designed **THE RURAL MAILBOX** for the Postal Service Department. Today, the mailbox's familiar tunnel shape is recognized by everyone, as intrinsic and homey a part of rural America as corn growing in the fields and cows grazing in the pasture.

WHEN COTTON WAS KING

By the mid-19th century, cotton had become the backbone of the economy of the American South. Cultivating and picking cotton became the leading occupation of slaves who had been torn from their homes in Africa. Cotton plantations required vast labor forces to handpick their crops. As the world flocked to buy our superior brand of cotton, the need for cheap labor encouraged the snowballing slave trade, directly leading to the American Civil War, a horrific yet glorious war fought to end slavery in America.

THE HUMBLE RAGGEDY ANN DOLL

Raggedy Ann-type dolls have been a favorite playmate of little girls since the 18th century (this one was made by hand, circa 1900). Before this populist child's companion could be store-bought, moms and grandmas sewed homespun versions of the floppy doll for the young girls of the family. Many have passed down from generation to generation and are cherished as a symbol and remembrance of a happy American childhood.

WHEN IT RAINS IT POURS

Since 1914 the **MORTON SALT** Umbrella Girl has been walking in the rain, accidentally pouring salt, charmingly driving home the point that Morton salt flowed freely in damp weather. She remains an enduring icon on Morton packaging.

THE UNFOLDING FANTASY OF THE PLAYBOY CENTERFOLD

More than Botticelli's *Venus*, Rubens's flesh goddesses, Manet's picnicking nude, more than even the immortal Betty Grable and Rita Hayworth World War II pinups, the American dream girl has been the **PLAYBOY PLAYMATE OF THE MONTH**, displayed on a three-page foldout poster long enough to fit the latest long-stemmed American beauty. Starting in 1954, the women in the foldouts in America's first classy "girlie" magazine have been the ideal of the wide-eyed young men of America. Centerfolds were plastered all over locker rooms, garages, teenagers' rooms, and many male-oriented workplaces. Since the feminist revolution in the U.S., posting a centerfold in the workplace may be viewed as a form of sexual harassment. But Hugh Hefner's parade of centerfolds continues in the naughty pages of *Playboy*. (Shown is the January 1971 Playmate, the pioneering Liv Lindeland, who demurely displays her pubic hair—a *Playboy* milestone. Basically shunned in the history of Western art as being either "unaesthetic" or "improper," this "first" in *Playboy* centerfolds may be regarded as an iconic moment. You be the judge.)

MISS JANUARY
PLAYBOY'S PLAYMATE OF THE MONTH

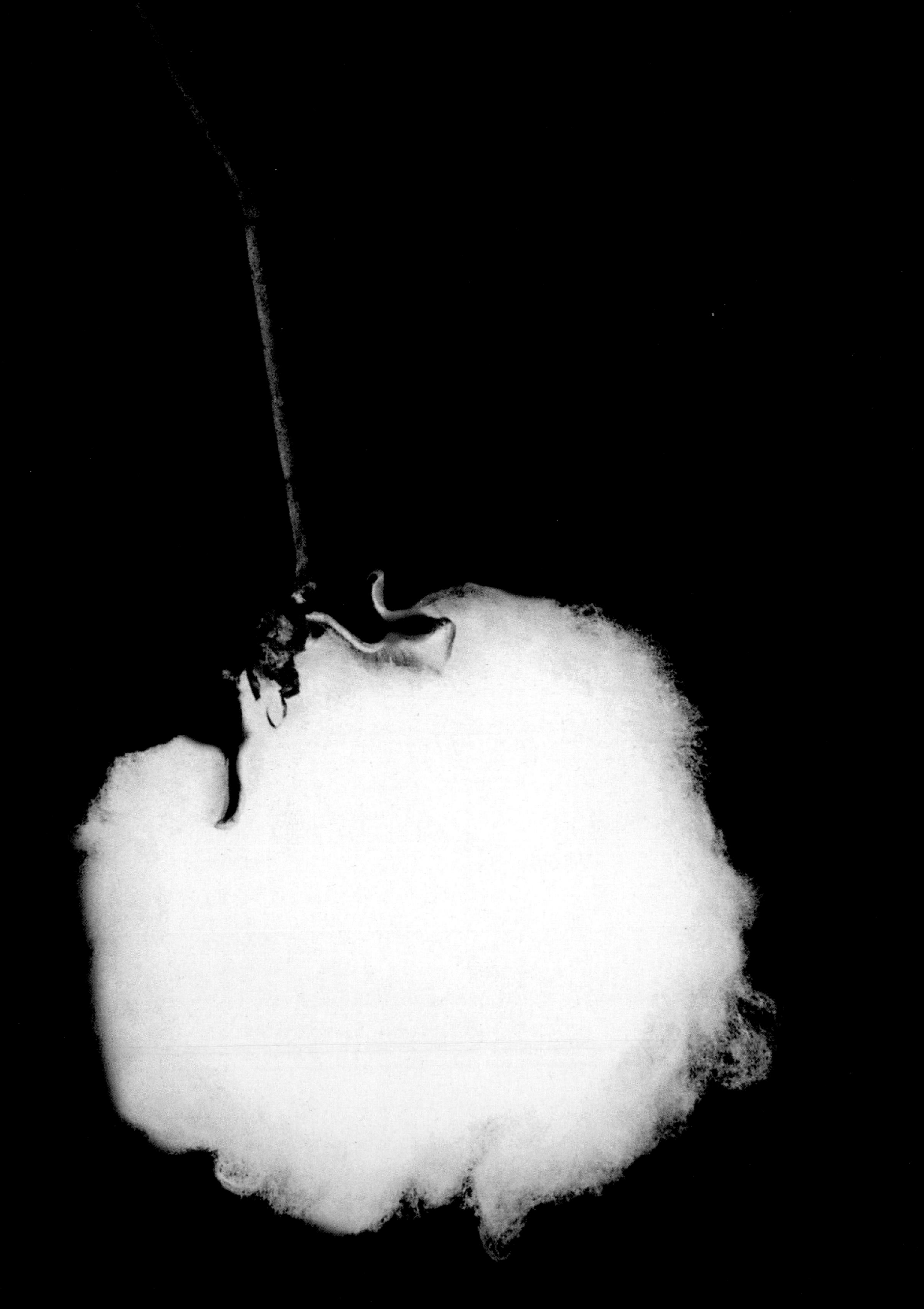

THE HOLY TRIO OF AMERICAN SPORTS

The tactile, hands-on shapes of the
BASKETBALL, **FOOTBALL**, and **BASEBALL**–
as different from one another as the
superbly functional shapes of each projectile–
are aerodynamically designed
for a specific grip:
Shoot a basketball with backspin,
throw a football in a perfect spiral,
creatively pitch a baseball.
Swish! Touchdown! Strike Three-e-e!

GUITAR ON FIRE

Even as a young man playing backup for the likes of James Brown, Little Richard, and Ike and Tina Turner, **JIMI HENDRIX** stood out. (And not just because he played his guitar left-handed.) He won over American music fans with a hot performance at the Monterey International Pop Music Festival in June 1967, which ended with Jimi lighting his guitar on fire–propelling him to superstardom. He had an incomparable musical talent and a flashy persona to match; whatever he wore, from band jackets to flowing scarfs, he was high-gloss cool. His electrified interpretation of *The Star Spangled Banner* at Woodstock was a seminal moment in rock. In his all-too-brief four-year reign, Hendrix expanded the vocabulary of the electric guitar more than anyone before or since. When drugs claimed him at 27 in 1970, the rock world lost the man that many have called the greatest musician in history.

YEE-HAAAA!

In 1867, when ranch hands started driving Longhorns to the railhead in Abilene, Kansas, the legendary lifestyle of the cowboy, and **THE COWBOY BOOT**, were born. In the 1930s, cowboy boots rose to a fashion status item, inspired by the film imagery of the cowboy hero–from Tom Mix to John Wayne. Then cowboy crooners such as Gene Autry and Roy Rogers, and the Nashville country music scene, added to the mass appeal that put cowboy boots on the feet of Americans of all ages, in all professions, all over America. Today classic American cowboy boots are going great guns, from Rodeo Drive to Madison Avenue, selling to strutting men and stylish women.

THE END OF THE CUTTHROAT RAZOR

In 1904 King Gillette, a traveling salesman, working with inventor William Emery Nickerson, received a patent for a **DOUBLE-EDGED SAFETY RAZOR BLADE**, which fit nicely into a specially designed holder with a handle and adjustable head. By giving customers an alternative to the traditional, and very dangerous, straight razor (still in use in barbershops) Gillette revolutionized the shaving industry, and the Gillette Company still dominates the market. Above all, Gillette's revolutionary blades were the first product designed to be thrown away (and bought again and again).

No. 775,134. PATENTED NOV. 15, 1904.
K. C. GILLETTE.
RAZOR.
APPLICATION FILED DEC. 3, 1901.
NO MODEL.

WHY CAN'T A WOMAN BE MORE LIKE A MAN?

This cheeky *Esquire* cover from early 1965 was pre-Steinem, pre-Abzug, pre-Friedan, before the hoopla about **THE FEMINIST MOVEMENT** had caught the public's eye. This spoof of a woman caught in a manly act as the budding feminist movement was about to ignite mainstream political thought in America brought smiles to the faces of (some) American women. A year later, the National Organization for Women (NOW) became the driving political power that ultimately effected changes for women in the U.S. in a few short decades: The right to initiate divorce proceedings, the right to choose whether to continue or terminate a pregnancy, and the right to receive equal pay for equal work.

A GENDER-BENDER ICON

To avoid being rubbed out after they witness the St. Valentine's Day Massacre, two musicians flee Chicago disguised as women in an all-girl orchestra on its way to a gig in Florida. Billy Wilder's **SOME LIKE IT HOT** is undoubtedly the hottest film comedy ever produced—one of the greatest treasures in the history of the movies—a film that's loaded with sex but pretends it's about crime and greed. The band's red-hot singer, Marilyn Monroe, wants only to marry a millionaire, and lipstick and eye-makeup-adorned **TONY CURTIS** wants only sex, and they end up wanting only each other. The other female impersonator, the tart **JACK LEMMON**, captivates a moneybags played by Joe E. Brown, and—while Jack's still in drag—they drive off into the sunset.

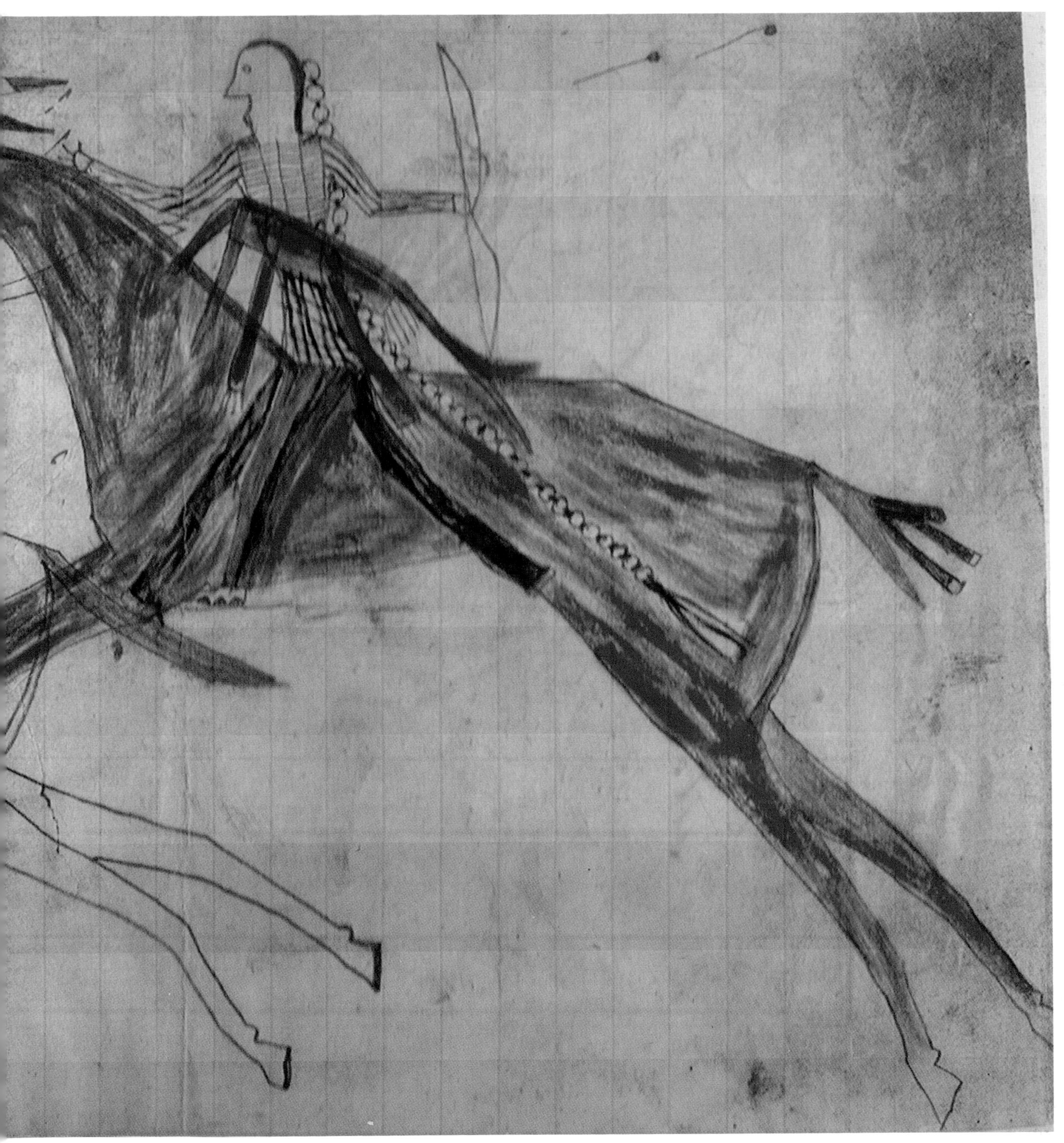

THE EXPLOITS OF THE GREAT PLAINS INDIANS ON THE WHITE MAN'S PAPER

A profound sense of history compelled Indians of the Great Plains in the late 19th century to chronicle the lives, struggles, and conquests of their people pictorially. They made startling drawings with colored pencils on the used ledger pages of the white settlers. This dramatic **PLAINS INDIAN DRAWING** depicts a Cheyenne warrior in pursuit of a U.S. Cavalryman firing a third shot from his revolver. When the tribe gathered to discuss noteworthy events of the recent or more distant past, these visual histories were passed amongst their people, and were soiled by repeated handling.

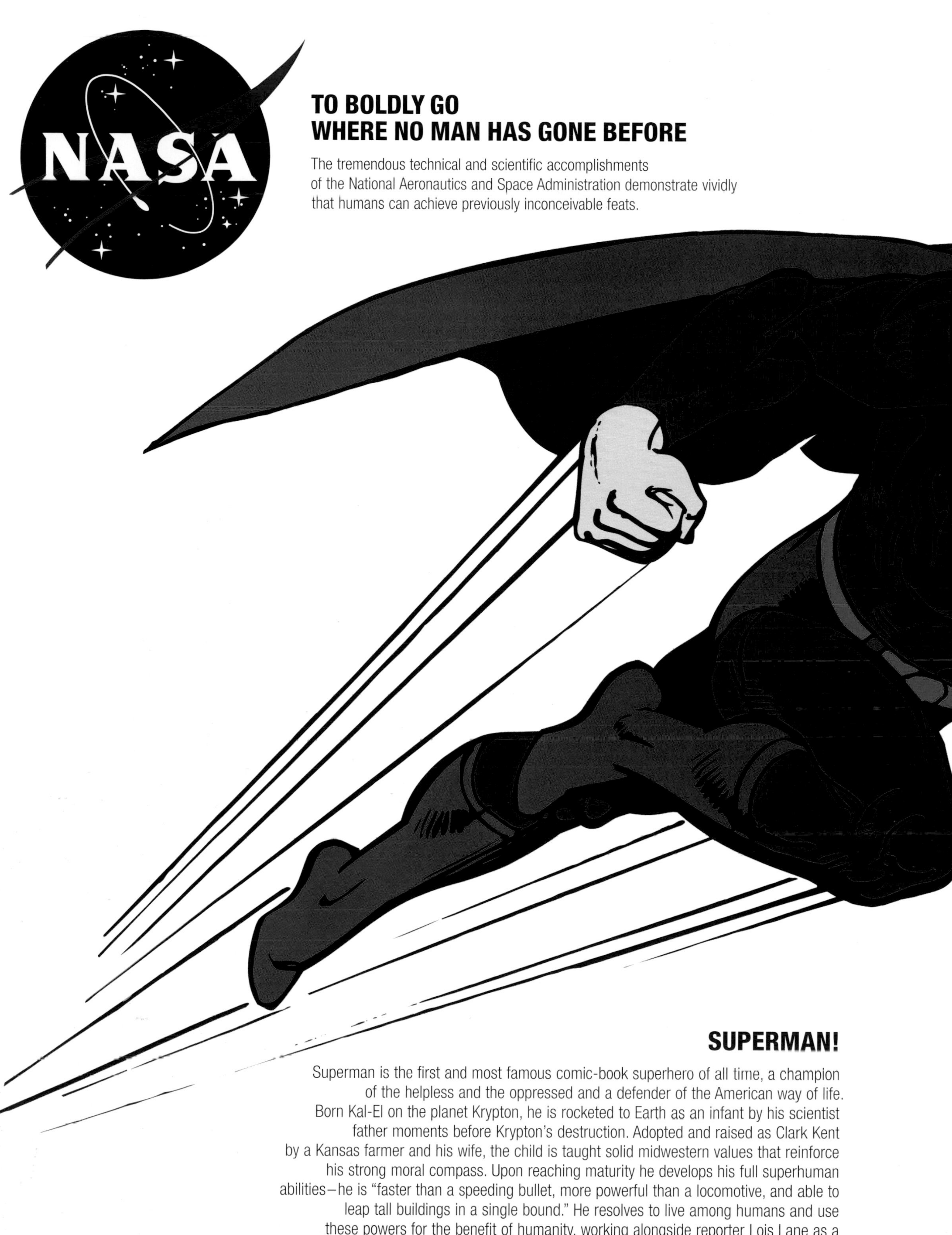

TO BOLDLY GO WHERE NO MAN HAS GONE BEFORE

The tremendous technical and scientific accomplishments of the National Aeronautics and Space Administration demonstrate vividly that humans can achieve previously inconceivable feats.

SUPERMAN!

Superman is the first and most famous comic-book superhero of all time, a champion of the helpless and the oppressed and a defender of the American way of life. Born Kal-El on the planet Krypton, he is rocketed to Earth as an infant by his scientist father moments before Krypton's destruction. Adopted and raised as Clark Kent by a Kansas farmer and his wife, the child is taught solid midwestern values that reinforce his strong moral compass. Upon reaching maturity he develops his full superhuman abilities—he is "faster than a speeding bullet, more powerful than a locomotive, and able to leap tall buildings in a single bound." He resolves to live among humans and use these powers for the benefit of humanity, working alongside reporter Lois Lane as a mild-mannered reporter for the Metropolis newspaper *The Daily Planet*. An awkward love triangle develops: Clark has a crush on Lois, but Lois is hot for Superman. (If anything you just read is news to you, you must just have come to Earth from another planet.)

SUPERSTAR!

Madonna Louise Ciccone, an Italian-American better known as the iconic pop singer **MADONNA**, is the most successful female recording artist of all time. Her iconoclastic music videos, elaborately mounted stage performances, and use of political, sexual, and religious themes and imagery in her work has made her the Queen of Pop throughout the world. Who can ever forget (or forgive) her performance of *Like a Virgin* at the first MTV Music Video Awards show in 1984, when she writhed on the stage on top of a wedding cake wearing a wedding gown, lacy stockings, garters, and her trademark Boy Toy belt.

THE WILD ONE

MARLON BRANDO was the most influential stage and film actor of the 20th century. Armed with the techniques of the Stanislavski Method of acting, the first six films of Brando's career featured performances of monumental proportions, raising the bar not just for other actors but for Brando himself. In *The Men* (1950) he played a bitter crippled vet; in *A Street Car Named Desire* (1951) he reprised his acclaimed stage role as Stanley Kowalski; in *Viva Zapata!* (1952) he played the Mexican revolutionary Emiliano Zapata; in *Julius Caesar* (1953) he was Marc Antony; in *The Wild One* (1953) he played the leader of a motorcycle gang; and in *On the Waterfront* (1954) he was an ex-prize fighter turned longshoreman. Brando became a hero for the younger generation for his role of motorcycle rebel Johnny Strabler in *The Wild One*, creating his unique rebel image for the rock 'n' roll era, directly inspiring Elvis Presley and James Dean. He seemed to have lost much of his energy and direction by the end of the 1950s–but his performance as Don Vito Corleone in *The Godfather* (1972) electrified the world, followed by another classic role as the tortured Colonel Kurtz in *Apocalypse Now* (1979), a metaphor for the insanity of the war in Vietnam. Marlon Brando forever changed the art of acting.

OUR BELOVED BUMS WERE HEADED WEST

In 1955 New York baseball fans were traumatized by rumors that **BROOKLYN DODGERS** owner Walter O'Malley would move the franchise to La-La Land. There wasn't one Dodger player who wished to leave the borough where dreams came true, where the team finally defeated the vaunted New York Yankees in the 1955 World Series. "Dem Bums" had broken the color barrier in 1947 when the previous Brooklyn owner, the heroic Branch Rickey, put the pioneering Jackie Robinson on the lush green grass of Ebbets Field, the most charming ballpark in Major League Baseball. But alas, the treacherous O'Malley did indeed take flight, with "Jackie, Pee Wee, Campy and The Duke." More than a half century later, the memory of Brooklyn's loss of their Beloved Bums still hoits.

225 PORTRAITS OF AMERICA

WALKER EVANS photographed, and made heroic, the American landscape. His oeuvre includes every aspect of proletarian life, forever recording the simple aspects of everyday American culture. This 1936 portrait of a Savannah, Georgia, storefront displaying 225 penny-pictures is a defining image of the art of Walker Evans.

MELTS IN YOUR MOUTH, NOT IN THE STOVE

In the early 1930s, a smart cookie invented **THE CHOCOLATE CHIP COOKIE**, by accident. Ruth Graves Wakefield and her hubby owned a tourist lodge named The Toll House Inn, where she gained a reputation for her home-cooked meals and swell desserts. One of her favorite recipes was for Butter Drop Do cookies. The recipe called for baker's chocolate. One day she ran out of it and substituted a Nestlé semi-sweet chocolate bar she had cut up into small pieces. But unlike the baker's chocolate, the small pieces softened but did not melt completely. Toll House cookies were born! Ruth struck a deal with Nestlé: she allowed her recipe to be used on Nestlé packages and was given a lifetime supply of Nestlé chocolate. Chocolate chip cookies soon became, and remain, the favorite cookie in America, and that's the truth, Ruth.

WHO SAYS A SCHLOCKY PAPER CUP CAN'T BE A DESIGN ICON?

Nothing says "New York" more than a cup of deli coffee served in a blue-and-white paper cup, one of the warmest and most comforting symbols of the city. Because of its use on TV shows such as *NYPD Blue* and *Law & Order*, even non-New Yorkers know that **THE ANTHORA** (a misspelling of *amphora*) is the authentic way to drink java on the streets of Manhattan.

STUDIO

LUCKY LINDY!

CHARLES LINDBERGH took off from New York in 1927 in his silver monoplane, the *Spirit of St. Louis*, and flew, solo, into history. The 25-year-old airmail pilot flew nonstop to Paris and took on the quality of myth. His first unassuming words when he climbed out of his cramped cockpit were, "Are there any mechanics here?" Overwhelming overnight celebrity followed him home from Paris, and as the century's first hero, Lindy unwittingly ushered in the age of mass-media celebrity.

LADY LINDY!

AMELIA EARHART, the first woman to fly the Atlantic solo, vanished in the Pacific during an attempted around-the-world flight. Her mysterious disappearance contributed to her legendary status. In a letter to her husband, George Putnam, she wrote: "Please know I am quite aware of the hazards. I want to do it because I want to do it. Women must try to do things as men have tried. When they fail, their failure must be but a challenge to others." Amelia Earhart was an early feminist whose life and achievements have provided inspiration to generations of young women.

HIS MASTER'S VOICE

This was the most famous logo in the world before Coca-Cola came along. This painting of **NIPPER**, doggedly listening to "his master's voice," was acquired in 1901 by the Victor Talking-Machine Company (which later became RCA Victor). The painting was a sort of mourning piece in memory of the brother of the artist, who depicted his brother's dog (Nipper) listening rapturously to the faithfully perfect sound of his departed brother's voice.

AN UDDERLY PERFECT LOGO: ELSIE THE COW

BORDEN created Elsie as their spokes-cow in 1936 when she starred in ads directed to doctors in medical journals extolling the purity of Borden Brand Condensed milk. (Her hubby is Elmer the Bull, in a prolific and happy union.) The fresh-as-a-daisy Elsie logo remains the imagery of Borden Brand milk (and numerous packaged cheeses and other Borden Brand products—but that's an udder story).

THE PIONEER OF RECORDED MUSIC

ENRICO CARUSO was as much an American as an Italian. When America discovered him, he discovered America, and he remained in New York until his untimely death in 1921 at the age of 48. (He was once arrested for pinching a lady's fanny, Italian style, in Central Park.) The Great Caruso was the most popular singer of any genre in the first 20 years of the 20th century. The Great Tenor pioneered recorded music with the Victor Talking-Machine Company, and they did much to promote each other throughout the world. His 1902 recording of *Pagliacci* was the first record to sell a million copies. His devoted fans may have imagined that Nipper was listening intently to the voice of the Great Caruso singing *Pagliacci.*

"IT'LL KNOCK BOTH YOUR EYES OUT!"

The Golden Era of **3-D MOVIES** began in 1952, with a film called *Bwana Devil.* (This photo by *Life* photographer J. R. Eyerman documented the rapt attention paid by a zombie-like Hollywood audience.) Following its success, a swarm of 3-D films giving the illusion of astonishing depth were produced. The process was a natural for out-of-this-world subjects: *It Came from Outer Space*, *Robot Monsters*, and *Creature from the Black Lagoon*, and horror films typecasting Vincent Price as the King of 3-D, and then movies like *The French Line*, starring the voluptuous Jane Russell in revealing costumes. The tag line for her 3-D film was "It'll knock *both* your eyes out!" But as fast as 3-D came, it went. In the mid-1950s, wide-screen formats knocked 3-D into the second dimension. But starting in the 1980s, IMAX introduced a new golden age with films such as *Ghosts of the Abyss* and *Aliens of the Deep*, played on giant screens that envelop the audience. There are ongoing attempts to invent a system that does not require the wearing of glasses, but watching a 3-D movie without them just wouldn't be as much fun.

THE LOLITA TABOO

The 1962 Stanley Kubrick film *Lolita* starred James Mason as a divorced British professor of French literature who travels to small-town America for a teaching position and pursues the underage **LOLITA**, played by 14-year-old Sue Lyon. Mason's charactor goes so far as to marry Lolita's loud, overbearing, status-seeking mother, so as to remain close to her daughter. Sue Lyon was banned from the gala premiere because of the film's "adults only" rating. This famous photo by **BERT STERN** of Lolita wearing Valentine glasses is not an image that appears in the movie, but it has become the classic image of a precocious teenage nymphet. In popular American culture the name "Lolita" has become a code word for an underage sex symbol.

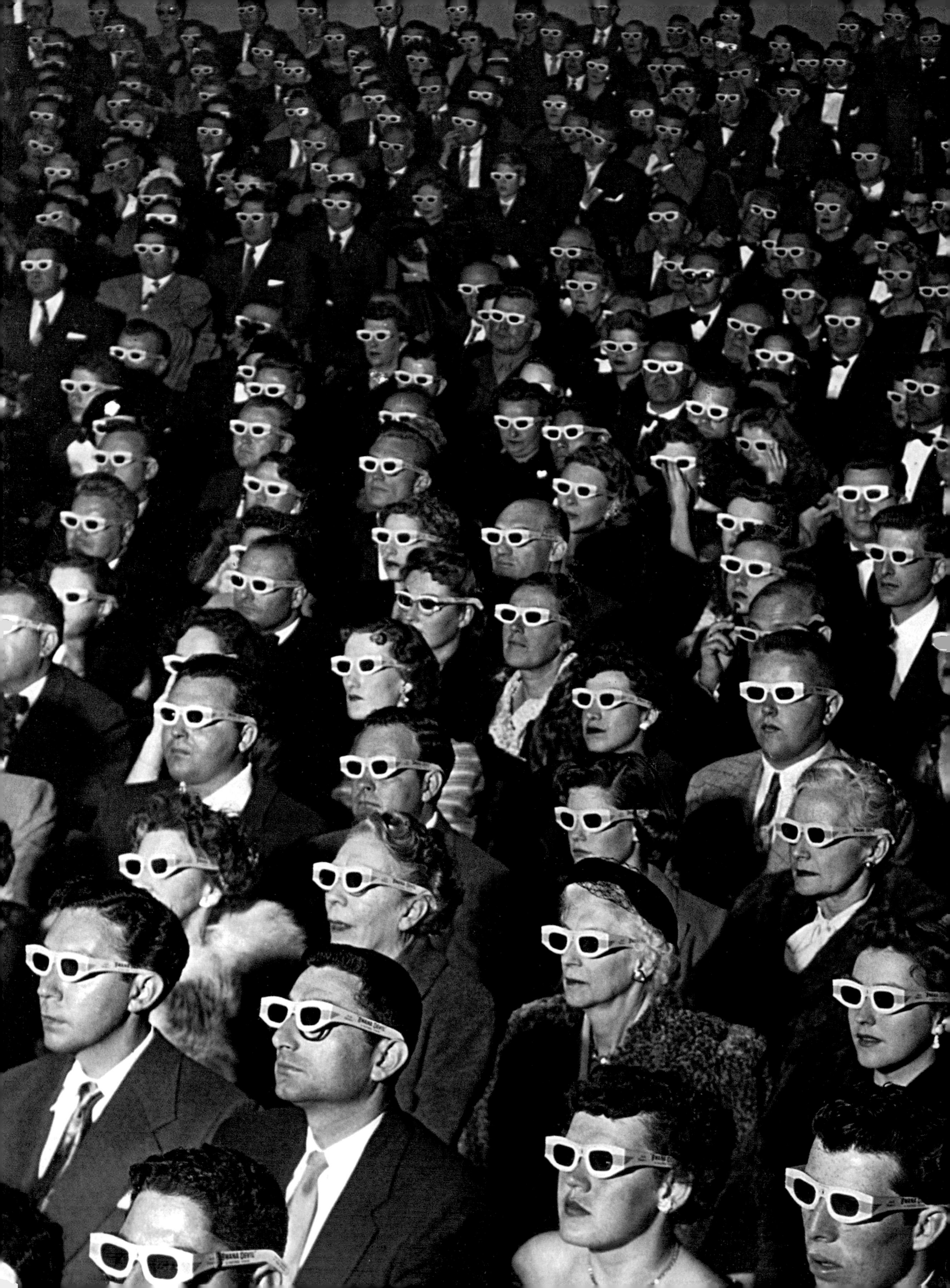

HATS OFF TO THE AMERICAN COWBOY (WHO EVEN WEARS HIS HAT WHEN HE SLEEPS)

Men spent days on horseback herding cattle, huddled in the saddle under a broiling sun, shivering in the midst of a driving blizzard, breaking broncs, fighting Indians and cattle rustlers—and all the time wearing the ubiquitous symbol of the American Cowboy, **THE COWBOY HAT** (from derbies to Stetsons to sombreros). They wore them outdoors and indoors—even in bed. These legendary cowpunchers on the Western frontier during the 19th century, were immortalized in some of the greatest films ever made.

THE LOST ICON

"Until the first blow fell," *The New York Times* wrote on October 30,1963, "no one was convinced that **PENN STATION** really would be demolished or that New York would permit this monumental act of vandalism... Any city gets what it admires, will pay for, and, ultimately, deserves...We will probably be judged not by the monuments we build but by those we have destroyed." When Penn Station was completed in 1910, behind its breathtaking Roman facade was the genuine majesty of its steel-ribbed, open, cathedral-like spaces and shafts of golden light. The great train concourse was covered with acres of glass in domes, arches, and vaults; it was an urban undertaking without precedent, exceeding the grandeur of any public edifice in history. This was the noble space the world saw when arriving by train to the greatest city in the world. The glorious structure was the heart of New York for half a century, destroyed by the real estate logic that dictates the demolition of the very essence that makes an area desirable. Civic-minded committees fought the good fight to save Penn Station but were rebuffed when the president of the Pennsylvania Railroad Company crassly said, "Does it make any sense to preserve a building merely as a monument?" The demolition of the McKim, Mead & White masterpiece left an indelible blot on the reputation of the railroad and the men who ran it.

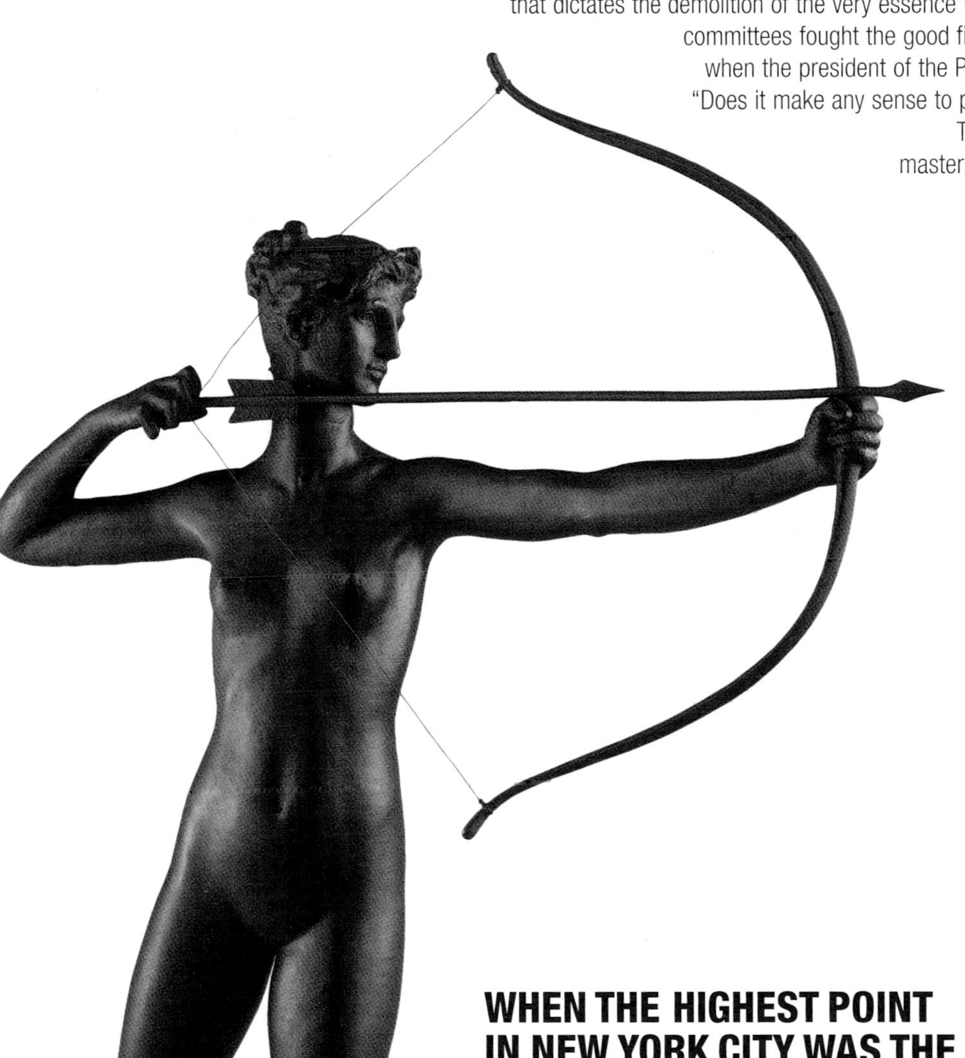

WHEN THE HIGHEST POINT IN NEW YORK CITY WAS THE GOLDEN DIANA

The great sculptor Augustus Saint-Gaudens transformed allegorical, neoclassical figures into images of heroic realism. In 1893, when his 13-foot-high gilded copper weathervane of **THE HUNTRESS DIANA** was installed at the apex of the original Madison Square Tower at Madison Square, she was the tallest point in New York City. Sixty-six incandescent lamps and ten arc spotlights illuminated the radiant figure at night, providing the most dynamic nocturnal vision in America. In 1925, when the first Madison Square Garden was torn down, the sculpture was given to the Philadelphia Museum of Art. Shown is a gilded-bronze reduction (1928) that grandly resides at New York's Metropolitan Museum of Art, a remembrance of the original Madison Square Garden, guarded by the lovely Diana.

THE DISCOVERY OF SPACE

The **BUCK ROGERS 25TH CENTURY ROCKET PISTOL, MODEL XZ-35** was the first, and most beautiful, toy ray-gun ever produced (1935), an exuberant Art Deco fantasy powered, with pure imagination, by America's almost unlimited capacity to wonder. The weapon that rocketed the Buck Rogers craze that swept America was intended to protect us from our deepest fears of the dark unknown, reminding us of our vulnerability in the face of an endless and mysterious cosmos. Anthony "Buck" Rogers was born in August 1928 in the pulp magazine *Amazing Stories*, an Air Force officer who lapses into a coma and awakens in the 25th century, where he finds America in ruins and the world dominated by Mongolians from inland China. Discovering the marvels of this future world, including antigravity belts, spaceships, and the Rocket Pistol, Buck sets out to free the world and battle evil and injustice. His exploits were chronicled in a syndicated comic strip, radio serial, movies, and later, a television series. In 1935 more than 2,000 people stood in line outside of Macy's to buy the Rocket Pistol. The craze extended to every toy store in America, and millions were sold. The American space hero became the greatest pop culture hero of all time. Followed by Flash Gordon, they transformed space into a popular and well-known adventure setting, teaching us what we know about space, until the advent of the space race with the Soviet Union in the 1950s and 1960s.

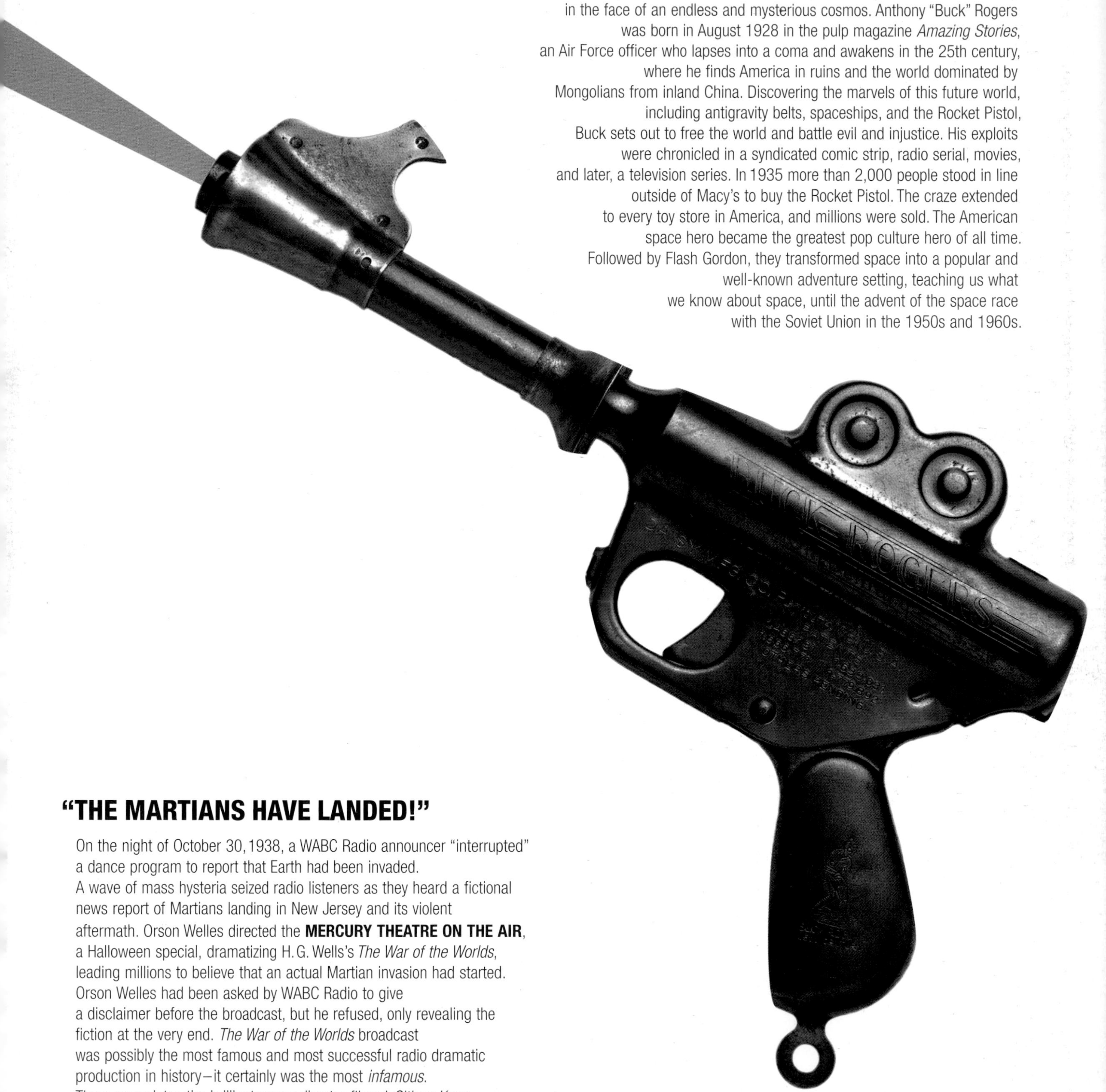

"THE MARTIANS HAVE LANDED!"

On the night of October 30, 1938, a WABC Radio announcer "interrupted" a dance program to report that Earth had been invaded. A wave of mass hysteria seized radio listeners as they heard a fictional news report of Martians landing in New Jersey and its violent aftermath. Orson Welles directed the **MERCURY THEATRE ON THE AIR**, a Halloween special, dramatizing H. G. Wells's *The War of the Worlds*, leading millions to believe that an actual Martian invasion had started. Orson Welles had been asked by WABC Radio to give a disclaimer before the broadcast, but he refused, only revealing the fiction at the very end. *The War of the Worlds* broadcast was possibly the most famous and most successful radio dramatic production in history–it certainly was the most *infamous*. Three years later, the brilliant young director filmed *Citizen Kane*, the greatest motion picture of all time.

The brute appeal of the world-famous

LOUISVILLE SLUGGER–

from the knob to steady the grip to the tapered handle swelling to display the branded label and growing into the "sweet spot" on the potent barrelhead– is one of the most splendidly tailored tools in all of sports! Today there are additional bat brands, but the name Louisville Slugger remains synonymous with baseball.

The magical world of

BROADWAY MUSICALS:

Bye Bye Birdie, *42nd Street*, *A Chorus Line*, *West Side Story*, *Chicago*, *The Producers*, *Anything Goes*...

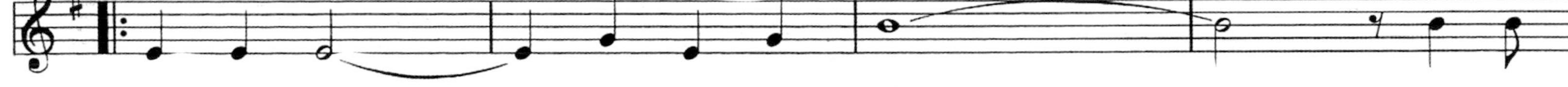

Come and meet those danc - ing feet, on the

GENUINE K55

av-e-nue I'm tak-ing you to, For-ty Sec-ond street.

Sitting Bull

"THE SLAYER OF CUSTER"

SITTING BULL led an estimated 2,500 Sioux and Cheyenne warriors against the 7th United States Cavalry under General George Armstrong Custer at the Battle of Little Bighorn on June 25, 1876. Custer's Last Stand was the worst defeat ever suffered by the U.S. Army at the hands of the Indians. Custer had led 220 men to their deaths. The nation was shocked, and the government vowed vengeance. "All my warriors were brave and knew no fear," Sitting Bull said later. "The soldiers who were killed were brave men too...but we did not go out of our country to kill them. They came to kill us and got killed themselves." With the might of the U.S. Cavalry seeking revenge, Sitting Bull led his tribe into Canada, and with the Army on his heels he finally surrendered. His status as a symbol in the white world earned him amnesty for a time, but he was gunned down a few years later. The last major battle of the Indian Wars (now known as the Wounded Knee Massacre) took place two weeks after the killing of Sitting Bull. The Indians had lost the West, but the spirit of the great Sitting Bull and his people will be remembered forever.

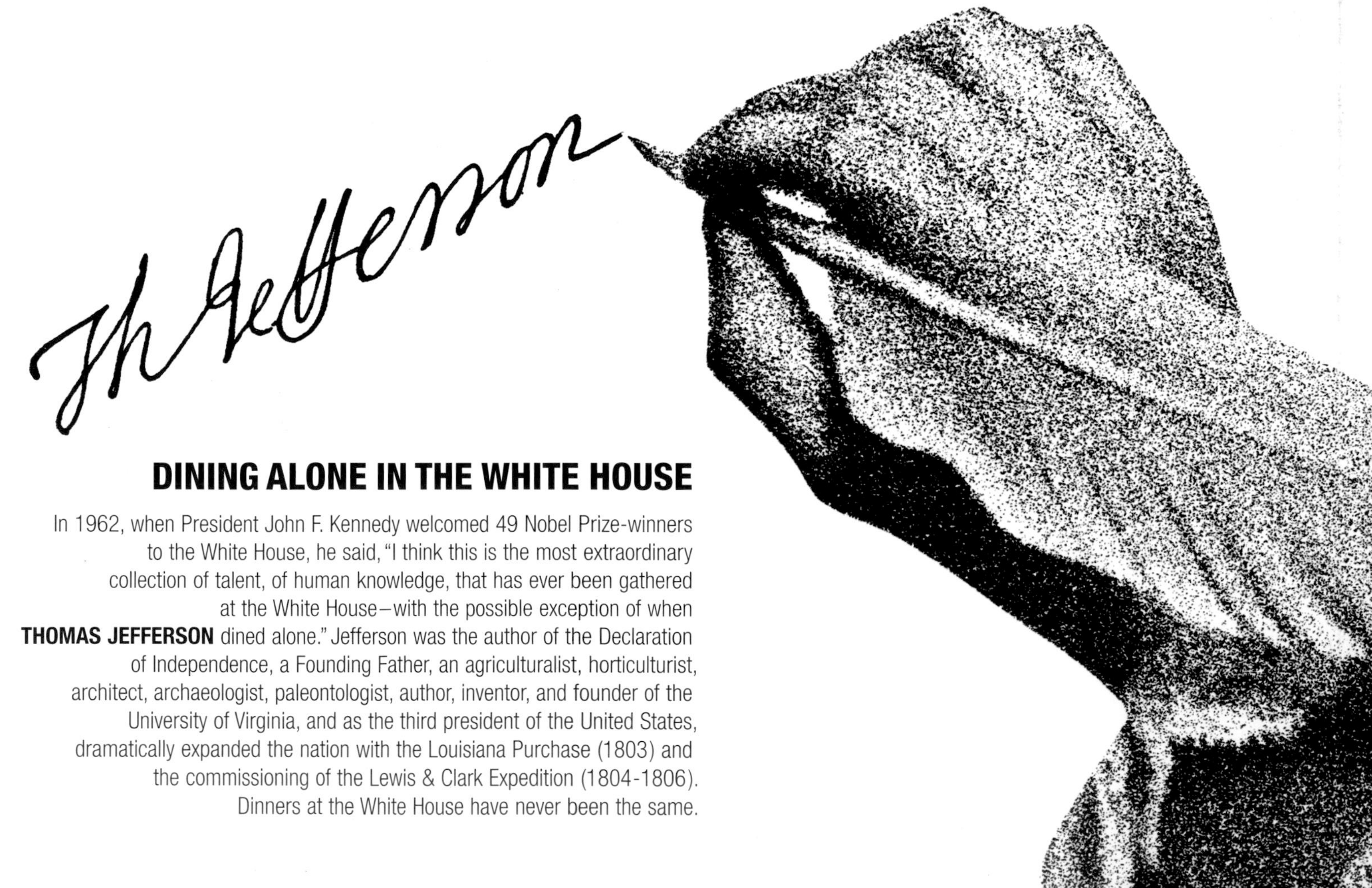

DINING ALONE IN THE WHITE HOUSE

In 1962, when President John F. Kennedy welcomed 49 Nobel Prize-winners to the White House, he said, "I think this is the most extraordinary collection of talent, of human knowledge, that has ever been gathered at the White House—with the possible exception of when **THOMAS JEFFERSON** dined alone." Jefferson was the author of the Declaration of Independence, a Founding Father, an agriculturalist, horticulturist, architect, archaeologist, paleontologist, author, inventor, and founder of the University of Virginia, and as the third president of the United States, dramatically expanded the nation with the Louisiana Purchase (1803) and the commissioning of the Lewis & Clark Expedition (1804-1806). Dinners at the White House have never been the same.

MAKING THE WORLD SAFE FOR DEMOCRACY

FRANKLIN DELANO ROOSEVELT lifted the U.S. out of economic despair and revolutionized the American way of life. Then he helped make the world safe for democracy, in the war against the Axis powers. Historian Arthur Schlesinger, Jr. profoundly observed that FDR was our best loved and most-hated president.

Loved because, though patrician by birth, he believed in and fought for plain people—for the "third of the nation, ill-housed, ill-clad, ill-nourished." But he was hated because he called for changes that reduced the power of those who profited from the old order, those who denounced him as "that traitor to his class." Historians like Schlesinger and political scientists are unanimous in placing FDR with Washington and Lincoln as one of our three greatest presidents.

THE FIRST VICTORY IN THE MAKING OF A DEMOCRACY

WASHINGTON CROSSING THE DELAWARE, Emanuel Gottlieb Leutze's gigantic, melodramatic canvas, is an image indelibly etched in the psyche of the American people. It was a desperate time for George Washington and his ragtag Continental Army. They were defeated, demoralized, and uncertain of the future. General Washington desperately needed a victory. During the bitter, freezing night of December 25, 1776, battered by raging winds, snow, sleet, and rain, Washington led his troops across the ice-swollen Delaware. Early in the morning, they surprised the Hessian troops encamped near Trenton, New Jersey, and after fierce fighting and the loss of the Hessian commander, the mercenaries surrendered. The news of the American victory spread rapidly through the colonies, reinvigorating the flagging spirit of the Revolution. It remains the most important victory in the history of the United States.

THE BOMB, DIMITRI!
THE HYDROGEN BOMB!

In the iconic 1964 film directed by Stanley Kubrick,
DR. STRANGELOVE OR: HOW I LEARNED TO STOP WORRYING AND LOVE THE BOMB,
President Merkin Muffley, played by Peter Sellers,
calls the premier of the Soviet Union to inform him that an insane renegade
American general is attempting to start a nuclear war.

President Muffley (on the phone):
Hello? Uh, hello? Hello, Dimitri? Listen, I can't hear too well,
do you suppose you could turn the music down just a little? (pause)
Oh, that's much better. Yes. Fine, I can hear you now, Dimitri.
Clear and plain and coming through fine. I'm coming through fine too, eh?
Good, then. Well then, as you say we're both coming through fine.
Good. Well, it's good that you're fine, and–and I'm fine. I agree with you.
It's great to be fine. (laughs) *Now then, Dimitri,*
you know how we've always talked about the possibility of something
going wrong with the bomb. (pause)
The BOMB, Dimitri! The hydrogen bomb!
Well now, what happened is, uh, one of our base commanders,
he had a sort of, well, he went a little funny in the head.
You know. Just a little...funny. And, uh, he went and did a silly thing.
Well, I'll tell you what he did, he ordered his planes...
to attack your country...

WORRYING ABOUT THE BOMB

The **CIVIL DEFENSE** logo
became ubiquitous in America–a stark, even forbidding design that
symbolized the Cold War. School air-raid drills were
conducted in which children were taught to "duck and cover" under their
desks to avoid atomic fallout; fallout shelters were built;
and thousands of steel drums were distributed containing biscuits for
emergency rations in case of an A-bomb attack.
This logo, designed by Charles Coiner, was born in 1939 and was
killed in action in 2006, replaced by a less
ominous EM symbol (Federal Emergency Management Agency).
P.S. The CD insignia still exists on countless metal drums full of stale biscuits,
still standing ready to help feed the nation in an emergency.

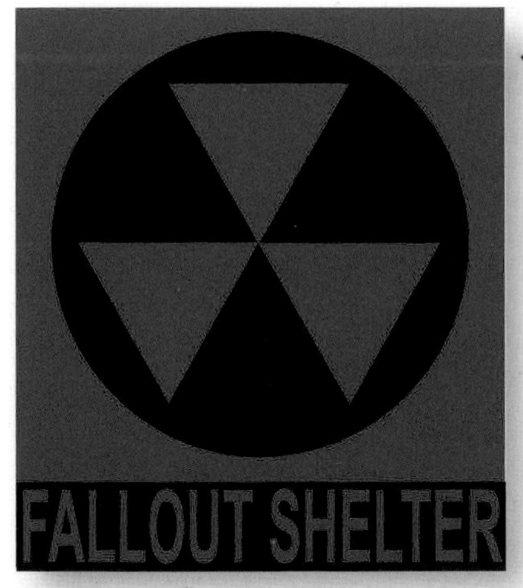

DR. STRANGELOVE TO THE RESCUE

This sign identified **NUCLEAR FALLOUT SHELTERS** built in the 1950s
during the Cold War between the U.S. and
the Soviet Union. Many were bunker-style shelters for high-ranking
officials and the military–but thousands
were merely basements of buildings (where a nuclear attack
would have buried them under tons of rubble).
The ludicrous logic of the fallout shelter was to protect against the
force of a nuclear explosion and exposure
to killer fallout until radioactivity "decayed to a safer level."

STEINWAY & SONS
NEW YORK HAMBURG
D
487189
N 0182
STEINWAY

THE MODERN PIANO: AN AMERICAN INVENTION

The piano is an American invention. America created the cast-iron frame, and by the middle of the 19th century the piano as we know it was built by Americans, becoming a symbol of culture in the American home. After the Civil War, every home had to have two things: a piano and a sewing machine. No young lady could be called educated unless she could play. Much of the social life at home revolved around the piano in those long-ago days before the automobile, the movies, radio, and television. **STEINWAY & SONS** was founded four generations ago, in 1853, by a large and ambitious family of German immigrants whose craftsmanship and technical innovation set the standards for the modern piano and brought acclaim for their remarkably beautiful instruments. The world's greatest pianists promoted the Steinway, bringing them to concert halls across America. Anton Rubinstein, Ignace Paderewski, Josef Hofmann, Sergei Rachmaninoff, Arthur Rubinstein, and Vladimir Horowitz made Steinway the instrument of the immortals.

THE SUITS AT IBM

IBM is a worldwide information-technology leader, and the only one with a continuous history dating back to the 19th century. This simple, bold, fresh logo for Big Blue was designed by Paul Rand in 1972. Eight stripes radiate throughout the logo to offer a dazzling visual effect suggesting speed and dynamism. For most of the 20th century, executives at IBM were subject to a dress code: a blue suit, white shirt, and dark tie, which made them the butt of many a joke. But IBM had the last laugh: IBM employees, wearing blue suits, white shirts, and dark ties, have earned five Nobel Prizes and five National Medals of Science!

THE MOST ENDURING BUSINESS TOOL EVER!

THE UNDERWOOD TYPEWRITER NO. 5 was one of the most successful business products in history, so well constructed and engineered for high-speed typists that its basic design remained unchanged from 1900 to 1961. Ding!

THE SIT-DOWN FIGHTER FOR CIVIL RIGHTS

In Montgomery, Alabama, in 1955, as a bus became crowded, a black woman returning home from her job was ordered by an imperious bus driver to give up her seat to a white man. When she remained seated, she dramatically humanized the struggle to dismantle Jim Crow segregation in the South. That simple decision made **ROSA PARKS** a legend and a heroic symbol of civil disobedience in the face of brute authority.

THE GODMOTHER OF THE FEMINIST MOVEMENT

The one-dollar gold coin issued in 1979 may have been unpopular because of its similar size to the quarter, but **SUSAN B. ANTHONY**, the drillmaster of the suffrage movement from the time of the Civil War, remains the greatest icon of womens rights in the history of America. Read her words: "We demand that women shall be given the means to assert herself, regardless of whether she uses it or not...For a people are only as great, as free, as lofty, as advanced, as its women are free, noble, and progressive." The great social activist had no patience when it came to dogma of the past, delivered by man or woman. She said, "I distrust those people who know so well what God wants them to do, because I notice it always coincides with their own desires." Amen.

THE MIRACLE WORKER

In 1955 **DR. JONAS SALK**, the physician and researcher, announced that he had developed the first vaccine to immunize human beings against the dreadful polio virus. (The most famous victim of the disease had been the intrepid Franklin Delano Roosevelt, who went on to become the president of the United States.) The continued development of polio vaccines has saved hundreds of thousands of lives, and spared millions around the world a life of debilitating paralysis. The great doctor did not seek wealth or fame through his great contribution to the human race, stating "Who owns my polio vaccine? The people! Could you patent the sun?"

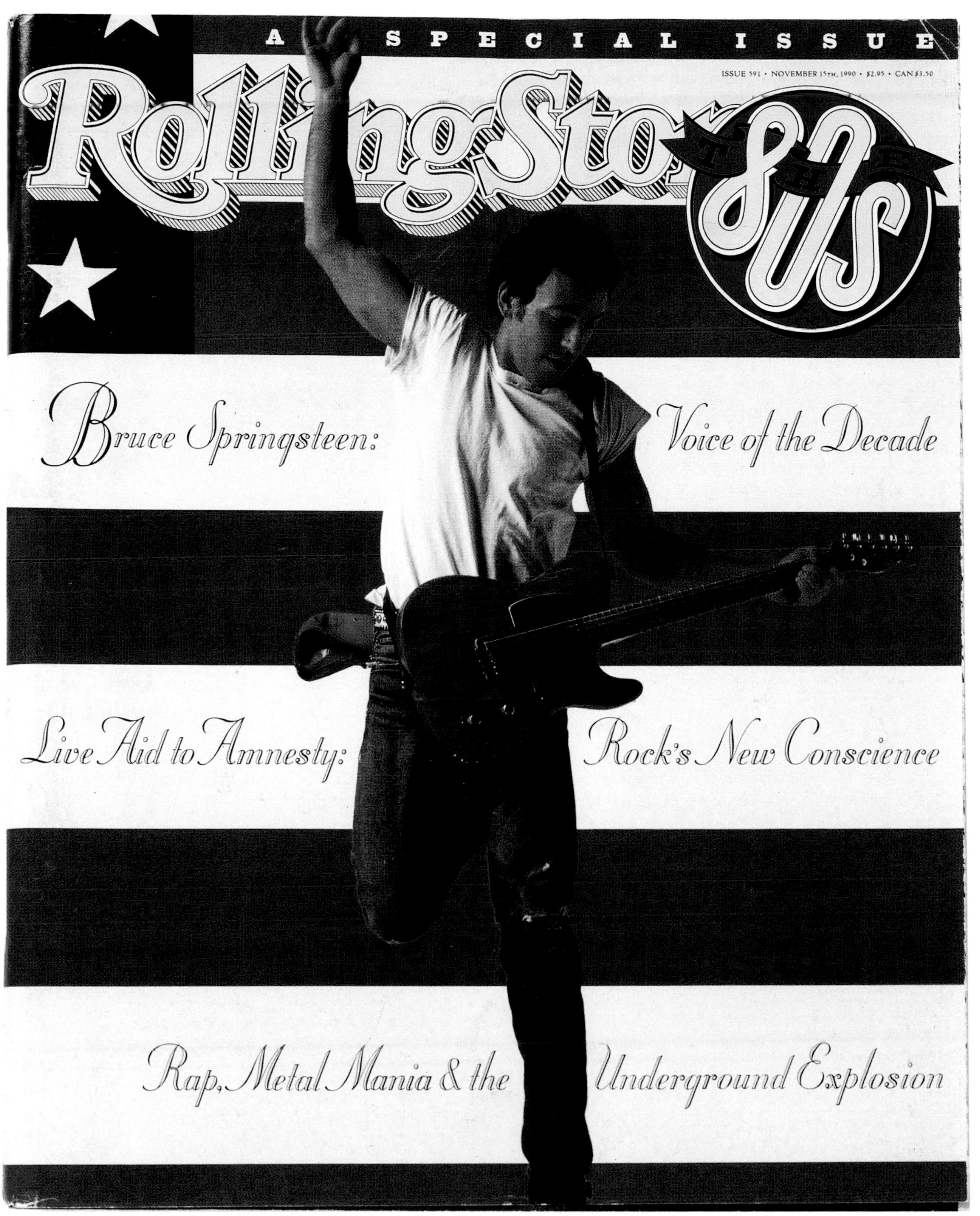
A SPECIAL ISSUE
ISSUE 591 • NOVEMBER 15TH, 1990 • $2.95 • CAN $3.50
Rolling Stone
THE 80'S
Bruce Springsteen: Voice of the Decade
Live Aid to Amnesty: Rock's New Conscience
Rap, Metal Mania & the Underground Explosion

WHAT KIND OF BABY WAS DR. SPOCK?

In 1904 Benjamin McLane Spock dressed up for his first birthday picture. Forty-two years later Benjamin wrote a book. Its first sentence read "You know more than you think you do." Parents had never heard anything like it, and Spock became America's best-loved baby doctor. Writing like a warm and welcome confidant, Dr. Spock put nervous mothers at ease, and they basked in the warmth of his advice. Parents may have produced the Baby Boomers, but Dr. Spock brought them up.

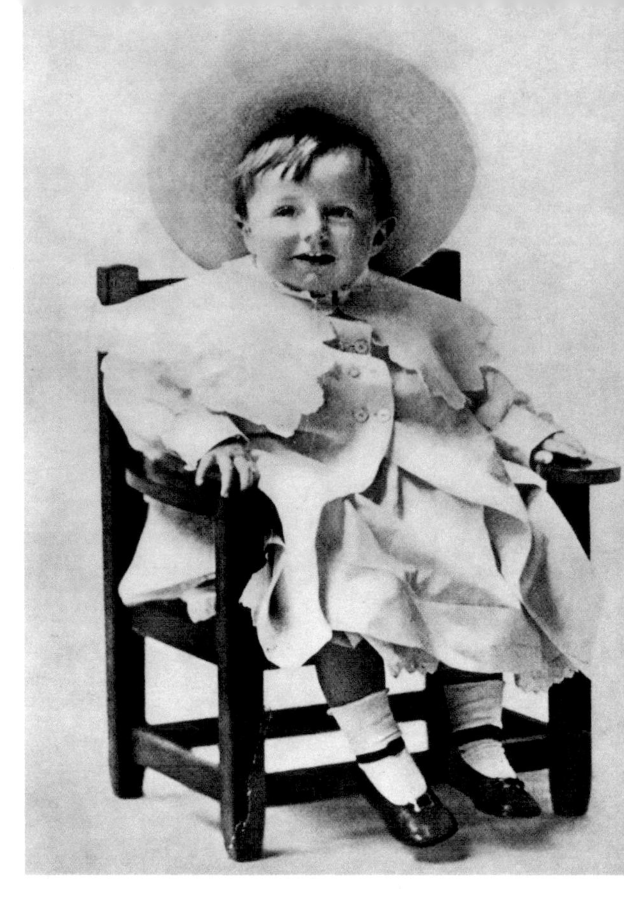

BORN IN THE U.S.A.

Devoted to music, politics, and popular culture, **ROLLING STONE** was founded in 1967 by Jann Wenner in San Francisco. Initially identified with the hippie counterculture of the era, the magazine made a mark with its political coverage and by launching the careers of many prominent writers in the 1970s, becoming a powerful influence on pop culture throughout America. In the 1990 issue shown, *Rolling Stone* celebrates the Voice of the Decade, **BRUCE SPRINGSTEEN**, for his stirring role in defining the struggles of ordinary Americans in the 1980s. *Born in the U.S.A.* has become a second national anthem, with its rousing sentiments of patriotism, over a dark criticism of American hubris.

AN EYE-POPPING ICON

LITTLE ORPHAN ANNIE was born in 1924 (she was ten years old and hasn't celebrated a birthday yet). Annie was taken in by Daddy Warbucks, a capitalist of unlimited wealth, who tackled international intrigue and neverending plots to kidnap or harm his beloved Annie. With her curly mop of carrot-topped hair and vacant circles for eyes, and her dog Sandy always at her side, Annie continues to win the hearts of audiences everywhere thanks to the musical *Annie*, first produced on Broadway in 1977. The lineup of Broadway Annies, including Andrea McArdle and Sarah Jessica Parker, has been eye-popping. The 1982 film version directed by John Huston is lovely—if you haven't seen it, *leapin' lizards*—go to Blockbuster tomorrow!

THE ROCKY HORROR PICTURE SHOW

FILM NOIR POP ART

TOM WESSELMANN,
best known for his "Great American Nudes,"
was a modern-day master of
sexy, luscious lips smoking with attitude.

A MIDNIGHT CULT MOVIE RUN AMOK

THE ROCKY HORROR PICTURE SHOW is a science-fiction/horror/comedy/musical film that was released in 1975, had a 30-week first run, and went on to become the cult hit that wouldn't go away, playing weekly midnight shows in theaters all over the country. Any showing is a hallucinatory happening, where fanatics dressed as characters from the film respond ritualistically to scenes by throwing rice and toast, squirting water, yelling, dancing, cursing, abusing the actors, and screaming puns, pop-culture references, and sex jokes at the screen. If you've never seen the show, you're a "virgin;" if you attend frequently, you're a "slut;" and if you've only seen the film on video or DVD, you're a "masturbator." It's the cult-film phenomenon of all time. You've got to see it to believe it.

S.W.A.K.

SEALED WITH A KISS
has been the traditional epistolary sign-off between
friends and lovers in America,
and a lipstick impression added by a loved one,
especially from a sweetheart to a GI
stationed overseas, was carried close to the heart.

THEY CALLED HIM "AMERICA'S ROBIN HOOD"

As a teenager, **JESSE JAMES** was a marauding Confederate bushwhacker, a guerrilla soaked in blood; later, he was harbored by the Ku Klux Klan. After the Civil War, Jesse and his brother Frank took up with the Younger Brothers gang, robbing banks, stagecoaches, and trains. The James Gang usually limited itself to stealing from the tellers in banks and the express safes in the baggage cars of trains. Jesse, not robbing "plain folk," gained a Robin Hood image that was perpetuated in the *Kansas City Times*. He was finally shot in the back as he stood on a chair hanging a picture—gang member Bob Ford did the dirty deed for the reward money. Jesse James became an icon, not only celebrated by former Confederates but portrayed as a folk hero in dozens of films. Shown is the figure of folklore in his coffin in 1882, mourned by America. (But Jesse James was no Robin Hood.)

"WHO ARE THOSE GUYS?"

Butch Cassidy and the Sundance Kid was a 1969 Western in which the main characters were more inclined to trade quips than gunfire. Paul Newman, who played Butch, was already a huge Hollywood star, but the film catapulted Robert Redford, who played the Sundance Kid, into stardom. (His Sundance Film Festival and Utah ski resort are named for his role in the film.) In 1973 the two were brought together again in *The Sting*—an Oscar-winning caper film, with a complicated plot revolving around two professional grifters conning a Chicago mob boss. Besides becoming the highest-grossing film of 1974, the film won Best Picture and seven other Oscars. The names of **PAUL NEWMAN & ROBERT REDFORD** are forever linked because of the chemistry of their charismatic talent.

A PAINTER OF THE PEOPLE

THOMAS HART BENTON painted the history of the American heartland by heroically depicting its people: black field hands loading cotton, weather-beaten cowboys and wildcatters, hillbillies, Indians, sharecroppers, folk musicians, politicos, steel workers, dance hall girls, fur trappers—all the robust characters of American folklore, mythology, and history. The painting shown, *Lord, Heal the Child* (1934), portrays a woman preacher praying for the healing of a child with rickets, driven by a chorus and the music of a lanky banjo player named Red, a guitar player named Homer Laverett of Galena, Missouri, a harmonica player, and Uncle Lawrence, an aged mountain fiddler from Tennessee.

THE METEOR OF COUNTRY MUSIC

The career of **HANK WILLIAMS**, singer, songwriter, Grand Ole Opry star, MGM recording artist, was only six years and 125 songs long. His short, blazing career was touched with gold—he earned 11 gold records for such singles as *Jambalaya*, *Your Cheatin' Heart*, and *Hey, Good-Lookin'.* Williams stopped the show at his first appearance at the Grand Ole Opry in 1949, with *Love Sick Blues*. After six encores, the audience was still applauding wildly. The beloved troubadour was equally at home with jivey novelty tunes, honky-tonk numbers, heartfelt religious songs, and ballads. Audiences found him electrifying. He was real. He was genuine. He broke your heart. On New Year's Day 1953, Hank Williams died while he was dozing in the back of a chauffeur-driven Cadillac convertible, bound for his next gig in Canton, Ohio. His death was pronounced a heart attack, but many believe it was the summation of a troubled life of drinking, drugs, and hard living. On country music charts that week was his hit, *I'll Never Get Out of This World Alive*. Hank Williams was 29.

THE YOUNG, PIONEERING WARNER BROS.

In 1924 four Jewish brothers from Poland put the Warner Bros. name on the Hollywood map with a dog—the great Rin Tin Tin. Then, in 1927, came the first talkie, *The Jazz Singer*, followed in 1929 with *Gold Diggers of Broadway*, one of the first all-color, all-talkie musicals. In the 1930s came glorified gangster films with James Cagney, Joan Blondell, and Edward G. Robinson. Then came melodramas, swashbucklers, and adaptions of best-selling novels with stars like Bette Davis, Olivia de Havilland, and Errol Flynn, followed by the zany Looney Tunes cartoons. Then the classics: *Casablanca*, *Yankee Doodle Dandy*, *The Treasure of the Sierra Madre*, *A Streetcar Named Desire*, *A Star is Born*, *Mister Roberts*, *The Searchers*, *My Fair Lady*, *Bonnie and Clyde*, *Unforgiven*, *GoodFellas*...

THE MOST MEMORABLE IMAGE IN FILM HISTORY

The sight of the silhouette of the Little Tramp—a derby hat, tight frock coat, baggy pants, oversized shoes, twitching moustache, and a flexible bamboo cane—is one of the most endearing in the history of moviemaking. **CHARLIE CHAPLIN** was the first creative genius of the motion picture industry, the conjuror of dazzling cinematic images, including some of the most touching scenes ever filmed. Chaplin's tramp celebrated the power of American creativity in the dawn of the film age, becoming an icon the world over.

"NO ONE IS AS GOOD AS BETTE WHEN SHE'S BAD"

This Warner Bros. publicity slogan said it all. **BETTE DAVIS**, with her Bette Davis eyes, clipped New England diction, and extravagant cigarette smoking, simply had no rival, with her spitfire acting, her refusal to prettify the gritty roles in her rogue's gallery of testy women—and her way with a kick-ass line: in *All About Eve* (1950), in an almost self-parodying grand gesture, she belted out her most famous line, "Fasten your seatbelts! It's going to be a bumpy night!"

Astor
20,000 LEAGUES
CINEMASCOPE
APPLIANCES
NO

IMMORTALITY!

JAMES DEAN, having personified youthful angst in a mere three films, was killed driving his Porsche 550 Spyder on U.S. Highway 466. His last words: "My fun days are over." In his first film, *East of Eden* (1955), directed by Elia Kazan, he played the son of a constantly disapproving father; for the role, Dean received the first posthumous acting nomination in Oscar history. Dean's mainstream status as a cultural phenomenon is embodied in the title of his second film, *Rebel Without a Cause* (1955). In his last film, *Giant* (1956), which was released after his death, he once again showed original creative talent playing an angry white-trash Texas youth clawing his way to fame and fortune. As with Buddy Holly, Bruce Lee, Marilyn Monroe, and many others, James Dean died prematurely at the young age of 24. He once said these prophetic words: "If a man can bridge the gap between life and death...I mean, if he can live on after he has died, then maybe he was a great man. To me the only success, the only greatness, is immortality."

I'D WALK A MILE FOR A CAMEL

CAMEL remained one of the top cigarette brands for 40 years. Introduced in 1913, R.J. Reynolds named their brand Camel as an allusion to the Turkish tobacco they contained (even though the camel is shown against an Egyptian backdrop). The camel illustration was fashioned after a photo of Old Joe, a one-humped dromedary in the Barnum & Bailey Circus, which happened to be visiting Winston-Salem at the time. In 1958, the R.J. Reynolds executives decided, disastrously, to upgrade the famous Camel pack. The outrage was so immediate and vociferous that the company pulled the packages off the shelves. The current design is one that has remained basically unchanged for almost a century, an example of "unprofessional" vernacular design at its best.

SCARED OF HIS OWN SHADOW

America's celebration of **GROUNDHOG DAY** began in Punxsutawney, Pennsylvania, on February 2, 1886, with festivities to witness a groundhog coming out of his winter burrow: if he cast a shadow it would be a sure sign that there would be six more weeks of winter. (On the groundhog's debut performance, there was no shadow—there would be an early spring!) The tradition has continued, and it was enshrined in popular culture with the 1993 film *Groundhog Day*, in which an obnoxious TV weatherman played by Bill Murray wakes up each morning and finds it's Groundhog Day, over and over and over again. The film made the term "Groundhog Day" synonymous with "It's déjà vu all over again." Watch Bill Murray and Andie MacDowell in *Groundhog Day* once, and you'll want to see it over and over and over again.

"I *AM* BIG. IT'S THE PICTURES THAT GOT SMALLER."

The very epitome of the movie queen, **GLORIA SWANSON** worked at being a star all her life. During the Roaring Twenties, Swanson was Hollywood's biggest star, earning thousands of dollars a week and with a lifestyle to match. Her curvaceous profile (which she flaunts in her autograph above) was everywhere in American pop culture, a symbol of the silent-picture era. She was at her peak in 1925, when she actually married a French marquis; she wrote to her studio, "Arriving with Marquis. Arrange ovation." Paramount dutifully complied. Her ascendancy waned with the Depression years, but Swanson made the screen's greatest comeback in 1950 with her magnificent performance as the aging star Norma Desmond in Billy Wilder's classic *Sunset Boulevard*. In the film on meeting Desmond, William Holden remarks: "...You used to be in pictures. You used to be big." "I *am* big," Gloria Swanson says in character. "It's the pictures that got smaller." That sad mixture of overblown pride and undeniable truth remains her epitaph.

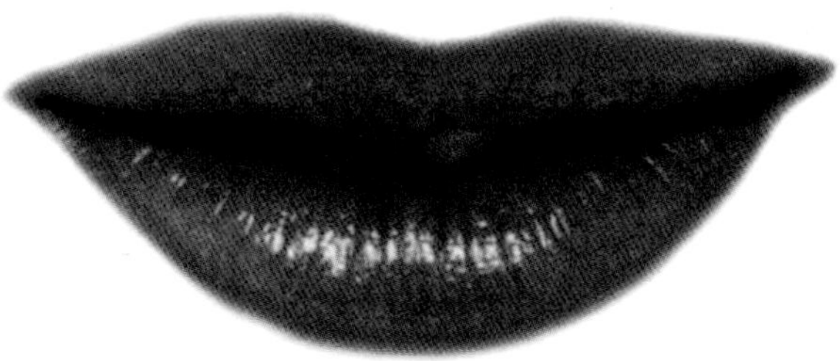

"AVON CALLING"

Since 1886, Avon products have been primarily sold by an **AVON LADY**, door-to-door, selling cosmetics to women in the comfort and privacy of their homes. Ringing doorbells from coast-to-coast, Avon is No. 1 in direct sales nationwide (and distributed in 135 countries worldwide) despite the existence of scores of expensive domestic and foreign brand-name cosmetics.

IS THE HAMBURGER AMERICA'S FAVORITE FAST FOOD?

FUGEDDABOUTIT!

PIZZA is the great equalizer. Everybody loves it—food snobs, octogenarians, picky kids, cops on the beat, construction workers, carnivores, vegetarians. The true cognoscenti of pizza are New Yorkers. Lombardi's pizzeria, opened by Gennaro Lombardi in 1905 on Spring Street, the heart of Little Italy in Manhattan, is the birthplace of pizza in the United States—a place of worship for many Americans. Made in coal-burning brick ovens and served piping hot, the pizza's crust is thin, the edges slightly burnt and crispy, the melted mozzarella cheese and spicy tomato sauce a fusion of indescribable taste. There are more than 500 pizzerias in New York City, and thousands of others all over America, but for pizza historians and aficionados, Lombardi's remains the sacred ground of America's most revered fast food. Go to Lombardi's or Patsy's or Pontillo's or Joe and Pat's or Una Pizza Napoletana or Totonno's or Grimaldi's or Gonzo or Nino's or Rosario's or John's of Bleecker Street and take a bite (but don't burn your tongue).

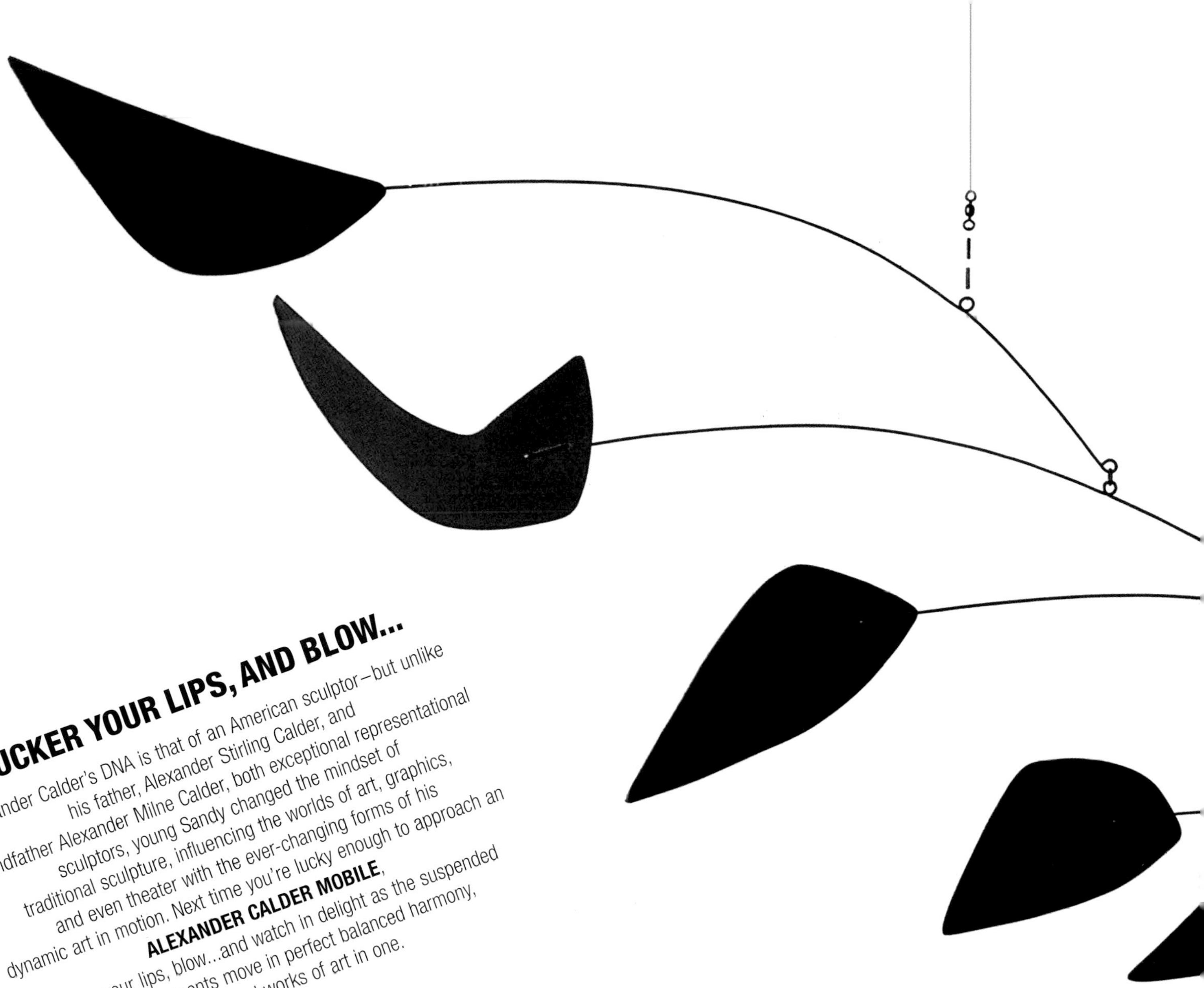

PUCKER YOUR LIPS, AND BLOW...

Alexander Calder's DNA is that of an American sculptor—but unlike his father, Alexander Stirling Calder, and grandfather Alexander Milne Calder, both exceptional representational sculptors, young Sandy changed the mindset of traditional sculpture, influencing the worlds of art, graphics, and even theater with the ever-changing forms of his dynamic art in motion. Next time you're lucky enough to approach an **ALEXANDER CALDER MOBILE**, pucker your lips, blow...and watch in delight as the suspended abstract elements move in perfect balanced harmony, a thousand works of art in one.

"KING GEORGE CAN READ THAT CLEAR ACROSS THE SEA,"

said **JOHN HANCOCK**, the president of the Continental Congress, thumbing his nose at King George III as he scrolled his signature under the Declaration of Independence (and added an arrogant paraph) on August 2,1776. His John Hancock was fully twice the size of the signature of any other of the brave band of brothers.

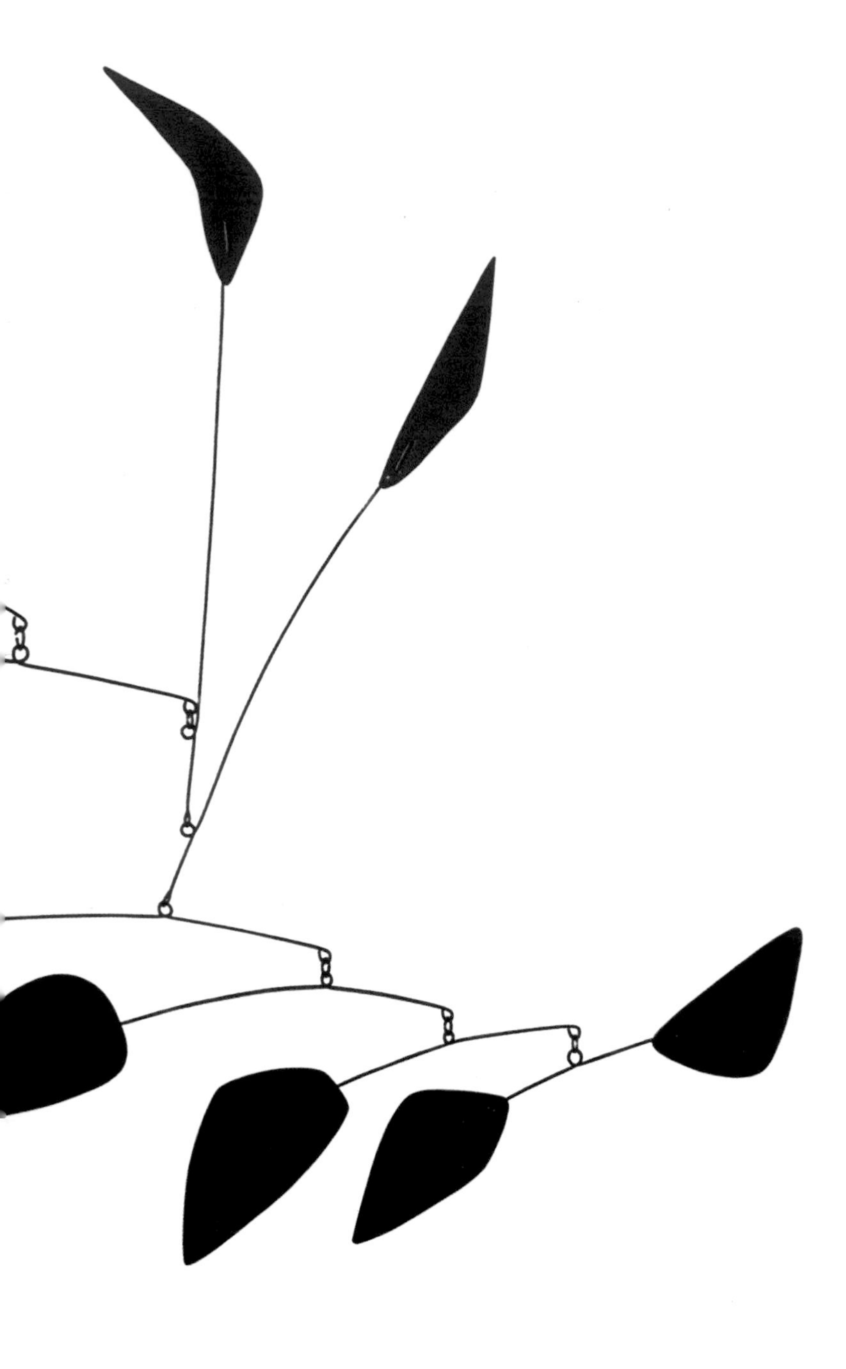

"YOU CAN'T POSSESS RADIANCE, YOU CAN ONLY ADMIRE IT."

ELIZABETH TAYLOR

Married eight times, yet no man has ever possessed her. But as an actress **ELIZABETH TAYLOR** captivated her audience—with her extraordinary beauty, innate talent, and courageous passion.

THE PACKAGE THAT PERSUADED WOMEN THAT SMOKING WAS HYGIENIC (COUGH, COUGH)

Arriving on the scene in the 1930s, a latecomer after Camel and Chesterfield, **LUCKY STRIKE** embarked on an ad campaign to persuade women that smoking was *good* for them (the italics are mine) and that smoking in public was fashionable. The only problem was that the bull's-eye package was muddy green and the brand name was only on one side (duh!). In 1941 Raymond Loewy was challenged by the infamous president of the American Tobacco Company, George Washington Hill, to design a better-selling package. Loewy merely replaced the green background with clean white, slapped the red circle and brand name on both sides, modernized the type, and tucked the nitty-gritty info onto the sides. From an old-fashioned, rather dingy look, it instantly acquired a modern aura: the bright red and brilliant white suggested freshness and hygiene. And the rest is history (along with millions of deaths since, attributed to cancer-causing tobacco).

THE DESPISED HOLLYWOOD GOSSIP ICON

HEDDA HOPPER hobnobbed with the biggest names in Hollywood, dug out scoops before her competition, spilled the beans on the high and mighty of Hollywood, and was totally vicious in dealing with those who displeased her, intentionally or not. Her long-running feud with rival Louella Parsons became as notorious as many of Hopper's columns. She was never seen without her trademark flamboyant hat (usually sporting a dead bird), pad and pen in hand, on the prowl for gossip. Besides being feared as a career-buster, she was despised as well for "naming names" of alleged Communists, many of them simply liberals, during the era when McCarthyism gripped the Hollywood community. The feared fictional columnist J.J. Hunsecker, played by Burt Lancaster in the film *Sweet Smell of Success*, is said to have been inspired by the malicious Queen of Hollywood. Weegee, the famous tabloid photographer, nailed her in this remarkable photograph.

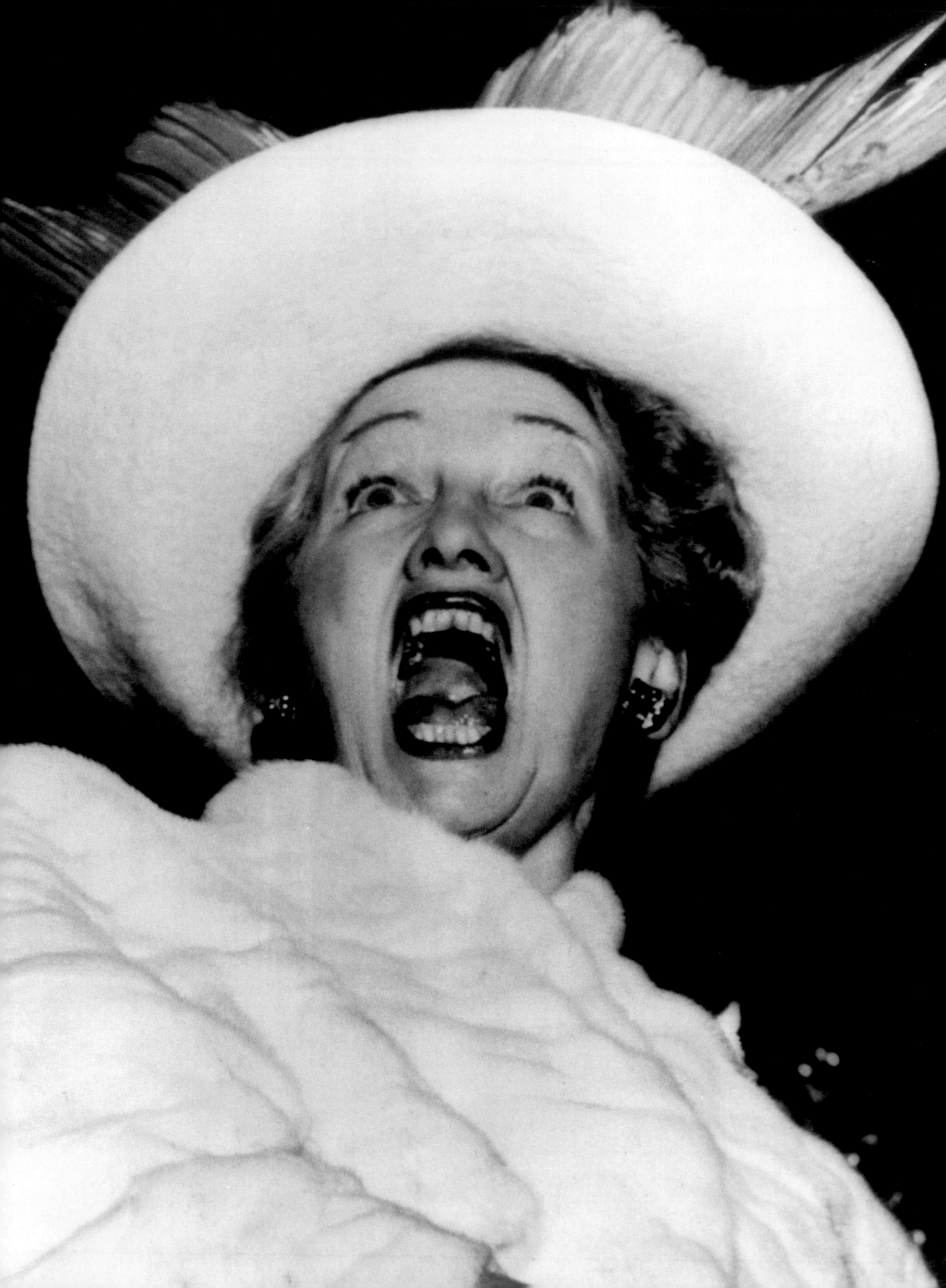

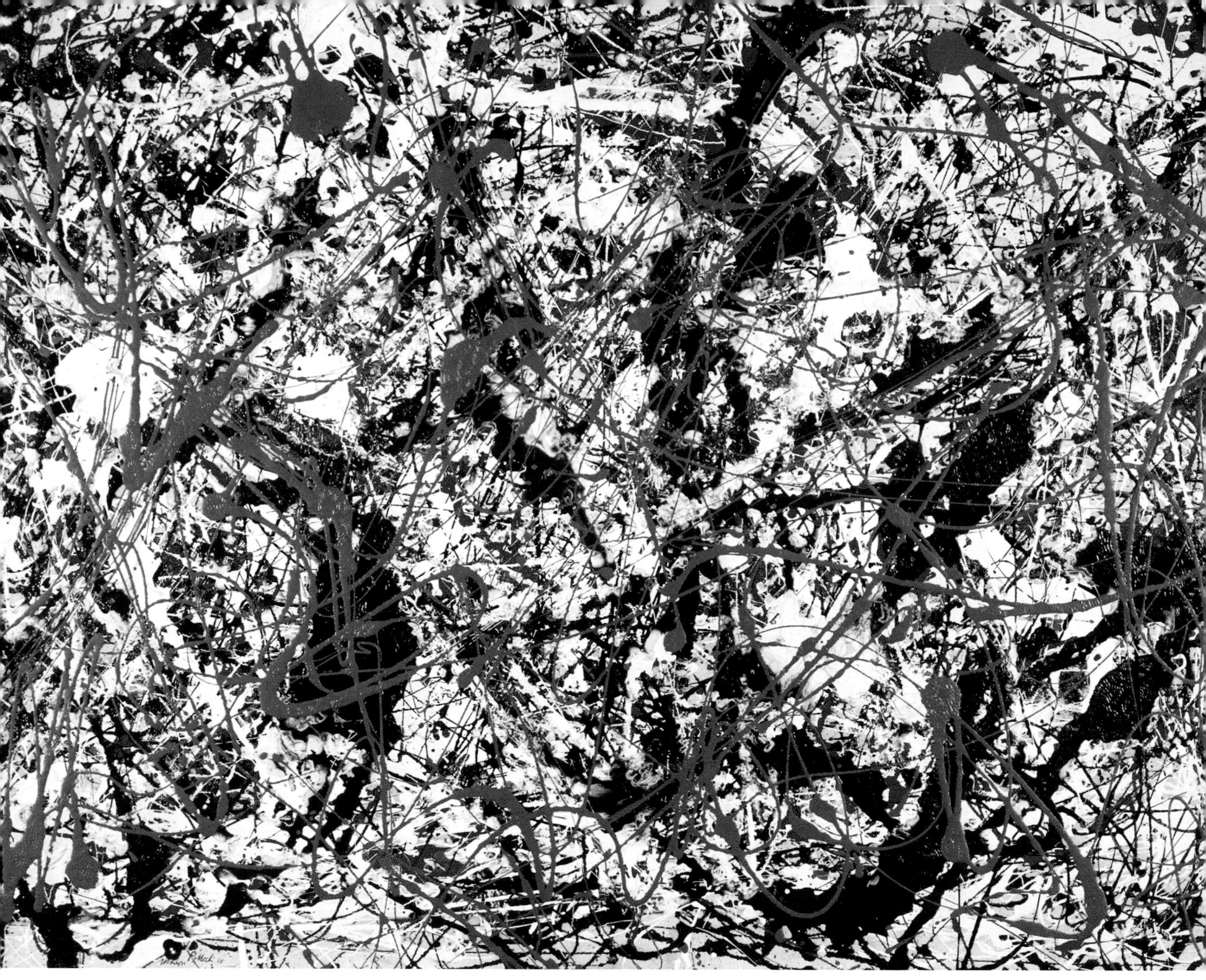

JACK THE DRIPPER

The many visual experiments of **JACKSON POLLOCK** finally led him, at the age of 35, to his "classic" style of poured, blotted, sprinkled, and dripped paint, creating apocalyptic canvases that made him a worldwide celebrity in 1947. His iconoclastic Abstract Expressionist paintings could be regarded as the destruction of art as we know it, or as a synthesis of a new creative energy. Pollock's floor paintings were ridiculed at first but profoundly influenced a re-examination by the avant-garde of the question, "What is art?"

THE MUTANT RIPPER

Conceived by Marvel Comics in the late 1970s, an international brotherhood of mutants named the X-Men formed lasting bonds—but the 5-foot, 3-inch **WOLVERINE** was a one-mutant show. After a scientist implants an unbreakable "adamantium" skeleton with retractable claws into Wolverine's miraculously healing body, he turns into a half-mad lethal weapon with a heightened sense of sight, hearing, and smell, and lives like an animal in a Canadian forest. Troubled by the experimental invasion of his body, the cocky, quarrelsome Wolverine joins the X-Men and becomes the archetypal hero who performs pain-defying feats, yet walks forever on a razor's edge.

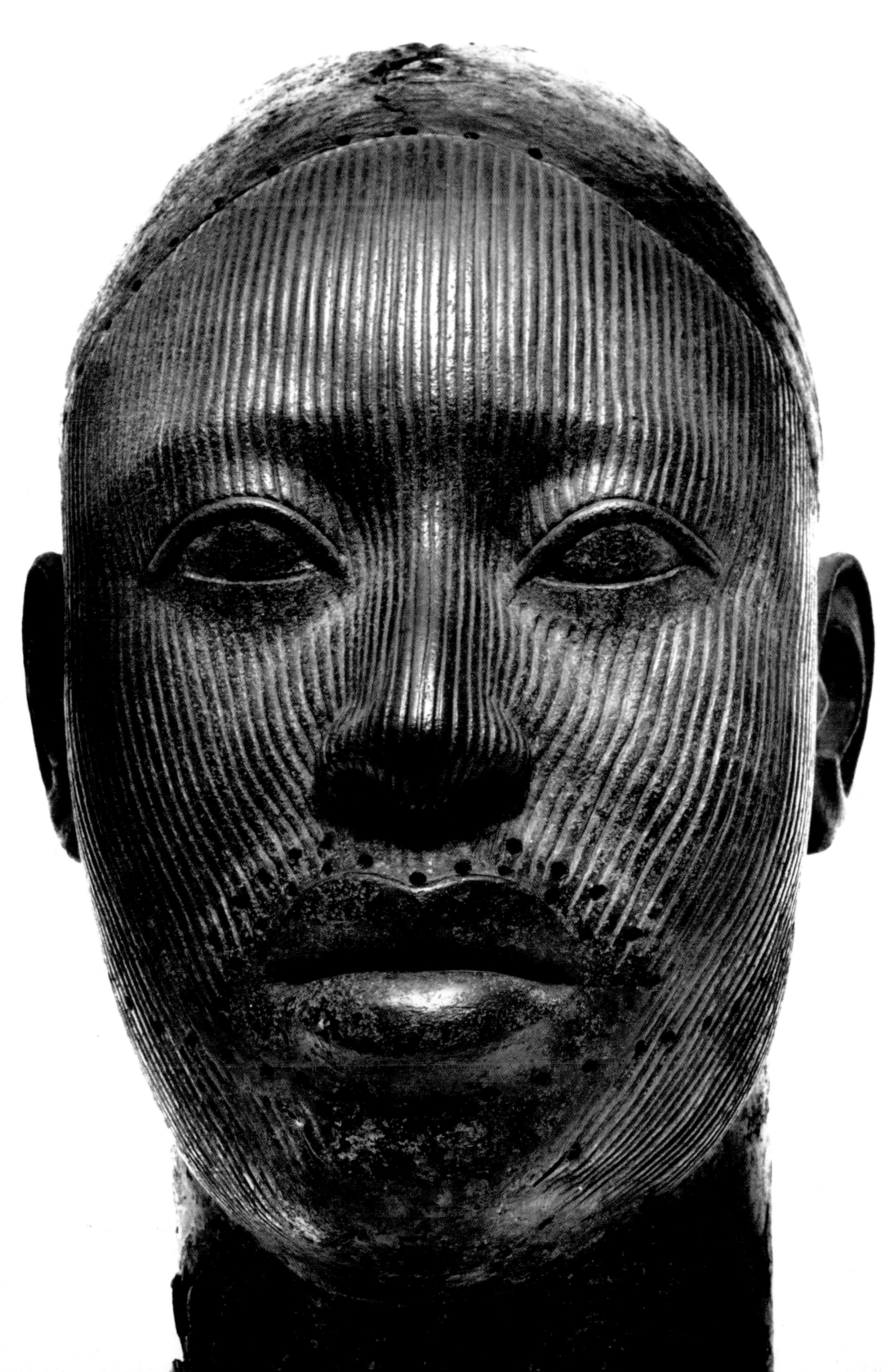

ROOTS (THE SEARCH FOR WHO WE ARE)

In 1976, after 12 years of intense research and many trips to Africa, **ALEX HALEY** wrote his book **ROOTS**, tracing his ancestry back seven generations to his African great-great-great-great-grandfather, Kunta Kinte, who had been kidnapped from Gambia in 1767, brought by slave ship to America, and given the name Tobey. Haley's *Roots: The Saga of an American Family* was adapted in 1977 for a TV miniseries that ran for eight consecutive nights, captivating America and inspiring families of all ethnic groups. The search for roots is deep in the consciousness of all people, especially immigrants to America, and most especially the offspring of African slaves. Haley's genealogical search inspired many to pursue African studies and sparked an intense interest in the oral history of slavery in America that continues, gloriously unabated to this day (leading African-Americans to bestow African names on their children, carrying on the tradition of their ancestors). The sculpture shown, photographed by Eliot Elisofon, is a late-12th-century bronze memorial head from the Yoruba tribe in Ife, Nigeria, a great work of art symbolizing the roots of a people.

ETCHED IN OUR HEARTS

Beautifully conceived and designed by Yale architecture student **MAYA LIN** and dedicated in 1982, the **VIETNAM VETERANS MEMORIAL** in Washington, D.C., lists the names of 58,249 brave patriots whose memory is forever etched in the American psyche, along with the sorrowful belief that we fought a morally wrong war.

LIVING WITH LIGHT

Visionary and prolific, **FRANK LLOYD WRIGHT** conceived leaded-glass windows for almost every one of his buildings between 1885 and 1923, his most celebrated years. His output was prodigious: an estimated 4,365 window designs for more than 160 structures. In revolutionizing a centuries-old art form with the highly abstract glass he called **LIGHT SCREENS**, the pioneering genius distanced himself from the Art Nouveau forms of Louis Comfort Tiffany and invented a fully modern language of design. Wright's windows were integral to his architectural conceptions, all designed with geometric patterns that echoed the ethos of the architecture, and giving each interior warm, natural, but theatrical illumination. This detail of a window design, which enhances the Darwin D. Martin house in Buffalo, New York, is called the *Tree of Life*, an abstraction of the natural wonders surrounding each of the great man's startling edifices.

THE INVISIBLE HOUSE

In 1949 **PHILIP JOHNSON** anchored **THE GLASS HOUSE**, his country retreat in New Canaan, Connecticut, with a central, cylindrical shape enclosing a rectangular fireplace, and surrounded it with invisible glass walls. From one side of the house one sees the moon, and the other side the sun—simultaneously. Stand in the living room and you are graced with a 360-degree vista of nature. In effect, Johnson's iconic statement took the International Style of architecture, conceived by Mies van der Rohe and Walter Gropius, to its absolute extreme of "invisibility." Floating on a quietly rolling hill, there followed a brick guest house, and over the years Johnson added a lake pavilion, a painting gallery, a sculpture gallery, a studio, a tower, a "ghost house," and a visitor's pavilion. Before he died in 2005, Philip Johnson bequeathed the property and all its buildings to the National Trust for Historic Preservation. If a heaven on earth exists, this 47-acre exploration of architecture, landscape design, and art, is it!

HO, HO, HO, GREEN GIANT

Wearing a tunic, wreath, and boots made of leaves, he has presided over his fertile valley with a watchful eye since 1925, as his deep, resonant voice echoes from hill to dale. The kind and gentle **JOLLY GREEN GIANT** embodied the delicious frozen vegetables produced by the Green Giant Company, a big, big brand in American households.

VA-VA-VA-VOOM!

She was famous as an actress, singer, and dancer, but **BETTY GRABLE** was immortalized in this cheesecake shot, the number one pinup of the World War II era and beyond. Grable's shapely gams were showcased in dozens of her Technicolor musicals, famously insured by 20th Century-Fox for one million bucks (per leg).

WHEN HAWAIIAN SHIRTS WALKED THE HALLS OF THE WHITE HOUSE

The popularity and status of **THE HAWAIIAN SHIRT** boomed in the U.S. after America's fighting men returned from the war in the South Pacific. The "Aloha" shirts, brilliantly colored with floral patterns or other island motifs, were worn by Harry S. Truman regularly during his tenure in the White House (and when he walked the streets of Independence, Missouri). Elvis Presley, Bing Crosby, Arthur Godfrey, and Johnny Weissmuller wore them for entertaining. When Hawaii became our 50th state, in 1959, the garment officially gained all-American status. They are basically men's attire, but there's nothing sexier than Sweet Lalani wearing only an Aloha shirt and a lei.

JAMES BROWN was always 25 years ahead of his time. His music was sweaty and complex, disciplined and wild, lusty and socially conscious. Beyond his dozens of rhythm-and-blues hits, Mister Dynamite forged an entire musical idiom that is now a foundation of pop music worldwide. His stage moves—the spins, the quick shuffles, the knee-drops, the splits—were imitated but never equaled by performers who tried to match his talent and stamina, from Mick Jagger to Michael Jackson. "I taught them everything they know, but not *everything* I know," said the Minister of Super Heavy Funk. James Brown made the world *feel good!*

The honchos at Paramount Pictures opposed the casting of the "has-been" Marlon Brando in the lead role of Godfather Don Vito Corleone in the cinematic masterpiece **THE GODFATHER**. But director Francis Ford Coppola wanted Brando. Fighting for survival, Coppola caved in to the demand that Brando–the *great* Brando–be required to perform in *multiple* screen tests. But despite intense pressure and threats of dismissal, Coppola was not fired, and got Brando, who gave an inspired performance, delivering the most memorable line in cinema history (with wads of cotton in his mouth), "I'm going to make him an offer he can't refuse."

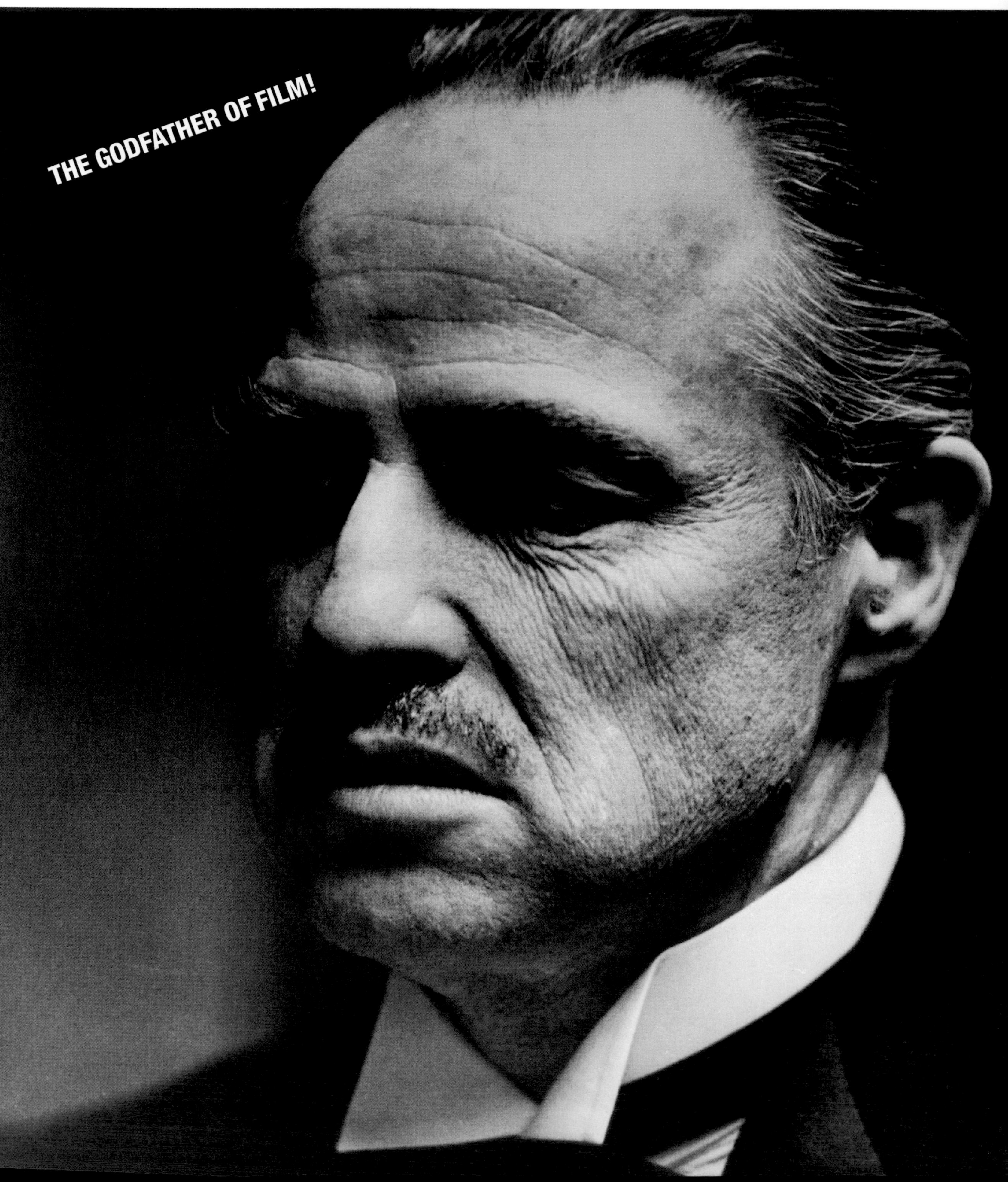

THE JOE LOUIS IMAGE OF AMERICA

On the night of June 22, 1938, in Yankee Stadium, the **JOE LOUIS** return-bout KO of Adolf Hitler's hero, Max Schmeling, was a seminal event in the beginning of America's fight against fascism. In that turbulent time in history, Joe's first-round knockout made him an instant popular and national hero. The iconic Brown Bomber made 25 defenses of his heavyweight title and was the world champ for almost 12 years. In those times, Joe Louis and America were synonymous. His life and his achievements prompted sportswriter Jimmy Cannon to write, "Joe Louis is a credit to his race–the human race." After the death of the great champion in 1981, Muhammad Ali said, "Howard Hughes dies, with all his billions, not a tear. Joe Louis, everybody cried."

THE JOHN WAYNE IMAGE OF AMERICA

Throughout the world, Duke rose far above recognition as a famous actor to status as an American icon. The 6-foot, 4-inch cowboy with the swaggering walk epitomized the rugged, individualistic man. A major star from the 1940s to the 1970s, he was most famous for his Westerns and World War II epics, but in real life Wayne never served in the military–deferred because he was 34 and had four children (while many famous Hollywood actors in a similar situation ran out and enlisted, including Henry Fonda, Jimmy Stewart, Clark Gable, and Tyrone Power). His role in *The Sands of Iwo Jima* made him the ultimate American patriot. (A recent pop song entitled *The Sands of Iwo Jima* reminisces about a young boy who loves John Wayne movies, and asks his great-uncle, a World War II veteran, if Wayne's Iwo Jima movie is really the way it happened. The old man smiles, shakes his head and says, "I never saw *John Wayne* on the beach at Iwo Jima.")

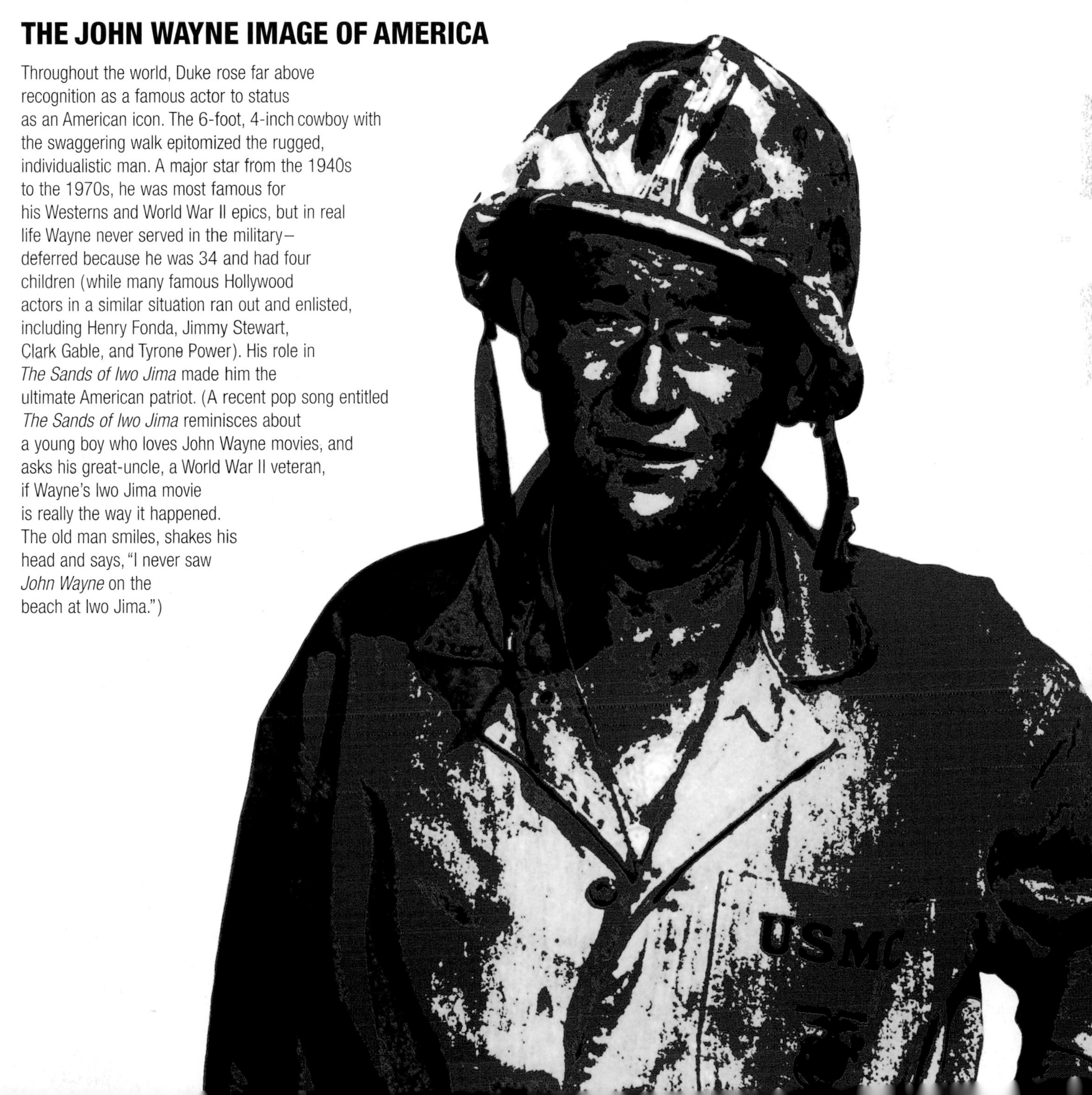

EVERLAST

SMILEY APPROVES

Smiley, usually in the form of a button, has at least four people laying claim to the credit for this happy face, which has become the symbol of contentment around the world since its introduction in the early 1960s. Introducing Smiley to any situation gets an immediate reaction as a stamp of approval. (And Smiley, with its variations, has become a staple in Internet chat rooms worldwide.)

THE MOST FAMOUS FASHION PHOTO OF ALL TIME

The most original, prophetic, and controversial American fashion designer of the 1950s, '60s, and '70s, **RUDI GERNREICH**, was fashion's bad boy and its oracle. He became world famous (along with his muse and model **PEGGY MOFFITT**) with his outrageous topless swimsuit, his equally shocking invisible "No Bra," his see-through shirt, and his startlingly graphic unisex look, infusing Seventh Avenue with a new kind of wit and intellect (and the beauty of surprise!). His topless swimsuit enlivened the summer of 1964 and was worn on California beaches by a brazen few.

VIAGRA TO THE RESCUE

It may have been invented in England by Pfizer Pharmaceutical researchers, but the famed male erectile-dysfunction remedy **VIAGRA** got really big stateside when it was famously hawked by 76-year-old Senator Bob Dole.

THE WETSUIT MAN...

In the 1950s surfing fanatic Jack O'Neill opened his first Surf Shop in San Francisco, where he sold his revolutionary **WETSUITS** that made cold-water surfing "always summer on the inside." Today, the surfing pioneer has a thriving international company that dominates the world's wetsuit and beach-sportswear markets.

...IN SEARCH OF THE PERFECT WAVE

For a full year cameraman Bruce Brown captured surfers Mike Hynson and Robert August hanging ten in the waters off their West Coast home, as well as off of Hawaii, Australia, Tahiti, Africa, and New Zealand. **THE ENDLESS SUMMER** (1966) is a documentary film of two blond California surfing buddies toting 10-foot surfboards, trekking from ocean to ocean, seeking deeper meaning of their lives, and searching for a spiritual understanding of life. The thoughtful and soulful young Americans challenged the stereotype of the brain-dead surfer dude and validated the desire of generations of (tanned) men and women to live life for that one moment, in search of the perfect wave.

DROWNING IN HIS OWN SOUP

The pervading image of the avant-garde Pop Art movement in the 1960s was the ubiquitous Campbell's soup can as immortalized by **ANDY WARHOL**. Maybe Andy was an innovator and an original thinker, but he was most certainly a major-league showman. His parlaying of a soup can (not to mention that mundane Brillo box) into personal stardom, was a defining act of instant celebrity status in America. "M'm! M'm! Good!"

SLAVE CHAINS (THE SHAME OF A NATION)

The United States of America endured
the bloodiest war in its history
as the Union Army defeated the Confederacy,
finally validating the revolutionary
words in our Declaration of Independence:
"All Men Are Created Equal..."

THE CITY THAT NEVER SLEEPS

The American city was the focus of much of the art of **EDWARD HOPPER**, one of our first representational painters to realize the pictorial power of the modern metropolis. He was never interested in the spectacular aspects of a city like New York–its skyscrapers and its famous skyline–yet his city is monumental; heartrending, with a penetrating sense of loneliness, with or without a human presence. For all his realism, Edward Hopper was essentially a poet. His oeuvre is totally American–the painting shown, *Nighthawks* (1942), an indelible image of the city that never sleeps, bathed in neon, recreated and parodied numerous times in pop culture, seems like the opening frame of the opening scene of a film noir we're breathlessly waiting to see unfold in a darkened movie theater.

Mar. 29, 1976 **THE NEW YORKER** Price 75 cents

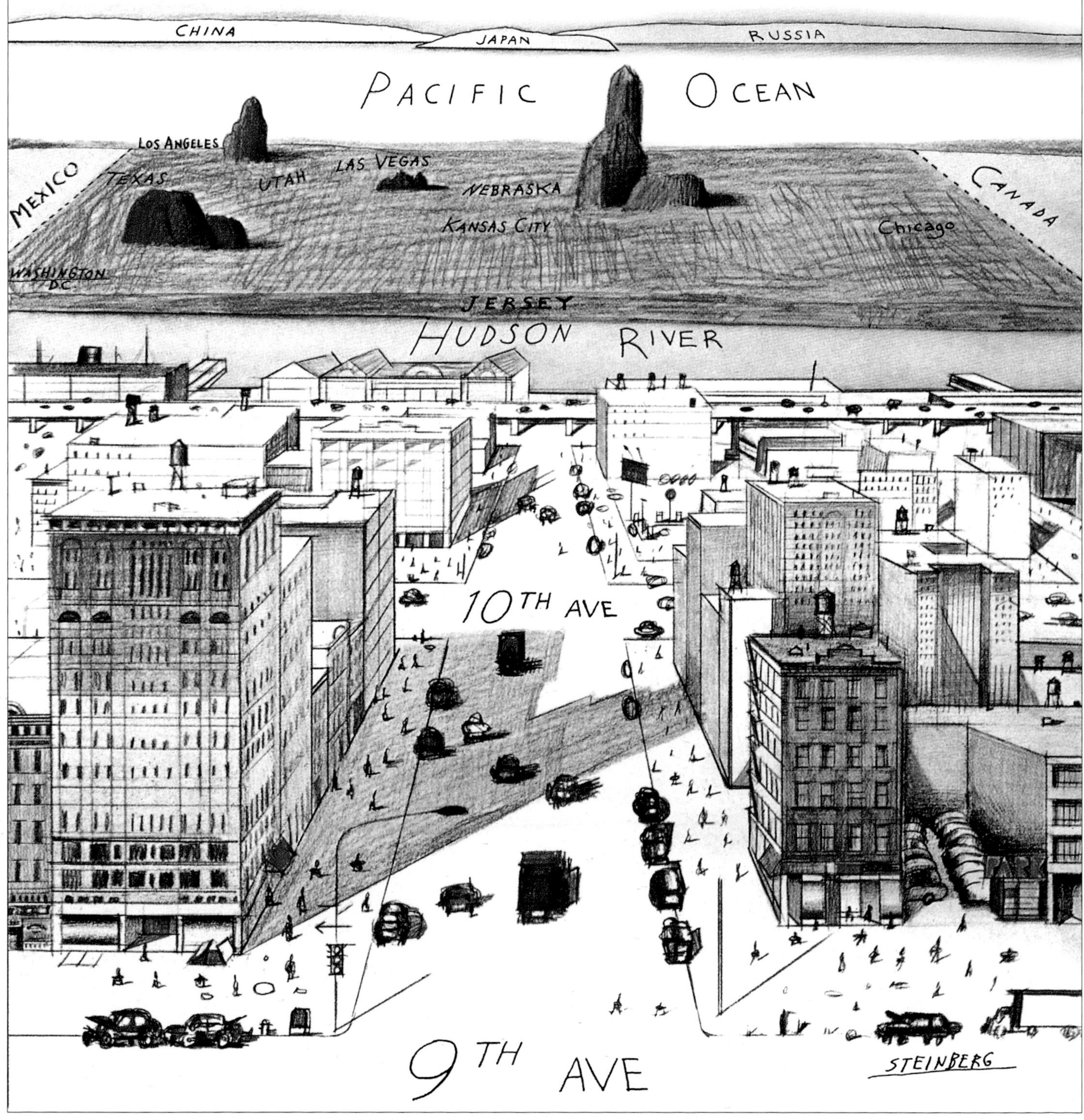

A NEW YORKER'S VIEW OF THE WORLD

The covers of **SAUL STEINBERG** for *The New Yorker* magazine parodied, and helped shape postwar visual culture in America. This famous drawing demonstrates a New Yorker's chauvinistic view of the world—satirically depicting Manhattan without its iconic Empire State and Chrysler buildings, but rather one of the city's pockets of nowhere, the vicinity of Hell's Kitchen. Imitations of this iconic cover are still being churned out for chambers of commerce the world over.

AMERICA'S MAIN SQUEEZE

In 1907 The Sunkist Growers, a marketing cooperative owned by 6,000 citrus growers in California and Arizona, wrapped their oranges in tissue printed with their trademark **SUNKIST**, the first branded fruit in America. In 1926 the Sunkist name was stamped on each and every succulent orange, a defining moment in American marketing history.

I HEAR AMERICA CLICKING

Designed in 1934 by Walter Dorwin Teague, the **KODAK BABY BROWNIE CAMERA**, ingenious in its simplicity, sold by the millions. Its clear, sharp images are still displayed proudly in America's family albums.

WHO COULD ASK FOR ANYTHING MORE?

No art is more American or more brilliant than the uniquely creative music of **GEORGE GERSHWIN**, and the simple, colloquial, rhymed conversational lyrics of his big brother **IRA GERSHWIN**.

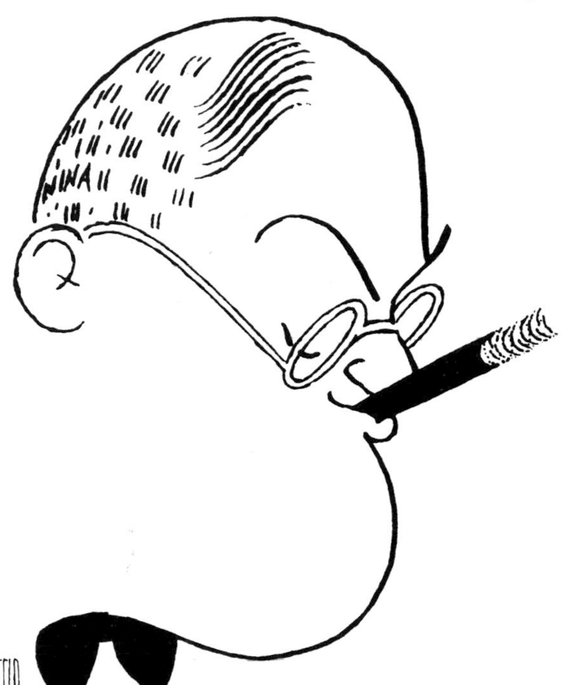

THE MOST QUOTED FOUNDING FATHER

BENJAMIN FRANKLIN was a publisher and printer (*The Pennsylvania Gazette*, *Poor Richard's Almanac*), scientist, inventor (the lightning rod, the Franklin stove, bifocal glasses), diplomat (minister to France), candlemaker, political writer and activist, linguist (fluent in five languages), abolitionist, and humorist. He established the University of Pennsylvania and Franklin & Marshall College, was the first Postmaster General, and even invented the *idea* of an American nation. And they call *Leonardo da Vinci* "the Renaissance Man."

THE FIRST ICONIC FOOD LABEL IN AMERICA

QUAKER OATS, with the instantly recognizable Quaker man, was introduced in 1887. For Americans at that time, the patriarchal Quaker was a strong homespun image, for Quakers were seen as upholding values of honesty and fair trading. The image became even more powerful in 1957 with this close-up portrait of a smiling Quaker who bore a faint resemblance to George Washington. On a cold morning, a hot bowl of Quaker Oats will bring a smile to your face.

"Remember that time is money."

"Never leave that till tomorrow which you can do today."

"Nothing can be said to be certain except death and taxes."

"Beer is proof that God loves us, and wants us to be happy."

"Three may keep a secret if two of them are dead."

"There is no little enemy."

"God helps them that help themselves."

"When the well's dry, we know the worth of water."

"Fish and visitors smell in three days."

"Little strokes, fell great oaks."

"There was never a good war or a bad peace."

"He that falls in love with himself will have no rivals."

DONNAKARAN

PERRY ELLIS

TOMMY HILFIGER

Oleg Cassini

liz claiborne

MICHAEL KORS

NORMA KAMALI

DIANE von FURSTENBERG

B

Gloria Vanderbilt

Carolina Herrera

Oscar de la Renta

BETSEY JOHNSON.

NORMAN NORELL

HALSTON

GEOFFREY BEENE

THE AMERICAN FASHION EXPLOSION

CLAIRE McCARDELL, a beautiful model turned designer, pioneered the creation of the American Look in the 1940s, with clothing that defined an American style of casual elegance. Rather than look to chic French fashion for inspiration, she recognized that American women had different needs than the European couture client—and she saw the potential of an enormous ready-to-wear market. Her free wheeling clothes reflected a modern lifestyle that was adapting to the pace of life in America. The beauty of her clothes came from new cuts that produced a clean, functional garment that comfortably flattered the wearer. In defining the American Look in the '40s and '50s, she inspired future generations of young, vibrant American designers, all unique and fresh in their contributions, establishing iconic brand names that continue to sell to both sexes of all ages, changing the world of mass fashion design forever.

THE METAMORPHOSIS OF AN ICON

From his spaghetti-western beginnings and his anti-hero tough guy role in the 1971 movie *Dirty Harry*, the development of **CLINT EASTWOOD** into an illustrious film director is one of the most stirring success stories in the annals of America. His films are lessons in humanity. Any viewing of his *Pale Rider*, *Unforgiven*, *Mystic River*, *Million Dollar Baby*, *Flags of Our Fathers*, or *Letters from Iwo Jima* would make your day. Clint Eastwood has reached the pinnacle of inspirational film directors. This intense photograph by Nigel Parry returns Eastwood to his "Go ahead—make my day" persona.

THE RETICENT NATIONAL HERO

After being picked by the Arizona Cardinals in the lowly seventh round of the 1998 NFL draft, **PAT TILLMAN** proved to be a relentlessly ferocious defensive halfback, becoming a fan favorite. But it is what Tillman did in 2002, after the terrorist attacks on America on September 11, 2001, that turned him into a national hero. Pat walked away from the Cardinals and their contract proposal of three years for $3.6 million...to join the U.S. Army instead, intent on doing his part in the war against the Al Qaeda terrorist organization that had masterminded the attacks. Pat Tillman, at the age of 27, was killed in Afghanistan by "friendly fire," instantly becoming an American hero. The awe he inspires is not related to the war in Iraq, nor is it associated with pro-war or antiwar sentiments; it is the story of a man who walked away from a lucrative career and took a courageous, principled stand in response to an attack on his country, something that most of us would not do.

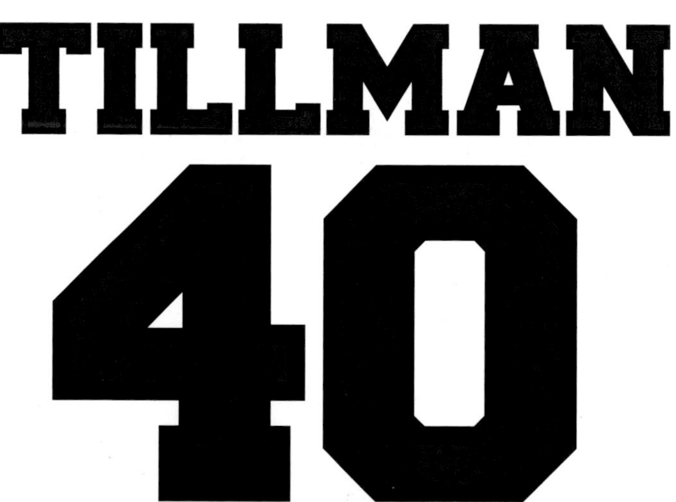

THE BEAUTY OF EXTREME SPORTS

In 1980 Scott and Brennan Olson, two brothers from Minnesota, adapted in-line skates and boldly branded them **ROLLERBLADES**. Styled like a ski boot and designed for supernatural mobility, the birth of Rollerblades helped inspire the Xtreme sports generation that expressed life in the fast lane.

THE PIONEERING AMERICAN MODERNIST

Out of the energy, vibrancy, change, and conflict of popular culture in the U.S., **STUART DAVIS** forged a personal iconography inspired by all things American he considered "hot," including introducing the use of consumer packaging, years before Pop Art hit the scene. (This explosive 1950 painting was inspired by a Champion Spark Plug matchbook cover.)

CHANGING THE WAY AMERICA CHANGED ITS OIL

In 1979 **JIFFY LUBE** pioneered the drive-thru quick-oil-change industry in America, where a team services a motorist on the go. This action logo, a circular "J" in the form of a directional sign, a striking curved red arrow, practically forces you to make a turn off the road into one of the 2,200 Jiffy Lube driveways in America.

THE STUDIO 54 PHENOMENON

It's hard to imagine now that people fueled by joints, cocaine, and LSD actually partied like that and were able to function the next day.

THE PIONEERING WOMAN ON THE FRONTIER OF ROCK

JANIS JOPLIN was a powerful, flamboyant original, a pulsating life force who exuded raw emotions that personified the 1960s and early '70s. Her rebellious, rasping sound was rich with expression; she pioneered an entirely new range of artistry for women in the male-dominated world of rock, transcending her role of a Texas-chick singer and becoming the first to front a full-fledged rock band and to become an internationally known star. The only female pop-rock star who had the balls never to wear makeup—which is just as well—her furious energy and themes of pain and loss were accompanied by streams of sweat flowing over the then startling sight of the tattoo of a heart on her ample left breast, a seminal act in the late 1970s that forged the acceptance of tattoos as art on entertainers and athletes. Everything about Joplin was original and over the top; she lost herself in drugs, speed, and booze, and sadly left us at the age of 27.

MALCOLM

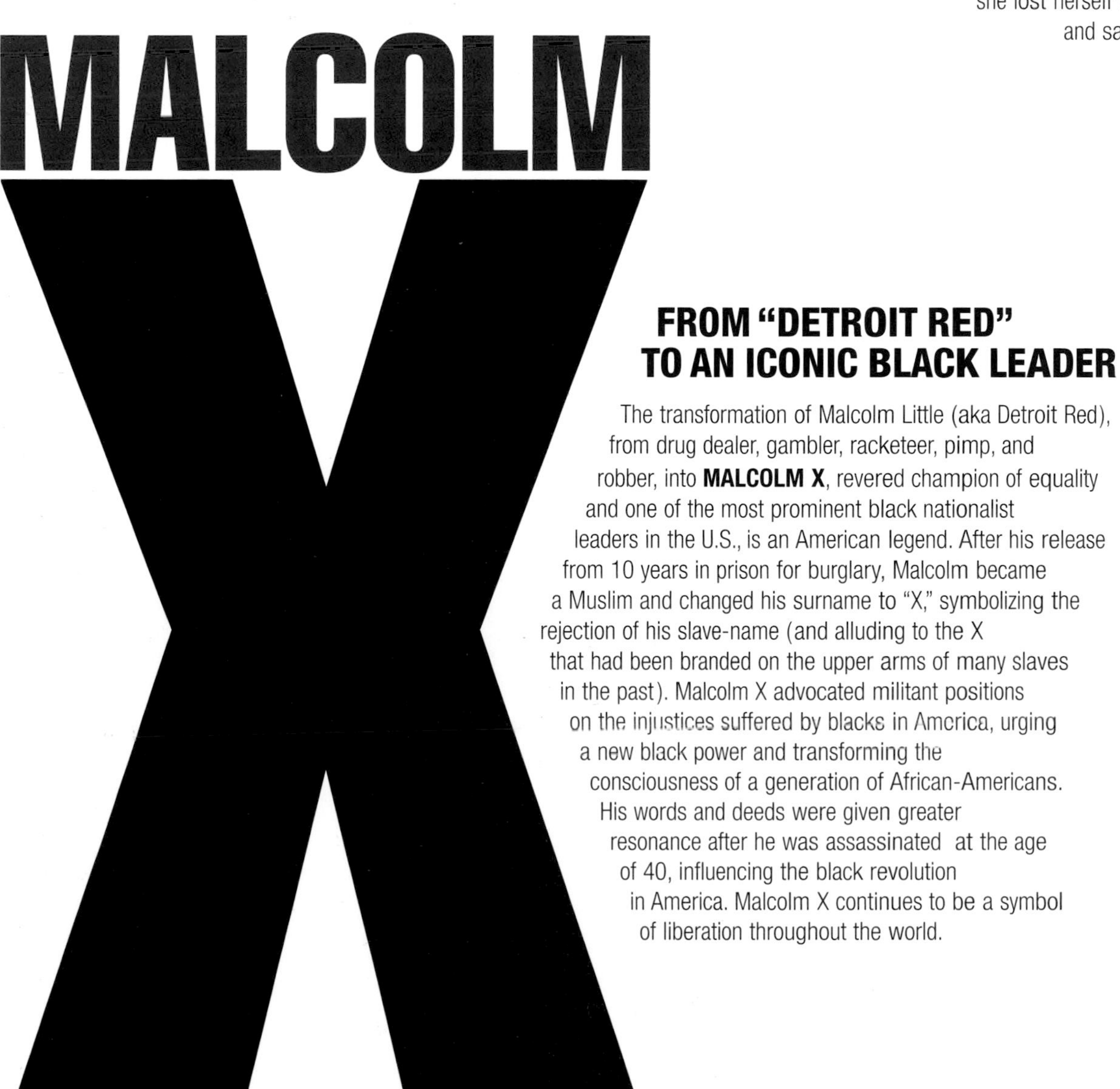

FROM "DETROIT RED" TO AN ICONIC BLACK LEADER

The transformation of Malcolm Little (aka Detroit Red), from drug dealer, gambler, racketeer, pimp, and robber, into **MALCOLM X**, revered champion of equality and one of the most prominent black nationalist leaders in the U.S., is an American legend. After his release from 10 years in prison for burglary, Malcolm became a Muslim and changed his surname to "X," symbolizing the rejection of his slave-name (and alluding to the X that had been branded on the upper arms of many slaves in the past). Malcolm X advocated militant positions on the injustices suffered by blacks in America, urging a new black power and transforming the consciousness of a generation of African-Americans. His words and deeds were given greater resonance after he was assassinated at the age of 40, influencing the black revolution in America. Malcolm X continues to be a symbol of liberation throughout the world.

THE TILLING OF AMERICA

In 1837 a young journeyman blacksmith named **JOHN DEERE** founded a farm-equipment company, that–foot by foot, acre by acre–aided the settlement and development of the midwestern United States, a vast, fertile land that the homesteaders of the 19th century transformed into a golden land of promise.

THE REAPER OF DEATH TRANSFORMED INTO A SYMBOL OF LIFE

The Civil War paintings of **WINSLOW HOMER** first brought his remarkable artistic mentality to public attention. Homer read an article in *The Atlantic Monthly* reflecting on the aftermath of the Battle of Gettysburg in 1863, leaving a total of over 43,000 casualties:
"The bodies of once living and brave men, slowly mouldering to dust in this sanctified soil, form but a small, a single sheaf from that great recent harvest reaped by Death with the sickle of war."
Profoundly moved by these words on the effect the war had on the nation, this encouraging, symbolic image of *The Veteran in a New Field* formed in Homer's mind in 1865.
From that harvest of war, Homer transformed the Grim Reaper into a symbol of life and abundance for the future of the Union.

THE EIGHT GREATEST CROONERS IN THE HISTORY OF AMERICAN POPULAR MUSIC

Caricatured by film and theater lover Al Hirschfeld are (clockwise from left) Tony Bennett, Ella Fitzgerald, Bing Crosby, Frank Sinatra, Lena Horne, Judy Garland, Nat "King" Cole, and Fred Astaire. Play it again, Sam...

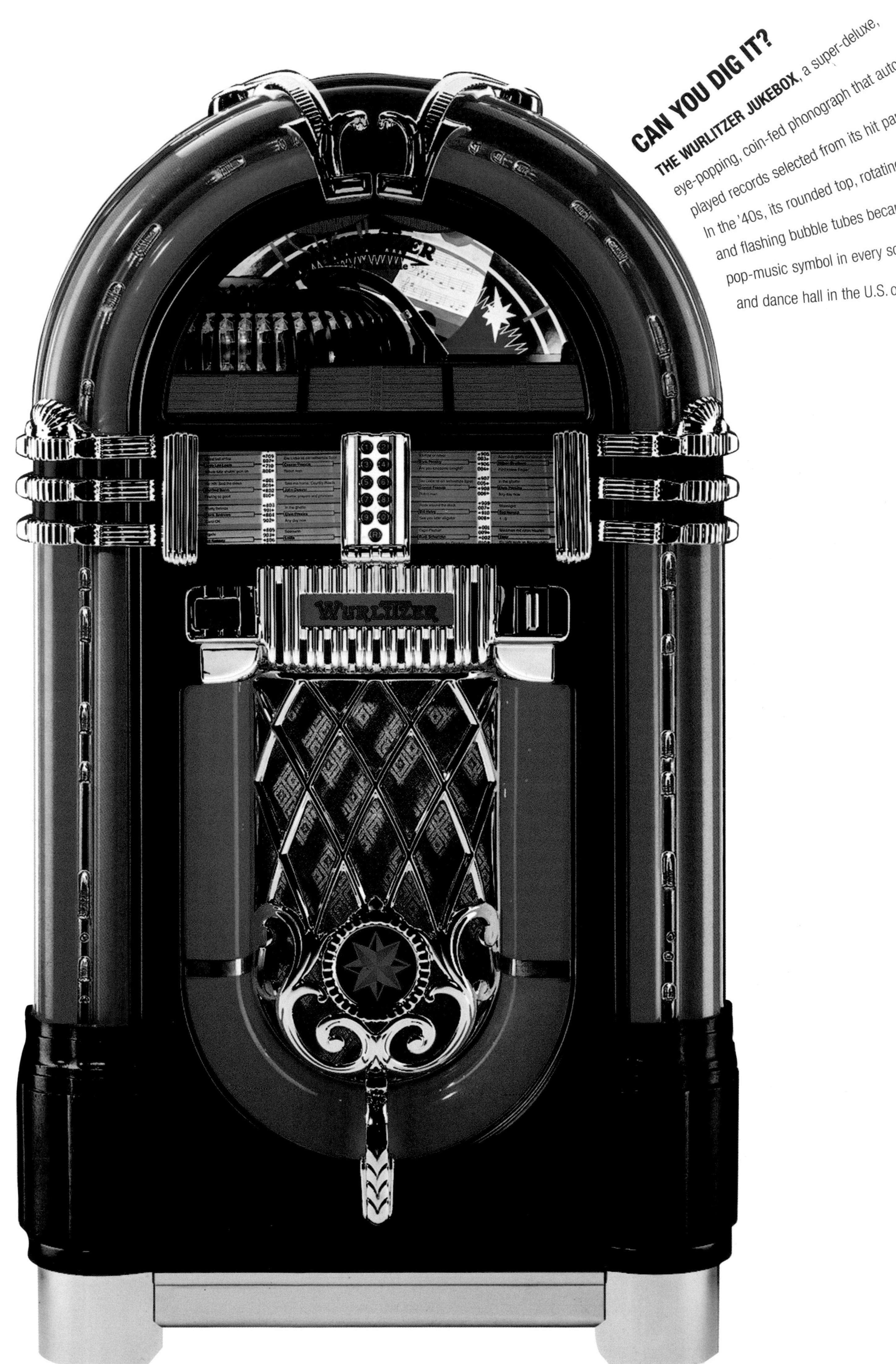

CAN YOU DIG IT?

THE WURLITZER JUKEBOX, a super-deluxe, eye-popping, coin-fed phonograph that automatically played records selected from its hit parade list. In the '40s, its rounded top, rotating color columns and flashing bubble tubes became the iconic pop-music symbol in every soda shop, bar, and dance hall in the U.S. of A.

YES, VIRGINIA, THERE REALLY IS NO BETTY CROCKER

In 1921 a group of food execs chose the name "Betty" because it seemed warm and friendly, and "Crocker" because it was the name of a retired executive. In 1924 Betty got a voice and took to the airwaves dishing out cooking advice, and in 1936 a kindly and caring portrait of her was presented to America. General Mills claims her current image is actually a combination of 75 real-life women of diverse backgrounds and ages who represent the true Betty Crocker.

"THE WOMAN EVEN WOMEN CAN ADORE"

In the early 1930s, the young femme fatale **MARLENE DIETRICH** would stride up the Champs-Elysées wearing her famous trouser suits, her hair smoothed into a neat bob. Parisians abandoned their cars and sidewalk tables and followed her up the avenue. Paramount turned Dietrich's masculine attire into a publicity triumph, touting its new star as "the woman even women can adore." She was a fashion icon as well as a film icon; no other actress brought so much taste and style to the business of glamour—not Joan Crawford, and not even Dietrich's Swedish rival, the great Garbo. All her long life, Dietrich blurred gender lines and looked the part of the modern, emancipated woman (with lovers chosen freely from both sexes). She was a woman's woman and a man's man. In this publicity shot of the young Marlene Dietrich for the 1930 movie *Morocco*, she is wearing one of her trademark tuxedos. It fits her to a T.

THE BIRTH OF RADIO

Radio station KDKA in Pittsburgh took to the airwaves in 1920, and a new culture of mass entertainment and advertising was born. This Walter Dorwin Teague *Bluebird* radio (1934) was just one of the eye-catching products of the American Machine Age.

SHE MAKES PEOPLE CARE BECAUSE *SHE* CARES

OPRAH WINFREY talks to millions of us in the privacy, and sometimes loneliness, of our homes. She empathizes, entertains, and educates. (Being selected for Oprah's Book Club means that the title will soar to the top of bestseller lists.) She edged out both Superman and Elvis to be named the greatest pop-culture icon of all time by VH1; she was named near the top of *Fortune's 50 Most Powerful Women in America* list; she has the highest rated daytime talk-show in television history; and she is one of the most famous and influential philanthropists in the world.

THE MOTHER OF ALL MODERN MUSEUMS

The first museum in the world built exclusively for Modern Art, the **MUSEUM OF MODERN ART** opened in New York in 1929, ten days after the Wall Street crash. Financed by the Rockefeller family, the iconic museum was designed in the International Style by modernist architects Philip Goodwin and Edward Durell Stone. The spectacular Abby Aldrich Rockefeller sculpture garden, designed by Philip Johnson, was added in 1953. In 1984 a major renovation, designed by Cesar Pelli, doubled the museum's size, and in 2004 another extensive addition, designed by Yoshio Taniguchi, made MoMA the mother of all museums.

THE EASTER BUNNY

Although originating in Western European culture, the Easter Bunny has become an American symbol reflecting the renewal of life in springtime and the Resurrection in the Christian religion. Each year a trustworthy rabbit leaves Easter baskets full of candy, gifts, and colored eggs (red, symbolizing the blood of the sacrificed Christ; green, emerging foliage; pastels, a rainbow of hope). The prolific fertility of rabbits, "breeding like bunnies," adds to the concept of the annual rebirth of mankind.

BUGS BUNNY

One of the most recognizable American images, real or imaginary, is Bugs Bunny, a street-smart gray rabbit with a Mel Blanc Brooklyn accent who stars in the Looney Tunes and Merrie Melodies animated films produced by Warner Bros. "Of course you realize, 'dis means War!" is his response to any bullying or threat in his constant feuds with Elmer Fudd, Yosemite Sam, Daffy Duck, and Marvin the Martian. With wit and guile, the carrot-chomping Bugs Bunny always comes out the winner. *What's up, doc?*

"SOME DRY WHITE TOAST, PLEASE"

John Belushi (as "Joliet" Jake Blues) and Dan Aykroyd (as Elwood Blues) made their television debut as **THE BLUES BROTHERS** in a 1978 episode of NBC's *Saturday Night Live*. The instant popular reaction to their schtick inspired them to assemble a talented band that melded jazz, soul, and blues, producing an album that went double platinum. Their rip-roaring success led to *The Blues Brothers* film, directed by John Landis, that has become an American cult phenomenon. The photograph shown is an interpretation in blue of the iconic pair by the iconic photographer **ANNIE LEIBOVITZ**. The tragic drug-induced death of John Belushi in 1982 robbed the world of a comic genius.

Jake: *Bring me four fried chickens and a Coke!*
Elwood: *For me, some dry white toast, please.*

POP ART IN 1926

Designed by Charles Strite, **THE TOASTMASTER** was the first toaster able to brown both sides of the bread simultaneously, pop up the toast, and turn itself off. Another technological breakthrough!

THE ICONIC STREET CON

Anybody walking the streets of a major city in America who runs into a group of con artists playing **THE SHELL GAME**, and who actually places a bet on which of three walnuts is covering a pea the "shell man" has quickly shuffled, is nuts. The player (otherwise known as a "victim") cannot possibly win. Consider yourself warned.

"I DID EVERYTHING FRED ASTAIRE DID, EXCEPT BACKWARDS AND IN HIGH HEELS"

GINGER ROGERS' stardom occurred when she was teamed with the gifted Fred Astaire, forming the greatest dancing duo ever to hit the silver screen. *Flying Down to Rio* (1933), *Roberta* (1935), and *Top Hat* (1935) made their names synonymous—even the grave of Ginger's screen partner is just yards away from hers. Together, from 1933 to 1939, they made nine musical films at RKO, revolutionizing the Hollywood musical, introducing dance routines of unprecedented elegance and virtuosity, set to songs specially composed for them by the greatest pop-song composers of the day, and performed in the most glamorous Art Deco sets ever seen on film. To this day, "Fred and Ginger" remains an automatic reference for any successful partnership. Katharine Hepburn said of the great dance duo, "Fred gave Ginger class, and Ginger gave Fred sex appeal."

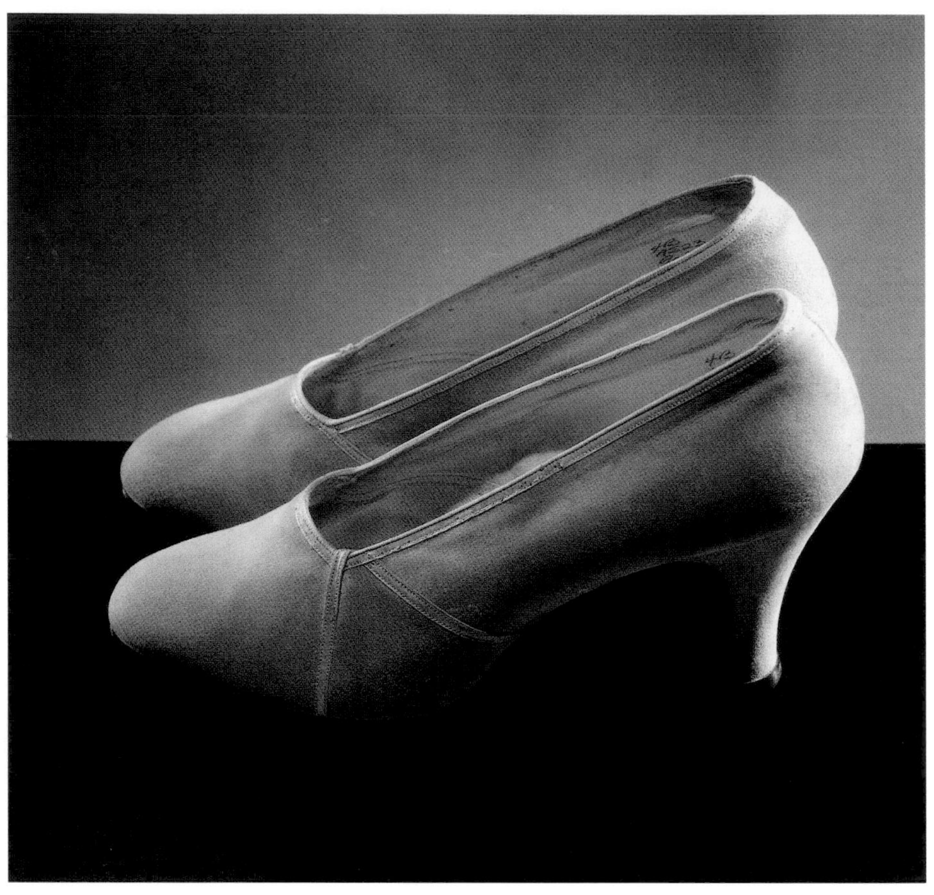

THE BEST ACTION AT A DALLAS COWBOYS GAME IS ON THE SIDELINE

Organized cheering first started at Princeton University in the late 1800s with the crowd chant *Rah Rah Rah, Tiger Tiger Tiger, Sis Sis Sis, Boom Boom Boom, Ahhhh, Princeton Princeton Princeton,* a way to get the football crowd into the game. In 1898 Johnny Campbell, a student at the University of Minnesota, stood in front of a crowd and directed them in a chant, making him the first cheerleader. But through the years, cheerleading has been mainly a female war dance at football games. Cheerleading in high schools and colleges remains a serious athletic activity, requiring gymnastic skills, partner stunts, pyramids, and breathtaking jumps. But in 1972 the **DALLAS COWBOYS CHEERLEADERS** made it a new ball game in the National Football League, with revealing costumes and provocative dance moves. "America's Sweethearts" are the sexiest gals in Texas.
Don't take our word for it–check them out at a Cowboys game.

BOOP-OOP-A-DOOP!

BETTY BOOP was the original flapper cartoon, making her appearance in 1933. The cartoon sex symbol was modeled on Helen Kane, a cutesy-pie singer at Paramount Pictures. Betty, a flapper with more heart than brains, became infamous in the 1932 short *Minnie the Moocher*, backed by the big-band orchestra of Cab Calloway.
Betty Boop was the first cartoon character to represent a sexpot as she exposed her panties (as shown, or rather as *not* shown), a garter, and breasts with ample cleavage. But Betty was finally done in when the production code censorship laws in the late 1930s forced her to cover up.
A sad day in America.

A REAL-LIFE SUPERHERO

Even before the death of **CHRISTOPHER REEVE** in 2004, his fight for research on new treatments for severe spinal cord injuries had won him the cultural status of an iconic symbol, not unlike the cinematic role he was most famous for, Superman. In 1995, Reeve, a fine stage and screen actor, was paralyzed from the neck down after falling from his horse in an equestrian competition. For the remainder of his life he was confined to a wheelchair (as shown in this powerful portrait by Herb Ritts), unable to breathe for long without the assistance of a mechanical respirator. Sitting in his wheelchair, Lincoln-like, with seemingly supernatural strength, speaking sporadically while sucking for air, Reeve gallantly became a spokesman for the disabled and a crusader for stem-cell research. Christopher Reeve was a magnificent human being, and a real-life superhero.

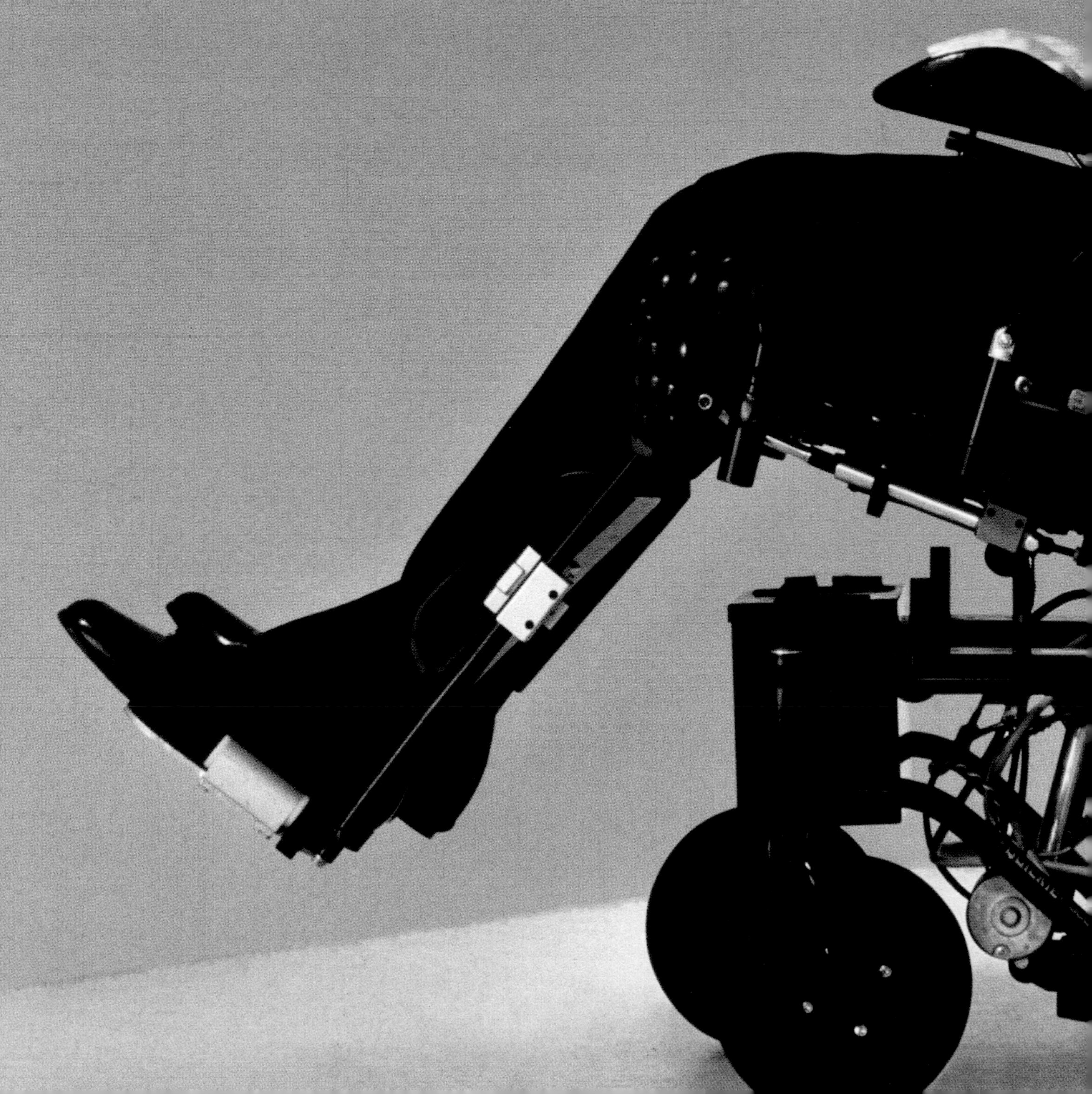

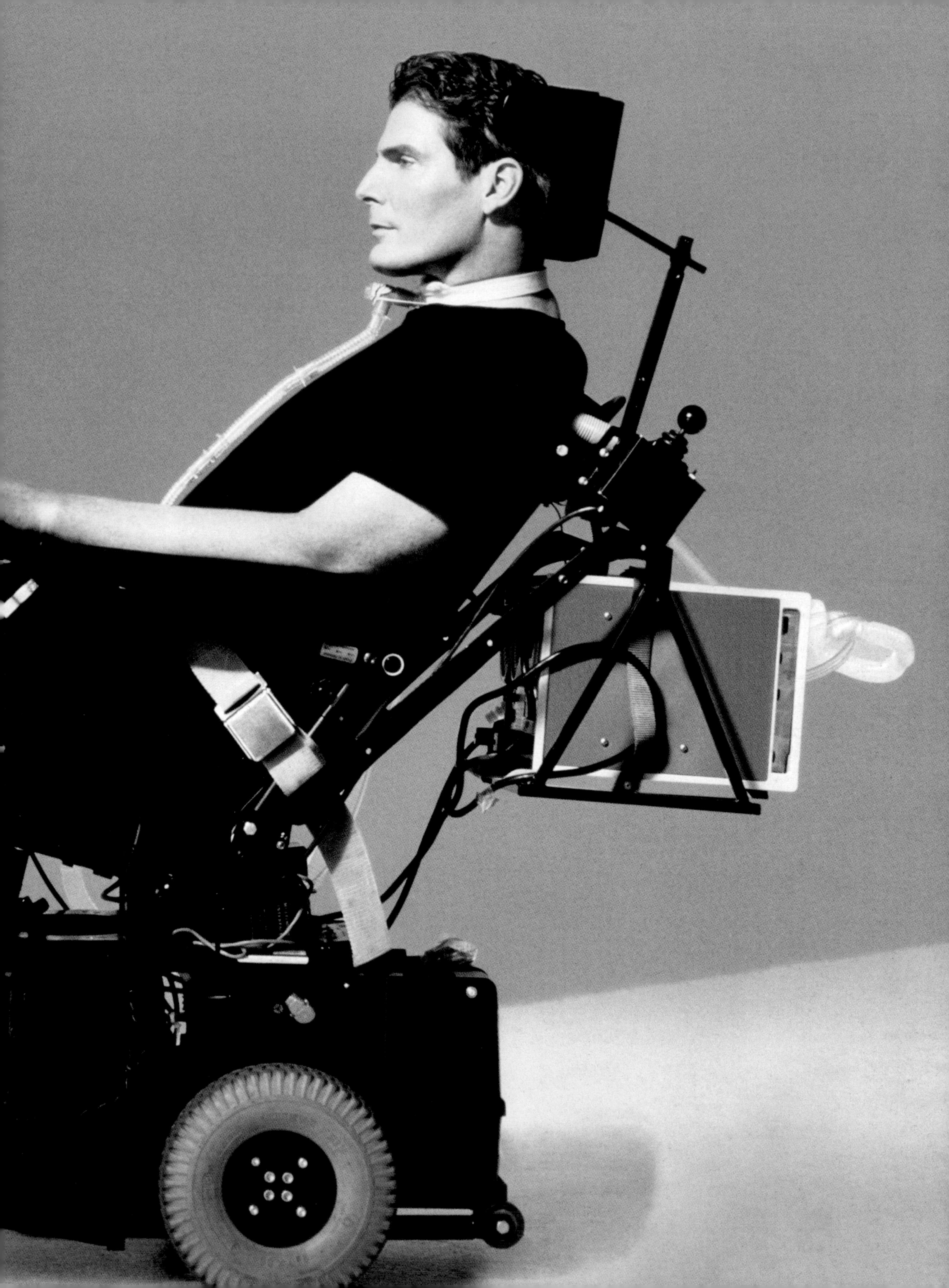

"AND A LITTLE CHILD SHALL LEAD THEM"

THE PEACEABLE KINGDOM (1847) one of the many variations painted by Edward Hicks, was a powerful spiritual and symbolic representation of "burying the hatchet," portraying the legendary William Penn in a friendly powwow with the Indians in the lands of Pennsylvania. The heartfelt charm of the popular image reflected a literal interpretation of the prophecy in Isaiah (11:6): "The Wolf also shall dwell with the lamb, and the leopard shall lie down with the kid; and the calf and the young lion and the fatling together; and a little child shall lead them." Hicks gives no clue as to whether the wolf represented the Indian—or the invading European.

AMERIKA'S FIRST IKONIK KOMIK STRIP

One of the earliest comic strips, created in 1913 by George Herriman, a kartoonist for the Hearst papers, was **KRAZY KAT**, a kat of indeterminate sex, who was in love with Ignatz Mouse, who demonstrated her (his?) affection by tossing "a heavy brick upon Krazy's knoodle." Meanwhile, Offissa Pupp, the local kanine konstable, also loved Krazy, and tried to protect him (her?) by attempting to katch Ignatz at her (his?) various kriminal kapers and throw the rat in the jug. The hoi polloi loved the strip, and the swells were big fans of Krazy Kat, among them: Pablo Picasso, Charlie Chaplin, Gertrude Stein, F. Scott Fitzgerald, James Joyce, Frank Kapra, and an impressionable young Walt Disney, years before Mickey Mouse. (Our spellcheck went krazy as this piece was being typed.)

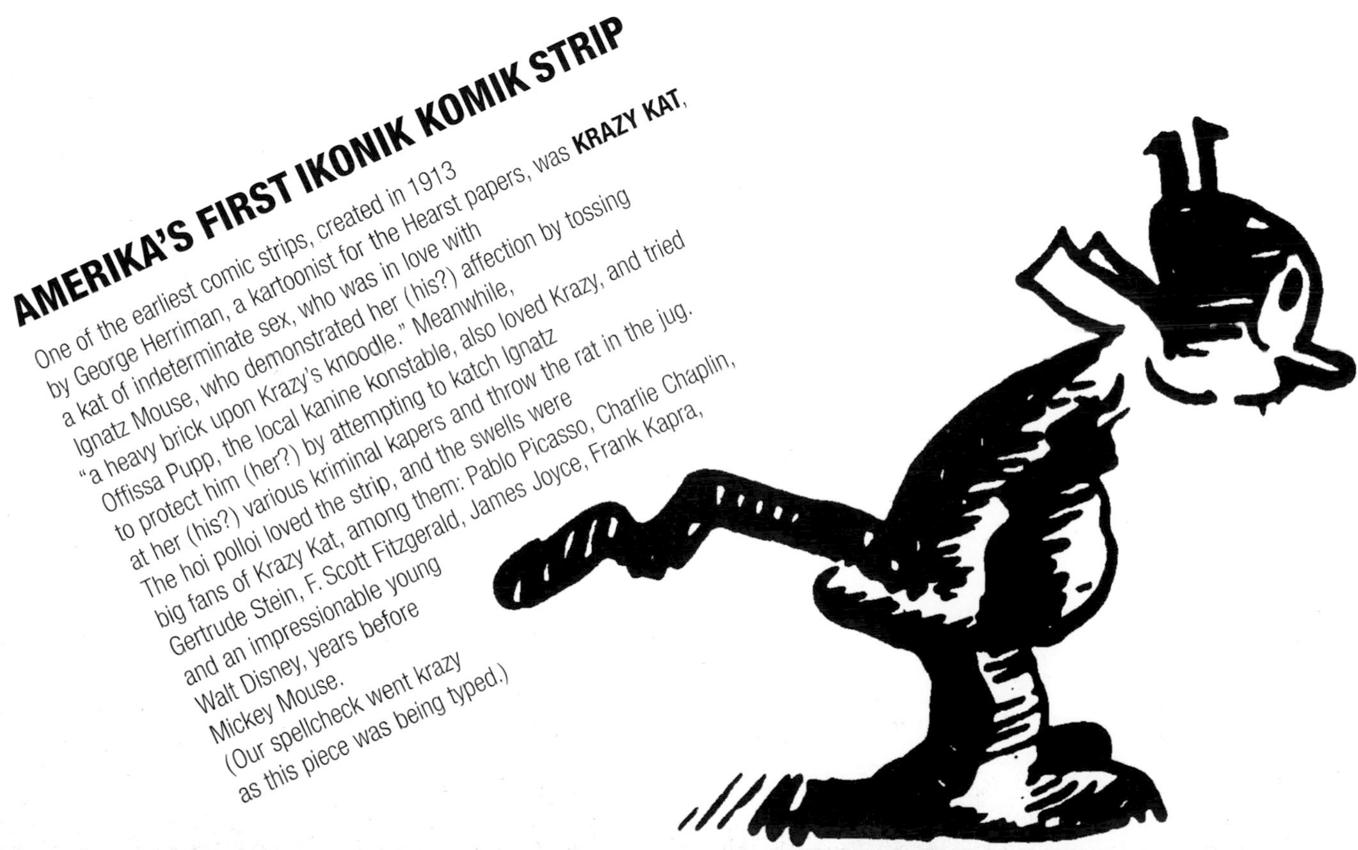

A NATION OF DOG LOVERS

The Old and New Testaments speak of dogs with contempt as "unclean beasts." Today, some cultures eat dogs, some cultures are afraid of dogs, and some cultures train dogs to fight. In America, dogs are regarded as residents of their homes, even members of the family, and those families spend billions of dollars a year to provide good food, shelter, and kind, loving attention. There are 65 million dogs owned in America. Thirty-nine percent of U.S. households (or 40.6 million) own at least one dog. Dogs in America are companions, guard dogs, guide dogs for the blind, bomb and drug sniffers, and a hunter's best friend. As objects of beauty, the pedigreed pooches are status symbols, primped and displayed for competitive dog shows. Some have even been pop stars: Rin Tin Tin, Lassie, Nipper, Beethoven, White Fang, Hooch, Spuds McKenzie, Sandy, Snoopy, Toto... (Marilyn is shown snuggling a lovable Pekingese – *the lucky dog!*)

THE WASHINGTON MONUMENT IN 1860 (THE SYMBOL OF A NATION DIVIDED)

As we built our nation we built our national icons. In 1836 a design was chosen for a lasting monument whose dimensions and magnificence would symbolize America's gratitude to and reverence for our first president. A 600-foot Egyptian-style obelisk was designed, then modified to 500 feet. The cornerstone of the Washington Monument was laid in 1848 and work progressed slowly, stone by stone; the monument had reached the height of 156 feet in 1854, when the impending crisis of a civil war interrupted the meticulous work. The obelisk remained truncated during the turbulent time of the Civil War. Then in 1876 work was resumed—but the exact stone could not be matched! Nevertheless, the glorious monument was completed in 1884, topped with an added 55-foot-tall pyramid. The monument reaches a height of 555 feet, the world's tallest masonry structure. Next time you visit Washington, when the light is just right, you can spot the exact point in our history when the United States of America was threatened with a heartrending physical and spiritual division. (This vintage image was taken by the great Matthew Brady, circa 1860.)

STEPPING INTO THE FUTURE

Augustus Saint-Gaudens was the greatest sculptor in American history. This figure of **VICTORY** (Nike) was part of a design for the monument to General William Tecumseh Sherman installed at the Fifth Avenue entrance to New York's Central Park in 1902. St. Gaudens' classically draped winged figure, striding boldly forward leading the victorious general on horseback, was the embodiment of a spiritual war to save the Union and end slavery, a symbol of the grandeur of a new age of freedom in the United States of America.

LIFE GIVES BIRTH TO THE WORLD OF JOURNALISM

In 1936 Henry Luce, the publisher of *Fortune* and *Time*, bought a successful magazine called **LIFE**, wanting only its name, and recreated it as the greatest weekly magazine in history. In the years following World War II, *Life* was so popular that President Truman, Sir Winston Churchill, and General Douglas MacArthur all serialized their memoirs in its lush 9"x12" pages. *Life* spawned many imitations, such as *Look*, but Luce's lineup of legendary photographers such as Edward Steichen, Alfred Eisenstaedt, Margaret Bourke-White, Eugene Smith, and Gordon Parks dazzled the eye and the mind, week after week, and *Life* dominated the news-magazine category for more than 40 years.

THREE MARTYRED LEGENDS

JOHN F. KENNEDY, **ROBERT F. KENNEDY** and **DR. MARTIN LUTHER KING, JR.**, the three most mourned Americans since FDR, were all assassinated within a fateful five-year period. Here they are seen hauntingly watching over the sacred ground of Arlington National Cemetery, in a hagiographic fantasy created for an *Esquire* cover in 1968, a short time after the death of Robert Kennedy. It was a sorry, dark period in American history.

MAKE LOVE NOT WAR

This rallying cry for youthful antiwar activists during the Vietnam War was used on dozens of poster and button designs in the U.S. Along with the worldwide peace symbol, which was originally designed as a logo for the Campaign for Nuclear Disarmament, it became the slogan for American counterculture during the Age of Aquarius.

dward R Murrow
Ben Shahn

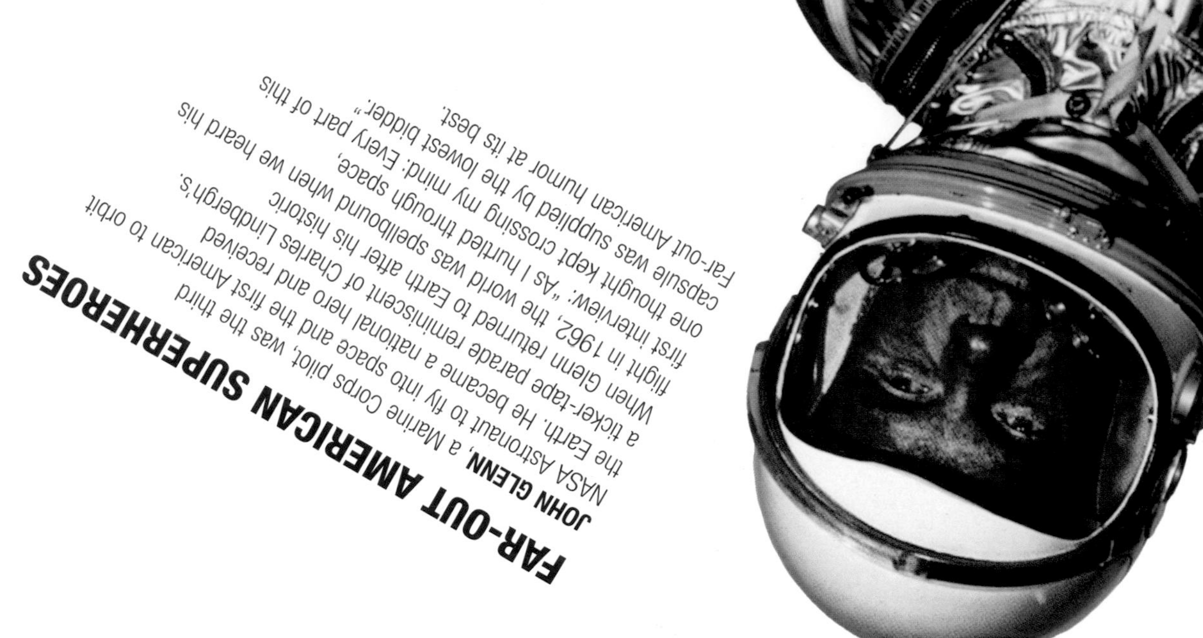

FAR-OUT AMERICAN SUPERHEROES

JOHN GLENN, a Marine Corps pilot, was the third NASA Astronaut to fly into space and the first American to orbit the Earth. He became a national hero and received a ticker-tape parade reminiscent of Charles Lindbergh's. When Glenn returned to Earth after his historic flight in 1962, the world was spellbound when we heard his first interview: "As I hurtled through space, one thought kept crossing my mind: Every part of this capsule was supplied by the lowest bidder." Far-out American humor at its best.

THE SLAYER OF McCARTHYISM

On March 9, 1954, during the shameful period of McCarthyism, legendary CBS newsman **EDWARD R. MURROW** looked dead into the eye of every American and said: "We will not walk in fear, one of another. We will not be driven by fear into an age of unreason, if we dig deep in our history and our doctrine, and remember that we are not descended from fearful men—not from men who feared to write, to speak, to associate and to defend causes that were, for the moment, unpopular... We can deny our heritage and our history, but we cannot escape responsibility for the result. There is no way for a citizen of the Republic to abdicate his responsibilities." With these words in his *Report on Senator Joseph McCarthy*, Edward R. Murrow, the pioneering television news broadcaster who had first come to prominence with his radio broadcasts during World War II, slayed the dragon of McCarthyism in America. "Good night, and good luck." (This drawing by **BEN SHAHN**, a blacklist victim during that period, was a stinging attack on McCarthy that ran in a CBS Television tune-in ad the morning of that fateful day.)

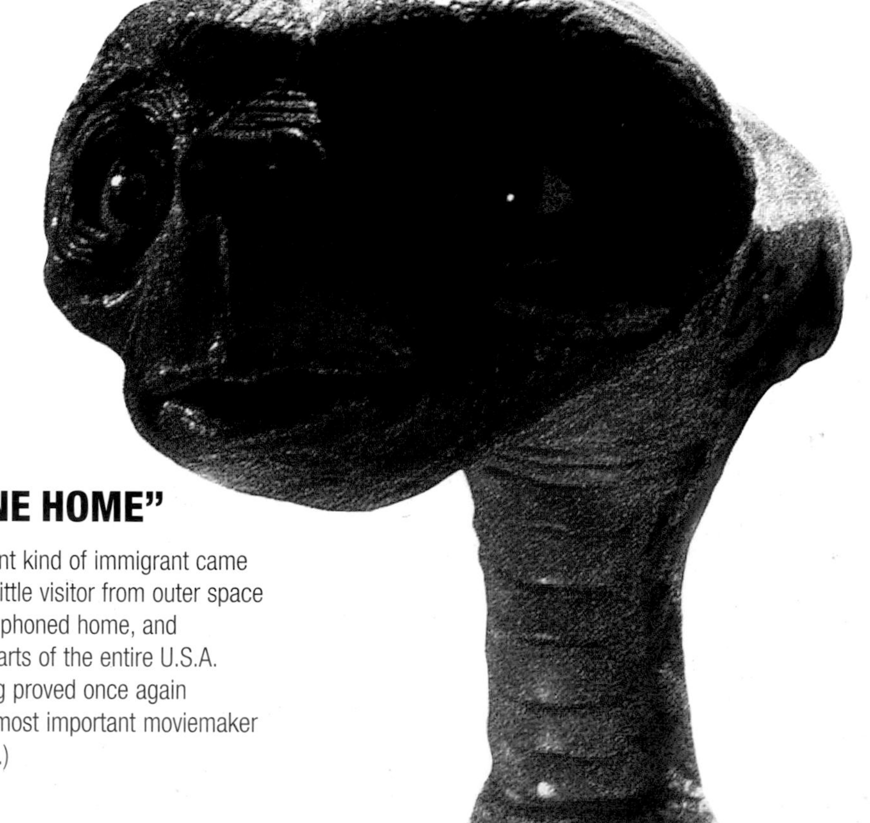

"E.T., PHONE HOME"

In 1982 a different kind of immigrant came to America; this little visitor from outer space landed on Earth, phoned home, and turned on the hearts of the entire U.S.A. (Steven Spielberg proved once again that he was the most important moviemaker of his generation.)

THE ICONIC, GALLOPING PONY EXPRESS

The Pony Express was a wildly romantic mail service made up of "young, skinny, wiry fellows, not over 18, expert riders, willing to risk death daily, orphans preferred," who carried the mail on horseback across the prairies, plains, deserts, and tortuous mountain paths of the Western United States. At the beginning of the Civil War, from the Missouri River to the Pacific Coast, riders drove their steeds at full gallop from station to station at intervals of ten miles, changing to a fresh horse at each station, carrying 20 pounds of mail, averaging ten mph for 100 miles each exhausting day. The arrival of the Iron Horse cut short the Pony Express after only 18 months, but the idea of a band of rugged individualists fighting against all odds to get the mail through from St. Joseph, Missouri, to the gold-mining communities of California, has lingered as one of our most romantic images of the West.

...REPLACED BY THE ICONIC IRON HORSE

THE FIRST TRANSCONTINENTAL RAILROAD, considered the greatest technological feat of the 19th century, linked the railway network of the eastern U.S. all the way to California on the Pacific Coast. It was one of the crowning achievements of Abraham Lincoln, completed four years after his assassination. The **UNION PACIFIC RAILROAD** built the railway *westward*, starting in Omaha, Nebraska; the Central Pacific Railroad, starting in Sacramento, California, headed *eastward*. They finally connected at Promontory Summit, Utah. On May 10, 1869, the last spike (a gold-plated Golden Spike) was driven in, symbolizing the completion of the transcontinental railroad, fulfilling Lincoln's dream of connecting the nation from sea to shining sea. Shown to the right is a rendition of the Union Pacific Railroad shield logo, a folk-art celebration of the great event.

75 MILLION ROARING FANS

America is a **NASCAR** nation—the fastest growing, most popular sports business in the U.S., attracting a fanatical down-home fan base and more sponsorship by corporate America than the powerful National Football League. Stock-car racing is now a multimillion-dollar business, the second-most-watched sport on television after pro football. NASCAR drivers are media-savvy, fan-friendly marketing machines—their roster includes such superstar drivers as Dale Earnhardt, Richard Petty, A. J. Foyt, Jeff Gordon, Jimmie Johnson, Dale Earnhardt, Jr., Kasey Kahane—as one-third of all American adults follow their pursuit of breakneck speed from the stands or from their sofas.

AHEAD OF THE PACK

American cars of the mid-1950s were pure Americana: streamlined aesthetics adorned with **HOOD ORNAMENTS** of sensuous goddesses, rocketships, or this spectacular incarnation of the Indian Chief Pontiac.

BULL'S-EYE!

There are numerous humongous mass-market discount retailers in America: Wal-Mart, Kmart, Kroger, Kohl's, Sears, and Costco among them. But in the matter of mass class, **TARGET** zeros in on upscale, trend-forward merchandise offered at low cost, as opposed to the marketing of low-cost, low-priced goods (where low prices strongly suggest low quality to the consumer). Giants like Wal-Mart are brutally efficient at selling basic necessities, but Target has Isaac Mizrahi clothes and Michael Graves housewares (on which, by the way, the margins are terrific). At the Wal-Marts of the world, you save two cents here, 19 cents there. Target is the *cool* mass-shopping destination for Americans who buy for taste as well as price.

THE FIRST CARTOON IN AN AMERICAN NEWSPAPER

In 1754, 20 years before the outbreak of the American Revolution, Benjamin Franklin urged the American colony to prepare for its own defense against both French and Indian forces on the frontier, who continually attacked the American subjects of Great Britain. The mother country appeared incapable or unwilling to protect them. Franklin's cartoon, *Join, or Die*, appeared in his **PENNSYLVANIA GAZETTE**, and called for the delegates to the Albany convention of 1754 to organize an inter-colonial council for defense, with taxing powers, an American army, fortifications, an expansion plan, and a Crown-appointed presiding officer. Every colony rejected his plan. Franklin believed until his death that if it had been adopted, it would have prevented the need for the American Revolution. Blimey!

®
AN AMERICAN ICON?
YUP!
Montana outdoorsman GARY COOPER transformed himself into Mr. America and played classic American film roles: John Doe (Meet John Doe), Longfellow Deeds (Mr. Deeds Goes to Town), Lou Gehrig (The Pride of The Yankees), Howard Roark (The Fountainhead), Robert Jordan (For Whom the Bell Tolls), and—terse to the point of being monosyllabic—Marshal Will Kane in High Noon. Cooper personified the strong and silent type, whose ethos demanded he courageously do the right thing no matter what the cost.

"I HAVE TWO LOVES, MY COUNTRY AND PAREE"

To Parisians, **JOSEPHINE BAKER** was America. The mischievous 19-year-old topless dancer, soon to be nicknamed "Black Venus," left her native St. Louis in 1925 and moved to Paris to perform her unique versions of American jazz, blues, and boogie-woogie. The slinky beauty's eroticism, humor, and courage are interwoven into the fabric of American music. Her new world was *La Revue Nègre* of Paris: bare-breasted, wearing high heels, and her famous banana skirt or revealing feathery outfits, often accompanied by her pet cheetah, Chiquita (who was adorned with a diamond collar). Baker helped make the Paris between the wars a magical, glittering city–the world capital of art and entertainment. Baker's sauciness and humor wowed the French–her signature song was *J'ai deux amours* ("I Have Two Loves"–my country and Paris)–and she became a muse for cultural mavericks such as Langston Hughes, Ernest Hemingway, F. Scott Fitzgerald, and Pablo Picasso. During visits to America both before and after World War II, she was never received with open arms–because she refused to perform in segregated nightclubs–but she was finally given her due at a celebration of her life at Carnegie Hall in 1973. But Josephine Baker was not without her affectations. At a dinner party held for her in New York, she stood up and gave a gracious thank-you talk, speaking French, as well as English with a French accent. A black maid went up to her and whispered, "Honey, you is full of shit. Speak the way yo' mouth was born." Josephine had her fired.

THE BIRTH OF INSTANT CELEBRITY

Celebrity is a 20th-century phenomenon. Cultural historians agree that the transformation of fame, which was once the result of some past *deed* (or misdeed) suddenly becoming an instantaneous act of unearned celebrity–was the result of the birth of mass media in the early decades of the 20th century. That phenomenon was led by the birth of **MOVIE FAN MAGAZINES**, making many a pretty face memorable and famous with repetition on their sycophantic covers. *Motion Picture Stories* was launched in 1911, followed by *Photoplay* and *Silver Screen*, all featuring movie stars on their covers, handsomely drawn or photographed. This parade of covers drove the star system through the Golden Age of Hollywood, with 60 popular culture magazines published between 1911 and 1940 in the U.S.A. alone. Today, almost every mass magazine on our newsstands has been captivated by the sicko-fan ethos of pop culture. This 1934 *Silver Screen* cover helped screen star Jean Harlow become the most famous woman in America.

IN AMERICA, NO MAN IS ABOVE THE LAW–NOT EVEN THE PRESIDENT

Just when you think democracy might be going haywire in America, we prove to ourselves and to the generations that follow that we have an innate American ability to right ourselves. In 1972, the administration of President Richard Milhous Nixon planned a break-in at the headquarters of the Democratic National Committee at the Watergate Hotel in Washington, D.C. The "plumbers unit," which included former members of the C.I.A., planted listening devices while disguised as common criminals to provide cover. A security guard saw signs of the break-in, called the D.C. police, and the five burglars were arrested. Investigative reporting by Bob Woodward and Carl Bernstein of the *Washington Post* led to hearings held by a senate committee. The burning question was "What did the President know, and when did he know it?," focusing attention on Nixon's involvement in **THE WATERGATE SCANDAL**. We learned that our president was up to his ears in criminal activities: He had evaded taxes, accepted illegal campaign contributions, ordered secret bombings, harassed his opponents, ordered wiretaps and break-ins, and when the shit hit the fan, stonewalled with an illegal cover-up. The smoking gun was when his secret conversations, which Nixon had recorded on audiotape, were revealed and subpoenaed, proving his complicity in the burglary and cover-up. Named by the grand jury as a co-conspirator, President Nixon resigned on August 9, 1974, the only president so disgraced. The Constitution and American democracy had prevailed. Nine months earlier, at a press conference, the President of the United States had faced the nation and said, "I am not a crook." He lied.

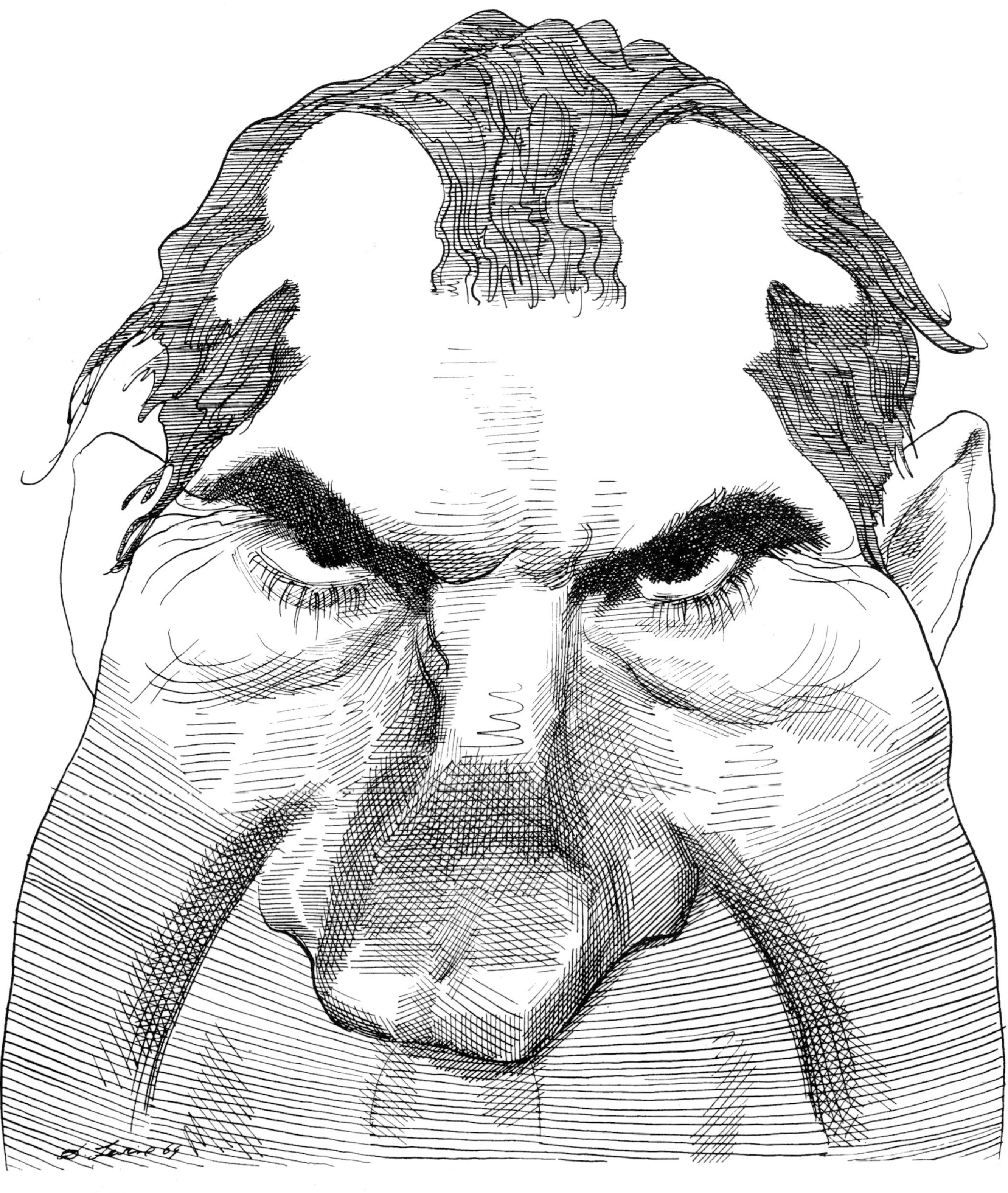

A NATION CRACKED AND IN NEED OF HEALING
(THE TRUE STORY OF AMERICA'S LIBERTY BELL)

The so-called **LIBERTY BELL** was cast in the early 1750s to toll in the Pennsylvania State House and to commemorate the 50-year anniversary of William Penn's 1701 Charter of Privileges, Pennsylvania's original Constitution—a powerful declaration of the rights and freedoms of Americans living under British rule. Penn's concept of religious freedom, his liberal stance on Native American rights, and his inclusion of citizens in the enacting of laws, were precursors of the future. The bell's inscription prophetically read: "Proclaim Liberty throughout all the land unto all the inhabitants thereof," a quarter of a century before our Declaration of Independence. Tradition tells us that the bell summoned citizens to hear the first public reading of the Declaration on July 8,1776. Not! The truth is that the bell only achieved iconic status when, in 1839, Abolitionists adapted it as a symbol for their struggle to bring liberty to America's slaves, and gave it the name *Liberty Bell.* As for the legendary crack, it seems the bell was a lemon—broken on the first stroke of the clapper in 1753! Looking back, the cracked Liberty Bell was a ringing metaphor for a country breaking apart with a civil war being fought for the freedom of its black slaves.
P.S. If this story about our heritage doesn't ring a bell, blame it on our history books.

80,000 SERVED AT THE KENTUCKY DERBY

In 1794 German and Scots-Irish farmers in Pennsylvania, who made whiskey from the rye they grew, refused to pay taxes on their product to the fledgling U.S. government. They took up arms in what became known as the Whiskey Rebellion and President George Washington sent in troops. Some farmers fled the tumult, landed in Kentucky, planted *corn* instead of rye, and distilled America's only native spirit: bourbon! When the Kentucky Derby, held at Churchill Downs in Louisville, became a tradition, everybody drank a combination of bourbon, locally harvested mint, sugar, and water (with well-crushed ice, of course) named **THE MINT JULEP**. 80,000 juleps are served each year during the Derby. Always served in a silver or pewter cup (as shown) the mint julep is synonymous with not only the Kentucky Derby, but the traditions of the old South.

THE INDOMITABLE UNDERDOG

At the peak of his celebrity in the late 1930s, **SEABISCUIT**, a runty, crooked-legged racehorse rescued from obscurity by a California car dealer and ridden by a one-eyed jockey with the help of a washed-up trainer, was more famous and beloved than President Franklin Delano Roosevelt. Seabiscuit-mania sprang from the horse's intrepid fighting spirit at a time of growth in a national mass culture fueled by rural electrification, photo-wire services, cheap radios, and the ardent connection of depression-weary Americans with a scrappy underdog. Seabiscuit's biggest win was "The Match of the Century" in 1938, the most eagerly anticipated sporting event of its time, when the stalwart racehorse pulled away from War Admiral, the Triple Crown Champion, and won by three clean lengths.

TEARS OF A NATION

On Friday, November 22, 1963, at 11:37, Air Force One touched down at Love Field, and Dallas' greeting, like the 76 degree temperature, was warm and refreshing. Because of the pleasant weather, the plastic bubble top of the Presidential Lincoln limousine was removed and the bullet-proof side windows rolled down. At 11:50 a.m., once Kennedy was seated, his motorcade began to roll on an 11-mile route through downtown Dallas. Mrs. John Connolly, seated in the jump seat with Texas Governor John Connolly, turned smilingly to the president and said, "You can't say that Dallas doesn't love you." Jack Kennedy's reply was cut off by the sharp, brutal sound of a gunshot. Three shots seem to have been fired, the last exploding the president's head on impact. First Lady Jacqueline Kennedy cried "Jack! Oh no! No!" as she reached for her stricken husband. **THE ASSASSINATION OF JOHN F. KENNEDY** was an act of horror that shook the world, forever haunting the American psyche.

B

BUCK ROGERS BLASTS OFF!

In the year 1928 **BUCK ROGERS** blasts off (in the year 2419) on the cover of one of America's popular pulp magazines.

"PSST, WANNA BUY A BRIDGE?"

Designed by John Augustus Roebling and built by hand from 1869 to 1883, **THE BROOKLYN BRIDGE** is a noble gateway between the boroughs of Brooklyn and Manhattan. Among many stunning photographic and painted images, Joseph Stella's expressionistic masterpiece depicts the spectacular, soaring, cathedral-like landmark with huge vaulted spaces and modernistic steel cables, still the most monumental bridge span ever built by man.

CHANGING THE FACE OF THE NATION

Baseball, America's Game, was a *segregated* game—until, in the spring of 1947, **JACKIE ROBINSON**, wearing a Brooklyn Dodger uniform, thrilled fans, shattered baseball's color barrier, and changed the face of the nation. Hank Aaron, a beneficiary of the pioneering Jackie Robinson, paid homage to his legacy with this glowing appreciation: "Jackie was bigger than life; bigger than the teammates who got up a petition to keep him off the club, bigger than the pitchers who threw at him or the base runners who dug their spikes into his skin, bigger than the bench jockey who hollered for him to carry his bags and shine his shoes, bigger than the so-called fans who mocked him with mops on their heads and made death threats." Jackie Robinson let his bat, his fielding, and his base running do the talking. When Jackie put on number 42 and started stealing bases in a Brooklyn uniform, he changed the sports world and America...forever. No one would ever have believed there could be another American athlete as iconic as Babe Ruth, but the accomplishments of Jackie Robinson surpassed even the god-like Bambino.

THE RURAL AMERICAN CHURCH

You needn't be a Christian, or a believer in any religion, to be in awe of the simple grandeur and symbolic power of the early churches of the pioneering West, places of comfort and hope for so many American families building new lives in a vast new land. (Shown is a rural church in California, photographed by the great chronicler of the American West, Ansel Adams.)

JACK RUBY SHOOTS LEE HARVEY OSWALD, LIVE

The killing of the assassin of President John F. Kennedy was the most astonishing scene ever projected, live, to a television audience of millions. On Sunday morning, November 24,1963, Jack Ruby, the proprietor of a Dallas strip joint, walked into the city prison, just one of the boys, to witness the president's killer being transferred to the county jail. Emerging from an elevator, Lee Harvey Oswald was led toward an armored car by a group of detectives. A burly form in a natty suit plunged forward, pointed a gun, and fired one shot. Oswald slumped as an astonished policeman shouted, "Jack, you son of a bitch!" Oswald had killed our president and our dreams for building a better America, and Ruby killed our chance to make any sense of what went down. May the two of them burn in Hell.

THE SINGING COWBOY

He was the first of the Singing Cowboys, followed by Roy Rogers and a bunkhouse of hundreds of other warblers. Riding his horse Champion, and with Smiley Burnette as his sidekick, **GENE AUTRY** was the most popular Western performer of all time, the only person to receive five stars on the Hollywood Walk of Fame (the Motion Picture, Radio, Recording, TV, and Theater stars). Autry went on to become a cowboy business tycoon, but he is still beloved for his Western movies as the "Bing Crosby on horseback."

THE URBAN COWBOY

Back in the good ol' days, spurred on by the popularity of the Singing Cowboy, a **STREET PHOTOGRAPHER** would often come into the working-class neighborhoods of urban cities, leading a pony and toting a Graphlex camera. Kids lined up, the photographer clicked the shots, printed them, and then tried to collect from the surprised mothers. The kids usually got a lickin' for blowing a hard-earned buck, but the charm of their little cowpoke on a chestnut steed usually won the moms over. (Below is a kid in the Bronx, with his big sister, getting ready to ride off into the sunset in 1936.)

THE ICONIC WINGED STEED

The ancient Greeks wrote that the mythological Pegasus sprang from the blood of Medusa when Perseus decapitated her. The winged horse reappeared in the late 19th century when Standard Oil Company of New York (SOCONY) used the inspirational, immortal Pegasus to identify gas stations in the U.S. and around the world. SOCONY became **MOBIL** in 1954, and the swift-winged steed still soars above Mobile service stations and on most packaged products.

YOU'RE BETTER OFF UNDER THE UMBRELLA

The red **TRAVELERS** umbrella is one of the great American business icons, a symbol of insurance protection for home, auto, and business that has its policy holders singin' in the rain.

SHAPING THE GOLDEN AGE OF THE HOLLYWOOD MUSICAL

Fred Astaire represented refinement; **GENE KELLY**, athleticism—a swaggeringly virile dancer of incomparable grace and charm.

THE ICONIC EYE

In the great American marketplace, **THE CBS LOGO**, designed by William Golden and Kurt Weihs, remains the unblinking eye of branding excellence throughout the world.

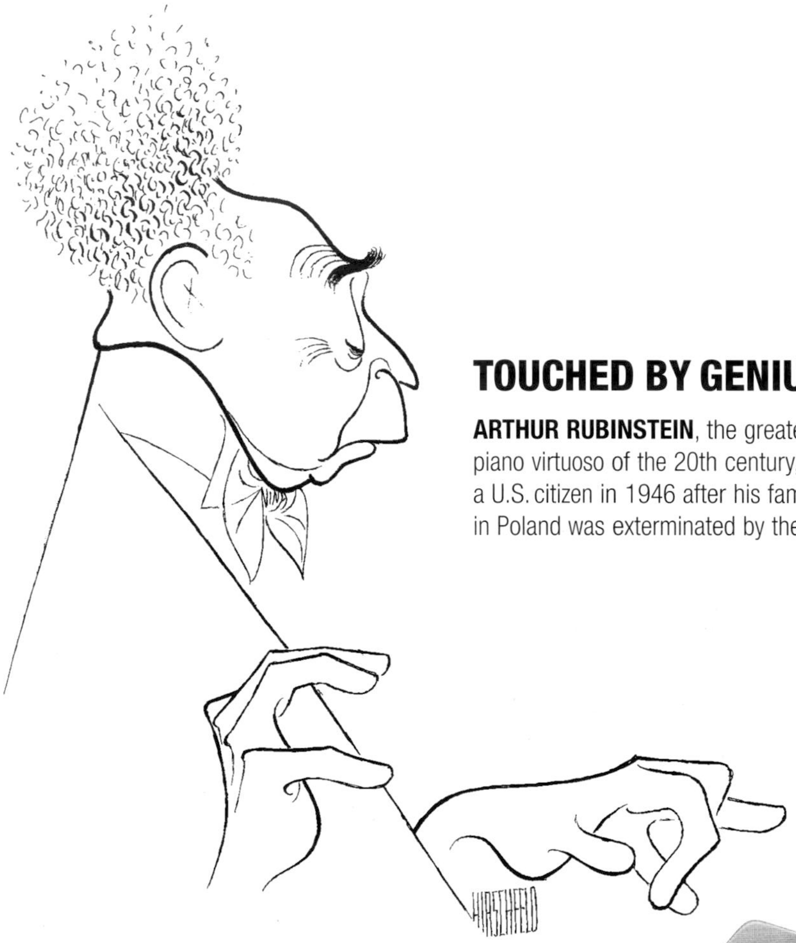

TOUCHED BY GENIUS

ARTHUR RUBINSTEIN, the greatest piano virtuoso of the 20th century, became a U.S. citizen in 1946 after his family in Poland was exterminated by the Nazis.

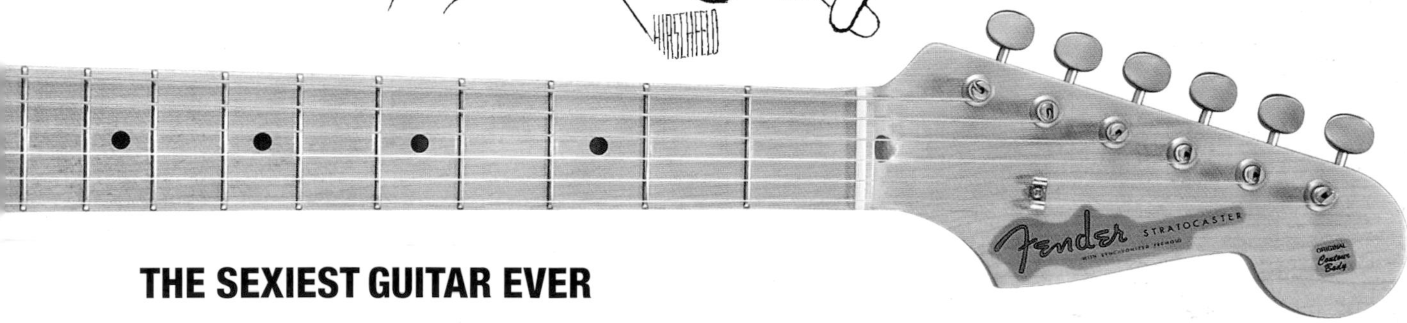

THE SEXIEST GUITAR EVER

The **1957 FENDER STRATOCASTER** is the most popular electric guitar ever made, with a sinuous shape that allows for free movement onstage—a guitar as sexy as the sexiest rock 'n' roller.

THE FRIENDLIEST GHOST YOU KNOW

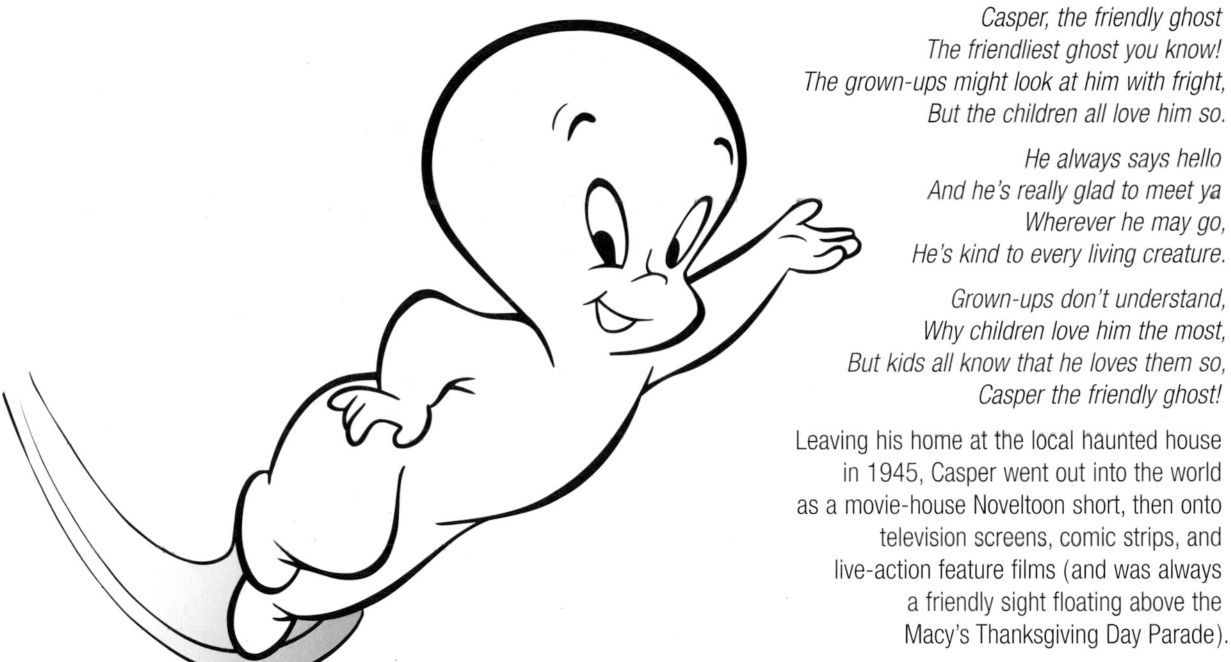

Casper, the friendly ghost
The friendliest ghost you know!
The grown-ups might look at him with fright,
But the children all love him so.

He always says hello
And he's really glad to meet ya
Wherever he may go,
He's kind to every living creature.

Grown-ups don't understand,
Why children love him the most,
But kids all know that he loves them so,
Casper the friendly ghost!

Leaving his home at the local haunted house in 1945, Casper went out into the world as a movie-house Noveltoon short, then onto television screens, comic strips, and live-action feature films (and was always a friendly sight floating above the Macy's Thanksgiving Day Parade).

THE NEW YORK TIMES CROSSWORD PUZZLE, created by freelance writers and edited by Will Shortz, appears daily, becoming increasingly more difficult throughout the week with the most challenging one on Sunday. The *Times* puzzles have become a daily addiction for Americans in the know.

POPULAR ACROSS THE COUNTRY AND UP AND DOWN THE COAST

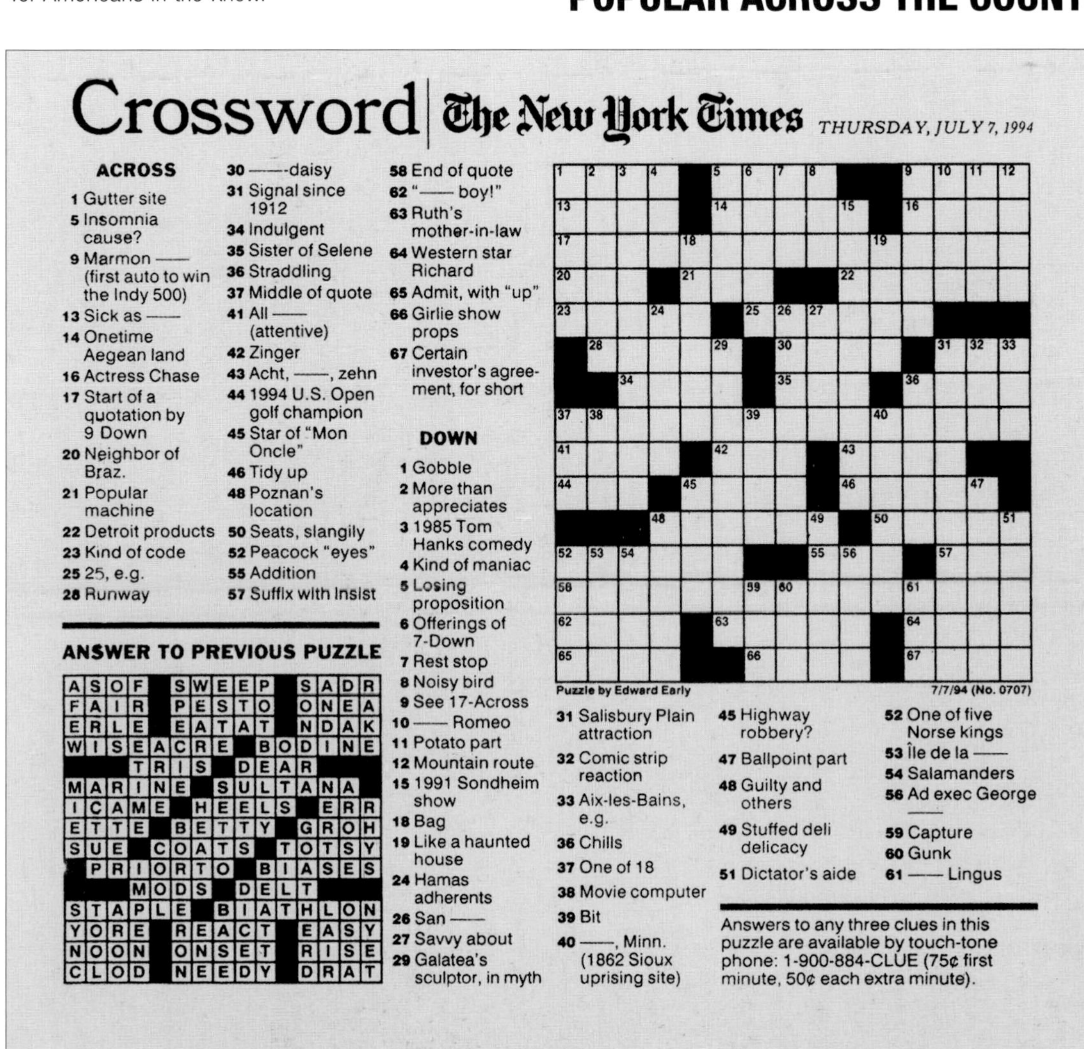

Crossword | The New York Times THURSDAY, JULY 7, 1994

ACROSS

1 Gutter site
5 Insomnia cause?
9 Marmon —— (first auto to win the Indy 500)
13 Sick as ——
14 Onetime Aegean land
16 Actress Chase
17 Start of a quotation by 9 Down
20 Neighbor of Braz.
21 Popular machine
22 Detroit products
23 Kind of code
25 25, e.g.
28 Runway
30 ——-daisy
31 Signal since 1912
34 Indulgent
35 Sister of Selene
36 Straddling
37 Middle of quote
41 All —— (attentive)
42 Zinger
43 Acht, ——, zehn
44 1994 U.S. Open golf champion
45 Star of "Mon Oncle"
46 Tidy up
48 Poznan's location
50 Seats, slangily
52 Peacock "eyes"
55 Addition
57 Suffix with insist
58 End of quote
62 "—— boy!"
63 Ruth's mother-in-law
64 Western star Richard
65 Admit, with "up"
66 Girlie show props
67 Certain investor's agreement, for short

DOWN

1 Gobble
2 More than appreciates
3 1985 Tom Hanks comedy
4 Kind of maniac
5 Losing proposition
6 Offerings of 7-Down
7 Rest stop
8 Noisy bird
9 See 17-Across
10 —— Romeo
11 Potato part
12 Mountain route
15 1991 Sondheim show
18 Bag
19 Like a haunted house
24 Hamas adherents
26 San ——
27 Savvy about
29 Galatea's sculptor, in myth
31 Salisbury Plain attraction
32 Comic strip reaction
33 Aix-les-Bains, e.g.
36 Chills
37 One of 18
38 Movie computer
39 Bit
40 ——, Minn. (1862 Sioux uprising site)
45 Highway robbery?
47 Ballpoint part
48 Guilty and others
49 Stuffed deli delicacy
51 Dictator's aide
52 One of five Norse kings
53 Île de la ——
54 Salamanders
56 Ad exec George ——
59 Capture
60 Gunk
61 —— Lingus

Puzzle by Edward Early 7/7/94 (No. 0707)

ANSWER TO PREVIOUS PUZZLE

ASOF SWEEP SADR
FAIR PESTO ONEA
ERLE EATAT NDAK
WISEACRE BODINE
TRIS DEAR
MARINE SULTANA
ICAME HEELS ERR
ETTE BETTY GROH
SUE COATS TOTSY
PRIORTO BIASES
MODS DELT
STAPLE BIATHLON
YORE REACT EASY
NOON ONSET RISE
CLOD NEEDY DRAT

Answers to any three clues in this puzzle are available by touch-tone phone: 1-900-884-CLUE (75¢ first minute, 50¢ each extra minute).

MASTER OF MANACLES

At the beginning of the 20th century, **HARRY HOUDINI** became world renowned as an illusionist, escapologist, and stunt performer. In plain sight of spellbound audiences, he would free himself from chains, handcuffs, ropes, locks, straitjackets, and sealed milk cans, often while hanging from a rope or suspended in water. His name today is synonymous with the word *magician*, and it's used to describe any baseball pitcher, politician, firefighter, or crooked corporate executive who escapes from a seemingly impossible situation. Houdini spent much of his life as a ghostbuster, debunking self-proclaimed psychics and mediums. Harry Houdini left this Earth on October 31, 1926—Halloween!

YOGI-ISMS

YOGI BERRA, the Hall of Fame Yankee catcher,
part-time right fielder and full-time malapropist, is one of the most
beloved cartoon characters in American culture:
cuddlier than Smokey the Bear,
funnier than Fred Flintstone,
more heroic than Buzz Lightyear,
better looking than Shrek,
and a *much* better hitter than Popeye.
His Yogi-isms have become an
iconic part of America's colloquial language.
It can be safely said that Yogi Berra
is more often quoted in America than
William Shakespeare.

You can observe a lot by watching.

The future ain't what it used to be.

80% of putts that fall short don't go in.

Nobody goes to that restaurant anymore—it's too crowded.

If you can't imitate him, don't copy him.

If the people don't want to come out to the park, nobody's going to stop them.

I thought they said "steak dinner," but then I found out it was a state dinner.

It gets late early out there.

When you come to a fork in the road, take it.

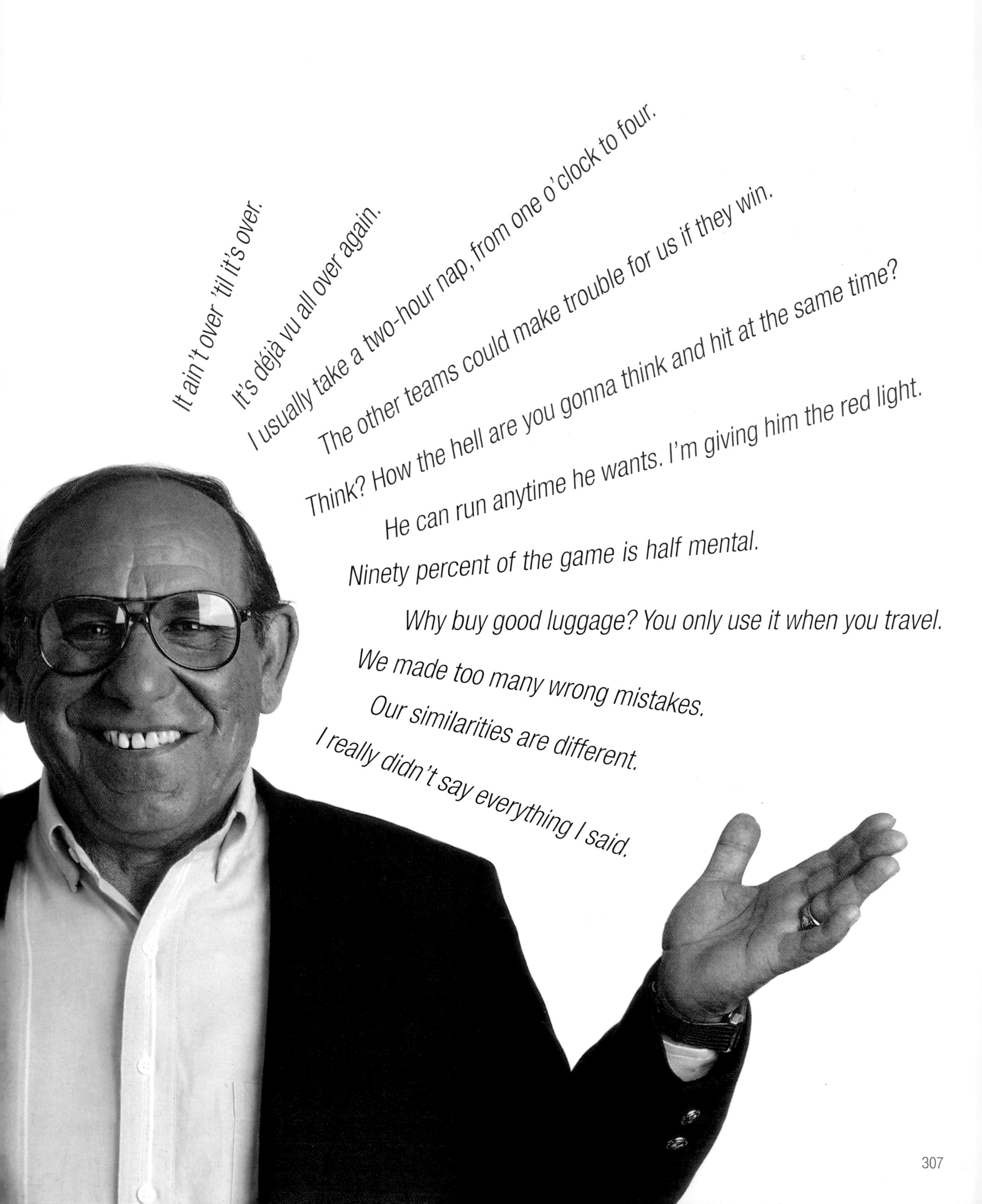
It ain't over 'til it's over.
It's déjà vu all over again.
I usually take a two-hour nap, from one o'clock to four.
The other teams could make trouble for us if they win.
Think? How the hell are you gonna think and hit at the same time?
He can run anytime he wants. I'm giving him the red light.
Ninety percent of the game is half mental.
Why buy good luggage? You only use it when you travel.
We made too many wrong mistakes.
Our similarities are different.
I really didn't say everything I said.

UNITED
STATES

THE APOLLO 11 MOON WALK (AND OUR PROPHETIC FLAG IN 1776)

On July 20, 1969, Astronaut Neil Armstrong took "One small step for man, one giant leap for mankind" as he set foot on the surface of the moon in the scientific achievement of the millennium, the impossible dream of all impossible dreams. When the 50-star American flag was planted, it was the unexpected fulfillment of what appears to have been prophesied by the use of a crescent moon on the "Liberty Flag" in 1776. One of the earliest flags of the American Patriots of the War of Independence, it was created before the conception of the Stars and Stripes.

"TO THE MOON, ALICE!"

Blustery Brooklyn bus driver Ralph Kramden in **THE HONEYMOONERS**, played by the rotund comedian Jackie Gleason (*Bang. Zoom. To the moon, Alice!*) was always devising harebrained schemes to get rich quick, aided and abetted by his dim-witted upstairs neighbor, sewer worker Ed Norton, played by the brilliant Art Carney (*The first time I took the test for the sewer, I flunked—I couldn't even float*). Audrey Meadows played Alice, Kramden's acerbic wife, and Joyce Randolph played Norton's temperamental spouse, Trixie. The half-hour working-class skits were a smash hit in 1955 and became iconized when they began to appear in syndicated reruns that are still running today. *The Honeymooners* has become America's most beloved, enduring, and immortal television comedy of all time. Har-ha, har-de-har-har!

TARZAN, LORD OF THE APES

Tarzan may have sprung from aristocratic English stock and been raised as an orphan by gorillas in the jungles of Africa, but American Olympic swimming champion Johnny Weissmuller made "The Lord of the Apes" an American screen star, swinging in the trees on a back lot in Hollywood. Twelve popular Weissmuller films (1932-48) followed the adventures of Tarzan the family man, his lovely Jane, their growing Boy, and their faithful, madcap companion, a chimp named Cheetah.

JASS! In 1917 the *first* "Jass" record was cut, and **THE JAZZ AGE** was *born!*

THE ULTIMATE '60s SPORT

Fads like the Hula Hoop went 'round and 'round and got nowhere. But the **FRISBEE** lives forever, sailing through the air, back and forth, into the grasping hands of millions of American men, women, children, and—often—their dogs.

AMERICA GOES APE FOR XEROX

The process of Xerography was conceived in 1938 by Chester Carlson, who made his momentous discovery in solitude and offered it to more than 20 major corporations, among them IBM, General Electric, Eastman Kodak, and RCA. The Abominable No-Men of Corporate America turned him down flat, passing up the opportunity to own what *Fortune* magazine would describe as "the most successful product ever manufactured in America." Carlson finally made a deal with the Haloid Company, an obscure maker of photographic paper, and produced the Xerox 914. In 1960, to show TV viewers how easily a Xerox copy could be made, a chimpanzee was cast to deftly lift the pad, slip an original in place, jab the correct buttons, and scratch its armpits while the Xerox 914 clicked out a perfect copy. When the outrageous chimp commercial ran, America went copy crazy—and the Xerox culture was born! Today, the world will make two trillion copies a year based on Xerography, made famous by the grandson of Cheetah the Chimp.

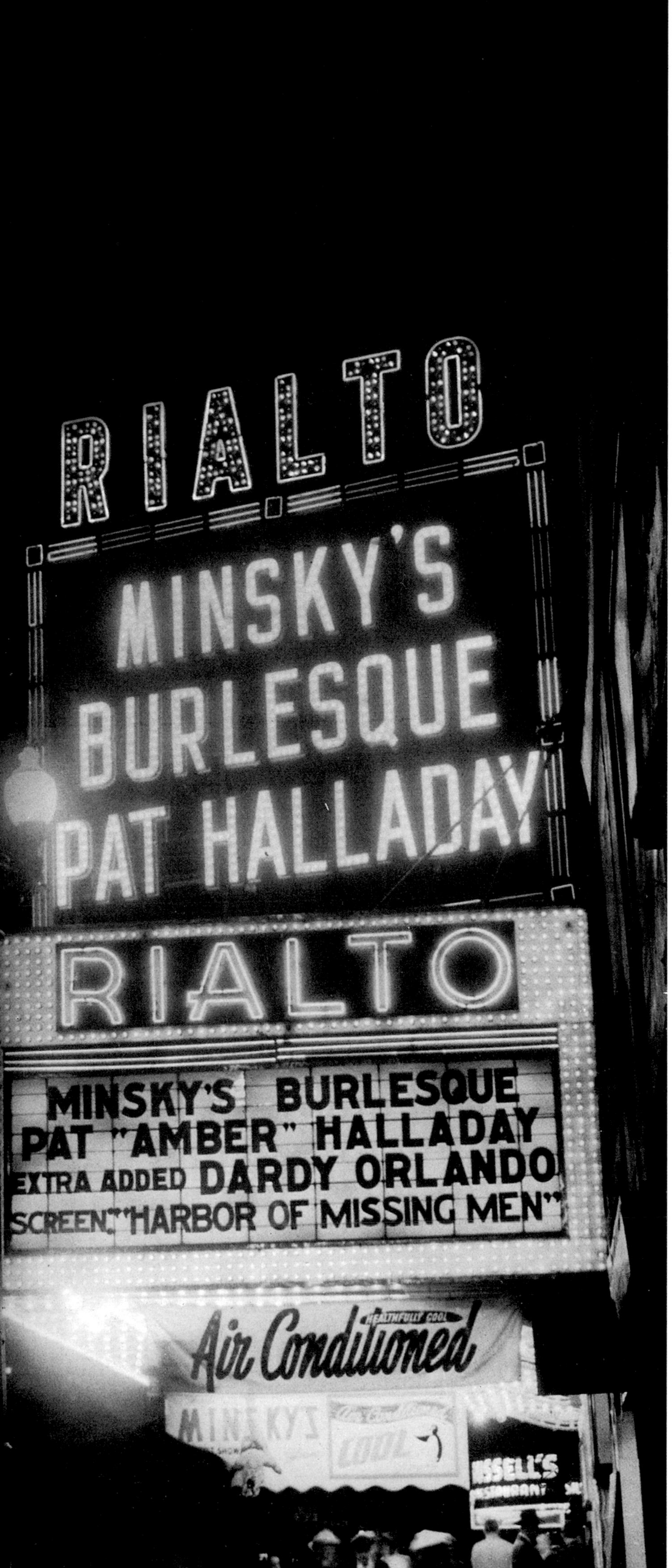

"TAKE IT OFF!"

Before there were sexually explicit television shows and movies, porno films, and videocassettes, adult bookstores and topless bars, sex shops, and massage parlors, there was **BURLESQUE**. The smoke-filled theater was always filled with camaraderie and risqué vaudeville comedians, with statuesque strippers bumping and grinding in time to loud brassy music. To the tune of *Take It Off*, men out for the night hooted and shouted, often accompanied by a wife or girlfriend trying to pretend she wasn't really enjoying the show (despite her squeals of feigned shock and maybe a tinge of envy).

THE ICONIC PASTIES OF TEMPEST STORM

When local decency laws were passed to limit nudity in Burlesque houses in the 1940s, women's nipples were deemed to be too erotic to be displayed in public—so the sequined, cone-shaped pastie was concocted, pasted with a special glue onto each offending nipple. Those exotic burlesque queens with special talents wore pasties with tassels to demonstrate their twirling techniques. Now *that's* entertainment.

THE CLASS ACT OF BURLESQUE

GYPSY ROSE LEE was the most famous stripper of her day, working nights at Minsky's Burlesque. Compared to the-bump-and-grind styles of the typical babes of burlesque, Gypsy slinked on stage, delivering a witty, intellectual recitation as she slowly revealed her charms. Her put-on routine (while taking it off) won her film and television exposure (heh-heh) and she became the world-famous Lady of Burlesque. In 1957 she published a scathing memoir about her monstrous stage mother that became a sensational, award-winning musical, adding to Gypsy's cultural status as the smartest American sexual icon ever.

THE LIGHT OF REVELATION AND MARTYRDOM

Just minutes before this photo was taken, on June 5, 1968, **SENATOR ROBERT F. KENNEDY** was thanking supporters who had helped him win the crucial 1968 primary election in California for the presidency of the United States. It had been a night of great promise and hope for the future. As RFK entered a corridor of the kitchen of the Ambassador Hotel in Los Angeles, shots rang out from a .22-caliber pistol, fired by the assassin Sirhan Sirhan. *Life* photographer Bill Eppridge's camera froze this moment immediately after the shooting, as Kennedy lay mortally wounded. The light appears to be a religious light of revelation and martyrdom, transforming the tableau into a pietà depicting the dying of the hope of a troubled nation.

THE LAST WORD IN FILM HISTORY

The story of William Randolph Hearst, thinly veiled by Orson Welles in the story of "Citizen Kane," is a parable of idealism corrupted by wealth and fame. Welles, the boy wonder of radio, made the leap to film and crafted the greatest film of all time. **CITIZEN KANE** opens with a depleted, destroyed Charles Foster Kane dying with his last word, "Rosebud," on his lips, as a sheet is drawn over him by a nurse. The narrative of the film is a search for the meaning of the newspaper tycoon's final word. As the film closes, we see the trivial junk of Kane's life thrown into a blazing furnace—and the secret is revealed—"Rosebud" is the name of his childhood sled, a burning metaphor for a man who had realized that he had lost his soul.

THE MOST RECOGNIZED PLANE IN AVIATION HISTORY

THE FLYING TIGERS were a heroic volunteer group that flew in Burma and China against the Japanese during the year *prior* to December 7, 1941. Before they were disbanded in 1942, this gallant group destroyed 299 Japanese planes. The shark-faced Curtiss P-40B Tomahawk fighter is a true graphic icon in the history of America.

YANKEE DOODLE DANDY

The staid, stiff Windsor chair was a staple of British nobility. In the 1730s, furniture makers in New England added a jauntier Yankee look, reaching a high point of sculptural zip and pizzazz in the 1790s. **THE AMERICAN WINDSOR CHAIR** remains the most popular vernacular seating in the U.S. The great furniture designer Charles Eames said in the 1970s that he much admired its buttock-hugging seat and bare-bones styling: "I have always hoped my chairs would be regarded as the Windsors of the 20th century." Shown is an 1810 fan-back Connecticut Windsor.

THE GLOBAL NEWS ICON

In 1980 media legend Ted Turner reinvented reporting and changed the face of TV news with **CABLE NEWS NETWORK (CNN)**, the world's first 24-hour news network. CNN had a meteoric success–becoming the largest, most trusted, most watched news network in the world.

THE HUMAN COMET

Samuel Langhorne Clemens was born–and died–in years in which Halley's Comet appeared (1835 and 1910)! Writing under the pen name **MARK TWAIN**, he created a distinctive American literature built on American themes and colloquial language. Ernest Hemingway once said: "All modern American literature comes from one book by Mark Twain called *Huckleberry Finn*... all American writing comes from that. There was nothing before. There has been nothing as good since." And William Faulkner wrote of Clemens, "...the first truly American writer, and all of us since are his heirs."

A WONDERFUL LIFE

JIMMY STEWART became instantly famous after starring in three heartwarming Depression-era Frank Capra films: *You Can't Take it With You*, *It's a Wonderful Life*, and *Mr. Smith Goes to Washington* (shown). His homey screen persona in film after film made him an American Icon, leaving a legacy of classic performances in great films including George Cukor's *Philadelphia Story*; Arthur Mann's *Winchester '73*; and Alfred Hitchcock's *Rear Window*, *The Man Who Knew Too Much*, and *Vertigo*. His memorable John Ford films included *The Man Who Shot Liberty Valance*. Stewart interrupted his career by joining the U.S. Army Air Corps nine months *before* the attack on Pearl Harbor, and rose to the rank of colonel, twice receiving the distinguished Flying Cross for missions over Germany and later as chief of staff of a Bombardment Wing of the Eighth Air Force. No make-believe for Jimmy Stewart–he was a movie superstar who became a real-life American combat hero! He died in 1997 at the age of 89 after a brilliant career. It was, truly, a wonderful life.

FROZEN FOOD TAKES OFF

When you crave fresh fruits and veggies in the middle of the winter, you can thank Clarence Birdseye for providing the next best thing. In 1922 Clarence invented flash-freezing, so food products could be preserved without altering their taste. Birds Eye—and convenient, delicious frozen food—have been synonymous ever since.

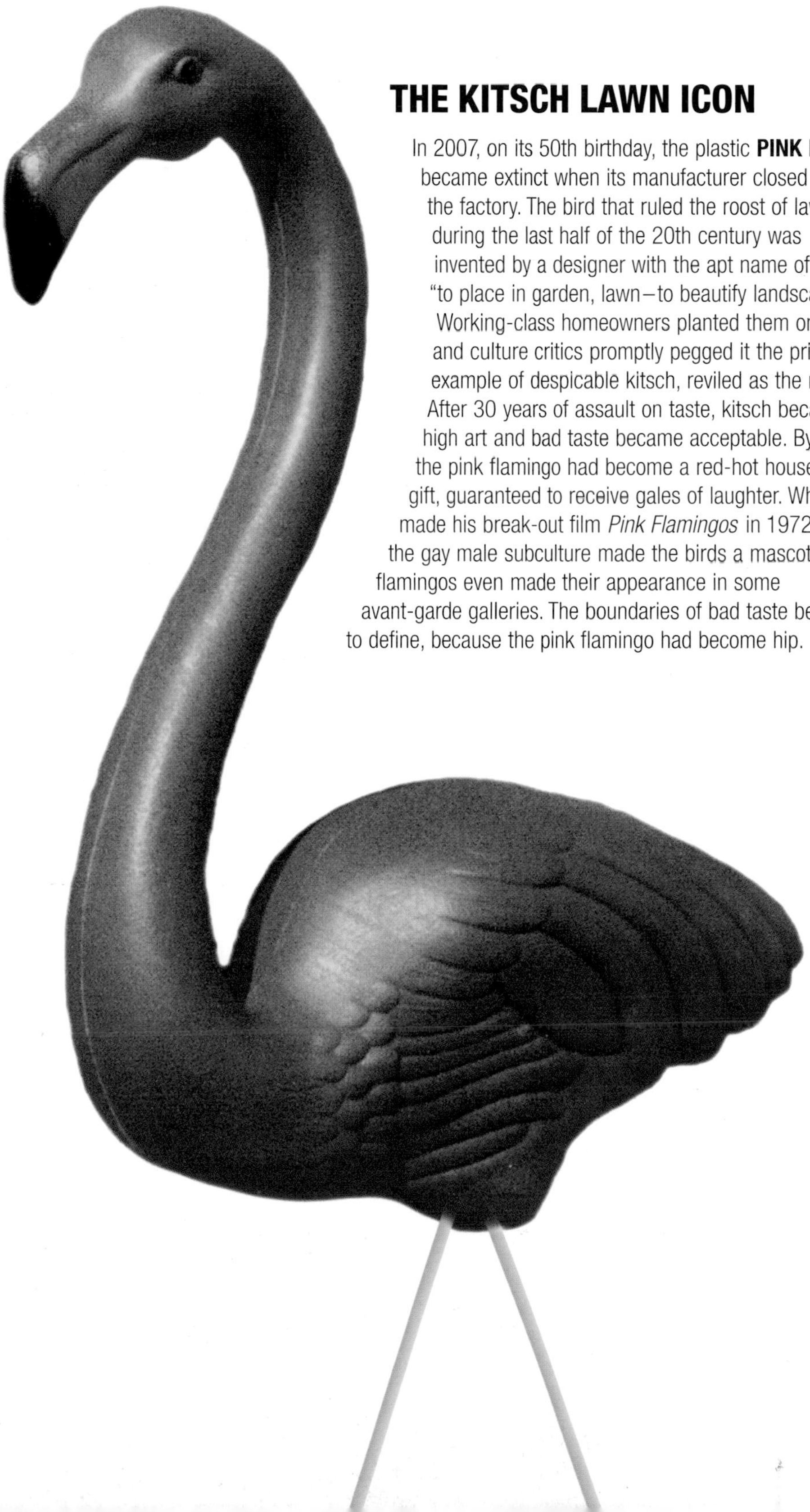

THE KITSCH LAWN ICON

In 2007, on its 50th birthday, the plastic **PINK FLAMINGO** became extinct when its manufacturer closed the factory. The bird that ruled the roost of lawn ornaments during the last half of the 20th century was invented by a designer with the apt name of Don Featherstone "to place in garden, lawn—to beautify landscape." Working-class homeowners planted them on their modest lawns—and culture critics promptly pegged it the prime example of despicable kitsch, reviled as the nadir of bad taste. After 30 years of assault on taste, kitsch became high art and bad taste became acceptable. By the 1990s, the pink flamingo had become a red-hot housewarming gift, guaranteed to receive gales of laughter. When John Waters made his break-out film *Pink Flamingos* in 1972, the gay male subculture made the birds a mascot, and pink flamingos even made their appearance in some avant-garde galleries. The boundaries of bad taste became hard to define, because the pink flamingo had become hip.

TURKEY DAY

The star of **THANKSGIVING DAY** is always a big, bountiful turkey, a tradition that supposedly began with the Pilgrims' first celebration of thanks to the Almighty, after their first harvest in 1621. "We are so far from want that we often wish you partakers of our plenty," was their invitation to fellow settlers and the Indians. The custom was sustained, then proclaimed a national Thanksgiving Day by President Abraham Lincoln. Since 1947 the National Turkey Federation has presented each president with one live turkey and two dressed turkeys each year. The live turkey is "pardoned," passing the rest of its days on a peaceful farm. (Some claim that the tradition began with Lincoln pardoning his son's pet turkey.) The big, bodacious one shown, from *Gourmet* magazine's 2006 Thanksgiving issue, wasn't so lucky.

THE BIG IDEA!

It's no wonder a **LIGHTBULB** is the worldwide symbol for the conception of an idea, because **THOMAS EDISON**'s invention shined the light on a new world of creativity, productivity, and commerce.

THE BRIGHTEST IMMIGRANT EVER

ALBERT EINSTEIN was arguably the most important immigrant to grace our shores, having dramatically changed the landscape of human knowledge.

BUBBLE IN THE SKY

The most beautiful helicopter ever, the American-made and designed bubble-headed **1945 BELL 47D1**.

LOOKING DOWN FROM THE TOP

The statuesque **EMPIRE STATE BUILDING**, completed in 1931, staunchly oversees New York's comings and goings. A witness to tragedy and triumph, it continues to stand supreme in the greatest city in the world.

THE GREAT AMERICAN T-SHIRT

Body-fitting or XXL, T-shirts have become high-fashion statements designed to fit each individual American lifestyle, telling the world who you are, on your chest.

"BOFFO BOX-OFFICE BIZ"

The style and the "slanguage" of *Variety*, the glossy newsmagazine for the show-biz crowd, helped keep it required reading for aspiring actors, superstars, and Hollywood moguls alike. For over a century *Variety* has delivered breaking news, exclusive scoops, and must-read features in a spunky industry-insider lingo, many of which have made their way into your dictionary: striptease, payola, boffo, hoofer, pix, syndie, ozoner, flop, arthouse, deejay, cliffhanger, tinseltown...

IF YOU'VE NEVER BEEN TO L.A., STEP ON IT!

Stroll along Hollywood Boulevard, then veer off onto Vine Street, and have fun spotting the names of 2,300 stars on **THE HOLLYWOOD WALK OF FAME**, immortalized by the Hollywood Chamber of Commerce for their lasting contributions to the entertainment industry. Since 1960 the Walk of Fame has become L.A.'s most popular tourist attraction–and the price is right. "Look! There's Rudolph Valentino–they called him the Latin Lover." "And there's Barbra Streisand! Sidney Poitier! Ava Gardner! And Bob Hope! Snow White? Didn't the Seven Dwarfs get a star?" "Susan Sarandon!–and she looks better than ever!"

THEY DON'T CALL BOSTON "BEANTOWN" FOR NOTHIN'!

Boston and beans are synonymous. **BOSTON BAKED BEANS**, slow-baked in molasses, have been a favorite Boston dish since Colonial days, when the city was swimming in molasses as a result of trade with the West Indies. Boston residents continued to be up to their asses in molasses: The Great Molasses Flood of 1919 killed 21 and injured 150 when a tank holding molasses exploded, inspiring jokes ever since on the digestive results of eating too many beans. A popular rhyme among kids in Boston is:

"Beans, beans. Good for your heart.
The more you eat, the more you fart.
The more you fart, the better you feel.
So eat your beans at every meal."

THE DELUSIONARY LOVER

The cerebral work of **WOODY ALLEN** explores paranoia, hypochondria, mortality, religion, crime, psychoanalysis, and, last but not least, male sexual fantasies. As a stand-up comic, actor, screenwriter, playwright, musician, and film director, the Brooklyn-born humorist brings a knowing, confessional spin to the anxieties of modern American life. His satirical film style draws on Jewish humor, classic literature, philosophy, European cinema, jazz, and his home-town, where he lives, works, and produces most of his movies. Though he's no Tyrone Power or George Clooney, the great American film auteur continues to attract the young, hot, female actors in Hollywood, who are intellectually, and (we are led to believe), sexually attracted to the wit and sophistication of his neurotic on-screen persona. For confirmation of his assumed role as a fanatical flirt, Woody Allen once famously said, "I took nine months trying to get out of the womb, and the rest of my life trying to get back in."

THE ICONIC NYLON STOCKINGS

In the 20th century, when it became socially acceptable for women to flash their gams in public, a peek at curvaceous legs shimmering in expensive silk stockings drove men wild. Then DuPont patented Nylon (a new synthetic fiber) and introduced it at the 1939 World's Fair. A year later, affordable, sexy nylon stockings came to market. On the first day 800,000 pairs were sold–64 million in the first year. America immediately became a land of leg lovers. Alas, when the U.S. joined World War II, all production of nylon went into the war effort for use in parachutes and tires, and nylon stockings took a walk. (Many women painted seams on the backs of their legs to stay in fashion.) When the war ended, women were again free to strut their stuff, to the delight of the leg lovers of America.

THE ICONIC GLOVE OF MICHAEL JACKSON

Each time Michael Jackson stepped on the stage he reinvented himself, not only in the clothes he chose but also in his constantly altering physical appearance. A star since his spectacular debut with The Jackson 5 in the late 1960s, he grew up in front of our eyes, an astonishing prodigy, stylistically wise beyond his years, expressing both the exuberance of a child and the swagger of a seasoned stage performer. At the time of his revolutionary *Thriller* album, he wore short, tight pants; a black sequined jacket; a black hat; black loafers; white socks—and a knockout, now iconic, sequined glove on his right hand. He went on to bondage and leather motifs, militaristic jackets, and glittering armbands—all looks Michael could hide behind, as If he desired protection, desperately wanting not to be exposed to his adoring fans.

THE ICONIC GLOVES OF THE CENTURY

During the nine months of the **O. J. SIMPSON** murder trial, which began in January 1995, only the police evidence photographs could convey the violence and bloodletting on Bundy Drive on the night of June 12, 1994. Nicole Brown Simpson had purchased for her husband two pairs of extra-large cashmere-lined, dark brown leather Aris Isotoner gloves on December 20, 1990. The gloves were part of a batch of 240 pairs that had been sold exclusively at Bloomingdale's in New York City. Videotape showed O. J. Simpson wearing them at two football games. Simpson's attorney, Johnnie Cochran, insisted that his client wear latex gloves while trying on a pair of gloves found at the crime scene and presented as evidence at court. TV and still cameras filmed Simpson struggling to get the gloves on, and audio equipment recorded him saying, "They're too tight." Although he was later able to slip on a new pair in the same size, the damage to the prosecution's case was done. Linking the gloves from the crime scene to Simpson was key in identifying him as the murderer of his former wife and Ronald Goldman. That the gloves could have shrunk because of blood and moisture, or that they did not fit because Simpson tried them on over sticky latex liners, did not seem to resonate with the jury. "You will always remember those gloves," Cochran said in his summation to the jury. "When [prosecuting attorney Christopher] Darden asked him to try them on...they didn't fit!" And, Cochran concluded with his mantra, "If it doesn't fit, you must acquit!" O. J. Simpson was acquitted.

THE WORLD'S MOST FAMOUS BRAND

The iconic **COCA-COLA CONTOUR BOTTLE** was designed in 1915, its shape based on a drawing by an unknown designer of a cocoa bean in an encyclopedia. The memorable bottle shape, the graceful script logo, and the pizzazz of sweetness and bubbles make Coca-Cola, still, America's favorite soft drink.

BARBIE NO.1

Barbie debuted in 1959 and became America's most famous doll, as well as a cult object and collector's item. Ostracized by many parents (and some feminists), this mini-mannequin with impossible proportions remains a marketing phenomenon throughout the world, as young girls continue to go ape for the plastic clotheshorse.

THE HEROISM OF SEPTEMBER 11, 2001

On the morning of 9/11, nineteen terrorists hijacked four American commercial jet airliners and wrought destruction on American land. In a series of coordinated terrorist suicide attacks, two hijacked jets plunged into the Twin Towers of the World Trade Center in Manhattan, destroying them within two hours and heavily damaging the surrounding buildings. The third hijacked jet crashed into the Pentagon in Arlington County, Virginia. Passengers and members of the crew of the fourth airliner heroically tried to take control of their plane from the hijackers, and the jet crashed into a field in Shanksville, Pennsylvania.
The Al Qaeda, a terrorist organization masterminded by Osama bin Laden, bore responsibility for the horrendous damage and deaths of 2,996 people.
Among the fatalities were:
23 New York City Police Department officers
37 Port Authority police officers
343 New York City Fire Department firefighters
The Acting Chief of Brooklyn Fire Department Ladder Co. 105 said of this Nigel Parry photo of his heroic brothers:
"Those jackets? They belong to the men who didn't make it out."

CREATING A NEW AMERICAN ICON

At Ground Zero, on the sacred ground where the Twin Towers fell, a new American icon is rising in lower Manhattan, a glorious image of rebirth and the symbolic start of the healing process of a wounded nation. Designed by Skidmore, Owings & Merrill, the asymmetrical, 1,776-foot-high, monolithic glass structure will reflect the sky and stand as the centerpiece of the new World Trade Center, with memorials to the thousands who perished there. At night, emanating from **FREEDOM TOWER** will be an intense beam of light that will rise a thousand feet in the air above New York, an added symbol of the undaunted strength of the American people.

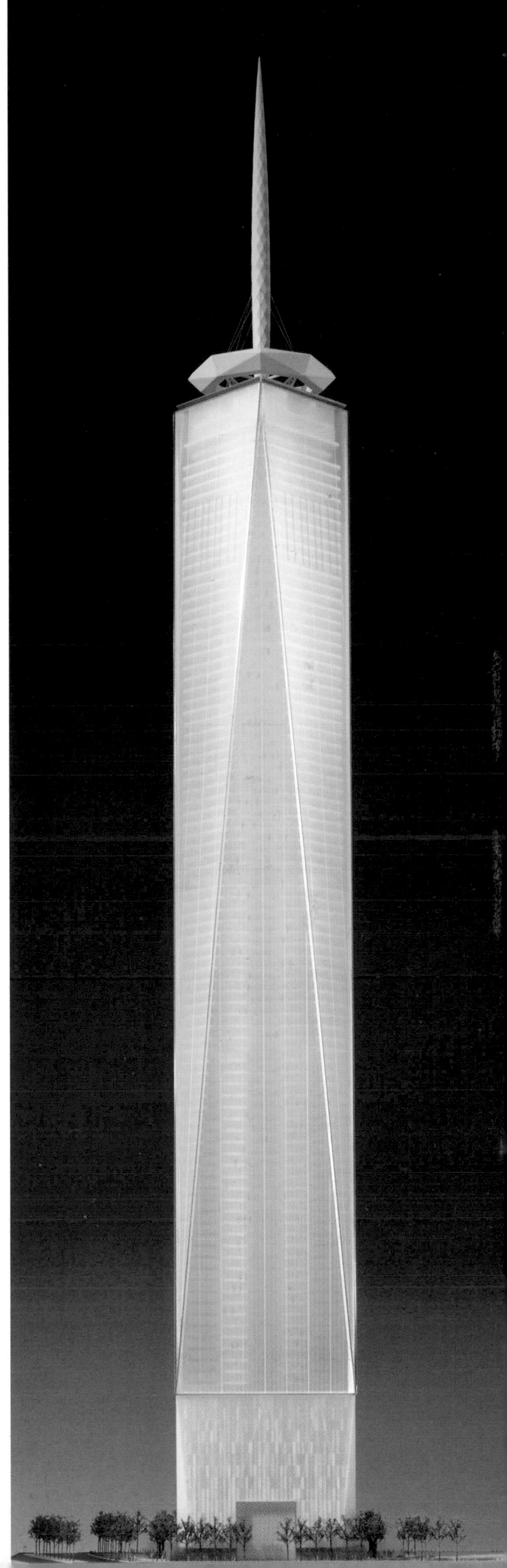

F.D.N.Y.
F.D.N.Y.
105
F.D.N.Y.
F.D.N.Y.
219
105
219
105
219

POP LOVE

Since the beginning of film, there has never been a shortage of famous Hollywood dynamite duos. Quickly dubbed "Brangelina" by the media when they began dating, the superstud **BRAD PITT** and the saintly, ultra-glamourous **ANGELINA JOLIE**, tireless workers for charity causes, became the most popular and most paparazzi-hounded celebrity couple since Douglas Fairbanks & Mary Pickford. Look at this list of star-studded red-carpet celebrity couples who have driven starstruck American movie fans wild throughout the years, some married–some living in sin:

Douglas Fairbanks & Mary Pickford
Charlie Chaplin & Paulette Goddard
Gilbert Roland & Constance Bennett
Irving Thalberg & Norma Shearer
Joseph Kennedy & Gloria Swanson
Mack Sennett & Mabel Normand
Johnny Weissmuller & Lupe Vélez
George S. Kaufman & Mary Astor
Clark Gable & Carole Lombard
Spencer Tracy & Katharine Hepburn
Howard Hughes & Katharine Hepburn
Howard Hughes & Ava Gardner
Humphrey Bogart & Lauren Bacall
Desi Arnaz & Lucille Ball
Paul Newman & Joanne Woodward
Tony Curtis & Janet Leigh
José Ferrer & Rosemary Clooney
Mel Brooks & Anne Bancroft
William Holden & Stefanie Powers
William Holden & Brenda Marshall
Louis Hayward & Ida Lupino
Howard Duff & Ida Lupino
Dick Powell & Joan Blondell
Dick Powell & June Allyson
Mickey Rooney & Ava Gardner
Artie Shaw & Ava Gardner
Frank Sinatra & Juliet Prowse
Frank Sinatra & Ava Gardner
Frank Sinatra & Mia Farrow
Woody Allen & Mia Farrow
Robert Wagner & Natalie Wood
Eli Wallach & Anne Jackson
Tony Martin & Alice Faye
Phil Harris & Alice Faye
Roberto Rossellini & Ingrid Bergman
Ronald Reagan & Jane Wyman
Ronald Reagan & Nancy Davis
Fred MacMurray & June Haver
Artie Shaw & Lana Turner
Lex Barker & Lana Turner
Tony Martin & Cyd Charisse
Mel Ferrer & Audrey Hepburn
Harry James & Betty Grable
Robert Walker & Jennifer Jones
David O. Selznick & Jennifer Jones
Joe DiMaggio & Marilyn Monroe
Arthur Miller & Marilyn Monroe
Vic Damone & Diahann Carroll
Michael Wilding & Elizabeth Taylor
Michael Todd & Elizabeth Taylor
Eddie Fisher & Elizabeth Taylor
Richard Burton & Elizabeth Taylor
Richard Burton & Elizabeth Taylor (again)

Ossie Davis & Ruby Dee
Tony Franciosa & Shelley Winters
Albert Finney & Audrey Hepburn
Jean-Pierre Aumont & Maria Montez
Ernest Borgnine & Katy Jurado
Garson Kanin & Ruth Gordon
Louis Malle & Candice Bergen
Vincente Minnelli & Judy Garland
Steve Allen & Jayne Meadows
Orson Welles & Rita Hayworth
Gary Cooper & Patricia Neal
Gary Cooper & Ingrid Bergman
Elvis Presley & Ann-Margret
Elvis Presley & Priscilla Presley
Johnny Cash & June Carter
Robert Mitchum & Shirley MacLaine
Rex Harrison & Carole Landis
Blake Edwards & Julie Andrews
Roman Polanski & Sharon Tate
Ryan O'Neal & Farrah Fawcett
Lee Majors & Farrah Fawcett
Lee Marvin & Michelle Triola
Sonny Bono & Cher
Burt Reynolds & Dinah Shore
Fernando Lamas & Arlene Dahl
Bing Crosby & Grace Kelly
Ray Milland & Grace Kelly
Cary Grant & Dyan Cannon
John Agar & Shirley Temple
Sammy Davis Jr. & May Britt
John Drew Barrymore & Bo Derek
Roger Vadim & Jane Fonda
Richard Gere & Cindy Crawford
Al Pacino & Diane Keaton
Woody Allen & Louise Lasser
George Burns & Gracie Allen
Peter Allen & Liza Minnelli
David Gest & Liza Minnelli
Bob Dylan & Joan Baez
John Lennon & Yoko Ono
Kevin Bacon & Kyra Sedgwick
Kevin Kline & Phoebe Cates
Mikhail Baryshnikov & Jessica Lange
Sam Shepard & Jessica Lange
Harvey Keitel & Lorraine Bracco
Edward James Olmos & Lorraine Bracco
Clint Eastwood & Sondra Locke
John Travolta & Kelly Preston
Gene Wilder & Gilda Radner
Matthew Broderick & Sarah Jessica Parker
Steve McQueen & Ali McGraw
Peter Bogdanovich & Cybil Shepherd
Jack Nicholson & Anjelica Huston

Warren Beatty & Annette Bening
Jon Peters & Barbra Streisand
Elliott Gould & Barbra Streisand
Don Johnson & Barbra Streisand
James Brolin & Barbra Streisand
John McEnroe & Tatum O'Neal
Brian De Palma & Nancy Allen
Andre Agassi & Brooke Shields
John Cassavetes & Gena Rowlands
Johnny Depp & Kate Moss
Johnny Depp & Winona Ryder
Don Johnson & Melanie Griffith
Steven Bauer & Melanie Griffith
Don Johnson & Melanie Griffith (again)
Antonio Banderas & Melanie Griffith
Kurt Russell & Goldie Hawn
Ted Danson & Whoopi Goldberg
Ted Danson & Mary Steenburgen
Michael Jackson & Lisa Marie Presley
Nicholas Cage & Lisa Marie Presley
Dennis Quaid & Meg Ryan
Lyle Lovett & Julia Roberts
Tim Robbins & Susan Sarandon
Jeff Goldblum & Geena Davis
Steven Spielberg & Kate Capshaw
Sean Penn & Madonna
Sean Penn & Robin Wright Penn
Michael Douglas & Catherine Zeta-Jones
Bruce Willis & Demi Moore
Ashton Kutcher & Demi Moore
Tom Hanks & Rita Wilson
Liam Neeson & Natasha Richardson
Alec Baldwin & Kim Basinger
Ethan Hawke & Uma Thurman
Jim Carrey & Lauren Holly
Ben Affleck & Jennifer Garner
Ben Affleck & Jennifer Lopez
P. Diddy & Jennifer Lopez
Marc Anthony & Jennifer Lopez
Chad Lowe & Hilary Swank
Ellen DeGeneres & Anne Heche
Nick Lachey & Jessica Simpson
Tom Cruise & Nicole Kidman
Tom Cruise & Penelope Cruz
Tom Cruise & Katie Holmes
David Arquette & Courteney Cox
Heath Ledger & Michelle Williams
Will Smith & Jada Pinkett Smith
Vince Vaughn & Jennifer Aniston
Brad Pitt & Gwyneth Paltrow
Brad Pitt & Jennifer Aniston
Billy Bob Thornton & Angelina Jolie
Brad Pitt & Angelina Jolie

(Editor's note: One-night stands not included.)

POP LOVE

Since the beginning of film, there has never been a shortage of famous Hollywood dynamite duos.
Quickly dubbed "Brangelina" by the media when they began dating, the superstud **BRAD PITT** and the saintly, ultra-glamourous **ANGELINA JOLIE**, tireless workers for charity causes, became the most popular and most paparazzi-hounded celebrity couple since
Douglas Fairbanks & Mary Pickford. Look at this list of star-studded red-carpet celebrity couples who have driven starstruck American movie fans wild throughout the years, some married–some living in sin:

Douglas Fairbanks & Mary Pickford
Charlie Chaplin & Paulette Goddard
Gilbert Roland & Constance Bennett
Irving Thalberg & Norma Shearer
Joseph Kennedy & Gloria Swanson
Mack Sennett & Mabel Normand
Johnny Weissmuller & Lupe Vélez
George S. Kaufman & Mary Astor
Clark Gable & Carole Lombard
Spencer Tracy & Katharine Hepburn
Howard Hughes & Katharine Hepburn
Howard Hughes & Ava Gardner
Humphrey Bogart & Lauren Bacall
Desi Arnaz & Lucille Ball
Paul Newman & Joanne Woodward
Tony Curtis & Janet Leigh
José Ferrer & Rosemary Clooney
Mel Brooks & Anne Bancroft
William Holden & Stefanie Powers
William Holden & Brenda Marshall
Louis Hayward & Ida Lupino
Howard Duff & Ida Lupino
Dick Powell & Joan Blondell
Dick Powell & June Allyson
Mickey Rooney & Ava Gardner
Artie Shaw & Ava Gardner
Frank Sinatra & Juliet Prowse
Frank Sinatra & Ava Gardner
Frank Sinatra & Mia Farrow
Woody Allen & Mia Farrow
Robert Wagner & Natalie Wood
Eli Wallach & Anne Jackson
Tony Martin & Alice Faye
Phil Harris & Alice Faye
Roberto Rossellini & Ingrid Bergman
Ronald Reagan & Jane Wyman
Ronald Reagan & Nancy Davis
Fred MacMurray & June Haver
Artie Shaw & Lana Turner
Lex Barker & Lana Turner
Tony Martin & Cyd Charisse
Mel Ferrer & Audrey Hepburn
Harry James & Betty Grable
Robert Walker & Jennifer Jones
David O. Selznick & Jennifer Jones
Joe DiMaggio & Marilyn Monroe
Arthur Miller & Marilyn Monroe
Vic Damone & Diahann Carroll
Michael Wilding & Elizabeth Taylor
Michael Todd & Elizabeth Taylor
Eddie Fisher & Elizabeth Taylor
Richard Burton & Elizabeth Taylor
Richard Burton & Elizabeth Taylor (again)

Ossie Davis & Ruby Dee
Tony Franciosa & Shelley Winters
Albert Finney & Audrey Hepburn
Jean-Pierre Aumont & Maria Montez
Ernest Borgnine & Katy Jurado
Garson Kanin & Ruth Gordon
Louis Malle & Candice Bergen
Vincente Minnelli & Judy Garland
Steve Allen & Jayne Meadows
Orson Welles & Rita Hayworth
Gary Cooper & Patricia Neal
Gary Cooper & Ingrid Bergman
Elvis Presley & Ann-Margret
Elvis Presley & Priscilla Presley
Johnny Cash & June Carter
Robert Mitchum & Shirley MacLaine
Rex Harrison & Carole Landis
Blake Edwards & Julie Andrews
Roman Polanski & Sharon Tate
Ryan O'Neal & Farrah Fawcett
Lee Majors & Farrah Fawcett
Lee Marvin & Michelle Triola
Sonny Bono & Cher
Burt Reynolds & Dinah Shore
Fernando Lamas & Arlene Dahl
Bing Crosby & Grace Kelly
Ray Milland & Grace Kelly
Cary Grant & Dyan Cannon
John Agar & Shirley Temple
Sammy Davis Jr. & May Britt
John Drew Barrymore & Bo Derek
Roger Vadim & Jane Fonda
Richard Gere & Cindy Crawford
Al Pacino & Diane Keaton
Woody Allen & Louise Lasser
George Burns & Gracie Allen
Peter Allen & Liza Minnelli
David Gest & Liza Minnelli
Bob Dylan & Joan Baez
John Lennon & Yoko Ono
Kevin Bacon & Kyra Sedgwick
Kevin Kline & Phoebe Cates
Mikhail Baryshnikov & Jessica Lange
Sam Shepard & Jessica Lange
Harvey Keitel & Lorraine Bracco
Edward James Olmos & Lorraine Bracco
Clint Eastwood & Sondra Locke
John Travolta & Kelly Preston
Gene Wilder & Gilda Radner
Matthew Broderick & Sarah Jessica Parker
Steve McQueen & Ali McGraw
Peter Bogdanovich & Cybil Shepherd
Jack Nicholson & Anjelica Huston

Warren Beatty & Annette Bening
Jon Peters & Barbra Streisand
Elliott Gould & Barbra Streisand
Don Johnson & Barbra Streisand
James Brolin & Barbra Streisand
John McEnroe & Tatum O'Neal
Brian De Palma & Nancy Allen
Andre Agassi & Brooke Shields
John Cassavetes & Gena Rowlands
Johnny Depp & Kate Moss
Johnny Depp & Winona Ryder
Don Johnson & Melanie Griffith
Steven Bauer & Melanie Griffith
Don Johnson & Melanie Griffith (again)
Antonio Banderas & Melanie Griffith
Kurt Russell & Goldie Hawn
Ted Danson & Whoopi Goldberg
Ted Danson & Mary Steenburgen
Michael Jackson & Lisa Marie Presley
Nicholas Cage & Lisa Marie Presley
Dennis Quaid & Meg Ryan
Lyle Lovett & Julia Roberts
Tim Robbins & Susan Sarandon
Jeff Goldblum & Geena Davis
Steven Spielberg & Kate Capshaw
Sean Penn & Madonna
Sean Penn & Robin Wright Penn
Michael Douglas & Catherine Zeta-Jones
Bruce Willis & Demi Moore
Ashton Kutcher & Demi Moore
Tom Hanks & Rita Wilson
Liam Neeson & Natasha Richardson
Alec Baldwin & Kim Basinger
Ethan Hawke & Uma Thurman
Jim Carrey & Lauren Holly
Ben Affleck & Jennifer Garner
Ben Affleck & Jennifer Lopez
P. Diddy & Jennifer Lopez
Marc Anthony & Jennifer Lopez
Chad Lowe & Hilary Swank
Ellen DeGeneres & Anne Heche
Nick Lachey & Jessica Simpson
Tom Cruise & Nicole Kidman
Tom Cruise & Penelope Cruz
Tom Cruise & Katie Holmes
David Arquette & Courteney Cox
Heath Ledger & Michelle Williams
Will Smith & Jada Pinkett Smith
Vince Vaughn & Jennifer Aniston
Brad Pitt & Gwyneth Paltrow
Brad Pitt & Jennifer Aniston
Billy Bob Thornton & Angelina Jolie
Brad Pitt & Angelina Jolie

(Editor's note: One-night stands not included.)

THE WORLD'S MOST FAMOUS BRAND

The iconic **COCA-COLA CONTOUR BOTTLE** was designed in 1915, its shape based on a drawing by an unknown designer of a cocoa bean in an encyclopedia. The memorable bottle shape, the graceful script logo, and the pizzazz of sweetness and bubbles make Coca-Cola, still, America's favorite soft drink.

BARBIE NO.1

Barbie debuted in 1959 and became America's most famous doll, as well as a cult object and collector's item. Ostracized by many parents (and some feminists), this mini-mannequin with impossible proportions remains a marketing phenomenon throughout the world, as young girls continue to go ape for the plastic clotheshorse.

THE DNA OF ALL-AMERICAN STYLE (IT'S IN OUR JEANS)

Since the early 1960s Americans have been brought up wearing the clean-cut Ivy League look: comfortable, casual, simple yet elegant blazers and sweaters from the college campus, chinos and denims from the blue-collar workforce—the essence of American sportswear and the foundation of our popular style. And we love our navy peacoats, motorcycle and bomber jackets, cool shades and horn-rim glasses, bowling shirts, football jerseys, baseball caps, golf shirts, and athletic shoes as much as we love our spiffy suits or dresses for the office and nights out on the town. With the advent of casual Fridays in America, the workplace became less formal, and our preoccupation with fitness and sports made athletic wear essential weekend wear. Americans with style and taste wore a T-shirt with a pair of jeans, socks, and tennis sneakers and looked cool. (Check out good ol' Uncle Sam, flaunting a beat-up pair of denim jeans.) In the late 1960s an awakened black pride inspired African-American fashion designs. Today America's hip-hop fans adopt popular preppy fashions, and suburban kids borrow looks and ideas from the urban fashionistas. Appropriation has become an art form in itself. Fashion in America remains a reflection of the many cultural sources in our tolerant democracy—the way we dress is its own everchanging language of personal style. Much of the imagery of the United States creates a widening gap between reality and the myth of American life and a book of flag-waving, jingoistic icons may add to that disparity, but we believe that the icons of our culture, and certainly the way we dress, reflect the values and principles of our popular American lifestyle.

CREDITS

End Paper © Charles Smith / CORBIS **4** Copyright Carl Fischer **5** Mica hand, Hopewell culture, 300 BC-500 CE. Werner Forman / Art Resource, NY. Field Museum of Natural History, Chicago, USA **6** Catlin, George (1796-1872) Buffalo Bull's Back Fat, head chief, Blood Tribe, 1832, Blackfoot oil on canvas, Smithsonian American Art Museum, Washington, DC / Art Resource, NY **7** Photo © Luke Lois **8** Photo © Luke Lois **10** Copyright Carl Fischer **11** The NBA logo is used with permission from NBA Properties, Inc. © 2007 NBA Properties, Inc. All Rights Reserved (Popcorn) Photo © Luke Lois **13** National Archives 111-B-3658 (Brady Collection) **14** Collection American Folk Art Museum, New York **15** (Indian) Smithsonian Institution Collections, National Museum of American History, Behring Center (Can opener) Photo © Luke Lois **16** Copyright Douglas Kent Hall **17** AP Photo **18** (Trylon & Perisphere) From George Lois (Eagle) Museum of the City of New York. Gift of Henry Rogers Benjamin **19** (Golf Ball) Photo © Luke Lois The Nike Swosh design is a trademark of Nike, Inc. **20** MONOPOLY® & ©2007 Hasbro, Inc. Used with permission **21** Printed with permission of Louis Armstrong Educational Foundation, Inc. Photograph by Bert Stern **22** (Medal) Photo © Luke Lois (Powder horn) Photographer Unknown **23** Google logo © Google Inc. and is used with permission **25** Whistler, James Abbott McNeill (1834-1903) Arrangement in Gray and Black No. 1, or The Artist's Mother 1871 RF 699 Photo: J.G. Berizzi Réunion des Musées Nationaux / Art Resource NY The Musee d'Orsay, Paris, France **26** International Quilt Study Center, University of Nebraska-Lincoln, 2003.003.0071 (Torch) Copyright Carl Fischer **27** (Ice cream) Copyright Carl Fischer Logo Courtesy of Jantzen Apparel, LLC (Camera) Photo © Luke Lois **28** Davies & Starr/ Getty Images **29** MTV's "I Want My MTV" used with permission by MTV ©2007 MTV Networks All Rights Reserved MTV, all related titles, characters and logos are trademarks owned by MTV Networks, a division of Viacom International Inc **30** Photograph courtesy of The Goodyear Tire & Rubber Company © 6/22/06 The Goodyear Tire & Rubber Company **31** (Petty Girl) George Lois **32** CORBIS Photograph by Gutzon Borglum **34** Jokerman Video / George Lois **35** (Chair) Photo © Luke Lois (Mantle) Photo by Dick Richards (Jeep) Willys-Overland Motors, Inc. (est 1909) Gift of Daimler Chrysler Corporation Fund. (261.2002) The Museum of Modern Art, New York, NY USA Digital Image © The Museum of Modern Art / Licensed by SCALA / Art Resource, NY. (Table) Isamu Noguchi (1904-1988) © ARS, NY. Table (IN-50) 1944 Gift of Robert Gruen (12.1980) The Museum of Modern Art, New York, NY U.S.A. Digital Image © The Museum of Modern Art / Licensed by SCALA / Art Resource, NY. © 2007 The Isamu Noguchi Foundation and Garden Museum, New York / Artists Rights Society (ARS), New York (Groucho Marx) © Al Hirschfeld Reproduced by arrangement with Hirschfeld's exclusive representative, The Margo Feiden Galleries Ltd., New York, www.alhirschfeld.com **36** AP Photo / Joe Rosenthal **38** O'Keefe, Georgia (1887-1986) © ARS, NY Cow's Skull: Red, White, and Blue 1931 Alfred Stieglitz Collection, 1952, 52.203. Image copyright © The Metropolitain Museum of Art / Art Resource The Metropolitan Museum of Art, New York, NY, USA. **39** (Shield) Courtesy Donald Ellis Gallery (Gold) Photo © Luke Lois Pac-Man® ©1980 Namco Bandai Games Inc. Courtesy of Namco Bandai Games America Inc. **40** © Carl Fischer / George Lois **41** ©A.M.P.A.S.® The OSCAR Statue is used with permission of the Academy of Motion Picture Arts and Science **42** (Lamb chop) Photo © Luke Lois (Ketchup) H.J. Heinz Company used with permission **43** © 1975 Universal Pictures **44** (Grapes) Gourmet Images / Fotosearch (Beard) Copyright Carl Fischer **45** Cock Weather Vane by Selma Sandler ca. 1938, Index of American Design, Image © 2004 Board of Trustees, National Gallery of Art, Washington The Nike Swosh design is a trademark of Nike, Inc. **46** Blanket courtesy of Andre Emmerich **47** Photo © Luke Lois **48** (Tiffany Lamp) Photo © Luke Lois (Mickey Mouse) © Disney Enterprises, Inc. **49** Edward Sorel **50** Balloon image is used by permission of Macy's **51** John James Audubon **52** © Bettman / CORBIS **53** The Rabbit Head Design is a trademark of Playboy and is used with permission (Beer) Used with the permission of Anheuser-Busch, Incorporated All Rights Reserved Photo © Luke Lois **54** (Red Cross) Printed with permission of The American National Red Cross (Frankenstein) © 1935 Universal Pictures Corporation **55** BAND-AID® is a registered trademark of Johnson & Johnson Westinghouse Logo printed with permission of Westinghouse Electric Corporation **56** Reprinted with Permission of Joanna T. Steichen **57** (Gold Coin, Nickel, Tennis balls) Photo © Luke Lois **58** Art © Jasper Johns / Licensed by VAGA, New York, NY **59** (Badges) Photo © Luke Lois **60** ™ 2007 Lou Gehrig by CMG Worldwide, Inc. / www.LouGehrig.com **61** Design & Art © Paul Davis **62** From The Charlotte Dinger Collection **63** (Snowboarder) Nick Latham / Getty Images Sport / Getty Images (Duck) FD 4-43 Anthony Elmer Crowell (1862-1951) Black Duck Decoy © Shelburne Museum, Shelburne, Vermont **65** (Tommy Gun) Reprinted with permission from: National Park Service / Golden Gate NRA, GOGA 55 (Chair) Photo © Luke Lois **66** Blondie © King Features Syndicate **67** © Philippe Halsman / Magnum Photos **68** Walter Iooss Jr. / National Basketball Association / Getty Images **69** Photo © Luke Lois **70** Courtesy Frederic Remington Art Museum, Ogdensburg, NY **71** (Logo) Copyright 1997-2006 Enron All Rights Reserved (Mouse) Photo © Luke Lois **72** Alvin Ailey American Dance Theater's Dwana Adiaha Smallwood Photo by Andrew Eccles For further information on Alvin Ailey American Dance Theater, Ailey II, The Ailey School, The Ailey Extension and Ailey Arts In Education and Community Programs, visit: www.alvinailey.org **72** National Archives LC-DIG-pprs-00626 **74** The Wizard of Oz © Turner Entertainment Co. A Warner Bros. Entertainment Company All Rights Reserved **75** (Barbed Wire) Photo © Luke Lois **76** John L. Sullivan, ca. 1885 / Everett Collection, Inc. (Cagney) John Kobal Foundation / Hulton Archive / Getty Images **77** Casablanca © Turner Entertainment Co. A Warner Bros. Entertainment Company All Rights Reserved **78** © Shell Brands International (Motorcycle) Randy Leffingwell **79** Photograph Courtesy of New Colt Holding Corp **80** MAD #154 © 1972 E.C. Publications, Inc. All Rights Reserved Used with Permission **81** © 1931 Universal Pictures Corporation **82** © Bob Adelman / Magnum Photos **83** AP Photo / files **84** (Pie) Photo © Luke Lois © Apple Inc. Used with permission All Rights Reserved Apple ® and the Apple logo are registered trademark of Apple Inc. **86** Courtesy of Lucasfilm Ltd. Copyright and Trademark Notice: Star Wars: Episode IV - A New Hope © 1977 and 1997 Lucasfilm Ltd. & ™ All Rights Reserved Used under authorization. Unauthorized duplication is a violation of applicable law **87** The Shadow character, copyrights, and trademarks are owned by The Condé Nast Publications Used with permission **88** Photo © Luke Lois **90** (Sign & Trophy) Photos © Tommy Steele **91** Courtesy Tommy Hilfiger with permission of The Elmira School District **92** Image of the Radio City Rockettes courtesy of MSG Entertainment, a division of Madison Square Garden, L.P. All Rights Reserved **93** © George Hinke **94** The Solomon R. Guggenheim Museum, New York Photograph by David Heald © The Solomon R. Guggenheim Foundation, New York **95** © The New Yorker Collection 1958 Alan Dunn from cartoonbank.com All Rights Reserved **96** Used with permission from McDonald's Corporation (Lucille Ball) Image used with the permission of Desilu, too LLC **97** Courtesy of Wheaties and General Mills **98** (Eye) Photo © Luke Lois **99** BATMAN ™ DC Comics All Rights Reserved Used with Permission Buffalo Bill Historical Center, Cody, Wyoming; Given in Memory of William R. Coe and Mai Rogers Coe; 8.66 **100** © Pete Saloutos / zefa / CORBIS **101** Photo by Richard Sexton © 1987 from American Style: Classic Product Design from Airstream to Zippo **102** National Archives LC-USZ62-134760 circa May 3, 1921 **103** Dorling Kindersley/Getty Images **104** Homage to Mae West © George Lois **106** ™ © 2007 Babe Ruth by CMG Worldwide, Inc. /www.BabeRuth.com **107** (Logo) Copyright © by The New York Times Co. Reprinted with Permission (Baby Ruth Bar) Printed with permission of Nestle North America **108** Peanuts: © United Feature Syndicate, Inc. **109** Printed by permission of the Norman Rockwell Family Agency Copyright © 1943 the Norman Rockwell Family Entities **110** Hollywood Steps Out © Turner Entertainment Co. A Warner Bros. Entertainment Company All Rights Reserved **111** Shirley Temple Starhead © Twentieth Century Fox All Rights Reserved Printed with permission of Shirley Temple Black **113** Spider-Man ™ & © 2007 Marvel Characters, Inc. Used with permission **115** Grant Wood American, 1891-1942 American Gothic, 1930 Friends of American Art Collection 1930.934 Photograph by Bob Hashimoto. Reproduction, The Art Institute of Chicago **116** Photograph by Jerry L. Thompson from the book Quarry: A Collection in Lieu of Memoirs by Lincoln Kirstein Published by Twelve Trees Press printed with permission **117** Photo © Luke Lois **118** Life Savers® is a registered trademark of

the Wrigley Company (Candy bar) © The Hershey Company **119** Photo © Frederic Winkowski **120** W. Eugene Smith / Time & Life Pictures / Getty Images (Prudential Rock) Logo used with permission of Prudential Financial **121** 2007 Y.A. Tittle by CMG Worldwide, Inc. / www.CMGWorldwide.com **122** © Carl Fischer / George Lois **123** © Andy Warhol Foundation / CORBIS **124** Popeye © King Features Syndicate (Kodak) Logo Used with permission of Eastman Kodak Company **125** Alfred Eisenstaedt / Time & Life Pictures / Getty Images **126** Buster Brown is a registered trademark of Brown Shoe Company, Inc. St. Louis, Missouri **127** ™ / © 2007 Maria Elena Holly by CMG Worldwide, Inc. / www.BuddyHolly.co **128** War Chief of the White Mountain Apache, 1906 Mary Evans Picture Library / Everett Collection (ME 10001305) **129** Marie Hansen / Time & Life Pictures / Getty Images **130** John Kobal Foundation / Hulton Archive / Getty Images **132** ™ 2007 Estate of Louis McKay by CMG Worldwide, Inc. / www.CMGWorldwide.com/ © Underwood & Underwood / CORBIS **133** Printed with permission of Ford Motor Company **135** Photo © Luke Lois **136** Thomas D. McAvoy / Time & Life Pictures / Getty Images **137** © Greyhound Lines, Inc. All Rights Reserved used with permission **138** Jimmy Durante photographer unknown, circa 1950s **139** Burma-Shave is a registered trademark of American Safety Razor Company **140** © (2007) Sesame Workshop "Sesame Street" and its characters are trademarks of Sesame Workshop All Rights Reserved **141** © image copyright Matthew Welch © Apple Inc. Use with permission All Rights Reserved Apple ® and the Apple logo are registered trademark of Apple Inc. **142** The trademark Jack Daniel's appears courtesy of Jack Daniel's Properties, Inc. Jack Daniel's & the Old No. 7 are registered trademarks of Jack Daniel's Properties, Inc. Photo © Luke Lois **143** Photo W.C. Fields Courtesy of W.C. Fields productions, Inc. **144** © Carl Fischer / George Lois **145** The I LOVE NY Logo is a registered trademark and service mark of New York State Department of Economic Development; used with permission **146** (T-Rex) © 1993 Universal City Studios, Inc. and Amblin Entertainment, Inc. Art by Chip Kidd **147** © Bettmann / CORBIS **148** AP Photo / Murray Becker **149** (Marshmallow) Photo © Luke Lois. (Lighter) zippo.com used with permission Photo © Luke Lois **150** (Giraffe) Benjamin Rabier, late 1800s **151** Copyright 2007 USA TODAY, a division of Gannett Co. Inc. USA TODAY Logo used with permission (Tupac) © Danny Clinch / CORBIS Outline **152** Gjon Mili / Time & Life Pictures / Getty Images **153** With permission of Illustration House Inc. for The Estate of Margaret Held **154** M&M's ® and The Milk Chocolate Melts In Your Mouth Not In Your Hand ® are registered trademarks of Mars, Incorporated These trademarks are used with permission Mars, Incorporated is not associated with Universe Publishing Image and trademarks used with permission of Mars, Incorporated © Mars, Inc. 2007 **155** Adam's Rib © Turner Entertainment Co. A Warner Bros. Entertainment Company All Rights Reserved **156** ™ / © 2007 Bettie Page / www.BettiePage.com **157** King Kong © RKO Pictures, Inc. Licensed by Warner Bros. Entertainment Inc. All Rights Reserved **158** George Lois **159** (Garbo) Clarence Sinclair Bull / Hulton Archive / Getty Images (Mailer) George Lois **160** Copyright Carl Fischer / George Lois **161** Chiquita Oval is a trademark of Chiquita Brands L.L.C. in the United States and other countries and is used with permission no other use of the Chiquita Oval is permitted without the prior, written permission of Chiquita Brands L.L.C. Photo © Luke Lois (Lean Cuisine) Printed with permission of Nestlé North America Photo © Luke Lois **162** Elvis Presley Stamp Design © 1993 United States Postal Service All Rights Reserved Used with Permission Printed with permission of Elvis Presley Enterprises, Inc **163** Photo © Luke Lois **164** Printed with permission of Starbucks U.S. Brands, LLC. (Pillsbury Doughboy) ©2007 and ®/™ General Mills All Rights Reserved Image courtesy of General Mills **165** Collection American Folk Art Museum, New York. **166** © The Sporting News / ZUMA **167** Photo by Richard Sexton © 1987 from American Style: Classic Product Design from Airstream to Zippo **168** (Raggedy Ann Doll) Collection American Folk Art Museum, New York (The Morton Salt Girl) A registered trademark of Morton International, Inc. used with permission **169** Photo by George Lois **170** Photograph reproduced by Special Permission of Playboy Magazine © 1970 by Playboy Miss January and Playmate of the Month are trademarks of Playboy and are used with permission **172** Published with permission of Spalding Sports. Photo © Luke Lois **173** (Baseball) Rawlings ® Photo © Luke Lois (Football) Printed with permission of NFL Properties LLC and Wilson Sporting Goods, Co. Photo © Luke Lois **174** Photograph by Gered Mankowitz © Bowstir Ltd 2007 / mankowitz.com Courtesy of Govinda Gallery **175** © Burke / Triolo Productions / Brand X / CORBIS **176** Copyright Carl Fischer / George Lois **177** © MGM **178** From the Diaries of John Gregory Bourke Volume 18 January 5, 1877–January 20, 1877 Courtesy of USMA **180** Logo Printed with permission of NASA (SUPERMAN™) DC Comics All Rights Reserved Used with Permission **181** Photograph by Bert Stern **182** Photo courtesy George Lois **183** ™ The Marlon Brando Living Trust by CMG Worldwide, www.Marlon Brando.com **184** Photos © Luke Lois **185** Evans, Walker (1903-1975) © Copyright Penny Picture Display, Savannah, Georgia 1936 Gift of Willard Van Dyke (1458.1968) Digital Image © The Museum of Modern Art / Licensed by SCALA / Art Resource, N. **186** Culver Pictures **187** ™ 2007 Amelia Earhart by CMG Worldwide, Inc. / www.AmeliaEarhart.com **188** Francis Barraud His Masters Voice 1898 Advertising Trademark used with permission of Thomson and RCA Trademark Management (Elsie the Cow) Trademark used by permission **190** Photograph by Bert Stern **191** J.R. Eyerman / Time & Life Pictures / Getty Images **192** Photocollage © Luke Lois **194** Augustus Saint-Gaudens (1848-1907), Diana, 1893-94 The Metropolitan Museum of Art, Gift of Lincoln Kirstein, 1985 (1985.353) Photograph © 1994 The Metropolitan Museum of Art **195** Avery Architectural and Fine Arts Library, Columbia University **196** Ralph L. Finn, 1951 Gaywood **197** Photo © Luke Lois / From the collection of George Lois **198** Thanks to Louisville Slugger **199** Forty Second Street (From "42nd Street") Words by Al Dubin Music by Harry Warren © 1932 (Renewed) Warner Bros. Inc. All Rights Reserved Used by Permission of Alfred Publishing Co., Inc. **200** WHS#4504: Portrait of Sitting Bull taken in the summer of 1890 Wisconsin Historical Society / Courtesy Everett Collection **202** Keystone / Hulton Archive / Getty Images **203** Leutze, Emanuel Gottlieb (1816-1868) Washington Crossing the Delaware 1851 Gift of John Stewart Kennedy, 1897, 97.34 Image copyright © The Metropolitan Museum of Art / Art Resource **204** ™ 2007 The Lynne Unger Children's Trust by CMG Worldwide, Inc. / www.PeterSellers.com **206** Courtesy of Steinway & Sons **207** The IBM Logo is printed with permission and is a registered trademark (Typewriter) Photo © Luke Lois **208** (Rosa Parks) © Bettman / CORBIS (Coin) Photo © Luke Lois **210** Photo by Annie Leibovitz Rolling Stone, November 15, 1990 © Rolling Stone LLC 1990 All Rights reserved Reprinted by Permission **211** Annie © Tribune Media Services, Inc. All Rights Reserved Reprinted with permission **212** The Rocky Horror Picture Show © 1975 Twentieth Century Fox All Rights Reserved **213** Tom Wesselmann (1931-2004) © VAGA, NY. Smoker, 1 (Mouth 12) 1967 Susan Morse Hilles Fund (226.1968) Digital Image © The Museum of Modern Art / Licensed by SCALA / Art Reource, NY. Art © Estate of Tom Wesselmann / Licensed by VAGA, New York, NY **214** © 1973, Universal Studios, Inc. **215** © Bettemann / CORBIS **216** The Hainsworth Collection, photo courtesy R.H. Love Galleries, Chicago **217** © Underwood & Underwood / CORBIS **218** ™ 2007 Bette Davis by CMG Worldwide, Inc. / www.BetteDavis.com. With permission from Warner Bros. Entertainment **219** Use of the WB in Shield Logo by permission from Warner Bros. Entertainment Inc. **220** ™ 2007 James Dean, Inc. by CMG Worldwide, Inc. / www.JamesDean.com / © Dennis Stock / Magnum Photos **221** (Camel) Photo by Richard Sexton © 1987 from American Style: Classic Product Design from Airstream to Zippo. Camel © R.J. Reynolds Tobacco Company **223** Photo © Luke Lois **224** Photo © Luke Lois **226** © 2007 Calder Foundation, New York / Artists Rights Society (ARS), New York. Photo © Luke Lois **227** Photo by Tim Galfas **228** Photo © Luke Lois **229** Weegee (Arthur Fellig) / International Center of Photography / Hulton Archive / Getty Images **230** Jackson Pollock (1912-1956) © ARS, NY. Silver over Black, White, Yellow and Red, 1948 Inv.: AM 1972-29 Photo: Jacqueline Hyde Musee National d'Art Moderne, Centre Georges Pompidou, Pars, France Photo credit CNAC / MNAM / Dist. Réunion des Musées Nationaux / Art Resource, NY 2007 The Pollock-Krasner Foundation / Artist Rights Society (ARS), New York **231** Wolverine™ & © 2007 Marvel Characters, Inc. Used with permission **232** IFE Male head, Nigeria 12th Century Copper alloy, Photograph by Eliot Elisofon, 1951 Courtesy of the Embassy of the Federal Republic of Nigeria on behalf of the National Commission for Museums

and Monuments of Nigeria **233** © Todd Gipstein / CORBIS **234** Printed with permission of The Philip Johnson Glass House, a National Trust for Historic Preservation site **235** Frank Lloyd Wright Tree of Life Window (detail) Grey Art Gallery, New York University Art Collection, Purchased with funds from the Cestaro Foundation, 1970 © 2007 Frank Lloyd Wright Foundation, Scottsdale, AZ / Artists Rights Society (ARS), NY **236** (Green Giant) Image courtesy of General Mills (Betty Grable) 1943 / Everett Collection, Inc. **237** Photo © Tommy Steele **238** © Thomas Brill / dpa / CORBIS **239** ™ The Marlon Brando Living Trust by CMG Worldwide, www.Marlon Brando.com / © Betteman / CORBIS **240** 1949 / Everett Collection, Inc. **241** ™2007 Joe Louis by CMG Worldwide, Inc. / www.CMGWorldwide.com / © Bettmann / CORBIS **242** Photograph by William Claxton / Courtesy Demont Photo Management **243** Viagra, Pfizer and the blue diamond tablet shape are registered trademarks of Pfizer Photo © Luke Lois **244** Logo © O'Neill, Inc. (Andy Warhol) Copyright Carl Fischer / George Lois **245** (Surfer) Photo © tonyrobertsphoto.com **246** Wrought iron coffle leg shackle: Dr. Sample Pittman collection Harlem NYC **248** Edward Hopper 1882-1967 Nighthawks, 1942 Friends of American Art Collection 1942.51 Photograph by Robert Hashimoto Reproduction, The Art Institute of Chicago **250** Steinberg / The New Yorker © 1976 Saul Steinberg, "View of the World from 9th Avenue" © 1976 The Saul Steinberg Foundation / Artists Rights Society (ARS), NY Cover reprinted with permission of The New Yorker magazine All Rights Reserved **251** Sunkist logo Reprinted with Permission of Sunkist Growers, Inc. All Rights Reserved (Camera) Photo Used with permission of Eastman Kodak Company **252** George and Ira Gershwin © Al Hirchfeld Reproduced by arrangement with Hirschfeld's exlusive representative, The Margo Feiden Galleries, Ltd., New York. www.alhirschfeld.com (Quaker Oats) Package image used with permission of The Quaker Oats Company **253** National Portrait Gallery, Smithsonian Institution / Art Resource, NY **254** Donna Karan logo printed with permission of The Donna Karan Company, LLC; Perry Ellis ® printed with permission of Licensor Apparel LLC & PEI Licensing Inc.; Printed with permission of Tommy Hilfiger, Geoffrey Beene, Oleg Cassini, Liz Claiborne, Michael Kors LLC, Norma Kamali, Diane von Furstenberg **255** Gloria Vanderbilt logo printed with permission of Jones Investment Co. Inc, a subsidiary of Jones Apparel Group, Inc.; Printed with permission of Carolina Herrera, Oscar de la Renta, Betsey Johnson; © Norman Norell; Printed with permission of Bill Blass, Halston **256** Nigel Parry / CPI **257** © Photography Plus C/O Stealth Media Solutions / CORBIS **258** Courtesy of Rollerblade ® USA **259** Little Giant Art © Estate of Stuart Davis / Licensed by VAGA, New York, NY. Jiffy Lube logo © 2007 Jiffy Lube ® International, Inc. **261** © Elliott Landy / Landyvision.com **262** The Veteran in a New Field Image copyright © The Metropolitan Museum of Art / Art Resource **263** Trademark furnished Courtesy of Deere & Company **264** © Al Hirschfeld. Reproduced by arrangement with Hirschfeld's exclusive representative, The Margo Feiden Galleries Ltd., New York, www.alhirschfeld.com **265** The Wurlitzer Jukebox image is copyrighted by and a trademark of Gibson Guitar Corp. The Wurlitzer Jukebox image is used with permission by Gibson Guitar Corp **266** Betty Crocker Spoon logo and images courtesy of General Mills. Bluebird Radio Photo © Luke Lois **267** Morocco, Marlene Dietrich, 1930. / Everett Collection, Inc. **268** Copyright: 2005 Harpo Productions, Inc / All Rights Reserved / Photographer: Cliff Watts **269** Ladies Home Journal printed with permission of Meredith Corporation, illustration by Frank S. Guild; MoMA is the registered trademark of The Museum of Modern Art NY and is used with permission; Bugs Bunny-"Looney Tunes" characters, names and all related indicia are ™ & © Warner Bros. Entertainment Inc. All Rights Reserved **270** © Annie Leibovitz / CONTACT Press Images **271** Toaster photograph courtesy of The Liliane and David M. Stewart Program for Modern Design, Gift of Eric Brill (shells) Photo © Luke Lois **272** Printed with permission of the Dallas Cowboy Cheerleaders **273** © Condé Nast Archive / CORBIS Betty Boop © King Features Syndicate. **274** © Herb Ritts / Lime Foto **276** Edward Hicks, 1780-1849 the Peacable Kingdom, ca 1846 Fine Arts Museums of San Francisco, gift of Mr. and Mrs. John D. Rockefeller 3rd, 19993.35.14 Krazy Kat © King Features Syndicate **277** Monroe Image by Milton H. Greene © 2007 Joshua Greene www.archiveimages.com **278** ©Library of Congress, Prints & Photographs Division, [LC-DIG-cwpbh-03248] **279** Augustus Saint-Gaudens American 1848-1907 Victory 1892-1903 Carnegie Museum of Art Pittspurgh: Purchase 19.5.2 **280** (logo) © LIFE Inc. printed with permission **281** Copyright Carl Fischer / George Lois **282** Art © Estate of Ben Shahn / Licensed by VAGA, New York, NY **283** John Glenn Photo credit: NASA; E.T. © 1982 Universal City Studios, Inc. **284** Photo © Luke Lois UP Shield Logo is a Registered trademark of Union Pacific Railroad Company printed with permission; The NASCAR Logo is printed with permission of National Association for Stock Car Auto Racing, Inc. **285** UP Tin Shield sign courtesy of G.K.S. Bush Antiques; (hood ornament) Photo by Rob d'Estrubé Copyright © 2000 by Ken Steacy **286** "Join or Die" cartoon in the Pennsylvania Gazette, Benjamin Franklin, Library Company of Philadelphia **287** © 2007 Target.com. All Rights Reserved. The Bullseye Design is a trademark of Target Brands, Inc. and is used with permission; Photograph of Gary Cooper by Bert Stern **288** © Bettman / CORBIS **290** © David Levine **292** Mint Julep photograph © Russell Kaye & Sandra-Lee Phipps **293** Photo © George Lois **294** AP Archive **295** Copyright Carl Fischer / George Lois **296** ™ 2007 Rachel Robinson by CMG Worldwide, Inc. /www.JackieRobinson.com / © The Sporting News / ZUMA **297** Stella, Joseph The Voice of the City of New York Interpreted: The Bridge, 1920-1922 The Newark Museum / Art Resource, NY **298** © Ansel Adams Publishing Rights Trust / CORBIS **299** Photograph by Dick Richards / George Lois **300** Gene Autry circa 1930s, photographer unknown **301** The Pegasus Logo is printed with Permission of ExxonMobil **302** (Kelly) Gjon Mili / Time & Life Pictures / Getty Images (logo) Printed with Permission of Travelers (guitar) Fender®, Stratocaster® and the distinctive headstock and body designs commonly found on the Stratocaster® guitar are trademarks owned by Fender Musical Instruments Corporation, and are used herein with express written permission **303** CBS Eye Logo printed with permission of CBS Broadcasting Inc. (Rubenstein) © Al Hirchfeld Reproduced by arrangement with Hirschfeld's exclusive representative, The Margo Feiden Galleries, Ltd., New York. www.alhirschfeld.com **304** Casper ™ & © Harvey Entertainment, Inc. (Puzzle) Copyright © 2007 by The New York Times Co. Reprinted with permission **305** Houdini circa early 1900's photo by John Mulholland **306** Photo © Luke Lois **308** NASA **309** Photo by Richard Sexton © 1987 from American Style: Classic Product Design from Airstream to Zippo Image of Jackie Gleason used with permission of Jaglea VIP Corp. The Honeymooners is a trademark used under license. Likeness permission granted by Audrey Meadows Six Trust **310** Tarzan and family, 1941 EV1765 / Everett Collection, Inc. First Jass Record printed courtesy of SONY BMG Music Entertainment **311** Photo © Luke Lois Used courtesy of Frisbee, Frisbee® is a registered trademark of Wham-O Inc. 2007 Xerox is a registered trademark of Xerox Corporation reprinted with permission **313** (Pasties) Photo © Luke Lois **314** (Buttons) Photo © Luke Lois **315** Bill Eppridge / Time & Life Pictures / Getty Images **316** © Photoservice Electa **317** Photo © Luke Lois Chair from the collection of George Lois **318** CNN Logo © 2007 Cable News Network. A Time Warner Company All Rights Reserved Mark Twain ™ / © 2007 Mark Twain by CMG Worldwide, Inc. / www.CMGWorldwide.com. **319** Mr. Smith Goes to Washington, James Stewart, 1939 / Everett Collection, Inc. **320** Pink Flamingo © Union products / Don Featherstone **321** Photo © Roland Bello **322** (light bulb) Photo © Luke Lois. (Einstein) HIP / Art Resource, N. **323** (helicopter) Digital Image © The Museum of Modern Art / Licensed by SCALA / Art Resource, NY. (Empire State Building) © Peter Mauss / Esto All Rights Reserved **324** Variety logo printed with permission of Variety Hollywood Walk of Fame™ & Design © 2007 Hollywood Chamber of Commerce All Rights Reserved **325** Photo by: André Baranowski **326** Copyright Carl Fischer / George Lois **327** Photo Wolfgang Eichler **328** © Reuters / CORBIS **329** Courtroom Pool Photography AP **330** © CORBIS **332** Nigel Parry / CPI **333** Rendering of the Freedom Tower courtesy of Skidmore, Owings and Merrill **334** Barbie® is a trademark owned by and used with permOission from Mattel, Inc. © 2007 Mattel, Inc. All Rights Reserved Mattel makes no representation as to the authenticity of the materials obtained herein The authors assume full responsibility for facts and information contained in this book All opinions expressed are those of the authors, and not of Mattel, Inc. ©2006 The Coca-Cola Company, All rights reserved. "Coca-Cola" is a registered trademark of The Coca-Cola Company **335** © James Montgomery Flagg / George Lois / Luke Lois

INDEX

D

E

F

G

M

N

O

THE FISHES

Although, at first we think the slogan "wonder in the living room" refers to an aquarium with esthetically beautiful plant decorations with changing colors, it also refers to the fishes that belong in the aquarium. In decorating an aquarium we can take two paths. First, we can choose to occupy ourselves with decorations composed of plants and think about which fishes we would like to have afterwards. Most of the time we choose a group of fish that we think are beautiful due to their form, shape and/or color. Then it is unimportant if the animals in this aquarium do nothing else than swim back and forth. The other option is to first think about the fishes we would like to care for. Then their beauty does not come first, but more their natural behavior in building a territory or the way they display during courtship and spawning. Of course, this fish community can also be very appealing. In this case the choice of plants is made afterwards, but with the functional use of certain species of plants, and how to group them together, in mind.

It is important that we know how many fishes can be accomodated. We should look for a certain balance between the number of fishes and healthy plants. In addition, we have the size of the aquarium, the illumination, the water temperature, the healthiness of the water, the feeding process, and the number of bacteria all playing an important role in the total life process. Every factor is as important as the other. If one is not correct, it can be the reason why our aquarium community will not function correctly. The combination of fish and plants is very important. Real water plants play a completely different role than the swamp plants, which are mostly used by us. Real water plants produce more oxygen when the environment is right, and most of the time they grow faster. If we have a lot of those plants in our aquarium, then the starting position is quite different than in an aquarium with swamp plants. This again influences the fish community which has been chosen.

In the esthetically pleasing aquarium we combine plants and fishes. In reality, many aquarists follow the ratio of one

"We should look for a certain balance between the number of fish and healthy plants..."

Frozen foods offer a wide range of choices to the aquarist. Photo courtesy of Ocean Nutrition.

gram of fish to two liters of water for small species, and one gram of fish to three or four or more liters of water when it is a larger fish. With the larger growing species an important issue is—how much food they digest and how much detritus has to be broken down. The rule of so many grams of fish per so much water is actually very inadequate, and can be confusing for beginners.

We should ask ourselves how much room a fish needs on the basis of its behavior, and we will find that out quickly enough: The more water the animal has at its disposal the better it is. Surely, there is a bottom line, otherwise we could hardly hold any fish in our aquarium. Often enough the hobbyist draws the line.

One may find a small number of fishes boring, while another may be completely content with them. You could have a very beautiful aquarium with a length of one and a half meters in which there are only four to six Discus, or a nice school of *Puntius tetrazona*, or a collection of a number of species. Here tastes are

You could have a very beautiful aquarium with a length of one and a half meters, in which there are only four to six Discus.

different. There is rarely a hobbyist who will enjoy looking behind the tail of a fish to see another. In this case we arrive at the other point.

In many cases the question of whether it is a 'schooling fish' or not plays a role. Of course, this also depends on the size of the aquarium. When a fish is not a 'schooling fish', it does not mean that two of them are enough. It is true that such species more or less live their own lives, but they also like to choose their partner when they spawn. Therefore, even from those species we buy more of the notorious 'spawning pairs.'

If you only put a community together from species that you like, the functional combination of fishes and plants does not play a role. The number of fishes and the form of the society almost always means that in this aquarium nothing interesting happens. Only when the aquarium is very large will the possibility arise that some fishes will build a territory at a certain spot and will spawn there. This is a stroke of luck that seldom happens.

Therefore, it is better to care for less species with more fish per species, but always less than the normal community aquarium. Aquariums populated by this rule distinguish themselves, and one often finds fry that are born in them. There are no fry without spawning and no spawning without courtship, and there is no courtship when the aquarium environment is not suitable. Actually, there is no suitable aquarium environment if we do not know what the fishes prefer. Without this knowledge it often happens that aquariums are supplied with wrong decorations. In this case, we may choose the wrong plants, put the right plants in the wrong spot, or choose the wrong lighting. The delight we could have from the aquarium never occurs. The sad thing about this is that we often do not know that we could have something completely different, namely an aquarium that can be fascinating and have the correct environment.

***Puntius tetrazona* is a nice schooling fish that looks very beautiful in an aquarium. Photo by K. Knaack.**

ILLUMINATION

Now we suddenly have arrived at another road, because what is "wrong lighting"? The fundamental lighting of a Dutch tank is related to the plants, but now we are referring to the fishes. Here we can ask ourselves if an aquarium could be illuminated too strongly. There are several starting points to answer this question.

Many aquarists point to the fierce lighting in the tropics, which is much stronger than we have to offer our plants. This may be true but these aquarists are thinking about the plants, and the fishes only play a minor part.

Other aquarists consider the fishes more, but also include the plants. They already have the knowledge that many plant species will thrive with much less light. Typical examples are: Java fern *(Microsorium pteropus)* and *Anubias barteri* var. *nana*, which will clearly have trouble at a light quantity that we need for a lush growth of Java moss *(Vesicularia dubyana)*. Do we turn down the illumination? If so, the Java moss *(Vesicularia dubyana)* will grow less lush, but the Java fern will grow well.

When we look into an aquarium in which the illumination is very strong (for the plants that need strong light), then we can observe that many fishes do not look as

colorful as they should. Even when the aquarium is healthy, functions well, and is well cared for, Bleeding Heart Tetras *(Hyphessobrycon erythrostigma)* do not show as much red as they should. The beautiful pastel tints are absent from *Hemigrammus ocellifer*, and even more so with *Hemigrammus pulcher* or *Hemigrammus caudovittatus*. This is also the case with *Hemmigrammus rhodostomus* and *Petitella georgiae*. A school of those fishes should not be combined with *Paracheirodon axelrodi*. When both schools mix together none of them show to their best advantage. There is more than one kind of

Above: The beautiful pastel tints are absent from _Hemigrammus ocellifer._ Photo by A. Roth. _Below:_ Even when the aquarium is healthy, functions well, and is well cared for the Bleeding Hearts do not appear as red as they could. Photo by M. P. & C. Piednoir.

A school of either *Hemigrammus rhodostomus* or *Petitella georgiae* should not be mixed with *Paracheirodon axelrodi*, because their best colors will not show. Photos by H.-J. Richter.

fish species that normally swim at lower, middle, or upper water layers. Moreover, many fishes behave shyly, something they normally do not do.

We call fishes "shy" when they withdraw among the plants. A typical example is the pretty *Puntius fasciolans* of Africa, or *Poecilocharax weitzmani* of South America. Very often we see how these species are withdrawing to an open spot between the plants, where the lighting is not as harsh as it is at other spots in the aquarium. Of course the "shyness" can also have other causes than poor lighting. A too small aquarium, or a wrongly combined fish community could also be the cause. If we leave this out of consideration, then the lighting is more often thought guilty than it naturally is.

I still speak of a normal and not of a so called "functional" community aquarium. A wonder in the living room with a beautiful, healthy plant balance is only truly beautiful when we also are concerned with the fishes. They should be living as a colorful contrasting point against the stillness of the rest. However, liveliness and color are influenced by light.

How does this appear in nature? We will give a few examples, otherwise we would need a completely new article about light.

Many fish live in very clear waters, which are exposed to the sun almost the whole day, and these waters can look everything from colorless to cola colored, or darker. At the banks we often find a very thick vegetative growth. Grasses and other plants hang into the water, but at the border we often find water plants or swamp plants. In other parts, these waters are, at least for a part of the day, in

When an embankment is densely grown with swamp plants, then there is only diffuse light at a depth of 20 to 30 centimeters.

Above: A typical example of a "shy" fish is *Poecilocharax weitzmani*, which wll withdraw into a secluded space in the aquarium. Photo by H.-J. Richter. *Below: Paracheirodon axelrodi* is one of the most popular fish to use in a Dutch aquarium because it does not bother other fishes or eat any of the plant life.

shadows or even in deep shadows, so that there are only a few water plants or none at all. All these habitats are separated into surface zone, bottom zone, embankment zone, and open water zone. Many fishes are found in all zones, and often the adults and juveniles are separate. There are also species that only live in a certain zone, and other species that are not to be found there.

The light in these zones is mostly of varying intensity. At the surface of the open water we find the highest intensity and at the bottom much less. When the embankment has a dense growth of swamp plants, then there is only

Above: Danio aequipinnatus **was found in clear water. Photo by M.P. & C. Piednoir.** ***Below:*** **The waterfall is from Sri Lanka during the dry season; it contradicts the jungle biotope.**

Above: **In the stagnant slow moving water these *Belontia signata* were found together with the *Danio aequipinnatus*. *Below:* In Southeast Asia *Rasbora borapetensis* live in very different habitats. Photos by M. P. & C. Piednoir.**

diffuse light at a depth of 20 to 30 centimeters. Cola colored water filters out even more light. Strong light above the water does not mean that it is as light everywhere in the water. There we find the border zone. This is where the light is less in much overshadowed jungle brooks with very cola colored water, where we often find very specific plants, or no plants at all in the water.

The waterfall was photographed in the dry season in Sri Lanka, and contradicts a jungle biotope. In the clear water we found *Danio aequipinnatus* and in the stagnant or slow moving sections we found it together with adult *Belontia signata*! In Southeast Asia we will find *Rasbora*, *Puntius* and *Danio* species, which if we talk about them in relationship to the light, live in very different habitats. Many only live in certain habitats, which are often in the shade, or flow through cola colored water, or live in water that is mixed with loam particles, so that we cannot see our hand anymore at a depth of 20 centimeters. Here they live in the upper water parts, but also at a depth of more than 1 meter. I will name only one *Rasbora heteromorpha*, that can be found in the darkest cola colored water. Here they look unbelievably red, just like *Rasbora kalochroma*, which can be so red that they look

_Rasbora heteromorph_a can be found in the darkest cola colored water, and here they look unbelievably red. Photo by M. P. & C. Piednoir.

***Puntius* species can hardly be found in cola colored water, and they are mostly encountered at a depth of at least 50 centimeters under the water surface, or in the upper part where there are enough plants. Photo by Dr. Herbert R. Axelrod**

almost black. In nature, *Rasbora heteromorpha* can also be found in much clearer, colorless water, but there they are less colorful. *Puntius tetrazona* is an example of a fish that can be found in many different habitats, but they usually show the same color. *Puntius pentazona*, or *P. hexazona* can hardly be found in cola colored water, and mostly at a depth of at least 50 centimeters under the water surface, or in the upper part where there are enough plants. For instance, in the aquarium we accompany *Danio aequipipinnatus*, for the upper and middle parts of a larger aquarium, with *Puntius pentazona*, which will not be as colorful when nothing is done about the lighting and the color of the bottom.

In principle, it can be said that all fishes with a deep, dark red, brownish red, or blackish red body color come from a dark environment. There are also other grounds on which these fishes never show their optimal color, if we do not apply special methods, like filtering through peat, or dimmed lighting, and such. This is very difficult to accomplish in an aquarium in the living room. So, we have to look for a compromise, or put together a very special fish community.

To compromise means that we must choose plants that need less light, and in this way accommodate the fishes. However, this reduces the choice of plants. It is too bad that these fast growing plants need a lot of light. In smaller aquariums nothing works except to combine such plants with fishes that tolerate less light. A mixture is rarely possible.

In larger aquariums, of 100 centimeters or more, it is possible to create shade and diffuse light as well as very well lit places. This can, for instance, be accomplished through plants that grow along the water surface, like *Myriophyllum, Rotala,* and many kinds of *Vallisneria.* Floating plants are less suitable, because they multiply too rapidly and we have to restrict them to a certain spot at the surface. The simplest thing to do is to use *Ceratopteris cornuta and Ceratopteris pteroides.* Their bushy roots can be pinned to the Styropor wall or to a floating piece of cork, which can be held in place by a thin bamboo shoot that gets fastened between the front and rear panes. This is done in such a way that the cork is pushed underwater a bit and held in place. Also, a piece of bogwood can be used. A piece of bogwood overgrown with Java fern (*Microsorium pteropus*), *Vesicularia dubyana* (Java-moss) or *Bolbitis heudelotii,* or with pinned down floating plants will create shadows or diffused light spots in the aquarium, especially at the top side of the open swimming space. This idea provides many possibilities, which moreover can be supported by a dark colored bottom or one that is overgrown. In the diffused light areas we plant those plants that stay low, and that do not need too much light.

We can get a very nice dark bottom when we spread basalt chips on the bottom layer of coarse sand. We can also mix both ingredients and just put them on the bottom and combine them with low growing plants like *Cryptocoryne parva, Echinodorus tenellus*, etc. This works on almost all fishes in a calming way, and they will also show better colors.

I would advise against using a peat filter, for this filter will color the water brown and much more light is needed to penetrate the water.

Therefore, we come to an

Aquarium:	*200x50x50 cm*
Light hood:	*5 cm high*
Lighting:	*1 Philips TL 65W/32*
past:	*1 Philips TL 65W/33*
	2 Philips TL 8W/33
later:	*1 Philips 'TL'D 58W/83 (12 hours)*
	1 Philips 'TL'D 58W/84 (9 hours)
	2 Philips TL 8W/33 (12 hours)
Decoration:	*bogwood between the plants, highest terrace 15 cm. Walls of Styropor, painted in several natural colors, partially grown over with Vesicularia dubyana.*
Filter:	*1 week per month. Every week 20% fresh water.*

aquarium with changes in the lighting that will be appreciated by many fishes. We can rearrange this with ordinary lamps in different wattages. Today this is much more difficult to arrange due to fluorescent lights, for their big disadvantage is that they give a flat uniform light. This light does not liven up the aquarium, so we must help

Plants used in the setup above:

Hygrophila stricta
Hygrophila difformis
Rotala rotundifolia
Lobelia cardinalis
Aponogeton undulatus
Cryptocoryne becketii
Nymphaea lotus **(green, red spotted)**
Nymphaea lotus **(red)**
Heteranthera zosterifolia
Vesicularia dubyana **(on walls)**
Hydrocoytle leucopetala
Cryptocoryne "petchii"
Aponogeton crispus
Saururus cernuus
Cryptocoryne willisii
Eichhornia azurea
Echinodorus tenellus
Microsorium pteropus
Limnophila aquatica
Ludwigia repens x palustris **(with bogwood)**
Echinodorus bleheri
Cryptocoryne undulata

with the grouping of plants. We also can lower the light intensity at certain spots with pieces of cardboard on the cover-pane under the fluorescent lights.

Many hobbyists already practice lighting differences as they choose their lamps. In Dutch aquariums we can see that instead of one 36 watt lamp and one 18 watt lamp, three 18 watt lamps are used, because the light quantity is different. Already, many top aquariums have as many lamps in their lighting hoods as necessary. In this way, we have light reserve and we can "play" with light, not only to please the plants, but also to please the fishes.

A normal or common community aquarium is divided into sunny and shady areas, more or less divided swimming room that can especially be accomplished in larger aquariums. In this way, we can establish particular spots that are preferred by many fishes. Thus, we have the transition to the functional aquarium.

The functional aquarium is a new expression. It is defined as: "A functional aquarium is an esthetically and decorative aquarium with plants, in which the plants are grouped in such a way that they invite the fishes to show more of their behavior climaxing in their breeding."

So, before we begin to make a choice of plants, make a drawing of how to plant the aquarium and we should have an idea about the fishes that we want to care for. The starting point is to bring the fishes to breed in the living room aquarium, without having the intention to do so. In this way, it becomes a beautiful aquarium in which we can

Above: Nematobrycon palmeri, a species of tetra, has been known to spontaneously spawn when living in an aquarium. Below: The _Pyrrhulina spilota_ male should have a quiet spot in the aquarium where he can build a preserve. Photo by W. Sommer.

***Moenkhausia pittieri* is a species that prefers dark spots; if these spots are not available it will do nothing in the aquarium. Photo above by M. P. & C. Piednoir, and below by R. Zukal.**

observe the lives of our fishes. This means also a limitation in choosing the fishes. If we care for many animals of one kind, then it must always be a community in which the different species disturb each other as little as possible. This is closely related to the size of the aquarium, because in a small aquarium we can only care for one species that lives at the bottom, with a few species gladly laying their eggs in the plants at the edges of the aquarium.

SPAWNING

We should know something about reproductive behavior and the way the fishes will exhibit it. In this way, species from the wild are distinguished from those species that are bred. Species from the wild will need a special tank, or we will have to use a breeding tank.

Let us limit ourselves, in the first place, to the community aquarium mainly with fishes from South America. We can compile a list of many different associations in which oftentimes a fish will one day spawn spontaneously. The tetras, for instance: *Nematobrycon* species and *Inpaichthys kerri*, *Moenkhausia pittieri*, *Copella arnoldi*, and many *Pyrrhulina* species. *Nematobrycon*, *Inpaichthys*, and *Moenkhausia pittieri* are typical examples of species that prefer dark spots. If those spots are not available, they will do nothing. They like to spawn at walls that are overgrown with Java moss or Java fern, but also at spots where the lighting is diffuse, for instance under bushy *Myriophyllum* and even *Blyxa echinosperma*. The sparkling *Moenkhausia pittieri* like to mate in plants at the border region, preferably in plants with fine leaves, but also in *Bacopa, Lobelia,* and *Rotala* leaves. They are not choosy, but prefer diffusely lit spots, and will even spawn in densely grown bottom plants or in *Cryptocoryne* species. *Hyphessobrycon callistus* prefer the same conditions as *Moenkhausia pittieri. Hasemania nana,* on the other hand, prefer to spawn in the evening, when the lights of the aquarium are turned a little lower. Here, the lowering of the light intensity plays a role. *Poptella orbicularis* loves to have a sunny, or well lit, aquarium, and will spawn at very well lit spots, many times free in the water, many times close to plants just like *Gymnocorymbus ternetzi.*

So far so good. All this will

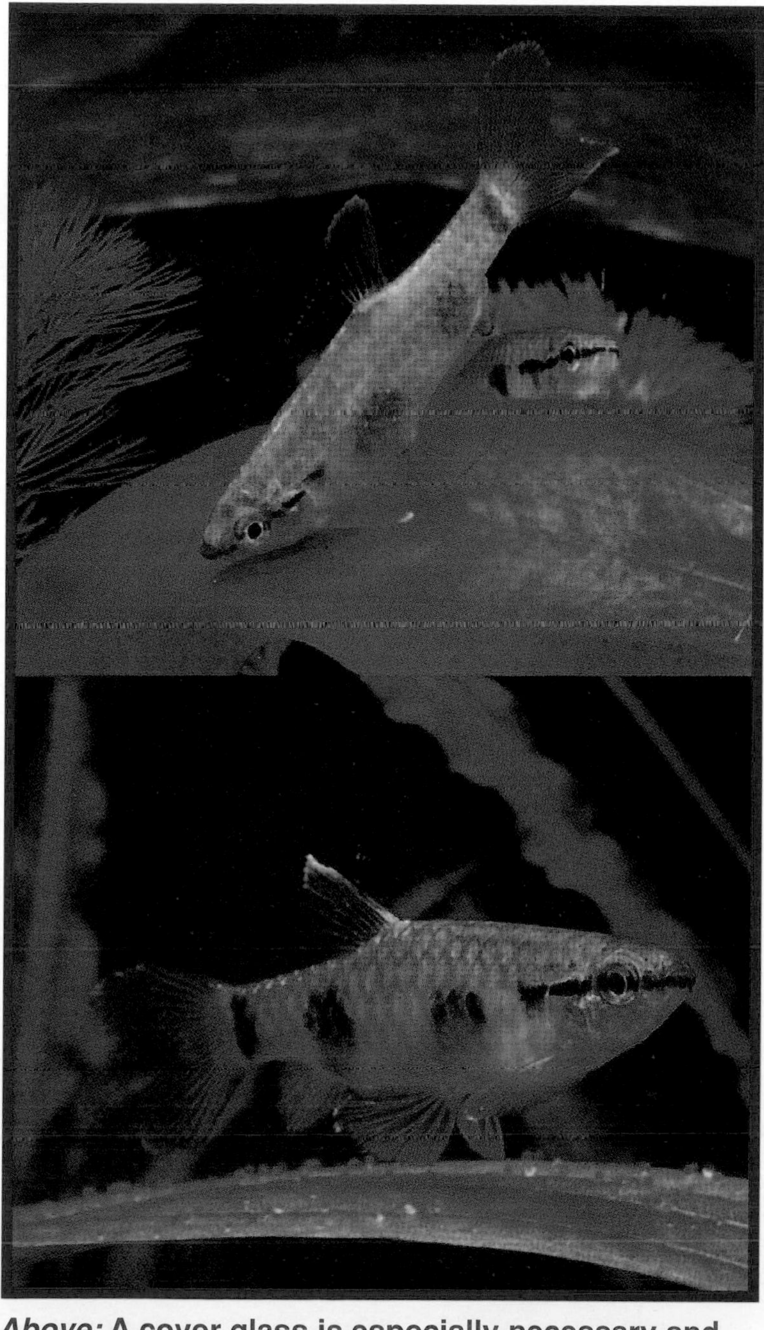

Above: **A cover glass is especially necessary and appreciated by many species, such as *Pyrrhulina vittata.***

Below: Copella arnoldi **likes to spawn on surfaces that are overgrown wih Java moss or Java fern.**

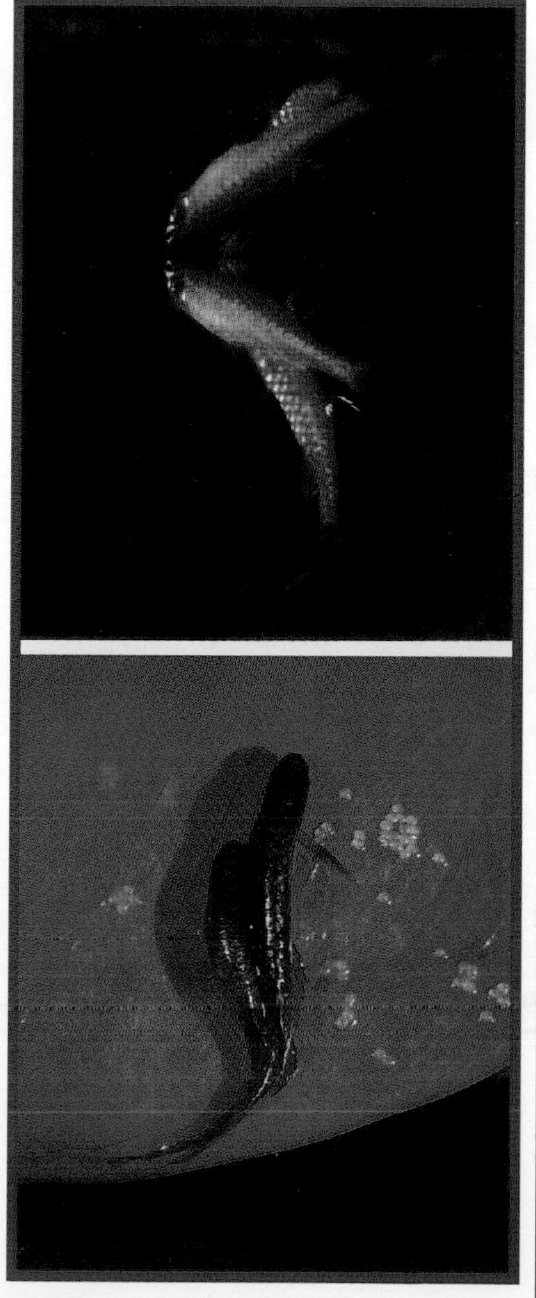

Danio malabarcus **works well in the upper and middle parts of the larger aquarium. Photo by H.-J. Richter.**

happen in a normal community aquarium with not too many fishes, or with more fishes when we can supply them with darker and quieter spots. It is different with *Copella arnoldi*, which will spawn outside the water, mostly on the cover glass. The male should also have a quiet spot in the aquarium where he can build a preserve, just like *Pyrrhulina* species. Large or small, they prefer spawning on a large leaf. The smaller species spawn on a leaf approximately 6 centimeters long and from 3 to 4 centimeters wide, while the larger ones use, of course, larger leaves. The leaves should also be strong enough. In the first place, the *Anubias* species are relevant as are *Echinodorus*, like *horizontalis, cordifolius* and such. These plants also have to grow in the right spot, which are somewhat away from places that are too often frequented by other fishes when they are swimming. These spots are somewhat away from the large swimming area. They are bordered with other plants. A cover glass is especially necessary and appreciated by many species, for instance, the small *Pyrrhulina* species. Are those plants missing those tetras, or are they just situated at the wrong spot? The fish will swim around them without utilizing them.

These fish can be perfectly placed together with *Gasteropelecus maculatus*, but also with *Rivulus* species. These fish will swim throughout the entire aquarium, but will spawn preferably just below the surface and even on the floating plants, like *Riccia fluitans*. They also use the roots, especially from, *Ceratopteris* species or the *Myriophyllum* garlands that grow along the surface. In this way, the plants have two functions. They serve as a light dimmer and as a spawning place.

Rasbora heteromorpha **can be found in much clearer water, but they are much less colorful. Photo by M. P. & C. Piednoir.**